WHITAKER'S ALMANACK
2006

A & C BLACK

LONDON

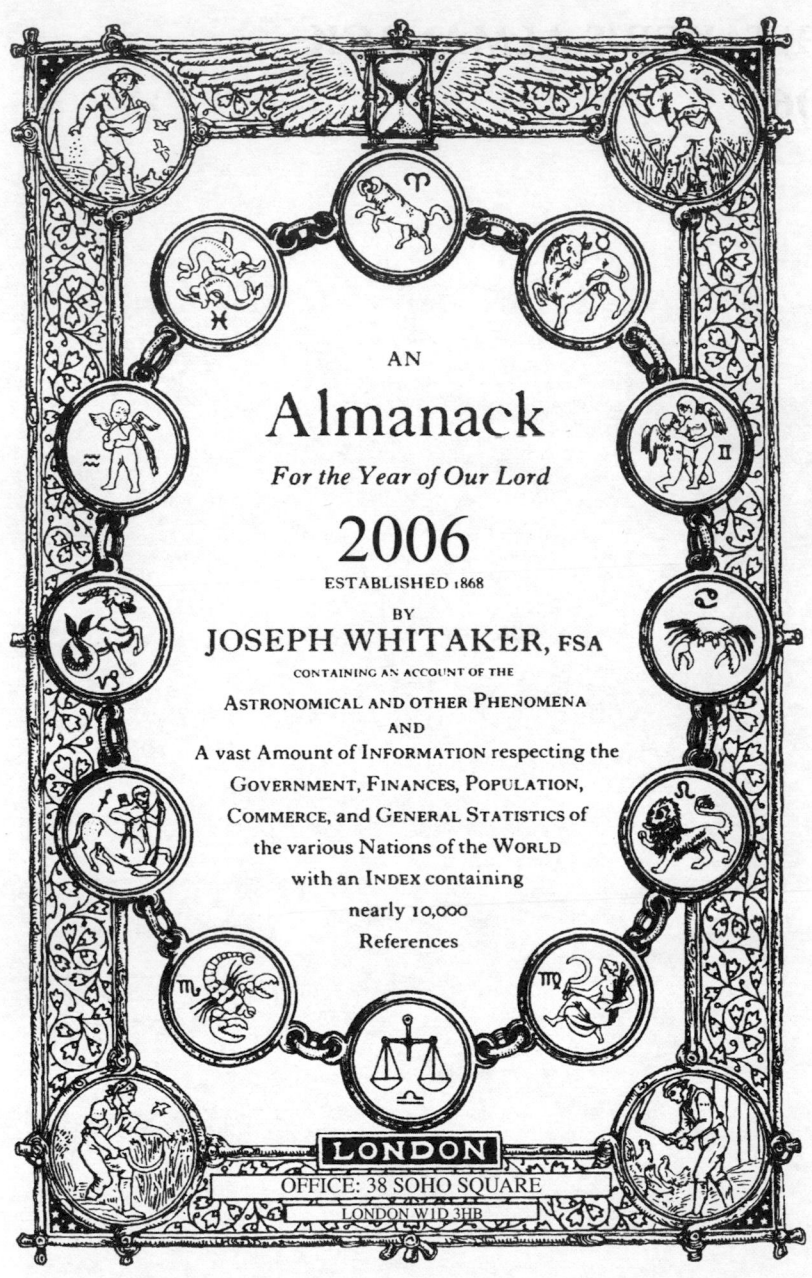

AN

Almanack

For the Year of Our Lord

2006

ESTABLISHED 1868

BY

JOSEPH WHITAKER, FSA

CONTAINING AN ACCOUNT OF THE

ASTRONOMICAL AND OTHER PHENOMENA

AND

A vast Amount of INFORMATION respecting the

GOVERNMENT, FINANCES, POPULATION,

COMMERCE, and GENERAL STATISTICS of

the various Nations of the WORLD

with an INDEX containing

nearly 10,000

References

LONDON

OFFICE: 38 SOHO SQUARE

LONDON W1D 3HB

The traditional design of the title page for Whitaker's Almanack which has appeared in each edition since 1868

WHITAKER'S ALMANACK

2006

A & C BLACK

LONDON

A & C BLACK (PUBLISHERS) LTD
38 Soho Square, London W1D 3HB

Whitaker's Almanack published annually since 1868
© 138th edition A & C Black (Publishers) Ltd 2005

STANDARD EDITION
Cloth covers   ISBN-10: 0-7136-7018-5
               ISBN-13: 978-0-7136-7018-9

CONCISE EDITION
Paperback   ISBN 10: 0-7136-7019-3
            ISBN 13: 978-0-7136-7019-6

Jacket photographs: © Corbis
Typeset in Great Britain by: RefineCatch Ltd,
   Bungay, Suffolk
Printed and bound in Great Britain by: William Clowes Ltd,
   Beccles, Suffolk

Whitaker's is a Registered trade mark of J. Whitaker and
Sons Ltd, Registered Trade Mark Nos. (UK)
1322125/09; 13422126/16 and 1322127/41; (EU)
19960401/09, 16, 41, licensed for use by A & C Black
(Publishers) Ltd.

Whitaker's Almanack was compiled with the assistance
of: Amnesty International; Christian Research; *The
Diplomatic List* © Crown Copyright; *International
Financial Statistics Year Book* © International Monetary
Fund; *Military Balance 2004–5*, published by Taylor &
Francis; *People in Power* © Cambridge International
Reference on Current Affairs (CIRCA); 2004 *World
Development Indicators*, published by The World Bank;
UK Hydrographic Office; The Met Office; Oxford
Cartographers; WM/Reuters; CIA World Factbook;
Keesings Worldwide. Crown copyright material is
reproduced with the permission of the Controller of Her
Majesty's Stationery Office.

EDITORIAL STAFF
Editor-in-Chief: Inna Ward
Project Editors: Luke Block, Ruth Northey
Editorial Assistants: Rob Hardy, Louise Reip

CONTRIBUTORS
Vanessa White (Editorial); Elizabeth Holmes
(Education); Gordon Taylor (Astronomy); Hemant
Kanitkar (Hindu calendar); Isabelle Kenning (Mobile
Communications); Karen Harries-Rees (Environment);
Dominic Orchard (Information Technology); Clive
Longhurst (Insurance); Roger Merrick (Mutual
Societies); Duncan Murray, Chris Priestley (Legal
Notes); Jill Papworth (Taxation); Dr Neil Faulker, Dr
Nadia Durrani (Archaeology); John Hitchman
(Architecture); Max Andrews (Art); Steve Clarke
(Broadcasting); Peter Marren, Matthew Saunders
(Conservation); Bridie Macmahon (Dance); Tom Charity
(Film); Jon Ashworth (Business and Finance); Nicolette
Jones (Literature); Pippa Murphy, Piers Martin (Music);
Elizabeth Forbes (Opera); Patrick Robathan
(Parliament); Erica Stary (Public Acts); Neil Bone
(Science and Discovery); Jane Edwardes (Theatre);
Edward Gibbes, Stan Greenberg (Sport), Hilary
Marsden (Countries of the World)

INDEX
Colin Izat, Fiona Smith - IndX Ltd

CONTENTS

6

FOREWORD BY JON SNOW

I am a journalist, my business is information. Say I am writing an article and I need to know how much it costs to send a child to Britain's most expensive private school, Eton. I can either get on the internet and deploy a search engine, or I can look it up in *Whitaker's Almanack*. But the reason I need the information is because I'm writing about a potential UK Conservative Party leader who went there. But what is his constituency and by how much did he win it? It's all here and amazingly easy to find.

Whitaker's Almanack remains the most accessible, the most comprehensive compendium of information in the English language. Despite the age of the internet there is no other place in the world that will tell me: how to address a Marchioness the next time I have to interview one (Lady); find the postcode for my daughter's university (LS2 9JT); and retrieve the rate of inflation in the Solomon Islands (1.8 per cent) – all in one breath, all in one place.

Whitaker's is a resource that I have had on my literal desktop ever since I can remember – it rarely, if ever, fails me. This is a book of both lateral and vertical information, holistic and rounded. There are the straight facts in abundance, but they are interwoven with the more eclectic facts and figures that complete the picture.

The *Almanack* is even more than that: for 138 years it has provided a snapshot of who we are, caught at one moment in time. The year recorded in this edition was one in which Britain was economically out of step with its European competitors, the nearly two decades of growth was sustained whilst France and Germany continued to stagnate. Europe appeared dogged by a failure to restructure and reform labour practices.

It was also a year in which Britain's Prime Minister Tony Blair won an unprecedented third term for a Labour government. To some extent he was the man the electorate loved to hate, or even hated to love. At one point in the campaign, his rival and Chancellor of the Exchequer, Gordon Brown had to ride to the rescue. The election was fought on an almost American style double ticket. Gordon Brown's eventual succession to the Premiership seemed to be agreed, but when it would happen remained a mystery. All that Mr Blair would say was that this was positively his last election. Almost immediately after his re-election, Blair's star went back into the ascendant in marked contrast to his major European colleagues. Germany's Chancellor Schroeder suffered so grievous a set back in regional state elections, that he brought forward his country's general election. Italy's Prime Minister Berlusconi remained embattled, struggling to keep one coalition together and then establishing another that looked no more robust. But it was France's president Jacques Chirac who seemed to have experienced the unhappiest of years. Forced to stage a referendum to approve the European Union's new constitution, his innate unpopularity contributed to wholesale defeat. Coming up for air, France was favourite to win the staging of the Olympic Games in 2012; he was knocked back again when the IOC awarded the Games to London. It was a body blow and talk of how to get rid of Chirac before his second seven-year term ends in 2007 became widespread.

In the United States, President George Bush's popularity faded too in 2005. The folksy charm that had secured his re-election in 2004 wore thin in the face of continuing military and political failure in Iraq and his handling of the aftermath of Hurricane Katrina. The war in Iraq provided a painful backdrop to world events. The 'coalition of the willing' became less willing and less of a coalition as the year unfolded. The Spanish pulled their troops out, Poland followed, Italy announced a departure date, and even Britain talked of pulling out most of her forces from southern Iraq. The wider 'war on terror' fared little better. Afghanistan's poppy harvest hit record highs as did her export of heroin to the West. The security situation there worsened. Suicide bombings fanned out from intense daily killings in Iraq, to terrifying transit attacks in London and car bombs in Egypt. Even the White House began to tone down its rhetoric about winning.

China continued to boom, with her voracious demand for fuel to drive her burgeoning economy beginning to impact on world record oil prices.

The most salutary signal of man's incapacity in the face of the elements came with the tsunami that swept across the Indian Ocean in the last days of December 2004, devastating coastal regions of Indonesia, Thailand, India and Sri Lanka. Many thousands died as entire villages were washed out to sea. The world's reaction was uplifting and hundreds of millions of dollars were raised for the victims in the biggest response to any natural catastrophe mankind has ever seen.

There was also an extraordinary response to the G8 industrialised nations' decision to focus on Africa. Billions of people are said to have watched the sequence of Live 8 concerts across the world as part of an exercise to raise awareness of the continent's needs.

A year then of optimism and vision set against a challenging backdrop of natural disaster, war and terrorism. Seventeen years after the Berlin Wall came down the world is still in search of a new order and new sense of equilibrium.

PREFACE

Welcome to the 138th edition of *Whitaker's Almanack*. As can be expected from a general election edition, readers will find complete results for the election of 5 May 2005, listing every candidate for every constituency together with the size of the electorate, turnout, majority, swing and the previous election outcome. In addition, included for the first time are the main three parties' manifesto pledges, as well as some interesting statistics on turnout, women MPs, smallest and largest majorities and declaration times.

Those of you regularly using the forms of address page will notice its absence; however, the relevant information can still be found throughout the peerage section. Other changes include the addition of a list of internet domain names for different countries and the expansion of the culture profiles in the countries of the world section. Due to its popularity, the periodic table has now become a permanent feature. The Public Offices section has been re-ordered alphabetically and is now decidedly easier to navigate.

As always the book has been scrupulously updated throughout, using the most authoritative of sources – the full list can be found on the imprint page. I would urge our readers to look over the excellent year in review section at the back of the book – the only place where subjective opinion is allowed to slip into *Whitaker's*.

Finally, I would like to sincerely thank the thousands of individuals who kindly help us update our database each year and to welcome two new team members on board. Please keep writing to us with your invaluable feedback and suggestions.

Inna Ward
Editor-in-Chief

Whitaker's Almanack
38 Soho Square
London
W1D 3HB

Email: whitakers@acblack.com
Web: www.whitakersalmanack.com

THE YEAR 2006

CHRONOLOGICAL CYCLES AND ERAS

Dominical Letter	A
Epact	30
Golden Number (Lunar Cycle)	XII
Julian Period	6719
Roman Indiction	14
Solar Cycle	27

	Beginning
Japanese year Heisei 18	1 January
Chinese year of the Dog	29 January
Regnal year 55	6 February
Hindu new year	30 March
Indian (Saka) year 1928	30 March
Muslim year AH 1427*	30 January
Sikh new year	14 March
Jewish year AM 5767*	22 September
Roman year 2759 AUC	

* Year begins at sunset

RELIGIOUS CALENDARS

CHRISTIAN

Epiphany	6 January
Presentation of Christ in the Temple	2 February
Ash Wednesday	1 March
The Annunciation	25 March
Maundy Thursday	13 April
Good Friday	14 April
Easter Day (western churches)	16 April
Easter Day (Eastern Orthodox)	23 April
Rogation Sunday	21 May
Ascension Day	25 May
Pentecost (Whit Sunday)	4 June
Trinity Sunday	11 June
Corpus Christi	15 June
All Saints' Day	1 November
Advent Sunday	3 December
Christmas Day	25 December

HINDU

Makara Sankranti	14 January
Vasant Panchami (Sarasvati-puja)	2 February
Mahashivaratri	26 February
Holi	14 March
Chaitra (Hindu new year)	30 March
Ramanavami	6 April
Raksha-bandhan	9 August
Janmashtami	15 August
Ganesh Chaturthi, first day	27 August
Ganesh festival, last day	6 September
Durga-puja	23 September
Navaratri festival, first day	23 September
Sarasvati-puja	1 October
Dasara	2 October
Diwali, first day	19 November
Diwali, last day	24 November

JEWISH

Purim,	14 March
Passover, first day	13 April
Feast of Weeks, first day	2 June
Jewish new year, first day	23 September
Yom Kippur (Day of Atonement)	2 October
Feast of Tabernacles, first day	7 October
Chanucah, first day	16 December

MUSLIM

Muslim new year	31 January
Ramadan, first day	24 September

SIKH

Birthday of Guru Gobind Singh Ji	5 January
Baisakhi Mela (Sikh new year)	14 March
Martyrdom of Guru Arjan Dev Ji	16 June
Birthday of Guru Nanak Dev Ji	5 November
Martyrdom of Guru Tegh Bahadur Ji	24 November

CIVIL CALENDAR

Accession of Queen Elizabeth II	6 February
Duke of York's birthday	19 February
St David's Day	1 March
Earl of Wessex birthday	10 March
Commonwealth Day	13 March
St Patrick's Day	17 March
Birthday of Queen Elizabeth II	21 April
St George's Day	23 April
Europe Day	9 May
Coronation of Queen Elizabeth II	2 June
Duke of Edinburgh's birthday	10 June
The Queen's Official Birthday	17 June
Princess Royal's birthday	15 August
Lord Mayor's Day	11 November
Remembrance Sunday	12 November
Prince of Wales's birthday	14 November
Wedding Day of Queen Elizabeth II	20 November
St Andrew's Day	30 November

LEGAL CALENDAR

LAW TERMS

Hilary Term	11 January to 12 April
Easter Term	25 April to 26 May
Trinity Term	6 June to 31 July
Michaelmas Term	2 October to 21 December

QUARTER DAYS

England, Wales and Northern Ireland

Lady	25 March
Midsummer	24 June
Michaelmas	29 September
Christmas	25 December

TERM DAYS

Scotland

Candlemas	28 February
Whitsunday	28 May
Lammas	28 August
Martinmas	28 November

2006

JANUARY					
Sunday	1	8	15	22	29
Monday	2	9	16	23	30
Tuesday	3	10	17	24	31
Wednesday	4	11	18	25	
Thursday	5	12	19	26	
Friday	6	13	20	27	
Saturday	7	14	21	28	

FEBRUARY					
Sunday		5	12	19	26
Monday		6	13	20	27
Tuesday		7	14	21	28
Wednesday	1	8	15	22	
Thursday	2	9	16	23	
Friday	3	10	17	24	
Saturday	4	11	18	25	

MARCH					
Sunday		5	12	19	26
Monday		6	13	20	27
Tuesday		7	14	21	28
Wednesday	1	8	15	22	29
Thursday	2	9	16	23	30
Friday	3	10	17	24	31
Saturday	4	11	18	25	

APRIL					
Sunday		2	9	16	23	30
Monday		3	10	17	24	
Tuesday		4	11	18	25	
Wednesday		5	12	19	26	
Thursday		6	13	20	27	
Friday		7	14	21	28	
Saturday	1	8	15	22	29	

MAY					
Sunday		7	14	21	28
Monday	1	8	15	22	29
Tuesday	2	9	16	23	30
Wednesday	3	10	17	24	31
Thursday	4	11	18	25	
Friday	5	12	19	26	
Saturday	6	13	20	27	

JUNE					
Sunday		4	11	18	25
Monday		5	12	19	26
Tuesday		6	13	20	27
Wednesday		7	14	21	28
Thursday	1	8	15	22	29
Friday	2	9	16	23	30
Saturday	3	10	17	24	

JULY					
Sunday		2	9	16	23	30
Monday		3	10	17	24	31
Tuesday		4	11	18	25	
Wednesday		5	12	19	26	
Thursday		6	13	20	27	
Friday		7	14	21	28	
Saturday	1	8	15	22	29	

AUGUST					
Sunday		6	13	20	27
Monday		7	14	21	28
Tuesday	1	8	15	22	29
Wednesday	2	9	16	23	30
Thursday	3	10	17	24	31
Friday	4	11	18	25	
Saturday	5	12	19	26	

SEPTEMBER					
Sunday		3	10	17	24
Monday		4	11	18	25
Tuesday		5	12	19	26
Wednesday		6	13	20	27
Thursday		7	14	21	28
Friday	1	8	15	22	29
Saturday	2	9	16	23	30

OCTOBER					
Sunday	1	8	15	22	29
Monday	2	9	16	23	30
Tuesday	3	10	17	24	31
Wednesday	4	11	18	25	
Thursday	5	12	19	26	
Friday	6	13	20	27	
Saturday	7	14	21	28	

NOVEMBER					
Sunday		5	12	19	26
Monday		6	13	20	27
Tuesday		7	14	21	28
Wednesday	1	8	15	22	29
Thursday	2	9	16	23	30
Friday	3	10	17	24	
Saturday	4	11	18	25	

DECEMBER					
Sunday		3	10	17	24	31
Monday		4	11	18	25	
Tuesday		5	12	19	26	
Wednesday		6	13	20	27	
Thursday		7	14	21	28	
Friday	1	8	15	22	29	
Saturday	2	9	16	23	30	

PUBLIC HOLIDAYS

	England and Wales	Scotland	Northern Ireland
New Year	† 2 January	2, †3 January	† 2 January
St Patrick's Day	–	–	‡ 17 March
* Good Friday	14 April	14 April	14 April
Easter Monday	17 April	–	17 April
Early May	† 1 May	1 May	† 1 May
Spring	29 May	† 29 May	29 May
Battle of the Boyne	–	–	‡ 12 July
Summer	28 August	7 August	28 August
* Christmas	25, 26 December	25, †26 December	25, 26 December

* In England, Wales and Northern Ireland, Christmas Day and Good Friday are common law holidays
In the Channel Islands, Liberation Day is a bank and public holiday
† Subject to royal proclamation
‡ Subject to proclamation by the Secretary of State for Northern Ireland

2007

JANUARY
Sunday			7	14	21	28
Monday	1	8	15	22	29	
Tuesday	2	9	16	23	30	
Wednesday	3	10	17	24	31	
Thursday	4	11	18	25		
Friday	5	12	19	26		
Saturday	6	13	20	27		

FEBRUARY
Sunday		4	11	18	25
Monday		5	12	19	26
Tuesday		6	13	20	27
Wednesday		7	14	21	28
Thursday	1	8	15	22	
Friday	2	9	16	23	
Saturday	3	10	17	24	

MARCH
Sunday		4	11	18	25
Monday		5	12	19	26
Tuesday		6	13	20	27
Wednesday		7	14	21	28
Thursday	1	8	15	22	29
Friday	2	9	16	23	30
Saturday	3	10	17	24	31

APRIL
Sunday	1	8	15	22	29
Monday	2	9	16	23	30
Tuesday	3	10	17	24	
Wednesday	4	11	18	25	
Thursday	5	12	19	26	
Friday	6	13	20	27	
Saturday	7	14	21	28	

MAY
Sunday		6	13	20	27
Monday		7	14	21	28
Tuesday	1	8	15	22	29
Wednesday	2	9	16	23	30
Thursday	3	10	17	24	31
Friday	4	11	18	25	
Saturday	5	12	19	26	

JUNE
Sunday		3	10	17	24
Monday		4	11	18	25
Tuesday		5	12	19	26
Wednesday		6	13	20	27
Thursday		7	14	21	28
Friday	1	8	15	22	29
Saturday	2	9	16	23	30

JULY
Sunday	1	8	15	22	29
Monday	2	9	16	23	30
Tuesday	3	10	17	24	31
Wednesday	4	11	18	25	
Thursday	5	12	19	26	
Friday	6	13	20	27	
Saturday	7	14	21	28	

AUGUST
Sunday		5	12	19	26
Monday		6	13	20	27
Tuesday		7	14	21	28
Wednesday	1	8	15	22	29
Thursday	2	9	16	23	30
Friday	3	10	17	24	31
Saturday	4	11	18	25	

SEPTEMBER
Sunday		2	9	16	23	30
Monday		3	10	17	24	
Tuesday		4	11	18	25	
Wednesday		5	12	19	26	
Thursday		6	13	20	27	
Friday		7	14	21	28	
Saturday	1	8	15	22	29	

OCTOBER
Sunday			7	14	21	28
Monday	1	8	15	22	29	
Tuesday	2	9	16	23	30	
Wednesday	3	10	17	24	31	
Thursday	4	11	18	25		
Friday	5	12	19	26		
Saturday	6	13	20	27		

NOVEMBER
Sunday		4	11	18	25
Monday		5	12	19	26
Tuesday		6	13	20	27
Wednesday		7	14	21	28
Thursday	1	8	15	22	29
Friday	2	9	16	23	30
Saturday	3	10	17	24	

DECEMBER
Sunday		2	9	16	23	30
Monday		3	10	17	24	31
Tuesday		4	11	18	25	
Wednesday		5	12	19	26	
Thursday		6	13	20	27	
Friday		7	14	21	28	
Saturday	1	8	15	22	29	

PUBLIC HOLIDAYS

	England and Wales	*Scotland*	*Northern Ireland*
New Year	† 1 January	1, †2 January	† 1 January
St Patrick's Day	–	–	‡ 17 March
* Good Friday	6 April	6 April	6 April
Easter Monday	9 April	–	9 April
Early May	† 7 May	7 May	† 7 May
Spring	28 May	† 28 May	28 May
Battle of the Boyne	–	–	‡ 12 July
Summer	27 August	6 August	27 August
* Christmas	25, 26 December	25, †26 December	25, 26 December

* In England, Wales and Northern Ireland, Christmas Day and Good Friday are common law holidays
In the Channel Islands, Liberation Day is a bank and public holiday
† Subject to royal proclamation
‡ Subject to proclamation by the Secretary of State for Northern Ireland

FORTHCOMING EVENTS

* Provisional dates
† Venue not confirmed

JANUARY

6–15	London Boat Show, Excel, London Docklands
11–29	London International Mime Festival
14	Russian Winter Festival, Trafalgar Square, London
17–19	UK Dance Championships, Bournemouth International Centre
18–22	London Art Fair, Business Design Centre, London
24–29	World Social Forum, various venues
28–5 February	MCN London Motorcycle Show, Alexandra Palace, London
29	Chinese New Year Celebrations, London

FEBRUARY

10–12	Labour Party Spring Conference, Blackpool
10–19	Leicester Comedy Festival
27–6 March	Kinofilm – Manchester International Short Film Festival

MARCH

2	World Book Day
3–5	Liberal Democrat Party Spring Conference, Harrogate
4–12	Bath Literature Festival
4–18 June	Designer of the Year Exhibition, Design Museum, London
5–7	London Book Fair, Excel, London Docklands
8	International Women's Day
8–2 April	Ideal Home Show, Earls Court, London
9–12	Crufts Dog Show, NEC, Birmingham
10–19	National Science Week
22–28	BADA Antiques and Fine Art Fair, Duke of York Square, London
25–2 April	The Sunday Times Oxford Literary Festival

APRIL

April–September	Chichester Festival Theatre season
20–23	Chelsea Art Fair, Chelsea Old Town Hall

MAY

12–14	Battersea Contemporary Art Fair
12–28 October	Pitlochry Festival Theatre season
18–28	Royal Society of British Artists Exhibition, Mall Galleries, London

19–4 June	Bath International Music Festival
19–27 August	Glyndebourne Festival Opera season
23–27	Chelsea Flower Show, Royal Hospital, Chelsea
26–4 June	The Hay Festival, Hay-on-Wye, Hereford

JUNE

9–25	The Aldeburgh Festival of Music and the Arts, Snape
12–20 August	Royal Academy of Arts Summer Exhibition
17	Trooping the Colour, Horseguards Parade, London
30–16 July	Cheltenham Music Festival

JULY

2–5	The Royal Show, National Agricultural Centre, Stoneleigh Park
4–9	Hampton Court Palace Flower Show, Surrey
7–15	York Early Music Festival
7–23	Buxton Festival, Derbyshire
14–9 September	BBC Promenade Concerts, Royal Albert Hall, London
19–23	RHS Flower Show, Tatton Park, Cheshire
20–29	The Welsh Proms, St David's Hall, Cardiff
*27–30	Cambridge Folk Festival
*28–30	WOMAD Festival, Rivermead, Reading
28–6 August	Edinburgh Jazz and Blues Festival

AUGUST

4–26	Edinburgh Military Tattoo, Edinburgh Castle
5–12	Royal National Eisteddfod of Wales, Swansea
6–11	Three Choirs Festival, Hereford
13–3 September	Edinburgh International Festival
22–24	Wisley Flower Show, RHS Garden, Wisley
26–28	Notting Hill Carnival, Notting Hill, London
26–28	Town and Country Festival, National Agricultural Centre, Stoneleigh Park

SEPTEMBER

1–5 November	Blackpool Illuminations, Promenade
2	Braemar Royal Highland Gathering, Aberdeenshire
8	International Literacy Day
11–14	TUC Annual Congress, Brighton Centre, Brighton

15–24	Southampton Boat Show, Mayflower Park, Southampton
16–21	Liberal Democrat Party Autumn Conference, Brighton
16–26 November	Liverpool Biennial International Festival of Contemporary Art
24–28	Labour Party Conference, Manchester

OCTOBER

October–January	Turner Prize Exhibition, Tate Britain, London
2–5	Conservative Party Conference, Bournemouth
5	National Poetry Day
12–16	Frieze Art Fair, Regent's Park, London
Mid-October	Man Booker Prize
*18–2 November	London Film Festival, NFT and other venues
*27–29	Classic Motor Show, NEC, Birmingham

NOVEMBER

5	London to Brighton Veteran Car Run
11	Lord Mayor's Procession and Show, City of London
*16–23	Northern Lights Film Festival, Newcastle
17–27	Huddersfield Contemporary Music Festival
*27–28	CBI Annual Conference, Business Design Centre, London

SPORTS EVENTS

JANUARY

| 15–22 | Snooker: Masters, Wembley Conference Centre |

FEBRUARY

4	Rugby Union: Six Nations Championship, Ireland v. Italy, Lansdowne Road
4	Rugby Union: Six Nations Championship, England v. Wales, Twickenham
5	Rugby Union: Six Nations Championship, Scotland v. France, Murrayfield
10–26	Olympic Winter Games, Torino, Italy
11	Rugby Union: Six Nations Championship, France v. Ireland, Stade de France
11	Rugby Union: Six Nations Championship, Italy v. England, Stadio Flaminio
12	Rugby Union: Six Nations Championship, Wales v. Scotland, Millennium Stadium
25	Rugby Union: Six Nations Championship, France v. Italy, Stade de France

| 25 | Rugby Union: Six Nations Championship, Scotland v. England, Murrayfield |
| 26 | Rugby Union: Six Nations Championship, Ireland v. Wales, Lansdowne Road |

MARCH

11	Rugby Union: Six Nations Championship, Wales v. Italy, Millennium Stadium
11	Rugby Union: Six Nations Championship, Ireland v. Scotland, Lansdowne Road
12	Rugby Union: Six Nations Championship, France v. England, Stade de France
15–26	Commonwealth Games, Melbourne, Australia
18	Rugby Union: Six Nations Championship, Italy v. Scotland, Stadio Flaminio
18	Rugby Union: Six Nations Championship, Wales v. France, Millennium Stadium
18	Rugby Union: Six Nations Championship, England v. Ireland, Twickenham

APRIL

2	Oxford and Cambridge Boat Race, Putney to Mortlake, London
15–1 May	Snooker: World Championship, Crucible Theatre, Sheffield
23	Athletics: Flora London Marathon

MAY

4–7	Mitsubishi Motors Badminton Horse Trials, Badminton
7	Football: Welsh FA Cup Final†
10	Football: UEFA Cup Final, Eindhoven, The Netherlands
11–14	Royal Windsor Horse Show, Home Park, Windsor
13	Football: The FA Cup Final, Wembley Stadium, London
13	Football: Scottish FA Cup Final, Hampden Park, Glasgow
17	Football: UEFA Champions League Final, Paris, France
20	Rugby Union: Heineken Cup Final, Millennium Stadium, Cardiff
27–9 June	TT Motorcycle Races, Isle of Man

JUNE

9–9 July	Football: FIFA World Cup, Germany
19–24	British Amateur Golf Championship, Royal St Georges Golf Club
25–2 July	Sailing: Rolex Commordores' Cup, Cowes, Isle of Wight
26–9 July	Tennis: Wimbledon Championship, All England Lawn Tennis Club, London

JULY

8–22	Shooting: NRA Imperial Meeting, Bisley Camp, Surrey
14–16	British Formula 1 Grand Prix, Silverstone, Northants
20–23	Golf: The Open Championship, Royal Liverpool Golf Club
29–5 August	Sailing: Skandia Cowes Week, Isle of Wight

AUGUST

3–6	Golf: The Women's British Open, Royal Lytham & St Annes Golf Club
26	Rugby League: Challenge Cup Final, Wembley Stadium, London

SEPTEMBER

7–10	Burghley Horse Trials, Stamford, Lincolnshire
*18	Athletics: Great North Run, Newcastle upon Tyne
22–24	Golf: The Ryder Cup, County Kildare, Ireland

OCTOBER

4–8	Horse of the Year Show, NEC, Birmingham

HORSE RACING

25 March	Lincoln Handicap, Doncaster
6–8 April	Grand National, Aintree, Liverpool
6 May	Two Thousand Guineas, Newmarket
7 May	One Thousand Guineas, Newmarket
2 June	The Oaks, Epsom Downs
2 June	Coronation Cup, Epsom Downs
3 June	The Derby, Epsom Downs
*20–24 June	Royal Ascot
*29 July	King George VI and Queen Elizabeth Diamond Stakes, Ascot
9 September	St Leger†
28–30 September	Cambridgeshire Meeting, Newmarket
12–14 October	Champions Meeting, Newmarket

CRICKET

12 August	Twenty20 Cup Final, Trent Bridge
26 August	C&G Trophy Final, Lord's

Npower Test Match Series

11–15 May	England v. Sri Lanka, 1st, Lord's
25–29 May	England v. Sri Lanka, 2nd, Edgbaston
2–6 June	England v. Sri Lanka, 3rd, Trent Bridge

Twenty20 International

15 June	England v. Sri Lanka, Rose Bowl

NatWest Series

17 June	England v. Sri Lanka, 1st, Lord's
20 June	England v. Sri Lanka, 2nd, The Oval
24 June	England v. Sri Lanka, 3rd, Riverside
28 June	England v. Sri Lanka, 4th, Old Trafford
1 July	England v. Sri Lanka, 5th, Headingley

Npower Test Match Series

13–17 July	England v. Pakistan, 1st, Lord's
27–31 July	England v. Pakistan, 2nd, Old Trafford
4–8 August	England v. Pakistan, 3rd, Headingley
17–21 August	England v. Pakistan, 4th, The Oval

Twenty20 International

28 August	England v. Pakistan, Bristol

NatWest Series

30 August	England v. Pakistan, 1st, Cardiff
2 September	England v. Pakistan, 2nd, Lord's
5 September	England v. Pakistan, 3rd, Rose Bowl
8 September	England v. Pakistan, 4th, Trent Bridge
10 September	England v. Pakistan, 5th, Edgbaston

THE UNITED KINGDOM

THE UK IN FIGURES

The United Kingdom comprises Great Britain (England, Wales and Scotland) and Northern Ireland. The Isle of Man and the Channel Islands are Crown dependencies with their own legislative systems, and not a part of the United Kingdom.

AREA OF THE UNITED KINGDOM	sq. km
United Kingdom	242,514
England	130,281
Wales	20,732
Scotland	77,925
Northern Ireland	13,576

Source: ONS – Annual Abstract of Statistics 2005 (Crown copyright)

POPULATION

The first official census of population in England, Wales and Scotland was taken in 1801 and a census has been taken every ten years since, except in 1941 when there was no census because of war. The last official census in the United Kingdom was taken on 29 April 2001 and the next is due in April 2011.

The first official census of population in Ireland was taken in 1841. However, all figures given below refer only to the area which is now Northern Ireland. Figures for Northern Ireland in 1921 and 1931 are estimates

based on the censuses taken in 1926 and 1937 respectively.

Estimates of the population of England before 1801, calculated from the number of baptisms, burials and marriages, are:

1570	4,160,221	1670	5,773,646
1600	4,811,718	1700	6,045,008
1630	5,600,517	1750	6,517,035

For further details see www.statistics.gov.uk

CENSUS RESULTS 1801–2001 (thousands)

	United Kingdom			England and Wales			Scotland			Northern Ireland		
	Total	Male	Female	Total	Male	Female	Total	Male	Female	Total	Male	Female
1801	—	—	—	8,893	4,255	4,638	1,608	739	869	—	—	—
1811	13,368	6,368	7,000	10,165	4,874	5,291	1,806	826	980	—	—	—
1821	15,472	7,498	7,974	12,000	5,850	6,150	2,092	983	1,109	—	—	—
1831	17,835	8,647	9,188	13,897	6,771	7,126	2,364	1,114	1,250	—	—	—
1841	20,183	9,819	10,364	15,914	7,778	8,137	2,620	1,242	1,378	1,649	800	849
1851	22,259	10,855	11,404	17,928	8,781	9,146	2,889	1,376	1,513	1,443	698	745
1861	24,525	11,894	12,631	20,066	9,776	10,290	3,062	1,450	1,612	1,396	668	728
1871	27,431	13,309	14,122	22,712	11,059	11,653	3,360	1,603	1,757	1,359	647	712
1881	31,015	15,060	15,955	25,974	12,640	13,335	3,736	1,799	1,936	1,305	621	684
1891	34,264	16,593	17,671	29,003	14,060	14,942	4,026	1,943	2,083	1,236	590	646
1901	38,237	18,492	19,745	32,528	15,729	16,799	4,472	2,174	2,298	1,237	590	647
1911	42,082	20,357	21,725	36,070	17,446	18,625	4,761	2,309	2,452	1,251	603	648
1921	44,027	21,033	22,994	37,887	18,075	19,811	4,882	2,348	2,535	1,258	610	648
1931	46,038	22,060	23,978	39,952	19,133	20,819	4,843	2,326	2,517	1,243	601	642
1951	50,225	24,118	26,107	43,758	21,016	22,742	5,096	2,434	2,662	1,371	668	703
1961	52,709	25,481	27,228	46,105	22,304	23,801	5,179	2,483	2,697	1,425	694	731
1971	55,515	26,952	28,562	48,750	23,683	25,067	5,229	2,515	2,714	1,536	755	781
1981	55,848	27,104	28,742	49,155	23,873	25,281	5,131	2,466	2,664	*1,533	750	783
1991	56,467	27,344	29,123	49,890	24,182	25,707	4,999	2,392	2,607	1,578	769	809
2001	58,789	28,581	30,208	52,042	25,327	26,715	5,062	2,432	2,630	1,685	821	864

* Figure includes 44,500 non-enumerated persons
Source: ONS – Census Reports (Crown copyright)

RESIDENT POPULATION: 2003 ESTIMATES AND FUTURE PROJECTIONS (MID-YEAR) (thousands)

	United Kingdom			England and Wales			Scotland			Northern Ireland		
	Total	Male	Female	Total	Male	Female	Total	Male	Female	Total	Male	Female
2003	59,554	29,108	30,446	52,794	25,841	26,953	5,057	2,435	2,623	1,703	833	870
2006	60,254	29,514	30,740	53,463	26,231	27,232	5,068	2,441	2,628	1,723	843	880
2011	61,401	30,160	31,241	54,615	26,880	27,735	5,034	2,423	2,611	1,753	857	895
2021	63,835	31,432	32,403	57,060	28,168	28,892	4,963	2,380	2,583	1,811	884	928
2026	64,902	31,995	32,947	58,163	28,718	29,445	4,907	2,346	2,562	1,832	891	940

Source: ONS – Annual Abstract of Statistics 2005 (Crown copyright)

ISLANDS: CENSUS RESULTS 1901–2001

	Isle of Man			Jersey			*Guernsey		
	Total	Male	Female	Total	Male	Female	Total	Male	Female;
1901	54,752	25,496	29,256	52,576	23,940	28,636	40,446	19,652	20,794
1911	52,016	23,937	28,079	51,898	24,014	27,884	41,858	20,661	21,197
1921	60,284	27,329	32,955	49,701	22,438	27,263	38,315	18,246	20,069
1931	49,308	22,443	26,865	50,462	23,424	27,038	40,643	19,659	20,984
1951	55,123	25,749	29,464	57,296	27,282	30,014	43,652	21,221	22,431
1961	48,151	22,060	26,091	57,200	27,200	30,000	45,068	21,671	23,397
1971	56,289	26,461	29,828	72,532	35,423	37,109	51,458	24,792	26,666
1981	64,679	30,901	33,778	77,000	37,000	40,000	53,313	25,701	27,612
1991	69,788	33,693	36,095	84,082	40,862	43,220	58,867	28,297	30,570
2001	76,315	37,372	38,943	87,186	42,485	44,701	59,807	29,138	30,669

* Population of Guernsey, Herm, Jethou and Lithou

Figures for 1901–71 record all persons present on census night; census figures for 1981–2001 record all persons resident in the islands on census night. The 2001 population census also recorded the population of Alderney as 2,294 and an informal census of Sark gave its population as 591.

Source: ONS – Census Reports (Crown copyright)

RESIDENT POPULATION

BY AGE AND SEX 2003 (MID-YEAR ESTIMATES)
Thousands

Age Range	Males	Females
Under 1	349	331
1–4	1,384	1,319
5–9	1,869	1,781
10–14	1,995	1,896
15–19	1,983	1,873
20–29	3,697	3,682
30–44	6,701	6,817
45–59	5,653	5,771
60–64	1,439	1,504
65–74	2,354	2,651
75–84	1,371	2,030
85+	313	791

Source: ONS – Annual Abstract of Statistics 2005 (Crown copyright)

BY ETHNIC GROUP AVERAGE SPRING 2002 – WINTER 2002/3

Ethnic group	Estimated population (thousands)
White	
British*	51,010
Other*	1,946
Mixed	
White and Black Caribbean	234
White and Black African	72
White and Asian	129
Other Mixed	74
Asian	
Indian	1,016
Pakistani	718
Bangladeshi	273
Other Asian	302
Black	
Black Caribbean	584
Black African	541
Black Other	59
Chinese	199
Other	458
All†	59,330

* Data excludes Northern Ireland as detailed level ethnicity questions are not asked of the White group in Northern Ireland
† Includes ethnic group not stated

Source: ONS – Annual Abstract of Statistics 2005 (Crown copyright)

IMMIGRATION

ACCEPTANCES FOR SETTLEMENT IN THE UK BY NATIONALITY
(Country specified only when the figure is over 1,000)

Region	Number of persons	
	2002	2003
Europe: total*	11,740	15,390
Poland	875	1,310
Turkey	2,920	4,340
Russia†	1,365	2,180
Serbia and Montenegro‡	1,540	1,140
Americas: total	11,680	16,735
Canada	1,300	1,730
Colombia	805	1,045
Jamaica	2,675	4,500
USA	4,355	5,695
Africa: total	39,165	45,835
Dem. Rep. Congo	1,260	1,475
Ghana	2,585	4,065
Kenya	1,055	1,600
Nigeria	5,325	7,695
Sierra Leone	855	1,380
Somalia	10,000	6,820
South Africa	6.135	8,930
Zimbabwe	3,530	3,510
Asia: total	46,585	55,190
Indian sub-continent: total	24,665	30,190
Bangladesh	4,725	5,610
India	8,005	11,460
Pakistan	11,935	13,120
Middle East: total	5,345	4,985
Iran	1,715	1,545
Iraq	1,955	1,415
Remainder of Asia: total	16,575	20,015
China	1,705	2,575
Japan	1,785	1,875
Philippines	1,505	3,845
Sri Lanka	2,935	2,560
Thailand	1,335	2,030
Oceania: total	6,250	7,185
Australia	3,500	4,160
New Zealand	2,645	2,940
British Overseas Citizens	330	830
Stateless§	215	320
All nationalities	115,965	141,490

* Excluding European Economic Area nationals
† Includes holders of passports of the former Soviet Union
‡ Includes holders of passports of the former Yugoslavia
§ Includes refugees from South East Asia

Source: ONS – Annual Abstract of Statistics 2005 (Crown copyright)

BIRTHS

2003

	Live births	Male	Female	Birth rate*
United Kingdom	696,000	357,000	339,000	11.7
England and Wales	621,000	318,000	303,000	11.8
Scotland	52,000	27,000	26,000	10.4
Northern Ireland	22,000	11,000	10,000	12.7

* Live births per 1,000 population
Source: ONS – Annual Abstract of Statistics 2005 (Crown copyright)

LEGAL ABORTIONS

	2000	2003
England and Wales	175,542	181,582
Scotland	11,997	12,217*

* provisional data
Source: ONS – Annual Abstract of Statistics 2005 (Crown copyright)

DEATHS

2003

Males	Deaths	Death Rate*
United Kingdom	288,604	9.9
England and Wales	253,852	
Scotland	27,832	
Northern Ireland	6,920	
Females		
United Kingdom	322,584	10.6
England and Wales	284,402	
Scotland	30,640	
Northern Ireland	7,542	

* per 1,000 population
Sources: ONS – Annual Abstract of Statistics 2005 (Crown copyright)

INFANT MORTALITY 2003
Deaths of infants under 1 year of age per 1,000 live births

	Number
United Kingdom	5.3
England and Wales	5.3
Scotland	5.1
Northern Ireland	5.2

Source: ONS – Annual Abstract of Statistics 2005 (Crown copyright)

MARRIAGE AND DIVORCE

2003

	Marriages	Divorces
United Kingdom	306,214*	166,737
England and Wales	267,700*	153,490
Scotland	30,757*	10,928
Northern Ireland	7,757*	2,319

* Provisional data
Source: ONS – Annual Abstract of Statistics 2005 (Crown copyright)

ENVIRONMENT

ESTIMATED TOTAL EMISSIONS OF GREENHOUSE GASES ON IPCC BASIS*
Million tonnes (Carbon dioxide equivalent[†])

	1990	1995	2000	2002
Carbon dioxide	603.6	564.0	557.9	551.0
Methane	76.9	64.3	48.8	44.1
Nitrous oxide	67.9	57.0	44.8	41.0
Hydrofluorocarbons	11.38	15.49	9.08	10.42
Perfluorocarbons	1.39	0.46	0.54	0.38
Sulphur hexafluoride	1.08	1.29	1.85	1.59
Total	762	703	663	648
1990 Baseline[‡]	766	—	—	—
Percentage change from 1990 baseline	—	−8.2	−13.4	−15.3

* based on the methodology developed by the Intergovernmental Panel on Climate Change (IPCC)
† 12 tonnes of carbon is equivalent to 44 tonnes of carbon dioxide.
‡ The sum of 1990 totals for carbon dioxide, methane and nitrous oxide and 1995 totals for hydrofluorocarbons, perfluorocarbons and sulphur hexafluoride. Used for comparison with the Kyoto target.
Source: ONS – Annual Abstract of Statistics 2005 (Crown copyright)

MATERIALS COLLECTED FROM HOUSEHOLDS FOR RECYCLING (ENGLAND)
Thousand tonnes

	1996/7	2000/1	2002/3
Compost	279	798	1,187
Paper and card	600	934	1,125
Glass	311	397	471
Scrap metal and white goods	199	310	422
Co-mingled (separated after collection)	77	206	267
Textiles	32	45	54
Cans (ferrous and aluminium)	18	26	27
Plastics	6	13	13
Other*	2	84	176
Total	1,687	2,812	3,742

* Includes oils, batteries, aluminium foil, books and shoes
Source: ONS – Social Trends 2005 (Crown copyright)

HOUSEHOLDS

BY TYPE OF HOUSEHOLD AND FAMILY IN GREAT BRITAIN 2004
Percentages

One Person	
Under state pension age	14
Over state pension age	15
One family households	
Couple	
No children	29
1–2 dependent children	18
3 or more dependent children	4
Non-dependent children only	6
Lone parent	
Dependent children	7
Non-dependent children only	3
Two or more unrelated adults	3
Multi-family households	1
All Households (=100%) *(millions)*	24.1

Source: ONS – Social Trends 2005 (Crown copyright)

HOUSEHOLDS BY SIZE IN GREAT BRITAIN 2004
Percentages

One person	29
Two people	35
Three people	16
Four people	14
Five people	5
Six or more people	2
All households (=100%) *(millions)*	24.1
Average household size *(number of people)*	2.4

Source: ONS – *Social Trends 2005* (Crown copyright)

PERCENTAGE OF DEPENDENT CHILDREN LIVING IN
DIFFERENT FAMILY TYPES IN GREAT BRITAIN

	1992	2001	2004
Couple families			
1 child	17	17	17
2 children	38	37	37
3 or more children	27	24	23
Lone mother families			
1 child	5	6	7
2 children	6	8	9
3 or more children	5	6	6
Lone father families			
1 child	1	1	1
2 or more children	1	1	1

Source: ONS – *Social Trends 2005* (Crown copyright)

ADULTS LIVING WITH THEIR PARENTS BY AGE AND
GENDER (ENGLAND)
Percentages

	2002	2003	2004
Males			
20–24	55	55	58
25–29	20	22	24
30–34	9	9	10
Females			
20–24	39	38	39
25–29	11	11	12
30–34	3	4	4

Source: ONS – *Social Trends 2005* (Crown copyright)

HOUSEHOLDS WITH INTERNET ACCESS BY
HOUSEHOLD TYPE
Percentages

	1998/9	2002/3
One person		
Over state pension age	1	7
Under state pension age	8	36
Couple without children		
Over state pension age	2	21
Under state pension age	14	55
All other adults without children	16	57
Lone parent	5	35
Couple with children	16	69
All other adults with children	20	52

Source: ONS – *Social Trends 2004* (Crown copyright)

HOUSEHOLD COMPOSITION BY TENURE (2003/4)
Percentages

	Owned outright	Owned with mortgage	Rented from social sector	Rented privately
One person				
Under pensionable age	15	43	23	19
Over pensionable age	58	5	31	6
One family households				
Couple				
No children	45	36	10	9
Dependent children	9	70	15	7
Non-dependent children only	32	55	10	3
Lone parent				
Dependent children	7	29	50	15
Non-dependent children only	34	31	28	8
Other households	20	25	15	40
All households	29	40	20	11

Source: ONS – *Social Trends 2005* (Crown copyright)

HEALTH

LIFE EXPECTANCY 2003

Males	76.2 years
Females	80.5 years

DEATHS: BY CAUSE 2003

	England and Wales	Scotland	N. Ireland
Total Deaths	538,254	58,472	14,462
Deaths from natural causes	519,297	56,161	13,912
Certain infectious and parasitic diseases	4,763	660	157
ntestinal infectious diseases	1,063	85	13
Respiratory & other tuberculosis	451	59	11
Meningococcal infection	118	5	4
Viral hepatitis	209	23	–
AIDS (HIV – disease)	224	33	2
Neoplasms	139,360	15,412	3,882
Malignant neoplasms	135,955	15,116	3,757
Malignant neoplasm of oesophagus	6,427	776	154
Malignant neoplasm of stomach	5,285	579	165

Malignant neoplasm of colon	9,152	966	313
Malignant neoplasm of rectum and anus	3,982	368	103
Malignant neoplasm of pancreas	6,242	641	173
Malignant neoplasm of trachea, bronchus and lung	28,765	3,893	810
Malignant neoplasm of skin	1,585	146	40
Malignant neoplasm of breast	11,276	1,149	291
Malignant neoplasm of cervix uteri	951	120	31
Malignant neoplasm of prostate	9,166	786	217
Leukaemia	3,916	367	85
Diseases of the blood and blood-forming organs and certain disorders involving the immune mechanism	1,065	148	37
Endocrine, nutritional and metabolic diseases	8,016	958	246
Diabetes mellitus	6,316	709	190
Mental and behavioural disorders	14,846	2,637	341
Vascular and unspecified dementia	13,401	1,997	284
Alcohol abuse	469	356	52
Drug dependence and non-dependent abuse of drugs	655	228	3
Diseases of the nervous system and sense organs	15,793	1,303	481
Meningitis (including meningococcal)	229	19	3
Alzheimer's disease	5,055	354	224
Diseases of the circulatory system	205,508	22,102	5,448
Ischaemic heart diseases	99,790	11,441	2,843
Cerebrovascular diseases	57,808	6,497	1,531
Diseases of the respiratory system	75,138	7,454	2,082
Influenza	77	15	4
Pneumonia	34,400	2,859	1,025
Bronchitis, emphysema and other chronic obstructive pulmonary diseases	25,765	3,014	660
Asthma	1,284	98	32
Diseases of the digestive system	24,948	3,215	587
Gastric and duodenal ulcer	3,678	316	77
Chronic liver disease	5,844	1,170	156
Diseases of the skin and subcutaneous tissue	1,661	131	15
Diseases of the musculo-skeletal system and connective tissue	4,634	369	93
Rheumatoid arthritis and juvenile arthritis	907	103	26
Osteoporosis	1,583	70	16
Diseases of the genito-urinary system	9,120	1,056	327
Diseases of the kidney and ureter	4,135	670	225
Complications of pregnancy, childbirth and the puerperium	45	7	3
Certain conditions originating in the perinatal period (excluding neonatals)	207	149	62
Congenital malformations, deformations and chromosomal abnormalities (excluding neonatals)	1,299	172	69
Congenital malformations of the nervous system	142	23	12
Congenital malformations of the circulatory system	540	63	16
Symptoms, signs and abnormal findings not classified elsewhere	12,894	388	82
Senility without mention of psychosis (old age)	11,394	236	63
Sudden infant death syndrome	136	43	–
Deaths from external causes	16,693	2,311	550
All accidents	10,979	1,326	364
Land transport accidents	2,943	357	120
Accidental falls	2,732	668	44
Accidental poisonings	835	30	30
Suicide and intentional self-harm	3,270	560	132
Homicide and assault	318	101	30
Event of undetermined intent	1,776	234	12

Source: ONS – *Annual Abstract of Statistics 2005* (Crown copyright)

NOTIFICATIONS OF INFECTIONS DISEASES (UK)

	2002	2003
Measles	3,675	2,726
Mumps	2,333	4,565
Rubella	2,002	1,525
Whooping cough	1,051	509
Scarlet fever	2,749	3,252
Dysentery	1,167	1,144
Food poisoning	81,562	79,073
Typhoid and paratyphoid fevers	183	277
Hepatitis	5,035	5,203
Tuberculosis	7,239	6,863
Malaria	866	820

Source: ONS – Annual Abstract of Statistics 2005 (Crown copyright)

IMMUNISATION OF CHILDREN BY THEIR SECOND BIRTHDAY (UK)
Percentages

	1991/2	2003/4
Tetanus	94	94
Diphtheria	94	94
Poliomyelitis	94	94
Whooping cough	88	94
Measles, mumps, rubella (MMR)	90	81

Source: ONS – Social Trends 2005 (Crown copyright)

ADULTS EXCEEDING SPECIFIED LEVELS* OF ALCOHOL BY AGE AND GENDER 2003/4 (GREAT BRITAIN)
Percentages

	16–24	25–44	45–64	65+	All 16+
Males					
4–8 units	14	17	21	14	17
8+ units	37	30	20	6	23
4+ units	51	47	41	19	40
Females					
3–6 units	14	18	15	4	13
6+ units	26	13	5	1	9
3+ units	40	30	20	4	23

* On at least one day in the previous week. Current Department of Health advice is that consumption of between 3 and 4 units a day for men and between 2 and 3 units a day for women should not lead to significant health risks. A unit of alcohol is 8 grams by weight or 10ml by volume of pure alcohol, i.e. the amount contained in half a pint of ordinary strength beer or lager, a single pub measure of spirits or a small glass of ordinary strength wine.
Source: ONS – Social Trends 2005 (Crown copyright)

PREVALENCE OF DRUG MISUSE BY YOUNG ADULTS* BY DRUG CATEGORY AND GENDER 2002/3 (ENGLAND AND WALES)
Percentages

	Males	Females
Cannabis	32	21
Ecstasy	7	4
Cocaine	7	3
Amphetamines	4	3
Magic mushrooms or LSD	3	1
Cocaine	7	2
All Class A drugs†	11	6
Any drug‡	35	23

* aged 16–24 years
† Includes heroin, cocaine (powder and 'crack'), ecstasy, magic mushrooms, LSD and unprescribed use of methadone
‡ Includes drugs not listed in the table
Source: ONS – Social Trends 2005 (Crown copyright)

THE NATIONAL FLAG

The national flag of the United Kingdom is the Union Flag, generally known as the Union Jack.

The Union Flag is a combination of the cross of St George, patron saint of England, the cross of St Andrew, patron saint of Scotland, and a cross similar to that of St Patrick, patron saint of Ireland.

Cross of St George: cross Gules in a field Argent (red cross on a white ground)

Cross of St Andrew: saltire Argent in a field Azure (white diagonal cross on a blue ground)

Cross of St Patrick: saltire Gules in a field Argent (red diagonal cross on a white ground)

The Union Flag was first introduced in 1606 after the union of the kingdoms of England and Scotland under one sovereign. The cross of St Patrick was added in 1801 after the union of Great Britain and Ireland.

FLYING THE UNION FLAG

The correct orientation of the Union Flag when flying is with the broader diagonal band of white uppermost in the hoist (i.e. near the pole) and the narrower diagonal band of white uppermost in the fly (i.e. furthest from the pole).

It is the practice to fly the Union Flag daily on some customs houses. In all other cases, flags are flown on government buildings by command of The Queen. It is now customary for the Union Flag to be flown at Buckingham Palace, Windsor Castle and Sandringham when The Queen is not in residence.

The flying of the Union Flag on public buildings is decided by the Department for Culture, Media and Sport at The Queen's command. On the days appointed, the Union Flag is flown on government buildings in the United Kingdom from 8 a.m. to sunset.

FLAGS AT HALF-MAST

Flags are flown at half-mast (i.e. two-thirds up between the top and bottom of the flagstaff) on the following occasions:

(a) From the announcement of the death up to the funeral of the Sovereign, except on Proclamation Day, when flags are hoisted right up from 11 a.m. to sunset
(b) The funerals of members of the royal family, subject to special commands from The Queen in each case
(c) The funerals of foreign rulers, subject to special commands from The Queen in each case
(d) The funerals of prime ministers and ex-prime ministers of the UK, subject to special commands from The Queen in each case
(e) Other occasions by special command of The Queen

On occasions when days for flying flags coincide with days for flying flags at half-mast, the following rules are observed. Flags are flown:

(a) although a member of the royal family, or a near relative of the royal family, may be lying dead, unless special commands are received from The Queen to the contrary
(b) although it may be the day of the funeral of a foreign ruler

If the body of a very distinguished subject is lying at a government office, the flag may fly at half-mast on that office until the body has left (provided it is a day on which the flag would fly) and then the flag is to be hoisted right up. On all other government buildings the flag will fly as usual.

THE ROYAL STANDARD

The Royal Standard is hoisted only when The Queen is actually present in the building, and never when Her Majesty is passing in procession.

DAYS FOR FLYING FLAGS

Birthday of The Countess of Wessex	20 January
The Queen's Accession	6 February
Birthday of The Duke of York	19 February
*St David's Day (in Wales only)	1 March
Birthday of The Earl of Wessex	10 March
**Commonwealth Day (2006)	13 March
Birthday of The Queen	21 April
*St George's Day (in England only)	23 April
†Europe Day	9 May
Coronation Day	2 June
Birthday of The Duke of Edinburgh	10 June
The Queen's Official Birthday (2006)	17 June
Birthday of The Princess Royal	15 August
Remembrance Sunday (2006)	12 November
Birthday of The Prince of Wales	14 November
The Queen's Wedding Day	20 November
*St Andrew's Day (in Scotland only)	30 November
‡The opening of Parliament by The Queen	
‡The prorogation of Parliament by The Queen	

* Where a building has two or more flagstaffs, the appropriate national flag may be flown in addition to the Union Flag, but not in a superior position
** Commonwealth Day is always the second Monday in March
† The Union Flag should fly alongside the European flag. On government buildings that have only one flagpole, the Union Flag should take precedence
‡ Flags are flown whether or not The Queen performs the ceremony in person. Flags are flown only in the Greater London area

THE ROYAL FAMILY

THE SOVEREIGN

ELIZABETH II, by the Grace of God, of the United Kingdom of Great Britain and Northern Ireland and of her other Realms and Territories Queen, Head of the Commonwealth, Defender of the Faith
Her Majesty Elizabeth Alexandra Mary of Windsor, elder daughter of King George VI and of HM Queen Elizabeth the Queen Mother
Born 21 April 1926, at 17 Bruton Street, London W1
Ascended the throne 6 February 1952
Crowned 2 June 1953, at Westminster Abbey
Married 20 November 1947, in Westminster Abbey, HRH The Prince Philip, Duke of Edinburgh
Official residences: Buckingham Palace, London SW1A 1AA; Windsor Castle, Berks; Palace of Holyroodhouse, Edinburgh
Private residences: Sandringham, Norfolk; Balmoral Castle, Aberdeenshire

HUSBAND OF THE QUEEN

HRH THE PRINCE PHILIP, DUKE OF EDINBURGH, KG, KT, OM, GBE, AC, QSO, PC, Ranger of Windsor Park
Born 10 June 1921, son of Prince and Princess Andrew of Greece and Denmark, naturalised a British subject 1947, created Duke of Edinburgh, Earl of Merioneth and Baron Greenwich 1947

CHILDREN OF THE QUEEN

HRH THE PRINCE OF WALES (Prince Charles Philip Arthur George), KG, KT, GCB, OM and Great Master of the Order of the Bath, AK, QSO, PC, ADC(P)
Born 14 November 1948, created Prince of Wales and Earl of Chester 1958, succeeded as Duke of Cornwall, Duke of Rothesay, Earl of Carrick and Baron Renfrew, Lord of the Isles and Great Steward of Scotland 1952
Married (1) 29 July 1981 Lady Diana Frances Spencer (Diana, Princess of Wales (1961–97), youngest daughter of the 8th Earl Spencer and the Hon. Mrs Shand Kydd), marriage dissolved 1996; (2) 9 April 2005 Mrs Camilla Rosemary Parker Bowles, now HRH The Duchess of Cornwall (*born* 17 July 1947, daughter of Major Bruce Shand and the Hon. Mrs Rosalind Shand)
Issue:
(1) HRH Prince William of Wales (Prince William Arthur Philip Louis), *born* 21 June 1982
(2) HRH Prince Henry of Wales (Prince Henry Charles Albert David), *born* 15 September 1984
Residences of the Prince of Wales: Clarence House, London SW1A 1BA; Highgrove, Doughton, Tetbury, Glos GL8 8TN; Birkhall, Ballater, Aberdeenshire

HRH THE PRINCESS ROYAL (Princess Anne Elizabeth Alice Louise), KG, KT, GCVO
Born 15 August 1950, declared The Princess Royal 1987
Married (1) 14 November 1973 Captain Mark Anthony Peter Phillips, CVO (*born* 22 September 1948); marriage dissolved 1992; (2) 12 December 1992 Captain Timothy James Hamilton Laurence, MVO, RN (*born* 1 March 1955)
Issue:
(1) Peter Mark Andrew Phillips, *born* 15 November 1977

(2) Zara Anne Elizabeth Phillips, *born* 15 May 1981
Residence: Gatcombe Park, Minchinhampton, Glos GL6 9AT

HRH THE DUKE OF YORK (Prince Andrew Albert Christian Edward), KCVO, ADC(P)
Born 19 February 1960, created Duke of York, Earl of Inverness and Baron Killyleagh 1986
Married 23 July 1986 Sarah Margaret Ferguson, now Sarah, Duchess of York (*born* 15 October 1959, younger daughter of Major Ronald Ferguson and Mrs Hector Barrantes), marriage dissolved 1996
Issue:
(1) HRH Princess Beatrice of York (Princess Beatrice Elizabeth Mary), *born* 8 August 1988
(2) HRH Princess Eugenie of York (Princess Eugenie Victoria Helena), *born* 23 March 1990
Residences: Buckingham Palace, London SW1A 1AA; Sunninghill Park, Ascot, Berks SL5 7TH

HRH THE EARL OF WESSEX (Prince Edward Antony Richard Louis), KCVO
Born 10 March 1964, created Earl of Wessex, Viscount Severn 1999
Married 19 June 1999 Sophie Helen Rhys-Jones, now HRH The Countess of Wessex (*born* 20 January 1965, daughter of Mr and Mrs Christopher Rhys-Jones)
Issue:
(1) Lady Louise Windsor (Louise Alice Elizabeth), *born* 8 November 2003
Residence: Bagshot Park, Bagshot, Surrey GU19 5HS

NEPHEW OF THE QUEEN

DAVID ALBERT CHARLES ARMSTRONG-JONES, VISCOUNT LINLEY, *born* 3 November 1961, *married* 8 October 1993 the Hon. Serena Stanhope, and has issue, Hon. Charles Patrick Inigo Armstrong-Jones, *born* 1 July 1999; Hon. Margarita Elizabeth Alleyne Armstrong-Jones, *born* 14 May 2002

NIECE OF THE QUEEN

LADY SARAH CHATTO (Sarah Frances Elizabeth), *born* 1 May 1964, *married* 14 July 1994 Daniel Chatto, and has issue, Samuel David Benedict Chatto, *born* 28 July 1996; Arthur Robert Nathaniel Chatto, *born* 5 February 1999

COUSINS OF THE QUEEN

HRH THE DUKE OF GLOUCESTER (Prince Richard Alexander Walter George), KG, GCVO, Grand Prior of the Order of St John of Jerusalem
Born 26 August 1944
Married 8 July 1972 Birgitte Eva van Deurs, now HRH The Duchess of Gloucester, GCVO (*born* 20 June 1946, daughter of Asger Henriksen and Vivian van Deurs)
Issue:
(1) Earl of Ulster (Alexander Patrick Gregers Richard), *born* 24 October 1974 *married* 22 June 2002 Dr Claire Booth
(2) Lady Davina Lewis (Davina Elizabeth Alice

Benedikte), *born* 19 November 1977 *married* 31 July 2004 Gary Lewis
(3) Lady Rose Windsor (Rose Victoria Birgitte Louise), *born* 1 March 1980
Residence: Kensington Palace, London W8 4PU

HRH THE DUKE OF KENT (Prince Edward George Nicholas Paul Patrick), KG, GCMG, GCVO, ADC(P)
Born 9 October 1935
Married 8 June 1961 Katharine Lucy Mary Worsley, now HRH The Duchess of Kent, GCVO (*born* 22 February 1933, daughter of Sir William Worsley, Bt.)
Issue:
(1) Earl of St Andrews (George Philip Nicholas), *born* 26 June 1962, *married* 9 January 1988 Sylvana Tomaselli, and has issue Baron Downpatrick (Edward Edmund Maximilian George), *born* 2 December 1988; Lady Marina-Charlotte Windsor (Marina-Charlotte Alexandra Katharine Helen), *born* 30 September 1992; Lady Amelia Windsor (Amelia Sophia Theodora Mary Margaret), *born* 24 August 1995
(2) Lady Helen Taylor (Helen Marina Lucy), *born* 28 April 1964, *married* 18 July 1992 Timothy Taylor, and has issue, Columbus George Donald Taylor, *born* 6 August 1994; Cassius Edward Taylor, *born* 26 December 1996; Eloise Olivia Katharine Taylor, *born* 3 March 2003; Estella Taylor, *born* 21 December 2004
(3) Lord Nicholas Windsor (Nicholas Charles Edward Jonathan), *born* 25 July 1970
Residence: Wren House, Palace Green, London W8 4PY

HRH PRINCESS ALEXANDRA, THE HON. LADY OGILVY (Princess Alexandra Helen Elizabeth Olga Christabel), KG, GCVO
Born 25 December 1936
Married 24 April 1963 The Rt. Hon. Sir Angus Ogilvy, KCVO (1928–2004), second son of 12th Earl of Airlie
Issue:
(1) James Robert Bruce Ogilvy, *born* 29 February 1964, *married* 30 July 1988 Julia Rawlinson, and has issue, Flora Alexandra Ogilvy, *born* 15 December 1994; Alexander Charles Ogilvy, *born* 12 November 1996
(2) Marina Victoria Alexandra, Mrs Mowatt, *born* 31 July 1966, *married* 2 February 1990 Paul Mowatt (marriage dissolved 1997), and has issue, Zenouska May Mowatt, *born* 26 May 1990; Christian Alexander Mowatt, *born* 4 June 1993
Residence: Thatched House Lodge, Richmond Park, Surrey TW10 5HP

HRH PRINCE MICHAEL OF KENT (Prince Michael George Charles Franklin), GCVO
Born 4 July 1942
Married 30 June 1978 Baroness Marie-Christine Agnes Hedwig Ida von Reibnitz, now HRH Princess Michael of Kent (*born* 15 January 1945, daughter of Baron Gunther von Reibnitz)

Issue:
(1) Lord Frederick Windsor (Frederick Michael George David Louis), *born* 6 April 1979
(2) Lady Gabriella Windsor (Gabriella Marina Alexandra Ophelia), *born* 23 April 1981
Residences: Kensington Palace, London W8 4PU; Nether Lypiatt Manor, Stroud, Glos GL6 7LS

ORDER OF SUCCESSION

1	HRH The Prince of Wales
2	HRH Prince William of Wales
3	HRH Prince Henry of Wales
4	HRH The Duke of York
5	HRH Princess Beatrice of York
6	HRH Princess Eugenie of York
7	HRH The Earl of Wessex
8	Lady Louise Windsor
9	HRH The Princess Royal
10	Peter Phillips
11	Zara Phillips
12	Viscount Linley
13	Hon. Charles Armstrong-Jones
14	Hon. Margarita Armstrong-Jones
15	Lady Sarah Chatto
16	Samuel Chatto
17	Arthur Chatto
18	HRH The Duke of Gloucester
19	Earl of Ulster
20	Lady Davina Lewis
21	Lady Rose Windsor
22	HRH The Duke of Kent
23	Lady Marina-Charlotte Windsor
24	Lady Amelia Windsor
25	Lady Helen Taylor
26	Columbus Taylor
27	Cassius Taylor
28	Eloise Taylor
29	Estella Taylor
30	Lord Frederick Windsor
31	Lady Gabriella Windsor
32	HRH Princess Alexandra, the Hon. Lady Ogilvy
33	James Ogilvy
34	Alexander Ogilvy
35	Flora Ogilvy
36	Marina, Mrs Paul Mowatt
37	Christian Mowatt
38	Zenouska Mowatt

HRH Prince Michael of Kent, and The Earl of St Andrews both lost the right of succession to the throne through marriage to a Roman Catholic. Lord Nicholas Windsor and Baron Downpatrick renounced their rights to the throne on converting to Roman Catholicism in 2001 and 2003 respectively. Their children remain in succession provided that they are in communion with the Church of England.

PRIVATE SECRETARIES TO THE ROYAL FAMILY

THE QUEEN

Office: Buckingham Palace, London SW1A 1AA
T 020-7930 4832 W www.royal.gov.uk
Private Secretary to The Queen, The Rt. Hon. Sir Robin Janvrin, KCB, KCVO

PRINCE PHILIP, THE DUKE OF EDINBURGH

Office: Buckingham Palace, London SW1A 1AA
T 020-7930 4832
Private Secretary, Brig. Sir Miles Hunt-Davis, KCVO, CBE

THE PRINCE OF WALES AND THE DUCHESS OF CORNWALL

Office: Clarence House, London SW1A 1BA T 020-7930 4832
Private Secretary, Sir Michael Peat, KCVO

THE DUKE OF YORK

Office: Buckingham Palace, London SW1A 1AA
T 020-7930 4832
Private Secretary, Alastair Watson

THE EARL AND COUNTESS OF WESSEX

Office: Bagshot Park, Surrey GU19 5PJ T 01276-707040
Private Secretary, Brig. J. Smedley

THE PRINCESS ROYAL

Office: Buckingham Palace, London SW1A 1AA
T 020-7930 4832
Private Secretary, Capt. N. P. Wright, LVO, RN

THE DUKE AND DUCHESS OF GLOUCESTER

Office: Kensington Palace, London W8 4PU T 020-7368 1000
Private Secretary, Alistair Wood, MBE

THE DUKE OF KENT

Office: St James's Palace, London SW1A 1BQ T 020-7930 4872
Private Secretary, N. Adamson, LVO, OBE

THE DUCHESS OF KENT

Office: Wren House, Palace Green, London W8 4PY
T 020-7937 2730
Personal Secretary, Miss V. Utley

PRINCE AND PRINCESS MICHAEL OF KENT

Office: Kensington Palace, London W8 4PU T 020-7938 3519
Private Secretary, N. Chance

PRINCESS ALEXANDRA, THE HON. LADY OGILVY

Office: Buckingham Palace, London SW1A 1AA
T 020-7024 4270
Private Secretary, Lt.-Col. Richard Macfarlane

ROYAL SALUTES

ENGLAND

The basic Royal Salute is 21 rounds with 41 rounds fired at Hyde Park because it is a royal park. At the Tower of London 62 rounds are fired on Royal anniversaries (21 plus a further 20 because the Tower is a royal palace and a further 21 'for the City of London'). Gun salutes occur on the following Royal anniversaries:

- Accession Day
- The Queen's birthday
- Coronation Day
- The birthday of the Duke of Edinburgh
- The Queen's official birthday
- State Opening of Parliament

Gun salutes also occur when Parliament is prorogued by the Sovereign, on royal births and when a visiting Head of State meets the Sovereign in London, Windsor or Edinburgh.

In London, salutes are fired at Hyde Park and The Tower of London although on some occasions (State visits, State Opening of Parliament and The Queen's Birthday Parade) Green Park is used instead.

Constable of the Royal Palace and Fortress of London, Gen. Sir Roger Wheeler, GCB, CBE

Lieutenant of the Tower of London, Lt.-Gen. Sir Hew Pike, KCB, DSO, MBE
Resident Governor and Keeper of the Jewel House, Maj.-Gen. Geoffrey Field, CB, CVO, OBE
Master Gunner of St James's Park, Gen. Sir Alex Harley, KBE, CB
Master Gunner within the Tower, Col. George Clarke, TD

SCOTLAND

Royal salutes are authorised at Edinburgh Castle and Stirling Castle, although in practice Edinburgh Castle is the only operating saluting station in Scotland. A salute of 21 guns is fired on the following occasions:

- the anniversaries of the birth, accession and coronation of the Sovereign
- the anniversary of the birth of HRH Prince Philip, Duke of Edinburgh

A salute of 21 guns is fired in Edinburgh on the occasion of the opening of the General Assembly of the Church of Scotland. A salute of 21 guns may also be fired in Edinburgh on the arrival of HM The Queen or a member of the royal family who is a Royal Highness on an official visit.

Other military saluting stations are at Cardiff and Belfast.

ROYAL HOUSEHOLD

PRIVATE SECRETARY'S OFFICE

The Private Secretary is responsible for:

- Informing and advising The Queen on constitutional, governmental and political matters in the UK, her other Realms and the wider Commonwealth, including communications with the Prime Minister and government departments
- Organising The Queen's domestic and overseas official programme
- The Queen's speeches, messages, patronage, photographs, and official presents and portraits of The Queen
- Communications in connection with the role of the royal family
- Dealing with correspondence to The Queen from members of the public
- Organising and co-ordinating royal travel
- Co-ordinating and initiating research to support engagements by members of the royal family

The Press Secretary is in charge of Buckingham Palace Press Office and reports to the Private Secretary. The Press Secretary is responsible for:

- Developing communications strategies to enhance the public understanding of the role of the monarchy
- Briefing the British and international media on the role and duties of The Queen and issues relating to the royal family
- Responding to media enquiries
- Arranging media facilities in the UK and overseas to support royal functions and engagements
- The management of the royal website

The Private Secretary is Keeper of the Royal Archives and is responsible for the care of the records of the Sovereign and the Royal Household from previous reigns. These papers are preserved in the Royal Archives at Windsor, where they are managed by the Registrar, reporting to the Assistant Keeper. As Keeper, it is the Private Secretary's responsibility to ensure the proper management of the records of the present reign with a view to their transfer to the archives as and when appropriate. The Private Secretary is an *ex officio* trustee of the Royal Collection Trust.

PRIVY PURSE AND TREASURER'S OFFICE

The Keeper of the Privy Purse and Treasurer to The Queen is responsible for:

- The Queen's Civil List, which is the money paid from the Government's Consolidated Fund to meet official expenditure relating to The Queen's duties as Head of State and Head of the Commonwealth
- Through the Director of Personnel, the planning and management of personnel policy across the Household, the administration of all pension schemes provided for the Household and private estates employees, and the allocation of employee and pensioner housing
- Information technology systems for the Household
- Internal audit services
- Health and safety
- All insurance matters
- The Privy Purse, which is mainly financed by the net income of the Duchy of Lancaster, and meets both official and private expenditure incurred by The Queen
- Liaison with other members of the royal family and their households on financial matters

- The Queen's private estates at Sandringham and Balmoral, The Queen's Racing Establishment and the Royal Studs and liaison with the Ascot Authority
- The Home Park at Windsor and liaison with the Crown Estate Commissioners concerning the Home Park and the Great Park at Windsor
- The Royal Philatelic Collection, managed by the Keeper of the Royal Philatelic Collection
- Administrative aspects of the Military Knights of Windsor and the Royal Almonry
- Administration of the Royal Victorian Order, of which the Keeper of the Privy Purse is Secretary, Long and Faithful Service Medals, and the Queen's Cups, Medals and Prizes, and policy on Commemorative Medals

The Keeper of the Privy Purse is one of three royal trustees (in respect of his responsibilities for the Civil List) and is Receiver-General of the Duchy of Lancaster and a member of the Duchy's Council.

The Keeper of the Privy Purse is also responsible for property services at occupied royal palaces in England, comprising Buckingham Palace, St James's Palace, Clarence House, Marlborough House Mews, the residential and office areas of Kensington Palace, Windsor Castle and buildings in the Home and Great Parks of Windsor and Hampton Court Mews and Paddocks. The costs of property services for occupied royal palaces are met from a grant-in-aid from the Department for Culture, Media and Sport.

The Director of Property Services, assisted by the Deputy Treasurer has day-to-day responsibility for the Royal Household's Property Section, which is responsible for:

- Fire safety issues
- Repairs and refurbishment of buildings and new buildings work
- Utilities and telecommunications
- Putting up stages, tents and other work in connection with ceremonial occasions, garden parties and other official functions

The Property Section is also responsible, in effect on a sub-contract basis from the Department for Culture, Media and Sport, for the maintenance of Marlborough House (which is occupied by the Commonwealth Secretariat).

The Keeper of the Privy Purse, assisted by the Deputy Treasurer, also oversees royal communications and information expenditure, which is met from the Property Services grant-in-aid, and the financial aspects of Royal Travel, which is met from a grant-in-aid provided by the Department for Transport.

The Keeper of the Privy Purse is an *ex officio* trustee of the Historic Royal Palaces Trust and the Royal Collection Trust.

The Queen's Civil List and the grants-in-aid for property services and royal travel are provided by the Government in return for the surrender by the Sovereign of the net surplus from the Crown Estate and other hereditary revenues.

MASTER OF THE HOUSEHOLD'S DEPARTMENT

The Master of the Household, assisted by two Deputy Masters of the Household (one of whom is also Equerry to the Queen), is responsible for the staff and domestic arrangements at Buckingham Palace, Windsor Castle, the

Palace of Holyroodhouse, Balmoral Castle and Sandringham House when The Queen is in residence. These arrangements include:

- The provision of meals for The Queen and other members of the royal family, their guests and Royal Household employees
- Service by liveried staff at meals, receptions and other events
- Travel arrangements for employees and the movement of baggage between the royal residences
- Cleaning and laundry
- Furnishings and the internal decorative appearance of occupied royal palaces in collaboration with the Director of the Royal Collection
- Liaison with the Royalty and Diplomatic Protection Department of the Metropolitan Police concerning security procedures at occupied royal palaces

The Master of the Household is responsible for The Queen's official entertaining, both at home and overseas, including preparation of guest lists, invitations and seating plans, and overseeing aspects of The Queen's private entertaining.

LORD CHAMBERLAIN'S OFFICE
The Comptroller, Lord Chamberlain's Office, assisted by the Deputy Comptroller, is responsible for:

- The organisation of all ceremonial engagements, including state visits to The Queen in the UK, royal weddings and funerals, the state opening of parliament, Guards of Honour at Buckingham Palace, Investitures, and the Garter and Thistle ceremonies
- Garden parties at Buckingham Palace and the Palace of Holyroodhouse (except for catering and tents)
- The Crown Jewels, which are part of the Royal Collection, when they are in use on state occasions
- Co-ordination of the arrangements for The Queen to be represented at funerals and memorial services and at the arrival and departure of visiting Heads of State
- Advising on matters of precedence, style and titles, dress, flying of flags, gun salutes, mourning and other ceremonial issues
- Supervising the applications from tradesmen for Royal Warrants of Appointment
- Advising on the commercial use of royal emblems and contemporary royal photographs
- The Ecclesiastical Household, the Medical Household, the Body Guards and certain ceremonial appointments such as Gentlemen Ushers and Pages of Honour
- The Lords in Waiting, who represent The Queen on various occasions and escort the visiting Head of State during incoming state visits
- The Queen's Bargemaster and Watermen and The Queen's swans

The Comptroller is also responsible for the Royal Mews, assisted by the Crown Equerry, who has day-to-day responsibility for:

- The provision of carriage processions for the State Opening of Parliament, state visits, Trooping of the Colour, Royal Ascot, the Garter Ceremony, the Thistle Service, the presentation of credentials to The Queen by incoming foreign Ambassadors and High Commissioners, and other state and ceremonial occasions
- The provision of chauffeur-driven cars
- Co-ordinating travel arrangements by road in respect of The Queen's official engagements

- Supervision and administration of the Royal Mews at Buckingham Palace, Windsor Castle, Hampton Court and the Palace of Holyroodhouse

The Comptroller also has overall responsibility for the Marshal of the Diplomatic Corps, who is responsible for the relationship between the Royal Household and the Diplomatic Heads of Mission in London; and the Secretary of the Central Chancery of the Orders of Knighthood, who administers the Orders of Chivalry, makes arrangements for investitures and the distribution of insignia, and ensures the proper public notification of awards through the *London Gazette*.

ROYAL COLLECTION DEPARTMENT
The Royal Collection, which contains a large number of works of art, is held by The Queen as Sovereign in trust for her successors and the nation and is not owned by her as an individual. The administration, conservation and presentation of the Royal Collection are funded by the Royal Collection Trust solely from income from visitors to Windsor Castle, Buckingham Palace and the Palace of Holyroodhouse. The Royal Collection Trust is chaired by the Prince of Wales. The Lord Chamberlain, the Private Secretary and the Keeper of the Privy Purse are *ex officio* trustees and there are three external trustees appointed by The Queen.

The Director of the Royal Collection is responsible for:

- The administration and custodial control of the Royal Collection in all royal residences
- The care, display, conservation and restoration of items in the Collection
- Initiating and assisting research into the Collection and publishing catalogues and books on the Collection
- Making the Collection accessible to the public and educating and informing the public about the Collection

The Director of the Royal Collection, who is at present also the Surveyor of The Queen's Works of Art, is assisted by the Surveyor of The Queen's Pictures, the Royal Librarian, the Deputy Surveyor of The Queen's Works of Art, the Managing Director, Royal Collection Enterprises, and the Finance Director, Royal Collection.

The Surveyor of The Queen's Pictures is responsible for pictures and miniatures, the Royal Librarian is responsible for all books, manuscripts, coins and medals, insignia and works of art on paper including the watercolours, prints and drawings in the Print Room at Windsor Castle, and the Surveyor of The Queen's Works of art is responsible for furniture, ceramics and the other decorative arts in the Collection.

The Director of the Royal Collection has overall responsibility for trading activities that fund the Royal Collection Department. These are administered by Royal Collection Enterprises Limited, the trading subsidiary of the Royal Collection Trust. The company, whose chair is the Keeper of the Privy Purse, is responsible for:

- Managing access by the public to Windsor Castle (including Frogmore House), Buckingham Palace (including the Royal Mews and The Queen's Gallery) and the Palace of Holyroodhouse
- Running shops at each location
- Managing the images and intellectual property rights of the Royal Collection

The Director of the Royal Collection is also an *ex officio* trustee of the Historic Royal Palaces Trust.

SENIOR MANAGEMENT

Lord Chamberlain, The Lord Luce

HEADS OF DEPARTMENT
Private Secretary to The Queen, The Rt. Hon. Sir Robin Janvin, KCB, KCVO
Keeper of the Privy Purse, Alan Reid
Master of the Household, Vice-Adm. Sir Tom Blackburn, KCVO, CB, LVO

Comptroller, Lord Chamberlain's Office, Lt.-Col. Sir Malcolm Ross, KCVO, OBE
Director of the Royal Collection, Sir Hugh Roberts, KCVO

NON-EXECUTIVE MEMBERS
Private Secretary to the Duke of Edinburgh, Brig. Sir Miles Hunt-Davis, KCVO, CBE
Private Secretary to the Prince of Wales, Sir Michael Peat, KCVO
The Poet Laureate, Prof. Andrew Motion

ROYAL FINANCES

FUNDING

CIVIL LIST
The Civil List dates back to the late 17th century. It was originally used by The Sovereign to supplement hereditary revenues for paying the salaries of judges, ambassadors and other government officers as well as the expenses of the Royal Household. In 1760 on the accession of George III it was decided that the Civil List would be provided by Parliament to cover all relevant expenditure in return for the King surrendering the hereditary revenues of the Crown. At that time Parliament undertook to pay the salaries of judges, ambassadors, etc. In 1831 Parliament agreed also to meet the costs of the royal palaces in return for a reduction in the Civil List. Each sovereign has agreed to continue this arrangement. The Civil List now meets the central staff costs and running expenses of The Queen's official household.

Until 1972, the amount of money allocated annually under the Civil List was set for the duration of a reign. The system was then altered to a fixed annual payment for ten years but from 1975 high inflation made an annual review necessary. The system of payments reverted to the practice of a fixed annual payment of £7.9m for a ten year period to 31 December 2000; during this period annual Civil List expenditure reached £6.5 million, and a reserve of £35 million was established. In order to draw down the reserve, the annual Civil List payment was left at £7.9 million for a further ten years, to 31 December 2010, and annual expenditure of approximately £2 million is transferred to the Civil List from the votes of government departments or from the Consolidated Fund.

In June 2002 the annual accounts for the Civil List were published for the first time and are to be published annually instead of at 10-yearly intervals.

	2004 £ thousand	2003 £ thousand
Civil List payment	7,900	7,900
Draw-down from the Civil List reserve	2,800	2,600
NET RECEIPTS	10,700	10,500
NET CIVIL LIST EXPENDITURE	(10,600)	(9,900)

PARLIAMENTARY ANNUITIES
The Civil List Acts provide for other members of the royal family to receive parliamentary annuities from government funds to meet the expenses of carrying out their official duties. Since 1993 The Queen has reimbursed all the annuities except those paid to the late Queen Elizabeth the Queen Mother and the Duke of Edinburgh.

The Prince of Wales does not receive a parliamentary annuity. He derives his income from the revenues of the Duchy of Cornwall and these monies meet the official and private expenses of the Prince of Wales and his family.

In 2000 the annual amounts payable to members of the royal family, excluding the Earl of Wessex, were reset at their 1990 levels for the next ten years. The Earl of Wessex had his annuity increased by £45,000 to £141,000 on the occassion of his marriage in 1999.

The annual payments remain as follows until December 2010:

	£
The Duke of Edinburgh	359,000
The Duke of York	249,000
The Earl of Wessex	141,000
The Princess Royal	228,000
The Duke and Duchess of Gloucester	175,000
The Duke and Duchess of Kent	236,000
Princess Alexandra	225,000
TOTAL	1,613,000
Refunded to the Treasury by the Queen	(1,254,000)
Total	359,000

GRANTS-IN-AID
Grants-in-aid are provided to the Royal Household annually by the Department for Culture, Media and Sport for Property Services and Communications and Information, and by the Department for Transport for Royal Travel. Property Services meets the cost of property maintenance, and of utilities, telephones and related services at the occupied royal palaces in England (*see* Royal Household section for a list of occupied palaces). Communications and Information meets the cost of communication and information services in connection with official royal functions and engagements in England and Scotland. Royal Travel meets the cost of official royal travel by air and rail.

GRANTS-IN-AID 2004–5:

	Grant-in-aid voted by parliament	Actual net expenditure
Property Services	£15,200,000*	£14,700,000
Communications and Information	£520,000	£500,000
Royal Travel	£5,700,000	£5,000,000

*Actual figure £14,500,000 – an advance was drawn on this sum in 2003–4 to fund the costs involved in the refurbishment of Clarence House and other Property Services' projects

THE PRIVY PURSE

The funds received by the Privy Purse pay for official expenses incurred by The Queen as head of state and for some of The Queen's private expenditure. The revenues of the Duchy of Lancaster are the principal source of income for the Privy Purse. The revenues of the Duchy were retained by George III in 1760 when the hereditary revenues were surrendered in exchange for the Civil List.

PERSONAL INCOME

The Queen's personal income derives mostly from investments, and is used to meet private expenditure.

EXPENDITURE MET BY GOVERNMENT DEPARTMENTS AND THE CROWN ESTATE 2004–5

	£ thousand
Administration of honours	500
Equerries, orderlies and other personnel support	1,000
Maintenance of the Palace of Holyroodhouse	1,900
State visits to and by The Queen and liaison with the Diplomatic Corps	900
Ceremonial occasions	500
Maintenance of Home Park, Windsor Castle	600
Other	100
Total	5,500

TAXATION

The Sovereign is not legally liable to pay income tax or capital gains tax. After income tax was reintroduced in 1842, some income tax was paid voluntarily by The Sovereign but over a long period these payments were phased out. In 1992 The Queen offered to pay tax on a voluntary basis from 6 April 1993, and the Prince of Wales offered to pay tax on a voluntary basis on his income from the Duchy of Cornwall (he was already taxed in all other respects).

The main provisions for The Queen and the Prince of Wales to pay tax, set out in a Memorandum of Understanding on Royal Taxation presented to Parliament on 11 February 1993, are that The Queen will pay income tax and capital gains tax in respect of her private income and assets, and on the proportion of the income and capital gains of the Privy Purse used for private purposes. Inheritance tax will be paid on The Queen's assets, except for those which pass to the next sovereign, whether automatically or by gift or bequest. The Prince of Wales will pay income tax on income from the Duchy of Cornwall used for private purposes.

The Prince of Wales has confirmed that he intends to pay tax on the same basis following his accession to the throne. Other members of the royal family are subject to tax as for any taxpayer.

MILITARY RANKS AND TITLES

THE QUEEN

ROYAL NAVY
Lord High Admiral of the United Kingdom

ARMY
Colonel-in-Chief
The Life Guards; The Blues and Royals (Royal Horse Guards and 1st Dragoons); The Royal Scots Dragoon Guards (Carabiniers and Greys); The Queen's Royal Lancers; Royal Tank Regiment; Corps of Royal Engineers; Grenadier Guards; Coldstream Guards; Scots Guards; Irish Guards; Welsh Guards; The Royal Welch Fusiliers; The Queen's Lancashire Regiment; The Argyll and Sutherland Highlanders (Princess Louise's); The Royal Green Jackets; Adjutant General's Corps; The Royal Mercian and Lancastrian Yeomanry; The Governor General's Horse Guards (of Canada); The King's Own Calgary Regiment (Royal Canadian Armoured Corps); Canadian Forces Military Engineers Branch; Royal 22e Régiment (of Canada); Governor General's Foot Guards (of Canada); The Canadian Grenadièr Guards; Le Régiment de la Chaudière (of Canada); 2nd Battalion Royal New Brunswick Regiment (North Shore); The 48th Highlanders of Canada; The Argyll and Sutherland Highlanders of Canada (Princess Louise's); The Calgary Highlanders; Royal Australian Engineers; Royal Australian Infantry Corps; Royal Australian Army Ordnance Corps; Royal Australian Army Nursing Corps; The Corps of Royal New Zealand Engineers; Royal New Zealand Infantry Regiment; The Malawi Rifles; The Royal Malta Artillery

Affiliated Colonel-in-Chief
The Queen's Gurkha Engineers

Captain General
Royal Regiment of Artillery; The Honourable Artillery Company; Combined Cadet Force; Royal Regiment of Canadian Artillery; Royal Regiment of Australian Artillery; Royal Regiment of New Zealand Artillery; Royal New Zealand Armoured Corps

Patron
Royal Army Chaplains' Department

ROYAL AIR FORCE
Air Commodore-in-Chief
Royal Auxiliary Air Force; Royal Air Force Regiment; Air Reserve of Canada; Royal Australian Air Force Reserve; Territorial Air Force (of New Zealand)

Commandant-in-Chief
Royal Air Force College, Cranwell

Hon. Air Commodore
Royal Air Force Marham; 603 (City of Edinburgh) Squadron Royal Auxiliary Air Force

HRH THE PRINCE PHILIP, DUKE OF EDINBURGH

ROYAL NAVY
Admiral of the Fleet
Admiral of the Fleet, Royal Australian Navy
Admiral of the Fleet, Royal New Zealand Navy
Admiral of the Royal Canadian Sea Cadets

ROYAL MARINES
Captain General, Royal Marines

ARMY
Field Marshal
Field Marshal, Australian Military Forces
Field Marshal, New Zealand Army

Colonel-in-Chief
The Queen's Royal Hussars (Queen's Own and Royal Irish); The Royal Gloucestershire, Berkshire and Wiltshire Regiment; The Highlanders (Seaforth, Gordons and Camerons); Corps of Royal Electrical and Mechanical Engineers; Intelligence Corps; Army Cadet Force; The Royal Canadian Regiment; The Royal Hamilton Light Infantry (Wentworth Regiment of Canada); The Cameron Highlanders of Ottawa; The Queen's Own Cameron Highlanders of Canada; The Seaforth Highlanders of Canada; The Royal Canadian Army Cadets; The Royal Australian Corps of Electrical and Mechanical Engineers; The Australian Army Cadet Corps

Colonel
Grenadier Guards

Hon. Colonel
City of Edinburgh University Officers' Training Corps; The Trinidad and Tobago Regiment

Member
Honourable Artillery Company

ROYAL AIR FORCE
Marshal of the Royal Air Force
Marshal of the Royal Australian Air Force
Marshal of the Royal New Zealand Air Force

Air Commodore-in-Chief
Air Training Corps; Royal Canadian Air Cadets

Hon. Air Commodore
Royal Air Force Kinloss

HRH THE PRINCE OF WALES

ROYAL NAVY
Vice Admiral

ARMY
Lieutenant-General

Colonel-in-Chief
The Royal Dragoon Guards; The 22nd Cheshire Regiment; The Royal Regiment of Wales (24th/41st Foot); The Parachute Regiment; The Royal Gurkha Rifles; Army Air Corps; The Royal Canadian Dragoons; Lord Strathcona's Horse (Royal Canadians); The Royal Regiment of Canada; Royal Winnipeg Rifles; Royal Australian Armoured Corps; The Royal Pacific Islands Regiment; 1st The Queen's Dragoon Guards; The Black Watch (Royal Highland Regiment); The King's Regiment

Deputy Colonel-in-Chief
The Highlanders (Seaforth, Gordons and Camerons)

Colonel
Welsh Guards

Royal Hon. Colonel
The Queen's Own Yeomanry

ROYAL AIR FORCE
Air Marshal

Hon. Air Commodore
Royal Air Force Valley

Air Commodore-in-Chief
Royal New Zealand Air Force

Colonel-in-Chief
Air Reserve Canada; The Black Watch (Royal Highland Regiment) of Canada; The Toronto Scottish Regiment (Queen Elizabeth The Queen Mother's Own)

HRH THE DUKE OF YORK

ROYAL NAVY
Commander
Admiral of the Sea Cadet Corps

ARMY
Colonel-in-Chief
The Staffordshire Regiment (The Prince of Wales's); The Royal Irish Regiment (27th (Inniskilling), 83rd, 87th and The Ulster Defence Regiment); 9th/12th Royal Lancers (The Prince of Wales's); The Royal Highland Fusiliers (Princess Margaret's Own Glasgow and Ayrshire Regiment); Small Arms School Corps; The Queen's York Rangers (First Americans); Royal New Zealand Army Logistics Regiment

ROYAL AIR FORCE
Hon. Air Commodore
Royal Air Force Lossiemouth

HRH THE EARL OF WESSEX

ARMY
Colonel-in-Chief
Hastings and Prince Edward Regiment; Saskatchewan Dragoons

Hon. Colonel
Royal Wessex Yeomanry

HRH THE COUNTESS OF WESSEX

ARMY
Colonel-in-Chief
Queen Alexandra's Royal Army Nursing Corps; The Lincoln and Welland Regiment

HRH THE PRINCESS ROYAL

ROYAL NAVY
Rear-Admiral (Chief Commandant for Women in the Royal Navy)

ARMY
Colonel-in-Chief
The King's Royal Hussars; Royal Corps of Signals; Royal Logistic Corps; The Worcestershire and Sherwood Foresters Regiment (29th/45th Foot); The Royal Scots (The Royal Regiment); The Royal Army Veterinary Corps; 8th Canadian Hussars (Princess

Louise's); Royal Newfoundland Regiment; Canadian Forces Communications and Electronics Branch; The Grey and Simcoe Foresters (Royal Canadian Armoured Corps); The Royal Regina Rifle Regiment; Canadian Forces Medical Branch; Royal Australian Corps of Signals; Royal New Zealand Corps of Signals; Royal New Zealand Nursing Corps

Affiliated Colonel-in-Chief
The Queen's Gurkha Signals; The Queen's Own Gurkha Transport Regiment

Colonel
The Blues and Royals (Royal Horse Guards and 1st Dragoons)

Hon. Colonel
University of London Officers' Training Corps

Commandant-in-Chief
First Aid Nursing Yeomanry (Princess Royal's Volunteer Corps)

ROYAL AIR FORCE
Hon. Air Commodore
Royal Air Force Lyneham; University of London Air Squadron

HRH THE DUKE OF GLOUCESTER

ARMY
Deputy Colonel-in-Chief
The Royal Gloucestershire, Berkshire and Wiltshire Regiment; The Royal Logistic Corps

Hon. Colonel
Royal Monmouthshire Royal Engineers (Militia)

ROYAL AIR FORCE
Hon. Air Marshal

Hon. Air Commodore
Royal Air Force Odiham; No. 501 (County of Gloucester) Squadron Royal Auxiliary Air Force

HRH THE DUCHESS OF GLOUCESTER

ARMY
Colonel-in-Chief
Royal Army Dental Corps; Royal Australian Army Educational Corps; Royal New Zealand Army Educational Corps

Deputy Colonel-in-Chief
Adjutant-General's Corps

HRH THE DUKE OF KENT

ARMY
Field Marshal

Colonel-in-Chief
The Royal Regiment of Fusiliers; The Devonshire and Dorset Regiment; Lorne Scots (Peel, Dufferin and Hamilton Regiment)

Deputy Colonel-in-Chief
The Royal Scots Dragoon Guards (Carabiniers and Greys)

Colonel
Scots Guards

ROYAL AIR FORCE
Hon. Air Chief Marshal

Hon. Air Commodore
Royal Air Force Leuchars

HRH THE DUCHESS OF KENT

ARMY
Hon. Major-General

Colonel-in-Chief
The Prince of Wales's Own Regiment of Yorkshire

Deputy Colonel-in-Chief
The Royal Dragoon Guards; Adjutant-General's Corps; The Royal Logistic Corps

HRH PRINCE MICHAEL OF KENT

ROYAL NAVY
Hon. Rear Admiral Royal Naval Reserve

ARMY
Major (retd)
The Royal Hussars (Prince of Wales's Own)

Colonel-in-Chief
Essex and Kent Scottish Regiment (Ontario)

ROYAL AIR FORCE
Hon. Air Commodore
RAF Benson

HRH PRINCESS ALEXANDRA, THE HON. LADY OGILVY

ROYAL NAVY
Patron
Queen Alexandra's Royal Naval Nursing Service

ARMY
Colonel-in-Chief
The King's Own Royal Border Regiment; The Light Infantry; The Queen's Own Rifles of Canada; The Canadian Scottish Regiment (Princess Mary's)

Deputy Colonel-in-Chief
The Queen's Royal Lancers

Hon. Colonel
The Royal Yeomanry

ROYAL AIR FORCE
Patron and Air Chief Commandant
Princess Mary's Royal Air Force Nursing Service

Hon. Air Commodore
Royal Air Force Cottesmore

THE HOUSE OF WINDSOR

King George V assumed by royal proclamation (17 July 1917) for his House and family, as well as for all descendants in the male line of Queen Victoria who are subjects of these realms, the name of Windsor.

KING GEORGE V

(George Frederick Ernest Albert), second son of King Edward VII, *born* 3 June 1865; *married* 6 July 1893 HSH Princess Victoria Mary Augusta Louise Olga Pauline Claudine Agnes of Teck (Queen Mary, *born* 26 May 1867; *died* 24 March 1953); *succeeded* to the throne 6 May 1910; *died* 20 January 1936. *Issue:*

1. HRH PRINCE EDWARD Albert Christian George Andrew Patrick David, *born* 23 June 1894, *succeeded* to the throne as King Edward VIII, 20 January 1936; *abdicated* 11 December 1936; created *Duke of Windsor* 1937; *married* 3 June 1937, Mrs Wallis Simpson (Her Grace The Duchess of Windsor, *born* 19 June 1896; *died* 24 April 1986), *died* 28 May 1972

2. HRH PRINCE ALBERT Frederick Arthur George, *born* 14 December 1895, *created* Duke of York 1920; *married* 26 April 1923, Lady Elizabeth Bowes-Lyon, youngest daughter of the 14th Earl of Strathmore and Kinghorne (HM Queen Elizabeth the Queen Mother, *born* 4 August 1900; *died* 30 March 2002), *succeeded* to the throne as King George VI, 11 December 1936; *died* 6 February 1952, *Issue:*
(1) HRH Princess Elizabeth Alexandra Mary, succeeded to the throne as Queen Elizabeth II, 6 February 1952 (*see* Royal Family)
(2) HRH Princess Margaret Rose (later HRH The Princess Margaret, Countess of Snowdon), *born* 21 August 1930: *married* 6 May 1960, Anthony Charles Robert Armstrong-Jones, GCVO, *created* Earl of Snowdon 1961 (marriage dissolved 1978), *died* 9 February 2002, having had issue (*see* Royal Family)

3. HRH PRINCESS (Victoria Alexandra Alice) MARY, *born* 25 April 1897, *created* Princess Royal 1932; *married* 28 February 1922, Viscount Lascelles, later the 6th Earl of Harewood (1882–1947), *died* 28 March 1965. *Issue:*
(1) George Henry Hubert Lascelles, 7th Earl of Harewood, KBE, *born* 7 February 1923; *married* (1) 1949, Maria (Marion) Stein (marriage dissolved 1967); *issue, (a)* David Henry George, Viscount Lascelles, *born* 1950; *(b)* James Edward, *born* 1953; *(c)* (Robert) Jeremy Hugh, *born* 1955; (2) 1967, Mrs Patricia Tuckwell; *issue, (d)* Mark Hubert, *born* 1964
(2) Gerald David Lascelles (1924–98), *married* (1) 1952, Miss Angela Dowding (marriage dissolved 1978); *issue, (a)* Henry Ulick, *born* 1953; (2) 1978, Mrs Elizabeth Colvin; *issue, (b)* Martin David, *born* 1962

4. HRH PRINCE HENRY William Frederick Albert, *born* 31 March 1900, *created* Duke of Gloucester, Earl of Ulster and Baron Culloden 1928, *married* 6 November 1935, Lady Alice Christabel Montagu-Douglas-Scott, daughter of the 7th Duke of Buccleuch and Queensbery (HRH Princess Alice, Duchess of Gloucester, *born* 25 December 1901: *died* 29 October 2004); *died* 10 June 1974. *Issue:*
(1) HRH Prince William Henry Andrew Frederick, *born* 18 December 1941; *accidentally killed* 28 August 1972
(2) HRH Prince Richard Alexander Walter George (HRH The Duke of Gloucester)

5. HRH PRINCE GEORGE Edward Alexander Edmund, *born* 20 December 1902, *created* Duke of Kent, Earl of St Andrews and Baron Downpatrick 1934, *married* 29 November 1934, HRH Princess Marina of Greece and Denmark (*born* 30 November, 1906; *died* 27 August 1968); *killed on active service*, 25 August 1942. *Issue:*
(1) HRH Prince Edward George Nicholas Paul Patrick (HRH The Duke of Kent)
(2) HRH Princess Alexandra Helen Elizabeth Olga Christabel (HRH Princess Alexandra, the Hon. Lady Ogilvy)
(3) HRH Prince Michael George Charles Franklin (HRH Prince Michael of Kent)

6. HRH PRINCE JOHN Charles Francis, *born* 12 July 1905; *died* 18 January 1919

DESCENDANTS OF QUEEN VICTORIA

QUEEN VICTORIA
(Alexandrina Victoria), *born* 24 May 1819; *succeeded* to the throne 20 June 1837; *married* 10 February 1840 (Francis) Albert Augustus Charles Emmanuel, Duke of Saxony, Prince of Saxe-Coburg and Gotha (HRH Albert, Prince Consort, *born* 26 August 1819, *died* 14 December 1861); *died* 22 January 1901. *Issue:*

I. HRH PRINCESS VICTORIA Adelaide Mary Louisa (Princess Royal) (1840–1901), *m.* 1858, Friedrich III (1831–88), German Emperor March–June 1888. *Issue:*

1. HIM Wilhelm II (1859–1941), German Emperor 1888–1918, *m.* (1) 1881 Princess Augusta Victoria of Schleswig-Holstein-Sonderburg-Augustenburg (1858–1921); (2) 1922 Princess Hermine of Reuss (1887–1947). *Issue:*

(a) Prince Wilhelm (1882–1951), *Crown Prince* 1888–1918, *m.* 1905 Duchess Cecilie of Mecklenburg-Schwerin; *issue:* Prince Wilhelm (1906–40); Prince Louis Ferdinand (1907–94), *m.* 1938 Grand Duchess Kira; Prince Hubertus (1909–50); Prince Friedrich Georg (1911–66); Princess Alexandrine Irene (1915–80); Princess Cecilie (1917–75)

(b) Prince Eitel-Friedrich (1883–1942), *m.* 1906 Duchess Sophie of Oldenburg (marriage dissolved 1926)

(c) Prince Adalbert (1884–1948), *m.* 1914 Princess Adelheid of Saxe-Meiningen; *issue:* Princess Victoria Marina (1917–81); Prince Wilhelm Victor (1919–89)

(d) Prince August Wilhelm (1887–1949), *m.* 1908 Princess Alexandra of Schleswig-Holstein-Sonderburg-Glücksburg (marriage dissolved 1920); *issue:* Prince Alexander (1912–85)

(e) Prince Oskar (1888–1958), *m.* 1914 Countess von Ruppin; *issue:* Prince Oskar (1915–39); Prince Burchard (1917–88); Princess Herzeleide (1918–89); Prince Wilhelm-Karl (b. 1922)

(f) Prince Joachim (1890–1920), *m.* 1916 Princess Marie of Anhalt; *issue:* Prince (Karl) Franz Joseph (1916–75), and has issue

(g) Princess Viktoria Luise (1892–1980), *m.* 1913 Ernst, Duke of Brunswick 1913–18 (1887–1953); *issue:* Prince Ernst (1914–87); Prince Georg (b. 1915), *m.* 1946 Princess Sophie of Greece and has issue (two sons, one daughter); Princess Frederika (1917–81), *m.* 1938 Paul I, King of the Hellenes; Prince Christian (1919–81); Prince Welf Heinrich (1923–97)

2. Princess Charlotte (1860–1919), *m.* 1878 Bernhard, Duke of Saxe-Meiningen 1914 (1851–1928). *Issue:* Princess Feodora (1879–1945), *m.* 1898 Prince Heinrich XXX of Reuss

3. Prince Heinrich (1862–1929), *m.* 1888 Princess Irene of Hesse. *Issue:*

(a) Prince Waldemar (1889–1945), *m.* Princess Calixta Agnes of Lippe

(b) Prince Sigismund (1896–1978), *m.* 1919 Princess Charlotte of Saxe-Altenburg;

issue: Princess Barbara (1920–94); Prince Alfred (b. 1924)

(c) Prince Heinrich (1900–4)

4. Prince Sigismund (1864–6)

5. Princess Victoria (1866–1929), *m.* (1) 1890, Prince Adolf of Schaumburg-Lippe (1859–1916); (2) 1927, Alexander Zubkov (1900–36)

6. Prince Waldemar (1868–79)

7. Princess Sophie (1870–1932), *m.* 1889 Constantine I (1868–1923), King of the Hellenes 1913–17, 1920–3. *Issue:*

(a) George II (1890–1947), King of the Hellenes 1923–4 and 1935–47, *m.* 1921 Princess Elisabeth of Roumania (marriage dissolved 1935)

(b) Alexander I (1893–1920), King of the Hellenes 1917–20, *m.* 1919 Aspasia Manos; *issue:* Princess Alexandra (1921–93), *m.* 1944 King Petar II of Yugoslavia

(c) Princess Helena (1896–1982), *m.* 1921 King Carol of Roumania, (marriage dissolved 1928) (*see* IV.2.(a))

(d) Paul I (1901–64), King of the Hellenes 1947–64, *m.* 1938 Princess Frederika of Brunswick; *issue:* King Constantine II (b. 1940), *m.* 1964 Princess Anne-Marie of Denmark, and has issue (three sons, two daughters); Princess Sophie (b. 1938), *m.* 1962 Juan Carlos I of Spain; Princess Irene (b. 1942)

(e) Princess Irene (1904–74), *m.* 1939 4th Duke of Aosta; *issue:* Prince Amedeo, 5th Duke of Aosta (b. 1943)

(f) Princess Katherine (Lady Katherine Brandram) (b. 1913), *m.* 1947 Major R. C. A. Brandram, MC, TD; *issue:* R. Paul G. A. Brandram (b. 1948)

8. Princess Margarethe (1872–1954), *m.* 1893 Prince Friedrich Karl of Hesse (1868–1940). *Issue:*

(a) Prince Friedrich Wilhelm (1893–1916)

(b) Prince Maximilian (1894–1914)

(c) Prince Philipp (1896–1980), *m.* 1925 Princess Mafalda of Italy; *issue:* Prince Moritz (b. 1926); Prince Heinrich (1927–99); Prince Otto (1937–98); Princess Elisabeth (b. 1940)

(d) Prince Wolfgang (1896–1989), *m.* (1) 1924 Princess Marie Alexandra of Baden; (2) 1948 Ottilie Möller

(e) Prince Richard (1901–69)

(f) Prince Christoph (1901–43), *m.* 1930 Princess Sophie of Greece (*see* III.1.(a)) and has issue (two sons, three daughters)

II. HRH PRINCE ALBERT EDWARD (HM KING EDWARD VII) (1841–1910), *m.* 1863 HRH Princess Alexandra of Denmark (1844–1925), *succeeded* to the throne 22 January 1901, *d.* 6 May 1910. *Issue:*

1. Albert Victor, Duke of Clarence and Avondale (1864–92)

2. George (KING GEORGE V) (1865–1936) (*see* House of Windsor)

3. Louise (1867–1931) Princess Royal 1905–31,

m. 1889 1st Duke of Fife (1849–1912). *Issue:*
(a) Princess Alexandra, Duchess of Fife (1891–
1959), *m.* 1913 Prince Arthur of Connaught
(b) Princess Maud (1893–1945), *m.* 1923 11th
Earl of Southesk (1893–1992); *issue:* The
Duke of Fife (*b.* 1929)
4. Victoria (1868–1935)
5. Maud (1869–1938), *m.* 1896 Prince Carl of
Denmark (1872–1957), later King Haakon VII
of Norway 1905–57. *Issue:*
(a) Olav V (1903–91), King of Norway 1957–
91, *m.* 1929 Princess Märtha of Sweden
(1901–54); *issue:* Princess Ragnhild (*b.*
1930); Princess Astrid (*b.* 1932); Harald V,
King of Norway (*b.* 1937)
6. Alexander (6–7 April 1871)
III. HRH PRINCESS ALICE Maud Mary (1843–78), *m.*
1862 Prince Ludwig (1837–92), Grand Duke of
Hesse 1877–92. *Issue:*
1. Victoria (1863–1950), *m.* 1884 *Admiral of the
Fleet* Prince Louis of Battenberg (1854–1921),
cr. 1st Marquess of Milford Haven 1917. *Issue:*
(a) Alice (1885–1969), *m.* 1903 Prince
Andrew of Greece (1882–1944); *issue:*
Princess Margarita (1905–81), *m.* 1931
Prince Gottfried of Hohenlohe-
Langenburg (*see* IV.4.(a)); Princess
Theodora (1906–69), *m.* Prince Berthold
of Baden (1906–63) and has issue (two
sons, one daughter); Princess Cecilie
(1911–37), *m.* George, Grand Duke of
Hesse (*see* III.4.(b)); Princess Sophie
(1914–2001), *m.* (1) 1930 Prince
Christoph of Hesse (*see* I.8.(f)); (2) 1946
Prince Georg of Hanover; Prince Philip,
Duke of Edinburgh (*b.* 1921)
(b) Louise (1889–1965), *m.* 1923 Gustaf VI
Adolf (1882–1973), King of Sweden
1950–73
(c) George, 2nd Marquess of Milford Haven
(1892–1938), *m.* 1916 Countess Nadejda,
daughter of Grand Duke Michael of Russia;
issue: Lady Tatiana (1917–88); David
Michael, 3rd Marquess (1919–70)
(d) Louis, 1st Earl Mountbatten of Burma
(1900–79), *m.* 1922 Edwina Ashley,
daughter of Lord Mount Temple; *issue:*
Patricia, Countess Mountbatten of Burma
(*b.* 1924); Pamela (*b.* 1929)
2. Elizabeth (1864–1918), *m.* 1884 Grand Duke
Sergius of Russia (1857–1905)
3. Irene (1866–1953), *m.* 1888 Prince Heinrich of
Prussia
4. Ernst Ludwig (1868–1937), Grand Duke of
Hesse 1892–1918, *m.* (1) 1894 Princess
Victoria Melita of Saxe-Coburg (*see* IV.3)
(marriage dissolved 1901); (2) 1905 Princess
Eleonore of Solms-Hohensolmslich. *Issue:*
(a) Princess Elizabeth (1895–1903)
(b) George, Hereditary Grand Duke of Hesse
(1906–37), *m.* Princess Cecilie of Greece
(*see* III.1.(a)), and had issue, two sons,
accidentally killed with parents, 1937
(c) Ludwig, Prince of Hesse (1908–68), *m.*
1937 Margaret, daughter of 1st Lord
Geddes
5. Frederick William (1870–3)
6. Alix (Tsaritsa of Russia) (1872–1918), *m.* 1894

Nicholas II (1868–1918) Tsar of All the Russias
1894–1917, assassinated 16 July 1918. *Issue:*
(a) Grand Duchess Olga (1895–1918)
(b) Grand Duchess Tatiana (1897–1918)
(c) Grand Duchess Marie (1899–1918)
(d) Grand Duchess Anastasia (1901–18)
(e) Alexis, Tsarevich of Russia (1904–18)
7. Marie (1874–8)
IV. HRH PRINCE ALFRED Ernest Albert, Duke of
Edinburgh, *Admiral of the Fleet* (1844–1900), *m.*
1874 Grand Duchess Marie Alexandrovna of Russia
(1853–1920), succeeded as Duke of Saxe-Coburg
and Gotha 22 August 1893. *Issue:*
1. Alfred, Prince of Saxe-Coburg (1874–99)
2. Marie (1875–1938), *m.* 1893 Ferdinand (1865–
1927), King of Roumania 1914–27. *Issue:*
(a) Carol II (1893–1953), King of Roumania
1930–40, *m.* (1) 1921 Princess Helena of
Greece (*see* I.7.(c)) (marriage dissolved
1928), *issue:* Michael (*b.* 1921), King of
Roumania 1927–30, 1940–7; (2) 1948
Princess Anne of Bourbon-Parma, and has
issue (five daughters)
(b) Elisabeth (1894–1956), *m.* 1921 George II,
King of the Hellenes
(c) Marie (1900–61), *m.* 1922 Alexander
(1888–1934), King of Yugoslavia 1921–
34; *issue:* Petar II (1923–70), King of
Yugoslavia 1934–45, *m.* 1944 Princess
Alexandra of Greece (*see* I.7.(b)) and has
issue (Crown Prince Alexander, *b.* 1945);
Prince Tomislav (1928–2000), *m.* (1)
1957 Princess Margarita of Baden
(daughter of Princess Theodora of Greece
and Prince Berthold of Baden, *see*
III.1.(a)); (2) 1982 Linda Bonney; and has
issue (three sons, one daughter); Prince
Andrej (1929–90), *m.* (1) 1956 Princess
Christina of Hesse (daughter of Prince
Christoph of Hesse and Princess Sophie
of Greece, *see* III.1.(a)); (2) 1963 Princess
Kira-Melita of Leiningen (*see* IV.3.(a)); and
has issue (three sons, two daughters)
(d) Prince Nicolas (1903–78)
(e) Princess Ileana (1909–91), *m.* (1) 1931
Archduke Anton of Austria; (2) 1954 Dr
Stefan Issarescu; *issue:* Archduke Stefan
(1932–98); Archduchess Maria Ileana
(1933–59); Archduchess Alexandra (*b.*
1935); Archduke Dominic (*b.* 1937);
Archduchess Maria Magdalena (*b.* 1939);
Archduchess Elisabeth (*b.* 1942)
(f) Prince Mircea (1913–16)
3. Victoria Melita (1876–1936), *m.* (1) 1894
Grand Duke Ernst Ludwig of Hesse (*see* III.4)
(marriage dissolved 1901); (2) 1905 the Grand
Duke Kirill of Russia (1876–1938). *Issue:*
(a) Marie Kirillovna (1907–51), *m.* 1925 Prince
Friedrich Karl of Leiningen; *issue:* Prince
Emich (1926–91); Prince Karl (1928–90);
Princess Kira-Melita (*b.* 1930), *m.* Prince
Andrej of Yugoslavia (*see* IV.2.(c)); Princess
Margarita (1932–96); Princess Mechtilde
(*b.* 1936); Prince Friedrich (1938–98)
(b) Kira Kirillovna (1909–67), *m.* 1938 Prince
Louis Ferdinand of Prussia; *issue:* Prince
Friedrich Wilhelm (*b.* 1939); Prince Michael
(*b.* 1940); Princess Marie (*b.* 1942); Princess

Kira (b. 1943–2004); Prince Louis Ferdinand (1944–77); Prince Christian (b. 1946); Princess Xenia (1949–92)

(c) Vladimir Kirillovich (1917–92), m. 1948 Princess Leonida Bagration-Mukhransky; issue: Grand Duchess Maria (b. 1953), and has issue

4. Alexandra (1878–1942), m. 1896 Ernst, Prince of Hohenlohe Langenburg. Issue:

(a) Gottfried (1897–1960), m. 1931 Princess Margarita of Greece (see III.1.(a)); issue: Prince Kraft (b. 1935–2004), Princess Beatrice (1936–97), Prince Georg Andreas (b. 1938), Prince Ruprecht (1944–76); Prince Albrecht (1944–92)

(b) Maria (1899–1967), m. 1916 Prince Friedrich of Schleswig-Holstein-Sonderburg-Glücksburg; issue: Prince Peter (1922–80); Princess Marie (1927–2000)

(c) Princess Alexandra (1901–63)

(d) Princess Irma (1902–86)

5. Princess Beatrice (1884–1966), m. 1909 Alfonso of Orleans, Infante of Spain. Issue:

(a) Prince Alvaro (1910–97), m. 1937 Carla Parodi-Delfino; issue: Doña Gerarda (b. 1939); Don Alonso (1941–75); Doña Beatriz (b. 1943); Don Alvaro (b. 1947)

(b) Prince Alonso (1912–36)

(c) Prince Ataulfo (1913–74)

V.   HRH PRINCESS HELENA Augusta Victoria (1846–1923), m. 1866 Prince Christian of Schleswig-Holstein-Sonderburg-Augustenburg (1831–1917). Issue:

1. Prince Christian Victor (1867–1900)

2. Prince Albert (1869–1931), Duke of Schleswig-Holstein 1921–31

3. Princess Helena (1870–1948)

4. Princess Marie Louise (1872–1956), m. 1891 Prince Aribert of Anhalt (marriage dissolved 1900)

5. Prince Harold (12–20 May 1876)

VI.   HRH PRINCESS LOUISE Caroline Alberta (1848–1939), m. 1871 the Marquess of Lorne, afterwards 9th Duke of Argyll (1845–1914); without issue

VII. HRH PRINCE ARTHUR William Patrick Albert, Duke of Connaught, Field Marshal (1850–1942), m. 1879 Princess Louisa of Prussia (1860–1917). Issue:

1. Margaret (1882–1920), m. 1905 Crown Prince Gustaf Adolf (1882–1973), afterwards King of Sweden 1950–73. Issue:

(a) Gustaf Adolf, Duke of Västerbotten (1906–47), m. 1932 Princess Sibylla of Saxe-Coburg-Gotha (see VIII.2.(b)); issue: Princess Margaretha (b. 1934); Princess Birgitta (b. 1937); Princess Désirée (b. 1938); Princess Christina (b. 1943); Carl XVI Gustaf, King of Sweden (b. 1946)

(h) Count Sigvard Bernadotte (1907–2002), m. (1) 1934 Erika Patzeck; (2) 1943 Sonja Robbert; (3) 1961 Marianne Lindberg; issue: Count Michael (b. 1944)

(c) Princess Ingrid (Queen Mother of Denmark) (1910–2000), m. 1935 Frederick IX (1899–1972), King of Denmark 1947–72; issue:

Margrethe II, Queen of Denmark (b. 1940); Princess Benedikte (b. 1944); Princess Anne-Marie (b. 1946), m. 1964 Constantine II of Greece

(d) Prince Bertil, Duke of Halland (1912–97), m. 1976 Mrs Lilian Craig

(e) Count Carl Bernadotte (1916–2003), m. (1) 1946 Mrs Kerstin Johnson; (2) 1988 Countess Gunnila Bussler

2. Arthur (1883–1938), m. 1913 HH the Duchess of Fife. Issue: Alastair Arthur, 2nd Duke of Connaught (1914–43)

3. (Victoria) Patricia (1886–1974), m. 1919 Adm. Hon. Sir Alexander Ramsay. Issue: Alexander Ramsay of Mar (1919–2000), m. 1956 Hon. Flora Fraser (Lady Saltoun)

VIII. HRH PRINCE LEOPOLD George Duncan Albert, Duke of Albany (1853–84), m. 1882 Princess Helena of Waldeck (1861–1922). Issue:

1. Alice (1883–1981), m. 1904 Prince Alexander of Teck (1874–1957), cr. 1st Earl of Athlone 1917. Issue:

(a) Lady May (1906–94), m. 1931 Sir Henry Abel-Smith, KCMG, KCVO, DSO; issue: Anne (b. 1932); Richard (b. 1933); Elizabeth (b. 1936)

(b) Rupert, Viscount Trematon (1907–28)

(c) Prince Maurice (March–September 1910)

2. Charles Edward (1884–1954), Duke of Albany 1884 until title suspended 1917, Duke of Saxe-Coburg-Gotha 1900–18, m. 1905 Princess Victoria Adelheid of Schleswig-Holstein-Sonderburg-Glücksburg. Issue:

(a) Prince Johann Leopold (1906–72), and has issue

(b) Princess Sibylla (1908–72), m. 1932 Prince Gustav Adolf of Sweden (see VII.1.(a))

(c) Prince Dietmar Hubertus (1909–43)

(d) Princess Caroline (1912–83), and has issue

(e) Prince Friedrich Josias (1918–98), and has issue

IX.   HRH PRINCESS BEATRICE Mary Victoria Feodore (1857–1944), m. 1885 Prince Henry of Battenberg (1858–96). Issue:

1. Alexander, 1st Marquess of Carisbrooke (1886–1960), m. 1917 Lady Irene Denison. Issue: (a) Lady Iris Mountbatten (1920–82), m.; issue: Robin A. Bryan (b. 1957)

2. Victoria Eugénie (1887–1969), m. 1906 Alfonso XIII (1886–1941) King of Spain 1886–1931. Issue:

(a) Prince Alfonso (1907–38)

(b) Prince Jaime (1908–75), and has issue

(c) Princess Beatriz (1909–2002), and has issue

(d) Princess Maria (1911–96), and has issue

(e) Prince Juan (1913–93), Count of Barcelona; issue: Princess Maria (b. 1936); Juan Carlos I, King of Spain (b. 1938), m. 1962 Princess Sophie of Greece and has issue (one son, two daughters); Princess Margarita (b. 1939)

(f) Prince Gonzalo (1914–34)

3. Major Lord Leopold Mountbatten (1889–1922)

4. Maurice (1891–1914), died of wounds received in action

KINGS AND QUEENS

ENGLISH KINGS AND QUEENS 927 TO 1603

HOUSES OF CERDIC AND DENMARK
Reign

927–939 ÆTHELSTAN
Son of Edward the Elder, by Ecgwynn, and grandson of Alfred
Acceded to Wessex and Mercia c.924, established direct rule over Northumbria 927, effectively creating the Kingdom of England
Reigned 15 years

939–946 EDMUND I
Born 921, son of Edward the Elder, by Eadgifu
Married (1) Ælfgifu (2) Æthelflæd
Killed aged 25, *reigned* 6 years

946–955 EADRED
Son of Edward the Elder, by Eadgifu
Reigned 9 years

955–959 EADWIG
Born before 943, son of Edmund and Ælfgifu
Married Ælfgifu
Reigned 3 years

959–975 EDGAR I
Born 943, son of Edmund and Ælfgifu
Married (1) Æthelflæd (2) Wulfthryth (3) Ælfthryth
Died aged 32, *reigned* 15 years

975–978 EDWARD I (the Martyr)
Born c.962, son of Edgar and Æthelflæd
Assassinated aged c.16, *reigned* 2 years

978–1016 ÆTHELRED (the Unready)
Born c.968/969, son of Edgar and Ælfthryth
Married (1) Ælfgifu (2) Emma, daughter of Richard I, Count of Normandy
1013–14 dispossessed of kingdom by Swegn Forkbeard (King of Denmark 987–1014)
Died aged c.47, *reigned* 38 years

1016 EDMUND II (Ironside)
Born before 993, son of Æthelred and Ælfgifu
Married Ealdgyth
Died aged over 23, *reigned* 7 months (April–November)

1016–1035 CNUT (Canute)
Born c.995, son of Swegn Forkbeard, King of Denmark, and Gunhild
Married (1) Ælfgifu (2) Emma, widow of Æthelred the Unready
Gained submission of West Saxons 1015, Northumbrians 1016, Mercia 1016, King of all England after Edmund's death, King of Denmark 1019–35, King of Norway 1028–35
Died aged c.40, *reigned* 19 years

1035–1040 HAROLD I (Harefoot)
Born c.1016/17, son of Cnut and Ælfgifu
Married Ælfgifu
1035 recognised as regent for himself and his brother Harthacnut; 1037 recognised as king
Died aged c.23, *reigned* 4 years

1040–1042 HARTHACNUT
Born c.1018, son of Cnut and Emma
Titular king of Denmark from 1028
Acknowledged King of England 1035–7 with Harold I as regent; effective king after Harold's death
Died aged c.24, *reigned* 2 years

1042–1066 EDWARD II (the Confessor)
Born between 1002 and 1005, son of Æthelred the Unready and Emma
Married Eadgyth, daughter of Godwine, Earl of Wessex
Died aged over 60, *reigned* 23 years

1066 HAROLD II (Godwinesson)
Born c.1020, son of Godwine, Earl of Wessex, and Gytha
Married (1) Eadgyth (2) Ealdgyth
Killed in battle aged c.46, *reigned* 10 months (January – October)

THE HOUSE OF NORMANDY

1066–1087 WILLIAM I (the Conqueror)
Born 1027/8, son of Robert I, Duke of Normandy; obtained the Crown by conquest
Married Matilda, daughter of Baldwin, Count of Flanders
Died aged c.60, *reigned* 20 years

1087–1100 WILLIAM II (Rufus)
Born between 1056 and 1060, third son of William I; succeeded his father in England only
Killed aged c.40, *reigned* 12 years

1100–1135 HENRY I (Beauclerk)
Born 1068, fourth son of William I
Married (1) Edith or Matilda, daughter of Malcolm III of Scotland (2) Adela, daughter of Godfrey, Count of Louvain
Died aged 67, *reigned* 35 years

1135–1154 STEPHEN
Born not later than 1100, third son of Adela, daughter of William I, and Stephen, Count of Blois
Married Matilda, daughter of Eustace, Count of Boulogne
1141 (February – November) held captive by adherents of Matilda, daughter of Henry I, who contested the crown until 1153
Died aged over 53, *reigned* 18 years

THE HOUSE OF ANJOU (PLANTAGENETS)

1154–1189 HENRY II (Curtmantle)
Born 1133, son of Matilda, daughter of Henry I, and Geoffrey, Count of Anjou
Married Eleanor, daughter of William, Duke of Aquitaine, and divorced queen of Louis VII of France
Died aged 56, *reigned* 34 years

1189–1199 RICHARD I (Coeur de Lion)
Born 1157, third son of Henry II
Married Berengaria, daughter of Sancho VI, King of Navarre
Died aged 42, *reigned* 9 years

1199–1216 JOHN (Lackland)
Born 1167, fifth son of Henry II

Married (1) Isabella or Avisa, daughter of William, Earl of Gloucester (divorced) (2) Isabella, daughter of Aymer, Count of Angoulême
Died aged 48, *reigned* 17 years

1216–1272   HENRY III
Born 1207, son of John and Isabella of Angoulême
Married Eleanor, daughter of Raymond, Count of Provence
Died aged 65, *reigned* 56 years

1272–1307   EDWARD I (Longshanks)
Born 1239, eldest son of Henry III
Married (1) Eleanor, daughter of Ferdinand III, King of Castile (2) Margaret, daughter of Philip III of France
Died aged 68, *reigned* 34 years

1307–1327   EDWARD II
Born 1284, eldest surviving son of Edward I and Eleanor
Married Isabella, daughter of Philip IV of France
Deposed January 1327, *killed* September 1327 aged 43, *reigned* 19 years

1327–1377   EDWARD III
Born 1312, eldest son of Edward II
Married Philippa, daughter of William, Count of Hainault
Died aged 64, *reigned* 50 years

1377–1399   RICHARD II
Born 1367, son of Edward (the Black Prince), eldest son of Edward III
Married (1) Anne, daughter of Emperor Charles IV (2) Isabelle, daughter of Charles VI of France
Deposed September 1399, *killed* February 1400 aged 33, *reigned* 22 years

THE HOUSE OF LANCASTER

1399–1413   HENRY IV
Born 1366, son of John of Gaunt, fourth son of Edward III, and Blanche, daughter of Henry, Duke of Lancaster
Married (1) Mary, daughter of Humphrey, Earl of Hereford (2) Joan, daughter of Charles, King of Navarre, and widow of John, Duke of Brittany
Died aged c.47, *reigned* 13 years

1413–1422   HENRY V
Born 1387, eldest surviving son of Henry IV and Mary
Married Catherine, daughter of Charles VI of France
Died aged 34, *reigned* 9 years

1422–1471   HENRY VI
Born 1421, son of Henry V
Married Margaret, daughter of René, Duke of Anjou and Count of Provence
Deposed March 1461, *restored* October 1470
Deposed April 1471, *killed* May 1471 aged 49, *reigned* 39 years

THE HOUSE OF YORK

1461–1483   EDWARD IV
Born 1442, eldest son of Richard of York (grandson of Edmund, fifth son of Edward III, and son of Anne, great-granddaughter of Lionel, third son of Edward iII)
Married Elizabeth Woodville, daughter of Richard, Lord Rivers, and widow of Sir John Grey

Acceded March 1461, *deposed* October 1470, *restored* April 1471
Died aged 40, *reigned* 21 years

1483   EDWARD V
Born 1470, eldest son of Edward IV
Deposed June 1483, *died* probably July – September 1483, aged 12, *reigned* 2 months (April – June)

1483–1485   RICHARD III
Born 1452, fourth son of Richard of York
Married Anne Neville, daughter of Richard, Earl of Warwick, and widow of Edward, Prince of Wales, son of Henry VI
Killed in battle aged 32, *reigned* 2 years

THE HOUSE OF TUDOR

1485–1509   HENRY VII
Born 1457, son of Margaret Beaufort (great-granddaughter of John of Gaunt, fourth son of Edward III) and Edmund Tudor, Earl of Richmond
Married Elizabeth, daughter of Edward IV
Died aged 52, *reigned* 23 years

1509–1547   HENRY VIII
Born 1491, second son of Henry VII
Married (1) Catherine, daughter of Ferdinand II, King of Aragon, and widow of his elder brother Arthur (divorced) (2) Anne, daughter of Sir Thomas Boleyn (executed) (3) Jane, daughter of Sir John Seymour (died in childbirth) (4) Anne, daughter of John, Duke of Cleves (divorced) (5) Catherine Howard, niece of the Duke of Norfolk (executed) (6) Catherine, daughter of Sir Thomas Parr and widow of Lord Latimer
Died aged 55, *reigned* 37 years

1547–1553   EDWARD VI
Born 1537, son of Henry VIII and Jane Seymour
Died aged 15, *reigned* 6 years

1553   JANE
Born 1537, daughter of Frances (daughter of Mary Tudor, the younger daughter of Henry VII) and Henry Grey, Duke of Suffolk
Married Lord Guildford Dudley, son of the Duke of Northumberland
Deposed July 1553, *executed* February 1554 aged 16, *reigned* 14 days

1553–1558   MARY I
Born 1516, daughter of Henry VIII and Catherine of Aragon
married Philip II of Spain
Died aged 42, *reigned* 5 years

1558–1603   ELIZABETH I
Born 1533, daughter of Henry VIII and Anne Boleyn
Died aged 69, *reigned* 44 years

BRITISH KINGS AND QUEENS SINCE 1603

THE HOUSE OF STUART
Reign

1603–1625   JAMES I (VI OF SCOTLAND)
Born 1566, son of Mary, Queen of Scots (granddaughter of Margaret Tudor, elder daughter of Henry VII), and Henry Stewart, Lord Darnley

Married Anne, daughter of Frederick II of Denmark
Died aged 58, *reigned* 22 years

1625–1649   CHARLES I
Born 1600, second son of James I
Married Henrietta Maria, daughter of Henry IV of France
Executed 1649 aged 48, *reigned* 23 years

COMMONWEALTH DECLARED 19 May 1649
1649–53 Government by a council of state
1653–8 Oliver Cromwell, *Lord Protector*
1658–9 Richard Cromwell, *Lord Protector*

Reign
1660–1685   CHARLES II
Born 1630, eldest son of Charles I
Married Catherine, daughter of John IV of Portugal
Died aged 54, *reigned* 24 years

1685–1688   JAMES II (VII OF SCOTLAND)
Born 1633, second son of Charles I
Married (1) Lady Anne Hyde, daughter of Edward, Earl of Clarendon (2) Mary, daughter of Alphonso, Duke of Modena
Reign ended with flight from kingdom December 1688
Died 1701 aged 67, *reigned* 3 years

INTERREGNUM
11 December 1688 to 12 February 1689

1689–1702   WILLIAM III
Born 1650, son of William II, Prince of Orange, and Mary Stuart, daughter of Charles I
Married Mary, elder daughter of James II
Died aged 51, *reigned* 13 years

1689–1694   MARY II
Born 1662, elder daughter of James II and Anne
Died aged 32, *reigned* 5 years

1702–1714   ANNE
Born 1665, younger daughter of James II and Anne
Married Prince George of Denmark, son of Frederick III of Denmark
Died aged 49, *reigned* 12 years

THE HOUSE OF HANOVER

1714–1727   GEORGE I (Elector of Hanover)
Born 1660, son of Sophia (daughter of Frederick, Elector Palatine, and Elizabeth Stuart, daughter of James I) and Ernest Augustus, Elector of Hanover
Married Sophia Dorothea, daughter of George William, Duke of Lüneburg-Celle
Died aged 67, *reigned* 12 years

1727–1760   GEORGE II
Born 1683, son of George I
Married Caroline, daughter of John Frederick, Margrave of Brandenburg-Anspach
Died aged 76, *reigned* 33 years

1760–1820   GEORGE III
Born 1738, son of Frederick, eldest son of George II
Married Charlotte, daughter of Charles Louis, Duke of Mecklenburg-Strelitz
Died aged 81, *reigned* 59 years

REGENCY 1811–20
Prince of Wales regent owing to the insanity of George III

Reign
1820–1830   GEORGE IV
Born 1762, eldest son of George III
Married Caroline, daughter of Charles, Duke of Brunswick-Wolfenbüttel
Died aged 67, *reigned* 10 years

1830–1837   WILLIAM IV
Born 1765, third son of George III
Married Adelaide, daughter of George, Duke of Saxe-Meiningen
Died aged 71, *reigned* 7 years

1837–1901   VICTORIA
Born 1819, daughter of Edward, fourth son of George III
Married Prince Albert of Saxe-Coburg and Gotha
Died aged 81, *reigned* 63 years

THE HOUSE OF SAXE-COBURG AND GOTHA

1901–1910   EDWARD VII
Born 1841, eldest son of Victoria and Albert
Married Alexandra, daughter of Christian IX of Denmark
Died aged 68, *reigned* 9 years

THE HOUSE OF WINDSOR

1910–1936   GEORGE V
Born 1865, second son of Edward VII
Married Victoria Mary, daughter of Francis, Duke of Teck
Died aged 70, *reigned* 25 years

1936   EDWARD VIII
Born 1894, eldest son of George V
Married (1937) Mrs Wallis Simpson
Abdicated 1936, *died* 1972 aged 77, *reigned* 10 months (20 January to 11 December)

1936–1952   GEORGE VI
Born 1895, second son of George V
Married Lady Elizabeth Bowes-Lyon, daughter of 14th Earl of Strathmore and Kinghorne
Died aged 56, *reigned* 15 years

1952–   ELIZABETH II
Born 1926, elder daughter of George VI
Married Philip, son of Prince Andrew of Greece

KINGS AND QUEENS OF SCOTS 1016 TO 1603

Reign
1016–1034   MALCOLM II
Born c.954, son of Kenneth II
Acceded to Alba 1005, secured Lothian c.1016, obtained Strathclyde for his grandson Duncan c.1016, thus reigning over an area approximately the same as that governed by later rulers of Scotland
Died aged c.80, *reigned* 18 years

THE HOUSE OF ATHOLL

1034–1040   DUNCAN I
Son of Bethoc, daughter of Malcolm II, and Crinan, Mormaer of Atholl
Married a cousin of Siward, Earl of Northumbria
Reigned 5 years

1040–1057   MACBETH
*Born c.*1005, son of a daughter of Malcolm II and Finlaec, Mormaer of Moray
Married Gruoch, granddaughter of Kenneth III
Killed aged *c.*52, *reigned* 17 years

1057–1058   LULACH
*Born c.*1032, son of Gillacomgan, Mormaer of Moray, and Gruoch (and stepson of Macbeth)
Died aged *c.*26, *reigned* 7 months (August – March)

1058–1093   MALCOLM III (Canmore)
*Born c.*1031, elder son of Duncan I
Married (1) Ingibiorg (2) Margaret (St Margaret), granddaughter of Edmund II of England
Killed in battle aged *c.*62, *reigned* 35 years

1093–1097   DONALD III BÁN
*Born c.*1033, second son of Duncan I
deposed May 1094, *restored* November 1094, *deposed* October 1097, *reigned* 3 years

1094   DUNCAN II
*Born c.*1060, elder son of Malcolm III and Ingibiorg
Married Octreda of Dunbar
Killed aged *c.*34, *reigned* 6 months (May–November)

1097–1107   EDGAR
*Born c.*1074, second son of Malcolm III and Margaret
Died aged *c.*32, *reigned* 9 years

1107–1124   ALEXANDER I (The Fierce)
*Born c.*1077, fifth son of Malcolm III and Margaret
Married Sybilla, illegitimate daughter of Henry I of England
Died aged *c.*47, *reigned* 17 years

1124–1153   DAVID I (The Saint)
*Born c.*1085, sixth son of Malcolm III and Margaret
Married Matilda, daughter of Waltheof, Earl of Huntingdon
Died aged *c.*68, *reigned* 29 years

1153–1165   MALCOLM IV (The Maiden)
*Born c.*1141, son of Henry, Earl of Huntingdon, second son of David I
Died aged *c.*24, *reigned* 12 years

1165–1214   WILLIAM I (The Lion)
*Born c.*1142, brother of Malcolm IV
Married Ermengarde, daughter of Richard, Viscount of Beaumont
Died aged *c.*72, *reigned* 49 years

1214–1249   ALEXANDER II
Born 1198, son of William I
Married (1) Joan, daughter of John, King of England (2) Marie, daughter of Ingelram de Coucy
Died aged 50, *reigned* 34 years

1249–1286   ALEXANDER III
Born 1241, son of Alexander II and Marie
Married (1) Margaret, daughter of Henry III of England (2) Yolande, daughter of the Count of Dreux
Killed accidentally aged 44, *reigned* 36 years

1286–1290   MARGARET (The Maid of Norway)
Born 1283, daughter of Margaret (daughter of Alexander III) and Eric II of Norway
Died aged 7, *reigned* 4 years

FIRST INTERREGNUM 1290–2
Throne disputed by 13 competitors. Crown awarded to John Balliol by adjudication of Edward I of England

THE HOUSE OF BALLIOL
1292–1296   JOHN (Balliol)
*Born c.*1250, son of Dervorguilla, great-great-great-granddaughter of David I, and John de Balliol
Married Isabella, daughter of John, Earl of Surrey
Abdicated 1296, *died* 1313 aged *c.*63, *reigned* 3 years

SECOND INTERREGNUM 1296–1306
Edward I of England declared John Balliol to have forfeited the throne for contumacy in 1296 and took the government of Scotland into his own hands

THE HOUSE OF BRUCE
1306–1329   ROBERT I (Bruce)
Born 1274, son of Robert Bruce and Marjorie, countess of Carrick, and great-grandson of the second daughter of David, Earl of Huntingdon, brother of William I
Married (1) Isabella, daughter of Donald, Earl of Mar (2) Elizabeth, daughter of Richard, Earl of Ulster
Died aged 54, *reigned* 23 years

1329–1371   DAVID II
Born 1324, son of Robert I and Elizabeth
Married (1) Joanna, daughter of Edward II of England (2) Margaret Drummond, widow of Sir John Logie (divorced)
Died aged 46, *reigned* 41 years
1332 Edward Balliol, son of John Balliol, crowned King of Scots September, expelled December
1333–6 Edward Balliol restored as King of Scots

THE HOUSE OF STEWART
1371–1390   ROBERT II (Stewart)
Born 1316, son of Marjorie (daughter of Robert I) and Walter, High Steward of Scotland
Married (1) Elizabeth, daughter of Sir Robert Mure of Rowallan (2) Euphemia, daughter of Hugh, Earl of Ross
Died aged 74, *reigned* 19 years

1390–1406   ROBERT III
*Born c.*1337, son of Robert II and Elizabeth
Married Annabella, daughter of Sir John Drummond of Stobhall
Died aged *c.*69, *reigned* 16 years

1406–1437   JAMES I
Born 1394, son of Robert III
Married Joan Beaufort, daughter of John, Earl of Somerset
Assassinated aged 42, *reigned* 30 years

1437–1460   JAMES II
Born 1430, son of James I
Married Mary, daughter of Arnold, Duke of Gueldres
Killed accidentally aged 29, *reigned* 23 years

1460–1488   JAMES III
Born 1452, son of James II
Married Margaret, daughter of Christian I of Denmark
Assassinated aged 36, *reigned* 27 years

1488–1513	JAMES IV *Born* 1473, son of James III *Married* Margaret Tudor, daughter of Henry VII of England *Killed* in battle aged 40, *reigned* 25 years
1513–1542	JAMES V *Born* 1512, son of James IV *Married* (1) Madeleine, daughter of Francis I of France (2) Mary of Lorraine, daughter of the Duc de Guise *Died* aged 30, *reigned* 29 years
1542–1567	MARY *Born* 1542, daughter of James V and Mary *Married* (1) the Dauphin, afterwards Francis II of France (2) Henry Stewart, Lord Darnley (3) James Hepburn, Earl of Bothwell *Abdicated* 1567, prisoner in England from 1568, *executed* 1587, *reigned* 24 years
1567–1625	JAMES VI (and I of England) *Born* 1566, son of Mary, Queen of Scots, and Henry, Lord Darnley Acceded 1567 to the Scottish throne, *reigned* 58 years Succeeded 1603 to the English throne, so joining the English and Scottish crowns in one person. The two kingdoms remained distinct until 1707 when the parliaments of the kingdoms became conjoined

WELSH SOVEREIGNS AND PRINCES

Wales was ruled by sovereign princes from the earliest times until the death of Llywelyn in 1282. The first English Prince of Wales was the son of Edward I, who was born in Caernarvon town on 25 April 1284. According to a discredited legend, he was presented to the Welsh chieftains as their prince, in fulfilment of a promise that they should have a prince who 'could not speak a word of English' and should be native born. This son, who afterwards became Edward II, was created 'Prince of Wales and Earl of Chester' at the Lincoln Parliament on 7 February 1301.

The title Prince of Wales is borne after individual conferment and is not inherited at birth, though some Princes have been declared and styled Prince of Wales but never formally so created (*s.*). The title was conferred on Prince Charles by The Queen on 26 July 1958. He was invested at Caernarvon on 1 July 1969.

INDEPENDENT PRINCES AD 844 TO 1282

844–878	Rhodri the Great
878–916	Anarawd, son of Rhodri
916–950	Hywel Dda, the Good
950–979	Iago ab Idwal (or Ieuaf)
979–985	Hywel ab Ieuaf, the Bad
985–986	Cadwallon, his brother
986–999	Maredudd ab Owain ap Hywel Dda
999–1008	Cynan ap Hywel ab Ieuaf
1018–1023	Llywelyn ap Seisyll
1023–1039	Iago ab Idwal ap Meurig
1039–1063	Gruffydd ap Llywelyn ap Seisyll
1063–1075	Bleddyn ap Cynfyn
1075–1081	Trahaern ap Caradog
1081–1137	Gruffydd ap Cynan ab Iago
1137–1170	Owain Gwynedd
1170–1194	Dafydd ab Owain Gwynedd
1194–1240	Llywelyn Fawr, the Great
1240–1246	Dafydd ap Llywelyn
1246–1282	Llywelyn ap Gruffydd ap Llywelyn

ENGLISH PRINCES SINCE 1301

1301	Edward (Edward II)
1343	Edward the Black Prince, son of Edward III
1376	Richard (Richard II), son of the Black Prince
1399	Henry of Monmouth (Henry V)
1454	Edward of Westminster, son of Henry VI
1471	Edward of Westminster (Edward V)
1483	Edward, son of Richard III (*d.* 1484)
1489	Arthur Tudor, son of Henry VII
1504	Henry Tudor (Henry VIII)
1610	Henry Stuart, son of James I (*d.* 1612)
1616	Charles Stuart (Charles I)
*c.*1638 (*s.*)	Charles Stuart (Charles II)
1688 (*s.*)	James Francis Edward Stuart (The Old Pretender), son of James II (*d.* 1766)
1714	George Augustus (George II)
1729	Frederick Lewis, son of George II (*d.* 1751)
1751	George William Frederick (George III)
1762	George Augustus Frederick (George IV)
1841	Albert Edward (Edward VII)
1901	George (George V)
1910	Edward (Edward VIII)
1958	Charles, son of Elizabeth II

PRINCESSES ROYAL

The style Princess Royal is conferred at the Sovereign's discretion on his or her eldest daughter. It is an honorary title, held for life, and cannot be inherited or passed on. It was first conferred on Princess Mary, daughter of Charles I, in approximately 1642.

*c.*1642	Princess Mary (1631–60), daughter of Charles I
1727	Princess Anne (1709–59), daughter of George II
1766	Princess Charlotte (1766–1828), daughter of George III
1840	Princess Victoria (1840–1901), daughter of Victoria
1905	Princess Louise (1867–1931), daughter of Edward VII
1932	Princess Mary (1897–1965), daughter of George V
1987	Princess Anne (b. 1950), daughter of Elizabeth II

PRECEDENCE

ENGLAND AND WALES

The Sovereign
The Prince Philip, Duke of
  Edinburgh
The Prince of Wales
The Sovereign's younger sons
The Sovereign's grandsons
The Sovereign's cousins
Archbishop of Canterbury
Lord High Chancellor
Archbishop of York
The Prime Minister
Lord President of the Council
Speaker of the House of Commons
Lord Privy Seal
Ambassadors and High
  Commissioners
Lord Great Chamberlain
Earl Marshal
Lord Chamberlain of the Household
Lord Steward of the Household
Master of the Horse
Dukes, according to their patent of
  creation:
  (1) of England
  (2) of Scotland
  (3) of Great Britain
  (4) of Ireland
  (5) those created since the Union
Eldest sons of Dukes of the Blood
  Royal
Marquesses, according to their patent
  of creation:
  (1) of England
  (2) of Scotland
  (3) of Great Britain
  (4) of Ireland
  (5) those created since the Union
Dukes' eldest sons
Earls, according to their patent of
  creation:
  (1) of England
  (2) of Scotland
  (3) of Great Britain
  (4) of Ireland
  (5) those created since the Union
Younger sons of Dukes of Blood Royal
Marquesses' eldest sons
Dukes' younger sons
Viscounts, according to their patent of
  creation:
  (1) of England
  (2) of Scotland
  (3) of Great Britain
  (4) of Ireland
  (5) those created since the Union
Earls' eldest sons
Marquesses' younger sons
Bishop of London
Bishop of Durham
Bishop of Winchester
Other English Diocesan Bishops
  according to seniority of
  consecration
Suffragan Bishops, according to
  seniority of consecration
Secretaries of State, if of the degree of
  a Baron
Barons, according to their patent of
  creation:

(1) of England
(2) of Scotland
(3) of Great Britain
(4) of Ireland
(5) those created since the Union,
  including Life Barons
Treasurer of the Household
Comptroller of the Household
Vice-Chamberlain of the Household
Secretaries of State under the degree of
  Baron
Viscounts' eldest sons
Earls' younger sons
Barons' eldest sons
Knights of the Garter
Privy Counsellors
Chancellor of the Exchequer
Chancellor of the Duchy of Lancaster
Lord Chief Justice of England
Master of the Rolls
President of the Family Division
Vice-Chancellor
Lords Justices of Appeal, according to
  seniority of appointment
Judges of the High Court, according
  to seniority of appointment
Viscounts' younger sons
Barons' younger sons
Sons of Life Peers and Lords of Appeal
  in Ordinary
Baronets, according to date of patent
Knights of the Thistle
Knights Grand Cross of the Bath
Knights Grand Commanders of the
  Star of India
Knights Grand Cross of St Michael
  and St George
Knights Grand Commanders of the
  Indian Empire
Knights Grand Cross of the Royal
  Victorian Order
Knights Grand Cross of the British
  Empire
Knights Commanders of the Bath
Knights Commanders of the Star of
  India
Knights Commanders of St Michael
  and St George
Knights Commanders of the Indian
  Empire
Knights Commanders of the Royal
  Victorian Order
Knights Commanders of the British
  Empire
Knights Bachelor
Vice-Chancellor of the County
  Palatine of Lancaster
Circuit Judges who held office as
  Official Referees to Supreme Court
  (immediately before 1 January
  1972)
Recorder of London
Recorders of Liverpool and
  Manchester, according to priority of
  appointment
Common Serjeant
Circuit Judges who held office
  immediately before 1 January
  1972, according to priority of
  appointment
Other Circuit Judges according to

priority or order of their respective
  appointments
Companions of the Bath
Companions of the Star of India
Companions of St Michael and St
  George
Companions of the Indian Empire
Commanders of the Royal Victorian
  Order
Commanders of the British Empire
Companions of the Distinguished
  Service Order
Lieutenants of the Royal Victorian
  Order
Officers of the British Empire
Companions of the Imperial Service
  Order
Eldest sons of younger sons of Peers
Baronets' eldest sons
Eldest sons of Knights, in the same
  order as their fathers
Members of the Royal Victorian
  Order
Members of the British Empire
Younger sons of Baronets
Younger sons of Knights, in the same
  order as their fathers
Esquires
Gentlemen

SCOTLAND

The Sovereign
The Prince Philip, Duke of Edinburgh
The Lord High Commissioner to the
  General Assembly of the Church of
  Scotland (while that Assembly is
  sitting)
The Duke of Rothesay (eldest son of
  the Sovereign)
The Sovereign's younger sons
Grandsons of the Sovereign
The Sovereign's cousins
Lord-Lieutenants
Lord Provosts of Cities being *ex-officio*
  Lord-Lieutenants of those Cities
  during their term of office
Sheriffs Principal, successively, within
  their own localities and during
  holding of office
Lord Chancellor of Great Britain
Moderator of the General Assembly of
  the Church of Scotland
Keeper of the Great Seal of Scotland
  (the First Minister)
The Presiding Officer
The Secretary of State for Scotland
Hereditary High Constable of
  Scotland
Hereditary Master of the Household in
  Scotland
Dukes, in same order as in England
Eldest sons of Dukes of the Blood
  Royal
Marquesses, as in England
Eldest sons of Dukes
Earls, as in England
Younger sons of Dukes of Blood
  Royal
Eldest sons of Marquesses

Dukes' younger sons
Lord Justice General
Lord Clerk Register
Lord Advocate
The Advocate-General
Lord Justice Clerk
Viscounts, as in England
Eldest sons of Earls
Marquesses' younger sons
Lord-Barons, as in England
Eldest sons of Viscounts
Earls' younger sons
Lord-Barons' eldest sons
Knights of the Garter
Knights of the Thistle
Privy Counsellors
Senators of College of Justice (Lords of
    Session)
Viscounts' younger sons
Lord-Barons' younger sons
Baronets
Knights Grand Cross and Knights
    Grand Commanders of Orders, as
    in England
Knights Commanders of Orders, as in
    England
Solicitor-General for Scotland
Lord Lyon King of Arms
Sheriffs Principal, when not within
    own county
Knights Bachelor
Sheriffs
Companions of Orders, as in England
Commanders of the Royal Victorian
    Order
Commanders of the British Empire
Companions of the Distinguished
    Service Order
Lieutenants of the Royal Victorian
    Order
Officers of the British Empire
Companions of the Imperial Service
    Order
Eldest sons of younger sons of Peers
Eldest sons of Baronets
Eldest sons of Knights, as in England
Members of the Royal Victorian Order
Members of the British Empire
Baronets' younger sons
Knights' younger sons
Esquires
Gentlemen

WOMEN

Women take the same rank as their husbands or as their brothers; but the daughter of a peer marrying a commoner retains her title as Lady or Honourable. Daughters of peers rank next immediately after the wives of their elder brothers, and before their younger brothers' wives. Daughters of peers marrying peers of lower degree take the same order of precedence as that of their husbands; thus the daughter of a Duke marrying a Baron becomes of the rank of Baroness only, while her sisters married to commoners retain their rank and take precedence of the Baroness. Merely official rank on the husband's part does not give any similar precedence to the wife.

Peeresses in their own right take the same precedence as peers of the same rank, i.e. from their date of creation.

LOCAL PRECEDENCE
Scotland
The Lord Provosts of the city districts of Aberdeen, Dundee, Edinburgh and Glasgow are Lord Lieutenants for those districts *ex officio* and take precedence as such.

THE PEERAGE

The rules which govern the creation and succession of peerages are extremely complicated. There are, technically, five separate peerages, the Peerage of England, of Scotland, of Ireland, of Great Britain, and of the United Kingdom. The Peerage of Great Britain dates from 1707 when an Act of Union combined the two kingdoms of England and Scotland and separate peerages were discontinued. The Peerage of the United Kingdom dates from 1801 when Great Britain and Ireland were combined under an Act of Union. Some Scottish peers have received additional peerages of Great Britain or of the United Kingdom since 1707, and some Irish peers additional peerages of the United Kingdom since 1801.

The Peerage of Ireland was not entirely discontinued from 1801 but holders of Irish peerages, whether pre-dating or created subsequent to the Union of 1801, were not entitled to sit in the House of Lords if they had no additional English, Scottish, Great Britain or United Kingdom peerage. However, they are eligible for election to the House of Commons and to vote in parliamentary elections. An Irish peer holding a peerage of a lower grade which enabled him to sit in the House of Lords was introduced there by the title which enabled him to sit, though for all other purposes he was known by his higher title.

In the Peerage of Scotland there is no rank of Baron; the equivalent rank is Lord of Parliament, abbreviated to 'Lord' (the female equivalent is 'Lady').

All peers of England, Scotland, Great Britain or the United Kingdom who are 21 years or over, and of British, Irish or Commonwealth nationality were entitled to sit in the House of Lords until the House of Lords Act 1999, when hereditary peers lost the right to sit. However, section two of the Act provided an exception for 90 hereditary peers plus the holders of the office of Earl Marshal and Lord Great Chamberlain to remain as Members of The House of Lords for their lifetime or pending further reform. Of the 90 hereditary peers, 75 were elected by the hereditary peers in their political party, or Crossbench grouping, and the remaining 15 by the whole House. Until 7 November 2002 any vacancy arising due to the death of one of the 90 excepted hereditary peers was filled by the runner-up to the original election. From 7 November 2002 any vacancy due to a death has been filled by holding a by-election. By-elections are conducted in accordance with arrangements made by the Clerk of the Parliaments and have to take place within three months of a vacancy occurring. If the vacancy is among the 75, only the excepted hereditary peers in the relevant party or Crossbench grouping are entitled to vote. If the vacancy is among the other 15, the whole House is entitled to vote.

In the list below, peers currently holding one of the 92 hereditary places in The House of Lords are indicated by **.

HEREDITARY WOMEN PEERS

Most hereditary peerages pass on death to the nearest male heir, but there are exceptions, and several are held by women.

A woman peer in her own right retains her title after marriage, and if her husband's rank is the superior she is designated by the two titles jointly, the inferior one second. Her hereditary claim still holds good in spite of any marriage whether higher or lower. No rank held by a woman can confer any title or even precedence upon her husband but the rank of a hereditary woman peer in her own right is inherited by her eldest son (or in some cases daughter).

After the Peerage Act 1963, hereditary women peers in their own right were entitled to sit in the House of Lords, subject to the same qualifications as men, until the House of Lords Act 1999.

LIFE PEERS

Since 1876 non-hereditary or life peerages have been conferred on certain eminent judges to enable the judicial functions of the House of Lords to be carried out. These Lords are known as Lords of Appeal in Ordinary or law lords. In 2004, Baroness Hale of Richmond became the first female law lord.

Since 1958 life peerages have been conferred upon distinguished men and women from all walks of life, giving them seats in the House of Lords in the degree of Baron or Baroness. They are addressed in the same way as hereditary Lords and Barons, and their children have similar courtesy titles.

PEERAGES EXTINCT SINCE THE LAST EDITION

VISCOUNTCIES: Cross (cr. 1886)
LIFE PEERAGES: Blatch (cr. 1987); Bruce of Donington (cr. 1974); Callaghan of Cardiff (cr. 1987); Campbell of Croy (cr. 1974); Carlisle of Bucklow (cr. 1987); Chapple (cr. 1985); Clark of Kempston (cr. 1992); Donaldson of Lymington (cr. 1988); Fitt (cr. 1983); Hanson (cr. 1983); King of Wartnaby (cr. 1983); Lane (cr. 1979); Orme (cr. 1997); Parry (cr. 1975); Roll of Ipsden (cr. 1977); Scarman (cr. 1977); Sheppard of Liverpool (cr. 1998); Trotman (cr. 1999); Whaddon (cr. 1978)

DISCLAIMER OF PEERAGES

The Peerage Act 1963 enables peers to disclaim their peerages for life. Peers alive in 1963 could disclaim within twelve months after the passing of the Act (31 July 1963); a person subsequently succeeding to a peerage may disclaim within 12 months (one month if an MP) after the date of succession, or of reaching 21, if later. The disclaimer is irrevocable but does not affect the descent of the peerage after the disclaimant's death, and children of a disclaimed peer may, if they wish, retain their precedence and any courtesy titles and styles borne as children of a peer. The disclaimer permitted the disclaimant to sit in the House of Commons if elected as an MP. As the House of Lords Act 1999 removed hereditary peers from the House of Lords, they are now entitled to sit in the House of Commons without having to disclaim their titles.

The following peerages are currently disclaimed:

EARLDOMS: Durham (1970); Selkirk (1994)
VISCOUNTCIES: Stansgate (1963)

BARONIES: Merthyr (1977); Reith (1972); Sanderson of
Ayot (1971)
PEERS WHO ARE MINORS (i.e. under 21 years of age)
  EARLS: Craven (*b.* 1989)
  VISCOUNTS: Selby (*b.* 1993)

FORMS OF ADDRESS

Forms of address are given under the style for each
individual rank of the peerage. Both formal and social
forms of address are given where usage differs; nowadays,
the social form is generally preferred to the formal, which
increasingly is used only for official documents and on
very formal occasions.

ABBREVIATIONS AND SYMBOLS

S.	Scottish title
I.	Irish title
**	Hereditary peer remaining in the House of Lords
°	there is no 'of' in the title
b.	Born
s.	Succeeded
m.	Married
w.	widower or widow
M.	Minor
†	heir not ascertained at time of going to press
F_	represents forename
S_	represents surname

HEREDITARY PEERS

PEERS OF THE BLOOD ROYAL

Style, His Royal Highness The Duke of _/His Royal Highness the Earl of_
Style of address (formal) May it please your Royal Highness; *(informal)* Sir

Created	Title, order of succession, name, etc.	Heir
	Dukes	
1947	*Edinburgh (1st),* HRH The Prince Philip, Duke of Edinburgh	The Prince of Wales §
1337	*Cornwall,* Charles, Prince of Wales, *s.* 1952	‡
1398 S.	*Rothesay,* Charles, Prince of Wales, *s.* 1952	‡
1986	*York (1st),* The Prince Andrew, Duke of York	None
1999	*Wessex (1st),* The Prince Edward, Earl of Wessex	None
1928	*Gloucester (2nd),* Prince Richard, Duke of Gloucester, *s.* 1974	Earl of Ulster
1934	*Kent (2nd),* Prince Edward, Duke of Kent, *s.* 1942	Earl of St Andrews

§ In June 1999, Buckingham Palace revealed that the current Earl of Wessex will succeed to the Dukedom of Edinburgh after the title
has returned to the crown. The Prince of Wales will only be able to confer the Dukedom on the Earl of Wessex when he succeeds his
mother as King.
‡ The title is held by the Sovereign's eldest son from the moment of his birth or the Sovereign's accession

DUKES

Coronet, Eight strawberry leaves

Style, His Grace the Duke of _
Envelope (formal), His Grace the Duke of _; *(social),* The Duke of _. *Letter (formal),* My Lord Duke; *(social),* Dear Duke.
Spoken (formal), Your Grace; *(social),* Duke
Wife's style, Her Grace the Duchess of _
Envelope (formal), Her Grace the Duchess of _; *(social),* The Duchess of _. *Letter (formal),* Dear Madam; *(social),* Dear
Duchess. *Spoken,* Duchess
Eldest son's style, Takes his father's second title as a courtesy title (*see* Courtesy titles)
Younger sons' style, 'Lord' before forename (F_) and surname (S_)
Envelope, Lord F_ S_. *Letter (formal),* My Lord; *(social),* Dear Lord F_. *Spoken (formal),* My Lord; *(social),* Lord F_
Daughters' style, 'Lady' before forename (F_) and surname (S_)
Envelope, Lady F_ S_. *Letter (formal),* Dear Madam; *(social),* Dear Lady F_. *Spoken,* Lady F_

Created	Title, order of succession, name, etc.	Heir
1868 I.	*Abercorn (5th),* James Hamilton, KG, *b.* 1934, *s.* 1979, *m.*, *Lord Steward*	Marquess of Hamilton, *b.* 1969
1701 S.	*Argyll (13th),* Torquhil Ian Campbell, *b.* 1968, *s.* 2001	Marquess of Lorne, *b.* 2004
1703 S.	*Atholl (11th),* John Murray, *b.* 1929, *s.* 1996, *m.*	Marquis of Tullibardine, *b.* 1960
1682	*Beaufort (11th),* David Robert Somerset, *b.* 1928, *s.* 1984, *w.*	Marquess of Worcester, *b.* 1952
1694	*Bedford (15th),* Andrew Ian Henry Russell, *b.* 1962, *s.* 2003, *m.*	Lord Robin L. H. R., *b.* 1963
1663 S.	*Buccleuch (9th) and Queensberry (11th) (S. 1684),* Walter Francis John Montagu Douglas Scott, KT, VRD, *b.* 1923, *s.* 1973, *m.*	Earl of Dalkeith, KBE, *b.* 1954

Created	Title, order of succession, name, etc.	Heir
1694	*Devonshire (12th),* Peregrine Andrew Morny Cavendish, *b.* 1944, *s.* 2004, *m.*	Marquess of Hartington, *b.* 1969
1900	*Fife (3rd),* James George Alexander Bannerman Carnegie, *b.* 1929, *s.* 1959	Earl of Southesk, *b.* 1961
1675	*Grafton (11th),* Hugh Denis Charles FitzRoy, KG, *b.* 1919, *s.* 1970, *m.*	Earl of Euston, *b.* 1947
1643 S.	*Hamilton (15th) and Brandon (12th) (1711),* Angus Alan Douglas Douglas-Hamilton, *b.* 1938, *s.* 1973 *Premier Peer of Scotland*	Marquis of Douglas and Clydesdale, *b.* 1978
1766 I.	*Leinster (9th),* Maurice FitzGerald, *b.* 1948, *s.* 2004, *m. Premier Duke, Marquess and Earl of Ireland*	Lord John F., *b.* 1952
1719	*Manchester (13th),* Alexander Charles David Drogo Montagu, *b.* 1962, *s.* 2002, *m.*	Viscount Mandeville, *b.* 1993
1702	*Marlborough (11th),* John George Vanderbilt Henry Spencer-Churchill, *b.* 1926, *s.* 1972, *m.*	Marquess of Blandford, *b.* 1955
1707 S.	** *Montrose (8th),* James Graham, *b.* 1935, *s.* 1992, *m.*	Marquis of Graham, *b.* 1973
1483	** *Norfolk (18th),* Edward Wiliam Fitzalan-Howard, *b.* 1956, *s.* 2002, *m. Premier Duke and Earl Marshal*	Earl of Arundel and Surrey, *b.* 1987
1766	*Northumberland (12th),* Ralph George Algernon Percy, *b.* 1956, *s.* 1995, *m.*	Earl Percy, *b.* 1984
1675	*Richmond (10th) and Gordon (5th) (1876),* Charles Henry Gordon Lennox, *b.* 1929, *s.* 1989, *m.*	Earl of March and Kinrara, *b.* 1955
1707 S.	*Roxburghe (10th),* Guy David Innes-Ker, *b.* 1954, *s.* 1974, *m. Premier Baronet of Scotland*	Marquis of Bowmont and Cessford, *b.* 1981
1703	*Rutland (11th),* David Charles Robert Manners, *b.* 1959, *s.* 1999, *m.*	Marquess of Granby, *b.* 1999
1684	*St Albans (14th),* Murray de Vere Beauclerk, *b.* 1939, *s.* 1988, *m.*	Earl of Burford, *b.* 1965
1547	*Somerset (19th),* John Michael Edward Seymour, *b.* 1952, *s.* 1984, *m.*	Lord Seymour, *b.* 1982
1833	*Sutherland (7th),* Francis Ronald Egerton, *b.* 1940, *s.* 2000, *m.*	Marquess of Stafford, *b.* 1975
1814	*Wellington (8th),* Arthur Valerian Wellesley, KG, LVO, OBE, MC, *b.* 1915, *s.* 1972, *m.*	Marquess of Douro, *b.* 1945
1874	*Westminster (6th),* Gerald Cavendish Grosvenor, KG, OBE, *b.* 1951, *s.* 1979, *m.*	Earl Grosvenor, *b.* 1991

MARQUESSES

Coronet, Four strawberry leaves alternating with four silver balls

Style, The Most Hon. the Marquess (of) _ . In Scotland the spelling 'Marquis' is preferred for pre-Union creations
Envelope (formal), The Most Hon. the Marquess of _; *(social),* The Marquess of _. *Letter (formal),* My Lord; *(social),* Dear Lord _. *Spoken (formal),* My Lord; *(social),* Lord _
Wife's style, The Most Hon. the Marchioness (of) _
Envelope (formal), The Most Hon. the Marchioness of _; *(social),* The Marchioness of _. *Letter (formal),* Madam; *(social),* Dear Lady _. *Spoken,* Lady _
Eldest son's style, Takes his father's second title as a courtesy title *(see* Courtesy titles)
Younger sons' style, 'Lord' before forename and surname, as for Duke's younger sons
Daughters' style, 'Lady' before forename and surname, as for Duke's daughter)

Created	Title, order of succession, name, etc.	Heir
1916	*Aberdeen and Temair (7th),* Alexander George Gordon, *b.* 1955, *s.* 2002, *m.*	Earl of Haddo, *b.* 1983
1876	*Abergavenny (6th) and 10th Earl, Abergavenny, 1784,* Christopher George Charles Nevill, *b.* 1955, *s.* 2000, *m.*	To Earldom only, David M. R. N., *b.* 1941
1821	*Ailesbury (8th),* Michael Sidney Cedric Brudenell-Bruce, *b.* 1926, *s.* 1974	Earl of Cardigan, *b.* 1952
1831	*Ailsa (8th),* Archibald Angus Charles Kennedy, *b.* 1956, *s.* 1994	Lord David Kennedy, *b.* 1958
1815	*Anglesey (7th),* George Charles Henry Victor Paget, *b.* 1922, *s.* 1947, *m.*	Earl of Uxbridge, *b.* 1950
1789	*Bath (7th),* Alexander George Thynn, *b.* 1932, *s.* 1992, *m.*	Viscount Weymouth, *b.* 1974
1826	*Bristol (8th),* Frederick William Augustus Hervey, *b.* 1979, *s.* 1999	Timothy H. H., *b.* 1960
1796	*Bute (7th),* John Colum Crichton-Stuart, *b.* 1958, *s.* 1993, *m.*	Lord Mount Stuart, *b.* 1989
1812	° *Camden (6th),* David George Edward Henry Pratt, *b.* 1930, *s.* 1983	Earl of Brecknock, *b.* 1965
1815	** *Cholmondeley (7th),* David George Philip Cholmondeley, *b.* 1960, *s.* 1990, *Lord Great Chamberlain*	Charles G. C., *b.* 1959
1816	° *Conyngham (7th),* Frederick William Henry Francis Conyngham, *b.* 1924, *s.* 1974, *m.*	Earl of Mount Charles, *b.* 1951

Created	Title, order of succession, name, etc.	Heir
1791 I.	*Donegall (7th),* Dermot Richard Claud Chichester, LVO, *b.* 1916, *s.* 1975, *w.*	Earl of Belfast, *b.* 1952
1789 I.	*Downshire (9th),* (Arthur Francis) Nicholas Wills Hill, *b.* 1959, *s.* 2003, *m.*	Earl of Hillsborough, *b.* 1996
1801 I.	*Ely (8th),* Charles John Tottenham, *b.* 1913, *s.* 1969, *w.*	Viscount Loftus, *b.* 1943
1801	*Exeter (8th),* (William) Michael Anthony Cecil, *b.* 1935, *s.* 1988, *m.*	Lord Burghley, *b.* 1970
1800 I.	*Headfort (6th),* Thomas Geoffrey Charles Michael Taylour, *b.* 1932, *s.* 1960, *m.*	Earl of Bective, *b.* 1959
1793	*Hertford (9th),* Henry Jocelyn Seymour, *b.* 1958, *s.* 1997, *m.*	Earl of Yarmouth, *b.* 1993
1599 S.	*Huntly (13th),* Granville Charles Gomer Gordon, *b.* 1944, *s.* 1987, *m.* *Premier Marquess of Scotland*	Earl of Aboyne, *b.* 1973
1784	*Lansdowne (9th),* Charles Maurice Mercer Nairne Petty-Fitzmaurice, *b.* 1941, *s.* 1999, *m.*	Earl of Shelburne, *b.* 1970
1902	*Linlithgow (4th),* Adrian John Charles Hope, *b.* 1946, *s.* 1987, *m.*	Earl of Hopetoun, *b.* 1969
1816 I.	*Londonderry (9th),* Alexander Charles Robert Vane-Tempest-Stewart, *b.* 1937, *s.* 1955, *m.*	Viscount Castlereagh, *b.* 1972
1701 S.	*Lothian (13th),* Michael Andrew Foster Jude Kerr (Michael Ancram), PC, *b.* 1945, *s.* 2004, *m.*	Lord Ralph W. F. J. K., *b.* 1957
1917	*Milford Haven (4th),* George Ivar Louis Mountbatten, *b.* 1961, *s.* 1970, *m.*	Earl of Medina, *b.* 1991
1838	*Normanby (5th),* Constantine Edmund Walter Phipps, *b.* 1954, *s.* 1994, *m.*	Earl of Mulgrave, *b.* 1994
1812	*Northampton (7th),* Spencer Douglas David Compton, *b.* 1946, *s.* 1978, *m.*	Earl Compton, *b.* 1973
1682 S.	*Queensberry (12th),* David Harrington Angus Douglas, *b.* 1929, *s.* 1954	Viscount Drumlanrig, *b.* 1967
1926	*Reading (4th),* Simon Charles Henry Rufus Isaacs, *b.* 1942, *s.* 1980, *m.*	Viscount Erleigh, *b.* 1986
1789	*Salisbury (7th) and Baron Gascoyne-Cecil (life peerage, 1999),* Robert Michael James Gascoyne-Cecil, PC, *b.* 1946, *s.* 2003, *m.*	Viscount Cranborne, *b.* 1970
1800 I.	*Sligo (11th),* Jeremy Ulick Browne, *b.* 1939, *s.* 1991, *m.*	Sebastian U. B., *b.* 1964
1787	° *Townshend (7th),* George John Patrick Dominic Townshend, *b.* 1916, *s.* 1921, *w.*	Viscount Raynham, *b.* 1945
1694 S.	*Tweeddale (14th),* Charles David Montagu Hay, *b.* 1947, *s.* 2005	Lord Andrew A. G. H., *b.* 1959
1789 I.	*Waterford (8th),* John Hubert de la Poer Beresford, *b.* 1933, *s.* 1934, *m.*	Earl of Tyrone, *b.* 1958
1551	*Winchester (18th),* Nigel George Paulet, *b.* 1941, *s.* 1968, *m. Premier Marquess of England*	Earl of Wiltshire, *b.* 1969
1892	*Zetland (4th),* Lawrence Mark Dundas, *b.* 1937, *s.* 1989, *m.*	Earl of Ronaldshay, *b.* 1965

EARLS

Coronet, Eight silver balls on stalks alternating with eight gold strawberry leaves

Style, The Right Hon. the Earl (of) _
Envelope (formal), The Right Hon. the Earl (of) _; *(social),* The Earl (of) _. *Letter (formal),* My Lord; *(social),* Dear Lord _.
Spoken (formal), My Lord; *(social),* Lord _.
Wife's style, The Right Hon. the Countess (of) _
Envelope (formal), The Right Hon. the Countess (of) _; *(social),* The Countess (of) _. *Letter (formal),* Madam; *(social),* Lady _. *Spoken (formal),* Madam; *(social),* Lady _.
Eldest son's style, Takes his father's second title as a courtesy title (*see* Courtesy Titles)
Younger sons' style, 'The Hon.' before forename and surname, as for Baron's children
Daughters' style, 'Lady' before forename and surname, as for Duke's daughter

Created	Title, order of succession, name, etc.	Heir
1639 S.	*Airlie (13th),* David George Coke Patrick Ogilvy, KT, GCVO, PC, Royal Victorian Chain, *b.* 1926, *s.* 1968, *m.*	Lord Ogilvy, *b.* 1958
1696	*Albemarle (10th),* Rufus Arnold Alexis Keppel, *b.* 1965, *s.* 1979, *m.*	Viscount Bury, *b.* 2003
1952	° *Alexander of Tunis (2nd),* Shane William Desmond Alexander, *b.* 1935, *s.* 1969, *m.*	Hon. Brian J. A., *b.* 1939
1662	*Annandale and Hartfell (11th),* Patrick Andrew Wentworth Hope Johnstone, *b.* 1941, *s.* 1983, *m.* claim established 1985	Lord Johnstone, *b.* 1971
1789	° *Annesley (11th),* Philip Harrison Annesley, *b.* 1927, *s.* 2001, *m.*	Hon. Michael R. A., *b.* 1933

Created	Title, order of succession, name, etc.	Heir
1785	*Antrim (9th)*, Alexander Randal Mark McDonnell, *b.* 1935, *s.* 1977, *m.*	Viscount Dunluce, *b.* 1967
1762	** *Arran (9th)*, Arthur Desmond Colquhoun Gore, *b.* 1938, *s.* 1983, *m.*	Paul A. G., CMG, CVO, *b.* 1921
1955	° ** *Attlee (3rd)*, John Richard Attlee, *b.* 1956, *s.* 1991, *m.*	None
1714	*Aylesford (11th)*, Charles Ian Finch-Knightley, *b.* 1918, *s.* 1958, *w.*	Lord Guernsey, *b.* 1947
1937	° ** *Baldwin of Bewdley (4th)*, Edward Alfred Alexander Baldwin, *b.* 1938, *s.* 1976, *w.*	Viscount Corvedale, *b.* 1973
1922	*Balfour (5th)*, Roderick Francis Arthur Balfour, *b.* 1948, *s.* 2003, *m.*	Charles G. Y. B., *b.* 1951
1772	° *Bathurst (8th)*, Henry Allen John Bathurst, *b.* 1927, *s.* 1943, *m.*	Lord Apsley, *b.* 1961
1919	° *Beatty (3rd)*, David Beatty, *b.* 1946, *s.* 1972, *m.*	Viscount Borodale, *b.* 1973
1797	*Belmore (8th)*, John Armar Lowry-Corry, *b.* 1951, *s.* 1960, *m.*	Viscount Corry, *b.* 1985
1739 I.	*Bessborough (12th)*, Myles Fitzhugh Longfield Ponsonby, *b.* 1941, *s.* 2002, *m.*	Viscount Duncannon, *b.* 1974
1815	*Bradford (7th)*, Richard Thomas Orlando Bridgeman, *b.* 1947, *s.* 1981, *m.*	Viscount Newport, *b.* 1980
1469	*Buchan (17th)*, Malcolm Harry Erskine, *b.* 1930, *s.* 1984, *m.*	Lord Cardross, *b.* 1960
1746	*Buckinghamshire (10th)*, (George) Miles Hobart-Hampden, *b.* 1944, *s.* 1983, *m.*	Sir John Hobart, Bt., *b.* 1945
1800	° *Cadogan (8th)*, Charles Gerald John Cadogan, *b.* 1937, *s.* 1997, *m.*	Viscount Chelsea, *b.* 1966
1878	° *Cairns (6th)*, Simon Dallas Cairns, CVO, CBE, *b.* 1939, *s.* 1989, *m.*	Viscount Garmoyle, *b.* 1965
1455	** *Caithness (20th)*, Malcolm Ian Sinclair, PC, *b.* 1948, *s.* 1965, *w.*	Lord Berriedale, *b.* 1981
1800	*Caledon (7th)*, Nicholas James Alexander, *b.* 1955, *s.* 1980, *m.*	Viscount Alexander, *b.* 1990
1661	*Carlisle (13th)*, George William Beaumont Howard, *b.* 1949, *s.* 1994	Hon. Philip C. W. H., *b.* 1963
1793	*Carnarvon (8th)*, George Reginald Oliver Molyneux Herbert, *b.* 1956, *s.* 2001, *m.*	Lord Porchester, *b.* 1992
1748 I.	*Carrick (10th)*, David James Theobald Somerset Butler, *b.* 1953, *s.* 1992, *m.*	Viscount Ikerrin, *b.* 1975
1800 I.	° *Castle Stewart (8th)*, Arthur Patrick Avondale Stuart, *b.* 1928, *s.* 1961, *w.*	Viscount Stuart, *b.* 1953
1814	° *Cathcart (7th)*, Charles Alan Andrew Cathcart, *b.* 1952, *s.* 1999, *m.*	Lord Greenock, *b.* 1986
1647 I.	*Cavan*, The 12th Earl died in 1988.	†Roger C. Lambart, *b.* 1944
1827	° *Cawdor (7th)*, Colin Robert Vaughan Campbell, *b.* 1962, *s.* 1993, *m.*	Viscount Emlyn, *b.* 1998
1801	*Chichester (9th)*, John Nicholas Pelham, *b.* 1944, *s.* 1944, *m.*	Richard A. H. P., *b.* 1952
1803 I.	*Clancarty (9th)*, Nicholas Power Richard Le Poer Trench, *b.* 1952, *s.* 1995	None
1776 I.	*Clanwilliam (7th)*, John Herbert Meade, *b.* 1919, *s.* 1989, *w.*	Lord Gillford, *b.* 1960
1776	*Clarendon (7th)*, George Frederick Laurence Hyde Villiers, *b.* 1933, *s.* 1955, *m.*	Lord Hyde, *b.* 1976
1620 I.	*Cork and Orrery (15th)*, John Richard Boyle, *b.* 1945, *s.* 2003, *m.*	Viscount Dungarvan, *b.* 1978
1850	*Cottenham (9th)*, Mark John Henry Pepys, *b.* 1983, *s.* 2000	Hon. Sam R. P., *b.* 1986
1762 I.	** *Courtown (9th)*, James Patrick Montagu Burgoyne Winthrop Stopford, *b.* 1954, *s.* 1975, *m.*	Viscount Stopford, *b.* 1988
1697	*Coventry (13th)*, George William Coventry, *b.* 1939, *s.* 2004, *m.*	David D. S. C., *b.* 1973
1857	° *Cowley (7th)*, Garret Graham Wellesley, *b.* 1934, *s.* 1975, *m.*	Viscount Dangan, *b.* 1965
1892	*Cranbrook (5th)*, Gathorne Gathorne-Hardy, *b.* 1933, *s.* 1978, *m.*	Lord Medway, *b.* 1968
1801 M.	*Craven (9th)*, Benjamin Robert Joseph Craven, *b.* 1989, *s.* 1990	Rupert J. E. C., *b.* 1926
1398 S.	*Crawford (29th) and Balcarres (12th) (S. 1651) and Baron Balniel (life peerage, 1974)*, Robert Alexander Lindsay, KT, GCVO, PC, *b.* 1927, *s.* 1975, *m. Premier Earl on Union Roll*	Lord Balniel, *b.* 1958
1861	*Cromartie (5th)*, John Ruaridh Blunt Grant Mackenzie, *b.* 1948, *s.* 1989, *m.*	Viscount Tarbat, *b.* 1987
1901	*Cromer (4th)*, Evelyn Rowland Esmond Baring, *b.* 1946, *s.* 1991, *m.*	Viscount Errington, *b.* 1994
1633 S.	*Dalhousie (17th)*, James Hubert Ramsay, *b.* 1948, *s.* 1999, *m.*	Lord Ramsay, *b.* 1981
1725 I.	*Darnley (11th)*, Adam Ivo Stuart Bligh, *b.* 1941, *s.* 1980, *m.*	Lord Clifton, *b.* 1968
1711	*Dartmouth (10th)*, William Legge, *b.* 1949, *s.* 1997	Hon. Rupert L., *b.* 1951
1761	° *De La Warr (11th)*, William Herbrand Sackville, *b.* 1948, *s.* 1988, *m.*	Lord Buckhurst, *b.* 1979
1622	*Denbigh (12th) and Desmond (11th) (I. 1622)*, Alexander Stephen Rudolph Feilding, *b.* 1970, *s.* 1995, *m.*	William D. F, *b.* 1939
1485	*Derby (19th)*, Edward Richard William Stanley, *b.* 1962, *s.* 1994, *m.*	Lord Stanley, *b.* 1998
1553	*Devon (18th)*, Hugh Rupert Courtenay, *b.* 1942, *s.* 1998, *m.*	Lord Courtenay, *b.* 1975
1800 I.	*Donoughmore (8th)*, Richard Michael John Hely-Hutchinson, *b.* 1927, *s.* 1981, *w.*	Viscount Suirdale, *b.* 1952
1661 I.	*Drogheda (12th)*, Henry Dermot Ponsonby Moore, *b.* 1937, *s.* 1989, *m.*	Viscount Moore, *b.* 1983
1837	*Ducie (7th)*, David Leslie Moreton, *b.* 1951, *s.* 1991, *m.*	Lord Moreton, *b.* 1981
1860	*Dudley (4th)*, William Humble David Ward, *b.* 1920, *s.* 1969, *m.*	Viscount Ednam, *b.* 1947
1660 S.	** *Dundee (12th)*, Alexander Henry Scrymgeour, *b.* 1949, *s.* 1983, *m.*	Lord Scrymgeour, *b.* 1982
1669 S.	*Dundonald (15th)*, Iain Alexander Douglas Blair Cochrane, *b.* 1961, *s.* 1986, *m.*	Lord Cochrane, *b.* 1991
1686 S.	*Dunmore (12th)*, Malcolm Kenneth Murray, *b.* 1946, *s.* 1995, *m.*	Hon. Geoffrey C. M., *b.* 1949

Created	Title, order of succession, name, etc.	Heir
1822 I.	*Dunraven and Mount-Earl (7th),* Thady Windham Thomas Wyndham-Quin, *b.* 1939, *s.* 1965, *m.*	None
1833	*Durham (6th),* Antony Claud Frederick Lambton, *b.* 1922, *s.* 1970, *m.* Disclaimed for life 1970	Hon. Edward R. L. (Baron Durham), *b.* 1961
1837	*Effingham (7th),* David Mowbray Algernon Howard, *b.* 1939, *s.* 1996, *m.*	Lord Howard of Effingham, *b.* 1971
1507 S.	*Eglinton (18th) and Winton (9th) (S. 1600),* Archibald George Montgomerie, *b.* 1939, *s.* 1966, *m.*	Lord Montgomerie, *b.* 1966
1733 I.	*Egmont (12th),* Thomas Frederick Gerald Perceval, *b.* 1934, *s.* 2001, *m.*	Hon. Donald W. P., *b.* 1954
1821	*Eldon (5th),* John Joseph Nicholas Scott, *b.* 1937, *s.* 1976, *m.*	Viscount Encombe, *b.* 1962
1633 S.	*Elgin (11th) and Kincardine (15th) (S. 1647),* Andrew Douglas Alexander Thomas Bruce, KT, *b.* 1924, *s.* 1968, *m.*	Lord Bruce, *b.* 1961
1789 I.	*Enniskillen (7th),* Andrew John Galbraith Cole, *b.* 1942, *s.* 1989, *m.*	Arthur G. C., *b.* 1920
1789 I.	*Erne (6th),* Henry George Victor John Crichton, *b.* 1937, *s.* 1940, *m.*	Viscount Crichton, *b.* 1971
1452 S.	** *Erroll (24th),* Merlin Sereld Victor Gilbert Hay, *b.* 1948, *s.* 1978, *m.* Hereditary Lord High Constable and Knight Marischal of Scotland	Lord Hay, *b.* 1984
1661	*Essex (11th),* Frederick Paul de Vere Capell, *b.* 1944, *s.* 2005	William J. C., *b.* 1952
1711	° ** *Ferrers (13th),* Robert Washington Shirley, PC, *b.* 1929, *s.* 1954, *m.*	Viscount Tamworth, *b.* 1952
1789	° *Fortescue (8th),* Charles Hugh Richard Fortescue, *b.* 1951, *s.* 1993, *m.*	John A. F. F., *b.* 1955
1841	*Gainsborough (5th),* Anthony Gerard Edward Noel, *b.* 1923, *s.* 1927, *m.*	Viscount Campden, *b.* 1950
1623 S.	*Galloway (13th),* Randolph Keith Reginald Stewart, *b.* 1928, *s.* 1978, *w.*	Andrew C. S., *b.* 1949
1703 S.	** *Glasgow (10th),* Patrick Robin Archibald Boyle, *b.* 1939, *s.* 1984, *m.*	Viscount of Kelburn, *b.* 1978
1806 I.	*Gosford (7th),* Charles David Nicholas Alexander John Sparrow Acheson, *b.* 1942, *s.* 1966, *m.*	Hon. Patrick B. V. M. A., *b.* 1915
1945	*Gowrie (2nd),* Alexander Patrick Greysteil Hore-Ruthven, PC, *b.* 1939, *s.* 1955, *m.*	Viscount Ruthven of Canberra, *b.* 1964
1684 I.	*Granard (10th),* Peter Arthur Edward Hastings Forbes, *b.* 1957, *s.* 1992, *m.*	Viscount Forbes, *b.* 1981
1833	° *Granville (6th),* Granville George Fergus Leveson-Gower, *b.* 1959, *s.* 1996, *m.*	Lord Leveson, *b.* 1999
1806	° *Grey (6th),* Richard Fleming George Charles Grey, *b.* 1939, *s.* 1963, *m.*	Philip K. G., *b.* 1940
1752	*Guilford (10th),* Piers Edward Brownlow North, *b.* 1971, *s.* 1999, *m.*	Lord North, *b.* 2002
1619	*Haddington (13th),* John George Baillie-Hamilton, *b.* 1941, *s.* 1986, *m.*	Lord Binning, *b.* 1985
1919	° *Haig (2nd),* George Alexander Eugene Douglas Haig, OBE, *b.* 1918, *s.* 1928, *m.*	Viscount Dawick, *b.* 1961
1944	*Halifax (3rd),* Charles Edward Peter Neil Wood, *b.* 1944, *s.* 1980, *m.*	Lord Irwin, *b.* 1977
1898	*Halsbury (4th),* Adam Edward Giffard, *b.* 1934, *s.* 2000, *m.*	None
1754	*Hardwicke (10th),* Joseph Philip Sebastian Yorke, *b.* 1971, *s.* 1974	Charles E. Y., *b.* 1951
1812	*Harewood (7th),* George Henry Hubert Lascelles, KBE, *b.* 1923, *s.* 1947, *m.*	Viscount Lascelles, *b.* 1950
1742	*Harrington (11th),* William Henry Leicester Stanhope, *b.* 1922, *s.* 1929, *m.*	Viscount Petersham, *b.* 1945
1809	*Harrowby (7th),* Dudley Danvers Granville Coutts Ryder, TD, *b.* 1922, *s.* 1987, *m.*	Viscount Sandon, *b.* 1951
1605	** *Home (15th),* David Alexander Cospatrick Douglas-Home, CVO, CBE, *b.* 1943, *s.* 1995, *m.*	Lord Dunglass, *b.* 1987
1821	° ** *Howe (7th),* Frederick Richard Penn Curzon, *b.* 1951, *s.* 1984, *m.*	Viscount Curzon, *b.* 1994
1529	*Huntingdon (16th),* William Edward Robin Hood Hastings Bass, LVO, *b.* 1948, *s.* 1990, *m.*	Hon. Simon A. R. H. H. B., *b.* 1950
1885	*Iddesleigh (5th),* John Stafford Northcote, *b.* 1957, *s.* 2004, *m.*	Viscount St Cyres, *b.* 1985
1756	*Ilchester (9th),* Maurice Vivian de Touffreville Fox-Strangways, *b.* 1920, *s.* 1970, *m.*	Robin M. F.-S., *b.* 1942
1929	*Inchcape (4th),* (Kenneth) Peter (Lyle) Mackay, *b.* 1943, *s.* 1994, *m.*	Viscount Glenapp, *b.* 1979
1919	*Iveagh (4th),* Arthur Edward Rory Guinness, *b.* 1969, *s.* 1992	Viscount Elveden, *b.* 2003
1925	° *Jellicoe (2nd) and Baron Jellicoe of Southampton (life peerage, 1999),* George Patrick John Rushworth Jellicoe, KBE, DSO, MC, PC, *b.* 1918, *s.* 1935, *m.*	Viscount Brocas, *b.* 1950
1697	*Jersey (10th),* George Francis William Child Villiers, *b.* 1976, *s.* 1998 *m.*	Hon. Jamie C. V., *b.* 1994
1822 I.	*Kilmorey (6th),* Sir Richard Francis Needham, PC, *b.* 1942, *s.* 1977, *m.,* (does not use title)	Viscount Newry and Mourne, *b.* 1966
1866	*Kimberley (5th),* John Armine Wodehouse, *b.* 1951, *s.* 2002, *m.*	Lord Wodehouse, *b.*1978
1768 I.	*Kingston (12th),* Robert Charles Henry King-Tenison, *b.* 1969, *s.* 2002, *m.*	Viscount Kingsborough, *b.* 2000
1633 S.	*Kinnoull (15th),* Arthur William George Patrick Hay, *b.* 1935, *s.* 1938, *m.*	Viscount Dupplin, *b.* 1962
1677 S.	*Kintore (14th),* James William Falconer Keith, *b.* 1976, *s.* 2004	Hon. Alexander D. B. K., *b.* 1946

Created	Title, order of succession, name, etc.	Heir
1914	° *Kitchener of Khartoum (3rd)*, Henry Herbert Kitchener, TD, *b.* 1919, *s.* 1937	None
1624	*Lauderdale (17th)*, Patrick Francis Maitland, *b.* 1911, *s.* 1968, *w.*	Viscount Maitland, *b.* 1937
1837	*Leicester (7th)*, Edward Douglas Coke, *b.* 1936, *s.* 1994, *m.*	Viscount Coke, *b.* 1965
1641 S.	*Leven (14th) and Melville (13th) (S. 1690)*, Alexander Robert Leslie Melville, *b.* 1924, *s.* 1947, *m.*	Lord Balgonie, *b.* 1954
1831	*Lichfield (5th)*, Thomas Patrick John Anson, *b.* 1939, *s.* 1960	Viscount Anson, *b.* 1978
1803 I.	*Limerick (7th)*, Edmund Christopher Pery, *b.* 1963, *s.* 2003, *m.*	Viscount Glentworth, *b.* 1991
1572	*Lincoln (19th)*, Robert Edward Fiennes-Clinton, *b.* 1972, *s.* 2001	Hon. William R. F.-C., *b.* 1980
1633 S.	** *Lindsay (16th)*, James Randolph Lindsay-Bethune, *b.* 1955, *s.* 1989, *m.*	Viscount Garnock, *b.* 1990
1626	*Lindsey (14th) and Abingdon (9th) (1682)*, Richard Henry Rupert Bertie, *b.* 1931, *s.* 1963, *m.*	Lord Norreys, *b.* 1958
1776 I.	*Lisburne (8th)*, John David Malet Vaughan, *b.* 1918, *s.* 1965, *m.*	Viscount Vaughan, *b.* 1945
1822 I.	** *Listowel (6th)*, Francis Michael Hare, *b.* 1964, *s.* 1997, *m.*	Hon. Timothy P. H., *b.* 1966
1905	** *Liverpool (5th)*, Edward Peter Bertram Savile Foljambe, *b.* 1944, *s.* 1969, *m.*	Viscount Hawkesbury, *b.* 1972
1945	° *Lloyd George of Dwyfor (3rd)*, Owen Lloyd George, *b.* 1924, *s.* 1968, *m.*	Viscount Gwynedd, *b.* 1951
1785 I.	*Longford (8th)*, Thomas Frank Dermot Pakenham, *b.* 1933, *s.* 2001, *m.*	Hon. Edward M. P., *b.* 1970
1807	*Lonsdale (7th)*, James Hugh William Lowther, *b.* 1922, *s.* 1953, *m.*	Viscount Lowther, *b.* 1949
1633 S.	*Loudoun (14th)*, Michael Edward Abney-Hastings, *b.* 1942, *s.* 2002, *m.*	Lord Mauchline, *b.* 1974
1838	*Lovelace (5th)*, Peter Axel William Locke King, *b.* 1951, *s.* 1964, *m.*	None
1795 I.	*Lucan (7th)*, Richard John Bingham, *b.* 1934, *s.* 1964, *m.* (missing since 8 November 1974)	Lord Bingham, *b.* 1967
1880	*Lytton (5th)*, John Peter Michael Scawen Lytton, *b.* 1950, *s.* 1985, *m.*	Viscount Knebworth, *b.* 1989
1721	*Macclesfield (9th)*, Richard Timothy George Mansfield Parker, *b.* 1943, *s.* 1992, *m.*	Hon. J. David G. P., *b.* 1945
1800	*Malmesbury (7th)*, James Carleton Harris, *b.* 1946, *s.* 2000, *m.*	Viscount FitzHarris, *b.* 1970
1776	*Mansfield and Mansfield (8th) (1792)*, William David Mungo James Murray, *b.* 1930, *s.* 1971, *m.*	Viscount Stormont, *b.* 1956
1565 S.	*Mar (14th) and Kellie (16th) (S. 1616) and Baron Erskine of Alloa Tower (life peerage, 2000)*, James Thorne Erskine, *b.* 1949, *s.* 1994, *m.*	Hon. Alexander D. E., *b.* 1952
1785 I.	*Mayo (10th)*, Terence Patrick Bourke, *b.* 1929, *s.* 1962	Lord Naas, *b.* 1953
1627 I.	*Meath (15th)*, John Anthony Brabazon, *b.* 1941, *s.* 1998, *m.*	Lord Ardee, *b.* 1977
1766	*Mexborough (8th)*, John Christopher George Savile, *b.* 1931, *s.* 1980, *m.*	Viscount Pollington, *b.* 1959
1813	*Minto (6th)*, Gilbert Edward George Lariston Elliot-Murray-Kynynmound, OBE, *b.* 1928, *s.* 1975, *m.*	Viscount Melgund, *b.* 1953
1562 S.	*Moray (20th)*, Douglas John Moray Stuart, *b.* 1928, *s.* 1974, *m.*	Lord Doune, *b.* 1966
1815	*Morley (6th)*, John St Aubyn Parker, KCVO, *b.* 1923, *s.* 1962, *m.*	Viscount Boringdon, *b.* 1956
1458	*Morton (22nd)*, John Charles Sholto Douglas, *b.* 1927, *s.* 1976, *m.*	Lord Aberdour, *b.* 1952
1789	*Mount Edgcumbe (8th)*, Robert Charles Edgcumbe, *b.* 1939, *s.* 1982	Piers V. E., *b.* 1946
1805	° *Nelson (9th)*, Peter John Horatio Nelson, *b.* 1941, *s.* 1981, *m.*	Viscount Merton, *b.* 1971
1660 S.	*Newburgh (12th)*, Don Filippo Giambattista Camillo Francesco Aldo Maria Rospigliosi, *b.* 1942, *s.* 1986, *m.*	Princess Donna Benedetta F. M. R., *b.* 1974
1827 I.	*Norbury (7th)*, Richard James Graham-Toler, *b.* 1967, *s.* 2000	None
1806 I.	*Normanton (6th)*, Shaun James Christian Welbore Ellis Agar, *b.* 1945, *s.* 1967, *m.*	Viscount Somerton, *b.* 1982
1647 S.	** *Northesk (14th)*, David John MacRae Carnegie, *b.* 1954, *s.* 1994, *m.*	Patrick C. C., *b.* 1940
1801	** *Onslow (7th)*, Michael William Coplestone Dillon Onslow, *b.* 1938, *s.* 1971, *m.*	Viscount Cranley, *b.* 1967
1696 S.	*Orkney (9th)*, (Oliver) Peter St John, *b.* 1938, *s.* 1998, *m.*	Viscount Kirkwall, *b.* 1969
1328 I.	*Ormonde and Ossory (I. 1527)*, The 25th/18th Earl (7th Marquess) died in 1988	†Viscount Mountgarret *b.* 1961 (*see* that title)
1925	*Oxford and Asquith (2nd)*, Julian Edward George Asquith, KCMG, *b.* 1916, *s.* 1928, *w.*	Viscount Asquith, OBE, *b.* 1952
1929	° ** *Peel (3rd)*, William James Robert Peel, *b.* 1947, *s.* 1969, *m.*	Viscount Clanfield, *b.* 1976
1551	*Pembroke (18th) and Montgomery (15th) (1605)*, William Alexander Sidney Herbert, *b.* 1978, *s.* 2003	Earl of Carnarvon *b.* 1956 (*see* that title)
1605	*Perth (18th)*, John Eric Drummond, *b.* 1935, *s.* 2002, *m.*	Viscount Strathallan, *b.* 1965
1905	*Plymouth (3rd)*, Other Robert Ivor Windsor-Clive, *b.* 1923, *s.* 1943, *m*	Viscount Windsor, *b.* 1951
1785	*Portarlington (7th)*, George Lionel Yuill Seymour Dawson-Damer, *b.* 1938, *s.* 1959, *m.*	Viscount Carlow, *b.* 1965
1689	*Portland (12th)*, Count Timothy Charles Robert Noel Bentinck, *b.* 1953, *s.* 1997, *m.*	Viscount Woodstock, *b.* 1984
1743	*Portsmouth (10th)*, Quentin Gerard Carew Wallop, *b.* 1954, *s.* 1984, *m.*	Viscount Lymington, *b.* 1981
1804	*Powis (8th)*, John George Herbert, *b.* 1952, *s.* 1993, *m.*	Viscount Clive, *b.* 1979
1765	*Radnor (8th)*, Jacob Pleydell-Bouverie, *b.* 1927, *s.* 1968, *w.*	Viscount Folkestone, *b.* 1955

Created	Title, order of succession, name, etc.	Heir
1831 I.	Ranfurly (7th), Gerald Françoys Needham Knox, b. 1929, s. 1988, m.	Viscount Northland, b. 1957
1771	Roden (10th), Robert John Jocelyn, b. 1938, s. 1993, m	Viscount Jocelyn, b. 1989
1801	Romney (8th), Julian Charles Marsham, b. 1948, s. 2004, m.	Viscount Marsham, b. 1977
1703 S.	Rosebery (7th), Neil Archibald Primrose, b. 1929, s. 1974, m.	Lord Dalmeny, b. 1967
1806 I.	Rosse (7th), William Brendan Parsons, b. 1936, s. 1979, m.	Lord Oxmantown, b. 1969.
1801	** Rosslyn (7th), Peter St Clair-Erskine, b. 1958, s. 1977, m.	Lord Loughborough, b. 1986
1457 S.	Rothes (22nd), James Malcolm David Leslie, b. 1958, s. 2005, m.	Alastair P. L., b. 1934
1861	° Russell (6th), Nicholas Lyulph Russell, b. 1968, s. 2004	Hon. John F. R., b. 1971
1915	° St Aldwyn (3rd), Michael Henry Hicks Beach, b. 1950, s. 1992, m.	Hon. David S. H. B., b. 1955
1815	St Germans (10th), Peregrine Nicholas Eliot, b. 1941, s. 1988	Lord Eliot, b. 1966
1660	** Sandwich (11th), John Edward Hollister Montagu, b. 1943, s. 1995, m.	Viscount Hinchingbrooke, b. 1969
1690	Scarbrough (13th), Richard Osbert Lumley, b. 1973, s. 2004	Hon. Thomas H. L., b. 1980
1701 S.	Seafield (13th), Ian Derek Francis Ogilvie-Grant, b. 1939, s. 1969, m.	Viscount Reidhaven, b. 1963
1882	** Selborne (4th), John Roundell Palmer, KBE, b. 1940, s. 1971, m.	Viscount Wolmer, b. 1971
1646 S.	Selkirk, Disclaimed for life 1994 (see Lord Selkirk of Douglas, page 70)	Master of Selkirk, b. 1978
1672	Shaftesbury (12th), Nicholas Edmund Anthony Ashley-Cooper, b. 1979, s. 2005, the 11th Earl died in May 2005 after succeeding his father who died sometime in November 2004	None
1756 I.	Shannon (9th), Richard Bentinck Boyle, b. 1924, s. 1963	Viscount Boyle, b. 1960
1442	** Shrewsbury and Waterford (22nd), Charles Henry John Benedict Crofton Chetwynd Chetwynd-Talbot, b. 1952, s. 1980, m. Premier Earl of England and Ireland	Viscount Ingestre, b. 1978
1961	Snowdon (1st) and Baron Armstrong-Jones (life peerage, 1999), Antony Charles Robert Armstrong-Jones, GCVO, b. 1930, m.	Viscount Linley, b. 1961
1765	° Spencer (9th), Charles Edward Maurice Spencer, b. 1964, s. 1992, m.	Viscount Althorp, b. 1994
1703 S.	Stair (14th), John David James Dalrymple, b. 1961, s. 1996	Hon. David H. D., b. 1963
1984	Stockton (2nd), Alexander Daniel Alan Macmillan, MEP, b. 1943, s. 1986, m.	Viscount Macmillan of Ovenden, b. 1974
1821	Stradbroke (6th), Robert Keith Rous, b. 1937, s. 1983, m.	Viscount Dunwich, b. 1961
1847	Strafford (8th), Thomas Edmund Byng, b. 1936, s. 1984, m.	Viscount Enfield, b. 1964
1606 S.	Strathmore and Kinghorne (18th) (S. 1677), Michael Fergus Bowes Lyon, b. 1957, s. 1987, m.	Lord Glamis, b. 1986
1603	Suffolk (21st) and Berkshire (14th) (1626), Michael John James George Robert Howard, b. 1935, s. 1941, m.	Viscount Andover, b. 1974
1955	Swinton (2nd), David Yarburgh Cunliffe-Lister, b. 1937, s. 1972, m.	Hon. Nicholas J. C.-L., b. 1939
1714	Tankerville (10th), Peter Grey Bennet, b. 1956, s. 1980	Revd the Hon. George A. G. B., b. 1925
1822	° Temple of Stowe (8th), (Walter) Grenville Algernon Temple-Gore-Langton, b. 1924, s. 1988, m.	Lord Langton, b. 1955
1815	Verulam (7th), John Duncan Grimston, b. 1951, s. 1973, m.	Viscount Grimston, b. 1978
1729	° Waldegrave (13th), James Sherbrooke Waldegrave, b. 1940, s. 1995, m.	Viscount Chewton, b. 1986
1759	Warwick (9th) and Brooke (9th) (1746), Guy David Greville, b. 1957, s. 1996, m.	Lord Brooke, b. 1982
1633 S.	Wemyss (12th) and March (8th), Francis David Charteris, KT, b. 1912, s. 1937, m.	Lord Neidpath, b. 1948
1621 I.	Westmeath (13th), William Anthony Nugent, b. 1928, s. 1971, m.	Hon. Sean C. W. N., b. 1965
1624	Westmorland (16th), Anthony David Francis Henry Fane, b. 1951, s. 1993, m.	Hon. Harry St C. F., b. 1953
1876	Wharncliffe (5th), Richard Alan Montagu Stuart Wortley, b. 1953, s. 1987, m.	Viscount Carlton, b. 1980
1801	Wilton (8th), Francis Egerton Grosvenor, b. 1934, s. 1999, m.	Viscount Grey de Wilton, b. 1959
1628	Winchilsea (17th) and Nottingham (12th) (1681), Daniel James Hatfield Finch Hatton, b. 1967, s. 1999, m.	Viscount Maidstone, b. 1998
1766	° Winterton (8th), (Donald) David Turnour, b. 1943, s. 1991, m.	Robert C. T., b. 1950
1956	Woolton (3rd), Simon Frederick Marquis, b. 1958, s. 1969, m.	None
1837	Yarborough (8th), Charles John Pelham, b. 1963, s. 1991, m.	Lord Worsley, b. 1990

COUNTESSES IN THEIR OWN RIGHT

Style, The Right Hon. the Countess (of) _
Envelope (formal), The Right Hon. the Countess (of) _; *(social),* The Countess (of) _. *Letter (formal),* Madam; *(social),* Lady _. *Spoken (formal),* Madam; *(social),* Lady _.
Husband, Untitled
Children's style, As for children of an Earl

Created	Title, order of succession, name, etc.	Heir
1643 S.	*Dysart (12th in line),* Katherine Grant of Rothiemurchus, *b.* 1918, *s.* 2003	Lord Huntingtower, *b.* 1946
c.1115 S. **	*Mar (31st in line),* Margaret of Mar, *b.* 1940, *s.* 1975, *m.* Premier Earldom of Scotland	Mistress of Mar, *b.* 1963
1947	° *Mountbatten of Burma (2nd in line),* Patricia Edwina Victoria Knatchbull, CBE, *b.* 1924, *s.* 1979, *m.*	Lord Romsey, *b.* 1947
c.1235 S.	*Sutherland (24th in line),* Elizabeth Millicent Sutherland, *b.* 1921, *s.* 1963, *m.*	Lord Strathnaver, *b.* 1947

VISCOUNTS

Coronet, Sixteen silver balls

Style, The Right Hon. the Viscount _
Envelope (formal), The Right Hon. the Viscount _; *(social),* The Viscount _. *Letter (formal),* My Lord; *(social),* Dear Lord _. *Spoken,* Lord _.
Wife's style, The Right Hon. the Viscountess _
Envelope (formal), The Right Hon. the Viscountess _; *(social),* The Viscountess _. *Letter (formal),* Madam; *(social),* Dear Lady _. *Spoken,* Lady _.
Children's style, 'The Hon.' before forename and surname, as for Baron's children
In Scotland, the heir apparent to a Viscount may be styled 'The Master of _ (title of peer)'

Created	Title, order of succession, name, etc.	Heir
1945	*Addison (4th),* William Matthew Wand Addison, *b.* 1945, *s.* 1992, *m.*	Hon. Paul W. A., *b.* 1973
1946	*Alanbrooke (3rd),* Alan Victor Harold Brooke, *b.* 1932, *s.* 1972	None
1919 **	*Allenby (3rd),* Lt.-Col. Michael Jaffray Hynman Allenby, *b.* 1931, *s.* 1984, *m.*	Hon. Henry J. H. A., *b.* 1968
1911	*Allendale (4th),* Wentworth Peter Ismay Beaumont, *b.* 1948, *s.* 2002, *m.*	Hon. Wentworth A. I. B., *b.* 1979
1642 S.	*Arbuthnott (16th),* John Campbell Arbuthnott, KT, CBE, DSC, *b.* 1924, *s.* 1966, *m.*	Master of Arbuthnott, *b.* 1950
1751 I.	*Ashbrook (11th),* Michael Llowarch Warburton Flower, *b.* 1935, *s.* 1995, *m.*	Hon. Rowland F. W. F., *b.* 1975
1917 **	*Astor (4th),* William Waldorf Astor, *b.* 1951, *s.* 1966, *m.*	Hon. William W. A., *b.* 1979
1781 I.	*Bangor (8th),* William Maxwell David Ward, *b.* 1948, *s.* 1993, *m.*	Hon. E. Nicholas W., *b.* 1953
1925	*Bearsted (5th),* Nicholas Alan Samuel, *b.* 1950, *s.* 1996, *m.*	Hon. Harry R. S., *b.* 1988
1963	*Blakenham (2nd),* Michael John Hare, *b.* 1938, *s.* 1982, *m.*	Hon. Caspar J. H., *b.* 1972
1935 **	*Bledisloe (3rd),* Christopher Hiley Ludlow Bathurst, QC, *b.* 1934, *s.* 1979	Hon. Rupert E. L. B., *b.* 1964
1712	*Bolingbroke (7th) and St John (8th) (1716),* Kenneth Oliver Musgrave St John, *b.* 1927, *s.* 1974	Hon. Henry F. St J, *h* 1957
1960	*Boyd of Merton (2nd),* Simon Donald Rupert Neville Lennox-Boyd, *b.* 1939, *s.* 1983, *m.*	Hon. Benjamin A. L.-B., *b.* 1964
1717 I	*Boyne (11th),* Gustavus Michael Stucley Hamilton-Russell, *b.* 1965, *s.* 1995, *m.*	Hon. Gustavus A. E. H.-R., *b.* 1999
1929	*Brentford (4th),* Crispin William Joynson-Hicks, *b.* 1933, *s.* 1983, *m.*	Hon. Paul W. J.-H., *b.* 1971
1929 **	*Bridgeman (3rd),* Robin John Orlando Bridgeman, *b.* 1930, *s.* 1982, *m.*	Hon. Luke R. O. B., *b.* 1971

Created	Title, order of succession, name, etc.	Heir
1868	*Bridport (4th) and 7th Duke, Bronte in Sicily, 1799,* Alexander Nelson Hood, *b.* 1948, *s.* 1969, *m.*	Hon. Peregrine A. N. H., *b.* 1974
1952	** *Brookeborough (3rd),* Alan Henry Brooke, *b.* 1952, *s.* 1987, *m.*	Hon. Christopher A. B., *b.* 1954
1933	*Buckmaster (3rd),* Martin Stanley Buckmaster, OBE, *b.* 1921, *s.* 1974	Adrian C. B., *b.* 1949
1939	*Caldecote (3rd),* Piers James Hampden Inskip, *b.* 1947, *s.* 1999, *m.*	Hon. Thomas J. H. I., *b.* 1985
1941	*Camrose (4th),* Adrian Michael Berry, *b.* 1937, *s.* 2001, *m.*	Hon. Jonathan W. B., *b.* 1970
1954	*Chandos (3rd) and Baron Lyttelton of Aldershot (life peerage, 2000),* Thomas Orlando Lyttelton, *b.* 1953, *s.* 1980, *m.*	Hon. Oliver A. L., *b.* 1986
1665 I.	*Charlemont (15th),* John Dodd Caulfeild, *b.* 1966, *s.* 2001, *m.*	Hon. Shane A. C., *b.* 1996
1921	*Chelmsford (4th) and UK Baron Chelmsford (1858),* Frederic Corin Piers Thesiger, *b.* 1962, *s.* 1999	To Barony only, Simon D. T., *b.* 1950
1717 I.	*Chetwynd (10th),* Adam Richard John Casson Chetwynd, *b.* 1935, *s.* 1965, *m.*	Hon. Adam D. C., *b.* 1969
1911	*Chilston (4th),* Alastair George Akers-Douglas, *b.* 1946, *s.* 1982, *m.*	Hon. Oliver I. A.-D., *b.* 1973
1902	*Churchill (3rd) and 5th UK Baron Churchill (1815),* Victor George Spencer, *b.* 1934, *s.* 1973	To Barony only, Richard H. R. S., *b.* 1926
1718	*Cobham (11th),* John William Leonard Lyttelton, *b.* 1943, *s.* 1977, *m.*	Hon. Christopher C. L., *b.* 1947
1902	** *Colville of Culross (4th),* John Mark Alexander Colville, QC, *b.* 1933, *s.* 1945, *m.*	Master of Colville, *b.* 1959
1826	*Combermere (6th),* Thomas Robert Wellington Stapleton-Cotton, *b.* 1969, *s.* 2000	Hon. David P. D. S.-C., *b.* 1932
1917	*Cowdray (4th),* Michael Orlando Weetman Pearson, *b.* 1944, *s.* 1995, *m.*	Hon. Peregrine J. D. P., *b.* 1994
1927	** *Craigavon (3rd),* Janric Fraser Craig, *b.* 1944, *s.* 1974	None
1943	*Daventry (4th),* James Edward FitzRoy Newdegate, *b.* 1960, *s.* 2000, *m.*	Hon. Humphrey J. F. N., *b.* 1995
1937	*Davidson (2nd),* John Andrew Davidson, *b.* 1928, *s.* 1970, *m.*	Hon. Malcolm W. M. D., *b.* 1934
1956	*De L'Isle (2nd),* Philip John Algernon Sidney, MBE, *b.* 1945, *s.* 1991, *m.*	Hon. Philip W. E. S., *b.* 1985
1776 I.	*De Vesci (7th),* Thomas Eustace Vesey, *b.* 1955, *s.* 1983, *m.*	Hon. Oliver I. V., *b.* 1991
1917	*Devonport (3rd),* Terence Kearley, *b.* 1944, *s.* 1973	Chester D. H. K., *b.* 1932
1964	*Dilhorne (2nd),* John Mervyn Manningham-Buller, *b.* 1932, *s.* 1980, *m.*	Hon. James E. M.-B., *b.* 1956
1622 I.	*Dillon (22nd),* Henry Benedict Charles Dillon, *b.* 1973, *s.* 1982	Hon. Richard A. L. D., *b.* 1948
1785 I.	*Doneraile (10th),* Richard Allen St Leger, *b.* 1946, *s.* 1983, *m.*	Hon. Nathaniel W. R. St J. St L., *b.* 1971
1680 I.	*Downe (12th),* Richard Henry Dawnay, *b.* 1967, *s.* 2002	Thomas P. D., *b.* 1978
1959	*Dunrossil (3rd),* Andrew William Reginald Morrison, *b.* 1953, *s.* 2000, *m.*	Hon. Callum A. B. M., *b.* 1994
1964	** *Eccles (2nd),* John Dawson Eccles, CBE, *b.* 1931, *s.* 1999, *m.*	Hon. William D. E., *b.* 1960
1897	*Esher (5th),* Christopher Lionel Baliol Brett, *b.* 1936, *s.* 2004, *m.*	Hon. Matthew C. A. B., *b.* 1963
1816	*Exmouth (10th),* Paul Edward Pellew, *b.* 1940, *s.* 1970, *m.*	Hon. Edward F. P., *b.* 1978
1620 S.	** *Falkland (15th),* Lucius Edward William Plantagenet Cary, *b.* 1935, *s.* 1984, *m. Premier Scottish Viscount on the Roll*	Master of Falkland, *b.* 1963
1720	*Falmouth (9th),* George Hugh Boscawen, *b.* 1919, *s.* 1962, *m.*	Hon. Evelyn A. H. B., *b.* 1955
1720 I.	*Gage (8th),* (Henry) Nicolas Gage, *b.* 1934, *s.* 1993, *m.*	Hon. Henry W. G., *b.* 1975
1727 I.	*Galway (12th),* George Rupert Monckton-Arundell, *b.* 1922, *s.* 1980, *m.*	Hon. J. Philip M., *b.* 1952
1478 I.	*Gormanston (17th),* Jenico Nicholas Dudley Preston, *b.* 1939, *s.* 1940, *w. Premier Viscount of Ireland*	Hon. Jenico F. T. P., *b.* 1974
1816 I.	*Gort (9th),* Foley Robert Standish Prendergast Vereker, *b.* 1951, *s.* 1995, *m.*	Hon. Robert F. P. V., *b.* 1993
1900	** *Goschen (4th),* Giles John Harry Goschen, *b.* 1965, *s.* 1977, *m.*	Hon. Alexander J. E. G., *b.* 2001
1849	*Gough (5th),* Shane Hugh Maryon Gough, *b.* 1941, *s.* 1951 None	
1929	*Hailsham (3rd),* Douglas Martin Hogg, PC, QC, MP, *b.* 1945, *s.* 2001, *m.*	Hon. Quintin J. N. M. H., *b.* 1973
1891	*Hambleden (4th),* William Herbert Smith, *b.* 1930, *s.* 1948, *m.*	Hon. William H. B. S., *b.* 1955
1884	*Hampden (6th),* Anthony David Brand, *b.* 1937, *s.* 1975, *m.*	Hon. Francis A. B., *b.* 1970
1936	*Hanworth (3rd),* David Stephen Geoffrey Pollock, *b.* 1946, *s.* 1996, *m.*	Harold W. C. P., *b.* 1988
1791 I.	*Harberton (11th),* Henry Robert Pomeroy, *b.* 1958, *s.* 2004, *m.* Hon. Patrick C. P., *b.* 1995	
1846	*Hardinge (7th),* Andrew Hartland Hardinge, *b.* 1960, *s.* 2004, *m.*	Hon. Thomas H. de M. H., *b.* 1993
1791 I.	*Hawarden (9th),* (Robert) Connan Wyndham Leslie Maude, *b.* 1961, *s.* 1991, *m.*	Hon. Varian J. C. E. M., *b.* 1997
1960	*Head (2nd),* Richard Antony Head, *b.* 1937, *s.* 1983, *m.*	Hon. Henry J. H., *b.* 1980

Created	Title, order of succession, name, etc.	Heir
1550	*Hereford (19th)*, Charles Robin De Bohun Devereux, *b.* 1975, *s.* 2004, Premier Viscount of England	Hon. Edward M. de B. D., *b.* 1977
1842	*Hill (9th)*, Peter David Raymond Charles Clegg-Hill, *b.* 1945, *s.* 2003	Hon. Paul A. R. C.-H., *b.* 1979
1796	*Hood (8th)*, Henry Lyttleton Alexander Hood, *b.* 1958, *s.* 1999, *m.*	Hon. Archibald L. S. H., *b.* 1993
1956	*Ingleby (2nd)*, Martin Raymond Peake, *b.* 1926, *s.* 1966, *w.*	None
1945	*Kemsley (3rd)*, Richard Gomer Berry, *b.* 1951, *s.* 1999, *m.*	Hon. Luke G. B., *b.* 1998
1911	*Knollys (3rd)*, David Francis Dudley Knollys, *b.* 1931, *s.* 1966, *m.*	Hon. Patrick N. M. K., *b.* 1962
1895	*Knutsford (6th)*, Michael Holland-Hibbert, *b.* 1926, *s.* 1986, *m.*	Hon. Henry T. H.-H., *b.* 1959
1954	*Leathers (3rd)*, Christopher Graeme Leathers, *b.* 1941, *s.* 1996, *m.*	Hon. James F. L., *b.* 1969
1781 I.	*Lifford (9th)*, (Edward) James Wingfield Hewitt, *b.* 1949, *s.* 1987, *m.*	Hon. James T. W. H., *b.* 1979
1921	*Long (4th)*, Richard Gerard Long, CBE, *b.* 1929, *s.* 1967, *m.*	Hon. James R. L., *b.* 1960
1957	*Mackintosh of Halifax (3rd)*, (John) Clive Mackintosh, *b.* 1958, *s.* 1980, *m.*	Hon. Thomas H. G. M., *b.* 1985
1955	*Malvern (3rd)*, Ashley Kevin Godfrey Huggins, *b.* 1949, *s.* 1978	Hon. M. James H., *b.* 1928
1945	*Marchwood (3rd)*, David George Staveley Penny, *b.* 1936, *s.* 1979, *w.*	Hon. Peter G. W. P., *b.* 1965
1942	*Margesson (2nd)*, Francis Vere Hampden Margesson, *b.* 1922, *s.* 1965, *m.*	Capt. Hon. Richard F. D. M., *b.* 1960
1660 I.	*Massereene (14th)*, John David Clotworthy Whyte-Melville Foster Skeffington, *b.* 1940, *s.* 1992, *m.*	Hon. Charles J. C. W.-M. F. S., *b.* 1973
1802	*Melville (9th)*, Robert David Ross Dundas, *b.* 1937, *s.* 1971, *m.*	Hon. Robert H. K. D., *b.* 1984
1916	*Mersey (4th)*, Richard Maurice Clive Bigham, *b.* 1934, *s.* 1979, *m.*	Master of Nairne, *b.* 1966
1717 I.	*Midleton (12th)*, Alan Henry Brodrick, *b.* 1949, *s.* 1988, *m.*	Hon. Ashley R. B., *b.* 1980
1962	*Mills (3rd)*, Christopher Philip Roger Mills, *b.* 1956, *s.* 1988, *m.*	None
1716 I.	*Molesworth (12th)*, Robert Bysse Kelham Molesworth, *b.* 1959, *s.* 1997	Hon. William J. C. M., *b.* 1960
1801 I.	*Monck (7th)*, Charles Stanley Monck, *b.* 1953, *s.* 1982 (Does not use title)	Hon. George S. M., *b.* 1957
1957	*Monckton of Brenchley (2nd)*, Maj.-Gen. Gilbert Walter Riversdale Monckton, CB, OBE, MC, *b.* 1915, *s.* 1965, *m.*	Hon. Christopher W. M., *b.* 1952
1946	** *Montgomery of Alamein (2nd)*, David Bernard Montgomery, CBE, *b.* 1928, *s.* 1976, *m.*	Hon. Henry D. M., *b.* 1954
1550 I.	*Mountgarret (18th)*, Piers James Richard Butler, *b.* 1961, *s.* 2004	Hon. Edmund H. R. B., *b.* 1962
1952	*Norwich (2nd)*, John Julius Cooper, CVO, *b.* 1929, *s.* 1954, *m.*	Hon. Jason C. D. B. C., *b.* 1959
1651 S.	*Oxfuird (14th)*, Ian Arthur Alexander Makgill, *b.* 1969, *s.* 2003	Hon. Robert E. G. M., *b.* 1969
1873	*Portman (10th)*, Christopher Edward Berkeley Portman, *b.* 1958, *s.* 1999, *m.*	Hon. Luke O. B. P., *b.* 1984
1743 I.	*Powerscourt (10th)*, Mervyn Niall Wingfield, *b.* 1935, *s.* 1973, *m.*	Hon. Mervyn A. W., *b.* 1963
1900	*Ridley (4th)*, Matthew White Ridley, KG, GCVO, TD, *b.* 1925, *s.* 1964, *m.*	Hon. Matthew W. R., *b.* 1958
1960	*Rochdale (2nd)*, St John Durival Kemp, *b.* 1938, *s.* 1993, *m.*	Hon. Jonathan H. D. K., *b.* 1961
1919	*Rothermere (4th)*, (Harold) Jonathan Esmond Vere Harmsworth, *b.* 1967, *s.* 1998, *m.*	Hon. Vere R. J. H. H., *b.* 1994
1937	*Runciman of Doxford (3rd)*, Walter Garrison Runciman (Garry), CBE, *b.* 1934, *s.* 1989, *m.*	Hon. David W. R., *b.* 1967
1918	*St Davids (3rd)*, Colwyn Jestyn John Philipps, *b.* 1939, *s.* 1991, *m.*	Hon. Rhodri C. P., *b.* 1966
1801	*St Vincent (7th)*, Ronald George James Jervis, *b.* 1905, *s.* 1940, *m.*	Hon. Edward R. J. J., *b.* 1951
1937	*Samuel (3rd)*, David Herbert Samuel, OBE, PHD, *b.* 1922, *s.* 1978, *m.*	Hon. Dan J. S., *b.* 1925
1911	*Scarsdale (4th)*, Peter Ghislain Nathaniel Curzon, *b.* 1949, *s.* 2000, *m.*	Hon. David J. N. C., *b.* 1958
1905 M.	*Selby (6th)*, Christopher Rolf Thomas Gully, *b.* 1993, *s.* 2001	Hon. (James) Edward H. G. G., *b.* 1945
1805	*Sidmouth (8th)*, Jeremy Francis Addington, *b.* 1947, *s.* 2005, *m.*	Hon. Steffan A., *b.* 1966
1940	** *Simon (3rd)*, Jan David Simon, *b.* 1940, *s.* 1993, *m.*	None
1960	** *Slim (2nd)*, John Douglas Slim, OBE, *b.* 1927, *s.* 1970, *m.*	Hon. Mark W. R. S., *b.* 1960
1954	*Soulbury (2nd)*, James Herwald Ramsbotham, *b.* 1915, *s.* 1971, *w.*	Hon. Sir Peter E. R., GCMG, GCVO, *b.* 1919
1776 I.	*Southwell (7th)*, Pyers Anthony Joseph Southwell, *b.* 1930, *s.* 1960, *m.*	Hon. Richard A. P. S., *b.* 1956
1942	*Stansgate*, Anthony Neil Wedgwood Benn, *b.* 1925, *s.* 1960, *w.* Disclaimed for life 1963.	Stephen M. W. B., *b.* 1951
1959	*Stuart of Findhorn (3rd)*, James Dominic Stuart, *b.* 1948, *s.* 1999, *m.*	Hon. Andrew M. S., *b.* 1957
1957	** *Tenby (3rd)*, William Lloyd George, *b.* 1927, *s.* 1983, *m.*	Hon. Timothy H. G. L. G., *b.* 1962
1952	*Thurso (3rd)*, John Archibald Sinclair, *b.* 1953, *s.* 1995, *m.*	Hon. James A. R. S., *b.* 1984
1721	*Torrington (11th)*, Timothy Howard St George Byng, *b.* 1943, *s.* 1961, *m.*	Colin H. C.-B., *b.* 1960
1936	** *Trenchard (3rd)*, Hugh Trenchard, *b.* 1951, *s.* 1987, *m.*	Hon. Alexander T. T., *b.* 1978
1921	** *Ullswater (2nd)*, Nicholas James Christopher Lowther, PC, LVO, *b.* 1942, *s.* 1949, *m.*	Hon. Benjamin J. L., *b.* 1975
1621 I.	*Valentia (15th)*, Richard John Dighton Annesley, *b.* 1929, *s.* 1983, *m.*	Hon. Francis W. D. A., *b.* 1959

Created	Title, order of succession, name, etc.	Heir
1952	** *Waverley (3rd)*, John Desmond Forbes Anderson, *b.* 1949, *s.* 1990	Hon. Forbes A. R. A., *b.* 1996
1938	*Weir (3rd)*, William Kenneth James Weir, *b.* 1933, *s.* 1975, *m.*	Hon. James W. H. W., *b.* 1965
1918	*Wimborne (4th)*, Ivor Mervyn Vigors Guest, *b.* 1968, *s.* 1993	Hon. Julien J. G., *b.* 1945
1923	*Younger of Leckie (5th)*, James Edward George Younger, *b.* 1955, *s.* 2003, *m.*	Hon. Alexander W. G. Y., *b.* 1993

BARONS/LORDS

Coronet, Six silver balls

Style, The Right Hon. the Lord _
Envelope (formal), The Right Hon. Lord _; *(social),* The Lord _. *Letter (formal),* My Lord, *(social),* Dear Lord _. *Spoken,* Lord _.
In the Peerage of Scotland there is no rank of Baron; the equivalent rank is Lord of Parliament (*see* page 44) and Scottish peers should always be styled 'Lord', never 'Baron'.
Wife's style, The Right Hon. the Lady _
Envelope (formal), The Right Hon. Lady _; *(social),* The Lady _. *Letter (formal),* My Lady; *(social),* Dear Lady _. *Spoken,* Lady _
Children's style, 'The Hon.' before forename (F_) and surname (S_)
Envelope, The Hon. F_ S_. *Letter,* Dear Mr/Miss/Mrs S_. *Spoken,* Mr/Miss/Mrs S_
In Scotland, the heir apparent to a Lord may be styled 'The Master of _ (title of peer)'

Created	Title, order of succession, name, etc.	Heir
1911	*Aberconway (4th),* (Henry) Charles McLaren, *b.* 1948, *s.* 2003, *m.*	Hon. Charles S. M., *b.* 1984
1873	*Aberdare (5th),* Alastair John Lyndhurst Bruce, *b.* 1947, *s.* 2005, *m.*	Hon. Hector M. N. B., *b.* 1974
1835	*Abinger (9th),* James Harry Scarlett, *b.* 1959, *s.* 2002, *m.*	Hon. Peter R. S., *b.* 1961
1869	*Acton (4th) and Acton of Bridgnorth (life peerage, 2000),* Richard Gerald Lyon-Dalberg-Acton, *b.* 1941, *s.* 1989, *m.*	Hon. John C. F. H. L.-D.-A., *b.* 1966
1887	** *Addington (6th),* Dominic Bryce Hubbard, *b.* 1963, *s.* 1982	Hon. Michael W. L. H., *b.* 1965
1896	*Aldenham (6th) and Hunsdon of Hunsdon (4th) (1923),* Vicary Tyser Gibbs, *b.* 1948, *s.* 1986, *m.*	Hon. Humphrey W. F. G., *b.* 1989
1962	*Aldington (2nd),* Charles Harold Stuart Low, *b.* 1948, *s.* 2000, *m.*	Hon. Philip T. A. L., *b.* 1990
1945	*Altrincham (3rd),* Anthony Ulick David Dundas Grigg, *b.* 1934, *s.* 2001, *m.*	Hon. (Edward) Sebastian G., *b.* 1965
1929	*Alvingham (2nd),* Maj.-Gen. Robert Guy Eardley Yerburgh, CBE, *b.* 1926, *s.* 1955, *m.*	Capt. Hon. Robert R. G. Y., *b.* 1956
1892	*Amherst of Hackney (4th),* William Hugh Amherst Cecil, *b.* 1940, *s.* 1980, *m.*	Hon. H. William A. C., *b.* 1968
1881	** *Ampthill (4th),* Geoffrey Denis Erskine Russell, CBE, PC *b.* 1921, *s.* 1973	Hon. David W. E. R., *b.* 1947
1947	*Amwell (3rd),* Keith Norman Montague, *b.* 1943, *s.* 1990, *m.*	Hon. Ian K. M., *b.* 1973
1863	*Annaly (6th),* Luke Richard White, *b.* 1954, *s.* 1990, *m.*	Hon. Luke H. W., *b.* 1990
1885	*Ashbourne (4th),* Edward Barry Greynville Gibson, *b.* 1933, *s.* 1983, *m.*	Hon. Edward C. d'O. G., *b.* 1967
1835	*Ashburton (7th),* John Francis Harcourt Baring, KG, KCVO, *b.* 1928, *s.* 1991, *m.*	Hon. Mark F. R. B., *b.* 1958
1892	*Ashcombe (4th),* Henry Edward Cubitt, *b.* 1924, *s.* 1962, *m.*	Mark E. C., *b.* 1964
1911	*Ashton of Hyde (3rd),* Thomas John Ashton, TD, *b.* 1926, *s.* 1983, *m.*	Hon. Thomas H. A., *b.* 1958
1800 I.	*Ashtown (7th),* Nigel Clive Crosby Trench, KCMG, *b.* 1916, *s.* 1990, *m.*	Hon. Roderick N. G. T., *b.* 1944
1956	** *Astor of Hever (3rd),* John Jacob Astor, *b.* 1946, *s.* 1984, *m.*	Hon. Charles G. J. A., *b.* 1990
1789 I.	*Auckland (10th) and Auckland (10th) (1793),* Robert Ian Burnard Eden, *b.* 1962, *s.* 1997, *m.*	Hon. Ronald J. E., *b.* 1931
1313	*Audley,* Barony in abeyance between three co-heiresses since 1997	
1900	** *Avebury (4th),* Eric Reginald Lubbock, *b.* 1928, *s.* 1971, *m.*	Hon. Lyulph A. J. L., *b.* 1954
1718 I.	*Aylmer (13th),* Michael Anthony Aylmer, *b.* 1923, *s.* 1982, *m.*	Hon. A. Julian A., *b.* 1951
1929	*Baden-Powell (3rd),* Robert Crause Baden-Powell, *b.* 1936, *s.* 1962, *m.*	Hon. David M. B.-P., *b.* 1940
1780	*Bagot (10th),* (Charles Hugh) Shaun Bagot, *b.* 1944, *s.* 2001, *m.*	Richard C. V. B., *b.* 1941
1953	*Baillieu (3rd),* James William Latham Baillieu, *b.* 1950, *s.* 1973, *m.*	Hon. Robert L. B., *b.* 1979
1607 S.	*Balfour of Burleigh (8th),* Robert Bruce, *b.* 1927, *s.* 1967, *m.*	Hon. Victoria B., *b.* 1973
1945	*Balfour of Inchrye (2nd),* Ian Balfour, *b.* 1924, *s.* 1988, *m.*	None

Created	Title, order of succession, name, etc.	Heir
1924	*Banbury of Southam (3rd)*, Charles William Banbury, *b.* 1953, *s.* 1981, *m.*	None
1698	*Barnard (11th)*, Harry John Neville Vane, TD, *b.* 1923, *s.* 1964	Hon. Henry F. C. V., *b.* 1959
1887	*Basing (5th)*, Neil Lutley Sclater-Booth, *b.* 1939, *s.* 1983, *m.*	Hon. Stuart W. S.-B., *b.* 1969
1917	*Beaverbrook (3rd)*, Maxwell William Humphrey Aitken, *b.* 1951, *s.* 1985, *m.*	Hon. Maxwell F. A., *b.* 1977
1647 S.	*Belhaven and Stenton (13th)*, Robert Anthony Carmichael Hamilton, *b.* 1927, *s.* 1961, *m.*	Master of Belhaven, *b.* 1953
1848 I.	*Bellew (7th)*, James Bryan Bellew, *b.* 1920, *s.* 1981, *w.*	Hon. Bryan E. B., *b.* 1943
1856	*Belper (5th)*, Richard Henry Strutt, *b.* 1941, *s.* 1999, *m.*	Hon. Michael H. S., *b.* 1969
1938	*Belstead (2nd) and Ganzoni (life peerage, 1999)*, John Julian Ganzoni, PC, *b.* 1932, *s.* 1958	None
1421	*Berkeley (18th) and Gueterbock (life peerage, 2000)*, Anthony Fitzhardinge Gueterbock, OBE, *b.* 1939, *s.* 1992, *m.*	Hon. Thomas F. G., *b.* 1969
1922	*Bethell (4th)*, Nicholas William Bethell, *b.* 1938, *s.* 1967, *m.*	Hon. James N. B., *b.* 1967
1938	*Bicester (3rd)*, Angus Edward Vivian Smith, *b.* 1932, *s.* 1968	Hugh C. V. S., *b.* 1934
1903	*Biddulph (5th)*, (Anthony) Nicholas Colin Maitland Biddulph, *b.* 1959, *s.* 1988, *m.*	Hon. Robert J. M. B., *b.* 1994
1938	*Birdwood (3rd)*, Mark William Ogilvie Birdwood, *b.* 1938, *s.* 1962, *m.*	None
1958	*Birkett (2nd)*, Michael Birkett, *b.* 1929, *s.* 1962, *w.*	Hon. Thomas B., *b.* 1982
1907	*Blyth (4th)*, Anthony Audley Rupert Blyth, *b.* 1931, *s.* 1977, *m.*	Hon. James A. I. B., *b.* 1970
1797	*Bolton (8th)*, Harry Algar Nigel Orde-Powlett, *b.* 1954, *s.* 2001, *m.*	Hon. Thomas O.-P., *b.* 1979
1452 S.	*Borthwick (24th)*, John Hugh Borthwick, *b.* 1940, *s.* 1996, *m.*	Hon. James H. A. B. of Glengelt, *b.* 1940
1922	*Borwick (4th)*, James Hugh Myles Borwick, MC, *b.* 1917, *s.* 1961, *m.*	(Geoffrey Robert) James B., *b.* 1955
1761	*Boston (10th)*, Timothy George Frank Boteler Irby, *b.* 1939, *s.* 1978, *m.*	Hon. George W. E. B. I., *b.* 1971
1942	** *Brabazon of Tara (3rd)*, Ivon Anthony Moore-Brabazon, *b.* 1946, *s.* 1974, *m.*	Hon. Benjamin R. M.-B., *b.* 1983
1880	*Brabourne (7th)*, John Ulick Knatchbull, CBE, *b.* 1924, *s.* 1943, *m.*	Lord Romsey, *b.* 1947
1925	*Bradbury (3rd)*, John Bradbury, *b.* 1940, *s.* 1994, *m.*	Hon. John B., *b.* 1973
1962	*Brain (2nd)*, Christopher Langdon Brain, *b.* 1926, *s.* 1966, *m.*	Hon. Michael C. B., *b.* 1928
1938	*Brassey of Apethorpe (3rd)*, David Henry Brassey, OBE, *b.* 1932, *s.* 1967, *m.*	Hon. Edward B., *b.* 1964
1788	*Braybrooke (10th)*, Robin Henry Charles Neville, *b.* 1932, *s.* 1990, *m.*	George N., *b.* 1943
1957	** *Bridges (2nd)*, Thomas Edward Bridges, GCMG, *b.* 1927, *s.* 1969, *m.*	Hon. Mark T. B., *b.* 1954
1945	*Broadbridge (4th)*, Martin Hugh Broadbridge, *b.* 1929, *s.* 2000, *m.*	Hon. Richard J. M. B., *b.* 1959
1933	*Brocket (3rd)*, Charles Ronald George Nall-Cain, *b.* 1952, *s.* 1967, *m.*	Hon. Alexander C. C. N.-C., *b.* 1984
1860	** *Brougham and Vaux (5th)*, Michael John Brougham, CBE, *b.* 1938, *s.* 1967	Hon. Charles W. B., *b.* 1971
1945	*Broughshane (3rd)*, (William) Kensington Davison, DSO, DFC, *b.* 1914, *s.* 1995	None
1776	*Brownlow (7th)*, Edward John Peregrine Cust, *b.* 1936, *s.* 1978, *m.*	Hon. Peregrine E. Q. C., *b.* 1974
1942	*Bruntisfield (2nd)*, John Robert Warrender, OBE, MC, TD, *b.* 1921, *s.* 1993, *m.*	Hon. Michael J. V. W., *b.* 1949
1950	*Burden (4th)*, Fraser William Elsworth Burden, *b.* 1964, *s.* 2000, *m.*	Hon. Ian S. B., *b.* 1967
1529	*Burgh (8th)*, (Alexander) Gregory Disney Leith, *b.* 1958, *s.* 2001, *m.*	Hon. Alexander J. S. L., *b.* 1986
1903	*Burnham (7th)*, Harry Frederick Alan Lawson, *b.* 1968, *s.* 2005	None
1897	*Burton (3rd)*, Michael Evan Victor Baillie, *b.* 1924, *s.* 1962, *m.*	Hon. Evan M. R. B., *b.* 1949
1643	*Byron (13th)*, Robert James Byron, *b.* 1950, *s.* 1989, *m.*	Hon. Charles R. G. B., *b.* 1990
1937	*Cadman (3rd)*, John Anthony Cadman, *b.* 1938, *s.* 1966, *m.*	Hon. Nicholas A. J. C., *b.* 1977
1945	*Calverley (3rd)*, Charles Rodney Muff, *b.* 1946, *s.* 1971, *m.*	Hon. Jonathan E. M., *b.* 1975
1383	*Camoys (7th)*, (Ralph) Thomas Campion George Sherman Stonor, GCVO, PC, *b.* 1940, *s.* 1976, *m.*	Hon. R. William R. T. S., *b.* 1974
1715 I.	*Carbery (11th)*, Peter Ralfe Harrington Evans-Freke, *b.* 1920, *s.* 1970, *m.*	Hon. Michael P. E.-F., *b.* 1942
1834 I.	*Carew (7th) and Carew (7th) (1838)*, Patrick Thomas Conolly-Carew, *b.* 1938, *s.* 1994, *m.*	Hon. William P. C.-C., *b.* 1973
1916	*Carnock (4th)*, David Henry Arthur Nicolson, *b.* 1920, *s.* 1982	Adam N., *b.* 1957
1796 I.	*Carrington (6th) and Carrington (6th) (1797) and Carington of Upton (life peerage, 1999)*, Peter Alexander Rupert Carington, KG, GCMG, CH, MC, PC, *b.* 1919, *s.* 1938, *m.*	Hon. Rupert F. J. C., *b.* 1948
1812	*Castlemaine (8th)*, Roland Thomas John Handcock, MBE, *b.* 1943, *s.* 1973, *m.*	Hon. Ronan M. E. H., *b.* 1989
1936	*Catto (3rd)*, Innes Gordon Catto, *b.* 1950, *s.* 2001, *m.*	Hon. Alexander G. C., *b.* 1952

Created	Title, order of succession, name, etc.	Heir
1918	Cawley (4th), John Francis Cawley, b. 1946, s. 2001, m.	Hon. William R. H. C., b. 1981
1937	Chatfield (2nd), Ernle David Lewis Chatfield, b. 1917, s. 1967, m.	None
1858	Chesham (6th), Nicholas Charles Cavendish, b. 1941, s. 1989, m.	Hon. Charles G. C. C., b. 1974
1945	Chetwode (2nd), Philip Chetwode, b. 1937, s. 1950, m.	Hon. Roger C., b. 1968
1945	** Chorley (2nd), Roger Richard Edward Chorley, b. 1930, s. 1978, m.	Hon. Nicholas R. D. C., b. 1966
1858	Churston (5th), John Francis Yarde-Buller, b. 1934, s. 1991, m.	Hon. Benjamin F. A. Y.-B., b. 1974
1946	Citrine (3rd), Ronald Eric Citrine, b. 1919, s. 1997, m. (Does not use title)	None
1800	Clanmorris (8th), Simon John Ward Bingham, b. 1937, s. 1988, m.	Robert D. de B. B., b. 1942
1672	Clifford of Chudleigh (14th), Thomas Hugh Clifford, b. 1948, s. 1988, m.	Hon. Alexander T. H. C., b. 1985
1299	Clinton (22nd), Gerard Nevile Mark Fane Trefusis, b. 1934, s. 1965, m.	Hon. Charles P. R. F. T., b. 1962
1955	Clitheroe (2nd), Ralph John Assheton, b. 1929, s. 1984, m.	Hon. Ralph C. A., b. 1962
1919	Clwyd (3rd), (John) Anthony Roberts, b. 1935, s. 1987, m.	Hon. J. Murray R., b. 1971
1948	Clydesmuir (3rd), David Ronald Colville, b. 1949, s. 1996, m.	Hon. Richard C., b. 1980
1960	** Cobbold (2nd), David Antony Fromanteel Lytton Cobbold, b. 1937, s. 1987, m.	Hon. Henry F. L. C., b. 1962
1919	Cochrane of Cults (4th), (Ralph Henry) Vere Cochrane, b. 1926, s. 1990, m.	Hon. Thomas II. V. C., b. 1957
1954	Coleraine (2nd), (James) Martin (Bonar) Law, b. 1931, s. 1980, m.	Hon. James P. B. L., b. 1975
1873	Coleridge (5th), William Duke Coleridge, b. 1937, s. 1984, m.	Hon. James D. C., b. 1967
1946	Colgrain (3rd), David Colin Campbell, b. 1920, s. 1973, m.	Hon. Alastair C. L. C., b. 1951
1917	** Colwyn (3rd), (Ian) Anthony Hamilton-Smith, CBE, b. 1942, s. 1966, m.	Hon. Craig P. H.-S., b. 1968
1956	Colyton (2nd), Alisdair John Munro Hopkinson, b. 1958, s. 1996, m.	Hon. James P. M. H., b. 1983
1841	Congleton (8th), Christopher Patrick Parnell, b. 1930, s. 1967, m.	Hon. John P. C. P., b. 1959
1927	Cornwallis (3rd), Fiennes Neil Wykeham Cornwallis, OBE, b. 1921, s. 1982, m.	Hon. F. W. Jeremy C., b. 1946
1874	Cottesloe (5th), Cdr. John Tapling Fremantle, b. 1927, s. 1994, m.	Hon. Thomas F. H. F., b. 1966
1929	Craigmyle (4th), Thomas Columba Shaw, b. 1960, s. 1998, m.	Hon. Alexander F. S., b. 1988
1899	Cranworth (3rd), Philip Bertram Gurdon, b. 1940, s. 1964, w.	Hon. Sacha W. R. G., b. 1970
1959	** Crathorne (2nd), Charles James Dugdale, b. 1939, s. 1977, m.	Hon. Thomas A. J. D., b. 1977
1892	Crawshaw (5th), David Gerald Brooks, b. 1934, s. 1997, m.	Hon. John P. B., b. 1938
1940	Croft (3rd), Bernard William Henry Page Croft, b. 1949, s. 1997, m.	None
1797 I.	Crofton (7th), Guy Patrick Gilbert Crofton, b. 1951, s. 1989, m.	Hon. E. Harry P. C., b. 1988
1375	Cromwell (7th), Godfrey John Bewicke-Copley, b. 1960, s. 1982, m.	Hon. David G. B.-C., b. 1997
1947	Crook (3rd), Robert Douglas Edwin Crook, b. 1955, s. 2001, m.	Hon. Matthew R. C., b. 1990
1920	Cullen of Ashbourne (3rd), Edmund Willoughby Marsham Cokayne, b. 1916, s. 2000, w.	(Hon.) John O'B. M. C., b. 1920
1914	Cunliffe (3rd), Roger Cunliffe, b. 1932, s. 1963, m.	Hon. Henry C., b. 1962
1927	Daresbury (4th), Peter Gilbert Greenall, b. 1953, s. 1996, m.	Hon. Thomas E. G., b. 1984
1924	Darling (3rd), (Robert) Julian Henry Darling, b. 1944, s. 2003, m.	Hon. Robert J. C. D., b. 1972
1946	Darwen (3rd), Roger Michael Davies, b. 1938, s. 1988, m.	Hon. Paul D., b. 1962
1932	Davies (3rd), David Davies, b. 1940, s. 1944, m.	Hon. David D. D., b. 1975
1812 I.	Decies (7th), Marcus Hugh Tristram de la Poer Beresford, b. 1948, s. 1992, m.	Hon. Robert M. D. de la P. B., b. 1988
1299	de Clifford (27th), John Edward Southwell Russell, b. 1928, s. 1982, m.	Hon. William S. R., b. 1930
1851	De Freyne (7th), Francis Arthur John French, b. 1927, s. 1935, m.	Hon. Fulke C. A. J. F., b. 1957
1821	Delamere (5th), Hugh George Cholmondeley, b. 1934, s. 1979, m.	Hon. Thomas P. G. C., b. 1968
1838	** de Mauley (7th), Rupert Charles Ponsonby, b. 1957, s. 2002, m.	Ashley G. P., b. 1959
1937	** Denham (2nd), Bertram Stanley Mitford Bowyer, KBE, PC, b. 1927, s. 1948, m.	Hon. Richard G. G. B., b. 1959
1834	Denman (5th), Charles Spencer Denman, CBE, MC, TD, b. 1916, s. 1971, w.	Hon. Richard T. S. D., b. 1946
1885	Deramore (6th), Richard Arthur de Yarburgh-Bateson, b. 1911, s. 1964, m.	None
1887	De Ramsey (4th), John Ailwyn Fellowes, b. 1942, s. 1993, m.	Hon. Freddie J. F., b. 1978
1264	de Ros (28th), Peter Trevor Maxwell, b. 1958, s. 1983, m. Premier Baron of England	Hon. Finbar J. M., b. 1988
1881	Derwent (5th), Robin Evelyn Leo Vanden-Bempde-Johnstone, LVO, b. 1930, s. 1986, m.	Hon. Francis P. H. V.-B.-J., b. 1965
1831	de Saumarez (7th), Eric Douglas Saumarez, b. 1956, s. 1991, m.	Hon. Victor T. S., b. 1956
1910	de Villiers (4th), Alexander Charles de Villiers, b. 1940, s. 2001, m.	None
1930	Dickinson (2nd), Richard Clavering Hyett Dickinson, b. 1926, s. 1943, m.	Hon. Martin H. D., b. 1961
1620 I.	Digby (12th) and Digby (5th) (1765), Edward Henry Kenelm Digby, KCVO, b. 1924, s. 1964, m.	Hon. Henry N. K. D., b. 1954

Created	Title, order of succession, name, etc.	Heir
1615	*Dormer (17th),* Geoffrey Henry Dormer, *b.* 1920, *s.* 1995, *m.*	Hon. William R. D., *b.* 1960
1943	*Dowding (3rd),* Piers Hugh Tremenheere Dowding, *b.* 1948, *s.* 1992	Hon. Mark D. J. D., *b.* 1949
1439	*Dudley (15th),* Jim Anthony Hill Wallace, *b.* 1930, *s.* 2002, *m.*	Hon. Jeremy W. G. W., *b.* 1964
1800 I.	*Dufferin and Clandeboye,*The 10th Baron died in 1991.	†Sir John Blackwood, Bt., *b.* 1944
1929	*Dulverton (3rd),* (Gilbert) Michael Hamilton Wills, *b.* 1944, *s.* 1992	Hon. Robert A. H. W., *b.* 1983
1800 I.	*Dunalley (7th),* Henry Francis Cornelius Prittie, *b.* 1948, *s.* 1992, *m.*	Hon. Joel H. P., *b.* 1981
1324 I.	*Dunboyne (29th),* John Fitzwalter Butler, *b.* 1951, *s.* 2004, *m.*	Hon. Richard P. T. B., *b.* 1983
1892	*Dunleath (6th),* Brian Henry Mulholland, *b.* 1950, *s.* 1997, *m.*	Hon. Andrew H. M., *b.* 1981
1439 I.	*Dunsany (20th),* Edward John Carlos Plunkett, *b.* 1939, *s.* 1999, *m.*	Hon. Randal P., *b.* 1983
1780	*Dynevor (9th),* Richard Charles Uryan Rhys, *b.* 1935, *s.* 1962	Hon. Hugo G. U. R., *b.* 1966
1963	*Egremont (2nd) and Leconfield (7th) (1859),* John Max Henry Scawen Wyndham, *b.* 1948, *s.* 1972, *m.*	Hon. George R. V. W., *b.* 1983
1643	*Elibank (14th),* Alan D'Ardis Erskine-Murray, *b.* 1923, *s.* 1973, *w.*	Master of Elibank, *b.* 1964
1802	*Ellenborough (8th),* Richard Edward Cecil Law, *b.* 1926, *s.* 1945, *m.*	Maj. Hon. Rupert E. H. L., *b.* 1955
1509 S.	*Elphinstone (19th) and Elphinstone (5th) (1885),* Alexander Mountstuart Elphinstone, *b.* 1980, *s.* 1994	Hon. Angus J. E., *b.* 1982
1934 **	*Elton (2nd),* Rodney Elton, TD, *b.* 1930, *s.* 1973, *m.*	Hon. Edward P. E., *b.* 1966
1627 S.	*Fairfax of Cameron (14th),* Nicholas John Albert Fairfax, *b.* 1956, *s.* 1964, *m.*	Hon. Edward N. T. F., *b.* 1984
1961	*Fairhaven (3rd),* Ailwyn Henry George Broughton, *b.* 1936, *s.* 1973, *m.*	Maj. Hon. James H. A. B., *b.* 1963
1916	*Faringdon (3rd),* Charles Michael Henderson, *b.* 1937, *s.* 1977, *m.*	Hon. James H. H., *b.* 1961
1756	*Farnham (13th),* Simon Kenlis Maxwell, *b.* 1933, *s.* 2001, *m.*	Hon. Robin S. M., *b.* 1965
1856	*Fermoy (6th),* Patrick Maurice Burke Roche, *b.* 1967, *s.* 1984, *m.*	Hon. E. Hugh B. R., *b.* 1972
1826	*Feversham (6th),* Charles Antony Peter Duncombe, *b.* 1945, *s.* 1963, *m.*	Hon. Jasper O. S. D., *b.* 1968
1798 I.	*ffrench (8th),* Robuck John Peter Charles Mario ffrench, *b.* 1956, *s.* 1986, *m.*	Hon. John C. M. J. F. ff., *b.* 1928
1909	*Fisher (3rd),* John Vavasseur Fisher, DSC, *b.* 1921, *s.* 1955, *m.*	Hon. Patrick V. F., *b.* 1953
1295	*Fitzwalter (22nd),* Julian Brook Plumptre, *b.* 1952, *s.* 2004, m.	Hon. Edward B. P., *b.* 1989
1776	*Foley (8th),* Adrian Gerald Foley, *b.* 1923, *s.* 1927, *m.*	Hon. Thomas H. F., *b.* 1961
1445	*Forbes (22nd),* Nigel Ivan Forbes, KBE, *b.* 1918, *s.* 1953, *m. Premier Lord of Scotland*	Master of Forbes, *b.* 1946
1821	*Forester (9th),* Charles Richard George Weld-Forester, *b.* 1975, *s.* 2004,	Wolstan W. W.-F., *b.* 1941
1922	*Forres (4th),* Alastair Stephen Grant Williamson, *b.* 1946, *s.* 1978, *m.*	Hon. George A. M. W., *b.* 1972
1917	*Forteviot (4th),* John James Evelyn Dewar, *b.* 1938, *s.* 1993, *w.*	Hon. Alexander J. E. D., *b.* 197
1951 **	*Freyberg (3rd),* Valerian Bernard Freyberg, *b.* 1970, *s.* 1993	None
1917	*Gainford (3rd),* Joseph Edward Pease, *b.* 1921, *s.* 1971, *m.*	Hon. George P., *b.* 1926
1818	*Garvagh (5th),* (Alexander Leopold Ivor) George Canning, *b.* 1920, *s.* 1956, *m.*	Hon. Spencer G. S. de R. C., *b.* 1953
1942 **	*Geddes (3rd),* Euan Michael Ross Geddes, *b.* 1937, *s.* 1975, *m.*	Hon. James G. N. G., *b.* 1969
1876	*Gerard (5th),* Anthony Robert Hugo Gerard, *b.* 1949, *s.* 1992, *m.*	Hon. Rupert B. C. G., *b.* 1981
1824	*Gifford (6th),* Anthony Maurice Gifford, *b.* 1940, *s.* 1961, *m.*	Hon. Thomas A. G., *b.* 1967
1917	*Gisborough (3rd),* Thomas Richard John Long Chaloner, *b.* 1927, *s.* 1951, *m.*	Hon. T. Peregrine L. C., *b.* 196
1960	*Gladwyn (2nd),* Miles Alvery Gladwyn Jebb, *b.* 1930, *s.* 1996	None
1899	*Glanusk (5th),* Christopher Russell Bailey, *b.* 1942, *s.* 1997, *m.*	Hon. Charles H. B., *b.* 1976
1918 **	*Glenarthur (4th),* Simon Mark Arthur, *b.* 1944, *s.* 1976, *m.*	Hon. Edward A. A., *b.* 1973
1911	*Glenconner (3rd),* Colin Christopher Paget Tennant, *b.* 1926, *s.* 1983, *m.*	Cody C. E. T., *b.* 1994
1964	*Glendevon (2nd),* Julian John Somerset Hope, *b.* 1950, *s.* 1996	Hon. Jonathan C. H., *b.* 1952
1922	*Glendyne (3rd),* Robert Nivison, *b.* 1926, *s.* 1967, *m.*	Hon. John N., *b.* 1960
1939 **	*Glentoran (3rd),* (Thomas) Robin (Valerian) Dixon, CBE, *b.* 1935, *s.* 1995, *m.*	Hon. Daniel G. D., *b.* 1959
1909	*Gorell (4th),* Timothy John Radcliffe Barnes, *b.* 1927, *s.* 1963, *m.*	Hon. Ronald A. H. B., *b.* 1931
1953 **	*Grantchester (3rd),* Christopher John Suenson-Taylor, *b.* 1951, *s.* 1995, *m.*	Hon. Jesse D. S.-T., *b.* 1977
1782	*Grantley (8th),* Richard William Brinsley Norton, *b.* 1956, *s.* 1995	Hon. Francis J. H. N., *b.* 1960
1794 I.	*Graves (10th),* Timothy Evelyn Graves, *b.* 1960, *s.* 2002	None
1445 S.	*Gray (23rd),* Andrew Godfrey Diarmid Stuart Campbell-Gray, *b.* 1964, *s.* 2003, *m.*	Master of Gray, *b.* 1996
1950	*Greenhill (3rd),* Malcolm Greenhill, *b.* 1924, *s.* 1989	None
1927 **	*Greenway (4th),* Ambrose Charles Drexel Greenway, *b.* 1941, *s.* 1975, *m.*	Hon. Nigel. P. G., *b.* 1944
1902	*Grenfell (3rd) and Grenfell of Kilvey (life peerage, 2000),* Julian Pascoe Francis St Leger Grenfell, *b.* 1935, *s.* 1976, *m.*	Francis P. J. G., *b.* 1938

Created	Title, order of succession, name, etc.	Heir
1944	*Gretton (4th)*, John Lysander Gretton, *b.* 1975, *s.* 1989	None
1397	*Grey of Codnor (6th)*, Richard Henry Cornwall-Legh, *b.* 1936, *s.* 1996, *m.*	Hon. Richard S. C. C.-L., *b.* 1976
1955	*Gridley (3rd)*, Richard David Arnold Gridley, *b.* 1956, *s.* 1996, *m.*	Hon. Carl R. G., *b.* 1981
1964	*Grimston of Westbury (3rd)*, Robert John Sylvester Grimston, *b.* 1951, *s.* 2003, *m.*	Hon. Gerald C. W. G., *b.* 1953
1886	*Grimthorpe (5th)*, Edward John Beckett, *b.* 1954, *s.* 2003, *m.*	Hon. Harry M. B., *b.* 1993
1945	*Hacking (3rd)*, Douglas David Hacking, *b.* 1938, *s.* 1971, *m.*	Hon. Douglas F. H., *b.* 1968
1950	*Haden-Guest (5th)*, Christopher Haden-Guest, *b.* 1948, *s.* 1996, *m.*	Hon. Nicholas H.-G., *b.* 1951
1886	*Hamilton of Dalzell (4th)*, James Leslie Hamilton, *b.* 1938, *s.* 1990, *m.*	Hon. Gavin G. H., *b.* 1968
1874	*Hampton (7th)*, John Humphrey Arnott Pakington, *b.* 1964, *s.* 2003, *m.*	None
1939	*Hankey (3rd)*, Donald Robin Alers Hankey, *b.* 1938, *s.* 1996, *m.*	Hon. Alexander M. A. H., *b.* 1947
1958	*Harding of Petherton (2nd)*, John Charles Harding, *b.* 1928, *s.* 1989, *m.*	Hon. William A. J. H., *b.* 1969
1910	*Hardinge of Penshurst (4th)*, Julian Alexander Hardinge, *b.* 1945, *s.* 1997	Hon. Hugh F. H., *b.* 1948
1876	*Harlech (6th)*, Francis David Ormsby-Gore, *b.* 1954, *s.* 1985, *m.*	Hon. Jasset D. C. O.-G., *b.* 1986
1939	*Harmsworth (3rd)*, Thomas Harold Raymond Harmsworth, *b.* 1939, *s.* 1990, *m.*	Hon. Dominic M. E. H., *b.* 1973
1815	*Harris (8th)*, Anthony Harris, *b* 1942, *s.* 1996, *m.*	Anthony J. T. H., *b.* 1915
1954	*Harvey of Tasburgh (2nd)*, Peter Charles Oliver Harvey, *b.* 1921, *s.* 1968, *w.*	Charles J. G. H., *b.* 1951
1295	*Hastings (22nd)*, Edward Delaval Henry Astley, *b.* 1912, *s.* 1956, *m.*	Hon. Delaval T. H. A., *b.* 1960
1835	*Hatherton (8th)*, Edward Charles Littleton, *b.* 1950, *s.* 1985, *m.*	Hon. Thomas E. L., *b.* 1977
1776	*Hawke (11th)*, Edward George Hawke, TD, *b.* 1950, *s.* 1992, *m.*	Hon. William M. T. H., *b.* 1995
1927	*Hayter (4th)*, George William Michael Chubb, *b.* 1943, *s.* 2003, *m.*	Hon. Thomas F. F. C., *b.* 1986
1945	*Hazlerigg (3rd)*, Arthur Grey Hazlerigg, *b.* 1951, *s.* 2002, *m.*	Hon. Arthur W. G. H., *b.* 1987
1943	*Hemingford (3rd)*, (Dennis) Nicholas Herbert, *b.* 1934, *s.* 1982, *m.*	Hon. Christopher D. C. H., *b.* 1973
1906	*Hemphill (5th)*, Peter Patrick Fitzroy Martyn Martyn-Hemphill, *b.* 1928, *s.* 1957, *m.*	Hon. Charles A. M. M.-H., *b.* 1954
1799 I.	** *Henley (8th) and Northington (6th) (1885)*, Oliver Michael Robert Eden, *b.* 1953, *s.* 1977, *m.*	Hon. John W. O. E., *b.* 1988
1800 I.	*Henniker (9th) and Hertsmere (5th) (1866)*, Mark Ian Philip Chandos Henniker-Major, *b.* 1947, *s.* 2004, *m.*	Hon. Frederick J. C. H.-M., *b.* 1983
1461	*Herbert (19th)*, David John Seyfried Herbert, *b.* 1952, *s.* 2002, *m.*	Hon. Oliver R. S. H., *b.* 1976
1886	*Herschell (3rd)*, Rognvald Richard Farrer Herschell, *b.* 1923, *s.* 1929, *m.*	None
1935	*Hesketh (3rd)*, Thomas Alexander Fermor-Hesketh, KBE, PC, *b.* 1950, *s.* 1955, *m.*	Hon. Frederick H. F.-H., *b.* 1988
1828	*Heytesbury (7th)*, James William Holmes à Court, *b.* 1967, *s.* 2004, *m.*	Peter M. H.. H. à. C., *b.* 1968
1886	*Hindlip (6th)*, Charles Henry Allsopp, *b.* 1940, *s.* 1993, *m.*	Hon. Henry W. A., *b.* 1973
1950	*Hives (3rd)*, Matthew Peter Hives, *b.* 1971, *s.* 1997	Hon. Michael B. H., *b.* 1926
1912	*Hollenden (4th)*, Ian Hampden Hope-Morley, *b.* 1946, *s.* 1999, *m.*	Hon. Edward H.-M., *b.* 1981
1897	*Holm Patrick (4th)*, Hans James David Hamilton, *b.* 1955, *s.* 1991, *m.*	Hon. Ion H. J. H., *b.* 1956
1797 I.	*Hotham (8th)*, Henry Durand Hotham, *b.* 1940, *s.* 1967, *m.*	Hon. William B. H., *b.* 1972
1881	*Hothfield (6th)*, Anthony Charles Sackville Tufton, *b.* 1939, *s.* 1991, *m.*	Hon. William S. T., *b.* 1977
1930	*Howard of Penrith (3rd)*, Philip Esme Howard, *b.* 1945, *s.* 1999, *m.*	Hon. Thomas Philip H., *b.* 1974
1960	*Howick of Glendale (2nd)*, Charles Evelyn Baring, *b.* 1937, *s.* 1973, *m.*	Hon. David E. C. B., *b.* 1975
1796 I.	*Huntingfield (7th)*, Joshua Charles Vanneck, *b.* 1954, *s.* 1994, *m.*	Hon. Gerard C. A. V., *b.* 1985
1866	** *Hylton (5th)*, Raymond Hervey Jolliffe, *b.* 1932, *s.* 1967, *m.*	Hon. William H. M. J., *b.* 1967
1933	*Iliffe (3rd)*, Robert Peter Richard Iliffe, *b.* 1944, *s.* 1996, *m.*	Hon. Edward R. I., *b.* 1968
1543 I.	*Inchiquin (18th)*, Conor Myles John O'Brien, *b.* 1943, *s.* 1982, *m.*	Conor J. A. O'B., *b.* 1952
1962	*Inchyra (2nd)*, Robert Charles Reneke Hoyer Millar, *b.* 1935, *s.* 1989, *m.*	Hon. C. James C. H. M., *b.* 1962
1964	** *Inglewood (2nd)*, (William) Richard Fletcher-Vane, *b.* 1951, *s.* 1989, *m.*	Hon. Henry W. F. F.-V., *b.* 1990
1919	*Inverforth (4th)*, Andrew Peter Weir, *b.* 1966, *s.* 1982	Hon. John V. W., *b.* 1935
1941	*Ironside (2nd)*, Edmund Oslac Ironside, *b.* 1924, *s.* 1959, *m.*	Hon. Charles E. G. I., *b.* 1956
1952	*Jeffreys (3rd)*, Christopher Henry Mark Jeffreys, *b.* 1957, *s.* 1986, *m.*	Hon. Arthur M. H. J., *b.* 1989
1906	*Joicey (5th)*, James Michael Joicey, *b.* 1953, *s.* 1993, *m.*	Hon. William J. J., *b.* 1990
1937	*Kenilworth (4th)*, (John) Randle Siddeley, *b.* 1954, *s.* 1981, *m.*	Hon. William R. J. S., *b.* 1992
1935	*Kennet (2nd)*, Wayland Hilton Young, *b.* 1923, *s.* 1960, *m.*	Hon. W. A. Thoby Y., *b.* 1957
1776 I.	*Kensington (8th) and Kensington (5th) (1886)*, Hugh Ivor Edwardes, *b.* 1933, *s.* 1981, *m.*	Hon. W. Owen A. E., *b.* 1964
1951	*Kenswood (2nd)*, John Michael Howard Whitfield, *b.* 1930, *s.* 1963, *m.*	Hon. Michael C. W., *b.* 1955
1788	*Kenyon (6th)*, Lloyd Tyrell-Kenyon, *b.* 1947, *s.* 1993, *m.*	Hon. Lloyd N. T.-K., *b.* 1972

Created	Title, order of succession, name, etc.	Heir
1947	*Kershaw (4th)*, Edward John Kershaw, *b.* 1936, *s.* 1962, *m.*	Hon. John C. E. K., *b.* 1971
1943	*Keyes (3rd)*, Charles William Packe Keyes, *b.* 1951, *s.* 2005, *m.*	Hon. Leopold R. J. K., *b.* 1956
1909	*Kilbracken (3rd)*, John Raymond Godley, DSC, *b.* 1920, *s.* 1950	Hon. Christopher J. G., *b.* 1945
1900	*Killanin (4th)*, (George) Redmond Fitzpatrick Morris, *b.* 1947, *s.* 1999, *m.*	Hon. Luke M. G. M., *b.* 1975
1943	*Killearn (3rd)*, Victor Miles George Aldous Lampson, *b.* 1941, *s.* 1996, *m.*	Hon. Miles H. M. L., *b.* 1977
1789 I.	*Kilmaine (7th)*, John David Henry Browne, *b.* 1948, *s.* 1978, *m.*	Hon. John F. S. B., *b.* 1983
1831	*Kilmarnock (7th)*, Alastair Ivor Gilbert Boyd, *b.* 1927, *s.* 1975, *m.*	Hon. Robin J. B., *b.* 1941
1941	*Kindersley (3rd)*, Robert Hugh Molesworth Kindersley, *b.* 1929, *s.* 1976, *m.*	Hon. Rupert J. M. K., *b.* 1955
1223 I.	*Kingsale (35th)*, John de Courcy, *b.* 1941, *s.* 1969, *Premier Baron of Ireland*	Nevinson M. de C., *b.* 1958
1902	*Kinross (5th)*, Christopher Patrick Balfour, *b.* 1949, *s.* 1985, *m.*	Hon. Alan I. B., *b.* 1978
1951	*Kirkwood (3rd)*, David Harvie Kirkwood, PHD, *b.* 1931, *s.* 1970, *m.*	Hon. James S. K., *b.* 1937
1800 I.	*Langford (9th)*, Col. Geoffrey Alexander Rowley-Conwy, OBE, *b.* 1912, *s.* 1953, *m.*	Hon. Owain G. R.-C., *b.* 1958
1942	*Latham (2nd)*, Dominic Charles Latham, *b.* 1954, *s.* 1970	Anthony M. L., *b.* 1954
1431	*Latymer (9th)*, Crispin James Alan Nevill Money-Coutts, *b.* 1955, *s.* 2003, *m.*	Hon. Drummond W. T. M.-C., *b.* 1986
1869	*Lawrence (5th)*, David John Downer Lawrence, *b.* 1937, *s.* 1968	None
1947	*Layton (3rd)*, Geoffrey Michael Layton, *b.* 1947, *s.* 1989, *m.*	Hon. David L., *b.* 1914
1839	*Leigh (6th)*, Christopher Dudley Piers Leigh, *b.* 1960, *s.* 2003, *m.*	Hon. Rupert D. L., *b.* 1994
1962	*Leighton of St Mellons (3rd)*, Robert William Henry Leighton Seager, *b.* 1955, *s.* 1998	Hon. Simon J. L. S., *b.* 1957
1797	*Lilford (8th)*, Mark Vernon Powys, *b.* 1975, *s.* 2005	Robert C. L. P., *b.* 1930
1945	*Lindsay of Birker (3rd)*, James Francis Lindsay, *b.* 1945, *s.* 1994, *m.*	Alexander S. L., *b.* 1940
1758 I.	*Lisle (9th)*, (John) Nicholas Geoffrey Lysaght, *b.* 1960, *s.* 2003	Hon. David J. L., *b.* 1963
1850	*Londesborough (9th)*, Richard John Denison, *b.* 1959, *s.* 1968, *m.*	Hon. James F. D., *b.* 1990
1541 I.	*Louth (16th)*, Otway Michael James Oliver Plunkett, *b.* 1929, *s.* 1950, *m.*	Hon. Jonathan O. P., *b.* 1952
1458 S.	*Lovat (16th) and Lovat (5th) (1837)*, Simon Fraser, *b.* 1977, *s.* 1995	Hon. Jack F., *b.* 1984
1946	*Lucas of Chilworth (3rd)*, Simon William Lucas, *b.* 1957, *s.* 2001, *m.*	Hon. John R. M. L., *b.* 1995
1663	** *Lucas (11th) and Dingwall (14th) (S. 1609)*, Ralph Matthew Palmer, *b.* 1951, *s.* 1991	Hon. Lewis E. P., *b.* 1987
1929	** *Luke (3rd)*, Arthur Charles St John Lawson-Johnston, *b.* 1933, *s.* 1996, *m.*	Hon. Ian J. St J. L.-J., *b.* 1963
1914	** *Lyell (3rd)*, Charles Lyell, *b.* 1939, *s.* 1943	None
1859	*Lyveden (7th)*, Jack Leslie Vernon, *b.* 1938, *s.* 1999, *m.*	Hon. Colin R. V., *b.* 1967
1959	*MacAndrew (3rd)*, Christopher Anthony Colin MacAndrew, *b.* 1945, *s.* 1989, *m.*	Hon. Oliver C. J. M., *b.* 1983
1776 I.	*Macdonald (8th)*, Godfrey James Macdonald of Macdonald, *b.* 1947, *s.* 1970, *m.*	Hon. Godfrey E. H. T. M., *b.* 1982
1937	*McGowan (4th)*, Harry John Charles McGowan, *b.* 1971, *s.* 2003, *m.*	Hon. Dominic J. W. McG., *b.* 1951
1922	*Maclay (3rd)*, Joseph Paton Maclay, *b.* 1942, *s.* 1969, *m.*	Hon. Joseph P. M., *b.* 1977
1955	*McNair (3rd)*, Duncan James McNair, *b.* 1947, *s.* 1989, *m.*	Hon. William S. A. M., *b.* 1958
1951	*Macpherson of Drumochter (2nd)*, (James) Gordon Macpherson, *b.* 1924, *s.* 1965, *m.*	Hon. James A. M., *b.* 1979
1937	** *Mancroft (3rd)*, Benjamin Lloyd Stormont Mancroft, *b.* 1957, *s.* 1987, *m.*	Hon. Arthur L. S. M., *b.* 1995
1807	*Manners (5th)*, John Robert Cecil Manners, *b.* 1923, *s.* 1972, *w.*	Hon. John H. R. M., *b.* 1956
1922	*Manton (4th)*, Miles Ronald Marcus Watson, *b.* 1958, *s.* 2003, *m.*	Hon. Thomas N. C. D. W., *b.* 1985
1908	*Marchamley (4th)*, William Francis Whiteley, *b.* 1968, *s.* 1994	None
1964	*Margadale (3rd)*, Alastair John Morrison, *b.* 1958, *s.* 2003, *m.*	Hon. Declan J. M., *b.* 1993
1961	*Marks of Broughton (3rd)*, Simon Richard Marks, *b.* 1950, *s.* 1998, *m.*	Hon. Michael M., *b.* 1989
1964	*Martonmere (2nd)*, John Stephen Robinson, *b.* 1963, *s.* 1989	David A. R., *b.* 1965
1776 I.	*Massy (10th)*, David Hamon Somerset Massy, *b.* 1947, *s.* 1995	Hon. John H. M., *b.* 1950
1935	*May (3rd)*, Michael St John May, *b.* 1931, *s.* 1950, *m.*	Hon. Jasper B. St J. M., *b.* 1965
1928	*Melchett (4th)*, Peter Robert Henry Mond, *b.* 1948, *s.* 1973	None
1925	*Merrivale (3rd)*, Jack Henry Edmond Duke, *b.* 1917, *s.* 1951, *w.*	Hon. Derek J. P. D., *b.* 1948
1911	Merthyr, Trevor Oswin Lewis, CBE, *b.* 1935, *s.* 1977, *m.* Disclaimed for life 1977	David T. L., *b.* 1977
1919	*Meston (3rd)*, James Meston, *b.* 1950, *s.* 1984, *m.*	Hon. Thomas J. D. M., *b.* 1977
1838	** *Methuen (7th)*, Robert Alexander Holt Methuen, *b.* 1931, *s.* 1994, *m.*	James P. A. M.-C., *b.* 1952
1711	*Middleton (12th)*, (Digby) Michael Godfrey John Willoughby, MC, *b.* 1921, *s.* 1970	Hon. Michael C. J. W., *b.* 1948

Created	Title, order of succession, name, etc.	Heir
1939	Milford (4th), Guy Wogan Philipps, b. 1961, s. 1999, m.	Hon. Archie S. P., b. 1997
1933	Milne (3rd), George Alexander Milne, b. 1941, s. 2005	Hon. Iain C. L. M., b. 1949
1951	Milner of Leeds (3rd), Richard James Milner, b. 1959, s. 2003, m.	None
1947	Milverton (2nd), Revd Fraser Arthur Richard Richards, b. 1930, s. 1978, m.	Hon. Michael H. R , b. 1936
1873	Moncreiff (6th), Rhoderick Harry Wellwood Moncreiff, b. 1954, s. 2002, m.	Hon. Harry J. W. M., b. 1986
1884	Monk Bretton (3rd), John Charles Dodson, b. 1924, s. 1933, m.	Hon. Christopher M. D., b. 1958
1885	Monkswell (5th), Gerard Collier, b. 1947, s. 1984, m.	Hon. James A. C., b. 1977
1728	** Monson (11th), John Monson, b. 1932, s. 1958, m.	Hon. Nicholas J. M., b. 1955
1885	** Montagu of Beaulieu (3rd), Edward John Barrington Douglas-Scott-Montagu, b. 1926, s. 1929, m.	Hon. Ralph D.-S.-M., b. 1961
1839	Monteagle of Brandon (6th), Gerald Spring Rice, b. 1926, s. 1946, m.	Hon. Charles J. S. R., b. 1953
1943	** Moran (2nd), (Richard) John (McMoran) Wilson, KCMG, b. 1924, s. 1977, m.	Hon. James M. W., b. 1952
1918	Morris (3rd), Michael David Morris, b. 1937, s. 1975, m.	Hon. Thomas A. S. M., b. 1982
1950	Morris of Kenwood (3rd), Jonathan David Morris, b. 1968, s. 2004, m.	None
1831	Mostyn (6th), Llewellyn Roger Lloyd-Mostyn, b. 1948, s. 2000, m.	Hon. Gregory P. R. L.-M., b. 1984
1933	Mottistone (4th), David Peter Seely, CBE, b. 1920, s. 1966, m.	Hon. Peter J. P. S., b. 1949
1945	Mountevans (3rd), Edward Patrick Broke Evans, b. 1943, s. 1974, m.	Hon. Jeffrey de C. R. E., b. 1948
1283	** Mowbray (26th), Segrave (27th) (1295) and Stourton (23rd) (1448), Charles Edward Stourton, CBE, b. 1923, s. 1965, m.	Hon. Edward W. S. S., b. 1953
1932	Moyne (3rd), Jonathan Bryan Guinness, b. 1930, s. 1992, m.	Hon. Jasper J. R. G., b. 1954
1929	** Moynihan (4th), Colin Berkeley Moynihan, b. 1955, s. 1997, m.	Hon. Nicholas E. B. M., b. 1994
1781 I.	Muskerry (9th), Robert Fitzmaurice Deane, b. 1948, s. 1988, m.	Hon. Jonathan F. D., b. 1986
1627 S.	Napier (14th) and Ettrick (5th) (1872), Francis Nigel Napier, KCVO, b. 1930, s. 1954, m.	Master of Napier, b. 1962
1868	Napier of Magdala (6th), Robert Alan Napier, b. 1940, s. 1987, m.	Hon. James R. N., b. 1966
1940	Nathan (2nd), Roger Carol Michael Nathan, b. 1922, s. 1963, m.	Hon. Rupert H. B. N., b. 1957
1960	Nelson of Stafford (3rd), Henry Roy George Nelson, b. 1943, s. 1995, m.	Hon. Alistair W. H. N., b. 1973
1959	Netherthorpe (3rd), James Frederick Turner, b. 1964, s. 1982, m.	Hon. Andrew J. E. T., b. 1993
1946	Newall (2nd), Francis Storer Eaton Newall, b. 1930, s. 1963, m.	Hon. Richard H. E. N., b. 1961
1776 I.	Newborough (8th), Robert Vaughan Wynn, b. 1949, s. 1998, m.	Hon. Charles H. R. W., b. 1923
1892	Newton (5th), Richard Thomas Legh, b. 1950, s. 1992, m.	Hon. Piers R. L., b. 1979
1930	Noel-Buxton (3rd), Martin Connal Noel-Buxton, b. 1940, s. 1980, m.	Hon. Charles C. N.-B., b. 1975
1957	Norrie (2nd), (George) Willoughby Moke Norrie, b. 1936, s. 1977, m.	Hon. Mark W. J. N., b. 1972
1884	** Northbourne (5th), Christopher George Walter James, b. 1926, s. 1982, m.	Hon. Charles W. H. J., b. 1960
1866	** Northbrook (6th), Francis Thomas Baring, b. 1954, s. 1990, m.	To the Baronetcy, Peter B. b. 1939
1878	Norton (8th), James Nigel Arden Adderley, b. 1947, s. 1993, m.	Hon. Edward J. A. A., b. 1982
1906	Nunburnholme (6th), Stephen Charles Wilson, b. 1973, s. 2000	Hon. David M. W., b. 1954
1950	Ogmore (3rd), Morgan Rees-Williams, b. 1937, s. 2004, m.	Hon. Tudor D. R.-W., b. 1991
1870	O'Hagan (4th), Charles Towneley Strachey, b. 1945, s. 1961	Hon. Richard T. S., b. 1950
1868	O'Neill (4th), Raymond Arthur Clanaboy O'Neill, TD, b. 1933, s. 1944, m.	Hon. Shane S. C. O'N., b. 1965
1836 I.	Oranmore and Browne (5th) and Mereworth (3rd) (1926), Dominick Geoffrey Thomas Browne, b. 1929, s. 2002	Hon. Martin M. D. B., b. 1931
1933	** Palmer (4th), Adrian Bailie Nottage Palmer, b. 1951, s. 1990, m.	Hon. Hugo B. R. P., b. 1980
1914	Parmoor (4th), (Frederick Alfred) Milo Cripps, b. 1929, s. 1977	Michael L. S. C., b. 1942
1937	Pender (3rd), John Willoughby Denison-Pender, b. 1933, s. 1965, m.	Hon. Henry J. R. D.-P., b. 1968
1866	Penrhyn (7th), Simon Douglas-Pennant, b. 1938, s. 2003, m.	Hon. Edward S. D.-P., b. 1966
1603	Petre (18th), John Patrick Lionel Petre, b. 1942, s. 1989, m.	Hon. Dominic W. P., b. 1966
1918	Phillimore (5th), Francis Stephen Phillimore, b. 1944, s. 1994, m.	Hon. Tristan A. S. P., b. 1977
1945	Piercy (3rd), James William Piercy, b. 1946, s. 1981	Hon. Mark E. P. P., b. 1953
1827	Plunket (8th), Robin Rathmore Plunket, b. 1925, s. 1975, m.	Hon. Shaun A. F. S. P., b. 1931
1831	Poltimore (7th), Mark Coplestone Bampfylde, b. 1957, s. 1978, m.	Hon. Henry A. W. B., b. 1985
1690 S.	Polwarth (11th), Andrew Walter Hepburne-Scott, b. 1947, s. 2005, m.	Master of Polwarth, b. 1973
1930	Ponsonby of Shulbrede (4th) and Ponsonby of Roehampton (life peerage, 2000), Frederick Matthew Thomas Ponsonby, b. 1958, s. 1990	None
1958	Poole (2nd), David Charles Poole, b. 1945, s. 1993, m.	Hon. Oliver J. P., b. 1972
1852	Raglan (5th), FitzRoy John Somerset, b. 1927, s. 1964	Hon. Geoffrey S., b. 1932
1932	Rankeillour (5th), Michael Richard Hope, b. 1940, s. 2005, m.	James F. H., b. 1968

Created	Title, order of succession, name, etc.	Heir
1953	*Rathcavan (3rd)*, Hugh Detmar Torrens O'Neill, *b.* 1939, *s.* 1994, *m.*	Hon. François H. N. O'N., *b.* 1984
1916	*Rathcreedan (3rd)*, Christopher John Norton, *b.* 1949, *s.* 1990, *m.*	Hon. Adam G. N., *b.* 1952
1868	*Rathdonnell (5th)*, Thomas Benjamin McClintock-Bunbury, *b.* 1938, *s.* 1959, *m.*	Hon. William L. M.-B., *b.* 1966
1911	*Ravensdale (3rd)*, Nicholas Mosley, MC, *b.* 1923, *s.* 1966, *m.*	Hon. Shaun N. M., *b.* 1949
1821	*Ravensworth (9th)*, Thomas Arthur Hamish Liddell, *b.* 1954, *s.* 2004, *m.*	Hon. Henry A. T. L., *b.* 1987
1821	*Rayleigh (6th)*, John Gerald Strutt, *b.* 1960, *s.* 1988, *m.*	Hon. John F. S., *b.* 1993
1937	** *Rea (3rd)*, John Nicolas Rea, MD, *b.* 1928, *s.* 1981, *m.*	Hon. Matthew J. R., *b.* 1956
1628 S.	** *Reay (14th)*, Hugh William Mackay, *b.* 1937, *s.* 1963, *m.*	Master of Reay, *b.* 1965
1902	*Redesdale (6th) and Mitford (life peerage 2000)*, Rupert Bertram Mitford, *b.* 1967, *s.* 1991, *m.*	Hon. Bertram D. M., *b.* 2000
1940	*Reith*, Christopher John Reith, *b.* 1928, *s.* 1971, *m.* Disclaimed for life 1972.	Hon. James H. J. R., *b.* 1971
1928	*Remnant (3rd)*, James Wogan Remnant, CVO, *b.* 1930, *s.* 1967, *m.*	Hon. Philip J. R., *b.* 1954
1806	*Rendlesham (9th)*, Charles William Brooke Thellusson, *b.* 1954, *s.* 1999, *m.*	Hon. Peter R. T., *b.* 1920
1933	*Rennell (3rd)*, (John Adrian) Tremayne Rodd, *b.* 1935, *s.* 1978, *m.*	Hon. James R. D. T. R., *b.* 1978
1964	*Renwick (2nd)*, Harry Andrew Renwick, *b.* 1935, *s.* 1973, *m.*	Hon. Robert J. R., *b.* 1966
1885	*Revelstoke (6th)*, James Cecil Baring, *b.* 1938, *s.* 2003, *m.*	Hon. Alexander R. B., *b.* 1970
1905	*Ritchie of Dundee (5th)*, (Harold) Malcolm Ritchie, *b.* 1919, *s.* 1978, *m.*	Hon. C. Rupert R. R., *b.* 1958
1935	*Riverdale (3rd)*, Anthony Robert Balfour, *b.* 1960, *s.* 1998	Hon. David R. B., *b.* 1938
1961	*Robertson of Oakridge (2nd)*, William Ronald Robertson, *b.* 1930, *s.* 1974, *m.*	Hon. William B. E. R., *b.* 1975
1938	*Roborough (3rd)*, Henry Massey Lopes, *b.* 1940, *s.* 1992, *m.*	Hon. Massey J. H. L., *b.* 1969
1931	*Rochester (2nd)*, Foster Charles Lowry Lamb, *b.* 1916, *s.* 1955, *w.*	Hon. David C. L., *b.* 1944
1934	*Rockley (3rd)*, James Hugh Cecil, *b.* 1934, *s.* 1976, *m.*	Hon. Anthony R. C., *b.* 1961
1782	*Rodney (10th)*, George Brydges Rodney, *b.* 1953, *s.* 1992, *m.*	Hon. John G. B. R., *b.*1999
1651 S.	*Rollo (14th) and Dunning (5th) (1869)*, David Eric Howard Rollo, *b.* 1943, *s.* 1997, *m.*	Master of Rollo, *b.* 1972
1959	*Rootes (3rd)*, Nicholas Geoffrey Rootes, *b.* 1951, *s.* 1992, *m.*	William B. R., *b.* 1944
1796 I.	*Rossmore (7th) and Rossmore (6th) (1838)*, William Warner Westenra, *b.* 1931, *s.* 1958, *m.*	Hon. Benedict W. W., *b.* 1983
1939	** *Rotherwick (3rd)*, (Herbert) Robin Cayzer, *b.* 1954, *s.* 1996, *m.*	Hon. H. Robin C., *b.* 1989
1885	*Rothschild (4th)*, (Nathaniel Charles) Jacob Rothschild, OM, GBE, *b.* 1936, *s.* 1990, *m.*	Hon. Nathaniel P. V. J. R., *b.* 1971
1911	*Rowallan (4th)*, John Polson Cameron Corbett, *b.* 1947, *s.* 1993	Hon. Jason W. P. C. C., *b.* 1972
1947	*Rugby (3rd)*, Robert Charles Maffey, *b.* 1951, *s.* 1990, *m.*	Hon. Timothy J. H. M., *b.* 1975
1919	*Russell of Liverpool (3rd)*, Simon Gordon Jared Russell, *b.* 1952, *s.* 1981, *m.*	Hon. Edward C. S. R., *b.* 1985
1876	*Sackville (7th)*, Robert Bertrand Sackville-West, *b.* 1958, *s.* 2004, *m.*	Hon. Arthur S-W., *b.* 2000
1964	*St Helens (2nd)*, Richard Francis Hughes-Young, *b.* 1945, *s.* 1980, *m.*	Hon. Henry T. H.-Y., *b.* 1986
1559	** *St John of Bletso (21st)*, Anthony Tudor St John, *b.* 1957, *s.* 1978, *m.*	Hon. Oliver B. St J., *b.* 1995
1887	*St Levan (4th)*, John Francis Arthur St Aubyn, DSC, *b.* 1919, *s.* 1978, *w.*	Hon. O. Piers St. A., *b.* 1920
1885	*St Oswald (6th)*, Charles Rowland Andrew Winn, *b.* 1959, *s.* 1999, *m.*	Hon. Rowland C. S. H. W., *b.* 1986
1960	*Sanderson of Ayot*, Alan Lindsay Sanderson, *b.* 1931, *s.* 1971, *m.* Disclaimed for life 1971.	Hon. Michael S., *b.* 1959
1945	*Sandford (2nd)*, Revd John Cyril Edmondson, DSC, *b.* 1920, *s.* 1959, *m.*	Hon. James J. M. E., *b.* 1949
1871	*Sandhurst (6th)*, Guy Rees John Mansfield, *b.* 1949, *s.* 2002, *m.*	Hon. Edward J. M., *b.* 1982
1802	*Sandys (7th)*, Richard Michael Oliver Hill, *b.* 1931, *s.* 1961, *m.*	The Marquess of Downshire
1888	*Savile (3rd)*, George Halifax Lumley-Savile, *b.* 1919, *s.* 1931	John A. T. L-S., *b.* 1947
1447	*Saye and Sele (21st)*, Nathaniel Thomas Allen Fiennes, *b.* 1920, *s.* 1968, *m.*	Hon. Martin G. F., *b.* 1961
1826	*Seaford (6th)*, Colin Humphrey Felton Ellis, *b.* 1946, *s.* 1999, *m.*	Hon. Benjamin F. T. E., *b.* 1976
1932	** *Selsdon (3rd)*, Malcolm McEacharn Mitchell-Thomson, *b.* 1937, *s.* 1963, *m.*	Hon. Callum M. M. M.-T., *b.* 1969
1489 S.	*Sempill (21st)*, James William Stuart Whitemore Sempill, *b.* 1949, *s.* 1995, *m.*	Master of Semphill, *b.* 1979
1916	*Shaughnessy (4th)*, Michael James Shaughnessy, *b.* 1946, *s.* 2003	Charles, G. P. S., *b.* 1955
1946	*Shepherd (3rd)*, Graham George Shepherd, *b.* 1949, *s.* 2001, *m.*	Hon. Patrick M. S., *b.* 19–
1964	*Sherfield (2nd)*, Christopher James Makins, *b.* 1942, *s.* 1996, *m.*	Hon. Dwight W. M., *b.* 1951
1902	*Shuttleworth (5th)*, Charles Geoffrey Nicholas Kay-Shuttleworth, *b.* 1948, *s.* 1975, *m.*	Hon. Thomas E. K.-S., *b.* 1976
1950	*Silkin (3rd)*, Christopher Lewis Silkin, *b.* 1947, *s.* 2001 Rory L. S., *b.* 1954	
1963	*Silsoe (2nd)*, David Malcolm Trustram Eve *b.* 1930, *s.* 1976, *m.*	Hon. Simon R. T. E., *b.* 1966

Created	Title, order of succession, name, etc.	Heir
1947	Simon of Wythenshawe (3rd), Matthew Simon, b. 1955, s. 2002	Martin S., b. 1944
1449 S.	Sinclair (18th), Matthew Murray Kennedy St Clair, b. 1968, s. 2004	Hugh A. C. St C., b. 1957
1957	Sinclair of Cleeve (3rd), John Lawrence Robert Sinclair, b. 1953, s. 1985	None
1919	Sinha (6th), Arup Kumar Sinha, b. 1966, s. 1999	Hon. Dilip K. S., b. 1967
1828	** Skelmersdale (7th), Roger Bootle-Wilbraham, b. 1945, s. 1973, m.	Hon. Andrew B.-W., b. 1977
1916	Somerleyton (3rd), Savile William Francis Crossley, GCVO, b. 1928, s. 1959, m.	Hon. Hugh F. S. C., b. 1971
1784	Somers (9th), Philip Sebastian Somers Cocks, b. 1948, s. 1995	Alan B. C., b. 1930
1780	Southampton (6th), Charles James FitzRoy, b. 1928, s. 1989, m.	Hon. Edward C. F., b. 1955
1959	Spens (4th), Patrick Nathaniel George Spens, b. 1968, s. 2001, m.	Hon. Peter L. S., b. 2000
1640	Stafford (15th), Francis Melfort William Fitzherbert, b. 1954, s. 1986, m.	Hon. Benjamin J. B. F., b. 1983
1938	Stamp (4th), Trevor Charles Bosworth Stamp, MD, b. 1935, s. 1987, m.	Hon. Nicholas C. T. S., b. 1978
1839	Stanley of Alderley (8th), Sheffield (8th) (I. 1738) and Eddisbury (7th) (1848), Thomas Henry Oliver Stanley, b. 1927, s. 1971, m.	Hon. Richard O. S., b. 1956
1318	** Strabolgi (11th), David Montague de Burgh Kenworthy, b. 1914, s. 1953, m.	Andrew D. W. K., b. 1967
1954	Strang (2nd), Colin Strang, b. 1922, s. 1978, m.	None
1628	Strange (17th), Adam Humphrey Drummond of Megginch, b. 1953, s. 2005 m.	Hon. John A. H. D. of M., b. 1992
1955	Strathalmond (3rd), William Roberton Fraser, b. 1947, s. 1976, m.	Hon. William G. F., b. 1976
1936	Strathcarron (2nd), David William Anthony Blyth Macpherson, b. 1924, s. 1937, m.	Hon. Ian D. P. M., b. 1949
1955	** Strathclyde (2nd), Thomas Galloway Dunlop du Roy de Blicquy Galbraith, PC, b. 1960, s. 1985, m.	Hon. Charles W. du R. de B. G., b. 1962
1900	Strathcona and Mount Royal (4th), Donald Euan Palmer Howard, b. 1923, s. 1959, m.	Hon. D. Alexander S. H., b. 1961
1836	Stratheden (6th) and Campbell (6th) (1841), Donald Campbell, b. 1934, s. 1987, m.	Hon. David A. C., b. 1963
1884	Strathspey (6th), James Patrick Trevor Grant of Grant, b. 1943, s. 1992, m.	Hon. Michael P. F. G., b. 1953
1838	Sudeley (7th), Merlin Charles Sainthill Hanbury-Tracy, b. 1939, s. 1941	D. Andrew J. H.-T., b. 1928
1786	Suffield (11th), Anthony Philip Harbord-Hamond, MC, b. 1922, s. 1951, w.	Hon. Charles A. A. H.-H., b. 1953
1893	Swansea (5th), Richard Anthony Hussey Vivian, b. 1957, s. 2005, m.	Hon. James H. H. V., b. 1999
1907	Swaythling (5th), Charles Edgar Samuel Montagu, b. 1954, s. 1998, m.	Hon. Anthony T. S. M., b. 1931
1919	** Swinfen (3rd), Roger Mynors Swinfen Eady, b. 1938, s. 1977, m.	Hon. Charles R. P. S. E., b. 1971
1935	Sysonby (3rd), John Frederick Ponsonby, b. 1945, s. 1956	None
1831 I.	Talbot of Malahide (10th), Reginald John Richard Arundell, b. 1931, s. 1987, m.	Hon. Richard J. T. A., b. 1957
1946	Tedder (3rd), Robin John Tedder, b. 1955, s. 1994, m.	Hon. Benjamin J. T., b. 1985
1884	Tennyson (5th), Cdr. Mark Aubrey Tennyson, DSC, b. 1920, s. 1991, m.	David H. A. T., b. 1960
1918	Terrington (6th), Christopher Richard James Woodhouse, MB, b. 1946, s. 2001, m.	Hon. Jack H. L. W., b. 1978
1940	Teviot (2nd), Charles John Kerr, b. 1934, s. 1968, m.	Hon. Charles R. K., b. 1971
1616	Teynham (20th), John Christopher Ingham Roper-Curzon, b. 1928, s. 1972, m.	Hon. David J. H. I. R.-C., b. 1965
1964	Thomson of Fleet (2nd), Kenneth Roy Thomson, b. 1923, s. 1976, m.	Hon. David K. R. T., b. 1957
1792	Thurlow (8th), Francis Edward Hovell-Thurlow-Cumming-Bruce, KCMG, b. 1912, s. 1971, w.	Hon. Roualeyn R. H.-T.-C.-B., b. 1952
1876	Tollemache (5th), Timothy John Edward Tollemache, b. 1939, s. 1975, m.	Hon. Edward J. H. T., b. 1976
1564 S.	Torphichen (15th), James Andrew Douglas Sandilands, b. 1946, s. 1975, m.	Robert P. S., b. 1950
1947	** Trefgarne (2nd), David Garro Trefgarne, PC, b. 1941, s. 1960, m.	Hon. George G. T., b. 1970
1921	Treverhin (4th) and Oaksey (2nd) (1947), John Geoffrey Tristram Lawrence, OBE, b. 1929, s. 1971, m.	Hon. Patrick J. T. L., b. 1960
1880	Trevor (5th), Marke Charles Hill-Trevor, b. 1970, s. 1997, m.	Hon. Iain R. H.-T., b. 1971
1461 I.	Trimlestown (21st), Raymond Charles Barnewall, b. 1930, s. 1997	None
1940	Tryon (3rd), Anthony George Merrik Tryon, b. 1940, s. 1976	Hon. Charles G. B. T., b. 1976
1935	Tweedsmuir (3rd), William de l'Aigle Buchan, b. 1916, s. 1996, m.	Hon. John W. H. de l'A. B., b. 1950
1523	Vaux of Harrowden (11th), Anthony William Gilbey, b. 1940, s. 2002, m.	Hon. Richard H. G. G., b. 1965
1800 I.	Ventry (8th), Andrew Wesley Daubeny de Moleyns, b. 1943, s. 1987, m.	Hon. Francis W. D. de M., b. 1965

Created	Title, order of succession, name, etc.	Heir
1762	Vernon (11th), Anthony William Vernon-Harcourt, b. 1939, s. 2000, m.	Hon. Simon A. V-H., b. 1969
1922	Vestey (3rd), Samuel George Armstrong Vestey, b. 1941, s. 1954, m.	Hon. William G. V., b. 1983
1841	Vivian (7th), Charles Crespigny Hussey Vivian, b. 1966, s. 2004	Hon. Victor A. R. B. V., b. 194C
1934	Wakehurst (3rd), (John) Christopher Loder, b. 1925, s. 1970, m.	Hon. Timothy W. L., b. 1958
1723	** Walpole (10th) and Walpole of Wolterton (8th) (1756), Robert Horatio Walpole, b. 1938, s. 1989, m.	Hon. Jonathan R. H. W., b. 1967
1780	Walsingham (9th), John de Grey, MC, b. 1925, s. 1965, m.	Hon. Robert de. G., b. 1969
1936	Wardington (3rd), William Simon Pease, b. 1925, s. 2005, m.	None
1792 I.	Waterpark (7th), Frederick Caryll Philip Cavendish, b. 1926, s. 1948, m.	Hon. Roderick A. C., b. 1959
1942	Wedgwood (4th), Piers Anthony Weymouth Wedgwood, b. 1954, s. 1970, m.	John W., b. 1919
1861	Westbury (6th), Richard Nicholas Bethell, MBE, b. 1950, s. 2001, m.	Hon. Alexander B., b. 1986
1944	Westwood (3rd), (William) Gavin Westwood, b. 1944, s. 1991, m.	Hon. W. Fergus W., b. 1972
1544/5	Wharton (12th), Myles Christopher David Robertson, b. 1964, s. 2000, m.	Hon. Christopher J. R., b. 1969
1935	Wigram (2nd), (George) Neville (Clive) Wigram, MC, b. 1915, s. 1960, w.	Maj. Hon. Andrew F. C. W., b. 1949
1491	** Willoughby de Broke (21st), Leopold David Verney, b. 1938, s. 1986, m.	Hon. Rupert G. V., b. 1966
1946	Wilson (2nd), Patrick Maitland Wilson, b. 1915, s. 1964, w.	None
1937	Windlesham (3rd) and Hennessy (life peerage, 1999), David James George Hennessy, CVO, PC, b. 1932, s. 1962, w.	Hon. James R. H., b. 1968
1951	Wise (2nd), John Clayton Wise, b. 1923, s. 1968, m.	Hon. Christopher J. C. W., b. 1949
1869	Wolverton (7th), Christopher Richard Glyn, b. 1938, s. 1988	Hon. Andrew J. G., b. 1943
1928	Wraxall (3rd), Eustace Hubert Beilby Gibbs, KCVO, CMG, b. 1929, s. 2001, w.	Hon. Anthony H. G., b. 1958
1915	Wrenbury (3rd), Revd John Burton Buckley, b. 1927, s. 1940, m.	Hon. William E. B., b. 1966
1838	Wrottesley (6th), Clifton Hugh Lancelot de Verdon Wrottesley, b. 1968, s. 1977, m.	Hon. Stephen J. W., b. 1955
1829	Wynford (9th), John Philip Robert Best, b. 1950, s. 2002, m.	Hon. Harry R. F. B., b. 1987
1308	Zouche (18th), James Assheton Frankland, b. 1943, s. 1965, m.	Hon. William T. A. F., b. 1984

BARONESSES/LADIES IN THEIR OWN RIGHT

Style, The Right Hon. the Lady _ , *or* The Right Hon. the Baroness _ , according to her preference. Either style may be used, except in the case of Scottish titles (indicated by S.), which are not baronies (*see* page 44) and whose holders are always addressed as Lady.
Envelope, may be addressed in same way as a Baron's wife or, if she prefers *(formal)*, The Right Hon. the Baroness _ *(social)*, The Baroness _. Otherwise as for a Baron's wife
Husband, Untitled
Children's style, As for children of a Baron

Created	Title, order of succession, name, etc.	Heir
1664	Arlington, Jennifer Jane Forwood, b. 1939, s. 1999, w. Title called out of abeyance 1999	Hon. Patrick J. D. F., b. 1967
1455	Berners (16th), Pamela Vivien Kirkham, b. 1929, s. 1995, m.	Hon. Rupert W. T. K., b. 1953
1529	Braye (8th), Mary Penelope Aubrey-Fletcher, b. 1941, s. 1985, m.	Two co-heiresses
1321	Dacre (27th), Rachel Leila Douglas-Home, b. 1929, s. 1970, w.	Hon. James T. A. D.-H., b. 195:
1332	** Darcy de Knayth (18th), Davina Marcia Ingrams, DBE, b. 1938, s. 1943, w.	Hon. Caspar D. I., b. 1962
1490 S.	Herries of Terregles (14th), Anne Elizabeth Fitzalan-Howard, b. 1938, s. 1975, w.	Lady Mary Mumford, b. 1940
1597	Howard de Walden (10th), Mary Hazel Caridwen Czernin, b. 1935, s. 2004, m. Title called out of abeyance 2004	Hon. Peter J. J. C. b. 1966
1602 S.	Kinloss (12th), Beatrice Mary Grenville Freeman-Grenville, b. 1922, s. 1944, m.	Master of Kinloss, b. 1953
1445 S.	** Saltoun (20th), Flora Marjory Fraser, b. 1930, s. 1979, w.	Hon. Katharine I. M. I. F., b. 1957
1313	Willoughby de Eresby (27th), (Nancy) Jane Marie Heathcote-Drummond-Willoughby, b. 1934, s. 1983	Two co-heiresses

LIFE PEERS

Style, The Right Hon. the Lord _ /The Right Hon. the Lady _ , *or* The Right Hon. the Baroness _ , according to her preference

Envelope (formal), The Right Hon. Lord _/Lady_/ Baroness_; *(social),* The Lord _/Lady_/Baroness_ *Letter (formal),* My Lord/Lady; *(social),* Dear Lord/ Lady _. *Spoken,* Lord/Lady _

Wife's style, The Right Hon. the Lady _

Husband, Untitled

Children's style, 'The Hon.' before forename (F_) and surname (S_)

Envelope, The Hon. F_ S_. *Letter,* Dear Mr/Miss/Mrs S_.

Spoken, Mr/Miss/Mrs S_

NEW LIFE PEERAGES

1 September 2004 to 31 August 2005:

Katherine Patricia Irene Adams; Andrew Adonis; Donald Anderson, PC; Anthony Louis Banks; Virginia Hilda Brunette Maxwell Bottomley, PC; David William George Chidgey; Dr. Lynda Margaret Clark, QC; Jean Ann Corston, PC; John Anderson Cunningham, PC; Dame Ruth Lynn Deech, DBE; Derek Foster, PC; George Foulkes, PC; Dame Irene Tordoff Fritchie, DBE; Sir Alastair Robertson Goodlad, KCMG; Sir Archibald Gavin Hamilton, PC; Michael John Hastings, CBE; Rt. Revd David Michael Hope, KCVO, PC; Alan Thomas Howarth, CBE, PC; Nicholas David Jones; Neil Gordon Kinnock, PC; Sir Archibald Johnstone Kirkwood; Sir Nicholas Walter Lyell, PC, QC; Sir Jonathan Hugh Mance, PC; Sir Brian Stanley Mawhinney, PC; Dr Lewis George Moonie; Estelle Morris, PC; Martin John O'Neill; Christopher Francis Patten, CH, PC; Gen. Sir David John Ramsbotham, GCB, CBE; *Prof.* Sir Martin John Rees; Gillian Patricia Shephard, PC; Christopher Robert Smith, PC; Clive Stafford Soley; Sir John Arthur Stevens; Winifred Ann Taylor, PC; Dr. Jennifer Louise Tonge; Sir Andrew Turnbull, KCB, CVO; Dennis Turner; Jonathan Adair Turner; Paul Archer Tyler, CBE; Josephine Clare Valentine

CREATED UNDER THE APPELLATE JURISDICTION ACT 1876 (AS AMENDED)

BARONS
Created

1986   *Ackner,* Desmond James Conrad Ackner, PC, *b.* 1920, *m.*

1980   *Bridge of Harwich,* Nigel Cyprian Bridge, PC, *b.* 1917, *m.*

1982   *Brightman,* John Anson, Brightman PC, *b.* 1911, *m.*

2004   *Brown of Eaton-under-Heywood,* Simon Denis Brown, PC, *b.* 1937, *m.,* *Lord of Appeal in Ordinary*

1991   *Browne-Wilkinson,* Nicolas Christopher Henry Browne-Wilkinson, PC, *b.* 1930, *m.*

2004   *Carswell,* Robert Douglas Carswell, PC, *b.* 1934, *m.,* *Lord of Appeal in Ordinary*

1996   *Clyde,* James John Clyde, PC, *b.* 1932, *m.*

1986   *Goff of Chieveley,* Robert Lionel Archibald Goff, PC, *b.* 1926, *m.*

1985   *Griffiths,* (William) Hugh Griffiths, MC, PC, *b.* 1923, *m.*

1995   *Hoffmann,* Leonard Hubert Hoffmann, PC, *b.* 1934, *m. Lord of Appeal in Ordinary*

1997   *Hutton,* (James) Brian (Edward) Hutton, PC, *b.* 1931, *m.*

1988   *Jauncey of Tullichettle,* Charles Eliot Jauncey, PC, *b.* 1925, *m.*

1993   *Lloyd of Berwick,* Anthony John Leslie Lloyd, PC, *b.* 1929, *m.*

2005   *Mance,* Jonathan Hugh, PC, *b.* 1943, *m. Lord of Appeal in Ordinary*

1998   *Millett,* Peter Julian Millett, PC, *b.* 1932, *m.*

1992   *Mustill,* Michael John Mustill, PC, *b.* 1931, *m.*

1994   *Nicholls of Birkenhead,* Donald James Nicholls, PC, *b.* 1933, *m. Second Senior Lord of Appeal in Ordinary*

1994   *Nolan,* Michael Patrick Nolan, PC, *b.* 1928, *m.*

1986   *Oliver of Aylmerton,* Peter Raymond Oliver, PC, *b.* 1921, *m.*

1999   *Phillips of Worth Matravers,* Nicholas Addison Phillips, b. 1938, *m. Lord Chief Justice of England and Wales*

1997   *Saville of Newdigate,* Mark Oliver Saville, PC, *b.* 1936, *m. Lord of Appeal in Ordinary*

1992   *Slynn of Hadley,* Gordon Slynn, PC, *b.* 1930, *m.*

1995   *Steyn,* Johan van Zyl Steyn, PC, *b.* 1932, *m. Lord of Appeal in Ordinary*

1982   *Templeman,* Sydney William Templeman, MBE, PC, *b.* 1920, *m.*

1992   *Woolf,* Harry Kenneth Woolf, PC, *b.* 1933, *m.*

BARONESSES
2004   *Hale of Richmond,* Brenda Marjorie Hale, DBE, PC, *b.* 1945, *m., Lord of Appeal in Ordinary*

CREATED UNDER THE LIFE PEERAGES ACT 1958

* Hereditary peer who has been granted a life peerage. For further details, please refer to the Hereditary Peers section, pages 45–64. For example, life peer *Balniel* can be found under his hereditary title *Earl of Crawford and Balcarres.*

‡ Title not confirmed at time of going to press.

BARONS
Created

2000   **Acton of Bridgnorth,* Lord Acton, *b.* 1941, *m.* (*see* Hereditary Peers)

2001   *Adebowale,* Victor Olufemi Adebowale, CBE, *b.* 1962

2005   *Adonis,* Andrew Adonis, *b.* 1963, *m.*

1998   *Ahmed,* Nazir Ahmed, *b.* 1957, *m.*

1996   *Alderdice,* John Thomas Alderdice, *b.* 1955, *m.*

1988   *Alexander of Weedon,* Robert Scott Alexander, QC, *b.* 1936, *m.*

1976   *Allen of Abbeydale,* Philip Allen, GCB, *b.* 1912, *w.*

1998   *Alli,* Waheed Alli, *b.* 1964

2004   *Alliance,* David Alliance, CBE, *b.* 1932

1997   *Alton of Liverpool,* David Patrick Paul Alton, *b.* 1951, *m.*

2005   *Anderson of Swansea,* Donald Anderson, PC, *b.* 1939, *m.*

1992   *Archer of Sandwell,* Peter Kingsley Archer, PC, QC, *b.* 1926, *m.*

1992   *Archer of Weston-super-Mare,* Jeffrey Howard Archer, *b.* 1940, *m.*

1988   *Armstrong of Ilminster,* Robert Temple Armstrong, GCB, CVO, *b.* 1927, *m.*

1999   *Armstrong-Jones, Earl of Snowdon, GCVO,
        b. 1930, m. (see Hereditary Peers)
2000   Ashcroft, Michael Anthony Ashcroft, KCMG,
2001   Ashdown of Norton-sub-Hamdon, Jeremy John
        Durham (Paddy) Ashdown, KBE, PC,
        b. 1941, m.
1992   Ashley of Stoke, Jack Ashley, CH, PC, b. 1922, w.
1993   Attenborough, Richard Samuel Attenborough,
        CBE, b. 1923, m.
1998   Bach, William Stephen Goulden Bach,
        b. 1946, m.
1997   Bagri, Raj Kumar Bagri, CBE, b. 1930, m.
1997   Baker of Dorking, Kenneth Wilfred Baker, CH,
        PC, b. 1934, m.
2004   Ballyedmond, Dr Edward Haughey, OBE,
        b. 1944, m.
1974   *Balniel, The Earl of Crawford and Balcarres,
        b. 1927, m. (see Hereditary Peers)
1974   Barber, Anthony Perrinott Lysberg Barber, TD,
        PC, b. 1920, m.
1992   Barber of Tewkesbury, Derek Coates Barber,
        b. 1918, m.
1983   Barnett, Joel Barnett, PC, b. 1923, m.
1997   Bassam of Brighton, (John) Steven Bassam,
        b. 1953
1967   Beaumont of Whitley, Revd Timothy Wentworth
        Beaumont, b. 1928, m.
1998   Bell, Timothy John Leigh Bell, b. 1941, m.
2000   Bernstein of Craigweil, Alexander Bernstein,
        b. 1936, m.
2001   Best, Richard Stuart Best, OBE, b. 1945, m.
2001   Bhatia, Amirali Alibhai Bhatia, OBE, b. 1932, m.
2004   Bhattacharyya, Prof. (Sushantha) Kumar
        Bhattacharyya, CBE, b. 1932, m.
1997   Biffen, (William) John Biffen, PC, b. 1930, m.
2005   Bilston, Dennis Turner, b. 1942, m.
1996   Bingham of Cornhill, Thomas Henry Bingham,
        KG, PC, b. 1933, m. Senior Lord of Appeal in
        Ordinary
2000   Birt, John Francis Hodgess Birt, b. 1944, m.
2001   Black of Crossharbour, Conrad Moffat Black,
        OC, PC, b. 1944, m.
1997   Blackwell, Norman Roy Blackwell, b. 1952, m.
1994   Blaker, Peter Allan Renshaw Blaker, KCMG, PC,
        b. 1922, m.
1978   Blease, William John Blease, b. 1914, m.
1995   Blyth of Rowington, James Blyth, b. 1940, m.
1996   Borrie, Gordon Johnson Borrie, QC, b. 1931, m.
1976   Boston of Faversham, Terence George Boston,
        QC, b. 1930, m.
1996   Bowness, Peter Spencer Bowness, CBE,
        b. 1943, m.
2003   Boyce, Michael Boyce, GCB, OBE, b. 1943
1999   Bradshaw, William Peter Bradshaw, b. 1936, m.
1998   Bragg, Melvyn Bragg, b. 1939, m.
1987   Bramall, Edwin Noel Westby Bramall, KG, GCB,
        OBE, MC, b. 1923, m.
2000   Brennan, Daniel Joseph Brennan, QC,
        b. 1942, m.
1999   Brett, William Henry Brett, b. 1942, m.
1976   Briggs, Asa Briggs, FBA, b. 1921, m.
2000   Brittan of Spennithorne, Leon Brittan, PC, QC,
        b. 1939, m.
2004   Broers, Prof. Alec (Nigel) Broers, b. 1938, m.
1997   Brooke of Alverthorpe, Clive Brooke, b. 1942, m.
2001   Brooke of Sutton Mandeville, Peter Leonard
        Brooke, CH, PC, b. 1934, m.
1998   Brookman, David Keith Brookman, b. 1937, m.

1979   Brooks of Tremorfa, John Edward Brooks,
        b. 1927, m.
2001   Browne of Madingley, Edmund John Phillip
        Browne, b. 1948
1997   Burlison, Thomas Henry Burlison, b. 1936, m.
1998   Burns, Terence Burns, GCB, b. 1944, m.
1998   Butler of Brockwell, (Frederick Edward) Robin
        Butler, KG, GCB, CVO, PC, b. 1938, m.
1978   Buxton of Alsa, Aubrey Leland Oakes Buxton,
        KCVO, MC, b. 1918, m.
2004   Cameron of Dillington, Ewen (James Hanning)
        Cameron, b. 1949, m.
1984   Cameron of Lochbroom, Kenneth John Cameron,
        PC, b. 1931, m.
1981   Campbell of Alloway, Alan Robertson Campbell,
        QC, b. 1917, m.
2001   Campbell-Savours, Dale Norman Campbell-
        Savours, b. 1943, m.
2002   Carey of Clifton, Rt. Revd George Leonard
        Carey, PC, b. 1935, m.
1999   *Carington of Upton, Lord Carrington, GCMG,
        b. 1919, m. (see Hereditary Peers)
1999   Carlile of Berriew, Alexander Charles Carlile,
        QC, b. 1948, m.
1975   Carr of Hadley, (Leonard) Robert Carr, PC,
        b. 1916, m.
1987   Carter, Denis Victor Carter, PC, b. 1932, m.
2004   Carter of Coles, Patrick Robert Carter, b. 1946, m.
1990   Cavendish of Furness, (Richard) Hugh Cavendish,
        b. 1941, m.
1996   Chadlington, Peter Selwyn Gummer, b. 1942, m.
1964   Chalfont, (Alun) Arthur Gwynne Jones, OBE,
        MC, PC, b. 1919, m.
2001   Chan, Michael Chew Koon Chan, MBE,
        b. 1940, m.
2005   Chidgey, David William George Chidgey,
        b. 1942, m.
1987   Chilver, (Amos) Henry Chilver, FRS, FRENG,
        b. 1926, m.
1977   Chitnis, Pratap Chidamber Chitnis, b. 1936, m.
1998   Christopher, Anthony Martin Grosvenor
        Christopher, CBE, b. 1925, m.
2001   Clark of Windermere, David George Clark, PC,
        PHD, b. 1939, m.
1998   Clarke of Hampstead, Anthony James Clarke,
        CBE, b. 1932, m.
1998   Clement-Jones, Timothy Francis Clement-Jones,
        CBE, b. 1949, m.
1990   Clinton-Davis, Stanley Clinton Clinton-Davis,
        PC, b. 1928, m.
1978   Cockfield, (Francis) Arthur Cockfield, PC,
        b. 1916, w.
2000   Coe, Sebastian Newbold Coe, OBE, b. 1956, m.
2001   Condon, Paul Leslie Condon, QPM, m.
1992   Cooke of Islandreagh, Victor Alexander Cooke,
        OBE, b. 1920, m.
1996   Cooke of Thorndon, Robin Brunskill Cooke,
        KBE, PC, PHD., b. 1926, m.
1997   Cope of Berkeley, John Ambrose Cope, PC,
        b. 1937, m.
2001   Corbett of Castle Vale, Robin Corbett, b. 1933, m.
1991   Craig of Radley, David Brownrigg Craig, GCB,
        OBE, b. 1929, m.
1987   Crickhowell, (Roger) Nicholas Edwards, PC,
        b. 1934, m.
1978   Croham, Douglas Albert Vivian Allen, GCB,
        b. 1917, w.
1995   Cuckney, John Graham Cuckney, b. 1925, w.

2003 *Cullen of Whitekirk,* William Douglas Cullen, PC, *b.* 1935, *m. Lord Justice General of Scotland and Lord President of the Court of Session*

2005 *Cunningham of Felling,* John Anderson Cunningham, PC, *b.* 1939, *m.*

1996 *Currie of Marylebone,* David Anthony Currie, *b.* 1946, *m.*

1993 *Dahrendorf,* Ralf Dahrendorf, KBE, PHD, DPHIL, FBA, *b.* 1929, *m.*

1997 *Davies of Coity,* (David) Garfield Davies, CBE, *b.* 1935, *m.*

1997 *Davies of Oldham,* Bryan Davies, *b.* 1939, *m.*

1993 *Dean of Harptree,* (Arthur) Paul Dean, PC, *b.* 1924, *m.*

1998 *Dearing,* Ronald Ernest Dearing, *b.* 1930, *m.*

1986 *Deedes,* William Francis Deedes, KBE MC, PC, *b.* 1913, *m.*

1991 *Desai,* Prof. Meghnad Jagdishchandra Desai, Ph.D., *b.* 1940, *m.*

1997 *Dholakia,* Navnit Dholakia, OBE, *b.* 1937, *m.*

1997 *Dixon,* Donald Dixon, PC, *b.* 1929, *m.*

1993 *Dixon-Smith,* Robert William Dixon-Smith, *b.* 1934, *m.*

1985 *Donoughue,* Bernard Donoughue, DPHIL, *b.* 1934

2004 *Drayson,* Paul Rudd Drayson, *b.* 1960, *m.*

1994 *Dubs,* Alfred Dubs, *b.* 1932, *m.*

2004 *Dykes,* Hugh John Maxwell Dykes, *b.* 1939, *m.*

1995 *Eames,* Robert Henry Alexander Eames, PHD, *b.* 1937, *m.*

1992 *Eatwell,* John Leonard Eatwell, PHD, *b.* 1945, *m.*

1983 *Eden of Winton,* John Benedict Eden, PC, *b.* 1925, *m.*

1999 *Elder,* Thomas Murray Elder, *b.* 1950

1992 *Elis-Thomas,* Dafydd Elis Elis-Thomas, PC, *b.* 1946, *m.*

1985 *Elliott of Morpeth,* Robert William Elliott, *b.* 1920, *m.*

1981 *Elystan-Morgan,* Dafydd Elystan Elystan-Morgan, *b.* 1932, *m.*

2000 **Erskine of Alloa Tower,* Earl of Mar and Kellie, *b.* 1949, *m.* (*see* Hereditary Peers)

1997 *Evans of Parkside,* John Evans, *b.* 1930, *m.*

2000 *Evans of Temple Guiting,* Matthew Evans, CBE, *b.* 1941, *m.*

1998 *Evans of Watford,* David Charles Evans, *b.* 1942, *m.*

1992 *Ewing of Kirkford,* Harry Ewing, *b.* 1931, *m.*

1983 *Ezra,* Derek Ezra, MBE, *b.* 1919, *m.*

1997 *Falconer of Thoroton,* Charles Leslie Falconer, QC, *b.* 1951, *m.*

1999 *Faulkner of Worcester,* Richard Oliver Faulkner, *b.* 1946, *m.*

2001 *Fearn,* Ronald Cyril Fearn, OBE, *b.* 1931, *m.*

1996 *Feldman,* Basil Feldman, *b.* 1926, *m.*

1999 *Fellowes,* Robert Fellowes, GCB, GCVO, PC, *b.* 1941, *m.*

1999 *Filkin,* David Geoffrey Nigel Filkin, CBE, *b.* 1944

1979 *Flowers,* Brian Hilton Flowers, FRS, *b.* 1924, *m.*

1999 *Forsyth of Drumlean,* Michael Bruce Forsyth, *b.* 1954, *m.*

1982 *Forte,* Charles Forte, *b.* 1908, *m.*

2005 *Foster of Bishop Auckland,* Derek Foster, PC, *b.* 1937, *m.*

1999 *Foster of Thames Bank,* Norman Robert Foster, OM, *b.* 1935, *m.*

2005 *Foulkes of Cumnock,* George Foulkes, PC, *b.* 1942, *m.*

2001 *Fowler,* (Peter) Norman Fowler, PC, *b.* 1938, *m.*

1989 *Fraser of Carmyllie,* Peter Lovat Fraser, PC, QC, *b.* 1945, *m.*

1997 *Freeman,* Roger Norman Freeman, PC, *b.* 1942, *m.*

2000 *Fyfe of Fairfield,* George Lennox Fyfe, *b.* 1941, *m.*

1999 **Ganzoni,* Lord Belstead, PC, *b.* 1932 (*see* Hereditary Peers)

2004 *Garden,* Timothy Garden, KCB, *b.* 1944, *m.*

1997 *Garel-Jones,* (William Armand) Thomas Tristan Garel-Jones, PC, *b.* 1941, *m.*

1999 **Gascoyne-Cecil,* The Marquess of Salisbury, PC, *b.* 1946, *m.* (*see* Hereditary Peers)

1999 *Gavron,* Robert Gavron, CBE, *b.* 1930, *m.*

2004 *George,* Edward (Alan John) George, GBE, PC, *b.* 1938, *m.*

2004 *Giddens,* Prof. Anthony Giddens, *b.* 1938, *m.*

1997 *Gilbert,* John William Gilbert, PC, PHD, *b.* 1927, *m.*

1992 *Gilmour of Craigmillar,* Ian Hedworth John Little Gilmour, PC, *b.* 1926, *m.*

1977 *Glenamara,* Edward Watson Short, CH, PC, *b.* 1912, *m.*

1999 *Goldsmith,* Peter Henry Goldsmith, QC, *b.* 1950, *m.*

1997 *Goodhart,* William Howard Goodhart, QC, *b.* 1933, *m.*

2005 *Goodlad,* Alastair Robertson Goodlad, KCMG, *b.* 1943, *m.*

1997 *Gordon of Strathblane,* James Stuart Gordon, CBE, *b.* 1936, *m.*

2004 *Gould of Brookwood,* Philip Gould *b.* 1950 *m.*

1999 *Grabiner,* Anthony Stephen Grabiner, QC, *b.* 1945, *m.*

1983 *Graham of Edmonton,* (Thomas) Edward Graham, *b.* 1925, *m.*

1983 *Gray of Contin,* James (Hamish) Hector Northey Gray, PC, *b.* 1927, *m.*

2000 *Greaves,* Anthony Robert Greaves, *b.* 1942, *m.*

1975 *Gregson,* John Gregson, *b.* 1924

2000 **Grenfell of Kilvey,* Lord Grenfell, *b.* 1935, *m..* (*see* Hereditary Peers)

2004 *Griffiths of Burry Port,* Revd. Dr Leslie John Griffiths, *b.* 1942, *m.*

1991 *Griffiths of Fforestfach,* Brian Griffiths, *b.* 1941, *m.*

2001 *Grocott,* Bruce Joseph Grocott, PC, *b.* 1940, *m.*

2000 **Gueterbock,* Lord Berkley, OBE, *b.* 1939, *m.* (*see* Hereditary Peers)

2000 *Guthrie of Craigiebank,* Charles Ronald Llewelyn Guthrie, GCB, LVO, OBE, *b.* 1938, *m.*

1995 *Habgood,* Rt. Revd John Stapylton Habgood, PC, PHD, *b.* 1927, *m.*

2005 *Hamilton of Epsom,* Archibald Gavin Hamilton, PC, *b.* 1941, *m.*

2001 *Hannay of Chiswick,* David Hugh Alexander Hannay, GCMG, CH, *b.* 1935, *m.*

1998 *Hanningfield,* Paul Edward Winston White, *b.* 1940

1997 *Hardie,* Andrew Rutherford Hardie, QC, PC, *b.* 1946, *m.*

1998 *Harris of Haringey,* (Jonathan) Toby Harris, *b.* 1953, *m.*

1979 *Harris of High Cross,* Ralph Harris, *b.* 1924, *m.*

1996   *Harris of Peckham*, Philip Charles Harris,
        b. 1942, m.

1999   *Harrison*, Lyndon Henry Arthur Harrison,
        b. 1947, m.

2004   *Hart of Chilton*, Garry Richard Rushby Hart,
        b. 1940, m.

1993   *Haskel*, Simon Haskel, b. 1934, m.

1998   *Haskins*, Christopher Robin Haskins, b. 1937, m.

2005   ‡*Hastings*, Michael John Hastings, CBE,
        b. 1958, m.

1997   *Hattersley*, Roy Sidney George Hattersley, PC,
        b. 1932, m.

2004   *Haworth*, Alan Robert Haworth, b. 1948, m.

1992   *Hayhoe*, Bernard John (Barney) Hayhoe, PC,
        b. 1925, m.

1992   *Healey*, Denis Winston Healey, CH, MBE, PC,
        b. 1917, m.

1999   **Hennessey*, Lord Windlesham, cvo, b. 1932, m.
        (*see* Hereditary Peers)

2001   *Heseltine*, Michael Ray Dibdin Heseltine, CH,
        PC, b. 1933, m.

1997   *Higgins*, Terence Langley Higgins, KBE, PC,
        b. 1928, m.

2000   *Hodgson of Astley Abbotts*, Robin Granville
        Hodgson, CBE, b. 1942, m.

1997   *Hogg of Cumbernauld*, Norman Hogg,
        b. 1938, m.

1991   *Hollick*, Clive Richard Hollick, b. 1945, m.

1990   *Holme of Cheltenham*, Richard Gordon Holme,
        CBE, b. 1936, m.

1979   *Hooson*, (Hugh) Emlyn Hooson, QC, b. 1925, m.

2005   *Hope of Thornes*, Rt. Revd David Michael Hope,
        KCVO, PC, b. 1940

1995   *Hope of Craighead*, (James Arthur) David Hope,
        PC, b. 1938, m. *Lord of Appeal in Ordinary*

2004   *Howard of Rising*, Greville Patrick Charles
        Howard, b. 1941, m.

2005   *Howarth of Newport*, Alan Thomas Howarth,
        CBE, PC, b. 1944

1992   *Howe of Aberavon*, (Richard Edward) Geoffrey
        Howe, CH, PC, QC, b. 1926, m.

1997   *Howell of Guildford*, David Arthur Russell
        Howell, PC, b. 1936, m.

1978   *Howie of Troon*, William Howie, b. 1924, w.

1997   *Hoyle*, (Eric) Douglas Harvey Hoyle,
        b. 1930, w.

1997   *Hughes of Woodside*, Robert Hughes,
        b. 1932, m.

2000   *Hunt of Chesterton*, Julian Charles Roland Hunt,
        CBE, b. 1941, m.

1997   *Hunt of Kings Heath*, Philip Alexander Hunt,
        OBE, b. 1949, m.

1980   *Hunt of Tanworth*, John Joseph Benedict Hunt,
        GCB, b. 1919, m.

1997   *Hunt of Wirral*, David James Fletcher Hunt,
        MBE, PC, b. 1942, m.

1997   *Hurd of Westwell*, Douglas Richard Hurd, CH,
        CBE, PC, b. 1930, m.

1996   *Hussey of North Bradley*, Marmaduke James
        Hussey, b. 1923, m.

1978   *Hutchinson of Lullington*, Jeremy Nicolas
        Hutchinson, QC, b. 1915, m.

1999   *Imbert*, Peter Michael Imbert, QPM, b. 1933, m.

1997   *Inge*, Peter Anthony Inge, KG, GCB, PC,
        b. 1935, m.

1987   *Irvine of Lairg*, Alexander Andrew Mackay
        Irvine, PC, QC, b. 1940, m.

1997   *Jacobs*, (David) Anthony Jacobs, b. 1931, m.

1997   *Janner of Braunstone*, Greville Ewan Janner, QC,
        b. 1928, w.

1999   **Jellicoe of Southampton*, Earl Jellicoe, KBE,
        b. 1918, w. (*see* Hereditary Peers)

1987   *Jenkin of Roding*, (Charles) Patrick (Fleeming)
        Jenkin, PC, b. 1926, m.

2000   *Joffe*, Joel Goodman Joffe, CBE, b. 1932, m.

2001   *Jones*, (Stephen) Barry Jones, b. 1937, m.

2005,   *Jones of Cheltenham*, Nigel David Jones,
        b. 1948, m.

1997   *Jopling*, (Thomas) Michael Jopling, PC,
        b. 1930, m.

2000   *Jordan*, William Brian Jordan, CBE,
        b. 1936, m.

1991   *Judd*, Frank Ashcroft Judd, b. 1935, m.

2004   *Kalms*, Harold Stanley Kalms, b. 1931 m.

1997   *Kelvedon*, (Henry) Paul Guinness Channon, PC,
        b. 1935, m.

2004   *Kerr of Kinlochard*, John (Olav) Kerr, GCMG,
        b. 1942, m.

2001   *Kilclooney*, John David Taylor, PC (NI),
        b. 1937, m.

1996   *Kilpatrick of Kincraig*, Robert Kilpatrick, CBE,
        b. 1926, m.

1985   *Kimball*, Marcus Richard Kimball, b. 1928, m.

2001   *King of Bridgwater*, Thomas Jeremy King, CH,
        PC, b. 1933, m.

1999   *King of West Bromwich*, Tarsem King, b. 1937

1993   *Kingsdown*, Robert (Robin) Leigh-Pemberton,
        KG, PC, b. 1927, m.

1994   *Kingsland*, Christopher James Prout, TD, PC,
        QC, b. 1942

2005   *Kinnock*, Neil Gordon Kinnock, PC, b. 1942, m.

1999   *Kirkham*, Graham Kirkham, b. 1944, m.

1975   *Kirkhill*, John Farquharson Smith,
        b. 1930, m.

2005   *Kirkwood of Kirkhope*, Archibald Johnstone
        Kirkwood, b. 1946, m.

1987   *Knights*, Philip Douglas Knights, CBE, QPM,
        b. 1920, m.

2004   *Laidlaw*, Irvine Alan Stewart Laidlaw,
        b. 1942, m.

1991   *Laing of Dunphail*, Hector Laing, b. 1923, m.

1999   *Laird*, John Dunn Laird, b. 1944, m.

1998   *Laming*, (William) Herbert Laming, CBE,
        b. 1936, m.

1998   *Lamont of Lerwick*, Norman Stewart Hughson
        Lamont, PC, b. 1942, m.

1990   *Lane of Horsell*, Peter Stewart Lane,
        b. 1925, w.

1997   *Lang of Monkton*, Ian Bruce Lang, PC,
        b. 1940, m.

1992   *Lawson of Blaby*, Nigel Lawson, PC, b. 1932, m.

2000   *Layard*, Peter Richard Grenville Layard,
        b. 1934, m.

1999   *Lea of Crondall*, David Edward Lea, OBE,
        b. 1937

2004   *Leitch*, Alexander Park Leitch, b. 1947, m.

1993   *Lester of Herne Hill*, Anthony Paul Lester, QC,
        b. 1936, m.

1997   *Levene of Portsoken*, Peter Keith Levene, KBE,
        b. 1941, m.

1997   *Levy*, Michael Abraham Levy, b. 1944, m.

1989   *Lewis of Newnham*, Jack Lewis, FRS,
        b. 1928, m.

1999   *Lipsey*, David Lawrence Lipsey, b. 1948, m.

2001   *Livsey of Talgarth*, Richard Arthur Lloyd Livsey,
        CBE, b. 1935, m.

1997 *Lloyd-Webber,* Andrew Lloyd Webber, b. 1948, m.

1997 *Lofthouse of Pontefract,* Geoffrey Lofthouse, b. 1925, w.

2000 *Luce,* Richard Napier Luce, GCVO, PC, b. 1936, m.

2005 *Lyell of Markyate,* Nicholas Walter Lyell, PC, QC, b. 1938, m.

2000 **Lyttleton of Aldershot,* The Viscount Chandos, b. 1953, m. (see Hereditary Peers)

1984 *McAlpine of West Green,* (Robert) Alistair McAlpine, b. 1942, m.

1988 *Macaulay of Bragar,* Donald Macaulay, QC, b. 1933, m.

1975 *McCarthy,* William Edward John McCarthy, DPHIL, b. 1925, m.

1976 *McCluskey,* John Herbert McCluskey, b. 1929, m.

1989 *McColl of Dulwich,* Ian McColl, CBE, FRCS, FRCSE, b. 1933, m.

1998 *Macdonald of Tradeston,* Angus John Macdonald, CBE, b. 1940, m.

1991 *Macfarlane of Bearsden,* Norman Somerville Macfarlane, KT, FRSE, b. 1926, m.

2001 *MacGregor of Pulham Market,* John Roddick Russell MacGregor, CBE, PC, b. 1937, m.

1982 *McIntosh of Haringey,* Andrew Robert McIntosh, b. 1933, m.

1979 *Mackay of Clashfern,* James Peter Hymers Mackay, KT, PC, FRSE, b. 1927, m.

1995 *Mackay of Drumadoon,* Donald Sage Mackay, PC, b. 1946, m.

2004 *McKenzie of Luton,* William David McKenzie, b. 1946, m.

1999 *Mackenzie of Culkein,* Hector Uisdean MacKenzie, b. 1940

1998 *Mackenzie of Framwellgate,* Brian Mackenzie, OBE, b. 1943, m.

1974 *Mackie of Benshie,* George Yull Mackie, CBE, DSO, DFC, b. 1919, m.

1996 *MacLaurin of Knebworth,* Ian Charter MacLaurin, b. 1937, m.

2001 *Maclennon of Rogart,* Robert Adam Ross Maclennan, PC, b. 1936, m.

1995 *McNally,* Tom McNally, PC, b. 1943, m.

2001 *Maginnis of Drumglass,* Kenneth Wiggins Maginnis, b. 1938, m.

1991 *Marlesford,* Mark Shuldham Schreiber, b. 1931, m.

1981 *Marsh,* Richard William Marsh, PC, b. 1928, m.

1998 *Marshall of Knightsbridge,* Colin Marsh Marshall, b. 1933, m.

1987 *Mason of Barnsley,* Roy Mason, PC, b. 1924, m.

2005 *Mawhinney,* Brian Stanley Mawhinney, PC, b. 1940, m.

2004 *Maxton,* John Alston Maxton, b. 1936, m.

2001 *May of Oxford,* Robert McCredie May, OM, b. 1936, m.

1997 *Mayhew of Twysden,* Patrick Barnabas Burke Mayhew, QC, PC, b. 1929, m.

1992 *Merlyn-Rees,* Merlyn Merlyn-Rees, PC, b. 1920, m.

1978 *Mishcon,* Victor Mishcon, QC, b. 1915, m.

2000 *Mitchell,* Parry Andrew Mitchell, b. 1943, m.

2000 **Mitford,* Lord Redesdale, b. 1967, m. (see Hereditary Peers)

1997 *Molyneaux of Killead,* James Henry Molyneaux, KBE, PC, b. 1920

1997 *Monro of Langholm,* Hector Seymour Peter Monro, AE, PC, b. 1922, m.

2005 *Moonie,* Dr. Lewis George Moonie, b. 1947, m.

1992 *Moore of Lower Marsh,* John Edward Michael Moore, PC, b. 1937, m.

1986 *Moore of Wolvercote,* Philip Brian Cecil Moore, GCB, GCVO, CMG, PC, b. 1921, m.

2000 *Morgan,* Kenneth Owen Morgan, b. 1934, m.

2001 *Morris of Aberavon,* John Morris, KG, QC, b. 1931, m.

1997 *Morris of Manchester,* Alfred Morris, PC, b. 1928, m.

2001 *Moser,* Claus Adolf Moser, KCB, CBE, b. 1922, m.

1979 *Murton of Lindisfarne,* (Henry) Oscar Murton, OBE, TD, PC, b. 1914, m.

1997 *Naseby,* Michael Wolfgang Laurence Morris, PC, b. 1936, m.

1997 *Neill of Bladen,* (Francis) Patrick Neill, QC, b. 1926, m.

1997 *Newby,* Richard Mark Newby, OBE, b. 1953, m.

1997 *Newton of Braintree,* Antony Harold Newton, OBE, PC, b. 1937, m.

1994 *Nickson,* David Wigley Nickson, KBE, FRSE, b. 1929, m.

1975 *Northfield,* (William) Donald Chapman, b. 1923

1998 *Norton of Louth,* Philip Norton, b. 1951

2000 *Oakeshott of Seagrove Bay,* Matthew Alan Oakeshott, b. 1947, m.

2005 *O'Neill of Clackmannan,* Martin John O'Neill, b. 1945, m.

2001 *Ouseley,* Herman George Ouseley, b. 1945, m.

1992 *Owen,* David Anthony Llewellyn Owen, CH, PC, b. 1938, m.

1999 *Oxburgh,* Ernest Ronald Oxburgh, KBE, FRS, PHD, b. 1934, m.

1991 *Palumbo,* Peter Garth Palumbo, b. 1935, m.

2000 *Parekh,* Bhikhu Chhotalal Parekh, b. 1935, m.

1992 *Parkinson,* Cecil Edward Parkinson, PC, b. 1931, m.

1999 *Patel,* Narendra Babubhai Patel, b. 1938

2000 *Patel of Blackburn,* Adam Hafejee Patel, b. 1940

2005 *Patten of Barnes,* Christopher Francis Patten, CH, PC, b. 1944, m.

1997 *Patten,* John Haggitt Charles Patten, PC, b. 1945, m.

1996 *Paul,* Swraj Paul, b. 1931, m.

1990 *Pearson of Rannoch,* Malcolm Everard MacLaren Pearson, b. 1942, m.

2001 *Pendry,* Thomas Pendry, b. 1934, m.

1987 *Peston,* Maurice Harry Peston, b. 1931, m.

1983 *Peyton of Yeovil,* John Wynne William Peyton, PC, b. 1919, m.

1998 *Phillips of Sudbury,* Andrew Wyndham Phillips, OBE, b. 1939, m.

1996 *Pilkington of Oxenford,* Revd Canon Peter Pilkington, b. 1933, w.

1992 *Plant of Highfield,* Prof. Raymond Plant, PHD, b. 1945, m.

1987 *Plumb,* (Charles) Henry Plumb, b. 1925, m.

1981 *Plummer of St Marylebone,* (Arthur) Desmond (Herne) Plummer, TD, b. 1914, m.

2000 **Ponsonby of Roehampton,* Lord Ponsonby of Shulbrede, b. 1958 (see Hereditary Peers)

2000 *Powell of Bayswater,* Charles David Powell, KCMG, b. 1941

1987　*Prior,* James Michael Leathes Prior, PC,
　　　b. 1927, *m.*

1982　*Prys-Davies,* Gwilym Prys Prys-Davies,
　　　b. 1923, *m.*

1997　*Puttnam,* David Terence Puttnam, CBE,
　　　b. 1941, *m.*

1987　*Pym,* Francis Leslie Pym, MC, PC, *b.* 1922, *m.*

1982　*Quinton,* Anthony Meredith Quinton, FBA,
　　　b. 1925, *m.*

1994　*Quirk,* Prof. (Charles) Randolph Quirk, CBE,
　　　FBA, *b.* 1920, *m.*

2001　*Radice,* Giles Heneage Radice, PC, *b.* 1936

2005　*Ramsbotham,* Gen. David John Ramsbotham,
　　　GCB, CBE, *b.* 1934, *m.*

2004　*Rana,* Dr Diljit Singh Rana, MBE, *b.* 1938, *m.*

1997　*Randall of St Budeaux,* Stuart Jeffrey Randall,
　　　b. 1938, *m.*

1978　*Rawlinson of Ewell,* Peter Anthony Grayson
　　　Rawlinson, PC, QC, *b.* 1919, *m.*

1997　*Razzall,* (Edward) Timothy Razzall, CBE,
　　　b. 1943, *m.*

1987　*Rees,* Peter Wynford Innes Rees, PC, QC,
　　　b. 1926, *m.*

2005　*Rees of Ludlow,* Prof. Sir Martin John,
　　　b. 1942, *m.*

1988　*Rees-Mogg,* William Rees-Mogg, *b.* 1928, *m.*

1991　*Renfrew of Kaimsthorn,* (Andrew) Colin Renfrew,
　　　FBA, *b.* 1937, *m.*

1999　*Rennard,* Christopher John Rennard, MBE,
　　　b. 1960

1979　*Renton,* David Lockhart-Mure Renton, KBE, TD,
　　　PC, QC, *b.* 1908, *w.*

1997　*Renton of Mount Harry,* (Ronald) Timothy
　　　Renton, PC, *b.* 1932, *m.*

1997　*Renwick of Clifton,* Robin William Renwick,
　　　KCMG, *b.* 1937, *m.*

1990　*Richard,* Ivor Seward Richard, PC, QC,
　　　b. 1932, *m.*

1983　*Richardson of Duntisbourne,* Gordon William
　　　Humphreys Richardson, KG, MBE, TD, PC,
　　　b. 1915, *m.*

1992　*Rix,* Brian Norman Roger Rix, CBE, *b.* 1924, *m.*

2004　*Roberts of Llandudno,* Revd John Roger Roberts,
　　　b. 1935, *m.*

1997　*Roberts of Conwy,* (Ieuan) Wyn (Pritchard)
　　　Roberts, PC, *b.* 1930, *m.*

1999　*Robertson of Port Ellen,* George Islay MacNeill
　　　Robertson, KT, GCMG, PC, *b.* 1946, *m.*

1992　*Rodger of Earlsferry,* Alan Ferguson Rodger, PC,
　　　QC, FBA, *b.* 1944, *Lord of Appeal in Ordinary*

1992　*Rodgers of Quarry Bank,* William Thomas
　　　Rodgers, PC, *b.* 1928, *m.*

1999　*Rogan,* Dennis Robert David Rogan, *b.* 1942, *m.*

1996　*Rogers of Riverside,* Richard George Rogers, RA,
　　　RIBA, *b.* 1933, *m.*

2001　*Rooker,* Jeffrey William Rooker, PC, *b.* 1941, *m.*

2000　*Roper,* John Francis Hodgess Roper, *b.* 1935, *m.*

2004　*Rosser,* Richard Andrew Rosser, *b.* 1944, *m.*

2004　*Rowlands,* Edward Rowlands, CBE, *b.* 1940, *m.*

1997　*Russell-Johnston,* (David) Russell Russell-
　　　Johnston, *b.* 1932, *m.*

1997　*Ryder of Wensum,* Richard Andrew Ryder, OBE,
　　　PC, *b.* 1949, *m.*

1996　*Saatchi,* Maurice Saatchi, *b.* 1946, *m.*

1989　*Sainsbury of Preston Candover,* John Davan
　　　Sainsbury, KG, *b.* 1927, *m.*

1997　*Sainsbury of Turville,* David John Sainsbury,
　　　b. 1940, *m.*

1987　*St John of Fawsley,* Norman Antony Francis St
　　　John-Stevas, PC, *b.* 1929

1997　*Sandberg,* Michael Graham Ruddock Sandberg,
　　　CBE, *b.* 1927, *m.*

1985　*Sanderson of Bowden,* Charles Russell Sanderson,
　　　b. 1933, *m.*

1998　*Sawyer,* Lawrence (Tom) Sawyer, *b.* 1943

2000　*Scott of Foscote,* Richard Rashleigh Folliott
　　　Scott, PC, *b.* 1934, *m. Lord of Appeal in
　　　Ordinary*

1997　*Selkirk of Douglas,* James Alexander Douglas-
　　　Hamilton, MSP, PC, QC, *b.* 1942, *m.*

1996　*Sewel,* John Buttifant Sewel, CBE, *b.* 1946

1999　*Sharman,* Colin Morven Sharman, OBE,
　　　b. 1943, *m.*

1994　*Shaw of Northstead,* Michael Norman Shaw,
　　　b. 1920, *m.*

2001　*Sheldon,* Robert Edward Sheldon, PC,
　　　b. 1923, *m.*

1994　*Sheppard of Didgemere,* Allan John George
　　　Sheppard, KCVO, *b.* 1932, *m.*

2000　*Shutt of Greetland,* David Trevor Shutt, OBE,
　　　b. 1942

1971　*Simon of Glaisdale,* Jocelyn Edward Salis Simon,
　　　PC, *b.* 1911, *m.*

1997　*Simon of Highbury,* David Alec Gwyn Simon,
　　　CBE, *b.* 1939, *m.*

1997　*Simpson of Dunkeld,* George Simpson,
　　　b. 1942, *m.*

1991　*Skidelsky,* Robert Jacob Alexander Skidelsky,
　　　DPHIL, *b.* 1939, *m.*

1997　*Smith of Clifton,* Trevor Arthur Smith,
　　　b. 1937, *m.*

2005　*Smith of Finsbury,* Christopher Robert Smith,
　　　PC, *b.* 1951

1999　*Smith of Leigh,* Peter Richard Charles Smith,
　　　b. 1945, *m.*

2004　*Snape,* Peter Charles Snape, *b.* 1942

2005　*Soley,* Clive Stafford Soley, *b.* 1939

1990　*Soulsby of Swaffham Prior,* Ernest Jackson
　　　Lawson Soulsby, PHD, *b.* 1926, *m.*

1983　*Stallard,* Albert William Stallard, *b.* 1921, *m.*

1997　*Steel of Aikwood,* David Martin Scott Steel, KT,
　　　KBE, PC, *b.* 1938, *m.*

2004　*Steinberg,* Leonard Steinberg, *b.* 1936

1991　*Sterling of Plaistow,* Jeffrey Maurice Sterling,
　　　GCVO, CBE, *b.* 1934, *m.*

2005　*Stevens of Kirkwhelpington,* John Arthur Stevens,
　　　b. 1942, *m.*

1987　*Stevens of Ludgate,* David Robert Stevens,
　　　b. 1936, *m.*

1999　*Stevenson of Coddenham,* Henry Dennistoun
　　　Stevenson, CBE, *b.* 1945, *m.*

1992　*Stewartby,* (Bernard Harold) Ian (Halley) Stewart,
　　　RD, PC, FBA, FRSE, *b.* 1935, *m.*

1983　*Stoddart of Swindon,* David Leonard Stoddart,
　　　b. 1926, *m.*

1969　*Stokes,* Donald Gresham Stokes, TD, FENG,
　　　b. 1914, *w.*

1997　*Stone of Blackheath,* Andrew Zelig Stone,
　　　b. 1942, *m.*

2005　*Stratford,* Anthony Louis Banks, *b.* 1943, *m.*

2001　*Sutherland of Houndwood,* Stewart Ross
　　　Sutherland, KT, *b.* 1941, *m.*

1971　*Tanlaw,* Simon Brooke Mackay, *b.* 1934, *m.*

1996　*Taverne,* Dick Taverne, QC, *b.* 1928, *m.*

1978　*Taylor of Blackburn,* Thomas Taylor, CBE,
　　　b. 1929, *m.*

1996   *Taylor of Warwick*, John David Beckett Taylor, b. 1952, m.

1992   *Tebbit*, Norman Beresford Tebbit, CH, PC, b. 1931, m.

2001   *Temple-Morris*, Peter Temple-Morris, b. 1938, m.

1996   *Thomas of Gresford*, Donald Martin Thomas, OBE, QC, b. 1937, m.

1987   *Thomas of Gwydir*, Peter John Mitchell Thomas, PC, QC, b. 1920, w.

1997   *Thomas of Macclesfield*, Terence James Thomas, CBE, b. 1937, m.

1981   *Thomas of Swynnerton*, Hugh Swynnerton Thomas, b. 1931, m.

1977   *Thomson of Monifieth*, George Morgan Thomson, KT, PC, b. 1921, m.

1990   *Tombs*, Francis Leonard Tombs, FENG, b. 1924, m.

1998   *Tomlinson*, John Edward Tomlinson, MEP, b. 1939

1994   *Tope*, Graham Norman Tope, CBE, b. 1943, m.

1981   *Tordoff*, Geoffrey Johnson Tordoff, b. 1928, m.

2004   *Triesman*, David Maxim Triesman, b. 1943

2004   *Truscott*, Dr Peter Derek Truscott, b. 1959 m.

1993   *Tugendhat*, Christopher Samuel Tugendhat, b. 1937, m.

2004   *Tunnicliffe*, Denis Tunnicliffe, CBE, b. 1943, m.

2000   *Turnberg*, Leslie Arnold Turnberg, MD, b. 1934, m.

2005   *Turnbull*, Andrew Turnbull, KCB, CVO, b. 1945, m.

2005   *Turner of Ecchinswell*, Jonathan Adair Turner, b. 1955, m.

2005   *Tyler*, Paul Archer Tyler, CBE, b. 1941, m.

2004   *Vallance of Tummel*, Iain (David Thomas) Vallance, b. 1943, m.

1990   *Varley*, Eric Graham Varley, PC, b. 1932, m.

1996   *Vincent of Coleshill*, Richard Frederick Vincent, GBE, KCB, DSO, b. 1931, m.

1985   *Vinson*, Nigel Vinson, LVO, b. 1931, m.

1990   *Waddington*, David Charles Waddington, GCVO, PC, QC, b. 1929, m.

1990   *Wade of Chorlton*, (William) Oulton Wade, b. 1932, m.

1992   *Wakeham*, John Wakeham, PC, b. 1932, m.

1999   *Waldegrave of North Hill*, William Arthur Waldegrave, PC, b. 1946, m.

2003   *Walker of Gestingthorpe*, Robert Walker, PC, b. 1938, m. Lord of Appeal in Ordinary

1992   *Walker of Worcester*, Peter Edward Walker, MBE, PC, b. 1932, m.

1995   *Wallace of Saltaire*, William John Lawrence Wallace, PHD, b. 1941, m.

1989   *Walton of Detchant*, John Nicholas Walton, TD, FRCP, b. 1922, m.

1998   *Warner*, Norman Reginald Warner, b. 1940, m.

1997   *Watson of Invergowrie*, Michael Goodall Watson, MSP, b. 1949, m.

1999   *Watson of Richmond*, Alan John Watson, CBE, b. 1941, m.

1992   *Weatherill*, (Bruce) Bernard Weatherill, PC, b. 1920, m.

1977   *Wedderburn of Charlton*, (Kenneth) William Wedderburn, FBA, QC, b. 1927, m.

1976   *Weidenfeld*, (Arthur) George Weidenfeld, b. 1919, m.

1996   *Whitty*, John Lawrence (Larry) Whitty, b. 1943, m.

1985   *Williams of Elvel*, Charles Cuthbert Powell Williams, CBE, b. 1933, m.

1999   *Williamson of Horton*, David (Francis) Williamson, GCMG, CB, b. 1934, m.

2002   *Wilson of Dinton*, Richard Thomas James Wilson, GCB, b. 1942, m.

1992   *Wilson of Tillyorn*, David Clive Wilson, KT, GCMG, PHD, b. 1935, m.

1995   *Winston*, Robert Maurice Lipson Winston, FRCOG, b. 1940, m.

1985   *Wolfson*, Leonard Gordon Wolfson, b. 1927, m.

1991   *Wolfson of Sunningdale*, David Wolfson, b. 1935, m.

1999   *Woolmer of Leeds*, Kenneth John Woolmer, b. 1940, m.

1994   *Wright of Richmond*, Patrick Richard Henry Wright, GCMG, b. 1931, m.

2004   *Young of Norwood Green*, Anthony (Ian) Young, b. 1942, m.

1984   *Young of Graffham*, David Ivor Young, PC, b. 1932, m.

BARONESSES
Created

2005   *Adams of Craigielea*, Katherine Patricia Irene Adams, b. 1947, w.

1997   *Amos*, Valerie Ann Amos, b. 1954

2000   *Andrews*, Elizabeth Kay Andrews, OBE, b. 1943, m.

1996   *Anelay of St Johns*, Joyce Anne Anelay, DBE, b. 1947, m.

1999   *Ashton of Upholland*, Catherine Margaret Ashton, b. 1956, m.

1999   *Barker*, Elizabeth Jean Barker, b. 1961

2000   *Billingham*, Angela Theodora Billingham, DPHIL, b. 1939, w.

1987   *Blackstone*, Tessa Ann Vosper Blackstone, PHD, b. 1942

1999   *Blood*, May Blood, MBE, b. 1938

2000   *Boothroyd*, Betty Boothroyd, OM, PC, b. 1929

2004   *Bonham-Carter of Yarnbury*, Jane Bonham Carter, b. 1957, w.

2005   *Bottomley of Nettlestone*, Virginia Hilda Brunette Maxwell Bottomley, PC, b. 1948, m.

1998   *Buscombe*, Peta Jane Buscombe, b. 1954, m.

1996   *Byford*, Hazel Byford, DBE, b. 1941, m.

1982   *Carnegy of Lour*, Elizabeth Patricia Carnegy of Lour, b. 1925

1992   *Chalker of Wallasey*, Lynda Chalker, PC, b. 1942, m.

2004   *Chapman*, Nicola Jane Chapman, b. 1961

2005   *Clark of Calton*, Dr Lynda Margaret Clark, QC, b. 1949

2000   *Cohen of Pimlico*, Janet Cohen, b. 1940, m.

2005   *Corston*, Jean Ann Corston, PC, b. 1942, m.

1982   *Cox*, Caroline Anne Cox, b. 1937, m.

1998   *Crawley*, Christine Mary Crawley, MEP, b. 1950, m.

1990   *Cumberlege*, Julia Frances Cumberlege, CBE, b. 1943, m.

1978   *David*, Nora Ratcliff David, b. 1913, w.

1993   *Dean of Thornton-le-Fylde*, Brenda Dean, PC, b. 1943, m.

2005   ‡*Deech*, Ruth Lynn Deech, DBE, b. 1943, m.

1974   *Delacourt-Smith of Alteryn,* Margaret Rosalind
Delacourt-Smith, *b.* 1916, *m.*

2004   *D'Souza,* Dr Frances Gertrude Claire D'Souza,
CMG, *b.* 1944 *m.*

1990   *Dunn,* Lydia Selina Dunn, DBE, *b.* 1940, *m.*

1990   *Eccles of Moulton,* Diana Catherine Eccles,
b. 1933, *m.*

1972   *Elles,* Diana Louie Elles, *b.* 1921, *m.*

1997   *Emerton,* Audrey Caroline Emerton, DBE,
b. 1935

1974   *Falkender,* Marcia Matilda Falkender, CBE,
b. 1932

2004   *Falkner of Margravine,* Kishwer Falkner,
b. 1955, *m.*

1994   *Farrington of Ribbleton,* Josephine Farrington,
b. 1940, *m.*

2001   *Finlay of Llandaff,* Ilora Gillian Finlay,
b. 1949, *m.*

1974   *Fisher of Rednal,* Doris Mary Gertrude Fisher,
b. 1919, *w.*

1990   *Flather,* Shreela Flather, *m.*

1997   *Fookes,* Janet Evelyn Fookes, DBE, *b.* 1936

2005   *Fritchie,* Irene Tordoff Fritchie, DBE,
b. 1942, *m.*

1999   *Gale,* Anita Gale, *b.* 1940

1981   *Gardner of Parkes,* (Rachel) Trixie (Anne)
Gardner, *b.* 1927, *m.*

2000   *Gibson of Market Rasen,* Anne Gibson, OBE,
b. 1940, *m*

2001   *Golding,* Llinos Golding, *b.* 1933, *m.*

1998   *Goudie,* Mary Teresa Goudie, *b.* 1946, *m.*

1993   *Gould of Potternewton,* Joyce Brenda Gould,
b. 1932, *m.*

2001   *Greenfield,* Susan Adele Greenfield, CBE,
b. 1950, *m.*

2000   *Greengross,* Sally Ralea Greengross, OBE,
b. 1935, *m.*

1991   *Hamwee,* Sally Rachel Hamwee, *b.* 1947

1999   *Hanham,* Joan Brownlow Hanham, CBE,
b. 1939, *m.*

1999   *Harris of Richmond,* Angela Felicity Harris,
b. 1944

1996   *Hayman,* Helene Valerie Hayman, PC,
b. 1949, *m.*

2004   *Henig,* Ruth Beatrice Henig, CBE, *b.* 1943, *m.*

1991   *Hilton of Eggardon,* Jennifer Hilton, QPM,
b. 1936

1995   *Hogg,* Sarah Elizabeth Mary Hogg, *b.* 1946, *m.*

1990   *Hollis of Heigham,* Patricia Lesley Hollis, DPHIL,
b. 1941, *m.*

1985   *Hooper,* Gloria Dorothy Hooper, CMG, *b.* 1939

2001   *Howarth of Breckland,* Valerie Georgina
Howarth, OBE, *b.* 1940

2001   *Howe of Idlicote,* Elspeth Rosamond Morton
Howe, CBE, *b.* 1932, *m.*

1999   *Howells of St Davids,* Rosalind Patricia-Anne
Howells, *b.* 1931, *m.*

1991   *James of Holland Park,* Phyllis Dorothy White (P.
D. James), OBE, *b.* 1920, *w.*

1992   *Jay of Paddington,* Margaret Ann Jay, PC,
b. 1939, *m.*

1979   *Jeger,* Lena May Jeger, *b.* 1915, *w.*

1997   *Kennedy of the Shaws,* Helena Ann Kennedy, QC,
b. 1950, *m.*

1997   *Knight of Collingtree,* (Joan Christabel) Jill
Knight, DBE, *b.* 1927, *w.*

1997   *Linklater of Butterstone,* Veronica Linklater,
b. 1943, *m.*

1996   *Lloyd of Highbury,* Prof. June Kathleen Lloyd,
DBE, FRCP, FRCPE, FRCGP, *b.* 1928

1978   *Lockwood,* Betty Lockwood, *b.* 1924, *w.*

1997   *Ludford,* Sarah Ann Ludford, *b.* 1951

2004   *McDonagh,* Margaret Josephine McDonagh

1979   *McFarlane of Llandaff,* Jean Kennedy
McFarlane, *b.* 1926

1999   *McIntosh of Hudnall,* Genista Mary McIntosh,
b. 1946

1997   *Maddock,* Diana Margaret Maddock,
b. 1945, *m.*

1991   *Mallalieu,* Ann Mallalieu, QC, *b.* 1945, *m.*

1970   *Masham of Ilton,* Susan Lilian Primrose
Cunliffe-Lister, *b.* 1935, *m.*

1999   *Massey of Darwen,* Doreen Elizabeth Massey,
b. 1938, *m.*

2001   *Michie of Gallanach,* Janet Ray Michie,
b. 1934, *m.*

1998   *Miller of Chilthorne Domer,* Susan Elizabeth
Miller, *b.* 1954

1993   *Miller of Hendon,* Doreen Miller, MBE,
b. 1933, *m.*

2004   *Morgan of Drefelin,* Delyth Jane Morgan,
b. 1961, *m.*

2001   *Morgan of Huyton,* Sally Morgan, *b.* 1959, *m.*

2004   *Morris of Bolton,* Patricia Morris, OBE,
b. 1953

2005   *Morris of Yardley,* Estelle Morris, PC,
b. 1952

2004   *Murphy,* Elaine Murphy, *b.* 1947, *m.*

2004   *Neuberger,* Rabbi Julia (Babette Sarah)
Neuberger, DBE, *b.* 1950, *m.*

1997   *Nicholson of Winterbourne,* Emma Harriet
Nicholson, MEP, *b.* 1941, *m.*

1982   *Nicol,* Olive Mary Wendy Nicol, *b.* 1923, *m.*

2000   *Noakes,* Shiela Valerie Masters, DBE,
b. 1949, *m.*

2000   *Northover,* Lindsay Patricia Granshaw,
b. 1954

1991   *O'Cathain,* Detta O'Cathain, OBE, *b.* 1938, *m.*

1999   *O'Neill of Bengarve,* Onora Sylvia O'Neill, CBE,
PHD, *b.* 1941

1989   *Oppenheim-Barnes,* Sally Oppenheim-Barnes,
PC, *b.* 1930, *m.*

1990   *Park of Monmouth,* Daphne Margaret Sybil
Désirée Park, CMG, OBE, *b.* 1921

1991   *Perry of Southwark,* Pauline Perry, *b.* 1931, *m.*

1997   *Pitkeathley,* Jill Elizabeth Pitkeathley, OBE,
b. 1940

1981   *Platt of Writtle,* Beryl Catherine Platt, CBE,
FENG, *b.* 1923, *m.*

1999   *Prashar,* Usha Kumari Prashar, CBE,
b. 1948, *m.*

2004   *Prosser,* Margaret Theresa Prosser, OBE,
b. 1937

1996   *Ramsay of Cartvale,* Margaret Mildred (Meta)
Ramsay, *b.* 1936

1994   *Rawlings,* Patricia Elizabeth Rawlings, *b.* 1939

1997   *Rendell of Babergh,* Ruth Barbara Rendell, CBE,
b. 1930, *m.*

1998   *Richardson of Calow,* Kathleen Margaret
Richardson, OBE, *b.* 1938, *m.*

2004   *Royall of Blaisdon,* Janet Anne Royall,
b. 1955, *m.*

1997   *Scotland of Asthal,* Patricia Janet Scotland, QC,
b. 1955, *m.*

2000   *Scott of Needham Market,* Rosalind Carol Scott,
b. 1957

1991	*Seccombe*, Joan Anna Dalziel Seccombe, DBE, b. 1930, m.
1998	*Sharp of Guildford*, Margaret Lucy Sharp, b. 1938, m.
1973	*Sharples*, Pamela Sharples, b. 1923, m.
2005	*Shephard of Northwold*, Gillian Patricia Shephard, PC, b. 1940, m.
1995	*Smith of Gilmorehill*, Elizabeth Margaret Smith, b. 1940, w.
1999	*Stern*, Vivien Helen Stern, CBE, b. 1941
1996	*Symons of Vernham Dean*, Elizabeth Conway Symons, b. 1951
2005	*Taylor of Bolton*, Winifred Ann Taylor, PC b. 1947, m.
1992	*Thatcher*, Margaret Hilda Thatcher, KG, OM, PC, FRS, b. 1925, w.
1994	*Thomas of Walliswood*, Susan Petronella Thomas, OBE, b. 1935, m.
1998	*Thornton*, (Dorothea) Glenys Thornton, b. 1952, m.
2005	*Tonge*, Dr. Jennifer Louise Tonge, b. 1941, m.
1980	*Trumpington*, Jean Alys Barker, PC, b. 1922, w.
1985	*Turner of Camden*, Muriel Winifred Turner, b. 1927, m.
1998	*Uddin*, Manzila Pola Uddin, b. 1959, m.
2005	‡*Valentine*, Josephine Clare Valentine
2004	*Wall of New Barnet*, Margaret Mary Wall, b. 1941, m.
2000	*Walmsley*, Joan Margaret Walmsley, b. 1943
1985	*Warnock*, Helen Mary Warnock, DBE, b. 1924, w.
1999	*Warwick of Undercliffe*, Diana Mary Warwick, b. 1945, m.
1999	*Whitaker*, Janet Alison Whitaker, b. 1936
1996	*Wilcox*, Judith Ann Wilcox, b. 1940, w.
1999	*Wilkins*, Rosalie Catherine Wilkins, b. 1946
1993	*Williams of Crosby*, Shirley Vivien Teresa Brittain Williams, PC, b. 1930, m.
2004	*Young of Hornsey*, Prof. Margaret Omolola Young, OBE, b. 1951, m.
1997	*Young of Old Scone*, Barbara Scott Young, b. 1948

LORDS SPIRITUAL

The Lords Spiritual are the Archbishops of Canterbury and York and 24 diocesan bishops of the Church of England. The Bishops of London, Durham and Winchester always have seats in the House of Lords; the other 21 seats are filled by the remaining diocesan bishops in order of seniority. The Bishop of Sodor and Man and the Bishop of Gibraltar are not eligible to sit in the House of Lords.

ARCHBISHOPS

Style, The Most Revd and Right Hon. the Lord Archbishop of_
Addressed as Archbishop *or* Your Grace

INTRODUCED TO HOUSE OF LORDS

2003 *Canterbury* (104th), Rowan Douglas Williams, PC, DPHIL, *b.* 1950, *m., cons.* 1992, *elected* 2002

* _ *York* (97th), John Mugabi Tucker Sentamu, PC, PHD, *b.* 1949, *cons.* 1996, *elected* 2005, *trans.* 2005

* At the time of going to press The Most Revd John Sentamu had not been introduced to the House of Lords, this is expected to take place sometime after his confirmation as Archbishop of York on 5 October 2005

BISHOPS

Style, The Right Revd the Lord Bishop of _
Addressed as My Lord
Elected date of confirmation as diocesan bishop

INTRODUCED TO HOUSE OF LORDS
(as at 31 August 2005)

1996 *London* (132nd), Richard John Carew Chartres, *b.* 1947, *m., cons.* 1992, *elected* 1995

2003 *Durham* (71st), Nicholas Thomas Wright, DPHIL, *b.* 1948, *m., cons.* 2003, *elected* 2003

1996 *Winchester* (96th), Michael Charles Scott-Joynt, *b.* 1943, *m., cons.* 1987, *elected* 1995

1993 *Oxford* (41st), Richard Douglas Harries, *b.* 1936, *m., cons.* 1987, *elected* 1987

1997 *Southwark* (9th), Thomas Frederick Butler, *b.* 1940, *m., cons.* 1985, *elected* 1991, *trans.* 1998

1997 *Manchester* (11th), Nigel Simeon McCulloch, *b.* 1942, *m., cons.* 1986, *elected* 1992, *trans.* 2002

1998 *Salisbury* (77th), David Staffurth Stancliffe, *b.* 1942, *m., cons.* 1993, *elected* 1993

1999 *Rochester* (106th), Michael James Nazir-Ali, PHD, *b.* 1949, *m., cons.* 1984, *elected* 1994

1999 *Chelmsford* (9th) John Warren Gladwin, *b.* 1942, *m., cons.* 1994, *elected* 1994, *trans.* 2003

1999 *Portsmouth* (8th), Kenneth William Stevenson, *b.* 1949, *m., cons.* 1995, *elected* 1995

1999 *St Albans* (9th), Christopher William Herbert, *b.* 1944, *m., cons.* 1995, *elected* 1995

2001 *Peterborough* (37th), Ian Cundy, *b.* 1945, *m., cons.* 1992, *elected* 1996

2001 *Chester* (40th), Peter Robert Forster, PHD, *b.* 1950, *cons.* 1996, *elected* 1996

2002 *St Edmundsbury and Ipswich* (9th), (John Hubert) Richard Lewis, *b.* 1943, *m., cons.* 1992, *elected* 1997

2002 *Truro* (14th), William Ind, *b.* 1942, *m., cons.* 1987, *elected* 1997

2002 *Worcester* (112th), Peter Stephen Maurice Selby, *b.* 1941, *cons.* 1984, *elected* 1997

2003 *Newcastle* (11th), (John) Martin Wharton, *b.* 1944, *m., cons.* 1992, *elected* 1997

2003 *Sheffield* (6th), John Nicholls, *b.* 1943, *m., cons.* 1990, *elected* 1997

2003 *Coventry* (8th), Colin J. Bennetts, *b.* 1940, *m., cons.* 1994, *elected* 1998

2003 *Liverpool* (7th), James Jones, *b.* 1948, *m., cons.* 1994, *elected* 1998

2003 *Leicester* (6th), Timothy John Stevens, *b.* 1946, *m., cons.* 1995, *elected* 1999

2004 *Southwell* (10th), George Henry Cassidy, *b.* 1942, *m., cons.* 1999, *elected* 1999

2004 *Norwich* (71st), Graham R. James, *b.* 1951, *m., cons.* 1993, *elected* 1999

2005 *Exeter* (70th), Michael L. Langrish, *b.* 1946, *m., cons.* 1993, *elected* 2000

BISHOPS AWAITING SEATS, in order of seniority
(as at 31 August 2005)

Ripon and Leeds (12th), John R. Packer, *b.* 1946, *m., cons.* 1996, *elected* 2000

Ely (68th) Dr. Anthony Russell, *b.* 1943, *m., cons.* 1988, *elected* 2000

Carlisle (65th) Graham Dow, *b.* 1942, *m., cons.* 1985, *elected* 2000

Chichester (102nd) John Hind, *b.* 1945, *cons.* 1991, *elected* 2001

Lincoln (71st) Dr John Saxbee, *b.* 1946, *cons.* 1994, *elected* 2001

Bath & Wells (77th) Peter Price, *b.* 1944, *m., cons.* 1997, *elected* 2002

Birmingham (8th) Dr John Tucker Mugabi Sentamu (Archbishop of York elect), PHD, *b.* 1949, m., *cons.* 1996, *elected* 2002

Bradford (9th) David James, *b.* 1945, *cons.* 1998, *elected* 2002

Wakefield (12th) Stephen G. Platten, *b.* 1947, *m., cons.* 2003, *elected* 2003

Bristol (55th) Michael A. Hill, *b.* 1947, *m., cons.* 1998, *elected* 2003

Lichfield (98th) Jonathan Gledhill, *b.* 1949, *m., cons.* 1996, *elected* 2003

Blackburn (8th) Nicholas Reade, *b.* 1946, *m., cons.* 2004, *elected* 2004

Hereford (104th) Anthony Martin Priddis, *b.* 1948, *m., cons.* 1996, *elected* 2004

Gloucester (40th) Michael Francis Perham, *b.* 1947, *m., cons.* 2004, *elected* 2004

Guildford (9th) Christopher John Hill, *b.* 1945, *cons.* 1996, *elected* 2004

Derby (7th) Alastair Llewellyn John Redfern, *b.* 1948, *m., cons.* 1997, *elected* 2005

COURTESY TITLES

The heir apparent to a Duke, Marquess or Earl uses the highest of his father's other titles as a courtesy title. For example, the Marquess of Blandford is heir to the Dukedom of Marlborough, and Viscount Amberley to the Earldom of Russell. Titles of second heirs (when in use) are also given, and the courtesy title of the father of a second heir is indicated by * e.g. Earl of Mornington, eldest son of *Marquess of Douro.

The holder of a courtesy title is not styled The Most Hon. or The Right Hon., and in correspondence 'The' is omitted before the title. The heir apparent to a Scottish title may use the title 'Master'.

MARQUESSES
*Blandford –
  Marlborough, D.
Bowmont and Cessford –
  Roxburghe, D.
Douglas and Clydesdale –
  Hamilton, D.
*Douro – Wellington, D.
Graham – Montrose, D.
Hamilton – Abercorn, D.
Hartington – Devonshire,
  D.
Lorne – Argyll, D.
Stafford – Sutherland, D.
Tullibardine – Atholl, D.
*Worcester – Beaufort, D.

EARLS
Aboyne – Huntly, M.
Arundel and Surrey –
  Norfolk, D.
*Bective – Headfort, M.
*Belfast – Donegall, M.
Brecknock – Camden, M.
Burford – St Albans, D.
*Cardigan – Ailesbury, M.
Compton – Northampton,
  M.
*Dalkeith – Buccleuch, D.
*Euston – Grafton, D.
Glamorgan – *Worcester,
  M.
Grosvenor – Westminster,
  D.
Haddo – Aberdeen and
  Temair, M.
Hillsborough – Downshire,
  M.
Hopetoun – Linlithgow, M.
March and Kinrara –
  Richmond, D.
Medina – Milford Haven,
  M.
*Mount Charles –
  Conyngham, M.
Mornington – *Douro, M.
Mulgrave – Normanby, M.
Percy – Northumberland,
  D.
Ronaldshay – Zetland, M.
*St Andrews – Kent, D.
Shelburne – Lansdowne,
  M.

*Southesk – Fife, D.
Sunderland – *Blandford,
  M.
*Tyrone – Waterford, M.
Ulster – Gloucester, D.
*Uxbridge – Anglesey, M.
Wiltshire – Winchester, M.
Yarmouth – Hertford, M.

VISCOUNTS
Alexander – Caledon, E.
Althorp – Spencer, E.
Andover – Suffolk and
  Berkshire, E.
Anson – Lichfield, E.
Asquith – Oxford and
  Asquith, E.
Boringdon – Morley, E.
Borodale – Beatty, E.
Boyle – Shannon, E.
Brocas – Jellicoe, E.
Bury – Albermarle, E.
Campden – Gainsborough,
  E.
Carlow – Portarlington, E.
Carlton – Wharncliffe, E.
Castlereagh – Londonderry,
  M.
Chelsea – Cadogan, E.
Chewton – Waldegrave, E.
Chichester – *Belfast, E.
Clanfield – Peel, E.
Clive – Powis, E.
Coke – Leicester, E.
Corry – Belmore, E.
Corvedale – Baldwin of
  Bewdley, E.
Cranborne – Salisbury, M.
Cranley – Onslow, E.
Crichton – Erne, E.
Curzon – Howe, E.
Dangan – Cowley, E.
Dawick – Haig, E.
Drumlanrig – Queensberry,
  M.
Duncannon – Bessborough,
  E.
Dungarvan – Cork and
  Orrery, E.
Dunluce – Antrim, E.
Dunwich – Stradbroke, E.
Dupplin – Kinnoull, E.
Ednam – Dudley, E.

Elveden – Iveagh, E.
Emlyn – Cawdor, E
Encombe – Eldon, E.
Enfield – Strafford, E.
Erleigh – Reading, M.
Errington – Cromer, E.
FitzHarris – Malmesbury,
  E.
Folkestone – Radnor, E.
Forbes – Granard, E.
Garmoyle – Cairns, E.
Garnock – Lindsay, E.
Glenapp – Inchcape, E.
Glentworth – Limerick, E.
Grey de Wilton – Wilton,
  E.
Grimstone – Verulam, E.
Gwynedd – Lloyd George
  of Dwyfor, E.
Hawkesbury – Liverpool,
  E.
Hinchingbrooke –
  Sandwich, E.
Ikerrin – Carrick, E.
Ingestre – Shrewsbury, E.
Ipswich – *Euston, E.
Jocelyn – Roden, E.
Kelburn – Glasgow, E.
Kingsborough – Kingston,
  E.
Kirkwall – Orkney, E.
Knebworth – Lytton, E.
Lascelles – Harewood, E.
Linley – Snowdon, E.
Loftus – Ely, M.
Lowther – Lonsdale, E.
Lymington – Portsmouth,
  E.
Macmillan of Ovenden –
  Stockton, E.
Maidstone – Winchilsea, E
Maitland – Lauderdale, E.
Mandeville – Manchester,
  D.
Marsham – Romney, E.
Melgund – Minto, E.
Merton – Nelson, E.
Moore – Drogheda, E.
Newport – Bradford, E.
Northland – Ranfurly, E
Newry and Morne –
  Kilmorey, E.
Petersham – Harrington, E.
Pollington – Mexborough,
  E
Raynham – Townshend,
  M.
Reidhaven – Seafield, E.
Ruthven of Canberra –
  Gowrie, E.
St Cyres – Iddesleigh, E.
Sandon – Harrowby, E.
Savernake – *Cardigan, E.
Slane – *Mount Charles, E.
Somerton – Normanton, E.
Stopford – Courtown, E.

Stormont – Mansfield, E.
Strathallan – Perth, E.
Stuart – Castle Stewart, E.
Suirdale – Donoughmore,
  E.
Tamworth – Ferrers, E.
Tarbat – Cromartie, E.
Vaughan – Lisburne, E.
Weymouth – Bath, M.
Windsor – Plymouth, E.
Wolmer – Selborne, E.
Woodstock – Portland, E.

BARONS (LORDS)
Aberdour – Morton, E.
Apsley – Bathurst, E.
Ardee – Meath, E.
Balgonie – Leven and
  Melville, E.
Balniel – Crawford and
  Balcarres, E.
Berriedale – Caithness, E.
Bingham – Lucan, E.
Binning – Haddington, E.
Brooke – Warwick, E.
Bruce – Elgin, E.
Buckhurst – De La Warr, E

Burghley – Exeter, M.
Cardross – Buchan, E.
Carnegie – *Southesk, E.
Clifton – Darnley, E.
Cochrane – Dundonald, E.
Courtenay – Devon, E.
Dalmeny – Rosebery, E.
Doune – Moray, E.
Downpatrick – *St
  Andrews, E.
Dunglass – Home, E.
Eliot – St Germans, E.
Eskdail – *Dalkeith, E.
Formartine – *Haddo, E.
Gillford – Clanwilliam, E.
Glamis – Strathmore, E.
Greenock – Cathcart, E.
Guernsey – Aylesford, E.
Hay – Erroll, E.
Howard of Effingham –
  Effingham, E.
Huntingtower – Dysart, C.
Hyde – Clarendon, E.
Irwin – Halifax, E.
Johnstone – Annandale and
  Hartfell, E.
Kenlis – *Bective, E.
Langton – Temple of
  Stowe, E.
La Poer – *Tyrone, E.
Leveson – Granville, E
Loughborough – Rosslyn,
  E.
Mauchline – Loudoun, C.
Medway – Cranbrook, E.
Montgomerie – Eglinton
  and Winton, E.
Moreton – Ducie, E.

Mount Stuart – *Bute, M*
Naas – *Mayo, E.*
Neidpath – *Wemyss and March, E.*
Norreys – *Lindsey and Abingdon, E.*

North – *Guilford, E.*
Ogilvy – *Airlie, E.*
Oxmantown – *Rosse, E.*
Paget de Beaudesert – *Uxbridge, E.*
Porchester – *Carnarvon, E.*

Ramsay – *Dalhousie, E.*
Romsey – *Mountbatten of Burma, C.*
Scrymgeour – *Dundee, E.*
Seymour – *Somerset, D.*
Stanley – *Derby, E.*

Strathnaver – *Sutherland, C.*
Wodehouse – *Kimberley, E.*
Worsley – *Yarborough, E.*

PEERS' SURNAMES

The following symbols indicate the rank of the peer holding each title:

C. Countess
D. Duke
E. Earl
M. Marquess
V. Viscount
*   Life Peer

Where no designation is given, the title is that of an hereditary Baron or Baroness

Abney-Hastings – *Loudoun, C.*
Acheson – *Gosford, E.*
Adams – *A. of Craigielea*
Adderley – *Norton*
Addington – *Sidmouth, V.*
Adebowale – *A. of Thornes*
Agar – *Normanton, E.*
Aitken – *Beaverbrook*
Akers-Douglas – *Chilston, V.*
Alexander – *A. of Tunis, E.*
Alexander – *A. of Weedon*
Alexander – *Caledon, E.*
Allen – *A. of Abbeydale*
Allen – *Croham*
Allsopp – *Hindlip*
Alton – *A. of Liverpool*
Anderson – *A. of Swansea*
Anderson – *Waverley, V.*
Anelay – *A. of St Johns*
Annesley – *Valentia, V.*
Anson – *Lichfield, E.*
Archer – *A. of Sandwell*
Archer – *A. of Weston-super-Mare*
Armstrong – *A. of Ilminster*
Armstrong-Jones – *Snowdon, E.*
Arthur – *Glenarthur*
Arundell – *Talbot of Malahide*
Ashdown – *A. of Norton-sub-Hamdon*
Ashley – *A. of Stoke*
Ashley-Cooper – *Shaftesbury, E.*
Ashton – *A. of Hyde*
Ashton – *A. of Upholland*
Asquith – *Oxford and Asquith, E.*

Assheton – *Clitheroe*
Astley – *Hastings*
Astor – *A. of Hever*
Aubrey-Fletcher – *Braye*
Bailey – *Glanusk*
Baillie – *Burton*
Baillie Hamilton – *Haddington, E.*
Baker – *B. of Dorking*
Baldwin – *B. of Bewdley, E.*
Balfour – *B. of Inchrye*
Balfour – *Kinross*
Balfour – *Riverdale*
Bampfylde – *Poltimore*
Banbury – *B. of Southam*
Banks – *Stratford*
Barber – *B. of Tewkesbury*
Baring – *Ashburton*
Baring – *Cromer, E.*
Baring – *Howick of Glendale*
Baring – *Northbrook*
Baring – *Revelstoke*
Barker – *Trumpington*
Barnes – *Gorell*
Barnewall – *Trimlestown*
Bassam – *B. of Brighton*
Bathurst – *Bledisloe, V.*
Beauclerk – *St Albans, D.*
Beaumont – *Allendale, V.*
Beaumont – *B. of Whitley*
Beckett – *Grimthorpe*
Benn – *Stansgate, V.*
Bennet – *Tankerville, E.*
Bentinck – *Portland, E.*
Beresford – *Decies*
Beresford – *Waterford, M.*
Bernstein – *B. of Craigweil*
Berry – *Camrose, V.*
Berry – *Kemsley, V.*
Bertie – *Lindsey, E.*
Best – *Wynford*
Bethell – *Westbury*
Bewicke-Copley – *Cromwell*
Bigham – *Mersey, V.*
Bingham – *B. of Cornhill*
Bingham – *Clanmorris*
Bingham – *Lucan, E.*
Black – *B. of Crossharbour*
Bligh – *Darnley, E.*
Blyth – *B. of Rowington*
Bonham Carter – *B.-C. of Yarnbury*

Bootle-Wilbraham – *Skelmersdale*
Boscawen – *Falmouth, V.*
Boston – *B. of Faversham*
Bottomley – *B. of Nettlestone*
Bourke – *Mayo, E.*
Bowes Lyon – *Strathmore, E.*
Bowyer – *Denham*
Boyd – *Kilmarnock*
Boyle – *Cork and Orrery, E.*
Boyle – *Glasgow, E.*
Boyle – *Shannon, E.*
Brabazon – *Meath, E.*
Brand – *Hampden, V.*
Brassey – *B. of Apethorpe*
Brett – *Esher, V.*
Bridge – *B. of Harwich*
Bridgeman – *Bradford, E.*
Brittan – *B. of Spennithorne*
Brodrick – *Midleton, V.*
Brooke – *Alanbrooke, V.*
Brooke – *B. of Alverthorpe*
Brooke – *Brookeborough, V.*
Brooke – *B. of Sutton Mandeville*
Brooks – *B. of Tremorfa*
Brooks – *Crawshaw*
Brougham – *Brougham and Vaux*
Broughton – *Fairhaven*
Brown – *B. of Eaton-under-Heywood*
Browne – *Kilmaine*
Browne – *B. of Madingley*
Browne – *Oranmore and Browne*
Browne – *Sligo, M.*
Bruce – *Aberdare*
Bruce – *Balfour of Burleigh*
Bruce – *Elgin and Kincardine, E.*
Brudenell-Bruce – *Ailesbury, M.*
Buchan – *Tweedsmuir*
Buckley – *Wrenbury*
Butler – *B. of Brockwell*
Butler – *Carrick, E.*
Butler – *Dunboyne*
Butler – *Mountgarret, V.*
Buxton – *B. of Alsa*
Byng – *Strafford, E.*

Byng – *Torrington, V.*
Cambell-Savours – *C.-S. of Allerdale*
Cameron – *C. of Dillington*
Cameron – *C. of Lochbroom*
Campbell – *Argyll, D.*
Campbell – *C. of Alloway*
Campbell – *Cawdor, E.*
Campbell – *Colgrain*
Campbell – *Stratheden and Campbell*
Campbell-Gray – *Gray*
Canning – *Garvagh*
Capell – *Essex, E.*
Carey – *C. of Clifton*
Carington – *Carrington*
Carlisle – *C. of Berriew*
Carnegie – *Fife, D.*
Carnegie – *Northesk, E.*
Carr – *C. of Hadley*
Carter – *C. of Coles*
Cary – *Falkland, V.*
Caulfeild – *Charlemont, V.*
Cavendish – *C. of Furness*
Cavendish – *Chesham*
Cavendish – *Devonshire, D.*
Cavendish – *Waterpark*
Cayzer – *Rotherwick*
Cecil – *Amherst of Hackney*
Cecil – *Exeter, M.*
Cecil – *Rockley*
Chalker – *C. of Wallasey*
Chaloner – *Gisborough*
Channon – *Kelvedon*
Chapman – *C. of Leeds*
Chapman – *Northfield*
Charteris – *Wemyss and March, E.*
Chetwynd-Talbot – *Shrewsbury, E.*
Chichester – *Donegall, M.*
Child Villiers – *Jersey, E.*
Cholmondeley – *Delamere*
Chubb – *Hayter*
Clark – *C. of Calton*
Clarke – *C. of Hampstead*
Clegg-Hill – *Hill, V.*
Clifford – *C. of Chudleigh*
Cochrane – *C. of Cults*
Cochrane – *Dundonald, E.*
Cocks – *Somers*
Cohen – *C. of Pimlico*
Cokayne – *Cullen of Ashbourne*

Coke – *Leicester, E.*
Cole – *Enniskillen, E.*
Collier – *Monkswell*
Colville – *Clydesmuir*
Colville – *C. of Culross, V.*
Compton –
 Northampton, M.
Conolly-Carew – *Carew*
Cooke – *C. of Islandreagh**
Cooke – *C. of Thorndon**
Cooper – *Norwich, V*
Cope – *C. of Berkeley**
Corbett – *C. of Castle*
 Vale*.
Corbett – *Rowallan*
Cornwall-Leigh – *Grey of*
 Condor
Courtenay – *Devon, E.*
Craig – *C. of Radley**
Craig – *Craigavon, V.*
Crichton – *Erne, E.*
Crichton-Stuart – *Bute, M.*
Cripps – *Parmoor*
Crossley – *Somerleyton*
Cubitt – *Ashcombe*
Cunliffe-Lister – *Masham*
 of Ilton*
Cunliffe-Lister – *Swinton,*
 E.
Cunningham – *C. of*
 Felling*
Currie – *C. of Marylebone**
Curzon – *Howe, E.*
Curzon – *Scarsdale, V.*
Cust – *Brownlow*
Czernin – *Howard de*
 Walden
Dalrymple – *Stair, E.*
Daubeny de Moleyns –
 Ventry
Davies – *D. of Coity**
Davies – *Darwen*
Davies – *D. of Oldham**
Davison – *Broughshane*
Dawnay – *Downe, V.*
Dawson-Damer –
 Portarlington, E.
Dean – *D. of Harptree**
Dean – *D. of Thornton-le-*
 Fylde*
Deane – *Muskerry*
de Courcy – *Kingsale*
de Grey – *Walsingham*
Delacourt-Smith –
 Delacourt Smith of
 Alteryn*
Denison – *Londesborough*
Denison-Pender – *Pender*
Devereux – *Hereford, V.*
Dewar – *Forteviot*
De Yarburgh-Bateson –
 Deramore
Dixon – *Glentoran*
Dodson – *Monk Bretton*
Douglas – *Morton, E.*
Douglas – *Queensberry, M.*
Douglas-Hamilton –
 Hamilton, D.

Douglas-Hamilton –
 Selkirk, E.
Douglas-Hamilton –
 Selkirk of Douglas*
Douglas-Home – *Dacre*
Douglas-Home – *Home, E.*
Douglas-Pennant –
 Penrhyn
Douglas-Scott-Montagu –
 Montagu of Beaulieu
Drummond – *Perth, E.*
Drummond of Megginch
 – *Strange*
Dugdale – *Crathorne*
Duke – *Merrivale*
Duncombe – *Feversham*
Dundas – *Melville, V.*
Dundas – *Zetland, M.*
Eady – *Swinfen*
Eccles – *E. of Moulton**
Eden – *Auckland*
Eden – *E. of Winton**
Eden – *Henley*
Edgcumbe – *Mount*
 Edgcumbe, E.
Edmondson – *Sandford*
Edwardes – *Kensington*
Edwards – *Crickhowell**
Egerton – *Sutherland, D.*
Eliot – *St Germans, E.*
Elliott – *E. of Morpeth**
Elliot-Murray-Kynyn-
 mound – *Minto, E.*
Ellis – *Seaford*
Erskine – *Buchan, E.*
Erskine – *Mar and Kellie,*
 E.
Erskine-Murray – *Elibank*
Evans – *E. of Parkside**
Evans – *E. of Temple*
 Guiting*
Evans – *E. of Watford**
Evans – *Mountevans*
Evans-Freke – *Carbery*
Eve – *Silsoe*
Ewing – *E. of Kirkford**
Fairfax – *F. of Cameron*
Falconer – *F. of Thoroton**
Falkner – *F. of*
 Margravine*
Fane – *Westmorland, E.*
Farrington – *F. of*
 Ribbleton*
Faulkner – *F. of Worcester**
Fearn – *F. of Southport**
Feilding – *Denbigh, E.*
Felton – *Seaford*
Fellowes – *De Ramsey*
Fermor-Hesketh – *Hesketh*
Fiennes – *Saye and Sele*
Fiennes-Clinton – *Lincoln,*
 E.
Finch Hatton – *Winchilsea,*
 E.
Finch-Knightley –
 Aylesford, E.
Finlay – *F. of Llandaff**
Fisher – *F. of Rednal**

Fitzalan-Howard – *Herries*
 of Terregles
Fitzalan-Howard –
 Norfolk, D.
FitzGerald – *Leinster, D.*
Fitzherbert – *Stafford*
FitzRoy – *Grafton, D.*
FitzRoy – *Southampton*
FitzRoy Newdegate –
 Daventry, V.
Fletcher-Vane – *Inglewood*
Flower – *Ashbrook, V.*
Foljambe – *Liverpool, E.*
Forbes – *Granard, E*
Forsyth – *F. of Drumlean*.*
Forwood – *Arlington*
Foster – *F. of Thames*
 Bank*
Foulkes – *F. of Cumnock**
Fowler – *F. of Sutton*
 Caulfield*
Fox-Strangways – *Ilchester,*
 E.
Frankland – *Zouche*
Fraser – *F. of Carmyllie**
Fraser – *F. of Kilmorack**
Fraser – *Lovat*
Fraser – *Saltoun*
Fraser – *Strathalmond*
Freeman-Grenville –
 Kinloss
Fremantle – *Cottesloe*
French – *De Freyne*
Fyfe – *F. of Fairfield**
Galbraith – *Strathclyde*
Ganzoni – *Belstead*
Gardner – *G. of Parkes**
Gascoyne-Cecil – *M. of*
 Salisbury*
Gathorne-Hardy –
 Cranbrook, E.
Gibbs – *Aldenham*
Gibbs – *Wraxall*
Gibson – *Ashbourne*
Gibson – *G. of Market*
 Rasen*
Giffard – *Halsbury, E.*
Gilbey – *Vaux of*
 Harrowden
Gilmour – *G. of*
 Craigmillar*
Glyn – *Wolverton*
Godley – *Kilbracken*
Goff – *G. of Chieveley**
Golding – *G. of Newcastle-*
 under-Lyme*
Gordon – *Aberdeen, M.*
Gordon – *G. of*
 Strathblane*
Gordon – *Huntly, M.*
Gordon Lennox –
 Richmond, D.
Gore – *Arran, E.*
Gould – *G. of Brookwood**
Gould – *G. of*
 Potternewton*
Graham – *G. of*
 Edmonton*

Graham – *Montrose, D.*
Graham-Toler – *Norbury,*
 F
Granshaw – *Northover**
Grant of Grant – *Strathspey*
Grant of Rothiemurchus –
 Dysart, C.
Granville – *G. of Eye**
Gray – *G. of Contin**
Greenall – *Daresbury*
Greville – *Warwick, E.*
Griffiths – *G. of Burry*
 Port*
Griffiths – *G. of*
 Fforestfach*
Grigg – *Altrincham*
Grimston – *G. of Westbury*
Grimston – *Verulam, E.*
Grosvenor – *Westminster, D.*
Grosvenor – *Wilton and*
 Ebury, E
Guest – *Wimborne, V*
Gueterbock – *Berkeley*
Guinness – *Iveagh, E.*
Guinness – *Moyne*
Gully – *Selby, V.*
Gummer – *Chadlington**
Gurdon – *Cranworth*
Guthrie – *G. of*
 Craigiebank*
Gwynne Jones – *Chalfont**
Hale – *H. of Richmond**
Hamilton – *Abercorn, D.*
Hamilton – *Belhaven and*
 Stenton
Hamilton – *H. of Dalzell*
Hamilton – *H. of Epsom**
Hamilton – *Holm Patrick*
Hamilton-Russell – *Boyne,*
 V.
Hamilton-Smith – *Colwyn*
Hanbury-Tracy – *Sudeley*
Handcock – *Castlemaine*
Hannay – *H. of Chiswick**
Harbord-Hamond –
 Suffield
Harding – *H. of Petherton*
Hardinge – *H. of Penshurst*
Hare – *Blakenham, V.*
Hare – *Listowel, E.*
Harmsworth – *Rothermere,*
 V.
Harris – *H. of Haringey**
Harris – *H. of High Cross**
Harris – *H. of Peckham**
Harris – *H. of Richmond**
Harris – *Malmesbury, E.*
Hart – *H. of Chilton**
Harvey – *H. of Tasburgh*
Hastings Bass –
 Huntingdon, E.
Haughey – *Ballyedmond**
Hay – *Erroll, E.*
Hay – *Kinnoull, E.*
Hay – *Tweeddale, M.*
Heathcote-Drummond-
 Willoughby –
 Willoughby de Eresby

Millar – *Inchyra*
Miller – *M. of Chiltorne Domer**
Miller – *M. of Hendon**
Milner – *M. of Leeds*
Mitchell-Thomson – *Selsdon*
Mitford – *Redesdale*
Molyneaux – *M. of Killead**
Monckton – *M. of Brenchley, V.*
Monckton-Arundell – *Galway, V.*
Mond – *Melchett*
Money-Coutts – *Latymer*
Monro – *M. of Langholm**
Montagu – *Manchester, D.*
Montagu – *Sandwich, E.*
Montagu – *Swaythling*
Montagu Douglas Scott – *Buccleuch, D.*
Montagu Stuart Wortley – *Wharncliffe, E.*
Montague – *Amwell*
Montgomerie – *Eglinton, E.*
Montgomery – *M. of Alamein, V.*
Moore – *Drogheda, E.*
Moore – *M. of Lower Marsh**
Moore – *M. of Wolvercote**
Moore-Brabazon – *Brabazon of Tara*
Moreton – *Ducie, E*
Morgan – *M. of Drefelin**
Morgan – *M. of Huyton**
Morris – *Killanin*
Morris – *M. of Aberavon**
Morris – *M. of Bolton**
Morris – *M. of Manchester**
Morris – *M. of Kenwood*
Morris – *M. of Yardley**
Morris – *Naseby**
Morrison – *Dunrossil, V.*
Morrison – *Margadale*
Moser – *M. of Regents Park**
Mosley – *Ravensdale*
Mountbatten – *Milford Haven, M.*
Muff – *Calverley*
Mulholland – *Dunleath*
Murray – *Atholl, D.*
Murray – *Dunmore, E.*
Murray – *Mansfield and Mansfield, E.*
Murton – *M. of Lindisfarne**
Nall-Cain – *Brocket*
Napier – *Napier and Ettrick*
Napier – *N. of Magdala*
Needham – *Kilmorey, E.*
Neill – *N. of Bladen**
Nelson – *N. of Stafford*

Nevill – *Abergavenny, M.*
Neville – *Braybrooke*
Newton – *N. of Braintree**
Nicholls – *N. of Birkenhead**
Nicolson – *Carnock*
Nicholson – *N. of Winterbourne**
Nivison – *Glendyne*
Noel – *Gainsborough, E.*
North – *Guilford, E.*
Northcote – *Iddesleigh, E.*
Norton – *Grantley*
Norton – *N. of Louth**
Norton – *Rathcreedan*
Nugent – *Westmeath, E.*
Oakeshott – *O. of Seagrove Bay**
O'Brien – *Inchiquin*
Ogilvie-Grant – *Seafield, E.*
Ogilvy – *Airlie, E.*
Oliver – *O. of Aylmerton**
O'Neill – *O'N. of Bengarve**
O'Neill – *O'N. of Clackmannan**
O'Neill – *Rathcavan*
Orde-Powlett – *Bolton*
Ormsby-Gore – *Harlech*
Ouseley – *O. of Peckham Rye**
Paget – *Anglesey, M.*
Pakenham – *Longford, E.*
Pakington – *Hampton*
Palmer – *Lucas and Dingwall*
Palmer – *Selborne, E.*
Park – *P. of Monmouth**
Parker – *Macclesfield, E.*
Parker – *Morley, E.*
Parnell – *Congleton*
Parsons – *Rosse, E.*
Patel – *P. of Blackburn**
Patten – *P. of Barnes**
Paulet – *Winchester, M.*
Peake – *Ingleby, V.*
Pearson – *Cowdray, V.*
Pearson – *P. of Rannoch**
Pease – *Gainford*
Pease – *Wardington*
Pelham – *Chichester, E.*
Pelham – *Yarborough, E.*
Pellew – *Exmouth, V*
Pendry – *P. of Stalybridge**.
Penny – *Marchwood, V.*
Pepys – *Cottenham, E.*
Perceval – *Egmont, E.*
Percy – *Northumberland, D.*
Perry – *P. of Southwark**
Pery – *Limerick, E.*
Peyton – *P. of Yeovil**
Philipps – *Milford*
Philipps – *St Davids, V.*
Phillips – *P. of Sudbury**
Phillips – *P. of Worth Matravers**

Phipps – *Normanby, M.*
Pilkington – *P. of Oxenford**
Plant – *P. of Highfield**
Platt – *P. of Writtle**
Pleydell-Bouverie – *Radnor, E.*
Plummer – *P. of St Marylebone**
Plumptre – *Fitzwalter*
Plunkett – *Dunsany*
Plunkett – *Louth*
Pollock – *Hanworth, V.*
Pomeroy – *Harberton, V.*
Ponsonby – *Bessborough, E.*
Ponsonby – *de Mauley*
Ponsonby – *P. of Shulbrede*
Ponsonby – *Sysonby*
Powell – *P. of Bayswater**
Powys – *Lilford*
Pratt – *Camden, M.*
Preston – *Gormanston, V.*
Primrose – *Rosebery, E.*
Prittie – *Dunalley*
Prout – *Kingsland**
Ramsay – *Dalhousie, E.*
Ramsay – *R. of Cartvale**
Ramsbotham – *Soulbury, V.*
Randall – *R. of St. Budeaux**
Rawlinson – *R. of Ewell**
Rees – *R. of Ludlow**
Rees-Williams – *Ogmore*
Rendell – *R. of Babergh**
Renfrew – *R. of Kaimsthorn**
Renton – *R. of Mount Harry**
Renwick – *R. of Clifton**
Rhys – *Dynevor*
Richards – *Milverton*
Richardson – *R. of Calow**
Richardson – *R. of Duntisbourne**
Ritchie – *R. of Dundee*
Roberts – *Clwyd*
Roberts – *R. of Conway**
Roberts – *R. of Llandudno**
Robertson – *R. of Oakridge*
Robertson – *R. of Port Ellen**
Robertson – *Wharton*
Robinson – *Martonmere*
Roche – *Fermoy*
Rodd – *Rennell*
Rodger – *R. of Earlsferry**
Rodgers – *R. of Quarry Bank**
Rogers – *R. of Riverside**
Roper-Curzon – *Teynham*
Rospigliosi – *Newburgh, E.*
Rous – *Stradbroke, E.*
Rowley-Conwy – *Langford*
Royall – *R. of Blaisdon**

Runciman – *R. of Doxford, V.*
Russell – *Ampthill*
Russell – *Bedford, D.*
Russell – *de Clifford*
Russell – *R. of Liverpool*
Ryder – *Harrowby, E.*
Ryder – *R. of Wensum**
Sackville – *De La Warr, E.*
Sackville-West – *Sackville*
Sainsbury – *S. of Preston Candover**
Sainsbury – *S. of Turville**
St Aubyn – *St Levan*
St Clair – *Sinclair*
St Clair-Erskine – *Rosslyn, E.*
St John – *Bolingbroke and St John, V.*
St John – *St John of Blesto*
St John-Stevas – *St John of Fawsley**
St Leger – *Doneraile, V.*
Samuel – *Bearsted, V.*
Sanderson – *S. of Ayot*
Sanderson – *S. of Bowden**
Sandilands – *Torphichen*
Saumarez – *De Saumarez*
Savile – *Mexborough, E.*
Saville – *S. of Newdigate**
Scarlett – *Abinger*
Schreiber – *Marlesford**
Sclater-Booth – *Basing*
Scotland – *S. of Asthal**
Scott – *Eldon, E*
Scott – *S. of Foscotte**
Scott – *S. of Needham Market**.
Scrymgeour – *Dundee, E.*
Seager – *Leighton of St Mellons*
Seely – *Mottistone*
Seyfried – *Herbert*
Seymour – *Hertford, M.*
Seymour – *Somerset, D.*
Sharp – *S. of Guildford**
Shaw – *Craigmyle*
Shaw – *S. of Northstead**
Sheldon – *S. of Ashdon-under-Lyne**
Shephard – *S. of Northwood**
Sheppard – *S. of Didgemere**
Shirley – *Ferrers, E.*
Short – *Glenamara**
Shutt – *S. of Greetland**
Siddeley – *Kenilworth*
Sidney – *De L'Isle, V.*
Simon – *S. of Glaisdale**
Simon – *S. of Highbury**
Simon – *S. of Wythenshawe*
Simpson – *S. of Dunkeld**
Sinclair – *Caithness, E.*
Sinclair – *S. of Cleeve*
Sinclair – *Thurso, V.*
Skeffington – *Massereene, V.*

Slynn – *S. of Hadley**
Smith – *Bicester*
Smith – *Hambleden, V.*
Smith – *Kirkhill**
Smith – *S. of Clifton**
Smith – *Smith of Finsbury**
Smith – *S. of Gilmorehill**
Smith – *S. of Leigh**
Somerset – *Beaufort, D.*
Somerset – *Raglan*
Soulsby – *S. of Swaffham Prior**
Spencer – *Churchill, V.*
Spencer-Churchill – *Marlborough, D.*
Spring Rice – *Monteagle of Brandon*
Stanhope – *Harrington, E.*
Stanley – *Derby, E.*
Stanley – *Stanley of Alderley and Sheffield*
Stapleton-Cotton – *Combermere, V.*
Steel – *S. of Aikwood**
Sterling – *S. of Plaistow**
Stevens – *S. of Kirkwhelpington**
Stevens – *S. of Ludgate**
Stevenson – *S. of Coddenham**
Stewart – *Galloway, E.*
Stewart – *Stewartby**
Stoddart – *S. of Swindon**
Stone – *S. of Blackheath**
Stonor – *Camoys*
Stopford – *Courtown, E.*
Stourton – *Mowbray*
Strachey – *O'Hagan*
Strutt – *Belper*
Strutt – *Rayleigh*
Stuart – *Castle Stewart, E.*
Stuart – *Moray, E.*
Stuart – *S. of Findhorn, V.*
Suenson-Taylor – *Grantchester*

Sutherland – *S. of Houndwood**
Symons – *S. of Vernham Dean**
Taylor – *Kilclooney**
Taylor – *T. of Blackburn**
Taylor – *T. of Bolton**
Taylor – *T. of Warwick**
Taylour – *Headfort, M.*
Temple-Gore-Langton – *Temple of Stowe, E*
Temple-Morris – *Temple-Morris of Llandaff**
Tennant – *Glenconner*
Thellusson – *Rendlesham*
Thesiger – *Chelmsford, V.*
Thomas – *T. of Gresford**
Thomas – *T. of Gwydir**
Thomas – *T. of Macclesfield**
Thomas – *T. of Swynnerton**
Thomas – *T. of Walliswood**
Thomson – *T. of Fleet*
Thomson – *T. of Monifieth**
Thynn – *Bath, M.*
Tottenham – *Ely, M.*
Trefusis – *Clinton*
Trench – *Ashtown*
Tufton – *Hothfield*
Turner – *Bilston**
Turner – *Netherthorpe*
Turner – *T. of Camden**
Turner – *T. of Ecchinswell**
Turnour – *Winterton, E.*
Tyrell-Kenyon – *Kenyon*
Vanden-Bempde-Johnstone – *Derwent*
Vane – *Barnard*
Vane-Tempest-Stewart – *Londonderry, M.*
Vanneck – *Huntingfield*

Vaughan – *Lisburne, E.*
Vereker – *Gort, V.*
Verney – *Willoughby de Broke*
Vernon – *Lyveden*
Vesey – *De Vesci, V.*
Villiers – *Clarendon, E.*
Vincent – *V. of Coleshill**
Vivian – *Swansea*
Wade – *W. of Chorlton**
Waldegrave – *W. of North Hill**
Walker – *W. of Gestingthorpe**
Walker – *W. of Worcester**
Wall – *W. of New Barnett**
Wallace – *Dudley*
Wallace – *W. of Saltaire**
Wallace – *W. of Tummel**
Wallop – *Portsmouth, E.*
Walton – *W. of Detchant**
Ward – *Bangor, V.*
Ward – *Dudley, E.*
Warrender – *Bruntisfield*
Warwick – *W. of Undercliffe**
Watson – *W. of Invergowrie**
Watson – *Manton*
Watson – *W. of Richmond**
Webber – *Lloyd-Webber**
Wedderburn – *W. of Charlton**
Weir – *Inverforth*
Weld-Forester – *Forester*
Wellesley – *Cowley, E.*
Wellesley – *Wellington, D.*
Westenra – *Rossmore*
White – *Annaly*
White – *Hanningfield**
Whiteley – *Marchamley*
Whitfield – *Kenswood*
Williams – *W. of Crosby**
Williams – *W. of Elve**
Williamson – *Forres*

Williamson – *W. of Horton**
Willoughby – *Middleton*
Wills – *Dulverton*
Wilson – *Moran*
Wilson – *Nunburnholme*
Wilson – *W. of Dinton**
Wilson – *W. of Tillyorn**
Windsor – *Gloucester, D.*
Windsor – *Kent, D.*
Windsor-Clive – *Plymouth, E.*
Wingfield – *Powerscourt, V.*
Winn – *St Oswald*
Wodehouse – *Kimberley, E.*
Wolfson – *W. of Sunningdale**
Wood – *Halifax, E.*
Woodhouse – *Terrington*
Woolmer – *W. of Leeds**
Wright – *W. of Richmond**
Wyndham – *Egremont and Leconfield*
Wyndham-Quin – *Dunraven, E.*
Wynn – *Newborough*
Yarde-Buller – *Churston*
Yerburgh – *Alvingham*
Yorke – *Hardwicke, E.*
Young – *Kennet*
Young – *Y. of Graffham**
Young – *Y. of Hornsey**
Young – *Y. of Norwood Green**
Young – *Y. of Old Scone**
Younger – *Y. of Leckie, V.*

ORDERS OF CHIVALRY

THE MOST NOBLE ORDER OF THE GARTER (1348)

KG
Ribbon, Blue
Motto, Honi soit qui mal y pense
(Shame on him who thinks evil of it)

The number of Knights and Lady Companions is limited to 24

SOVEREIGN OF THE ORDER
The Queen

LADIES OF THE ORDER
HRH The Princess Royal, 1994
HRH Princess Alexandra, The Hon. Lady Ogilvy, 2003

ROYAL KNIGHTS
HRH The Prince Philip, Duke of Edinburgh, 1947
HRH The Prince of Wales, 1958
HRH The Duke of Kent, 1985
HRH The Duke of Gloucester, 1997

EXTRA KNIGHT COMPANIONS AND LADIES
Grand Duke Jean of Luxembourg, 1972
HM The Queen of Denmark, 1979
HM The King of Sweden, 1983
HM The King of Spain, 1988
HM The Queen of the Netherlands, 1989
HIM The Emperor of Japan, 1998
HM The King of Norway, 2001

KNIGHTS AND LADY COMPANIONS
The Duke of Grafton, 1976
The Lord Richardson of Duntisbourne, 1983
The Lord Carrington, 1985
The Duke of Wellington, 1990
Field Marshal the Lord Bramall, 1990
The Viscount Ridley, 1992
The Lord Sainsbury of Preston Candover, 1992
The Lord Ashburton, 1994
The Lord Kingsdown, 1994
Sir Ninian Stephen, 1994
The Baroness Thatcher, 1995
Sir Edmund Hillary, 1995
Sir Timothy Colman, 1996
The Duke of Abercorn, 1999
Sir William Gladstone, 1999
Field Marshal The Lord Inge, 2001
Sir Anthony Acland, 2001

The Duke of Westminster, 2003
The Lord Butler of Brockwell, 2003
The Lord Morris of Aberavon, 2003
The Lady Soames, 2005
The Lord Bingham of Cornhill, 2005
Sir John Major, 2005
Prelate, The Bishop of Winchester

Chancellor, The Lord Carrington, KG, GCMG, CH, MC
Register, The Dean of Windsor
Garter King of Arms, P. Gwynn-Jones, CVO
Gentleman Usher of the Black Rod, Lt.-Gen. Sir Michael Willcocks, KCB
Secretary, P. L. Dickinson

THE MOST ANCIENT AND MOST NOBLE ORDER OF THE THISTLE (REVIVED 1687)

KT
Ribbon, Green
Motto, Nemo me impune lacessit
(No one provokes me with impunity)

The number of Knights and Ladies of the Thistle is limited to 16

SOVEREIGN OF THE ORDER
The Queen

ROYAL LADY OF THE ORDER
HRH The Princess Royal, 2000

ROYAL KNIGHTS
HRH The Prince Philip, Duke of Edinburgh, 1952
HRH The Prince of Wales, Duke of Rothesay, 1977

KNIGHTS AND LADIES
The Earl of Wemyss and March, 1966
The Duke of Buccleuch and Queensberry, 1978
The Earl of Elgin and Kincardine, 1981
The Lord Thomson of Monifieth, 1981
The Earl of Airlie, 1985
Sir Iain Tennant, 1986
The Viscount of Arbuthnott, 1996
The Earl of Crawford and Balcarres, 1996
Lady Marion Fraser, 1996
The Lord Macfarlane of Bearsden, 1996

The Lord Mackay of Clashfern, 1997
The Lord Wilson of Tillyorn, 2000
The Lord Sutherland of Houndwood, 2002
Sir Eric Anderson, 2002
The Lord Steel of Aikwood, 2004
The Lord Robertson of Port Ellen, 2004

Chancellor, The Duke of Buccleuch and Queensberry, KT, VRD
Dean, The Very Revd G. I. Macmillan, CVO
Secretary and Lord Lyon King of Arms, R. O. Blair, LVO, WS
Gentleman Usher of the Green Rod, Rear-Adm. C. H. Layman, CB, DSO, LVO

THE MOST HONOURABLE ORDER OF THE BATH (1725)

GCB *Military* GCE *Civil*

GCB	Knight (or Dame) Grand Cross
KCB	Knight Commander
DCB	Dame Commander
CB	Companion

Ribbon, Crimson
Motto, Tria juncta in uno
(Three joined in one)

Remodelled 1815, and enlarged many times since. The Order is divided into civil and military divisions. Women became eligible for the Order from 1 January 1971.

THE SOVEREIGN

GREAT MASTER AND FIRST OR PRINCIPAL KNIGHT GRAND CROSS
HRH The Prince of Wales, KG, KT, GCB, OM

Dean of the Order, The Dean of Westminster
Bath King of Arms, Gen. Sir Brian Kenny, GCB, CBE
Registrar and Secretary, Air Vice-Marshal Sir Richard Peirse, KCVO, CB
Genealogist, P. Gwynn-Jones, cvo
Gentleman Usher of the Scarlet Rod, Rear-Adm. I. R. Henderson, CB, CBE

Deputy Secretary, The Secretary of the Central Chancery of the Orders of Knighthood

Chancery, Central Chancery of the Orders of Knighthood, St James's Palace, London SW1A 1BH

THE ORDER OF MERIT (1902)

OM *Military*　　OM *Civil*

OM
Ribbon, Blue and crimson

This Order is designed as a special distinction for eminent men and women without conferring a knighthood upon them. The Order is limited in numbers to 24, with the addition of foreign honorary members.

THE SOVEREIGN

HRH The Prince Philip, Duke of Edinburgh, 1968
Revd Prof. Owen Chadwick, KBE, 1983
Sir Andrew Huxley, 1983
Dr. Frederick Sanger, 1986
The Baroness Thatcher, 1990
Dame Joan Sutherland, 1991
Sir Michael Atiyah, 1992
Lucian Freud, 1993
Sir Aaron Klug, 1995
The Lord Foster of Thames Bank, 1997
Sir Denis Rooke, 1997
Sir James Black, 2000
Sir Anthony Caro, 2000
Prof. Sir Roger Penrose, 2000
Sir Tom Stoppard, 2000
HRH The Prince of Wales, 2002
The Lord May of Oxford, 2002
The Lord Rothschild, 2002
Sir David Attenborough, 2005
The Baroness Boothroyd, 2005
Sir Michael Howard, 2005

Honorary Member, Nelson Mandela, 1995

Secretary and Registrar, The Lord Fellowes, GCB, GCVO, PC, QSO
Chancery, Central Chancery of the Orders of Knighthood, St James's Palace, London SW1A 1BH

THE MOST DISTINGUISHED ORDER OF ST MICHAEL AND ST GEORGE (1818)

GCMG　　　KCMG

GCMG	Knight (or Dame) Grand Cross
KCMG	Knight Commander
DCMG	Dame Commander
CMG	Companion

Ribbon, Saxon blue, with scarlet centre

Motto, Auspicium melioris aevi *(Token of a better age)*

THE SOVEREIGN

GRAND MASTER
HRH The Duke of Kent, KG, GCMG, GCVO, ADC

Prelate, The Rt. Revd David Urquhart
Chancellor, Sir Christopher Mallaby, GCMG, GCVO
Secretary, The Permanent Under-Secretary of State at the Foreign and Commonwealth Office and Head of the Diplomatic Service
Registrar, Lord Wilson of Tillyorn, KT, GCMG
King of Arms, Sir Ewen Fergusson, GCMG, GCVO
Gentleman Usher of the Blue Rod, Sir Anthony Figgis, KCVO, CMG
Dean, The Dean of St Paul's
Deputy Secretary, The Secretary of the Central Chancery of the Orders of Knighthood
Chancery, Central Chancery of the Orders of Knighthood, St James's Palace, London SW1A 1BH

THE MOST EMINENT ORDER OF THE INDIAN EMPIRE (1878)

GCIE	Knight Grand Commander
KCIE	Knight Commander
CIE	Companion

Ribbon, Imperial purple
Motto, Imperatricis auspiciis *(Under the auspices of the Empress)*

THE SOVEREIGN

Registrar, The Secretary of the Central Chancery of the Orders of Knighthood

No conferments have been made since 1947

THE IMPERIAL ORDER OF THE CROWN OF INDIA (1877) FOR LADIES

CI
Badge, the royal cipher of Queen Victoria in jewels within an oval, surmounted by an heraldic crown and attached to a bow of light blue watered ribbon, edged white

The honour does not confer any rank or title upon the recipient
No conferments have been made since 1947

HM The Queen, 1947

THE ROYAL VICTORIAN ORDER (1896)

GCVO　　　KCVO

GCVO	Knight or Dame Grand Cross
KCVO	Knight Commander
DCVO	Dame Commander
CVO	Commander
LVO	Lieutenant
MVO	Member

Ribbon, Blue, with red and white edges
Motto, Victoria

THE SOVEREIGN

Chancellor, The Lord Chamberlain
Secretary, The Keeper of the Privy Purse
Registrar, The Secretary of the Central Chancery of the Orders of Knighthood
Chaplain, The Chaplain of the Queen's Chapel of the Savoy
Hon. Genealogist, D. H. B. Chesshyre, CVO

THE MOST EXCELLENT ORDER OF THE BRITISH EMPIRE (1917)

GBE   KBE

The Order was divided into military and civil divisions in December 1918

GBE   Knight or Dame Grand Cross
KBE   Knight Commander
DBE   Dame Commander
CBE   Commander
OBE   Officer
MBE   Member

Ribbon, Rose pink edged with pearl grey with vertical pearl stripe in centre (military division); without vertical pearl stripe (civil division)
Motto, For God and the Empire

THE SOVEREIGN

GRAND MASTER
HRH The Prince Philip, Duke of Edinburgh, KG, KT, OM, GBE, PC

Prelate, The Bishop of London
King of Arms, Air Chief Marshal Sir Patrick Hine, GCB, GBE
Registrar, The Secretary of the Central Chancery of the Orders of Knighthood
Secretary, The Secretary of the Cabinet and Head of the Home Civil Service
Dean, The Dean of St Paul's
Gentleman Usher of the Purple Rod, Sir Alexander Michael Graham, GBE, DCL
Chancery, Central Chancery of the Orders of Knighthood, St James's Palace, London SW1A 1BH

ORDER OF THE COMPANIONS OF HONOUR (1917)

CH

Ribbon, Carmine, with gold edges

This Order consists of one class only and carries with it no title. The number of awards is limited to 65 (excluding honorary members).

Anthony, Rt. Hon. John, 1981
Ashley of Stoke, The Lord, 1975
Attenborough, Sir David, 1995
Baker, Dame Janet, 1993
Baker of Dorking, The Lord, 1992
Birtwistle, Sir Harrison, 2000
Brenner, Sydney, 1986
Brook, Peter, 1998
Brooke of Sutton Mandeville, The Lord, 1992
Carrington, The Lord, 1983
Christie, Sir George, 2001
Davis, Sir Colin, 2001
De Chastelain, Gen. John, 1999
Dench, Dame Judi, 2005
Fraser, Rt. Hon. Malcolm, 1977
Freud, Lucian, 1983
Glenamara, The Lord, 1976
Hamilton, Richard, 1999
Hannay of Chiswick, The Lord, 2003
Hawking, Prof. Stephen, 1989
Healey, The Lord, 1979
Heseltine, The Lord, 1997
Hobsbawm, Prof. Eric, 1998
Hockney, David, 1997
Hodgkin, Sir Howard, 2002
Howard, Sir Michael, 2002
Howe of Aberavon, The Lord, 1996
Hurd of Westwell, The Lord, 1995
Jones, James, 1977
King of Bridgewater, The Lord, 1992
Lange, Rt. Hon. David, 1989
Lessing, Doris, 1999
Lovelock, Prof. James, 2002
McKenzie, Prof. Dan Peter, 2003
MacKerras, Sir Charles, 2003
Mahon, Sir Denis, 2002
Major, Rt. Hon. Sir John, 1998
Owen, The Lord, 1994
Patten, Rt, Hon., The Lord, 1997
Pinter, Harold, 2002
Riley, Bridget, 1998
Sanger, Dr. Frederick, 1981
Scofield, Paul, 2000
Smith, Sir John, 1993
Somare, Rt. Hon. Sir Michael, 1978
Talboys, Rt. Hon. Sir Brian, 1981
Tebbit, The Lord, 1987
Varah, Revd Dr Chad, 1999

Honorary Members, Lee Kuan Yew, 1970; Prof. Amartya Sen, 2000; Bernard Haitink, 2002
Secretary and Registrar, The Secretary of the Central Chancery of the Orders of Knighthood

THE DISTINGUISHED SERVICE ORDER (1886)

DSO

Ribbon, Red, with blue edges

Bestowed in recognition of especial services in action of commissioned officers in the Navy, Army and Royal Air Force and (since 1942) Mercantile Marine. The members are Companions only. A Bar may be awarded for any additional act of service.

THE IMPERIAL SERVICE ORDER (1902)

ISO

Ribbon, Crimson, with blue centre

Appointment as Companion of this Order is open to members of the Civil Services whose eligibility is determined by the grade they hold. The Order consists of The Sovereign and Companions to a number not exceeding 1,900, of whom 1,300 may belong to the Home Civil Services and 600 to Overseas Civil Services. The then prime minister announced in March 1993 that he would make no further recommendations for appointments to the Order.

Secretary, The Secretary of the Cabinet and Head of the Home Civil Service
Registrar, The Secretary of the Central Chancery of the Orders of Knighthood

THE ROYAL VICTORIAN CHAIN (1902)

It confers no precedence on its holders

HM THE QUEEN

HM The King of Thailand, 1960
HM King Zahir Shah of Afghanistan, 1971
HM The Queen of Denmark, 1974
HM The King of Sweden, 1975
HM The Queen of the Netherlands, 1982
Gen. Antonio Eanes, 1985
HM The King of Spain, 1986
HM The King of Saudi Arabia, 1987
Dr Richard von Weizsäcker, 1992
HM The King of Norway, 1994
The Earl of Airlie, 1997
The Rt. Revd and Rt. Hon. Lord Carey of Clifton, 2002

BARONETAGE AND KNIGHTAGE

BARONETS

Style, 'Sir' before forename and surname, followed by 'Bt'.
Envelope, Sir F_ S_, Bt. *Letter (formal),* Dear Sir; *(social),*
Dear Sir F_. *Spoken,* Sir F_
Wife's style, 'Lady' followed by surname
Envelope, Lady S_. *Letter (formal),* Dear Madam; *(social),*
Dear Lady S_. *Spoken,* Lady S_

There are five different creations of baronetcies: Baronets
of England (creations dating from 1611); Baronets of
Ireland (creations dating from 1619); Baronets of
Scotland or Nova Scotia (creations dating from 1625);
Baronets of Great Britain (creations after the Act of Union
1707 which combined the kingdoms of England and
Scotland); and Baronets of the United Kingdom (creations
after the union of Great Britain and Ireland in 1801).

Badge of Baronets of the   *Badge of Baronets*
United Kingdom   *of Nova Scotia*

Badge of Ulster

The patent of creation limits the destination of a
baronetcy, usually to male descendants of the first
baronet, although special remainders allow the baronetcy
to pass, if the male issue of sons fail, to the male issue of
daughters of the first baronet. In the case of baronetcies of
Scotland or Nova Scotia, a special remainder of 'heirs
male and of tailzie' allows the baronetcy to descend to
heirs general, including women. There are four existing
Scottish baronets with such a remainder.

The Official Roll of the Baronetage is kept at the
Department for Constitutional Affairs by the Registrar of
the Baronetage. Anyone who considers that he is entitled
to be entered on the Roll may petition the Crown through
the Lord Chancellor. Every person succeeding to a
baronetcy must exhibit proofs of succession to the Lord
Chancellor. A person whose name is not entered on the
Official Roll will not be addressed or mentioned by the
title of baronet in any official document, nor will he be
accorded precedence as a baronet.

BARONETCIES EXTINCT SINCE THE LAST EDITION
Blount (cr. 1642); Larcom (cr. 1868)

Registrar of the Baronetage, vacant
Assistant Registrar, Steven Johnson
Office, Department for Constitutional Affairs,
  Constitutional Policy Division, 6th Floor, Selborne
  House, 54 Victoria Street, London SW1E 6QW
  T 020-7210 8564

KNIGHTS

Style, 'Sir' before forename and surname, followed by
  appropriate post-nominal initials if a Knight Grand
  Cross, Knight Grand Commander or Knight
  Commander
Envelope, Sir F_ S_. *Letter (formal),* Dear Sir; *(social),* Dear
  Sir F_. *Spoken,* Sir F_
Wife's style, 'Lady' followed by surname
Envelope, Lady S_. *Letter (formal),* Dear Madam; *(social),*
  Dear Lady S_. *Spoken,* Lady S_

The prefix 'Sir' is not used by knights who are clerics of
the Church of England, who do not receive the accolade.
Their wives are entitled to precedence as the wife of a
knight but not to the style of 'Lady'.

ORDERS OF KNIGHTHOOD
Knight Grand Cross, Knight Grand Commander, and
Knight Commander are the higher classes of the Orders
of Chivalry (*see* page 81). Honorary knighthoods of these
Orders may be conferred on men who are citizens of
countries of which The Queen is not head of state. As a
rule, the prefix 'Sir' is not used by honorary knights.

KNIGHTS BACHELOR

The Knights Bachelor do not constitute a Royal Order
but comprise the surviving representation of the ancient
State Orders of Knighthood. The Register of Knights
Bachelor, instituted by James I in the 17th century, lapsed
and in 1908 a voluntary association under the title of The
Society of Knights (now The Imperial Society of Knights
Bachelor by Royal Command) was formed with the
primary objects of continuing the various registers dating
from 1257 and obtaining the uniform registration of
every created Knight Bachelor. In 1926 a design for a
badge to be worn by Knights Bachelor was approved and
adopted; in 1974 a neck badge and miniature were added

Knight Principal, Sir Richard Gaskell
Prelate, Rt. Revd and Rt. Hon. The Bishop of London
Registrar, Sir Robert Balchin
Hon. Treasurer, Sir Paul Judge
Clerk to the Council, R. L. Jenkins, LVO, TD
Office, 1 Throgmorton Avenue, London EC2N 2BY

LIST OF BARONETS AND KNIGHTS

Revised to 31 August 2005

Peers are not included in this list

† Not registered on the Official Roll of the Baronetage at the time of going to press

() The date of creation of the baronetcy is given in parenthesis

I Baronet of Ireland
NS Baronet of Nova Scotia
S Baronet of Scotland

A full entry in italic type indicates that the recipient of a knighthood died during the year in which the honour was conferred. The name is included for purposes of record.

Abbott, Sir Albert Francis, Kt., CBE
Abbott, *Adm.* Sir Peter Charles, GBE, KCB
Abdy, Sir Valentine Robert Duff, Bt. (1850)
Acheson, *Prof.* Sir (Ernest) Donald, KBE
Ackers, Sir James George, Kt.
Ackers-Jones, Sir David, KBE, CMG
Ackroyd, Sir Timothy Robert Whyte, Bt. (1956)
Acland, Sir Antony Arthur, KG, GCMG, GCVO
Acland, *Lt.-Col.* Sir (Christopher) Guy (Dyke), Bt., MVO (1890)
Acland, Sir John Dyke, Bt. (1644)
Acland, *Maj.-Gen.* Sir John Hugh Bevil, KCB, CBE
Adam, Sir Christopher Eric Forbes, Bt. (1917)
Adam, Sir Kenneth Hugo, Kt., OBE
Adams, Sir William James, KCMG
Adsetts, Sir William Norman, Kt., OBE
Adye, Sir John Anthony, KCMG
Aga Khan IV, HH Prince Karim, KBE
Agnew, Sir Crispin Hamlyn, Bt. (S. 1629)
Agnew, Sir John Keith, Bt. (1895)
Agnew, Sir Rudolph Ion Joseph, Kt.
Agnew-Somerville, Sir Quentin Charles Somerville, Bt. (1957)
Aikens, *Hon.* Sir Richard John Pearson, Kt.
†Ainsworth, Sir Anthony Thomas Hugh, Bt. (1916)
Aird, *Capt.* Sir Alastair Sturgis, GCVO
Aird, Sir (George) John, Bt. (1901)
Airy, *Maj.-Gen.* Sir Christopher John, KCVO, CBE
Aitchison, Sir Charles Walter de Lancey, Bt. (1938)
Akehurst, *Gen.* Sir John Bryan, KCB, CBE
Alberti, *Prof.* Sir Kurt George Matthew Mayer, Kt.
Albu, Sir George, Bt. (1912)
Alcock, *Air Chief Marshal* Sir (Robert James) Michael, GCB, KBE
Aldous, *Rt. Hon.* Sir William, Kt.
Alexander, Sir Charles Gundry, Bt. (1945)
Alexander, Sir Douglas, Bt. (1921)
Allen, *Prof.* Sir Geoffrey, Kt., PHD, FRS
Allen, Sir John Derek, Kt., CBE
Allen, Sir Mark John Spurgeon, Kt., CMG
Allen, *Hon.* Sir Peter Austin Philip Jermyn, Kt.
Allen, Sir Thomas Boaz, Kt., CBE

Allen, *Hon.* Sir William Clifford, KCMG
Allen, Sir William Guilford, Kt.
Alleyne, Sir George Allanmoore Ogarren, Kt.
Alleyne, *Revd* John Olpherts Campbell, Bt. (1769)
Allinson, Sir (Walter) Leonard, KCVO, CMG
Alliott, *Hon.* Sir John Downes, Kt.
Allison, *Air Chief Marshal* Sir John Shakespeare, KCB, CBE
Althaus, Sir Nigel Frederick, Kt.
Alun-Jones, Sir (John) Derek, Kt.
Ambo, *Rt. Revd* George, KBE
Amet, *Hon.* Sir Arnold Karibone, Kt.
Amory, Sir Ian Heathcoat, Bt. (1874)
Anderson, Sir John Anthony, KBE
Anderson, *Maj.-Gen.* Sir John Evelyn, KBE
Anderson, Sir Leith Reinsford Steven, Kt., CBE
Anderson, *Vice-Adm.* Sir Neil Dudley, KBE, CB
Anderson, Sir (William) Eric Kinloch, Kt.
Anderson, *Prof.* Sir (William) Ferguson, Kt., OBE
Anderton, Sir (Cyril) James, Kt., CBE, QPM
Andrew, Sir Robert John, KCB
Andrews, Sir Derek Henry, KCB, CBE
Andrews, *Hon.* Sir Dormer George, Kt.
Angus, Sir Michael Richardson, Kt.
Annesley, Sir Hugh Norman, Kt., QPM
Anson, *Vice-Adm.* Sir Edward Rosebery, KCB
Anson, Sir John, KCB
Anson, *Rear-Adm.* Sir Peter, Bt., CB (1831)
Anstruther, Sir Ian Fife Campbell, Bt. (S. 1694)
Anstruther-Gough-Calthorpe, Sir Euan Hamilton, Bt. (1929)
Antico, Sir Tristan Venus, Kt.
Antrobus, Sir Edward Philip, Bt. (1815)
Appleyard, Sir Leonard Vincent, KCMG
Appleyard, Sir Raymond Kenelm, KBE
Arbib, Sir Martyn, Kt.
Arbuthnot, Sir Keith Robert Charles, Bt. (1823)
Arbuthnot, Sir William Reierson, Bt. (1964)
Arbuthnott, *Prof.* Sir John Peebles, Kt., PHD, FRSE
Archdale, *Capt.* Sir Edward Folmer, Bt., DSC, RN (1928)

Arculus, Sir Ronald, KCMG, KCVO
Arculus, Sir Thomas David Guy, Kt.
Armitage, *Air Chief Marshal* Sir Michael John, KCB, CBE
Armour, *Prof.* Sir James, Kt., CBE
Armstrong, Sir Christopher John Edmund Stuart, Bt., MBE (1841)
Armstrong, Sir Patrick John, Kt., CBE
Armstrong, Sir Richard, Kt., CBE
Armytage, Sir John Martin, Bt. (1738)
Arnold, Sir Malcolm Henry, Kt., CBE
Arnold, Sir Thomas Richard, Kt.
Arnott, Sir Alexander John Maxwell, Bt. (1896)
Arrindell, Sir Clement Athelston, GCMG, GCVO, QC
Arthur, Sir Gavyn Farr, Kt.
Arthur, *Lt.-Gen.* Sir (John) Norman Stewart, KCB
Arthur, Sir Michael Anthony, KCMG
Arthur, Sir Stephen John, Bt. (1841)
Ash, *Prof.* Sir Eric Albert, Kt., CBE, FRS, FRENG
Ashburnham, Sir James Fleetwood, Bt. (1661)
Ashley, Sir Bernard Albert, Kt.
Ashmore, *Admiral of the Fleet* Sir Edward Beckwith, GCB, DSC
Aske, Sir Robert John Bingham, Bt. (1922)
Askew, Sir Bryan, Kt.
Asscher, *Prof.* Sir (Adolf) William, Kt., MD, FRCP
Astill, *Hon.* Sir Michael John, Kt.
Astley-Cooper, Sir Alexander Paston, Bt. (1821)
Aston, Sir Harold George, Kt., CBE
Astwood, *Hon.* Sir James Rufus, KBE
Atcherley, Sir Harold Winter, Kt.
Atiyah, Sir Michael Francis, Kt., OM, PHD, FRS
Atkins, *Rt. Hon.* Sir Robert James, Kt.
Atkinson, *Prof.* Sir Anthony Barnes, Kt.
Atkinson, *Air Marshal* Sir David William, KBE
Atkinson, Sir Frederick John, KCB
Atkinson, Sir John Alexander, KCB, DFC
Atkinson, Sir Robert, Kt., DSC, FRENG
Atopare, Sir Sailas, GCMG
Attenborough, Sir David Frederick, Kt., OM, CH, CVO, CBE, FRS
Aubrey-Fletcher, Sir Henry Egerton, Bt. (1782)
Audland, Sir Christopher John, KCMG
Audley, Sir George Bernard, Kt.
Augier, *Prof.* Sir Fitz-Roy Richard, Kt.

Auld, *Rt. Hon.* Sir Robin Ernest, Kt.

Austin, Sir Anthony Leonard, Bt. (1894)

Austin, *Air Marshal* Sir Roger Mark, KCB, AFC

Austen-Smith, *Air Marshal* Sir Roy David, KBE, CB, CVO, DFC

Avei, Sir Moi, KBE

Axford, Sir William Ian, Kt.

Ayckbourn, Sir Alan, Kt., CBE

Aykroyd, Sir James Alexander Frederic, Bt. (1929)

Aykroyd, Sir William Miles, Bt., MC (1920)

Aylmer, Sir Richard John, Bt. (I. 1622)

Bacha, Sir Bhinod, Kt., CMG

Backhouse, Sir Jonathan Roger, Bt. (1901)

Bacon, Sir Nicholas Hickman Ponsonby, Bt. *Premier Baronet of England* (1611 and 1627)

Bacon, Sir Sidney Charles, Kt., CB, FRENG.

Baddeley, Sir John Wolsey Beresford, Bt. (1922)

Baddiley, *Prof.* Sir James, Kt., PHD, FRS, FRSE

Badge, Sir Peter Gilmour Noto, Kt.

Baer, Sir Jack Mervyn Frank, Kt.

Bagge, Sir (John) Jeremy Picton, Bt. (1867)

Bagnall, *Air Chief Marshal* Sir Anthony, GBE, KCB

Bailey, Sir Alan Marshall, KCB

Bailey, Sir Brian Harry, Kt., OBE

Bailey, Sir Derrick Thomas Louis, Bt., DFC (1919)

Bailey, Sir John Bilsland, KCB

Bailey, Sir Richard John, Kt., CBE

Bailey, Sir Stanley Ernest, Kt., CBE, QPM

Bailhache, Sir Philip Martin, Kt.

Baillie, Sir Adrian Louis, Bt. (1823)

Bain, *Prof.* Sir George Sayers, Kt.

Baird, Sir Charles William Stuart, Bt. (1809)

†Baird, Sir James Andrew Gardiner, Bt. (S. 1695)

Baird, *Lt.-Gen.* Sir James Parlane, KBE, MD

Baird, *Air Marshal* Sir John Alexander, KBE

Baird, *Vice-Adm.* Sir Thomas Henry Eustace, KCB

Bairsto, *Air Marshal* Sir Peter Edward, KBE, CB

Baker, Sir Bryan William, Kt.

Baker, *Prof.* Sir John Hamilton, Kt., QC

Baker, *Rt. Hon.* Sir (Thomas) Scott (Gillespie), Kt.

Balchin, Sir Robert George Alexander, Kt.

Balderstone, Sir James Schofield, Kt.

Baldwin, *Prof.* Sir Jack Edward, Kt., FRS

Baldwin, Sir Peter Robert, KCB

Ball, *Air Marshal* Sir Alfred Henry Wynne, KCB, DSO, DFC

Ball, Sir Christopher John Elinger, Kt.

Ball, Sir Richard Bentley, Bt. (1911)

Ball, *Prof.* Sir Robert James, Kt., PHD

Ballantyne, *Dr* Sir Frederick Nathaniel, GCMG

Bamford, Sir Anthony Paul, Kt.

Band, *Adm.* Sir Jonathon, KCB

Banham, Sir John Michael Middlecott, Kt.

Bannerman, Sir David Gordon, Bt., OBE (S. 1682)

Bannister, Sir Roger Gilbert, Kt., CBE, DM, FRCP

Barber, Sir Michael Bayldon, Kt.

Barber, Sir (Thomas) David, Bt. (1960)

Barbour, *Very Revd* Robert Alexander Stewart, KCVO, MC

Barclay, Sir Colville Herbert Sanford, Bt. (S. 1668)

Barclay, Sir David Rowat, Kt.

Barclay, Sir Frederick Hugh, Kt.

Barclay, Sir Peter Maurice, Kt., CBE

Barder, Sir Brian Leon, KCMG

Baring, Sir John Francis, Bt. (1911)

Barker, Sir Colin, Kt.

Barker, *Hon.* Sir (Richard) Ian, Kt.

Barlow, Sir Christopher Hilaro, Bt. (1803)

Barlow, Sir Frank, Kt., CBE

Barlow, Sir (George) William, Kt., FRENG

Barlow, Sir James Alan, Bt. (1902)

Barlow, Sir John Kemp, Bt. (1907)

Barnard, Sir Joseph Brian, Kt.

Barnes, *The Most Revd.* Brian James, KBE

Barnes, Sir (James) David (Francis), Kt., CBE

Barnes, Sir Kenneth, KCB

Barnewall, Sir Reginald Robert, Bt. (I. 1623)

Baron, Sir Thomas, Kt., CBE

Barraclough, *Air Chief Marshal* Sir John, KCB, CBE, DFC, AFC

Barran, Sir John Napoleon Ruthven, Bt. (1895)

Barratt, Sir Lawrence Arthur, Kt.

Barratt, Sir Richard Stanley, Kt., CBE, QPM

Barratt-Boyes, Sir Brian Gerald, KBE

Barrett, Sir Stephen Jeremy, KCMG

Barrett-Lennard, *Revd* Hugh Dacre, Bt. (1801)

Barrington, Sir Benjamin, Bt. (1831)

Barrington, Sir Nicholas John, KCMG, CVO

Barrington-Ward, *Rt. Revd* Simon, KCMG

Barron, Sir Donald James, Kt.

Barrow, *Capt.* Sir Richard John Uniacke, Bt. (1835)

Barry, Sir (Lawrence) Edward (Anthony Tress), Bt. (1899)

Barter, Sir Peter Leslie Charles, Kt., OBE

†Bartlett, Sir Andrew Alan, Bt. (1913)

Barttelot, *Col.* Sir Brian Walter de Stopham, Bt., OBE (1875)

Bate, Sir David Lindsay, KBE

†Bates, Sir Edward Robert, Bt. (1880)

Bates, Sir Malcolm Rowland, Kt.

Bates, Sir Richard Dawson Hoult, Bt. (1937)

Bateson, *Prof.* Sir Patrick, Kt.

Batho, Sir Peter Ghislain, Bt. (1928)

Bathurst, *Admiral of the Fleet* Sir (David) Benjamin, GCB

Batten, Sir John Charles, KCVO

Battersby, *Prof.* Sir Alan Rushton, Kt., FRS

Battishill, Sir Anthony Michael William, GCB

Baxendell, Sir Peter Brian, Kt., CBE, FRENG

Bayliss, Sir Richard Ian Samuel, KCVO, MD, FRCP

Bayne, Sir Nicholas Peter, KCMG

Baynes, Sir John Christopher Malcolm, Bt. (1801)

Bazley, Sir Thomas John Sebastian, Bt. (1869)

Beach, *Gen.* Sir (William Gerald) Hugh, GBE, KCB, MC

Beache, *Hon.* Sir Vincent Ian, KCMG

Beale, *Lt.-Gen.* Sir Peter John, KBE, FRCP

Beamish, Sir Adrian John, KCMG

Bean, *Hon.* Sir David Michael, Kt

Beaumont, *Capt.* the Hon. Sir (Edward) Nicholas (Canning), KCVO

Beaumont, Sir George (Howland Francis), Bt. (1661)

Beaumont, Sir Richard Ashton, KCMG, OBE

Beaumont-Dark, Sir Anthony Michael, Kt.

Beatson, *Hon.* Sir Jack, Kt.

Beavis, *Air Chief Marshal* Sir Michael Gordon, KCB, CBE, AFC

Beck, Sir Edgar Philip, Kt.

Beckett, Sir Richard Gervase, Bt., QC (1921)

Beckett, Sir Terence Norman, KBE, FRENG

Beckwith, Sir John Lionel, Kt., CBE

Bedser, Sir Alec Victor, Kt., CBE

Beecham, Sir Jeremy Hugh, Kt.

Beecham, Sir John Stratford Roland, Bt. (1914)

Beetham, *Marshal of the Royal Air Force* Sir Michael James, GCB, CBE, DFC, AFC

Beevor, Sir Thomas Agnew, Bt. (1784)

Beldam, *Rt. Hon.* Sir (Alexander) Roy (Asplan), Kt.

Belich, Sir James, Kt.

Bell, Sir Brian Ernest, KBE

Bell, Sir David Charles Maurice, Kt.

Bell, Sir John Lowthian, Bt. (1885)

Bell, *Prof.* Sir Peter Robert Frank, Kt

Bell, *Hon.* Sir Rodger, Kt.

Bell, Sir Stuart, Kt.

Bellamy, *Hon.* Sir Christopher William, Kt.

Bellingham, Sir Anthony Edward Norman, Bt. (1796)

Bender, Sir Brian Geoffrey, KCB

Benn, Sir (James) Jonathan, Bt. (1914)

Bennett, *Air Vice-Marshal* Sir Erik Peter, KBE, CB

Bennett, *Hon.* Sir Hugh Peter Derwyn, Kt.

Bennett, *Gen.* Sir Phillip Harvey, KBE, DSO

Bennett, Sir Richard Rodney, Kt., CBE

Bennett, Sir Ronald Wilfrid Murdoch, Bt. (1929)

Benson, Sir Christopher John, Kt.

Benyon, Sir William Richard, Kt.

Beresford, Sir (Alexander) Paul, Kt.,

Beresford-Peirse, Sir Henry Grant de la Poer, Bt. (1814)

Berghuser, *Hon.* Sir Eric, Kt., MBE

Beringer, *Prof.* Sir John Evelyn, Kt., CBE

Berman, Sir Franklin Delow, KCMG

Berners-Lee, Sir Timothy John, KBE

Bernard, Sir Dallas Edmund, Bt. (1954)

Bernstein, Sir Howard, Kt.

Berney, Sir Julian Reedham Stuart, Bt. (1620)

Berridge, *Prof.* Sir Michael John, Kt., FRS

Berrill, Sir Kenneth Ernest, GBE, KCB

Berriman, Sir David, Kt.

Berry, *Prof.* Sir Colin Leonard, Kt., FRCPATH

Berry, *Prof.* Sir Michael Victor, Kt., FRS

Berthon, *Vice-Adm.* Sir Stephen Ferrier, KCB

Berthoud, Sir Martin Seymour, KCVO, CMG

Best, Sir Richard Radford, KCVO, CBE

Best-Shaw, Sir John Michael Robert, Bt. (1665)

Bethune, *Hon.* Sir (Walter) Angus, Kt.

Bett, Sir Michael, Kt., CBE

Bevan, Sir Martyn Evan Evans, Bt. (1958)

Bevan, Sir Nicolas, Kt., CB

Bevan, Sir Timothy Hugh, Kt.

Beverley, *Lt.-Gen.* Sir Henry York La Roche, KCB, OBE, RM

Bibby, Sir Michael James, Bt. (1959)

Bichard, Sir Michael George, KCB

Bickersteth, *Rt. Revd* John Monier, KCVO

Biddulph, Sir Ian D'Olier, Bt. (1664)

Bide, Sir Austin Ernest, Kt.

Bidwell, Sir Hugh Charles Philip, GBE

Biggam, Sir Robin Adair, Kt.

Biggs, Sir Norman Paris, Kt.

Bilas, Sir Angmai Simon, Kt., OBE

Billière, *Gen.* Sir Peter Edgar de la Cour de la, KCB, KBE, DSO, MC

Bingham, *Hon.* Sir Eardley Max, Kt.

Birch, Sir John Allan, KCVO, CMG

Birch, Sir Roger, Kt., CBE, QPM

Bird, Sir Richard Geoffrey Chapman, Bt. (1922)

Birkin, Sir John Christian William, Bt. (1905)

Birkin, Sir (John) Derek, Kt., TD

Birkmyre, Sir James, Bt. (1921)

Birrell, Sir James Drake, Kt.

Birtwistle, Sir Harrison, Kt., CH

Bischoff, Sir Winfried Franz Wilhelm, Kt.

Bishop, Sir Michael David, Kt., CBE

Bisson, *Rt. Hon.* Sir Gordon Ellis, Kt.

Bjelke-Petersen, Sir Johannes, KCMG

Black, Sir James Whyte, Kt., OM, FRCP, FRS

Black, *Adm.* Sir (John) Jeremy, GBE, KCB, DSO

Black, Sir Robert David, Bt. (1922)

Blackburn, *Vice-Adm.* Sir David Anthony James, KCVO, CB, LVO

Blackburne, *Hon.* Sir William Anthony, Kt.

Blackett, Sir Hugh Francis, Bt. (1673)

Blackman, *Vice-Adm.* Sir Jeremy Joe, KCB

Blacklock, *Surgeon Capt. Prof.* Sir Norman James, KCVO, OBE

Blackman, Sir Frank Milton, KCVO, OBE

Blackwood, Sir John Francis, Bt. (1814)

Blair, *Lt.-Gen.* Sir Chandos, KCVO, OBE, MC

Blair, Sir Edward Thomas Hunter, Bt. (1786)

Blair, Sir Ian Warwick, Kt., QPM

Blake, Sir Alfred Lapthorn, KCVO, MC

Blake, Sir Francis Michael, Bt. (1907)

Blake, Sir Peter Thomas, Kt., CBE

Blake, Sir (Thomas) Richard (Valentine), Bt. (I. 1622)

Blaker, Sir John, Bt. (1919)

Blakiston, Sir Ferguson Arthur James, Bt. (1763)

Blanch, Sir Malcolm, KCVO

Bland, Sir (Francis) Christopher (Buchan), Kt.

Bland, *Lt.-Col.* Sir Simon Claud Michael, KCVO

Blank, Sir Maurice Victor, Kt.

Blatherwick, Sir David Elliott Spiby, KCMG, OBE

Blelloch, Sir John Nial Henderson, KCB

Blennerhassett, Sir (Marmaduke) Adrian Francis William, Bt. (1809)

Blewitt, *Maj.* Sir Shane Gabriel Basil, GCVO

Blofeld, *Hon.* Sir John Christopher Calthorpe, Kt.

Blois, Sir Charles Nicholas Gervase, Bt. (1686)

Blom-Cooper, Sir Louis Jacques, Kt., QC

Blomefield, Sir Thomas Charles Peregrine, Bt. (1807)

Bloomfield, Sir Kenneth Percy, KCB

Blundell, Sir Thomas Leon, Kt., FRS

Blunden, Sir George, Kt.

Blunden, Sir Philip Overington, Bt. (I. 1766)

Blunt, Sir David Richard Reginald Harvey, Bt. (1720)

Blyth, Sir Charles (Chay), Kt., CBE, BEM

Boardman, *Prof.* Sir John, Kt., FSA, FBA

Bodey, *Hon.* Sir David Roderick Lessiter, Kt.

Bodmer, Sir Walter Fred, Kt., PHD, FRS

Body, Sir Richard Bernard Frank Stewart, Kt., MP

Bogan, Sir Nagora, KBE

Boileau, Sir Guy (Francis), Bt. (1838)

Boles, Sir Jeremy John Fortescue, Bt. (1922)

Boles, Sir John Dennis, Kt., MBE

Bolland, Sir Edwin, KCMG

Bollers, *Hon.* Sir Harold Brodie Smith, Kt.

Bolt, *Air Marshal* Sir Richard Bruce, KBE, CB, DFC, AFC

Bolton, Sir Frederic Bernard, Kt., MC

Bona, Sir Kina, KBE

Bonallack, Sir Michael Francis, Kt., OBE

Bond, Sir John Reginald Hartnell, Kt.

Bond, Sir Kenneth Raymond Boyden, Kt.

Bond, *Prof.* Sir Michael Richard, Kt., FRCPSYCH, FRCPGLAS, FRCSE

Bondi, *Prof.* Sir Hermann, KCB, FRS

Bone, Sir Roger Bridgland, KCMG

Bonfield, Sir Peter Leahy, Kt., CBE, FRENG

Bonham, *Maj.* Sir Antony Lionel Thomas, Bt. (1852)

Bonington, Sir Christian John Storey, Kt., CBE

Bonsall, Sir Arthur Wilfred, KCMG, CBE

Bonsor, Sir Nicholas Cosmo, Bt. (1925)

Boolell, Sir Satcam, Kt.

Boord, Sir Nicolas John Charles, Bt. (1896)

Boorman, *Lt.-Gen.* Sir Derek, KCB

Booth, Sir Christopher Charles, Kt., MD, FRCP

Booth, Sir Douglas Allen, Bt. (1916)

Booth, Sir Gordon, KCMG, CVO

Boothby, Sir Brooke Charles, Bt. (1660)

Bore, Sir Albert, Kt.

Boreel, Sir Stephan Gerard, Bt. (1645)

†Borthwick, Sir Anthony Thomas, Bt. (1908)

Borysiewicz, *Prof.* Sir Leszek Krzysztof, Kt.

Bossom, *Hon.* Sir Clive, Bt. (1953)

Boswell, *Lt.-Gen.* Sir Alexander Crawford Simpson, KCB, CBE

Bosworth, Sir Neville Bruce Alfred, Kt., CBE

Booth, Sir Clive, Kt.

Bottoms, *Prof.* Sir Anthony Edward, Kt.

Bottomley, Sir James Reginald Alfred, KCMG

Boughey, Sir John George Fletcher, Bt. (1798)

Boulton, Sir Clifford John, GCB

Boulton, Sir William Whytehead, Bt., CBE, TD (1944)

Bourn, Sir John Bryant, KCB

Bouraga, Sir Phillip, KBE

Bourne, Sir Clive John, Kt.

Bowater, Sir Euan David Vansittart, Bt. (1939)

Bowater, Sir (John) Vansittart, Bt. (1914)

Bowden, Sir Andrew, Kt., MBE

Bowden, Sir Nicholas Richard, Bt. (1915)

Bowen, Sir Geoffrey Fraser, Kt.

Bowen, Sir Mark Edward Mortimer, Bt. (1921)

Bowes Lyon, Sir Simon Alexander, KCVO

Bowett, *Prof.* Sir Derek William, Kt., CBE, QC, FBA

†Bowlby, Sir Richard Peregrine Longstaff, Bt. (1923)

Bowman, Sir Edwin Geoffrey, KCB

Bowman, Sir Jeffery Haverstock, Kt.

Bowman-Shaw, Sir (George) Neville, Kt.

Bowness, Sir Alan, Kt., CBE

Bowyer-Smyth, Sir Thomas Weyland, Bt. (1661)

Boyce, Sir Graham Hugh, KCMG

Boyce, Sir Robert Charles Leslie, Bt. (1952)

Boyd, Sir Alexander Walter, Bt. (1916)

Boyd, Sir John Dixon Iklé, KCMG

Boyd, *Prof.* Sir Robert David Hugh, Kt.

Boyd-Carpenter, Sir (Marsom) Henry, KCVO

Boyd-Carpenter, *Lt.-Gen. Hon.* Sir Thomas Patrick John, KBE

Boyle, Sir Stephen Gurney, Bt. (1904)

Boynton, Sir John Keyworth, Kt., MC

Boyson, *Rt. Hon.* Sir Rhodes, Kt.

Brabham, Sir John Arthur, Kt., OBE

Bracewell-Smith, Sir Charles, Bt. (1947)

Bradbeer, Sir John Derek Richardson, Kt., OBE, TD

Bradford, Sir Edward Alexander Slade, Bt. (1902)

Bradshaw, Sir Kenneth Anthony, KCB

Brady, *Prof.* Sir John Michael Kt. FRS

Braithwaite, *Rt. Hon.* Sir Nicholas Alexander, Kt., OBE

Braithwaite, Sir Rodric Quentin, GCMG

Bramley, *Prof.* Sir Paul Anthony, Kt.

Branson, Sir Richard Charles Nicholas, Kt.

Bratza, *Hon.* Sir Nicolas Dušan, Kt.

Breckenridge, *Prof.* Sir Alasdair Muir, Kt. CBE

Brennan, *Hon.* Sir (Francis) Gerard, KBE

Brett, Sir Charles Edward Bainbridge, Kt., CBE

Brickwood, Sir Basil Greame, Bt. (1927)

Bridges, *Hon.* Sir Phillip Rodney, Kt., CMG

Brierley, Sir Ronald Alfred, Kt.

Bright, Sir Graham Frank James, Kt.

Bright, Sir Keith, Kt.

Brigstocke, *Adm.* Sir John Richard, KCB

Brinckman, Sir Theodore George Roderick, Bt. (1831)

†Brisco, Sir Campbell Howard, Bt. (1782)

Briscoe, Sir Brian Anthony, Kt.

Briscoe, Sir John Geoffrey James, Bt. (1910)

Brittan, Sir Samuel, Kt.

†Broadbent, Sir Andrew George, Bt. (1893)

Broadbent, Sir Richard John, KCB

Brocklebank, Sir Aubrey Thomas, Bt. (1885)

Brodie, Sir Benjamin David Ross, Bt. (1834)

Brodie-Hall, Sir Laurence Charles, Kt., AO, CMG

Brokking, Sir Trevor, Kt., CBE

Bromhead, Sir John Desmond Gonville, Bt. (1806)

Bromley, Sir Michael Roger, KBE

Bromley, Sir Rupert Charles, Bt. (1757)

Brook, *Prof.* Sir Richard John, Kt. OBE

†Brooke, Sir Alistair Weston, Bt. (1919)

Brooke, Sir Francis George Windham, Bt. (1903)

Brooke, *Rt. Hon.* Sir Henry, Kt.

Brooke, Sir (Richard) David Christopher, Bt. (1662)

Brooking, Sir Trevor David, Kt., CBE

Brooks, Sir Timothy Gerald Martin, KCVO

Brooksbank, Sir (Edward) Nicholas, Bt. (1919)

Broomfield, Sir Nigel Hugh Robert Allen, KCMG

†Broughton, Sir David Delves, Bt. (1661)

Broun, Sir William Windsor, Bt. (S. 1686)

Brown, Sir (Austen) Patrick, KCB

Brown, *Adm.* Sir Brian Thomas, KCB, CBE

Brown, Sir (Cyril) Maxwell Palmer, KCB, CMG

Brown, Sir David, Kt.

Brown, Sir Douglas Denison, Kt.

Brown, *Hon.* Sir Douglas Dunlop, Kt.

Brown, Sir George Francis Richmond, Bt. (1863)

Brown, Sir George Noel, Kt.

Brown, Sir Mervyn, KCMG, OBE

Brown, Sir Peter Randolph, Kt.

Brown, *Rt. Hon.* Sir Stephen, GBE

Brown, Sir Stephen David Reid, KCVO

Browne, Sir Nicholas Walker, KBE, CMG

Brownrigg, Sir Nicholas (Gawen), Bt. (1816)

Browse, *Prof.* Sir Norman Leslie, Kt., MD, FRCS

Bruce, Sir (Francis) Michael Ian, Bt. (S. 1628)

Bruce, Sir Hervey James Hugh, Bt. (1804)

Bruce-Gardner, Sir Robert Henry, Bt. (1945)

Bruce-Lockhart, Sir Alexander John (Sandy), Kt., OBE

Buckworth-Herne-Soame, Sir Charles John, Bt. (1697)

Brunner, Sir John Henry Kilian, Bt. (1895)

Brunton, Sir (Edward Francis) Lauder, Bt. (1908)

Brunton, Sir Gordon Charles, Kt.

Bryan, Sir Arthur, Kt.

Buchan-Hepburn, Sir John Alastair Trant Kidd, Bt. (1815)

Buchanan, Sir Andrew George, Bt. (1878)

Buchanan, *Vice-Adm.* Sir Peter William, KBE

Buchanan, Sir Robert Wilson (Robin), Kt.

Buchanan-Jardine, *Maj.* Sir (Andrew) Rupert (John), Bt., MC (1885)

Buckland, Sir Ross, Kt.

Buckley, Sir Michael Sidney, Kt.

Buckley, *Lt.-Cdr.* Sir (Peter) Richard, KCVO

Buckley, *Hon.* Sir Roger John, Kt.

Budd, Sir Alan Peter, Kt.

Budd, Sir Colin Richard, KCMG

Bull, Sir George Jeffrey, Kt.

Bull, Sir Simeon George, Bt. (1922)

Bullard, Sir Julian Leonard, GCMG

Bultin, Sir Bato, Kt., MBE

Bunbury, Sir Michael William, Bt. (1681), KCVO

Bunch, Sir Austin Wyeth, Kt., CBE

Bunyard, Sir Robert Sidney, Kt., CBE, QPM

Burbidge, Sir Peter Dudley, Bt. (1916)

Burden, Sir Anthony Thomas, Kt., QPM

Burdett, Sir Savile Aylmer, Bt. (1665)

Burgen, Sir Arnold Stanley Vincent, Kt., FRS

Burgess, *Gen.* Sir Edward Arthur, KCB, OBE

Burgess, Sir (Joseph) Stuart, Kt., CBE, PHD, FRSC

Burgh, Sir John Charles, KCMG, CB

Burke, Sir James Stanley Gilbert, Bt. (I. 1797)

Burke, Sir (Thomas) Kerry, Kt.

Burnell-Nugent, *Vice-Adm.* Sir James Michael, KCB, CBE, ADC

Burnet, Sir James William Alexander (Sir Alastair Burnet), Kt.

Burnett, *Air Chief Marshal* Sir Brian Kenyon, GCB, DFC, AFC

Burnett, Sir Charles David, Bt., (1913)

Burnett, Sir John Harrison, Kt.

Burnett, Sir Walter John, Kt.

Burney, Sir Nigel Dennistoun, Bt. (1921)

Burns, Sir (Robert) Andrew, KCMG

Burnton, *Hon.* Sir Stanley Jeffrey, Kt.

Burrell, Sir John Raymond, Bt. (1774)

Burridge, *Air Chief Marshal* Sir Brian Kevin, KCB, CBE, ADC

Burston, Sir Samuel Gerald Wood, Kt., OBE

Burt, Sir Peter Alexander, Kt.

Burton, Sir Carlisle Archibald, Kt., OBE

Chisholm, Sir John Alexander Raymond, Kt., FRENG

Chitty, Sir Thomas Willes, Bt. (1924)

Cholmeley, Sir Hugh John Frederick Sebastian, Bt. (1806)

Chow, Sir Chung Kong, Kt.

Chow, Sir Henry Francis, Kt., OBE

Christie, Sir George William Langham, Kt., CH

Christie, Sir William, Kt., MBE

Christopher, Sir Duncan Robin Carmichael, KBE, CMG

Chung, Sir Sze-yuen, GBE, FRENG

Clark, Sir Francis Drake, Bt. (1886)

Clark, Sir John Arnold, Kt.

Clark, Sir Jonathan George, Bt. (1917)

Clark, Sir Robert Anthony, Kt., DSC

Clark, Sir Terence Joseph, KBE, CMG, CVO

Clark, Sir Thomas Edwin, Kt.

Clarke, Rt. Hon. Sir Anthony Peter, Kt.

Clarke, Sir Arthur Charles, Kt., CBE

Clarke, Sir (Charles Mansfield) Tobias, Bt. (1831)

Clarke, Hon. Sir Christopher Simon Courtenay Stephenson, Kt.

Clarke, Sir Christopher James, Kt., OBE

Clarke, Hon. Sir David Clive, Kt.

Clarke, Sir Ellis Emmanuel Innocent, GCMG

Clarke, Sir Jonathan Dennis, Kt.

Clarke, Maj. Sir Peter Cecil, KCVO

Clarke, Sir Robert Cyril, Kt.

†Clarke, Sir Rupert Grant Alexander, Bt. (1882)

Clay, Sir Edward, KCMG

Clay, Sir Richard Henry, Bt. (1841)

Clayton, Sir David Robert, Bt. (1732)

Cleaver, Sir Anthony Brian, Kt.

Clementi, Sir David Cecil, Kt.

Cleminson, Sir James Arnold Stacey, KBE, MC

Clerk, Sir Robert Maxwell, Bt. (1679), OBE

Clerke, Sir John Edward Longueville, Bt. (1660)

Clifford, Sir Roger Joseph, Bt. (1887)

Clifford, Sir Timothy Peter Plint, Kt.

Clothier, Sir Cecil Montacute, KCB, QC

Clucas, Sir Kenneth Henry, KCB

Clutterbuck, Vice-Adm. Sir David Granville, KBE, CB

Coates, Sir Anthony Robert Milnes, Bt. (1911)

Coates, Sir David Frederick Charlton, Bt. (1921)

Coats, Sir Alastair Francis Stuart, Bt. (1905)

Coats, Sir William David, Kt.

Cobham, Sir Michael John, Kt., CBE

Cochrane, Sir (Henry) Marc (Sursock), Bt. (1903)

Cockburn, Sir John Elliot, Bt. (S. 1671)

Cockburn-Campbell, Sir Alexander Thomas, Bt. (1821)

Cockshaw, Sir Alan, Kt., FRENG

†Codrington, Sir Christopher George Wayne, Bt. (1876)

Codrington, Sir William Alexander, Bt. (1721)

Coghill, Sir Patrick Kendal Farley, Bt. (1778)

Coghlin, Hon. Sir Patrick, Kt.

Cohen, Sir Edward, Kt.

Cohen, Sir Ivor Harold, Kt., CBE, TD

Cohen, Prof. Sir Philip, Kt., PHD, FRS

Cohen, Sir Ronald, Kt.

Cole, Sir (Robert) William, Kt.

Coleman, Sir Robert John, KCMG

Coleridge, Hon. Sir Paul James Duke, Kt.

Coles, Sir (Arthur) John, GCMG

Colfox, Sir (William) John, Bt. (1939)

Collett, Sir Christopher, GBE

Collett, Sir Ian Seymour, Bt. (1934)

Collins, Hon. Sir Andrew David, Kt.

Collins, Sir Bryan Thomas Alfred, Kt., OBE, QFSM

Collins, Sir John Alexander, Kt

Collins, Sir Kenneth Darlington, Kt.

Collins, Hon. Sir Lawrence Antony, Kt.

Collyear, Sir John Gowen, Kt.

Colman, Hon. Sir Anthony David, Kt.

Colman, Sir Michael Jeremiah, Bt. (1907)

Colman, Sir Timothy, KG

Colquhoun of Luss, Sir Ivar Iain, Bt. (1786)

Colt, Sir Edward William Dutton, Bt. (1694)

Colthurst, Sir Charles St John, Bt. (1744)

Colvin, Sir Howard Montagu, Kt., CVO, CBE, FBA

Compton, Rt. Hon. Sir John George Melvin, KCMG

Conant, Sir John Ernest Michael, Bt. (1954)

Connell, Hon. Sir Michael Bryan, Kt.

Connery, Sir Sean, Kt.

Connor, Sir William Joseph, Kt.

Conran, Sir Terence Orby, Kt.

Cons, Hon. Sir Derek, Kt.

Constantinou, Sir Georkios, Kt., OBE

Conway, Prof. Sir Gordon Richard, KCMG, FRS

Cook, Sir Christopher Wymondham Rayner Herbert, Bt. (1886)

Cooke, Col. Sir David William Perceval, Bt. (1661)

Cooke, Sir Howard Felix Hanlan, GCMG, GCVO

Cooke, Hon. Sir Jeremy Lionel, Kt.

Cooke, Prof. Sir Ronald Urwick, Kt.

Cooksey, Sir David James Scott, Kt.

Cooper, Gen. Sir George Leslie Conroy, GCB, MC

Cooper, Sir Henry, Kt.

Cooper, Sir Richard Powell, Bt. (1905)

Cooper, Sir Robert George, Kt., CBE

Cooper, Maj.-Gen. Sir Simon Christie, GCVO

Cooper, Sir William Daniel Charles, Bt. (1863)

Coote, Sir Christopher John, Bt. (I. 1621), Premier Baronet of Ireland

Copas, Most Revd Virgil, KBE, DD

Copisarow, Sir Alcon Charles, Kt.

Corbett, Maj.-Gen. Sir Robert John Swan, KCVO, CB

Corby, Sir (Frederick) Brian, Kt.

Cordy-Simpson, Lt.-Gen. Sir Roderick Alexander, KBE, CB

Corfield, Sir Kenneth George, Kt., FRENG

Cormack, Sir Patrick Thomas, Kt., MP

Corness, Sir Colin Ross, Kt.

Cornforth, Sir John Warcup, Kt., CBE, DPHIL, FRS

Corry, Sir James Michael, Bt. (1885)

Cortazzi, Sir (Henry Arthur) Hugh, GCMG

Cory, Sir (Clinton Charles) Donald, Bt. (1919)

Cory-Wright, Sir Richard Michael, Bt. (1903)

Cossons, Sir Neil, Kt., OBE

Cotter, Sir Patrick Laurence Delaval, Bt. (I. 1763)

Cotterell, Sir John Henry Geers, Bt. (1805)

Cotton, Hon. Sir Robert Carrington, KCMG

Cotton, Sir William Frederick, Kt., CBE

Cottrell, Sir Alan Howard, Kt., PHD, FRS, FRENG

†Cotts, Sir Richard Crichton Mitchell, Bt. (1921)

Couper, Sir James George, Bt. (1841)

Court, Hon. Sir Charles Walter Michael, KCMG, OBE

Courtenay, Sir Thomas Daniel, Kt.

Cousins, Air Chief Marshal Sir David, KCB, AFC

Coville, Air Marshal Sir Christopher Charles Cotton, KCB

Cowan, Gen. Sir Samuel, KCB, CBE

Coward, Vice-Adm. Sir John Francis, KCB, DSO

Cowen, Rt. Hon. Prof. Sir Zelman, GCMG, GCVO

Cowie, Sir Thomas (Tom), Kt., OBE

Cowper-Coles, Sir Sherard Louis, KCMG, LVO

Cowperthwaite, Sir John James, KBE, CMG

Cox, Sir Alan George, Kt., CBE

Cox, Prof. Sir David Roxbee, Kt.,

Cox, Sir Geoffrey Sandford, Kt., CBE

Cox, Sir George Edwin, Kt.

Cox, Vice-Adm. Sir John Michael Holland, KCB

Cradock, Rt. Hon. Sir Percy, GCMG

Craft, Prof. Sir Alan William, Kt.

Craig, Sir (Albert) James (Macqueen), GCMG

Craig-Cooper, Sir (Frederick Howard) Michael, Kt., CBE, TD

Crane, Hon. Sir Peter Francis, Kt.

Crane, Prof. Sir Peter Robert, Kt.

Craufurd, Sir Robert James, Bt. (1781)

Craven, Sir John Anthony, Kt.

Craven, Sir Philip Lee, Kt., MBE

Crawford, *Prof.* Sir Frederick William, Kt., FRENG

Crawley-Boevey, Sir Thomas Michael Blake, Bt. (1784)

Crew, Sir (Michael) Edward, Kt., QPM

Cresswell, *Hon.* Sir Peter John, Kt.

Crichton-Brown, Sir Robert, KCMG, CBE, TD

Crick, *Prof.* Sir Bernard, Kt.

Crill, Sir Peter Leslie, KBE

Crisp, Sir Edmund Nigel Ramsay, KCB

Crisp, Sir (John) Peter, Bt. (1913)

†Critchett, Sir Charles George Montague, Bt. (1908)

Crockett, Sir Andrew Duncan, Kt.

Croft, Sir Owen Glendower, Bt. (1671)

Croft, Sir Thomas Stephen Hutton, Bt. (1818)

†Crofton, Sir Hugh Denis, Bt. (1801)

Crofton, *Prof.* Sir John Wenman, Kt.

†Crofton, Sir Julian Malby, Bt. (1838)

Crompton, Sir Dan, Kt., CBE, QPM

Crossland, *Prof.* Sir Bernard, Kt., CBE, FRENG

Crossley, Sir Sloan Nicholas, Bt. (1909)

Crowe, Sir Brian Lee, KCMG

Cruthers, Sir James Winter, Kt.

Cubbon, Sir Brian Crossland, GCB

Cubitt, Sir Hugh Guy, Kt., CBE

Cullen, Sir (Edward) John, Kt., FRENG

Culme-Seymour, Sir Michael Patrick, Bt. (1809)

Culpin, Sir Robert Paul, Kt.

Cummins, Sir Michael John Austin, Kt.

Cunliffe, Sir David Ellis, Bt. (1759)

Cunliffe-Owen, Sir Hugo Dudley, Bt. (1920)

Cunningham, *Lt.-Gen.* Sir Hugh Patrick, KBE

Cunynghame, Sir Andrew David Francis, Bt. (S. 1702)

†Currie, Sir Donald Scott, Bt. (1847)

Curry, Sir Donald Thomas Younger, Kt., CBE

Curtain, Sir Michael, KBE

Curtis, Sir Barry John, Kt.

Curtis, *Hon.* Sir Richard Herbert, Kt.

Curtis, Sir William Peter, Bt. (1802)

Curtiss, *Air Marshal* Sir John Bagot, KCB, KBE

Curwen, Sir Christopher Keith, KCMG

Cuschieri, *Prof.* Sir Alfred, Kt.

Cutler, Sir Charles Benjamin, KBE, ED

Dain, Sir David John Michael, KCVO

Dales, Sir Richard Nigel, KCVO

Dalrymple-Hay, Sir James Brian, Bt. (1798)

Dalrymple-White, *Wg Cdr.* Sir Henry Arthur, Bt., DFC (1926)

Dalton, Sir Alan Nugent Goring, Kt., CBE

Dalton, *Vice-Adm.* Sir Geoffrey Thomas James Oliver, KCB

Dalton, Sir Richard John, KCMG

Dalyell, Sir Tam (Thomas), Bt. (NS 1685)

Daniel, Sir John Sagar, Kt., DSC

Dannatt, *Lt.-Gen.* Sir Francis Richard, KCB, CBE

Darby, Sir Peter Howard, Kt., CBE, QFSM

Darell, Sir Jeffrey Lionel, Bt., MC (1795)

Darling, Sir Clifford, GCVO

Darrington, Sir Michael John, Kt.

Dasgupta, *Prof.* Sir Partha Sarathi, Kt.

†Dashwood, Sir Edward John Francis, Bt. (1707), *Premier Baronet of Great Britain*

Dashwood, Sir Richard James, Bt. (1684)

Daunt, Sir Timothy Lewis Achilles, KCMG

Davenport-Handley, Sir David John, Kt., OBE

David, Sir Jean Marc, Kt., CBE, QC

David, *His Hon.* Sir Robin (Robert) Daniel George, Kt.,

Davidson, Sir Robert James, Kt., FRENG

Davies, Sir Alan Seymour, Kt.

Davies, *Hon.* Sir (Alfred William) Michael, Kt.

Davies, Sir (Charles) Noel, Kt.

Davies, *Prof.* Sir David Evan Naughton, Kt., CBE, FRS, FRENG

Davies, *Hon.* Sir (David Herbert) Mervyn, Kt., MC, TD

Davies, Sir David John, Kt.

Davies, Sir Frank John, Kt., CBE

Davies, *Prof.* Sir Graeme John, Kt., FRENG

Davies, Sir John Howard, Kt.

Davies, Sir John Michael, KCB

Davies, *Vice-Adm.* Sir Lancelot Richard Bell, KBE

Davies, Sir Peter Maxwell, Kt., CBE

Davies, *Prof. Sir Robert Rees, Kt., CBE*

Davies, Sir Rhys Everson, Kt., QC

Davis, Sir Andrew Frank, Kt., CBE

Davis, Sir Colin Rex, Kt., CH, CBE

Davis, Sir Crispin Henry Lamert, Kt.

Davis, Sir John Gilbert, Bt. (1946)

Davis, *Hon.* Sir Nigel Anthony Lambert, Kt.

Davis, Sir Peter John, Kt.

Davis, *Hon.* Sir Thomas Robert Alexander Harries, KBE

Davis-Goff, Sir Robert (William), Bt. (1905)

Davison, *Rt. Hon.* Sir Ronald Keith, GBE, CMG

†Davson, Sir George Trenchard Simon, Bt. (1927)

Dawanincura, Sir John Norbert, Kt., OBE

Dawbarn, Sir Simon Yelverton, KCVO, CMG

Dawson, *Hon.* Sir Daryl Michael, KBE, CB

Dawson, Sir Hugh Michael Trevor, Bt. (1920)

Dawtry, Sir Alan (Graham), Kt., CBE, TD

Day, Sir Derek Malcolm, KCMG

Day, *Air Chief Marshal* Sir John Romney, KCB, OBE, ADC

Day, Sir (Judson) Graham, Kt.

Day, Sir Michael John, Kt., OBE

Day, Sir Simon James, Kt.

Deane, *Hon.* Sir William Patrick, KBE

Dear, Sir Geoffrey James, Kt., QPM

Dearlove, Sir Richard Billing, KCMG, OBE

de Bellaigue, Sir Geoffrey, GCVO

†Debenham, Sir Thomas Adam, Bt. (1931)

de Deney, Sir Geoffrey Ivor, KCVO

Deeny, *Hon.* Sir Donnell Justin Patrick, Kt.

de Hoghton, Sir (Richard) Bernard (Cuthbert), Bt. (1611)

De la Bère, Sir Cameron, Bt. (1953)

de la Rue, Sir Andrew George Ilay, Bt. (1898)

Dellow, Sir John Albert, Kt., CBE

Delves, *Lt.-Gen.* Sir Cedric Norman George, KBE

Denholm, Sir John Ferguson (Ian), Kt., CBE

Denison-Smith, *Lt.-Gen.* Sir Anthony Arthur, KBE

Denman, Sir (George) Roy, KCB, CMG

Denny, Sir Anthony Coningham de Waltham, Bt. (I. 1782)

Denny, Sir Charles Alistair Maurice, Bt. (1913)

Denton, *Prof.* Sir Eric James, Kt., CBE, FRS

Derbyshire, Sir Andrew George, Kt.

Derham, Sir Peter John, Kt.

de Trafford, Sir Dermot Humphrey, Bt. (1841)

Deverell, *Gen.* Sir John Freegard, KCB, OBE

Devesi, Sir Baddeley, GCMG, GCVO

De Ville, Sir Harold Godfrey Oscar, Kt., CBE

Devitt, Sir James Hugh Thomas, Bt. (1916)

de Waal, Sir (Constant Henrik) Henry, KCB, QC

Dewey, Sir Anthony Hugh, Bt. (1917)

Dewhurst, *Prof.* Sir (Christopher) John, Kt.

De Witt, Sir Ronald Wayne, Kt.

Dhenin, *Air Marshal* Sir Geoffrey Howard, KBE, AFC, GM, MD

Dhrangadhra, HH the Maharaja Raj Saheb of, KCIE

Dick-Lauder, Sir Piers Robert, Bt. (S. 1690)

Dickinson, Sir Harold Herbert, Kt.

Dilke, Sir Charles John Wentworth, Bt. (1862)

Dillwyn-Venables-Llewelyn, Sir John Michael, Bt. (1890)

Dixon, Sir Jeremy, Kt.

Dixon, Sir Jonathan Mark, Bt. (1919)

Djanogly, Sir Harry Ari Simon, Kt., CBE

Dobson, *Vice-Adm.* Sir David Stuart, KBE

Dodds, Sir Ralph Jordan, Bt. (1964)
Dodds-Parker, Sir (Arthur) Douglas, Kt.
Dollery, Sir Colin Terence, Kt.
Don-Wauchope, Sir Roger (Hamilton), Bt. (S. 1667)
Donald, Sir Alan Ewen, KCMG
Donald, Air Marshal Sir John George, KBE
Donaldson, Prof. Sir Liam Joseph, Kt.
Donne, Hon. Sir Gaven John, KBE
Donne, Sir John Christopher, Kt.
Donnelly, Sir Joseph Brian, KBE, CMG
Dookun, Sir Dewoonarain, Kt.
Dorey, Sir Graham Martyn, Kt.
Dorman, Sir Philip Henry Keppel, Bt. (1923)
Doughty, Sir Graham Martin, Kt.
Doughty, Sir William Roland, Kt.
Douglas, Hon. Sir Roger Owen, Kt.
Dover, Prof. Sir Kenneth James, Kt., DLITT, FBA, FRSE
Dowell, Sir Anthony James, Kt., CBE
Dowling, Sir Robert, Kt.
Downes, Sir Edward Thomas, Kt., CBE
Downey, Sir Gordon Stanley, KCB
Downs, Sir Diarmuid, Kt., CBE, FRENG
Downward, Maj.-Gen. Sir Peter Aldcroft, KCVO, CB, DSO, DFC
Dowson, Sir Philip Manning, Kt., CBE, PRA
Doyle, Sir Reginald Derek Henry, Kt., CBE
D'Oyly, Sir Hadley Gregory Bt. (1663)
Drake, Hon. Sir (Frederick) Maurice, Kt., DFC
Drewry, Lt.-Gen. Sir Christopher Francis, KCB, CBE
Drinkwater, Sir John Muir, Kt., QC
Driver, Sir Eric William, Kt.
Drummond, Sir John Richard Gray, Kt., CBE
Drury, Sir (Victor William) Michael, Kt., OBE
Dryden, Sir John Stephen Gyles, Bt. (1733 and 1795)
du Cann, Rt. Hon. Sir Edward Dillon Lott, KBE
†Duckworth, Sir Edward Richard Dyce, Bt. (1909)
du Cros, Sir Claude Philip Arthur Mallet, Bt. (1916)
Dudley-Williams, Sir Alastair Edgcumbe James, Bt. (1964)
Duff-Gordon, Sir Andrew Cosmo Lewis, Bt. (1813)
Duffell, Lt.-Gen. Sir Peter Royson, KCB, CBE, MC
Duffy, Sir (Albert) (Edward) Patrick, Kt., PHD
Dugdale, Sir William Stratford, Bt., MC (1936)
Duggin, Sir Thomas Joseph, Kt.
Dummett, Prof. Sir Michael Anthony Eardley, Kt., FBA
Dunbar, Sir Archibald Ranulph, Bt. (S. 1700)

Dunbar, Sir Robert Drummond Cospatrick, Bt. (S. 1698)
Dunbar, Sir James Michael, Bt. (S. 1694)
Dunbar of Hempriggs, Sir Richard Francis, Bt. (S. 1706)
Dunbar-Nasmith, Prof. Sir James Duncan, Kt., CBE
Duncan, Sir James Blair, Kt.
Dunlop, Sir Thomas, Bt. (1916)
Dunn, Air Marshal Sir Eric Clive, KBE, CB, BEM
Dunn, Rt. Hon. Sir Robin Horace Walford, Kt., MC
Dunne, Sir Thomas Raymond, KCVO
Dunning, Sir Simon William Patrick, Bt. (1930)
Dunnington-Jefferson, Sir Mervyn Stewart, Bt. (1958)
Dunstan, Lt.-Gen. Sir Donald Beaumont, KBE, CB
Dunt, Vice-Adm. Sir John Hugh, KCB
Duntze, Sir Daniel Evans, Bt. (1774)
Dupre, Sir Tumun, Kt., MBE
Dupree, Sir Peter, Bt. (1921)
Durand, Sir Edward Alan Christopher David Percy, Bt. (1892)
Durant, Sir (Robert) Anthony (Bevis), Kt.
Durie, Sir David Robert Campbell, KCMG
Durrant, Sir William Alexander Estridge, Bt. (1784)
Duthie, Prof. Sir Herbert Livingston, Kt.
Duthie, Sir Robert Grieve (Robin), Kt., CBE
Dwyer, Sir Joseph Anthony, Kt.
Dyke, Sir David William Hart, Bt. (1677)
Dyson, Rt. Hon. Sir John Anthony, Kt.
Eady, Hon. Sir David, Kt.
Eardley-Wilmot, Sir Michael John Assheton, Bt. (1821)
Earle, Sir (Hardman) George (Algernon), Bt. (1869)
Easton, Sir Robert William Simpson, Kt., CBE
Eaton, Adm. Sir Kenneth John, GBE, KCB
Eberle, Adm. Sir James Henry Fuller, GCB
Ebrahim, Sir (Mahomed) Currimbhoy, Bt. (1910)
Echlin, Sir Norman David Fenton, Bt. (I. 1721)
Eckersley, Sir Donald Payze, Kt., OBE
Eddington, Sir Roderick Ian, Kt.
Edge, Capt. Sir (Philip) Malcolm, KCVO
†Edge, Sir William, Bt. (1937)
Edmonstone, Sir Archibald Bruce Charles, Bt. (1774)
Edward, Sir David Alexander Ogilvy, KCMG
Edwardes, Sir Michael Owen, Kt.
Edwards, Sir Christopher John Churchill, Bt. (1866)

Edwards, Sir Llewellyn Roy, Kt.
Edwards, Prof. Sir Samuel Frederick, Kt., FRS
†Edwards-Moss, Sir David John, Bt. (1868)
Egan, Sir John Leopold, Kt.
Egerton, Sir Stephen Loftus, KCMG
Eichelbaum, Rt. Hon. Sir Thomas, GBE
Elias, Hon. Sir Patrick, Kt.
Eliott of Stobs, Sir Charles Joseph Alexander, Bt. (S. 1666)
Elliot, Sir Gerald Henry, Kt.
Elliott, Sir Clive Christopher Hugh, Bt. (1917)
Elliott, Sir David Murray, KCMG, CB
Elliott, Prof. Sir John Huxtable, Kt., FBA
Elliott, Sir Randal Forbes, KBE
Elliott, Prof. Sir Roger James, Kt., FRS
Ellis, Sir Ronald, Kt., FRENG
Elphinstone, Sir John, Bt. (S. 1701)
Elphinstone, Sir John Howard Main, Bt. (1816)
Elsmore, Sir Lloyd, Kt., OBE
Elton, Sir Arnold, Kt., CBE
Elton, Sir Charles Abraham Grierson, Bt. (1717)
Elton, Sir Leslie, Kt.
Elwes, Sir Jeremy Vernon, Kt., CBE
Elwood, Sir Brian George Conway, Kt., CBE
Elworthy, Air Cdre. Hon. Sir Timothy Charles, KCVO, CBE
Empey, Sir Reginald Norman Morgan, Kt., OBE
Enderby, Prof. Sir John Edwin, Kt. CBE, FRS
Engle, Sir George Lawrence Jose, KCB, QC
English, Sir Terence Alexander Hawthorne, KBE, FRCS
Epstein, Prof. Sir (Michael) Anthony, Kt., CBE, FRS
Errington, Col. Sir Geoffrey Frederick, Bt. (1963), OBE
Errington, Sir Lancelot, KCB
Erskine, Sir (Thomas) David, Bt. (1821)
Erskine-Hill, Sir Alexander Rodger, Bt. (1945)
Esmonde, Sir Thomas Francis Grattan, Bt. (I. 1629)
Esplen, Sir John Graham, Bt. (1921)
Essenhigh, Adm. Sir Nigel Richard, GCB
Etherton, Hon. Sir Terence Michael Elkan Barnet, Kt.
Evans, Sir Anthony Adney, Bt. (1920)
Evans, Rt. Hon. Sir Anthony Howell Meurig, Kt., RD
Evans, Prof. Sir Christopher Thomas, Kt., OBE
Evans, Air Chief Marshal Sir David George, GCB, CBE
Evans, Hon. Sir David Roderick, Kt.
Evans, Sir Harold Matthew, Kt.
Evans, Hon. Sir Haydn Tudor, Kt.
Evans, Prof. Sir John Grimley, Kt., FRCP
Evans, Sir John Stanley, Kt., QPM

Evans, *Prof.* Sir Martin John, Kt., FRS

Evans, Sir Richard Harry, Kt., CBE

Evans, Sir Richard Mark, KCMG, KCVO

Evans, Sir Robert, Kt., CBE, FRENG

Evans, Sir (William) Vincent (John), GCMG, MBE, QC

Evans-Lombe, *Hon.* Sir Edward Christopher, Kt.

†Evans-Tipping, Sir David Gwynne, Bt. (1913)

Eveleigh, *Rt. Hon.* Sir Edward Walter, Kt., ERD

Everard, Sir Robin Charles, Bt. (1911)

Every, Sir Henry John Michael, Bt. (1641)

Ewans, Sir Martin Kenneth, KCMG

†Ewart, Sir William Michael, Bt. (1887)

Ewbank, *Hon.* Sir Anthony Bruce, Kt.

Eyre, Sir Reginald Edwin, Kt.

Eyre, Sir Richard Charles Hastings, Kt., CBE

Faber, Sir Richard Stanley, KCVO, CMG

Fagge, Sir John Christopher Frederick, Bt. (1660)

Fairbairn, Sir (James) Brooke, Bt. (1869)

Fairhall, *Hon.* Sir Allen, KBE

Fairlie-Cuninghame, Sir Robert Henry, Bt. (S. 1630)

Fairweather, Sir Patrick Stanislaus, KCMG

Falconer, *Hon.* Sir Douglas William, Kt., MBE

†Falkiner, Sir Benjamin Simon Patrick, Bt. (I. 1778)

Fall, Sir Brian James Proetel, GCVO, KCMG

Falle, Sir Samuel, KCMG, KCVO, DSC

Fang, *Prof.* Sir Harry, Kt., CBE

Fareed, Sir Djamil Sheik, Kt.

Farmer, Sir Thomas, Kt., CBE

Farquhar, Sir Michael Fitzroy Henry, Bt. (1796)

Farquharson, *Rt. Hon.* Sir Donald Henry, Kt.

Farrar-Hockley, *Gen.* Sir Anthony Heritage, GBE, KCB, DSO, MC

Farrell, Sir Terence, Kt., CBE

Farrer, Sir (Charles) Matthew, GCVO

†Farrington, Sir Henry William, Bt. (1818)

Fat, Sir (Maxime) Edouard (Lim Man) Lim, Kt.

Faulkner, Sir (James) Dennis (Compton), Kt., CBE, VRD

Fay, Sir (Humphrey) Michael Gerard, Kt.

Fayrer, Sir John Lang Macpherson, Bt. (1896)

Fearn, Sir (Patrick) Robin, KCMG

Feilden, Sir Bernard Melchior, Kt., CBE

Feilden, Sir Henry Wemyss, Bt. (1846)

Fell, Sir David, KCB

Fender, Sir Brian Edward Frederick, Kt., CMG, PHD

Fenn, Sir Nicholas Maxted, GCMG

Fennell, *Hon.* Sir (John) Desmond Augustine, Kt., OBE

Fennessy, Sir Edward, Kt., CBE

Fergus, Sir Howard Archibald, KBE

Ferguson, Sir Alexander Chapman, Kt., CBE

Ferguson-Davie, Sir Michael, Bt. (1847)

Fergusson of Kilkerran, Sir Charles, Bt. (S. 1703)

Fergusson, Sir Ewan Alastair John, GCMG, GCVO

Fermor, Sir Patrick Michael Leigh, Kt., DSO, OBE

Feroze, Sir Rustam Moolan, Kt., FRCS

Fersht, *Prof.* Sir Alan Roy, Kt., FRS

Ferris, *Hon.* Sir Francis Mursell, Kt., TD

ffolkes, Sir Robert Francis Alexander, Bt., OBE (1774)

Field, Sir Malcolm David, Kt.

Field, *Hon.* Sir Richard Alan, Kt.

Fielding, Sir Colin Cunningham, Kt., CB

Fielding, Sir Leslie, KCMG

Fields, Sir Allan Clifford, KCMG

Fieldsend, *Hon.* Sir John Charles Rowell, KBE

Fiennes, Sir Ranulph Twisleton-Wykeham, Bt. (1916), OBE

Figg, Sir Leonard Clifford William, KCMG

Figgis, Sir Anthony St John Howard, KCVO, CMG

Figures, Sir Colin Frederick, KCMG, OBE

Finch, Sir Robert Gerard, Kt.

Finlay, Sir David Ronald James Bell, Bt. (1964)

Finney, Sir Thomas, Kt., OBE

Fisher, Sir George Read, Kt., CMG

Fison, Sir (Richard) Guy, Bt. (1905), DSC

Fitzalan-Howard, *Maj.-Gen.* Lord Michael, GCVO, CB, CBE, MC

†Fitzgerald, *Revd* Daniel Patrick, Bt. (1903)

FitzGerald, Sir Adrian James Andrew, Bt. (1880)

FitzHerbert, Sir Richard Ranulph, Bt. (1784)

Fitzpatrick, *Air Marshal* Sir John Bernard, KBE, CB

Flanagan, Sir Ronald, GBE

Fletcher, Sir James Muir Cameron, Kt.

Floissac, *Hon.* Sir Vincent Frederick, Kt., CMG, OBE

Floud, *Prof.* Sir Roderick Castle, Kt.

Floyd, Sir Giles Henry Charles, Bt. (1816)

Foley, *Lt.-Gen.* Sir John Paul, KCB, OBE, MC

Foley, Sir (Thomas John) Noel, Kt., CBE

Follett, *Prof.* Sir Brian Keith, Kt., FRS

Foot, Sir Geoffrey James, Kt.

Foots, Sir James William, Kt.

Forbes, *Maj.* Sir Hamish Stewart, Bt. (1823), MBE, MC

Forbes, *Adm.* Sir Ian Andrew, KCB, CBE

Forbes of Craigievar, Sir John Alexander Cumnock, Bt. (S. 1630)

Forbes, *Vice-Adm.* Sir John Morrison, KCB

Forbes, *Hon.* Sir Thayne John, Kt.

Forbes-Leith, Sir George Ian David, Bt. (1923)

Ford, Sir Andrew Russell, Bt. (1929)

Ford, Sir David Robert, KBE, LVO

Ford, *Maj.* Sir Edward William Spencer, GCVO, KCB, ERD

Ford, *Air Marshal* Sir Geoffrey Harold, KBE, CB, FRENG

Ford, *Prof.* Sir Hugh, Kt., FRS, FRENG

Ford, Sir John Archibald, KCMG, MC

Ford, *Gen.* Sir Robert Cyril, GCB, CBE

Foreman, Sir Philip Frank, Kt., CBE, FRENG

Forestier-Walker, Sir Michael Leolin, Bt. (1835)

Forman, Sir John Denis, Kt., OBE

Forrest, *Prof.* Sir (Andrew) Patrick (McEwen), Kt.

Forte, *Hon.* Sir Rocco John Vincent, Kt.

Forwood, Sir Peter Noel, Bt. (1895)

Foster, Sir Andrew William, Kt.

Foster, *Prof.* Sir Christopher David, Kt.

Foster, Sir John Gregory, Bt. (1930)

Foster, Sir Robert Sidney, GCMG, KCVO

Foulkes, Sir Arther Alexander, KCMG

Foulkes, Sir Nigel Gordon, Kt.

Fountain, *Hon.* Sir Cyril Stanley Smith, Kt.

Fowden, Sir Leslie, Kt., FRS

Fowke, Sir David Frederick Gustavus, Bt. (1814)

Fowler, Sir (Edward) Michael Coulson, Kt.

Fox, *Rt. Hon.* Sir Michael John, Kt.

Fox, Sir Paul Leonard, Kt., CBE

France, Sir Christopher Walter, GCB

Francis, Sir Horace William Alexander, Kt., CBE, FRENG

Frank, Sir Robert Andrew, Bt. (1920)

Franklin, Sir Michael David Milroy, KCB, CMG

Franks, Sir Arthur Temple, KCMG

Fraser, Sir Alasdair MacLeod, Kt.

Fraser, Sir Charles Annand, KCVO

Fraser, *Gen.* Sir David William, GCB, OBE

Fraser, Sir Iain Michael Duncan, Bt. (1943)

Fraser, Sir (James) Campbell, Kt.

Fraser, Sir James Murdo, KBE

Fraser, Sir William Kerr, GCB

Frayling, *Prof.* Sir Christopher John, Kt.

Frederick, Sir Christopher St John, Bt. (1723)

Freedman, *Prof.* Sir Lawrence David, KCMG, GBE

Freeland, Sir John Redvers, KCMG

Freeman, Sir James Robin, Bt. (1945)

Freer, *Air Chief Marshal* Sir Robert William George, GBE, KCB

French, *Air Marshal* Sir Joseph
  Charles, KCB, CBE
Frere, *Vice-Adm.* Sir Richard Tobias,
  KCB
Fretwell, Sir (Major) John (Emsley),
  GCMG
Freud, Sir Clement Raphael, Kt.
Friend *Prof.* Sir Richard Henry, Kt.
Froggatt, Sir Leslie Trevor, Kt.
Froggatt, Sir Peter, Kt.
Frossard, Sir Charles Keith, KBE
Frost, Sir David Paradine, Kt., OBE
Fry, Sir Peter Derek, Kt.
Fry, *Lt.-Gen.* Sir Robert Allan, KCB,
  CBE
Fulford, *Hon.* Sir Adrian Bruce, Kt.
Fuller, Sir James Henry Fleetwood,
  Bt. (1910)
Fuller, *Hon.* Sir John Bryan Munro,
  Kt.
Fulton, *Lt.-Gen.* Sir Robert Henry
  Gervase, KBE
Furness, Sir Stephen Roberts, Bt.
  (1913)
Gadsden, Sir Peter Drury
  Haggerston, GBE, FRENG
Gage, *Hon.* Sir William Marcus, Kt.,
  PC
Gains, Sir John Christopher, Kt.
Gainsford, Sir Ian Derek, Kt., DDS
Gaius, *Rt. Revd* Saimon, KBE
Galsworthy, Sir Anthony Charles,
  KCMG
Galway, Sir James, Kt., OBE
Gamble, Sir David Hugh Norman,
  Bt. (1897)
Gambon, Sir Michael John, Kt., CBE
Gardiner, Sir John Eliot, Kt., CBE
Gardner, *Prof.* Sir Richard Lavenham,
  Kt.
Gardner, Sir Roy Alan, Kt.
Garland, *Hon.* Sir Patrick Neville, Kt.
Garland, *Hon.* Sir Ransley Victor,
  KBE
Garner, Sir Anthony Stuart, Kt.
Garnett, *Adm.* Sir Ian David Graham,
  KCB
Garnier, *Rear-Adm.* Sir John, KCVO,
  CBE
Garrard, Sir David Eardley, Kt.
Garrett, Sir Anthony Peter, Kt., CBE
Garrick, Sir Ronald, Kt., CBE,
  FRENG
Garrioch, Sir (William) Henry, Kt.
Garrod, *Lt.-Gen.* Sir (John) Martin
  Carruthers, KCB, OBE
Garthwaite, Sir (William) Mark
  (Charles), Bt. (1919)
Gaskell, Sir Richard Kennedy
  Harvey, Kt.
Geno, Sir Makena Viora, KBE
Gent, Sir Christopher Charles, Kt.
George, Sir Arthur Thomas, Kt.
George, *Prof.* Sir Charles Frederick,
  MD, FRCP
George, Sir Richard William, Kt.,
  CVO
Gerken, *Vice-Adm.* Sir Robert
  William Frank, KCB, CBE
Gershon, Sir Peter Oliver, Kt., CBE
Gethin, Sir Richard Joseph St
  Lawrence, Bt. (I. 1665)

Ghurburrun, Sir Rabindrah, Kt.
Gibb, Sir Francis Ross (Frank), Kt.,
  CBE, FRENG
Gibbings, Sir Peter Walter, Kt.
Gibbons, Sir (John) David, KBE
Gibbons, Sir William Edward Doran,
  Bt. (1752)
Gibbs, *Hon.* Sir Richard John Hedley,
  Kt.
Gibbs, Sir Roger Geoffrey, Kt.
†Gibson, *Revd* Christopher Herbert,
  Bt. (1931)
Gibson, Sir Ian, Kt., CBE
Gibson, *Rt. Hon.* Sir Peter Leslie, Kt.
Gibson-Craig-Carmichael, Sir David
  Peter William, Bt. (S. 1702 and
  1831)
Giddings, *Air Marshal* Sir (Kenneth
  Charles) Michael, KCB, OBE, DFC,
  AFC
Gieve, Sir Edward John Watson, KCB
Giffard, Sir (Charles) Sydney
  (Rycroft), KCMG
Gilbart-Denham, *Lt.-Col.* Sir
  Seymour Vivian, KCVO
Gilbert, *Air Chief Marshal* Sir Joseph
  Alfred, KCB, CBE
Gilbert, Sir Martin John, Kt., CBE
†Gilbey, Sir Walter Gavin, Bt. (1893)
Gill, Sir Anthony Keith, Kt.
Gill, Sir Arthur Benjamin Norman,
  Kt., CBE
Gillam, Sir Patrick John, Kt.
Gillen, *Hon.* Sir John de Winter, Kt.
Gillett, Sir Robin Danvers Penrose,
  Bt. (1959), GBE, RD
Gillinson, Sir Clive Daniel, Kt., CBE
Gilmour, Sir John Edward, Bt.
  (1897), DSO, TD
Gina, Sir Lloyd Maepeza, KBE
Gingell, *Air Chief Marshal* Sir John,
  GBE, KCB, KCVO
Girolami, Sir Paul, Kt.
Girvan, *Hon.* Sir (Frederick) Paul, Kt.
Gladstone, Sir (Erskine) William, Bt.
  (1846), KG
Glenn, Sir (Joseph Robert) Archibald,
  Kt., OBE
Glidewell, *Rt. Hon.* Sir Iain Derek
  Laing, Kt.
Glover, Sir Victor Joseph Patrick, Kt.
Glyn, Sir Richard Lindsay, Bt. (1759
  and 1800)
Gobbo, Sir James Augustine, Kt., AC
Godber, Sir George Edward, GCB,
  DM
Goldberg, *Prof.* Sir Abraham, Kt.,
  MD, DSC, FRCP
Goldberg, *Prof.* Sir David Paul
  Brandes, Kt.
Goldman, Sir Samuel, KCB
Goldring, *Hon.* Sir John Bernard, Kt.
Gomersall, Sir Stephen John, KCMG
Gonsalves-Sabola, *Hon.* Sir Joaquim
  Claudino, Kt
†Gooch, Sir Miles Peter, Bt. (1866)
Gooch, Sir Timothy Robert, Bt.
  (1746), MBE
Goodall, Sir (Arthur) David Saunders,
  GCMG
Goodall, *Air Marshal* Sir Roderick
  Harvey, KBE, CB, AFC

Goode, *Prof.* Sir Royston Miles, Kt.,
  CBE, QC
Goodenough, Sir Anthony Michael,
  KCMG
Goodenough, Sir William McLernon,
  Bt. (1943)
Goodhart, Sir Philip Carter, Kt.
Goodhart, Sir Robert Anthony
  Gordon, Bt. (1911)
Goodhew, Sir Victor Henry, Kt.
Goodison, Sir Alan Clowes, KCMG
Goodison, Sir Nicholas Proctor, Kt.
Goodman, Sir Patrick Ledger, Kt.,
  CBE
Goodson, Sir Mark Weston Lassam,
  Bt. (1922)
Goodwin, Sir Frederick, KBE
Goodwin, Sir Frederick Anderson, Kt.
Goodwin, Sir Matthew Dean, Kt.,
  CBE
Goody, *Prof.* Sir John Rankine, Kt.
†Goold, Sir George William, Bt.
  (1801)
Gordon, Sir Charles Addison
  Somerville Snowden, KCB
Gordon, Sir Donald, Kt.
Gordon, Sir Gerald Henry, Kt., CBE,
  QC
Gordon, Sir Robert James, Bt.
  (S. 1706)
Gordon, Sir Sidney Samuel, Kt., CBE
Gordon-Cumming, Sir Alexander
  Penrose, Bt. (1804)
Gordon Lennox, Lord Nicholas
  Charles, KCMG, KCVO
†Gore, Sir Nigel Hugh St George, Bt.
  (I. 1622)
Gore-Booth, Sir Josslyn Henry
  Robert, Bt. (I. 1760)
Gorham, Sir Richard Masters, Kt.,
  CBE, DFC
Goring, Sir William Burton Nigel, Bt.
  (1627)
Gorman, Sir John Reginald, Kt., CVO,
  CBE, MC
Gorst, Sir John Michael, Kt.
Goschen, Sir (Edward) Alexander, Bt.
  (1916)
Gosling, Sir (Frederick) Donald,
  KCVO
Goswell, Sir Brian Lawrence, Kt.
Gough, Sir Charles Brandon, Kt.
Goulden, Sir (Peter) John, GCMG
Goulding, Sir Marrack Irvine,
  KCMG
Goulding, Sir (William) Lingard
  Walter, Bt. (1904)
Gourlay, *Gen.* Sir (Basil) Ian
  (Spencer), KCB, OBE, MC, RM
Gourlay, Sir Simon Alexander, Kt.
Govan, Sir Lawrence Herbert, Kt.
Gow, *Gen.* Sir (James) Michael, GCB
Gowans, Sir James Learmonth, Kt.,
  CBE, FRCP, FRS
†Graaff, Sir David de Villiers, Bt.
  (1911)
Grabham, Sir Anthony Henry, Kt.
Graham, Sir Alexander Michael, GBE
Graham, Sir James Bellingham, Bt.
  (1662)
Graham, Sir James Fergus Surtees, Bt.
  (1783)

Graham, Sir James Thompson, Kt.,
CMG
Graham, Sir John Alexander Noble,
Bt. (1906), GCMG
Graham, Sir John Alistair, Kt.
Graham, Sir John Moodie, Bt. (1964)
Graham, Sir Norman William, Kt., CB
Graham, Sir Peter, KCB, QC
Graham, Sir Peter Alfred, Kt., OBE
Graham, *Lt.-Gen.* Sir Peter Walter,
KCB, CBE
†Graham, Sir Ralph Stuart, Bt.
(1629)
Graham-Moon, Sir Peter Wilfred
Giles, Bt. (1855)
Graham-Smith, *Prof.* Sir Francis, Kt.
Granger, *Prof.* Sir Clive William John,
Kt.
Grant, Sir Archibald, Bt. (S. 1705)
Grant, Sir Clifford, Kt.
Grant, Sir (John) Anthony, Kt.
Grant, Sir John Douglas Kelso,
KCMG
Grant, Sir Patrick Alexander
Benedict, Bt. (S. 1688)
Grant, *Lt.-Gen.* Sir Scott Carnegie,
KCB
Grant-Suttie, Sir James Edward, Bt.
(S. 1702)
Granville-Chapman, *Lt.-Gen.* Sir
Timothy John, KCB, CBE
Gratton-Bellew, Sir Henry Charles,
Bt. (1838)
Gray, *Hon.* Sir Charles Anthony St
John, Kt.
Gray, *Prof.* Sir Denis John Pereira,
Kt., OBE, FRCGP
Gray, Sir John Archibald Browne, Kt.,
SCD, FRS
Gray, *Dr.* Sir John Armstrong Muir,
Kt., CBE
Gray, *Lt. Gen.* Sir Michael Stuart,
KCB, OBE
Gray, Sir Robert McDowall (Robin),
Kt.
Gray, Sir William Hume, Bt. (1917)
Graydon, *Air Chief Marshal* Sir
Michael James, GCB, CBE
Grayson, Sir Jeremy Brian Vincent
Harrington, Bt. (1922)
Green, Sir Allan David, KCB, QC
Green, Sir Andrew Fleming, KCMG
†Green, Sir Edward Patrick Lycett,
Bt. (1886)
Green, Sir Gregory David, KCMG
Green, *Hon.* Sir Guy Stephen
Montague, KBE
Green, Sir Kenneth, Kt.
Green, Sir Owen Whitley, Kt.
Green-Price, Sir Robert John, Bt.
(1874)
Greenaway, Sir John Michael
Burdick, Bt. (1933)
Greenbury, Sir Richard, Kt.
Greener, Sir Anthony Armitage, Kt.
Greengross, Sir Alan David, Kt.
Greening, *Rear-Adm.* Sir Paul
Woollven, GCVO
Greenstock, Sir Jeremy Quentin,
GCMG
Greenwell, Sir Edward Bernard, Bt.
(1906)

Gregson, Sir Peter Lewis, GCB
Greig, Sir (Henry Louis) Carron,
KCVO, CBE
Grey, Sir Anthony Dysart, Bt. (1814)
Grey-Egerton, Sir (Philip) John
(Caledon), Bt. (1617)
Grierson, Sir Michael John Bewes,
Bt. (S. 1685)
Grierson, Sir Ronald Hugh, Kt.
Griffin, *Maj.* Sir (Arthur) John
(Stewart), KCVO
Griffiths, Sir Eldon Wylie, Kt.
Grigson, *Hon.* Sir Geoffrey Douglas,
Kt.
Grimshaw, Sir Nicholas Thomas, Kt.,
CBE
Grimwade, Sir Andrew Sheppard,
Kt., CBE
Grindrod, *Most Revd* John Basil
Rowland, KBE
Grinstead, Sir Stanley Gordon, Kt.
Grose, *Vice-Adm.* Sir Alan, KBE
Gross, *Hon.* Sir Peter Henry, Kt.
Grossart, Sir Angus McFarlane
McLeod, Kt., CBE
Grotrian, Sir Philip Christian Brent,
Bt. (1934)
Grove, Sir Charles Gerald, Bt.
(1874)
Grove, Sir Edmund Frank, KCVO
Grugeon, Sir John Drury, Kt.
Guinness, Sir Howard Christian
Sheldon, Kt., VRD
Guinness, Sir John Ralph Sidney, Kt.,
CB
Guinness, Sir Kenelm Ernest Lee, Bt.
(1867)
Guise, Sir John Grant, Bt. (1783)
Gull, Sir Rupert William Cameron,
Bt. (1872)
Gumbs, Sir Emile Rudolph, Kt.
Gun-Munro, Sir Sydney Douglas,
GCMG, MBE
Gunn, Sir Robert Norman, Kt.
†Gunning, Sir Charles Theodore, Bt.
(1778)
Gunston, Sir John Wellesley, Bt.
(1938)
Gurdon, *Prof.* Sir John Bertrand, Kt.,
DPHIL, FRS
Guthrie, Sir Malcolm Connop,
Bt. (1936)
Guy, *Gen.* Sir Roland Kelvin, GCB,
CBE, DSO
Haddacks, *Vice-Adm.* Sir Paul
Kenneth, KCB
Hadfield, Sir Ronald, Kt., QPM
Hadlee, Sir Richard John, Kt., MBE
Hagart-Alexander, Sir Claud, Bt.
(1886)
Hague, *Prof.* Sir Douglas Chalmers,
Kt., CBE
Haines, *Prof.* Sir Andrew Paul, Kt.
Halberg, Sir Murray Gordon, Kt.,
MBE
Hall, Sir Basil Brodribb, KCB, MC,
TD
Hall, *Prof.* Sir David Michael
Baldock, Kt.
Hall, Sir Ernest, Kt., OBE
Hall, Sir Graham Joseph, Kt.
Hall, Sir Iain Robert, Kt.

Hall, Sir (Frederick) John (Frank), Bt.
(1923)
Hall, Sir John, Kt.
Hall, Sir John Bernard, Bt. (1919)
†Hall, Sir John Douglas Hoste, Bt.
(S. 1687)
Hall, Sir Peter Edward, KBE, CMG
Hall, *Prof.* Sir Peter Geoffrey, Kt.,
FBA
Hall, Sir Peter Reginald Frederick,
Kt., CBE
Hall, Sir Robert de Zouche, KCMG
Halliday, *Vice-Adm.* Sir Roy William,
KBE, DSC
Halpern, Sir Ralph Mark, Kt.
Halsey, *Revd* John Walter Brooke, Bt.
(1920)
Halstead, Sir Ronald, Kt., CBE
Hambling, Sir (Herbert) Hugh, Bt.
(1924)
Hamer, *Hon.* Sir Rupert James,
KCMG, ED
Hamilton, Sir Andrew Caradoc, Bt.
(S. 1646)
Hamilton, Sir Edward Sydney, Bt.
(1776 and 1819)
Hamilton, Sir James Arnot, KCB,
MBE, FRENG
Hamilton-Dalrymple, *Maj.* Sir Hew
Fleetwood, Bt. (S. 1697),
GCVO
Hamilton-Spencer-Smith, Sir John,
Bt. (1804)
Hammick, Sir Stephen George, Bt.
(1834)
Hammond, Sir Anthony Hilgrove,
KCB, QC
Hampel, Sir Ronald Claus, Kt.
Hampson, Sir Stuart, Kt.
Hampton, Sir (Leslie) Geoffrey, Kt.
Hanbury-Tenison, Sir Richard,
KCVO
Hancock, Sir David John Stowell,
KCB
Hand, *Most Revd* Geoffrey David,
KBE
Hanham, Sir Michael William, Bt.
(1667), DFC
Hanley, *Rt. Hon.* Sir Jeremy James,
KCMG
Hanmer, Sir John Wyndham Edward,
Bt. (1774)
Hannam, Sir John Gordon, Kt.
Hanson, Sir (Charles) Rupert
(Patrick), Bt. (1918)
Hanson, Sir John Gilbert, KCMG,
CBE
Harcourt-Smith, *Air Chief Marshal*
Sir David, GBE, KCB, DFC
Hardie, Sir Douglas Fleming, Kt.,
CBE
Hardie Boys, *Rt. Hon.* Sir Michael,
GCMG
Harding, Sir George William, KCMG,
CVO
Harding, *Marshal of the Royal Air
Force* Sir Peter Robin, GCB
Harding, Sir Roy Pollard, Kt., CBE
Hardy, Sir David William, Kt.
Hardy, Sir James Gilbert, Kt., OBE
Hardy, Sir Richard Charles Chandos,
Bt. (1876)

Hare, Sir David, Kt., FRSL

Hare, Sir Nicholas Patrick, Bt. (1818)

Harford, Sir (John) Timothy, Bt. (1934)

Hargroves, *Brig.* Sir Robert Louis, Kt., CBE

Harington, *Gen.* Sir Charles Henry Pepys, GCB, CBE, DSO, MC

Harington, Sir Nicholas John, Bt. (1611)

Harland, *Air Marshal* Sir Reginald Edward Wynyard, KBE, CB

Harley, *Gen.* Sir Alexander George Hamilton, KBE, CB

Harman, *Gen.* Sir Jack Wentworth, GCB, OBE, MC

Harman, *Hon.* Sir Jeremiah LeRoy, Kt.

Harman, Sir John Andrew, Kt.

Harmsworth, Sir Hildebrand Harold, Bt. (1922)

Harper, Sir Ewan William, Kt. CBE

Harper, *Prof.* Sir Peter Stanley, Kt., CBE

Harris, *Prof.* Sir Henry, Kt., FRCP, FRCPATH, FRS

Harris, Sir Jack Wolfred Ashford, Bt. (1932)

Harris, *Air Marshal* Sir John Hulme, KCB, CBE

Harris, *Prof.* Sir Martin Best, Kt., CBE

Harris, Sir Thomas George, KBE, CMG

Harrison, *Prof.* Sir Brian Howard, Kt.

Harrison, Sir David, Kt., CBE, FRENG

Harrison, Sir Ernest Thomas, Kt., OBE

Harrison, *Surgeon Vice-Adm.* Sir John Albert Bews, KBE

Harrison, *Hon.* Sir Michael Guy Vicat, Kt.

Harrison, Sir Michael James Harwood, Bt. (1961)

Harrison, Sir (Robert) Colin, Bt. (1922)

Harrison, Sir Terence, Kt., FRENG

Harrop, Sir Peter John, KCB

Hart, *Hon.* Sir Anthony Ronald, Kt.

Hart, Sir Graham Allan, KCB

Hart, *Hon.* Sir Michael Christopher Campbell, Kt.

Hartwell, Sir (Francis) Anthony Charles Peter, Bt. (1805)

Harvey, Sir Charles Richard Musgrave, Bt. (1933)

Harvey-Jones, Sir John Henry, Kt., MBE

Harvie, Sir John Smith, Kt., CBE

Harvie-Watt, Sir James, Bt. (1945)

Haselhurst, *Rt. Hon.* Sir Alan Gordon Barraclough, Kt.

Haskard, Sir Cosmo Dugal Patrick Thomas, KCMG, MBE

Haslam, *Rear-Adm.* Sir David William, KBE, CB

Hassett, *Gen.* Sir Francis George, KBE, CB, DSO, LVO

Hastings, Sir Max Macdonald, Kt.

Hatch, Sir David Edwin, Kt., CBE

Hatter, Sir Maurice, Kt.

Havelock-Allan, Sir (Anthony) Mark David, Bt. (1858)

Hawkins, Sir Richard Caesar, Bt. (1778)

Hawley, Sir Donald Frederick, KCMG, MBE

†Hawley, Sir Henry Nicholas, Bt. (1795)

Haworth, Sir Philip, Bt. (1911)

Hawthorne, *Prof.* Sir William Rede, Kt., CBE, SCD, FRS, FRENG

Hay, Sir David Osborne, Kt., CBE, DSO

Hay, Sir David Russell, Kt., CBE, FRCP, MD

Hay, Sir Hamish Grenfell, Kt.

Hay, Sir John Erroll Audley, Bt. (S. 1663)

†Hay, Sir Ronald Frederick Hamilton, Bt. (S. 1703)

Hayes, Sir Brian, Kt., CBE, QPM

Hayes, Sir Brian David, GCB

Hayman-Joyce, *Lt.-Gen.* Sir Robert John, KCB, CBE

Hayward, Sir Anthony William Byrd, Kt.

Hayward, Sir Jack Arnold, Kt., OBE

Haywood, Sir Harold, KCVO, OBE

Head, Sir Francis David Somerville, Bt. (1838)

Heap, Sir Peter William, KCMG

Heap, *Prof.* Sir Robert Brian, Kt., CBE, FRS

Hearne, Sir Graham James, Kt., CBE

Heath, Sir Mark Evelyn, KCVO, CMG

Heathcote, *Brig.* Sir Gilbert Simon, Bt., CBE (1733)

Heathcote, Sir Michael Perryman, Bt. (1733)

Heatley, Sir Peter, Kt., CBE

Hedley, *Hon.* Sir Mark, Kt.

Heiser, Sir Terence Michael, GCB

Henao, Revd Ravu, Kt., OBE

Henderson, Sir Denys Hartley, Kt.

Henderson, Sir (John) Nicholas, GCMG, KCVO

Hennessy, Sir James Patrick Ivan, KBE, CMG

†Henniker, Sir Adrian Chandos, Bt. (1813)

Henniker-Heaton, Sir Yvo Robert, Bt. (1912)

Henriques, *Hon.* Sir Richard Henry Quixano, Kt.

Henry, *Rt. Hon.* Sir Denis Robert Maurice, Kt.

Henry, *Hon.* Sir Geoffrey Arama, KBE

†Henry, Sir Patrick Denis, Bt. (1923)

Henry, *Hon.* Sir Trevor Ernest, Kt.

Henshaw, Sir David George, Kt.

Hepple, *Prof.* Sir Bob Alexander, Kt.

Herbecq, Sir John Edward, KCB

Herbert, *Adm.* Sir Peter Geoffrey Marshall, KCB, OBE

Herbert, Sir Walter William, Kt.

Hermon, Sir John Charles, Kt., OBE, QPM

Heron, Sir Conrad Frederick, KCB, OBE

Heron, Sir Michael Gilbert, Kt.

Heron-Maxwell, Sir Nigel Mellor, Bt. (S. 1683)

Hervey, Sir Roger Blaise Ramsay, KCVO, CMG

Hervey-Bathurst, Sir Frederick John Charles Gordon, Bt. (1818)

Heseltine, *Rt. Hon.* Sir William Frederick Payne, GCB, GCVO

Hetherington, Sir Thomas Chalmers, KCB, CBE, TD, QC

Hewetson, Sir Christopher Raynor, Kt., TD

Hewett, Sir Richard Mark John, Bt. (1813)

Hewitt, Sir (Cyrus) Lenox (Simson), Kt., OBE

Hewitt, Sir Nicholas Charles Joseph, Bt. (1921)

Heygate, Sir Richard John Gage, Bt. (1831)

Heywood, Sir Peter, Bt. (1838)

Hezlet, *Vice-Adm.* Sir Arthur Richard, KBE, CB, DSO, DSC

Hibbert, Sir Jack, KCB

Hickey, Sir Justin, Kt.

Hickman, Sir (Richard) Glenn, Bt. (1903)

Hicks, Sir Robert, Kt.

Hidden, *Hon.* Sir Anthony Brian, Kt.

Hielscher, Sir Leo Arthur, Kt.

Higgins, *Hon.* Sir Malachy Joseph, Kt.

Higginson, Sir Gordon Robert, Kt., PHD, FRENG

Higgs, Sir Derek Alan, Kt.

Hill, Sir Arthur Alfred, Kt., CBE

Hill, Sir Brian John, Kt.

Hill, Sir James Frederick, Bt. (1917)

Hill, Sir John Alfred Rowley, Bt. (I. 1779)

Hill, Sir John McGregor, Kt., PHD, FRENG

Hill, *Vice-Adm.* Sir Robert Charles Finch, KBE, FRENG

Hill-Norton, *Vice-Adm. Hon.* Sir Nicholas John, KCB

Hill-Wood, Sir Samuel Thomas, Bt. (1921)

Hillary, Sir Edmund, KG, KBE

Hillhouse, Sir (Robert) Russell, KCB

Hills, Sir Graham John, Kt.

Hine, *Air Chief Marshal* Sir Patrick Bardon, GCB, GBE

Hirsch, *Prof.* Sir Peter Bernhard, Kt., PHD, FRS

Hirst, *Rt. Hon.* Sir David Cozens-Hardy, Kt.

Hirst, Sir Michael William, Kt.

Hoare, *Prof.* Sir Charles Anthony Richard, Kt., FRS

Hoare, Sir David John, Bt. (1786)

Hoare, Sir Timothy Edward Charles, Bt. (I. 1784), OBE

Hobart, Sir John Vere, Bt. (1914)

Hobbs, *Maj.-Gen.* Sir Michael Frederick, KCVO, CBE

Hobday, Sir Gordon Ivan, Kt.

Hobhouse, Sir Charles John Spinney, Bt. (1812)

†Hodge, Sir Andrew Rowland, Bt. (1921)

Hodge, *Hon.* Sir Henry Egar Garfield, Kt.

Hodge, Sir James William, KCVO, CMG

Hodges, *Air Chief Marshal* Sir Lewis MacDonald, KCB, CBE, DSO, DFC

Hodgkin, Sir (Gordon) Howard (Eliot), Kt., CH, CBE

Hodgkinson, Sir Michael Stewart, Kt.

Hodgkinson, *Air Chief Marshal* Sir (William) Derek, KCB, CBE, DFC, AFC

Hodgson, Sir Maurice Arthur Eric, Kt., FRENG

Hodson, Sir Michael Robin Adderley, Bt. (I. 1789)

Hoffenberg, *Prof.* Sir Raymond, KBE

Hogg, Sir Christopher Anthony, Kt.

†Hogg, Sir Piers Michael James, Bt. (1846)

Holcroft, Sir Peter George Culcheth, Bt. (1921)

Holderness, Sir Martin William, Bt. (1920)

Holden, Sir Edward, Bt. (1893)

Holden, Sir John David, Bt. (1919)

Holden-Brown, Sir Derrick, Kt.

Holder, Sir John Henry, Bt. (1898)

Holdgate, Sir Martin Wyatt, Kt., CB, PHD

Holdsworth, Sir (George) Trevor, Kt., CVO

Holland, *Hon.* Sir Alan Douglas, Kt.

Holland, *Hon.* Sir Christopher John, Kt.

Holland, Sir Clifton Vaughan, Kt.

Holland, Sir Geoffrey, KCB

Holland, Sir John Anthony, Kt.

Holland, Sir Philip Welsby, Kt.

Holliday, *Prof.* Sir Frederick George Thomas, Kt., CBE, FRSE

Hollings, *Hon.* Sir (Alfred) Kenneth, Kt., MC

Hollom, Sir Jasper Quintus, KBE

Holloway, *Hon.* Sir Barry Blyth, KBE

Holm, Sir Ian (Ian Holm Cuthbert), Kt., CBE

Holman, *Hon.* Sir (Edward) James, Kt.

Holmes, *Prof.* Sir Frank Wakefield, Kt.

Holmes, Sir John Eaton, GCVO, KBE, CMG

Holmes-Sellors, Sir Patrick John, KCVO

Holroyd, *Air Marshal* Sir Frank Martyn, KBE, CB

Holt, *Prof.* Sir James Clarke, Kt.

Holt, Sir Michael, Kt., CBE

Home, Sir William Dundas, Bt. (S. 1671)

Honeycombe, *Prof.* Sir Robert William Kerr, Kt., FRS, FRENG

Honywood, Sir Filmer Courtenay William, Bt. (1660)

Hood, Sir Harold Joseph, Bt., TD (1922)

Hookway, Sir Harry Thurston, Kt.

Hooper, *Hon.* Sir Anthony, Kt., PC

Hope, Sir Colin Frederick Newton, Kt.

Hope, Sir John Carl Alexander, Bt. (S. 1628)

Hope-Dunbar, Sir David, Bt. (S. 1664)

Hopkin, Sir Royston Oliver, KCMG

Hopkin, Sir (William Aylsham) Bryan, Kt., CBE

Hopkins, Sir Anthony Philip, Kt., CBE

Hopkins, Sir Michael John, Kt., CBE, RA, RIBA

Hopwood, *Prof.* Sir David Alan, Kt., FRS

Hordern, *Rt. Hon.* Sir Peter Maudslay, Kt.

Horlick, *Vice-Adm.* Sir Edwin John, KBE, FRENG

Horlick, Sir James Cunliffe William, Bt. (1914)

Horlock, *Prof.* Sir John Harold, Kt., FRS, FRENG

Horn, *Prof.* Sir Gabriel, Kt., FRS

Horn-Smith, Sir Julian Michael, Kt.

Hornby, Sir Derek Peter, Kt.

Hornby, Sir Simon Michael, Kt.

Horne, Sir Alan Gray Antony, Bt. (1929)

Horne, *Dr* Sir Alistair Allan, Kt. CBE

Horsbrugh-Porter, Sir John Simon, Bt. (1902)

Horsfall, Sir John Musgrave, Bt. (1909), MC, TD

†Hort, Sir Andrew Edwin Fenton, Bt. (1767)

Horton, Sir Robert Baynes, Kt.

Hosker, Sir Gerald Albery, KCB, QC

Hoskyns, Sir Benedict Leigh, Bt. (1676)

Hoskyns, Sir John Austin Hungerford Leigh, Kt.

Hotung, Sir Joseph Edward, Kt.

Houghton, Sir John Theodore, Kt., CBE, FRS

Houldsworth, Sir Richard Thomas Reginald, Bt. (1887)

Hourston, Sir Gordon Minto, Kt.

House, *Lt.-Gen.* Sir David George, GCB, KCVO, CBE, MC

Houssemayne du Boulay, Sir Roger William, KCVO, CMG

Houstoun-Boswall, Sir (Thomas) Alford, Bt. (1836)

Howard, Sir David Howarth Seymour, Bt. (1955)

Howard, *Prof.* Sir Michael Eliot, Kt., OM, CH, CBE, MC

Howard-Dobson, *Gen.* Sir Patrick John, GCB

Howard-Lawson, Sir John Philip, Bt. (1841)

Howell, Sir Ralph Frederic, Kt.

Howells, Sir Eric Waldo Benjamin, Kt., CBE

Howes, Sir Christopher Kingston, KCVO, CB

Howlett, *Gen.* Sir Geoffrey Hugh Whitby, KBE, MC

Huggins, *Hon.* Sir Alan Armstrong, Kt.

Hugh-Jones, Sir Wynn Normington, Kt., LVO

Hugh-Smith, Sir Andrew Colin, Kt.

Hughes, *Hon.* Sir Anthony Philip Gilson, Kt.

Hughes, Sir Jack William, Kt.

Hughes, Sir Thomas Collingwood, Bt. (1773)

Hughes, Sir Trevor Poulton, KCB

Hughes-Morgan, *His Hon. Maj.-Gen.* Sir David John, Bt. (1925), CB, CBE

Hull, *Prof.* Sir David, Kt.

Hulse, Sir Edward Jeremy Westrow, Bt. (1739)

Hum, Sir Christopher Owen, KCMG

Hume, Sir Alan Blyth, Kt., CB

Hunt, Sir John Leonard, Kt.

Hunt, *Adm.* Sir Nicholas John Streynsham, GCB, LVO

Hunt, *Hon.* Sir Patrick James, Kt.

Hunt, Sir Rex Masterman, Kt., CMG

Hunt-Davis, *Brig.* Sir Miles Garth, KCVO, CBE

Hunter, Sir Alistair John, KCMG

Hunter, *Prof.* Sir Laurence Colvin, Kt., CBE, FRSE

Hunter, Sir Thomas Blane, Kt.

Huntington-Whiteley, Sir Hugo Baldwin, Bt. (1918)

Hurn, Sir (Francis) Roger, Kt.

Hurrell, Sir Anthony Gerald, KCVO, CMG

Hurst, Sir Geoffrey Charles, Kt., MBE

Husbands, Sir Clifford Straugh, GCMG

Hutchinson, *Hon.* Sir Ross, Kt., DFC

Hutchison, Sir James Colville, Bt. (1956)

Hutchison, *Rt. Hon.* Sir Michael, Kt.

Hutchison, Sir Robert, Bt. (1939)

Hutt, Sir Dexter Walter, Kt.

Huxley, *Prof.* Sir Andrew Fielding, Kt., OM, FRS

Huxtable, *Gen.* Sir Charles Richard, KCB, CBE

Ibbs, Sir (John) Robin, KBE

Imbert-Terry, Sir Michael Edward Stanley, Bt. (1917)

Imray, Sir Colin Henry, KBE, CMG

Ingham, Sir Bernard, Kt.

Ingilby, Sir Thomas Colvin William, Bt. (1866)

Inglefield-Watson, Sir John Forbes, Bt. (1895)

Inglis, Sir Brian Scott, Kt.

Inglis of Glencorse, Sir Roderick John, Bt. (S. 1703)

Ingram, Sir James Herbert Charles, Bt. (1893)

Ingram, Sir John Henderson, Kt., CBE

Inkin, Sir Geoffrey David, Kt., OBE

†Innes, Sir David Charles Kenneth Gordon, Bt. (NS 1686)

Innes of Edingight, Sir Malcolm Rognvald, KCVO

Innes, Sir Peter Alexander Berowald, Bt. (S. 1628)

Irvine, Sir Donald Hamilton, Kt., CBE, MD, FRCGP

Irving, *Prof.* Sir Miles Horsfall, Kt., MD, FRCS, FRCSE

Irwin, *Lt.-Gen.* Sir Alistair Stuart Hastings, KCB, CBE

Isaacs, Sir Jeremy Israel, Kt.

Isham, Sir Ian Vere Gyles, Bt. (1627)

Jack, *Hon.* Sir Alieu Sulayman, Kt.

Jack, Sir David, Kt., CBE, FRS, FRSE

Jack, Sir David Emmanuel, GCMG, MBE

Jack, *Hon.* Sir Raymond Evan, Kt.

Jackling, Sir Roger Tustin, KCB. CBE

Jackson, Sir Barry Trevor, Kt.

Jackson, Sir Kenneth Joseph, Kt.

Jackson, *Gen.* Sir Michael David, GCB, CBE

Jackson, Sir Michael Roland, Bt. (1902)

Jackson, Sir Nicholas Fane St George, Bt. (1913)

Jackson, Sir Keith Arnold, Bt. (1815)

Jackson, *Hon.* Sir Rupert Matthew, Kt.

†Jackson, Sir (William) Roland Cedric, Bt. (1869)

Jacob, *Hon.* Sir Robert Raphael Hayim (Robin), Kt., PC

Jacobi, Sir Derek George, Kt., CBE

Jacobi, *Dr* Sir James Edward, Kt., OBE

Jacobs, Sir Cecil Albert, Kt., CBE

Jacobs, *Hon.* Sir Kenneth Sydney, KBE

Jacomb, Sir Martin Wakefield, Kt.

Jaffray, Sir William Otho, Bt. (1892)

Jagger, Sir Michael Philip, Kt.

James, Sir Cynlais Morgan, KCMG

James, Sir Jeffrey Russell, KBE

James, Sir John Nigel Courtenay, KCVO, CBE

James, Sir Stanislaus Anthony, GCMG, OBE

Jamieson, *Air Marshal* Sir David Ewan, KBE, CB

Jansen, Sir Ross Malcolm, KBE

Janvrin, *Rt. Hon.* Sir Robin Berry, KCB, KCVO

Jardine of Applegirth, Sir Alexander Maule, Bt. (S. 1672)

Jardine, Sir Andrew Colin Douglas, Bt. (1916)

Jarman, *Prof.* Sir Brian, Kt., OBE

Jarratt, Sir Alexander Anthony, Kt., CB

Jarvis, Sir Gordon Ronald, Kt.

Jason, Sir David, Kt., OBE

Jawara, *Hon.* Sir Dawda Kairaba, Kt.

Jay, Sir Antony Rupert, Kt., CVO

Jay, Sir Michael Hastings, KCMG

Jeewoolall, Sir Ramesh, Kt.

Jefferson, Sir George Rowland, Kt., CBE, FRENG

Jeffreys, *Prof.* Sir Alec John, Kt., FRS

Jeffries, *Hon.* Sir John Francis, Kt.

Jehangir, Sir Cowasji, Bt. (1908)

Jejeebhoy, Sir Jamsetjee, Bt. (1857)

Jenkins, Sir Brian Garton, GBE

Jenkins, Sir Elgar Spencer, Kt., OBE

Jenkins, Sir James Christopher, KCB, QC

Jenkins, Sir Michael Nicholas Howard, Kt., OBE

Jenkins, Sir Michael Romilly Heald, KCMG

Jenkins, Sir Simon, Kt.

Jenkinson, Sir John Banks, Bt. (1661)

Jenks, Sir Maurice Arthur Brian, Bt. (1932)

Jenner, *Air Marshal* Sir Timothy Ivo, KCB

Jennings, Sir John Southwood, Kt., CBE, FRSE

Jennings, Sir Peter Neville Wake, Kt., CVO

Jephcott, Sir Neil Welbourn, Bt. (1962)

Jessel, Sir Charles John, Bt. (1883)

Jewkes, Sir Gordon Wesley, KCMG

Job, Sir Peter James Denton, Kt.

John, Sir David Glyndwr, KCMG

John, Sir Elton Hercules (Reginald Kenneth Dwight), Kt., CBE

Johns, *Air Chief Marshal* Sir Richard Edward, GCB, CBE, LVO

Johnson, Sir Colpoys Guy, Bt. (1755)

Johnson, *Gen.* Sir Garry Dene, KCB, OBE, MC

Johnson, Sir John Rodney, KCMG

†Johnson, Sir Patrick Eliot, Bt. (1818)

Johnson, *Hon.* Sir Robert Lionel, Kt.

Johnson, Sir Vassel Godfrey, Kt., CBE

Johnson-Ferguson, Sir Ian Edward, Bt. (1906)

Johnston, Sir John Baines, GCMG, KCVO

Johnston, *Lt.-Col.* Sir John Frederick Dame, GCVO, MC

Johnston, *Lt.-Gen.* Sir Maurice Robert, KCB, OBE

Johnston, Sir Thomas Alexander, Bt. (S. 1626)

Johnstone, Sir Geoffrey Adams Dinwiddie, KCMG

Johnstone, Sir (George) Richard Douglas, Bt. (S. 1700)

Johnstone, Sir (John) Raymond, Kt., CBE

Jolliffe, Sir Anthony Stuart, GBE

Jolly, Sir Aurthur Richard, KCMG

Jonas, Sir John Peter Jens, Kt., CBE

Jones, Sir Alan Jeffrey, Kt.

Jones, *Gen.* Sir (Charles) Edward Webb, KCB, CBE

Jones, Sir Digby Marritt, Kt.

Jones, *Air Marshal* Sir Edward Gordon, KCB, CBE, DSO, DFC

Jones, Sir Harry George, Kt., CBE

Jones, Sir John Francis, Kt.

Jones, Sir Keith Stephen, Kt.

Jones, Sir Lyndon, Kt.

Jones, Sir (Owen) Trevor, Kt.

Jones, Sir Richard Anthony Lloyd, KCB

Jones, Sir Robert Edward, Kt.

Jones, Sir Roger Spencer, Kt., OBE

Jones, Sir Simon Warley Frederick Benton, Bt. (1919)

†Joseph, *Hon.* Sir James Samuel, Bt. (1943)

Jowitt, *Hon.* Sir Edwin Frank, Kt.

Judge, *Rt. Hon.* Sir Igor, Kt.

Judge, Sir Paul Rupert, Kt.

Jugnauth, *Rt. Hon.* Sir Anerood, KCMG

Jungius, *Vice-Adm.* Sir James George, KBE

Kaberry, *Hon.* Sir Christopher Donald, Bt. (1960)

Kadoorie, *Hon.* Sir Michael David, Kt.

Kakaraya, Sir Pato, KBE

Kalo, Sir Kwamala, Kt., MBE

Kan Yuet-Keung, Sir, GBE

Kapi, *Hon.* Sir Mari, Kt., CBE

Kaputin, Sir John Rumet, KBE, CMG

Kaufman, *Rt. Hon.* Sir Gerald Bernard, Kt., PC

Kausimae, Sir David Nanau, KBE

Kavali, Sir Thomas, Kt., OBE

Kawharu, *Prof.* Sir Ian Hugh, Kt.

Kay, *Prof.* Sir Andrew Watt, Kt.

Kay, *Hon.* Sir Maurice Ralph, Kt., PC

Kaye, Sir Paul Henry Gordon, Bt. (1923)

Keane, Sir Richard Michael, Bt. (1801)

Kearney, *Hon.* Sir William John Francis, Kt., CBE

Keeble, Sir (Herbert Ben) Curtis, GCMG

Keegan, Sir John Desmond Patrick, Kt., OBE

Keene, *Rt. Hon.* Sir David Wolfe, Kt.

Keith, *Hon.* Sir Brian Richard, Kt.

Keith, *Prof.* Sir James, KBE

†Kellett, Sir Stanley Charles, Bt. (1801)

Kelly, Sir Christopher William, KCB

Kelly, Sir David Robert Corbett, Kt., CBE

Kelly, *Rt. Hon.* Sir (John William) Basil, Kt.

Kemakeza, Sir Allan, Kt.

Kemball, *Air Marshal* Sir (Richard) John, KCB, CBE

Kemp, Sir (Edward) Peter, KCB

Kemp-Welch, Sir John, Kt.

Kenilorea, *Rt. Hon.* Sir Peter, KBE

Kennaway, Sir John Lawrence, Bt. (1791)

Kennedy, Sir Francis, KCMG, CBE

Kennedy, *Hon.* Sir Ian Alexander, Kt.

Kennedy, *Prof.* Sir Ian McColl, Kt.

Kennedy, Sir Ludovic Henry Coverley, Kt.

†Kennedy, Sir Michael Edward, Bt., (1836)

Kennedy, *Rt. Hon.* Sir Paul Joseph Morrow, Kt.

Kennedy, *Air Chief Marshal* Sir Thomas Lawrie, GCB, AFC

Kennedy-Good, Sir John, KBE

Kenny, Sir Anthony John Patrick, Kt., DPHIL, DLITT, FBA

Kenny, *Gen.* Sir Brian Leslie Graham, GCB, CBE

Kentridge, Sir Sydney Woolf, KCMG, QC

Kenyon, Sir George Henry, Kt.

Kermode, Sir (John) Frank, Kt., FBA

Kermode, Sir Ronald Graham Quale, KBE

Kerr, *Hon.* Sir Brian Francis, Kt., PC

Kerr, *Adm.* Sir John Beverley, GCB

Kerry, Sir Michael James, KCB, QC

Kershaw, *Prof.* Sir Ian, Kt.

Kershaw, Sir (John) Anthony, Kt., MC

Kerslake, Sir Robert Walker, Kt.

Keswick, Sir John Chippendale Lindley, Kt.
Kevau, *Prof.* Sir Isi Henao, Kt., CBE
Kikau, *Ratu* Sir Jone Latianara, KBE
Killen, *Hon.* Sir Denis James, KCMG
Kimber, Sir Charles Dixon, Bt. (1904)
King, *Prof.* Sir David Anthony, Kt., FRS
King, Sir John Christopher, Bt. (1888)
King, *Vice-Adm.* Sir Norman Ross Dutton, KBE
King, Sir Wayne Alexander, Bt. (1815)
Kingman, *Prof.* Sir John Frank Charles, Kt., FRS
Kingsland, Sir Richard, Kt., CBE, DFC
Kingsley, Sir Ben, Kt.
Kinloch, Sir David, Bt. (S. 1686)
Kinloch, Sir David Oliphant, Bt. (1873)
Kipalan, Sir Albert, Kt.
Kirkpatrick, Sir Ivone Elliott, Bt. (S. 1685)
Kirkwood, *Hon.* Sir Andrew Tristram Hammett, Kt.
Kiszely, *Lt.-Gen.* Sir John Panton, KCB, MC
Kitcatt, Sir Peter Julian, Kt., CB
Kitson, *Gen.* Sir Frank Edward, GBE, KCB, MC
Kitson, Sir Timothy Peter Geoffrey, Kt.
Kleinwort, Sir Richard Drake, Bt. (1909)
Klug, Sir Aaron, Kt., OM
Kneller, Sir Alister Arthur, Kt.
Knight, Sir Harold Murray, KBE, DSC
Knight, *Air Chief Marshal* Sir Michael William Patrick, KCB, AFC
Knight, *Prof.* Sir Peter, Kt.
†Knill, Sir Thomas John Pugin Bartholomew, Bt. (1893)
Knowles, Sir Charles Francis, Bt. (1765)
Knowles, Sir Durward Randolph, Kt., OBE
Knowles, Sir Richard Marchant, Kt.
Knox, Sir David Laidlaw, Kt.
Knox, *Hon.* Sir John Leonard, Kt.
Knox-Johnston, Sir William Robert Patrick (Sir Robin), Kt., CBE, RD
Koraea, Sir Thomas, Kt.
Kornberg, *Prof.* Sir Hans Leo, Kt., DSC, SCD, PHD, FRS
Korowi, Sir Wiwa, GCMG
Krebs, *Prof.* Sir John Richard, Kt., DPHIL, FRS
Kroto, *Prof.* Sir Harold Walter, Kt., FRS
Kulukundis, Sir Elias George (Eddie), Kt., OBE
Kurongku, *Most Revd* Peter, KBE
Kwok-Po, *Dr.* Sir David Li, Kt., OBE
Lachmann, *Prof.* Sir Peter Julius, Kt.
Lacon, Sir Edmund Vere, Bt. (1818)
Lacy, Sir Patrick Brian Finucane, Bt. (1921)

Lacy, Sir John Trend, Kt., CBE
Laddie, *Hon.* Sir Hugh Ian Lang, Kt.
Laidlaw, Sir Christopher Charles Fraser, Kt.
Laing, Sir (John) Martin (Kirby), Kt., CBE
Laing, Sir (John) Maurice, Kt.
Laing, Sir (William) Kirby, Kt., FRENG
Laird, Sir Gavin Harry, Kt., CBE
Lake, Sir (Atwell) Graham, Bt. (1711)
Laker, Sir Frederick Alfred, Kt.
Lakin, Sir Michael, Bt. (1909)
Laking, Sir George Robert, KCMG
Lamb, Sir Albert Thomas, KBE, CMG, DFC
Lambert, Sir Anthony Edward, KCMG
Lambert, Sir John Henry, KCVO, CMG
†Lambert, Sir Peter John Biddulph, Bt. (1711)
Lampl, Sir Frank William, Kt.
Lampl, Sir Peter, Kt., OBE
Lamport, Sir Stephen Mark Jeffrey, KCVO
Landale, Sir David William Neil, KCVO
Landau, Sir Dennis Marcus, Kt.
Lander, Sir Stephen James, KCB
Lane, Prof. Sir David Philip, Kt.
†Langham, Sir John Stephen, Bt. (1660)
Langlands, Sir Robert Alan, Kt.
Langley, *Hon.* Sir Gordon Julian Hugh, Kt.
Langley, *Maj.-Gen.* Sir Henry Desmond Allen, KCVO, MBE
Langrishe, Sir James Hercules, Bt. (I. 1777)
Lankester, Sir Timothy Patrick, KCB
Lapli, Sir John Ini, GCMG
Large, Sir Andrew McLeod Brooks, Kt.
Latham, *Rt. Hon.* Sir David Nicholas Ramsey, Kt.
Latham, Sir Michael Anthony, Kt.
Latham, Sir Richard Thomas Paul, Bt. (1919)
Latimer, Sir (Courtenay) Robert, Kt., CBE
Latimer, Sir Graham Stanley, KBE
Latour-Adrien, *Hon.* Sir Maurice, Kt.
Laughton, Sir Anthony Seymour, Kt.
Laurence, Sir Peter Harold, KCMG, MC
Laurie, Sir Robert Bayley Emilius, Bt. (1834)
Lauterpacht, Sir Elihu, Kt., CBE, QC
Lauti, *Rt. Hon.* Sir Toaripi, GCMG
Lavan, *Hon.* Sir John Martin, Kt.
Lawes, Sir (John) Michael Bennet, Bt. (1882)
Lawler, Sir Peter James, Kt., OBE
†Lawrence, Sir Clive Wyndham, Bt. (1906)
Lawrence, Sir Henry Peter, Bt. (1858)
Lawrence, Sir Ivan John, Kt., QC
Lawrence, Sir John Patrick Grosvenor, Kt., CBE
Lawrence, Sir William Fettiplace, Bt. (1867)

Lawrence-Jones, Sir Christopher, Bt. (1831)
Laws, *Rt. Hon.* Sir John Grant McKenzie, Kt.
Lawson, Sir Christopher Donald, Kt.
Lawson, Sir Charles John Patrick, Bt. (1900)
Lawson, *Gen.* Sir Richard George, KCB, DSO, OBE
Lawson-Tancred, Sir Henry, Bt. (1662)
Lawton, *Prof.* Sir John Hartley, Kt., CBE, FRS
Layard, *Adm.* Sir Michael Henry Gordon, KCB, CBE
Lea, *Vice-Adm.* Sir John Stuart Crosbie, KBE
Lea, Sir Thomas William, Bt. (1892)
Leach, *Admiral of the Fleet* Sir Henry Conyers, GCB
Leahy, Sir Daniel Joseph, Kt.
Leahy, Sir John Henry Gladstone, KCMG
Leahy, Sir Terence Patrick, Kt.
Learmont, *Gen.* Sir John Hartley, KCB, CBE
Leaver, Sir Christopher, GBE
Le Bailly, *Vice-Adm.* Sir Louis Edward Stewart Holland, KBE, CB
Le Cheminant, *Air Chief Marshal* Sir Peter de Lacey, GBE, KCB, DFC
Lechmere, Sir Reginald Anthony Hungerford, Bt. (1818)
Ledger, Sir Philip Stevens, Kt., CBE, FRSE
Lee, Sir Arthur James, KBE, MC
Lee, *Brig.* Sir Leonard Henry, Kt.,
Lee, Sir Quo-wei, Kt., CBE
Leeds, Sir Christopher Anthony, Bt. (1812)
Lees, Sir David Bryan, Kt.
Lees, Sir Thomas Edward, Bt. (1897)
Lees, Sir Thomas Harcourt Ivor, Bt. (1804)
Lees, Sir (William) Antony Clare, Bt. (1937)
Le Fanu, *Maj.* Sir (George) Victor (Sheridan), KCVO
le Fleming, Sir David Kelland, Bt. (1705)
Legard, Sir Charles Thomas, Bt. (1660)
Legg, Sir Thomas Stuart, KCB, QC
Leggatt, *Rt. Hon.* Sir Andrew Peter, Kt.
Leggatt, Sir Hugh Frank John, Kt.
Leggett, *Prof.* Sir Anthony James, KBE
Leigh, Sir Geoffrey Norman, Kt.
Leigh, Sir Richard Henry, Bt. (1918)
Leighton, Sir Michael John Bryan, Bt. (1693)
Leitch, Sir George, KCB, OBE
Leith-Buchanan, Sir Gordon Kelly McNicol, Bt. (1775)
Le Marchant, Sir Francis Arthur, Bt. (1841)
Leng, *Gen.* Sir Peter John Hall, KCB, MBE, MC
Lennox-Boyd, The Hon. Sir Mark Alexander, Kt.

Leon, Sir John Ronald, Bt. (1911)
Leonard, *Rt. Revd Monsignor* and *Rt. Hon.* Graham Douglas, KCVO
Lepping, Sir George Geria Dennis, GCMG, MBE
Le Quesne, Sir (John) Godfray, Kt., QC
Lee-Steere, Sir Ernest Henry, KBE
Leslie, Sir Colin Alan Bettridge, Kt.
Leslie, Sir John Norman Ide, Bt. (1876)
Leslie, Sir Peter Evelyn, Kt.
Lester, Sir James Theodore, Kt.
Lethbridge, Sir Thomas Periam Hector Noel, Bt. (1804)
Lever, Sir Jeremy Frederick, KCMG, QC
Lever, Sir Paul, KCMG
Lever, Sir (Tresham) Christopher Arthur Lindsay, Bt. (1911)
Leveson, *Hon.* Sir Brian Henry, Kt.
Levey, Sir Michael Vincent, Kt., LVO
Levine, Sir Montague Bernard, Kt.
Levinge, Sir Richard George Robin, Bt. (I. 1704)
Lewinton, Sir Christopher, Kt.
Lewis, Sir David Courtenay Mansel, KCVO
Lewis, Sir John Anthony, Kt., OBE
Lewis, Sir Terence Murray, Kt., OBE, GM, QPM
Lewison, *Hon.* Sir Kim Martin Jordan, Kt.
Ley, Sir Ian Francis, Bt. (1905)
Li, Sir Ka-Shing, KBE
Lickiss, Sir Michael Gillam, Kt.
Liddington, Sir Bruce, Kt.
Liggins, *Prof.* Sir Graham Collingwood, Kt., CBE, FRS
Lightman, *Hon.* Sir Gavin Anthony, Kt.
Lighton, Sir Thomas Hamilton, Bt. (I. 1791)
Likierman, *Prof.* Sir John Andrew, Kt.
Lilleyman, *Prof.* Sir John Stuart, Kt.
Limon, Sir Donald William, KCB
Linacre, Sir (John) Gordon (Seymour), Kt., CBE, AFC, DFM
Lindop, Sir Norman, Kt.
Lindsay, Sir James Harvey Kincaid Stewart, Kt.
Lindsay, *Hon.* Sir John Edmund Frederic, Kt.
†Lindsay, Sir James Martin Evelyn, Bt, (1962)
†Lindsay-Hogg, Sir Michael Edward, Bt. (1905)
Lipton, Sir Stuart Anthony, Kt.
Lipworth, Sir (Maurice) Sydney, Kt.
Lister-Kaye, Sir John Phillip Lister, Bt. (1812)
Liston-Foulis, Sir Ian Primrose, Bt. (S. 1634)
Lithgow, Sir William James, Bt. (1925)
Little, *Most Revd* Thomas Francis, KBE
Littler, Sir (James) Geoffrey, KCB
Llewellyn, Sir David St Vincent, Bt. (1922)
Llewellyn-Smith, *Prof.* Sir Christopher Hubert, Kt.

Lloyd, *Prof.* Sir Geoffrey Ernest Richard, Kt., FBA
Lloyd, Sir Ian Stewart, Kt.
Lloyd, Sir Nicholas Markley, Kt.
Lloyd, *Rt. Hon.* Sir Peter Robert Cable, Kt., MP
Lloyd, Sir Richard Ernest Butler, Bt. (1960)
Lloyd, *Hon.* Sir Timothy Andrew Wigram, Kt.
Lloyd-Hughes, Sir Trevor Denby, Kt.
Lloyd-Jones, Sir (Peter) Hugh (Jefferd), Kt.
Loane, *Most Revd* Marcus Lawrence, KBE
Lobo, Sir Rogerio Hyndman, Kt., CBE
†Loder, Sir Edmund Jeune, Bt. (1887)
Logan, Sir David Brian Carleton, KCMG
Logan, Sir Donald Arthur, KCMG
Lokoloko, Sir Tore, GCMG, GCVO, OBE
Longmore, *Rt. Hon.* Sir Andrew Centlivres, Kt.
Loram, *Vice-Adm.* Sir David Anning, KCB, CVO
Lord, Sir Michael Nicholson, Kt.
Lorimer, Sir (Thomas) Desmond, Kt.
Los, *Hon.* Sir Kubulan, Kt., CBE
Loughran, Sir Gerald Finbar, KCB
Louisy, Sir Allan Fitzgerald Laurent, KCMG, PC
Lovell, Sir (Alfred Charles) Bernard, Kt., OBE, FRS
Lovelock, Sir Douglas Arthur, KCB
Loveridge, Sir John Warren, Kt.
Lovill, Sir John Roger, Kt., CBE
Lowe, *Air Chief Marshal* Sir Douglas Charles, GCB, DFC, AFC
Lowe, Sir Frank Budge, Kt.
Lowe, Sir Thomas William Gordon, Bt. (1918)
Lowson, Sir Ian Patrick, Bt. (1951)
Lowther, *Col.* Sir Charles Douglas, Bt. (1824)
Lowther, Sir John Luke, KCVO, CBE
Loyd, Sir Francis Alfred, KCMG, OBE
Loyd, Sir Julian St John, KCVO
Lu, Sir Tseng Chi, Kt.
Lucas, *Prof.* Sir Colin Renshaw, Kt.
Lucas, Sir Thomas Edward, Bt. (1887)
Lucas-Tooth, Sir (Hugh) John, Bt. (1920)
Luddington, Sir Donald Collin Cumyn, KBE, CMG, CVO
Lumsden, Sir David James, Kt.
Lushington, Sir John Richard Castleman, Bt. (1791)
Luttrell, *Col.* Sir Geoffrey Walter Fownes, KCVO, MC
Lygo, *Adm.* Sir Raymond Derek, KCB
Lyle, Sir Gavin Archibald, Bt. (1929)
Lynch-Blosse, *Capt.* Sir Richard Hely, Bt. (1622)
Lynch-Robinson, Sir Dominick Christopher, Bt. (1920)
Lyne, Sir Roderic Michael John, KBE, CMG

Lyons, Sir James Reginald, Kt.
Lyons, Sir John, Kt.
Lyons, Sir Michael Thomas, Kt.
McAlpine, Sir William Hepburn, Bt. (1918)
Macara, Sir Alexander Wiseman, Kt., FRCP, FRCGP
†Macara, Sir Hugh Kenneth, Bt. (1911)
McCaffrey, Sir Thomas Daniel, Kt.
McCallum, Sir Donald Murdo, Kt., CBE, FRENG
McCamley, Sir Graham Edward, KBE
McCarthy, Sir Callum, Kt.
McCartney, Sir (James) Paul, Kt., MBE
Macartney, Sir John Barrington, Bt. (I. 1799)
McClintock, Sir Eric Paul, Kt.
McColl, Sir Colin Hugh Verel, KCMG
McCollum, *Rt. Hon.* Sir William, Kt.
McCombe, *Hon.* Sir Richard George Bramwell, Kt.
McConnell, Sir Robert Shean, Bt. (1900)
McCorkell, *Col.* Sir Michael William, KCVO, OBE, TD
MacCormac, Sir Richard Cornelius, Kt., CBE
MacCormick, *Prof.* Sir Donald Neil, Kt., MEP, QC
†McCowan, Sir David William, Bt. (1934)
McCullough, *Hon.* Sir (Iain) Charles (Robert), Kt.
MacDermott, *Rt. Hon.* Sir John Clarke, Kt.
Macdonald of Sleat, Sir Ian Godfrey Bosville, Bt. (S. 1625)
Macdonald, Sir Kenneth Carmichael, KCB
McDonald, Sir Trevor, Kt., OBE
McDowell, Sir Eric Wallace, Kt., CBE
Mace, *Lt.-Gen.* Sir John Airth, KBE, CB
McEwen, Sir John Roderick Hugh, Bt. (1953)
McFarland, Sir John Talbot, Bt. (1914)
MacFarlane, *Prof.* Sir Alistair George James, Kt., CBE, FRS
Macfarlane, Sir (David) Neil, Kt.
Macfarlane, Sir George Gray, Kt., CB FRENG
McFarlane, Sir Ian, Kt.
McGeoch, *Vice-Adm.* Sir Ian Lachlan Mackay, KCB, DSO, DSC
McGrath, Sir Brian Henry, GCVO
Macgregor, Sir Edwin Robert, Bt. (1828)
McGregor, Sir Ian Alexander, Kt., CBE
McGregor, Sir James David, Kt., OBE
MacGregor of MacGregor, Sir Malcolm Gregor Charles, Bt. (1795)
McGrigor, *Capt.* Sir Charles Edward, Bt. (1831)
McIntosh, Sir Neil William David, Kt., CBE
McIntosh, Sir Ronald Robert Duncan, KCB

McIntyre, Sir Donald Conroy, Kt., CBE

McIntyre, Sir Meredith Alister, Kt.

Mackay, *Hon.* Sir Colin Crichton, Kt.

MacKay, *Prof.* Sir Donald Iain, Kt.

MacKay, Sir Francis Henry, Kt.

McKay, Sir John Andrew, Kt., CBE

McKay, Sir William Robert, KCB

Mackay-Dick, *Maj.-Gen.* Sir Iain Charles, KCVO, MBE

Mackechnie, Sir Alistair John, Kt.

McKellen, Sir Ian Murray, Kt., CBE

Mackenzie, Sir (James William) Guy, Bt. (1890)

Mackenzie, *Gen.* Sir Jeremy John George, GCB, OBE

†Mackenzie, Sir Peter Douglas, Bt. (S. 1673)

†Mackenzie, Sir Roderick McQuhae, Bt. (S. 1703)

McKenzie, Sir Roy Allan, KBE

Mackerras, Sir (Alan) Charles (MacLaurin), Kt., CH, CBE

Mackeson, Sir Rupert Henry, Bt. (1954)

McKillop, Sir Thomas Fulton Wilson, Kt.

McKinnon, Sir James, Kt.

McKinnon, *Hon.* Sir Stuart Neil, Kt.

Mackintosh, Sir Cameron Anthony, Kt.

Mackworth, Sir Digby (John), Bt. (1776)

McLaren, Sir Robin John Taylor, KCMG

McLaughlin, *Hon.* Mr Justice, Sir Richard, Kt.

Maclean of Dunconnell, Sir Charles Edward, Bt. (1957)

Maclean, Sir Donald Og Grant, Kt.

Maclean, Sir Lachlan Hector Charles, Bt. (NS 1631)

Maclean, Sir Murdo, Kt.

McLeod, Sir Charles Henry, Bt. (1925)

MacLeod, Sir (John) Maxwell Norman, Bt. (1924)

Macleod, Sir (Nathaniel William) Hamish, KBE

McLintock, Sir (Charles) Alan, Kt.

McLintock, Sir Michael William, Bt. (1934)

Maclure, Sir John Robert Spencer, Bt. (1898)

McMahon, Sir Brian Patrick, Bt. (1817)

McMahon, Sir Christopher William, Kt.

McMaster, Sir Brian John, Kt., CBE

Macmillan, Sir (Alexander McGregor) Graham, Kt.

MacMillan, *Lt.-Gen.* Sir John Richard Alexander, KCB, CBE

McMullin, *Rt. Hon.* Sir Duncan Wallace, Kt.

McMurtry, Sir David, Kt., CBE

Macnaghten, Sir Patrick Alexander, Bt. (1836)

McNair-Wilson, Sir Patrick Michael Ernest David, Kt.

McNamara, *Air Chief Marshal* Sir Neville Patrick, KBE

Macnaughton, *Prof.* Sir Malcolm Campbell, Kt.

McNee, Sir David Blackstock, Kt., QPM

McNulty, Sir (Robert William) Roy, Kt., CBE

MacPhail, Sir Bruce Dugald, Kt.

Macpherson, Sir Ronald Thomas Steward (Tommy), CBE, MC, TD

Macpherson of Cluny, *Hon.* Sir William Alan, Kt., TD

McQuarrie, Sir Albert, Kt.

MacRae, Sir (Alastair) Christopher (Donald Summerhayes), KCMG

Macready, Sir Nevil John Wilfrid, Bt. (1923)

MacSween, *Prof.* Sir Roderick Norman McIver, Kt.

Mactaggart, Sir John Auld, Bt. (1938)

Macwhinnie, Sir Gordon Menzies, Kt., CBE

McWilliam, Sir Michael Douglas, KCMG

McWilliams, Sir Francis, GBE

Madden, Sir David Christopher Andrew, KCMG

Madden, Sir Peter John, Bt. (1919)

Maddox, Sir John Royden, Kt.

Madel, Sir (William) David, Kt., MP

Magnus, Sir Laurence Henry Philip, Bt. (1917)

Mahon, Sir (John) Denis, Kt., CH, CBE

Mahon, Sir William Walter, Bt. (1819)

Maiden, Sir Colin James, Kt., DPHIL

Main, Sir Peter Tester, Kt., ERD

Maingard de la Ville ès Offrans, Sir Louis Pierre René, Kt., CBE

Maini, *Prof.* Sir Ravinder Nath, Kt.

Maino, Sir Charles, KBE

†Maitland, Sir Charles Alexander, Bt. (1818)

Maitland, Sir Donald James Dundas, GCMG, OBE

Major, Sir John, KG, CH, PC

Malbon, *Vice-Adm.* Sir Fabian Michael, KBE

Malcolm, Sir James William Thomas Alexander, Bt. (S. 1665)

Malet, Sir Harry Douglas St Lo, Bt. (1791)

Mallaby, Sir Christopher Leslie George, GCMG, GCVO

Mallet, Sir William George, GCMG, CBE

Mallick, *Prof.* Sir Netar Prakash, Kt.

Mallinson, Sir William James, Bt. (1935)

Malpas, Sir Robert, Kt., CBE

Mamo, Sir Anthony Joseph, Kt., OBE

Mancham, Sir James Richard Marie, KBE

Mander, Sir Charles Marcus, Bt. (1911)

Manduell, Sir John, Kt., CBE

Mann, *Hon.* Sir George Anthony, Kt.

Mann, *Rt. Revd* Michael Ashley, KCVO

Mann, Sir Rupert Edward, Bt. (1905)

Manning, Sir David Geoffrey, KCMG

Mansel, Sir Philip, Bt. (1622)

Mansfield, *Vice-Adm.* Sir (Edward) Gerard (Napier), KBE, CVO

Mansfield, *Prof.* Sir Peter, Kt.

Mantell, *Rt. Hon.* Sir Charles Barrie Knight, Kt.

Manton, Sir Edwin Alfred Grenville, Kt.

Manuella, Sir Tulaga, GCMG, MBE

Manzie, Sir (Andrew) Gordon, KCB

Margetson, Sir John William Denys, KCMG

Mark, Sir Robert, GBE

Markesinis, *Prof.* Sir Basil Spyridonos, Kt., QC

Markham, Sir Charles John, Bt. (1911)

Marling, Sir Charles William Somerset, Bt. (1882)

Marmot, Prof. Sir Michael Gideon, Kt.

Marr, Sir Leslie Lynn, Bt. (1919)

Marriner, Sir Neville, Kt., CBE

†Marsden, Sir Simon Neville Llewelyn, Bt. (1924)

Marsh, *Prof.* Sir John Stanley, Kt., CBE

Marshall, Sir Arthur Gregory George, Kt., OBE

Marshall, Sir Denis Alfred, Kt.

Marshall, *Prof.* Sir (Oshley) Roy, Kt., CBE

Marshall, Sir Peter Harold Reginald, KCMG

Marshall, Sir (Robert) Michael, Kt.

Martin, Sir Clive Haydon, Kt., OBE

Martin, Sir George Henry, Kt., CBE

Martin, *Vice-Adm.* Sir John Edward Ludgate, KCB, DSC

Martin, *Prof.* Sir Laurence Woodward, Kt.

Martin, Sir (Robert) Bruce, Kt., QC

Marychurch, Sir Peter Harvey, KCMG

Masefield, Sir Charles Beech Gordon, Kt.

Masefield, Sir Peter Gordon, Kt.

Mason, *Hon.* Sir Anthony Frank, KBE

Mason, Sir (Basil) John, Kt., CB, DSC, FRS

Mason, *Prof.* Sir David Kean, Kt., CBE

Mason, Sir Frederick Cecil, KCVO, CMG

Mason, Sir Gordon Charles, Kt., OBE

Mason, Sir John Charles Moir, KCMG

Mason, Sir John Peter, Kt., CBE

Mason, Sir Peter James, KBE

Mason, *Prof.* Sir Ronald, KCB, FRS

Massy-Greene, Sir (John) Brian, Kt.

Matane, HE Sir Paulias Nguna, GCMG, OBE

Mather, Sir (David) Carol (Macdonell), Kt., MC

Mathers, Sir Robert William, Kt.

Matheson of Matheson, Sir Fergus John, Bt. (1882)

Mathewson, Sir George Ross, Kt., CBE, PHD, FRSE

Matthews, Sir Peter Alec, Kt.

Matthews, Sir Terence Hedley, Kt., OBE

Maud, *Hon.* Sir Humphrey John Hamilton, KCMG

Maughan, Sir Deryck, Kt.

Mawer, Sir Philip John Courtney, Kt.

Maxwell, Sir Michael Eustace George, Bt. (S. 1681)

Maxwell-Hyslop, Sir Robert John (Robin), Kt.

Maxwell-Scott, Sir Dominic James, Bt. (1642)

May, *Rt. Hon.* Sir Anthony Tristram Kenneth, Kt.

Mayhew-Sanders, Sir John Reynolds, Kt.

Maynard, *Hon.* Sir Clement Travelyan, Kt.

Mayne, *Very Revd* Michael Clement Otway, KCVO

Meadow, *Prof.* Sir (Samuel) Roy, Kt., FRCP, FRCPE

Medlycott, Sir Mervyn Tregonwell, Bt. (1808)

Megarry, *Rt. Hon.* Sir Robert Edgar, Kt., FBA

Meldrum, Sir Graham, Kt., CBE, QFSM

Melhuish, Sir Michael Ramsay, KBE, CMG

Mellon, Sir James, KCMG

Melmoth, Sir Graham John, Kt.

Menter, Sir James Woodham, Kt., PHD, SCD, FRS

Merifield, Sir Anthony James, KCVO, CB

†Meyer, Sir (Anthony) Ashley Frank, Bt. (1910)

Meyer, Sir Christopher John Rome, KCMG

Meyjes, Sir Richard Anthony, Kt.

†Meyrick, Sir Timothy Thomas Charlton, Bt. (1880)

Miakwe, *Hon.* Sir Akepa, KBE

Michael, Sir Duncan, Kt.

Michael, *Dr* Sir Jonathan, Kt.

Michael, Sir Peter Colin, Kt., CBE

Middleton, Sir John Maxwell, Kt.

Middleton, Sir Peter Edward, GCB

Miers, Sir (Henry) David Alastair Capel, KBE, CMG

Milbank, Sir Anthony Frederick, Bt. (1882)

Milborne-Swinnerton-Pilkington, Sir Thomas Henry, Bt. (S. 1635)

Milburn, Sir Anthony Rupert, Bt. (1905)

Miles, Sir Peter Tremayne, KCVO

Miles, Sir William Napier Maurice, Bt. (1859)

Millais, Sir Geoffrey Richard Everett, Bt. (1885)

Millar, Sir Oliver Nicholas, GCVO, FBA

Millard, Sir Guy Elwin, KCMG, CVO

Miller, Sir Albert Joel, KCMG, MVO, MBE, QPM, CPM

Miller, Sir Donald John, Kt., FR.SE, FRENG

Miller, Sir Harry Holmes, Bt. (1705)

Miller, Sir Hilary Duppa (Hal), Kt.

Miller, *Lt.-Col.* Sir John Mansel, GCVO, DSO, MC

Miller, Sir Jonathan Wolfe, Kt., CBE

Miller, Sir Peter North, Kt.

Miller, Sir Robin Robert William, Kt.

Miller, Sir Ronald Andrew Baird, Kt., CBE

Miller of Glenlee, Sir Stephen William Macdonald, Bt. (1788)

Mills, *Vice-Adm.* Sir Charles Piercy, KCB, CBE, DSC

Mills, Sir Ian, Kt.

Mills, Sir Frank, KCVO, CMG

Mills, Sir Peter Frederick Leighton, Bt. (1921)

Milman, Sir David Patrick, Bt. (1800)

Milne, Sir John Drummond, Kt.

Milne-Watson, Sir Andrew Michael, Bt. (1937)

Milner, Sir Timothy William Lycett, Bt. (1717)

Milton-Thompson, *Surgeon Vice-Adm.* Sir Godfrey James, KBE

Mirrlees, *Prof.* Sir James Alexander, Kt., FBA

Mitchell, Sir David Bower, Kt.

Mitchell, Sir Derek Jack, KCB, CVO

Mitchell, *Rt. Hon.* Sir James FitzAllen, KCMG

Mitchell, *Very Revd* Patrick Reynolds, KCVO

Mitchell, *Hon.* Sir Stephen George, Kt.

Mitting, *Hon.* Sir John Edward, Kt.

Moate, Sir Roger Denis, Kt.

Mobbs, Sir (Gerald) Nigel, Kt.

Moberly, Sir Patrick Hamilton, KCMG

Moffat, Sir Brian Scott, Kt., OBE

Moffat, *Lt.-Gen.* Sir (William) Cameron, KBE

Mogg, Sir John Frederick, KCMG

Moir, Sir Christopher Ernest, Bt. (1916)

†Molesworth-St Aubyn, Sir William, Bt. (1689)

†Molony, Sir Thomas Desmond, Bt. (1925)

Monck, Sir Nicholas Jeremy, KCB

Money-Coutts, Sir David Burdett, KCVO

Montagu, Sir Nicholas Lionel John, KCB

Montagu-Pollock, Sir Giles Hampden, Bt. (1872)

Montague-Browne, Sir Anthony Arthur Duncan, KCMG, CBE, DFC

Montgomery, Sir (Basil Henry) David, Bt. (1801)

Montgomery, Sir (William) Fergus, Kt.

Montgomery-Cuninghame, Sir John Christopher Foggo, Bt. (NS 1672)

Moody-Stuart, Sir Mark, KCMG

Moollan, Sir Abdool Hamid Adam, Kt.

Moollan, *Hon.* Sir Cassam (Ismael), Kt.

†Moon, Sir Roger, Bt. (1887)

Moore, *Most Revd* Desmond Charles, KBE

Moore, Sir Francis Thomas, Kt.

Moore, *Maj.-Gen.* Sir (John) Jeremy, KCB, OBE, MC

Moore, Sir John Michael, KCVO, CB, DSC

Moore, *Vice Adm.* Sir Michael Antony Claës, KBE, LVO

Moore, *Prof.* Sir Norman Winfrid, Bt. (1919)

Moore, Sir Patrick Alfred Caldwell, Kt., CBE

Moore, Sir Patrick William Eisdell, Kt., OBE

Moore, Sir Roger George, KBE

Moore, Sir William Roger Clotworthy, Bt. (1932), TD

Moore-Bick, *Hon.* Sir Martin James, Kt., PC

Moores, Sir Peter, Kt., CBE

Morauta, Sir Mekere, Kt.

Mordaunt, Sir Richard Nigel Charles, Bt. (1611)

Moreton, Sir John Oscar, KCMG, KCVO, MC

Morgan, *Vice-Adm.* Sir Charles Christopher, KBE

Morgan, *Hon.* Sir Charles Declan, Kt.

Morgan, Sir Graham, Kt.

Morgan, Sir John Albert Leigh, KCMG

Morgan-Giles, *Rear-Adm.* Sir Morgan Charles, Kt., DSO, OBE, GM

Morison, *Hon.* Sir Thomas Richard Atkin, Kt.

Morland, *Hon.* Sir Michael, Kt.

Morland, Sir Robert Kenelm, Kt.

Morpeth, Sir Douglas Spottiswoode, Kt., TD

†Morris, Sir Allan Lindsay, Bt. (1806)

Morris, *Air Marshal* Sir Arnold Alec, KBE, CB

Morris, Sir Derek James, Kt.

Morris, Sir (James) Richard (Samuel), Kt., CBE

Morris, Sir Keith Elliot Hedley, KBE, CMG

Morris, *Prof.* Sir Peter John, Kt.

Morris, Sir Trefor Alfred, Kt., CBE, QPM

Morris, Sir William, Kt.

Morris, *Very Revd* William James, KCVO

Morrison, Sir (Alexander) Fraser, Kt., CBE

Morrison, Sir Howard Leslie, Kt., OBE

Morrison, Sir Kenneth Duncan, Kt., CBE

Morrison-Bell, Sir William Hollin Dayrell, Bt. (1905)

Morrison-Low, Sir James Richard, Bt. (1908)

Morritt, *Rt. Hon.* Sir (Robert) Andrew, Kt., CVO

Morrow, Sir Ian Thomas, Kt.

Morse, Sir Christopher Jeremy, KCMG

Mortimer, Sir John Clifford, Kt., CBE, QC

Morton, *Adm.* Sir Anthony Storrs, GBE, KCB

Moseley, Sir George Walker, KCB

Moses, *Hon.* Sir Alan George, Kt.

Moss, Sir David Joseph, KCVO, CMG

Moss, Sir Stirling Craufurd, Kt., OBE
Mostyn, *Gen.* Sir (Joseph) David Frederick, KCB, CBE
Mostyn, Sir William Basil John, Bt, (1670)
Mott, Sir John Harmer, Bt. (1930)
Mottram, Sir Richard Clive, KCB
†Mount, Sir (William Robert) Ferdinand, Bt. (1921)
Mountain, Sir Denis Mortimer, Bt. (1922)
Mountfield, Sir Robin, KCB
Mowbray, Sir John, Kt.
Mowbray, Sir John Robert, Bt. (1880)
Muir, Sir Laurence Macdonald, Kt.
†Muir, Sir Richard James Kay, Bt. (1892)
Muir-Mackenzie, Sir Alexander Alwyne Henry Charles Brinton, Bt. (1805)
Mulcahy, Sir Geoffrey John, Kt.
Mullens, *Lt.-Gen.* Sir Anthony Richard Guy, KCB, OBE
Mummery, *Rt. Hon.* Sir John Frank, Kt.
Munby, *Hon.* Sir James Lawrence, Kt.
Munn, Sir James, Kt., OBE
Munro, Sir Alan Gordon, KCMG
†Munro, Sir Kenneth Arnold William, Bt. (S. 1634)
†Munro, Sir Keith Gordon, Bt. (1825)
Muria, *Hon.* Sir Gilbert John Baptist, Kt.
Murphy, Sir Leslie Frederick, Kt.
Murray, *Rt. Hon.* Sir Donald Bruce, Kt.
Murray, Sir James, KCMG
Murray, *Prof.* Sir Kenneth, Kt.
Murray, Sir Nigel Andrew Digby, Bt. (S. 1628)
Murray, Sir Patrick Ian Keith, Bt. (S. 1673)
†Murray, Sir Rowland William, Bt. (S. 1630)
Mursell, Sir Peter, Kt., MBE
Musgrave, Sir Christopher John Shane, Bt. (1782)
Musgrave, Sir Christopher Patrick Charles, Bt. (1611)
Musson, *Gen.* Sir Geoffrey Randolph Dixon, GCB, CBE, DSO
Myers, Sir Philip Alan, Kt., OBE, QPM
Myers, *Prof.* Sir Rupert Horace, KBE
Mynors, Sir Richard Baskerville, Bt. (1964)
Naipaul, Sir Vidiadhar Surajprasad, Kt.
Nairn, Sir Michael, Bt. (1904)
Nairne, *Rt. Hon.* Sir Patrick Dalmahoy, GCB, MC
Naish, Sir (Charles) David, Kt.
Nall, Sir Edward William Joseph Bt. (1954)
Namaliu, *Rt. Hon.* Sir Rabbie Langanai, KCMG
†Napier, Sir Charles Joseph, Bt. (1867)
Napier, Sir John Archibald Lennox, Bt. (S. 1627)

Napier, Sir Oliver John, Kt.
Naylor-Leyland, Sir Philip Vyvyan, Bt. (1895)
Neal, Sir Eric James, Kt., CVO
Neal, Sir Leonard Francis, Kt., CBE
Neale, Sir Gerrard Anthony, Kt.
Neave, Sir Paul Arundell, Bt. (1795)
Neill, *Rt. Hon.* Sir Brian Thomas, Kt.
Neill, Sir (James) Hugh, KCVO, CBE, TD
†Nelson, Sir Jamie Charles Vernon Hope, Bt. (1912)
Nelson, *Hon.* Sir Robert Franklyn, Kt.
Neuberger, *Hon.* Sir David Edmond, Kt., PC
Neubert, Sir Michael John, Kt.
Neville, Sir Roger Albert Gartside, Kt.
New, *Maj.-Gen.* Sir Laurence Anthony Wallis, Kt., CB, CBE
Newall, Sir Paul Henry, Kt., TD
Newby, *Prof.* Sir Howard Joseph, Kt., CBE
Newington, Sir Michael John, KCMG
Newman, Sir Francis Hugh Cecil, Bt. (1912)
Newman, Sir Geoffrey Robert, Bt. (1836)
Newman, *Hon.* Sir George Michael, Kt.
Newman, Sir Kenneth Leslie, GBE, QPM
Newman, *Vice-Adm.* Sir Roy Thomas, KCB
Newsam, Sir Peter Anthony, Kt.
†Newson-Smith, Sir Peter Frank Graham, Bt. (1944)
Newton, Sir (Charles) Wilfred, Kt., CBE
Newton, Sir (Harry) Michael (Rex), Bt. (1900)
Newton, Sir Kenneth Garnar, Bt. (1924), OBE, TD
Ngata, Sir Henare Kohere, KBE
Nichol, Sir Duncan Kirkbride, Kt., CBE
Nicholas, Sir David, Kt., CBE
Nicholas, Sir John William, KCVO, CMG
Nicholls, *Air Marshal* Sir John Moreton, KCB, CBE, DFC, AFC
Nicholls, Sir Nigel Hamilton, KCVO, CBE
Nichols, Sir Richard Everard, Kt.
Nicholson, Sir Bryan Hubert, Kt. GBE
†Nicholson, Sir Charles Christian, Bt. (1912)
Nicholson, *Rt. Hon.* Sir Michael, Kt.
Nicholson, Sir Paul Douglas, Kt.
Nicholson, Sir Robin Buchanan, Kt., PHD, FRS, FRENG
Nicoll, Sir William, KCMG
Nightingale, Sir Charles Manners Gamaliel, Bt. (1628)
Nixon, Sir Simon Michael Christopher, Bt. (1906)
Nixon, Sir Edwin Ronald, Kt., CBE
Noble, Sir David Brunel, Bt. (1902)
Noble, Sir Iain Andrew, Bt., OBE (1923)

Nombri, Sir Joseph Karl, Kt., ISO, BEM
Noon, Sir Gulam Kaderbhoy, Kt., MBE
Norman, Sir Arthur Gordon, KBE, DFC
Norman, Sir Mark Annesley, Bt. (1915)
Norman, Sir Robert Henry, Kt., OBE
Norman, Sir Ronald, Kt., OBE
Normington, Sir David John, KCB
Norrington, Sir Roger Arthur Carver, Kt., CBE
Norriss, *Air Marshal* Sir Peter Coulson, KBE, CB, AFC
North, Sir Peter Machin, Kt., CBE, QC, DCL, FBA
North, Sir Thomas Lindsay, Kt.
North, Sir (William) Jonathan (Frederick), Bt. (1920)
Norton-Griffiths, Sir John, Bt. (1922)
Nossal, Sir Gustav Joseph Victor, Kt., CBE
Nott, *Rt. Hon.* Sir John William Frederic, KCB
Nourse, *Rt. Hon.* Sir Martin Charles, Kt.
Nugent, Sir John Edwin Lavallin, Bt. (I. 1795)
Nugent, Sir Robin George Colborne, Bt. (1806)
†Nugent, Sir (Walter) Richard Middleton, Bt. (1831)
Nunn, Sir Trevor Robert, Kt., CBE
Nunneley, Sir Charles Kenneth Roylance, Kt.
Nursaw, Sir James, KCB, QC
Nurse, Sir Paul Maxime, Kt.
Nuttall, Sir Nicholas Keith Lillington, Bt. (1922)
Nutting, Sir John Grenfell, Bt. (1903), QC
Oakeley, Sir John Digby Atholl, Bt. (1790)
Oakes, Sir Christopher, Bt. (1939)
Oakshott, *Hon.* Sir Anthony Hendrie, Bt. (1959)
Oates, Sir Thomas, Kt., CMG, OBE
O'Brien, Sir Frederick William Fitzgerald, Kt.
O'Brien, Sir Richard, Kt., DSO, MC
O'Brien, Sir Timothy John, Bt. (1849)
O'Brien, *Adm.* Sir William Donough, KCB, DSC
O'Connell, Sir Bernard, Kt.
O'Connell, Sir Maurice James Donagh MacCarthy, Bt. (1869)
O'Dea, Sir Patrick Jerad, KCVO
Odell, Sir Stanley John, Kt.
Odgers, Sir Graeme David William, Kt.
O'Donnell, Sir Augustine Thomas, KCB
O'Donnell, Sir Christopher John, Kt.
O'Donoghue, *Lt.-Gen.* Sir Kevin, KCB, CBE
O'Dowd, Sir David Joseph, Kt., CBE, QPM
Ogden, *Dr* Sir Peter James, Kt.
Ogden, Sir Robert, Kt., CBE

Ogilvy, Sir Francis Gilbert Arthur, Bt. (S. 1626)

Ogilvy-Wedderburn, Sir Andrew John Alexander, Bt. (1803)

Ognall, *Hon.* Sir Harry Henry, Kt.

Ohlson, Sir Brian Eric Christopher, Bt. (1920)

Oldham, *Dr* Sir John, Kt., OBE

Oliver, Sir James Michael Yorrick, Kt.

O'Loghlen, Sir Colman Michael, Bt. (1838)

Olver, Sir Stephen John Linley, KBE, CMG

Omand, Sir David Bruce, GCB

O'Nions, Prof. Sir Robert Keith, Kt., FRS, PHD

Ondaatje, Sir Christopher, Kt., CBE

Onslow, Sir John Roger Wilmot, Bt. (1797)

Oppenheimer, Sir Michael Bernard Grenville, Bt. (1921)

Orde, Sir Hugh Stephen Roden, Kt., OBE

O'Regan, *Dr* Sir Stephen Gerard (Tipene), Kt.

O'Reilly, Sir Anthony John Francis, Kt.

Orr, Sir David Alexander, Kt., MC

Orr, Sir John, Kt., OBE

Orr-Ewing, Sir (Alistair) Simon, Bt. (1963)

Orr-Ewing, Sir Archibald Donald, Bt. (1886)

Osborn, Sir John Holbrook, Kt.

Osborn, Sir Richard Henry Danvers, Bt. (1662)

Osborne, Sir Peter George, Bt. (I. 1629)

Osmond, Sir Douglas, Kt., CBE

Osmotherly, Sir Edward Benjamin Crofton, Kt., CB

O'Sullevan, Sir Peter John, Kt., CBE

Oswald, *Admiral of the Fleet* Sir (John) Julian Robertson, GCB

Oswald, Sir (William Richard) Michael, KCVO

Otton, Sir Geoffrey John, KCB

Otton, *Rt. Hon.* Sir Philip Howard, Kt.

Oulton, Sir Antony Derek Maxwell, GCB, QC

Ouseley, *Hon.* Sir Brian Walter, Kt.

Outram, Sir Alan James, Bt. (1858)

Owen, Sir Geoffrey, Kt.

Owen, *Hon.* Sir John Arthur Dalziel, Kt.

Owen, *Hon.* Sir Robert Michael, Kt.

Owen-Jones, Sir Lindsay Harwood, KBE

Packer, Sir Richard John, KCB

Page, Sir (Arthur) John, Kt.

Page, Sir John Joseph Joffre, Kt., OBE

Paget, Sir Julian Tolver, Bt. (1871), CVO

Paget, Sir Richard Herbert, Bt. (1886)

Paine, Sir Christopher Hammon, Kt., FRCP, FRCR

Pakenham, *Hon.* Sir Michael Aiden, KBE, CMG

Palin, *Air Chief Marshal* Sir Roger Hewlett, KCB, OBE

Palliser, *Rt. Hon.* Sir (Arthur) Michael, GCMG

Palmar, Sir Derek James, Kt.

Palmer, Sir Albert Rocky, Kt.

Palmer, Sir (Charles) Mark, Bt. (1886)

Palmer, Sir Geoffrey Christopher John, Bt. (1660)

Palmer, *Rt. Hon.* Sir Geoffrey Winston Russell, KCMG

Palmer, Sir John Edward Somerset, Bt. (1791)

Palmer, *Maj.-Gen.* Sir (Joseph) Michael, KCVO

Palmer, Sir Reginald Oswald, GCMG, MBE

Pantlin, Sir Dick Hurst, Kt., CBE

Parbo, Sir Arvi Hillar, Kt.

Park, *Hon.* Sir Andrew Edward Wilson, Kt.

Parker, Sir Alan William, Kt., CBE

Parker, Sir Eric Wilson, Kt.

Parker, *Rt. Hon.* Sir Jonathan Frederic, Kt.

Parker, *Maj.* Sir Michael John, KCVO, CBE

Parker, Sir Richard (William) Hyde, Bt. (1681)

Parker, *Rt. Hon.* Sir Roger Jocelyn, Kt.

Parker, Sir (Thomas) John, Kt.

Parker, Sir William Peter Brian, Bt. (1844)

Parkes, Sir Edward Walter, Kt., FRENG

Parry, Sir Emyr Jones, KCMG

Parry-Evans, *Air Chief Marshal* Sir David, GCB, CBE

Parsons, Sir John Christopher, KCVO

Parsons, Sir (John) Michael, Kt.

Parsons, Sir Richard Edmund (Clement Fownes), KCMG

Partridge, Sir Michael John Anthony, KCB

Pascoe, *Gen.* Sir Robert Alan, KCB, MBE

†Pasley, Sir Robert Killigrew Sabine, Bt. (1794)

Paston-Bedingfeld, *Capt.* Sir Edmund George Felix, Bt. (1661)

Paterson, Sir Dennis Craig, Kt.

Patnick, Sir (Cyril) Irvine, Kt., OBE

Patten, *Hon.* Mr Justice, Sir Nicholas John, Kt.

Pattie, *Rt. Hon.* Sir Geoffrey Edwin, Kt.

Pattinson, Sir (William) Derek, Kt.

Pattison, *Prof.* Sir John Ridley, Kt., DM, FRCPATH

Pattullo, Sir (David) Bruce, Kt., CBE

Pauncefort-Duncombe, Sir Philip Digby, Bt. (1859)

Payne, Sir Norman John, Kt., CBE, FRENG

Payne-Gallwey, Sir Philip Frankland, Bt. (1812)

Peach, Sir Leonard Harry, Kt.

Peacock, *Prof.* Sir Alan Turner, Kt., DSC

Pearce, Sir (Daniel Norton) Idris, Kt., CBE, TD

Pearse, Sir Brian Gerald, Kt.

Pearson, Sir Francis Nicholas Fraser, Bt. (1964)

Pearson, *Gen.* Sir Thomas Cecil Hook, KCB, CBE, DSO

Peart, *Prof.* Sir William Stanley, Kt., MD, FRS

Pease, Sir (Alfred) Vincent, Bt. (1882)

Pease, Sir Richard Thorn, Bt. (1920)

Peat, Sir Gerrard Charles, KCVO

Peat, Sir Michael Charles Gerrard, KCVO

Peck, Sir Edward Heywood, GCMG

Peckham, *Prof.* Sir Michael John, Kt.,

Pedelty, Sir Mervyn Kay, Kt.

Peek, *Vice-Adm.* Sir Richard Innes, KBE, CB, DSC

†Peek, Sir Richard Grenville, Bt. (1874)

Peel, Sir John Harold, KCVO

Peirse, *Air Vice-Marshal* Sir Richard Charles Fairfax, KCVO, CB

Pelgen, Sir Harry Friedrich, Kt., MBE

Peliza, Sir Robert John, KBE, ED

Pelly, Sir Richard John, Bt. (1840)

Pemberton, Sir Francis Wingate William, Kt., CBE

Pendry, *Prof.* Sir John Brian, Kt., FRS

Penrose, *Prof.* Sir Roger, Kt., OM, FRS

Penry-Davey, *Hon.* Sir David Herbert, Kt.

Pepper, *Dr.* Sir David Edwin, KCMG

Perowne, *Vice-Adm.* Sir James Francis, KBE

Perring, Sir John Raymond, Bt. (1963)

Perris, Sir David (Arthur), Kt., MBE

Perry, Sir David Howard, KCB

Perry, Sir (David) Norman, Kt., MBE

Perry, Sir Michael Sydney, GBE

Pervez, Sir Mohammed Anwar, Kt., OBE

Pestell, Sir John Richard, KCVO

Peters, *Prof.* Sir David Keith, Kt., FRCP

Petersen, Sir Jeffrey Charles, KCMG

Peterson, Sir Christopher Matthew, Kt., CBE, TD

†Petit, Sir Jehangir, Bt. (1890)

Peto, Sir Henry George Morton, Bt. (1855)

Peto, Sir Michael Henry Basil, Bt. (1927)

Peto, *Prof.* Sir Richard, Kt., FRS

Petrie, Sir Peter Charles, Bt. (1918), CMG

Pettigrew, Sir Russell Hilton, Kt.

Pettit, Sir Daniel Eric Arthur, Kt.

Pettitt, Sir Dennis, Kt.

Philips, *Prof.* Sir Cyril Henry, Kt.

Philipson-Stow, Sir Christopher, Bt. (1907), DFC

Phillips, Sir Fred Albert, Kt., CVO

Phillips, Sir (Gerald) Hayden, GCB

Phillips, Sir John David, Kt., QPM

Phillips, Sir Peter John, Kt., OBE

Phillips, Sir Robin Francis, Bt. (1912)

Phillis, Sir Robert Weston, Kt.

Pickard, Sir (John) Michael, Kt.

Pickthorn, Sir James Francis Mann, Bt. (1959)

Pidgeon, Sir John Allan Stewart, Kt.

†Piers, Sir James Desmond, Bt. (I. 1661)

Piggott-Brown, Sir William Brian, Bt. (1903)

Pigot, Sir George Hugh, Bt. (1764)

Pigott, Lt.-Gen. Sir Anthony David, KCB, CBE

Pigott, Sir Berkeley Henry Sebastian, Bt. (1808)

Pike, Lt.-Gen. Sir Hew William Royston, KCB, DSO, MBE

Pike, Sir Michael Edmund, KCVO, CMG

Pike, Sir Philip Ernest Housden, Kt., QC

Pilditch, Sir Richard Edward, Bt. (1929)

Pile, Sir Frederick Devereux, Bt. (1900), MC

Pill, Rt. Hon. Sir Malcolm Thomas, Kt.

Pilling, Sir Joseph Grant, KCB

Pinker, Sir George Douglas, KCVO

Pinsent, Sir Christopher Roy, Bt. (1938)

Pinsent, Sir Matthew Clive, Kt., CBE

Pippard, Prof. Sir (Alfred) Brian, Kt., FRS

Pitakaka, Sir Moses Puibangara, GCMG

Pitcher, Sir Desmond Henry, Kt.

Pitchers, Hon. Sir Christopher (John), Kt.

Pitchford, Hon. Sir Christopher John, Kt.

Pitman, Sir Brian Ivor, Kt.

Pitoi, Sir Sere, Kt., CBE

Pitt, Sir Harry Raymond, Kt., PHD, FRS

Pitt, Sir Michael Edward, Kt.

Pitts, Sir Cyril Alfred, Kt.

Plastow, Sir David Arnold Stuart, Kt.

Platt, Sir Harold Grant, Kt.

Platt, Sir Martin Philip, Bt. (1959)

Pledger, Air Chief Marshal Sir Malcolm David, KCB, OBE, AFC

Plumbly, Sir Derek John, KCMG

Pogo, Most Revd. Ellison Leslie, KBE

Pohai, Sir Timothy, Kt., MBE

Pole, Sir (John) Richard (Walter Reginald) Carew, Bt. (1628)

Pole, Sir Peter Van Notten, Bt. (1791)

Polkinghorne, Revd Canon John Charlton, KBE, FRS

Pollard, Sir Charles, Kt.

†Pollen, Sir Richard John Hungerford, Bt. (1795)

Pollock, Sir George Frederick, Bt. (1866)

Pollock, Admiral of the Fleet Sir Michael Patrick, GCB, LVO, DSC

Ponsonby, Sir Ashley Charles Gibbs, Bt., KCVO, MC (1956)

Poole, Hon. Sir David Anthony, Kt.

Poore, Sir Roger Ricardo, Bt. (1795)

Pope, Sir Joseph Albert, Kt., DSC, PHD

Popplewell, Hon. Sir Oliver Bury, Kt.

†Porritt, Sir Jonathon Espie, Bt. (1963)

Portal, Sir Jonathan Francis, Bt. (1901)

Porter, Sir Robert Wilson, Kt., PC (NI)

Posnett, Sir Richard Neil, KBE, CMG

Potter, Rt. Hon. Sir Mark Howard, Kt.

Potter, Maj.-Gen. Sir (Wilfrid) John, KBE, CB

Potts, Hon. Sir Francis Humphrey, Kt.

Pound, Sir John David, Bt. (1905)

Povey, Sir Keith, Kt., QPM

Powell, Sir Nicholas Folliott Douglas, Bt. (1897)

Powell, Sir Richard Royle, GCB, KBE, CMG

Power, Sir Alastair John Cecil, Bt. (1924)

Power, Hon. Sir Noel Plunkett, Kt.

Prance, Prof. Sir Ghillean Tolmie, Kt., FRS

Prendergast, Sir (Walter) Kieran, KCVO, CMG

Prescott, Sir Mark, Bt. (1938)

†Preston, Sir Philip Charles Henry Hulton, Bt. (1815)

Prevost, Sir Christopher Gerald, Bt. (1805)

Price, Sir David Ernest Campbell, Kt.

Price, Sir Francis Caradoc Rose, Bt. (1815)

Price, Sir Frank Leslie, Kt.

Price, Sir Norman Charles, KCB

Prickett, Air Chief Marshal Sir Thomas Other, KCB, DSO, DFC

Prideaux, Sir Humphrey Povah Treverbian, Kt., OBE

†Primrose, Sir John Ure, Bt. (1903)

Prince-Smith, Sir (William) Richard, Bt. (1911)

Pringle, Air Marshal Sir Charles Norman Seton, KBE, FRENG

Pringle, Hon. Sir John Kenneth, Kt.

Pringle, Lt.-Gen. Sir Steuart (Robert), Bt. (S. 1683), KCB

Pritchard, Sir Neil, KCMG

Prichard-Jones, Sir John, Bt. (1910)

†Proby, Sir William Henry, Bt. (1952)

Proctor-Beauchamp, Sir Christopher Radstock, Bt. (1745)

Prosser, Sir David John, Kt.

Prosser, Sir Ian Maurice Gray, Kt.

Pryke, Sir Christopher Dudley, Bt. (1926)

Puapua, Rt. Hon. Sir Tomasi, GCMG, KBE

Pugh, Sir Idwal Vaughan, KCB

Pumfrey, Hon. Sir Nicholas Richard, Kt.

Pumphrey, Sir (John) Laurence, KCMG

Purves, Sir William, Kt., CBE, DSO

Purvis, Vice-Adm. Sir Neville, KCB

Quan, Sir Henry (Francis), KBE

Quicke, Sir John Godolphin, Kt., CBE

Quigley, Sir (William) George (Henry), Kt., CB, PHD

Quilliam, Hon. Sir (James) Peter, Kt.

Quilter, Sir Anthony Raymond Leopold Cuthbert, Bt. (1897)

Quinlan, Sir Michael Edward, GCB

Quinton, Sir James Grand, Kt.

Radcliffe, Sir Sebastian Everard, Bt. (1813)

Radda, Prof. Sir George Karoly, Kt., CBE, FRS

Rae, Hon. Sir Wallace Alexander Ramsay, Kt.

Rae, Sir William, Kt., QPM

Raeburn, Sir Michael Edward Norman, Bt. (1923)

Raikes, Vice-Adm. Sir Iwan Geoffrey, KCB, CBE, DSC

Raison, Rt. Hon. Sir Timothy Hugh Francis, Kt.

Ralli, Sir Godfrey Victor, Bt., TD (1912)

Ramdanee, Sir Mookteswar Baboolall Kailash, Kt.

Ramphal, Sir Shridath Surendranath, GCMG

Ramphul, Sir Baalkhristna, Kt.

Ramphul, Sir Indurduth, Kt.

Ramsay, Sir Alexander William Burnett, Bt. (1806)

Ramsay, Sir Allan John (Hepple), KBE, CMG

Ramsay-Fairfax-Lucy, Sir Edmund John William Hugh, Bt. (1836)

Ramsbotham, Hon. Sir Peter Edward, GCMG, GCVO

Ramsden, Sir John Charles Josslyn, Bt. (1689)

Randle, Prof. Sir Philip John, Kt.

Rankin, Sir Ian Niall, Bt. (1898)

Rasch, Sir Simon Anthony Carne, Bt. (1903)

Rashleigh, Sir Richard Harry, Bt. (1831)

Ratford, Sir David John Edward, KCMG, CVO

Rattee, Hon. Sir Donald Keith, Kt.

Rattle, Sir Simon Dennis, Kt., CBE

Rawlins, Surgeon Vice-Adm. Sir John Stuart Pepys, KBE

Rawlins, Prof. Sir Michael David, Kt., FRCP, FRCPED

Rawlinson, Sir Anthony Henry John, Bt. (1891)

Rea, Prof. Sir Desmond, Kt., OBE

Read, Air Marshal Sir Charles Frederick, KBE, CB, DFC, AFC

Read, Sir John Emms, Kt.

†Reade, Sir Kenneth Ray, Bt. (1661)

Reardon-Smith, Sir (William) Antony (John), Bt. (1920)

Reay, Lt.-Gen. Sir (Hubert) Alan John, KBE

Redgrave, Maj.-Gen. Sir Roy Michael Frederick, KBE, MC

Redgrave, Sir Steven Geoffrey, Kt., CBE

Redmayne, Sir Nicholas, Bt. (1964)

Redwood, Sir Peter Boverton, Bt. (1911)

Reece, Sir Charles Hugh, Kt.

Rees, Sir David Allan, Kt., PHD, DSC, FRS

Reeve, Sir Anthony, KCMG, KCVO

Reeves, Most Revd Paul Alfred, GCMG, GCVO

Reffell, Adm. Sir Derek Roy, KCB

Refshauge, Maj.-Gen. Sir William Dudley, Kt., CBE

Reid, Sir Alexander James, Bt. (1897)

Reid, Sir (Harold) Martin (Smith), KBE, CMG

Reid, Sir Hugh, Bt. (1922)

Reid, Sir Norman Robert, Kt.

Reid, Sir Robert Paul, Kt.

Reid, Sir William Kennedy, KCB

Reiher, Sir Frederick Bernard Carl, KBE, CMG

Reilly, Lt.-Gen. Sir Jeremy Calcott, KCB, DSO

Renals, Sir Stanley, Bt. (1895)

Renouf, Sir Clement William Bailey, Kt.

Renshaw, Sir John David Bine, Bt. (1903)

Renwick, Sir Richard Eustace, Bt. (1921)

Reporter, Sir Shapoor Ardeshirji, KBE

Reynolds, Sir David James, Bt. (1923)

Reynolds, Sir Peter William John, Kt., CBE

Rhodes, Sir John Christopher Douglas, Bt. (1919)

Rice, Maj.-Gen. Sir Desmond Hind Garrett, KCVO, CBE

Rice, Sir Timothy Miles Bindon, Kt.

Richard, Sir Cliff, Kt., OBE

Richards, Sir Brian Mansel, Kt., CBE, PHD

Richards, Hon. Sir David Anthony Stewart, Kt.

Richards, Sir Francis Neville, KCMG, CVO

Richards, Sir Rex Edward, Kt., DSC, FRS

Richards, Hon. Sir Stephen Price, Kt.

Richardson, Sir Anthony Lewis, Bt. (1924)

Richardson, Rt. Hon. Sir Ivor Lloyd Morgan, Kt.

Richardson, Sir (John) Eric, Kt., CBE

Richardson, Lt.-Gen. Sir Robert Francis, KCB, CVO, CBE

Richardson, Sir Thomas Legh, KCMG

Richardson-Bunbury, Sir (Richard David) Michael, Bt. (I. 1787)

Richmond, Prof. Sir Mark Henry, Kt., FRS

Ricketts, Sir Robert Cornwallis Gerald St Leger, Bt. (1828)

Riddell, Sir John Charles Buchanan, Bt. (S. 1628), CVO

Ridley, Sir Adam (Nicholas), Kt.

Ridley, Sir Michael Kershaw, KCVO

Rifkind, Rt. Hon. Sir Malcolm Leslie, KCMG

Rigby, Sir Anthony John, Bt. (1929)

Rigby, Sir Peter, Kt.

Rimer, Hon. Sir Colin Percy Farquharson, Kt.

†Ripley, Sir William Hugh, Bt. (1880)

Risk, Sir Thomas Neilson, Kt.

Ritako, Sir Thomas Baha, Kt., MBE

Rivett-Carnac, Sir Miles James, Bt. (1836)

Rix, Rt. Hon. Sir Bernard Anthony, Kt.

Rix, Sir John, Kt., MBE, FRENG

Robati, Sir Pupuke, KBE

Robb, Sir John Weddell, Kt.

Roberts, Hon. Sir Denys Tudor Emil, KBE,

Roberts, Sir Derek Harry, Kt., CBE, FRS, FRENG

Roberts, Prof. Sir Edward Adam, KCMG

Roberts, Prof. Sir Gareth Gwyn, Kt., FRS

Roberts, Sir Gilbert Howland Rookehurst, Bt. (1809)

Roberts, Sir Hugh Ashley, KCVO

Roberts, Sir Ivor Anthony, KCMG

Roberts, Sir Samuel, Bt. (1919)

Roberts, Sir William James Denby, Bt. (1909)

Robertson, Sir Lewis, Kt., CBE, FRSE

Robins, Sir Ralph Harry, Kt., FRENG

Robinson, Sir Albert Edward Phineas, Kt.

†Robinson, Sir Christopher Philipse, Bt. (1854)

Robinson, Sir Gerrard Jude, Kt.

Robinson, Sir Ian, Kt.

Robinson, Sir John James Michael Laud, Bt. (1660)

Robinson, Dr Sir Kenneth, Kt.

Robinson, Sir Wilfred Henry Frederick, Bt. (1908)

Robson, Prof. Sir James Gordon, Kt., CBE

Robson, Sir John Adam, KCMG

Robson, Sir Stephen Arthur, Kt., CB

Robson, Sir Robert William, Kt., CBE

Roch, Rt. Hon. Sir John Ormond, Kt.

Roche, Sir David O'Grady, Bt. (1838)

Roche, Sir Henry John, Kt.

Rodgers, Sir (Andrew) Piers (Wingate Aikin-Sneath), Bt. (1964)

Rodley, Prof. Sir Nigel, KBE

Rodrigues, Sir Alberto Maria, Kt., CBE, ED

Rogers, Air Chief Marshal Sir John Robson, KCB, CBE

Rooke, Sir Denis Eric, Kt., OM, CBE, FRS, FRENG

Ropner, Sir John Bruce Woollacott, Bt. (1952)

†Ropner, Sir Robert Clinton, Bt. (1904)

Rose, Rt. Hon. Sir Christopher Dudley Roger, Kt.

Rose, Sir Clive Martin, GCMG

Rose, Sir David Lancaster, Bt. (1874)

Rose, Gen. Sir (Hugh) Michael, KCB, CBE, DSO, QGM

Rose, Sir John Edward Victor, Kt.

Rose, Sir Julian Day, Bt. (1872 and 1909)

Ross, Maj. Sir Andrew Charles Paterson, Bt. (1960)

Ross, Lt.-Gen. Sir Robert Jeremy, KCB, OBE

Ross, Lt.-Col. Sir Walter Hugh Malcolm, KCVO, OBE

Rossi, Sir Hugh Alexis Louis, Kt.

Roth, Prof. Sir Martin, Kt., MD, FRCP

Rothschild, Sir Evelyn Robert Adrian de, Kt.

Rougier, Hon. Sir Richard George, Kt.

Rove, Revd Ikan, KBE

Rowe, Rear-Adm. Sir Patrick Barton, KCVO, CBE

Rowe-Beddoe, Sir David Sydney, Kt.

Rowe-Ham, Sir David Kenneth, GBE

Rowland, Sir (John) David, Kt.

Rowlands, Air Marshal Sir John Samuel, GC, KBE

Rowley, Sir Charles Robert, Bt. (1836)

Rowling, Sir John Reginald, Kt.

Rowlinson, Prof. Sir John Shipley, Kt., FRS

Royce, Hon. Sir Roger John, Kt.

Royden, Sir Christopher John, Bt. (1905)

Rudd, Sir (Anthony) Nigel (Russell), Kt.

Rudge, Sir Alan Walter, Kt., CBE, FRS

Rugge-Price, Sir James Keith Peter, Bt. (1804)

Ruggles-Brise, Sir John Archibald, Bt. (1935), CB, OBE, TD

Rumbold, Sir Henry John Sebastian, Bt. (1779)

Runchorelal, Sir (Udayan) Chinubhai Madhowlal, Bt. (1913)

Rusby, Vice-Adm. Sir Cameron, KCB, LVO

†Russell, Sir (Arthur) Mervyn, Bt. (1812)

Russell, Sir Charles Dominic, Bt. (1916)

Russell, Sir George, Kt., CBE

Russell, Sir Muir, KCB

Russell, Prof. Sir Peter Edward Lionel, Kt., DLITT, FBA

Rutter, Prof. Sir Michael Llewellyn, Kt., CBE, MD, FRS

Ryan, Sir Derek Gerald, Bt. (1919)

Rycroft, Sir Richard John, Bt. (1784)

Ryder, Hon. Sir Ernest Nigel Ryder, Kt., TD

Ryrie, Sir William Sinclair, KCB

Sacks, Chief Rabbi Dr Jonathan, Kt.

Sacranie, Sir Iqbal Abdul Karim Mussa, Kt., OBE

Sainsbury, Rt. Hon. Sir Timothy Alan Davan, Kt.

St Clair-Ford, Sir James Anson, Bt. (1793)

St George, Sir John Avenel Bligh, Bt. (I. 1766)

St John-Mildmay, Sir Walter John Hugh, Bt. (1772)

St Johnston, Sir Kerry, Kt.

Sainty, Sir John Christopher, KCB

Salisbury, Sir Robert William, Kt.

Salt, Sir Patrick MacDonnell, Bt. (1869)

Salt, Sir (Thomas) Michael John, Bt. (1899)

Salusbury-Trelawny, Sir John Barry, Bt. (1628)

Sampson, Sir Colin, Kt., CBE, QPM

Samuel, Sir John Michael Glen, Bt. (1898)

Samuelson, Sir (Bernard) Michael (Francis), Bt. (1884)

Samuelson, Sir Sydney Wylie, Kt., CBE
Sanders, Sir Robert Tait, KBE, CMG
Sanders, Sir Ronald Michael, KCMG
Sanderson, Sir Frank Linton, Bt. (1920)
Sarei, Sir Alexis Holyweek, Kt., CBE
Satchwell, Sir Kevin Joseph, Kt.
Savage, Sir Ernest Walter, Kt.
Savile, Sir James Wilson Vincent, Kt., OBE
Saxby, Prof. Sir Robin Keith, Kt.
Say, Rt. Revd Richard David, KCVO
Scheele, Sir Nicholas Vernon, KCMG
Schiemann, Rt. Hon. Sir Konrad Hermann Theodor, Kt.
Scholar, Sir Michael Charles, KCB
Scholey, Sir David Gerald, Kt., CBE
Scholey, Sir Robert, Kt., CBE, FRENG
Scholtens, Sir James Henry, KCVO
Schreier, Sir Bernard, Kt.
Schubert, Sir Sydney, Kt.
Scipio, Sir Hudson Rupert, Kt.
Scoon, Sir Paul, GCMG, GCVO, OBE
Scott, Sir Anthony Percy, Bt. (1913)
Scott, Sir David Aubrey, GCMG
Scott, Sir James Jervoise, Bt. (1962)
Scott, Sir Kenneth Bertram Adam, KCVO, CMG
Scott, Sir Oliver Christopher Anderson, Bt. (1909)
Scott, Prof. Sir Philip John, KBE
Scott, Sir Ridley, Kt.
Scott, Sir Robert David Hillyer, Kt.
Scott, Sir Walter John, Bt. (1907)
Scott, Rear-Adm. Sir (William) David (Stewart), KBE, CB
Seale, Sir Clarence David, Kt.
Seale, Sir John Henry, Bt. (1838)
Seaman, Sir Keith Douglas, KCVO, OBE
Sebastian, Sir Cuthbert Montraville, GCMG, OBE
†Sebright, Sir Rufus Hugo Giles, Bt. (1626)
Seccombe, Sir (William) Vernon Stephen, Kt.
Seconde, Sir Reginald Louis, KCMG, CVO
Sedley, Rt. Hon. Sir Stephen John, Kt.
Seely, Sir Nigel Edward, Bt. (1896)
Seeto, Sir Ling James, Kt., MBE
Seeyave, Sir Rene Sow Choung, Kt., CBE
Seligman, Sir Peter Wendel, Kt., CBE
Semple, Sir John Laughlin, KCB
Sergeant, Sir Patrick, Kt.
Series, Sir (Joseph Michel) Emile, Kt., CBE
Serota, Sir Nicholas Andrew, Kt.
Serpell, Sir David Radford, KCB, CMG, OBE
†Seton, Sir Charles Wallace, Bt. (S. 1683)
Seton, Sir Iain Bruce, Bt. (S. 1663)
Severne, Air Vice-Marshal Sir John de Milt, KCVO, OBE, AFC
Shackleton, Prof. Sir Nicholas John, Kt., PHD, FRS
Shaffer, Sir Peter Levin, Kt., CBE
Shakerley, Sir Geoffrey Adam, Bt. (1838)

Shakespeare, Sir Thomas William, Bt. (1942)
Sharp, Sir Adrian, Bt. (1922)
Sharp, Sir Kenneth Johnston, Kt., TD
Sharp, Sir Leslie, Kt., QPM
Sharp, Sir Sheridan Christopher Robin, Bt. (1920)
Sharples, Sir James, Kt., QPM
Shattock, Sir Gordon, Kt.
Shaw, Sir Brian Piers, Kt.
Shaw, Sir (Charles) Barry, Kt., CB, QC
Shaw, Sir Charles De Vere, Bt. (1821)
Shaw, Prof. Sir John Calman, Kt., CBE
Shaw, Sir Neil McGowan, Kt.
Shaw, Sir Roy, Kt.
Shaw, Sir Run Run, Kt., CBE
†Shaw-Stewart, Sir Ludovic Houston, Bt. (S. 1667)
Shebbeare, Sir Thomas Andrew, KCVO
Sheehy, Sir Patrick, Kt.
Sheen, Hon. Sir Barry Cross, Kt.
Sheffield, Sir Reginald Adrian Berkeley, Bt. (1755)
Shehadie, Sir Nicholas Michael, Kt., OBE
Sheil, Hon. Sir John, Kt., PC
Sheinwald, Sir Nigel Elton, KCMG
Shelley, Sir John Richard, Bt. (1611)
Shepherd, Sir Colin Ryley, Kt.
Shepherd, Sir John Alan, KCVO, CMG
Shepperd, Sir Alfred Joseph, Kt.
Sher, Sir Antony, KBE
Sherston-Baker, Sir Robert George Humphrey, Bt. (1796)
Sherman, Sir Alfred, Kt.
Shields, Prof. Sir Robert, Kt., MD
Shiffner, Sir Henry David, Bt. (1818)
Silber, Hon. Sir Stephen Robert, Kt.
Shinwell, Sir (Maurice) Adrian, Kt.
Shock, Sir Maurice, Kt.
Short, Sir Apenera Pera, KBE
Shortridge, Sir Jon Deacon, KCB
Shuckburgh, Sir Rupert Charles Gerald, Bt. (1660)
Sieff, Hon. Sir David, Kt.
Silber, Rt. Hon. Sir Stephen Robert, Kt.
Simeon, Sir John Edmund Barrington, Bt. (1815)
Simmonds, Dr Sir Kennedy Alphonse, KCMG, PC
Simmons, Air Marshal Sir Michael George, KCB, AFC
Simmons, Sir Stanley Clifford, Kt.
Simms, Sir Neville Ian, Kt., FRENG
Simon, Hon. Sir Peregrine Charles Hugh, Kt.
Simonet, Sir Louis Marcel Pierre, Kt., CBE
Sims, Sir Roger Edward, Kt.
Sinclair, Sir Clive Marles, Kt.
Sinclair, Sir George Evelyn, Kt., CMG, OBE
Sinclair, Sir Ian McTaggart, KCMG, QC
Sinclair, Sir Patrick Robert Richard, Bt. (S. 1704)
Sinclair, Sir Robert John, Kt.
Sinclair-Lockhart, Sir Simon John Edward Francis, Bt. (S. 1636)

Sinden, Sir Donald Alfred, Kt., CBE
Singer, Prof. Sir Hans Wolfgang, Kt.
Singer, Hon. Sir Jan Petci, Kt.
Singh, Sir Pritpal, Kt.
Sione, Sir Tomu Malaefone, GCMG, OBE
Sitwell, Sir (Sacheverell) Reresby, Bt. (1808)
Skate, Hon. Sir William Jack, KCMG
Skeggs, Sir Clifford George, Kt.
Skehel, Sir John James, Kt., FRS
Skingsley, Air Chief Marshal Sir Anthony Gerald, GBE, KCB
Skinner, Sir (Thomas) Keith (Hewitt), Bt. (1912)
Skipwith, Sir Patrick Alexander d'Estoteville, Bt. (1622)
Slack, Sir William Willatt, KCVO, FRCS
Slade, Sir Benjamin Julian Alfred, Bt. (1831)
Slade, Rt. Hon. Sir Christopher John, Kt.
Slaney, Prof. Sir Geoffrey, KBE
Slater, Adm. Sir John (Jock) Cunningham Kirkwood, GCB, LVO
Sleight, Sir Richard, Bt. (1920)
Sloan, Sir Andrew Kirkpatrick, Kt., QPM
Sloman, Sir Albert Edward, Kt., CBE
Smart, Sir Jack, Kt., CBE
Smedley, Hon. Sir (Frank) Brian, Kt.
Smiley, Lt.-Col. Sir John Philip, Bt. (1903)
Smith, Sir Alan, Kt., CBE, DFC
Smith, Hon. Sir Andrew Charles, Kt.
Smith, Sir Andrew Thomas, Bt. (1897)
†Smith, Sir Robert Christopher Sydney Winwood, Bt. (1809)
Smith, Prof. Sir Colin Stansfield, Kt., CBE
Smith, Sir Cyril, Kt., MBE
Smith, Prof. Sir David Cecil, Kt., FRS
Smith, Sir David Iser, KCVO
Smith, Sir Dudley (Gordon), Kt.
Smith, Prof. Sir Eric Brian, Kt., PHD
Smith, Sir Geoffrey Johnson, Kt.
Smith, Sir John Alfred, Kt., QPM
Smith, Sir John Lindsay Eric, Kt., CH, CBE
Smith, Sir Joseph William Grenville, Kt.
Smith, Sir Leslie Edward George, Kt.
Smith, Sir Michael John Llewellyn, KCVO, CMG
Smith, Sir (Norman) Brian, Kt., CBE, PHD
Smith, Sir Paul Brierley, Kt., CBE
Smith, Hon. Sir Peter (Winston), Kt.
Smith, Sir Robert Courtney, Kt., CBE
Smith, Sir Robert Haldane, Kt
Smith, Sir Robert Hill, Bt. (1945)
Smith, Gen. Sir Rupert Anthony, KCB, DSO, OBE, QGM
Smith-Dodsworth, Sir John Christopher, Bt. (1784)
Smith-Gordon, Sir (Lionel) Eldred (Peter), Bt. (1838)
Smith-Marriott, Sir Hugh Cavendish, Bt. (1774)

Smithers, Sir Peter Henry Berry Otway, Kt., VRD, DPHIL

Smurfit, *Dr.* Sir Michael William Joseph, KBE

Smyth, Sir Timothy John, Bt. (1955)

Sobers, Sir Garfield St Auburn, Kt.

Solomon, Sir Harry, Kt.

Somare, *Rt. Hon.* Sir Michael Thomas, GCMG, CH

Somerville, *Brig.* Sir John Nicholas, Kt., CBE

Sorrell, Sir Martin Stuart, Kt.

Soulsby, Sir Peter Alfred, Kt.

Soutar, *Air Marshal* Sir Charles John Williamson, KBE

Southby, Sir John Richard Bilbe, Bt. (1937)

Southern, *Prof.* Sir Edwin Mellor, Kt.

Southgate, Sir Colin Grieve, Kt.

Southgate, Sir William David, Kt.

Southward, Sir Leonard Bingley, Kt., OBE

Southward, *Dr* Sir Nigel Ralph, KCVO

Southwood, *Prof.* Sir (Thomas) Richard (Edmund), Kt., FRS

Souyave, *Hon.* Sir (Louis) Georges, Kt.

Sowrey, *Air Marshal* Sir Frederick Beresford, KCB, CBE, AFC

Sparkes, Sir Robert Lyndley, Kt.

Sparrow, Sir John, Kt.

Spearman, Sir Alexander Young Richard Mainwaring, Bt. (1840)

Spedding, *Prof.* Sir Colin Raymond William, Kt., CBE

Speed, Sir (Herbert) Keith, Kt., RD

Speelman, Sir Cornelis Jacob, Bt. (1686)

Speight, *Hon.* Sir Graham Davies, Kt.

Spencer, Sir Derek Harold, Kt., QC

Spencer, *Vice-Adm.* Sir Peter, KCB

Spencer-Nairn, Sir Robert Arnold, Bt. (1933)

Spicer, Sir James Wilton, Kt.

Spicer, Sir Nicholas Adrian Albert, Bt. (1906)

Spicer, Sir (William) Michael Hardy, Kt.

Spiers, Sir Donald Maurice, Kt., CB, TD

Spooner, Sir James Douglas, Kt.

Spratt, *Col.* Sir Greville Douglas, GBE, TD

Spring, Sir Dryden Thomas, Kt.

Squire, *Air Chief Marshal* Sir Peter Ted, GCB, DFC, AFC, ADC

Stainton, Sir (John) Ross, Kt., CBE

Staite, Sir Richard John, Kt., OBE

Stamer, Sir (Lovelace) Anthony, Bt. (1809)

Standard, Sir Kenneth Livingstone, Kt., MD

Stanhope, *Adm.* Sir Mark, KCB, OBE

Stanier, Sir Beville Douglas, Bt. (1917)

Stanier, *Field Marshal* Sir John Wilfred, GCB, MBE

Stanley, *Rt. Hon.* Sir John Paul, Kt., MP

Staples, Sir Richard Molesworth, Bt. (I. 1628)

Stark, Sir Andrew Alexander Steel, KCMG, CVO

Starkey, Sir John Philip, Bt. (1935)

Staughton, *Rt. Hon.* Sir Christopher Stephen Thomas Jonathan Thayer, Kt.

Staveley, Sir John Malfroy, KBE, MC

Stear, *Air Chief Marshal* Sir Michael James Douglas, KCB, CBE

Steel, *Hon.* Sir David William, Kt.

Steer, Sir Alan William, Kt.

Stephen, *Rt. Hon.* Sir Ninian Martin, KG, GCMG, GCVO, KBE

Stephens, Sir (Edwin) Barrie, Kt.

Stephenson, Sir Henry Upton, Bt. (1936)

Stern, *Prof.* Sir Nicholas Herbert, Kt.

Sternberg, Sir Sigmund, Kt.

Stevens, Sir Jocelyn Edward Greville, Kt., CVO

Stevens, Sir Laurence Houghton, Kt., CBE

Stevenson, Sir Simpson, Kt.

Stewart, Sir Alan, KBE

Stewart, Sir Alan d'Arcy, Bt. (I. 1623)

Stewart, Sir Brian John, Kt., CBE

Stewart, Sir David James Henderson, Bt. (1957)

Stewart, Sir David John Christopher, Bt. (1803)

Stewart, Sir Edward Jackson, Kt.

Stewart, Sir James Douglas, Kt.

Stewart, Sir James Moray, KCB

Stewart, Sir (John) Simon (Watson), Bt. (1920)

Stewart, Sir John Young, Kt., OBE

Stewart, *Lt.-Col.* Sir Robert Christie, KCVO, CBE, TD

Stewart, Sir Robertson Huntly, Kt., CBE

Stewart, Sir Robin Alastair, Bt. (1960)

Stewart, *Prof.* Sir William Duncan Paterson, Kt., FRS, FRSE

Stewart-Clark, Sir John, Bt. (1918)

Stewart-Richardson, Sir Simon Alaisdair, Bt. (S. 1630)

Stewart-Wilson, *Lt.-Col.* Sir Blair Aubyn, KCVO

Stibbon, *Gen.* Sir John James, KCB, OBE

Stirling, Sir Alexander John Dickson, KBE, CMG

Stirling, Sir Angus Duncan Aeneas, Kt.

Stirling-Hamilton, Sir Malcolm William Bruce, Bt. (S. 1673)

Stirrup, *Air Chief Marshal* Sir Graham Eric (Jock), GCB, AFC, ADC

Stockdale, Sir Thomas Minshull, Bt. (1960)

Stoddart, *Wg Cdr.* Sir Kenneth Maxwell, KCVO, AE

Stoker, *Prof.* Sir Michael George Parke, Kt., CBE, FRCP, FRS, FRSE

Stones, Sir William Frederick, Kt., OBE

Stonhouse, *Revd* Michael Philip, Bt. (1628 and 1670)

Stonor, *Air Marshal* Sir Thomas Henry, KCB

Stoppard, Sir Thomas, Kt., OM, CBE

Storey, *Hon.* Sir Richard, Bt. (1960), CBE

Stothard, Sir Peter Michael, Kt.

Stott, Sir Adrian George Ellingham, Bt. (1920)

Stoute, Sir Michael Ronald, Kt.

Stowe, Sir Kenneth Ronald, GCB, CVO

Stracey, Sir John Simon, Bt. (1818)

Strachan, Sir Curtis Victor, Kt., CVO

Strachey, Sir Charles, Bt. (1801)

Strang Steel, Sir (Fiennes) Michael, Bt. (1938)

Strawson, *Prof.* Sir Peter Frederick, Kt., FBA

Street, *Hon.* Sir Laurence Whistler, KCMG

Streeton, Sir Terence George, KBE, CMG

Strickland-Constable, Sir Frederic, Bt. (1641)

Stringer, Sir Donald Edgar, Kt., CBE

Stringer, Sir Howard, Kt.

Strong, Sir Roy Colin, Kt., PHD, FSA

Stronge, Sir James Anselan Maxwell, Bt. (1803)

Stroud, *Prof.* Sir (Charles) Eric, Kt., FRCP

Stuart, Sir James Keith, Kt.

Stuart, Sir Kenneth Lamonte, Kt.

†Stuart, Sir Phillip Luttrell, Bt. (1660)

†Stuart-Forbes, Sir William Daniel, Bt. (S. 1626)

Stuart-Menteth, Sir James Wallace, Bt. (1838)

Stuart-Paul, *Air Marshal* Sir Ronald Ian, KBE

Stuart-Smith, *Rt. Hon.* Sir Murray, Kt.

Stubbs, Sir William Hamilton, Kt., PHD

Stucley, *Lt.* Sir Hugh George Coplestone Bampfylde, Bt. (1859)

Studd, Sir Edward Fairfax, Bt. (1929)

Studholme, Sir Henry William, Bt. (1956)

†Style, Sir William Frederick, Bt. (1627)

Sugar, Sir Alan Michael, Kt.

Sullivan, *Hon.* Sir Jeremy Mirth, Kt.

Sullivan, Sir Richard Arthur, Bt. (1804)

Sulston, Sir John Edward, Kt.

Sumner, *Hon.* Sir Christopher John, Kt.

Sutherland, Sir John Brewer, Bt. (1921)

Sutherland, Sir William George MacKenzie, Kt.

Sutton, Sir Frederick Walter, Kt., OBE

Sutton, *Air Marshal* Sir John Matthias Dobson, KCB

Sutton, Sir Richard Lexington, Bt. (1772)

Swaffield, Sir James Chesebrough, Kt., CBE, RD

Swaine, Sir John Joseph, Kt., CBE

Swan, Sir Conrad Marshall John Fisher, KCVO, PHD

Swan, Sir John William David, KBE

Swann, Sir Michael Christopher, Bt. (1906), TD

Swartz, *Hon.* Sir Reginald William Colin, KBE, ED

Sweeney, Sir George, Kt.

Sweeting, *Prof.* Sir Martin Nicholas, Kt., OBE, FRS

Sweetnam, Sir (David) Rodney, KCVO, CBE, FRCS

Swinburn, *Lt.-Gen.* Sir Richard Hull, KCB

Swinnerton-Dyer, *Prof.* Sir (Henry) Peter (Francis), Bt. (1678), KBE, FRS

Swinton, *Maj.-Gen.* Sir John, KCVO, OBE

Swire, Sir Adrian Christopher, Kt.

Swire, Sir John Anthony, Kt., CBE

Sykes, Sir David Michael, Bt. (1921)

Sykes, Sir Francis John Badcock, Bt. (1781)

Sykes, Sir Hugh Ridley, Kt.

Sykes, *Prof.* Sir (Malcolm) Keith, Kt.

Sykes, Sir Richard, Kt.

Sykes, Sir Tatton Christopher Mark, Bt. (1783)

Symington, *Prof.* Sir Thomas, Kt., MD, FRSE

Symons, *Vice-Adm.* Sir Patrick Jeremy, KBE

Synge, Sir Robert Carson, Bt. (1801)

Synnott, Sir Hilary Nicholas Hugh, KCMG

Talboys, *Rt. Hon.* Sir Brian Edward, CH, KCB

Tangaroa, *Hon.* Sir Tangoroa, Kt., MBE

Tapps-Gervis-Meyrick, Sir George Christopher Cadafael, Bt. (1791)

Tapsell, Sir Peter Hannay Bailey, Kt., MP

Tate, Sir (Henry) Saxon, Bt. (1898)

Tavare, Sir John, Kt., CBE

Tavener, *Prof.* Sir John Kenneth, Kt.

Taylor, Sir (Arthur) Godfrey, Kt.

Taylor, Sir Cyril Julian Hebden, GBE

Taylor, Sir Edward Macmillan (Teddy), Kt.

Taylor, *Rt. Revd* John Bernard, KCVO

Taylor, *Dr.* Sir John Michael, Kt., OBE

Taylor, Sir Nicholas Richard Stuart, Bt. (1917)

Taylor, *Prof.* Sir William, Kt., CBE

Taylor, Sir William George, Kt.

Teagle, *Vice-Adm.* Sir Somerford Francis, KBE

Tebbit, Sir Donald Claude, GCMG

Tebbit, Sir Kevin Reginald, KCB, CMG

Telford, Sir Robert, Kt., CBE, FRENG

Temple, *Prof.* Sir John Graham, Kt.

Temple, *Maj.* Sir Richard Anthony Purbeck, Bt. (1876), MC

Templeton, Sir John Marks, Kt.

Tennant, Sir Anthony John, Kt.

Tennant, *Capt.* Sir Iain Mark, Kt.

Tennyson-D'Eyncourt, Sir Mark Gervais, Bt. (1930)

Terry, *Air Marshal* Sir Colin George, KBE, CB

Terry, *Air Chief Marshal* Sir Peter David George, GCB, AFC

Thatcher, Sir Mark, Bt. (1990)

Thomas, Sir David John Godfrey, Bt. (1694)

Thomas, Sir Derek Morison David, KCMG

Thomas, Sir Jeremy Cashel, KCMG

Thomas, Sir (John) Alan, Kt.

Thomas, *Prof.* Sir John Meurig, Kt., FRS

Thomas, Sir Keith Vivian, Kt.

Thomas, Sir Philip Lloyd, KCVO, CMG

Thomas, Sir Quentin Jeremy, Kt., CB

Thomas, *Hon.* Sir Roger John Laugharne, Kt., PC

Thomas, *Hon.* Sir Swinton Barclay, Kt.

Thomas, Sir William James Cooper, Bt. (1919), TD

Thomas, Sir (William) Michael (Marsh), Bt. (1918)

Thompson, Sir Christopher Peile, Bt. (1890)

Thompson, Sir Clive Malcolm, Kt.

Thompson, Sir David Albert, KCMG

Thompson, Sir Gilbert Williamson, Kt., OBE

Thompson, *Prof.* Sir Michael Warwick, Kt., DSC

Thompson, Sir Nicholas Annesley, Bt. (1963)

Thompson, Sir Nigel Cooper, KCMG, CBE

Thompson, Sir Paul Anthony, Bt. (1963)

Thompson, Sir Peter Anthony, Kt.

Thompson, *Dr* Sir Richard Paul Hepworth, KCVO

Thompson, Sir Thomas d'Eyncourt John, Bt. (1806)

Thomson, Sir (Frederick Douglas) David, Bt. (1929)

Thomson, Sir John Adam, GCMG

Thomson, Sir John (Ian) Sutherland, KBE, CMG

Thomson, Sir Mark Wilfrid Home, Bt. (1925)

Thomson, Sir Thomas James, Kt., CBE, FRCP

Thorn, Sir John Samuel, Kt., OBE

Thorne, Sir Neil Gordon, Kt., OBE, TD

Thornton, Sir (George) Malcolm, Kt.

Thornton, Sir Peter Eustace, KCB

Thornton, Sir Richard Eustace, KCVO, OBE

†Thorold, Sir (Anthony) Oliver, Bt. (1642)

Thorpe, *Rt. Hon.* Sir Mathew Alexander, Kt.

Thouron, Sir John Rupert Hunt, KBE

Thwaites, Sir Bryan, Kt., PHD

Tickell, Sir Crispin Charles Cervantes, GCMG, KCVO

Tikaram, Sir Moti, KBE

Tilt, Sir Robin Richard, Kt.

Tiltman, Sir John Hessell, KCVO

Timmins, *Col.* Sir John Bradford, KCVO, OBE, TD

Tims, Sir Michael David, KCVO

Tindle, Sir Ray Stanley, Kt., CBE

Tippet, *Vice-Adm.* Sir Anthony Sanders, KCB

Tirvengadum, Sir Harry Krishnan, Kt.

Tod, *Vice-Adm.* Sir Jonathan James Richard, KCB, CBE

Todd, *Prof.* Sir David, Kt., CBE

Todd, Sir Ian Pelham, KBE, FRCS

Tollemache, Sir Lyonel Humphry John, Bt. (1793)

Tomkins, Sir Edward Emile, GCMG, CVO

Tomkys, Sir (William) Roger, KCMG

Tomlinson, *Prof.* Sir Bernard Evans, Kt., CBE

Tomlinson, Sir John Rowland, Kt., CBE

Tomlinson, Sir Michael John, Kt., CBE

Tomlinson, *Hon.* Sir Stephen Miles, Kt.

Tooley, Sir John, Kt.

ToRobert, Sir Henry Thomas, KBE

Torpy, *Air Marshal* Sir Glenn Lester, KCB, CBE, DSO

Torry, Sir Peter James, GCVO, KCMG

Tory, Sir Geofroy William, KCMG

Touche, Sir Anthony George, Bt. (1920)

Touche, Sir Rodney Gordon, Bt. (1962)

Toulson, *Hon.* Sir Roger Grenfell, Kt.

Tovadek, Sir Martin, Kt. CMG

Tovey, Sir Brian John Maynard, KCMG

ToVue, Sir Ronald, Kt., OBE

Towneley, Sir Simon Peter Edmund Cosmo William, KCVO

Townsend, Sir Cyril David, Kt.

Traill, Sir Alan Towers, GBE

Trant, *Gen.* Sir Richard Brooking, KCB

Treacher, *Adm.* Sir John Devereux, KCB

Treacy, *Hon.* Sir Colman Maurice, Kt.

Treitel, *Prof.* Sir Guenter Heinz, Kt., FBA, QC

Trench, Sir Peter Edward, Kt., CBE, TD

Trescowthick, Sir Donald Henry, KBE

†Trevelyan, Sir Edward (Norman), Bt. (1662)

Trevelyan, Sir Geoffrey Washington, Bt. (1874)

Trezise, Sir Kenneth Bruce, Kt., OBE

Trippier, Sir David Austin, Kt., RD

Tritton, Sir Anthony John Ernest, Bt. (1905)

Trollope, Sir Anthony Simon, Bt. (1642)

Trotman-Dickenson, Sir Aubrey Fiennes, Kt.

Trotter, Sir Neville Guthrie, Kt.

Trotter, Sir Ronald Ramsay, Kt.

Troubridge, Sir Thomas Richard, Bt. (1799)

Troup, *Vice-Adm.* Sir (John) Anthony (Rose), KCB, DSC

Trousdell, *Lt.-Gen.* Sir Philip Charles Cornwallis, KBE, CB

Truscott, Sir Ralph Eric Nicholson, Bt. (1909)

Tsang, Sir Donald Yam-keun, KBE

Tuck, Sir Bruce Adolph Reginald, Bt. (1910)

Tucker, Hon. Sir Richard Howard, Kt.

Tuckey, Rt. Hon. Sir Simon Lane, Kt.

Tugendhat, Hon. Sir Michael George, Kt.

Tuita, Sir Mariano Kelesimalefo, KBE

Tuite, Sir Christopher Hugh, Bt. (1622), PHD

Tuivaga, Sir Timoci Uluiburotu, Kt.

Tully, Sir William Mark, KBE

Tupper, Sir Charles Hibbert, Bt. (1888)

Turbott, Sir Ian Graham, Kt., CMG, CVO

Turing, Sir John Dermot, Bt. (S. 1638)

Turner, Sir Colin William Carstairs, Kt., CBE, DFC

Turner, Hon. Sir Michael John, Kt.

Turnquest, Sir Orville Alton, GCMG, QC

Tusa, Sir John, Kt.

Tuti, Revd Dudley, KBE

Tweedie, Prof. Sir David Philip, Kt.

Tyree, Sir (Alfred) William, Kt., OBE

Tyrwhitt, Sir Reginald Thomas Newman, Bt. (1919)

Underwood, Prof. Sir James Cressee Elphinstone, Kt.

Unsworth, Hon. Sir Edgar Ignatius Godfrey, Kt., CMG

Unwin, Sir (James) Brian, KCB

Ure, Sir John Burns, KCMG, LVO

Urquhart, Sir Brian Edward, KCMG, MBE

Urwick, Sir Alan Bedford, KCVO, CMG

Usher, Sir Andrew John, Bt. (1899)

Utting, Sir William Benjamin, Kt., CB

Vallat, Sir Francis Aimé, GBE, KCMG, QC

Vallings, Vice-Adm. Sir George Montague Francis, KCB

Vanderfelt, Sir Robin Victor, KBE

Vardy, Sir Peter, Kt.

Vasquez, Sir Alfred Joseph, Kt., CBE, QC

Vassar-Smith, Sir John Rathbone, Bt. (1917)

Vavasour, Sir Eric Michael Joseph Marmaduke, Bt. (1828)

Veale, Sir Alan John Ralph, Kt., FRENG

Veness, Sir David, Kt., CBE, QPM

Venner, Sir Kenneth Dwight Vincent, KBE

Vereker, Sir John Michael Medlicott, KCB

†Verney, Sir John Sebastian, Bt. (1946)

Verney, Hon. Sir Lawrence John, Kt., TD

†Verney, Sir Edmund Ralph, Bt. (1818)

Vernon, Sir Nigel John Douglas, Bt. (1914)

Vernon, Sir (William) Michael, Kt.

Vestey, Sir (John) Derek, Bt. (1921)

Vickers, Sir John Stuart, Kt.

Vickers, Lt.-Gen. Sir Richard Maurice Hilton, KCB, CVO, OBE

Vincent, Sir William Percy Maxwell, Bt. (1936)

Vineall, Sir Anthony John Patrick, Kt.

Vinelott, Hon. Sir John Evelyn, Kt.

Vines, Sir William Joshua, Kt., CMG

von Schramek, Sir Eric Emil, Kt.

†Vyvyan, Sir Ralph Ferrers Alexander, Bt. (1645)

Wade-Gery, Sir Robert Lucian, KCMG, KCVO

Waena, Sir Nathaniel Rahumaea, GCMG

Waine, Rt. Revd John, KCVO

Waite, Rt. Hon. Sir John Douglas, Kt.

Waka, Sir Lucas Joseph, Kt., OBE

Wake, Sir Hereward, Bt. (1621), MC

Wakefield, Sir (Edward) Humphry (Tyrell), Bt. (1962)

Wakefield, Sir Norman Edward, Kt.

Wakefield, Sir Peter George Arthur, KBE, CMG

Wakeford, Sir Geoffrey Michael Montgomery, Kt., OBE

Wakeford, Air Marshal Sir Richard Gordon, KCB, OBE, LVO, AFC

Wakeley, Sir John Cecil Nicholson, Bt. (1952), FRCS

†Wakeman, Sir Edward Offley Bertram, Bt. (1828)

Wakerley, Hon. Sir Richard MacLennon, Kt.

Wales, Sir Robert Andrew, Kt.

Waley-Cohen, Sir Stephen Harry, Bt. (1961)

Walford, Sir Christopher Rupert, Kt.

Walker, Sir Alfred Cecil, Kt.

Walker, Gen. Sir Antony Kenneth Frederick, KCB

Walker, Sir Baldwin Patrick, Bt. (1856)

Walker, Sir David Alan, Kt.

Walker, Sir Harold Berners, KCMG

†Walker, Sir Robert Cecil, Bt. (1906)

Walker, Sir James Graham, Kt., MBE

Walker, Sir John Ernest, Kt., DPHIL, FRS

Walker, Air Marshal Sir John Robert, KCB, CBE, AFC

Walker, Gen. Sir Michael John Dawson, GCB, CMG, CBE, ADC

Walker, Sir Miles Rawstron, Kt., CBE

Walker, Sir Patrick Jeremy, KCB

Walker, Hon. Sir Paul James, Kt.

Walker, Sir Rodney Myerscough, Kt.

Walker, Hon. Sir Timothy Edward, Kt.

Walker, Sir Victor Stewart Heron, Bt. (1868)

Walker-Okeover, Sir Andrew Peter Monro, Bt. (1886)

Walker-Smith, Sir John Jonah, Bt. (1960)

Wall, Sir John Anthony, Kt., CBE

Wall, Sir (John) Stephen, GCMG, LVO

Wall, Hon. Sir Nicholas Peter Rathbone, Kt., PC

Wall, Sir Robert William, Kt., OBE

Wallace, Lt.-Gen. Sir Christopher Brooke Quentin, KBE

Wallace, Prof. David James, Kt., CBE, FRS

Wallace, Sir Ian James, Kt., CBE

Waller, Rt. Hon. Sir (George) Mark, Kt.

Waller, Sir John Michael, Bt. (I. 1780)

Wallis, Sir Peter Gordon, KCVO

Wallis, Sir Timothy William, Kt.

Walmsley, Vice-Adm. Sir Robert, KCB

†Walsham, Sir Timothy John, Bt. (1831)

Walters, Prof. Sir Alan Arthur, Kt.

Walters, Sir Dennis Murray, Kt., MBE

Walters, Sir Frederick Donald, Kt.

Walters, Sir Peter Ingram, Kt.

Walters, Sir Roger Talbot, KBE, FRIBA

Wamiri, Sir Akapite, KBE

Wan, Sir Wamp, Kt., MBE

Wanless, Sir Derek, Kt.

Ward, Rt. Hon. Sir Alan Hylton, Kt.

Ward, Sir John Devereux, Kt., CBE

Ward, Prof. Sir John MacQueen, Kt., CBE

Ward, Sir Joseph James Laffey, Bt. (1911)

Ward, Sir Timothy James, Kt.

Wardale, Sir Geoffrey Charles, KCB

Wardlaw, Sir Henry (John), Bt. (S. 1631)

Waring, Sir (Alfred) Holburt, Bt. (1935)

Warmington, Sir David Marshall, Bt. (1908)

Warner, Sir (Edward Courtenay) Henry, Bt. (1910)

Warner, Prof. Sir Frederick Edward, Kt., FRS, FRENG

Warner, Sir Gerald Chierici, KCMG

Warren, Sir (Frederick) Miles, KBE

Warren, Sir Kenneth Robin, Kt.

†Warren, Sir Michael Blackley, Bt. (1784)

Wass, Sir Douglas William Gretton, GCB

Waterhouse, Hon. Sir Ronald Gough, GBE

Waterlow, Sir Christopher Rupert, Bt. (1873)

Waterlow, Sir (James) Gerard, Bt. (1930)

Waters, Gen. Sir (Charles) John, GCB, CBE

Waters, Sir (Thomas) Neil (Morris), Kt.

Wates, Sir Christopher Stephen, Kt.

Watkins, Rt. Hon. Sir Tasker, VC, GBE

Watson, Sir Bruce Dunstan, Kt.

Watson, Prof. Sir David John, Kt., PHD

Watson, Sir (James) Andrew, Bt. (1866)

Watson, Vice-Adm. Sir Philip Alexander, KBE, LVO

Watson, Sir Ronald Matthew, Kt., CBE

Watt, Lt.-Gen. Sir Charles Redmond, KCVO, CBE

Watt, Surgeon Vice-Adm. Sir James, KBE, FRCS

Watts, Sir Arthur Desmond, KCMG
Watts, Sir John Augustus Fitzroy, KCMG, CBE
Watts, Sir Philip Beverley, KCMG
Weatherall, *Prof.* Sir David John, Kt., FRS
Weatherall, *Vice-Adm.* Sir James Lamb, KCVO, KBE
Weatherstone, Sir Dennis, KBE
Weatherup, *Hon.* Sir Ronald Eccles, Kt.
Webb, *Prof.* Sir Adrian Leonard, Kt.
Webb, Sir Thomas Langley, Kt.
Webb-Carter, *Gen.* Sir Evelyn John, KCVO, OBE
Webster, *Very Revd* Alan Brunskill, KCVO
Webster, *Vice-Adm.* Sir John Morrison, KCB
Webster, *Hon.* Sir Peter Edlin, Kt.
Wedgwood, Sir (Hugo) Martin, Bt. (1942)
Weekes, Sir Everton DeCourcey, KCMG, OBE
Weinberg, Sir Mark Aubrey, Kt.
Weir, Sir Michael Scott, KCMG
Weir, *Hon.* Sir Reginald George, Kt.
Weir, Sir Roderick Bignell, Kt.
Welby, Sir (Richard) Bruno Gregory, Bt. (1801)
Welch, Sir John Reader, Bt. (1957)
Weldon, Sir Anthony William, Bt. (I. 1723)
Weller, Sir Arthur Burton, Kt., CBE
Wellings, Sir Jack Alfred, Kt., CBE
†Wells, Sir Christopher Charles, Bt. (1944)
Wells, Sir John Julius, Kt.
Wells, Sir William Henry Weston, Kt., FRICS
West, *Adm.* Sir Alan William John, GCB, DSC, ADC
Westbrook, Sir Neil Gowanloch, Kt., CBE
Westmacott, Sir Peter John, KCMG
Weston, Sir Michael Charles Swift, KCMG, CVO
Weston, Sir (Philip) John, KCMG
Whalen, Sir Geoffrey Henry, Kt., CBE
Wheeler, Sir Harry Anthony, Kt., OBE
Wheeler, *Air Chief Marshal* Sir (Henry) Neil (George), GCB, CBE, DSO, DFC, AFC
Wheeler, *Rt. Hon.* Sir John Daniel, Kt.
Wheeler, Sir John Hieron, Bt. (1920)
Wheeler, *Gen.* Sir Roger Neil, GCB, CBE
Wheeler-Booth, Sir Michael Addison John, KCB
Wheler, Sir Edward Woodford, Bt. (1660)
Whishaw, Sir Charles Percival Law, Kt.
Whitaker, Sir John James Ingham (Jack), Bt. (1936)
White, *Prof.* Sir Christopher John, Kt., CVO
White, Sir Christopher Robert Meadows, Bt. (1937)
White, Sir David Harry, Kt.

White, *Hon.* Sir Frank John, Kt.
White, Sir George Stanley James, Bt. (1904)
White, *Adm.* Sir Hugo Moresby, GCB, CBE
White, *Hon.* Sir John Charles, Kt., MBE
White, Sir John Woolmer, Bt. (1922)
White, Sir Nicholas Peter Archibald, Bt. (1802)
White, *Adm.* Sir Peter, GBE
White, Sir Willard Wentworth, Kt., CBE
Whitehead, Sir John Stainton, GCMG, CVO
Whitehead, Sir Rowland John Rathbone, Bt. (1889)
Whiteley, *Gen.* Sir Peter John Frederick, GCB, OBE, RM
Whitfield, Sir William, Kt., CBE
Whitmore, Sir Clive Anthony, GCB, CVO
Whitmore, Sir John Henry Douglas, Bt. (1954)
Whitney, Sir Raymond William, Kt., OBE, MP
Whitson, Sir Keith Roderick, Kt.
Wickerson, Sir John Michael, Kt.
Wicks, Sir Nigel Leonard, GCB, CVO, CBE
†Wigan, Sir Michael Iain, Bt. (1898)
Wiggin, Sir Alfred William (Jerry), Kt., TD
†Wiggin, Sir Charles Rupert John, Bt. (1892)
†Wigram, Sir John Woolmore, Bt. (1805)
Wilbraham, Sir Richard Baker, Bt. (1776)
Wiles, *Prof.* Sir Andrew John, KBE
Wilford, Sir (Kenneth) Michael, GCMG
Wilkes, *Prof.* Sir Maurice Vincent, Kt.
Wilkes, *Gen.* Sir Michael John, KCB, CBE
Wilkie, *Hon.* Sir Alan Fraser, Kt.
Wilkinson, Sir (David) Graham (Brook) Bt. (1941)
Wilkinson, *Prof.* Sir Denys Haigh, Kt., FRS
Wilkinson, Sir Philip William, Kt.
Willcocks, Sir David Valentine, Kt., CBE, MC
Willcocks, *Lt.-Gen.* Sir Michael Alan, KCB
Williams, Sir Arthur Dennis Pitt, Kt.
Williams, Sir (Arthur) Gareth Ludovic Emrys Rhys, Bt. (1918)
Williams, *Prof.* Sir Bruce Rodda, KBE
Williams, Sir Charles Othniel, Kt.
Williams, Sir Daniel Charles, GCMG, QC
Williams, *Adm.* Sir David, GCB
Williams, *Prof.* Sir David Glyndwr Tudor, Kt.
Williams, Sir David Innes, Kt.
Williams, Sir David Reeve, Kt., CBE
Williams, *Hon.* Sir Denys Ambrose, KCMG
Williams, Sir Donald Mark, Bt. (1866)

Williams, *Prof.* Sir (Edward) Dillwyn, Kt., FRCP
Williams, Sir Francis Owen Garbett, Kt., CBE
Williams, Sir (John) Kyffin, Kt., OBE, DL, RA
Williams, Sir (Lawrence) Hugh, Bt. (1798)
Williams, Sir Leonard, KBE, CB
Williams, Sir Osmond, Bt. (1909), MC
Williams, Sir Peter Michael, Kt.
Williams, Sir (Robert) Philip Nathaniel, Bt. (1915)
Williams, Sir Robin Philip, Bt. (1953)
Williams, Sir (William) Maxwell (Harries), Kt.
Williams-Bulkeley, Sir Richard Thomas, Bt. (1661)
Williams-Wynn, Sir David Watkin, Bt. (1688)
Williamson, *Marshal of the Royal Air Force* Sir Keith Alec, GCB, AFC
Williamson, Sir Robert Brian, Kt., CBE
Willink, Sir Charles William, Bt. (1957)
Willis, *Air Chief Marshal* Sir John Frederick, GBE, KCB
Willison, *Lt.-Gen.* Sir David John, KCB, OBE, MC
Wills, Sir David James Vernon, Bt. (1923)
Wills, Sir David Seton, Bt. (1904)
Wilmot, Sir David, Kt., QPM
Wilmot, Sir Henry Robert, Bt. (1759)
Wilsey, *Gen.* Sir John Finlay Willasey, GCB, CBE
Wilshaw, Sir Michael, Kt.
Wilson, *Prof.* Sir Alan Geoffrey, Kt.
Wilson, Sir Anthony, Kt.
Wilson, *Vice-Adm.* Sir Barry Nigel, KCB
Wilson, *Prof.* Sir Colin Alexander St John, Kt., RA, FRIBA
Wilson, Sir David, Bt. (1920)
Wilson, Sir David Mackenzie, Kt.
Wilson, Sir James William Douglas, Bt. (1906)
Wilson, *Brig.* Sir Mathew John Anthony, Bt. (1874), OBE, MC
Wilson, *Hon.* Sir Nicholas Allan Roy, Kt.
Wilson, Sir Robert Peter, KCMG
Wilson, *Air Chief Marshal* Sir (Ronald) Andrew (Fellowes), KCB, AFC
Wilson, *Hon.* Sir Ronald Darling, KBE, CMG
Wilton, Sir (Arthur) John, KCMG, KCVO, MC
Wingate, *Capt.* Sir Miles Buckley, KCVO
Winkley, Sir David Ross, Kt.
Winnington, Sir Anthony Edward, Bt. (1755)
Winship, Sir Peter James Joseph, Kt., CBE
Winter, *Dr* Sir Gregory Winter, Kt., CBE

Winterton, Sir Nicholas Raymond, Kt.

Winton, Sir Nicholas George, Kt., MBE

Wisdom, Sir Norman, Kt., OBE

Wiseman, Sir John William, Bt. (1628)

Wolfendale, *Prof.* Sir Arnold Whittaker, Kt., FRS

Wolfson, Sir Brian Gordon, Kt.

Wolseley, Sir Charles Garnet Richard Mark, Bt. (1628)

†Wolseley, Sir James Douglas, Bt. (I. 1745)

†Wombell, Sir George Philip Frederick, Bt. (1778)

Womersley, Sir Peter John Walter, Bt. (1945)

Woo, Sir Leo Joseph, Kt.

Woo, Sir Po-Shing, Kt.

Wood, Sir Alan Marshall Muir, Kt., FRS, FRENG

Wood, Sir Andrew Marley, GCMG

Wood, Sir Anthony John Page, Bt. (1837)

Wood, Sir Ian Clark, Kt., CBE

Wood, *Hon.* Sir John Kember, Kt., MC

Wood, Sir Martin Francis, Kt., OBE

Wood, Sir Michael Charles, KCMG

Wood, *Hon.* Sir Roderic Lionel James, Kt.

Wood, Sir Russell Dillon, KCVO, VRD

Wood, Sir William Alan, KCVO, CB

Woodard, *Rear Adm.* Sir Robert Nathaniel, KCVO

Woodcock, Sir John, Kt., CBE, QPM

Woodhead, *Vice-Adm.* Sir (Anthony) Peter, KCB

Woodhouse, *Rt. Hon.* Sir (Arthur) Owen, KBE, DSC

Woodroffe, *Most Revd* George Cuthbert Manning, KBE

Woods, Sir Robert Kynnersley, Kt., CBE

Woodward, *Hon.* Sir (Albert) Edward, Kt., OBE

Woodward, Sir Clive Ronald, Kt., OBE

Woodward, *Adm.* Sir John Forster, GBE, KCB

Worsley, *Gen.* Sir Richard Edward, GCB, OBE

Worsley, Sir (William) Marcus (John), Bt. (1838)

Worsthorne, Sir Peregrine Gerard, Kt.

Wratten, *Air Chief Marshal* Sir William John, GBE, CB, AFC

Wraxall, Sir Charles Frederick Lascelles, Bt. (1813)

Wrey, Sir George Richard Bourchier, Bt. (1628)

Wrigglesworth, Sir Ian William, Kt.

Wright, Sir Allan Frederick, KBE

Wright, Sir David John, GCMG, LVO

Wright, *Hon.* Sir (John) Michael, Kt.

Wright, Sir (John) Oliver, GCMG, GCVO, DSC

Wright, Sir Peter Robert, Kt., CBE

Wright, *Air Marshal* Sir Robert Alfred, KBE, AFC

Wrightson, Sir Charles Mark Garmondsway, Bt. (1900)

Wrigley, *Prof.* Sir Edward Anthony (Sir Tony), Kt., PHD, PBA

Wrixon-Becher, Sir John William Michael, Bt. (1831)

Wu, Sir Gordon Ying Sheung, KCMG

Wyldbore-Smith, *Maj.-Gen.* Sir (Francis) Brian, Kt., CB, DSO, OBE

Yacoub, *Prof.* Sir Magdi Habib, Kt., FRCS

Yaki, Sir Roy, KBE

Yang, *Hon.* Sir Ti Liang, Kt.

Yapp, Sir Stanley Graham, Kt.

Yardley, Sir David Charles Miller, Kt., LLD

Yarrow, Sir Eric Grant, Bt. (1916), MBE

Yellowlees, Sir Henry, KCB

Yocklunn, Sir John (Soong Chung), KCVO

Yoo Foo, Sir (François) Henri, Kt.

Young, Sir Brian Walter Mark, Kt.

Young, Sir Colville Norbert, GCMG, MBE

Young, Sir Dennis Charles, KCMG

Young, *Rt. Hon.* Sir George Samuel Knatchbull, Bt. (1813)

Young, *Hon.* Sir Harold William, KCMG

Young, Sir Jimmy Leslie Ronald, Kt., CBE

Young, Sir John Kenyon Roe, Bt. (1821)

Young, *Hon.* Sir John McIntosh, KCMG

Young, Sir John Robertson, GCMG

Young, Sir Leslie Clarence, Kt., CBE

Young, Sir Nicholas Charles, Kt.

Young, Sir Richard Dilworth, Kt.

Young, Sir Robin Urquhart, KCB

Young, Sir Roger William, Kt.

Young, Sir Stephen Stewart Templeton, Bt. (1945)

Young, Sir William Neil, Bt. (1769)

Younger, Sir Julian William Richard, Bt. (1911)

Yuwi, Sir Matiabe, KBE

Zeeman, *Prof.* Sir (Erik) Christopher, Kt., FRS

Zissman, Sir Bernard Philip, Kt.

Zochonis, Sir John Basil, Kt.

Zunz, Sir Gerhard Jacob (Jack), Kt., FRENG

Zurenuoc, Sir Zibang, KBE

THE ORDER OF ST JOHN

THE MOST VENERABLE ORDER OF THE HOSPITAL OF
ST JOHN OF JERUSALEM (1888)

GCStJ	Bailiff/Dame Grand Cross
KStJ	Knight of Justice/Grace
DStJ	Dame of Justice/Grace
CStJ	Commander
OstJ	Officer
SBStJ	Serving Brother
SSStJ	Serving Sister
EsqStJ	Esquire

Motto, Pro Fide, Pro Utilitate Hominum

The Order of St John, founded in the early 12th century
in Jerusalem, was a religious order with a particular duty
to care for the sick. In Britain the Order was dissolved by
Henry VIII in 1540 but the British branch was revived in
the early 19th century. The branch was not accepted by
the Grand Magistracy of the Order in Rome but its search
for a role in the tradition of the Hospitallers led to the
founding of the St John Ambulance Association in 1877
and later the St John Ambulance Brigade; in 1882 the St
John Ophthalmic Hospital was founded in Jerusalem. A
royal charter was granted in 1888 establishing the British
Order of St John as a British Order of Chivalry with the
Sovereign as its head. Since October 1999, a separate
Priory of England and the Islands has governed the Order
in England, the Channel Islands and the Isle of Man, with
a Commandery in Northern Ireland.

The whole Order world-wide is now governed by a
Grand Council including the representatives of all 8
Priories (England, Scotland, Wales, South Africa, New
Zealand, Canada, Australia and the United States). There
are also branches in about 30 other countries, mostly in
the Commonwealth. Apart from the St John Ambulance
Foundation, the Order is also responsible for the
Jerusalem Eye Hospital. Admission to the Order is
conferred in recognition of service, usually in St John
Ambulance or the Eye Hospital. Membership does not
confer any rank, style, title or precedence on a recipient.

SOVEREIGN HEAD OF THE ORDER
HM The Queen

GRAND PRIOR
HRH The Duke of Gloucester, KG, GCVO
Lord Prior, Eric Barry
Prelate, The Rt. Revd John Waine, KCVO
Vice Lord Prior, Prof. Anthony Mellows, OBE, TD
Deputy Lord Prior (Establishments), John Strachan
Deputy Lord Prior (Finance), Capt. Norman Lloyd-
Edwards
Secretary General, Rear-Adm. Andrew Gough, CB
Headquarters, Priory House, 25 St John's Lane, London
EC1M 4PP

DAMES

DAMES GRAND CROSS AND DAMES COMMANDERS

Style, 'Dame' before forename and surname, followed by appropriate post-nominal initials. Where such an award is made to a lady already in possession of a higher title, the appropriate initials follow her name
Envelope, Dame F_ S_, followed by appropriate post-nominal letters. *Letter (formal),* Dear Madam; *(social),* Dear Dame F_. *Spoken,* Dame F
Husband, Untitled

Dame Grand Cross and Dame Commander are the higher classes for women of the Order of the Bath, the Order of St Michael and St George, the Royal Victorian Order, and the Order of the British Empire. Dames Grand Cross rank after the wives of Baronets and before the wives of Knights Grand Cross. Dames Commanders rank after the wives of Knights Grand Cross and before the wives of Knights Commanders.

Honorary Dames Commanders may be conferred on women who are citizens of countries of which The Queen is not head of state.

LIST OF DAMES
Revised to 31 August 2005

Women peers in their own right and life peers are not included in this list. Female members of the royal family are not included in this list; details of the orders they hold can be found within the Royal Family section.

If a dame has a double barrelled or hyphenated surname, she is listed under the first element of the name. *A full entry in italic type* indicates that the recipient of an honour died during the year in which the honour was conferred. The name is included for the purposes of record.

Abaijah, Dame Josephine, DBE
Airlie, The Countess of, DCVO
Albemarle, The Countess of, DBE
Allen, *Prof.* Dame Ingrid Victoria, DBE
Anderson, *Brig. Hon.* Dame Mary Mackenzie (Mrs Pihl), DBE
Andrews, Dame Julie, DBE
Anglesey, The Marchioness of, DBE
Anson, Lady (Elizabeth Audrey), DBE
Anstee, Dame Margaret Joan, DCMG
Arden, *Rt. Hon.* Dame Mary Howarth (Mrs Mance), DBE
Atkins, Dame Eileen, DBE
Bainbridge, Dame Beryl, DBE
Baker, Dame Janet Abbott (Mrs Shelley), CH, DBE
Baron, *Hon.* Dame Florence Jacqueline, DBE
Barrow, Dame Jocelyn Anita (Mrs Downer), DBE
Barstow, Dame Josephine Clare (Mrs Anderson), DBE
Bassey, Dame Shirley, DBE
Beaurepaire, Dame Beryl Edith, DBE
Beer, *Prof.* Dame Gillian Patricia Kempster, DBE, FBA
Bergquist, *Prof.* Dame Patricia Rose, DBE
Bewley, Dame Beulah Rosemary, DBE
Bibby, Dame Enid, DBE

Black, *Prof.* Dame Carol Mary, DBE
Black, *Hon.* Dame Jill Margaret, DBE
Blackadder, Dame Elizabeth Violet, DBE
Blaize, Dame Venetia Ursula, DBE
Blaxland, Dame Helen Frances, DBE
Booth, *Hon.* Dame Margaret Myfanwy Wood, DBE
Bowtell, Dame Ann Elizabeth, DCB
Boyd, Dame Vivienne Myra, DBE
Barbour, Dame Margaret (Mrs Ash), DBE
Bracewell, *Hon.* Dame Joyanne Winifred (Mrs Copeland), DBE
Brain, Dame Margaret Anne (Mrs Wheeler), DBE
Brennan, Dame Maureen, DBE
Bridges, Dame Mary Patricia, DBE
Brittan, Dame Diana (Lady Brittan of Spennithorne), DBE
Browne, Lady Moyra Blanche Madeleine, DBE
Browne-Evans, Dame Lois Marie, DBE
Buckland, Dame Yvonne Helen Elaine, DBE
Burslem, Dame Alexandra Vivien, DBE
Butler-Sloss, *Rt. Hon.* Dame (Ann) Elizabeth (Oldfield), GBE
Buttfield, Dame Nancy Eileen, DBE
Byatt, Dame Antonia Susan, DBE, FRSL
Bynoe, Dame Hilda Louisa, DBE
Caldicott, Dame Fiona, DBE, FRCP, FRCPSYCH
Campbell-Preston, Dame Frances Olivia, DCVO
Cartwright, Dame Silvia Rose, DBE
Charles, Dame (Mary) Eugenia, DBE
Clark, *Prof.* Dame Jill MacLeod, DBE
Clark, *Prof.* Dame (Margaret) June, DBE, PHD
Clay, Dame Marie Mildred, DBE
Clayton, Dame Barbara Evelyn (Mrs Klyne), DBE
Collarbone, Dame Patricia, DBE
Corsar, *The Hon.* Dame Mary Drummond, DBE
Coward, Dame Pamela Sarah, DBE
Cox, Dame Laura Mary (The Hon. Mrs Justice), DBE
Davies, Dame Wendy Patricia, DBE
Davis, Dame Karlene Cecile, DBE
Daws, Dame Joyce Margaretta, DBE
Dawson, *Prof.* Dame Sandra Jane Noble, DBE
Dell, Dame Miriam Patricia, DBE
Dench, Dame Judith Olivia (Mrs Williams), CH, DBE
Descartes, Dame Marie Selipha Sesenne, DBE, BEM
Devonshire, The Duchess of, DCVO
Digby, Lady, DBE
Dobbs, Dame Linda Penelope (The Hon. Mrs Justice), DBE
Docherty, Dame Jacqueline, DBE
Duffield, Dame Vivien Louise, DBE
Dumont, Dame Ivy Leona, DCMG
Dyche, Dame Rachael Mary, DBE
Elcoat, Dame Catherine Elizabeth, DBE
Ellison, Dame Jill, DBE
Else, Dame Jean, DBE
Engel, Dame Pauline Frances (Sister Pauline Engel), DBE
Esteve-Coll, Dame Elizabeth Anne Loosemore, DBE
Evans, Dame Anne Elizabeth Jane, DBE
Evans, Dame Madeline Glynne Dervel, DBE, CMG
Evison, Dame Helen June Patricia, DBE
Fenner, Dame Peggy Edith, DBE
Fielding, Dame Pauline, DBE

Fort, Dame Maeve Geraldine, DCMG, DCVO
Fraser, Dame Dorothy Rita, DBE
Friend, Dame Phyllis Muriel, DBE
Frost, Dame Phyllis Irene, DBE
Fry, Dame Margaret Louise, DBE
Gallagher, Dame Monica Josephine, DBE
Gardiner, Dame Helen Louisa, DBE, MVO
Giles, *Air Comdt.* Dame Pauline (Mrs Parsons), DBE, RRC
Glen-Haig, Dame Mary Alison, DBE
Gloster, *Hon.* Dame Elisabeth (Mrs Brodie), DBE
Glover, Dame Audrey Frances, DBE, CMG
Goodall, *Dr* Dame (Valerie) Jane, DBE
Goodman, Dame Barbara, DBE
Gordon, Dame Minita Elmira, GCMG, GCVO
Gordon, *Hon.* Dame Pamela Felicity, DBE
Gow, Dame Jane Elizabeth (Mrs Whiteley), DBE
Grafton, The Duchess of, GCVO
Grant, Dame Mavis, DBE
Green, Dame Pauline, DBE
Grey, Dame Beryl Elizabeth (Mrs Svenson), DBE
Grey-Thompson, Dame Tanni Carys Davina, DBE
Grimthorpe, The Lady, DCVO
Guilfoyle, Dame Margaret Georgina Constance, DBE
Guthardt, *Revd Dr* Dame Phyllis Myra, DBE
Hallett, *Hon.* Dame Heather Carol, DBE
Harbison, Dame Joan Irene, DBE
Harper, Dame Elizabeth Margaret Way, DBE
Harris, Lady Pauline, DBE
Hedley-Miller, Dame Mary Elizabeth, DCVO, CB
Heilbron, *Hon.* Dame Rose, DBE
Herbison, Dame Jean Marjory, DBE, CMG
Hercus, *Hon.* Dame (Margaret) Ann, DCMG
Higgins, *Prof.* Dame Julia Stretton, DBE, FRS
Higgins, *Prof.* Dame Rosalyn, DBE, QC
Hill, *Air Cdre* Dame Felicity Barbara, DBE
Hine, Dame Deirdre Joan, DBE, FRCP
Hodgson, Dame Patricia Anne, DBE
Hogg, *Hon.* Dame Mary Claire (Mrs Koops), DBE
Hollows, Dame Sharon, DBE
Holmes, Dame Kelly, DBE
Hoodless, Dame Elisabeth Anne, DBE
Hufton, *Prof.* Dame Olwen, DBE
Hussey, Dame Susan Katharine (Lady Hussey of North Bradley), DCVO
Hutton, Dame Deirdre Mary, DBE
Imison, Dame Tamsyn, DBE
Isaacs, Dame Albertha Madeline, DBE
James, Dame Naomi Christine (Mrs Haythorne), DBE
Jenkins, Dame (Mary) Jennifer (Lady Jenkins of Hillhead), DBE
Johnson, *Prof.* Dame Louise Napier, DBE, FRS
Jonas, Dame Judith Mayhew
Jones, Dame Gwyneth (Mrs Haberfeld-Jones), DBE
Keegan, Dame Geraldine Mary Marcella, DBE
Kekedo, Dame Rosalina Violet, DBE
Kelleher, Dame Joan, DBE
Kellett-Bowman, Dame (Mary) Elaine, DBE
Kelly, Dame Lorna May Boreland, DBE
Kershaw, Dame Janet Elizabeth Murray (Dame Betty), DBE
Kettlewell, *Comdt.* Dame Marion Mildred, DBE
Kidu, Lady, DBE
King, Dame Thea, DBE
Kirby, Dame Georgina Kamiria, DBE
Kramer, *Prof.* Dame Leonie Judith, DBE
Laine, Dame Cleo (Clementine) Dinah (Mrs Dankworth), DBE
Lamb, Dame Dawn Ruth, DBE

Legge-Schwarzkopf, Dame Elisabeth Friederike Marie Olga, DBE
Lewis, Dame Edna Leofrida (Lady Lewis), DBE
Lott, Dame Felicity Ann Emwhyla (Mrs Woolf), DBE
Louisy, Dame (Calliopa) Pearlette, GCMG
Lynn, Dame Vera (Mrs Lewis), DBE
MacArthur, Dame Ellen Patricia, DBE
Macdonald, Dame Mary Beaton, DBE
McDonald, Dame Mavis, DCB
Mackinnon, Dame (Una) Patricia, DBE
McLaren, Dame Anne Laura, DBE, FRCOG, FRS
Macmillan of Ovenden, Katharine, Viscountess, DBE
Mayhew, Dame Judith, DBE
Major, Dame Malvina Lorraine (Mrs Fleming), DBE
Major, Dame Norma Christina Elizabeth, DBE
Manningham-Buller, *Hon.* Dame Elizabeth, DCB
Metge, *Dr* Dame (Alice) Joan, DBE
Middleton, Dame Elaine Madoline, DCMG, MBE
Mills, Dame Barbara Jean Lyon, DBE, QC
Mirren, Dame Helen, DBE
Moores, Dame Yvonne, DBE
Morgan, *Dr* Dame Gillian Margaret, DBE
Morrison, *Hon.* Dame Mary Anne, DCVO
Muirhead, Dame Lorna Elizabeth Fox, DBE
Muldoon, Lady Thea Dale, DBE, QSO
Mullally, *Revd* Dame Sarah Elisabeth, DBE
Mumford, Lady Mary Katharine, DCVO
Munro, Dame Alison, DBE
Murdoch, Dame Elisabeth Joy, DBE
Neville, Dame Elizabeth, DBE, QPM
Neville-Jones, Dame (Lilian) Pauline, DCMG
Ogilvie, Dame Bridget Margaret, DBE, PHD, DSC
Oliver, Dame Gillian Frances, DBE
Ollerenshaw, Dame Kathleen Mary, DBE, DPHIL
Oxenbury, Dame Shirley Anne, DBE
Park, Dame Merle Florence (Mrs Bloch), DBE
Pauffley, *Hon.* Dame Anna Evelyn Hamilton, DBE
Penhaligon, Dame Annette (Mrs Egerton), DBE
Peters, Dame Mary Elizabeth, DBE
Platt, Dame Denise, DBE
Plowright, Dame Joan Ann, DBE
Polak, *Prof.* Dame Julia Margaret, DBE
Poole, Dame Avril Anne Barker, DBE
Porter, Dame Shirley (Lady Porter), DBE
Powell, Dame Sally Ann Vickers, DBE
Prendergast, Dame Simone Ruth, DBE
Prentice, Dame Winifred Eva, DBE
Price, Dame Margaret Berenice, DBE
Pugh, *Dr* Dame Gillian Mary, DBE
Purves, Dame Daphne Helen, DBE
Quinn, Dame Sheila Margaret Imelda, DBE
Rafferty, *Hon.* Dame Anne Judith, DBE
Rawson, *Prof.* Dame Jessica Mary, DBE
Rees, *Prof.* Dame Lesley Howard, DBE
Reeves, Dame Helen May, DBE
Richardson, Dame Mary, DBE
Riddelsdell, Dame Mildred, DCB, CBE
Ridsdale, Dame Victoire Evelyn Patricia (Lady Ridsdale), DBE
Rigg, Dame Diana, DBE
Rimington, Dame Stella, DCB
Ritterman, Dame Janet, DBE
Roberts, Dame Jane Elisabeth, DBE
Robins, Dame Ruth Laura, DBE
Robottom, Dame Marlene, DBE
Roddick, Dame Anita Lucia, DBE
Roe, Dame Marion Audrey, DBE
Roe, Dame Raigh Edith, DBE

Ronson, Dame Gail, DBE
Rothwell, *Prof.* Dame Nancy Jane, DBE
Rumbold, *Rt. Hon.* Dame Angela Claire Rosemary, DBE
Runciman of Doxford, The Viscountess, DBE
Salas, Dame Margaret Laurence, DBE
Salmond, *Prof.* Dame Mary Anne, DBE
Sawyer, *Hon.* Dame Joan Augusta, DBE
Scardino, Dame Marjorie, DBE
Scott, Dame Catherine Margaret (Mrs Denton), DBE
Seward, Dame Margaret Helen Elizabeth, DBE
Shirley, Dame Stephanie, DBE
Shovelton, Dame Helena, DBE
Sibley, Dame Antoinette (Mrs Corbett), DBE
Smith, Dame Dela, DBE
Smith, *Rt. Hon.* Dame Janet Hilary (Mrs Mathieson), DBE
Smith, *Hon.* Dame Jennifer Meredith, DBE
Smith, Dame Margaret Natalie (Maggie) (Mrs Cross), DBE
Smith, Dame Margot, DBE
Soames, Lady Mary, KG, DBE
Southgate, *Prof.* Dame Lesley Jill, DBE
Spark, Dame Muriel Sarah, DBE
Spencer, Dame Rosemary Jane, DCMG
Steel, *Hon.* Dame (Anne) Heather (Mrs Beattie), DBE
Strachan, Dame Valerie Patricia Marie, DCB
Strathern, *Prof.* Dame Anne Marilyn, DBE
Street, Dame Susan Ruth, DCB
Sutherland, Dame Joan (Mrs Bonynge), OM, DBE
Sutherland, Dame Veronica Evelyn, DBE, CMG
Symmonds, Dame Olga Patricia, DBE
Taylor, Dame Elizabeth, DBE

Taylor, Dame Meg, DBE
Te Atairangikaahu, Te Arikinui, Dame, DBE
Te Kanawa, Dame Kiri Janette, DBE
Thomas, *Prof.* Dame Jean Olwen, DBE
Thomas, Dame Maureen Elizabeth (Lady Thomas), DBE
Thorneycroft, Lady Carla, DBE
Tinson, Dame Sue, DBE
Tizard, Dame Catherine Anne, GCMG, GCVO, DBE
Tokiel, Dame Rosa, DBE
Trotter, Dame Janet Olive, DBE
Turner-Warwick, Dame Margaret Elizabeth Harvey, DBE, FRCP, FRCPED
Uprichard, Dame Mary Elizabeth, DBE
Varley, Dame Joan Fleetwood, DBE
Wagner, Dame Gillian Mary Millicent (Lady Wagner), DBE
Wall, Dame (Alice) Anne, (Mrs Michael Wall), DCVO
Wallis, Dame Sheila Ann, DBE
Warburton, Dame Anne Marion, DCVO, CMG
Waterhouse, Dame Rachel Elizabeth, DBE, PHD
Waterman, *Dr* Dame Fanny, DBE
Webb, *Prof.* Dame Patricia, DBE
Weir, Dame Gillian Constance (Mrs Phelps), DBE
Weller, Dame Rita, DBE
Weston, Dame Margaret Kate, DBE
Wheldon, Dame Juliet Louise, DCB, QC
Wilson-Barnett, *Prof.* Dame Jenifer, DBE
Winstone, Dame Dorothy Gertrude, DBE, CMG
Wong Yick-ming, Dame Rosanna, DBE

DECORATIONS AND MEDALS

PRINCIPAL DECORATIONS AND MEDALS
In order of wear

VICTORIA CROSS (VC), 1856 (*see* below)
GEORGE CROSS (GC), 1940 (*see* below)

BRITISH ORDERS OF KNIGHTHOOD (*see* Orders of Chivalry)
BARONET'S BADGE
KNIGHT BACHELOR'S BADGE

INDIAN ORDER OF MERIT (MILITARY)

DECORATIONS
Conspicuous Gallantry Cross (CGC), 1995
Royal Red Cross Class I (RRC), 1883
Distinguished Service Cross (DSC), 1914
Military Cross (MC), December 1914
Distinguished Flying Cross (DFC), 1918
Air Force Cross (AFC), 1918
Royal Red Cross Class II (ARRC)
Order of British India
Kaisar-i-Hind Medal
Order of St John

MEDALS FOR GALLANTRY AND DISTINGUISHED CONDUCT
Union of South Africa Queen's Medal for Bravery, in Gold
Distinguished Conduct Medal (DCM), 1854
Conspicuous Gallantry Medal (CGM), 1874
Conspicuous Gallantry Medal (Flying)
George Medal (GM), 1940
Queen's Police Medal for Gallantry
Queen's Fire Service Medal for Gallantry
Royal West African Frontier Force Distinguished Conduct Medal
King's African Rifles Distinguished Conduct Medal
Indian Distinguished Service Medal
Union of South Africa Queen's Medal for Bravery, in Silver
Distinguished Service Medal (DSM), 1914
Military Medal (MM), 1916
Distinguished Flying Medal (DFM), 1918
Air Force Medal (AFM)
Constabulary Medal (Ireland)
Medal for Saving Life at Sea (Sea Gallantry Medal)
Indian Order of Merit (Civil)
Indian Police Medal for Gallantry
Ceylon Police Medal for Gallantry
Sierra Leone Police Medal for Gallantry
Sierra Leone Fire Brigades Medal for Gallantry
Colonial Police Medal for Gallantry (CPM)
Queen's Gallantry Medal (QGM), 1974
Royal Victorian Medal (RVM), Gold, Silver and Bronze
British Empire Medal (BEM)
Canada Medal
Queen's Police Medal for Distinguished Service (QPM)
Queen's Fire Service Medal for Distinguished Service (QFSM)
Queen's Volunteer Reserves Medal
Queen's Medal for Chiefs

CAMPAIGN MEDALS AND STARS
Including authorised United Nations, European Community/Union and North Atlantic Treaty Organisation medals (in order of date of campaign for which awarded)

POLAR MEDALS (in order of date)

IMPERIAL SERVICE MEDAL

POLICE MEDALS FOR VALUABLE SERVICE
Indian Police Medal for Meritorious Service
Ceylon Police Medal for Merit
Sierra Leone Police Medal for Meritorious Service
Sierra Leone Fire Brigades Medal for Meritorious Service
Colonial Police Medal for Meritorious Service

BADGE OF HONOUR

JUBILEE, CORONATION AND DURBAR MEDALS
Queen Victoria, King Edward VII, King George V, King George VI, Queen Elizabeth II and Long and Faithful Service Medals

EFFICIENCY AND LONG SERVICE DECORATIONS AND MEDALS
Medal for Meritorious Service
Accumulated Campaign Service Medal
Medal for Long Service and Good Conduct (Military)
Naval Long Service and Good Conduct Medal
Medal for Meritorious Service (Royal Navy 1918–28)
Indian Long Service and Good Conduct Medal
Indian Meritorious Service Medal
Royal Marines Meritorious Service Medal (1849–1947)
Royal Air Force Meritorious Service Medal (1918–1928)
Royal Air Force Long Service and Good Conduct Medal
Medal for Long Service and Good Conduct (Ulster Defence Regiment)
Indian Long Service and Good Conduct Medal
Royal West African Frontier Force Long Service and Good Conduct Medal
Royal Sierra Leone Military Forces Long Service and Good Conduct Medal
King's African Rifles and Long Service and Good Conduct Medal
Indian Meritorious Service Medal
Police Long Service and Good Conduct Medal
Fire Brigade Long Service and Good Conduct Medal
African Police Medal for Meritorious Service
Royal Canadian Mounted Police Long Service Medal
Ceylon Police Long Service Medal
Ceylon Fire Services Long Service Medal
Sierra Leone Police Long Service Medal
Colonial Police Long Service Medal
Sierra Leone Fire Brigades Long Service Medal
Mauritius Police Long Service and Good Conduct Medal
Mauritius Fire Services Long Service and Good Conduct Medal
Mauritius Prisons Service Long Service and Good Conduct Medal
Colonial Fire Brigades Long Service Medal

Colonial Prison Service Medal
Hong Kong Disciplined Services Medal
Army Emergency Reserve Decoration (ERD)
Volunteer Officers' Decoration (VD)
Volunteer Long Service Medal
Volunteer Officers' Decoration (for India and the Colonies)
Volunteer Long Service Medal (for India and the Colonies)
Colonial Auxiliary Forces Officers' Decoration
Colonial Auxiliary Forces Long Service Medal
Medal for Good Shooting (Naval)
Militia Long Service Medal
Imperial Yeomanry Long Service Medal
Territorial Decoration (TD), 1908
Ceylon Armed Services Long Service Medal
Efficiency Decoration (ED)
Territorial Efficiency Medal
Efficiency Medal
Special Reserve Long Service and Good Conduct Medal
Decoration for Officers of the Royal Navy Reserve (RD), 1910
Decoration for Officers of the Royal Naval Volunteer Reserve (VRD)
Royal Naval Reserve Long Service and Good Conduct Medal
Royal Naval Volunteer Reserve Long Service and Good Conduct Medal
Royal Naval Auxiliary Sick Berth Reserve Long Service and Good Conduct Medal
Royal Fleet Reserve Long Service and Good Conduct Medal
Royal Naval Wireless Auxiliary Reserve Long Service and Good Conduct Medal
Royal Naval Auxiliary Service Medal
Air Efficiency Award (AE), 1942
Volunteer Reserves Service Medal
Ulster Defence Regiment Medal
Northern Ireland Home Service Medal
Queen's Medal (for Champion Shots of the RN and RM)
Queen's Medal (for Champion Shots of the New Zealand Naval Forces)
Queen's Medal (for Champion Shots in the Military Forces)
Queen's Medal (for Champion Shots of the Air Forces)
Cadet Forces Medal, 1950
Coastguard Auxiliary Service Long Service Medal
Special Constabulary Long Service Medal
Canadian Forces Decoration
Royal Observer Corps Medal
Civil Defence Long Service Medal
Ambulance Service (Emergency Duties) Long Service and Good Conduct Medal
Royal Fleet Auxiliary Service Medal Rhodesia Medal
Royal Ulster Constabulary Service Medal
Northern Ireland Prison Service Medal
Union of South Africa Commemoration Medal
Indian Independence Medal
Pakistan Medal
Ceylon Armed Services Inauguration Medal
Ceylon Police Independence Medal (1948)
Sierra Leone Independence Medal
Jamaica Independence Medal
Uganda Independence Medal
Malawi Independence Medal
Fiji Independence Medal
Papua New Guinea Independence Medal
Solomon Islands Independence Medal
Service Medal of the Order of St John
Badge of the Order of the League of Mercy
Voluntary Medical Service Medal (1932)
Women's Royal Voluntary Service Medal

South African Medal for War Services
Colonial Special Constabulary Medal

HONORARY MEMBERSHIP OF COMMONWEALTH ORDERS

OTHER COMMONWEALTH MEMBERS' ORDERS, DECORATIONS AND MEDALS

FOREIGN ORDERS

FOREIGN DECORATIONS

FOREIGN MEDALS

THE VICTORIA CROSS (1856)
FOR CONSPICUOUS BRAVERY

VC

Ribbon, Crimson, for all Services (until 1918 it was blue for the Royal Navy)

Instituted on 29 January 1856, the Victoria Cross was awarded retrospectively to 1854, the first being held by Lt. C. D. Lucas, RN, for bravery in the Baltic Sea on 21 June 1854 (gazetted 24 February 1857). The first 62 Crosses were presented by Queen Victoria in Hyde Park, London, on 26 June 1857.

The Victoria Cross is worn before all other decorations on the left breast, and consists of a cross-pattée of bronze one-and-a-half inches in diameter, with the Royal Crown surmounted by a lion in the centre, and beneath there is the inscription For Valour. Holders of the VC currently receive a tax-free annuity of £1,500, irrespective of need or other conditions. In 1911, the right to receive the Cross was extended to Indian soldiers, and in 1920 to matrons, sisters and nurses, and the staff of the Nursing Services and other services pertaining to hospitals and nursing, and to civilians of either sex regularly or temporarily under the orders, direction or supervision of the naval, military, or air forces of the Crown.

SURVIVING RECIPIENTS OF THE VICTORIA CROSS
as at August 2005

Beharry, Pte. J. G. (Princess of Wales's Royal Regiment)
   2005 Iraq
Bhan Bhagta Gurung, Havildar (2nd Gurkha Rifles)
   1945 World War
Cruickshank, Flt. Lt. J. A. (RAFVR)
   1944 World War
Fraser, Lt.-Cdr. I. E., DSC, RD and bar (RNR)
   1945 World War
Kenna, Pte. E. (Australian Military Forces, 2/4th (NSW))
   1945 World War
Lachhiman Gurung, Havildar (8th Gurkha Rifles)
   1945 World War
Payne, WO K., DSC (USA) (Australian Army Training Team)
   1969 Vietnam
Rambahadur Limbu, Capt., MVO (10th Princess Mary's Gurkha Rifles)
   1965 Sarawak

Smith, *Sgt.* E. A., CM, CD (Seaforth Highlanders of Canada)
1944 *World War*
Speakman-Pitts, *Sgt.* W. (Black Watch, attached KOSB)
1951 *Korea*
Tulbahadur Pun, *Lt.* (6th Gurkha Rifles)
1944 *World War*
Umrao Singh, *Sub Major* (Royal Indian Artillery)
1944 *World War*
Watkins, *Maj. Rt. Hon.* Sir Tasker, GBE (Welch Regiment)
1944 *World War*
Wilson, *Lt.-Col.* E. C. T. (East Surrey Regiment)
1940 *World War*

THE GEORGE CROSS (1940)
FOR GALLANTRY

GC

Ribbon, Dark blue, threaded through a bar adorned with laurel leaves
Instituted 24 September 1940 (with amendments, 3 November 1942)

The George Cross is worn before all other decorations (except the VC) on the left breast (when worn by a woman it may be worn on the left shoulder from a ribbon of the same width and colour fashioned into a bow). It consists of a plain silver cross with four equal limbs, the cross having in the centre a circular medallion bearing a design showing St George and the Dragon. The inscription *For Gallantry* appears round the medallion and in the angle of each limb of the cross is the Royal cypher 'G VI' forming a circle concentric with the medallion. The reverse is plain and bears the name of the recipient and the date of the award. The cross is suspended by a ring from a bar adorned with laurel leaves on dark blue ribbon one-and-a-half inches wide.

The cross is intended primarily for civilians; awards to the fighting services are confined to actions for which purely military honours are not normally granted. It is awarded only for acts of the greatest heroism or of the most conspicuous courage in circumstances of extreme danger. From 1 April 1965, holders of the Cross have received a tax-free annuity, which is currently £1,500. The cross has twice been awarded collectively rather than to an individual: to Malta (1942) and the Royal Ulster Constabulary (1999).

The royal warrant which ordained that the grant of the Empire Gallantry Medal should cease authorised holders of that medal to return it to the Central Chancery of the Orders of Knighthood and to receive in exchange the George Cross. A similar provision applied to posthumous awards of the Empire Gallantry Medal made after the outbreak of war in 1939. In October 1971 all surviving holders of the Albert Medal and the Edward Medal exchanged those decorations for the George Cross.

SURVIVING RECIPIENTS OF THE GEORGE CROSS
as at August 2005

If the recipient originally received the Albert Medal (AM) or the Edward Medal (EM), this is indicated by the initials in parenthesis.

Archer, *Col.* B. S. T., GC, OBE, ERD, 1941
Bamford, J., GC, 1952
Beaton, J., GC, CVO, 1974
Bridge, *Lt.-Cdr.* J., GC, GM and bar, 1944
Butson, *Lt.-Col.* A. R. C., GC, CD, MD (AM), 1948
Farrow, K., GC (AM), 1948
Finney, Trooper C., GC, 2003
Flintoff, H. H., GC (EM), 1944
Gledhill, A. J., GC, 1967
Gregson, J. S., GC (AM), 1943
Johnson, *WO1 (SSM)* B., GC, 1990
Kinne, D. G., GC, 1954
Lowe, A. R., GC (AM), 1949
Lynch, J., GC, BEM (AM), 1948
Pratt, M. K., GC, 1978
Purves, Mrs M., GC (AM), 1949
Raweng, Awang anak, GC, 1951
Rowlands, *Air Marshal* Sir John, GC, KBE, 1943
Stevens, H. W., GC, 1958
Styles, *Lt.-Col.* S. G., GC, 1972
Walker, C., GC, 1972
Walker, C. H., GC (AM), 1942
Walton, E. W. K., GC (AM), DSO, 1948
Wilcox, C., GC (EM), 1949
Wooding, E. A., GC (AM), 1945

CHIEFS OF CLANS IN SCOTLAND

Only chiefs of whole Names or Clans are included, except certain special instances (marked *) who, though not chiefs of a whole Name, were or are for some reason (eg the Macdonald forfeiture) independent. Under decision (*Campbell-Gray*, 1950) that a bearer of a 'double or triple-barrelled' surname cannot be held chief of a part of such, several others cannot be included in the list at present.

THE ROYAL HOUSE: HM THE QUEEN
AGNEW: Sir Crispin Agnew of Lochnaw, Bt.
ANSTRUTHER: Tobias Anstruther of Anstruther and Balcaskie
ARBUTHNOTT: The Viscount of Arbuthnott, KT, CBE, DSC
BANNERMAN: Sir David Bannerman of Elsick, Bt.
BARCLAY: Peter C. Barclay of Towie Barclay and of that Ilk
BORTHWICK: The Lord Borthwick
BOYD: The Lord Kilmarnock, MBE
BOYLE: The Earl of Glasgow
BRODIE: Alexander Brodie of Brodie
BROUN OF COLSTOUN: Sir William Broun of Colstoun, Bt.
BRUCE: The Earl of Elgin and Kincardine, KT
BUCHAN: David Buchan of Auchmacoy
BURNETT: J. C. A. Burnett of Leys
CAMERON: Donald Cameron of Lochiel
CAMPBELL: The Duke of Argyll
CARMICHAEL: Richard Carmichael of Carmichael
CARNEGIE: The Duke of Fife
CATHCART: The Earl Cathcart
CHARTERIS: The Earl of Wemyss and March, KT
CLAN CHATTAN: K. Mackintosh of Clan Chattan
CHISHOLM: Hamish Chisholm of Chisholm (*The Chisholm*)
COCHRANE: The Earl of Dundonald
COLQUHOUN: Sir Ivar Colquhoun of Luss, Bt.
CRANSTOUN: David Cranstoun of that Ilk
CUMMING: Sir Alastair Cumming of Altyre, Bt.
DARROCH: Capt. Duncan Darroch of Gourock
DAVIDSON: Alister Davidson of Davidston
DEWAR: Michael Dewar of that Ilk and Vogrie
DRUMMOND: The Earl of Perth
DUNBAR: Sir James Dunbar of Mochrum, Bt.
DUNDAS: David Dundas of Dundas
DURIE: Andrew Durie of Durie, CBE
ELIOTT: Mrs Margaret Eliott of Redheugh
ERSKINE: The Earl of Mar and Kellie
FARQUHARSON: Capt. A. Farquharson of Invercauld, MC
FERGUSSON: Sir Charles Fergusson of Kilkerran, Bt.
FORBES: The Lord Forbes, KBE
FORSYTH: Alistair Forsyth of that Ilk
FRASER: The Lady Saltoun
*FRASER (OF LOVAT): The Lord Lovat
GAYRE: R. Gayre of Gayre and Nigg
GORDON: The Marquess of Huntly
GRAHAM: The Duke of Montrose
GRANT: The Lord Strathspey
GRIERSON: Sir Michael Grierson of Lag, Bt.
GUTHRIE: Alexander Guthrie of Guthrie
HAIG: The Earl Haig, OBE

HALDANE: Martin Haldane of Gleneagles
HANNAY: David Hannay of Kirkdale and of that Ilk
HAY: The Earl of Erroll
HENDERSON: Alistair Henderson of Fordell
HUNTER: Pauline Hunter of Hunterston
IRVINE OF DRUM: David Irvine of Drum
JARDINE: Sir Alexander Jardine of Applegirth, Bt.
JOHNSTONE: The Earl of Annandale and Hartfell
KEITH: The Earl of Kintore
KENNEDY: The Marquess of Ailsa
KERR: The Marquess of Lothian, KCVO
KINCAID: Madam Arabella Kincaid of Kincaid
LAMONT: Revd Peter Lamont of that Ilk
LEASK: Madam Leask of Leask
LENNOX: Edward Lennox of that Ilk
LESLIE: The Earl of Rothes
LINDSAY: The Earl of Crawford and Balcarres, KT, GCVO, PC
LIVINGSTONE OR MACLEA: Alastair Livingstone of Bachuil
LOCKHART: Angus Lockhart of the Lee
LUMSDEN: Gillem Lumsden of that Ilk and Blanerne
MACALESTER: William St J. McAlester of Loup and Kennox
MACARTHUR; John MacArthur of that Ilk
MCBAIN: J. H. McBain of McBain
MACDONALD: The Lord Macdonald (*The Macdonald of Macdonald*)
*MACDONALD OF CLANRANALD: Ranald Macdonald of Clanranald
*MACDONALD OF SLEAT (CLAN HUSTEAIN): Sir Ian Macdonald of Sleat, Bt.
*MACDONELL OF GLENGARRY: Ranald MacDonell of Glengarry
MACDOUGALL: Morag MacDougall of MacDougall
MACDOWALL: Fergus Macdowall of Garthland
MACGREGOR: Sir Malcolm MacGregor of MacGregor, Bt.
MACINTYRE: Donald MacIntyre of Glenoe
MACKAY: The Lord Reay
MACKENZIE: The Earl of Cromartie
MACKINNON: Anne Mackinnon of Mackinnon
MACKINTOSH: John Mackintosh of Mackintosh (*The Mackintosh of Mackintosh*)
MACLACHLAN: Euan MacLachlan of MacLachlan
MACLAREN: Donald MacLaren of MacLaren and Achleskine
MACLEAN: The Hon. Sir Lachlan Maclean of Duart, Bt., CVO
MACLENNAN: Ruaraidh MacLennan of MacLennan
MACLEOD: John MacLeod of MacLeod
MACMILLAN: George MacMillan of MacMillan
MACNAB: J. C. Macnab of Macnab (*The Macnab*)
MACNAGHTEN: Sir Patrick Macnaghten of Macnaghten and Dundarave, Bt.
MACNEACAIL: John Macneacail of Macneacail and Scorrybreac
MACNEIL OF BARRA: Ian Macneil of Barra (*The Macneil of Barra*)
MACPHERSON: The Hon. Sir William Macpherson of Cluny, TD

MACTHOMAS: Andrew MacThomas of Finegand
MAITLAND: The Earl of Lauderdale
MAKGILL: The Viscount of Oxfuird
MALCOLM (MACCALLUM): Robin N. L. Malcolm of Poltalloch
MAR: The Countess of Mar, St Michael's Farm
MARJORIBANKS: Andrew Marjoribanks of that Ilk
MATHESON: Maj. Sir Fergus Matheson of Matheson, Bt.
MENZIES: David Menzies of Menzies
MOFFAT: Madam Moffat of that Ilk
MONCREIFFE: The Hon. Peregrine Moncreiffe of that Ilk
MONTGOMERIE: The Earl of Eglinton and Winton
MORRISON: Dr Iain Morrison of Ruchdi
MUNRO: Hector Munro of Foulis
MURRAY: The Duke of Atholl
NESBITT (or NISBET): Mark Nesbitt of that Ilk
NICOLSON: The Lord Carnock
OGILVY: The Earl of Airlie, KT, GCVO, PC
OLIPHANT: Richard Oliphant of that Ilk
RAMSAY: The Earl of Dalhousie
RATTRAY: James Rattray of Rattray
RIDDELL: Sir John Riddell of Riddell, CB, CVO

ROBERTSON: Alexander Robertson of Struan *(Struan-Robertson)*
ROLLO: The Lord Rollo
ROSE: Miss Elizabeth Rose of Kilravock
ROSS: David Ross of that Ilk and Balnagowan
RUTHVEN: The Earl of Gowrie, PC
SCOTT: The Duke of Buccleuch and Queensberry, KT, VRD
SCRYMGEOUR: The Earl of Dundee
SEMPILL: The Lord Sempill
SHAW: John Shaw of Tordarroch
SINCLAIR: The Earl of Caithness
SKENE: Danus Skene of Skene
STIRLING: Fraser Stirling of Cader
STRANGE: Maj. Timothy Strange of Balcaskie
SUTHERLAND: The Countess of Sutherland
SWINTON: John Swinton of that Ilk
TROTTER: Alexander Trotter of Mortonhall
URQUHART: Kenneth Urquhart of Urquhart
WALLACE: Ian Wallace of that Ilk
WEDDERBURN: The Master of Dundee
WEMYSS: Michael Wemyss of that Ilk

THE PRIVY COUNCIL

The Sovereign in Council, or Privy Council, was the chief source of executive power until the system of cabinet government developed in the 18th century. Now the Privy Council's main functions are to advise the Sovereign and to exercise its own statutory responsibilities independent of the Sovereign in Council.

Membership of the Privy Council is automatic upon appointment to certain government and judicial positions in the United Kingdom, eg Cabinet ministers may be Privy Counsellors and are sworn in on first assuming office. Membership is also accorded by The Queen to eminent people in the UK and independent countries of the Commonwealth of which Her Majesty is Queen, on the recommendation of the British prime minister. Membership of the Council is retained for life, except for very occasional removals.

The administrative functions of the Privy Council are carried out by the Privy Council Office under the direction of the President of the Council, who is always a member of the Cabinet.

President of the Council, The Rt. Hon.
Baroness Amos
Clerk of the Council, A. Galloway

MEMBERS *as at August 2005*

Style The Right (or Rt.) Hon._
Envelope, The Right (or Rt.) Hon.
F_ S_. *Letter,* Dear Mr/Miss/Mrs
S_. *Spoken,* Mr/Miss/Mrs S_
It is incorrect to use the letters PC after the name in conjunction with the prefix The Right Hon., unless the Privy Counsellor is a peer below the rank of Marquess and so is styled The Right Hon. because of his/her rank. In this case only, the post-nominal letters may be used in conjunction with the prefix The Right Hon.

HRH The Duke of Edinburgh, 1951
HRH The Prince of Wales, 1977

Abernethy, *Hon.* Lord (John Alastair Cameron), 2005
Ackner, Lord, 1980
Ainsworth, Robert, 2005
Airlie, Earl of, 1984
Aldous, Sir William, 1995
Alebua, Ezekiel, 1988
Alexander, Douglas, 2005

Amos, Baroness, 2003
Ampthill, Lord, 1995
Ancram, Michael, 1996
Anderson of Swansea, Lord, 2000
Anthony, Douglas, 1971
Arbuthnot, James, 1998
Archer of Sandwell, Lord, 1977
Arden, Dame Mary, 2000
Armstrong, Hilary, 1999
Arthur, *Hon.* Owen, 1995
Ashdown of Norton-sub-Hamdon, Lord, 1989
Ashley of Stoke, Lord, 1979
Atkins, Sir Robert, 1995
Auld, Sir Robin, 1995
Baker, Sir Thomas, 2002
Baker of Dorking, Lord, 1984
Barber, Lord, 1963
Barnett, Lord, 1975
Barron, Kevin, 2001
Battle, John, 2002
Beckett, Margaret, 1993
Beith, Alan, 1992
Beldam, Sir Roy, 1989
Belstead, Lord, 1983
Benn, Anthony, 1964
Benn, Hilary, 2003
Biffen, Lord, 1979
Bingham of Cornhill, Lord, 1986
Birch, William, 1992
Bisson, Sir Gordon, 1987
Blackstone, Baroness, 2001
Blair, Tony, 1994
Blaker, Lord, 1983
Blanchard, Peter, 1998
Blears, Hazel, 2005
Blunkett, David, 1997
Boateng, Paul, 1999
Bolger, James, 1991
Booth, Albert, 1976
Boothroyd, Baroness, 1992
Boscawen, *Hon.* Robert, 1992
Bottomley of Nettlestone, Baroness, 1992
Boyd, Colin, 2000
Boyson, Sir Rhodes, 1987
Bradley, Keith, 2001
Brathwaite, Sir Nicholas, 1991
Bridge of Harwich, Lord, 1975
Brightman, Lord, 1979
Brittan of Spennithorne, Lord, 1981
Brook, Sir Henry, 1996
Brooke of Sutton Mandeville, Lord, 1988
Brown, Gordon, 1996
Brown, Nicholas, 1997
Brown, Sir Stephen, 1983
Brown of Eaton-under-Heywood, Lord, 1992
Browne, Desmond, 2005
Browne-Wilkinson, Lord, 1983
Butler, Sir Adam, 1984
Butler of Brockwell, Lord, 2004
Butler-Sloss, Dame Elizabeth, 1988
Buxton, Sir Richard, 1997
Byers, Stephen, 1998
Bryon, Sir Dennis, 2004
Caborn, Richard, 1999
Caithness, Earl of, 1990

Cameron of Lochbroom, Lord, 1984
Camoys, Lord, 1997
Campbell, Sir Walter Menzies, 1999
Campbell, Sir William, 1999
Canterbury, The Archbishop of, 2002
Carey of Clifton, Lord, 1991
Carnwath, Sir Robert, 2002
Carr of Hadley, Lord, 1963
Carrington, Lord, 1959
Carswell, Lord, 1993
Carter, Lord, 1997
Casey, Sir Maurice, 1986
Chadwick, Sir John, 1997
Chalfont, Lord, 1964
Chalker of Wallasey, Baroness, 1987
Chan, Sir Julius, 1981
Chataway, Sir Christopher, 1970
Chilcot, Sir John, 2004
Christie, Perry, 2004
Clark of Windermere, Lord, 1997
Clark, Helen, 1990
Clarke, Sir Anthony, 1998
Clarke, Charles, 2001
Clarke, Kenneth, 1984
Clarke, Thomas, 1997
Clinton-Davis, Lord, 1998
Clwyd, Ann, 2004
Clyde, Lord, 1996
Cockfield, Lord, 1982
Colman, Fraser, 1986
Compton, Sir John, 1983
Cooke of Thorndon, Lord, 1977
Cope of Berkeley, Lord, 1988
Corston, Baroness, 2003
Cosgrove, *Hon.* Lady (Hazel Cosgrove), 2003
Coulsfield, *Hon.* Lord (John Coulsfield), 2000
Cowen, Sir Zelman, 1981
Cradock, Sir Percy, 1993
Crawford and Balcarres, Earl of, 1972
Creech, *Hon.* Wyatt, 1999
Crickhowell, Lord, 1979
Croom-Johnson, Sir David, 1984
Cullen of Whitekirk, *Hon.* Lord, 1997
Cunningham of Felling, Lord, 1993
Curry, David, 1996
Darling, Alistair, 1997
Davies, Denzil, 1978
Davies, Ronald, 1997
Davis, David, 1997
Davis, Terence, 1999
Davison, Sir Ronald, 1978
de la Bastide, Michael, 2004
Dean of Harptree, Lord, 1991
Dean of Thornton-le-Fylde, Baroness, 1998
Deedes, Lord, 1962
Denham, John, 2000
Denham, Lord, 1981
Dixon, Lord, 1996
Dobson, Frank, 1997
Dorrell, Stephen, 1994
du Cann, Sir Edward, 1964
Duncan Smith, Iain, 2001
Dunn, Sir Robin, 1980
Dyson, Sir John, 2001

Mustill, Lord, 1985
Nairne, Sir Patrick, 1982
Namaliu, Sir Rabbie, 1989
Naseby, Lord, 1994
Needham, Sir Richard, 1994
Neill, Sir Brian, 1985
Neuberger, Sir David, 2004
Newton of Braintree, Lord, 1988
Nicholls of Birkenhead, Lord, 1995
Nicholson, Sir Michael, 1995
Nimmo Smith, *Hon.* Lord (William Nimmo Smith), 2005
Nolan, Lord, 1991
Nott, Sir John, 1979
Nourse, Sir Martin, 1985
Oakes, Gordon, 1979
O'Connor, Sir Patrick, 1980
O'Donnell, Turlough, 1979
Oliver of Aylmerton, Lord, 1980
Oppenheim-Barnes, Baroness, 1979
Osborne, *Hon.* Lord (Kenneth Osborne), 2001
Otton, Sir Philip, 1995
Owen, Lord, 1976
Paeniu, Bikenibeu, 1991
Palliser, Sir Michael, 1983
Palmer, Sir Geoffrey, 1986
Parker, Sir Jonathan, 2000
Parker, Sir Roger, 1983
Parkinson, Lord, 1981
Patten, Lord, 1990
Patten of Barnes, Lord, 1989
Patterson, Percival, 1993
Pattie, Sir Geoffrey, 1987
Pendry, Lord, 2000
Penrose, *Hon.* Lord (George Penrose), 2000
Peters, Winston, 1998
Peyton of Yeovil, Lord, 1970
Phillips of Worth Matravers, Lord, 1995
Pill, Sir Malcolm, 1995
Pindling, Sir Lynden, 1976
Portillo, Michael, 1992
Potter, Sir Mark, 1996
Prescott, John, 1994
Price, George, 1982
Primarolo, Dawn, 2002
Prior, Lord, 1970
Prosser, *Hon.* Lord (William Prosser), 2000
Puapua, Sir Tomasi, 1982
Pym, Lord, 1970
Quin, Joyce, 1998
Radice, Lord, 1999
Raison, Sir Timothy, 1982
Ramsden, James, 1963
Rawlinson of Ewell, Lord, 1964
Raynsford, Nick, 2001

Redwood, John, 1993
Rees, Lord, 1983
Reid, George, 2004
Reid, John, 1998
Renton, Lord, 1962
Renton of Mount Harry, Lord, 1989
Richard, Lord, 1993
Richardson, Sir Ivor, 1978
Richardson of Duntisbourne, Lord, 1976
Rifkind, Sir Malcolm, 1986
Rix, Sir Bernard, 2000
Roberts of Conwy, Lord, 1991
Robertson of Port Ellen, Lord, 1997
Roch, Sir John, 1993
Rodger of Earlsferry, Lord, 1992
Rodgers of Quarry Bank, Lord, 1975
Rooker, Lord, 1999
Rose, Sir Christopher, 1992
Ross, *Hon.* Lord (Donald MacArthur), 1985
Rumbold, Dame Angela, 1991
Ryder of Wensum, Lord, 1990
Sainsbury, Sir Timothy, 1992
St John of Fawsley, Lord, 1979
Salisbury, Marquess of, 1994
Sandiford, Erskine, 1989
Saville of Newdigate, Lord, 1994
Sawyer, Dame Joan, 2004
Schiemann, Sir Konrad, 1995
Scotland of Asthal, Baroness, 2001
Scott of Foscote, Lord, 1991
Seaga, Edward, 1981
Sedley, Sir Stephen, 1999
Selkirk of Douglas, Lord, 1996
Shearer, Hugh, 1969
Sheldon, Lord, 1977
Shephard of Northwold, Baroness, 1992
Shiel, Sir John, 2005
Shipley, Jennifer, 1998
Short, Clare, 1997
Simmonds, Sir Kennedy, 1984
Simon of Glaisdale, Lord, 1961
Sinclair, Ian, 1977
Slade, Sir Christopher, 1982
Slynn of Hadley, Lord, 1992
Smith, Andrew, 1997
Smith, Dame Janet, 2002
Smith, Jacqueline, 2003
Smith of Finsbury, Lord, 1997
Somare, Sir Michael, 1977
Spellar, John, 2001
Stanley, Sir John, 1984
Staughton, Sir Christopher, 1988
Steel of Aikwood, Lord, 1977
Stephen, Sir Ninian, 1979
Stewartby, Lord, 1989
Steyn, Lord, 1992

Strang, Gavin, 1997
Strathclyde, Lord, 1995
Straw, Jack, 1997
Stuart-Smith, Sir Murray, 1988
Sutherland, *Hon.* Lord (Ranald Sutherland), 2000
Symons of Vernham Dean, Baroness, 2001
Talboys, Sir Brian, 1977
Taylor of Bolton, Baroness, 1997
Tebbit, Lord, 1981
Templeman, Lord, 1978
Thatcher, Baroness, 1970
Thomas, Edmund, 1996
Thomas of Gwydir, Lord, 1964
Thomas, Sir Roger, 2003
Thomas, Sir Swinton, 1994
Thomson of Monifieth, Lord, 1966
Thorpe, Jeremy, 1967
Thorpe, Sir Matthew, 1995
Tipping, Andrew, 1998
Tizard, Robert, 1986
Trefgarne, Lord, 1989
Trimble, David, 1997
Trumpington, Baroness, 1992
Tuckey, Sir Simon, 1998
Ullswater, Viscount, 1994
Upton, Simon, 1999
Varley, Lord, 1974
Waddington, Lord, 1987
Waite, Sir John, 1993
Wakeham, Lord, 1983
Waldegrave of North Hill, Lord, 1990
Walker of Gestingthorpe, Lord, 1997
Walker of Worcester, Lord, 1970
Wall, Sir Nicholas, 2004
Wallace, James, 2000
Waller, Sir Mark, 1996
Ward, Sir Alan, 1995
Watkins, Sir Tasker, 1980
Weatherill, Lord, 1980
Wheeler, Sir John, 1993
Widdecombe, Ann, 1997
Wigley, Dafydd, 1997
Williams, Alan, 1977
Williams of Crosby, Baroness, 1974
Wilson, Brian, 2003
Windlesham, Lord, 1973
Winti, Paias, 1987
Withers, Reginald, 1977
Woodhouse, Sir Owen, 1974
Woolf, Lord, 1986
Wylie, *Hon.* Lord (Norman Wylie), 1970
York, The Archbishop of, 2005
Young, Sir George, 1993
Young of Graffham, Lord, 1984
Zacca, Edward, 1992

PRIVY COUNCIL OF NORTHERN IRELAND

The Privy Council of Northern Ireland had responsibilities in Northern Ireland similar to those of the Privy Council in Great Britain until the Northern Ireland Act 1974 instituted direct rule and a UK Cabinet minister became responsible for the functions previously exercised by the Northern Ireland government.

Membership of the Privy Council of Northern Ireland is retained for life. Since the Northern Ireland Constitution Act 1973 no further appointments have been made. The postnominal initials PC (NI) are used to differentiate its members from those of the Privy Council.

MEMBERS *as at August 2005*

Bailie, Robin, 1971
Bleakley, David, 1971

Craig, William, 1963
Dobson, John, 1969
Kelly, Sir Basil, 1969
Kilclooney, Lord, 1970
Kirk, Herbert, 1962
Long, William, 1966
Porter, Sir Robert, 1969

PARLIAMENT

The United Kingdom constitution is not contained in any single document but has evolved over time, formed partly by statute, partly by common law and partly by convention. A constitutional monarchy, the United Kingdom is governed by Ministers of the Crown in the name of the Sovereign, who is head both of the state and of the government.

The organs of government are the legislature (Parliament), the executive and the judiciary. The executive consists of HM Government (Cabinet and other Ministers), government departments and local authorities (see Local Government, Government Departments and Public Offices). The judiciary (see Law Courts and Offices) pronounces on the law, both written and unwritten, interprets statutes and is responsible for the enforcement of the law; the judiciary is independent of both the legislature and the executive.

THE MONARCHY

The Sovereign personifies the state and is, in law, an integral part of the legislature, head of the executive, head of the judiciary, commander-in-chief of all armed forces of the Crown and 'Supreme Governor' of the Church of England. The seat of the monarchy is in the United Kingdom. In the Channel Islands and the Isle of Man, which are Crown dependencies, the Sovereign is represented by a Lieutenant-Governor. In the member states of the Commonwealth of which the Sovereign is head of state, her representative is a Governor-General; in UK dependencies the Sovereign is usually represented by a Governor, who is responsible to the British Government.

Although in practice the powers of the monarchy are now very limited, restricted mainly to the advisory and ceremonial, there are important acts of government which require the participation of the Sovereign. These include summoning, proroguing and dissolving Parliament, giving royal assent to bills passed by Parliament, appointing important office-holders, eg government ministers, judges, bishops and governors, conferring peerages, knighthoods and other honours, and granting pardon to a person wrongly convicted of a crime. The Sovereign appoints the prime minister; by convention this office is held by the leader of the political party which enjoys, or can secure, a majority of votes in the House of Commons. In international affairs the Sovereign as head of state has the power to declare war and make peace, to recognise foreign states and governments, to conclude treaties and to annex or cede territory. However, as the Sovereign entrusts executive power to Ministers of the Crown and acts on the advice of her Ministers, which she cannot ignore, royal prerogative powers are in practice exercised by Ministers, who are responsible to Parliament.

Ministerial responsibility does not diminish the Sovereign's importance to the smooth working of government. She holds meetings of the Privy Council (see below), gives audiences to her Ministers and other officials at home and overseas, receives accounts of Cabinet decisions, reads dispatches and signs state papers; she must be informed and consulted on every aspect of national life; and she must show complete impartiality.

COUNSELLORS OF STATE

In the event of the Sovereign's absence abroad, it is necessary to appoint Counsellors of State under letters patent to carry out the chief functions of the Monarch, including the holding of Privy Councils and giving royal assent to acts passed by Parliament. The normal procedure is to appoint as Counsellors three or four members of the royal family among those remaining in the UK.

In the event of the Sovereign on accession being under the age of 18 years, or at any time unavailable or incapacitated by infirmity of mind or body for the performance of the royal functions, provision is made for a regency.

THE PRIVY COUNCIL

The Sovereign in Council, or Privy Council, was the chief source of executive power until the system of Cabinet government developed. Its main function is to advise the Sovereign to approve Orders in Council and to advise on the issue of royal proclamations. The Council's own statutory responsibilities (independent of the powers of the Sovereign in Council) include powers of supervision over the registering bodies for the medical and allied professions. A full Council is summoned only on the death of the Sovereign or when the Sovereign announces his or her intention to marry. (For a full list of Privy Counsellors, see The Privy Council section.)

There are a number of advisory Privy Council committees, whose meetings the Sovereign does not attend. Some are prerogative committees, such as those dealing with legislative matters submitted by the legislatures of the Channel Islands and the Isle of Man or with applications for charters of incorporation; and some are provided for by statute, e.g. those for the universities of Oxford and Cambridge and the Scottish universities.

The Judicial Committee of the Privy Council is the court of final appeal from courts of the UK dependencies, courts of independent Commonwealth countries which have retained the right of appeal and courts of the Channel Islands and the Isle of Man.

It also has certain jurisdiction within the United Kingdom, the most important of which is that it is the court of final appeal for 'devolution issues', i.e. issues as to the legal competences and functions of the legislative and executive authorities established in Scotland, Wales and Northern Ireland by the devolution legislation of 1998.

The Committee is composed of Privy Counsellors who hold, or have held, high judicial office, although usually only three or five hear each case.

Administrative work is carried out by the Privy Council Office under the direction of the Lord President of the Council, a Cabinet Minister.

PARLIAMENT

Parliament is the supreme law-making authority and can legislate for the UK as a whole or for any parts of it separately (the Channel Islands and the Isle of Man are Crown dependencies and not part of the UK). The main functions of Parliament are to pass laws, to provide (by voting taxation) the means of carrying on the work of government and to scrutinise government policy and administration, particularly proposals for expenditure. International treaties and agreements are by custom presented to Parliament before ratification.

Parliament emerged during the late 13th and early 14th centuries. The officers of the King's household and the King's judges were the nucleus of early Parliaments, joined by such ecclesiastical and lay magnates as the King might summon to form a prototype 'House of Lords', and occasionally by the knights of the shires, burgesses and proctors of the lower clergy. By the end of Edward III's reign a 'House of Commons' was beginning to appear; the first known Speaker was elected in 1377.

Parliamentary procedure is based on custom and precedent, partly formulated in the Standing Orders of both Houses of Parliament, and each House has the right to control its own internal proceedings and to commit for contempt. The system of debate in the two Houses is similar; when a motion has been moved, the Speaker proposes the question as the subject of a debate. Members speak from wherever they have been sitting. Questions are decided by a vote on a simple majority. Draft legislation is introduced, in either House, as a bill. Bills can be introduced by a Government Minister or a private Member, but in practice the majority of bills which become law are introduced by the government. To become law, a bill must be passed by each House (for parliamentary stages, see Bill, page 131) and then sent to the Sovereign for the royal assent, after which it becomes an Act of Parliament.

Proceedings of both Houses are public, except on extremely rare occasions. The minutes (called *Votes and Proceedings in the Commons,* and *Minutes of Proceedings in the Lords*) and the speeches (*The Official Report of Parliamentary Debates,* Hansard) are published daily. Proceedings are also recorded for transmission on radio and television and stored in the Parliamentary Recording Unit before transfer to the National Sound Archive. Television cameras have been allowed into the House of Lords since 1985 and into the House of Commons since 1989; committee meetings may also be televised.

By the Parliament Act of 1911, the maximum duration of a Parliament is five years (if not previously dissolved), the term being reckoned from the date given on the writs for the new Parliament. The maximum life has been prolonged by legislation in such rare circumstances as the two world wars (31 January 1911 to 25 November 1918; 26 November 1935 to 15 June 1945). Dissolution and writs for a general election are ordered by the Sovereign on the advice of the prime minister. The life of a Parliament is divided into sessions, usually of one year in length, beginning and ending most often in October or November.

DEVOLUTION

The Scottish Parliament has legislative power over all devolved matters, i.e. matters not reserved to Westminster or otherwise outside its powers. The National Assembly for Wales has power to make secondary legislation in the areas where executive functions have been transferred to it. The Northern Ireland Assembly has legislative authority in the fields previously administered by the Northern Ireland departments. The Assembly was suspended in October 2002 and dissolved in April 2003. For further information, see the Regional Government section.

THE HOUSE OF LORDS

London SW1A 0PW
T 020-7219 3000 Information Office 020-7219 3107
E hlinfo@parliament.uk W www.parliament.uk

The House of Lords is the second chamber, or 'Upper House' of the UK's bicameral parliament. Until the beginning of the twentieth century, the House of Lords had considerable power, being able to veto any bill submitted to it by the House of Commons. Today the main functions of the House of Lords are to revise legislation, to act as a check on the government, to provide a forum of independent expertise and to act as a final court of appeal.

The House of Lords has a number of Select Committees. Some relate to the internal affairs of the House – such as its management and administration – while others carry out important investigative work on matters of public interest. There are four main areas of work – Europe, science, the economy and the constitution. House of Lords investigative committees look at broader issues and do not mirror government departments as the Select Committees in the Commons do.

The House of Lords has judicial powers as the ultimate court of appeal for courts in Great Britain and Northern Ireland, except for criminal cases in Scotland. These powers are exercised by the Lords of Appeal in Ordinary (the Law Lords) (see Law Courts and Officers section). On 12 June 2003 the government announced reforms affecting the role of the Lord Chancellor as a judge and Speaker of the House of Lords and establishing a separate Supreme Court (see Government Departments section).

Members of the House of Lords comprise life peers created under the Life Peerages Act 1958, 92 hereditary peers under the House of Lords Act 1999 and Lords of Appeal in Ordinary, i.e. Law Lords, under the Appellate Jurisdiction Act 1876. The Archbishops of Canterbury and York, the Bishops of London, Durham and Winchester, and the 21 senior diocesan bishops of the Church of England are also members.

The House of Lords Act provides for 90 elected hereditary peers to remain in the House of Lords until longer-term reform of the House has been carried out; 42 Conservative, 28 crossbench, three Liberal Democrat and two Labour. Elections for each of the party groups and crossbenches were held in October and November 1999. Fifteen office holders were elected by the Whole House. Two Hereditary Peers, the Earl Marshal and the Lord Great Chamberlain are also members.

Peers are disqualified from sitting in the House if they are:
– aliens, i.e. any peer who is not a British citizen, a Commonwealth citizen (under the British Nationality Act 1981) or a citizen of the Republic of Ireland
– under the age of 21
– undischarged bankrupts or, in Scotland, those whose estate is sequestered
– convicted of treason
Bishops retire at the age of 70 and cease to be members of the House at that time.

Peers who do not wish to attend sittings of the House of Lords may apply for Leave of Absence for the duration of a Parliament.

Members of the House of Lords are unpaid but are entitled to allowances for attendance at sittings of the House. The daily maxima are £132.00 for overnight subsistence, £66.00 for day subsistence and incidental travel, and £55.00 for secretarial costs (as at August 2005).

COMPOSITION *as at 1 July 2005*

Archbishops and Bishops	25
Life peers under the Appellate Jurisdiction Act 1876	28 (1 woman)
Life peers under the Life Peerages Act 1958	586 (129 women)
Peers under the House of Lords Act 1999	92 (3 women)
Total	731

STATE OF THE PARTIES *as at 1 July 2005**

Conservative	208
Labour	215
Liberal Democrat	74
Crossbench	187
Archbishops and Bishops	25
Other	14
Total	723

* Excluding 8 peers on leave of absence from the House

OFFICERS

The House is presided over by the Lord Chancellor, who is *ex officio* Speaker of the House. (On 12 June 2003 the government announced proposals to end the role of the Lord Chancellor as a judge and Speaker of the House of Lords, *see* description of Lord Chancellor's role below and Government Departments section).

A panel of deputy Speakers is appointed by Royal Commission. The first deputy Speaker is the Chairman of Committees, appointed at the beginning of each session, who is a salaried officer of the House. He takes the chair when the whole House is in Committee and in some select committees. He is assisted by a panel of deputy chairmen, headed by the salaried Principal Deputy Chairman of Committees, who is also chairman of the European Communities Committee of the House.

The Clerk of the Parliaments is the Accounting Officer and the chief permanent official responsible for the administration of the House. The Gentleman Usher of the Black Rod is responsible for security and other services and also has royal duties as secretary to the Lord Great Chamberlain.

Secretary of State for Constitutional Affairs and Lord Chancellor (The Lord Chancellor's salary is paid by the Department for Constitutional Affairs and no salary is claimed as Lord Chancellor or Speaker of the House of Lords), The Rt. Hon. Lord Falconer of Thoroton, QC
Private Secretary, Mrs S. Albon
Chairman of Committees (£79,382), The Lord Brabazon of Tara
Principal Deputy Chairman of Committees (£74,265), The Lord Grenfell

HOUSE OF LORDS MANAGEMENT BOARD
Staff are placed in the following pay bands according to their level of responsibility and taking account of other factors such as experience and marketability.

Judicial Group 4	£155,404
Senior Band 3	£93,139–£133,233
Senior Band 2	£75,607–£122,882
Senior Band 1A	£63,655–£85,469
Senior Band 1	£54,788–£91,384
Band A1	£46,911–£66,844
Band A2	£38,618–£55,303

Clerk of the Parliaments (Judicial Group 4), P. D. G. Hayter, LVO
Clerk Assistant (Senior Band 3), M. G. Pownall
Reading Clerk and Clerk of the Journals (Senior Band 2), D. R. Beamish, LLM
Clerk of the Committees and Clerk of the Overseas Office (Senior Band 2), Dr R. H. Walters, DPHIL
Finance Director (Senior Band 1A), E. C. Ollard
Head of Human Resources (Senior Band 1A), Dr F. P. Tudor
Clerk of the Judicial Office and Registrar of Lords Interests (Senior Band 1A), B. P. Keith
Librarian (Senior Band 1A), D. L. Jones
Clerk of Public and Private Bill Office and Examiner of Petitions for Private Bills in the House of Lords (Senior Band 1), T. V. Mohan
Editor of the Official Report (Senior Band 1), Miss J. A. Bradshaw
Clerk of the Records (Senior Band 1), S. K. Ellison
Financial Adviser (Senior Band 1), M. J. Barram
Deputy Finance Director and Head of Finance (Senior Band 1), A. D. Underwood
Director of Public Information (Band A1), Miss M. L. Morgan
Counsel to the Chairman of Committees (Senior Band 2), A. Roberts
Second Counsel to the Chairman of Committees (Senior Band 2), Dr C. S. Kerse, CB, PHD
Legal Adviser to the Human Rights Committee (Senior Band 2), M. Hunt
Clerk of the Procedure Committee (Senior Band 1), M. E. Ollard
Clerks of Select Committees (Senior Band 1), S. P. Burton; J. A. Vaughan

DEPARTMENT OF THE GENTLEMAN USHER OF THE BLACK ROD
Gentleman Usher of the Black Rod and Serjeant-at-Arms (Senior Band 2), Lt.-Gen. Sir Michael Willcocks, KCB
Yeoman Usher of the Black Rod and Deputy Serjeant-at-Arms (Band A2), Brig. H. D. C. Duncan, MBE

SELECT COMMITTEES
The main House of Lords select committees, *as at June 2005,* are as follows:
European Union – Chair, Lord Grenfell; *Clerk,* S. Burton
European Union – Sub-committees:
   A (Economic and Financial Affairs and International Trade) – Chair, Lord Radice; *Clerk,* E. Lock
   B (Internal Market) – Chair, Lord Woolmer of Leeds; *Clerk,* A. Murphy
   C (Foreign Affairs, Defence and Development Policy) – Chair, Lord Bowness; *Clerk,* E. Baldock
   D (Agriculture and the Environment) – Chair, Lord Renton of Mount Harry; *Clerk,* S. Todd

E *(Law and Institutions)* – *Chair,* Lord Brown of
Eaton-under-Heywood; *Clerk,* S. Price
F *(Home Affairs)* – *Chair,* Lord Wright of
Richmond; *Clerk,* T. Rawsthorne
G *(Social and Consumer Affairs)* – *Chair,* Baroness
Thomas of Walliswood; *Clerk,* G. Baker
Constitution Committee – *Chair,* Lord Holme of
Cheltenham; *Clerk,* I. Mackley
Delegated Powers and Regulatory Reform – *Chair,* Lord
Dahrendorf; *Clerk,* C. Salmon
Economic Affairs – *Chair,* Lord Wakeham; *Clerk,* R.
Graham-Harrison
Science and Technology – *Chair,* Lord Broers; *Clerk,* Dr
C. S. Johnson
I – *Chair,* Lord Sutherland of Houndwood; *Clerk,*
M. Collon
II – *Chair,* Baroness Perry of Southwark; *Clerk,* Dr
C. S. Johnson
Human Rights Joint Committee – *Chair,* Andrew Dismore,
MP; *Lords Clerk,* E. Lock

THE HOUSE OF COMMONS

London SW1A 0AA
T 020-7219 3000
Information Office 020-7219 4272
Forthcoming business 020-7219 5532
E hcinfo@parliament.uk W www.parliament.uk

The members of the House of Commons are elected by
universal adult suffrage. For electoral purposes, the United
Kingdom is divided into constituencies, each of which
returns one member to the House of Commons, the
member being the candidate who obtains the largest
number of votes cast in the constituency. To ensure
equitable representation, the four Boundary Commissions
keep constituency boundaries under review and
recommend any redistribution of seats which may seem
necessary because of population movements, etc. The
number of seats was raised to 640 in 1945, reduced to
625 in 1948, and subsequently rose to 630 in 1955, 635
in 1970, 650 in 1983, 651 in 1992 and 659 in 1997,
before falling to 646 in 2005. Of the present 646 seats,
there are 529 for England, 40 for Wales, 59 for Scotland
and 18 for Northern Ireland.

An electoral reform commission headed by Lord
Jenkins of Hillhead proposed in October 1998 that the
'first-past-the-post' system of electing members of the
House of Commons should be replaced by an alternative
vote top-up system, under which 80–85 per cent of
Members of Parliament (MPs) would be elected by an
alternative vote method and the remaining 15–20 per
cent by an open-list system of proportional
representation.

ELECTIONS

Elections are by secret ballot, each elector casting one
vote; voting is not compulsory. For entitlement to vote in
parliamentary elections, *see* Legal Notes section. When a
seat becomes vacant between general elections, a by-
election is held.

British subjects and citizens of the Irish Republic can
stand for election as MPs provided they are 21 or over and
not subject to disqualification. Those disqualified from
sitting in the House include:
– undischarged bankrupts
– people sentenced to more than one year's imprisonment
– members of the House of Lords (but hereditary peers
not sitting in the Lords are eligible)

– holders of certain offices listed in the House of
Commons Disqualification Act 1975, e.g. members of
the judiciary, civil service, regular armed forces, police
forces, some local government officers and some
members of public corporations and government
commissions.

A candidate does not require any party backing but his or
her nomination for election must be supported by the
signatures of ten people registered in the constituency. A
candidate must also deposit with the returning officer
£500, which is forfeit if the candidate does not receive
more than 5 per cent of the votes cast. All election
expenses at a general election, except the candidate's
personal expenses, are subject to a statutory limit of
£7,150, plus five pence for each elector in a borough
constituency or seven pence for each elector in a county
constituency.

See pages 137–180 for an alphabetical list of MPs,
results of the last general election and results of
by-elections since the general election.

STATE OF THE PARTIES *as at 1 September 2005*

Conservative, 196 (17 women)
Labour, 353 (97 women)
Liberal Democrats, 62 (9 women)
Plaid Cymru, 3
Scottish National Party, 6
Sinn Fein (have not taken their seats), 5 (1 woman)
Social Democratic Labour Party, 3
Democratic Unionist Party, 9 (1 woman)
Ulster Unionist, 1 (1 woman)
Respect, 1
Independent, 2
The Speaker and three Deputy Speakers, 4 (1 woman)
Vacant, 1
Total, 645 (127 women)

BUSINESS

The week's business of the House is outlined each
Thursday by the Leader of the House, after consultation
between the Chief Government Whip and the Chief
Opposition Whip. A quarter to a third of the time will be
taken up by the government's legislative programme and
the rest by other business. As a rule, bills likely to raise
political controversy are introduced in the Commons
before going on to the Lords, and the Commons claims
exclusive control in respect of national taxation and
expenditure. Bills such as the Finance Bill, which impose
taxation, and the Consolidated Fund Bills, which
authorise expenditure, must begin in the Commons. A bill
of which the financial provisions are subsidiary may begin
in the Lords; and the Commons may waive its rights in
regard to Lords' amendments affecting finance.

The Commons has a public register of MPs' financial
and certain other interests; this is published annually as a
House of Commons paper. Members must also disclose
any relevant financial interest or benefit in a matter before
the House when taking part in a debate, in certain other
proceedings of the House, or in consultations with other
MPs, with Ministers or with civil servants.

MEMBERS' PAY AND ALLOWANCES

Since 1911 members of the House of Commons have
received salary payments; facilities for free travel were
introduced in 1924. Salary rates since 1911 are as
follows:

1911	£400	1986 Jan	£17,702
1931	360	1987 Jan	18,500
1934	380	1988 Jan	22,548
1935	400	1989 Jan	24,107
1937	600	1990 Jan	26,701
1946	1,000	1991 Jan	28,970
1954	1,250	1992 Jan	30,854
1957	1,750	1994 Jan	31,687
1964	3,250	1995 Jan	33,189
1972 Jan	4,500	1996 Jan	34,085
1975 June	5,750	1996 July	43,000
1976 June	6,062	1997 April	43,860
1977 July	6,270	1998 April	45,066
1978 June	6,897	1999 April	47,008
1979 June	9,450	2000 April	48,371
1980 June	11,750	2001 April	49,822
1981 June	13,950	2002 April	55,118
1982 June	14,510	2003 April	56,358
1983 June	15,308	2004 April	57,485
1984 Jan	16,106	2005 April	59,095
1985 Jan	16,904		

In 1969 MPs were granted an annual allowance for secretarial and research expenses, revised in July 2001. Members receive an Incidental Expenses Provision (£20,000) and a staffing allowance (up to £84,081).

Since 1972 MPs have been able to claim reimbursement for the additional cost of staying overnight away from their main residence while on parliamentary business; this is known as the Additional Costs Allowance and from April 2005 is £21,634 a year.

Members of staff who are paid out of the allowances can benefit from a sum not exceeding 10 per cent of their gross salary which is paid into the Portcullis Pension Plan. This sum comes from a central budget.

MEMBERS' PENSIONS

Pension arrangements for MPs were first introduced in 1964. The arrangements currently provide a pension of one-fiftieth of salary for each year of pensionable service with a maximum of two-thirds of salary at age 65. Pension is payable normally at age 65, for men and women, or on later retirement. Pensions may be paid earlier, e.g. on retirement due to ill health or at age 60 after 20 years' service. The widow/widower of a former MP receives a pension of five-eighths of the late MP's pension. Pensions are index-linked. Members currently contribute six or nine per cent of salary to the pension fund; there is an Exchequer contribution, currently 24 per cent of an MPs salary.

The House of Commons Members' Fund provides for annual or lump sum grants to ex-MPs, their widows or widowers, and children whose incomes are below certain limits or who are experiencing severe hardship. Members contribute £24 a year and the Exchequer £215,000 a year to the fund.

HOUSE OF COMMONS PAY BANDS

Staff are placed in the following Senior Civil Service pay bands. These pay bands apply to the most senior staff in departments and agencies.

Pay Band 1	£54,787–£91,831
Pay Band 1A	£63,554–£103,063
Pay Band 2	£75,606–£122,882
Pay Band 3	£93,139–£133,233

OFFICERS AND OFFICIALS

The House of Commons is presided over by the Speaker, who has considerable powers to maintain order in the House. A Deputy Speaker, called the Chairman of Ways and Means, and two Deputy Chairmen may preside over sittings of the House of Commons; they are elected by the House, and, like the Speaker, neither speak nor vote other than in their official capacity.

The staff of the House are employed by a Commission chaired by the Speaker. The heads of the six House of Commons departments are permanent officers of the House, not MPs. The Clerk of the House is the principal adviser to the Speaker on the privileges and procedures of the House, the conduct of the business of the House, and committees. The Serjeant-at-Arms is responsible for security, ceremonial, and for accommodation in the Commons part of the Palace of Westminster.

Speaker (£133,997), The Rt. Hon. Michael J. Martin, MP (Glasgow Springburn)

Chairman of Ways and Means (£97,949), Sir Alan Haselhurst, MP (Saffron Walden)

First Deputy Chairman of Ways and Means (£93,243), Sylvia Heal, MP (Halesowen and Rowley Regis)

Second Deputy Chairman of Ways and Means (£93,243), Sir Michael Lord, MP (Suffolk Central and Ipswich North)

OFFICES OF THE SPEAKER AND CHAIRMAN OF WAYS AND MEANS

Speaker's Secretary (£63,554–£103,063), A. Sinclair

Chaplain to the Speaker, Revd Canon R. Wright

Secretary to the Chairman of Ways and Means (£40,284–£54,940), J. Whatley

DEPARTMENT OF THE CLERK OF THE HOUSE

Clerk of the House of Commons (£155,404), R. B. Sands

Clerk Assistant (£93,139–£133,233), D. G. Millar

Clerk of Committees (£93,139–£133,233), Ms H. E. Irwin

Clerk of Legislation (£93,139–£133,233), Dr M. R. Jack

Principal Clerks (£75,606–£122,882)

Table Office, R. J. Rogers

Journals, Ms J. Sharpe

Principal Clerk and Deputy Head of Committee Office, R. W. G. Wilson

Principal Clerks (£63,554–£103,063)

Overseas Office, L. C. Laurence Smyth

Bills, F. A. Cranmer

Clerk of Domestic Committees / Secretary to the Commission, D. L. Natzler

Select Committees, D. W. N. Doig; A. R. Kennon

Delegated Legislation, P. A. Evans

Deputy Principal Clerks (£54,787–£91,831), J. S. Benger, DPHIL; Mrs S. A. R. Davies; A. H. Doherty; Mrs E. J. Flood; K. C. Fox; Miss L. M. Gardner; D. J. Gerhold; M. D. Hamlyn; D. F. Harrison; T. W. P. Healey; Ms P. A. Helme; M. Hennessy; Mrs E. S. Hunt; B. M. Hutton; Dr R. G. James; C. G. Lee; D. R. Lloyd; S. Mark; Mrs C. Oxborough; S. J. Patrick; R. I. S. Phillips; C. J. Poyser; S. J. Priestly; F. J. Reid; Mrs J. N. St J. Mulley; Ms E. C. Samson; A. Sandall; C. A. Shaw; C. D. Stanton; N. P. Walker; Dr C. R. M. Ward

Senior Clerks (£40,284–£54,940), M. P. Atkins; D. Bates; T. Byrne; M. Clark; G. K. Clarke; R. C. A. Cooke; J. H. Davies; M. Egan; Ms K. Emms; M. Etherton; G. F. J. Farrar; Miss T. S. Garratty; J. Gearson; T. Goldsmith; D. H. Griffiths; P. Harborne; M. Hillyard; Miss S. F. Ioannou; T. Jarvis; Ms S. Jones; Ms C. A. Littleboy; G.

McKee; Miss F. McLean; Sir Edward Osmotherly; J.
Patterson; C. Porro; J. D. W. Rhys; I. Rogers; Ms L.
Spiers; Ms N. Welfoot; J. D. Whatley; N. P. Wright; H.
A. Yardley
Examiners of Petitions for Private Bills, F. A. Cranmer; T.
Mohan
Registrar of Members' Interests (£54,787–£91,831), Ms
A. Barry
Taxing Officer, F. A. Cranmer

VOTE OFFICE
Deliverer of the Vote (£54,787–£91,831), J. F. Collins
Deputy Deliverers of the Vote (£40,284–£54,940), O. B.
T. Sweeney *(Parliamentary)*; R. Brook *(Development)*;
Ms J. Pitt *(Production)*; A. Powell *(Systems)*

LEGAL SERVICES OFFICE
Speaker's Counsel and Head of Legal Services Office
(£75,606–£122,882), J. E. G. Vaux
Counsel for European Legislation (£63,554–£103,064), M.
Carpenter
Counsel for Legislation (£63,554–£103,063), Peter Davis
Deputy Counsel (£54,787–£91,831), A. Akbar; P.
Brooksbank; Ms V. Rose
Assistant Counsel (£40,284–£54,940), Ms V. Daly

DEPARTMENT OF THE SERJEANT-AT-ARMS
Serjeant-at-Arms (£75,606–£122,882), P. Grant Peterkin
Deputy Serjeant-at-Arms (£63,554–£103,063), R. M.
Morton
Assistant Serjeants-at-Arms, (£40,284–£66,614), Ms R.
Beech; Mrs J. Pay; J. M. Robertson

DEPARTMENT OF THE LIBRARY
Librarian (£75,606–£122,882), J. Pullinger
Directors (£54,787–£91,831), R. Clements *(Research
Services)*; K. G. Cuninghame *(Resources)*; Miss E. M.
McInnes *(PIMS Project Director)*; S. Wise *(Service
Delivery and Development)*; E. Wood *(Information
Services)*
Heads of Sections (£40,284–£66,614), C. Barclay; R.
Cracknell; T. Edmonds; O. Gay; Mrs C. Gillie; Ms J.
Lourie; V. Miller; B. Morgan; Dr C. Pond; Ms P. J.
Strickland
Senior Library Clerks (£40,284–£54,940), G. Berman; P.
Bolton; P. Bowers; Ms B. Brevitt; Ms S. Broadbridge;
Ms D. Clark; Ms L. Conway; R. Elton; C. Fairbairn; V.
Gialias; Ms D. Gore; Ms H. Holden; J. Hough; T. Jarrett;
R. Kelly; S. Kennedy; V. Keter; S. McGinness; A.
Mellows-Facer; K. Parry; M. Peck; Ms F. Poole; Ms J.
Roll; P. Ryan; A. Seely; C. Taylor; Ms A. Thorp; I.
Townsend; P. Ward; D. Webb; Ms I. White; Ms F.
Whittle; Ms W. Wilson; R. Winstone; R. Young; T.
Youngs

DEPARTMENT OF FINANCE AND ADMINISTRATION
Director of Finance and Administration (£75,606–
£122,882), A. J. Walker
Director of Operations (£54,787–£91,831), T. M. Bird
Director of Human Resource Management (£54,787–
£91,831), Ms S. Craig
Director of Finance Policy (£54,787–£91,831), C. Ridley
Director of Internal Review Services (£48,859–£66,614),
R. Russell

DEPARTMENT OF THE OFFICIAL REPORT
Editor (£63,554–£103,063), Miss L. Sutherland
Deputy Editors (£54,787–£91,831), Ms C. Fogarty; V. A.
Widgery

REFRESHMENT DEPARTMENT
Director of Catering Services (£63,554–£103,063), Mrs S.
Harrison
Business Development Manager (£48,859–£66,614), Miss
M. Akingbola
Catering Operations Manager (Outbuildings) (£40,284–
£54,940), Ms D. Herd
*Food and Beverage Operations Manager, Palace of
Westminster* (£40,284–£54,940), R. Gibbs
Executive Chef (£40,284–£54,940), D. Dorricott
Retail Manager (£40,284–£54,940), Mrs M. DeSouza
Human Resources and Development Manager (£40,284–
£54,940), J. van den Broek

SELECT COMMITTEES
The more significant committees, as at July 2005, are:

DEPARTMENTAL COMMITTEES
Constitutional Affairs – Chair, The Rt. Hon. Alan Beith,
MP; *Clerk,* Roger Phillips
Culture, Media and Sport – Chair, John Whittingdale, MP;
Clerk, Kenneth Fox
Defence – Chair, The Rt. Hon. James Arbuthnot, MP; *Clerk,*
Mark Hutton
Education and Skills – Chair, Barry Sheerman, MP; *Clerk,*
David Lloyd
Environment, Food and Rural Affairs – Chair, The Rt. Hon.
Michael Jack, MP; *Clerk,* Matthew Hamlyn
Foreign Affairs – Chair, Mike Gapes, MP; *Clerk,* Steve
Priestley
Health – Chair, The Rt. Hon. Kevin Barron, MP; *Clerk,*
Dr David Harrison
Home Affairs – Chair, The Rt. Hon. John Denham, MP;
Clerk, Dr Robin James
International Development – Chair, Malcolm Bruce, MP;
Clerk, Alistair Doherty
Northern Ireland Affairs – Chair, Sir Patrick Cormack, MP;
Clerk, Dr John Patterson
*Office of the Deputy Prime Minister: Housing, Planning,
Local Government and the Regions* – Chair, Dr Phyllis
Starkey, MP; *Clerks,* Elizabeth Hunt; Jessica
Mulley
Scottish Affairs – Chair, Mohammad Sarwar, MP; *Clerk,*
Mike Clark
Standards and Privileges – Chair, The Rt. Hon. Sir George
Young, BT, MP; *Clerk,* Dr Christopher Ward
Trade and Industry – Chair, Peter Luff, MP; *Clerk,*
Elizabeth Flood
Transport – Chair, Gwyneth Dunwoody, MP; *Clerk,*
Dr John Patterson
Treasury – Chair, The Rt. Hon. John McFall, MP; *Clerk,*
Crispin Poyser
Welsh Affairs – Chair, Dr Hywel Francis, MP; *Clerk,* Jame
Davies
Work and Pensions – Chair, Terry Rooney, MP; *Clerk,*
Sarah Davies

NON-DEPARTMENTAL COMMITTEES
Environmental Audit – Chair, Peter Ainsworth, MP; *Clerk,*
Mike Hennessy
European Scrutiny – Chair, Jimmy Hood, MP; *Clerks,*
Dorian Gerhold; Jane Fox
Finance and Services – Chair, Sir Stuart Bell, MP; *Clerk,*
David Natzler
Human Rights (Joint Committee) – Chair, Andrew Dismore
MP; *Clerks,* Ed Lock; Nick Walker
Intelligence and Security (Cabinet Office) – Chair, The Rt.
Hon. Paul Murphy, MP; *Clerk,* Alistair Corbett

Modernisation of the House of Commons – *Chair,* The Rt. Hon. Geoffrey Hoon, MP; *Clerk,* George Cubie
Procedure – *Chair,* Sir Nicholas Winterton, MP; *Clerk,* Simon Patrick
Public Accounts – *Chair,* Edward Leigh, MP; *Clerk,* Nick Wright
Public Administration – *Chair,* Dr Tony Wright, MP; *Clerk,* Eve Sampson
Regulatory Reform – *Chair,* Andrew Miller, MP; *Clerk,* Mick Hillyard
Science and Technology – *Chair,* Phil Willis, MP; *Clerk,* Chris Shaw
Statutory Instruments (Joint Committee) – *Chair,* Eric Forth, MP; *Clerks,* Mick Hillyard; Kath Kavanagh

DOMESTIC COMMITTEE
Administration – *Chair,* Frank Doran, MP; *Clerk,* Steven Mark

PARLIAMENTARY INFORMATION

The following is a short glossary of aspects of the work of Parliament. Unless otherwise stated, references are to House of Commons procedures.

BILL – Proposed legislation is termed a bill. The stages of a public bill (for private bills, *see* below) in the House of Commons are as follows:
First Reading: This stage merely constitutes an order to have the bill printed.
Second Reading: The debate on the principles of the bill.
Committee Stage: The detailed examination of a bill, clause by clause. In most cases this takes place in a standing committee, or the whole House may act as a committee. A special standing committee may take evidence before embarking on detailed scrutiny of the bill. Very rarely, a bill may be examined by a select committee.
Report Stage: Detailed review of a bill as amended in committee.
Third Reading: Final debate on a bill. Public bills go through the same stages in the House of Lords, except that in almost all cases the committee stage is taken in committee of the whole House.
A bill may start in either House, and has to pass through both Houses to become law. Both Houses have to agree the same text of a bill, so that the amendments made by the second House are then considered in the originating House, and if not agreed, sent back or themselves amended, until agreement is reached.
CHILTERN HUNDREDS – A nominal office of profit under the Crown, the acceptance of which requires an MP to vacate his/her seat. The Manor of Northstead is similar. These are the only means by which an MP may resign.
CONSOLIDATED FUND BILL – A bill to authorise issue of money to maintain government services. The bill is dealt with without debate.
EARLY DAY MOTION – A motion put on the notice paper by an MP without, in general, the real prospect of its being debated. Such motions are expressions of back-bench opinion.
FATHER OF THE HOUSE – The Member whose continuous service in the House of Commons is the longest. The present Father of the House is the Rt. Hon. Alan Williams.
HOURS OF MEETING – The House of Commons normally meets on Mondays and Tuesdays at 2.30 p.m., Wednesdays at 11.30 a.m., Thursdays at 10.30 a.m. and some Fridays at 9.30 a.m. (*See also* Westminster Hall Sittings, below.) The House of Lords normally meets at 2.30 p.m. Monday to Wednesday and at 11 a.m. on Thursdays. In the latter part of the session, the House of Lords sometimes sits on Fridays at 11 a.m.
LEADER OF THE OPPOSITION – In 1937 the office of Leader of the Opposition was recognised and a salary was assigned to the post. Since April 2005 this has been £127,757 (including a parliamentary salary of £59,095). The present Leader of the Opposition is Michael Howard, who at the time of writing had announced that he would be standing down from the post before the end of 2005.
THE LORD CHANCELLOR – The Lord High Chancellor of Great Britain is (*ex officio*) the Speaker of the House of Lords. Unlike the Speaker of the House of Commons, he is a member of the government, takes part in debates and votes in divisions. He does not have the same powers as the Speaker of the House of Commons, for example he is not responsible for maintaining order during debates, as this is the responsibility of the Lords as a whole. The Lord Chancellor sits in the Lords on one of the Woolsacks, which are couches covered with red cloth and stuffed with wool. If he wishes to address the House in any way except formally as Speaker, he leaves the Woolsack.
Under the Constitutional Reform Act 2005, the Lord Chancellor's role as head of the judiciary will end. A new Supreme Court (separate from the House of Lords) will be established, and a new Judicial Appointments Commission created. It is also expected that the House of Lords will make new arrangements for its speakership.
The current Lord Chancellor is Lord Falconer of Thoroton, who is also Secretary of State for Constitutional Affairs. The Department for Constitutional Affairs was created in 2003, incorporating most of the responsibilities of the Lord Chancellor's Department.
NORTHERN IRELAND GRAND COMMITTEE – The Northern Ireland Grand Committee consists of all MPs representing constituencies in Northern Ireland, together with not more than 25 other MPs nominated by the Committee of Selection. The business of the committee includes questions, short debates, ministerial statements, bills, legislative proposals and other matters relating exclusively to Northern Ireland, and delegated legislation.
The Northern Ireland Affairs Committee is one of the departmental select committees, empowered to examine the expenditure, administration and policy of the Northern Ireland Office and the administration and expenditure of the Crown Solicitor's Office.
OPPOSITION DAY – A day on which the topic for debate is chosen by the Opposition. There are 20 such days in a normal session. On 17 days, subjects are chosen by the Leader of the Opposition; on the remaining three days by the leader of the next largest opposition party.
PARLIAMENT ACTS 1911 AND 1949 – Under these Acts, bills may become law without the consent of the Lords, though the House of Lords has the power to delay a public bill for 13 months from its first second reading in the House of Commons.
PRIME MINISTER'S QUESTIONS – The prime minister answers questions from 12.00 to 12.30 p.m. on Wednesdays.
PRIVATE BILL – A bill promoted by a body or an individual to give powers additional to, or in conflict with, the general law, and to which a special procedure applies to enable people affected to object.
PRIVATE MEMBER'S BILL – A public bill promoted by a Member who is not a member of the government.
PRIVATE NOTICE QUESTION – A question adjudged of urgent importance on submission to the Speaker (in the

Lords, the Leader of the House), answered at the end of oral questions.

PRIVILEGE – The House of Commons has rights and immunities to protect it from obstruction in carrying out its duties. These are known as parliamentary privilege and enable Members of Parliament to debate freely. The most important privilege is that of freedom of speech. MPs cannot be prosecuted for sedition or sued for libel or slander over anything said during proceedings in the House. This enables them to raise in the House questions affecting the public good which might be difficult to raise outside owing to the possibility of being sued. The House of Lords has similar privileges.

QUESTION TIME – Oral questions are answered by Ministers in the Commons from 2.30 to 3.30 p.m. on Mondays and Tuesdays, 11.30 a.m. to 12.30 p.m. on Wednesdays, and 10.30 to 11.30 a.m. on Thursdays. Questions are also taken at the start of the Lords sittings, with a daily limit of four oral questions.

ROYAL ASSENT – The royal assent is signified by letters patent to such bills and measures as have passed both Houses of Parliament (or bills which have been passed under the Parliament Acts 1911 and 1949). The Sovereign has not given royal assent in person since 1854. On occasion, for instance in the prorogation of Parliament, royal assent may be pronounced to the two Houses by Lords Commissioners. More usually royal assent is notified to each House sitting separately in accordance with the Royal Assent Act 1967. The old French formulae for royal assent are then endorsed on the acts by the Clerk of the Parliaments.

The power to withhold assent resides with the Sovereign but has not been exercised in the UK since 1707.

SELECT COMMITTEES – Consisting usually of 10 to 15 members of all parties, select committees are a means used by both Houses in order to investigate certain matters.

Most select committees in the House of Commons are tied to departments: each committee investigates subjects within a government department's remit. There are other select committees dealing with matters such as public accounts (i.e. the spending by the government of money voted by Parliament) and European legislation, and also committees advising on procedures and domestic administration of the House. Major select committees usually take evidence in public; their evidence and reports are published on the Parliament website and in hard copy by TSO (The Stationery Office). House of Commons select committees are reconstituted after a general election. For main committees, see page 130.

In the House of Lords, select committees do not mirror government departments but cover broader issues. There is a select committee on the European Union (EU), which

has seven sub-committees dealing with specific areas of EU policy. The House of Lords also has a select committee on science and technology, which appoints sub-committees to deal with specific subjects, and a select committee on delegated powers and regulatory reform. For committees, see pages 127–8. In addition, ad hoc select committees have been set up from time to time to investigate specific subjects. There are also some joint committees of the two Houses, e.g. the committees on statutory instruments and on human rights.

THE SPEAKER – The Speaker of the House of Commons is the spokesperson and chair of the Chamber. He or she is elected by the House at the beginning of each Parliament or when the previous Speaker retires or dies. The Speaker neither speaks in debates nor votes in divisions except when the voting is equal.

VACANT SEATS – When a vacancy occurs in the House of Commons during a session of Parliament, the writ for the by-election is moved by a Whip of the party to which the member whose seat has been vacated belonged. If the House is in recess, the Speaker can issue a warrant for a writ, should two members certify to him that a seat is vacant.

WELSH AFFAIRS COMMITTEE — The Welsh Affairs Committee is one of the departmental select committees, empowered to examine matters within the responsibility of the Secretary of State for Wales (including relations with the National Assembly for Wales).

WESTMINSTER HALL SITTINGS – Following a report by the Modernisation of the House of Commons Select Committee, the Commons decided in May 1999 to set up a second debating forum. It is known as 'Westminster Hall' and sittings are in the Grand Committee Room on Tuesdays from 9.30 a.m. to 2 p.m., Wednesdays from 9.30 to 11.30 a.m. and from 2.30 to 5 p.m., and Thursdays from 2.30 to 5.30 p.m. Sittings will be open to the public at the times indicated.

WHIPS – In order to secure the attendance of Members of a particular party in Parliament, particularly on the occasion of an important vote, Whips (originally known as 'Whippers-in') are appointed. The written appeal or circular letter issued by them is also known as a 'whip', its urgency being denoted by the number of times it is underlined. Failure to respond to a three-line whip is tantamount in the Commons to secession (at any rate temporarily) from the party. Whips are provided with office accommodation in both Houses, and government and some opposition Whips receive salaries from public funds.

PARLIAMENTARY EDUCATION UNIT
Norman Shaw Building (North), London SW1A 2TT
T 020-7219 2105 E edunit@parliament.uk
W www.explore.parliament.uk

GOVERNMENT OFFICE

The government is the body of Ministers responsible for the administration of national affairs, determining policy and introducing into Parliament any legislation necessary to give effect to government policy. The majority of Ministers are members of the House of Commons but members of the House of Lords, or of neither House, may also hold ministerial responsibility. The Lord Chancellor is always a member of the House of Lords. The prime minister is, by current convention, always a member of the House of Commons.

THE PRIME MINISTER

The office of prime minister, which had been in existence for nearly 200 years, was officially recognised in 1905 and its holder was granted a place in the table of precedence. The prime minister, by tradition also First Lord of the Treasury and Minister for the Civil Service, is appointed by the Sovereign and is usually the leader of the party which enjoys, or can secure, a majority in the House of Commons. Other Ministers are appointed by the Sovereign on the recommendation of the prime minister, who also allocates functions amongst Ministers and has the power to obtain their resignation or dismissal individually.

The prime minister informs the Sovereign of state and political matters, advises on the dissolution of Parliament, and makes recommendations for important Crown appointments, the award of honours, etc.

As the chairman of Cabinet meetings and leader of a political party, the prime minister is responsible for translating party policy into government activity. As leader of the government, the prime minister is responsible to Parliament and to the electorate for the policies and their implementation.

The prime minister also represents the nation in international affairs, e.g. summit conferences.

THE CABINET

The Cabinet developed during the 18th century as an inner committee of the Privy Council, which was the chief source of executive power until that time. The Cabinet is composed of about 20 Ministers chosen by the prime minister, usually the heads of government departments (generally known as Secretaries of State unless they have a special title, e.g. Chancellor of the Exchequer), the leaders of the two Houses of Parliament, and the holders of various traditional offices.

The Cabinet's functions are the final determination of policy, control of government and co-ordination of government departments. The exercise of its functions is dependent upon enjoying majority support in the House of Commons. Cabinet meetings are held in private, taking place once or twice a week during parliamentary sittings and less often during a recess. Proceedings are confidential, the members being bound by their oath as Privy Counsellors not to disclose information about the proceedings.

The convention of collective responsibility means that the Cabinet acts unanimously even when Cabinet Ministers do not all agree on a subject. The policies of departmental Ministers must be consistent with the policies of the government as a whole, and once the government's policy has been decided, each Minister is expected to support it or resign.

The convention of ministerial responsibility holds a Minister, as the political head of his or her department, accountable to Parliament for the department's work. Departmental Ministers usually decide all matters within their responsibility, although on matters of political importance they normally consult their colleagues collectively. A decision by a departmental Minister is binding on the government as a whole.

POLITICAL PARTIES

Before the reign of William and Mary the principal officers of state were chosen by and were responsible to the Sovereign alone, and not to Parliament or the nation at large. Such officers acted sometimes in concert with one another but more often independently, and the fall of one did not, of necessity, involve that of others, although all were liable to be dismissed at any moment.

In 1693 the Earl of Sunderland recommended to William III the advisability of selecting a ministry from the political party which enjoyed a majority in the House of Commons, and the first united ministry was drawn in 1696 from the Whigs, to which party the King owed his throne. This group became known as the Junto and was regarded with suspicion as a novelty in the political life of the nation, being a small section meeting in secret apart from the main body of Ministers. It may be regarded as the forerunner of the Cabinet and in the course of time it led to the establishment of the principle of joint responsibility of Ministers, so that internal disagreement caused a change of personnel or resignation of the whole body of Ministers.

The accession of George I, who was unfamiliar with the English language, led to a disinclination on the part of the Sovereign to preside at meetings of his Ministers and caused the appearance of a prime minister, a position first acquired by Robert Walpole in 1721 and retained by him without interruption for 20 years and 326 days.

DEVELOPMENT OF PARTIES

In 1828 the Whigs became known as Liberals, a name originally given by its opponents to imply laxity of principles, but gradually accepted by the party to indicate its claim to be pioneers and champions of political reform and progressive legislation. In 1861 a Liberal Registration Association was founded and Liberal Associations became widespread. In 1877 a National Liberal Federation was formed, with its headquarters in London. The Liberal Party was in power for long periods during the second half of the 19th-century and for several years during the first quarter of the 20th-century, but after a split in the party in 1931, the numbers elected remained small. In 1988, a majority of the Liberals agreed on a merger with the Social Democratic Party under the title Social and Liberal Democrats; since 1989 they have been known as the Liberal Democrats. A minority continue separately as the Liberal Party.

Soon after the change from Whig to Liberal the Tory Party became known as Conservative, a name believed to have been invented by John Wilson Croker in 1830 and to have been generally adopted around the time of the passing of the Reform Act of 1832 – to indicate that the preservation of national institutions was the leading principle of the party. After the Home Rule crisis of 1886 the dissentient Liberals entered into a compact with the Conservatives, under which the latter undertook not to contest their seats, but a separate Liberal Unionist organisation was maintained until 1912, when it was united with the Conservatives.

Labour candidates for Parliament made their first appearance at the general election of 1892, when there were 27 standing as Labour or Liberal-Labour. In 1900 the Labour Representation Committee (LRC) was set up in order to establish a distinct Labour group in Parliament, with its own whips, its own policy, and a readiness to co-operate with any party which might be engaged in promoting legislation in the direct interests of labour. In 1906 the LRC became known as the Labour Party.

The Council for Social Democracy was announced by four former Labour Cabinet Ministers in January 1981 and in March 1981 the Social Democratic Party (SDP) was launched. Later that year the SDP and the Liberal Party formed an electoral alliance. In 1988 a majority of the SDP agreed on a merger with the Liberal Party but a minority continued as a separate party under the SDP title. In 1990 it was decided to wind up the party organisation and its three sitting MPs were known as independent social democrats. None were returned at the 1992 general election.

Plaid Cymru was founded in 1926 to provide an independent political voice for Wales and to campaign for self-government in Wales.

The Scottish National Party was founded in 1934 to campaign for independence for Scotland.

The Social Democratic and Labour Party was founded in 1970, emerging from the civil rights movement of the 1960s, with the aim of promoting reform, reconciliation and partnership across the sectarian divide in Northern Ireland, and of opposing violence from any quarter.

The Democratic Unionist Party was founded in 1971 to resist moves by the Ulster Unionist Party which were considered a threat to the Union. Its aim is to maintain Northern Ireland as an integral part of the UK.

The Ulster Unionist Council first met formally in 1905. Its objectives are to maintain Northern Ireland as an integral part of the UK and to promote the aims of the Ulster Unionist Party.

Sinn Fein first emerged in the 1900s as a federation of nationalist clubs. It is a left-wing republican and labour party that seeks to end British governance in Ireland and achieve a 32-county republic.

GOVERNMENT AND OPPOSITION

The government of the day is formed by the party which wins the largest number of seats in the House of Commons at a general election, or which has the support of a majority of members in the House of Commons. By tradition, the leader of the majority party is asked by the Sovereign to form a government, while the largest minority party becomes the official Opposition with its own leader and a 'Shadow Cabinet'. Leaders of the Government and Opposition sit on the front benches of the Commons with their supporters (the back-benchers) sitting behind them.

FINANCIAL SUPPORT

Financial support for Opposition parties in the House of Commons was introduced in 1975 and is commonly known as Short Money, after Edward Short, the Leader of the House at that time, who introduced the scheme. Short Money allocation for 2005–6 is:

Conservative	£3,576,789
Liberal Democrats	£1,524,291
Plaid Cymru	£59,404
SNP	£126,633
SDLP	£53,254
Democratic Unionists	£142,887

A specific allocation for the Leader of the Opposition' office was introduced in April 1999 and has been set at £583,169 for the years 2005–6.

Financial support for Opposition parties in the House of Lords was introduced in 1996 and is commonly known as Cranborne Money.

The parties included here are those with MPs sitting in the House of Commons in the present Parliament.

CONSERVATIVE PARTY
Conservative Campaign Headquarters, 25 Victoria Street, London SW1H 0DL
T 020-7222 9000 F 020-7222 1135
E ccoffice@conservatives.com
W www.conservatives.com

SHADOW CABINET *as at June 2005*
Leader of the Opposition, The Rt. Hon. Michael Howard, QC, MP
Deputy Leader and Secretary of State for Defence, The Rt. Hon. Michael Ancram, QC, MP
Chancellor of the Exchequer, George Osborne, MP
Secretary of State for Home Affairs, The Rt. Hon. David Davis, MP
Party Chair, The Rt. Hon. Francis Maude, MP
Secretary of State for Constitutional Affairs, Oliver Heald, MP
Secretary of State for Deregulation, The Rt. Hon. John Redwood, MP
Secretary of State for Education and Skills, David Cameron, MP
Secretary of State for Environment, Food and Rural Affairs, The Rt. Hon. Oliver Letwin, MP
Secretary of State for the Family and for Culture, Media and Sport, The Rt. Hon. Theresa May, MP
Secretary of State for Foreign Affairs, Dr Liam Fox, MP
Secretary of State for Health, Andrew Lansley, CBE, MP
Secretary of State for International Development, Andrew Mitchell, MP
Leader in the House of Commons, Chris Grayling, MP
Leader in the House of Lords, The Rt. Hon. Lord Strathclyde
Secretary of State for Local Government Affairs and Communities, Caroline Spelman, MP
Secretary of State for Northern Ireland, David Lidington, MP
Secretary of State for Trade and Industry, David Willetts, MP
Secretary of State for Transport, Alan Duncan, MP
Chief Secretary to the Treasury, Philip Hammond, MP
Secretary of State for Work and Pensions, The Rt. Hon. Malcolm Rifkind, MP

CONSERVATIVE WHIPS
House of Lords, The Rt. Hon. Lord Cope of Berkeley
House of Commons, The Rt. Hon. David Mclean, MP

LABOUR PARTY
16 Old Queen Street, London SW1H 9HP
T 0870-590 0200 E info@new.labour.org.uk
W www.labour.org.uk
Parliamentary Party Leader, The Rt. Hon. Tony Blair, MP
Deputy Party Leader, The Rt. Hon. John Prescott, MP
Leader in the Lords, The Rt. Hon. Baroness Amos
Chair, The Rt. Hon. Ian McCartney, MP
General Secretary, Matt Carter
General Secretary, Scottish Labour Party, L. Quinn

LIBERAL DEMOCRATS
4 Cowley Street, London SW1P 3NB
T 020-7222 7999 F 020-7799 2170
E info@libdems.org.uk
W www.libdems.org.uk
President, Simon Hughes, MP
Hon. Treasurer, Lord Razzall
Chief Executive, Lord Chris Rennard
Parliamentary Party Leader, The Rt. Hon. Charles Kennedy, MP
Leader in the House of Commons, David Heath, MP
Leader in the House of Lords, The Rt. Hon. Lord McNally of Blackpool

LIBERAL DEMOCRAT SPOKESMEN *as at July 2005*
Deputy Leader and Foreign Secretary, The Rt. Hon. Menzies Campbell, QC, MP
Chancellor and Treasury, Dr Vincent Cable, MP
Communities and Local Government, Sarah Teather, MP
Culture, Media and Sport, Don Foster, MP
Defence, Michael Moore, MP
Education and Skills, Edward Davey, MP
Environment and Rural Affairs, Norman Baker, MP
Health, Prof. Steve Webb, MP
Home Affairs, Mark Oaten, MP
International Development, Andrew George, MP
Office of the Deputy Prime Minister, Simon Hughes, MP
Scotland, John Thurso, MP
Trade and Industry, Norman Lamb, MP
Transport, Tom Brake, MP
Wales and Northern Ireland, Lembit Opik, MP
Women and Older People, Sandra Gidley, MP
Work and Pensions, David Laws, MP
Chair of the Parliamentary Party, Matthew Taylor, MP
Chair of Campaigns and Communications Committee, Lord Razzall

LIBERAL DEMOCRAT WHIPS
House of Lords, Lord Shutt
House of Commons, Andrew Stunell, MP

RESPECT – THE UNITY COALITION
Room 207–208, Coborn House, 3 Coborn Row, London E3 2DA
T 020-8980 3507 F 020-8981 5862
E office@respectcoalition.org W www.respectcoalition.org
Chair, Linda Smith
Vice-Chair, Salma Yaqoob
National Secretary, John Rees
Treasurer, Elaine Graham-Leigh

PLAID CYMRU - THE PARTY OF WALES
Ty Gwynfor, 18 Park Grove, Cardiff CF10 3BN
T 029-2064 6000 F 029-2064 6001
E post@plaidcymru.org W www.plaidcymru.org
Party President, Dafydd Iwan
Chair, John Dixon
Hon. Treasurer, Jeff Canning
Chief Executive/General Secretary, Dafydd Trystan

SCOTTISH NATIONAL PARTY

107 McDonald Road, Edinburgh EH7 4NW
T 0131-525 8900 F 0131-525 8901
E snp.hq@snp.org W www.snp.org
Westminster Parliamentary Party Leader, Alex Salmond, MP
Westminster Parliamentary Party Chief Whip, Pete Wishart, MP
Scottish Parliamentary Party Leader, Nicola Sturgeon, MSP
Scottish Parliamentary Party Chief Whip, Tricia Warwick, MSP
National Treasurer, Colin Beattie
National Secretary, Alasdair Allan
Chief Executive, Peter Murrell

NORTHERN IRELAND DEMOCRATIC UNIONIST PARTY

91 Dundela Avenue, Belfast BT4 3BU
T 028-9065 4479 F 028-9065 4480
E info@dup.org.uk W www.dup2win.com
Parliamentary Party Leader, Ian Paisley, MP, MEP, MLA
Deputy Leader, Peter Robinson, MP, MLA
Chair, Maurice Morrow, MLA
Chief Executive, Allan Ewart
Hon. Treasurer, Gregory Campbell, MP, MLA
Party Secretary, Nigel Dodds, MP, MLA

SINN FEIN

53 Falls Road, Belfast BT12 4PD
T 028-9022 3000 F 028-9022 3001
E sfadmin@eircom.net W www.sinnfein.ie
Party President, Gerry Adams, MP, MLA
Vice-President, Pat Doherty, MP, MLA
Chief Negotiator, Martin McGuinness, MP, MLA
General Secretary, Mitchel McLaughlin

SOCIAL DEMOCRATIC AND LABOUR PARTY

121 Ormeau Road, Belfast BT7 1SH
T 028-9024 7700 F 028-9023 6699
E sdlp@indigo.ie W www.sdlp.ie
Parliamentary Party Leader, Mark Durkan, MLA
Deputy Leader, Dr Alasdair McDonnell, MLA
Chief Whip, John Dallat, MLA
Chair, Patricia Lewsley, MLA
Treasurer, Peter McEvoy
General Secretary, Geraldine Cosgrove

ULSTER UNIONIST PARTY

429 Holywood Road, Belfast BT4 2LN
T 028-9076 5500 F 028-9076 9419
E uup@uup.org W www.uup.org
Party Leader, Sir Reg Empey, OBE, MLA
Chief Whip, Ald. Roy Beggs, MP

ULSTER UNIONIST COUNCIL
President, Lord Rogan of Lower Iveagh
Leader, Sir Reg Empey, OBE, MLA
Chair of the Executive Committee, James Cooper
Hon. Treasurer, Jack Allen, OBE
Vice-Chair, David Campbell
Vice-Presidents, Lord Maginnis of Drumglass; Jim Nicholson, MEP; Cllr. Jim Rodgers, OBE; Mrs May Steele, MBE, JP
Hon. Secretaries, Mrs Joan Carson; Cllr. Danny Kennedy, MLA; Cllr. Bertie Kerr; David McClarty, MLA
Assistant Hon. Treasurer, Edward Keown

The following parties have sitting MEPs

GREEN PARTY

1a Waterlow Road, London N19 5NJ
T 020-7272 4474 F 020-7272 6653
E office@greenparty.org.uk
W www.greenparty.org.uk
Chair, Hugo Charlton
Principle Speakers, Caroline Lucas, MEP; Keith Taylor
Registered Treasurer, Anthony Cooper

UK INDEPENDENCE PARTY

PO Box 9876, Birmingham B6 4DN
T 0121-333 7737 F 0121-333 1520
E mail@ukip.org W www.ukip.org
Party Leader, Roger Knapman, MEP
Deputy Leader, Michael Nattrass, MEP
Chair, Petrina Holdsworth
General Secretary, Geoffrey Kingscott

MEMBERS OF PARLIAMENT

*New MP
†Previously MP in another seat
‡Previously MP for another party

Abbott, Diane (b. 1953) Lab., Hackney North & Stoke Newington, Maj. 7,427

Adams, Gerry (b. 1948) SF, Belfast West, Maj. 19,315

***Afriyie, Adam** (b. 1965) C., Windsor, Maj. 10,292

Ainger, Nick (b. 1949) Lab., Carmarthen West & Pembrokeshire South, Maj. 1,910

Ainsworth, Peter (b. 1956) C., Surrey East, Maj. 15,921

Ainsworth, Rt. Hon. Robert (b. 1952) Lab., Coventry North East, Maj. 14,222

***Alexander, Danny** (b. 1972) LD, Inverness, Nairn, Badenoch & Strathspey, Maj. 4,148

Alexander, Douglas (b. 1967) Lab., Paisley & Renfrewshire South, Maj. 13,232

Allen, Graham (b. 1953) Lab., Nottingham North, Maj. 12,171

Amess, David (b. 1952) C., Southend West, Maj. 8,959

Ancram, Rt. Hon. Michael (b. 1945) C., Devizes, Maj. 13,194

***Anderson, David** (b. 1953) Lab., Blaydon, Maj. 5,335

Anderson, Janet (b. 1949) Lab., Rossendale & Darwen, Maj. 3,676

Arbuthnot, Rt. Hon. James (b. 1952) C., Hampshire North East, Maj. 12,549

Armstrong, Rt. Hon. Hilary (b. 1945) Lab., Durham North West, Maj. 13,443

Atkins, Charlotte (b. 1950) Lab., Staffordshire Moorlands, Maj. 2,438

Atkinson, Peter (b. 1943) C., Hexham, Maj. 5,020

***Austin, Ian** (b. 1965) Lab., Dudley North, Maj. 5,432

Austin, John (b. 1944) Lab., Erith & Thamesmead, Maj. 11,500

Bacon, Richard (b. 1962) C., Norfolk South, Maj. 8,782

Bailey, Adrian (b. 1945) Lab. (Co-op), West Bromwich West, Maj. 10,894

Baird, Vera (b. 1950) Lab., Redcar, Maj. 12,116

Baker, Norman (b. 1957) LD, Lewes, Maj. 8,474

Baldry, Tony (b. 1950) C., Banbury, Maj. 10,797

***Balls, Ed** (b. 1967) Lab. (Co-op), Normanton, Maj. 10,002

***Banks, Gordon** (b. 1955) Lab., Ochil & Perthshire South, Maj. 688

Barker, Gregory (b. 1966) C., Bexhill & Battle, Maj. 13,449

***Barlow, Celia** (b. 1955) Lab., Hove, Maj. 420

Baron, John (b. 1959) C., Billericay, Maj. 11,206

Barrett, John (b. 1954) LD, Edinburgh West, Maj. 13,600

Barron, Rt. Hon. Kevin (b. 1946) Lab., Rother Valley, Maj. 14,224

Battle, Rt. Hon. John (b. 1951) Lab., Leeds West, Maj. 12,810

Bayley, Hugh (b. 1952) Lab., York, City of, Maj. 10,472

Beckett, Rt. Hon. Margaret (b. 1943) Lab., Derby South, Maj. 5,657

Begg, Anne (b. 1955) Lab., Aberdeen South, Maj. 1,348

Beith, Rt. Hon. Alan (b. 1943) LD, Berwick-upon-Tweed, Maj. 8,632

Bell, Sir Stuart (b. 1938) Lab., Middlesbrough, Maj. 12,567

Bellingham, Henry (b. 1955) C., Norfolk North West, Maj. 9,180

Benn, Rt. Hon. Hilary (b. 1953) Lab., Leeds Central, Maj. 11,866

Benton, Joe (b. 1933) Lab., Bootle, Maj. 16,357

***Benyon, Richard** (b. 1960) C., Newbury, Maj. 3,460

Bercow, John (b. 1963) C., Buckingham, Maj. 18,129

Beresford, Sir Paul (b. 1946) C., Mole Valley, Maj. 11,997

Berry, Dr Roger (b. 1948) Lab., Kingswood, Maj. 7,873

Betts, Clive (b. 1950) Lab., Sheffield Attercliffe, Maj. 15,967

***Binley, Brian** (b. 1942) C., Northampton South, Maj. 4,419

Blackman, Liz (b. 1949) Lab., Erewash, Maj. 7,084

***Blackman-Woods, Dr Roberta** (b. 1957) Lab., Durham, City of, Maj. 3,274

Blair, Rt. Hon. Tony (b. 1953) Lab., Sedgefield, Maj. 18,449

Blears, Rt. Hon. Hazel (b. 1956) Lab., Salford, Maj. 7,945

Blizzard, Bob (b. 1950) Lab., Waveney, Maj. 5,915

Blunkett, Rt. Hon. David (b. 1947) Lab., Sheffield Brightside, Maj. 13,644

Blunt, Crispin (b. 1960) C., Reigate, Maj. 10,988

***Bone, Peter** (b. 1952) C., Wellingborough, Maj. 687

Borrow, David (b. 1952) Lab., Ribble South, Maj. 2,184

Boswell, Tim (b. 1942) C., Daventry, Maj. 14,686

Bottomley, Peter (b. 1944) C., Worthing West, Maj. 9,379

Bradshaw, Ben (b. 1960) Lab., Exeter, Maj. 7,665

Brady, Graham (b. 1967) C., Altrincham & Sale West, Maj. 7,159

Brake, Tom (b. 1962) LD, Carshalton & Wallington, Maj. 1,068

Brazier, Julian (b. 1953) C., Canterbury, Maj. 7,471

Breed, Colin (b. 1947) LD, Cornwall South East, Maj. 6,507

Brennan, Kevin (b. 1959) Lab., Cardiff West, Maj. 8,167

***Brokenshire, James** (b. 1968) C., Hornchurch, Maj. 480

Brooke, Annette (b. 1947) LD, Dorset Mid & Poole North, Maj. 5,482

Brown, Rt. Hon. Gordon (b. 1951) Lab., Kirkcaldy & Cowdenbeath, Maj. 18,216

***Brown, Lyn** (b. 1960) Lab., West Ham, Maj. 9,801

Brown, Rt. Hon. Nick (b. 1950) Lab., Newcastle upon Tyne East & Wallsend, Maj. 7,565

Brown, Russell (b. 1951) Lab., Dumfries & Galloway, Maj. 2,922

Browne, Rt. Hon. Desmond (b. 1952) Lab., Kilmarnock & Loudoun, Maj. 8,703

***Browne, Jeremy** (b. 1970) LD, Taunton, Maj. 573

Browning, Angela (b. 1946) C., Tiverton & Honiton, Maj. 11,051

Bruce, Malcolm (b. 1944) LD, Gordon, Maj. 11,026

Bryant, Chris (b. 1962) Lab., Rhondda, Maj. 16,242

Buck, Karen (b. 1958) Lab., Regent's Park & Kensington North, Maj. 6,131

Burden, Richard (b. 1954) Lab., Birmingham Northfield, Maj. 6,454

Burgon, Colin (b. 1948) Lab., Elmet, Maj. 4,528

Burnham, Andy (b. 1970) Lab., Leigh, Maj. 17,272

Burns, Simon (b. 1952) C., Chelmsford West, Maj. 9,620

***Burrowes, David** (b. 1969) C., Enfield Southgate, Maj. 1,747

Burstow, Paul (b. 1962) LD, Sutton & Cheam, Maj. 2,846

Burt, Alistair (b. 1955) C., Bedfordshire North East, Maj. 12,251

***Burt, Lorely** (b. 1957) LD, Solihull, Maj. 279

***Butler, Dawn** (b. 1969) Lab., Brent South, Maj. 11,326

Butterfill, Sir John (b. 1941) C., Bournemouth West, Maj. 4,031

Byers, Rt. Hon. Stephen (b. 1953) Lab., Tyneside North, Maj. 15,037

Byrne, Liam (b. 1970) Lab., Birmingham Hodge Hill, Maj. 5,449

Cable, Dr Vincent (b. 1943) LD, Twickenham, Maj. 9,965

Caborn, Rt. Hon. Richard (b. 1943) Lab., Sheffield Central, Maj. 7,055

Cairns, David (b. 1966) Lab., Inverclyde, Maj. 11,259

Cameron, David (b. 1966) C., Witney, Maj. 14,156

Campbell, Alan (b. 1957) Lab., Tynemouth, Maj. 4,143

Campbell, Gregory (b. 1953) DUP, Londonderry East, Maj. 7,727

Campbell, Rt. Hon. Sir Menzies (b. 1941) LD, Fife North East, Maj. 12,571

Campbell, Ronnie (b. 1943) Lab., Blyth Valley, Maj. 8,527

Carmichael, Alistair (b. 1965) LD, Orkney & Shetland, Maj. 6,627

*Carswell, Douglas (b. 1971) C., Harwich, Maj. 920

Cash, Bill (b. 1940) C., Stone, Maj. 9,089

Caton, Martin (b. 1951) Lab., Gower, Maj. 6,703

Cawsey, Ian (b. 1960) Lab., Brigg & Goole, Maj. 2,894

Challen, Colin (b. 1953) Lab., Morley & Rothwell, Maj. 12,343

Chapman, Ben (b. 1940) Lab., Wirral South, Maj. 3,724

Chaytor, David (b. 1949) Lab., Bury North, Maj. 2,926

Chope, Christopher (b. 1947) C., Christchurch, Maj. 15,559

Clapham, Michael (b. 1943) Lab., Barnsley West & Penistone, Maj. 11,314

Clappison, James (b. 1956) C., Hertsmere, Maj. 11,093

*Clark, Greg (b. 1967) C., Tunbridge Wells, Maj. 9,988

*Clark, Katy (b. 1967) Lab., Ayrshire North & Arran, Maj. 11,296

Clark, Paul (b. 1957) Lab., Gillingham, Maj. 254

Clarke, Rt. Hon. Charles (b. 1950) Lab., Norwich South, Maj. 3,653

Clarke, Rt. Hon. Kenneth (b. 1940) C., Rushcliffe, Maj. 12,974

Clarke, Rt. Hon. Thomas (b. 1941) Lab., Coatbridge, Chryston & Bellshill, Maj. 19,519

*Clegg, Nick (b. 1967) LD, Sheffield Hallam, Maj. 8,682

Clelland, David (b. 1943) Lab., Tyne Bridge, Maj. 10,400

Clifton-Brown, Geoffrey (b. 1953) C., Cotswold, Maj. 9,688

Clwyd, Rt. Hon. Ann (b. 1937) Lab., Cynon Valley, Maj. 13,259

Coaker, Vernon (b. 1953) Lab., Gedling, Maj. 3,811

Coffey, Ann (b. 1946) Lab., Stockport, Maj. 9,163

Cohen, Harry (b. 1949) Lab., Leyton & Wanstead, Maj. 6,857

Connarty, Michael (b. 1947) Lab., Linlithgow & Falkirk East, Maj. 11,202

Conway, Derek (b. 1953) C., Old Bexley & Sidcup, Maj. 9,920

Cook, Frank (b. 1935) Lab., Stockton North, Maj. 12,437

*Cooper, Rosie (b. 1950) Lab., Lancashire West, Maj. 6,084

Cooper, Yvette (b. 1969) Lab., Pontefract & Castleford, Maj. 15,246

Corbyn, Jeremy (b. 1949) Lab., Islington North, Maj. 6,716

Cormack, Sir Patrick (b. 1939) C., Staffordshire South, Maj. 8,847

Cousins, Jim (b. 1944) Lab., Newcastle upon Tyne Central, Maj. 3,982

*Cox, Geoffrey (b. 1960) C., Devon West & Torridge, Maj. 3,236

*Crabb, Stephen (b. 1973) C., Preseli Pembrokeshire, Maj. 607

Crausby, David (b. 1946) Lab., Bolton North East, Maj. 4,103

*Creagh, Mary (b. 1967) Lab., Wakefield, Maj. 5,154

Cruddas, Jonathan (b. 1965) Lab., Dagenham, Maj. 7,605

Cryer, Ann (b. 1939) Lab., Keighley, Maj. 4,852

Cummings, John (b. 1943) Lab., Easington, Maj. 18,636

Cunningham, Jim (b. 1941) Lab., Coventry South, Maj. 6,255

Cunningham, Tony (b. 1952) Lab., Workington, Maj. 6,895

Curry, Rt. Hon. David (b. 1944) C., Skipton & Ripon, Maj. 11,620

Curtis-Thomas, Claire (b. 1958) Lab., Crosby, Maj. 5,840

Darling, Rt. Hon. Alistair (b. 1953) Lab., Edinburgh South West, Maj. 7,242

Davey, Edward (b. 1965) LD, Kingston & Surbiton, Maj. 8,966

David, Wayne (b. 1957) Lab., Caerphilly, Maj. 15,359

Davidson, Ian (b. 1950) Lab. (Co-op), Glasgow South West, Maj. 13,896

*Davies, David (b. 1970) C., Monmouth, Maj. 4,527

*Davies, Philip (b. 1972) C., Shipley, Maj. 422

Davies, Quentin (b. 1944) C., Grantham & Stamford, Maj. 7,445

Davis, Rt. Hon. David (b. 1948) C., Haltemprice & Howden, Maj. 5,116

Dean, Janet (b. 1949) Lab., Burton, Maj. 1,421

Denham, Rt. Hon. John (b. 1953) Lab., Southampton Itchen, Maj. 9,302

Dhanda, Parmjit (b. 1971) Lab., Gloucester, Maj. 4,271

Dismore, Andrew (b. 1954) Lab., Hendon, Maj. 2,699

Djanogly, Jonathan (b. 1965) C., Huntingdon, Maj. 12,847

Dobbin, Jim (b. 1941) Lab. (Co-op), Heywood & Middleton, Maj. 11,083

Dobson, Rt. Hon. Frank (b. 1940) Lab., Holborn & St Pancras, Maj. 4,787

Dodds, Nigel (b. 1958) DUP, Belfast North, Maj. 5,188

Doherty, Pat (b. 1945) SF, Tyrone West, Maj. 5,005

‡Donaldson, Jeffrey (b. 1962) DUP, Lagan Valley, Maj. 14,117

Donohoe, Brian (b. 1948) Lab., Ayrshire Central, Maj. 10,423

Doran, Frank (b. 1949) Lab., Aberdeen North, Maj. 6,795

Dorrell, Rt. Hon. Stephen (b. 1952) C., Charnwood, Maj. 8,809

*Dorries, Nadine (b. 1958) C., Bedfordshire Mid, Maj. 11,355

Dowd, Jim (b. 1951) Lab., Lewisham West, Maj. 9,932

Drew, David (b. 1952) Lab. (Co-op), Stroud, Maj. 350

*Duddridge, James (b. 1971) C., Rochford & Southend East, Maj. 5,494

Duncan Smith, Rt. Hon. Iain (b. 1954) C., Chingford & Woodford Green, Maj. 10,641

Duncan, Alan (b. 1957) C., Rutland & Melton, Maj. 12,930

*Dunne, Philip (b. 1958) C., Ludlow, Maj. 2,027

Heald, Oliver (*b.* 1954) *C., Hertfordshire North East,* Maj. 9,138

Healey, John (*b.* 1960) *Lab., Wentworth,* Maj. 15,056

Heath, David (*b.* 1954) *LD, Somerton & Frome,* Maj. 812

Heathcoat-Amory, Rt. Hon. David (*b.* 1949) *C., Wells,* Maj. 3,040

*Hemming, John (*b.* 1960) *LD, Birmingham Yardley,* Maj. 2,672

Henderson, Doug (*b.* 1949) *Lab., Newcastle upon Tyne North,* Maj. 7,023

Hendrick, Mark (*b.* 1958) *Lab. (Co-op), Preston,* Maj. 9,407

Hendry, Charles (*b.* 1959) *C., Wealden,* Maj. 15,921

Hepburn, Stephen (*b.* 1959) *Lab., Jarrow,* Maj. 13,904

Heppell, John (*b.* 1948) *Lab., Nottingham East,* Maj. 6,939

*Herbert, Nick (*b.* 1963) *C., Arundel & South Downs,* Maj. 11,309

Hermon, Lady Sylvia (*b.* 1956) *UUP, Down North,* Maj. 4,944

Hesford, Stephen (*b.* 1957) *Lab., Wirral West,* Maj. 1,097

Hewitt, Rt. Hon. Patricia (*b.* 1948) *Lab., Leicester West,* Maj. 9,070

Heyes, David (*b.* 1946) *Lab., Ashton-under-Lyne,* Maj. 13,952

Hill, Rt. Hon. Keith (*b.* 1943) *Lab., Streatham,* Maj. 7,466

*Hillier, Meg (*b.* 1969) *Lab. (Co-op), Hackney South & Shoreditch,* Maj. 10,204

Hoban, Mark (*b.* 1964) *C., Fareham,* Maj. 11,702

Hodge, Rt. Hon. Margaret (*b.* 1944) *Lab., Barking,* Maj. 8,883

*Hodgson, Sharon (*b.* 1966) *Lab., Gateshead East & Washington West,* Maj. 13,407

Hoey, Kate (*b.* 1946) *Lab., Vauxhall,* Maj. 9,977

Hogg, Rt. Hon. Douglas (*b.* 1945) *C., Sleaford & North Hykeham,* Maj. 12,705

*Hollobone, Philip (*b.* 1964) *C., Kettering,* Maj. 3,301

*Holloway, Adam (*b.* 1965) *C., Gravesham,* Maj. 654

Holmes, Paul (*b.* 1957) *LD, Chesterfield,* Maj. 3,045

Hood, Jimmy (*b.* 1948) *Lab., Lanark & Hamilton East,* Maj. 11,947

Hoon, Rt. Hon. Geoff (*b.* 1953) *Lab., Ashfield,* Maj. 10,213

Hope, Phil (*b.* 1955) *Lab. (Co-op), Corby,* Maj. 1,517

Hopkins, Kelvin (*b.* 1941) *Lab., Luton North,* Maj. 6,487

Horam, John (*b.* 1939) *C., Orpington,* Maj. 4,947

*Horwood, Martin (*b.* 1962) *LD, Cheltenham,* Maj. 2,303

*Hosie, Stewart (*b.* 1963) *SNP, Dundee East,* Maj. 383

Howard, Rt. Hon. Michael (*b.* 1941) *C., Folkestone & Hythe,* Maj. 11,680

*Howarth, David (*b.* 1958) *LD, Cambridge,* Maj. 4,339

Howarth, George (*b.* 1949) *Lab., Knowsley North & Sefton East,* Maj. 16,269

Howarth, Gerald (*b.* 1947) *C., Aldershot,* Maj. 5,334

Howells, Dr Kim (*b.* 1946) *Lab., Pontypridd,* Maj. 13,191

Hoyle, Lindsay (*b.* 1957) *Lab., Chorley,* Maj. 7,625

Hughes, Rt. Hon. Beverley (*b.* 1950) *Lab., Stretford & Urmston,* Maj. 7,851

Hughes, Simon (*b.* 1951) *LD, Southwark North & Bermondsey,* Maj. 5,406

*Huhne, Chris (*b.* 1954) *LD, Eastleigh,* Maj. 568

Humble, Joan (*b.* 1951) *Lab., Blackpool North & Fleetwood,* Maj. 5,062

*Hunt, Jeremy (*b.* 1966) *C., Surrey South West,* Maj. 5,711

*Hunter, Mark (*b.* 1957) *LD, Cheadle,* Maj. 3,657

*Hurd, Nick (*b.* 1962) *C., Ruislip-Northwood,* Maj. 8,910

Hutton, Rt. Hon. John (*b.* 1955) *Lab., Barrow & Furness,* Maj. 6,037

Iddon, Dr Brian (*b.* 1940) *Lab., Bolton South East,* Maj. 11,638

Illsley, Eric (*b.* 1955) *Lab., Barnsley Central,* Maj. 12,732

Ingram, Rt. Hon. Adam (*b.* 1947) *Lab., East Kilbride, Strathaven & Lesmahagow,* Maj. 14,723

Irranca-Davies, Huw (*b.* 1963) *Lab., Ogmore,* Maj. 13,703

Jack, Rt. Hon. Michael (*b.* 1946) *C., Fylde,* Maj. 12,459

Jackson, Glenda (*b.* 1936) *Lab., Hampstead & Highgate,* Maj. 3,729

*Jackson, Stewart (*b.* 1965) *C., Peterborough,* Maj. 2,740

*James, Sian (*b.* 1959) *Lab., Swansea East,* Maj. 11,249

Jenkin, Bernard (*b.* 1959) *C., Essex North,* Maj. 10,903

Jenkins, Brian (*b.* 1942) *Lab., Tamworth,* Maj. 2,569

Johnson, Boris (*b.* 1964) *C., Henley,* Maj. 12,793

Johnson, Rt. Hon. Alan (*b.* 1950) *Lab., Hull West & Hessle,* Maj. 9,450

*Johnson, Diana (*b.* 1966) *Lab., Hull North,* Maj. 7,351

*Jones, David (*b.* 1952) *C., Clwyd West,* Maj. 133

Jones, Helen (*b.* 1954) *Lab., Warrington North,* Maj. 12,204

Jones, Kevan (*b.* 1964) *Lab., Durham North,* Maj. 16,781

Jones, Dr Lynne (*b.* 1951) *Lab., Birmingham Selly Oak,* Maj. 8,851

Jones, Martyn (*b.* 1947) *Lab., Clwyd South,* Maj. 6,348

Jowell, Rt. Hon. Tessa (*b.* 1947) *Lab., Dulwich & West Norwood,* Maj. 8,807

Joyce, Eric (*b.* 1960) *Lab., Falkirk,* Maj. 13,475

Kaufman, Rt. Hon. Sir Gerald (*b.* 1930) *Lab., Manchester Gorton,* Maj. 5,808

*Kawczynski, Daniel (*b.* 1972) *C., Shrewsbury & Atcham,* Maj. 1,808

Keeble, Sally (*b.* 1951) *Lab., Northampton North,* Maj. 3,960

*Keeley, Barbara (*b.* 1952) *Lab., Worsley,* Maj. 9,368

Keen, Alan (*b.* 1937) *Lab. (Co-op), Feltham & Heston,* Maj. 6,820

Keen, Ann (*b.* 1948) *Lab., Brentford & Isleworth,* Maj. 4,411

Keetch, Paul (*b.* 1961) *LD, Hereford,* Maj. 962

Kelly, Rt. Hon. Ruth (*b.* 1968) *Lab., Bolton West,* Maj. 2,064

Kemp, Fraser (*b.* 1958) *Lab., Houghton & Washington East,* Maj. 16,065

Kennedy, Rt. Hon. Charles (*b.* 1959) *LD, Ross, Skye & Lochaber,* Maj. 14,249

Kennedy, Rt. Hon. Jane (*b.* 1958) *Lab., Liverpool Wavertree,* Maj. 5,173

Key, Robert (*b.* 1945) *C., Salisbury,* Maj. 11,142

Khabra, Piara (*b.* 1922) *Lab., Ealing Southall,* Maj. 11,440

*Khan, Sadiq (*b.* 1970) *Lab., Tooting,* Maj. 5,381

Kidney, David (*b.* 1955) *Lab., Stafford,* Maj. 2,121

Kilfoyle, Peter (*b.* 1946) *Lab., Liverpool Walton,* Maj. 15,957

Kirkbride, Julie (*b.* 1960) *C., Bromsgrove,* Maj. 10,080

Knight, Rt. Hon. Greg (*b.* 1949) *C., Yorkshire East,* Maj. 6,283

Knight, Jim (*b.* 1965) *Lab., Dorset South,* Maj. 1,812

*Kramer, Susan (*b.* 1950) *LD, Richmond Park,* Maj. 3,731

Kumar, Dr Ashok (*b.* 1956) *Lab., Middlesbrough South & Cleveland East,* Maj. 8,000

Ladyman, Dr Stephen (*b.* 1952) *Lab., Thanet South,* Maj. 664

Laing, Eleanor (*b.* 1958) *C., Epping Forest,* Maj. 14,358

Lait, Jacqui (*b.* 1947) *C., Beckenham,* Maj. 8,401

Lamb, Norman (*b.* 1957) *LD, Norfolk North,* Maj. 10,606

Lammy, David (*b.* 1972) *Lab., Tottenham,* Maj. 13,034

*Lancaster, Mark (*b.* 1970) *C., Milton Keynes North East,* Maj. 1,665

Lansley, Andrew (*b.* 1956) *C., Cambridgeshire South,* Maj. 8,001

*Law, Peter (*b.* 1948) *Ind., Blaenau Gwent,* Maj. 9,121

Laws, David (*b.* 1965) *LD, Yeovil,* Maj. 8,562

Laxton, Bob (*b.* 1944) *Lab., Derby North,* Maj. 3,757

Lazarowicz, Mark (*b.* 1953) *Lab. (Co-op), Edinburgh North & Leith,* Maj. 2,153

*Leech, John (*b.* 1971) *LD, Manchester Withington,* Maj. 667

Leigh, Edward (*b.* 1950) *C., Gainsborough,* Maj. 8,003

Lepper, David (*b.* 1945) *Lab. (Co-op), Brighton Pavilion,* Maj. 5,030

Letwin, Rt. Hon. Oliver (*b.* 1956) *C., Dorset West,* Maj. 2,461

Levitt, Tom (*b.* 1954) *Lab., High Peak,* Maj. 735

Lewis, Ivan (*b.* 1967) *Lab., Bury South,* Maj. 8,912

Lewis, Dr Julian (*b.* 1951) *C., New Forest East,* Maj. 6,551

Liddell-Grainger, Ian (*b.* 1959) *C., Bridgwater,* Maj. 8,469

Lidington, David (*b.* 1956) *C., Aylesbury,* Maj. 11,065

Lilley, Rt. Hon. Peter (*b.* 1943) *C., Hitchin & Harpenden,* Maj. 11,393

Linton, Martin (*b.* 1944) *Lab., Battersea,* Maj. 163

Lloyd, Tony (*b.* 1950) *Lab., Manchester Central,* Maj. 9,776

Llwyd, Elfyn (*b.* 1951) *PC, Meirionnydd Nant Conwy,* Maj. 6,614

Lord, Sir Michael (*b.* 1938) *C., Suffolk Central & Ipswich North,* Maj. 7,856

Loughton, Tim (*b.* 1962) *C., Worthing East & Shoreham,* Maj. 8,183

Love, Andy (*b.* 1949) *Lab. (Co-op), Edmonton,* Maj. 8,075

Lucas, Ian (*b.* 1960) *Lab., Wrexham,* Maj. 6,819

Luff, Peter (*b.* 1955) *C., Worcestershire Mid,* Maj. 13,327

McAvoy, Rt. Hon. Thomas (*b.* 1943) *Lab. (Co-op), Rutherglen & Hamilton West,* Maj. 16,112

McCabe, Stephen (*b.* 1955) *Lab., Birmingham Hall Green,* Maj. 5,714

McCafferty, Christine (*b.* 1945) *Lab., Calder Valley,* Maj. 1,367

*McCarthy, Kerry (*b.* 1965) *Lab., Bristol East,* Maj. 8,621

*McCarthy-Fry, Sarah (*b.* 1955) *Lab. (Co-op), Portsmouth North,* Maj. 1,139

McCartney, Rt. Hon. Ian (*b.* 1951) *Lab., Makerfield,* Maj. 18,149

†McCrea, Dr William (*b.* 1948) *DUP, Antrim South,* Maj. 3,448

McDonagh, Siobhain (*b.* 1960) *Lab., Mitcham & Morden,* Maj. 12,560

*McDonnell, Dr Alasdair (*b.* 1949) *SDLP, Belfast South,* Maj. 1,235

McDonnell, John (*b.* 1951) *Lab., Hayes & Harlington,* Maj. 10,847

MacDougall, John (*b.* 1947) *Lab., Glenrothes,* Maj. 10,664

*McFadden, Pat (*b.* 1965) *Lab., Wolverhampton South East,* Maj. 10,495

McFall, Rt. Hon. John (*b.* 1944) *Lab. (Co-op), Dunbartonshire West,* Maj. 12,553

*McGovern, James (*b.* 1956) *Lab., Dundee West,* Maj. 5,379

McGrady, Edward (*b.* 1935) *SDLP, Down South,* Maj. 9,140

McGuinness, Martin (*b.* 1950) *SF, Ulster Mid,* Maj. 10,976

McGuire, Anne (*b.* 1949) *Lab., Stirling,* Maj. 4,767

McIntosh, Anne (*b.* 1954) *C., Vale of York,* Maj. 13,712

McIsaac, Shona (*b.* 1960) *Lab., Cleethorpes,* Maj. 2,642

Mackay, Rt. Hon. Andrew (*b.* 1949) *C., Bracknell,* Maj. 12,036

McKechin, Ann (*b.* 1961) *Lab., Glasgow North,* Maj. 3,338

McKenna, Rosemary (*b.* 1941) *Lab., Cumbernauld, Kilsyth & Kirkintilloch East,* Maj. 11,562

Mackinlay, Andrew (*b.* 1949) *Lab., Thurrock,* Maj. 6,375

Maclean, Rt. Hon. David (*b.* 1953) *C., Penrith & The Border,* Maj. 11,904

McLoughlin, Patrick (*b.* 1957) *C., Derbyshire West,* Maj. 10,753

*MacNeil, Angus (*b.* 1970) *SNP, Na h-Eileanan an Iar,* Maj. 1,441

McNulty, Tony (*b.* 1958) *Lab., Harrow East,* Maj. 4,730

MacShane, Rt. Hon. Denis (*b.* 1948) *Lab., Rotherham,* Maj. 10,681

Mactaggart, Fiona (*b.* 1953) *Lab., Slough,* Maj. 7,851

Mahmood, Khalid (*b.* 1961) *Lab., Birmingham Perry Barr,* Maj. 7,948

*Main, Anne (*b.* 1957) *C., St Albans,* Maj. 1,361

*Malik, Shahid (*b.* 1967) *Lab., Dewsbury,* Maj. 4,615

Malins, Humfrey (*b.* 1945) *C., Woking,* Maj. 6,612

Mallaber, Judith (*b.* 1951) *Lab., Amber Valley,* Maj. 5,275

Mann, John (*b.* 1960) *Lab., Bassetlaw,* Maj. 10,837

Maples, John (*b* 1943) *C., Stratford-upon-Avon,* Maj. 12,184

Marris, Rob (*b.* 1955) *Lab., Wolverhampton South West,* Maj. 2,879

Marsden, Gordon (*b.* 1953) *Lab., Blackpool South,* Maj. 7,922

Marshall, David (*b.* 1941) *Lab., Glasgow East,* Maj. 13,507

Marshall-Andrews, Bob (*b.* 1944) *Lab., Medway,* Maj. 213

Martin, Rt. Hon. Michael (*b.* 1945) *The Speaker, Glasgow North East,* Maj. 10,134

Martlew, Eric (*b.* 1949) *Lab., Carlisle,* Maj. 5,695

Mates, Rt. Hon. Michael (*b.* 1934) *C., Hampshire East,* Maj. 5,509

Maude, Rt. Hon. Francis (*b.* 1953) *C., Horsham,* Maj. 12,627

May, Rt. Hon. Theresa (*b.* 1956) *C., Maidenhead,* Maj. 6,231

Meacher, Rt. Hon. Michael (*b.* 1939) *Lab., Oldham West & Royton,* Maj. 10,454

Meale, Alan (*b.* 1949) *Lab., Mansfield,* Maj. 11,365

Mercer, Patrick (*b.* 1956) *C., Newark,* Maj. 6,464

Merron, Gillian (*b.* 1959) *Lab., Lincoln,* Maj. 4,614

Michael, Rt. Hon. Alun (*b.* 1943) *Lab. (Co-op), Cardiff South & Penarth,* Maj. 9,237

Milburn, Rt. Hon. Alan (b. 1958) Lab., Darlington, Maj. 10,404

Miliband, Rt. Hon. David (b. 1966) Lab., South Shields, Maj. 12,312

*Miliband, Edward (b. 1969) Lab., Doncaster North, Maj. 12,656

Miller, Andrew (b. 1949) Lab., Ellesmere Port & Neston, Maj. 6,486

*Miller, Maria (b. 1964) C., Basingstoke, Maj. 4,680

*Milton, Anne (b. 1955) C., Guildford, Maj. 347

Mitchell, Andrew (b. 1956) C., Sutton Coldfield, Maj. 12,283

Mitchell, Austin (b. 1934) Lab., Great Grimsby, Maj. 7,654

Moffatt, Laura (b. 1954) Lab., Crawley, Maj. 37

Mole, Chris (b. 1958) Lab., Ipswich, Maj. 5,332

*Moon, Madeleine (b. 1950) Lab., Bridgend, Maj. 6,523

Moore, Michael (b. 1965) LD, Berwickshire, Roxburgh & Selkirk, Maj. 5,901

Moran, Margaret (b. 1955) Lab., Luton South, Maj. 5,650

*Morden, Jessica (b. 1968) Lab., Newport East, Maj. 6,838

Morgan, Julie (b. 1944) Lab., Cardiff North, Maj. 1,146

Morley, Elliot (b. 1952) Lab., Scunthorpe, Maj. 8,963

Moss, Malcolm (b. 1943) C., Cambridgeshire North East, Maj. 8,901

Mountford, Kali (b. 1954) Lab., Colne Valley, Maj. 1,501

Mudie, George (b. 1945) Lab., Leeds East, Maj. 11,578

*Mulholland, Greg (b. 1970) LD, Leeds North West, Maj. 1,877

Mullin, Chris (b. 1947) Lab., Sunderland South, Maj. 11,059

*Mundell, David (b. 1962) C., Dumfriesshire, Clydesdale & Tweeddale, Maj. 1,738

Munn, Meg (b. 1959) Lab. (Co-op), Sheffield Heeley, Maj. 11,370

*Murphy, Conor (b. 1963) SF, Newry & Armagh, Maj. 8,195

Murphy, Denis (b. 1948) Lab., Wansbeck, Maj. 10,581

Murphy, Jim (b. 1967) Lab., Renfrewshire East, Maj. 6,657

Murphy, Rt. Hon. Paul (b. 1948) Lab., Torfaen, Maj. 14,791

Murrison, Dr Andrew (b. 1961) C., Westbury, Maj. 5,349

Naysmith, Dr Doug (b. 1941) Lab. (Co-op), Bristol North West, Maj. 8,962

*Newmark, Brooks (b. 1958) C., Braintree, Maj. 3,893

Norris, Dan (b. 1960) Lab., Wansdyke, Maj. 1,839

Oaten, Mark (b. 1964) LD, Winchester, Maj. 7,476

O'Brien, Mike (b. 1954) Lab., Warwickshire North, Maj. 7,553

O'Brien, Stephen (b. 1957) C., Eddisbury, Maj. 6,195

O'Hara, Eddie (b. 1937) Lab., Knowsley South, Maj. 17,688

Olner, Bill (b. 1942) Lab., Nuneaton, Maj. 2,280

Opik, Lembit (b. 1965) LD, Montgomeryshire, Maj. 7,173

Osborne, George (b. 1971) C., Tatton, Maj. 11,731

Osborne, Sandra (b. 1956) Lab., Ayr, Carrick & Cumnock, Maj. 9,997

Ottaway, Richard (b. 1945) C., Croydon South, Maj. 13,528

Owen, Albert (b. 1960) Lab., Ynys Mon, Maj. 1,242

Paice, James (b. 1949) C., Cambridgeshire South East, Maj. 8,624

Paisley, Revd Ian (b. 1926) DUP, Antrim North, Maj. 17,965

Palmer, Dr Nick (b. 1950) Lab., Broxtowe, Maj. 2,296

Paterson, Owen (b. 1956) C., Shropshire North, Maj. 11,020

Pearson, Ian (b. 1959) Lab., Dudley South, Maj. 4,244

*Pelling, Andrew (b. 1959) C., Croydon Central, Maj. 75

*Penning, Michael (b. 1957) C., Hemel Hempstead, Maj. 499

*Penrose, John (b. 1964) C., Weston-Super-Mare, Maj. 2,079

Picking, Anne (b. 1958) Lab., East Lothian, Maj. 7,620

Pickles, Eric (b. 1952) C., Brentwood & Ongar, Maj. 11,612

Plaskitt, James (b. 1954) Lab., Warwick & Leamington, Maj. 266

Pope, Greg (b. 1960) Lab., Hyndburn, Maj. 5,587

Pound, Stephen (b. 1948) Lab., Ealing North, Maj. 7,059

Prentice, Bridget (b. 1952) Lab., Lewisham East, Maj. 6,751

Prentice, Gordon (b. 1951) Lab., Pendle, Maj. 2,180

Prescott, Rt. Hon. John (b. 1938) Lab., Hull East, Maj. 11,747

Price, Adam (b. 1968) PC, Carmarthen East & Dinefwr, Maj. 6,718

Primarolo, Rt. Hon. Dawn (b. 1954) Lab., Bristol South, Maj. 11,142

Prisk, Mark (b. 1962) C., Hertford & Stortford, Maj. 13,097

*Pritchard, Mark (b. 1966) C., Wrekin, The, Maj. 942

Prosser, Gwyn (b. 1943) Lab., Dover, Maj. 4,941

Pugh, Dr John (b. 1949) LD, Southport, Maj. 3,838

Purchase, Ken (b. 1939) Lab. (Co-op), Wolverhampton North East, Maj. 8,156

Purnell, James (b. 1970) Lab., Stalybridge & Hyde, Maj. 8,348

Rammell, Bill (b. 1959) Lab., Harlow, Maj. 97

Randall, John (b. 1955) C., Uxbridge, Maj. 6,171

Raynsford, Rt. Hon. Nick (b. 1945) Lab., Greenwich & Woolwich, Maj. 10,146

Redwood, Rt. Hon. John (b. 1951) C., Wokingham, Maj. 7,240

Reed, Andy (b. 1964) Lab. (Co-op), Loughborough, Maj. 1,996

*Reed, Jamie (b. 1973) Lab., Copeland, Maj. 6,320

Reid, Alan (b. 1954) LD, Argyll & Bute, Maj. 5,636

Reid, Rt. Hon. Dr John (b. 1947) Lab., Airdrie & Shotts, Maj. 14,084

†Rifkind, Rt. Hon. Sir Malcolm (b. 1946) C., Kensington & Chelsea, Maj. 12,418

*Riordan, Linda (b. 1953) Lab. (Co-op), Halifax, Maj. 3,417

Robathan, Andrew (b. 1951) C., Blaby, Maj. 7,873

Robertson, Angus (b. 1969) SNP, Moray, Maj. 5,676

Robertson, Hugh (b. 1962) C., Faversham & Kent Mid, Maj. 8,720

Robertson, John (b. 1952) Lab., Glasgow North West, Maj. 10,093

Robertson, Laurence (b. 1958) C., Tewkesbury, Maj. 9,892

Robinson, Geoffrey (b. 1938) Lab., Coventry North West, Maj. 9,315

Robinson, Iris (b. 1949) DUP, Strangford, Maj. 13,049

Robinson, Peter (b. 1948) DUP, Belfast East, Maj. 5,877

*Rogerson, Dan (b. 1975) LD, Cornwall North, Maj. 3,076

Rooney, Terry (b. 1950) Lab., Bradford North,
Maj. 3,511
Rosindell, Andrew (b. 1966) C., Romford, Maj. 11,589
*Rowen, Paul (b. 1955) LD, Rochdale, Maj. 442
Roy, Frank (b. 1958) Lab., Motherwell & Wishaw,
Maj. 15,222
Ruane, Christopher (b. 1958) Lab., Vale of Clwyd,
Maj. 4,669
Ruddock, Joan (b. 1943) Lab., Lewisham Deptford,
Maj. 11,811
Ruffley, David (b. 1962) C., Bury St Edmunds, Maj. 9,930
Russell, Bob (b. 1946) LD, Colchester, Maj. 6,277
Russell, Christine (b. 1945) Lab., Chester, City of,
Maj. 915
Ryan, Joan (b. 1955) Lab., Enfield North, Maj. 1,920
Salmond, Alex (b. 1954) SNP, Banff & Buchan,
Maj. 11,837
Salter, Martin (b. 1954) Lab., Reading West, Maj. 4,682
Sanders, Adrian (b. 1959) LD, Torbay, Maj. 2,029
Sarwar, Mohammad (b. 1952) Lab., Glasgow Central,
Maj. 8,531
*Scott, Lee (b. 1956) C., Ilford North, Maj. 1,653
*Seabeck, Alison (b. 1954) Lab., Plymouth Devonport,
Maj. 8,103
Selous, Andrew (b. 1962) C., Bedfordshire South West,
Maj. 8,277
*Shapps, Grant (b. 1968) C., Welwyn Hatfield,
Maj. 5,946
Shaw, Jonathan (b. 1966) Lab., Chatham & Aylesford,
Maj. 2,332
Sheerman, Barry (b. 1940) Lab. (Co-op), Huddersfield,
Maj. 8,351
Shepherd, Richard (b. 1942) C., Aldridge-Brownhills,
Maj. 5,507
Sheridan, James (b. 1952) Lab., Paisley & Renfrewshire
North, Maj. 11,001
Short, Rt. Hon. Clare (b. 1946) Lab., Birmingham
Ladywood, Maj. 6,801
Simmonds, Mark (b. 1964) C., Boston & Skegness,
Maj. 5,907
Simon, Sion (b. 1969) Lab., Birmingham Erdington,
Maj. 9,575
Simpson, Alan (b. 1948) Lab., Nottingham South,
Maj. 7,486
*Simpson, David (b. 1959) DUP, Upper Bann,
Maj. 5,298
Simpson, Keith (b. 1949) C., Norfolk Mid, Maj. 7,560
Singh, Marsha (b. 1954) Lab., Bradford West,
Maj. 3,026
Skinner, Dennis (b. 1932) Lab., Bolsover, Maj. 18,437
*Slaughter, Andrew (b. 1960) Lab., Ealing, Acton &
Shepherd's Bush, Maj. 5,520
Smith, Rt. Hon. Andrew (b. 1951) Lab., Oxford East,
Maj. 963
*Smith, Angela (b. 1961) Lab., Sheffield Hillsborough,
Maj. 11,243
Smith, Angela (b. 1959) Lab. (Co-op), Basildon,
Maj. 3,142
Smith, Geraldine (b. 1961) Lab., Morecambe &
Lunesdale, Maj. 4,768
Smith, Rt. Hon. Jacqui (b. 1962) Lab., Redditch,
Maj. 2,716
Smith, John (b. 1951) Lab., Vale of Glamorgan,
Maj. 1,808
Smith, Sir Robert (b. 1958) LD, Aberdeenshire West &
Kincardine, Maj. 7,471
*Snelgrove, Anne (b. 1957) Lab., Swindon South,
Maj. 1,353

Soames, Hon. Nicholas (b. 1948) C., Sussex Mid,
Maj. 5,890
*Soulsby, Sir Peter (b. 1948) Lab., Leicester South,
Maj. 3,717
Southworth, Helen (b. 1956) Lab., Warrington South,
Maj. 3,515
Spellar, Rt. Hon. John (b. 1947) Lab., Warley,
Maj. 10,147
Spelman, Caroline (b. 1958) C., Meriden, Maj. 7,009
Spicer, Sir Michael (b. 1943) C., Worcestershire West,
Maj. 2,475
Spink, Dr Robert (b. 1948) C., Castle Point, Maj. 8,201
Spring, Richard (b. 1946) C., Suffolk West, Maj. 8,909
Squire, Rachel (b. 1954) Lab., Dunfermline & West Fife,
Maj. 11,562
Stanley, Rt. Hon. Sir John (b. 1942) C., Tonbridge &
Malling, Maj. 13,352
Starkey, Dr Phyllis (b. 1947) Lab., Milton Keynes South
West, Maj. 4,010
Steen, Anthony (b. 1939) C., Totnes, Maj. 1,947
Stewart, Ian (b. 1950) Lab., Eccles, Maj. 12,886
Stoate, Dr Howard (b. 1954) Lab., Dartford, Maj. 706
Strang, Rt. Hon. Gavin (b. 1943) Lab., Edinburgh East,
Maj. 6,202
Straw, Rt. Hon. Jack (b. 1946) Lab., Blackburn,
Maj. 8,009
Streeter, Gary (b. 1955) C., Devon South West,
Maj. 10,141
Stringer, Graham (b. 1950) Lab., Manchester Blackley,
Maj. 12,027
Stuart, Gisela (b. 1955) Lab., Birmingham Edgbaston,
Maj. 2,349
*Stuart, Graham (b. 1962) C., Beverley & Holderness,
Maj. 2,580
Stunell, Andrew (b. 1942) LD, Hazel Grove, Maj. 7,748
Sutcliffe, Gerry (b. 1953) Lab., Bradford South,
Maj. 9,167
Swayne, Desmond (b. 1956) C., New Forest West,
Maj. 17,285
*Swinson, Jo (b. 1980) LD, Dunbartonshire East,
Maj. 4,061
Swire, Hugo (b. 1959) C., Devon East, Maj. 7,936
Syms, Robert (b. 1956) C., Poole, Maj. 5,988
Tami, Mark (b. 1963) Lab., Alyn & Deeside, Maj. 8,378
Tapsell, Sir Peter (b. 1930) C., Louth & Horncastle,
Maj. 9,896
Taylor, Dari (b. 1944) Lab., Stockton South, Maj. 6,139
Taylor, David (b. 1946) Lab. (Co-op), Leicestershire North
West, Maj. 4,477
Taylor, Ian (b. 1945) C., Esher & Walton, Maj. 7,727
Taylor, Matthew (b. 1963) LD, Truro & St Austell,
Maj. 7,403
Taylor, Dr Richard (b. 1935) KHHC, Wyre Forest,
Maj. 5,250
Teather, Sarah (b. 1974) LD, Brent East, Maj. 2,712
Thomas, Gareth (b. 1967) Lab. (Co-op), Harrow West,
Maj. 2,028
*Thornberry, Emily (b. 1960) Lab., Islington South &
Finsbury, Maj. 484
Thurso, John (b. 1953) LD, Caithness, Sutherland &
Easter Ross, Maj. 8,168
Timms, Stephen (b. 1955) Lab., East Ham, Maj. 13,155
Tipping, Paddy (b. 1949) Lab., Sherwood, Maj. 6,652
Todd, Mark (b. 1954) Lab., Derbyshire South, Maj. 4,495
Touhig, Don (b. 1947) Lab. (Co-op), Islwyn,
Maj. 15,740
Tredinnick, David (b. 1950) C., Bosworth, Maj. 5,319
Trickett, Jon (b. 1950) Lab., Hemsworth, Maj. 13,481

Truswell, Paul (b. 1955) Lab., Pudsey, Maj. 5,870
Turner, Andrew (b. 1953) C., Isle of Wight, Maj. 12,978
Turner, Dr Desmond (b. 1939) Lab., Brighton
Kemptown, Maj. 2,737
Turner, Neil (b. 1945) Lab., Wigan, Maj. 11,767
Twigg, Derek (b. 1959) Lab., Halton, Maj. 14,606
Tyrie, Andrew (b. 1957) C., Chichester, Maj. 10,860
*Ussher, Kitty (b. 1971) Lab., Burnley, Maj. 5,778
*Vaizey, Ed (b. 1969) C., Wantage, Maj. 8,017
*Vara, Shailesh (b. 1960) C., Cambridgeshire North West,
Maj. 9,833
Vaz, Keith (b. 1956) Lab., Leicester East, Maj. 15,876
Viggers, Peter (b. 1938) C., Gosport, Maj. 5,730
*Villiers, Theresa (b. 1968) C., Chipping Barnet,
Maj. 5,960
Vis, Dr Rudi (b. 1941) Lab., Finchley & Golders Green,
Maj. 741
*Walker, Charles (b. 1967) C., Broxbourne, Maj. 11,509
*Wallace, Ben (b. 1970) C., Lancaster & Wyre,
Maj. 4,171
Walley, Joan (b. 1949) Lab., Stoke-on-Trent North,
Maj. 10,036
Walter, Robert (b. 1948) C., Dorset North, Maj. 2,244
*Waltho, Lynda (b. 1960) Lab., Stourbridge, Maj. 407
Ward, Claire (b. 1972) Lab., Watford, Maj. 1,148
Wareing, Robert (b. 1930) Lab., Liverpool West Derby,
Maj. 15,225
Waterson, Nigel (b. 1950) C., Eastbourne, Maj. 1,124
Watkinson, Angela (b. 1941) C., Upminster, Maj. 6,042
Watson, Tom (b. 1967) Lab., West Bromwich East,
Maj. 11,652
Watts, Dave (b. 1951) Lab., St Helens North, Maj. 13,962
Webb, Prof. Steve (b. 1965) LD, Northavon, Maj. 11,033
Weir, Michael (b. 1957) SNP, Angus, Maj. 1,601
Whitehead, Dr Alan (b. 1950) Lab., Southampton Test,
Maj. 7,018
Whittingdale, John (b. 1959) C., Maldon & Chelmsford
East, Maj. 12,573
Wicks, Malcolm (b. 1947) Lab., Croydon North,
Maj. 13,888
Widdecombe, Rt. Hon. Ann (b. 1947) C., Maidstone &
The Weald, Maj. 14,856
Wiggin, Bill (b. 1966) C., Leominster, Maj. 13,187
Willetts, David (b. 1956) C., Havant, Maj. 6,508
Williams, Rt. Hon. Alan (b. 1930) Lab., Swansea West,
Maj. 4,269
Williams, Betty (b. 1944) Lab., Conwy, Maj. 3,081

Williams, Hywel (b. 1953) PC, Caernarfon,
Maj. 5,209
*Williams, Mark (b. 1966) LD, Ceredigion, Maj. 219
Williams, Roger (b. 1948) LD, Brecon & Radnorshire,
Maj. 3,905
*Williams, Stephen (b. 1966) LD, Bristol West,
Maj. 5,128
Willis, Phil (b. 1941) LD, Harrogate & Knaresborough,
Maj. 10,429
*Willott, Jenny (b. 1974) LD, Cardiff Central,
Maj. 5,593
Wills, Michael (b. 1952) Lab., Swindon North,
Maj. 2,571
Wilshire, David (b. 1943) C., Spelthorne, Maj. 9,936
*Wilson, Rob (b. 1965) C., Reading East, Maj. 475
*Wilson, Sammy (b. 1953) DUP, Antrim East,
Maj. 7,304
Winnick, David (b. 1933) Lab., Walsall North,
Maj. 6,640
Winterton, Lady Ann (b. 1941) C., Congleton,
Maj. 8,246
Winterton, Sir Nicholas (b. 1938) C., Macclesfield,
Maj. 9,401
Winterton, Rosie (b. 1958) Lab., Doncaster Central,
Maj. 9,802
Wishart, Peter (b. 1962) SNP, Perth & Perthshire North,
Maj. 1,521
Wood, Mike (b. 1946) Lab., Batley & Spen, Maj. 5,788
Woodward, Shaun (b. 1958) Lab., St Helens South,
Maj. 9,309
Woolas, Phil (b. 1959) Lab., Oldham East & Saddleworth,
Maj. 3,590
Wright, Anthony (b. 1954) Lab., Great Yarmouth,
Maj. 3,055
Wright, David (b. 1967) Lab., Telford, Maj. 5,406
Wright, Iain (b. 1972) Lab., Hartlepool, Maj. 7,478
*Wright, Jeremy (b. 1972) C., Rugby & Kenilworth,
Maj. 1,556
Wright, Dr Tony (b. 1948) Lab., Cannock Chase,
Maj. 9,227
Wyatt, Derek (b. 1949) Lab., Sittingbourne & Sheppey,
Maj. 79
Yeo, Tim (b. 1945) C., Suffolk South, Maj. 6,606
Young, Rt. Hon. Sir George (b. 1941) C., Hampshire
North West, Maj. 13,264
Younger-Ross, Richard (b. 1953) LD, Teignbridge,
Maj. 6,215

GENERAL ELECTION RESULTS

The results of voting in each parliamentary division at the general election of 5 May 2005 are given below. The majority in the 2001 general election and any by-election between 2001 and 2005 is given below the 2005 result.

SCOTTISH BOUNDARY CHANGES

The number of Scottish constituencies was reduced from 72 to 59 for the 2005 general election, bringing the average electorate of each constituency in line with that of England.

Although 23 constituencies are known by names that existed in the 2001 general election, their boundaries have moved to incorporate parts of other old seats and now bear little relation to those of 2001. Three seats remain geographically unaffected by the boundary changes: Orkney & Shetland, Western Isles (now known by its Gaelic name of Na h-Eileanan an Iar), and Eastwood (renamed Renfrewshire East).

For the large majority of constituencies where a boundary change has taken place, it is not appropriate to make a straight comparison between the results of 2001 and 2005. The seat of Dundee East, for example, comprises 80 per cent of the old Dundee East constituency and 30 per cent of the old Angus constituency; it cannot therefore be described as a simple gain for the Scottish National Party from Labour. The term 'notional' used here refers to a theoretical set of results, published by Professors Rallings and Thrasher of Plymouth University, that estimates the way each new constituency might have voted in the 2001 general election.

KEY

*New MP
†Previously MP in another seat
‡Previously MP for another party
§Notional result; *see* explanation of Scottish boundary changes
E. Electorate   T. Turnout

Abbreviations of parties standing in the General Election in 2005:

AFC	Alliance for Change
Alliance	Alliance
AP	Alternative Party
Baths	Save the Bristol North Baths Party
Bean	New Millennium Bean
BMG	Blair Must Go Party
BNP	British National Party
BPP	British Public Party
Bridges	Build Duddon and Morecambe Bridges
Burnley	Burnley First Independent
C.	Conservative
CAP	Community Action Party
CG	Community Group
CL	Communist League
Clause 28	Clause 28 Children's Protection Christian Democrats
Comm.	Communist Party
Comm. Brit.	Communist Party of Britain
Community	Community
CP	Civilisation Party
CPA	Christian Peoples Alliance
Croydon	Croydon Pensions Alliance
Currency	Virtue Currency Cognitive Appraisal Party
DDTP	Death, Dungeons & Taxes Party
Dem. Lab.	Democratic Labour Party
Dem. Soc. All.	Democratic Socialist Alliance – People Before Profit
DUP	Democratic Unionist Party
EDP	English Democratic Party
EPP	English Parliamentary Party
Elvis	Church of the Militant Elvis Party
Eng. Dem.	English Democrats Party
Eng. Ind.	English Independence Party
FF	familiesfirst.uk.net
Fit	Fit Party For Integrity And Trust
Forum	Open-Forum
FP	Freedom Party
Free Scot.	Free Scotland Party
FWP	Forward Wales Party
GBB	Get Britain Back Party
Good	Common Good
Green	Green

Green Soc.	Alliance for Green Socialism
Honesty	Demanding Honesty in Politics and Whitehall
Ind. Green	Independent Green Voice
Ind.	Independent
Ind. Pr. Lab.	Independent Progressive Labour
IP	Imperial Party
Iraq	Iraq War, Not in My Name
IWCA	Independent Working Class Association
IZB	Islam Zinda Baad Platform
JP	Justice Party
KHHC	Kidderminster Hospital and Health Concern
Lab.	Labour
Lab. (Co-op)	Labour (Co-operative)
LCA	Legalise Cannabis Alliance
LD	Liberal Democrat
Lib.	Liberal
Local	Local Community Party
Loony	Monster Raving Loony Party
Masts	Removal of Tetra Masts in Cornwall
MC	The Millenium Council
Meb. Kcr.	Mebyon Kernow
MNP	Motorcycle News Party
NACVP	Newcastle Academy with Christian Values Party
NEP	New England Party
NF	National Front
Northern	Northern Progress for You
OCV	Operation Christian Vote
OFD	Organisation of Free Democrats
Online	Seeks a Worldwide Online Participatory Directory
Paisley	Pride in Paisley Party
PC	Plaid Cymru
PDP	Progressive Democratic Party
PHF	People of Horsham First
Power	Max Power Party
PPN-V	Peace Party, Non-Violence, Justice, Environment
PPS	Pensioners Party Scotland
Progress	Peace and Progress Party
Protest	Protest Vote Party
PRTYP	Personality and Rational Thinking? Yes! Party
Publican	Publican Party - Free to Smoke (Pubs)
RA	Residents Association

R & R Loony	Rock & Roll Loony Party
Respect	Respect – the Unity Coalition
RP	The Resolutionist Party
St Albans	St Albans Party
Scot. Green	Scottish Green Party
Scot. Ind.	Scottish Independence Party
Scot. Senior	Scottish Senior Citizens Party
Scot. U.	Scottish Unionist
SDLP	Social Democratic and Labour Party
Senior	Senior Citizens Party
SF	Sinn Fein
Silent	Silent Majority Party
SNH	Safeguard the National Health Service
SNP	Scottish National Party
Soc. All.	Socialist Alliance
Soc. Alt.	Socialist Alternative Party
Socialist	Socialist
Soc. Lab.	Socialist Labour Party
Soc. Unity	Socialist Unity Network
SOS	SOS! Voters Against Overdevelopment of Northampton
Speaker	The Speaker
SSCUP	Scottish Senior Citizens Unity Party
SSP	Scottish Socialist Party
Tele.	telepathicpartnership.com
TEPK	Tigers Eye the Party for Kids
Third	Third Way
TP	Their Party
UKC	UK Community Issues Party
UKIP	UK Independence Party
UK Path	UK Pathfinders
UKPP	UK Pensioners Party
UUP	Ulster Unionist Party
Veritas	Veritas
Vote Dream	Vote for Yourself Rainbow Dream Ticket
Wessex Reg.	Wessex Regionalist
Work	The People's Choice Making Politicians Work
WP	Workers' Party
WRP	Workers' Revolutionary Party
XPP	Xtraordinary People Party
YPB	Your Party (Banbury)

PARLIAMENTARY CONSTITUENCIES AS AT 5 MAY 2005

ENGLAND

ALDERSHOT
E. 78,553 T. 48,141 (61.28%)   C. hold
Gerald Howarth, C.   20,572
Adrian Collett, LD   15,238
Howard Linsley, Lab.   9,895
Derek Rumsey, UKIP   1,182
Gary Cowd, Eng. Dem.   701
Howling Lord Hope, Loony   553
C. maj. 5,334 (11.08%)
1.74% swing C. to LD
(2001: C. maj. 6,564 (14.49%))

ALDRIDGE-BROWNHILLS
E. 61,761 T. 39,556 (64.05%)   C. hold
Richard Shepherd, C.   18,744
Jon Phillips, Lab.   13,237
Roy Sheward, LD   4,862
William Vaughan, BNP   1,620
Graham Eardley, UKIP   1,093
C. maj. 5,507 (13.92%)
1.98% swing Lab. to C.
(2001: C. maj. 3,768 (9.97%))

ALTRINCHAM & SALE WEST
E. 67,247 T. 44,310 (65.89%)   C. hold
Graham Brady, C.   20,569
John Stockton, Lab.   13,410
Ian Chappell, LD   9,595
Gary Peart, UKIP   736
C. maj. 7,159 (16.16%)
4.70% swing Lab. to C.
(2001: C. maj. 2,941 (6.75%))

AMBER VALLEY
E. 75,376 T. 47,391 (62.87%) Lab. hold
Judy Mallaber, Lab.   21,593
Gillian Shaw, C.   16,318
Kate Smith, LD   6,225
Paul Snell, BNP   1,243
Alexander Stevenson, Veritas   1,224
Hugh Price, UKIP   788
Lab. maj. 5,275 (11.13%)
2.55% swing Lab. to C.
(2001: Lab. maj. 7,227 (16.24%))

ARUNDEL & SOUTH DOWNS
E. 72,535 T. 49,690 (68.50%)   C. hold
*Nick Herbert, C.   24,752
Derek Deedman, LD   13,443
Sharon Whitlam, Lab.   8,482
Andrew Moffat, UKIP   2,700
Mark Stack, Protest   313
C. maj. 11,309 (22.76%)
3.55% swing C. to LD
(2001: C. maj. 13,704 (29.86%))

ASHFIELD
E. 73,403 T. 42,051 (57.29%) Lab. hold
Rt. Hon. Geoff Hoon, Lab.   20,433
Giles Inglis-Jones, C.   10,220
Wendy Johnson, LD   5,829
Roy Adkins, Ind.   2,292
Kathryn Allsop, Ind.   1,900
Sarah Hemstock, Veritas   1,108
Eddie Grenfell, Ind.   269
Lab. maj. 10,213 (24.29%)
4.72% swing Lab. to C.
(2001: Lab. maj. 13,268 (33.72%))

ASHFORD
E. 79,493 T. 51,685 (65.02%)   C. hold
Damian Green, C.   26,651
Valerie Whitaker, Lab.   13,353
Chris Took, LD   8,308
Richard Boden, Green   1,753
Bernard Stroud, UKIP   1,620
C. maj. 13,298 (25.73%)
5.19% swing Lab. to C.
(2001: C. maj. 7,359 (15.35%))

ASHTON UNDER LYNE
E. 72,000 T. 36,967 (51.34%) Lab. hold
David Heyes, Lab.   21,211
Graeme Brown, C.   7,259
Les Jones, LD   5,108
Anthony Jones, BNP   2,051
Dr John Whittaker, UKIP   768
Jack Crossfield, Local   570
Lab. maj. 13,952 (37.74%)
2.82% swing Lab. to C.
(2001: Lab. maj. 15,518 (43.39%))

AYLESBURY
E. 82,428 T. 51,458 (62.43%)   C. hold
David Lidington, C.   25,252
Peter Jones, LD   14,187
Mohammed Khaliel, Lab.   9,540
Christopher Adams, UKIP   2,479
C. maj. 11,065 (21.50%)
0.56% swing LD to C.
(2001: C. maj. 10,009 (20.39%))

BANBURY
E. 87,168 T. 56,209 (64.48%)   C. hold
Tony Baldry, C.   26,382
Les Sibley, Lab.   15,585
Zoe Patrick, LD   10,076
Alyson Duckmanton, Green   1,590
Dianna Heimann, UKIP   1,241
James Starkey, NF   918
Christopher Rowe, YPB   417
C. maj. 10,797 (19.21%)
4.54% swing Lab. to C.
(2001: C. maj. 5,219 (10.13%))

BARKING
E. 57,658 T. 28,906 (50.13%) Lab. hold
Rt. Hon. Margaret Hodge, Lab.   13,826
Keith Prince, C.   4,943
Richard Barnbrook, BNP   4,916
Toby Wickenden, LD   3,211
Terry Jones, UKIP   803
Laurie Cleeland, Green   618
Demetrious Panton, Ind.   530
Michael Saxby, WRP   59
Lab. maj. 8,883 (30.73%)
3.61% swing Lab. to C.
(2001: Lab. maj. 9,534 (37.94%))

BARNSLEY CENTRAL
E. 60,592 T. 28,615 (47.23%) Lab. hold
Eric Illsley, Lab.   17,478
Miles Crompton, LD   4,746
Peter Morel, C.   3,813
Geoff Broadley, BNP   1,403
Donald Wood, Ind.   1,175
Lab. maj. 12,732 (44.49%)
5.22% swing Lab. to LD
(2001: Lab. maj. 15,130 (54.93%))

BARNSLEY EAST & MEXBOROUGH
E. 66,941 T. 33,026 (49.34%) Lab. hold
Jeff Ennis, Lab.   20,779
Sharron Brook, LD   6,654
Carolyn Abbott, C.   4,853
Terence Robinson, Soc. Lab.   740
Lab. maj. 14,125 (42.77%)
4.44% swing Lab. to LD
(2001: Lab. maj. 16,789 (51.64%))

BARNSLEY WEST & PENISTONE
E. 66,985 T. 36,852 (55.02%) Lab. hold
Michael Clapham, Lab.   20,372
Clive Watkinson, C.   9,058
Alison Brelsford, LD   7,422
Lab. maj. 11,314 (30.70%)
2.52% swing Lab. to C.
(2001: Lab. maj. 12,352 (35.74%))

BARROW & FURNESS
E. 61,883 T. 36,493 (58.97%) Lab. hold
Rt. Hon. John Hutton, Lab.   17,360
Bill Dorman, C.   11,323
Barry Rabone, LD   6,130
Alan Beach, UKIP   758
Timothy Bell, Bridges   409
Brian Greaves, Veritas   306
Helene Young, Ind.   207
Lab. maj. 6,037 (16.54%)
4.40% swing Lab. to C.
(2001: Lab. maj. 9,889 (25.34%))

BASILDON
E. 73,912 T. 43,141 (58.37%)
Lab. (Co-op) hold
Angela Smith, Lab. (Co-op)   18,720
Aaron Powell, C.   15,578
Martin Thompson, LD   4,473
Emma Colgate, BNP   2,055
Alix Blythe, UKIP   1,143
Vikki Copping, Green   662
Kim Gandy, Eng. Dem.   510
Lab. (Co-op) maj. 3,142 (7.28%)
5.82% swing Lab. (Co-op) to C.
(2001: Lab. (Co-op) maj. 7,738
(18.93%))

BASINGSTOKE
E. 76,404 T. 48,123 (62.98%)   C. gain
*Maria Miller, C.   19,955
Paul Harvey, Lab.   15,275
Jen Smith, LD   9,952
Peter Effer, UKIP   1,044
Darren Shirley, Green   928
Roger Robertson, BNP   821
Roger Macnair, MC   148
C. maj. 4,680 (9.73%)
3.95% swing Lab. to C.
(C. gain because previous MP defected to
DUP in 2004)
(2001: C. maj. 880 (1.83%))

BASSETLAW
E. 69,389 T. 40,342 (58.14%) Lab. hold
John Mann, Lab.   22,847
Jonathan Sheppard, C.   12,010
David Dobbie, LD   5,485
Lab. maj. 10,837 (26.86%)
0.90% swing C. to Lab.
(2001: Lab. maj. 9,748 (25.06%))

BATH
E. 66,824 T. 45,836 (68.59%) LD hold
Don Foster, LD   20,101
Sian Dawson, C.   15,463
Harriet Ajderian, Lab.   6,773
Eric Lucas, Green   2,494
Richard Crowder, UKIP   770
Patrick Cobbe, Ind.   177
Graham Walker, Ind.   58
LD maj. 4,638 (10.12%)
5.63% swing LD to C.
(2001: LD maj. 9,894 (21.37%))

BATLEY & SPEN
E. 62,948 T. 39,208 (62.29%) Lab. hold
Mike Wood, Lab.   17,974
Robert Light, C.   12,186
Neil Bentley, LD   5,731
Colin Auty, BNP   2,668
Clive Lord, Green   649
Lab. maj. 5,788 (14.76%)
0.81% swing C. to Lab.
(2001: Lab. maj. 5,064 (13.14%))

BATTERSEA
E. 69,548 T. 41,049 (59.02%) Lab. hold
Martin Linton, Lab.   16,569
Dominic Schofield, C.   16,406
Norsheen Bhatti, LD   6,006
Hugo Charlton, Green   1,735
Terence Jones, UKIP   333
Lab. maj. 163 (0.40%)
6.67% swing Lab. to C.
(2001: Lab. maj. 5,053 (13.73%))

BEACONSFIELD
E. 68,083 T. 43,523 (63.93%) C. hold
Dominic Grieve, C.   24,126
Peter Chapman, LD   8,873
Alex Sobel, Lab.   8,422
John Fagan, UKIP   2,102
C. maj. 15,253 (35.05%)
1.96% swing LD to C.
(2001: C. maj. 13,065 (31.07%))

BECKENHAM
E. 74,738 T. 48,964 (65.51%) C. hold
Jacqui Lait, C.   22,183
Liam Curran, Lab.   13,782
Jef Foulger, LD   10,862
James Cartwright, UKIP   1,301
Roderick Reed, Ind.   836
C. maj. 8,401 (17.16%)
3.14% swing Lab. to C.
(2001: C. maj. 4,959 (10.88%))

BEDFORD
E. 70,629 T. 42,072 (59.57%) Lab. hold
Patrick Hall, Lab.   17,557
Richard Fuller, C.   14,174
Michael Headley, LD   9,063
Peter Conquest, UKIP   995
John McCready, Ind.   283
Lab. maj. 3,383 (8.04%)
3.57% swing Lab. to C.
(2001: Lab. maj. 6,157 (15.17%))

BEDFORDSHIRE MID
E. 73,768 T. 50,420 (68.35%) C. hold
*Nadine Dorries, C.   23,345
Mark Chapman, LD   11,990
Martin Lindsay, Lab.   11,351
Richard Joselyn, UKIP   1,372
Ben Foley, Green   1,292
Howard Martin, Veritas   769
Saqhib Ali, Ind.   301
C. maj. 11,355 (22.52%)
2.55% swing C. to LD
(2001: C. maj. 8,066 (17.29%))

BEDFORDSHIRE NORTH EAST
E. 72,757 T. 49,505 (68.04%) C. hold
Alistair Burt, C.   24,725
Keith White, Lab.   12,474
Stephen Rutherford, LD   10,320
James May, UKIP   1,986
C. maj. 12,251 (24.75%)
2.9% swing Lab. to C.
(2001: C. maj. 8,577 (18.96%))

BEDFORDSHIRE SOUTH WEST
E. 74,096 T. 45,814 (61.83%) C. hold
Andrew Selous, C.   22,114
Joyce Still, Lab.   13,837
Andy Strange, LD   7,723
Tom Wise, UKIP   1,923
Kenson Gurney, Forum   217
C. maj. 8,277 (18.07%)
8.15% swing Lab. to C.
(2001: C. maj. 776 (1.77%))

BERWICK-UPON-TWEED
E. 56,944 T. 36,090 (63.38%) LD hold
Rt. Hon. Alan Beith, LD   19,052
Mike Elliott, C.   10,420
Glen Reynolds, Lab.   6,618
LD maj. 8,632 (23.92%)
0.31% swing C. to LD
(2001: LD maj. 8,458 (23.30%))

BETHNAL GREEN & BOW
E. 85,950 T. 44,007 (51.20%)
                               Respect gain
†‡George Galloway, Respect   15,801
Oona King, Lab.   14,978
Shahagir Bakth Faruk, C.   6,244
Syed Nurul Islam Dulu, LD   4,928
John Foster, Green   1,950
Ejiro Etefia, AFC   68
Celia Pugh, CL   38
Respect maj. 823 (1.87%)
26.20% swing Lab. to Respect
(2001: Lab. maj. 10,057 (26.14%))

BEVERLEY & HOLDERNESS
E. 77,460 T. 50,202 (64.81%) C. hold
*Graham Stuart, C.   20,434
George McManus, Lab.   17,854
Brian Willie, LD   9,578
Oliver Marriott, UKIP   2,336
C. maj. 2,580 (5.14%)
1.73% swing Lab. to C.
(2001: C. maj. 781 (1.68%))

BEXHILL & BATTLE
E. 69,676 T. 46,834 (67.22%) C. hold
Greg Barker, C.   24,629
Mary Varrall, LD   11,180
Michael Jones, Lab.   8,457
Anthony Smith, UKIP   2,568
C. maj. 13,449 (28.72%)
2.63% swing LD to C.
(2001: C. maj. 10,503 (23.45%))

BEXLEYHEATH & CRAYFORD
E. 65,025 T. 42,580 (65.48%) C. gain
†David Evennett, C.   19,722
Nigel Beard, Lab.   15,171
David Raval, LD   5,144
John Dunford, UKIP   1,302
Jay Lee, BNP   1,241
C. maj. 4,551 (10.69%)
7.17% swing Lab. to C.
(2001: Lab. maj. 1,472 (3.65%))

BILLERICAY
E. 79,537 T. 48,858 (61.43%) C. hold
John Baron, C.   25,487
Anneliese Dodds, Lab.   14,281
Mike Hibbs, LD   6,471
Bryn Robinson, BNP   1,435
Seantino Callaghan, UKIP   1,184
C. maj. 11,206 (22.94%)
5.97% swing Lab. to C.
(2001: C. maj. 5,013 (10.99%))

BIRKENHEAD
E. 57,097 T. 27,786 (48.66%) Lab. hold
Rt. Hon. Frank Field, Lab.   18,059
Stuart Kelly, LD   5,125
Howard Morton, C.   4,602
Lab. maj. 12,934 (46.55%)
5.54% swing Lab. to LD
(2001: Lab. maj. 15,591 (53.82%))

BIRMINGHAM EDGBASTON
E. 64,893 T. 37,631 (57.99%) Lab. hold
Gisela Stuart, Lab.   16,465
Deirdre Alden, C.   14,116
Mike Dixon, LD   5,185
Peter Beck, Green   1,116
Stephen White, UKIP   749
Lab. maj. 2,349 (6.24%)
3.10% swing Lab. to C.
(2001: Lab. maj. 4,698 (12.45%))

BIRMINGHAM ERDINGTON
E. 64,951 T. 31,746 (48.88%) Lab. hold
Sion Simon, Lab.   16,810
Victoria Elvidge, C.   7,235
Jerry Evans, LD   5,027
Sharon Ebanks, BNP   1,512
Rannal Hepburn, UKIP   746
Terry Williams, NF   416
Lab. maj. 9,575 (30.16%)
1.20% swing Lab. to C.
(2001: Lab. maj. 9,962 (32.55%))

BIRMINGHAM HALL GREEN
E. 57,222 T. 34,536 (60.35%) Lab. hold
Stephen McCabe, Lab.   16,304
Eddie Hughes, C.   10,590
Roger Harmer, LD   6,682
David Melhuish, UKIP   960
Lab. maj. 5,714 (16.55%)
1.77% swing Lab. to C.
(2001: Lab. maj. 6,648 (20.09%))

BIRMINGHAM HODGE HILL
E. 53,903 T. 28,417 (52.72%) Lab. hold
Liam Byrne, Lab.   13,822
Nicola Davies, LD   8,373
Deborah Thomas, C.   3,768
Denis Adams, BNP   1,445
Adrian Duffen, UKIP   680
Azmat Begg, Progress   329
Lab. maj. 5,449 (19.18%)
18.29% swing Lab. to LD
(2004 July by-election: Lab. maj. 460
(2.25%))
(2001: Lab. maj. 11,618 (43.90%))

BIRMINGHAM LADYWOOD
E. 70,977 T. 33,246 (46.84%) Lab. hold
Rt. Hon. Clare Short, Lab.   17,262
Ayoub Khan, LD   10,461
Philippa Stroud, C.   3,515
Lynette Nazemi-Afshar, UKIP   2,008
Lab. maj. 6,801 (20.46%)
20.11% swing Lab. to LD
(2001: Lab. maj. 18,143 (57.61%))

BIRMINGHAM NORTHFIELD
E. 54,868 T. 31,056 (56.60%) Lab. hold
Richard Burden, Lab.   15,419
Vicky Ford, C.   8,965
Trevor Sword, LD   4,171
Mark Cattell, BNP   1,278
Gillian Chant, UKIP   641
Richard Rodgers, Good   428
Louise Houldey, Soc. Alt.   120
Francis Sweeney, WRP   34
Lab. maj. 6,454 (20.78%)
2.81% swing Lab. to C.
(2001: Lab. maj. 7,798 (26.40%))

BIRMINGHAM PERRY BARR
E. 70,126 T. 38,911 (55.49%) Lab. hold
Khalid Mahmood, Lab.   18,269
Jon Hunt, LD   10,321
Naweed Khan, C.   6,513
Dr Mohammad Naseem, Respect   2,173
Rajinder Clair, Soc. Lab.   890
Bimla Balu, UKIP   745
Lab. maj. 7,948 (20.43%)
1.61% swing Lab. to LD
(2001: Lab. maj. 8,753 (23.39%))

BIRMINGHAM SELLY OAK
E. 70,162 T. 41,740 (59.49%) Lab. hold
Dr Lynne Jones, Lab.   19,226
Joe Tildesley, C.   10,375
Richard Brighton, LD   9,591
Barney Smith, Green   1,581
Ronan Burnett, UKIP   967
Lab. maj. 8,851 (21.21%)
2.29% swing Lab. to C.
(2001: Lab. maj. 10,339 (25.78%))

**BIRMINGHAM SPARKBROOK &
SMALL HEATH**
E. 73,721 T. 38,192 (51.81%) Lab. hold
Roger Godsiff, Lab.   13,787
Salma Yaqoob, Respect   10,498
Talib Hussain, LD   7,727
Sameer Mirza, C.   3,480
Jennifer Brookes, UKIP   1,342
Ian Jamieson, Green   855
Abdul Chaudhary, Ind.   503
Lab. maj. 3,289 (8.61%)
24.4% swing Lab. to Respect
(2001: Lab. maj. 16,246 (44.33%))

BIRMINGHAM YARDLEY
E. 50,975 T. 29,431 (57.74%) LD gain
*John Hemming, LD   13,648
Jayne Innes, Lab.   10,976
Paul Uppal, C.   2,970
Robert Purcell, BNP   1,523
Mohammed Yaqub, UKIP   314
LD maj. 2,672 (9.08%)
8.83% swing Lab. to LD
(2001: Lab. maj. 2,578 (8.59%))

BISHOP AUCKLAND
E. 67,534 T. 38,128 (56.46%) Lab. hold
*Helen Goodman, Lab.   19,065
Chris Foote-Wood, LD   9,018
Richard Bell, C.   8,736
Margaret Hopson, UKIP   1,309
Lab. maj. 10,047 (26.35%)
8.36% swing Lab. to LD
(2001: Lab. maj. 13,926 (36.12%))

BLABY
E. 75,444 T. 49,388 (65.46%)   C. hold
Andrew Robathan, C.   22,487
David Morgan, Lab.   14,614
Jeff Stephenson, LD   9,382
Michael Robinson, BNP   1,704
Delroy Young, UKIP   1,201
C. maj. 7,873 (15.94%)
1.45% swing Lab. to C.
(2001: C. maj. 6,209 (13.03%))

BLACKBURN
E. 73,494 T. 41,805 (56.88%) Lab. hold
Rt. Hon. Jack Straw, Lab.   17,562
Imtiaz Ameen, C.   9,553
Tony Melia, LD   8,608
Nicholas Holt, BNP   2,263
Craig Murray, Ind.   2,082
Dorothy Baxter, UKIP   954
Graham Carter, Green   783
Lab. maj. 8,009 (19.16%)
1.90% swing Lab. to C.
(2001: Lab. maj. 9,249 (22.85%))

**BLACKPOOL NORTH &
FLEETWOOD**
E. 74,975 T. 43,290 (57.74%) Lab. hold
Joan Humble, Lab.   20,620
Gavin Williamson, C.   15,558
Steven Bate, LD   5,533
Roy Hopwood, UKIP   1,579
Lab. maj. 5,062 (11.69%)
0.87% swing Lab. to C.
(2001: Lab. maj. 5,721 (13.44%))

BLACKPOOL SOUTH
E. 73,529 T. 38,342 (52.15%) Lab. hold
Gordon Marsden, Lab.   19,375
Michael Winstanley, C.   11,453
Doreen Holt, LD   5,552
Roy Goodwin, BNP   1,113
John Porter, UKIP   849
Lab. maj. 7,922 (20.66%)
0.32% swing Lab. to C.
(2001: Lab. maj. 8,262 (21.30%))

BLAYDON
E. 62,413 T. 39,053 (62.57%) Lab. hold
*David Anderson, Lab.   20,120
Peter Maughan, LD   14,785
Dorothy Luckhurst, C.   3,129
Norman Endacott, UKIP   1,019
Lab. maj. 5,335 (13.66%)
3.70% swing Lab. to LD
(2001: Lab. maj. 7,809 (21.06%))

BLYTH VALLEY
E. 63,640 T. 35,773 (56.21%) Lab. hold
Ronnie Campbell, Lab.   19,659
Jeffrey Reid, LD   11,132
Michael Windridge, C.   4,982
Lab. maj. 8,527 (23.84%)
5.72% swing Lab. to LD
(2001: Lab. maj. 12,188 (35.28%))

**BOGNOR REGIS &
LITTLEHAMPTON**
E. 65,591 T. 40,747 (62.12%)   C. hold
Nick Gibb, C.   18,183
George O'Neill, Lab.   10,361
Simon McDougall, LD   8,927
Adrian Lithgow, UKIP   3,276
C. maj. 7,822 (19.20%)
2.36% swing Lab. to C.
(2001: C. maj. 5,643 (14.48%))

BOLSOVER
E. 67,568 T. 38,699 (57.27%) Lab. hold
Dennis Skinner, Lab.   25,217
Denise Hawksworth, LD   6,780
Hasan Imam, C.   6,702
Lab. maj. 18,437 (47.64%)
4.53% swing Lab. to LD
(2001: Lab. maj. 18,777 (49.06%))

BOLTON NORTH EAST
E. 67,394 T. 36,911 (54.77%) Lab. hold
David Crausby, Lab.   16,874
Paul Brierley, C.   12,771
Adam Killeya, LD   6,044
Kevin Epsom, UKIP   640
Alan Ainscow, Veritas   375
Lynne Lowe, Soc. Lab.   207
Lab. maj. 4,103 (11.12%)
5.25% swing Lab. to C.
(2001: Lab. maj. 8,422 (21.62%))

BOLTON SOUTH EAST
E. 63,697 T. 31,850 (50.00%) Lab. hold
Dr Brian Iddon, Lab.   18,129
Deborah Dunleavy, C.   6,491
Frank Harasiwka, LD   6,047
Florence Bates, UKIP   840
David Jones, Veritas   343
Lab. maj. 11,638 (36.54%)
0.57% swing Lab. to C.
(2001: Lab. maj. 12,871 (37.69%))

BOLTON WEST
E. 63,836 T. 40,543 (63.51%) Lab. hold
Rt. Hon. Ruth Kelly, Lab.   17,239
Philip Allott, C.   15,175
Tim Perkins, LD   7,241
Marjorie Ford, UKIP   524
Michael Ford, Veritas   290
Kate Griggs, XPP   74
Lab. maj. 2,064 (5.09%)
4.15% swing Lab. to C.
(2001: Lab. maj. 5,518 (13.39%))

BOOTLE
E. 53,700 T. 25,622 (47.71%) Lab. hold
Joe Benton, Lab.   19,345
Chris Newby, LD   2,988
Wafik Moustafa, C.   1,580
Paul Nuttall, UKIP   1,054
Peter Glover, Soc. Alt.   655
Lab. maj. 16,357 (63.84%)
2.59% swing Lab. to LD
(2001: Lab. maj. 19,043 (69.01%))

BOSTON & SKEGNESS
E. 71,212 T. 41,869 (58.79%)   C. hold
Mark Simmonds, C.   19,329
Paul Kenny, Lab.   13,422
Dr Richard Horsnell, UKIP   4,024
Alan Riley, LD   3,649
Wendy Russell, BNP   1,025
Marcus Petz, Green   420
C. maj. 5,907 (14.11%)
6.42% swing Lab. to C.
(2001: C. maj. 515 (1.28%))

BOSWORTH
E. 71,596 T. 47,499 (66.34%) C. hold
David Tredinnick, C. 20,212
Rupert Heid, Lab. 14,893
James Moore, LD 10,528
Denis Walker, UKIP 1,866
C. maj. 5,319 (11.20%)
3.07% swing Lab. to C.
(2001: C. maj. 2,280 (5.05%))

BOURNEMOUTH EAST
E. 63,426 T. 37,599 (59.28%) C. hold
*Tobias Ellwood, C. 16,925
Andrew Garratt, LD 11,681
David Stokes, Lab. 7,191
Thomas Collier, UKIP 1,802
C. maj. 5,244 (13.95%)
2.18% swing LD to C.
(2001: C. maj. 3,434 (9.59%))

BOURNEMOUTH WEST
E. 63,658 T. 33,924 (53.29%) C. hold
Sir John Butterfill, C. 14,057
Richard Renaut, LD 10,026
Dafydd Williams, Lab. 7,824
Michael Maclaire-Hillier, UKIP 2,017
C. maj. 4,031 (11.88%)
2.90% swing C. to LD
(2001: C. maj. 4,718 (14.02%))

BRACKNELL
E. 80,657 T. 51,141 (63.41%) C. hold
Rt. Hon. Andrew Mackay, C. 25,412
Janet Keene, Lab. 13,376
Lee Glendon, LD 10,128
Vincent Pearson, UKIP 1,818
Dominica Roberts, Ind. 407
C. maj. 12,036 (23.53%)
4.95% swing Lab. to C.
(2001: C. maj. 6,713 (13.64%))

BRADFORD NORTH
E. 64,515 T. 34,397 (53.32%) Lab. hold
Terry Rooney, Lab. 14,622
David Ward, LD 11,111
Teck Khong, C. 5,569
Lynda Cromie, BNP 2,061
Steve Schofield, Green 560
Umit Yildiz, Respect 474
Lab. maj. 3,511 (10.21%)
9.88% swing Lab. to LD
(2001: Lab. maj. 8,969 (25.61%))

BRADFORD SOUTH
E. 67,576 T. 36,605 (54.17%) Lab. hold
Gerry Sutcliffe, Lab. 17,954
Geraldine Carter, C. 8,787
Mike Doyle, LD 5,334
Dr James Lewthwaite, BNP 2,862
Derek Curtis, Green 695
Jason Smith, UKIP 552
Therese Muchewicz, Veritas 421
Lab. maj. 9,167 (25.04%)
1.23% swing Lab. to C.
(2001: Lab. maj. 9,662 (27.50%))

BRADFORD WEST
E. 67,356 T. 36,369 (54.00%) Lab. hold
Marsha Singh, Lab. 14,570
Haroon Rashid, C. 11,544
Mukhtar Ali, LD 6,620
Paul Cromie, BNP 2,525
Parvez Darr, Green 1,110
Lab. maj. 3,026 (8.32%)
1.27% swing Lab. to C.
(2001: Lab. maj. 4,165 (10.85%))

BRAINTREE
E. 80,458 T. 53,055 (65.94%) C. gain
*Brooks Newmark, C. 23,597
Alan Hurst, Lab. 19,704
Peter Turner, LD 7,037
James Abbott, Green 1,308
Roger Lord, UKIP 1,181
Buster Michael Nolan, Ind. 228
C. maj. 3,893 (7.34%)
4.02% swing Lab. to C.
(2001: Lab. maj. 358 (0.71%))

BRENT EAST
E. 56,227 T. 31,068 (55.25%) LD hold
Sarah Teather, LD 14,764
Yasmin Qureshi, Lab. 12,052
Kwasi Kwarteng, C. 3,193
Shahrar Ali, Green 905
Michelle Weininger, Ind. 115
Rainbow George Weiss, Vote Dream 39
LD maj. 2,712 (8.73%)
30.68% swing Lab. to LD
(2003 Sept. by-election: LD maj. 1,118
(5.36%))
(2001: Lab. maj. 13,047 (45.00%))

BRENT NORTH
E. 60,148 T. 35,682 (59.32%) Lab. hold
Barry Gardiner, Lab. 17,420
Bob Blackman, C. 11,779
Havard Hughes, LD 5,672
Babar Ahmad, Progress 685
Rainbow George Weiss, Vote Dream 126
Lab. maj. 5,641 (15.81%)
7.13% swing Lab. to C.
(2001: Lab. maj. 10,205 (30.07%))

BRENT SOUTH
E. 56,508 T. 29,764 (52.67%) Lab. hold
*Dawn Butler, Lab. 17,501
James Allie, LD 6,175
Rishi Saha, C. 4,485
Rowan Langley, Green 957
Shaun Wallace, Ind. 297
Rocky Fernandez, Ind. 288
Rainbow George Weiss, Vote Dream 61
Lab. maj. 11,326 (38.05%)
12.20% swing Lab. to LD
(2001: Lab. maj. 17,380 (60.69%))

BRENTFORD & ISLEWORTH
E. 84,366 T. 46,017 (54.54%) Lab. hold
Ann Keen, Lab. 18,329
Alexander Northcote, C. 13,918
Andrew Dakers, LD 10,477
John Hunt, Green 1,652
Phillip Andrews, Community 1,118
Michael Stoneman, NF 523
Lab. maj. 4,411 (9.59%)
6.80% swing Lab. to C.
(2001: Lab. maj. 10,318 (23.18%))

BRENTWOOD & ONGAR
E. 64,496 T. 44,145 (68.45%) C. hold
Eric Pickles, C. 23,609
Gavin Stollar, LD 11,997
John Adams, Lab. 6,579
Stuart Gulleford, UKIP 1,805
Anthony Appleton, Ind. 155
C. maj. 11,612 (26.30%)
1.91% swing LD to C.
(2001: C. maj. 2,821 (6.48%))

BRIDGWATER
E. 75,790 T. 48,109 (63.48%) C. hold
Ian Liddell-Grainger, C. 21,240
Matthew Burchell, Lab. 12,771
James Main, LD 10,940
Ray Weinstein, UKIP 1,767
Charlie Graham, Green 1,391
C. maj. 8,469 (17.60%)
1.96% swing Lab. to C.
(2001: C. maj. 4,987 (10.42%))

BRIGG & GOOLE
E. 67,364 T. 42,578 (63.21%) Lab. hold
Ian Cawsey, Lab. 19,257
Matthew Bean, C. 16,363
Gary Johnson, LD 5,690
Stephen Martin, UKIP 1,268
Lab. maj. 2,894 (6.80%)
1.43% swing Lab. to C.
(2001: Lab. maj. 3,961 (9.65%))

BRIGHTON KEMPTOWN
E. 65,985 T. 39,719 (60.19%) Lab. hold
Dr Desmond Turner, Lab. 15,858
Judith Symes, C. 13,121
Marina Pepper, LD 6,560
Simon Williams, Green 2,800
Dr James Chamberlain-Webber, UKIP 758
Caroline O'Reilly, PPN-V 172
John McLeod, Soc. Lab. 163
Elaine Cook, Ind. 127
Phil Clarke, Soc. Alt. 113
Gene Dobbs, Ind. 47
Lab. maj. 2,737 (6.89%)
2.83% swing Lab. to C.
(2001: Lab. maj. 4,922 (12.56%))

BRIGHTON PAVILION
E. 68,087 T. 43,578 (64.00%)
Lab. (Co-op) hold
David Lepper, Lab. (Co-op) 15,427
Mike Weatherley, C. 10,397
Keith Taylor, Green 9,571
Hazel Thorpe, LD 7,171
Kimberley Crisp-Comotto, UKIP 508
Tony Greenstein, Green Soc. 188
Ian Fyvie, Soc. Lab. 152
Christopher Rooke, Ind. 122
Keith Jago, Ind. 42
Lab. (Co-op) maj. 5,030 (11.55%)
6.06% swing Lab. (Co-op) to C.
(2001: Lab. (Co-op) maj. 9,643
(23.68%))

BRISTOL EAST
E. 68,096 T. 41,720 (61.27%) Lab. hold
*Kerry McCarthy, Lab. 19,152
Philip James, LD 10,531
Julia Manning, C. 8,787
Arjuna Krishna-Das, Green 1,586
Jean Smith, UKIP 1,132
Paulette North, Respect 532
Lab. maj. 8,621 (20.66%)
8.59% swing Lab. to LD
(2001: Lab. maj. 13,392 (33.20%))

BRISTOL NORTH WEST
E. 77,703 T. 47,492 (61.12%)
                    Lab. (Co-op) hold
Dr Doug Naysmith, Lab. (Co-op) 22,192
Alastair Watson, C.   13,230
Bob Hoyle, LD   9,545
Christopher Lees, UKIP   1,132
Michael Blundell, EDP   828
Graeme Jones, Soc. Alt.   565
Lab. (Co-op) maj. 8,962 (18.87%)
2.28% swing Lab. (Co-op) to C.
(2001: Lab. (Co-op) maj. 11,087
(23.74%))

BRISTOL SOUTH
E. 70,835 T. 42,328 (59.76%) Lab. hold
Rt. Hon. Dawn Primarolo, Lab.   20,778
Kay Barnard, LD   9,636
Graham Hill, C.   8,466
Charlie Bolton, Green   2,127
Mark Dent, UKIP   1,321
Lab. maj. 11,142 (26.32%)
7.86% swing Lab. to LD
(2001: Lab. maj. 14,181 (34.61%))

BRISTOL WEST
E. 81,382 T. 57,396 (70.53%) LD gain
*Stephen Williams, LD   21,987
Valerie Davey, Lab.   16,859
David Martin, C.   15,429
Justin Quinnell, Green   2,163
Simon Muir, UKIP   439
Bernard Kennedy, Soc. Lab.   329
Doug Reid, Baths   190
LD maj. 5,128 (8.93%)
8.44% swing Lab. to LD
(2001: Lab. maj. 4,426 (7.95%))

BROMLEY & CHISLEHURST
E. 71,173 T. 46,137 (64.82%) C. hold
Rt. Hon. Eric Forth, C.   23,583
Rachel Reeves, Lab.   10,241
Peter Brooks, LD   9,368
David Hooper, UKIP   1,475
Ann Garrett, Green   1,470
C. maj. 13,342 (28.92%)
4.01% swing Lab. to C.
(2001: C. maj. 9,037 (20.90%))

BROMSGROVE
E. 70,762 T. 47,810 (67.56%) C. hold
Julie Kirkbride, C.   24,387
David Jones, Lab.   14,307
Sue Haswell, LD   7,197
Paul Buckingham, UKIP   1,919
C. maj. 10,080 (21.08%)
1.63% swing Lab. to C.
(2001: C. maj. 8,138 (17.81%))

BROXBOURNE
E. 68,106 T. 40,628 (59.65%) C. hold
*Charles Walker, C.   21,878
Jamie Bolden, Lab.   10,369
Andrew Porrer, LD   4,973
Dr Andrew Emerson, BNP   1,929
Martin Harvey, UKIP   1,479
C. maj. 11,509 (28.33%)
2.28% swing Lab. to C.
(2001: C. maj. 8,993 (23.76%))

BROXTOWE
E. 71,121 T. 48,806 (68.62%) Lab. hold
Dr Nick Palmer, Lab.   20,457
Bob Seely, C.   18,161
David Watts, LD   7,837
Paul Anderson, Green   896
Patricia Wolfe, UKIP   695
Damian Hockney, Veritas   590
Mark Gregory, Ind.   170
Lab. maj. 2,296 (4.70%)
3.64% swing Lab. to C.
(2001: Lab. maj. 5,873 (11.98%))

BUCKINGHAM
E. 70,265 T. 48,307 (68.75%) C. hold
John Bercow, C.   27,748
David Greene, Lab.   9,619
Luke Croydon, LD   9,508
David Williams, UKIP   1,432
C. maj. 18,129 (37.53%)
4.05% swing Lab. to C.
(2001: C. maj. 13,325 (29.43%))

BURNLEY
E. 65,869 T. 38,983 (59.18%) Lab. hold
*Kitty Ussher, Lab.   14,999
Gordon Birtwistle, LD   9,221
Harry Brooks, Burnley   5,786
Yousuf Miah, C.   4,206
Len Starr, BNP   4,003
Dr Jeff Slater, Ind.   392
Robert McDowell, UKIP   376
Lab. maj. 5,778 (14.82%)
9.15% swing Lab. to LD
(2001: Lab. maj. 10,498 (28.46%))

BURTON
E. 78,556 T. 47,882 (60.95%) Lab. hold
Janet Dean, Lab.   19,701
Adrian Pepper, C.   18,280
Sandra Johnson, LD   6,236
Julie Russell, BNP   1,840
Philip Lancaster, UKIP   913
Brian Buxton, Veritas   912
Lab. maj. 1,421 (2.97%)
3.73% swing Lab. to C.
(2001: Lab. maj. 4,849 (10.44%))

BURY NORTH
E. 72,268 T. 44,439 (61.49%) Lab. hold
David Chaytor, Lab.   19,130
David Nuttall, C.   16,204
Wilf Davison, LD   6,514
Stewart Clough, BNP   1,790
Philip Silver, UKIP   476
Ryan O'Neill, Soc. Lab.   172
Ian Upton, Veritas   153
Lab. maj. 2,926 (6.58%)
4.00% swing Lab. to C.
(2001: Lab. maj. 6,532 (14.58%))

BURY SOUTH
E. 66,898 T. 39,154 (58.53%) Lab. hold
Ivan Lewis, Lab.   19,741
Alex Williams, C.   10,829
Victor D'Albert, LD   6,968
Jim Greenhalgh, UKIP   1,059
Yvonne Hossack, Ind.   557
Lab. maj. 8,912 (22.76%)
4.77% swing Lab. to C.
(2001: Lab. maj. 12,772 (32.30%))

BURY ST EDMUNDS
E. 79,658 T. 52,619 (66.06%) C. hold
David Ruffley, C.   24,332
David Monaghan, Lab.   14,402
David Chappell, LD   10,423
Dr John Howlett, UKIP   1,859
Graham Manning, Green   1,603
C. maj. 9,930 (18.87%)
6.95% swing Lab. to C.
(2001: C. maj. 2,503 (4.98%))

CALDER VALLEY
E. 71,325 T. 47,770 (66.98%) Lab. hold
Christine McCafferty, Lab.   18,426
Liz Truss, C.   17,059
Liz Ingleton, LD   9,027
John Gregory, BNP   1,887
Paul Palmer, Green   1,371
Lab. maj. 1,367 (2.86%)
1.83% swing Lab. to C.
(2001: Lab. maj. 3,094 (6.52%))

CAMBERWELL & PECKHAM
E. 55,739 T. 28,991 (52.01%) Lab. hold
Rt. Hon. Harriet Harman, Lab.   18,933
Richard Porter, LD   5,450
Jessica Lee, C.   2,841
Paul Ingram, Green   1,172
Derek Penhallow, UKIP   350
Margaret Sharkey, Soc. Lab.   132
Sanjay Kulkarni, WRP   113
Lab. maj. 13,483 (46.51%)
4.88% swing Lab. to LD
(2001: Lab. maj. 14,123 (56.26%))

CAMBRIDGE
E. 70,154 T. 43,569 (62.10%) LD gain
*David Howarth, LD   19,152
Anne Campbell, Lab.   14,813
Ian Lyon, C.   7,193
Martin Lucas-Smith, Green   1,245
Helene Davies, UKIP   569
Tom Woodcock, Respect   477
Suzon Forscey-Moore, Ind.   60
Graham Wilkinson, Ind.   60
LD maj. 4,339 (9.96%)
14.99% swing Lab. to LD
(2001: Lab. maj. 8,579 (20.03%))

CAMBRIDGESHIRE NORTH EAST
E. 85,079 T. 50,877 (59.80%) C. hold
Malcolm Moss, C.   24,181
Ffinlo Costain, Lab.   15,280
Alan Dean, LD   8,693
Leonard Baynes, UKIP   2,723
C. maj. 8,901 (17.50%)
2.12% swing Lab. to C.
(2001: C. maj. 6,373 (13.26%))

CAMBRIDGESHIRE NORTH WEST
E. 79,694 T. 49,092 (61.60%) C. hold
*Shailesh Vara, C.   22,504
Ayfer Orhan, Lab.   12,671
John Souter, LD   11,232
Robert Brown, UKIP   2,685
C. maj. 9,833 (20.03%)
0.80% swing Lab. to C.
(2001: C. maj. 8,101 (18.43%))

CAMBRIDGESHIRE SOUTH
E. 77,022 T. 52,648 (68.35%) C. hold
Andrew Lansley, C.   23,676
Andrew Dickson, LD   15,675
Sandra Wilson, Lab.   10,189
Robin Page, UKIP   1,556
Simon Saggers, Green   1,552
C. maj. 8,001 (15.20%)
1.09% swing C. to LD
(2001: C. maj. 8,403 (17.38%))

CAMBRIDGESHIRE SOUTH EAST
E. 85,901 T. 56,060 (65.26%) C. hold
James Paice, C.   26,374
Jonathan Chatfield, LD   17,750
Fiona Ross, Lab.   11,936
C. maj. 8,624 (15.38%)
0.97% swing C. to LD
(2001: C. maj. 8,990 (17.33%))

CANNOCK CHASE
E. 75,194 T. 43,155 (57.39%) Lab. hold
Dr Tony Wright, Lab.   22,139
Ian Collard, C.   12,912
Jenny Pinkett, LD   5,934
Roy Jenkins, UKIP   2,170
Lab. maj. 9,227 (21.38%)
2.34% swing Lab. to C.
(2001: Lab. maj. 10,704 (26.07%))

CANTERBURY
E. 72,046 T. 47,587 (66.05%) C. hold
Julian Brazier, C.   21,113
Alex Hilton, Lab.   13,642
Jenny Barnard-Langston, LD   10,059
Geoff Meaden, Green   1,521
John Moore, UKIP   926
Rocky van de Benderskum, LCA   326
C. maj. 7,471 (15.70%)
5.56% swing Lab. to C.
(2001: C. maj. 2,069 (4.58%))

CARLISLE
E. 59,508 T. 35,394 (59.48%) Lab. hold
Eric Martlew, Lab.   17,019
Mike Mitchelson, C.   11,324
Steven Tweedie, LD   5,916
Steven Cochrane, UKIP   792
Lezley Gibson, LCA   343
Lab. maj. 5,695 (16.09%)
0.12% swing Lab. to C.
(2001: Lab. maj. 5,702 (16.33%))

CARSHALTON & WALLINGTON
E. 67,844 T. 43,061 (63.47%) LD hold
Tom Brake, LD   17,357
Ken Andrew, C.   16,289
Andrew Theobald, Lab.   7,396
Francis Day, UKIP   1,111
Bob Steel, Green   908
LD maj. 1,068 (2.48%)
4.36% swing LD to C.
(2001: LD maj. 4,547 (11.20%))

CASTLE POINT
E. 69,480 T. 45,802 (65.92%) C. hold
Dr Robert Spink, C.   22,118
Luke Akehurst, Lab.   13,917
James Sandbach, LD   4,719
Neil Hamper, UKIP   3,431
Irene Willis, Green   1,617
C. maj. 8,201 (17.91%)
7.71% swing Lab. to C.
(2001: C. maj. 985 (2.48%))

CHARNWOOD
E. 76,274 T. 50,616 (66.36%) C. hold
Rt. Hon. Stephen Dorrell, C.   23,571
Richard Robinson, Lab.   14,762
Sue King, LD   9,057
Andrew Holders, BNP   1,737
Jamie Bye, UKIP   1,489
C. maj. 8,809 (17.40%)
0.68% swing Lab. to C.
(2001: C. maj. 7,739 (16.03%))

CHATHAM & AYLESFORD
E. 70,515 T. 42,080 (59.68%) Lab. hold
Jonathan Shaw, Lab.   18,387
Anne Jobson, C.   16,055
Debra Enever, LD   5,744
Jeffrey King, UKIP   1,226
Michael Russell, Eng. Dem.   668
Lab. maj. 2,332 (5.54%)
2.69% swing Lab. to C.
(2001: Lab. maj. 4,340 (10.92%))

CHEADLE
E. 68,123 T. 47,437 (69.63%) LD hold
Patsy Calton, LD   23,189
Stephen Day, C.   19,169
Martin Miller, Lab.   4,169
Vincent Cavanagh, UKIP   489
Richard Chadfield, BNP   421
LD maj. 4,020 (8.47%)
4.20% swing C. to LD
(2001: LD maj. 33 (0.08%))

CHELMSFORD WEST
E. 82,489 T. 51,052 (61.89%) C. hold
Simon Burns, C.   22,946
Stephen Robinson, LD   13,326
Russell Kennedy, Lab.   13,236
Kenneth Wedon, UKIP   1,544
C. maj. 9,620 (18.84%)
0.18% swing C. to LD
(2001: C. maj. 6,261 (13.01%))

CHELTENHAM
E. 71,541 T. 43,621 (60.97%) LD hold
*Martin Horwood, LD   18,122
Dr Vanessa Gearson, C.   15,819
Christopher Evans, Lab.   4,988
Dr Robert Hodges, Ind.   2,651
Keith Bessant, Green   908
Niall Warry, UKIP   608
Dancing Ken Hanks, Loony   525
LD maj. 2,303 (5.28%)
3.64% swing LD to C.
(2001: LD maj. 5,255 (12.56%))

CHESHAM & AMERSHAM
E. 69,217 T. 47,097 (68.04%) C. hold
Cheryl Gillan, C.   25,619
John Ford, LD   11,821
Rupa Huq, Lab.   6,610
Nick Wilkins, Green   1,656
David Samuel-Camps, UKIP   1,391
C. maj. 13,798 (29.30%)
1.53% swing LD to C.
(2001: C. maj. 11,882 (26.24%))

CHESTER, CITY OF
E. 69,785 T. 44,903 (64.34%) Lab. hold
Christine Russell, Lab.   17,458
Paul Offer, C.   16,543
Mia Jones, LD   9,818
Allan Weddell, UKIP   776
Ed Abrams, Eng. Dem.   308
Lab. maj. 915 (2.04%)
6.66% swing Lab. to C.
(2001: Lab. maj. 6,894 (15.36%))

CHESTERFIELD
E. 74,007 T. 44,121 (59.62%) LD hold
Paul Holmes, LD   20,875
Simon Rich, Lab.   17,830
Mark Kreling, C.   3,605
Christopher Brady, UKIP   997
Ian Jerram, Eng. Dem.   814
LD maj. 3,045 (6.90%)
0.54% swing Lab. to LD
(2001: LD maj. 2,586 (5.82%))

CHICHESTER
E. 78,645 T. 52,401 (66.63%) C. hold
Andrew Tyrie, C.   25,302
Alan Hilliar, LD   14,442
Jonathan Austin, Lab.   9,632
Douglas Denny, UKIP   3,025
C. maj. 10,860 (20.72%)
1.09% swing C. to LD
(2001: C. maj. 11,355 (22.93%))

CHINGFORD & WOODFORD
GREEN
E. 61,386 T. 38,648 (62.96%) C. hold
Rt. Hon. Iain Duncan Smith, C.   20,555
Simon Wright, Lab.   9,914
John Beanse, LD   6,832
Michael McGough, UKIP   1,078
Barry White, Ind.   269
C. maj. 10,641 (27.53%)
6.35% swing to C.
(2001: C. maj. 5,487 (14.84%))

CHIPPING BARNET
E. 66,143 T. 42,381 (64.07%) C. hold
*Theresa Villiers, C.   19,744
Pauline Coakley-Webb, Lab.   13,784
Sean Hooker, LD   6,671
Audrey Poppy, Green   1,199
Victor Kaye, UKIP   924
Rainbow George Weiss, Vote Dream   59
C. maj. 5,960 (14.06%)
3.85% swing Lab. to C.
(2001: C. maj. 2,701 (6.36%))

CHORLEY
E. 78,838 T. 49,569 (62.87%) Lab. hold
Lindsay Hoyle, Lab.   25,131
Simon Mallett, C.   17,506
Alexander Wilson-Fletcher, LD   6,932
Lab. maj. 7,625 (15.38%)
1.11% swing Lab. to C.
(2001: Lab. maj. 8,444 (17.61%))

CHRISTCHURCH
E. 74,109 T. 51,565 (69.58%) C. hold
Christopher Chope, C.   28,208
Leslie Coman, LD   12,649
Jim King, Lab.   8,051
David Hughes, UKIP   2,657
C. maj. 15,559 (30.17%)
1.42% swing LD to C.
(2001: C. maj. 13,544 (27.32%))

CITIES OF LONDON &
WESTMINSTER
E. 72,577 T. 36,487 (50.27%) C. hold
Mark Field, C. 17,260
Hywel Lloyd, Lab. 9,165
Marie-Louise Rossi, LD 7,306
Tristan Smith, Green 1,544
Colin Merton, UKIP 399
Brian Haw, Ind. 298
Jill McLachlan, CPA 246
David Harris, Veritas 218
Cass Jean-Claude Cass-Horne, Ind. 51
C. maj. 8,095 (22.19%)
4.47% swing Lab. to C.
(2001: C. maj. 4,499 (13.24%))

CLEETHORPES
E. 70,746 T. 43,589 (61.61%) Lab. hold
Shona McIsaac, Lab. 18,889
Martin Vickers, C. 16,247
Geoff Lowis, LD 6,437
Bill Hardie, UKIP 2,016
Lab. maj. 2,642 (6.06%)
3.59% swing Lab. to C.
(2001: Lab. maj. 5,620 (13.25%))

COLCHESTER
E. 79,010 T. 44,899 (56.83%) LD hold
Bob Russell, LD 21,145
Kevin Bentley, C. 14,868
Laura Bruni, Lab. 8,886
LD maj. 6,277 (13.98%)
0.64% swing C. to LD
(2001: LD maj. 5,553 (12.70%))

COLNE VALLEY
E. 74,121 T. 48,920 (66.00%) Lab. hold
Kali Mountford, Lab. 17,536
Maggie Throup, C. 16,035
Elisabeth Wilson, LD 11,822
Barry Fowler, BNP 1,430
Lesley Hedges, Green 1,295
Helen Martinek, Veritas 543
Ian Mumford, Loony 259
Lab. maj. 1,501 (3.07%)
3.40% swing Lab. to C.
(2001: Lab. maj. 4,639 (9.87%))

CONGLETON
E. 72,770 T. 46,682 (64.15%) C. hold
Lady Ann Winterton, C. 21,189
Nicholas Milton, Lab. 12,943
Eleanor Key, LD 12,550
C. maj. 8,246 (17.66%)
0.92% swing Lab. to C.
(2001: C. maj. 7,134 (15.82%))

COPELAND
E. 54,206 T. 33,757 (62.28%) Lab. hold
*Jamie Reed, Lab. 17,033
Chris Whiteside, C. 10,713
Frank Hollowell, LD 3,880
Edward Caley-Knowles, UKIP 735
Brian Earley, Ind. 734
Alan Mossop, Eng. Dem. 662
Lab. maj. 6,320 (18.72%)
2.22% swing C. to Lab.
(2001: Lab. maj. 4,964 (14.28%))

CORBY
E. 73,000 T. 48,527 (66.48%)
Lab. (Co-op) hold
Phil Hope, Lab. (Co-op) 20,913
Andrew Griffith, C. 19,396
David Radcliffe, LD 6,184
Ian Gillman, UKIP 1,278
Steve Carey, Soc. Lab. 499
John Morris, Ind. 257
Lab. (Co-op) maj. 1,517 (3.13%)
4.47% swing Lab. (Co-op) to C.
(2001: Lab. (Co-op) maj. 5,700
(12.07%))

CORNWALL NORTH
E. 86,841 T. 55,982 (64.46%) LD hold
*Dan Rogerson, LD 23,842
Mark Formosa, C. 20,766
David Acton, Lab. 6,636
David Campbell-Bannerman, UKIP
3,063
Dick Cole, Meb. Ker. 1,351
Alan Eastwood, Veritas 324
LD maj. 3,076 (5.49%)
6.36% swing LD to C.
(2001: LD maj. 9,832 (18.21%))

CORNWALL SOUTH EAST
E. 80,704 T. 53,455 (66.24%) LD hold
Colin Breed, LD 24,986
Ashley Gray, C. 18,479
Colin Binley, Lab. 6,069
David Lucas, UKIP 2,693
Graham Sandercock, Meb. Ker. 769
Anne Assheton-Salton, Veritas 459
LD maj. 6,507 (12.17%)
0.89% swing C. to LD
(2001: LD maj. 5,375 (10.39%))

COTSWOLD
E. 71,039 T. 47,351 (66.65%) C. hold
Geoffrey Clifton-Brown, C. 23,326
Philip Beckerlegge, LD 13,638
Mark Dempsey, Lab. 8,457
Richard Buckley, UKIP 1,538
James Derieg, Ind. 392
C. maj. 9,688 (20.46%)
2.80% swing C. to LD
(2001: C. maj. 11,983 (26.06%))

COVENTRY NORTH EAST
E. 70,225 T. 37,195 (52.97%) Lab. hold
Rt. Hon. Robert Ainsworth, Lab. 21,178
Jaswant Singh Birdi, C. 6,956
Russell Field, LD 6,123
Dave Nellist, Soc. Alt. 1,874
Paul Sootheran, UKIP 1,064
Lab. maj. 14,222 (38.24%)
2.02% swing Lab. to C.
(2001: Lab. maj. 15,751 (42.27%))

COVENTRY NORTH WEST
E. 73,180 T. 43,438 (59.36%) Lab. hold
Geoffrey Robinson, Lab. 20,942
Brian Connell, C. 11,627
Iona Anderson, LD 7,932
David Clarke, BNP 1,556
Sandra List, UKIP 766
Nicola Downes, Soc. Alt. 615
Lab. maj. 9,315 (21.44%)
2.06% swing Lab. to C.
(2001: Lab. maj. 10,874 (25.56%))

COVENTRY SOUTH
E. 68,884 T. 40,685 (59.06%) Lab. hold
Jim Cunningham, Lab. 18,649
Heather Wheeler, C. 12,394
Vincent McKee, LD 7,228
Rob Windsor, Soc. Alt. 1,097
William Brown, UKIP 829
Irene Rogers, Ind. 344
James Rooney, FF 144
Lab. maj. 6,255 (15.37%)
2.64% swing Lab. to C.
(2001: Lab. maj. 8,279 (20.65%))

CRAWLEY
E. 71,911 T. 41,973 (58.37%) Lab. hold
Laura Moffatt, Lab. 16,411
Henry Smith, C. 16,374
Rupert Sheard, LD 6,503
Richard Trower, BNP 1,277
Ronald Walters, UKIP 935
Robin Burnham, Dem. Soc. All. 263
Arshad Khan, JP 210
Lab. maj. 37 (0.09%)
8.52% swing Lab. to C.
(2001: Lab. maj. 6,770 (17.13%))

CREWE & NANTWICH
E. 72,472 T. 43,485 (60.00%) Lab. hold
Gwyneth Dunwoody, Lab. 21,240
Eveleigh Moore-Dutton, C. 14,162
Paul Roberts, LD 8,083
Lab. maj. 7,078 (16.28%)
3.78% swing Lab. to C.
(2001: Lab. maj. 9,906 (23.84%))

CROSBY
E. 54,255 T. 36,194 (66.71%) Lab. hold
Claire Curtis-Thomas, Lab. 17,463
Debi Jones, C. 11,623
Jim Murray, LD 6,298
Dr John Whittaker, UKIP 454
Geoffrey Bottoms, Comm. Brit. 199
David Braid, Clause 28 157
Lab. maj. 5,840 (16.14%)
3.26% swing Lab. to C.
(2001: Lab. maj. 8,353 (22.66%))

CROYDON CENTRAL
E. 80,825 T. 48,957 (60.57%) C. gain
*Andrew Pelling, C. 19,974
Geraint Davies, Lab. 19,899
Jeremy Hargreaves, LD 6,384
Ian Edwards, UKIP 1,066
Bernice Golberg, Green 1,036
Marianne Bowness, Veritas 304
John Cartwright, Loony 193
Janet Stears, Work 101
C. maj. 75 (0.15%)
4.42% swing Lab. to C.
(2001: Lab. maj. 3,984 (8.69%))

CROYDON NORTH
E. 83,796 T. 43,847 (52.33%) Lab. hold
Malcolm Wicks, Lab. 23,555
Tariq Ahmad, C. 9,667
Adrian Gee-Turner, LD 7,560
Shasha Khan, Green 1,248
Henry Pearce, UKIP 770
Peter Gibson, Croydon 394
Winston McKenzie, Veritas 324
Farhan Rasheed, Ind. 197
Michelle Chambers, Work 132
Lab. maj. 13,888 (31.67%)
4.29% swing Lab. to C.
(2001: Lab. maj. 16,858 (40.25%))

CROYDON SOUTH
E. 76,872 T. 48,897 (63.61%)   C. hold
Richard Ottaway, C. 25,320
Paul Smith, Lab. 11,792
Sandra Lawman, LD 10,049
James Feisenberger, UKIP 1,054
Graham Dare, Veritas 497
Mark Samuel, Work 185
C. maj. 13,528 (27.67%)
4.18% swing Lab. to C.
(2001: C. maj. 8,697 (19.30%))

DAGENHAM
E. 60,141 T. 30,841 (51.28%) Lab. hold
Jonathan Cruddas, Lab. 15,446
Michael White, C. 7,841
James Kempton, LD 3,106
Lawrence Rustem, BNP 2,870
Gerard Batten, UKIP 1,578
Lab. maj. 7,605 (24.66%)
3.43% swing Lab. to C.
(2001: Lab. maj. 8,693 (31.52%))

DARLINGTON
E. 65,281 T. 39,388 (60.34%) Lab. hold
Rt. Hon. Alan Milburn, Lab. 20,643
Anthony Frieze, C. 10,239
Robert Adamson, LD 7,269
John Hoodless, UKIP 730
Dai Davies, Veritas 507
Lab. maj. 10,404 (26.41%)
0.19% swing C. to Lab.
(2001: Lab. maj. 9,529 (23.38%))

DARTFORD
E. 74,028 T. 46,779 (63.19%) Lab. hold
Dr Howard Stoate, Lab. 19,909
Gareth Johnson, C. 19,203
Peter Bucklitsch, LD 5,036
Mark Croucher, UKIP 1,407
Michael Tibby, NEP 1,224
Lab. maj. 706 (1.51%)
2.94% swing Lab. to C.
(2001: Lab. maj. 3,306 (7.39%))

DAVENTRY
E. 88,758 T. 60,439 (68.09%)   C. hold
Tim Boswell, C. 31,206
Andrew Hammond, Lab. 16,520
Hannah Saul, LD 9,964
Barry Mahoney, UKIP 1,927
Barrie Wilkins, Veritas 822
C. maj. 14,686 (24.30%)
3.64% swing Lab. to C.
(2001: C. maj. 9,649 (17.02%))

DENTON & REDDISH
E. 68,267 T. 35,442 (51.92%) Lab. hold
*Andrew Gwynne, Lab. 20,340
Alex Story, C. 6,842
Allison Seabourne, LD 5,814
John Edgar, BNP 1,326
Gerald Price, UKIP 1,120
Lab. maj. 13,498 (38.08%)
3.77% swing Lab. to C.
(2001: Lab. maj. 15,330 (45.63%))

DERBY NORTH
E. 68,173 T. 43,818 (64.27%) Lab. hold
Bob Laxton, Lab. 19,272
Richard Aitken-Davies, C. 15,515
Jeremy Beckett, LD 7,209
Martin Bardoe, Veritas 958
Michelle Medgyesy, UKIP 864
Lab. maj. 3,757 (8.57%)
3.64% swing Lab. to C.
(2001: Lab. maj. 6,982 (15.85%))

DERBY SOUTH
E. 70,397 T. 43,373 (61.61%) Lab. hold
Rt. Hon. Margaret Beckett, Lab. 19,683
Lucy Care, LD 14,026
David Brackenbury, C. 8,211
David Black, UKIP 845
Frank Leeming, Veritas 608
Lab. maj. 5,657 (13.04%)
12.05% swing Lab. to LD
(2001: Lab. maj. 13,855 (32.16%))

DERBYSHIRE NORTH EAST
E. 70,981 T. 43,434 (61.19%) Lab. hold
*Natascha Engel, Lab. 21,416
Dominic Johnson, C. 11,351
Tom Snowdon, LD 8,812
Kenneth Perkins, UKIP 1,855
Lab. maj. 10,065 (23.17%)
2.96% swing Lab. to C.
(2001: Lab. maj. 12,258 (29.10%))

DERBYSHIRE SOUTH
E. 85,049 T. 55,820 (65.63%) Lab. hold
Mark Todd, Lab. 24,823
Simon Spencer, C. 20,328
Deborah Newton-Cook, LD 7,600
David Joines, BNP 1,797
Edward Spalton, Veritas 1,272
Lab. maj. 4,495 (8.05%)
3.53% swing Lab. to C.
(2001: Lab. maj. 7,851 (15.11%))

DERBYSHIRE WEST
E. 73,865 T. 51,143 (69.24%)   C. hold
Patrick McLoughlin, C. 24,378
David Menon, Lab. 13,625
Ray Dring, LD 11,408
Michael Cruddas, UKIP 1,322
Nick Delves, Loony 405
Martin Kyslun, Ind. 5
C. maj. 10,753 (21.03%)
3.23% swing Lab. to C.
(2001: C. maj. 7,370 (14.57%))

DEVIZES
E. 86,168 T. 56,146 (65.16%)   C. hold
Rt. Hon. Michael Ancram, C. 27,253
Fiona Hornby, LD 14,059
Sharon Charity, Lab. 12,519
Alan Wood, UKIP 2,315
C. maj. 13,194 (23.50%)
0.84% swing C. to LD
(2001: C. maj. 11,896 (22.34%))

DEVON EAST
E. 71,000 T. 49,247 (69.36%)   C. hold
Hugo Swire, C. 23,075
Tim Dumper, LD 15,139
James Court, Lab. 7,598
Colin McNamee, UKIP 3,035
Christopher Way, Ind. 400
C. maj. 7,936 (16.11%)
0.51% swing C. to LD
(2001: C. maj. 8,195 (17.13%))

DEVON NORTH
E. 76,203 T. 51,930 (68.15%)   LD hold
Nick Harvey, LD 23,840
Orlando Fraser, C. 18,868
Mark Cann, Lab. 4,656
John Browne, UKIP 2,740
Richard Knight, Green 1,826
LD maj. 4,972 (9.57%)
1.76% swing C. to LD
(2001: LD maj. 2,984 (6.06%))

DEVON SOUTH WEST
E. 71,307 T. 48,885 (68.56%)   C. hold
Gary Streeter, C. 21,906
Judy Evans, LD 11,765
Christopher Mavin, Lab. 11,545
Hugh Williams, UKIP 3,669
C. maj. 10,141 (20.74%)
3.86% swing C. to LD
(2001: C. maj. 7,144 (15.23%))

DEVON WEST & TORRIDGE
E. 83,489 T. 58,584 (70.17%)   C. gain
*Geoffrey Cox, C. 25,013
David Walter, LD 21,777
Rebecca Richards, Lab. 6,001
Matthew Jackson, UKIP 3,790
Peter Christie, Green 2,003
C. maj. 3,236 (5.52%)
3.83% swing LD to C.
(2001: LD maj. 1,194 (2.14%))

DEWSBURY
E. 62,243 T. 38,595 (62.01%) Lab. hold
*Shahid Malik, Lab. 15,807
Sayeeda Warsi, C. 11,192
Kingsley Hill, LD 5,624
David Exley, BNP 5,066
Brenda Smithson, Green 593
Alan Girvan, Ind. 313
Lab. maj. 4,615 (11.96%)
4.18% swing Lab. to C.
(2001: Lab. maj. 7,449 (20.32%))

DON VALLEY
E. 66,993 T. 36,864 (55.03%) Lab. hold
Caroline Flint, Lab. 19,418
Adam Duguid, C. 10,820
Stewart Arnold, LD 6,626
Lab. maj. 8,598 (23.32%)
1.33% swing Lab. to C.
(2001: Lab. maj. 9,520 (25.99%))

DONCASTER CENTRAL
E. 65,731 T. 34,351 (52.26%) Lab. hold
Rosie Winterton, Lab. 17,617
Patrick Wilson, LD 7,815
Stefan Kerner, C. 6,489
John Wilkinson, BNP 1,239
Alan Simmons, UKIP 1,191
Lab. maj. 9,802 (28.53%)
8.80% swing Lab. to LD
(2001: Lab. maj. 11,999 (35.39%))

DONCASTER NORTH
E. 61,741 T. 31,578 (51.15%) Lab. hold
*Ed Miliband, Lab. 17,531
Martin Drake, C. 4,875
Doug Pickett, LD 3,800
Martin Williams, CG 2,365
Lee Hagan, BNP 1,506
Robert Nixon, UKIP 940
Michael Cassidy, Eng. Dem. 561
Lab. maj. 12,656 (40.08%)
4.17% swing Lab. to C.
(2001: Lab. maj. 15,187 (48.42%))

DORSET MID & POOLE NORTH
E. 65,924 T. 45,159 (68.50%)   LD hold
Annette Brooke, LD 22,000
Simon Hayes, C. 16,518
Philip Murray, Lab. 5,221
Avril King, UKIP 1,420
LD maj. 5,482 (12.14%)
5.63% swing C. to LD
(2001: LD maj. 384 (0.88%))

DORSET NORTH
E. 74,286 T. 52,815 (71.10%)   C. hold
Robert Walter, C.   23,714
Emily Gasson, LD   21,470
John Yarwood, Lab.   4,596
Richard Frampton Hobbs, UKIP   1,918
Ralph Arliss, Green   1,117
C. maj. 2,244 (4.25%)
1.85% swing C. to LD
(2001: C. maj. 3,797 (7.94%))

DORSET SOUTH
E. 70,668 T. 48,584 (68.75%) Lab. hold
Jim Knight, Lab.   20,231
Ed Matts, C.   18,419
Graham Oakes, LD   7,647
Hugh Chalker, UKIP   1,571
Vic Hamilton, LCA   282
Bernard Parkes, Respect   219
Andrew Kirkwood, PRTYP   107
Colin Bex, Wessex Reg.   83
David Marchesi, Soc. Lab.   25
Lab. maj. 1,812 (3.73%)
1.70% swing C. to Lab.
(2001: Lab. maj. 153 (0.34%))

DORSET WEST
E. 69,764 T. 53,225 (76.29%)   C. hold
Rt. Hon. Oliver Letwin, C.   24,763
Justine McGuinness, LD   22,302
Dave Roberts, Lab.   4,124
Linda Guest, UKIP   1,084
Susan Greene, Green   952
C. maj. 2,461 (4.62%)
0.89% swing LD to C.
(2001: C. maj. 1,414 (2.85%))

DOVER
E. 70,884 T. 47,884 (67.55%) Lab. hold
Gwyn Prosser, Lab.   21,680
Paul Watkins, C.   16,739
Antony Hook, LD   7,607
Mike Wiltshire, UKIP   1,252
Vic Matcham, Ind.   606
Lab. maj. 4,941 (10.32%)
0.62% swing Lab. to C.
(2001: Lab. maj. 5,199 (11.56%))

DUDLEY NORTH
E. 68,766 T. 41,408 (60.22%) Lab. hold
*Ian Austin, Lab.   18,306
Ian Hillas, C.   12,874
Gerry Lewis, LD   4,257
Simon Darby, BNP   4,022
Malcolm Davis, UKIP   1,949
Lab. maj. 5,432 (13.12%)
2.26% swing Lab. to C.
(2001: Lab. maj. 6,800 (17.63%))

DUDLEY SOUTH
E. 65,228 T. 39,276 (60.21%) Lab. hold
Ian Pearson, Lab.   17,800
Marco Longhi, C.   13,556
Jonathan Bramall, LD   4,808
John Salvage, BNP   1,841
Andrew Benion, UKIP   1,271
Lab. maj. 4,244 (10.81%)
3.98% swing Lab. to C.
(2001: Lab. maj. 6,817 (18.76%))

DULWICH & WEST NORWOOD
E. 72,232 T. 41,989 (58.13%) Lab. hold
Rt. Hon. Tessa Jowell, Lab.   19,059
Jonathan Mitchell, LD   10,252
Kim Humphreys, C.   9,200
Jenny Jones, Green   2,741
Ralph Atkinson, UKIP   290
David Heather, Veritas   241
Amanda Rose, Soc. Lab.   149
Judy Weleminsky, Fit   57
Lab. maj. 8,807 (20.97%)
9.37% swing Lab. to LD
(2001: Lab. maj. 12,310 (32.19%))

DURHAM NORTH
E. 67,506 T. 37,341 (55.32%) Lab. hold
Kevan Jones, Lab.   23,932
Philip Latham, LD   7,151
Mark Watson, C.   6,258
Lab. maj. 16,781 (44.94%)
4.12% swing Lab. to LD
(2001: Lab. maj. 18,683 (48.44%))

DURHAM NORTH WEST
E. 68,130 T. 39,509 (57.99%) Lab. hold
Rt. Hon. Hilary Armstrong, Lab.   21,312
Alan Ord, LD   7,869
Jamie Devlin, C.   6,463
Watts Stelling, Ind.   3,865
Lab. maj. 13,443 (34.03%)
6.80% swing Lab. to LD
(2001: Lab. maj. 16,333 (41.64%))

DURHAM, CITY OF
E. 71,441 T. 44,364 (62.10%) Lab. hold
*Dr Roberta Blackman-Woods, Lab.
                                       20,928
Carol Woods, LD   17,654
Ben Rogers, C.   4,179
Anthony Martin, Veritas   1,603
Lab. maj. 3,274 (7.38%)
12.51% swing Lab. to LD
(2001: Lab. maj. 13,441 (32.40%))

EALING ACTON & SHEPHERD'S
BUSH
E. 70,454 T. 39,623 (56.24%) Lab. hold
*Andrew Slaughter, Lab.   16,579
Jonathan Gough, C.   11,059
Gary Malcolm, LD   9,986
Geoff Burgess, Green   1,999
Lab. maj. 5,520 (13.93%)
7.54% swing Lab. to C.
(2001: Lab. maj. 10,789 (29.00%))

EALING NORTH
E. 78,298 T. 46,507 (59.40%) Lab. hold
Stephen Pound, Lab.   20,956
Roger Curtis, C.   13,897
Francesco Fruzza, LD   9,148
Alan Outten, Green   1,319
Robin Lambert, UKIP   692
David Malindine, Veritas   495
Lab. maj. 7,059 (15.18%)
5.58% swing Lab. to C.
(2001: Lab. maj. 11,837 (26.33%))

EALING SOUTHALL
E. 83,738 T. 47,045 (56.18%) Lab. hold
Piara Khabra, Lab.   22,937
Nigel Bakhai, LD   11,497
Mark Nicholson, C.   10,147
Sarah Edwards, Green   2,175
Malkiat Bilku, WRP   289
Lab. maj. 11,440 (24.32%)
6.59% swing Lab. to LD
(2001: Lab. maj. 13,683 (29.22%))

EASINGTON
E. 61,084 T. 31,855 (52.15%) Lab. hold
John Cummings, Lab.   22,733
Christopher Ord, LD   4,097
Lucille Nicholson, C.   3,400
Ian McDonald, BNP   1,042
Dave Robinson, Soc. Lab.   583
Lab. maj. 18,636 (58.50%)
4.00% swing Lab. to LD
(2001: Lab. maj. 21,949 (66.49%))

EAST HAM
E. 78,104 T. 39,569 (50.66%) Lab. hold
Stephen Timms, Lab.   21,326
Abdul Khaliq Mian, Respect   8,171
Sarah Macken, C.   5,196
Ann Haigh, LD   4,296
David Bamber, CPA   580
Lab. maj. 13,155 (33.25%)
19.95% swing Lab. to Respect
(2001: Lab. maj. 21,032 (56.42%))

EASTBOURNE
E. 74,628 T. 48,392 (64.84%)   C. hold
Nigel Waterson, C.   21,033
Stephen Lloyd, LD   19,909
Andrew Jones, Lab.   5,268
Andrew Meggs, UKIP   1,233
Clive Gross, Green   949
C. maj. 1,124 (2.32%)
1.24% swing C. to LD
(2001: C. maj. 2,154 (4.81%))

EASTLEIGH
E. 76,844 T. 49,771 (64.77%) LD hold
*Christopher Huhne, LD   19,216
Conor Burns, C.   18,648
Chris Watt, Lab.   10,238
Christopher Murphy, UKIP   1,669
LD maj. 568 (1.14%)
2.64% swing LD to C.
(2001: LD maj. 3,058 (6.43%))

ECCLES
E. 69,006 T. 34,632 (50.19%) Lab. hold
Ian Stewart, Lab.   19,702
Thelma Matuk, C.   6,816
Jane Brophy, LD   6,429
Peter Reeve, UKIP   1,685
Lab. maj. 12,886 (37.21%)
3.29% swing Lab. to C.
(2001: Lab. maj. 14,528 (43.78%))

EDDISBURY
E. 72,249 T. 45,674 (63.22%)   C. hold
Stephen O'Brien, C.   21,181
Mark Green, Lab.   14,986
Joanne Crotty, LD   8,182
Steve Roxborough, UKIP   1,325
C. maj. 6,195 (13.56%)
1.64% swing Lab. to C.
(2001: C. maj. 4,568 (10.29%))

EDMONTON
E. 58,764 T. 34,703 (59.05%)
                          Lab. (Co-op) hold
Andy Love, Lab. (Co-op)   18,456
Lionel Zetter, C.   10,381
Dr Iarla Kilbane-Dawe, LD   4,162
Nina Armstrong, Green   889
Gwyneth Rolph, UKIP   815
Lab. (Co-op) maj. 8,075 (23.27%)
2.42% swing Lab. (Co-op) to C.
(2001: Lab. (Co-op) maj. 9,772
(28.10%))

ELLESMERE PORT & NESTON
E. 68,249 T. 42,069 (61.64%) Lab. hold
Andrew Miller, Lab.   20,371
Myles Hogg, C.   13,885
Steve Cooke, LD   6,607
Henry Crocker, UKIP   1,206
Lab. maj. 6,486 (15.42%)
5.37% swing Lab. to C.
(2001: Lab. maj. 10,861 (26.15%))

ELMET
E. 68,514 T. 47,146 (68.81%) Lab. hold
Colin Burgon, Lab.   22,260
Andrew Millard, C.   17,732
Madeleine Kirk, LD   5,923
Tracy Andrews, BNP   1,231
Lab. maj. 4,528 (9.60%)
0.26% swing C. to Lab.
(2001: Lab. maj. 4,171 (9.08%))

ELTHAM
E. 57,236 T. 35,305 (61.68%) Lab. hold
Clive Efford, Lab.   15,381
Spencer Drury, C.   12,105
Ian Gerrard, LD   5,669
Jeremy Elms, UKIP   1,024
Barry Roberts, BNP   979
Andrew Graham, Ind.   147
Lab. maj. 3,276 (9.28%)
5.71% swing Lab. to C.
(2001: Lab. maj. 6,996 (20.70%))

ENFIELD NORTH
E. 66,460 T. 40,749 (61.31%) Lab. hold
Joan Ryan, Lab.   18,055
Nick de Bois, C.   16,135
Simon Radford, LD   4,642
Terence Farr, BNP   1,004
Gary Robbens, UKIP   750
Patrick Burns, Ind.   163
Lab. maj. 1,920 (4.71%)
0.63% swing Lab. to C.
(2001: Lab. maj. 2,291 (6.01%))

ENFIELD SOUTHGATE
E. 63,613 T. 42,210 (66.35%) C. gain
*David Burrowes, C.   18,830
Stephen Twigg, Lab.   17,083
Ziz Kakoulakis, LD   4,724
Trevor Doughty, Green   1,083
Brian Hall, UKIP   490
C. maj. 1,747 (4.14%)
8.69% swing Lab. to C.
(2001: Lab. maj. 5,546 (13.23%))

EPPING FOREST
E. 72,776 T. 44,860 (61.64%) C. hold
Eleanor Laing, C.   23,783
Bambos Charalambous, Lab.   9,425
Michael Heavens, LD   8,279
Julian Leppert, BNP   1,728
Andrew Smith, UKIP   1,014
Robin Tilbrook, Eng. Dem.   631
C. maj. 14,358 (32.01%)
6.07% swing Lab. to C.
(2001: C. maj. 8,426 (19.87%))

EPSOM & EWELL
E. 75,515 T. 49,879 (66.05%) C. hold
Chris Grayling, C.   27,146
Jonathan Lees, LD   10,699
Charles Mansell, Lab.   10,265
Peter Kefford, UKIP   1,769
C. maj. 16,447 (32.97%)
3.50% swing LD to C.
(2001: C. maj. 10,080 (21.61%))

EREWASH
E. 78,376 T. 50,553 (64.50%) Lab. hold
Liz Blackman, Lab.   22,472
David Simmonds, C.   15,388
Martin Garnett, LD   7,073
Robert Kilroy-Silk, Veritas   2,957
Sadie Graham, BNP   1,319
Geoffrey Kingscott, UKIP   941
R. U. Seerius, Loony   287
David Bishop, Elvis   116
Lab. maj. 7,084 (14.01%)
0.13% swing Lab. to C.
(2001: Lab. maj. 6,932 (14.26%))

ERITH & THAMESMEAD
E. 72,058 T. 37,651 (52.25%) Lab. hold
John Austin, Lab.   20,483
Chris Bromby, C.   8,983
Steven Toole, LD   5,088
Brian Ravenscroft, BNP   1,620
Barrie Thomas, UKIP   1,477
Lab. maj. 11,500 (30.54%)
1.47% swing Lab. to C.
(2001: Lab. maj. 11,167 (33.48%))

ESHER & WALTON
E. 76,926 T. 47,878 (62.24%) C. hold
Ian Taylor, C.   21,882
Mark Marsh, LD   14,155
Richard Taylor, Lab.   9,309
Bernard Collignon, UKIP   1,582
Chinners Chinnery, Loony   608
Richard Cutler, Soc. Lab.   342
C. maj. 7,727 (16.14%)
5.17% swing C. to LD
(2001: C. maj. 11,538 (25.34%))

ESSEX NORTH
E. 73,037 T. 47,959 (65.66%) C. hold
Bernard Jenkin, C.   22,811
Elizabeth Hughes, Lab.   11,908
James Raven, LD   9,831
Christopher Fox, Green   1,718
George Curtis, UKIP   1,691
C. maj. 10,903 (22.73%)
3.37% swing Lab. to C.
(2001: C. maj. 7,186 (15.99%))

EXETER
E. 84,964 T. 55,068 (64.81%) Lab. hold
Ben Bradshaw, Lab.   22,619
Peter Cox, C.   14,954
Jon Underwood, LD   11,340
Margaret Danks, Lib.   2,214
Tim Brenan, Green   1,896
Mark Fitzgeorge-Parker, UKIP   1,854
John Stuart, Ind.   191
Lab. maj. 7,665 (13.92%)
4.21% swing Lab. to C.
(2001: Lab. maj. 11,759 (22.35%))

FALMOUTH & CAMBORNE
E. 71,509 T. 48,015 (67.15%) LD gain
*Julia Goldsworthy, LD   16,747
Candy Atherton, Lab.   14,861
Ashley Crossley, C.   12,644
Michael Mahon, UKIP   1,820
David Mudd, Ind.   961
Paul Holmes, Lib.   423
Hilda Wasley, Meb. Ker.   370
Peter Gifford, Veritas   128
Richard Smith, Masts   61
LD maj. 1,886 (3.93%)
9.52% swing Lab. to LD
(2001: Lab. maj. 4,527 (9.67%))

FAREHAM
E. 72,599 T. 48,576 (66.91%) C. hold
Mark Hoban, C.   24,151
James Carr, Lab.   12,449
Richard De Ste-Croix, LD   10,551
Peter Mason-Apps, UKIP   1,425
C. maj. 11,702 (24.09%)
4.33% swing Lab. to C.
(2001: C. maj. 7,009 (15.42%))

FAVERSHAM & KENT MID
E. 66,411 T. 43,626 (65.69%) C. hold
Hugh Robertson, C.   21,690
Andrew Bradstock, Lab.   12,970
David Naghi, LD   7,204
Robert Thompson, UKIP   1,152
Norman Davidson, Loony   610
C. maj. 8,720 (19.99%)
4.90% swing Lab. to C.
(2001: C. maj. 4,183 (10.19%))

FELTHAM & HESTON
E. 75,391 T. 37,282 (49.45%)
                           Lab. (Co-op) hold
Alan Keen, Lab. (Co-op)   17,741
Mark Bowen, C.   10,921
Satnam Kaur Khalsa, LD   6,177
Graham Kemp, NF   975
Elizabeth Anstis, Green   815
Leon Mullett, UKIP   612
Warwick Prachar, Ind.   41
Lab. (Co-op) maj. 6,820 (18.29%)
8.35% swing Lab. (Co-op) to C.
(2001: Lab. (Co-op) maj. 12,657
(34.99%))

FINCHLEY & GOLDERS GREEN
E. 69,808 T. 43,214 (61.90%) Lab. hold
Dr Rudi Vis, Lab.   17,487
Andrew Mennear, C.   16,746
Sue Garden, LD   7,282
Noel Lynch, Green   1,136
Jeremy Jacobs, UKIP   453
Rainbow George Weiss, Vote Dream 110
Lab. maj. 741 (1.71%)
3.40% swing Lab. to C.
(2001: Lab. maj. 3,716 (8.51%))

FOLKESTONE & HYTHE
E. 70,914 T. 48,503 (68.40%) C. hold
Rt. Hon. Michael Howard, C.   26,161
Peter Carroll, LD   14,481
Maureen Tomison, Lab.   6,053
Dr Hazel Dawe, Green   688
Petrina Holdsworth, UKIP   619
Lord Toby Jug, Loony   175
Rodney Hylton-Potts, GBB   153
Grahame Leon-Smith, Senior   151
Sylvia Dunn, Progress   22
C. maj. 11,680 (24.08%)
5.60% swing LD to C.
(2001: C. maj. 5,907 (12.88%))

FOREST OF DEAN
E. 67,225 T. 47,640 (70.87%) C. gain
*Mark Harper, C.   19,474
Isabel Owen, Lab.   17,425
Christopher Coleman, LD   8,185
Patricia Hill, UKIP   1,140
Stephen Tweedie, Green   991
Anthony Reeve, Ind.   300
Gerald Morgan, EPP   125
C. maj. 2,049 (4.30%)
4.45% swing Lab. to C.
(2001: Lab. maj. 2,049 (4.59%))

FYLDE
E. 75,703 T. 45,510 (60.12%)   C. hold
Rt. Hon. Michael Jack, C.   24,287
William Parbury, Lab.   11,828
Bill Winlow, LD   7,748
Tim Akeroyd, Lib.   1,647
C. maj. 12,459 (27.38%)
2.95% swing Lab. to C.
(2001: C. maj. 9,610 (21.48%))

GAINSBOROUGH
E. 70,733 T. 45,681 (64.58%)   C. hold
Edward Leigh, C.   20,040
Adrian Heath, LD   12,037
John Knight, Lab.   11,744
Steven Pearson, UKIP   1,860
C. maj. 8,003 (17.52%)
1.02% swing C. to LD
(2001: C. maj. 8,071 (19.07%))

GATESHEAD EAST & WASHINGTON WEST
E. 61,421 T. 34,668 (56.44%) Lab. hold
*Sharon Hodgson, Lab.   20,997
Frank Hindle, LD   7,590
Lee Martin, C.   4,812
Jim Batty, UKIP   1,269
Lab. maj. 13,407 (38.67%)
7.29% swing Lab. to LD
(2001: Lab. maj. 17,904 (53.26%))

GEDLING
E. 68,917 T. 44,069 (63.95%) Lab. hold
Vernon Coaker, Lab.   20,329
Anna Soubry, C.   16,518
Raymond Poynter, LD   6,070
Alan Margerison, UKIP   741
Deborah Johnson, Veritas   411
Lab. maj. 3,811 (8.65%)
2.06% swing Lab. to C.
(2001: Lab. maj. 5,598 (12.78%))

GILLINGHAM
E. 72,223 T. 45,167 (62.54%) Lab. hold
Paul Clark, Lab.   18,621
Tim Butcher, C.   18,367
Andrew Stamp, LD   6,734
Craig MacKinlay, UKIP   1,191
Gordon Bryan, Ind.   254
Lab. maj. 254 (0.56%)
2.41% swing Lab. to C.
(2001: Lab. maj. 2,272 (5.38%))

GLOUCESTER
E. 82,500 T. 51,803 (62.79%) Lab. hold
Parmjit Dhanda, Lab.   23,138
Paul James, C.   18,867
Jeremy Hilton, LD   7,825
Gary Phipps, UKIP   1,116
Bryan Meloy, Green   857
Lab. maj. 4,271 (8.24%)
0.10% swing C. to Lab.
(2001: Lab. maj. 3,880 (8.05%))

GOSPORT
E. 71,119 T. 43,034 (60.51%)   C. hold
Peter Viggers, C.   19,268
Richard Williams, Lab.   13,538
Roger Roberts, LD   7,145
John Bowles, UKIP   1,825
Andrea Smith, Green   1,258
C. maj. 5,730 (13.32%)
3.36% swing Lab. to C.
(2001: C. maj. 2,621 (6.59%))

GRANTHAM & STAMFORD
E. 74,074 T. 47,147 (63.65%)   C. hold
Quentin Davies, C.   22,109
Ian Selby, Lab.   14,664
Patrick O'Connor, LD   7,838
Stuart Rising, UKIP   1,498
Benedict Brown, Eng. Dem.   774
John Andrews, OFD   264
C. maj. 7,445 (15.79%)
3.02% swing Lab. to C.
(2001: C. maj. 4,518 (9.76%))

GRAVESHAM
E. 68,705 T. 45,179 (65.76%)   C. gain
*Adam Holloway, C.   19,739
Chris Pond, Lab.   19,085
Bruce Parmenter, LD   4,851
Geoff Coates, UKIP   850
Christopher Nickerson, Eng. Ind.   654
C. maj. 654 (1.45%)
6.29% swing Lab. to C.
(2001: Lab. maj. 4,862 (11.14%))

GREAT GRIMSBY
E. 63,711 T. 32,964 (51.74%) Lab. hold
Austin Mitchell, Lab.   15,512
Giles Taylor, C.   7,858
Andrew de Freitas, LD   6,356
Stephen Fyfe, BNP   1,338
Martin Grant, UKIP   1,239
David Brooks, Green   661
Lab. maj. 7,654 (23.22%)
5.78% swing Lab. to C.
(2001: Lab. maj. 11,484 (34.78%))

GREAT YARMOUTH
E. 68,887 T. 41,378 (60.07%) Lab. hold
Anthony Wright, Lab.   18,850
Mark Fox, C.   15,795
Stephen Newton, LD   4,585
Bertie Poole, UKIP   1,759
Michael Skipper, LCA   389
Lab. maj. 3,055 (7.38%)
1.96% swing Lab. to C.
(2001: Lab. maj. 4,564 (11.31%))

GREENWICH & WOOLWICH
E. 64,033 T. 35,615 (55.62%) Lab. hold
Rt. Hon. Nick Raynsford, Lab.   17,527
Christopher Le Breton, LD   7,381
Alistair Craig, C.   7,142
David Sharman, Green   1,579
Garry Bushell, Eng. Dem.   1,216
Stanley Gain, UKIP   709
Puvarani Nagalingam, Ind.   61
Lab. maj. 10,146 (28.49%)
8.21% swing Lab. to LD
(2001: Lab. maj. 13,433 (41.29%))

GUILDFORD
E. 75,566 T. 51,631 (68.33%)   C. gain
*Anne Milton, C.   22,595
Sue Doughty, LD   22,248
Karen Landles, Lab.   5,054
John Pletts, Green   811
Martin Haslam, UKIP   645
John Morris, PPN-V   166
Victoria Lavin, Ind.   112
C. maj. 347 (0.67%)
0.90% swing LD to C.
(2001: LD maj. 538 (1.12%))

HACKNEY NORTH & STOKE NEWINGTON
E. 59,260 T. 29,380 (49.58%) Lab. hold
Diane Abbott, Lab.   14,268
James Blanchard, LD   6,841
Ertan Hurer, C.   4,218
Mischa Borris, Green   2,907
David Vail, Ind.   602
Nusrat Sen, Soc. Lab.   296
Nigel Barrow, Loony   248
Lab. maj. 7,427 (25.28%)
10.84% swing Lab. to LD
(2001: Lab. maj. 13,651 (46.09%))

HACKNEY SOUTH & SHOREDITCH
E. 64,818 T. 32,237 (49.73%)
                        Lab. (Co-op) hold
*Meg Hillier, Lab. (Co-op)   17,048
Gavin Baylis, LD   6,844
John Moss, C.   4,524
Ipemndoh dan Iyan, Green   1,779
Dean Ryan, Respect   1,437
Benjamin Rae, Lib.   313
Monty Goldman, Comm.   200
Jonty Leff, WRP   92
Lab. (Co-op) maj. 10,204 (31.65%)
8.97% swing Lab. (Co-op) to LD
(2001: Lab. (Co-op) maj. 15,049 (49.59%))

HALESOWEN & ROWLEY REGIS
E. 65,748 T. 41,327 (62.86%) Lab. hold
Sylvia Heal, Lab.   19,243
Les Jones, C.   14,906
Martin Turner, LD   5,204
Nikki Sinclaire, UKIP   1,974
Lab. maj. 4,337 (10.49%)
4.12% swing Lab. to C.
(2001: Lab. maj. 7,359 (18.74%))

HALIFAX
E. 64,861 T. 39,659 (61.14%)
                        Lab. (Co-op) hold
*Linda Riordan, Lab. (Co-op)   16,579
Kris Hopkins, C.   13,162
Michael Taylor, LD   7,100
Geoff Wallace, BNP   2,627
Thomas Holmes, NF   191
Lab. (Co-op) maj. 3,417 (8.62%)
3.28% swing Lab. (Co-op) to C.
(2001: Lab. (Co-op) maj. 6,129 (15.17%))

HALTEMPRICE & HOWDEN
E. 68,471 T. 48,029 (70.15%)   C. hold
Rt. Hon. David Davis, C.   22,792
Jon Neal, LD   17,676
Edward Hart, Lab.   6,104
Jonathan Mainprize, BNP   798
Philip Lane, UKIP   659
C. maj. 5,116 (10.65%)
3.16% swing LD to C.
(2001: C. maj. 1,903 (4.33%))

HALTON
E. 64,379 T. 34,183 (53.10%) Lab. hold
Derek Twigg, Lab.   21,460
Colin Bloom, C.   6,854
Roger Barlow, LD   5,869
Lab. maj. 14,606 (42.73%)
3.92% swing Lab. to C.
(2001: Lab. maj. 17,428 (50.56%))

HAMMERSMITH & FULHAM
E. 79,082 T. 49,327 (62.37%)   C. gain
*Greg Hands, C.   22,407
Melanie Smallman, Lab.   17,378
Alan Bullion, LD   7,116
Fiona Harrold, Green   1,933
Giles Fisher, UKIP   493
C. maj. 5,029 (10.20%)
7.35% swing Lab. to C.
(2001: Lab. maj. 2,015 (4.51%))

HAMPSHIRE EAST
E. 79,801 T. 53,139 (66.59%)   C. hold
Rt. Hon. Michael Mates, C.   24,273
Ruth Bright, LD   18,764
Marjory Broughton, Lab.   8,519
David Samuel, UKIP   1,583
C. maj. 5,509 (10.37%)
3.66% swing C. to LD
(2001: C. maj. 8,890 (17.68%))

HAMPSHIRE NORTH EAST
E. 72,939 T. 47,287 (64.83%)   C. hold
Rt. Hon. James Arbuthnot, C.   25,407
Adam Carew, LD   12,858
Kevin McGrath, Lab.   7,630
Paul Birch, UKIP   1,392
C. maj. 12,549 (26.54%)
1.81% swing C. to LD
(2001: C. maj. 13,257 (30.17%))

HAMPSHIRE NORTH WEST
E. 79,763 T. 51,265 (64.27%)   C. hold
Rt. Hon. Sir George Young, C.   26,005
Martin Tod, LD   12,741
Michael Mumford, Lab.   10,594
Peter Sumner, UKIP   1,925
C. maj. 13,264 (25.87%)
1.50% swing C. to LD
(2001: C. maj. 12,009 (24.69%))

HAMPSTEAD & HIGHGATE
E. 68,737 T. 38,173 (55.53%) Lab. hold
Glenda Jackson, Lab.   14,615
Piers Wauchope, C.   10,886
Ed Fordham, LD   10,293
Sian Berry, Green   2,013
Magnus Nielsen, UKIP   275
Rainbow George Weiss, Vote Dream 91
Lab. maj. 3,729 (9.77%)
6.24% swing Lab. to C.
(2001: Lab. maj. 7,876 (22.24%))

HARBOROUGH
E. 74,583 T. 47,922 (64.25%)   C. hold
Edward Garnier, C.   20,536
Jill Hope, LD   16,644
Peter Evans, Lab.   9,222
Marietta King, UKIP   1,520
C. maj. 3,892 (8.12%)
1.60% swing C. to LD
(2001: C. maj. 5,252 (11.31%))

HARLOW
E. 63,500 T. 39,733 (62.57%) Lab. hold
Bill Rammell, Lab.   16,453
Robert Halfon, C.   16,356
Lorna Spenceley, LD   5,002
John Felgate, UKIP   981
Anthony Bennett, Veritas   941
Lab. maj. 97 (0.24%)
6.39% swing Lab. to C.
(2001: Lab. maj. 5,228 (13.03%))

HARROGATE & KNARESBOROUGH
E. 65,622 T. 42,858 (65.31%) LD hold
Phil Willis, LD   24,113
Maggie Punyer, C.   13,684
Lorraine Ferris, Lab.   3,627
Chris Royston, UKIP   845
Colin Banner, BNP   466
John Allman, AFC   123
LD maj. 10,429 (24.33%)
1.68% swing C. to LD
(2001: LD maj. 8,845 (20.97%))

HARROW EAST
E. 84,033 T. 50,823 (60.48%) Lab. hold
Tony McNulty, Lab.   23,445
David Ashton, C.   18,715
Pash Nandhra, LD   7,747
Paul Cronin, UKIP   916
Lab. maj. 4,730 (9.31%)
6.92% swing Lab. to C.
(2001: Lab. maj. 11,124 (23.14%))

HARROW WEST
E. 74,228 T. 47,759 (64.34%)
                           Lab. (Co-op) hold
Gareth Thomas, Lab. (Co-op)   20,298
Mike Freer, C.   18,270
Christopher Noyce, LD   8,188
Janice Cronin, UKIP   576
Berjis Daver, Ind.   427
Lab. (Co-op) maj. 2,028 (4.25%)
4.48% swing Lab. (Co-op) to C.
(2001: Lab. (Co-op) maj. 6,156
(13.20%))

HARTLEPOOL
E. 68,776 T. 35,436 (51.52%) Lab. hold
Iain Wright, Lab.   18,251
Jody Dunn, LD   10,773
Amanda Vigar, C.   4,058
George Springer, UKIP   1,256
Frank Harrison, Soc. Lab.   373
Iris Ryder, Green   288
John Hobbs, Ind.   275
Sausage Supremo Headbanger, Loony
                                                  162
Lab. maj. 7,478 (21.10%)
11.51% swing Lab. to LD
(2004 Sept. by-election: Lab. maj. 2,033
(6.48%))
(2001: Lab. maj. 14,571 (38.29%))

HARWICH
E. 80,474 T. 50,408 (62.64%)   C. gain
*Douglas Carswell, C.   21,235
Ivan Henderson, Lab.   20,315
Keith Tully, LD   5,913
Jeffrey Titford, UKIP   2,314
John Tipple, Respect   477
Christopher Humphrey, Ind.   154
C. maj. 920 (1.83%)
3.61% swing Lab. to C.
(2001: Lab. maj. 2,596 (5.40%))

HASTINGS & RYE
E. 72,765 T. 43,004 (59.10%) Lab. hold
Michael Foster, Lab.   18,107
Mark Coote, C.   16,081
Richard Stevens, LD   6,479
Terry Grant, UKIP   1,098
Sally Phillips, Green   1,032
John Ord-Clarke, Loony   207
Lab. maj. 2,026 (4.71%)
2.87% swing Lab. to C.
(2001: Lab. maj. 4,308 (10.45%))

HAVANT
E. 68,545 T. 41,351 (60.33%)   C. hold
David Willetts, C.   18,370
Sarah Bogle, Lab.   11,862
Alex Bentley, LD   8,358
Timothy Dawes, Green   1,006
Steve Harris, UKIP   998
Ian Johnson, BNP   562
Russell Thomas, Veritas   195
C. maj. 6,508 (15.74%)
2.67% swing Lab. to C.
(2001: C. maj. 4,207 (10.40%))

HAYES & HARLINGTON
E. 57,493 T. 32,389 (56.34%) Lab. hold
John McDonnell, Lab.   19,009
Richard Worrall, C.   8,162
Jon Ball, LD   3,174
Tony Hazel, BNP   830
Martin Haley, UKIP   552
Brian Outten, Green   442
Paul Goddard, Ind.   220
Lab. maj. 10,847 (33.49%)
4.03% swing Lab. to C.
(2001: Lab. maj. 13,466 (41.56%))

HAZEL GROVE
E. 64,376 T. 39,117 (60.76%) LD hold
Andrew Stunell, LD   19,355
Alan White, C.   11,607
Andrew Graystone, Lab.   6,834
Keith Ryan, UKIP   1,321
LD maj. 7,748 (19.81%)
1.06% swing LD to C.
(2001: LD maj. 8,435 (21.92%))

HEMEL HEMPSTEAD
E. 73,095 T. 47,108 (64.45%)   C. gain
*Michael Penning, C.   19,000
Tony McWalter, Lab. (Co-op)   18,501
Dr Richard Grayson, LD   8,089
Barry Newton, UKIP   1,518
C. maj. 499 (1.06%)
4.61% swing Lab. (Co-op) to C.
(2001: Lab. (Co-op) maj. 3,742 (8.16%))

HEMSWORTH
E. 67,339 T. 36,792 (54.64%) Lab. hold
Jon Trickett, Lab.   21,630
Jonathan Mortimer, C.   8,149
David Hall-Matthews, LD   5,766
John Burdon, Veritas   1,247
Lab. maj. 13,481 (36.64%)
3.87% swing Lab. to C.
(2001: Lab. maj. 15,636 (44.39%))

HENDON
E. 71,764 T. 41,839 (58.30%) Lab. hold
Andrew Dismore, Lab.   18,596
Dr Richard Evans, C.   15,897
Nahid Boethe, LD   5,831
David Williams, Green   754
Melvyn Smallman, UKIP   637
Rainbow George Weiss, Vote Dream 68
Michael Stewart, PDP   56
Lab. maj. 2,699 (6.45%)
5.85% swing Lab. to C.
(2001: Lab. maj. 7,417 (18.16%))

HENLEY
E. 68,538 T. 46,537 (67.90%)   C. hold
Boris Johnson, C.   24,894
David Turner, LD   12,101
Kaleem Saeed, Lab.   6,862
Mark Stevenson, Green   1,518
Delphine Gray-Fisk, UKIP   1,162
C. maj. 12,793 (27.49%)
4.22% swing LD to C.
(2001: C. maj. 8,458 (19.05%))

HEREFORD
E. 71,813 T. 46,894 (65.30%) LD hold
Paul Keetch, LD   20,285
Virginia Taylor, C.   19,323
Tom Calver, Lab.   4,800
Brian Lunt, Green   1,052
Christopher Kingsley, UKIP   1,030
Peter Morton, Ind.   404
LD maj. 962 (2.05%)
0.06% swing LD to C.
(2001: LD maj. 968 (2.17%))

HERTFORD & STORTFORD
E. 73,394 T. 49,692 (67.71%)   C. hold
Mark Prisk, C.   25,074
Richard Henry, Lab.   11,977
James Lucas, LD   9,129
Peter Hart, Green   1,914
David Sodey, UKIP   1,026
Debbie Le May, Veritas   572
C. maj. 13,097 (26.36%)
7.24% swing Lab. to C.
(2001: C. maj. 5,603 (11.88%))

HERTFORDSHIRE NORTH EAST
E. 72,190 T. 47,374 (65.62%)   C. hold
Oliver Heald, C.   22,402
Andrew Harrop, Lab.   13,264
Iain Coleman, LD   10,147
David Hitchman, UKIP   1,561
C. maj. 9,138 (19.29%)
5.79% swing Lab. to C.
(2001: C. maj. 3,444 (7.71%))

HERTFORDSHIRE SOUTH WEST
E. 73,170 T. 50,088 (68.45%)   C. hold
*David Gauke, C.   23,494
Ed Featherstone, LD   15,021
Kerron Cross, Lab.   10,466
Colin Rodden, UKIP   1,107
C. maj. 8,473 (16.92%)
0.54% swing C. to LD
(2001: C. maj. 8,181 (17.31%))

HERTSMERE
E. 67,572 T. 42,572 (63.00%)   C. hold
James Clappison, C.   22,665
Kelly Tebb, Lab.   11,572
Jonathan Davies, LD   7,817
James Dry, Soc. Lab.   518
C. maj. 11,093 (26.06%)
7.12% swing Lab. to C.
(2001: C. maj. 4,902 (11.81%))

HEXHAM
E. 60,374 T. 41,513 (68.76%)   C. hold
Peter Atkinson, C.   17,605
Kevin Graham, Lab.   12,585
Andrew Duffield, LD   10,673
Ian Riddell, Eng. Dem.   521
Thomas Davison, IP   129
C. maj. 5,020 (12.09%)
3.06% swing Lab. to C.
(2001: C. maj. 2,529 (5.96%))

HEYWOOD & MIDDLETON
E. 71,510 T. 39,053 (54.61%)   Lab.
(Co-op) hold
Jim Dobbin, Lab. (Co-op)   19,438
Stephen Pathmarajah, C.   8,355
Crea Lavin, LD   7,261
Gary Aronsson, BNP   1,855
Phil Burke, Lib.   1,377
Dr John Whittaker, UKIP   767
Lab. (Co-op) maj. 11,083 (28.38%)
0.86% swing Lab. (Co-op) to C.
(2001: Lab. (Co-op) maj. 11,670
(30.09%))

HIGH PEAK
E. 75,275 T. 49,989 (66.41%) Lab. hold
Tom Levitt, Lab.   19,809
Andrew Bingham, C.   19,074
Marc Godwin, LD   10,000
Michael Schwartz, UKIP   1,106
Lab. maj. 735 (1.47%)
3.93% swing Lab. to C.
(2001: Lab. maj. 4,489 (9.33%))

HITCHIN & HARPENDEN
E. 67,207 T. 47,387 (70.51%)   C. hold
Rt. Hon. Peter Lilley, C.   23,627
Hannah Hedges, LD   12,234
Paul Orrett, Lab.   10,499
John Saunders, UKIP   828
Peter Rigby, Ind.   199
C. maj. 11,393 (24.04%)
2.66% swing C. to LD
(2001: C. maj. 6,663 (14.83%))

HOLBORN & ST PANCRAS
E. 68,237 T. 34,359 (50.35%) Lab. hold
Rt. Hon. Frank Dobson, Lab.   14,857
Jill Fraser, LD   10,070
Margot James, C.   6,482
Adrian Oliver, Green   2,798
Rainbow George Weiss, Vote Dream 152
Lab. maj. 4,787 (13.93%)
10.98% swing Lab. to LD
(2001: Lab. maj. 11,175 (35.90%))

HORNCHURCH
E. 59,773 T. 38,169 (63.86%)   C. gain
*James Brokenshire, C.   16,355
John Cryer, Lab.   15,875
Nat Green, LD   2,894
Ian Moore, BNP   1,313
Lawrence Webb, UKIP   1,033
Malvin Brown, RA   395
Graham Williamson, Third   304
C. maj. 480 (1.26%)
2.71% swing Lab. to C.
(2001: Lab. maj. 1,482 (4.17%))

HORNSEY & WOOD GREEN
E. 76,621 T. 47,330 (61.77%)   LD gain
*Lynne Featherstone, LD   20,512
Barbara Roche, Lab.   18,117
Peter Forrest, C.   6,014
Jayne Forbes, Green   2,377
Roy Freshwater, UKIP   310
LD maj. 2,395 (5.06%)
14.57% swing Lab. to LD
(2001: Lab. maj. 10,614 (24.09%))

HORSHAM
E. 80,974 T. 54,495 (67.30%)   C. hold
Rt. Hon. Francis Maude, C.   27,240
Rosie Sharpley, LD   14,613
Rehman Chishti, Lab.   9,320
Hugo Miller, UKIP   2,552
Jim Duggan, Ind.   416
Martin Jeremiah, PHF   354
C. maj. 12,627 (23.17%)
1.87% swing C. to LD
(2001: C. maj. 13,666 (26.92%))

HOUGHTON & WASHINGTON EAST
E. 67,089 T. 34,694 (51.71%) Lab. hold
Fraser Kemp, Lab.   22,310
Mark Greenfield, LD   6,245
Anthony Devenish, C.   4,772
John Richardson, BNP   1,367
Lab. maj. 16,065 (46.30%)
7.20% swing Lab. to LD
(2001: Lab. maj. 19,818 (58.91%))

HOVE
E. 69,939 T. 44,796 (64.05%) Lab. hold
*Celia Barlow, Lab.   16,786
Nicholas Boles, C.   16,366
Paul Elgood, LD   8,002
Anthea Ballam, Green   2,575
Stuart Bower, UKIP   575
Paddy O'Keeffe, Respect   268
Bob Dobbs, Ind.   95
Richard Franklin, Silent   78
Brian Ralfe, Ind.   51
Lab. maj. 420 (0.94%)
3.31% swing Lab. to C.
(2001: Lab. maj. 3,171 (7.55%))

HUDDERSFIELD
E. 61,723 T. 34,940 (56.61%)
                        Lab. (Co-op) hold
Barry Sheerman, Lab. (Co-op)   16,341
Emma Bone, LD   7,990
David Meacock, C.   7,597
Julie Stewart-Turner, Green   1,651
Karl Hanson, BNP   1,036
Theresa Quarmby, Ind.   325
Lab. (Co-op) maj. 8,351 (23.90%)
7.18% swing Lab. (Co-op) to LD
(2001: Lab. (Co-op) maj. 10,046
(28.39%))

HULL EAST
E. 65,407 T. 31,022 (47.43%) Lab. hold
Rt. Hon. John Prescott, Lab.   17,609
Andy Sloan, LD   5,862
Katy Lindsay, C.   4,038
Alan Siddle, BNP   1,022
Janet Toker, Lib.   1,018
Graham Morris, Veritas   750
Ronald Noon, Ind.   334
Linda Muir, Soc. Lab.   207
Carl Wagner, LCA   182
Lab. maj. 11,747 (37.87%)
5.88% swing Lab. to LD
(2001: Lab. maj. 15,325 (49.64%))

HULL NORTH
E. 62,590 T. 29,584 (47.27%) Lab. hold
*Diana Johnson, Lab.   15,364
Denis Healy, LD   8,013
Lydia Rivlin, C.   3,822
Martin Deane, Green   858
Brian Wainwright, BNP   766
Tineke Robinson, Veritas   389
Christopher Veasey, Northern   193
Carl Wagner, LCA   179
Lab. maj. 7,351 (24.85%)
6.30% swing Lab. to LD
(2001: Lab. maj. 10,721 (37.44%))

HULL WEST & HESSLE
E. 61,494 T. 27,818 (45.24%) Lab. hold
Rt. Hon. Alan Johnson, Lab.   15,305
David Nolan, LD   5,855
Karen Woods, C.   5,769
Stephen Wallis, Veritas   889
Lab. maj. 9,450 (33.97%)
4.66% swing Lab. to LD
(2001: Lab. maj. 10,951 (37.87%))

HUNTINGDON
E. 83,843 T. 52,418 (62.52%)   C. hold
Jonathan Djanogly, C.   26,646
Julian Huppert, LD   13,799
Stephen Sartain, Lab.   9,821
Derek Norman, UKIP   2,152
C. maj. 12,847 (24.51%)
0.78% swing C. to LD
(2001: C. maj. 12,792 (26.06%))

HYNDBURN
E. 67,086 T. 39,449 (58.80%) Lab. hold
Greg Pope, Lab.   18,136
James Mawdsley, C.   12,549
Bill Greene, LD   5,577
Christian Jackson, BNP   2,444
Dr John Whittaker, UKIP   743
Lab. maj. 5,587 (14.16%)
3.66% swing Lab. to C.
(2001: Lab. maj. 8,219 (21.49%))

ILFORD NORTH
E. 70,718 T. 43,000 (60.80%)   C. gain
*Lee Scott, C.   18,781
Linda Perham, Lab.   17,128
Mark Gayler, LD   5,896
Andrew Cross, UKIP   902
Martin Levin, Ind.   293
C. maj. 1,653 (3.84%)
4.55% swing Lab. to C.
(2001: Lab. maj. 2,115 (5.26%))

ILFORD SOUTH
E. 79,639 T. 42,693 (53.61%)
                          Lab. (Co-op) hold
Mike Gapes, Lab. (Co-op)   20,856
Stephen Metcalfe, C.   11,628
Matthew Lake, LD   8,761
Kashif Rana, BPP   763
Colin Taylor, UKIP   685
Lab. (Co-op) maj. 9,228 (21.61%)
6.14% swing Lab. (Co-op) to C.
(2001: Lab. (Co-op) maj. 13,997
(33.90%))

IPSWICH
E. 68,825 T. 41,878 (60.85%) Lab. hold
Chris Mole, Lab.   18,336
Paul West, C.   13,004
Richard Atkins, LD   8,464
Alison West, UKIP   1,134
Jervis Kay, Eng. Dem.   641
Sally Wainman, Ind.   299
Lab. maj. 5,332 (12.73%)
4.03% swing Lab. to C.
(2001 Nov. by-election: Lab. maj. 4,087
(14.91%))
(2001: Lab. maj. 8,081 (20.79%))

ISLE OF WIGHT
E. 109,046 T. 66,843 (61.30%) C. hold
Andrew Turner, C.   32,717
Anthony Rowlands, LD   19,739
Mark Chiverton, Lab.   11,484
Michael Tarrant, UKIP   2,352
Edward Corby, Ind.   551
C. maj. 12,978 (19.42%)
7.48% swing LD to C.
(2001: C. maj. 2,826 (4.45%))

ISLINGTON NORTH
E. 58,427 T. 31,494 (53.90%) Lab. hold
Jeremy Corbyn, Lab.   16,118
Laura Willoughby, LD   9,402
Nicola Talbot, C.   3,740
Jon Nott, Green   2,234
Lab. maj. 6,716 (21.32%)
10.78% swing Lab. to LD
(2001: Lab. maj. 12,958 (42.88%))

ISLINGTON SOUTH & FINSBURY
E. 57,748 T. 30,961 (53.61%) Lab. hold
*Emily Thornberry, Lab.   12,345
Bridget Fox, LD   11,861
Melanie McLean, C.   4,594
James Humphries, Green   1,471
Patricia Theophanides, UKIP   470
Andy the Hat Gardner, Loony   189
Chris Gidden, Ind.   31
Lab. maj. 484 (1.56%)
12.12% swing Lab. to LD
(2001: Lab. maj. 7,280 (25.81%))

JARROW
E. 61,814 T. 33,978 (54.97%) Lab. hold
Stephen Hepburn, Lab.   20,554
Bill Schardt, LD   6,650
Linkson Jack, C.   4,807
Alan Badger, UKIP   1,567
Roger Nettleship, SNH   400
Lab. maj. 13,904 (40.92%)
5.06% swing Lab. to LD
(2001: Lab. maj. 17,595 (51.03%))

KEIGHLEY
E. 68,229 T. 46,312 (67.88%) Lab. hold
Ann Cryer, Lab.   20,720
Karl Poulsen, C.   15,868
Nader Fekri, LD   5,484
Nick Griffin, BNP   4,240
Lab. maj. 4,852 (10.48%)
0.62% swing C. to Lab.
(2001: Lab. maj. 4,005 (9.24%))

KENSINGTON & CHELSEA
E. 62,662 T. 31,336 (50.01%)   C. hold
†Rt. Hon. Sir Malcolm Rifkind, C.
                                    18,144
Jennifer Kingsley, LD   5,726
Catherine Atkinson, Lab.   5,521
Julia Stephenson, Green   1,342
Mildred Eilorat, UKIP   395
Alfred Bovill, Ind.   107
Eddie Adams, Green Soc.   101
C. maj. 12,418 (39.63%)
0.46% swing LD to C.
(2001: C. maj. 8,771 (31.28%))

KETTERING
E. 81,887 T. 55,646 (67.95%)   C. gain
*Philip Hollobone, C.   25,401
Phil Sawford, Lab.   22,100
Roger Aron, LD   6,882
Rosemarie Clark, UKIP   1,263
C. maj. 3,301 (5.93%)
3.58% swing Lab. to C.
(2001: Lab. maj. 665 (1.24%))

KINGSTON & SURBITON
E. 72,671 T. 49,750 (68.46%) LD hold
Edward Davey, LD   25,397
Kevin Davis, C.   16,431
Nick Parrott, Lab.   6,553
Barry Thornton, UKIP   657
John Hayball, Soc. Lab.   366
David Henson, Veritas   200
Rainbow George Weiss, Vote Dream 146
LD maj. 8,966 (18.02%)
6.95% swing LD to C.
(2001: LD maj. 15,676 (31.93%))

KINGSWOOD
E. 84,400 T. 56,311 (66.72%) Lab. hold
Dr Roger Berry, Lab.   26,491
Owen Inskip, C.   18,618
Geoff Brewer, LD   9,089
John Knight, UKIP   1,444
David Burnside, Ind.   669
Lab. maj. 7,873 (13.98%)
6.26% swing Lab. to C.
(2001: Lab. maj. 13,962 (26.51%))

KNOWSLEY NORTH & SEFTON
EAST
E. 70,403 T. 37,053 (52.63%) Lab. hold
George Howarth, Lab.   23,461
Flo Clucas, LD   7,192
Naman Purewal, C.   5,064
Michael McDermott, BNP   872
Stephen Whatham, Soc. Lab.   464
Lab. maj. 16,269 (43.91%)
4.52% swing Lab. to LD
(2001: Lab. maj. 18,927 (50.45%))

KNOWSLEY SOUTH
E. 70,726 T. 36,444 (51.53%) Lab. hold
Eddie O'Hara, Lab.   24,820
David Smithson, LD   7,132
Andrea Leadsom, C.   4,492
Lab. maj. 17,688 (48.53%)
4.86% swing Lab. to LD
(2001: Lab. maj. 21,316 (58.26%))

LANCASHIRE WEST
E. 74,777 T. 43,155 (57.71%) Lab. hold
*Rosie Cooper, Lab.	20,746
Alf Doran, C.	14,662
Richard Kemp, LD	6,059
Alan Freeman, UKIP	871
Stephen Garrett, Eng. Dem.	525
David Braid, Clause 28	292

Lab. maj. 6,084 (14.10%)
4.17% swing Lab. to C.
(2001: Lab. maj. 9,643 (22.44%))

LANCASTER & WYRE
E. 80,739 T. 52,061 (64.48%)   C. gain
*Ben Wallace, C.	22,266
Anne Sacks, Lab.	18,095
Stuart Langhorn, LD	8,453
Jon Barry, Green	2,278
John Mander, UKIP	969

C. maj. 4,171 (8.01%)
4.47% swing Lab. to C.
(2001: Lab. maj. 481 (0.92%))

LEEDS CENTRAL
E. 62,939 T. 29,186 (46.37%) Lab. hold
Rt. Hon. Hilary Benn, Lab.	17,526
Ruth Coleman, LD	5,660
Brian Cattell, C.	3,865
Mark Collett, BNP	1,201
Peter Sewards, UKIP	494
Mick Dear, Ind.	189
Oluwole Taiwo, Ind.	126
Julian Fitzgerald, AFC	125

Lab. maj. 11,866 (40.66%)
6.53% swing Lab. to LD
(2001: Lab. maj. 14,381 (52.67%))

LEEDS EAST
E. 54,691 T. 30,077 (54.99%) Lab. hold
George Mudie, Lab.	17,799
Andrew Tear, LD	6,221
Dominic Ponniah, C.	5,557
Peter Socrates, Ind.	500

Lab. maj. 11,578 (38.49%)
5.48% swing Lab. to LD
(2001: Lab. maj. 12,643 (43.51%))

LEEDS NORTH EAST
E. 63,304 T. 41,467 (65.50%) Lab. hold
Fabian Hamilton, Lab.	18,632
Matthew Lobley, C.	13,370
Jonathan Brown, LD	8,427
Celia Foote, Green Soc.	1,038

Lab. maj. 5,262 (12.69%)
2.57% swing Lab. to C.
(2001: Lab. maj. 7,089 (17.82%))

LEEDS NORTH WEST
E. 71,644 T. 44,711 (62.41%)   LD gain
*Greg Mulholland, LD	16,612
Judith Blake, Lab.	14,735
George Lee, C.	11,510
Martin Hemingway, Green	1,128
Adrian Knowles, Eng. Dem.	545
Jeannie Sutton, Green Soc.	181

LD maj. 1,877 (4.20%)
9.59% swing Lab. to LD
(2001: Lab. maj. 5,236 (12.33%))

LEEDS WEST
E. 62,882 T. 33,718 (53.62%) Lab. hold
Rt. Hon. John Battle, Lab.	18,704
Darren Finlay, LD	5,894
Tim Metcalfe, C.	4,807
David Blackburn, Green	2,519
Julie Day, BNP	1,166
David Sewards, UKIP	628

Lab. maj. 12,810 (37.99%)
6.85% swing Lab. to LD
(2001: Lab. maj. 14,935 (46.54%))

LEICESTER EAST
E. 66,383 T. 41,306 (62.22%) Lab. hold
Keith Vaz, Lab.	24,015
Suella Fernandes, C.	8,139
Susan Cooper, LD	7,052
Colin Brown, Veritas	1,666
Valerie Smalley, Soc. Lab.	434

Lab. maj. 15,876 (38.44%)
2.69% swing C. to Lab.
(2001: Lab. maj. 13,442 (33.06%))

LEICESTER SOUTH
E. 72,310 T. 42,411 (58.65%) Lab. gain
*Sir Peter Soulsby, Lab.	16,688
Parmjit Singh Gill, LD	12,971
Martin McElwee, C.	7,549
Yvonne Ridley, Respect	2,720
Matthew Follett, Green	1,379
Ken Roseblade, Veritas	573
Dave Roberts, Soc. Lab.	315
Paul Lord, Ind.	216

Lab. maj. 3,717 (8.76%)
14.26% swing Lab. to LD
(2004 July by-election: LD maj.1,654 (5.62%))
(2001: Lab. maj. 13,243 (31.43%))

LEICESTER WEST
E. 62,389 T. 33,224 (53.25%) Lab. hold
Rt. Hon. Patricia Hewitt, Lab.	17,184
Sarah Richardson, C.	8,114
Zuffar Haq, LD	5,803
Geoff Forse, Green	1,571
Steve Score, Soc. Alt.	552

Lab. maj. 9,070 (27.30%)
0.86% swing Lab. to C.
(2001: Lab. maj. 9,639 (29.02%))

LEICESTERSHIRE NORTH WEST
E. 70,519 T. 47,140 (66.85%)
Lab. (Co-op) hold
David Taylor, Lab. (Co-op)	21,449
Nicola Le Page, C.	16,972
Rod Keyes, LD	5,682
John Blunt, UKIP	1,563
Clive Potter, BNP	1,474

Lab. (Co-op) maj. 4,477 (9.50%)
4.31% swing Lab. (Co-op) to C.
(2001: Lab. (Co-op) maj. 8,157 (18.12%))

LEIGH
E. 72,473 T. 36,488 (50.35%) Lab. hold
Andy Burnham, Lab.	23,097
Laurance Wedderburn, C.	5,825
Dave Crowther, LD	4,962
Ian Franzen, CAP	2,189
Thomas Hampson, LCA	415

Lab. maj. 17,272 (47.34%)
0.49% swing C. to Lab.
(2001: Lab. maj. 16,362 (46.35%))

LEOMINSTER
E. 70,587 T. 48,793 (69.12%)   C. hold
Bill Wiggin, C.	25,407
Caroline Williams, LD	12,220
Paul Bell, Lab.	7,424
Felicity Norman, Green	2,191
Peter Venables, UKIP	1,551

C. maj. 13,187 (27.03%)
2.42% swing LD to C.
(2001: C. maj. 10,367 (22.19%))

LEWES
E. 67,073 T. 46,552 (69.40%)   LD hold
Norman Baker, LD	24,376
Rory Love, C.	15,902
Richard Black, Lab.	4,169
Susan Murray, Green	1,071
John Petley, UKIP	1,034

LD maj. 8,474 (18.20%)
1.58% swing LD to C.
(2001: LD maj. 9,710 (21.37%))

LEWISHAM DEPTFORD
E. 59,018 T. 30,393 (51.50%) Lab. hold
Joan Ruddock, Lab.	16,902
Columba Blango, LD	5,091
James Cartlidge, C.	3,773
Darren Johnson, Green	3,367
Ian Page, Soc. Alt.	742
Dr David Holland, UKIP	518

Lab. maj. 11,811 (38.86%)
7.21% swing Lab. to LD
(2001: Lab. maj. 15,293 (52.54%))

LEWISHAM EAST
E. 59,135 T. 31,127 (52.64%) Lab. hold
Bridget Prentice, Lab.	14,263
James Cleverly, C.	7,512
Richard Thomas, LD	6,787
Anna Baker, Green	1,243
Arnold Tarling, UKIP	697
Bernard Franklin, NF	625

Lab. maj. 6,751 (21.69%)
4.12% swing Lab. to C.
(2001: Lab. maj. 8,959 (29.82%))

LEWISHAM WEST
E. 58,349 T. 31,923 (54.71%) Lab. hold
Jim Dowd, Lab.	16,611
Alex Feakes, LD	6,679
Evett McAnuff, C.	6,396
Nick Long, Green	1,464
Jens Winton, UKIP	773

Lab. maj. 9,932 (31.11%)
8.25% swing Lab. to LD
(2001: Lab. maj. 11,920 (38.68%))

LEYTON & WANSTEAD
E. 60,444 T. 33,272 (55.05%) Lab. hold
Harry Cohen, Lab.	15,234
Meher Khan, LD	8,377
Julien Foster, C.	7,393
Ashley Gunstock, Green	1,522
Nick Jones, UKIP	591
Marc Robertson, Ind.	155

Lab. maj. 6,857 (20.61%)
10.71% swing Lab. to LD
(2001: Lab. maj. 12,904 (38.27%))

LICHFIELD
E. 65,565 T. 43,744 (66.72%)   C. hold
Michael Fabricant, C.	21,274
Nigel Gardner, Lab.	14,194
Ian Jackson, LD	6,804
Malcolm McKenzie, UKIP	1,472

C. maj. 7,080 (16.19%)
2.78% swing Lab. to C.
(2001: C. maj. 4,426 (10.62%))

LINCOLN
E. 65,203 T. 36,857 (56.53%) Lab. hold
Gillian Merron, Lab.   16,724
Karl McCartney, C.   12,110
Lisa Gabriel, LD   6,715
Nicholas Smith, UKIP   1,308
Lab. maj. 4,614 (12.52%)
5.08% swing Lab. to C.
(2001: Lab. maj. 8,420 (22.68%))

LIVERPOOL GARSTON
E. 63,669 T. 34,974 (54.93%) Lab. hold
Maria Eagle, Lab.   18,900
Paula Keaveney, LD   11,707
Amber Rudd, C.   3,424
Kevin Kearney, UKIP   780
David Oatley, WRP   163
Lab. maj. 7,193 (20.57%)
8.85% swing Lab. to LD
(2001: Lab. maj. 12,494 (38.27%))

LIVERPOOL RIVERSIDE
E. 75,171 T. 31,191 (41.49%)
                          Lab. (Co-op) hold
Louise Ellman, Lab. (Co-op)   17,951
Richard Marbrow, LD   7,737
Gabrielle Howatson, C.   2,843
Peter Cranie, Green   1,707
Beth Marshall, Soc. Lab.   498
Ann Irving, UKIP   455
Lab. (Co-op) maj. 10,214 (32.75%)
10.98% swing Lab. (Co-op) to LD
(2001: Lab. (Co-op) maj. 13,950
(54.70%))

LIVERPOOL WALTON
E. 62,044 T. 27,930 (45.02%) Lab. hold
Peter Kilfoyle, Lab.   20,322
Kiron Reid, LD   4,365
Sharon Buckle, C.   1,655
Joseph Moran, UKIP   1,108
Daniel Wood, Lib.   480
Lab. maj. 15,957 (57.13%)
3.05% swing Lab. to LD
(2001: Lab. maj. 17,996 (63.24%))

LIVERPOOL WAVERTREE
E. 69,189 T. 35,171 (50.83%) Lab. hold
Rt. Hon. Jane Kennedy, Lab.   18,441
Colin Eldridge, LD   13,268
Jason Steen, C.   2,331
Mark Bill, UKIP   660
Gary Theys, Soc. Lab.   244
Paul Filby, Dem. Soc. All.   227
Lab. maj. 5,173 (14.71%)
11.81% swing Lab. to LD
(2001: Lab. maj. 12,319 (38.33%))

LIVERPOOL WEST DERBY
E. 64,591 T. 30,464 (47.16%) Lab. hold
Robert Wareing, Lab.   19,140
Patrick Maloney, LD   3,915
Steve Radford, Lib.   3,606
Peter Garrett, C.   2,567
Kai Andersen, Soc. Lab.   698
Peter Baden, UKIP   538
Lab. maj. 15,225 (49.98%)
2.66% swing Lab. to LD
(2001: Lab. maj. 15,853 (51.29%))

LOUGHBOROUGH
E. 72,351 T. 46,140 (63.77%)
                          Lab. (Co-op) hold
Andy Reed, Lab. (Co-op)   19,098
Nicky Morgan, C.   17,102
Graeme Smith, LD   8,258
Bernard Sherratt, UKIP   1,094
John McVay, Veritas   588
Lab. (Co-op) maj. 1,996 (4.33%)
5.04% swing Lab. (Co-op) to C.
(2001: Lab. (Co-op) maj. 6,378
(14.41%))

LOUTH & HORNCASTLE
E. 75,313 T. 46,683 (61.99%)   C. hold
Sir Peter Tapsell, C.   21,744
Frank Hodgkiss, Lab.   11,848
Fiona Martin, LD   9,480
Christopher Pain, UKIP   3,611
C. maj. 9,896 (21.20%)
2.10% swing Lab. to C.
(2001: C. maj. 7,554 (16.99%))

LUDLOW
E. 64,572 T. 46,540 (72.07%)   C. gain
*Philip Dunne, C.   20,979
Matthew Green, LD   18,952
Nigel Knowles, Lab.   4,974
Jim Gaffney, Green   852
Michael Zuckerman, UKIP   783
C. maj. 2,027 (4.36%)
4.07% swing LD to C.
(2001: LD maj. 1,630 (3.78%))

LUTON NORTH
E. 68,175 T. 39,122 (57.38%) Lab. hold
Kelvin Hopkins, Lab.   19,062
Hannah Hall, C.   12,575
Linda Jack, LD   6,081
Colin Brown, UKIP   1,255
Kayson Gurney, Forum   149
Lab. maj. 6,487 (16.58%)
4.46% swing Lab. to C.
(2001: Lab. maj. 9,977 (25.50%))

LUTON SOUTH
E. 71,949 T. 38,918 (54.09%) Lab. hold
Margaret Moran, Lab.   16,610
Richard Stay, C.   10,960
Qurban Hussain, LD   8,778
Charles Lawman, UKIP   957
Marc Scheimann, Green   790
Mohammed Ilyas, Respect   725
Arthur Lynn, WRP   98
Lab. maj. 5,650 (14.52%)
5.62% swing Lab. to C.
(2001: Lab. maj. 10,133 (25.75%))

MACCLESFIELD
E. 72,267 T. 45,621 (63.13%)   C. hold
Sir Nicholas Winterton, C.   22,628
Stephen Carter, Lab.   13,227
Catherine O'Brien, LD   8,918
John Scott, Veritas   848
C. maj. 9,401 (20.61%)
2.41% swing Lab. to C.
(2001: C. maj. 7,200 (15.79%))

MAIDENHEAD
E. 63,978 T. 45,850 (71.67%)   C. hold
Rt. Hon. Theresa May, C.   23,312
Kathryn Newbound, LD   17,081
Janet Pritchard, Lab.   4,144
Tim Rait, BNP   704
Douglas Lewis, UKIP   609
C. maj. 6,231 (13.59%)
3.00% swing LD to C.
(2001: C. maj. 3,284 (7.58%))

MAIDSTONE & THE WEALD
E. 74,054 T. 48,755 (65.84%)   C. hold
Rt. Hon. Ann Widdecombe, C.   25,670
Beth Breeze, Lab.   10,814
Mark Corney, LD   10,808
Anthony Robertson, UKIP   1,463
C. maj. 14,856 (30.47%)
3.92% swing Lab. to C.
(2001: C. maj. 10,318 (22.64%))

MAKERFIELD
E. 69,039 T. 35,580 (51.54%) Lab. hold
Rt. Hon. Ian McCartney, Lab.   22,494
Kulveer Ranger, C.   4,345
Trevor Beswick, LD   3,789
Peter Franzen, CAP   2,769
Dennis Shambley, BNP   1,221
Gregory Atherton, UKIP   962
Lab. maj. 18,149 (51.01%)
0.04% swing C. to Lab.
(2001: Lab. maj. 17,750 (50.92%))

MALDON & CHELMSFORD EAST
E. 69,502 T. 46,091 (66.32%)   C. hold
John Whittingdale, C.   23,732
Sue Tibballs, Lab.   11,159
Matthew Lambert, LD   9,270
Jesse Pryke, UKIP   1,930
C. maj. 12,573 (27.28%)
4.05% swing Lab. to C.
(2001: C. maj. 8,462 (19.19%))

MANCHESTER BLACKLEY
E. 60,229 T. 27,591 (45.81%) Lab. hold
Graham Stringer, Lab.   17,187
Iain Donaldson, LD   5,160
Amar Ahmed, C.   3,690
Roger Bullock, UKIP   1,554
Lab. maj. 12,027 (43.59%)
6.99% swing Lab. to LD
(2001: Lab. maj. 14,464 (54.53%))

MANCHESTER CENTRAL
E. 69,656 T. 29,264 (42.01%) Lab. hold
Tony Lloyd, Lab.   16,993
Marc Ramsbottom, LD   7,217
Tom Jackson, C.   2,504
Steven Durrant, Green   1,292
Richard Kemp, NF   421
Damien O'Connor, Ind. Pr. Lab.   382
Dr John Whittaker, UKIP   272
Ronald Sinclair, Soc. Lab.   183
Lab. maj. 9,776 (33.41%)
9.80% swing Lab. to LD
(2001: Lab. maj. 13,742 (53.00%))

MANCHESTER GORTON
E. 64,696 T. 29,123 (45.02%) Lab. hold
Rt. Hon. Sir Gerald Kaufman, Lab.
                                15,480
Qassim Afzal, LD   9,672
Amanda Byrne, C.   2,848
Gregory Beaman, UKIP   783
Dan Waller, WRP   181
Matthew Kay, RP   159
Lab. maj. 5,808 (19.94%)
10.79% swing Lab. to LD
(2001: Lab. maj. 11,304 (41.51%))

MANCHESTER WITHINGTON
E. 67,781 T. 37,458 (55.26%) LD gain
*John Leech, LD   15,872
Rt. Hon. Keith Bradley, Lab. 15,205
Karen Bradley, C.   3,919
Brian Candeland, Green   1,595
Dr Robert Gutfreund-Walmsley, UKIP
                                 424
Ivan Benett, Ind.   243
Yasmin Zalzala, Ind.   153
Richard Reed, TP   47
LD maj. 667 (1.78%)
17.33% swing Lab. to LD
(2001: Lab. maj. 11,524 (32.88%))

MANSFIELD
E. 69,131 T. 38,276 (55.37%) Lab. hold
Alan Meale, Lab.   18,400
Anne Wright, C.   7,035
Stewart Rickersey, Ind.   6,491
Roger Shelley, LD   5,316
Michael Harvey, Veritas   1,034
Lab. maj. 11,365 (29.69%)
0.13% swing Lab. to C.
(2001: Lab. maj. 11,038 (29.95%))

MEDWAY
E. 67,251 T. 41,093 (61.10%) Lab. hold
Bob Marshall-Andrews, Lab.   17,333
Mark Reckless, C.   17,120
Geoffrey Juby, LD   5,152
Robert Oakley, UKIP   1,488
Lab. maj. 213 (0.52%)
4.64% swing Lab. to C.
(2001: Lab. maj. 3,780 (9.79%))

MERIDEN
E. 77,342 T. 46,503 (60.13%) C. hold
Caroline Spelman, C.   22,416
Jim Brown, Lab.   15,407
William Laitinen, LD   7,113
Denis Brookes, UKIP   1,567
C. maj. 7,009 (15.07%)
3.29% swing Lab. to C.
(2001: C. maj. 3,784 (8.49%))

MIDDLESBROUGH
E. 65,924 T. 32,140 (48.75%) Lab. hold
Sir Stuart Bell, Lab.   18,562
Joe Michna, LD   5,995
Caroline Flynn-Macleod, C.   5,263
Ron Armes, BNP   819
Michael Landers, UKIP   768
Jackie Elder, Ind.   503
Derrick Arnott, Ind.   230
Lab. maj. 12,567 (39.10%)
9.03% swing Lab. to LD
(2001: Lab. maj. 16,330 (48.43%))

MIDDLESBROUGH SOUTH &
CLEVELAND EAST
E. 71,883 T. 43,696 (60.79%) Lab. hold
Dr Ashok Kumar, Lab.   21,945
Mark Brooks, C.   13,945
Carl Minns, LD   6,049
Geoffrey Groves, BNP   1,099
Charlotte Bull, UKIP   658
Lab. maj. 8,000 (18.31%)
1.47% swing Lab. to C.
(2001: Lab. maj. 9,351 (21.26%))

MILTON KEYNES NORTH EAST
E. 78,758 T. 50,104 (63.62%)   C. gain
*Mark Lancaster, C.   19,674
Brian White, Lab.   18,009
Jane Carr, LD   9,789
Michael Phillips, UKIP   1,400
Peter Richardson, Green   1,090
Anant Vyas, Ind.   142
C. maj. 1,665 (3.32%)
3.60% swing Lab. to C.
(2001: Lab. maj. 1,829 (3.88%))

MILTON KEYNES SOUTH WEST
E. 82,228 T. 48,709 (59.24%) Lab. hold
Dr Phyllis Starkey, Lab.   20,862
Iain Stewart, C.   16,852
Neil Stuart, LD   7,909
George Harlock, UKIP   1,750
Alan Francis, Green   1,336
Lab. maj. 4,010 (8.23%)
3.57% swing Lab. to C.
(2001: Lab. maj. 6,978 (15.38%))

MITCHAM & MORDEN
E. 65,172 T. 39,868 (61.17%) Lab. hold
Siobhain McDonagh, Lab.   22,489
Andrew Shellhorn, C.   9,929
Jo Christie-Smith, LD   5,583
Tom Walsh, Green   1,395
Adrian Roberts, Veritas   286
Rathy Alagaratnam, Ind.   186
Lab. maj. 12,560 (31.50%)
2.40% swing Lab. to C.
(2001: Lab. maj. 13,785 (36.31%))

MOLE VALLEY
E. 68,181 T. 49,415 (72.48%)   C. hold
Sir Paul Beresford, C.   27,060
Nasser Butt, LD   15,063
Farmida Bi, Lab.   5,310
David Payne, UKIP   1,475
Roger Meekins, Veritas   507
C. maj. 11,997 (24.28%)
1.35% swing LD to C.
(2001: C. maj. 10,153 (21.57%))

MORECAMBE & LUNESDALE
E. 67,775 T. 41,635 (61.43%) Lab. hold
Geraldine Smith, Lab.   20,331
James Airey, C.   15,563
Alex Stone, LD   5,741
Lab. maj. 4,768 (11.45%)
0.39% swing Lab. to C.
(2001: Lab. maj. 5,092 (12.22%))

MORLEY & ROTHWELL
E. 72,248 T. 42,495 (58.82%) Lab. hold
Colin Challen, Lab.   20,570
Nick Vineall, C.   8,227
Stewart Golton, LD   6,819
Robert Finnigan, Ind.   4,608
Chris Beverley, BNP   2,271
Lab. maj. 12,343 (29.05%)
1.20% swing Lab. to C.
(2001: Lab. maj. 12,090 (31.45%))

NEW FOREST EAST
E. 68,633 T. 45,235 (65.91%)   C. hold
Dr Julian Lewis, C.   21,975
Brian Dash, LD   15,424
Stephen Roberts, Lab.   5,492
Katy Davies, UKIP   2,344
C. maj. 6,551 (14.48%)
2.70% swing LD to C.
(2001: C. maj. 3,829 (9.08%))

NEW FOREST WEST
E. 69,232 T. 46,067 (66.54%)   C. hold
Desmond Swayne, C.   26,004
Murari Kaushik, LD   8,719
Janice Hurne, Lab.   7,590
Brian Lawrence, UKIP   1,917
Janet Richards, Green   1,837
C. maj. 17,285 (37.52%)
3.80% swing LD to C.
(2001: C. maj. 13,191 (29.92%))

NEWARK
E. 72,249 T. 45,696 (63.25%)   C. hold
Patrick Mercer, C.   21,946
Jason Reece, Lab.   15,482
Stuart Thompstone, LD   7,276
Charlotte Creasy, UKIP   992
C. maj. 6,464 (14.15%)
2.56% swing Lab. to C.
(2001: C. maj. 4,073 (9.02%))

NEWBURY
E. 75,903 T. 54,673 (72.03%)   C. gain
*Richard Benyon, C.   26,771
David Rendel, LD   23,311
Oscar Van Nooijen, Lab.   3,239
David McMahon, UKIP   857
Nicholas Cornish, Ind.   409
Barrie Singleton, Ind.   86
C. maj. 3,460 (6.33%)
5.54% swing LD to C.
(2001: LD maj. 2,415 (4.75%))

NEWCASTLE-UNDER-LYME
E. 68,414 T. 39,788 (58.16%) Lab. hold
Paul Farrelly, Lab.   18,053
Jeremy Lefroy, C.   9,945
Trevor Johnson, LD   7,528
David Nixon, UKIP   1,436
John Dawson, BNP   1,390
Prof. Andrew Dobson, Green   918
Marian Harvey-Lover, Veritas   518
Lab. maj. 8,108 (20.38%)
2.72% swing Lab. to C.
(2001: Lab. maj. 9,986 (25.82%))

NEWCASTLE UPON TYNE CENTRAL
E. 62,734 T. 35,920 (57.26%) Lab. hold
Jim Cousins, Lab.   16,211
Greg Stone, LD   12,229
Wendy Morton, C.   5,749
Joe Hulm, Green   1,254
Clive Harding, NACVP   477
Lab. maj. 3,982 (11.09%)
11.10% swing Lab. to LD
(2001: Lab. maj. 11,605 (33.28%))

NEWCASTLE UPON TYNE EAST &
WALLSEND
E. 56,900 T. 31,678 (55.67%) Lab. hold
Rt. Hon. Nick Brown, Lab.   17,462
David Ord, LD   9,897
Norma Dias, C.   3,532
William Hopwood, Soc. Alt.   582
Martin Levy, Comm. Brit.   205
Lab. maj. 7,565 (23.88%)
9.81% swing Lab. to LD
(2001: Lab. maj. 14,223 (43.50%))

NEWCASTLE UPON TYNE NORTH
E. 64,599 T. 38,444 (59.51%) Lab. hold
Doug Henderson, Lab.	19,224
Ron Beadle, LD	12,201
Neil Hudson, C.	6,022
Roland Wood, NF	997
Lab. maj. 7,023 (18.27%)
11.22% swing Lab. to LD
(2001: Lab. maj. 14,450 (39.73%))

NORFOLK MID
E. 81,738 T. 54,734 (66.96%) C. hold
Keith Simpson, C.	23,564
Daniel Zeichner, Lab.	16,004
Vivienne Clifford-Jackson, LD	12,988
Simon Fletcher, UKIP	2,178
C. maj. 7,560 (13.81%)
2.57% swing Lab. to C.
(2001: C. maj. 4,562 (8.68%))

NORFOLK NORTH
E. 80,784 T. 58,965 (72.99%) LD hold
Norman Lamb, LD	31,515
Iain Dale, C.	20,909
Philip Harris, Lab.	5,447
Stuart Agnew, UKIP	978
Justin Appleyard, Ind.	116
LD maj. 10,606 (17.99%)
8.56% swing C. to LD
(2001: LD maj. 483 (0.86%))

NORFOLK NORTH WEST
E. 82,171 T. 50,649 (61.64%) C. hold
Henry Bellingham, C.	25,471
Damien Welfare, Lab.	16,291
Simon Higginson, LD	7,026
Michael Stone, UKIP	1,861
C. maj. 9,180 (18.12%)
5.66% swing Lab. to C.
(2001: C. maj. 3,485 (6.81%))

NORFOLK SOUTH
E. 85,896 T. 58,974 (68.66%) C. hold
Richard Bacon, C.	26,399
Dr Ian Mack, LD	17,617
John Morgan, Lab.	13,262
Philip Tye, UKIP	1,696
C. maj. 8,782 (14.89%)
1.28% swing LD to C.
(2001: C. maj. 6,893 (12.32%))

NORFOLK SOUTH WEST
E. 88,260 T. 55,127 (62.46%) C. hold
†Christopher Fraser, C.	25,881
Charmaine Morgan, Lab.	15,795
April Pond, LD	10,207
Delia Hall, UKIP	2,738
Kim Hayes, Ind.	506
C. maj. 10,086 (18.30%)
0.30% swing Lab. to C.
(2001: C. maj. 9,366 (17.69%))

NORMANTON
E. 65,129 T. 37,424 (57.46%)
	Lab. (Co-op) hold
*Ed Balls, Lab. (Co-op)	19,161
Andrew Percy, C.	9,159
Simone Butterworth, LD	6,357
John Aveyard, BNP	1,967
Mark Harrop, Ind.	780
Lab. (Co-op) maj. 10,002 (26.73%)
1.18% swing Lab. (Co-op) to C.
(2001: Lab. (Co-op) maj. 9,937 (29.09%))

NORTHAMPTON NORTH
E. 73,926 T. 42,048 (56.88%) Lab. hold
Sally Keeble, Lab.	16,905
Damian Collins, C.	12,945
Andrew Simpson, LD	10,317
John Howsam, UKIP	1,050
Paul Withrington, SOS	495
Andrew Otchie, CPA	336
Lab. maj. 3,960 (9.42%)
4.80% swing Lab. to C.
(2001: Lab. maj. 7,893 (19.02%))

NORTHAMPTON SOUTH
E. 89,722 T. 54,481 (60.72%) C. gain
*Brian Binley, C.	23,818
Tony Clarke, Lab.	19,399
Kevin Barron, LD	8,327
Derek Clark, UKIP	1,032
Anthony Green, Veritas	508
John Harrisson, SOS	437
John Percival, Loony	354
Fitzy Fitzpatrick, Ind.	346
Tim Webb, CPA	260
C. maj. 4,419 (8.11%)
4.92% swing Lab. to C. \
(2001: Lab. maj. 885 (1.73%))

NORTHAVON
E. 81,800 T. 59,056 (72.20%) LD hold
Prof. Steve Webb, LD	30,872
Chris Butt, C.	19,839
Patricia Gardener, Lab.	6,277
Adrian Blake, UKIP	1,032
Alan Pinder, Green	922
Thomas Beacham, Ind.	114
LD maj. 11,033 (18.68%)
0.48% swing C. to LD
(2001: LD maj. 9,877 (17.71%))

NORWICH NORTH
E. 76,992 T. 47,033 (61.09%) Lab. hold
Dr Ian Gibson, Lab.	21,097
James Tumbridge, C.	15,638
Robin Whitmore, LD	7,616
Adrian Holmes, Green	1,252
John Youles, UKIP	1,122
Bill Holden, Ind.	308
Lab. maj. 5,459 (11.61%)
0.62% swing Lab. to C.
(2001: Lab. maj. 5,863 (12.85%))

NORWICH SOUTH
E. 70,409 T. 42,190 (59.92%) Lab. hold
Rt. Hon. Charles Clarke, Lab.	15,904
Andrew Aalders-Dunthorne, LD	12,251
Antony Little, C.	9,567
Adrian Ramsay, Green	3,101
Vandra Ahlstrom, UKIP	597
Christine Constable, Eng. Dem.	466
Don Barnard, LCA	219
Roger Blackwell, WRP	85
Lab. maj. 3,653 (8.66%)
7.09% swing Lab. to LD
(2001: Lab. maj. 8,816 (20.70%))

NOTTINGHAM EAST
E. 60,634 T. 30,091 (49.63%) Lab. hold
John Heppell, Lab.	13,787
Issan Ghazni, LD	6,848
Jim Thornton, C.	6,826
Ashley Baxter, Green	1,517
Anthony Ellwood, UKIP	740
Pete Ratcliff, Soc. Unity	373
Lab. maj. 6,939 (23.06%)
11.44% swing Lab. to LD
(2001: Lab. maj. 10,320 (34.71%))

NOTTINGHAM NORTH
E. 61,894 T. 30,383 (49.09%) Lab. hold
Graham Allen, Lab.	17,842
Priti Patel, C.	5,671
Tim Ball, LD	5,190
Irena Marriott, UKIP	1,680
Lab. maj. 12,171 (40.06%)
0.34% swing Lab. to C.
(2001: Lab. maj. 12,240 (40.74%))

NOTTINGHAM SOUTH
E. 68,921 T. 34,840 (50.55%) Lab. hold
Alan Simpson, Lab.	16,506
Sudesh Mattu, C.	9,020
Tony Sutton, LD	7,961
Ken Browne, UKIP	1,353
Lab. maj. 7,486 (21.49%)
2.90% swing Lab. to C.
(2001: Lab. maj. 9,989 (27.29%))

NUNEATON
E. 73,440 T. 45,280 (61.66%) Lab. hold
Bill Olner, Lab.	19,945
Mark Pawsey, C.	17,665
Ali Asghar, LD	5,884
Keith Tyson, UKIP	1,786
Lab. maj. 2,280 (5.04%)
6.18% swing Lab. to C.
(2001: Lab. maj. 7,535 (17.40%))

OLD BEXLEY & SIDCUP
E. 68,227 T. 44,572 (65.33%) C. hold
Derek Conway, C.	22,191
Gavin Moore, Lab.	12,271
Nickolas O'Hare, LD	6,564
Michael Barnbrook, UKIP	2,015
Claire Sayers, BNP	1,227
Gregory Peters, Ind.	304
C. maj. 9,920 (22.26%)
7.16% swing Lab. to C.
(2001: C. maj. 3,345 (7.94%))

OLDHAM EAST & SADDLEWORTH
E. 75,680 T. 43,367 (57.30%) Lab. hold
Phil Woolas, Lab.	17,968
Tony Dawson, LD	14,378
Keith Chapman, C.	7,901
Michael Treacy, BNP	2,109
Valerie Nield, UKIP	873
Philip O'Grady, Ind.	138
Lab. maj. 3,590 (8.28%)
1.14% swing LD to Lab.
(2001: Lab. maj. 2,726 (6.00%))

OLDHAM WEST & ROYTON
E. 70,496 T. 37,562 (53.28%) Lab. hold
Rt. Hon. Michael Meacher, Lab.	18,452
Sean Moore, C.	7,998
Stuart Bodsworth, LD	7,519
Anita Corbett, BNP	2,606
David Short, UKIP	987
Lab. maj. 10,454 (27.83%)
2.81% swing Lab. to C.
(2001: Lab. maj. 13,365 (33.44%))

ORPINGTON
E. 78,276 T. 54,734 (69.92%) C. hold
John Horam, C.	26,718
Chris Maines, LD	21,771
Emily Bird, Lab.	4,914
Mick Greenhough, UKIP	1,331
C. maj. 4,947 (9.04%)
4.25% swing LD to C.
(2001: C. maj. 269 (0.53%))

OXFORD EAST
E. 72,234 T. 41,790 (57.85%) Lab. hold
Rt. Hon. Andrew Smith, Lab.	15,405
Steve Goddard, LD	14,442
Virginia Morris, C.	6,992
Jacob Sanders, Green	1,813
Honest Blair, Ind.	1,485
Maurice Leen, IWCA	892
Peter Gardner, UKIP	715
Pat Mylvaganam, Ind.	46

Lab. maj. 963 (2.30%)
11.83% swing Lab. to LD
(2001: Lab. maj. 10,344 (25.96%))

OXFORD WEST & ABINGDON
E. 80,195 T. 52,600 (65.59%) LD hold
Dr Evan Harris, LD	24,336
Amanda McLean, C.	16,653
Antonia Bance, Lab.	8,725
Tom Lines, Green	2,091
Marcus Watney, UKIP	795

LD maj. 7,683 (14.61%)
1.60% swing LD to C.
(2001: LD maj. 9,185 (17.81%))

PENDLE
E. 64,917 T. 41,132 (63.36%) Lab. hold
Gordon Prentice, Lab.	15,250
Jane Ellison, C.	13,070
Shazad Anwar, LD	9,528
Thomas Boocock, BNP	2,547
Graham Cannon, UKIP	737

Lab. maj. 2,180 (5.30%)
2.73% swing Lab. to C.
(2001: Lab. maj. 4,275 (10.76%))

PENRITH & THE BORDER
E. 70,922 T. 46,882 (66.10%) C. hold
Rt. Hon. David Maclean, C.	24,046
Geyve Walker, LD	12,142
Michael Boaden, Lab.	8,958
William Robinson, UKIP	1,187
Mark Gibson, LCA	549

C. maj. 11,904 (25.39%)
3.89% swing C. to LD
(2001: C. maj. 14,677 (33.17%))

PETERBOROUGH
E. 67,499 T. 41,204 (61.04%) C. gain
*Stewart Jackson, C.	17,364
Rt. Hon. Helen Clark, Lab.	14,624
Nick Sandford, LD	6,876
Mary Herdman, UKIP	1,242
Terry Blackham, NF	931
Marc Potter, MNP	167

C. maj. 2,740 (6.65%)
6.91% swing Lab. to C.
(2001: Lab. maj. 2,854 (7.17%))

PLYMOUTH DEVONPORT
E. 72,848 T. 42,013 (57.67%) Lab. hold
*Alison Seabeck, Lab.	18,612
Richard Cuming, C.	10,509
Judith Jolly, LD	8,000
Bill Wakeham, UKIP	3,324
Keith Greene, Ind.	747
Robert Hawkins, Soc. Lab.	445
Tony Staunton, Respect	376

Lab. maj. 8,103 (19.29%)
5.98% swing Lab. to C.
(2001: Lab. maj. 13,033 (31.24%))

PLYMOUTH SUTTON
E. 67,202 T. 38,192 (56.83%)
Lab. (Co-op) hold
Linda Gilroy, Lab. (Co-op)	15,497
Oliver Colvile, C.	11,388
Karen Gillard, LD	8,685
Robert Cumming, UKIP	2,392
Rob Hawkins, Soc. Lab.	230

Lab. (Co-op) maj. 4,109 (10.76%)
4.24% swing Lab. (Co-op) to C.
(2001: Lab. (Co-op) maj. 7,517
(19.24%))

PONTEFRACT & CASTLEFORD
E. 61,871 T. 32,947 (53.25%) Lab. hold
Yvette Cooper, Lab.	20,973
Simon Jones, C.	5,727
Wesley Paxton, LD	3,942
Suzy Cass, BNP	1,835
Bob Hague, Green Soc.	470

Lab. maj. 15,246 (46.27%)
2.95% swing Lab. to C.
(2001: Lab. maj. 16,378 (52.17%))

POOLE
E. 64,178 T. 40,513 (63.13%) C. hold
Robert Syms, C.	17,571
Mike Plummer, LD	11,583
Darren Brown, Lab.	9,376
John Barnes, UKIP	1,436
Peter Pirnie, BNP	547

C. maj. 5,988 (14.78%)
2.42% swing C. to LD
(2001: C. maj. 7,166 (18.27%))

POPLAR & CANNING TOWN
E. 81,544 T. 39,010 (47.84%) Lab. hold
Jim Fitzpatrick, Lab.	15,628
Tim Archer, C.	8,499
Oliur Rahman, Respect	6,573
Janet Ludlow, LD	5,420
Terry McGrenera, Green	955
Aminul Hoque, Ind.	815
Tony Smith, Veritas	650
Simeon Ademolake, CPA	470

Lab. maj. 7,129 (18.27%)
11.55% swing Lab. to C.
(2001: Lab. maj. 14,104 (41.35%))

PORTSMOUTH NORTH
E. 62,884 T. 37,717 (59.98%)
Lab. (Co-op) hold
*Sarah McCarthy-Fry, Lab. (Co-op)	
	15,412
Penny Mordaunt, C.	14,273
Gary Lawson, LD	6,684
Mike Smith, UKIP	1,348

Lab. (Co-op) maj. 1,139 (3.02%)
5.45% swing Lab. (Co-op) to C.
(2001: Lab. (Co-op) maj. 5,134
(13.93%))

PORTSMOUTH SOUTH
E. 70,969 T. 40,374 (56.89%) LD hold
Mike Hancock, LD	17,047
Caroline Dinenage, C.	13,685
Mark Button, Lab.	8,714
Dennis Pierson, UKIP	928

LD maj. 3,362 (8.33%)
3.60% swing LD to C.
(2001: LD maj. 6,094 (15.54%))

PRESTON
E. 63,351 T. 34,081 (53.80%)
Lab. (Co-op) hold
Mark Hendrick, Lab. (Co-op)	17,210
Fiona Bryce, C.	7,803
William Parkinson, LD	5,701
Michael Lavalette, Respect	2,318
Ellen Boardman, UKIP	1,049

Lab. (Co-op) maj. 9,407 (27.60%)
3.22% swing Lab. (Co-op) to C.
(2001: Lab. (Co-op) maj. 12,268
(34.04%))

PUDSEY
E. 70,411 T. 46,444 (65.96%) Lab. hold
Paul Truswell, Lab.	21,261
Pamela Singleton, C.	15,391
James Keeley, LD	8,551
David Daniel, UKIP	1,241

Lab. maj. 5,870 (12.64%)
0.09% swing C. to Lab.
(2001: Lab. maj. 5,626 (12.45%))

PUTNEY
E. 61,498 T. 36,574 (59.47%) C. gain
*Justine Greening, C.	15,497
Tony Colman, Lab.	13,731
Jeremy Ambache, LD	5,965
Keith Magnum, Green	993
Anthony Gahan, UKIP	388

C. maj. 1,766 (4.83%)
6.46% swing Lab. to C.
(2001: Lab. maj. 2,771 (8.09%))

RAYLEIGH
E. 71,996 T. 46,193 (64.16%) C. hold
Mark Francois, C.	25,609
Julian Ware-Lane, Lab.	10,883
Sid Cumberland, LD	7,406
Janet Davies, UKIP	2,295

C. maj. 14,726 (31.88%)
6.25% swing Lab. to C.
(2001: C. maj. 8,290 (19.38%))

READING EAST
E. 72,806 T. 43,912 (60.31%) C. gain
*Rob Wilson, C.	15,557
Tony Page, Lab.	15,082
Prof. John Howson, LD	10,619
Rob White, Green	1,548
David Lamb, UKIP	849
Jan Lloyd, Ind.	135
Rex Hora, Ind.	122

C. maj. 475 (1.08%)
6.95% swing Lab. to C.
(2001: Lab. maj. 5,588 (12.81%))

READING WEST
E. 69,011 T. 42,103 (61.01%) Lab. hold
Martin Salter, Lab.	18,940
Ewan Cameron, C.	14,258
Denise Gaines, LD	6,663
Peter Williams, UKIP	1,180
Adrian Windisch, Green	921
Dave Boyle, Veritas	141

Lab. maj. 4,682 (11.12%)
4.98% swing Lab. to C.
(2001: Lab. maj. 8,849 (21.08%))

REDCAR
E. 66,947 T. 38,861 (58.05%) Lab. hold
Vera Baird, Lab. 19,968
Ian Swales, LD 7,852
Jonathan Lehrle, C. 6,954
Christopher McGlade, Ind. 2,379
Andrew Harris, BNP 985
Edward Walker, UKIP 564
John Taylor, Soc. Lab. 159
Lab. maj. 12,116 (31.18%)
8.25% swing Lab. to LD
(2001: Lab. maj. 13,443 (35.19%))

REDDITCH
E. 64,121 T. 40,291 (62.84%) Lab. hold
Rt. Hon. Jacqui Smith, Lab. 18,012
Karen Lumley, C. 15,296
Nigel Hicks, LD 5,602
John Ison, UKIP 1,381
Lab. maj. 2,716 (6.74%)
0.02% swing C. to Lab.
(2001: Lab. maj. 2,484 (6.71%))

REGENT'S PARK & KENSINGTON
NORTH
E. 78,975 T. 40,680 (51.51%) Lab. hold
Karen Buck, Lab. 18,196
Jeremy Bradshaw, C. 12,065
Rabi Martins, LD 7,569
Dr Paul Miller, Green 1,985
Pamela Perrin, UKIP 456
Rezouk Boufas, CP 227
Abby Dharamsey, Ind. 182
Lab. maj. 6,131 (15.07%)
6.32% swing Lab. to C.
(2001: Lab. maj. 10,266 (27.71%))

REIGATE
E. 65,719 T. 42,605 (64.83%) C. hold
Crispin Blunt, C. 20,884
Jane Kulka, LD 9,896
Sam Townend, Lab. 8,896
Jeremy Wraith, UKIP 1,921
Harold Green, EDP 600
Michael Selby, Ind. 408
C. maj. 10,988 (25.79%)
0.46% swing C. to LD
(2001: C. maj. 8,025 (20.33%))

RIBBLE SOUTH
E. 75,357 T. 47,511 (63.05%) Lab. hold
David Borrow, Lab. 20,428
Lorraine Fullbrook, C. 18,244
Mark Alcock, LD 7,634
Kenneth Jones, UKIP 1,205
Lab. maj. 2,184 (4.60%)
1.82% swing Lab. to C.
(2001: Lab. maj. 3,792 (8.22%))

RIBBLE VALLEY
E. 75,692 T. 49,766 (65.75%) C. hold
Nigel Evans, C. 25,834
Julie Young, LD 11,663
Jack Davenport, Lab. 10,924
Kevin Henry, UKIP 1,345
C. maj. 14,171 (28.48%)
2.81% swing LD to C.
(2001: C. maj. 11,238 (22.85%))

RICHMOND (YORKS)
E. 69,521 T. 45,200 (65.02%) C. hold
Rt. Hon. William Hague, C. 26,722
Neil Foster, Lab. 8,915
Jacquie Bell, LD 7,982
Leslie Rowe, Green 1,581
C. maj. 17,807 (39.40%)
1.17% swing Lab. to C.
(2001: C. maj. 16,319 (37.06%))

RICHMOND PARK
E. 70,555 T. 51,374 (72.81%) LD hold
*Susan Kramer, LD 24,011
Marco Forgione, C. 20,280
James Butler, Lab. 4,768
James Page, Green 1,379
Peter Dul, UKIP 458
Peter Flower, CPA 288
Margaret Harrison, Ind. 83
Rainbow George Weiss, Vote Dream 63
Richard Meacock, Ind. 44
LD maj. 3,731 (7.26%)
1.42% swing LD to C.
(2001: LD maj. 4,964 (10.10%))

ROCHDALE
E. 69,894 T. 40,836 (58.43%) LD gain
*Paul Rowen, LD 16,787
Lorna Fitzsimons, Lab. 16,345
Khalid Hussain, C. 4,270
Derek Adams, BNP 1,773
Dr John Whittaker, UKIP 499
Samir Chatterjee, Green 448
Mohammed Salim, IZB 361
Carl Faulkner, Veritas 353
LD maj. 442 (1.08%)
7.72% swing Lab. to LD
(2001: Lab. maj. 5,655 (14.35%))

ROCHFORD & SOUTHEND EAST
E. 71,186 T. 39,462 (55.44%) C. hold
*James Duddridge, C. 17,874
Fred Grindrod, Lab. 12,380
Graham Longley, LD 5,967
John Croft, UKIP 1,913
Andrew Vaughan, Green 1,328
C. maj. 5,494 (13.92%)
2.43% swing C. to Lab.
(2001: C. maj. 7,034 (18.78%))

ROMFORD
E. 58,571 T. 36,482 (62.29%) C. hold
Andrew Rosindell, C. 21,560
Margaret Mullane, Lab. 9,971
Geoffrey Seeff, LD 3,066
John McCaffrey, BNP 1,088
Terry Murray, UKIP 797
C. maj. 11,589 (31.77%)
7.51% swing Lab. to C.
(2001: C. maj. 5,977 (16.74%))

ROMSEY
E. 72,177 T. 50,311 (69.71%) LD hold
Sandra Gidley, LD 22,465
Caroline Nokes, C. 22,340
Matthew Stevens, Lab. 4,430
Michael Wigley, UKIP 1,076
LD maj. 125 (0.25%)
2.32% swing LD to C.
(2001: LD maj. 2,370 (4.89%))

ROSSENDALE & DARWEN
E. 72,207 T. 44,437 (61.54%) Lab. hold
Janet Anderson, Lab. 19,073
Nigel Adams, C. 15,397
Mike Carr, LD 6,670
Anthony Wentworth, BNP 1,736
Graeme McIver, Green 821
David Duthie, UKIP 740
Lab. maj. 3,676 (8.27%)
1.85% swing Lab. to C.
(2001: Lab. maj. 5,223 (12.63%))

ROTHER VALLEY
E. 67,973 T. 39,495 (58.10%) Lab. hold
Rt. Hon. Kevin Barron, Lab. 21,871
Colin Phillips, C. 7,647
Phillip Bristow, LD 6,272
Nicholas Cass, BNP 2,020
Gordon Brown, UKIP 1,685
Lab. maj. 14,224 (36.01%)
2.21% swing Lab. to C.
(2001: Lab. maj. 14,882 (40.44%))

ROTHERHAM
E. 54,410 T. 29,978 (55.10%) Lab. hold
Rt. Hon. Denis MacShane, Lab. 15,840
Timothy Gordon, LD 5,159
Lee Rotherham, C. 4,966
Marlene Guest, BNP 1,986
David Cutts, UKIP 1,122
Richard Penycate, Green 905
Lab. maj. 10,681 (35.63%)
8.83% swing Lab. to LD
(2001: Lab. maj. 13,077 (44.55%))

RUGBY & KENILWORTH
E. 83,303 T. 56,949 (68.36%) C. gain
*Jeremy Wright, C. 23,447
Andy King, Lab. 21,891
Richard Allanach, LD 10,143
John Thurley, UKIP 911
Brian Hadland, Ind. 299
Lillian Pallikaropoulos, Ind. 258
C. maj. 1,556 (2.73%)
4.04% swing Lab. to C.
(2001: Lab. maj. 2,877 (5.35%))

RUISLIP-NORTHWOOD
E. 60,774 T. 39,670 (65.27%) C. hold
*Nick Hurd, C. 18,939
Mike Cox, LD 10,029
Ashley Riley, Lab. 8,323
Graham Lee, Green 892
Ian Edward, NF 841
Roland Courtenay, UKIP 646
C. maj. 8,910 (22.46%)
3.49% swing C. to LD
(2001: C. maj. 7,537 (20.29%))

RUNNYMEDE & WEYBRIDGE
E. 74,172 T. 43,524 (58.68%) C. hold
Philip Hammond, C. 22,366
Paul Greenwood, Lab. 10,017
Henry Bolton, LD 7,771
Anthony Micklethwait, UKIP 1,719
Charles Gilman, Green 1,180
Mad Crab Collett, Loony 358
Katrina Osman, UKC 113
C. maj. 12,349 (28.37%)
4.33% swing Lab. to C.
(2001: C. maj. 8,360 (19.70%))

RUSHCLIFFE
E. 79,913 T. 56,311 (70.47%) C. hold
Rt. Hon. Kenneth Clarke, C. 27,899
Edward Gamble, Lab. 14,925
Karrar Khan, LD 9,813
Simon Anthony, Green 1,692
Matthew Faithfull, UKIP 1,358
Daniel Moss, Veritas 624
C. maj. 12,974 (23.04%)
4.76% swing Lab. to C.
(2001: C. maj. 7,357 (13.51%))

RUTLAND & MELTON
E. 75,823 T. 49,284 (65.00%)   C. hold
Alan Duncan, C.   25,237
Linda Arnold, Lab.   12,307
Grahame Hudson, LD   9,153
Peter Baker, UKIP   1,554
Duncan Shelley, Veritas   696
Helen Pender, Ind.   337
C. maj. 12,930 (26.24%)
3.97% swing Lab. to C.
(2001: C. maj. 8,612 (18.30%))

RYEDALE
E. 67,770 T. 44,120 (65.10%)   C. hold
John Greenway, C.   21,251
Gordon Beever, LD   10,782
Paul Blanchard, Lab.   9,148
Stephen Feaster, UKIP   1,522
John Clarke, Lib.   1,417
C. maj. 10,469 (23.73%)
6.31% swing LD to C.
(2001: C. maj. 4,875 (11.11%))

SAFFRON WALDEN
E. 77,600 T. 53,020 (68.32%)   C. hold
Rt. Hon. Sir Alan Haselhurst, C.   27,263
Elfreda Tealby-Watson, LD   14,255
Swatantra Nandanwar, Lab.   8,755
Raymond Tyler, UKIP   1,412
Raymond Brown, Eng. Dem.   860
Trevor Hackett, Veritas   475
C. maj. 13,008 (24.53%)
0.27% swing LD to C.
(2001: C. maj. 12,004 (23.99%))

ST ALBANS
E. 64,595 T. 45,462 (70.38%)   C. gain
*Anne Main, C.   16,953
Kerry Pollard, Lab.   15,592
Michael Green, LD   11,561
Richard Evans, UKIP   707
Janet Girsman, St Albans   430
Mark Reynolds, Ind.   219
C. maj. 1,361 (2.99%)
6.60% swing Lab. to C.
(2001: Lab. maj. 4,466 (10.21%))

ST HELENS NORTH
E. 69,834 T. 39,271 (56.23%) Lab. hold
Dave Watts, Lab.   22,329
John Beirne, LD   8,367
Paul Oakley, C.   7,410
Sylvia Hall, UKIP   1,165
Lab. maj. 13,962 (35.55%)
3.99% swing Lab. to LD
(2001: Lab. maj. 15,901 (42.29%))

ST HELENS SOUTH
E. 65,441 T. 35,473 (54.21%) Lab. hold
Shaun Woodward, Lab.   19,345
Brian Spencer, LD   10,036
Una Riley, C.   4,602
Malcolm Nightingale, UKIP   847
Michael Perry, Soc. Lab.   643
Lab. maj. 9,309 (26.24%)
0.17% swing Lab. to LD
(2001: Lab. maj. 8,985 (26.58%))

ST IVES
E. 74,716 T. 50,417 (67.48%)   LD hold
Andrew George, LD   25,577
Christian Mitchell, C.   13,968
Michael Dooley, Lab.   6,583
Michael Faulkner, UKIP   2,551
Katrina Slack, Green   1,738
LD maj. 11,609 (23.03%)
1.31% swing C. to LD
(2001: LD maj. 10,053 (20.41%))

SALFORD
E. 53,294 T. 22,600 (42.41%) Lab. hold
Rt. Hon. Hazel Blears, Lab.   13,007
Norman Owen, LD   5,062
Laetitia Cash, C.   3,440
Lisa Duffy, UKIP   1,091
Lab. maj. 7,945 (35.15%)
6.88% swing Lab. to LD
(2001: Lab. maj. 11,012 (48.91%))

SALISBURY
E. 80,385 T. 54,322 (67.58%)   C. hold
Robert Key, C.   25,961
Richard Denton-White, LD   14,819
Clare Moody, Lab.   9,457
Frances Howard, UKIP   2,290
Hamish Soutar, Green   1,555
John Holme, Ind.   240
C. maj. 11,142 (20.51%)
1.98% swing LD to C.
(2001: C. maj. 8,703 (16.54%))

SCARBOROUGH & WHITBY
E. 73,806 T. 46,912 (63.56%)   C. gain
*Robert Goodwill, C.   19,248
Lawrence Quinn, Lab.   18,003
Tania Exley-Moore, LD   7,495
Jonathan Dixon, Green   1,214
Paul Abbott, UKIP   952
C. maj. 1,245 (2.65%)
5.10% swing Lab. to C.
(2001: Lab. maj. 3,585 (7.54%))

SCUNTHORPE
E. 62,669 T. 32,664 (52.12%) Lab. hold
Elliot Morley, Lab.   17,355
Julian Sturdy, C.   8,392
Neil Poole, LD   5,556
David Baxendale, UKIP   1,361
Lab. maj. 8,963 (27.44%)
1.70% swing Lab. to C.
(2001: Lab. maj. 10,372 (30.85%))

SEDGEFIELD
E. 66,666 T. 41,475 (62.21%) Lab. hold
Rt. Hon. Tony Blair, Lab.   24,421
Grp Capt Al Lockwood, C.   5,972
Robert Browne, LD   4,935
Reg Keys, Ind.   4,252
William Brown, UKIP   646
Mark Farrell, NF   253
Fiona Luckhurst-Matthews, Veritas   218
Berony Abraham, Ind.   209
Boney Maroney, Loony   157
Jonathan Cockburn, BMG   103
Terry Pattinson, Senior   97
Cherri Gilham, UKPP   82
Helen John, Ind.   68
John Barker, Ind.   45
Julian Brennan, Ind.   17
Lab. maj. 18,449 (44.48%)
0.24% swing C. to Lab.
(2001: Lab. maj. 17,713 (44.00%))

SELBY
E. 78,111 T. 52,549 (67.27%) Lab. hold
John Grogan, Lab.   22,623
Mark Menzies, C.   22,156
Ian Cuthbertson, LD   7,770
Lab. maj. 467 (0.89%)
1.68% swing Lab. to C.
(2001: Lab. maj. 2,138 (4.25%))

SEVENOAKS
E. 65,109 T. 43,298 (66.50%)   C. hold
Michael Fallon, C.   22,437
Ben Abbotts, LD   9,467
Tim Stanley, Lab.   9,101
Robert Dobson, UKIP   1,309
John Marshall, Eng. Dem.   751
Mark Ellis, UK Path   233
C. maj. 12,970 (29.96%)
1.09% swing LD to C.
(2001: C. maj. 10,154 (23.83%))

SHEFFIELD ATTERCLIFFE
E. 67,815 T. 37,019 (54.59%) Lab. hold
Clive Betts, Lab.   22,250
Kevin Moore, LD   6,283
Tracy Critchlow, C.   5,329
Jonathan Arnott, UKIP   1,680
Beverley Jones, BNP   1,477
Lab. maj. 15,967 (43.13%)
5.22% swing Lab. to LD
(2001: Lab. maj. 18,844 (52.60%))

SHEFFIELD BRIGHTSIDE
E. 51,379 T. 24,629 (47.94%) Lab. hold
Rt. Hon. David Blunkett, Lab.   16,876
Jonathan Harston, LD   3,232
Tim Clark, C.   2,205
Christopher Hartigan, BNP   1,537
Judith Clarke, UKIP   779
Lab. maj. 13,644 (55.40%)
6.37% swing Lab. to LD
(2001: Lab. maj. 17,049 (66.72%))

SHEFFIELD CENTRAL
E. 59,862 T. 29,985 (50.09%) Lab. hold
Rt. Hon. Richard Caborn, Lab.   14,950
Ali Qadar, LD   7,895
Samantha George, C.   3,094
Bernard Little, Green   1,808
Maxine Bowler, Respect   1,284
Mark Payne, BNP   539
Charlotte Arnott, UKIP   415
Lab. maj. 7,055 (23.53%)
9.09% swing Lab. to LD
(2001: Lab. maj. 12,544 (41.72%))

SHEFFIELD HALLAM
E. 59,606 T. 40,427 (67.82%)   LD hold
*Nick Clegg, LD   20,710
Spencer Pitfield, C.   12,028
Mahroof Hussain, Lab.   5,110
Rob Cole, Green   1,331
Sid Cordle, CPA   441
Nigel James, UKIP   438
Ian Senior, BNP   369
LD maj. 8,682 (21.48%)
1.48% swing LD to C.
(2001: LD maj. 9,347 (24.44%))

SHEFFIELD HEELEY
E. 59,748 T. 34,093 (57.06%)
                          Lab. (Co-op) hold
Meg Munn, Lab. (Co-op)   18,405
Colin Ross, LD   7,035
Aster Crawshaw, C.   4,987
John Beatson, BNP   1,314
Rob Unwin, Green   1,312
Mark Suter, UKIP   775
Mark Dunnell, Soc. Alt.   265
Lab. (Co-op) maj. 11,370 (33.35%)
0.47% swing Lab. (Co-op) to LD
(2001: Lab. (Co-op) maj. 11,704
(34.28%))

SHEFFIELD HILLSBOROUGH
E. 75,706 T. 45,884 (60.61%) Lab. hold
*Angela Smith, Lab.   23,477
John Commons, LD   12,234
Jackie Doyle-Price, C.   6,890
David Wright, BNP   2,010
Maurice Patterson, UKIP   1,273
Lab. maj. 11,243 (24.50%)
4.87% swing Lab. to LD
(2001: Lab. maj. 14,569 (34.25%))

SHERWOOD
E. 75,913 T. 47,117 (62.07%) Lab. hold
Paddy Tipping, Lab.   22,824
Bruce Laughton, C.   16,172
Peter Harris, LD   6,384
Moritz Dawkins, UKIP   1,737
Lab. maj. 6,652 (14.12%)
3.15% swing Lab. to C.
(2001: Lab. maj. 9,373 (20.42%))

SHIPLEY
E. 69,575 T. 47,666 (68.51%)   C. gain
*Philip Davies, C.   18,608
Christopher Leslie, Lab.   18,186
John Briggs, LD   7,018
Tom Linden, BNP   2,000
Quentin Deakin, Green   1,665
David Crabtree, Iraq   189
C. maj. 422 (0.89%)
1.99% swing Lab. to C.
(2001: Lab. maj. 1,428 (3.10%))

SHREWSBURY & ATCHAM
E. 73,193 T. 50,296 (68.72%)   C. gain
*Daniel Kawczynski, C.   18,960
Michael Ion, Lab.   17,152
Richard Burt, LD   11,487
Peter Lewis, UKIP   1,349
Emma Bullard, Green   1,138
James Gollins, Ind.   126
Nigel Harris, Online   84
C. maj. 1,808 (3.59%)
5.38% swing Lab. to C.
(2001: Lab. maj. 3,579 (7.17%))

SHROPSHIRE NORTH
E. 73,477 T. 46,510 (63.30%)   C. hold
Owen Paterson, C.   23,061
Sandra Samuels, Lab.   12,041
Steven Bourne, LD   9,115
Ian Smith, UKIP   2,233
C. maj. 11,020 (23.69%)
5.14% swing Lab. to C.
(2001: C. maj. 6,241 (13.42%))

SITTINGBOURNE & SHEPPEY
E. 62,950 T. 40,803 (64.82%) Lab. hold
Derek Wyatt, Lab.   17,051
Gordon Henderson, C.   16,972
Jane Nelson, LD   5,183
Stephen Dean, UKIP   926
Mad MikeYoung, R & R Loony   479
David Cassidy, Veritas   192
Lab. maj. 79 (0.19%)
4.54% swing Lab. to C.
(2001: Lab. maj. 3,509 (9.27%))

SKIPTON & RIPON
E. 76,485 T. 50,521 (66.05%)   C. hold
Rt. Hon. David Curry, C.   25,100
Paul English, LD   13,480
Paul Baptie, Lab.   9,393
Ian Bannister, UKIP   2,274
Robert Leakey, Currency   274
C. maj. 11,620 (23.00%)
1.66% swing C. to LD
(2001: C. maj. 12,930 (26.32%))

SLEAFORD & NORTH HYKEHAM
E. 79,612 T. 53,397 (67.07%)   C. hold
Rt. Hon. Douglas Hogg, C.   26,855
Katrina Bull, Lab.   14,150
David Harding-Price, LD   9,710
Guy Croft, UKIP   2,682
C. maj. 12,705 (23.79%)
3.05% swing Lab. to C.
(2001: C. maj. 8,622 (17.70%))

SLOUGH
E. 71,595 T. 37,095 (51.81%) Lab. hold
Fiona Mactaggart, Lab.   17,517
Sheila Gunn, C.   9,666
Thomas McCann, LD   5,739
Ajaz Khan, Respect   1,632
Geoff Howard, UKIP   1,415
David Wood, Green   759
Paul Janik, Ind.   367
Lab. maj. 7,851 (21.16%)
5.45% swing Lab. to C.
(2001: Lab. maj. 12,508 (32.07%))

SOLIHULL
E. 77,910 T. 52,313 (67.15%)   LD gain
*Lorely Burt, LD   20,896
John Taylor, C.   20,617
Rory Vaughan, Lab.   8,058
Diane Carr, BNP   1,752
Andrew Moore, UKIP   990
LD maj. 279 (0.53%)
10.01% swing C. to LD
(2001: C. maj. 9,407 (19.49%))

SOMERTON & FROME
E. 77,806 T. 54,102 (69.53%)   LD hold
David Heath, LD   23,759
Clive Allen, C.   22,947
Joseph Pestell, Lab.   5,865
William Lukins, UKIP   1,047
Carleton Beaman, Veritas   484
LD maj. 812 (1.50%)
0.12% swing C. to LD
(2001: LD maj. 668 (1.27%))

SOUTH HOLLAND & THE DEEPINGS
E. 77,453 T. 48,249 (62.29%)   C. hold
John Hayes, C.   27,544
Linda Woodings, Lab.   11,764
Steve Jarvis, LD   6,244
Jamie Corney, UKIP   1,950
Paul Poll, Ind.   747
C. maj. 15,780 (32.71%)
4.34% swing Lab. to C.
(2001: C. maj. 11,099 (24.02%))

SOUTH SHIELDS
E. 59,403 T. 30,206 (50.85%) Lab. hold
Rt. Hon. David Miliband, Lab.   18,269
Stephen Psallidas, LD   5,957
Richard Lewis, C.   5,207
Nader Afshari-Naderi, Ind.   773
Lab. maj. 12,312 (40.76%)
2.78% swing Lab. to LD
(2001: Lab. maj. 14,090 (46.28%))

SOUTHAMPTON ITCHEN
E. 78,818 T. 43,225 (54.84%) Lab. hold
Rt. Hon. John Denham, Lab.   20,871
Flick Drummond, C.   11,569
David Goodall, LD   9,162
Kim Rose, UKIP   1,623
Lab. maj. 9,302 (21.52%)
2.80% swing Lab. to C.
(2001: Lab. maj. 11,223 (27.13%))

SOUTHAMPTON TEST
E. 72,833 T. 41,783 (57.37%) Lab. hold
Dr Alan Whitehead, Lab.   17,845
Stephen MacLoughlin, C.   10,827
Steve Sollitt, LD   10,368
John Spottiswoode, Green   1,482
Peter Day, UKIP   1,261
Lab. maj. 7,018 (16.80%)
5.08% swing Lab. to C.
(2001: Lab. maj. 11,207 (26.96%))

SOUTHEND WEST
E. 64,915 T. 39,830 (61.36%)   C. hold
David Amess, C.   18,408
Peter Wexham, LD   9,449
Jan Etienne, Lab.   9,072
Carole Sampson, UKIP   1,349
Dr Marimuthu Velmurugan, Ind.   745
Jeremy Moss, Eng. Dem.   701
Dan Anslow, Power   106
C. maj. 8,959 (22.49%)
0.55% swing LD to C.
(2001: C. maj. 7,941 (21.25%))

SOUTHPORT
E. 67,977 T. 41,201 (60.61%)   LD hold
Dr John Pugh, LD   19,093
Mark Bigley, C.   15,255
Paul Brant, Lab.   5,277
Terry Durrance, UKIP   749
Bill Givens, YPB   589
Harry Forster, Veritas   238
LD maj. 3,838 (9.32%)
1.00% swing C. to LD
(2001: LD maj. 3,007 (7.31%))

SOUTHWARK NORTH & BERMONDSEY
E. 77,084 T. 37,959 (49.24%)   LD hold
Simon Hughes, LD   17,874
Kirsty McNeill, Lab.   12,468
David Branch, C.   4,752
Storm Poorun, Green   1,137
Linda Robson, UKIP   791
Paul Winnett, NF   704
Simi Lawanson, CPA   233
LD maj. 5,406 (14.24%)
5.94% swing LD to Lab.
(2001: LD maj. 9,632 (26.13%))

SPELTHORNE
E. 69,650 T. 42,829 (61.49%)   C. hold
David Wilshire, C.   21,620
Keith Dibble, Lab.   11,684
Simon James, LD   7,318
Christopher Browne, UKIP   1,968
Caroline Schwark, UKC   239
C. maj. 9,936 (23.20%)
7.70% swing Lab. to C.
(2001: C. maj. 3,262 (7.80%))

STAFFORD
E. 70,359 T. 45,554 (64.75%) Lab. hold
David Kidney, Lab.   19,889
David Chambers, C.   17,768
Barry Stamp, LD   6,390
Frederick Goode, UKIP   1,507
Lab. maj. 2,121 (4.66%)
3.34% swing Lab. to C.
(2001: Lab. maj. 5,032 (11.34%))

STAFFORDSHIRE MOORLANDS
E. 69,136 T. 44,253 (64.01%) Lab. hold
Charlotte Atkins, Lab.   18,126
Marcus Hayes, C.   15,688
John Fisher, LD   6,927
Steve Povey, UKIP   3,512
Lab. maj. 2,438 (5.51%)
4.09% swing Lab. to C.
(2001: Lab. maj. 5,838 (13.69%))

STAFFORDSHIRE SOUTH
By-election held 23 June 2005 due to
the death of the Liberal Democrat
candidate during the general election
campaign

STALYBRIDGE & HYDE
E. 66,013 T. 35,314 (53.50%) Lab. hold
James Purnell, Lab.   17,535
Lisa Boardman, C.   9,187
Viv Bingham, LD   5,532
Nigel Byrne, BNP   1,399
Mike Smee, Green   1,088
Dr John Whittaker, UKIP   573
Lab. maj. 8,348 (23.64%)
2.00% swing Lab. to C.
(2001: Lab. maj. 8,859 (27.64%))

STEVENAGE
E. 66,889 T. 41,934 (62.69%) Lab. hold
Barbara Follett, Lab.   18,003
George Freeman, C.   14,864
Julia Davies, LD   7,610
Victoria Peebles, UKIP   1,305
Antal Losonczi, Ind.   152
Lab. maj. 3,139 (7.49%)
6.35% swing Lab. to C.
(2001: Lab. maj. 8,566 (20.18%))

STOCKPORT
E. 65,593 T. 35,771 (54.53%) Lab. hold
Ann Coffey, Lab.   18,069
Elizabeth Berridge, C.   8,906
Lyn-Su Floodgate, LD   7,832
Richard Simpson, UKIP   964
Lab. maj. 9,163 (25.62%)
3.54% swing Lab. to C.
(2001: Lab. maj. 11,569 (32.70%))

STOCKTON NORTH
E. 63,271 T. 36,428 (57.57%) Lab. hold
Frank Cook, Lab.   20,012
Harriett Baldwin, C.   7,575
Neil Hughes, LD   6,869
Kevin Hughes, BNP   986
Gordon Parkin, UKIP   986
Lab. maj. 12,437 (34.14%)
3.60% swing Lab. to C.
(2001: Lab. maj. 14,647 (41.34%))

STOCKTON SOUTH
E. 71,286 T. 44,923 (63.02%) Lab. hold
Dari Taylor, Lab.   21,480
James Gaddas, C.   15,341
Mike Barker, LD   7,171
Sandra Allison, UKIP   931
Lab. maj. 6,139 (13.67%)
3.44% swing Lab. to C.
(2001: Lab. maj. 9,086 (20.55%))

STOKE-ON-TRENT CENTRAL
E. 57,643 T. 27,907 (48.41%) Lab. hold
Mark Fisher, Lab.   14,760
John Redfern, LD   4,986
Esther Baroudy, C.   4,823
Michael Coleman, BNP   2,178
Joseph Bonfiglio, UKIP   914
Jim Cessford, Soc. Alt.   246
Lab. maj. 9,774 (35.02%)
5.50% swing Lab. to LD
(2001: Lab. maj. 11,845 (41.86%))

STOKE-ON-TRENT NORTH
E. 58,422 T. 30,760 (52.65%) Lab. hold
Joan Walley, Lab.   16,191
Benjamin Browning, C.   6,155
Henry Jebb, LD   4,561
Spencer Cartlidge, BNP   2,132
Eileen Braithwaite, UKIP   696
Ian Taylor, Veritas   689
Harry Chesters, Ind.   336
Lab. maj. 10,036 (32.63%)
3.25% swing Lab. to C.
(2001: Lab. maj. 11,784 (39.13%))

STOKE-ON-TRENT SOUTH
E. 70,612 T. 37,820 (53.56%) Lab. hold
*Robert Flello, Lab.   17,727
Mark Deaville, C.   9,046
Andrew Martin, LD   5,894
Mark Leat, BNP   3,305
Neville Benson, UKIP   1,043
Grant Allen, Veritas   805
Lab. maj. 8,681 (22.95%)
3.08% swing Lab. to C.
(2001: Lab. maj. 10,489 (29.11%))

STONE
E. 70,359 T. 47,036 (66.85%) C. hold
Bill Cash, C.   22,733
Mark Davis, Lab.   13,644
Peter Stevens, LD   9,111
Michael Nattrass, UKIP   1,548
C. maj. 9,089 (19.32%)
3.05% swing Lab. to C.
(2001: C. maj. 6,036 (13.22%))

STOURBRIDGE
E. 64,479 T. 41,708 (64.68%) Lab. hold
*Lynda Waltho, Lab.   17,089
Diana Coad, C.   16,682
Chris Bramall, LD   6,850
Daniel Pui Chai Mau, UKIP   1,087
Lab. maj. 407 (0.98%)
4.29% swing Lab. to C.
(2001: Lab. maj. 3,812 (9.55%))

STRATFORD-UPON-AVON
E. 84,591 T. 58,240 (68.85%) C. hold
John Maples, C.   28,652
Dr Susan Juned, LD   16,468
Rachel Blackmore, Lab. (Co-op)   10,145
Harry Cottam, UKIP   1,621
Mick Davies, Green   1,354
C. maj. 12,184 (20.92%)
0.29% swing C. to LD
(2001: C. maj. 11,802 (21.49%))

STREATHAM
E. 79,193 T. 40,615 (51.29%) Lab. hold
Rt. Hon. Keith Hill, Lab.   18,950
Darren Sanders, LD   11,484
James Sproule, C.   7,238
Shane Collins, Green   2,245
Trevor Gittings, UKIP   396
William Colvill, WRP   127
Philippa Stone, Ind.   100
Robert West, Ind.   40
Sarah Acheng, Ind.   35
Lab. maj. 7,466 (18.38%)
10.09% swing Lab. to LD
(2001: Lab. maj. 14,270 (38.57%))

STRETFORD & URMSTON
E. 61,979 T. 38,101 (61.47%) Lab. hold
Rt. Hon. Beverley Hughes, Lab.   19,417
Damian Hinds, C.   11,566
Faraz Bhatti, LD   5,323
Mark Krantz, Respect   950
Michael McManus, UKIP   845
Lab. maj. 7,851 (20.61%)
6.71% swing Lab. to C.
(2001: Lab. maj. 13,239 (33.97%))

STROUD
E. 79,748 T. 56,875 (71.32%)
                             Lab. (Co-op) hold
David Drew, Lab. (Co-op)   22,527
Neil Carmichael, C.   22,177
Peter Hirst, LD   8,026
Martin Whiteside, Green   3,056
Edward Noble, UKIP   1,089
Lab. (Co-op) maj. 350 (0.62%)
4.26% swing Lab. (Co-op) to C.
(2001: Lab. (Co-op) maj. 5,039 (9.13%))

SUFFOLK CENTRAL & IPSWICH
NORTH
E. 76,271 T. 50,866 (66.69%) C. hold
Sir Michael Lord, C.   22,333
Neil MacDonald, Lab.   14,477
Andrew Houseley, LD   10,709
John West, UKIP   1,754
Martin Wolfe, Green   1,593
C. maj. 7,856 (15.44%)
4.04% swing Lab. to C.
(2001: C. maj. 3,469 (7.36%))

SUFFOLK COASTAL
E. 77,423 T. 52,557 (67.88%) C. hold
Rt. Hon. John Gummer, C.   23,415
David Rowe, Lab.   13,730
David Young, LD   11,637
Richard Curtis, UKIP   2,020
Paul Whitlow, Green   1,755
C. maj. 9,685 (18.43%)
4.92% swing Lab. to C.
(2001: C. maj. 4,326 (8.58%))

SUFFOLK SOUTH
E. 70,237 T. 48,707 (69.35%) C. hold
Tim Yeo, C.   20,471
Kathy Pollard, LD   13,865
Kevin Craig, Lab.   11,917
James Carver, UKIP   2,454
C. maj. 6,606 (13.56%)
1.45% swing C. to LD
(2001: C. maj. 5,081 (11.22%))

SUFFOLK WEST
E. 72,856 T. 44,205 (60.67%)   C. hold
Richard Spring, C.   21,682
Michael Jefferys, Lab.   12,773
Adrian Graves, LD   7,573
Ian Smith, UKIP   2,177
C. maj. 8,909 (20.15%)
5.02% swing Lab. to C.
(2001: C. maj. 4,295 (10.12%))

SUNDERLAND NORTH
E. 58,146 T. 28,913 (49.72%) Lab. hold
Bill Etherington, Lab.   15,719
Stephen Daughton, C.   5,724
James Hollern, LD   4,277
Neil Herron, Ind.   2,057
Debra Hiles, BNP   1,136
Lab. maj. 9,995 (34.57%)
5.11% swing Lab. to C.
(2001: Lab. maj. 13,354 (44.78%))

SUNDERLAND SOUTH
E. 62,256 T. 30,712 (49.33%) Lab. hold
Chris Mullin, Lab.   17,982
Robert Oliver, C.   6,923
Gareth Kane, LD   4,492
David Guynan, BNP   1,166
Rosalyn Warner, Loony   149
Lab. maj. 11,059 (36.01%)
3.91% swing Lab. to C.
(2001: Lab. maj. 13,667 (43.82%))

SURREY EAST
E. 73,948 T. 49,253 (66.60%)   C. hold
Peter Ainsworth, C.   27,659
Jeremy Pursehouse, LD   11,738
James Bridge, Lab.   7,288
Tony Stone, UKIP   2,158
Winston Matthews, LCA   410
C. maj. 15,921 (32.32%)
2.13% swing LD to C.
(2001: C. maj. 13,203 (28.06%))

SURREY HEATH
E. 76,090 T. 47,858 (62.90%)   C. hold
*Michael Gove, C.   24,642
Rosalyn Harper, LD   13,797
Chris Lowe, Lab.   7,989
Steve Smith, UKIP   1,430
C. maj. 10,845 (22.66%)
0.66% swing C. to LD
(2001: C. maj. 10,819 (23.99%))

SURREY SOUTH WEST
E. 72,977 T. 52,409 (71.82%)   C. hold
*Jeremy Hunt, C.   26,420
Simon Cordon, LD   20,709
Thomas Sleigh, Lab.   4,150
Timothy Clark, UKIP   958
Glenn Platt, Veritas   172
C. maj. 5,711 (10.90%)
4.58% swing LD to C.
(2001: C. maj. 861 (1.74%))

SUSSEX MID
E. 72,114 T. 49,494 (68.63%)   C. hold
Hon. Nicholas Soames, C.   23,765
Serena Tierney, LD   17,875
Robert Fromant, Lab.   6,280
Harold Piggott, UKIP   1,574
C. maj. 5,890 (11.90%)
1.58% swing C. to LD
(2001: C. maj. 6,898 (15.05%))

SUTTON & CHEAM
E. 63,319 T. 41,932 (66.22%) LD hold
Paul Burstow, LD   19,768
Richard Willis, C.   16,922
Anand Shukla, Lab.   4,954
Rainbow George Weiss, Vote Dream 288
LD maj. 2,846 (6.79%)
2.02% swing LD to C.
(2001: LD maj. 4,304 (10.84%))

SUTTON COLDFIELD
E. 72,995 T. 46,318 (63.45%)   C. hold
Andrew Mitchell, C.   24,308
Robert Pocock, Lab.   12,025
Craig Drury, LD   7,710
Stephen Shorrock, UKIP   2,275
C. maj. 12,283 (26.52%)
1.63% swing Lab. to C.
(2001: C. maj. 10,104 (23.25%))

SWINDON NORTH
E. 73,636 T. 44,885 (60.96%) Lab. hold
Michael Wills, Lab.   19,612
Justin Tomlinson, C.   17,041
Mike Evemy, LD   6,831
Robert Tingey, UKIP   998
Andy Newman, Soc. Unity   208
Ernest Reynolds, Ind.   195
Lab. maj. 2,571 (5.73%)
6.71% swing Lab. to C.
(2001: Lab. maj. 8,105 (19.15%))

SWINDON SOUTH
E. 72,267 T. 43,472 (60.15%) Lab. hold
*Anne Snelgrove, Lab.   17,534
Robert Buckland, C.   16,181
Sue Stebbing, LD   7,322
Bill Hughes, Green   1,234
Stephen Halden, UKIP   955
Alan Hayward, Ind.   193
John Williams, Ind.   53
Lab. maj. 1,353 (3.11%)
6.90% swing Lab. to C.
(2001: Lab. maj. 7,341 (16.92%))

TAMWORTH
E. 71,675 T. 43,740 (61.03%) Lab. hold
Brian Jenkins, Lab.   18,801
Christopher Pincher, C.   16,232
Phillip Bennion, LD   6,175
Patrick Eston, Veritas   1,320
Tom Simpson, UKIP   1,212
Lab. maj. 2,569 (5.87%)
2.78% swing Lab. to C.
(2001: Lab. maj. 4,598 (11.42%))

TATTON
E. 64,140 T. 41,414 (64.57%)   C. hold
George Osborne, C.   21,447
Justin Madders, Lab.   9,716
Ainsley Arnold, LD   9,016
Diane Bowler, UKIP   996
Michael Gibson, Ind.   239
C. maj. 11,731 (28.33%)
3.73% swing Lab. to C.
(2001: C. maj. 8,611 (20.86%))

TAUNTON
E. 85,466 T. 59,528 (69.65%) LD gain
*Jeremy Browne, LD   25,764
Adrian Flook, C.   25,191
Andrew Govier, Lab.   7,132
Helen Miles, UKIP   1,441
LD maj. 573 (0.96%)
0.69% swing C. to LD
(2001: C. maj. 235 (0.43%))

TEIGNBRIDGE
E. 88,674 T. 60,898 (68.68%) LD hold
Richard Younger-Ross, LD   27,808
Stanley Johnson, C.   21,593
Chris Sherwood, Lab.   6,931
Trevor Colman, UKIP   3,881
Reginald Wills, Lib.   685
LD maj. 6,215 (10.21%)
2.56% swing C. to LD
(2001: LD maj. 3,011 (5.08%))

TELFORD
E. 59,277 T. 34,206 (57.71%) Lab. hold
David Wright, Lab.   16,506
Stella Kyriazis, C.   11,100
Ian Jenkins, LD   4,941
Tom McCartney, UKIP   1,659
Lab. maj. 5,406 (15.80%)
5.67% swing Lab. to C.
(2001: Lab. maj. 8,383 (27.15%))

TEWKESBURY
E. 72,145 T. 45,453 (63.00%)   C. hold
Laurence Robertson, C.   22,339
Alistair Cameron, LD   12,447
Charles Mannan, Lab.   9,179
Robert Rendell, Green   1,488
C. maj. 9,892 (21.76%)
0.96% swing LD to C.
(2001: C. maj. 8,663 (19.17%))

THANET NORTH
E. 72,734 T. 43,732 (60.13%)   C. hold
Roger Gale, C.   21,699
Iris Johnston, Lab.   14,065
Mark Barnard, LD   6,279
Timothy Stocks, UKIP   1,689
C. maj. 7,634 (17.46%)
0.79% swing Lab. to C.
(2001: C. maj. 6,650 (15.88%))

THANET SOUTH
E. 63,436 T. 41,242 (65.01%) Lab. hold
Dr Stephen Ladyman, Lab.   16,660
Mark MacGregor, C.   15,996
Guy Voizey, LD   5,431
Nigel Farage, UKIP   2,079
Howard Green, Green   888
Maude Kinsella, Ind.   188
Lab. maj. 664 (1.61%)
1.47% swing Lab. to C.
(2001: Lab. maj. 1,792 (4.54%))

THURROCK
E. 79,545 T. 43,692 (54.93%) Lab. hold
Andrew Mackinlay, Lab.   20,636
Garry Hague, C.   14,261
Earnshaw Palmer, LD   4,770
Nick Geri, BNP   2,526
Carol Jackson, UKIP   1,499
Lab. maj. 6,375 (14.59%)
6.08% swing Lab. to C.
(2001: Lab. maj. 9,997 (26.76%))

TIVERTON & HONITON
E. 83,375 T. 58,168 (69.77%)   C. hold
Angela Browning, C.   27,838
David Nation, LD   16,787
Fiona Bentley, Lab.   7,944
Robert Edwards, UKIP   2,499
Roy Collins, Lib.   1,701
Colin Matthews, Green   1,399
C. maj. 11,051 (19.00%)
3.87% swing LD to C.
(2001: C. maj. 6,284 (11.26%))

TONBRIDGE & MALLING
E. 68,444 T. 46,063 (67.30%)   C. hold
Rt. Hon. Sir John Stanley, C.   24,357
Victoria Hayman, Lab.   11,005
John Barstow, LD   8,980
David Waller, UKIP   1,721
C. maj. 13,352 (28.99%)
4.77% swing Lab. to C.
(2001: C. maj. 8,250 (19.44%))

TOOTING
E. 70,504 T. 41,568 (58.96%) Lab. hold
*Sadiq Khan, Lab.   17,914
James Bethell, C.   12,533
Stephanie Dearden, LD   8,110
Siobhan Vitelli, Green   1,695
Ali Zaidi, Respect   700
Strachan McDonald, UKIP   424
Ian Perkin, Ind.   192
Lab. maj. 5,381 (12.95%)
7.36% swing Lab. to C.
(2001: Lab. maj. 10,400 (27.67%))

TORBAY
E. 76,474 T. 47,303 (61.86%) LD hold
Adrian Sanders, LD   19,317
Marcus Wood, C.   17,288
David Pedrick-Friend, Lab.   6,972
Graham Booth, UKIP   3,726
LD maj. 2,029 (4.29%)
4.91% swing LD to C.
(2001: LD maj. 6,708 (14.10%))

TOTNES
E. 74,744 T. 50,575 (67.66%)   C. hold
Anthony Steen, C.   21,112
Michael Treleaven, LD   19,165
Valerie Burns, Lab.   6,185
Roger Knapman, UKIP   3,914
Michael Thompson, Ind.   199
C. maj. 1,947 (3.85%)
1.73% swing C. to LD
(2001: C. maj. 3,597 (7.30%))

TOTTENHAM
E. 66,231 T. 31,664 (47.81%) Lab. hold
David Lammy, Lab.   18,343
Wayne Hoban, LD   5,309
William MacDougall, C.   4,278
Janet Alder, Respect   2,014
Pete McAskie, Green   1,457
Jaamit Durrani, Soc. Lab.   263
Lab. maj. 13,034 (41.16%)
8.39% swing Lab. to LD
(2001: Lab. maj. 16,916 (53.53%))

TRURO & ST AUSTELL
E. 80,256 T. 51,564 (64.25%) LD hold
Matthew Taylor, LD   24,089
Dr Fiona Kemp, C.   16,686
Dr Charlotte Mackenzie, Lab.   6,991
David Noakes, UKIP   2,736
Conan Jenkin, Meb. Ker.   1,062
LD maj. 7,403 (14.36%)
0.84% swing LD to C.
(2001: LD maj. 8,065 (16.04%))

TUNBRIDGE WELLS
E. 64,630 T. 42,482 (65.73%)   C. hold
*Greg Clark, C.   21,083
Laura Murphy, LD   11,095
Jacqui Jedrzejewski, Lab.   8,736
Victor Webb, UKIP   1,568
C. maj. 9,988 (23.51%)
0.35% swing C. to LD
(2001: C. maj. 9,730 (24.20%))

TWICKENHAM
E. 72,015 T. 51,687 (71.77%) LD hold
Dr Vincent Cable, LD   26,696
Paul Maynard, C.   16,731
Brian Whitington, Lab.   5,868
Henry Gower, Green   1,445
Douglas Orchard, UKIP   766
Brian Gilbert, Ind.   117
Rainbow George Weiss, Vote Dream   64
LD maj. 9,965 (19.28%)
1.98% swing C. to LD
(2001: LD maj. 7,655 (15.33%))

TYNE BRIDGE
E. 53,565 T. 26,383 (49.25%) Lab. hold
David Clelland, Lab.   16,151
Chris Boyle, LD   5,751
Tom Fairhead, C.   2,962
Kevin Scott, BNP   1,072
Jill Russell, Respect   447
Lab. maj. 10,400 (39.42%)
9.35% swing Lab. to LD
(2001: Lab. maj. 14,889 (57.19%))

TYNEMOUTH
E. 64,023 T. 42,859 (66.94%) Lab. hold
Alan Campbell, Lab.   20,143
Michael McIntyre, C.   16,000
Colin Finlay, LD   6,716
Lab. maj. 4,143 (9.67%)
5.05% swing Lab. to C.
(2001: Lab. maj. 8,678 (19.77%))

TYNESIDE NORTH
E. 64,634 T. 36,939 (57.15%) Lab. hold
Rt. Hon. Stephen Byers, Lab.   22,882
Duncan McLellan, C.   7,845
Gillian Ferguson, LD   6,212
Lab. maj. 15,037 (40.71%)
7.09% swing Lab. to C.
(2001: Lab. maj. 20,668 (55.01%))

UPMINSTER
E. 55,075 T. 34,676 (62.96%)   C. hold
Angela Watkinson, C.   16,820
Keith Darvill, Lab.   10,778
Peter Truesdale, LD   3,128
Ronald Ower, RA   1,455
Chris Roberts, BNP   1,173
Alan Hindle, UKIP   701
Melanie Collins, Green   543
David Durant, Third   78
C. maj. 6,042 (17.42%)
6.88% swing Lab. to C.
(2001: C. maj. 1,241 (3.67%))

UXBRIDGE
E. 57,878 T. 34,378 (59.40%)   C. hold
John Randall, C.   16,840
Rod Marshall, Lab.   10,669
Dr Tariq Mahmood, LD   4,544
Cliff Le May, BNP   763
Stephen Young, Green   725
Robert Kerby, UKIP   553
Peter Shaw, NF   284
C. maj. 6,171 (17.95%)
5.84% swing Lab. to C.
(2001: C. maj. 2,098 (6.28%))

VALE OF YORK
E. 76,000 T. 50,378 (66.29%)   C. hold
Anne McIntosh, C.   26,025
David Scott, Lab.   12,313
Jeremy Wilcock, LD   12,040
C. maj. 13,712 (27.22%)
0.70% swing Lab. to C.
(2001: C. maj. 12,517 (25.81%))

VAUXHALL
E. 79,637 T. 37,353 (46.90%) Lab. hold
Kate Hoey, Lab.   19,744
Charles Anglin, LD   9,767
Edward Heckels, C.   5,405
Tim Summers, Green   1,705
Robert McWhirter, UKIP   271
Daniel Lambert, Socialist   240
Janus Polenceus, Eng. Dem.   221
Lab. maj. 9,977 (26.71%)
6.14% swing Lab. to LD
(2001: Lab. maj. 13,018 (38.99%))

WAKEFIELD
E. 73,118 T. 43,381 (59.33%) Lab. hold
*Mary Creagh, Lab.   18,802
Alec Shelbrooke, C.   13,648
David Ridgway, LD   7,063
Grant Rowe, BNP   1,328
Derek Hardcastle, Green   1,297
John Upex, UKIP   467
Paul McEnhill, Eng. Dem.   356
Mick Griffiths, Soc. Alt.   319
Linda Sheridan, Soc. Lab.   101
Lab. maj. 5,154 (11.88%)
3.70% swing Lab. to C.
(2001: Lab. maj. 7,954 (19.28%))

WALLASEY
E. 63,764 T. 36,671 (57.51%) Lab. hold
Angela Eagle, Lab.   20,085
Leah Fraser, C.   10,976
Joanna Pemberton, LD   4,770
Philip Griffiths, UKIP   840
Lab. maj. 9,109 (24.84%)
4.02% swing Lab. to C.
(2001: Lab. maj. 12,276 (32.87%))

WALSALL NORTH
E. 63,268 T. 33,428 (52.84%) Lab. hold
David Winnick, Lab.   15,990
Ian Lucas, C.   9,350
Douglas Taylor, LD   4,144
William Locke, BNP   1,992
Anthony Lenton, UKIP   1,182
Peter Smith, Dem. Lab.   770
Lab. maj. 6,640 (19.86%)
4.60% swing Lab. to C.
(2001: Lab. maj. 9,391 (29.06%))

WALSALL SOUTH
E. 60,370 T. 35,315 (58.50%) Lab. hold
Rt. Hon. Bruce George, Lab.   17,633
Kabir Sabar, C.   9,687
Mohamed Hanif Asmal, LD   3,240
Derek Bennett, UKIP   1,833
Kevin Smith, BNP   1,776
Nadia Fazal, Respect   1,146
Lab. maj. 7,946 (22.50%)
2.98% swing Lab. to C.
(2001: Lab. maj. 9,931 (28.46%))

WALTHAMSTOW
E. 63,079 T. 34,444 (54.60%) Lab. hold
Neil Gerrard, Lab.   17,323
Farid Ahmed, LD   9,330
Jane Wright, C.   6,254
Robert Brock, UKIP   810
Nancy Taaffe, Soc. Alt.   727
Lab. maj. 7,993 (23.21%)
12.18% swing Lab. to LD
(2001: Lab. maj. 15,181 (44.09%))

WANSBECK
E. 63,096 T. 36,809 (58.34%) Lab. hold
Denis Murphy, Lab.   20,315
Simon Reed, LD   9,734
Ginny Scrope, C.   5,515
Dr Nic Best, Green   1,245
Lab. maj. 10,581 (28.75%)
3.13% swing Lab. to LD
(2001: Lab. maj. 13,101 (35.01%))

WANSDYKE
E. 70,359 T. 50,933 (72.39%) Lab. hold
Dan Norris, Lab.   20,686
Chris Watt, C.   18,847
Gail Coleshill, LD   10,050
Peter Sandell, UKIP   1,129
Geoffrey Parkes, Ind.   221
Lab. maj. 1,839 (3.61%)
3.86% swing Lab. to C.
(2001: Lab. maj. 5,113 (10.42%))

WANTAGE
E. 76,156 T. 51,931 (68.19%) C. hold
*Ed Vaizey, C.   22,354
Andrew Crawford, LD   14,337
Mark McDonald, Lab.   12,464
Adam Twine, Green   1,332
Nikolai Tolstoy-Miloslavsky, UKIP   798
Gerald Lambourne, Eng. Dem.   646
C. maj. 8,017 (15.44%)
1.92% swing LD to C.
(2001: C. maj. 5,600 (11.40%))

WARLEY
E. 56,171 T. 32,087 (57.12%) Lab. hold
Rt. Hon. John Spellar, Lab.   17,462
Karen Bissell, C.   7,315
Tony Ferguson, LD   4,277
Simon Smith, BNP   1,761
Malcolm Conniglale, Soc. Lab.   637
David Matthews, UKIP   635
Lab. maj. 10,147 (31.62%)
3.05% swing Lab. to C.
(2001: Lab. maj. 11,850 (37.72%))

WARRINGTON NORTH
E. 73,352 T. 40,418 (55.10%) Lab. hold
Helen Jones, Lab.   21,632
Andrew Ferryman, C.   9,428
Peter Walker, LD   7,699
John Kirkham, UKIP   1,086
Mike Hughes, CAP   573
Lab. maj. 12,204 (30.19%)
4.38% swing Lab. to C.
(2001: Lab. maj. 15,156 (38.95%))

WARRINGTON SOUTH
E. 75,724 T. 46,797 (61.80%) Lab. hold
Helen Southworth, Lab.   18,972
Fiona Bruce, C.   15,457
Ian Marks, LD   11,111
Gerald Kelley, UKIP   804
Paul Kennedy, Ind.   453
Lab. maj. 3,515 (7.51%)
4.37% swing Lab. to C.
(2001: Lab. maj. 7,387 (16.24%))

WARWICK & LEAMINGTON
E. 81,205 T. 54,784 (67.46%) Lab. hold
James Plaskitt, Lab.   22,238
Chris White, C.   21,972
Linda Forbes, LD   8,119
Ian Davison, Green   1,534
Greville Warwick, UKIP   921
Lab. maj. 266 (0.49%)
5.32% swing Lab. to C.
(2001: Lab. maj. 5,953 (11.12%))

WARWICKSHIRE NORTH
E. 75,435 T. 46,939 (62.22%) Lab. hold
Mike O Brien, Lab.   22,561
Ian Gibb, C.   15,008
Jerry Roodhouse, LD   6,212
Michaela Mackenzie, BNP   1,910
Iain Campbell, UKIP   1,248
Lab. maj. 7,553 (16.09%)
2.81% swing Lab. to C.
(2001: Lab. maj. 9,639 (21.71%))

WATFORD
E. 76,280 T. 49,394 (64.75%) Lab. hold
Claire Ward, Lab.   16,575
Sal Brinton, LD   15,427
Ali Miraj, C.   14,634
Steve Rackett, Green   1,466
Kenneth Wight, UKIP   1,292
Lab. maj. 1,148 (2.32%)
12.75% swing Lab. to LD
(2001: Lab. maj. 5,555 (11.98%))

WAVENEY
E. 77,138 T. 49,653 (64.37%) Lab. hold
Bob Blizzard, Lab.   22,505
Peter Aldous, C.   16,590
Nick Bromley, LD   7,497
Brian Aylett, UKIP   1,861
Graham Elliott, Green   1,200
Lab. maj. 5,915 (11.91%)
3.11% swing Lab. to C.
(2001: Lab. maj. 8,553 (18.13%))

WEALDEN
E. 82,261 T. 55,653 (67.65%) C. hold
Charles Hendry, C.   28,975
Christopher Wigley, LD   13,054
Dudley Rose, Lab.   9,360
Julian Salmon, Green   2,150
Keith Riddle, UKIP   2,114
C. maj. 15,921 (28.61%)
1.25% swing LD to C.
(2001: C. maj. 13,772 (26.11%))

WEAVER VALE
E. 69,072 T. 39,420 (57.07%) Lab. hold
Mike Hall, Lab.   18,759
Jonathan Mackle, C.   11,904
Nigel Griffiths, LD   7,723
Brenda Swinscoe, UKIP   1,034
Lab. maj. 6,855 (17.39%)
3.58% swing Lab. to C.
(2001: Lab. maj. 9,637 (24.54%))

WELLINGBOROUGH
E. 79,679 T. 53,005 (66.52%) C. gain
*Peter Bone, C.   22,674
Paul Stinchcombe, Lab.   21,987
Richard Church, LD   6,147
James Wrench, UKIP   1,214
Nicholas Alex, Veritas   749
Andy Dickson, Soc. Lab.   234
C. maj. 687 (1.30%)
2.96% swing Lab. to C.
(2001: Lab. maj. 2,355 (4.62%))

WELLS
E. 77,842 T. 52,965 (68.04%) C. hold
Rt. Hon. David Heathcoat-Amory, C.
                                      23,071
Tessa Munt, LD   20,031
Dan Whittle, Lab.   8,288
Steven Reed, UKIP   1,575
C. maj. 3,040 (5.74%)
0.15% swing LD to C.
(2001: C. maj. 2,796 (5.45%))

WELWYN HATFIELD
E. 65,617 T. 44,716 (68.15%) C. gain
*Grant Shapps, C.   22,172
Melanie Johnson, Lab.   16,226
Sara Bedford, LD   6,318
C. maj. 5,946 (13.30%)
8.05% swing Lab. to C.
(2001: Lab. maj. 1,196 (2.79%))

WENTWORTH
E. 63,561 T. 35,596 (56.00%) Lab. hold
John Healey, Lab.   21,225
Mark Hughes, C.   6,169
Keith Orrell, LD   4,800
Jonathan Pygott, BNP   1,798
John Wilkinson, UKIP   1,604
Lab. maj. 15,056 (42.30%)
3.20% swing Lab. to C.
(2001: Lab. maj. 16,449 (48.70%))

WEST BROMWICH EAST
E. 60,565 T. 35,512 (58.63%) Lab. hold
Tom Watson, Lab.   19,741
Rosemary Bromwich, C.   8,089
Ian Garrett, LD   4,386
Carl Butler, BNP   2,329
Steven Grey, UKIP   607
Judith Sambrook, Soc. Lab.   200
Margaret Macklin, Ind.   160
Lab. maj. 11,652 (32.81%)
1.46% swing C. to Lab.
(2001: Lab. maj. 9,763 (29.89%))

WEST BROMWICH WEST
E. 66,752 T. 34,917 (52.31%)
                         Lab. (Co-op) hold
Adrian Bailey, Lab. (Co-op)   18,951
Mimi Harker, C.   8,057
Martyn Smith, LD   3,583
James Lloyd, BNP   3,456
Kevin Walker, UKIP   870
Lab. (Co-op) maj. 10,894 (31.20%)
2.23% swing Lab. (Co-op) to C.
(2001: Lab. (Co-op) maj. 11,355
(35.66%))

WEST HAM
E. 62,184 T. 30,966 (49.80%) Lab. hold
*Lyn Brown, Lab.   15,840
Lindsey German, Respect   6,039
Chris Whitbread, C.   3,618
Alexandra Sugden, LD   3,364
Jane Lithgow, Green   894
Stephen Hammond, CPA   437
Henry Mayhew, UKIP   409
Generoso Alcantara, Veritas   365
Lab. maj. 9,801 (31.65%)
19.12% swing Lab. to Respect
(2001: Lab. maj. 15,645 (53.45%))

WESTBURY
E. 83,039 T. 55,604 (66.96%) C. hold
Dr Andrew Murrison, C.   24,749
Duncan Hames, LD   19,400
Phil Gibby, Lab.   9,640
Lincoln Williams, UKIP   1,815
C. maj. 5,349 (9.62%)
0.42% swing C. to LD
(2001: C. maj. 5,294 (10.46%))

WESTMORLAND & LONSDALE
E. 69,363 T. 49,636 (71.56%) LD gain
*Tim Farron, LD 22,569
Tim Collins, C. 22,302
John Reardon, Lab. 3,796
Robert Gibson, UKIP 660
Anthony Kemp, Ind. 309
LD maj. 267 (0.54%)
3.55% swing C. to LD
(2001: C. maj. 3,147 (6.57%))

WESTON-SUPER-MARE
E. 74,900 T. 49,095 (65.55%) C. gain
*John Penrose, C. 19,804
Brian Cotter, LD 17,725
Damien Egan, Lab. 9,169
Paul Spencer, UKIP 1,207
Clive Courtney, BNP 778
William Human, Ind. 225
Paul Hemingway-Arnold, Honesty 187
C. maj. 2,079 (4.23%)
2.48% swing LD to C.
(2001: LD maj. 338 (0.72%))

WIGAN
E. 64,267 T. 34,278 (53.34%) Lab. hold
Neil Turner, Lab. 18,901
John Coombes, C. 7,134
Denise Capstick, LD 6,051
Dr John Whittaker, UKIP 1,166
Kevin Williams, CAP 1,026
Lab. maj. 11,767 (34.33%)
3.29% swing Lab. to C.
(2001: Lab. maj. 13,743 (40.91%))

WILTSHIRE NORTH
E. 80,896 T. 56,061 (69.30%) C. hold
James Gray, C. 26,282
Paul Fox, LD 20,979
David Nash, Lab. 6,794
Neil Dowdney, UKIP 1,428
Philip Allnatt, Ind. 578
C. maj. 5,303 (9.46%)
1.07% swing LD to C.
(2001: C. maj. 3,878 (7.32%))

WIMBLEDON
E. 63,714 T. 43,404 (68.12%) C. gain
*Stephen Hammond, C. 17,886
Roger Casale, Lab. 15,585
Stephen Gee, LD 7,868
Giles Barrow, Green 1,374
Andrew Mills, UKIP 408
Christopher Coverdale, Ind. 211
Alastair Wilson, TEPK 50
Rainbow George Weiss, Vote Dream 22
C. maj. 2,301 (5.30%)
7.20% swing Lab. to C.
(2001: Lab. maj. 3,744 (9.11%))

WINCHESTER
E. 85,810 T. 61,658 (71.85%) LD hold
Mark Oaten, LD 31,225
George Hollingbery, C. 23,749
Patrick Davies, Lab. 4,782
Dr David Abbott, UKIP 1,321
Arthur Uther Pendragon, Ind. 581
LD maj. 7,476 (12.12%)
2.08% swing LD to C.
(2001: LD maj. 9,634 (16.29%))

WINDSOR
E. 68,290 T. 43,693 (63.98%) C. hold
*Adam Afriyie, C. 21,646
Antony Wood, LD 11,354
Mark Muller, Lab. 8,339
David Black, UKIP 1,098
Derek Wall, Green 1,074
Peter Hooper, Ind. 182
C. maj. 10,292 (23.56%)
1.22% swing LD to C.
(2001: C. maj. 8,889 (21.11%))

WIRRAL SOUTH
E. 58,834 T. 39,704 (67.48%) Lab. hold
Ben Chapman, Lab. 16,892
Carl Cross, C. 13,168
Simon Holbrook, LD 8,568
David Scott, UKIP 616
Laurence Jones, Ind. 460
Lab. maj. 3,724 (9.38%)
1.65% swing Lab. to C.
(2001: Lab. maj. 5,049 (12.68%))

WIRRAL WEST
E. 61,050 T. 41,233 (67.54%) Lab. hold
Stephen Hesford, Lab. 17,543
Esther McVey, C. 16,446
Jeff Clarke, LD 6,652
John Moore, UKIP 429
Roger Taylor, AP 163
Lab. maj. 1,097 (2.66%)
3.65% swing Lab. to C.
(2001: Lab. maj. 4,035 (9.97%))

WITNEY
E. 78,053 T. 53,869 (69.02%) C. hold
David Cameron, C. 26,571
Liz Leffman, LD 12,415
Tony Gray, Lab. 11,845
Richard Dossett-Davies, Green 1,682
Paul Wesson, UKIP 1,356
C. maj. 14,156 (26.28%)
0.79% swing LD to C.
(2001: C. maj. 7,973 (16.20%))

WOKING
E. 72,676 T. 46,045 (63.36%) C. hold
Humfrey Malins, C. 21,838
Anne Lee, LD 15,226
Ellie Blagbrough, Lab. 7,507
Matthew Davies, UKIP 1,324
Michael Osman, UKC 150
C. maj. 6,612 (14.36%)
0.70% swing C. to LD
(2001: C. maj. 6,759 (15.75%))

WOKINGHAM
E. 68,614 T. 46,072 (67.15%) C. hold
Rt. Hon. John Redwood, C. 22,174
Prue Bray, LD 14,934
David Black, Lab. 6,991
Frank Carstairs, UKIP 994
Top Cat Owen, Loony 569
Richard Colborne, BNP 376
Michael Hall, Tele. 34
C. maj. 7,240 (15.71%)
1.02% swing LD to C.
(2001: C. maj. 5,994 (13.67%))

WOLVERHAMPTON NORTH EAST
E. 60,595 T. 32,956 (54.39%)
Lab. (Co-op) hold
Ken Purchase, Lab. (Co-op) 17,948
Alexandra Robson, C. 9,792
David Jack, LD 3,845
Lydia Simpson, UKIP 1,371
Lab. (Co-op) maj. 8,156 (24.75%)
3.45% swing Lab. (Co-op) to C.
(2001: Lab. (Co-op) maj. 9,965
(31.64%))

WOLVERHAMPTON SOUTH EAST
E. 54,047 T. 28,251 (52.27%) Lab. hold
*Pat McFadden, Lab. 16,790
James Fairbairn, C. 6,295
David Murray, LD 3,682
Kevin Simmons, UKIP 1,484
Lab. maj. 10,495 (37.15%)
4.26% swing Lab. to C.
(2001: Lab. (Co-op) maj. 12,464
(45.66%))

WOLVERHAMPTON SOUTH WEST
E. 67,096 T. 41,679 (62.12%) Lab. hold
Rob Marris, Lab. 18,489
Sandy Verma, C. 15,610
Colin Ross, LD 5,568
Douglas Hope, UKIP 1,029
Edward Mullins, BNP 983
Lab. maj. 2,879 (6.91%)
0.81% swing Lab. to C.
(2001: Lab. maj. 3,487 (8.53%))

WOODSPRING
E. 71,662 T. 51,618 (72.03%) C. hold
Dr Liam Fox, C. 21,587
Mike Bell, LD 15,571
Chanel Stevens, Lab. 11,249
Rebecca Lewis, Green 1,309
Anthony Butcher, UKIP 1,269
Michael Howson, BNP 633
C. maj. 6,016 (11.65%)
3.90% swing C. to LD
(2001: C. maj. 8,798 (18.04%))

WORCESTER
E. 72,384 T. 46,388 (64.09%) Lab. hold
Michael Foster, Lab. 19,421
Margaret Harper, C. 16,277
Mary Dhonau, LD 7,557
Richard Chamings, UKIP 1,113
Martin Roberts, BNP 980
Chris Lennard, Green 921
Prudence Dowson, Ind. 119
Lab. maj. 3,144 (6.78%)
3.13% swing Lab. to C.
(2001: Lab. maj. 5,766 (13.04%))

WORCESTERSHIRE MID
E. 71,546 T. 48,127 (67.27%) C. hold
Peter Luff, C. 24,783
Matt Gregson, Lab. 11,456
Margaret Rowley, LD 9,796
Tony Eaves, UKIP 2,092
C. maj. 13,327 (27.69%)
2.01% swing Lab. to C.
(2001: C. maj. 10,627 (23.67%))

WORCESTERSHIRE WEST
E. 66,999 T. 47,077 (70.27%) C. hold
Sir Michael Spicer, C.	20,959
Tom Wells, LD	18,484
Qamar Bhatti, Lab.	4,945
Caroline Bovey, UKIP	1,590
Malcolm Victory, Green	1,099

C. maj. 2,475 (5.26%)
3.37% swing C. to LD
(2001: C. maj. 5,374 (11.99%))

WORKINGTON
E. 61,441 T. 39,737 (64.68%) Lab. hold
Tony Cunningham, Lab.	19,554
Judith Pattinson, C.	12,659
Kate Clarkson, LD	5,815
Mark Richardson, UKIP	1,328
John Peacock, LCA	381

Lab. maj. 6,895 (17.35%)
4.30% swing Lab. to C.
(2001: Lab. maj. 10,850 (25.94%))

WORSLEY
E. 69,534 T. 36,946 (53.13%) Lab. hold
*Barbara Keeley, Lab.	18,859
Graham Evans, C.	9,491
Richard Clayton, LD	6,902
Bernard Gill, UKIP	1,694

Lab. maj. 9,368 (25.36%)
3.99% swing Lab. to C.
(2001: Lab. maj. 11,787 (33.33%))

WORTHING EAST & SHOREHAM
E. 72,302 T. 44,543 (61.61%) C. hold
Tim Loughton, C.	19,548
Daniel Yates, Lab.	11,365
James Doyle, LD	10,844
Richard Jelf, UKIP	2,109
Chris Baldwin, LCA	677

C. maj. 8,183 (18.37%)
2.06% swing Lab. to C.
(2001: C. maj. 6,139 (14.25%))

WORTHING WEST
E. 71,780 T. 44,941 (62.61%) C. hold
Peter Bottomley, C.	21,383
Claire Potter, LD	12,004
Antony Bignell, Lab.	8,630
Timothy Cross, UKIP	2,374
Chris Baldwin, LCA	550

C. maj. 9,379 (20.87%)
0.02% swing C. to LD
(2001: C. maj. 9,037 (20.91%))

WREKIN, THE
E. 67,291 T. 45,054 (66.95%) C. gain
*Mark Pritchard, C.	18,899
Peter Bradley, Lab.	17,957
Bill Tomlinson, LD	6,608
Bruce Lawson, UKIP	1,590

C. maj. 942 (2.09%)
5.37% swing Lab. to C.
(2001: Lab. maj. 3,587 (8.65%))

WYCOMBE
E. 71,464 T. 44,427 (62.17%) C. hold
Paul Goodman, C.	20,331
Julia Wassell, Lab.	13,280
James Oates, LD	8,780
Robert Davis, UKIP	1,735
David Fitton, Ind.	301

C. maj. 7,051 (15.87%)
4.41% swing Lab. to C.
(2001: C. maj. 3,168 (7.04%))

WYRE FOREST
E. 73,192 T. 46,987 (64.20%)
KHHC hold
Dr Richard Taylor, KHHC	18,739
Mark Garnier, C.	13,489
Marc Bayliss, Lab.	10,716
Fran Oborski, Lib.	2,666
Rustie Lee, UKIP	1,074
Bert Priest, Loony	303

KHHC maj. 5,250 (11.17%)
13.92% swing KHHC to C.
(2001: KHHC maj. 17,630 (35.93%))

WYTHENSHAWE & SALE EAST
E. 71,766 T. 36,184 (50.42%) Lab. hold
Paul Goggins, Lab.	18,878
Jane Meehan, C.	8,051
Alison Firth, LD	7,766
William Ford, UKIP	1,120
Lynn Worthington, Soc. Alt.	369

Lab. maj. 10,827 (29.92%)
3.02% swing Lab. to C.
(2001: Lab. maj. 12,608 (35.97%))

YEOVIL
E. 77,668 T. 49,913 (64.26%) LD hold
David Laws, LD	25,658
Ian Jenkins, C.	17,096
Colin Rolfe, Lab.	5,256
Graham Livings, UKIP	1,903

LD maj. 8,562 (17.15%)
4.50% swing C. to LD
(2001: LD maj. 3,928 (8.16%))

YORK, CITY OF
E. 75,555 T. 46,597 (61.67%) Lab. hold
Hugh Bayley, Lab.	21,836
Clive Booth, C.	11,364
Andrew Waller, LD	10,166
Andy D'Agorne, Green	2,113
Richard Jackson, UKIP	832
Ken Curran, Ind.	121
Damien Fleck, DDTP	93
Andrew Hinkles, Ind.	72

Lab. maj. 10,472 (22.47%)
3.12% swing Lab. to C.
(2001: Lab. maj. 13,779 (28.72%))

YORKSHIRE EAST
E. 76,648 T. 46,925 (61.22%) C. hold
Rt. Hon. Greg Knight, C.	21,215
Emma Hoddinott, Lab.	14,932
Jim Wastling, LD	9,075
Christopher Tresidder, UKIP	1,703

C. maj. 6,283 (13.39%)
1.29% swing Lab. to C.
(2001: C. maj. 4,682 (10.81%))

WALES

ABERAVON
E. 51,080 T. 30,104 (58.94%) Lab. hold
Dr Hywel Francis, Lab.	18,077
Claire Waller, LD	4,140
Philip Evans, PC	3,545
Annunziata Rees-Mogg, C.	3,064
Walter Wright, Veritas	768
Miranda La Vey, Green	510

Lab. maj. 13,937 (46.30%)
3.57% swing Lab. to LD
(2001: Lab. maj. 16,108 (53.36%))

ALYN & DEESIDE
E. 58,939 T. 35,496 (60.22%) Lab. hold
Mark Tami, Lab.	17,331
Lynne Hale, C.	8,953
Paul Brighton, LD	6,174
Richard Coombs, PC	1,320
William Crawford, UKIP	918
Klaus Armstrong-Braun, FWP	378
Judith Kilshaw, Ind.	215
Glyn Davies, Comm Brit	207

Lab. maj. 8,378 (23.60%)
1.22% swing Lab. to C.
(2001: Lab. maj. 9,222 (26.04%))

BLAENAU GWENT
E. 53,301 T. 35,251 (66.14%) Ind. gain
*Peter Law, Ind.	20,505
Maggie Jones, Lab.	11,384
Brian Thomas, LD	1,511
John Price, PC	843
Dr Phillip Lee, C.	816
Peter Osborne, UKIP	192

Ind. maj. 9,121 (25.87%)
43.38% swing Lab. to Ind.
(2001: Lab. maj. 19,313 (60.88%))

BRECON & RADNORSHIRE
E. 55,171 T. 38,341 (69.49%) LD hold
Roger Williams, LD	17,182
Andrew Davies, C.	13,277
Leighton Veale, Lab.	5,755
Mabon ap Gwynfor, PC	1,404
Elizabeth Phillips, UKIP	723

LD maj. 3,905 (10.18%)
4.09% swing C. to LD
(2001: LD maj. 751 (2.00%))

BRIDGEND
E. 63,936 T. 37,859 (59.21%) Lab. hold
*Madeleine Moon, Lab.	16,410
Helen Baker, C.	9,887
Paul Warren, LD	7,949
Gareth Clubb, PC	2,527
Jonathan Spink, Green	595
Kunnathur Rajan, UKIP	491

Lab. maj. 6,523 (17.23%)
4.96% swing Lab. to C.
(2001: Lab. maj. 10,045 (27.15%))

CAERNARFON
E. 46,393 T. 27,999 (60.35%) PC hold
Hywel Williams, PC	12,747
Martin Eaglestone, Lab.	7,538
Melfyn ab Owain, LD	3,508
Guy Opperman, C.	3,483
Elwyn Williams, UKIP	723

PC maj. 5,209 (18.60%)
3.26% swing Lab. to PC
(2001: PC maj. 3,511 (12.08%))

CAERPHILLY
E. 66,939 T. 39,229 (58.60%) Lab. hold
Wayne David, Lab.   22,190
Lindsay Whittle, PC   6,831
Stephen Watson, C.   5,711
Ashgar Ali, LD   3,861
Graeme Beard, FWP   636
Lab. maj. 15,359 (39.15%)
1.00% swing PC to Lab.
(2001: Lab. maj. 14,425 (37.15%))

CARDIFF CENTRAL
E. 61,001 T. 36,132 (59.23%) LD gain
*Jenny Willott, LD   17,991
Jon Owen Jones, Lab. (Co-op)   12,398
Gotz Mohindra, C.   3,339
Richard Grigg, PC   1,271
Raja Gul Raiz, Respect   386
Frank Hughes, UKIP   383
Anne Savoury, Ind.   168
Captain Beany, Bean   159
Catherine Taylor-Dawson, Vote
Dream   37
LD maj. 5,593 (15.48%)
8.69% swing Lab. (Co-op) to LD
(2001: Lab. (Co-op) maj. 659 (1.89%))

CARDIFF NORTH
E. 64,341 T. 45,360 (70.50%) Lab. hold
Julie Morgan, Lab.   17,707
Jonathan Morgan, C.   16,561
John Dixon, LD   8,483
John Rowlands, PC   1,936
Don Hulston, UKIP   534
Alison Hobbs, FWP   138
Catherine Taylor-Dawson, Vote Dream   1
Lab. maj. 1,146 (2.53%)
5.87% swing Lab. to C.
(2001: Lab. maj. 6,165 (14.26%))

CARDIFF SOUTH & PENARTH
E. 65,710 T. 36,912 (56.17%)
                        Lab. (Co-op) hold
Rt. Hon. Alun Michael, Lab. (Co-op)
                                     17,447
Victoria Green, C.   8,210
Gavin Cox, LD   7,529
Jason Toby, PC   2,023
John Matthews, Green   729
Jennifer Tuttle, UKIP   522
Dave Bartlett, Soc. Alt.   269
Andrew Taylor, Ind.   104
Catherine Taylor-Dawson, Vote
Dream   79
Lab. (Co-op) maj. 9,237 (25.02%)
4.67% swing Lab. (Co-op) to C.
(2001: Lab. (Co-op) maj. 12,287
(34.37%))

CARDIFF WEST
E. 59,847 T. 34,561 (57.75%) Lab. hold
Kevin Brennan, Lab.   15,729
Simon Baker, C.   7,562
Alison Goldsworthy, LD   6,060
Neil McEvoy, PC   4,316
Joe Callan, UKIP   727
Catherine Taylor-Dawson, Vote
Dream   167
Lab. maj. 8,167 (23.63%)
4.79% swing Lab. to C.
(2001: Lab. maj. 11,321 (33.22%))

CARMARTHEN EAST & DINEFWR
E. 53,484 T. 38,291 (71.59%) PC hold
Adam Price, PC   17,561
Ross Hendry, Lab.   10,843
Suzy Davies, C.   5,235
Juliana Hughes, LD   3,719
Mike Squires, UKIP   661
Sid Whitworth, LCA   272
PC maj. 6,718 (17.54%)
5.37% swing Lab. to PC
(2001: PC maj. 2,590 (6.81%))

CARMARTHEN WEST &
PEMBROKESHIRE SOUTH
E. 56,245 T. 37,863 (67.32%) Lab. hold
Nick Ainger, Lab.   13,953
David Morris, C.   12,043
John Dixon, PC   5,582
John Allen, LD   5,399
Josie MacDonald, UKIP   545
Alex Daszak, LCA   237
Nick Turner, Ind.   104
Lab. maj. 1,910 (5.04%)
3.62% swing Lab. to C.
(2001: Lab. maj. 4,538 (12.29%))

CEREDIGION
E. 53,493 T. 35,947 (67.20%) LD gain
*Mark Williams, LD   13,130
Simon Thomas, PC   12,911
John Harrison, C.   4,455
Alun Davies, Lab.   4,337
Dave Bradney, Green   846
Iain Sheldon, Veritas   268
LD maj. 219 (0.61%)
6.00% swing PC to LD
(2001: PC maj. 3,944 (11.40%))

CLWYD SOUTH
E. 52,353 T. 32,931 (62.90%) Lab. hold
Martyn Jones, Lab.   14,808
Tom Biggins, C.   8,460
Deric Burnham, LD   5,105
Mark Strong, PC   3,111
Alwyn Humphreys, FWP   803
Nick Powell, UKIP   644
Lab. maj. 6,348 (19.28%)
3.64% swing Lab. to C.
(2001: Lab. maj. 8,898 (26.56%))

CLWYD WEST
E. 55,642 T. 35,614 (64.01%)   C. gain
*David Jones, C.   12,909
Gareth Thomas, Lab.   12,776
Frank Taylor, LD   4,723
Eilian Williams, PC   3,874
Warwick Nicholson, UKIP   512
Jimmy James, Ind.   507
Patrick Keenan, Soc. Lab.   313
C. maj. 133 (0.37%)
1.80% swing Lab. to C.
(2001: Lab. maj. 1,115 (3.22%))

CONWY
E. 53,987 T. 33,657 (62.34%) Lab. hold
Betty Williams, Lab.   12,479
Guto Bebb, C.   9,398
Gareth Roberts, LD   6,723
Paul Rowlinson, PC   3,730
Jim Killock, Green   512
David Lloyd Jones, Soc. Lab.   324
Kenneth Khambatta, UKIP   298
Tim Evans, LCA   193
Lab. maj. 3,081 (9.15%)
4.47% swing Lab. to C.
(2001: Lab. maj. 6,219 (18.10%))

CYNON VALLEY
E. 45,369 T. 26,647 (58.73%) Lab. hold
Rt. Hon. Ann Clwyd, Lab.   17,074
Geraint Benney, PC   3,815
Margaret Phelps, LD   2,991
Antonia Dunn, C.   2,062
Susan Davies, UKIP   705
Lab. maj. 13,259 (49.76%)
0.77% swing PC to Lab.
(2001: Lab. maj. 12,998 (48.22%))

DELYN
E. 52,766 T. 34,004 (64.44%) Lab. hold
David Hanson, Lab.   15,540
John Bell, C.   8,896
Tudor Jones, LD   6,089
Phil Thomas, PC   2,524
May Crawford, UKIP   533
Nigel Williams, Ind.   422
Lab. maj. 6,644 (19.54%)
2.65% swing Lab. to C.
(2001: Lab. maj. 8,605 (24.84%))

GOWER
E. 60,925 T. 39,542 (64.90%) Lab. hold
Martin Caton, Lab.   16,786
Mike Murray, C.   10,083
Nick Tregoning, LD   7,291
Sian Caiach, PC   3,089
Richard Lewis, UKIP   1,264
Rhodri Griffiths, Green   1,029
Lab. maj. 6,703 (16.95%)
1.42% swing Lab. to C.
(2001: Lab. maj. 7,395 (19.80%))

ISLWYN
E. 50,595 T. 30,865 (61.00%)
                        Lab. (Co-op) hold
Don Touhig, Lab. (Co-op)   19,687
Jim Criddle, PC   3,947
Lee Dillon, LD   3,873
Phillip Howells, C.   3,358
Lab. (Co-op) maj. 15,740 (51.00%)
0.67% swing PC to Lab. (Co-op)
(2001: Lab. (Co-op) maj. 15,309
(48.31%))

LLANELLI
E. 55,678 T. 35,344 (63.48%) Lab. hold
*Nia Griffith, Lab.   16,592
Neil Baker, PC   9,358
Adrian Phillips, C.   4,844
Ken Rees, LD   4,550
Lab. maj. 7,234 (20.47%)
1.39% swing PC to Lab.
(2001: Lab. maj. 6,403 (17.69%))

MEIRIONNYDD NANT CONWY
E. 33,443 T. 20,640 (61.72%) PC hold
Elfyn Llwyd, PC   10,597
Rhodri Jones, Lab.   3,983
Dan Munford, C.   3,402
Adrian Fawcett, LD   2,192
Francis Wykes, UKIP   466
PC maj. 6,614 (32.04%)
2.53% swing Lab. to PC
(2001: PC maj. 5,684 (26.98%))

MERTHYR TYDFIL & RHYMNEY
E. 54,579 T. 29,976 (54.92%) Lab. hold
Dai Havard, Lab.   18,129
Ceirion Rees, LD   4,195
Noel Turner, PC   2,972
Roger Berry, C.   2,680
Neil Greer, FWP   1,030
Gwyn Parry, UKIP   699
Ina Marsden, Soc. Lab.   271
Lab. maj. 13,934 (46.48%)
3.88% swing Lab. to LD
(2001: Lab. maj. 14,923 (47.10%))

MONMOUTH
E. 63,093 T. 45,653 (72.36%)   C. gain
*David Davies, C.   21,396
Huw Edwards, Lab.   16,869
Phil Hobson, LD   5,852
Jonathan Clark, PC   993
John Bufton, UKIP   543
C. maj. 4,527 (9.92%)
5.39% swing Lab. to C.
(2001: Lab. maj. 384 (0.86%))

MONTGOMERYSHIRE
E. 46,766 T. 30,097 (64.36%)   LD hold
Lembit Opik, LD   15,419
Simon Baynes, C.   8,246
David Tinline, Lab.   3,454
Ellen ap Gwynn, PC   2,078
Clive Easton, UKIP   900
LD maj. 7,173 (23.83%)
1.16% swing C. to LD
(2001: LD maj. 6,234 (21.51%))

NEATH
E. 57,607 T. 35,817 (62.17%) Lab. hold
Rt. Hon. Peter Hain, Lab.   18,835
Geraint Owen, PC   6,125
Sheila Waye, LD   5,112
Harri Lloyd Davies, C.   4,136
Susan Jay, Green   658
Gerry Brienza, Ind.   360
Pat Tabram, LCA   334
Heather Falconer, Respect   257
Lab. maj. 12,710 (35.49%)
3.41% swing Lab. to PC
(2001: Lab. maj. 14,816 (42.31%))

NEWPORT EAST
E. 54,956 T. 31,825 (57.91%) Lab. hold
*Jessica Morden, Lab.   14,389
Ed Townsend, LD   7,551
Matthew Collings, C.   7,459
Mohammad Asghar, PC   1,221
Roger Thomas, UKIP   945
Liz Screen, Soc. Lab.   260
Lab. maj. 6,838 (21.49%)
9.60% swing Lab. to LD
(2001: Lab. maj. 9,874 (31.56%))

NEWPORT WEST
E. 60,287 T. 35,732 (59.27%) Lab. hold
Paul Flynn, Lab.   16,021
Dr William Morgan, C.   10,563
Nigel Flanagan, LD   6,398
Tony Salkeld, PC   1,278
Hugh Moelwyn Hughes, UKIP   848
Peter Varley, Green   540
Saeid Arjomand, Ind.   84
Lab. maj. 5,458 (15.27%)
5.63% swing Lab. to C.
(2001: Lab. maj. 9,304 (26.54%))

OGMORE
E. 52,349 T. 30,278 (57.84%) Lab. hold
Huw Irranca-Davies, Lab.   18,295
Jackie Radford, LD   4,592
Dr Norma Lloyd-Nesling, C.   4,243
John Williams, PC   3,148
Lab. maj. 13,703 (45.26%)
2.01% swing Lab. to LD
(2002 Feb. by-election: Lab maj. 5,721
(31.13%))
(2001: Lab. maj. 14,574 (48.02%))

PONTYPRIDD
E. 65,074 T. 39,634 (60.91%) Lab. hold
Dr Kim Howells, Lab.   20,919
Mike Powell, LD   7,728
Quentin Gwynne Edwards, C.   5,321
Julie Richards, PC   4,420
David Bevan, UKIP   1,013
Robert Griffiths, Comm.   233
Lab. maj. 13,191 (33.28%)
7.91% swing Lab. to LD
(2001: Lab. maj. 17,684 (46.16%))

PRESELI PEMBROKESHIRE
E. 55,502 T. 38,587 (69.52%)   C. gain
*Stephen Crabb, C.   14,106
Sue Hayman, Lab.   13,499
Dewi Smith, LD   4,963
Matt Mathias, PC   4,752
James Carver, UKIP   498
Molly Scott-Cato, Green   494
Trish Bowen, Soc. Lab.   275
C. maj. 607 (1.57%)
4.79% swing Lab. to C.
(2001: Lab. maj. 2,946 (8.01%))

RHONDDA
E. 51,041 T. 31,148 (61.03%) Lab. hold
Chris Bryant, Lab.   21,198
Layton Percy Jones, PC   4,956
Karen Roberts, LD   3,264
Paul Stuart-Smith, C.   1,730
Lab. maj. 16,242 (52.14%)
2.48% swing PC to Lab.
(2001: Lab. maj. 16,047 (47.19%))

SWANSEA EAST
E. 58,813 T. 30,834 (52.43%) Lab. hold
*Sian James, Lab.   17,457
Robert Speht, LD   6,208
Ellenor Bland, C.   3,103
Carolyn Shan Couch, PC   2,129
Kevin Holloway, BNP   770
Timothy Jenkins, UKIP   674
Tony Young, Green   493
Lab. maj. 11,249 (36.48%)
9.27% swing Lab. to LD
(2001: Lab. maj. 16,148 (53.70%))

SWANSEA WEST
E. 57,946 T. 33,086 (57.10%) Lab. hold
Rt. Hon. Alan Williams, Lab.   13,833
Rene Kinzett, LD   9,564
Mohammed Abdel-Haq, C.   5,285
Harri Roberts, PC   2,150
Martyn Shrewsbury, Green   738
Martyn Ford, UKIP   609
Yvonne Holley, Veritas   401
Robert Williams, Soc. Alt.   288
Steve Pank, LCA   218
Lab. maj. 4,269 (12.90%)
9.64% swing Lab. to LD
(2001: Lab. maj. 9,550 (29.75%))

TORFAEN
E. 60,669 T. 35,979 (59.30%) Lab. hold
Rt. Hon. Paul Murphy, Lab.   20,472
Nick Ramsay, C.   5,681
Veronica Watkins, LD   5,678
Aneurin Preece, PC   2,242
David Rowlands, UKIP   1,145
Richard Turner-Thomas, Ind.   761
Lab. maj. 14,791 (41.11%)
2.54% swing Lab. to C.
(2001: Lab. maj. 16,280 (46.19%))

VALE OF CLWYD
E. 51,982 T. 32,313 (62.16%) Lab. hold
Christopher Ruane, Lab.   14,875
Felicity Elphick, C.   10,206
Elizabeth Jewkes, LD   3,820
Mark Jones, PC   2,309
Mark Young, Ind.   442
Edna Khambatta, UKIP   375
Jeff Ditchfield, LCA   286
Lab. maj. 4,669 (14.45%)
1.68% swing Lab. to C.
(2001: Lab. maj. 5,761 (17.81%))

VALE OF GLAMORGAN
E. 68,657 T. 47,324 (68.93%) Lab. hold
John Smith, Lab.   19,481
Alun Cairns, C.   17,673
Mark Hooper, LD   6,140
Barry Shaw, PC   2,423
Richard Suchorzewski, UKIP   840
Karl-James Langford, Lib.   605
Paul Mules, Soc. Lab.   162
Lab. maj. 1,808 (3.82%)
3.29% swing Lab. to C.
(2001: Lab. maj. 4,700 (10.40%))

WREXHAM
E. 48,016 T. 30,385 (63.28%) Lab. hold
Ian Lucas, Lab.   13,993
Tom Rippeth, LD   7,174
Dr Therese Coffey, C.   6,079
Sion Owen, PC   1,744
John Walker, BNP   919
Janet Williams, FWP   476
Lab. maj. 6,819 (22.44%)
6.72% swing Lab. to LD
(2001: Lab. maj. 9,188 (30.58%))

YNYS MON
E. 52,512 T. 35,462 (67.53%) Lab. hold
Albert Owen, Lab.   12,278
Eurig Wyn, PC   11,036
Peter Rogers, Ind.   5,216
James Roach, C.   3,915
Sarah Green, LD   2,418
Elaine Gill, UKIP   367
Tim Evans, LCA   232
Lab. maj. 1,242 (3.50%)
0.58% swing PC to Lab.
(2001: Lab. maj. 800 (2.35%))

SCOTLAND

ABERDEEN NORTH
E. 65,714 T. 36,634 (55.75%) Lab. hold
Frank Doran, Lab.	15,557
Steve Delaney, LD	8,762
Kevin Stewart, SNP	8,168
David Anderson, C.	3,456
John Connon, SSP	691

Lab. maj. 6,795 (18.55%)
§ 9.25% swing Lab. to LD
(§ 2001 Lab. maj. 9,294 (23.66%))

ABERDEEN SOUTH
E. 67,012 T. 41,621 (62.11%) Lab. hold
Anne Begg, Lab.	15,272
Vicki Harris, LD	13,924
Stewart Whyte, C.	7,134
Maureen Watt, SNP	4,120
Rhonda Reekie, Scot. Green	768
Donald Munro, SSP	403

Lab. maj. 1,348 (3.24%)
§ 3.13% swing Lab. to LD
(§ 2001 Lab. maj. 3,931 (9.49%))

ABERDEENSHIRE WEST & KINCARDINE
E. 65,548 T. 41,648 (63.54%) LD hold
Sir Robert Smith, LD	19,285
Alex Johnstone, C.	11,814
James Barrowman, Lab.	5,470
Caroline Little, SNP	4,700
Lorna Grant, SSP	379

LD maj. 7,471 (17.94%)
§ 2.25% swing C. to LD
(§ 2001 LD maj. 5,146 (13.44%))

AIRDRIE & SHOTTS
E. 61,955 T. 33,158 (53.52%) Lab. hold
Rt. Hon. Dr John Reid, Lab.	19,568
Malcolm Balfour, SNP	5,484
Helen Watt, LD	3,792
Stuart Cottis, C.	3,271
Fraser Coats, SSP	706
Joseph Rowan, Scot. Ind.	337

Lab. maj. 14,084 (42.48%)
§ 1.51% swing SNP to Lab.
(§ 2001 Lab. maj. 13,545 (39.46%))

ANGUS
E. 63,093 T. 38,186 (60.52%)
SNP hold
Mike Weir, SNP	12,840
Sandy Bushby, C.	11,280
Douglas Bradley, Lab.	6,850
Scott Rennie, LD	6,660
Alan Manley, SSP	556

SNP maj. 1,601 (4.20%)
§ 1.34% swing C. to SNP
(§ 2001 SNP maj. 532 (1.52%))

ARGYLL & BUTE
E. 67,325 T. 43,229 (64.21%) LD hold
Alan Reid, LD	15,786
James McGrigor, C.	10,150
Carolyn Manson, Lab.	9,696
Isobel Strong, SNP	6,716
Deirdre Henderson, SSP	881

LD maj. 5,636 (13.04%)
§ 1.94% swing C. to LD
(§ 2001 LD maj. 3,832 (9.16%))

AYR, CARRICK & CUMNOCK
E. 73,448 T. 45,048 (61.33%) Lab. hold
Sandra Osborne, Lab.	20,433
Mark Jones, C.	10,436
Colin Waugh, LD	6,341
Charles Brodie, SNP	5,932
Donald Sharp, SSCUP	592
Murray Steele, SSP	554
James McDaid, Soc. Lab.	395
Bryan McCormack, UKIP	365

Lab. maj. 9,997 (22.19%)
§ 2.18% swing Lab. to C.
(§ 2001 Lab. maj. 12,387 (26.56%))

AYRSHIRE CENTRAL
E. 68,643 T. 42,871 (62.46%) Lab. hold
Brian Donohoe, Lab.	19,905
Garry Clark, C.	9,482
Iain Kennedy, LD	6,881
Jahangir Hanif, SNP	4,969
Denise Morton, SSP	820
Robert Cochrane, Soc. Lab.	468
Jim Groves, UKIP	346

Lab. maj. 10,423 (24.31%)
§ 0.68% swing C. to Lab.
(§ 2001 Lab. maj. 9,772 (22.96%))

AYRSHIRE NORTH & ARRAN
E. 72,986 T. 44,205 (60.57%) Lab. hold
*Katy Clark, Lab.	19,417
Stewart Connell, C.	8,121
Tony Gurney, SNP	7,938
George White, LD	7,264
Colin Turbett, SSP	780
John Pursley, UKIP	382
Louise McDaid, Soc. Lab.	303

Lab. maj. 11,296 (25.55%)
§ 2.68% swing Lab. to C.
(§ 2001 Lab. maj. 12,140 (27.33%))

BANFF & BUCHAN
E. 65,570 T. 37,216 (56.76%)
SNP hold
Alex Salmond, SNP	19,044
Sandy Wallace, C.	7,207
Eleanor Anderson, LD	4,952
Rami Okasha, Lab.	4,476
Victor Ross, OCV	683
Kathleen Kemp, UKIP	442
Steve Will, SSP	412

SNP maj. 11,837 (31.81%)
§ 2.22% swing C. to SNP
(§ 2001 SNP maj. 9,744 (27.37%))

BERWICKSHIRE, ROXBURGH & SELKIRK
E. 71,702 T. 45,388 (63.30%) LD hold
Michael Moore, LD	18,993
John Lamont, C.	13,092
Sam Held, Lab.	7,206
Aileen Orr, SNP	3,885
John Hein, Lib.	916
Graeme McIver, SSP	695
Peter Neilson, UKIP	601

LD maj. 5,901 (13.00%)
§ 5.90% swing LD to C.
(§ 2001 LD maj. 10,770 (24.80%))

CAITHNESS, SUTHERLAND & EASTER ROSS
E. 46,837 T. 27,663 (59.06%) LD hold
John Thurso, LD	13,957
Alan Jamieson, Lab.	5,789
Karen Shirron, SNP	3,686
Angus Ross, C.	2,835
Gordon Campbell, Ind.	848
Luke Ivory, SSP	548

LD maj. 8,168 (29.53%)
§ 7.60% swing Lab. to LD
(§ 2001 LD maj. 4,078 (14.33%))

COATBRIDGE, CHRYSTON & BELLSHILL
E. 67,385 T. 38,344 (56.90%) Lab. hold
Rt. Hon. Thomas Clarke, Lab.	24,725
Duncan Ross, SNP	5,206
Rodney Ackland, LD	4,605
Lindsay Paterson, C.	2,775
Joan Kinloch, SSP	1,033

Lab. maj. 19,519 (50.90%)
§ 1.82% swing Lab. to SNP
(§ 2001 Lab. maj. 22,092 (54.55%))

CUMBERNAULD, KILSYTH & KIRKINTILLOCH EAST
E. 64,748 T. 39,088 (60.37%) Lab. hold
Rosemary McKenna, Lab.	20,251
James Hepburn, SNP	8,689
Hugh O'Donnell, LD	5,817
James Boswell, C.	2,718
Willie O'Neill, SSP	1,141
Patrick Elliott, OCV	472

Lab. maj. 11,562 (29.58%)
§ 1.11% swing Lab. to SNP
(§ 2001 Lab. maj. 12,667 (31.79%))

DUMFRIES & GALLOWAY
E. 74,273 T. 50,891 (68.52%) Lab. hold
Russell Brown, Lab.	20,924
Peter Duncan, C.	18,002
Douglas Henderson, SNP	6,182
Keith Legg, LD	4,259
John Schofield, Scot. Green	745
John Dennis, SSP	497
Mark Smith, OCV	282

Lab. maj. 2,922 (5.74%)
§ 2.73% swing C. to Lab.
(§ 2001 Lab. maj. 141 (0.28%))

DUMFRIESSHIRE, CLYDESDALE & TWEEDDALE
E. 66,045 T. 44,616 (67.55%) C. gain
*David Mundell, C.	16,141
Sean Marshall, Lab.	14,403
Patsy Kenton, LD	9,046
Andrew Wood, SNP	4,075
Sarah MacTavish, SSP	521
Tony Lee, UKIP	430

C. maj. 1,738 (3.90%)
§ 7.98% swing Lab. to C.
(§ 2001 Lab. maj. 5,254 (12.06%))

DUNBARTONSHIRE EAST
E. 64,763 T. 46,724 (72.15%) LD gain
*Jo Swinson, LD	19,533
John Lyons, Lab.	15,472
David Jack, C.	7,708
Chris Sagan, SNP	2,716
Stuart Callison, Scot. Green	876
Pamela Page, SSP	419

LD maj. 4,061 (8.69%)
§ 7.49% swing Lab. to LD
(§ 2001 Lab. maj. 2,601 (6.29%))

DUNBARTONSHIRE WEST
E. 67,805 T 41,589 (61 34%)
Lab. (Co-op) hold
Rt. Hon. John McFall, Lab. (Co-op)
21,600
Tom Chalmers, SNP   9,047
Niall Walker, LD   5,999
Campbell Murdoch, C.   2,679
Les Robertson, SSP   1,708
Bryan Maher, UKIP   354
Marlon Dawson, OCV   202
Lab. (Co-op) maj. 12,553 (30.18%)
§ 4.65% swing Lab. (Co-op) to SNP
(§ 2001 Lab. (Co-op) maj. 18,169
(39.49%))

DUNDEE EAST
E. 63,335 T. 39,540 (62.43%)
SNP gain
*Stewart Hosie, SNP   14,708
Iain Luke, Lab.   14,325
Christopher Bustin, C.   5,061
Clive Sneddon, LD   4,498
Harvey Duke, SSP   537
Donald Low, UKIP   292
David Allison, Ind.   119
SNP maj. 383 (0.97%)
§ 1.13% swing Lab. to SNP
(§ 2001 Lab. maj. 496 (1.29%))

DUNDEE WEST
E. 65,857 T. 36,936 (56.09%) Lab. hold
*James McGovern, Lab.   16,468
Joe Fitzpatrick, SNP   11,089
Nykoma Garry, LD   5,323
Christopher McKinlay, C.   3,062
Jim McFarlane, SSP   994
Lab. maj. 5,379 (14.56%)
§ 3.99% swing Lab. to SNP
(§ 2001 Lab. maj. 8,410 (22.54%))

DUNFERMLINE & FIFE WEST
E. 70,775 T. 42,394 (59.90%) Lab. hold
Rachel Squire, Lab.   20,111
David Herbert, LD   8,549
Douglas Chapman, SNP   8,026
Roger Smillie, C.   4,376
Susan Archibald, SSP   689
Ian Borland, UKIP   643
Lab. maj. 11,562 (27.27%)
§ 6.47% swing Lab. to LD
(§ 2001 Lab. maj. 14,845 (36.64%))

EAST KILBRIDE, STRATHAVEN &
LESMAHAGOW
E. 75,132 T. 47,733 (63.53%) Lab. hold
Rt. Hon. Adam Ingram, Lab.   23,264
Douglas Edwards, SNP   8,541
John Oswald, LD   7,904
Tony Lewis, C.   4,776
Kirsten Robb, Scot. Green   1,575
Rose Gentle, Ind.   1,513
John Houston, Ind.   160
Lab. maj. 14,723 (30.84%)
§ 0.78% swing SNP to Lab.
(§ 2001 Lab. maj. 13,999 (29.29%))

EAST LOTHIAN
E. 70,989 T. 45,776 (64.48%) Lab. hold
Anne Picking, Lab.   18,983
Chris Butler, LD   11,363
William Stevenson, C.   7,315
Paul McLennan, SNP   5,995
Michael Collie, Scot. Green   1,132
Gary Galbraith, SSP   504
Eric Robb, UKIP   306
William Thompson, OCV   178
Lab. maj. 7,620 (16.65%)
§ 7.54% swing Lab. to LD
(§ 2001 Lab. maj. 14,011 (31.73%))

EDINBURGH EAST
E. 64,826 T. 39,709 (61.25%) Lab. hold
Rt. Hon. Gavin Strang, Lab.   15,899
Gordon Mackenzie, LD   9,697
Stefan Tymkewycz, SNP   6,760
Mev Brown, C.   4,093
Cara Gillespie, Scot. Green   2,266
Catriona Grant, SSP   868
Brett Harris, DDTP   89
Peter Clifford, Ind.   37
Lab. maj. 6,202 (15.62%)
§ 8.47% swing Lab. to LD
(§ 2001 Lab. maj. 12,808 (32.56%))

EDINBURGH NORTH & LEITH
E. 68,038 T. 42,640 (62.67%)
Lab. (Co-op) hold
Mark Lazarowicz, Lab. (Co-op)   14,597
Mike Crockart, LD   12,444
Iain Whyte, C.   7,969
Davie Hutchison, SNP   4,344
Mark Sydenham, Scot. Green   2,482
Bill Scott, SSP   804
Lab. (Co-op) maj. 2,153 (5.05%)
§ 8.26% swing Lab. (Co-op) to LD
(§ 2001 Lab. maj. 8,688 (21.56%))

EDINBURGH SOUTH
E. 60,993 T. 42,698 (70.00%) Lab. hold
Nigel Griffiths, Lab.   14,188
Marilyne MacLaren, LD   13,783
Gavin Brown, C.   10,291
Graham Sutherland, SNP   2,635
Dr Steve Burgess, Scot. Green   1,387
Morag Robertson, SSP   414
Lab. maj. 405 (0.95%)
§ 6.50% swing Lab. to LD
(§ 2001 Lab. maj. 5,785 (13.95%))

EDINBURGH SOUTH WEST
E. 67,135 T. 43,926 (65.43%) Lab. hold
Rt. Hon. Alistair Darling, Lab.   17,476
Gordon Buchan, C.   10,234
Simon Clark, LD   9,252
Nick Elliott-Cannon, SNP   4,654
John Blair-Fish, Scot. Green   1,520
Pat Smith, SSP   585
William Boys, UKIP   205
Lab. maj. 7,242 (16.49%)
§ 0.71% swing Lab. to C.
(§ 2001 Lab. maj. 7,951 (17.91%))

EDINBURGH WEST
E. 65,741 T. 45,265 (68.85%) LD hold
John Barrett, LD   22,417
David Brogan, C.   8,817
Navraj Singh Ghaleigh, Lab.   8,433
Sheena Cleland, SNP   4,124
Ailsa Spindler, Scot. Green   964
Gary Clark, SSP   510
LD maj. 13,600 (30.05%)
§ 6.71% swing C. to LD
(§ 2001 LD maj. 5,320 (11.86%))

FALKIRK
E. 76,784 T. 45,750 (59.58%) Lab. hold
Eric Joyce, Lab.   23,261
Laura Love, SNP   9,789
Callum Chomczuk, LD   7,321
David Potts, C.   4,538
Danny Quinlan, SSP   838
Lab. maj. 13,475 (29.45%)
§ 0.36% swing Lab. to SNP
(§ 2001 Lab. maj. 13,555 (30.17%))

FIFE NORTH EAST
E. 62,057 T. 38,556 (62.13%) LD hold
Rt. Hon. Sir Menzies Campbell, LD
20,088
Mike Scott-Hayward, C.   7,517
Anthony King, Lab.   4,920
Rod Campbell, SNP   4,011
Jim Park, Scot. Green   1,071
Dr Duncan Pickard, UKIP   533
Jack Ferguson, SSP   416
LD maj. 12,571 (32.60%)
§ 3.20% swing C. to LD
(§ 2001 LD maj. 9,686 (26.20%))

GLASGOW CENTRAL
E. 64,053 T. 28,037 (43.77%) Lab. hold
Mohammad Sarwar, Lab.   13,518
Isabel Nelson, LD   4,987
Bill Kidd, SNP   4,148
Richard Sullivan, C.   1,757
Gordon Masterton, Scot. Green   1,372
Marie Gordon, SSP   1,110
Walter Hamilton, BNP   671
Ian Johnson, Soc. Lab.   255
Thomas Greig, OCV   139
Elinor McKenzie, Comm. Brit.   80
Lab. maj. 8,531 (30.43%)
§ 7.36% swing Lab. to LD
(§ 2001 Lab. maj. 9,382 (33.82%))

GLASGOW EAST
E. 64,130 T. 30,939 (48.24%) Lab. hold
David Marshall, Lab.   18,775
Lachlan McNeill, SNP   5,268
David Jackson, LD   3,665
Carl Thomson, C.   2,135
George Savage, SSP   1,096
Lab. maj. 13,507 (43.66%)
§ 1.48% swing Lab. to SNP
(§ 2001 Lab. maj. 15,238 (46.62%))

GLASGOW NORTH
E. 55,419 T. 27,921 (50.38%) Lab. hold
Ann McKechin, Lab.   11,001
Amy Rodger, LD   7,663
Kenneth McLean, SNP   3,614
Brian Pope, C.   2,441
Martin Bartos, Scot. Green   2,135
Nick Tarlton, SSP   1,067
Lab. maj. 3,338 (11.96%)
§ 8.70% swing Lab. to LD
(§ 2001 Lab. maj. 8,023 (29.36%))

GLASGOW NORTH EAST
E. 62,042 T. 28,418 (45.80%)
Speaker hold
Rt. Hon. Michael Martin, Speaker15,153
John McLaughlin, SNP   5,019
Doris Kelly, Soc. Lab.   4,036
Graham Campbell, SSP   1,402
Daniel Houston, Scot. U.   1,266
Scott McLean, BNP   920
Joe Chambers, Ind.   622
Speaker maj. 10,134 (35.66%)
§ 6.62% swing Speaker to SNP
(§ 2001 Speaker maj. 15,203 (48.90%))

GLASGOW NORTH WEST

E. 61,880 T. 34,061 (55.04%) Lab. hold

John Robertson, Lab.	16,748
Paul Graham, LD	6,655
Graeme Hendry, SNP	4,676
Murray Roxburgh, C.	3,262
Martha Wardrop, Scot. Green	1,333
Anthea Irwin, SSP	1,108
Colin Muir, Soc. Lab.	279

Lab. maj. 10,093 (29.63%)
§ 6.80% swing Lab. to LD
(§ 2001 Lab. maj. 13,231 (38.83%))

GLASGOW SOUTH

E. 68,837 T. 38,431 (55.83%) Lab. hold

Tom Harris, Lab.	18,153
Arthur Sanderson, LD	7,321
Finlay MacLean, SNP	4,860
Dr Janette McAlpine, C.	4,836
Kay Allan, Scot. Green	1,692
Ronnie Stevenson, SSP	1,303
Dorothy Entwistle, Soc. Lab.	266

Lab. maj. 10,832 (28.19%)
§ 4.93% swing Lab. to LD
(§ 2001 Lab. maj. 13,042 (33.15%))

GLASGOW SOUTH WEST

E. 62,005 T. 30,977 (49.96%)
Lab. (Co-op) hold

Ian Davidson, Lab. (Co-op)	18,653
James Dornan, SNP	4,757
Katy Gordon, LD	3,593
Scott Brady, C.	1,786
Keith Baldassara, SSP	1,666
Alistair McConnachie, Ind. Green	379
Violet Shaw, Soc. Lab.	143

Lab. (Co-op) maj. 13,896 (44.86%)
§ 0.22% swing SNP to Lab. (Co-op)
(§ 2001 Lab. (Co-op) maj. 14,687
(44.42%))

GLENROTHES

E. 66,563 T. 37,366 (56.14%) Lab. hold

John MacDougall, Lab.	19,395
John Beare, SNP	8,731
Elizabeth Riches, LD	4,728
Belinda Don, C.	2,651
George Rodger, PPS	716
Morag Balfour, SSP	705
Paul Smith, UKIP	440

Lab. maj. 10,664 (28.54%)
§ 2.71% swing Lab. to SNP
(§ 2001 Lab. maj. 12,988 (33.95%))

GORDON

E. 71,925 T. 44,438 (61.78%) LD hold

Malcolm Bruce, LD	20,008
Iain Brotchie, Lab.	8,982
Philip Atkinson, C.	7,842
Joanna Strathdee, SNP	7,098
Tommy Paterson, SSP	508

LD maj. 11,026 (24.81%)
§ 3.73% swing Lab. to LD
(§ 2001 LD maj. 6,845 (17.36%))

INVERCLYDE

E. 59,291 T. 36,098 (60.88%) Lab. hold

David Cairns, Lab.	18,318
Stuart McMillan, SNP	7,059
Douglas Herbison, LD	6,123
Gordon Fraser, C.	3,692
David Landels, SSP	906

Lab. maj. 11,259 (31.19%)
§ 2.51% swing Lab. to SNP
(§ 2001 Lab. maj. 11,314 (29.06%))

INVERNESS, NAIRN, BADENOCH & STRATHSPEY

E. 69,636 T. 44,255 (63.55%) LD gain

*Danny Alexander, LD	17,830
David Stewart, Lab.	13,682
David Thompson, SNP	5,992
Robert Rowantree, C.	4,579
Donnie MacLeod, Scot. Green	1,065
Donald Lawson, Publican	678
George MacDonald, SSP	429

LD maj. 4,148 (9.37%)
§ 6.01% swing Lab. to LD
(§ 2001 Lab. maj. 1,134 (2.65%))

KILMARNOCK & LOUDOUN

E. 72,851 T. 44,383 (60.92%) Lab. hold

Rt. Hon. Desmond Browne, Lab.	20,976
Daniel Coffey, SNP	12,273
Gary Smith, C.	5,026
Kevin Lang, LD	4,945
Hugh Kerr, SSP	833
Ronnie Robertson, UKIP	330

Lab. maj. 8,703 (19.61%)
§ 5.45% swing Lab. to SNP
(§ 2001 Lab. maj. 13,621 (30.51%))

KIRKCALDY & COWDENBEATH

E. 71,606 T. 41,796 (58.37%) Lab. hold

Rt. Hon. Gordon Brown, Lab.	24,278
Alan Bath, SNP	6,062
Alex Cole-Hamilton, LD	5,450
Stuart Randall, C.	4,308
Steve West, SSP	666
Peter Adams, UKIP	516
James Parker, Scot. Senior	425
Elizabeth Kwantes, Ind.	47
Pat Sargent, Ind.	44

Lab. maj. 18,216 (43.58%)
§ 1.84% swing SNP to Lab.
(§ 2001 Lab. maj. 16,238 (39.91%))

LANARK & HAMILTON EAST

E. 73,736 T. 43,589 (59.11%) Lab. hold

Jimmy Hood, Lab.	20,072
Fraser Grieve, LD	8,125
John Wilson, SNP	7,746
Robert Pettigrew, C.	5,576
Dennis Reilly, SSP	802
Donald Mackay, UKIP	437
Duncan McFarlane, Ind.	416
Robin Mawhinney, OCV	415

Lab. maj. 11,947 (27.41%)
§ 5.89% swing Lab. to LD
(§ 2001 Lab. maj. 12,861 (28.59%))

LINLITHGOW & FALKIRK EAST

E. 76,739 T. 46,389 (60.45%) Lab. hold

Michael Connarty, Lab.	22,121
Gordon Guthrie, SNP	10,919
Stephen Glenn, LD	7,100
Michael Veitch, C.	5,486
Ally Hendry, SSP	763

Lab. maj. 11,202 (24.15%)
§ 1.16% swing Lab. to SNP
(§ 2001 Lab. maj. 11,796 (26.46%))

LIVINGSTON

E. 76,353 T. 44,337 (58.07%) Lab. hold

Rt. Hon. Robin Cook, Lab.	22,657
Angela Constance, SNP	9,560
Charles Dundas, LD	6,832
Alison Ross, C.	4,499
Steven Nimmo, SSP	789

Lab. maj. 13,097 (29.54%)
§ 1.17% swing Lab. to SNP
(§ 2001 Lab. maj. 13,638 (31.88%))

MIDLOTHIAN

E. 60,644 T. 37,704 (62.17%) Lab. hold

David Hamilton, Lab.	17,153
Fred Mackintosh, LD	9,888
Colin Beattie, SNP	6,400
Iain McGill, C.	3,537
Norman Gilfillan, SSP	726

Lab. maj. 7,265 (19.27%)
§ 6.98% swing Lab. to LD
(§ 2001 Lab. maj. 12,017 (31.29%))

MORAY

E. 66,463 T. 38,793 (58.37%)
SNP hold

Angus Robertson, SNP	14,196
Jamie Halcro-Johnston, C.	8,520
Kevin Hutchens, Lab.	7,919
Linda Gorn, LD	7,460
Norma Anderson, SSP	698

SNP maj. 5,676 (14.63%)
§ 4.07% swing C. to SNP
(§ 2001 SNP maj. 1,852 (5.06%))

MOTHERWELL & WISHAW

E. 66,987 T. 37,109 (55.40%) Lab. hold

Frank Roy, Lab.	21,327
Ian MacQuarrie, SNP	6,105
Conor Snowden, LD	4,464
Peter Finnie, C.	3,440
Gregor MacEwan, SSP	1,019
Dallas Carter, Free Scot.	384
Coral Thompson, OCV	370

Lab. maj. 15,222 (41.02%)
§ 2.35% swing SNP to Lab.
(§ 2001 Lab. maj. 13,778 (36.33%))

NA H-EILEANAN AN IAR

E. 21,576 T. 13,836 (64.13%)
SNP gain

*Angus MacNeil, SNP	6,213
Calum MacDonald, Lab.	4,772
Dr Jean Davis, LD	1,096
James Hargreaves, OCV	1,048
Andy Maciver, C.	610
Joanne Telfer, SSP	97

SNP maj. 1,441 (10.41%)
9.29% swing Lab. to SNP
(2001: Lab. maj. 1,074 (8.16%))

OCHIL & PERTHSHIRE SOUTH

E. 70,731 T. 46,697 (66.02%) Lab. hold

*Gordon Banks, Lab.	14,645
Annabelle Ewing, SNP	13,957
Elizabeth Smith, C.	10,021
Catherine Whittingham, LD	6,218
George Baxter, Scot. Green	978
Iain Campbell, SSP	420
David Bushby, UKIP	275
Maitland Kelly, Free Scot.	183

Lab. maj. 688 (1.47%)
§ 0.18% swing Lab. to SNP
(§ 2001 Lab. maj. 821 (1.83%))

ORKNEY & SHETLAND

E. 33,048 T. 17,742 (53.69%) LD hold

Alistair Carmichael, LD	9,138
Richard Meade, Lab.	2,511
Frank Nairn, C.	2,357
John Mowat, SNP	1,833
John Aberdein, SSP	992
Scott Dyble, UKIP	424
Paul Cruickshank, LCA	311
Brian Nugent, Free Scot.	176

LD maj. 6,627 (37.35%)
8.29% swing Lab. to LD
(2001: LD maj. 3,475 (20.77%))

PAISLEY & RENFREWSHIRE NORTH
E. 63,076 T. 40,005 (64.82%) Lab. hold
James Sheridan, Lab.   18,697
Bill Wilson, SNP   7,696
Lewis Hutton, LD   7,464
Philip Lardner, C.   5,566
Angela McGregor, SSP   646
Katharine McGavigan, Soc. Lab.   444
John Pearson, UKIP   372
Lab. maj. 11,001 (26.91%)
§ 1.34% swing Lab. to SNP
(§ 2001 Lab. maj. 12,417 (29.58%))

PAISLEY & RENFREWSHIRE SOUTH
E. 60,181 T. 37,860 (62.91%) Lab. hold
Douglas Alexander, Lab.   19,904
Eileen McCartin, LD   6,672
Andrew Doig, SNP   6,653
Thomas Begg, C.   3,188
Iain Hogg, SSP   789
Gordon Matthew, Paisley   381
Robert Rodgers, Ind.   166
Howard Broadbent, Soc. Lab.   107
Lab. maj. 13,232 (34.95%)
§ 6.24% swing Lab. to LD
(§ 2001 Lab. maj. 13,968 (36.10%))

PERTH & PERTHSHIRE NORTH
E. 70,895 T. 45,930 (64.79%)
           SNP hold
Peter Wishart, SNP   15,469
Douglas Taylor, C.   13,948
Doug Maughan, Lab.   8,601
Gordon Campbell, LD   7,403
Philip Stott, SSP   509
SNP maj. 1,521 (3.31%)
§ 3.85% swing SNP to C.
(§ 2001 SNP maj. 5,020 (11.01%))

RENFREWSHIRE EAST
E. 65,714 T. 47,405 (72.14%) Lab. hold
Jim Murphy, Lab.   20,815
Richard Cook, C.   14,158
Dr Gordon Macdonald, LD   8,659
Osama Bhutta, SNP   3,245
Ian Henderson, SSP   528
Lab. maj. 6,657 (14.04%)
2.43% swing Lab. to C.
(2001: Lab. maj. 9,141 (18.90%))

ROSS, SKYE & LOCHABER
E. 50,507 T. 32,538 (64.42%) LD hold
Rt. Hon. Charles Kennedy, LD   19,100
Christine Conniff, Lab.   4,851
John Hodgson, C.   3,275
Mhairi Will, SNP   3,119
David Jardine, Scot. Green   1,097
Phillip Anderson, UKIP   500
Anne Macleod, SSP   412
Morris Grant, Ind.   184
LD maj. 14,249 (43.79%)
§ 11.27% swing Lab. to LD
(§ 2001 LD maj. 6,567 (21.26%))

RUTHERGLEN & HAMILTON WEST
E. 73,998 T. 43,261 (58.46%)
           Lab. (Co-op) hold
Rt. Hon. Thomas McAvoy, Lab. (Co-op)
    24,054
Ian Robertson, LD   7,942
Margaret Park, SNP   6,023
Peter Crerar, C.   3,621
Bill Bonnar, SSP   1,164
Janice Murdoch, UKIP   457
Lab. (Co-op) maj. 16,112 (37.24%)
§ 5.37% swing Lab. (Co-op) to LD
(§ 2001 Lab. maj. 18,504 (44.42%))

STIRLING
F. 64,554 T. 43,691 (67.68%) Lab. hold
Anne McGuire, Lab.   15,729
Stephen Kerr, C.   10,962
Kelvin Holdsworth, LD   9,052
Frances McGlinchey, SNP   5,503
Duncan Illingworth, Scot. Green   1,302
Rowland Sheret, SSP   458
James McDonald, Ind.   261
Michael Willis, OCV   215
Matthew Desmond, UKIP   209
Lab. maj. 4,767 (10.91%)
§ 4.18% swing Lab. to C.
(§ 2001 Lab. maj. 8,303 (19.28%))

NORTHERN IRELAND

ANTRIM EAST
E. 58,335 T. 31,767 (54.46%)
           DUP gain
*Sammy Wilson, DUP   15,766
Roy Beggs, UUP   8,462
Sean Neeson, Alliance   4,869
Danny O'Connor, SDLP   1,695
James McKeown, SF   828
David Kerr, Vote Dream   147
DUP maj. 7,304 (22.99%)
11.67% swing UUP to DUP
(2001: UUP maj. 128 (0.36%))

ANTRIM NORTH
E. 74,450 T. 45,926 (61.69%)
           DUP hold
Revd Ian Paisley, DUP   25,156
Philip McGuigan, SF   7,191
Rodney McCune, UUP   6,637
Sean Farren, SDLP   5,585
Jayne Dunlop, Alliance   1,357
DUP maj. 17,965 (39.12%)
0.47% swing DUP to SF
(2001: DUP maj. 14,224 (28.90%))

ANTRIM SOUTH
E. 66,931 T. 37,957 (56.71%)
           DUP gain
†Revd William McCrea, DUP   14,507
David Burnside, UUP   11,059
Noreen McClelland, SDLP   4,706
Henry Cushnan, SF   4,407
David Ford, Alliance   3,278
DUP maj. 3,448 (9.08%)
5.69% swing UUP to DUP
(2001: UUP maj. 1,011 (2.29%))

BELFAST EAST
E. 53,176 T. 30,831 (57.98%)
           DUP hold
Peter Robinson, DUP   15,152
Sir Reg Empey, UUP   9,275
Naomi Long, Alliance   3,746
Deborah Devenny, SF   1,029
Mary Muldoon, SDLP   844
Alan Greer, C.   434
Joe Bell, WP   179
Lynda Gilby, Vote Dream   172
DUP maj. 5,877 (19.06%)
0.13% swing DUP to UUP
(2001: DUP maj. 7,117 (19.32%))

BELFAST NORTH
E. 52,853 T. 30,540 (57.78%)
           DUP hold
Nigel Dodds, DUP   13,935
Gerry Kelly, SF   8,747
Alban Maginness, SDLP   4,950
Fred Cobain, UUP   2,154
Marjorie Hawkins, Alliance   438
Marcella Delaney, WP   165
Lynda Gilby, Vote Dream   151
DUP maj. 5,188 (16.99%)
0.69% swing SF to DUP
(2001: DUP maj. 6,387 (15.60%))

BELFAST SOUTH
E. 52,668 T. 32,028 (60.81%)
           SDLP gain
*Dr Alasdair McDonnell, SDLP   10,339
James Spratt, DUP   9,104
Michael McGimpsey, UUP   7,263
Alex Maskey, SF   2,882
Geraldine Rice, Alliance   2,012
Lynda Gilby, Vote Dream   235
Paddy Lynn, WP   193
SDLP maj. 1,235 (3.86%)
11.91% swing UUP to SDLP
(2001: UUP maj. 5,399 (14.23%))

BELFAST WEST
E. 53,831 T. 34,545 (64.17%) SF hold
Gerry Adams, SF   24,348
Alex Attwood, SDLP   5,033
Diane Dodds, DUP   3,652
Chris McGimpsey, UUP   779
John Lowry, WP   432
Lynda Gilby, Vote Dream   154
Liam Kennedy, Ind.   147
SF maj. 19,315 (55.91%)
4.36% swing SDLP to SF
(2001: SF maj. 19,342 (47.20%))

DOWN NORTH
E. 59,748 T. 32,290 (54.04%)
           UUP hold
Lady Sylvia Hermon, UUP   16,268
Peter Weir, DUP   11,324
David Alderdice, Alliance   2,451
Liam Logan, SDLP   1,009
Julian Robertson, C.   822
Christopher Carter, Ind.   211
Janet McCrory, SF   205
UUP maj. 4,944 (15.31%)
20.35% swing UUP to DUP
(2001: UUP maj. 7,324 (19.69%))

DOWN SOUTH
E. 73,668 T. 48,177 (65.40%)
           SDLP hold
Edward McGrady, SDLP   21,557
Caitriona Ruane, SF   12,417
Jim Wells, DUP   8,815
Dermot Nesbitt, UUP   4,775
Julian Crozier, Alliance   613
SDLP maj. 9,140 (18.97%)
3.82% swing SDLP to SF
(2001: SDLP maj. 13,858 (26.61%))

FERMANAGH & SOUTH TYRONE
E. 67,174 T. 48,793 (72.64%) SF hold
Michelle Gildernew, SF   18,638
Arlene Foster, DUP   14,056
Tom Elliott, UUP   8,869
Tommy Gallagher, SDLP   7,230
SF maj. 4,582 (9.39%)
12.35% swing SF to DUP
(2001: SF maj. 53 (0.10%))

FOYLE
E. 69,207 T. 45,609 (65.90%)

		SDLP hold
*Mark Durkan, SDLP	21,119	
Mitchel McLaughlin, SF	15,162	
William Hay, DUP	6,557	
Eammon McCann, Soc EA	1,649	
Earl Storey, UUP	1,091	
Ben Reel, Vote Dream	31	

SDLP maj. 5,957 (13.06%)
5.28% swing SDLP to SF
(2001: SDLP maj. 11,550 (23.63%))

LAGAN VALLEY
E. 70,742 T. 42,572 (60.18%)DUP gain

‡Jeffrey Donaldson, DUP	23,289
Basil McCrea, UUP	9,172
Seamus Close, Alliance	4,316
Paul Butler, SF	3,197
Patricia Lewsley, SDLP	2,598

DUP maj. 14,117 (33.16%)
38.13% swing UUP to DUP
(2001: UUP maj. 18,342 (39.93%))

LONDONDERRY EAST
E. 58,861 T. 35,504 (60.32%)

		DUP hold
Gregory Campbell, DUP	15,225	
David McClarty, UUP	7,498	
John Dallat, SDLP	6,077	
Billy Leonard, SF	5,709	
Yvonne Boyle, Alliance	924	
Malcolm Samuel, Ind.	71	

DUP maj. 7,727 (21.76%)
8.50% swing UUP to DUP
(2001: DUP maj. 1,901 (4.77%))

NEWRY & ARMAGH
E. 72,448 T. 50,696 (69.98%)   SF gain

*Conor Murphy, SF	20,965
Dominic Bradley, SDLP	12,770
Paul Berry, DUP	9,311
Danny Kennedy, UUP	7,025
Gerry Markey, Ind.	625

SF maj. 8,195 (16.16%)
11.30% swing SDLP to SF
(2001: SDLP maj. 3,575 (6.43%))

STRANGFORD
E. 69,040 T. 37,032 (53.64%)

		DUP hold
Iris Robinson, DUP	20,921	
Gareth McGimpsey, UUP	7,872	
Kieran McCarthy, Alliance	3,332	
Joe Boyle, SDLP	2,496	
Terry Dick, C.	1,462	
Dermot Kennedy, SF	949	

DUP maj. 13,049 (35.24%)
16.34% swing UUP to DUP
(2001: DUP maj. 1,110 (2.57%))

TYRONE WEST
E. 60,286 T. 43,487 (72.13%)   SF hold

Pat Doherty, SF	16,910
Dr Kieran Deeny, Ind.	11,905
Thomas Buchanan, DUP	7,742
Eugene McMenamin, SDLP	3,949
Derek Hussey, UUP	2,981

SF maj. 5,005 (11.51%)
14.65% swing SF to Ind.
(2001: SF maj. 5,040 (10.39%))

ULSTER MID
E. 62,666 T. 45,426 (72.49%)   SF hold

Martin McGuinness, SF	21,641
Ian McCrea, DUP	10,665
Patsy McGlone, SDLP	7,922
Billy Armstrong, UUP	4,853
Francis Donnelly, WP	345

SF maj. 10,976 (24.16%)
2.12% swing DUP to SF
(2001: SF maj. 9,953 (19.93%))

UPPER BANN
E. 72,402 T. 44,422 (61.35%)

		DUP gain
*David Simpson, DUP	16,679	
David Trimble, UUP	11,381	
John O'Dowd, SF	9,305	
Dolores Kelly, SDLP	5,747	
Alan Castle, Alliance	955	
Tom French, WP	355	

DUP maj. 5,298 (11.93%)
7.98% swing UUP to DUP
(2001: UUP maj. 2,058 (4.03%))

BY-ELECTIONS 2005

CHEADLE
(14 July 2005)
E. 68,051 T. 37,567 (55.20%)   LD hold

*Mark Hunter, LD	19,593
Stephen Day, C.	15,936
Martin Miller, Lab.	1,739
Leslie Leggett, Veritas	218
John Allman, AFC	81

LD. maj. 3,657 (9.73%)
0.63% swing C. to LD
(2005: LD. maj. 4,020 (8.47%))

STAFFORDSHIRE SOUTH
(23 June 2005)
E. 68,763 T. 25,635 (37.28%)   C. hold

Sir Patrick Cormack, C.	13,343
Paul Kalinauckas, Lab.	4,496
Joanne Crotty, LD	3,540
Malcolm Hurst, UKIP	2,675
Garry Bushell, Eng. Dem.	643
Katherine Spohrer, Green	437
Adrian Davies, FP	434
Revd David Braid, Clause 28	67

C. maj. 8,847 (34.51%)
9.10% swing Lab to C.
(2001: C. maj. 6,881 (16.31%))

LIVINGSTON
(29 September 2005)
See Stop Press

MANIFESTO COMMITMENTS 2005

LABOUR, *Britain Forward Not Back*
- No increase in the basic or higher rates of income tax
- No extension of VAT to food, children's clothes, books, newspapers or public transport fares
- Increase the minimum hourly wage to £5.35 by October 2006
- Reform incapacity benefit by 2008 in order to encourage a return to work
- Every school in the country to offer 'enterprise education' by 2006
- Over £180 billion investment in the transport network over the next ten years
- Free off-peak local bus travel for those over 60 and the disabled
- New powers to Ofsted (Office for Standards in Education) to deal with parental complaints and to close failing schools where necessary
- A neighbourhood policing team for every community
- 24,000 extra community support officers and 12,000 police officers freed up for frontline duties
- Increase, by at least a half, programmes for young people at risk of offending, and expand drug treatment for young people
- A Violent Crime Reduction Bill to restrict the sale of replica guns, raise the age limit for the purchase of knives to 18 and allow headteachers to search pupils for knives and guns
- Supervision of every offender following release from prison
- Changes to the way fraud trials are conducted in order to make them quicker and more effective
- Reform of the legal aid system to provide better help for the vulnerable
- Legislation for the new offence of corporate manslaughter
- Establishment of a points system for immigrants based upon skills
- Penalties for employers of up to £2,000 for each illegal immigrant employed
- All entrants requiring visas to be fingerprinted by 2008
- Identity cards for all visitors planning to stay in the country for longer than three months
- Introduce identity cards that incorporate biometric data such as fingerprints
- Eject more failed asylum seekers
- New laws and control orders to help catch and convict those involved in terrorist activity or who condone acts of terror
- Triple NHS spending by 2008
- No patient to wait longer than 18 weeks from referral to operation
- Release of £250 million each year from NHS bureaucracy to be used on the 'frontline'
- NHS patients' right to choose, by 2008, any hospital offering operations at NHS prices
- Extra £210 million investment in school meals
- Legislate for higher standards of nutrition for school meals
- Legislate to ban smoking in all restaurants, as well as pubs and bars where food is served
- The right of all employees over the age of 65 to request of their employer that they carry on in employment
- Child poverty halved by 2010
- Increase in free childcare for parents of three- and four-year-olds

- Paid maternity leave increased to nine months from 2007
- Increase supply of council property by 10,000 each year by 2008
- A referendum on the new European Union (EU) constitution

CONSERVATIVE, *Are You Thinking What We're Thinking?*
- Spend the same as Labour on the NHS, schools, transport and international development and more on police, defence and pensions
- Save £12 billion a year by 2007–8 by freezing civil service recruitment, remove 235,000 bureaucratic posts and cut or abolish 168 public bodies
- Use £8 billion from savings to reduce borrowing, and use the remaining £4 billion to cut taxes
- Increase government spending by 1 per cent less than Labour by 2011–12
- Reduce council tax bills by up to £500 for households where all residents are over 65
- Increase the basic state pension in line with earnings rather than prices, on top of increases in line with inflation
- Create a Lifetime Savings Account in which government contributions top up personal savings
- Use of financial institutions' unclaimed assets to replenish failed pension schemes
- No adoption of the Euro
- More flexible maternity pay: choice of whether to receive it over nine months or a higher amount over six months
- All families who qualify for the Working Tax Credit to receive up to £50 a week for each child under the age of five
- An extra £15 billion each year for schools by 2009–10
- Give headteachers and governors full control over admissions and expulsions
- 300,000 grants of £1,000 each for pupils wishing to undertake vocational study alongside GCSEs
- Two hours of free after-school sport per week for every child
- Ban on junk food in schools
- An additional 600,000 school places to allow parents to choose the school that best suits their child
- Abolition of university fees
- Increase NHS budget by £34 billion a year during first parliament
- Reduce bureaucracy and government targets
- Give patients and GPs the ability to choose their hospital or care provider
- Full medical tests for those from outside the EU staying in the United Kingdom for longer than a year
- Recruit 5,000 new police officers each year
- 20,000 extra prison places and no early release from prison
- 25,000 residential drug rehabilitation places
- Establish a British border control police force
- Introduce a points system based on skills for work permits
- Withdraw from the 1951 Geneva Convention
- Set an annual limit on the number of entrants into Britain, including a fixed quota of asylum seekers
- Abolish regional assemblies, returning powers to local authorities
- Cut the number of MPs by 20 per cent

- Introduce a bill to overturn the ban on hunting with dogs
- Spend £2.7 billion more than Labour on the 'frontline' of the armed forces
- Referendum on the EU Constitution

LIBERAL DEMOCRAT, *The Real Alternative*
- Free personal care for the elderly and disabled
- Fifty per cent income tax over £100,000
- More tests and scans available in GPs' surgeries and pharmacies and at flexible times
- Publish waiting times for tests and scans
- Free eye and dental check-ups
- An extra 8,000 more doctors, 12,000 more nurses and 18,000 more therapists and scientists by 2008
- Abolish centralised NHS targets
- Introduce minimum nutritional standards and increase funding for school meals
- Restrict advertising of unhealthy food during children's television programmes
- Ban smoking in all enclosed public spaces
- More cycle routes
- Abolish university fees and make grants available to poorer students
- 21,000 more nursery and junior school teachers
- Increase maternity pay for the first six months
- Reduce external testing of children
- Opportunity for all students over 14 years of age to study both academic and vocational subjects
- 10,000 extra police officers and 20,000 more community support officers
- Large late-night entertainment venues to contribute to the cost of extra late-night policing
- Increase resources for education and training in prisons to tackle reoffending
- Establish a UK border force to protect the borders against terrorism, people-trafficking and drug smuggling
- Repeal the Prevention of Terrorism Act
- Work with the EU to ensure that all EU countries accept their fair share of refugees
- Allow asylum seekers to work legally to end their dependence upon benefits
- Introduce a Single Equality Act to criminalise all unfair discrimination
- Allow the National Audit Office to scrutinise the budget, including public borrowing
- Replace the council tax with a local income tax based upon the ability to pay
- Raise the stamp duty threshold from £120,000 to £150,000
- Reduce the regulation of businesses
- Rate relief for businesses with a rateable value of less than £25,000
- Abolish the Department of Trade and Industry
- Simplify the pension system by abolishing means-testing
- Abolish the Child Support Agency
- Restore independence of the National Lottery fund
- Heighten scrutiny of arms sales including a code of conduct for arms brokers
- Increase British aid spending to at least 0.5 per cent of Gross National Income by 2007–8
- Cut road tax on cars that are the least polluting and increase it on those that pollute more
- Free rail discount cards for the elderly, young people, the disabled and families
- Free off-peak local bus travel for all pensioners and the disabled
- A new War Powers Act that would require Parliament's authority before the governement goes to war
- Strengthen the powers of Parliament to scrutinise the actions of the government
- Reduce the number of government ministers by over a third and move government bureaucracy out of London
- Introduce the Single Transferable Vote electoral system for local and general elections, and lower the voting age
- Replace the House of Lords with a predominantly elected second chamber

GENERAL ELECTION FACTS AND FIGURES

MPS DEFEATED AT THE 2005 GENERAL ELECTION

CONSERVATIVE
Collins, Tim, *Westmorland and Lonsdale*
Duncan, Peter, *Dumfries and Galloway*
Flook, Adrian, *Taunton*
Taylor, John, *Solihull*

LABOUR
Atherton, Candy, *Falmouth and Camborne*
Beard, Nigel, *Bexleyheath and Crayford*
Bradley, Rt. Hon. Keith, *Manchester Withington*
Bradley, Peter, *Wrekin, The*
Campbell, Anne, *Cambridge*
Casale, Roger, *Wimbledon*
Clark, Rt. Hon. Helen, *Peterborough*
Clarke, Tony, *Northampton South*
Colman, Tony, *Putney*
Cryer, John, *Hornchurch*
Davey, Valerie, *Bristol West*
Davies, Geraint, *Croydon Central*
Edwards, Huw, *Monmouth*
Fitzsimons, Lorna, *Rochdale*
Henderson, Ivan, *Harwich*
Hurst, Alan, *Braintree*
Johnson, Melanie, *Welwyn Hatfield*
Jones, Jon Owen, *Cardiff Central*
King, Andy, *Rugby and Kenilworth*
King, Oona, *Bethnal Green and Bow*
Leslie, Christopher, *Shipley*
Luke, Iain, *Dundee East*
Lyons, John, *Dunbartonshire East*
MacDonald, Calum, *Na h-Eileanan an Iar*
McWalter, Tony, *Hemel Hempstead*
Perham, Linda, *Ilford North*
Pollard, Kerry, *St Albans*
Pond, Chris, *Gravesham*
Quinn, Lawrie, *Scarborough and Whitby*
Roche, Barbara, *Hornsey and Wood Green*
Sawford, Phil, *Kettering*
Stewart, David, *Inverness East, Nairn, Badenoch and Strathspey*
Stinchcombe, Paul, *Wellingborough*
Thomas, Gareth, *Clwyd West*
Twigg, Stephen, *Enfield Southgate*
White, Brian, *Milton Keynes North East*

LIBERAL DEMOCRAT
Cotter, Brian, *Weston-Super-Mare*
Doughty, Sue, *Guildford*
Gill, Parmjit Singh, *Leicester South*
Green, Matthew, *Ludlow*
Rendel, David, *Newbury*

OTHER
Beggs, Roy, UUP, *Antrim East*
Burnside, David, UUP, *Antrim South*
Ewing, Annabelle, SNP, *Ochil and Perthshire South*
Thomas, Simon, PC, *Ceredigion*
Trimble, Rt. Hon. David, UUP, *Upper Bann*

MPS WHO RETIRED AT THE 2005 GENERAL ELECTION
CONSERVATIVE
Atkinson, David, *Bournemouth East*

Bottomley, Rt. Hon. Virginia, *Surrey South West*
Chapman, Sir Sydney, *Chipping Barnet*
Cran, James, *Beverley and Holderness*
Flight, Howard, *Arundel and South Downs*
Hawkins, Nick, *Surrey Heath*
Mawhinney, Rt. Hon. Sir Brian, *Cambridgeshire North West*
Norman, Archie, *Tunbridge Wells*
Page, Richard, *Hertfordshire South West*
Portillo, Rt. Hon. Michael, *Kensington and Chelsea*
Roe, Dame Marion, *Broxbourne*
Sayeed, Jonathan, *Bedfordshire Mid*
Shephard, Rt. Hon. Gillian, *Norfolk South West*
Taylor, Sir Teddy, *Rochford and Southend East*
Trend, Hon. Michael, *Windsor*
Wilkinson, John, *Ruislip-Northwood*

LABOUR
Adams, Irene, *Paisley North*
Anderson, Rt. Hon. Donald, *Swansea East*
Banks, Tony, *West Ham*
Barnes, Harry, *Derbyshire North East*
Bennett, Andrew, *Denton and Reddish*
Best, Harold, *Leeds North West*
Boateng, Rt. Hon. Paul, *Brent South*
Caplin, Ivor, *Hove*
Clark, Dr Lynda, *Edinburgh Pentlands*
Coleman, Iain, *Hammersmith and Fulham*
Corston, Rt. Hon. Jean, *Bristol East*
Cox, Tom, *Tooting*
Cranston, Ross, *Dudley North*
Cunningham, Rt. Hon. Dr Jack, *Copeland*
Dalyell, Tam, *Linlithgow*
Davies, Rt. Hon. Denzil, *Llanelli*
Dawson, Hilton, *Lancaster and Wyre*
Drown, Julia, *Swindon South*
Foster, Rt. Hon. Derek, *Bishop Auckland*
Foulkes, Rt. Hon. George, *Carrick, Cumnock and Doon Valley*
Griffiths, Jane, *Reading East*
Griffiths, Win, *Bridgend*
Hinchliffe, David, *Wakefield*
Howarth, Rt. Hon. Alan, *Newport East*
Hughes, Kevin, *Doncaster North*
Jackson, Helen, *Sheffield Hillsborough*
Jackson, Robert, *Wantage*
Jamieson, David, *Plymouth Devonport*
Lawrence, Jackie, *Preseli Pembrokeshire*
Lewis, Terry, *Worsley*
Liddell, Rt. Hon. Helen, *Airdrie and Shotts*
Mahon, Alice, *Halifax*
McNamara, Kevin, *Hull North*
McWilliam, John, *Blaydon*
Moonie, Lewis, *Kirkcaldy*
Morris, Rt. Hon. Estelle, *Birmingham Yardley*
O'Brien, William, *Normanton*
O'Neill, Martin, *Ochil*
Organ, Diana, *Forest of Dean*
Pickthall, Colin, *Lancashire West*
Pike, Peter, *Burnley*
Quin, Rt. Hon. Joyce, *Gateshead East and Washington West*
Rapson, Syd, *Portsmouth North*
Ross, Ernie, *Dundee West*
Savidge, Malcolm, *Aberdeen North*
Sedgemore, Brian, *Hackney South and Shoreditch*
Shipley, Debra, *Stourbridge*

Smith, Rt. Hon. Chris, *Islington South and Finsbury*
Smith, Llewellyn, *Blaenau Gwent*
Soley, Clive, *Ealing Acton and Shepherd's Bush*
Steinberg, Gerry, *Durham, City of*
Stevenson, George, *Stoke-on-Trent South*
Taylor, Rt. Hon. Ann, *Dewsbury*
Turner, Dennis, *Wolverhampton South East*
Tynan, Bill, *Hamilton South*
Wilson, Rt. Hon. Brian, *Cunninghame North*
Worthington, Tony, *Clydebank and Milngavie*
Wray, James, *Glasgow Baillieston*

LIBERAL DEMOCRAT
Allan, Richard, *Sheffield Hallam*
Burnett, John, *Devon West and Torridge*
Chidgey, David, *Eastleigh*
Jones, Nigel, *Cheltenham*
Kirkwood, Sir Archibald, *Roxborough and Berwickshire*
Marsden, Paul, *Shrewsbury and Atcham*
Tonge, Dr Jenny, *Richmond Park*
Tyler, Paul, *Cornwall North*

OTHER
Hume, John, SDLP, *Foyle*
Hunter, Andrew, DUP, *Basingstoke*
Mallon, Seamus, SDLP, *Newry and Armagh*
Smyth, Revd Martin, UUP, *Belfast South*

NEW MPS

CONSERVATIVE
Afriyie, Adam, *Windsor*
Benyon, Richard, *Newbury*
Binley, Brian, *Northampton South*
Bone, Peter, *Wellingborough*
Brokenshire, James, *Hornchurch*
Burrowes, David, *Enfield Southgate*
Carswell, Douglas, *Harwich*
Clark, Greg, *Tunbridge Wells*
Cox, Geoffrey, *Devon West and Torridge*
Crabb, Stephen, *Preseli Pembrokeshire*
Davies, David, *Monmouth*
Davies, Philip, *Shipley*
Dorries, Nadine, *Bedfordshire Mid*
Duddridge, James, *Rochford and Southend East*
Dunne, Philip, *Ludlow*
Ellwood, Tobias, *Bournemouth East*
Gauke, David, *Hertfordshire South West*
Goodwill, Robert, *Scarborough and Whitby*
Gove, Michael, *Surrey Heath*
Greening, Justine, *Putney*
Hammond, Stephen, *Wimbledon*
Hands, Greg, *Hammersmith and Fulham*
Harper, Mark, *Forest of Dean*
Herbert, Nick, *Arundel and South Downs*
Hollobone, Philip, *Kettering*
Holloway, Adam, *Gravesham*
Hunt, Jeremy, *Surrey South West*
Hurd, Nick, *Ruislip-Northwood*
Jackson, Stewart, *Peterborough*
Jones, David, *Clwyd West*
Kawczynski, Daniel, *Shrewsbury and Atcham*
Lancaster, Mark, *Milton Keynes North East*
Main, Anne, *St Albans*
Miller, Maria, *Basingstoke*
Milton, Anne, *Guildford*
Mundell, David, *Dumfriesshire, Clydesdale and Tweeddale*
Newmark, Brooks, *Braintree*

Pelling, Andrew, *Croydon Central*
Penning, Michael, *Hemel Hempstead*
Penrose, John, *Weston-Super-Mare*
Pritchard, Mark, *The Wrekin*
Scott, Lee, *Ilford North*
Shapps, Grant, *Welwyn Hatfield*
Stuart, Graham, *Beverley and Holderness*
Vaizey, Ed, *Wantage*
Vara, Shailesh, *Cambridgeshire North West*
Villiers, Theresa, *Chipping Barnet*
Walker, Charles, *Broxbourne*
Wallace, Ben, *Lancaster and Wyre*
Wilson, Rob, *Reading East*
Wright, Jeremy, *Rugby and Kenilworth*

LABOUR
Balls, Ed, *Normanton*
Hillier, Meg, *Hackney South and Shoreditch*
McCarthy-Fry, Sarah, *Portsmouth North*
Riordan, Linda, *Halifax*
Anderson, David, *Blaydon*
Austin, Ian, *Dudley North*
Banks, Gordon, *Ochil and Perthshire South*
Barlow, Celia, *Hove*
Blackman-Woods, Dr Roberta, *City of Durham*
Brown, Lyn, *West Ham*
Butler, Dawn, *Brent South*
Clark, Katy, *Ayrshire North and Arran*
Cooper, Rosie, *Lancashire West*
Creagh, Mary, *Wakefield*
Engel, Natascha, *Derbyshire North East*
Flello, Robert, *Stoke-on-Trent South*
Goodman, Helen, *Bishop Auckland*
Griffith, Nia, *Llanelli*
Gwynne, Andrew, *Denton and Reddish*
Hodgson, Sharon, *Gateshead East and Washington West*
James, Sian, *Swansea East*
Johnson, Diana, *Hull North*
Keeley, Barbara, *Worsley*
Khan, Sadiq, *Tooting*
Malik, Shahid, *Dewsbury*
McCarthy, Kerry, *Bristol East*
McFadden, Pat, *Wolverhampton South East*
McGovern, James, *Dundee West*
Miliband, Edward, *Doncaster North*
Moon, Madeleine, *Bridgend*
Morden, Jessica, *Newport East*
Reed, Jamie, *Copeland*
Seabeck, Alison, *Plymouth Devonport*
Slaughter, Andrew, *Ealing, Acton and Shepherd's Bush*
Smith, Angela, *Sheffield Hillsborough*
Snelgrove, Anne, *Swindon South*
Soulsby, Sir Peter, *Leicester South*
Thornberry, Emily, *Islington South and Finsbury*
Ussher, Kitty, *Burnley*
Waltho, Lynda, *Stourbridge*

LIBERAL DEMOCRAT
Alexander, Danny, *Inverness, Nairn, Badenoch and Strathspey*
Browne, Jeremy, *Taunton*
Burt, Lorely, *Solihull*
Clegg, Nick, *Sheffield Hallam*
Farron, Tim, *Westmorland and Lonsdale*
Featherstone, Lynne, *Hornsey and Wood Green*
Goldsworthy, Julia, *Falmouth and Camborne*
Hemming, John, *Birmingham Yardley*
Horwood, Martin, *Cheltenham*

Howarth, David, *Cambridge*
Huhne, Chris, *Eastleigh*
Kramer, Susan, *Richmond Park*
Leech, John, *Manchester Withington*
Mulholland, Greg, *Leeds North West*
Rogerson, Dan, *Cornwall North*
Rowen, Paul, *Rochdale*
Swinson, Jo, *Dunbartonshire East*
Williams, Mark, *Ceredigion*
Williams, Stephen, *Bristol West*
Willott, Jenny, *Cardiff Central*

OTHER
Durkan, Mark, SDLP, *Foyle*
Hosie, Stewart, SNP, *Dundee East*
Law, Peter, Ind., *Blaenau Gwent*
McDonnell, Dr Alasdair, SDLP, *Belfast South*
MacNeil, Angus, SNP, *Na h-Eileanan an Iar*
Murphy, Conor, SF, *Newry and Armagh*
Simpson, David, DUP, *Upper Bann*
Wilson, Sammy, DUP, *Antrim East*

WOMEN MPS
by party

Labour	98 (28 per cent)
Conservative	17 (9 per cent)
Liberal Democrat	10 (16 per cent)
DUP	1 (11 per cent)
Sinn Fein	1 (20 per cent)
UUP	1 (100 per cent)
Plaid Cymru	0
SNP	0
Other	0
Total	128 (20 per cent)

VOTES CAST 1997, 2001 AND 2005

	1997	2001	2005
Conservative	9,600,940	8,357,622	8,772,599
Labour	13,517,911	10,724,895	9,547,876
Liberal Democrats	5,243,440	4,812,833	5,982,164
UK Independence Party	—	—	602,498
Scottish Nationalist	622,260	464,305	412,267
Plaid Cymru	161,030	195,892	174,838
N. Ireland Parties	780,920	635,735	669,426
Others	1,361,701	1,177,516	962,029
Total	31,287,702	26,368,798	27,123,697

PARLIAMENTS SINCE 1970

Assembled	Dissolved	yr	m.	d.
29 June 1970	8 February 1974	3	7	10
6 March 1974	20 September 1974	0	6	14
22 October 1974	7 April 1979	4	5	16
9 May 1979	13 May 1983	4	0	4
15 June 1983	18 May 1987	3	11	3
17 June 1987	16 March 1992	4	8	28
27 April 1992	8 April 1997	4	11	12
7 May 1997	14 May 2001	4	0	7
13 June 2001	11 April 2005	3	9	29
11 May 2005				

SEATS CHANGING HANDS

CONSERVATIVE GAINS

From Labour	31
From Liberal Democrats	5
Total	36

LIBERAL DEMOCRAT GAINS

From Conservative	3
From Labour	12
From Plaid Cymru	1
Total	16

DEMOCRATIC UNIONIST PARTY GAINS

From Ulster Unionist Party	4
Total	4

SCOTTISH NATIONAL PARTY GAINS

From Labour	2
Total	2

INDEPENDENT GAIN

From Labour	1
Total	1

LABOUR GAIN

From Liberal Democrats	1
Total	1

RESPECT GAIN

From Labour	1
Total	1

SDLP GAIN

From Ulster Unionist Party	1
Total	1

SINN FEIN GAIN

From SDLP	1
Total	1

TURNOUT

The UK Parliamentary electorate at 1 December 2004 was 44,180,243. Excluding the 69,461 electors in South Staffordshire, the total electorate in the 645 seats contested on 5 May 2005 was 44,110,782.

HIGHEST TURNOUT

Constituency	Turnout	Percentage turnout
Dorset West	53,225	76.29
Norfolk North	58,965	72.99
Richmond Park	51,374	72.81
Fermanagh and South Tyrone	48,793	72.64
Ulster Mid	45,426	72.49
Mole Valley	49,415	72.48
Wansdyke	50,933	72.39
Monmouth	45,653	72.36
Northavon	59,056	72.20
Dunbartonshire East	46,724	72.15

LOWEST TURNOUT

Constituency	Turnout	Percentage turnout
Liverpool Riverside	31,191	41.49
Manchester Central	29,264	42.01
Salford	22,600	42.41
Glasgow Central	28,037	43.77
Liverpool Walton	27,930	45.02
Manchester Gorton	29,123	45.02
Hull West and Hessle	27,818	45.24
Glasgow North East	28,418	45.80
Manchester Blackley	27,591	45.81
Leeds Central	29,186	46.37

MAJORITIES

SMALLEST MAJORITIES

Crawley, Laura Moffatt, Lab.	37
Croydon Central, Andrew Pelling, C.	75
Sittingbourne and Sheppey, Derek Wyatt, Lab.	79
Harlow, Bill Rammell, Lab.	97
Romsey, Sandra Gidley, LD	125
Clwyd West, David Jones, C.	133
Battersea, Martin Linton, Lab.	163
Medway, Bob Marshall-Andrews, Lab.	213
Ceredigion, Mark Williams, LD	219
Gillingham, Paul Clark, Lab.	254

LARGEST MAJORITIES

Coatbridge, Chryston and Bellshill, Rt. Hon. Thomas Clarke, Lab.	19,519
Belfast West, Gerry Adams, SF	19,315
Easington, John Cummings, Lab.	18,636
Sedgefield, Rt. Hon. Tony Blair, Lab.	18,449
Bolsover, Dennis Skinner, Lab.	18,437
Kirkcaldy and Cowdenbeath, Rt. Hon. Gordon Brown, Lab.	18,216
Makerfield, Rt. Hon. Ian McCartney, Lab.	18,149
Buckingham, John Bercow, C.	18,129
Antrim North, Revd Ian Paisley, DUP	17,965
Richmond (Yorks), Rt. Hon. William Hague, C.	17,807

CANDIDATES

The youngest person to stand for election in 2005 was Hannah Hedges, who was the Liberal Democrat candidate for Hitchin and Harpenden at the age of 21, whilst the oldest was Robert Leakey, who stood for the Virtue Currency and Cognitive Appraisal Party in Skipton and Ripon at the age of 90.

Sedgefield broke the UK general election record for the most candidates, with 14 standing against Tony Blair; the previous record-holder was Finchley in 1983, when Margaret Thatcher was one of 11 candidates.

Catherine Taylor-Dawson, Vote for Yourself Dream Ticket candidate in four Cardiff seats, set a new record for the fewest votes in a general election by winning just one vote in Cardiff North; the previous record was 13 votes for an independent candidate in Finchley in 1983.

DECLARATION TIMES

Counts in Northern Ireland take place on the day after polling day, so they are shown separately.

Sunderland South was the first to declare its results for the fourth consecutive election; the two other constituencies that make up the fastest three are also in Sunderland.

EARLIEST	Time	Date
Great Britain		
Sunderland South	22:44	5 May
Sunderland North	23:25	5 May
Houghton & Washington East	23:32	5 May
Northern Ireland		
Belfast West	14:18	6 May
Belfast South	16:34	6 May
Antrim North	16:44	6 May

LATEST	Time	Date
Great Britain		
Harlow	11:31	7 May
Crawley	14:00	6 May
Wirral West	13:31	6 May
Northern Ireland		
Ulster Mid	21:41	6 May
Down South	21:23	6 May
Foyle	20:08	6 May

THE GOVERNMENT

THE CABINET *as at 1 September 2005*

Prime Minister, First Lord of the Treasury and Minister for the Civil Service
The Rt. Hon. Tony Blair, MP (since May 1997)
Deputy Prime Minister (since May 1997) and First Secretary of State (since June 2001)
The Rt. Hon. John Prescott, MP
Chancellor of the Exchequer
The Rt. Hon. Gordon Brown, MP (since May 1997)
Leader of the House of Commons and Lord Privy Seal
The Rt. Hon. Geoff Hoon, MP (since May 2005)
Secretary of State for Constitutional Affairs and Lord Chancellor
The Rt. Hon. Lord Falconer of Thoroton, QC (since June 2003)
Secretary of State for Foreign and Commonwealth Affairs
The Rt. Hon. Jack Straw, MP (since June 2001)
Secretary of State for the Home Department
The Rt. Hon. Charles Clarke, MP (since December 2004)
Secretary of State for Environment, Food and Rural Affairs
The Rt. Hon. Margaret Beckett, MP (since June 2001)
Secretary of State for International Development
The Rt. Hon. Hilary Benn, MP (since October 2003)
Secretary of State for Transport (since May 2002) and Secretary of State for Scotland (since June 2003)
The Rt. Hon. Alistair Darling, MP
Secretary of State for Health
The Rt. Hon. Patricia Hewitt, MP (since May 2005)
Secretary of State for Northern Ireland (since May 2005) and Secretary of State for Wales (since October 2002)
The Rt. Hon. Peter Hain, MP
Secretary of State for Defence
The Rt. Hon. Dr John Reid, MP (since May 2005)
Secretary of State for Work and Pensions
The Rt. Hon. David Blunkett, MP (since May 2005)
Leader of the House of Lords and President of the Council
The Rt. Hon. Baroness Amos (since October 2003)
Secretary of State for Trade and Industry
The Rt. Hon. Alan Johnson, MP (since May 2005)
Secretary of State for Education and Skills
The Rt. Hon. Ruth Kelly, MP (since December 2004)
Secretary of State for Culture, Media and Sport
The Rt. Hon. Tessa Jowell, MP (since June 2001)
Parliamentary Secretary to the Treasury (Chief Whip)
The Rt. Hon. Hilary Armstrong, MP (since June 2001)
Minister Without Portfolio and Party Chair
The Rt. Hon. Ian McCartney, MP (since April 2003)
Chancellor of the Duchy of Lancaster
The Rt. Hon. John Hutton, MP (since May 2005)
Chief Secretary to the Treasury
The Rt. Hon. Des Browne, MP (since May 2005)
Minister of Communities and Local Government
The Rt. Hon. David Miliband, MP (since May 2005)

The Attorney-General (The Rt. Hon. Lord Goldsmith, QC), the Minister of State for Europe in the Foreign and Commonwealth Office (Douglas Alexander, MP) and the Government Chief Whip in the House of Lords and Captain of the Gentlemen-at-Arms (The Rt. Hon. Lord Grocott) attend Cabinet meetings although they are not members of the Cabinet.

LAW OFFICERS

Attorney-General
The Rt. Hon. Lord Goldsmith, QC (since June 2001)
Solicitor-General
The Hon. Mike O'Brien, QC, MP (since May 2005)
Advocate-General for Scotland
Baroness Clark of Calton, QC (since May 1999)

MINISTERS OF STATE

Cabinet Office
The Rt. Hon. John Hutton, MP *(Chancellor of the Duchy of Lancaster)*
Constitutional Affairs
The Rt. Hon. Harriet Harman, QC, MP
Culture, Media and Sport
The Rt. Hon. Richard Caborn, MP *(Sport)*
Defence
The Rt. Hon. Adam Ingram, MP *(Armed Forces)*
Office of the Deputy Prime Minister
Yvette Cooper, MP *(Housing and Planning)*
The Rt. Hon. David Miliband, MP *(Communities and Local Government)*
Phil Woolas, MP *(Local Government)*
Education and Skills
The Rt. Hon. Beverley Hughes, MP *(Children and Families)*
Bill Rammell, MP *(Higher Education and Lifelong Learning)*
The Rt. Hon. Jacqui Smith, MP *(Schools)*
Environment, Food and Rural Affairs
Elliot Morley, MP *(Climate Change and Environment)*
Foreign and Commonwealth Office
The Rt. Hon. Douglas Alexander, MP *(Europe)*
Dr Kim Howells, MP *(Middle East)*
Ian Pearson, MP *(Trade)*
Health
The Rt. Hon. Jane Kennedy, MP *(Quality and Patient Safety)*
Lord Warner *(NHS Delivery)*
Rosie Winterton, MP *(Health Services)*
Home Office
The Rt. Hon. Hazel Blears, MP *(Security, Policing and Community Safety)*
Tony McNulty, MP *(Citizenship, Immigration and Nationality)*
The Rt. Hon. Baroness Scotland of Asthal, QC *(Criminal Justice and Offender Management)*
Northern Ireland Office
David Hanson, MP
The Rt. Hon. Lord Rooker
Trade and Industry
The Rt. Hon. Alun Michael, MP *(Industry and the Regions)*
Ian Pearson, MP *(Trade)*
Malcolm Wicks, MP *(Energy)*

Transport
  Dr Stephen Ladyman, MP
Treasury
  John Healey, MP *(Financial Secretary)*
  Ivan Lewis, MP *(Economic Secretary)*
  The Rt. Hon. Dawn Primarolo, MP *(Paymaster-General)*
Work and Pensions
  The Rt. Hon. Margaret Hodge, MBE, MP *(Employment and Welfare Reform)*
  Stephen Timms, MP *(Pensions Reform)*

UNDER-SECRETARIES OF STATE

Cabinet Office
  Jim Murphy, MP
Constitutional Affairs
  Nick Ainger, MP *(Wales)*
  Baroness Ashton of Upholland
  David Cairns, MP *(Scotland)*
  Bridget Prentice, MP
Culture, Media and Sport
  David Lammy, MP *(Culture)*
  James Purnell, MP *(Creative Industries and Tourism)*
Defence
  Lord Drayson *(Defence Procurement)*
  Don Touhig, MP *(Veterans)*
Office of the Deputy Prime Minister
  Baroness Andrews, OBE
  Jim Fitzpatrick, MP
Education and Skills
  Lord Adonis *(Schools)*
  Maria Eagle, MP *(Children, Young People and Families)*
  Phil Hope, MP *(Skills)*
Environment, Food and Rural Affairs
  Lord Bach *(Sustainable Farming and Food)*
  Ben Bradshaw, MP *(Local Environment, Marine and Animal Welfare)*
  Jim Knight, MP *(Rural Affairs, Landscape and Biodiversity)*
Foreign and Commonwealth Office
  Lord Triesman
Health
  Liam Byrne, MP *(Care Services)*
  Caroline Flint, MP *(Public Health)*
Home Office
  Andy Burnham, MP
  Paul Goggins, MP
  Fiona Mactaggart, MP
International Development
  Gareth Thomas, MP
Northern Ireland Office
  Angela Smith, MP
  Shaun Woodward, MP

Trade and Industry
  Barry Gardiner, MP *(Competitiveness)*
  Meg Munn, MP *(Women and Equality)*
  Lord Sainsbury of Turville, KG *(Science and Innovation)*
  Gerry Sutcliffe, MP *(Employment Relations and Consumer Affairs)*
Transport
  Karen Buck, MP
  Derek Twigg, MP
Work and Pensions
  Lord Hunt of Kings Heath, OBE *(Lords)*
  Anne McGuire, MP *(Disabled People)*
  James Plaskitt, MP *(Commons)*

GOVERNMENT WHIPS

HOUSE OF LORDS
Captain of the Honourable Corps of the Gentlemen-at-Arms (Chief Whip)
  The Rt. Hon. Lord Grocott
Captain of The Queen's Bodyguard of the Yeomen of the Guard (Deputy Chief Whip)
  Lord Davies of Oldham
Lords-in-Waiting
  Lord Bassam of Brighton
  Lord Evans of Temple Guiting, CBE
  Lord McKenzie of Luton
Baronesses-in-Waiting
  Baroness Crawley
  Baroness Farrington of Ribbleton
  Baroness Royall of Blaisdon

HOUSE OF COMMONS
Parliamentary Secretary to the Treasury (Chief Whip)
  The Rt. Hon. Hilary Armstrong, MP
Treasurer of HM Household (Deputy Chief Whip)
  The Rt. Hon. Bob Ainsworth, MP
Comptroller of HM Household
  The Rt. Hon. Thomas McAvoy, MP
Vice-Chamberlain of HM Household
  John Heppell, MP
Lords Commissioners of HM Treasury
  Vernon Coaker, MP; Gillian Merron, MP; Joan Ryan, MP; Tom Watson, MP; Dave Watts, MP
Assistant Whips
  Kevin Brennan, MP; Alan Campbell, MP; Ian Cawsey, MP; Tony Cunningham, MP; Parmjit Dhanda, MP; Frank Roy, MP; Claire Ward, MP

GOVERNMENT DEPARTMENTS

THE CIVIL SERVICE

Under the Next Steps programme, launched in 1988, many semi-autonomous executive agencies were established to carry out much of the work of the Civil Service. Executive agencies operate within a framework set by the responsible minister which specifies policies, objectives and available resources. All executive agencies are set annual performance targets by their minister. Each agency has a chief executive, who is responsible for the day-to-day operations of the agency and who is accountable to the minister for the use of resources and for meeting the agency's targets. The minister accounts to Parliament for the work of the agency. Nearly 75 per cent of civil servants now work in executive agencies. In April 2004 there were about 544,110 permanent civil servants.

The Senior Civil Service was created in 1996 and on 1 April 2004 comprised about 4,000 staff from Permanent Secretary to the former grade 5 level, including all agency chief executives. All government departments and executive agencies are now responsible for their own pay and grading systems for civil servants outside the Senior Civil Service.

SALARIES 2005–6

MINISTERIAL SALARIES *from 1 April 2005*
Ministers who are Members of the House of Commons receive a parliamentary salary (£59,095) in addition to their ministerial salary.

Prime Minister	£124,837
Cabinet Minister (Commons)	£74,902
Cabinet Minister (Lords)	£101,668
Minister of State (Commons)	£38,854
Minister of State (Lords)	£79,382
Parliamentary Under-Secretary (Commons)	£29,491
Parliamentary Under-Secretary (Lords)	£69,138

SPECIAL ADVISERS' SALARIES *from 1 April 2005*
Special advisers to government ministers are paid out of public funds; their salaries are negotiated individually, but are usually in the range of £37,365 to £98,907.

CIVIL SERVICE SALARIES *from 1 April 2005*

Senior Civil Servants	
Permanent Secretary	£130,350–£264,250
Band 3	£93,139–£198,197
Band 2	£75,607–£159,659
Band 1A	£63,555–£126,627
Band 1	£54,788–£115,616

Staff are placed in pay bands according to their level of responsibility and taking account of other factors such as experience and marketability. Movement within and between bands is based on performance. Following the delegation of responsibility for pay and grading to government departments and agencies from 1 April 1996, it is no longer possible to show service-wide pay rates for staff outside the Senior Civil Service.

GOVERNMENT DEPARTMENTS

CABINET OFFICE

70 Whitehall, London SW1A 2AS
Switchboard 020-7276 3000 T 020-7276 1234
W www.cabinet-office.gov.uk

The Cabinet Office has four main roles: to support the prime minister in leading the government; to support the government in transacting its business; to lead and support the reform and delivery programme; and to co-ordinate security and intelligence. The department is headed by the Chancellor of the Duchy of Lancaster and has one Minister of State. The Cabinet Office has two executive agencies: the Government Car and Despatch Agency (GCDA) and the Central Office of Information (COI Communications), which is a department in its own right and operates as a Trading Fund.

Prime Minister and Minister for the Civil Service,
The Rt. Hon. Tony Blair, MP
Principal Private Secretary to the Prime Minister and Head of Policy Directorate, Ivan Rogers
Chancellor of the Duchy of Lancaster and Minister for the Cabinet Office, The Rt. Hon. John Hutton, MP
Parliamentary Private Secretary, Adrian Bailey, MP
Principal Private Secretary, Sue Pither
Assistant Private Secretary, Tom Harris
Private Secretary, Lee O'Rourke
Parliamentary Secretary, Jim Murphy, MP
Private Secretary, Michelle Duncan
Secretary of the Cabinet and Head of the Home Civil Service, Sir Gus O'Donnell
Principal Private Secretary, Penny Ciniewicz
Private Secretary, Mark Talbot
Assistant Private Secretaries, Jeanne Bilbrough; Rebecca Mupita
Security and Intelligence Co-ordinator and Permanent Secretary, Bill Jeffrey
Principal Private Secretary, Dominic Fagan
Private Secretary, Timo Pocock
Minister without Portfolio and Party Chair, The Rt. Hon. Ian McCartney, MP
Parliamentary Private Secretary, Neil Turner, MP

CEREMONIAL SECRETARIAT
35 Great Smith Street, London SW1P 3BQ T 020-7276 2770
Ceremonial Officer, Denis Brennan

CIVIL CONTINGENCIES SECRETARIAT
10 Great George Street, London SW1P 3AE
Head, Bruce Mann
Deputy Head, Peter Tallantire, CMG

DEFENCE AND OVERSEAS AFFAIRS SECRETARIAT
Prime Minister's Foreign Policy Adviser and Head of Secretariat, Sir Nigel Sheinwald, KCMG
Deputy Head, Margaret Aldred, CBE

ECONOMIC AND DOMESTIC SECRETARIAT
Director, Paul Britton, CB
Deputy Head, Robin Fellgett

EUROPEAN SECRETARIAT
Prime Minister's European Policy Adviser and Head of Secretariat, Kim Darroch, CMG
Deputy Head, Katrina Williams

INTELLIGENCE AND SECURITY SECRETARIAT
Director, Chris Wright
Chief of the Assessments Staff, Tim Dowse

OFFICE OF THE COMMISSIONER FOR PUBLIC APPOINTMENTS (OCPA)
35 Great Smith Street, London SW1P 3BQ T 020-7276 2625
The Commissioner for Public Appointments is responsible for monitoring, regulating, reporting and advising on ministerial appointments to public bodies. The Commissioner publishes a code of practice and an annual report. The Commissioner can investigate complaints about the way in which appointments were made or applicants treated. By a separate order in council, Northern Ireland has its own Commissioner for Public Appointments; this post is also currently held by Baroness Fritchie, DBE.
Commissioner for Public Appointments, Baroness Fritchie, DBE
Senior Policy Adviser, Pam Cooke
Secretary to the Commissioner and Head of the Office, Jim Barron

OFFICE OF THE CIVIL SERVICE COMMISSIONERS (OCSC)
35 Great Smith Street, London SW1P 3BQ T 020-7276 2615
The independent Civil Service Commissioners are the custodians of the principle of selection on merit by fair and open competition; they publish a recruitment code and audit departments' and agencies' compliance. When the most senior posts are opened to people from outside the Service, the Commissioners normally chair the recruitment process. The Commissioners also advise departments on how to promote the Civil Service Code, and act as an independent appeals body under it. There is a separate body of Civil Service Commissioners for Northern Ireland.
First Commissioner, Baroness Prashar, CBE
Commissioners (part-time), R. Ayre; Sir D. Bell; P. Bounds; Dame A. Burslem, DBE; Ms B. Curtis; Ms S. Forbes, CBE; Baroness Fritchie, DBE; Prof. E. Gallagher, CBE; H. Hamill, CB; Ms M. J. Jacobi; G. Lemos, CMG; J. MacAuslan; A. MacDonald, CB; Ms E. McMeikan; Ms S. Pantelides; Dr M. Semple, OBE; C. Stephens
Secretary to the Commissioners and Head of the Office, Jim Barron

BETTER REGULATION EXECUTIVE (BRE)
22 Whitehall, London SW1A 2WH T 020-7276 2193
The Better Regulation Executive (BRE) is responsible for delivering better regulation and reducing unnecessary bureaucracy; it covers the private, public and voluntary sectors, across both domestic and European issues. The BRE deals with the flow of new regulations and the stock of existing regulations, including the particulars of how inspection and enforcement activities are carried out.
Director (acting), Simon Virley

THE PRIME MINISTER'S DELIVERY UNIT
1 Horse Guards Road, London SW1A 2HQ T 020-7270 5876
The Prime Minister's Delivery Unit was established in June 2001. Its main role is to ensure the delivery of the prime minister's top priority outcomes in the public services sector by 2008. The Unit reports to the prime minister through the Head of the Civil Service and the

Minister for the Cabinet Office. The Unit's work is carried out by a team of staff with experience of successful delivery in the public and private sectors.
Prime Minister's Chief Adviser on Delivery (acting), Peter Thomas
Directors, Richard Page-Jones; Nick Ville

E-GOVERNMENT UNIT
Stockley House, 130 Wilton Road, London SW1V 1LQ
T 020-7276 3285
The e-Government Unit works with departments to efficiently deliver, and improve, public services via better understanding and use of information technology. It does this by implementing the Government IT Strategy, promoting best practice across government and providing citizen-centred online services (such as www.direct.gov.uk). The e-Government Unit takes on the work previously undertaken by the Office of the e-Envoy.
Head of e-Government, Ian Watmore
Private Secretary, Ryan Heath

PRIME MINISTER'S STRATEGY UNIT (PMSU)
Admiralty Arch, The Mall, London SW1A 2WH
T 020-7276 1881
The Prime Minister's Strategy Unit (PMSU) was established in June 2002, although predecessor units date back to 1998. The PMSU has three main roles: to carry out strategic reviews and provide policy advice in accordance with the prime minister's policy priorities; to promote strategic thinking across government; and to conduct occasional strategic audits of the progress made by, and challenges facing, the UK and UK government. The Unit reports directly to the prime minister (who takes final decisions about its work programme) through the Cabinet Secretary, and can work in any area of domestic policy. Currently, the Unit's focus is public service reform; opportunity and welfare reform; infrastructure issues; and local governance. Since its inception the Unit has published over 50 reports, discussion papers and analytical pieces on its website www.strategy.gov.uk.
Director (acting), Stephen Aldridge

THE PRIME MINISTER'S OFFICE OF PUBLIC SERVICES REFORM (OPSR)
22 Whitehall, London SW1A 2WH T 020-7276 3600
F 020-7276 3530 E opsr@cabinet-office.x.gsi.gov.uk
W www.cabinetoffice.gov.uk/opsr
The prime minister established the Office of Public Services Reform (OPSR) in 2001, based within the Cabinet Office. The Unit reports directly to the prime minister through the Cabinet Secretary. Its role is to advise and work with the prime minister and departments on the reform of public services (the NHS, schools, local policing and local government). It is responsible for communicating the principles and values of public service reform and customer focus; models for improving public service delivery; solving pay and recruitment problems in the public sector; developing systems for managing cross-cutting issues affecting service delivery; and devising methods of management that reduce the impact of regulation on front-line services.
Prime Minister's Adviser on Public Services Reform, Dr Wendy Thomson, CBE

CENTRAL SPONSOR FOR INFORMATION ASSURANCE (CSIA)
Stockley House, 130 Wilton Road, London SW1V 1LQ
T 020-7276 3267

The CSIA was established on 1 April 2003 to assure the government that risks to the national information infrastructure are managed appropriately. It works with partners in the public and private sectors, as well as its international counterparts, to help safeguard the nation's IT and telecommunications services.
Director, Dr Steve Marsh

CORPORATE DEVELOPMENT GROUP (CDG)
Admiralty Arch, The Mall, London SW1A 2WH
T 020-7276 1566 F 020-7276 1404
CDG is responsible for recruiting and developing staff and raising the capability of HR management throughout the Civil Service. CDG encompasses the Centre for Management and Policy Studies (CMPS) and Civil Service Pensions.
Director-General, Ms A. Perkins, CB
Directors, John Barker, CB; Richard Furlong; Tim Kemp; Anne-Marie Lawlor; Jonathan Slater; David Spencer; Mike Watts

GOVERNMENT COMMUNICATION GROUP (GCG)
67 Tufton Street, London SW1P 3QS T 020-7276 2709
The Office of the Head of the Government Communication Group (GCG) is responsible for the standards of the service provided by the GCG to Whitehall departments and their agencies. It supports the Head of the Civil Service's work and provides guidance on the strategic development of the GCG, its professional practice, recruitment and promotion. Its focus is on cross-departmental communication and management of the central GCG units.
Director, Government Communication, Sue Jenkins
Director, Government Communication Network, Lyn Salisbury
Director, Professional Development, Tim Dunmore
Head of Media Monitoring Unit, Clarence Mitchell
Permanent Secretary, Howell James, CBE

CORPORATE MANAGEMENT
Managing Director Accounting Officer, Colin Balmer
Director, Finance, Jerry Page
Director, Business Development, Steve Cullen
Director, Human Resources, Anne Copeland
Deputy Director, Histories, Openness and Records, Tessa Stirling
Deputy Director, Infrastructure, Eric Hepburn

OFFICE OF PUBLIC SECTOR INFORMATION (OPSI)
St Clements House, 2–16 Colegate, Norwich NR3 1BQ
T 01603-621000 Enquiries 01603-723013 W www.opsi.gov.uk
The Office of Public Sector Information (OPSI) is responsible for policy in relation to access and re-use of UK public sector information. The legal and statutory responsibilities of Her Majesty's Stationery Office (HMSO), in relation to statutory publishing and the management of Crown copyright, operate from within the OPSI's wider remit.
Director/Controller, Carol Tullo

COMMUNICATION GROUP
70 Whitehall, London SW1A 2AS T 020-7270 3000
Advises on presentation of departmental policy and activity. Handles media and public relations activities other than recruitment publicity and advertising.
Director of Communication, John Worne
Deputy Director and Head of News, John Bretherton

Deputy Director and Head of Strategic Communications, Ann Hall

PRIME MINISTER'S OFFICE
10 Downing Street, London SW1A 2AA T 020-7270 3000
F 020-7925 0918 W www.number-10.gov.uk
Prime Minister, The Rt. Hon Tony Blair, MP
Parliamentary Private Secretary, Keith Hill, MP
Chief of Staff, Jonathan Powell
Deputy Chief of Staff, Liz Lloyd
Principal Private Secretary, Ivan Rogers
Private Secretaries, Miles Gibson; Kate Gross; Simon Morys; Nikhil Rathi; Daniel Thornton
Diary Secretary, Parna Taylor
Head of Policy Directorate, David Bennett
Policy Directorate, Vicki Bakhshi; Kieran Brent; Phil Collins; Gareth Davies; Ian Dodge; Tom Ellis; Bernadette Kelly; Alex Martin; Geoffrey Norris; Nick Rowley; Conor Ryan
Chief Strategy Adviser, Matthew Taylor
Research and Information Unit, Catherine Rimmer
Director of Communications and Strategy, David Hill
Strategic Communications Unit, Benjamin Wegg Prosser; Godric Smith
Direct Communications Unit, Tina Sampson
Prime Minister's Official Spokesman, Tom Kelly
Director of Events and Visits, Jo Gibbons
Director of Government Relations, Ruth Turner
Director of Political Operations, John McTernan
Secretary for Appointments, William Chapman
Adviser on Foreign Policy and Head of the Overseas and Defence Secretariat, Sir Nigel Sheinwald, KCMG
Foreign Policy, Grace Cassy; Justin Forsyth; Laurie Lee; Antony Philipson; David Quarrey
Adviser on European Union Affairs and Head of the European Secretariat, Kim Darroch
Parliamentary Clerk, Nicholas Howard

OFFICE OF THE DEPUTY PRIME MINISTER
26 Whitehall, London SW1A 2WH T 020-7944 4400
W www.odpm.gov.uk
The Office of the Deputy Prime Minister (ODPM) was created in May 2002 and took on responsibility for policy areas from both the Department for Transport, Local Government and the Regions, and the Cabinet Office. The ODPM brings together regional and local government (including the Regional Government Offices), housing, planning and regeneration, social exclusion and neighbourhood renewal.

Regional and local government and the government's cross-cutting agenda for neighbourhood renewal and social inclusion are administered by a single department under the Deputy Prime Minister, who also has responsibility for implementing regional government and local government white papers. The Deputy Prime Minister will continue to act as the Prime Minister's deputy across the full range of domestic and international business, chairing a range of key Cabinet committees.
Deputy Prime Minister and First Secretary of State, The Rt. Hon. John Prescott, MP
Private Secretary, Peter Betts
Minister of State, The Rt. Hon. David Miliband, MP *(Communities and Local Government)*
Private Secretary, Angela Kerr
Minister of State, The Rt. Hon. Philip Woolas *(Local Government)*
Private Secretary, Justin Homer

Minister of State, Yvette Cooper, MP *(Housing and Planning)*
Private Secretary, Mark Livesey
Parliamentary Under-Secretary of State, Jim Fitzpatrick, MP
Private Secretary, Sue Beaumont
Parliamentary Under-Secretary of State, Baroness Andrews, MP
Private Secretary, Patrick Owen
Permanent Secretary, Mavis McDonald
Private Secretary, Andrew Vaughan
Chief Scientist, David Fisk

DIRECTORATE OF COMMUNICATION
Director of Communication Directorate, Derek Plews
Deputy Director of Communications, Jane Groom

CORPORATE STRATEGY AND RESOURCES GROUP
Director-General, Peter Unwin
Directors, Peter Walton *(HR and Workplace Services)*; Andrew Lean *(Finance)*; Michael Kell *(Analysis and Research)*; Sarah Cox *(Business Change and Delivery)*
Heads of Departments, Alan Beard; David Buttress; Duncan Campbell; Steph Coster; Caroline Cousin; Shona Dunn; Meg Green; Wendy Jarvis; Amanda McFeeters; Andrew Morrison; Cath Shaw; Steve Simmonds; Chris Smith; David Smith; Jan White; Philip White; Jane Williams

LEGAL DIRECTORATE
Director, Sandra Unerman
Heads of Departments, Pamela Conlan; Fred Croft; Denise Fowler; Gloria Hedley-Dent; David Jordan; Donatella Phillips; Bernard Wilson

LOCAL GOVERNMENT AND FIRE GROUP
Director-General, Neil Kinghan
Directors, Lindsay Bell *(Local Government Finance)*; Clive Norris *(Fire and Rescue Service)*; John O'Brien *(Local Government Performance and Practice)*; David Prout *(Local Government Policy)*
Heads of Departments, Andrew Allberry; Stephen Claughton; Terry Crossley; Robert Davies; Paul Downie; Diana Kahn; Dave Lawrence; Kevin Lloyd; Sir Graham Meldrum; Shelagh Prosser; Cath Reynolds; Paul Rowsell; Mandy Skinner; Sarah Sturrock; Geoff Tierney; Marie Winckler

REGIONAL DEVELOPMENT GROUP
Director-General, Rob Smith
Directors, Richard Allan *(Regional Policy)*; Andrew Campbell *(Regional Co-ordination Unit)*; Alun Evans *(Civil Resilience)*
Heads of Departments, Julie Anderson; Christopher Bowden; Vince Brady; Richard Bruce; Philip Cox; Nick Dexter; Ian Jones; Mike Reed; Pam Temple
Regional Directors, Liz Meek *(London)*; Paul Martin *(South-East)*; Bronwyn Hill *(South-West)*; Keith Barnes *(North-West)*; Felicity Everiss *(Yorkshire and the Humber)*; Jonathon Blackie *(North-East)*; Jane Todd *(East Midlands)*; Graham Garbutt *(West Midlands)*; Caroline Bowdler *(East of England)*

SUSTAINABLE COMMUNITIES GROUP
Director-General, Richard McCarthy
Directors, Jeff Channing *(Thames Gateway)*; Brian Hackland *(Planning)*; Su Bonfanti *(Urban Policy)*; Neil McDonald *(Housing)*; Andrew Wells *(Sustainable Communities)*

Heads of Departments, Mike Ash; Joan Bailey; Michelle Banks; Henry Cleary; Mark Coulshed; Nick Dexter; Mitesh Dhanak; Dawn Eastmead; David Edwards; Richard Footitt; Richard Goodwin; Lester Hicks; Joanna Key; Anne Kirkham; Bob Ledsome; Peter Matthew; Peter Ruback; Ian Scotter; Lisette Simcock; John Stambollouian; Carol Sweetenham

TACKLING DISADVANTAGE GROUP
Director-General, Joe Montgomery
Directors, Terrie Alafat *(Homelessness and Housing Support)*; Alan Davis *(Neighbourhood Strategy)*; Alan Riddell *(Neighbourhood Operations)*

SOCIAL EXCLUSION UNIT
Director, Claire Tyler
Heads of Departments, Susan Acland-Hood; Lisa Barker; Marcus Bell; Allan Bowman; John Bright; Carol Hayden; Martin Joseph; Stephen Martin; Neil O'Connor; Bert Provan; Vanessa Scarborough; Rosie Seymour; Ruth Stainer; Teresa Vokes

REGIONAL CO-ORDINATION UNIT
River Walk House, Millbank, London SW1P 4RR
T 020-7217 3550
Director-General, Rob Smith
Director, Andrew Campbell

DEPARTMENT FOR CONSTITUTIONAL AFFAIRS (DCA)
Selbourne House, 54–60 Victoria Street, London SW1E 6QW
T 020-7210 8500 W www.dca.gov.uk
Created in June 2003, the Department for Constitutional Affairs (DCA) is responsible for justice, rights and democracy. It brought together most of the Lord Chancellor's Department, the UK devolution settlements and, for administrative purposes only, the staff of the Scotland Office and the Wales Office. Its role is to drive forward the reform and improvement of the legal and justice system in England and Wales, to uphold the rule of law, and to reform and safeguard the constitution so that it serves the public effectively. Priority issues for the department are to: fight crime and anti-social behaviour; provide improved support for the victims of crime and for magistrates; engender respect for the authority of the courts; ensure the efficiency and effectiveness of fraud trials; provide a more diverse judiciary and an improved experience for jurors; support the rights of the disadvantaged; ensure a fairer deal for legal aid; reform legal services; tackle the 'compensation culture'; continue reform of the House of Lords; and improve electoral administration.

The department is responsible for the administration of the courts and tribunals in England and Wales, and for the overall management of legal aid (through its sponsorship of the Legal Services Commission). The annual budget for 2004–5 was around £3.4 billion – approximately £1 billion was spent on the courts and £2 billion on legal aid. The department employs approximately 24,000 staff, around 20,000 of whom work in tribunals and courts (including, since April 2005, the magistrates' courts). The courts support the independent judiciary, which is comprised of 2,450 judges. The DCA also oversees the work of the 42 Magistrates' Courts Committees, which support around 28,700 magistrates across England and Wales. Four sister departments – Her Majesty's Court Service, the Northern Ireland Court Service, Her Majesty's Land Registry and the National Archives –

report directly to the Secretary of State for Constitutional Affairs. Also associated with the DCA are a number of organisations such as: the Public Guardianship Office; the Office of the Official Solicitor and Public Trustee; the Law Commission; the Office of the Legal Services Ombudsman; Her Majesty's Inspectorate of Court Administration; and the Judicial Studies Board. From April 2006, the DCA will be responsible for the newly formed Tribunals Service (*see* Tribunals section), which will bring together the administration of all the major tribunals across government. Responsibilities for the maintenance of the relationship between Westminster and the devolved administrations in Edinburgh and Cardiff remain with the Secretary of State for Scotland and the Secretary of State for Wales respectively.

Secretary of State for Constitutional Affairs and Lord Chancellor, The Rt. Hon. Lord Falconer of Thoroton, QC
Principal Private Secretary, Mike Anderson
Special Adviser, Philip Bassett
Expert Adviser, Garry Hart
Parliamentary Clerk, Ann Nixon
Minister of State, The Rt. Hon. Harriet Harman, QC, MP
Private Secretary, Grant Morris
Parliamentary Under-Secretary, Baroness Ashton of Upholland
Private Secretary, Nicola Westmore
Parliamentary Under-Secretary, Bridget Prentice, MP
Private Secretary, Edward Bowles
Permanent Secretary, Alex Allan
Private Secretary, Jade Cortes
Head of the Crown Office, Ian Denyer

COMMUNICATIONS DIRECTORATE
T 020-7210 8512
Director, Lucian Hudson
Head of News, Peter Wilkinson

STRATEGY GROUP
Director, General Strategy, Rod Clark
Director, Consumer Strategy Directorate, Jane Frost
Director, Corporate Management, Kevin Sadler
Director, Constitution Directorate, Andrew McDonald
Director, Legal Aid Strategy, Amanda Finlay
Director, Council on Tribunals, Ray Burningham
Heads of Divisions, Edward Adams; Sarah Albon; Belinda Crowe; Tony Donaldson; Colin Myerscough; Antonia Romeo; John Sills; Judith Simpson; Mark Taylor; Peter Thompson

FINANCE
T 020-7210 2801
Director-General, Barbara Moorhouse
Director, Commercial Group, Colin Lyne
Head of Financial Operation, Nick Sharman
Head of Internal Assurance, Alan Rummins
Heads of Divisions, Richard Atkinson; Ken Cooney; Alicia O'Neill; Adam Skinner

LEGAL AND JUDICIAL SERVICES
T 020-7210 8010
Director-General, John Lyon
Director, Judicial Appointments, Clare Pelham
Director, Judicial Policy, Liz Grimsey
Director, Legal Group, Richard Heaton
Director, Corporate Diversity, Nick Smedley
Heads of Divisions, Anita Bharucha; Rowena Collins Rice; Lee Hughes, CBE; Anunay Jha; Claire Johnston; Judith

Killick; Michael Kron; Maggy Pigott; Emma Robinson; Ray Sams; Alistair Shaw; Mary Shaw; Jonathan Solly; David Staff; Kate Todman; Alasdair Wallace; Valerie Willer

CHIEF EXECUTIVE OPERATIONS
T 020-7210 8001
Chief Executive Operations and Second Permanent Secretary, Ian Magee

CROWN OFFICE
House of Lords, London SW1A 0PW T 020-7219 4713

SUPREME COURT GROUP
Royal Courts of Justice, Strand, London WC2A 2LL
T 020-7947 6000

DEPARTMENT FOR CULTURE, MEDIA AND SPORT

2–4 Cockspur Street, London SW1Y 5DH T 020-7211 6200
F 020-7211 6032 W www.culture.gov.uk

The Department for Culture, Media and Sport was established in July 1997 and is responsible for government policy relating to the arts, broadcasting, press freedom and regulation, the film and music industries, museums and galleries, libraries, architecture and the historic environment, sport and recreation, tourism, the National Lottery, gambling, and alcohol and entertainment licensing.

Secretary of State for Culture, Media and Sport, The Rt. Hon. Tessa Jowell, MP
Principal Private Secretary, Helen MacNamara
Special Advisers, Nick Bent; Sara Latham; Roger Sharp
Parliamentary Private Secretary, Barbara Follett, MP
Minister of State, The Rt. Hon. Richard Caborn, MP *(Sport and Olympics)*
Private Secretary, Amy Ward
Parliamentary Private Secretary, Ben Chapman, MP
Parliamentary Under-Secretary of State, David Lammy, MP *(Arts and Heritage)*
Private Secretary, David McLaren
Parliamentary Under-Secretary of State, James Purnell, MP *(Creative Industries and Tourism)*
Private Secretary, Rachel Streatton
Permanent Secretary, Dame Sue Street, DCB
Director-General, Children, Young People and Communities, Jeff Jacobs

STRATEGY AND COMMUNICATIONS DIRECTORATE
Head of News, Paddy Feeny
Head of Promotions and Publicity, Penny Dolby
Head of Strategy Division, David Roe

CORPORATE SERVICES DIRECTORATE
Head of Group, Nicholas Holgate
Head, Evidence and Analysis Unit, Ian Wood
Head, Finance and Planning Division, Keith Smith
Head, Internal Audit, Michael Kirk
Head, Personnel and Central Services Division, Shaun Cove

ARTS AND CULTURE DIRECTORATE
Head of Group, Alan Davey
Director, Government Art Collection, Penny Johnson
Head, Architecture and Historic Environment Division, Harry Reeves
Head, Arts Division, Phil Clapp
Head, Museums and Cultural Property, Nigel Pittman

Head, Museums and Libraries Sponsorship, Richard
  Hartman
Head, Public Bodies Division, Janet Evans

CREATIVE INDUSTRIES, BROADCASTING, GAMBLING
AND LOTTERY DIRECTORATE
Head of Group, Andrew Ramsay
Head, Broadcasting Division, Jon Zeff
Head, Creative Industries Division, Mark Ferrero
Head, Gambling and National Lottery Licensing, Elliot
  Grant
Head, National Lottery Distribution and Communities,
  Simon Broadley

TOURISM, LIBRARIES AND COMMUNITIES
DIRECTORATE
Head of Group, Brian Leonard
Head, Alcohol and Entertainment Licensing, Andrew
  Cunningham
Head, Libraries and Communities, Vanessa Brand
Head, Tourism Division, Kevin Williamson

SPORT DIRECTORATE
Head of Group, Nicky Roche
Head, Sports Division, Paul Heron

DEPARTMENT FOR EDUCATION AND SKILLS

Sanctuary Buildings, Great Smith Street, London SW1P 3BT
Caxton House, Tothill Street, London SW1H 9NA
Wellington House, Waterloo Road, London SE1 8UG
Castle View House, East Lane, Runcorn WA7 2GJ
Mowden Hall, Staindrop Road, Darlington DL3 9BG
Moorfoot, Sheffield S1 4PQ T 0870-001 2345 Public
Enquiries 0870-000 2288 E info@dfes.gsi.gov.uk
W www.dfes.gov.uk
The Department for Education and Skills aims to help
build a competitive economy and inclusive society, by
creating opportunities for everyone to develop their
learning potential and achieve excellence in standards of
education and levels of skills. The department's main
objectives are to give children an excellent start in
education and to enable young people and adults to
develop and equip themselves with the skills, knowledge
and personal qualities needed for life and work. The
department also sponsors 23 non-departmental public
bodies across a variety of professional disciplines and
educational services.
Secretary of State for Education and Skills, The Rt. Hon.
  Ruth Kelly, MP
Principal Private Secretary, Mela Watts
Private Secretaries, Francesca Orpen; Kirsty Pearce
Special Advisers, Dan Corry; Richard Darlington
Parliamentary Private Secretary, Jonathan Shaw, MP
Minister of State, The Rt. Hon. Jacqui Smith, MP *(Schools)*
Private Secretary, Charles Deighton-Fox
Parliamentary Private Secretary, Ann McKechin, MP
Minister of State, Bill Rammell, MP *(Higher Education and
  Lifelong Learning)*
Private Secretary, Jane Mardell
Parliamentary Private Secretary, Ian Lucas, MP
Minister of State, The Rt. Hon. Beverly Hughes, MP
  (Children and Families)
Private Secretary, Jenny Preece
Parliamentary Private Secretary, Christine Russell, MP
Parliamentary Under-Secretary of State, Lord Adonis
  (Schools)
Private Secretary, Rebecca Beeton

Parliamentary Under-Secretary of State, Maria Eagle, MP
  (Children and Families)
Private Secretary, Nicola Sams
Parliamentary Under-Secretary of State, Phil Hope, MP
  (Skills)
Private Secretary, Jonathan Duff
Permanent Secretary, David Normington, CB
Private Secretary, Paul Price
Parliamentary Clerk, Mike Watts
Spokesman in the House of Lords, Lord Adonis

STRATEGY AND COMMUNICATIONS DIRECTORATE
Director, Michael Stevenson
Heads of Divisions, John Shield *(News)*; Vanessa Wilson
  (Strategic Communications Planning)
Divisional Managers, Stuart Dickenson *(acting; Corporate
  Communications)*; Diana Laurillard *(e-Learning Strategy
  Unit)*; Trevor Cook *(Public Affairs)*; Mohammad
  Haroon *(Regions, Delivery Support and Regeneration)*

CHILDREN, YOUNG PEOPLE AND FAMILIES
DIRECTORATE
Director-General, Tom Jeffery
Director, Children's Workforce Unit, Jeanette Pugh
Director, Safeguarding Children Group, Althea Efunshile
Director, Supporting Children and Young People Group,
  Anne Weinstock
Director, Sure Start, Naomi Eisenstadt

SCHOOLS DIRECTORATE
Director-General, Peter Housden
Directors, School Standards Group, Chris Wormald
  (Academies); Andrew McCully *(Delivery)*; Jon Coles
  (London Challenge Programme); Helen Williams *(Primary
  Education)*; Peter Wanless *(Secondary Education)*
Chief Adviser on School Standards, vacant
Director, School Resources Group, Stephen Crowne
Director, School Workforce Group, Stephen Hillier

SCHOOLS DIRECTORATE AND CHILDREN, YOUNG
PEOPLE AND FAMILIES DIRECTORATE JOINT
COMMANDS
Director, Local Transformation Group, Sheila Scales
Director, Strategy Group, Anne Jackson

HIGHER EDUCATION DIRECTORATE
Director-General, Sir Alan Wilson
Director, Higher Education Strategy, Ruth Thompson
Director, Student Finance Strategy, Michael Hipkins

LIFELONG LEARNING DIRECTORATE
Director-General, Steven Marston
Director, FE, Learning and Skills Performance Group, Susan
  Pember
Director, Joint International Unit, Clive Tucker
Director, Qualifications and Young People Group, Jon Coles
Director, Skills Group, vacant
Director, Standards Unit, Jane Williams

FINANCE AND ANALYTICAL SERVICES DIRECTORATE
Director-General, Peter Makeham
Director and Chief Economist, John Elliot
Director, Centre for Procurement Performance, Ian Taylor
Director, Finance, Stephen Kershaw

CORPORATE SERVICES AND DEVELOPMENT
DIRECTORATE
Director-General, Susan Thomas
Director, Mike Daly

TECHNOLOGY DIRECTORATE
Director, Michael Stevenson

LEGAL ADVISER'S OFFICE
Legal Adviser, David Noble

DEPARTMENT FOR ENVIRONMENT, FOOD AND RURAL AFFAIRS

Nobel House, 17 Smith Square, London SW1P 3JR
T 020-7238 3000 **F** 020-7238 6591 **W** www.defra.gov.uk
The Department for Environment, Food and Rural Affairs (Defra) is responsible for government policy on the environment, rural matters, farming and food production. In association with the agriculture departments of the Scottish Executive, the National Assembly for Wales and the Northern Ireland Office, and with the Intervention Board, the department is responsible for negotiations in the EU on the common agricultural and fisheries policies, and for single European market questions relating to its responsibilities. Its remit includes international agricultural and food trade policy.

The department's priority is the sustainable use of natural resources, specifically to ensure economic prosperity through sustainable methods of farming, fishing, food and water supply, and other industries that meet consumer requirements. Defra also exercises responsibilities for policies on climate change, a range of pollution issues relating to waste and recycling, the protection and enhancement of the countryside and the marine environment, flood defence, GM crops, hunting, rural development and other rural issues. It is the licensing authority for veterinary medicines and the registration authority for pesticides. It administers policies relating to the control of animal, plant and fish diseases. It provides scientific, technical and professional services and advice to farmers, growers and ancillary industries, and also commissions research to assist in the formulation and assessment of policy and to underpin applied research and development work done by industry.

Secretary of State for Environment, Food and Rural Affairs, The Rt. Hon. Margaret Beckett, MP
Principal Private Secretary, Gavin Ross
Private Secretaries, Sophia Brecknell; Richard Chapman; Deborah Petterson
Special Advisers, Stephen Hale; Hazell Phillips; Sheila Watson
Minister of State, Elliot Morley, MP *(Climate Change and Environment)*
Senior Private Secretary, Bradley Bates
Private Secretary, Emma Webbon
Parliamentary Under-Secretary of State (Commons), Jim Knight, MP *(Rural Affairs, Landscape and Biodiversity)*
Private Secretaries, Mike Burbridge; Palminder Kaur
Assistant Private Secretaries, Lewis Mortimer; Nina Roney
Parliamentary Private Secretary, Peter Bradley, MP
Parliamentary Under-Secretary of State (Commons), Ben Bradshaw, MP *(Local Environment, Marine and Animal Welfare)*
Principal Private Secretary, Kathleen Cameron
Private Secretary, Tristan Crago
Parliamentary Under-Secretary of State (Lords), Lord Bach *(Sustainable Farming and Food)*
Senior Private Secretary, Lee Harbord
Private Secretary, Emma Harding
Assistant Private Secretaries, Alice Cohen; Naomi Williams
Permanent Secretary, Brian Bender, CB
Private Secretary, Tim Lord
Assistant Private Secretary, Nasrine Amzour

FINANCE, PLANNING AND RESOURCES DIRECTORATE
Nobel House, 17 Smith Square, London SW1P 3JR
T 020-7270 6000
Finance Director, Andrew Burchell
Deputy Director, Ian Grattidge
Heads of Division, Roger Atkinson; Jane Bloodworth; Julie Flint; Lee McDonough; David Rabey; Richard Wilkinson

STRATEGY AND SUSTAINABLE DEVELOPMENT
Director, Jill Rutter
Heads of Division, Scott Ghagan; Bronwen Jones; Andy Taylor; Prashant Vaze

SOLICITOR AND LEGAL SERVICES DIRECTORATE GENERAL
Solicitor and Director-General Legal Services, Donald Macrae
Directors, Gill Aitken; Robert Humm
Heads of Division, Charles Allen; Chris Burke; Linda Dann; Gisela Davis; Peter Davis; Brian Dickinson; Sally Lewis; Alistair McGlone; Jonathan Robinson; Anne Sachs; Sue Spence; Clare Sylvester; Mark Wilson
Chief Investigation Officer, Jan Panting

GOVERNMENT OFFICES, RURAL DIRECTORS
East of England, Building A, Westbrook Centre, Milton Road, Cambridge CB4 1YG **T** 01223-372759 *Rural Director,* Mark Edwards
East Midlands, The Belgrave Centre, Talbot Street, Nottingham NG1 5GG **T** 0115-971 9971 *Rural Director,* Graham Norbury
North East, Welbar House, Gallowgate, Newcastle-upon-Tyne NE1 4TD **T** 0191-201 3300 *Rural Director,* John Bainton
North West, Sunley Tower, Piccadilly Plaza, Manchester M1 4BE **T** 0161-952 4000 *Regional Director,* Neil Cumberlidge
South East, Bridge House, 1 Walnut Tree Close, Guildford GU1 4GA **T** 01483-882255 *Regional Director,* Mark Bilsborough
South West, 4th and 5th Floors, The Pithay, Bristol BS1 2PB **T** 0117-900 1700 *Regional Director,* Tim Render
West Midlands, 77 Paradise Circus, Queensway, Birmingham B1 2DT **T** 0121-212 5000 *Regional Director,* Chris Marsh
Yorkshire and the Humber, PO Box 213, City House, New Station Street, Leeds LS1 4US **T** 0113-280 0600 *Regional Director,* Felicity Everiss

RURAL DEVELOPMENT SERVICE
T 020-7238 3000
Head of Group, John Adams
Head of Technical Advice, Alan Hooper
Business Planning, Jeff Robinson
ERDPIT Programme Director, Ann Tarran
Strategy Delivery and Implementation, Paul Egginton
RDS HQ, Phil Cutts
Operations, Ian Fugler

RURAL DEVELOPMENT CENTRES AND MANAGERS
East of England, Block B, Government Buildings, Brooklands Avenue, Cambridge CB2 2DR **T** 01223-462727 *Regional Manager,* Martin Edwards
East Midlands, Block 7, Government Buildings, Chalfont Drive, Nottingham NG8 3SN **T** 0115-929 1191 *Regional Manager,* Sue Buckenham
North East, Government Buildings, Kenton Bar, Newcastle-upon-Tyne NE5 3EW **T** 0191-214 1800 *Regional Manager,* Fiona Gough

North West, Electra Way, Crewe Business Park, Crewe CW1 6GJ T 01270-754000 *Regional Manager,* Tony Percival
South East, Block A, Government Buildings, Coley Park, Reading RG1 6DT T 0118-958 1222 *Regional Manager,* Terry Bradfield
South West, Block 3, Government Buildings, Burghill Road, Westbury-on-Trym, Bristol BS10 6NJ T 0117-959 1000 *Regional Manager,* Mark Watson
West Midlands, Block C, Government Buildings, Whittington Road, Worcester WR5 2LQ T 01905-763355 *Regional Manager,* Geoff Sansome
Yorkshire and the Humber, Government Buildings, Otley Road, Lawnswood, Leeds LS16 5QT T 0113-230 3750 *Regional Manager,* Peter Nottage

SUSTAINABLE FARMING, FOOD AND FISHERIES DIRECTORATE GENERAL
9 Millbank, c/o 17 Smith Square, London SW1P 3JR
T 020-7238 3000
Director-General, Andrew Lebrecht

FOOD CHAIN ANALYSIS AND FARMING
Director, Mike Segal
Deputy Director, Economics and Statistics, Simon Harding
Heads of Division, Ray Anderson; Peter Helm; Stuart Platt; Katherine Riggs; John Watson; Andrea Young

EU AND INTERNATIONAL POLICY
Director, David Hunter
Heads of Division, Andrew Lawrence; Sarah Thomas

SUSTAINABLE AGRICULTURE AND LIVESTOCK PRODUCTS DIRECTORATE
Director, Sonia Phippard
Heads of Division, Jeremy Eppel; Nafees Meah; Andrew Slade

FOOD INDUSTRY AND CROPS DIRECTORATE
Director, John Robbs
Heads of Division, Jeremy Cowper; Dr Stephen Hunter; David Jones; Andrew Kuyk; Andrew Perrins; Mike Wray; Callton Young

FISHERIES DIRECTORATE
Director, Rodney Anderson
Heads of Division, Peter Boyling; Richard Cowan; Linsay Harris; Chris Ryder; Anne Sharp
Sea Fisheries Inspectorate and Chief Executive Designate, Nigel Gooding

NATURAL RESOURCES AND RURAL AFFAIRS DIRECTORATE GENERAL
Ergon House, Horseferry Road, London SW1P 2AL
T 020-7238 3000
Director-General, Ursula Brennan

MODERNISING RURAL DEVELOPMENT AND DELIVERY
Director, Jane Brown
Heads of Division, Tim Allen; Peter Cleasy; Martin Nesbit; Andrew Robinson

RURAL POLICIES AND COMMUNITIES
Director, John Mills
Heads of Division, Collette Backwell; James Bradley; Robin Mortimer; Katheryn Packer; Richard Pullen

WILDLIFE, COUNTRYSIDE AND LAND USE DIRECTORATE
Director, Brian Harding
Heads of Division, Martin Brasher; David Coleman; Peter Costigan; Sheila McCabe; Hilary Thompson; Sue Townsend

ANIMAL HEALTH AND WELFARE DIRECTORATE GENERAL
1A Page Street, London SW1P 4PQ T 020-7904 6000
Chief Veterinary Officer and Director-General, Debby Reynolds
Deputy Chief Veterinary Officer, Fred Landeg
Heads of Division, Nick Coulson; Nigel Gibbens; Ruth Lysons; David Mouat; David Pritchard; Peter Stevenson; Vic Verma

ANIMAL HEALTH AND WELFARE DIRECTORATE
Director, David Dawson
Heads of Division, John Bourne; Simon Hewitt; Malcolm Hunt; Diana Linskey; Alison Reeves

TSE GROUP
Director, Peter Nash
Heads of Division, Sue Eades; Nigel Gibbens; Francis Marlow; Kate Richards

ENVIRONMENT DIRECTORATE GENERAL
Ashdown House, 123 Victoria Street, London SW1E 6DE
T 020-7238 6000
Director-General, Bill Stow, CB

ENVIRONMENT QUALITY AND WASTE DIRECTORATE
Director, Neil Thornton
Heads of Division, John Burns; Lindsay Cornish; Sue Ellis Ivor Llewelyn; Martin Williams

CLIMATE, ENERGY AND ENVIRONMENTAL RISK DIRECTORATE
Director, Henry Derwent
Heads of Division, Robert Bettley-Smith; Colin Church; Chris De Grouchy; Stephen De Souza; Sarah Hendry; Chris Leigh; Jackie Stone

ENVIRONMENTAL STRATEGY DIRECTORATE
Director, Robert Lowson
Heads of Division, Nigel Atkinson; John Custance; Bob Davies; Roy Hathaway; Terence Ilot; Helen Marquard; Sabine Mosner

WATER DIRECTORATE
Director, Richard Bird
Heads of Division, Dave Bench; Prof. Jeni Colbourne; Daniel Instone; Sarah Nason; John Roberts; Richard Wood

SCIENCE DIRECTORATE
Cromwell House, Dean Stanley Street, London SW1P 3JH
T 020-7238 6000
Chief Scientific Adviser and Head of Directorate, Prof. Howard Dalton, FRS
Deputy Chief Scientific Adviser, Dr Miles Parker
Heads of Division, Catherine Boyle; Mike Tas

CENTRAL ANALYTICAL DIRECTORATE
Director, David Thompson
Head of Division, Dave Cawley

OPERATIONS AND SERVICE DELIVERY
DIRECTORATE GENERAL
9 Millbank, c/o 17 Smith Square, London SW1P 3JR
T 020-7238 3000
Director-General, Mark Addison

CORPORATE SERVICES DIRECTORATE
3–8 Whitehall Place, London SW1A 2HH T 020-7270 6000
Director, Richard Allen
Heads of Division, Wendy Cartwright; Neil MacIntosh;
  Teresa Newell; Tony Nickson; John Nodder; Caroline
  Smith; Mike Watkins

COMMUNICATIONS DIRECTORATE
Director of Communications, Yasmin Diamond
Head of Corporate Communications, Kelly Freeman
Head of News, Jean Ward

IMPROVEMENT AND DELIVERY GROUP
Cromwell House, Dean Bradley Street, London SW1P 3JH
T 020-7238 6000
Director, Francesca Okosi
Heads of Division, Mark Ace; Richard Chalk

INTELLIGENT CUSTOMER FUNCTION DIRECTORATE
Government Buildings, Epsom Road, Guildford GU1 2LD
T 01483-568121
Director, David Myers
Deputy Director, Denise McDonagh
Heads of Division, Peter Barber; Ray Boguslawski; David
  Brown; Andy Dowell; David Penhallurick; Iain Walker

FOREIGN AND COMMONWEALTH OFFICE

King Charles Street, London SW1A 2AH T 020-7008 1500
W www.fco.gov.uk
The Foreign and Commonwealth Office (FCO) provides,
through its staff in the UK and through its diplomatic
missions abroad, the means of communication between
the British government and other governments – and
international governmental organisations – on all matters
falling within the field of international relations.

It is responsible for: alerting the British government to
the implications of developments overseas; promoting
British interests overseas; protecting British citizens
abroad; explaining British policies to, and cultivating
relationships with, governments overseas; the discharge of
British responsibilities to the overseas territories; entry
clearance UK Visas (with the Home Office); and
promoting British business overseas (jointly with the
Department of Trade and Industry through UK Trade and
Investment).

Secretary of State for Foreign and Commonwealth Affairs,
  The Rt. Hon. Jack Straw, MP
Principal Private Secretary, Geoffrey Adams, CMG
Special Advisers, Ed Owen; Dr Michael Williams
Team Parliamentary Private Secretary, Lawrie Quinn, MP
Minister of State, Douglas Alexander, MP *(Europe)*
Private Secretary, Nick Leake
Parliamentary Private Secretary, Phyllis Starkey, MP
Minister of State, Dr Kim Howells, MP *(Middle East)*
Private Secretary, Emma Wade
Parliamentary Private Secretary, Mark Todd, MP
Minister of State, Ian Pearson, MP *(Trade)*
Private Secretary, Georgia Hutchinson
Parliamentary Private Secretary, Lawrie Quinn, MP
Parliamentary Under-Secretary of State, Lord Triesman
Private Secretary, Bharat Joshi

*Permanent Under-Secretary of State and Head of HM
  Diplomatic Service*, Sir Michael Jay, KCMG
Private Secretary, Matthew Lodge
Group Chief Executive, UK Trade and Investment, Sir
  Stephen Brown, KCVO
Directors-General, Nicola Brewer, CMG *(EU Policy)*;
  Martin Donnelly, CMG *(Economic)*; David Richmond,
  CMG *(Defence/Intelligence)*; John Sawers, CMG
  (Political); Dickie Stagg, CMG *(Corporate Affairs)*; Sir
  Michael Wood, KCMG *(Legal Adviser)*

DIRECTORS
Africa, James Bevan
Americas/Overseas Territories, Robert Culshaw, MVO
Asia Pacific, Nigel Cox
Chief Executive, FCO Services, Stephen Sage
Communications, John Williams
Consular Services, Paul Sizeland
Defence and Strategic Threats, Edward Oakden
Economic Policy, Creon Butler
Finance, Ric Todd
Global Issues, Philippa Drew
Human Resources, Darren Warren
International Security, Stephen Pattison
Iraq, Dominic Asquith, CMG
Mediterranean Europe, Bilateral, Resources, Dominick
  Chilcott
Middle East and North Africa, Peter Gooderham
South Asia and Afghanistan, Tom Phillips, CMG
Strategy and Information, Anne Pringle, CMG
UK Visas, Robin Barnett

UK SPECIAL REPRESENTATIVES
Afghanistan, Tom Phillips, CMG
Nepal, Jeffrey James
South Caucasus, Sir Brian Fall, KCMG
Sudan, Dr Alastair McPhail, OBE

HEADS OF DEPARTMENTS
Afghanistan Group, Richard Codrington
Africa Department (Equatorial), Tim Hitchens
Africa Department (Southern), Andrew Lloyd
Association of South-East Asian Nations and Oceania Group,
  Michael Reilly
Climate Change and Energy Group, Valerie Caton
Consular Directorate, Paul Sizeland *(Director of Consular
  Services)*; Janet Douglas *(Assistance Group)*; David
  Fitton *(Crisis Group)*; David Clegg, MVO *(Passports and
  Documentary Services Group)*; Tim Flear, MVO *(Policy,
  Communications and Training Group)*; David
  Popplestone *(Resources Group)*
Counter-Proliferation Department, David Landsman
Counter-Terrorism Policy Department, Philip Parham
Diplomatic Service Families Association, Emilie Salvesen
Drugs and International Crime Department, Lesley Pallett
Eastern Department, Simon Smith
Eastern Adriatic Department, Karen Pierce, CVO
Economic Policy Directorate, Creon Butler *(Director and
  Chief Economist)*; Charles Hay *(G8 Presidency Team)*;
  Graham Minter *(Global Business Group)*; Hasan
  Bakhshi *(Global Economy Group)*; Fiona Clouder
  Richards *(Science and Innovation Group)*
Estate Strategy Unit, Geoff Gillham
European Union (External) Assistant Directorate, Tim
  Barrow, LVO, MBE *(Assistant Director)*; Dominic
  Schroeder *(Common Foreign and Security Policy Team)*;
  Andrew Key *(EU Northern Europe and International
  Team)*; Martin Reynolds *(Enlargement Team)*

European Union (Internal), David Frost
Far East Group, Denis Keefe
Financial Planning and Performance Department, Tristan Price
FCO Services, Stephen Sage *(Chief Executive);* Joy Herring *(Client Services);* Nigel Morris *(Facilities Service Delivery);* Kerry Simmonds *(Finance);* Elaine Kennedy *(Human Resources);* Patrick Cullen *(ICT Service Delivery);* Dr Vanessa L. Davies *(People and Best Practice Service Delivery);* Sarah Squires *(Positive Image UK Service Delivery);* Rod Peters *(Supply Chain Service Delivery)*
Grant-Aided Public Bodies and Scholarships Team, Public Diplomacy Group, Charles Winnington-Ingram
Human Resources Directorate, David Warren *(Head of HR Directorate);* Carole Sweeney *(Employment Policy Team);* Greg Dorey *(HR Direct);* Andrew George *(Health and Welfare Policy Team);* David Powell *(Pay and Benefits Policy Team);* Gerry Reffo *(Professional Development);* Simon Pease *(Workforce Planning Team)*
Human Rights, Democracy and Governance Group, Alex Hall Hall
Information Management Group, Heather Yasamee
Internal Audit Department, Jon Hews
International Organisations Department, Tim Morris
IT Strategy Unit, Nick Westcott
Latin America and Caribbean Department, Stephen Williams
Legal Adviser, Sir Michael Wood, KCMG
Middle East and North Africa Directorate, Peter Gooderham *(Director);* Nick Banner *(Arab/Israel and North Africa Group);* Jolyon Welsh *(Arabian Peninsula Group);* Frances Guy *(Engaging with the Islamic World Group);* Charles Gray *(Iran Coordination Group)*
North America Team, Anne Jarrett; Martin Rickerd, OBE, MVO
Overseas Territories Department, Tony Crombie, OBE
Parliamentary Relations and Devolution Team, Chris Stanton
Press Office, John Williams *(Press Secretary);* Peter Reid *(Head of News Room)*
Prism Programme, Andy Tucker
Procurement Policy Department, Roger Seager
Protocol Division, Charles de Chassiron, CVO
Public Diplomacy, Timothy Livesey
Research Analysts, Robin Hoggard, CMG
Resource Accounting Department, Iain Morgan
Security Policy Group, Hugh Powell
Security Strategy Unit, Peter Millett
South Asia Group, James Dauris
Strategy Group, Vivien Life
Sudan Unit, Anna Bewes
Sustainable Development and Commonwealth Group, Andrew Soper
Trade Union Side, Stephen Watson *(TUS Chair);* Pam Chapman *(TUS Secretary)*
UK Outreach Team, Graeme Thomas
Whitehall Liaison Department, Claire Smith

UK TRADE AND INVESTMENT
Joint Board Chair, Douglas Alexander, MP
Group Chief Executive, Sir Stephen Brown, KCVO
Chief Executive, Inward Investment Group, William Pedder
Group Directors, John Reynolds *(E-Transformation Group);* Peter Tibber *(International Sectors Group);* Ian Fletcher *(International Trade Development Group);* Susan Haird *(Strategy and Corporate Group)*

UK VISAS (JOINT FCO/HOME OFFICE DIRECTORATE)
Superintending Directors, Bill Jeffrey; Dickie Stagg, CMG
Director, UK Visas, Robin Barnett
Head of Directorate, Mandie Campbell

DEPARTMENT OF HEALTH

Richmond House, 79 Whitehall, London SW1A 2NS
T 020-7210 3000 W www.dh.gov.uk
The Department of Health is responsible for the provision of the National Health Service (NHS) in England and for social care. The department's aims are: to support, protect, promote and improve the nation's health; to secure the provision of comprehensive, high-quality care for all those who need it, regardless of their ability to pay, where they live or their age; and to provide responsive social care and child protection for those who lack the support they need.

The Department of Health is responsible for setting health and social care policy in England. The department's work sets standards and drives modernisation across all areas of the NHS, social care and public health.

Secretary of State for Health, The Rt. Hon. Patricia Hewitt, MP
Principal Private Secretary, Dominic Hardy
Private Secretaries, Helena Feinstein; Luisa Stewart
Assistant Private Secretary, Kate Bowe
Parliamentary Private Secretary, Tom Harris, MP
Minister of State, The Rt. Hon. Jane Kennedy, MP *(Quality and Patient Safety)*
Private Secretary, Sally Warren
Minister of State, Rosie Winterton, MP *(Health Services)*
Private Secretary, Alistair Finney
Parliamentary Under-Secretary of State, Liam Byrne, MP *(Care Services)*
Private Secretary (acting), Yvette Gyampoh
Minister of State, Lord Warner *(NHS Delivery)*
Private Secretary, Frances Smethurst
Parliamentary Under-Secretary of State, Caroline Flint, MP *(Public Health)*
Private Secretary, Anna Norris
Parliamentary Clerk, Neil Townley
Permanent Secretary, Sir Nigel Crisp, KCB
Head of Sir Nigel Crisp's Office, Shaun Gallagher
Private Secretary, David Cockayne
Assistant Private Secretaries, Helen Davies; Greg Madden; Clare Osborne

MANAGEMENT BOARD
Permanent Secretary and Chief Executive of the NHS, Sir Nigel Crisp KCB
Director of User Experience and Involvement/Professional Leadership, and Chief Nursing Officer, Prof. Christine Beasley, CBE
Group Director and Chief Medical Officer of Standards and Quality, Prof. Sir Liam Donaldson
Group Director of Delivery, John Bacon
Group Director, Strategy and Business Development, Hugh Taylor, CB
Director of Communications, Sian Jarvis
Director of Finance and Investment, Richard Douglas
Director of Strategy, Stephen O'Brien

HEALTH AND SOCIAL CARE STANDARDS AND QUALITY GROUP
Group Director, Prof. Sir Liam Donaldson, KB
Director/Deputy Chief Medical Officer for Health Improvement, Dr Fiona Adshead

Director/Deputy Chief Medical Officer for Healthcare Quality, Dr Bill Kirkup
Director, Care Services Directorate, Prof. Antony Sheehan
Director, Children and Mental Health, Mark Davies
Director, Group Business Team, Alan Doran
Director, Health Protection, International Health and Scientific Development, Dr David Harper, CB
Director, Older People and Disability, Craig Muir
Directors, Regional Public Health, Dr Gina Radford *(East of England);* Prof. Lindsey Davies *(East Midlands);* Dr Sue Atkinson *(London);* Dr Bill Kirkup *(North-East);* Prof. John Ashton, CBE *(North-West);* Dr Mike Gill *(South-East);* Dr Gabriel Scally *(South-West);* Dr Rashmi Shukla *(West Midlands);* Prof. Paul Johnstone *(Yorkshire and Humberside)*
Director, Research and Development, Sally Davies
Deputy Director, Group Business Team, Maggie King
Deputy Director, Delivery, Noreen Caine
Deputy Director, Research Policy Strategy, Russell Hamilton
Division Head, Health Improvement and Prevention, Imogen Sharp
Division Head, Clinical Governance, Ron Cullen
Division Head, Sexual Health and Substance Misuse, Cathy Hamlyn
Division Head, Standards, Investigation, and Healthcare Quality, Jane Moore
Division Heads, Penny Bevan; Nick Boyd; Gerard Hetherington; Liz Woodeson
Branch Heads, Ian Berry; Richard Campbell; Dr Jennie Carpenter; Dr Gillian Chapman; Dr Caroline Davies; Catherine Jones; Gavin Larner; Susan Londsdale; Anne McDonald; Dr Hugh Markowe; Dr William Maton-Howarth; Dr Robert Maynard, CBE; Neil Paterson; Claire Phillips; Dr Mary Piper; Anne Richardson; Wendy Russell; Hilary Samson-Barry; Adrian Sieff; Dr Peter Sneddon; Dr John Stephenson; Jonathan Stopes-Roe; Janet Walden; Dr Hilary Walker; Dr Ailsa Wight; Lindsay Wilkinson; Dr Sandra Williams; Patience Wilson; Dr Louise Wood

STRATEGY AND BUSINESS DEVELOPMENT GROUP
Group Director, Hugh Taylor, CB
Director, Communications, Sian Jarvis
Director, Corporate Management and Development, Hugh Taylor, CB
Director, Equality and Human Rights, Surinder Sharma
Director, Social Care, Kathryn Hudson
Director, Strategy, Stephen O'Brien
Director, User Experience and Involvement/Professional Leadership, Prof. Christine Beasley, CBE
Deputy Chief Nursing Officer, Kate Billingham
Head, Corporate Human Resources, Anne Rainsberry
Head, Customer Services Centre, Linda Percival
Head, Group Business Team, Peter Allanson
Head, Information Services, Beverley Bryant
Head, Medicines, Pharmacy and Industry, Dr Felicity Harvey
Head, Patients and the Public, Harry Cayton
Head, Secretariat, Heather Gwynn, CBE
Head, User Experience and Involvement, Flora Goldhill
Programme Director, Organisation Review, Chris Outram
Chief Economic Adviser, Corporate Analytical Team, Prof. Barry McCormick
Chief Health Professions Officer, Kay East
Chief Pharmaceutical Officer for England, Dr Jim Smith
Chief Scientific Officer, Sue Hill
Deputy Chief Pharmaceutical Officer, Jeanette Howe
Branch Heads, Jim Allwood; Emma Back; Tim Baxter; Caroline Brock; Mike Brownlee; Richard Carter; Judith Dainty; Sharon Davidson; Gill Eastabrook; Melanie Field; Donald Franklin, Marion Purt; Jon Hibbs; Chris Horsey; Andrea Humphrey; Peter Kendall; David Mowat; Barry Mussenden; Keith Nurse; Pip Parr, Lindy Petts; Bill Phillips; Simon Reeve; Wynn Roberts; Geoff Royston; Aileen Simkins; David Stemp; Mark Sudbury; Stephen Warburton; John Weeks; Linda Wishart; Lydia Yee

HEALTH AND SOCIAL CARE SERVICES DELIVERY GROUP
Group Director, John Bacon
Chief Dental Officer, Prof. Raman Bedi
Director, Access, Margaret Edwards
Director, Commercial, Ken Anderson
Director, Counter Fraud and Security Management, Jim Gee
Director, Development, Kate Barnard
Director, Finance and Investment, Richard Douglas
Director, Programmes and Performance, Duncan Selbie
Director, System Reform, Julie Taylor
Director, Workforce, Andrew Foster
National Director, Widening Participation in Learning, Prof. Bob Fryer
Deputy Director, Access Policy Development and Capacity Planning, Bob Ricketts
Deputy Director, Accounting and Governance, Anne-Marie Millar
Deputy Director, Delivery and Programmes, Ivan Ellul
Deputy Directors, Financial System Reforms, Liz Eccles, CBE; Bill McCarthy
Deputy Director, Investment, Peter Coates, CBE
Deputy Director, Model Career Portfolio, Nic Greenfield
Deputy Director, National Leadership Network, Peter Houghton
Deputy Director, NHS and Social Care Finance, Alastair MacLellan
Deputy Director, Planning and Performance Review, Sally Campbell
Deputy Director, Primary Care, Gary Belfield
Deputy Director, Recovery and Support Unit, Richard Gleave
Deputy Director, Secondary Care, Matthew Coats
Deputy Director, Workforce Capacity Portfolio, Rob Webster
Head of Group Business Team, Richard Mundon
Senior Performance Manager, Recovery and Support Unit, Tim Young
Account Managers, Recovery and Support Unit, Nick Chapman; Martin Robson
Deputy Account Managers, Recovery and Support Unit, Ian Dodge; Chris Garrett; Helen Robinson
Branch Heads, Richard Armstrong; Miles Ayling; Patsy Bailey; Martin Campbell; Steve Catling; Keith Derbyshire; Ben Dyson; Mike Evershed; Julie Hall; John Holden; Paul Loveland; Jonathan Marron; Debbie Mellor, OBE; Ian Mills; Stephen Mitchell; Richard Murray; Simon Peck; Jeff Peers; Amanda Phillips; Dean Royles; Keith Smith; Paul Stocks; Mark Svenson; Jeff Tomlinson; Carl Vincent; Stephen Waring; Chris Watson; Giles Wilmore
National Clinical Director of Emergency Access, Prof. Sir George Alberti
National Clinical Director of Patient Experience in Accident and Emergency, Jonathan Asbridge
National Clinical Director of Primary Care, David Colin-Thome, OBE

SOLICITOR'S OFFICE, DEPARTMENT FOR WORK AND PENSIONS
Solicitor, Paul Jenkins
Director of Legal Services, John Catlin

SPECIAL HEALTH AUTHORITIES

COUNTER FRAUD AND SECURITY MANAGEMENT SERVICE
W www.cfsms.nhs.uk

DENTAL PRACTICE BOARD
W www.dpb.nhs.uk

DENTAL VOCATIONAL TRAINING AUTHORITY
W www.dvta.nhs.uk

FAMILY HEALTH SERVICES APPEAL AUTHORITY
W www.fhsaa.nhs.uk

HEALTH PROTECTION AGENCY
W www.hpa.org.uk

MENTAL HEALTH ACT COMMISSION
W www.mhac.org.uk

NATIONAL BLOOD SERVICE
W www.blood.co.uk

NATIONAL CLINICAL ASSESSMENT AUTHORITY
W www.ncaa.nhs.uk

NATIONAL INSTITUTE FOR CLINICAL EXCELLENCE
W www.nice.org.uk

NATIONAL TREATMENT AGENCY FOR SUBSTANCE MISUSE
W www.nta.nhs.uk

NATIONAL PATIENT SAFETY AGENCY
W www.npsa.nhs.uk

NHS APPOINTMENTS COMMISSION
W www.appointments.org.uk

NHS DIRECT
W www.nhsdirect.nhs.uk

NHS LITIGATION AUTHORITY
W www.nhsla.com

NHS LOGISTICS AUTHORITY
W www.logistics.nhs.uk

NHS PENSIONS AGENCY
W www.nhspa.gov.uk

PRESCRIPTION PRICING AUTHORITY
W www.ppa.org.uk

UK TRANSPLANT
W www.uktransplant.org.uk

HOME OFFICE
2 Marsham Street, London SW1P 4DF T 0870-000 1585
W www.homeoffice.gov.uk
The Home Office deals with those internal affairs in England and Wales which have not been assigned to other government departments. The Home Secretary is the link between The Queen and the public and exercises certain powers on her behalf, including that of the royal pardon.

The Home Office's objectives are: to build a safe, just and tolerant society and to maintain and enhance public security and protection; to support and mobilise communities so that they are able to shape policy and improvement for their locality, overcome nuisance and anti-social behaviour, maintain and enhance social cohesion and enjoy their homes and public spaces peacefully; to deliver departmental policies and responsibilities fairly, effectively and efficiently; and to make the best use of resources. These objectives reflect the priorities of the government and the Home Secretary in areas of crime, citizenship and communities, namely: to reduce crime and the fear of crime; to reduce organised and international crime; to combat terrorism and other threats to national security; to ensure the effective delivery of justice; to deliver effective custodial and community sentences; to reduce re-offending and protect the public; to reduce the availability and abuse of dangerous drugs; to regulate entry to, and settlement in, the UK in the interests of sustainable growth and social inclusion; and to support strong, active communities in which people of all races and backgrounds are valued and participate on equal terms.

The Home Office delivers these aims through the prison, probation and immigration services; its agencies and non-departmental public bodies, and by working with partners in private, public and voluntary sectors, individuals and communities. The Home Secretary is also the link between the UK government and the governments of the Channel Islands and the Isle of Man.
Secretary of State for the Home Department, The Rt. Hon. Charles Clarke, MP
Principal Private Secretary, Jonathan Sedgwick
Private Secretaries, Nicola Carnie; Emma Churchill; Kate Hipwell; Abbie Lloyd; Lai Chi Ng; Mark Williams
Special Advisers, Matt Cavanagh; Huw Evans; Katherine Raymond; Matthew Seward
Minister of State, The Rt. Hon. Hazel Blears, MP *(Security, Policing and Community Safety)*
Private Secretary, Debbie Gibson
Minister of State, Tony McNulty, MP *(Citizenship, Immigration and Nationality)*
Private Secretary, Neil Roberts
Minister of State, The Rt. Hon. Baroness Scotland of Asthal, QC *(Criminal Justice and Offender Management)*
Private Secretary, Anna Hodgson
Parliamentary Under-Secretary of State, Andy Burnham, MP *(Anti-Drugs Co-ordination and Organised and International Crime)*
Private Secretary, Simon Peachey
Parliamentary Under-Secretary of State, Paul Goggins, MP *(Correctional Services and Reducing Re-Offending)*
Private Secretary, Hannah Gregory
Parliamentary Under-Secretary of State, Fiona Mactaggart, MP *(Race Equality, Community Policy and Civil Renewal)*
Private Secretary, Jill Wanliss
Permanent Secretary of State, John Gieve
Private Secretary, Roy Middleton
Parliamentary Clerk, Tony Strutt

COMMUNICATION DIRECTORATE
Director, Julia Simpson
Assistant Director and Head of Direct Communications Unit, Geoff Sampher
Customer Communications Manager, Katie Kerr

Deputy Director and Head of News (Press Office), John Toker
Deputy Director and Head of Marketing and Strategic Communications, Anne Nash
Head of Internal Communications Unit, Bill Reay
Head of Information Services Unit, Peter Griffiths

COMMUNITIES GROUP
Director-General, Helen Edwards
Director, Active Community Unit, Jitinder Kohli
Chair, Commission for Racial Equality, Trevor Phillips
Heads of Units, Dr Jon Richmond *(Animal Procedures and Coroners Unit);* Judith Lempriere *(Community Cohesion Unit);* Helen Judge *(Race Equality Unit);* John Curtis and Betty Moxon *(Regions and Renewals Unit);* Katherine Courtney *(Identity Cards Programme Director);* Richard Jenkins *(Service Delivery Workstrand Assistant Director)*

CORPORATE DEVELOPMENT AND SERVICES DIRECTORATE
Director, Charles Everett
Heads of Units, Andrew Hyslop and David Palmer *(Agreement and Service Delivery);* Tony Edwards *(Building and Estate Management);* Nigel Arkle *(Commercial and Procurement Unit);* Tony Fitzpatrick *(Home Office Pay and Pensions Service);* Carol Anderson *(Programme Project Management Support Services);* Peter Lowe *(Information Management Technology Unit)*
President of HO Sports and Social Association, John Gieve

CRIME REDUCTION AND COMMUNITY SAFETY GROUP
Director-General, Mark Neale
Directors, Richard Kornicki *(Organised Crime);* Peter Storr *(International);* Vic Hogg *(Drugs)*
Heads of Units, Judith Lempriere *(Cohesion and Faith Unit);* Vic Hogg *(Communities and Law Enforcement Drugs Unit);* Win Harris *(European and International Unit);* Jim Bradley *(Financial Crime Team);* Paul Regan *(HR Transition Team);* Richard Bradley *(Judicial Co-operation Unit);* Stephen Webb *(Organised and Financial Crime Unit);* Judy Youell *(Strategic Co-ordination and Planning Unit)*

OFFICE FOR CRIMINAL JUSTICE REFORM (OCJR)
Chief Executive, Moira Wallace, OBE
Director-General, Criminal Justice IT (CJIT), John Suffolk
Director, Criminal Case Management, Jane Furniss
Director, Performance and Planning, Jonathan Sedgwick
Director, Confidence, Customers and Communication, vacant
Heads of Units, vacant *(Claims Assessment Team);* Nicola Murray *(acting) (Communications Unit);* Paul Morrison *(Criminal Justice System Race Unit);* Deborah Grice *(Criminal Law Policy Unit);* vacant *(Criminal Procedure and Evidence Unit);* Paul A. David *(Faith and Citizenship);* James Quinault *(Finance and Strategy Unit);* Tim Bianek *(Governance and Planning Unit);* Catherine Lee *(Justice and Enforcement Unit);* Ann-Marie Field *(Local Performance and Delivery Support);* Tyson Hepple *(Programme Management);* Dr Tony Munton *(Research Development and Statistics);* Mark De Paul *(Trial Policy and Procedures Unit);* Joanne Drean *(Victims and Confidence Unit)*
Chair, Youth Justice Board, Sean Larkins

HUMAN RESOURCES DIRECTORATE
Director, John Marsh
Personnel Director, Deborah Louden

Heads of Units, Felicity Clarkson *(Career Development and Assessment Unit);* Nigel Benger *(Corporate Support Services Unit);* David McDonough *(Departmental Security Unit);* Jill Douglas *(HRO Performance and Delivery Team);* Tony Williams *(Human Resources Operations);* Tom Randle *(Policy and Employment Relations Unit)*

IMMIGRATION AND NATIONALITY DIRECTORATE
Director-General, Bill Jeffrey
Senior Directors, Ken Sutton *(Asylum Support, Casework and Appeals);* Mark Tanzer *(Change and Reform Strategy);* David Stephens *(Finance and Services);* Paul Paglian *(Human Resources);* Paula Higson *(Managed Migration);* Brodie Clark *(Operations and Projects);* Nick Baird *(Policy)*
Directors, Joyce Irvine *(Appeals Directorate);* Terry Neale *(Asylum Casework Directorate);* Dave Roberts *(Enforcements and Removals);* Stephen Calvard *(Business Information Systems and Technology Directorate);* Mary Shaw *(Department for Constitutional Affairs Asylum Division);* Peter Topping *(FOI Act);* Brian Pollett *(Detention Services);* Mark Goulding *(e-Border);* Colin Allars *(International Development);* Tony Arber *(Finance);* Christina Parry *(General Group, Managed Migration);* Ros McCool *(Human Resources Services);* Lorraine Rogerson *(Immigration and Nationality Policy Directorate);* Don Ingham *(Immigration Service Major Projects);* Stacy Thornton *(Special Casework Project);* David Wilson *(Intelligence);* Susannah Simon *(European Policy Directorate);* Emma de-la-Haye *(Joint Delivery Programme);* Freda Chaloner *(National Asylum Support Service);* Digby Griffith *(National Asylum Support Service: Accommodation);* Jeremy Oppenheim *(National Asylum Support Service: Casework and Appeals);* Chris Hudson *(Operations Manager, Managed Migration)*

WORK PERMITS UK
Director, Kevin Faulkner
Heads of Units, Neil Hughes *(Customer Relations, Intelligence and Post Issue Checking);* Paula Higson *(Managed Migration);* Steve Lamb *(Operations Manager);* Mick Seals *(Policy, Reviews, Sector Schemes Evaluation)*

LEGAL ADVISERS' BRANCH
Senior Legal Adviser, David Seymour
Deputy Legal Adviser, Clive Osborne
Assistant Legal Advisers, Stephen Braviner-Roman; Harry Carter; Richard Clayton; Rosemary Davies; Andrew Dodsworth; Peter Fish; Nasrin Khan; Robert Messenger; Anne Morris; Kevan Norris

PERFORMANCE AND FINANCE DIRECTORATE
Director, Andrew Wren
Heads of Units, Carl Moynehan *(Accounting and Finance Unit);* Tim Hurdle *(Audit and Assurance Unit);* Alison Barnett *(Performance and Finance Support)*

RESEARCH, DEVELOPMENT AND STATISTICS DIRECTORATE
Director, Mark Greenhorn
Directors, Jon Simmons *(CRCSG);* Mark De Pulford *(Office for Criminal Justice Reform)*
Assistant Directors, David Pyle; Carole F. Willis *(Crime and Policing Group);* Gary Raw *(Immigration and Community Group)*

CENTRAL POLICE TRAINING AND DEVELOPMENT
AUTHORITY (CENTREX)
Chief Executive, Norman Bettison

DEPARTMENT FOR INTERNATIONAL DEVELOPMENT

1 Palace Street, London SW1 5HE **T** 020-7023 0000
F 020-7023 0016 **E** enquiry@dfid.gov.uk **W** www.dfid.gov.uk
Abercrombie House, Eaglesham Road, East Kilbride, Glasgow
G75 8EA **T** 01355-844000 **F** 01355-844099
Public Enquiries 0845-300 4100

The Department for International Development (DFID) is responsible for promoting sustainable development and reducing poverty. The central focus of the government's policy, based on the 1997 and 2000 White Papers on International Development, is a commitment to the internationally agreed Millennium Development Goals, to be achieved by 2015. These seek to: eradicate extreme poverty and hunger; achieve universal primary education; promote gender equality and empower women; reduce child mortality; improve maternal health; combat HIV/AIDS, malaria and other diseases; ensure environmental sustainability; and encourage a global partnership for development.

DFID's assistance is concentrated in the poorest countries of sub-Saharan Africa and Asia, but also contributes to poverty reduction and sustainable development in middle-income countries, including those in Latin America and Eastern Europe. DFID works in partnership with governments committed to the Millennium Development Goals, and with the private sector and the research community. It also works with multilateral institutions, including the World Bank, United Nations agencies, and the European Commission. DFID has headquarters in London and East Kilbride, offices in many developing countries, and staff based in British embassies and high commissions around the world.

Secretary of State for International Development, Hilary Benn, MP
Principal Private Secretary, Moazzam Malik
Private Secretary, Melanie Speight
Special Advisers, Alex Evans; Beatrice Stern
Parliamentary Private Secretaries, Tom Levitt, MP; Dr Ashok Kumar, MP
Parliamentary Clerk, Peter Gordon
Parliamentary Under-Secretary of State, Gareth R. Thomas, MP
Private Secretary, Judith Herbertson
Assistant Private Secretary, Sarah White
House of Lords Spokespeople, Baroness Amos; Lord Triesman
Liaison Peer, Baroness Whitaker
Permanent Secretary, Suma Chakrabarti
Private Secretary, Rebecca Goddard
Director-General, Corporate Performance and Knowledge Sharing, Mark Lowcock
Director-General, Policy and International, Masood Ahmed
Director-General, Regional Programmes, Minouche Shafik
Non-Executive Directors, Helen Ghosh; Bill Griffiths

REGIONAL PROGRAMMES

AFRICA DIVISION
Director, Dave Fish
Director of Africa Policy, Graham Teskey
East and Central Africa, Heads of Departments, David Batt *(Deputy Director);* Desmond Curran *(Africa Great Lakes and Horn)*

East and Central Africa, Heads of Offices, Paul Ackroyd *(Ethiopia);* Simon Bland *(Kenya);* Dr Colin Kirk *(Rwanda);* David Stanton *(Tanzania);* Eric Hawthorne *(Uganda)*
East and Central Africa, Heads of Field Offices, Martin Johnston *(Angola);* Sue Hogwood *(Burundi);* Bronte Flecker *(Democratic Republic of Congo);* David Bell *(Somalia)*
Southern Africa, Head of Department, Anthony Smith *(Deputy Director)*
Southern Africa, Heads of Offices, Roger Wilson *(Malawi);* Eamon Cassidy *(Mozambique);* Beverly Warmington *(Zambia);* John Barrett *(Zimbabwe)*
Southern Africa, Heads of Field Offices, Sue Wardell *(South Africa, SACU, SADC);* Diana Webster *(Lesotho)*
West Africa, Sudan, Conflict and Humanitarian Policy, Head of Department, Marcus Manuel *(Deputy Director)*
West Africa, Heads of Offices, Mike Hammond *(Ghana);* William Kingsmill *(Nigeria)*
West Africa, Heads of Field Offices, Richard Hogg *(Sierra Leone);* Jonathan Lingham *(Sudan)*

ASIA AND PACIFIC DIVISION
Director, Charlotte Seymour Smith
Heads of Departments, Jeremy Clarke *(Asia Directorate);* Pam Jenkins *(Director's Cabinet);* Stephen McCelland *(Strategy and Country Group)*
Heads of Offices, Alistair Fernie *(Afghanistan);* David Wood *(Bangladesh);* Elizabeth Smith *(Cambodia);* Adrian Davis *(China);* Susanna Moorehead *(India);* Sarah Richards *(Indonesia);* Mark Mallalieu *(Nepal);* Yusaf Samiullah *(Pakistan);* Marshall Elliot *(South-East Asia);* Mandeep Kaur-Grewal *(Sri Lanka);* Bela Bird *(Vietnam)*

EUROPE, MIDDLE EAST AND AMERICAS DIVISION
Director, Martin Dinham
Heads of Departments, Brenda Killen *(Europe, Middle East and Americas);* Jessica Irvine *(Europe and Central Asia);* Richard Teuten *(Latin America);* Michael Anderson *(Middle East and North Africa);* Clive Warren *(Overseas Territories)*
Heads of Offices, Sam Bickersteth *(Bolivia);* Miranda Munro *(Brazil);* Joanne Alston *(Caribbean);* Gregory Briffa *(Guyana);* Vic Heard *(Honduras);* Elizabeth Carrire *(Jamaica);* Georgia Taylor *(Nicaragua);* Mark Lewis *(Peru);* Simon Bland *(Russia);* Doug Houston *(Ukraine)*
UK Delegation to the European Bank of Reconstruction and Development, Simon Ray

POLICY AND INTERNATIONAL

POLICY DIVISION
Director, Sharon White
Group Heads, Joanne Alston; Hans-Martin Boehmer; Richard Boulter; Deborah Hermer; Sam Sharpe; Graham Teskey
Heads of Profession, Desmond Bermingham *(Education);* John Burton *(Economics);* Siobhan Carey *(Statistics and Chief Statistician);* Gordon Conway *(Chief Scientist);* Jim Harvey *(Rural Livelihoods; Environment (acting));* Dr Andrew Norton *(Social Development);* Stewart Tyson *(Health);* Tony Venables *(Chief Economist);* Alistair Wray *(Infrastructure and Urban Development)*

INTERNATIONAL DIVISION
Director, Peter Grant
Heads of Departments, Margaret Cund *(International Financial Institutions)*; Nick Dyer *(European Union)*; Dianna Melrose *(International Trade)*; Michael Mosselmans *(Conflict and Humanitarian Affairs)*; Carol Robson *(United Nations and Commonwealth)*
Team Leader, Rachel Turner *(International Division Advisory Team)*
UK Permanent Representative, Anthony Beattie *(FAO)*
UK Permanent Delegate, David Leslie Stanton *(UNESCO)*

CORPORATE PERFORMANCE AND
KNOWLEDGE SHARING

CORPORATE PERFORMANCE AND KNOWLEDGE
SHARING DIVISION
Heads of Departments, Mike Hammond *(Evaluation)*; Gavin McGillivray *(Private Sector Infrastructure/CDC)*; Paul Spray *(Policy Research)*

FINANCE AND CORPORATE PERFORMANCE DIVISION
Director, Richard Calvert
Heads of Departments, Gordon Alexander *(ARIES)*; Stephen Chard *(Programme Guidance and Support)*; Mike Noronha *(Internal Audit)*; Mike Smithson *(Accounts)*; Kevin Sparkhall *(Strategy and Finance)*

HUMAN RESOURCES DIVISION
Director, Liz Davies
Heads of Departments, John Anning *(Human Resources Operations)*; Peter Brough *(Overseas Pensions)*; Ian McKendry *(Human Resources Policy)*

INFORMATION, KNOWLEDGE AND
COMMUNICATIONS DIVISION
Director, Joy Hutcheon
Heads of Departments, David Gillett *(Special Projects)*; Michael Green *(Information and Civil Society)*; Gary James *(Office Services and Security)*; Simon Jones *(Information Systems and Services)*

CDC GROUP PLC

CDC CAPITAL PARTNERS
6 Duke Street, London SW1Y 6BN **T** 020-7484 7700
F 020-7484 7750 **E** info@cdcgroup.com
W www.cdcgroup.com
Founded in 1948, CDC provides finance for the government to invest through third-party fund managers in the private sector in developing economies; it covers countries in Africa, Asia and Latin America. CDC is a public limited company with the Department for International Development as its 100 per cent shareholder.
Chair, Malcolm Williamson
Chief Executive, Richard Laing

OFFICE OF THE LEADER OF THE HOUSE OF COMMONS
2 Carlton Gardens, London SW1Y 5AA **T** 020-7210 1025
W www.commonsleader.gov.uk
The Office of the Leader of the House of Commons is responsible for the arrangement of government business in the House of Commons and for planning and supervising the government's legislative programme. The Leader upholds the rights and privileges of the House and acts as a spokesperson for the government as a whole.

The Leader reports regularly to Cabinet on parliamentary business and the legislative programme. In his capacity as Leader of the House, he is a member of the Public Accounts Commission and of the House of Commons Commission. He also chairs Cabinet Committees on Parliamentary Modernisation and the Legislative Programme. As Lord Privy Seal, he is trustee of the Chevening Estate.
The Deputy Leader of the House of Commons supports the Leader in handling the government's business in the House of Commons. He is responsible for monitoring MPs' and Peers' correspondence and is a member of several Committees, including the Committees on the Legislative Programme, Parliamentary Modernisation, and Local Government Strategy and Performance.
Leader of the House of Commons, The Rt. Hon. Geoff Hoon, MP
Principal Private Secretary, Glynne Jones
Private Secretaries, Stephen Hillcoat; James Newman; Mike Newman
Deputy Leader of the House of Commons, Nigel Griffiths, MP
Private Secretary, Frances Slee

LORD CHANCELLOR'S DEPARTMENT
see Department for Constitutional Affairs

NORTHERN IRELAND OFFICE
11 Millbank, London SW1P 4PN **T** 020-7210 3000
Castle Buildings, Stormont, Belfast BT4 3SG **T** 028-9052 0700
W www.nio.gov.uk
The Northern Ireland Office was established in 1972, when the Northern Ireland (Temporary Provisions) Act transferred the legislative and executive powers of the Northern Ireland Parliament and government to the UK Parliament and a Secretary of State.
The Northern Ireland Office is responsible primarily for security issues, law and order and prisons, and for matters relating to the political and constitutional future of the province. It also deals with international issues as they affect Northern Ireland.
Under the terms of the 1998 Good Friday Agreement, power was devolved to the Northern Ireland Assembly in 1999. The Assembly took on responsibility for the relevant areas of work previously undertaken by the departments of the Northern Ireland Office, covering agriculture and rural development, the environment, regional development, social development, education, higher education, training and employment, enterprise, trade and investment, culture, arts and leisure, health, social services, public safety and finance and personnel. On 14 October 2002 the Northern Ireland Assembly was suspended and Northern Ireland returned to direct rule. For further details, *see* Regional Government section.
Secretary of State for Northern Ireland, The Rt. Hon. Peter Hain, MP
Minister of State, The Rt. Hon. Lord Rooker
Minister of State, David Hanson, MP
Parliamentary Under-Secretaries of State, Angela Smith, MP; Shaun Woodward, MP
Permanent Under-Secretary, Sir Joseph Pilling, KCB
Head of the Northern Ireland Civil Service, Nigel Hamilton

NORTHERN IRELAND INFORMATION SERVICE
Stormont Castle, Stormont Estate, Belfast BT4 3TT
T 028-9052 0700

SCOTLAND OFFICE AND OFFICE OF THE ADVOCATE-GENERAL FOR SCOTLAND

Dover House, Whitehall, London SW1A 2AU T 020-7270 6754
F 020-7270 6812
1 Melville Crescent, Edinburgh EH3 7HW T 0131-244 9010
F 0131-244 9028 E scottish.secretary@scotland.gov.uk
W www.scotlandoffice.gov.uk

The Scotland Office is the department of the Secretary of State for Scotland, who promotes the devolution settlement for Scotland and also represents Scottish interests in the Cabinet on matters reserved to the UK Parliament under the terms of the Scotland Act 1998, i.e. constitutional matters, foreign affairs, defence, international development, the civil service, financial and economic matters, national security, immigration and nationality, misuse of drugs, trade and industry, various aspects of energy regulation and transport, social security, employment, abortion, genetics, surrogacy, medicines, broadcasting and equal opportunities.

The Advocate-General is the legal adviser to the UK government on Scottish law and is supported by staff in the Office of the Advocate-General for Scotland. *See also* Regional Government section and Department for Constitutional Affairs.

Secretary of State for Scotland, The Rt. Hon Alistair Darling, MP
Private Secretary, Chloe Squires
Parliamentary Under-Secretary of State, David Cairns, MP
Private Secretary, Chloe Squires
Parliamentary Private Secretary, Russel Brown, MP
Spokesperson in the House of Lords, Lord Evans of Temple Guiting, CBE
Advocate-General for Scotland, Baroness Clark of Calton, QC
Private Secretary, James Johnston

DEPARTMENT OF TRADE AND INDUSTRY

1 Victoria Street, London SW1H 0ET T 020-7215 5000
F 020-7215 0105 W www.dti.gov.uk

The Department of Trade and Industry (DTI) works with businesses, employees and consumers to increase UK productivity and competitiveness. The department's aim is to make the UK a more prosperous country and close the gap with its international competitors by making it easier and more attractive to start and develop new businesses in the UK. The DTI focuses on innovation, to help more firms to grow and capture new markets, ensuring fair and open markets at home and overseas to support successful UK businesses and the creation of jobs, and better support for scientific excellence It also aims to ensure that the economy is underpinned by secure, sustainable and affordable energy sources.

Secretary of State for Trade and Industry, The Rt. Hon. Alan Johnson, MP
Principal Private Secretary, Matthew Hilton
Private Secretaries, Matthew Bilson; Ian Gibbons; Spencer Mahoney; Louise Proudlove
Parliamentary Private Secretary, Bob Laxton, MP
Minister of State, Ian Pearson, MP *(Trade)*
Private Secretary, Nick Leake
Parliamentary Private Secretary, Lawrie Quinn, MP
Minister of State, Malcolm Wicks, MP *(Energy)*
Private Secretary, Brian Payne
Parliamentary Private Secretary, Eric Joyce, MP

Minister of State, The Rt. Hon. Alun Michael, MP *(Industry and the Regions)*
Private Secretary, Emma Briggs
Parliamentary Private Secretary, Andy Love, MP
Parliamentary Under-Secretary of State, Gerry Sutcliffe, MP *(Employment Relations and Consumer Affairs)*
Private Secretary, Dominic Scullard
Parliamentary Under-Secretary of State, Lord Sainsbury of Turville *(Science and Innovation)*
Private Secretary, Joe Burns
Parliamentary Under-Secretary of State, Barry Gardiner, MP *(Competitiveness)*
Private Secretary, Dr Matthew Clarke
Parliamentary Under-Secretary of State, Megg Munn, MP, *(Women and Equality)*
Private Secretary, Helen Dwyer
Permanent Secretary, Sir Brian Bender, KCB
Private Secretary, Amita Randhawa
Parliamentary Clerk, Tim Williams

STRATEGY AND COMMUNICATIONS UNIT
Directors, John Doherty *(E-Comms)*; Sheree Dodd *(Media Relations)*; Sheila Morris *(Secretariat)*; Margaret Porteus *(Strategic Marketing)*; Neil Feinson *(Strategic Planning)*

STRATEGIC POLICY ANALYSIS UNIT
Chief Economic Adviser and Director-General, Economics, Vicky Pryce
Directors, Ken Warwick *(Deputy Chief Economic Adviser)*; Mark Conaty *(Economic Analysis)*; Brian Titley *(Performance and Evaluation)*; Tim Andrews *(Statistics and Analysis)*

INNOVATION GROUP
Director-General, David Hughes
Deputy Director-General, Rolande Anderson
Directors, Dr Colin Hicks *(Director-General of British National Space Centre)*; Jeff Llewellyn *(Director and Chief Executive of National Weights and Measures Laboratory)*; Ron Marchant *(Chief Executive of Patent Office)*; Patrick McDonald *(Technology Director)*

ENERGY GROUP
Director-General, Joan MacNaughton
Director, Export Control and Non-Proliferation, Rob Wright
Heads of Units, Peter Waller *(Energy Industries and Technologies)*; Claire Durkin *(Energy Markets)*; Jim Campbell *(Energy Resources and Development)*; Paul McIntyre *(Energy Strategy)*

BUSINESS GROUP
Director-General, Mark Gibson
Executive Team, Martin Wyn-Griffith *(Chief Executive of Small Business Service)*; John Alty *(Head of Business Relations 1)*; David Hendon *(Head of Business Relations 2)*; Adam Dawson *(Head of Business Support)*; Stephen Speed *(Head of Regions)*
Directors, Regional Offices, Jonathan Blackie *(North-East)*; Keith Barnes *(North-West)*; Felicity Everiss *(Yorkshire and the Humber)*; Graham Garbutt *(West Midlands)*; Jane Todd *(East Midlands)*; Bronwyn Hill *(South-West)*; Paul Martin *(South-East)*; Liz Meek *(London)*; Caroline Bowdler *(East of England)*

SERVICES GROUP
Director-General, David Evans
Directors, John Reynolds *(Capabilities Manager)*; Claire

Clancy *(Companies House)*; Ian Jones *(Efficiency Directorate)*; Jeanne Spinks *(Employment Tribunals Service)*; Adam Jackson *(Finance and Resource Management)*, Shirley Pointer *(Human Resources and Change Management)*; Yvonne Gallagher *(Information and Workplace Services)*; Desmond Flynn *(Insolvency Service)*

FAIR MARKETS GROUP
Director-General, Edmund Hosker
Directors, John Taylor *(Chief Executive of ACAS)*; Graeme Charles *(Central Arbitration Committee)*; Bernadette Kelly *(Company Law and Governance)*; David Saunders *(Consumer and Competition Policy)*; Janice Munday *(Employment Relations)*; Neil McMillan *(Europe and Better Regulation)*; Chris Dee *(Low Pay Commission)*; Tim Abraham *(Trade Policy)*; Angela Mason *(Women and Equality Unit)*

LEGAL SERVICES GROUP
The Solicitor and Director-General, Anthony Inglese
Director of Legal Resource Management and Legislation, and International Policy Unit, Carl Warren
Director of Legal Services A (Business and Consumers), Mike Thomas
Director of Legal Services B (Employment, Discrimination, Equality and Intellectual Property), Rachel Sandby-Thomas
Director of Legal Services C (Energy, Companies and Insolvency), Scott Milligan
Director of Legal Services D (Enforcement), Deborah Collins

OFFICE OF SCIENCE AND TECHNOLOGY
1 Victoria Street, London SW1H 0ET **W** www.ost.gov.uk
The Office of Science and Technology supports the development of science, engineering and technology in the UK, and aims to maximise their uses to best benefit society and the economy.
Chief Scientific Adviser and Head of Office of Science and Technology, Prof. Sir David King, KB
Director-General, Research Councils, Sir Keith O'Nions
Director, Science and Engineering Base Group, John Neilson
Director, Transdepartmental Science and Technology Group, Jeremy Clayton

UK TRADE AND INVESTMENT
Kingsgate House, 66–74 Victoria Street, London SW1E 6SW
T 020-7215 8000 **W** www.uktradeinvest.gov.uk
UK Trade and Investment is the government organisation that supports both companies in the UK trading internationally and overseas enterprises seeking to locate in the UK. The organisation brings together the work of the DTI and the Foreign and Commonwealth Office.
Chief Executive, Sir Stephen Brown, KCVO
Deputy Chief Executive, Director for Corporate Planning, Susan Haird
Directors, Paul Madden *(International Sectors and e-Transformation)*; Ian Fletcher *(International Trade Development)*; William Pedder *(Inward Investment)*
Directors (Shareholder Executive), Richard Gillingwater *(Chief Executive)*; Mark Higson *(Deputy Chief Executive)*; Mark Russell *(Industrial Development Unit)*; Peter Schofield *(MoD/HMT Shareholdings/Liaison)*; Christina McCombe *(Royal Mail and Postal Service)*

DEPARTMENT FOR TRANSPORT
Great Minster House, 76 Marsham Street, London SW1P 4DR
Ashdown House, 123 Victoria Street, London SW1E 6DE
T 020-7944 8300/4873 **W** www.dft.gov.uk
The Department for Transport was established in May 2002 following the de-merger of the Department of Transport, Local Government and the Regions.
The department's main responsibilities are aviation, freight, health and safety, integrated and local transport, London Underground, maritime, mobility and inclusion, railways, roads and road safety, shipping and vehicles.
Secretary of State for Transport, The Rt. Hon Alistair Darling, MP
Principal Private Secretary, Scott McPherson
Minister of State, Dr Stephen Ladyman, MP
Private Secretary, Jenny Laber
Parliamentary Under-Secretary of State, Derek Twigg, MP
Private Secretary, Dr Adam Simmons
Parliamentary Under-Secretary of State, Karen Buck, MP
Private Secretary, Paul Anderson
Permanent Secretary, David Rowlands
Private Secretary, Rosie Snashall

DRIVER, VEHICLE AND OPERATOR GROUP
Director-General, Stephen Hickey

LEGAL SERVICES DIRECTORATE
Director, Christopher Muttukumaru
Divisional Managers, Martin Bedford *(Employment and Corporate Services)*; Robert Caune *(Railways, Track and Safety)*; Ginny Harrison *(Marine)*; David Ingham *(Secondary Legislation)*; Alan Jones *(Aviation)*; Hussein Kaya *(Highways)*; Julie Murnane *(Road Vehicles)*; Stephen Rock *(Driving and Road Safety)*; Elizabeth Walsh *(Railways, Operations and Construction)*

RAILWAYS, AVIATION, LOGISTICS, MARITIME AND SECURITY GROUP
Director-General, Sue Killen
Directors, Stephen Bligh *(Maritime and Coastguard Agency)*; Vivien Bodnar *(Rail Performance Directorate)*; Mark Lambirth *(Rail Directorate)*; David McMillan *(Aviation Directorate)*; Brian Wadsworth *(Logistics and Maritime Transport Directorate)*
Deputy Director, John Grubb *(Transport Security Division)*
Chief Inspectors, David King *(Air Accidents Investigation Branch)*; Stephen Meyer *(Marine Accidents Investigation Branch)*
Principal Investigator of Rail Accidents, Carolyn Griffiths *(Rail Accidents Investigation Branch)*

ROADS, REGIONAL AND LOCAL TRANSPORT GROUP
Director-General, Robert Devereux
Directors, Steve Gooding *(Roads and Vehicle Directorate)*; Bob Linnard *(Integrated and Local Transport Directorate)*

DELIVERY AND SECURITY GROUP
Director-General, Simon Webb
Directors, Ken Beeton *(Transport Finance Directorate)*; Rod Eddington *(Eddington Transport Study Team)*; Ann Frye *(Mobility and Inclusion Unit)*; Mike Fuhr *(Major Projects Directorate)*; Michael Herron *(Business Delivery Services Directorate)*; Prof. Frank Kelly *(Chief Scientific Adviser)*; Kate Mingay *(Corporate Finance Directorate)*; Jeremy Mooney *(Communication Directorate)*; Niki Thompkinson *(Transport Security and Contingencies Directorate)*; David Thompson *(Analysis and Strategy*

Directorate); Ian Woodman *(Planning and Performance Directorate)*

HM TREASURY

1 Horse Guards Road, London SW1A 2HQ **T** 020-7270 5000
E public.enquiries@hm-treasury.gov.uk
W www.hm-treasury.gov.uk

The Office of the Lord High Treasurer has been continuously in commission for well over 200 years. The Lord High Commissioners of HM Treasury are the First Lord of the Treasury (who is also the prime minister), the Chancellor of the Exchequer and five junior Lords. This Board of Commissioners is assisted at present by the Chief Secretary, the Parliamentary Secretary (who is also the Government Chief Whip in the House of Commons), the Paymaster-General, the Financial Secretary, and the Economic Secretary. The prime minister as First Lord is not primarily concerned with the day-to-day aspects of Treasury business; neither are the Parliamentary Secretary and the Junior Lords as Government Whips. Treasury business is managed by the Chancellor of the Exchequer and the other Treasury Ministers, assisted by the Permanent Secretary.

The Chief Secretary is responsible for expenditure, including: spending reviews and strategic planning; in-year control; public sector pay and pensions; efficiency in public services; capital investment; and public service delivery and Public Service Agreement (PSA) targets. He also has responsibility for the Treasury's interest in devolution, and for financial services – including strategic oversight of banking, financial services and insurance – working in conjunction with the Economic Secretary.

The Paymaster-General has oversight of the UK tax system as a whole – including direct, indirect and corporate taxation, capital gains tax, inheritance tax, and VAT. She is the Departmental Minister for HM Revenue and Customs, and has overall responsibility for the Finance Bill. She is also responsible for European and international tax issues, tax credits, the Treasury's interest in childcare issues, and the welfare reform group.

The Financial Secretary is the Departmental Minister for HM Treasury, and has ministerial responsibility for the Office for National Statistics and the Royal Mint. He is also responsible for enterprise and productivity, competition and better regulation, science policy, regional economic policy, urban regeneration and social exclusion, environmental issues, excise duties and gambling, and public/private partnerships.

The Economic Secretary works with the Chief Secretary on matters relating to financial services. He has responsibility for: personal savings policy; supporting the Chancellor on EU and international finance issues; EMU preparations; the voluntary sector; charities; corporate social responsibility; and foreign exchange reserves and debt management policy (with responsibility for National Savings and Investments, the Debt Management Office and the Government Actuary's Department).

Prime Minister and First Lord of the Treasury, The Rt. Hon. Tony Blair, MP
Chancellor of the Exchequer, The Rt. Hon. Gordon Brown, MP
Principal Private Secretary, James Bowler
Private Secretaries, Jonathan Black; John-Christophe Gray
Parliamentary Private Secretary, Ann Keen, MP
Director of Policy and Planning, Michael Ellam
Special Advisers, Paul Gregg; Michael Jacobs; Spencer Livermore; Damian McBride; Shriti Vadera; Stewart Wood

Chief Secretary to the Treasury, The Rt. Hon. Desmond Browne, MP
Private Secretary, Matthew Style
Parliamentary Private Secretary, Kali Mountford, MP
Special Advisers, Jonathan Ashworth; Cathy Koester
Paymaster-General, The Rt. Hon. Dawn Primarolo, MP
Private Secretary, Kathryn Morgan
Parliamentary Private Secretary, Andrew Reed, MP
Financial Secretary to the Treasury, John Healey, MP
Private Secretary, Sarah Rees
Parliamentary Private Secretary, Mark Tami, MP
Economic Secretary to the Treasury, Ivan Lewis, MP
Private Secretary, Guy Davison
Permanent Secretary to the Treasury, Nick Macpherson
Private Secretary, Ciaran Martin
Parliamentary Secretary to the Treasury and Government Chief Whip, The Rt. Hon. Hilary Armstrong, MP
Private Secretary, Roy Stone
Treasurer of HM Household and Deputy Chief Whip, Bob Ainsworth, MP
Comptroller of HM Household, The Rt. Hon. Thomas McAvoy, MP
Vice-Chamberlain of HM Household, John Heppell, MP
Lords Commissioners of HM Treasury (Whips), Vernon Coaker, MP; Gillian Merron, MP; Joan Ryan, MP; Tom Watson, MP; Dave Watts, MP
Assistant Whips, Kevin Brennan, MP; Alan Campbell, MP; Ian Cawsey, MP; Tony Cunningham, MP; Parmjit Dhanda, MP; Frank Roy, MP; Claire Ward, MP

DIRECTORATES
Head of Ministerial Support Team, James Bowler
Head of Communications and Strategy Team, Paul Kissack

MACROECONOMIC POLICY AND INTERNATIONAL FINANCE
Managing Director, Jon Cunliffe
Directors, Simon Brooks; Melanie Dawes; Sue Owen; Stephen Pickford

BUDGET AND PUBLIC FINANCE
Managing Director, vacant
Directors, Tony Orhnial; Dave Ramsden; Edward Troup; Mike Williams

PUBLIC SERVICES
Managing Director, Jonathan Stephens
Directors, Mridul Brivati; Anita Charlesworth; Paul Johnson; Sarah Mullen; Ray Shostak

MINISTERIAL AND CORPORATE SERVICES
Director of Operations, Tamara Finkelstein

GOVERNMENT FINANCIAL MANAGEMENT
Managing Director, Mary Keegan
Directors, Ian Carruthers; Brian Glicksman; Geoff Russell

FINANCE, REGULATION AND INDUSTRY
Managing Director, James Sassoon
Directors, John Kingman; Clive Maxwell

OTHER BODIES

OFFICE OF GOVERNMENT COMMERCE (OGC)
Trevelyan House, 26–30 Great Peter Street, London SW1P 2BY
T 0845-000 4999 **W** www.ogc.gov.uk
The Office of Government Commerce was set up on 1 April 2000. It is a unique body within government, overseen by a supervisory board of Ministers and officials

from across the departments of government. Its aims are to achieve the best value for money for the government's commercial relationships and to ensure coherence of purchasing activity across 200 government departments, non-governmental bodies and agencies. The OGC is an office of HM Treasury
Chief Executive, John Oughton

TREASURY SOLICITOR'S DEPARTMENT

DEPARTMENT OF HM PROCURATOR-GENERAL AND TREASURY SOLICITOR
1 Kemble Street, London WC2B 4TS T 020-7210 3000
F 020-7210 3004
The Treasury Solicitor's Department, which became an executive agency in 1996, provides legal services for many government departments and is answerable to the Attorney-General. Those departments without their own lawyers are provided with legal advice, and both they and other departments are provided with litigation services. The Treasury Solicitor is also the Queen's Proctor, and is responsible for collecting ownerless goods (*bona vacantia*) on behalf of the Crown.
HM Procurator-General and Treasury Solicitor, Permanent Secretary, Dame Juliet Wheldon, DCB, QC

BONA VACANTIA DIVISION
Head of Division, Valerie Cain

CABINET OFFICE AND CENTRAL ADVISORY DIVISION
Head of Division, Rosemary Jeffreys

DEPARTMENT OF CULTURE, MEDIA AND SPORT DIVISION
Legal Adviser, Isabel Letwin

DEPARTMENT FOR EDUCATION AND SKILLS DIVISION
Legal Adviser, David Noble

DIRECTORATE OF CORPORATE STRATEGY
Director, Hilary Jackson

EMPLOYMENT AND COMMERCIAL CONTRACTS DIVISION
Head of Division, Simon Harker

EUROPEAN DIVISION
Head of Division, Frances Nash

HM TREASURY ADVISORY DIVISION
Legal Adviser, Stephen Parker

LITIGATION DIVISION
Head of Division, David Pearson

WALES OFFICE
Gwydyr House, Whitehall, London SW1A 2ER T 020-7270 0549
F 020-7270 0568 E walesoffice@walesoffice.gsi.gov.uk
W www.walesoffice.gov.uk
The Wales Office is the department of the Secretary of State for Wales, who represents Welsh interests in the Cabinet. *See* also Regional Government section and Department for Constitutional Affairs.
Secretary of State for Wales, The Rt. Hon. Peter Hain, MP
Principal Private Secretary, Glynne Jones
Parliamentary Private Secretary, Chris Ruane, MP
Parliamentary Under-Secretary, Nick Ainger, MP
Head of Office, Alan Cogbill

DEPARTMENT FOR WORK AND PENSIONS
Richmond House, 79 Whitehall, London SW1A 2NS
T 020-7238 0800 F 020-7238 0763
E ministers@dwp.gsi.gov.uk W www.dwp.gov.uk
The Department for Work and Pensions was formed on 8 June 2001 from parts of the former Department of Social Security, the Department for Education and Employment and the Employment Service. The department helps unemployed people of working age into work, helps employers to fill their vacancies and provides financial support to people unable to help themselves, through back-to-work programmes. The department also administers the child support system, social security benefits and the social fund. In addition, the department has reciprocal social security arrangements with other countries.
In April 2002 the Benefits Agency and the Employment Service were replaced by the Jobcentre Plus network (responsible for helping people to find jobs and paying benefits to people of working age), and the Pension Service which administers the Benefits Agency's pension-related services.
Secretary of State for Work and Pensions, The Rt. Hon. David Blunkett, MP
Principal Private Secretary, Susan Park
Private Secretaries, Matt Adams; Barry Cassels; Robin Gordon-Farleigh; Georgina Hill
Special Advisers, Matthew Doyle; Katherine Raymond; Sue Regan; Anne Turley
Parliamentary Private Secretary, Laura Moffat, MP
Minister of State, The Rt. Hon. Margaret Hodge, MP *(Employment and Welfare Reform)*
Parliamentary Private Secretary, Eric Joyce, MP
Private Secretary, Paul Fisher
Minister of State, Stephen Timms, MP *(Pensions Reform)*
Private Secretary, Paul Todd
Assistant Private Secretary, Helen Hutchings; Naeem Rahman
Parliamentary Under-Secretary of State (Commons), James Plaskitt, MP
Private Secretary, Helen Daniels
Parliamentary Under-Secretary of State (Lords), Lord Hunt of Kings Heath, OBE
Private Secretary, Sarah Thompson
Parliamentary Under-Secretary of State, Anne McGuire, MP *(Disabled People)*
Private Secretary, Laura Timms
Assistant Private Secretaries, Kerry Smith; Paul Warren
Permanent Secretary, Sir Richard Mottram, KCB
Private Secretary, Judith Tunstall
Parliamentary Clerk, Tim Elms

WORK, WELFARE AND EQUALITY GROUP
Group Director, Adam Sharples
Director, Fraud, Planning and Presentation Strategy, R. Clark
Director, National Employment Panel, Ms C. Stratton
Director, Work and Welfare Strategy, M. Richardson
Divisional Manager, Family Poverty and Employment Division, Julia Sweeney

DISABILITY AND CARERS DIRECTORATE
Chief Executive, Disability and Carers Service, Terry Moran
Director, Disability and Carers, Bruce Calderwood
Director, Strategic Analysis, Robert Laslett
Director, Presentation and External Relations, Liz Tillett

Director, Joint International Unit, C. Tucker
Director, Pensions Client Directorate, Phil Wynn Owen
Director, Pensions Stewardship Division, Richard d'Souza
Director, State/Private Pension Reform, Charles Ramsden
Director, Private Pensions Programme, Ms Hilary Reynolds
Divisional Manager, Financial Assistance Scheme,
  Christopher Evans
Divisional Manager, Pensions Strategy, Chris Capella
Head of Division, Private Pensions, Pension Protection Team,
  Charlie Massey

CORPORATE AND SHARED SERVICES GROUP
FINANCE
Group Director and Principal Finance Officer, J. Codling
Director, Commercial, D. Smith
Director, Corporate Management Information, Sue Rice
Director, Financial Management, M. Davison
Director, Financial Services, P. Robinson
Director, Internal Assurance Services, C. Turner

PROGRAMME AND SYSTEMS DELIVERY GROUP
Group Director, Joe Harley
Head, Programme and Systems Delivery, Stephen Holt
Director, External Supply, John Priest
Director, Planning and Finance Strategy, Keith Palmer

HUMAN RESOURCES GROUP
Group Director, Kevin White
Diversity Director, Debbie Heigh
Head of Department, HR Services, G. Adey
Head of Department, Occupational Psychology, Dr M.
  Dalgliesh
Head of Department, Senior Civil Service, Doug Watkins
Head of Department, Training Services, Mick Holbrook
Head of Department, Workforce Planning, Clarissa
  Poulson

MEDICAL POLICY AND CORPORATE MEDICAL
GROUP
Chief Medical Adviser and Medical Director, Dr Bill
  Gunnyeon
Contractorisation of Medical Services (IMPACT) Project,
  Dr M. Henderson
EU of Medical Advisers in Social Security (UEMASS), Dr P.
  Stidolph
Policy Manager, Disability and Carer Benefits, Dr R.
  Thomas
Policy Manager, State Incapacity Benefits, Dr P. Sawney

LAW AND SPECIAL POLICY GROUP
Head of Group, Paul Jenkins
Director of Legal Services, J. Catlin
Assistant Director, Commercial Branch, R. Powell
Assistant Director, SOL Litigation, Ms A. James
Assistant Director, SOL Prosecutions, Amanda
  de Blaquiere

INFORMATION AND ANALYSIS DIRECTORATE
Director, David Frazer
Director, Work, Welfare and Poverty, Michael Richardson
Policy Manager, Adjudicational and Constitutional Reform, J.
  Griffiths
Policy Manager, Welfare to Work Strategy, Jonathan Portes

COMMUNICATIONS DIRECTORATE
Group Director, Simon MacDowall
Head of Corporate Communications, Ken Young
Head of Marketing, Steve O'Neill
Head of Media Relations and News, Lindsey French

EXECUTIVE AGENCIES

CABINET OFFICE

GOVERNMENT CAR AND DESPATCH AGENCY
46 Ponton Road, London SW8 5AX
T 020-7217 3839 F 020-7217 3840
The agency provides secure transport and mail
distribution to government and the public sector.
Chief Executive, Roy Burke

COI COMMUNICATIONS
Hercules Road, London SE1 7DU
T 020-7928 2345 F 020-7928 5037
COI (the Central Office of Information) is a government
agency which offers consultancy, procurement and project
management services to central government.
Administrative responsibility for the COI rests with the
Minister for the Cabinet Office.
Chief Executive, A. Bishop
Deputy Chief Executive, P. Buchanan
Senior Personal Secretary, Mrs I. MacMull

MANAGEMENT BOARD
Members, G. Beasant; I. Hamilton; Ms E. Lochhead; A.
  Wade; Mrs S. Whetton

OFFICE OF THE DEPUTY PRIME MINISTER

FIRE SERVICE COLLEGE
Moreton-in-Marsh, Gloucestershire GL56 0RH T 01608-650831
F 01608-651788 W www.fireservicecollege.ac.uk
The Fire Service College provides unique facilities for
both practical and theoretical fire fighting, fire safety and
accident and emergency training, including urban search
and rescue and community safety.
Chief Executive, Gill Newton

ORDNANCE SURVEY
Romsey Road, Southampton SO16 4GU T 08456-050505
F 023-8079 2615 W www.ordnancesurvey.co.uk
The Ordnance Survey department carries out official
surveying and definitive mapping of Great Britain.
Chief Executive, V. Lawrence

PLANNING INSPECTORATE
Temple Quay House, 2 The Square, Temple Quay, Bristol
BS1 6PN T 0117-372 6372
Crown Buildings, Cathays Park, Cardiff CF10 3NQ
T 029-2082 3866 F 029-2082 5150
W www.planning-inspectorate.gov.uk

The issues the Inspectorate deals with include: appeals
against the decisions of local authorities on planning
applications; appeals against local authority enforcement
notices; listed building consent appeals; advertisement
appeals; rights of way cases; and cases arising from the
Environmental Protection and Water Acts, and the
Transport and Works Act.
Chief Executive, Katrine Sporle

THE QUEEN ELIZABETH II CONFERENCE CENTRE
Broad Sanctuary, London SW1P 3EE T 020-7222 5000
F 020-7798 4200 W www.qeiicc.co.u
The Centre provides secure conference facilities for
national and international government and private sector
use.
Chief Executive, Ernest Vincent

DEPARTMENT OF CONSTITUTIONAL AFFAIRS

HER MAJESTY'S COURTS SERVICE
see Law Courts and Offices section

HM LAND REGISTRY
see Public Offices section

NATIONAL ARCHIVES
see Public Offices section

NORTHERN IRELAND COURT SERVICE
Windsor House, Bedford Street, Belfast BT2 7LT
T 028-9032 8594

DEPARTMENT FOR CULTURE, MEDIA AND SPORT

ROYAL PARKS AGENCY
The Old Police House, Hyde Park, London W2 2UH
T 020-7298 2000 F 020-7298 2005
E hq@royalparks.gsi.gov.uk W www.royalparks.gov.uk
The agency is responsible for maintaining and developing over 2,000 hectares (5,000 acres) of urban parkland contained within the eight royal parks in London, which are: Bushy Park (with the Longford River); Green Park; Greenwich Park; Hyde Park; Kensington Gardens; Regent's Park (with Primrose Hill); Richmond Park; and St James's Park.
Chief Executive, Mark Camley

DEPARTMENT FOR ENVIRONMENT, FOOD AND RURAL AFFAIRS

CENTRE FOR ENVIRONMENT, FISHERIES AND AQUACULTURE SCIENCE (CEFAS)
Pakefield Road, Lowestoft, Suffolk NR33 0HT T 01502-562244
F 01502-513865 W www.cefas.co.uk
The agency, established in April 1997, provides research and consultancy services in fisheries science and management, aquaculture, fish health and hygiene, environmental impact assessment, and environmental quality assessment.
Chief Executive, Mark Farrar, FCA

CENTRAL SCIENCE LABORATORY (CSL)
Sand Hutton, York YO41 1LZ T 01904-462000
F 01904-462111 E science@csl.gov.uk W www.csl.gov.uk
The Central Science Laboratory (CSL) specialises in the sciences underpinning agriculture for sustainable crop production; environmental management and conservation; and food safety and quality. As a result of research carried out, CSL provides a wide range of analytical, diagnostic and consultancy services to organisations in both the public and private sectors, designed to support the international land-based and food industries.
Chief Executive, Prof. Michael Roberts

PESTICIDES SAFETY DIRECTORATE
Mallard House, Kings Pool, 3 Peasholme Green, York YO1 7PX
T 01904-640500 F 01904-455733
E information@psd.defra.gsi.gov.uk W www.pesticides.gov.uk
The Pesticides Safety Directorate is responsible for the evaluation and approval of agricultural pesticides and the development of policies relating to them, in order to protect consumers, users and the environment.
Chief Executive, Dr H. K. Wilson
Director, Approvals, R. Davis
Director, Finance, IT and Corporate Services, Ms K. Dyson
Director, Policy, Dr S. Popple

RURAL PAYMENTS AGENCY
see Public Offices section

STATE VETERINARY SERVICE
Corporate Centre, Spur 11, Block C, Government Buildings, Whittington Road, Worcester WR5 2LQ
T 01905-768862/768865 F 01905-768851
W www.svs.gov.uk
The State Veterinary Service (SVS) was established as an executive agency on 1 April 2005. It is the government's delivery agent for animal health and welfare in England, Scotland and Wales, and is responsible for the prevention, detection and management of diseases in livestock. The SVS's main responsibilities include import and export certification, animal by-products and catering waste, and emergency preparedness.
Chief Executive, Glenys Stacey

VETERINARY LABORATORIES AGENCY
Woodham Lane, New Haw, Addlestone, Surrey KT15 3NB
T 01932-341111 F 01932-347046
E enquiries@vla.defra.gov.uk W www.vla.gov.uk
The Veterinary Laboratories Agency safeguards public and animal health through veterinary research and surveillance of farmed livestock and wildlife.
Chief Executive, Prof. S. Edwards
Director of Finance, C. Morrey
Director of Research (acting), Prof. C. J. Thorns
Director of Science Strategy, Prof. J. A. Morris
Director of Surveillance and Laboratory Services, R. D. Hancock

VETERINARY MEDICINES DIRECTORATE
Woodham Lane, New Haw, Addlestone, Surrey KT15 3LS
T 01932-336911 F 01932-336618 W www.vmd.gov.uk
The Veterinary Medicines Directorate is responsible for all aspects of the authorisation and control of veterinary medicines, including post-authorisation surveillance of residues in animals and animal products, and also for the provision of policy advice to ministers.
Chief Executive, Steve Dean
Director, Corporate Business, Chris Bean
Director, Licensing, John O'Brien
Director, Policy, John Fitzgerald

FOREIGN AND COMMONWEALTH OFFICE

CORPS OF QUEEN'S MESSENGERS
Support Group, Foreign and Commonwealth Office, London SW1A 2AH T 020-7008 2779
Superintendent of the Corps of Queen's Messengers, A. C. Brown
Queen's Messengers, S. J. Addy; P. Allen; R. Allen; Maj. J. E. A. Andre; Maj. A. N. D. Bols; Lt.-Col. R. I. S. Burgess; Maj. P. C. H. Dening-Smitherman; Sqn. Ldr. J. S. Frizzell; J. A. Hatfield; Sqn Ldr P. J. Hearn; Sqn Ldr A. Hill; W. Lisle; R. Long; Maj. K. J. Rowbottom; Maj. M. R. Senior; Maj. J. H. Steele

WILTON PARK CONFERENCE CENTRE
Wiston House, Steyning, W. Sussex BN44 3DZ T 01903-815020
F 01903-816373
Wilton Park organises international affairs conferences and is hired out to government departments and commercial users.
Chief Executive, Colin Jennings

DEPARTMENT OF HEALTH

MEDICINES AND HEALTHCARE PRODUCTS REGULATORY AGENCY (MHRA)
Market Towers, 1 Nine Elms Lane, London SW8 5NQ
T 020-7084 2000 F 020-7084 2353 E info@mhra.gsi.gov.uk
W www.mhra.gov.uk
The MHRA is responsible for protecting and promoting public and patient safety by ensuring that medicines, healthcare products and medical equipment meet appropriate standards of safety, quality, performance and effectiveness, and are used safely.
Chair, Prof. Alasdair Breckenridge
Chief Executive, Prof. Kent Woods

NHS PURCHASING AND SUPPLY AGENCY
Premier House, 60 Caversham Road, Reading RG1 7EB
T 0118-980 8600 F 0118-980 8650 E pasa@pasa.nhs.uk
W www.pasa.nhs.uk
The agency is responsible for ensuring that the NHS makes the most effective use of its resources by getting the best value for money possible when purchasing goods and services. It works with around 400 NHS trusts and health authorities, and manages in the region of 3,000 national purchasing contracts.
Chief Executive, Duncan Eaton

HOME OFFICE

UK PASSPORT SERVICE
Globe House, 89 Ecclestone Square, London SW1V 1PN
Advice Line 0870-521 0410
Chief Executive, Christine Nickles

CRIMINAL RECORDS BUREAU
Shannon Court, 10 Princes Parade, Princes Dock, Liverpool
L2 1QY T 0870-909 0811
Chief Executive, Vincent Gaskill

FORENSIC SCIENCE SERVICE
Corporate and Policy Office, 2920 Solihull Parkway, Trident Court, Birmingham Business Park, Birmingham B37 7YN
T 0121-329 5200
Chief Executive, David Werrett

HM PRISON SERVICE
Cleland House, Page Street, London SW1P 4LN
Director-General, Phil Wheatley

PAROLE BOARD FOR ENGLAND AND WALES
see Prison Service section

PRISONS AND PROBATIONS OMBUDSMAN FOR ENGLAND AND WALES
see Prison Service section

NORTHERN IRELAND OFFICE

COMPENSATION AGENCY
Royston House, Upper Queen Street, Belfast BT1 6FD
T 028-9024 9944

FORENSIC SCIENCE NORTHERN IRELAND
Seapark, 151 Belfast Road, Carrickfergus, Co. Antrim BT38 8PL
T 028-9036 5744

YOUTH JUSTICE AGENCY
Corporate Headquarters, 4143 Waring Street, Belfast BT1 2DY
T 028-9031 6 400

NORTHERN IRELAND PRISON SERVICE
Dundonald House, Upper Newtownards Road, Belfast BT4 3SU
T 028-9052 5065

DEPARTMENT OF TRADE AND INDUSTRY

COMPANIES HOUSE
Crown Way, Cardiff CF14 3UZ T 0870-333 3636
F 029-2038 0900
London Information Centre, 21 Bloomsbury Street, London
WC1B 3XD T 0870-333 3636 F 029-2038 0517
Edinburgh Information Centre, 37 Castle Terrace, Edinburgh
EH1 2EB T 0870-333 3636 F 0131-535 5820
E enquiries@companieshouse.gov.uk
W www.companieshouse.gov.uk
Companies House incorporates companies, registers company documents and provides company information.
Registrar of Companies for England and Wales, Claire Clancy
Registrar of Companies for Scotland, Jim Henderson

EMPLOYMENT TRIBUNALS SERVICE
19–29 Woburn Place, London WC1H 0LU T 0845-795 9775
F 020-7273 8670
The Service became an executive agency in 1997 and brought together the administrative support for the employment tribunals and the Employment Appeal Tribunal.
Chief Executive, Jeanne Spinks

THE INSOLVENCY SERVICE
PO Box 203, 21 Bloomsbury Street, London WC1B 3QW
T 020-7637 1110 F 020-7636 4709
Insolvency Enquiry Line 020-7291 6895
Redundancy Enquiry Line 0845-145 0004
W www.insolvency.gov.uk
The role of the Service includes: administration and investigation of the affairs of bankrupts, partners and companies in compulsory liquidation; dealing with the disqualification of directors in all corporate failures authorising and regulating the insolvency profession providing banking and investment services for bankruptcy and liquidation estate funds; assessing and paying statutory entitlement to redundancy payments when an employer cannot, or will not, pay its employees and advising ministers on insolvency, redundancy and related issues.
Inspector-General and Chief Executive, Desmond Flynn
Deputy Inspectors-General, L. T. Cramp; G. Hornee

NATIONAL WEIGHTS AND MEASURES LABORATORY
Stanton Avenue, Teddington, Middx TW11 0JZ
T 020-8943 7272 F 020-8943 7270 E info@nwml.dti.gov.uk
W www.nwml.gov.uk

The Laboratory administers weights and measures legislation, carries out type examination, calibration and testing, and runs courses on legal metrology.
Chief Executive, Dr Jeff Llewellyn

PATENT OFFICE
see Intellectual Property section

DEPARTMENT FOR TRANSPORT

DRIVER AND VEHICLE LICENSING AGENCY (DVLA)
Longview Road, Swansea SA6 7JL T 01792-782341
F 0870-850 1285 E press.dvla@gtnet.gov.uk
W www.dvla.gov.uk
The agency is responsible for registering and licensing drivers and vehicles, and the collection and enforcement of vehicle excise duty. The DVLA also maintains records of all those who are entitled to drive various types of vehicle (currently 39 million people), all vehicles entitled to travel on public roads (currently 32 million), and drivers' endorsements, disqualifications and medical conditions.
Chief Executive, Clive Bennett

DRIVING STANDARDS AGENCY
Stanley House, 56 Talbot Street, Nottingham NG1 5GU
T 0115-901 2500 F 0115-901 2510 W www.dsa.gov.uk
The agency is responsible for carrying out theory and practical driving tests for car drivers, motorcyclists, bus and lorry drivers, and for maintaining the registers of approved driving instructors and large goods vehicle instructors. It also supervises Compulsory Basic Training (CBT) for learner motorcyclists. There are five area offices, which manage over 400 practical driving test centres across Britain.
Chief Executive, Gary Austin

HIGHWAYS AGENCY
123 Buckingham Palace Road, London SW1W 9HA
T 0845-955 6575 W www.highways.gov.uk
The agency is responsible for delivering the Department for Transport's road programme and for maintaining the 7,754 km (4,818 miles) of motorways and trunk roads in England.
Chief Executive, Archie Robertson

MARITIME AND COASTGUARD AGENCY
Spring Place, 105 Commercial Road, Southampton SO15 1EG
T 023-8032 9100 F 023-8032 9298 W www.mcga.gov.uk
The agency's aims are to prevent loss of life, continuously improve maritime safety and protect the marine environment.
Chief Executive, Capt. Stephen Bligh
Chief Coastguard, J. Astbury

VEHICLE CERTIFICATION AGENCY
Eastgate Office Centre, Eastgate Road, Bristol BS5 6XX
T 0117-952 4235 F 0117-952 4104 E enquiries@vca.gov.uk
W www.vca.gov.uk
The agency is the UK authority responsible for ensuring that vehicles and vehicle parts have been designed and constructed to meet internationally agreed standards of safety and environmental protection.
Chief Executive, P. Markwick

VEHICLE AND OPERATOR SERVICES AGENCY
Berkeley House, Croydon Street, Bristol BS5 0DA
T 0117-954 3200 F 0117 954 3212 E enquiries@vosa.gov.uk
W www.vosa.gov.uk
The Vehicle and Operator Services Agency was formed on 1 April 2003 from the merger of the Vehicle Inspectorate and the Traffic Area Network. The agency is responsible for: processing applications for licences to operate heavy goods and public service vehicles; registering bus services; operating and administering testing schemes for all vehicles, including statutory annual testing of commercial vehicles, single vehicle approval of imported vehicles and vehicle identity checks; supervision of the MOT scheme; enforcement checks of vehicle safety, drivers' hours and emissions levels; supporting the independent Traffic Commissioners in carrying out their responsibilities for operator licensing, vocational drivers and bus registration; providing training and advice for commercial operators and MOT testers; and investigating vehicle accidents, defects and recalls.
Chief Executive, Stephen J. Tetlow

HM TREASURY

NATIONAL SAVINGS AND INVESTMENTS
see Finance section

OFFICE FOR NATIONAL STATISTICS
see Public Offices section

OGC BUYING SOLUTIONS
Royal Liver Building, Pier Head, Liverpool L3 1PE
T 0870-268 2222 F 0151-227 3315
W www.ogcbuyingsolutions.gov.uk
The agency provides a professional purchasing service to government departments and other public bodies. From April 2000 it became part of the Office of Government Commerce reporting to the Chief Secretary to the Treasury.
Chief Executive, Hugh Barrett

ROYAL MINT
see Public Offices section

UK DEBT MANAGEMENT OFFICE
Eastcheap Court, 11 Philpot Lane, London EC3M 8UD
T 020-7862 6500 F 020-7862 6509 W www.dmo.gov.uk
The UK Debt Management Office (DMO) was launched as an executive agency of HM Treasury in April 1998. The office has two main functions: it carries out the government's debt management policy (by minimising financing costs over the long term); and it is the government's cash manager, balancing the Exchequer's cash flow on a daily basis through the issue of Treasury Bills, buying and selling securities in the money markets, and securing cost-effective short-term asset or liability management. On 1 July 2002 the operations of the Public Works Loan Board (PWLB) and the Commissioners for the Reduction of the National Debt (CRND) were integrated with the DMO.
Chief Executive, Robert Stheeman

DEPARTMENT FOR WORK AND PENSIONS

APPEALS SERVICE AGENCY
see Tribunals section

CHILD SUPPORT AGENCY
PO Box 55, Brierly Hill, West Midlands DY5 1YL CSA
Helpline 08457-133133 W www.csa.gov.uk
The agency was set up in April 1993. It is responsible for the administration of the Child Support Act and for the assessment, collection and enforcement of maintenance payments for all new cases.
Chief Executive, Stephen Geraghty
Non-Executive Directors, John Cross; Mary Hay; Barney McGahan; Barbara Moorhouse
Deputy Chief Executive and Director of Business Development, Mike Isaac
Directors, Ron Eagle; Jim Edgar; Elaine Fox; Mark Grimshaw; Shirley Trundle, CBE

DISABILITY AND CARERS SERVICE
Room 8208, Northfylde Central Offices, Norcross, Blackpool, Lancs FY5 3TA T 01253-333112 W www.dwp.gov.uk
The Disability and Carers Service (DCS) aims to enable the independence of disabled people and carers through the financial support available from the Disability Living Allowance, Attendance Allowance and Carer's Allowance. The DCS also deliver payments to those who have become disabled as a result of vaccine damage. Currently the service provides in excess of £13 billion per year to over 4 million disabled people and carers.
Chief Executive, Terry Moran
Chief Operating Officer, Vivien Hopkins

JOBCENTRE PLUS
Level 6b, Caxton House, Tothill Street, London SW1H 9NA
T 020-7273 6102 F 020-7273 6099
W www.jobcentreplus.gov.uk
Jobcentre Plus was formed in April 2002 following the merger of the Employment Service and some parts of the Benefits Agency. The agency administers claims for, and payment of, social security benefits to help people gain employment or improve their prospects for work, as well as helping employers to fill their vacancies. Jobcentre Plus currently pays more than £100 million per day in working-age benefits.
Chief Executive (acting), Lesley Strathie

THE PENSION SERVICE
Trevelyan House, 30 Great Peter Street, London SW1P 2BY
T 0207-271 2601 Public Enquiries 0845-606 0265
W www.thepensionservice.gov.uk
The Pension Service was launched in April 2002 as an organisation dedicated to understanding the wishes and needs of today's and future pensioners, and providing State financial support for pensioners.
Chief Executive, Alexis Cleveland

THE RENT SERVICE
5 Welbeck Street, London W1G 9YQ T 020-7023 6000
F 020-7023 6222 W www.therentservice.gov.uk
The agency combines 77 independent units previously administered by local authorities.
Chief Executive, Ms C. Copeland

VETERANS AGENCY
Norcross, Blackpool, Lancs FY5 3WP T 0800-169 2277
E help@veteransagency.gsi.gov.uk
W www.veteransagency.mod.uk
The Veterans Agency provides information and advice on issues of concern to veterans and their families. The agency also administers the War Pension Scheme and the Armed Forces Compensation Scheme, and provide welfare support to war pensioners and war widow(er)s. It is also responsible for the management of the Ilford Park Polish Home.
Chief Executive, A. Burnham

PUBLIC OFFICES

ADJUDICATOR'S OFFICE

Haymarket House, 28 Haymarket, London SW1Y 4SP
T 020-7930 2292 E adjudicators@gtnet.gov.uk
W www.adjudicatorsoffice.gov.uk

The Adjudicator's Office opened in 1993 and investigates complaints about the way HM Revenue and Customs, the Valuation Office Agency, the Public Guardianship Office and the Insolvency Service have handled a person's affairs.
The Adjudicator, Dame Barbara Mills, DBE, QC
Head of Office, Simon Oakes

ADVISORY, CONCILIATION AND ARBITRATION SERVICE

Brandon House, 180 Borough High Street, London SE1 1LW
T 020-7210 3613 F 020-7210 3708
W www.acas.org.uk

The Advisory, Conciliation and Arbitration Service (ACAS) was set up under the Employment Protection Act 1975 (the provisions now being found in the Trade Union and Labour Relations (Consolidation) Act 1992).

ACAS is directed by a Council consisting of a full-time chair and part-time employer, trade union and independent members, all appointed by the Secretary of State for Trade and Industry. The functions of the Service are to promote the improvement of industrial relations in general, to provide facilities for conciliation, mediation and arbitration as means of avoiding and resolving industrial disputes, and to provide advisory and information services on industrial relations matters to employers, employees and their representatives.

ACAS has regional offices in Birmingham, Bury St Edmonds, Bristol, Cardiff, Fleet, Glasgow, Kent, Leeds, Liverpool, London, Manchester, Newcastle upon Tyne and Nottingham.
Chair, R. Donaghy, OBE
Chief Executive, J. Taylor

ADVISORY COUNCIL ON NATIONAL RECORDS AND ARCHIVES

Secretariat: The National Archives, Kew, Surrey TW9 4DU
020-8392 5381 F 020-8392 5286

Following the bringing together of the Public Record Office and the Historical Manuscripts Commission to form the National Archives, the Advisory Council advises on all matters relating to the preservation, use of, and access to historical manuscripts, records and archives of all kinds. The new Advisory Council on National Records and Archives encompasses the statutory Advisory Council on Public Records, and advises on public records issues as before.
Chair, The Rt. Hon. Lord Phillips, Master of the Rolls
Secretary, T. R. Padfield

ANCIENT MONUMENTS BOARD FOR WALES (CADW)

Plas Carew, Unit 5–7 Cefn Coed, Parc Nantgarw, Cardiff CF15 7QQ
T 01443-336000 F 01443-336001
E cadw@wales.gsi.gov.uk
W www.cadw.wales.gov.uk

The Ancient Monuments Board for Wales advises the Welsh Assembly Government on its statutory functions in respect of ancient monuments and historic buildings.
Chair, Richard Brewer
Members, Prof. Miranda Aldhouse-Green, FSA; Dr Nancy Edwards; Prof. Ralph Griffiths, DLITT; John Hilling; Christopher Musson, MBE, FSA; Dr Emma Plunkett Dillon; Dr Anthony Ward; Prof. Alasdair Whittle, FBA, DPHIL

ARCHITECTURE AND DESIGN SCOTLAND

Bakehouse Close, 146 Canongate, Edinburgh EH8 8DD
T 0131-556 6699 F 0131-556 6633
E info@ads.org.uk W www.ads.org.uk

Architecture and Design Scotland (ADS) was established in 2005 by the Scottish Executive as the national champion for good architecture, design and planning in the built environment. ADS also assumed the independent design review and advisory role of the Royal Fine Art Commission for Scotland.
Chair, Raymond Young
Deputy Chairs, Prof. Brian Evans; Malcolm Fraser
Chief Executive, Sebastian Tombs

ARMED FORCES' PAY REVIEW BODY

8th Floor, Oxford House, 76 Oxford Street, London W1D 1BS
T 020-7467 7244 W www.ome.uk.com

The Armed Forces' Pay Review Body was appointed in 1971. It advises the prime minister and government on the pay and allowances of members of naval, military and air forces of the Crown.
Chair, Prof. David Greenaway
Members, Robert Burgin; Alison Gallico; Dr Peter Knight; Prof. Derek Leslie; Prof. Lord Patel of Dunkeld; Neil Sherlock; Air Vice-Marshall (retd) Ian Stewart, CB; Dr Anne Wright

ARTS COUNCIL ENGLAND

14 Great Peter Street, London SW1P 3NQ
T 0845-300 6200
E enquiries@artscouncil.org.uk
W www.artscouncil.org.uk

Arts Council England is the national development agency for the arts in England, distributing public money from government and the National Lottery. Between 2003 and 2006 Arts Council England invested £2 billion of public funds in the arts in England. Arts Council Grants for the arts are for individuals, arts organisations, national touring and other people who use the arts in their work.

On 1 April 2002, the Arts Council of England and nine regional arts boards joined together to form a single development organisation for the arts. The nine regions are East, East Midlands, London, North East, North West, South East, South West, West Midlands and Yorkshire.

Chair, Prof. Sir Christopher Frayling
Members, Diran Adebayo; Janet Barnes; Tom Bloxham, MBE; Deborah Bull, CBE; Deborah Grubb; Lady Sue Woodford Hollick; Prof. Alan Livingston; Stephen Lowe; Sir Brian McMaster, CBE; Elsie Owusu, OBE; Dr Tom Shakespeare; William Sieghart; Prof. Stuart Timperley; Dorothy Wilson
Chief Executive, Peter Hewitt

ARTS COUNCIL OF NORTHERN IRELAND

MacNeice House, 77 Malone Road, Belfast BT9 6AQ
T 028-9038 5200
E info@artscouncil-ni.org
W www.artscouncil-ni.org

The Arts Council of Northern Ireland is the prime distributor of government funds in support of the arts in Northern Ireland. It is funded by the Department of Culture, Arts and Leisure, and the grant for 2005–6 was over £10 million.

Chair, Ms R. Kelly
Vice-Chair, M. Bradley
Members, Mrs E. M. Benson; Mrs K. Bond; W. Chamberlain; Ms L. Finnegan; Ms J. A. Holmes; A. Kennedy; T. Kerr; B. J. Milligan; W. H. C. Montgomery; Ms S. M. O'Connor; G. O'Heara; P. Spratt
Chief Executive, Ms R. McDonough

ARTS COUNCIL OF WALES

9 Museum Place, Cardiff CF10 3NX
T 029-2037 6500 F 029-2022 1447
E feedback@artswales.org.uk
W www.artswales.org.uk

The Arts Council of Wales is the development body for the arts in Wales. It funds arts organisations with funding from the National Assembly for Wales and is the distributor of National Lottery funds to the arts in Wales. The grant for 2005–6 is £26.2 million from the National Assembly and £11.3 million from the National Lottery.

Chair, Geraint Talfan Davies
Members, Simon Dancey; Dai Davies; Meg Elis; Harry James; John Metcalf; Christopher O'Neill; Dr Francesca Rhydderch; Huw Roberts; Janet Roberts; Prof. Dai Smith; Ruth Till; David Vokes; Rhiannon Wyn Hughes
Chief Executive, Peter Tyndall

ASSEMBLY OMBUDSMAN FOR NORTHERN IRELAND AND NORTHERN IRELAND COMMISSIONER FOR COMPLAINTS

Progressive House, 33 Wellington Place, Belfast BT1 6HN
T 028-9023 3821 F 028-9023 4912
E ombudsman@ni-ombudsman.org.uk
W www.ni-ombudsman.org.uk

The Ombudsman is appointed under legislation with powers to investigate complaints by people claiming to have sustained injustice in consequence of maladministration arising from action taken by a Northern Ireland government department, or any other public body within his remit. Staff are presently seconded from the Northern Ireland Civil Service.

Ombudsman, Tom Frawley
Deputy Ombudsman, J. MacQuarrie
Directors, P. Gibson; I. Houston; H. Mallon; C. O'Hare

AUDIT COMMISSION

1st Floor, Millbank Tower, London SW1P 4HQ
T 020-7828 1212
E enquiries@audit-commission.gov.uk
W www.audit-commission.gov.uk

The Audit Commission was set up in 1983 and is responsible for appointing external auditors to local authorities, including the Greater London Authority, and local National Health Service bodies. It is also responsible for promoting the proper stewardship of public finance and value for money in the services provided by local authorities and health bodies.

The Commission has a chairman, a deputy chairman and up to 18 members who are appointed by the Office of the Deputy Prime Minister in consultation with the Secretary of State for Wales and the Health Secretaries in England and Wales.

Chair, J. Strachan
Members, S. Bundred; J. Coulter; Dr J. Dixon; R. Hoyle; P. Jones; Dr. P. Lane; T. Legg; Sir Michael Lyons; D. Moss; B. Pomeroy; Ms S. Drew Smith; B. Pomeroy; Prof. P. C. Smith; C. White
Chief Executive, Steve Bundred

AUDIT SCOTLAND

110 George Street, Edinburgh EH2 4LH
T 0131-477 1234 F 0131-477 4567
W www.audit-scotland.gov.uk

Audit Scotland was set up on 1 April 2000 to provide services to the Accounts Commission and the Auditor General for Scotland. Together they help to ensure that the Scottish Executive and public sector bodies in Scotland are held accountable for the proper, efficient and effective use of around £18 billion of public funds.

Audit Scotland's work covers over 200 bodies including local authorities; police and fire boards; NHS boards; further education colleges; Scottish Water; departments of the Scottish Executive; executive agencies such as the Prison Service and non-departmental public bodies such as Scottish Enterprise.

Audit Scotland carries out financial and regularity audits to ensure that public sector bodies adhere to the highest standards of financial management and governance. It also performs audits to ensure that these bodies achieve the best value for money. All of Audit Scotland's work in connection with local authorities, fire and police boards is carried out for the Accounts Commission, while its other work is undertaken for the Auditor General.

Auditor General, R. W. Black
Accounts Commission Chair, A. MacNish

BANK OF ENGLAND

Threadneedle Street, London EC2R 8AH
T 020-7601 4444 F 020-7601 4771
E enquiries@bankofengland.co.uk
W www.bankofengland.co.uk

The Bank of England was incorporated in 1694 under royal charter. It is the banker of the government and manages the issue of banknotes. Since May 1997 it has been operationally independent and its Monetary Policy Committee has had responsibility for setting short-term interest rates to meet the government's inflation target. As the central reserve bank of the country, the Bank keeps the accounts of British banks, who maintain with it a proportion of their cash resources, and of most overseas central banks. The Bank has three main areas of activity: monetary stability, market operations and financial stability. Its responsibility for banking supervision has been transferred to the Financial Services Authority.

Governor, M. A. King
Deputy Governors, Sir Andrew Large; Ms R. Lomax
Non-Executive Directors, B. Barber; Ms A. C. Fawcett, CBE; Mrs M. Francis, LVO; Sir Graham Hall; The Hon. Peter Jay; Prof. Sir John Likierman; C. McCarthy; Sir Brian Moffat, OBE; Sir William Morris; P. Myners; Sir Thomas Parker; Dr D. Potter, CBE; Mrs L. Powers-Freeling; Ms H. Rabbats, CBE; A. Sarin; G. Wilkinson
Monetary Policy Committee, The Governor; the Deputy Governors; Mrs K. Barker; C. Bean; Ms M. Bell; R. Lambert; Prof. S. Nickell; P. Tucker
Advisers to the Governor, L. Berkowitz; A. Clark; M. Glover
Chief Cashier and Executive Director, Banking Services, A. Bailey
Secretary, A. Wardlow
The Auditor, S. Brown

BIG LOTTERY FUND
1 Plough Place, London EC4A 1DE
T 020-7211 1800; Advice Line 0845-410 2030
F 020-7211 1750
E general.enquiries@biglotteryfund.org.uk
W www.biglotteryfund.org.uk

The Big Lottery Fund was launched on 1 June 2004, merging the New Opportunities Fund and the Community Fund. The Fund receives 50 per cent of the proceeds raised for good causes through the sale of lottery tickets, which is currently between £600 and £700 million per year (this level of funding is guaranteed until the current Camelot licence expires in 2009). The money is distributed to charitable, benevolent and philanthropic organisations in the voluntary and community sectors, as well as health, education and environmental projects. The Big Lottery Fund also assumed the Millennium Commission's role of supporting large-scale regenerative projects.

Chair, Prof. Sir Clive Booth
Members, Dr Samuel Burnside; Paul Cavanagh; David Campbell, CBE; Tom Davies; Roland Doven, MBE; Breidge Gadd, CBE; John Gartside, OBE; Douglas Graham; Taha Idris; Dugald Mackie; John Naylor, OBE; Esther O'Callaghan; Anna Southall; Huw Vaughan Thomas; Diana Whitworth
Chief Executive, Stephen Dunmore
Director, Wales, Ceri Doyle
Director, Northern Ireland, Walter Rader
Director, Scotland, Dharmendra Kanani

BOUNDARY COMMISSIONS
The Commissions are constituted under the Parliamentary Constituencies Act 1986. The Speaker of the House of Commons is *ex officio* chairman of all four commissions in the UK. Each of the four commissions is required by law to keep the parliamentary constituencies in their part of the UK under review. The latest Boundary Commission report for England was completed in April 1995 and its

proposals took effect at the 1997 general election. The next report must be submitted before April 2006. The latest Scottish report was completed in December 2004, with the European constituencies completed in April 1996.

ENGLAND
1 Drummond Gate, London SW1V 2QQ
T 020-7533 5177 F 020-7533 5176
W www.statistics.gov.uk/pbc/
Deputy Chair, The Hon. Mr Justice Sullivan

WALES
1st Floor, Caradog House, 1–6 St Andrews Place, Cardiff CF10 3BE
T 029-2039 5031 F 029-2039 5250
W www.lgbc-wales.gov.uk
Deputy Chair, John Davies

SCOTLAND
3 Drumsheugh Gardens, Edinburgh EH3 7QJ
T 0131-538 7200 F 0131-538 7240
W www.bcomm-scotland.gov.uk
Deputy Chair, The Rt. Hon. Lady Cosgrove, CBE

NORTHERN IRELAND
2nd Floor, Forestview, Purdy's Lane, Newtownbreda, Belfast BT8 7AR
T 028-9069 4800 F 028-9069 4801
W www.boundarycommission.org.uk
Deputy Chair, The Hon. Mr Justice Coghlin

BRITISH BROADCASTING CORPORATION (BBC)
Television Centre, Wood Lane, London W12 7RJ
T 020-8743 8000; BBC Information Line 0870-010 0222
W www.bbc.co.uk

The BBC was incorporated under royal charter in 1926 as successor to the British Broadcasting Company Ltd. The BBC's current charter came into force on 1 May 1996 and extends to 31 December 2006. The chair, vice-chair and other governors are appointed by The Queen-in-Council. The BBC is financed by revenue from receiving licences for the home services and by grant-in-aid from Parliament for the World Service (radio).

BOARD OF GOVERNORS
Chair, Michael Grade, CBE
Vice-Chair, Anthony Salz
National Governors, Prof. F. Monds *(N. Ireland)*; Prof. M. Jones *(Wales)*; Jeremy Peat *(Scotland)*; R. Sondhi, CBE *(England)*
Governors, Deborah Bull, CBE; Dame Ruth Deech; D. Gleeson; Angela Sarkis, CBE; R. Tait

BOARD OF MANAGEMENT

EXECUTIVE COMMITTEE
Director-General and Editor-in-Chief, M. Thompson
Deputy Director-General, M. Byford
Directors, Ms J. Abramsky *(Radio and Music)*; Ms J. Bennett *(Television)*; Ms H. Boaden *(News)*; S. Dando *(Human Resources and Internal)*; Tim Davie *(Marketing, Communications and Audiences)*; Ms C. Fairbairn *(Strategy and Distribution)*; A. Highfield *(New Media)*; P. Loughrey *(Nations and Regions)*; P. Salmon *(Sport)*; John Smith *(Chief Executive, BBC Worldwide)*; J. Smith *(Chief Operating Officer)*; Ms C. Thomson

(Policy and Legal); J. Willis *(Factual and Learning)*;
A. Yentob *(Drama, Entertainment and Children)*

OTHER SENIOR STAFF
Controller, BBC1, P. Fincham
Controller, BBC2, R. Keating
Controller, BBC3, S. Murphy
Controller, BBC4, J. Hadlow
Controller, Factual, G. Benson
Controller, BBC Daytime, Ms A. Sharman
Controller, Radio 1, A. Parfitt
Controller, Radio 2, L. Douglas
Controller, Radio 3, R. Wright
Controller, Radio 4, M. Damazer
Controller, Radio 5 Live, B. Shennan
*Controller, BBC Proms, Live Events and Television Classical
   Music,* N. Kenyon
Controller, Network Development, Nations and Regions,
   C. Cameron

BRITISH COUNCIL
10 Spring Gardens, London SW1A 2BN
T 020-7930 8466 F 020-7389 6347
E generalenquiries@britishcouncil.org
W www.britishcouncil.org
Bridgewater House, 58 Whitworth Street, Manchester M1 6BB
T 0161-957 7000

The British Council was established in 1934, incorporated by Royal Charter in 1940 and granted a supplemental charter in 1993. It is an independent, non-political organisation which promotes Britain abroad and is the UK's international organisation for educational and cultural relations. The British Council is represented in 216 towns and cities in 109 countries. Turnover in 2004–5, including Foreign and Commonwealth Office grants and contracted money, was in the region of £485.5 million.
Chair, Lord Kinnock, PC
Director-General, D. Green, CMG

BRITISH FILM INSTITUTE
21 Stephen Street, London W1T 1LN
T 020-7255 1444 F 020-7436 0439
W www.bfi.org.uk

The British Film Institute (BFI) offers opportunities for people throughout the UK to experience, learn and discover more about the world of film and moving image culture. The BFI incorporates the National Film and Television Archive, the BFI National Library, the monthly magazine *Sight and Sound,* BFI Publishing, BFI Video/DVD, the BFI National Film Theatre, the annual London Film Festival and the BFI London IMAX, and provides advice and support for regional cinemas and film festivals across the UK.
Chair, Anthony Minghella, CBE
Director, Amanda Nevill

BRITISH LIBRARY
96 Euston Road, London NW1 2DB
T 0870-444 1500
E visitor-services@bl.uk W www.bl.uk

The British Library was established in 1973. It is the UK's national library and occupies a key position in the library and information network. The Library aims to serve scholarship, research, industry, commerce and all other

major users of information. Its services are based on collections which include over 16 million volumes, 1 million discs, and 55,000 hours of tape recordings. The Library is now based at two sites: London (St Pancras and Colindale) and Boston Spa, W. Yorks. The Library's sponsoring department is the Department for Culture, Media and Sport.

Access to the reading rooms at St Pancras is limited to holders of a British Library Reader's Pass; information about eligibility is available from the Reader Admissions Office. The exhibition galleries and public areas are open to all, free of charge. Opening hours of services vary and should be checked by telephone.

BRITISH LIBRARY BOARD
Chair, Lord Eatwell of Stratton
Chief Executive and Deputy Chair, Mrs L. Brindley
Members, H. Boyd-Carpenter, KCVO; R. S. Broadhurst, CBE; Prof. R. Burgess; Ms S. Forbes, CBE; D. Lewis; Sir Colin Lucas; Ms E. Mackay; S. Olswang; Dr G. W. Roberts

BRITISH LIBRARY, BOSTON SPA
Boston Spa, Wetherby, W. Yorks LS23 7BQ
T 01937-546000

BRITISH LIBRARY, ST PANCRAS
96 Euston Road, London NW1 2DB
T 020-7412 7000
Press and Public Relations, T 020-7412 7111
Visitor Services, T 020-7412 7332
Education Service, T 020-7412 7797

SCHOLARSHIP AND COLLECTIONS
Reader Services, T 020-7412 7676
Asia, Pacific and Africa Collections, **T 020-7412 7873**
British Collections, T 020-7412 7676
Western Manuscripts, T 020-7412 7513
Map Library, T 020-7412 7702
Music Library, T 020-7412 7772
Philatelic Collections, T 020-7412 7635
British Library Sound Archive, T 020-7412 7676
British Library Newspapers, Colindale Avenue, London NW9 5HE T 020-7412 7353
European and American Collections, T 020-7412 7676

OPERATIONS AND SERVICES
Reader Admissions, T 020-7412 7677

SCIENCE, TECHNOLOGY AND INNOVATION
Science and Technology, T 020-7412 7494/7288
Patents, T 020-7412 7919
Business, T 020-7412 7454
Social Science, Law and Official Publications, T 020-7412 7536
National Preservation Office, T 020-7412 7612

BRITISH MUSEUM
Great Russell Street, London WC1B 3DG
T 020-7323 8000 F 020-7323 8616
E information@thebritishmuseum.ac.uk
W www.thebritishmuseum.ac.uk

The British Museum houses the national collection of antiquities, ethnography, coins and paper money, medals, prints and drawings. The British Museum may be said to date from 1753, when Parliament approved the holding of a public lottery to raise funds for the purchase of the collections of Sir Hans Sloane and the Harleian manuscripts, and for their proper housing and maintenance. The building (Montagu House) was opened in 1759. The existing buildings were erected between 1823 and the present day, and the original collection has increased to its current dimensions by gifts and purchases. Total government grant-in-aid for 2005–6 is £37.3 million.

BOARD OF TRUSTEES

Appointed by the Sovereign, HRH The Duke of Gloucester, KG, GCVO

Appointed by the Prime Minister, Hasan Askari; Sir John Boyd, KCMG *(Chair);* Lord Browne of Madingley; Sir Ronald Cohen; Prof. Barry Cunliffe; Francis Finlay; Val Gooding, OBE; Bonnie Greer; Prof. Martin Kemp; Baroness Helena Kennedy; Richard Lambert; David Lindsell; Dr David Norgrove; Eric Salama; Vikram Seth, CBE

Appointed by the Trustees of the British Museum, The Hon. Phillip Lader; Lord Powell of Bayswater, KCMG; Sir John Tusa

Appointed by the Royal Society, Dr Olga Kennard; Ms Edmee P. Leventis

Appointed by the Royal Academy, Tom Phillips

Appointed by the British Academy, Sir Keith Thomas

OFFICERS

Director, Neil MacGregor
Deputy Director, Andrew Burnett
Deputy Director, Dawn Austwick, OBE
Director of Marketing and Public Affairs, Honor Wilson-Fletcher
Director of Operations, Chris Rofe
Director of Resources, D. Austwick, OBE
Head of Communications, Joanna Mackle
Head of Building and Estates, K. T. Stannard
Head of Education, Gareth Binns
Head of Finance, Chris Herring
Head of Membership Development, vacant

KEEPERS

Keeper of Ancient Near East Antiquities, Dr John Curtis
Keeper of Coins and Medals, Joe Cribb
Keeper of Department of Asia, Robert Knox
Keeper of Ancient Egypt and Sudan, Vivian Davies
Keeper of Africa, Oceania and the Americas, Jonathan King
Keeper of Greek and Roman Antiquities, Dr Dyfri Williams
Keeper of Prehistory and Europe, Leslie Webster
Keeper of Prints and Drawings, Antony Griffiths
Conservation, Documentation and Science, Sheridan Bowman

BRITISH PHARMACOPOEIA COMMISSION

Market Towers, 1 Nine Elms Lane, London SW8 5NQ
T 020-7084 2561 E bpcom@mhra.gsi.gov.uk
W www.pharmacopoeia.org.uk

The British Pharmacopoeia Commission sets standards for medicinal products used in human and veterinary medicines and is responsible for publication of *British Pharmacopoeia* (a publicly available statement of the standard that a product must meet throughout its shelf-life), *British Pharmacopoeia (Veterinary)* and the *British Approved Names.* It has 15 members who are appointed by the Secretary of State for Health, the Minister for Environment, Food and Rural Affairs, the Scottish

Ministers, the National Assembly for Wales, and the relevant Northern Ireland departments.
Chair, Prof. D. Calam, OBE, DPhil
Vice-Chair, Prof. J. A. Goldsmith
Secretary and Scientific Director, Dr M. G. Lee

BRITISH STANDARDS INSTITUTION, BSI GROUP

389 Chiswick High Road, London W4 4AL
T 020-8996 9001 F 020-8996 7001
E cservices@bsi-global.com W www.bsi-global.com

British Standards – a part of the BSI Group – was the world's first national standards-making body, and is the recognised authority in the UK for the preparation and publication of national standards, both for products and for the service sector. About 90 per cent of its standards work is internationally linked. British Standards are issued for voluntary adoption, though in some cases compliance with a British Standard is required by legislation. Industrial and consumer products and services certified as complying with the relevant British Standard and operating an assessed quality management system are eligible to carry BSI's certification trade mark, known as the 'Kitemark'.
Chair, Sir David John, KCMG
Chief Executive, Stevan Breeze

BRITISH WATERWAYS

Willow Grange, Church Road, Watford WD17 4QA
T 01923-201120 F 01923-201300
E enquiries.hq@britishwaterways.co.uk
W www.britishwaterways.co.uk

British Waterways conserves and manages the network of over 2,000 miles of canals and rivers in England, Scotland and Wales. It is accountable to the Department for Environment, Food and Rural Affairs in England and Wales, and the Scottish Executive in Scotland.

Its responsibilities include maintaining the waterways and structures on and around them; looking after wildlife and the waterway environment; and ensuring that canals and rivers are safe and enjoyable places to visit.
Chair, Tony Hales
Vice-Chair, Dr Campbell Christie
Board Members, Ms S. Achmatowicz; Richard Bowker; I. Darling; G. Fleming; Ms H. Gordon; D. Langslow; T. Tricker
Chief Executive, R. Evans

THE BROADS AUTHORITY

18 Colegate, Norwich NR3 1BQ
T 01603-610734 F 01603-765710
E broads@broads-authority.gov.uk
W www.broads-authority.gov.uk

The Broads Authority is a special statutory authority set up under the Norfolk and Suffolk Broads Act 1988. The functions of the Authority are to conserve and enhance the natural beauty of the Broads; to provide integrated management of the land and water space of the area; to promote the enjoyment of the Broads by the public; and to protect the interests of navigation. The Authority comprises 35 members, appointed by the local authorities in the area covered, environmental conservation bodies, the Environment Agency, and the Great Yarmouth Port Authority.
Chair, Prof. K. Turner
Chief Executive, Dr J. Packman

CENTRAL ARBITRATION COMMITTEE

PO Box 51547, London SE1 1ZG
T 020-7904 2300 F 020-7904 2301
E enquiries@cac.gov.uk W www.cac.gov.uk

The Central Arbitration Committee is a permanent independent body which determines claims for statutory recognition and de-recognition of trade unions for collective bargaining purposes where such recognition or de-recognition cannot be agreed voluntarily. It also adjudicates on disclosure of information cases, deals with claims and complaints relating to European Works Councils in Great Britain, and arbitrates in industrial disputes.
Chair, Sir Michael Burton
Chief Executive, Graeme Charles

CERTIFICATION OFFICE FOR TRADE UNIONS AND EMPLOYERS' ASSOCIATIONS

Brandon House, 180 Borough High Street, London SE1 1LW
T 020-7210 3734/5 F 020-7210 3612
E info@certoffice.org W www.certoffice.org

The Certification Office is an independent statutory authority. The Certification Officer is appointed by the Secretary of State for Trade and Industry and is responsible for receiving and scrutinising annual returns from trade unions and employers' associations; for determining complaints concerning trade union elections, certain ballots and certain breaches of trade union rules; for ensuring observance of statutory requirements governing mergers between trade unions and employers' associations; for overseeing the political funds and finances of trade unions and employers' associations; and for certifying the independence of trade unions.
Certification Officer, David Cockburn

SCOTLAND
54–66 Frederick Street, Edinburgh EH2 1NB
T 0131-200 1200
Certification Officer for Scotland, Christine Stuart

CHARITY COMMISSION

Harmsworth House, 13–15 Bouverie Street, London EC4Y 8DP
2nd Floor, 20 King's Parade, Queen's Dock, Liverpool L3 4DQ
Woodfield House, Tangier, Taunton, Somerset TA1 4BL
8th Floor, Clarence House, Clarence Place, Newport NP19 7AA
T 0870-333 0123 W www.charitycommission.gov.uk

The Charity Commission for England and Wales is the government department whose aim is to give the public confidence in the integrity of charities. It also carries out the functions of the registration, monitoring and support of charities and the investigation of alleged wrongdoing. The Commission maintains a computerised register of some 187,000 charities. It is accountable to the courts and, for its efficiency, to the Home Secretary. There are five Commissioners appointed by the Home Office for a fixed term and the Commission has Offices in London, Liverpool, Taunton and Newport.
Chief Executive, Andrew Hind
Chair, Geraldine Peacock
Acting Legal Commissioner, K. M. Dibble
Commissioners (part-time), Lindsay Driscoll; D. Taylor; D. Unwin; John Williams; Tess Woodcraft
Heads of Legal Section, K. M. Dibble; G. S. Goodchild; J. Kilby

Head of Human Resources, Ms S. Bailey
Head of Policy Division, Ms R. Chapman
Information Systems Controller, K. Chown

CHURCH COMMISSIONERS

1 Millbank, London SW1P 3JZ
T 020-7898 1000 F 020-7898 1131
E commissioners.enquiry@c-of-e.org
W www.churchcommissioners.org

The Church Commissioners were established in 1948 by the amalgamation of Queen Anne's Bounty (established 1704) and the Ecclesiastical Commissioners (established 1836). They are responsible for the management of the majority of the Church of England's assets, the income from which is predominantly used to help pay for the stipend and pension of the clergy. The Commissioners own over 120,000 acres of agricultural land, a number of residential estates in central London, and commercial property across Great Britain. They also carry out administrative duties in connection with pastoral reorganisation and redundant churches.

The Commissioners are: the Archbishops of Canterbury and of York; four bishops, three clergy and four lay persons elected by the respective houses of the General Synod; two deans or provosts elected by all the deans and provosts; three persons nominated by The Queen; three persons nominated by the Archbishops of Canterbury and York; three persons nominated by the Archbishops after consultation with others including the lord mayors of London and York and the vice-chancellors of the universities of Oxford and Cambridge; the First Lord of the Treasury; the Lord President of the Council; the Home Secretary; the Lord Chancellor; the Secretary of State for Culture, Media and Sport; and the Speaker of the House of Commons.

CHURCH ESTATES COMMISSIONERS
First, A. Whittam Smith
Second, Sir Stuart Bell, MP
Third, vacant

OFFICERS
Secretary, A. C. Brown
Deputy Secretary (Finance and Investment), C. W. Daws

ASSISTANT SECRETARIES
Chief Surveyor, P. Clark
Chief Investments Manager, M. Chaloner
Pastoral and Redundant Churches, P. Lewis
Official Solicitor, S. Jones

CIVIL AVIATION AUTHORITY (CAA)

CAA House, 45–59 Kingsway, London WC2B 6TE
T 020-7379 7311 W www.caa.co.uk

The CAA is the UK's specialist aviation regulator. Its responsibilities include ensuring that the aviation industry meets the highest technical and operational safety standards; preventing holidaymakers from being stranded abroad or losing money because of tour operator insolvency; planning and regulating all UK airspace; regulating airports, air traffic services and airlines; and providing advice on aviation policy from an economic standpoint.
Chair, Sir Roy McNulty
Secretary and Legal Adviser, R. J. Britton

THE COAL AUTHORITY

200 Lichfield Lane, Mansfield, Notts NG18 4RG
T 01623-427162 F 01623-622072
E thecoalauthority@coal.gov.uk
W www.coal.gov.uk

The Coal Authority was established under the Coal Industry Act 1994 to manage certain functions previously undertaken by British Coal, including ownership of unworked coal. It is responsible for licensing coal mining operations and for providing information on coal reserves and past and future coal mining. It settles subsidence claims not falling on coal mining operators. It deals with the management and disposal of property, and with surface hazards such as abandoned coal mine shafts.
Chair, J. Harris
Chief Executive, A. Schofield, OBE

COLLEGE OF ARMS (HERALDS' COLLEGE)

Queen Victoria Street, London EC4V 4BT
T 020-7248 2762 F 020-7248 6448
E enquiries@college-of-arms.gov.uk
W www.college-of-arms.gov.uk

The Sovereign's Officers of Arms (Kings, Heralds and Pursuivants of Arms) were first incorporated by Richard III. The powers vested by the Crown in the Earl Marshal (the Duke of Norfolk) with regard to state ceremonial are largely exercised through the College. The College is also the official repository of the arms and pedigrees of English, Welsh, Northern Irish and Commonwealth (except Canadian) families and their descendants, and its records include official copies of the records of Ulster King of Arms, the originals of which remain in Dublin. The 13 officers of the College specialise in genealogical and heraldic work for their respective clients.

Arms have always been, and still are, granted by letters patent from the Kings of Arms. A right to arms can only be established by the registration in the official records of the College of Arms of a pedigree showing direct male line descent from an ancestor already appearing therein as being entitled to arms, or by making application through the College of Arms for a grant of arms. Grants are made to corporations as well as to individuals.
Earl Marshal, The Duke of Norfolk

KINGS OF ARMS
Garter, P. L. Gwynn-Jones, CVO, FSA
Clarenceux, D. H. B. Chesshyre, CVO, FSA
Norroy and Ulster, T. Woodcock, LVO, FSA

HERALDS
Richmond (and Earl Marshal's Secretary), P. L. Dickinson
York, H. E. Paston-Bedingfeld
Chester (and Registrar), T. H. S. Duke
Lancaster, R. J. B. Noel
Windsor, W. G. Hunt, TD
Somerset, D. V. White

PURSUIVANTS
Rouge Dragon, C. E. A. Cheesman
Bluemantle, M. P. D. O'Donoghue

COMMISSION FOR ARCHITECTURE AND THE BUILT ENVIRONMENT

The Tower Building, 11 York Road, London SE1 7NX
T 020-7960 2400 F 020-7960 2444
E enquiries@cabe.org.uk W www.cabe.org.uk

The Commission for Architecture and the Built Environment (CABE) is responsible for promoting the importance of high quality architecture and urban design, and encouraging the understanding of architecture through educational and regional initiatives. CABE offers free advice to local authorities, public sector clients and others embarking on building projects of any size or purpose.
Chief Executive, Richard Simmons

COMMISSION FOR INTEGRATED TRANSPORT

Zone F16, 1st Floor, Ashdown House, 123 Victoria Street, London SW1E 6DE
E cfit@dft.gsi.gov.uk
W www.cfit.gov.uk

The Commission for Integrated Transport (CfIT) was proposed in the 1998 Transport White Paper and was set up in June 1999. Its role is to provide independent expert advice to the government in order to achieve a transport system that supports sustainable development. The CfIT also encourages best practice amongst local authorities and delivery agencies, and assesses both the impact of new technology on future policy options and transport policy initiatives from outside the UK. Members of the Commission are appointed by the Secretary of State for Transport.
Chair, Peter Hendy
Vice-Chair, David Leeder
Members, John Armitt; Neil Betteridge; Garrett Emmerson; Sir Michael Hodgkinson; Helen Holland; Sir Roy McNulty, CBE; Michael Roberts; Archie Robinson; Neil Scales; Baroness Ros Scott; Richard Turner

COMMISSION FOR LOCAL ADMINISTRATION IN ENGLAND

10th Floor, Millbank Tower, Millbank, London SW1P 4QP
T 020-7217 4620 F 020-7217 4621
Enquiry line 0845-602 1983 E enquiries@lgo.org.uk
W www.lgo.org.uk

Local Commissioners (local government ombudsmen) are responsible for investigating complaints from members of the public against local authorities (but not town and parish councils); English Partnerships (planning matters only); Housing Action Trusts; education appeal panels; police authorities and certain other authorities. The Commissioners are appointed by the Crown on the recommendation of the Deputy Prime Minister.

Certain types of action are excluded from investigation, including personnel matters and commercial transactions unless they relate to the purchase or sale of land. Complaints can be sent direct to the Local Government Ombudsman or through a councillor, although the Local Government Ombudsman will not consider a complaint unless the council has had an opportunity to investigate and reply to a complainant.

A free leaflet, *Complaint about the council? How to complain to the Local Government Ombudsman*, is available from the Commission's offices.

Chair and Chief Executive of the Commission and Local Commissioner (£150,878), T. Redmond
Local Commissioner (£113,121), J. R. White
Member (ex officio), The Parliamentary Commissioner for Administration
Deputy Chief Executive and Secretary (£77,497), N. J. Karney

COMMISSION FOR RACIAL EQUALITY

St Dunstan's House, 201–211 Borough High Street, London SE1 1GZ
T 020-7939 0000 F 020-7939 0001
E info@cre.gov.uk W www.cre.gov.uk

The Commission for Racial Equality (CRE) was set up under the 1976 Race Relations Act. It receives an annual grant from the Home Office but works independently of government. The CRE is run by commissioners appointed by the Home Secretary, and has support from all the main political parties.

The CRE has three main duties: to work towards the elimination of racial discrimination and to promote equality of opportunity; to encourage good relations between people from different racial and ethnic backgrounds; and to monitor the way the Race Relations Act is working and recommend ways in which it can be improved.

The CRE is the only government-appointed body with statutory power to enforce the Race Relations Act, and can provide legal advice and assistance to those who think they have been discriminated against. It also has a reference library which is open to the public (by appointment only).
Chair, Trevor Phillips
Deputy Chair, Kay Hampton

COMMITTEE ON STANDARDS IN PUBLIC LIFE

35 Great Smith Street, London SW1P 3BQ
T 020-7276 2595 F 020-7276 2585
W www.public-standards.gov.uk

The Committee on Standards in Public Life was set up in October 1994. It is a standing body whose chair and members are appointed by the prime minister; three members are nominated by the leaders of the three main political parties. The Committee's remit is to examine concerns about standards of conduct of all holders of public office, including arrangements relating to financial and commercial activities, and to make recommendations as to any changes in present arrangements which might be required to ensure the highest standards of propriety in public life. It is also charged with reviewing issues in relation to the funding of political parties. The Committee does not investigate individual allegations of misconduct.
Chair, Sir Alistair Graham
Members, Lloyd Clark, QPM; Rita Donaghy, OBE; Prof. Hazel Genn, CBE; Dame Patricia Hodgson, DBE; The Rt. Hon. Baroness Jay of Paddington; Baroness Maddock; The Rt. Hon. Baroness Shephard; Dr Elizabeth Vallance; Dr Brian Woods-Scawen

COMMONWEALTH INSTITUTE

New Zealand House, 80 Haymarket, London SW1Y 4TQ
T 020-7603 4535 F 020-7602 4525
E information@commonwealth.org.uk
W www.commonwealth.org.uk

The Commonwealth Institute is an educational trust. Its members are the member states of the Commonwealth who elect a Board of Trustees responsible to them. The Trustees have entered a joint venture with Cambridge University to create a Centre for Commonwealth Education.
Chair, Miss J. Hanratty, OBE
Vice-Chair, The Rt. Hon. Lord Fellowes, GCB, GCVO

COMMONWEALTH WAR GRAVES COMMISSION

2 Marlow Road, Maidenhead, Berks SL6 7DX
T 01628-634221 F 01628-771208
E casualty.enq@cwgc.org
W www.cwgc.org

The Commonwealth War Graves Commission (formerly Imperial War Graves Commission) was founded by royal charter in 1917. It is responsible for the commemoration of 1,694,883 members of the forces of the Commonwealth who lost their lives in the two world wars. More than one million graves are maintained in 23,274 burial grounds throughout the world. Over three-quarters of a million men and women who have no known grave or who were cremated are commemorated by name on memorials built by the Commission.

The funds of the Commission are derived from the six participating governments, i.e. the UK, Canada, Australia, New Zealand, South Africa and India.
President, HRH The Duke of Kent, KG, GCMG, GCVO, ADC
Chair, The Secretary of State for Defence (UK)
Vice-Chair, Air Chief Marshall Sir Peter Squire, GCB, DFC, AFC, DSC
Members, The High Commissioners in London for Australia, Canada, South Africa, New Zealand and India; Adm. Sir Peter Abbott, GBE, KCB; Ian Henderson, CBE, FRICS; Sir John Keegan, OBE; Alan Meale, MP; The Hon. Nicholas Soames, MP; Sir Rob Young, GCMG
Director-General and Secretary to the Commission, R. E. Kellaway, CBE
Deputy Director-General, M. S. Johnson, OBE
Legal Adviser and Solicitor, G. C. Reddie
Directors, D. R. Parker *(Information and Secretariat)*; B. Davidson, MBE *(Works)*; John Tooke *(Horticulture)*; Ms C. Cecil *(Personnel)*; P. J. Haysom *(Finance)*

COMMUNITIES SCOTLAND

Thistle House, 91 Haymarket Terrace, Edinburgh EH12 5HE
T 0131-313 0044 F 0131-313 2680
W www.communitiesscotland.gov.uk

Communities Scotland is a Scottish Executive agency reporting directly to Ministers. Its overall aim is to improve the quality of life for people in Scotland by working with others to create sustainable, healthy and attractive communities. They do this by regenerating neighbourhoods, empowering communities and improving the effectiveness of investment.
Chief Executive, Angiolina Foster

COMPETITION COMMISSION

Victoria House, Southampton Row, London WC1B 4AD
T 020-7271 0100 F 020-7271 0367
E info@competition-commission.gsi.gov.uk
W www.competition-commission.org.uk

The Commission was established in 1948 as the Monopolies and Restrictive Practices Commission (later the Monopolies and Mergers Commission); it became the Competition Commission in April 1999 under the Competition Act 1998. The Commission conducts in-depth inquiries into mergers (anticipated and completed); markets; and the regulation of major industries. Every inquiry the Commission undertakes is in response to a reference made to it by another authority, usually the Office of Fair Trading, but in certain circumstances by a Minister or by the regulators under sector-specific legislative provisions relating to regulated industries. The Commission has no power to conduct inquiries on its own initiative.

The Commission has a full-time chairman and three deputy chairmen. There are usually around 50 Commission members to carry out investigations. All are appointed by the Secretary of State for Trade and Industry for single eight-year terms.

Chair, Prof P. A. Geroski
Deputy Chairs, C. A. Clarke; Mrs D. Guy; P. J. Freeman
Members, S. Ahmed; Ms J. Almond; Prof. J. Baillie; Mrs S. E. Brown, OBE; Mrs L. Carstensen; Miss L. I. Christmas; Dr J. Collings; Dr D. Coyle; R. Davis; Mrs C. Dobson; Ms B. Donoghue; L. D. Elks; R. Farrant; N. Garthwaite; W. Gibson; C. F. W. Goodall; Prof. C. Graham; Prof. A. Gregory; I. Grey; G. H. Hadley; Prof. A. Hamlin; Prof. J. Haskel; P. F. Hazell; C. E. Henderson, CB; Mrs J. Hill; G. L . Holbrook, MBE; R. N. Holroyd; Mrs M. J. Hopkirk; A. Johnston; I. Jones; P. N. Jones; Prof. P. D. Klemperer; Prof. B. Lyons; Dame Barbara Mills, DBE, QC; Prof. P. Moizer; Sir Derek Morris; R. Murray; D. Newkirk; Prof. D. Parker; J. A. Peat; Ms E. Pollard; Prof. M. Raj; E. J. Seddon; C. R. Smallwood; J. Smith; A. Stern; P. Stoddart; Prof. P. Sudarsanam; R. Taylor; Prof. D. G. Trelford; R. Turgoose; Prof. C. Waddams; S. D. Walzer; Prof. M Waterson; M. R. Webster; J. Whiticar; Prof. S. R. M. Wilks; Mrs C. F. Woolf, CBE; C. Wilson; A. M. Young
Non-Executive Directors, A. P. Foster; Dame Patricia Hodgson, DBE
Chief Executive and Secretary, M. E. Stanley

COMPETITION SERVICE

Victoria House, Bloomsbury Place, London WC1A 2EB
T 020-7979 7979 F 020-7979 7978
E info@catribunal.org.uk
W www.catribunal.org.uk

The Enterprise Act 2002 created the Competition Service, a non-departmental public body whose purpose is to fund and provide support services to the Competition Appeal Tribunal. Support services include everything necessary to facilitate the carrying out by the Competition Appeal Tribunal of its statutory functions such as administration, accommodation and office equipment.
Director, Operations, Jeremy Straker

CONSUMER COUNCIL FOR WATER (CCW)

Victoria Square House, Victoria Square, Birmingham B2 4AJ
T 0121-345 1000
E enquiries@ccwater.org.uk W www.ccwater.org.uk

The Consumer Council for Water (CCW) was established on 1 October 2005 under the Water Act 2003, and took over the functions of WaterVoice to represent customers' interests in respect of price, service and value for money from their water and sewerage services, and to investigate complaints from customers about their water company. There are nine regional committees in England and one in Wales.
Chair, Dame Yve Buckland, DBE

CORPORATION OF LONDON JOINT ARCHIVE SERVICE

40 Northampton Road, London EC1R 0HB
T 020-7332 3820 F 020-7833 9136
E ask.lma@corpoflondon.gov.uk
W www.cityoflondon.gov.uk/lma

The Corporation of London Joint Archive Service was established in 2003 and comprises the London Metropolitan Archives and the Corporation of London Records Office to form the largest local authority record office in the UK. Records deposited include those of the administrative bodies for the former counties of London and Middlesex, as well as archives from numerous associations, businesses, charities, hospitals, Anglican parishes and families and individuals from the Greater London area. In addition, the municipal archives of the City of London, regarded as the most complete collection of ancient municipal records in existence, are available for consultation. These include collections of statutes; continuous series of judicial rolls; books from 1252 and Council minutes from 1275; records of the Old Bailey and Guildhall sessions from 1603; financial records from the 16th century; the records of London Bridge from the 12th century; and numerous subsidiary series and miscellanea of historical interest.
Head Archivist, D. Jenkins, PHD

CORPORATION OF TRINITY HOUSE

Trinity House, Tower Hill, London EC3N 4DH
T 020-7481 6900 F 020-7480 7662
W www.trinityhouse.co.uk

The Corporation of Trinity House, the General Lighthouse Authority for England, Wales and the Channel Islands, was granted its first charter by Henry VIII in 1514. Trinity House maintains 71 lighthouses, 13 major floating aids to navigation (e.g. light vessels) and more than 420 buoys. The Corporation also has certain statutory jurisdiction over aids to navigation maintained by local harbour authorities and is responsible for marking or dispersing wrecks dangerous to navigation, except those occurring within port limits or wrecks of HM ships.

Trinity House is maintained out of the General Lighthouse Fund, which is provided from light dues levied on ships calling at ports of the UK and the Republic of Ireland. The Corporation is also a deep-sea pilotage authority, authorised by the Secretary of State for Transport to license deep-sea pilots, and a charitable organisation, which funds a cadet training scheme and retirement homes for mariners and their dependants.

The affairs of the Corporation are controlled by a board of Elder Brethren and the Secretary. A separate board, which comprises Elder Brethren, senior staff and outside representatives, currently controls the Lighthouse Service. The Elder Brethren also act as nautical assessors in marine cases in the Admiralty Division of the High Court of Justice.

ELDER BRETHREN
Master, HRH The Prince Philip, Duke of Edinburgh, KG, KT, PC
Deputy Master and Executive Chair, Rear-Adm. J. M. de Halpert, CB
Wardens, Capt. C. M. C. Stewart *(Rental)*; Cdre. P. J. Melson, CBE, RN *(Nether)*
Elder Brethren, HRH The Prince of Wales, KG, KT; HRH The Duke of York, KCVO, ADC; Sir Brian Shaw; Capt. J. E. Bury; Capt. D. J. Cloke; Capt. Sir Miles Wingate, KCVO; Capt. P. F. Mason, CBE; Capt.T. Woodfield, OBE; The Rt. Hon. Lord Simon of Glaisdale; Capt. D. T. Smith, OBE, RN; Cdr. Sir Robin Gillett, BT, GBE, RD, RNR; Capt. Sir Malcolm Edge, KCVO; The Rt. Hon. Lord Cuckney of Millbank; Capt. D. J. Orr; The Rt. Hon. Lord Carrington, KG, GCMG, CH, MC, PC; The Rt. Hon. Lord Mackay of Clashfern, KT; Sir Adrian Swire; The Rt. Hon. Lord Sterling of Plaistow, CBE, GCVO; Cdr. M. J. Rivett-Carnac, RN, DL; Adm. Sir Jock Slater, GCB, LVO; Capt. J. R. Burton-Hall, RD, Capt. I. Gibb; Capt. D. C. Glass; D. F. Potter; Capt. D. P. Richards, RD, RNR; S. P. Sherard; Lord Brown of Madingley; The Rt. Hon. Lord Robertson of Port Ellen, GCMG; Rear-Adm. Sir Patrick Rowe, KCVO, CBE; The Hon. C. C. Lyttelton; Capt. N. R. Pryke, MCIT

OFFICERS
Secretary, P. Galloway
Director of Finance, J. S. Wedge
Director of Operations and Asset Management, Cdre. P. J. Melson, CBE, RN
Technical Director, David Golden
Director of Navigation, Capt. Duncan Glass

COUNCIL ON TRIBUNALS
81 Chancery Lane, London WC2A 1BQ
T 020-7855 5200 F 020-7855 5201
E enquiries@cot.gsi.gov.uk
W www.council-on-tribunals.gov.uk

The Council on Tribunals is an independent body that operates under the Tribunals and Inquiries Act 1992. It consists of 15 members appointed by the Lord Chancellor/Secretary of State for Constitutional Affairs and the Scottish Ministers; one member is appointed to represent the interests of people in Wales. The Scottish Committee of the Council generally considers Scottish tribunals and matters relating only to Scotland. The Parliamentary Commissioner for administration is an *ex officio* member of the Council and the Scottish Committee.

The Council advises on, and keeps under review, the constitution and working of the tribunals listed in the Tribunals and Inquiries Act, and considers and reports on administrative procedures relating to statutory inquiries. Some 80 tribunals are currently under the Council's supervision. It is consulted by and advises government departments on a wide range of subjects relating to adjudicative procedures.

Chair, The Rt. Hon. Lord Newton of Braintree, OBE
Members, The Parliamentary Commissioner *(ex officio)*, Ann Abraham; Carolyn Berkeley, JP; Elizabeth Cameron; Judith Edwards; Rosalind Hepplewhite; Susan Howdle; Penny Letts; Prof. A. MacLeary; Stephen Mannion; Bernard Quoroll; Prof. Genevra Richardson; Dr Adrian Stokes; Heather Wilcox

SCOTTISH COMMITTEE OF THE COUNCIL ON TRIBUNALS
44 Palmerston Place, Edinburgh EH12 5BJ
T 0131-220 1236 F 0131-225 4271
E sccot@gtnet.gov.uk
Chair, Prof. A. MacLeary
Members, The Parliamentary Commissioner for Administration *(ex officio)*; Elizabeth C. Cameron; Douglas Graham; Stephen Mannion; Lyndy Roberts; Audrey Watson; Mary Wood

COUNTRYSIDE AGENCY
John Dower House, Crescent Place, Cheltenham GL50 3RA
T 01242-521381 E info@countryside.gov.uk
W www.countryside.gov.uk

The Countryside Agency was set up in April 1999 by the merger of the Countryside Commission with parts of the Rural Development Commission. It is a statutory body which promotes the conservation and enhancement of the countryside in England, and undertakes activities aimed at stimulating job creation and the provision of essential services in the countryside. It also designates national parks and maps open land for public access (right to roam). The Agency is funded by an annual grant from the Department for Environment, Food and Rural Affairs and board members are appointed by the Secretary of State.
Chair, Dr Stuart Burgess
Deputy Chair, Pam Warhurst
Members, Dr Tayo Adebowale; Kate Ashbrook; Prof. Sheena Asthana; Richard Burge; Dr Jim Cox, OBE; Peter Fane; Norman Glass, CB; Tony Hams, OBE; Rt. Revd Graham James; Prof. Philip Lowe, OBE; Alison McLean; Howard Petch, CBE; Prof. Mark Shucksmith; John Varley; Prof. Michael Winter
Chief Executive, Graham Garbutt
Directors, Tracey Slaven; Andrew Wood

COUNTRYSIDE COUNCIL FOR WALES/ CYNGOR CEFN GWLAD CYMRU
Maes y Ffynnon, Penrhosgarnedd, Bangor, Gwynedd LL57 2DW
T 0845-130 6229 F 01248-355782
E enquiries@ccw.gov.uk W www.ccw.gov.uk

The Countryside Council for Wales is the government's statutory adviser on sustaining natural beauty, wildlife and the opportunity for outdoor enjoyment in Wales and its inshore waters. It is funded by the National Assembly for Wales and accountable to the First Secretary, who appoints its members.
Chair, J. Lloyd Jones, OBE
Chief Executive, R. Thomas
Director, Corporate Services, L. Warmington
Director, Countryside Policy, Dr J. Taylor
Director of Science, Dr D. Parker

COURT OF THE LORD LYON
HM New Register House, Edinburgh EH1 3YT
T 0131-556 7255 F 0131-557 2148
W www.lyon-court.com

The Court of the Lord Lyon is the Scottish Court of Chivalry (including the genealogical jurisdiction of the *Ri-Sennachie* of Scotland's Celtic Kings). The Lord Lyon King of Arms has jurisdiction, subject to appeal to the Court of Session and the House of Lords, in questions of heraldry and the right to bear arms. The Court also administers the Scottish Public Register of All Arms and Bearings and the Public Register of All Genealogies. Pedigrees are established by decrees of Lyon Court and by letters patent. As Royal Commissioner in Armory, the Lord Lyon grants patents of arms (which constitute the grantee and heirs noble in the Noblesse of Scotland) to virtuous and well-deserving Scotsmen and to petitioners (personal or corporate) in The Queen's overseas realms of Scottish connection, and issues birthbrieves.
Lord Lyon King of Arms, R. O. Blair, LVO, WS

HERALDS
Albany, J. A. Spens, MVO, RD, WS
Rothesay, Sir Crispin Agnew of Lochnaw, BT, QC
Ross, C. J. Burnett, FSA SCOT

PURSUIVANTS
Unicorn, Alastair Campbell of Airds
Carrick, Mrs C. G. W. Roads, MVO, FSA SCOT
Bute, W. D. H. Sellar
Orkney Herald Extraordinary, Sir Malcolm Innes of Edinqight, KCVO, WS
Linlithgow Pursuivant Extraordinary, J. C. G. George, KSG
Lyon Clerk and Keeper of Records, Mrs C. G. W. Roads, MVO, FSA SCOT
Procurator-Fiscal, George Way of Plean, SSC
Herald Painter, Mrs Y. Holton
Macer, H. M. Love

COVENT GARDEN MARKET AUTHORITY
Covent House, New Covent Garden Market, London SW8 5NX
T 020-7720 2211 F 020-7622 5307
E info@cgma.gov.uk
W www.cgma.gov.uk

The Covent Garden Market Authority is constituted under the Covent Garden Market Acts 1961 to 1977, the members being appointed by the Minister of Environment, Food and Rural Affairs. The Authority owns and operates the 56-acre New Covent Garden Markets (fruit, vegetables, flowers), which have been trading since 1974.
Chair (part-time), Baroness Dean of Thornton-le-Fylde
General Manager, Dr P. M. Liggins

CRIMINAL CASES REVIEW COMMISSION
Alpha Tower, Suffolk Street, Queensway, Birmingham B1 1TT
T 0121-633 1800 F 0121-633 1823/1804
E info@ccrc.gov.uk W www.ccrc.gov.uk

The Criminal Cases Review Commission is an independent body set up under the Criminal Appeal Act 1995. It is a non-departmental public body reporting to Parliament via the Home Secretary. It is responsible for investigating suspected miscarriages of justice in England, Wales and Northern Ireland, and deciding whether or not to refer cases back to an appeal court. Membership of the Commission is by royal appointment; the senior executive staff are appointed by the Commission.
Chair, Prof. Graham Zellick
Members, M. Allen; B. Capon; L. Elks; M. Emerton; A. Foster; D. Jessel; D. Kyle; Prof. L. Leigh; J. MacKeith; I. Nicholl; K. Singh; B. Skitt; J. Weeden
Director of Finance and IT, C. Albert
Director of HR and Administration, P. Wilkinson
Head of Communication, B. Worrall
Legal Advisers, Ms A. Flower; J. Wagstaff
Investigations Advisers, R. Barrington; C. Harding

CRIMINAL INJURIES COMPENSATION APPEALS PANEL (CICAP)
11th Floor, Cardinal Tower, 12 Farringdon Road, London EC1M 3HS
T 020-7549 4600 F 020-7549 4643
E info@cicap.gsi.gov.uk W www.cicap.gov.uk
Chair, R. Goodier
Chief Executive and Secretary to the Panel, Miss J. Martin

CRIMINAL INJURIES COMPENSATION AUTHORITY (CICA)
Morley House, 26–30 Holborn Viaduct, London EC1A 2JQ
T 020-7842 6800 F 020-7436 0804
Tay House, 300 Bath Street, Glasgow G2 4LN
T 0141-331 2726 F 0141-331 2287
W www.cica.gov.uk Freephone 0800-358 3601

All applications for compensation for personal injury arising from crimes of violence in England, Scotland and Wales are dealt with at the above locations. (Separate arrangements apply in Northern Ireland.) Applications received up to 31 March 1996 are assessed on the basis of common law damages under the 1990 compensation scheme. Applications received on or after 1 April 1996 are assessed under a tariff-based scheme, made under the Criminal Injuries Compensation Act 1995, by the Criminal Injuries Compensation Authority (CICA). There is a separate avenue of appeal to the Criminal Injuries Compensation Appeals Panel (CICAP).
Chief Executive, Howard Webber
Deputy Chief Executive, Edward McKeown
Head of Legal Services, Anne Johnstone

CROFTERS COMMISSION
4–6 Castle Wynd, Inverness IV2 3EQ
T 01463-663450 F 01463-711820
E info@crofterscommission.org.uk
W www.crofterscommission.org.uk

The Crofters Commission, established in 1955 under the Crofters (Scotland) Act, is a government-funded organisation whose overall objective is the promotion of thriving and sustainable crofting communities. It works with communities to develop, reorganise and regulate crofting, and advises Scottish Ministers on crofting matters. The Commission administers the Crofting Counties Agricultural Grants Scheme, the Croft Entrant Scheme, the Cattle Improvement Scheme and the Crofting Community Development Scheme. It also provides a free enquiry service.
Chair, David Green
Chief Executive, Shane Rankin

CROWN ESTATE
16 Carlton House Terrace, London SW1Y 5AH
T 020-7210 4377 F 020-7930 8187
W www.crownestate.co.uk

The Crown Estate is valued at more than £5 billion, and includes substantial blocks of urban property, primarily in London, almost 110,000 hectares of rural land, almost half the foreshore, and the sea bed out to the twelve nautical mile territorial limit throughout the United Kingdom. The Crown Estate is part of the hereditary possessions of the Sovereign 'in right of the Crown', managed under the provisions of the Crown Estate Act 1961. The Crown Estate has a duty to maintain and enhance the capital value of estate and the income obtained from it. Under the terms of the 1961 Act, the Crown Estate pays its revenue surplus to the Treasury every year.
Chair, Ian Grant, CBE
Chief Executive, Roger Bright
Board Members, Sir Donald Curry, KB, CBE; Hugh
    Duberly, CBE; Jenefer Greenwood, FRICS; Martin
    Moore; Dinah Nichols, CB; Ronald Spinney, FRICS
Directors, Chris Bourchier *(Rural Estate)*; Giles Clarke
    (Investment and Asset Management); Martin Gravestock
    (Corporate Operations); John Lelliot *(Finance and
    Information Services)*; Frank Parrish *(Marine Estate)*

HEADS OF DEPARTMENTS
Communications, Emma Twyman
Customer Management, Elspeth Miller
Development Management, Liam Colgan
Internal Audit, John Ford
Legal, David Harris
Office Portfolio, Charles Gardner
Regional Portfolio, Jim Yates
Residential Portfolio, Giles Clarke
Retail Portfolio, David Shaw

EDINBURGH OFFICE
6 Bell's Brae, Edinburgh EH4 3BJ
T 0131-260 6070 F 0131-260 6090
Edinburgh Office Manager, Ian Pritchard

WINDSOR ESTATE
The Crown Estate Office, The Great Park, Windsor, Berks
SL4 2HT
T 01753-860222 F 01753-859617
Deputy Ranger, P. Everett

DEER COMMISSION FOR SCOTLAND
Knowsley, 82 Fairfield Road, Inverness IV3 5LH
T 01463-231751 F 01463-712931
E enquiries@deercom.com
W www.dcs.gov.uk

The Deer Commission for Scotland has the general functions of furthering the conservation and control of deer in Scotland. It has the statutory duty, with powers, to prevent damage to agriculture, forestry and the habitat by deer. It is funded by the Scottish Executive.
Chair (part-time), Prof. J. Milne, MBE
Director, N. Reiter
Technical Director, D. Balharry

DESIGN COUNCIL
34 Bow Street, London WC2E 7DL
T 020-7420 5200 F 020-7420 5300
E info@designcouncil.org.uk
W www.design-council.org.uk

The Design Council is a campaigning organisation which works with partners in business, education and government to promote the effective use of good design. It is a registered charity with a Royal Charter and is funded by grant-in-aid from the Department of Trade and Industry.
Chair, Sir George Cox
Chief Executive, David Kester

DISABILITY RIGHTS COMMISSION
Freepost MID 02164, Stratford-upon-Avon CV37 9BR
T 0845-762 2633
W www.drc-gb.org

The Commission is an executive non-departmental public body established in April 2000. Its role is to advise government on issues of discrimination against disabled people and the operation of the Disability Discrimination Act 1995. It promotes good practice to employers and service providers and provides advice, information and legal support to disabled people.
Chair, Bert Massie, CBE
Deputy Chair, John Hougham, CBE
Chief Executive, Bob Niven
Commissioners, Saghir Alam; Stephen Alambritis; Michael
    Burton; Jane Campbell, MBE; Susan Daniels; Richard
    Exell, OBE; Dr Kevin Fitzpatrick; Christopher Holmes,
    MBE; Elaine Noad; Eve Rank; Lakhvir Rellon; Philippa
    Russel, CBE; Jenny White, MBE

ECGD (EXPORT CREDITS GUARANTEE DEPARTMENT)
PO Box 2200, 2 Exchange Tower, Harbour Exchange Square,
London E14 9GS
T 020-7512 7000 F 020-7512 7649
W www.ecgd.gov.uk

ECGD, the Export Credits Guarantee Department, is the UK's official export credit agency. A separate government department reporting to the Secretary of State for Trade and Industry, it has more than 80 years' experience of working closely with exporters, project sponsors, banks and buyers to help UK exporters of capital equipment and project-related goods and services. ECGD does this by providing: help in arranging finance packages for buyers of UK goods by guaranteeing bank loans; insurance against non-payment to UK exporters; and, oversea investment insurance – a facility that gives UK investors up to 15 years' insurance against political risks such as war, expropriation and restrictions on remittances.

EXECUTIVE COMMITTEE
Chief Executive and Accounting Officer, P. Crawford
Non-Executive Chair, G. Pimlott
Group Directors, Nigel Addison-Smith *(Finance)*; S. R.
    Dodgson *(Human Resources)*; V. Lunn-Rockliffe *(Credit
    Risk Group)*; D. N. Ridley *(General Counsel)*; J. R. Weiss
    (Deputy Chief Executive and Director of Business Group)

NON-EXECUTIVE DIRECTORS
D. Godfrey; D. Harrison; J. Wright

DIRECTORS
Business Divisions, R. Gotts; G. G. Welsh
Recoveries Division, R. Lethbridge
Guarantee Policy and Administration Division, A. Faulkner
Head of Business Principles Unit, D. Allwood
Credit Risk Analysis Division, P. Radford
Capital Control and Portfolio Management Division,
  J. Croall
Infrastructure Division, L. Woods
Treasury Division, J. Cross
Financial Controller, T. Read
Internal Audit and Assurance Division, G. Cassell
Operational Research, Strategy and Change Division,
  R. Kaufman
Head of International Relations, R. Mayer
Head of Communications, R. Watson

EXPORT GUARANTEES ADVISORY COUNCIL
Chair, E. P. Airey
Other Members, Sir S. Brown; J. Elkington; Prof. J. Kydd;
  M. Roberts; A. Shepherd; P. Talbot; Dr R.
  Thamotheram

ENGLISH HERITAGE (HISTORIC BUILDINGS AND MONUMENTS COMMISSION FOR ENGLAND)
23 Savile Row, London W1S 2ET
T 020-7973 3000 F 020-7973 3001
W www.english-heritage.org.uk

English Heritage was established under the National Heritage Act 1983. On 1 April 1999 it merged with the Royal Commission on the Historical Monuments of England to become the new lead body for England's historic environment. Its duties are to carry out and sponsor archaeological, architectural and scientific surveys and research designed to increase the understanding of England's past and its changing condition; to identify buildings, monuments and landscapes for protection whilst also offering expert advice, skills and grants to conserve these sites; to encourage town planners to make imaginative re-use of historic buildings to aid regeneration of the centres of cities, towns and villages; to manage and curate selected sites; and to curate and make publicly accessible the National Monuments Record, whose records of over one million historic sites and buildings, and extensive collections of photographs, maps, drawings and reports constitute the central database and archive of England's historic environment.
Chair, Sir Neil Cossons, OBE, FSA, FMA
Commissioners, Maria Adebowale; Joyce Bridges, CBE; Bill
  Bryson; Michael Cairns; Prof. David Cannadine,
  DPHIL, LITT D, FBA; Manish Chande; Gilly
  Drummond; Marquess of Douro, OBE; Piers Gough,
  CBE, FRSA; Jane Grenville, FSA; Michael Jolly, CBE;
  Earl of Leicester; Richard Morris, OBE, FSA; Les Sparks,
  OBE, FRSA; Elizabeth Williamson, FSA
Chief Executive, Dr Simon Thurley
CUSTOMER SERVICES, Customer Services Department,
  PO Box 569, Swindon SN2 2YP T 0870-333 1181
  E customers@english-heritage.org.uk
NATIONAL MONUMENTS RECORD, National Monuments
  Record Centre, Kemble Drive, Swindon SN2 2GZ
  T 01793-414600 F 01793-414606

ENGLISH NATURE
Northminster House, Peterborough PE1 1UA
T 01733-455000 F 01733-568834
Enquiry Service 01733-455100
E enquiries@english-nature.org.uk
W www.english-nature.org.uk

English Nature was established in 1991 and is responsible for advising the Department of the Environment, Food and Rural Affairs on nature conservation in England. It promotes, directly and through others, the conservation of England's wildlife and natural features. It selects, establishes and manages National Nature Reserves and identifies and notifies Sites of Special Scientific Interest. It provides advice and information about nature conservation, and supports and conducts research relevant to these functions. Through the Joint Nature Conservation Committee, it works with its sister organisations in Scotland and Wales on UK and international nature conservation issues. Free publications are available by contacting the Enquiry Service.
Chair, M. Doughty
Chief Executive, Dr A. Brown
Directors, A. Clements; Ms S. Collins; Dr K. L. Duff;
  P. Newby; Miss C. E. M. Wood

ENVIRONMENT AGENCY
Rio House, Waterside Drive, Aztec West, Almondsbury, Bristol
BS32 4UD
T 0870-850 6506 F 01709-312820
E enquiries@environment-agency.gov.uk
W www.environment-agency.gov.uk

The Environment Agency was established in 1996 under the Environment Act 1995 and is a non-departmental public body sponsored by the Department of the Environment, Food and Rural Affairs and the National Assembly for Wales. The Agency is responsible for pollution prevention and control in England and Wales, and for the management and use of water resources, including flood defences, fisheries and navigation. It has head offices in London and Bristol, and eight regional offices.

THE BOARD
Chair, Sir John Harman
Members, P. Bye; Ted Cantle, CBE; John Edmonds; Peter
  Matthews; Sara Parkin, OBE; Richard Percy; Dr
  Lyndon Stanton; Cllr Kay Twitchen, OBE; Dr Malcolm
  Smith; Prof. Lynda Warren

THE EXECUTIVE
Chief Executive, Barbara Young
Director of Corporate Affairs, Helen McCallum
Director of Environmental Protection, Tricia Henton
Director of Finance, Nigel Reader
Director of Legal Services, Ric Navarro
Director of Operations, Dr Paul Leinster
Director of Performance and Innovation, Chris Bale
Director of Personnel, Giles Duncan
Director of Water Management, David King

EQUALITY COMMISSION FOR NORTHERN IRELAND

Equality House, 7–9 Shaftesbury Square, Belfast BT2 7DP
T 028-9050 0600 F 028-9024 8687
E information@equalityni.org
W www.equalityni.org

The Equality Commission was set up in 1999 under the Northern Ireland Act 1998 and is responsible for promoting equality, eliminating discrimination on the grounds of race, disability, sexual orientation, gender, religion and political opinion and for overseeing the statutory duty on public authorities to promote equality of opportunity.

Chief Commissioner, Joan Harbison
Deputy Chief Commissioner, Anne O'Reilly
Chief Executive, Evelyn Collins

EQUAL OPPORTUNITIES COMMISSION

Arndale House, Arndale Centre, Manchester M4 3EQ
T 0845-601 5901 F 0161-838 1733
E info@eoc.org.uk
W www.eoc.org.uk
Media Enquiries, 36 Broadway, London SW1H 0BH
T 020-7222 0004

Other Offices, St Stephens House, 279 Bath Street,
Glasgow G2 4JL
T 0845-601 5901
Windsor House, Windsor Lane, Cardiff CF10 3GE
T 029-2034 3552

The Equal Opportunities Commission was established under the Sex Discrimination Act in 1975. It was set up as an independent statutory body with the following powers: to work towards the elimination of discrimination on the grounds of sex or marriage; to promote equality of opportunity for women and men; to keep under review the Sex Discrimination Act and the Equal Pay Act; and to provide legal advice and assistance to individuals who have been discriminated against.

Chair, Ms J. Mellor
Deputy Chair, Ms J. Watson
Commissioners, Ms R. Arshad, OBE; Evelyn Asante-Mensah; Ms S. Ashtiany; Mohammad Aziz; Catherine Brown; Ms F. Cannon; Ms K. Carberry; Ms J. Drake; Duncan Fisher; Frances Hasler; Ms D. Mattinson; N. Rhys Wooding; S. Sharma; Ms T. Woodcraft
Chief Executive, C. Slocock

FOOD STANDARDS AGENCY (UK)

Aviation House, 125 Kingsway, London WC2B 6NH
T 020-7276 8000 F 020-7276 8004
E helpline@foodstandards.gsi.gov.uk
W www.food.gov.uk

The Food Standards Agency (FSA) was established in April 2000 to protect public health from risks arising in connection with the consumption of food, and otherwise to protect the interests of consumers in relation to food. The Agency has the general function of developing policy in these areas and provides information and advice to the government, other public bodies and consumers. It also sets standards for and monitors food law enforcement by local authorities. The Agency is a UK-wide non-ministerial government body, led by a board which has been appointed to act in the public interest. It has executive offices in Scotland, Wales and Northern Ireland.

It is advised by advisory committees on food safety matters of special interest to each of these areas.

Chair, Dame Deirdre Hutton, CBE
Deputy Chair, Julia Unwin, OBE
Chief Executive, Dr Jon Bell
FOOD STANDARDS AGENCY NORTHERN IRELAND, 10c Clarendon Road, Belfast BT1 3BG T 028-9041 7700
E infosani@foodstandards.gsi.gov.uk
FOOD STANDARDS AGENCY SCOTLAND, St Magnus House, 6th Floor, 25 Guild Street, Aberdeen AB11 6NJ T 01224-285100
E scotland@foodstandards.gsi.gov.uk
FOOD STANDARDS AGENCY WALES, 11th Floor, Southgate House, Wood Street, Cardiff CF10 1EW T 029-2067 8999
E wales@foodstandards.gsi.gov.uk

EXECUTIVE AGENCY

MEAT HYGIENE SERVICE
Kings Pool, Peasholme Green, York YO1 7PR
T 01904-455501 F 01904-455502

The Meat Hygiene Service was launched on 1 April 1995 as an agency of the former Ministry of Agriculture, Fisheries and Food, and became an Executive Agency of the Food Standards Agency on 1 April 2000. It protects public health and animal welfare at slaughter through veterinary supervision and meat inspection in licensed fresh meat premises in Great Britain.

Chief Executive, C. J. Lawson

FOREIGN COMPENSATION COMMISSION

Room SG/111, Old Admiralty Building, Spring Gardens, London SW1A 2PA
T 020-7008 1321 F 020-7008 0160

The Foreign Compensation Commission (FCC) was set up by the Foreign Compensation Act 1950 primarily to distribute, under Orders in Council, funds received from other governments in accordance with agreements to pay compensation for expropriated British property and other losses sustained by British nationals. The FCC carries out both judicial and administrative functions, including the adjudication of claims by applicants and the investment and management of compensation funds.

Chair, Dr John Barker
Secretary, Barrie England, LVO

FORESTRY COMMISSION

Silvan House, 231 Corstorphine Road, Edinburgh EH12 7AT
T 0845-367 3787 F 0131-334 3047
E enquiries@forestry.gsi.gov.uk
W www.forestry.gov.uk

The Forestry Commission is the government department responsible for forestry policy in Great Britain. It reports directly to forestry Ministers (i.e. the Secretary of State for Environment, Food and Rural Affairs, the Scottish Ministers and the National Assembly for Wales), to whom it is responsible for advice on forestry policy and for the implementation of that policy.

The Commission's principal objectives are to protect Britain's forests and woodlands; expand Britain's forest area; enhance the economic value of forest resources; conserve and improve the biodiversity, landscape and cultural heritage of forests and woodlands; develop opportunities for woodland recreation; and increase public understanding of, and community participation in, forestry. Forest Enterprise, an executive agency of the Forestry Commission, ceased to exist on 1 April 2003. Three new bodies, one each for England, Scotland and Wales, have been created in its place.

Chair (part-time), The Rt. Hon. Lord Clark of Windermere
Director-General and Deputy Chair (G2), T. Rollinson
FORESTRY COMMISSION ENGLAND, Great Eastern House, Tenison Road, Cambridge CB1 2BU T 01223-314546
FORESTRY COMMISSION SCOTLAND, 231 Corstorphine Road, Edinburgh EH12 7AT T 0131-334 0303
FORESTRY COMMISSION WALES, Victoria Terrace, Aberystwyth, Ceredigion SY23 2DQ T 01970-625866
FOREST RESEARCH, Alice Holt Lodge, Wrecclesham, Farnham, Surrey GU10 4LU T 01420-222555
NORTHERN RESEARCH STATION, Roslin, Midlothian EH25 9SY T 0131-445 2176

GAMING BOARD FOR GREAT BRITAIN
Berkshire House, 168–173 High Holborn, London WC1V 7AA
T 020-7306 6200 F 020-7306 6266
E enqs@gbgb.org.uk
W www.gbgb.org.uk

The Board was established in 1968 and is responsible to the Secretary of State for Culture, Media and Sport. It is the regulatory body for casinos, bingo clubs, gaming machines and the larger society, and all local authority, lotteries in Great Britain. Its functions are to ensure that those involved in organising gaming and lotteries are fit and proper to do so and to keep gaming free from criminal infiltration; to ensure that gaming and lotteries are run fairly and in accordance with the law; and to advise the Secretary of State on developments in gaming and lotteries.

Chair, Peter Dean, CBE
Chief Executive, Jenny Williams

GOVERNMENT ACTUARY'S DEPARTMENT
Finlaison House, 15–17 Furnival Street, London EC4A 1AB
T 020-7211 2601 F 020-7211 2650
E enquiries@gad.gov.uk
W www.gad.gov.uk

The Government Actuary's Department provides a consulting service to government departments, the public sector, and overseas governments. The actuaries advise on social security schemes and superannuation arrangements in the public sector at home and abroad, on population and other statistical studies, and on supervision of insurance companies and pension funds.

Government Actuary, C. D. Daykin, CB
Directing Actuaries, A. I. Johnston
Chief Actuaries, E. I. Battersby; I. A. Boonin; S. R. Humphrey; D. Lewis; G. T. Russell

GOVERNMENT COMMUNICATIONS HEADQUARTERS (GCHQ)
Priors Road, Cheltenham GL52 5AJ
T 01242-221491 F 01242-574349
E pressoffice@gchq.gsi.gov.uk W www.gchq.gov.uk

GCHQ produces signals intelligence in support of national security and the UK's economic wellbeing, and in the prevention or detection of serious crime. Additionally, GCHQ Communications-Electronics Security Group (CESG) is the national authority for information assurance, and provides advice and assistance

to government departments, the armed forces and other national infrastructure bodies on the security of their communications and information systems. GCHQ was placed on a statutory footing by the Intelligence Services Act 1994 and is headed by a director who is directly accountable to the Foreign Secretary.

Director, D. E. Pepper

GOVERNMENT HOSPITALITY
Lancaster House, Stable Yard, St James's, London SW1A 1BB
T 020-7008 8517 F 020-7008 8526

The Government Hospitality Fund was instituted in 1908 for the purpose of organising official hospitality on a regular basis with a view to the promotion of international goodwill.

Government Hospitality is now incorporated as part of the Foreign and Commonwealth Office's Services Directorate.

Manager of Government Hospitality, Robert Alexander

GOVERNMENT OFFICES FOR THE REGIONS
The nine Government Offices for the Regions (GOs) are the primary means by which a wide range of government policies are delivered in the English regions. The Government Offices bring together the activities and interests of ten 'sponsor' government departments: the Office of the Deputy Prime Minister; the Department for Education and Skills; the Department of Trade and Industry; the Department for Environment, Food and Rural Affairs; the Home Office; the Department for Culture, Media and Sport; the Department for Work and Pensions; the Department for Transport; the Department of Health; and the Cabinet Office.

GOs contribute to the delivery of over 40 Public Service Agreements (PSAs) on behalf of their sponsor departments. These PSAs cover a diverse range of tasks including regenerating communities, fighting crime, tackling housing needs, improving public health, raising standards in education and skills, tackling countryside issues, and reducing unemployment. GOs also manage European funds.

GOs directly manage the spending programmes of the government departments listed above. They oversee budgets and contracts delegated to regional organisations, as well as carrying out regulatory functions and sponsoring Regional Development Agencies. As part of central government, their role also includes providing a regional perspective to inform the development and evaluation of policy. In 2003–4, the GOs were responsible for approximately £9 billion of government expenditure.

The Government Office Network comprises the nine regional Government Offices, and the Regional Co-ordination Unit.

REGIONAL CO-ORDINATION UNIT
2nd Floor, Riverwalk House, 157–161 Millbank, London SW1P 4RR
T 020-7217 3595 F 020-7217 3590
W www.rcu.gov.uk
Director-General, Rob Smith
Director, Andrew Campbell
Directors, Ian Jones *(Corporate Communications)*; Ann-Marie Field *(Strategy)*; Julie Anderson *(Business Development)*; Vince Brady *(Human Resources)*

EAST MIDLANDS
The Belgrave Centre, Stanley Place, Talbot Street, Nottingham
NG1 5GG
T 0115-971 9971 F 0115-971 2404
E enquiries.goem@go-regions.gov.uk
W www.go-em.gov.uk
Regional Director, Jane Todd

EAST OF ENGLAND
Eastbrook, Shaftesbury Road, Cambridge CB2 2DF
T 01223-372500 F 01223-372501
W www.go-east.gov.uk
Regional Director, Caroline Bowdler

LONDON
Riverwalk House, 157–161 Millbank, London SW1P 4RR
T 020-7217 3111 F 020-7217 3450
W www.go-london.gov.uk
Regional Director, Liz Meek

NORTH-EAST
Citygate, Gallowgate, Newcastle upon Tyne NE1 4WH
T 0191-201 3300 F 0191-202 3998
W www.go-ne.gov.uk
Regional Director, Jonathan Blackie

NORTH-WEST
City Tower, Piccadilly Plaza, Manchester M1 4BE
T 0161-952 4000 F 0161-952 4099
W www.go-nw.gov.uk
Regional Director, Keith Barnes

SOUTH-EAST
Bridge House, 1 Walnut Tree Close, Guildford GU1 4GA
T 01483-882255 F 01483-882259
W www.go-se.gov.uk
Regional Director, Paul Martin

SOUTH-WEST
2 Rivergate, Temple Quay, Bristol BS1 6ED
T 0117-900 1700 F 0117-900 1900
W www.gosw.gov.uk
Regional Director, Bronwyn Hill

WEST MIDLANDS
5 St Phillips Place, Colmore Row, Birmingham B3 2PW
T 0121-352 5050 F 0121-352 5194
E enquiries.gowm@go-regions.gsi.gov.uk
W www.go-wm.gov.uk
Regional Director, Graham Garbutt

YORKSHIRE AND THE HUMBER
PO Box 213, City House, New Station Street, Leeds LS1 4US
T 0113-283 8301 F 0113-283 6394
E enquiries.goyh@go-regions.gsi.gov.uk W www.goyh.gov.uk
Regional Director, Felicity Everiss

HEALTH AND SAFETY COMMISSION
Rose Court, 2 Southwark Bridge, London SE1 9HS
T 020-7717 6000 F 020-7717 6644
E hseinformationservices@natbrit.com
W www.hse.gov.uk

The Health and Safety Commission was created under the
Health and Safety at Work etc. Act 1974, with duties to
reform health and safety law, to propose new regulations,
and generally to promote the protection of people at work
and the public from hazards arising from industrial and
commercial activity, including major industrial accidents
and the transportation of hazardous materials.
　Its members are nominated by organisations representing
employers, employees, local authorities and others.
Chair, B. Callaghan
Members, Ms M. Burns; D. Carrigan; Ms J. Donovan; Ms J.
　Edmond-Smith; Ms J. Hackitt; S. Khan; J. Longworth;
　H. Robertson; Ms E. Snape

HEALTH AND SAFETY EXECUTIVE
Rose Court, 2 Southwark Bridge, London SE1 9HS
T 020-7717 6000 F 020-7717 6717

The Health and Safety Executive is the Health and Safety
Commission's major instrument. Through its
inspectorates it enforces health and safety law in the
majority of industrial premises. The Executive advises the
Commission in its major task of laying down safety
standards through regulations and practical guidance for
many industrial processes. The Executive is also the
licensing authority for nuclear installations, the reporting
officer on the severity of nuclear incidents in Britain, and
it is responsible for the Channel Tunnel Safety Authority.
Chief Executive, Jeffrey Podger
Deputy Director-General, Operations, J. McCracken
Deputy Director-General, Policy, J. Rees
*Director and HM Chief Inspector of the Nuclear
　Installations Inspectorate*, Dr M. Weightman
*Director, Corporate Science and Analytical Service
　Directorate and Chief Scientist*, Dr P. Davies
Director, Field Operations Directorate, S. Caldwell
Director, Hazardous Installations Directorate, K. Myers
Director, Strategic Programme, J. Willis
Director, Resource Planning Directorate, V. Dews
Director, Policy Programmes, G. Denham

HEALTH PROTECTION AGENCY
Central Office: 7th Floor, Holborn Gate, 330 High Holborn,
London WC1V 7BA
T 020-7759 2700 F 020-7759 2733
E firstname.surname@hpa.org.uk
W www.hpa.org.uk

The Health Protection Agency (HPA) was set up on 1
April 2003 and is responsible for protecting the health
and well-being of the population of England and Wales. It
provides up-to-date, impartial and authoritative advice for
government, health professionals and the public. The HPA
works at local, regional, national and international levels
to reduce the impact of infectious diseases and reduce
exposure to chemicals, radiation and poisons, as well as
ensuring a rapid response when hazards occur. The HPA
provides services in Northern Ireland and works closely
with similar organisations in Scotland, so that there is a
co-ordinated response to incidents, trends and outbreaks
on a national level. Research and development projects
conducted by HPA scientists are primarily concerned with
new methods of treating illness and assessing exposure to
chemicals or radiation, i.e. developing new vaccines and
biomarkers of chemical exposure.
Chair, Sir William Stewart
Chief Executive, Prof. Pat Troop
Directors, Prof. Pete Borriello *(Centre for Infections)*; Dr
　Roger Cox *(Radiation and Environmental Hazards)*;
　Prof. Roger Gilmour *(Business)*; Dr Nigel Lightfoot
　(Emergency Response); Dr Mary O'Mahony *(Local and
　Regional Services)*; Prof. Stephen Palmer *(Chemical
　Hazards and Poisons)*

HIGHLANDS AND ISLANDS ENTERPRISE
Cowan House, Inverness Retail and Business Park, Inverness
IV2 7GF
T 01463-234171 F 01463-244469
E hie.general@hient.co.uk
W www.hie.co.uk

Highlands and Islands Enterprise (HIE) was set up under
the Enterprise and New Towns (Scotland) Act 1991. Its
role is to design, direct and deliver enterprise
development, training and environmental and social
projects and services. HIE is made up of a strategic core
body and ten Local Enterprise Companies (LECs), to
which many of its individual functions are delegated.
Chair, W. Roe
Chief Executive, I. J. R. S. Cumming

HISTORIC ENVIRONMENT ADVISORY COUNCIL FOR SCOTLAND
Longmore House, Salisbury Place, Edinburgh EH9 1SH
T 0131-668 8810 F 0131-668 8987
E heacs@scotland.gsi.gov.uk
W www.heacs.org.uk

The Historic Environment Advisory Council for Scotland
is the advisory body set up to provide Scottish Ministers
with advice on issues affecting the historic environment
and how the functions of the Scottish Ministers may be
exercised effectively for the benefit of said historic
environment. In this context the historic environment
means any or all structures and places in Scotland of
historical, archaeological or architectural interest or
importance.
Chair, Elizabeth Burns, CMG, OBE

HISTORIC ROYAL PALACES
Hampton Court Palace, Surrey KT8 9AU
T 0870-751 5172 F 020-8781 9754
W www.hrp.org.uk

Historic Royal Palaces is a non-departmental public body
with charitable status. The Secretary of State for Culture,
Media and Sport is still accountable to Parliament for the
care, conservation and presentation of the palaces, which
are owned by the Sovereign in right of the Crown. The
chair of the trustees is appointed by The Queen on the
advice of the Secretary of State. Historic Royal Palaces is
responsible for the Tower of London, Hampton Court
Palace, Kensington Palace State Apartments, the Royal
Ceremonial Dress Collection, Kew Palace, Queen
Charlotte's Cottage, and the Banqueting House,
Whitehall.

TRUSTEES
Chair, Sir Nigel Mobbs
Appointed by The Queen, A. Reid; Sir Hugh Roberts,
   KCVO, FSA; Field Marshal Lord Inge, KG, GCB
Appointed by the Secretary of State, Dr B. Cherry, FSA;
   J. Hamer; Ms A. Heylin, OBE; Malcolm Reading
Ex officio, Sir Roger Wheeler, GCB, CBE *(Constable of the
   Tower of London)*

OFFICERS
Chief Executive, M. Day
Director of Conservation, J. Barnes
Director of Finance, Ms S. O'Neill
Director of Human Resources, G. Josephs
Director, Palaces Group, R. Giddins

Director of Communications and Development, D. Homan
Resident Governor, HM Tower of London, Maj.-Gen.
   G. Field, CD, CVO, OBE
Retail Director, Ms A. Boyes

HM REVENUE AND CUSTOMS
Board of HM Revenue and Customs, 100 Parliament Street,
London SW1A 2BQ
W www.hmrc.gov.uk

HM Revenue and Customs was formed following the
integration of the Inland Revenue and HM Customs and
Excise, which was made formal by Parliament on 18 April
2005. It administers, and advises the Chancellor of the
Exchequer on any matters connected with the following
areas: income, corporation, capital gains, inheritance,
insurance premium, stamp, land and petroleum revenue
taxes; environmental taxes (climate change and aggregates
levy, landfill tax); value added tax (VAT); customs duties
and frontier protection; excise duties; National Insurance;
tax credits, child benefit and the Child Trust Fund;
enforcement of the minimum wage; and recovery of
student loan repayments.

THE BOARD OF HM REVENUE AND CUSTOMS
Chair, David Varney
Deputy Chair, Paul Gray, CB
Director, General Policy and Technical, Dave Hartnett, CB
*Director, General Enforcement, Compliance and Central
   Policy,* Mike Eland
Director, General Corporate Services, Helen Ghosh
*Director (acting), General Processes, Frontiers and Large
   Business Services,* Mike Hanson, MBE
Director, Finance, Stephen Jones
Director, Organisation Development, Steve Heminsley
Chief Information Officer, Steve Lamey
General Counsel and Solicitor (acting), David Hogg

VALUATION OFFICE AGENCY
New Court, 48 Carey Street, London WC2A 2JE
T 020-7506 1700 F 020-7506 1998
E customerservices@voa.gsi.gov.uk
W www.voa.gov.uk

The Valuation Office is an executive agency of HM
Revenue and Customs, and is responsible for valuing
property for tax purposes.
Chief Executive, Andrew Hudson

HOME-GROWN CEREALS AUTHORITY
Caledonia House, 223 Pentonville Road, London N1 9HY
T 020-7520 3926 F 020-7520 3954
E communications@hgca.com
W www.hgca.com

Set up under the Cereals Marketing Act 1965, the Home-
Grown Cereals Authority (HGCA) Board consists of:
seven members representing UK cereal growers; seven
representing dealers in, or processors of, grain; and two
independent members. HGCA's functions are to improve
the production and marketing of UK-grown cereals and
oilseeds through a research and development programme,
to provide a market information service and to promote
UK cereals in export markets.
Chair, J. Page
Chief Executive, J. Cowens

HORSERACE TOTALISATOR BOARD

Douglas House, Chapel Lane, Wigan WN3 4HS
T 01942-617500 F 01942-617701
W www.totesport.com

The Horserace Totalisator Board (the Tote) was established by the Betting, Gaming and Lotteries Act 1963. Its function is to operate totalisators on approved racecourses in Great Britain, and it also provides on and off-course cash and credit offices. Under the Horserace Totalisator and Betting Levy Board Act 1972, it is further empowered to offer bets at starting price (or other bets at fixed odds) on any sporting event, and under the Horserace Totalisator Board Act 1997 to take bets on any event, except the National Lottery. The chair and members of the Board are appointed by the Secretary of State for Culture, Media and Sport.

The government announced in March 2001 that the Tote would eventually be sold to a racing trust, subject to the necessary legislation going through Parliament. The privatisation of the Tote is expected to be completed during the new parliamentary term.

Chair, P. I. Jones
Chief Executive, T. Beaumont
Chief Operating Officer, T. Phillips

HOUSE OF LORDS RECORD OFFICE (THE PARLIAMENTARY ARCHIVES)

The Parliamentary Archives, London SW1A 0PW
T 020-7219 3074 F 020-7219 2570
E hlro@parliament.uk
W www.portcullis.parliament.uk

Since 1497, the records of Parliament have been kept within the Palace of Westminster. They are in the custody of the Clerk of the Parliaments. In 1946 the Record Office was established to supervise their preservation and their availability to the public.

Some three million documents are preserved, including Acts of Parliament from 1497, journals of the House of Lords from 1510, minutes and committee proceedings from 1610, and papers laid before Parliament from 1531. Amongst the records are the Petition of Right, the Death Warrant of Charles I, the Declaration of Breda, and the Bill of Rights. The House of Lords Record Office also has charge of the journals of the House of Commons (from 1547), and other surviving records of the Commons (from 1572), including documents relating to private bill legislation from 1818. Among other documents are the records of the Lord Great Chamberlain, the political papers of certain members of the two Houses, and documents relating to Parliament acquired on behalf of the nation. The Record Office makes the records available through a public search room and answers enquiries concerning the archives and history of Parliament.

Clerk of the Records, S. K. Ellison
Assistant Clerks of the Records, Ms F. P. Grey *(Freedom of Information Officer)*; D. L. Prior; Dr C. Shenton

HOUSING CORPORATION

Maple House, 149 Tottenham Court Road, London W1T 7BN
T 0845-230 7000 F 020-7393 2111
E enquiries@housingcorp.gsx.gov.uk
W www.housingcorp.gov.uk

Established by Parliament in 1964, the Housing Corporation regulates and funds registered social landlords, which are non-profit making bodies run by voluntary committees. There are over 2,000 registered social landlords, most of which are housing associations, who provide homes for more than 2.9 million people. Under the Housing Act 1996, the Corporation's regulatory role was widened to embrace new types of landlords, in particular local housing companies. The Corporation is funded by the Office of the Deputy Prime Minister.

Chair, Peter Dixon
Deputy Chair, Shaukat Moledina
Chief Executive, Jon Rouse

HOUSING OMBUDSMAN SERVICE

Norman House, 105–109 Strand, London WC2R 0AA
T 020-7836 3630 F 020-7836 3900
E ombudsman@ihos.org.uk
W www.ihos.org.uk

The Housing Ombudsman Service deals with complaints from residents concerning shortcomings in the way homes are managed by landlords and housing agents. The Ombudsman has a statutory jurisdiction over all registered social landlords in England. Private and other landlords can join the Service on a voluntary basis.

Ombudsman, Dr Mike Biles
Deputy Ombudsman, Rafael Runco

HUMAN FERTILISATION AND EMBRYOLOGY AUTHORITY

21 Bloomsbury Street, London WC1B 3HF
T 020-7291 8200 F 020-7291 8201
E admin@hfea.gov.uk
W www.hfea.gov.uk

The Human Fertilisation and Embryology Authority (HFEA) was established under the Human Fertilisation and Embryology Act 1990. Its function is to license the following activities: the creation or use of embryos outside the body in the provision of infertility treatment services; the use of donated gametes in infertility treatment; the storage of gametes or embryos; and research on human embryos. It maintains a confidential database of all such treatments and of egg and sperm donors, and provides information to patients, clinics and the public. The HFEA also produces a code of practice that provides guidelines to infertility clinics about the proper conduct of licensed activities, keeps under review information about embryos and, when requested to do so, gives advice to the Secretary of State for Health.

Chair, Suzi Leather
Members, Hossam Abdalla; Prof. Tom Baldwin; Prof. David Barlow; Prof. Christopher Barratt; Ivor Brecker; Clare Brown; Prof. Iain Cameron; Prof. Neva Haites; Rt. Revd Richard Harries; Baroness Hayman; Jennifer Hunt; Emily Jackson; Dr Maybeth Jamieson; Simon Jenkins; Walter Merricks; Sara Nathan; Sharmila Nebhrajani

HUMAN GENETICS COMMISSION

Area 652C, Skipton House, 80 London Road, London SE1 6LH
T 020-7972 1518 F 020-7972 1717
E hgc@doh.gov.uk W www.hgc.gov.uk

The Human Genetics Commission was established in 1999, subsuming three previous advisory committees. Its remit is to give Ministers strategic advice on how developments in human genetics will impact on people and health care, focusing in particular on the special and ethical implications.

Chair, Baroness H. Kennedy of the Shaws, QC
Members, Dr W. Albert; Prof. Emerita Brenda Almond; Dr S. Bain; Dr Celia Brazell; Prof. Angus Clarke; Dr Paul Darragh; Prof. J. Harris; Michael Harrison; Dr Iona Heath; Dr Susan Johnson; A. Kent; Ms S. Leather; Dr Patrick Morrison; Ms H. Newiss; Mrs C. Patch; Prof. M. Richards; P. Sayers; Dr S. Singleton; Dr R. Skinner; Sir John Sulston; Prof. V. van Heyningen; Mr G. Watts
Head of Secretariat, Gwen Nightingale

IMPERIAL WAR MUSEUM

Lambeth Road, London SE1 6HZ
T 020-7416 5320
F 020-7416 5374

The Museum, founded in 1917, illustrates and records all aspects of the two world wars and other military operations involving Britain and the Commonwealth since 1914. It was opened in its present home, formerly Bethlem Hospital, in 1936. The Museum is a multi-branch organisation which also includes: the Churchill Museum and Cabinet War Rooms in Whitehall; HMS Belfast in the Pool of London; Imperial War Museum Duxford in Cambridgeshire; and Imperial War Museum North in Trafford, Manchester.

The total grant-in-aid (including grants for special projects) for 2005–6 is £17.8 million.

OFFICERS
Chair of Trustees, Adm. Sir Jock Slater, GCB, LVO
Director-General, R. W. K. Crawford, CBE
Director of Collections, M. Whitmore
Director of Corporate Services, A. Stoneman
Director of HMS Belfast, B. King
Director of Public Services, Miss A. Godwin
Director, Churchill Museum and Cabinet War Rooms, P. Reed
Director, Imperial War Museum Duxford, R. Ashton
Director, Imperial War Museum North, J. Forrester
Secretary and Director of Finance, J. Card

INDEPENDENT INTERNATIONAL COMMISSION ON DECOMMISSIONING

Dublin Castle, Block M, Ship Street, Dublin 2
T 00 353 1-478 0111 F 00 353 1-478 0600
Rosepark House, Upper Newtownards Road, Belfast BT4 3NX
T 028-9048 8600
F 028-9048 8601

The Commission was established by agreement between the British and Irish governments in August 1997. Its objective is to facilitate the decommissioning of illegally-held firearms and explosives in accordance with the relevant legislation in both jurisdictions. Its members are appointed jointly by the two governments; staff are appointed by the Commission. All are drawn from countries other than the UK and the Republic of Ireland.
Commissioners, Gen. J. de Chastelain *(Chair, Canada)*; A. D. Sens *(USA)*
Staff Director, A. Suonio *(Finland)*

INDEPENDENT POLICE COMPLAINTS COMMISSION (IPCC)

90 High Holborn, London WC1V 6BH
T 0845-300 2002 F 020-7404 0430
E enquiries@ipcc.gsi.gov.uk
W www.ipcc.gov.uk

The Independent Police Complaints Commission succeeded the Police Complaints Authority on 1 April 2004. It was established under the Police Reform Act 2002 following responses to the government document *Complaints Against Police; Framework for a New System,* published in December 2000. The IPCC is an independent public body and is not part of any government department. The IPCC has teams of investigators headed by Regional Directors in each of its regions to assist with the supervision and management of some police investigations. They also carry out independent investigations into serious incidents or allegations of misconduct by persons serving with the police. The 17 commissioners of the IPCC must not previously have worked for the police.
Chair, N. Hardwick
Deputy Chair, J. Wadham
Commissioners, I. Bynoe; J. Crawley; T. Davies; M. Franklin; G. Garland; Ms D. Glass; L. Jackson; N. Long; L. Lustgarten; Ms N. Malik; Ms R. Marsh; D. Petch; Ms M. Mian Pritchard; Ms A. Somal; Ms N. Williams
Chief Executive, Susan Atkins

INDEPENDENT REVIEW SERVICE FOR THE SOCIAL FUND

4th Floor, Centre City Podium, 5 Hill Street, Birmingham B5 4UB
T 0800-096 1926 E sfc@irs-review.org.uk
W www.irs-review.org.uk

The Social Fund Commissioner is appointed by the Secretary of State for Work and Pensions. The Commissioner appoints Social Fund Inspectors, who provide an independent review for customers dissatisfied with decisions made in Jobcentre Plus offices throughout England, Scotland and Wales regarding the grants and loans available from the Discretionary Social Fund.
Social Fund Commissioner, Sir Richard Tilt

INDUSTRIAL INJURIES ADVISORY COUNCIL

6th Floor, The Adelphi, 1–11 John Adam Street, London WC2N 6HT
T 020-7962 8066 F 020-7712 2255
E iiac@dwp.gsi.gov.uk W www.iiac.org.uk

The Industrial Injuries Advisory Council was established under the Social Security Administration Act 1992, with statutory provisions governing its work set out in section 171 of the Act. The Council consists of 15 members appointed by the Secretary of State, and has three roles: to advise on the prescription of diseases; to advise on matters referred to the Council by the Secretary of State or proposals concerning the Industrial Injuries Disablement Benefit Scheme; and to advise on any other matter relating to industrial injuries benefit or its administration.
Chair, Prof. A. J. Newman Taylor, OBE, FRCP

INFORMATION COMMISSIONER'S OFFICE

Wycliffe House, Water Lane, Wilmslow, Cheshire SK9 5AF
T 01625-545745 F 01625-524510
E mail@ico.gsi.gov.uk
W www.informationcommissioner.gov.uk

The Information Commissioner's Office oversees and enforces the Freedom of Information Act 2000 and the Data Protection Act 1998, with the objective of promoting public access to official information and protecting personal information.

The Data Protection Act 1998 sets out rules for the processing of personal information and applies to records held on computers and some paper files. It works in two ways; it dictates that those who record and use personal information (data controllers) must be open about how the information is used and must follow the eight principles of 'good information handling'; and it gives individuals certain rights to access their personal information.

The Freedom of Information Act 2000 is designed to help end the culture of unnecessary secrecy and open up the inner working of the public sector to citizens and businesses. Under the Freedom of Information Act, public authorities must produce a publication scheme that sets out what information the public authority is obliged to publish by law.

The Information Commissioner reports annually to Parliament on the performance of his functions under the Acts and has obligations to assess breaches of the Acts.
Information Commissioner, Richard Thomas

INTELLIGENCE SERVICES COMMISSIONER

c/o PO Box 33220, London SW1H 9ZQ
T 020-7035 3711

The Commissioner is appointed by the prime minister. He keeps under review the issue of warrants by the Secretaries of State as detailed under the Regulation of Investigatory Powers Act (RIPA) 2000 and sections 5, 6 and 7 of the Intelligence Services Act 1994. The Commissioner is also required to submit an annual report on the discharge of his functions to the prime minister.
Commissioner, The Rt. Hon. Lord Brown of Eaton-under-Heywood

INTERCEPTION OF COMMUNICATIONS COMMISSIONER

c/o PO Box 33220, London SW1H 9ZQ
T 020-7035 3711

The Interception of Communications Commissioner is appointed by the prime minister for a period of three years. The Commissioner's job is to keep under review the issue of interception warrants and the adequacy of the arrangements for ensuring the product of interception is properly handled. He does this by reviewing the warrant applications that the intercepting agencies have made to the Secretary of State, in order to be certain that the Secretary of State was right to sign the warrants. He also visits the security, intelligence and law enforcement agencies to examine his selection of interception warrants with the officers responsible for the relevant investigations. At the end of each reporting year, the Commissioner submits a report to the prime minister which is subsequently published and laid before Parliament.
Commissioner, The Rt. Hon. Sir Swinton Thomas

INVESTIGATORY POWERS TRIBUNAL

PO Box 33220, London, SW1H 9ZQ
T 020-7035 3711 W www.ipt-uk.com

The Investigatory Powers Tribunal replaced the Interception of Communications Tribunal, the Intelligence Services Tribunal, the Security Services Tribunal and the complaints function of the Commissioner appointed under the Police Act 1997.

The Regulation of Investigatory Powers Act 2000 provides for a Tribunal made up of senior members of the legal profession, independent of the government and appointed by The Queen, to consider all complaints against the intelligence services and those against public authorities in respect of powers covered by RIPA; and to consider proceedings brought under section 7 of the Human Rights Act 1998 against the intelligence services and law enforcement agencies in respect of these powers.
President, The Rt. Hon. Lord Justice John Mummery
Vice-President, Mr Justice Michael Burton
Members, W. Carmichael; Sir Richard Gaskell; Sheriff Principal J. McInnes, QC; Sir John Pringle, QC; P. Scott, QC; R. Seabrook, QC

JOINT NATURE CONSERVATION COMMITTEE

Monkstone House, City Road, Peterborough PE1 1JY
T 01733-562626 F 01733-555948
E comment@jncc.gov.uk W www.jncc.gov.uk

The Committee was established under the Environmental Protection Act 1990. It advises the government and others on UK and international nature conservation issues and disseminates knowledge on these subjects. It establishes common standards for the monitoring of nature conservation and research, and provides guidance to English Nature, Scottish Natural Heritage, the Countryside Council for Wales and the Department of the Environment for Northern Ireland.
Chair, Adrian Darby, OBE
Director of Resources and External Affairs, M. Yeo
Director of Science, Dr M. A. Vincent
Managing Director, D. Steer

LAND REGISTRY

Lincoln's Inn Fields, London WC2A 3PH
T 020-7917 8888 F 020-7955 0110
E propertyinformationteam@landregistry.gsi.gov.uk
W www.landregistry.gov.uk

The registration of title to land was first introduced in England and Wales by the Land Registry Act 1862. The Land Registry keeps and maintains the Land Register for England and Wales, and is an executive agency and trading fund responsible to the Secretary of State for Constitutional Affairs and Lord Chancellor. There are 24 offices in England and Wales, each of which provides land registration services for different counties and unitary authorities. The Land Register has been open to public inspection since 1990.

Details of all Land Registry offices, telephone numbers, opening times and senior staff can be found on its website. *Land Registry Practice Guide 51 (Feb 2005)* also lists the contact details of the offices and the areas they serve. It is available from any of the offices and can be viewed and downloaded from the website.

DIRECTING BOARD
Chief Land Registrar and Chief Executive, Peter Collis
Director of Legal Services, Joe Timothy
Director for Business Development and Deputy Chief
Executive, Ted Beardsall, CBE
Director of Operations, Andy Howarth

LAW COMMISSION
Conquest House, 37–38 John Street, London WC1N 2BQ
T 020-7453 1220 F 020-7453 1297
W www.lawcom.gov.uk

The Law Commission was set up in 1965, under the Law Commissions Act 1965, to make proposals to the government for the examination of the law in England and Wales and for its revision where it is unsuited to modern requirements, obscure, or otherwise unsatisfactory. It recommends to the Lord Chancellor programmes for the examination of different branches of the law and suggests whether the examination should be carried out by the Commission itself or by some other body. The Commission is also responsible for the preparation of Consolidation and Statute Law (Repeals) Bills.
Chair, The Hon. Mr Justice Toulson
Commissioners, Prof. H. Beale, QC; S. Bridge; Dr Jeremy Horder; Prof. M. Partington, CBE
Chief Executive, S. Humphreys

LAW OFFICERS' DEPARTMENTS
Legal Secretariat to the Law Officers, Attorney-General's Chambers, 9 Buckingham Gate, London SW1E 6JP
T 020-7271 2492 F 020-7271 2494
E lslo@gtnet.gov.uk W www.lslo.gov.uk
Attorney-General's Chambers, Royal Courts of Justice, Belfast BT1 3JY
T 028-9054 6082 F 028-9054 6049

The Law Officers of the Crown for England and Wales are the Attorney-General and the Solicitor-General. The Attorney-General, assisted by the Solicitor-General, is the chief legal adviser to the government and is also ultimately responsible for all Crown litigation. He has overall responsibility for the work of the Law Officers' Departments (the Treasury Solicitor's Department, the Crown Prosecution Service, the Serious Fraud Office, the Revenue and Customs Prosecution Office and the Legal Secretariat to the Law Officers). He has a specific statutory duty to superintend the discharge of their duties by the Director of Public Prosecutions (who heads the Crown Prosecution Service) and the Director of the Serious Fraud Office. The Director of Public Prosecutions for Northern Ireland and the Crown Solicitor for Northern Ireland are also responsible to the Attorney-General for the performance of their functions. The Attorney-General has additional responsibilities in relation to aspects of the civil and criminal law.
Attorney-General, The Rt. Hon. Lord Goldsmith, QC
Private Secretary, F. McElroy
Solicitor-General, The Hon. Mike O'Brien, QC, MP
Legal Secretary, J. Jones
Deputy Legal Secretary, H. Heycock

LEARNING AND SKILLS COUNCIL
Cheylesmore House, Quinton Road, Coventry CV1 2WT
T 0845-019 4170 F 024-7682 3675
Helpline 0870-900 6800
E info@lsc.gov.uk W www.lsc.gov.uk

The Learning and Skills Council (LSC) was established in April 2001 to replace the Further Education Funding and the Training and Enterprise Councils. It is a non-departmental public body responsible for the planning and funding of post-16 education and training. Its remit is to ensure that high-quality post-16 provision is available to meet the needs of employers, individuals and communities. The LSC operates through a national office based in Coventry and 47 local departments, which work to promote the equality of opportunity in the workplace, aiming to ensure that the needs of the most disadvantaged people in the labour market are met. These local departments in most cases have coterminous boundaries with Small Business Service franchises.
Chair, Chris Banks
Vice-Chair, Sandra Burslem, OBE
Chief Executive, Mark Haysom

LEGAL SERVICES COMMISSION
85 Gray's Inn Road, London WC1X 8TX
T 020-7759 0000 Directory Information Line 0845-608 1122
W www.legalservices.gov.uk

The Legal Services Commission was created under the Access to Justice Act 1999 and replaced the Legal Aid Board in April 2000. It is a non-departmental public body which is accountable to the Department for Constitutional Affairs.

The Commission is responsible for two schemes. The Community Legal Service (CLS) funds the delivery of civil legal and advice services, identifies priorities and unmet needs, and develops suppliers and services to meet those needs. The Criminal Defence Service (CDS) provides free legal advice and representation for people involved in criminal investigations or proceedings.

The Commission produces free information leaflets which are available from solicitors' and advisory offices and on the Commission's website.
Chief Executive, Clare Dodgson
Chair, Sir Michael Bichard
Members, A. Andrew; D. Edmonds; A. Edwards; T. Fahm; Ms J. Herzog; T. Jones; L. Joyce; B. Seaman; L. M. Segerman-Peck

LORD GREAT CHAMBERLAIN'S OFFICE
House of Lords, London SW1A 0PW
T 020-7219 3100 F 020-7219 2500

The Lord Great Chamberlain is a Great Officer of State, the office being hereditary since the grant of Henry I to the family of De Vere, Earls of Oxford. It is now a joint hereditary office rotating on the death of the Sovereign between the Cholmondeley, Carington and the Ancaster families. The Lord Great Chamberlain is responsible for the royal apartments in the Palace of Westminster, i.e. the Sovereign's Robing Room, the Royal Gallery, the administration of the Chapel of St Mary Undercroft and, in conjunction with the Lord Chancellor and the Speaker, Westminster Hall. The Lord Great Chamberlain has the right to perform specific services at a Coronation, he carries out ceremonial duties in the Palace of Westminster when the Sovereign visits the Palace and has particular responsibility for the internal administrative arrangements within the House of Lords for State Openings of Parliament.

Lord Great Chamberlain, The Marquess of Cholmondeley
Secretary to the Lord Great Chamberlain, Lt.-Gen. Sir Michael Willcocks, KCB
Clerks to the Lord Great Chamberlain, Ms J. Perodeau; Ms Rebecca Russel Ponte

LORD PRESIDENT OF THE COUNCIL'S OFFICE

2 Carlton Gardens, London SW1Y 5AA
T 020-7210 1056
W www.privy-council.org.uk

The Lord President of the Council is a member of the Cabinet and Leader of the House of Lords. She has no departmental portfolio, but is a member of a number of Cabinet committees. She is responsible to the prime minister for the organisation of government business in the House and has a responsibility to the House itself to advise it on procedural matters and other difficulties which arise. She is the Lords' spokesperson on international development issues.

Lord President of the Council, Leader of the House of Lords, The Rt. Hon. Baroness Amos
Principal Private Secretary, Sue Ball

MENTAL HEALTH ACT COMMISSION

Maid Marian House, 56 Hounds Gate, Nottingham NG1 6BG
T 0115-943 7100 F 0115-943 7101
E chiefexec@mhac.org.uk
W www.mhac.org.uk

The Mental Health Act Commission was established in 1983. Its functions are to keep under review the operation of the Mental Health Act 1983; to visit and meet patients detained under the Act; to investigate complaints falling within the Commission's remit; to operate the 'consent to treatment' safeguards in the Mental Health Act; to publish a biennial report on its activities; to monitor the implementation of the Code of Practice; and to advise Ministers. Commissioners are appointed by the Secretary of State for Health.

Chair, Prof. Kamlesh Patel
Vice-Chair, Deborah Jenkins
Chief Executive, Chris Heginbotham

MUSEUM OF LONDON

London Wall, London EC2Y 5HN
T 0870-444 3852 F 0870-444 3853
E info@museumoflondon.org.uk
W www.museumoflondon.org.uk

The Museum of London illustrates the history of London from prehistoric times to the present day. It opened in 1976 and is based on the amalgamation of the former Guildhall Museum and London Museum. The Museum is controlled by a Board of Governors, appointed (nine each) by the government and the Corporation of London. The Museum is currently funded by grants from the Department for Culture, Media and Sport and the Corporation of London. The total grant-in-aid for 2005–6 is £11 million.

Chair of Board of Governors, Michael Cassidy, CBE
Director, Prof. J. Lohman

MUSEUMS, LIBRARIES AND ARCHIVES COUNCIL

16 Queen Anne's Gate, London SW1H 9AA
T 020-7273 1444 F 020-7273 1404
E info@mla.gov.uk W www.mla.gov.uk

The Museums, Libraries and Archives Council (MLA) was launched in April 2000 in order to provide strategic guidance, advice and advocacy across the whole of government on museum, archive and library matters. It is a non-departmental public body sponsored by the Department for Culture, Media and Sport. The MLA replaced the Museums and Galleries Commission (MGC) and the Library and Information Commission (LIC), and now includes archives within its portfolio.

Chair, Mark Wood
Chief Executive, Chris Batt, OBE
Board Members, David Barrie; Lynne Brindley; Ajay Chowdhury; Dr Maurna Crozier; Loyd Grossman; Sir David Henshaw; Sir Geoffrey Holland; Mark Jones; Nicholas Kingsley; Neil MacGregor; Bill MacNaught; Bob McKee; Michael Stevenson; Virginia Tandy; Alan Watkin

NATIONAL ARCHIVES

Kew, Richmond, Surrey TW9 4DU
T 020-8876 3444 F 020-8878 8905
W www.nationalarchives.gov.uk

The National Archives, a government department and an executive agency reporting to the Lord Chancellor/Secretary of State for Constitutional Affairs, was formed in April 2003 by bringing together the Public Record Office (founded in 1838) and the Historical Manuscripts Commission (founded in 1869).

The National Archives for England, Wales and the United Kingdom acts as the custodian of the nation's collective memory as revealed in the records of government. It also collects and disseminates information about archives relating to British history wherever they are held.

Its aims are: to assist and promote the study of the past through the public records and other archives in order to inform the present and the future; to act as chief source of authoritative advice and guidance on records management, archive policy and related information policy matters within government; to provide impartial advice to custodians of records and papers throughout the public and private sectors on records and archives management.

The National Archives administers the UK's public records system under the Public Records Acts of 1958 and 1967. The records it holds span 1,000 years – from the Domesday Book to the latest government papers to be released – and fill more than 100 miles of shelving. The records held by the National Archives are available to the public, without charge, in the reading rooms.

The National Archives also provides free expert advice to owners, custodians and users of archives throughout the UK. They include central and local government, universities, business and industry, many other individuals and institutions, and a range of public and private grant-awarding bodies.

Director of National Advisory and Public Services, Dr E. Hallam-Smith
Director of Government and Technology Group, Dr D. Thomas

Director of Strategy, Finance and Resources, Mrs W. Jones
Head of Online Services and Strategic Marketing, J. Strachan

NATIONAL ARCHIVES OF SCOTLAND
HM General Register House, Edinburgh EH1 3YY
T 0131-535 1314 F 0131-535 1360
E enquiries@nas.gov.uk W www.nas.gov.uk

The history of the National Archives of Scotland can be traced back to the 13th century. The National Archives of Scotland (formerly the Scottish Record Office) is an executive agency of the Scottish Executive and keeps the administrative records of pre-Union Scotland, the registers of central and local courts of law, the public registers of property rights and legal documents, and many collections of local and church records and private archives. Certain groups of records, mainly the modern records of government departments in Scotland, the Scottish railway records, the plans collection, and private archives of an industrial or commercial nature, are preserved in the branch repository at West Register House in Charlotte Square. The National Register of Archives for Scotland is based in the West Register House.
Keeper of the Records of Scotland, G. P. MacKenzie
Deputy Keepers, Dr P. D. Anderson; D. Brownlee

NATIONAL ARMY MUSEUM
Royal Hospital Road, London SW3 4HT
T 020-7730 0717
E info@national-army-museum.ac.uk
W www.national-army-museum.ac.uk

The National Army Museum covers the history of five centuries of the British Army, chronicling the campaigns and battles fought over this time as well as the social history and development of the Army. The museum houses a wide array of artefacts, paintings, photographs, uniforms and equipment. It was established by royal charter in 1960.
Chair, General Sir John Waters, GCB, CBE
Director, Dr A. J. Guy
Assistant Directors, Dr P. B. Boyden; D. K. Smurthwaite

NATIONAL AUDIT OFFICE
157 197 Buckingham Palace Road, London SW1W 9SP
T 020-7798 7000 F 020-7798 7070
E enquiries@nao.gsi.gov.uk
W www.nao.org.uk

The National Audit Office came into existence under the National Audit Act 1983 to replace and continue the work of the former Exchequer and Audit Department. The Act reinforced the Office's total financial and operational independence from the government and brought its head, the Comptroller and Auditor-General, into a closer relationship with Parliament as an officer of the House of Commons.
The National Audit Office provides independent information, advice and assurance to Parliament and the public about all aspects of the financial operations of government departments and many other bodies receiving public funds. It does this by examining and certifying the accounts of these organisations. It also regularly publishes reports to Parliament on the results of its value for money investigations of the economy, namely the efficiency and effectiveness with which public resources have been used. The National Audit Office is also the auditor by agreement of the accounts of certain international and other organisations. In addition, the Office authorises the issue of public funds to government departments.
Comptroller and Auditor-General, Sir John Bourne, KCB
Private Secretary, Neil Sayers
Deputy Comptroller and Auditor-General, Tim Burr
Assistant Auditors-General, Gabrielle Cohen; Wendy Kenway-Smith; Caroline Mawhood; Jim Rickleton; Anna Simons; Martin Sinclair; Michael Whitehouse

NATIONAL CONSUMER COUNCIL
20 Grosvenor Gardens, London SW1W 0DH
T 020-7730 3469 F 020-7730 0191
E info@ncc.org.uk W www.ncc.org.uk

The National Consumer Council (NCC) was set up by the government in 1975 to give an independent voice to consumers in the UK. Its role is to advocate the consumer interest to decision-makers in national and local government, industry and regulatory bodies, business and the professions. It does this through a combination of research and campaigning. NCC is a non-profit making company limited by guarantee and is largely funded by grant-in-aid from the Department of Trade and Industry. The Council is not a consumer advice or complaints body.
Chair (acting), Dr Robert Chilton
Chief Executive, Ed Mayo

NATIONAL CRIMINAL INTELLIGENCE SERVICE (NCIS)
PO Box 8000, London SE11 5EN
T 020-7238 8000
W www.ncis.gov.uk

The National Criminal Intelligence Service (NCIS) provides intelligence about serious and organised crime to law enforcement, government and other relevant national and international agencies. Following the Serious Organised Crime and Police Bill, the Serious Organised Crime Agency is due to come into being in April 2006, at which point the NCIS and the National Crime Squad, and their respective Service Authorities, will cease to exist.
Director-General, P. Hampson, QPM, CBE
Deputy Director General, D. Bolt
Director, Finance and Administration, Ms M. Ashworth
Director, Intelligence Services Division, N. Bailey
Director, International Division, R. Wainwright
Director, Resources Division, N. Beard
Director, UK Division, I. Cruxton *(acting)*

SERVICE AUTHORITY
PO Box 2600, London SW1V 2WG
T 020-7238 2600

The Service Authority for NCIS is responsible for ensuring its effective operation. It operates with the Service Authority for the National Crime Squad. There are 12 members of the authorities, of whom the chairman and seven others serve as 'core members' on both authorities.
Chair, P. Lever
Clerk, A. Mulholland
Finance Officer, P. Hampshire

NATIONAL ENDOWMENT FOR SCIENCE, TECHNOLOGY AND THE ARTS (NESTA)
Fishmongers' Chambers, 110 Upper Thames Street, London EC4R 3TW
T 020-7645 9500
E nesta@nesta.org.uk W www.nesta.org.uk

The National Endowment for Science, Technology and the Arts (NESTA) was established under the National Lottery Act 1998 with a £200 million (raised in 2003 to £250 million) endowment from the proceeds of the National Lottery. Its four main funding programmes are: *Invention and Innovation* takes original ideas with commercial or social potential and helps them get to market; *Fellowship* supports exceptionally talented and innovative people, and enables them to pursue a tailor-made programme of personal creative development; *Learning* researches and pioneers initiatives, which will drive education and encourage public engagement with science, technology and the arts; and the *Creative Pioneer Programme* helps recent graduates from the creative industries to develop their entrepreneurial skills.
Chair, Chris Powell
Chief Executive (acting), Janet Morrison

NATIONAL GALLERIES OF SCOTLAND
The Dean Gallery, 73 Bedford Road, Edinburgh EH4 3DS
T 0131-624 6200 F 0131-623 7133
E enquiries@nationalgalleries.org W www.natgalscot.ac.uk

The National Galleries of Scotland comprise the National Gallery of Scotland, the Scottish National Portrait Gallery, the Scottish National Gallery of Modern Art, the Dean Gallery and the Royal Scottish Academy Building. There are also outstations at Paxton House, Berwickshire, and Duff House, Banffshire. Total government grant-in-aid for 2004–5 was £10.51 million.

TRUSTEES
Chair of the Trustees, Mr B. Ivory, CBE
Trustees, Ms V. Atkinson; Ms A. Bonnar; Bailie E. Cameron; G. J. N. Gemmell, CBE; M. Ellington; Dr I. McKenzie Smith, OBE; Prof. R. Thomson; G. Weaver; Dr Ruth Wishart

OFFICERS
Director-General, Sir T. Clifford, FRSE
Director, National Gallery of Scotland (G6), M. Clarke
Director, Scottish National Portrait Gallery (G6), J. Holloway
Director, Scottish National Gallery of Modern Art and Dean Gallery (G6), R. Calvocoressi

NATIONAL GALLERY
Trafalgar Square, London WC2N 5DN
T 020-7747 2885 F 020-7747 2423
W www.nationalgallery.org.uk

The National Gallery, which houses a permanent collection of western painting from the 13th to the 20th century, was founded in 1824, following a parliamentary grant of £60,000 for the purchase and exhibition of the Angerstein collection of pictures. The present site was first occupied in 1838; an extension to the north of the building with a public entrance in Orange Street was opened in 1975; the Sainsbury wing was opened in 1991; and the Getty Entrance opened off Trafalgar Square at the east end of the main building in September 2004. Total government grant-in-aid for 2005–6 is £22.316 million.

BOARD OF TRUSTEES
Chair, P. Scott, QC
Trustees, V. Barnsley; S. Burke; J. Fenton; M. Getty; Prof. J. Higgins; Lady Hopkins; Lord Kerr of Kinlochard; Prof. M. King; J. Lessore; D. A. Moore; Lady Normanby; J. Snow; R. Sondhi

OFFICERS
Director, Dr C. Saumarez Smith
Director of Administration, J. MacAuslan
Director of Conservation, M. H. Wyld, CBE
Director of Communications, Clare Gough
Director of Collections and Media, Dr S. Foister
Director of Education, K. Adler
Director of Scientific Research, Dr A. Roy
Senior Curator, D. Jaffé

NATIONAL HERITAGE MEMORIAL FUND
7 Holbein Place, London SW1W 8NR
T 020-7591 6000 F 020-7591 6001
W www.nhmf.org.uk

The National Heritage Memorial Fund was set up under the National Heritage Act 1980 in memory of people who have given their lives for the United Kingdom. The Fund provides grants (and sometimes loans) to organisations based in the United Kingdom, mainly so they can buy items of outstanding interest and of importance to the national heritage. These must either be at risk or have a memorial character. The Fund is administered by 14 trustees who are appointed by the prime minister.

The National Lottery etc. Act 1993 designated the Fund as distributor of the heritage share of proceeds from the National Lottery. As a result, the Fund now operates two funds: the National Heritage Memorial Fund and the Heritage Lottery Fund. The National Heritage Memorial Fund receives an annual grant from the Department for Culture, Media and Sport.
Chair, Liz Forgan, OBE
Trustees, Madhu Anjali; The Earl of Dalkeith; Nicholas Dodd; Mike Emmerich; Catherine Graham-Harrison; Tristram Hunt; Dr Brian Lang; Dr Derek Langslow; Dr Mike Phillips; Matthew Saunders; Giles Waterfield; Primrose Wilson; James Wright, CBE
Director, Carole Souter

NATIONAL LIBRARY OF SCOTLAND
George IV Bridge, Edinburgh EH1 1EW
T 0131-623 3700 F 0131-623 3701
E enquiries@nls.uk W www.nls.uk

The Library, which was founded as the Advocates' Library in 1682, became the National Library of Scotland in 1925. It is funded by the Scottish Executive. It contains about 13 million books and pamphlets, two million maps, 20,000 current periodicals, 350 newspaper titles and 120,000 manuscripts. It has an unrivalled Scottish collection.

The Reading Room is for reference and research which cannot conveniently be pursued elsewhere. Admission is by ticket.
Chair of the Trustees, Prof. Michael Anderson, OBE, FBA, FRSE
National Librarian and Secretary to the Trustees, M. Wade
Director of Collection Development, C. Newton
Director of Corporate Services, D. Campbell

Director of Customer Services, G. Hunt
Director of Development and Marketing, A. Miller

NATIONAL LIBRARY OF WALES/
LLYFRGELL GENEDLAETHOL CYMRU

Aberystwyth SY23 3BU
T 01970-632800 F 01970-615709
W www.llgc.org.uk

The National Library of Wales was founded by royal charter in 1907, and is funded by the National Assembly for Wales. It contains about four million printed books, 40,000 manuscripts, four million deeds and documents, numerous maps, prints and drawings, and a sound and moving image collection. It specialises in manuscripts and books relating to Wales and the Celtic peoples. It is the repository for pre-1858 Welsh probate records, manorial records and tithe documents, and certain legal records. Admission is by reader's ticket to the Reading Rooms but entry to the exhibition programme is free.

President, Dr R. Brinley Jones
Heads of Departments, M. W. Mainwaring *(Corporate Services)*; G. Jenkins *(Collection Services)*; Dr W. R. M. Griffiths *(Public Services)*
Librarian, A. M. W. Green

NATIONAL LOTTERY COMMISSION

101 Wigmore Street, London W1U 1QU
T 020-7016 3400 F 020-7016 3401
W www.natlotcomm.gov.uk

The National Lottery Commission replaced the Office of the National Lottery (OFLOT) in April 1999 under the National Lottery Act 1998. The Commission is responsible for the granting, varying and enforcing of licences to run the National Lottery. Its duties are to ensure that the National Lottery is run with all due propriety, that the interests of players are protected, and, subject to these two objectives, that returns to the good causes are maximised. The Commission does not have a role in the distribution of funds to good causes, this is undertaken by 14 distributors, visit www.lotterygoodcauses.org.uk for further information. Gaming and lotteries in the UK are officially regulated and may only be run by licensed operators or in licensed premises.

The Department of Culture, Media and Sport is responsible for gaming and lottery policy and laws. The National Lottery is the most heavily regulated part of the gaming market. Empowered by the National Lottery Act 1993 (as amended), the Department of Culture, Media and Sport directs the National Lottery Commission, who in turn regulates Camelot, the lottery operator. Camelot, a private company wholly owned by five shareholders, was granted a second seven-year licence to run the Lottery, which began on 27 January 2002.

Chair, Timothy Hornsby
Chief Executive, Mark Harris
Commissioners, Robert Foster; Brian Pomeroy; Jo Valentine; Anne Wright
Director of Compliance, Marta Phillips
Director of Licensing, Annette Lovell
Director of Performance and Communications, Catherine Forrester
Director of Resources, Clare McCullough
Director of Competition Programme, Colin Perry

NATIONAL MARITIME MUSEUM

Park Row, Greenwich, London SE10 9NF
T 020-8858 4422 F 020-8312 6632

Established by Act of Parliament in 1934, the National Maritime Museum illustrates the maritime history of Great Britain in the widest sense, underlining the importance of the sea and its influence on the nation's power, wealth, culture, technology and institutions. The Museum is in three groups of buildings in Greenwich Park: the main building, the Queen's House (built by Inigo Jones, 1616–35) and the Royal Observatory (including Wren's Flamsteed House). In May 1999, a £20 million Heritage Lottery-supported project opened 16 new galleries in a glazed courtyard in the Museum's west wing. Total government grant-in-aid for 2005–6 is £15,236,000.

Director, R. Clare
Chair, Rt. Hon. The Lord Sterling of Plaistow

NATIONAL MUSEUMS AND GALLERIES
OF WALES

Cathays Park, Cardiff CF10 3NP
T 029-2039 7951 F 029-2057 3321
E post@nmgw.ac.uk W www.nmgw.ac.uk

The National Museums and Galleries of Wales comprise: the National Museum and Gallery, Cardiff; the Museum of Welsh Life, St Fagans; Big Pit National Museum of Wales, Blaenafon; the Roman Legionary Museum, Caerleon; Turner House Gallery, Penarth; National Waterfront Museum, Swansea; the Welsh Slate Museum, Llanberis; the Segontium Roman Museum, Caernarfon; and the National Woollen Museum, Dre-fach Felindre. Total funding from the Welsh Assembly government for 2004–5 was £18.7 million.

President, Paul E. Loveluck, CBE, JP
Vice-President, Dr Susan J. Davies
Treasurer, G. Wyn Howells, ACIB

OFFICERS
Director-General, Michael Houlihan
Directors, R. Gwyn *(Communications)*; M. Richards *(Operations)*; J. Sheppard *(Finance and IT)*; M. Tooby *(National Museum and Gallery)*; Dr E. Wiliam *(Collections and Research, and Deputy Director)*; J. Williams-Davies *(Museum of Welsh Life)*

Council Members, D. Bowen Lewis; Dr Iolo ap Gwynn; Prof. Colin L. Jones, OBE; Prof. J. W. Last; J. E. Peirson Jones, CBE; M.C. T. Prichard, CBE; Dr Peter Warren, CBE; H. R. C. Williams; Dr Brian Willott; Rhiannon Wyn Hughes, MBE; J. Wynford Evans, CBE

NATIONAL MUSEUMS LIVERPOOL

127 Dale Street, Liverpool L2 2JH
T 0151-207 0001 F 0151-478 4790
W www.nationalmuseumsliverpool.org.uk

The Board of Trustees of the National Museums Liverpool (formerly National Museums and Galleries on Merseyside) is responsible for the World Museum Liverpool, the Merseyside Maritime Museum (incorporating HM Customs and Excise National Museum), the Museum of Liverpool Life, the Lady Lever Art Gallery, the Walker, Sudley House and the Conservation Centre. Total government grant-in-aid for 2005–6 is £17,256,000.

Chair of the Board of Trustees, Loyd Grossman
Director, Dr David Fleming

Keeper of Art Galleries, J. Treuherz
Keeper of Conservation, vacant
Keeper, World Museum Liverpool, J. Millard
Keeper, Merseyside Maritime Museum, T. Tibbles
Keeper, Museum of Liverpool Life, J. Dugdale

NATIONAL MUSEUMS OF SCOTLAND

Chambers Street, Edinburgh EH1 1JF
T 0131-247 4422 F 0131-220 4819
E info@nms.ac.uk W www.nms.ac.uk

The National Museums of Scotland comprise the Royal Museum of Scotland, the National War Museum of Scotland, the Museum of Scottish Country Life, the Museum of Flight, Shambellie House Museum of Costume and the Museum of Scotland. Total funding from the Scottish Executive is an annual grant of £18 million.

BOARD OF TRUSTEES
Chair, Lord Wilson of Tillyorn, KT, GCMG, PHD, FRSE
Members, James Fiddes, OBE, FRICS; Lesley Hart, MBE; Grenville Shaw Johnston, OBE, TD, KCSG, CA; Michael Kirwan, CA; Prof. Michael Lynch, PHD, FRSE, FSA (SCOT); Christina Macaulay; Anne MacLean; Neena Mahal, DCG; Sir Neil McIntosh, CBE; Prof. Malcolm McLeod; Dr Stuart Munro; Ian Ritchie, CBE, FRENG, FRSE; A. J. C. Smith, FFA, FCIA; Sir John Ward, CBE, CA; Mrs N. Mahal, DCG; Prof. A. Manning, OBE, DPHIL, FRSE, FIBIOL; Prof. J. Murray, CENG

OFFICERS
Director, Dr Gordon Rintoul, PHD
Director of Collections, Jane Carmichael
Director of Facilities Management and Projects, Stephen Elson
Director of Finance and Resources, Andrew Patience
Director of Marketing and Development, Catherine Holden
Director of Public Programmes, Mary Bryden
Head of Corporate Policy and Performance, Sheila McClure
Managing Director of NMS Enterprises, Peter Williamson

NATIONAL PHYSICAL LABORATORY

Hampton Road, Teddington, Middx TW11 0LW
T 020-8977 3222 F 020-8943 6458
E enquiry@npl.co.uk W www.npl.co.uk

The Laboratory is the UK's national standards laboratory. It develops, maintains and disseminates national measurement standards for physical quantities such as mass, length, time, temperature, voltage, force and pressure. It also conducts underpinning research on engineering materials and information technology, and disseminates good measurement practice. It is government-owned but contractor-operated.
Managing Director, Dr B. McGuiness
Director of Business Development, D. C. Richardson

NATIONAL PORTRAIT GALLERY

St Martin's Place, London WC2H 0HE
T 020-7306 0055 F 020-7306 0056
W www.npg.org.uk

A grant was made in 1856 to form a gallery of the portraits of the most eminent persons in British history. The present building was opened in 1896 and the Ondaatje Wing (including a new Balcony Gallery, Tudor Gallery, IT Gallery, Lecture Theatre and roof-top restaurant) opened in May 2000. There are three regional partnerships displaying portraits at Montacute House, Beningbrough Hall and Bodelwyddan Castle. Total government grant-in-aid for 2005–6 is £6,385,000.

BOARD OF TRUSTEES
Chair, Sir David Scholey, CBE
Trustees, The Rt. Hon. Baroness Amos; Zeinab Badawi; Prof. R. Boucher, CBE, FRENG; Prof. David Cannadine; The Marchioness of Douro; Amelia Fawcett, CBE; Flora Fraser; Sir Nicholas Grimshaw, CBE, PRA; Prof. Ludmilla Jordanova; Sir Christopher Ondaatje, CBE, OC; Tom Phillips, CBE, RA; Prof. Sara Selwood; Alexandra Shulman, OBE; Sir John Weston, KCMG; Prof. The Earl Russell, FBA; Baroness Willoughby de Eresby
Director, S. Nairne

NATIONAL SAVINGS AND INVESTMENTS

375 Kensington High Street, London W14 8SD
T 020-7348 9200 F 020-7048 9698
W www.nsandi.com

National Savings and Investments came into being in 1861 when the Palmerston government set up the Post Office Savings Bank, a savings scheme which aimed to encourage ordinary wage earners 'to provide for themselves against adversity and ill health'. National Savings and Investments was established as a government department in 1969. It became an executive agency of the Treasury in 1996 and is responsible for the design, marketing and administration of savings and investment products for personal savers and investors. In April 1999 Siemens Business Services took over all the back office functions at National Savings and Investments.
Chief Executive, A. Cook
Finance Director, T. Bayley
Marketing Director, Karen Jones
Partnerships and Operations Director, S. Owen
Sales Director, J. Prout

NATURAL HISTORY MUSEUM

Cromwell Road, London SW7 5BD
T 020-7942 5000

The Natural History Museum originates from the natural history departments of the British Museum, which grew extensively during the 19th century; in 1860 the natural history collection was moved from Bloomsbury to a new location. Part of the site of the 1862 International Exhibition in South Kensington was acquired for the new museum, and the Museum opened to the public in 1881. In 1963 the Natural History Museum became completely independent with its own board of trustees. The Walter Rothschild Zoological Museum, Tring, bequeathed by the second Lord Rothschild, has formed part of the Museum since 1938. The Geological Museum merged with the Natural History Museum in 1985. Total government grant-in-aid for 2005–6 is £40.8 million.
Trustees, Prof. Sir Keith O'Nions, FRS *(Chair)*; Sir William Castell; Prof. Dianne Edwards, CBE, FRS; Prof. M. Hassell, CBE, FRS; Ian Henderson, CBE, FRICS; Prof. C. Leaver, CBE, FRS; Prof. Georgina Mace, OBE; Dame Judith Mayhew, DBE; Prof. J. McGlade; Lord Palumbo; Prof. Linda Partridge, FRS, FRSE; O. Stocken; Sir Richard Sykes, FRS

SENIOR STAFF

Director, Dr Michael Dixon
Director of Public Engagement Group, Sharon Ament
Head of Estates, K. Rellis
Director of Finance, N. Greenwood
Director of Human Resources, P. Brereton
Director of Science, R. Lane
Director, Tring Zoological Museum, Mrs T. Wild
Head of Audit and Review, D. Thorpe
Head of Library and Information Services, G. Higley
Head of Visitor Services, I. Jenkinson
Keeper of Botany, Dr J. Vogel
Keeper of Entomology, Dr Q. Wheeler
Keeper of Mineralogy, Prof. A. Fleet
Keeper of Palaeontology, Dr N. MacLeod
Keeper of Zoology, Prof. P. Rainbow

NORTHERN IRELAND AUDIT OFFICE

106 University Street, Belfast BT7 1EU
T 028-9025 1000 F 028-9025 1106
E info@niauditoffice.gov.uk
W www.niauditoffice.gov.uk

The primary aim of the Northern Ireland Audit Office is to provide independent assurance, information and advice to the Northern Ireland Assembly (or to parliament during the suspension of devolution) on the proper accounting for Northern Ireland departmental and certain other public expenditure, revenue, assets and liabilities; on regularity and propriety; and on the economy, efficiency and effectiveness of the use of resources.
Comptroller and Auditor-General for Northern Ireland, J. M. Dowdall, CB

NORTHERN IRELAND AUTHORITY FOR ENERGY REGULATION

Queens House, 10–18 Queen Street, Belfast BT1 6ED
T 028-9031 1575 F 028-9031 1740
E ofreg@nics.gov.uk
W http://ofreg.nics.gov.uk

The Northern Ireland Authority for Energy Regulation (NIAER), formerly the Office for the Regulation of Electricity and Gas (Ofreg), is the regulatory body for the electricity and gas supply industries in Northern Ireland.
Chair and Chief Executive, Douglas McIldoon

NORTHERN IRELAND HUMAN RIGHTS COMMISSION

Temple Court, 39 North Street, Belfast BT1 1NA
T 028-9024 3987 F 028-9024 7844
E information@nihrc.org
W www.nihrc.org

The Northern Ireland Human Rights Commission was set up in March 1999. Its main functions are to keep under review the law and practice relating to human rights in Northern Ireland, to advise the government and to promote an awareness of human rights in Northern Ireland. It can also take cases to court. The members of the Commission are appointed by the Secretary of State for Northern Ireland.
Chief Commissioner, Prof. Monica McWilliams
Commissioners, Jonathan Bell; Thomas Duncan; Lady Christine Eames; Prof. Colin Harvey; Alan Henry; Ann Hope; Kevin McLaughlin; Eamonn O'Neill; Geraldine Rice

NORTHERN LIGHTHOUSE BOARD

84 George Street, Edinburgh EH2 3DA
T 0131-473 3100 F 0131 220 2093
E enquiries@nlb.org.uk W www.nlb.org.uk

The Lighthouse Board is the general lighthouse authority for Scotland and the Isle of Man and owes its origin to an Act of Parliament passed in 1786. At present there are 19 Commissioners who operate under the Merchant Shipping Act 1995.

The Commissioners control 210 lighthouses, many lighted and unlighted buoys and a DGPS system.

COMMISSIONERS

The Lord Advocate; the Solicitor-General for Scotland; the Lord Provosts of Edinburgh, Glasgow and Aberdeen; the Convener of Highland Council; the Convener of Argyll and Bute Council; the Sheriffs-Principal of North Strathclyde, Tayside, Central and Fife, Grampian, Highlands and Islands, South Strathclyde, Dumfries and Galloway, Lothians and Borders and Glasgow and Strathkelvin; Peter MacKay, CB, *(Chair);* Capt. Kenneth MacLeod; Dr Andrew Cubie, CBE, FRSE; Robert Quayle; Alistair Whyte; George Sutherland

OFFICERS

Chief Executive, Capt. James Taylor, RN
Director of Finance, Douglas Gorman
Director of Engineering, Moray Waddell
Director of Operations and Navigational Requirements, Guy Platten

OFFICE OF COMMUNICATIONS (OFCOM)

Riverside House, 2A Southwark Bridge Road, London SE1 9HA
T 020-7981 3040 F 020-7981 3043
E contact@ofcom.org.uk
W www.ofcom.org.uk

The Office of Communications (Ofcom) was established in 2003 under the Office of Communications Act 2002 as the independent regulator for the UK communications industries with responsibility for television, radio, telecommunications and wireless communications services. It merged the functions of five regulatory bodies: the Independent Television Commission (ITC), The Broadcasting Standards Commission (BSC), the Office of Telecommunications (Oftel), the Radio Authority (RAu) and the Radiocommunications Agency (RA). Members of the board are appointed by the Secretaries of State for Trade and Industry and for Culture, Media and Sport.
Chief Executive, Stephen Carter
Chair, David Currie
Deputy Chair, Richard Hooper
Board Members, Millie Banerjee; Ian Hargreaves; Kip Meek; Sara Nathan; Ed Richards

OFFICE OF FAIR TRADING

Fleetbank House, 2–6 Salisbury Square, London EC4Y 8JX
T 0845-722 4499 F 020-7211 8800
E enquiries@oft.gsi.gov.uk
W www.oft.gov.uk

The Office of Fair Trading (OFT) is a non-ministerial government department established as a corporate body. It pursues its primary goal of making markets work better for consumers through enforcement of competition and consumer legislation, market studies and communication.

The Consumer Regulation Enforcement Division pursues the Office's consumer protection duties principally through the Enterprise Act 2002, the Consumer Credit Act 1974, the Estate Agents Act 1979, the Control of Misleading Advertisements Regulations Act 1988, the Consumer Protection (Distance Selling) Regulations 2000 and the Unfair Terms in Consumer Contracts Regulations 1999.

The Competition Enforcement Division is responsible for investigating and taking action against agreements that restrict competition and conduct abusing a dominant position, under both the UK Competition Act 1998, as amended by the Enterprise Act 2002, and European competition legislation. The Division also assumes an important role in reviewing mergers under the UK and EC merger control regimes. It has additional responsibilities for competition matters arising under other legislation, including the Financial Services and Markets Act 2000 and the Transport Act 2000.

The Markets and Policy Initiatives Division conducts market studies, which are made public, helping the Office assess whether action is needed to make markets work better for consumers. It negotiates and reviews undertakings following certain Competition Commission reports; provides advice to government departments on the potential effects of new policy and legislation on competition and consumers; co-ordinates the Office's overall relationships with government departments, devolved administrations and other bodies; and leads on payment systems work.

The Communications Division's work entails the empowerment of consumers through campaigns, advice and education. It also informs businesses of their rights and duties under competition and consumer laws, giving an opportunity for law-abiding businesses to complain about anti-competitive behaviour of others.

The Office of Fair Trading also liaises with the European Commission on competition and consumer protection initiatives.

Chair, Philip Collins
Chief Executive Officer, John Singleton
Non-Executive Directors, Allan Asher; Lord Blackwell; Christine Farnish; Richard Whish; Rosalind Wright
Director of Communications, Mike Ricketts
Director of Competition Enforcement, Vincent Smith
Director of Consumer Regulation Enforcement, Christine Wade
Solicitor to the OFT, Brian McHenry
Director of Markets and Policy Initiatives, Jonathan May
Director of Resources and Services, Bart Smith

BOARD SECRETARIAT
Head of the Secretariat, Erik Wilson
Board Secretary, Francesca Seymour

OFFICE OF GAS AND ELECTRICITY MARKETS (OFGEM)

9 Millbank, London SW1P 3GE
T 020-7901 7000 F 020-7901 7066
Regents Court, 70 West Regent Street, Glasgow G2 2QZ
T 0141-331 2678 F 0141-331 2777
W www.ofgem.gov.uk

The Office of Gas and Electricity Markets (Ofgem) is the regulator for Britain's gas and electricity industries. Its role is to protect and advance the interests of consumers by promoting competition where possible, and through regulation only where necessary. Ofgem operates under the direction and governance of the Gas and Electricity Markets Authority, which makes all major decisions and sets policy priorities for Ofgem. Ofgem's powers are provided for under the Gas Act 1986 and the Electricity Act 1989, as amended by the Utilities Act 2000. It also has enforcement powers under the Competition Act 1998.

Chief Executive, A. Buchanan
Managing Directors, D. Gray *(Networks)*; Sarah Harrison *(Corporate Affairs)*; S. Smith *(Markets)*
Chief Operating Officer, R. Field

OFFICE OF THE LEGAL SERVICES OMBUDSMAN

3rd Floor, Sunlight House, Quay Street, Manchester M3 3JZ
T 0161-839 7262; 0845-601 0794 F 0161-832 5446
E lso@olso.gsi.gov.uk
W www.olso.org

The Legal Services Ombudsman is appointed by the Lord Chancellor under the Courts and Legal Services Act 1990 to oversee the handling of complaints against solicitors, barristers, licensed conveyancers, legal executives and patent agents by their professional bodies. A complainant must first complain to the relevant professional body before raising the matter with the Ombudsman, who will then check that all complaints were addressed within a reasonable time. The Ombudsman is independent of the legal profession and her services are free of charge.

Legal Services Ombudsman, Zahida Manzoor, CBE
Operations Director, Steve Lees

OFFICE OF THE SCOTTISH LEGAL SERVICES OMBUDSMAN

17 Waterloo Place, Edinburgh EH1 3DL
T 0131-556 9123 F 0131-556 9292
E ombudsman@slso.org.uk
W www.slso.org.uk

The Ombudsman investigates complaints about the way in which Scottish professional bodies have handled a complaint against a practitioner.

The Ombudsman also examines complaints about the unwillingness of a professional body to investigate a complaint against a practitioner.

Scottish Legal Services Ombudsman, Linda Costelloe Baker

OFFICE OF THE LORD ADVOCATE

Crown Office, 25 Chambers Street, Edinburgh EH1 1LA
T 0131-226 2626 F 0131-226 6564
W www.crownoffice.gov.uk

The Law Officers for Scotland are the Lord Advocate and the Solicitor-General for Scotland.

Lord Advocate, The Rt. Hon. Colin Boyd, QC
Solicitor-General for Scotland, Elish Angiolini, QC
Crown Agent and Chief Executive, Norman McFadyen

OFFICE OF MANPOWER ECONOMICS

8th Floor, Oxford House, 76 Oxford Street, London W1D 1BS
T 020-7467 7244 F 020-7467 7208
W www.ome.uk.com

The Office of Manpower Economics (OME) was set up in 1971. It is an independent non-statutory organisation which is responsible for servicing independent review bodies which advise on the pay of various public service groups, the Police Negotiating Board and the Police

Advisory Board for England and Wales. The Office is also responsible for servicing *ad hoc* bodies of inquiry and for undertaking research into pay and associated matters as requested by the government.

OME Director, Dr R. A. Wright

Director, Health Secretariats, Research and Analysis Group and OME Deputy Director, D. A. Miner

Director, Armed Forces' and Prison Service Secretariats, Mrs C. Haworth

Director, Senior Salaries Secretariat, K. Masson

Director, School Teachers', Police Negotiating Board and Police Advisory Board for England and Wales Secretariats, D. J. T. Wilson

Press Liaison Officer, C. P. Jordan

OFFICE FOR NATIONAL STATISTICS

1 Drummond Gate, London SW1V 2QQ
T 0845-601 3034
E info@statistics.gov.uk
W www.statistics.gov.uk

The Office for National Statistics (ONS) was created in 1996 by the merger of the Central Statistical Office and the Office of Population Censuses and Surveys. It is both a government department and an executive agency of the Treasury and is responsible for preparing, interpreting and publishing key statistics on the government, economy and society of the UK. Its key responsibilities include: the provision of population estimates and projections and statistics on health and other demographic matters in England and Wales; the production of the UK National Accounts and other key economic indicators; the organisation of population censuses in England and Wales and surveys for government departments and public bodies; and the promotion of these functions within the UK, the European Union and internationally to provide a statistical service to meet European Union and international requirements.

The General Register Office is part of the ONS and is responsible for administering marriage laws, and for local registration of births, marriages and deaths in England and Wales.

The National Statistics initiative was launched in June 2000, headed by the National Statistician, with an independent Statistics Commission, providing assurance to Parliament about the integrity of official statistics and statistical practice. The National Statistics brand encompasses the statistical output of the ONS, plus many of the key public interest statistics produced by other government departments.

National Statistician, Registrar-General for England and Wales, Karen Dunnell

Chief Operating Officer, Hilary Douglas

Executive Directors, Cynthia Clark *(Methodology)*; Karen Dunnell *(Surveys and Administrative Sources)*; Joe Grice *(Measurement of Government Activity)*; Jil Matheson *(Economic and Social Reporting)*; Colin Mowl *(Macroeconomics and Labour Market)*; Dennis Roberts *(Registration Services)*

Parliamentary Clerks, Alex Elton-Wall; Robert Smith

OFFICE OF THE PENSIONS OMBUDSMAN

6th Floor, 11 Belgrave Road, London SW1V 1RB
T 020-7834 9144 F 020-7821 0065
E enquiries@pensions-ombudsman.org.uk
W www.pensions-ombudsman.org.uk

The Pensions Ombudsman is appointed by the Secretary of State for Work and Pensions, under the Pension Schemes Act 1993 as amended by the Pensions Act 1995. He independently investigates and decides complaints and disputes concerning pension schemes. The Pension Ombudsman's decision is final and binding to all parties concerned in the complaint or dispute, and it can be legally enforced.

Pensions Ombudsman, David Laverick

OFFICE OF RAIL REGULATION

1 Waterhouse Square, 138–142 Holborn, London EC1N 2TQ
T 020-7282 2000 F 020-7282 2047
E rail.library@orr.gsi.gov.uk W www.rail-reg.gov.uk

The Office of the Rail Regulator was set up under the Railways Act 1993. It became the Office of Rail Regulation (ORR) on 5 July 2004, under the provisions of the Railways and Transport Safety Act 2003. The board and chair are appointed by the Secretary of State for Transport. The Office's principal function is to regulate Network Rail's stewardship of the national network and to provide the economic regulation of the monopoly and dominant elements of the rail industry. The Office also licenses operators of railway assets, approves agreements for access by those operators to track, stations and light maintenance depots, and enforces domestic competition law. The International Rail Regulator is a statutory office separate from that of the Office of Rail Regulation. The International Rail Regulator licenses the operation of certain international rail services in the European Economic Area, and access to railway infrastructure in Great Britain for the purpose of the operation of such services. The Office of The International Rail Regulator is co-located with the Office of Rail Regulation, which fulfils both functions. Under the Railways Act 2005, responsibility for railway safety regulation was transferred to the Office of Rail Regulation from the Health and Safety Executive.

Chair, Chris Bolt

Chief Executive, Keith Webb

Non-Executive Directors, Peter Bucks; Jeffrey Jowell, QC; Jane May; Jim O'Sullivan; Chris Stokes

OFFICE FOR STANDARDS IN EDUCATION (OFSTED)

Alexandra House, 33 Kingsway, London WC2B 6SE
T 020-7421 6800
E geninfo@ofsted.gov.uk
W www.ofsted.gov.uk

Ofsted is a non-ministerial government department established under the Education (Schools Act) 1992. Since April 2001 Ofsted has been responsible for inspecting all educational provision for 16–19 year olds to establish and monitor an independent inspection system for maintained schools in England. Its inspection role also includes the inspection of local education authorities, teacher training institutions and youth work. In September 2001, Ofsted took over the regulation of childcare providers, from 150 local authorities.

HM Chief Inspector, David Bell
Directorate of Education, Miriam Rosen
Director of Corporate Services, Robert Green
Director of Early Years, Maurice Smith
Director of Finance, Jonathan Thompson

OFFICE OF WATER SERVICES
Centre City Tower, 7 Hill Street, Birmingham B5 4UA
T 0121-625 1300 F 0121-625 1400
E enquiries@ofwat.gsi.gov.uk
W www.ofwat.gov.uk

The Office of Water Services (Ofwat) was set up under the Water Act 1989 and is a non-ministerial government department headed by the Director-General of Water Services. It is the independent economic regulator of the water and sewerage companies in England and Wales. Ofwat's main duties are to ensure that the companies can finance and carry out the functions specified in the Water Industry Act 1991 and to protect the interests of water customers.
Director-General of Water Services, P. Fletcher

ORDNANCE SURVEY
Romsey Road, Maybush, Southampton SO16 4GU
T 023-8030 5030 Helpline 0845-605 0505 F 023-8079 2615
E customerservices@ordnancesurvey.co.uk

Ordnance Survey is the national mapping agency for Great Britain. It is a government department and executive agency operating as a Trading Fund and reporting to the Office of the Deputy Prime Minister.
Director-General and Chief Executive, Ms V. Lawrence

PARADES COMMISSION
Windsor House, 9–15 Bedford Street, Belfast BT2 7EL
T 028-9089 5900 F 028-9032 2988
E info@paradescommission.com
W www.paradescommission.org

The Parades Commission was set up under the Public Processions (Northern Ireland) Act 1998. Its function is to encourage and facilitate local accommodation on contentious parades; where this is not possible, the Commission is empowered to make legal determinations about such parades, which may include imposing conditions on aspects of the notified parade (such as restrictions on routes/areas and exclusion of certain groups with a record of bad behaviour).

The chairman and members are appointed by the Secretary of State for Northern Ireland; the membership must, as far as is practicable, be representative of the community in Northern Ireland.
Chair, Sir Anthony Holland
Members, John Cousins; Revd Roy Magee; Billy Martin; Peter Osborne; Sir John Pringle; Peter Quinn

PARLIAMENTARY AND HEALTH SERVICE OMBUDSMAN
Millbank Tower, Millbank, London SW1P 4QP
T 0845-015 4033 F 020-7217 4160
E opca.enquiries@ombudsman.org.uk
W www.ombudsman.org.uk
Health Service Ombudsman T 0845-015 4033 F 020-7217 4000
E ohsc.enquiries@ombudsman.gsi.gov.uk

The Parliamentary Ombudsman (also known as the Parliamentary Commissioner for Administration) is independent of government and is an officer of Parliament. She is responsible for investigating complaints referred to her by MPs from members of the public who claim to have sustained injustice in consequence of maladministration by or on behalf of government departments and certain non-departmental public bodies. In March 1999 an additional 158 public bodies were brought within the jurisdiction of the Parliamentary Ombudsman. Certain types of action by government departments or bodies are excluded from investigation. The Parliamentary Ombudsman is also responsible for investigating complaints, referred by MPs, alleging that access to official information has been wrongly refused under the Code of Practice on Access to Government Information 1994.

The Health Service Ombudsman (also known as the Health Service Commissioner) for England and for Wales is responsible for investigating complaints against National Health Service authorities and trusts that are not dealt with by those authorities to the satisfaction of the complainant. Complaints can be referred direct by the member of the public who claims to have sustained injustice or hardship in consequence of the failure in a service provided by a relevant body, failure of that body to provide a service or in consequence of any other action by that body. The Ombudsman's jurisdiction now covers complaints about family doctors, dentists, pharmacists and opticians, and complaints about actions resulting from clinical judgement.

The Health Service Ombudsman is also responsible for investigating complaints that information has been wrongly refused under the Code of Practice on Openness in the National Health Service 1995. The two offices are presently held by the Parliamentary Ombudsman.
Parliamentary Ombudsman and Health Service Ombudsman, Ms A. Abraham
Deputy Parliamentary Commissioner, Ms T. Longdon
Directors, Health Service Commissioners, D. R. G. Pinchin; L. Charlton
Directors, Parliamentary Commissioner, Ms C. Corrigan; N. Jordan
Finance and Establishment Officer, I. Walker

PARLIAMENTARY COMMISSIONER FOR STANDARDS
House of Commons, London SW1A 0AA
T 020-7219 0311
F 020-7219 0490

Following the recommendations of the Committee on Standards in Public Life, the House of Commons agreed to the appointment of an independent Parliamentary Commissioner for Standards with effect from November 1995. The Commissioner has responsibility for maintaining and monitoring the operation of the Register of Members' Interests and other parliamentary registers; advising Members of Parliament and the Select Committee on Standards and Privileges on questions of propriety; and interpreting the Code of Conduct and related rules of the House. The Commissioner also receives and investigates complaints about the conduct of MPs.
Parliamentary Commissioner for Standards, Sir Philip Mawer

PARLIAMENTARY COUNSEL
36 Whitehall, London SW1A 2AY
T 020-7210 6644 F 020-7210 0963
W www.parliamentary-counsel.gov.uk

Parliamentary Counsel draft all government bills (i.e. primary legislation) except those relating exclusively to Scotland. They also advise on all aspects of parliamentary procedure in connection with such bills and draft government amendments to them, as well as any motions (including financial resolutions) necessary to secure their introduction into, and passage through, Parliament.
First Parliamentary Counsel, Sir Geoffrey Bowman, KCB
Counsel, Sir Edward Caldwell, KCB, QC; Helen Caldwell;
    David Cook; Philip Davies, CB; Elizabeth Gardiner;
    Daniel Greenberg; Adrian Hogarth; Catherine
    Johnston, CB; Peter Knowles, CB; Stephen Laws, CB;
    Léonie McLaughlin; Robert Parker, CB; Douglas
    Ramsay; David Saunders, CB; Geoffrey Sellers, CB;
    John Sellers, CB

PAROLE BOARD FOR ENGLAND AND WALES
Abell House, John Islip Street, London SW1P 4LH
T 0870-420 3505 F 0870-420 3506
E info@paroleboard.gov.uk
W www.paroleboard.gov.uk

The duty of the Parole Board is to advise the Home Secretary with respect to matters referred to it by him which are connected with the early release or recall of prisoners. Its functions include giving directions concerning the release on licence of prisoners serving discretionary life sentences and of certain prisoners serving long-term determinate sentences.
Chair, Prof. Sir Duncan Nichol, CBE
Vice-Chair, The Hon. Mr Justice Butterfield
Chief Executive, Christine Glenn

PAROLE BOARD FOR SCOTLAND
Saughton House, Broomhouse Drive, Edinburgh EH11 3XD
T 0131-244 8373 F 0131-244 6974

The Board directs and advises the Scottish Ministers on the release of prisoners on licence, and related matters.
Chair, Prof. J. J. McManus
Vice-Chair, Sheriff Rita Rae, QC

PATENT OFFICE
Concept House, Cardiff Road, Newport NP10 8QQ
T 0845-950 0505 F 01633-814444
E enquiries@patent.gov.uk
W www.patent.gov.uk

The Patent Office is an executive agency of the Department of Trade and Industry. The Office is responsible for intellectual property (IP) policy and operation in the UK, and aims to educate business, researchers and the public about the IP system; facilitate the appropriate protection and use of rights; design and provide commercial services to assist business use of the IP system; and create a domestic and international legal and political framework, which balances the interests of rights holders with the need for open competition and free markets.
Comptroller-General and Chief Executive, R. Marchant
Director, Finance, Dr K. Woodrow
Director, Intellectual Property and Innovation, P. Lawrence

Director, HR and Corporate Administrative Support,
    L. Smyth
Director, Patents, S. Dennehey
Director, Trade Marks and Designs, R. Webb
Director, Information and Communications, M. Pacey

PENSION PROTECTION FUND
Knollys House, 17 Addiscombe Road, Croydon CR0 6SR
T 0845-600 2541 F 020-8633 4903
E information@ppf.gsi.gov.uk
W www.pensionprotectionfund.org.uk

The Pension Protection Fund (PPF) became operational on 6 April 2005. It was established to pay compensation to members of eligible defined-benefit pension schemes where a qualifying insolvency event in relation to the employer occurs, or where there is a lack of sufficient assets in the pension scheme. The chair and board of the PPF are appointed by, and accountable to, the Secretary of State for Work and Pensions, and are responsible for: paying compensation; calculating annual levies; and setting and overseeing investment strategy.
Chair, Lawrence Churchill
Chief Executive, Myra Kinghorn
Board Members, Ian Abrams; Mark Baker, CBE; Partha
    Dasgupta; Michael Deakin; Jeannie Drake; Alan
    Duncan; Christopher Hughes

THE PENSIONS REGULATOR
Napier House, Trafalgar Place, Brighton BN1 4DW
T 0870-606 3636 F 0870-241 1144
E customersupport@thepensionsregulator.gov.uk
W www.thepensionsregulator.gov.uk

The Pensions Regulator was established in April 2005 as the new regulator of work-based pensions in the UK, replacing the Occupational Pensions Regulatory Authority (OPRA). It aims to protect the benefits of occupational and personal pension scheme members, while reducing the risk of situations leading to claims on the Pension Protection Fund. The Regulator is able to issue improvement notices and third party notices, disqualify trustees deemed unfit to carry out their duties, and freeze a scheme at risk while it investigates.
Chair, David Norgrove
Chief Executive, Tony Hobman

POLICE ADVISORY BOARD FOR ENGLAND AND WALES
8th Floor, Oxford House, 76 Oxford Street, London W1D 1BS
T 020-7467 7244
W www.ome.uk.com

The Police Advisory Board for England and Wales provides advice to the Secretary of State on general questions affecting the police in England and Wales. It also considers draft regulations which the Secretary of State proposes to make with respect to matters other than hours of duty, leave, pay and allowances or the issue, use and return of police clothing, personal equipment and other effects.
Independent Chair, John Randall
Independent Deputy Chair, Prof. Gillian Morris

POLICE NEGOTIATING BOARD

8th Floor, Oxford House, 76 Oxford Street, London W1D 1BS
T 020-7467 7244 W www.ome.uk.com

The Police Negotiating Board (PNB) was established by Act of Parliament in 1980 to negotiate pay, allowances, hours of duty, leave and pensions of United Kingdom police officers and to make recommendations on these matters to the Home Secretary, Secretary of State for Northern Ireland, and Scottish Ministers.
Independent Chair, John Randall
Independent Deputy Chair, Prof. Gillian Morris

POLICE OMBUDSMAN FOR NORTHERN IRELAND

New Cathedral Buildings, St Anne's Square, Belfast BT1 1PG
T 028-9082 8600 F 028-9082 8659
E info@policeombudsman.org
W www.policeombudsman.org

Founded in November 2000 under the Police (Northern Ireland) Act 1998, the function of the Office of the Police Ombudsman for Northern Ireland is to investigate complaints against the police in an impartial, efficient, effective and (as far as is possible) transparent way, to win the confidence of the public and the police. It must report on trends in complaints and react to incidents involving the police, where it is in the public interest, even if no individual complaint has been made.
Police Ombudsman, N. O'Loan

PORT OF LONDON AUTHORITY

Bakers' Hall, 7 Harp Lane, London EC3R 6LB
T 020-7743 7900 F 020-7743 7999
W www.portoflondon.co.uk

The Port of London Authority (PLA) is the port authority for the 93 miles of the tidal River Thames from the Estuary to Teddington. It provides navigational and pilotage services for ships using the Port of London, including the maintenance of shipping channels. The PLA is also actively engaged in the promotion of the Port of London, which handles over 53 million tonnes of cargo each year.

The PLA is a public trust constituted under the Port of London Act 1908 and subsequent legislation.
Chair, Simon Sherrard
Chief Executive, Richard Everitt

POSTAL SERVICES COMMISSION

Hercules House, 6 Hercules Road, London SE1 7DB
T 020-7593 2100 F 020-7593 2142
E info@psc.gov.uk W www.psc.gov.uk

The Postal Services Commission (Postcomm) is an independent regulator set up by the Postal Services Act 2000 to secure the universal postal service, introduce competition to the UK postal market, and ensure that postal operators, including Royal Mail, meet the needs of their customers throughout the UK. Postcomm also monitors – and reports to the Department of Trade and Industry – on the network of post offices in the UK.
Chair, Nigel Stapleton

PRISONS AND PROBATION OMBUDSMAN FOR ENGLAND AND WALES

Ashley House, 2 Monck Street, London SW1P 2BQ
T 020-7035 2876 F 020-7035 2860
E mail@ppo.gsi.gov.uk
W www.ppo.gov.uk

The Ombudsman is appointed by the Home Secretary. He provides a free and independent adjudication service for prisoners and those under probation supervision who have been unable to resolve their grievances with the Prison and Probation Services. He also conducts independent investigations into the deaths of prisoners, residents of probation hostels and people detained by the immigration authorities.
Ombudsman, Stephen Shaw, CBE

PRISON SERVICE PAY REVIEW BODY

8th Floor, Oxford House, 76 Oxford Street, London W1D 1BS
T 020-7467 7244 W www.ome.uk.com

The Prison Service Pay Review Body (PSPRB) was set up in 2001. It makes independent recommendations on the pay of prison governors, prison officers and related grades for the Prison Service in England and Wales and for the Northern Ireland Prison Service.
Chair, Jerry Cope
Members, Derek Bourn; Beryl Brewer; Peter Heard; Frank Horisk; Sarah Murray; Dr Peter Riach; Ann Robinson; Peter Tett

PRIVY COUNCIL OFFICE

2 Carlton Gardens, London SW1Y 5AA
T 020-7210 1033 F 020-7210 1071
W www.privycouncil.gov.uk

The Office is responsible for the arrangements leading to the making of all royal proclamations and Orders in Council; for certain formalities connected with ministerial changes; for considering applications for the granting (or amendment) of royal charters; for the scrutiny and approval of by-laws and statutes of chartered bodies; and for the appointment of high sheriffs and many Crown and Privy Council appointments to governing bodies.
Lord President of the Council (and Leader of the House of Lords), The Rt. Hon. Baroness Amos, PC
Principal Private Secretary, Sue Ball
Private Secretary, Paul Clark
Clerk of the Council, Alex Galloway
Deputy Clerk of the Council and Director of Corporate Services, Graham Donald
Senior Clerk, Meriel McCullagh
Senior Clerk, Ruth Williams
Registrar of the Judicial Committee, Mary MacDonald

PUBLIC GUARDIANSHIP OFFICE

Archway Tower, 2 Junction Road, London N19 5SZ
T 0845-330 2900 F 0870-739 5780
E custserv@guardianship.gsi.gov.uk
W www.guardianship.gov.uk

The Public Guardianship Office (PGO) is the administrative arm of the Court of Protection and is part of the Department for Constitutional Affairs.

Established on 1 April 2001, it has taken over the mental health functions previously undertaken by the Public Trust Office (PTO). The PGO provides service

that promote the financial and social well-being of people with mental incapacity throughout England and Wales.
Chief Executive (acting) David Thompson
Director of Operations, Craig McIlwrath
Director of Business Strategy and Innovation, Glenn Dalton
Management Accountant, Stephen Taylor

PUBLIC RECORD OFFICE OF NORTHERN IRELAND

66 Balmoral Avenue, Belfast BT9 6NY
T 028-9025 5905 F 028-9025 5999
E proni@dcalni.gov.uk W www.proni.gov.uk

The Public Record Office of Northern Ireland is responsible for identifying and preserving Northern Ireland's archival heritage and making it available to the public. It is an executive agency of the Department of Culture, Arts and Leisure.
Chief Executive, Dr G. Slater

PUBLIC SERVICES OMBUDSMAN FOR WALES

1 Ffordd Yr Hen Gae, Pencoed CF35 5LJ
T 01656-641150 F 01656-641199
E ask@ombudsman-wales.org.uk
W www.ombudsman-wales.org.uk

The office of Public Service Ombudsman for Wales was established, with effect from 1 April 2006, by the Public Services Ombudsman (Wales) Act 2005. The Ombudsman, who is appointed by The Queen, investigates complaints of injustice caused by maladministration or service failure by the National Assembly for Wales (and public bodies sponsored by the Assembly); National Health Service bodies, including GPs; registered social landlords; local authorities, including community councils; fire and rescue authorities; police authorities; national park authorities; and countryside and environmental organisations. Free leaflets explaining the process of making a complaint are available from the Ombudsman's office.
Ombudsman-Designate, Adam Peat

RAIL SAFETY AND STANDARDS BOARD

Evergreen House, 160 Euston Road, London NW1 2DX
T 020-7904 7777 F 020-7557 9072
E enquiries@rssb.co.uk
W www.rssb.co.uk

The Rail Safety and Standards Board was established on 1 April 2003 to help focus the rail industry on the continuous improvement in the safety performance of Britain's railways, through facilitating the reduction in risk to passengers and railway workers. Its objectives include: the development of a long-term industry safety strategy; the effective representation of the UK rail industry in the development of EU legislation and standards that impact on the safe interworking of trains and infrastructure; to propose change through facilitation of a research and development programme, and through education and awareness of safety issues. The Rail Safety and Standards Board is a not-for-profit organisation.
Chief Executive, Len Porter
Director, Policy and Strategic Initiatives, Aidan Nelson
Director, Standards, Anson Jack

REGIONAL DEVELOPMENT AGENCIES

Broadway House, Tothill Street, London SW1H 9NQ
T 020-7222 8180 F 020-7222 8182
W www.englandsrdas.com

Regional Development Agencies (RDAs) were established to help the English regions improve their relative economic performance and reduce social and economic disparities within and between regions. Their five statutory objectives are to further economic development and regeneration; to promote business efficiency and competitiveness; to promote employment; to enhance the development and application of skills relevant to employment; and to contribute to sustainable development. There are nine RDAs in England, and they are financed through a single fund provided by contributing government departments (DTI, ODPM, DfES, DEFRA and DCMS). In 2004–5 the RDAs' budget was £1.8 billion.

RDA REGIONS

NORTH WEST – PO Box 37, Renaissance House, Centre Park, Warrington WA1 1XB T 01925-400100 *Chair,* Bryan Gray, MBE, DL
YORKSHIRE – Victoria House, 2 Victoria Place, Leeds LS11 5AE T 0113-394 9600 *Chair,* Terry Hodgkinson
NORTH EAST – Stella House, Goldcrest Way, Newburn Riverside, Newcastle upon Tyne NE15 8NY T 0191-229 6200 *Chair,* Margaret Fay
WEST MIDLANDS – 3 Priestley Wharf, Holt Street, Aston Science Park, Birmingham B7 4BN T 0121-380 3500 *Chair,* Nick Paul
EAST MIDLANDS – Apex Court, City Link, Nottingham NG2 4LA T 0115-988 8300 *Chair,* Bryan Jackson
EAST OF ENGLAND – The Business Centre, Station Road, Histon, Cambridge CB4 9LQ T 01223-713900 *Chair,* Richard Ellis
SOUTH WEST – Sterling House, Dix's Field, Exeter EX1 1QA T 01392-214747 *Chair,* Juliet Williams
LONDON – Devon House, 58–60 St Katharines Way, London E1W 1JX T 020-7680 2000 *Chair,* Mary Reilly
SOUTH EAST – Cross Lanes, Guildford GU1 1YA T 01483-484200 *Chair,* Jim Braithwaite

REGISTERS OF SCOTLAND

Meadowbank House, 153 London Road, Edinburgh EH8 7AU
Customer Service Centres 0845-607 0161/0164
E customer.services@ros.gov.uk
W www.ros.gov.uk

Registers of Scotland is the executive agency responsible for framing and maintaining records relating to property and other legal documents in Scotland. The agency holds 16 registers: two property registers (General Register of Sasines and Land Register of Scotland) and the remainder grouped under the Chancery and Judicial registers (Register of Deeds in the Books of Council and Session; Register of Protests; Register of Judgements; Register of Service of Heirs; Register of the Great Seal; Register of the Quarter Seal; Register of the Prince's Seal; Register of Crown Grants; Register of Sheriffs' Commissions; Register of the Cachet Seal; Register of Inhibitions and Adjudications; Register of Entails; Register of Hornings; and Register of Community Interests in Land).
Chief Executive and Keeper of the Registers of Scotland, J. Meldrum
Deputy Keeper, B. Beveridge
Managing Director, F. Manson

REGISTRAR OF PUBLIC LENDING RIGHT

Richard House, Sorbonne Close, Stockton on Tees TS17 6DA
T 01642-604699 F 01642-615641
E authorservices@plr.uk.com
W www.plr.uk.com

Under the Public Lending Right system, in operation since 1983, payment is made from public funds to authors whose books are lent out from public libraries. Payment is made once a year and the amount each author receives is proportionate to the number of times (established from a sample) that each registered book has been lent out during the previous year. The Registrar of PLR, who is appointed by the Secretary of State for Culture, Media and Sport, compiles the register of authors and books. Authors resident in all EC countries are eligible to apply. (The term 'author' covers writers, illustrators, translators, and some editors/compilers.)

A payment of 5.26 pence was made in 2004–5 for each estimated loan of a registered book, up to a top limit of £6,000 for the books of any one registered author; the money for loans above this level is used to augment the remaining PLR payments. In 2005, the sum of £6.55 million was paid out to 18,686 registered authors and assignees as the annual payment of PLR.
Registrar, Dr J. G. Parker
Chair of Advisory Committee, S. Brett

REVIEW BODY FOR NURSING AND OTHER HEALTH PROFESSIONS

8th Floor, Oxford House, 76 Oxford Street, London W1D 1BS
T 020-7467 7244 W www.ome.uk.com

The Review Body for nursing staff, midwives, health visitors and professions allied to medicine was set up in 1983. Following the Agenda for Change the review body changed its name. It advises the prime minister and the Secretaries of State for Health, Scotland and Wales on the remuneration of nursing staff and other health professions employed in the National Health Service.
Chair, Prof. Gillian Morris
Members, Lucinda Bolton; Prof. Richard Disney; Wilma MacPherson, CBE; Prof. Alan Manning; Prof. Pauline Weetman; Sharon Whitlam

REVIEW BODY ON DOCTORS' AND DENTISTS' REMUNERATION

8th Floor, Oxford House, 76 Oxford Street, London W1D 1BS
T 020-7467 7244 W www.ome.uk.com

The Review Body on Doctors' and Dentists' Remuneration was set up in 1971. It advises the prime minister and the Secretaries of State for Health, Scotland and Wales on the remuneration of doctors and dentists taking any part in the National Health Service.
Chair, Michael Blair, QC
Members, Prof. John Beath; Prof. Frank Burchill; Dr Margaret Collingwood, TD; Prof. Peter Dolton; Hugh Donaldson; David Grafton

ROYAL AIR FORCE MUSEUM

Grahame Park Way, London NW9 5LL
T 020-8205 2266 F 020-8200 1751
W www.rafmuseum.org

The Museum has two sites, one at the former airfield at Hendon and the second at Cosford, in the West Midlands, both of which illustrate the development of aviation from before the Wright brothers to the present-day RAF. Total government grant-in-aid for 2004–5 was £6,796,000.
Director-General, Dr M. A. Fopp

ROYAL BOTANIC GARDEN EDINBURGH

20A Inverleith Row, Edinburgh EH3 5LR
T 0131-552 7171 F 0131-248 2901
E info@rbge.org.uk
W www.rbge.org.uk

The Royal Botanic Garden Edinburgh (RBGE) originated as the Physic Garden, established in 1670 beside the Palace of Holyroodhouse. The Garden moved to its present 28-hectare site at Inverleith, Edinburgh, in 1821. There are also three Regional Gardens: Benmore Botanic Garden, near Dunoon, Argyll; Logan Botanic Garden, near Stranraer, Wigtownshire; and Dawyck Botanic Garden, near Stobo, Peeblesshire. Since 1986 RBGE has been administered by a board of trustees established under the National Heritage (Scotland) Act 1985. It receives an annual grant from the Environment and Rural Affairs Department of the Scottish Executive.

RBGE is an international centre for scientific research on plant diversity and for horticulture education and conservation. It has an extensive library, a herbarium with over two million preserved plant specimens, and over 16,500 species in the living collections.
Chair of the Board of Trustees, Dr P. Nicholson
Regius Keeper, Prof. S. Blackmore, FRSE

ROYAL BOTANIC GARDENS KEW

Richmond, Surrey TW9 3AB
T 020-8332 5000 F 020-8332 5197
Wakehurst Place, Ardingly, W. Sussex RH17 6TN
T 01444-89000 F 01444-894069
E info@kew.org W www.kew.org

The Royal Botanic Gardens (RBG) Kew were originally laid out as a private garden for Kew House for George III's mother, Princess Augusta, in 1759. The gardens were much enlarged in the 19th century, notably by the inclusion of the grounds of the former Richmond Lodge. In 1965 the garden at Wakehurst Place was acquired; it i owned by the National Trust and managed by RBG Kew. Under the National Heritage Act 1983 a board of trustee was set up to administer the gardens, which in 198 became an independent body supported by grant-in-aid from the Department of Environment, Food and Rural Affairs.

The functions of RBG Kew are to carry out research into plant sciences, to disseminate knowledge about plants and to provide the public with the opportunity to gain knowledge and enjoyment from the gardens collections. There are extensive national reference collections of living and preserved plants and comprehensive library and archive. The main emphasis is on plant conservation and biodiversity.

BOARD OF TRUSTEES
Chair, Lord Selborne
Members, Denise Bradley; Tanya Burman; Andrew Cahn; Richard Deverell; Prof. Charles Godfray; Dr Sandy Harrison; Baroness Helene Hayman; Richard Lapthorne, CBE; David Norman; Marion Regan; Sir Richard Sykes
Director, Prof. Peter Crane, FRS

ROYAL COMMISSION FOR THE EXHIBITION OF 1851

Sherfield Building, Imperial College, London SW7 2AZ
T 020-7594 8790 F 020-7594 8794
E royalcom1851@ic.ac.uk
W www.royalcommission1851.org.uk

The Royal Commission was incorporated by supplemental charter as a permanent commission after winding up the affairs of the Great Exhibition of 1851. Its object is to promote scientific and artistic education by means of funds derived from its Kensington estate, purchased with the surplus left over from the Great Exhibition. Annual charitable expenditure on educational grants is about £1 million.

President, HRH The Prince Philip, Duke of Edinburgh, KG, KT, OM, GBE, AC, QSO, PC
Chair, Board of Management, Sir Alan Rudge, CBE, FRS, FRENG

ROYAL COMMISSION ON ENVIRONMENTAL POLLUTION

3rd Floor, The Sanctuary, Westminster, London SW1P 3JS
T 020-7799 8970 F 020-7799 8971
E enquiries@rcep.org.uk W www.rcep.org.uk

The Commission was set up in 1970 to advise on national and international matters concerning the pollution of the environment.

Chair, Prof. Sir John Lawton, CBE, FRS
Members, Prof. Nicholas Cumpsty; Prof. P. Elkins; Dr I. Graham-Bryce, CBE; Prof. S. Holgate; Prof. J. Jowell; Prof. Peter Liss; Dr S. Owens, OBE; Prof. Judith Petts; Prof. J. Plant, CBE; Prof. S. Rayner; J. Speirs; Prof. J. Sprent

ROYAL COMMISSION ON THE ANCIENT AND HISTORICAL MONUMENTS OF SCOTLAND

John Sinclair House, 16 Bernard Terrace, Edinburgh EH8 9NX
T 0131-662 1456 F 0131-662 1499
E nmrs@rcahms.gov.uk W www.rcahms.gov.uk

The Royal Commission was established in 1908 and is appointed to provide for the survey and recording of ancient and historical monuments connected with the culture, civilisation and conditions of life of the people in Scotland from the earliest times. It is funded by the Scottish Executive. The Commission compiles and maintains the National Monuments Record of Scotland as the national record of the archaeological and historical environment.

Chair, Prof. John Hume
Commissioners, Kate Byrne; Prof. John Hunter, FSA; Prof. Angus Macdonald; Dr M. A. Mackay; G. Masterton, CENG; Prof. C. D. Morris, FSA, FRSE; Dr J. Murray; Dr S. Nenadic; J. W. T. Simpson

ROYAL COMMISSION ON THE ANCIENT AND HISTORICAL MONUMENTS OF WALES

Crown Building, Plas Crug, Aberystwyth SY23 1NJ
T 01970-621200 F 01970-627701
E nmr.wales@rcahmw.gov.uk
W www.rcahmw.gov.uk

The Royal Commission was established in 1908 and is currently empowered by a Royal Warrant of 2001 to survey, record, publish and maintain a database of ancient and historical and maritime sites and structures, and landscapes, in Wales. The Commission is funded by the National Assembly for Wales and is also responsible for the National Monuments Record of Wales, which is open daily for public reference, for the supply of archaeological information to the Ordnance Survey, for the co-ordination of archaeological aerial photography in Wales, and for sponsorship of the regional Sites and Monuments Records.

Chair, Prof. Ralph A. Griffiths, DLITT, FRHISTS
Vice-Chair, Dr Eurwyn Williams, FSA
Commissioners, Prof. Anthony D. Carr, FSA, FRHISTS; David W. Crossley, FSA; Mrs A. Eastham; Neil Harries; John W. Lloyd, CB; John Newman, FSA; Prof. Patrick Sims-Williams, FBA; Dr Llinos Smith, FRHISTS

ROYAL MAIL GROUP PLC

148 Old Street, London EC1V 9HQ
T 020-7250 2888
W www.royalmailgroup.com

Crown services for the carriage of government dispatches were set up in about 1516. The conveyance of public correspondence began in 1635 and the mail service was made a parliamentary responsibility with the setting up of a Post Office in 1657. Telegraphs came under Post Office control in 1870 and the Post Office Telephone Service began in 1880. The National Girobank service of the Post Office began in 1968. The Post Office ceased to be a government department in 1969 when responsibility for the running of the postal, telecommunications, giro and remittance services was transferred to a public authority called The Post Office.

The 1981 British Telecommunications Act separated the functions of the Post Office, making it solely responsible for postal services and Girobank. Girobank was privatised in 1990. The Postal Services Act 2000 turned The Post Office into a wholly owned public limited company establishing a regulatory regime under the Postal Service Commission. The Post Office Group changed its name to Consignia plc on 26 March 2001 when its new corporate structure took effect. On 4 November the name was changed to Royal Mail Group plc.

The chairman, chief executive and members of the board are appointed by the Secretary of State for Trade and Industry but responsibility for the running of Royal Mail Group plc as a whole rests with the board in its corporate capacity.

BOARD
Chair, Allan Leighton
Chief Executive (Royal Mail), Adam Crozier
Chief Executive (Post Office Ltd), David Mills
Members, David Burden *(Chief Information Officer)*; Marisa Cassoni *(Director, Finance)*; Tony McCarthy *(Director, People and Organisational Development)*
Non-Executive Directors, David Fish; Richard Handover; Mike Hodgkinson; John Neill; Baroness Prosser; Bob Wigley
Company Secretary, Jonathan Evans

ROYAL MINT

Llantrisant, Pontyclun CF72 8YT
T 01443-222111 F 01443-623148
E judith.nicholas@royalmint.gov.uk
W www.royalmint.gov.uk

The prime responsibility of the Royal Mint is the provision of United Kingdom coinage but it actively competes in world markets for a share of the available circulating coin business and about half of the coins and blanks it produces annually are exported. The Mint also manufactures special proof and uncirculated quality coins in gold, silver and other metals; military and civil decorations and medals; commemorative and prize medals; and royal and official seals. It also markets a range of gifts and collectible items.

The Royal Mint became an executive agency of the Treasury in 1990. The government announced in July 1999 that the Royal Mint would be given greater commercial freedom to expand its business into new areas and develop partnerships with the private sector.
Master of the Mint, The Chancellor of the Exchequer *(ex officio)*
Chief Executive, G. Sheehan

ROYAL NATIONAL THEATRE

South Bank, London SE1 9PX
T 020-7452 3333 E info@nationaltheatre.org.uk
W www.nationaltheatre.org.uk

The Royal National Theatre was designed by modernist architect Denys Lasdun, and opened in 1976. It houses three distinct theatres: the Olivier, the Lyttleton and the Cottesloe. In 1997 the building underwent extensive renovation and development, and a new exterior performance space was added.
Chair, Sir Hayden Phillips, GCB
Members, Susan Chinn; James Hill; Nicola Horlick; Rachel Lomax; Caragh Merrick; Grahame Morris; Caro Newling; Ben Okri, OBE; André Ptaszynski; Rt. Hon. Chris Smith, MP; Edward Walker-Arnott; Nicholas Wright
Director, Nicholas Hytner
Executive Director, Nick Starr

ROYAL NAVAL MUSEUM

HM Naval Base (PP66), Portsmouth PO1 3NH
T 023-9272 7562 F 023-9272 7575
E information@royalnavalmuseum.org
W www.royalnavalmuseum.org

The Royal Naval Museum is a non-departmental public body of the Ministry of Defence, and is a registered charity. Nelson's flagship, the HMS *Victory*, is in dry dock and is part of the museum. The Museum aims to provide an effective and accessible repository for the heritage of the Navy, and to raise public awareness, and encourage scholarship and research into, the history and achievements of the Royal Navy.
Chair of Board of Trustees, Adm. Sir Peter Abbott, GBE, KCB

RURAL PAYMENTS AGENCY (RPA)

Kings House, 33 Kings Road, Reading RG1 3BU
T 0118-958 3626 F 0118-959 7736
E enquiries@rpa.gsi.gov.uk
W www.rpa.gov.uk

The Rural Payments Agency (RPA) is as an executive agency of the Department for Environment, Food and Rural Affairs. It is the single paying agency responsible for Common Agricultural Policy (CAP) schemes in England and for certain schemes throughout the UK.
Chief Executive, Johnston McNeill
Directors, Richard Gregg *(Human Resources)*; Alex Kerr *(Finance)*; Ian Hewitt *(Operations)*; Alan McDermott *(Information Systems)*; Martin Truran *(Legal)*; Simon Vry *(Business Development)*

SCHOOL TEACHERS' REVIEW BODY

8th Floor, Oxford House, 76 Oxford Street, London W1D 1BS
T 020-7467 7244 W www.ome.uk.com

The School Teachers' Review Body (STRB) was set up under the School Teachers' Pay and Conditions Act 1991. It is required to examine and report on such matters relating to the statutory conditions of employment of school teachers in England and Wales as may be referred to it by the Secretary of State for Education and Skills.
Chair, Bill Cockburn, CBE, TD
Members, Monojit Chatterji; Rodney East; Ros Gardner; Mark Goodridge; Dr Bleddyn Bryn Roberts, John Singh; Jo Stephens; Bruce Warman

SCIENCE MUSEUM

Exhibition Road, London SW7 2DD
T 0870-870 4868 F 020-7942 4447
W www.sciencemuseum.org.uk

The Science Museum, part of the National Museum of Science and Industry, houses the national collections of science, technology, industry and medicine. The Museum began as the science collection of the South Kensington Museum and first opened in 1857. In 1883 it acquired the collections of the Patent Museum and in 1909 the science collections were transferred to the new Science Museum, leaving the art collections with the Victoria and Albert Museum. The Wellcome Wing was opened in July 2000.

Some of the Museum's commercial aircraft, agricultural machinery, and road and rail transport collections are at Wroughton, Wilts. The National Museum of Science and Industry also incorporates the National Railway Museum, York, the National Museum of Photography, Film and Television, Bradford, and Locomotion: the National Railway Museum at Shildon.

Total government grant-in-aid for 2005–6 is £34,093,000.

BOARD OF TRUSTEES

Chair, The Rt. Hon. Lord Waldegrave of North Hill
Members, Prof. Sir Ron U. Cooke, DSC; Prof. A. Dowling, CBE, FRENG, G. Dyke; Dr A. Grocock; Dr D. Gurr; R. Haythornthwaite; D. E. Rayner, CBE; Prof. Sir Martin Rees; Dr Maggie Semple, OBE; S. Singh, MBE; M. G. Smith; Prof. R. A. Smith, PHD, FRENG; Prof. Kathy Sykes; Sir William Wells

OFFICERS
Director (acting), J. Tucker
Head of Corporate Communications, M. Pudney
Head of Design, T. Molloy
Head of Estates, J. Bevin
Head of Finance, Ms A. Caine
Head of Human Resources, Ms A. McAllister
Head of IT, Ms M. Burns
Head of National Museum of Photography, Film and Television, C. Philpott
Managing Director, NMSI Trading Ltd, Ms M. Jackson
Head of National Railway Museum, A. Scott
Head of Planning and Development, A. Leitch
Head of Science Museum, J. Tucker
Head of Sustainable Development and Master Planning, C. Gordon

SCOTTISH ARTS COUNCIL

2 Manor Place, Edinburgh EH3 7DD
T 0131-226 6051 F 0131-225 9833
E help.desk@scottisharts.org.uk
W www.scottisharts.org.uk

The Scottish Arts Council is the main arts development agency in Scotland. It is a non-departmental public body, accountable to Scottish Ministers. The Scottish Arts Council invests funds from the Scottish Executive and National Lottery and works with partners to support and develop artistic excellence and creativity throughout Scotland.
Chair, Richard Holloway
Members, Joanna Baker; Arthur Cormack; Bob Downes; Steven Grimmond; Jennifer Hawksworth; Arthur Herman; Jane Jeffrey; Annie Marrs; Roy McEwan; James McSharry; Louise Mitchell; John Mulgrew; Rab Noakes; Ben Twist; Jennifer Waterton
Chief Executive, Graham Berry

SCOTTISH CRIMINAL CASES REVIEW COMMISSION

5th Floor, Portland House, 17 Renfield Street, Glasgow G2 5AH
T 0141-270 7030 F 0141-270 7040/23
E info@sccrc.org.uk
W www.sccrc.org.uk

The Commission is a non-departmental public body which started operating on 1 April 1999. It assumed the role previously performed by the Secretary of State for Scotland to consider alleged miscarriages of justice in Scotland and refer cases meeting the relevant criteria to the High Court for determination. Members are appointed by The Queen on the recommendation of the First Minister; senior executive staff are appointed by the Commission.
Chair, The Very Revd G. Forbes, CBE
Members, R. Anderson, QC; D. Belfall; G. Bell, QC; Prof. P. Duff; Sir Gerald Gordon, CBE, QC; J. Mackay, QPM
Chief Executive, Gerard Sinclair

SCOTTISH ENTERPRISE

Atlantic Quay, 150 Broomielaw, Glasgow G2 8LU
T 0141-248 2700 Helpline 0845-607 8787 F 0141-221 3217
E network.helpline@scotent.co.uk
W www.scottish-enterprise.com

Scottish Enterprise was established in 1991 and its purpose is to create jobs and prosperity for the people of Scotland. It is funded by the Scottish Executive and is responsible to the Scottish Ministers. Working in partnership with the private and public sectors, Scottish Enterprise aims to further the development of Scotland's economy, to enhance the skills of the Scottish workforce and to promote Scotland's international competitiveness. Scottish Enterprise is concerned with attracting firms to Scotland and, through Scottish Trade International, it helps Scottish companies to compete in world export markets. Scottish Enterprise has a network of Local Enterprise Companies that deliver economic development services at local level.
Chair, Sir John Ward, CBE
Chief Executive, Jack Perry

SCOTTISH ENVIRONMENT PROTECTION AGENCY

Erskine Court, The Castle Business Park, Stirling FK9 4TR
T 01786-457700 Hotline 0800-807060
F 01786-446885 W www.sepa.org.uk

The Scottish Environment Protection Agency (SEPA) is the public body responsible for environmental protection in Scotland. It regulates potential pollution to land, air and water, the storage, transport and disposal of controlled waste and the safekeeping and disposal of radioactive materials. It does this within a complex legislative framework of Acts of Parliament, EC Directives and Regulations, granting licences to operations of industrial processes and waste disposal. SEPA also operates Floodline, 0845-988 1188, a public service providing information on possible risk of flooding 24 hours a day, 365 days a year.
Chair, Sir Ken Collins
Chief Executive, Campbell Gemmell
Director of Environmental Regulation and Improvement, Colin Bayes
Director of Environmental and Organisational Development, Calum MacDonald
Director of Environmental Science, Chris Spray

SCOTTISH LAW COMMISSION

140 Causewayside, Edinburgh EH9 1PR
T 0131-668 2131 F 0131-662 4900
E info@scotlawcom.gov.uk
W www.scotlawcom.gov.uk

The Commission keeps the law in Scotland under review and makes proposals for its development and reform. It is responsible to the Scottish Ministers through the Scottish Executive Justice Department.
Chair (part-time), The Hon. Lord Eassie
Chief Executive, Miss J. McLeod
Commissioners, Prof. G. Maher, QC; Prof. K. G. C. Reid; Prof. J. M. Thomson; C. J. Tyre, QC

SCOTTISH LEGAL AID BOARD

44 Drumsheugh Gardens, Edinburgh EH3 7SW
T 0131-226 7061
E general@slab.org.uk
W www.slab.org.uk

The Scottish Legal Aid Board was set up under the Legal Aid (Scotland) Act 1986 to manage legal aid in Scotland. It reports to the Scottish Executive. Board members are appointed by Scottish Ministers.
Chair, Jean Couper
Members, William Gallagher; Peter Gray, QC; Graeme McKinstry; Susan McPhee; Ellen Morton; David Nicol;

Prof. Ian Percy, CBE; Elaine Rosie; Margaret Scanlan; Sheriff Kenneth Ross; Malcolm Thomson, QC
Chief Executive, Lindsay Montgomery

SCOTTISH NATURAL HERITAGE
12 Hope Terrace, Edinburgh EH9 2AS
T 0131-447 4784 F 0131-446 2277
E enquiries@snh.gov.uk
W www.snh.org.uk

Scottish Natural Heritage was established in 1992 under the Natural Heritage (Scotland) Act 1991. It provides advice on nature conservation to all those whose activities affect wildlife, landforms and features of geological interest in Scotland, and seeks to develop and improve facilities for the enjoyment and understanding of the Scottish countryside. It is funded by the Scottish Executive.
Chair, Dr J. Markland, CBE
Chief Executive, I. Jardine
Chief Scientific Adviser, C. Galbraith
Directors of Operations, J. Thomson *(West)*; A. Bachell *(East)*; J. Watson *(North)*
Director of Corporate Services, I. Edgeler

SCOTTISH PRISONS COMPLAINTS COMMISSION
Government Buildings, Broomhouse Drive, Edinburgh EH11 3XD
T 0131-244 8423 F 0131-244 8430
E spcc@scotland.gsi.gov.uk W www.scotland.gov.uk/spcc

The Commission was established in 1994. It is an independent body to which prisoners in Scottish prisons can make application in relation to any matter where they have failed to obtain satisfaction from the Scottish Prison Service's internal grievance procedures. Clinical judgements made by medical officers, matters which are the subject of legal proceedings and matters relating to sentence, conviction and parole decision-making are excluded from the Commission's jurisdiction. The Commissioner is appointed by the Scottish Ministers.
Commissioner, V. Barrett

SCOTTISH PUBLIC SERVICES OMBUDSMAN
4 Melville Street, Edinburgh EH3 7NS
T 0870-011 5378 F 0870-011 5379
E enquiries@scottishombudsman.org.uk
W www.scottishombudsman.org.uk

The Scottish Public Services Ombudsman was established in 2002. The Ombudsman investigates complaints about Scottish government departments, councils, housing associations, the National Health Service and other public bodies. The public bodies which the Scottish Public Services Ombudsman may consider investigating are taken from a list of such bodies outlined in the Scottish Public Services Ombudsman Act 2002. The Ombudsman's remit was extended in 2005 to cover Scotland's further education (FE) colleges and higher education institutions (HEIs). Complaints considered by the Ombudsman can range from complaints about poor service, failure to provide a service, administrative failure and complaints about the NHS including hospital staff, GPs, dentists and other health professionals.
Scottish Public Services Ombudsman, Prof. Alice Brown

SCOTTISH RECORDS ADVISORY COUNCIL
HM General Register House, Edinburgh EH1 3YY
T 0131-535 1403 F 0131-535 1430
W www.nas.gov.uk/srac

The Council was established under the Public Record (Scotland) Act 1937. Its members are appointed by the First Minister and it may submit proposals or make representations to the First Minister, the Lord Justice General or the Lord President of the Court of Session on questions relating to the public records of Scotland.
Chair, Prof. H. MacQueen
Secretary, Dr A. Rosie

SEAFISH INDUSTRY AUTHORITY
18 Logie Mill, Logie Green Road, Edinburgh EH7 4HG
T 0131-558 3331 F 0131-558 1442
E seafish@seafish.co.uk
W www.seafish.org

Established under the Fisheries Act 1981, Seafish work with the seafood industry to satisfy consumers, raise standards, improve efficiency and secure a sustainable future. It is sponsored by the four UK fisherie departments and is funded by a levy on seafood.
Chair, Andrew Dewar-Durie
Chief Executive, John Rutherford

SECRET INTELLIGENCE SERVICE (MI6)
PO Box 1300, London SE1 1BD

The Secret Intelligence Service produces secret intelligence in support of the government's security defence, foreign and economic policies. It was placed on statutory footing by the Intelligence Services Act 1994 and is headed by a chief, known as 'C', who is directly accountable to the Foreign Secretary.
Chief, J. M. Scarlett, CMG, OBE

SECURITY SERVICE (MI5)
PO Box 3255, London SW1P 1AE
T 020-7930 9000
W www.mi5.gov.uk

The Security Service is responsible for security intelligence work against covertly organised threats to the UK. These include terrorism, espionage and the proliferation of weapons of mass destruction. The Service also supports the police and other law enforcement agencies in their work against serious crime and provides security advice to a wide range of organisations to help reduce vulnerability to threats from individuals, groups countries hostile to UK interests. The Home Secretary has parliamentary accountability for the Security Service.
Director-General, Eliza Manningham-Buller

SENIOR SALARIES REVIEW BODY
8th Floor, Oxford House, 76 Oxford Street, London W1D 1BS
T 020-7467 7244 W www.ome.uk.com

The Senior Salaries Review Body (formerly the Top Salaries Review Body) was set up in 1971 to advise the prime minister on the remuneration of the judiciary, senior civil servants and senior officers of the armed forces. In 1993 its remit was extended to cover the pay, pensions and allowances of MPs, Ministers and other whose pay is determined by a Ministerial and Other

Salaries Order and the allowances of peers. It also advises on the pay of officers and members of the devolved Parliament and Assemblies.

Chair, John Baker, CBE

Members, Mark Baker, CBE; David Clayman; Mary Galbraith; Prof. David Greenaway; Jim McKenna; Mei Sim Lai, OBE, FCA, FCCA; Sir Peter North, CBE, QC; Richard Pearson; Janet Rubin

SENTENCE REVIEW COMMISSIONERS
5th Floor, Windsor House, 12–16 Bedford Street, Belfast BT2 7SR
T 028-9054 9412 F 028-9054 9427
E sentrev@belfast.org.uk
W www.sentencereview.org.uk

The Sentence Review Commissioners are appointed by the Secretary of State for Northern Ireland to consider applications from prisoners serving sentences in Northern Ireland for declarations that they are entitled to early release in accordance with the provisions of the Northern Ireland (Sentences) Act 1998. The commissioners have been appointed until 31 July 2005 and are served by staff seconded from the Northern Ireland Office.

Joint Chairs, Sir John Belloch, KCB; B. Currin

Commissioners, Dr S. Casale; Dr P. Curran; I. Dunbar, CB; Mrs M. Gilpin; Dr A. Grounds; Ms C. McGrory; Dr D. Morrow

SERIOUS FRAUD OFFICE
Elm House, 10–16 Elm Street, London WC1X 0BJ
T 020-7239 7272 F 020-7837 1689
E public.enquiries@sfo.gsi.gov.uk

The Serious Fraud Office (SFO) is an independent government department that investigates and prosecutes serious or complex fraud. It is part of the UK Criminal Justice System. The Office is headed by the Director who is appointed by and accountable to the Attorney-General. The SFO has jurisdiction over England, Wales and Northern Ireland but not Scotland, the Isle of Man or the Channel Islands.

Director, Robert Wardle

SMALL BUSINESS COUNCIL
5th Floor, Kingsgate House, 66–74 Victoria Street, London SW1E 6SW
T 020-7215 8519
E sbcsecretariat@sbs.gsi.gov.uk
W www.sbs.gov.uk/sbc

The Small Business Council was set up in May 2000. It is a non-departmental public body reporting to the Secretary of State for Trade and Industry on the needs of existing and potential small businesses.

Chair, Julie Kenny, CBE

Members, Simon Bartley; Sue Brownson, OBE; Grant Burton; Elsa Caleb; Peter Donaldson; Lorraine Gradwell; Teresa Graham, OBE; Paul Harrod; Caroline Hughes; Andrew Ive; Scott Johnson; John McLaren-Stewart; Ilyas Patel; Sally Preston; Fiona Price; Dr John Reynolds; Prof. Monder Ram; Michael Robinson; Sean Taggart; Simon Topman; Janice Ward; Candida Whitmill

SMALL BUSINESS SERVICE
Kingsgate House, 66–74 Victoria Street, London SW1E 6SW
T 020-7215 5000
W www.sbs.gov.uk
Business Link T 0845 600 9006 W www.businesslink.gov.uk

The Small Business Service was set up in March 2000 as an agency of the Department of Trade and Industry. The Service works with the public, private and voluntary sectors. Working through the Business Link network, the Small Business Service provides information, advice or access to experts for small businesses.

Chair, Nigel Griffiths, MP
Chief Executive, Martin Wyn Griffith
Strategy Board Members, Rodney Buse; Mark Gibson; Teresa Graham, OBE; Stephen Lyle Smythe; Richard Price; Andrew Summers, CMG; Martin Wyn Griffith

STATISTICS COMMISSION
Artillery House, 11–19 Artillery Row, London SW1P 1RT
T 020-7273 8008 F 020-7273 8019
E statscom@statscom.org.uk
W www.statscom.org.uk

The Statistics Commission has been set up to advise on the quality, quality assurance and priority-setting for official statistics, and on the procedures designed to deliver statistical integrity, to help ensure official statistics are trustworthy and responsive to public needs. It is independent of both Ministers and the producers of National Statistics. It operates in a transparent way with the minutes of its meetings, correspondence and evidence it receives, and advice it gives, all normally publicly available for scrutiny.

Chair, Prof. D. Rhind, CBE, FRS, FBA
Vice-Chair, D. Wanless
Members, Ian Beesley; Miss C. Bowe; Sir Kenneth Calman, KCB; Ms P. Hodgson; Mrs J. Trewsdale; M. Weale

THE STUDENT LOANS COMPANY LTD
100 Bothwell Street, Glasgow G2 7JD
T 0800-405010 F 0141-306 2005
W www.slc.co.uk

The Student Loans Company Ltd is wholly owned by the government. It administers the Student Loan Scheme (established in 1990) and the Income Contingent Loans Scheme (established in 1998), and provides loans to eligible students in higher education in the United Kingdom. In the region of £2,500,000 of loans were distributed during 2004–5 to 780,000 students.

Chair, Keith Bedell-Pearce
Chief Executive, Ralph Seymour-Jackson

TATE BRITAIN
Millbank, London SW1P 4RG
T 020-7887 8008 F 020-7887 8007
W www.tate.org.uk

Tate Britain displays the national collection of British art. The gallery opened in 1897, the cost of building (£80,000) being defrayed by Sir Henry Tate, who also contributed the nucleus of the present collection. The Turner wing was opened in 1910, and further galleries and a new sculpture hall followed in 1937. In 1979 a further extension was built, and the Clore Gallery, for the Turner collection, was opened in 1987. The Centenary Development was opened in 2001. There are four Tate galleries: Tate Britain and Tate Modern in London, Tate Liverpool and Tate St Ives.

BOARD OF TRUSTEES

Chair, Paul Myners, CBE
Trustees, Helen Alexander; Victoria Barnsley; Melanie Clore; Sir Howard Davies; Patricia Lankester; Prof. Jennifer Latto; Chris Ofili; Julian Opie; Fiona Rae; Jon Snow; John Studzinski

OFFICERS

Director, Sir Nicholas Serota
Deputy Director, Alex Beard
Director of Collections, Jan Debbaut
Director, Tate Britain, Stephen Deuchar
Director, Tate Liverpool, Christoph Gruneberg
Director, Tate Modern, Vicente Todoli
Director, Tate St Ives, Susan Daniel-McElvoy

TATE MODERN

Bankside, London SE1 9TG
T 020-7887 8008 Booking 020-7887 8888
W www.tate.org.uk

Opened on 11 May 2000, Tate Modern displays the Tate collection of international modern art dating from 1900 to the present day. It includes works by Dalí, Picasso, Matisse and Warhol as well as many contemporary works. It is housed in the former Bankside Power Station in London, which was redesigned by the Swiss architects Herzog and de Meuron.
Director, Vicente Todoli

TOURISM BODIES

Visit Britain, Visit Scotland, the Wales Tourist Board and the Northern Ireland Tourist Board are responsible for developing and marketing the tourist industry in their respective countries.

VISIT BRITAIN

Thames Tower, Black's Road, London W6 9EL T 020-8846 9000
F 020-8563-0302 W www.visitbritain.com
Chief Executive, T. Wright

VISIT SCOTLAND

94 Ocean Drive, Leith, Edinburgh EH6 6JH T 0131-472 2222
Thistle House, Beechwood Park North, Inverness IV2 3ED
T 01463-716996 E info@visitscotland.com
W www.visitscotland.com
Chair, P. Lederer; *Chief Executive,* P. Riddle

WALES TOURIST BOARD

Brunel House, 2 Fitzalan Road, Cardiff CF24 0UY T 029-2049 9909 F 029-2048 5031 E info@visitwales.co.uk
W www.visitwales.com
Chief Executive, Jonathan Jones

NORTHERN IRELAND TOURIST BOARD

59 North Street, Belfast BT1 1NB T 028-9023 1221
F 028-9024 0960 E info@nitb.com
W www.discovernorthernireland.com
Chief Executive, Alan Clarke

TRAINING AND DEVELOPMENT AGENCY (TDA)

Portland House, Stag Place, London SW1E 5TT
T 0870-4960 123
W www.tda.gov.uk

The Training and Development Agency (TDA) was launched on 1 September 2005 and took on the role, and expanded the remit of, the Teacher Training Agency. It is funded and overseen by the Department for Education and Skills. The TDA aims to: attract able and committed people to teaching, concentrating specifically on subjects where teachers are in short supply; provide schools and their staff with good information on training and development opportunities; and ensure that new teachers enter schools with appropriate skills and knowledge, through working closely with providers of initial teacher training.
Chief Executive, Ralph Tabberer

TRANSPORT FOR LONDON

Windsor House, 42–50 Victoria Street, London SW1H 0TL
T 020-7941 4500
E enquiries@tfl.gov.uk W www.tfl.gov.uk/tfl/

Transport for London (TfL) was formed in July 2000 as a functional body of the Greater London Authority and is responsible for the capital's transport system. Its role is to implement the Mayor of London's Transport Strategy and manage the transport services across London for which the Mayor has responsibility.
Chair, Ken Livingstone
Vice-Chair, Dave Wetzel
Commissioner of Transport for London, Bob Kiley

UK ATOMIC ENERGY AUTHORITY

Harwell, Didcot, Oxon OX11 0RA
T 01235-820220
W www.ukaea.org.uk

The UK Atomic Energy Authority (UKAEA) was established by the Atomic Energy Authority Act 1954 and took over responsibility for the research and development of the civil nuclear power programme. The Authority's commercial arm, AEA Technology PLC, was privatised in 1996. UKAEA is now responsible for the safe management and decommissioning of its radioactive plants and for maximising the income from the buildings and land on its sites. UKAEA also undertakes the UK's contribution to the international fusion programme.
Chair, Hon. Mrs Barbara Thomas
Chief Executive, Dipesh Shah

UK FILM COUNCIL

10 Little Portland Street, London W1W 7JG
T 020-7861 7861 F 020-7861 7862
E info@ukfilmcouncil.org.uk W www.ukfilmcouncil.org.uk

The Council was created in April 2000 by the Department for Culture, Media and Sport to develop a strategy for the development and leadership of film culture and the film industry, as well as to promote the widest possible enjoyment and understanding of cinema throughout the nations and regions of the UK.
Chair, Stewart Till, CBE
Deputy Chair, Andrew Eaton
Chief Executive, John Woodward

UK FILM COUNCIL INTERNATIONAL

10 Little Portland Street, London W1W 7JG
T 020-7861 7861 F 020-7861 7864
E internationalinfo@ukfilmcouncil.org.uk
W www.ukfilmcouncil.org.uk

UK Film Council International (formerly the British Film Commission) was originally established in 1991. Its remit is to attract inward investment by promoting the UK as a international production centre to the film and television industries and encouraging the use of British locations, services, facilities and personnel. Working with the UK Screen Agencies, UK Film Concil International also provides overseas producers with a bespoke information service and offers practical help and advice to those filming in the UK.

British Film Commissioner, S. Norris
Director, Ms C. Wise

UNITED KINGDOM SPORTS COUNCIL (UK SPORT)

40 Bernard Street, London WC1N 1ST
T 020-7211 5100 F 020-7211 5246
W www.uksport.gov.uk

The UK Sports Council (UK Sport) was established by Royal Charter in 1996. Its role is to lead the UK to sporting excellence by supporting winning athletes, world-class events, world-class standards and ethically fair and drug-free sport. UK Sport is responsible for managing and distributing public investment (£29 million annually) and is a statutory distributor of funds raised by the National Lottery.

Chair, Sue Campbell, CBE
Chief Executive (acting), Liz Nicholl, MBE

UNRELATED LIVE TRANSPLANT REGULATORY AUTHORITY

Room 423, Wellington House, 133–155 Waterloo Road, London SE1 8UG
T 020-7972 4812 F 020-7972 4790
E dhmail@doh.gsi.gov.uk
W www.advisorybodies.doh.gov.uk/ultra

The Unrelated Live Transplant Regulatory Authority (ULTRA) is a statutory body established in 1990. In every case where the transplant of an organ within the definition of the Human Organ Transplants Act 1989 is proposed between a living donor and a recipient who are not genetically related, the proposal must be referred to ULTRA. Applications must be made by registered medical practitioners.

The Authority comprises a chair and ten members appointed by the Secretary of State for Health. The secretariat is provided by Department of Health officials.

Chair, Prof. Sir Roddy MacSween
Members, Deborah Bowman; Prof. Andrew Bradley; Dr James Douglas; Dr Susan Fuggle; Antony Hooker; Anne Keogh; Prof. Andrew Rees; Keith Rigg; Susanne Roff; Stephanie Sullivan

VICTORIA AND ALBERT MUSEUM

Cromwell Road, London SW7 2RL
T 020-7942 2000 W www.vam.ac.uk

The Victoria and Albert Museum is the national museum of fine and applied art and design. It descends directly from the Museum of Manufactures, which opened in Marlborough House in 1852 after the Great Exhibition of 1851. The Museum was moved in 1857 to become part of the South Kensington Museum. It was renamed the Victoria and Albert Museum in 1899. It also houses the National Art Library and Print Room.

The Museum administers two branch museums: the Museum of Childhood at Bethnal Green and the Theatre Museum in Covent Garden. The museum in Bethnal Green was opened in 1872 and the building is the most important surviving example of the type of glass and iron construction used by Paxton for the Great Exhibition. Total government grant-in-aid for 2005–6 is £37.7 million.

OFFICERS
Director, M. Jones
Deputy Director, I. Blatchford
Director of Collections and Keeper of Sculpture, Metalwork, Ceramics and Glass Department, Dr P. E. D. Williamson
Director of Collections Services, N. Umney
Director of Learning and Interpretation, D. Anderson, OBE
Director of Projects and Estate, Mrs G. F. Miles
Director of Public Affairs, D. Whitmore
Director of Development, Miss J. Lawson
Director of the Museum of Childhood, Ms D. Lees
Director of the Theatre Museum, G. Marsh
Managing Director of V&A Enterprises Ltd, Ms J. Prosser

WALLACE COLLECTION

Hertford House, Manchester Square, London W1U 3BN
T 020-7563 9500 F 020-7224 2155
E enquiries@wallacecollection.org
W www.wallacecollection.org

The Wallace Collection was bequeathed to the nation by the widow of Sir Richard Wallace, in 1897, and Hertford House was subsequently acquired by the government. Total government grant-in-aid for 2005–6 is £2.58 million.

Director, Rosalind Savill

WELSH DEVELOPMENT AGENCY

Plas Glyndwr, Kingsway, Cardiff CF10 3AH
T 01443-845500 F 01443-845589
E enquiries@wda.co.uk W www.wda.co.uk

The Agency was established under the Welsh Development Agency Act 1975. Its remit is to help further the regeneration of the economy and improve the environment in Wales. Under the Government of Wales Act 1998, the Land Authority for Wales and the Development Board for Rural Wales merged with the Welsh Development Agency. The Agency is sponsored by the National Assembly for Wales.

The Agency's priorities are to create new businesses and to encourage existing small firms to grow. Its main activities include promoting Wales as a location for inward investment, helping to boost the growth, profitability and competitiveness of indigenous Welsh companies, providing investment capital for industry, encouraging investment by the private sector in property development, grant-aiding land reclamation, and stimulating quality urban and rural development.

Chair, Sir Roger Jones, OBE
Chief Executive, Gareth Hall

WINE STANDARDS BOARD

Five Kings House, 1 Queen Street Place, London EC4R 1QS
T 020-7236 9512 F 020-7236 7908
E enquiries@wsb.org.uk
W www.wsb.org.uk

The Wine Standards Board (WSB), established in 1973, is
an executive non-departmental public body responsible to
the Department for Environment, Food and Rural Affairs.
The WSB enforces EU wine regulations in the UK and
manages the UK Vineyard Register, which records the
area under vine and the annual harvest and production
returns required from growers and producers.
Chair, Christopher Roberts, CB

WOMEN'S NATIONAL COMMISSION

1 Victoria Street, London SW1H 0ET
T 020-7215 6933 F 020-7215 2840
E wnc@dti.gsi.gov.uk
W www.thewnc.org.uk

The Women's National Commission was established in
1969 as an independent advisory committee to the
government. Its remit is to ensure that the informed
opinions of women are given their due weight in the
deliberations of the government and in public debate on
matters of public interest, including those of special
interest to women. The Commission is based within the
Department of Trade and Industry alongside the Women
and Equality Unit.
Chair, Baroness Margaret Prosser, OBE
Director, Janet Veitch

REGIONAL GOVERNMENT

LONDON

GREATER LONDON AUTHORITY (GLA)
City Hall, The Queen's Walk, London SE1 2AA
T 020-7983 4000
Press Office 020-7983 4070
E mayor@london.gov.uk W www.london.gov.uk

On 7 May 1998 London voted in favour of the formation of the Greater London Authority (GLA). The first elections to the GLA took place on 4 May 2000 and the new Authority took over its responsibilities on 3 July 2000. On 15 July 2002 the GLA moved to one of London's most spectacular buildings, newly built on a brownfield site on the south bank of the river Thames, adjacent to Tower Bridge. The second election to the GLA took place on 10 June 2004.

The structure and objectives of the GLA stem from its eight main areas of responsibility. These are transport, planning, economic development and regeneration, environment, police, fire and emergency planning, culture and health. The bodies that co-ordinate these functions and report to the GLA are: Transport for London (TfL); the London Development Agency (LDA); the Metropolitan Police Authority (MPA); and the London Fire and Emergency Planning Authority (LFEPA). The GLA also absorbed a number of other London bodies, such as the London Planning Advisory Committee, the London Ecology Unit and the London Research Centre.

The GLA consists of a directly elected mayor, the Mayor of London, and a separately elected assembly, the London Assembly. The Mayor has the key role of decision making, with the Assembly performing the tasks of regulating and scrutinising these decisions. In addition, the GLA has around 600 permanent staff to support the activities of the Mayor and the Assembly, which are overseen by a Head of Paid Service. The Mayor may appoint two political advisors, though does not necessarily exercise this power, but he may not appoint the Chief Executive, the Monitoring Officer or the Chief Finance Officer. These must be appointed by the assembly.

Every aspect of the Assembly and its activities must be open to public scrutiny and therefore accountable. The Assembly holds the Mayor to account through scrutiny of its strategies, decisions and actions. This is carried out by direct questioning at Assembly meetings and by conducting detailed investigations in committee.

People's Question Time gives Londoners the chance to question the Mayor and the London Assembly about plans, priorities and policies for London. It is held twice a year in different areas of London. A People's Question Time meeting was scheduled to take place in October 2005.

The role of the Mayor can be broken down into a number of key areas: to represent and promote London at home and abroad and speak up for Londoners; to devise strategies and plans to tackle London-wide issues, such as transport, economic development and regeneration, air quality, environment, noise, waste, bio-diversity, planning and culture; and to set budgets for Transport for London,

the London Development Agency, the Metropolitan Police Authority and the London Fire and Emergency Planning Authority. The Mayor is Chair of Transport for London and has the power to appoint the members of their board and those of the London Development Agency; he also makes appointments to the police and fire authorities. With London's successful bid to host the 2012 Olympic and Paralympic Games, the Mayor is the signatory to the contract with the International Olympic Committee undertaking that the Games will be delivered.

The role of the Assembly can be broken down into a number of key areas:
– to check on and balance the Mayor
– to scrutinise the Mayor
– to have the power to amend the Mayor's budget by a majority of two-thirds
– to investigate issues of London-wide significance and make proposals to the Mayor
– to provide the Deputy Mayor and the members serving on the police, fire and emergency planning authorities with advice

Mayor, Ken Livingstone
Deputy Mayor, Nicky Gavron
Chair of the London Assembly, Sally Hamwee
Deputy Chair of the Assembly, Brian Coleman

ELECTIONS AND THE VOTING SYSTEMS
The Assembly is elected every four years at the same time as the Mayor, and consists of 25 members. There is one member from each of the 14 GLA constituencies topped up with 11 London members who are representatives of political parties or individuals standing as independent candidates. The next election will be in May 2008.

The GLA constituencies are: Barnet and Camden; Bexley and Bromley; Brent and Harrow; City and East, covering Barking and Dagenham, the City of London, Newham and Tower Hamlets; Croydon and Sutton; Ealing and Hillingdon; Enfield and Haringey; Greenwich and Lewisham; Havering and Redbridge; North East, covering Hackney, Islington and Waltham Forest; Lambeth and Southwark; West Central, covering Hammersmith and Fulham, Kensington and Chelsea and Westminster; South West, covering Hounslow, Kingston upon Thames and Richmond upon Thames; Merton and Wandsworth.

Two distinct voting systems are used to appoint the existing Mayor and the Assembly. The Mayor is elected using the Supplementary Vote System (SVS). With SVS electors have two votes: one to give a first choice for Mayor and one to give a second choice. Electors cannot vote twice for the same candidate. If one candidate gets more than half of all the first choice votes, he or she becomes Mayor. If no candidate gets more than half the first choice votes, the two candidates with the most first choice votes remain in the election and all the other candidates drop out. The second choice votes on the ballot papers of the candidates who drop out are then counted. Where these second choice votes are for the two remaining candidates they are added to the first choice votes these candidates already have. The candidate with the most first and second choice votes combined becomes the Mayor of London.

The Assembly is appointed using the Additional Member System (AMS). Under AMS, electors have two votes. The first vote is for a constituency candidate. The second vote is for a party list or individual candidate contesting the London-wide Assembly seats. The 14 constituency members are elected under the first-past-the-post system, the same system used in general and local elections. Electors vote for one candidate and the candidate with the most votes wins. The Additional (London) Members are drawn from party lists or are independent candidates who stand as London Members.

The Greater London Returning Officer (GLRO) is the independent official responsible for running the first election in London. The GLRO has overall responsibility for running a free, fair and efficient election. He is supported in this by Returning Officers in each of the 14 London Constituencies.
GLRO, Anthony Mayer

TRANSPORT FOR LONDON (TfL)

TfL is the integrated body responsible for London's transport system. Its role is to implement the Mayor's transport strategy for London and manage transport services across the capital for which the Mayor has responsibility. TfL is directed by a management board whose members are chosen for their understanding of transport matters and are appointed by the Mayor, who chairs the board. TfL's role is:
- to manage the London Underground, buses, Croydon Tramlink and the Docklands Light Railway (DLR)
- to manage a 580 km network of main roads and all of London's 4,600 traffic lights
- to regulate taxis and minicabs
- to run the London River Services, Victoria Coach Station and London's Transport Museum
- to help to co-ordinate the Dial-a-Ride and Taxicard schemes for door-to-door services for transport users with mobility problems

The London Borough Councils maintain the role of highway and traffic authorities for 95 per cent of London's roads. A £5 congestion charge for motorists driving into central London between the hours of 7 a.m. and 6.30 p.m., Monday to Friday (excluding public holidays) was introduced on 17 February 2003, and was subsequently raised to £8 on 4 July 2005.
Transport Commissioner for London, Robert Kiley

LONDON DEVELOPMENT AGENCY (LDA)

The LDA promotes economic development and regeneration. It is one of the nine regional development agencies set up around the country to perform this task. It is run by a board of 14 members appointed by the Mayor. The key aspects of the LDA's role are:
- to promote business efficiency, investment and competitiveness
- to promote employment
- to enhance the skills of local people
- to create sustainable development

The London Boroughs retain powers to promote economic development in their local areas.
Chair, Mary Reilly

THE ENVIRONMENT

The Mayor is required to formulate strategies to tackle London's environmental issues including: the quality of water, air and land; the use of energy and London's contribution to climate change targets; ground water levels and traffic emissions; and municipal waste management.

METROPOLITAN POLICE AUTHORITY (MPA)

This body, which oversees the policing of London consists of 12 members of the assembly, including the Deputy Mayor, four magistrates and seven independents. One of the independents is appointed directly by the Home Secretary. The role of the MPA is:
- to maintain an efficient and effective police force
- to publish an annual policing plan
- to set police targets and monitor performance
- to be part of the appointment, discipline and removal of senior officers
- to be responsible for the performance budget
- to oversee formal inquiries and the implementation of their recommendations

The boundaries of the metropolitan police districts have been changed to be consistent with the 32 London boroughs. Areas beyond the GLA remit have been incorporated into the Surrey, Hertfordshire and Essex police areas. The City of London has its own police force.
Chair, Len Duvall

LONDON FIRE AND EMERGENCY PLANNING AUTHORITY (LFEPA)

On 3 July 2000 the London Fire and Civil Defence Authority became the London Fire and Emergency Planning Authority. It consists of 17 members, 9 drawn from the assembly and 8 from the London Boroughs. The role of LFEPA is:
- to set the strategy for the provision of fire services
- to ensure that the fire brigade can meet all the normal requirements efficiently
- to ensure that effective arrangements are made for the fire brigade to receive emergency calls and deal with them promptly
- to ensure that information useful to the development of the fire brigades is gathered
- to assist the boroughs with their emergency planning training and exercises
Chair, Valerie Shawcross

SALARIES *as at August 2005*

Mayor	£115,79
Deputy Mayor	£71,99
Assembly Member	£49,26

LONDON ASSEMBLY COMMITTEES

Chair, 2005 Elections Review Committee, Brian Coleman
Chair, Audit Panel, Peter Hulme Cross
Chair, Budget Committee, Sally Hamwee
Chair, Business Management and Appointments Committee, Brian Coleman
Chair, Economic Development, Culture, Sport and Tourism Committee, Dee Doocey
Chair, Environment Committee, Darren Johnson
Chair, Health and Public Services Committee, Joanne McCartney
Chair, Planning and Spatial Development Committee, Tony Arbour
Chair, Transport Committee, Roger Evans
Commission on London Governance (Advisory Committee)
Standards Committee

LONDON ASSEMBLY ORGANISATIONAL STRUCTURE

MAYOR'S OFFICE
Public Affairs (International and European Relations, London Stakeholders, Government and Parliamentary Liaison, Public Consultation, Public Affairs Publications)
Best Value Partnership (Borough Liaison)
Economic and Business Policy (Private Sector, Strategic Evaluation Unit)
Equalities and Policing
Environment
Tourism and Creative Industries
London House (Brussels)
Administration Manager

SECRETARIAT
Assembly Support
Scrutiny and Investigations
Committee Services
Assembly's Media Relations

CHIEF EXECUTIVE'S OFFICE
Governance
Marketing
Mayor's Media Relations

POLICY AND PARTNERSHIPS
Spatial Development Strategy
Planning Decisions
Architecture and Urbanism Unit
Environment
Culture
Policy Support (Health, Housing and Homelessness, Social Inclusion, Sustainable Development)
Business Support

CORPORATE SERVICES
GLA Economics
Information and Communication Technology
Legal
HR and Administration (Facilities Management and Internal Communications)
Research Library
Data Management
Public Liaison
Business Support

FINANCE AND PERFORMANCE
Core Performance and Project Management
Strategic Performance
Core Finance
Strategic Finance

LONDON ASSEMBLY MEMBERS
as at 20 July 2005
Arbour, Anthony, *C., South West*, Maj. 4,067
Arnold, Jennette Sarah Alfreda, *Lab., North East*, Maj. 13,338
Barnes, Richard Michael, *C., Ealing and Hillingdon*, Maj. 11,016
Biggs, John Robert, *Lab., City and East*, Maj. 14,336
Blackman, Robert, *C., Brent and Harrow*, Maj. 4,686
Bray, Angela Lavinia, *C., West Central*, Maj. 29,944
Coleman, Brian, *C., Barnet and Camden*, Maj. 11,519
Doocey, Dee, *LD, London List*
Duvall, Leonard Lloyd, *Lab., Greenwich and Lewisham*, Maj. 14,083

Evans, Jeremy Roger, *C., Havering and Redbridge*, Maj. 16,706
Gavron, Felicia Nicolette, *Lab., London List*
Hamwee, Sally Rachel, *LD, London List*
Hockney, Nicholas Damian, *UKIP, London List*
Howlett, Elizabeth, *C., Merton and Wandsworth*, Maj. 16,878
Hulme Cross, Peter Kenneth, *UKIP, London List*
Johnson, Darren, *Green, London List*
Jones, Jenny, *Green, London List*
McCartney, Joanne, *Lab., Enfield and Haringey*, Maj. 1,574
Neill, Robert James Macgillivray, *C., Bexley and Bromley*, Maj. 34,254
Pelling, Andrew John, *C., Croydon and Sutton*, Maj. 23,694
Pope, Geoff, *LD, London List*
Qureshi, Murad, *Lab., London List*
Shawcross, Valerie, *Lab., Lambeth and Southwark*, Maj. 5,475
Tope, Graham Norman, *LD, London List*
Tuffrey, Michael William, *LD, London List*

STATE OF THE PARTIES *as at 20 July 2005*

Party	Seats	Gain/Loss
Conservative (C.)	9	0
Labour (Lab.)	7	−2
Liberal Democrats (LD)	5	+1
Green (Green)	2	−1
UK Independence (UKIP)	2	+2

MAYORAL ELECTION RESULTS
10 June 2004
E. 5,197,647 *T.* 1,920,533 (36.95%)
Change in turnout from 2000 +2.52%
Good votes 1st choice 1,863,671 (97.04%); 2nd choice 1,591,443 (82.86%)
Rejected votes 1st choice 56,862 (2.96%); 2nd choice 329,090 (17.14%)

First	Party	Votes	%
Ken Livingstone	Lab.	685,541	35.70
Steven Norris	C.	542,423	28.24
Simon Hughes	LD	284,645	14.82
Frank Maloney	UKIP	115,665	6.02
Lindsey German	Respect	61,731	3.21
Julian Leppert	BNP	58,405	3.04
Darren Johnson	Green	57,331	2.99
Ram Gidoomal	CPA	41,696	2.17
Lorna Reid Ind. Working Class		9,542	0.50
Tammy Nagalingam	Ind.	6,692	0.35

Second	Party	Votes	%
Simon Hughes	LD	465,704	24.25
Ken Livingstone	Lab.	250,517	13.04
Steven Norris	C.	222,559	11.59
Darren Johnson	Green	208,686	10.87
Frank Maloney	UKIP	193,157	10.06
Julian Leppert	BNP	70,736	3.68
Lindsey German	Respect	63,294	3.30
Ram Gidoomal	CPA	56,721	2.95
Lorna Reid Ind. Working Class		39,678	2.07
Tammy Nagalingam	Ind.	20,391	1.06

LONDON ASSEMBLY ELECTION RESULTS

10 June 2004

CONSTITUENCIES

BARNET AND CAMDEN
E. 371,186 T. 38.41%

Brian Coleman, C.	47,640
Lucy Anderson, Lab.	36,121
Jonathan Simpson, LD	23,603
Miranda Dunn, Green	11,921
Magnus Nielsen, UKIP	8,685
Elisabeth Wheatley, Respect	5,150
Humberto Heliotrope, CPA	1,914

C. majority 11,519

BEXLEY AND BROMLEY
E. 397,075 T. 41.48%

Robert Neill, C.	64,246
Duncan Borrowman, LD	29,992
Heather Bennett, UKIP	26,703
Charles Mansell, Lab.	24,848
Ann Garrett, Green	8,069
Miranda Suit, CPA	3,397
Alun Morinan, Respect	1,673

C. majority 34,254

BRENT AND HARROW
E. 332,723 T. 38.03%

Robert Blackman, C.	39,900
Toby Harris, Lab.	35,214
Havard Hughes, LD	20,782
Daniel Moss, UKIP	7,199
Mohammad Ali, Green	6,975
Albert Harriott, Respect	4,586
Gladstone Macaulay, CPA	2,734

C. majority 4,686

CITY AND EAST
E. 437,298 T. 33.43%

John Biggs, Lab.	38,085
Shafi Choudhury, C.	23,749
Oliur Rahman, Respect	19,675
Guy Burton, LD	18,255
Christopher Pratt, UKIP	17,997
Terry McGrenera, Green	8,687
Christopher Gill, CPA	4,461

Lab. majority 14,336

CROYDON AND SUTTON
E. 376,175 T. 37.82%

Andrew Pelling, C.	52,330
Steven Gauge, LD	28,636
Sean Fitzsimons, Lab.	25,861
James Feisenberger, UKIP	15,203
Shasha Khan, Green	6,175
David Campanale, CPA	4,234
Waqas Hussain, Respect	3,108

C. majority 23,694

EALING AND HILLINGDON
E. 397,564 T. 37.28%

Richard Barnes, C.	45,230
Gurcharan Singh, Lab.	34,214
Michael Cox, LD	23,440
David Malindine, UKIP	14,698
Sarah Edwards, Green	9,395
Dalawar Chaudhry, Ind.	5,285
Salvinder Dhillon, Respect	4,229
Genevieve Hibbs, CPA	3,024

C. majority 11,016

ENFIELD AND HARINGEY
E. 343,617 T. 36.14%

Joanne McCartney, Lab.	33,955
Peter Forrest, C.	32,381
Wayne Hoban, LD	19,720
Brian Hall, UKIP	10,652
Jayne Forbes, Green	10,310
Sait Akgul, Respect	6,855
Peter Wolstenholme, CPA	2,365

Lab. majority 1,574

GREENWICH AND LEWISHAM
E. 329,450 T. 35.10%

Leonard Duvall, Lab.	36,251
Gareth Bacon, C.	22,168
Alexander Feakes, LD	19,183
Timothy Reynolds, UKIP	13,454
Susan Luxton, Green	11,271
Stephen Hammond, CPA	3,619
Ian Page, Respect/Soc. Alt.	2,825

Lab. majority 14,083

HAVERING AND REDBRIDGE
E. 350,652 T. 38.96%

Jeremy Evans, C.	44,723
Keith Darvill, Lab.	28,017
Lawrence Webb, UKIP	18,297
Matthew Lake, LD	13,646
Malvin Brown, Residents Assn. of London	6,925
Ashley Gunstock, Green	6,006
Abdurahman Jafar, Respect	5,185
Juliet Hawkins, CPA	2,917
David Stephens, Third Way	2,031
Peter Thorogood, Ind.	1,591

C. majority 16,706

LAMBETH AND SOUTHWARK
E. 373,293 T. 33.38%

Valerie Shawcross, Lab.	36,286
Caroline Pidgeon, LD	30,808
Bernard Gentry, C.	17,379
Shane Collins, Green	11,906
Frank Maloney, UKIP	8,775
Janet Noble, Respect	4,934
Simisola Lawanson, CPA	3,653
Navindh Baburam, Ind.	609

Lab. majority 5,475

MERTON AND WANDSWORTH
E. 340,792 *T.* 38.55%

Elizabeth Howlett, C.	48,295
Kathryn Smith, Lab.	31,417
Andrew Martin, LD	17,864
Roy Vickery, Green	10,163
Adrian Roberts, UKIP	8,327
Ruairidh Maclean, Respect	4,291
Ellen Greco, CPA	2,782
Rathy Alagaratnam, Ind.	1,240
C. majority 16,878	

NORTH EAST
E. 410,719 *T.* 33.93%

Jennette Arnold, Lab.	37,380
Terry Stacy, LD	24,042
Andrew Boff, C.	23,264
Jon Nott, Green	16,739
Robert Selby, UKIP	11,459
Dean Ryan, Respect	11,184
Andrew Otchie, CPA	3,219
James Beavis, Comm.	1,378
Lab. majority 13,338	

SOUTH WEST
E. 384,450 *T.* 40.31%

Tony Arbour, C.	48,858
Dee Doocey, LD	44,791
Seema Malhotra, Lab.	25,225
Alan Hindle, UKIP	12,477
Judy Maciejowska, Green	9,866
Omar Waraich, Respect	3,785
Peter Flower, CPA	3,008
C. majority 4,067	

WEST CENTRAL
E. 352,653 *T.* 35.28%

Angela Bray, C.	51,884
Ansuya Sodha, Lab.	21,940
Francesco Fruzza, LD	17,478
Julia Stephenson, Green	10,762
Nicholas Hockney, UKIP	7,219
Kevin Cobham, Respect	4,825
Jillian McLachlan, CPA	1,993
C. majority 29,944	

TOP-UP MEMBERS

LABOUR
Felicia Nicolette Gavron
Murad Qureshi

LIBERAL DEMOCRAT
Dee Doocey
Lynne Featherstone
Sally Hamwee
Graham Tope
Michael Tuffrey

UK INDEPENDENCE PARTY
Peter Cross
Nicholas Hockney

GREEN PARTY
Darren Johnson
Jenny Jones

WALES

NATIONAL ASSEMBLY FOR WALES
Cathays Park, Cardiff CF1 3NQ
T 029-2082 5111
National Assembly Information Line 029-2089 8200
E webmaster@wales.gov.uk
W www.wales.gov.uk

In July 1997 the government announced plans to establish a National Assembly for Wales. In a referendum on 18 September 1997 about 50 per cent of the electorate voted, of whom 50.3 per cent voted in favour of the Assembly. Elections are to be held every four years. The first elections were held on 6 May 1999 when approximately 46 per cent of the electorate voted. On 1 May 2003 the second Welsh Assembly elections took place. The next election will take place in May 2007.

The Assembly has 60 members (including the Presiding Officer), comprising 40 constituency members and 20 additional regional members from party lists. It can introduce only secondary legislation and has no power to raise or lower income tax.

The National Assembly for Wales has responsibility in Wales for ministerial functions relating to health and personal social services; education, except for terms and conditions of service and student awards; training; the Welsh language, arts and culture; the implementation of the Citizen's Charter in Wales; local government; housing; water and sewerage; environmental protection; sport; agriculture and fisheries; forestry; land use, including town and country planning and countryside and nature conservation; new towns; non-departmental public bodies and appointments in Wales; ancient monuments and historic buildings and the Welsh Arts Council; roads; tourism; financial assistance to industry; the Strategic Development Scheme in Wales and the Programme for the Valleys; and the operation of the European Regional Development Fund in Wales and other European Union matters.

SALARIES *as at 1 April 2005*
†First Minister	£72,863
†Minister/Presiding Officer	£37,797
Assembly Members (AM)	£44,000*

*Reduced by two-thirds if the member is already an MP or an MEP
†First Minister, Ministers and Presiding Officer also receive the Assembly Member salary

THE PRESIDING OFFICER
Lord Dafydd Elis-Thomas, AM

WELSH ASSEMBLY GOVERNMENT
First Minister of the Assembly, Rhodri Morgan, AM
Principal Private Secretary, Lawrence Conway
Special Advisers, Paul Griffiths; Mark Drakeford; Dr Rachel Jones; Cathy Owens; Martin Mansfield; Jane Runeckles
Minister for Assembly Business, Jane Hutt, AM
Minister for Business, Karen Sinclair, AM
Minister for Culture, Welsh Language and Sport, Alun Pugh, AM
Minister for Economic Development and Transport, Andrew Davies, AM
Minister for Education and Lifelong Learning, Jane Davidson, AM
Minister for Environment, Planning and Countryside, Carwyn Jones, AM

Minister for Finance, Local Government and Public Services, Sue Essex, AM
Minister for Health and Social Services, Dr Brian Gibbons, AM
Minister for Social Justice and Regeneration, Edwina Hart, AM
Deputy Minister for Communities, Huw Lewis, AM
Deputy Minister for Economic Development and Transport, Tamsin Dunwoody-Kneafsey, AM
Deputy Minister for Finance, Local Government and Public Services, and Education and Lifelong Learning, Christine Chapman, AM
Deputy Minister for Older People, John Griffiths
Permanent Secretary, Sir Jon Shortridge
Clerk to the Assembly, Paul Silk

EXECUTIVE BOARD
Senior Director, Policy, Derek Jones
Director, Business and Information Management, Bryan Mitchell
Director, Economic Development and Transport, David Pritchard
Director, Education and Training, Richard Davies
Director, Environment, Planning and Countryside, Gareth Jones
Director, Health and Social Care, Ann Lloyd
Director, Human Resources, Bernard Galton
Director, Local Government, Public Service and Culture, Hugh Rawlings
Director, Public Service Development, Barbara Wilson
Director, Regulation/Inspection Review, Helen Thomas
Director, Social Justice and Regeneration, John Bader
Director, Spending Review, Martin Evans
Director, Strategy and Communications, Huw Brodie
Chief Medical Officer, Dr Ruth Hall
Principal Finance Officer, David Richards
Non-Executive Directors, Adrian Webb; Kathryn Bishop

DEPARTMENTS AND OFFICES
Agriculture and Rural Affairs Department
Assembly Parliamentary Service
Communications Directorate
Economic Development Department
Finance Group
Health Protection and Improvement Directorate
Local Government Group
NHS Directorate
Office of the Counsel General
Social Services and Communities Group
Strategic Policy Unit
Training and Education Department
Transport, Planning and Environment Group

EXECUTIVE AGENCIES
Cadw: Welsh Historic Monuments
Planning Inspectorate
Welsh European Funding Office

COMMITTEES

SUBJECT COMMITTEES
Culture, Welsh Language and Sport
Economic Development and Transport
Education and Lifelong Learning
Environment, Planning and Countryside
Health and Social Services
Local Government and Public Services
Social Justice and Regeneration

STANDING COMMITTEES
Audit
Business
Equality of Opportunity
European and External Affairs
House
Legislation
Standards of Conduct

MEMBERS OF THE WELSH ASSEMBLY
as at July 2004
Andrews, Leighton, *Lab., Rhondda,* Maj. 7,954
Barrett, Lorraine Jayne, *Lab., Cardiff South and Penarth,*
Maj. 4,114
Bates, Michael, *LD, Montgomeryshire,* Maj. 12,297
Black, Peter, *LD, South Wales West region*
Bourne, Prof. Nicholas, *C., Mid and West Wales region*
Burnham, Eleanor, *LD, North Wales region*
Butler, Rosemary Janet Mair, *Lab., Newport West,*
Maj. 3,752
Cairns, Alun, *C., South Wales West region*
Chapman, Christine, *Lab., Cynon Valley,* Maj. 7,117
Cuthbert, Jeffrey, *Lab., Caerphilly,* Maj. 4,974
Davidson, Jane Elizabeth, *Lab., Pontypridd,* Maj. 6,920
Davies, Andrew David, *Lab., Swansea West,* Maj. 2,562
Davies, David Thomas Charles, *C., Monmouth,* Maj. 8,510
Davies, Edward, *C., Mid and West Wales region*
Davies, Janet, *PC, South Wales West region*
Davies, Jocelyn, *PC, South Wales East region*
Dunwoody-Kneafsey, Moyra Tamsin, *Lab., Preseli
Pembrokeshire,* Maj. 1,326
Elis-Thomas, Lord Dafydd, *PC, Meirionnydd Nant Conwy,*
Maj. 8,742
Essex, Susan Linda, *Lab., Cardiff North,* Maj. 540
Francis, Elizabeth Ann (Lisa), *C., Mid and West Wales
region*
German, Michael, *LD, South Wales East region*
Gibbons, Brian, *Lab., Aberavon,* Maj. 7,813
Graham, William, *C., South Wales East region*
Gregory, Janice, *Lab., Ogmore,* Maj. 6,504
Griffiths, Albert John, *Lab., Newport East,* Maj. 3,464
Gwyther, Christine Margery, *Lab., Carmarthen West and
South Pembrokeshire,* Maj. 515
Hart, Edwina, *Lab., Gower,* Maj. 5,688
Hutt, Jane, *Lab., Vale of Glamorgan,* Maj. 2,653
Idris Jones, Denise, *Lab., Conwy,* Maj. 72
Isherwood, Mark, *C., North Wales region*
James, Irene, *Lab., Islwyn,* Maj. 7,320
Jones, Alun, *PC, Caernarfon,* Maj. 5,905
Jones, Carwyn Howell, *Lab., Bridgend,* Maj. 2,421
Jones, Elin, *PC, Ceredigion,* Maj. 4,618
Jones, Helen, *PC, Mid and West Wales region*
Jones, Laura Anne, *C., South Wales East region*
Jones, Margaret Ann (Ann), *Lab., Vale of Clwyd,*
Maj. 3,341
Law, Peter, *Ind., Blaenau Gwent,* Maj. 11,736
Lewis, Huw, *Lab., Merthyr Tydfil and Rhymney,* Maj. 8,160
Lloyd, Dr David, *PC, South Wales West region*
Lloyd, Val, *Lab., Swansea East,* Maj. 3,997
Marek, Dr John, *Forward Wales, Wrexham,* Maj. 973
Melding, David, *C., South Wales Central region*
Mewies, Sandra Elaine, *Lab., Delyn,* Maj. 1,624
Morgan, Hywel Rhodri, *Lab., Cardiff West,* Maj. 6,837
Morgan, Jonathan, *C., South Wales Central region*
Neagle, Lynne, *Lab., Torfaen,* Maj. 6,964
Pugh, Alun John, *Lab., Clwyd West,* Maj. 436
Randerson, Jennifer Elizabeth, *LD, Cardiff Central,*
Maj. 7,156

Ryder, Janet, *PC, North Wales region*
Sergeant, Carl, *Lab., Alyn and Deeside,* Maj. 3,503
Sinclair, Karen, *Lab., Clwyd South,* Maj. 2,891
Thomas, Catherine, *Lab., Llanelli,* Maj. 21
Thomas, Gwenda, *Lab., Neath,* Maj. 4,946
Thomas, Owen, *PC, South Wales Central region*
Thomas, Rhodri, *PC, Carmarthen East and Dinefwr,*
Maj. 4,614
Williams, Brynle, *C., North Wales region*
Williams, Kirsty, *LD, Brecon and Radnorshire,*
Maj. 5,308
Wood, Leanne, *PC, South Wales Central region*
Wyn Jones, Ieuan, *PC, Ynys Mon,* Maj. 2,255

STATE OF THE PARTIES *as at May 2005*

	Constituency AMs	Regional AMs	AM Total
Labour (Lab.)	29	0	29
Plaid Cymru (PC)	4†	7	11†
Conservative (C.)	1	10	11
Liberal Democrats (LD)	3	3	6
Others	2	0	2
The Presiding Officer	1	0	1

† Excludes the Presiding Officer, who has no party
allegiance while in post

WELSH ASSEMBLY ELECTION RESULTS
1 May 2003

CONSTITUENCIES

ABERAVON (S. WALES WEST)
E. 50,208 T. 37.6%

Brian Gibbons, Lab.	11,137
Geraint Owen, PC	3,324
Claire Waller, LD	1,840
Myr Boult, C.	1,732
Robert Williams, Soc. Alt.	608
Gwenno Saunders, Ind. Wales	114

Lab. majority 7,813

ALYN AND DEESIDE (WALES N.)
E. 60,518 T. 25.1%

Carl Sergeant, Lab.	7,036
Matthew Wright, C.	3,533
Paul Brighton, LD	2,509
Richard Coombs, PC	1,160
William Crawford, UKIP	826

Lab. majority 3,503

BLAENAU GWENT (S. WALES EAST)
E. 52,927 T. 37.8%

Peter Law, Lab.	13,884
Stephen Bard, LD	2,148
Rhys Ab Elis, PC	1,889
Barrie O'Keefe, C.	1,131
Roger Thomas, UKIP	719

Lab. majority 11,736

BRECON AND RADNORSHIRE (WALES MID AND W.)
E. 53,739 T. 50.0%

Kirsty Williams, LD	13,325
Nicholas Bourne, C.	8,017
David Rees, Lab.	3,130
Brynach Parri, PC	1,329
Elizabeth Phillips, UKIP	1,042

LD majority 5,308

BRIDGEND (S. WALES WEST)
E. 62,540 T. 35.4%

Carwyn Howell Jones, Lab.	9,487
Alun Hugh Cairns, C.	7,066
Cheryl Anne Green, LD	2,980
Keith Parry, PC	1,939
Timothy Charles Jenkins, UKIP	677

Lab. majority 2,421

CAERNARFON (WALES N.)
E. 47,173 T. 45.0%

Alun Ffred Jones, PC	11,675
Martin Robert Eaglestone, Lab.	5,770
Goronwy Owen Edwards, C.	2,402
Stephen William Churchman, LD	1,392

PC majority 5,905

CAERPHILLY (S. WALES EAST)
E. 68,152 T. 37.3%

Jeffrey Cuthbert, Lab.	11,893
Lindsay Whittle, PC	6,919
Laura Jones, C.	2,570
Rob Roffe, LD	1,281
Anne Blackman, Ind.	1,204
Ann, Dafydd-Lewis, Ind.	930
Brenda Vipass, UKIP	590

Lab. majority 4,974

CARDIFF CENTRAL (S. WALES CENTRAL)
E. 62,470 T. 33.7%

Jennifer Elizabeth Randerson, LD	11,256
Geoff Miles Mungham, Lab.	4,100
Craig Stuart Piper, C.	2,378
Owen John Thomas, PC	1,795
Raja Gul Raiz, Soc. All.	541
Captain Beany, Bean	289
Madeleine Elise Jeremy, ProLife	239

LD majority 7,156

CARDIFF NORTH (S. WALES CENTRAL)
E. 64,528 T. 43.9%

Susan Linda Essex, Lab.	10,413
Jonathan Morgan, C.	9,873
John Leslie Dixon, LD	3,474
Hewel William Wyn Jones, PC	2,679
Donald Edwin Hulston, UKIP	1,295

Lab. majority 540

CARDIFF SOUTH AND PENARTH (S. WALES CENTRAL)
E. 65,505 T. 31.0%

Lorraine Jayne Barrett, Lab.	8,978
Dianne Elizabeth Rees, C.	4,864
Rodney Simon Berman, LD	3,154
Richard Rhys Grigg, PC	2,538
David Charles Bartlett, Soc. Alt.	585

Lab. majority 4,114

CARDIFF WEST (S. WALES CENTRAL)
E. 60,523 T. 35.4%

Hywel Rhodri Morgan, Lab.	10,420
Heather Douglas, C.	3,583
Jacqueline-Anne Gasson, LD	2,914
Eluned Mary Bush, PC	2,859
Frank Roger Wynne Hughes, UKIP	929

Lab. majority 6,837

CARMARTHEN EAST AND DINEFWR
(WALES MID AND W.)
E. 54,110 T. 49.5%

Rhodri Thomas, PC	12,969
Anthony Cooper, Lab.	8,355
Harri Lloyd-Davies, C.	3,576
Steffan John, LD	1,866

PC majority 4,614

CARMARTHEN WEST AND SOUTH PEMBROKESHIRE
(WALES MID AND W.)
E. 56,403 T. 43.0%

Christine Margery Gwyther, Lab.	8,384
Llyr Hughes Griffiths, PC	7,869
David Nicholas Thomas, C.	4,917
Mary Kathleen Megarry, LD	2,222
Arthur Ronald Williams, Ind.	580

Lab. majority 515

CEREDIGION (WALES MID AND W.)
E. 52,940 T. 50.0%

Elin Jones, PC	11,883
John Davies, LD	7,265
Rhianon Passmore, Lab.	3,308
Owen Williams, C.	2,923
Ian Sheldon, UKIP	940

PC majority 4,618

CLWYD SOUTH (WALES N.)
E. 53,452 T. 35.1%

Karen Sinclair, Lab.	6,814
Dyfed Edwards, PC	3,923
Albert Fox, C.	3,548
Marc Jones, John Marek Ind.	2,210
Derek Burnham, LD	1,666
Edwina Theunissen, UKIP	501

Lab. majority 2,891

CLWYD WEST (WALES N.)
E. 54,463 T. 40.6%

Alun John Pugh, Lab.	7,693
Brynle Williams, C.	7,257
Janet Ryder, PC	4,715
Eleanor Burnham, LD	1,743
Peter Murray, UKIP	715

Lab. majority 436

CONWY (WALES N.)
E. 54,443 T. 38.7%

Denise Idris Jones, Lab.	6,467
Gareth Jones, PC	6,395
Guto Bebb, C.	5,152
Graham Rees, LD	2,914

Lab. majority 72

CYNON VALLEY (S. WALES CENTRAL)
E. 44,473 T. 37.5%

Christine Chapman, Lab.	10,841
David Alun Walters, PC	3,724
Robert Owen Humphreys, LD	1,120
Daniel Clive Byron Thomas, C.	984

Lab. majority 7,117

DELYN (WALES N.)
E. 54,426 T. 31.4%

Sandra Elaine Mewies, Lab.	6,520
Mark Isherwood, C.	4,896
David Lloyd, LD	2,880
Paul Rowlinson, PC	2,588

Lab. majority 1,624

GOWER (S. WALES WEST)
E. 60,523 T. 39.9%

Edwina Hart, Lab.	10,334
Stephen James, C.	4,646
Sian Caiach, PC	3,502
Nicholas Tregoning, LD	2,775
Richard Lewis, UKIP	2,444

Lab. majority 5,688

ISLWYN (S. WALES EAST)
E. 51,170 T. 40.3%

Irene James, Lab.	11,246
Brian Hancock, PC	3,926
Paul Taylor, Tinker against the Assembly	2,201
Terri-Anne Matthews, C.	1,848
Huw Price, LD	1,268

Lab. majority 7,320

LLANELLI (WALES MID AND W.)
E. 57,428 T. 40.9%

Catherine Thomas, Lab.	9,916
Helen Mary Jones, PC	9,895
Gareth Jones, C.	1,712
Kenneth Rees, LD	1,644

Lab. majority 21

MEIRIONNYDD NANT CONWY (WALES MID AND W.)
E. 33,742 T. 45.5%

Lord Dafydd Elis-Thomas, PC	8,717
Edwin Woodward, Lab.	2,891
Lisa Francis, C.	2,485
Kenneth Harris, LD	1,100

PC majority 5,826

MERTHYR TYDFIL AND RHYMNEY (S. WALES EAST)
E. 55,768 T. 33.5%

Huw Lewis, Lab.	11,148
Alun Cox, PC	2,988
John Prosser, C.	1,539
Neil Greer, Ind.	1,423
John Ault, LD	1,324

Lab. majority 8,160

MONMOUTH (S. WALES EAST)
E. 62,451 T. 44.9%

David Thomas Charles Davies, C.	15,989
Sian Catherine James, Lab.	7,479
Alison Leyland Willott, LD	2,973
Stephen Vaughan Thomas, PC	1,355

C. majority 8,510

MONTGOMERYSHIRE (WALES MID AND W.)
E. 45,598 T. 43.0%

Michael Bates, LD	7,869
Edward Davies, C.	5,572
Rina Clarke, Lab.	2,039
David Senior, PC	1,918
David Rowlands, UKIP	1,107
Robert Mills, Ind.	985

LD majority 2,297

NEATH (S. WALES WEST)
E. 56,759 T. 39.4%

Gwenda Thomas, Lab.	11,332
Alun Llewelyn, PC	6,386
Helen Jones, LD	2,048
Chris Smart, C.	2,011
Huw Pudner, WSA	410

Lab. majority 4,946

NEWPORT EAST (S. WALES EAST)
E. 56,563 T. 30.4%

Albert John Griffiths, Lab.	7,621
Matthew Robert Hatton Evans, C.	4,157
Charles Edward Townsend, LD	2,768
Mohammad Asghar, PC	1,555
Neal John Reynolds, UKIP	987

Lab. majority 3,464

NEWPORT WEST (S. WALES EAST)
E. 61,238 T. 35.3%

Rosemary Janet Mair Butler, Lab.	10,053
William Graham, C.	6,301
Phylip Andrew David Hobson, LD	2,094
Anthony Michael Salkeld, PC	1,678
Hugh Moelwyn Hughes, UKIP	1,102
Richard Morse, WSA	198

Lab. majority 3,752

OGMORE (S. WALES WEST)
E. 49,565 T. 34.3%

Janice Gregory, Lab.	9,874
Janet Marion Davies, PC	3,370
Jacqueline Radford, LD	1,567
Richard John Hill, C.	1,532
Christopher Herriott, Soc. Lab.	410

Lab. majority 6,504

PONTYPRIDD (S. WALES CENTRAL)
E. 63,204 T. 38.8%

Jane Elizabeth Davidson, Lab.	12,206
Delme Ifor Bowen, PC	5,286
Michael John Powell, LD	3,443
Jayne Louise Cowan, C.	2,438
Peter Manuel Gracia, UKIP	1,025

Lab. majority 6,920

PRESELI PEMBROKESHIRE (WALES MID AND W.)
E. 55,195 T. 41.7%

Moyra Tamsin Dunwoody-Kneafsey, Lab.	8,067
Paul Windsor Davies, C.	6,741
Sion Tomos Jobbins, PC	5,227
Michael Ian Warden, LD	2,799

Lab. majority 1,326

RHONDDA (S. WALES CENTRAL)
E. 50,463 T. 46.0%

Leighton Andrews, Lab.	14,170
Geraint Davies, PC	6,216
Jeff Gregory, Ind.	909
Veronica Watkins, LD	680
Dr K. T. Rajan, UKIP	524
Paul Williams, C.	504

Lab. majority 7,954

SWANSEA EAST (S. WALES WEST)
E. 57,252 T. 30.7%

Val Lloyd, Lab.	8,221
Peter Black, LD	4,224
Dr Dewi Evans, PC	2,223
David Alan Robinson, UKIP	1,474
Peter Morris, C.	1,135
Alan Thomson, WSA	133

Lab. majority 3,997

SWANSEA WEST (S. WALES WEST)
E. 58,749 T. 33.3%

Andrew David Davies, Lab.	7,023
Dr David Rees Lloyd, PC	4,461
Arthur Michael Day, LD	3,510
Dorian Rowbottom, C.	3,106
David Charles Evans, UKIP	1,040
David Leigh Richards, WSA	272

Lab. majority 2,562

TORFAEN (S. WALES EAST)
E. 61,264 T. 32.1%

Lynne Neagle, Lab.	10,152
Nicholas Ramsay, C.	3,188
Michael German, LD	2,746
Aneurin Preece, PC	2,092
David Rowlands, UKIP	1,377

Lab. majority 6,964

VALE OF CLWYD (WALES N.)
E. 49,319 T. 36.5%

Margaret Ann Jones, Lab.	8,256
Darren Millar, C.	5,487
Malcom Evans, PC	2,516
Robina Feeley, LD	1,630

Lab. majority 2,769

VALE OF GLAMORGAN (S. WALES CENTRAL)
E. 68,947 T. 40.7%

Jane Hutt, Lab.	12,267
David Melding, C.	9,614
Christopher Franks, PC	3,921
Nilmini de Silva, LD	2,049

Lab. majority 2,653

WREXHAM (WALES N.)
E. 50,508 T. 34.5%

Dr John Marek, John Marek Ind.	6,539
Susan Lesley Griffiths, Lab.	5,566
Janet Finch-Saunders, C.	2,228
Tom Ripperth, LD	1,701
Peter Ryder, PC	1,329

John Marek Ind. majority 973

YNYS MON (WALES N.)
E. 49,998 T. 51.0%

Ieuan Wyn Jones, PC	9,452
Peter Rogers, C.	7,197
William Jones, Lab.	6,024
Nicholas Bennett, LD	2,089
Francis Charles Wykes, UKIP	481

PC majority 2,255

REGIONS

MID AND WEST WALES
E. 409,155 T. 184,198

PC	51,874 (28.2%)
Lab.	46,451 (25.2%)
C.	35,566 (19.3%)
LD	30,177 (16.4%)
Green	7,794 (4.2%)
UKIP	5,945 (3.2%)
Mid and West Wales Pensioners	3,968 (2.2%)
Ind. Wales	1,324 (0.7%)
Vote 2 Stop The War	716 (0.4%)
ProLife	383 (0.2%)

PC majority 5,423
(1999 PC Majority 30,712)
Additional Members: Prof. N. Bourne, C., G. Davies, C., L. Francis, C., H. Jones, PC

NORTH WALES
E. 474,300 T. 175,028

Lab.	55,250 (31.6%)
PC	41,640 (23.8%)
C.	38,543 (22.0%)
LD	17,503 (10.0%)
John Marek Ind.	11,008 (6.3%)
UKIP	4,500 (2.6%)
Green	4,200 (2.4%)
Ind. Wales	1,552 (0.9%)
Comm.	522 (0.3%)
ProLife	310 (0.2%)

Lab. majority 13,610
(1999 Lab. Majority 4,155)
Additional Members: E. Burnham, LD, M. Isherwood, C., J. Ryder, PC, B. Williams, C.

SOUTH WALES CENTRAL
E. 480,113 T. 181,047

Lab.	74,369 (41.1%)
C.	33,404 (18.5%)
PC	27,956 (15.4%)
LD	24,926 (13.8%)
UKIP	6,920 (3.8%)
Green	6,047 (3.3%)
Soc. Lab.	3,217 (1.8%)
Bean	1,027 (0.6%)
Ind. Wales	1,018 (0.6%)
Vote 2 Stop The War	1,013 (0.6%)
Comm.	577 (0.3%)
ProLife	573 (0.3%)

Lab. majority 40,965
(1999 Lab. Majority 21,484)
Additional Members: D. Melding, C., J. Morgan, C., O. Thomas, PC, L. Wood, PC

SOUTH WALES EAST
E. 469,533 *T.* 169,731

Lab.	76,522 (45.1%)
C.	34,231 (20.2%)
PC	21,384 (12.6%)
LD	17,661 (10.4%)
UKIP	5,949 (3.5%)
Green	5,291 (3.1%)
Soc. Lab.	3,695 (2.2%)
BNP	3,210 (1.9%)
Ind Wales	1,226 (0.7%)
ProLife	562 (0.3%)

Lab. majority 42,291
(1999 Lab. Majority 34,814)
Additional Members: J. Davies, *PC,* M. German, *LD,* W. Graham, *C.,* L. A. Jones, *C.*

SOUTH WALES WEST
E. 395,596 *T.* 23,541

Lab.	58,066 (41.6%)
PC	24,799 (17.8%)
C.	20,981 (15.0%)
LD	17,746 (12.7%)
Green	6,696 (4.8%)
UKIP	6,113 (4.4%)
Soc. Lab.	3,446 (2.5%)
Ind. Wales	1,346 (1.0%)
ProLife	355 (0.3%)

Lab. majority 33,267
(1999 Lab. Majority 19,868)
Additional Members: P. Black, *LD,* A. Cairns, *C.,* J. Davies, *PC,* D. Lloyd, *PC*

SCOTLAND

SCOTTISH PARLIAMENT

Edinburgh EH99 1SP
T 0131-348 5000/0845-278 1999 F 0131-348 5601
Textphone 0845-270 0152
E sp.info@scottish.parliament.uk
W www.scottish.parliament.uk

In July 1997 the government announced plans to establish a Scottish Parliament. In a referendum on 11 September 1997 about 60 per cent of the electorate voted. Of those who voted, 74.3 per cent voted in favour of the Parliament and 63.5 in favour of it having tax-raising powers. Elections are to be held every four years. The first elections were held on 6 May 1999, when about 59 per cent of the electorate voted. The first meeting was held on 12 May 1999 and the Scottish Parliament was officially opened on 1 July 1999 at the Assembly Hall, Edinburgh. A new building to house Parliament was opened, in the presence of The Queen, at Holyrood on 9 September 2004. On 1 May 2003 the second elections to the Scottish Parliament took place.

The Scottish Parliament has 129 members (including the Presiding Officer), comprising 73 constituency members and 56 additional regional members, mainly from party lists. It can introduce primary legislation and has the power to raise or lower the basic rate of income tax by up to three pence in the pound.

The areas for which the Scottish Parliament is responsible include: education, health, law, environment, economic development, local government, housing, police, fire services, planning, financial assistance to industry, tourism, some transport, heritage and the arts, agriculture, forestry and food standards.

SALARIES *as at 1 April 2005*

First Minister	£74,903*
Ministers	£38,857*
Lord Advocate	£50,765*
Solicitor-General for Scotland	£36,707*
Junior Ministers	£24,338*
MSPs	£51,709†
Presiding Officer	£38,857*
Deputy Presiding Officers	£24,338*

*In addition to the MSP salary
†Reduced by two-thirds if the member is already an MP or an MEP

SCOTTISH EXECUTIVE

St Andrew's House, Regent Road, Edinburgh EH1 3DG
T 0845-774 1741 Enquiry Line 0131-556 8400
E ceu@scotland.gov.uk
W www.scotland.gov.uk

The Scottish Executive is the devolved government for Scotland. It is responsible for most of the issues of day-to-day concern to the people of Scotland, including health, education, justice, rural affairs and transport, and manages an annual budget of around £20 billion.

The Executive was established in 1999, following the first elections to the Scottish Parliament. It is a coalition between the Scottish Labour Party and the Scottish Liberal Democrats.

The Executive is led by a First Minister who is nominated by the Parliament and in turn appoints the other Scottish Ministers.

Scottish Executive civil servants are accountable to Scottish Ministers, who are themselves accountable to the Scottish Parliament.

First Minister, The Rt. Hon. Jack McConnell, MSP *(Lab.)*
Deputy First Minister and Minister for Enterprise and Lifelong Learning, Nicol Stephen, MSP *(LD)*
Minister for Communities, Malcolm Chisholm, MSP *(Lab.)*
Minister for Education and Young People, Peter Peacock, MSP *(Lab.)*
Minister for Environment and Rural Development, Ross Finnie, MSP *(LD)*
Minister for Finance and Public Services, Tom McCabe, MSP *(Lab.)*
Minister for Health and Community Care, Andy Kerr, MSP *(Lab.)*
Minister for Justice, Cathy Jamieson, MSP *(Lab.)*
Minister for Parliamentary Business, Margaret Curran, MSP *(Lab.)*
Minister for Tourism, Culture and Sport, Patricia Ferguson, MSP *(Lab.)*
Minister for Transport and Telecommunications, Tavish Scott, MSP *(LD)*
Lord Advocate, The Rt. Hon. Colin Boyd, QC

JUNIOR MINISTERS (NOT MEMBERS OF THE SCOTTISH EXECUTIVE)
Deputy Minister for Communities, Johann Lamont, MSP *(Lab.)*
Deputy Minister for Education and Young People, Euan Robson, MSP *(LD)*
Deputy Minister for Enterprise, and Lifelong Learning, Allan Wilson, MSP *(Lab.)*
Deputy Minister for Environment and Rural Development, Lewis Macdonald, MSP *(Lab.)*
Deputy Minister for Finance and Parliamentary Business, Tavish Scott, MSP *(LD)*
Deputy Minister for Health and Community Care, Rhona Brankin, MSP *(Lab.)*
Deputy Minister for Justice, Hugh Henry, MSP *(Lab.)*
Solicitor-General for Scotland, Elish Angiolini, QC

CHANGE AND CORPORATE SERVICES
Saughton House, Broomhouse Drive, Edinburgh EH11 3XD
T 0845-774 1741
Director of Change and Corporate Services, Sally Carruthers

FINANCE AND CENTRAL SERVICES DEPARTMENT (FCSD)
Victoria Quay, Edinburgh EH6 6QQ
T 0845-774 1741/0131-556 8400
Head of Department, Dr Andrew Goudie

EXECUTIVE AGENCY
Scottish Public Pensions Agency

ENVIRONMENT AND RURAL AFFAIRS DEPARTMENT
Pentland House, 47 Robb's Loan, Edinburgh EH14 1TY
T 0845-774 1741/0131-556 8400 F 0131-244 8240
Head of Department, Richard Wakeford

EXECUTIVE AGENCIES
Animal Health Veterinary Unit
Fisheries Research Services
Scottish Agricultural Science Agency
Scottish Fisheries Protection Agency

DEVELOPMENT DEPARTMENT
Victoria Quay, Edinburgh EH6 6QQ
T 0131-244 0763
Head of Department, Nicola Munro

EXECUTIVE AGENCY
Communities Scotland

EDUCATION DEPARTMENT
Victoria Quay, Edinburgh EH6 6QQ
T 0845-774 1741/0131-556 8400
Head of Department, Mike Ewart

EXECUTIVE AGENCIES
Historic Scotland
HM Inspectorate of Education

ENTERPRISE, TRANSPORT AND LIFELONG
LEARNING DEPARTMENT
Meridian Court, Cadogan Street, Glasgow G2 7AB
T 0131-556 8400 F 0131-244 8240
Head of Department, Eddie Frizzell, CB

EXECUTIVE AGENCY
Student Awards Agency for Scotland

HEALTH DEPARTMENT
St Andrew's House, Edinburgh EH1 3DG
T 0131-244 2440
Chief Executive, Dr Kevin Woods

JUSTICE DEPARTMENT
St Andrew's House, Regent Road, Edinburgh EH1 3DG
T 0131-244 2120 F 0131-244 2121
Head of Department, Robert Gordon, CB

EXECUTIVE AGENCIES
Accountant in Bankruptcy
General Register Office for Scotland
Registers of Scotland
Scottish Court Service
Scottish Prison Service

LEGAL AND PARLIAMENTARY SERVICES
25 Chambers Street, Edinburgh EH1 1LA
T 0845-774 1741 F 0131-225 7473
Head of Department, Robert Gordon, CB

CROWN OFFICE AND PROCURATOR FISCAL
SERVICE
29 Chambers Street, Edinburgh EH1 1LD
T 0131-226 4962
Chief Executive and Crown Agent, Norman McFadyen

OFFICE OF THE PERMANENT SECRETARY
St Andrew's House, Regent Road, Edinburgh EH1 3DG
T 0131-244 4028 F 0131-244 2756
Head of Department, John Elvidge

MEMBERS OF THE SCOTTISH PARLIAMENT
as at May 2005
Adam, Brian, *SNP, Aberdeen North,* Maj. 457
Aitken, Bill, *C., Glasgow region*
Alexander, Wendy, *Lab., Paisley North,* Maj. 4,310
Arbuckle, Andrew, *LD, Mid Scotland and Fife region*
Baillie, Jackie, *Lab., Dumbarton,* Maj. 6,612

Baird, Shiona, *Scot. Green, North East Scotland region*
Baker, Richard, *Lab., North East Scotland region*
Ballance, Chris, *Scot. Green, South of Scotland region*
Ballard, Mark, *Scot. Green, Lothians region*
Barrie, Scott, *Lab., Dunfermline West,* Maj. 4,080
Boyack, Sarah, *Lab., Edinburgh Central,* Maj. 2,666
Brankin, Rhona, *Lab. Co-op, Midlothian,* Maj. 5,542
Brocklebank, Ted, *C., Mid Scotland and Fife region*
Brown, Robert E., *LD, Glasgow region*
Brownlee, Derek, *C., South of Scotland region*
Butler, Bill, *Lab., Glasgow Anniesland,* Maj. 6,253
Byrne, Rosemary, *SSP, South of Scotland region*
Canavan, Dennis, *Ind., Falkirk West,* Maj. 10,000
Chisholm, Malcolm, *Lab., Edinburgh North and Leith,* Maj. 5,414
Craigie, Cathie, *Lab., Cumbernauld and Kilsyth,* Maj. 520
Crawford, Bruce, *SNP, Mid Scotland and Fife region*
Cunningham, Roseanna, *SNP, Perth,* Maj. 727
Curran, Frances, *SSP, West of Scotland region*
Curran, Margaret, *Lab., Glasgow Baillieston,* Maj. 6,178
Davidson, David, *C., North East Scotland region*
Deacon, Susan, *Lab., Edinburgh East and Musselburgh,* Maj. 6,157
Douglas-Hamilton, James, *C., Lothians region*
Eadie, Helen, *Lab. Co-op, Dunfermline East,* Maj. 7,290
Ewing, Fergus, *SNP, Inverness East, Nairn and Lochaber,* Maj. 1,046
Ewing, Margaret, *SNP, Moray,* Maj. 5,312
Fabiani, Linda, *SNP, Central Scotland region*
Ferguson, Patricia, *Lab., Glasgow Maryhill,* Maj. 5,368
Fergusson, Alex, *C., Galloway and Upper Nithsdale,* Maj. 99
Finnie, Ross, *LD, West of Scotland region*
Fox, Colin, *SSP, Lothians region*
Fraser, Murdo, *C., Mid Scotland and Fife region*
Gallie, Phil, *C., South of Scotland region*
Gibson, Rob, *SNP, Highlands and Islands region*
Gillon, Karen, *Lab., Clydesdale,* Maj. 6,671
Glen, Marlyn, *Lab., North East Scotland region*
Godman, Trish, *Lab., Renfrewshire West,* Maj. 2,492
Goldie, Annabel, *C., West of Scotland region*
Gorrie, Donald, *LD, Central Scotland region*
Grahame, Christine, *SNP, South of Scotland region*
Harper, Robin, *Scot. Green, Lothians region*
Harvie, Patrick, *Scot. Green, Glasgow region*
Henry, Hugh, *Lab., Paisley South,* Maj. 2,453
Home Robertson, John, *Lab., East Lothian,* Maj. 8,175
Hughes, Janis, *Lab., Glasgow Rutherglen,* Maj. 6,303
Hyslop, Fiona, *SNP, Lothians region*
Ingram, Adam, *SNP, South of Scotland region*
Jackson, Gordon, *Lab., Glasgow Govan,* Maj. 1,235
Jackson, Dr Sylvia, *Lab., Stirling,* Maj. 2,880
Jamieson, Cathy, *Lab. Co-op, Carrick, Cumnock and Doon Valley,* Maj. 7,454
Jamieson, Margaret, *Lab., Kilmarnock and Loudoun,* Maj. 1,240
Johnstone, Alex, *C., North East Scotland region*
Kane, Rosie, *SSP, Glasgow region*
Kerr, Andy, *Lab., East Kilbride,* Maj. 5,281
Lamont, Johann, *Lab. Co-op, Glasgow Pollok,* Maj. 3,341
Leckie, Carolyn, *SSP, Central Scotland region*
Livingstone, Marilyn, *Lab., Kirkcaldy,* Maj. 4,824
Lochhead, Richard, *SNP, North East Scotland region*
Lyon, George, *LD, Argyll and Bute,* Maj. 4,196
MacAskill, Kenny, *SNP, Lothians region*
Macdonald, Lewis, *Lab., Aberdeen Central,* Maj. 1,242
MacDonald, Margo, *Ind., Lothians region*
Macintosh, Kenneth, *Lab., Eastwood,* Maj. 3,702

Maclean, Kate, *Lab., Dundee West,* Maj. 1,066
Macmillan, Maureen, *Lab., Highlands and Islands region*
Martin, Campbell, *Ind., West of Scotland region*
Martin, Paul, *Lab., Glasgow Springburn,* Maj. 8,007
Marwick, Tricia, *SNP, Mid Scotland and Fife region*
Mather, Jim, *SNP, Highlands and Islands region*
Matheson, Michael, *SNP, Central Scotland region*
Maxwell, Stewart, *SNP, West of Scotland*
May, Christine, *Lab. Co-op, Fife Central,* Maj. 2,762
McAveety, Frank, *Lab., Glasgow Shettleston,* Maj. 6,347
McCabe, Tom, *Lab., Hamilton South,* Maj. 4,824
McConnell, Jack, *Lab., Motherwell and Wishaw,* Maj. 9,259
McFee, Bruce, *SNP, West of Scotland region*
McGrigor, Jamie, *C., Highlands and Islands region*
McLetchie, David, *C., Edinburgh Pentlands,* Maj. 2,111
McMahon, Michael, *Lab., Hamilton North and Bellshill,* Maj. 7,905
McNeil, Duncan, *Lab., Greenock and Inverclyde,* Maj. 3,009
McNeill, Pauline, *Lab., Glasgow Kelvin,* Maj. 3,289
McNulty, Des, *Lab., Clydebank and Milngavie,* Maj. 4,534
Milne, Nanette, *C., North East Scotland region*
Mitchell, Margaret, *C., Central Scotland region*
Monteith, Brian, *C., Mid Scotland and Fife region*
Morgan, Alasdair, *SNP, South of Scotland region*
Morrison, Alasdair, *Lab., Western Isles,* Maj. 720
Muldoon, Bristow, *Lab., Livingston,* Maj. 3,670
Mulligan, Mary, *Lab., Linlithgow,* Maj. 1,970
Munro, John F., *LD, Ross, Skye and Inverness West,* Maj. 6,848
Murray, Dr Elaine, *Lab., Dumfries,* Maj. 1,096
Neil, Alex, *SNP, Central Scotland region*
Oldfather, Irene, *Lab., Cunninghame South,* Maj. 6,076
Peacock, Peter, *Lab., Highlands and Islands region*
Peattie, Cathy, *Lab., Falkirk East,* Maj. 6,659
Pringle, Mike, *LD, Edinburgh South,* Maj. 158
Purvis, Jeremy, *LD, Tweeddale, Ettrick and Lauderdale,* Maj. 538
Radcliffe, Nora, *LD, Gordon,* Maj. 4,071
Reid, George, *SNP, Ochil,* Maj. 296
Robison, Shona, *SNP, Dundee East,* Maj. 90
Robson, Euan, *LD, Roxburgh and Berwickshire,* Maj. 2,490
Rumbles, Mike, *LD, Aberdeenshire West Kincardine,* Maj. 5,399
Ruskell, Mark, *Scot. Green, Mid Scotland and Fife region*
Scanlon, Mary, *C., Highlands and Islands region*
Scott, Eleanor, *Scot. Green, Highlands and Islands region*
Scott, John, *C., Ayr,* Maj. 1,890
Scott, Tavish, *LD, Shetland,* Maj. 2,260
Sheridan, Tommy, *SSP, Glasgow region*
Smith, Elaine, *Lab., Coatbridge and Chryston,* Maj. 8,571
Smith, Iain, *LD, Fife North East,* Maj. 5,055
Smith, Margaret, *LD, Edinburgh West,* Maj. 5,914
Stephen, Nicol, *LD, Aberdeen South,* Maj. 8,016
Stevenson, Stewart, *SNP, Banff and Buchan,* Maj. 8,364
Stone, Jamie, *LD, Caithness, Sutherland and Easter Ross,* Maj. 2,092
Sturgeon, Nicola, *SNP, Glasgow region*
Swinburne, John, *SSCUP, Central Scotland region*
Swinney, John, *SNP, North Tayside,* Maj. 4,503
Tosh, Murray, *C., West of Scotland region*
Turner, Dr Jean, *Ind., Strathkelvin and Bearsden,* Maj. 438
Wallace, Jim, *LD, Orkney,* Maj. 1,755
Watson, Mike (Lord Watson of Invergowrie), *Lab., Glasgow Cathcart,* Maj. 5,112

Welsh, Andrew, *SNP, Angus,* Maj. 6,687
White, Sandra, *SNP, Glasgow region*
Whitefield, Karen, *Lab., Airdrie and Shotts,* Maj. 8,977
Wilson, Allan, *Lab., Cunninghame North,* Maj. 3,390

STATE OF THE PARTIES *as at May 2005*

	Constituency MSPs	Regional MSPs	Total
Scottish Labour Party (Lab.)	46	4	50
Scottish National Party (SNP)	9*	17	26*
Scottish Conservative and Unionist Party (C.)	3	15	18
Scottish Liberal Democrats (LD)	13	4	17
Scottish Green Party (Scot. Green)	0	7	7
Scottish Socialist Party (SSP)	0	6	6
Scottish Senior Citizens' Unity Party (SSCUP)	0	1	1
Independent† (Ind.)	2	2	4
Total	73	56	129

* The Presiding Officer was elected as a constituency member for the SNP but has no party allegiance while in post
† Independents are: Dennis Canavan, Margo MacDonald, Campbell Martin and Dr Jean Turner
The Presiding Officer, George Reid, MSP
Deputy Presiding Officers, Trish Godman, MSP *(Lab.);* Murray Tosh, MSP *(C.)*

SCOTTISH PARLIAMENT CONSTITUENCIES
as at May 2003

ABERDEEN CENTRAL
(Scotland North East Region)
E. 49,477. T. 20,964 (42.37%)

Lewis Macdonald, Lab.	6,835
Richard Lochhead, SNP	5,593
Eleanor Anderson, LD	4,744
Alan Butler, C.	2,616
Andy Cumbers, SSP	1,176

Lab. majority 1,242 (5.92%)
2.13% swing Lab. to SNP

ABERDEEN NORTH
(Scotland North East Region)
E. 52,898. T. 25,027 (47.31%)

Brian Adam, SNP	8,381
Elaine Thomson, Lab.	7,924
John Reynolds, LD	5,767
Jim Gifford, C.	2,311
Katrine Trolle, SSP	644

SNP majority 457 (1.83%)
1.63% swing Lab. to SNP

ABERDEEN SOUTH
(Scotland North East Region)
E. 58,204. T. 30,124 (51.76%)

Nicol Stephen, LD	13,821
Richard Baker, Lab.	5,805
Ian Duncan, C.	5,230
Maureen Watt, SNP	4,315
Keith Farnsworth, SSP	953

LD majority 8,016 (26.61%)
10.77% swing Lab. to LD

ABERDEENSHIRE WEST AND KINCARDINE
(Scotland North East Region)
E. 62,542 T. 31,636 (50.58%)

Mike Rumbles, LD	14,553
David Davidson, C.	9,154
Ian Angus, SNP	4,489
Kevin Hutchens, Lab.	2,727
Alan Manley, SSP	713

LD majority 5,399 (17.07%)
5.33% swing C. to LD

AIRDRIE AND SHOTTS
(Scotland Central Region)
E. 56,680 T. 25,086 (44.26%)

Karen Whitefield, Lab.	14,209
Gil Paterson, SNP	5,232
Alan Melville, C.	2,203
Fraser Coats, SSP	2,096
Kevin Lang, LD	1,346

Lab. majority 8,977 (35.78%)
4.37% swing SNP to Lab.

ANGUS
(Scotland North East Region)
E. 60,608 T. 29,789 (49.15%)

Andrew Welsh, SNP	13,251
Alex Johnstone, C.	6,564
John Denning, Lab.	4,871
Dick Speirs, LD	3,802
Bruce Wallace, SSP	1,301

SNP majority 6,687 (22.45%)
1.66% swing SNP to C.

ARGYLL AND BUTE
(Highlands and Islands Region)
E. 48,330 T. 27,948 (57.83%)

George Lyon, LD	9,817
David Petrie, C.	5,621
Jim Mather, SNP	5,485
Hugh Raven, Lab.	5,107
Des Divers, SSP	1,667
David Walker, SPA	251

LD majority 4,196 (15.01%)
1.68% swing LD to C.

AYR
(Scotland South Region)
E. 55,523 T. 31,591 (56.90%)

John Scott, C.	12,865
Rita Miller, Lab.	10,975
James Dornan, SNP	4,334
Stuart Ritchie, LD	1,769
James Stewart, SSP	1,648

C. majority 1,890 (5.98%)
3.02% swing Lab. to C.

BANFF AND BUCHAN
(Scotland North East Region)
E. 55,358 T. 26,149 (47.24%)

Stewart Stevenson, SNP	13,827
Stewart Whyte, C.	5,463
Ian Brotchie, Lab.	2,885
Debra Storr, LD	2,227
Alan Buchan, SPA	907
Alice Rowan, SSP	840

SNP majority 8,364 (31.99%)
1.80% swing SNP to C.

CAITHNESS, SUTHERLAND AND EASTER ROSS
(Highlands and Islands Region)
E. 40,462 T. 21,127 (52.21%)

Jamie Stone, LD	7,742
Deirdre Steven, Lab.	5,650
Rob Gibson, SNP	3,692
Alan McLeod, C.	2,262
Gordon Campbell, Ind.	953
Frank Ward, SSP	828

LD majority 2,092 (9.90%)
3.48% swing LD to Lab.

CARRICK, CUMNOCK AND DOON VALLEY
(Scotland South Region)
E. 65,102 T. 34,366 (52.79%)

Cathy Jamieson, Lab. Co-op	16,484
Phil Gallie, C.	9,030
Adam Ingram, SNP	5,822
Murray Steele, SSP	1,715
Caron Howden, LD	1,315

Lab. Co-op majority 7,454 (21.69%)
3.20% swing Lab. Co-op to C.

CLYDEBANK AND MILNGAVIE
(Scotland West Region)
E. 51,327 T. 26,514 (51.66%)

Des McNulty, Lab.	10,585
Jim Yuill, SNP	6,051
Rod Ackland, LD	3,224
Mary Leishman, C.	2,885
Dawn Brennan, SSP	1,902
Danny McCafferty, Ind.	1,867

Lab. majority 4,534 (17.10%)
1.49% swing SNP to Lab.

CLYDESDALE
(Scotland South Region)
E. 63,675 T. 32,442 (50.95%)

Karen Gillon, Lab.	14,800
John Brady, SNP	8,129
Alastair Campbell, C.	5,174
Fraser Grieve, LD	2,338
Owen Meharry, SSP	1,422
David Morrison, SPA	579

Lab. majority 6,671 (20.56%)
5.30% swing SNP to Lab.

COATBRIDGE AND CHRYSTON
(Scotland Central Region)
E. 51,521 T. 23,862 (46.32%)

Elaine Smith, Lab.	13,422
James Gribben, SNP	4,851
Donald Reece, C.	2,041
Gordon Martin, SSP	1,911
Doreen Nisbet, LD	1,637

Lab. majority 8,571 (35.92%)
0.73% swing SNP to Lab.

CUMBERNAULD AND KILSYTH
(Scotland Central Region)
E. 48,667 T. 24,404 (50.14%)

Cathie Craigie, Lab.	10,146
Andrew Wilson, SNP	9,626
Kenny McEwan, SSP	1,823
Hugh O'Donnell, LD	1,264
Margaret McCulloch, C.	978
Christopher Donohue, Ind.	567

Lab. majority 520 (2.13%)
5.89% swing Lab. to SNP.

CUNNINGHAME NORTH
(Scotland West Region)
E. 55,319 T. 28,634 (51.76%)

Allan Wilson, Lab.	11,145
Campbell Martin, SNP	7,755
Peter Ramsay, C.	5,542
John Boyd, LD	2,333
Sean Scott, SSP	1,859

Lab. majority 3,390 (11.84%)
1.25% swing Lab. to SNP

CUNNINGHAME SOUTH
(Scotland South Region)
E. 49,877 T. 22,772 (45.66%)

Irene Oldfather, Lab.	11,165
Michael Russell, SNP	5,089
Rosemary Byrne, SSP	2,677
Andrew Brocklehurst, C.	2,336
Iain Dale, LD	1,505

Lab. majority 6,076 (26.68%)
1.78% swing SNP to Lab.

DUMBARTON
(Scotland West Region)
E. 55,575 T. 28,823 (51.86%)

Jackie Baillie, Lab.	12,154
Iain Docherty, SNP	5,542
Eric Thompson, LD	4,455
Murray Tosh, C.	4,178
Les Robertson, SSP	2,494

Lab. majority 6,612 (22.94%)
4.61% swing SNP to Lab.

DUMFRIES
(Scotland South Region)
E. 61,517 T. 32,110 (52.20%)

Elaine Murray, Lab.	12,834
David Mundell, C.	11,738
Andrew Wood, SNP	3,931
Clare Hamblen, LD	2,394
John Dennis, SSP	1,213

Lab. majority 1,096 (3.41%)
3.05% swing Lab. to C.

DUNDEE EAST
(Scotland North East Region)
E. 53,876 T. 26,348 (48.90%)

Shona Robison, SNP	10,428
John McAllion, Lab.	10,338
Edward Prince, C.	3,133
Clive Sneddon, LD	1,584
James Gourlay, Ind.	865

SNP majority 90 (0.34%)
4.68% swing Lab. to SNP

DUNDEE WEST
(Scotland North East Region)
E. 51,387 T. 25,003 (48.66%)

Kate McLean, Lab.	8,234
Irene McGugan, SNP	7,168
Ian Borthwick, Ind.	4,715
Shona Ferrier, LD	1,878
Jim McFarland, SSP	1,501
Victoria Roberts, C.	1,376
Morag MacLachlan, SPA	131

Lab. majority 1,066 (4.26%)
1.92% swing SNP to Lab.

DUNFERMLINE EAST
(Scotland Mid and Fife Region)
E. 51,220 T. 23,154 (45.20%)

Helen Eadie, Lab. Co-op	11,552
Janet Law, SNP	4,262
Stuart Randall, C.	2,485
Brian Stewart, Local Hospital	1,890
Linda Graham, SSP	1,537
Rodger Spillane, LD	1,428

Lab. Co-op majority 7,290 (31.48%)
1.08% swing SNP to Lab. Co-op

DUNFERMLINE WEST
(Scotland Mid and Fife Region)
E. 53,915 T. 25,240 (46.81%)

Scott Barrie, Lab.	8,664
David Wishart, Local Hospital	4,584
Brian Goodall, SNP	4,392
Jim Tolson, LD	3,636
Jim Mackie, C.	1,868
Andy Jackson, SSP	923
Alastair Harper, Ind.	714
Damien Quigg, Ind.	459

Lab. majority 4,080 (16.16%)

EAST KILBRIDE
(Scotland Central Region)
E. 65,472 T. 34,087 (52.06%)

Andy Kerr, Lab.	13,825
Linda Fabiani, SNP	8,544
Grace Campbell, C.	3,785
Carolyn Leckie, SSP	2,736
Colin McCartney, Ind.	2,597
Alex Mackie, LD	2,181
John Houston, Ind.	419

Lab. majority 5,281 (15.49%)
0.08% swing Lab. to SNP

EAST LOTHIAN
(Scotland South Region)
E. 59,227 T. 31,204 (52.69%)

John Home Robertson, Lab.	13,683
Judy Hayman, LD	5,508
Stewart Thomson, C.	5,459
Tom Roberts, SNP	5,174
Hugh Kerr, SSP	1,380

Lab. majority 8,175 (26.20%)
6.95% swing Lab. to LD

EASTWOOD
(Scotland West Region)
E. 67,051 T. 38,889 (58.00%)

Ken Macintosh, Lab.	13,946
Jackson Carlaw, C.	10,244
Allan Steele, LD	5,056
Stewart Maxwell, SNP	4,736
Margaret Hinds, Local Health	3,163
Steve Oram, SSP	1,504
Martyn Greene, SPA	240

Lab. majority 3,702 (9.52%)
2.42% swing C. to Lab.

EDINBURGH CENTRAL
(Lothians Region)
E. 60,824 *T.* 28,014 (46.06%)
Sarah Boyack, Lab.	9,066
Andy Myles, LD	6,400
Kevin Pringle, SNP	4,965
Peter Finnie, C.	4,802
Catriona Grant, SSP	2,552
James O'Neill, SPA	229

Lab. majority 2,666 (9.52%)
5.98% swing Lab. to LD

EDINBURGH EAST AND MUSSELBURGH
(Lothians Region)
E. 57,704 *T.* 29,043 (50.33%)
Susan Deacon, Lab.	12,654
Kenny MacAskill, SNP	6,497
John Smart, C.	3,863
Gary Peacock, LD	3,582
Derek Durkin, SSP	2,447

Lab. majority 6,157 (21.20%)
1.53% swing SNP to Lab.

EDINBURGH NORTH AND LEITH
(Lothians Region)
E. 60,501 *T.* 28,734 (47.49%)
Malcolm Chisholm, Lab.	10,979
Anne Dana, SNP	5,565
Ian Mowat, C.	4,821
Sebastian Tombs, LD	4,785
Bill Scott, SSP	2,584

Lab. majority 5,414 (18.84%)
1.13% swing Lab. to SNP

EDINBURGH PENTLANDS
(Lothians Region)
E. 58,534 *T.* 33,382 (57.03%)
David McLetchie, C.	12,420
Iain Gray, Lab.	10,309
Ian McKee, SNP	5,620
Simon Clark, LD	3,943
Frank O'Donnell, SSP	1,090

C. majority 2,111 (6.32%)
6.80% swing Lab. to C.

EDINBURGH SOUTH
(Lothians Region)
E. 60,366 *T.* 31,196 (51.68%)
Mike Pringle, LD	10,005
Angus Mackay, Lab.	9,847
Gordon Buchan, C.	5,180
Alex Orr, SNP	4,396
Shirley Gibb, SSP	1,768

LD majority 158 (0.51%)
7.61% swing Lab. to LD

EDINBURGH WEST
(Lothians Region)
E. 60,136 *T.* 33,301 (55.38%)
Margaret Smith, LD	14,434
James Douglas-Hamilton, C.	8,520
Carol Fox, Lab.	5,046
Alyn Smith, SNP	4,133
Pat Smith, SSP	993
Bruce Skivington, SPA	175

LD majority 5,914 (17.76%)
3.37% swing C. to LD

FALKIRK EAST
(Scotland Central Region)
E. 56,175 *T.* 27,559 (49.06%)
Cathy Peattie, Lab.	14,235
Keith Brown, SNP	7,576
Thomas Calvert, C.	2,720
Karen Utting, LD	1,651
Mhairi McAlpine, SSP	1,377

Lab. majority 6,659 (24.16%)
6.20% swing SNP to Lab.

FALKIRK WEST
(Scotland Central Region)
E. 52,122 *T.* 26,400 (50.65%)
Dennis Canavan, Ind.	14,703
Michael Matheson, SNP	4,703
Lee Whitehill, Lab.	4,589
Iain Mitchell, C.	1,657
Jacqueline Kelly, LD	748

Ind. majority 10,000 (37.88%)
0.34% swing SNP to Ind.

FIFE CENTRAL
(Scotland Mid and Fife Region)
E. 57,633 *T.* 25,597 (44.41%)
Christine May, Lab. Co-op	10,591
Tricia Marwick, SNP	7,829
Andrew Rodger, Ind.	2,258
James North, C.	1,803
Elizabeth Riches, LD	1,725
Morag Balfour, SSP	1,391

Lab. Co-op majority 2,762 (10.79%)
7.81% swing Lab. Co-op to SNP

FIFE NORTH EAST
(Scotland Mid and Fife Region)
E. 58,695 *T.* 29,282 (49.89%)
Iain Smith, LD	13,479
Ted Brocklebank, C.	8,424
Capre Ross-Williams, SNP	3,660
Gregor Poynton, Lab.	2,353
Carlo Morelli, SSP	1,366

LD majority 5,055 (17.26%)
1.59% swing C. to LD

GALLOWAY AND UPPER NITHSDALE
(Scotland South Region)
E. 51,651 *T.* 29,635 (57.38%)
Alex Fergusson, C.	11,332
Alasdair Morgan, SNP	11,233
Norma Hart, Lab.	4,299
Neil Wallace, LD	1,847
Joy Cherkaoui, SSP	709
Graham Brockhouse, SPA	215

C. majority 99 (0.33%)
4.70% swing SNP to C.

GLASGOW ANNIESLAND
(Glasgow Region)
E. 50,795 *T.* 22,165 (43.64%)
Bill Butler, Lab. Co-op	10,141
Bill Kidd, SNP	3,888
Bill Aitken, C.	3,186
Charlie McCarthy, SSP	2,620
Iain Brown, LD	2,330

Lab. Co-op majority 6,253 (28.21%)
5.19% swing Lab. Co-op to SNP

GLASGOW BAILLIESTON
(Glasgow Region)
E. 46,346 T. 18,270 (39.42%)

Margaret Curran, Lab.	9,657
Lachlan McNeill, SNP	3,479
Jim McVicar, SSP	2,461
Janette McAlpine, C.	1,472
David Jackson, LD	1,201

Lab. majority 6,178 (33.81%)
10.43% swing SNP to Lab.

GLASGOW CATHCART
(Glasgow Region)
E. 49,017 T. 22,307 (45.51%)

Mike Watson, Lab.	8,742
David Ritchie, SNP	3,630
Richard Cook, C.	2,888
Malcolm Wilson, SSP	2,819
Pat Lally, Local Health	2,419
Tom Henery, LD	1,741
Robert Wilson, Parent Ex	68

Lab. majority 5,112 (22.92%)
1.50% swing SNP to Lab.

GLASGOW GOVAN
(Glasgow Region)
E. 48,635 T. 21,136 (43.46%)

Gordon Jackson, Lab.	7,834
Nicola Sturgeon, SNP	6,599
Jimmy Scott, SSP	2,369
Faisal Butt, C.	1,878
Paul Graham, LD	1,807
Razaq Dean, Ind.	226
John Foster, CPPDS	215
Asif Nasir, SPA	208

Lab. majority 1,235 (5.84%)
0.41% swing Lab. to SNP

GLASGOW KELVIN
(Glasgow Region)
E. 56,038 T. 22,080 (39.40%)

Pauline McNeill, Lab.	7,880
Sandra White, SNP	4,591
Douglas Herbison, LD	3,334
Andy Harvey, SSP	3,159
Gawain Towler, C.	1,816
Alistair McConnachie, Ind.	1,300

Lab. majority 3,289 (14.90%)
0.32% swing Lab. to SNP

GLASGOW MARYHILL
(Glasgow Region)
E. 49,119 T. 18,243 (37.14%)

Patricia Ferguson, Lab.	8,997
Bill Wilson, SNP	3,629
Donnie Nicolson, SSP	2,945
Arthur Sanderson, LD	1,785
Robert Erskine, C.	887

Lab. majority 5,368 (29.42%)
5.31% swing SNP to Lab.

GLASGOW POLLOK
(Glasgow Region)
E. 47,134 T. 21,538 (45.70%)

Johann Lamont, Lab. Co-op	9,357
Tommy Sheridan, SSP	6,016
Kenneth Gibson, SNP	4,118
Ashraf Anjum, C.	1,012
Isabel Nelson, LD	962
Robert Ray, Parent Ex	73

Lab. Co-op majority 3,341 (15.51%)
3.35% swing Lab. Co-op to SSP

GLASGOW RUTHERGLEN
(Glasgow Region)
E. 49,512 T. 23,554 (47.57%)

Janis Hughes, Lab.	10,794
Robert Brown, LD	4,491
Anne McLaughlin, SNP	3,511
Gavin Brown, C.	2,499
Bill Bonnar, SSP	2,259

Lab. majority 6,303 (26.76%)
0.21% swing LD to Lab.

GLASGOW SHETTLESTON
(Glasgow Region)
E. 46,730 T. 16,547 (35.41%)

Francis McAveety, Lab. Co-op	9,365
Jim Byrne, SNP	3,018
Rosie Kane, SSP	2,403
Dorothy Luckhurst, C.	982
Lewis Hutton, LD	779

Lab. Co-op majority 6,347 (38.36%)
5.87% swing SNP to Lab. Co-op

GLASGOW SPRINGBURN
(Glasgow Region)
E. 49,551 T. 18,573 (37.48%)

Paul Martin, Lab.	10,963
Frank Rankin, SNP	2,956
Margaret Bean, SSP	2,653
Alan Rodger, C.	1,233
Charles Dundas, LD	768

Lab. majority 8,007 (43.11%)
5.36% swing SNP to Lab.

GORDON
(Scotland North East Region)
E. 60,686 T. 28,798 (47.45%)

Nora Radcliffe, LD	10,963
Nanette Milne, C.	6,892
Alasdair Allan, SNP	6,501
Ellis Thorpe, Lab.	2,973
John Sangster, SSP	780
Steven Mathers, Ind.	689

LD majority 4,071 (14.14%)
1.48% swing LD to C.

GREENOCK AND INVERCLYDE
(Scotland West Region)
E. 46,045 T. 23,781 (51.65%)

Duncan McNeil, Lab.	9,674
Ross Finnie, LD	6,665
Tom Chalmers, SNP	3,532
Tricia McCafferty, SSP	2,338
Charles Dunlop, C.	1,572

Lab. majority 3,009 (12.65%)
1.20% swing Lab. to LD

HAMILTON NORTH AND BELLSHILL
(Scotland Central Region)
E. 51,965 *T.* 24,195 (46.56%)

Michael McMahon, Lab.	12,812
Alex Neil, SNP	4,907
Charles Ferguson, C.	2,625
Shareen Blackhall, SSP	1,932
Siobhan Mathers, LD	1,477
Gordon McIntosh, SPA	442

Lab. majority 7,905 (32.67%)
7.36% swing SNP to Lab.

HAMILTON SOUTH
(Scotland Central Region)
E. 45,749 *T.* 20,518 (44.85%)

Tom McCabe, Lab.	9,546
John Wilson, SNP	4,722
Margaret Mitchell, C.	2,601
Willie O'Neil, SSP	1,893
John Oswald, LD	1,756

Lab. majority 4,824 (23.51%)
2.09% swing Lab. to SNP

INVERNESS EAST, NAIRN AND LOCHABER
(Highlands and Islands Region)
E. 66,694 *T.* 34,795 (52.17%)

Fergus Ewing, SNP	10,764
Rhoda Grant, Lab.	9,718
Mary Scanlon, C.	6,205
Patsy Kenton, LD	5,622
Steve Arnott, SSP	1,661
Thomas Lamont, Ind.	825

SNP majority 1,046 (3.01%)
0.98% swing Lab. to SNP

KILMARNOCK AND LOUDOUN
(Scotland Central Region)
E. 61,055 *T.* 31,520 (51.63%)

Margaret Jamieson, Lab.	12,633
Danny Coffey, SNP	11,423
Robin Traquair, C.	3,295
Ian Gibson, LD	1,571
Colin Rutherford, SSP	1,421
May Anderson, Ind.	404
Matthew Donnelly, Ind.	402
Lyndsay McIntosh, SPA	371

Lab. majority 1,240 (3.93%)
1.59% swing Lab. to SNP

KIRKCALDY
(Scotland Mid and Fife Region)
E. 49,653 *T.* 21,939 (44.18%)

Marilyn Livingstone, Lab. Co-op	10,235
Colin Welsh, SNP	5,411
Alex Cole-Hamilton, LD	2,417
Mike Scott-Hayward, C.	2,332
Rudi Vogels, SSP	1,544

Lab. Co-op majority 4,824 (21.99%)
1.10% swing SNP to Lab. Co-op

LINLITHGOW
(Lothians Region)
E. 54,113 *T.* 27,645 (51.09%)

Mary Mulligan, Lab.	11,548
Fiona Hyslop, SNP	9,578
Gordon Lindhurst, C.	3,059
Martin Oliver, LD	2,093
Steve Nimmo, SSP	1,367

Lab. majority 1,970 (7.13%)
0.77% swing Lab. to SNP

LIVINGSTON
(Lothians Region)
E. 65,421 *T.* 30,557 (46.71%)

Bristow Muldoon, Lab.	13,327
Peter Johnston, SNP	9,657
Lindsay Paterson, C.	2,848
Paul McGreal, LD	2,714
Robert Richard, SSP	1,640
Stephen Milburn, SPA	371

Lab. majority 3,670 (12.01%)
0.67% swing SNP to Lab.

MIDLOTHIAN
(Lothians Region)
E. 48,319 *T.* 23,556 (48.75%)

Rhona Brankin, Lab. Co-op	11,139
Graham Sutherland, SNP	5,597
Jacqui Bell, LD	2,700
Rosemary MacArthur, C.	2,557
Bob Goupillot, SSP	1,563

Lab. Co-op majority 5,542 (23.53%)
2.48% swing SNP to Lab. Co-op

MORAY
(Highlands and Islands Region)
E. 58,242 *T.* 26,981 (46.33%)

Margaret Ewing, SNP	11,384
Tim Wood, C.	6,072
Peter Peacock, Lab.	5,157
Linda Gorn, LD	3,283
Norma Anderson, SSP	1,085

SNP majority 5,312 (19.69%)
3.24% swing C. to SNP

MOTHERWELL AND WISHAW
(Scotland Central Region)
E. 51,785 *T.* 25,388 (49.03%)

Jack McConnell, Lab.	13,739
Lloyd Quinan, SNP	4,480
Mark Nolan, C.	2,542
John Milligan, SSP	1,961
John Swinburne, SSCUP	1,597
Keith Legg, LD	1,069

Lab. majority 9,259 (36.47%)
9.92% swing SNP to Lab.

OCHIL
(Scotland Mid and Fife Region)
E. 55,596 *T.* 30,416 (54.71%)

George Reid, SNP	11,659
Richard Simpson, Lab.	11,363
Malcolm Parkin, C.	2,946
Catherine Whittingham, LD	2,536
Felicity Garvie, SSP	1,102
Flash Gordon Approaching, Loony	432
William Whyte, Ind.	378

SNP majority 296 (0.97%)
2.25% swing Lab. to SNP

ORKNEY
(Highlands and Islands Region)
E. 15,487 T. 8,004 (51.68%)
Jim Wallace, LD	3,659
Christopher Zawadski, C.	1,904
John Mowat, SNP	1,056
John Aberdein, SSP	914
Richard Meade, Lab.	471

LD majority 1,755 (21.93%)
14.93% swing LD to C.

PAISLEY NORTH
(Scotland West Region)
E. 44,999 T. 22,206 (49.35%)
Wendy Alexander, Lab.	10,631
George Adam, SNP	6,321
Allison Cook, C.	1,871
Brian O'Malley, LD	1,705
Sean Hurl, SSP	1,678

Lab. majority 4,310 (19.41%)
1.39% swing SNP to Lab.

PAISLEY SOUTH
(Scotland West Region)
E. 49,818 T. 24,984 (50.15%)
Hugh Henry, Lab.	10,190
Bill Martin, SNP	7,737
Eileen McCartin, LD	3,517
Mark Jones, C.	1,775
Frances Curran, SSP	1,765

Lab. majority 2,453 (9.82%)
2.42% swing Lab. to SNP

PERTH
(Scotland and Mid Fife Region)
E. 61,957 T. 31,614 (51.03%)
Roseanna Cunningham, SNP	10,717
Alexander Stewart, C.	9,990
Robert Ball, Lab.	5,629
Gordon Campbell, LD	3,530
Philip Stott, SSP	982
Thomas Burns, Ind.	509
Ken Buchanan, SPA	257

SNP majority 727 (2.30%)
1.56% swing SNP to C.

RENFREWSHIRE WEST
(Scotland West Region)
E. 50,963 T. 28,302 (55.53%)
Trish Godman, Lab.	9,671
Bruce McFee, SNP	7,179
Annabel Goldie, C.	6,867
Alison King, LD	2,902
Gerry MaCartney, SSP	1,683

Lab. majority 2,492 (8.81%)
0.15% swing SNP to Lab.

ROSS, SKYE AND INVERNESS WEST
(Highlands and Islands Region)
E. 55,777 T. 28,971 (51.94%)
John Farquhar Munro, LD	12,495
David Thompson, SNP	5,647
Maureen MacMillan, Lab.	5,464
Jamie McGrigor, C.	3,772
Anne McLeod, SSP	1,593

LD majority 6,848 (23.64%)
6.66% swing SNP to LD

ROXBURGH AND BERWICKSHIRE
(Scotland South Region)
E. 45,625 T. 22,511 (49.34%)
Euan Robson, LD	9,280
Sandy Scott, C.	6,790
Roderick Campbell, SNP	2,816
Sam Held, Lab.	2,802
Graeme McIver, SSP	823

LD majority 2,490 (11.06%)
0.90% swing LD to C.

SHETLAND
(Highlands and Islands Region)
E. 16,677 T. 8,645 (51.84%)
Tavish Scott, LD	3,989
Willie Ross, SNP	1,729
John Firth, C.	1,281
Peter Hamilton, Lab.	880
Peter Andrews, SSP	766

LD majority 2,260 (26.14%)
7.00% swing LD to SNP

STIRLING
(Scotland and Mid Fife Region)
E. 52,087 T. 29,647 (56.92%)
Sylvia Jackson, Lab.	10,661
Brian Monteith, C.	7,781
Bruce Crawford, SNP	5,645
Kenyon Wright, LD	3,432
Margaret Stewart, SSP	1,486
Keith Harding, SPA	642

Lab. majority 2,880 (9.71%)
1.25% swing Lab. to C.

STRATHKELVIN AND BEARSDEN
(Scotland West Region)
E. 61,905 T. 35,736 (57.73%)
Jean Turner, Ind.	10,983
Brian Fitzpatrick, Lab.	10,556
Jo Swinson, LD	4,956
Fiona McLeod, SNP	4,846
Rory O'Brien, C.	4,005

Ind. majority 438 (1.23%)

TAYSIDE NORTH
(Scotland Mid and Fife Region)
E. 62,697 T. 33,343 (53.18%)
John Swinney, SNP	14,960
Murdo Fraser, C.	10,463
Gordon MacRae, Lab.	3,521
Bob Forrest, LD	3,200
Rosie Adams, SSP	942
George Ashe, SPA	231

SNP majority 4,503 (13.51%)
1.24% swing C. to SNP

TWEEDDALE, ETTRICK AND LAUDERDALE
(Scotland South Region)
E. 50,912 T. 26,700 (52.44%)
Jeremy Purvis, LD	7,191
Christine Grahame, SNP	6,653
Catherine Maxwell Stuart, Lab.	5,757
Derek Brownlee, C.	5,687
Norman Lockhart, SSP	1,053
Alex Black, SPA	349

LD majority 538 (2.01%)
5.63% swing LD to SNP

WESTERN ISLES
(Highlands and Islands Region)
E. 21,205 *T.* 12,387 (58.42%)

Alasdair Morrison, Lab.	5,825	
Alasdair Nicholson, SNP	5,105	
Frank Warren, C.	612	
Conor Snowden, LD	498	
Joanne Telfer, SSP	347	

Lab. majority 720 (5.81%)
4.59% swing Lab. to SNP

REGIONS

GLASGOW
E. 492,877 *T.* 39.42%

Lab.	77,040	(39.65%)
SNP	34,894	(17.96%)
SSP	31,116	(16.02%)
C.	15,299	(7.87%)
LD	14,839	(7.64%)
Scot. Green	14,570	(7.50%)
SSCUP	4,750	(2.44%)
Soc. Lab.	3,091	(1.59%)
ProLife	2,477	(1.27%)
SUP	2,349	(1.21%)
BNP	2,344	(1.21%)
SPA	612	(0.32%)
UKIP	552	(0.28%)
CPPDS	345	(0.18%)
Lab. majority	42,146	(21.69%)

.64% swing *SNP* to *Lab.*

ADDITIONAL MEMBERS

Bill Aitken	*C.*
Robert Brown	*LD*
Sandra White	*SNP*
Nicola Sturgeon	*SNP*
Patrick Harvie	*Scot. Green*
Tommy Sheridan	*SSP*
Rosie Kane	*SSP*

HIGHLANDS AND ISLANDS
E. 322,874 *T.* 52.22%

SNP	39,497	(23.43%)
Lab.	37,605	(22.30%)
LD	31,655	(18.78%)
C.	26,989	(16.01%)
Scot. Green	13,935	(8.27%)
SSP	9,000	(5.34%)
UKIP	1,947	(1.15%)
ASSDR	1,822	(1.08%)
PFRI	1,768	(1.05%)
Soc. Lab.	1,617	(0.96%)
RSP	1,438	(0.85%)
SPA	793	(0.47%)
Ind.	353	(0.21%)
Rural	177	(0.10%)
SNP majority	1,892	(1.12%)

.57% swing *SNP* to *Lab.*

ADDITIONAL MEMBERS

Jamie McGrigor	*C.*
Mary Scanlon	*C.*
Peter Peacock	*Lab.*
Maureen MacMillan	*Lab.*
Jim Mather	*SNP*
Rob Gibson	*SNP*
Eleanor Scott	*Scot. Green*

LOTHIANS
E. 525,918 *T.* 50.52%

Lab.	65,102	(24.50%)
SNP	43,142	(16.24%)
C.	40,173	(15.12%)
Scot. Green	31,908	(12.01%)
LD	29,237	(11.01%)
Ind.	27,144	(10.22%)
SSP	14,448	(5.44%)
PP	5,609	(2.11%)
Lib	2,573	(0.97%)
Soc. Lab.	2,181	(0.82%)
UKIP	1,057	(0.40%)
Witchery	964	(0.36%)
SPA	879	(0.33%)
ProLife	608	(0.23%)
Ind. C.	383	(0.14%)
Ind. A.	184	(0.07%)
Ind. Gatensbury	78	(0.03%)
Lab. majority	21,960	(8.27%)

1.89% swing *SNP* to *Lab.*

ADDITIONAL MEMBERS

Lord James Douglas-Hamilton	*C.*
Kenny MacAskill	*SNP*
Fiona Hyslop	*SNP*
Robin Harper	*Scot. Green*
Mark Ballard	*Scot. Green*
Margo MacDonald	*Ind.*
Colin Fox	*SSP*

SCOTLAND CENTRAL
E. 541,191 *T.* 48.61%

Lab.	106,318	(40.41%)
SNP	59,274	(22.53%)
C.	24,121	(9.17%)
SSP	19,016	(7.23%)
SSCUP	17,146	(6.52%)
LD	15,494	(5.89%)
Scot. Green	12,248	(4.66%)
Soc. Lab.	3,855	(1.47%)
SUP	2,147	(0.82%)
Ind.	1,265	(0.48%)
SPA	1,192	(0.45%)
UKIP	1,009	(0.38%)
Lab. majority	47,044	(17.88%)

3.19% swing *SNP* to *Lab.*

ADDITIONAL MEMBERS

Margaret Mitchell	*C.*
Donald Gorrie	*LD*
Alex Neil	*SNP*
Michael Matheson	*SNP*
Linda Fabiani	*SNP*
John Swinburne	*SSCUP*
Carolyn Leckie	*SSP*

SCOTLAND MID AND FIFE
E. 503,453 *T.* 49.68%

Lab.	63,239	(25.29%)
SNP	57,631	(23.04%)
C.	43,941	(17.57%)
LD	30,112	(12.04%)
Scot. Green	17,147	(6.86%)
SSP	11,401	(4.56%)
PP	8,380	(3.35%)
FHC	5,064	(2.02%)
SLH	4,662	(1.86%)
UKIP	2,355	(0.94%)
Soc. Lab.	2,273	(0.91%)
SPA	1,191	(0.48%)
Christian	1,064	(0.43%)
Ind. Gray	996	(0.40%)
Ind.	637	(0.25%)
Lab. majority	5,608	(2.24%)

1.22% swing *Lab.* to *SNP*

ADDITIONAL MEMBERS

Murdo Fraser	*C.*
Brian Monteith	*C.*
Ted Brocklebank	*C.*
Keith Raffan	*LD*
Bruce Crawford	*SNP*
Tricia Marwick	*SNP*
Mark Ruskell	*Scot. Green*

SCOTLAND NORTH EAST
E. 505,036 *T.* 48.25%

SNP	66,463	(27.28%)
Lab.	49,189	(20.19%)
LD	45,831	(18.81%)
C.	42,318	(17.37%)
Scot. Green	12,724	(5.22%)
SSP	10,226	(4.20%)
PP	5,584	(2.29%)
Fishing	5,566	(2.28%)
Soc. Lab.	2,431	(1.00%)
UKIP	1,498	(0.61%)
SPA	941	(0.39%)
Ind.	902	(0.37%)
SNP majority	17,274	(7.09%)

0.10% swing *Lab.* to *SNP*

ADDITIONAL MEMBERS

David Davidson	*C.*
Alex Johnstone	*C.*
Nanette Milne	*C.*
Marlyn Glen	*Lab.*
Richard Baker	*Lab.*
Richard Lochhead	*SNP*
Shiona Baird	*Scot. Green*

SCOTLAND SOUTH
E. 503,109 *T.* 52.33%

Lab.	78,955	(29.99%
C.	63,827	(24.24%
SNP	48,371	(18.37%
LD	27,026	(10.26%
Scot. Green	15,062	(5.72%
SSP	14,228	(5.40%
PP	9,082	(3.45%
Soc. Lab.	3,054	(1.16%
UKIP	1,889	(0.72%
SPA	1,436	(0.55%
Rural	355	(0.13%
Lab. majority	15,128	(5.75%

1.83% swing *Lab.* to *C.*

ADDITIONAL MEMBERS

Phil Gallie	*C.*
David Mundell	*C.*
Christine Grahame	*SNP*
Alasdair Morgan	*SNP*
Adam Ingram	*SNP*
Chris Ballance	*Scot. Green*
Rosemary Byrne	*SSP*

SCOTLAND WEST
E. 483,002 *T.* 61.53%

Lab.	83,931	(28.24%
LD	71,580	(24.09%
SNP	50,387	(16.96%
C.	40,261	(13.55%
SSP	18,591	(6.26%
Scot. Green	14,544	(4.89%
SSCUP	7,100	(2.39%
ProLife	3,674	(1.24%
Soc. Lab.	3,155	(1.06%
UKIP	1,662	(0.56%
SUP	1,617	(0.54%
SPA	674	(0.23%
Lab. majority	12,351	(4.16%

11.70% swing *Lab.* to *LD*

ADDITIONAL MEMBERS

Annabel Goldie	*C.*
Murray Tosh	*C.*
Ross Finnie	*LD*
Campbell Martin	*SNP*
Bruce McFee	*SNP*
Stewart Maxwell	*SNP*
Frances Curran	*SSP*

NORTHERN IRELAND

NORTHERN IRELAND ASSEMBLY

Parliament Buildings, Stormont, Belfast BT4 3XX
T 028-9052 1333 F 028-9052 1961
W www.ni-assembly.gov.uk

The Assembly was suspended from midnight on 14 October 2002 and was dissolved on 28 April 2003. On 26 November 2003 elections to the Assembly were held but the Assembly remains suspended at the time of going to press (August 2005). The Secretary of State assumed responsibility for the direction of the Northern Ireland departments. The following is an overview of the organisation and structure of the Assembly, which applied when it was operational. Talks to discuss the future of the Assembly are ongoing.

The Assembly has 108 members elected by the single transferable vote system (six from each of the 18 Westminster constituencies). The first elections took place on 25 June 1998 and members met for the first time on 1 July. The executive powers of the Assembly are discharged by an Executive Committee comprising a First Minister and Deputy First Minister (jointly elected by the Assembly on a cross-community basis) and up to ten ministers with departmental responsibilities. Ministerial posts are allocated on the basis of the number of seats each party holds. Ministers receive 70 per cent of full pay during suspension of the Assembly.

The Assembly met in shadow form pending the establishment of an Executive and the transfer of powers from Parliament. Following devolution it has executive and legislative authority over those areas formerly the responsibility of the government's Northern Ireland departments.

Power was initially due to be transferred to the new executive on 10 March 1999, but disagreements emerged over whether Sinn Fein should be allowed to enter the executive before Irish Republican Army (IRA) weapons had been decommissioned. Further deadlines were also missed and on 15 July the Assembly met to nominate ministers, with the transfer of power to follow on 18 July. However, as the decommissioning issue had still not been resolved, Unionists failed to nominate ministers (the Ulster Unionist Party (UUP) boycotting the meeting itself) and the process collapsed. On 20 July the two prime ministers announced a review of the implementation of the Good Friday Agreement to be facilitated by US Senator George Mitchell. The timing of the review dovetailed with the inevitably sensitive publication of the Patten Commission's report on policing.

On 18 November 1999, following statements from the UUP, Sinn Fein and the IRA, Senator Mitchell indicated in his review that he now believed there was a basis for devolution to occur, for the institutions to be established and for decommissioning to take place as soon as possible. On 20 November the Secretary of State announced support for the Mitchell proposals and stated that the assembly should meet on 29 November for the purpose of running the d'Hondt procedure for appointing shadow ministers, and devolution should take effect after the necessary parliamentary procedures had been completed on 2 December 1999.

Powers were devolved to the Assembly and other institutions established on 2 December 1999 on a basis agreed by the parties during the Mitchell review. The review created the expectation that the establishment of the institutions and the appointment of authorised representatives produced conditions in which Sinn Fein could influence bringing about the start of decommissioning. But it was a matter of political reality that if decommissioning did not occur by the end of January it would be very difficult for David Trimble to continue as leader of the Ulster Unionist Party. In late November the Council of the UUP endorsed the Mitchell outcome but also recommended that progress on the timing and modalities of decommissioning be reviewed at the end of January 2000.

Sufficient cross-community support enabled devolution and the institutions to flourish, but that support began to ebb when the anticipated progress on decommissioning failed to materialise at the end of January. The two governments took receipt of General de Chastelain's 31 January report but held back publication in order to explore any hope of credible progress on decommissioning. Both governments tried further efforts to gain clarity on the decommissioning issue. No deal was struck and on 11 February the Secretary of State signed the order to suspend the Assembly. Parliament buildings remained open for use by Assembly Members for the purpose of carrying out constituency work and they continued to be paid salaries and allowances – set at the lower pre-devolution shadow rate to reflect the suspension of Assembly business.

Following a period of intensive discussions with pro-Agreement parties during 4 and 5 May 2000 at Hillsborough, the prime minister and Taoiseach issued a joint statement committing both government's proposals. On 6 May the IRA responded with a significant and forthcoming statement that revealed an intention to pursue their political objectives peacefully – contact with the Decommissioning Commission would be renewed, and a process would be initiated to put arms verifiably beyond use. The pro-Agreement parties welcomed these developments. The Prime Minister and the Taoiseach announced on 8 May that they would ask the former Finnish president Martti Ahtisaari and Cyril Ramaphosa, the African National Congress (ANC) negotiator, to become the independent inspectors. On 9 May, the Chief Constable of the Royal Ulster Constabulary (RUC) recognised that the IRA statement marked a significant reduction in the overall threat and announced a number of measures, spread across Northern Ireland, designed as a return to more normal policing. Devolved power was restored at midnight on 29 May 2000.

Following the resignation of First Minister David Trimble on 1 July 2001 in protest against lack of progress in the decommissioning issue, the situation turned critical and the British and Irish governments issued a package of proposals in an attempt to break the political deadlock. With no sign of the IRA decommissioning its weapons, Northern Ireland Secretary John Reid suspended the devolved institutions for 24 hours on 11 July and 21 September, insisting it would be the last time he carried out the technical order. Following a police raid of Sinn Fein's offices at Stormont, investigating alleged intelligence gathering, Unionists walked out of the Executive and the Assembly was suspended again. The election of 2003 saw an increase of seats held by both the DUP and Sinn Fein, but failed to bring about the desired restoration of the Assembly.

On 28 July 2005 the leadership of the IRA formally ordered an end to its armed campaign. A statement released by the group read: 'All IRA units have been ordered to dump arms. All volunteers have been instructed to assist the development of purely political and democratic programmes through exclusively peaceful means. Volunteers must not engage in any other activities whatsoever.' The IRA leadership authorised a representative to engage with the Independent International Commission on Decommissioning, in order to verifiably put the arms beyond use and therefore to further enhance public confidence in the peace process.

The Independent Monitoring Commission (a body established in 2004 consisting of nominees of the British, Irish and US governments) will play a major role in the decommissioning process. In October 2005 it was expected to provide an interim assessment of the first few weeks following the IRA statement. A further, more expansive, report was due to be delivered to the government in January 2006.

During late 2005 the government was due to introduce legislation to allow the return of paramilitary fugitives to Northern Ireland, while at the same time reducing security levels in the province – watchtowers and bases will be demolished, and troop numbers are due to fall from 10,500 to 5,000 by 1 August 2007. The restoration of the Assembly, however – either in real or shadow form – will require further negotiations involving the main political parties.

SALARIES *as at December 2003**
Assembly Member   £31,817
*In 2005 the salaries remained frozen at the 2003 level until the Assembly is reinstated.

NORTHERN IRELAND EXECUTIVE
Castle Buildings, Stormont, Belfast BT4 3SG
T 028-9052 0700 F 028-9052 8195
W www.northernireland.gov.uk

During suspension the following departments fall under the control of the Secretary of State for Northern Ireland and his Northern Ireland Office ministerial team.
Secretary of State for Northern Ireland, The Rt. Hon. Peter Hain, MP
Minister of State, The Rt. Hon. Lord Rooker
    (Security and Policing, Finance and Personnel, Environment, Agriculture and Rural Development and Office of the First Minister and Deputy First Minister)
Minister of State, David Hanson, MP *(Social Development, Political Development, Criminal Justice and Culture, Arts and Leisure)*
Parliamentary Under-Secretary, Angela Smith, MP *(Employment and Learning, Education, Enterprise, Trade and Investment)*
Parliamentary Under-Secretary, Shaun Woodward, MP *(Health, Social Services and Public Safety, Security and Policing, Prisons, Organised Crime Task Force, Assets Recovery Agency, Regional Development)*

OFFICE OF THE FIRST MINISTER AND DEPUTY FIRST MINISTER
Castle Buildings, Stormont Estate, Belfast BT4 3SR
T 028-9052 0000 W www.ofmdfmni.gov.uk

DEPARTMENT OF AGRICULTURE AND RURAL DEVELOPMENT
Dundonald House, Upper Newtownards Road, Belfast BT4 3SB
T 028-9052 0100 W www.dardni.gov.uk

EXECUTIVE AGENCIES
RIVERS AGENCY, 4 Hospital Road, Belfast BT8 8JP
T 028-9025 3355
FOREST SERVICE, Dundonald House, Belfast BT4 3SB
T 028-9052 4288

DEPARTMENT OF CULTURE, ARTS AND LEISURE
3rd Floor, Interpoint, 20–24 York Street, Belfast BT15 1AQ
T 028-9025 8825 F 028-9025 8906 W www.dcalni.gov.uk

EXECUTIVE AGENCIES
THE PUBLIC RECORD OFFICE OF NORTHERN IRELAND, 66 Balmoral Avenue, Belfast BT9 6NY T 028-9025 1318 F 028-9025 5999
THE ORDNANCE SURVEY OF NORTHERN IRELAND, Colby House, Stranmillis Court, Belfast BT9 5BJ T 028-9025 5755
F 028-9025 5700

DEPARTMENT OF EDUCATION
Rathgael House, 43 Balloo Road, Bangor, Co. Down BT19 7PR
T 028-9127 9100 W www.deni.gov.uk

DEPARTMENT FOR EMPLOYMENT AND LEARNING
39–49 Adelaide House, Adelaide Street, Belfast BT2 8FD
T 028-9025 7777 W www.delni.gov.uk

DEPARTMENT OF ENTERPRISE, TRADE AND INVESTMENT
Netherleigh, Massey Avenue, Belfast BT4 2JP T 028-9052 9900
F 028-9052 9550

DEPARTMENT OF THE ENVIRONMENT
Clarence Court, 10 18 Adelaide Street, Belfast BT2 8GB
T 028-9054 0013 W www.doeni.gov.uk

EXECUTIVE AGENCIES
Driver and Vehicle Licensing Agency (Northern Ireland)
Driver and Vehicle Testing Agency (Northern Ireland)
Environment and Heritage Service
Planning Service

DEPARTMENT OF FINANCE AND PERSONNEL
Rathgael House, Balloo Road, Bangor BT19 7NA
T 028-9127 9279 W www.dfpni.gov.uk

EXECUTIVE AGENCIES
BUSINESS DEVELOPMENT SERVICE, Craiganlet Buildings, Stoney Road, Belfast BT4 3SX T 028-9052 0444
LAND REGISTERS OF NORTHERN IRELAND, Lincoln Building, 27–45 Great Victoria Street, Belfast BT2 7SL T 028-9025 1515
NORTHERN IRELAND STATISTICS AND RESEARCH AGENCY*, McAuley House, 2–14 Castle Street, Belfast BT1 1SA
T 028-9034 8100
RATE COLLECTION AGENCY, Oxford House, 49–55 Chichester Street, Belfast BT1 4HH T 028-9025 2252
VALUATION AND LANDS AGENCY, Queen's Court, 56–66 Upper Queen Street, Belfast BT1 6FD T 028-9025 0700
*Incorporates the General Register Office (Northern Ireland Oxford House, 49–55 Chichester Street, Belfast BT1 4H
T 028-9025 2000

DEPARTMENT OF HEALTH, SOCIAL SERVICES AND PUBLIC SAFETY
Castle Buildings, Stormont, Belfast BT4 3SJ T 028-9052 0500
F 028-9052 0572 W www.dhsspsni.gov.uk

EXECUTIVE AGENCIES
Northern Ireland Health and Social Services Estate Agency

DEPARTMENT FOR REGIONAL DEVELOPMENT
Clarence Court, 10–18 Adelaide Street, Belfast BT2 8GB
T 028-9054 0540 F 028-9054 0064 W www.drdni.gov.uk

DEPARTMENT FOR SOCIAL DEVELOPMENT
Lighthouse Building, 1 Cromac Place, Gasworks Business Park,
Ormeau Road, Belfast BT7 2JB T 028-9082 9492
W www.dsdni.gov.uk

NORTHERN IRELAND ASSEMBLY MEMBERS
as at 1 August 2005

Adams, Gerry, *SF, Belfast West*
Armstrong, Billy, *UUP, Ulster Mid*
Attwood, Alex, *SDLP, Belfast West*
Beare, Norah, *DUP, Lagan Valley*
Beggs, Roy, *UUP, Antrim East*
Bell, Billy, *UUP, Lagan Valley*
Bell, Eileen, *All., Down North*
Berry, Paul, *DUP, Newry and Armagh*
Birnie, Dr Esmond, *UUP, Belfast South*
Bradley, Dominic, *SDLP, Newry and Armagh*
Bradley, Mary, *SDLP, Foyle*
Bradley, P. J., *SDLP, Down South*
Brolly, Francis, *SF, East Londonderry*
Buchanan, Thomas, *DUP, West Tyrone*
Burns, Thomas, *SDLP, Antrim South*
Burnside, David, *UUP, Antrim South*
Campbell, Gregory, *DUP, Londonderry East*
Clarke, Willie, *SF, Down South*
Close, Seamus, *All., Lagan Valley*
Clyde, Wilson, *DUP, Antrim South*
Cobain, Fred, *UUP, Belfast North*
Copeland, Michael, *UUP, Belfast East*
Coulter, Revd Robert, *UUP, Antrim North*
Cree, Leslie, *UUP, Down North*
Dallat, John, *SDLP, Londonderry East*
Dawson, George, *DUP, Antrim East*
Deeny, Kieran, *Ind., Tyrone West*
Dodds, Diane, *DUP, Belfast West*
Dodds, Nigel, *DUP, Belfast North*
Doherty, Pat, *SF, Tyrone West*
Donaldson, Jeffrey, *DUP, Lagan Valley*
Dougan, Geraldine, *SF, Ulster Mid*
Durkan, Mark, *SDLP, Foyle*
Easton, Alex, *DUP, Down North*
Elliot, Tom, *UUP, Fermanagh and South Tyrone*
Empey, Sir Reg, *UUP, Belfast East*
Ennis, George, *DUP, Strangford*
Irvine, David, *PUP, Belfast East*
Farren, Dr Sean, *SDLP, Antrim North*
Ferguson, Michael, *SF, Belfast West*
Ford, David, *All., Antrim South*
Foster, Arlene, *DUP, Fermanagh and South Tyrone*
Gallagher, Tommy, *SDLP, Fermanagh and South Tyrone*
Gardiner, Samuel, *UUP, Upper Bann*
Gildernew, Michelle, *SF, Fermanagh and South Tyrone*
Girvan, Paul, *DUP, Antrim South*
Hanna, Carmel, *SDLP, Belfast South*
Hay, William, *DUP, Foyle*
Hilditch, David, *DUP, Antrim East*
Hillis, Norman, *UUP, Londonderry East*
Hussey, Derek, *UUP, Tyrone West*
Hyland, Davy, *SF, Newry and Armagh*
Kelly, Dolores, *SDLP, Upper Bann*
Kelly, Gerry, *SF, Belfast North*
Kennedy, Danny, *UUP, Newry and Armagh*
Kilclooney, Lord, *UUP, Strangford*
Lewsley, Patricia, *SDLP, Lagan Valley*
Long, Naomi, *All., Belfast East*
Maginness, Alban, *SDLP, Belfast North*
Maskey, Alex, *SF, Belfast South*
McCann, Fra, *SF, Belfast West*

McCarthy, Kieran, *All., Strangford*
†**McCartney**, Raymond, *SF, Foyle*
McCartney, Robert, *UKUP, Down North*
McCausland, Nelson, *DUP, Belfast North*
McClarty, David, *UUP, Londonderry East*
McCrea, Revd William, *DUP, Ulster Mid*
McDonnell, Dr Alasdair, *SDLP, Belfast South*
McElduff, Barry, *SF, Tyrone West*
McFarland, Alan, *UUP, Down North*
McGimpsey, Michael, *UUP, Belfast South*
McGlone, Patsy, *SDLP, Ulster Mid*
McGuigan, Philip, *SF, Antrim North*
McGuinness, Martin, *SF, Ulster Mid*
McLaughlin, Mitchel, *SF, Foyle*
McMenamin, Eugene, *SDLP, Tyrone West*
McNarry, David, *UUP, Strangford*
Molloy, Francis, *SF, Ulster Mid*
Morrow, Maurice, *DUP, Fermanagh and South Tyrone*
Moutray, Stephen, *DUP, Upper Bann*
Murphy, Conor, *SF, Newry and Armagh*
Neeson, Sean, *All., Antrim East*
Nesbitt, Dermot, *UUP, Down South*
Newton, Robin, *DUP, Belfast East*
O'Dowd, John, *SF, Upper Bann*
O'Rawe, Patricia, *SF, Newry and Armagh*
O'Reilly, Tom, *SF, Fermanagh and South Tyrone*
Paisley, Revd Dr Ian, *DUP, Antrim North*
Paisley, Ian Jnr., *DUP, Antrim North*
Poots, Edwin, *DUP, Lagan Valley*
Ramsey, Pat, *SDLP, Foyle*
‡**Ramsey**, Sue, *SF, Belfast West*
Ritchie, Margaret, *SDLP, Down South*
Robinson, George, *DUP, Londonderry East*
Robinson, Iris, *DUP, Strangford*
Robinson, Ken, *UUP, Antrim East*
Robinson, Mark, *DUP, Belfast South*
Robinson, Peter, *DUP, Belfast East*
Ruane, Caitriona, *SF, Down South*
Shannon, Jim, *DUP, Strangford*
Simpson, David, *DUP, Upper Bann*
Stanton, Kathy, *SF, Belfast North*
Storey, Mervyn, *DUP, Antrim North*
Trimble, The Rt. Hon. David, *UUP, Upper Bann*
Weir, Peter, *DUP, Down North*
Wells, Jim, *DUP, Down South*
Wilson, Jim, *UUP, Antrim South*
Wilson, Sammy, *DUP, Antrim East*

* Elected as UUP candidate, became a member of the DUP with effect from 15 January 2004
† Mary Nelis resigned from the Northern Ireland Assembly and was replaced by Raymond McCartney, whose appointment was notified by the Chief Electoral Officer with effect from 15 July 2004
‡ Bairbre de Brun resigned from the Northern Ireland Assembly and was relpaced by Sue Ramsey, whose appointment was notified by the Chief Electoral Officer with effect from 29 November 2004

POLITICAL COMPOSITION

Democratic Unionist Party (DUP)	33
Sinn Fein (SF)	24
Ulster Unionist Party (UUP)	24
Social Democratic and Labour Party (SDLP)	18
Alliance Party (All.)	6
Progressive Unionist Party (PUP)	1
UK Unionist Party (UKUP)	1
Independent (Ind.)	1

NORTHERN IRELAND ASSEMBLY ELECTION RESULTS
as at November 2003
* Indicates those who were elected

ANTRIM EAST
E. 55,473 *T.* 56.50%
Total Valid Poll: 30,952
Quota: 4,422
*Roy Beggs, UUP
*Sammy Wilson, DUP
*George Dawson, DUP
*David Hilditch, DUP
Daniel O'Connor, SDLP
*Sean Neeson, All.
*Ken Robinson, UUP
Roy McCune, UUP
Jack McKee, Ind.
Stewart Dickson, All.
Roger Hutchinson, Ind.
Oliver McMullan, SF
Tom Robinson, UKUP
Carolyn Howarth, PUP
Robert Mason, Ind.
John Anderson, Ind.
Anne Monaghan, NIWC
Alan Greer, C.
Andrew Frew, Green

ANTRIM NORTH
E. 70,489 *T.* 63.32%
Total Valid Poll: 44,099
Quota: 6,300
*Revd Dr Ian Paisley, DUP
*Ian Paisley Jnr., DUP
*Revd Robert Coulter, UUP
*Philip McGuigan, SF
*Sean Farren, SDLP
*Mervyn Storey, DUP
James Currie, UUP
Declan O'Loan, SDLP
Jayne Dunlop, All.
Kane Gardiner, Ind.
Nathaniel Small, UKUP
Billy McCaughey, PUP

ANTRIM SOUTH
E. 63,640 *T.* 59.49%
Total Valid Poll: 37,421
Quota: 5,346
*David Burnside, UUP
*Wilson Clyde, DUP
*Paul Girvan, DUP
Martin Meehan, SF
*David Ford, All.
*Jim Wilson, UUP
*Thomas Burns, SDLP
Donovan McClelland, SDLP
John Smyth, DUP

Adrian Cochrane-Watson, UUP
Norman Boyd, NIUP
Joan Cosgrove, NIWC
Ken Wilkinson, PUP
Jason Docherty, C.

BELFAST EAST
E. 51,937 *T.* 60.70%
Total Valid Poll: 30,965
Quota: 4,424
*Peter Robinson, DUP
*Sir Reg Empey, UUP
*David Ervine, PUP
*Naomi Long, All.
*Michael Copeland, UUP
Jim Rodgers, UUP
*Robin Newton, DUP
Harry Toan, DUP
Joe O'Donnell, SF
Leo Van Es, SDLP
Terry Dick, C.
Thomas Black, Soc.
Joseph Bell, WP
John McBlain, Ind.
George Weiss, VFYS

BELFAST NORTH
E. 51,353 *T.* 62.31%
Total Valid Poll: 31,532
Quota: 4,505
*Nigel Dodds, DUP
*Gerry Kelly, SF
*Alban Maginness, SDLP
*Kathy Stanton, SF
*Fred Cobain, UUP
Pat Convery, SDLP
*Nelson McCausland, DUP
William Hutchinson, PUP
Fraser Agnew, UUC
Frank McCoubrey, Ind.
Eliz Byrne McCullough, NIWC
Marjorie Hawkins, All.
Peter Emerson, Green
Raymond McCord, Ind.
Marcella Delaney, WP
John Gallagher, VFYP

BELFAST SOUTH
E. 50,707 *T.* 62.59%
Total Valid Poll: 31,330
Quota: 4,476
*Michael McGimpsey, UUP
*Mark Robinson, DUP
*Alex Maskey, SF
*Carmel Hanna, SDLP
*Alasdair McDonnell, SDLP
Ruth Patterson, DUP
*Esmond Birnie, UUP
Monica McWilliams, NIWC
Geraldine Rice, All.
John Hiddleston, UUP
Tom Ekin, All.
Thomas Morrow, PUP
John Wright, Green
James Barbour, SP
Roger Lomas, C.
Patrick Lynn, WP
Linsay Steven, VFYP

BELFAST WEST
E. 50,861 *T.* 65.92%
Total Valid Poll: 32,854
Quota: 4,694
*Gerry Adams, SF
*Fra McCann, SF
*Bairbre de Brun, SF†
*Michael Ferguson, SF
*Alex Attwood, SDLP
Sue Ramsey, SF
Joe Hendron, SDLP
*Diane Dodds, DUP
Chris McGimpsey, UUP
Hugh Smyth, PUP
John Lowry, WP
John MacVicar, Ind.
Kathryn Ayers, All.
David Kerr, Ulster Third Way
† Bairbre de Brun resigned from the Northern Ireland Assembly and was replaced by Sue Ramsey, whose appointment was notified by the Chief Electoral Officer with effect from 29 November 2004

DOWN NORTH
E. 57,422 *T.* 54.54%
Total Valid Poll: 30,835
Quota: 4,406
*Leslie Cree, UUP
*Peter Weir, DUP
*Alex Easton, DUP
*Alan McFarland, UUP
*Robert McCartney, UKUP
Diana Peacocke, UUP
*Eileen Bell, All.
Liam Logan, SDLP
Brian Wilson, Ind.
Jane Morrice, NIWC
Ann Chambers, Ind. Unionist
John Barry, Green
Stephen Farry, All.
Julian Robertson, C.
Alan Field, Ind.
David Rose, PUP
Maria George, SF
Tom Sheridan, UKUP
Chris Carter, Ind.

DOWN SOUTH
E. 70,149 *T.* 65.59%
Total Valid Poll: 45,346
Quota: 6,479
*Jim Wells, DUP
*Dermot Nesbitt, UUP
*P. J. Bradley, SDLP
*Catriona Ruane, SF
*Margaret Ritchie, SDLP
*Willie Clarke, SF
Eamonn O'Neill, SDLP
Jim Donaldson, UUP
Eamonn McConvey, SF
Marian Fitzpatrick, SDLP
Raymond Blaney, Green
Trudy Miller, NIWC
Neil Powell, All.
Nelson Wharton, UKUP
Malachi Curran, Ind.
Desmond O'Hagan, WP

FERMANAGH AND SOUTH TYRONE
E. 64,336 *T.* 72.86%
Total Valid Poll: 46,160
Quota: 6,595
*Michelle Gildernew, SF
*Tom Elliot, UUP
*Maurice Morrow, DUP
*Tom O'Reilly, SF
*Arlene Foster, UUP†
*Tommy Gallagher, SDLP
Gerry McHugh, SF
Bert Johnston, DUP
Frank Britton, SDLP
Robert Mulligan, UUP
Eithne McNulty, NIWC
Linda Cleland, All.
† elected as UUP candidate, became a member of the DUP with effect from 15 January 2004

FOYLE
E. 65,303 *T.* 63.45%
Total Valid Poll: 40,806
Quota: 5,830
*Mark Durkan, SDLP
*William Hay, DUP
*Mitchel McLaughlin, SF
Raymond McCartney, SF
*Mary Nelis, SF†
*Mary Bradley, SDLP
Mary Hamilton, UUP
*Pat Ramsey, SDLP
Eamonn McCann, SEA
Gerard Diver, SDLP
Annie Courtney, Ind.
Alan Castle, All.
Danny McBrearty, Ind.
† Mary Nelis resigned from the Northern Ireland Assembly and was replaced by Raymond McCartney, whose appointment was notified by the Chief Electoral Officer with effect from 15 July 2004

LAGAN VALLEY
E. 67,910 *T.* 61.44%
Total Valid Poll: 41,254
Quota: 5,894
*Jeffrey Donaldson, UUP†
*Edwin Poots, DUP
*Seamus Close, All.
Andrew Hunter, DUP
Paul Butler, SF
*Patricia Lewsley, SDLP
*Billy Bell, UUP
Ivan Davis, Ind.
*Norah Beare, UUP
Jim Kirkpatrick, UUP
Joanne Johnston, C.
Andrew Park, PUP
Frances McCarthy, WP
† elected as UUP candidate, became a member of the DUP with effect from 15 January 2004

LONDONDERRY EAST
E. 56,203 *T.* 61.75%
Total Valid Poll: 34,273
Quota: 4,897
*Gregory Campbell, DUP
*David McClarty, UUP
*Francis Brolly, SF

*George Robinson, DUP
*John Dallat, SDLP
Maurice Bradley, DUP
Michael Coyle, SDLP
*Norman Hillis, UUP
Cliona O'Kane, SF
Boyd Douglas, UUC
Edwin Stevenson, UUP
Pauline Armitage, UKUP
Yvonne Boyle, All.
Marion Baur, SEA

NEWRY AND ARMAGH
E. 68,731 T. 70.18%
Total Valid Poll: 47,378
Quota: 6,769
*Paul Berry, DUP
*Conor Murphy, SF
*Danny Kennedy, UUP
*Davy Hyland, SF
*Patricia O'Rawe, SF
Jim Lennon, SDLP
*Dominic Bradley, SDLP
John Fee, SDLP
William Frazer, Ind.
Freda Donnelly, DUP
Peter Whitcroft, All.

STRANGFORD
E. 66,308 T. 57.06%
Total Valid Poll: 37,250
Quota: 5,322
*Iris Robinson, DUP
*Lord Kilclooney, UUP
*Jim Shannon, DUP
*George Ennis, DUP
*David McNarry, UUP
Joe Boyle, SDLP
*Kieran McCarthy, All.
Bob Little, UUP
Dermot Kennedy, SF
Cedric Wilson, NIUP
Colin Neill, PUP
Philip Orr, Green
Danny McCarthy, Ind.

TYRONE WEST
E. 57,795 T. 73.24%
Total Valid Poll: 41,729

Quota: 5,962
*Dr Kieran Deeny, Ind.
*Pat Doherty, SF
*Barry McElduff, SF
*Thomas Buchanan, DUP
Brian McMahon, SF
*Derek Hussey, UUP
*Eugene McMenamin, SDLP
Joe Byrne, SDLP
Derek Reaney, DUP
Bert Wilson, UUP
Roy Reid, PUP
Steven Alexander, All.

ULSTER MID
E. 60,095 T. 74.92%
Total Valid Poll: 44,362
Quota: 6,338
*Revd Dr William McCrea, DUP
*Martin McGuinness, SF
*Geraldine Dougan, SF
*Francie Molloy, SF
*Billy Armstrong, UUP
*Patsy McGlone, SDLP
Dennis Haughey, SDLP
Trevor Wilson, UUP
Alan Miller, DUP
Cora Groogan, SF
Francis Donnelly, WP
James Holmes, All.

UPPER BANN
E. 68,814 T. 64.15%
Total Valid Poll: 43,482
Quota: 6,212
*David Trimble, UUP
*David Simpson, DUP
*John O'Dowd, SF
*Stephen Moutray, DUP
Dara O'Hagan, SF
*Dolores Kelly, SDLP
Kieran Corr, SDLP
*Samuel Gardiner, UUP
Denis Watson, DUP
George Savage, UUP
David Jones, Ind.
Sidney Anderson, Ind.
Francis McQuaid, All.
Tom French, WP

LOCAL GOVERNMENT

Major changes in local government were introduced in England and Wales in 1974 and in Scotland in 1975 by the Local Government Act 1972 and the Local Government (Scotland) Act 1973. Further significant alterations were made in England by the Local Government Acts of 1985, 1992 and 2000.

The structure in England was based on two tiers of local authorities (county councils and district councils) in the non-metropolitan areas; and a single tier of metropolitan councils in the six metropolitan areas of England and London borough councils in London.

Following reviews of the structure of local government in England by the Local Government Commission, 46 unitary (all-purpose) authorities were created between April 1995 and April 1998 to cover certain areas in the non-metropolitan counties. The remaining county areas continue to have two tiers of local authorities. The county and district councils in the Isle of Wight were replaced by a single unitary authority on 1 April 1995; the former counties of Avon, Cleveland, Humberside and Berkshire were replaced by unitary authorities; and Hereford and Worcester was replaced by a new county council for Worcestershire (with district councils) and a unitary authority for Herefordshire.

The Local Government (Wales) Act 1994 and the Local Government etc (Scotland) Act 1994 abolished the two-tier structure in Wales and Scotland with effect from 1 April 1996, replacing it with a single tier of unitary authorities.

ELECTIONS

Local elections are normally held on the first Thursday in May, although in 2004 they were held on 10 June to coincide with the European Parliament elections. Generally, all British subjects, citizens of the Republic of Ireland, Commonwealth and other European Union citizens who are 18 years or over and resident on the qualifying date in the area for which the election is being held, are entitled to vote at local government elections. A register of electors is prepared and published annually by local electoral registration officers.

A returning officer has the overall responsibility for an election. Voting takes place at polling stations, arranged by the local authority and under the supervision of a presiding officer specially appointed for the purpose. Candidates, who are subject to various statutory qualifications and disqualifications designed to ensure that they are suitable to hold office, must be nominated by electors for the electoral area concerned.

In England, the Boundary Committee for England is responsible for carrying out periodic reviews of electoral arrangements and making recommendations to the Electoral Commission. Following the Deputy Prime Minister's announcement on 16 June 2003 that referendums would be held on the establishment of three elected regional assemblies in the North East, North West and Yorkshire and the Humber, the Boundary Committee for England commenced a major review of local government structure in these areas. Final recommendations were submitted to the Deputy Prime Minister on 25 May 2004 and provide for a minimum of two different options for the establishment of unitary authorities in each county area. In a referendum in the North East region, held on 4 November 2004, the electorate voted against the establishment of a regional assembly.

In Wales and Scotland these matters are the responsibility of the Local Government Boundary Commission for Wales and the Boundary Commission for Scotland respectively. The Local Government Act 2000 provided for the Secretary of State to change the frequency and phasing of elections.

THE BOUNDARY COMMITTEE FOR ENGLAND, Trevelyan House, Great Peter Street, London SW1P 2HW
T 020-7271 0500 W www.boundarycommittee.org.uk
LOCAL GOVERNMENT BOUNDARY COMMISSION FOR WALES, Caradog House, 1–6 St Andrew's Place, Cardiff CF10 3BE
T 029-2039 5031 W www.lgbc-wales.gov.uk
THE BOUNDARY COMMISSION FOR SCOTLAND,
3 Drumsheugh Gardens, Edinburgh EH3 7QJ
T 0131-538 7200 W www.bcomm-scotland.gov.uk

INTERNAL ORGANISATION

The council as a whole is the final decision-making body within any authority. Councils are free to a great extent to make their own internal organisational arrangements. The Local Government Act, given royal assent on 28 July 2000, allows councils to adopt one of three broad categories of a new constitution which include a separate executive.

These three categories are:
– A directly elected mayor with a cabinet selected by that mayor
– A cabinet, either elected by the council or appointed by its leader
– A directly elected mayor and council manager
Normally, questions of policy are settled by the full council, while the administration of the various services is the responsibility of committees of councillors. Day-to-day decisions are delegated to the council's officers, who act within the policies laid down by the councillors.

FINANCE

Local government in England, Wales and Scotland is financed from four sources: the council tax, non-domestic rates, government grants, and income from fees and charges for services.

COUNCIL TAX

Under the Local Government Finance Act 1992, from 1 April 1993 the council tax replaced the community charge (which had been introduced in April 1989 in Scotland and April 1990 in England and Wales in place of domestic rates).

The council tax is a local tax levied by each local council. Liability for the council tax bill usually falls on the owner-occupier or tenant of a dwelling which is their sole or main residence. Council tax bills may be reduced because of the personal circumstances of people resident in a property, and there are discounts in the case of dwellings occupied by fewer than two adults.

In England, each county council, each district council and each police authority sets its own council tax rate. The district councils collect the combined council tax, and the county councils and police authorities claim their share from the district councils' collection funds. In Wales, each unitary authority and each police authority sets its own council tax rate. The unitary authorities collect the combined council tax and the police authorities claim their share from the funds. In Scotland, each local authority sets its own rate of council tax.

The tax relates to the value of the dwelling. Each dwelling is placed in one of eight valuation bands, ranging from A to H, based on the property's estimated market value as at 1 April 1991. Wales recently underwent a revaluation of bands based on the estimated market value of property as at 1 April 2003. The new band structure took effect from 1 April 2005 and will be used to calculate council tax bills in Wales from 1 April 2005.

The valuation bands and ranges of values in England, Wales and Scotland are:

England

A	Up to £40,000	E	£88,001–£120,000
B	£40,001–£52,000	F	£120,001–£160,000
C	£52,001–£68,000	G	£160,001–£320,000
D	£68,001–£88,000	H	Over £320,000

Wales

A	Up to £44,000	F	£162,001–£223,000
B	£44,001–£65,000	G	£223,001–£324,000
C	£65,001–£91,000	H	£324,001–£424,000
D	£91,001–£123,000	I	Over £424,000
E	£123,001–£162,000		

Scotland

A	Up to £27,000	E	£58,001–£80,000
B	£27,001–£35,000	F	£80,001–£106,000
C	£35,001–£45,000	G	£106,001–£212,000
D	£45,001–£58,000	H	Over £212,000

The council tax within a local area varies between the different bands according to proportions laid down by law. The charge attributable to each band as a proportion of the Band D charge set by the council is approximately:

A	67%	F	144%
B	78%	G	167%
C	89%	H	200%
D	100%	I	233%*
E	122%		

* Wales only

The Band D rate is given in the tables on the following pages. There may be variations from the given figure within each district council area because of different parish or community precepts being levied.

NON-DOMESTIC RATES

Non-domestic (business) rates are collected by billing authorities; these are the district councils in those areas of England with two tiers of local government and unitary authorities in other parts of England, in Wales and in Scotland. In respect of England and Wales, the Local Government Finance Act 1988 provides for liability for rates to be assessed on the basis of a poundage (multiplier) tax on the rateable value of property (hereditaments). Separate multipliers are set by the Office of the Deputy Prime Minister in England, the National Assembly for Wales and the Scottish Executive, and rates are collected by the billing authority for the area where a property is located. Rate income collected by billing authorities is paid into a national non-domestic rating (NNDR) pool and redistributed to individual authorities on the basis of the adult population figure as prescribed by the Office of the Deputy Prime Minister, the National Assembly for Wales or the Scottish Executive. The rates pools are maintained separately in England, Wales and Scotland. Actual payment of rates in certain cases is subject to transitional arrangements, to phase in the larger increases and reductions in rates resulting from the effects of the latest revaluation.

Rates are levied in Scotland in accordance with the Local Government (Scotland) Act 1975. For 1995–6, the Secretary of State for Scotland prescribed a single non-domestic rates poundage to apply throughout the country at the same level as the uniform business rate (UBR) in England. Rate income is pooled and redistributed to local authorities on a per capita basis.

Rateable values for the 2005 rating lists come into effect on 1 April 2005. They are derived from the rental value of property as at 1 April 2003 and determined on certain statutory assumptions by the Valuation Office Agency in England and Wales, and by Regional Assessors in Scotland. New property which is added to the list, and significant changes to existing property, necessitate amendments to the rateable value on the same basis. Rating lists (valuation rolls in Scotland) remain in force until the next general revaluation. Such revaluations take place every five years, the next being in 2010.

Certain types of property are exempt from rates, eg agricultural land and buildings, certain businesses and places of public religious worship. Charities and other non-profit-making organisations may receive full or partial relief. Empty property is liable to pay rates at 50 per cent, except for certain specified classes which are entirely exempt.

GOVERNMENT GRANTS

In addition to specific grants in support of revenue expenditure on particular services, central government pays revenue support grant to local authorities. This grant is paid to each local authority so that if each authority spends at the level of its standard spending assessment, all authorities in the same class can set broadly the same council tax.

COMPLAINTS

In England the Local Government Ombudsman is responsible for investigating complaints from members of the public who claim to have suffered as a consequence of maladministration in local government or in certain local bodies. The Public Services Ombudsman for Wales and the Scottish Public Services Ombudsman fulfil similar roles in their respective regions.

The Northern Ireland Commissioner for Complaints fulfils a similar function in Northern Ireland, investigating complaints about local authorities and certain public bodies.

Complaints are made to the relevant local authority in the first instance and complainants may approach the

Ombudsmen or Commissioners if not satisfied. Complaints may also be made directly to the Ombudsmen or Commissioners.

The Local Government Act 2000 established a Standards Board and an independent tribunal known as the Adjudication Panel for England. The Standards Board investigates any allegations that councillors have breached the council's Code of Conduct. At the end of the investigation, the case may be referred to either the relevant local authority's standards committee or the Adjudication Panel, which has a number of sanctions at its disposal, up to and including the disqualification of a member from holding office for five years.

THE QUEEN'S REPRESENTATIVES

The Lord-Lieutenant of a county is the permanent local representative of the Crown in that county. The appointment of Lords-Lieutenant is now regulated by the Lieutenancies Act 1997. They are appointed by the Sovereign on the recommendation of the Prime Minister. The retirement age is 75. The office of Lord-Lieutenant dates from 1551, and its holder was originally responsible for the maintenance of order and for local defence in the county. The duties of the post include attending on royalty during official visits to the county, performing certain duties in connection with armed forces of the Crown (and in particular the reserve forces), and making presentations of honours and awards on behalf of the Crown. In England, Wales and Northern Ireland, the Lord-Lieutenant usually also holds the office of *Custos Rotulorum*. As such, he or she acts as head of the county's commission of the peace (which recommends the appointment of magistrates).

The office of Sheriff (from the Old English shire-reeve) of a county was created in the tenth century. The Sheriff was the special nominee of the Sovereign, and the office reached the peak of its influence under the Norman kings. The Provisions of Oxford (1258) laid down a yearly tenure of office. Since the mid-16th century the office has been purely civil, with military duties taken over by the Lord-Lieutenant of the county. The Sheriff (commonly known as 'High Sheriff') attends on royalty during official visits to the county, acts as the returning officer during parliamentary elections in county constituencies, attends the opening ceremony when a High Court judge goes on circuit, executes High Court writs, and appoints under-sheriffs to act as deputies. The appointments and duties of the High Sheriffs in England and Wales are laid down by the Sheriffs Act 1887.

The serving High Sheriff submits a list of names of possible future sheriffs to a tribunal which chooses three names to put to the Sovereign. The tribunal nominates the High Sheriff annually on 12 November and the Sovereign picks the name of the Sheriff to succeed in the following year. The term of office runs from 25 March to the following 24 March (the civil and legal year before 1752). No person may be chosen twice in three years if there is any other suitable person in the county.

CIVIC DIGNITIES

District councils in England may petition for a royal charter granting borough or 'city' status to the district. Local councils in Wales may petition for a royal charter granting county borough or 'city' status to the council.

In England and Wales the chairman of a borough or county borough council may be called a mayor, and the chairman of a city council may be called a Lord Mayor if Lord Mayoralty has been conferred on that city. Parish councils in England and community councils in Wales may call themselves 'town councils', in which case their chairman is the town mayor.

In Scotland the chairman of a local council may be known as a convenor; a provost is the mayoral equivalent. The chairmen of the councils for the cities of Aberdeen, Dundee, Edinburgh and Glasgow are Lord Provosts.

ENGLAND

There are currently 34 counties; all are divided into districts. In addition, there are 46 unitary authorities and 238 district councils. The populations of most of the unitary authorities are in the range of 100,000 to 300,000. The district councils have populations broadly in the range of 60,000 to 100,000; some, however, have larger populations, because of the need to avoid dividing large towns, and some in mainly rural areas have smaller populations.

The main conurbations outside Greater London – Tyne and Wear, West Midlands, Merseyside, Greater Manchester, West Yorkshire and South Yorkshire – are divided into 36 metropolitan boroughs, most of which have a population of over 200,000.

There are also about 10,000 parishes, in 219 of the district councils and 18 of the metropolitan boroughs.

ELECTIONS
For districts, counties and for about 8,000 parishes, there are elected councils, consisting of directly elected councillors. The councillors elect annually one of their number as chairman.

Generally, councillors serve four years and there are no elections of district and parish councillors in county election years. In metropolitan boroughs, one-third of the councillors for each ward are elected each year except in the year when county elections take place elsewhere. District councils can choose whether to have elections by thirds or whole council elections. In the former case, one-third of the council, as nearly as may be, is elected in each year of metropolitan borough elections. If whole council elections are chosen, these are held in the year midway between county elections.

FUNCTIONS
In non-metropolitan areas, functions are divided between the districts and counties (those requiring the larger area or population are generally the responsibility of the county). The metropolitan councils, with the larger population in their areas, already had wider functions than non-metropolitan councils, and following abolition of the metropolitan county councils were also given most of their functions. A few functions continue to be exercised over the larger area by joint bodies, made up of councillors from each district.

The allocation of functions is as follows:

County councils: education; strategic planning; traffic, transport and highways; fire service; consumer protection; refuse disposal; smallholdings; social services; libraries

District councils: local planning; housing; highways (maintenance of certain urban roads and off-street car parks); building regulations; environmental health; refuse collection; cemeteries and crematoria

Unitary and metropolitan councils: their functions are all those listed above, except that the fire service is exercised by a joint body

Concurrently by county and district councils: recreation (parks, playing fields, swimming pools); museums; encouragement of the arts, tourism and industry

The Police and Magistrates Court Act 1994 set up police authorities in England and Wales separate from the local authorities.

PARISH COUNCILS

Parishes with 200 or more electors must generally have parish councils, which means that over three-quarters of the parishes have councils. A parish council comprises at least five members, the number being fixed by the district council. Elections are held every four years, at the time of the election of the district councillor for the ward including the parish. All parishes have parish meetings comprising the electors of the parish. Where there is no council, the meeting must be held at least twice a year.

Parish council functions include: allotments; encouragement of arts and crafts; community halls, recreational facilities (e.g. open spaces, swimming pools); cemeteries and crematoria; and many minor functions. They must also be given an opportunity to comment on planning applications. They may, like county and district councils, spend limited sums for the general benefit of the parish. They levy a precept on the district councils for their funds.

REGIONAL CHAMBERS/ASSEMBLIES

Voluntary, multi-party and inclusive Regional Chambers have been established in each of the eight english regions outside London. The Chambers operate within the same boundaries as the Government Offices in the Regions and the Regional Development Agencies (RDAs). Regional Chambers have been formally recognised by the government as being representative of the interests of the region in relation to the work of their respective RDAs.

All of the Chambers have adopted the title 'assembly' and each Chamber strives to be representative of the region it serves. Under guidance issued by the Secretary of State, this representation comprises 70 per cent local authority members and 30 per cent drawn from other sectors, including higher and further education, the small business sector, parish and town councils, the NHS, voluntary organisations, Learning and Skills Councils, regional cultural consortia, rural and environmental groups and other regional stakeholders.

ROLE OF THE CHAMBERS

The Regional Chambers' initial focus, under the Regional Development Agencies Act 1998, was to act as consultative bodies for the RDA's regional economic strategies. The Chambers have been actively involved in the production of regional sustainable development frameworks (RSDFs). Further details can be found on the Department for Environment, Food and Rural Affairs website: www.defra.gov.uk

The Regional Assemblies (Preparations) Act received royal assent on 8 May 2003, giving the Chambers responsibility to act as regional planning bodies and to receive direct funding from central government for fulfilling this role.

EAST MIDLANDS REGIONAL ASSEMBLY, First Floor Suite, Council Offices, Nottingham Road, Melton Mowbray, Leicestershire LE13 0UL T 01664-502555 W www.emra.gov.uk
EAST OF ENGLAND REGIONAL ASSEMBLY, Flempton House, Flempton, Bury St Edmunds, Suffolk IP28 6EG T 01284-728151 W www.eera.gov.uk

NORTH EAST ASSEMBLY, The Guildhall, Quayside, Newcastle upon Tyne NE1 3AF T 0191-261 7388
W www.northeastassembly.gov.uk
NORTH WEST REGIONAL ASSEMBLY, Wigan Investment Centre, Waterside Drive, Wigan WN3 5BA T 01942-737916
W www.nwra.gov.uk
SOUTH EAST ENGLAND REGIONAL ASSEMBLY, Berkeley House, Cross Lanes, Guildford, Surrey GU1 1UN T 01483-555200
W www.southeast-ra.gov.uk
SOUTH WEST REGIONAL ASSEMBLY, Dennett House, 11 Middle Street, Taunton, Somerset TA1 1SH T 01823-270101
W www.southwest-ra.gov.uk
WEST MIDLANDS REGIONAL ASSEMBLY, Regional Partnership Centre, 3rd Floor, Albert House, Quay Place, 92–93 Edward Street, Birmingham B12 RA T 0121-245 0200
W www.wmra.gov.uk
YORKSHIRE AND HUMBER ASSEMBLY, 18 King Street, Wakefield, West Yorkshire WF1 2SQ T 01924-331555
W www.yhassembly.gov.uk

The English Regions Network, a representative body for the Chambers, was formed in early 2000.
THE ENGLISH REGIONS NETWORK, c/o West Midlands Regional Assembly (*see above*) T 0117-924 9465
W ern.smartregion.org.uk

FINANCE

Budgeted revenue expenditure in 2005–6 is £84 billion, 25 per cent of this is to be raised through council tax, 58 per cent from formula grant (revenue support grant, re-distributed business rates and police grant) and 16 per cent from specific grants. Formula grant totalled £49 billion (26,663 million in respect of revenue support grant and £18,004 million from the national non-domestic rate pool). Specific grants are estimated to amount to £13 billion and £21.3 billion is being raised locally through council tax.

In England, the average council tax per dwelling for 2005–6 is £1,009, up from £967 in 2004–5, an increase of 4.3 per cent. The average council tax for 2005–6 is £1,048 in shire areas, £1,078 in London and £840 in metropolitan areas. In England, the average council tax bill for a band D dwelling (occupied by two adults, including parish precepts) for 2005–6 is £1,214, an average increase of 1.4 per cent from 2004–5. The average band D council tax is £1,234 in shire areas, £1,162 in London and £1,190 in metropolitan areas. The assumed council tax yield for 2005–6 is £21,320 million.

The provisional amount estimated to be raised from national non-domestic rates from central and local lists is £18,004 million. The national non-domestic rating multiplier, or poundage, for 2005–6 is 42.2p (41.5p for small businesses).

Under the Local Government and Housing Act 1989, local authorities have four main ways of paying for capital expenditure: borrowing and other forms of extended credit; capital grants from central government towards some types of capital expenditure; 'usable' capital receipts from the sale of land, houses and other assets; and revenue.

The amount of capital expenditure which a local authority can finance by borrowing (or other forms of credit) is effectively limited by the credit approvals issued to it by central government. Most credit approvals can be used for any kind of local authority capital expenditure; these are known as basic credit approvals. Others (supplementary credit approvals) can be used only for the kind of expenditure specified in the approval, and so are often given to fund particular projects or services.

Local authorities can use all capital receipts from the sale of property or assets for capital spending, except in the case of sales of council houses. Generally, the 'usable' part of a local authority's capital receipts consists of 25 per cent of receipts from the sale of council houses and 50 per cent of other housing assets such as shops or vacant land. The balance has to be set aside as provision for repaying debt and meeting other credit liabilities.

EXPENDITURE

Local authority budgeted net revenue expenditure for 2005–6 is:

Service	£m
Education	34,960
Highways and transport	4,984
Social Services	16,874
Housing (excluding HRA)	2,314
Cultural, environment and planning	8,772
Police	10,313
Fire	2,110
Courts	57
Central services	3,457
Other	156
Mandatory rent allowances	7,201
Mandatory rent rebates	466
Rent rebates granted to HRA tenants	3,783
Net current expenditure	95,446
Capital financing	2,721
Capital expenditure charged to revenue account	868
Council tax benefit	2,994
Discretionary non-domestic rate relief	26
Bad debt provision	20
Flood defence payments to Environment Agency	27
Less interest receipts	(834)
Less specific grants outside AEF	(17,274)
Gross revenue expenditure	83,995
Less specific grants inside AEF	(13,014)
Net revenue expenditure	70,980
Less appropriations from reserves	(510)
Less adjustments	(12)
BUDGET REQUIREMENT	70,481

HRA = Housing Revenue Account
AEF = aggregate external finance

LONDON

The Greater London Council was abolished in 1986 and London is divided into 32 borough councils, which have a status similar to the metropolitan borough councils in the rest of England, and the Corporation of the City of London.

In March 1998 the government announced proposals for a Greater London Authority (GLA) covering the area of the 32 London boroughs and the City of London, which would comprise a directly elected mayor and a 25-member assembly. A referendum was held in London on 7 May 1998; the turnout was approximately 34 per cent and 72 per cent of electors voted in favour of the GLA. The independent candidate for London Mayor, Ken Livingstone, was elected on 4 May 2000 and the Authority assumed its responsibilities on 3 July 2000. He was re-elected on 10 June 2004 as a Labour candidate.

The GLA is responsible for transport, economic development, strategic planning, culture, health, the environment, the police and fire and emergency planning. The separately elected assembly scrutinises the mayor's activities and approves plans and budgets. There are 14 constituency assembly members, each representing a separate area of London (each constituency is made up of two or three complete London boroughs). Eleven additional members, making up the total assembly complement of 25 members, are elected on a London-wide basis, either as independents or from party political lists on the basis of proportional representation. Parties or independent candidates must secure at least five per cent of the vote to be entitled to additional seats.

LONDON BOROUGH COUNCILS

The London boroughs have whole council elections every four years, in the year immediately following the county council election year. The most recent elections took place on 2 May 2002.

The borough councils have responsibility for the following functions: building regulations; cemeteries and crematoria; consumer protection; youth employment; environmental health; electoral registration; food; drugs; housing; leisure services; libraries; local planning; local roads; museums; parking; recreation (parks, playing fields, swimming pools); refuse collection and street cleansing; social services; town planning; and traffic management.

CORPORATION OF LONDON

The Corporation of London is the local authority for the City of London. Its legal definition is 'The Mayor and Commonalty and Citizens of the City of London'. It is governed by the Court of Common Council, which consists of the Lord Mayor, 25 other aldermen, and about 100 common councilmen. The Lord Mayor and two sheriffs are nominated annually by the City guilds (the livery companies) and elected by the Court of Aldermen. Aldermen and councilmen are elected from the 25 wards into which the City is divided; councilmen must stand for re-election annually. The Council is a legislative assembly, and there are no political parties.

The Corporation has the same functions as the London borough councils. In addition, it runs the City of London Police; is the health authority for the Port of London; has health control of animal imports throughout Greater London, including at Heathrow airport; owns and manages public open spaces throughout Greater London; runs the Central Criminal Court; and runs Billingsgate, Smithfield and Spitalfields markets.

THE CITY GUILDS (LIVERY COMPANIES)

The livery companies of the City of London grew out of early medieval religious fraternities and began to emerge as trade and craft guilds, retaining their religious aspect, in the 12th century. From the early 14th century, only members of the trade and craft guilds could call themselves citizens of the City of London. The guilds began to be called livery companies, because of the distinctive livery worn by the most prosperous guild members on ceremonial occasions, in the late 15th century.

By the early 19th century the power of the companies within their trades had begun to wane, but those wearing the livery of a company continued to play an important role in the government of the City of London. Liverymen still have the right to nominate the Lord Mayor and sheriffs, and most members of the Court of Common Council are liverymen.

WALES

The Local Government (Wales) Act 1994 abolished the two-tier structure of eight county and 37 district councils which had existed since 1974, and replaced it, from 1 April 1996, with 22 unitary authorities. The new authorities were elected in May 1995. Each unitary authority inherited all the functions of the previous county and district councils, except fire services (which are provided by three combined fire authorities, composed of representatives of the unitary authorities) and National Parks (which are the responsibility of three independent National Park Authorities).

COMMUNITY COUNCILS

In Wales community councils are the equivalent of parishes in England. Unlike England, where many areas are not in any parish, communities have been established for the whole of Wales, forming approximately 865 communities in all. Community meetings may be convened as and when desired.

Community councils exist in 737 communities and further councils may be established at the request of a community meeting. Community councils have broadly the same range of powers as English parish councils. Community councillors are elected for a term of four years.

FINANCE

Non-hypothecated funding for 2005–6 is £3,345.6 million. This comprises revenue support grant of £2,675 million, support from the national non-domestic rate pool of £605 million, deprivation grant of £21.5 million and performance incentive grant of £30.7 million. The non-domestic rating multiplier or poundage for Wales for 2005–6 is 42.1p. The average Band D council tax levied in Wales for 2005–6 is £921, comprising unitary authorities £762, police authorities £138 and community councils £21.

EXPENDITURE

Local authority budgeted net revenue expenditure for 2005–6 is:

Service	£m
Education	2,100.9
Social services	1,114.5
Council fund housing, including housing benefit	404.0
Rent rebates granted to HRA tenants	275.1
Local environmental services	331.6
Roads and transport	260.2
Libraries, culture, heritage, sport and recreation	169.6
Planning, economic and community development and tourism	112.9
Coroners' and other courts*	2.8
Council tax benefit and administration	28.0
Debt financing costs	288.2
Central administrative and other revenue expenditure	294.0
Police	568.7
Fire	136.1
National Parks	17.2
Gross revenue expenditure	6,103.8
Less specific government grants	(1,366.3)
Net revenue expenditure	4,737.5

HRA = Housing Revenue Account

* Responsibility for magistrates' courts transferred to the Department for Constitutional Affairs on 1 April 2005

SCOTLAND

The Local Government etc. (Scotland) Act 1994 abolished the two-tier structure of nine regional and 53 district councils which had existed since 1975 and replaced it, from 1 April 1996, with 29 unitary authorities on the mainland; the three islands councils remained. The new authorities were elected in April 1995.

In July 1999 the Scottish Parliament assumed responsibility for legislation on local government. The government had established a Commission on Local Government and the Scottish Parliament (the McIntosh Commission) to make recommendations on the relationship between local authorities and the new Parliament and on increasing local authorities' accountability. The Commission published its reports in July 1999.

Following this report, the Scottish Executive established the 'Renewing Local Democracy' working group to consider ways in which to make council membership more attractive and councils more representative of their communities. The group would also advise on appropriate membership levels for each council, looking at modernising management practices and local concerns. They also investigated which method of election would be most appropriate, taking account of proportionality and the councillor-ward link, fair provision for independents, allowance for geographical diversity and a close fit between council wards and natural communities, and advised on an appropriate system of remuneration for councillors, taking account of available resources.

The Scottish Executive also set up the Leadership Advisory Panel in August 1999 following the recommendations of the McIntosh Report. The panel worked closely with Scottish local authorities, helping them to conduct a review of their political management structures and to implement its recommendations.

The Local Government in Scotland Bill was introduced to the Scottish Parliament in May 2002. The bill focused on three integrated core elements:

– A power for local authorities to promote and improve the well-being of their area and/or persons in it
– Statutory underpinning for community planning through the introduction of a duty on local authorities and key partners, including police, health boards and enterprise agencies
– A duty to secure best value.

ELECTIONS

The unitary authorities consist of directly elected councillors. The Scottish Local Government (Elections) Act 2002 moved elections from a three-year to a four-year cycle; the last elections took place in May 2003.

FUNCTIONS

The functions of the councils and islands councils are: education; social work; strategic planning; the provision of infrastructure such as roads; consumer protection; flood prevention; coast protection; valuation and rating; the police and fire services; civil defence; electoral registration; public transport; registration of births, deaths and marriages; housing; leisure and recreation; development and building control; environmental health; licensing; allotments; public conveniences; and the administration of district courts.

COMMUNITY COUNCILS

Scottish community councils differ from those in England and Wales. Their purpose as defined in statute is to ascertain and express the views of the communities they represent, and to take in the interests of their communities such action as appears to be expedient or practicable. Over 1,100 community councils have been established under schemes drawn up by local authorities in Scotland.

FINANCE

Budgeted aggregate external finance for 2005–6 is £8,087 million, comprising; £5,455 million revenue support grant, non-domestic rate income of £1,897 million and specific grants of £735 million. The non-domestic rate multiplier or poundage for 2005–6 is 46.1p. In 2005–6 a single owned property with a rateable value of £5,000 is eligible for 30 per cent small business rate relief. The average Band D council tax for 2005–6 is £1,094.

EXPENDITURE

The 2005–6 net expenditure budget estimates for local authorities in Scotland were:

Service	£m
Education	4,071.7
Cultural and related services	523.6
Social work services	1,982.9
Police	1,005.9
Roads and transport	515.4
Environmental services	463.6
Fire	276.8
Planning and development services	162.2
Other	1,243.0
Total	10,245.4

NORTHERN IRELAND

For the purpose of local government Northern Ireland has a system of 26 single-tier district councils.

ELECTIONS

Council members are elected for periods of four years at a time on the principle of proportional representation.

FUNCTIONS

The district councils have three main roles. These are:

Executive: responsibility for a wide range of local services including building regulations; community services; consumer protection; cultural facilities; environmental health; miscellaneous licensing and registration provisions, including dog control; litter prevention; recreational and social facilities; refuse collection and disposal; street cleaning; and tourist development

Representative: nominating representatives to sit as members of the various statutory bodies responsible for the administration of regional services such as drainage, education, fire, health and personal social services, housing, and libraries

Consultative: acting as the medium through which the views of local people are expressed on the operation in their area of other regional services – notably conservation (including water supply and sewerage services), planning and roads – provided by those departments of central government which have an obligation, statutory or otherwise, to consult the district councils about proposals affecting their areas

FINANCE

Local government in Northern Ireland is funded by a system of rates. The ratepayer receives a combined tax bill consisting of the regional rate and the district rate, which is set by each district council. The regional and district rates are both collected by the Rate Collection Agency. The product of the district rates is paid over to each council whilst the product of the regional rate supports expenditure by the departments of the Executive and Assembly. Rate bills are calculated by multiplying the property's Net Annual Value (NAV) by the regional and district rate poundages respectively. A general revaluation of non-domestic properties became effective from 1 April 2003, based on 2001 rental values, however the values of domestic properties continue to be based on 1976 rental values.

For 2005–6 the overall average domestic poundage is 315.61p and the overall average non-domestic rate poundage is 45.78p.

POLITICAL COMPOSITION OF LOCAL COUNCILS

As at July 2005

Abbreviations

All.	Alliance
BNP	British National Party
C.	Conservative
DUP	Democratic Unionist Party
Green	Green
Ind.	Independent
Ind. Un.	Independent Unionist
IF	Island First
Lab.	Labour
LD	Liberal Democrat
Lib.	Liberal
O.	Other
PC	Plaid Cymru
R	Residents Associations/Ratepayers
SD	Social Democrat
SDLP	Social Democratic and Labour Party
SF	Sinn Fein
SNP	Scottish National Party
Soc.	Socialist
UUP	Ulster Unionist Party
v.	Vacant
WP	Workers Party

Total number of seats is given in brackets after council name

ENGLAND

COUNTY COUNCILS

Bedfordshire (52)	C. 36; LD 9; Lab. 7
Buckinghamshire (57)	C. 44; LD 11; Lab. 2
Cambridgeshire (62)	C. 42; LD 16; Lab. 4
Cheshire (51)	C. 26; Lab. 16; LD 8; Ind. 1
Cornwall (82)	LD 48; Ind. 20; C. 9; Lab. 5
Cumbria (84)	Lab. 39; C. 32; LD 11; Ind. 2
Derbyshire (64)	Lab. 38; C. 15; LD 10; Ind. 1
Devon (62)	LD 33; C. 22; Lab. 4; Ind. 2
Dorset (45)	C. 24; LD 16; Lab. 4; Ind. 1
Durham (63)	Lab. 54; LD 5; C. 2; Ind. 2
East Sussex (49)	C. 28; LD 14; Lab. 5; Ind. 1
Essex (75)	C. 52; Lab. 13; LD 8; Ind. 2
Gloucestershire (63)	C. 33; Lab. 13; LD 13; O. 2; Ind. 1; R. 1
Hampshire (78)	C. 46; LD 28; Lab. 4
Hertfordshire (77)	C. 46; Lab. 15; LD 14; Green 1; v. 1
Kent (84)	C. 57; Lab. 21; LD 6
Lancashire (84)	Lab. 44; C. 31; LD 6; Green 1; Ind. 1; O. 1
Leicestershire (55)	C. 30; Lab. 13; LD 12
Lincolnshire (77)	C. 45; Lab. 21; LD 8; Ind. 3
Norfolk (84)	C. 46; Lab. 22; LD 14; Green 2
North Yorkshire (72)	C. 43; LD 18; Lab. 9; Ind. 2
Northamptonshire (73)	C. 45; Lab. 21; LD 7
Northumberland (67)	Lab. 35; C. 14; LD 14; Ind. 4
Nottinghamshire (67)	Lab. 38; C. 25; LD 4
Oxfordshire (74)	C. 43; LD 17; Lab. 9; Green 5
Shropshire (48)	C. 25; LD 11; Lab. 9; Ind. 3
Somerset (58)	LD 30; C. 24; Lab. 4
Staffordshire (62)	Lab. 36; C. 22; LD 4
Suffolk (75)	C. 45; Lab. 22; LD 7; Ind. 1
Surrey (80)	C. 58; LD 12; R. 8; Lab. 2
Warwickshire (62)	C. 27; Lab. 23; LD 11; Ind. 1

West Sussex (70)	C. 46; LD 17; Lab. 7
Wiltshire (49)	C. 28, LD 16; Lab. 3; Ind. 2
Worcestershire (57)	C. 29; Lab. 17; LD 8; Ind. 3

DISTRICT COUNCILS

Adur (29)	C. 25; Ind. 2; Lab. 2
Allerdale (56)	Lab. 27; C. 15; LD 5; Ind. 4
Alnwick (30)	Ind. 18; LD 10; Lab. 2
Amber Valley (45)	C. 24; Lab. 21
Arun (56)	C. 35; LD 10; Lab. 8; Ind. 3
Ashfield (33)	Lab. 18; Ind. 12; Green 2; C. 1
Ashford (43)	C. 25; Ind. 9; LD 5; Lab. 4
Aylesbury Vale (59)	C. 30; LD 25; Ind. 4
Babergh (43)	LD 18; C. 11; Ind. 7; Lab. 6; O. 1
Barrow-in-Furness (38)	Lab. 24; C. 12; Ind. 2
Basildon (42)	C. 24; Lab. 15; LD 3
Basingstoke and Deane (60)	C. 28; LD 17; Lab. 12; Ind. 3
Bassetlaw (48)	C. 24; Lab. 17; Ind. 5; LD 1; O. 1
Bedford (54)	C. 16; Lab. 15; LD 13; Ind. 10
Berwick-upon-Tweed (29)	C. 14; Ind. 8; LD 7
Blaby (39)	C. 25; LD 9; Lab. 4; Ind. 1
Blyth Valley (50)	Lab. 35; LD 9; C. 3; Ind. 3
Bolsover (37)	Lab. 31; Ind. 4; R. 2
Boston (32)	C. 12; Lab. 11; Ind. 5; LD 4
Braintree (60)	C. 27; Lab. 20; Ind 7; LD 4; Green 2
Breckland (54)	C. 42; Lab. 8; Ind. 4
Brentwood (37)	C. 21; LD 13; Lab. 3
Bridgnorth (34)	C. 17; LD 8; Ind. 7; Lab. 2
Broadland (47)	C. 31; LD 11; Ind. 5
Bromsgrove (39)	C. 21; Ind. 7; Lab. 6; R. 4; LD 1
Broxbourne (38)	C. 35; Lab. 2; BNP 1
Broxtowe (44)	Lab. 15; C. 13; LD 12; Ind. 3; v. 1
Burnley (45)	Lab. 21; LD 11; BNP 6; C. 4; Ind. 3
Cambridge (42)	LD 28; Lab. 13; C. 1
Cannock Chase (41)	Lab. 17; LD 13; C. 10; v. 1
Canterbury (50)	C. 26; LD 17; Lab. 7
Caradon (42)	Ind. 22; LD 16; C. 3; Lab. 1
Carlisle (52)	Lab. 24; C. 20; LD 7; Ind. 1
Carrick (47)	LD 29; Ind. 9; C. 8; Lab. 1
Castle Morpeth (33)	C. 10; Lab. 9; Ind. 7; LD 6; Green 1
Castle Point (41)	C. 34; Ind. 6; v. 1
Charnwood (52)	C. 24; Lab. 21; LD 7
Chelmsford (57)	C. 35; LD 19; Lab. 2; Ind. 1
Cheltenham (40)	LD 18; C. 15; O. 5; Lab. 2
Cherwell (50)	C. 37; Lab. 10; LD 3
Chester (60)	LD 23; C. 20; Lab 16; Ind. 1
Chester-le-Street (34)	Lab. 29; Ind. 4; C. 1
Chesterfield (48)	LD 36; Lab. 12
Chichester (48)	C. 24; LD 21; Ind. 2; v. 1
Chiltern (40)	C. 27; LD 12; Ind. 1
Chorley (47)	Lab. 21; C. 20; Ind. 3; LD 3
Christchurch (24)	C. 16; LD 7; Ind. 1
Colchester (60)	C. 28; LD 22; Lab. 7; Ind. 3
Congleton (48)	C. 27; LD 14; O. 4; Ind. 3
Copeland (51)	Lab. 30; C. 16; Ind. 4; v. 1
Corby (29)	Lab. 18; C. 9; LD 2
Cotswolds (44)	C. 26; Ind. 9; LD 8; v. 1

Craven (30)	C. 13; Ind. 11; LD 6
Crawley (37)	Lab. 19; C. 16; LD 2
Crewe and Nantwich (56)	Lab. 22; C. 21; Ind. 7; LD 6
Dacorum (52)	C. 31; Lab. 14; LD 6; v. 1
Dartford (44)	C. 21; Lab. 16; R. 5; O. 2
Daventry (38)	C. 34; Lab. 3; LD 1
Derbyshire Dales (39)	C. 24; LD 9; Lab. 5; Ind. 1
Derwentside (55)	Lab. 38; Ind. 16; LD 1
Dover (45)	C. 22; Lab. 20; LD 3
Durham (50)	LD 30; Lab. 17; Ind. 3
Easington (51)	Lab. 45; Ind. 4; LD 2
East Cambridgeshire (39)	LD 17; C. 15; Ind. 7
East Devon (59)	C. 33; LD 17; Ind. 7; v. 2
East Dorset (36)	C. 24; LD 11; Ind. 1
East Hampshire (44)	C. 25; LD 18; v. 1
East Hertfordshire (50)	C. 40; LD 5; Ind. 4; v. 1
East Lindsey (60)	Ind. 30; C. 12; Lab. 12; LD 6
East Northamptonshire (36)	C. 33; Lab. 3
East Staffordshire (39)	C. 22; Lab. 16; LD 1
Eastbourne (27)	C. 14; LD 13
Eastleigh (44)	LD 32; C. 9; Lab. 3
Eden (38)	Ind. 26; C. 8; LD 4
Ellesmere Port and Neston (43)	Lab. 27; C. 13; LD 2; Ind. 1
Elmbridge (60)	R. 30; C. 21; LD 8; O. 1
Epping Forest (58)	C. 26; LD 14; R. 6; Ind. 5; Lab. 4; BNP 3
Epsom and Ewell (38)	R. 27; LD 6; Lab. 3; C. 2
Erewash (51)	C. 27; Lab. 20; LD 2; Ind. 1; v. 1
Exeter (40)	Lab. 18; LD 13; C. 5; Lib. 4
Fareham (31)	C. 22; LD 9
Fenland (40)	C. 36; Lab. 3; Ind. 1
Forest Heath (27)	C. 22; Ind. 5
Forest of Dean (48)	C. 17; Lab. 14; Ind. 10; LD 4; O. 2; v. 1
Fylde (51)	C. 26; Ind. 15; R. 8; Lib. 2
Gedling (50)	C. 21; Lab. 21; LD 7; Ind. 1
Gloucester (36)	C. 16; LD 12; Lab. 8
Gosport (34)	C. 18; Lab. 11; LD 5
Gravesham (44)	Lab. 23; C. 21
Great Yarmouth (39)	C. 26; Lab. 13
Guildford (48)	C. 25; LD 20; Lab. 2; Ind. 1
Hambleton (44)	C. 36; Ind. 4; LD 3; Lab. 1
Harborough (37)	LD 18; C. 16; Ind. 2; Lab. 1
Harlow (33)	C. 13; Lab. 11; LD 9
Harrogate (54)	C. 29; LD 21; Ind. 2; O. 2
Hart (35)	C. 17; LD 12; O. 4; Ind. 2
Hastings (32)	Lab. 14; C. 13; LD 5
Havant (38)	C. 27; Lab. 6; LD 5
Hertsmere (39)	C. 26; Lab. 7; LD 6
High Peak (43)	Lab. 17; C. 12; LD 8; Ind. 5; v. 1
Hinckley and Bosworth (34)	C. 19; LD 9; Lab. 6
Horsham (44)	C. 22; LD 19; Ind. 2; v. 1
Huntingdonshire (52)	C. 39; LD 10; Ind. 3
Hyndburn (35)	C. 18; Lab. 16; v. 1
Ipswich (48)	Lab. 23; C. 18; LD 7
Kennet (43)	C. 28; Ind. 8; LD 3; O. 3; Lab. 1
Kerrier (44)	Ind. 21; LD 9; Lab. 5; C. 4; O. 4; Lib. 1
Kettering (45)	C. 30; Lab. 13; Ind. 2
King's Lynn and West Norfolk (62)	C. 38; Lab. 14; LD 7; Ind. 3
Lancaster (60)	Lab. 20; Ind. 14; C. 11; LD 8; Green 7
Lewes (41)	LD 27; C. 11; Ind. 3
Lichfield (56)	C. 35; Lab. 16; LD 5
Lincoln City (33)	Lab. 25; C. 7; LD 1
Macclesfield (60)	C. 35; LD 14; Lab. 6; R. 3; Ind. 2
Maidstone (55)	C. 23; LD 20; Lab. 8; Ind. 4
Maldon (31)	C. 21; Ind. 8; Lab. 2
Malvern Hills (38)	LD 20; C. 12; Ind. 5; Green 1
Mansfield (46)	Ind. 26; Lab. 13; LD 4; O. 2; C. 1
Melton (28)	C. 18; Ind. 6; Lab. 4
Mendip (46)	C. 29; LD 12; Ind. 5
Mid Bedfordshire (53)	C. 38; LD 11; Ind. 4
Mid Devon (42)	Ind. 20; C. 13; LD 8; Green 1
Mid Suffolk (40)	C. 20; LD 10; Ind. 5; Green 2, Lab. 2; v. 1
Mid Sussex (54)	C. 28; LD 24; Lab. 2
Mole Valley (41)	C. 19; LD 17; Ind. 5
New Forest (60)	C. 32; LD 27; Ind. 1
Newark and Sherwood (46)	C. 23; Lab. 12; Ind. 7; LD 4
Newcastle-under Lyme (60)	Lab. 32; C. 14; LD 12; Ind. 2
North Cornwall (36)	Ind. 19; LD 13; C. 3; O. 1
North Devon (43)	LD 21; Ind. 12; C. 9; v. 1
North Dorset (33)	C. 15; LD 12; Ind. 6
North East Derbyshire (53)	Lab. 35; C. 8; LD 6; Ind. 3; v. 1
North Hertfordshire (49)	C. 28; Lab. 14; LD 7
North Kesteven (40)	C. 18; Ind. 13; LD 5; Lab. 4
North Norfolk (48)	LD 28; O. 15; Ind. 4, v.1
North Shropshire (40)	Ind. 20; C. 16; Lab. 4
North Warwickshire (35)	Lab. 16; C. 15; LD 4
North West Leicestershire (38)	Lab. 21; C. 12; LD 3; Ind. 2
North Wiltshire (53)	LD 26; C. 25; Ind. 1; Lab. 1
Northampton (47)	C. 20; LD 16; Lab. 10; Ind. 1
Norwich (39)	LD 18; Lab. 15; Green 5; C. 1
Nuneaton and Bedworth (34)	Lab. 22; C. 10; LD 1; v. 1
Oadby and Wigston (26)	LD 17; C. 9
Oswestry (29)	Ind. 10; C. 7; LD 7; O. 4; Lab. 1
Oxford (48)	Lab. 20; LD 18; Green 7; Ind. 3
Pendle (49)	LD 30; C. 12; Lab. 7
Penwith (35)	LD 14; C. 12; Ind. 9
Preston (57)	Lab. 23; C. 18; LD 11; Ind. 3; O. 2
Purbeck (24)	C. 14; LD 8; Ind. 2
Redditch (29)	Lab. 16; C. 10; LD 3
Reigate and Banstead (51)	C. 36; R 6; LD 5; Lab. 3; Ind. 1
Restormel (45)	LD 23; Ind. 13; C. 8; O. 1
Ribble Valley (40)	C. 22; LD 15; Ind. 2; Lab. 1
Richmondshire (34)	Ind. 14; C. 11; LD 8; SD 1
Rochford (39)	C. 31; LD 4; Ind. 1; Lab. 1; R 1; v. 1
Rossendale (36)	C. 24; Lab. 9; LD 2; Ind. 1
Rother (38)	C. 25; LD 7; Ind. 3; Lab. 3
Rugby (48)	C. 21; Lab. 14; LD 10; Ind. 3
Runnymede (42)	C. 33; Ind. 6; Lab. 3
Rushcliffe (50)	C. 33; LD 10; Lab. 4; Ind. 2; Green 1
Rushmoor (42)	C. 23; LD 11; Lab. 5; Ind. 3
Ryedale (30)	C. 12; Ind. 7; LD 7; Lib. 2; R. 2
St Albans (58)	LD 29; C. 17; Lab. 11; Ind. 1
St Edmundsbury (45)	C. 28; Lab. 10; Ind. 5; LD 2
Salisbury (55)	C. 30; Lab. 11; LD 9; Ind. 5

Scarborough (50) | C. 26; Ind. 14; Lab. 8; LD 2
Sedgefield (50) | Lab. 34; Ind. 8; LD 7; C. 1
Sedgemoor (50) | C. 35; Lab. 14; LD 1
Selby (41) | C. 23; Lab. 14; Ind. 3; LD 1
Sevenoaks (54) | C. 33; Lab. 10; LD 8; Ind. 3
Shepway (46) | C. 17; LD 15; O. 10; Green 1; Ind. 1; v. 2
Shrewsbury and Atcham (40) | C. 20; Lab. 11; LD 6; Ind. 3
South Bedfordshire (50) | C. 34; LD 12; Lab. 4
South Bucks (40) | C. 32; Ind. 6; LD 1; v. 1
South Cambridgeshire (57) | C. 23; LD 19; Ind. 13; Lab. 2
South Derbyshire (36) | Lab. 21; C. 14; Ind. 1
South Hams (40) | C. 28; LD 7; Ind. 2; Lab. 2; O. 1
South Holland (38) | C. 27; Ind. 10; O. 1
South Kesteven (58) | C. 32; Ind. 12; Lab. 10; LD 4
South Lakeland (52) | LD 22; C. 20; Lab. 8; Ind. 2
South Norfolk (46) | LD 28; C. 18
South Northamptonshire (42) | C. 29; Ind. 9; Lab. 4
South Oxfordshire (48) | C. 28; LD 9; Lab. 4; R. 4; Ind. 3
South Ribble (55) | C. 18; Lab. 17; LD 15; O. 4; Ind. 1
South Shropshire (34) | LD 14; C. 10; Ind. 8; O. 2
South Somerset (60) | LD 37; C. 16; Ind. 7
South Staffordshire (49) | C. 35; Lab. 8; Ind. 4; LD 1; O. 1
Spelthorne (39) | C. 35; LD 4
Stafford (59) | C. 40; Lab. 14; LD 5
Staffordshire Moorlands (56) | C. 21; R. 13; LD 11; Lab. 7; Ind. 3; O. 1
Stevenage (39) | Lab. 32; LD 4; C. 3
Stratford-on-Avon (53) | C. 30; LD 20; Ind. 3
Stroud (51) | C. 27; Lab. 11; LD 6; Green 4; Ind. 3
Suffolk Coastal (55) | C. 42; LD 11; Lab. 2
Surrey Heath (40) | C. 22; LD 13; Lab. 3; Ind. 2
Swale (47) | C. 26; Lab. 11; LD 10
Tamworth (30) | C. 16; Lab. 13; Ind. 1
Tandridge (42) | C. 27; LD 11; Ind. 2; Lab. 2
Taunton Deane (54) | C. 31; LD 15; Lab. 5; Ind. 3
Teesdale (32) | Ind. 11; Lab. 9; O. 9; C. 3
Teignbridge (46) | LD 17; Ind. 15; C. 14
Tendring (60) | C. 25; LD 13; Lab. 11; Ind. 7; O. 4
Test Valley (48) | C. 30; LD 17; Ind. 1
Tewkesbury (38) | C. 18; LD 9; Ind. 5; Lab. 3; R. 3
Thanet (56) | C. 31; Lab. 23; Ind. 1; LD. 1
Three Rivers (48) | LD 29; C. 12; Lab. 7
Tonbridge and Malling (53) | C. 34; LD 12; Lab. 7
Torridge (36) | Ind. 19; O. 8; LD 7; C. 2
Tunbridge Wells (48) | C. 36; LD 10; Lab. 1; v. 1
Tynedale (52) | C. 27; LD 11; Lab. 10; Ind. 4
Uttlesford (44) | LD 31; C. 10; Ind. 3
Vale of White Horse (51) | LD 30; C. 20; Ind. 1
Vale Royal (57) | C. 24; Lab. 20; LD 11; Ind. 2
Wansbeck (45) | Lab. 37; LD 8
Warwick (46) | C. 16; Lab. 14; LD 10; Ind. 6
Watford (37) | LD 28; C. 4; Lab. 3; Green 2
Waveney (48) | C. 25; Lab. 13; Ind. 7; LD 3
Waverley (57) | LD 28; C. 27; Ind. 2
Wealden (55) | C. 34; LD 15; Ind. 6
Wear Valley (40) | Lab. 25; LD 10; Ind. 5

Wellingborough (36) | C. 26; Lab. 9; Ind. 1
Welwyn & Hatfield (48) | C. 31; Lab. 13; Green; 1; Lib. 1; v. 2
West Devon (31) | C. 12; Ind. 11; LD 8
West Dorset (48) | C. 26; LD 12; Ind. 10
West Lancashire (54) | C. 29; Lab. 25
West Lindsey (37) | C. 19; LD 16; Ind. 2
West Oxfordshire (49) | C. 28; LD 13; Ind. 7; Lab. 1
West Somerset (31) | C. 18; Ind. 8; Lab. 2; LD 2; v. 1
West Wiltshire (44) | C. 19; LD 18; Ind. 4; Lab. 3
Weymouth and Portland (36) | LD 14; Lab. 9; C. 8; Ind. 5
Winchester (57) | LD 26; C. 21; Ind. 6; Lab. 4
Woking (36) | C. 17; LD 15; Lab. 4
Worcester (35) | C. 18; Lab. 10; Ind. 4; LD 3
Worthing (37) | C. 26; LD 11
Wychavon (45) | C. 31; LD 12; Lab. 2
Wycombe (60) | C. 45; Lab. 9; Ind. 3; LD 2; v. 1
Wyre (55) | C. 33; Lab. 21; LD 1
Wyre Forest (42) | C. 18; O. 16; Lab. 4; Ind. 2; LD 2

LONDON BOROUGH COUNCILS

Barking and Dagenham (51) | Lab. 41; C. 3; LD 3; R. 2; v. 2
Barnet (63) | C. 33; Lab. 24; LD 6
Bexley (63) | Lab. 32; C. 30; LD 1
Brent (63) | Lab. 34; C. 17; LD 10; v. 2
Bromley (60) | C. 40; LD 13; Lab. 6; Ind. 1
Camden (54) | Lab. 35; C. 11; LD 8
Croydon (70) | Lab. 37; C. 31; LD 2
Ealing (69) | Lab. 48; C. 17; LD 4
Enfield (63) | C. 39; Lab. 24
Greenwich (51) | Lab. 38; C. 9; LD 4
Hackney (57) | Lab. 46; C. 8; LD 3
Hammersmith and Fulham (46) | Lab. 29; C. 17
Haringey (57) | Lab. 41; LD 16
Harrow (63) | Lab. 30; C. 28; LD 3; Ind. 2
Havering (54) | C. 26; R 17; Lab. 11
Hillingdon (65) | C. 30; Lab. 27; LD 8
Hounslow (60) | Lab. 36; C. 13; LD 5; O. 4; Ind. 1; v. 1
Islington (48) | LD 36; Lab. 10; Ind. 2
Kensington and Chelsea (54) | C. 41; Lab. 12; LD 1
Kingston upon Thames (48) | LD 30; C. 15; Lab. 3
Lambeth (63) | Lab. 29; LD 27; C. 7
Lewisham (54) | Lab. 40; LD 8; C. 2; Soc. 2; Ind. 1; Green 1
Merton (60) | Lab. 33; C. 24; R 3
Newham (60) | Lab. 59; O. 1
Redbridge (63) | C. 33; Lab. 20; LD 9; Ind. 1
Richmond upon Thames (54) | C. 34; LD 19; Ind. 1
Southwark (63) | LD 29; Lab. 26; C. 6; Ind. 2
Sutton (54) | LD 43; C. 8; Lab. 3
Tower Hamlets (51) | Lab. 31; LD 15; Ind. 2; O. 2; C. 1
Waltham Forest (60) | Lab. 27; C. 18; LD 15
Wandsworth (60) | C. 50; Lab. 10
Westminster (60) | C. 48; Lab. 11; v. 1

METROPOLITAN BOROUGH COUNCILS

Barnsley (63) | Lab. 33; Ind. 22; C. 5; LD 3
Birmingham (120) | Lab. 46; C. 39; LD 31; O. 3; v. 1
Bolton (60) | LD 21; Lab. 20; C. 19
Bradford (90) | C. 38; Lab. 29; LD 15; BNP 4; Green 4

Bury (51) Lab. 27; C. 19; LD 5
Calderdale (51) C. 21; LD 15; Lab. 9; BNP 3; Ind. 3
Coventry (54) C. 27; Lab. 20; LD 3; Ind. 2; Soc. 2
Doncaster (63) Lab. 28; LD 12; C. 9; Ind. 9; O. 5
Dudley (72) C. 40; Lab. 25; LD 6; Ind. 1
Gateshead (66) Lab. 43; LD 22; Lib. 1
Kirklees (69) LD 24; C. 22; Lab. 18; Green 3; BNP 1; Ind. 1
Knowsley (63) Lab. 51; LD 11; v. 1
Leeds (99) Lab. 40; LD 26; C. 24; Ind. 6; Green 3
Liverpool (90) LD 60; Lab 27; Lib. 3
Manchester (96) Lab. 57; LD 38; Green 1
Newcastle-upon-Tyne (78) LD 48; Lab. 30
North Tyneside (60) C. 27; Lab. 24; LD 7; Ind. 1; v. 1
Oldham (60) Lab 33; LD 25; C. 2
Rochdale (60) LD 27; Lab. 24; C. 9
Rotherham (63) Lab. 53; C. 7; Ind. 3
St Helens (48) Lab. 24; LD 18; C. 6
Salford (60) Lab. 44; C. 8; LD 7; v. 1
Sandwell (72) Lab. 53; C. 12; LD 5; BNP 1; Ind. 1
Sefton (66) LD 27; Lab. 20; C. 19
Sheffield (84) Lab. 44; LD 37; C. 2; Green 1
Solihull (51) C. 26; LD 15; Lab. 8; Ind 1; v. 1
South Tyneside (54) Lab. 35; Ind. 6; O. 6; LD 4; C. 3
Stockport (63) LD 35; Lab. 14; C. 10; R. 3; Ind. 1
Sunderland (75) Lab. 61; C. 12; LD 2
Tameside (57) Lab. 43; C. 8; LD 3; Ind. 1
Trafford (63) C. 40; Lab. 20; LD 3
Wakefield (63) Lab. 44; C. 10; Ind. 6; LD 3
Walsall (60) C. 36; Lab. 15; LD 6; Ind. 1; v. 2
Wigan (75) Lab. 41; O. 18; LD 8; C. 7; v. 1
Wirral (66) Lab. 26; C. 21; LD 19
Wolverhampton (60) Lab. 41; C. 16; LD 3

UNITARY COUNCILS

Bath and North East Somerset (65) LD 29; C. 26; Lab. 6; Ind. 4
Blackburn with Darwen (64) Lab. 34; C. 17; LD 12; Ind. 1
Blackpool (42) Lab. 25; C. 13; LD 4
Bournemouth (54) LD 31; C. 18; Lab. 3; Ind. 2
Bracknell Forest (42) Lab. 34; C. 6; Ind. 1; LD 1
Brighton and Hove (54) Lab. 23; C. 20; Green 6; LD 3; Ind. 2
Bristol (70) LD 32; Lab. 27; C. 11
Darlington (53) Lab. 35; C. 16; LD 2
Derby (51) Lab. 26; LD 13; C. 11; O. 1
East Riding of Yorkshire (67) C. 28; LD 23; Lab. 8; Ind. 6; SD 2
Halton (55) Lab. 34; LD 14; C. 7
Hartlepool (47) Lab. 25; Ind. 9; LD 9; C. 4
Herefordshire (58) C. 21; Ind. 17; LD 16; Lab. 4
Isle of Wight (48) C. 35; LD 5; Ind. 4; Lab. 2; O. 2
Kingston-upon-Hull (59) Lab. 27; LD 22; Ind. 5; Lib. 3; C. 2
Leicester (54) LD 23; Lab. 20; C. 10; Ind. 1
Luton (48) Lab. 22; LD 20; C. 4; Ind. 2
Medway (55) C. 30; Lab. 17; LD 6; Ind. 2
Middlesbrough (48) Lab. 29; C. 7; Ind. 6; LD 6
Milton Keynes (51) LD 27; Lab. 16; C. 7; Ind. 1
North East Lincolnshire (42) C. 16; LD 15; Lab. 7; Ind. 4

North Lincolnshire (43) C. 23; Lab. 20
North Somerset (61) LD 24; C. 23; Lab. 10; Ind. 3; Green 1
Nottingham (55) Lab. 38; LD 9; C. 7; Ind. 1
Peterborough (57) C. 33, Lab. 7; Ind. 6; O. 6; LD 4; v. 1
Plymouth (57) Lab. 35; C. 19; LD 2; Ind. 1
Poole (42) C. 26; LD 16
Portsmouth (42) LD 21; C. 14; Lab. 7
Reading (46) Lab. 35; C. 6; LD 5
Redcar and Cleveland (59) Lab. 23; LD 16; C. 13; Ind. 7
Rutland (26) C. 14; Ind. 6; LD 4; O. 2
Slough (41) Lab. 15; Ind. 10; C. 7; LD 6; Lib. 3
South Gloucestershire (70) LD 32; C. 21; Lab 16; Ind. 1
Southampton (48) LD 18; C. 15; Lab. 15
Southend-on-Sea (51) C. 31; Lab. 9; LD 7; Ind. 4
Stockton-on-Tees (56) Lab. 27; C. 12; Ind. 9; LD 8
Stoke-on-Trent (60) Lab. 33; Ind. 11; C. 5; LD 5; O. 4; BNP 2
Swindon (59) C. 33; Lab. 18; LD 5; Ind. 3
Telford and Wrekin (54) Lab. 27; C. 14; Ind. 8; LD 5
Thurrock (49) C. 28; Lab. 19; Ind. 2
Torbay (36) LD 23; C. 11; Ind. 2
Warrington (57) Lab. 30; LD 21; C. 6
West Berkshire (52) C. 27; LD 25
Windsor and Maidenhead (57) LD 34; C. 16; Ind 6; Lab. 1
Wokingham (54) C. 38; LD 16
York (47) LD 29; Lab. 15; Green 2; Ind. 1

WALES

Blaenau Gwent (42) Lab. 31; Ind. 8; LD 3
Bridgend (54) Lab. 22; LD 13; Ind. 10; C. 8; PC 1
Caerphilly (73) Lab. 39; PC 26; Ind. 8
Cardiff (75) LD 32; Lab. 27; C. 12; PC 4
Carmarthenshire (74) Ind. 31; Lab. 25; PC 16; C. 1; O. 1
Ceredigion (42) Ind. 16; PC 16; LD 9; Lab. 1
Conwy (59) Ind. 18; C. 12; Lab. 12; PC 10; LD 6; v. 1
Denbighshire (47) Ind. 19; C. 8; Lab. 8; PC 7; O. 3; LD 2
Flintshire (70) Lab. 37; Ind. 17; LD 10; C. 4; PC 1; O. 1
Gwynedd (75) PC 43; Ind. 16; Lab. 9; LD 6; O. 1
Merthyr Tydfil (33) Lab. 16; Ind. 9; O. 8
Monmouthshire (43) C. 23; Lab. 9; Ind. 5; LD 4; PC 2
Neath Port Talbot (64) Lab. 36; PC 10; R. 9; Ind. 4; SD 3; LD 2
Newport (50) Lab. 31; C. 11; LD 6; Ind. 1; PC 1
Pembrokeshire (60) Ind. 38; Lab. 12; PC 5; LD 3; O. 2
Powys (73) Ind. 55; LD 14; Lab. 4
Rhondda Cynon Taff (75) Lab. 57; PC 13; Ind. 3; LD 2
Swansea (72) Lab. 32; LD 20; Ind. 11; C. 4; PC 4; O. 1
Torfaen (44) Lab. 34; Ind. 8; C. 1; LD 1
Vale of Glamorgan (47) C. 20; Lab. 16; PC 8; Ind. 3
Wrexham (52) Ind. 25; Lab. 19; C. 4; O. 4
YNYS MON (Isle of Anglesey) (40) Ind. 28; PC 7; C. 2; Lab. 1; LD 1; O. 1

SCOTLAND

Aberdeen (43)	LD 20; Lab. 14; SNP 6; C. 3
Aberdeenshire (68)	LD 28; SNP 15; Ind. 14; C. 11
Angus (29)	SNP 17; Ind. 6; LD 3; C. 2; Lab. 1
Argyll and Bute (36)	Ind. 24; LD 7; SNP 3; C. 2
Clackmannanshire (18)	Lab. 10; SNP 7; C. 1
Dumfries and Galloway (47)	Lab. 14; Ind. 12; O. 11; LD 5; SNP 5
Dundee (29)	SNP 11; Lab. 10; C. 5; LD 2; Ind. 1
East Ayrshire (32)	Lab. 23; SNP 8; C. 1
East Dunbartonshire (24)	LD 12; Lab. 7; C. 3; Ind. 2
East Lothian (23)	Lab. 16; C. 4; LD 1; SNP 1; Ind. 1
East Renfrewshire (20)	Lab. 8; C. 7; LD 3; Ind. 2
Edinburgh (58)	Lab. 30; LD 15; C. 13
Eilean Siar (Western Isles) (31)	O. 31; Lab. 4; SNP 3
Falkirk (32)	Lab. 13; SNP 10; Ind. 6; C. 2; v. 1
Fife (78)	Lab. 36; LD 23; SNP 11; Ind. 3; O. 3; C. 2
Glasgow (79)	Lab. 71; LD 3; SNP 3; C. 1; Soc. 1
Highland (80)	Ind. 57; LD 9; Lab. 8; SNP 6
Inverclyde (20)	LD 13; Lab. 6; Ind. 1
Midlothian (18)	Lab. 14; LD 3; Ind. 1
Moray (26)	Ind. 16; Lab. 5; SNP 3; C. 1; LD 1
North Ayrshire (30)	Lab. 20; C. 5; SNP 3; Ind. 2
North Lanarkshire (70)	Lab. 54; SNP 11; Ind. 4; v. 1
Orkney Islands (21)	Ind. 21
Perth and Kinross (41)	SNP 15; C. 10; LD 9; Lab. 5; Ind. 2
Renfrewshire (40)	Lab. 21; SNP 15; LD 3; C. 1
Scottish Borders (34)	C. 11; Ind. 11; LD 8; SNP 2; O. 2
Shetland Islands (22)	Ind. 17; LD 5
South Ayrshire (30)	C. 15; Lab. 15
South Lanarkshire (67)	Lab. 50; SNP 10; C. 3; LD 2; Ind. 2
Stirling (22)	Lab. 12; C. 10
West Dunbartonshire (22)	Lab. 17; SNP 2; Ind. 2; Soc. 1
West Lothian (32)	Lab. 18; SNP 11; Ind. 2; C. 1

NORTHERN IRELAND

Antrim (19)	DUP 6; UUP 5; SF 3; All. 2; SDLP 2; Ind. 1
Ards (23)	DUP 12; UUP 7; All. 3; SDLP 1
Armagh City (22)	DUP 6; SDLP 6; SF 5; UUP 5
Ballymena (24)	DUP 14; UUP 5; SDLP 3; Ind. 1; SF 1
Ballymoney (16)	DUP 8; SF 3; SDLP 2; UUP 2; Ind. 1
Banbridge (17)	DUP 7; UUP 5; SDLP 3; All. 1; SF 1
Belfast (51)	DUP 15; SF 14; SDLP 8; UUP 7; All. 4; O. 2; Ind. 1
Carrickfergus (17)	DUP 8; UUP 4; All. 3; Ind. 2
Castlereagh (23)	DUP 13; All. 4; UUP 4; SDLP 2
Coleraine (22)	DUP 10; UUP 8; SDLP 3; Ind. 1
Cookstown (16)	SDLP 5; SF 5; DUP 3; UUP 3
Craigavon (26)	DUP 9; SF 6; UUP 6; SDLP 4; Ind. Un. 1
Derry City (30)	SDLP 14; SF 10; DUP 5; UUP 1
Down (23)	SDLP 10; SF 5; UUP 4; DUP 3; Green 1
Dungannon and South Tyrone (22)	SF 9; DUP 5; SDLP 4; UUP 4
Fermanagh (23)	SF 9; SDLP 5; UUP 5; DUP 4
Larne (15)	DUP 5; UUP 4; All. 2; Ind. 2; SDLP 2
Limavady (15)	SF 6; DUP 3; SDLP 3; UUP 2; Ind. 1
Lisburn (30)	DUP 13; UUP 7; SF 4; All. 3; SDLP 3
Magherafelt (16)	SF 8; DUP 4; SDLP 2; UUP 2
Moyle (15)	SF 4; DUP 3; Ind. 3; SDLP 3; UUP 2
Newry and Mourne (30)	SF 13; SDLP 9; UUP 3; DUP 2; Ind. 2; Green 1
Newtownabbey (25)	DUP 12; UUP 6; All. 2; R. 2; Ind. 1; SDLP 1; SF 1
North Down (25)	DUP 8; UUP 8; All. 6; Ind. 2; Green 1
Omagh (21)	SF 10; DUP 3; SDLP 3; UUP 3; Ind. 2
Strabane (16)	SF 8; DUP 3; SDLP 2; UUP 2; Ind. 1

ENGLAND

The Kingdom of England lies between 55° 46′ and 49° 57′ 30″ N. latitude (from a few miles north of the mouth of the Tweed to the Lizard), and between 1° 46′ E. and 5° 43′ W. longitude (from Lowestoft to Land's End). England is bounded on the north by the Cheviot Hills; on the south by the English Channel; on the east by the Straits of Dover (Pas de Calais) and the North Sea; and on the west by the Atlantic Ocean, Wales and the Irish Sea. It has a total area of 130,410 sq. km (50,351 sq. miles): land 129,652 sq. km (50,058 sq. miles); inland water 758 sq. km (293 sq. miles).

POPULATION
The population at the 2001 census was 49,138,831. The average density of the population in 2001 was 3.8 persons per hectare.

FLAG
The flag of England is the cross of St George, a red cross on a white field (cross gules in a field argent). The cross of St George, the patron saint of England, has been used since the 13th century.

RELIEF
There is a marked division between the upland and lowland areas of England. In the extreme north the Cheviot Hills (highest point, the Cheviot, 815 m/2,674 ft) form a natural boundary with Scotland. Running south from the Cheviots, though divided from them by the Tyne Gap, is the Pennine range (highest point, Cross Fell, 893 m/2,930 ft), the main orological feature of the country. The Pennines culminate in the Peak District of Derbyshire (Kinder Scout, 636 m/2,088 ft). West of the Pennines are the Cumbrian mountains, which include Scafell Pike (978 m/3,210 ft), the highest peak in England, and to the east are the Yorkshire Moors, their highest point being Urra Moor (454 m/1,490 ft).

In the west, the foothills of the Welsh mountains extend into the bordering English counties of Shropshire (the Wrekin, 407 m/1,334 ft; Long Mynd, 516 m/1,694 ft) and Hereford and Worcester (the Malvern Hills – Worcestershire Beacon, 425 m/1,394 ft). Extensive areas of highland and moorland are also to be found in the south-western peninsula formed by Somerset, Devon and Cornwall, principally Exmoor (Dunkery Beacon, 519 m/1,704 ft), Dartmoor (High Willhays, 621 m/2,038 ft) and Bodmin Moor (Brown Willy, 420 m/1,377 ft). Ranges of low, undulating hills run across the south of the country, including the Cotswolds in the Midlands and south-west, the Chilterns to the north of London, and the North (Kent) and South (Sussex) Downs of the south-east coastal areas.

The lowlands of England lie in the Vale of York, East Anglia and the area around the Wash. The lowest-lying are the Cambridgeshire Fens in the valleys of the Great Ouse and the River Nene, which are below sea-level in places. Since the 17th century extensive drainage has brought much of the Fens under cultivation. The North Sea coast between the Thames and the Humber, low-lying and formed of sand and shingle for the most part, is subject to erosion and defences against further incursion have been built along many stretches.

HYDROGRAPHY
The Severn is the longest river in Great Britain, rising in the north-eastern slopes of Plynlimon (Wales) and entering England in Shropshire with a total length of 354 km (220 miles) from its source to its outflow into the Bristol Channel, where it receives the Bristol Avon on the east and the Wye on the west; its other tributaries are the Vyrnwy, Tern, Stour, Teme and Upper (or Warwickshire) Avon. The Severn is tidal below Gloucester, and a high bore or tidal wave sometimes reverses the flow as high as Tewkesbury (21.75 km/13.5 miles above Gloucester). The scenery of the greater part of the river is very picturesque, and the Severn is a noted salmon river, with some of its tributaries being famous for trout. Navigation is assisted by the Gloucester and Berkeley Ship Canal (26 km/16.25 miles), which admits vessels of 350 tons to Gloucester. The Severn Tunnel was begun in 1873 and completed in 1886 at a cost of £2 million and after many difficulties caused by flooding. It is 7 km (4 miles 628 yards) in length (of which 3.67 km/2.25 miles are under the river). The Severn road bridge between Haysgate, Gwent, and Almondsbury, Glos, with a centre span of 988 m (3,240 ft), was opened in 1966.

The longest river wholly in England is the Thames, with a total length of 346 km (215 miles) from its source in the Cotswold hills to the Nore, and is navigable by ocean-going ships to London Bridge. The Thames is tidal to Teddington (111 km/69 miles from its mouth) and forms county boundaries almost throughout its course; on its banks are situated London, Windsor Castle, Eton College and Oxford University. Of the remaining English rivers, those flowing into the North Sea are the Tyne, Wear, Tees, Ouse and Trent from the Pennine Range, Great Ouse (257 km/160 miles), which rises in Northamptonshire, and the Orwell and Stour from the hills of East Anglia. Flowing into the English Channel are the Sussex Ouse from the Weald, the Itchen from the Hampshire Hills, and the Axe, Teign, Dart, Tamar and Exe from the Devonian hills. Flowing into the Irish Sea are the Mersey, Ribble and Eden from the western slopes of the Pennines and the Derwent from the Cumbrian mountains.

The English Lakes, noteworthy for their picturesque scenery and poetic associations, lie in Cumbria's Lake District; the largest are Windermere (16 km/10 miles long), Ullswater and Derwent Water.

ISLANDS
The Isle of Wight is separated from Hampshire by the Solent. The capital, Newport, stands at the head of the estuary of the Medina, and Cowes (at the mouth) is the chief port. Other centres are Ryde, Sandown, Shanklin, Ventnor, Freshwater, Yarmouth, Totland Bay, Seaview and Bembridge.

Lundy (the name means Puffin Island), 18 km (11 miles) north-west of Hartland Point, Devon, is about five km (three miles) long and almost one km (half a mile) wide on average, with a total area of about 452 hectares (1,116 acres), and a population of about 18. It became the property of the National Trust in 1969 and is now principally a bird sanctuary.

The Isles of Scilly comprise about 140 islands and skerries (total area, 10 sq. km/6 sq. miles) situated 45 km

(28 miles) south-west of Land's End in Cornwall. Only five are inhabited: St Mary's, St Agnes, Bryher, Tresco and St Martin's. The population at the 2001 census was 2,153. The entire group has been designated a Conservation Area, a Heritage Coast, and an Area of Outstanding Natural Beauty, and has been given National Nature Reserve status by the Nature Conservancy Council because of its unique flora and fauna. Tourism and the winter/spring flower trade for the home market form the basis of the economy of the Isles. The island group is a recognised rural development area.

EARLY HISTORY

Archaeological evidence suggests that England has been inhabited since at least the Palaeolithic period, though the extent of the various Palaeolithic cultures was dependent upon the degree of glaciation. The succeeding Neolithic and Bronze Age cultures have left abundant remains throughout the country; the best-known of these are the henges and stone circles of Stonehenge (ten miles north of Salisbury, Wilts) and Avebury (Wilts), both of which are believed to have been of religious significance. In the latter part of the Bronze Age the Goidels, a people of Celtic race, invaded the country and brought with them Celtic civilisation and dialects; as a result place names in England bear witness to the spread of the invasion over the whole kingdom.

THE ROMAN CONQUEST
The Roman conquest of Gaul (57–50 BC) brought Britain into close contact with Roman civilisation, but although Julius Caesar raided the south of Britain in 55 and 54 BC, conquest was not undertaken until nearly 100 years later. In AD 43 the Emperor Claudius dispatched Aulus Plautius, with a well-equipped force of 40,000, and himself followed with reinforcements in the same year. Success was delayed by the resistance of Caratacus (Caractacus), the British leader from AD 48–51, who was finally captured and sent to Rome, and by a great revolt in AD 61 led by Boudicca (Boadicea), Queen of the Iceni, but the south of Britain was secured by AD 70, and Wales and the area north to the Tyne by about AD 80.

In AD 122, the Emperor Hadrian visited Britain and built a continuous rampart, since known as Hadrian's Wall, from Wallsend to Bowness (Tyne to Solway). The work was entrusted by the Emperor Hadrian to Aulus Platorius Nepos, legate of Britain from AD 122 to 126, and it was intended to form the northern frontier of the Roman Empire.

The Romans administered Britain as a province under a Governor, with a well-defined system of local government, each Roman municipality ruling itself and its surrounding territory, while London was the centre of the road system and the seat of the financial officials of the Province of Britain. Colchester, Lincoln, York, Gloucester and St Albans stand on the sites of five Roman municipalities, and Wroxeter, Caerleon, Chester, Lincoln and York were at various times the sites of legionary fortresses. Well-preserved Roman towns have been uncovered at or near Silchester (Calleva Atrebatum), ten miles south of Reading, Wroxeter (Viroconium Cornoviorum), near Shrewsbury, and St Albans (Verulamium) in Hertfordshire.

Four main groups of roads radiated from London, and a fifth (the Fosse) ran obliquely from Lincoln through Leicester, Cirencester and Bath to Exeter. Of the four groups radiating from London, one ran south-east to Canterbury and the coast of Kent, a second to Silchester and thence to parts of western Britain and south Wales, a third (later known as Watling Street) ran through Verulamium to Chester, with various branches, and the fourth reached Colchester, Lincoln, York and the eastern counties.

In the fourth century Britain was subject to raids along the east coast by Saxon pirates, which led to the establishment of a system of coastal defences from the Wash to Southampton Water, with forts at Brancaster, Burgh Castle (Yarmouth), Walton (Felixstowe), Bradwell, Reculver, Richborough, Dover, Lympne, Pevensey and Porchester (Portsmouth). The Irish (Scoti) and Picts in the north were also becoming more aggressive and from about AD 350 incursions became more frequent and more formidable. As the Roman Empire came under attack increasingly towards the end of the fourth century, many troops were removed from Britain for service in other parts of the empire. The island was eventually cut off from Rome by the Teutonic conquest of Gaul, and with the withdrawal of the last Roman garrison early in the fifth century, the Romano-British were left to themselves.

SAXON SETTLEMENT
According to legend, the British King Vortigern called in the Saxons to defend him against the Picts, the Saxon chieftains being Hengist and Horsa, who landed at Ebbsfleet, Kent, and established themselves in the Isle of Thanet; but the events during the one-and-a-half centuries between the final break with Rome and the re-establishment of Christianity are unclear. However, it would appear that in the course of this period the raids turned into large-scale settlement by invaders traditionally known as Angles (England north of the Wash and East Anglia), Saxons (Essex and southern England) and Jutes (Kent and the Weald), which pushed the Romano-British into the mountainous areas of the north and west. Celtic culture outside Wales and Cornwall survives only in topographical names. Various kingdoms established at this time attempted to claim overlordship of the whole country, hegemony finally being achieved by Wessex (capital, Winchester) in the ninth century. This century also saw the beginning of raids by the Vikings (Danes), which were resisted by Alfred the Great (871–899), who fixed a limit to the advance of Danish settlement by the Treaty of Wedmore (878), giving them the area north and east of Watling Street on the condition that they adopt Christianity.

In the tenth century the kings of Wessex recovered the whole of England from the Danes, but subsequent rulers were unable to resist a second wave of invaders. England paid tribute (Danegeld) for many years, and was invaded in 1013 by the Danes and ruled by Danish kings from 1016 until 1042, when Edward the Confessor was recalled from exile in Normandy. On Edward's death in 1066 Harold Godwinson (brother-in-law of Edward and son of Earl Godwin of Wessex) was chosen to be King of England. After defeating (at Stamford Bridge, Yorkshire, 25 September) an invading army under Harald Hadraada, King of Norway (aided by the outlawed Earl Tostig of Northumbria, Harold's brother), Harold was himself defeated at the Battle of Hastings on 14 October 1066, and the Norman conquest secured the throne of England for Duke William of Normandy, a cousin of Edward the Confessor.

CHRISTIANITY

Christianity reached the Roman province of Britain from Gaul in the third century (or possibly earlier). Alban, traditionally Britain's first martyr, was put to death as a Christian during the persecution of Diocletian (22 June 303) at his native town *Verulamium*, and the Bishops of *Londinium*, *Eboracum* (York), and *Lindum* (Lincoln) attended the Council of Arles in 314. However, the Anglo-Saxon invasions submerged the Christian religion in England until the sixth century: conversion was undertaken in the north from 563 by Celtic missionaries from Ireland led by St Columba, and in the south by a mission sent from Rome in 597 which was led by St Augustine, who became the first archbishop of Canterbury. England appears to have been converted again by the end of the seventh century and followed, after the Council of Whitby in 663, the practices of the Roman Church, which brought the kingdom into the mainstream of European thought and culture.

PRINCIPAL CITIES

There are 50 cities in England and, as space constraints prevent us from including profiles of them all, the profiles below represent just a selection of England's principal cities (with date city status conferred). Other cities are: Chichester (pre-1900), Derby (1977), Ely (pre-1900), Exeter (pre-1900), Gloucester (pre-1900), Hereford (pre-1900), Lancaster (1937), Lichfield (pre-1900), London (pre-1900), Peterborough (pre-1900), Plymouth (1928), Portsmouth (1926), Preston (2002), Ripon (pre-1900), Salford (1926), Sunderland (1992), Truro (pre-1900), Wakefield (pre-1900), Wells (pre-1900), Westminster (pre-1900), Wolverhampton (2000) and Worcester (pre-1900).

Certain cities have also been granted a Lord Mayoralty – this grant confers no additional powers or functions and is purely honorific. Cities with Lord Mayors are: Birmingham, Bradford, Bristol, Canterbury, Chester, Coventry, Exeter, Kingston-upon-Hull, Leeds, Leicester, Liverpool, London, Manchester, Newcastle-upon-Tyne, Norwich, Nottingham, Oxford, Plymouth, Portsmouth, Sheffield and Stoke-on-Trent.

BATH (PRE-1900)

Bath stands on the River Avon between the Cotswold Hills to the North and the Mendips to the south. In the early 18th century, Bath became England's premier spa town where the rich and celebrated members of fashionable society gathered to 'take the waters' and enjoy the town's theatres and concert rooms. During this period the architect John Wood laid the foundations for a new Georgian city to be built using the honey-coloured stone for which Bath is famous today.

Contemporary Bath is a thriving tourist destination and remains a leading cultural, religious and historical centre with many art galleries and historic sites including: the Pump Room (1790); the Royal Crescent (1767); the Circus (1754); the 18th-century Assembly Rooms (housing the Museum of Costume); Pulteney Bridge (1771); the Guildhall and the Abbey, now over 500 years old, which is built on the site of the Saxon monastery.

BIRMINGHAM (PRE-1900)

Birmingham is Britain's second largest city, with a population of nearly one million. The generally accepted derivation of 'Birmingham' is the *ham* (dwelling-place) of the *ing* (family) of *Beorma*, presumed to have been Saxon.

During the Industrial Revolution the town grew into a major manufacturing centre and in 1889 was granted city status.

Recent developments include Millennium Point, which houses Thinktank, the Birmingham museum of science and discovery, and Brindleyplace, a development of shops, offices and leisure facilities on a former industrial site clustered around canals. In 2003 the Bullring shopping centre was officially opened as part of the city's urban regeneration programme.

The principal buildings are the Town Hall (1834–50), the Council House (1879), Victoria Law Courts (1891), Birmingham University (1906–9), the 13th-century Church of St Martin-in-the-Bull-Ring (rebuilt 1873), the Cathedral (formerly St Philip's Church) (1711), the Roman Catholic Cathedral of St Chad (1839–41), the Assay Office (1773), the Rotunda (1964) and the National Exhibition Centre (1976). There is also the Birmingham Museum and Art Gallery which was founded in 1885 and is home to a collection of Pre-Raphaelite paintings.

BRIGHTON AND HOVE (2000)

Brighton and Hove is situated on the south coast of England, around 96 km (60 miles) south of London. Originally a fishing village called Brighthelmstone, it was transformed into a fashionable seaside resort in the 18th century when Dr Richard Russell popularised the benefits of his 'sea-water cure'; as one of the closest beaches to London, Brighton began to attract wealthy visitors. One of these was the Prince Regent (the future King George IV), who first visited in 1783 and became so fond of the city that in 1807 he bought the former farmhouse he had been renting, and gradually turned it into Brighton's most recognisable building, the Royal Pavilion. The Pavilion is renowned for its Indo-Saracenic exterior, featuring minarets and an enormous central dome designed by John Nash, combined with the lavish chinoiserie of Frederick Crace's and Robert Jones' interiors.

Brighton and Hove's Regency heritage can also be seen in the numerous elegant squares and crescents designed by Amon Wilds and Augustin Busby that dominate the seafront.

Brighton and Hove is once again a fashionable resort, known for its cafe culture, lively nightlife and large gay scene.

BRADFORD (PRE-1900)

During the Industrial Revolution of the 18th and 19th centuries Bradford expanded rapidly and a great deal of wealth was generated by the wool industry.

Bradford city centre has a host of buildings with historical and cultural interest, including: City Hall, with its 19th-century Lord Mayor's rooms and Victorian law court; Bradford Cathedral; the Priestley, a theatre and arts centre originally established as the Bradford Civic Playhouse by J. B. Priestley and friends; the Colour Museum; the National Museum of Photography, Film and Television which houses five floors of interactive displays and three cinemas; and Piece Hall Yard which incorporates the Bradford Club, a Victorian Gothic style club dating from 1837; and the Peace Museum.

BRISTOL (PRE-1900)

Bristol was a Royal Borough before the Norman Conquest. The earliest form of the name is *Bricgstow*. In 1373 Edward III granted Bristol county status.

The principal buildings include the 12th-century

Cathedral with Norman chapter house and gateway, the 14th-century Church of St Mary Redcliffe, Wesley's Chapel, Broadmead, the Merchant Venturers' Almshouses, the Council House (1956), Guildhall, Exchange (erected from the designs of John Wood in 1743), Cabot Tower, the University and Clifton College. The Roman Catholic Cathedral at Clifton was opened in 1973.

The Clifton Suspension Bridge, with a span of 702 feet over the Avon, was projected by Isambard Kingdom Brunel in 1836 but was not completed until 1864. Brunel's SS *Great Britain,* the first ocean-going propeller-driven ship, is now being restored in the City Docks from where she was launched in 1843. The docks themselves have been extensively restored and redeveloped; the 19th-century two-storey former tea warehouse is now the Arnolfini centre for contemporary arts, and an 18th-century sail loft houses the Architecture Centre. Behind the baroque-domed facade of the former 'E' Shed are shops, cafes, restaurants and the Watershed Media Centre, and on Princes Wharf disused transit sheds house the Industrial Museum.

CAMBRIDGE (1951)

Cambridge, a settlement far older than its ancient University, lies on the River Cam or Granta. The city is a county town and regional headquarters. Its industries include technology research and development, and biotechnology. Among its open spaces are Jesus Green, Sheep's Green, Coe Fen, Parker's Piece, Christ's Pieces, the University Botanic Garden, and the 'Backs' – lawns and gardens through which the Cam winds behind the principal line of college buildings. Historical sites east of the Cam include; King's Parade, Great St Mary's Church, Gibbs' Senate House and King's College Chapel.

University and college buildings provide the outstanding features of Cambridge's architecture but several churches (especially St Benet's, the oldest building in the city, and St Sepulchre's, the Round Church) are also notable. The Guildhall (1937) stands on a site, of which at least part, has held municipal buildings since 1224.

CANTERBURY (PRE-1900)

Canterbury, seat of the Archbishop of Canterbury, the primate of the Church of England, dates back to prehistoric times. It was the Roman *Durovernum Cantiacorum* and the Saxon *Cant-wara-byrig* (stronghold of the men of Kent). Here in 597 St Augustine began the conversion of the English to Christianity, when Ethelbert, King of Kent, was baptised.

Of the Benedictine St Augustine's Abbey, burial place of the Jutish Kings of Kent, only ruins remain. St Martin's Church, on the eastern outskirts of the city, is stated by Bede to have been the place of worship of Queen Bertha, the Christian wife of King Ethelbert, before the advent of St Augustine.

In 1170 the rivalry of Church and State culminated in the murder in Canterbury Cathedral, by Henry II's knights, of Archbishop Thomas Becket. His shrine became a great centre of pilgrimage, as described in Chaucer's *Canterbury Tales.* After the Reformation pilgrimages ceased, but the prosperity of the city was strengthened by an influx of Huguenot refugees, who introduced weaving. The poet and playwright Christopher Marlowe was born and raised in Canterbury, and there are also literary associations with Defoe, Dickens, Joseph Conrad and Somerset Maugham.

The Cathedral, with architecture ranging from the 11th to the 15th centuries, is famous worldwide. Modern pilgrims are attracted particularly to the Martyrdom, the Black Prince's Tomb, the Warriors' Chapel and the many examples of medieval stained glass.

The medieval city walls are built on Roman foundations and the 14th-century West Gate is one of the finest buildings of its kind in the country.

The 1,000-seat Marlowe Theatre is a centre for the Canterbury Arts Festival each autumn.

CARLISLE (PRE-1900)

Carlisle is situated at the confluence of the River Eden and River Caldew, 309 miles north-west of London and about ten miles from the Scottish border. It was granted a charter in 1158.

The city stands at the western end of Hadrian's Wall and dates from the original Roman settlement of *Luguvalium.* Granted to Scotland in the tenth century, Carlisle is not included in the Domesday Book. William Rufus reclaimed the area in 1092 and the castle and city walls were built to guard Carlisle and the western border; the citadel is a Tudor addition to protect the south of the city. Border disputes were common until the problem of the Debateable Lands was settled in 1552. During the Civil War the city remained Royalist; in 1745 Carlisle was besieged for the last time by the Young Pretender (Bonnie Prince Charlie).

The Cathedral, originally a 12th-century Augustinian priory, was enlarged in the 13th and 14th centuries after the diocese was created in 1133. To the south is a restored Tithe Barn and nearby the 18th-century church of St Cuthbert, the third to stand on a site dating from the seventh century.

Carlisle is the major shopping, commercial and agricultural centre for the area, and industries include the manufacture of metal goods, biscuits and textiles. However, the largest employer is the services sector, most notably in central and local government, retailing and transport. The city has an important communications position at the centre of a network of major roads, as a stage on the main west coast rail services, and with its own airport at Crosby-on-Eden.

CHESTER (PRE-1900)

Chester is situated on the River Dee. Its recorded history dates from the first century when the Romans founded the fortress of *Deva.* The city's name is derived from the Latin *castra* (a camp or encampment). During the Middle Ages, Chester was the principal port of north-west England but declined with the silting of the Dee estuary and competition from Liverpool. The city was also an important military centre, notably during Edward I's Welsh campaigns and the Elizabethan Irish campaigns. During the Civil War, Chester supported the King and was besieged from 1643 to 1646. Chester's first charter was granted *c.* 1175 and the city was incorporated in 1506. The office of Sheriff is the earliest created in the country (*c.* 1120s), and in 1992 the Mayor was granted the title of Lord Mayor. He/she also enjoys the title 'Admiral of the Dee'.

The city's architectural features include the city walls (an almost complete two-mile circuit), the unique 13th-century Rows (covered galleries above the street-level shops), the Victorian Gothic Town Hall (1869), the Castle (rebuilt 1788 and 1822) and numerous half-timbered buildings. The Cathedral was a Benedictine abbey until the Dissolution. Remaining monastic buildings include the chapter house, refectory and cloisters and there is a modern free-standing bell tower. The Norman church of

St John the Baptist was a cathedral church in the early Middle Ages.

COVENTRY (PRE 1900)

Coventry is an important industrial centre, producing vehicles, machine tools, agricultural machinery, man-made fibres, aerospace components and telecommunications equipment. New investment has come from financial services, power transmission, professional services, leisure and education.

The city owes its beginning to Leofric, Earl of Mercia, and his wife Godiva who, in 1043, founded a Benedictine monastery. The guildhall of St Mary dates from the 14th century, three of the city's churches date from the 14th and 15th centuries, and 16th-century almshouses may still be seen. Coventry's first cathedral was destroyed at the Reformation, its second in the 1940 blitz (the walls and spire remain) and the new cathedral designed by Sir Basil Spence, consecrated in 1962, now draws numerous visitors.

Coventry is the home of the University of Warwick, Coventry University, the Westwood Business Park, the Cable and Wireless Technical Training College, the Museum of British Road Transport and the Skydome Arena.

DURHAM (PRE-1900)

The city of Durham is a major tourist attraction and its prominent Norman Cathedral and castle are set high on a wooded peninsula overlooking the River Wear. The Cathedral was founded as a shrine for the body of St Cuthbert in 995. The present building dates from 1093 and among its many treasures is the tomb of the Venerable Bede (673–735). Durham's Prince Bishops had unique powers up to 1836, being lay rulers as well as religious leaders. As a palatinate, Durham could have its own army, nobility, coinage and courts. The Castle was the main seat of the Prince Bishops for nearly 800 years; it is now used as a college by the University of Durham. The University, founded in the early 19th century on the initiative of Bishop William Van Mildert, is England's third oldest.

Among other buildings of interest is the Guildhall in the Market Place which dates from the 14th century. Work has been carried out to conserve this area as part of the city's contribution to the Council of Europe's Urban Renaissance Campaign. Annual events include Durham's Regatta in June (claimed to be the oldest rowing event in Britain) and the Annual Gala (formerly Durham Miners' Gala) in July.

The economy has undergone a significant change with the replacement of mining as the dominant industry by 'white collar' employment. Although still a predominantly rural area, the industrial and commercial sector is growing and a wide range of manufacturing and service industries are based on industrial estates in and around the city. A research and development centre, linked to the University, also plays an important role in the local economy.

KINGSTON-UPON-HULL (PRE-1900)

Hull (officially Kingston-upon-Hull) lies at the junction of the River Hull with the Humber, 22 miles from the North Sea. It is one of the major seaports of the United Kingdom. The port provides a wide range of cargo services, including ro-ro and container traffic, and handles an estimated million passengers annually on daily sailings to Rotterdam and Zeebrugge. There is a variety of manufacturing and service industries. Kingston-upon-Hull was so named by Edward I. City status was accorded in 1897 and the office of Mayor raised to the dignity of Lord Mayor in 1914.

The city, restored after heavy air raid damage during the Second World War, has good educational facilities with both the University of Hull and the University of Lincoln being within its boundaries. Hull is home to the world's only submarium, The Deep, a £45.5 million project which opened in 2002, and the Kingston Communications Stadium, with a seating capacity for 25,000, which was also completed in 2002.

Tourism is a major growth industry; the old town area has been renovated and includes museums, a marina and a shopping complex. Just west of the city is the Humber Bridge, the fourth-largest suspension bridge in the world.

LEEDS (PRE-1900)

Leeds, situated in the lower Aire Valley, is a junction for road, rail, canal and air services and an important commercial centre. It was first incorporated by Charles I in 1626. The earliest forms of the name are *Loidis* or *Ledes*, the origins of which are obscure.

The principal buildings are the Civic Hall (1933), the Town Hall (1858), the Municipal Buildings and Art Gallery (1884) with the Henry Moore Gallery (1982), the Corn Exchange (1863) and the University. The Parish Church (St Peter's) was rebuilt in 1841; the 17th-century St John's Church has a fine interior with a famous English Renaissance screen; the last remaining 18th-century church in the city is Holy Trinity in Boar Lane (1727). Kirkstall Abbey (about three miles from the centre of the city), founded by Henry de Lacy in 1152, is one of the most complete examples of a Cistercian house now remaining. Temple Newsam, birthplace of Lord Darnley and largely rebuilt by Sir Arthur Ingram c. 1620, was acquired by the Council in 1922. Adel Church, about five miles from the centre of the city, is a fine Norman structure. The new Royal Armouries Museum houses the collection of antique arms and armour formerly held at the Tower of London.

LEICESTER (1919)

Leicester is situated in central England. The city was an important Roman settlement and also one of the five Danish boroughs of Danelaw. In 1485 Richard III was buried in Leicester following his death at the nearby Battle of Bosworth. In 1589 Queen Elizabeth I granted a charter to the city and the ancient title was confirmed by letters patent in 1919.

The textile industry, responsible for Leicester's early expansion, has declined in recent years, although the city still maintains a strong manufacturing base. Cotton mills and factories are now undergoing extensive regeneration and are being converted into offices, apartments, bars and restaurants. The principal buildings include the two universities (the University of Leicester and De Montfort University), as well as the Town Hall, the 13th-century Guildhall, De Montfort Hall, Leicester Cathedral, the Jewry Wall (the UK's highest standing Roman wall), St Nicholas Church and St Mary de Castro church. The motte and Great Hall of Leicester can be seen from the castle gardens, situated next to the ancient River Soar.

Leicester today, is one of the UK's most ethnically diverse cities, home to the only Jain temple in the western world and hosts the country's second-largest Carribean carnival.

LINCOLN (PRE-1900)

Situated 40 miles inland on the River Witham, Lincoln derives its name from a contraction of *Lindum Colonia,* the settlement founded in AD 48 by the Romans to command the crossing of Ermine Street and Fosse Way. Sections of the third-century Roman city wall can be seen, including an extant gateway (Newport Arch), and excavations have discovered traces of a sewerage system unique in Britain. The Romans also drained the surrounding fenland and created a canal system, laying the foundations of Lincoln's agricultural prosperity and also the city's importance in the medieval wool trade as a port and Staple town.

As one of the Five Boroughs of Danelaw, Lincoln was an important trading centre in the ninth and tenth centuries and medieval prosperity from the wool trade lasted until the 14th century. This wealth enabled local merchants to build parish churches, of which three survive, and there are also remains of a 12th century Jewish community (Jew's House and Court, Aaron's House). However, the removal of the Staple to Boston in 1369 heralded a decline, from which the city only recovered fully in the 19th century, when improved fen drainage made Lincoln agriculturally important. Improved canal and rail links led to industrial development, mainly in the manufacture of machinery, components and engineering products.

The castle was built shortly after the Conquest and is unusual in having two mounds; on one motte stands a Keep (Lucy's Tower) added in the 12th century. It currently houses one of the four surviving copies of the Magna Carta. The Cathedral was begun c.1073 when the first Norman bishop moved the see of Lindsey to Lincoln, but was mostly destroyed by fire and earthquake in the 12th century. Rebuilding was begun by St Hugh and completed over a century later. Other notable architectural features are the 12th-century High Bridge, the oldest in Britain still to carry buildings, and the Guildhall, situated above the 15th–16th-century Stonebow gateway.

LIVERPOOL (PRE-1900)

Liverpool, on the north bank of the River Mersey, three miles from the Irish Sea, is the United Kingdom's foremost port for Atlantic trade. Tunnels link Liverpool with Birkenhead and Wallasey.

There are 2,100 acres of dockland on both sides of the river and the Gladstone and Royal Seaforth Docks can accommodate tanker-sized vessels. Liverpool Free Port was opened in 1984.

Liverpool was created a free borough in 1207 and a city in 1880. From the early 18th century it expanded rapidly with the growth of industrialisation and Atlantic trade. Surviving buildings from this period include the Bluecoat Chambers (1717, formerly the Bluecoat School), the Town Hall (1754, rebuilt to the original design 1795), and buildings in Rodney Street, Canning Street and the suburbs. Notable from the 19th and 20th centuries are the Anglican Cathedral, built from the designs of Sir Giles Gilbert Scott (the foundation stone was laid in 1904, but the building was only completed in 1980); the Catholic Metropolitan Cathedral (designed by Sir Frederick Gibberd, consecrated 1967) and St George's Hall (1842), regarded as one of the finest modern examples of classical architecture. The refurbished Albert Dock (designed by Jesse Hartley) contains the Merseyside Maritime Museum and Tate Gallery, Liverpool.

In 1852 an Act was obtained for establishing a public library, museum and art gallery; as a result Liverpool had one of the first public libraries in the country. The Brown,

Picton and Hornby libraries form one of the country's major collections. The Victoria Building of Liverpool University, the Royal Liver, Cunard and Mersey Docks & Harbour Company buildings at the Pier Head, the Municipal Buildings and the Philharmonic Hall are other examples of the city's fine architecture.

Six areas of Liverpool's maritime mercantile city were designated as UNESCO World Heritage Sites in 2004, and Liverpool has been elected as European Capital of Culture for 2008.

MANCHESTER (PRE-1900)

Manchester (the *Mamucium* of the Romans, who occupied it in AD 79) is a commercial and industrial centre with a population engaged in the engineering, chemical, clothing, food processing and textile industries and in education. Banking, insurance and a growing leisure industry are among the prime commercial activities. The city is connected with the sea by the Manchester Ship Canal, opened in 1894, 35.5 miles long, and accommodating ships up to 15,000 tons. In 2004 Manchester Airport handled just over 21 million terminal, transit, scheduled and charter passengers, making it the UK's third largest by number of passengers.

The principal buildings are: the Town Hall, erected in 1877 from the designs of Alfred Waterhouse, with a large extension of 1938; the Royal Exchange (1869, enlarged 1921); the Central Library (1934); Heaton Hall; the 17th-century Chetham Library; the Rylands Library (1900), which includes the Althorp collection; the University precinct; the 15th-century cathedral (formerly the parish church) and G-MEX exhibition centre. Recent developments include the Manchester Arena, the largest indoor arena in Europe, and the Bridgewater Hall. Manchester is the home of the Hallé Orchestra, the Royal Northern College of Music, the Royal Exchange Theatre and seven public art galleries.

To accommodate the Commonwealth Games held in Manchester in 2002, new sports facilities were built including a stadium, swimming pool complex and the National Cycling Centre.

The town received its first charter of incorporation in 1838 and was created a city in 1853.

NEWCASTLE UPON TYNE (PRE-1900)

Newcastle upon Tyne, on the north bank of the River Tyne, is eight miles from the North Sea. A cathedral and university city, it is the administrative, commercial and cultural centre for north-east England and the principal port. It is an important manufacturing centre with a wide variety of industries.

The principal buildings include the Castle Keep (12th century), Black Gate (13th century), Blackfriars (13th century), West Walls (13th century), St Nicholas's Cathedral (15th century, fine lantern tower), St Andrew's Church (12th–14th century), St John's (14th–15th century), All Saints (1786 by Stephenson), St Mary's Roman Catholic Cathedral (1844), Trinity House (17th century), Sandhill (16th-century houses), Guildhall (Georgian), Grey Street (1834–9), Central Station (1846–50), Laing Art Gallery (1904), University of Newcastle Physics Building (1962) and Medical Building (1985), Civic Centre (1963), Central Library (1969) and Eldon Square Shopping Development (1976). Open spaces include the Town Moor (927 acres) and Jesmond Dene. Ten bridges span the Tyne at Newcastle, including the tilting Millennium Bridge (2001), which links the city with Gateshead to the south.

The city's name is derived from the 'new castle' (1080) erected as a defence against the Scots. In 1400 it was made a county, and in 1882 a city.

NORWICH (PRE-1900)

Norwich grew from an early Anglo-Saxon settlement near the confluence of the Rivers Yare and Wensum, and now serves as provincial capital for the predominantly agricultural region of East Anglia. The name is thought to relate to the most northerly of a group of Anglo-Saxon villages or *wics*. The city's first known charter was granted in 1158 by Henry II.

Norwich serves its surrounding area as a market town and commercial centre, banking and insurance being prominent among the city's businesses. From the 14th century until the Industrial Revolution, Norwich was the regional centre of the woollen industry, but now the biggest single industry is financial services and principal trades are engineering, printing, shoemaking, the production of chemicals and clothing, food processing and technology. Norwich is accessible to seagoing vessels by means of the River Yare, entered at Great Yarmouth, 20 miles to the east.

Among many historic buildings are the Cathedral (completed in the 12th century and surmounted by a 15th-century spire 315 feet in height); the keep of the Norman castle (now a museum and art gallery); the 15th-century flint-walled Guildhall; some thirty medieval parish churches; St Andrew's and Blackfriars' Halls; the Tudor houses preserved in Elm Hill and the Georgian Assembly House. The University of East Anglia is on the city's western boundary.

NOTTINGHAM (PRE-1900)

Nottingham stands on the River Trent. *Snotingaham* or *Notingeham*, literally the homestead of the people of Snot, is the Anglo-Saxon name for the Celtic settlement of *Tigguocobauc*, or the house of caves. In 878, Nottingham became one of the Five Boroughs of Danelaw. William the Conqueror ordered the construction of Nottingham Castle, while the town itself developed rapidly under Norman rule. Its laws and rights were later formally recognised by Henry II's charter in 1155. The Castle became a favoured residence of King John. In 1642 King Charles I raised his personal standard at Nottingham Castle at the start of the Civil War.

Nottingham is home to Notts County FC (the world's oldest football league side), Nottingham Forest FC, Nottingham Racecourse, Trent Bridge cricket ground and the National Watersports Centre. The principal industries include textiles, pharmaceuticals, food manufacturing, engineering and telecommunications. There are two universities within the city boundaries.

Architecturally, Nottingham has a wealth of notable buildings, particularly those designed in the Victorian era by T. C. Hine and Watson Fothergill. The City Council owns the castle, of Norman origin but restored in 1878, Wollaton Hall (1580–8), Newstead Abbey (home of Lord Byron), the Guildhall (1888) and Council House (1929). St Mary's, St Peter's and St Nicholas's Churches are of interest, as is the Roman Catholic Cathedral (Pugin, 1842–4). Nottingham was granted city status in 1897.

OXFORD (PRE-1900)

Oxford is a university city, an important industrial centre, and a market town. Industry played a minor part in Oxford until the motor industry was established in 1912.

Oxford is known for its architecture, its oldest specimens being the reputedly Saxon tower of St Michael's Church, the remains of the Norman castle and city walls, and the Norman church at Iffley. It also has many Gothic buildings, such as the Divinity Schools, the Old Library at Merton College, William of Wykeham's New College, Magdalen College and Christ Church and many other college buildings. Later centuries are represented by the Laudian quadrangle at St John's College, the Renaissance Sheldonian Theatre by Wren, Trinity College Chapel, and All Saints Church, Hawksmoor's mock-Gothic at All Souls College, and the 18th-century Queen's College. In addition to individual buildings, High Street and Radcliffe Square both form interesting architectural compositions. Most of the colleges have gardens, those of Magdalen, New College, St John's and Worcester being the largest.

ST ALBANS (PRE-1900)

The origins of St Albans, situated on the River Ver, stem from the Roman town of *Verulamium*. Named after the first Christian martyr in Britain, who was executed here, St Albans has developed around the Norman Abbey and Cathedral Church (consecrated 1115), built partly of materials from the old Roman city. The museums house Iron Age and Roman artefacts and the Roman Theatre, unique in Britain, has a stage as opposed to an amphitheatre. Archaeological excavations in the city centre have revealed evidence of pre-Roman, Saxon and medieval occupation.

The town's significance grew to the extent that it was a signatory and venue for the drafting of the Magna Carta. It was also the scene of riots during the Peasants' Revolt, the French King John was imprisoned there after the Battle of Poitiers, and heavy fighting took place there during the Wars of the Roses.

Previously controlled by the Abbot, the town achieved a charter in 1553 and city status in 1877. The street market, first established in 1553, is still an important feature of the city, as are many hotels and inns, surviving from the days when St Albans was an important coach stop. Tourist attractions include historic churches and houses, and a 15th-century clock tower.

The city is now home to a wide range of businesses, with special emphasis on information and legal services. In addition, it is the home of the Royal National Rose Society, and of Rothamsted Park, the agricultural research centre.

SALISBURY (PRE-1900)

The history of Salisbury centres around the Cathedral and Cathedral Close. The city evolved from an Iron Age camp a mile to the north of its current position which was strengthened by the Romans and called *Serviodunum*. The Normans built a castle and cathedral on the site and renamed it Sarum. In AD 1220, Bishop Richard Poore and the architect Elias de Derham decided to build a new Gothic style cathedral. The cathedral was completed 38 years later and a community known as New Sarum, now called Salisbury, grew around it. Originally the cathedral had a squat tower; the 404 ft spire that makes the cathedral the tallest medieval structure in the world was added c.1315. A walled close with houses for the clergy was built around the cathedral; the Medieval Hall still stands today, alongside buildings dating from the 13th to the 20th century, including some designed by Sir Christopher Wren.

A prosperous wool and cloth trade allowed Salisbury to flourish until the 17th century. When the wool trade declined new crafts were established including cutlery, leather and basket work, saddlery, lacemaking, joinery and malting. By 1750 it had become an important road junction and coaching centre and in the Victorian era the railways created a new age of expansion and prosperity. Today Salisbury is a thriving tourist centre.

SHEFFIELD (PRE-1900)

Sheffield is situated at the junction of the Sheaf, Porter, Rivelin and Loxley valleys with the River Don and was created a city in 1893. Though its cutlery, silverware and plate have long been famous, Sheffield has other and now more important industries: special and alloy steels, engineering, tool-making, medical equipment and media-related industries (in its new Cultural Industries Quarter). Sheffield has two universities and is an important research centre.

The parish church of St Peter and St Paul, founded in the 12th century, became the Cathedral Church of the Diocese of Sheffield in 1914. The Roman Catholic Cathedral Church of St Marie (founded 1847) was created a cathedral for the new diocese of Hallam in 1980. Parts of the present building date from c.1435. The principal buildings are the Town Hall (1897), the Cutlers' Hall (1832), City Hall (1932), Graves Art Gallery (1934), Mappin Art Gallery, the Crucible Theatre and the restored 19th-century Lyceum theatre, which dates from 1897 and was reopened in 1990. Three major sports venues were opened between 1990 and 1991: Sheffield Arena, Don Valley Stadium and Pond's Forge. The Millennium Galleries opened in 2001.

SOUTHAMPTON (1964)

Southampton is a major seaport on the south coast of England, situated between the mouths of the Test and Itchen rivers. Southampton's natural deep-water harbour has made the area an important settlement since the Romans built the first port (known as *Clausentum*) in the first century, and Southampton's port has witnessed several important departures, including those of King Henry V in 1415 for the Battle of Agincourt, RMS *Titanic* in 1912, and the *Mayflower* in 1620.

The city's strategic importance, not only as a seaport but also as a centre for aircraft production, meant that it was heavily bombed during the Second World War; however, many historically significant structures remain, including the Wool House, dating from 1417 and now used as the Maritime Museum; parts of the Norman city walls which are among the most complete in the UK; the Bargate, which was originally the main gateway into the city; God's House Tower, now the Museum of Archaeology; St Michael's, the city's oldest church; and the Tudor Merchants Hall.

Home to the National Oceanography Centre, the International Boat Show and some of the country's principal watersports venues, Southampton's coastal setting and maritime history remain its main focus, but it also features extensive parks and a thriving entertainment scene.

STOKE-ON-TRENT (1925)

Stoke-on-Trent, standing on the River Trent and familiarly known as the Potteries, is the main centre of employment for the population of north Staffordshire. The city is the largest clayware producer in the world (china, earthenware, sanitary goods, refractories, bricks and tiles) and also has a wide range of other manufacturing industries, including steel, chemicals, engineering and tyres. Extensive reconstruction has been carried out in recent years.

The city was formed by the federation of the separate municipal authorities of Tunstall, Burslem, Hanley, Stoke, Fenton, and Longton in 1910 and received its city status in 1925.

WINCHESTER (PRE-1900)

Winchester, the ancient capital of England, is situated on the River Itchen. The city is rich in architecture of all types but the Cathedral takes pride of place. Built in 1079–93 the cathedral exhibits examples of Norman, Early English and Perpendicular styles and is the burial place of author Jane Austen. Winchester College, founded in 1382, is one of the country's most famous public schools, and the original building (1393) remains largely unaltered. St Cross Hospital, another great medieval foundation, lies one mile south of the city. The almshouses were founded in 1136 by Bishop Henry de Blois, and Cardinal Henry Beaufort added a new almshouse of 'Noble Poverty' in 1446. The chapel and dwellings are of great architectural interest, and visitors may still receive the 'Wayfarer's Dole' of bread and ale.

Excavations have done much to clarify the origins and development of Winchester. Part of the forum and several of the streets from the Roman town have been discovered. Excavations in the Cathedral Close have uncovered the entire site of the Anglo-Saxon cathedral (known as the Old Minster) and parts of the New Minster which was built by Alfred's son, Edward the Elder, and is the burial place of the Alfredian dynasty. The original burial place of St Swithun, before his remains were translated to a site in the present cathedral, was also uncovered.

Excavations in other parts of the city have thrown much light on Norman Winchester, notably on the site of the Royal Castle (adjacent to which the new Law Courts have been built) and in the grounds of Wolvesey Castle, where the great house built by Bishops Giffard and Henry de Blois in the 12th century has been uncovered. The Great Hall, built by Henry III between 1222 and 1236, survives and houses the Arthurian Round Table.

YORK (PRE-1900)

The city of York is an archiepiscopal seat. Its recorded history dates from AD 71, when the Roman Ninth Legion established a base under Petilius Cerealis that would later become the fortress of *Eburacum,* or *Eboracum.* In Anglo-Saxon times the city was the royal and ecclesiastical centre of Northumbria, and after capture by a Viking army in AD 866 it became the capital of the Viking kingdom of Jorvik. By the 14th century the city had become a great mercantile centre, mainly because of its control of the wool trade, and was used as the chief base against the Scots. Under the Tudors its fortunes declined, although Henry VIII made it the headquarters of the Council of the North. Excavations on many sites, including Coppergate, have greatly expanded knowledge of Roman, Viking and medieval urban life.

With its development as a railway centre in the 19th century the commercial life of York expanded, and today the city is home to the award-winning National Railway Museum. The principal industries are the manufacture of chocolate, scientific instruments and sugar.

The city is rich in examples of architecture of all periods. The earliest church was built in AD 627 and, in the 12th to 15th centuries, the present Minster was built in a succession of styles. Other examples within the city are the medieval city walls and gateways, churches and guildhalls. Domestic architecture includes the Georgian mansions of The Mount, Micklegate and Bootham.

LORDS-LIEUTENANT AND HIGH SHERIFFS

County/Shire	Lord-Lieutenant	High Sheriff, 2005–6
Bedfordshire	S. Whitbread	Angela Farnbrough
Berkshire	P. Wroughton	Hon. Mary Bayliss
Bristol	J. Tidmarsh	Roger Baird
Buckinghamshire	Sir Nigel Mobbs	Mrs Paddy Hopkirk
Cambridgeshire	Archibald Duberly	Simon Leatham
Cheshire	W. Bromley-Davenport	Carolin Paton-Smith
Cornwall	Lady Mary Holborow	Peter Hodgson, CBE
Cumbria	J. Cropper	Adam Taylor
Derbyshire	J. Bather	Robert Shields
Devon	E. Dancer, CBE	Sir John Cave
Dorset	Capt. M. Fulford-Dobson	Hon. Charlotte Townshend
Durham	Sir Paul Nicholson	Simon Still
East Riding of Yorkshire	R. Marriott, TD	Elizabeth Rymer
East Sussex	Mrs P. Stewart-Roberts	David Tate
Essex	Lord Petre	Jennifer Tolhurst
Gloucestershire	H. Elwes	Michael Stone
Greater London	Lord Imbert, QPM	Andrew Smith
Greater Manchester	Col. J. Timmins, OBE, TD	Sir David Wilmot, QPM
Hampshire	Mrs F. Fagan	Peter Andreae
Herefordshire	Sir Thomas Dunne, KCVO	Andrew Grant
Hertfordshire	S. Bowes Lyon, KCVO	David McMullen
Isle of Wight	C. Bland	John Fisher
Kent	A. Willett, CBE	William Wells
Lancashire	Lord Shuttleworth	James Armfield, OBE
Leicestershire	Lady Gretton	James Buxton
Lincolnshire	Mrs B. Cracroft-Eley	Nigel Brown
Merseyside	A. Waterworth	Rosemary Hawley
Norfolk	Richard Jewson	Sir Nicholas Bacon, Bt.
North Yorkshire	Lord Crathorne	Catherine Mackinlay
Northamptonshire	Lady Juliet Townsend	Hereward Wake
Northumberland	Sir John Riddell, CVO	Ian Speke
Nottinghamshire	Sir Andrew Buchanan, Bt.	Anthony Wilkinson
Oxfordshire	H. Brunner	Ian Laing
Rutland	Dr Laurence Howard	Robert Boyle
Shropshire	A. Heber-Percy	Michael Lowe
Somerset	Lady Gass	Fiona Densham
South Yorkshire	David Moody	Sarah Lee
Staffordshire	J. Hawley, TD	Lord Stafford
Suffolk	Lord Tollemache	Maj. Phillip Hope-Cobbold
Surrey	Mrs S. Goad	David Hypher
Tyne and Wear	N. Sherlock	Dr Margaret Appleby
Warwickshire	M. Dunne	Dr Balraj Dhesi
West Midlands	R. Taylor, OBE	Roger Dickens
West Sussex	H. Wyatt	Vyvyan Tregear
West Yorkshire	Dr Ingrid Roscoe	Timothy Hare
Wiltshire	John Bush, OBE	David Margesson
Worcestershire	M. Brinton	Andrew Grant

ENGLISH COUNTIES AND SHIRES

COUNTY COUNCILS: CONTACT DETAILS, AREA

Council	Administrative Headquarters	Telephone	Area (Hectares)
Bedfordshire	County Hall, Bedford	01234-363222	119,220
Buckinghamshire	County Hall, Aylesbury	01296-395000	156,509
Cambridgeshire	Shire Hall, Cambridge	01223-717111	304,357
Cheshire	County Hall, Chester	01244-602424	208,344
Cornwall	County Hall, Truro	01872-322000	354,810
Cumbria	The Courts, Carlisle	01228-606060	676,780
Derbyshire	County Hall, Matlock	01629-580000	255,000
Devon	County Hall, Exeter	01392-382000	656,085
Dorset	County Hall, Dorchester	01305-251000	254,181
Durham	County Hall, Durham	0191-383 3000	223,181
East Sussex	County Hall, Lewes	01273-481000	179,530
Essex	County Hall, Chelmsford	01245-492211	345,619
Gloucestershire	Shire Hall, Gloucester	01452-425000	279,875
Hampshire	The Castle, Winchester	01962-841841	367,896
Hertfordshire	County Hall, Hertford	01992-555555	163,416
Kent	County Hall, Maidstone	01622-671411	373,063
Lancashire	County Hall, Preston	01772-254868	289,780
Leicestershire	County Hall, Leicester	0116-232 3232	208,300
Lincolnshire	County Offices, Lincoln	01522-552222	591,470
Norfolk	County Hall, Norwich	0844-800 8020	537,234
Northamptonshire	County Hall, Northampton	01604-236236	235,966
Northumberland	County Hall, Morpeth	01670-533000	502,594
North Yorkshire	County Hall, Northallerton	01609-780780	803,741
Nottinghamshire	County Hall, Nottingham	0115-982 3823	208,519
Oxfordshire	County Hall, Oxford	01865-792422	260,595
Shropshire	The Shirehall, Shrewsbury	01743-251000	318,761
Somerset	County Hall, Taunton	01823-355455	345,233
Staffordshire	County Buildings, Stafford	01785-223121	262,355
Suffolk	County Hall, Ipswich	01473-583000	380,207
Surrey	County Hall, Kingston upon Thames	020-8541 8800	167,011
Warwickshire	Shire Hall, Warwick	01926-410410	197,854
West Sussex	County Hall, Chichester	01243-777100	198,936
Wiltshire	County Hall, Trowbridge	01225-713000	325,548
Worcestershire	County Hall, Worcester	01905-763763	173,529

COUNTY COUNCILS: POPULATION, BAND D COUNCIL TAX, CHIEF EXECUTIVES

Council & Administrative Headquarters	Population	Average Band D Council Tax for the Shire Area	Chief Executive
Bedfordshire, Bedford	381,600	£989	Andrea Hill
Buckinghamshire, Aylesbury	479,000	£889	Chris Williams
Cambridgeshire, Cambridge	552,700	£846	Ian Stewart
Cheshire, Chester	673,800	£912	Jeremy Taylor
Cornwall, Truro	501,300	£880	Peter Stethridge
Cumbria, Carlisle	487,600	£971	Peter Stybelski
Derbyshire, Matlock	734,600	£917	Nick Hodgson
Devon, Exeter	704,500	£932	Philip Jenkinson
Dorset, Dorchester	391,000	£953	David Jenkins
Durham, Durham	493,500	£925	Ken Manto
East Sussex, Lewes	492,300	£959	Cheryl Miller
Essex, Chelmsford	1,310,900	£918	Paul Coen
Gloucestershire, Gloucester	564,600	£923	Peter Bungard
Hampshire, Winchester	1,240,000	£869	Peter Robertson
Hertfordshire, Hertford	1,034,000	£938	Caroline Tapster
Kent, Maidstone	1,329,700	£877	Peter Gilroy
Lancashire, Preston	1,135,000	£950	Chris Trinick
Leicestershire, Leicester	609,600	£890	J. Sinnott
Lincolnshire, Lincoln	646,600	£900	Tony McArdle
Norfolk, Norwich	796,700	£957	Tim Byles
North Yorkshire, Northallerton	569,700	£857	John Marsden
Northamptonshire, Northampton	629,700	£857	Rory Borealis
Northumberland, Morpeth	307,200	£1,072	Mark Henderson
Nottinghamshire, Nottingham	748,500	£1,033	Roger Latham
Oxfordshire, Oxford	605,500	£966	Joanna Simons
Shropshire, Shrewsbury	283,200	£890	Carolyn Downs
Somerset, Taunton	489,100	£939	Alan Jones
Staffordshire, Stafford	806,700	£860	Nigel Pursey
Suffolk, Ipswich	668,500	£948	Mike More
Surrey, Kingston upon Thames	1,059,000	£921	Richard Shaw
Warwickshire, Warwick	505,900	£950	Jim Graham
West Sussex, Chichester	753,600	£954	Mark Hammond
Wiltshire, Trowbridge	433,000	£885	Keith Robinson
Worcestershire, Worcester	542,100	£857	Rob Sykes

DISTRICT COUNCILS

District Council	Telephone	Population	Band D Council Tax*	Chief Executive
Adur	01273-263000	59,600	£1,299	Ian Lowrie
Allerdale	01900-326333	93,500	£1,275	Gillian Bishop
Alnwick	01665-510505	31,000	£1,318	William Batey
Amber valley	01773-570222	116,500	£1,261	Peter Carney
Arun	01903-737500	140,800	£1,249	Ian Sumnall
Ashfield	01623-450000	111,500	£1,370	Alan Mellor
Ashford	01233-637311	102,700	£1,171	David Hill
Aylesbury Vale	01296-585858	165,700	£1,223	Richard Carr
Babergh	01473-822801	83,500	£1,242	Patricia Rockall
Barrow-in-Furness	01229-894900	72,000	£1,312	Tom Campbell
Basildon	01268-533333	165,700	£1,298	Bala Mahendran
Basingstoke and Deane	01256-844844	152,600	£1,140	Gordon Hoadcroft
Bassetlaw	01909-533533	107,700	£1,369	James Molloy
Bedford	01234-267422	147,900	£1,319	Shaun Field
Berwick-upon-Tweed	01289-330044	25,900	£1,311	Jane Pannell
Blaby	0116-275 0555	90,300	£1,231	Sandra Whiles
Blyth Valley	01670-542322	81,300	£1,291	Geoff Paul
Bolsover	01246-240000	71,800	£1,311	Wes Lumley
Boston	01205-314200	55,700	£1,178	Nicola Bulbeck
Braintree	01376-552525	132,200	£1,242	Allan Reid
Breckland	01362-695333	121,400	£1,202	Mrs R. Hellard
Brentwood	01277-261111	68,400	£1,232	Bob McLintock
Bridgnorth	01746-713100	52,500	£1,257	John Harmeston
Broadland	01603-431133	118,500	£1,246	Colin Bland
Bromsgrove	01527-873232	87,800	£1,228	Sue Nixon
Broxbourne	01992-785555	87,100	£1,152	Mike Walker
Broxtowe	0115-917 7777	107,600	£1,370	Mel Brown
Burnley	01282-425011	89,500	£1,329	Dr Gillian Taylor
CAMBRIDGE CITY	01223-457000	108,900	£1,167	Rob Hammond
Cannock Chase	01543-462621	92,100	£1,241	Stephen Brown
CANTERBURY CITY	01227-862000	135,300	£1,202	Colin Carmichael
Caradon	01579-341000	79,600	£1,192	Byron Davies
CARLISLE CITY	01228-817000	100,700	£1,302	Maggie Mooney
Carrick	01872-224400	87,900	£1,193	John Winskill
Castle Morpeth	01670-535000	49,000	£1,352	Ken Dunbar
Castle Point	01268-882200	86,600	£1,279	David Marchant
Charnwood	01509-263151	153,500	£1,209	Brian Hayes
Chelmsford	01245-606606	157,100	£1,239	Steve Packham
Cheltenham	01242-262626	110,000	£1,248	Chris Huckle *(acting)*
Cherwell	01295-252535	131,800	£1,269	Grahame Handley
CHESTER CITY	01244-324324	118,200	£1,238	Paul Durham
Chesterfield	01246-345345	98,900	£1,225	David Shaw
Chester-le-Street	0191-387 1919	53,700	£1,265	Roy Templeman
Chichester	01243-785166	106,400	£1,212	John Marsland
Chiltern	01494-729000	89,200	£1,242	Alan Goodrum
Chorley	01257-515151	100,400	£1,286	Jeffrey Davies
Christchurch	01202-495000	44,900	£1,286	Michael Turvey
Colchester	01206-282222	155,800	£1,242	Adrian Pritchard
Congleton	01270-763231	90,700	£1,242	Glyn Chambers
Copeland	01946-852585	69,300	£1,295	Dr. John Stanforth
Corby	01536-464000	53,200	£1,164	Chris Mallender
Cotswold	01285-623000	80,400	£1,253	Robert Austin
Craven	01756-700600	53,600	£1,254	Gill Dixon
Crawley	01293-438000	99,800	£1,235	Michael Coughlin
Crewe and Nantwich	01270-537777	111,000	£1,220	Alan Wenham
Dacorum	01442-228000	137,800	£1,205	Daniel Zammit

* Average Band D council tax bill for 2005–6. Average Band D council tax in the county area, which are exclusive of precepts for fire and police authorities, are given on the previous page, county councils claim their share of the combined funds from their district authorities.

District Council	Telephone	Population	Band D Council Tax*	Chief Executive
Dartford	01322-343434	85,900	£1,195	Graham Harris
Daventry	01327-871100	71,800	£1,178	Mrs J. Gregory
Derbyshire Dales	01629-761100	69,500	£1,287	David Wheatcroft
Derwentside	01207-218000	85,100	£1,345	Mike Clark
Dover	01304-821199	104,500	£1,204	Nadeem Aziz
DURHAM CITY	0191-386 6111	87,700	£1,286	Brian Spears
Easington	0191-527 0501	94,000	£1,404	Janet Johnson
East Cambridgeshire	01353-665555	73,200	£1,183	John Hill
East Devon	01395-516551	125,500	£1,237	Mark Williams
East Dorset	01202-886201	83,800	£1,324	Alan Breakwell
East Hampshire	01730-266551	109,300	£1,204	Will Godfrey
East Hertfordshire	01279-655261	128,900	£1,235	Miranda Steward; Rachel Stopard
East Lindsey	01507-601111	130,500	£1,138	Nigel Howells
East Northamptonshire	01832-742000	76,500	£1,166	Stephen Baker
East Staffordshire	01283-508000	103,800	£1,248	William Saunders
Eastbourne	01323-410000	89,700	£1,330	Martin Ray
Eastleigh	023-8068 8000	116,200	£1,201	Chris Tapp
Eden	01768-864671	49,800	£1,281	Ian Bruce
Ellesmere Port and Neston	0151-356 6789	81,700	£1,234	S. Ewbank
Elmbridge	01372-474474	121,900	£1,258	Michael Lockwood
Epping Forest	01992-564000	120,900	£1,256	John Scott; Peter Hayward
Epsom and Ewell	01372-732000	67,100	£1,208	David Smith
Erewash	0115-907 2244	110,100	£1,250	John Rice
EXETER CITY	01392-277888	111,100	£1,214	Philip Bostock
Fareham	01329-236100	108,000	£1,162	Alan Davies
Fenland	01354-654321	83,500	£1,249	Tim Pilsbury
Forest Heath	01638-719000	55,500	£1,250	David Burnip
Forest of Dean	01594-810000	80,000	£1,273	Tim Perrin
Fylde	01253-721222	73,200	£1,259	Ken Lee
Gedling	0115-901 3901	111,800	£1,351	Peter Murdoch
GLOUCESTER CITY	01452-522232	109,900	£1,243	Paul Smith
Gosport	023-9258 4242	76,400	£1,214	Ian Lycett
Gravesham	01474-564422	95,700	£1,184	Jim Wintour
Great Yarmouth	01493-856100	90,800	£1,231	Richard Packham
Guildford	01483-505050	129,700	£1,223	David Williams
Hambleton	01609-779977	84,100	£1,188	Peter Simpson
Harborough	01858-821100	76,600	£1,223	Sue Smith
Harlow	01279-446611	78,900	£1,304	Malcolm Morley
Harrogate	01423-500600	151,300	£1,279	Mick Walsh
Hart	01252-622122	83,500	£1,210	Jules Samuels
Hastings	01424-781066	85,000	£1,340	Roy Mawford
Havant	023-9247 4174	116,900	£1,197	Gwen Andrews
Hertsmere	020-8207 2277	94,500	£1,210	Eden Lee
High Peak	0845-129 7777	89,400	£1,269	Peter Sloman
Hinckley and Bosworth	01455-238141	100,100	£1,185	Steve Atkinson
Horsham	01403-215100	122,100	£1,214	Tom Crowley
Huntingdonshire	01480-388388	157,000	£1,191	David Monks
Hyndburn	01254-388111	81,500	£1,300	David Welsby
Ipswich	01473-432000	117,100	£1,348	James Hehir
Kennet	01380-724911	74,800	£1,220	Mark Boden
Kerrier	01209-614000	92,500	£1,200	Barry Manning
Kettering	01536-410333	81,800	£1,176	David Cook
King's Lynn and West Norfolk	01553-616200	135,300	£1,240	Ray Harding
LANCASTER CITY	01524-582000	133,900	£1,272	Mark Cullinan
Lewes	01273-471600	92,200	£1,350	John Crawford
Lichfield	01543-308000	93,200	£1,208	Nina Dawes
LINCOLN CITY	01522-881188	85,600	£1,212	Andrew Taylor
Macclesfield	01625-500500	150,100	£1,227	Vivienne Horton
Maidstone	01622-602000	139,000	£1,245	David Petford
Maldon	01621-854477	59,400	£1,258	Delwyn Burbidge
Malvern Hills	01684-892700	72,200	£1,224	Chris Bocock
Mansfield	01623-463463	98,100	£1,386	Richard Goad
Melton	01664-502502	47,900	£1,224	Mrs L. Aisbett
Mendip	01749-343399	103,900	£1,235	David Thomson
Mid Bedfordshire	01525-402051	121,000	£1,336	Jaki Salisbury
Mid Devon	01884-255255	69,800	£1,288	Paul Edwards

District Council	Telephone	Population	Band D Council Tax*	Chief Executive
Mid Suffolk	01449-720711	86,800	£1,241	Andrew Good
Mid Sussex	01444-458166	127,400	£1,234	John Jory
Mole Valley	01306-885001	80,300	£1,207	Heather Kerswell
New Forest	02380-285000	169,300	£1,223	David Yates
Newark and Sherwood	01636-650000	106,300	£1,418	Richard Dix
Newcastle-under-Lyme	01782-717717	122,000	£1,220	Felix Harley
North Cornwall	01208-893333	80,500	£1,201	Mark Hall
North Devon	01271-327711	87,500	£1,280	John Sunderland
North Dorset	01258-454111	61,900	£1,289	Elizabeth Goodall
North East Derbyshire	01246-231111	96,900	£1,312	James Gravenor *(acting)*
North Hertfordshire	01462-474000	116,900	£1,236	John Campbell
North Kesteven	01529-414155	94,000	£1,184	Ruth Marlow
North Norfolk	01263-513811	98,400	£1,245	Philip Burton
North Shropshire	01939-232771	57,100	£1,290	Nicola Yates
North Warwickshire	01827-715341	61,900	£1,305	Jerry Hutchinson
North West Leicestershire	01530-454545	85,500	£1,249	Christine Fisher
North Wiltshire	01249-706111	125,400	£1,254	R. Marshall
Northampton	01604-837837	194,500	£1,192	Mairi McLean
NORWICH CITY	01603-212212	121,600	£1,292	Anne Seex
Nuneaton and Bedworth	02476-376376	119,100	£1,274	Christine Kerr
Oadby and Wigston	0116-2888961	55,800	£1,237	Ruth Hyde
Oswestry	01691-671111	37,300	£1,322	Paul Shevlin
OXFORD CITY	01865-249811	134,200	£1,317	Caroline Bull
Pendle	01282-661661	89,300	£1,335	Stephen Barnes
Penwith	01736-362341	63,000	£1,152	Jim McKenna
PRESTON CITY	01772-906000	129,600	£1,325	James Carr
Purbeck	01929-556561	44,400	£1,311	Steve Mackenzie
Redditch	01527-64252	78,800	£1,234	Christopher Smith
Reigate and Banstead	01737-276000	126,500	£1,243	Nigel Clifford
Restormel	01726-223300	95,500	£1,159	Patricia Crowson
Ribble Valley	01200-425111	54,000	£1,245	David Morris
Richmondshire	01748-829100	47,000	£1,277	Harry Tabiner
Rochford	01702-546366	78,500	£1,269	Paul Warren
Rossendale	01706-217777	65,700	£1,340	Owen Williams
Rother	01424-787878	85,400	£1,305	Derek Stevens
Rugby	01788-533533	87,400	£1,249	Diane Colley
Runnymede	01932-838383	78,000	£1,193	Tim Williams
Rushcliffe	0115-981 9911	105,600	£1,364	Keith Beaumont
Rushmoor	01252-398398	91,000	£1,194	Andrew Lloyd
Ryedale	01653-600666	50,900	£1,268	Harold Mosley
ST ALBANS CITY	01727-866100	129,000	£1,242	Patricia Adley
St Edmundsbury	01284-763233	98,200	£1,252	Deborah Cadman
SALISBURY	01722-336272	114,600	£1,203	Richard Sheard
Scarborough	01723-232323	106,200	£1,277	John Trebble
Sedgefield	01388-816166	87,200	£1,428	N. Vaulks
Sedgemoor	01278-435435	105,900	£1,212	Kerry Rickards
Selby	01757-705101	76,500	£1,260	Martin Connor
Sevenoaks	01732-227000	109,300	£1,242	Robin Hales
Shepway	01303-850388	96,200	£1,272	Alistair Stewart
Shrewsbury and Atcham	01743-281000	95,900	£1,247	Robin Hooper
South Bedfordshire	01582-472222	112,600	£1,396	Jon Ruddick
South Bucks	01753-533333	61,900	£1,214	Chris Furness
South Cambridgeshire	01223-443000	130,000	£1,216	John Ballantyne
South Derbyshire	01283-221000	81,600	£1,244	Frank McArdle
South Hams	01803-861234	81,800	£1,255	Ruth Bagley
South Holland	01775-761161	76,500	£1,174	Terry Huggins
South Kesteven	01476-406080	124,800	£1,152	Duncan Kerr
South Lakeland	01539-733333	102,300	£1,293	Mike Jones
South Norfolk	01508-533633	110,700	£1,262	Geoffrey Rivers
South Northamptonshire	01327-322322	79,300	£1,190	Jean Morgan
South Oxfordshire	01491-823000	128,200	£1,265	David Buckle
South Ribble	01772-421491	103,900	£1,294	Jean Hunter
South Shropshire	01584-813000	40,400	£1,323	Graham Biggs
South Somerset	01935-462462	151,000	£1,244	Philip Dolan
South Staffordshire	01902-696000	105,900	£1,185	Rolf Levesley
Spelthorne	01784-451499	90,400	£1,216	Karen Satterford

District Council	Telephone	Population	Band D Council Tax*	Chief Executive
Stafford	01785-619000	120,700	£1,204	David Rawlings
Staffordshire Moorlands	01538-483483	94,500	£1,224	Simon Baker
Stevenage	01438-242242	79,700	£1,223	Ian Paske
Stratford-on-Avon	01789-267575	111,500	£1,230	Paul Lankester
Stroud	01453-766321	107,900	£1,293	David Hagg
Suffolk Coastal	01394-383789	115,100	£1,229	Jeremy Schofield *(acting)*
Surrey Heath	01276-707100	80,300	£1,244	Barry Catchpole
Swale	01795-424341	122,800	£1,188	Chris Edwards
Tamworth	01827-709709	74,500	£1,181	David Weatherley
Tandridge	01883-722000	79,300	£1,245	Stephen Weigel
Taunton Deane	01823-356356	102,300	£1,201	Penny James
Teesdale	01833-690000	24,500	£1,298	Charles Anderson
Teignbridge	01626-361101	121,000	£1,264	Howard Davis
Tendring	01255-425501	138,600	£1,227	John Hawkins
Test Valley	01264-368000	109,800	£1,158	Roger Tetstall
Tewkesbury	01684-295010	76,400	£1,196	Teri Turner
Thanet	01843-577000	126,700	£1,228	Richard Samuel
Three Rivers	01923-776611	82,800	£1,235	Steven Halls
Tonbridge and Malling	01732-844522	107,600	£1,213	David Hughes
Torridge	01237-428700	59,000	£1,252	John van Delaarschot
Tunbridge Wells	01892-526121	104,000	£1,188	Philip Thomas *(acting)*
Tynedale	01434-652200	58,800	£1,329	Richard Robson
Uttlesford	01799-510510	68,900	£1,250	Alasdair Bovaird
Vale of White Horse	01235-520202	115,600	£1,226	Terry Stock
Vale Royal	01606-862862	122,100	£1,237	Anne Bingham-Holmes
Wansbeck	01670-532200	61,100	£1,306	R. Stephenson
Warwick	01926-450000	126,000	£1,218	Janie Barrett
Watford	01923-226400	79,700	£1,293	Alastair Robertson
Waveney	01502-562111	112,300	£1,207	Glenn Garrod
Waverley	01483-523333	115,600	£1,248	Christine Pointer
Wealden	01892-653311	140,000	£1,343	Charles Lant
Wear Valley	01388-765555	61,300	£1,290	Iain Phillips
Wellingborough	01933-229777	72,500	£1,139	Tony McArdle
Welwyn Hatfield	01707-357000	97,500	£1,260	Michel Saminaden
West Devon	01822-813600	48,800	£1,305	David Incoll
West Dorset	01305-251010	92,400	£1,307	David Clarke
West Lancashire	01695-577177	108,400	£1,284	William Taylor
West Lindsey	01427-676676	79,500	£1,216	Duncan Sharkey
West Oxfordshire	01993-861000	95,600	£1,206	Geoff Bonner
West Somerset	01984-632291	35,200	£1,220	Timothy Howes
West Wiltshire	01225-776655	118,200	£1,243	Andrew Pate
Weymouth and Portland	01305-838000	63,700	£1,367	Tom Grainger
WINCHESTER CITY	01962-840222	107,200	£1,189	Simon Eden
Woking	01483-755855	89,800	£1,249	Paul Russell
WORCESTER CITY	01905-723471	93,400	£1,197	David Wareing
Worthing	01903-239999	97,500	£1,242	Sheryl Grady
Wychavon	01386-565000	112,900	£1,188	Jack Hegarty
Wycombe	01494-461000	162,100	£1,207	Richard Cummins
Wyre	01253-891000	105,600	£1,263	Jim Corry
Wyre Forest	01562-820505	96,900	£1,244	Walter Delin

Councils in CAPITAL LETTERS have city status

METROPOLITAN BOROUGH COUNCILS

District Council	Telephone	Population	Band D Council Tax*	Chief Executive
Barnsley	01226-770770	218,100	£1,162	Phil Coppard
BIRMINGHAM CITY	0121-303 9944	977,100	£1,139	Stephen Hughes (acting)
Bolton	01204-333333	261,000	£1,216	Bernard Knight
BRADFORD CITY	01274-432001	467,700	£1,105	Philip Robinson
Bury	0161-2535000	180,600	£1,172	Mark Sanders
Calderdale	01422-357257	192,400	£1,237	Paul Sheehan
COVENTRY CITY	02476-833333	300,800	£1,258	Stella Manzie
Doncaster	01302-734444	286,900	£1,102	Susan Law
Dudley	01384-818181	305,200	£1,064	Andrew Sparke
Gateshead	0191-433 3000	191,200	£1,362	Roger Kelly
Kirklees	01484-221000	388,600	£1,190	Rob Vincent
Knowsley	0151-489 6000	150,500	£1,197	Sheena Ramsey
LEEDS CITY	0113-247 4554	715,400	£1,086	Paul Rogerson
LIVERPOOL CITY	0151-233 3000	439,500	£1,282	David Henshaw
MANCHESTER CITY	0161-234 5000	392,800	£1,167	Howard Bernstein
NEWCASTLE UPON TYNE CITY	0191-232 8520	259,600	£1,329	Ian Stratford
North Tyneside	0191-200 6565	191,700	£1,260	vacant
Oldham	0161-911 3000	217,400	£1,346	Andrew Kilburn
Rochdale	01706-647474	205,200	£1,211	Roger Ellis
Rotherham	01709-382121	248,200	£1,200	Mike Cuff
St Helens	01744-456000	176,800	£1,211	Carole Hudson
SALFORD CITY	0161-794 4711	216,100	£1,329	John Willis
Sandwell	0121-569 2200	282,900	£1,175	Nigel Summers
Sefton	0151-922 4040	283,000	£1,245	Graham Haywood
SHEFFIELD CITY	0114-272 6444	513,200	£1,274	Bob Kerslake
Solihull	0121-704 6000	199,500	£1,095	Katherine Kerswell
South Tyneside	0191-427 1717	152,800	£1,242	Irene Lucas
Stockport	0161-480 4949	284,500	£1,252	John Schultz
SUNDERLAND CITY	0191-553 1000	280,800	£1,154	Jed Fitzgerald
Tameside	0161-342 8355	213,000	£1,180	Janet Calendar
Trafford	0161-912 1212	210,100	£1,046	David McNulty
WAKEFIELD CITY	01924-306090	315,200	£1,090	John Foster
Walsall	01922-650000	253,500	£1,282	Annie Shepperd
Wigan	01942-244991	301,400	£1,192	Joyce Redfern
Wirral	0151-638 7070	312,300	£1,222	Stephen Maddox
WOLVERHAMPTON CITY	01902-556556	236,600	£1,227	Derrick Anderson

Councils in CAPITAL LETTERS have city status
* Average B and D council tax bill for 2005–6

UNITARY COUNCILS

District Council	Telephone	Population	Band D Council Tax*	Chief Executive
Bath and North East Somerset	01225-477000	169,000	£1,195	John Everitt
Blackburn with Darwen	01254-585585	137,500	£1,274	Philip Watson
Blackpool	01253-477477	142,300	£1,239	Steve Weaver
Bournemouth	01202-451451	163,400	£1,240	Paul Godier
Bracknell Forest	01344-424642	109,600	£1,099	Timothy Weadon
BRIGHTON AND HOVE CITY	01273-290000	247,800	£1,219	Alan McCarthy
BRISTOL CITY	0117-922 2000	380,600	£1,296	Nick Gurney
Darlington	01325-380651	97,800	£1,148	Ada Burns
DERBY CITY	01332-293111	221,700	£1,128	Ray Cowlishaw
East Riding of Yorkshire	01482-887700	314,100	£1,241	Nigel Pearson
Halton	0151-424 2061	118,200	£1,123	David Parr
Hartlepool	01429-266522	88,600	£1,361	Paul Walker
Herefordshire	01432-260000	174,800	£1,229	Neil Pringle
Isle of Wight	01983-821000	132,700	£1,248	Mike Fisher
KINGSTON UPON HULL CITY	01482-609100	243,600	£1,143	Kim Riley
LEICESTER CITY	0116-254 9922	279,900	£1,176	Rodney Green
Luton	01582-546000	184,400	£1,122	Kevin Crompton
Medway	01634-306000	249,500	£1,070	Judith Armitt
Middlesbrough	01642-245432	134,800	£1,230	Jan Richmond
Milton Keynes	01908-691691	207,100	£1,153	John Best
North East Lincolnshire	01472-313131	158,000	£1,325	George Krawiec
North Lincolnshire	01724-296296	152,800	£1,294	Simon Driver
North Somerset	01934-888888	188,600	£1,216	Graham Turner
NOTTINGHAM CITY	0115-915 5555	267,000	£1,315	Gordon Mitchell
PETERBOROUGH CITY	01733-563141	156,100	£1,163	Gillian Beasley
PLYMOUTH CITY	01752-668000	240,700	£1,176	Barry Keel
Poole	01202-633633	138,300	£1,189	John McBride
PORTSMOUTH CITY	023-9282 2251	186,700	£1,122	Marion Headicar
Reading	0118-939 0900	143,100	£1,270	Trish Haines
Redcar and Cleveland	01642-444000	139,100	£1,273	Colin Moore
Rutland	01572-722577	34,600	£1,410	K. Franklin
Slough	01753-552288	119,100	£1,107	Cheryl Coppell
South Gloucestershire	01454-868686	245,600	£1,239	Amanda Deeks
SOUTHAMPTON CITY	023-8022 3855	217,500	£1,223	Brad Roynon
Southend-on-Sea	01702-215000	160,300	£1,068	Robert Tinlin
Stockton-on-Tees	01642-393939	178,400	£1,213	George Garlick
STOKE-ON-TRENT CITY	01782-234567	240,600	£1,146	Ita O'Donovan
Swindon	01793-463000	180,100	£1,170	Michael Pitt
Telford and Wrekin	01952-202100	158,300	£1,196	Michael Frater
Thurrock	01375-390000	143,000	£1,099	David White
Torbay	01803-201201	129,700	£1,212	Richard Painter
Warrington	01925-444400	191,100	£1,106	David Whitehead
West Berkshire	01635-42400	144,400	£1,280	Jim Graham
Windsor and Maidenhead	01628-798888	133,600	£1,112	David Lunn
Wokingham	0118-974 6000	150,300	£1,225	Doug Patterson
YORK CITY	01904-613161	181,100	£1,127	David Atkinson

Councils in CAPITAL LETTERS have city status
* Average B and D council tax bill for 2005–6

1 Stockton-on-Tees
2 Middlesbrough
3 Blackpool
4 Blackburn
  with Darwen
5 Bolton
6 Bury
7 Rochdale
8 Salford
9 Oldham
10 Liverpool
11 Knowsley
12 St Helens
13 Halton
14 Warrington
15 Trafford
16 Manchester
17 Tameside
18 Stockport
19 Nottingham
20 Telford and
   Wrekin
21 Wolverhampton
22 Walsall
23 Sandwell
24 Dudley
25 Birmingham
26 Solihull
27 Coventry
28 Peterborough
29 South Glos
30 Bristol
31 Bath and
   NE Somerset
32 Windsor and
   Maidenhead
33 Slough
34 Reading
35 Wokingham
36 Bracknell Forest
37 Thurrock
38 Southend
39 Medway
40 Plymouth
41 Torbay

LONDON

1 Hillingdon
2 Harrow
3 Barnet
4 Enfield
5 Waltham Forest
6 Redbridge
7 Barking and Dagenham
8 Havering
9 Ealing
10 Brent
11 Camden
12 Haringey
13 Islington
14 Hackney
15 Newham
16 Hounslow
17 Hammersmith and Fulham
18 Kensington and Chelsea
19 City of Westminster
20 City of London
21 Tower Hamlets
22 Richmond upon Thames
23 Wandsworth
24 Lambeth
25 Southwark
26 Lewisham
27 Greenwich
28 Bexley
29 Kingston upon Thames
30 Merton
31 Sutton
32 Croydon
33 Bromley

LONDON

THE CORPORATION OF LONDON

The City of London is the historic centre at the heart of London known as 'the square mile' around which the vast metropolis has grown over the centuries. The City's residential population at census day 2001 was 7,186, in addition, about 300,000 people work in the City. The civic government is carried on by the Corporation of London through the Court of Common Council.

The City is an international financial and business centre, generating about £30 billion a year for the British economy. It includes the head offices of the principal banks, insurance companies and mercantile houses, in addition to buildings ranging from the historic Roman Wall and the 15th-century Guildhall, to the massive splendour of St Paul's Cathedral and the architectural beauty of Wren's spires.

The City of London was described by Tacitus in AD 62 as 'a busy emporium for trade and traders'. Under the Romans it became an important administration centre and hub of the road system. Little is known of London in Saxon times, when it formed part of the kingdom of the East Saxons. In 886 Alfred recovered London from the Danes and reconstituted it a burgh under his son-in-law. In 1066 the citizens submitted to William the Conqueror who in 1067 granted them a charter, which is still preserved, establishing them in the rights and privileges they had hitherto enjoyed.

THE MAYORALTY

The Mayoralty was probably established about 1189, the first Mayor being Henry Fitz Ailwyn who filled the office for 23 years and was succeeded by Fitz Alan (1212–14). A new charter was granted by King John in 1215, directing the Mayor to be chosen annually, which has been done ever since, though in early times the same individual often held the office more than once. A familiar instance is that of 'Whittington, thrice Lord Mayor of London' (in reality four times, 1397, 1398, 1406, 1419); and many modern cases have occurred. The earliest instance of the phrase 'Lord Mayor' in English is in 1414. It was used more generally in the latter part of the 15th century and became invariable from 1535 onwards. At Michaelmas the liverymen in Common Hall choose two Aldermen who have served the office of Sheriff for presentation to the Court of Aldermen, and one is chosen to be Lord Mayor for the following mayoral year.

LORD MAYOR'S DAY

The Lord Mayor of London was previously elected on the feast of St Simon and St Jude (28 October), and from the time of Edward I, at least, was presented to the King or to the Barons of the Exchequer on the following day, unless that day was a Sunday. The day of election was altered to 16 October in 1346, and after some further changes was fixed for Michaelmas Day in 1546, but the ceremonies of admittance and swearing-in of the Lord Mayor continued to take place on 28 and 29 October respectively until 1751. In 1752, at the reform of the calendar, the Lord Mayor was continued in office until 8 November, the 'new style' equivalent of 28 October. The Lord Mayor is now presented to the Lord Chief Justice at the Royal Courts of Justice on the second Saturday in November to make the final declaration of office, having been sworn in at Guildhall on the preceding day. The procession to the Royal Courts of Justice is popularly known as the Lord Mayor's Show.

REPRESENTATIVES

Aldermen are mentioned in the 11th century and their office is of Saxon origin. They were elected annually between 1377 and 1394, when an Act of Parliament of Richard II directed them to be chosen for life.

The Common Council was, at an early date, substituted for a popular assembly called the *Folkmote*. At first only two representatives were sent from each ward, but now each of the City's 25 wards is represented by an Alderman and at least two Common Councilmen (the number depending on the size of the ward).

OFFICERS

Sheriffs were Saxon officers; their predecessors were the *wic-reeves* and *portreeves* of London and Middlesex. At first they were officers of the Crown, and were named by the Barons of the Exchequer; but Henry I (in 1132) gave the citizens permission to choose their own Sheriffs, and the annual election of Sheriffs became fully operative under King John's charter of 1199. The citizens lost this privilege, as far as the election of the Sheriff of Middlesex was concerned, by the Local Government Act 1888; but the liverymen continue to choose two Sheriffs of the City of London, who are appointed on Midsummer Day and take office at Michaelmas.

The office of Chamberlain is an ancient one, the first contemporary record of which is 1237. The Town Clerk (or Common Clerk) is first mentioned in 1274.

ACTIVITIES

The work of the Corporation is assigned to a number of committees which present reports to the Court of Common Council. These Committees are: Barbican Centre; Barbican Residential; Board of Governors of the City of London Freeman's School, the City of London School, London School for Girls, the Guildhall School of Music and Drama and the Museum of London; Bridge House Trust; City Lands and Bridge House Estates Managers of West Ham Park; Community Services Education; Epping Forest and Open Spaces Establishment; Finance; Gresham (city side); Guildhall Yard East Building; Hampstead Heath Management Libraries; Guildhall Art Galleries and Archives; Livery Markets; Planning and Transportation; Police; Policy and Resources; Port Health and Environmental Services Queen's Park and Highgate Wood Management and Standards Committees.

The City's estate, in the possession of which the Corporation of London differs from other municipalities is managed by the City Lands and Bridge House Estate Committee, the chairmanship of which carries with it the title of Chief Commoner.

The Honourable the Irish Society, which manages the Corporation's estates in Ulster, consists of a Governor and five other Aldermen, the Recorder, and 19 Common Councilmen, of whom one is elected Deputy Governor.

THE LORD MAYOR 2005–6
The Rt. Hon. the Lord Mayor, Alderman Rt. Hon. David Brewer
Private Secretary, Kay Brock

THE SHERIFFS 2005–6
John Stuttard *(Alderman, Lime Street)*; Kevin Kearney

OFFICERS, ETC.
Town Clerk, Chris Duffield
Chamberlain, Peter Derrick
Chief Commoner (2005), Christopher Mitchell, OBE
Clerk, The Honourable the Irish Society, S. Waley

THE ALDERMEN
with office held and date of appointment to that office

Name and Ward	CC	Ald.	Shff	Lord Mayor
Sir Richard Nichols, Candlewick	1983	1984	1994	1997
Lord Levene of Portsoken, KBE, Portsoken	1983	1984	1995	1998
Sir Clive Martin, OBE, Aldgate	–	1985	1996	1999
Sir David Howard, Bt., Cornhill	1972	1986	1997	2000
Sir Michael Oliver, Bishopsgate	1980	1987	1997	2001
Sir Gavyn Arthur, Cripplegate	1988	1991	1998	2002
Sir Robert Finch, Coleman Street	–	1992	1999	2003
Michael Savory, Bread Street	1980	1996	2001	2004

All the above have passed the Civic Chair

David Brewer, *Bassishaw*	1992	1996	2002
Nicholas Anstee, *Aldersgate*	1987	1996	2003
John Hughesdon, *Billingsgate*	1991	1997	2004
John Stuttard, *Lime Street*	–	2001	
David Lewis, *Broad Street*	–	2001	
Dr Andrew Parmley, *Vintry*	1992	2001	
Simon Walsh, *Farringdon Wt.*	1989	2000	
Robert Hall, *Farringdon Wn.*	1995	2002	
Mrs Alison Gowman, *Dowgate*	1991	2002	
Richard Walduck, OBE, *Tower*	–	2003	
Gordon Haines, *Queenhithe*	–	2004	
Colin Hart, *Cheap*	–	2004	
Daniel Caspi, *Bridge*	1994	2004	
Roger Gifford, *Cordwainer*	–	2004	
David Mauleverer, *Walbrook*	–	2005	2002
Ian Luder, *Castle Baynard*	1998	2005	

THE COMMON COUNCIL
Deputy: Each Common Councilman so described serves as deputy to the Alderman of her/his ward.

Abrahams, G. C. (2000) — *Farringdon Wt.*
Absalom, J. D. (1994) — *Farringdon Wt.*
Altman, L. P., CBE (1996) — *Cripplegate*
Angell, E. H. (1991) — *Cripplegate*
Ayers, K. E. (1996) — *Bassishaw*
Barker, *Deputy* J. A. (1981) — *Cripplegate*
Bear, M. D. (2003) — *Portsoken*
Bennett, J. A. (2005) — *Broad Street*
Bird, J. L., OBE (1977) — *Tower*

Boleat, M. J. (2002) — *Cordwainer*
Bradshaw, D. J. (1991) — *Cripplegate Wn.*
Branson, N. A. C. (2002) — *Langbourn*
Brewster, J. W., OBE (1994) — *Bassishaw*
Burleigh, I. R. (2005) — *Portsoken*
Carrington, M. L. (2004) — *Lime Street*
Cassidy, *Deputy* M. J. (1989) — *Coleman Street*
Catt, R. M. (2004) — *Castle Baynard*
Cenci Di Bello, Mrs P. J. (2004) — *Farringdon Wn.*
Chadwick, R. A. H. (1994) — *Tower*
Cohen, Mrs C. M., OBE (1986) — *Lime Street*
Cotgrove, D. (1991) — *Lime Street*
Currie, *Deputy* Miss S. E. M. (1985) — *Cripplegate*
Day, M. J. (2005) — *Bishopsgate*
Dove, W. H., MBE (1993) — *Bishopsgate*
Duckworth, S. (2000) — *Bishopsgate*
Dudley, The Revd Dr M. R. (2002) — *Aldersgate*
Duffield, R. W. (2004) — *Farringdon Wn*
Eskenzi, *Deputy* A. N., CBE (1970) — *Farringdon Wn.*
Eve, R. A. (1980) — *Cheap*
Everett, K. M. (1984) — *Candlewick*
Farr, M. C. (1998) — *Walbrook*
Farrow, *Deputy* M. W. W. (1996) — *Farringdon Wt.*
Farthing, R. B. C. (1981) — *Aldgate*
FitzGerald, *Deputy* R. C. A. (1981) — *Bread Street*
Fraser, S. J. (1993) — *Coleman Street*
Fraser, *Deputy* W. B. (1981) — *Vintry*
Galloway, *Deputy* A. D. (1981) — *Broad Street*
Gillon, G. M. F. (1995) — *Cordwainer*
Ginsburg, S. (1990) — *Bishopsgate*
Graves, A. C. (1985) — *Bishopsgate*
Halliday, *Deputy* Mrs P. A. (1992) — *Walbrook*
Hardwick, Dr P. B. (1987) — *Aldgate*
Harris, B. N. (2004) — *Bridge*
Haynes, J. E. H. (1986) — *Cornhill*
Henderson-Begg, M. (1977) — *Coleman Street*
Hilliars, N. R. M. (2005) — *Farringdon Wt.*
Hoffman, T. D. D.(2002) — *Vintry*
Holland, *Deputy* J., CBE (1972) — *Aldgate*
Hughes-Penney, R. C. (2004) — *Farringdon Wn.*
Hunt, W. G. (2004) — *Castle Baynard*
Jackson, L. St J. T. (1978) — *Bread Street*
Jones, H. L. M. (2004) — *Portsoken*
Kellett, Mrs M. W. F. (1986) — *Tower*
Kemp, D. L. (1984) — *Coleman Street*
King, A. J. N. (1999) — *Queenhithe*
Knowles, *Deputy* S. K. (1984) — *Candlewick*
Lawrence, G. A. (2002) — *Farringdon Wt.*
Leck, P. (1998) — *Aldersgate*
Lee, The Revd Dr B. J. (2001) — *Portsoken*
Lord, C. E. (2001) — *Coleman Street*
Luder, I. D. (1998) — *Castle Baynard*
McGuinness, C. S. (1997) — *Castle Baynard*
Malins, J. H., QC (1981) — *Farringdon Wt.*
Martinelli, *Deputy* P. J. (1994) — *Bassishaw*
Mayhew, J. P. (1996) — *Aldersgate*
Mead, Mrs W. (1997) — *Farringdon Wt.*
Mitchell, *Deputy* C. R. (1971) — *Castle Baynard*
Mobsby, *Deputy* D. J. L. (1985) — *Billingsgate*
Mooney, B. D. F. (1998) — *Queenhithe*
Moss, A. D. (1989) — *Tower*
Moys, Mrs S. D. (2001) — *Aldgate*
Nash, *Deputy* Mrs J. C. (1983) — *Aldersgate*
Newman, Mrs P. B. (1989) — *Aldersgate*
Nove, P. R. (2004) — *Castle Baynard*
Owen, Mrs J. (1975) — *Langbourn*
Owen-Ward, J. R. (1983) — *Bridge*
Page, M. (2002) — *Farringdon Wn.*

Pembroke, *Deputy* Mrs A. M. F. (1978) *Cheap*
Pollard, J. H. G. (2002) *Dowgate*
Price, E. E. (1996) *Farringdon Wt.*
Pulman, *Deputy* G. A. G. (1983) *Tower*
Punter, C. (1993) *Cripplegate*
Quilter, S. D. (1998) *Cripplegate*
Regan, R. D. (1998) *Farringdon Wn.*
Robinson, Mrs D. C. (1989) *Bishopsgate*
Roney, *Deputy* E. P. T., CBE (1974) *Bishopsgate*
Scott, J. G. S. (1999) *Broad Street*
Shalit, *Deputy* D. M. (1972) *Farringdon Wn.*
Sherlock, *Deputy* M. R. C. (1992) *Dowgate*
Simons, J. L. (2004) *Castle Baynard*
Snyder, *Deputy* M. J. (1986) *Cordwainer*
Spanner, J. H., TD (2001) *Farringdon Wt.*
Stevenson, F. P. (1994) *Cripplegate*
Thompson, D. J. (2004) *Aldgate*
Tomlinson, J. (2004) *Cripplegate*
Twogood, M. (2004) *Farringdon Wt.*
Wang, Mrs C. A. M. (2004) *Cornhill*
Welbank, J. M. (2005) *Billingsgate*
Willoughby, *Deputy* P. J. (1985) *Bishopsgate*
Wooten, D. H. (2002) *Farringdon Wn.*

THE CITY GUILDS (LIVERY COMPANIES)

The constitution of the livery companies has been unchanged for centuries. There are three ranks of membership: freemen, liverymen and assistants. A person can become a freeman by patrimony (through a parent having been a freeman); by servitude (through having served an apprenticeship to a freeman); or by redemption (by purchase).

Election to the livery is the prerogative of the company, who can elect any of its freemen as liverymen. Assistants are usually elected from the livery and form a Court of Assistants which is the governing body of the company. The Master (in some companies called the Prime Warden) is elected annually from the assistants.

The register for 2005–6 listed 24,733 liverymen of the guilds entitled to vote at elections at Common Hall.

The order of precedence, omitting extinct companies, is given in parenthesis after the name of each company in the list below. In certain companies the election of Master or Prime Warden for the year does not take place until the autumn. In such cases the Master or Prime Warden for 2004–5, rather than 2005–6, is given.

THE TWELVE GREAT COMPANIES
In order of civic precedence

MERCERS *(1). Hall,* Mercers' Hall, Ironmonger Lane, London EC2V 8HE *Livery,* 231. *Clerk,* Charles Parker *Master,* A. Lane

GROCERS *(2). Hall,* Grocers' Hall, Princes Street, London EC2R 8AD *Livery,* 349. *Clerk,* Brig. P. P. Rawlins, MBE *Master,* M. A. Hedley

DRAPERS *(3). Hall,* Drapers' Hall, Throgmorton Avenue, London EC2N 2DQ *Livery,* 283. *Clerk,* Rear-Adm. A. B. Ross, CB, CBE *Master,* David Handley

FISHMONGERS *(4). Hall,* Fishmongers' Hall, London Bridge, London EC4R 9EL *Livery,* 319. *Clerk,* Keith Waters *Prime Warden,* Andrew Scott

GOLDSMITHS *(5). Hall,* Goldsmiths' Hall, Foster Lane, London EC2V 6BN *Livery,* 275. *Clerk,* R. G. Melly *Prime Warden,* M. Dru Drury, CBE, FSA

SKINNERS *(6/7). Hall,* Skinners' Hall, 8 Dowgate Hill, London EC4R 2SP *Livery,* 400. *Clerk,* B. P. Plummer, CBE *Master,* J. L. Cohen, QC

MERCHANT TAYLORS *(6/7). Hall,* 30 Threadneedle Street, London EC2R 8JB *Livery,* 332. *Clerk,* David Peck *Master,* John Hall

HABERDASHERS *(8). Hall,* 18 West Smithfield, London EC1A 9HQ *Livery,* 290. *Clerk,* Rear-Adm. Richard Phillips, CB *Master,* Anthony Miller (until 24 November 2005) *Master,* Peter Davidson (from 25 November 2005, subject to election)

SALTERS *(9). Hall,* Salters' Hall, 4 Fore Street, London EC2Y 5DE *Livery,* 167. *Clerk,* Col. Michael Barneby *Master,* William Christopher

IRONMONGERS *(10). Hall,* Ironmongers' Hall, Shaftesbury Place, Barbican, London EC2Y 8AA *Livery,* 133. *Clerk,* Col. Hamon Massey *Master,* Sir Graeme Davies

VINTNERS *(11). Hall,* Vintners' Hall, Upper Thames Street, London EC4V 3BG *Livery,* 312. *Clerk,* Brig. M. Smythe, OBE *Master,* W. D. Robson

CLOTHWORKERS *(12). Hall,* Clothworkers' Hall, Dunster Court, Mincing Lane, London EC3R 7AH *Livery,* 240. *Clerk,* Andrew Blessley *Master,* John Harding Jones

OTHER CITY GUILDS
In alphabetical order

ACTUARIES *(91). Hall,* The Cote, Old Gloucester Road, Alveston, Bristol BS35 3LQ *Livery,* 213. *Clerk,* Michael Turner *Master,* Jeremy Goford

AIR PILOTS AND AIR NAVIGATORS *(81). Hall,* Cobham House, 9 Warwick Court, Gray's Inn, London WC1R 5DJ *Livery,* 500. *Grand Master,* HRH The Duke of York, KCVO, ADC *Clerk,* Paul Tacon *Master,* Capt. Peter Buggé, FRAES

APOTHECARIES *(58). Hall,* Apothecaries' Hall, 14 Black Friars Lane, London EC4V 6EJ *Livery,* 1,282. *Clerk,* A. M. Wallington-Smith *Master,* Prof. B. Livesley

ARBITRATORS *(93).* 13 Hall Gardens, Colney Heath, St Albans, Herts AL4 0QF *Livery,* 150. *Clerk,* Mrs G. Duffy *Master,* Michael Stephens

ARMOURERS AND BRASIERS *(22). Hall,* Armourers' Hall, 81 Coleman Street, London EC2R 5BJ *Livery,* 123. *Clerk,* Cdre Christopher Waite *Master,* Stephen Martin

BAKERS *(19). Hall,* Bakers' Hall, Harp Lane, London EC3R 6DP *Livery,* 300. *Clerk,* John Tompkins *Master,* Alan Willis

BARBERS *(17). Hall,* Barber-Surgeons' Hall, Monkwell Square, Wood Street, London EC2Y 5BL *Livery,* 210. *Clerk* Col. P. J. Durrant, MBE *Prime Warden,* Prof. J. W. Last CBE, DLITT

BASKETMAKERS *(52).* 29 Ingram House, Park Road, Hampton Wick, Surrey KT1 4BA *Livery,* 300. *Clerk,* Roger de Pilkyngton *Prime Warden,* Ronald Bartle

BLACKSMITHS *(40).* 48 Upwood Road, London SE12 8AN *Livery,* 223. *Clerk,* Christopher Jeal *Prime Warden,* Joh Smith

BOWYERS *(38).* 5 Archer House, Vicarage Crescent, Londor SW11 3LF *Livery,* 101. *Clerk,* Richard Wilkinson *Master* Peter Seaton

BREWERS *(14). Hall,* Brewers' Hall, Aldermanbury Square, London EC2V 7HR *Livery,* 175. *Clerk,* Brig. D. J. Ross, CBE *Master,* C. P. Lees-Jones, FRICS

BRODERERS *(48).* Ember House, 35–37 Creek Road, East Molesey, Surrey KT8 9BE *Livery,* 178. *Clerk,* P. J. C. Crouch *Master,* M. Whitfeld

BUILDERS MERCHANTS *(88)*. 4 College Hill, London
EC4R 2RB *Livery*, 206. *Clerk*, Sheila Robinson, TD
Master F H Robertson

BUTCHERS *(24)*. *Hall*, Butchers' Hall, 87 Bartholomew Close,
London EC1A 7EB *Livery*, 664. *Clerk*, Anthony Morrow,
CVO *Master*, G. John Edkins

CARMEN *(77)*. 8 Little Trinity Lane, London EC4V 2AN *Livery*,
500. *Clerk*, Walter Gill *Master*, Michael Power

CARPENTERS *(26)*. *Hall*, Carpenters' Hall, 1 Throgmorton
Avenue, London EC2N 2JJ *Livery*, 184. *Clerk*, Maj.-Gen. P.
T. Stevenson, OBE *Master*, M. O. P. May

CHARTERED ACCOUNTANTS *(86)*. The Rustlings, Valley
Close, Studham, Dunstable LU6 2QN *Livery*, 333. *Clerk*,
Clifford Bygrave *Master*, Sir Hugh Collum

CHARTERED ARCHITECTS *(98)*. 82A Muswell Hill Road,
London N10 3JR *Livery*, 135. *Clerk*, David Cole-Adams
Master, Richard Saxon, CBE

CHARTERED SECRETARIES AND ADMINISTRATORS
(87). 3rd Floor, Saddlers' House, 40 Gutter Lane, London
EC2V 6BR *Livery*, 228. *Clerk*, Col. M. J. Dudding, OBE,
TD *Master*, Sir Clive Martin, OBE, TD

CHARTERED SURVEYORS *(85)*. 75 Meadway Drive, Horsell,
Woking, Surrey GU21 4TF *Livery*, 345. *Clerk*, Mrs A. L.
Jackson *Master*, Brian Lamden

CLOCKMAKERS *(61)*. Salters' Hall, 4 Fore Street, London
EC2Y 5DE *Livery*, 263. *Clerk*, Joe Buxton *Master*, Maj.-
Gen. D. A. Pennefather, CB, OBE

COACHMAKERS AND COACH-HARNESS MAKERS *(72)*.
Woodlands House, The Clump, Chorleywood, Hertfordshire
WD3 4BB *Livery*, 400. *Clerk*, Gp Capt. Gerry Bunn, CBE
Master, Roger Smith

CONSTRUCTORS *(99)*. Forge Farmhouse, Glassenbury,
Cranbrook, Kent TN17 2QE *Livery*, 135. *Clerk*, Tim
Nicholson *Master*, Robert Craig

COOKS *(35)*. Coombe Ridge, Thursley Road, Churt, Farnham,
Surrey GU10 2LQ *Livery*, 78. *Clerk*, Michael Thatcher
Master, G. A. V. Rees

COOPERS *(36)*. *Hall*, Coopers' Hall, 13 Devonshire Square,
London EC2M 4TH *Livery*, 260. *Clerk*, Lt.-Col. Adrian
Carroll *Master*, G. C. Sutton

CORDWAINERS *(27)*. Clothworkers' Hall, Dunster Court,
Mincing Lane, London EC3R 7AH *Livery*, 164. *Clerk*, Lt.-
Col. J. R. Blundell, RM *Master*, R. P. D. Brown

CURRIERS *(29)*. Hedgerley, 10 The Leaze, Ashton Keynes, ,
Wiltshire SN6 6PE *Livery*, 88. *Clerk*, Gp Capt. David Moss
Master, Anthony Steinthal

CUTLERS *(18)*. *Hall*, Cutlers' Hall, Warwick Lane, London
EC4M 7BR *Livery*, 100. *Clerk*, J. P. Allen *Master*, Hon.
Michael Donaldson

DISTILLERS *(69)*. 71 Lincoln's Inn Fields, London WC2A 3JF
Livery, 260. *Clerk*, C. V. Hughes *Master*, David Grant

DYERS *(13)*. *Hall*, Dyers' Hall, 10 Dowgate Hill, London
EC4R 2ST *Livery*, 129. *Clerk*, J. R. Vaizey *Prime
Warden*, N. P. Blair

ENGINEERS *(94)*. Wax Chandlers' Hall, Gresham Street,
London EC2V 7AD *Livery*, 285. *Clerk*, Air Vice-Marshal
Graham Skinner, CBE *Master*, Dr Robert Hawley, CBE,
FRSE, FRENG

ENVIRONMENTAL CLEANERS *(97)*. 6 Grange Meadows,
Elmswell, Bury St Edmunds, Suffolk IP30 9GE *Livery*, 241.
Clerk, Michael Bizley *Master*, Michael Poulter

FAN MAKERS *(76)*. Skinners' Hall, 8 Dowgate Hill, London
EC4R 2SP *Livery*, 202. *Clerk*, Keith Patterson *Master*,
Lawrence Turner, OBE

FARMERS *(80)*. *Hall*, 3 Cloth Street, London EC1 *Livery*, 300.
Clerk, Col. D. King *Master*, Lord Plumb

FARRIERS *(55)*. 19 Queen Street, Chipperfield, Kings Langley,
Herts WD4 9BT *Livery*, 310. *Clerk*, Charlotte Clifford
Master, David Short

FELTMAKERS *(63)*. The Old Post House, Upton Grey,
Basingstoke, Hampshire RG25 2RL *Livery*, 171. *Clerk*, Maj.
J. T. H. Coombs *Master*, Cdr. J. M. D. Curtsis RD

FIREFIGHTERS *(103)*. The Insurance Hall, 20 Aldermanbury,
London EC2V 7HY *Livery*, 70. *Clerk*, Mrs M. Holland
Prior *Master*, Alan Wells QFSM

FLETCHERS *(39)*. *Hall*, The Farmers' and Fletchers' Hall, 3
Cloth Street, London EC1A 7LD *Livery*, 143. *Clerk*, M.
Johnson *Master*, D. H. Wootton

FOUNDERS *(33)*. *Hall*, Founders' Hall, Number One, Cloth
Fair, London EC1A 7JQ *Livery*, 155. *Clerk*, A. J. Gillett
Master, P. J. M. Prain

FRAMEWORK KNITTERS *(64)*. 86 Park Drive, Upminster,
Essex RM14 3AS *Livery*, 215. *Clerk*, Alan Clark *Master*,
Lord Sanderson of Bowden

FRUITERERS *(45)*. Chapelstones, 84 High Street, Codford St
Mary, Warminster BA12 0ND *Livery*, 283. *Clerk*, Lt.-Col.
L. G. French *Master*, P. Y. Bartlett

FUELLERS *(95)*. 26 Merrick Square, London SE1 4JB *Livery*,
109. *Clerk*, Sir Anthony Reardon Smith, Bt. *Master*,
Cyril McCombe, MBE

FURNITURE MAKERS *(83)*. Painters' Hall, 9 Little Trinity
Lane, London EC4V 2AD *Livery*, 287. *Clerk*, Mrs J. A.
Wright *Master*, Edward Tadros

GARDENERS *(66)*. 25 Luke Street, London EC2A 4AR *Livery*,
267. *Clerk*, Col. N. G. S. Gray *Master*, G. R. C. Petty

GIRDLERS *(23)*. *Hall*, Girdlers' Hall, Basinghall Avenue,
London EC2V 5DD *Livery*, 80. *Clerk*, Lt.-Col. Richard
Sullivan *Master*, D. A. F. Gibbes

GLASS SELLERS *(71)*. 57 Witley Court, Coram Street, London
WC1N 1HD *Livery*, 230. *Hon. Clerk*, Col. Audrey Smith
Master, B. J. Rawles

GLAZIERS AND PAINTERS OF GLASS *(53)*. *Hall*, Glaziers'
Hall, 9 Montague Close, London SE1 9DD *Livery*, 290.
Clerk, David Eking *Master*, Phillida Shaw

GLOVERS *(62)*. 73 Clapham Manor Street, London SW4 6DS
Livery, 261. *Clerk*, Monique Hood *Master*, Walter
Demuth

GOLD AND SILVER WYRE DRAWERS *(74)*. Bee Cottage,
North Heath, Chieveley, Berkshire RG20 8UA *Livery*, 313.
Clerk, Cdr. R. E. D. House *Master*, James Walker

GUNMAKERS *(73)*. The Proof House, 48–50 Commercial
Road, London E1 1LP *Livery*, 256. *Clerk*, Col. W. F.
Chesshyre *Master*, C. D. Price

HACKNEY CARRIAGE DRIVERS *(104)*. 25 The Grove,
Parkfield, Latimer, Buckinghamshire HP5 1UE *Livery*, 98.
Clerk, Mary Whitworth *Master*, John Beesley

HORNERS *(54)*. c/o Clergy House, Hide Place, London
SW1P 4NJ *Livery*, 220. *Clerk*, Raymond Layard *Master*,
Dr Brian Ridgewell

INFORMATION TECHNOLOGISTS *(100)*. *Hall*,
Information Technologists' Hall, 39A Bartholomew Close,
London EC1A 7JN *Livery*, 245. *Clerk*, Michael Grant
Master, John Leighfield, CBE

INNHOLDERS *(32)*. *Hall*, Innholders' Hall, 30 College Street,
London EC4R 2RH *Livery*, 114. *Clerk*, Dougal Bulger
Master, Anthony Mellery-Pratt, FRICS

INSURERS *(92)*. The Hall, 20 Aldermanbury, London
EC2V 7HY *Livery*, 380. *Clerk*, L. J. Walters *Master*, Roger
Taylor

INTERNATIONAL BANKERS *(106)*. 1 Bengal Court, London
EC3V 9DD *Livery*, 100. *Clerk*, Tim Woods, BEM *Master*,
Michael Kirkwood, CMG

JOINERS AND CEILERS *(41)*. 75 Meadway Drive, Horsell, Woking, Surrey GU21 4TF *Livery*, 128. *Clerk*, Mrs A. L. Jackson *Master*, Alastair MacQueen

LAUNDERERS *(89)*. *Hall*, Launderers' Hall, 9 Montague Close, London Bridge, London SE1 9DD *Livery*, 250. *Clerk*, Mrs J. Polek *Master*, Paul Woolfenden

LEATHERSELLERS *(15)*. *Hall*, Leathersellers' Hall, 15 St Helen's Place, London EC3A 6DQ *Livery*, 150. *Clerk*, Jonathan Cooke, OBE *Master*, John Newton

LIGHTMONGERS *(96)*. Crown Wharf, 11a Coldharbour, Blackwall Reach, London E14 9NS *Livery*, 165. *Clerk*, Derek Wheatley *Master*, John Otten

LORINERS *(57)*. 8 Portland Square, London E1W 2QR *Livery*, 344. *Clerk*, Graham Forbes, FRICS *Master*, David Lancaster

MAKERS OF PLAYING CARDS *(75)*. 2 Cannon Way, West Molesey, Surrey KT8 2NB *Livery*, 146. *Clerk*, Paul Bowen *Master*, Mark Ladd

MANAGEMENT CONSULTANTS *(105)*. Copperfield, The Ridgeway, Cranleigh, GN6 7HR *Livery*, 148. *Clerk*, Dennis Hall *Master*, Barrie Collins

MARKETORS *(90)*. 13 Hall Gardens, Colney Heath, St Albans, Herts AL4 0QF *Livery*, 250. *Clerk*, Mrs G. Duffy *Master*, Sir Paul Judge

MASONS *(30)*. 22 Cannon Hill, Southgate, London N14 6LG *Livery*, 125. *Clerk*, P. F. Clark *Master*, J. W. Wilson

MASTER MARINERS *(78)*. *Hall*, HQS Wellington, Temple Stairs, Victoria Embankment, London WC2R 2PN *Livery*, 197. *Admiral*, HRH The Prince Philip, Duke of Edinburgh, KG, KT, OM, GBE, PC *Clerk*, Cdr. Rod Craig *Master*, HRH The Princess Royal, KG, GCVO

MUSICIANS *(50)*. 6th Floor, 2 London Wall Building, London EC2M 5PP *Livery*, 381. *Clerk*, Col. Tim Hoggarth *Master*, Peter Fowler

NEEDLEMAKERS *(65)*. 5 Staple Inn, London WC1V 7QH *Livery*, 220. *Clerk*, Michael Cook *Master*, Michael Snyder

PAINTER-STAINERS *(28)*. *Hall*, Painters' Hall, 9 Little Trinity Lane, London EC4V 2AD *Livery*, 320. *Clerk*, Chris Twyman *Master*, Nigel Lindsay-Fynn

PATTENMAKERS *(70)*. 3 The High Street, Sutton Valence, Kent ME17 3AG *Livery*, 200. *Clerk*, Col. R. W. Murfin, TD *Master*, Christopher Stone

PAVIORS *(56)*. 3 Ridgemount Gardens, Enfield, Middx EN2 8QL *Livery*, 251. *Clerk*, John White *Master*, John Carpenter

PEWTERERS *(16)*. *Hall*, Pewterers' Hall, Oat Lane, London EC2V 7DE *Livery*, 80. *Clerk*, Lt.-Col. Thomas Reeve-Tucker, OBE *Master*, Paul Wildash

PLAISTERERS *(46)*. *Hall*, Plaisterers' Hall, 1 London Wall, London EC2Y 5JU *Livery*, 210. *Clerk*, Hilary Machtus *Master*, Michael Hall

PLUMBERS *(31)*. Wax Chandlers' Hall, 6 Gresham Street, London EC2V 7AD *Livery*, 337. *Clerk*, Lt.-Col. R. J. A. Paterson-Fox *Master*, John Lockyer

POULTERS *(34)*. The Old Butchers, Station Road, Groombridge, Kent TN3 9QX *Livery*, 204. *Clerk*, Gwen Butcher *Master*, J. Greville Cater

SADDLERS *(25)*. *Hall*, Saddlers' Hall, 40 Gutter Lane, London EC2V 6BR *Livery*, 73. *Clerk*, W. S. Brereton-Martin, CBE *Master*, J. R. Vant

SCIENTIFIC INSTRUMENT MAKERS *(84)*. 9 Montague Close, London SE1 9DD *Livery*, 230. *Clerk*, N. J. Watson *Master*, C. Saunders Singer

SCRIVENERS *(44)*. HQS Wellington, Temple Stairs, Victoria Embankment, London WC2R 2PN *Livery*, 199. *Clerk*, Andrew Hill *Master*, R. A. Reeve

SHIPWRIGHTS *(59)*. Ironmongers Hall, Barbican, London EC2Y 8AA *Livery*, 414. *Grand Master*, HRH The Prince Philip, Duke of Edinburgh, KG, KT, OM, GBE, PC *Clerk*, Rear Adm. Derek Anthony, MBE *Prime Warden*, Richard Fayer

SOLICITORS *(79)*. 4 College Hill, London EC4R 2RB *Livery*, 350. *Clerk*, Neil Cameron *Master*, Nigel Bamping

SPECTACLE MAKERS *(60)*. Apothecaries' Hall, Black Friars Lane, London EC4V 6EL *Livery*, 380. *Clerk*, Lt.-Col. J. A. B. Salmon, OBE *Master*, J. R. S. Baker

STATIONERS AND NEWSPAPER MAKERS *(47)*. *Hall*, Stationers' Hall, Ave Maria Lane, London EC4M 7DD *Livery*, 429. *Clerk*, Brig. D. G. Sharp, AFC *Master*, R. P. F. Shorten

TALLOW CHANDLERS *(21)*. *Hall*, Tallow Chandlers' Hall, 4 Dowgate Hill, London EC4R 2SH *Livery*, 175. *Clerk*, Brig. R. M. Wilde, CBE *Master*, R. B. Yates

TAX ADVISERS *(107)*. 191 West End Road, Ruislip, Middlesex HA4 6LD *Freemen*, 94. *Clerk*, Paul Herbage *Master*, Erica Stary

TIN PLATE WORKERS (ALIAS WIRE WORKERS) *(67)*. Bartholomew House, 66 Westbury Road, New Malden, Surrey KT3 5AS *Livery*, 205. *Clerk*, Michael Henderson-Begg *Master*, Bruce Gilson

TOBACCO PIPE MAKERS AND TOBACCO BLENDERS *(82)*. Hackhurst Farm, Lower Dicker, Hailsham, E. Sussex BN27 4BP *Livery*, 150. *Clerk*, Nick Hallings-Pott *Master*, Richard Yeo

TURNERS *(51)*. 182 Temple Chambers, Temple Avenue, London EC4Y 0HP *Livery*, 174. *Clerk*, Edward Windsor Clive *Master*, A. G. Ciclitira

TYLERS AND BRICKLAYERS *(37)*. 30 Shelley Avenue, Tiptree CO5 0SF *Livery*, 151. *Clerk*, Barry Blumson *Master*, Philip Parris

UPHOLDERS *(49)*. Hall in the Wood, 46 Quail Gardens, Selsdon Vale, Croydon CR2 8TF *Livery*, 213. *Clerk*, Mrs J. R. Cody *Master*, J. P. Cody

WATER CONSERVATORS *(102)*. 22 Broadfields, Headstone Lane, Hatch End, Middlesex HA2 6NH *Livery*, 189. *Clerk*, Ralph Riley *Master*, David Jones

WAX CHANDLERS *(20)*. *Hall*, Wax Chandlers' Hall, 6 Gresham Street, London EC2V 7AD *Livery*, 128. *Clerk*, R. J Percival *Master*, D. G. Jefferies CBE, FRENG

WEAVERS *(42)*. Saddlers' House, Gutter Lane, London EC2V 6BR *Livery*, 125. *Clerk*, John Snowdon *Upper Bailiff*, J. F. M. Monkhouse

WHEELWRIGHTS *(68)*. Ember House, 35–37 Creek Road, East Molesey, Surrey KT8 9BE *Livery*, 214. *Clerk*, P. Crouch *Master*, T. Hopcroft

WOOLMEN *(43)*. 22 Broomfields, Headstone Lane, Hatch End, Middlesex HAZ 6WH *Livery*, 141. *Clerk*, Ralph Riley *Master*, Richard Pickance

WORLD TRADERS *(101)*. 36 Ladbroke Grove, London W11 2PA *Livery*, 185. *Clerk*, Nigel Pullman *Master*, William King

SECURITY PROFESSIONALS *(No Livery)*. 1 Wallis Mews, Guildford Road, Leatherhead, Surrey KT22 9DQ *Freemen*, 210. *Clerk*, John Maddock *Master*, Trevor Gray

PARISH CLERKS *(No Livery*)*. Acreholt, 33 Medstead Road, Beech, Alton, Hampshire GU34 4AD *Members*, 95. *Clerk*, Lt.-Col. B. J. N. Coombes *Master*, R. M. J. Stewart

WATERMEN AND LIGHTERMEN *(No Livery*)*. *Hall*, Watermen's Hall, 16 St Mary-at-Hill, London EC3R 8EF *Owning Freemen*, 324. *Clerk*, Colin Middlemiss *Master*, Andrew Howard

* Parish Clerks and Watermen and Lightermen have requested to remain with no livery.

LONDON BOROUGH COUNCILS

Council	Administrative Headquarters	Telephone	Population*	Band D†	Chief Executive
Barking and Dagenham	Dagenham, RM10 7BN	020-8592 4500	163,900	£1,153	Graham Farrant
Barnet	Hendon, NW4 4BG	020-8359 2000	314,600	£1,246	Leo Boland
Bexley	Bexleyheath, DA6 7LB	020-8303 7777	218,300	£1,243	Nick Johnson
Brent	Wembley, HA9 9EZ	020-8937 1234	263,500	£1,184	Gareth Daniel
Bromley	Bromley, BR1 3UH	020-8464 3333	295,500	£1,093	David Bartlett
Camden	Judd Street, WC1H 9JE	020-7278 4444	198,000	£1,233	Moira Gibb, CBE
CORPORATION OF LONDON	Guildhall, EC2P 2EJ	020-7606 3030	7,200	£806	Chris Duffield
Croydon	Park Lane, Croydon, CR9 3JS	020-8686 4433	330,700	£1,225	David Wechsler
Ealing	New Broadway, W5 2BY	020-8825 5000	300,900	£1,251	Darra Singh
Enfield	Silver Street, EN1 3XA	020-8379 1000	273,600	£1,229	Rob Leak
Greenwich	Wellington Street, SE18 6PW	020-8854 8888	214,500	£1,180	Mary Ney
Hackney	Mare Street, E8 1EA	020-8356 5000	202,800	£1,253	Penny Thompson
Hammersmith and Fulham	King Street, W6 9JU	020-8748 3020	165,200	£1,158	Geoff Alltimes
Haringey	High Road, N22 8LE	020-8489 0000	216,500	£1,323	Max Caller
Harrow	Harrow, HA1 2UJ	020-8863 5611	207,400	£1,296	Joyce Markham
Havering	Romford, RM1 3BD	01708-434343	224,200	£1,328	Stephen Evans
Hillingdon	Uxbridge, UB8 1UW	01895-250111	242,400	£1,267	Dorian Leatham
Hounslow	Lampton Road, Hounslow TW3 4DN	020-8583 2000	212,300	£1,321	Mark Gilks
Islington	Upper Street, N1 2UD	020-7527 2000	175,800	£1,157	Helen Bailey
Kensington and Chelsea	Hornton Street, W8 7NX	020-7937 5464	158,900	£992	Derek Myers
Kingston upon Thames	Kingston upon Thames, KT1 1EU	020-8546 2121	147,300	£1,375	Bruce McDonald
Lambeth	Brixton, SW2 1RW	020-7926 1000	266,200	£1,096	Stuart Holton
Lewisham	Catford Road, SE6 4RU	020-8314 6000	248,900	£1,199	Barry Quirk, CBE
Merton	London Road, Morden SM4 5DX	020-8543 2222	187,900	£1,247	Ged Curran
Newham	East Ham, E6 2RP	020-8430 2000	243,700	£1,112	Dave Burbage
Redbridge	Ilford, IG1 1DD	020-8554 5000	238,600	£1,197	Roger Hampson
Richmond upon Thames	Twickenham, TW1 3BZ	020-8891 1411	172,300	£1,386	Gillian Norton
Southwark	Peckam Road, SE5 8UB	020-7525 5000	244,900	£1,099	Robert Coomber
Sutton	St. Nicholas Way, Sutton, SM1 1EA	020-8770 5000	179,700	£1,238	Patricia Hughes *acting*
Tower Hamlets	Clove Crescent, E14 2BG	020-7364 5000	196,100	£1,052	Christine Gilbert
Waltham Forest	Forest Road, E17 4JF	020-8496 3000	218,300	£1,305	Jacquie Dean
Wandsworth	Wandsworth High Street, SW18 2PU	020-8871 6000	260,400	£614	Gerald Jones
WESTMINSTER	Victoria Street, SW1E 6QP	020-7641 6000	181,300	£618	Peter Rogers

* Census 2001 (Crown copyright)
† Average Band D council tax bill 2005–6
Councils in CAPITAL LETTERS have City status

WALES

The Principality of Wales (Cymru) occupies the extreme west of the central southern portion of the island of Great Britain, with a total area of 20,758 sq. km (8,015 sq. miles): land 20,628 sq. km (7,965 sq. miles); inland water 130 sq. km (50 sq. miles). It is bounded on the north by the Irish Sea, on the south by the Bristol Channel, on the east by the English counties of Cheshire, Shropshire, Herefordshire and Gloucestershire, and on the west by St George's Channel.

Across the Menai Straits is the island of Anglesey (Ynys Môn) (715 sq. km/276 sq. miles), communication with which is facilitated by the Menai Suspension Bridge (305 m/1,000 ft long) built by Telford in 1826, and by the tubular railway bridge (335 m/1,100 ft long) built by Stephenson in 1850. Holyhead harbour, on Holy Isle (north-west of Anglesey), provides accommodation for ferry services to Dublin (113 km/70 miles).

POPULATION
The population at the 2001 census was 2,903,085 (males 1,403,782; females 1,499,303). The average density of population in 2001 was 1.4 persons per hectare (0.6 persons per acre).

RELIEF
Wales is a country of extensive tracts of high plateau and shorter stretches of mountain ranges deeply dissected by river valleys. Lower-lying ground is largely confined to the coastal belt and the lower parts of the valleys. The highest mountains are those of Snowdonia in the north west (Snowdon, 1,085 m/3,559 ft), Berwyn (Aran Fawddwy, 906 m/2,971 ft), Cader Idris (Pen y Gadair, 892 m/2,928 ft), Dyfed (Plynlimon, 752 m/2,467 ft), and the Black Mountain, Brecon Beacons and Black Forest ranges in the south-east (Pen y Fan, 886 m/2,906 ft; Waun Fâch, 811 m/2,660 ft; Carmarthen Van, 802 m/2,630 ft).

HYDROGRAPHY
The principal river in Wales is the Severn, which flows from the slopes of Plynlimon to the English border. The Wye (209 km/130 miles) also rises in the slopes of Plynlimon. The Usk (90 km/56 miles) flows into the Bristol Channel, through Gwent. The Dee (113 km/70 miles) rises in Bala Lake and flows through the Vale of Llangollen, where an aqueduct (built by Telford in 1805) carries the Pontcysyllte branch of the Shropshire Union Canal across the valley. The estuary of the Dee is the navigable portion, 23 km (14 miles) in length and about 8 km (5 miles) in breadth, and the tide rushes in with dangerous speed over the 'Sands of Dee'. The Towy (109 km/68 miles), Teifi (80 km/50 miles), Taff (64 km/40 miles), Dovey (48 km/30 miles), Taf (40 km/25 miles) and Conway (39 km/24 miles) are wholly Welsh rivers.

The largest natural lake is Bala (Llyn Tegid) in Gwynedd, nearly 7 km (4 miles) long and 1.6 km (1 mile) wide. Lake Vyrnwy is an artificial reservoir, about the size of Bala, and forms the water supply of Liverpool; Birmingham is supplied from reservoirs in the Elan and Claerwen valleys.

WELSH LANGUAGE
According to the 2001 census results, the percentage of people aged three years and over, able to speak Welsh is:

Blaenau Gwent	9.1	Neath Port Talbot	17.8
Bridgend	10.6	Newport	9.6
Caerphilly	10.9	Pembrokeshire	21.5
Cardiff	10.9	Powys	20.8
Carmarthenshire	50.1	Rhondda Cynon Taf	12.3
Ceredigion	51.8	Swansea	13.2
Conwy	29.2	Torfaen	10.7
Denbighshire	26.1	Vale of Glamorgan	11.1
Flintshire	14.1	Wrexham	14.4
Gwynedd	68.7	Ynys Mon (Isle of	59.8
Merthyr Tydfil	10.0	Anglesey)	
Monmouthshire	9.0		
Wales	*20.5*		

FLAG
The flag of Wales, the Red Dragon (Y Ddraig Goch), is a red dragon on a field divided white over green (per fess argent and vert a dragon passant gules). The flag was augmented in 1953 by a royal badge on a shield encircled with a riband bearing the words *Ddraig Goch Ddyry Cychwyn* and imperially crowned, but this augmented flag is rarely used.

EARLY HISTORY

The earliest inhabitants of whom there is any record appear to have been subdued or exterminated by the Goidels (a people of Celtic race) in the Bronze Age. A further invasion of Celtic Brythons and Belgae followed in the ensuing Iron Age. The Roman conquest of southern Britain and Wales was for some time successfully opposed by Caratacus (Caractacus or Caradog), chieftain of the Catuvellauni and son of Cunobelinus (Cymbeline). South-east Wales was subjugated and the legionary fortress at Caerleon-on-Usk established by about AD 75–7; the conquest of Wales was completed by Agricola about AD 78. Communications were opened up by the construction of military roads from Chester to Caerleon-on-Usk and Caerwent, and from Chester to Conwy (and thence to Carmarthen and Neath). Christianity was introduced during the Roman occupation, in the fourth century.

ANGLO-SAXON ATTACKS
The Anglo-Saxon invaders of southern Britain drove the Celts into the mountain stronghold of Wales, and into Strathclyde (Cumberland and south-west Scotland) and Cornwall, giving them the name of *Waelisc* (Welsh) meaning 'foreign'. The West Saxons' victory of Deorham (AD 577) isolated Wales from Cornwall and the battle of Chester (AD 613) cut off communication with Strathclyde and northern Britain. In the eighth century the boundaries of the Welsh were further restricted by the annexations of Offa, King of Mercia, and counter-attacks were largely prevented by the construction of an artificial boundary from the Dee to the Wye (Offa's Dyke).

In the ninth century Rhodri Mawr (844–878) united the country and successfully resisted further incursions of the Saxons by land and raids of Norse and Danish pirates by sea, but at his death his three provinces of Gwynedd (north), Powys (mid) and Deheubarth (south) were divided among his three sons, Anarawd, Mervyn and Cadell. Cadell's son Hywel Dda ruled a large part of Wales and codified its laws but the provinces were not united again until the rule of Llewelyn ap Seisyllt (husband of the heiress of Gwynedd) from 1018 to 1023.

THE NORMAN CONQUEST

After the Norman conquest of England, William I created palatine counties along the Welsh frontier, and the Norman barons began to make encroachments into Welsh territory. The Welsh princes recovered many of their losses during the civil wars of Stephen's reign, and in the early 13th century Owen Gruffydd, prince of Gwynedd, was the dominant figure in Wales. Under Llywelyn ap Iorwerth (1194–1240) the Welsh united in powerful resistance to English incursions and Llywelyn's privileges and de facto independence were recognised in the Magna Carta. His grandson, Llywelyn ap Gruffydd, was the last native prince; he was killed in 1282 during hostilities between the Welsh and English, allowing Edward I of England to establish his authority over the country. On 7 February 1301, Edward of Caernarvon, son of Edward I, was created Prince of Wales, a title subsequently borne by the eldest son of the sovereign.

Strong Welsh national feeling continued, expressed in the early 15th century in the rising led by Owain Glyndwr, but the situation was altered by the accession to the English throne in 1485 of Henry VII of the Welsh House of Tudor. Wales was politically assimilated to England under the Act of Union of 1535, which extended English laws to the Principality and gave it parliamentary representation for the first time.

EISTEDDFOD

The Welsh are a distinct nation, with a language and literature of their own, and the national bardic festival (Eisteddfod), instituted by Prince Rhys ap Griffith in 1176, is still held annually. These Eisteddfodau (sessions) form part of the Gorsedd (assembly) and are believed to date from the time of Prydian, a ruling prince in an age many centuries before the Christian era.

PRINCIPAL CITIES

There are five cities in Wales (with date city status conferred): Bangor (pre-1900), Cardiff (1905), St David's (1994), Newport (2002) and Swansea (1969).

Cardiff and Swansea have also been granted Lord Mayoralties.

CARDIFF

Cardiff, at the mouth of the Rivers Taff, Rhymney and Ely, is the capital city of Wales and at the 2001 census had a population of 305,353. The city has changed dramatically in recent years following the regeneration of Cardiff Bay and construction of a barrage, which has created a permanent freshwater lake and waterfront for the city. As the capital city, Cardiff is home to the National Assembly for Wales and is a major administrative, retail, business and cultural centre.

The civic centre is home to many fine buildings including: the City Hall, Castell Coch, Cardiff Castle, Llandaff Cathedral, the National Museum of Wales, University buildings, Law Courts and the Temple of Peace and Health. The Millennium Stadium opened in 1999;

the largest stadium in the UK until the rebuilding of Wembley Stadium is complete, the Millennium Stadium has hosted FA Cup finals and other high-profile English football matches since 2001.

SWANSEA

Swansea (Abertawe) is a seaport with a population of 223,293 at the 2001 census. The Gower peninsula was brought within the city boundary under local government reform in 1974.

The principal buildings are the Norman Castle (rebuilt c. 1330), the Royal Institution of South Wales, founded in 1835 (including library), the University of Wales Swansea at Singleton, and the Guildhall, containing Frank Brangwyn's British Empire panels. The Dylan Thomas Centre, formerly the old Guildhall, was restored in 1995. More recent buildings include the County Hall, the Maritime Quarter Marina, the Wales National Pool and the National Waterfront Museum.

Swansea was chartered by the Earl of Warwick, c. 1158–84, and further charters were granted by King John, Henry III, Edward II, Edward III and James II, Oliver Cromwell (two) and the Marcher Lord William de Breos. It was formally invested with city status in 1969 by HRH The Prince of Wales.

LOCAL COUNCILS

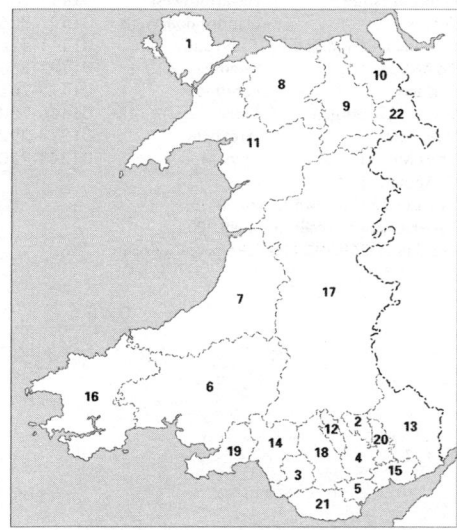

Key	Council	Key	Council
1	Anglesey (Ynys Mon)	12	Merthyr Tydfil
2	Blaenau Gwent	13	Monmouthshire
3	Bridgend	14	Neath Port Talbot
4	Caerphilly	15	Newport
5	Cardiff	16	Pembrokeshire
6	Carmarthenshire	17	Powys
7	Ceredigion	18	Rhondda, Cynon, Taff
8	Conwy	19	Swansea
9	Denbighshire	20	Torfaen
10	Flintshire	21	Vale of Glamorgan
11	Gwynedd	22	Wrexham

LORDS-LIEUTENANT AND HIGH SHERIFFS

County/Shire	Lord-Lieutenant	High Sheriff, 2005–6
Clwyd	T. Jones, CBE	Harold Cunningham
Dyfed	Lord Morris of Aberavon, PC, QC	John Thomas
Gwent	S. Boyle	Cdre Tobin Elliott
Gwynedd	vacant	Jessamy Alexander
Mid Glamorgan	Mrs K. Thomas	Clive Thomas

LOCAL COUNCILS

Council	Administrative Headquarters	Telephone	Population*	Band D Council Tax†	Chief Executive
Blaenau Gwent	Ebbw Vale	01495-350555	70,100	£1,101	R. Morrison
Bridgend	Bridgend	01656-643643	128,700	£995	Keri Lewis
Caerphilly	Hengoed	01443-815588	169,500	£902	Malgwyn Davies
CARDIFF CITY	Cardiff	029-2087 2000	305,300	£872	Byron Davies
Carmarthenshire	Carmarthen	01267-234567	173,600	£941	Mark James
Ceredigion	Aberaeron	01545-570881	75,400	£901	Owen Watkin
Conwy	Conwy	01492-574000	109,600	£827	C. Barker
Denbighshire	Ruthin	01824-706000	93,100	£1,051	Ian Miller
Flintshire	Mold	01352-752121	148,600	£921	Philip McGreevy
Gwynedd	Caernarfon	01286-672255	116,800	£961	Harry Thomas
Merthyr Tydfil	Merthyr Tydfil	01685-725000	56,000	£1,090	Alistair Neill
Monmouthshire	Cwmbran	01633-644644	84,900	£954	Colin Berg
Neath Port Talbot	Port Talbot	01639-763333	134,500	£1,128	Ken Sawyers
NEWPORT CITY	Newport	01633-656656	137,000	£772	Chris Freegard
Pembrokeshire	Haverfordwest	01437-764551	112,900	£734	Bryn Parry-Jones
Powys	Llandrindod Wells	01597-826000	126,300	£901	Mark Kerr
Rhondda Cynon Taff	Tonypandy	01443-424000	232,000	£1,002	Keith Griffiths
SWANSEA	Swansea	01792-636000	223,300	£910	Tim Thorogood
Torfaen	Pontypool	01495-762200	91,000	£940	Alison Ward
Vale of Glamorgan	Barry	01446-700111	119,300	£866	John Maitland-Evans
Wrexham	Wrexham	01978-292000	128,500	£931	Isobel Garner
Ynys Mon (Isle of Anglesey)	Ynys Mon	01248-750057	66,800	£877	Geraint Edwards

* Census 2001 (Crown copyright)
† Average Band D council tax bill 2005–6
Councils in CAPITAL LETTERS have City status

SCOTLAND

he Kingdom of Scotland occupies the northern portion
f the main island of Great Britain and includes the Inner
nd Outer Hebrides, Orkney, Shetland, and many other
slands. It lies between 60° 51′ 30″ and 54° 38′ N.
ititude and between 1° 45′ 32″ and 6° 14′ W.
ongitude, with England to the south, the Atlantic Ocean
n the north and west, and the North Sea on the east.

The greatest length of the mainland (Cape Wrath to the
Iull of Galloway) is 441 km (274 miles), and the greatest
readth (Buchan Ness to Applecross) is 248 km (154
ailes). The customary measurement of the island of Great
ritain is from the site of John o' Groats house, near
Juncansby Head, Caithness, to Land's End, Cornwall, a
otal distance of 970 km (603 miles) in a straight line and
approximately 1,448 km (900 miles) by road.

The total area of Scotland is 78,789 sq. km (30,420 sq.
iles): land 77,097 sq. km (29,767 sq. miles), inland
ater 1,692 sq. km (653 sq. miles).

OPULATION
he population at the 2001 census was 5,062,011 (males
432,494; females 2,629,517). The average density of
e population in 2001 was 0.65 persons per hectare (0.3
rsons per acre).

ELIEF
here are three natural orographic divisions of Scotland.
he southern uplands have their highest points in Merrick
43 m/2,766 ft), Rhinns of Kells (814 m/2,669 ft) and
airnsmuir of Carsphairn (797 m/2,614 ft), in the west;
d the Tweedsmuir Hills in the east (Broad Law 840 m/
756 ft; Dollar Law 817 m/2,682 ft; Hartfell 808 m/
651 ft).

The central lowlands, formed by the valleys of the
yde, Forth and Tay, divide the southern uplands from
e northern Highlands, which extend almost from the
treme north of the mainland to the central lowlands,
d are divided into a northern and a southern system by
e Great Glen.

The Grampian Mountains, which entirely cover the
uthern Highland area, include in the west Ben Nevis
,343 m/4,406 ft), the highest point in the British Isles,
d in the east the Cairngorm Mountains (Ben Macdui
309 m/4,296 ft; Braeriach 1,295 m/4,248 ft; Cairn
orm 1,245 m/4,084 ft). The north-western Highland
ea contains the mountains of Wester and Easter Ross
arn Eige 1,183 m/3,880 ft; Sgurr na Lapaich 1,151 m/
775 ft).

Created, like the central lowlands, by a major
ological fault, the Great Glen (97 km/60 miles long)
is between Inverness and Fort William, and contains
ch Ness, Loch Oich and Loch Lochy. These are linked
each other and to the north-east and south-west coasts
Scotland by the Caledonian Canal, providing a
vigable passage between the Moray Firth and the Inner
brides.

DROGRAPHY
e western coast is fragmented by peninsulas and
inds, and indented by fjords (sea-lochs), the longest of
ich is Loch Fyne (68 km/42 miles long) in Argyll.
hough the east coast tends to be less fractured and

lower, there are several great drowned inlets (firths), e.g.
Firth of Forth, Firth of Tay, Moray Firth, as well as the
Firth of Clyde in the west.

The lochs are the principal hydrographic feature. The
largest in Scotland and in Britain is Loch Lomond (70 sq.
km/27 sq. miles), in the Grampian valleys and the longest
and deepest is Loch Ness (39 km/24 miles long and 244
m/800 ft deep), in the Great Glen.

The longest river is the Tay (188 km/117 miles), noted
for its salmon. It flows into the North Sea, with Dundee
on the estuary, which is spanned by the Tay Bridge (3,136
m/10,289 ft) opened in 1887 and the Tay Road Bridge
(2,245 m/7,365 ft) opened in 1966. Other noted salmon
rivers are the Dee (145 km/90 miles) which flows into
the North Sea at Aberdeen, and the Spey (177 km/110
miles), the swiftest flowing river in the British Isles, which
flows into Moray Firth. The Tweed, which gave its name
to the woollen cloth produced along its banks, marks in
the lower stretches of its 154-km (96-mile) course the
border between Scotland and England.

The most important river commercially is the Clyde
(171 km/106 miles), formed by the junction of the Daer
and Portrail water, which flows through the city of
Glasgow to the Firth of Clyde. During its course it passes
over the picturesque Falls of Clyde, Bonnington Linn
(9 m/30 ft), Corra Linn (26 m/84 ft), Dundaff Linn
(3 m/10 ft) and Stonebyres Linn (24 m/80 ft), above and
below Lanark. The Forth (106 km/66 miles), upon which
stands Edinburgh, the capital, is spanned by the Forth
Railway Bridge (1890), which is 1,625 m (5,330 ft) long,
and the Forth Road Bridge (1964), which has a total
length of 1,876 m (6,156 ft) (over water) and a single
span of 914 m (3,000 ft).

The highest waterfall in Scotland, and the British Isles,
is Eas a'Chùal Aluinn with a total height of 201 m (658
ft), which falls from Glas Bheinn in Sutherland. The Falls
of Glomach, on a head-stream of the Elchaig in Wester
Ross, have a drop of 113 m (370 ft).

GAELIC LANGUAGE
According to the 2001 census, 1.2 per cent of the
population of Scotland, mainly in Western Isles, were able
to speak the Scottish form of Gaelic.

LOWLAND SCOTTISH LANGUAGE
Several regional Lowland Scottish dialects, known
variously as Scots, Scotch, Lallans or Doric, are widely
spoken. The General Register Office (Scotland) estimated
in 1996 that 1.5 million people, or 30 per cent of the
population, are Scots speakers. A question on Scots was
not included in the 2001 census.

FLAG
The flag of Scotland is known as the Saltire. It is a white
diagonal cross on a blue field (saltire argent in a field
azure) and represents St Andrew, the patron saint of
Scotland.

THE SCOTTISH ISLANDS

ORKNEY

The Orkney Islands (total area 972 sq. km/376 sq. miles) lie about ten km (six miles) north of the mainland, separated from it by the Pentland Firth. Of the 90 islands and islets (holms and skerries) in the group, about one-third are inhabited.

The total population at the 2001 census was 19,245; the 2001 populations of the islands shown here include those of smaller islands forming part of the same council district.

Mainland, 15,339	Rousay, 267
Burray, 357	Sanday, 478
Eday, 121	Shapinsay, 300
Flotta, 81	South Ronaldsay, 854
Hoy, 392	Stronsay, 358
North Ronaldsay, 70	Westray, 563
Papa Westray, 65	

The islands are rich in prehistoric and Scandinavian remains, the most notable being the Stone Age village of Skara Brae, the burial chamber of Maes Howe, the many brochs (towers) and the 12th-century St Magnus Cathedral. Scapa Flow, between the Mainland and Hoy, was the war station of the British Grand Fleet from 1914 to 1919 and the scene of the scuttling of the surrendered German High Seas Fleet (21 June 1919).

Most of the islands are low-lying and fertile, and farming (principally beef cattle) is the main industry. Flotta, to the south of Scapa Flow, is the site of the oil terminal for the Piper, Claymore and Tartan fields in the North Sea.

The capital is Kirkwall (population 6,206) situated on Mainland.

SHETLAND

The Shetland Islands have a total area of 1,427 sq. km (551 sq. miles) and a population at the 2001 census of 21,988. They lie about 80 km (50 miles) north of the Orkneys, with Fair Isle about half way between the two groups. Out Stack, off Muckle Flugga, 1.6 km (one mile) north of Unst, is the most northerly part of the British Isles (60° 51′ 30″ N. lat.).

There are over 100 islands, of which 16 are inhabited. Populations at the 2001 census were:

Mainland, 17,575	Muckle Roe, 104
Bressay, 384	Trondra, 133
East Burra, 66	Unst, 720
Fair Isle, 69	West Burra, 784
Fetlar, 86	Whalsay, 1,034
Housay, 76	Yell, 957

Shetland's many archaeological sites include Jarlshof, Mousa and Clickhimin, and its long connection with Scandinavia has resulted in a strong Norse influence on its place-names and dialect.

Industries include fishing, knitwear and farming. In addition to the fishing fleet there are fish processing factories, and the traditional handknitting of Fair Isle and Unst is supplemented now with machine-knitted garments. Farming is mainly crofting, with sheep being raised on the moorland and hills of the islands. Latterly the islands have become a centre of the North Sea oil industry, with pipelines from the Brent and Ninian fields running to the terminal at Sullom Voe, the largest of its kind in Europe. Lerwick is the main centre for supply services for offshore oil exploration and development.

The capital is Lerwick (population 6,830) situated o Mainland.

THE HEBRIDES

Until the late 13th century the Hebrides included othe Scottish islands in the Firth of Clyde, the peninsula c Kintyre (Argyll), the Isle of Man, and the (Irish) Isle c Rathlin. The origin of the name is stated to be th Greek *Eboudai*, latinised as *Hebudes* by Pliny, an corrupted to its present form. The Norwegian nam *Sudreyjar* (Southern Islands) was latinised as *Sodorenses,* name that survives in the Anglican bishopric of Sodc and Man.

There are over 500 islands and islets, of which abou 100 are inhabited, though mountainous terrain an extensive peat bogs mean that only a fraction of the tot area is under cultivation. Stone, Bronze and Iron Ag settlement has left many remains, including those Callanish on Lewis, and Norse colonisation influence language, customs and place-names. Occupations incluc farming (mostly crofting and stock-raising), fishing an the manufacture of tweeds and other woollens. Tourism also an important part of the economy.

The Inner Hebrides lie off the west coast of Scotlar and are relatively close to the mainland. The largest ar best-known is Skye (area 1,665 sq. km/643 sq. mile pop. 9,251; chief town, Portree), which contains th Cuillin Hills (Sgurr Alasdair 993 m/3,257 ft); Bla Bheir (928 m/3,046 ft); the Storr (719 m/2,358 ft) and th Red Hills (Beinn na Caillich 732 m/2,403 ft). Oth islands in the Highland council area include Raasay (pc 194), Rum, Eigg (pop. 131) and Muck.

Further south the Inner Hebridean islands inclue Arran (pop. 5,058) containing Goat Fell (874 m/2,8(ft); Coll and Tiree (pop. 934); Colonsay and Orons (pop. 113); Easdale (pop. 58); Gigha (pop. 110); Isl (area 608 sq. km/235 sq. miles; pop. 3,457); Jura (ar 414 sq. km/160 sq. miles; pop. 188) with a range of h culminating in the Paps of Jura (Beinn-an-Oir, 785 n 2,576 ft, and Beinn Chaolais, 755 m/2,477 ft); Lismc (pop. 146); Luing (pop. 220); and Mull (area 950 sq. kn 367 sq. miles; pop. 2,696; chief town Tobermor containing Ben More (967 m/3,171 ft).

The Outer Hebrides, separated from the mainland the Minch, now form the Eilean Siar Western Isles Islan Council area (area 2,897 sq. km/1,119 sq. mil population at the 2001 census 26,502). The main islan are Lewis with Harris (area 1,994 sq. km/770 sq. mil pop. 19,918), whose chief town, Stornoway, is t administrative headquarters; North Uist (pop. 1,32 South Uist (pop. 1,818); Benbecula (pop. 1,249) a Barra (pop. 1,078). Other inhabited islands inclu Bernera (233), Berneray (136), Eriskay (133), Grims (201), Scalpay (322) and Vatersay (94).

EARLY HISTORY

There is evidence of human settlement in Scotland dati from the third millennium BC, the earliest settlers bei Middle Stone Age hunters and fishermen. Early in second millennium BC, New Stone Age farmers began cultivate crops and rear livestock; their settlements w on the west coast and in the north, and included Sk Brae and Maeshowe (Orkney). Settlement by the Ea Bronze Age 'Beaker Folk', so-called from the shape their drinking vessels, in eastern Scotland dates fr about 1800 BC. Further settlement is believed to h occurred from 700 BC onwards, as tribes were displa rom further south by new incursions from the Continent and the Roman invasions from AD 43.

Julius Agricola, the Roman governor of Britain AD 77–84, extended the Roman conquests in Britain by advancing into Caledonia, culminating with a victory at Mons Graupius, probably in AD 84; he was recalled to Rome shortly afterwards and his forward policy was not pursued. Hadrian's Wall, mostly completed by AD 30, marked the northern frontier of the Roman empire except for the period between about AD 144 and 190 when the frontier moved north to the Forth-Clyde isthmus and a turf wall, the Antonine Wall, was manned.

After the Roman withdrawal from Britain, there were centuries of warfare between the Picts, Scots, Britons, Angles and Vikings. The Picts, believed to be a non-Indo-European race, occupied the area north of the Forth. The Scots, a Gaelic-speaking people of northern Ireland, colonised the area of Argyll and Bute (the kingdom of Dalriada) in the fifth century AD and then expanded eastwards and northwards. The Britons, speaking a Brythonic Celtic language, colonised Scotland from the south from the first century BC; they lost control of south-eastern Scotland (incorporated into the kingdom of Northumbria) to the Angles in the early seventh century but retained Strathclyde (south-western Scotland and Cumbria). Viking raids from the late eighth century were followed by Norse settlement in the western and northern Isles, Argyll, Caithness and Sutherland from the mid-ninth century onwards.

UNIFICATION

The union of the areas which now comprise Scotland began in AD 843 when Kenneth mac Alpin, king of the Scots from c.834, also became king of the Picts, joining the two lands to form the kingdom of Alba (comprising Scotland north of a line between the Forth and Clyde rivers). Lothian, the eastern part of the area between the Forth and the Tweed, seems to have been leased to Kenneth II of Alba (reigned 971–995) by Edgar of England c.973/4, and Scottish possession was confirmed by Malcolm II's victory over a Northumbrian army at Carham c.1016. At about this time Malcolm II (reigned 1005–34) placed his grandson Duncan on the throne of the British kingdom of Strathclyde, bringing under Scots rule virtually all of what is now Scotland.

The Norse possessions were incorporated into the kingdom of Scotland from the 12th century onwards. An uprising in the mid-12th century drove the Norse from most of mainland Argyll. The Hebrides were ceded to Scotland by the Treaty of Perth in 1266 after a Norwegian expedition in 1263 failed to maintain Norse authority over the islands. Orkney and Shetland fell to Scotland in 1468–9 as a pledge for the unpaid dowry of Margaret of Denmark, wife of James III, although Danish claims of suzerainty were relinquished only with the marriage of Anne of Denmark to James VI in 1590.

From the 11th century, there were frequent wars between Scotland and England over territory and the extent of England's political influence. The failure of the Scottish royal line with the death of Margaret of Norway in 1290 led to disputes over the throne which were resolved by the adjudication of Edward I of England. He awarded the throne to John Balliol in 1292 but Balliol's refusal to be a puppet king led to war. Balliol surrendered to Edward I in 1296 and Edward attempted to rule Scotland himself. Resistance to Scotland's loss of independence was led by William Wallace, who defeated the English at Stirling Bridge (1297), and Robert Bruce,

crowned in 1306, who held most of Scotland by 1311 and routed Edward II's army at Bannockburn (1314). England recognised the independence of Scotland in the Treaty of Northampton in 1328. Subsequent clashes include the disastrous battle of Flodden (1513) in which James IV and many of his nobles fell.

THE UNION

In 1603 James VI of Scotland succeeded Elizabeth I on the throne of England (his mother, Mary Queen of Scots, was the great-granddaughter of Henry VII), his successors reigning as sovereigns of Great Britain. Political union of the two countries did not occur until 1707.

THE JACOBITE REVOLTS

After the abdication (by flight) in 1688 of James VII and II, the crown devolved upon William III (grandson of Charles I) and Mary II (elder daughter of James VII and II). In 1689 Graham of Claverhouse roused the Highlands on behalf of James VII and II, but died after a military success at Killiecrankie.

After the death of Anne (younger daughter of James VII and II), the throne devolved upon George I (great-grandson of James VI and I). In 1715, armed risings on behalf of James Stuart (the Old Pretender, son of James VII and II) led to the indecisive battle of Sheriffmuir, and the Jacobite movement died down until 1745, when Charles Stuart (the Young Pretender) defeated the Royalist troops at Prestonpans and advanced to Derby (1746). From Derby, the adherents of 'James VIII and III' (the title claimed for his father by Charles Stuart) fell back on the defensive and were finally crushed at Culloden (16 April 1746).

PRINCIPAL CITIES

ABERDEEN

Aberdeen, 209 km (130 miles) north-east of Edinburgh, received its charter as a Royal Burgh in 1124. Scotland's third largest city, Aberdeen lies between two rivers, the Dee and the Don, facing the North Sea; the city has a strong maritime history and is today a major centre for offshore oil exploration and production. It is also an ancient university town and distinguished research centre. Other industries include engineering, food processing, textiles, paper manufacturing and chemicals.

Places of interest include King's College, St Machar's Cathedral, Brig o' Balgownie, Duthie Park and Winter Gardens, Hazlehead Park, the Kirk of St Nicholas, Mercat Cross, Marischal College and Marischal Museum, Provost Skene's House, Art Gallery, Gordon Highlanders Museum, Satrosphere Hands-On Discovery Centre, and Aberdeen Maritime Museum.

DUNDEE

The Royal Burgh of Dundee is situated on the north bank of the Tay estuary. The city's port and dock installations are important to the offshore oil industry and the airport also provides servicing facilities. Principal industries include textiles, biotechnology and digital media, lasers, printing, tyre manufacture, food processing, engineering and tourism.

The unique City Churches – three churches under one roof, together with the 15th-century St Mary's Tower – are the most prominent architectural feature. Dundee is home to two historic ships: the Dundee-built RRS *Discovery* which took Capt. Scott to the Antarctic lies alongside Discovery Quay, and the frigate *Unicorn,* the only British-built wooden warship still afloat, is moored in Victoria Dock. Places of interest include Mills Public Observatory, the Tay road and rail bridges, Dundee Contemporary Arts Centre, McManus Galleries, Claypotts Castle, Broughty Castle, Verdant Works (Textile Heritage Centre) and the Sensation Science Centre.

EDINBURGH
Edinburgh is the capital city and seat of government in Scotland. The city is built on a group of hills and contains in Princes Street one of the most beautiful thoroughfares in the world. Edinburgh has many strong literary associations and was named UNESCO City of Literature in 2005.

The principal buildings are the Castle, which now houses the Stone of Scone and also includes St Margaret's Chapel, the oldest building in Edinburgh, and near it, the Scottish National War Memorial; the Palace of Holyroodhouse; Parliament House, the present seat of the judicature; three universities (Edinburgh, Heriot-Watt, Napier); St Giles' Cathedral; St Mary's (Scottish Episcopal) Cathedral (Sir George Gilbert Scott); the General Register House (Robert Adam); the National and the Signet Libraries; the National Gallery of Scotland; the Royal Scottish Academy; the Scottish National Portrait Gallery; and the Edinburgh International Conference Centre.

GLASGOW
Glasgow, a Royal Burgh, is Scotland's largest city and its principal commercial and industrial centre. The city occupies the north and south banks of the Clyde, formerly one of the chief commercial estuaries in the world. The main industries include engineering, electronics, finance, chemicals and printing. The city is also a key tourist and conference destination.

The chief buildings are the 13th-century Gothic Cathedral, the University (Sir George Gilbert Scott), the City Chambers, the Royal Concert Hall, St Mungo Museum of Religious Life and Art, Pollok House, the School of Art (Charles Rennie Mackintosh), Kelvingrove Art Galleries, the Gallery of Modern Art, the Burrell Collection museum and the Mitchell Library. The city is home to the Scottish National Orchestra, Scottish Opera, Scottish Ballet and BBC Scotland and Scottish Television.

INVERNESS
Inverness was granted city status in 2000. The city's name is derived from the Gaelic for 'the mouth of the Ness', referring to the river on which it lies. Inverness is recorded as being at the junction of the old trade routes since AD 565. Today the city is the main administrative centre for the north of Scotland and is the capital of the Highlands. Tourism is one of the city's main industries.

Among the city's most notable buildings is Abertarff House, built in 1593 and the oldest secular building remaining in Inverness. Balnain House, built as a town house in 1726, is a fine example of early Georgian architecture. Once a hospital for Hanoverian soldiers after the battle of Culloden and as billets for the Royal Engineers when completing the first Ordnance Survey, today Balnain House is the National Trust for Scotland regional HQ. The Old High Church, on St Michael's Mount, is the original Parish Church of Inverness and built on the site of the earliest Christian church in the city. Parts of the church date back to the 14th century.

Stirling was granted city status in 2002. Aberdeen, Dundee, Edinburgh and Glasgow have also been granted Lord Mayoralty/Lord Provostship.

LORDS-LIEUTENANT

Title	Name
Aberdeenshire	A. D. M. Farquharson, OBE
Angus	Mrs G. L. Osborne
Argyll and Bute	K. A. Mackinnon
Ayrshire and Arran	Maj. R. Y. Henderson, TD
Banffshire	Mrs Clare N. Russell
Berwickshire	Maj. A. R. Trotter
Caithness	Miss M. A. G. Dunnett
Clackmannan	Mrs S. C. Cruickshank
Dumfries	Capt. R. C. Cunningham-Jardine
Dunbartonshire	Brig. D. D. G. Hardie, TD
East Lothian	W. Garth Morrison, CBE
Eilean Siar/Western Isles	A. Matheson, OBE
Fife	Mrs C. M. Dean
Inverness	Donald Angus Cameron of Lochiel
Kincardineshire	J. D. B. Smart
Lanarkshire	G. K. Cox, MBE
Midlothian	Patrick Robert Prenter, CBE
Moray	Grenville Shaw Johnston, OBE, TD

Title	Name
Nairn	E. J. Brodie
Orkney	G. R. Marwick
Perth and Kinross	Sir David Montgomery, Bt.
Renfrewshire	C. H. Parker, OBE
Ross and Cromarty	Capt. R. W. K. Stirling of Fairburn, TD
Roxburgh, Ettrick and Lauderdale	Dr June Paterson-Brown, CB
Shetland	J. H. Scott
Stirling and Falkirk	vacant
Sutherland	Dr Monica Maitland Main
The Stewartry of Kirkcudbright	Lt.-Gen. Sir Norman Arthur, KCB
Tweeddale	Capt. D. Younger
West Lothian	Mrs I. G. Brydie, MBE
Wigtown	Maj. E. S. Orr-Ewing

The Lord Provosts of the four city districts of Aberdeen, Dundee, Edinburgh and Glasgow are Lords-Lieutenant for the districts *ex officio*.

LOCAL COUNCILS

Council	Administrative Headquarters	Telephone	Population*	Band D Council Tax†	Chief Executive
ABERDEEN	Aberdeen	01224-522000	212,125	£1,162	Douglas Paterson
Aberdeenshire	Aberdeen	01467-620981	226,871	£1,065	Alan Campbell
Angus	Forfar	01307-461460	108,400	£1,037	David Sawers
Argyll and Bute	Lochgilphead	01546-602127	91,306	£1,117	James McLellan
Clackmannanshire	Alloa	01259-452000	48,077	£1,074	Keir Bloomer
Dumfries and Galloway	Dumfries	01387-260000	147,765	£988	Philip Jones
DUNDEE	Dundee	01382-434000	145,663	£1,180	Alex Stephen
East Ayrshire	Kilmarnock	01563-576000	120,235	£1,116	Fiona Lees
East Dunbartonshire	Kirkintilloch	0141-578 8000	108,243	£1,078	Sue Bruce
East Lothian	Haddington	01620-827827	90,088	£1,069	John Lindsay
East Renfrewshire	Giffnock	0141-577 3000	89,311	£1,053	David Dippie
EDINBURGH	Edinburgh	0131-200 2000	448,624	£1,126	Tom Aitchison
Eilean Siar (Western Isles)	Stornoway	01851-703773	26,502	£956	Bill Howat
Falkirk	Falkirk	01324-506070	145,191	£999	Mary Pitcaithly
Fife	Glenrothes	01592-414141	349,429	£1,050	Douglas Sinclair, CBE
GLASGOW	Glasgow	0141-287 2000	577,869	£1,213	George Black
Highland	Inverness	01463-702000	208,914	£1,086	Arthur McCourt
Inverclyde	Greenock	01475-717171	84,203	£1,176	Robert Cleary
Midlothian	Dalkeith	0131-270 7500	80,941	£1,176	Trevor Muir
Moray	Elgin	01343-543451	86,940	£1,045	Alastair Keddie
North Ayrshire	Irvine	01294-324100	135,817	£1,075	Ian Snodgrass, OBE
North Lanarkshire	Motherwell	01698-302222	321,067	£1,041	Gavin Whitefield
Orkney	Kirkwall	01856-873535	19,245	£973	Alistair Buchan
Perth and Kinross	Perth	01738-475000	134,949	£1,088	Bernadette Malone
Renfrewshire	Paisley	0141-842 5000	172,867	£1,091	Tom Scholes
Scottish Borders	Melrose	01835-824000	106,764	£1,019	David Hume
Shetland	Lerwick	01595-744511	21,988	£981	Morgan Goodlad
South Ayrshire	Ayr	01292-612000	112,097	£1,063	Tom Cairns
South Lanarkshire	Hamilton	01698-454444	302,216	£1,040	Michael Docherty
STIRLING	Stirling	0845-277 700	86,212	£1,149	Keith Yates
West Dunbartonshire	Dumbarton	01389-737000	93,378	£1,113	Tim Huntingford
West Lothian	Livingston	01506-777000	158,714	£1,074	Alex Linkston

Census 2001 (Crown copyright). Councils in CAPITAL LETTERS have City status
Average Band D bill 2005–6

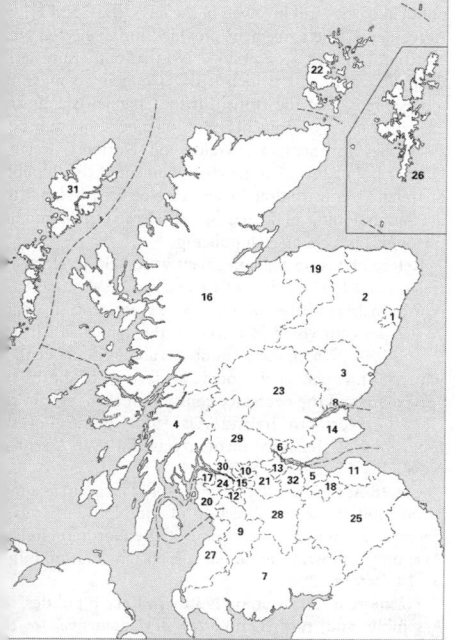

Key	Council	Key	Council
1	Aberdeen City	17	Inverclyde
2	Aberdeenshire	18	Midlothian
3	Angus	19	Moray
4	Argyll and Bute	20	North Ayrshire
5	City of Edinburgh	21	North Lanarkshire
6	Clackmannanshire	22	Orkney
7	Dumfries and Galloway	23	Perth and Kinross
8	Dundee City	24	Renfrewshire
9	East Ayrshire	25	Scottish Borders
10	East Dunbartonshire	26	Shetland
11	East Lothian	27	South Ayrshire
12	East Renfrewshire	28	South Lanarkshire
13	Falkirk	29	Stirling
14	Fife	30	West Dunbartonshire
15	Glasgow City	31	Western Isles (Eilean Siar)
16	Highland	32	West Lothian

NORTHERN IRELAND

Northern Ireland has a total area of 14,144 sq. km (5,467 sq. miles): land, 13,532 sq. km (5,225 sq. miles); inland water and tideways, 628 sq. km (249 sq. miles).

The population of Northern Ireland at the 2001 census was 1,685,267 (males, 821,449; females, 863,818).

In 2001 the number of persons in the various religious denominations (expressed as percentages of the total population) were: Catholic, 40.26; Presbyterian, 20.69; Church of Ireland, 15.30; Methodist Church in Ireland, 3.51; other Christian (including Christian related) 6.07; other religions and philosophies, 0.3; no religion or religion not stated, 13.88.

FLAG

The official national flag of Northern Ireland is now the Union Flag. The flag formerly in use (a white, six-pointed star in the centre of a red cross on a white field, enclosing a red hand and surmounted by a crown) has not been used since the imposition of direct rule.

PRINCIPAL CITIES

BELFAST

Belfast, the administrative centre of Northern Ireland, is situated at the mouth of the River Lagan at its entrance to Belfast Lough. The city grew, owing to its easy access by sea to Scottish coal and iron, to be a great industrial centre.

The principal buildings are of a relatively young age and include the Parliament Buildings at Stormont, the City Hall, Waterfront Hall, the Law Courts, the Public Library and the Museum and Art Gallery.

Belfast received its first charter of incorporation in 1613 and was created a city in 1888; the title of Lord Mayor was conferred in 1892.

LONDONDERRY

Londonderry (originally Derry) is situated on the River Foyle, and has important associations with the City of London. The Irish Society was created by the City of London in 1610, and under its royal charter of 1613 it fortified the city and was for a long time closely associated with its administration. Because of this connection the city was incorporated in 1613 under the new name of Londonderry.

The city is famous for the great siege of 1688–9, when for 105 days the town held out against the forces of James II. The city walls are still intact and form a circuit of 1.6 km (one mile) around the old city.

Interesting buildings are the Protestant Cathedral of St Columb's (1633) and the Guildhall, reconstructed in 1912 and containing a number of beautiful stained glass windows, many of which were presented by the livery companies of London.

Three other places in Northern Ireland have been granted city status: Armagh (1994), Newry (2002) and Lisburn (2002).

CONSTITUTIONAL DEVELOPMENTS

Northern Ireland is subject to the same fundamental constitutional provisions which apply to the rest of the United Kingdom. It had its own parliament and government from 1921 to 1972, but after increasing civil unrest the Northern Ireland (Temporary Provisions) Act 1972 transferred the legislative and executive powers of the Northern Ireland parliament and government to the UK Parliament and a Secretary of State. The Northern Ireland Constitution Act 1973 provided for devolution in Northern Ireland through an assembly and executive, but a power-sharing executive formed by the Northern Ireland political parties in January 1974 collapsed in May 1974. Following the collapse of the power-sharing executive Northern Ireland returned to direct rule governance under the provisions of the Northern Ireland Act 1974, placing the Northern Ireland department under the direction and control of the Secretary of State for Northern Ireland.

In December 1993 the British and Irish governments published the Joint Declaration complementing their political talks, and making clear that any settlement would need to be founded on principles of democracy and consent. The declaration also stated that a democratically mandated parties could be involved in political talks as long as they permanently renounce paramilitary violence.

On 12 January 1998 the British and Irish governments issued a joint document, *Propositions on Heads of Agreement,* proposing the establishment of various new cross-border bodies; further proposals were presented on 27 January. A draft peace settlement was issued by the talks' chairman, the US Sen. George Mitchell, on 6 April 1998 but was rejected by the Unionists the following day. On 10 April agreement was reached between the British and Irish governments and the eight Northern Ireland political parties still involved in the talks (the Good Friday Agreement). The agreement provided for an elected New Northern Ireland Assembly; a North/South Ministerial Council, and a British-Irish Council comprising representatives of the British, Irish, Channel Islands and Isle of Man governments and members of the new assemblies for Scotland, Wales and Northern Ireland. Further points included the abandonment of the Republic of Ireland's constitutional claim to Northern Ireland; the decommissioning of weapons; the release of paramilitary prisoners; and changes in policing.

Referendums on the agreement were held in Northern Ireland and the Republic of Ireland on 22 May 1998. Northern Ireland the turnout was 81 per cent, of which 71.12 per cent voted in favour of the agreement. In the Republic of Ireland, the turnout was about 55 per cent, which 94.4 per cent voted in favour of both the agreement and the necessary constitutional change. In the UK, the Northern Ireland Act 1998, enshrining the provisions of the Agreement, received Royal Assent November 1998.

On 28 April 2003 the Secretary of State again assumed responsibility for the direction of the Northern Ireland departments on the dissolution of the Northern Ireland Assembly, following its initial suspension from midnight on 14 October 2002.

For more information on Northern Ireland politics, the Assembly and further political developments, *see* the Regional Government section.

FINANCE

Northern Ireland's expenditure is funded through the Northern Ireland Consolidated Fund (NICF). Up until devolution on 2 December 1999, the NICF was largely financed by Northern Ireland's attributed share of UK taxation and supplemented by a grant-in-aid. From devolution, these separate elements have been subsumed into a single Block Grant. The Northern Ireland Departmental Expenditure Limit for 2005–6 is £7,578.8 million.

LORDS-LIEUTENANT AND HIGH SHERIFFS

County	Lord-Lieutenant	High Sheriff 2005
Antrim	The Lord O'Neill, TD	David Reade
Armagh	The Earl of Caledon	Leslie Johnston
Belfast City	Lady Carswell, OBE	David Browne
Down	William Hall	James Shaw
Fermanagh	The Earl of Erne	Archie Birrell
Londonderry	Denis Desmond, CBE	Rosemary O'Donnell
Londonderry City	Dr Donal Keegan, OBE	Ian Young, OBE
Tyrone	The Duke of Abercorn	Sydney Gamble

DISTRICT COUNCILS

Council	Telephone	Population*	Chief Executive
Antrim, Co. Down	028-9446 3113	48,366	David McCammick
Ards, Co. Down	028-9182 4000	73,244	Ashley Boreland
ARMAGH CITY, Co. Armagh	028-3752 9600	54,263	Victor Brownlees
Ballymena, Co. Antrim	028-2566 0300	58,610	Mervyn Rankin
Ballymoney, Co. Antrim	028-2766 0200	26,894	John Dempsey
Banbridge, Co. Down	028-4066 0600	41,392	Robert Gilmore
BELFAST CITY, Co. Antrim and Co. Down	028-9032 0202	277,391	Peter McNaney
Carrickfergus, Co. Antrim	028-9335 1604	37,659	Alan Cardwell
Castlereagh, Co. Down	028-9046 4500	66,488	Adrian Donaldson
Coleraine, Co. Londonderry	028-7034 7034	56,315	Wavell Moore
Cookstown, Co. Tyrone	028-8676 2205	32,581	Michael McGuckin
Craigavon, Co. Armagh	028-3831 2400	80,671	Francis Rock
DERRY CITY, Co. Londonderry	028-7136 5151	105,066	Anthony McGurk
Down, Co. Down	028-4461 0800	63,828	John McGrillen
Dungannon & South Tyrone, Co. Tyrone	028-8772 0300	47,735	John Campbell
Fermanagh, Co. Fermanagh	028-6632 5050	57,527	Rodney Connor
Larne, Co. Antrim	028-2827 2313	30,832	Colm McGarry
Limavady, Co. Londonderry	028-7772 2226	32,422	Liam Flanigan
LISBURN CITY, Co. Antrim	028-9250 9250	108,694	Norman Davidson
Magherafelt, Co. Londonderry	028-7939 7979	39,780	John McLaughlin
Moyle, Co. Antrim	028-2076 2225	15,933	Richard Lewis
NEWRY and Mourne, Co. Down and Co. Armagh	028-3031 3031	87,058	Thomas McCall
Newtownabbey, Co. Antrim	028-9034 0000	79,995	Norman Dunn
North Down, Co. Down	028-9127 0371	76,323	Trevor Polley
Omagh, Co. Tyrone	028 8224 5321	47,952	Daniel McSorley
Strabane, Co. Tyrone	028-7138 2204	38,248	Philip Faithfull

Census 2001 (Crown copyright)
Councils in CAPITAL LETTERS have City Status

THE ISLE OF MAN
Ellan Vannin

The Isle of Man is an island situated in the Irish Sea, in latitude 54° 3'–54° 25' N. and longitude 4° 18'–4° 47' W., nearly equidistant from England, Scotland and Ireland. Although the early inhabitants were of Celtic origin, the Isle of Man was part of the Norwegian Kingdom of the Hebrides until 1266, when this was ceded to Scotland. Subsequently granted to the Stanleys (Earls of Derby) in the 15th century and later to the Dukes of Atholl, it was brought under the administration of the Crown in 1765. The island forms the bishopric of Sodor and Man.

The total land area is 572 sq. km (221 sq. miles). The 2001 census showed a resident population of 76,315 (males, 37,372; females, 38,943). The main language in use is English. There are no remaining native speakers of Manx Gaelic but 1,527 people are able to speak the language.

CAPITAL ΨDouglas; population (2001), 25,347. ΨCastletown (3,100) is the ancient capital; the other towns are ΨPeel (3,785) and ΨRamsey (7,322)

FLAG – A red flag charged with three conjoined armoured legs in white and gold

TYNWALD DAY – 5 July

GOVERNMENT

The Isle of Man is a self-governing Crown dependency, having its own parliamentary, legal and administrative system. The British government is responsible for international relations and defence. Under the UK Act of Accession, Protocol 3, the island's relationship with the European Union is limited to trade alone and does not extend to financial aid. The Lieutenant-Governor is The Queen's personal representative on the island.

The legislature, Tynwald, is the oldest parliament in the world in continuous existence. It has two branches: the Legislative Council and the House of Keys. The Council consists of the President of Tynwald, the Bishop of Sodor and Man, the Attorney-General (who does not have a vote) and eight members elected by the House of Keys. The House of Keys has 24 members, elected by universal adult suffrage. The branches sit separately to consider legislation and sit together, as Tynwald Court, for most other parliamentary purposes.

The presiding officer of Tynwald Court is the President of Tynwald, elected by the members, who also presides over sittings of the Legislative Council. The presiding officer of the House of Keys is Mr Speaker, who is elected by members of the House.

The principal members of the Manx government are the Chief Minister and nine departmental ministers, who comprise the Council of Ministers.

Lieutenant-Governor, HE Vice-Adm. Sir Paul Kenneth Haddacks, KCB

ADC to the Lieutenant-Governor, C. J. Tummon

President of Tynwald, The Hon. Noel Cringle

Speaker, House of Keys, The Hon. James Brown, SHK

The First Deemster and Clerk of the Rolls, John Michael Kerruish

Clerk of Tynwald, Secretary to the House of Keys and Counsel to the Speaker, Mr Malachy Cornwell-Kelly

Clerk of the Legislative Council and Deputy Clerk of Tynwald, Mrs M. Cullen

Attorney-General, W. J. H. Corlett, QC

Chief Minister, The Hon. Donald Gelling, MLC

Chief Secretary, Mrs M. Williams

ECONOMY

Most of the income generated in the island is earned in the services sector with financial and professional services accounting for just over half of the national income. Tourism and manufacturing are also major generators of income whilst the island's other traditional industries of agriculture and fishing now play a smaller role in the economy. Under the terms of Protocol 3, the island has tariff-free access to EU markets for its goods.

In May 2005 the island's unemployment rate was 1.4 per cent and inflation (RPI) was 3.7 per cent.

FINANCE

The budget for 2005–6 provides for net revenue expenditure of £483 million. The principal sources of government revenue are taxes on income and expenditure. Income tax is payable at a rate of 10 per cent on the first £10,300 of taxable income for single resident individuals and 18 per cent on the balance, after personal allowances of £8,500. These bands are doubled for married couples. The rate of income tax is 10 per cent on the first £100 million of taxable income of trading companies, rising to 15 per cent on the balance. By agreement with the British government, the island keeps most of its rates of indirect taxation (VAT and duties) the same as those in the United Kingdom. However, VAT on tourist accommodation, property, repairs and renovation is charged at 5 per cent. A reciprocal agreement of national insurance benefits and pensions exists between the governments of the Isle of Man and the United Kingdom. Taxes are also charged on property (rates), but these are comparatively low.

The major government expenditure items are health, social security and education, which account for 58 per cent of the government budget. The island makes an annual contribution to the United Kingdom for defence and other external services.

THE CHANNEL ISLANDS

The Channel Islands, situated off the north-west coast of France (at distances from 16 to 48 km (10 to 30 miles) are the only portions of the Dukedom of Normandy still belonging to the Crown, to which they have been attached since the Norman Conquest of 1066. They were the only British territory to come under German occupation during the Second World War, following invasion on 30 June to 1 July 1940. The islands were relieved by British forces on 9 May 1945, and 9 May (Liberation Day) is now observed as a bank and public holiday.

The islands consist of Jersey (11,630 ha/28,717 acres), Guernsey (6,340 ha/15,654 acres), and the dependencies of Guernsey: Alderney (795 ha/1,962 acres), Brecqhou (30/74), Great Sark (419/1,035), Little Sark (97/239), Herm (130/320), Jethou (18/44) and Lihou (15/38) – total of 19,474 ha/48,083 acres, or 194 sq. km/75 sq. miles. The 2001 census showed the population of Jersey as 87,186; Guernsey, 59,807 and Alderney 2,294. Sark did not complete the same census but a recent informal census gave its population figure 591. The official languages are English and French. country districts of Jersey and Guernsey and throughout Sark a Norman-French *patois* is also in use, though to a declining extent.

GOVERNMENT

The islands are Crown dependencies with their own legislative assemblies (the States in Jersey, Guernsey and Alderney, and the Court of Chief Pleas in Sark), and systems of local administration and of law, and their own courts. Acts passed by the States require the sanction of The Queen-in-Council. The British government is responsible for defence and international relations. The Channel Islands have trading rights alone within the European Union; these rights do not include financial aid.

In both Bailiwicks the Lieutenant-Governor and Commander-in-Chief, who is appointed by the Crown, is the personal representative of The Queen and the channel of communication between the Crown (via the Privy Council) and the island's government.

In 2001 the States of Jersey took the decision to move to a ministerial system of government combined with a system of scrutiny. This system is expected to be fully implemented by the end of December 2005. On 1 May 2004 Guernsey also introduced a ministerial governance system consisting of a Policy Council comprising a chief minister and ten departmental ministers. Justice is administered by the Royal Courts of Jersey and Guernsey, each consisting of the Bailiff and 12 elected Jurats. The Bailiffs of Jersey and Guernsey, appointed by the Crown, are President of the States and of the Royal Courts of their respective islands.

Each Bailiwick constitutes a deanery under the jurisdiction of the Bishop of Winchester.

ECONOMY AND TRADE

A mild climate and good soil have led to the development of intensive systems of agriculture and horticulture, which form a significant part of the economy. Equally important are earnings from tourism and banking and finance, the low rate of income tax (20p in the £ in Jersey and Guernsey; no tax of any kind in Sark) and the absence of super-tax and death duties, make the islands an important offshore financial centre.

Principal exports are agricultural produce and flowers; imports are chiefly machinery, manufactured goods, food, fuel and chemicals. Trade with the UK is regarded as internal.

British currency is legal tender in the Channel Islands but each Bailiwick issues its own coins and notes (*see* Finance section). They also issue their own postage stamps; UK stamps are not valid.

JERSEY

Lieutenant-Governor and Commander-in-Chief of Jersey, Air Chief Marshal Sir John Cheshire, KBE, CB, *apptd* 2001
Secretary and ADC, Lt.-Col. A. J. C. Woodrow, OBE, MC
Bailiff of Jersey, Sir Philip Bailhache, Kt.

Deputy Bailiff, M. C. St J. Birt
Attorney-General, W. J. Bailhache, QC
Receiver-General, P. Lewin
Solicitor-General, Miss S. C. Nicolle, QC
Greffier of the States, M. N. de la Haye
States Treasurer, Mr I. Black

FINANCE

Year to 31 December	2003	2004
Revenue income	£568,005,000	£564,065,000
Revenue expenditure	£526,837,000	£565,691,000
Capital expenditure	£62,730,000	£53,669,000

CHIEF TOWN – ΨSt Helier, on the south coast of Jersey
FLAG – A white field charged with a red saltire cross, and the arms of Jersey in the upper centre

GUERNSEY AND DEPENDENCIES

Lieutenant-Governor and Commander-in-Chief of the Bailiwick of Guernsey and its Dependencies, HE Lt.-Gen. Sir John Foley, KCB, OBE, MC, *apptd* 2000
Secretary and ADC, Colonel R. H. Graham, MBE
Bailiff of Guernsey, Geoffrey Rowland
Deputy Bailiff, Richard Collas
HM Procureur and Receiver-General, J. N. van Leuven, QC
HM Comptroller, H. E. Roberts, QC
Chief Executive, States of Guernsey, M. J. Brown
Chief Minister, Deputy Laurie Morgan

FINANCE

Year to 31 Dec.	2003	2004
Revenue	£287,969,000	£284,879,000
Expenditure	£254,390,000	£275,656,000

CHIEF TOWNS – ΨSt Peter Port, on the east coast of Guernsey; St Anne on Alderney
FLAG – White, bearing a red cross of St George, with a gold cross overall in the centre

ALDERNEY

President of the States, Sir Norman Browse
Clerk of the States, David Jeremiah, OBE
Clerk of the Court, Mrs S. Kelly

SARK

Seigneur of Sark, J. M. Beaumont, OBE
The Seneschal, Lt.-Col. R. J. Guille, MBE
The Greffier, J. P. Hamon

OTHER DEPENDENCIES

Herm and Lihou are owned by the States of Guernsey; Herm is leased. Jethou is leased by the Crown to the States of Guernsey and is sub-let by the States. Brecqhou is within the legislative and judicial territory of Sark.

EUROPEAN PARLIAMENT

European Parliament elections take place at five-yearly intervals; the first direct elections to the Parliament were held in 1979. In mainland Britain Members of the European Parliament (MEPs) were elected in all constituencies on a first-past-the-post basis until the elections of June 1999 when a regional system of proportional representation was introduced (see below); in Northern Ireland three MEPs have been elected by the single transferable vote system of proportional representation since 1979. From 1979 to 1994 the number of seats held by the UK in the European Parliament was 81. At the June 1994 election the number of seats increased to 87. Following EU enlargement in May 2004, the number of seats at the June 2004 election decreased to 78 (England 64, Wales 4, Scotland 7, Northern Ireland 3).

At the European Parliament elections held on 10 June 2004, all British MEPs were elected under a 'closed-list' regional system of proportional representation, with England being divided into nine regions and Scotland and Wales each constituting a region. Parties submitted a list of candidates for each region in their own order of preference. Voters voted for a party or an independent candidate, and the first seat in each region was allocated to the party or candidate with the highest number of votes. The rest of the seats in each region were then allocated broadly in proportion to each party's share of the vote. Each region returned the following number of members: East Midlands, 6; Eastern, 7; London, 9; North East, 3; North West, 9; South East, 10; South West, 7; West Midlands, 7; Yorkshire and the Humber, 6; Wales, 4; Scotland, 7.

If a vacancy occurs due to the resignation or death of an MEP, the vacancy is filled by the next available person on that party's list. If an independent MEP resigns or dies, a by-election is held. Where an MEP leaves the party on whose list he/she was elected, there is no requirement to resign and he/she can remain in office until the next election.

British subjects and nationals of member states of the European Union are eligible for election to the European Parliament provided they are 21 or over and not subject to disqualification. Since 1994, eligible citizens have had the right to vote in elections to the European Parliament in the UK as long as they are entered on the electoral register.

MEPs currently receive a salary from the parliaments or governments of their respective member states, set at the level of the national parliamentary salary and subject to national taxation. British MEPs receive a salary of £59,095.

A proposal that all MEPs should be paid the same rate of salary out of the EU budget, and be subject to the EU tax rate, is under negotiation between the European Parliament and the Council of Ministers but has yet to be agreed.

The next elections to the European Parliament will take place in June 2009.

UK MEMBERS *as at June 2005*

*Denotes membership of the last European Parliament
†Replacements since the last election
‡Previously a member of UKIP
** Previously a member of DUP

**Allister, James (b. 1953), *NI, Northern Ireland*
Ashworth, Richard (b. 1947), *C., South East*
*Atkins, Rt. Hon. Sir Robert (b. 1946), *C., North West*
*Attwooll, Elspeth M. A. (b. 1943), *LD, Scotland*
Batten, Gerard (b. 1972), *UKIP, London*
*Beazley, Christopher J. P. (b. 1952), *C., Eastern*
Bloom, Godfrey (b. 1949), *UKIP, Yorkshire and the Humber*
*Booth, Graham (b. 1940), *UKIP, South West*
*Bowis, John C., OBE (b. 1945), *C., London*
†Bowles, Sharon M. (b. 1953), *LD, South East*
*Bradbourn, Philip, OBE (b. 1951), *C., West Midlands*
*Bushill-Matthews, Philip (b. 1943), *C., West Midlands*
*Callanan, Martin (b. 1961), *C., North East*
*Cashman, Michael (b. 1950), *Lab., West Midlands*
*Chichester, Giles B. (b. 1946), *C., South West*
Clark, Derek (b. 1933), *UKIP, East Midlands*
*Corbett, Richard (b. 1955), *Lab., Yorkshire and the Humber*
*Davies, Christopher G. (b. 1954), *LD, North West*
de Brún, Bairbre (b. 1954), *SF, Northern Ireland*
*Deva, Niranjan J. A. (Nirj), FRSA (b. 1948), *C., South East*
*Dover, Densmore (b. 1938), *C., North West*
*Duff, Andrew N. (b. 1950), *LD, Eastern*
*Elles, James E. M. (b. 1949), *C., South East*
*Evans, Jillian R. (b. 1959), *PC, Wales*
*Evans, Jonathan P., FRSA (b. 1950), *C., Wales*
*Evans, Robert J. E. (b. 1956), *Lab., London*
*Farage, Nigel P. (b. 1964), *UKIP, South East*
*Ford, Glyn J. (b. 1950), *Lab., South West*
*Gill, Neena (b. 1956), *Lab., West Midlands*
Hall, Fiona (b. 1955), *LD, North East*
*Hannan, Daniel J. (b. 1971), *C., South East*
*Harbour, Malcolm (b. 1947), *C., West Midlands*
*Heaton-Harris, Christopher (b. 1967), *C., East Midlands*
*Helmer, Roger (b. 1944), *C., East Midlands*
*Honeyball, Mary (b. 1952), *Lab., London*
*Howitt, Richard (b. 1961), *Lab., Eastern*
*Hudghton, Ian (b. 1951), *SNP, Scotland*
*Hughes, Stephen (b. 1952), *Lab., North East*
*Jackson, Caroline F., DPHIL (b. 1946), *C., South West*
†Kamall, Syed S. (b.1967), *C., London*
Karim, Sajjad (b. 1970), *LD, North West*
‡Kilroy-Silk, Robert (b. 1942), *NI, East Midlands*
*Kinnock, Glenys (b. 1944), *Lab., Wales*
*Kirkhope, Timothy J. R. (b. 1945), *C., Yorkshire and the Humber*
Knapman, Roger (b. 1944), *UKIP, South West*
*Lambert, Jean D. (b. 1950), *Green, London*
*Lucas, Dr Caroline (b. 1960), *Green, South East*
*Ludford, Baroness (b. 1951), *LD, London*
*Lynne, Elizabeth (b. 1948), *LD, West Midlands*
*McAvan, Linda (b. 1962), *Lab., Yorkshire and the Humber*
*McCarthy, Arlene (b. 1960), *Lab., North West*

*McMillan-Scott, Edward H. C. (b. 1949), *C., Yorkshire and the Humber*
*Martin, David W. (b. 1954), *Lab., Scotland*
*Moraes, Claude (b. 1965), *Lab., London*
*Morgan, Eluned (b. 1967), *Lab., Wales*
‡Mote, Ashley (b. 1936), *NI, South East*
Nattrass, Mike (b. 1945), *UKIP, West Midlands*
*Newton Dunn, William F. (Bill) (b. 1941), *LD, East Midlands*
*Nicholson, James (b. 1945), *UUP, Northern Ireland*
*Nicholson of Winterbourne, Baroness (b. 1941), *LD, South East*
*Parish, Neil (b. 1956), *C., South West*
*Purvis, John R., CBE (b. 1938), *C., Scotland*
*Skinner, Peter W. (b. 1959), *Lab., South East*

Smith, Alyn (b. 1973), *SNP, Scotland*
*Stevenson, Struan (b. 1948), *C., Scotland*
*Stihler, Catherine D. (b. 1973), *Lab., Scotland*
*Sturdy, Robert W. (b. 1944), *C., Eastern*
*Sumberg, David (b. 1941), *C., North West*
*Tannock, Dr Charles (b. 1957), *C., London*
*Titford, Jeffrey (b. 1933), *UKIP, Eastern*
*Titley, Gary (b. 1950), *Lab., North West,*
*Van Orden, Geoffrey (b. 1945), *C., Eastern*
*Wallis, Diana (b. 1954), *LD, Yorkshire and the Humber*
*Watson, Graham R. (b. 1956), *LD, South West*
*Whitehead, Phillip (b. 1937), *Lab., East Midlands*
Whittaker, John (b. 1945), *UKIP, North West*
Wise, Tom (b. 1948), *UKIP, Eastern*
*Wynn, Terence (Terry) (b. 1946), *Lab., North West*

UK REGIONS *as at 10 June 2004*

Abbreviations

AGS	Alliance for Green Socialism
Common	The Common Good
ED	English Democrats
EFP	English Freedom Party
FW	Forward Wales
NI	Non-attached Members
OCV	Operation Christian Vote
Peace	Peace Party
PPBG	People's Party for Better Government
Respect	Respect – Unity Coalition
SEA	Socialist Environmental Alliance
Senior	Senior Citizens
Soc. All.	Socialist Alliance
SSP	Scottish Socialist Party
SWW	Scottish Wind Watch

For other abbreviations, *see* UK General Election Results

EASTERN

(Bedfordshire, Cambridgeshire, Essex, Hertfordshire, Luton, Norfolk, Peterborough, Southend-on-Sea, Suffolk, Thurrock)

E. 4,137,210		T. 36.73%
C.	465,526	(30.8%)
UKIP	296,160	(19.6%)
Lab.	244,929	(16.2%)
LD	211,378	(14.0%)
Ind.	93,028	(6.2%)
Green	84,068	(5.6%)
BNP	65,557	(4.3%)
ED	26,807	(1.8%)
Respect	13,904	(0.9%)
Ind.	5,137	(0.3%)
ProLife	3,730	(0.3%)
C. majority		169,366

(June 1999, C. maj. 174,959)

MEMBERS ELECTED
*G. van Orden, *C.*
*J. Titford, *UKIP*
*R. Howitt, *Lab.*
*R. Sturdy, *C.*
A. Duff, *LD*
*C. Beazley, *C.*
T. Wise, *UKIP*

EAST MIDLANDS

(Derby, Derbyshire, Leicester, Leicestershire, Northamptonshire, Nottingham, Nottinghamshire, Rutland)

E. 3,220,019		T. 43.88%
C.	371,362	(26.4%)
UKIP	366,498	(26.1%)
Lab.	294,918	(21.0%)
LD	181,964	(12.9%)
BNP	91,860	(6.5%)
Green	76,633	(5.5%)
Respect	20,009	(1.4%)
Ind.	2,615	(0.2%)
Ind.	847	(0.1%)
C. majority		4,864

(June 1999, C. maj. 78,906)

MEMBERS ELECTED
*R. Helmer, *C.*
‡R. Kilroy-Silk, *NI*
*P. Whitehead, *Lab.*
*C. Heaton-Harris, *C.*
D. Clark, *UKIP*
*W. Newton Dunn, *LD*

LONDON

E. 5,054,957		T. 37.65%
C.	504,941	(26.5%)
Lab.	466,584	(24.5%)
LD	288,790	(15.2%)
UKIP	232,633	(12.2%)
Green	158,986	(8.4%)
Respect	91,175	(4.8%)
BNP	76,152	(4.0%)
CPA	45,038	(2.4%)
ED	15,945	(0.8%)
PPBG	5,205	(0.3%)
C. majority		38,357

(June 1999, Lab. maj. 26,477)

MEMBERS ELECTED
†S. Kamall, *C.*
*C. Moraes, *Lab.*
*Baroness Ludford, *LD*
*J. Bowis, *C.*
*M. Honeyball, *Lab.*
G. Batten, *UKIP*
*C. Tannock, *C.*

*J. Lambert, *Green*
*R. Evans, *Lab.*

NORTH EAST

(Co. Durham, Darlington, Hartlepool, Middlesbrough, Northumberland, Redcar and Cleveland, Stockton-on-Tees, Tyne and Wear)

E. 1,905,132		T. 41.54%
Lab.	266,057	(34.1%)
C.	144,969	(18.6%)
LD	138,791	(17.8%)
UKIP	94,887	(12.2%)
BNP	50,249	(6.4%)
Ind.	39,658	(5.1%)
Green	37,247	(4.8%)
Respect	8,633	(1.1%)
Lab. majority		121,088

(June 1999, Lab. maj. 57,000)

MEMBERS ELECTED
*S. Hughes, *Lab.*
*M. Callanan, *C.*
Ms F. Hall, *LD*

NORTHERN IRELAND

(Northern Ireland forms a three-member seat with a single transferable vote system)

E. 1,072,669		T. 51.72%
Jim Allister, *NI*	175,761	(31.9%)
Bairbre de Brún, *SF*	144,541	(26.3%)
Jim Nicholson, *UUP*	91,164	(16.6%)
Martin Morgan, *SDLP*	87,559	(15.9%)
John Gilliland, *Ind.*	36,270	(6.6%)
Eamonn McCann, *SEA*	9,172	(1.6%)
Lindsay Whitcroft, *Green*	4,810	(0.9%)

MEMBERS ELECTED
**J. Allister, *NI*
B. de Brún, *SF*
*J. Nicholson, *UUP*

NORTH WEST

(Blackburn-with-Darwen, Blackpool, Cheshire, Cumbria, Greater Manchester, Halton, Lancashire, Merseyside, Warrington)

E. 5,151,488	T. 41.46%
Lab.	576,388 (27.3%)
C.	509,446 (24.1%)
LD	335,063 (15.8%)
UKIP	257,158 (12.2%)
BNP	134,959 (6.4%)
Green	117,393 (5.6%)
Lib.	96,325 (4.6%)
ED	34,110 (1.6%)
Respect	24,636 (1.2%)
Country	11,283 (0.5%)
ProLife	10,084 (0.5%)
Ind.	8,318 (0.4%)
Lab. majority	66,942

(June 1999, C. maj. 9,516)

MEMBERS ELECTED

*G. Titley, Lab.
*D. Dover, C.
*C. Davies, LD
*A. McCarthy, Lab.
J. Whittaker, UKIP
*D. Sumberg, C.
*T. Wynn, Lab.
*Sir Robert Atkins, C.
S. Karim, LD

SCOTLAND

E. 3,839,952	T. 30.75%
Lab.	310,865 (26.4%)
SNP	231,505 (19.7%)
C.	209,028 (17.8%)
LD	154,178 (13.1%)
Green	79,695 (6.8%)
UKIP	78,828 (6.7%)
SSP	61,356 (5.2%)
OCV	21,056 (1.8%)
BNP	19,427 (1.6%)
SWW	7,255 (0.6%)
Ind.	3,624 (0.3%)
Lab. majority	79,360

(June 1999, Lab. maj. 14,962)

MEMBERS ELECTED

*D. Martin, Lab.
*I. Hudghton, SNP
*S. Stevenson, C.
*C. Stihler, Lab.
*E. Attwooll, LD
A. Smith, SNP
*J. Purvis, C.

SOUTH EAST

(Bracknell Forest, Brighton and Hove, Buckinghamshire, East Sussex, Hampshire, Isle of Wight, Kent, Medway, Milton Keynes, Oxfordshire, Portsmouth, Reading, Slough, Southampton, Surrey, West Berkshire, West Sussex, Windsor and Maidenhead, Wokingham)

E. 6,034,549	T. 36.78%
C.	776,370 (35.2%)
UKIP	431,111 (19.5%)
LD	338,342 (15.3%)
Lab.	301,398 (13.7%)
Green	173,351 (7.9%)
BNP	64,877 (2.9%)
Senior	42,681 (1.9%)
ED	29,126 (1.3%)
Respect	13,426 (0.9%)
Peace	12,572 (0.6%)
CPA	11,733 (0.5%)
ProLife	6,579 (0.3%)
Ind.	5,671 (0.3%)
C. majority	345,259

(June 1999, C. maj. 369,785)

MEMBERS ELECTED

*D. Hannan, C.
*N. Farage, UKIP
*N. Deva, C.
†S. Bowles, LD
*P. Skinner, Lab.
*J. Elles, C.
‡A. Mote, NI
R. Ashworth, C.
*Dr Caroline Lucas, Green
*Baroness Nicholson of Winterbourne, LD

SOUTH WEST

(Bath and North East Somerset, Bournemouth, Bristol, Cornwall, Devon, Dorset, Gloucestershire, North Somerset, South Gloucestershire, Swindon, Torbay, Wiltshire)

E. 3,845,210	T. 37.80%
C.	457,371 (31.6%)
UKIP	326,784 (22.5%)
LD	265,619 (18.3%)
Lab.	209,908 (14.5%)
Green	103,821 (7.2%
BNP	43,653 (3.0%)
Country	30,824 (2.1%)
Respect	10,437 (0.7%)
C. majority	130,587

(June 1999, C. maj. 246,283)

MEMBERS ELECTED

*N. Parish, C.
G. Booth, UKIP
*G. Watson, LD
*Dr Caroline Jackson, C.
*G. Ford, Lab.
R. Knapman, UKIP
*G. Chichester, C.

WALES

E. 2,218,649	T. 41.86%
Lab.	297,810 (32.1%)
C.	177,771 (19.1%)
PC	159,888 (17.2%)
UKIP	96,677 (10.4%)
LD	96,116 (10.4%)
Green	32,761 (3.5%)
BNP	27,135 (2.9%)
FW	17,280 (1.9%)
Ch. D	6,821 (0.7%)
Respect	5,427 (0.6%)
Lab. majority	120,039

(June 1999, Lab. maj. 14,455)

MEMBERS ELECTED

*G. Kinnock, Lab.
*J. Evans, C.
*J. Evans, PC
*E. Morgan, Lab.

WEST MIDLANDS

(Herefordshire, Shropshire, Staffordshire, Stoke-on-Trent, Telford and Wrekin, Warwickshire, West Midlands Metropolitan area, Worcestershire)

E. 3,957,848	T. 36.63%
C.	392,937 (27.3%)
Lab.	336,613 (23.4%)
UKIP	251,366 (17.5%)
LD	197,479 (13.7%)
BNP	107,794 (7.5%)
Green	73,991 (5.2%)
Respect	34,704 (2.4%)
Pensioner	33,501 (2.3%)
Common	8,650 (0.6%)
C. majority	56,324

(June 1999, C. maj. 84,048)

MEMBERS ELECTED

*P. Bushill-Matthews, C.
*M. Cashman, Lab.
M. Nattrass, UKIP
*E. Lynne, LD
*P. Bradbourn, C.
*N. Gill, Lab.
*M. Harbour, C.

YORKSHIRE AND THE HUMBER

(East Riding of Yorkshire, Kingston-upon-Hull, North East Lincolnshire, North Lincolnshire, North Yorkshire, South Yorkshire, West Yorkshire, York)

E. 3,719,717	T. 42.93%
Lab.	413,213 (26.3%)
C.	387,369 (24.6%)
LD	244,607 (15.6%)
UKIP	228,666 (14.0%)
BNP	126,538 (8.0%)
Green	90,337 (5.7%)
Respect	29,865 (1.9%)
ED	24,068 (1.5%)
Ind.	14,762 (0.9%)
AGS	13,776 (0.9%)

(June 1999, C. maj. 39,629)

MEMBERS ELECTED
*Linda McAvan, Lab.
*T. Kirkhope, C.
*D. Wallis, LD
G. Bloom, UKIP
*R. Corbett, Lab.
*E. McMillan-Scott, C.

For further information about the European Parliament, visit www.europarl.org.uk

The county and unitary authority areas listed after each European parliamentary constituency name are a guide to the areas covered by each constituency.

For detailed information about which areas of the country are covered by a particular region, please contact the Home Office.

LAW COURTS AND OFFICES

JUDICIAL COMMITTEE OF THE PRIVY COUNCIL

The Judicial Committee of the Privy Council is the final court of appeal for the United Kingdom Overseas Territories (see pages 1046–52) and Crown Dependencies and those independent Commonwealth countries which have retained this avenue of appeal (Antigua and Barbuda, The Bahamas, Barbados, Belize, Brunei, Cook Islands and Niue, Dominica, Grenada, Jamaica, Kiribati, Mauritius, St Christopher and Nevis, St Lucia, St Vincent and the Grenadines, Trinidad and Tobago, and Tuvalu) and the sovereign base areas of Akrotiri and Dhekelia in Cyprus. The Committee also hears appeals against pastoral schemes under the Pastoral Measure 1983.

Under the devolution legislation enacted in 1998, the Judicial Committee of the Privy Council is the final arbiter in disputes as to the legal competence of matters done or proposed by the devolved legislative and executive authorities in Scotland, Wales and Northern Ireland.

In 2004 the Judicial Committee dealt with a total of 66 appeals and 71 petitions for special leave to appeal.

The members of the Judicial Committee include past and present Lord Chancellors and Lords of Appeal in Ordinary, and other Privy Counsellors who hold or have held high judicial office in the United Kingdom or in certain designated courts of Commonwealth countries from which appeals are taken to the Judicial Committee.

JUDICIAL COMMITTEE OF THE PRIVY COUNCIL
Downing Street, London SW1A 2AJ T 020-7276 0483/5
Registrar of the Privy Council, Mary Macdonald
Chief Clerk, Jackie Lindsay

JUDICATURE OF ENGLAND AND WALES

The legal system of England and Wales is separate from those of Scotland and Northern Ireland and differs from them in law, judicial procedure and court structure, although there is a common distinction between civil law (disputes between individuals) and criminal law (acts harmful to the community).

The supreme judicial authority for England and Wales is the House of Lords, which is the ultimate court of appeal from all courts in Great Britain and Northern Ireland (except criminal courts in Scotland) for all cases except those concerning the interpretation and application of European Community law, including preliminary rulings requested by British courts and tribunals, which are decided by the European Court of Justice (see European Union section). Under the Human Rights Act 1998, which came into force on 2 October 2000, the European Convention on Human Rights is incorporated into British law; unresolved cases are still referred to the European Court of Human Rights. As a court of appeal the House of Lords consists of the Lord Chancellor and the Lords of Appeal in Ordinary (law lords).

SUPREME COURT OF JUDICATURE

The Supreme Court of Judicature comprises the Court of Appeal, the High Court of Justice and the Crown Court. The High Court of Justice is the superior civil court and is divided into three divisions. The Chancery Division is concerned mainly with equity, bankruptcy and contentious probate business. The Queen's Bench Division deals with commercial and maritime law, serious personal injury and medical negligence cases, cases involving a breach of contract and professional negligence actions. The Family Division deals with matters relating to family law. Sittings are held at the Royal Courts of Justice in London or at 126 District Registries outside the capital. High Court judges sit alone to hear cases at first instance. The Technology and Construction Court, which deals with cases that require expert evidence on technical and other issues concerning mainly the construction industry, is also currently part of the High Court. Appeals from the High Court are heard in the Court of Appeal (Civil Division), presided over by the Master of the Rolls, and may go on to the House of Lords.

In December 1999 the Lord Chancellor began a wide-ranging, independent review of the criminal courts in England and Wales. Lord Justice Auld led the review into how the criminal courts work at every level. The report *Review of the Criminal Courts of England and Wales* was published in October 2001 and assessed what should be done to modernise and improve the criminal justice system so that its aims can be achieved more effectively.

CRIMINAL CASES

In criminal matters the decision to prosecute in the majority of cases rests with the Crown Prosecution Service, the independent prosecuting body in England and Wales. The Service is headed by the Director of Public Prosecutions, who works under the superintendence of the Attorney-General. Certain categories of offence continue to require the Attorney-General's consent for prosecution.

The Crown Court sits in about 90 centres, divided into seven regions, and is presided over by High Court judges, full-time circuit judges, and part-time recorders, sitting with a jury in all trials which are contested. Since 12 April 2000, the distinction between assistant recorders and recorders has changed. Consequently, there are now only full recorders. The post of assistant recorder remains on the statute book but appointments are no longer made. There were 1,241 full recorders at 1 October 2003. The Crown Court deals with trials of the more serious criminal offences, the sentencing of offenders committed for sentence by magistrates' courts (when magistrates consider their own power of sentence inadequate), and appeals from magistrates' courts. Magistrates usually sit with a circuit judge or recorder to deal with appeals and committals for sentence. Appeals from the Crown Court, either against sentence or conviction, are made to the Court of Appeal (Criminal Division), presided over by the Lord Chief Justice. A further appeal from the Court of Appeal to the House of Lords can be brought if a point of law of general public importance is considered to be involved.

Minor criminal offences (summary offences) are dealt with in magistrates' courts, which usually consist of three unpaid lay magistrates (justices of the peace) sitting without a jury, who are advised on points of law and procedure by a legally qualified clerk to the justices. There were around 28,000 justices of the peace in July 2004. In busier courts a full-time, salaried and legally qualified district judge (magistrates' court) – formerly known as a stipendiary judge – presides alone. There were 137 district judges (magistrates' courts) in June 2005. Cases involving people under 18 are heard in youth courts (specially constituted magistrates' courts). Preliminary proceedings in a serious case to decide whether there is evidence to justify committal for trial in the Crown Court are also dealt with in the magistrates' courts. Appeals from magistrates' courts against sentence or conviction are made to the Crown Court. Appeals upon a point of law are made to the High Court, and may go on to the House of Lords.

CIVIL CASES

Most minor civil cases are dealt with by the county courts, of which there are 218 (see the Court Service website, www.courtservice.gov.uk, for further details). Cases are heard by circuit judges or district judges. For cases involving small claims there are special simplified procedures. Where there are financial limits on county court jurisdiction, claims which exceed those limits may be tried in the county courts with the consent of the parties, subject to the Court's agreement, or in certain circumstances on transfer from the High Court. Outside London, bankruptcy proceedings can be heard in designated county courts. Magistrates' courts can deal with certain classes of civil case and committees of magistrates license public houses, clubs and betting shops. For the implementation of the Children Act 1989, a new structure of hearing centres was set up in 1991 for family proceedings cases, involving magistrates' courts (family proceedings courts), divorce county courts, family hearing centres and care centres. Appeals in family matters heard in the family proceedings courts go to the Family Division of the High Court; affiliation appeals and appeals from decisions of the licensing committees of magistrates go to the Crown Court. Appeals from county courts may be heard in the High Court of Appeal (civil division) and may go on to the House of Lords.

CORONERS' COURT

Coroners' courts investigate violent and unnatural deaths, or sudden deaths where the cause is unknown. Cases may be brought before a local coroner (a senior lawyer or doctor) by doctors, the police, various public authorities or members of the public. Where a death is sudden and the cause is unknown, the coroner may order a post-mortem examination to determine the cause of death rather than hold an inquest in court.

Judicial appointments are made by The Queen; the most senior appointments are made on the advice of the prime minister and other appointments on the advice of the lord chancellor.

Under the provisions of the Criminal Appeal Act 1995, a commission was set up to direct and supervise investigations into possible miscarriages of justice and to refer cases to the courts on the grounds of conviction and sentence; these functions were formerly the responsibility of the home secretary.

HOUSE OF LORDS
AS FINAL COURT OF APPEAL

The Lord High Chancellor and Secretary of State for Constitutional Affairs (£213,899, this is the statutory entitlement, however, Lord Falconer currently receives only a salary equivalent to that received by other Secretaries of State in the House of Lords), The Rt. Hon. Lord Falconer of Thoroton, *born* 1951, *apptd* 2003

LORDS OF APPEAL IN ORDINARY *as at 1 August 2005* (each £184,814)
Style, The Rt. Hon. Lord/Lady–

Rt. Hon. Lord Bingham of Cornhill, KG, *born* 1933, *apptd* 2000
Rt. Hon. Lord Nicholls of Birkenhead, *born* 1933, *apptd* 1994
Rt. Hon. Lord Steyn, *born* 1932, *apptd* 1995
Rt. Hon. Lord Hoffmann, *born* 1934, *apptd* 1995
Rt. Hon. Lord Hope of Craighead, *born* 1938, *apptd* 1996
Rt. Hon. Lord Saville of Newdigate, *born* 1936, *apptd* 1997
Rt. Hon. Lord Scott of Foscote, *born* 1934, *apptd* 2000
Rt. Hon. Lord Rodger of Earlsferry, *born* 1944, *apptd* 2001
Rt. Hon. Lord Walker of Gestingthorpe, *born* 1938, *apptd* 2002
Rt. Hon. Lady Hale of Richmond, *born* 1945, *apptd* 2004
Rt. Hon. Lord Carswell, *born* 1934, *apptd* 2004
Rt. Hon. Lord Brown of Eaton-under-Heywood, *born* 1937, *apptd* 2004

JUDICIAL OFFICE OF THE HOUSE OF LORDS
House of Lords, London SW1A 0PW T 020-7219 3111
Registrar, The Clerk of the Parliaments

SUPREME COURT OF JUDICATURE

COURT OF APPEAL
The Master of the Rolls (£191,276), The Rt. Hon. Lord Justice Clarke, *born* 1943, *apptd* 2005
Secretary, Mrs L. Francis
Clerk, Miss L. Turvey

LORDS JUSTICES OF APPEAL *as at 1 August 2005* (each £175,671)
Style, The Rt. Hon. Lord/Lady Justice [surname]

Rt. Hon. Sir Paul Kennedy, *born* 1935, *apptd* 1992
Rt. Hon. Sir Christopher Rose, *born* 1937, *apptd* 1992
Rt. Hon. Sir Robin Auld, *born* 1937, *apptd* 1995
Rt. Hon. Sir Malcolm Pill, *born* 1938, *apptd* 1995
Rt. Hon. Sir Alan Ward, *born* 1938, *apptd* 1995
Rt. Hon. Sir Mathew Thorpe, *born* 1938, *apptd* 1995
Rt. Hon. Sir Henry Brooke, *born* 1936, *apptd* 1996
Rt. Hon. Sir Igor Judge, *born* 1941, *apptd* 1996
Rt. Hon. Sir George Waller, *born* 1940, *apptd* 1996
Rt. Hon. Sir John Mummery, *born* 1938, *apptd* 1996
Rt. Hon. Sir John Chadwick, ED, *born* 1941, *apptd* 1997
Rt. Hon. Sir Richard Buxton, *born* 1938, *apptd* 1997
Rt. Hon. Sir Anthony May, *born* 1940, *apptd* 1997
Rt. Hon. Sir Simon Tuckey, *born* 1941, *apptd* 1998
Rt. Hon. Sir John Laws, *born* 1945, *apptd* 1999
Rt. Hon. Sir Stephen Sedley, *born* 1939, *apptd* 1999
Rt. Hon. Sir Jonathan Mance, *born* 1943, *apptd* 1999
Rt. Hon. Sir David Latham, *born* 1942, *apptd* 2000

Rt. Hon. Sir Bernard Rix, *born* 1944, *apptd* 2000
Rt. Hon. Sir Jonathan Parker, *born* 1937, *apptd* 2000
Rt. Hon. Dame Mary Arden, DBE, *born* 1947, *apptd* 2000
Rt. Hon. Sir David Keene, *born* 1941, *apptd* 2000
Rt. Hon. Sir John Dyson, *born* 1943, *apptd* 2001
Rt. Hon. Sir Andrew Longmore, *born* 1944, *apptd* 2001
Rt. Hon. Sir Robert Carnwath, CVO, *born* 1945, *apptd* 2002
Rt. Hon. Sir Scott Baker, *born* 1937, *apptd* 2002
Rt. Hon. Dame Janet Smith, DBE, *born* 1940, *apptd* 2002
Rt. Hon. Sir John Thomas, *born* 1947, *apptd* 2003
Rt. Hon. Sir Robin Jacob, *born* 1941, *apptd* 2003
Rt. Hon. Sir Nicholas Wall, *born* 1945, *apptd* 2004
Rt. Hon. Sir David Neuberger, *born* 1948, *apptd* 2004
Rt. Hon. Sir Maurice Kay, *born* 1942, *apptd* 2004
Rt. Hon. Sir Anthony Hooper, *born* 1937, *apptd* 2004
Rt. Hon. Sir William Gage, *born* 1938, *apptd* 2004
Rt. Hon. Sir Martin Moore-Bick, *born* 1948, *apptd* 2005
Rt. Hon. Sir Timothy Lloyd, *born* 1946, *apptd* 2005

Ex officio Judges, The Lord High Chancellor and Secretary of State for Constitutional Affairs; the Lord Chief Justice of England and Wales; the Master of the Rolls; the President of the Family Division; and the Vice-Chancellor

COURT OF APPEAL (CIVIL DIVISION)
Vice-President, The Rt. Hon. Lord Justice Brooke

COURT OF APPEAL (CRIMINAL DIVISION)
Vice-President, The Rt. Hon. Lord Justice Rose
Judges, The Lord Chief Justice of England; the Master of the Rolls; Lords Justices of Appeal; and Judges of the High Court of Justice

COURTS-MARTIAL APPEAL COURT
Judges, The Lord Chief Justice of England; the Master of the Rolls; Lords Justices of Appeal; and Judges of the High Court of Justice

HIGH COURT OF JUSTICE

CHANCERY DIVISION
President, The Lord High Chancellor and Secretary of State for Constitutional Affairs
The Vice-Chancellor (£184,814), The Rt. Hon. Sir Andrew Morritt, CVO, *born* 1938, *apptd* 2000
Secretary, Miss E. Harbert
Clerk, Chris James

JUDGES *as at 1 August 2005* (each £155,404)
Style, The Hon. Mr/Mrs Justice [surname]

Hon. Sir John Lindsay, *born* 1935, *apptd* 1992
Hon. Sir Edward Evans-Lombe, *born* 1937, *apptd* 1993
Hon. Sir William Blackburne, *born* 1944, *apptd* 1993
Hon. Sir Gavin Lightman, *born* 1939, *apptd* 1994
Hon. Sir Colin Rimer, *born* 1944, *apptd* 1994
Hon. Sir Hugh Laddie, *born* 1946, *apptd* 1995
Hon. Sir Andrew Park, *born* 1939, *apptd* 1997
Hon. Sir Nicholas Pumfrey, *born* 1951, *apptd* 1997
Hon. Sir Michael Hart, *born* 1948, *apptd* 1998
Hon. Sir Lawrence Collins, *born* 1941, *apptd* 2000
Hon. Sir Nicholas Patten, *born* 1950, *apptd* 2000
Hon. Sir Terrence Etherton, *born* 1951, *apptd* 2001
Hon. Sir Peter Smith, *born* 1952, *apptd* 2002
Hon. Sir Kim Lewison, *born* 1952, *apptd* 2003
Hon. Sir David Richards, *born* 1951, *apptd* 2003

Hon. Sir George Mann, *born* 1951, *apptd* 2004
Hon. Sir Nicholas Warren, *born* 1949, *apptd* 2005

HIGH COURT OF JUSTICE IN BANKRUPTCY
Judges, The Vice-Chancellor and Judges of the Chancery Division of the High Court

COMPANIES COURT
Judges, The Vice-Chancellor and Judges of the Chancery Division of the High Court

PATENT COURT (APPELLATE SECTION)
Judge, Judges of the Chancery Division of the High Court

QUEEN'S BENCH DIVISION
The Lord Chief Justice of England and Wales (£211,399),
The Rt. Hon. Lord Phillips of Worth Matravers, *born* 1938, *apptd* 2005
Private Secretary, Michèle Souris
Clerk, Mrs J. Jones
President, The Rt. Hon. Lord Justice Judge, *born* 1941, *apptd* 2005
Vice-President, The Rt. Hon. Lord Justice May, *born* 1940, *apptd* 2002

JUDGES *as at 1 August 2005* (each £155,404)
Style, The Hon. Mr/Mrs Justice [surname]

Hon. Sir Stuart McKinnon, *born* 1938, *apptd* 1988
Hon. Sir Peter Cresswell, *born* 1944, *apptd* 1991
Hon. Sir Christopher Holland, *born* 1937, *apptd* 1992
Hon. Sir Richard Curtis, *born* 1933, *apptd* 1992
Hon. Sir Anthony Colman, *born* 1938, *apptd* 1992
Hon. Sir John Forbes, *born* 1938, *apptd* 1993
Hon. Sir Rodger Bell, *born* 1939, *apptd* 1993
Hon. Sir Thomas Morison, *born* 1939, *apptd* 1993
Hon. Sir Andrew Collins, *born* 1942, *apptd* 1994
Hon. Sir Alexander Butterfield, *born* 1942, *apptd* 1995
Hon. Sir George Newman, *born* 1941, *apptd* 1995
Hon. Sir David Poole, *born* 1938, *apptd* 1995
Hon. Sir Martin Moore-Bick, *born* 1946, *apptd* 1995
Hon. Sir Gordon Langley, *born* 1943, *apptd* 1995
Hon. Sir Robert Nelson, *born* 1942, *apptd* 1996
Hon. Sir Roger Toulson, *born* 1946, *apptd* 1996
Hon. Sir Alan Moses, *born* 1945, *apptd* 1996
Hon. Sir David Eady, *born* 1943, *apptd* 1997
Hon. Sir Jeremy Sullivan, *born* 1945, *apptd* 1997
Hon. Sir David Penry-Davey, *born* 1942, *apptd* 1997
Hon. Sir Stephen Richards, *born* 1950, *apptd* 1997
Hon. Sir David Steel, *born* 1943, *apptd* 1998
Hon. Sir Charles Gray, *born* 1942, *apptd* 1998
Hon. Sir Nicolas Bratza, *born* 1945, *apptd* 1998
Hon. Sir Michael Burton, *born* 1946, *apptd* 1998
Hon. Sir Rupert Jackson, *born* 1948, *apptd* 1999
Hon. Dame Heather Hallett, DBE, *born* 1949, *apptd* 1999
Hon. Sir Patrick Elias, *born* 1947, *apptd* 1999
Hon. Sir Richard Aikens, *born* 1948, *apptd* 1999
Hon. Sir Stephen Silber, *born* 1944, *apptd* 1999
Hon. Sir John Goldring, *born* 1944, *apptd* 1999
Hon. Sir Peter Crane, *born* 1940, *apptd* 2000
Hon. Dame Anne Rafferty, DBE, *born* 1950, *apptd* 2000
Hon. Sir Geoffrey Grigson, *born* 1944, *apptd* 2000
Hon. Sir Richard Gibbs, *born* 1941, *apptd* 2000
Hon. Sir Richard Henriques, *born* 1943, *apptd* 2000
Hon. Sir Stephen Tomlinson, *born* 1952, *apptd* 2000
Hon. Sir Andrew Smith, *born* 1947, *apptd* 2000
Hon. Sir Stanley Burnton, *born* 1942, *apptd* 2000
Hon. Sir Patrick Hunt, *born* 1943, *apptd* 2000

Hon. Sir Christopher Pitchford, *born* 1947, *apptd* 2000
Hon. Sir Brian Leveson, *born* 1949, *apptd* 2000
Hon. Sir Duncan Ouseley, *born* 1950, *apptd* 2000
Hon. Sir Richard McCombe, *born* 1952, *apptd* 2001
Hon. Sir Raymond Jack, *born* 1942, *apptd* 2001
Hon. Sir Robert Owen, *born* 1944, *apptd* 2001
Hon. Sir Colin Mackay, *born* 1943, *apptd* 2001
Hon. Sir John Mitting, *born* 1947, *apptd* 2001
Hon. Sir Roderick Evans, *born* 1946, *apptd* 2001
Hon. Sir Nigel Davis, *born* 1951, *apptd* 2001
Hon. Sir Peter Gross, *born* 1952, *apptd* 2001
Hon. Sir Brian Keith, *born* 1944, *apptd* 2001
Hon. Sir Jeremy Cooke, *born* 1949, *apptd* 2001
Hon. Sir Richard Field, *born* 1947, *apptd* 2002
Hon. Sir Christopher Pitchers, *born* 1942, *apptd* 2002
Hon. Sir Colman Treacy, *born* 1949, *apptd* 2002
Hon. Sir Peregrine Simon, *born* 1950, *apptd* 2002
Hon. Sir Roger Royce, *born* 1944, *apptd* 2002
Hon. Dame Laura Cox, DBE, *born* 1951, *apptd* 2002
Hon. Sir Adrian Fulford, *born* 1953, *apptd* 2002
Hon. Sir Jack Beatson, *born* 1948, *apptd* 2003
Hon. Sir Michael Tugendhat, *born* 1944, *apptd* 2003
Hon. Sir David Clarke, *born* 1942, *apptd* 2003
Hon. Sir Richard Wakerley, *born* 1942, *apptd* 2003
Hon. Sir Anthony Hughes, *born* 1948, *apptd* 2004
Hon. Dame Elizabeth Gloster, DBE, *born* 1949, *apptd* 2004
Hon. Sir David Bean, *born* 1954, *apptd* 2004
Hon. Sir Alan Wilkie, *born* 1947, *apptd* 2004
Hon. Dame Linda Dobbs, DBE, *born* 1951, *apptd* 2004
Hon. Sir Henry Hodge, OBE, *born* 1944, *apptd* 2004
Hon. Sir Paul Walker, *born* 1954, *apptd* 2004
Hon. Sir David Calvert-Smith, *born* 1945, *apptd* 2005
Hon. Sir Christopher Clarke, *born* 1947, *apptd* 2005
Hon. Sir Peter Openshaw, *born* 1947, *apptd* 2005

FAMILY DIVISION
President (£184,814), The Rt. Hon. Sir Mark Potter, *born* 1937, *apptd* 2005
Secretary, Mrs S. Leung
Clerk, Miss Ayo Onatade

JUDGES *as at 1 August 2005* (each £155,404)
Style, The Hon. Mr/Mrs Justice [surname]

Hon. Dame Joyanne Bracewell, DBE, *born* 1934, *apptd* 1990
Hon. Sir Jan Singer, *born* 1944, *apptd* 1993
Hon. Sir Nicholas Wilson, *born* 1945, *apptd* 1993
Hon. Sir Andrew Kirkwood, *born* 1944, *apptd* 1993
Hon. Sir Hugh Bennett, *born* 1943, *apptd* 1995
Hon. Sir Edward Holman, *born* 1947, *apptd* 1995
Hon. Dame Mary Hogg, DBE, *born* 1947, *apptd* 1995
Hon. Sir Christopher Sumner, *born* 1939, *apptd* 1996
Hon. Sir Arthur Charles, *born* 1948, *apptd* 1998
Hon. Sir David Bodey, *born* 1947, *apptd* 1999
Hon. Dame Jill Black, DBE, *born* 1954, *apptd* 1999
Hon. Sir James Munby, *born* 1948, *apptd* 2000
Hon. Sir Paul Coleridge, *born* 1949, *apptd* 2000
Hon. Sir Mark Hedley, *born* 1946, *apptd* 2002
Hon. Dame Anna Pauffley, DBE, *born* 1956, *apptd* 2003
Hon. Sir Roderic Wood, *born* 1951, *apptd* 2004
Hon. Dame Florence Baron, DBE, *born* 1952, *apptd* 2004
Hon. Sir Ernest Ryder, *born* 1957, *apptd* 2004
Hon. Sir Andrew McFarlane, *born* 1954, *apptd* 2005

TECHNOLOGY AND CONSTRUCTION COURT
St Dunstan's House, 133–137 Fetter Lane, London EC4A 1HD
T 020-7947 6022

JUDGES (each £125,803, Presiding Judge, £155,404)
The Hon. Mr Justice Jackson *(Presiding Judge)*
His Hon. Judge Havery, QC
His Hon. Judge Thornton, QC
His Hon. Judge Wilcox
His Hon. Judge Toulmin, CMG, QC
His Hon. Judge Coulson, QC
Court Manager, Kevin Johnson

LORD CHANCELLOR'S DEPARTMENT
see Government Departments section

SUPREME COURT DEPARTMENTS AND OFFICES
Royal Courts of Justice, London WC2A 2LL
T 020-7947 6000

DIRECTOR'S OFFICE
T 020-7947 6159
Director, Alistair Clegg
Group Manager and Deputy Director, J. Selch
Group Manager, Probate Service, R. P. Knight
Group Manager, Family Proceedings, J. Miller
Finance and Performance Officer, K. Richardson
Criminal Appeals and Administration Court Manager, Helen Smith

ADMIRALTY AND COMMERCIAL REGISTRY AND MARSHAL'S OFFICE
T 020-7947 6112
Registrar, P. Miller
Admiralty Marshal and Court Manager, K. Houghton

BANKRUPTCY AND COMPANIES COURT
T 020-7947 6441
Chief Registrar, S. Baister
Bankruptcy Registrars, C. Derrett; G. W. Jaques; W. Nicholls; P. J. S. Rawson; J. A. Simmonds
Court Manager, Jane O'Connor

CENTRAL OFFICE OF THE SUPREME COURT
Senior Master of the Supreme Court (QBD), and Queen's Remembrancer, R. L. Turner
Masters of the Supreme Court (QBD), P. G. A. Eyre; B. J. F. Fontaine; I. H. Foster; H. J. Leslie; P. Miller; G. H. Rose; J. G. G. Ungley; S. Whittaker; B. Yoxall
Court Manager, M. A. Brown

CHANCERY CHAMBERS
T 020-7947 7785
Chief Master of the Supreme Court, J. I. Winegarten
Masters of the Supreme Court, T. J. Bowles; N. W. Bragge; J. A. Moncaster; N. S. Price; P. R. Teverson
Court Manager, Jane O'Connor

COURT OF APPEAL CIVIL DIVISION
T 020-7947 6533
Head of the Civil Appeals Office, David Gladwell
Court Manager, Judy Anckorn

COURT OF APPEAL CRIMINAL DIVISION
T 020-7947 6011
Registrar, R. A. Venne
Deputy Registrar, Ms P. Donelly
Group Manager, Helen Smith

ADMINISTRATIVE OFFICE OF THE SUPREME COURT
T 020-7947 6655
*Master of the Crown Office, and Queen's Coroner and
  Attorney,* R. A. Venne
Head of Crown Office, Mrs L. G. Knapman
Group Manager, Helen Smith

EXAMINERS OF THE COURT
Empowered to take examination of witnesses in all
divisions of the High Court.
Examiners, M. W. M. Chism; A. G. Dyer; A. W. Hughes;
  Mrs G. M. Kenne; R. M. Planterose

SUPREME COURT COSTS OFFICE
T 020-7947 7314
Senior Cost Judge, P. T. Hurst
Masters of the Supreme Court, C. D. N. Campbell;
  A. Gordon-Saker; J. E. O'Hare; P. R. Rogers;
  T. H. Seager-Berry; J. Simons; C. C. Wright
Court Manager, Geoff Waterhouse

COURT OF PROTECTION
Archway Towers, 11th Floor, 2 Junction Road, London N19 5SZ
T 020-7664 7317
Master, D. A. Lush

ELECTION PETITIONS OFFICE
Room E08, Royal Courts of Justice, London WC2A 2LL
T 020-7947 6956
The office accepts petitions and deals with all matters
relating to the questioning of parliamentary, European
Parliament and local government elections, and with
applications for relief under the Representation of the
People legislation.
Prescribed Officer, R. L. Turner
Chief Clerk, Ms C. Bowstead

OFFICE OF THE LORD CHANCELLOR'S VISITORS
Archway Towers, 11th Floor, 2 Junction Road, London N19 5SZ
T 020-7664 7317
Legal Visitor, A. R. Tyrrell
Medical Visitors, Dr T. S. Ananthanarayanan; Dr A. Bailey;
  Dr N. Choudry; Dr T. Heads; Dr R. Lucas; Dr S. B.
  Mahapatra; Dr P. Saleem; Dr J. Waite

OFFICIAL RECEIVERS' DEPARTMENT
21 Bloomsbury Street, London WC1B 3QW
T 020-7637 1110
Inspector-General, D. Flynn
Deputies, L. Gramp; G. Horna

OFFICIAL SOLICITOR'S DEPARTMENT
81 Chancery Lane, London WC2A 1DD
T 020-7911 7127
Official Solicitor to the Supreme Court, L. C. Oates
Deputy Official Solicitor, E. Solomons

PRINCIPAL REGISTRY (FAMILY DIVISION)
First Avenue House, 42–49 High Holborn, London WC1V 6NP
T 020-7947 6000
Senior District Judge, P. Waller
District Judges, A. R. S. Bassett-Cross; M. C. Berry; Ms H.
  Black; Ms S. M. Bowman; Ms H. C. Bradley; G. C.
  Brasse; Ms P. Cushing; Ms K. E. Green; P. Greene; R.
  Harper; G. Maple; Ms H. McGregor; C. Million; Ms D.
  Redgrave; Ms L. D. Roberts; R. Robinson; M. J. Segal;
  K. J. White
Family and Probate Service Group Manager, R. P. Knight

DISTRICT PROBATE REGISTRARS:
Probate Manager of London, Kevin Donnelly
Birmingham District, Pam Walbeoff
Brighton District, Phil Ellwood
Bristol District, Russell Joyce
Ipswich District, Helen Whitby
Leeds District, Angela Parry
Liverpool District, Karen Clark-Rimmer
Manchester District, Paul Burch
Newcastle District, Christine Riley
Oxford District, Roland Da Costa
Wales District, Paul Curran
Winchester District, Alan Butler

JUDGE ADVOCATES

THE JUDGE ADVOCATE OF THE FLEET
c/o Chichester Combined Court, Southgate, Chichester
PO19 1SX T 01243-520741
Judge Advocate of the Fleet (£116,515), His Hon. Judge
  Sessions

**OFFICE OF THE JUDGE ADVOCATE-GENERAL OF THE
FORCES**
(Joint Service for the Army and the Royal Air Force)
81 Chancery Lane, London WC2A IBQ
T 020-7218 8089
Judge Advocate-General (£116,515), His Hon. Judge
  Blackett
Vice-Judge Advocate-General (£112,116), Michael Hunter
Judge Advocates (£97,483),* J. F. T. Bayliss; C. R. Burn;
  J. P. Camp; M. R. Elsom; R. C. C. Seymour
Style for Judge Advocates, Judge Advocate [surname]
* salary includes £4,000 inner London weighting

HIGH COURT AND CROWN COURT CENTRES

First-tier centres deal with both civil and criminal cases
and are served by High Court and circuit judges. Second-
tier centres deal with criminal cases only and are served
by High Court and circuit judges. Third-tier centres deal
with criminal cases only and are served only by circuit
judges.

LONDON REGION
First-tier – None
Second-tier – Central Criminal Court
Third-tier – Blackfriars, Harrow, Inner London Sessions
  House, Isleworth, Kingston, Middlesex Guildhall,
  Snaresbrook, Southwark, Wood Green, Woolwich and
  Croydon
Regional Director, Nicola Bastin, 1st Floor, 10 Maltravers
  Street, London WC2A 3EU T 020-7947 6072
Area Directors (London Crown): Sarah McAdam, *Central;*
  Sandra Aston, *North-East;* Rachel Cerfontyne, *North-
  West;* Bertie Pincheria, *South-East;* Danny Sullivan,
  South-West
Area Director (London Civil), Linda Lennon
Area Director (London Family), Sheridan Greenland

The High Court in Greater London sits at the Royal
Courts of Justice.

MIDLAND REGION
First-tier – Birmingham, Lincoln, Nottingham, Stafford,
  Warwick
Second-tier – Leicester, Northampton, Shrewsbury,
  Worcester, Wolverhampton

Third-tier – Coventry, Derby, Hereford, Stoke-on-Trent
Regional Director, Alan Eccles, PO Box 11772, 6th Floor, Temple Court, Bull Street, Birmingham B4 6WF
T 0121-681 3213
Area Directors: Dave Bennett, *Staffordshire*; Judith Cashmore-James, *West Mercia*; Lin Hunnigan, *West Midlands*; Kevin Launchbury, *Warwickshire*; Robin Lovell, *Northamptonshire*; Linda Mayhew, *Derbyshire*; Alan Philips, *Nottinghamshire*; Richard Redgrave, *Lincolnshire*; Mark Swales, *Leicestershire/Warwickshire Group*; D. Bennett, *Staffordshire/West Mercia Group*; A. Phillips, *East Midlands Group*

NORTH-EASTERN REGION

First-tier – Leeds, Newcastle upon Tyne, Sheffield, Teesside
Second-tier – Bradford, York
Third-tier – Doncaster, Durham, Kingston-upon-Hull, Great Grimsby
Regional Director, S. Caven, 18th Floor, West Riding House, Albion Street, Leeds LS1 5AA T 0113-251 1200
Area Directors: Paul Bradley, *North Yorkshire*; Dyfed Foulkes, *Humberside*; Sharon Greenhough, *South Yorkshire*; David Keane, *Durham*; Colin Monson, *Cleveland*; Sheila Proudlock, *Northumbria*; Patrick Traynor, *West Yorkshire*

NORTH-WESTERN REGION

First-tier – Carlisle, Liverpool, Manchester (Crown Square), Preston
Third-tier – Barrow-in-Furness, Bolton, Burnley, Manchester (Minshull Street)
Regional Director, Mrs C. A. Mayer, 15 Quay Street, Manchester M60 9FD T 0161-833 1005
Area Directors: S. Evans, *Cumbria*; Miss G. Hague, *Lancashire*; R. Knott, *Greater Manchester*; S. McNally, *Merseyside*

SOUTH-EASTERN REGION

First-tier – Chelmsford, Lewes, Norwich, Oxford
Second-tier – Ipswich, Luton, Maidstone, Reading, St Albans
Third-tier – Aylesbury, Basildon, Bury St Edmunds, Cambridge, Canterbury, Chichester, Croydon, Guildford, King's Lynn, Peterborough, Southend
Regional Director, Kevin Pogson, New Cavendish House, 18 Maltravers Street, London WC2R 3EU T 020-7947 6006
Area Directors: Stephen Fash, *Bedfordshire*; Pat Lloyd, *Cambridgeshire*; Mike Littlewood, *Essex*; Jonathan Lane, *Hertfordshire*; Stephen Savage, *Kent*; Pauline Cornford, *Norfolk*; John Rodley, *Suffolk*; Simon Townley, *Surrey*; Dave Weston, *Sussex*; Peter Hammersley, *Thames Valley*

WALES AND CHESHIRE REGION

First-tier – Caernarfon, Cardiff, Chester, Mold, Swansea
Second-tier – Carmarthen, Merthyr Tydfil, Newport, Welshpool
Third-tier – Dolgellau, Haverfordwest, Knutsford, Warrington
Regional Director, N. Chibnall, Churchill House, Churchill Way, Cardiff CF10 4HH T 029-2041 5505
Area Directors: A. Davies, *South Wales*; Julia Eeles, *Cheshire*; Howard Matthews, *Gwent*; Clare Pillman, *North Wales*; Luigi Strinati, *Dyfed Powys*

SOUTH-WESTERN REGION

First-tier – Bristol, Exeter, Truro, Winchester
Second-tier – Dorchester and Weymouth, Gloucester, Plymouth
Third-tier – Barnstaple, Bournemouth, Newport (IOW), Portsmouth, Salisbury, Southampton, Swindon, Taunton
Regional Director, Peter Risk, 5th Floor, Greyfriars, Lewins Mead, Bristol BS1 2NR T 0117-910 3600
Area Directors: N. Jeffery, *Wiltshire*; D. Gentry, *Devon and Cornwall*; R. White, *Avon and Somerset*; R. Brummitt, *Dorset*; M. Speller, *Gloucestershire*; S. Williamson, *Hampshire and Isle of Wight*

CIRCUIT JUDGES

Senior Circuit Judges, each £125,803
Circuit Judges at the Central Criminal Court, London (Old Bailey Judges), each £125,803
Circuit Judges, each £116,515
Style, His/Her Hon. Judge [surname]
Senior Presiding Judge, The Rt. Hon. Lord Justice Thomas

LONDON REGION

Presiding Judges, The Hon. Mr Justice Bell; The Hon. Mrs Justice Rafferty; The Hon. Mr Justice Gross

P. C. Ader; Ms S. A. Anwyl, QC; B. J. Barker, QC; Ms S. Barnes; P. J. L. Beaumont, QC *(Common Serjeant)*; R. V. M. E. Behar; Mrs C. V. Bevington; I. G. Bing; M. G. Binning; W. J. Birtles; H. O. Blacksell, QC; L. S. Burn; C. W. Byers; A. Campbell; J. Q. Campbell; M. J. Carroll; S. H. Colgan; P. E. Copley; Mrs P. M. T. Dangor; G. Davis; P. N. De Mille; M. Dean, QC; P. Dodgson; W. H. Dunn, QC; C. Elwen; Miss D. Faber; P. E. J. Focke, QC; G. C. F. Forrester; Ms D. A. Freedman; M. Fysh, QC; C. A. H. Gibson; C. G. M. Gordon; A. A. Goymer; P. Grobel; TD, VRD; C. R. H. Hardy, QC; R. G. Hawkins, QC; J. M. Haworth; D. E. A. Higgins; A. N. Hitching; R. Hone, QC; M. Hucker; D. A. Inman; A. B. Issard-Davies; Dr P. J. E. Jackson; N. Jones; T. J. C. Joseph; I. G. F. Karsten, QC; S. S. Katkhuda; W. A. Kennedy; G. M. P. F. Khayat, QC; T. R. King; B. J. Knight, QC; Ms P. E. Knowles; S. Kramer, QC; T. Lawrence; D. M. Levy, QC; C. C. D. Lindsay, QC; N. G. E. Loraine-Smith; J. A. M. Lowen; Capt. S. Lyons, CBE; K. C. MacRae; N. Madge; D. N. N. Martineau; D. Matheson, QC; A. G. McDowall; R. J. McGregor-Johnson; R. G. McKinnon; N. A. Medawar, QC; Miss A. E. Mitchell; F. I. Mitchell; D. Mole, QC; A. P. Morris, QC; C. J. Moss, QC; P. Moss; A. P. Norris, OBE; J. O'Mahony; D. C. J. Paget, QC; A. Pardoe, QC; W. Pawlak; Miss V. A. Pearlman; N. A. J. Philpot; T. D. Pillay; D. C. Pitman; A. B. Pitts; T. G. Pontius; S. Pratt; R. J. C. V. Prendergast; J. Price; D. W. Radford; M. P. Reynolds; D. J. Richardson; G. Rivlin, QC; S. D. Robbins; J. Roberts, QC; J. M. Roberts; P. Rook; R. B. Sanders; A. G. Simmons; C. M. Smith, QC; S. A. R. Smith; E. Southwell; P. R. Statman; S. M. Stephens, QC; Mrs L. J. Stern, QC; N. A. Stewart; G. Stone, QC; T. M. F. Stow, QC; J. B. C. Tanzer; Ms A. M. Tapping; P. Testar; C. H. Tilling; J. P. Wadsworth, QC; R. Walker; S. P. Waller; C. S. Welchman; J. E. van der Werff; S. R. Wilkinson; R. J. Winstanley; Ms S. E. Woollam; M. K. Zeidman, QC

MIDLAND REGION

Presiding Judges, The Hon. Mr Justice Goldring; The Hon. Mr Justice Gibbs

I. D. G. Alexander, QC; Miss C. Alton; C. Bellamy; D. Bennett; R. Bray; D. Brunning; J. Burgess; Miss J. Butler,

QC; M. Cardinal; J. Cavell; M. Challinor; *F. Chapman; P. Clark; M. Coates; R. Cole; N. B. Coles, QC; I. Collis; T. Corrie; P. De Mille (shared with South-Eastern Circuit); Miss P. Deeley; M. J. Dudley; M. R. Eades; P. Eccles, QC; T. Faber; Miss E. Fisher; J. Fletcher; A. Geddes; P. Glenn; P. Gregory; R. Griffith-Jones; A. Hamilton; D. Hamilton; S. Hammond; Miss A. W. Hampton; C. Harris, QC (shared with South-Eastern Circuit); P. Head; M. Heath; E. Hindley, QC; C. Hodson; H. Hughes; R. Inglis; R. Jenkins; F. Kirkham; J. Lea; A. MacDuff, QC; P. McCahill, QC; D. McCarthy; A. McCreath; D. McEvoy, QC; M. McKenna; J. Machin; W. D. Matthews; H. R. Mayor, QC; C. Metcalf; J. Milmo, QC; A. Mitchell; N. Mitchell; P. Morrell; I. Morris; H. Morrison; M. Mott; A. H. Norris, QC; R. O'Rorke; S. Oliver-Jones, QC; R. Onions; R. Orme; J. Orrell; O. Pearce-Higgins, QC; M. Pert, QC; *R. Pollard; O. Price; D. Pugsley; J. Pyke; P. Ross; J. Rubery; R. Rundell; J. H. B. Saunders, QC *(Recorder of Birmingham)*; J. Shand; D. Stanley; M. Stokes, QC; G. Styler; A. Taylor; J. Teare; S. Tonking; S. Waine; J. Wait; J. Warner; N. Webb; C. Wide, QC; W. Wood, QC

NORTH-EASTERN REGION

Presiding Judges, The Hon. Mr Justice Grigson; The Hon. Mr Justice Andrew Smith

NORTH AND WEST YORKSHIRE AREAS

S. Ashurst; J. E. Barry; R. Bartfield; C. O. J. Behrens; P. Benson; S. Cahill; G. Cliffe; P. J. Cockroft; J. Dobkin; A. C. Finnerty; R. A. Grant; S. P. Grenfell; S. J. Gullick; T. S. A. Hawkesworth, QC; P. M. L. Hoffman; P. Hunt; R. Ibbotson; N. H. Jones, QC; G. H. Kamil; T. D. Kent-Jones, TD; J. Kershaw; P. Langan, QC; K. M. P. Macgill; A. G. McCallum; R. M. Scott; J. Spencer, QC; S. M. Spencer, QC; J. S. H. Stewart, QC; L. Sutcliffe; T. Walsh; J. S. Wolstenholme

NORTHUMBRIA, DURHAM, CLEVELAND AREAS

P. J. B. Armstrong; B. Bolton; P. H. Bowers; A. N. J. Briggs; D. M. A. Bryant; M. L. Cartlidge; M. J. Evans; E. J. Faulks; P. J. Fox, QC; T. Hewitt; D. Hodson; A. T. Lancaster; P. R. Lowden; J. T. Milford, QC; J. P. Moir; M. G. C. Moorhouse; L. Spittle; M. J. Taylor; C. T. Walton; J. De G. Walford; G. Whitburn, QC; D. R. Wood

HUMBERSIDE AND SOUTH YORKSHIRE AREAS

T. W. Barber; J. W. Bullimore; E. A. Carr; M. T. Cracknell; J. Davies; J. Dowse; A. R. Goldsack, QC; L. Hull; S. M. Jack; P. F. H. Jones; K. R. Keen, QC; S. W. Lawler, QC; M. K. Mettyear; R. J. Moore; M. J. A. Murphy, QC; J. H. Reddihough; P. E. Robertshaw; G. Robinson; J. Shipley; J. A. Swanson; R. E. Thorn, QC

NORTH-WESTERN REGION

Presiding Judges, The Hon. Mr Justice Leveson; The Hon. Mr Justice McCombe

M. P. Allweis; J. M. Appleby; J. F. Appleton; E. K. Armitage, QC; R. K. Atherton; Miss P. H. Badley; S. W. Baker; P. Batty; A. N. H. Blake; C. Bloom, QC; D. Boulton; L. F. M. Brown; R. Brown; M. D. Byrne; B. I. Caulfield; D. Clark; T. Clayson; G. M. Clifton; C. J. Cornwall; Miss J. M. P. Daley; S. B. Duncan; Miss D. B. Eaglestone; T. K. Earnshaw; G. A. Ensor; P. S. Fish; D. Fletcher; Miss B. A. Forrester; J. R. Foster, QC; J. R. B. Geake; D. S. Gee; H. Gee, QC; W. George; A. J. Gilbart, QC; *J. A. D. Gilliland, QC; N. B. D. Gilmour; *H. B. Globe, QC *(Recorder of Liverpool)*; C. L. Goldstone, QC; M. de Haas, QC; I. M.

Hamilton; J. A. Hammond; D. Harris, QC; *T. B. Hegarty, QC; M. J. Henshell; D. Hernandez; F. R. B. Holloway; *R. C. Holman; *N. J. G. Howarth; C. James; *M. Kershaw, QC *(Commercial Circuit Judge)*; E. M. Knopf; Miss L. J. Kushner, QC; P. M. Lakin; B. L. Lever; B. Lewis; J. Lewis; A. C. Lowcock; B. Lunt; A. P. Lyon; D. I. Mackay; J. B. Macmillan; *D. G. Maddison *(Recorder of Manchester)*; *B. C. Maddocks; C. J. Mahon; W. P. Morris; T. J. Mort; L. A. Newton; F. D. Owen; J. A. Phillips; J. C. Phipps; G. Platts; P. R. Raynor, QC; J. H. Roberts; Miss M. Roddy; Miss G. D. Ruaux; M. W. Rudland; A. A. Rumbelow, QC; A. Russel, QC; E. Slinger; A. Smith; P. Smith; Miss E. M. Steel; M. T. Steiger, QC; *S. Stewart, QC; D. R. Swift; P. Sycamore; C. B. Tetlow; R. Thomas, QC; I. J. C. Trigger; A. R. Warnock; Miss B. J. Watson; K. Wilkinson; B. Woodward

SOUTH-EASTERN REGION

Presiding Judges, The Hon. Mr Justice Bell; The Hon. Mrs Justice Rafferty; The Hon. Mr Justice Gross

M. F. Addison; J. Altman; A. R. L. Ansell; M. G. Anthony; C. Atkins; E. H. Bailey; F. Baker, QC; C. G. Ball, QC; A. F. Balston; G. S. Barham; W. E. Barnett, QC; R. A. Barratt, QC; J. Bevan, QC; N. C. van der Bijl; A. V. Bradbury; G. B. Breen; M. Brooke, QC; R. G. Brown, DL; J. M. Bull, QC, DL; J. P. Burke, QC; D. Caddick; Ms A. Campbell, DL; J. Carey; Ms M. T. Catterson; R. Chapple; P. C. Clegg; Miss S. Coates; N. J. Coleman; *P. H. Collins, CBE; S. S. Coltart; C. D. Compston; T. A. C. Coningsby, QC; A. Cooper; T. G. E. Corrie; Dr E. Cotran; P. R. Cowell; K. Cox; M. L. S. Cripps; C. A. Critchlow; J. F. Crocker; D. M. Cryan; P. Curl; A. M. Darroch; P. G. Dedman; J. E. Devaux; P. H. Downes; C. M. Edwards; D. R. Ellis; R. C. Elly; J. D. Farnworth; R. Foster; A. Goldstaub, QC; D. N. Goodin; J. B. Gosschalk; C. Gratwicke; A. E. Greenwood; G. H. Gypps; J. Hall; Miss G. Hallon; J. Hamilton; Miss S. Hamilton, QC; C. Harris, QC; W. G. Hawkesworth; R. J. Haworth; R. M. Hayward; R. Hayward-Smith, QC; K. M. J. Hollis; J. F. Holt; K. A. D. Hornby; M. Horowitz, QC; Ms J. C. A. Hughes, QC; P. Jacobs; S. Kay, QC; C. J. B. Kemp; A. W. P. King; P. H. Latham; M. Lawson, QC; M. Levy; S. H. Lloyd; Mrs C. M. Ludlow; B. M. McIntyre; W. N. McKinnon; N. A. McKittrick; D. Mackie, QC, CBE; T. Maher; F. J. M. Marr-Johnson; Ms S. Matthews, QC; V. Mayer; D. J. Mellor; C. R. Mitchell; D. C. Mitchell; H. M. Morgan; D. Morton Jack; R. T. Moss; Miss M. J. S. Mowat; G. S. Murdoch, QC; T. M. E. Nash; R. Newton; A. I. Niblett; Mrs M. F. Norrie-Walker; Brig. P. W. O'Brien; A. Oppenheimer; M.O'Sullivan; A. Patience, QC; Mrs N. Pearce; J. R. Platt; J. R. Playford, QC; Miss I. M. Plumstead; D. J. Rennie; J. R. Reid, QC; M. S. Rich, QC; J. Richards; N. P. Riddell; W. M. Rose; J. Rylance; T. R. G. Ryland; J. E. A. Samuels, QC; A. R. G. Scott-Gall; J. S. Sennitt; D. Serota, QC; J. L. Sessions; J. Simpkiss; P. R. Simpson; S. P. Sleeman; Miss Z. P. Smith; S. B. Spence; P. J. Thompson; A. G. Y. Thorpe; T. L. Viljoen; R. Wakefield; A. R. Webb; Miss J. A. Williams; Ms S. Williams; P. Wulwik

WALES AND CHESHIRE REGION

Presiding Judges, The Hon. Mr Justice Roderick Evans; The Hon. Mr Justice Pitchford

K. Barnett; N. Bidder, QC; M. R. Burr; J. R. Case; N. M. Chambers, QC; S. Clarke; J. Curran; D. L. Daniel; J. Davies; R. L. Denyer, QC; J. B. S. Diehl, QC; J. D. Durham Hall, QC; R. Dutton; D. Edwards; G. O. Edwards, QC; M.

Farmer, QC; M. Furness; W. Gaskell; J. Griffith Williams, QC; D. Halbert; D. Hale; S. Hopkins, QC; D. Hughes; R. P. Hughes; T. M. Hughes, QC; C. Llewellyn-Jones, QC; C. Masterman; D. W. Morgan; D. G. Morris; D. C. Morton; I. C. Parry; G. A. L. Price, QC; P. Price, QC; E. M. Rees; D. W. Richards; P. Richards; J. M. T. Rogers, QC; K. Thomas; W. Williams, QC; N. F. Woodward

SOUTH-WESTERN REGION

Presiding Judges, The Hon. Mr Justice David Steel; The Hon. Mr Justice Owen

P. R. Barclay; A. J. Barnett; J. F. Beashel; R. Bond; J. G. Boggis, QC; G. Boney, QC; J. Bonvin; *M. J. L. Brodrick; J. M. Burford, QC; *R. D. Bursell, QC; G. W. A. Cottle; M. G. Cotterill; T. G. Cowling; *T. Crowther, QC; K. C. Cutler; P. Darlow; Simon Darwall Smith; Susan P. Darwall Smith; Mrs L. Davies; J. W. Dixon; J. Foley; F. Gilbert, QC; D. L. Griffiths; J. D. Griggs; C. M. A. Hagen; J. M. Harrow; A. M. Havelock-Allan, QC; P. J. Hooton; D. Hope; M. K. Harington; R. Hetherington; I. Hughes, QC; G. Hume Jones; J. R. Jarvis; P. Lambert; C. Leigh, QC; T. Longbotham; I. S. McKintosh; J. G. McNaught; The Lord Meston, QC; T. J. Milligan; J. O. Neligan; S. K. O'Malley; S. K. Overend; I. Pearson; R. Price; M. W. Roach; R. Rucker; A. Rutherford; R. M. Shawcross; J. Tabor, QC; W. E. M. Taylor; D. K. Ticehurst, QC; D. I. H. Tyzack, QC; N. Vincent; R. C. B. Wade; P. Wassall; J. H. Weeks, QC; J. S. Wiggs

DISTRICT JUDGES

District Judges (each £93,483)

LONDON REGION

Ms J. C. Allen; A. W. Armon-Jones; I. M. Avent; J. D. Banks; Ms J. L. Beattie; T. P. Bowles; T. G. Brett; J. H. G. Chrispin; E. Cohen; B. R. J. Cole; C. F. Dabezies; Ms S. H. D. Fink; N. G. Freeborough; S. M. Gerlis; M. C. Gilchrist; S. G. Gold; N. J. Gregory; Ms R. Fine; J. Gittens; Ms E. J. M. Habershon; S. Hasan; M. J. Haselgrove; R. M. Jacey; T. N. Jenkins; H. E. Kemp; Ms M. T. Langley; M. Lee; B. G. Lightman; H. L. Manners; M. J. Marin; Ms L. D. Millard; A. J. Mills; R. J. Mitchell; S. I. Morley; A. J. Morris; R. W. Mullis; R. H. Naqvi; M. Nicholson; Ms M. J. Parker; S. Plaskow; K. A. Price; Ms S. K. Sethi; I. V. Sheratte; G. M. Silverman; H. A. Silverman; R. Southcombe; Ms E. F. M. Stary; Ms S. Stephenson; Ms P. A. Sturdy; J. E. Taylor; A. D. Thomas; I. G. Tilbury; M. F. Trent; C. W. Vokes; M. J. Walker; A. N. Wicks; F. J. Wilkinson; A. J. Worthington; Ms J. E. Wright; M. Zimmels

MIDLAND REGION

M. Anson; M. Asokan; P. Atkinson; C. Beale; A. Brown; A. Butler; D. Cernik; R. Chapman; A. Cleary; R. Cole; D. J. Cooke; T. Cotterill; T. Davies; E. Dickinson; D. D. Douce; P. Dowling; L. Eaton; M. Ellery; A. Elliott; S. Gailey; F. Goddard; R. Hearne; R. L. Hudson; J. Ilsley; J. Jack; A. Jones; P. Kesterton; I. Knifton; K. Lacy; D. Lipman, P. McHale; P. Mackenzie; A. Marston; A. Maw; R. Merriman; S. Middleton; D. Millard; A. Mithani; R. J. Morton; D. O'Regan; B. Oliver; D. Owen; M. Parry; P. Rank; F. Reeson; T. Ridgway; S. Rogers; P. Sanghera; R. Savage; L. H. Schroeder; V. Sehdev; S. C. W. Smith; V. Stamenkovich; A. Stark; A. F. Suckling; P. Thompson; R. J. Toombs; Ms K. A. Venables; P. Waterworth; R. Whitehurst

NORTH-EASTERN REGION

S. T. Alderson; H. Anderson; C. A. Arkless; I. D. Atherton; A. M. Babbington; H. J. Bailey; R. Barraclough; I. P. Besford; C. M. Birkby; J. Bower; J. A. Buchan; P. E. Bullock; I. L. Buxton; S. Chesterfield; P. Cuthbertson; G. J. Edwards; I. S. Fairwood; J. Flanagan; P. R. Giles; M. M. Glentworth; N. W. Goudie; S. J. Greenwood; M. F. Handley; R. V. M. Hall; J. E. Harrison, H. F. Heath; N. G. Hickinbottom; R. N. Hill; T. W. Hill; J. R. A. Howard; R. A. Jordan; C. Khan; D. Kirkham; A. M. Large; D. E. Lascelles; P. E. Lawton; G. Y. Lingard; R. Loomba; G. Lord; J. E. Mainwaring-Taylor; G. M. Marley; P. C. Mort; D. A. Oldham; A. P. Powell; M. F. Rhodes; D. M. Robertson; J. S. Robinson; S. Rodgers; A. M. Saffman; D. Scott-Phillips; I. F. Slim; S. E. Spencer; B. D. Stapely; D. M. Stocken; J. A. Taylor; P. W. J. Traynor; D. J. R. Weston; P. J. E. Wildsmith; J. S. Wilson; H. P. Wood; M. J. Young

NORTH-WESTERN REGION

R. R. P. Ackroyd; G. R. Ashton; P. G. Bellamy; I. Bennett; Ms A. J. C. Brazier; R Bryce; M. E. Buckley; Ms V. Buckley; D. B. Chapman; J L. Clark; J. R. Clegg; J. F. Coffey; P. St J. Dignan; E. Donnelly; J. F. Duerden; C. R. Fairclough; G. J. Fitzgerald; R. M. Forrester; C. R. Fox; C. E. Freeman; B. N. Gaunt; J. M. Geddes; M. Gosnell; M. Griffiths; A. J. J. Harrison; N. Harrison; L. Henthorn; J. D. Heyworth; J. Horan; M. A. Hovington; G. A. Humphreys-Roberts; S. C. Jackson; J. A. James; E. Johnson; A. Jones; E. R. Jones; G. A. Needham; G. Nuttall; N. A. Law; R. A. McCullagh; B. V. McGrath; Ms M. A. Mornington; L. C. Osborne; J. K. Park; M. I. Peake; I. J. Pickup; J. J. B. Rawkins; D. J. Shannon; Ms J. Shaw; M. J. Simpson; R. Smedley; G. D. Smith; L. S. Stephens; Ms P. S. Stockton; L. G. Sykes; C. M. Swindley; R. Talbot; B. W. Travers; M. W. Turner; M. J. Wilby; P. T. Wilby; S. Wright

SOUTH-EASTERN REGION

V. S. Batcup; P. R. Bazley-White; D. S. Beck; M. Birchall; R. H. L. Blomfield; A. J. Blunsdon; N. J. Brookes; G. H. Burgess; Ms L. M. Burgess; P. R. Carr; C. B. Chandler; Ms J. I. Collier; C. N. Darbyshire; R. A. Davis; S. A. F. Davies; J. R. Davidson; I. M. Diamond; R. Dudley; C. M. Edwards; I. Evans; D. M. Eynon; Ms M. Fawcett; Ms G. B. Field; J. M. Fortgang; Ms V. W. Gatter; P. Gamba; P. S. Gill; P. M. L. Glover; G. A. Green; D. F. Hallett; Ms C. M. Hamilton; D. N. Hayes; Ms R. M. Henry; Ms S. Henson; P. F. Hewetson-Brown; N. E. Hickman; R. S. Hicks; N. E. Jackson; W. Jackson; Ms H. K. Johns; Ms S. Jones; Ms R. V. Karp; Ms I. A. Kubiak; J. L. C. Kirby; D. C. Lamdin; C. J. Lethem; H. A. J. Letts; A. D. Levey; S. E. Levinson; R. R. Matthews; T. P. McLoughlin; J. S. Merrick; Ms E. C. Millward; S. R. Mitchell; C. B. Molle; P. Mostyn; T. J. R. Parker; M. J. Payne; Ms G. L. Pearl; Ms P. Pearl; P. H. Pelly; P. R. Pescod; R. Polden; Ms A. L. Raeside; J. M. Rhodes; J. T. Robinson; P. C. Rogers; M. Royall; B. I. Rutland; Ms W. F. Shanks; M. N. Skerratt; Ms E. J. Silverwood-Cope; Ms M. M. Short; R. G. Sparrow; D. V. Steel; J. R. K. Taylor; A. K. Taylor; E. R. W. Temple; R. C. Tetlow; A. S. Wharton; Ms E. Willers

SOUTH-WESTERN REGION

C. M. Ackner; C. E. H. Ackroyd; R. D. I. Adam; J. D. Ainsworth; D. Carney; B. R. Carron; G. F. Cawood; M. T. Cooper; P. W. Corrigan; J. P. Crosse; M. Dancey; M. P. H. Daniel; J. M. R. Dowell; Ms J. Exton; D. J. Field; J. Freeman; J. W. Frenkel; C. Fuller; F. Goddard; R. A. F. Griggs; A. M. Harvey; J. Hurley; R. D. S. James; P. D. Jolly; B. G. Meredith; P. Mildred; P. Mitchell; A. D. Moon; N. J. Murphy; R. F. D. Naylor; M. Reid; M. Rutherford; A. L. Simons; P. N. Singleton; B. J. A. Smith; J. Sparrow; Mrs G. Stuart Brown; M. H. Tennant; A. B. Thomas; J. L. Thomas;

C. J. Tromans; A. J. Wainwright; A. Walker; I. E. Weintroub; D. R. White; R. A. Wilson

WALES AND CHESHIRE REGION

D. J. Asplin; C. F. Beattie; G. H. F. Carson; J. L. Davies; C. R. Dawson; Mrs H. Dawson; J. M. Doel; P. M. Evans; Miss R. Evans; Mrs J. E. Garland-Thomas; W. H. Godwin; S. G. Harrison; R. L. Hendicott; R. A. Hoffman; D. P. Jenkins; T. A. John; T. J. Lewis; G. W. Little; P. H. Llewellyn, OBE; C. W. Newman; A. T. North; Mrs C. E. O'Leary; C. G. Perry; T. M. Phillips; V. Reeves; J. E. Regan; S. Rogers; R. Singh, CBE; J. G. Thomas; A. A. Wallace; A. J. P. Weaver; O. W. Williams; D. Wyn Rees

DISTRICT JUDGES (MAGISTRATES' COURTS)

The Provisional and Metropolitan Division has been changed; all former Provincial and Metropolitan Stipendiary Magistrates can serve nationally within any district and are now called District Judges (Magistrates' Courts).

District Judges (each £97,483, salary includes £4,000 inner London weighting)

M. A. Abelson; Mrs J. H. Alderson; R. W. Anderson; Mrs A. Arnold; G. B. Babington-Browne; A. Berg; J. S. Bennett; A. Bopa-Rai; M. Brown; J. A. Browne; P. H. R. Browning; N. R. Cadbury; G. Chalk; J. J. Charles; T. M. Chatelier; D. J. Chinery; R. F. S. Clancy; M. Cooper; S. N. Cooper; C. R. Darnton; Mrs S. E. Driver; S. Earl; R. Elsey; T. English; P. R. Farmer; J. Finestein; P. J. Firth; J. G. Foster; M. J. Friel; I. Gillespie; P. Gillibrand; C. Goulborn; K. Gray; R. House; M. L. R. Harris; Ms K. Harrison; R. Holland; J. A. Jellema; R. D. Kitson; Ms B. A. Knight; A. N. H. Leigh-Smith; I. S. Lomax; B. Loosley; C. M. McColl; D. V. Manning-Davies; D. M. Meredith; B. Morgan; Mrs L. Morgan; M. C. Morris; P. F. Nuttall; D. Parsons; J. B. Prowse; S. Qureshi; P. B. Richardson; P. G. G. Richards; M. A. Rosenberg; F. J. Rutherford; N. Sanders; A. Shaw; Mrs E. M. Shelvey; J. Stobart; P. C. Tain; D. R. G. Tapp; D. L. Thomas; W. D. Thomas; A. Vickers; M. J. Walker; P. Ward; G. R. Watkins; Ms P. J. Watkins; R. E. H. Williams; M. Wood; J. I. Woollard; R. J. Zara

METROPOLITAN BASE COURTS

Bow Street, T. H. Workman *(Senior District Judge)*; H. N. Evans; C. L. Pratt; Ms D. E. Wickham
Brent Magistrates' Court, Ms K. J. Marshall
Camberwell Green, A. C. Baldwin; A. Callaway; Ms S. V. Green; Ms A. L. Sawetz; P. Wain; J. A. Zani
Croydon Magistrates' Court, A. P. Carr; M. Hunter
Greenwich, M. Kelly; D. Lynch; H. C. F. Riddle; P. S. Wallis
Feltham Magistrates' Court, S. N. Day
Hendon Magistrates' Court, C. S. Wiles
Highbury Corner, I. M. Baker; J. Henderson; R. A. McPhee; J. V. Perkins; Ms D. Quick
Horseferry Road, A. T. Evans; Q. A. Purdy; M. Snow; Ms C. S. R. Tubbs
Inner London and City, N. Crichton
Marylebone, G. Parsons; Ms E. J. Roscoe
South-Western, S. Bayne; Ms M. Coleman; K. I. Grant
Stratford Magistrates' Court, C. A. Dawson; H. Gott; Ms S. L. Sims
Thames, Ms J. R. Comyns; S. E. Dawson; Ms F. J. McIvor; M. J. Read; Ms A. M. Rose
Tower Bridge, G. S. F. Black; S. Somjee; T. R. Stone
West London Magistrates' Court, P. Clark; J. B. Coleman; D.

K. Lachlar; J. R. D. Philips; D. Simpson; A. Sweet; Ms S. F. Williams

CROWN PROSECUTION SERVICE

50 Ludgate Hill, London EC4M 7EX T 020-7796 8000
E enquiries@cps.gov.uk
W www.cps.gov.uk

The Crown Prosecution Service (CPS) is responsible for the independent review and conduct of criminal proceedings instituted by police forces in England and Wales, with the exception of cases conducted by the Serious Fraud Office and certain minor offences.

The Service is headed by the Director of Public Prosecutions (DPP), who works under the superintendence of the Attorney-General, and a Chief Executive. The Service comprises a headquarters and 42 areas, each area corresponding to a police area in England and Wales. Each area is headed by a Chief Crown Prosecutor, supported by an Area Business Manager.

Director of Public Prosecutions, Ken Macdonald, QC
Chief Executive, R. Foster
Directors, C. Newell *(Casework)*; P. Geering *(Policy)*; J. Graham *(Finance)*; Ms C. Hamon *(Business Information Systems)*; Ms A. O'Connor *(Human Resources)*
Head of Communications, P. Teare
Head of Management Audit Services, R. Capstick

CPS AREAS ENGLAND

AVON AND SOMERSET, 2nd Floor, Froomsgate House, Rupert Street, Bristol BS1 2QJ T 0117-930 2800
Chief Crown Prosecutor, D. Archer
BEDFORDSHIRE, Sceptre House, 7–9 Castle Street, Luton LU1 3AJ T 01582-816600
Chief Crown Prosecutor, R. Newcombe
CAMBRIDGESHIRE, Justinian House, Spitfire Close, Ermine Business Park, Huntingdon, Cambs PE29 6XY T 01480-825200
Chief Crown Prosecutor, R. Crowley
CHESHIRE, 2nd Floor, Windsor House, Pepper Street, Chester CH1 1TD T 01244-408600
Chief Crown Prosecutor, C. Lindley
CLEVELAND, 5 Linthorpe Road, Middlesbrough, Cleveland TS1 1TX T 01642-204500
Chief Crown Prosecutor, M. Goldman
CUMBRIA, 1st Floor, Stocklund House, Castle Street, Carlisle CA3 8SY T 01228-882900
Chief Crown Prosecutor, D. Farmer
DERBYSHIRE, 7th Floor, St Peter's House, Gower Street, Derby DE1 1SB T 01332-614000
Chief Crown Prosecutor, B. Gunn
DEVON AND CORNWALL, Hawkins House, Pynes Hill, Rydon Lane, Exeter EX2 5SS T 01392-288000
Chief Crown Prosecutor, A. Cresswell
DORSET, Ground Floor, Oxford House, Oxford Road, Bournemouth BH8 8HA T 01202-498700
Chief Crown Prosecutor, J. Revell
DURHAM, Elvet House, Hallgarth Street, Durham DH1 3AT T 0191-383 5800
Chief Crown Prosecutor, Ms P. Ragnauth
ESSEX, County House, 100 New London Road, Chelmsford CM2 0RG T 01245-455800
Chief Crown Prosecutor, J. Bell
GLOUCESTERSHIRE, 2 Kimbrose Way, Gloucester GL1 2DB T 01452-872400
Chief Crown Prosecutor, R. Coe-Salazar

GREATER MANCHESTER, PO Box 237, 8th Floor, Sunlight House, Quay Street, Manchester M60 3PS T 0161-827 4700
Chief Crown Prosecutor, J. Holt

HAMPSHIRE AND ISLE OF WIGHT, 3rd Floor, Black Horse House, 8–10 Leigh Road, Eastleigh, Hants SO50 9FH T 023-8067 3800
Chief Crown Prosecutor, N. Hawkins

HERTFORDSHIRE, Queen's House, 58 Victoria Street, St Albans, Herts AL1 3HZ T 01727-798700
Chief Crown Prosecutor, C. Ingham

HUMBERSIDE, Citadel House, 58 High Street, Kingston-upon-Hull HU1 1QD T 01482-621000
Chief Crown Prosecutor, N. Cowgill

KENT, Priory Gate, 29 Union Street, Maidstone ME14 1PT T 01622-356300
Chief Crown Prosecutor, Ms E. Howe

LANCASHIRE, Guildhall House, Guildhall Street, Preston PR1 3NU T 01772-272770
Chief Crown Prosecutor, R. Marshall

LEICESTERSHIRE, Mansfield House, 74 Belgrave Gate, Leicester LE1 3GG T 0116-204 6700
Chief Crown Prosecutor, M. Howard

LINCOLNSHIRE, Crosstrend House, 10A Newport, Lincoln LN1 3DF T 01522-585900
Chief Crown Prosecutor, Ms A. Kerr

LONDON, 7th Floor, CPS HQ, 50 Ludgate Hill, London EC4M 7EX T 020-7796 8000
Chief Crown Prosecutor, Ms D. Sharpling

MERSEYSIDE, 7th Floor (South), Royal Liver Building, Pier Head, Liverpool L3 1HN T 0151-239 6400
Chief Crown Prosecutor, Paul Whittaker

NORFOLK, Carmelite House, St James Court, Whitefriars, Norwich NR3 1SL T 01603-693000
Chief Crown Prosecutor, P. Tidey

NORTH YORKSHIRE, Athena House, Kettlestring Lane, Clifton Moor, York YO30 4XF T 01904-731700
Chief Crown Prosecutor, R. Turnbull

NORTHAMPTONSHIRE, Beaumont House, Cliftonville, Northampton NN1 5BE T 01604-823600
Chief Crown Prosecutor, Grace Ononiwu

NORTHUMBRIA, St Ann's Quay, 122 Quayside, Newcastle upon Tyne NE1 3BD T 0191-260 4200
Chief Crown Prosecutor, Ms N. Reasbeck

NOTTINGHAMSHIRE, 2 King Edward Court, King Edward Street, Nottingham NG1 1EL T 0115-852 3300
Chief Crown Prosecutor, Ms K. Carty

SOUTH YORKSHIRE, Greenfield House, 32 Scotland Street, Sheffield S3 7DQ T 0114-229 8600
Chief Crown Prosecutor, Mrs J. Walker

STAFFORDSHIRE, 11A Princes Street, Stafford ST16 2EU T 01785-272200
Chief Crown Prosecutor, H. Ireland

SUFFOLK, 9th Floor, St Vincent's House, 1 Cutler Street, Ipswich IP1 1UL T 01473-282100
Chief Crown Prosecutor, C. Yule

SURREY, Saxon House, 3 Onslow Street, Guildford, Surrey GU1 4YA T 01483-468200
Chief Crown Prosecutor, Ms S. Hebblethwaite

SUSSEX, City Gates, 185 Dyke Road, Brighton BN3 1TL T 01273-765600
Chief Crown Prosecutor, Mrs S. J. Gallagher

THAMES VALLEY, The Courtyard, Lombard Street, Abingdon, Oxon OX14 5SE T 01235-551900
Chief Crown Prosecutor, B. Ubhey

WARWICKSHIRE, Rossmore House, 10 Newbold Terrace, Leamington Spa CV32 4EA T 01926-455000
Chief Crown Prosecutor, M. Lynn

WEST MERCIA, Artillery House, Heritage Way, Droitwich, Worcester WR9 8YB T 01905-825000
Chief Crown Prosecutor, J. England

WEST MIDLANDS, Colmore Gate, 2 Colmore Row, Birmingham B3 2QA T 0121-262 1300
Chief Crown Prosecutor, D. Blundell

WEST YORKSHIRE, Oxford House, Oxford Row, Leeds LS1 3BE T 0113-290 2700
Chief Crown Prosecutor, N. Franklin

WILTSHIRE, 2nd Floor, Fox Talbot House, Bellinger Close, Malmesbury Road, Chippenham SN15 1BN T 01249-766100
Chief Crown Prosecutor, Ms K. Harrold

CPS AREAS WALES

DYFED POWYS, Heol Penlanffos, Tanerdy, Carmarthen, Dyfed SA31 2EZ T 01267-242100
Chief Crown Prosecutor, S. Rowlands

GWENT, 6th Floor, Chartist Tower, Upper Dock Street, Newport, Gwent NP20 1DW T 01633-261100
Chief Crown Prosecutor, Madhu Rai

NORTH WALES, Bromfield House, Ellice Way, Wrexham LL13 7YW T 01978-346000
Chief Crown Prosecutor, E. Beltrami

SOUTH WALES, 20th Floor, Capital House, Greyfriars Road, Cardiff CF10 3PL T 029-2080 3900
Chief Crown Prosecutor, C. Woolley

HER MAJESTY'S COURTS SERVICE

5th Floor, Clive House, Petty France, London SW1H 9HD
T 020-7189 2000 F 020-7189 2732
E customerservicecshq@hmcourts-service.gsi.gov.uk
W www.hmcourts-service.gov.uk

Her Majesty's Courts Service (HMCS) was launched on 1 April 2005, bringing together the Magistrates' Courts Service and the Court Service into a single organisation, and is responsible for the administration of the Court of Appeal, the High Court, the Crown Court, the magistrates' courts, the county courts and the Probate Service. HMCS is an executive agency of the Department for Constitutional Affairs, and provides information on procedures and processes for the public, hearing lists, and address details for all relevant courts.
Chief Executive, Sir Ron De Witt, KB
Field Services Director, Kevin Pogson

SCOTTISH JUDICATURE

Scotland has a legal system separate from, and differing greatly from, the English legal system in enacted law, judicial procedure and the structure of courts.

In Scotland the system of public prosecution is headed by the Lord Advocate and is independent of the police, who have no say in the decision to prosecute. The Lord Advocate, discharging his functions through the Crown Office in Edinburgh, is responsible for prosecutions in the High Court, sheriff courts and district courts. Prosecutions in the High Court are prepared by the Crown Office and conducted in court by one of the law officers, by an advocate-depute, or by a solicitor advocate. In the inferior courts the decision to prosecute is made and prosecution is preferred by procurators fiscal, who are lawyers and full-time civil servants subject to the directions of the Crown Office. A permanent legally qualified civil servant, known as the Crown Agent, is responsible for the running of the Crown Office and the organisation of the Procurator Fiscal Service, of which he is the head.

Scotland is divided into six sheriffdoms, each with a full-time sheriff principal. The sheriffdoms are further divided into sheriff court districts, each of which has a legally qualified resident sheriff or sheriffs, who are the judges of the court.

In criminal cases sheriffs principal and sheriffs have the same powers; sitting with a jury of 15 members, they may try more serious cases on indictment, or, sitting alone, may try lesser cases under summary procedure. Minor summary offences are dealt with in district courts which are administered by the district and the islands local government authorities and presided over by lay justices of the peace (of whom there were 3,465 in June 2005) and, in Glasgow only, by district judges (magistrates' courts). Juvenile offenders (children under 16) may be brought before an informal children's hearing comprising three local lay people. The superior criminal court is the High Court of Justiciary which is both a trial and an appeal court. Cases on indictment are tried by a High Court judge, sitting with a jury of 15, in Edinburgh and on circuit in other towns. Appeals from the lower courts against conviction or sentence are also heard by the High Court, which sits as an appeal court only in Edinburgh. There is no further appeal to the House of Lords in criminal cases.

In civil cases the jurisdiction of the sheriff court extends to most kinds of action. Appeals against decisions of the sheriff may be made to the sheriff principal and thence to the Court of Session, or direct to the Court of Session, which sits only in Edinburgh. The Court of Session is divided into the Inner and the Outer House. The Outer House is a court of first instance in which cases are heard by judges sitting singly, sometimes with a jury of 12. The Inner House, itself subdivided into two divisions of equal status, is mainly an appeal court. Appeals may be made to the Inner House from the Outer House as well as from the sheriff court. An appeal may be made from the Inner House to the House of Lords.

The judges of the Court of Session are the same as those of the High Court of Justiciary, the Lord President of the Court of Session also holding the office of Lord Justice General in the High Court. Senators of the College of Justice are Lords Commissioners of Justiciary as well as judges of the Court of Session. On appointment, a Senator takes a judicial title, which is retained for life. Although styled The Hon./Rt. Hon. Lord, the Senator is not a peer.

The office of coroner does not exist in Scotland. The local procurator fiscal inquires privately into sudden or suspicious deaths and may report findings to the Crown Agent. In some cases a fatal accident inquiry may be held before the sheriff.

COURT OF SESSION AND HIGH COURT OF JUSTICIARY

The Lord President and Lord Justice General (£191,276), The Rt. Hon. Lord Cullen of Whitekirk, *born* 1935, *apptd* 2001
Private Secretary, A. Maxwell

INNER HOUSE
Lords of Session (each £175,671)

FIRST DIVISION
The Lord President

Rt. Hon. Lord Penrose, (George Penrose), *born* 1938, *apptd* 1990

Rt. Hon. Lord Hamilton (Arthur Hamilton), *born* 1942, *apptd* 1995
Rt. Hon. Lady Cosgrove (Hazel Aronson), *born* 1946, *apptd* 1996
Rt. Hon. Lord Nimmo Smith (William Nimmo Smith), *born* 1942, *apptd* 1996

SECOND DIVISION
Lord Justice Clerk (£184,814), The Rt. Hon. Lord Gill (Brian Gill), *born* 1942, *apptd* 2001
Rt. Hon. Lord Osborne (Kenneth Osborne), *born* 1937, *apptd* 1990
Rt. Hon. Lord MacFadyen (Donald MacFadyen), *born* 1945, *apptd* 1995
Rt. Hon. Lord Abernethy (Alistair Cameron), *born* 1938, *apptd* 1992
Rt. Hon. Lord Johnston (Alan Johnston), *born* 1942, *apptd* 1994

OUTER HOUSE
Lords of Session (each £155,404)

Hon. Lord Dawson (Thomas Dawson), *born* 1948, *apptd* 1995
Hon. Lord Philip (Alexander Philip), *born* 1942, *apptd* 1996
Hon. Lord Kingarth (Derek Emslie), *born* 1949, *apptd* 1997
Hon. Lord Eassie (Ronald Mackay), *born* 1945, *apptd* 1997
Hon. Lord Reed (Robert Reed), *born* 1956, *apptd* 1998
Hon. Lord Wheatley (John Wheatley), *born* 1941, *apptd* 2000
Hon. Lady Paton (Ann Paton), *born* 1952, *apptd* 2000
Hon. Lord Carloway (Colin Sutherland), *born* 1954, *apptd* 2000
Hon. Lord Clarke (Matthew Clarke), *born* 1947, *apptd* 2000
Rt. Hon. The Lord Hardie (Andrew Hardie), *born* 1946, *apptd* 2000
Rt. Hon. The Lord Mackay of Drumadoon (Donald Mackay), *born* 1946, *apptd* 2000
Hon. Lord McEwan (Robin McEwan), *born* 1943, *apptd* 2000
Hon. Lord Menzies (Duncan Menzies), *born* 1953, *apptd* 2001
Hon. Lord Drummond Young (James Drummond Young), *born* 1950, *apptd* 2001
Hon. Lord Emslie (Nigel Emslie), *born* 1947, *apptd* 2001
Hon. Lady Smith (Anne Smith), *born* 1955, *apptd* 2001
Hon. Lord Brodie (Philip Brodie), *born* 1950, *apptd* 2002
Hon. Lord Bracadale (Alastair Campbell), *born* 1949, *apptd* 2003
Hon. Lady Dorrian (Leeona J.), *born* 1959, *apptd* 2005
Hon. Lord Hodge (Patrick S.), *born* 1953, *apptd* 2005
Hon. Lord Macphail (Iain Duncan), *born* 1938, *apptd* 2005
Hon. Lord Glennie (Angus), *born* 1950, *apptd* 2005
Hon. Lord Kinclaven (Alexander F. Wylie), *born* 1951, *apptd* 2005

COURT OF SESSION AND HIGH COURT OF JUSTICIARY
Parliament House, Parliament Square, Edinburgh EH1 1HQ
T 0131-225 2595
Principal Clerk of Session and Justiciary, David Shand
Deputy Principal Clerk of Justiciary, N. Dowie

Deputy Principal Clerk of Session and Principal Extractor,
R. Cockburn
Deputy in Charge of Offices of Court, Y. Anderson
Deputy Principal Clerk (Keeper of the Rolls), A. Moffat
Deputy Clerks of Session and Justiciary, D. Bruton; G.
Combe; T. Cruickshank; E. Dickson; N. Dowie; W.
Dunn; A. Finlayson; J. Lynn; L. Maclachlan; D.
MacLeod; R. MacPherson; I. Martin; L. McFarlane; N.
McGinley; A. McKay; J. McLean; J. Moyes; J.
O'Donnell; Q. Oliver; C. Reid; R. Sinclair; A.
Thompson; M. Weir

SCOTTISH EXECUTIVE JUSTICE DEPARTMENT

Hayweight House, 23 Lauriston Street, Edinburgh EH3 9DQ
T 0131-229 9200

The Judicial Appointments and Finance Division is
responsible for the provision of sufficient judges and
sheriffs to meet the needs of the business of the supreme
and sheriffs court in Scotland. It is also responsible for
providing the secretariat for the independent Judicial
Appointments Board for Scotland as well as providing
resources for the efficient administration of a number of
specialist courts and tribunals.
Head of Judicial Appointments and Finance Division, D.
Stewart

SCOTTISH COURT SERVICE

Hayweight House, 23 Lauriston Street, Edinburgh EH3 9DQ
T 0131-229 9200 W www.scotcourts.gov.uk

The Scottish Court Service is an executive agency within
the Scottish Executive Justice Department. It is
responsible to the Scottish Ministers for the provision of
staff, court houses and associated services for the supreme
and sheriff courts.
Chief Executive, Eleanor Emberson

SHERIFF COURT OF CHANCERY

27 Chambers Street, Edinburgh EH1 1LB
T 0131-225 2525

The Court deals with service of heirs and completion of
title in relation to heritable property.
Sheriff Principal, Edward F. Bowen, QC

HM COMMISSARY OFFICE

27 Chambers Street, Edinburgh EH1 1LB
T 0131-225 2525

The Office is responsible for issuing confirmation, a legal
document entitling a person to execute a deceased
person's will, and other related matters.
Commissary Clerk, David Shand

SCOTTISH LAND COURT

1 Grosvenor Crescent, Edinburgh EH12 5ER
T 0131-225 3595

The court deals with disputes relating to agricultural and
crofting land in Scotland.
Chair (£125,803), The Hon. Lord McGhie (James
McGhie), QC
Members, D. J. Houston; A. Macdonald *(part-time);* J.
Kinloch *(part-time)*
Principal Clerk, K. H. R. Graham, WS

SHERIFFDOMS
SALARIES

Sheriff Principal	£125,803
Sheriff	£116,515
*Floating Sheriff	

GLASGOW AND STRATHKELVIN
Sheriff Principal, vacant
Area Director West, David Forrester

SHERIFFS AND SHERIFF CLERK
Glasgow, J. A. Baird; *Mrs P. M. M. Bowman; S. Cathcart;
D. Convery; Mrs A. L. A. Duncan; J. D. Friel; A. C.
Henry; W. H. Holligan; A. G. Johnston; B. Kearney; B.
A. Lockhart; Mrs D. M. MacNeill, QC; H. Matthews,
QC; C. W. McFarlane, QC; I. H. L. Miller; J. K. Mitchell;
A. W. Noble; A. C. Normand; *M. G. O'Grady, QC; I. A.
S. Peebles, QC; Miss R. E. A. Rae, QC; Miss S. A. O.
Raeburn, QC; Mrs F. L. Reith, QC; *Ms L. M. Ruxton;
C. A. L. Scott; J. A. Taylor; W. J. Totten
Sheriff Clerk, E. A. Cumming

GRAMPIAN, HIGHLANDS AND ISLANDS
Sheriff Principal, Sir Stephen S. T. Young, Bt., QC
Area Director North, Eric McQueen

SHERIFFS AND SHERIFF CLERKS
Aberdeen and Stonehaven, G. K. Buchanan; Mrs A. M.
Cowan; D. J. Cusine; *P. P. Davies; C. J. Harris, QC; A. S.
Jessop; K. A. McLernan; *K. M. Stewart; J. K. Tierney
Sheriff Clerks, Mrs E. Laing *(Aberdeen);* A. Hempseed
(Stonehaven)
Banff, A. McLernan; *Sheriff Clerk Depute,* David Altman
Dingwall, A. L. MacFadyen; *Sheriff Clerk Depute,* M.
McBey
Dornoch, D. O. Sutherland; *Sheriff Clerk Depute,* Ken Kerr
Elgin, I. A. Cameron; *Sheriff Clerk,* W. M. Cochrane
Fort William, W. D. Small *(also Oban); Sheriff Clerk
Depute,* S. McKenna
Inverness, Portree, Stornoway, Tain and Wick, D. Booker-
Milburn; A. Pollock; *Sheriff Clerk,* A. Bayliss
(Inverness); Sheriff Clerks Depute, Miss M. Campbell
(Lochmaddy and Portree); Miss L. Hughes *(Stornoway);*
R. M. Hughes *(Tain);* Mrs J. McEwan *(Wick)*
Kirkwall and Lerwick, G. Napier; *Sheriff Clerks Depute,* A.
Moore *(Kirkwall);* B. Reid *(Lerwick)*
Peterhead, *M. Garden; *Sheriff Clerk,* R. Cantwell
(Peterhead)
Lochmaddy, A. L. MacFadyen; *Sheriff Clerk Depute,* Miss
M. Campbell

LOTHIAN AND BORDERS
Sheriff Principal, E. F. Bowen, QC
Area Director East, M. Bonar

SHERIFFS AND SHERIFF CLERKS
Edinburgh, J. D. Allan; R. G. Craik, QC *(also Peebles);* J. A.
Farrell; J. M. S. Horsburgh, QC; Mrs M. L. E. Jarvie, QC;
G. W. M. Liddle; A. Lothian; *Mrs K. E. C. Mackie; *N.
J. MacKinnon; K. M. MacIver; I. McColl; *D. W. M.
McIntyre; M. McPartlin; *J. C. C. McSherry; N. M. P.
Morrison, QC; Miss I. A. Poole; G. W. S. Presslie *(also
Haddington);* *J. P. Scott; Miss M. M. Stephen; C. N.
Stoddart; *Sheriff Clerk,* D. Shand
Linlithgow, G. R. Fleming; P. Gillam; W. D. Muirhead; *M.
G. R. Edington; *Sheriff Clerk,* D. Lynn

Haddington, G. W. S. Presslie *(also Edinburgh)*; *Sheriff Clerk*, I. Munro

Jedburgh and Duns, T. A. K. Drummond, QC; *Sheriff Clerk*, I. W. Williamson

Peebles, R. G. Craik, QC *(also Edinburgh)*; *Sheriff Clerk Depute*, G. Sutherland

Selkirk, T. A. K. Drummond, QC; *Sheriff Clerk Depute*, M. McCabe

NORTH STRATHCLYDE

Sheriff Principal, B. A. Kerr, QC
Area Director West, D. Forrester

SHERIFFS AND SHERIFF CLERKS

Campbeltown, *W. Dunlop *(also Paisley)*; *Sheriff Clerk Depute*, Miss E. Napier

Dumbarton, J. T. Fitzsimons; T. Scott; S. W. H. Fraser; *Sheriff Clerk*, S. Bain

Dunoon, Mrs C. M. A. F. Gimblett; *Sheriff Clerk Depute*, J. McGraw

Greenock, J. Herald *(also Rothesay)*; V. J. Canavan; *Mrs R. Swanney; *Sheriff Clerk*, Ms J. G. Blackstock

Kilmarnock, T. M. Croan; W. S. Ireland; Mrs I. S. McDonald; C. G. McKay; *A. G. Watson; *Sheriff Clerk*, A. P. Johnston

Oban, W. D. Small *(also Fort William)*; *Sheriff Clerk Depute*, K. Carter

Paisley, *A. M. Cubie; N. Douglas; *W. Dunlop *(also Campbeltown)*; G. C. Kavanagh; D. J. Pender; *C. W. Pettigrew; Ms S. M. Sinclair; J. Spy; *Ms S. A. Waldron; *Sheriff Clerk*, Miss C. Cockburn

Rothesay, J. Herald *(also Greenock)*; *Sheriff Clerk Depute*, Mrs C. K. McCormick

SOUTH STRATHCLYDE, DUMFRIES AND GALLOWAY

Sheriff Principal, J. C. McInnes, QC
Area Director West, D. Forrester

SHERIFFS AND SHERIFF CLERKS

Airdrie, R. H. Dickson; Mrs M. M. Galbraith *(also Lanark)*; J. C. Morris, QC; A. D. Vannet; *Sheriff Clerk*, J. Hamilton

Ayr, N. Gow, QC; J. McGowan; C. B. Miller; *Sheriff Clerk*, O. McShane

Dumfries, K. G. Barr; K. A. Ross; *Sheriff Clerk*, E. Young

Hamilton, D. M. Bicket; W. E. Gibson; *W. S. S. Ireland; *Ms C. A. Kelly; *J. Montgomery; H. S. Neilson; Miss J. Powrie; H. K. Small; Mrs M. Smart; J. H. Stewart; T. Welsh, QC; *Sheriff Clerk*, F. Petrie

Lanark, Mrs M. M. Galbraith *(also Airdrie)*; Ms N. C. Stewart; *Sheriff Clerk*, Mrs M. McLean

Stranraer and Kirkcudbright, J. R. Smith; *Sheriff Clerks*, W. McIntosh *(Stranraer)*; B. Lindsay *(Kirkcudbright)*

TAYSIDE, CENTRAL AND FIFE

Sheriff Principal, R. A. Dunlop, QC
Area Director East, M. Bonar
SHERIFFS AND SHERIFF CLERKS
Alloa, W. M. Reid; *Sheriff Clerk*, L. Reid

Arbroath, C. N. R. Stein; *Sheriff Clerks*, S. Munro *(Arbroath)*; A. Pirie *(Forfar)*

Cupar, G. J. Evans; *Sheriff Clerk*, C. Donald

Dundee, R. A. Davidson; A. J. M. Duff; I. D. Dunbar; J. G. Hughes; A. G. McCulloch; *L. Wood; *Sheriff Clerk*, R. McMillan

Dunfermline, I. C. Simpson; *D. M. Mackie; *Sheriff Clerk*, J. Murphy

Falkirk, *C. Caldwell; A. J. Murphy; A. V. Sheehan; *Sheriff Clerk*, R. McMillan

Forfar, K. A. Veal; *Sheriff Clerk*, Alan Pirie

Kirkcaldy, B. G. Donald; R. J. MacLeod; *Sheriff Clerk*, S. Walker

Perth, M. J. Fletcher; L. D. R. Foulis; R. A. McCreadie, QC; *D. C. W. Pyle; *Sheriff Clerk*, A. Nicol

Stirling, A. Cubie; A. W. Robertson; *Sheriff Clerk*, R. Sinclair

STIPENDIARY MAGISTRATES

GLASGOW
R. Hamilton, *apptd* 1984; J. B. C. Nisbet, *apptd* 1984; R. B. Christie, *apptd* 1985; Mrs J. A. M. MacLean, *apptd* 1990

CROWN OFFICE AND PROCURATOR FISCAL SERVICE

CROWN OFFICE
25 Chambers Street, Edinburgh EH1 1LA
T 0131-226 2626 W www.crownoffice.gov.uk

Crown Agent, Norman McFadyen
Deputy Crown Agent, James Brisbane

PROCURATORS FISCAL

SALARIES	
Area Fiscals	£53,451–£155,008
District Procurator Fiscal	£38,500–£56,600

GRAMPIAN AREA
Area Procurator Fiscal, Ms C. Frame (acting) *(Aberdeen)*
Procurators Fiscal, A. B. Hutchinson; S. Ralph

HIGHLAND AND ISLANDS AREA
Area Procurator Fiscal, A. Laing *(Inverness)*
Procurators Fiscal, G. Aitken; Ms S. Foard; A. MacDonald; D. S. Teale; R. W. Urquhart; Ms A. Wyllie

LANARKSHIRE AREA
Area Procurator Fiscal, Ms J. Cameron *(Hamilton)*
Procurators Fiscal, Mrs A. C. Donaldson; S. Houston; D. Spiers

CENTRAL AREA
Area Procurator Fiscal, Mrs G. W. Watt *(Stirling)*
Procurators Fiscal, Ms R. McQuaid; N. Bowie (acting)

DUNDEE AREA
Area Procurator Fiscal, D. Howdle *(Dundee)*
Procurators Fiscal, Ms B. Bott; D. Griffiths; Ms E. Miller

FIFE AREA
Area Procurator Fiscal, C. Ritchie *(Kirkcaldy)*
Procurators Fiscal, J. Robertson; E. B. Russell

LOTHIAN AND BORDERS AREA
Area Procurator Fiscal, W. A. Gilchrist *(Edinburgh)*
Procurators Fiscal, A. R. G. Fraser; W. Gallacher; M. Paterson; A. J. P. Reith; R. Stott

AYRSHIRE AREA
Area Procurator Fiscal, John Dunn *(Kilmarnock)*
Procurators Fiscal, K. Donnelly; I. L. Murray

ARGYLL AND CLYDE AREA
Area Procurator Fiscal, J. Watt *(Paisley)*
Procurators Fiscal, W. S. Carnegie; C. Most; M. Ramage;
   G. F. Williams

DUMFRIES AND GALLOWAY AREA
Area Procurator Fiscal, T. Dysart *(Dumfries)*
Procurators Fiscal, N. Patrick; J. Service

GLASGOW AREA
Area Procurator Fiscal, Ms C. Dyer *(Glasgow)*
Procurators Fiscal, A. Currie; D. Green; Ms J. Harrower; M.
   Watson

NORTHERN IRELAND JUDICATURE

In Northern Ireland the legal system and the structure of
courts closely resemble those of England and Wales; there
are, however, often differences in enacted law.
   The Supreme Court of Judicature of Northern Ireland
comprises the Court of Appeal, the High Court of Justice
and the Crown Court. The practice and procedure of
these courts is similar to that in England. The superior
civil court is the High Court of Justice, from which an
appeal lies to the Northern Ireland Court of Appeal; the
House of Lords is the final civil appeal court.
   The Crown Court, served by High Court and county
court judges, deals with criminal trials on indictment.
Cases are heard before a judge and, except those involving
offences specified under emergency legislation, a jury.
Appeals from the Crown Court against conviction or
sentence are heard by the Northern Ireland Court of
Appeal; the House of Lords is the final court of appeal.
   The decision to prosecute in cases tried on indictment
and in summary cases of a serious nature rests in Northern
Ireland with the Director of Public Prosecutions, who is
responsible to the Attorney-General. Minor summary
offences are prosecuted by the police.
   Minor criminal offences are dealt with in magistrates'
courts by a legally qualified resident magistrate and,
where an offender is under the age of 17, by juvenile
courts each consisting of a resident magistrate and two lay
members specially qualified to deal with juveniles (at least
one of whom must be a woman). On 1 August 2005 there
were 802 justices of the peace in Northern Ireland.
Appeals from magistrates' courts are heard by the county
court, or by the Court of Appeal on a point of law or an
issue as to jurisdiction.
   Magistrates' courts in Northern Ireland can deal with
certain classes of civil case but most minor civil cases are
dealt with in county courts. Judgments of all civil courts
are enforceable through a centralised procedure
administered by the Enforcement of Judgments Office.

SUPREME COURT OF JUDICATURE
The Royal Courts of Justice, Belfast BT1 3JF T 028-9023 5111
Lord Chief Justice of Northern Ireland (£191,276), The Rt.
   Hon. Sir Brian Kerr, *born* 1948, *apptd* 2004
Principal Secretary, S. T. A. Rogers

LORDS JUSTICES OF APPEAL (each £175,671)
Style, The Rt. Hon. Lord Justice [surname]

Rt. Hon. Sir Michael Nicholson, *born* 1933, *apptd* 1995
Rt. Hon. Sir Anthony Campbell, *born* 1936, *apptd* 1998
Rt. Hon. Sir John Shiel, *born* 1938, *apptd* 2004

PUISNE JUDGES (each £155,404)
Style, The Hon. Mr Justice [surname]

Hon. Sir Malachy Higgins, *born* 1944, *apptd* 1993
Hon. Sir Paul Girvan, *born* 1948, *apptd* 1995
Hon. Sir Patrick Coghlin, *born* 1945, *apptd* 1997
Hon. Sir John Gillen, *born* 1947, *apptd* 1998
Hon. Sir Richard McLaughlin, *born* 1947, *apptd* 1999
Hon. Sir Ronald Weatherup, *born* 1947, *apptd* June 2001
Hon. Sir Reginald Weir, *born* 1947, *apptd* 2003
Hon. Sir Declan Morgan, *born* 1952, *apptd* 2004
Hon. Sir Donnell Deeny, *born* 1950, *apptd* 2004
Hon. Sir Anthony Hart, *born* 1946, *apptd* 2005

MASTERS OF THE SUPREME COURT (each £93,483)
Master, Queen's Bench and Appeals and Clerk of the Crown,
   J. W. Wilson, QC
Master, High Court, C. J. McCorry
Master, Office of Care and Protection, F. B. Hall
Master, Chancery Office, R. A. Ellison
Master, High Court with Matrimonial, C. W. G. Redpath
Master, Taxing Office, J. C. Napier

OFFICIAL SOLICITOR
Official Solicitor to the Supreme Court of Northern Ireland,
   Miss B. M. Donnelly

COUNTY COURTS

JUDGES (each £116,515)
Style, His/Her Hon. Judge [surname]

Judge Babington; Judge Finnegan; Judge Gibson, QC; Her
Hon. Judge Kennedy; Judge Lockie; Judge Loughran;
Judge Lynch; Judge McFarland; Judge McKay, QC; Judge
McReynolds; Judge Markey, QC; Judge Marrinan, QC;
Judge Martin *(Chief Social Security and Child Support
Commissioner);* Judge Rodgers; Judge Smyth, QC

RECORDERS
Belfast (£135,867), Judge Burgess
Londonderry, Her Hon. Judge Philpott, QC

MAGISTRATES' COURTS

RESIDENT MAGISTRATES (each £93,483)
There are 19 resident magistrates in Northern Ireland.

CROWN SOLICITORS' OFFICE
PO Box 410, Royal Courts of Justice, Belfast BT1 3JY
T 028-9054 2555
Crown Solicitor, O. G. Paulin

DEPARTMENT OF THE DIRECTOR OF PUBLIC
PROSECUTIONS
93 Chichester Street, Belfast BT1 3TR
T 028-9054 2444
Director of Public Prosecutions, Sir Alasdair Fraser, CB, QC
Deputy Director of Public Prosecutions, W. R. Junkin

NORTHERN IRELAND COURT SERVICE
Windsor House, Bedford Street, Belfast BT2 7LT
T 028-9032 8594
Director, D. A. Lavery

TRIBUNALS

THE TRIBUNALS SERVICE

The Tribunals Service is a new executive agency within the Department for Constitutional Affairs that will bring the largest central government tribunals together in a single organisation and provide them with common administrative support. The Service also aims to deliver greater consistency in practice and procedure, ensure tribunals are manifestly independent from those whose decisions are being reviewed and provide increased access to information for the public. The Tribunals Service entered its transition year in April 2005 and will formally launch in April 2006, when it will be responsible for hearing appeals relating to immigration, tax, freedom of information, employment disputes, benefits, special educational needs and disability, criminal injuries compensation and mental health. A number of other government tribunals are expected to join the Tribunals Service in the future.

Chief Executive, Peter Handcock

AGRICULTURAL LAND TRIBUNALS

c/o DEFRA, Ergon House, c/o Nobel House, London SW1P 3JR
T 020-7238 6811 W www.defra.gov.uk

Agricultural Land Tribunals settle disputes and other issues between agricultural landlords and tenants, and drainage disputes between neighbours.

There are seven tribunals covering England and one covering Wales. For each tribunal the Lord Chancellor appoints a chair and one or more deputies (barristers or solicitors of at least seven years' standing). The Lord Chancellor also appoints lay members to three statutory panels: the 'landowners' panel, the 'farmers' panel and the 'drainage' panel.

Each tribunal is an independent statutory body with jurisdiction only within its own geographical area. A separate tribunal is constituted for each case, and consists of a chair and two lay members nominated by the chair.

Chairmen (England), His Hon. Judge Machin, QC;
George Newsom; Paul de la Piquerie; His Hon.
Robert Taylor; Nigel Thomas; John Weatherill;
Martin Wood
Chair (Wales), John Owen

APPEALS SERVICE

5th Floor, 14 Grays Inn Road, Fox Court, London WC1X 8HN
T 020-7712 2600 W www.appeals-service.gov.uk

The Appeals Service arranges and hears appeals on decisions concerned with social security, child support, child tax credit, pensions credit, housing benefit, council tax benefit, vaccine damage, tax credits and compensation recovery.

Judicial authority for the Service rests with the president, while administrative responsibility is exercised by the Appeals Service Agency, which is an executive agency of the Department for Work and Pensions.

President, His Hon. Judge Harris
Chief Executive, Appeals Service Agency, Christina Townsend

ASYLUM AND IMMIGRATION TRIBUNAL

Arnhem Support Centre, PO Box 6987, Leicester LE1 6ZX
T 0845-6000 877 W www.ait.gov.uk

The Asylum and Immigration Tribunal (AIT) hears appeals against decisions made by the Home Secretary (and his officials) and its powers are derived from the Immigration and Asylum Act 1999. This tribunal replaced the two-tiered Immigration Appellate Authority on 4 April 2005 by merging the Immigration Adjudicators and the Immigration Appeal Tribunal under Section 26 of the Asylum and Immigration (Treatment of Claimants, etc) Act 2004. Immigration judges hear appeals from decisions concerning the need for, and the refusal of, leave to enter or remain in the UK, refusals to grant asylum, decisions to make deportation orders and directions to remove persons subject to immigration control from the UK. An appeal against a decision by the Home Secretary will go before a case management review hearing in the first instance, where the appellant, his/her representative and a representative from the Home Office will attend before an immigration judge who will, if practicable, identify the key issues of the appeal.

The appeal will then proceed to the substantive hearing stage, which all parties must attend, where it will be heard by a single immigration judge – or for more complex cases before a panel of Tribunal members. The panel is a combination of one or more immigration judges and lay members. Appellants can apply for a review of the Tribunal decision on a point of law only. Immigration judges are appointed by the Lord Chancellor.

President, The Hon. Mr Justice Hodge, OBE
Deputy Presidents, Libby Arfon-Jones; Mark Ockelton

CARE STANDARDS TRIBUNAL

18 Pocock Street, London SE1 0BW T 020-7960 0660
E cst@cst.gsi.gov.uk W www.carestandardstribunal.gov.uk

The Tribunal considers appeals in relation to decisions made about the inclusion of individuals' names on the list of those considered unsuitable to work with children, restrictions from teaching, and general registration decisions made about care homes, children's homes, nurses' agencies, residential family centres and fostering agencies. The Tribunal's president appoints the panels for each case and each appeal is heard by a legally qualified chair and two lay members with expertise in the field.

President, His Hon. Judge Pearl

CIVIL AVIATION AUTHORITY

CAA House, 45–49 Kingsway, London WC2B 6TE T 020-7453
6172 E legal@caa.co.uk W www.caa.co.uk

The Civil Aviation Authority (CAA) does not have a separate tribunal department as such, however for certain purposes the CAA must conform to tribunal requirements. For example, to deal with appeals against the refusal or revocation of aviation licences and certificates issued by the CAA, and the allocation of routes outside of the EU to airlines.

The chairman and four non-executive members who may sit on panels for tribunal purposes are appointed by the Secretary of State for Transport.
Chair, Sir Roy McNulty, CBE

COMMONS COMMISSIONERS
Room Zone 1/05b, Temple Quay House, 2 The Square, Temple Quay, Bristol BS1 6EB T 0117-372 8973
E commons.commissioners@defra.gsi.gov.uk
The Commons Commissioners are responsible for deciding disputes arising under the Commons Registration Act 1965. They also enquire into the ownership of unclaimed common land and village greens. Commissioners must be barristers or solicitors of at least seven years' standing and are appointed by the Lord Chancellor.
Chief Commons Commissioner, Edward Cousins

COMPETITION APPEAL TRIBUNAL
Victoria House, Bloomsbury Place, London WC1A 2EB
T 020-7979 7979 E catribunal@catribunal.org.uk
W www.catribunal.org.uk
The Competition Appeal Tribunal (CAT) is a specialist tribunal established to hear certain cases in the sphere of UK competition and economic regulatory law. The CAT hears appeals against decisions of the Office of Fair Trading and the regulators in the electricity, gas, water, railways and air traffic services sectors under the Competition Act 1998, and the Competition Commission under the merger control and market investigation provisions of the Enterprise Act 2002. The CAT also has jurisdiction under the Competition Act 1998 to award damages in respect of infringements of EC or UK competition law and to hear appeals against decisions of OFCOM under the Communications Act 2003. The CAT is headed by a president and has a panel of 18 chairmen and a panel of 19 ordinary members with backgrounds in law, economics, business, accountancy and regulation. The president and chairmen are appointed by the Lord Chancellor, the ordinary members are appointed by the Secretary of State.
President, Sir Christopher Bellamy

COPYRIGHT TRIBUNAL
Harmsworth House, 13–15 Bouverie Street, London EC4Y 8DP
T 020-7596 6510 E copyright.tribunal@patent.gov.uk
W www.patent.gov.uk/copy/tribunal/
The Copyright Tribunal resolves disputes over copyright licences, principally where there is collective licensing.
The chair and two deputy chairmen are appointed by the Lord Chancellor. Up to eight ordinary members are appointed by the Secretary of State for Trade and Industry.
Chair, C. P. Tootal

CRIMINAL INJURIES COMPENSATION APPEALS PANEL
11th Floor, Cardinal Tower, Farringdon Road, London EC1M 3HS
T 020-7549 4600 E info@cicap.gsi.gov.uk W www.cicap.gov.uk
The Criminal Injuries Compensation Appeals Panel determines appeals against review decisions made by the Criminal Injuries Compensation Authority on applications for compensation received from victims of crimes of violence. The chair and members of the panel are appointed by the Home Secretary. Each hearing panel consists of two or three members, one of which will be a qualified lawyer.
Chair, Roger Goodier

EMPLOYMENT APPEAL TRIBUNAL
Central Office: Audit House, 58 Victoria Embankment, London EC4Y 0DS T 020-7273 1041 *Divisional Office:* 52 Melville Street, Edinburgh EH3 7HS T 0131-225 3963
W www.employmentappeals.gov.uk
The Employment Appeal Tribunal hears appeals on a question of law arising from any decision of an employment tribunal. A tribunal consists of a judge and two lay members. They are appointed by The Queen on the recommendation of the Lord Chancellor and the Secretary of State for Trade and Industry. Administrative support is provided by the Employment Tribunals Service.
President, The Hon. Mr Justice Burton
Scottish Chair, The Hon. Lady Smith

EMPLOYMENT TRIBUNALS (ENGLAND AND WALES)
Victory House, 30–34 Kingsway, London WC2B 6EX
T 0845-795 9775 W www.employmenttribunals.gov.uk
Employment Tribunals for England and Wales sit in 12 regions. The tribunals deal with matters of employment law, redundancy, dismissal, contract disputes, sexual, racial and disability discrimination and related areas of dispute which may arise in the workplace. A public register of applications and decisions is held at 100 Southgate Street, Bury St Edmunds, Suffolk IP33 2AQ . The tribunals are funded by the Department of Trade and Industry; administrative support is provided by the Employment Tribunals Service.
Chairmen, who may be full-time or part-time, are legally qualified. They are appointed by the Lord Chancellor. Tribunal members are appointed by the Secretary of State for Trade and Industry.
President, G. Meeran

EMPLOYMENT TRIBUNALS (SCOTLAND)
Eagle Building, 215 Bothwell Street, Glasgow G2 7TS
T 0141-204 0730
Tribunals in Scotland have the same remit as those in England and Wales. Chairmen are appointed by the Lord President of the Court of Session and lay members by the Secretary of State for Trade and Industry.
President, C. M. Milne

FAMILY HEALTH SERVICES APPEAL AUTHORITY
30 Victoria Avenue, Harrogate HG1 5PR T 01423-530280
E mail@fhsaa.nhs.co.uk W www.fhsaa.nhs.uk
The Family Health Services Appeal Authority (FHSAA) considers appeals against the decisions of Primary Care Trusts (PCTs), for example appeals by GPs, dentists, pharmacists and opticians against disciplinary action taken against them. The FHSAA aims to resolve contract disputes between GPs and PCTs and also deals with appeals relating to the vocational training of GPs. The president allocates appeals and applications to panels normally consisting of a legal chair, a professional member and a lay member. The FHSAA's president and members are appointed by the Lord Chancellor.
Chair, Alan Crute

FINANCIAL SERVICES AND MARKETS TRIBUNAL
15–19 Bedford Avenue, London WC1B 3AS T 020-7612 9700
E vatlon@dca.gsi.gov.uk
The Financial Services and Markets Tribunal hears cases arising from decisions issued by the Financial Services Authority against financial service providers, including banks, clearing houses, stockbrokers and pension advisers.

The president, a panel of legally qualified chairmen and a panel of lay members are all appointed by the Lord Chancellor.

President, His Hon. Stephen Oliver, QC

GENERAL COMMISSIONERS OF INCOME TAX

Department for Constitutional Affairs, Selborne House, 54–60 Victoria Street, London SW1E 6QW **T** 020-7210 8990

General commissioners of income tax operate under the Taxes Management Act 1970. They are unpaid judicial officers who sit in some 392 divisions throughout the United Kingdom to hear appeals against decisions by the HM Revenue & Customs on a variety of taxation matters. The commissioners' jurisdiction was extended in 1999 to hear National Insurance appeals. The Lord Chancellor appoints general commissioners (except in Scotland, where they are appointed by the Scottish Executive). There are approximately 2,100 general commissioners appointed throughout the United Kingdom. In each division, commissioners appoint a clerk, who is normally legally qualified, who makes the administrative arrangements for appeal hearings and advises the commissioners on points of law and procedure. The Department for Constitutional Affairs pays the clerks' remuneration.

Appeals from the general commissioners are by way of case stated, on a point of law, to the High Court (the Court of Session in Scotland or the Court of Appeal in Northern Ireland).

In 2004, approximately 33,800 cases were listed before the general commissioners.

IMMIGRATION SERVICES TRIBUNAL

Procession House, 55 Ludgate Hill, London EC4M 7JW

T 020-7029 9790 **E** imset@dca.gsi.gov.uk

W www.immigrationservicestribunal.gov.uk

The Immigration Services Tribunal is an independent judicial body set up to provide a forum in which appeals against decisions of the Immigration Services Commissioner and complaints made by the Immigration Services Commissioner can be heard and determined. The cases exclusively concern people providing advice and representation services in connection with immigration matters.

The Tribunal forms part of the Court Service. It is the responsibility of the Lord Chancellor. There is a president, who is the judicial head; other judicial members, who must be legally qualified; lay members who must have substantial experience in immigration services or in the law and procedure relating to immigration; and a secretary who is responsible for administration. The tribunal can sit anywhere in the UK.

President, His Hon. Judge Cripps

INDUSTRIAL TRIBUNALS AND THE FAIR EMPLOYMENT TRIBUNAL (NORTHERN IRELAND)

Long Bridge House, 20–24 Waring Street, Belfast BT1 2EB

T 028-9032 7666

W www.industrialfairemploymenttribunalsni.gov.uk

The industrial tribunal system in Northern Ireland was set up in 1965 and has a similar remit to the employment tribunals in the rest of the UK. There is also a Fair Employment Tribunal, which hears and determines individual cases of alleged religious or political discrimination in employment. Employers can appeal to the Fair Employment Tribunal if they consider the directions of the Equality Commission to be unreasonable, inappropriate or unnecessary, and the Equality Commission can make application to the Tribunal for the enforcement of undertakings or directions with which an employer has not complied.

The president, vice-president and part-time chairmen of the Fair Employment Tribunal are appointed by the Lord Chancellor. The full-time chair and the part-time chairmen of the industrial tribunals and the panel members to both the industrial tribunals and the Fair Employment Tribunal are appointed by the Department for Employment and Learning.

President of the Industrial Tribunals and the Fair Employment Tribunal, Eileen McBride

INFORMATION TRIBUNAL

Arnhem House Support Centre, PO Box 6987, Leicester LE1 6ZX

T 0845-6000 877 **E** linformationtribunal@dca.gsi.gov.uk

W www.informationtribunal.gov.uk

The Information Tribunal determines appeals against notices issued by the Information Commissioner. The chair and deputy chair are appointed by the Lord Chancellor and must be legally qualified. Lay members are appointed by the Lord Chancellor to represent the interests of data users or data subjects. A tribunal consists of a chair sitting with equal numbers of the lay members. There is a separate panel of the tribunal which hears national security appeals; the president of this panel is Sir Stephen Mitchell.

Chair, John Angel

LANDS TRIBUNAL

Procession House, 55 Ludgate Hill, London EC4M 7JW

T 020-7029 9780 **E** lands@dca.gsi.gov.uk

W www.landstribunal.gov.uk

The Lands Tribunal is an independent judicial body which determines questions relating to the valuation of land, rating appeals from valuation tribunals, appeals from leasehold valuation tribunals, the discharge or modification of restrictive covenants, and compulsory purchase compensation. The tribunal may also arbitrate under references by consent. The president and members are appointed by the Lord Chancellor. Cases are usually heard by a single member but they may sometimes be heard by two members.

President, G. R. Bartlett, QC

LANDS TRIBUNAL FOR SCOTLAND

1 Grosvenor Crescent, Edinburgh EH12 5ER **T** 0131-225 7996

E mailbox@lands-tribunal-scotland.org.uk

W www.lands-tribunal-scotland.org.uk

The Lands Tribunal for Scotland has the same remit as the tribunal for England and Wales but also covers questions relating to tenants' rights to buy their homes under the Housing (Scotland) Act 1987. The president is appointed by the Lord President of the Court of Session.

President, The Hon. Lord McGhie, QC

MENTAL HEALTH REVIEW TRIBUNALS

Secretariat: Health Service Directorate, 11 Belgrave Road, London SW1V 1RB **W** www.mhrt.org.uk

The Mental Health Review Tribunals are independent judicial bodies which review the cases of patients compulsorily detained under the provisions of the Mental Health Act 1983. They have the power to discharge the patient, to recommend leave of absence, delayed discharge, transfer to another hospital or that a guardianship order be made, to reclassify both restricted and unrestricted patients, and to recommend

consideration of a supervision application. There are three tribunals in England and Wales, each headed by a regional chair who is appointed by the Lord Chancellor on a part-time basis. Each tribunal is made up of at least three members, and must include a lawyer, who acts as president, a medical member and a lay member.
Liaison Judge, His Hon. Judge Sycamore

NATIONAL HEALTH SERVICE TRIBUNAL (SCOTLAND)

40 Craiglockhart Road North, Edinburgh EH14 1BT
T 0131-443 2575
The Scottish National Health Service Tribunal considers representations that the continued inclusion of a doctor, dentist, optometrist or pharmacist on a health board's list would be prejudicial to the efficiency of the service concerned. The Tribunal sits when required and is composed of a chair, one lay member, and one practitioner member drawn from a representative professional panel. The chair is appointed by the Lord President of the Court of Session, and the lay member and the members of the professional panel are appointed by the Scottish Ministers.
Chair, John Graham

NATIONAL PARKING ADJUDICATION SERVICE

6th Floor, Barlow House, Minshull Street, Manchester M1 3DZ
T 0161-242 5252 E npas@parking-appeals.gov.uk
W www.parking-appeals.gov.uk
The National Parking Adjudication Service considers appeals from motorists against Penalty Charge Notices issued by councils in England and Wales under the Road Traffic Act 1991. Parking adjudicators are appointed by the Lord Chancellor and must be lawyers of five years' standing. Cases are decided by a single adjudicator, either in a postal or a personal hearing.
Service Director, Bob Tinsley

PENSIONS APPEAL TRIBUNAL

Procession House, 55 Ludgate Hill, London EC4M 7JW
T 020-7029 9800 F 020-7029 9801
W www.pensionsappealtribunals.gov.uk
The Pensions Appeal Tribunals are responsible for hearing appeals from ex-servicemen or women and widows who have had their claims for a war pension rejected by the Secretary of State for Work and Pensions. The Entitlement Appeal Tribunals hear appeals in cases where the Secretary of State has refused to grant a war pension. The Assessment Appeal Tribunals hear appeals against the Secretary of State's assessment of the degree of disablement caused by an accepted condition. The tribunal members are appointed by the Secretary of State for Constitutional Affairs.
President, Dr H. M. G. Concannon, LLM

PENSIONS APPEAL TRIBUNALS FOR SCOTLAND
20 Walker Street, Edinburgh EH3 7HS T 0131-220 1404
President, C. N. McEachran, QC

OFFICE OF THE SOCIAL SECURITY AND CHILD SUPPORT COMMISSIONERS

3rd Floor, Procession House, 55 Ludgate Hill, London EC4A 7JW
T 020-7029 9850
23 Melville Street, Edinburgh EH3 7PW T 0131-225 2201
E osscs@courtservice.gsi.gov.uk W www.osscsc.gov.uk
The Social Security Commissioners are the final statutory authority to decide appeals relating to entitlement to

social security benefits. The Child Support Commissioners are the final statutory authority to decide appeals relating to child support. Appeals may be made in relation to both matters only on a point of law. The Commissioners' jurisdiction covers England, Wales and Scotland. There are 18 commissioners, all of which are qualified lawyers.
Chief Social Security Commissioner and Chief Child Support Commissioner, His Hon. Judge Hickinbottom

OFFICE OF THE SOCIAL SECURITY COMMISSIONERS AND CHILD SUPPORT COMMISSIONERS FOR NORTHERN IRELAND

1st Floor, Headline Building, 1014 Victoria Street, Belfast BT1 3GG T 028-9033 2344
E socialsecuritycommissioners@courtsni.gov.uk
W www.courtsni.gov.uk
The role of Northern Ireland Social Security Commissioners and Child Support Commissioners is similar to that of the Commissioners in Great Britain. There are two commissioners for Northern Ireland.
Chief Commissioner, His Hon. Judge Martin, QC
Commissioner, Mrs M. F. Brown, LLB

RESIDENTIAL PROPERTY TRIBUNAL SERVICE

10 Alfred Place, London WC1E 7LR T 0845-600 3178
W www.rpts.gov.uk
The Residential Property Tribunal Service provides members to sit on panels for the Rent Assessment Committees and Leasehold Valuation Tribunals, and serves the private-rented and leasehold housing market in England by resolving disputes between leaseholders, tenants and landlords. The president and chairmen are appointed by the Lord Chancellor and other members are appointed by the Office of the Deputy Prime Minister.
President, Siobhan McGrath

SOLICITORS' DISCIPLINARY TRIBUNAL

3rd Floor, Gate House, 1 Farringdon Street, London EC4M 7NS
T 020-7329 4808 E enquiries@solicitorsdt.com
W www.solicitorstribunal.org.uk
The Solicitors' Disciplinary Tribunal is an independent statutory body whose members are appointed by the Master of the Rolls. The Tribunal considers applications made to it alleging either professional misconduct and/or a breach of the statutory rules by which solicitors are bound against an individually named solicitor, former solicitor, registered foreign lawyer, or solicitor's clerk. The Tribunal has around 30 members, two thirds are solicitor members and one third lay members. The president and solicitor members do not receive remuneration and lay members are remunerated by the Department for Constitutional Affairs.
President, A. Isaacs

SOLICITORS' DISCIPLINE TRIBUNAL (SCOTTISH)

Unit 3.5, The Granary Business Centre, Coal Road, Cuper, Fife KY15 5YQ T 01334-659088 W www.ssdt.org.uk
The Scottish Solicitors' Discipline Tribunal is an independent statutory body with a panel of 22 members, 14 of whom are solicitors; members are appointed by the Lord President of the Court of Session. Its principal function is to consider complaints of misconduct against solicitors in Scotland.
Chair, G. F. Ritchie

SPECIAL COMMISSIONERS

15–19 Bedford Avenue, London WC1B 3AS T 020-7612 9700
W www.financeandtaxtribunals.gov.uk

The Special Commissioners are an independent body appointed by the Lord Chancellor to hear complex appeals against decisions of the Board of Inland Revenue and its officials.

Presiding Special Commissioner, His Hon. Judge Oliver, QC

SPECIAL EDUCATIONAL NEEDS AND DISABILITY TRIBUNAL

Central Office, Procession House, 55 Ludgate Hill, London EC4M 7JW T 0870-241 2555

Darlington Office, Ground Floor, Mowden Hall, Staindrop Road DL3 9BG W www.sendist.gov.uk

The Special Educational Needs and Disability Tribunal considers parents' appeals against the decisions of Local Education Authorities (LEAs) about children's special educational needs if parents cannot reach agreement with the LEA. Its president and chairmen are appointed by the Lord Chancellor. Specialist members are appointed by the Secretary of State for Education and Skills.

President, Lady Rosemary Hughes

SPECIAL IMMIGRATION APPEALS COMMISSION

15 Breams Buildings, London EC4A 1DZ T 020-7073 4200

The Commission was set up under the Special Immigration Appeals Commission Act 1997. Its main function is to consider appeals against orders for deportations in cases which involve, in the main, considerations of national security. Members are appointed by the Lord Chancellor.

Chair, The Hon. Mr Justice Ouseley

TRAFFIC COMMISSIONERS

c/o Scottish Traffic Area, Argyle House, 3 Lady Lawson Street, Edinburgh EH3 9SE T 0131-200 4955 W www.vosa.gov.uk

The Traffic Commissioners are responsible for licensing operators of heavy goods and public service vehicles. There are eight Commissioners, each constituting a tribunal for the purposes of the Tribunals and Inquiries Act 1992.

Traffic Commissioner, Miss J. N. Aitken

TRANSPORT TRIBUNAL

Procession House, 55 Ludgate Hill, London EC4M 7JW
T 020-7029 9780 E transport@dca.gsi.gov.uk
W www.transporttribunal.gov.uk

The Transport Tribunal has three jurisdictions: it hears appeals against decisions made by Traffic Commissioners at public inquiries, appeals against decisions of the Registrar of Approved Driving Instructors and is able to resolve disputes under the Postal Services Act 2000. The Tribunal consists of a legally qualified president, other judicial members, and lay members. The president and legal members are appointed by the Lord Chancellor and the lay members by the Secretary of State for Transport.

Members of the Transport Tribunal also act as the London Service Permit Appeals Panel.

President, H. B. H. Carlisle, QC

VALUATION TRIBUNAL SERVICE

Chief Executive's Office, Block 1, Angel Square, 1 Torren's Street, London EC1V 1NY T 020-7841 8700
W www.valuation-tribunals.gov.uk

The Valuation Tribunal Service (VTS) was created as a corporate body by the Local Government Finance Act 2003, and is responsible for providing or arranging the services required for the operation of valuation tribunals in England. The VTS is comprised of a chair and members appointed by the Secretary of State. There are 56 tribunals in England and four in Wales, which hear appeals concerning council tax and non-domestic rating and land drainage rates in England and Wales. There are 56 tribunals in England and four in Wales; those in England are funded by the Office of the Deputy Prime Minister and those in Wales by the National Assembly for Wales. A separate tribunal is constituted for each hearing, and normally consists of a clerk and two or three other members. Members are appointed by a representative of the local authorities and the Valuation Tribunal president and serve on a voluntary basis. The Valuation Tribunal Management Board considers all matters affecting valuation tribunals in England, and the Council of Wales Valuation Tribunals performs the same function in Wales.

Chair, Valuation Tribunal Management Board, N. Galbraith
Valuation Tribunals Chief Executive Officer, Laurence Barnes
President, Council of Wales Valuation Tribunals, J. H. Owens

VAT AND DUTIES TRIBUNALS

15–19 Bedford Avenue, London WC1B 3AS T 020-7612 9700
W www.financeandtaxtribunals.gov.uk

VAT and Duties Tribunals are administered by the Department for Constitutional Affairs in England and Wales, and by the First Minister in Scotland. They are independent and decide disputes between taxpayers and HM Revenue and Customs. In England and Wales, the president and chairmen are appointed by the Lord Chancellor and members by the Treasury. Chairmen in Scotland are appointed by the Lord President of the Court of Session.

President, His Hon. Stephen Oliver, QC
Vice-President, England and Wales, J. D. Demack
Vice-President, Scotland, T. G. Coutts, QC

TRIBUNAL CENTRES

EDINBURGH, 44 Palmerston Place, Edinburgh EH12 5BJ
T 0131-226 3551

LONDON (including Belfast), 15–19 Bedford Avenue, London WC1B 3AS T 020-7612 9700

MANCHESTER, 9th Floor, Westpoint, 501 Chester Road, Manchester M16 5HU T 0161-868 6600

THE POLICE SERVICE

There are 52 police forces in the United Kingdom. Most forces' areas are coterminous with one or more local authority areas. Policing in London is carried out by the Metropolitan Police and the City of London Police; in Northern Ireland by the Police Service of Northern Ireland; and by the Isle of Man, States of Jersey and Guernsey forces in their respective islands and bailiwicks. National services include the National Crime Squad (NCS) and the National Criminal Intelligence Service (NCIS).

Police Authorities are independent bodies, responsible for the supervision of local policing. There are 43 police authorities in England and Wales, most with 17 members comprising nine local councillors, three magistrates and five independent members. Authorities which are responsible for larger areas may have more members, such as the Metropolitan Police Authority which has 23 members: 12 drawn from the London Assembly, four magistrates and seven independent members. The Corporation of London acts as the police authority for the City of London Police. In Scotland, six of the forces are maintained by joint police boards, made up of local councillors from each council in the force area; the other two constabularies (Dumfries and Galloway and Fife) are directly administered by their respective councils. The Northern Ireland Policing Board is an independent public body consisting of 19 political and independent members.

Police forces in England, Scotland and Wales are financed by central and local government grants and a precept on the council tax. The Police Service of Northern Ireland is wholly funded by central government. The police authorities, subject to the approval of the Home Secretary (in England and Wales), the Secretary of State for Northern Ireland and to regulations, are responsible for appointing the Chief Constable. In England and Wales they are responsible for publishing annual policing plans and reports, setting local objectives and a budget, and levying the precept. The police authorities in Scotland are responsible for setting a budget, providing the resources necessary to police the area adequately, appointing officers of the rank of Assistant Chief Constable and above, and determining the number of officers and civilian staff in the force. The Northern Ireland Policing Board exercises these functions in Northern Ireland.

The Home Secretary, the Secretary of State for Northern Ireland and the Scottish Executive are responsible for the organisation, administration and operation of the police service. They make regulations covering matters such as police ranks, discipline, hours of duty and pay and allowances. All police forces are subject to inspection by HM Inspectors of Constabulary, who report to the Home Secretary, Scottish Executive or Secretary of State for Northern Ireland.

COMPLAINTS

The Independent Police Complaints Commission (IPCC) has overall responsibility for the system of complaints against the police. The IPCC has the power to initiate, carry out and oversee investigations and is also responsible for the way complaints are handled by local police forces. An officer who is dismissed, required to resign or reduced in rank, whether as a result of a complaint or not, may appeal to a police appeals tribunal established by the relevant police authority. In Scotland, Chief Constables are obliged to investigate a complaint against one of their officers; if there is a suggestion of criminal activity, the complaint is investigated by an independent public prosecutor. In Northern Ireland complaints are investigated by the Police Ombudsman.

RATES OF PAY

BASIC RATES OF PAY *at 1 April 2005*

Chief Constables of Greater Manchester, Strathclyde and West Midlands**	£151,926–£154,500
Chief Constable**	£108,150–£144,201
Deputy Chief Constable**	£92,700–£118,452
Assistant Chief Constable**	£77,250–£90,126
Chief Superintendent	£63,345–£66,951
–Superintendent Range 2*	£60,735–£64,635
Superintendent	£53,046–£61,800
Chief Inspector[†§]	£44,094 (£45,852)–£45,909 (£47,664)
Inspector[†§]	£39,840 (£41,586)–£43,212 (£44,970)
Sergeant[†]	£31,092–£34,944
Constable[†]	£19,803–£31,092

* For Superintendents who were not given the rank of Chief Superintendent on its re-introduction on 1 January 2002
† Officers who have been on the highest available salary for one year will have access to a competence-related threshold payment of £1,032 per annum
§ London salary in parenthesis, applicable only to officers in the Metropolitan and City of London police forces
** Chief Officers may receive a bonus of at least 5 per cent of pensionable pay if their performance is deemed exceptional

*Metropolitan Police**	
Commissioner	£221,451
Deputy Commissioner	£182,826
*City of London Police**	
Commissioner	£137,000
Assistant Commissioner	£113,000
Police Service of Northern Ireland	
Chief Constable	£164,799
Deputy Chief Constable	£133,899

* London weighting from 1 July 2004 is £1,938 per annum

POLICE FORCES

Strength: size of force as known at February 2005
Source: Police and Constabulary Almanac 2005, Hazell & Co.

ENGLAND

AVON AND SOMERSET CONSTABULARY, PO Box 37, Portishead, Bristol BS20 8QJ T 0845-456 7000
  Strength, 3,276
  Chief Constable, S. Pilkington, QPM
BEDFORDSHIRE POLICE, Police Headquarters, Woburn Road, Kempston, Bedford MK43 9AX T 01234-841212
  Strength, 1,254
  Chief Constable, Gillian Parker

CAMBRIDGESHIRE CONSTABULARY, Hinchingbrooke Park, Huntingdon PE29 6NP T 0845-456 4564
Strength, 1,419
Chief Constable, T. Lloyd, QPM

CHESHIRE CONSTABULARY, Clemonds Hey, Oakmere Road, Winsford CW7 2UA T 01244-350000
Strength, 2,210
Chief Constable, P. Fahy, QPM

CLEVELAND POLICE, PO Box 70, Ladgate Lane, Middlesbrough TS8 9EH T 01642-326326
Strength, 1,675
Chief Constable, Sean Price

CUMBRIA CONSTABULARY, Carleton Hall, Penrith, Cumbria CA10 2AU T 01768-891999
Strength, 1,256
Chief Constable, Michael Baxter

DERBYSHIRE CONSTABULARY, Butterley Hall, Ripley, Derbyshire DE5 3RS T 0845-123 3333
Strength, 2,084
Chief Constable, D. F. Coleman, QPM

DEVON AND CORNWALL CONSTABULARY, Middlemoor, Exeter EX2 7HQ T 08452-777444
Strength, 3,383
Chief Constable, Maria Wallis, QPM

DORSET POLICE, Winfrith, Dorchester, Dorset DT2 8DZ
T 01929-462727
Strength, 1,402
Chief Constable, M. Baker

DURHAM CONSTABULARY, Aykley Heads, Durham DH1 5TT T 0845-606 0365 W www.durham.police.uk
Strength, 1,685
Chief Constable, P. Garvin, QPM

ESSEX POLICE, PO Box 2, Springfield, Chelmsford, Essex CM2 6DA T 01245-491491 W www.essex.police.uk
Strength, 3,159
Chief Constable, D. F. Stevens, QPM

GLOUCESTERSHIRE CONSTABULARY, Holland House, Lansdown Road, Cheltenham, Glos GL51 6QH
T 0845-090 1234 W www.gloucestershire.police.uk
Strength, 1,174
Chief Constable, T. Brain, QPM, PHD

GREATER MANCHESTER POLICE, PO Box 22 (S West PDO), Chester House, Boyer Street, Manchester M16 0RE
T 0161-872 5050
Strength, 8,170
Chief Constable, Michael Todd, QPM

HAMPSHIRE CONSTABULARY, West Hill, Winchester, Hants SO22 5DB T 0845-045 4545
Strength, 3,500
Chief Constable, Paul Kernaghan, QPM

HERTFORDSHIRE CONSTABULARY, Stanborough Road, Welwyn Garden City, Herts AL8 6XF T 01707-354200
Strength, 2,131
Chief Constable, Frank Whiteley

HUMBERSIDE POLICE, Priory Road Police Station, Priory Road, Hull HU1 5SF T 01482-326111
Strength, 2,260
Chief Constable, D. Westwood, QPM, PHD

KENT POLICE, Sutton Road, Maidstone, Kent ME15 9BZ
T 01622-690690
Strength, 3,555
Chief Constable, M. Fuller, QPM

LANCASHIRE CONSTABULARY, PO Box 77, Hutton, Nr. Preston, Lancs PR4 5SB T 01772-614444
W www.lancashire.police.uk
Strength, 3,451
Chief Constable, vacant

LEICESTERSHIRE CONSTABULARY, St John's, Enderby, Leicester LE19 2BX T 0116-222 2222
Strength, 2,211
Chief Constable, Matthew Baggott, QPM

LINCOLNSHIRE POLICE, PO Box 999, Lincoln LN5 7PH
T 01522-532222 W www.lincs.police.uk
Strength, 1,264
Chief Constable, Tony Lake, QPM

MERSEYSIDE POLICE, PO Box 59, Liverpool L69 1JD
T 0151-709 6010
Strength, 4,386
Chief Constable, B. Hogan-Howe, QPM

NORFOLK CONSTABULARY, Operations and Communications Centre, Falconers Chase, Wymondham, Norfolk NR18 0WW T 01953-424242
Strength, 1,580
Chief Constable, vacant

NORTHAMPTONSHIRE POLICE, Wootton Hall, Northampton NN4 0JQ T 01604-700700
Strength, 1,308
Chief Constable, Peter Maddison

NORTHUMBRIA POLICE, Ponteland, Newcastle upon Tyne NE20 0BL T 01661-872555
Strength, 4,031
Chief Constable, J. Strachan, CBE, QPM

NORTH YORKSHIRE POLICE, Newby Wiske Hall, Northallerton, N. Yorks DL7 9HA T 0845-606 0247
W www.northyorkshire.police.uk
Strength, 1,427
Chief Constable, Ms. D. Cannings

NOTTINGHAMSHIRE POLICE, Sherwood Lodge, Arnold, Nottingham NG5 8PP T 0115-967 0999
Strength, 2,458
Chief Constable, S. Green, QPM

SOUTH YORKSHIRE POLICE, Snig Hill, Sheffield S3 8LY
T 0114-220 2020
Strength, 3,336
Chief Constable, M. Hughes

STAFFORDSHIRE POLICE, Cannock Road, Stafford ST17 0QG T 0845-302010
Strength, 2,218
Chief Constable, John Giffard, CBE, QPM

SUFFOLK CONSTABULARY, Martlesham Heath, Ipswich IP5 3QS T 01473-613500
Strength, 1,309
Chief Constable, Alastair McWhirter, QPM

SURREY POLICE, Mount Browne, Sandy Lane, Guildford, Surrey GU3 1HG T 0845-125 2222
W www.surrey.police.uk
Strength, 1,967
Chief Constable, Robert Quick, QPM

SUSSEX POLICE, Malling House, Lewes, E. Sussex BN7 2DZ
T 0845-607 0999
Strength, 3,140
Chief Constable, Ken Jones, QPM

THAMES VALLEY POLICE, Kidlington, Oxon OX5 2NZ
T 0845-8505 505
Strength, 3,821
Chief Constable, Peter Neyroud, QPM

WARWICKSHIRE POLICE, Leek Wootton, Warwick CV35 7QB T 01926-415000
Strength, 1,008
Chief Constable, John Burbeck, QPM

WEST MERCIA CONSTABULARY, Hindlip Hall, Hindlip, PO Box 55, Worcester WR3 8SP T 08457-444888
W www.westmercia.police.uk
Strength, 2,408
Chief Constable, P. West, QPM

WEST MIDLANDS POLICE, PO Box 52, Lloyd House, Colmore Circus, Queensway, Birmingham B4 6NQ
T 0845-113 5000
Strength, 7,573
Chief Constable, Paul Scott-Lee, QPM
WEST YORKSHIRE POLICE, PO Box 9, Wakefield, W. Yorks WF1 3QP T 01924-375222
Strength, 5,598
Chief Constable, C. Cramphorn
WILTSHIRE CONSTABULARY, London Road, Devizes, Wilts SN10 2DN T 01380-722341
Strength, 1,243
Chief Constable, M. Richards

WALES
DYFED-POWYS POLICE, PO Box 99, Llangunnor, Carmarthen SA31 2PF T 01267-222020
Strength, 1,170
Chief Constable, T. Grange, QPM
GWENT POLICE, Croesyceiliog, Cwmbran, Torfaen NP44 2XJ
T 01633-838111 W www.gwent.police.uk
Strength, 1,261
Chief Constable, Michael Tonge
NORTH WALES POLICE, Colwyn Bay, Conwy LL29 8AW
T 01492-517171
Strength, 1,528
Chief Constable, R. Brunstrom
SOUTH WALES POLICE, Cowbridge Road, Bridgend CF31 3SU T 01656-655555
Strength, 3,324
Chief Constable, Barbara Wilding, QPM

SCOTLAND
CENTRAL SCOTLAND POLICE, Police Headquarters, Randolphfield, Stirling FK8 2HD T 01786-456000
W www.centralscotland.police.uk
Strength, 768
Chief Constable, Andrew Cameron, QPM
DUMFRIES AND GALLOWAY CONSTABULARY, Police Headquarters, Cornwall Mount, Dumfries DG1 1PZ
T 01387-252112 W www.dumfriesandgalloway.police.uk
Strength, 478
Chief Constable, D. Strang, QPM
FIFE CONSTABULARY, Detroit Road, Glenrothes, Fife KY6 2RJ T 01592-418888 W www.fife.police.uk
Strength, 953
Chief Constable, Peter Wilson, QPM
GRAMPIAN POLICE, Queen Street, Aberdeen AB10 1ZA
T 0845-600 5700 W www.grampian.police.uk
Strength, 1,315
Chief Constable, Colin McKerracher
LOTHIAN AND BORDERS POLICE, Fettes Avenue, Edinburgh EH4 1RB T 0131-311 3131
Strength, 2,819
Chief Constable, Paddy Tomkins
NORTHERN CONSTABULARY, Old Perth Road, Inverness IV2 3SY T 01463-715555
Strength, 680
Chief Constable, Ian Latimer
STRATHCLYDE POLICE, Police Headquarters, 173 Pitt Street, Glasgow G2 4JS T 0141-532 2000
W www.strathclyde.police.uk
Strength, 7,433
Chief Constable, William Rae, QPM
TAYSIDE POLICE, PO Box 59, West Bell Street, Dundee DD1 9JU T 01382-223200 W www.tayside.police.uk
Strength, 1,180
Chief Constable, John Vine, QPM

NORTHERN IRELAND
POLICE SERVICE OF NORTHERN IRELAND, Brooklyn, Knock Road, Belfast BT5 6LE T 028-9065 0222
W www.psni.police.uk
Strength, 9,851
Chief Constable, H. Orde

ISLANDS
GUERNSEY POLICE, Police Headquarters, Hospital Lane, St Peter Port, Guernsey GY1 2QN T 01481-725111
Strength, 177
Chief Officer, G. LePage
ISLE OF MAN CONSTABULARY, Police Headquarters, Glencrutchery Road, Douglas, Isle of Man IM2 4RG
T 01624-631212
Strength, 236
Chief Constable, M. Culverhouse
STATES OF JERSEY POLICE, PO Box 789, St Helier, Jersey JE4 3ZD T 01534-612612
Strength, 241
Chief Officer, Graham Power, QPM

METROPOLITAN POLICE SERVICE
New Scotland Yard, 8–10 Broadway, London SW1H 0BG
T 020-7230 1212 W www.met.police.uk
Strength (April 2005), 31,057
Commissioner, Sir Ian Blair, QPM
Deputy Commissioner, Paul Stephenson, QPM
Chief of Staff, Deputy Assistant Commissioner, Carole Howlett

TERRITORIAL POLICING
Most of the day-to-day policing of London is the responsibility of Territorial Policing which comprises 33 Borough Operational Command Units (BOCU).
Assistant Commissioner, Tim Godwin, OBE
Assistant Commissioner (Central Operations), Stephen House, QPM

SPECIALIST OPERATIONS
Police units which make up Specialist Operations are responsible for intelligence, security, protection of politicians, embassies and royalty, and the investigation of certain categories of serious crimes, including racial and violent crime and terrorism.
Assistant Commissioners, Sir David Venness, CBE, QPM; Andy Hayman

SPECIALIST CRIME
The Specialist Crime Directorate's main areas of focus are safeguarding children and young people; Class 'A' drugs; dismantling organised criminal networks and seizing their assets; gun-enabled crime; and the investigation and prevention of homicide.
Assistant Commissioner, Tarique Ghaffur, CBE, QPM
Service Improvement Assistant Commissioner, Alan Brown
Human Resources Director, Martin Tiplady
Director of Resources, Keith Luck
Director of Public Affairs and Internal Communication, Dick Fedorico
Director of Information, Ailsa Beaton

CITY OF LONDON POLICE
37 Wood Street, London EC2P 2NQ
T 020-7601 2222 W www.cityoflondon.police.uk
Strength (February 2005), 720

Though small, the City of London has one of the most

important financial centres in the world and the force has particular expertise in areas such as fraud investigation as well as the areas required of any police force. The force has a wholly elected police authority, the police committee of the Corporation of London, which appoints the Commissioner.

Commissioner, James Hart, QPM, PHD
Assistant Commissioner, Mike Bowron
Commander, Frank Armstrong

BRITISH TRANSPORT POLICE
15 Tavistock Place, London WC1H 9SJ T 020-7388 7541 W www.btp.police.uk
Strength (March 2005), 2,493

British Transport Police is the national police force for the railways in England, Wales and Scotland, including the London Underground system, Docklands Light Railway, Midland Metro Tram system and Croydon Tramlink. The Chief Constable reports to the British Transport Police Authority. The members of the Authority are appointed by the Secretary of State for Transport and include representatives from the rail industry as well as independent members. Officers are paid the same as other police forces.

Chief Constable, Ian Johnston, CBE, QPM
Deputy Chief Constable, Andy Trotter, QPM

MINISTRY OF DEFENCE POLICE
MDP Wethersfield, Braintree, Essex CM7 4AZ T 01371-854000
Strength (April 2005), 3,396

The Ministry of Defence Police is a civilian police force with specific responsibility for meeting the requirements of the MOD and associated customers, including visiting forces and the Royal Mint. Other specialist services include marine policing, dogs, firearms and Police Search Teams. The Force also has its own Criminal Investigation Department with specialist officers working in the field of fraud investigation and can also offer crime prevention advice. MDP officers are also serving as a part of the British contingent of police officers supporting the United Nations policing operations.

Chief Constable, S. Love
Deputy Chief Constable, D. A. Ray, QPM, MA, LLM
Director of Resources and Planning, S. Beedle
Assistant Chief Constables: Director of Personnel and Professional Development, R. Chidley; *Director of Operational Support,* J. P. Bligh; *Director of Divisional Operations,* G. P. McAuley

CIVIL NUCLEAR CONSTABULARY
Building F6, Culham Science Centre, Abingdon, Oxon OX14 3DB T 01235-463760
Strength (March 2005), 584

The Constabulary is responsible for policing UK civil nuclear industry facilities and for escorting nuclear material between establishments within the UK and worldwide. The Chief Constable is responsible, through the Civil Nuclear Police Authority, to the President of the Board of Trade.

Chief Constable, W. F. Pryke
Deputy Chief Constable, vacant

NATIONAL POLICE SERVICES

The Serious Organised Crime and Police Act 2005 provided for the establishment of the Serious Organised Crime Agency (SOCA). From 1 April 2006, NCS and NCIS, together with parts of HM Customs and Excise and the UK Immigration Service will be amalgamated to form SOCA.

NATIONAL CRIME SQUAD
Headquarters: PO Box 2500, London SW1V 2WF
T 020-7238 2500 E contact@ncs.police.uk
W www.nationalcrimesquad.police.uk

The National Crime Squad (NCS) investigates national and international organised and serious crime, typically, drugs trafficking, illegal arms dealing, money laundering, contract killings, counterfeit currency as well as kidnap and extortion. It also supports police forces investigating serious crime.

Director-General, Trevor Pearce

NATIONAL CRIMINAL INTELLIGENCE SERVICE
Headquarters: PO Box 8000, London SE11 5EN
T 020-7238 8000 W www.ncis.co.uk

The National Criminal Intelligence Service (NCIS) provides strategic intelligence overviews for national targeting of organised criminality and supplies operational intelligence on the most difficult and dangerous criminal organisations. It provides criminal intelligence to all UK police forces, the National Crime Squad and other law enforcement agencies.

Director-General, Peter Hampton, CBE, QPM

NCS AND NCIS SERVICE AUTHORITIES
Headquarters: PO Box 2600, London SW1V 2WG
T 020-7238 2600

The Service Authorities are responsible for ensuring the effective operation of the National Crime Squad (NCS) and the National Criminal Intelligence Service (NCIS). The NCS Service Authority has nine members and the NCIS Service Authority has eleven members. Eight members sit on both Authorities. The Service Authorities are non-departmental public bodies.

Chair, Paul Lever
Clerk, Andrew Mulholland

FORENSIC SCIENCE SERVICE
Headquarters: Trident Court, 2920 Solihull Parkway, Birmingham Business Park B37 3YN T 0121-329 5200

The Forensic Science Service (FSS) provides forensic science services to the police forces in England and Wales. It employs over 2,500 people, including over 1,600 trained scientists, and has seven laboratories throughout the country.

Chief Executive, David Werrett, PHD

POLICE INFORMATION TECHNOLOGY ORGANISATION
Headquarters: New Kings Beam House, 22 Upper Ground, London SE1 9QY T 020-8358 5555 W www.pito.org.uk

The Police Information Technology Organisation (PITO) is a non-departmental public body funded by grant-in-aid from central Government and by charges from the services

provided. It provides information technology, communications systems and services to the police and other criminal justice organisations in the UK, and also has a role in the purchasing of goods and services for the police.
Chair, Chris Earnshaw
Chief Executive, Phillip Webb

THE SPECIAL CONSTABULARY

Each police force has its own special constabulary, made up of volunteers who work in their spare time. Special Constables have full constabulary powers and perform police duties under the supervision of, and supported by, regular officers. Visit www.specialconstables.gov.uk for further information.

UK POLICE NATIONAL MISSING PERSONS BUREAU

Headquarters: Room 209, New Scotland Yard, Broadway, London SW1H 0BG **T** 0207-230 4029
E nationalmissingpersons@met.police.uk
W www.missingpersons.police.uk

The Police National Missing Persons Bureau (PNMPB) acts as a central clearing house of information, receiving reports about missing persons that are still outstanding after 14 days (or earlier if it is felt that some harm may have befallen them). Reports of unidentified persons who are unable or unwilling to identify themselves, unidentified bodies or remains within 48 hours of being found are also recorded with a view to cross-matching the missing against the found. Information is forwarded to the PNMPB from all forces in the UK and from foreign police forces via Interpol. The Bureau also manages the Missing Kids website http://uk.missingkids.com

STAFF ASSOCIATIONS

Police officers are not permitted to join a trade union or to take strike action. All ranks have their own staff associations.

ASSOCIATION OF CHIEF POLICE OFFICERS OF
ENGLAND, WALES AND NORTHERN IRELAND,
7th Floor, 25 Victoria Street, London SW1H 0EX
T 020-7227 3434
Negotiating Secretary, N. Yeo
POLICE SUPERINTENDENTS' ASSOCIATION OF
ENGLAND AND WALES, 67A Reading Road, Pangbourne,
Reading RG8 7JD **T** 0118-984 4005
National Secretary, Chief Supt. Philip Aspey
POLICE FEDERATION OF ENGLAND AND WALES, 15–17
Langley Road, Surbiton, Surrey KT6 6LP **T** 020-8335 1000
W www.polfed.org
General Secretary, John Francis
ASSOCIATION OF CHIEF POLICE OFFICERS IN
SCOTLAND, Police Headquarters, 173 Pitt Street, Glasgow
G2 4JS **T** 0141-532 2052
E acpos.secretariat@strathclyde.pnn.police.uk
Hon. Secretary, William Rae, QPM
ASSOCIATION OF SCOTTISH POLICE
SUPERINTENDENTS, Secretariat, 173 Pitt Street,
Glasgow G2 4JS **T** 0141-221 5796
W www.scottishpolicesupers.co.uk
General Secretary, Carol Forfar
SCOTTISH POLICE FEDERATION, 5 Woodside Place,
Glasgow G3 7QF **T** 0141-332 5234 **W** www.spf.org.uk
General Secretary, Douglas Keil, QPM
SUPERINTENDENTS' ASSOCIATION OF NORTHERN
IRELAND, 77–79 Garnerville Road, Belfast BT4 2NX
T 028-909 22201 **E** mail@psani.org **W** www.psani.org
Hon. Secretary, Supt. G. Thomson
POLICE FEDERATION FOR NORTHERN IRELAND, 77–79
Garnerville Road, Belfast BT4 2NX **T** 028-9076 4200
E office.pfni@btconnect.com **W** www.policefed-ni.org.uk
Secretary, T. Spence

THE PRISON SERVICE

The prison services in the United Kingdom are the responsibility of the Home Secretary, the Scottish Executive Justice Department and the Secretary of State for Northern Ireland. The chief director-generals (chief executive in Scotland), officers of the Prison Service, the Scottish Prison Service and the Northern Ireland Prison Service are responsible for the day-to-day running of the system.

There are 140 prison establishments in England and Wales, 16 in Scotland and three in Northern Ireland. Convicted prisoners are classified according to their assessed security risk and are housed in establishments appropriate to that level of security. There are no open prisons in Northern Ireland. Female prisoners are housed in women's establishments or in separate wings of mixed prisons. Remand prisoners are, where possible, housed separately from convicted prisoners. Offenders under the age of 21 are usually detained in a Young Offender Institution, which may be a separate establishment or part of a prison. Appellant and failed asylum seekers are held in Immigration Removal Centres, or in separate units of other prisons.

Eleven prisons are now run by the private sector, and in England, Wales and Scotland all escort services have been contracted out to private companies. In Scotland, one prison (Kilmarnock) was built and financed by the private sector and is being operated by private contractors.

There are independent prison inspectorates in England, Wales and Scotland which report annually on conditions and the treatment of prisoners. The Chief Inspector of Criminal Justice in Northern Ireland and HM Chief Inspector of Prisons for England and Wales perform an inspectorate role for prisons in Northern Ireland. Every prison establishment also has an Independent Monitoring Board made up of local volunteers.

Any prisoner whose complaint is not satisfied by the internal complaints procedures may complain to the Prisons Ombudsman for England and Wales, the Scottish Prisons Complaints Commission or the Prisoner Ombudsman for Northern Ireland (a new post created in May 2005).

The 11 private sector prisons in England and Wales are the direct responsibility of the chief executive of the National Offender Management Service (NOMS). The NOMS was created in January 2004, with Martin Narey named as its chief executive, in order to integrate prisons and probation into a system whereby end-to-end management of offenders is provided; this is expected to reduce re-offending and cut the growth rate of the prison population. The chief executive also has responsibility for public prisons, the National Probation Service, the Youth Justice Board and NOMS policy. The prisons and probation inspectorates, the Prisons Ombudsman and the Independent Monitoring Boards report to the Home Secretary.

PRISON POPULATION (UK)
as at March 2005

	Remand	Sentenced	Other
ENGLAND AND WALES			
Male	11,417	58,134	1,028
Female	930	3,406	47
Total	12,347	61,540	1,075
*SCOTLAND			
Male	—	—	—
Female	—	—	—
Total	1,245	5,375	—
N. IRELAND			
Male	436	799	—
Female	13	20	—
Total	449	819	—
UK TOTAL	14,041	67,734	1,075

The projected 'high scenario' prison population for 2011 in England and Wales is 90,780; the 'low scenario' is 76,520
* Figures for Scotland are an average for 2003–4
Sources: Home Office – *Research Development Statistics*; Scottish Prison Service – *Annual Report and Accounts 2003–4*; Northern Ireland Prison Service – www.niprisonservice.gov.uk

SENTENCED PRISON POPULATION BY SEX AND OFFENCE (ENGLAND AND WALES)
as at 31 March 2005

	Male	Female
Violence against the person	14,210	621
Sexual offences	6,030	32
Burglary	8,099	228
Robbery	8,066	373
Theft, handling	3,639	393
Fraud and forgery	1,136	128
Drugs offences	9,385	1,207
Motoring offences	2,125	39
Other offences	4,729	335
Offence not recorded	668	45
*Total	58,087	3,401

*Figures do not include civil (non-criminal) prisoners or fine defaulters
Source: Home Office – *Research Development Statistics*

SENTENCED POPULATION BY LENGTH OF SENTENCE (ENGLAND AND WALES)
as at 31 March 2005

	Adults	Young Offenders
Less than 12 months	6,155	1,851
12 months to less than 4 years	17,120	4,200
4 years to less than life	24,530	1,825
Life	5,613	194
*Total	53,418	8,070

*Figures do not include civil (non-criminal) prisoners or fine defaulters
Source: Home Office – *Research Development Statistics*

AVERAGE DAILY SENTENCED POPULATION BY LENGTH
OF SENTENCE 2004–5 (SCOTLAND)

	Adults	Young Offenders
Less than 4 years	2,237	402
4 years or over (including life)	2,766	158
Total	5,003	560

Source: Scottish Prison Service – Annual Report and Accounts 2004–5

SELF-INFLICTED DEATHS IN PRISON APRIL 2004–
MARCH 2005 (ENGLAND AND WALES)

Males	73
Females	12
Total	85
Rate per 100,000 prisoners in custody	114

Source: Home Office – Research Development Statistics

OPERATING COSTS OF PRISON SERVICE IN ENGLAND
AND WALES 2004–5

	£
Staff costs	1,439,882,000
Other administrative costs	989,738,000
Operating income	430,491,000
Net operating costs for the year	2,203,524,000
Average cost per prison place	27,854

Source: HM Prison Service – Annual Report and Accounts 2004–5

OPERATING COSTS OF SCOTTISH PRISON SERVICE
2004–5

	£
Total income	2,856,000
Total expenditure	258,568,000
Staff costs	123,575,000
Running costs	92,226,000
Other current expenditure	42,767,000
Operating cost	255,712,000
Cost of capital charges	14,721,000
Interest payable and similar charges	6,000
Interest receivable	21,000
Cost for financial year	270,418,000

Source: Scottish Prison Service – Annual Report and Accounts 2004–5

OPERATING COSTS OF NORTHERN IRELAND PRISON
SERVICE 2004–5

	£
Income	201,000
Staff costs	82,237,000
Depreciation	8,531,000
Other current expenditure	24,222,000
Total expenditure	115,227,000
Net operating costs for the year	115,495,000

Source: Northern Ireland Prison Service – Annual Report and Accounts
2004–5

THE PRISON SERVICES

HM PRISON SERVICE
Cleland House, Page Street, London SW1P 4LN
T 0870-000 1397 E public.enquiries@hmps.gsi.gov.uk
W www.hmprisonservice.gov.uk

SALARIES FROM 1 APRIL 2005

Senior Manager A	£53,043–£75,583
Senior Manager B	£50,968–£72,265
Senior Manager C	£45,444–£65,080
Senior Manager D	£40,524–£59,490
Manager E	£27,876–£42,170
Manager F	£24,365–£35,771
Manager G	£21,723–£29,302

THE PRISON SERVICE MANAGEMENT BOARD
Director-General (SCS), Phil Wheatley, CB
Deputy Director-General (SCS), Director of High Security
    Prisons (SCS), Peter Atherton
Director of Operations (SCS), Michael Spurr
Director of Personnel (SCS), Gareth Hadley
Director of Finance (SCS), Ann Beasley
Head of Prison Health (SCS), Richard Bradshaw
Board Secretary and Head of Secretariat (SMB), Ken Everett
Race Equality Adviser, Beverly Thompson
Legal Adviser, Harry Carter
Media Relations, Michael Winders

AREA MANAGERS
Niall Clifford (North-East); Ian Lockwood (North-West);
Steve Wagstaffe (Yorkshire and Humberside); Bob Perry
(East Midlands); John May (Wales); Alan Scott (West
Midlands); Danny McAllister (Eastern); Sue McAllister
(South-West); Nick Pascoe (Thames Valley, Hampshire
and Isle of Wight); Keith Munns (London); Colin
McConnell (Surrey and Sussex); Adrian Smith (Kent);
Trevor Williams (Contracted Prisons)

PRISON ESTABLISHMENTS – ENGLAND AND
WALES

POPULATION STATISTICS
as at 29 July 2005

Male prisoners	72,004
Female prisoners	4,534
*Useable operational capacity	77,897
Number under home detention curfew	3,264

*The sum of all establishments' capacity less a 1,700-place operating
 margin

ACKLINGTON, nr. Morpeth, Northumberland NE65 9XF
    Prisoners, 863 Governor, Mike Kirby
ALBANY, 55 Parkhurst Road, Newport, Isle of Wight PO30 5RS
    Prisoners, 518 Governor, Mel Jones
††ALTCOURSE (private prison), Higher Lane, Fazakerley,
    Liverpool L9 7LH Prisoners, 933 Director, John
    McLaughlin
†‡ASHFIELD (private prison), Shortwood Road,
    Pucklechurch, Bristol BS16 9QJ Prisoners, 319 Director,
    Vicky O'Dea
ASHWELL, Oakham, Rutland, Leics LE15 7LF
    Prisoners, 542 Governor, Chris Di Paolo
*ASKHAM GRANGE, Askham Richard, York YO23 3FT
    Prisoners, 99 Governor, Alec McCrystal
‡AYLESBURY, Bierton Road, Aylesbury, Bucks HP20 1EH
    Prisoners, 432 Governor, David Kennedy

†BEDFORD, Loyes, Bedford MK40 1HG
  Prisoners, 480 *Governor,* Paul Kempster
†BELMARSH, Western Way, Thamesmead, London SE28 0EB
  Prisoners, 901 *Governor,* Geoff Hughes
†BIRMINGHAM, Winson Green Road, Birmingham B18 4AS
  Prisoners, 1,387 *Governor,* Mike Shann
†BLAKENHURST, Hewell Lane, Redditch, Worcs B97 6QS
  Prisoners, 1,056 *Governor,* Ferdie Parker
BLANTYRE HOUSE, Horden, Goudhurst, Kent TN17 2NH
  Prisoners, 118 *Governor,* Kieron Taylor
BLUNDESTON, Lowestoft, Suffolk NR32 5BG
  Prisoners, 461 *Governor,* Teresa Clarke
†‡BRINSFORD, New Road, Featherstone, Wolverhampton
  WV10 7PY *Prisoners,* 454 *Governor,* Tom Watson
†BRISTOL, 19 Cambridge Road, Bristol BS7 8PS
  Prisoners, 591 *Governor,* Suzy Dymond-White
†BRIXTON, Jebb Avenue, London SW2 5XF
  Prisoners, 811 *Governor,* John Podmore
*†‡BROCKHILL, Hewell Lane, Redditch, Worcs B97 6RD
  Prisoners, 119 *Governor,* Alison Gomme
*†BRONZEFIELD (private prison), Woodthorpe Road,
  Ashford, Middlesex TW15 3JZ
  Prisoners, 408 *Director,* Janine McDowell
*†‡BUCKLEY HALL, Buckley Hall Road, Rochdale, Lancs
  OL12 9DP *Prisoners,* 347 *Governor,* Susan Morrison
†BULLINGDON, PO Box 50, Bicester, Oxon OX25 1WD
  Prisoners, 968 *Governor,* Sue Saunders
*‡BULLWOOD HALL, High Road, Hockley, Essex SS5 4TE
  Prisoners, 154 *Governor,* Mukhtar Posclay
CAMP HILL, Newport, Isle of Wight PO30 5PB
  Prisoners, 592 *Governor,* Robert Bennett
CANTERBURY, 46 Longport, Canterbury, Kent CT1 1PJ
  Prisoners, 309 *Governor,* Helen Rinaldi
†CARDIFF, Knox Road, Cardiff CF24 0UG
  Prisoners, 750 *Governor,* Paul Tidball
‡CASTINGTON, Morpeth, Northumberland NE65 9XG
  Prisoners, 387 *Governor,* Matthew Spencer
CHANNINGS WOOD, Denbury, Newton Abbott, Devon
  TQ12 6DW *Prisoners,* 658 *Governor,* Jeannine Hendrick
†‡CHELMSFORD, 200 Springfield Road, Chelmsford, Essex
  CM2 6LQ *Prisoners,* 581 *Governor,* Nigel Smith
COLDINGLEY, Shaftesbury Road, Bisley, Woking, Surrey
  GU24 9EX *Prisoners,* 391 *Governor,* Paul McDowell
*COOKHAM WOOD, Rochester, Kent ME1 3LU
  Prisoners, 151 *Governor,* Ed Tullet
DARTMOOR, Princetown, Yelverton, Devon PL20 6RR
  Prisoners, 621 *Governor,* Serena Watts
‡DEERBOLT, Bowes Road, Barnard Castle, Co. Durham DL12
  9BG *Prisoners,* 402 *Governor,* Alan Tallentire
†‡DONCASTER (private prison), off North Bridge Road,
  Marshgate, Doncaster DN5 8UX *Prisoners,* 1,087
  Director, Rod MacFarquar
†DORCHESTER, North Square, Dorchester, Dorset DT1 1JD
  Prisoners, 252 *Governor,* Steve Holland
DOVEGATE (private prison), Uttoxeter, Staffs ST14 8XR
  Prisoners, 791 *Director,* Kevin Rogers
§DOVER, The Citadel, Western Heights, Dover, Kent CT17
  9DR *Prisoners,* 304 *Governor,* Val Whitecross
*DOWNVIEW, Sutton Lane, Sutton, Surrey SM2 5PD
  Prisoners, 244 *Governor,* Peter Dawson
*DRAKE HALL, Eccleshall, Staffs ST21 6LQ
  Prisoners, 276 *Governor,* John Huntington
*†DURHAM, Old Elvet, Durham DH1 3HU
  Prisoners, 693 *Governor,* Sandy McEwan
*EAST SUTTON PARK, Sutton Valence, Maidstone, Kent
  ME17 3DF *Prisoners,* 96 *Governor,* Robin Carter
*†‡EASTWOOD PARK, Falfield, Wotton-under-Edge, Glos
  GL12 8DB *Prisoners,* 276 *Governor,* Tim Beeston

EDMUNDS HILL, Stradishall, Newmarket, Suffolk CB8 9YN
  Prisoners, 155 *Governor,* Norma King
†‡ELMLEY, Church Road, Eastchurch, Sheerness, Kent ME12
  4DZ *Prisoners,* 975 *Governor,* Chris Bartlett
ERLESTOKE, Devizes, Wilts SN10 5TU
  Prisoners, 420 *Governor,* Doug Moon
EVERTHORPE, Beck Road, Brough, E. Yorks HU15 1RB
  Prisoners, 546 *Governor,* Gary Monaghan
†EXETER, 30 New North Road, Exeter EX4 4EX
  Prisoners, 511 *Governor,* Mark Flinton
FEATHERSTONE, New Road, Featherstone,
  Wolverhampton WV10 7PU
  Prisoners, 612 *Governor,* Michael Bolton
†‡FELTHAM, Bedfont Road, Feltham, Middx TW13 4ND
  Prisoners, 610 *Governor,* Andrew Cross
FORD, Arundel, W. Sussex BN18 0BX
  Prisoners, 535 *Governor,* Fiona Radford
‡FOREST BANK (private prison), Agecroft Road,
  Pendlebury, Manchester M27 8FB
  Prisoners, 1,045 *Director,* Ivor Woods
*†FOSTON HALL, Foston, Derby DE65 5DN
  Prisoners, 215 *Governor,* Paddy Scriven
FRANKLAND, Brasside, Durham DH1 5YD
  Prisoners, 703 *Governor,* Phil Copple
FULL SUTTON, York YO41 1PS
  Prisoners, 605 *Governor,* Bob Mullen
GARTH, Ulnes Walton Lane, Leyland, Preston PR26 8NE
  Prisoners, 651 *Governor,* Bob McColm
GARTREE, Gallow Field Road, Market Harborough, Leics LE16
  7RP *Prisoners,* 451 *Governor,* Julia Morgan
†‡GLEN PARVA, 10 Tigers Road, Wigston, Leicester LE18 4TN
  Prisoners, 794 *Governor,* Brian Edwards
†GLOUCESTER, Barrack Square, Gloucester GL1 2JN
  Prisoners, 281 *Governor,* David Chalmers
GRENDON, Grendon Underwood, Bucks HP18 0TL
  Prisoners, 225 *Governor,* Dr Peter Bennett
‡GUYS MARSH, Shaftesbury, Dorset SP7 0AH
  Prisoners, 567 *Governor,* Barry Greenbury
§HASLAR, 2 Dolphin Way, Gosport, Hampshire PO12 2AW
  Prisoners, 125 *Manager,* Carole Draper
HAVERIGG, Millom, Cumbria LA18 4NA
  Prisoners, 542 *Governor,* Sue McCullagh
HEWELL GRANGE, Redditch, Worcs B97 6QQ
  Prisoners, 169 *Governor,* Alison Gomme
†‡HIGH DOWN, High Down Lane, Sutton, Surrey SM2 5PJ
  Prisoners, 741 *Governor,* Peter Dawson
†‡HIGHPOINT, Stradishall, Newmarket, Suffolk CB8 9YG
  Prisoners, 789 *Governor,* Sue Doolan
†‡HINDLEY, Gibson Street, Bickershaw, Wigan, Lancs WN2
  5TH *Prisoners,* 407 *Governor,* Jayne Blake
‡HOLLESLEY BAY, Woodbridge, Suffolk IP12 3JW
  Prisoners, 282 *Governor,* Ken Kan
*†‡HOLLOWAY, Parkhurst Road, London N7 0NU
  Prisoners, 424 *Governor,* Tony Hassall
HOLME HOUSE, Holme House Road, Stockton-on-Tees TS18
  2QU *Prisoners,* 974 *Governor,* Mick Lees
†HULL, Hedon Road, Hull HU9 5LS
  Prisoners, 964 *Governor,* Steve Tilley
‡HUNTERCOMBE, Nuffield, Henley-on-Thames, Oxon RG9
  5SB *Prisoners,* 352 *Governor,* Elaine Jones
KINGSTON, 122 Milton Road, Portsmouth PO3 6AS
  Prisoners, 193 *Governor,* John Robinson
KIRKHAM, Freckleton Road, Kirkham, Preston, Lancs PR4 2RN
  Prisoners, 537 *Governor,* Steve Lawrence
KIRKLEVINGTON GRANGE, Yarm, Cleveland TS15 9PA
  Prisoners, 220 *Governor,* Alan Richer
LANCASTER, The Castle, Lancaster LA1 1YL
  Prisoners, 241 *Governor,* Derek Harrison

†‡LANCASTER FARMS, Far Moor Lane, Stone Row Head,
Off Quernmore Road, Lancaster LA1 3QZ
Prisoners, 528 *Governor,* Paul Holland
LATCHMERE HOUSE, Church Road, Ham Common,
Richmond, Surrey TW10 5HH
Prisoners, 204 *Governor,* Ruth Kringle
†LEEDS, 2 Gloucester Terrace, Stanningley Road, Leeds LS12
2TJ *Prisoners,* 1,226 *Governor,* Ian Blakeman
LEICESTER, Welford Road, Leicester LE2 7AJ
Prisoners, 340 *Governor,* Steve Turner
†LEWES, Brighton Road, Lewes, E. Sussex BN7 1EA
Prisoners, 523 *Governor,* Eoin McLennan-Murray
LEYHILL, Wotton-under-Edge, Glos GL12 8BT
Prisoners, 485 *Governor,* Richard Booty
†LINCOLN, Greetwell Road, Lincoln LN2 4BD
Prisoners, 474 *Governor,* Lynne Saunders
§LINDHOLME, Bawtry Road, Hatfield Woodhouse, Doncaster
DN7 6EE *Prisoners,* 801 *Governor,* Martin Ward
LITTLEHEY, Perry, Huntingdon, Cambs PE28 0SR
Prisoners, 706 *Governor,* David Taylor
†LIVERPOOL, 68 Hornby Road, Liverpool L9 3DF
Prisoners, 1,368 *Governor,* Cathy James
LONG LARTIN, South Littleton, Evesham, Worcs WR11 8TZ
Prisoners, 442 *Governor,* Nick Leader
*†‡LOW NEWTON, Brasside, Durham DH1 5YA
Prisoners, 279 *Governor,* Andrea Whitfield
LOWDHAM GRANGE (private prison), Lowdham, Notts
NG14 7DA *Prisoners,* 503 *Director,* Peter Wright
MAIDSTONE, 36 County Road, Maidstone, Kent ME14 1UZ
Prisoners, 546 *Governor,* Jane Galbally
MANCHESTER, 1 Southall Street, Manchester M60 9AH
Prisoners, 1,244 *Governor,* Chris Sheffield
‡MOORLAND CLOSED, Bawtry Road, Hatfield Woodhouse,
Doncaster DN7 6BW *Prisoners,* 758 *Governor,* Jacqui Tilley
‡MOORLAND OPEN, Thorne Road, Hatfield, Doncaster DN7
6EL *Prisoners,* 237 *Governor,* Jacqui Tilley
*MORTON HALL, Swinderby, Lincoln LN6 9PT
Prisoners, 296 *Governor,* Damian Evans
THE MOUNT, Molyneaux Avenue, Bovingdon, Hemel
Hempstead, Herts HP3 0NZ
Prisoners, 698 *Governor,* Steve Rodford
*†‡NEW HALL, Dial Wood, Flockton, Wakefield, W. Yorks
WF4 4XX *Prisoners,* 307 *Governor,* Sara Snell
NORTH SEA CAMP, Freiston, Boston, Lincs PE22 0QX
Prisoners, 279 *Governor,* Norman Warwick
‡NORTHALLERTON, East Road, Northallerton, N. Yorks DL6
1NW *Prisoners,* 220 *Governor,* Bill Shaw
†‡NORWICH, Knox Road, Norwich, Norfolk NR1 4LU
Prisoners, 775 *Governor,* James Shanley
†NOTTINGHAM, Perry Road, Sherwood, Nottingham NG5
3AG *Prisoners,* 508 *Governor,* Wendy Sinclair-Gieben
‡ONLEY, Willoughby, Rugby, Warks CV23 8AP
Prisoners, 517 *Governor,* Alison Perry
†‡PARC (private prison), Heol Hopcyn John, Bridgend, S.
Wales CF35 6AR *Prisoners,* 953 *Director,* Roy Woolford
†PARKHURST, Newport, Isle of Wight PO30 5NX
Prisoners, 506 *Governor,* Steve Metcalf
†PENTONVILLE, Caledonian Road, London N7 8TT
Prisoners, 1,187 *Governor,* Gary Deighton
*†PETERBOROUGH (private prison), Saville Road,
Westfield, Peterborough PE3 7PD
Prisoners, 680 *Director,* Mike Conway
‡PORTLAND, Easton, Portland, Dorset DT5 1DL
Prisoners, 389 *Governor,* Stephen Twinn
‡PRESCOED, Coed-y-Paen, Pontypool, Monmouthshire
NP4 0TB *Prisoners,* 169 *Governor,* Phil Morgan
†PRESTON, 2 Ribbleton Lane, Preston, Lancs PR1 5AB
Prisoners, 593 *Governor,* Alan Brown

RANBY, Retford, Notts DN22 8EU
Prisoners, 1,000 *Governor,* Phil Wragg
†‡READING, Forbury Road, Reading, Berks RG1 3HY
Prisoners, 291 *Governor,* Pauline Bryant
RISLEY, Warrington Road, Risley, Warrington, Cheshire WA3
6BP *Prisoners,* 1,059 *Governor,* Paul Norbury
‡ROCHESTER, 1 Fort Road, Rochester, Kent ME1 3QS
Prisoners, 389 *Governor,* Stephen O'Connell
RYE HILL (private prison), Willoughby, nr. Rugby, Warks
CV23 8SZ *Prisoners,* 584 *Director,* Stuart Mitson
*SEND, Ripley Road, Woking, Surrey GU23 7LJ
Prisoners, 211 *Governor,* Brian Ritchie
SHEPTON MALLET, Cornhill, Shepton Mallet, Somerset BA4
5LU *Prisoners,* 184 *Governor,* Nick Evans
†SHREWSBURY, The Dana, Shrewsbury, Shropshire SY1 2HR
Prisoners, 292 *Governor,* Gerry Hendry
SPRING HILL, Grendon Underwood, nr. Aylesbury, Bucks
HP18 0TL *Prisoners,* 315 *Governor,* Dr Peter Bennett
STAFFORD, 54 Gaol Road, Stafford ST16 3AW
Prisoners, 671 *Governor,* Louise Taylor
STANDFORD HILL, Church Road, Eastchurch, Sheerness,
Kent ME12 4AA *Prisoners,* 463 *Governor,* John Wilson
STOCKEN, Stocken Hall Road, Stretton, nr. Oakham, Leics
LE15 7RD *Prisoners,* 618 *Governor,* Moira Bartlett
‡STOKE HEATH, Market Drayton, Shropshire TF9 2JL
Prisoners, 633 *Governor,* Peter Small
*†‡STYAL, Wilmslow, Cheshire SK9 4HR
Prisoners, 387 *Governor,* Steve Hall
SUDBURY, Ashbourne, Derbyshire DE6 5HW
Prisoners, 550 *Governor,* Chris Davidson
SWALESIDE, Brabazon Road, Eastchurch, Isle of Sheppey,
Kent ME12 4AX *Prisoners,* 771 *Governor,* Tony Robson
†SWANSEA, 200 Oystermouth Road, Swansea SA1 3SR
Prisoners, 420 *Governor,* Phil Taylor
‡SWINFEN HALL, Lichfield, Staffs WS14 9QS
Prisoners, 602 *Governor,* Peter Knapton
‡THORN CROSS, Arley Road, Appleton Thorn, Warrington,
Cheshire WA4 4RL
Prisoners, 252 *Governor,* Clive Chatterton
USK, 47 Maryport Street, Usk, Monmouthshire NP15 1XP
Prisoners, 250 *Governor,* Phil Morgan
THE VERNE, Portland, Dorset DT5 1EQ
Prisoners, 585 *Governor,* Mike Cook
WAKEFIELD, 5 Love Lane, Wakefield, West Yorks WF2 9AG
Prisoners, 555 *Governor,* David Thompson
†§WANDSWORTH, PO Box 757, Heathfield Road, London
SW18 3HS *Prisoners,* 1,436 *Governor,* Ian Mulholland
‡WARREN HILL, Hollesley, Woodbridge, Suffolk IP12 3JW
Prisoners, 206 *Governor,* Stuart Robinson
WAYLAND, Griston, Thetford, Norfolk IP25 6RL
Prisoners, 700 *Governor,* Michael Wood
WEALSTUN, Wetherby, W. Yorks LS23 7AZ
Prisoners, 766 *Governor,* Amy Rice
WELLINGBOROUGH, Millers Park, Doddington Road,
Wellingborough, Northants NN8 2NH
Prisoners, 573 *Governor,* Jim Lewis
‡WERRINGTON, Stoke-on-Trent ST9 0DX
Prisoners, 140 *Governor,* Frank Flynn
‡WETHERBY, York Road, Wetherby, W. Yorks LS22 5ED
Prisoners, 340 *Governor,* Paul Foweather
WHATTON, 14 Cromwell Road, Whatton, Nottingham NG13
9FQ *Prisoners,* 353 *Governor,* Mrs V. Hart
WHITEMOOR, Longhill Road, March, Cambs PE15 0PR
Prisoners, 439 *Governor,* Martin Lomas
WINCHESTER, Romsey Road, Winchester SO22 5DF
Prisoners, 687 *Governor,* Cathy Allison
WOLDS (private prison), Everthorpe, Brough, E. Yorks HU15
2JZ *Prisoners,* 298 *Director,* Dave McDonnell

†‡§WOODHILL, Tattenhoe Street, Milton Keynes, Bucks MK4
   4DA *Prisoners,* 766 *Governor,* Edd Willetts
‡WORMWOOD SCRUBS, PO Box 757, Du Cane Road,
   London W12 0AE
   Prisoners, 1,247 *Governor,* Luke Serjeant
WYMOTT, Ulnes Walton Lane, Leyland, Preston PR26 8LW
   Prisoners, 1,050 *Governor,* Alan Scott

SCOTTISH PRISON SERVICE (SPS)

Calton House, 5 Redheughs Rigg, Edinburgh EH12 9HW
T 0131-556 8400 E gaolinfo@sps.gov.uk W www.sps.gov.uk

SALARIES 2005–6
Senior managers in the Scottish Prison Service, including
governors and deputy governors of prisons, are paid
across three pay bands:

Band I	£48,000–£59,800
Band H	£38,100–£49,550
Band G	£30,000–£41,200

SPS BOARD
Chief Executive, Tony Cameron
Director, Human Resources, Barbara Allison
Director, Finance and Business Services, Willie Pretswell
Director, Corporate Services, Ken Thomson
Director, Rehabilitation and Care, Alec Spencer
Director, Prisons, Mike Duffy
Director, Prison Services, Peter Withers
Non-Executive Directors, Bill Carr; Elinor Smith

PRISON ESTABLISHMENTS
Average prisoner numbers 2004–5
*†ABERDEEN, 4 Grampian Place, Aberdeen AB11 8FN
   Prisoners, 225 *Governor,* Audrey Mooney
‡BARLINNIE, Glasgow G33 2QX
   Prisoners, 1,195 *Governor,* Bill McKinlay
CASTLE HUNTLY, Longforgan, nr. Dundee DD2 5HL
   Prisoners, 155 *Governor,* Ian Whitehead
*†‡CORNTON VALE, Cornton Road, Stirling FK9 5NU
   Prisoners, 246 *Governor,* Sue Brookes
*†‡DUMFRIES, Terregles Street, Dumfries DG2 9AX
   Prisoners, 182 *Governor,* Chrissie McGeever
†EDINBURGH, 33 Stenhouse Road, Edinburgh EH11 3LN
   Prisoners, 701 *Governor,* David Croft
GLENOCHIL, King O'Muir Road, Tullibody, Clackmannanshire
   FK10 3AD *Prisoners,* 485 *Governor,* Kate Donegan
†GREENOCK, Gateside, Greenock PA16 9AH
   Prisoners, 323 *Governor,* Derek McGill
*†INVERNESS, Duffy Drive, Inverness IV2 3HH
   Prisoners, 150 *Governor,* Alastair MacDonald

‡KILMARNOCK (private prison), Mauchline Road,
   Kilmarnock KA1 5AA
   Prisoners, 583 *Director,* Nick Cameron
LOW MOSS, Crosshill Road, Bishopbriggs, Glasgow G64 2QB
   Prisoners, 298 *Governor,* Eric Fairbairn
NORANSIDE, Fern By Forfar, Angus DD8 3QY
   Prisoners, 135 *Governor,* Ian Whitehead
‡PERTH, 3 Edinburgh Road, Perth PH2 8AT
   Prisoners, 655 *Governor,* Stephen Swan
PETERHEAD, Aberdeenshire AB24 2YY
   Prisoners, 298 *Governor,* Ian Gunn
‡POLMONT, Falkirk, Stirlingshire FK2 0AB
   Prisoners, 632 *Governor,* Bill Millar
SHOTTS, Newmill/Canthill Road, Lanarkshire ML7 4LE
   Prisoners, 515 *Governor,* Audrey Park

NORTHERN IRELAND PRISON SERVICE

Dundonald House, Upper Newtownards Road, Belfast BT4 3SU
T 028-9052 5065 E info@niprisonservice.gov.uk
W www.niprisonservice.gov.uk

SALARIES 2005–6

Governor 1	£61,220–£65,976
Governor 2	£55,407–£59,118
Governor 3	£47,705–£51,156
Governor 4	£40,066–£43,828
Governor 5	£34,671–£39,276

A Northern Ireland allowance is also payable

STAFF
Director-General, Robin Masefield, CBE
Director, Finance and Personnel, Pauline Shepherd
Director, Operations, Max Murray
Director, Services, Douglas Bain

PRISON ESTABLISHMENTS
Prisoners *as at 28 July 2005*
*†‡§HYDEBANK WOOD YOC, Hospital Road, Belfast BT8
   8NA *Prisoners,* 233 *Governor,* Stephen Davis
†§MAGHABERRY, Old Road, Ballinderry Upper, Lisburn, Co.
   Antrim BT28 2PT *Prisoners,* 718 *Governor,* Alan Longwell
MAGILLIGAN, Point Road, Limavady, Co. Londonderry
   BT49 0LR *Prisoners,* 369 *Governor,* Alan Craig

* Women's establishment or establishment with units for women
† Remand Centre or establishment with units for remand
prisoners
‡ Young Offender Institution or establishment with units for
young offenders
§ Immigration Removal Centre or establishment with units for
immigration detainees

DEFENCE

The armed forces of the United Kingdom comprise the Royal Navy, the Army and the Royal Air Force (RAF). The Queen is Commander-in-Chief of all the armed forces. The Secretary of State for Defence is responsible for the formulation and content of defence policy and for providing the means by which it is conducted. The formal legal basis for the conduct of defence in the UK rests on a range of powers vested by statute and Letters Patent in the Defence Council, chaired by the Secretary of State for Defence. Beneath the ministers lies the top management of the Ministry of Defence (MoD), headed jointly by the Permanent Secretary and the Chief of Defence Staff. The Permanent Secretary is the government's principal civilian adviser on defence and has the primary responsibility for policy, finance, management and administration. He is also personally accountable to Parliament for the expenditure of all public money voted for defence purposes. The Chief of the Defence Staff is the professional head of the armed forces in the UK and the principal military adviser to the Secretary of State and the government.

The Defence Management Board (DMB) is the executive board of the Defence Council. Chaired by the Permanent Secretary, it acts as the main executive board of the Ministry of Defence, providing senior level leadership and strategic management of defence.

The Central Staff, headed by the Vice-Chief of the Defence Staff and the Second Permanent Under-Secretary of State, is the policy core of the department. The Defence Procurement Agency is responsible for purchasing equipment. The Defence Logistics Organisation has responsibility for logistic support.

A permanent Joint Headquarters for the conduct of joint operations was set up at Northwood in 1996. The Joint Headquarters connects the policy and strategic functions of the MoD Head Office with the conduct of operations and is intended to strengthen the policy/executive division.

Britain pursues its defence and security policies through its membership of NATO (to which most of its armed forces are committed), the European Union, the Organisation for Security and Co-operation in Europe and the UN (*see* International Organisations section).

ARMED FORCES STRENGTH *as at 1 July 2005*
Figures are for UK Regular Forces including both trained and untrained personnel and nursing services, but excludes Gurkhas, full-time Reserve Service personnel, the Home Service battalions of the Royal Irish Regiment, mobilised reservists and Naval Activated Reservists.

All Services	198,750
Men	180,700
Women	18,050
Royal Naval Services	39,710
Army	107,800
Royal Air Force	51,240

Source: MOD Defence Analytical Services Agency *National Statistics* (Crown copyright)

SERVICE PERSONNEL

	Royal Navy	Army	RAF	All Services
1975 strength	76,200	167,100	95,000	338,300
1990 strength	63,210	152,810	89,680	305,700
1999 strength	43,700	109,720	55,210	208,630
2001 strength	42,420	109,530	53,700	205,650
2002 strength	41,630	110,050	53,000	204,680
2003 strength	41,550	112,130	53,240	206,920
2004 strength	40,510	111,500	53,130	205,140
2005 strength	39,710	107,800	51,240	198,750

Source: MOD Defence Analytical Services Agency *National Statistics* (Crown copyright)

CIVILIAN PERSONNEL

1993 level	159,600
1999 level	123,000
2000 level	121,300
2001 level	118,200
2002 level	110,100
2003 level	107,600
2004 level	108,990
2005 level	107,680

As of 1 April 2004 the definition of the civilian workforce changed to include permanent and casual personnel, Royal Fleet Auxiliaries, Trading Funds and Locally Engaged civilians. Figures above reflect the revised definition.
Source: MOD Defence Analytical Services Agency *National Statistics* (Crown copyright)

UK DEFENCE: SERVICE MANPOWER STRENGTHS
as at 1 April 2004

	Thousands
Full-time trained strength	190.1
Trained Naval Service	37.5
UK regulars	36.4
Full-time reserve service	1.1
Trained Army	103.5
UK regulars	99.4
Full-time reserve service	0.7
Gurkhas	3.4
Trained RAF	49.1
UK regulars	48.7
Full-time reserve service	0.4
Untrained UK regulars	22.5
Naval Service	4.5
Army	13.3
RAF	4.7
Locally entered personnel (excluding Gurkhas)	0.4
Royal Irish Regiment Home Service battalions	3.4
Reserve personnel	246.7
Regular Reserves	201.4
Naval Services	22.8
Army	141.9
of which mobilised	0.1
RAF	36.6
of which mobilised	–
Volunteer Reserves	45.4
Royal Naval Reserve & Royal Marine Reserve	4.5
of which mobilised	0.1

Territorial Army					38.3
of which mobilised					2.9
Royal Auxiliary Air Force					2.6
of which mobilised					–
Cadet Forces					155.6
Naval Service					22.6
Army					80.5
RAF					52.5

Source: ONS – *Annual Abstract of Statistics 2005* (Crown copyright)

UK REGULAR FORCES: DEATHS

	1995	2000	2001	2002	2003
Deaths					
Total Number	201	148	140	148	170
Male	192	144	137	139	163
Female	9	4	3	9	7
Rates per thousand					
Tri-service	0.94	0.72	0.68	0.72	0.82
Navy	0.57	0.62	0.79	0.66	0.90
Army	0.98	0.81	0.71	0.85	0.79
RAF	0.83	0.62	0.48	0.52	0.75

Source: ONS – *Annual Abstract of Statistics 2005* (Crown copyright)

NUCLEAR FORCES

Britain's strategic forces comprise four ballistic missile Vanguard class nuclear-powered submarines, each capable of carrying 16 Trident missiles equipped with nuclear warheads. There is a Ballistic Missile Early Warning System station at Fylingdales.

ARMS CONTROL

The 1990 Conventional Armed Forces in Europe (CFE) Treaty, which commits all NATO and former Warsaw Pact members to limiting their holdings of five major classes of conventional weapons, has been adapted to reflect the changed geo-strategic environment and negotiations continue for its implementation. The Open Skies Treaty, which the UK signed in 1992 and entered into force in 2002, allows for the overflight of States Parties by other States Parties using unarmed observation aircraft.

In 1968 the UK signed and ratified the Nuclear Non-Proliferation Treaty, which came into force in 1970 and was indefinitely and unconditionally extended in 1995. In 1996 the UK signed the Comprehensive Nuclear Test Ban Treaty and ratified it in 1998. The UK is a party to the 1972 Biological and Toxin Weapons Convention, which provides for a worldwide ban on biological weapons, and the 1993 Chemical Weapons Convention, which came into force in 1997 and provides for a verifiable worldwide ban on chemical weapons.

DEFENCE BUDGET DEPARTMENTAL EXPENDITURE LIMITS (DEL)

Year	£ billion Resource Budget	Capital Budget	Total DEL
2003–4 (outturn)	31.3	6.1	37.4
2004–5 (estimate)	32.6	6.6	39.2
Projections			
2005–6	32.7	6.9	39.6
2006–7	32.7	7.0	39.7
2007–8	33.0	7.6	40.6

Source: The Budget 2005

MINISTRY OF DEFENCE

Old War Office, Whitehall, London SW1A 2EU
T 020-7218 9000 Public Enquiry Office 0870-607 4455
W www.mod.uk
Officers promoted in an acting capacity to a more senior rank are listed under the more senior rank. Promotion to five-star rank is no longer usual in peacetime.

GRADE EQUIVALENTS

Grade 1 equivalents: (5*) Admiral of the Fleet, (5*) Field Marshal, (5*) Marshal of the RAF, (4*) Admiral, (4*) General, (4*) Air Chief Marshal
Grade 2 equivalents: (3*) Vice Admiral, (3*) Lieutenant-General, (3*) Air Marshal
Secretary of State for Defence, The Rt. Hon. Dr John Reid, MP
Private Secretary, C. Baker
Special Advisers, J. Arnold-Forster; S. Bates
Parliamentary Private Secretary, Siobhain McDonagh, MP
Minister of State for the Armed Forces, The Rt. Hon. Adam Ingram, MP
Parliamentary Private Secretary, Wayne David, MP
Private Secretary, R. Johnson
Parliamentary Under-Secretary of State for Defence and Minister for Defence Procurement, Lord Drayson
Private Secretary, C. Bailey
Parliamentary Under-Secretary of State for Defence and Minister for Veterans, Don Touhig, MP
Private Secretary, J. Williams
Permanent Under-Secretary of State, Sir Kevin Tebbit, KCB, CMG
Chief of Defence Staff, Gen. Sir Michael Walker GCB, CMG, CBE, ADC, GEN
Second Permanent Under-Secretary, Ian Andrews, CBE, TD

THE DEFENCE COUNCIL

The Defence Council is the Senior Committee of the Ministry of Defence, which was established by Royal Prerogative under the Letters Patent in April 1964. The Letters Patent confer on the Defence Council the command over all of the Armed Forces and charge the Council with such matters relating to the administration of the Armed Forces as the Secretary of State for Defence should direct them to execute. It is chaired by the Secretary of State for Defence and consists of the Minister of State for the Armed Forces, the Parliamentary Under-Secretary of State for Defence and Minister for Defence Procurement, the Parliamentary Under-Secretary of State for Defence and Minister for Veterans, the Permanent Under-Secretary of State, the Chief of the Defence Staff, the Chief of the Naval Staff and First Sea Lord, the Chief of the General Staff, the Chief of the Air Staff, the Vice-Chief of the Defence Staff, the Second Permanent Under-Secretary of State, the Chief Scientific Adviser, the Chief of Defence Procurement and the Chief of Defence Logistics.

CHIEFS OF STAFF

CHIEF OF THE NAVAL STAFF
First Sea Lord and Chief of the Naval Staff (4*), Adm. Sir Alan West, GCB, DSC, ADC
Asst Chief of the Naval Staff (2*), Rear-Adm. A. M. Massey, CBE

CHIEF OF THE GENERAL STAFF
Chief of the General Staff (4*), Gen. Sir Mike Jackson, KCB, CBE, DSO, ADC
Asst Chief of the General Staff (2*), Maj.-Gen. W. R. Rollo, CBE, ADC

CHIEF OF THE AIR STAFF
Chief of the Air Staff (4*), Air Chief Marshal Sir Jock Stirrup, KCB, AFC, ADC
Asst Chief of the Air Staff (2*), Air Vice-Marshal C. Moran, OBE, MVO

CENTRAL STAFFS
Vice-Chief of the Defence Staff, Gen. Sir Timothy Granville-Chapman, KCB, CBE, ADC
Second Permanent Under-Secretary, Ian Andrews, CBE, TD

DEFENCE INTELLIGENCE STAFF
Old War Office, Whitehall, London SW1A 2EU
T 020-7218 6645 F 020-7218 1562
Chief of Defence Intelligence (3*), Lt.-Gen. A. P. Ridgway, CB, CBE
Deputy Chief of Defence Intelligence, Anthony Pawson

DEFENCE SCIENTIFIC STAFF
Chief Scientific Adviser, Prof. Roy Anderson, FRS
Science and Technology Director and Director-General of Research and Technology, M. Markin, OBE

COMMANDER-IN-CHIEF FLEET
C.-in-C Fleet, Adm. Sir Jonathon Band, KCB
Deputy C.-in-C. Fleet, Vice-Adm. T. McClement, OBE

SECOND SEA LORD/COMMANDER-IN-CHIEF NAVAL HOME COMMAND
Second Sea Lord and C.-in-C. Naval Home Command, Vice-Adm. Sir James Burnell-Nugent, KCB, CBE, ADC
Chief of Staff to Second Sea Lord and C.-in-C. Naval Home Command, Rear-Adm. M. Kimmons

ADJUTANT-GENERAL'S DEPARTMENT
Adjutant-General, Lt.-Gen. F. R. Viggers, CMG, MBE
Deputy Adjutant-General and Director-General Service Conditions, Maj.-Gen. T. Tyler

COMMANDER-IN-CHIEF LAND COMMAND
C.-in-C., Land Command, Gen. Sir Richard Dannatt, KCB
Chief of Staff, HQ Land Command, Maj.-Gen. B. W. B. White-Spunner, CBE

HQ STRIKE COMMAND
Air Officer Commanding-in-Chief, Air Chief Marshal Sir Brian Burridge, KCB, CBE, ADC
Deputy Commander-in-Chief Strike Command, Air Marshal C. R. Loader, OBE, FRAES

HQ PERSONNEL AND TRAINING COMMAND
Air Member for Personnel and Commander-in-Chief Personnel and Training Command, Air Marshal Sir Joe French, KCB, CBE
Chief of Staff and Deputy Commander-in-Chief Personnel and Training Command, Air Vice-Marshal P. J. Dye

EXECUTIVE AGENCIES

ARMED FORCES PERSONNEL ADMINISTRATION AGENCY (AFPAA)
Building 182, RAF Innsworth, Gloucester GL3 1HW
T 01452-712612, ext. 7347
ARMY BASE REPAIR ORGANISATION (ABRO)
Building 203, Portway, Monxton Road, Andover, Hampshire SP11 8HT T 01264-383295
ARMY PERSONNEL CENTRE (APC)
Kentigern House, 65 Brown Street, Glasgow G2 8EX
T 0845-4600 9663
ARMY TRAINING AND RECRUITING AGENCY
Building 370, Trenchard Lines, Upavon, Pewsey, Wilts SN9 6BE T 01980-615220
DEFENCE ANALYTICAL SERVICES AGENCY (DASA)
1st Floor, Zone 1B, St George's Court, 2–12 Bloomsbury Way, London WC1A 2SH T 020-7305 2192
DEFENCE AVIATION REPAIR AGENCY (DARA)
Building 145, RAF St Athan, Barry, Vale of Glamorgan CF62 4WA T 01446-798834
DEFENCE BILLS AGENCY (DBA)
Mersey House, Drury Lane, Liverpool L2 7PX
T 0151-242 2225
DEFENCE DENTAL AGENCY (DDA)
RAF Halton, Aylesbury, Bucks HP22 5PG T 01296-623535, ext. 6851
DEFENCE ESTATES (DE)
Kingston Road, Sutton Coldfield B75 7RL T 0121-311 2140
DEFENCE GEOGRAPHIC AND IMAGERY INTELLIGENCE AGENCY (DGIA)
Watson Building, Elmwood Avenue, Feltham, Middx TW13 7AH T 020-8818 2133
DEFENCE INTELLIGENCE AND SECURITY CENTRE (DISC)
Chicksands, Shefford, Beds SG17 5PR T 01462-752181
DEFENCE LOGISTICS ORGANISATION (DLO)
DLO Headquarters, Spur 5, E Block, Granville Road, Ensleigh, Bath BA1 5AB T 01225-467764
Chief of Defence Logistics, Gen. Sir Kevin O'Donoghue
DLO SECRETARIAT (LAND), Building 300, Monxton Road, Andover, Hampshire SP11 8HT T 01264-383512
DLO SECRETARIAT (STRIKE), Room J103, Cranswick House, RAF Wynton, Huntingdon, Cambridgeshire PE28 2EA
T 01480-52451, ext. 6976

Business Units:
BRITISH FORCES POST OFFICE (BFPO), Inglis Barracks, Mill Hill, London NW7 1PX T 020-8818 6310
CORPORATE TECHNICAL SERVICES (CTS), DLO Andover, Building 300/2, Monxton Road, Andover SP11 8HT
T 01264-383499
DEFENCE CATERING GROUP (DCG), Block B, Spur 6, Ensleigh, Bath BA1 5AB T 01225-467943
DEFENCE CLOTHING INTEGRATED PROJECT TEAM (DC IPT), DLO Caversfield, Skimmingdish Lane, Caversfield, Bicester, Oxon OX27 9TS T 01869-875552
DEFENCE COMMUNICATION SERVICES AGENCY (DCSA), HQ, Basil Hill Site, Park Lane, Corsham, Wilts SN13 9NR T 01225-814750
DEFENCE FUELS GROUP (DFG), West Moors, Wimborne, Dorset BH21 6QS T 01202-654474
DEFENCE MUNITIONS GROUP (DMG), Spur 10, Block B, Ensleigh, Bath T 01225-467097
DEFENCE STORAGE AND DISTRIBUTION AGENCY (DSDA), Ploughley Road, Lower Arncott, Bicester, Oxon OX25 2LD T 01869-256842

DEFENCE SUPPLY CHAIN, T 01264-383762

DEFENCE TRANSPORT AND MOVEMENTS AGENCY, (DTMA), Building 400, DLO Andover, Monxton Road, Andover, Hampshire SP11 8HJ T 01264-381135

FUTURE DEFENCE SUPPLY CHAIN INITIATIVE (FDSCI), Spur 2, Block D, Foxhill, Bath BA1 5AB T 9355-83145

MEDICAL SUPPLIES AGENCY (MSA), Drummond Barracks, Ludgershall, Andover, Hants SP11 9RU T 01264-798451

NUCLEAR/WARSHIP SUPPORT AGENCY, Management Suite, Birch 1C, Abbey Wood, Bristol BS34 8JH T 0117-913 7512

PAY AS YOU DINE PROJECT (PAYD), Building 209, DLO Andover, Monxton Road, Andover, Hants SP11 8HT T 01264-348051

DEFENCE MEDICAL EDUCATION AND TRAINING AGENCY (DMETA)
MacKenzie Building, Royal Hospital Haslar & Fort Blockhouse, Gosport, Hampshire PO12 2AB T 023-9276 5284

DEFENCE PROCUREMENT AGENCY (DPA)
Maple 2120, MOD Abbey Wood, Bristol BS34 8JH T 0117-913 0000

DEFENCE SCIENCE AND TECHNOLOGY LABORATORY (DSTL)
Ively Road, Farnborough, Hampshire GU14 0LX T 01980-613121

DEFENCE VETTING AGENCY
Building 107, Imphal Barracks, Fulford Road, York YO10 4AS T 01904–665820

DISPOSAL SERVICES AGENCY
2nd Floor, St George's Court, 2–12 Bloomsbury Way, London WC1A 2SH T 020-7305 3147

THE DUKE OF YORK'S ROYAL MILITARY SCHOOL (DYRMS)
Dover, Kent CT15 5EQ T 01304-245024

MET OFFICE
Fitzroy Road, Exeter EX1 3PB T 0870-900 0100

MINISTRY OF DEFENCE POLICE AND GUARDING AGENCY (MDPGA)
Wethersfield, Braintree, Essex CM7 4AZ T 01371-854000

NAVAL RECRUITING AND TRAINING AGENCY (NRTA)
Victory Building, HM Naval Base Portsmouth, Hampshire PO1 3LS T 023-9272 7600

PAY AND PERSONNEL AGENCY (PPA)
PO Box 99, Bath BA1 1YT T 01225-828105

QUEEN VICTORIA SCHOOL
Dunblane, Perthshire FK15 0JY T 01786-822288

RAF TRAINING GROUP DEFENCE AGENCY (RAF TGDA)
RAF Innsworth, Gloucester GL3 1EZ T 01452-712612, ext. 5346

SERVICE CHILDREN'S EDUCATION (SCE)
Building 5, Wegberg Military Complex BFPO 40 T 2161-908 2295

UK HYDROGRAPHIC OFFICE
Admiralty Way, Taunton, Somerset TA1 2DN T 01823-337900

UK NATIONAL CODIFICATION BUREAU (UK NCB)
Room 2.4.23, Kentigern House, 65 Brown Street, Glasgow G2 8EX T 0141-224 2164

VETERANS AGENCY (VA)
Tomlinson House, Norcross, Blackpool FY5 3WP T 0800-169 2277

THE ROYAL NAVY

LORD HIGH ADMIRAL OF THE UNITED KINGDOM
HM The Queen

ADMIRALS OF THE FLEET
HRH The Prince Philip, Duke of Edinburgh, KG, KT, OM, GBE, AC, QSO, PC, *apptd* 1953
Sir Michael Pollock, GCB, LVO, DSC, *apptd* 1974
Sir Edward Ashmore, GCB, DSC, *apptd* 1977
Sir Henry Leach, GCB, *apptd* 1982
Sir Julian Oswald, GCB, *apptd* 1993
Sir Benjamin Bathurst, GCB, *apptd* 1995

ADMIRALS
West, Sir Alan, GCB, DSC, ADC *(First Sea Lord and Chief of Naval Staff)*
Band, Sir Jonathon, KCB *(C.-in-C. Fleet, Commander Allied Naval Forces North)*
Stanhope, Sir Mark, KCB, OBE *(Deputy Supreme Allied Commander Transformation)*

VICE-ADMIRALS
Dunt, Peter Arthur, CB *(Chief Executive Defence Estate/ Chief Naval Logistics Officer (Head of Specialisation))*
Burnell-Nugent, Sir James, KCB, CBE, ADC *(Second Sea Lord and Cincnavhome))*
McClement, Timothy, OBE *(Deputy C.-in-C. Fleet/Chief Naval Welfare Officer (Head of Specialisation))*
McLean, Rory, CB, OBE *(Deputy Chief of Defence Staff (Health))*

REAR-ADMIRALS
HRH The Princess Royal, KG, KT, GCVO *(Chief Commandant for Women in the Royal Navy)*
Stevens, Robert Patrick, CB *(Chief of Staff to the Maritime Cdr. Allied Forces, Southern Europe)*
Ward, Rees Graham John, CB *(Chief Executive, Defence Communications Services Agency)*
Guild, Nigel Charles Forbes, CB *(Director-General Capability (Carrier Strike)/Chief Naval Engineering Officer (Head of Specialisation)*
Dymock, Anthony Knox, CB *(Head of British Defence Staff, Washington)*
Rapp, James Campsie *(Director-General Trafalgar 200)*
Style, Charles Rodney, CBE *(Cdr. UK Maritime Force)*
Boissier, Robin Paul *(Director-General Logistics Fleet)*
Cheadle, Richard Frank *(Director Land & Maritime/ Controller of the Navy)*
Goodall, Simon Richard James, CBE *(Director-General Training and Education)*
Snelson, David George, CB *(Chief of Staff (Warfare) to C.-in-C.-Fleet, Rear-Adm. Surface Ships (Head of Fighting Arm))*
Harris, Nicholas Henry Linton, MBE *(Flag Officer Scotland & N. Ireland/Chief of Staff (Maritime Port Security) to C.-in-C.-Fleet)*
Johns, Adrian James, CBE *(Rear-Adm. Fleet Air Arm (Head of Fighting Arm))*
Chittenden, Timothy Clive *(Chief of Staff (Support) to C.-in-C.-Fleet)*
Spires, Trevor Allan *(Chief Executive Armed Forces Personnel Administration Agency)*
Wilcocks, Philip Lawrence, DSC *(Deputy Chief of Joint Operations (Operational Support))*
Ainsley, Roger Stewart *(Flag Officer Sea Training)*
Soar, Trevor Alan, OBE *(Capability Manager (Precision Attack))*
Lambert, Paul *(Cdr. (Operations) to C.-in-C.-Fleet, Rear-Adm. Submarines (Head of Fighting Arm))*
Laurence, Timothy James Hamilton, MVO *(Assistant Chief of Defence Staff (Resources & Planning))*
Cooke, David John, MBE *(Deputy Cdr. Strike Force South)*
Wilkinson, Peter John *(Defence Services Secretary)*
Clayton, Christopher Hugh Trevor *(Assistant Director Intelligence Division, NATO International Military Staff)*
Raby, Nigel John Francis, OBE *(STLB Merger Project Team Leader)*
Borley, Kim John *(Flag Officer Training & Recruiting/ Chief Executive Naval Recruiting & Training Agency)*
Mark, Robert Alan *(Senior Naval Member of the Directing Staff of the Royal College of Defence Studies)*
Parry, Christopher John, CBE *(Director-General Joint Doctrine & Concepts)*
Latham, Neil Degge *(Commandant, College of Management and Technology)*
Kimmons, Michael *(Chief of Staff to Second Sea Lord/C.-in-C. Naval Home Command)*
Mathews, Andrew David Hugh *(Director-General (Nuclear))*
Ibbotson, Richard Jeffery, DSC *(Naval Secretary)*
Massey, Alan Michael, CBE *(Assistant Chief of the Naval Staff)*

HM FLEET *as at 1 June 2005*

Submarines	
Vanguard Class	Vanguard, Vengeance, Victorious, Vigilant
Swiftsure Class	Sceptre, Sovereign, Spartan, Superb
Trafalgar Class	Talent, Tireless, Torbay, Trafalgar, Trenchant, Triumph, Turbulent
Aircraft Carriers	Ark Royal, Illustrious, Invincible
Amphibious Assault Ships	Ocean, Albion, Bulwark
Destroyers	
Type 42 Batch 2	Exeter, Liverpool, Nottingham, Southampton
Type 42 Batch 3	Edinburgh, Gloucester, Manchester, York
Frigates	
Type 23	Argyll, Grafton, Iron Duke, Kent, Lancaster, Monmouth, Montrose, Northumberland, Portland, Richmond, St Albans, Somerset, Sutherland, Westminster
Type 22	Campbeltown, Chatham, Cornwall, Cumberland
Minehunters	
Hunt Class	Atherstone, Brocklesby, Cattistock, Chiddingfold, Hurworth, Ledbury, Middleton, Quorn
Sandown Class	Bangor, Blyth, Grimsby, Pembroke, Penzance, Ramsey, Shoreham, Walney
Patrol Craft	
Archer Class P2000 Fast Training Boats	Archer, Biter, Blazer, Charger, Dasher, Example, Exploit, Explorer, Express,

Gibraltar Squadron	Puncher, Pursuer, Raider, Ranger, Smiter, Tracker, Trumpeter Sabre, Scimitar
16 m Fast Patrol Class	
Castle Class Patrol Vessels	Dumbarton Castle
River Class Patrol Vessels	Mersey, Severn, Tyne,

Survey Vessels

Antarctic Patrol Ship	Endurance
Ocean Survey Vessels	Scott
Coastal Survey Vessels	Gleaner, Roebuck
Multi-Role Survey Vessels	HMS Echo, HMS Enterprise

OTHER PARTS OF THE NAVAL SERVICE

ROYAL MARINES

The Royal Marines were formed in 1664 and are part of the Naval Service. Their primary purpose is to conduct amphibious and land warfare. The principal operational units are:
- Three Commando Brigade Royal Marines, an amphibious all-arms brigade trained to operate in arduous environments (a core element of the UK's Joint Rapid Reaction Force)
- Fleet Protection Group Royal Marines (responsible for the security of nuclear weapon facilities)
- Special Boat Service, the maritime special forces.

The Royal Marines also provide detachments for warships and land-based naval parties as required. The headquarters of the Royal Marines is at Portsmouth and principal bases are at Plymouth, Arbroath, Poole, Taunton and Chivenor. The Corps of Royal Marines is about 6,500 strong.

CAPTAIN-GENERAL
HRH The Prince Philip, Duke of Edinburgh, KG, KT, OM, GBE, AC, QSO

COLONELS-COMMANDANT
Lt.-Gen. R. H. G. Fulton *(Representative Col. Commandant Royal Marines)*
Brig. S. P. Hill, OBE *(Col. Commandant Royal Marines)*

LIEUTENANT-GENERALS
Fulton, R. H. G. *(Deputy Chief of Defence Staff (Equipment Capability))*
Fry, R. A., CBE *(Deputy Chief of Defence Staff (Commitments))*

MAJOR-GENERALS
Lane, R. G. T., CBE
Dutton, J. B., CBE

ROYAL MARINES RESERVES (RMR)
The Royal Marines Reserve is a commando-trained volunteer force with the principal role, when mobilised, of supporting the Royal Marines. The current strength of the RMR is about 1,000.
Commanding Officer, RMR, Lt.-Col. E. C. Musto

ROYAL FLEET AUXILIARY SERVICE (RFA)
The Royal Fleet Auxiliary Service is a civilian-manned flotilla of 22 ships. Its primary role is to supply the Royal Navy with fuel, ammunition, food and stores, enabling it to maintain operations away from its home ports. It also provides secure logistic support and amphibious operations for the Army and Royal Marines, and forward ship maintenance and repair and sea-borne aviation training facilities for the Royal Navy.

FLEET AIR ARM
The Fleet Air Arm (FAA) provides the Royal Navy with a multi-role aviation combat capability able to operate autonomously at short notice worldwide in all environments, over the sea and land. The FAA has some 6,200 people, which comprises 11.5 per cent of the total Royal Naval strength. It operates some 200 combat aircraft and more than 50 support/training aircraft.

ROYAL NAVAL RESERVE (RNR)
The Royal Naval Reserve is an integral part of the Naval Service. It comprises up to 3,250 men and women nation-wide who volunteer to train in their spare time to enable the Royal Navy to meet its operational commitments, at sea and ashore, in crisis or war.

The standard annual training commitment is 24 days, including 12 days' continuous operational training.
Director, Naval Reserve, Capt. S. J. Timms, OBE

QUEEN ALEXANDRA'S ROYAL NAVAL NURSING SERVICE
The first nursing sisters were appointed to naval hospitals in 1884 and the Queen Alexandra's Royal Naval Nursing Service (QARNNS) gained its current title in 1902. Nursing ratings were introduced in 1960 and men were integrated into the Service in 1982; QARNNS recruits qualified nurses as both officers and ratings, and student nurse training can be undertaken in the Service.
Patron, HRH Princess Alexandra, the Hon. Lady Ogilvy, KG, GCVO
Director of Naval Nursing Services and Matron-in-Chief, Capt. L. Gibbon, ARRC, QHN, QARNNS

THE ARMY

THE QUEEN

FIELD MARSHALS
HRH The Prince Philip, Duke of Edinburgh, KG, KT, OM, GBE, AC, QSO, PC, *apptd* 1953
HRH The Duke of Kent, KG, GCMG, GCVO, ADC, *apptd* 1993
Lord Bramall, KG, GCB, OBE, MC, *apptd* 1982
Lord Vincent of Coleshill, GBE, KCB, DSO, *apptd* 1991
Sir John Stanier, GCB, MBE, *apptd* 1985
Sir John Chapple, GCB, CBE, *apptd* 1992
Lord Inge, KG, GCB, DL, *apptd* 1994

GENERALS
Walker, Sir Michael, GCB, CMG, CBE, ADC Gen *(Chief of the Defence Staff)*
Jackson, Sir Mike, GCB, CBE, DSO, ADC Gen *(Chief of the General Staff)*
Granville-Chapman, Sir Timothy, KCB, CBE, ADC Gen *(Vice Chief of the Defence Staff)*
O'Donoghue, Sir Kevin, KCB, CBE *(Chief of Defence Logistics)*
Dannat, Sir Richard, KCB, CBE, MC *(C.-in-C. Land Command)*
Reith, Sir John, KCB, CBE *(Deputy Supreme Allied Cdr. Europe)*

LIEUTENANT GENERALS
HRH The Prince of Wales, KG, KT, GCB, AK, OM, QSO, PC, ADC
McColl, J. C., CBE, DSO *(Cdr. Regional Forces, Land Command)*
Kiszely, Sir John, KCB, MC *(Director Defence Academy)*
Ridgway, A. P., CB, CBE *(Chief of Defence Intelligence)*
Watt, Sir Redmond, KVCO, CBE *(General Officer Commanding Northern Ireland)*
Judd, D. L., CB *(Deputy Cdr. Joint Force Command, Brunssum)*
Brims, R. V., CBE, DSO *(Cdr. Field Army, Land Command)*
Richards, D. J., CBE, DSO *(Cdr. Allied Rapid Reaction Corps)*
Viggers, F. R., CMG, MBE *(Adj.-Gen.)*
Houghton, J. N. R., CBE *(Deputy Commanding Gen. Multi-National Force Iraq & Senior British Military Representative (Iraq))*

MAJOR-GENERALS
Raper, A. J., CBE *(Defence Logistics Transformation Programme Team Leader/Quartermaster General)*
Gilchrist, P., CBE *(Head of British Defence Staff, Washington)*
Cross, T., CBE *(GOC Theatre Troops, Land Command)*
Figgures, A. C., CBE *(Technical Director, Defence Procurement Agency/Master-General of the Ordnance)*
Gamon, J. A., CBE, QHDS *(Special Project Officer, Deputy Chief of Defence Staff (Health))*
Baxter, R., CBE *(Director-General Development and Doctrine)*

Ritchie, A. S., CBE *(Commandant Royal Military Academy, Sandhurst)*
Cima, K. H. *(HQ Land Command/HQ Adj. Gen. Co-Location Implementation Team Leader)*
Lamb, G. C. M., CMG, OBE, DSO *(Director-General Training Support)*
Rollo, W. R., CBE *(Assistant Chief of the Defence Staff)*
Leakey, A. D., CBE *(Cdr. European Union Force)*
Wood, M. D., CBE *(Director-General Logistics (Supply Chain))*
Huntley, M. *(Director-General Logistics (Land))*
Wall, P. A., CBE *(Deputy Chief Joint Operations (Operations), Permanent Joint HQ)*
Cottam, N. J., OBE *(Military Secretary)*
Shirreff, A. R. D., CBE *(General Officer Commanding 3 (UK) Division)*
Pearson, P. T. C., CBE *(Cdr. British Forces Cyprus)*
Howell, D. M., OBE *(Director Army Legal Services)*
Lillywhite, L. P., MBE, QHS *(Director-General Medical Operational Capability)*
The Duke of Westminster, KG, OBE, TD, DL *(Assistant Chief of the Defence Staff (Reserves and Cadets))*
Applegate, R. A. D., OBE *(Capability Manager (Battlefield Manoeuvre))*
Tyler, T. N. *(Deputy Adj.-Gen. and Director-General Service Conditions (Army))*
Loudon, W. E. B., CBE *(GOC 2nd Division)*
Kerr, J. S., CBE *(GOC 4th Division)*
Roberts, S. J. L., OBE *(GOC London District)*
Bill, D. R. *(GOC United Kingdom Support Command (Germany))*
Whitley, A. E., CBE, CMG *(Senior British Loan Service Officer, Oman)*
Graham, A. J. N., CBE *(Director-General Army Training and Recruiting)*
Stewart, A. R. E. de C., CBE *(Assistant Chief of the Defence Staff (Policy))*
Cooper, J., DSO, MBE *(GOC 1st (UK) Armoured Division)*
Brown, C. C., CBE *(Chief of Staff Allied Rapid Reaction Corps)*
Wilkes, Revd D. E., OBE, QHC *(Chaplain General)*
Farquhar, A. P., CBE *(GOC 5th Division)*
White-Spunner, B. W. B., CBE *(Chief of Staff, HQ Land Command)*
Wilson, C. C., CBE *(Senior Army Member, Royal College of Defence Studies)*
Parker, N. R., CBE *(Deputy Commanding General Multi-National Corps, Iraq)*
Balfour, J. M. J., CBE *(Kosovo Protection Corps Co-ordinator)*
Mans, M. F. N. *(between postings)*
Riley, J. P., DSO *(Senior British Military Advisor Central Command)*
Coward, G. R., OBE *(Cdr. Joint Helicopter Command)*
Hawley, A., OBE *(Director-General Army Medical Services)*

CONSTITUTION OF THE ARMY

The Army consists of the Regular Army, the Regular Reserve and the Territorial Army (TA). It is commanded by the Chief of the General Staff, who is the professional Head of Service and Chairman of the Executive Committee of the Army Board, which provides overall strategic policy and direction to the Commands. These are: Land Command, which includes the Field Army, Regional Forces and the Joint Helicopter Command; Northern Ireland; and the Personnel and Training Command. The Army is divided into functional Arms and Services, sub-divided into Regiments and Corps (listed below in order of precedence). The Army is currently undergoing a major reform programme known as the Future Army Structure (FAS), which will incorporate changes in tactical doctrine, organisational structure, personnel terms and conditions of service and the introduction of new equipment. In particular, the Infantry are being re-structured into large multi-battalion regiments, which in some cases will involve amalgamations and changes in title. The timescale of the changes was still to be confirmed at the time of going to press.

Further information in the public domain on the composition of the Army Board, Headquarters, Arms and Services, including addresses, can be obtained from the Army List, which is published annually by the Stationery Office and held in most public libraries. Members of the public can write for general information to: Headquarters Adjutant General Secretariat, Trenchard Lines, Upavon, Wiltshire SN9 6BE. Information on how to make requests for information under the Freedom of Information Act 2000 can be found at: www.foi.mod.uk, which includes an electronic request form. All enquiries with regard to records of serving personnel (Regular and Territorial Army) should be directed to: The Army Personnel Centre Help Desk, Kentigern House, 65 Brown Street, Glasgow G2 8EX T 0141–224 2023/3303. Enquirers should note that the Army is governed in the release of personal information by various Acts of Parliament.

ORDER OF PRECEDENCE OF CORPS AND REGIMENTS OF THE BRITISH ARMY

ARMS

HOUSEHOLD CAVALRY
The Life Guards
The Blues and Royals (Royal Horse Guards and 1st Dragoons)

ROYAL HORSE ARTILLERY
(when on parade with their guns, the Royal Horse Artillery take precedence over the Household Cavalry)

ROYAL ARMOURED CORPS
1st The Queen's Dragoon Guards
The Royal Scots Dragoon Guards (Carabiniers and Greys)
The Royal Dragoon Guards
The Queen's Royal Hussars (The Queen's Own and Royal Irish)
9th/12th Royal Lancers (Prince of Wales')
The King's Royal Hussars
The Light Dragoons
The Queen's Royal Lancers
Royal Tank Regiment

ROYAL REGIMENT OF ARTILLERY
(with the exception of the Royal Horse Artillery (see above))

CORPS OF ROYAL ENGINEERS
ROYAL CORPS OF SIGNALS
REGIMENTS OF FOOT GUARDS
Grenadier Guards
Coldstream Guards
Scots Guards
Irish Guards
Welsh Guards

REGIMENTS OF INFANTRY
(Regiments marked with * are to be formed)

The Royal Regiment of Scotland*
The Princess of Wales' Royal Regiment (The Queen and Royal Hampshire's)
The King's, Lancashire and Border Regiment*
The Royal Regiment of Fusiliers
The Royal Anglian Regiment
The Light Infantry
The Yorkshire Regiment*
The Mercian Regiment*
The Royal Welsh*
The Royal Irish Regiment
The Parachute Regiment
The Royal Ghurka Rifles
The Royal Green Jackets

SPECIAL AIR SERVICE REGIMENT
ARMY AIR CORPS

SERVICES

ROYAL ARMY CHAPLAINS' DEPARTMENT
THE ROYAL LOGISTIC CORPS
Regimental HQ, Dettingen House, The Princess Royal Barracks, Deepcut, Camberley, Surrey GU16 6RW
ROYAL ARMY MEDICAL CORPS
Regimental HQ, Slim Road, Camberley, Surrey GU15 4NP
CORPS OF ROYAL ELECTRICAL AND MECHANICAL ENGINEERS
Regimental HQ, Hazebrouck Barracks, Isaac Newton Road, Arborfield, Reading, Berkshire RG2 9NJ
ADJUTANT-GENERAL'S CORPS
Regimental HQ, Worthy Down, Winchester, Hants SO21 2RG
ROYAL ARMY VETERINARY CORPS
Regimental HQ, The Former Army Staff College, Slim Road, Camberley, Surrey GU15 4NP
SMALL ARMS SCHOOL CORPS
Regimental HQ, Land Warfare Centre, Warminster, Wiltshire BA12 0DJ
ROYAL ARMY DENTAL CORPS
Regimental HQ, The Former Army Staff College, Slim Road, Camberley, Surrey GU15 4NP
INTELLIGENCE CORPS
Regimental HQ, Chicksands, Shefford, Beds SG17 5PR
ARMY PHYSICAL TRAINING CORPS
Regimental HQ, Fox Lines, Queen's Avenue, Aldershot, Hants GU11 2LB
QUEEN ALEXANDRA'S ROYAL ARMY NURSING CORPS
Regimental HQ, Slim Road, Camberley, Surrey GU15 4NP
CORPS OF ARMY MUSIC
Regimental HQ, Kneller Hall, Twickenham, Middx TW2 7DU
THE ROYAL MONMOUTHSHIRE ROYAL ENGINEERS (MILITIA) (TA)
THE HONOURABLE ARTILLERY COMPANY (TA)
Regimental HQ, Finsbury Barracks, City Road, London EC1Y 2BQ
REST OF THE TERRITORIAL ARMY (TA)

ARMY EQUIPMENT

Tanks	543
Challenger 2	386
Challenger	156
Chieftan	1
Armoured Infantry Fighting Vehicle	575
Armoured Personnel Carrier	1,121
Artillery pieces	407
Surface-to-air missile	339
Anti-tank guided weapon	902
Helicopters	274
Attack	126
Apache	17
Lynx	109
Support	148
Reconnaissance	475
Fuchs	11
Scimitar	327
Sabre	137
Aircraft	6

Source: Military Balance 2004–5

THE TERRITORIAL ARMY (TA)

The Territorial Army provides formed units and individuals as an essential part of the Army's order of battle for operations across all military tasks in order to ensure that the Army is capable of mounting and sustaining operations at nominated states of readiness. It also provides a basis for regeneration, while at the same time maintaining links with the local community and society at large. Since 1 December 2002 its established strength has been 41,914.

Inspector-General, Lt.-Gen. J. C. McColl, CBE, DSO

QUEEN ALEXANDRA'S ROYAL ARMY NURSING CORPS

The Queen Alexandra's Royal Army Nursing Corps (QARANC) was founded in 1902 as Queen Alexandra's Imperial Military Nursing Service and gained its present title in 1949. The QARANC has trained nurses for the register since 1950 and also trains and employs Health Care Assistants to Level 2 NVQ, with the option to train to Level 3. The Corps recruits qualified nurses as Officers and other ranks and in 1992 male nurses already serving in the Army were transferred to the QARANC.

Col.-in-Chief, HRH The Countess of Wessex
Director of Army Nursing Services (DANS), Col. J. D. F. Quinn

THE ROYAL AIR FORCE

THE QUEEN

MARSHAL OF THE ROYAL AIR FORCE
HRH The Prince Philip, Duke of Edinburgh, KG, KT, OM, GBE, AC, QSO, PC, *apptd* 1953

AIR CHIEF MARSHALS
Burridge, Sir Brian, KCB, CBE, ADC *(C.-in-C. RAF Strike Command)*
Stirrup, Sir Jock, KCB, AFC, ADC *(Chief of the Air Staff)*

AIR MARSHALS
HRH The Prince of Wales, KG, KT, OM, GCB, AK, QSO, ADC
French, Sir Joe, KCB, CBE *(Air Member for Personnel and C.-in-C. Personnel & Training Command)*
Loader, C. R., OBE *(Deputy C.-in-C. Strike Command)*
Miller, G. A., CBE *(Deputy Cdr. Joint Force Command, Naples)*
Pocock, D. J., CVO *(Deputy Chief of the Defence Staff (Personnel))*
Thompson, J. H., CB *(Director-General Saudi Arabia Armed Forces Project)*
Torpy, Sir Glenn, KCB, CBE, DSO *(Chief of Joint Operations, PJHQ)*
Walker, P. B., CB, CBE *(Director Joint Welfare Centre, Stavanger)*
Wright, Sir Robert, KBE, AFC *(UK Military Representative to NATO and the EU)*

AIR VICE-MARSHALS
Charles, R. A. *(Director RAF Legal Services)*
Chisnall, S. *(Senior Directing Staff (Air), Royal College of Defence Studies)*
Cliffe, J. A., OBE *(Director-General Training & Education, MOD)*
Dalton, S. G. G. *(Capability Manager (Information Superiority), MOD & Controller Aircraft)*
Dougherty, S. R. C., QHP *(Director-General RAF Medical Services)*
Dye, P. J., OBE *(Chief of Staff to Air Member for Personnel & Deputy C.-in-C. Personnel & Training Command)*
Harper, C. N., CBE *(Chief of Staff (Operations) Strike Command)*
Heath, M. C., CBE *(between appointments)*
The Ven. Hesketh, R. D., CB, QHC *(Director-General RAF Chaplaincy Services)*
Leeson, K. J., CBE *(Assistant Chief of the Defence Staff (Logistics Operations))*
Luker, P. D., OBE *(Deputy Commander Coalition Force Command, Afghanistan)*
McNicoll, I. W., CBE *(Air Officer Commanding No 2 Group)*
Maddox, N. D. A., CBE *(Commandant Joint Services Command & Staff College)*
Moran, C. H., OBE, MVO *(Assistant Chief of the Air Staff)*
Ness, C. W. *(Process & Organisation Review Team Leader)*
Nickols, C. M., CBE *(Assistant Chief of the Defence Staff (Operations))*
Peach, S. W., CBE *(Director-General Intelligence Collection)*
Ponsonby, J. M. M., OBE *(Air Officer Commanding Training Group)*
Rennison, D. R. G. *(Chief of Staff (Support) Strike Command)*
Ruddock, P. W. D., CBE *(Air Secretary)*

Thornton, B. M., CB *(Director-General Logistics (Strike))*
Thornton, E. J., QHP *(Director-General Healthcare)*
Walker, D., CBE, AFC *(Air Officer Commanding No 1 Group)*
Walker, D. A., OBE, MVO *(Master of the Royal Household from January 2005)*
White, A. D., CB *(Air Officer Commanding No 3 Group)*

CONSTITUTION OF THE ROYAL AIR FORCE
The RAF consists of two commands, Strike Command and Personnel and Training Command. Three RAF stations – Aldergrove, Benson and Odiham – are part of Joint Helicopter Command.

Strike Command's mission is to deliver, sustain and develop air power in the most effective manner to meet the UK's Foreign and Security Policy. Consisting of three groups, each organised around specific operational duties, the Command is responsible for all of the RAF's front-line forces. No 1 Group comprises the tactical fast-jet forces responsible for attack, offensive support and air defence operations. No 2 Group provides air combat support and includes enabling forces such as Air Transport and Air Refuelling, and the RAF Regiment. No 3 Group is the Air Battle management group and includes Airborne Early Warning, Maritime Patrol, and Search and Rescue aircraft.

Personnel and Training Command (PTC) is responsible for recruiting, training, supporting and retaining the servicemen and women needed to sustain the Royal Air Force. The Command consists of two agencies. The RAF Training Group Defence Agency deals with the recruitment and selection of all RAF personnel, as well as providing RAF non-operational flying and ground training. The RAF Personnel Management Agency (RAF PMA) is responsible for managing the careers of uniformed personnel serving in the Regular and Reserve Air Forces. It also assigns and deploys personnel to meet the military tasks in times of war, crisis and peace.

RAF EQUIPMENT

Aircraft	
BAe 125	6
BAe 146	2
Canberra	7
C-17A	4
Dominie	9
Harrier	79
Hawk	115
Hercules	51
Islander	2
Jaguar	62
King Air (leased)	7
Nimrod	24
Sentry E-3D	6
Tornado	254
Tristar	9
Tucano	73
Tutor	99
Typhoon	11
VC10	19

Helicopters

Bell	4
Chinook	38
Merlin	22
Puma	39
Sea King	23
Squirrel	38
Twin Squirrel	3

Source: Military Balance 2004–5

ROYAL AUXILIARY AIR FORCE (RAUXAF)

The Auxiliary Air Force was formed in 1924 to train an elite corps of civilians to serve their country in flying squadrons in their spare time. In 1947 the Force was awarded the prefix 'Royal' in recognition of its distinguished war service and the Sovereign's Colour for the Royal Auxiliary Air Force was presented in 1989. The RAuxAF continues to recruit civilians who undertake military training in their spare time to support the Royal Air Force in times of emergency or war.

Air Commodore-in-Chief, HM The Queen

Honorary Inspector-General Royal Auxiliary Air Force, Air Vice-Marshal B. H. Newton, CB, CVO, OBE, FCMI
Inspector Royal Auxiliary Air Force, Gp Capt. R. G. Kemp, QVRM, AE, ADC, FRIN

PRINCESS MARY'S ROYAL AIR FORCE NURSING SERVICE

The Princess Mary's Royal Air Force Nursing Service (PMRAFNS) was formed on 1 June 1918 as the Royal Air Force Nursing Service. In June 1923, His Majesty King George V gave his Royal Assent for the Royal Air Force Nursing Service to be known as the Princess Mary's Royal Air Force Nursing Service. Men were integrated into the PMRAFNS in 1980 and now serve as officers and other ranks.

Patron and Air Chief Commandant, HRH Princess Alexandra, The Hon. Lady Ogilvy, KG, GCVO
Director of Nursing Services and Matron-in-Chief, Gp Capt. W. B. Williams, RRC, QHN

SERVICE SALARIES

The following rates of pay apply from 1 April 2005.

The pay rates shown are for Army personnel. The rates apply also to personnel of equivalent rank and pay band in the other services (*see* below for table of relative ranks).

Rank	Daily	Annual
SECOND LIEUTENANT	£58.36	£21,301.40
LIEUTENANT		
On appointment	£70.15	£25,604.75
After 1 year in rank	£72.00	£26,280.00
After 2 years in rank	£73.84	£26,951.60
After 3 years in rank	£75.68	£27,623.20
After 4 years in rank	£77.53	£28,298.45
CAPTAIN		
On appointment	£89.89	£32,809.85
After 1 year in rank	£92.30	£33,689.50
After 2 years in rank	£94.74	£34,580.10
After 3 years in rank	£97.18	£35,470.70
After 4 years in rank	£99.60	£36,354.00
After 5 years in rank	£102.04	£37,244.60
After 6 years in rank	£104.46	£38,127.90
After 7 years in rank	£105.69	£38,576.85
After 8 years in rank	£106.90	£39,018.50
MAJOR		
On appointment	£113.23	£41,328.95
After 1 year in rank	£116.03	£42,350.95
After 2 years in rank	£118.81	£43,365.65
After 3 years in rank	£121.62	£44,391.30
After 4 years in rank	£124.41	£45,409.65
After 5 years in rank	£127.22	£46,435.30
After 6 years in rank	£130.02	£47,457.30
After 7 years in rank	£132.81	£48,475.65
After 8 years in rank	£135.61	£49,497.65
LIEUTENANT-COLONEL		
On appointment	£158.92	£58,005.80
After 1 year in rank	£161.03	£58,775.95
After 2 years in rank	£163.12	£59,538.80
After 3 years in rank	£165.20	£60,298.00
After 4 years in rank	£167.29	£61,060.85
After 5 years in rank	£169.38	£61,823.70
After 6 years in rank	£171.47	£62,586.55
After 7 years in rank	£173.57	£63,353.05
After 8 years in rank	£175.68	£64,123.20
COLONEL		
On appointment	£184.04	£67,174.60
After 1 year in rank	£186.46	£68,057.90
After 2 years in rank	£188.88	£68,941.20
After 3 years in rank	£191.30	£69,824.50
After 4 years in rank	£193.72	£70,707.80
After 5 years in rank	£196.14	£71,591.10
After 6 years in rank	£198.55	£72,470.75
After 7 years in rank	£200.98	£73,357.70
After 8 years in rank	£203.41	£74,244.65
BRIGADIER		
On appointment	£220.75	£80,573.75
After 1 year in rank	£223.10	£81,431.50
After 2 years in rank	£225.45	£82,289.25
After 3 years in rank	£227.79	£83,143.35
After 4 years in rank	£230.16	£84,008.40

PAY SYSTEM FOR SENIOR MILITARY OFFICERS

Revised pay rates effective from 1 April 2005 for all military officers of 2* rank and above (excluding medical and dental officers).

MAJOR-GENERAL (2*)	Daily	Annual
Scale 1	£247.08	£90,186
Scale 2	£250.80	£91,543
Scale 3	£255.72	£93,337
Scale 4	£260.95	£95,247
Scale 5	£266.19	£97,158
Scale 6	£271.42	£99,068
Scale 7	£276.65	£100,978

LIEUTENANT-GENERAL (3*)	Daily	Annual
Scale 1	£291.43	£106,372
Scale 2	£298.90	£109,099
Scale 3	£306.57	£111,897
Scale 4	£314.43	£114,766
Scale 5	£322.49	£117,709
Scale 6	£330.76	£120,728
Scale 7	n/a	n/a

GENERAL (4*)	Daily	Annual
Scale 1	£370.92	£135,386
Scale 2	£378.34	£138,094
Scale 3	£385.91	£140,857
Scale 4	£393.62	£143,673
Scale 5	£401.50	£146,546
Scale 6	£409.53	£149,477
Scale 7	n/a	n/a

Field Marshal – appointments to this rank will not usually be made in peacetime. The salary for holders of the rank is equivalent to the salary of a 5-star General, a salary created only in times of war. In peacetime, the equivalent rank to Field Marshal is the Chief of the Defence Staff. From 1 April 2005, the annual salary range for the Chief of the Defence Staff is £193,327–£205,160.

OFFICERS COMMISSIONED FROM THE SENIOR RANKS

Rank	Daily	Annual
Level 15	£120.16	£43,858.40
Level 14	£119.37	£43,570.05
Level 13	£118.54	£43,267.10
Level 12	£116.94	£42,683.10
Level 11	£115.35	£42,102.75
Level 10	£113.74	£41,515.10
Level 9	£112.14	£40,931.10
Level 8	£110.53	£40,343.45
Level 7*	£108.53	£39,613.45
Level 6	£107.30	£39,164.50
Level 5	£106.05	£38,708.25
Level 4**	£103.57	£37,803.05
Level 3	£102.34	£37,354.10
Level 2	£101.08	£36,894.20
Level 1†	£98.61	£35,992.65

* Minimum entry point for SUY, SCCs and LEs with over 15 years' service

** Minimum entry point for SUY, SCCs and LEs with between 12–15 years' service

† Minimum entry point for SUY, SCCs and LEs with under 12 years' service

SOLDIERS' SALARIES

The pay structure below officer level is divided into pay bands. Jobs at each rank are allocated to bands according to their score in the job evaluation system. Length of service is from age 18.

Scale A: committed to serve for less than 6 years, or those with less than 9 years' service who are serving on Open Engagement

Scale B: committed to serve for 6 years but less than 9 years

Scale C: committed to serve for 9 years or more, or those with more than 9 years' service who are serving on Open Engagement

Rates of pay effective from 1 April 2005 are:

	Lower Band		Higher Band	
	Daily	Annual	Daily	Annual
PRIVATE				
Level 1	£37.99	£13,866.35	£37.99	£13,866.35
Level 2	£40.22	£14,680.30	£43.49	£15,873.85
Level 3	£42.45	£15,494.25	£48.01	£17,523.65
Level 4	£46.17	£16,852.05	£51.62	£18,841.30
LANCE CORPORAL (levels 5–7 also applicable to Privates)				
Level 5	£48.65	£17,757.25	£57.08	£20,834.20
Level 6	£50.69	£18,501.85	£59.85	£21,845.25
Level 7	£52.86	£19,293.90	£62.60	£22,849.00
Level 8	£55.28	£20,177.20	£65.42	£23,878.30
Level 9	£57.28	£20,907.20	£68.61	£25,042.65

	Lower Band		Higher Band	
	Daily	Annual	Daily	Annual
CORPORAL				
Level 1	£62.60	£22,849.00	£65.42	£23,878.30
Level 2	£65.42	£23,878.30	£68.61	£25,042.65
Level 3	£68.61	£25,042.65	£71.97	£26,269.05
Level 4	£69.14	£25,236.10	£73.65	£26,882.25
Level 5	£69.68	£25,433.20	£75.43	£27,531.95
Level 6	£70.23	£25,633.95	£76.99	£28,101.35
Level 7	£70.75	£25,823.75	£78.67	£28,714.55

	Lower Band		Higher Band	
	Daily	Annual	Daily	Annual
SERGEANT				
Level 1	£71.16	£25,973.40	£77.66	£28.345.90
Level 2	£73.02	£26,652.30	£79.67	£29,079.55
Level 3	£74.85	£27,320.25	£81.69	£29,816.85
Level 4	£75.61	£27,597.65	£82.72	£30,192.80
Level 5	£77.58	£28,316.70	£84.33	£30,780.45
Level 6	£80.26	£29,294.90	£85.94	£31,368.10
Level 7	£80.87	£29,517.55	£87.55	£31,955.75

	Lower Band		Higher Band	
	Daily	Annual	Daily	Annual
STAFF SERGEANT				
Level 1	£78.77	£28,751.05	£87.61	£31,977.65
Level 2	£79.80	£29,127.00	£89.73	£32,751.45
Level 3	£82.39	£30,072.35	£91.87	£33,532.55
Level 4	£84.32	£30,776.80	£94.00	£34,310.00

WARRANT OFFICER II (levels 5–7 also applicable to Staff Sergeants)

Level 5	£85.47	£31,196.55	£96.14	£35,091.10
Level 6	£89.33	£32,605.45	£98.26	£35,864.90
Level 7	£90.70	£33,105.50	£99.68	£36,383.20
Level 8	£91.87	£33,532.55	£101.10	£36,901.50
Level 9	£93.95	£34,291.75	£102.54	£37,427.10

	Lower Band		Higher Band	
	Daily	Annual	Daily	Annual
WARRANT OFFICER I				
Level 1	£91.51	£33,401.15	£99.77	£36,416.05
Level 2	£93.29	£34,050.85	£101.73	£37,131.45
Level 3	£95.17	£34,737.05	£103.48	£37,770.20
Level 4	£97.06	£35,426.90	£105.38	£38,463.70
Level 5	£98.95	£36,116.75	£107.26	£39,149.90
Level 6	£101.73	£37,131.45	£109.17	£39,847.05
Level 7	£104.60	£38,179.00	£110.84	£40,456.60

RELATIVE RANK – ARMED FORCES

Royal Navy	Army	Royal Air Force
1 Admiral of the Fleet	1 Field Marshal	1 Marshal of the RAF
2 Admiral (Adm.)	2 General (Gen.)	2 Air Chief Marshal
3 Vice-Admiral (Vice-Adm.)	3 Lieutenant-General (Lt.-Gen.)	3 Air Marshal
4 Rear-Admiral (Rear-Adm.)	4 Major-General (Maj.-Gen.)	4 Air Vice-Marshal
5 Commodore (Cdre)	5 Brigadier (Brig.)	5 Air Commodore (Air Cdre)
6 Captain (Capt.)	6 Colonel (Col.)	6 Group Captain (Gp Capt.)
7 Commander (Cdr.)	7 Lieutenant-Colonel (Lt.-Col.)	7 Wing Commander (Wg Cdr.)
8 Lieutenant-Commander (Lt. Cdr.)	8 Major (Maj.)	8 Squadron Leader (Sqn Ldr)
9 Lieutenant (Lt.)	9 Captain (Capt.)	9 Flight Lieutenant (Flt. Lt.)
10 Sub-Lieutenant (Sub-Lt.)	10 Lieutenant (Lt.)	10 Flying Officer (FO)
11 Acting Sub-Lieutenant (Acting Sub-Lt.)	11 Second Lieutenant (2nd Lt.)	11 Pilot Officer (PO)

SERVICE RETIRED PAY
on compulsory retirement

Those who leave the services having served at least five years, but not long enough to qualify for the appropriate immediate pension, now qualify for a preserved pension and terminal grant, both of which are payable at age 60. The tax-free resettlement grants shown below are payable on release to those who qualify for a preserved pension and who have completed nine years' service from age 21 (officers) or 12 years from age 18 (other ranks).

The annual rates for Army personnel are given. The rates apply also to personnel of equivalent rank in the other services, including the nursing services.

OFFICERS
Applicable to officers who give full pay service on the active list on or after 31 March 2005. Pensionable earnings for senior officers (*) is defined as the total amount of basic pay received during the year ending on the day prior to retirement, or the amount of basic pay received during any 12-month period within 3 years prior to retirement, whichever is the higher. Figures for Senior Officers are percentage rates of pensionable earnings on final salary arrangements on or after 31 March 2005.

No of years reckonable service over age 21	Capt. and below	Major	Lt-Col.	Colonel	Brigadier General*	Major-General*	Lieutenant-General*	General*
16	£10,866	£12,942	£16,969	£19,648	£23,452	—	—	—
17	£11,367	£13,556	£17,754	£20,557	£24,367	—	—	—
18	£11,868	£14,171	£18,539	£21,466	£25,281	—	—	—
19	£12,369	£14,786	£19,324	£22,375	£26,195	—	—	—
20	£12,870	£15,401	£20,109	£23,284	£27,110	—	—	—
21	£13,371	£16,015	£20,894	£24,193	£28,024	—	—	—
22	£13,872	£16,630	£21,679	£25,102	£28,938	—	—	—
23	£14,372	£17,245	£22,464	£26,011	£29,853	—	—	—
24	£14,873	£17,859	£23,249	£26,920	£30,767	38.5%	—	—
25	£15,374	£18,474	£24,034	£27,828	£31,681	39.7%	—	—
26	£15,875	£19,089	£24,819	£28,737	£32,596	40.8%	—	—
27	£16,376	£19,703	£25,604	£29,646	£33,510	42.0%	42.0%	—
28	£16,877	£20,318	£26,389	£30,555	£34,424	43.1%	43.1%	—
29	£17,377	£20,933	£27,174	£31,464	£35,339	44.3%	44.3%	—
30	£17,878	£21,548	£27,959	£32,373	£36,253	45.4%	45.4%	45.4%
31	£18,379	£22,162	£28,745	£33,282	£37,167	46.6%	46.6%	46.6%
32	£18,880	£22,777	£29,530	£34,191	£38,082	47.7%	47.7%	47.7%
33	£19,381	£23,392	£30,315	£35,100	£38,996	48.9%	48.9%	48.9%
34	£19,882	£24,006	£31,100	£36,009	£39,910	50.0%	50.0%	50.0%

WARRANT OFFICERS, NCOS AND PRIVATES
(Applicable to soldiers who give full pay service on or after 31 March 2005)

No. of years reckonable service	Below Corporal	Corporal	Sergeant	Staff Sergeant	Warrant Officer Level II	Warrant Officer Level I
22	£6,422	£8,296	£9,094	£10,360	£11,060	£11,761
23	£6,646	£8,586	£9,412	£10,721	£11,446	£12,171
24	£6,870	£8,875	£9,729	£11,083	£11,832	£12,582
25	£7,094	£9,165	£10,047	£11,444	£12,218	£12,992
26	£7,318	£9,454	£10,364	£11,806	£12,604	£13,403
27	£7,543	£9,744	£10,681	£12,168	£12,990	£13,813
28	£7,767	£10,033	£10,999	£12,529	£13,377	£14,224
29	£7,991	£10,323	£11,316	£12,891	£13,763	£14,634
30	£8,215	£10,613	£11,634	£13,252	£14,149	£15,045
31	£8,439	£10,902	£11,951	£13,614	£14,535	£15,455
32	£8,663	£11,192	£12,269	£13,976	£14,921	£15,866
33	£8,888	£11,481	£12,586	£14,337	£15,307	£16,276
34	£9,112	£11,771	£12,903	£14,699	£15,693	£16,687
35	£9,336	£12,060	£13,221	£15,060	£16,079	£17,097
36	£9,560	£12,350	£13,538	£15,422	£16,465	£17,508
37	£9,784	£12,640	£13,856	£15,784	£16,851	£17,918

RESETTLEMENT GRANTS
Terminal grants are in each case three times the rate of retired pay or pension. There are special rates of retired pay for certain other ranks not shown above. Lower rates are payable in cases of voluntary retirement.

A gratuity of £3,695 is payable for officers with short service commissions for each year completed. Resettlement grants are: officers £12,709; non-commissioned ranks £8,687.

THE EDUCATION SYSTEM

Responsibility for education in England lies with the Secretary of State for Education and Skills; in Wales, with the National Assembly for Wales and the Minister for Education and Lifelong Learning; in Scotland, with Scottish Ministers; and in Northern Ireland with the Education Minister and the Minister for Employment and Learning.

The main concerns of the education departments are the formulation of national policies for education and the maintenance of consistency in educational standards. They are responsible for the broad allocation of revenue and capital resources for education, and for the supply and training of teachers. The Secretary of State is responsible for determining the rates of pay and conditions of employment of teachers in England and in Wales. In Scotland and Northern Ireland these are matters for the respective ministers. The Teacher Training Agency in England promotes teaching as a career on behalf of the Secretary of State and for a limited range of matters on the request of the Welsh Assembly Government.

EXPENDITURE

In the UK in 2004–5, total expenditure on education and training was:

	2004–5 outturn accruals £m	2004–5 estimated outturn accruals £m
Under fives	3,724	4,118
Primary schools	16,455	17,313
Secondary schools	15,098	19,304
Higher education	7,211	7,384
Further education	7,088	7,702
Student support	1,155	1,838
Training	1,658	1,845
Other education and training	5,592	6,265
Total education and training	60,980	65,770

Total managed expenditure on education and training in real terms from 1995–6 to 2004–5 was:

	£bn		£bn
1995–6	44.5	2000–1	50.0
1996–7	44.9	2001–2	54.4
1997–8	44.8	2002–3	56.5
1998–9	45.2	2003–4	61.0
1999–2000	46.7	2004–5 (estimated)	64.5

Of which education:

	£bn		£bn
1995–6	44.1	2000–1	48.4
1996–7	43.4	2001–2	53.0
1997–8	43.4	2002–3	54.9
1998–9	43.8	2003–4	59.3
1999–2000	45.1	2004–5 (estimated)	62.7

Most of this expenditure, except that for higher and further education in England, Wales and Scotland (which is met by the respective funding agencies), is incurred by local authorities, which make their own expenditure decisions according to their local situations and needs. Expenditure on education by central government and local authorities in the UK in £m was:

	2003–4
Local education authorities	
Current	36,362
Capital	2,852
Total	39,214
Central government	
Current	20,494
Capital	1,272
Total	21,766
All public authorities	
Current	56,856
Capital	4,124
Total	60,980

The following table shows total managed expenditure on education and training as a percentage of GDP:

	2002–3 outturn	2003–4 outturn	2004–5 estimated outturn
Education and training	5.2	5.5	5.6
Of which education	5.0	5.3	5.4

Statistics are published by each of the home education departments through press notices, bulletins and statistical volumes. These can be found on the relevant websites: England: W www.dfes.gov.uk; Wales: W www.wales.gov.uk; Scotland: W www.scotland.gov.uk N. Ireland: W www.deni.gov.uk

The bulk of direct expenditure by the DfES, the Welsh Assembly Government and the Scottish Executive is directed towards supporting post-16 education. Funding for higher education in universities and colleges is channelled through the Higher Education Funding Councils (HEFCs). Funding for further education, sixth form provision, and adult and community education is channelled through the funding councils for that sector and, in Wales, through the National Council for Education and Training (ELWa). ELWa is to be merged with the Assembly Government on 1 April 2006. In addition, the DfES currently funds student support in England and Wales (although Wales is taking over responsibility for its own student support), the City Technology Colleges, the City College for the Technology of the Arts, and pays grants under the specialist schools programme.

In Wales the Assembly Government also funds curriculum development, educational services and research. In Scotland the main elements of central government expenditure, in addition to those outlined above, are grant-aided special schools, student awards and bursaries (through the Student Awards Agency for Scotland), teachers, curriculum development, special educational needs and community education. In Northern Ireland the Department of Education also administers the teachers' superannuation scheme, pays teachers' salaries and funds grant-maintained integrated and voluntary grammar schools. The Department for Employment and

Learning directly funds higher education, student awards and further education.

LOCAL EDUCATION ADMINISTRATION

In England and Wales the school education service is administered by local education authorities (LEAs), which have day-to-day responsibility for providing most state primary and secondary education in their areas. They share with the appropriate funding bodies the duty to provide adult education to meet local needs. The LEAs own and maintain most schools and some colleges, build new ones and provide equipment. LEAs are financed largely from the council tax and aggregate external finance from the Office of the Deputy Prime Minister in England and the National Assembly for Wales. LEA-maintained schools usually manage their own budgets. The LEA allocates funds to the school, largely on the basis of pupil numbers, and the school governing body is responsible for overseeing spending and for most aspects of staffing, including appointments and dismissals. LEAs also have intervention powers to add additional governors, take back control of a school's budget or replace the governing body of a school with an interim executive when a school is placed in special measures, is judged to have serious weaknesses or is causing concern and has not complied with a formal warning from the LEA. The duty of providing education locally in Scotland rests with the education authorities. They are responsible for the construction of buildings, the employment of teachers and other staff, and the provision of equipment and materials. Devolved School Management is in place for all primary, secondary and special schools. Education authorities are required to establish school boards consisting of parents and teachers as well as co-opted members whose responsibilities include staff appointments.

> The Standards in Scotland Schools etc. Act 2000 set out a School Improvement Framework which gives strategic direction to school education through five National Priorities in Education. These define the outcomes that education authorities and their schools have to deliver for young people. The National Priorities cover: attainment and achievement; framework for learning; inclusion and equality; values and citizenship; and learning for life.

Education, with the exception of further and higher education, is administered locally in Northern Ireland by five education and library boards, which fund controlled and maintained schools and whose costs are met in full by the Northern Ireland Executive. All grant-aided schools include elected parents and teachers on their boards of governors. Provision has been made for schools wishing to provide integrated education to have grant-maintained integrated status, funded directly by the Department of Education. All schools and colleges of further education have full responsibility for their own budgets, including staffing costs.

THE INSPECTORATE

ENGLAND

The Office for Standards in Education (Ofsted) is a non-ministerial government department in England headed by HM Chief Inspector of Schools (HMCI). Ofsted's remit is to help improve the quality and standards of childcare through regular independent inspection and regulation. It must also provide advice to the Secretary of State based on inspection evidence. Ofsted must report on all maintained schools in England, local education authorities (supported by the Audit Commission), initial teacher training courses, the private, voluntary and independent nursery sector (including childminders and day-care establishments), independent schools, (including independent special schools), youth services, service children's education, and all education and training for ages 16–19 in sixth form and further education colleges. Ofsted also reports on the impact of government initiatives such as the national numeracy and literacy strategies. Since September 2005 Ofsted has worked with a number of other inspectorates to inspect children's services in England.

The current inspection framework, *Framework 2003 – Inspecting Schools*, came into effect in September 2003. Schools are inspected at least once every six years. As at August 2005, there are currently 755 Registered Inspectors, 4,943 Team Inspectors (including Registered Inspectors) and 338 Lay Inspectors.

W www.ofsted.gov.uk

WALES

Estyn: Arolygiaeth Ei Mawrhydi dros Addysg a Hyfforddiant yng Nghymru (Her Majesty's Inspectorate for Education and Training in Wales) is responsible for inspecting early years' provision in the non-maintained sector, primary schools, secondary schools, special schools (including independent special schools), pupil referral units, independent schools, further education, youth support services, local education authorities, teacher education and training, work-based learning, Careers Wales companies, the education, guidance and training elements of the New Deal and adult community based learning. Its remit from the Department of Training and Education also includes providing advice on a wide range of education and training matters.

W www.estyn.gov.uk

SCOTLAND

HM Inspectorate of Education (HMIE) is an executive agency of the Scottish Executive. HM Inspectors (HMI) inspect or review and report on education provision in primary, secondary and special schools, further education institutions (under contract to the Scottish Further Education Funding Council), initial teacher education, community learning and development, care and welfare of pupils, the education functions of local authorities, prison education, children's services and in other contexts as necessary. They work in collaboration with the Care Commission in integrated inspection of pre-school education centres and residential schools. They work with Audit Scotland on the inspection of education authorities and on behalf of the Scottish Further Education Funding Council in the review of Scotland's 43 further education colleges. The HMI work in teams alongside lay members (who are volunteer members of the public) and associate assessors (who are practising teachers or senior educationalists seconded for the inspection). HMIE is led by the senior chief inspector, supported by six chief inspectors (five of whom head inspectorates) and twelve assistant chief inspectors. There are approximately 80 HMI in Scotland. The Scottish Higher Education Funding Council has a duty to assess quality in higher education institutions and universities, a responsibility which it sub-contracts to the Quality Assurance Agency for Higher Education (QAA) Scotland Office. The Further and Higher Education (Scotland) Act 2005 extends this duty on the Council to secure that provision is made for assessing and enhancing the quality of education provided.

W www.hmie.gov.uk

NORTHERN IRELAND

Inspection is carried out in Northern Ireland by the Education and Training Inspectorate, which provides inspection services for the Department of Education, the Department for Employment and Learning and the Department of Culture, Arts and Leisure. Schools are inspected currently once every five to seven years. In further education and training, extended inspections are carried out once every eight years and focused inspections at least every four years. In addition, the Inspectorate provides evidence-based advice to ministers and departments to assist in the formulation and evaluation of policies in education, training and youth. The Inspectorate comprises one chief inspector, four assistant chief inspectors, 10 managing inspectors and 51 inspectors.

W www.deni.gov.uk/inspection_services

SCHOOLS AND PUPILS

Full-time education is compulsory in Great Britain for all children between five and 16 years and between four and 16 years in Northern Ireland. About 93 per cent of children in the United Kingdom receive free education from public funds and the rest attend fee-charging schools or are educated at home. Provision is being increased for pre-school children and many pupils remain at school after the minimum leaving age. No fees are charged in any publicly maintained school in England, Wales and Scotland. In Northern Ireland, fees may be charged in voluntary schools and are paid by pupils in preparatory departments of grammar schools, but pupils admitted to the secondary departments of grammar schools, unless they come from outside Northern Ireland, do not pay fees. Students under 19 years of age attending courses at further education colleges are not charged course fees.

PUPIL NUMBERS

In the maintained sector in the UK in 2004 there were:

Nursery pupils	150,500
Primary pupils	5,111,400
Secondary pupils	4,013,100
Pupils in Special Schools	103,200
Pupils in pupil referral units	13,400
Total pupils in all maintained schools	9,391,400

ENGLAND AND WALES

There are two main types of school in England and Wales: schools maintained by the state, which charge no fees; and independent schools, which charge fees. Schools maintained by the state, with the exception of the Academies and City Technology Colleges, which exist in England alone, are maintained by local education authorities (LEAs). Schools maintained by the state are classified as community, voluntary or foundation schools. Community schools are owned by LEAs and wholly funded by them (although sixth forms have separate funding arrangements). They are non-denominational and provide primary and secondary education. Schools in the voluntary category provide primary and secondary education and many have a particular religious ethos.

Although the school buildings are in many cases provided by the voluntary body, the LEA financially maintains them. There are two subdivisions in the voluntary category: voluntary controlled, and voluntary aided. In the case of voluntary controlled schools, the LEA bears all the costs. In voluntary aided schools, the governing body is responsible for the buildings, perimeter walls and fences, playgrounds, furniture fixtures and fittings, the Secretary of State for Education and Skills may pay capital grant of up to 90 per cent of approved capital expenditure, while the LEA is responsible for playing fields and buildings on those fields related to their use as playing fields. The arrangements in Wales are different, and the rate of grant support is 85 per cent. Foundation schools provide primary and secondary education. They can have a religious character, although most do not. They are funded by the LEA, and, via the LEA, by the relevant funding bodies in respect of sixth form provision, although the land and buildings will be owned by a foundation or by the governors.

The number of schools by category in 2004 was:

	England	Wales
Maintained nursery schools (inc. two Direct Grant for England)	470	34
Total maintained primary and secondary schools	21,171	1,815
Of which:		
Community	13,283	1,532
Voluntary aided	4,304	163
Voluntary controlled	2,706	108
Foundation	878	12
Pupil referral units	426	31
Maintained special schools	1,078	43
Non-maintained special schools	70	–
CTC's and CCTA's (England only)*	14	–
Academies	12	–
Independent schools	2,302	60
Total	25,543	1,983

* City Technology Colleges and City Colleges for the Technology of the Arts

LEAs are required to provide the schools that they maintain with a delegated budget to cover their running costs, including staffing costs. LEAs can retain funding of various centrally provided services, including transport and some special educational needs. The LEA acts as admission authority for most community and some voluntary schools.

Governing bodies – All publicly maintained schools have a governing body, usually made up of a number of parent and local community representatives, governors appointed by the LEA if the school is LEA-maintained, the head teacher (unless he or she chooses otherwise) and serving teachers and other staff. All schools can appoint up to two sponsor governors and, since August 2005, maintained secondary schools can appoint up to four sponsor governors. Sponsor governors are persons who give substantial assistance to the school, financially or in kind, or who provide services to the school. Governing bodies are responsible for the overall policies of schools and their academic aims and objectives.

City Technology Colleges (CTCs) and City Colleges for the Technology of the Arts (CCTAs) are found in England only, and are state-aided but independent of LEAs. Their aim is to widen the choice of secondary education in disadvantaged urban areas and to teach a broad curriculum with an emphasis on science, technology, business understanding and arts technologies. Capital costs are shared by government and business sponsors, and running costs are covered by a per capita grant from the DfES in line with an average of the comparable costs in LEA-maintained schools in the areas where CTCs are located.

The *Specialist Schools Programme* is open to all maintained secondary schools in England, including special schools with secondary aged pupils, that wish to develop a curriculum specialism in one of ten specialist areas: arts, business and enterprise, engineering, humanities, languages, mathematics and computing, music, science, sports, and technology. Schools can also combine two specialisms. Schools must raise £50,000 in unconditional private/business sponsorship, except smaller schools (schools with 500 pupils or fewer) which must raise at least £20,000 depending on pupil numbers. There are two application rounds a year. Schools must also prepare four-year development plans. These must include measurable targets for how they intend to raise attainment and extend opportunities for pupils in the specialist area and improve teaching and learning, thereby securing improvement across the whole school. Schools must also share expertise, resources and good practice with other schools and the wider community. Specialist schools receive additional recurrent funding to support the targets within their plan. This is currently calculated at a rate of £129 per pupil per annum up to 1000 pupils and over 1,200 pupils (eg a school with 1600 pupils will receive £129 × 1400). In addition, specialist schools receive a one-off capital grant of £100,000 supplemented by sponsorship raised, to improve their specialist facilities. Specialist schools are encouraged to include sponsors and local businesses on their governing bodies. All maintained schools are able to appoint two sponsor governors and specialist schools will be expected to appoint some sponsor/business/employer governors. Specialist schools can apply for redesignation at the end of the four-year phase to extend specialist status for a further four years. In July 2005 there were 2,383 designated specialist schools. Over three-quarters of England's secondary schools have now achieved specialist status.

Academies – Academies (England only) are independent state schools open to all abilities. They are usually in disadvantaged areas and are established by sponsors from business or faith or voluntary groups. Sponsors and the DfES provide capital costs, and running costs are met in full by the DfES, but funded in recurrent terms at comparable levels to other local schools. Academies either replace seriously failing schools with poor examination results or are established to meet local demand for places. The first three academies opened in September 2002 and a further nine opened in September 2003. Five more academies opened in September 2004 and 10 more were due to open in September 2005.

Excellence in Cities (EiC) is a programme of support in England designed to raise school standards and pupil expectations in disadvantaged urban communities. *Excellence Clusters* bring the core strands of the EiC programme to smaller pockets of deprivation elsewhere.

Federations are groups of two or more schools with a formal agreement to work together to raise standards.

The *Beacon Schools Programme* was set up in England to help raise standards across primary and secondary education by sharing and spreading locally and nationally the good practice identified in successful schools. The programme is currently being phased out and the last contracts ended in August 2005. A new programme at secondary level, the *Leading Edge Partnership Programme*, builds on the success of the Beacon Schools Programme and supports innovative approaches to addressing critical learning challenges; 103 partnerships began in September 2003 and a further 102 partnerships were announced in early 2004. Groups of primary schools identify a learning focus to help to raise standards of attainment through the *Primary Strategy Learning Networks*.

Independent/State School Partnerships were launched in 1998 and forge links between independent and state schools to enhance the opportunities on offer to pupils. In 2004–5, a £1.4 million government package funded 46 new partnership projects.

Education Action Zones (EAZs) were established in England from 1998 to develop local partnerships between schools, parents, the community, businesses and local authorities to find solutions to educational underachievement. They were set up as statutory bodies with a maximum five-year lifespan. After five years EAZs in rural areas have changed into Excellence Clusters and those in EiC areas have changed into EiC Action Zones.

SCOTLAND

Education authority schools (known as publicly-funded schools) are financed by local government, partly through revenue support grants from central government, and partly from local taxation. Devolved management from the local authority to the school is in place for more than 88 per cent of all school-level expenditure. A small number of grant-aided schools, mainly in the special sector, are conducted by boards of managers and receive grants direct from the Scottish Executive Education Department. Independent schools charge fees and receive no direct grant, but are subject to inspection and registration. The number of schools by category in September 2004 was:

Publicly funded schools	2,793
Independent schools	152
Total	2,945

NORTHERN IRELAND

Controlled schools are managed by the education and library boards (ELBs) through boards of governors consisting of representatives of transferors (mainly the Protestant churches), parents, teachers and the ELB. Within the controlled sector there is a small number of controlled integrated schools. Voluntary maintained schools are managed by boards of governors consisting of members nominated by trustees (mainly Roman Catholic) with representatives of teachers, parents and the ELB. Voluntary schools receive grants towards capital costs and running costs in whole or in part. A majority are entitled to capital grants at 100 per cent. Voluntary non-maintained schools are mainly voluntary grammar schools managed by boards of governors consisting of representatives of parents, teachers and, in most cases, the Department of Education and the ELB, as well as those appointed as provided in each school's scheme of management. Integrated schools exist to educate Protestant and Roman Catholic children, as well as those of other faiths and none, together. Latest figures show that there are currently 55 integrated schools, comprising 19 integrated second level colleges and 36 integrated primary schools. There are a number of Irish-language schools and units, and, as at August 2005, there were 18 Irish-medium schools and 12 Irish-medium units attached to schools in the English language sector. Of the 18 schools, 17 are Irish-medium primary schools. There are also 3 Irish-medium nursery units. The number of schools in Northern Ireland by type in 2004–5 was:

Grant-Aided Mainstream	
Nursery*	99
Primary	894
Secondary: total	232
grammar	70
other	162
Non-maintained mainstream	17
Special (maintained)	45
Total all schools	1,287

*Excludes voluntary and private pre-school education centres

THE STATE SYSTEM

SURE START
All early years services in England, including pre-school education, now come under the Sure Start banner. Sure Start programmes increase the availability of childcare for all children; improve health, education and emotional development for young people; and support parents in their role including increasing their chances to work, train and study. To do this, it operates both programmes open to all children and families and others concentrated on disadvantaged areas, although children's centres providing integrated services for under 5s are now being rolled out to all communities. There will be 3,500 across England by 2010. Sure Start's remit is usually confined to the under 5s, but in the case of childcare it is responsible for ensuring that accessible and affordable care is available for all children up to the age of 14, or 16 for children with a special need.

    W www.surestart.gov.uk

PRE-SCHOOL EDUCATION
Pre-school education is for children from three to five years. It is not compulsory, although a free place is available for every three and four-year-old whose parents want one. From 2006, all 3 and 4 year olds will receive their free early education over 38 weeks of the year instead of 33 and from 2007, they will begin to receive an enhanced entitlement of 15 hours per week instead of 12½, with all of them receiving it by 2010, In Wales, a free part-time place in a maintained or non-maintained setting is available for each child from the term following their third birthday. In Scotland, pre-school education places are available for all three- and four-year-olds whose parents request one. Northern Ireland has a compulsory school-starting age of four, and since March 2003 sufficient places have been available, on request of the parents, for each child in its' immediate pre-school year.

    Free, part-time, pre-school, or early education is funded by the Government via local authorities but takes place variously in nursery schools, nursery classes in primary schools, private schools, voluntary sector groups and some childminder networks in England. All providers, whatever their sector, can receive Government funding through local authorities to provide free places if they can demonstrate, via Ofsted inspections, that curricular goals are being met. In Northern Ireland approximately 30 per cent of pre-school education takes place in voluntary/ private sector playgroups funded by the Department of education. The proportion of all pre-school places taken by three- and four-year-olds in the UK as at January 2004, by sector, was:

	Public sector %	Public and voluntary sector %	All providers %
UK	65	35	100
England	64	39	103
Wales	81	–	81
Scotland	65	28	93
Northern Ireland	58	13	71

PRIMARY EDUCATION
Primary education begins at five years in Great Britain and four years in Northern Ireland. In England, Wales and Northern Ireland the transfer to secondary school is generally made at 11 years. In Scotland, the primary school course lasts for seven years and pupils transfer to secondary courses at about the age of 12.

    Primary schools consist mainly of infant schools for children aged five to seven, junior schools for those aged seven to 11, and combined junior and infant schools for both age groups. First schools in some parts of England cater for ages five to ten as the first stage of a three-tier system of first, middle and secondary schools. Unlike England, Scotland has only primary schools.

PRIMARY SCHOOLS (UK) 2003–4
No. of primary schools	22,509
No. of pupils (including nursery classes)	5,111,400
No. of pupils (excluding nursery classes)	4,796,700

Pupil-teacher ratios in public sector mainstream primary schools:

	2001–2	2002–3	2003–4
UK	22.0	21.0	21.0
England	22.5	22.6	22.7
Wales	21.0	20.7	21.1
Scotland	18.9	18.0	18.2
Northern Ireland	19.8	19.6	19.9

The average size of classes 'as taught' was 25.9 in 2003–4, a slight reduction from 2002–3. (Figures refer to 'all classes' rather than 'one-teacher classes' only.)

MIDDLE SCHOOLS
Middle schools take children from first schools, mostly in England, cover varying age ranges between eight and 14 and usually lead on to comprehensive upper schools.

SECONDARY EDUCATION
Secondary schools are for children aged 11 to 16 and for those who choose to stay on to 18. At 16, many students prefer to move on to tertiary or sixth form colleges or into further education colleges or work-based training. Most secondary schools in England, Wales and Scotland are co-educational. The largest secondary schools have over 1,500 pupils, but only 5.3 per cent of schools in the United Kingdom take over 1,000 pupils.

	England	Wales	Scotland	Northern Ireland
No. of pupils (000s)	3,970.7	254.7	406.0	165.3
Average class size	21.9	20.6	–	–
Pupil-teacher ratio	17.0	16.6	12.8	14.6

In England and Wales the main types of maintained secondary schools are: comprehensive schools, whose admission arrangements are without reference to ability or aptitude; deemed middle schools (in England), for children aged between eight and 14 years who then move on to senior comprehensive schools at 12, 13 or 14; and (in England) secondary grammar schools, with selective intake, providing an academic course from 11 to 16–18 years.

In Scotland all pupils in education authority secondary schools attend schools with a comprehensive intake. Most of these schools provide a full range of courses appropriate to all levels of ability from first to sixth year.

In Northern Ireland the process of selection (currently the 11-plus examination) is at the heart of the education system. Children are placed in either grammar (38 per cent of pupils in 2004) or secondary (62 per cent of pupils in 2004) based on a test taken during their seventh year at school when they are ten or eleven years of age. Following research into the selective education system in Northern Ireland, extensive consultation and recommendations from the Post-Primary Review Working Group (Costello), the Northern Ireland education system is currently undergoing major reform, and in particular, post-primary education and the means by which pupils transfer from primary to post-primary schools. The key aspects of the new arrangements are:

• The last Transfer Tests will be held in Autumn 2008
• Transfer from primary to post-primary will be based on informed parental choice
• A Pupil Profile will be developed for each child, detailing his or her progress

The new post-primary arrangements will guarantee all pupils access to a much wider range of academic and vocational courses, with a minimum of 24 courses at Key stage 4, and 27 at post-16. At least one third of the courses on offer will be academic in nature, and at least one third will be vocational.

SPECIAL EDUCATION

Wherever possible, taking parents' wishes into account, children with special educational needs (SEN) are educated in ordinary schools, which are required to publish their policy for pupils with such needs. Local education authorities in England and Wales and education and library boards in Northern Ireland are required to identify and secure provision for children with special educational needs and to involve the parents in any decision.

In Scotland, school placing is a matter of agreement between education authorities and parents. Parents have the right to say which school they want their child to attend, and a right of appeal where their wishes are not being met.

Maintained special schools are run by education authorities which pay all the costs of maintenance, but under the terms of local management, all maintained schools must have a delegated budget including maintained special schools. Non-maintained special schools are run by voluntary bodies; they may receive some grant from central government for capital expenditure and for equipment but their current expenditure is met primarily from the fees charged to education authorities for pupils placed in the schools. Some independent schools provide education wholly or mainly for children with special educational needs. The number of pupils in all schools with statements of special needs in 2003–4 was:

	No.	Percentage
UK	290,700	2.9
England	247,600	3.0
Wales	15,000	3.4
Scotland	16,100	1.9
Northern Ireland	11,000	3.2

Of all the pupils with statements of special educational needs in 2003–4, 64 per cent were educated in mainstream schools (nursery, primary, secondary and independent schools).

ELECTIVE HOME EDUCATION

There is no legal obligation on parents in the UK to educate their children at school provided that the local education authority is satisfied that the child is receiving full-time education suited to its age, abilities and aptitudes. The education authority need not be informed that a child is being educated at home unless the child is already registered at a state school. In that case the parents must arrange for the child's name to be removed from the school's register (by writing to the head teacher) before education at home can begin. Failure to do so leaves the parents liable to prosecution for condoning non-attendance. There are no official figures on the numbers of pupils educated outside school but estimates suggest that between 100,000 and 170,000 children are being educated at home.

INDEPENDENT SCHOOLS

Independent schools charge fees and are owned and managed under special trusts, with profits being used for the benefit of the schools concerned. There are 2,300 independent schools in Britain, educating over 624,000 pupils, or 7 per cent of the total school-age population. The number of pupils at independent schools in 2004 was:

UK	624,000
England	573,100
Wales	9,600
Scotland	32,000
Northern Ireland	9,200

The annual survey carried out by the Independent Schools Council (ISC) shows that 0.6 per cent fewer pupils were being educated in ISC accredited independent schools in 2005 than in 2004. The Independent Schools Council, formed in 1974, acts on behalf of the seven independent schools' associations which constitute it. These associations are: Headmasters' and Headmistresses' Conference, the Girls' Schools Association, the Independent Schools Association, the Society of Headmasters and Headmistresses of Independent Schools, the Incorporated Association of Preparatory Schools, the Association of Governing Bodies of Independent Schools and the Independent Schools Bursars Association. There are 1,275 schools in membership of the ISC, educating 80 per cent of all children educated outside the state sector. Most of the schools outside ISC membership are likely to be privately owned. The ISC has overall responsibility for the Independent Schools Inspectorate (ISI), which works under a framework agreed with the DfES and Ofsted. A school must pass an ISI accreditation inspection to qualify for membership of an association within ISC. Schools are evaluated on their educational standards (including attainment, learning and behaviour), quality of teaching, assessment and recording, curriculum, staffing, premises and resources, links with parents and the community, pupils' personal development and pastoral care, management, efficiency, aims and ethos. ISC schools are subject to inspection every six years. In 2004 over half of the 11-year-olds who took national curriculum key stage 2 tests at preparatory schools achieved the level expected of 14-year-olds. At GCSE, 55.5 per cent of all exams taken by independent school candidates achieve either an A* or A grade (compared to the national average of 17.4 per cent) and at A-level, about 70.9 per cent of entries were awarded an A or B grade (national average, 45.1 per cent). In 2004, over 118,000 pupils at ISC schools received help with their fees in the form of bursaries and scholarships from the schools. In 2004, ISC member schools spent £547.6 million (an average of £1,091 per pupil) on new and improved buildings and equipment.

W www.isc.co.uk

THE CURRICULUM

ENGLAND

The national curriculum was introduced in primary and secondary schools between autumn 1989 and autumn 1996, for the period of compulsory schooling from five to 16. It is mandatory in all maintained schools. Following a review in 1999, a revised curriculum was introduced in schools from September 2000.

The Foundation Stage was introduced in September 2000 for children aged 3–5. It sets out six areas of learning:

- Personal, social and emotional development
- Communication
- Mathematical development
- Knowledge and understanding of the world
- Physical development
- Creative development

The Education Act 2002 extended the national curriculum to include the Foundation Stage. This Act also established a single national assessment system for the Foundation Stage called the Foundation Stage Profile. The statutory subjects in the national curriculum are:

Core subjects	Foundation subjects
English	Design and Technology
Mathematics	Information and Communication Technology
	History
	Geography
	Art and Design
	Music
	Physical Education
	Citizenship
	Modern Foreign Language

At key stage three (11- to 14-year-olds) a modern foreign language is introduced. At key stage four (14- to 16-year-olds) pupils are required to continue to study the core subjects, plus physical education, information and communication technology, work-related learning and careers education. Citizenship and sex education are compulsory subjects for all secondary pupils. In addition, schools must provide access for each KS4 pupil to a minimum of one course in the arts (art and design, music, dance, drama and media arts), one course in the humanities (history and geography), at least one modern foreign language and design and technology. Other subjects, such as drama, dance and classical languages, are taught when the resources of individual schools permit. Religious education must be taught across all key stages. Parents have the right to withdraw their children from religious education and sex education classes.

Statutory assessment takes place on entry to primary school and national tests and tasks in English and mathematics at key stage one (five- to seven-year-olds), with the addition of science at key stages two (seven- to 11-year-olds) and three (11- to 14-year-olds), are in place. Teachers make their own assessments of their pupils' progress to set alongside the test results. At key stage four, the GCSE and vocational equivalents are the main form of assessment.

The DfES in England publishes tables showing pupils' performance in A-level, AS-level, GCSE, GNVQ and Vocational A-level examinations school by school. LEAs are required to publish similar information in November each year showing the results of national curriculum tests and teacher assessments for seven, 11- and 14-year-olds.

The Qualifications and Curriculum Authority (QCA) is an independent government agency funded by the DfES. It is responsible for setting the National Curriculum, and for ensuring that the curriculum and qualifications available to young people and adults are of high quality, coherent and flexible and its remit ranges from the under-fives to higher level vocational qualifications.

W www.qca.org.uk

WALES

The national curriculum was introduced simultaneously in Wales and, although it is broadly similar to the National Curriculum of England, has separate and distinctive characteristics which are reflected in the programmes of study where appropriate. Following a review of the curriculum in Wales, changes were introduced from September 2000. Welsh is compulsory for pupils at all key stages, either as a first or as a second language. According to the January 2003 schools' census 21 per cent of primary school pupils are taught in classes where Welsh is used as a medium of teaching to some degree. In November 2002, additional funding of £9.5 million was announced for Welsh language education; £7 million has been used to support bilingual nursery education between 2004–6. The percentage of children speaking Welsh fluently in primary school has increased from 13.2 per cent in 1988 to 16.8 per cent in 2002. In July 2003 the Minister for Education and Lifelong Learning in Wales announced that statutory testing would be removed for pupils in Wales at the end of Key Stage 2 from 2004–5 and from 2005–6 for Key Stage 3. Statutory teacher assessment remains and will be strengthened by moderation and accreditation arrangements. Assessment at the end of Key Stage 1 remains by teacher assessment only.

Awdurdod Cymwysterau, Cwricwlwm ac Asesu Cymru (ACCAC – the Qualifications, Curriculum and Assessment Authority for Wales) advises government on the matters within its remit. ACCAC is funded by the National Assembly for Wales through the Department for Training and Education.

W www.accac.org.uk

SCOTLAND

The content and management of the curriculum in Scotland are not prescribed by statute but are the responsibility of education authorities and individual head teachers. Advice and guidance are provided by the Scottish Executive Education Department and Learning and Teaching Scotland, which also has a developmental role. Those bodies have produced guidelines on the structure and balance of the curriculum as well as for each of five broad curriculum areas for the five to 14 age group. There are also guidelines on, assessment across the whole curriculum, on reporting to parents, and on the use of national tests for reading, writing and mathematics at six levels. Testing is carried out by the school when the teacher judges that a pupil has completed a level; most pupils are expected to move from one level to the next at roughly 18-month to two-year intervals. Guidance on the curriculum for 14- to 16-year-olds recommends study within each of eight modes: language and communication; mathematical studies; science; technology; social studies; creative activities; physical education; and religious and moral education. There is also a recommended percentage of time to be devoted to each area over the two years. Provision is also made for teaching in Gaelic in many parts of Scotland and the number of pupils, at all levels from nursery to secondary, in Gaelic-medium Education is growing. Local authorities must ensure that local education provision meets demand and consider whether they need a Gaelic-medium class, school or unit. For 16- to 18-year-olds, National Qualifications, a unified framework of courses and awards which brings together both academic and vocational courses, was introduced in 1999. The Scottish Qualifications Authority awards the certificates.

W www.sqa.org.uk

NORTHERN IRELAND

The statutory Northern Ireland curriculum is made up of religious education and five broad areas of study at primary level and six at secondary level. Provided the requirements of the statutory curriculum are met, it is for each school to decide what additional subjects should be made available for pupils. Pupils at key stages 1 and 2 study religious education, English, mathematics, science, history and geography (known as the environment and society area of study), art and design, music and PE (the creative and expressive area of study), Irish (in Irish-language schools only) and four educational cross-curricular themes (education for mutual understanding, cultural heritage, health education and information technology). At key stage 3, pupils also study technology and design, plus a foreign language (pupils in Irish-language schools can study a foreign language or continue studying Irish) and two extra cross-curricular themes (economic awareness and careers education). At key stage 4, pupils can drop technology and design, art and design, and music and can choose one subject from history, geography, business studies, home economics, economics, political studies or social and environmental studies. The Government accepted proposals from The Northern Ireland Council for the Curriculum Examinations and Assessment (CCEA) for a revised Northern Ireland Curriculum in June 2004. The necessary legislation to implement the revised curriculum will be in place by September 2006, and the new curriculum will be phased in over a number of years to allow schools to plan for and implement the changes. A number of elements of the revised curriculum are being piloted in advance of implementation. The revised curriculum will be less prescriptive in terms of content, and more holistic and flexible. There will be greater emphasis on developing skills (such as communication, numeracy and ICT, along with thinking skills such as creativity, team-work and problem-solving) and a new area of Learning for Life and Work at key stages 3 and 4 that will include Education for Employability, Citizenship and Personal, Social and Health Education (PSHE). In addition to RE, the other Learning Areas (which will replace Areas of Study) are:

Key Stages 1 and 2	Key Stages 3 and 4
The Arts	Learning for Life and Work
Language and Literacy	The Arts
Mathematics and Numeracy	Language and Literacy
Personal Development and	Mathematics
Mutual Understanding	Modern Languages
Physical Education	Physical Education
The World Around Us	Science and Technology

The assessment of pupils is broadly in line with practice in England and Wales and takes place at the ages of eight, 11 and 14, i.e. end of key stage assessment. With the introduction of the revised curriculum, this will be replaced by annual reporting in the form of a Pupil Profile. Teachers will assess pupils in the skills of communication, numeracy and ICT and assign a numerical level of progression. Teachers will also comment on a pupil's progress and areas for future development in the other thinking skills and in the learning areas. The GCSE is used to assess 16-year-olds. The CCEA is a unique education body in the UK in that it combines the three functions of a curriculum advisory body, an awarding body and a qualifications regulatory body. It monitors and advises the Department of Education and teachers on all matters relating to the curriculum, assessment arrangements and examinations in grant-aided schools. It conducts GCSE, A- and AS-level examinations, pupil assessment at key stages one, two and three and administers the transfer procedure tests. It also ensures that qualifications offered by awarding bodies in Northern Ireland are of an appropriate quality and standard.

W www.ccea.org.uk

PUBLIC EXAMINATIONS AND QUALIFICATIONS

ENGLAND, WALES AND NORTHERN IRELAND

In 1988 a single system of examinations, the General Certificate of Secondary Education (GCSE), which is usually taken after five years of secondary education, was introduced. The GCSE is the main method of assessing the performance of pupils on a subject-specific basis. The structure of the examination reflects National Curriculum requirements where these apply. GCSE short-course qualifications are available in some subjects. As a rule the syllabus comprises half the content of a full GCSE course. In September 2002 eight GCSEs in vocational subjects were introduced (known as Applied GCSEs) and they are: Applied Art and Design, Applied Business, Engineering, Health and Social Care, Applied ICT, Leisure and Tourism, Manufacturing, and Applied Science.

The GCSE differs from its predecessors in that there are syllabuses based on national criteria covering course objectives, content and assessment methods; differentiated assessment (i.e. different papers or questions for different ranges of ability) and grade-related criteria (i.e. grades awarded on absolute rather than relative performance). The GCSE certificates are awarded on an eight-point scale, A* to G. All GCSE syllabuses, assessments and grading procedures are monitored by the Qualifications and Curriculum Authority to ensure that they conform to the national criteria. In England in 2004, 53.7 per cent of 15- to 16-year olds gained at least five results at grade C or better at GCSE or General National Vocational Qualification (GNVQ) equivalent (59.5 per cent in Northern Ireland), while 88.8 per cent achieved five or more at grade G or above. Students are increasingly encouraged to continue their education post-16. For those who do so, in addition to the vocational qualifications outlined below, there are GCE (General Certificate of Education), AS (Advanced Subsidiary) and A (Advanced) Levels and the advanced Vocational Certificate of Education (VCE). Since September 2005 VCEs will have AS/A2 units, bringing them into line with GCE A-levels. At the same time the formal distinction between GCEs and VCEs was dropped and both vocational and academic qualifications are now known as GCEs. However, a small number of subjects – Art and Design, Business, ICT and science – are currently available as GCEs and VCEs. In order to distinguish between the different patterns of study and assessment in these qualifications, the term applied' will be introduced into the current vocational qualification in these subjects: for example, the current VCE in Art and Design will be known as the GCE A-level in Applied Art and Design. A-level courses usually last two years and have traditionally provided the foundation for entry to higher education. AS-level qualifications were introduced in September 2000 and represent the first half of a full A-level and is assessed accordingly. Following extensive consultations in 1996 and 1997 which indicated the need to broaden the post-16 curriculum, new A-level qualifications were introduced in September 2000. The new A-level qualification consists of six units (three AS units and three A2 units). Students who go on to complete the full A-level will be assessed on their attainment in all six units, which may be taken either in stages or at the end of the course. A-levels and AS-levels are marked on a six-point scale from A to E. There is also the opportunity for A-level candidates to take additional papers known as Advanced Extension Awards (which replaced Special papers) and these are designed to challenge the most able A-level students.

VOCATIONAL QUALIFICATIONS

National Vocational Qualifications (NVQs) in the form of General NVQs (GNVQs) are gradually being phased out and replaced with vocational GCSEs in schools. The Advanced GNVQ has been replaced by the Advanced Vocational Certificate of Education (AVCE) or vocational A-Level which exists in three, six or 12-unit forms, equivalent to an AS-level, an A-level and 2 A-levels respectively. Many maintained schools offer BTEC Firsts and an increasing number offer BTEC Nationals.

There are three unitary awarding bodies (UABs) in England offering GNVQs, GCSEs, AS- and A-levels. The bodies are the Assessment and Qualifications Alliance (AQA), Edexcel, and Oxford, Cambridge and RSA Examinations (OCR). The Joint Council for Qualifications (JCQ) co-ordinates the work of the three English UABs, the Welsh Joint Education Committee and the Northern Ireland Council for the Curriculum, Examinations and Assessment.

SCOTLAND

Scotland has its own system of public examinations, and in 1999 a new system of National Qualifications was introduced. Five levels of study are offered: Access, Intermediate 1, Intermediate 2, Higher and Advanced Higher. The new Higher National course and Advanced Higher National course are direct replacements for the old SCE Higher grade and the Certificate of Sixth Year Studies respectively. National Qualifications are included on the Scottish Credit and Qualifications Framework (SCQF) (see below), with Access equating to levels 1 to 3, Intermediate 1 to level 4, Intermediate 2 to level 5, Higher to level 6 and Advanced Higher to level 7.

National Courses consist of blocks of study called National Units. A unit usually consists of around 40 hours of study and there are three units in a course. Unit awards demonstrate that a learner has achieved competence in a particular area of study. National Course awards are graded by external assessment, which consists of an examination, coursework or performance, or a combination of two or more of these. National Course awards also require candidates to pass all unit assessments of the course. A typical National Course external assessment requires candidates to demonstrate long-term retention of knowledge, high levels of problem solving, integration of knowledge across a whole course and an ability to apply knowledge and skills in novel situations. The range of subjects has been expanded to include vocational qualifications.

A number of schools use the new National Qualifications system for pupils in their fourth year of secondary education, but the majority of this lower age group still take the traditional Standard Grade examinations at the end of a two-year course. Awards at Standard Grade are set at three levels: Credit (leading to awards at grade 1 or 2); General (leading to awards at grade 3 or 4); and Foundation (leading to awards at grade 5 or 6). Grade 7 is awarded to those who, although they have completed the course, have not attained any of these levels. Normally pupils will take examinations covering two pairs of grades, either grades 1–4 or grades 3–6. Most candidates take seven or eight Standard Grade examinations. The three levels of Standard Grade equate to levels 3 to 5 of the SCQF.

THE INTERNATIONAL BACCALAUREATE

The International Baccalaureate (IB) Organization is a non-profit foundation that offers three challenging educational programmes – the Primary Years Programme for students aged 3 to 12, the Middle Years Programme for students aged 11 to 16 and the Diploma Programme for students aged 16 to 19. Each programme can be taught in its own right, but, when linked together, they form a continuum of education for students aged 3 to 19. The programmes consist of a curriculum or curriculum framework and a pedagogy promoting good teaching practice; methods of student assessment appropriate to the age range; professional development and support opportunities for educators; and an ongoing process of school evaluation. The programmes are offered through IB World Schools (of which there are 79 in the UK and over 1,500 worldwide) and are well recognised by governments and universities around the world. More than half of the 200,000 students currently participating in IB programmes are in state funded schools.

W www.ibo.org

PROGRESS FILE

Progress File is the successor to the National Record of Achievement. Progress File is an interactive set of guides designed to help young people and adults identify their skills. It enables individuals to manage their learning through promoting ongoing reviewing, planning and development, and recording achievement as part of lifelong learning. The Progress File objectives are to equip people to plan and manage their learning and make effective transitions; to increase motivation and confidence to achieve; and to stimulate learning to gain knowledge and skills, in areas perhaps not otherwise recognised in national qualifications.

W www.dfes.gov.uk/progressfile/

TEACHERS

ENGLAND AND WALES

All teachers working in maintained primary, special and secondary schools, non-maintained special schools and pupil referral units are required to register with the General Teaching Council for England (GTCE) in England and the General Teaching Council for Wales (GTCW) in Wales. GTCE: W www.gtce.org.uk GTCW: W www.gtcw.org.uk

New entrants to the teaching profession in state primary and secondary schools are required to be graduates and to have Qualified Teacher Status (QTS). QTS is achieved by successfully completing a course of initial teacher training, traditionally either a Bachelor of Education (BEd) degree, BA with QTS, BSc with QTS or the Postgraduate Certificate of Education (PGCE) at an accredited institution. New entrants are statutorily required to serve a three term (full-time, pro rata part-time) induction period during which they will have a structured programme of support. All initial teacher training has a strong element of practical school-based work, with student teachers spending significant periods of their training in the classroom.

In addition to the traditional routes, in recent years various employment-based routes to QTS have been developed. The Graduate Teacher Programme (GTP) is designed for mature, well-qualified people who can quickly take on teaching responsibilities and who need to earn a living while they train. Trainees are paid a salary and undergo up to a year of school-based training. The Registered Teacher Programme (RTP) is designed for people without a degree or formal teaching qualification but with at least two years of higher education; entrants are paid a salary and complete a degree while undergoing training for up to two years. Employment-based training routes account for about 15 per cent of all teacher training places.

Teachers in further education are not required to have QTS, though roughly half have a teaching qualification and most have industrial, commercial or professional experience. Since July 2002, all new entrants to FE teaching in Wales are required to have, or to be working towards, a specified FE teaching qualification. A qualification for aspiring head teachers, the National Professional Qualification for Headship (NPQH), has been introduced. The National College for School Leadership administers this qualification and others and acts as a focus for development and support. In Wales, the NPQH and other headship programmes are administered by the Welsh Assembly Government and consideration is being given to establishing a similar scheme in respect of FE principals, in association with

powers under the Education Act 2002 allowing the making of regulations requiring FE principals to have a specified qualification.

New financial incentives for trainee teachers are being introduced from September 2006. Maths and science postgraduate trainees may be eligible for a £9,000 tax free bursary while they train, and a £5,000 taxable 'golden hello' after successfully completing the induction period. Modern languages, English or drama, design and technology, ICT, music and religious education Postgraduate trainees may be eligible for a £9,000 training bursary and a £2,500 'golden hello'. A £6,000 training bursary is available for other postgraduate secondary and primary trainees. In Wales a similar scheme operates, on a pilot basis, for those undertaking the full-time PGCE (FE) or PGCE (PcET) (Post-compulsory Education and Training). Eligible students receive a bursary of £6,000 (£7,000 for mathematics and science courses since September 2005), paid in instalments whilst studying. In England, other training awards may be available through the Secondary Shortage Subject Scheme (SSSS). This is an additional, means-tested hardship fund from the Teacher Training and Development Agency for Schools. The subjects currently included are: design and technology, geography, information technology, mathematics, modern languages, music, religious education and science.

In Wales, placement grants supported by the Higher Education Funding Council for Wales (HEFCW) provide £1,000 per funded student on undergraduate priority courses – the same subjects that attract the £4,000 training grant – and £600 to students on other undergraduate courses.

The Teacher Training Agency became the Training and Development Agency for Schools (TDA) in September 2005. In addition to attracting quality people to initial teacher training (ITT), funding universities, colleges and schools to deliver ITT and working to improve the quality of training, the agency's new role will be to work with schools to help them develop and train their whole school team. The TDA administers returners' programme for qualified teachers who wish to refresh their skills before returning to the profession. Participants are entitled to a bursary of up to £150 a week to a total of £1,500 and additional childcare support. The TDA supports the sharing of good practice in teacher training, encourages schools to offer placements for trainee teachers, and funds training and assessment for higher level teaching assistant (HLTA) status.

In Wales funding of ITT is undertaken by the HEFCW. On an integrated England and Wales basis the TDA also acts as a central source of information and advice on entry to teaching.

The General Teaching Council for England, an independent professional council, acts as a disciplinary body dealing with cases of misconduct and incompetence in England. It is also responsible for promoting the profession and professional standards and for advising the Secretary of State. The separate General Teaching Council for Wales fulfils a similar role in Wales and provides advice to the Welsh Assembly Government.

The Specialist Teacher Assistant scheme provides trained support to qualified teachers in the teaching of reading, writing and arithmetic to young pupils.

TDA: W www.teach.gov.uk; HLTA: W www.hlta.gov.uk NPQH: W www.teachernet.gov.uk/management/profession development/npqh

In January 2003 the DfES, Welsh Assembly Government, employers and teaching unions signed a national agreement, 'Raising Standards and Tackling Workload', setting out a three-year programme of reforms to provide more classroom support for teachers.

SCOTLAND

The General Teaching Council (GTC) for Scotland advises central government on matters relating to teacher supply and the professional suitability of all teacher training courses. The GTC is also the body responsible for disciplinary procedures in cases of professional misconduct. All teachers in maintained schools must be registered with the GTC. Only graduates are accepted as entrants to the profession; primary school teachers undertake either a four-year vocational degree course or a one-year postgraduate course, while teachers of academic subjects in secondary schools undertake the latter. There is also a combined degree sometimes known as a concurrent degree.

The Scottish Qualification for Headship has been introduced for aspiring head teachers. Universities with specialist education departments provide both in-service and pre-service training for teachers. The universities are funded by the Scottish Higher Education Funding Council, which also sets intake levels for teacher education courses in line with guidance provided by the Scottish Executive.

GTCS: W www.gtcs.org.uk; Scottish Qualification for Headship: W www.sqh.ed.ac.uk

NORTHERN IRELAND

All new entrants to teaching in grant-aided schools are graduates and hold an approved teaching qualification. A fully integrated programme of Initial Teacher Education (ITE), induction and early professional development as well as the Professional Qualification for Headship (PQH(NI)) programme, is in place in Northern Ireland. ITE is provided by Queen's University, Belfast, University of Ulster, Stranmillis University College, St Mary's University College and the Open University (NI). The university colleges are concerned with teacher education mainly for the primary school sector and the universities mainly for the post-primary sector. The General Teaching Council for Northern Ireland advises government on professional issues, maintains a register of professional teachers and acts as a disciplinary body.

GTCNI: W www.gtcni.org.uk; PQH(NI): W www.rtuni.org.pqhni.cfm

QUALIFIED TEACHERS 2002–3 (Full-time (*thousands**))

	E&W	Scotland	NI	Total UK
Maintained nursery and primary schools	179.5	21.5	8.1	209.1
Maintained secondary schools	197.3	23.1	10.1	230.5
Non-maintained mainstream schools	51.0	2.5	0.1	53.6
All special schools	14.3	2.1	0.7	17.1
Total	442.1	49.1	19.0	510.2

*Provisional

SALARIES

Qualified teachers in England, Wales and Northern Ireland, other than the leadership group (which includes head teachers, deputy head teachers and advanced skills teachers) are paid on a six-point main pay scale. Teachers who demonstrate exceptional ability have the opportunity to be assessed against national standards and moving to the three point upper scale. An 'Excellent Teacher' scheme is being developed now which, subject to consideration by the School Teachers' Review Body, would allow further salary progression. Entry points and placement depend on relevant experience. There are additional cash allowances for management responsibilities, special needs work and recruitment and retention factors which may be awarded at the discretion of the relevant body, i.e. the governing body or the LEA. The 'advanced skills teacher' grade was introduced to enhance prospects in the classroom for the most able teachers; this grade does not apply in Northern Ireland. Experienced teachers are assessed against national standards to move onto the upper pay scale, after which they receive performance-related pay increases. There is a statutory superannuation scheme. Teachers working in the London area are paid on separate pay scales. Teachers in Northern Ireland have, with a few exceptions, the same pay and working conditions as teachers in England and Wales under a long-established principle of parity negotiated at the Teachers' Salaries and Conditions of Service Committee (Schools) which comprises the employing authorities, the Department of Education and the five recognised teacher unions. In Northern Ireland the Teachers' Negotiating Committee will consider both the Excellent Teachers' Scheme and the introduction of Teaching and Learning Responsibility payments in due course. A Performance Review and Staff Development scheme has been agreed and was implemented from September 2005 in Northern Ireland. This will be used as part of a body of evidence to inform progression up the upper pay scale. As at September 2005, salary scales for teachers in England, Wales and Northern Ireland were:

Head teacher	£37,344–£92,619+
Principal (Northern Ireland)	£37,617–£88,797
Deputy-head/Vice-principal (Northern Ireland)	from £33,249
Advanced skills teacher	£31,263–£49,872
Teacher (Northern Ireland)	£19,161–£32,628
Inner London	
Head teacher	£43,587–£98,862+
Deputy head teacher	from £39,249
Advanced skills teacher	£37,509–£56,115
Teacher	£22,611–£38,634

Teachers in Scotland are paid on a seven-point scale. The entry point depends on type of qualification and additional allowances are payable under a range of circumstances. As at 1 April 2005, salary scales for teachers in Scotland were:

Head teacher/deputy head teacher	£37,590–£73,377
Principal teacher	£33,141–£42,780
Chartered teacher	£31,341–£37,269
Main grade	£19,059–£30,399

POST-16 EDUCATION

In the United Kingdom in 2001–2, 77 per cent of 16-year-olds and 65 per cent of 17-year-olds were in post-compulsory education, either at school or in full-time further education or in Government supported training. There were over 4.75 million further education students in the UK during the academic year 2002–3, of which 78 per cent were part-time. The number of students by country of study in 2002–3 was (in thousands):

	Full-time	Part-time
UK	1,026.7	3,701.6
England	914.5	3,104.7
Wales	44.85	213.7
Scotland*	46.0	329.3
Northern Ireland	21.5	54.0
* Enrolments, not head count		

In 2003–4, there were 465 further education colleges in the UK of which 102 were sixth form colleges. In 2002–3, there were 59,000 full-time academic staff in further education institutions.

ENGLAND AND WALES

Further education and sixth form colleges are funded directly by central government through the Learning and Skills Council in England, which operates through 47 local offices, nine regions and a National Office in Coventry, and Education and Learning Wales (ELWa), in Wales. Further education colleges are controlled by autonomous further education corporations, which include substantial representation from industry and commerce, and which own their own assets and employ their own staff. Their funding is determined in part by the number of students enrolled and their level of achievement.

Further education tends to be broadly vocational in purpose and employers are often involved in designing courses. It ranges from lower-level technical and commercial courses and government-sponsored training, through courses for those aiming at higher-level posts in industry, commerce and administration, to professional courses. Facilities exist for GCE A- and AS-levels, GCSEs, GNVQs and a full range of vocational qualifications. These courses can form the foundation for progress to higher education qualifications. Many students attend part-time, either through day or block release from employment, or in the evenings. Adult learners usually form the largest proportion of students in further education colleges, often studying part-time in the evening or at weekends. The main courses and examinations in the vocational field, all of which link in with the National Qualification Framework, are offered by a wide and diverse range of awarding bodies.

Details of the awarding bodies offering vocational qualifications can be found at the QCA website: W www.qca.org.uk; the Learning and Skills Council, England: W www.lsc.gov.uk; ELWa, Wales: W www.elwa.ac.uk

WORK-BASED LEARNING

Apprenticeships are a way for learners to get practical experience while gaining nationally recognised qualifications. The Learning and Skills Council in England and ELWa in Wales contribute towards the cost of the training and assessment. Apprenticeships normally last between one and three years (four in Wales) and there are two levels: Foundation Modern Apprenticeships and Advanced Apprenticeships at Levels 2 and 3 respectively. Both of these lead to:

• National Vocational Qualifications
• Key Skills qualifications – transferable work-related skills like IT and communication, problem solving, application of number and IT, improving learning, and performance and teamwork.

• Technical certificates – vocationally related qualifications that provide the basic knowledge of the NVQ

There are currently over 255,500 young people aged between 16 to 24 on Apprenticeships in England alone with similar programmes in place in Scotland, Northern Ireland and Wales

In May 2004 the new family of Apprenticeships was announced, incorporating Young Apprenticeships for 14–16 year olds, which was launched in September 2004 with 1,000 young people. A further 2,000 young people will join the programme from September 2005. The reforms also led to the opening up of Adult Apprenticeships by scrapping the arbitrary 25 year old age limit. Trials have now begun in the Engineering, Construction and Health sectors. There are no plans for any more trials at present.

Since January 2004 the Apprenticeship programme in Wales have been open to all people irrespective of age and who have left full-time statutory education W www.realworkrealpay.info

SCOTLAND

Since Autumn 2005, the Scottish Further and Higher Education Funding Council has been the statutory body responsible for funding the 44 further education colleges. The Scottish Qualifications Authority (SQA) is the statutory awarding body for qualifications in the national education and training system in Scotland. It is both the main awarding body for qualifications for work including Scottish Vocational Qualifications (SVQs) and is also the accrediting body. The SQA is by statute required clearly to separate its awarding and accrediting functions. There are three main qualification 'families' in Scottish further education: National Qualifications; Higher National Qualifications (HNC and HND); and SVQs. In addition to Standard Grade qualifications, National Qualifications are available at five levels: Access, Intermediate 1, Intermediate 2, Higher and Advanced Higher. Another feature of the qualifications system is the Scottish Group Award (SGA). SGAs are built up unit by unit and allow opportunity for credit transfer from other qualifications (such as Standard Grade or SVQ), providing a further option for learners, especially adult learners. SVQs are competence-based qualifications suitable for workplace delivery but they can also be taken in further education colleges and other centres where work-place conditions can be simulated. The Scottish Credit and Qualifications Framework includes qualifications across academic and vocational sectors in a single credit-based framework. It comprises 12 levels, covering mainstream qualifications from Access level in National Qualifications to postgraduate qualifications, and including SVQs. In the academic year 2003–4 there were 467,895 student enrolments on vocational and non-vocational courses in further education colleges. Of the total, higher educational courses accounted for 26 per cent of college activity.

Scottish Further Education Funding Council W www.sfefc.ac.uk; SQA: W www.sqa.org.uk

NORTHERN IRELAND

All further education colleges are independent corporate bodies like their counterparts in the rest of the UK. Responsibility for the sector lies with the Department for

Employment and Learning (DELNI), which funds the colleges directly. The colleges own their own property, are responsible for their own services and employ their own staff.

The governing bodies of the colleges must include at least 50 per cent membership from those who are engaged or employed in business, industry, or any profession.

Northern Ireland has 16 institutions of further education, and in 2002–3 there were 21,464 full-time and 53,989 part-time enrolments on vocational further education courses.

W www.delni.gov.uk

STUDENT SUPPORT

Education Maintenance Allowance (EMA) is a means-tested allowance to support young people in post-16 education. It was introduced in England, Scotland and Northern Ireland in September 2004 and is now available in Wales. EMA consists of a weekly allowance of up to £30, plus periodic bonus payments and is available to students from low-income households who are aged 16 and 17 in the academic year 2005–6 and staying on at school and college. EMA is normally available for up to 3 years. Also available to students in England in that age group are Learner Support Funds. These funds, which are targeted at those students in greatest need, have four separate strands: Transport, Childcare (Care2Learn), Residential and General funding. Whilst the funding for both transport and childcare are universal, the discretionary nature of the other funds allows local learning institutions to provide targeted help and support where it is needed. In England, the Adult Learning Grant (ALG) is a grant of up to £30 per week for adults who are on low incomes. It is paid to learners who are studying full time for their first full level 2 (five GCSEs or equivalent) or first full level 3 qualification (two A levels or equivalent). ALG aims to encourage adults to participate and to stay in learning, by providing a regular source of financial support during term time. ALG is administered by the Learning Skills Council and piloted in over one hundred and fifty further education providers across 19 Learning and Skills Council areas. Eligible Welsh-domiciled students aged over 18 on further education courses, whether full-time or part-time subject to a minimum contact requirement), receive a means-tested non-repayable Assembly Learning Grant. The grant is administered by local education authorities. Discretionary Financial Contingency Funds are also available to all students suffering hardship and are administered by the institutions themselves. In addition, individual Learning Accounts are available in Wales, which provide adults with means-tested support of up to £200 to undertake a wide range of learning. Eligible Scottish-domiciled further education students can apply to their college for discretionary support in the form of bursaries. These can include allowances for maintenance, travel, study, dependants and additional support needs. College students receiving EMAs may also be eligible for the non-maintenance elements. Colleges administer discretionary funds in the form of hardship funds. They also have a childcare fund which is used to pay for registered childcare. Some colleges may offer different methods of childcare support and provision, for example on-site nurseries or childcare vouchers.

Full-time students over 19 years of age and resident in Northern Ireland, on certain vocational courses, may benefit from discretionary non-repayable further education bursaries. The bursaries are administered by the education and library boards. Support for further education students in Northern Ireland includes free tuition to all full-time students up to age 18 and to all full-time students over 18 undertaking a vocational course at level 3 or below. In addition, financial help is provided by colleges through a discretionary support fund for both full-time and part-time students whose access to and participation in further education is inhibited by financial considerations.

VOCATIONAL QUALIFICATIONS

National Vocational Qualifications (NVQs) are work-related competence-based qualifications. They are designed to reflect the skills and knowledge needed to do a job effectively, and represent national standards recognised by employers. General National Vocational Qualifications (GNVQs) are now being replaced by vocational GCSEs. These are available in the following subjects: applied art and design, applied business, engineering, health and social care, applied ICT, leisure and tourism, manufacturing, applied science.

The Advanced Vocational Certificate of Education (VCE), replaced Advanced GNVQs. It is available in different forms: the three-unit Advanced Subsidiary (equivalent to one GCE AS-level), the six-unit Advanced Level (equivalent to one GCE A-level), and the 12-unit Double Award (equivalent to two GCE A-levels). The timetable for the withdrawal of the individual 6-unit GNVQ titles was issued by the Qualifications and Curriculum Authority in November 2003. The withdrawal is taking place in three stages from 2005 to 2007, starting with titles with extremely low numbers of candidate entries. QCA has identified and advised schools and colleges of alternative qualifications for each of the GNVQ subject areas.

'New Deal' is a government programme administered by the Department of Work and Pensions. It aims to help unemployed people to get off benefits and into employment, and to improve the skills base of the workforce. The New Deal for Young People is mandatory for all 18–24 year olds who have been claiming Jobseeker's Allowance (JSA) for 6 months. New Deal 25 Plus is mandatory for those aged 25 and over who have been claiming Jobseeker's Allowance for 18 months or 18 out of the last 21 months. There are also voluntary New Deal programmes for lone parents; people aged 50 and over; disabled people, and partners of those claiming benefits.

HIGHER EDUCATION

The term higher education is used to describe education above A-level, Higher and Advanced Higher Grade and their equivalent, which is provided in universities, colleges of higher education and in some further education colleges.

The main purposes of higher education are:
• To enable people to develop their capabilities and fulfil their potential, both personally and at work
• To advance knowledge and understanding through scholarship and research
• To contribute to an economically successful and culturally diverse nation.

STUDENT NUMBERS IN THE UK

Higher Education student numbers in the UK (including UK, other European Union, and non-European-Union students) in 2003–4 were:

	Total	Full-time	Part-time
Total HE students	2,247,440	–	–
Total post-graduate students	523,830	220,395	303,435
Total undergraduate students	1,723,610	1,141,850	581,760

Higher Education qualifications obtained in the UK in 2003–4 were:

	Full-time	Part-time
HE qualifications obtained	425,260	170,380
First degrees	260,450	31,640
Higher degrees	79,020	31,690
Other postgraduate	39,785	31,585
Other graduate	46,000	75,465

Advice to government on matters relating to higher education is provided by the separate Higher Education Funding Councils for England, Wales and Scotland, and by the Northern Ireland Higher Education Council. The former receive a block grant from central government which they allocate to the universities and colleges. In Northern Ireland the grant is allocated directly to institutions by the Department for Employment and Learning.

England: **W** www.hefc.ac.uk; Wales: **W** www.hefcw.ac.uk; Scotland: **W** www.shefc.ac.uk; Northern Ireland: **W** www.delni.gov.uk

TYPES OF HIGHER EDUCATION INSTITUTION

The Further and Higher Education Act 1992 and parallel legislation in Scotland removed the distinction between higher education provided by the universities and that provided in England and Wales by the former polytechnics and colleges of higher education and in Scotland by the former polytechnics, central institutions and others. It allowed all polytechnics, and other higher education institutions which satisfy the necessary criteria, to award their own taught course and research degrees and to adopt the title of university. All the polytechnics, and some colleges of higher education have since done so. The change of name does not affect the legal constitution of the institutions. Funding is by the Higher Education Funding Councils for England, Wales and Scotland and directly by the Department for Employment and Learning in Northern Ireland. There are now 89 universities in the UK whereas only 48 existed prior to the Further and Higher Education Acts 1992. Of the 89, 72 are in England (including the University of London, which has a federal structure), two in Wales (one a federal institution comprising six constituent institutions and two university colleges), 13 in Scotland (14 including the Open University in Scotland) and two in Northern Ireland. There are also 64 colleges of higher education, some of which are multidisciplinary while others specialise, for example, in teacher training. Some award their own degrees and qualifications, while others are validated by a university or a national body.

GOVERNANCE OF UNIVERSITIES AND COLLEGES

The pre-1992 universities each have their own system of internal governance but broad similarities exist. Most are run by two main bodies: the senate, which deals primarily with academic issues and consists of members elected from within the university; and the council, which is the executive governing body and is responsible for all appointments and promotions, and bidding for and allocation of financial resources. At least half the members of the council are drawn from outside the university. Many of the council's functions are carried out through committees. Joint committees of senate and council are common. The 1992 Act, and the Education reform Act 1988, set out the system of governance for universities which were formerly polytechnics or other higher education institutions and for the colleges of higher education. Each institution also has articles of government that are approved by the Privy Council. These post-1992 institutions are run by boards of governors, which are responsible for the mission, finances and all appointments. Much of the board's business is delegated to committees. In particular, there is usually an academic board that deals with all matters relating to teaching and research.

OPEN UNIVERSITY AND THE UNIVERSITY FOR INDUSTRY

The non-residential Open University provides a modular programme of courses throughout the UK leading to first and higher degrees, diplomas and certificates. Students are taught through distance learning, using written and audio-visual materials and the internet, supported by tutorials and short residential courses. No qualification are needed for entry at undergraduate level. The Open University received £174.1 million in public funding 2003–4. In 2003–4, 160,000 undergraduates were registered. The University for Industry (Ufi) Ltd operate the learndirect and UK online network and services and i the largest government backed supported e-learning organisation in the world. Ufi aims to boost people' employability, by helping them gain skills and qualifications, as well as improve organisations' productivity and competitiveness. Through the nationa network of over 2,000 learndirect centres in England Wales and Northern Ireland and 6,000 UK onlin centres in England, Ufi provides access and support to range of services from taster and skills-check activities t e-learning courses which are linked to qualifications. I addition, learndirect – the National Learning Advic Service provides impartial information, advice an guidance to callers on more than 900,000 course nationally from thousands of providers. There is on private university in England, the University c Buckingham, which receives no public funding.

SCOTLAND

The Scottish Higher Education Funding Counc (SHEFC) funds 20 institutions of higher educatio including 14 universities. The universities are broadl managed as described above and the remaining colleg are managed by independent governing bodies whic include representatives of industrial, commercia professional and educational interests.

NORTHERN IRELAND
In Northern Ireland higher education is provided in the 16 colleges of further education, the two universities and the two university colleges. These institutions offer a range of courses, including first and postgraduate degrees, PGCEs, undergraduate diplomas and certificates, and professional qualifications.

ACADEMIC STAFF
Each university and college appoints its own academic staff. The Universities and Colleges Employers Association (UCEA) is the employers' association for subscribing universities and other higher education institutions in the UK. It provides a framework within which representatives of institutions can discuss salaries, conditions of service, employee relations and all matters connected with the employment of staff and employees. The services of the UCEA include collective bargaining and an annual salary survey. Teaching staff in higher education require no formal teaching qualification. However, the Higher Education Academy leads, supports and informs the professional development and recognition of staff in higher education as well as promoting good practice and providing information, advice and resources. Teacher trainers are required to spend a certain amount of time in schools to ensure that they have sufficient recent practical experience.

W www.heacademy.ac.uk

In the academic year 2002–3 there were 137,000 full-time academic staff in all further and higher education institutions in the UK. Of these, 84,000 were male and 54,000 were female.

> As a result of the National Framework Agreement, staff working in higher education should be, since August 2004, paid to a single national pay scale. The Framework sought to unify pay arrangements as well as address concerns about equal pay. At a local level, universities and colleges are able to negotiate variants according to need.

Lecturers' Common Interest Group Higher Education Pay Scales since 1 August 2004, assuming assimilation to new pay scales. However, for many institutions this has been phased in between August 2004 and, in some cases, July 2006.

Grade Lecturer	£ p.a.
9	24,886
10	24,886
11	25,633
12	27,194
13	28,009
14	28,850
15	29,715
Senior Lecturer	
(b)	28,850
0	28,850
1	29,715
2	30,607
3	31,544
4	32,471
5	33,445
6	34,448
7	35,482
8	36,546

Principal lecturer	
0	37,643
1	37,643
2	37,643
3	37,643
4	38,772
5	39,935
6	41,133
7	42,367
8	42,367
9	43,638
Researcher A	
1	12,987
2	14,192
3	15,056
4	15,973
5	16,946
6	17,978
Researcher B	
1	19,645
2	19,645
3	20,842
4	22,111
5	22,774
6	24,161
7	24,868
8	25,633
9	27,194
10	28,009
11	28,850
Part-time hourly rates (£)	
I/II/III	32.42
IV	26.77
V	19.59

FINANCE
The total income of institutions of higher education in the UK in 2003–4 was (in £ thousands):

	£	% of total
Funding council grants	6,516,597	38.6
Tuition fees, education grants and contracts	4,078,976	24.2
Research grants and contracts	2,714,591	16.1
Other income	3,320,439	19.7
Endowment and investment income	236,438	1.4
Total	16,867,041	100

The total expenditure of institutions of higher education in the UK in 2003–4 was (in £ thousands):

	£	% of total
Staff costs	9,728,675	58.5
Other operating expenses	5,904,120	35.5
Depreciation	791,329	4.8
Interest payable	201,588	1.2
Total	16,625,712	100

COURSES
In the UK all universities and some colleges award their own degrees and other qualifications and may act as awarding and validating bodies for colleges. The power to award degrees is regulated by law and it is an offence to purport to award a UK degree unless authorised to do so. The Quality Assurance Agency for Higher Education advises government on applications for degree-awarding powers.

The Quality Assurance Agency for Higher Education is funded by subscriptions from universities and higher education institutions and through contracts with the main higher education funding bodies. It is governed by a board representing a range of interests. Of its 14 members, four are appointed by the representative bodies of the heads of higher education institutions, four are appointed by the funding bodies in higher education and six are independent directors with experience of industry, commerce or finance or the practice of a profession.

Facilities exist for full-time and part-time study, day release, sandwich or block release. Credit accumulation and transfer systems (CATS) allow a student to achieve a final qualification by accumulating credits for courses of study successfully achieved, or even professional experience, over a period.

Higher education courses comprise: first degree and postgraduate (including research); Diploma in Higher Education (DipHE); BTEC Higher National Diplomas (HND) and Higher National Certificates (HNC); and preparation for professional examinations.

The DipHE is commonly a two-year diploma usually intended to serve as a stepping stone to a degree course or other further study. The DipHE is awarded by the institution itself if it is accredited; by an accredited institution of its choice if not. The HNCs are awarded after two years' part-time study. The HNDs are awarded after two years' full-time, or three years' sandwich-course or part-time study.

The foundation degree, launched in 2001, is a two-year vocational higher education qualification which forms either a self-contained qualification or a basis for further study leading to an honours degree or further professional qualifications.

Undergraduate courses lead to the title of Bachelor, Bachelor of Arts (BA) and Bachelor of Science (BSc) being the most common, except in certain Scottish universities where Master is sometimes used for a first degree in arts subjects. For a higher degree the titles are Master of Arts (MA), Master of Science (MSc) and the research degrees of Master of Philosophy (MPhil) and Doctor of Philosophy (PhD or, at a few universities, DPhil).

Most undergraduate courses at universities and colleges of higher education run for three years, but some take four years or longer. Postgraduate studies vary in length.

Post-experience short courses form a significant part of higher education provision, reflecting the demand for professional and technical training. Most of these courses fund themselves.

W www.qaa.ac.uk

ADMISSIONS

The target proportion of 18- to 30-year-olds entering full-time higher education by 2010 is set in England at 50 per cent. Institutions suffer financial penalties if the number of students laid down for them by the funding councils is exceeded, but the individual university or college decides which students to accept. The formal entry requirements to most degree courses are two or more A-levels at grade E or above (or equivalent), and to HND courses one A-level (or equivalent). In practice, most offers of places require qualifications in excess of this, higher requirements usually reflecting the popularity of a course or institution. These requirements do not, however, exclude applications from students with a variety of non-GCSE qualifications or unquantified experience and skills. For admission to a degree, DipHE or HND, potential students apply through the Universities and Colleges Admission Service (UCAS), the organisation responsible for managing applications to higher education courses in the UK. UCAS operates an online application system. The aim is that by 2006, 100 per cent of applications will be received electronically. UCAS handles over 450,000 applications a year as the UK's only central admissions service for full-time higher education courses. The only exception among universities is the Open University, which conducts its own admissions. Applications for undergraduate teacher training courses are made through UCAS and for postgraduate teacher training, through the Graduate Teacher Training Registry. (Details of initial teacher training courses in Scotland can be obtained from those universities offering such courses, from Universities Scotland, and from the website created by the Scottish Executive to promote teaching: www.teachinginscotland.com. Since 2005, applications for postgraduate social work are also made through UCAS. For admission as a postgraduate student, universities and colleges normally require a good first degree in a subject related to the proposed course of study or research. Most applications are made to individual institutions, except for teaching and social work.

W www.ucas.ac.uk

FEES

Entrants to undergraduate courses living in England and Northern Ireland pay, directly to the institution, an annual contribution to their tuition fees (up to £1,175 in 2005–6) depending on their own level of income and that of their household. Those whose household's residual income is less than £22,010 pay nothing and those whose households have a residual income of £32,745 or more pay the full £1,175. The tuition fee contribution represents some 25 per cent of the average cost of a higher education course in the UK and the balance is paid out of public funds. Students from EU member countries pay fees at home student rates and, if studying at institutions in England, Wales and Northern Ireland, are liable to make an annual contribution to fees assessed against household income. Among the classes of students exempt from payment are eligible: Scottish-domiciled and EU students at Scottish institutions; students from England, Wales and Northern Ireland may be eligible in the fourth year for fee waiver support if they meet certain criteria while studying a degree course at a Scottish institution; existing students with mandatory awards (see below), for whom the grant-awarding body pays; students on certain courses of initial teacher training; medical students in the fifth year of their course; health professionals on National Health Service bursaries; and students in receipt of full fee support. For access courses fees payable can range from zero to several hundred pounds, depending on the learner's circumstances (e.g. they are on means-tested benefits), the provider's (FE college or university) fee remission policies, and the type of course (full- or part-time, and subject studied).

From 2006, support for students who normally live in Wales can apply to Student Finance Wales for a mean tested Assembly Learning Grant of up to £2,700 and a maintenance loan, the level of which will depend on family income and whether or not a student lives with their parents whilst studying, but 75 per cent is available to all students.

Students who normally live in Wales and who start studying in Wales in 2006–7 will pay an annual deferred fixed fee of £1,200. Students who normally live in Wales but choose to study elsewhere in the UK will be charged fees according to the fee regime of the country in which they study and that set by the institution. Student Finance Wales will provide a loan to defer this fee – but these students will not be entitled to a fee grant.

Fee levels in Wales will be the same for students who normally live elsewhere in the UK and hope to begin studying in Wales in academic year 2006–7. However, these students are not eligible to receive Student Finance Wales services. They should seek advice from their local funding bodies in respect of fee loans available.

STUDENT SUPPORT

LOANS

Since September 1998, the means-tested loan has been the main form of support for most undergraduate students in the UK on full-time or sandwich undergraduate courses of higher education. Students apply through LEAs in England and Wales, education and library boards in Northern Ireland and the Students Awards Agency in Scotland. Of the maximum loan, 75 per cent is available to all eligible students regardless of income; the remaining 25 per cent is means tested by the LEA. The loan rates for 2005–6 are:

Living in college/lodgings in London area	£5,175
Living in college/lodgings elsewhere	£4,195
Living in parental home	£3,320

In Scotland the loan is income-assessed and the maximum loan for 2005–6 is £4,195 for students living outside the parental home, and £3,320 for those living at home. An additional loan of up to £545 will be available to young students from families with an income of up to £19,730.

Extra income assessed loans are available to students whose courses last more than 30 term-time weeks or who need to study abroad in certain high-cost countries. Loans are available to students on designated courses. Certain residency conditions also apply. In 2003–4, 847,000 student support scheme students took out loans to the value of £2,705 million.

Repayment of income contingent loans begins in the April after the student has left their course. Those who pay tax through PAYE have repayments deducted from their salaries once they earn more than £15,000 a year. The self-employed make repayments through their tax returns. Repayments are calculated at 9 per cent of income over the threshold. If income falls below the threshold, repayments cease until income rises above it.

NON-REPAYABLE GRANTS AND ALLOWANCES

Higher Education Grants of £1,000 are available to students whose household income is £15,580 or less. Partial grants are available to those whose household income is between £15,581 and £21,561. Eligible Welsh-domiciled undergraduates from low-income families, whether on full-time or part-time courses, receive a means-tested non-repayable Assembly Learning Grant of up to £1,500 per year. The grant is administered by local education authorities. Eligible Scottish-domiciled students from low income families at institutions in Scotland may apply for a Young Students' Bursary. The maximum available in 2005–6 is £2,395. Full-time

students on a low income who are resident in Northern Ireland may benefit from discretionary non-repayable Access Bursaries of up to £2,000. The award of a bursary carries a reduction in student loan entitlement. The bursaries are administered by the education and library boards. Some students, such as those with children or other dependants, or those leaving care, can apply for additional means-tested help. Disabled students are eligible for non means-tested Disabled Students' Allowances.

HELP FOR PART-TIME STUDENTS

Part-time students on courses in England and Wales that are 50 per cent or more of an equivalent full-time course can apply for support towards their fee costs and their course costs. This help does not have to be repaid, and entitlement to the grants depends on the students' income and that of their husband, wife or partner.

CHANGES TO STUDENT FINANCE FROM 2006
New full-time students
From 2006, universities and colleges in England can charge new full-time undergraduate students up to £3,000 in tuition fees. But from September 2006, no eligible full-time undergraduate student will have to pay fees before they start their course or whilst they are studying, as they do now. Instead a Student Loan for Fees can be taken out, which does not have to be repaid until the course is finished and earnings are over £15,000.

Other aspects of the 2006 student support arrangements for 2006 starters include:
- A new Maintenance Grant worth up to £2,700 for eligible students from low income households
- Institutional bursaries – these will be at least £300 for students eligible for the full £2,700 grant and on courses charging £3,000, but many institutions are offering much more. Many bursaries are in the region of £1,000.
- All eligible students can also continue to apply for a Student Loan for Maintenance to help with living costs.

2006 existing students or gap year students
Existing full-time students or students who took a gap year from an English institution in 2005 and qualified for the gap year exemption will continue to be charged up to around £1,200 in tuition fees. Students from low-income households can continue to apply for the £1,000 higher education grant for help with tuition fees. These students will not be eligible for the new maintenance grant worth up to £2,700.

From 2006 all eligible full-time students – new and existing – can apply for a Student Loan for Fees to defer payment of their tuition fees.

LEARNER SUPPORT AND ACCESS FUNDS

Funds, known as the Access to Learning Fund in England (Hardship Funds in Scotland, Financial Contingency Funds in Wales and Support Funds in Northern Ireland) are allocated by central government to the appropriate funding councils in England and Wales and to the Student Awards Agency in Scotland, and are administered by further and higher education institutions. In Northern Ireland they are allocated by central government directly to the institution. Their purpose is to provide help for individual students facing financial difficulties. Generally, full-time or part-time undergraduates or postgraduates may apply. Universities and colleges manage their own procedures within national frameworks. The amount payable depends on individual circumstances and on the amount the institution has available.

POSTGRADUATE AWARDS

In general, postgraduate students do not qualify for mandatory support (including student loans and tuition fee assistance). An exception to this is the postgraduate Certificate in Education Studies for those wishing to become teachers.

Awards for postgraduate courses are the responsibility of the Research Councils, depending on the field of study. The Research Councils are independent bodies and make their own decisions about expenditure on postgraduate support according to the resources available to them. The fact that a course lies within its remit does not oblige the Research Councils to support all or indeed any student applying for awards.

It is for institutions to decide the level of their fees. The Government is raising the levels of award available to postgraduates under the competitive merit-based system provided by the Research Councils: the minimum PhD stipend will be £12,000 by 2005–6.

Targeted support is also available to meet particular needs: postgraduate students can apply through their colleges for discretionary help from the Access to Learning Fund. Disabled Students Allowances are also available to eligible students undertaking postgraduate study.

There is support available to students in Scotland for postgraduate study through the Postgraduate Students' Allowances Scheme (PSAS), which is administered by the Student Awards Agency for Scotland (SAAS). Eligible students can apply for an award consisting of a means tested maintenance grant and payment of tuition fees. Courses supported under PSAS are generally nine month taught postgraduate diploma courses on largely vocational subjects. Awards from PSAS are discretionary, not mandatory, so there is no guarantee of an award at postgraduate level.

ADULT AND CONTINUING EDUCATION

In the UK, the duty of securing adult and continuing education leading to academic or vocational qualifications is statutory. The Learning and Skills Council in England, the National Council for Education and Training in Wales and the Further Education Funding Council in Scotland are responsible for and fund those courses which take place in their sector and lead to academic and vocational qualifications, prepare students to undertake further or higher education courses, or confer basic skills; the Higher Education Funding Councils fund advanced courses of continuing education. The LEAs have the power, although not the duty, to provide those courses which do not fall within the remit of the funding bodies. In Northern Ireland the Department for Employment and

Learning is responsible for the funding of the statutory further education sector.

The involvement of universities in adult education and continuing education has diversified considerably. Birkbeck College, part of the University of London, offers a range of degree and other courses designed specifically to meet the needs of mature students. The post-1992 universities and the colleges of higher education, because of their range of courses and flexible patterns of student attendance, provide opportunities in the field of adult and continuing education. The Forum for the Advancement of Continuing Education promotes collaboration between institutions of higher education active in this area. The Open University, in partnership with the BBC, provides distance teaching leading to first degrees, and also offers post-experience and higher degree courses. Of the voluntary bodies providing adult education, the biggest is the Workers' Educational Association (WEA), which operates throughout the UK and provides over 10,000 courses each year, reaching more than 95,000 adults. The WEA is a charity supported by funding from the Learning and Skills Council in England, ELWa and by the Scottish Executive and local authorities in Scotland. NIACE, the National Institute of Adult Continuing Education, has a broad remit to promote lifelong learning opportunities for adults. NIACE works to develop increased participation in education and training in England and Wales, particularly for those currently under-represented. It does this through research and project work, conferences, publications and the provision of an information service to educational providers. NIACE and the Basic Skills Agency together manage the Community Learning Fund on behalf of the DfES. NIACE Dysgu Cymru, the Welsh committee, receives financial support from the National Assembly for Wales, support in kind from local authorities, and advises government, voluntary bodies and education providers on adult continuing education and training matters in Wales. In Scotland, policy responsibility for community learning and development lies with Learning Connections in Communities Scotland. In Northern Ireland, those functions are undertaken by the Department for Employment and Learning.

WEA: W www.wea.org.uk; NIACE: W www.niace.org.uk

The Adult Learning Inspectorate (ALI) is a non-departmental government-funded public body established under the Learning and Skills Act 2000 with the responsibility of raising the standards of education and training for young people and adults in England. It inspects and reports on the quality of education and training and can also be commissioned to inspect private training provision in the UK.

ALI: W www.ali.gov.uk

The Universities' Association for Continuing Education (UACE) represents and promotes the interests of continuing education and lifelong learning providers within higher education.

UACE: W www.uace.org.uk

EDUCATION DIRECTORY

LOCAL EDUCATION AUTHORITIES

ENGLAND

COUNTY COUNCILS

BEDFORDSHIRE County Hall, Cauldwell Street, Bedford
MK42 9AP **T** 01234-363222 **W** www.bedfordshire.gov.uk
Chief Executive, Andrea Hill

BUCKINGHAMSHIRE County Hall, Walton Street, Aylesbury
HP20 1UA **T** 01296-395000 **W** www.buckscc.gov.uk
Chief Education Officer, Sue Imbriano

CAMBRIDGESHIRE Box RES 1101, Shire Hall, Castle Hill,
Cambridge CB3 0AF **T** 01223-717111
W www.cambridgeshire.gov.uk
Chief Executive, Ian Stewart

CHESHIRE County Hall, Chester CH1 1SQ **T** 01244-602424
W www.cheshire.gov.uk
Chief Executive, Jeremy Taylor

CORNWALL County Hall, Treyew Road, Truro TR1 3AY
T 01872-322032 **W** www.cornwall.gov.uk
Director, Geoff Aver

CUMBRIA Cumbria Education Department, 5 Portland
Square, Carlisle CA1 1PU **T** 01228-606877
W www.cumbria.gov.uk/education
Corporate Director of Education, Ms V. Ashfield

DERBYSHIRE County Hall, Matlock DE4 3AG
T 01629-585814 **W** www.derbyshire.gov.uk
Chief Education Officer (acting), David Shaw

DEVON County Hall, Topsham Road, Exeter EX2 4QG
T 01392-382059 **W** www.devon.gov.uk
Director of Education, Phil Norrey

DORSET County Hall, Colliton Park, Dorchester DT1 1XJ
T 01305-224110 **W** www.dorsetforyou.com
Director, D. Goddard

DURHAM County Hall, Durham DH1 5UF **T** 0191-386 4411
W www.durham.gov.uk
Director, Keith Mitchell

EAST SUSSEX PO Box 4, County Hall, St Anne's Crescent,
Lewes BN7 1SG **T** 01273-481000
W www.eastsussexcc.gov.uk
Director of Children's Services, Matt Dunkley

ESSEX PO Box 47, Chelmsford CM2 6WN **T** 01245-492211
W www.essexcc.gov.uk
Head of Schools Service, Dr Carey Bennet

GLOUCESTERSHIRE Shire Hall, Westgate Street, Gloucester
GL1 2TG **T** 01452-425000 **W** www.gloucestershire.gov.uk
Chief Education Officer, Peter Bungard

HAMPSHIRE County Office, Education Department, The
Castle, Winchester SO23 8UG **T** 01962-846452
W www.hants.gov.uk/education
Director of Education, John Coughlan

HERTFORDSHIRE County Hall, Pegs Lane, Hertford
SG13 8DE **T** 01438-737500 **W** www.hertsdirect.org
Director, J. Harris

ISLE OF WIGHT County Hall, High Street, Newport
PO30 1UD **T** 01983-823400 **W** www.iwight.com
Director of Children's Services, D. Pettitt

KENT Sessions House, County Hall, Maidstone ME14 1XG
T 01622-671411 **W** www.kent.gov.uk
Strategic Director, Graham Badman

LANCASHIRE PO Box 61, County Hall, Preston PR1 8RJ
T 0845-0530000 **W** www.lancashire.gov.uk
Director, S. Mulvany

LEICESTERSHIRE County Hall, Glenfield, Leicester LE3 8RF
T 0116-265 6631 **W** www.leics.gov.uk
Director, Gareth Williams

LINCOLNSHIRE County Offices, Newland, Lincoln LN1 1YQ
T 01522-552222 **W** www.lincolnshire.gov.uk
Director, Dr C. Berry

NORFOLK County Hall, Martineau Lane, Norwich NR1 2DL
T 0844-800 8001 **W** www.norfolk.gov.uk
Director of Children's Services, Lisa Christensen

NORTHAMPTONSHIRE John Dryden House, 8–10 The Lakes,
Northampton NN4 7DD **T** 01604-236236
W www.northamptonshire.gov.uk
Director for Children and Young People, Andrew Sortwell

NORTHUMBERLAND County Hall, Morpeth NE61 2EF
T 01670-533000 **W** www.northumberland.gov.uk
Director of Children's Services, Trevor Doughty

NORTH YORKSHIRE County Hall, Northallerton, N. Yorks
DL7 8AE **T** 01609-780780 **W** www.northyorks.gov.uk
Corporate Director, Cynthia Welbourn , FRSA

NOTTINGHAMSHIRE County Hall, West Bridgford,
Nottingham NG2 7QP **T** 0115-982 3823
W www.nottinghamshire.gov.uk
Director, P. Tulley

OXFORDSHIRE Education Department, Macclesfield House,
New Road, Oxford OX1 1NA **T** 01865-815449
W www.oxfordshire.gov.uk
Director for Learning and Culture, Keith Bartley

SHROPSHIRE The Shirehall, Abbey Foregate, Shrewsbury
SY2 6ND **T** 01743-254307 **W** www.shropshireonline.gov.uk
Director, Children and Young People, Liz Nicholson

SOMERSET County Hall, Taunton TA1 4DY **T** 0845-345 9122
W www.somerset.gov.uk
County Education Officer, Jon Rose

STAFFORDSHIRE Staffordshire County Council, Tipping
Street, Stafford ST16 2DH **T** 01785-223121
W www.staffordshire.gov.uk
Director, Peter Traves

SUFFOLK Suffolk County Council, Endeavour House, Russell
Road, Ipswich IP1 2BX **T** 01473-583000
W www.suffolkcc.gov.uk
Director for Children and Young People, Rosalind Turner

SURREY County Hall, Penrhyn Road, Kingston upon Thames
KT1 2DJ **T** 0845-600 9009 **W** www.surreycc.gov.uk
Executive Director for Children and Young People,
Dr P. Gray

WARWICKSHIRE 22 Northgate Street, Warwick CV34 4SP
T 01926-410410 **W** www.warwickshire.gov.uk
County Education Officer, E. Wood

WEST SUSSEX County Hall, Chichester PO19 1RF
T 01243-777100 **W** www.westsussex.gov.uk
Director, Mark Hammond

WILTSHIRE County Hall, Bythesea Road, Trowbridge
BA14 8JB **T** 01225-713000 **W** www.wiltshire.gov.uk
Director for Children and Education, R. W. Wolfson

WORCESTERSHIRE Educational Services Directorate, PO Box 73, Worcester WR5 2YA T 01905-766859 W www.worcestershire.gov.uk
Director of Educational Services, Julien Kramer

UNITARY AND METROPOLITAN BOROUGH COUNCILS

BARNSLEY Berneslai Close, Barnsley S70 2HS
T 01226-773500 W www.barnsley.gov.uk
Executive Director, Education, E. Sutton

BATH AND NORTH EAST SOMERSET PO Box 25, Riverside, Temple Street, Keynsham, Bristol BS31 1DN
T 01225-394210 W www.bathnes.gov.uk
Education Director, Mike Young

BIRMINGHAM Education Offices, Margaret Street, Birmingham B3 3BU T 0121-303 2590 W www.bgfl.org
Strategic Director, Tony Howell

BLACKBURN WITH DARWEN Town Hall, Blackburn BB1 7DY T 01254-477477 W www.blackburn.gov.uk
Director, Peter Morgan

BLACKPOOL Progress House, Clifton Road, Blackpool FY4 4US T 01253-477477
Director of Children's Services, David Lund

BOLTON PO Box 53, Paderborn House, Civic Centre, Bolton BL1 1JW T 01204-332010 W www.boltonlea.org.uk
Director, Margaret Blenkinsop

BOURNEMOUTH Dorset House, 20–22 Christchurch Road, Bournemouth BH1 3NL T 01202-456219
W www.bournemouth.gov.uk
Director of Children's Services, P. Deshpande

BRACKNELL FOREST Seymour House, 38 Broadway, Bracknell, Berks RG12 1AU T 01344-424642
W www.bracknell-forest.gov.uk
Director of Education, Children's Services and Libraries, T. Eccleston

BRADFORD Future House, Bolling Road, Bradford BD4 7EB T 01274-385500 W www.educationbradford.com
Education Director, Phil Green

BRIGHTON AND HOVE Children, Families and Schools, Kings House, Grand Avenue, Hove BN3 2SR
T 01273-294267 W www.brighton-hove.gov.uk
Director of Education, David Hawker

BRISTOL The Council House, College Green, Bristol BS99 7EB T 0117-903 7900 W www.bristol-lea.org.uk
Director of Education and Children's Services, Heather Tomlinson

BURY Athenaeum House, Market Street, Bury BL9 0BN T 0161-253 5652 W www.bury.gov.uk
Executive Director of Children's Services, Eleni Ioannides

CALDERDALE Schools and Children's Services, Town Hall, Halifax HX1 1UJ T 01422-392500 W www.calderdale.gov.uk
Group Director, Caroline Gruen

COVENTRY Council Offices, Earl Street, Coventry CV1 5RR T 024-7683 1511 W www.coventry.gov.uk
Director of Education, Roger Edwardson

DARLINGTON Darlington Borough Council, Town Hall, Darlington DL1 5QT T 01325-380651
W www.darlington.gov.uk
Director, Ada Burns

DERBY Middleton House, 27 St Mary's Gate, Derby DE1 3NN T 01332-716924 W www.derby.gov.uk
Director, A. Flack

DONCASTER The Council House, College Road, Doncaster DN1 3AD T 01302-737103
Executive Director, Mark Eales

DUDLEY Westox House, 1 Trinity Road, Dudley DY1 1JQ T 01384-818181 W www.dudley.gov.uk
Director of Children's Services, John Freeman

EAST RIDING OF YORKSHIRE East Riding of Yorkshire Council, County Hall, Beverley HU17 9BA T 01482-392020
W www.eastriding.gov.uk
Director of Children, Family and Adult Services, Jon Mager

GATESHEAD Civic Centre, Regent Street, Gateshead NE8 1HH T 0191-433 3000 W www.gateshead.gov.uk
Director, Roger Kelly

HALTON Halton Borough Council, Grosvenor House, Halton Lea, Runcorn WA7 2ED T 0151-424 2061
Strategic Director, Children and Young People, Diana Terris

HARTLEPOOL Civic Centre, Victoria Road, Hartlepool TS24 8AY T 01429-266522 W www.hartlepool.gov.uk
Director of Children's Services, Adrienne Simcock

HEREFORDSHIRE Children's Services Directorate, PO Box 185, Blackfriars Street, Hereford HR4 9ZR T 01432-260900
W www.herefordshire.gov.uk
Director of Education, Ms S. Fiennes

KINGSTON UPON HULL Essex House, Manor Street, Kingston upon Hull HU1 1YD T 01482-613007
Corporate Director, Helen McMullen

KIRKLEES Oldgate House, 2 Oldgate, Huddersfield HD1 6QW T 01484-225242 W www.kirklees.gov.uk
Director of Lifelong Learning, G. Tonkin

KNOWSLEY Education Offices, Huyton Hey Road, Huyton, Knowsley L36 5YH T 0151-443 3232
W www.knowsley.gov.uk
Director, Damian Allen

LEEDS 10th Floor West, 110 Merrion Centre, Leeds LS2 8DT T 0113-247 5590 W www.educationleeds.co.uk
Chief Executive, Chris Edwards

LEICESTER Marlborough House, 38 Welford Road, Leicester LE2 7AA T 0116-252 7700 W www.leicester.gov.uk
Director of Education, Steven Andrews

LIVERPOOL Education Department, Municipal Buildings, Dale Street, Liverpool L69 2DH T 0151-233 3006
W www.liverpool.gov.uk
Executive Director, Colin Hilton

LUTON Unity House, 111 Stuart Street, Luton LU1 5NP T 01582-548001 W www.luton.gov.uk
Corporate Director Children and Learning, T. Dessent

MANCHESTER Overseas House, Quay Street, Manchester M3 3BB T 0161-234 5000
Chief Education Officer (acting), Dr Barbara Comiskey

MEDWAY Civic Centre, Strood, Rochester, Kent ME2 4AU T 01634-306000 W www.medway.gov.uk
Director of Education, Rose Collinson

MIDDLESBROUGH PO Box 99, Town Hall, Russell Street, Middlesbrough TS1 2QQ T 01642-245432
Corporate Director, Terry Redmayne

MILTON KEYNES Civic Offices, Saxon Court, 505 Avebury Boulevard, Milton Keynes MK9 3HS T 01908-691691
W www.mkweb.co.uk
Head of Education, John Best

NEWCASTLE UPON TYNE Newcastle Springfield Centre, Off Blakelaw Road, Newcastle upon Tyne NE5 3HU
T 0191-277 4401 W www.newcastle.gov.uk
Executive Director of Children's Services, Catherine Fitt

NORTH EAST LINCOLNSHIRE Municipal Offices, Town Hall Square, Grimsby DN31 1HU T 01472-323021
W www.nelincs.gov.uk
Executive Director (interim), Barbara Hughes

NORTH LINCOLNSHIRE PO Box 35, Hewson House, Station Road, Brigg DN20 8XJ T 01724-296296
W www.northlincs.gov.uk
Head of Education, Learning and Achievement, D. Lea

NORTH SOMERSET PO Box 51, Town Hall, Weston-super-Mare BS23 1DY **T** 01934-888888 **W** www.n-somerset.gov.uk
Director, Graham Turner

NORTH TYNESIDE Stephenson House, Stephenson Street, North Shields, Tyne and Wear NE30 1QA **T** 0191-200 5006 **W** www.northtyneside.gov.uk
Education Director, Gill Alexander

NOTTINGHAM Sandfield Centre, Sandfield Road, Lenton, Nottingham NG7 1QH **T** 0115-915 0800 **W** www.nottinghamschools.co.uk
Corporate Director of Education and Children's Services, Edwina Grant

OLDHAM PO Box 40, Civic Centre, West Street, Oldham OL1 1XJ **T** 0161-911 4260 **W** www.oldham.gov.uk
Executive Director, Children's Services (acting), P. Makin

PETERBOROUGH Children's Services Department, Bayard Place, Broadway, Peterborough PE1 1FB **T** 01733-748444 **W** www.thelearningcity.co.uk
Director, Children's Services, Mohammed Mehmet

PLYMOUTH Windsor House, Tavistock Road, Plymouth PL6 5UF **T** 01752-307400 **W** www.pgfl.plymouth.gov.uk
Director, Bronwen Lacey

POOLE Civic Centre, Poole, Dorset BH15 2RU **T** 01202-633633 **W** www.boroughofpoole.com
Policy Director, Children's Services, John Nash

PORTSMOUTH Civic Offices, Guildhall Square, Portsmouth PO1 2AL **T** 023-9282 2251 **W** www.portsmouthcc.gov.uk
Strategic Director, Children, Families and Learning, Lynda Fisher

READING Civic Centre, PO Box 2623, Reading RG1 7WA **T** 0118-939 0900 **W** www.reading.gov.uk
Director of Education and Children's Services, David Williams

REDCAR AND CLEVELAND Redcar and Cleveland House, Kirkleatham Street, Redcar TS10 1YA **T** 01642-444121 **W** www.redcar-cleveland.gov.uk
Director of Education, Jenny Lewis

ROCHDALE PO Box 70, Municipal Offices, Smith Street, Rochdale OL16 1YD **T** 01706-647474 **W** www.rochdale.gov.uk
Director of Education, Terry Piggott

ROTHERHAM Education Office, Norfolk House, Walker Place, Rotherham S65 1AS **T** 01709-382121 **W** www.rotherham.gov.uk
Senior Executive Director, Children and Young People's Services, Sonia Sharp

ROYAL BOROUGH OF WINDSOR AND MAIDENHEAD Town Hall, St Ives Road, Maidenhead, Berks SL6 1RF **T** 01628-798888 **W** www.rbwm.gov.uk
Director of Education, Malcolm Peckham

RUTLAND Catmose, Oakham, Rutland LE15 6HP **T** 01572-722577 **W** www.rutland.gov.uk
Director of Children's Services, Ms C. Chambers

SALFORD Minerva House, Pendlebury Road, Swinton, Manchester **T** 0161-778 0123 **W** www.salford.gov.uk
Director, Mrs J. Baker

SANDWELL PO Box 41, Shaftesbury House, 402 High Street, West Bromwich, West Midlands B70 9LT **T** 0121-569 2200 **W** www.lea.sandwell.gov.uk
Executive Director, Eric Griffiths

SEFTON Town Hall, Oriel Road, Bootle, Merseyside L20 7AE **T** 0151-922 4040 **W** www.sefton.gov.uk/education
Strategic Director, Bryn Marsh

SHEFFIELD Education Directorate, Town Hall, Pinstone Street, Sheffield S1 2HH **T** 0114-273 5722 **W** www.sheffield.gov.uk
Executive Director, Jonathan Crossley-Holland

SLOUGH Town Hall, Bath Road, Slough SL1 3UQ **T** 01753-875700
Strategic Director of Education and Children's Services, Janet Tomlinson

SOLIHULL PO Box 20, Council House, Homer Road, Solihull B91 3QU **T** 0121-704 6000 **W** www.solihull.gov.uk
Director of Education and Children's Services, Kevin Crompton

SOUTHAMPTON Southampton City Council, 5th Floor, Frobisher House, Nelson Gate, Southampton SO15 1BZ **T** 023-8083 2417 **W** www.southampton.gov.uk
Chief Executive, Brad Roynon

SOUTHEND-ON-SEA Children and Learning, Civic Centre, Victoria Avenue, Southend-on-Sea SS2 6ER **T** 01702-215000 **W** www.southend.gov.uk
Director, Paul Greenhalgh

SOUTH GLOUCESTERSHIRE Bowling Hill, Chipping Sodbury, S. Glos BS37 6JX **T** 01454-868686 **W** www.southglos.gov.uk
Director of Children and Young People, Therese Gillespie

SOUTH TYNESIDE Town Hall and Civic Offices, Westoe Road, South Shields NE33 2RL **T** 0191-427 1717
Executive Director, Children's Services, Kim Bromley-Derrey

ST HELENS Rivington Centre, Rivington Road, St Helens WA10 4ND **T** 01744-455328 **W** www.sthelens.gov.uk
Director, Mrs S. Richardson

STOCKPORT 3rd Floor, Stopford House, Stockport SK1 3XE **T** 0161-474 3813 **W** www.stockport.gov.uk
Director for Education, Ed Blundell

STOCKTON-ON-TEES Municipal Buildings, Church Road, Stockton-on-Tees TS18 1LD **T** 01642-393939 **W** www.stockton.gov.uk
Director of Children, Education and Social Care, Ann Baxter

STOKE-ON-TRENT Floor 2, Civic Centre, Glebe Street, Stoke-on-Trent ST4 1HH **T** 01782-232014 **W** www.stoke.gov.uk/education
Director, N. Rigby

SUNDERLAND PO Box 101, Civic Centre, Sunderland SR2 7DN **T** 0191-553 1000 **W** www.sunderland.gov.uk
Director of Education (acting), Terry Walsh

SWINDON Sanford House, Sanford Street, Swindon SN1 1QH **T** 01793-463902 **W** www.swindon.gov.uk
Director of Education, Hilary Pitts

TAMESIDE Council Offices, Wellington Road, Ashton under Lyne, Lancs OL6 6DL **T** 0161-342 8355 **W** www.tameside.gov.uk
Executive Director, Ian Smith

TELFORD AND WREKIN PO Box 440, Civic Offices, Telford, Shropshire TF3 4WF **T** 01952-202100 **W** www.telford.gov.uk
Corporate Director, Christine Davies, CBE

THURROCK PO Box 118, Grays, Essex RM17 6GF **T** 01375-652652 **W** www.thurrock.gov.uk/education
Corporate Director for Children Education and Families, Steve Beynon

TORBAY Oldway Mansion, Paignton, Devon TQ3 2TE **T** 01803-208227
Chief Executive of Children's Services, Tony Smith

TRAFFORD Children's and Young People's Service, PO Box 22, Trafford Town Hall, Talbot Road, Stretford, Trafford M32 0ES **T** 0161-912 2000 **W** www.trafford.gov.uk
Chief Executive, Chris Pratt

WAKEFIELD County Hall, Bond Street, Wakefield WF1 2QL **T** 01924-306090 **W** www.wakefield.gov.uk
Corporate Director (Education), J. McLeod

WALSALL Civic Centre, Darwall Street, Walsall WS1 1TP
T 01922-652081 W www.walsall.gov.uk
Chief Education Officer, David Brown

WARRINGTON Warrington Borough Council, New Town
House, Buttermarket Street, Warrington, Cheshire WA1 2NJ
T 01925-444400 W www.warrington.gov.uk
Director, Malcolm Roxburgh

WEST BERKSHIRE Avonbank House, West Street, Newbury,
Berks RG14 1BZ T 01635-42400 W www.westberks.gov.uk
Corporate Director, Richard Hubbard

WIGAN Progress House, Westwood Park Drive, Wigan, Lancs
WN3 4HH T 01942-486125 W www.wiganmbc.gov.uk
Director of Education, Ged Rowney

WIRRAL Hamilton Building, Conway Street, Birkenhead,
Wirral CH41 4FD T 0151-606 2000 W www.wirral.gov.uk
Director, Howard Cooper

WOKINGHAM Wokingham District Council, Shute End,
Wokingham, Berks RG40 1WN T 0118-974 6100
W www.wokingham.gov.uk
Corporate Head of Education, David Hawthorne

WOLVERHAMPTON Wolverhampton Civic Centre, Wulfruna
Street, Wolverhampton WV1 1RR T 01902-556556
W www.wolverhampton.gov.uk
Director of Education, Roy Lockwood

YORK Mill House, North Street, York YO1 6JD
T 01904-613161 W www.york.gov.uk
Director of Education, Patrick Scott

LONDON

*Inner London borough

BARKING AND DAGENHAM Town Hall, Barking, Essex
IG11 7LU T 020-8227 3181 W www.lbbd.gov.uk
Director of Education, Arts and Libraries, Roger
Luxton, OBE

BARNET Building 4, North London Business Park, Oakleigh
Road South, London N11 1NP T 020-8359 7618
W www.barnet.gov.uk
Chief Education Officer, Gillian Palmer

BEXLEY Hill View, Hill View Drive, Welling, Kent DA16 3RY
T 020-8303 7777 W www.bexley.gov.uk
Director of Education, Deborah Absalom

BRENT Chesterfield House, 9 Park Lane, Wembley, Middx
HA9 7RW T 020-8937 3000 W www.brent.gov.uk
Director of Education, John Christie

BROMLEY Civic Centre, Stockwell Close, Bromley BR1 3UH
T 020-8464 3333 W www.bromley.gov.uk
Director of Education, Ken Davis

*CAMDEN Crowndale Centre, 218–220 Eversholt Street,
London NW1 1BD T 020-7974 1525
W www.camden.gov.uk
Director, Yvette Stanley

*CITY OF LONDON Education Service, Corporation of
London, PO Box 270, Guildhall, London EC2P 2EJ
T 020-7332 1750
City Education Officer, Ian Comfort

*CITY OF WESTMINSTER City Hall, 13th Floor, 64 Victoria
Street, London SW1E 6QP T 020-7641 6000
W www.westminster.gov.uk
Director of Education, Phyl Crawford

CROYDON Taberner House, Park Lane, Croydon CR9 1TP
T 020-8686 4433 W www.croydon.gov.uk
Director, P. Wylie

EALING Education Service, Perceval House, 14–16 Uxbridge
Road, London W5 2HL T 020-8825 5599
W www.ealing.gov.uk
Director of Education, Nick Jarman

ENFIELD 7th Floor, Civic Centre, Silver Street, Enfield, Middx
EN1 3XA T 020-8379 3201 W www.enfield.gov.uk
Director of Education, Peter Lewis

*GREENWICH Riverside House, Woolwich High Street,
London SE18 6DF T 020-8921 8230
W www.greenwich.gov.uk
Director of Education, Paul Burnett

*HACKNEY Hackney Technology and Learning Centre,
1 Reading Lane, London E8 1GQ T 020-8820 7000
W www.learningtrust.co.uk
Chief Executive, Alan Wood

*HAMMERSMITH AND FULHAM Education Department,
Town Hall, King Street, London W6 9JU T 020-8753 3625
W www.lbhf.gov.uk
Education Director, Sandy Adamson

HARINGEY Education Department, Civic Centre, High Road,
London N22 8LE T 020-8489 0000 W www.haringey.gov.uk
Director of the Children's Service, Sharon Shoesmith

HILLINGDON Civic Centre, High Street, Uxbridge UB8 1UW
T 01895-250529
Corporate Director, Christopher Spencer

HARROW PO Box 22, Civic Centre, Station Road, Harrow
HA1 2UW T 020-8863 5611 W www.harrow.gov.uk
Director of Learning and Community Development, Javed
Khan

HOUNSLOW Civic Centre, Lampton Road, Hounslow, Middx
TW3 4DN T 020-8583 2000 W www.hounslow.gov.uk
Director of Children and Lifelong Learning, Robert
Garnett

HAVERING Town Hall, Main Road, Romford RM1 3BC
T 01708-432488
Executive Director of Education, David Maclean

*ISLINGTON Laycock Street, Islington, London N1 1TH
T 020-7527 5566 W www.islington.gov.uk
Director of Children's Services, Paul Curran

*KENSINGTON AND CHELSEA The Royal Borough of
Kensington and Chelsea, Town Hall, Hornton Street, London
W8 7NX T 020-7361 3334 W www.rbkc.gov.uk
Executive Director for Education, Libraries and Arts,
Jacky Griffin

KINGSTON UPON THAMES Guildhall 2, Kingston upon
Thames KT1 1EU T 020-8546 2121
W www.kingston.gov.uk
Director of Learning and Children's Services, P. Leeson

*LAMBETH International House, Canterbury Crescent, London
SW9 7QE T 020-7926 1000 W www.lambeth.gov.uk
Executive Director of Education, Phyllis Dunipace

*LEWISHAM Department of Children and Young People,
Laurence House, 1 Catford Road, London SE6 4RU
T 020-8314 8221 W www.lewisham.gov.uk
Executive Director, Frankie Sulke

MERTON Civic Centre, London Road, Morden, Surrey
SM4 5DX T 020-8274 4901 W www.merton.gov.uk
Director of Children, Schools and Families (acting),
Sue Ross

NEWHAM Broadway House, 322 High Street, Stratford,
London E15 1AJ T 020-8430 2000
Executive Director, Children and Young People,
Ms P. Maddison

REDBRIDGE Lynton House, 255–259 High Road, Ilford, Essex
IG1 1NN T 020-8478 3020 W www.redbridge.gov.uk
Director of children's services (interim), Liz Graham

RICHMOND UPON THAMES London Borough of Richmond
upon Thames, 1st Floor, Regal House, London Road,
Twickenham TW1 3QB T 020-8891 7500
W www.richmond.gov.uk
Director of Education and Leisure Services, Anji Phillips

*SOUTHWARK John Smith House, 144–152 Walworth Road, London SE17 1JL T 020 7525 5050/5001
W www.southwark.gov.uk
Strategic Director of Education, Alison Delyth
SUTTON The Grove, Carshalton, Surrey SM5 3AL
T 020-8770 5000 W www.sutton.gov.uk
Strategic Director, Dr I. Birnbaum
*TOWER HAMLETS Mulberry Place, 5 Clove Crescent, London E14 2BG T 020-7364 4954
W www.towerhamlets.org.uk
Corporate Director of Education (acting), Christine Whatford
WALTHAM FOREST Education Centre, 97 Queens Road, London E17 8QS T 020-8496 5900 W www.eduaction.com
Chief Education Officer, Christopher Kiernan
*WANDSWORTH Town Hall, Wandsworth High Street, London SW18 2PU T 020-8871 8013
W www.wandsworth.gov.uk
Director, Paul Robinson

WALES

ANGLESEY Park Mount, Glanhwfa Road, Llangefni, Anglesey LL77 7EY T 01248-752980
Director of Education and Leisure, Richard Parry Jones
BLAENAU GWENT Festival House, Victoria Business Park, Ebbw Vale, Blaenau Gwent NP23 6ER T 01495-355337
Director of Lifelong Learning and Strategic Partnerships (acting), B. Pugh
BRIDGEND Bridgend County Borough Council, Sunnyside, Bridgend CF31 4AR T 01656-642600
W www.bridgend.gov.uk
Director (acting), Graham Avery
CAERPHILLY Education Offices, Caerphilly Road, Ystrad Mynach, Hengoed CF82 7EP T 01443-815588
Director of Education, David Hopkins
CARDIFF County Hall, Atlantic Wharf, Cardiff CF10 4UW
T 029-2087 2000 W www.cardiff.gov.uk
Head of Service, Byron Davies
CARMARTHENSHIRE Pibwrlwyd, Carmarthen SA31 2NH
T 01267-224532 W www.carmarthenshire.gov.uk
Director of Education and Children's Services, Vernon Morgan
CEREDIGION Swyddfa'r Sir, Marine Terrace, Aberystwyth SY23 2DE T 01970-633656
Director, T. G. Jones
CONWY Government Buildings, Dinerth Road, Colwyn Bay LL28 4UL T 01492-575031 W www.conwy.gov.uk
Director of Lifelong Learning, R. Elwyn Williams
DENBIGHSHIRE Denbighshire County Council, Wynnstay Road, Ruthin, LL15 1YN T 01824-706777
W www.denbighshire.gov.uk
Director, H. Griffith
FLINTSHIRE County Hall, Mold CH7 6ND T 01352-704023
W www.flintshire.gov.uk
Director of Education and Children's Services, John R. Clutton
GWYNEDD Schools Service Development Directorate, Council Offices, Caernarfon LL55 1SH T 01286-672255
W www.gwynedd.gov.uk
Head of Lifelong Learning, Rhys Wynn Parri
MERTHYR TYDFIL Ty Keir Hardie, Riverside Court, Avenue De Clichy, Merthyr Tydfil CF47 8XD T 01685-724600
W www.mnet2000.org.uk
Director of Integrated Children's Services, C. A. Abbott
MONMOUTHSHIRE Monmouthshire County Council, Floor 5, County Hall, Cwmbran NP44 2XH T 01633-644487
W www.monmouthshire.gov.uk
Director, P. Cooke

NEATH PORT TALBOT Civic Centre, Port Talbot SA13 1PJ
T 01639-763298 W www.neath-porttalbot.gov.uk
Director of Education, Leisure and Lifelong Learning, K. Napieralla
NEWPORT Civic Centre, Newport NP20 4UR T 01633-656656
W www.newport.gov.uk
Chief Education Officer, Ms S. Menghini
PEMBROKESHIRE County Hall, Haverfordwest SA61 1TP
T 01437-764551 W www.pembrokeshire.gov.uk
Director, B. Parry-Jones
POWYS County Hall, Llandrindod Wells LD1 5LG
T 01597-826422 W www.education.powys.gov.uk Group
Director, vacant
RHONDDA CYNON TAFF Ty Trevithick, Abercynon, Mountain Ash, CF45 4UQ T 01443-744000
Director of Education, Dewi Jones
SWANSEA County Hall, Oystermouth Road, Swansea SA1 3SN
T 01792 636351 W www.swansea.gov.uk/education
Director, R. Parry
TORFAEN County Hall, Croesyceiliog, Cwmbran, Torfaen NP44 2WN T 01633-648105 W www.torfaen.gov.uk
Director, Mike de Val
VALE OF GLAMORGAN The Vale of Glamorgan Council, Civic Offices, Holton Road, Barry CF63 4RU
T 01446-700111 W www.valeofglamorgan.gov.uk
Director, B. Jeffreys
WREXHAM Wrexham County Borough Council, Ty Henblas, Queen's Square, Wrexham LL13 8AZ T 01978-297505
W www.wrexham.gov.uk
Director, Isobel Garner

SCOTLAND

ABERDEEN Summerhill Education Centre, Stronsay Drive, Aberdeen AB15 6JA T 01224-522000
W www.aberdeencity.gov.uk
Corporate Director for Learning and Leisure, J. Stodter
ABERDEENSHIRE Woodhill House, Westburn Road, Aberdeen AB16 5GJ T 01224-664630
W www.aberdeenshire.gov.uk
Director of Education and Recreation, Sohail Faruqi
ANGUS County Buildings, Market Street, Forfar DD8 3WE
T 01307-461460 W www.angus.gov.uk
Director of Education, Jim Anderson
ARGYLL AND BUTE Argyll House, Alexandra Parade, Dunoon, Argyll PA23 8AJ T 01369-704000
W www.argyll-bute.gov.uk
Director of Education, Ronald Gould
CLACKMANNANSHIRE Education and Community Services, Lime Tree House, Alloa FK10 1EX T 01259-452374
T councils W www.clacksweb.org.uk
Head of Education, Jim Goodall
DUMFRIES AND GALLOWAY Woodbank, 30 Edinburgh Road, Dumfries DG1 1NW T 01387-260400
Corporate Director of Education and Community Services, Fraser Sanderson
DUNDEE Floor 8, Tayside House, Crichton Street, Dundee DD1 3RJ T 01382-433111 W www.dundeecity.gov.uk
Director of Education, Mrs A. Wilson
EAST AYRSHIRE Council Headquarters, London Road, Kilmarnock KA3 7BU T 01563-576109
W www.east-ayrshire.gov.uk
Director, John Mulgrew, OBE
EAST DUNBARTONSHIRE Boclair House, 100 Milngavie Road, Bearsden, Glasgow G61 2TQ T 0141-578 8000
W www.eastdunbarton.gov.uk
Strategic Director, Community, David Anderson

EAST LOTHIAN East Lothian Council, John Muir House, Haddington EH41 3HA **T** 01620-827631 **W** www.eastlothian.gov.uk
Director of Education and Children's Services, Alan Blackie
EAST RENFREWSHIRE Council Offices, 211 Main Street, Barrhead, G78 1SY **T** 0141-577 3404 **W** www.eastrenfrewshire.gov.uk
Director of Education, John Wilson
EDINBURGH Wellington Court, 10 Waterloo Place, Edinburgh EH1 3EG **T** 0131-469 3000
Director, Children and Families, R. Jobson
EILEAN SIAR/WESTERN ISLES Council Offices, Sandwick Road, Stornoway, Isle of Lewis HS1 2BW **T** 01851-703773 **W** www.cne-siar.gov.uk
Director of Education, Murdo Macleod
FALKIRK McLaren House, Marchmont Avenue, Polmont, Falkirk FK2 0NZ **T** 01324-506600 **W** www.falkirk.gov.uk
Director, Julia Swan
FIFE Rothesay House, Rothesay Place, Glenrothes KY7 5PN **T** 01592-413656 **W** www.fife.gov.uk
Head of Education, Roger Stewart
GLASGOW Wheatley House, 25 Cochrane Street, Merchant City, Glasgow G1 1HL **T** 0141-287 2000 **W** www.glasgow.gov.uk
Director, Ronnie O'Connor
HIGHLAND Council Buildings, Glenurquhart Road, Inverness IV3 5NX **T** 01463-702802 **W** www.highland.gov.uk
Director of Education, Culture and Sport, B. Robertson
INVERCLYDE 105 Dalrymple Street, Greenock PA15 1HT **T** 01475-712824
Director, Jim Sutherland
MIDLOTHIAN Fairfield House, 8 Lothian Road, Dalkeith EH22 3ZG **T** 0131-270 7500 **W** www.midlothian.gov.uk
Director, D. MacKay
MORAY Council Offices, High Street, Elgin IV30 1BX **T** 01343-563001 **W** www.moray.gov.uk
Director, Alastair Keddie
NORTH AYRSHIRE Cunninghame House, Friarscroft, Irvine KA12 8DB **T** 01294-324400 **W** www.north-ayrshire.gov.uk
Director of Education, John Travers
NORTH LANARKSHIRE Municipal Buildings, Kildonan Street, Coatbridge ML5 3BT **T** 01236-812222 **W** www.northlan.gov.uk
Director of Education, Michael O'Neill
ORKNEY ISLANDS Council Offices, School Place, Kirkwall, Orkney KW15 1NY **T** 01856-873535 **W** www.orkney.gov.uk
Director, Leslie Manson
PERTH AND KINROSS Pullar House, 35 Kinnoull Street, Perth PH1 5GD **T** 01738-476200 **W** www.perthshire.com
Executive Director, George Waddell
RENFREWSHIRE Council Headquarters, South Building, Cotton Street, Paisley PA1 1LE **T** 0141-842 5663 **W** www.renfrewshire.gov.uk
Director of Education, Shelagh Rae
SCOTTISH BORDERS Scottish Borders Council, Council Headquarters, Newtown St Boswells, Melrose, Roxburghshire TD6 0SA **T** 01835-824000 **W** www.scotborders.gov.uk
Director, David Hume

SHETLAND ISLANDS Education Service, Hayfield House, Hayfield Lane, Lerwick, Shetland ZE1 0QD **T** 01595-744000 **W** www.shetland.gov.uk
Head of Education, Alex Jamieson
SOUTH AYRSHIRE County Buildings, Wellington Square, Ayr KA7 1DR **T** 01292-612201 **W** www.south-ayrshire.gov.uk
Director, Mike McCabe
SOUTH LANARKSHIRE Council Offices, Almada Street, Hamilton ML3 0AA **T** 01698-454444 **W** www.southlanarkshire.gov.uk
Executive Director of Education Resources, Ken Arthur
STIRLING Stirling Council, Viewforth, Stirling FK8 2ET **T** 01786-442666 **W** www.stirling.gov.uk
Director, David Cameron
WEST DUNBARTONSHIRE Council Offices, Garshake Road, Dumbarton G82 3PU **T** 01389-737309
Director, Bob Cook
WEST LOTHIAN West Lothian House, Almondvale Boulevard, Livingston EH54 6QG **T** 01506-776000
Director of Education and Cultural Services, Mrs K. Reid

NORTHERN IRELAND

BELFAST 40 Academy Street, Belfast BT1 2NQ **T** 028-9056 4000 **W** www.belb.org.uk
Chief Executive, David Cargo
NORTH EAST County Hall, 182 Galgorm Road, Ballymena, Co. Antrim BT42 1HN **T** 028-2565 3333 **W** www.neelb.org.uk
Chief Executive, G. Topping
SOUTH 3 Charlemont Place, The Mall, Armagh BT61 9AX **T** 028-3751 2200 **W** www.selb.org
Chief Executive, Helen McClenaghan
SOUTH EAST Headquarters Offices, Grahamsbridge Road, Dundonald, Belfast BT16 2HS **T** 028-9056 6200 **W** www.seelb.org.uk
Chief Executive, J. B. Fitzsimons
WEST Western Education and Library Board, 1 Hospital Road, Omagh, Co. Tyrone BT79 0AW **T** 028-8241 1411 **W** www.welbni.org
Chief Executive, B. Mulholland

ISLANDS

GUERNSEY The Grange, St Peter Port, Guernsey GY1 1RQ **T** 01481-710821
Director, D. T. Neale
ISLE OF MAN St. George's Court, Upper Church Street, Douglas, Isle of Man IM1 2SG **T** 01624-685820 **W** www.gov.im
Director, John Cain
ISLES OF SCILLY Town Hall, St Mary's, Isles of Scilly TR21 0LW **T** 01720-422537 **W** www.scilly.gov.uk
General Schools Adviser, Suzanne Pender
JERSEY PO Box 142, Jersey JE4 8QJ **T** 01534-509500
Director of Education, Sport and Culture, T. W. McKeon

ADVISORY BODIES

SCHOOLS

BRITISH EDUCATIONAL COMMUNICATIONS AND TECHNOLOGY AGENCY Milburn Hill Road, Science Park, Coventry CV4 7JJ **T** 024-7641 6994 **W** www.becta.org.uk
Chief Executive, Owen Lynch

EDUCATION OTHERWISE PO Box 7420, London N9 9SG
T Helpline: 0870-730 0074
W www.education-otherwise.org

INTERNATIONAL BACCALAUREATE ORGANISATION Peterson House, Malthouse Avenue, Cardiff Gate, Cardiff CF23 8GL **T** 029-2054 7777 **W** www.ibo.org
Academic Director, Monique Conn

LEARNING AND SKILLS COUNCIL Cheylesmore House, Quinton Road, Coventry CV1 2WT **T** 0845-019 4170
W www.lsc.gov.uk
Chief Executive, Mark Haysom

SPECIAL EDUCATIONAL NEEDS AND DISABILITY TRIBUNAL Procession House, 55 Ludgate Hill, London EC4M 7JW **T** Helpline: 0870-241 2555
W www.sendist.gov.uk
President, Lady Rosemary Hughes

INDEPENDENT SCHOOLS

ASSOCIATION OF GOVERNING BODIES OF INDEPENDENT SCHOOLS Field House, Newton Tony, Salisbury, Wilts SP4 0HF **W** www.agbis.org.uk
Secretary, Shane Rutter-Jerome

INDEPENDENT SCHOOLS COUNCIL St Vincent House, 30 Orange Street, London WC2H 7HH **T** 020-7766 7070
W www.isc.co.uk
General Secretary, Jonathan Shephard

INDEPENDENT SCHOOLS EXAMINATIONS BOARD Jordan House, Christchurch Road, New Milton, Hants BH25 6QJ **T** 01425-621111 **W** www.iseb.co.uk
General Secretary, Mrs J. Williams

FURTHER EDUCATION

ACER (ASSOCIATION OF COLLEGES IN THE EASTERN REGION) Suite 1, Lancaster House, Meadow Lane, St Ives, Cambs PE27 4LG **T** 01480-468198 **W** www.acer.ac.uk
Chief Executive, Veronica Windmill

AOSEC (ASSOCIATION OF SOUTH EAST COLLEGES) Building 33, University of Reading, London Road, Reading RG1 5AQ **T** 0118-378 6325 **W** www.aosec.org.uk
Chief Executive, Breyan Knowles

CENTRA EDUCATION AND TRAINING Duxbury Park, Duxbury Hall Road, Chorley, Lancs PR7 4AT
T 01257-241428 **W** www.centra.org.uk
Chief Executive, Mike Frain

EMFEC (EAST MIDLANDS FURTHER EDUCATION COUNCIL) Robins Wood House, Robins Wood Road, Aspley, Nottingham NG8 3NH **T** 0115-854 1616
W www.emfec.co.uk
Chief Executive, Jennie Gardiner

LEARNING AND SKILLS DEVELOPMENT AGENCY Regent Arcade House, 19–25 Argyll Street, London W1F 7LS **T** 020-7297 9000 **W** www.lsda.org.uk
Chief Executive, Andrew Thomson

LEARNING SOUTH WEST Bishops Hull House, Bishops Hull, Taunton, Somerset TA1 5EP **T** 01823-335491
W www.learning-southwest.org.uk
Chief Executive, Liz McGrath

NCFE Citygate, St James' Boulevard, Newcastle upon Tyne NE1 4JE **T** 0191-239 8000 **W** www.ncfe.org.uk
Chief Executive, Isabel Sutcliffe

WELSH JOINT EDUCATION COMMITTEE 245 Western Avenue, Cardiff CF5 2YX **T** 029-2026 5000
W www.wjec.co.uk
Chief Executive, Gareth Pierce

HIGHER EDUCATION

ASSOCIATION OF COMMONWEALTH UNIVERSITIES 36 Gordon Square, London WC1H 0PF **T** 020-7380 6700
W www.acu.ac.uk
Secretary-General, Dr John Rowett

NORTHERN IRELAND HIGHER EDUCATION COUNCIL 39–49 Adelaide Street, Belfast BT2 8FD **T** 02890-257949
Chair, Tony Hopkins, CBE

QUALITY ASSURANCE AGENCY FOR HIGHER EDUCATION Southgate House, Southgate Street, Gloucester GL1 1UB **T** 01452-557000 **W** www.qaa.ac.uk
Chief Executive, Peter Williams

UNIVERSITIES SCOTLAND 53 Hanover Street, Edinburgh EH2 2PJ **T** 0131-226 1111
W www.universities-scotland.ac.uk
Director, David Caldwell

UNIVERSITIES UK Woburn House, 20 Tavistock Square, London WC1H 9HQ **T** 020-7419 4111
W www.universitiesuk.ac.uk
Chief Executive, Baroness Warwick of Undercliffe

CURRICULUM COUNCILS

COUNCIL FOR THE CURRICULUM, EXAMINATIONS AND ASSESSMENT 29 Clarendon Road, Clarendon Dock, Belfast BT1 3BG **T** 028-9026 1200 **W** www.ccea.org.uk
Chief Executive, Gavin Boyd

LEARNING AND TEACHING SCOTLAND 74 Victoria Crescent Road, Glasgow G12 9JN **T** 0141-337 5000
W www.ltscotland.org.uk
Chief Executive, Bernard McLeary

QUALIFICATIONS, CURRICULUM AND ASSESSMENT AUTHORITY FOR WALES (ACCAC) Castle Buildings, Womanby Street, Cardiff CF10 1SX **T** 029-2037 5400
W www.accac.org.uk
Chief Executive, John Valentine Williams

QUALIFICATIONS AND CURRICULUM AUTHORITY 83 Piccadilly, London W1J 8QA **T** 020-7509 5555
W www.qca.org.uk
Chief Executive, Dr Ken Boston

EXAMINING BODIES

ENGLAND

ASSESSMENT AND QUALIFICATIONS ALLIANCE (AQA) Devas Street, Manchester M15 6EX **T** 0161-953 1180
W www.aqa.org.uk
Director-General, Dr Mike Cresswell

EDEXCEL 190 High Holborn, London, WC1V 7BH
T 0870-240 9800 **W** www.edexcel.org.uk
Managing Director, Jerry Jarvis

OXFORD CAMBRIDGE AND RSA EXAMINATIONS (OCR) 9 Hills Road, Cambridge CB2 1PB **T** 01223-553311
W www.ocr.org.uk
Chief Executive, Greg Watson, FRSA

SCOTLAND

SCOTTISH QUALIFICATIONS AUTHORITY Hanover House, 24 Douglas Street, Glasgow G2 7NQ
T 0845-279 1000 **W** www.sqa.org.uk
Chief Executive, Anton Colella

WALES

WELSH JOINT EDUCATION COMMITTEE 245 Western
Avenue, Cardiff CF5 2YX **T** 029-2026 5000
W www.wjec.co.uk
Chief Executive, Gareth Pierce

NORTHERN IRELAND

COUNCIL FOR THE CURRICULUM, EXAMINATIONS
AND ASSESSMENT 29 Clarendon Road, Clarendon Dock,
Belfast, County Antrim BT1 3BG **T** 028-9026 1200
W www.ccea.org.uk
Chief Executive, Gavin Boyd

INTERNATIONAL

UNIVERSITY OF CAMBRIDGE INTERNATIONAL
EXAMINATIONS (CIE) 1 Hills Road, Cambridge CB1 2EU
T 01223-553554 **W** www.cie.org.uk
Chief Executive (acting), Ann Puntis

GCSE AND A-LEVEL
See above: AQA; CIE; EDEXCEL; COUNCIL FOR THE
CURRICULUM, EXAMINATIONS AND ASSESSMENT;
WELSH JOINT EDUCATION COMMITTEE

FURTHER EDUCATION
See above: CIE; EDEXCEL; OCR
CITY & GUILDS 1 Giltspur Street, London EC1A 9DD
T 020-7294 2800 **W** www.city-and-guilds.co.uk
Director-General, Chris Humphries, CBE

FUNDING COUNCILS

FURTHER EDUCATION
EDUCATION AND LEARNING WALES (ELWA) Linden
Court, The Orchards, Ilex Close, Cardiff CF14 5DZ
T 029-2076 1861 **W** www.elwa.org.uk
Chief Executive (acting), Sheila Drury
LEARNING AND SKILLS COUNCIL Cheylesmore House,
Quinton Road, Coventry CV1 2WT **T** 0845-019 4170
W www.lsc.gov.uk
Chief Executive, Mark Haysom
SCOTTISH FUNDING COUNCILS FOR FURTHER AND
HIGHER EDUCATION Donaldson House, 97 Haymarket
Terrace, Edinburgh EH12 5HD **T** 0131-313 6500
W www.sfc.ac.uk
Chief Executive, Roger McClure

HIGHER EDUCATION
HIGHER EDUCATION FUNDING COUNCIL FOR
ENGLAND Northavon House, Coldharbour Lane, Bristol
BS16 1QD **T** 0117-931 7317 **W** www.hefce.ac.uk
Chief Executive, Prof. Sir Howard Newby, CBE
HIGHER EDUCATION FUNDING COUNCIL FOR WALES
Linden Court, The Orchards, Ilex Close, Cardiff CF14 5DZ
T 029-2076 1861 **W** www.elwa.org.uk
Chief Executive, Prof. Philip Gummett
SCOTTISH FUNDING COUNCILS FOR FURTHER AND
HIGHER EDUCATION Donaldson House, 97 Haymarket
Terrace, Edinburgh EH12 5HD **T** 0131-313 6500
W www.sfc.ac.uk
Chief Executive, Roger McClure
STUDENT AWARDS AGENCY FOR SCOTLAND Gyleview
House, 3 Redheughs Rigg, Edinburgh EH12 9HH
T 0845-111 1711 **W** www.saas.gov.uk
Chief Executive, David Stephen
STUDENT LOANS COMPANY LTD 100 Bothwell Street,
Glasgow G2 7JD **T** 0141-306 2000 **W** www.slc.co.uk
Chief Executive, Ralph Seymour-Jackson
TRAINING AND DEVELOPMENT AGENCY FOR
SCHOOLS Portland House, Stag Place, London SW1E 5TT
T 0845-606 0323 **W** www.tda.gov.uk
Chief Executive, Ralph Tabberer

ADMISSIONS AND COURSE INFORMATION

CAREERS RESEARCH AND ADVISORY CENTRE 2nd Floor,
Sheraton House, Castle Park, Cambridge CB3 0AX
T 01223-460277 **W** www.crac.org.uk
Chief Executive (acting), Gill Wilson
SOCIAL WORK ADMISSIONS SYSTEM Rosehill, New Barn
Lane, Cheltenham, Glos GL52 3LZ **T** 0870-112 2207
SWAS Unit Manager, Janet Pearce
UNIVERSITIES AND COLLEGES ADMISSIONS SERVICE
(UCAS) Rosehill, New Barn Lane, Cheltenham, Glos
GL52 3LZ **T** 0870-1122211 **W** www.ucas.com
Chief Executive, Anthony McClaran
UNIVERSITIES SCOTLAND 53 Hanover Street,
Edinburgh EH2 2PJ **T** 0131-226 1111
W www.universities-scotland.ac.uk
Director, David Caldwell

UNIVERSITIES

The following is a list of universities, which have been granted degree awarding powers by either a Royal Charter or an Act of Parliament. There are other recognised bodies in the UK with degree awarding powers, as well as institutions offering courses leading to a degree of a recognised body. For further information please visit www.dfes.gov.uk.

UNIVERSITY OF ABERDEEN (1495)
King's College, Aberdeen AB24 3FX T 01224-272000
E communications@abdn.ac.uk W www.abdn.ac.uk
Full-time students (2004–5), 11,403
Chancellor, Lord Wilson of Tillyorn, KT, GCMG, PHD
Principal and Vice-Chancellor, Prof. C. Duncan Rice
Academic Registrar, Dr Trevor Webb
Secretary to the University, Steve Cannon

UNIVERSITY OF ABERTAY DUNDEE (1994)
Bell Street, Dundee DD1 1HG T 01382-308000
E enquiries@abertay.ac.uk W www.abertay.ac.uk
Full-time students (2004–5), 3,382
Chancellor, The Rt. Hon. the Earl of Airlie, KT, GCVO, PC
Vice-Chancellor, Prof. Bernard King
Academic Registrar, Dr C. Fraser

ANGLIA POLYTECHNIC UNIVERSITY (1992)
Rivermead Campus, Bishop Hall Lane, Chelmsford, Essex
CM1 1SQ T 01245-493131 E info@anglia.ac.uk
W www.anglia.ac.uk
Full-time students (2004–5), 6,952
Chancellor, Lord Ashcroft, KCMG
Vice-Chancellor, Prof. David Tidmarsh
Secretary, Stephen Bennett

ASTON UNIVERSITY (1895)
Aston Triangle, Birmingham B4 3ET T 0121-204 3000
W www.aston.ac.uk
Full-time students (2004–5), 6,000
Chancellor, Sir Michael Bett, CBE
Vice-Chancellor, Prof. Mike Wright, PHD, FRENG
Registrar, David Packham, FRSA

UNIVERSITY OF BATH (1966)
Bath BA2 7AY T 01225-388388 W www.bath.ac.uk
Full-time students (2004–5), 9,525
Chancellor, Lord Tugendhat
Vice-Chancellor, Prof. Glynis Breakwell, PHD, FRSA
Registrar, Mr J. A. Bursey

UNIVERSITY OF BIRMINGHAM (1900)
Edgbaston, Birmingham B15 2TT T 0121-414 3344
W www.bham.ac.uk
Full-time students (2004–5), 32,000
Chancellor, Sir Dominic Cadbury
Vice-Chancellor, Prof. Michael Sterling, FRENG
Registrar and Secretary, Dr Jonathan Nicholls

BOURNEMOUTH UNIVERSITY (1992)
Fern Barrow, Poole, Dorset BH12 5BB T 01202-524111
E enquiries@bournemouth.ac.uk W www.bournemouth.ac.uk
Full-time students (2004–5), 14,579
Chancellor, Lord Taylor of Warwick
Vice-Chancellor, Prof. Paul Curran
Registrar, Noel Richardson

UNIVERSITY OF BRADFORD (1966)
Richmond Building, Richmond Road, Bradford, W. Yorks
BD7 1DP T 01274-232323 W www.brad.ac.uk
Full-time students (2004–5), 7,958
Chancellor, Baroness Lockwood of Dewsbury
Vice-Chancellor, Prof. C. M. Taylor
Registrar and Secretary, N. J. Andrew

UNIVERSITY OF BRIGHTON (1992)
Mithras House, Lewes Road, Brighton BN2 4AT
T 01273-600900 E postmaster@bton.ac.uk
W www.bton.ac.uk
Full-time students (2004–5), 17,000
Chair of the Board, Sir Michael Checkland
Vice-Chancellor, Prof. Julian Crampton
Head of Registry, Sharon Jones
Registrar and Secretary, Christine Moon

UNIVERSITY OF BRISTOL (1876)
Senate House, Tyndall Avenue, Bristol BS8 1TH
T 0117-928 9000 W www.bristol.ac.uk
Full-time students (2003–4), 14,500
Chancellor, Baroness Hale of Richmond, DBE, PC
Vice Chancellor, Prof. Eric Thomas
Registrar, Lynn Robinson
University Secretary, Dr Kate McKenzie

BRUNEL UNIVERSITY (1966)
Uxbridge, Middx UB8 3PH T 01895-274000
W www.brunel.ac.uk
Full-time students (2004–5), 12,903
Chancellor, The Rt. Hon. Lord Wakeham, DL
Vice-Chancellor, Prof. Stephen Schwartz
Secretary and Registrar, Ms E. J. Weale

UNIVERSITY OF BUCKINGHAM (1983)
Buckingham MK18 1EG T 01280-814080
E reception@buckingham.ac.uk W www.buckingham.ac.uk
Full-time students (2004–5), 650
Chancellor, Sir Martin Jacomb
Vice-Chancellor, Dr Terence Kealey
Registrar, Prof. Len Evans
Secretary, Prof. John Clarke

UNIVERSITY OF CAMBRIDGE (1209)
The Old Schools, Trinity Lane, Cambridge CB2 1TN
T 01223-337733 W www.cam.ac.uk
Undergraduates (2004–5), 11,982
Chancellor, HRH The Prince Philip, Duke of Edinburgh,
    KG, KT, OM, GBE, PC, FRS
Vice-Chancellor, Prof. Alison Richard (Newnham), PHD
High Steward, Dame Bridget Ogilvie (Girton), FRS
Deputy High Steward, Lord Richardson of Duntisbourne,
    MBE, TD, PC
Comissary, Lord Mackay of Clashfern, KT, PC, FRSE
Pro-Vice-Chancellors, Prof. A. D. Cliff, Prof. I. M. Leslie,
    Prof. M. C. McKendrick, Prof. A. C. Minson, Dr K. B.
    Pretty
Proctors, Dr J. A. Little (St Catherine's), Dr N. C. Pyper
    (Fitzwilliam)
Orator, A. J. Bowen (Jesus)
Registrary, T. J. Mead, PHD (Wolfson)
Librarian, P. K. Fox (Selwyn)
Director of the Fitzwilliam Museum, D. D. Robinson
    (Magdalene)
Academic Secretary, G. P. Allen (Wolfson)
Director of Finance, A. M. Reid (Wolfson)

COLLEGES AND HALLS *with dates of foundation*

CHRIST'S (1505) *Master,* Prof. Malcolm Bowie, DPHIL, FBA
CHURCHILL (1960) *Master,* Sir John Boyd, KCMG
CLARE (1326) *Master,* Prof. A. J. Badger, PHD
CORPUS CHRISTI (1352) *Master,* Prof. H. Ahmed, FRENG
DARWIN (1964) *Master,* Prof. W. A. Brown, CBE
DOWNING (1800) *Master,* Prof. B. J. Everitt, PHD
EMMANUEL (1584) *Master,* Lord Wilson of Dinton, GCB, LLB
FITZWILLIAM (1966) *Master,* Prof. R. D. Lethbridge
GIRTON (1869) *Mistress,* Prof. Dame Marilyn Strathern, PHD, FBA
GONVILLE AND CAIUS (1348) *Master,* N. McKendrick
HOMERTON (1824) *Principal,* Dr K. B. Pretty
HUGHES HALL (1985) *President,* Prof. P. Richards, MD, PHD
JESUS (1496) *Master,* Prof. R. Mair, PHD, FRENG
KING'S (1441) *Provost,* Dame Judith Mayhew Jonas
LUCY CAVENDISH COLLEGE (1965) *President,* Dame Veronica Sutherland, CMG
MAGDALENE (1542) *Master,* D. D. Robinson
NEW HALL (1954) *President,* Mrs A. Lonsdale, CBE
NEWNHAM (1871) *Principal,* Baroness O'Neill of Bengarve, CBE
PEMBROKE (1347) *Master,* Sir Richard Dearlove, KCMG, OBE
PETERHOUSE (1284) *Master,* Lord Wilson of Tillyorn, KT, GCMG
QUEENS' (1448) *President,* Prof. Lord Eatwell
ROBINSON (1977) *Warden,* A. D. Yates
ST CATHARINE'S (1473) *Master,* Prof. D. S. Ingram, CBE
ST EDMUND'S (1896) *Master,* Prof. J. P. Luzio
ST JOHN'S (1511) *Master,* Prof. R. N. Perham, SCD, FRS
SELWYN (1882) *Master,* Prof. R. J. Bowring, LITTD
SIDNEY SUSSEX (1596) *Master,* Prof. Dame Sandra Dawson
TRINITY (1546) *Master,* Prof. Lord Rees, FRS
TRINITY HALL (1350) *Master,* Prof. M. J. Daunton, FBA
WOLFSON (1965) *President,* G. Johnson, PHD

UNIVERSITY OF CENTRAL ENGLAND IN BIRMINGHAM (1992)
Perry Barr, Birmingham B42 2SU **T** 0121-331 5000
E info@ucechoices.com **W** www.uce.ac.uk
Full-time students (2004–5), 24,592
Chancellor, Cllr Michael Nangle
Vice-Chancellor, Dr Peter Knight
Secretary and Registrar, Maxine Penlington

UNIVERSITY OF CENTRAL LANCASHIRE (1992)
Preston PR1 2HE **T** 01772-201201 **W** www.uclan.ac.uk
Full-time students (2004–5), 35,000
Chancellor, Sir Richard Evans, CBE (2002)
Vice-Chancellor, Dr Malcolm McVicar
Head of Student Affairs, Ian McMillan

CITY UNIVERSITY (1966)
Northampton Square, London EC1V 0HB **T** 020-7040 5060
E registry@city.ac.uk **W** www.city.ac.uk
Full-time students (2004–5), 12,996
Chancellor, Michael Savory
Vice-Chancellor, Prof. David Rhind, PHD, DSC
Registrar, Eamon Martin
Secretary, Ian Creagh

COVENTRY UNIVERSITY (1992)
Priory Street, Coventry CV1 5FB **T** 024-7688 7688
W www.coventry.ac.uk
Full-time students (2004–5), 9,481
Vice-Chancellor, Prof. Madeleine Atkins, CBE
Academic Registrar, Kate Quantrell

CRANFIELD UNIVERSITY (1969)
Cranfield, Beds MK43 0AL **T** 01234-750111
E info@cranfield.ac.uk **W** www.cranfield.ac.uk
Students (2004–5), 3,059
Chancellor, Lord Vincent of Coleshill, GBE, KCB, DSO
Vice-Chancellor, Prof. Frank Hartley, DSC
Academic Registrar and Secretary, David Buck

DE MONTFORT UNIVERSITY (1992)
The Gateway, Leicester LE1 9BH **T** 08459-454647
E enquiry@dmu.ac.uk **W** www.dmu.ac.uk
Full-time students (2004–5), 12,500
Chancellor, Baroness Prashar, CBE
Vice-Chancellor, Prof. Philip Tasker
Registrar, Eugene Critchlow
Clerk to the Board of Governors, Alison Wells

UNIVERSITY OF DERBY (1992)
Kedleston Road, Derby DE22 1GB **T** 01332-590500
W www.derby.ac.uk
Full-time students (2004–5), 8,200
Chancellor, Leslie Wagner
Vice-Chancellor, Prof. John Coyne
Registrar, June Hughes

UNIVERSITY OF DUNDEE (1967)
Nethergate, Dundee DD1 4HN **T** 01382-344000
E university@dundee.ac.uk **W** www.dundee.ac.uk
Full-time students (2004–5), 11,579
Chancellor, Sir James Black, OM, FRCP, FRS, FRSE
Vice-Chancellor, Sir Alan Langlands
Academic Secretary, Dr David Duncan

UNIVERSITY OF DURHAM (1832)
The University Office, Durham DH1 3HP **T** 0191-334 2000
W www.dur.ac.uk
Full-time students (2004–5), 14,200
Chancellor, Dr Bill Bryson
Vice-Chancellor and Warden, Prof. Sir Kenneth Calman, KCB, MD, PHD
Registrar and Secretary, L. Sanders

COLLEGES
COLLINGWOOD *Principal,* Prof. Jane H. M. Taylor, DPHIL
GEORGE STEPHENSON *Principal,* Prof. A. C. Darnell
GREY *Master,* Prof. J. M. Chamberlain, DPHIL
HATFIELD *Acting Master,* Angel B. Scott
JOHN SNOW *Principal,* Prof. H. M. Evans, PHD
ST AIDAN'S *Principal,* J. S. Ashworth
ST CHAD'S *Principal,* Revd J. P. M. Cassidy, PHD
ST CUTHBERT'S SOCIETY *Principal,* Prof. R. D. Boyne, PHD
ST HILD AND ST BEDE *Principal,* J. A. Pearson, PHD
ST. JOHN'S *Principal,* Rt. Revd Prof. S. W. Sykes
ST MARY'S *Principal,* Miss J. L. Hobbs
TREVELYAN *Principal,* N. Martin, PHD
UNIVERSITY *Master,* Prof. M. E. Tucker, PHD
USHAW *Rector,* Revd T. Drainey
USTINOV COLLEGE *Principal,* Penelope B. Wilson, DPHIL
VAN MILDERT *Principal,* Prof. P. O'Meara, DPHIL

UNIVERSITY OF EAST ANGLIA (1963)

Norwich NR4 7TJ T 01603-456161 E press@uea.ac.uk
W www.uea.ac.uk
Full-time students (2004–5), 13,692
Chancellor, Sir Brandon Gough
Vice-Chancellor, Prof. David Eastwood
Registrar, Shelagh Cottrell
Registrar and Secretary, Brian Summers

UNIVERSITY OF EAST LONDON (1898)

Longbridge Road, Dagenham, Essex RM8 2AS T 020-8223 3000
E publicity@uel.ac.uk W www.uel.ac.uk
Full-time students (2004–5), 18,000
Chancellor, Lord Rix, CBE, DL
Vice-Chancellor, Prof. Michael Thorne
Registrar and Secretary, Alan Ingle

UNIVERSITY OF EDINBURGH (1583)

Old College, South Bridge, Edinburgh EH8 9YL T 0131-650 1000
E communications.office@ed.ac.uk W www.cd.ac.uk
Full-time students (2004–5), 22,363
Chancellor, HRH The Prince Philip, Duke of Edinburgh,
   KG, KT, OM, GBE, PC, FRS
Principal and Vice-Chancellor, Prof. Timothy O'Shea, PHD
Registrar, Dr Bruce D. Nelson
Secretary, Melvyn Cornish

UNIVERSITY OF ESSEX (1965)

Wivenhoe Park, Colchester CO4 3SQ T 01206-873333
W www.essex.ac.uk
Full-time students (2004–5), 5,710
Chancellor, Lord Phillips of Sudbury, OBE
Vice-Chancellor, Prof. Ivor Crewe
Registrar and Secretary, Tony Rich, PHD

UNIVERSITY OF EXETER (1955)

The Queen's Drive, Exeter, Devon EX4 4QJ T 01392-661000
E www.ex.ac.uk
Full-time students (2004–5), 8,460
Chancellor, Lord Alexander of Weedon, QC
Vice-Chancellor, Prof. Steve Smith, PHD
Registrar and Secretary, David J. Allen

UNIVERSITY OF GLAMORGAN (1992)

Pontypridd CF37 1DL T 01443-828812 E enquiries@glam.ac.uk
W www.glam.ac.uk
Full-time students (2004–5), 9,741
Chancellor, Lord Morris of Aberavon KG, PC, QC
Vice-Chancellor, Prof. David Halton
Academic Registrar, John O'Shea
Secretary, Leigh Bracegirdle

UNIVERSITY OF GLASGOW (1451)

Gilbert Scott Building, University Avenue, Glasgow G12 8QQ
T 0141-330 2000 E publicity.services@gla.ac.uk
W www.gla.ac.uk
Full-time students (2004–5), 18,972
Chancellor, Sir William Kerr Fraser, GCB, LLD, FRSE
Vice-Chancellor, Sir Muir Russell, KCB, FRSE
Secretary, David Newall

GLASGOW CALEDONIAN UNIVERSITY (1993)

City Campus, 70 Cowcaddens Road, Glasgow G4 0BA
T 0141-331 3000 E helpline@gcal.ac.uk
W www.caledonian.ac.uk
Full-time students (2004–5), 15,000
Chancellor, Magnus Magnusson, KBE
Vice-Chancellor, Dr Ian Johnston, CB
Registrar, Brendan Ferguson
Secretary, Alison Rooney

UNIVERSITY OF GLOUCESTERSHIRE (2001)

Park Campus Cheltenham GL50 2RH T 01242-532710
W www.glos.ac.uk
Full-time students (2004–5), 6,800
Chancellor, Lord Carey of Clifton, PC
Vice-Chancellor, Dame Janet Trotter
Academic Registrar, Julie Smalls
Secretary, Paul Van Rossum

UNIVERSITY OF GREENWICH (1992)

Old Royal Naval College, Park Row, Greenwich, London
SE10 9LS T 020-8331 8000 E courseinfo@gre.ac.uk
W www.gre.ac.uk
Full-time students (2004–5), 15,305
Chancellor, Lord Holme of Cheltenham, CBE, PC
Vice-Chancellor, Baroness Blackstone, PHD
Registrar and Secretary, Linda Cording

HERIOT-WATT UNIVERSITY (1966)

Edinburgh EH14 4AS T 0131-449 5111 E enquires@hw.ac.uk
W www.hw.ac.uk
Full-time students (2004–5), 5,445
Chancellor, Lord Mackay of Clashfern, KT, PC, FRSE
Vice-Chancellor, Prof. John Archer,
   CBE, PHD, FRSE, FRENG
Secretary, Peter Wilson

UNIVERSITY OF HERTFORDSHIRE (1992)

College Lane, Hatfield, Herts AL10 9AB T 01707-284000
E admissions@herts.ac.uk W www.herts.ac.uk
Full-time students (2004–5), 16,286
Chancellor, Marquess of Salisbury, PC
Vice-Chancellor, Prof. R. J. T. Wilson
Registrar, Mrs S. C. Grant

UNIVERSITY OF HUDDERSFIELD (1992)

Queensgate, Huddersfield HD1 3DH T 01484-422288
W www.hud.ac.uk
Full-time students (2004–5), 11,527
Chancellor, Patrick Stewart, OBE
Vice-Chancellor, Prof. John Tarrant
Academic Registrar, Kathy Sherlock
Secretary, Tony Mears

UNIVERSITY OF HULL (1927)

Cottingham Road, Hull HU6 7RX T 01482-346311
W www.hull.ac.uk
Full-time students (2004–5), 12,982
Chancellor, Lord Armstrong of Ilminster, GCB, CVO
Vice-Chancellor, Prof. David J. Drewry
Deputy Vice-Chancellor, Prof. J. W. Bruce
Registrar and Secretary, Mrs F. J. Owen

KEELE UNIVERSITY (1962)

Keele, Staffs ST5 5BG T 01782-621111 W www.keele.ac.uk
Full-time students (2003–4), 5,636
Chancellor, Prof. Sir David Weatherall, FRS
Vice-Chancellor, Prof. Janet Finch, CBE
Secretary and Registrar, Mr S. J. Morris

UNIVERSITY OF KENT AT CANTERBURY (1965)

Canterbury, Kent CT2 7NZ T 01227-764000
W www.kent.ac.uk
Full-time students (2004–5), 14,280
Chancellor, Sir Crispin Tickell, GCMG, KCVO, DCL
Vice-Chancellor, Prof. David Melville, CBE, PHD
Registrar and Secretary, Nick McHard

KINGSTON UNIVERSITY (1992)
River House, 53–57 High Street, Kingston upon Thames, Surrey
KT1 1LQ **T** 020-8547 2000 **W** www.kingston.ac.uk
Full-time students (2004–5), 17,719
Chancellor, Sir Peter Hall
Vice-Chancellor, Prof. Peter Scott
University Secretary, Raficq Abdulla, MBE

UNIVERSITY OF LANCASTER (1964)
Bailrigg, Lancaster LA1 4YW **T** 01524-65201
W www.lancs.ac.uk
Full-time students (2004–5), 10,641
Chancellor, Sir Christian Bonington
Vice-Chancellor, Prof. Paul Wellings
Registrar, Marion McClintock
Secretary, Fiona Aiken

UNIVERSITY OF LEEDS (1904)
Leeds LS2 9JT **T** 0113-243 1751 **W** www.leeds.ac.uk
Full-time students (2004–5), 29,424
Chancellor, Lord Bragg
Vice-Chancellor, Prof. Michael Arthur
Secretary, Roger Gair

LEEDS METROPOLITAN UNIVERSITY (1992)
Civic Quarter, Leeds LS1 3HE **T** 0113-283 2600
W www.lmu.ac.uk
Full-time students (2004–5), 14,866
Chancellor, Brendan Foster, MBE
Vice-Chancellor, Prof. Simon Lee
Registrar and Secretary, Stephen Denton

UNIVERSITY OF LEICESTER (1957)
University Road, Leicester LE1 7RH **T** 0116-252 2522
W www.le.ac.uk
Full-time students (2004–5), 18,005
Chancellor, Sir Michael Atiyah, OM, FRS, PHD
Vice-Chancellor, Prof. Robert Burgess, PHD
Registrar and Secretary, Keith Julian

UNIVERSITY OF LINCOLN (1992)
Brayford Pool, Lincoln, LN6 7TS **T** 01522-882000
W www.lincoln.ac.uk
Full-time students (2004–5), 8,365
Chancellor, Dame Elizabeth Esteve-Coll
Vice-Chancellor, Prof. David Chiddick
Registrar, Edmund Fitzpatrick

UNIVERSITY OF LIVERPOOL (1903)
Senate House, Abercromby Square, Liverpool L69 3BX **T** 0151-
794 2000 **W** www.liv.ac.uk
Full-time students (2004–5), 17,521
Chancellor, Lord Owen, CH, PC
Vice-Chancellor, Prof. Drummond Bone
Chief Operating Officer, John Latham

LIVERPOOL JOHN MOORES UNIVERSITY (1992)
Egerton Court, 2 Rodaney Street, Liverpool L3 5UX **T** 0151-231
2121 **W** www.livjm.ac.uk
Full-time students (2004–5), 13,556
Chancellor, Cherie Booth, QC
Vice-Chancellor, Prof. Michael Brown
Secretary, Alison Wild

UNIVERSITY OF LONDON (1836)
Senate House, Malet Street, London WC1E 7HU **T** 020-7862
8000 **E** enquiries@lon.ac.uk **W** www.lon.ac.uk
Full-time students (2004–5), 96,862
Chancellor, HRH The Princess Royal, KG, GCVO, FRS
Vice-Chancellor, Prof. Sir Graeme Davies
Chair of the Council, Rt. Hon. Lord Brooke of Sutton
    Mandeville, CH, PC
Academic Registrar, Gillian Roberts
Director of Administration, Catherine Swarbrick

COLLEGES
BIRKBECK COLLEGE Malet Street, London WC1E 7HX
    Master, Prof. D. Latchman
CENTRAL SCHOOL OF SPEECH AND DRAMA Embassy
    Theatre, Eton Avenue, London NW3 3HY
    Principal, Prof. Gary Crossley
COURTAULD INSTITUTE OF ART North Block, Somerset
    House, Strand, London WC2R 0RN
    Director, Dr Deborah Swallow
GOLDSMITHS COLLEGE Lewisham Way, New Cross,
    London SE14 6NW
    Warden, Prof. Geoffrey Crossick
HEYTHROP COLLEGE Kensington Square, London
    W8 5HQ
    Principal, Revd Dr J. McDade, SJ, BD
IMPERIAL COLLEGE (includes Imperial College Schools of
    Medicine at Charing Cross, Hammersmith and St Mary's
    hospitals and at the National Heart and Lung Institute),
    South Kensington, London SW7 2A7
    Rector, Prof. Sir Richard Sykes, FRS
INSTITUTE OF CANCER RESEARCH Royal Cancer Hospital,
    Chester Beatty Laboratories, 237 Fulham Road, London
    SW3 6JB
    Chief Executive, Prof. P. Rigby
INSTITUTE OF EDUCATION 20 Bedford Way, London
    WC1H 0AL
    Director, Prof. G. Whitty
KING'S COLLEGE LONDON (includes Guy's, King's and St
    Thomas's Schools of Medicine, Dentistry and Biomedical
    Sciences), Strand, London WC2R 2LS
    Principal, Prof. R. Trainor
LONDON BUSINESS SCHOOL Sussex Place, Regent's
    Park, London NW1 4SU
    Principal, Prof. L. D'Andrea Tyson
LONDON SCHOOL OF ECONOMICS AND POLITICAL
    SCIENCE Houghton Street, London WC2A 2AE
    Director, Sir Howard Davies
LONDON SCHOOL OF HYGIENE AND TROPICAL
    MEDICINE Keppel Street, London WC1E 7HT
    Dean, Prof. A. Haines
QUEEN MARY (incorporating St Bartholomew's and the Royal
    London School of Medicine and Dentistry), Mile End Road,
    London E1 4NS
    Principal, Prof. A. Smith, FRS
ROYAL ACADEMY OF MUSIC Marylebone Road, London
    NW1 5HT
    Principal, Prof. Curtis Price, KBE
ROYAL HOLLOWAY Egham Hill, Egham, Surrey TW20 0EX
    Principal, Prof. S. Hill, MPHIL
ROYAL VETERINARY COLLEGE Royal College Street,
    London NW1 0TU
    Principal and Dean, Prof. Q. McKellar
ST GEORGE'S HOSPITAL MEDICAL SCHOOL Cranmer
    Terrace, London SW17 0RE
    Principal, Prof. Michael Farthing, FRCP

SCHOOL OF ORIENTAL AND AFRICAN STUDIES
Thornhaugh Street, Russell Square, London WC1H 1AX
Director, Prof. C. Bundy
SCHOOL OF PHARMACY 29–39 Brunswick Square, London
WC1N 1AX
Dean, Prof. A. T. Florence, CBE, PHD, FRSE
UNIVERSITY COLLEGE LONDON (including UCL Medical
School), Gower Street, London WC1E 6BT
Provost and President, Prof. Malcolm Grant

INSTITUTES
UNIVERSITY OF LONDON INSTITUTE IN PARIS
9–11 rue de Constantine, 75340 Paris, Cedex 07
Director, Prof. David Shepheard
UNIVERSITY MARINE BIOLOGICAL STATION Millport,
Isle of Cumbrae KA28 0EG
Director, Dr Rupert Ormond

SCHOOL OF ADVANCED STUDY
Senate House, Malet Street, London WC1E 7HU
Dean, Prof. Nicholas Mann
INSTITUTE OF ADVANCED LEGAL STUDIES Charles Clore
House, 17 Russell Square, London WC1B 5DR
Director, Prof. Avrom Sherr
INSTITUTE OF CLASSICAL STUDIES Senate House, Malet
Street, London WC1E 7HU
Director, Prof. Tim Cornell
INSTITUTE OF COMMONWEALTH STUDIES
27–28 Russell Square, London WC1B 5DS
Director, Prof. T. Shaw
INSTITUTE OF ENGLISH STUDIES Senate House, Malet
Street, London WC1E 7HU
Director, Prof. W. Gould
INSTITUTE OF GERMANIC AND ROMANCE STUDIES
Senate House, Malet Street, London WC1E 7HU
Director, Prof. Naomi Segal
INSTITUTE OF HISTORICAL RESEARCH Senate House,
Malet Street, London WC1E 7HU
Director, Prof. David Bates
INSTITUTE OF MUSICAL STUDIES Senate House, Malet
Street, London WC1E 7HU
Director, vacant
INSTITUTE OF PHILOSOPHY Senate House, Malet Street,
London WC1E 7HU
Director, Prof. Tim Crane
INSTITUTE FOR THE STUDY OF THE AMERICAS
31 Tavistock Square, London WC1H 9HA
Director, Prof. J. Dunkerley
WARBURG INSTITUTE Woburn Square, London WC1H 0AB
Director, Prof. C. Hope

DISTANCE LEARNING
EXTERNAL PROGRAMME Senate House, Malet Street,
London WC1E 7HU
Director, J. M. McConnell

LONDON METROPOLITAN UNIVERSITY (2002)
31 Jewry Street, London EC3N 2EY T 020-7423 0000
W www.londonmet.ac.uk
Full-time students (2004–5), 15,065
President, Prof. Sir Roderick Floud
Vice-Chancellor and Chief Executive, Brian Roper
Secretary, John McParland

LONDON SOUTH BANK UNIVERSITY (1992)
103 Borough Road, London SE1 0AA T 020-7928 8989
W www.sbu.ac.uk
Full-time students (2004–5), 19,000
Chancellor, Sir Trevor McDonald
Vice-Chancellor, Prof. Deian Hopkin
Pro-Vice Chancellor, Dr Ruth Farwell
Secretary, Karen Stephenson

LOUGHBOROUGH UNIVERSITY (1966)
Ashby Road, Loughborough, Leics LE11 3TU T 01509-263171
W www.lboro.ac.uk
Full-time students (2004–5), 12,600
Chancellor, Sir John Jennings, CBE, FRSE
Vice-Chancellor, Prof. Sir David Wallace,
CBE, FRS, FRENG
Academic Registrar, Dr J. C. Nutkins
Registrar and Secretary, John Town

UNIVERSITY OF LUTON (1993)
Park Square, Luton LU1 3JU T 01582-734111
W www.luton.ac.uk
Full-time students (2004–5), 12,500
Chancellor, Sir Robin Biggam
Vice-Chancellor, Prof. Les Ebdon
Academic Registrar, Dr Jim Franklin
Secretary, Arthur Sullivan

UNIVERSITY OF MANCHESTER (1824)
Oxford Road, Manchester M13 9PL T 0161-306 6000
E enquiry@manchester.ac.uk W www.manchester.ac.uk
Full-time students (2004–5), 28,802
Co-Chancellors, Anna Ford and Sir Terry Leahy
Vice-Chancellor, Prof. Alan Gilbert
Registrar and Secretary, Dugald Mackie

MANCHESTER METROPOLITAN UNIVERSITY
(1992)
All Saints, Manchester M15 6BH T 0161-247 2000
E enquiries@mmu.ac.uk W www.mmu.ac.uk
Full-time students (2004–5), 27,587
Chancellor, Dame Janet Smith, DBE, PC
Vice-Chancellor, Prof. J. Brooks, PHD
Registrar, K. Karczewski-Slowikowski
University Secretary, K. Hughes

MIDDLESEX UNIVERSITY (1992)
North London Business Park, Oakleigh Road, London N11 1QS
T 020-8411 5000 W www.mdx.ac.uk
Full-time students (2004–5), 24,166
Chancellor, Lord Sheppard of Didgemere, KCVO
Vice-Chancellor, Prof. Michael Driscoll
Registrar, Colin Davis

NAPIER UNIVERSITY (1992)
Craighouse Road, Edinburgh EH10 5LG T 0500-353570
E info@napier.ac.uk W www.napier.ac.uk
Full-time students (2004–5), 10,182
Vice-Chancellor, Prof. Joan Stringer, CBE
Registrar and Secretary, Dr Gerry Webber

UNIVERSITY OF NEWCASTLE UPON TYNE (1963)
6 Kensington Terrace, Newcastle upon Tyne NE17 7RU
T 0191-222 6000 E postmaster@ncl.ac.uk W www.ncl.ac.uk
Full-time students (2004–5), 13,158
Chancellor, Rt. Hon. Lord Patten of Barnes, CH, PC
Vice-Chancellor, Prof. Christopher Edwards
Registrar, Dr John Hogan

NORTHUMBRIA UNIVERSITY AT NEWCASTLE (1992)
Ellison Building, Ellison Place, Newcastle upon Tyne NE1 8ST
T 0191-232 6002 W www.northumbria.ac.uk
Full-time students (2004–5), 20,515
Pro-Chancellors, Gavin Black and Haydn Biddle
Vice-Chancellor, Prof. Kel Fidler
Registrar, Cheryl Penna
Secretary, Richard Bott

UNIVERSITY OF NOTTINGHAM (1948)
University Park, Nottingham NG7 2RD T 0115-951 5151
W www.nottingham.ac.uk
Full-time students (2004–5), 23,740
Chancellor, Prof. Yang Fujia, LITTD
Vice Chancellor, Prof. Sir Colin Campbell
Registrar, Keith Jones

NOTTINGHAM TRENT UNIVERSITY (1992)
Burton Street, Nottingham NG1 4BU T 0115-941 8418
W www.ntu.ac.uk
Full-time students (2004–5), 17,000
Chair, Prof. Neil T. Gorman
Academic Registrar, David Samson

OPEN UNIVERSITY (1969)
Walton Hall,Milton Keynes MK7 6AA T 01908-274066
E general-enquiries@open.ac.uk W www.open.ac.uk
Full-time students (2004–5), 72,617
Chancellor, Baroness Boothroyd, PC
Vice-Chancellor, Prof. Brenda Gourley
Secretary, Fraser Woodburn

UNIVERSITY OF OXFORD (c. 12th century)
University Offices, Wellington Square, Oxford OX1 2JD
T 01865-270000 W www.ox.ac.uk
Full-time students (2004–5), 18,113
Chancellor, Lord Patten of Barnes, CH, PC
High Steward, Lord Bingham of Cornhill, PC (Balliol, Nuffield)
Vice-Chancellor, Dr J. A. Hood
Pro-Vice-Chancellors, Dr Bill Macmillan, Dr Jon Dellandrea, Prof. Nigel Thrift, Prof. Elizabeth Fallaize, Dame Fiona Caldicott
Registrar, D. R. Holmes (St John's)
Secretary of the Faculties and Academic Registrar, A. P. Weale (Worcester)
Proctors, Prof. A. Grafen (St John's), Prof. R. W. Daniel (Brasenose)
Assessor, Dr F. N. Pieke (St Cross)
Public Orator, R. H. A. Jenkyns
Director of University Library Services and Bodley's Librarian, R. P. Carr (Balliol)
Director of the Ashmolean Museum, Dr C. Brown (Worcester)
Keeper of Archives, S. Bailey
Director of Estates, Ms J. Wood
Director of Finance, G. F. B. Kerr

COLLEGES AND HALLS *with dates of foundation*

ALL SOULS (1438) *Warden*, Prof. J. Davis, FBA, PHD
BALLIOL (1263) *Master*, A. Graham
BLACKFRIARS (1221) *Regent*, Revd Richard Finn, DPHIL
BRASENOSE (1509) *Principal*, Prof. R. Cashmore, FRS
CAMPION HALL (1896) *Master*, Revd Dr G. J. Hughes
CHRIST CHURCH (1546) *Dean*, Very Revd C. A. Lewis
CORPUS CHRISTI (1517) *President*, Timothy Lankester, KCB

EXETER (1314) *Rector*, Ms Frances Cairncross, CBE
GREEN (1979) *Warden*, Sir John Hanson, KCMG, CBE
GREYFRIARS (1910) *Warden*, Dr Nicholas Richardson
HARRIS MANCHESTER (1786) *Principal*, Revd R. Waller, PHD
HERTFORD (1974) *Principal*, Dr John Landers
JESUS (1571) *Principal*, Sir John Krebs, FRS
KEBLE (1868) *Warden*, Prof. A. Cameron, CBE, PHD, FBA
KELLOGG (1990) *President*, Dr G. P. Thomas
LADY MARGARET HALL (1878) *Principal*, Dr Frances Lannon
LINACRE (1962) *Principal*, Prof. P. A. Slack, FBA
LINCOLN (1427) *Rector*, Prof. P. Langford
MAGDALEN (1458) *President*, Prof. David Clary, FRS
MANSFIELD (1886) *Principal*, Dr. D. Walford, FRCP
MERTON (1264) *Warden*, Prof. Dame J. Rawson, CBE, FBA
NEW COLLEGE (1379) *Warden*, Prof. A. J. Ryan, FBA
NUFFIELD (1958) *Warden*, Prof. Stephen Nickell, FBA
ORIEL (1326) *Provost*, Sir Derek Morris
PEMBROKE (1624) *Master*, Giles Henderson, CBE
QUEEN'S (1340) *Provost*, Sir Alan Budd
REGENT'S PARK (1820) *Principal*, Revd Dr P. S. Fiddes
ST ANNE'S (1952) *Principal*, Tim Gardam
ST ANTONY'S (1953) *Warden*, Sir Marrack Goulding, KCMG
ST BENET'S HALL (1897) *Master*, Father Leo Chamberlain
ST CATHERINE'S (1963) *Master*, Prof. Roger Ainsworth
ST CROSS (1965) *Master*, Prof. Andrew Goudie
ST EDMUND HALL (c.1278) *Principal*, Prof. D. M. P. Mingos, FRS
ST HILDA'S (1893) *Principal*, Lady Judith English
ST HUGH'S (1886) *Principal*, A. Dilnot, CBE
ST JOHN'S (1555) *President*, Sir Michael Scholar, KCB
ST PETER'S (1929) *Master*, Prof. Bernard Silverman, FRS
SOMERVILLE (1879) *Principal*, Dame Fiona Caldicott, DBE, FRCP, FRCPSYCH
TEMPLETON (1965) *Dean*, Prof. Michael Earl
TRINITY (1554) *President*, The Hon. Michael J. Beloff, FRSA
UNIVERSITY (1249) *Master*, Lord Butler of Brockwell, GCB, CVO
WADHAM (1610) *Warden*, Sir Neil Chalmers, CBE
WOLFSON (1966) *President*, Prof. Sir Gareth Roberts, FRS, PHD
WORCESTER (1714) *Provost*, R. G. Smethurst
WYCLIFFE HALL (1877) *Principal*, Revd Dr Richard Turnbull

OXFORD BROOKES UNIVERSITY (1992)
Gipsy Lane, Oxford OX3 0BP T 01865-741111
E query@brookes.ac.uk W www.brookes.ac.uk
Full-time students (2004–5), 13,242
Chancellor, Jon Snow
Vice-Chancellor, Prof. Graham Upton
Academic Registrar, Stephen Marshall

UNIVERSITY OF PAISLEY (1992)
Paisley PA1 2BE T 0141-848 3000 E uni-direct@paisley.ac.uk
W www.paisley.ac.uk
Full-time students (2004–5), 7,534
Chancellor, Sir Robert Smith
Principal and Vice-Chancellor (acting), Prof. Seamus McDaid
Secretary and Registrar, David Rigg

UNIVERSITY OF PLYMOUTH (1992)
Drake Circus,Plymouth PL4 8AA **T** 01752-600600
W www.plymouth.ac.uk
Full-time students (2004–5), 16,180
Vice-Chancellor, Prof. Roland Levinsky
Academic Registrar and Secretary, Jane Hopkinson

UNIVERSITY OF PORTSMOUTH (1992)
University House, Winston Churchill Avenue, Portsmouth
PO1 2UP **T** 023-9284 8484 **E** info.centre@port.ac.uk
W www.port.ac.uk
Full-time students (2004–5), 14,145
Chancellor, Lord Palumbo
Vice-Chancellor, Prof. John Craven
Registrar, Andy Rees

QUEEN'S UNIVERSITY BELFAST (1908)
University Road, Belfast BT7 1NN **T** 028-9024 5133
W www.qub.ac.uk
Full-time students (2004–5), 17,000
Chancellor, Senator George Mitchell
Vice-Chancellor, Prof. Peter Gregson
Registrar, James O'Kane

UNIVERSITY OF READING (1926)
Whiteknights, PO Box 217, Reading RG6 6AH **T** 0118-987 5123
W www.reading.ac.uk
Full-time students (2004–5), 10,536
Chancellor, Lord Carington of Upton, KG, GCMG, CH, MC
Vice-Chancellor, Prof. Gordon Marshall
Director of Student Services, W. D. Watts
Director of Academic Services, Keith Hodgson

ROBERT GORDON UNIVERSITY (1992)
Schoolhill, Aberdeen AB10 1FR **T** 01224-262000
E admissions@rgu.ac.uk **W** www.rgu.ac.uk
Full-time students (2004–5), 11,500
Chancellor, Sir Ian Wood
Vice-Chancellor, Prof. Mike Pittilo
Registrar, Hilary Douglas
Secretary, Dr Adrian Graves

ROYAL COLLEGE OF ART (1837)
Kensington Gore, London SW7 2EU **T** 020-7590 4444
E admissions@rca.ac.uk **W** www.rca.ac.uk
Full-time students (2004–5), 800
Provost, Sir Terence Conran
Rector and Vice-Provost, Prof. Sir Christopher Frayling, PHD
Registrar, Alan Selby

ROYAL COLLEGE OF MUSIC (1882)
Prince Consort Road, London SW7 2BS **T** 020-7589 3643
E info@rcm.ac.uk **W** www.rcm.ac.uk
Full-time students (2004–5), 600
Director, Dr Colin Lawson
Dean and Deputy Director, Jeremy Cox
Registrar and Sectretary, Kevin Porter

UNIVERSITY OF ST ANDREWS (1413)
College Gate, St Andrews, Fife KY16 9AJ **T** 01334-476161
W www.st-andrews.ac.uk
Full-time students (2004–5), 6,042
Chancellor, Sir Kenneth Dover
Principal, Dr Brian Lang
Secretary and Registrar, Alastair Work

UNIVERSITY OF SALFORD (1967)
Salford, Greater Manchester M5 4WT **T** 0161-295 5000
W www.salford.ac.uk
Full-time students (2004–5), 12,497
Chancellor, Prof. Sir Martin Harris
Vice-Chancellor, Prof. Michael Harloe
Academic Registrar, Dr Kathleen Whyte
Secretary, Stephanie MacPherson

UNIVERSITY OF SHEFFIELD (1905)
Western Bank, Sheffield S10 2TN **T** 0114-222 2000
W www.shef.ac.uk
Full-time students (2004–5), 15,742
Chancellor, Sir Peter Middleton, GCB
Vice-Chancellor, Prof. R. F. Boucher, CBE, PHD, FRENG
Registrar and Secretary, D. E. Fletcher, PHD

SHEFFIELD HALLAM UNIVERSITY (1992)
City Campus, Howard Street, Sheffield S1 1WB
T 0114-225 5555 **W** www.shu.ac.uk
Full-time students (2004–5), 22,000
Chancellor, Prof. Lord Winston
Vice-Chancellor, Prof. Diana Green
Registrar, Gwyn Arnold
Secretary, Liz Winders

UNIVERSITY OF SOUTHAMPTON (1952)
Highfield, Southampton SO17 1BJ **T** 023-8059 5000
E external@soton.ac.uk **W** www.soton.ac.uk
Full-time students (2004–5), 17,534
Chancellor, The Earl of Selborne, KBE, FRS
Vice-Chancellor, Prof. Bill Wakeham
Secretary and Registrar, John Lauwerys

STAFFORDSHIRE UNIVERSITY (1992)
Stoke-on-Trent, Staffs ST4 2DE **T** 01782-294000
W www.staffs.ac.uk
Full-time students (2004–5), 8,766
Chancellor, Sir Bill Morris
Vice-Chancellor, Prof. Christine King
Secretary, Ken Sproston

UNIVERSITY OF STIRLING (1967)
Stirling FK9 4LA **T** 01786-473171 **W** www.stir.ac.uk
Full-time students (2004–5), 7,060
Chancellor, Dame Diana Rigg
Vice-Chancellor, Prof. Christine Hallet
Registrar, Douglas Wood
University Secretary, Kevin Clarke

UNIVERSITY OF STRATHCLYDE (1964)
16 Richmond Street,Glasgow G1 1XQ **T** 0141-552 4400
W www.strath.ac.uk
Full-time students (2004–5), 10,659
Chancellor, Lord Hope of Craighead, PC, FRSE
Vice-Chancellor and Principal, Prof. Andrew Hamnett, DPHIL, FRSE
Secretary, Dr Peter West

UNIVERSITY OF SUNDERLAND (1992)
Edinburgh Building, Chester Road, Sunderland SR1 3SD
T 0191-515 2000 **W** www.sunderland.ac.uk
Full-time students (2004–5), 8,800
Chancellor, Lord Puttnam, CBE
Vice-Chancellor, Prof. Peter Fidler
Secretary, John Pacey

UNIVERSITY OF SURREY (1966)
Guildford, Surrey GU2 7XH T 01483-300800
E information@surrey.ac.uk W www.surrey.ac.uk
Full-time students (2004–5), 9,858
Chancellor, HRH the Duke of Kent,
    KG, GCMG, GCVO, ADC(P)
Vice-Chancellor, Prof. Christopher M. Snowden, FRENG
Registrar, P. W. Beardsley
Secretary, J. W. A. Strawson

UNIVERSITY OF SUSSEX (1961)
Sussex House, Falmer, Brighton BN1 9RHT 01273-606755
E information@sussex.ac.uk W www.sussex.ac.uk
Full-time students (2004–5), 10,511
Chancellor, Lord Attenborough, CBE
Vice-Chancellor, Prof. Alasdair Smith
Registrar, Owen Richards

UNIVERSITY OF TEESSIDE (1992)
Middlesbrough, Tees Valley TS1 3BA T 01642-218121
W www.tees.ac.uk
Full-time students (2004–5), 8,553
Chancellor, Lord Sawyer
Vice-Chancellor, Prof. Graham Henderson
Academic Registrar, Kathryn Turnbull
University Secretary, Morgan McClintock

THAMES VALLEY UNIVERSITY (1992)
St Mary's Road, Ealing, London W5 5RF T 020-8579 5000
W www.tvu.ac.uk
Full-time students (2004–5), 7,000
Vice-Chancellor, Prof. Geoff Crispin
Secretary, Ann-Marie Dalton

UNIVERSITY OF WALES (1893)
King Edward VII Avenue, Cathays Park, Cardiff CF10 3NS
T 029-2038 2656 E uniwales@wales.ac.uk
W www.wales.ac.uk
Full-time students (2004–5), 75,000
Chancellor, HRH The Prince of Wales,
    KG, KT, GCB, OM, PC
Senior Vice-Chancellor, Prof. A. J. Chapman
Secretary-General, Dr L. E. Williams

SWANSEA INSTITUTE OF HIGHER EDUCATION Mount
    Pleasant, Swansea T 01792-481000
    Principal, Prof. D. Warner

MEMBER INSTITUTES
TRINITY COLLEGE, CARMARTHEN Carmarthen SA31 3EP
    T 01267-676767
    Principal, Dr M. Hughes
UNIVERSITY OF WALES, ABERYSTWYTH Old College,
    King Street,Aberystwyth SY23 2AX T 01970-623111
    Vice-Chancellor, Prof. N. G. Lloyd
UNIVERSITY OF WALES, BANGOR Gwynedd LL57 2DG
    T 01248-351151
    Vice-Chancellor, Prof. R. M. Jones
NORTH EAST WALES INSTITUTE OF HIGHER
    EDUCATION Plas Coch, Mold Road,Wrexham LL11 2AW
    T 01978-290666
    Principal, Prof. M. Scott
ROYAL WELSH COLLEGE OF MUSIC AND DRAMA
    Maes y Castell, Cathays Park,Cardiff CF10 3ER
    Principal, Edmond Fivet

UNIVERSITY OF WALES, NEWPORT Caerleon Campus PO
    Box 179 Newport NP6 1YG T 01633-430088
    Vice-Chancellor, Prof. J. R. Lusty, PHD, FRSC
UNIVERSITY OF WALES INSTITUTE, CARDIFF Llandaff
    Centre, Western Avenue, Cardiff CF5 2SG T 029-2041 6070
    Vice-Chancellor, Prof. A. J. Chapman
UNIVERSITY OF WALES, LAMPETER Lampeter, SA48 7ED
    T 01570-422351
    Vice-Chancellor, Prof. R. A. Pearce
UNIVERSITY OF WALES, SWANSEA Singleton Park,
    SA2 8PP T 01792-205678
    Vice-Chancellor, Prof. R. B. Davies

UNIVERSITY OF WARWICK (1965)
Coventry CV4 7AL T 024-7652 3523 W www.warwick.ac.uk
Full-time students (2004–5), 10,346
Chancellor, Sir Nicholas Scheele
Vice-Chancellor, Prof. David Vandelinde, PHD, FRS
Academic Registrar, Dr D. Law, PHD
Secretary, C. E. Charlton

UNIVERSITY OF WESTMINSTER (1992)
309 Regent Street, London W1B 2UW T 020-7911 5000
W www.wmin.ac.uk
Full-time students (2004–5), 10,463
Chair of the Court of Governors, Dr Terry Wright
Vice-Chancellor and Rector, Dr Geoffrey Copland
University Secretary and Clerk to the Court, Carole
    Mainstone

UNIVERSITY OF THE WEST OF ENGLAND (1992)
Frenchay Campus, Coldharbour Lane, Bristol BS16 1QY
T 0117-965 6261 E enquiries@uwe.ac.uk W www.uwe.ac.uk
Full-time students (2004–5), 18,988
Chancellor, Dame Elizabeth Butler-Sloss, GBE, PC
Vice-Chancellor, A. C. Morris, CBE
Assistant Academic Secretary, Maureen McLaughlin

UNIVERSITY OF WOLVERHAMPTON (1992)
Wulfruna Street, Wolverhampton WV1 1SB T 01902-321000
W www.wlv.ac.uk
Full-time students (2004–5), 9,944
Chancellor, Lord Paul
Vice-Chancellor, Prof. Caroline Gipps, PHD
Registrar, Jane Nelson
Secretary, Antony W. Lee

UNIVERSITY OF YORK (1963)
Heslington, York YO10 5DD T 01904-430000
W www.york.ac.uk
Full-time students (2004–5), 9,767
Chancellor, Greg Dyke
Vice-Chancellor, Prof. Brian Cantor, PHD, FRENG
Registrar and Secretary, Sally Neocosmos

UNIVERSITY OF ULSTER (1984)
Cromore Road, Coleraine, Co. Londonderry BT52 1SA T 08700
400 700 W www.ulster.ac.uk
Full-time students (2004–5), 16,497
Chancellor, Sir Richard Nichols
Vice-Chancellor (acting), Prof. Richard Barnett, PHD
Head of Academic Registry, Dr Alan Scott

PROFESSIONAL EDUCATION

The organisations listed below are those which, by providing specialist training or conducting examinations, control entry into a profession, or are responsible for maintaining a register of those with professional qualifications in their sector.

EU RECOGNITION
It is possible for those with professional qualifications obtained in the UK to have these recognised in other European countries. Further information can be obtained from www.dfes.gov.uk/europeopen or:

DEPARTMENT FOR EDUCATION AND SKILLS Moorfoot, Sheffield S1 4PQ **T** 0870-001 2345 **E** info@dfes.gsi.gov.uk **W** www.dfes.gov.uk

ACCOUNTANCY
The main bodies granting membership on examination after a period of practical work are:
ASSOCIATION OF CHARTERED CERTIFIED ACCOUNTANTS (ACCA) 29 Lincoln's Inn Fields, London WC2A 3EE **T** 020-7059 5700 **E** info@accaglobal.com **W** www.accaglobal.com
Chief Executive, Allen Blewitt
CHARTERED INSTITUTE OF PUBLIC FINANCE AND ACCOUNTANCY (CIPFA) 3 Robert Street, London WC2N 6RL **T** 020-7543 5600 **E** www.cipfa.org.uk
Chief Executive, Steve Freer
INSTITUTE OF CHARTERED ACCOUNTANTS IN ENGLAND AND WALES Chartered Accountants' Hall, PO Box 433, London EC2P 2BJ **T** 020-7920 8100 **W** www.icaew.co.uk
Chief Executive, Eric Anstee
INSTITUTE OF CHARTERED ACCOUNTANTS IN IRELAND 11 Donegall Square South, Belfast BT1 5JE **T** 028-9032 1600 **E** ca@icai.ie **W** www.icai.ie
Chief Executive, Pat Costello
INSTITUTE OF CHARTERED ACCOUNTANTS OF SCOTLAND (ICAS) CA House, 21 Haymarket Yards, Edinburgh EH12 5BH **T** 0131-347 0100 **E** enquiries@icas.org.uk **W** www.icas.org.uk
Chief Executive, Desmond Hudson
THE CHARTERED INSTITUTE OF MANAGEMENT ACCOUNTANTS (CIMA) 26 Chapter Street, London SW1P 4NP **T** 020-8849 2456 **W** www.cimaglobal.com
Chief Executive, Charles Tilley

ACTUARIAL SCIENCE
The UK actuarial profession is controlled by the Institute of Actuaries in London and the Faculty of Actuaries in Edinburgh. The Faculty and Institute together issue technical guidance, develop actuarial techniques and set examinations, professional codes and disciplinary standards. UK qualified actuaries may be Fellows of either organisation. Practising certificates are issued on certain actuaries for their statutory role in the financial management of life offices and most pension schemes.
FACULTY OF ACTUARIES IN SCOTLAND Maclaurin House, 18 Dublin Street, Edinburgh EH1 3PP **T** 0131-240 1300 **E** faculty@actuaries.org.uk **W** www.actuaries.org.uk
Secretary, Richard Maconachie
INSTITUTE OF ACTUARIES Staple Inn Hall, High Holborn, London WC1V 7QJ **T** 020-7632 2100 **E** institute@actuaries.org.uk **W** www.actuaries.org.uk
Secretary-General, Caroline Instance

ARCHITECTURE
The Education Committee of the Royal Institute of British Architects sets standards and, by means of validation criteria held in common with the Architects Registration Board, guides the whole system of architectural education throughout the UK. RIBA recognises courses at 38 schools of architecture in the UK for exemption from their own examinations as well as courses at 53 overseas schools.
ARCHITECTS REGISTRATION BOARD 8 Weymouth Street, London W1W 5BU **T** 020-7580 5861 **E** info@arb.org.uk **W** www.arb.org.uk
Chief Executive and Registrar, Robin Vaughan
ARCHITECTURAL ASSOCIATION 36 Bedford Square, London WC1B 3ES **T** 020-7887 4000 **E** arch-assoc@arch-assoc.org.uk **W** www.arch-assoc.org.uk
Chief Executive, Brett Steele
ROYAL INSTITUTE OF BRITISH ARCHITECTS 66 Portland Place, London W1B 1AD **T** 020-7580 5533 **E** info@inst.riba.org **W** www.riba.org
Chief Executive, Richard Hastilow, CBE

BANKING
CHARTERED INSTITUTE OF BANKERS IN SCOTLAND Drumsheugh House, 38b Drumsheugh Gardens, Edinburgh EH3 7SW **T** 0131-473 7777 **E** info@ciobs.org.uk **W** www.ciobs.org.uk
Chief Executive, Prof. Charles Munn, OBE
INSTITUTE OF FINANCIAL SERVICES IFS House, 4–9 Burgate Lane, Canterbury CT1 2XJ **T** 01227-818609 **E** customerservices@ifslearning.com **W** www.ifslearning.com
Chief Executive, Gavin Shreeve

BUILDING
CHARTERED INSTITUTE OF BUILDING Englemere, Kings Ride, Ascot, Berks SL5 7TB **T** 01344-630700 **E** reception@ciob.org.uk **W** www.ciob.org.uk
Chief Executive, Chris Blythe
INSTITUTE OF CLERKS OF WORKS OF GREAT BRITAIN Equinox, 28 Commerce Road, Lynch Wood, Peterborough PE2 6LR **T** 01733-405160 **W** www.icwgb.org
Chief Executive, Don McGeorge
ROYAL INSTITUTION OF CHARTERED SURVEYORS 12 Great George Street, Parliament Square, London SW1P 3AD **T** 020-7222 7000 **E** contactrics@rics.org **W** www.rics.org
Chief Executive, J. A. H. J. Armstrong

BUSINESS MANAGEMENT AND ADMINISTRATION
ASSOCIATION OF MBAS 25 Hosier Lane, London EC1A 9LQ **T** 020-7246 2686 **E** info@mbaworld.org.uk **W** www.mbaworld.org.uk
Chief Executive, Jeanette Purcell
CHARTERED INSTITUTE OF HOUSING Octavia House, Westwood Business Park, Westwood Way, Coventry CV4 8JP **T** 024-7685 1700 **E** customer.services@cih.org **W** www.cih.org
Chief Executive, D. Butler
CHARTERED INSTITUTE OF MARKETING Moor Hall, Cookham, Maidenhead, Berks SL6 9QH **T** 01628-427500 **W** www.cim.co.uk
Chief Executive, Christine Cryne
CHARTERED INSTITUTE OF PERSONNEL AND DEVELOPMENT 151 The Broadway, London, SW19 1JQ **T** 020-8612 6200 **E** cipd@cipd.co.uk **W** www.cipd.co.uk
Director General, Geoff Armstrong

CHARTERED INSTITUTE OF PURCHASING AND SUPPLY
Easton House, Easton on the Hill, Stamford, Lincs PE9 3NZ
T 01780-756777 E info@cips.org W www.cips.org
Chief Executive, Ken James

CHARTERED MANAGEMENT INSTITUTE
Management House, Cottingham Road, Corby, Northants
NN17 1TT T 01536-204222 E enquiries@managers.org.uk
W www.managers.org.uk
Chief Executive, Mary Chapman

INSTITUTE OF ADMINISTRATIVE MANAGEMENT
Caroline House, 55–57 High Holborn, London WC1V 6DX
T 020-7841 1100 E info@instam.org W www.instam.org
Chief Executive Officer, David Woodgate

INSTITUTE OF CHARTERED SECRETARIES AND
ADMINISTRATORS (1891) 16 Park Crescent, London
W1B 1AH T 020-7580 4741 E info@icsa.co.uk
W www.icsa.org.uk
Chief Executive and Secretary, John Ainsworth

INSTITUTE OF EXPORT (1935) Export House, Minerva
Business Park, Lynch Wood, Peterborough PE2 6FT
T 01733-404400 E institute@export.org.uk
W www.export.org.uk
Chair, Andy Nemes

INSTITUTE OF QUALITY ASSURANCE 12 Grosvenor
Crescent, London SW1X 7EE T 020-7245 6722
E iqa@iqa.org W www.iqa.org
Director-General, Frank Steer

CHIROPRACTIC
The General Chiropractic Council (GCC) is the statutory
regulatory body for chiropractors and its role and remit is
defined in the Chiropractors Act 1994. It is illegal for
anyone in the UK to use the title 'chiropractor' unless
registered with the GCC.

BRITISH CHIROPRACTIC ASSOCIATION Blagrave House,
17 Blagrave Street, Reading, Berks RG1 1QB
T 0118-950 5950 E enquiries@chiropractic-uk.co.uk
W www.chiropractic-uk.co.uk
Executive Director, Sue Wakefield

GENERAL CHIROPRACTIC COUNCIL 44 Wicklow Street,
London WC1X 9HL T 020-7713 5155
E enquiries@gcc-uk.org W www.gcc-uk.org
Chief Executive, Margaret Coats

SCOTTISH CHIROPRACTIC ASSOCIATION Laigh Hatton
Farm, Old Greenock Road, Bishopton, Renfrewshire PA7 5PB
T 01505-863151 W www.sca-chiropractic.org

DANCE
The Council for Dance Education and Training (CDET)
accredits courses at the following: ArtsEdLondon; Arts
Education Tring Park; Central School of Ballet; Bird
College of Performing Arts; Elmhurst School for Dance;
The Hammond School; The Italia Conti Academy of
Theatre Arts Limited; Laban; Laine Theatre Arts Ltd;
London Contemporary Dance School; London Studio
Centre; Northern Ballet School; Performers College;
Stella Mann College; The Urdang Academy.

The accreditation of a course in a school does not
necessarily imply that other courses of a different type or
duration in the same school are also accredited. CDET has
approved the teacher registration systems of the
following: British Ballet Organisation; British Theatre
Dance Association; Imperial Society of Teachers of
Dancing; Royal Academy of Dancing.

COUNCIL FOR DANCE EDUCATION AND TRAINING
Toynbee Hall, 28 Commercial Street, London E1 6LS
T 020-7247 4030 E info@cdet.org.uk W www.cdet.org.uk
Director, Sean Williams

IMPERIAL SOCIETY OF TEACHERS OF DANCING
Imperial House, 22–26 Paul Street, London EC2A 4QE
T 020-7377 1577 W www.istd.org
Chief Executive, Michael J. Browne, FRSA

INTERNATIONAL DANCE TEACHERS' ASSOCIATION
International House, 76 Bennett Road, Brighton BN2 5JL
T 01273-685652 E info@idta.co.uk W www.idta.co.uk
Chief Executive, Keith Holmes

ROYAL ACADEMY OF DANCE 36 Battersea Square, London
SW11 3RA T 020-7326 8000 E info@rad.org.uk
W www.rad.org.uk
Chief Executive, Luke Rittner

ROYAL BALLET SCHOOL 46 Floral Street, London
WC2E 9DA T 020-7836 8899
E enquiries@royalballetschool.co.uk
W www.royalballetschool.co.uk
Director, Gailene Stock

DEFENCE
The Joint Services Command and Staff College, the Royal
College of Defence Studies and the Defence College of
Management and Technology are all colleges of the Defence
Academy, which was formed in 2002 to bring together the
research and training capabilities of a number of colleges.
Further information available at www.da.mod.uk.

DEFENCE COLLEGE OF MANAGEMENT AND
TECHNOLOGY (DCMT) Cranfield University, Shrivenham,
Swindon SN6 8LA T 01793-782551
W www.rmcs.cranfield.ac.uk

JOINT SERVICES COMMAND AND STAFF COLLEGE (JSC)
Faringdon Road, Watchfield, Swindon, Wilts SN6 8TS
T 01793-788000 E registry@jscsc.org.uk
W www.jscsc.org.uk
Commandant, Air Vice-Marshal N. D. A. Maddox, CBE

ROYAL COLLEGE OF DEFENCE STUDIES (RCDS) Seaford
House, 37 Belgrave Square, London SW1X 8NS
T 020-7915 4800 E dsupport@rcds.mod.uk
W www.da.mod.uk/rcds
Commandant, Adm. Sir Ian Garnett, KCB

ROYAL NAVAL COLLEGE
BRITANNIA ROYAL NAVAL COLLEGE Dartmouth, Devon
TQ6 0HJ T 01803-677108 E brnc-commodore@nrta.mod.uk
W www.britannia.ac.uk
Commodore, Cdre Tim Harris, RN

MILITARY COLLEGES
DIRECTORATE OF EDUCATIONAL AND TRAINING
SERVICES (ARMY) Trenchard Lines, Upavon, Pewsey, Wilts
SN9 6BE T 01980-618719/618701 E enquiries@detsa.co.uk
W www.ets.mod.uk
Director, Brig. A. W. E. Brister

ROYAL MILITARY ACADEMY SANDHURST Camberley,
Surrey GU15 4PQ T 01276-63344
W www.sandhurst.mod.uk
Commandant, Maj.-Gen. A. S. Ritchie, CBE

ROYAL AIR FORCE COLLEGES
ROYAL AIR FORCE COLLEGE RAF Cranwell, Sleaford, Lincs
NG34 8HB T 01400-261201 W www.cranwell.raf.mod.uk
Commandant, Cdre Mike Barter

ROYAL AIR FORCE HALTON Aylesbury, Bucks HP22 5PG
T 01296-623535

DENTISTRY
In order to practise in the UK, a dentist must be registered
with the General Dental Council. To be registered a
person must be qualified in one of the following ways:

hold the degree or diploma in dental surgery of a university in the UK or hold the licentiate in dental surgery awarded by one of the Royal Surgical Colleges in the UK; have completed the Council's International Qualifying Examination (IQE); be a European Community or European Economic Area national holding an appropriate European diploma; hold a registered overseas diploma or be an EEA national holding a primary dental qualification from outside the EEA but having acquired the right to practise in the EEA. The holder of a dental degree or diploma other than those referred to above may be eligible for temporary registration to enable him or her to practise dentistry in the United Kingdom for a limited period and in specified posts without the need to take further examinations. The Dentists Register and Rolls of Dental Auxiliaries are maintained by:

GENERAL DENTAL COUNCIL 37 Wimpole Street, London W1G 8DQ T 020-7887 3800 E information@gdc-uk.org W www.gdc-uk.org
Chief Executive, Antony Townsend

DRAMA
The national accrediting body for courses providing training in drama for the professional theatre is the National Council for Drama Training (NCDT). NCDT accredits courses at 21 drama schools in England, Scotland and Wales. It also sponsors annual seminars on graduate showcases, television training and skills needs in the small sector. There are two useful guides for students entering drama school: *A Practical Guide to Vocational Training in Dance and Drama* and *An Applicant's Guide to Auditioning and Interviewing at Dance and Drama*. These publications and numerous information sheets and useful links are available on the NCDT's website (*see* below).

NATIONAL COUNCIL FOR DRAMA TRAINING 1–7 Woburn Walk, London WC1H 0JJ T 020-7387 3650 E info@ncdt.co.uk W www.ncdt.co.uk
Director, Adele Bailey

ENGINEERING
The Engineering Council UK (ECUK) sets standards of professional competence and ethics for engineers, technologists and technicians, and regulates the profession through the 36 Licensed Members listed below.

ENGINEERING COUNCIL (UK) (2002) 10 Maltravers Street, London WC2R 3ER T 020-7240 7891 E staff@engc.org.uk W www.engc.org.uk
Executive Director, Andrew Ramsay
BRITISH COMPUTER SOCIETY W www.bcs.org.uk
BRITISH INSTITUTE OF NON-DESTRUCTIVE TESTING W www.bindt.org
CHARTERED INSTITUTION OF BUILDING SERVICES ENGINEERS W www.cibse.org
CHARTERED INSTITUTION OF WATER AND ENVIRONMENTAL MANAGEMENT W www.ciwem.org.uk
ENERGY INSTITUTE W www.energyinst.org.uk
INSTITUTE OF ACOUSTICS W www.ioa.org.uk
INSTITUTE OF CAST METALS ENGINEERS W www.icme.org.uk
INSTITUTE OF HEALTHCARE ENGINEERING AND ESTATE MANAGEMENT W www.iheem.org.uk
INSTITUTE OF HIGHWAY INCORPORATED ENGINEERS W www.ihie.org.uk
INSTITUTE OF THE MOTOR INDUSTRY W www.motor.org.uk
INSTITUTE OF MATERIALS, MINERALS AND MINING W www.iom3.org

INSTITUTE OF MARINE ENGINEERING, SCIENCE AND TECHNOLOGY W www.imarest.org
INSTITUTE OF MEASUREMENT AND CONTROL W www.instmc.org.uk
INSTITUTE OF PHYSICS W www.iop.org
INSTITUTE OF PHYSICS AND ENGINEERING IN MEDICINE W www.ipem.org.uk
INSTITUTE OF PLUMBING AND HEATING ENGINEERING W www.iphe.org.uk
INSTITUTION OF AGRICULTURAL ENGINEERS W www.iagre.org
INSTITUTION OF CHEMICAL ENGINEERS W www.icheme.org
INSTITUTION OF CIVIL ENGINEERS W www.ice.org.uk
INSTITUTION OF ELECTRICAL ENGINEERS W www.iee.org.uk
INSTITUTION OF ENGINEERING DESIGNERS W www.ied.org.uk
INSTITUTION OF FIRE ENGINEERS W www.ife.org.uk
INSTITUTION OF GAS ENGINEERS AND MANAGERS W www.igem.org.uk
INSTITUTION OF HIGHWAYS AND TRANSPORTATION W www.iht.org
INSTITUTION OF INCORPORATED ENGINEERS W www.iie.org.uk
INSTITUTION OF LIGHTING ENGINEERS W www.ile.org.uk
INSTITUTION OF MECHANICAL ENGINEERS W www.imeche.org.uk
INSTITUTION OF NUCLEAR ENGINEERS W www.inuce.org.uk
INSTITUTION OF RAILWAY SIGNAL ENGINEERS W www.irse.org
INSTITUTION OF STRUCTURAL ENGINEERS W www.istructe.org.uk
INSTITUTION OF WATER OFFICERS W www.iwo.org.uk
ROYAL AERONAUTICAL SOCIETY W www.raes.org.uk
ROYAL INSTITUTION OF NAVAL ARCHITECTS W www.rina.org.uk
SOCIETY OF ENVIRONMENTAL ENGINEERS W www.environmental.org.uk
SOCIETY OF OPERATIONS ENGINEERS W www.soe.org.uk
WELDING INSTITUTE W www.twi.co.uk

FILM AND TELEVISION
The Sector Skills Council for the audio visual industries in the UK is Skillset, an independent organisation that aims to promote high standards of training, provide career advice, recognise and certificate the skills the industries require. Mid-2005 saw the establishment of the Broadcast Training and Skills Regulator (BTSR), a collaboration between Ofcom, Skillset and broadcasters, designed to promote training across the broadcasting industry (see www.ofcom.org.uk).

BKSTS – the Moving Image Society also accredits short and full-time courses relevant and practical experience to provide beneficial to the media industry.

BKSTS – THE MOVING IMAGE SOCIETY Pinewood Studios, Iver Heath, Bucks SL0 0NH T 01753-656656 E info@bksts.com W www.bksts.com
Director, Wendy Laybourn
SKILLSET Prospect House, 80–110 New Oxford Street, London WC1A 1HB T 020-7520 5757 E info@skillset.org W www.skillset.org
Chief Executive, Dinah Caine

HOTELKEEPING, CATERING AND INSTITUTIONAL MANAGEMENT

HOTEL AND CATERING INTERNATIONAL
MANAGEMENT ASSOCIATION Trinity Court, 34 West
Street, Sutton, Surrey SM1 1SH T 020-8661 4900
W www.hcima.org.uk
Chief Executive, *Philippe Rossiter*
BRITISH INSITITUTE OF INNKEEPING Wessex House, 80
Park Street, Camberley, Surrey GU15 3PT T 01276-684449
W www.bii.org

INSURANCE

ASSOCIATION OF AVERAGE ADJUSTERS The Baltic
Exchange, St Mary Axe, London EC3A 8BH
T 020-7623 5501 E aaa@balticexchange.com
W www.average-adjusters.com
Chair, Nigel Rogers
CHARTERED INSTITUTE OF LOSS ADJUSTERS Peninsular
House, 36 Monument Street, London EC3R 8LJ
T 020-7337 9960 E info@cila.co.uk W www.cila.co.uk
Executive Director, Graham Cave
CHARTERED INSURANCE INSTITUTE 20 Aldermanbury,
London EC2V 7HY T 020-7417 4415 E is@cii.co.uk
W www.cii.co.uk
Director-General, Sandy Scott

JOURNALISM

Courses for trainee newspaper journalists are available at
30 centres. One-year full time courses are available for
selected students, three-year degree programmes and 18-
week courses for graduates. Particulars for all these
courses are available from the National Council for the
Training of Journalists (NCTJ). Short courses for mid-
career development are available, as are various distance
learning courses.

The Broadcast Journalism Training Council (BJTC) is
an association of the UK's main broadcast journalism
employers, and it accredits 30 courses at 18 colleges and
universities.

For periodical journalists, there are twelve centres
running courses approved by the Periodicals Training
Council (PTC), the training arm of the Periodical
Publishers Association (PPA). The PTC also provides
career information for people wishing to join the industry.
BROADCAST JOURNALISM TRAINING COUNCIL (BJTC)
18 Miller's Close, Rippingale, Nr. Bourne, Lincs PE10 0TH
T 01778-440025 W www.bjtc.org.uk
The Secretary, Jim Latham
NATIONAL COUNCIL FOR THE TRAINING OF
JOURNALISTS (NCTJ) Latton Bush Centre, Southern Way,
Harlow, Essex CM18 7BL T 01279-430009 E info@nctj.com
W www.nctj.com
Chief Executive, Joanne Butcher
PERIODICALS TRAINING COUNCIL Queens House, 28
Kingsway, London WC2B 6JR T 020-7404 4166
W www.ppa.co.uk
Director, Loraine Davies

LAW

THE BAR

The governing body of the Bar of England and Wales is
the General Council of the Bar, also known as the Bar
Council. All practising barristers pay an annual
subscription fee to support the Bar Council. Its functions
include dealing with disciplinary matters, acting as the
public voice of the profession, and regulating the
education and training requirements for those wishing to
enter the profession.

In the first (or 'academic') stage, aspiring barristers must
obtain a law degree of a good standard (at least second
class). Alternatively, a non-law degree (at least second
class) followed by a one-year full-time or two-year part-
time Common Professional Examination (CPE) or an
approved Postgraduate Diploma in Law (PgDL).

The second (vocational) stage is the completion of the
Bar Vocational Course (BVC), which is available at eight
validated institutions in the UK and must be applied
for around one year in advance through
www.bvconline.co.uk. All barristers must join one of the
four Inns of Court prior to commencing the BVC.

Students are 'Called to the Bar' by their Inn after
completion of the vocational stage, but cannot practise as a
barrister until completion of the third stage, which is called
'pupillage'. Call to the Bar does not entitle a person to
practise as a barrister – successful completion of pupillage
is now a pre-requisite. Pupillage lasts for two six-month
periods: the 'non-practising six' and the 'practising six'.
The former consists of shadowing an experienced
barrister, while the latter involves appearing in court as a
barrister. From 2008 Call will only take place after a
period of pupillage. Further information can be found on
the Bar Council's website and www.legaleducation.org.uk.

Admission to the Bar of Northern Ireland is controlled
by the Honorable Society of the Inn of Court of Northern
Ireland and admission as an Advocate of the Scottish Bar
by the Faculty of Advocates.

FACULTY OF ADVOCATES Parliament House, Edinburgh
EH1 1RF T 0131-226 5071 W www.advocates.org.uk
Chief Executive Officer, Tony Parker
GENERAL COUNCIL OF THE BAR 289–293 High Holborn,
London WC1V 7HZ T 020-7242 0082
E chiefexec@barcouncil.org.uk W www.barcouncil.org.uk
Chief Executive, David Hobart
HONORABLE SOCIETY OF THE INN OF COURT OF
NORTHERN IRELAND The Under-Treasurer's Office, Royal
Courts of Justice, Belfast BT1 3JF T 028-9072 4699
T 028-9072 4786
Under-Treasurer, J. W. Wilson, QC
INNS OF COURT SCHOOL OF LAW 4 Gray's Inn Place,
Gray's Inn, London WC1R 5DX T 020-7404 5787
W www.city.ac.uk/icsl
Dean, Prof. Adrian Keane

THE INNS OF COURT

HONOURABLE SOCIETY OF GRAY'S INN 8 South Square,
London WC1R 5ET T 020-7458 7800
W www.graysinn.org.uk
Treasurer, Sir Alan Ward, PC
HONOURABLE SOCIETY OF LINCOLN'S INN Treasury
Office, Lincoln's Inn, London WC2A 3TL T 020-7405 1393
E mail@lincolnsinn.org.uk W www.lincolnsinn.org.uk
Under Treasurer, Col. D. Hills, MBE
HONOURABLE SOCIETY OF THE INNER TEMPLE Inner
Temple, London EC4Y 7HL T 020-7797 8250
E enquiries@innertemple.org.uk
W www.innertemple.org.uk
Sub-Treasurer, Patrick Maddams
HONOURABLE SOCIETY OF THE MIDDLE TEMPLE
Middle Temple Lane,London EC4Y 9AT T 020-7427 4800
E studentenquiries@middletemple.org.uk
W www.middletemple.org.uk
Under Treasurer, Air Cdre Peter Hilling

SOLICITORS

The College of Law is the oldest and largest provider of
vocational legal education and training for students
wishing to become solicitors and barristers in England

and Wales. It also offers training after qualification and a wide range of distance-learning courses. There are a number of other institutions offering the necessary courses, namely the Legal Practice Course and the Common Professional Examination/Graduate Diploma in Law (conversion courses for non-law graduates). The Law Society of England and Wales, the Law Society of Scotland and the Law Society of Northern Ireland regulate the education and examination of trainee solicitors and control admission to the roll of solicitors.

COLLEGE OF LAW Braboeuf Manor, Portsmouth Road, St Catherine's, Guildford, Surrey GU3 1HA T 0800-328 0153 W www.college-of-law.co.uk
 Chief Executive, Prof. Nigel Savage
LAW SOCIETY OF ENGLAND AND WALES The Law Society's Hall, 113 Chancery Lane, London WC2A 1PL T 020-7242 1222 W www.lawsociety.org.uk
 Chief Executive, Janet Paraskeva
LAW SOCIETY OF NORTHERN IRELAND 98 Victoria Street, Belfast BT1 3JZ T 028-9023 1614 E info@lawsoc-ni.org W www.lawsoc-ni.org
 Chief Executive and Secretary, John Bailie
LAW SOCIETY OF SCOTLAND 26 Drumsheugh Gardens, Edinburgh EH3 7YR T 0131-226 7411 E lawscot@lawscot.org.uk W www.lawscot.org.uk
 Chief Executive, Douglas Mill

LIBRARIANSHIP AND INFORMATION SCIENCE

The Chartered Institute of Library and Information Professionals (CILIP) is the leading professional membership body for librarians, information specialists and knowledge managers. It accredits degree and postgraduate courses in library and information science which are offered by 17 universities in the UK. Further information is available on the Institute's website (*see* below).

CHARTERED INSTITUTE OF LIBRARY AND INFORMATION PROFESSIONALS 7 Ridgmount Street, London WC1E 7AE T 020-7255 0500 E info@cilip.org.uk W www.cilip.org.uk
 Chief Executive, Bob McKee, PHD, FRSA

MEDICINE

All doctors must be registered with the General Medical Council (GMC), which is responsible for protecting the public by setting standards for professional practice, overseeing medical education, keeping a register of qualified doctors and taking action where a doctor's fitness to practise is in doubt.

The GMC's Education Committee has a statutory general function of promoting high standards of medical education and co-ordinating the stages of medical education. The Committee has specific powers set by the Medical Act in relation to undergraduate medical education in the UK, and the training of provisionally registered doctors in the period that follows graduation. Specialist training is provided by the royal colleges, faculties and societies listed below.

The United Examining Board runs qualifying examinations for candidates who have trained overseas. These candidates must also have spent a period at a UK medical school.

FACULTY OF PHARMACEUTICAL MEDICINE 1 St Andrew's Place, Regents Park, London NW1 4LB T 020-7224 0343 E fpm@fpm.org.uk W www.fpm.org.uk
 Chief Executive, Kathryn Swanston

GENERAL MEDICAL COUNCIL 178 Great Portland Street, London W1N 6JE T 0845-357 3456 E qmc@gmc-uk.org W www.gmc-uk.org
 Chief Executive, Finlay Scott
ROYAL COLLEGE OF GENERAL PRACTITIONERS 14 Princes Gate, London SW7 1PU T 020-7581 3232 E ino@rcgp.org.uk W www.rcgp.org.uk
 Chief Executive, Hilary De Lyon
UNITED EXAMINING BOARD Apothecaries Hall, Black Friars Lane, London EC4V 6EJ T 020-7236 1180 E examoffice@apothecaries.org
 Chair, Prof. J. S. P. Lumley

COLLEGES/SOCIETIES HOLDING POSTGRADUATE MEMBERSHIP AND DIPLOMA

FACULTY OF ACCIDENT AND EMERGENCY MEDICINE 35–43 Lincoln's Inn Fields, London WC2A 3PE T 020-7405 7071 E faem@emergencymedicine.uk.net W www.faem.org.uk
 President, Jim Wardrope
FACULTY OF PUBLIC HEALTH MEDICINE 4 St Andrews Place, London NW1 4LB T 020-7935 0243 E enquiries@fphm.org.uk W www.fphm.org.uk
 Chief Executive, Paul Scourfield
ROYAL COLLEGE OF ANAESTHETISTS 48–49 Russell Square, London WC1B 4JY T 020-7813 1900 E info@rcoa.ac.uk W www.rcoa.ac.uk
 The College Secretary, Kevin Storey
ROYAL COLLEGE OF OBSTETRICIANS AND GYNAECOLOGISTS 27 Sussex Place, Regent's Park, London NW1 4RG T 020-7772 6200 W www.rcog.org.uk
 Secretary, Kim Dawson
ROYAL COLLEGE OF PAEDIATRICS AND CHILD HEALTH 50 Hallam Street, London W1W 6DE T 020-7307 5600 E enquiries@rcpch.ac.uk W www.rcpch.ac.uk
 College Secretary, Len Tyler
ROYAL COLLEGE OF PATHOLOGISTS 2 Carlton House Terrace, London SW1Y 5AF T 020-7451 6700 E info@rcpath.org W www.rcpath.org
 President, Sir James Underwood
ROYAL COLLEGE OF PHYSICIANS 11 St Andrews Place, Regent's Park, London NW1 4LE T 020-7935 1174 W www.rcplondon.ac.uk
 President, Prof. Dame Carol Black
ROYAL COLLEGE OF PHYSICIANS AND SURGEONS OF GLASGOW 232–242 St Vincent Street, Glasgow G2 5RJ T 0141-221 6072 W www.rcpsglasg.ac.uk
 President, Prof. G. M. Teasdale
ROYAL COLLEGE OF PHYSICIANS OF EDINBURGH 9 Queen Street, Edinburgh EH2 1JQ T 0131-225 7324 E info@rcpe.ac.uk W www.rcpe.ac.uk
 President, Prof. N. J. Douglas
ROYAL COLLEGE OF PSYCHIATRISTS 17 Belgrave Square, London SW1X 8PG T 020-7235 2351 E rcpsych@rcpsych.ac.uk W www.rcpsych.ac.uk
 President, Prof. Sheila Hollins
ROYAL COLLEGE OF RADIOLOGISTS 38 Portland Place, London W1B 1JQ T 020-7636 4432 E enquiries@rcr.ac.uk W www.rcr.ac.uk
 President, Prof. J. E. S. Husband, OBE
ROYAL COLLEGE OF SURGEONS OF EDINBURGH Nicolson Street, Edinburgh EH8 9DW T 0131-527 1600 E information@rcsed.ac.uk W www.rcsed.ac.uk
 Chief Executive, J. R. C. Foster
ROYAL COLLEGE OF SURGEONS OF ENGLAND 35–43 Lincoln's Inn Fields, London WC2A 3PE T 020-7405 3474 W www.rcseng.ac.uk
 Chief Executive, Craig Duncan

SOCIETY OF APOTHECARIES OF LONDON 14 Black Friars
  Lane, London EC4V 6EJ **T** 020-7236 1189
  E clerk@apothecaries.org **W** www.apothecaries.org
  The Clerk, A. M. Wallington-Smith

MEDICINE, COMPLEMENTARY

Complementary medicine, known as 'alternative
medicine', includes such professions as aromatherapy,
counselling, hypnotherapy, reflexology, massage and
physical therapy.

In order to gain entry to the British Register of
Complementary Practitioners, administered by
the Institute for Complementary Medicine (ICM),
practitioners must either complete an ICM approved
course or be assessed by the registration panel.

Professional courses are validated by:
INSTITUTE FOR COMPLEMENTARY MEDICINE
  PO Box 194, London SE16 7QZ **T** 020-7237 5165
  E info@i-c-m.org.uk **W** www.i-c-m.org.uk

MEDICINE, SUPPLEMENTARY PROFESSIONS

The standard of professional education for arts therapists,
biomedical scientists, chiropodists and podiatrists, clinical
scientists, dietitians, occupational therapists, operating
department practitioners, orthoptists, paramedics,
prosthetists and orthotists, physiotherapists,
radiographers, and speech and language therapists is
regulated by the Health Professions Council, who only
register those practitioners who meet certain standards of
training, performance and conduct.
HEALTH PROFESSIONS COUNCIL Park House, 184
  Kennington Park Road, London SE11 4BU **T** 020-7582 0866
  E info@hpc-uk.org **W** www.hpc-uk.org
  Chief Executive and Registrar, Marc Seale

ART, DRAMA AND MUSIC THERAPIES

A postgraduate qualification in the relevant therapy is
required. Details of accredited training programmes in the
UK can be obtained from the following organisations:
ASSOCIATION OF PROFESSIONAL MUSIC THERAPISTS
  25 Cranbrook Road, East Barnet, Herts EN4 8SY **T** 020-8440
  4153 **E** apmtoffice@aol.com **W** www.apmt.org
  Administrator, Louise Karena
BRITISH ASSOCIATION OF ART THERAPISTS Mary Ward
  House, 24–27 White Lion Street, London N1 9PD
  T 020-7686 4216 **E** info@baat.org **W** www.baat.org
  President, Prof. Diana Waller
BRITISH ASSOCIATION OF DRAMATHERAPISTS
  41 Broomhouse Lane, London SW6 3DP **T** 020-7731 0160
  E info@badth.org.uk **W** www.badth.org.uk

BIOMEDICAL SCIENCES

Qualifications from higher education establishments and
training in medical laboratories are required for
membership of the Institute of Biomedical Science.
INSTITUTE OF BIOMEDICAL SCIENCE 12 Coldbath
  Square, London EC1R 5HL **T** 020-7713 0214
  E mail@ibms.org **W** www.ibms.org
  Chief Executive, Alan Potter

CHIROPODY AND PODIATRY

The Society of Chiropodists and Podiatrists is the
professional body and trade union for chiropodists and
podiatrists. Professional recognition is granted by the
Society to students who are awarded BSc degrees in
Podiatry or Podiatric Medicine after attending a course of
full-time training for three or four years at one of the

recognised schools in the UK. Qualifications granted and
degrees recognised by the Society are approved for the
purpose of State Registration, which is a condition of
employment within the National Health Service.
SOCIETY OF CHIROPODISTS AND PODIATRISTS
  1 Fellmonger's Path, Tower Bridge Road, London SE1 3LY
  T 020-7234 8620 **W** www.feetforlife.org
  Chief Executive, Joanna Brown

CLINICAL SCIENCE

ASSOCIATION OF CLINICAL SCIENTISTS c/o Association
  for Clinical Biochemistry, 130–132 Tooley Street, London
  SE1 2TU **T** 020-7940 8960 **E** info@assclinsci.org
  W www.assclinsci.org

DIETETICS

The British Dietetic Association (BDA), established in
1936, is the professional association for dietitians. Full
membership is open to UK Registered dietitians, who
must also be registered with the Health Professions
Council (*see* Professions Supplementary to Medicine).
BRITISH DIETETIC ASSOCIATION 5th Floor, Charles
  House, 148–149 Great Charles Street, Queensway,
  Birmingham B3 3HT **T** 0121-200 8080 **E** info@bda.uk.com
  W www.bda.uk.com
  Chief Executive, Andy Burman

OCCUPATIONAL THERAPY

The professional qualification and eligibility for
registration may be obtained upon successful completion
of a validated course in any of the educational institutions
approved by the College of Occupational Therapists,
which is the professional body for occupational therapy in
the UK. The courses are normally degree-level courses
based in higher education institutions.
COLLEGE OF OCCUPATIONAL THERAPISTS 106–114
  Borough High Street, London SE1 1LB **T** 020-7357 6480
  W www.cot.org.uk

ORTHOPTICS

Orthoptists undertake the diagnosis and treatment of all
types of squint and other anomalies of binocular vision,
working in close collaboration with ophthalmologists.
The professional body is the British and Irish Orthoptic
Society and training is at degree level.
BRITISH AND IRISH ORTHOPTIC SOCIETY Tavistock
  House North, Tavistock Square, London WC1H 9HX
  T 020-7387 7992 **W** www.orthoptics.org.uk
  Chair, Rosemary Auld

PARAMEDICAL SERVICES

BRITISH PARAMEDIC ASSOCIATION 28 Wilfred Street,
  Derby, DE23 8GF **T** 01332-746356
  E www.britishparamedic.org
  Chief Executive, Roland Furber

PHYSIOTHERAPY

Full-time three- or four-year degree courses are available
at over 30 higher education institutions in the UK.
Information about courses leading to to State Registration
is available from the Chartered Society of Physiotherapy.
CHARTERED SOCIETY OF PHYSIOTHERAPY 14 Bedford
  Row, London WC1R 4ED **T** 020-7306 6666
  W www.csp.org.uk
  Chief Executive, Phil Gray

PROSTHETICS AND ORTHOTICS

Prosthetists provide artificial limbs, while orthotists provide devices to support or control a part of the body. It is necessary to obtain an honours degree to become a prosthetist or orthotist. Training is centred at University of Salford and University of Strathclyde.

BRITISH ASSOCIATION OF PROSTHETISTS AND
   ORTHOTISTS Sir James Clark Building, Abbey Mill Business Centre, Paisley PA1 1TJ T 0141-561 7217
   E admin@bapo.com W www.bapo.com
   Executive Professional Officer, Ken Andrew

RADIOGRAPHY

In order to practise both diagnostic and therapeutic radiography in the UK, it is necessary to have successfully completed a course of education and training recognised by the Privy Council. Such courses are offered by universities throughout the UK and lead to the award of a degree in radiography. Further information is available from the Society and College of Radiographers.

SOCIETY AND COLLEGE OF RADIOGRAPHERS
   207 Providence Square, Mill Street, London SE1 2EW
   T 020-7740 7200 E info@sor.org W www.sor.org
   Chief Executive, Richard Evans

SPEECH AND LANGUAGE THERAPY

The Royal College of Speech and Language Therapists accredits education and training courses leading to qualification.

ROYAL COLLEGE OF SPEECH AND LANGUAGE
   THERAPISTS 2 White Hart Yard, London SE1 1NX
   T 020-7378 3012 T 020-7403 7254 E info@rcslt.org
   W www.rcslt.org
   Chief Executive, Kamini Gadhok

MERCHANT NAVY TRAINING OFFICERS

WARSASH MARITIME CENTRE Southampton Institute, Newtown Road, Warsash, Southampton SO31 9ZL
   T 01489-576161 E wmc@solent.ac.uk
   W www.solent.ac.uk/wmc/
   Director, John Millican

SEAFARERS

NATIONAL SEA TRAINING CENTRE North West Kent College, Dering Way, Gravesend, Kent DA12 2JJ
   T 01322-629600 W www.nwkcollege.ac.uk/nstc
   Head of School, Paul Russell

MUSIC

Education and training for a career in musical performance and composition are provided by the institutions and conservatoires listed below. Professional organisations granting qualifications after examination are the Associated Board of the Royal Schools of Music and the Trinity College Examination Board.

ASSOCIATED BOARD OF THE ROYAL SCHOOLS OF
   MUSIC 24 Portland Place, London W1B 1LU
   T 020-7636 5400 E abrsm@abrsm.ac.uk W www.abrsm.org
BIRMINGHAM CONSERVATOIRE Paradise Place,
   Birmingham B3 3HG T 0121-331 5901
   E conservatoire@uce.ac.uk W www.conservatoire.uce.ac.uk
   Principal, Prof. George Caird
GUILDHALL SCHOOL OF MUSIC AND DRAMA Silk Street,
   Barbican, London EC2Y 8DT T 020-7628 2571
   E music@gsmd.ac.uk W www.gsmd.ac.uk
   Principal, Prof. Barry Ife, CBE
LEEDS COLLEGE OF MUSIC 3 Quarry Hill, Leeds LS2 7PD
   T 0113-222 3400 E enquiries@lcm.ac.uk W www.lcm.ac.uk
   Principal, David Hoult

NATIONAL OPERA STUDIO The Clore Building, 2 Chapel Yard, Wandsworth High Street, London SW18 4HZ
   T 020-8874 8811 E info@nationaloperastudio.org.uk
   W www.nationaloperastudio.org.uk
   Director, Donald Maxwell
ROYAL ACADEMY OF MUSIC Marylebone Road, London
   NW1 5HT T 020-7873 7373 W www.ram.ac.uk
   Principal, Prof. Curtis Price, KBE
ROYAL COLLEGE OF MUSIC Prince Consort Road, London
   SW7 2BS T 020-7589 3643 E info@rcm.ac.uk
   W www.rcm.ac.uk
   Director, Dr Colin Lawson
ROYAL COLLEGE OF ORGANISTS Millennium Point, Curzon
   Street, Birmingham B4 7XG T 0121-331 7222
   E admin@rco.org.uk W www.rco.org.uk
   General Manager, Kim Gilbert
ROYAL NORTHERN COLLEGE OF MUSIC 124 Oxford
   Road, Manchester M13 9RD T 0161-907 5200
   E info@rncm.ac.uk W www.rncm.ac.uk
   Principal, Prof. E. Gregson
ROYAL SCOTTISH ACADEMY OF MUSIC AND DRAMA
   100 Renfrew Street, Glasgow G2 3DB T 0141-332 4101
   E registry@rsamd.ac.uk W www.rsamd.ac.uk
   Principal, John Wallace, OBE
ROYAL WELSH COLLEGE OF MUSIC AND DRAMA Maes y
   Castell, Cathays Park, Cardiff CF10 3ER T 029-2034 2854
   W www.rwcmd.ac.uk
   Principal, Edmond Fivet
TRINITY COLLEGE OF MUSIC King Charles Court, Old
   Royal Naval College, London SE10 9JF T 020-8305 4444
   E enquiries@tcm.ac.uk W www.tcm.ac.uk
   Principal and Chief Executive, Gavin Henderson, CBE

NURSING

All nurses and midwives must be registered with the Nursing and Midwifery Council (NMC). Courses leading to registration as a nurse or midwife are at least three years in length. Most courses are at diploma level, but some are at degree level, and students study in colleges of nursing or in institutions of higher education. Different courses lead to different types of registration, including Registered General Nurse (RGN), Registered Mental Nurse (RMN), Registered Nurse for Learning Disabilities (RNLD), Registered Sick Children's Nurse (RSCN) and Registered Midwife (RM). The NMC is responsible for validating courses in nursing and midwifery.

The Royal College of Nursing is the largest professional union representing nurses, and provides higher education through its Institute.

NURSING AND MIDWIFERY COUNCIL 23 Portland Place,
   London W1B 1PZ T 020-7637 7181
   E communications@nmc-uk.org W www.nmc-uk.org
   Chief Executive, Sarah Thewlis
ROYAL COLLEGE OF NURSING 20 Cavendish Square,
   London W1G 0RN T 020-7409 3333 W www.rcn.org.uk
   General Secretary, Dr Beverly Malone

OPHTHALMIC AND DISPENSING OPTICS

Professional bodies are:
ASSOCIATION OF BRITISH DISPENSING OPTICIANS
   199 Gloucester Terrace, London W2 6LD T 020-7298 5100
   E general@abdo.org.uk W www.abdo.org.uk
   General Secretary, Sir Anthony Garrett, CBE
COLLEGE OF OPTOMETRISTS 42 Craven Street,
   London WC2N 5NG T 020-7839 6000
   W www.college-optometrists.org
   Chief Executive, Bryony Pawinska

OSTEOPATHY

Osteopathy was the first profession previously outside conventional medical services to achieve statutory recognition under a new body: the General Osteopathic Council (GOsC). Since May 2000 all practising osteopaths have had to be registered with the GOsC and the title 'osteopath' is protected by law. To gain entry to the register, all newly qualified osteopaths have to be in possession of a recognised qualification from a course accredited by the GOsC.

GENERAL OSTEOPATHIC COUNCIL Osteopathy House, 176 Tower Bridge Road, London SE1 3LU **T** 020-7357 6655 **E** info@osteopathy.org.uk **W** www.osteopathy.org.uk
Chief Executive, Madeleine Craggs

PHARMACY

The Royal Pharmaceutical Society of Great Britain is the regulatory and professional body for pharmacists in all aspects of practice. It has a statutory duty to maintain the registers of pharmacists and pharmacy premises. In order to register, students must have a degree in pharmacy followed by one year pre-registration training at a premises recognised by the Society and must pass an entrance examination.

ROYAL PHARMACEUTICAL SOCIETY OF GREAT BRITAIN 1 Lambeth High Street,London SE1 7JN **T** 020-7735 9141 **E** enquiries@rpsgb.org **W** www.rpsgb.org
Secretary and Registrar, Ann Lewis

PHOTOGRAPHY

BRITISH INSTITUTE OF PROFESSIONAL PHOTOGRAPHY Fox Talbot House, Amwell End, Ware, Herts SG12 9HN **T** 01920-464011 **E** info@bipp.com **W** www.bipp.com
Executive Officer, M. Berry

PRINTING

Details of training courses in printing can be obtained from the Institute of Paper, Printing and Publishing and the British Printing Industries Federation. Examinations are also held by various independent further education examining boards.

BRITISH PRINTING INDUSTRIES FEDERATION Farringdon Point, 29–35 Farringdon Road, London EC1M 3JF **T** 0870-240 4085 **W** www.britishprint.com
Chief Executive, Michael Johnson
INSTITUTE OF PAPER, PRINTING AND PUBLISHING 83 Guildford Street, Chertsey, Surrey KT16 9AS **T** 0870-330 8625 **E** info@ip3.org.uk **W** www.ip3.org.uk

SURVEYING

ASSOCIATION OF BUILDING ENGINEERS Lutyens House, Billing Brook Road, Weston Favell, Northampton NN3 8NW **T** 01604-404121 **E** building.engineers@abe.org.uk **W** www.abe.org.uk
Chief Executive, David Gibson
INSTITUTE OF REVENUES, RATING AND VALUATION 41 Doughty Street, London WC1N 2LF **T** 020-7831 3505 **W** www.irrv.org.uk
Director, David Magor
ROYAL INSTITUTION OF CHARTERED SURVEYORS 12 Great George Street, Parliament Square, London SW1P 3AD **T** 020-7222 7000 **E** info@rics.org.uk **W** www.rics.org
Chief Executive, J. H. A. J. Armstrong

TEACHING

To work as a qualified teacher in a school in England and Wales, Qualified Teacher Status (QTS) must be acquired by completing a programme of Initial Teacher Training. Teaching is an all-graduate profession. Those without a first degree may take a Bachelor of Education (BEd) or a Bachelor of Arts/Science (BA/BSc) with QTS, full time for three or four years, depending on the programme followed. These degrees combine subject and professional studies with teaching practice.

For those who already have a first degree, the most common route is through a one-year Postgraduate Certificate in Education (PGCE). This may be taken full time or part time, or as a distance learning programme. Postgraduates may also gain QTS through training in a school (School-Centred Initial Teacher Training). Graduates aged 24 or above can apply to train through the Graduate Teacher Programme, which offers a salary while employed in a school as a trainee teacher, usually for one year.

Further information on how to become a teacher in England and Wales is available on the Training and Development Agency for Schools website (*see* below). Further personal advice is available from the Teaching Information Line, 0845-600 0991 (0845-600 0992 for Welsh speakers). Details on courses in Scotland can be obtained from universities and the Graduate Teacher Training Registry (GTTR). Details of the courses in Northern Ireland can be obtained from individual universities and the Department of Education for Northern Ireland.

DEPARTMENT OF EDUCATION NORTHERN IRELAND Rathgael House, 43 Balloo Road, Bangor, Co. Down BT19 7PR **T** 028-9127 9279 **E** mail@deni.gov.uk **W** www.deni.gov.uk
GRADUATE TEACHER TRAINING REGISTRY (GTTR) Rosehill, New Barn Lane, Cheltenham, Glos GL52 3LZ **T** 0870-1122205 **E** enquiries@gttr.ac.uk **W** www.gttr.ac.uk
Chief Executive, Anthony McClaran
TRAINING AND DEVELOPMENT AGENCY FOR SCHOOLS Portland House, Stag Place, London SW1E 5TT **T** 0845-606 0323 **W** www.tda.gov.uk
Chief Executive, Ralph Tabberer

VETERINARY MEDICINE

The regulatory body for veterinary medicine is the Royal College of Veterinary Surgeons, which keeps the register of those entitled to practise veterinary medicine. Holders of recognised degrees from any of the six UK university veterinary schools or from certain EU or overseas universities are entitled to be registered, and holders of certain other degrees may take a statutory membership examination.

The British Veterinary Association is the professional body representing veterinary surgeons. The British Veterinary Nursing Association is the professional body representing veterinary nurses.

BRITISH VETERINARY ASSOCIATION 7 Mansfield Street, London W1G 9NQ **T** 020-7636 6541 **E** bvahq@bva.co.uk **W** www.bva.co.uk
President, Dr Bob McCracken, CBE, PHD
BRITISH VETERINARY NURSING ASSOCIATION Suite 11, Shenval House, South Road, Harlow, Essex CM20 2BD **T** 01279-450567 **W** www.bvna.org.uk
ROYAL COLLEGE OF VETERINARY SURGEONS Belgravia House, 62–64 Horseferry Road, London SW1P 2AF **T** 020-7222 2001 **E** admin@rcvs.org.uk **W** www.rcvs.org.uk
Chief Executive, Jane Hern

INDEPENDENT SCHOOLS

School	Web Address	Termly fees Day	Board	Head
ENGLAND				
The Abbey School, Berks	www.theabbey.co.uk	£2,980	–	Mrs B. Stanley
Abbey Gate College, Cheshire	www.abbeygatecollege.co.uk	£2,596	–	E. W. Mitchell
Abbots Bromley, Girls, Staffs	www.abbotsbromley.staffs.sch.uk	£3,620	£6,195	Mrs P. J. Woodhouse
Abbotsholme School, Derbys	www.abbotsholme.com	£4,800	£7,000	S. Fairclough
Abingdon School, Oxon	www.abingdon.org.uk	£3,589	£6,548	M. Turner
Ackworth School, W. Yorks	www.ackworthschool.com	£2,971	£5,093	P. J. Simpson
Aldenham School, Herts	www.aldenham.com	£4,484	£6,499	R. S. Harman
Alderley Edge, Girls, Cheshire	www.aesg.info	£2,268	–	Mrs K. Mills
The Alice Ottley School, Worcs	www.thealiceottleyschool.co.uk	£2,895	–	Mrs M. Chapman
Alleyn's School, London SE22	www.alleyns.org.uk	£3,560	–	C. Diggory
Amberfield School, Suffolk	www.amberfield.suffolk.sch.uk	£2,435	–	Mrs H. Kay
Ampleforth College, N. Yorks	www.ampleforthcollege.york.sch.uk	£3,650	£6,840	Revd C. G. Everitt
Ardingly College, W. Sussex	www.ardingly.com	£5,120	£6,840	J. Franklin
Arnold School, Lancs	www.arnoldschool.com	£2,332	–	B. M. Hughes
Arts Educational School, Herts	www.aes-tring.com	£5,380	£6,800	S. Anderson
Ashford School (UCST), Kent	www.ashfordschool.co.uk	£3,483	£6,043	M. Buchanan
Ashville College, N. Yorks	www.ashville.co.uk	£2,920	£5,495	A. A. P. Fleck
The Atherley School (UCST), Hants	www.atherley.hants.sch.uk	£2,730	–	Mrs H. Crawford
Austin Friars, Cumbria	www.austinfriars.cumbria.sch.uk	£2,869	–	C. J. Lumb
Bablake School, W. Midlands	www.bablake.com	£2,345	–	Dr S. Nuttall
Badminton School, Bristol	www.badminton.bristol.sch.uk	£4,060	£7,220	Mrs J. A. Scarrow
Bancroft's School, Essex	www.bancrofts.essex.sch.uk	£3,252	–	P. R. Scott
Barnard Castle School, Durham	www.barneyschool.org.uk	£2,980	£5,131	D. H. Ewart
Batley Grammar School, W. Yorks	www.batleygrammar.co.uk	£2,360	–	B. Battye
Battle Abbey School, E. Sussex	www.battleabbeyschool.com	£3,632	£5,935	R. C. Clark
Bearwood College, Berks	www.bearwoodcollege.berks.sch.uk	£4,340	£6,880	S. G. G. Aiano
Bedales School, Hants	www.bedales.org.uk	£6,040	£7,845	K. J. Budge
Bedford High School, Beds	www.bedfordhigh.co.uk	£3,095	£5,673	Mrs G. Piotrowska
Bedford Modern School, Beds	www.bedmod.co.uk	£2,786	–	S. Smith
Bedford School, Beds	www.bedfordschool.org.uk	£4,200	£6,604	I. P. Evans
Bedgebury School, Kent	www.bedgeburyschool.co.uk	£3,880	£6,245	Mrs H. M. Moriarty
Bedstone College, Shrops	www.bedstone.org	£3,250	£5,998	M. S. Symonds
Beechwood Sacred Heart, Kent	www.beechwood.org.uk	£3,750	£6,075	N. Beesley
The Belvedere School (GDST), Merscyside	www.gdst.net/belvedere	£2,455	–	Mrs A. Sherman
Benenden School, Kent	www.benenden.kent.sch.uk	£7,450	–	Mrs C. M. Oulton
Berkhamsted Collegiate, Herts	www.berkhamstedcollegiateschool.org.uk	£4,175	£6,618	Dr P. Chadwick
Bethany School, Kent	www.bethanyschool.org.uk	£3,886	£6,045	N. D. B. Dorey
Birkdale School, S. Yorks	www.birkdaleschool.org.uk	£2,577	–	R. J. Court
Birkenhead High School (GDST), Merseyside	www.gdst.net/birkenheadhigh	£2,455	–	Mrs C. H. Evans
Birkenhead School, Merseyside	www.birkenheadschool.co.uk	£2,549	–	D. J. Clark
Bishop's Stortford College, Herts	www.bishops-stortford-college.herts.sch.uk	£3,990	£5,536	J. G. Trotman
Blackheath High School (GDST), London SE3	www.blackheathhighschool.gdst.net	£3,063	–	Mrs E. A. Laws
Bloxham School, Oxon	www.bloxhamschool.com	£5,515	£7,145	M. E. Allbrook
Blundell's School, Devon	www.blundells.org	£4,400	£6,825	I. R. Davenport
Bolton School Boys' Division, Lancs	www.boys.bolton.sch.uk	£2,471	–	M. E. W. Brooker
Bolton School Girls' Division, Lancs	www.girls.bolton.sch.uk	£2,611	–	Mrs G. Richards
Bootham School, N. Yorks	www.bootham.york.sch.uk	£3,850	£6,072	J. F. J. Taylor
Box Hill School, Surrey	www.boxhillschool.org.uk	£3,775	£6,225	M. Eagers
Bradfield College, Berks	www.bradfieldcollege.org.uk	£5,800	£7,250	P. J. M. Roberts
Bradford Girls' Grammar School, W. Yorks	www.bggs.com	£2,880	–	Mrs L. J. Warrington
Bradford Grammar School, W. Yorks	www.bradfordgrammar.com	£8,339	–	S. R. Davidson
Brentwood School, Essex	www.brentwoodschool.co.uk	£3,647	£6,318	D. I. Davies
Brighton and Hove High School (GDST), E. Sussex	www.gdst.net/bhhs	£2,455	–	Mrs A. Greatorex

School	Web Address	Termly fees Day	Board	Head
Brighton College, E. Sussex	www.brightoncollege.net	£4,401	£6,822	A. F. Seldon
Brigidine School Windsor, Berks	www.brigidine.org.uk	£3,045	–	Mrs J. Dunn
Bristol Cathedral School, Bristol	www.bristolcathedral.bristol.sch.uk	£2,666	–	Mrs Anne Davey
Bristol Grammar School, Bristol	www.bristolgrammarschool.co.uk	£2,705	–	Dr D. J. Mascord
Bromley High School (GDST), Kent	www.gdst.net/bromleyhigh	£3,063	–	Mrs L. Duggleby
Bromsgrove School, Worcs	www.bromsgrove-school.co.uk	£3,520	£6,330	C. J. Edwards
Bruton School for Girls, Somerset	www.brutonschool.co.uk	£3,225	£5,425	Mrs B. Bates
Bryanston School, Dorset	www.bryanston.co.uk	–	£7,269	Ms S. J. Thomas
Burgess Hill, Girls, W. Sussex	www.burgesshill-school.com	£3,390	£5,885	Mrs S. Gorham
Bury Grammar School, Lancs	www.burygrammarschoolboys.co.uk	£2,120	–	K. Richards
Bury Grammar School (Girls), Lancs	www.bgsg.bury.sch.uk	£2,120	–	Mrs R. Georghiou
Canford School, Dorset	www.canford.com	£5,525	£7,360	J. D. Lever
Casterton School, Lancs	www.castertonschool.co.uk	£3,473	£5,805	P. McLaughlin
Caterham School, Surrey	www.caterhamschool.co.uk	£3,660	£6,827	R. A. E. Davey
Central Newcastle High School (GDST), Tyne and Wear	www.newcastlehigh.gdst.net	£2,455	–	M. Tippett
Channing School, London N6	www.channing.co.uk	£3,480	–	Mrs B. Elliott
Charterhouse, Surrey	www.charterhouse.org.uk	£6,112	£7,394	Revd J. S. Witheridge
Cheadle Hulme School, Cheshire	www.cheadlehulmeschool.co.uk	£2,490	–	P. V. Dixon
Cheltenham College, Glos	www.cheltcoll.gloucs.sch.uk	£5,360	£7,150	J. S. Richardson
The Cheltenham Ladies', Glos	www.cheltladiescollege.org	£4,863	£7,243	Mrs V. Tuck
Chetham's School of Music, Manchester	www.chethams.com	£5,667	£7,321	Mrs C. Hickman
Chigwell School, Essex	www.chigwell-school.org	£3,699	£5,622	D. F. Gibbs
Christ's Hospital, W. Sussex	www.christs-hospital.org.uk	–	£5,966	P. C. D. Southern
Churcher's College, Hants	www.churcherscollege.com	£2,795	–	S. H. L. Williams
City of London Freemen's, Surrey	www.clfs.surrey.sch.uk	£3,834	£6,098	D. C. Haywood
City of London School, EC4	www.clsb.org.uk	£3,612	–	D. R. Levin
City of London, Girls, EC2	www.clsg.org.uk	£3,528	–	Dr Y. A. Burne
Claremont Fan Court School, Surrey	www.claremont-school.co.uk	£3,430	–	Mrs P. B. Farrar
Clayesmore School, Dorset	www.clayesmore.com	£5,060	£6,915	M. G. Cooke
Clifton College, Bristol	www.cliftoncollegeuk.com	£4,560	£6,890	M. J. Moore
Clifton High School, Bristol	www.cliftonhigh.bristol.sch.uk	£2,660	£4,600	Mrs C. Culligan
Cobham Hall, Kent	www.cobhamhall.com	£4,900	£7,100	Mrs H. Davy
Cokethorpe School, Oxon	www.cokethorpe.org.uk	£3,940	–	D. J. Ettinger
Colfe's School, London SE12	www.colfes.com	£3,174	–	R. F. Russell
Colston's Girls' School, Bristol	www.colstonsgirls.bristol.sch.uk	£2,278	–	Mrs L. Jones
Colston's School, Bristol	www.colstons.bristol.sch.uk	£2,510	£5,315	P. T. Fraser
Combe Bank School, Kent	www.combebank.kent.sch.uk	£3,720	–	Mrs R. Martin
Concord College, Shrops	www.concordcollegeuk.com	£3,000	£6,312	N. G. Hawkins
Cranford House School, Oxon	www.cranfordhouse.oxon.sch.uk	£3,010	–	Mrs C. Hamilton
Cranleigh School, Surrey	www.cranleigh.org	£6,053	£7,450	G. Waller
Croham Hurst School, Surrey	www.crohamhurst.com	£3,095	–	Mrs E. J. Abbotts
Croydon High (GDST), Surrey	www.gdst.net/croydonhigh	£3,063	–	Miss L. M. Ogilvie
Culford School, Suffolk	www.culford.co.uk	£4,279	£6,566	J. F. Johnson-Munday
Dame Alice Harpur School, Beds	www.dahs.co.uk	£2,767	–	Mrs J. Berry
Dame Allan's Boys' School, Tyne and Wear	www.dameallans.co.uk	£2,413	–	Dr J. R. Hind
Dame Allan's Girls' School, Tyne and Wear	www.dameallans.co.uk	£2,413	–	Dr J. R. Hind
Dauntsey's School, Wilts	www.dauntseys.co.uk	£3,790	£6,345	S. Roberts
Dean Close School, Glos	www.deanclose.co.uk	£5,295	£7,495	Revd T. M. Hastie-Smith
Denstone College, Staffs	www.denstonecollege.org	£3,160	£5,000	D. M. Derbyshire
Derby High School, Derbys	www.dbyhigh.demon.co.uk	£2,395	–	C. T. Callaghan
Dover College, Kent	www.dovercollege.org.uk	£2,995	£5,995	S. Jones
Downe House, Berks	www.downehouse.net	£5,520	£7,625	E. McKendrick
Downside School, Somerset	www.downside.co.uk	£3,408	£6,530	Leo Maidlow Davis
Duke of York's Royal Military School, Kent	www.doyrms.mod.uk	–	£1,500	J. A. Cummings
Dulwich College, London SE21	www.dulwich.org.uk	£3,775	£7,605	G. G. Able
Dunottar School, Surrey	www.dunottar.surrey.sch.uk	£3,225	–	Mrs J. Hobson

School	Web Address	Termly fees Day	Board	Head
Durham High School for Girls, Durham	www.dhsfg.org.uk	£2,435	–	Mrs A. J. Templeman
Durham School, Durham	www.durhamschool.co.uk	£3,832	£5,832	N. G. Kern
Eastbourne College, E. Sussex	www.eastbourne-college.co.uk	£4,390	£6,695	S. P. Davies
Edgbaston High School, W. Midlands	www.edgbastonhigh.bham.sch.uk	£2,370	–	Miss E. M. Mullenger
Ellesmere College, Shrops	www.ellesmere.com	£4,056	£6,290	B. J. Wignall
Elmhurst School for Dance, W. Midlands	www.elmhurstdance.co.uk	£4,200	£5,400	J. J. McNamara
Eltham College, London SE9	www.eltham-college.org.uk	£3,302	–	P. J. Henderson
Emanuel School, London SW11	www.emanuel.org.uk	£3,387	–	M. D. Hanley-Browne
Embley Park School (UCST), Hants	www.embleypark.org.uk	£3,501	£5,794	D. F. Chapman
Epsom College, Surrey	www.epsomcollege.org.uk	£5,266	£7,463	S. R. Borthwick
Eton College, Berks	www.etoncollege.com	–	£7,896	A R. M. Little
Ewell Castle School, Surrey	www.ewellcastle.co.uk	£2,975	–	A. J. Tibble
Exeter School, Devon	www.exeterschool.org.uk	£2,660	–	R. Griffin
Farlington School, W. Sussex	www.farlingtonschool.net	£3,525	£5,605	Mrs P. M. Mawer
Farnborough Hill, Hants	www.farnborough-hill.org.uk	£2,760	–	Miss J. Thomas
Farringtons School, Kent	www.farringtons.org.uk	£3,090	£5,680	Mrs C. James
Felsted School, Essex	www.felsted.org	£4,857	£6,584	S. C. Roberts
Forest School, London E17	www.forest.org.uk	£3,377	–	A. G. Boggis
Framlingham College, Suffolk	www.framlingham.suffolk.sch.uk	£3,753	£5,839	Mrs G. M. Randall
Francis Holland (C of E) School, London NW1	www.francisholland.org	£3,625	–	Mrs V. M. Durham
Francis Holland (C of E) School, London SW1	www.fhs-sw1.org.uk	£3,725	–	Miss S. J. Pattenden
Frensham Heights, Surrey	www.frensham-heights.org.uk	£4,515	£6,720	A. Fisher
Friends' School, Essex	www.friends.org.uk	£3,590	£5,790	A. Waters
Fulneck School, W. Yorks	www.fulneckschool.co.uk	£2,775	£5,095	T. Kernohan
Gateways School, W. Yorks	www.gatewayschool.co.uk	£2,655	–	Mrs D. Davidson
Giggleswick School, N. Yorks	www.giggleswick.org.uk	£4,400	£6,557	G. P. Boult
The Godolphin and Latymer School, London W6	www.godolphinandlatymer.com	£3,700	–	Miss M. Rudland
The Godolphin School, Wilts	www.godolphin.org	£4,295	£6,600	Miss M. J. Horsburgh
The Grange School, Cheshire	www.grange.org.uk	£2,195	–	C. P. Jeffery
Greenacre School for Girls, Surrey	www.greenacre.surrey.sch.uk	£3,040	–	Mrs P. M. Wood
Grenville College, Devon	www.grenville.devon.sch.uk	£2,995	£5,995	Dr S. J. Wormleighton
Gresham's School, Norfolk	www.greshams.com	£5,340	£6,890	A. R. Clark
Guildford High (UCST), Surrey	www.guildfordhigh.surrey.sch.uk	£3,117	–	Mrs F. J. Boulton
The Haberdashers' Aske's Boys' School, Herts	www.habsboys.org.uk	£3,600	–	P. B. Hamilton
The Haberdashers' Aske's School for Girls, Herts	www.habsgirls.org.uk	£2,800	–	Mrs E. Radice
Haileybury, Herts	www.haileybury.com	£5,245	£6,985	S. A. Westley
Halliford School, Middx	www.hallifordschool.co.uk	£2,900	–	P. V. Cottam
Hampton School, Middx	www.hamptonschool.org.uk	£3,530	–	B. R. Martin
Harrogate Ladies' College, N. Yorks	www.hlc.org.uk	£3,500	£5,900	Dr M. J. Hustler
Harrow School, Middx	www.harrowschool.org.uk	–	£7,875	B. J. Lenon
Headington School, Oxon	www.headington.org	£3,230	£6,150	Mrs A. Coutts
Heathfield School, Berks	www.heathfieldschool.net	–	£7,270	Mrs F. King
Heathfield School (GDST), Middx	www.heathfield.gdst.net	£3,063	–	Miss C. M. Juett
Hereford Cathedral School, Herefordshire	www.hcsch.org	£2,785	–	P. A. Smith
Hethersett Old Hall School, Norfolk	www.hohs.co.uk	£2,995	£5,900	Mrs J. M. Mark
Highclare School, W. Midlands	www.highclareschool.co.uk	£2,635	–	Mrs M. Viles
Highgate School, London N6	www.highgateschool.org.uk	£4,195	–	R. P. Kennedy
Hipperholme Grammar, W. Yorks	www.hipperholmegrammar.org	£2,320	–	Dr J. Scarth
Hollygirt School, Notts	www.hollygirt.notts.sch.uk	£2,395	–	Mrs M. I. Connolly
Holy Trinity College, Kent	www.holytrinitycollegebromley.co.uk	£3,013	–	Mrs P. A. Lightfoot
Holy Trinity School, Worcs	www.holytrinity.co.uk	£2,595	–	Mrs Y. Wilkinson

School	Web Address	Termly fees Day	Board	Head
Hull Collegiate (UCST), E. Yorks	www.hullcollegiateschool.co.uk	£2,240	–	R. Haworth
The Hulme Grammar School for Boys, Lancs	www.hulmegrammarschools.org.uk	£2,099	–	K. E. Jones
The Hulme Grammar School for Girls, Lancs	www.hulme-grammar.oldham.sch.uk	£2,099	–	Miss M. S. Smolenski
Hurstpierpoint College, W. Sussex	www.hppc.co.uk	£5,035	£6,595	T. J. Manly
Hymers College, Humberside	www.hymerscollege.co.uk	£2,151	–	J. C. Morris
Immanuel College, Herts		£3,317	–	P. Skelker
Ipswich High (GDST), Suffolk	www.ipswichhigh.gdst.net	£2,455	–	Miss V. C. MacCuish
Ipswich School, Suffolk	www.ipswich.suffolk.sch.uk	£3,019	£5,258	I. G. Galbraith
James Allen's Girls' School (JAGS), London SE22	www.jags.org.uk	£3,435	–	Mrs M. Gibbs
The John Lyon School, Middx	www.johnlyon.org	£3,395	–	K. J. Riley
Kelly College, Devon	www.kellycollege.com	£4,050	£6,900	M. S. Steed
Kent College, Kent	www.kentcollege.com	£4,005	£6,845	G. G. Carminati
Kent College Pembury, Kent	www.kent-college.co.uk	£4,115	£6,640	Mrs A. Upton
Kimbolton School, Cambs	www.kimbolton.cambs.sch.uk	£3,165	£5,265	J. Belbin
King Edward VI High School for Girls, W. Midlands	www.kehs.org.uk	£2,420	–	Miss S. H. Evans
King Edward VI School, Hants	www.kes.hants.sch.uk	£2,962	–	A. J. Thould
King Edward VII and Queen Mary School, Lancs	www.keqms.co.uk	£2,240	–	R. J. Karling
King Edward's School, Surrey	www.kesw.surrey.sch.uk	£4,480	£6,320	P. K. Fulton-Peebles
King Edward's School, W. Midlands	www.kes.bham.sch.uk	£2,460	–	R. M. Dancey
King Edward's School, Somerset	www.kesbath.com	£2,832	–	C. Rowe
King Henry VIII School, W. Midlands	www.khviii.com	£2,345	–	George Fisher
King William's College, Isle of Man	www.kwc.sch.im	£4,600	£6,700	P. D. John
King's College, Somerset	www.kings-taunton.co.uk	£4,550	£6,660	C. D. Ramsey
King's College School, London SW19	www.kcs.org.uk	£4,350	–	A. C. V. Evans
The King's High, Girls, Warks	www.khsw.warwks.sch.uk	£2,673	–	Mrs E. Surber
The King's School, Ely	www.kings-ely.cambs.sch.uk	£4,470	£6,470	Mrs S. E. Freestone
The King's School, Macclesfield, Cheshire	www.kingsmac.co.uk	£2,332	–	S. Coyne
The King's School, Canterbury	www.kings-school.co.uk	£5,760	£7,760	Revd Canon K. H. Wilkinson
The King's School, Chester	www.kingschester.co.uk	£2,475	–	T. J. Turvey
The King's School, Gloucester	www.thekingsschool.co.uk	£3,800	–	P. R. Lacey
King's School, Rochester, Kent	www.kings-school-rochester.co.uk	£4,470	£7,520	Dr I. R. Walker
King's School, Bruton, Somerset	www.kingsbruton.com	£4,910	£6,700	N. M. Lashbrook
The King's School, Tyne and Wear	www.kings-tynemouth.org.uk	£2,326	–	P. J. S. Cantwell
The King's School, Worcester	www.ksw.org.uk	£2,906	–	T. H. Keyes
Kingham Hill School, Oxon	www.kingham-hill.oxon.sch.uk	£4,638	£6,718	M. J. Morris
The Kingsley School, Warks	www.thekingsleyschool.org	£2,530	–	Mrs C. A. Mannion Watson
Kingston Grammar School, Surrey	www.kingston-grammar.surrey.sch.uk	£3,595	–	C. D. Baxter
Kingswood School, Somerset	www.kingswood.bath.sch.uk	£2,918	£6,537	G. M. Best
Kirkham Grammar School, Lancs	www.kirkhamgrammar.co.uk	£2,299	£4,233	D. R. Walker
The Lady Eleanor Holles, Middx	www.lehs.org.uk	£3,401	–	Mrs G. Low
La Retraite Swan, Wilts	www.la-retraite-swan.org.uk	£2,915	–	Mrs R. A. Simmons
La Sagesse School, Tyne and Wear	www.lasagesse.org.uk	£2,620	–	Miss L. Clark
Lancing College, W. Sussex	www.lancingcollege.co.uk	£5,075	£7,295	P. M. Tinniswood
Langley School, Norfolk	www.langleyschool.co.uk	£2,810	£5,590	J. G. Malcolm
Latymer Upper School, London W6	www.latymer-upper.org	£3,995	–	P. J. Winter
Lavant House, W. Sussex	www.lavanthouse.org.uk	£3,365	£5,330	Mrs M. Scott
Leeds Girls' High School, N. Yorks	www.lghs.org	£2,736	–	Ms S. Fishburn
Leeds Grammar School, W. Yorks	www.leedsgrammar.com	£2,685	–	M. Bailey
Leicester Grammar School, Leics	www.leicestergrammar.org.uk	£2,635	–	C. P. M. King
Leicester High, Girls, Leics	www.leicesterhigh.co.uk	£2,520	–	Mrs J. Burns

School	Web Address	Termly fees Day	Board	Head
Leighton Park School, Berks	www.leightonpark.reading.sch.uk	£4,618	£6,950	J. H. Dunston
The Leys School, Cambs	www.theleys.cambs.sch.uk	£4,475	£6,990	M. Slater
The Licensed Victuallers', Berks	www.lvs.ascot.sch.uk	£3,270	£5,745	I. A. Mullins
Lincoln Minster (UCST), Lincs	www.lincolnminsterschool.co.uk	£2,675	£5,062	C. J. Rickart
Liverpool College, Merseyside	www.liverpoolcollege.org.uk	£2,530	–	J. D. B. Christian
Lodge School, Surrey	www.lodgeschool.co.uk	£2,750	–	Miss P. A. Maynard
Longridge Towers School, Northumberland	www.lts.org.uk	£2,390	£4,950	A. E. Clemit
Lord Wandsworth College, Hants	www.lordwandsworth.org	£4,840	£6,495	I. G. Power
Loughborough Grammar, Leics	www.loughgs.leics.sch.uk	£2,715	£4,824	P. B. Fisher
Loughborough High School, Leics	www.loughhs.leics.sch.uk	£2,493	–	Miss B. A. O'Connor
Luckley-Oakfield School, Berks	www.luckley.wokingham.sch.uk	£3,186	£5,438	Miss V. A. Davis
Magdalen College School, Oxon	www.mcsoxford.org	£3,293	–	A. D. Halls
Malvern College, Worcs	www.malcol.org	£4,740	£7,330	H. C. K. Carson
Malvern Girls' College, Worcs	www.mgc.worcs.sch.uk	£3,300	£6,780	Mrs P. M. C. Leggate
The Manchester Grammar School, Manchester	www.mgs.org	£2,413	–	C. Ray
Manchester High School for Girls, Manchester	www.manchesterhigh.co.uk	£2,412	–	Mrs C. Lee-Jones
Manor House School, Surrey	www.manorhouse.surrey.sch.uk	£3,214	–	Mrs A. Morris
The Marist Senior School, Berks	www.themaristschools.com	£2,825	–	K. McCloskey
Marlborough College, Wilts	www.marlboroughcollege.org	£5,475	£7,300	N. A. Sampson
Marymount International School, Surrey	www.marymountlondon.com	£4,583	£7,717	C. Channing
The Maynard School, Devon	www.maynard.co.uk	£2,698	–	Dr D. West
Merchant Taylors' School, Merseyside	www.merchanttaylors.sefton.sch.uk	£2,184	–	D. H. I. Cook
Merchant Taylors' School, Middx	www.mtsn.org.uk	£3,995	–	S. N. Wright
Merchant Taylors' School for Girls, Merseyside	www.mtgs.co.uk	£2,292	–	Mrs J. C. Moon
Mill Hill School, London NW7	www.millhill.org.uk	£4,195	£6,580	W. R. Winfield
Millfield, Somerset	www.millfieldschool.com	£5,000	£7,500	P. M. Johnson
Milton Abbey School, Dorset	www.miltonabbey.co.uk	£5,620	£7,490	W. J. Hughes-D'Aeth
Moira House Girls School, E. Sussex	www.moirahouse.co.uk	£3,850	£6,625	Mrs A. Harris
Monkton Combe School, Somerset	www.monktoncombeschool.com	£4,983	£7,102	R. P. Backhouse
More House School, London SW1	www.morehouse.org.uk	£3,525	–	Mrs L. Falconer
Moreton Hall, Shrops	www.moretonhall.org	£4,860	£6,650	J. Forster
Mount St Mary's College, Derbys	www.msmcollege.co.uk	£2,895	£5,220	P. MacDonald
The Mount School, N. Yorks	www.mount.n-yorks.sch.uk	£3,780	£5,865	Mrs D. J. Gant
The Mount School, London NW7	www.mountschool.com	£2,493	–	Mrs J. K. Jackson
New Hall School, Essex	www.newhallschool.co.uk	£4,060	£6,100	Mrs K. Jeffrey
Newcastle-under-Lyme, Staffs	www.nuls.org.uk	£2,328	–	R. S. Dillow
The Newcastle upon Tyne Church High School, Tyne and Wear	www.churchhigh.com	£2,400	–	Mrs L. G. Smith
North Cestrian Grammar School, Cheshire	www.ncgs.co.uk	£2,090	–	D. G. Vanstone
North London Collegiate, Middx	www.nlcs.org.uk	£3,339	–	Mrs B. McCabe
Northampton High School, Northants	www.northamptonhigh.northants.sch.uk	£2,660	–	Mrs L. A. Mayne
Northwood College, Middx	www.northwoodcollege.co.uk	£3,291	–	Mrs R. Mercer
Norwich High (GDST), Norfolk	www.gdst.net/norwich/	£2,455	–	Mrs V. C. Bidwell
Norwich School, Norfolk	www.norwich-school.org.uk	£2,667	–	J. B. Hawkins
Notre Dame Senior School, Surrey	www.notredame.co.uk	£3,180	–	Mrs B. Williams
Notting Hill and Ealing High School (GDST), London W13	www.nhehs.gdst.net	£3,063	–	Mrs S. M. Whitfield
Nottingham High School, Notts	www.nottinghamhigh.co.uk	£2,798	–	C. S. Parker
Nottingham High School for Girls (GDST), Notts	www.gdst.net/nottinghamgirlshigh	£2,455	–	Mrs A. C. Rees
Oakham School, Leics	www.oakham.rutland.sch.uk	£4,270	£7,140	Dr J. A. F. Spence
Ockbrook School, Derbys	www.ockbrook.derby.sch.uk	£2,471	£4,568	Ms D. P. Bolland

School	Web Address	Termly fees		Head
		Day	Board	
The Old Palace School of John Whitgift, Surrey	www.oldpalace.croydon.sch.uk	£2,698	–	Ms J. Harris
The Oratory School, Berks	www.oratory.co.uk	£4,930	£6,835	C. I. Dytor
Oswestry School, Shrops	www.oswestryschool.org.uk	£3,310	£5,570	P. D. Stockdale
Oundle School, Northants	www.oundleschool.org.uk	£3,995	£6,897	C. M. P. Bush
Our Lady of Sion School, W. Sussex	www.sionschool.org.uk	£2,685	–	M. Scullion
Our Lady's Convent Senior, Oxon	www.olcss.org.uk	£2,660	–	Mrs L. Renwick
Oxford High School (GDST), Oxon	www.gdst.net/oxfordhigh	£2,455	–	Miss O. F. S. Lusk
Palmers Green High School, London N21	www.pghs.co.uk	£2,795	–	Mrs C. Edmundson
Pangbourne College, Berks	www.pangbournecollege.com	£4,815	£6,865	T. J. C. Garnier
Parsons Mead, Surrey	www.parsonsmeadsurrey.co.uk	£3,330	–	Mrs P. Taylor
The Perse School, Cambs	www.perse.co.uk	£3,465	–	N. P. V. Richardson
The Perse School for Girls, Cambs	www.perse.cambs.sch.uk	£3,300	–	Miss P. M. Kelleher
Peterborough High School, Cambs	www.peterboroughhigh.co.uk	£2,989	£5,468	Mrs S. A. Dixon
Pipers Corner School, Bucks	www.piperscorner.co.uk	£3,395	£5,610	Mrs V. M. Stattersfield
Plymouth College, Devon	www.plymouthcollege.com	£2,852	£5,456	A. J. Morsley
Pocklington School, E. Yorks	www.pocklingtonschool.com	£3,071	£5,444	N. Clements
Polam Hall School, Durham	www.polamhall.com	£2,920	£5,625	Miss M. Green
The Portsmouth Grammar, Hants	www.pgs.org.uk	£2,989	–	T. R. Hands
Portsmouth High (GDST), Hants	www.gdst.net/portsmouthhigh	£2,455	–	Miss P. Hulse
The Princess Helena College, Herts	www.phc.herts.sch.uk	£4,410	£6,370	Mrs A-M. Hodgkiss
Princethorpe College, Warks	www.princethorpe.co.uk	£2,425	–	J. M. Shinkwin
Prior Park College, Somerset	www.priorpark.co.uk	£3,310	£5,968	R. G. G. Mercer
Prior's Field, Surrey	www.priorsfield.surrey.sch.uk	£3,695	£5,950	Mrs J. Dwyer
Priory School, W. Midlands	www.prioryschool.net	£2,535	–	Mrs E. Brook
The Purcell School, Herts	www.purcell-school.org	£6,434	£8,229	J. N. Tolputt
Putney High School (GDST), London SW15	www.gdst.net/putneyhigh	£3,063	–	Dr D. V. Lodge
Queen Anne's School, Berks	www.qas.org.uk	£4,778	£7,074	Mrs D. Forbes
Queen Elizabeth Grammar, W. Yorks	www.wgsf.org.uk	£2,497	–	M. R. Gibbons
Queen Elizabeth's Grammar, Lancs	www.qegs.blackburn.sch.uk	£2,567	–	D. S. Hempsall
Queen Elizabeth's Hospital, Bristol	www.qehbristol.co.uk	£2,664	£4,909	S. W. Holliday
Queen Margaret's School, N. Yorks	www.queenmargaretsschool.co.uk	£3,945	£6,225	G. A. H. Chapman
Queen's College, London W13	www.qcl.org.uk	£3,800	–	Miss M. M. Connell
Queen's College, Somerset	www.queenscollege.org.uk	£3,792	£5,724	C. J. Alcock
Queen's Gate School, London SW7	www.queensgate.org	£3,625	–	Mrs A. Holyoak
The Queen's School, Cheshire	www.queens.cheshire.sch.uk	£2,645	–	Mrs C. M. Buckley
Queenswood, Herts	www.queenswood.herts.sch.uk	£5,480	£7,265	Ms C. M. Farr
Radley College, Oxon	www.radley.org.uk	£7,120	–	A. W. McPhail
Ratcliffe College, Leics	www.ratcliffecollege.com	£3,539	£5,331	P. Farrar
The Read School, N. Yorks	www.readschool.co.uk	£2,232	£4,830	R. A. Hadfield
Reading Blue Coat School, Berks	www.blue-coat.reading.sch.uk	£3,085	–	S. J. W. McArthur
The Red Maids' School, Bristol	www.redmaids.bristol.sch.uk	£2,525	–	Mrs I. Tobias
Redland High, Girls, Bristol	www.redland.bristol.sch.uk	£2,715	–	Dr R. A. Weeks
Reed's School, Surrey	www.reeds.surrey.sch.uk	£4,604	£6,090	D. W. Jarrett
Reigate Grammar School, Surrey	www.reigategrammar.org	£3,303	–	D. S. Thomas
Rendcomb College, Glos	www.rendcombcollege.co.uk	£4,500	£5,675	G. Holden
Repton School, Derbys	www.repton.org.uk	£4,955	£6,675	R. A. Holroyd
Rishworth School, W. Yorks	www.rishworth-school.co.uk	£2,790	£5,425	R. A. Baker
Roedean School, E. Sussex	www.roedean.co.uk	£4,450	£7,800	Mrs C. Shaw
Rossall School, Lancs	www.rossallschool.org.uk	£2,493	£6,350	T. J. Wilbur
The Royal Grammar School, Surrey	www.rgs-guildford.co.uk	£3,305	–	T. M. S. Young
Royal Grammar, Tyne and Wear	www.rgs.newcastle.sch.uk	£2,283	–	J. F. X. Miller
Royal Grammar School, Worcs	www.rgsw.org.uk	£2,664	–	A. R. Rattue
The Royal High School Bath (GDST), Somerset	www.gdst.net/royalhighbath	£2,455	£4,814	J. Graham-Brown
The Royal Hospital School, Suffolk	www.royalhospitalschool.org	£3,380	£5,636	H. W. Blackett
The Royal Masonic, Girls, Herts	www.royalmasonic.herts.sch.uk	£3,235	£5,240	Mrs D. Rose
Royal Russell School, Surrey	www.royalrussell.co.uk	£3,480	£6,925	J. R. Jennings

School	Web Address	Termly fees Day	Board	Head
The Royal School, Surrey	www.royal-school.org	£3,956	£6,281	Mrs L. Taylor-Gooby
The Royal Wolverhampton School, W. Midlands	www.theroyalschool.co.uk	£3,315	£6,600	T. Waters
Rugby School, Warks	www.rugbyschool.net	£4,600	£7,250	P. S. J. Derham
Ryde School with Upper Chine, Isle of Wight	www.rydeschool.org.uk	£2,600	£5,315	Dr N. J. England
Rye St Antony School, Oxon	www.ryestantony.co.uk	£3,055	£5,185	Miss A. M. Jones
St Albans High School, Herts	www.sahs.org.uk	£2,955	–	Ms J. Pain
St Albans School, Herts	www.st-albans.herts.sch.uk	£3,514	–	A. R. Grant
St Antony's Leweston School, Dorset	www.leweston.co.uk	£3,925	£5,925	H. J. MacDonald
St Bede's College, Manchester	www.stbedescollege.co.uk	£2,260	–	J. Byrne
St Bede's School, E. Sussex	www.stbedesschool.org	£4,055	£6,595	S. Cole
St Bees School, Cumbria	www.st-bees-school.org	£3,822	£6,377	P. J. Capes
St Benedict's School, London W5	www.stbenedictscaling.org.uk	£3,310	–	C. J. Cleugh
St Catherine's School, Surrey	www.stcatherines.info	£3,585	£5,900	Mrs A. Phillips
St Catherine's School, Middx	www.stcatherineschool.co.uk	£2,820	–	Mrs Z. M. Braganza
St Christopher School, Herts	www.stchris.co.uk	£3,585	£6,300	D. Wilkinson
St Columba's College, Herts	www.scc.herts.sch.uk	£2,570	–	N. J. B. O'Sullivan
St David's School, Middx	www.stdavidsschool.com	£3,175	£5,880	Ms P. Bristow
St Dominic's Priory School, Staffs		£2,302	–	A. Egan
St Dominic's School, Staffs	www.st-dominics-brewood.co.uk	£2,910	–	Mrs S. White
St Dunstan's College, London SE6	www.stdunstans.org.uk	£3,420	–	Mrs F. Cordeaux
St Edmund's College, Herts	www.stedmundscollege.org	£3,810	£6,175	C. P. Long
St Edmund's School, Kent	www.stedmunds.org.uk	£4,311	£6,677	J. M. Gladwin
St Edward's School, Oxon	www.stedwards.oxon.sch.uk	£5,694	£7,208	A. F. Trotman
St Edward's School, Glos	www.stedwards.co.uk	£3,245	–	A. J. Nash
Saint Felix Schools, Suffolk	www.stfelix.co.uk	£3,750	£5,850	D. A. T. Ward
St Francis' College, Herts	www.st-francis.herts.sch.uk	£3,030	£5,960	Miss M. Hegarty
St Gabriel's School, Berks	www.st-gabriels.w-berks.sch.uk	£2,950	–	A. Jones
St George's College, Surrey	www.st-georges-college.co.uk	£3,770	–	J. A. Peake
St George's School, Berks	www.stgeorges-ascot.org.uk	£4,650	£7,200	Mrs C. L. Jordan
St George's School, W. Midlands	www.sgse.co.uk	£2,450	–	Miss H. Phillips
The School of St Helen and St Katharine, Oxon	www.sthelens.oxon.sch.uk	£2,837	–	Mrs C. L. Hall
St Helen's School for Girls, Middx	www.sthelensnorthwood.co.uk	£3,230	£5,986	Mrs M. Morris
St James Independent School for Senior Girls, London W14	www.stjamesschools.co.uk	£3,045	–	Mrs L. Hyde
St James's School, Worcs	www.st-james-school.co.uk	£3,995	£6,580	Mrs R. Hayes
St John's College, Hants	www.stjohnscollege.co.uk	£2,375	£5,100	N. W. Thorne
St John's School, Surrey	www.stjohnsleatherhead.co.uk	£5,050	£6,950	N. J. R. Haddock
St Joseph's College, Suffolk	www.stjos.co.uk	£2,965	£5,140	Mrs S. Grant
St Joseph's Convent School, Berks	www.st-josephs.reading.sch.uk	£2,910	–	Mrs M. Sheridan
St Lawrence College, Kent	www.slcuk.com	£4,321	£7,260	Revd M. Aitken
St Leonards Mayfield School, E. Sussex	www.stlm.e-sussex.sch.uk	£4,400	£6,600	Mrs J. Dalton
St Margaret's School, Herts	www.stmargaretsbushey.co.uk	£3,515	£6,295	M. Ferris
St Margaret's School, Devon	www.stmargarets-school.co.uk	£2,414	–	Miss R. Edbrooke
Saint Martin's, W. Midlands	www.saintmartins-school.com	£2,625	–	Mrs J. Carwithen
St Mary's College, Merseyside	www.stmaryscrosby.co.uk	£2,113	–	Mrs J. M. Marsh
St Mary's Convent School, Worcs	www.stmarys.org.uk	£2,475	–	Mrs S. K. Cookson
St Mary's Hall, E. Sussex	www.stmaryshall.co.uk	£3,528	£5,825	Mrs S. M. Meek
St Mary's School, Berks	www.st-marys-ascot.co.uk	£4,770	£6,990	Mrs M. Breen
St Mary's School, Bucks	www.stmarys-gx.org	£3,245	–	Mrs F. A. Balcombe
St Mary's School, Cambs	www.stmaryscambridge.co.uk	£3,290	£6,550	Mrs J. Triffitt
St Mary's School, Dorset	www.st-marys-shaftesbury.co.uk	£4,105	£6,085	Mrs M. McSwiggan
St Mary's School, Essex	www.stmarysschool.org.uk	£2,405	–	Mrs G. M. G. Mouser
St Mary's School, Oxon	www.stmarys.oxon.sch.uk	£4,900	£7,330	Mrs S. Sowden
St Mary's School, Wilts	www.stmaryscalne.org	£5,180	£7,580	Mrs H. Wright
St Nicholas' School, Hants	www.st-nicholas.hants.sch.uk	£2,840	–	Mrs A. V. Whatmough

School	Web Address	Day	Board	Head
		Termly fees		
St Paul's Girls' School, London W6	www.spgs.org	£3,948	–	Miss E. Diggory
St Paul's School, London SW13	www.stpaulsschool.org.uk	£4,680	£6,965	G. M. Stephen
St Peter's School, N. Yorks	www.st-peters.york.sch.uk	£3,462	£5,813	R. I. Smyth
St Swithun's School, Hants	www.stswithuns.com	£3,950	£6,510	Dr H. L. Harvey
St Teresa's School, Surrey	www.stteresas.surrey.sch.uk	£3,700	£6,285	Mrs M. E. Prescott
Scarborough College and Lisvane, N. Yorks	www.scarboroughcollege.co.uk	£2,712	£4,137	T. L. Kirkup
Seaford College, W. Sussex	www.seaford.org	£4,180	£6,370	T. J. Mullins
Sedbergh School, Cumbria	www.sedbergh.cumbria.sch.uk	£5,140	£6,900	C. H. Hirst
Sevenoaks School, Kent	www.sevenoaksschool.org	£4,179	£6,733	Mrs C. L. Ricks
Shebbear College, Devon	www.shebbearcollege.co.uk	£2,640	£4,930	R. S. Barnes
Sheffield High (GDST), S. Yorks	www.sheffieldhighschool.org.uk	£2,455	–	Mrs V. A. Dunsford
Sherborne School, Dorset	www.sherborne.org	£5,635	£7,225	S. F. Eliot
Sherborne School for Girls, Dorset	www.sherborne.com	£5,575	£7,625	Mrs G. Kerton-Johnson
Shiplake College, Oxon	www.shiplake.org.uk	£4,445	£6,590	A. G. S. Davies
Shrewsbury High (GDST), Shrops	www.gdst.net/shrewsburyhigh	£2,455	–	Mrs M. Cass
Shrewsbury School, Shrops	www.shrewsbury.org.uk	£5,290	£7,530	J. W. R. Goulding
Sibford School, Oxon	www.sibford.oxon.sch.uk	£2,817	£5,579	M. Goodwin
Sidcot School, Somerset	www.sidcot.org.uk	£3,330	£7,200	J. Walmsley
Silcoates School, W. Yorks	www.silcoates.com	£2,952	–	A. P. Spillane
Sir William Perkins's School, Surrey	www.swps.org.uk	£3,111	–	Miss S. A. Ross
Solihull School, W. Midlands	www.solsch.org.uk	£2,515	–	J. A. Claughton
South Hampstead High School (GDST), London NW3	www.gdst.net/shhs	£3,063	–	Mrs J. E. Stephen
Stafford Grammar School, Staffs	www.stafford-grammar.co.uk	£2,386	–	M. R. Darley
Stamford High School, Lincs	www.ses.lincs.sch.uk	£3,004	£5,700	Dr P. R. Mason
Stamford School, Lincs	www.ses.lincs.sch.uk	£3,004	£5,700	Dr P. R. Mason
Stanbridge Earls School, Hants	www.stanbridgeearls.co.uk	£5,000	£6,745	G. P. Link
Stockport Grammar School, Cheshire	www.stockportgrammar.co.uk	£2,319	–	A. H. Chicken
Stonar School, Wilts	www.stonarschool.com	£3,125	£5,550	Mrs M. Murray
Stonyhurst College, Lancs	www.stonyhurst.ac.uk	£3,884	£6,636	A. J. F. Aylward
Stover School, Devon	www.stover.co.uk	£2,715	£5,545	T. A. Packer
Stowe School, Bucks	www.stowe.co.uk	£5,665	£7,660	A. K. Wallersteiner
Streatham and Clapham High School (GDST), London SW16	www.gdst.net/streathamhigh	£3,063	–	Mrs S. Mitchell
Sunderland High School (UCST), Tyne and Wear	www.sunderlandhigh.co.uk	£2,191	–	Dr A. Slater
Surbiton High (UCST), Surrey	www.surbitonhigh.com	£3,199	–	Dr J. Longhurst
Sutton High School for Girls (GDST), Surrey	www.gdst.net/suttonhigh	£3,063	–	S. J. Callaghan
Sutton Valence School, Kent	www.svs.org.uk	£4,688	£7,150	J. S. Davies
Sydenham High School (GDST), London SE26	www.gdst.net/sydenhamhigh	£3,063	–	Mrs K. E. Pullen
Talbot Heath, Dorset	www.talbotheath.org.uk	£2,900	£4,830	Mrs C. Dipple
Taunton School, Somerset	www.tauntonschool.co.uk	£4,115	£6,400	Dr J. H. Newton
Teesside Preparatory and High School, Cleveland	www.teessidehigh.co.uk	£2,569	–	Mrs H. French
Tettenhall College, W. Midlands	www.tettenhallcollege.co.uk	£3,040	£5,283	P. C. Bodkin
Thetford Grammar School, Norfolk	www.thetgram.norfolk.sch.uk	£2,627	–	G. J. Price
Thornton College, Bucks	www.thorntoncollege.com	£2,775	£4,600	Miss A. T. Williams
Thorpe House School, Norfolk	www.thorpehouseschool.com	£2,090	–	A. Todd
Tonbridge School, Kent	www.tonbridge-school.org	£5,210	£7,374	T. H. P. Haynes
Tormead School, Surrey	www.tormeadschool.org.uk	£3,145	–	Mrs S. E. Marks
Trent College, Notts	www.trentcollege.net	£3,745	£5,644	J. S. Lee
Trinity School, Surrey	www.trinity-school.org	£3,325	–	C. J. Tarrant
Truro High School for Girls, Cornwall	www.trurohigh.co.uk	£2,728	£5,143	M. A. McDowell
Truro School, Cornwall	www.truroschool.com	£2,809	£5,479	P. K. Smith
Tudor Hall, Oxon	www.tudorhall.oxon.sch.uk	£4,200	£6,515	Miss W. Griffiths
University College School, London NW3	www.ucs.org.uk	£4,165	–	K. J. Durham

| | | Termly fees | | |
School	Web Address	Day	Board	Head
Uppingham School, Leics	www.uppingham.co.uk	£5,250	£7,500	Dr S. C. Winkley
Wakefield Girls' High School, W. Yorks	www.wgsf.org.uk	£2,497	–	Mrs P. A. Langham
Walthamstow Hall, Kent	www.walthamstow-hall.co.uk	£3,920	–	Mrs J. Milner
Warminster School, Wilts	www.warminsterschool.org.uk	£3,220	£5,600	D. M. Dowdles
Warwick School, Warks	www.warwickschool.org	£2,888	£6,163	E. B. Halse
Wellingborough School, Northants	www.wellingboroughschool.org	£3,147	–	G. R. Bowe
Wellington College, Berks	www.wellingtoncollege.org.uk	£6,132	£7,665	R. I. H. B. Dyer
Wellington School, Somerset	www.wellington-school.org.uk	£2,794	£4,967	A. J. Rogers
Wells Cathedral School, Somerset	www.wells-cathedral-school.com	£3,860	£6,450	Mrs E. C. Cairncross
Wentworth College, Dorset	www.wentworthcollege.com	£3,225	£5,190	Miss S. Coe
West Buckland School, Devon	www.westbuckland.devon.sch.uk	£3,035	£5,290	J. F. Vick
Westfield School, Tyne and Wear	www.westfield.newcastle.sch.uk	£2,551	–	Mrs M. Farndale
Westholme School, Lancs	www.westholmeschool.com	£1,969	–	Mrs L. Croston
Westminster School, London SW1	www.westminster.org.uk	£5,496	£7,316	M. S. Spurr
Westonbirt, Glos	www.westonbirt.gloucs.sch.uk	£4,760	£6,860	Mrs M. Henderson
Whitford Hall and Dodderhill, Worcs	www.whitford-dodderhillschool.co.uk	£2,590	–	Mrs J. M. Mumby
Whitgift School, Surrey	www.whitgift.co.uk	£3,541	–	C. A. Barnett
William Hulme's Grammar School, Manchester	www.whgs.co.uk	£2,372	–	S. R. Patriarca
Wimbledon High School (GDST), London SW19	www.gdst.net/wimbledon	£3,063	–	Mrs P. H. Wilkes
Winchester College, Hants	www.winchestercollege.org	£7,442	£7,833	R. D. Townsend
Windermere St Anne's School, Cumbria	www.wsaschool.com	£3,020	£5,460	Miss W. A. Ellis
Wisbech Grammar School, Cambs	www.wgs.cambs.sch.uk	£2,620	–	R. S. Repper
Wispers School for Girls, Surrey	www.wispers.org.uk	£3,960	£6,280	L. H. Beltran
Withington Girls' School, Manchester	www.withington.manchester.sch.uk	£2,370	–	Mrs J. D. Pickering
Woldingham School, Surrey	www.woldingham.surrey.sch.uk	£4,230	£7,080	Miss D. Vernon
Wolverhampton Grammar School, W. Midlands	www.wgs.org.uk	£2,764	–	B. St J. Trafford
Woodbridge School, Suffolk	www.woodbridge.suffolk.sch.uk	£3,458	£6,022	S. H. Cole
Woodhouse Grove School, W. Yorks	www.woodhousegrove.co.uk	£2,875	£5,250	D. C. Humphreys
Worksop College, Notts	www.worksopcollege.notts.sch.uk	£3,945	£5,765	R. A. Collard
Worth School, W. Sussex	www.worthschool.co.uk	£5,226	£7,055	P. Armstrong
Wrekin College, Shrops	www.wrekincollege.ac.uk	£3,745	£6,195	S. G. Drew
Wychwood School, Oxon	www.wychwood-school.org.uk	£2,975	£4,800	Mrs S. Wingfield Digby
Wycliffe College, Glos	www.wycliffe.co.uk	£4,465	£6,600	Mrs M. E. Burnet Ward
Wycombe Abbey School, Bucks	www.wycombeabbey.com	£5,775	£7,700	Mrs P. E. Davies
Wykeham House School, Hants	www.wykehamhouse.hants.sch.uk	£2,331	–	Mrs R. M. Kamaryc
Yarm School, Cleveland	www.yarmschool.org	£2,797	–	D. M. Dunn
The Yehudi Menuhin School, Surrey	www.yehudimenuhinschool.co.uk	£9,662	£9,924	N. Chisholm

WALES

School	Web Address	Day	Board	Head
Christ College, Brecon	www.christcollegebrecon.com	£3,975	£5,940	D. P. Jones
Haberdashers' Monmouth School for Girls, Monmouth	www.habs-monmouth.org	£3,116	£5,571	Dr B. Despontin
Howell's School, Denbigh	www.howells.org	£2,990	£4,590	Mrs L. A. Robinson
Howell's School Llandaff (GDST), Cardiff	www.howells.cardiff.sch.uk	£2,471	–	Mrs C. J. Fitz
Llandovery College, Llandovery	www.llandoverycollege.com	£3,505	£5,290	P. A. Hogan
Monmouth School, Monmouth	www.habs-monmouth.org	£3,168	£5,282	S. G. Connors
Rougemont School, Newport	www.rsch.co.uk	£2,550	–	Dr J. Tribbick
Ruthin School, Ruthin	www.ruthinschool.co.uk	£3,340	£5,420	J. S. Rowlands
Rydal Penrhos School, Colwyn Bay	www.rydal-penrhos.com	£3,541	£5,935	M. S. James
St David's College, Llandudno	www.stdavidscollege.co.uk	£3,553	£5,465	W. Seymour

School	Web Address	Termly fees Day	Board	Head
SCOTLAND				
Dollar Academy, Dollar	www.dollaracademy.org.uk	£2,568	£5,850	J. S. Robertson
The High School of Dundee, Dundee	www.highschoolofdundee.co.uk	£2,475	–	A. M. Duncan
The Edinburgh Academy, Edinburgh	www.edinburghacademy.org.uk	£2,950	£6,200	J. V. Light
Fettes College, Edinburgh	www.fettes.com	£4,629	£6,733	M. C. B. Spens
George Heriot's School, Edinburgh	www.george-heriots.com	£2,462	–	A. G. Hector
George Watson's College, Edinburgh	www.gwc.org.uk	£2,606	–	G. Edwards
The Glasgow Academy, Glasgow	www.theglasgowacademy.org.uk	£2,460	–	P. J. Brodie
Glenalmond College, Perth	www.glenalmondcollege.co.uk	£4,575	£6,720	G. C. Woods
The High School of Glasgow, Glasgow	www.glasgowhigh.com	£2,232	–	C. D. R. Mair
Hutchesons' Grammar School, Glasgow	www.hutchesons.org	£7,572	–	Dr K. M. Greig
Kelvinside Academy, Glasgow	www.kelvinsideacademy.org.uk	£2,573	–	J. L. Broadfoot
Kilgraston School, Perthshire	www.kilgraston.com	£3,500	£5,930	M. Farmer
Lomond School, Helensburgh	www.lomond-school.org	£2,445	£5,230	A. D. Macdonald
Loretto School, Midlothian	www.loretto.com	£4,455	£6,676	M. B. Mavor
The Mary Erskine School, Edinburgh	www.esms.edin.sch.uk	£2,668	£4,823	J. N. D. Gray
Merchiston Castle School, Edinburgh	www.merchiston.co.uk	£4,950	£6,925	A. R. Hunter
Morrison's Academy, Crieff	www.morrisonsacademy.org	£2,573	£6,274	G. S. H. Pengelley
Robert Gordon's College, Aberdeen	www.rgc.aberdeen.sch.uk	£7,600	–	H. Ouston
St Aloysius' College, Glasgow	www.staloysius.org	£6,940	–	J. Stoer
St Columba's School, Kilmacolm	www.st-columbas.org	£2,400	–	D. G. Girdwood
St George's School for Girls, Edinburgh	www.st-georges.edin.sch.uk	£2,735	£5,460	Dr J. McClure
St Margaret's School, Edinburgh	www.st-margarets.edin.sch.uk	£2,525	£5,222	Mrs E. M. Davis
St Margaret's School for Girls, Aberdeen	www.st-margaret.aberdeen.sch.uk	£2,551	–	Mrs L. McKay
Stewart's Melville College, Edinburgh	www.esms.edin.sch.uk	£2,418	£4,823	J. N. D. Gray
Strathallan School, Forgandenny	www.strathallan.co.uk	£4,396	£6,504	B. K. Thompson
NORTHERN IRELAND				
Bangor Grammar School, Bangor		£95	–	S. D. Connolly
Belfast Royal Academy, Belfast	www.belfastroyalacademy.com	£80	–	W. S. F. Young
Campbell College, Belfast	www.campbellcollege.co.uk	£575	£2,775	R. J. I. Pollock
Coleraine Academical Institution, Coleraine	www.coleraineai.demon.co.uk	£120	–	L. F. Quigg
Methodist College, Belfast	www.methody.org	–	£2,325	T. W. Mulryne
Portora Royal School, Enniskillen	www.portoraroyal.co.uk	£45	–	J. N. Morton
The Royal Belfast Academical Institution, Belfast	www.rbai.org.uk	£230	–	R. M. Ridley
The Royal School Dungannon, Dungannon	www.royaldungannon.com	£37	£1,667	P. D. Hewitt
CHANNEL ISLANDS				
Elizabeth College, Guernsey	www.elizcoll.org	£1,720	–	N. D. Argent
The Ladies' College, Guernsey	www.ladiescollege.sch.gg	£1,240	–	Miss M. E. Macdonald
Victoria College, Jersey	www.vcj.sch.je	£1,200	–	R. G. Cook

NATIONAL ACADEMIES OF SCHOLARSHIP

BRITISH ACADEMY (1902)
10 Carlton House Terrace, London SW1Y 5AH
T 020-7969 5200
W www.britac.ac.uk

The British Academy is an independent, self-governing learned society for the promotion of the humanities and social sciences. It supports advanced academic research and is a channel for the Government's support of research in those disciplines.

The Fellows are scholars who have attained distinction in one of the branches of study that the Academy exists to promote. Candidates must be nominated by existing Fellows. There are 770 Ordinary Fellows, 15 Honorary Fellows and 306 Corresponding Fellows overseas.
President, Baroness O'Neill, FBA
Treasurer, Prof. R. J. P. Kain, FBA
Foreign Secretary, Prof. C. N. J. Mann, FBA
Publications Secretary, Dr D. J. McKitterick, FBA
Secretary, P. W. H. Brown, CBE

ROYAL ACADEMY OF ARTS (1768)
Burlington House, Piccadilly, London W1J OBD
T 020-7300 8000
W www.royalacademy.org.uk

The Royal Academy of Arts is an independent, self-governing society devoted to the encouragement and promotion of the fine arts.

Membership of the Academy is limited to 80 Royal Academicians, all being painters, engravers, sculptors or architects. Candidates are nominated and elected by the existing Academicians. There is also a limited class of honorary membership and there were 20 honorary members as at June 2004.
President, Sir Nicholas Grimshaw, PRA
Treasurer, Prof. Paul Huxley, RA
Keeper, Prof. Maurice Cockrill, RA
Secretary (acting), Mary Anne Stevens

ROYAL ACADEMY OF ENGINEERING (1976)
29 Great Peter Street, London SW1P 3LW
T 020-7227 0500
W www.raeng.org.uk

The Royal Academy of Engineering was established as the Fellowship of Engineering in 1976. It was granted a royal charter in 1983 and its present title in 1992. It is an independent, self-governing body whose object is the pursuit, encouragement and maintenance of excellence in the whole field of engineering, in order to promote the advancement of the science, art and practice of engineering for the benefit of the public.

Election to the Fellowship is by invitation only, from nominations supported by the body of Fellows. At June 2005 there were 1,335 Fellows. The Duke of Edinburgh is the Senior Fellow and the Duke of Kent is a Royal Fellow.
President, Lord Broers, FRS, FRENG
Senior Vice-President, Sir Duncan Michael, FRENG

Vice-Presidents, G. A. Campbell, FRENG; Prof. W. R. Eatock Taylor, FRENG; Dr S. E. Ion, OBE, FRENG; P. C. Ruffles, CBE, FRS, FRENG; P. Saraga, OBE, FRENG; Dr R. S. Steedman, FRENG; Sir Peter Williams, CBE, FRS, FRENG
Hon. Treasurer, F. C. Price, FRENG
Hon. Secretaries, P. Saraga, OBE, FRENG *(International Activities)*; Dr J. E. King, CBE, FRENG *(Education and Training)*
Chief Executive, P. D. Greenish, CBE

ROYAL SCOTTISH ACADEMY (1838)
The Mound, Edinburgh EH2 2EL
T 0131-225 6671 W www.royalscottishacademy.org

The Scottish Academy was founded in 1826 to arrange exhibitions of contemporary paintings and to establish a society of fine art in Scotland. The Academy was granted a royal charter in 1838.

Members are elected from the disciplines of art and architecture. Elections are from nominations put forward by the existing membership. A recent change to the constitution has led to the creation of two classes of membership: Honorary Academicians and Academicians; at mid-2005 there were 28 Honorary Academicians and 98 Academicians.
President, I. McKenzie Smith, OBE, PRSA
Secretary, W. Scott, RSA
Treasurer, I. Metzstein, OBE, RSA
Administrative Secretary, B. Laidlaw, ACIS

ROYAL SOCIETY (1660)
6–9 Carlton House Terrace, London SW1Y 5AG
T 020-7451 2500
W www.royalsoc.ac.uk

The Royal Society is an independent academy promoting the natural and applied sciences. Founded in 1660, the Society has three roles, as the UK academy of science, as a learned Society and as a funding agency. It is an independent, self-governing body under a royal charter, promoting and advancing all fields of physical and biological sciences, of mathematics and engineering, medical and agricultural sciences and their application.

Fellows are elected for their contributions to science, both in fundamental research resulting in greater understanding, and also in leading and directing scientific and technological progress in industry and research establishments. A maximum of 44 new Fellows, who must be citizens or residents of the British Commonwealth countries or Ireland, may be elected annually.

Up to six Foreign Members, who are selected from those not eligible to become Fellows because of citizenship or residency, are elected annually for their contributions to science.

One Honorary Fellow may be elected each year from those not eligible for election as Fellows or Foreign members. There are approximately 1,400 Fellows and Foreign Members covering all scientific disciplines.
President, Prof. Lord May of Oxford, OM, PRS
Treasurer, Prof. Sir D. Wallace, CBE, FRS, FRENG

Biological Secretary, Prof. D. Read, FRS
Physical Secretary, Prof. M. Taylor, FRS
Foreign Secretary, Prof. Dame J. Higgins, DBE, FRS, FRENG
Executive Secretary, S. Cox, CVO

ROYAL SOCIETY OF EDINBURGH (1783)

22–26 George Street, Edinburgh EH2 2PQ
T 0131-240 5000
W www.royalsoced.org.uk

The Royal Society of Edinburgh (RSE) is Scotland's National Academy of Science and Letters. An independent body with charitable status, its multidisciplinary membership of around 1400 fellows represents a knowledge resource for the people of Scotland. Granted its Royal Charter in 1783 for the 'advancement of learning and useful knowledge', the Society organises conferences and lectures both for the specialist and for the general public; provides independent, expert advice to key decision-makers in Scotland; strengthens links between academia and industry and produces academic journals of international standing. The Society also awards over £1.5 million annually to Scotland's top young academics to promote research in Scotland.

At May 2005 there were 1410 Fellows.
President, Lord Sutherland of Houndwood, KT, FBA, FRSE
Vice-Presidents, Prof. J. Coggins, FRSE; Prof. Gavin McCrone, CB, FRSE; Prof. John Mavor, FRSE
Treasurer, Edward Cunningham, CBE, FRSE
General Secretary, Prof. A. Miller, CBE, FRSE

RESEARCH COUNCILS

The government funds basic and applied civil science research, mostly through the eight research councils, which are established under Royal Charter and supported by the Department of Trade and Industry. The councils support research and training in universities and other higher education establishments. The science budget, administered by the Department of Trade and Industry's Office of Science and Technology (OST), contributes around 30 per cent of public sector investment in research, with funding from other government departments (including higher education funding) and regional development making up the remaining investment. The councils also receive income for research commissioned by government departments and the private sector, in addition to income from charitable sources. The annual science budget is set to rise to £3.45 billion by 2007–8, from £2.73 billion in 2004–5, with the total 2005–6 allocation at £3.09 billion.

The government science budget for 2005–6 includes the following allocations:

	£000s
AHRC	80,536
BBSRC	336,186
CLRC	167,004
EPSRC	568,193
ESRC	123,465
MRC	478,787
NERC	334,047
PPARC	293,916
Royal Society	32,520
Royal Academy of Engineering	5,850
British Academy	14,050
Higher Education Innovation Fund	69,425
Science Research Investment Fund	300,000

Source: Department of Trade and Industry – *Science Budget Allocations 2005–6 to 2007–8* (Crown Copyright)

BIOTECHNOLOGY AND BIOLOGICAL SCIENCES RESEARCH COUNCIL (BBSRC)

Polaris House, North Star Avenue, Swindon SN2 1UH
T 01793-413200

The BBSRC promotes and supports research training relating to the understanding and exploitation of biological systems; advances knowledge and technology; provides trained scientists to meet the needs of biotechnological-related industries; and provides advice, disseminates knowledge, and promotes public understanding of biotechnology and the biological sciences.
Chair, Dr P. Ringose
Chief Executive, Prof. J. Goodfellow, CBE

INSTITUTES
BABRAHAM INSTITUTE, Babraham Hall, Babraham, Cambridge CB2 4AT T 01223-496000
Director, Dr R. G. Dyer

INSTITUTE FOR ANIMAL HEALTH, Compton Laboratory, Compton, Newbury, Berks RG20 7NN T 01635-578411
Director (acting), Prof. M. Shirley

BBSRC / MRC NEUROPATHOGENESIS UNIT, Ogston Building, West Mains Road, Edinburgh EH9 3JF
T 0131-667 5204

PILBRIGHT LABORATORY, Ash Road, Pilbright, Woking, Surrey GU24 0NF T 01483-232441
Head, Dr David Mackay

ROTHAMSTED RESEARCH, Rothamsted, Harpenden, Herts AL5 2JQ T 01582-763133 *Director*, Prof. I. R. Crute

BROOM'S BARN, Higham, Bury St. Edmunds, Suffolk IP28 6NP T 01284-812200 *Director*, Dr J. D. Pidgeon

INSTITUTE OF FOOD RESEARCH, Norwich Research Park, Colney Lane, Norwich NR4 7UA T 01603-255000
Director, Prof. D. White

INSTITUTE OF GRASSLAND AND ENVIRONMENTAL RESEARCH, Aberystwyth Research Centre, Plas Gogerddan, Aberystwyth SY23 3EB T 01970-823000
Director, Prof. C. Pollock, OBE

NORTH WYKE RESEARCH STATION, Okehampton, Devon EX20 2SB T 01837-883500 *Head*, Prof. S. Jarvis

JOHN INNES CENTRE, Norwich Research Park, Colney, Norwich NR4 7UH T 01603-452571 *Director*, Prof. C. Lamb

ROSLIN INSTITUTE, Roslin, Midlothian EH25 9PS
T 0131-527 4200 *Director*, Dr Harry Griffin

SILSOE RESEARCH INSTITUTE, West Park, Silsoe, Bedford MK45 4HS T 01525-860000 *Director*, Prof. B. Day

SCOTTISH EXECUTIVE ENVIRONMENT AND RURAL AFFAIRS DEPARTMENT

Through its Science and Research Group, the Scottish Executive Environment and Rural Affairs Department (SEERAD) funds a programme of environmental, biological and agricultural research, which forms a significant part of the UK science base in this area. A large proportion of SEERAD's research is implemented by its Main Research Providers (MRPs), with the remaining work carried out by universities and private research organisations.

The MRPs receive core funding from SEERAD Science and Research Group to support identified research activities, in addition to capital funding. They also compete for funding from other sources in the public and private sectors.

BIOMATHEMATICS AND STATISTICS SCOTLAND BioSS (administered by SCRI), University of Edinburgh, James Clerk Maxwell Building, The King's Buildings, Mayfield Road, Edinburgh EH9 3JZ T 0131-650 4900 *Director (acting)*, David Elston

HANNAH RESEARCH INSTITUTE, Hannah Research Park, Ayr KA6 5HL T 01292-674000 *Director (acting)*, Prof. Chris Knight

MACAULAY LAND USE RESEARCH INSTITUTE,
Craigiebuckler, Aberdeen AB15 8QH T 01224-498200
Director, Prof. E. M. Gill
MOREDUN RESEARCH INSTITUTE, Pentlands Science Park,
Bush Loan, Penicuik, Midlothian EH26 0PZ T 0131-445 5111
Director, Prof. Julie Fitzpatrick
ROWETT RESEARCH INSTITUTE, Greenburn Road,
Bucksburn, Aberdeen AB21 9SB T 01224-712751
Director, Prof. P. J. Morgan
ROYAL BOTANIC GARDEN EDINBURGH (RGBE),
20a Inverleith Row, Edinburgh EH3 5LP T 0131-552 7171
Regius Keeper, Prof. Stephen Blackmore, FRSE
SCOTTISH AGRICULTURAL COLLEGE (SAC), West Mains
Road, Edinburgh EH9 3JG T 0131-535 4000
Chief Executive, Prof. W. McKelvie
SCOTTISH CROP RESEARCH INSTITUTE (SCRI),
Invergowrie, Dundee DD2 5DA T 01382-562731
Director, Prof. P. Gregory

COUNCIL FOR THE CENTRAL LABORATORY OF THE RESEARCH COUNCILS (CCLRC)

Rutherford Appleton Laboratory, Chilton,
Didcot, Oxon OX11 0QX
T 01235-445553
W www.cclrc.ac.uk

The CCLRC is a non-departmental body of the Office of Science and Technology, which is part of the Department of Trade and Industry. It is the national portal and centre for key, large-scale research facilities in support of science and engineering research. In particular, the CCLRC has strategic and operational roles in respect of neutron scattering, synchrotron radiation and high power laser facilities. These will enable UK researchers to carry out world-leading science. As well as providing strategic advice, the CCLRC also provides facilities for scientists to research a broad spectrum of applications, from the molecular structure of drugs enabling them to be targeted to maximise efficiency and minimise side effects, to the discovery of planets in distant galaxies.

The CCLRC operates the Rutherford Appleton Laboratory in Oxfordshire, the Daresbury Laboratory in Cheshire and the Chilbolton Observatory in Hampshire.
Chair, Prof. Sir Graeme Davies
Chief Executive, Prof. J. Wood

CHILBOLTON OBSERVATORY, Stockbridge, Hampshire
SO20 6BJ T 01264-860391
DARESBURY LABORATORY, Daresbury, Warrington,
Cheshire WA4 4AD T 01925-603000
RUTHERFORD APPLETON LABORATORY, Chilton, Didcot,
Oxon OX11 0QX T 01235-445000

ECONOMIC AND SOCIAL RESEARCH COUNCIL (ESRC)

Polaris House, North Star Avenue, Swindon SN2 1UJ
T 01793-413000
E comms@esrc.ac.uk W www.esrcsocietytoday.ac.uk

The purpose of the ESRC is to promote and support research and postgraduate training in the social sciences; to advance knowledge and provide trained social scientists; to provide advice on, and disseminate knowledge and promote public understanding of the social sciences.
Chair, F. Cairncross, CBE
Chief Executive, I. Diamond

RESEARCH CENTRES
CENTRE FOR ANALYSIS OF RISK AND RELEGATION,
London School of Economics and Political Science,
Houghton Street, London WC2A 2AE T 020-7955 6577
Directors, Prof. M. Power; Prof. B. Hutter
CENTRE FOR THE ANALYSIS OF SOCIAL EXCLUSION,
London School of Economics, Houghton Street, London
WC2A 2AE T 020-7955 6679 *Director*, Prof. J. Hills
CENTRE FOR BUSINESS RELATIONSHIPS,
ACCOUNTABILITY, SUSTAINABILITY AND SOCIETY,
Cardiff University, 54 Park Place, Cardiff CF10 3AT
T 029-2087 6562, *Director*, Prof. K. Peattie
CENTRE FOR BUSINESS RESEARCH, Department of
Applied Economics, University of Cambridge, Sidgwick
Avenue, Cambridge CB3 9DE T 01223-765320
Director, Prof. A. Hughes
CENTRE FOR ECONOMIC AND SOCIAL ASPECTS OF
GENOMICS, Lancaster University, Furness College,
Lancaster, RA1 4YG T 01524-59270
Director, Prof. R. Chadwick
CENTRE FOR ECONOMIC LEARNING AND SOCIAL
EVOLUTION, Department of Economics, University College
London, Gower Street, London WC1E 6BT T 020-7679 5879
Research Director, Prof. T. Börgers
CENTRE FOR ECONOMIC PERFORMANCE, London
School of Economics, Houghton Street, London WC2A 2AE
T 020-7955 7284 *Director*, Prof. J. Van Reenan
CENTRE FOR GENOMICS IN SOCIETY, University of
Exeter, Amory Building, Rennes Drive, Exeter, Devon EX4 4RJ
T 01392-262053 *Director*, J. Dupré
CENTRE FOR MICROECONOMIC ANALYSIS OF PUBLIC
POLICY (CMAPP), Institute for Fiscal Studies, 7 Ridgmount
Street, London WC1E 7AE T 020-7636 3784
Director, Prof. R. Blundell
CENTRE FOR ORGANISATION AND INNOVATION,
Institute of Work Psychology, University of Sheffield,
Sheffield S10 2TN T 0114-222 3287 *Director*, Prof. T. Wall
CENTRE FOR RESEARCH ON INNOVATION AND
COMPETITION, Faculty of Economic and Social Studies,
University of Manchester M13 9PL T 0161-275 2000
Directors, Prof. S. Metcalfe; Prof. R. Coombs
CENTRE FOR SKILLS, KNOWLEDGE AND
ORGANISATIONAL PERFORMANCE (SKOPE),
University of Oxford, Department of Economics, Manor Road,
Oxford OX1 3UP T 01865-271087 *Director*, K. Mayhew
CENTRE FOR SOCIAL AND ECONOMIC RESEARCH ON
INNOVATION IN GENOMICS, University of Edinburgh,
Old Surgeon's Hall, High School Yards, Edinburgh EH1 1LZ
T 0131-650 9113 *Director*, Prof. J. Tait
CENTRE FOR SOCIAL AND ECONOMIC RESEARCH ON
THE GLOBAL ENVIRONMENT, School of Environmental
Sciences, University of East Anglia, Norwich NR4 7TJ
T 01603-593738 *Director*, Prof. R. K. Turner
CENTRE FOR THE STUDY OF GLOBALISATION AND
REGIONALISATION, Department of Political Science,
University of Warwick, Coventry CV4 7AL T 024-7657 2533
Directors, Prof. R. Higgott; Prof. J. A. Scholte
CENTRE ON MICRO-SOCIAL CHANGE, University of Essex,
Wivenhoe Park, Colchester, Essex CO4 3SQ
T 01206-872734 *Directors*, Prof. J. Ermisch;
Prof. J. Gershuny
CENTRE ON MIGRATION, POLICY AND SOCIETY,
University of Oxford, 58 Banbury Road, Oxford OX2 6QS
T 01865-274711 *Director*, Dr S. Vertovec
COMPLEX PRODUCT SYSTEMS INNOVATION CENTRE,
SPRU, Mantell Building, University of Sussex, Brighton
BN1 9RF T 01273-678177 *Directors*, Prof. M. Hobday;
Prof. H. Rush

FINANCIAL MARKETS CENTRE, London School of
Economics, Houghton Street, London WC2A 2AE
T 020-7955 7002 *Director*, Prof. D. Webb

RESOURCE CENTRES

CENTRE FOR APPLIED SOCIAL SURVEYS, Social and
Community Planning Research, 35 Northampton Square,
London EC1V 0AX T 020-8059 2533 *Director*, R. Thomas
CENTRE FOR ECONOMIC POLICY RESEARCH, 90–98
Goswell Road, London EC1V 7DB T 020-7878 2900
Director, Prof. R. Portes
ESRC DATA ARCHIVE, University of Essex, Wivenhoe Park,
Colchester, Essex CO4 3SQ T 01206-872001
Director, K. Schurer
ESRC UK CENTRE FOR EVIDENCE BASED POLICY,
Queen Mary and Westfield College, Department of Politics,
Mile End Road, London E1 4NS T 020-7882 7657
Director, Prof. K. Young
INTERNATIONAL BIBLIOGRAPHY OF THE SOCIAL
SCIENCES, British Library of Political and Economic Science,
London School of Economics, Houghton Street, London
WC2A 2AE T 020-7955 7000 *Director*, Ms J. Sykes
INTERNATIONAL BIBLIOGRAPHY OF THE SOCIAL
SCIENCES: ON-LINE RESOURCE CENTRE, L, ondon
School of Economics, 10 Portugal Street, London WC2A 2HD
T 020-7955 7455
Director, Ms. L. Brindley
QUALITATIVE DATA ARCHIVAL RESOURCE CENTRE,
Department of Sociology, University of Essex, Colchester,
Essex CO4 3SQ T 01206-873058
Director, Prof. P. Thompson
RESOURCE CENTRE FOR ACCESS TO DATA IN EUROPE,
Department of Geography, University of Durham, Durham
DH1 3HP T 0191-374 7350 *Director*, Prof. R. Hudson

ENGINEERING AND PHYSICAL SCIENCES RESEARCH COUNCIL (EPSRC)

Polaris House, North Star Avenue, Swindon SN2 1ET
T 01793-444000 W www.epsrc.ac.uk

The EPSRC is the UK government's main funding agency
for research and training in engineering and the physical
sciences in universities and other organisations throughout
the UK. It also provides advice, disseminates knowledge
and promotes public understanding in these areas.
Chair, Prof. Dame Julia Higgins, FRS, FRENG
Chief Executive, Prof. J. O'Reilly, FRENG, CENG

MEDICAL RESEARCH COUNCIL (MRC)

20 Park Crescent, London W1B 1AL
T 020-7636 5422 W www.mrc.ac.uk

The purpose of the MRC is to promote medical and
related biological research. The council employs its own
research staff and funds research by other institutions and
individuals, complementing the research resources of the
universities and hospitals.
Chair, Sir Anthony Cleaver
Chief Executive, Prof. Colin Blakemore
Chair, Neurosciences and Mental Health Board, Prof. A.
North
Chair, Molecular and Cellular Medicine Board, Prof. M.
Wakelam
Chair, Infections and Immunity Board, Prof. A. McMichael
Chair, Health Services and Public Health Research Board, Dr
D. Armstrong
Chair, Physiological and Clinical Sciences Board, Prof. John
Savill

MRC RESEARCH CENTRES

Biostatistics Unit W www.mrc-bsu.cam.ac.uk
Cambridge Centre for Behavioural and Clinical Neuroscience
T 01223-333558
Cancer Cell Unit W www.hutchison-mrc.cam.ac.uk
Cell Biology Unit W www.ucl.ac.uk/lmcb
*MRC/UCL Centre Development for Medical Molecular
Virology* T 020-7679 9119
*MRC/University of Newcastle Centre Development in
Clinical Brain Ageing*
Centre for Developmental Neurobiology
W www.kcl.ac.uk/depsta/biomedical/mrcdevbiol
*MRC/University of Edinburgh Centre for Inflammation
Research* W www.cir.med.ed.ac.uk
Centre for Protein Engineering W www.mrc-cpe.cam.ac.uk
MRC/University of Bristol Centre for Synaptic Plasticity
W www.bris.ac.uk/depts/synaptic
Clinical Sciences Centre W www.csc.mrc.ac.uk
Clinical Trials Unit W www.ctu.mrc.ac.uk
Cognition and Brain Sciences Unit
W www.mrc-cbu.cam.ac.uk
Dunn Human Nutrition Unit W www.mrc-dunn.cam.ac.uk
Epidemiology Unit T 01223-330315
Epidemiology Resource Centre T 023-8077 7624
Functional Genetics Unit W www.mrcfgu.ox.ac.uk
*MRC/University of Sussex Genome Damage and Stability
Centre* W www.lifesci.sussex.ac.uk/gdsc
Health Services Research Collaboration W www.hsrc.ac.uk
Human Genetics Unit W www.hgu.mrc.ac.uk
Human Immunology Unit T 01865-222336
Human Reproductive Sciences Unit W www.hrsu.mrc.ac.uk
Immunochemistry Unit W www.bioch.ox.ac.uk/immunoch
*MRC/University of Birmingham Centre for Immune
Regulation* W www.bham.ac.uk/mrcbcir
Institute for Environment and Health W www.le.ac.uk/ieh
Institute of Hearing Research W www.ihr.mrc.ac.uk
Laboratories Fajara, The Gambia
W www.extra.mrc.ac.uk/gambia
Laboratory of Molecular Biology T 01223-248011
W www.mrc-lmb.cam.ac.uk
MRC/UCL Laboratory for Molecular Virology
T 020-7679 9119
Mammalian Genetics Unit T 01235-841000
W www.mgu.har.mrc.ac.uk
Molecular Haemotology Unit T 01865-222443
W www.imm.ox.ac.uk/groups/mrc_molhaem
National Institute for Medical Research
W www.nimr.mrc.ac.uk
Prion Unit W www.prion.ucl.ac.uk
Protein Phosphorylation Unit
W www.dundee.ac.uk/lifesciences/mrcppu
Radiation and Genome Stability Unit
W www.ragsu.har.mrc.ac.uk
Resource Centre for Human Nutrition Research
W www.mrc-hnr.cam.ac.uk
Rosalind Franklin Centre for Genomics Research
W www.hgmp.mrc.ac.uk
Social and Public Health Sciences Unit
W www.msoc-mrc.gla.ac.uk
Social, Genetic and Developmental Psychiatry Centre
T 020-7836 5454
Toxicology Unit W www.le.ac.uk/cmht
Virology Unit W www.vir.gla.ac.uk

NATURAL ENVIRONMENT RESEARCH COUNCIL (NERC)

Polaris House, North Star Avenue, Swindon SN2 1EU
T 01793-411500
W www.nerc.ac.uk

The UK's Natural Environment Research Council (NERC) funds and carries out impartial scientific research in the sciences of the environment. Its work covers the full range of atmospheric, earth, biological, terrestrial and aquatic sciences, from the depths of the oceans to the upper atmosphere. Its mission is to gather and apply knowledge, create understanding and predict the behaviour of the natural environment and its resources.

Chair, Rob Margetts, CBE, FRENG
Chief Executive, Prof. Alan Thorpe

RESEARCH CENTRES

BRITISH ANTARCTIC SURVEY, High Cross, Madingley Road, Cambridge CB3 OET T 01223-221400
Director, Prof. Chris Rapley
BRITISH GEOLOGICAL SURVEY, Kingsley Dunham Centre, Keyworth, Nottingham NG12 5GG T 0115-936 3100
Executive Director, Dr David Falvey
CENTRE FOR ECOLOGY AND HYDROLOGY, Polaris House, North Star Avenue, Swindon SN2 1EU
T 01793-442516 *Director*, Prof. Patricia Nuttall, OBE
PROUDMAN OCEANOGRAPHIC LABORATORY, Joseph Proudman Building, 6 Brownlow Street, Liverpool L3 5DA
T 0151-795 4800 *Director*, Prof. Andrew Willmott

COLLABORATIVE CENTRES

CENTRE FOR OBSERVATION OF AIR-SEA INTERACTIONS AND FLUXES, Plymouth Marine Laboratory, Prospect Place, Plymouth PL1 3DH
T 01752-633429 *Director*, Prof. Jim Aiken
CENTRE FOR OBSERVATION AND MODELLING OF EARTHQUAKES AND TECTONICS, Department of Earth Sciences, University of Oxford, Parks Road, Oxford OX1 3PR
T 01865-272030 *Director*, Prof. Barry Parsons
CENTRE FOR POLAR OBSERVATION AND MODELLING, Department of Space and Climate Physics, Pearson Building, University College London, Gower Street, London WC1E 6BT T 020-7679 3031
Director, Prof. Duncan Wingham
CENTRE FOR POPULATION BIOLOGY, Imperial College London, Silwood Park Campus, Ascot SL5 7PY
T 020-7594 2475 *Director*, Prof. Charles Godfray, FRS
CLIMATE AND LAND SURFACE SYSTEMS INTERACTION CENTRE, Department of Geography, University of Wales Swansea, Singleton Park, Swansea SA2 8PP
T 01792-295647 *Director*, Prof. Mike Barnsley
DATA ASSIMILATION RESEARCH CENTRE, Department of Meteorology, University of Reading, PO Box 243, Earley Gate, Reading RG6 6BB T 0118-378 6728
Director, Prof. Alan O'Neill
ENVIRONMENTAL SYSTEMS SCIENCE CENTRE, University of Reading, Harry Pitt Building, 3 Earley Gate, PO Box 238, Reading RG6 6AL T 0118-378 8741 *Director*, Prof. Robert Gurney
NATIONAL INSTITUTE FOR ENVIRONMENTAL E-SCIENCE, Centre for Mathematical Science, Wilberforce Road, Cambridge CB3 0WA T 01223-764289
Director, Dr Martin Dove
NATIONAL OCEANOGRAPHY CENTRE, SOUTHAMPTON, University of Southampton, Waterfront Campus, European Way, Southampton SO14 3ZH
T 023-8059 6100 *Director*, Prof. Ed Hill

NERC CENTRES FOR ATMOSPHERIC SCIENCE, University of Reading, Earley Gate, PO Box 243, Reading RG6 6BB
T 0118-378 6979 *Director*, Prof. Stephen Mobbs
NCAS ATMOSPHERIC CHEMISTRY MODELLING SUPPORT UNIT, Department of Chemistry, University of Cambridge, Lensfield Road, Cambridge CB2 1EW
T 01223-336473 *Director*, Prof. John Pyle
NCAS BRITISH ATMOSPHERIC DATA CENTRE, Rutherford Appleton Laboratory, Chilton, Didcot OX11 0QX
T 01235-445012 *Director*, Dr Bryan Lawrence
NCAS CENTRE FOR GLOBAL ATMOSPHERIC MODELLING, Department of Meteorology, University of Reading, PO Box 243, Earley Gate, Reading RG6 6BB
T 0118-378 8424 *Director*, Prof. Julia Slingo
NCAS DISTRIBUTED INSTITUTE FOR ATMOSPHERIC COMPOSITION, School of Chemistry, University of Leeds, Leeds LS2 9JT T 0113-343 6450
Director, Prof. Mike Pilling
NCAS FACILITY FOR AIRBORNE ATMOSPHERIC MEASUREMENTS, Building 125, Cranfield University, Cranfield, Bedford MK43 0AL T 01234-754411
Head of Facility, Steve Ball
NCAS UNIVERSITIES FACILITY FOR ATMOSPHERIC MEASUREMENTS, School of Earth and Environment, University of Leeds, Leeds LS2 9JT T 0113-343 6461
Director, Dr Alan Blyth
NCAS UNIVERSITIES WEATHER RESEARCH NETWORK, Department of Meteorology, University of Reading, PO Box 243, Earley Gate, Reading, RG6 6BB T 0118-378 8957
Director, Prof. P. Mason
NERC CENTRE FOR TERRESTRIAL CARBON DYNAMICS, University of Sheffield, Hicks Building, Hounsfield Road, Sheffield S3 7RH T 0114-222 3803
Director, Prof. Shaun Quegan
PLYMOUTH MARINE LABORATORY, Prospect Place, Plymouth PL1 3DH T 01752-633100
Director, Prof. Nicholas Owens
SCOTTISH ASSOCIATION FOR MARINE SCIENCE, Dunstaffnage Marine Laboratory, Oban PA37 1QA
T 01631-559000 *Director*, Prof. Graham Shimmield
SEA MAMMAL RESEARCH UNIT, Gatty Marine Laboratory, University of St Andrews, St Andrews KY16 8LB
T 01334-462630 *Director*, Prof. Ian Boyd
TYNDALL CENTRE FOR CLIMATE CHANGE RESEARCH, School of Environmental Sciences, University of East Anglia, Norwich, Norfolk NR4 7TJ T 01603-593900
Executive Director, Prof. Mike Hulme

PARTICLE PHYSICS AND ASTRONOMY RESEARCH COUNCIL (PPARC)

Polaris House, North Star Avenue, Swindon SN2 1SZ
T 01793-442000
E pr.pus@pparc.ac.uk

The Particle Physics and Astronomy Research Council (PPARC) is the UK's strategic science investment agency. It funds research, education and public understanding in four broad areas of science – particle physics, astronomy, cosmology and space sciences.

PPARC is government funded and provides research grants and studentships to scientists in British universities, gives researchers access to world-class facilities and funds the UK membership of international bodies such as the European Laboratory for Particle Physics (CERN), the European Space Agency (ESA) and the European Southern Observatory (ESO). It also contributes money to the UK telescopes overseas on La Palma, Hawaii, Australia and in Chile, the UK Astronomy Technology Centre at

the Royal Observatory, Edinburgh and the MERLIN/
VLBI National Facility.
Chair, P. Warry
Chief Executive, Prof. Richard Wade
ISAAC NEWTON GROUP OF TELESCOPES, Apartado de
Coreos 321, 38770 Santa Cruz de la Palma, Tenerife, Canary
Islands T +34 922-425401 *Director*, Dr R. Rutten
JOINT ASTRONOMY CENTRE, 660 North A'ohoku Place,
University Park, Hilo, Hawaii 96720, USA T +1 808 961 3756
Director, Prof. G. Davies
UK ASTRONOMY TECHNOLOGY CENTRE, Blackford Hill,
Edinburgh EH9 3HJ T 0131-668 8100
Director, Prof. Ian Robson

ARTS AND HUMANITIES RESEARCH COUNCIL (AHRC)

Whitefriars, Lewins Mead, Bristol BS1 2AE
T 0117-987 6500 W www.ahrc.ac.uk

Launched in April 2005 as the successor organisation to
the Arts and Humanities Research Board, the Arts and
Humanities Research Council (AHRC) funds postgraduate
training and research in the arts and humanities,
encompassing discplines such as English literature,
history, modern languages, archaeology, music and drama.

Each year the AHRC is to provide around £70 million
to support research and postgraduate study in the arts and
humanities. It will also provide funding of around £10
million a year to museums, galleries and other collections
in English universities.
Chair, Prof. Sir Brian Follett
Chief Executive, Prof. Geoffrey Crossick

RESEARCH AND TECHNOLOGY ORGANISATIONS

The following industrial and technological research
bodies are members of the Association of Independent
Research and Technology Organisations Limited
(AIRTO). Members' activities span a wide range of
disciplines from life sciences to engineering. Their work
includes basic research, development and design of
innovative products or processes, instrumentation testing
and certification, and technology and management
consultancy. AIRTO publishes a directory to help clients
identify the organisations that might be able to assist them.

AIRTO LTD, c/o CCFRA, Station Road, Chipping Campden,
Glos, GL55 6LD T 01386-842247 *President*, Prof. R. Brook
ADVANCED MANUFACTURING TECHNOLOGY
RESEARCH INSTITUTE, Hulley Road, Macclesfield,
Cheshire SK10 2NE T 01625-425421
Managing Director, P. Sholl
AIRCRAFT RESEARCH ASSOCIATION LTD, Manton Lane,
Bedford MK41 7PF T 01234-350681
Chief Executive, B. Timmins
BLC (THE LEATHER TECHNOLOGY CENTRE), Leather
Trade House, Kings Park Road, Moulton Park, Northants
NN3 6JD T 01604-679999 *Chief Executive*, M. Parsons
BRE (BUILDING RESEARCH ESTABLISHMENT), Garston,
Watford, Hertfordshire WD25 9XX T 01923-664000
Chief Executive, Dr M. Wyatt
BREWING RESEARCH INTERNATIONAL,
Lyttel Hall, Coopers Hill Road, Nutfield, Surrey
RH1 4HY T 01737-822272
Director-General, Dr M. Kierstan
BRITISH MARITIME TECHNOLOGY LTD, Orlando House,
1 Waldegrave Road, Teddington, Middx TW11 8LZ
T 020-8943 5544 *Chief Executive*, R. Swann

BUILDING SERVICES RESEARCH AND INFORMATION
ASSOCIATION, Old Bracknell Lane West, Bracknell,
Berks RG12 7AH T 01344-426511
Chief Executive, A. Eastwell
CAMPDEN AND CHORLEYWOOD FOOD RESEARCH
ASSOCIATION, Chipping Campden, Glos GL55 6LD
T 01386-842000 *Director-General*, Prof. C. Dennis
CASTINGS TECHNOLOGY INTERNATIONAL, 7 East Bank
Road, Sheffield, S2 3PT T 0114-272 8647
Chief Executive, Dr Mike Ashton
CENTRAL LABORATORY OF THE RESEARCH
COUNCILS, Chilton, Didcot, Oxfordshire, OX11 OQX
T 01235-445000 *Chief Executive*, Prof. J. Wood
CERAM RESEARCH (BRITISH CERAMIC RESEARCH
LTD), Queen's Road, Penkhull, Stoke-on-Trent ST4 7LQ
T 01782-764444 *Chief Executive*, Dr N. E. Sanderson
CIRIA (CONSTRUCTION INDUSTRY RESEARCH AND
INFORMATION ASSOCIATION), Classic House, 174–180
Old Street, London EC1V 9BP T 020-7549 3300
Director-General, Dr T. Broyd
FIRA INTERNATIONAL LTD (FURNITURE INDUSTRY
RESEARCH ASSOCIATION), Maxwell Road, Stevenage,
Herts SG1 2EW T 01438-777700
Managing Director, H. Davies
HR WALLINGFORD GROUP LTD (hydroinformatics and
engineering), Howbery Park, Wallingford, Oxon OX10 8BA
T 01491-835381 *Chief Executive*, Dr S. W. Huntington
ITRI LTD, (tin and chemicals), Unit 3, Curo Park, Frogmore,
St Albans, Herts AL2 2DD T 01727-875544
Chief Executive, D. Bishop
LGC, Queens Road, Teddington, Middx TW11 0LY
T 020-8943 7000 *Chief Executive and Government
Chemist*, Dr R. Worswick
LEATHERHEAD FOOD INTERNATIONAL, Randalls Road,
Leatherhead, Surrey KT22 7RY T 01372-376761
Director, J. Bevington
MATERIALS ENGINEERING RESEARCH LABORATORY
LTD, Tamworth Road, Hertford SG13 7DG T 01992-500120
Managing Director, Dr. R. H. Martin
MOTOR INDUSTRY RESEARCH ASSOCIATION, Watling
Street, Nuneaton, Warks CV10 0TU T 024-7635 5000
Managing Director, J. R. Wood
MOTOR INSURANCE REPAIR RESEARCH CENTRE,
Colthorp Lane, Thatcham, Berks RG19 4NP
T 01635-868855 *Chief Executive*, P. Roberts
NATIONAL COMPUTING CENTRE LTD, Oxford House,
Oxford Road, Manchester M1 7ED T 0161-242 2499
Chief Executive, M. Gough
NATIONAL METALS TECHNOLOGY CENTRE (NAMTEC),
Q Block, Swindon Technology Centre, Moorgate, Rotherham
S60 3AR T 01709-724990
Chief Executive (acting), Dr Alan Partridge
NATIONAL PHYSICAL LABORATORY, Hampton Road,
Teddington, Middx TW11 0LW T 020-8977 3222
Chief Executive, Dr B. McGuiness
NCIMB LIMITED (microbiological supply and bacterial culture
collection), 23 St Machar Drive, Aberdeen AB24 3RY
T 01224-273332 *Chief Executive*, Dr A. Syms
PRA COATINGS TECHNOLOGY CENTRE, 14 Castle Mews,
High Street, Hampton, Middx TW12 2NP T 020-8487 0800
Managing Director and Company Secretary, J. Marshall
PERA GROUP (multi-disciplinary research, design,
development and consultancy), Pera Innovation Park,
Melton Mowbray, Leics LE13 0PB T 01664-501501
Chief Executive, Dr P. Davies, CBE
QINETIQ (science consultancy), Cody Building, Ively Road,
Farnborough, Hants GU14 OLX T 08700-100 942
Chief Executive, Sir John Chisholm, FRENG

RAPRA TECHNOLOGY LTD (rubber and plastics), Shawbury, Shrewsbury SY4 4NR **T** 01939-250383 North East Centre, 18 Belasis Court, Belasis Technology Park, Billingham TS23 4AZ **T** 01642-370406 *Managing Director*, A. Ward

SATRA TECHNOLOGY CENTRE (footwear, apparel, safety products and furniture), Satra House, Rockingham Road, Kettering, Northants NN16 9JH **T** 01536-410000 *Chief Executive*, Dr R. E. Whittaker

SCOTCH WHISKY RESEARCH INSTITUTE, The Robertson Trust Building, Research Park North, Riccarton, Edinburgh EH14 4AP **T** 0131 449-8900 *Director*, Dr G. M. Steele

SIRA LTD (measurement, instrumentation, control and optical systems technology), South Hill, Chislehurst, Kent BR7 5EH **T** 020-8467 2636 *Managing Director*, Prof. R. A. Brook

SMITH INSTITUTE (mathematics and computing), PO Box 183, Guildford, Surrey GU2 5GG **T** 01483-579108 *Chair of the Council*, Dr B. Smith, CBE

SPORTS TURF RESEARCH INSTITUTE, St Ives Estate, Bingley, W. Yorks BD16 1AU **T** 01274-565131 *Chief Executive*, Dr G. McKillop

STEEL CONSTRUCTION INSTITUTE, Silwood Park, Ascot, Berks SL5 7QN **T** 01344-623345 *Director*, Dr G. Owens

TRADA TECHNOLOGY LTD (timber and wood-based products), Chiltern House, Stocking Lane, Hughenden Valley, High Wycombe, Bucks HP14 4ND **T** 01494-563091 *Managing Director*, A. Abbott

TWI LTD Granta Park, Great Abington, Cambridge CB1 6AL **T** 01223-891162 *Chief Executive*, Dr R. John

UNIVERSITY OF SURREY (UNIS), Guildford, Surrey GU2 7XH **T** 01483-689065 *Vice Chancellor and Chief Executive*, Prof. Patrick Dowling

SOCIAL WELFARE

NATIONAL HEALTH SERVICE

The National Health Service (NHS) came into being on 5 July 1948 under the National Health Service Act 1946, covering England and Wales and, under separate legislation, Scotland and Northern Ireland. The NHS is now administered by the Secretary of State for Health (in England), the National Assembly for Wales, the Scottish Executive and the Secretary of State for Northern Ireland.

The function of the NHS is to provide a comprehensive health service designed to secure improvement in the physical and mental health of the people and to prevent, diagnose and treat illness. It was founded on the principle that treatment should be provided according to clinical need rather than ability to pay, and should be free at the point of delivery.

Hospital, mental, dental, nursing, ophthalmic and ambulance services and facilities for the care of expectant and nursing mothers and young children are provided by the NHS to meet all reasonable requirements. Rehabilitation services such as occupational therapy, physiotherapy, speech therapy and surgical and medical appliances are supplied where appropriate. Specialists and consultants who work in NHS hospitals can also engage in private practice, including the treatment of their private patients in NHS hospitals.

STRUCTURE

The structure of the NHS remained relatively stable for the first 30 years of its existence. In 1974, a three-tier management structure comprising Regional Health Authorities, Area Health Authorities and District Management Teams was introduced in England, and the NHS became responsible for community health services. In 1979 Area Health Authorities were abolished and District Management Teams were replaced by District Health Authorities.

The National Health Service and Community Care Act 1990 provided for more streamlined Regional Health Authorities and District Health Authorities, and for the establishment of Family Health Services Authorities (FHSAs) and NHS Trusts. The concept of the 'internal market' was introduced into health care, whereby care was provided through NHS contracts where health authorities or boards and GP fundholders (the purchasers) were responsible for buying health care from hospitals, non-fundholding GPs, community services and ambulance services (the providers). The Act also paved the way for the Community Care reforms, which were introduced in April 1993, and changed the way care is administered for older people, the mentally ill, the physically handicapped and people with learning disabilities.

ENGLAND

Regional Health Authorities in England were abolished in April 1996 and replaced by eight regional offices which, together with the headquarters in Leeds, formed the NHS Executive (which has since been merged with the Department of Health). In April 2002, as an interim arrangement, the eight regional offices were replaced by

four Directorates of Health and Social Care (DsHSC). In April 2003, the DsHSCs were abolished.

STRATEGIC HEALTH AUTHORITIES

In April 1996 the District Health Authorities and Family Health Service Authorities were merged to form 100 unified Health Authorities (HAs) in England. In April 2002, 28 new health authorities were formed from the existing HAs. In October 2002, as part of the new arrangements set out in the NHS Reform and Health Care Professions Act 2002, these new health authorities were renamed Strategic Health Authorities (SHAs) and charged with creating a strategic framework for managing the performance of Primary Care Trusts and building the capacity of health services locally.

PRIMARY CARE TRUSTS

The first 17 Primary Care Trusts (PCTs) became operational in England on 1 April 2000. There are currently around 300 PCTs covering all areas of England. PCTs were created to give primary care professionals greater control over how resources are best used to benefit patients. PCTs are responsible for tackling health inequalities, developing primary and community health services and commissioning secondary care services. They are free-standing statutory bodies undertaking many of the functions previously exercised by former Health Authorities, such as securing the provision of services and integrating health and social care.

Each PCT is overseen by a lay board, comprising a chairman and non-executive directors who are appointed by the NHS Appointments Commission and who are members of the local community to be served by the PCT. The Board's role is to provide strategic oversight and verification to the work of the Executive, which is made up of health professionals.

NHS TRUSTS AND FOUNDATION TRUSTS

Hospitals are managed by NHS Trusts (also known as Acute Trusts) that are responsible for the quality of hospital health care and for spending funds efficiently.

The first ten NHS Foundation Trusts were established on 1 April 2004 with a further ten established on 1 July 2004. NHS Foundation Trusts are NHS hospitals, but have their own accountability and governance systems, which function outside of the Department of Health's framework, giving them greater freedom to run their own affairs. NHS Foundation Trusts treat patients according to NHS principles and standards and are inspected by the Commission for Healthcare Audit and Improvement (CHAI). The government's aim is that by 2008, all NHS Trusts will have reached a standard which will enable them to apply for NHS Foundation Trust status.

Contact details for all the SHAs, PCTs and other NHS organisations in England can be found in the *NHS England, Authorities and Trusts* section on the NHS website: www.nhs.uk or by calling the Department of Health Public Enquiry Office on 020-7210 4850.

WALES

LOCAL HEALTH BOARDS AND COMMUNITY HEALTH COUNCILS

In Wales there were five HAs which replaced the former 17 HAs and FHSAs in April 1996. The HAs set up 22 Local Health Groups (LHGs), coterminous with local authority areas (see Local Government section), which began work in April 1999. Originally they advised HAs, but in March 2003 the five HAs were abolished and the LHGs were renamed Local Health Boards (LHBs) and took up a role similar to PCTs, assuming responsibility for commissioning services and devising strategies for improving health. They also integrate the delivery of primary and community care. Each Local Health Board has a governing body made up of local doctors, a nurse, other health professionals, members of the local authority and voluntary organisations and others to represent the interests of patients. There is also a small executive team to take action on decisions and provide services for the public.

There is also a Community Health Council (CHC) for each of the 22 local government areas.

SPECIALISED SERVICES AND PUBLIC HEALTH

Although LHBs plan and fund most hospital and family health services there are a few specialised services which are overseen at national level. These services are the responsibility of the Health Commission Wales (Specialised Services), which was set up in April 2003. The National Public Health Service also gives advice and guidance to LHBs on a range of issues such as disease protection and control as well as child protection.

NHS TRUSTS AND HOSPITALS

There are 14 NHS Trusts in Wales, including one all-Wales Ambulance Trust. Between them, the Trusts are responsible for managing 135 hospitals.

REGIONAL OFFICES

There are three regional offices of the National Assembly based in mid, north and south-east Wales. The regional offices support co-ordination, at local level, between LHBs, local authorities and NHS Trusts. They have a specific role in ensuring that Assembly initiatives are carried out.

Contact details for the LHBs, Community Health Councils, NHS Trusts and all other NHS national and local services in Wales are available in the NHS Wales Directory section on the Welsh NHS website: www.wales.nhs.uk.

SCOTLAND

In Scotland, the Scottish Executive Health Department leads the central management of the NHS, heading a Management Executive, which oversees the work of 15 area Health Boards responsible for planning health services for their area.

HEALTH BOARDS

ARGYLL AND CLYDE, Ross House, Hawkhead Road, Paisley PA2 7BN T 0141-842 7200 W www.nhsac.scot.nhs.uk

AYRSHIRE AND ARRAN, 3 Lister Street, Crosshouse Hospital, Crosshouse KA2 0BE T 01563-577037
W www.nhsayrshireandarran.com

BORDERS, Newstead, Melrose, Roxburghshire TD6 9BD T 01896-825500 W www.nhsborders.org.uk

DUMFRIES AND GALLOWAY, Mid North, Crichton Hall, Dumfries DG1 4TG T 01387-246246
W www.nhsdg.scot.nhs.uk

FIFE, Hayfield House, Hayfield Road, Kirkcaldy, Fife KY2 5AH T 01592-643355 W www.show.scot.nhs.uk/fhb

FORTH VALLEY, 33 Spittal Street, Stirling FK8 1DX T 01786-463031 W www.forthvalley.scot.nhs.uk

GRAMPIAN, Summerfield House, 2 Eday Road, Aberdeen AB15 6RE T 0845-456 6000 W www.nhsgrampian.org

GREATER GLASGOW, Dalian House, 350 St Vincent Street, Glasgow G3 8YU T 0141-201 4444 W www.nhsgg.org.uk

HIGHLAND, Assynt House, Beechwood Park, Inverness IV2 3HG T 01463-717123
W www.show.scot.nhs.uk/nhshighland

LANARKSHIRE, 14 Beckford Street, Hamilton, Lanarkshire ML3 0TA T 01698-281313
W www.show.scot.nhs.uk/nhslanarkshire

LOTHIAN, Deaconess House, 148 Pleasance, Edinburgh EH8 9RS T 0131-536 9000 W www.nhslothian.scot.nhs.uk

ORKNEY, Garden House, New Scapa Road, Kirkwall, Orkney KW15 1BQ T 01856-888000 W www.show.scot.nhs.uk/ohb

SHETLAND, Brevik House, South Road, Lerwick ZE1 0TG T 01595-696767 W www.show.scot.nhs.uk/shb

TAYSIDE, Kings Cross, Clepington Road, Dundee DD3 8EA T 01382-818479 W www.nhstayside.scot.nhs.uk

WESTERN ISLES, 37 South Beach Street, Stornoway, Isle of Lewis HS1 2BB T 01851-702997
W www.show.scot.nhs.uk/wihb

NORTHERN IRELAND

In Northern Ireland there are four Health and Social Services Boards responsible for commissioning services to meet the needs of their respective populations. They are also responsible for assessing the needs of that population, establishing objectives and developing policies and priorities to meet these objectives.

EASTERN, Champion House, 12–22 Linenhall Street, Belfast BT2 8BS T 028-9032 1313 W www.ehssb.n-i.nhs.uk

NORTHERN, County Hall, 182 Galgorm Road, Ballymena BT42 1QB T 028-2565 3333 W www.nhssb.n-i.nhs.uk

SOUTHERN, Tower Hill, Armagh BT61 9DR T 028-3741 0041
W www.shssb.org

WESTERN, 15 Gransha Park, Clooney Road, Londonderry BT47 6FN T 0800-585 329 W www.whssb.org

THE NHS PLAN

In July 2000 the government launched the NHS Plan, a ten year strategy to modernise the health service. In June 2004 it also launched the NHS Improvement Plan, which set out the next stage of NHS reform, moving the focus from access to services towards the broader issues of public health and chronic disease management. The core aims are to sustain increased levels of investment in the NHS and to continue to focus on the improvements outlined in the NHS Plan, while delivering greater levels of choice and information to patients. In July 2004, the Department of Health published National Standards, Local Action: Health and Social Care Standards and Planning Framework 2005/6–2007/8, which cut the number of national targets that NHS providers must comply with from 62 to 20. These national targets, which cover areas such as waiting times for accident and emergency treatment, will become national core standards which all providers of care must maintain from April 2005. Alongside this, NHS providers will be given power to set more locally relevant targets.

FINANCE

The NHS is still funded mainly through general taxation, although in recent years more reliance has been placed on the NHS element of National Insurance contributions, patient charges and other sources of income.

In the April 2002 Budget, the Chancellor announced a five-year spending plan for the NHS. Over the years 2003–4 to 2007–8, these plans mean that expenditure on the NHS in the UK will increase on average by 7.2 per cent a year over and above inflation, 7.4 per cent a year for England. The spending plans are set out in the table below:

	UK £ millions	% real terms increase*	England £ millions	% real terms increase*
2003–4	74,800	7.0	61,300	7.1
2004–5	82,200	7.1	67,400	7.2
2005–6	90,500	7.4	74,400	7.6
2006–7	99,400	7.2	81,800	7.3
2007–8	109,400	7.4	90,200	7.5

* Calculated using GDP deflator at 27 June 2003
Source: Department of Health

PRIVATE FINANCE INITIATIVE

The Private Finance Initiative (PFI) was launched in 1992, and involves the private sector in designing, building, financing and operating new hospitals and primary care premises, which are then leased to the NHS. The NHS Plan committed the NHS to entering into a new public private partnership, Partnerships for Health, a joint venture between the Department of Health and Partnerships UK plc (PUK) established in September 2001. Its role is to support the development of NHS Local Improvement Finance Trusts (LIFT) by implementing a standard approach to procurement as well as providing some equity. LIFTs are set up as limited companies with the local NHS, Partnerships for Health and the private sector as shareholders. LIFT schemes build and refurbish primary care premises, which the schemes own and then rent to GPs on a lease basis (as well as other parties such as chemists, opticians, dentists etc).

There are currently 51 approved LIFT projects in England; of these, 37 have reached financial close. Eight of these schemes now have buildings open to patients. By the end of 2004–5 NHS LIFT had attracted around £490 million of private capital investment. In addition, the Department of Health provided £175 million of public capital up to the end of 2004–5, and will provide another £31 million in 2005–6 to help PCTs with the start-up costs of their LIFT schemes.

EMPLOYEES AND SALARIES

EMPLOYEES

NHS HOSPITAL AND COMMUNITY HEALTH SERVICE STAFF *(Great Britain) 2003*
Full-time equivalent

Hospital medical staff	80,537
Community health medical staff	1,756
Hospital dental staff	1,981
Community health dental staff	1,448
Nursing and midwifery staff	474,263
General medical practitioners	40,013
General dental practitioners	22,891

Source: ONS – *Annual Abstract of Statistics 2005* (Crown copyright)

SALARIES

General Practitioners (GPs), dentists, optometrists and pharmacists are self-employed, and are employed by the NHS under contract. On 20 June 2003 GPs accepted a new practice-based contract which rewards practices for delivering quality and a wider range of services. Dentists receive payment for items of treatment for individual adult patients and, in addition, a continuing care payment for those registered with them. Optometrists receive approved fees for each sight test they carry out. Pharmacists receive professional fees from the NHS and are refunded the cost of prescriptions supplied. Doctors in training receive additional supplements reflecting the intensity and out-of-hours elements of their duties, these can range from 20–100 per cent of the basic salary.

SALARIES FOR HOSPITAL MEDICAL AND DENTAL STAFF AND NURSES*
As at 1 April 2005

Consultant (2003 contract)	£69,298–£93,768
Consultant (pre-2003 contract)	£57,370–£74,658
Senior Registrar	£32,607–£42,985
Specialist Registrar	£28,307–£42,985
Registrar	£28,307–£34,337
Senior House Officer	£25,324–£35,511
House Officer	£20,295–£22,907
Nursing Grades H–I (Nurse Specialist/Modern Matron)	£27,509–£36,046
Nursing Grade G (Charge Nurse)	£24,629–£29,971
Nursing Grade F (Senior Nurse)	£20,872–£27,024
Nursing Grade E (Experienced Staff Nurse)	£18,818–£22,725
Nursing Grade D (Newly Qualified Nurse)	£17,610–£19,437
Nursing Grade C (Enrolled Nurse and some nursing auxiliary staff)	£14,348–£17,610
Nursing Grades A–B (Nursing auxiliary staff and nursing assistants)	£10,710–£14,833

* These figures do not include merit awards, discretionary points or banding supplements

HEALTH SERVICES

PRIMARY AND COMMUNITY HEALTH CARE

Primary and community health care services comprise the family health services (i.e. the general medical, personal medical, pharmaceutical, dental, and ophthalmic services) and community services (including preventive activities such as vaccination, immunisation and fluoridation). Nursing services including practice nurses, community nurses and health visitors and ante- and post-natal care.

PRIMARY MEDICAL SERVICES

In England, Primary Medical Services are the responsibility of Primary Care Trusts (PCTs) who contract with GPs to provide the service to the NHS. They do so in one of two ways: by providing general medical services (GMS) under national rules or by successfully applying to become a personal medical service (PMS) pilot, with a contract that is largely locally determined. As at 1 October 2003, just over 40 per cent of GPs were in PMS.

In Wales, responsibility for primary medical services rests with Local Health Boards (LHBs), in Scotland with the 15 Health Boards and in Northern Ireland with the four Health and Social Services Boards (*see* Structure section).

Any vocationally trained doctor may provide general or personal medical services. GPs may also have private fee-paying patients, but not if that patient is already an NHS patient on that doctor's patient list.

A person who is ordinarily resident in the UK is eligible to register with a GP (or PMS provider) for free primary care treatment. Should a patient have difficulty in registering with a doctor, he or she should contact the local PCT for help. When a person is away from home he/she can still access primary care treatment from a GP if they ask to be treated as a temporary resident. In an emergency any doctor in the service will give treatment and advice.

GPs are responsible for the care of their patients 24 hours a day, seven days a week, but can fulfil the terms of their contract by delegating or transferring responsibility for out-of-hours (OOH) care to an accredited provider. Under the new GMS contract, practices will be able to opt out of responsibility for patient care during the OOH period. When they do so, it will become a Primary Care Trust (PCT) responsibility. PCTs will be able to provide the OOH cover themselves or commission the service from an OOH provider.

Increasingly, some secondary care services, such as minor operations and consultations, can be provided in a primary care setting. The number of such practitioners is growing and the new GMS contract provides a platform for further expansion.

In addition, drop-in services are being developed. A total of 62 NHS Walk-in Centres are operational across the country, with a further 17 centres under development. They are nurse-led and provide treatment for minor ailments and injuries, health information and self-help advice with extended opening hours (normally every day of the year from 7 a.m.–10 p.m. Monday to Friday, and 9 a.m.–10 p.m. Saturday and Sunday).

HEALTH COSTS

Some people are exempt from, or entitled to help with, health costs such as prescription charges, ophthalmic and dental costs, and in some cases help towards travel costs to and from hospital.

The following list is intended as a general guide to those who may be entitled to help, or who are exempt from some of the charges relating to the above:

– children under 16 and young people in full time education who are under 19
– people aged 60 or over
– pregnant women and women who have had a baby in the last 12 months
– people, or their partners, who are in receipt of Income Support and/or income-based Jobseeker's Allowance
– people in receipt of the Pension Credit Guarantee Credit
– people with a specified medical condition or disability
– diagnosed glaucoma patients and immediate family members
– diagnosed diabetic patients
– NHS in-patients
– NHS out-patients for all medication given at a hospital or NHS walk-in centre
– patients of the Community Dental Service or an out-patient of the NHS Hospital Dental Service
– people registered blind or partially sighted
– people who need complex lenses
– war pensioners whose treatment/prescription is for their accepted disablement

People in other circumstances may also be eligible for help; Booklet HC11, available from main post offices and local social security offices gives further details or visit www.dh.gov.uk.

WALES
People aged under 25 living in Wales get free NHS prescriptions and dental examinations.

PHARMACEUTICAL SERVICES
Patients may obtain medicines and appliances under the NHS from any pharmacy whose owner has entered into arrangements with the PCT to provide this service. There are also some suppliers who only provide special appliances. In rural areas, where access to a pharmacy may be difficult, patients may be able to obtain medicines, etc, from a dispensing doctor.

In England, a charge of £6.50 is payable for each item supplied (except for contraceptives for which there is no charge), unless the patient is exempt and the declaration on the back of the prescription form is completed. Prepayment certificates (£33.90 valid for four months, £93.20 valid for a year) may be purchased by those patients not entitled to exemption who require frequent prescriptions. Prescription charges in Scotland and Northern Ireland are currently the same. In Wales NHS prescription charges differ: a charge of £4 is payable for each item dispensed and pre-payment certificates cost £20.93 for four months and £57.46 for 12 months.

DENTAL SERVICES
Dentists, like doctors, may take part in the NHS and also have private patients. Dentists are responsible to the local health provider in whose areas they provide services. Patients may go to any dentist who is taking part in the NHS and is willing to accept them. Patients are required to pay 80 per cent of the cost of NHS dental treatment. Since 1 April 2005 the maximum patient charge allowed for an NHS course of treatment stands at £384 in England, Scotland and Northern Ireland and £354 in Wales. There is no charge for arrest of bleeding or repairs to dentures; home visits by the dentist or re-opening a surgery in an emergency are charged for as treatment given in the normal way.

In July 2004 the government announced a £368 million funding injection for NHS dentistry in England. The Department of Health plans to recruit the equivalent of an extra 1,000 dentists by October 2005, of which around 650 will be new recruits. This funding was accompanied by a package of reforms to modernise the dentistry profession and ensure continued local expenditure on dentistry through PCTs.

In April 2005 the Welsh Assembly announced that £5 million extra in funding would be allocated for the 2005–6 financial year to modernise dental practice in Wales. The extra funding would mainly be used to fund the introduction of Personal Dental Service (PDS) schemes. These schemes will allow dentists and LHBs to work in partnership to meet local needs and to make commissioning decisions in line with local plans.

In March 2005 the Scottish Executive announced that £150 million would be invested in NHS dentistry in Scotland over the next three years. Part of the investment would be used for the education and training of dentists within the NHS.

GENERAL OPHTHALMIC SERVICES

General Ophthalmic Services are administered by local health providers. Testing of sight may be carried out by any ophthalmic medical practitioner or ophthalmic optician (optometrist). The optician must give the prescription to the patient, who can take this to any supplier of glasses to have them dispensed. Only registered opticians can supply glasses to children and to people registered as blind or partially sighted. At the end of December 2003 there were around 9,000 ophthalmic opticians and 700 ophthalmic medical practitioners in Great Britain.

The NHS sight test costs £18.39 throughout the UK. Free eyesight tests and help towards the cost are available to people in certain circumstances. Help is also available for the purchase of glasses. (*see* Health Costs section or booklet HC11)

COMMUNITY CHILD HEALTH SERVICE

Pre-school services at GP surgeries or child health clinics provide regular monitoring of children's physical, mental and emotional health and development, and advice to parents on their children's health and welfare.

The School Health Service provides for the medical and dental examination of schoolchildren, and advises the local education authority, the school, the parents and the pupil of any health factors which may require special consideration during the pupil's school life. GPs are increasingly undertaking child health monitoring in order to improve the preventive health care of children.

NHS DIRECT AND NHS 24

NHS Direct is a 24-hour nurse-led advice telephone service for England and Wales. It provides medical advice as well as directing people to the appropriate part of the NHS for treatment if necessary. T 0845-46 47

NHS 24 provides an equivalent service for Scotland. T 08454-24 24 24

SECONDARY CARE AND OTHER SERVICES

HOSPITALS

NHS hospitals provide acute and specialist care services, treating conditions which normally cannot be dealt with by primary care specialists and medical emergencies.

NUMBER OF BEDS AND PATIENT ACTIVITY 2003–4

	England*	Wales
In-patients:		
Average daily available beds	184,000	14,200
Average daily occupation of beds	157,000	11,800
Out-patient attendances:		
New patients	13,032,000	739,500
Total attendances	44,598,000	2,868,300

*Scotland**	
In-patients:	
Average available staffed beds	30,900
Average occupied beds	25,100
Out-patient attendances:	
New patients	2,743,000
Total attendances	6,291,000

Northern Ireland	
In-patients:	
Beds available	8,358
Average daily occupation of beds	7,037
Out-patients:	
New cases	1,014,000
Total attendances	2,161,000

* 2002–3 figures

Source: ONS – *Annual Abstract of Statistics 2005* (Crown copyright)

CHARGES

NHS Trusts can provide accommodation in single rooms or small wards, if not required for patients who need privacy for medical reasons. The patient is still an NHS patient, but there may be a charge for these additional facilities. NHS Trusts can charge for certain patient services that are considered to be additional treatments over and above the normal service provision. There is no blanket policy to cover this and each case is considered in the light of the patient's clinical need. However, if an item or service is considered to be an integral part of a patient's treatment by their clinician, then a charge should not be made.

In some NHS hospitals, accommodation and services are available for the treatment of private patients where it does not interfere with care for NHS patients. Income generated by treating private patients is then put back into local NHS services. Private patients undertake to pay the full costs of medical treatment, accommodation, medication and other related services. Charges for private patients are set locally.

WAITING LISTS

England

At the end of May 2005 the total number of patients waiting to be admitted to NHS hospitals in England was 826,300, a decrease of 7.6 per cent on the previous year. The number of patients who had been waiting more than six months was 49,600, a decrease of 42.2 per cent from May 2004, when the total was 85,900. No patients had been waiting longer than 12 months at the end of May 2005 and only 17 patients had been waiting over nine months. Under the charter *Your Guide to the NHS,* patients are guaranteed admission within 18 months of being placed on a waiting list. In July 2004 a new target, of an 18 week maximum wait from start time (i.e. seeing a GP) to treatment, was set to be achieved by 2008.

Wales

In Wales the number of patients waiting for in-patient or day case treatment totalled 65,492 on 30 June 2005, a 13.3 per cent decrease from 75,517 in June 2004; of these, 123 had been waiting over 18 months, 1,073 over 12 months and 14,310 over six months.

Scotland

Numbers of patients waiting for in-patient or day case treatment totalled 112,639 as at 31 March 2005, compared with 110,277 patients in 2004, an increase of 2.1 per cent. At March 2005 admittance rates were as follows: 86.7 per cent of patients were admitted within six months, 96.1 per cent within nine months and 98.4 per cent within 12 months. NHS Scotland has pledged that by the end of 2007 no patient will wait more than 18 weeks between a decision being made to undertake treatment, to the start of that treatment.

Northern Ireland
In June 2004 around 51,000 people were waiting for in-patient treatment in Northern Ireland, with 3,235 of these waiting for more than 18 months.

COMPARATIVE UK IN-PATIENT WAITING LISTS, JUNE 2004

	Number of in-patients waiting for treatment per 1,000 population	Number of in-patients waiting 12+ months per 1,000 population
England	17.87	0.01
Wales	25.87	3.06
Scotland	22.23	0
Northern Ireland	30.4	4.04

AMBULANCE SERVICE

The NHS provides emergency ambulance services free of charge via the 999 emergency telephone service. Air ambulances, provided through local charities and partially funded by the NHS, are used throughout the UK. They assist with cases where access may be difficult or heavy traffic could hinder road progress. Non-emergency ambulance services are provided free of charge to patients who are deemed to require them on medical grounds.

In 2004–5 in England approximately 5.6 million emergency calls were made to the ambulance service, an increase of 5 per cent on the previous year. There were about 3.5 million emergency patient journeys. Since 1 April 2001 all services have had a system of call prioritisation. The prioritisation procedures require all emergency calls to be classified as either immediately life threatening (category A) or other emergency (category B/C). Services are expected to reach 75 per cent of Category A (life threatening) calls within eight minutes and 95 per cent of category B/C calls within 19 minutes in rural areas and 14 minutes in urban areas. In 2004–5, 76.2 per cent of life threatening calls resulted in emergency response arriving at the scene of the incident within eight minutes (75.7 per cent in 2003–4). For category B/C calls, 87.8 per cent of incidents were responded to within 14–19 minutes.

BLOOD SERVICES

There are four national bodies which co-ordinate the blood donor programme in the UK. Donors give blood at local centres on a voluntary basis.
NATIONAL BLOOD SERVICE, Oak House, Reeds Crescent, Watford, Herts WD24 4QN T 01923-486800
  W www.blood.co.uk
SCOTTISH NATIONAL BLOOD TRANSFUSION SERVICE, 21 Ellens Glen Road, Edinburgh EH17 7QT T 0131-536 5700
  W www.scotblood.co.uk
WELSH BLOOD SERVICE, Ely Valley Road, Talbot Green, Pontyclun CF72 9WB T 01443-622000
  W www.welsh-blood.org.uk
NORTHERN IRELAND BLOOD TRANSFUSION SERVICE, Belfast City Hospital Complex, Lisburn Road, Belfast BT9 7TS
  T 028-9032 1414 W www.nibts.org

HOSPICES

Hospice or palliative care may be available for patients with life-threatening illnesses. It may be provided at the patient's home or in a voluntary or NHS hospice or in hospital, and is intended to ensure the best possible

quality of life for the patient during their illness, and to provide help and support to both the patient and the patient's family. The National Council for Palliative Care co-ordinates NHS and voluntary services in England, Wales and Northern Ireland; the Scottish Partnership for Palliative Care performs the same function in Scotland.
NATIONAL COUNCIL FOR PALLIATIVE CARE, The Fitzpatrick Building, 188–194 York Way N7 9AS
  T 020-7697 1520 W www.ncpc.org.uk
SCOTTISH PARTNERSHIP FOR PALLIATIVE CARE, 1A Cambridge Street, Edinburgh EH1 2DY T 0131-229 0538
  W www.palliativecarescotland.org.uk

NHS CHARTERS

The original Patient's Charter was published in 1991 and came into force in 1992; an expanded version was published in 1995. The Charter set out the rights of patients in relation to the standards of service they should expect to receive at all times and standards of service that the NHS aimed to provide.

The Patient's Charter was replaced nationally in 2001 with *Your Guide to the NHS,* which provided information on how to get treatment and gave specific details on minimum standards for patients, targets for the NHS and improvements in the NHS Plan. It also detailed what patients had a right to expect from the NHS and what is expected from patients.

Information for patients about all aspects of the NHS has now been reorganised and is available on the NHS website www.nhs.uk.

COMPLAINTS

Firstly, an attempt must be made to resolve the complaint at a local level directly with the healthcare provider concerned. Patient Advice and Liaison Services (PALS) have been established for every NHS and Primary Care Trust in England. PALS are not part of the complaint procedure itself, but can give advice on local complaints procedure, or resolve concerns informally. Secondly, if the case is not resolved locally, an independent review can be requested by the Healthcare Commission in England or by the relevant Health and Social Services Board in Northern Ireland. As a final resort, complainants may approach the Health Service Ombudsman in England, the Scottish Public Services Ombudsman, Public Services Ombudsman for Wales or the Commissioner for Complaints in Northern Ireland.

RECIPROCAL ARRANGEMENTS

Citizens of countries in the European Economic Area (EEA – *see* European Union section) who are resident in the UK are entitled to receive emergency health care either free of charge or for a reduced charge when they are temporarily visiting other member states of the EEA. Form E111, available at post offices, should be obtained before travelling (to be replaced by the European Health Insurance Card from 31 December 2005). There are also bilateral agreements with several other countries, including Australia and New Zealand, for the provision of urgent medical treatment free of charge.

EEA nationals visiting the UK and visitors from other countries with which the UK has bilateral health care agreements, are entitled to receive emergency health care on the NHS on the same terms as it is available to UK residents.

PERSONAL SOCIAL SERVICES

The Secretary of State for Health (in England), the National Assembly for Wales, the Scottish Executive and the Secretary of State for Northern Ireland are responsible, under the Local Authority Social Services Act 1970, for the provision of social services for older people, disabled people, families and children, and those with mental disorders. Personal Social Services are administered by local authorities according to policies, with standards set by central and devolved government. Each authority has a Director of Social Services and a Social Services Committee responsible for the social services functions placed upon them. Local authorities provide, enable and commission care after assessing the needs of their population. The private and voluntary sectors also play an important role in the delivery of social services, and an estimated six million people in Great Britain provide substantial regular care for a member of their family.

Under the Care Standards Act 2000, the National Care Standards Commission (NCSC) was set up on 1 April 2002 to regulate social, private and voluntary care services throughout England. In April 2004, under the Health and Social Care (Community Health and Standards) Act 2003, the NCSC was replaced by the Commission for Social Care Inspection (CSCI). The CSCI was established as a single, regulatory authority, incorporating the work formerly carried out by the Social Services Inspectorate (SSI), the SSI/Audit Commission Joint Review Team and the NCSC. Services such as care homes and children's homes managed by local authorities, domiciliary care services, independent fostering agencies and residential family centres, that were previously regulated by the NCSC, are now registered and inspected by the CSCI. The CSCI ensures that care services are run in accordance with national minimum standards and regulations that have been set by the Government. As well as regulating care services, the CSCI assesses all areas of care services provided by local authorities in England against a national agenda, ensuring they meet their social services responsibilities through a system of inspections and self-assessment. The CSCI collates information on local services from May to July each year and makes this information available to the public.

COMMISSION FOR SOCIAL CARE INSPECTION (CSCI),
33 Greycoat Street, London SW1P 2QF T 020-7979 2000
W www.csci.org.uk

FINANCE
The Personal Social Services programme is financed partly by central and devolved governments, with decisions on expenditure allocations being made at local authority level.

STAFF
PERSONAL SOCIAL SERVICES STAFF 2003 (Great Britain)

Full-time equivalent	
Home help service	35,000
Field social workers	37,200
Residential care staff	51,400
Day care establishments staff	28,900
All other staff (including management and administration and ancillary staff)	59,500
Total staff	212,000

Source: ONS – Annual Abstract of Statistics 2005 (Crown copyright)

OLDER PEOPLE
Services for older people are designed to enable them to remain living in their own homes for as long as possible. Local authority services include advice, domestic help, meals in the home, alterations to the home to aid mobility, emergency alarm systems, day and/or night attendants, laundry services and the provision of day centres and recreational facilities. Charges may be made for these services. Respite care may also be provided in order to allow carers temporary relief from their responsibilities.

Local authorities and the private sector also provide 'sheltered housing' for older people, sometimes with resident wardens.

If an older person is admitted to a residential home, charges are made according to a means test; if the person cannot afford to pay, the costs are met by the local authority.

In March 2001 a National Service Framework for Older People was published. The framework set national standards and service models of care across health and social service for older people whether they live at home, in residential care or are being cared for in hospital.

DISABLED PEOPLE
Services for disabled people are designed to enable them to remain living in their own homes wherever possible. Local authority services include advice, adaptations to the home, meals in the home, help with personal care, occupational therapy, educational facilities and recreational facilities. Respite care may also be provided in order to allow carers temporary relief from their responsibilities.

Special housing may be available for disabled people who can live independently, and residential accommodation for those who cannot.

FAMILIES AND CHILDREN
Local authorities are required to provide services aimed at safeguarding the welfare of children in need and, wherever possible, allowing them to be brought up by their families. Services include advice, counselling, help in the home and the provision of family centres. Many authorities also provide short-term refuge accommodation for women and children.

DAY CARE
In allocating day care places to children, local authorities give priority to children with special needs, whether in terms of their health, learning abilities or social needs. Since September 2001 the Office for Standards in Education (Ofsted) has been responsible for the regulation and registration of all early years childcare and education provision in England (previously the responsibility of the local authorities). All day care and childminding services which care for children under eight years of age for more than two hours a day must register with Ofsted and are inspected at least every two years. As at 31 March 2005 there were 1,468,300 childcare places and 104,700 childcare providers in England.

In Wales, Scotland and Northern Ireland local authorities have responsibility for registration and inspection of day care facilities.

CHILD PROTECTION
Children considered to be at risk of physical injury, neglect or sexual abuse are placed on the local authority's child protection register. Local authority social services staff, schools, health visitors and other agencies work

together to prevent and detect cases of abuse. In England as at 31 March 2004 there were 26,300 children on child protection registers, a 1.13 per cent decrease from March 2003. Of the children registered during 2003–4, 12,600 were at risk of neglect, 5,700 of physical abuse, 2,800 of sexual abuse and 5,600 of emotional abuse. On 31 March 2004 there were 2,135 children on child protection registers in Wales, 2,245 in Scotland and 1,417 in Northern Ireland.

LOCAL AUTHORITY CARE
Local authorities are required to provide accommodation for children who have no parents or guardians or whose parents or guardians are unable or unwilling to care for them. A family proceedings court may also issue a care order where a child is being neglected or abused, or is not attending school; the court must be satisfied that this would positively contribute to the well-being of the child.

The welfare of children in local authority care must be properly safeguarded. Children may be placed with foster families, who receive payments to cover the expenses of caring for the child or children, or in residential care.

Children's homes may be run by the local authority or by the private or voluntary sectors; all homes are subject to inspection procedures. In England as at 31 March 2004, 61,100 children were in the care of local authorities. Of these, 41,600 were in foster placements. In Wales 4,315 children were being looked after by local authorities on 31 March 2004, 11,675 in Scotland and 2,510 children in Northern Ireland.

ADOPTION
Local authorities are required to provide an adoption service, either directly or via approved voluntary societies. In the UK, in 2003, 5,429 children (under 18 years of age) were entered onto the Adopted Children Register; 4,821 in England and Wales, 468 in Scotland and 140 in Northern Ireland.

PEOPLE WITH LEARNING DISABILITIES
Services for people with learning disabilities are designed to enable them to remain living in the community wherever possible. Local authority services include short-term care, support in the home, the provision of day care centres, and help with other activities outside the home. Residential care is provided for the severely or profoundly disabled.

MENTALLY ILL PEOPLE
Under the Care Programme Approach, mentally ill people should be assessed by specialist services, receive a care plan and a key worker should be appointed for each patient. Regular reviews of the patient's progress should be conducted. Local authorities provide help and advice to mentally ill people and their families, and places in day centres and social centres. Social workers can apply for a mentally disturbed person to be compulsorily detained in hospital. Where appropriate, mentally ill people are provided with accommodation in special hospitals, local authority accommodation, or at homes run by private or voluntary organisations. Patients who have been discharged from hospitals may be placed on a supervision register. A Mental Health National Service Framework was published in September 1999 setting national standards on how to prevent and treat mental illness.

NATIONAL INSURANCE

The National Insurance (NI) scheme operates under the Social Security Contributions and Benefits Act 1992 and the Social Security Administration Act 1992, and orders and regulations made thereunder. The scheme is financed by contributions payable by earners, employers and others (*see* below) and by a Treasury grant. Money collected under the scheme is used to finance the National Insurance Fund (from which contributory benefits are paid) and to contribute to the cost of the National Health Service.

NATIONAL INSURANCE FUND
Estimated receipts, payments and statement of balances of the National Insurance Fund for 2005–6:

Receipts	£000s
Net National Insurance contributions	66,195,000
Compensation from Consolidated Fund for Statutory Sick Pay and Statutory Maternity Pay recoveries	1,397,000
Income from investments	1,605,000
State scheme premiums	137,000
Other receipts	68,000
Total receipts	69,403,000

Payments	£000s
Benefits	58,530,000
Benefits increase due to proposed changes	1,802,000
Personal and stakeholder pensions contracted-out rebates	3,347,000
Age-related rebates for contracted-out money purchase schemes	290,000
Transfers to Northern Ireland	255,000
Administration	1,515,000
Redundancy fund payments (net)	267,000
Other payments	20,000
Total receipts	65,996,000

Balances	£000s
Opening balance	31,198
Excess of receipts over payments	3,407,000
Balance at end of year	34,605,000

CONTRIBUTIONS
There are six classes of National Insurance contributions (NICs):

Class 1	paid by employees and their employers
Class 1A	paid by employers who provide employees with certain benefits in kind for private use, such as company cars
Class 1B	paid by employers who enter into a Pay As You Earn (PAYE) Settlement Agreement with the HM Revenue and Customs
Class 2	paid by self-employed people
Class 3	voluntary contributions paid to protect entitlement to the State Pension for those who do not pay enough NI contributions in another class
Class 4	paid by the self-employed on their taxable profits over a set limit. These are normally paid by self-employed people in addition to Class 2 contributions. Class 4 contributions do not count towards benefits.

The lower and upper earnings limits and the percentage rates referred to below apply from April 2005 to April 2006.

CLASS 1

Class 1 contributions are paid where a person:
- is an employed earner (employee), office holder (e.g. company director) or employed under a contract of service in Great Britain or Northern Ireland
- is 16 or over and under state pension age
- earns at or above the earnings threshold of £94.00 per week (including overtime pay, bonus, commission, etc, without deduction of superannuation contributions)

Class 1 contributions are made up of primary and secondary contributions. Primary contributions are those paid by the employee and these are deducted from earnings by the employer. Since 6 April 2001 the employee's and employer's earnings thresholds have been the same and are referred to as the earnings threshold. Primary contributions are not paid on earnings below the earnings threshold of £94.00. Contributions are payable at the rate of 11 per cent on earnings between the earnings threshold and the upper earnings limit of £630.00 per week (9.4 per cent for contracted-out employment). Above the upper earnings limit 1 per cent is payable.

Some married women or widows pay a reduced rate of 4.85 per cent on earnings between the earnings threshold and upper earnings limits and 1 per cent above this. It is no longer possible to elect to pay the reduced rate but those who had reduced liability before 12 May 1977 may retain it so long as certain conditions are met. See leaflet CA09 (widows or widowers) or leaflet CA13 (married women).

Secondary contributions are paid by employers of employed earners at the rate of 12.8 per cent on all earnings above the earnings threshold of £94.00 per week. There is no upper earnings limit for employers' contributions. Employers operating contracted-out salary related schemes pay reduced contributions of 9.3 per cent; those with contracted-out money-purchase schemes pay 11.8 per cent. The contracted-out rate applies only to that portion of earnings between the earnings threshold and the upper earnings limits. Employers' contributions below and above those respective limits are assessed at the appropriate not contracted-out rate.

CLASS 2

Class 2 contributions are paid where a person is self-employed and is 16 or over and under state pension age. Contributions are paid at a flat rate of £2.10 per week regardless of the amount earned. However, those with earnings of less than £4,345 a year can apply for Small Earnings Exception, e.g. exemption from liability to pay Class 2 contributions. Those granted exemption from Class 2 contributions may pay Class 2 or Class 3 contributions voluntarily. Self-employed earners (whether or not they pay Class 2 contributions) may also be liable to pay Class 4 contributions based on profits. There are special rules for those who are concurrently employed and self-employed.

Married women and widows can no longer choose not to pay Class 2 contributions but those who elected not to pay Class 2 contributions before 12 May 1977 may retain the right so long as certain conditions are met.

Class 2 contributions are collected by the National Insurance Contributions Office (NICO), an executive agency of the HM Revenue and Customs, by direct debit or quarterly bills. See leaflets CWL2 and CA02.

CLASS 3

Class 3 contributions are voluntary flat-rate contributions of £7.35 per week payable by persons over the age of 16 who would otherwise be unable to qualify for retirement pension and certain other benefits because they have an insufficient record of Class 1 or Class 2 contributions. This may include those who are not working, those not liable for Class 1 or Class 2 contributions or those excepted from Class 2 contributions. Married women and widows who on or before 11 May 1977 elected not to pay Class 1 (full rate) or Class 2 contributions cannot pay Class 3 contributions while they retain this right. Class 3 contributions are collected by the NICO by quarterly bills or direct debit. See leaflet CA08.

CLASS 4

Self-employed people whose profits and gains are over £4,895 a year pay Class 4 contributions in addition to Class 2 contributions. This applies to self-employed earners over 16 and under the state pension age. Class 4 contributions are calculated at 8 per cent of annual profits or gains between £4,895 and £32,760 and 1 per cent above. Class 4 contributions are assessed and collected by the HM Revenue and Customs together with Schedule D tax. It is possible, in some circumstances, to apply for exceptions from liability to pay Class 4 contributions or to have the amount of contribution reduced (where Class 1 contributions are payable on earnings assessed for Class 4 contributions). See leaflet CWL2.

PENSIONS

Many people will qualify for a State Pension; however, there are further pension choices available, such as personal and stakeholder pensions. There are also other non-pension savings and investment options. The following section provides background information on existing pension schemes.

STATE PENSION SCHEME

The state pension scheme consists of:
- basic State Pension
- additional State Pension

People may be able to get both or either when they reach State Pension age and meet the qualifying conditions.

The State Pension does not have to be claimed at State Pension age, people can delay claiming it to earn extra weekly State Pension or a lump sum payment.

Basic State Pension (see also Benefits, State Pension: Categories A and B)

The amount of basic State Pension paid is dependent on the number of 'qualifying years' a person has established during their 'working life'. In 2005–6, the full basic State Pension is £82.05 a week and the minimum basic State Pension is £20.51 a week.

Qualifying Years

A 'qualifying year' is a tax year in which a person has enough earnings on which they have paid, are treated as having paid, or have been credited with National Insurance (NI) contributions (*see* National Insurance Credits section). By State Pension age, a person needs to have one qualifying year from NI contributions paid or from NI contributions treated as being paid to be eligible for any basic State Pension. The number of qualifying years can be reduced if a person qualifies for Home Responsibilities Protection (*see* below).

National Insurance Credits
Those in receipt of Carer's Allowance, Working Tax Credit (with a disability element), Jobseeker's Allowance, Incapacity Benefit, Statutory Sick Pay or Statutory Maternity Pay may have Class 1 NI contributions credited to them. Persons undertaking certain training courses or jury service or who have been wrongly imprisoned for a conviction which is quashed on appeal may also get Class 1 NI credits for each week they receive benefit or fulfil certain conditions. Class 1 NI credits count toward all future contributory benefits. A Class 3 NI credit for basic State Pension and bereavement benefit purposes is awarded, where required, for each week the Working Tax Credit (without a disability element) has been received. However, a State Pension will not be paid based on a record of NI credits alone.

Working Life
'Working life' is counted from the start of the tax year in which a person reaches 16 to the end of the tax year before the one in which they reach State Pension age: for men this is normally 49 years and for women this varies between 44 and 49 years depending on their birth date (*see* State Pension Age). To get the full rate (100 per cent) basic State Pension a person must normally have qualifying years for about 90 per cent of their working life. To get the minimum basic State Pension (25 per cent) a person will normally need ten or eleven qualifying years.

State Pension Age
State Pension Age is:
– 65 for men
– 60 for women born on or before 5 October 1950
– 61 for women born on 6 October 1950 or any day through to and including 5 October 1951
– 62 for women born on 6 October 1951 or any day through to and including 5 October 1952
– 63 for women born on 6 October 1952 or any day through to and including 5 October 1953
– 64 for women born on 6 October 1953 or any day through to and including 5 October 1954
– 65 for women born on 6 October 1954 or later

Using the NI contribution record of another to claim a State Pension
Married women who are not entitled to a State Pension on their own NI contributions may get a basic State Pension calculated using their husband's NI contribution record. A basic State Pension may be paid of up to 60 per cent of the husband's entitlement (up to £49.15 a week in 2005–6). From 6 April 2010, married men will be able to claim a basic State Pension based on their spouse's NI contributions if better than one based on their own record and if their wife was born after 1950. A State Pension is also payable to widows, widowers and people who are divorced, based on their late or ex-spouse's NI contributions.

Non-contributory State Pensions (see also Benefits, State Pension: Category D)
A non-contributory State Pension may be payable to those aged 80 or over who live in England, Scotland or Wales, and have done so for a total of ten years or more for any continuous period in the 20 years after their 60th birthday, if they are not entitled to another category of State Pension, or are entitled to one below the rate of £49.15 a week in 2005–6.

Graduated Retirement Benefit
Graduated Retirement Benefit (GRB) is based on the amount of graduated NI contributions paid into the GRB scheme between April 1961 and April 1975.

Home Responsibilities Protection
It is possible for people who are unable to work because they care for children or a sick or disabled person at home to reduce the number of qualifying years required. This is called Home Responsibilities Protection (HRP) and can be given for any tax year since April 1978; the number of years for which HRP is given is deducted from the number of qualifying years needed. From April 2002, HRP may, in some cases, also qualify the recipient for additional State Pension.

Additional State Pension
The amount of additional State Pension paid depends on the amount of earnings a person has, or is treated as having, between the lower and upper earnings limits for each complete tax year between 6 April 1978 (when the scheme started) and the tax year before they reach State Pension age. The right to additional State Pension does not depend on the person's right to basic State Pension.

From 1978 to 2002, additional State Pension was called the State Earnings-Related Pension Scheme (SERPS). SERPS covered all earnings by employees from 6 April 1978 to 5 April 1997 on which standard rate Class 1 NI contributions had been paid, and earnings between 6 April 1997 and 5 April 2002 if the standard rate Class 1 NI contributions had been contracted-in.

In 2002, SERPS was reformed through the State Second Pension, by improving the pension available to low and moderate earners and extending access to certain carers and people with long-term illness or disability. If earnings on which Class 1 NI contributions have been paid or can be treated as paid are above the annual NI Lower Earnings Limit (£4,264 for 2005–6) but below the statutory Low Earnings Threshold (£12,100 for 2005–6), the State Second Pension regards this as earnings of £12,100 and it is treated as equivalent. Certain carers and people with long-term illness and disability will be considered as having earned at the Low Earnings Threshold for each complete tax year since 2002–3 even if they do not work at all, or earn less than the annual NI Lower Earnings Limit.

The amount of additional State Pension paid also depends on when a person reaches state pension age; changes phased in from 6 April 1999 mean that pensions are calculated differently from that date.

Inheritance
Men or women widowed before 6 October 2002 can inherit all of their late spouse's SERPS pension. From 6 October 2002, the maximum percentage of SERPS pension that a person can inherit from a late spouse depends on their late spouse's date of birth:

Maximum % SERPS entitlement for surviving spouse	d.o.b (men)	d.o.b (women)
100%	5/10/37 or earlier	5/10/42 or earlier
90%	6/10/37 to 5/10/39	6/10/42 to 5/10/44
80%	6/10/39 to 5/10/41	6/10/44 to 5/10/46
70%	6/10/41 to 5/10/43	6/10/46 to 5/10/48
60%	6/10/43 to 5/10/45	6/10/48 to 5/7/50
50%	6/10/45 or later	6/7/50 or later

The maximum State Second Pension a person can inherit from a late spouse is 50 per cent.

Pension Forecasts
The Pension Service provides a State Pension forecasting service: T 0845-300 0168 or www.thepensionservice.gov.uk

CONTRACTED-OUT PENSION SCHEMES
Personal Pension Schemes
Since July 1988, an employee has been able to start a personal pension which, if it meets certain conditions, can be used in place of the additional State Pension. These pensions are known as Appropriate Personal Pensions (APPs). The part of an APP derived from the protected rights (rights comprising mainly the NIC rebate and its investment return) is intended to provide benefits broadly equivalent to those given up in the additional State Pension. At retirement, a contracted-out deduction will be made from additional State Pension built up from 6 April 1987 to 5 April 1997. The reduction may be more or less than that part of the pension derived from the protected rights. From 6 April 1997 to 5 April 2002, members of an APP scheme will not have built up any entitlement to additional State Pension during the period of their membership. From 6 April 2002, employees contracted-out into a personal pension and earning between the lower earnings limit and the low earnings threshold (£4,264 and £12,100 in 2005–6) will be entitled to a reduced amount of additional State Pension.

Stakeholder Pension Schemes
Introduced in 2001, Stakeholder pensions are available to everyone but are principally for moderate earners who do not have access to a good value company pension scheme. Stakeholder pensions must meet a number of minimum standards to make sure they are flexible, portable and annual management charges are capped. The minimum contribution is £20 per month.
 As with personal pensions it is possible to invest up to £3,600 (including tax relief) into stakeholder pensions each year without evidence of earnings. Contributions can be made on someone else's behalf, for example, a non-working partner. Some people who are already members of occupational pension schemes can also contribute to a stakeholder pension scheme. If it meets certain conditions, it can be used to contract out of the additional State Pension (formerly SERPS). When someone contracts out of the State scheme with either an APP or a Stakeholder Pension, both the employee and their employers pay NI contributions at the full not contracted-out rate. At the end of the tax year to which those NI contributions relate, HM Revenue and Customs (HMRC) pays an age-related rebate (which increases with age) and tax relief on the employee's share of the rebate directly into the scheme for investment on behalf of the employee.

OCCUPATIONAL PENSION SCHEMES
Contracted-Out Salary-Related (COSR) Scheme
- these schemes provide a pension related to earnings
- any notional additional State Pension built up from 6 April 1978 to 5 April 1997 will be reduced by the amount of Guaranteed Minimum Pension (GMP) built up during that period (the contracted-out deduction)
- from 6 April 1997 these schemes no longer provide a GMP. Instead, as a condition of contracting out they have to satisfy a reference scheme test to ensure that the benefits provided are at least as good as a prescribed standard
- when someone contracts out of the additional State Pension through a COSR scheme, both the scheme member and the employer pay a reduced rate of NI contributions (known as the rebate) to compensate for the State Pension given up

Contracted-Out Money Purchase (COMP) Scheme
- these schemes provide a pension based on the value of the fund at retirement, i.e. the money paid in, along with the investment return
- the part of the COMP fund derived from protected rights is intended to provide benefits broadly equivalent to those given up in the additional State Pension
- a contracted-out deduction, which may be more or less than that part of the pension derived from the protected rights, will be made from any additional pension built up from 6 April 1988 to 5 April 1997. Between 6 April 1997 and 5 April 2002 members of a COMP scheme will not have built up any entitlement to additional State Pension during the period of their membership
- as with a COSR scheme, when someone contracts out of the additional State Pension through a COMP scheme, both the scheme member and the employer pay a reduced rate of NI contributions to compensate for the State Pension given up. In addition, at the end of the tax year to which the NI contributions relate, the Inland Revenue pays an additional age-related rebate direct to the scheme for investment on behalf of the employee

Contracted-Out Mixed Benefit (COMB) Scheme
A mixed benefit scheme has two active sections, one salary related and the other money purchase. Scheme rules set out which section individual employees may join and the circumstances (if any), in which members may move between sections. Each section must satisfy the respective contracting-out conditions for COSR and COMP schemes.
 From April 2002, members of contracted-out occupational schemes earning between £4,264 and £27,800 (in 2005–6) may build up entitlement to a reduced amount of additional State Pension as well as that built up in their occupational pension.

COMPLAINTS
The Pensions Advisory Service (OPAS) gives free help and advice to people who have problems with occupational or personal pensions. There are two bodies for pension complaints. The Financial Ombudsman Service deals with complaints which predominantly concern the sale and/or marketing of occupational, stakeholder and personal pensions. The Pensions Ombudsman deals with complaints which predominantly concern the management (after sale or marketing) of occupational, stakeholder and personal pensions. From April 2005, the Occupational Pensions Regulatory Authority (OPRA) was replaced with the Pensions Regulator, a new body for work-based pensions. The Pensions Regulator concentrates its resources on schemes where there is the greatest risk to the security of members' benefits, promotes effective governance for all pension schemes and works with trustees, employers and professional advisers to put things right when necessary.

TAX CREDITS

From April 2003 Working Families' Tax Credit, Disabled Person's Tax Credit and the Children's Tax Credit were replaced with Working Tax Credit and Child Tax Credit. Tax Credits are administered by HM Revenue and

Customs (HMRC) and are awarded for up to 12 months, although they can be adjusted during the year to reflect changes of income or circumstances.

WORKING TAX CREDIT

Working Tax Credit is made up of a basic payment with additional payments for couples, lone parents, people working over 30 hours a week, disabled workers and people aged 50 or over returning to work after a period of benefits. The tax credit will be paid with wages to people who are employed and directly to the self-employed. It is available to:
- People with dependent children and/or a disability, working at least 16 hours a week
- People aged 25 or over and working at least 30 hours a week

The aim of the tax credit system is to provide a guaranteed minimum income from full-time work for those aged 25 or over, of £200 a week for couples, and £169 a week for single people. This is increased for those with a disability or for those with children.

WORKING TAX CREDIT 2005–6
£ per year

Annual Income/status*	Tax Credit per annum
5,000	
Single	–
Couple	–
Single adult with a disability	3,785
8,000	
Single	1,250
Couple	2,845
Single adult with a disability	3,420
10,000	
Single	510
Couple	2,105
Single adult with a disability	2,680
15,000	
Single	–
Couple	255
Single adult with a disability	830

* Those with incomes of £5,000 a year are assumed to work part-time (working between 16 and 30 hours a week). In families with an income of £8,000 a year or more, at least one adult is assumed to be working 30 or more hours a week.

CHILD CARE

In families with children where a lone parent or both partners in a couple work for at least 16 hours a week, or where one partner works and the other is disabled, the family is entitled to the childcare element of Working Tax Credit. This payment can contribute up to 70 per cent of childcare costs up to a maximum of £175 a week for one child and up to £300 a week for two or more children. Families can only claim if they use an approved or registered childcare provider.

CHILD TAX CREDIT

Child Tax Credit combines all income-related support for children and is paid direct to the main carer. The credit is made up of a main 'family' payment with additional payments for each extra child in the household, for children with a disability and an extra payment for children who are severely disabled. Child Tax Credit is available to households where:
- There is at least one dependant under 16 years old
- There is at least one dependant under 19 years old and

in full-time non-advanced education or registered with the Careers or Connexions Service (does not include Scotland or Northern Ireland)

CHILD TAX CREDIT AND WORKING TAX CREDIT (FOR HOUSEHOLDS WITH CHILDREN) 2005–6
£ per year

Annual Income*	One Child		Two Children	
	No Childcare	Maximum Childcare	No Childcare	Maximum Childcare
0	2,240	2,240	3,930	3,930
5,000†	5,455	11,840	7,150	18,100
8,000†	5,085	11,457	6,780	17,730
10,000‡	4,345	10,735	6,040	16,990
15,000	2,495	8,885	4,190	15,140
20,000	645	7,035	2,340	13,290
25,000	545	5,185	545	11,440
30,000	545	3,335	545	9,590
35,000	545	1,485	545	7,740
40,000	545	545	545	5,890
45,000	545	545	545	4,040
50,000	545	545	545	2,190
60,000	–	–	–	175
65,000	–	–	–	–

* Those with incomes of £5,000 a year are assumed to work part-time (working between 16 and 30 hours a week). In families with an income of £8,000 a year or more, at least one adult is assumed to be working 30 or more hours a week.
† At income levels of £5,000 and £8,000 awards are shown for lone parents.
‡ At an income level of £10,000 awards are shown for two parents working part-time (between 16 and 30 hours per week) or one parent working full-time.

BENEFITS

The following is intended as a comprehensive and detailed guide to the benefits system. However, terms and conditions of entitlement and benefit rates are constantly changing and all prospective claimants should check exact entitlements and rates of benefit directly with their local social security office or online at www.dwp.gov.uk. Leaflets relating to the various benefits and contribution conditions for different benefits are available from local social security offices; leaflet GL23 *Social Security Benefit Rates* is a general guide to benefit rates and contributions.

CONTRIBUTORY BENEFITS

Entitlement to contributory benefits depends on National Insurance contribution conditions being satisfied either by the claimant or by some other person (depending on the kind of benefit). The class or classes of National Insurance contribution which for this purpose are relevant to each benefit are:

Jobseeker's Allowance (contribution-based)	Class 1
Incapacity Benefit	Class 1 or 2
Maternity Allowance	Class 1 or 2
Widow's Benefit and Bereavement Benefit	Class 1, 2 or 3
State Pensions, categories A and B	Class 1, 2 or 3

The system of contribution conditions relates to yearly levels of earnings on which National Insurance contributions have been paid.

JOBSEEKER'S ALLOWANCE

Jobseeker's Allowance (JSA) replaced unemployment benefit and income support for unemployed people under pension age from 7 October 1996. There are two routes of entitlement. Contribution-based JSA is paid as a personal rate (i.e. additional benefit for dependants is not paid) to those who have made sufficient NI contributions in two particular tax years. Savings and partner's earnings are not taken into account and payment can be made for up to six months. Rates of JSA correspond to income support rates.

Claims for this benefit are made through Jobcentre Plus offices and Jobcentres. A person wishing to claim JSA must generally be unemployed or a JSA claimant working on average less than 16 hours a week, capable of work and available for any work which they can reasonably be expected to do, usually for at least 40 hours per week. They must agree and sign a 'jobseeker's agreement', which will set out each claimant's plans to find work, and must actively seek work. If they refuse work or training their benefit may be sanctioned for between one and 26 weeks.

A person will be sanctioned from JSA for up to 26 weeks if they have left a job voluntarily without just cause or through misconduct. In these circumstances, it may be possible to receive hardship payments, particularly where the claimant or their family is vulnerable, e.g. if sick or pregnant, or for those with children or caring responsibilities. *See* leaflet JSAL5 *JSA – Helping You Back to Work.*

INCAPACITY BENEFIT

Incapacity Benefit is available to those who are incapable of work but cannot get statutory sick pay from their employer. It is not payable to those over State Pension age. However, people who are already in receipt of short-term Incapacity Benefit when they reach State Pension age may continue to receive this benefit for up to 52 weeks. Apart from those people who qualify under the special provisions for people incapacitated in youth, entitlement is based on a person's NI contribution record. In order to qualify for Incapacity Benefit, two contribution conditions, based on the last three tax years before the year in which benefit is claimed, must be satisfied. The amount of Incapacity Benefit payable may be reduced where a claimant receives more than a specified amount of occupational or personal pension. Severely disabled people aged between 16 and 19 should receive Incapacity Benefit without meeting the NI contribution conditions. There are three rates of Incapacity Benefit:
– short-term lower rate for the first 28 weeks of sickness
– short-term higher rate from weeks 29 to 52
– long-term rate from week 53 onwards

The terminally ill and those entitled to the highest rate care component of disability living allowance are paid the long-term rate after 28 weeks. Incapacity benefit is taxable after 28 weeks.

Two rates of age addition are paid with long-term benefit based on the claimant's age when incapacity started. The higher rate is payable where incapacity for work commenced before the age of 35, and the lower rate where incapacity commenced before the age of 45. Increases for dependants are payable for those claiming for any period prior to 6 April 2003 and who are entitled to short-term Incapacity Benefit at the higher rate, basic State Pension rate or long-term Incapacity Benefit. For all periods after 6 April 2003 claimants should enquire about Child Tax Credits.

There are two medical tests of incapacity: the 'own occupation' test and the 'personal capability' assessment. Those who worked before becoming incapable of working will be assessed, for the first 28 weeks of incapacity, on their ability to do their own job. After 28 weeks (or from the start of incapacity for those who were not working) claimants are assessed on their ability to carry out a range of work related activities. *See* leaflets IB1 and IB214. Since October 2001 all new benefit claimants in Jobcentre Plus areas receive a service combining jobs and benefits advice and support. The government plans to extend this as Jobcentre Plus is rolled out nationally by 2006. New Incapacity Benefit claimants will be invited back for work-focused interviews at intervals of not longer than three years. The interviews do not include medical tests, but if the claimant is due for a medical test around the same time, their local office will aim to schedule both together. People who are severely disabled and those who are terminally ill will not be asked to attend these interviews.

BEREAVEMENT BENEFITS

Bereavement benefits replaced widow's benefit on 9 April 2001. Those claiming widow's benefit before this date will continue to receive them under the old scheme for as long as they qualify. The new system provides bereavement benefits for widows and widowers providing that their deceased spouse paid NI contributions. The new system offers benefits in three forms:

Bereavement Payment – may be received by a man or woman who is under the State Pension age at the time of their spouse's death, or whose husband or wife was not entitled to a Category A retirement pension when he or she died. It is a single tax-free lump sum of £2,000 payable immediately on becoming a widow or widower

Widowed Parent's Allowance – a taxable benefit payable to the surviving partner if he or she is entitled or treated as entitled to child benefit, or to a widow if she is expecting her husband's baby at the time of his death

Bereavement Allowance – a taxable weekly benefit paid for 52 weeks after the spouse's death. If aged over 55 and under State Pension age the full allowance is payable, if aged between 45 and 54 a percentage of the full rate is paid. A widow or widower may receive this allowance if his or her Widowed Parent's Allowance ends before 52 weeks.

It is not possible to receive Widowed Parent's Allowance and Bereavement Allowance at the same time. Bereavement benefits and widow's benefit, in any form, cease upon remarriage or are suspended during a period of cohabitation as man and wife without being legally married. *See* leaflets GL14 and D49 (D49S for deaths that occur in Scotland).

STATE PENSION: CATEGORIES A AND B

Category A pension is payable for life to men and women who reach State Pension age and who satisfy the contributions conditions. Category B pension is payable for life to married women, widows and widowers and is based on their wife or husband's contributions. It is payable to a married woman only when both the wife and husband have claimed their State Pension and they have both reached State Pension age. From April 2010, a married man will be able to qualify for a Category B pension from his wife's contributions providing she was born on or after 6 April 1950. Category B pension is also payable on widowhood after State Pension age. Category B pension is payable to widows regardless of the age of their husband when he died, although at present, it is only paid to widowers if their wife had reached State Pension age when she died. Widowers who reach State Pension age on or after 6 April 2010 will be able to get a Category B pension on the same terms as widows. There are special rules for those who are widowed before reaching State Pension age.

Where a person is entitled to both a Category A and Category B pension then they can be combined to give a composite pension, but this cannot be more than the full rate pension. Where a person is entitled to more than one Category A or Category B pension then only one can be paid. In such cases the person can choose which to get; if no choice is made, the most favourable one is paid.

A person may defer claiming their pension beyond State Pension age. In doing so they may earn increments which will increase the weekly amount paid by one per cent per five weeks of deferral (equivalent to 10.4 per cent/year) when they claim their State Pension. If a person delays claiming for at least 12 months they are given the option of a one-off taxable lump sum, instead of a pension increase, based on the weekly pension deferred, plus interest. If a married man defers his Category A pension, his wife cannot claim a Category B pension on his contributions but she may earn increments on her State Pension during this time. A woman can defer her Category B pension, and earn increments, even if her husband is claiming his Category A pension.

The basic State Pension is £82.05 per week plus any additional (earnings-related) State Pension the person may be entitled to. An increase of £49.15 is paid for an adult dependant, providing the dependant's earnings do not exceed the rate of Jobseeker's Allowance for a single person (see below) and the couple are living together. If the couple are not living together an increase is payable if the dependant's earnings are not above £49.15. Before April 2003 it was also possible to get an increase of Category A and B pensions for a child or children. Since April 2003 provision for children has been made through Child Tax Credits. An age addition of 25p per week is payable with a State Pension if a pensioner is aged 80 or over.

The Category B pension provides up to £49.15 a week for a married woman and up to £82.05 a week for a widow/widower.

Since 1989 pensioners have been allowed to have unlimited earnings without affecting their State Pension.

For further information see Pensions section.

GRADUATED RETIREMENT BENEFIT
Graduated NI contributions were first payable from April 1961 and were calculated as a percentage of earnings between certain bands. The Graduated Retirement Benefit scheme existed until April 1975, however it is still paid, in addition to any State Pension, to those who made the relevant contributions. A person will receive Graduated Retirement Benefit based on their own contributions, even if not entitled to a basic State Pension. Widows and widowers may inherit half of their deceased spouses entitlement, but none that the deceased spouse may have been eligible for from a former spouse.

Graduated Retirement Benefit is calculated using a weekly rate for each 'unit' of graduated contributions paid by the employee (half a unit or more counts as a whole unit); the rate varies from person to person. A unit of graduated Retirement Benefit can be calculated by adding together all graduated contributions and dividing by 7.5 (men) or 9.0 (women). If a person defers making a claim beyond State Pension age, they may earn an increase or a one-off lump sum payment in respect of their deferred Graduated Retirement Benefit; calculated in the same way as for the Category A or B State Pension.

WEEKLY RATES OF BENEFIT *from April 2005*

Jobseeker's Allowance (JSA) (contribution-based)

Person under 18	£33.85
Person aged 18–24	£44.50
Person aged 25 to State Pension age	£56.20

From October 2003 people between 60 and State Pension age can choose to claim Pension Credits instead of JSA.

Short-term Incapacity Benefit

Person under State Pension age – lower rate	£57.65
Person under State Pension age – higher rate	£68.20
Increase for adult dependant	£35.65
Person over State Pension age	£73.35
Person over State Pension age – higher rate	£76.45
Increase for adult dependant	£43.95

Long-term Incapacity Benefit

Person under State Pension age	£76.45
Increase for adult dependant	£45.70
Age addition – lower rate	£8.05
Age addition – higher rate	£10.05

Widow's Benefits (from April 2005)

Widowed mother's allowance	£82.05
Widow's pension, full entitlement (aged 55 and over at time of spouse's death)	£82.05

Amount of widow's pension by age of widow at spouse's death (for deaths occurring before 11 April 1988 refer to the age-points in brackets):

aged 54 (49)	£76.31
aged 53 (48)	£70.56
aged 52 (47)	£64.82
aged 51 (46)	£59.08
aged 50 (45)	£53.33
aged 49 (44)	£47.59
aged 48 (43)	£41.85
aged 47 (42)	£36.10
aged 46 (41)	£30.36
aged 45 (40)	£24.62

Bereavement Benefit (from April 2005)

Bereavement Payment (lump sum)	£2,000.00
Widowed Parent's Allowance	£82.05
Bereavement Allowance, full entitlement (aged 55 and over at time of spouse's death)	£82.05

Amount of Bereavement Allowance by age of widow/widower at spouse's death:

aged 54	£76.31
aged 53	£70.56
aged 52	£64.82
aged 51	£59.08

aged 50	£53.33
aged 49	£47.59
aged 48	£41.05
aged 47	£36.10
aged 46	£30.36
aged 45	£24.62

State Pension: Categories A and B

Category A or B pension for a single person	£82.05
Category B pension (married women)	£49.15
Increase for adult dependant	£49.15
Age addition at age 80	£0.25

NON-CONTRIBUTORY BENEFITS

These benefits are paid from general taxation and are not dependent on NI contributions. Unless otherwise stated, a benefit is tax-free and is not means tested.

JOBSEEKER'S ALLOWANCE (INCOME-BASED)

Those who do not qualify for contribution-based Jobseeker's Allowance (JSA(c)), those who have exhausted their entitlement to contribution-based JSA or those for whom contribution-based JSA provides insufficient income may qualify for income-based JSA. The amount paid depends on age, number of dependants, amount of income and savings. Income-based JSA is comprised of three parts:
- A personal allowance for the jobseeker and his/her partner and an allowance for each child or young person for whom they are responsible (*see* below)
- Premiums for people with special needs
- Premiums for housing costs

The rules of entitlement are the same as for contribution-based JSA.

If one person in a couple was born after 28 October 1957 and neither person in the couple has responsibility for a child or children, then the couple will have to make a joint claim for JSA if they wish to receive income-based JSA.

Since April 2003 claimants have had the option to choose to claim Child Tax Credit instead of an increase of JSA for children.

MATERNITY ALLOWANCE

Maternity Allowance (MA) covers women who are self-employed or otherwise do not qualify for Statutory Maternity Pay (SMP). In order to qualify for payment, a woman must have been employed and/or self-employed for at least 26 weeks in the 66 week period up to and including the week before the baby is due (test period). She must also have average weekly earning of at least £30 (Maternity Allowance Threshold) in any 13 weeks of the test period. Women who are self-employed will be deemed to have earnings at or above the Maternity Allowance Threshold. A woman can choose to start receiving MA from the 11th week before the week in which the baby is due up to the day following the day of birth. This will depend on when the woman stops work to have her baby or if the baby is born before she stops work. However, where the woman is absent from work for pregnancy related illness on or after the Sunday of the 4th week before the baby is due to be born, MA will start the day following the first day of absence from work for a pregnancy-related illness. MA is paid up to 26 weeks and is only paid while the woman is not working.

CHILD BENEFIT

Child Benefit is payable for virtually all children aged under 16, and for those aged 16 to 18 who are studying full-time up to and including A-level or equivalent standard. It is also payable for a short period if the child has left school recently and is registered for work or work-based training for young people at a careers office or with the Connexions Service (in Northern Ireland, Training and Employment Agency).

GUARDIAN'S ALLOWANCE

Where the parents of a child are dead, the person who has the child in his/her family may claim a Guardian's Allowance in addition to Child Benefit. In specified circumstances the allowance is payable on the death of only one parent. *See* leaflet NI14.

CARER'S ALLOWANCE

Carer's Allowance (CA) is a benefit payable to people who spend at least 35 hours per week caring for a severely disabled person. To qualify for CA a person must be caring for someone in receipt of one of the following benefits:
- the middle or highest rate of disability living allowance care component
- either rate of attendance allowance
- constant attendance allowance, paid at not less than the normal maximum rate, under the industrial injuries or war pension schemes

See leaflets SD1 and SD4.

SEVERE DISABLEMENT ALLOWANCE

Since April 2001 Severe Disablement Allowance (SDA) has not been available to new claimants. Those claiming SDA before that date will continue to receive it for as long as they qualify.

ATTENDANCE ALLOWANCE

This is payable to disabled people who claim after the age of 65 and who need a lot of care or supervision because of physical or mental disability, and who have needed help for a period of at least six months. Attendance Allowance has two rates: the lower rate is for day or night care, and the higher rate is for day and night care. People not expected to live for more than six months because of an illness can receive the highest rate of Attendance Allowance straight away. *See* leaflets DS702 and SD1.

DISABILITY LIVING ALLOWANCE

This is payable to disabled people who claim before the age of 65 who have personal care and/or mobility needs because of an illness or disability for a period of at least three months and are likely to have those needs for a further six months or more. The allowance has two components: the care component, which has three rates, and the mobility component, which has two rates. The rates depend on the care and mobility needs of the claimant. People not expected to live for more than six months because of an illness will automatically receive the highest rate of the care component. *See* leaflets DS704 and SD1.

STATE PENSION: CATEGORY D

Category D pension is provided for people aged 80 and over if they are not entitled to another category of pension or are entitled to a State Pension that is less than the Category D rate. The person must also normally live in Great Britain and have done so for a continuous period of ten years within any 20-year period since their 60th birthday (for further information *see* Pensions section).

WEEKLY RATES OF BENEFIT *from April 2005*

Jobseeker's Allowance (income-based)

Person under 18, living with family	£33.85
Person under 18, living away from home	£44.50
Person aged 18–24	£44.50
Person aged 25 to state pension age	£56.20
Couple with one or both under 18	£33.85–£88.15
	(depending on circumstances)
Couple aged 18 to state pension age	£88.15
Dependent children and young persons premium up to 16	£43.88
16–19 years	£43.88
Family premium	£16.10
Family premium (lone parent)	£16.10

Maternity Allowance

Standard rate	£106 or 90% of the women's average weekly earnings if less than £106
Increase for adult dependant	£35.65

Child Benefit

Eldest child	£16.50
Each subsequent child	£11.05

Guardian's allowance

Each child	£11.85

Carer's Allowance

	£45.70
Increase for dependent adult	£27.30

Severe Disablement Allowance

Basic rate	£46.20
*Age related addition:	
Under 40	£16.05
40–49	£10.30
50–59	£5.15

* The age addition applies to the age when incapacity began

Additions may be payable for dependent adults

Attendance Allowance

Higher rate	£60.60
Lower rate	£40.55

Disability Living Allowance
Care component

Higher rate	£60.60
Middle rate	£40.55
Lowest rate	£16.05

Mobility component

Higher rate	£42.30
Lower rate	£16.05

State Pension: Category D

Single person	£49.15
Age addition to State Pension at age 80	£0.25

INCOME SUPPORT

Income Support is a benefit for those aged 16 and over whose income is below a certain level. It can be paid to people who are not expected to sign on as unemployed (Income Support for unemployed people was replaced by Jobseeker's Allowance in October 1996) and who are:

– incapable of work due to sickness or disability
– bringing up children alone
– looking after a person who has a disability
– registered blind

Pension Credit replaced Income Support for people aged 60 or over on 6 October 2003. Some people who are not in these categories may also be able to claim income support.

Income Support is also payable to people who work fewer than 16 hours a week on average (or 24 hours for a partner). Some people can claim Income Support if they work longer hours.

Income Support is not payable if the claimant, or claimant and partner, have capital or savings in excess of £8,000. For capital and savings in excess of £3,000, a deduction of £1 a week is made for every £250 or part of £250 held. Different limits apply to people permanently in residential care and nursing homes: the upper limit is £16,000 and deductions apply for capital in excess of £10,000.

Sums payable depend on fixed allowances laid down by law for people in different circumstances. If both partners are eligible for Income Support, either may claim it for the couple. People receiving Income Support may be able to receive Housing Benefit, help with mortgage or home loan interest and help with health care. They may also be eligible for help with exceptional expenses from the Social Fund. Special rates may apply to some people living in residential care or nursing homes. Leaflet IS20 gives a detailed explanation of income support.

In October 1998 the government's voluntary New Deal for Lone Parents programme became available throughout the UK. All lone parents receiving Income Support are assigned a personal adviser at a Jobcentre who will provide guidance and support with a view to enabling the claimant to find work.

INCOME SUPPORT PREMIUMS

Income Support premiums are additional weekly payments for those with special needs. People qualifying for more than one premium will normally only receive the highest single premium for which they qualify. However, family premium, disabled child premium, severe disability premium and carer premium are payable in addition to other premiums.

People with children may qualify for:
– the family premium if they have at least one child (a higher rate is paid to lone parents, although from 6 April 1998 it has not been available to new claimants)
– the disabled child premium if they have a child who

receives Disability Living Allowance or is registered blind

Carers may qualify for:
- the carer premium if they or their partner are in receipt of Carer's Allowance

Long-term sick or disabled people may qualify for:
- the disability premium if they or their partner are receiving certain benefits because they are disabled or cannot work; are registered blind; or if the claimant has been incapable of work or receiving Statutory Sick Pay for at least 364 days (196 days if the person is terminally ill), including periods of incapacity separated by eight weeks or less
- the severe disability premium if the person lives alone and receives Attendance Allowance or the middle or higher rate of Disability Living Allowance care component and no one receives Carer's Allowance for caring for that person. This premium is also available to couples where both partners meet the above conditions

WEEKLY RATES OF BENEFIT *from April 2005*

Income Support

Single person

under 18	£33.85
under 18 (higher)	£44.50
aged 18–24	£44.50
aged 25 and over	£56.20
aged under 18 and a single parent (lower)	£33.85
aged under 18 and a single parent (higher)	£44.50
aged 18 and over and a single parent	£56.20

Couples

Both under 18 (with responsibility for a child)	£67.15
one or both aged 18 or over	£88.15
For each child in a family from birth to day before 19th birthday	£43.88

Premiums

Family premium	£16.10
Family (lone parent) premium	£16.10
Disabled child premium	£43.89
Carer premium	£25.80

Disability premium

Single	£23.95
Couple	£34.20

Enhanced disability premium

Single	£11.70
Enhanced disabled child premium	£17.71
Severe disability premium	
Lower rate (single person and some couples)	£45.50
Higher rate (couples)	£91.00

PENSION CREDIT

Pension Credit was introduced on 6 October 2003 and replaces Income Support for those aged 60 and over.

There are two elements to Pension Credit:

The Guarantee Credit

The guarantee credit provides a guaranteed minimum income, with additional elements for people who have:
- relevant housing costs
- severe disabilities
- caring responsibilities

Income from State Pension, private pensions, earnings and certain benefits are taken into account when calculating the guarantee credit. For savings and capital in excess of £6,000 a deduction of £1 per week is made for every £500 or part of £500 held.

People receiving the guarantee credit element of Pension Credit will be able to receive Housing Benefit, Council Tax Benefit and help with health care costs.

The Savings Credit

Single people aged 65 or over (and couples where one member is 65 or over) may be entitled to a savings credit which will reward pensioners who have modest income or savings. The savings credit is calculated by taking into account any qualifying income above the savings credit threshold. For 2005–6 the threshold is £82.05 for single people and £131.20 for couples. The savings credit gives pensioners a cash addition calculated at 60p for every pound of qualifying income they have between the savings credit threshold and the guarantee credit. After this, the maximum reward will be reduced by 40p for every pound of income above the guarantee level. The maximum savings credit is £16.44 per week (£21.51 a week for couples).

Income that qualifies towards the savings credit includes State Pensions, earnings, second pensions and capital above £6,000.

Some people will be entitled to the guarantee credit, some to the savings credit and some to both.

Where only the savings credit is in payment, people need to claim standard Housing Benefit or Council Tax Benefit. Although local authorities take any savings credit into account in the Housing Benefit/Council Tax Benefit assessment, for people aged 65 and over Housing Benefit/Council Tax Benefit is enhanced to ensure that gains in Pension Credit are not depleted.

WEEKLY RATES OF BENEFIT *From April 2005*

Standard minimum guarantee:	
Single	£109.45
Couple	£167.05
Additional amount for:	
Severe disability	£45.50
Carers	£25.80
Savings credit threshold:	
Single	£82.05
Couple	£131.20

HOUSING BENEFIT

Housing Benefit is designed to help people with rent (including rent for accommodation in guesthouses, lodgings or hostels). It does not cover mortgage payments. The amount of benefit paid depends on:
- the income of the claimant, and partner if there is one, including earned income, unearned income (any other income including some other benefits) and savings
- number of dependants
- certain extra needs of the claimant, partner or any dependants
- number and gross income of people sharing the home who are not dependent on the claimant

– how much rent is paid

Housing Benefit is not payable if the claimant, or claimant and partner, have savings of over £16,000. The amount of benefit is affected if savings held exceed £3,000 (£6,000 for pensioners and £10,000 for people living in care homes). Housing Benefit is not paid for meals, fuel or certain service charges that may be included in the rent. Deductions are also made for most non-dependants who live in the same accommodation as the claimant (and their partner).

The maximum amount of benefit (which is not necessarily the same as the amount of rent paid) may be paid where the claimant is in receipt of Income Support or income-based Jobseeker's Allowance or where the claimant's income is less than the amount allowed for their needs. Any income over that allowed for their needs will mean that their benefit is reduced. See leaflets GL16 and RR2.

COUNCIL TAX BENEFIT

Nearly all the rules which apply to Housing Benefit apply to Council Tax Benefit, which helps people on low incomes to pay council tax bills. The amount payable depends on how much council tax is paid and who lives with the claimant. The benefit may be available to those receiving Income Support or income-based Jobseeker's Allowance or to those whose income is less than that allowed for their needs. Any income over that allowed for their needs will mean that their Council Tax Benefit is reduced. Deductions are made for non-dependants.

The maximum amount that is payable for those living in properties in council tax bands A to E is 100 per cent of the claimant's council tax liability. This also applies to those living in properties in bands F to H who were in receipt of the benefit at 31 March 1998 if they have remained in the same property.

If a person shares a home with one or more adults (not their partner) who are on a low income, it may be possible to claim a second adult rebate. Those who are entitled to both Council Tax Benefit and second adult rebate will be awarded whichever is the greater. Second adult rebate may be claimed by those not in receipt of Council Tax Benefit.

AGE-RELATED PAYMENTS 2005

During winter 2005–6 the Government is making two one-off age-related payments.

The first is a payment of £200 to households with someone aged 65 or over, not in receipt of the guarantee credit element of Pension Credit, to help with the cost of council tax bills.

The second is a payment of £50 to households with someone aged 70 or over, in receipt of the guarantee credit element of Pension Credit, to help with the cost of additional living expenses.

These payments will be made together with Winter Fuel Payments.

THE SOCIAL FUND

REGULATED PAYMENTS
Sure Start Maternity Grant

The Sure Start Maternity Grant (SSMG) is a one-off payment of £500 for parents on low incomes to buy essential items for new babies. To qualify, mothers and expectant mothers must also receive health and welfare advice for themselves and their child from an approved health professional. SSMG can be claimed any time from the 29th week of pregnancy until the child is three months old. Those eligible are mothers or their partners in receipt of Income Support, income-based Jobseeker's Allowance, Pension Credit, Child Tax Credit at a rate higher than the family element or Working Tax Credit where a disability or severe disability element is in payment.

Funeral Payments

Payable for the necessary cost of burial or cremation, plus other funeral expenses incurred up to £700, to people receiving Income Support, income-based Jobseeker's Allowance, Pension Credit, Child Tax Credit at a higher rate than the family element, Working Tax Credit where a disability or severe disability element is in payment, Council Tax Benefit or Housing Benefit who have good reason for taking responsibility for the funeral expenses. These payments are recoverable from any estate of the deceased.

Cold Weather Payments

A payment of £8.50 when the average temperature over seven consecutive days is recorded at or forecast to be 0°C or below in the qualifying person's area. Payments are made to people on Pension Credit, as well as those on Income Support, income-based Jobseeker's Allowance and those who have a child under five or disabled, or whose benefit includes a pensioner or disability premium. Payments do not have to be repaid.

Winter Fuel Payments

An annual payment of at least £200 per household paid to most people aged 60 or over. Where the household includes someone aged 80 or over, the amount is £300. The majority of eligible people are paid automatically before Christmas, although a few need to claim. Payments do not have to be repaid.

DISCRETIONARY PAYMENTS
Community Care Grants

These are intended to help people on Income Support, income-based Jobseeker's Allowance, in receipt of Pension Credit, or receiving payments on account of such benefits (or those likely to receive these benefits or leaving residential or institutional accommodation) to live as independently as possible in the community; ease exceptional pressures on families; care for a prisoner or young offender released on temporary licence; help people set up home as part of a resettlement programme and/or assist with certain travelling expenses. They do not have to be repaid.

Budgeting Loans

These are interest-free loans to people who have been receiving Income Support, income-based Jobseeker's Allowance, Pension Credit or payments on account of such benefits for at least 26 weeks, for intermittent expenses that may be difficult to budget for.

Crisis Loans

These are interest-free loans to anyone, whether receiving benefits or not, who is without resources in an emergency or due to a disaster, where there is no other means of preventing serious damage or serious risk to their, or their family member's, health or safety.

SAVINGS

Savings over £500 (£1,000 for people aged 60 or over) are taken into account for Community Care Grants and

Budgeting Loans. All savings are taken into account for Crisis Loans. Savings are not taken into account for Sure Start Maternity Grants, Funeral Payments, Cold Weather or Winter Fuel Payments.

INDUSTRIAL INJURIES AND DISABLEMENT BENEFITS

The Industrial Injuries Scheme, administered under the Social Security Contributions and Benefits Act 1992, provides a range of benefits designed to compensate for disablement resulting from an industrial accident (i.e. an accident arising out of and in the course of an employed earner's employment) or from a prescribed disease due to the nature of a person's employment. Those who are self-employed are not covered by this scheme.

INDUSTRIAL INJURIES DISABLEMENT BENEFIT

A person must be at least 14 per cent disabled (except for certain respiratory diseases) in order to qualify for this benefit. The amount paid depends on the degree of disablement:

- those assessed as 14–19 per cent disabled are paid at the 20 per cent rate
- those with disablement of over 20 per cent will have the percentage rounded up or down to the nearest ten per cent, e.g. a disablement of 44 per cent will be paid at the 40 per cent rate while a disablement of 45 per cent will be paid at the 50 per cent rate

Benefit is payable 15 weeks (90 days) after the date of the accident or onset of the disease (subject to backdating limits) and may be payable for a limited period or for life. The benefit is payable whether the person works or not and those who are incapable of work are entitled to draw Statutory Sick Pay or Incapacity Benefit in addition to industrial injuries disablement benefit. It may also be possible to claim the following allowances:

- Reduced Earnings Allowance for those who are unable to return to their regular work or work of the same standard and who had their accident (or whose disease started) before 1 October 1990. At State Pension age this is converted to Retirement Allowance
- Constant Attendance Allowance for those with a disablement of 100 per cent who need constant care. There are four rates of allowance depending on how much care the person needs
- Exceptionally Severe Disablement Allowance for those who are entitled to constant care attendance allowance at one of the higher rates and who need constant care permanently

See leaflets SD6, SD7 and SD8.

OTHER BENEFITS

People who are disabled because of an accident or disease that was the result of work that they did before 5 July 1948 are not entitled to Industrial Injuries Disablement benefit. They may, however, be entitled to payment under the Workmen's Compensation Scheme or the Pneumoconiosis, Byssinosis and Miscellaneous Diseases Benefit Scheme. See leaflet GL23. People who suffer from certain industrial diseases caused by dust, or their dependants, can make a claim for an additional payment under the Pneumoconiosis etc (Workers' Compensation) Act 1979 if they are unable to get damages from the employer who caused or contributed to the disease.

WEEKLY RATES OF BENEFIT *from April 2005*

* *Disablement Benefit/pension*

Degree of disablement:	
100 per cent	£123.80
90	£111.42
80	£99.04
70	£86.66
60	£74.28
50	£61.90
40	£49.52
30	£37.14
20	£24.76
Unemployability Supplement	£76.75
Addition for adult dependant (subject to earnings rule)	£45.70
Reduced Earnings Allowance (maximum)	£49.52
Retirement Allowance (maximum)	£12.38
Constant Attendance Allowance (normal maximum rate)	£49.60
Exceptionally Severe Disablement Allowance	£49.60

* There is a weekly benefit for those under 18 with no dependants which is set at a lower rate

CLAIMS AND QUESTIONS

Entitlement to benefit and regulated Social Fund payments is determined by a decision maker on behalf of the Secretary of State for the Department of Work and Pensions. A claimant who is dissatisfied with that decision can ask for an explanation. They can dispute the decision by applying to have it revised or, in particular circumstances, superseded. If they are still dissatisfied they can go to the Appeals Service where it will be heard by an independent tribunal. There is a further right of appeal to a Social Security Commissioner against the tribunal's decision but this is on a point of law only and leave to appeal must first be obtained.

Decisions on claims and applications for Housing Benefit and Council Tax Benefit are made by Local Authority decision makers. The explanation, dispute and appeals process is the same as for other benefits. See leaflets GL24 and NI260DMA.

All decisions on applications to the discretionary Social Fund are made by Jobcentre Plus Social Fund decision makers. Applicants can ask for a review of the decision within 28 days of the date on the decision letter. The Social Fund Review Officer will review the case and there is a further right of review by an independent Social Fund Inspector.

EMPLOYER PAYMENTS

STATUTORY MATERNITY PAY

Employers pay Statutory Maternity Pay (SMP) to pregnant women who have been employed by them full or part-time for at least 26 weeks into the 15th week before the week the baby is due, and whose earnings on average at least equal the Lower Earnings Limit applied to NI contributions (£82 per week from April 2005). All women who meet these conditions receive payment of 90 per cent of their average earnings for the first six weeks, followed by a maximum of 20 weeks at £106 or 90 per cent of the woman's average weekly earnings if this is less than £106. SMP can be paid, at the earliest, 11 weeks before the week in which the baby is due, up to the day following the birth. Women can decide when they wish their maternity leave to start and can work until the baby is born. However, where the woman is absent from work for a pregnancy-related illness on or after the Sunday of the 4th week before the baby is due to be born, SMP will start the day following the first day of absence from work for the pregnancy-related illness. SMP is not payable for any week in which the woman works. Employers are reimbursed for 92 per cent of the SMP they pay. Small employers with annual gross NI payments of £45,000 or less recover 100 per cent of the SMP paid out plus 4.5 per cent in compensation for the secondary NI contributions paid on SMP. *See* Leaflet NI17A and HM Revenue and Customs guide for employers E15.

STATUTORY PATERNITY PAY

Employers pay Statutory Paternity Pay (SPP) to employees who are taking leave when a child is born or placed for adoption. To qualify the employee must:
– have responsibility for the child's upbringing
– be the biological father of the child (or the child's adopter), or the husband/partner of the mother or adopter
– be taking time off work to care for the child and/or support the mother or adopter
– have been employed by the same employer for at least 26 weeks ending with the 15th week before the baby is due (or the week in which the adopter is notified of having been matched with a child)
– continue working for the employer up to the child's birth (or placement for adoption)
– have earnings on average at least equal to the Lower Earnings Limit applied to NI contributions (£82 per week from April 2005)

Employees who meet these conditions receive payment of £106 or 90 per cent of the employee's average weekly earnings if this is less than £106. The employee can choose to be paid for one or two consecutive weeks. The earliest the SPP period can begin is the date of the child's birth or placement for adoption. The SPP period must be completed within eight weeks of that date. SPP is not payable for any week in which the employee works. Employers are reimbursed in the same way as for Statutory Maternity Pay. *See* Department of Trade and Industry leaflets PL514 and PL515.

STATUTORY ADOPTION PAY

Employers pay Statutory Adoption Pay (SAP) to employees taking adoption leave from their employers. To qualify for SAP the employee must:
– be newly matched with a child by an adoption agency
– have been employed by the same employer for at least 26 weeks ending the week in which they have been notified of being matched with a child
– have earnings at least equal to the lower earnings limit applied to NI contributions (£82 per week from April 2005)

Employees who meet these conditions receive payment of £106 or 90 per cent of their average weekly earnings if this is less than £106 for up to 26 weeks. The SAP period can start from the date of the child's placement. SAP is not payable for any week in which the employee works. Where a couple adopt a child only one of them may receive SAP, the other may be able to receive Statutory Paternity Pay (SPP) if they meet the eligibility criteria. Employers are reimbursed in the same way as for Statutory Maternity Pay. *See* Department of Trade and Industry leaflet PL515.

STATUTORY SICK PAY

Employers pay Statutory Sick Pay (SSP) for up to 28 weeks to any employee incapable of work for four or more consecutive days. SSP is payable to employees between the ages of 16 and 65 who have average earnings at or above the point at which earnings become relevant for NI purposes (£82 from April 2005) in a specified period. SSP is paid at £68.20 per week and is subject to PAYE and NI contributions. Employees who cannot obtain SSP may be able to claim Incapacity Benefit. Employers may be able to recover some SSP costs. *See* HM Revenue and Customs Leaflets CA86 *Employees* and CA30 *Employer Manual.*

WAR PENSIONS AND THE ARMED FORCES COMPENSATION SCHEME

The Veteran's Agency (previously known as The War Pensions Agency) became an executive agency of the Ministry of Defence in June 2001. The Agency is responsible for the administration of war pensions and the Armed Forces Compensation Scheme (AFCS) to members of the armed forces in respect of disablement or death due to service. There is also a scheme for civilians and civil defence workers in respect of the 1939–45 war, and other schemes for groups such as merchant seamen and Polish armed forces who served under British command during World War II.

PENSIONS

War Disablement Pension is awarded for the disabling effects of any injury, wound or disease which was the result of, or was aggravated by, conditions of service in the armed forces prior to 6 April 2005. Claims are only considered once the person has left the armed forces. The amount of pension paid depends on the severity of disablement, which is assessed by comparing the health of the claimant with that of a healthy person of the same age and sex. The person's earning capacity or occupation are not taken into account in this assessment. A pension is awarded if the person has a disablement of 20 per cent or more and a lump sum is usually payable to those with a disablement of less than 20 per cent. No award is made for noise-induced sensorineural hearing loss where the assessment of disablement is less than 20 per cent.

War Widow/Widower's Pension is payable where the spouse's death was due to, or hastened by, service in the armed forces, prior to 6 April 2005, or where the spouse was in receipt of a War Disablement Pension constant attendance allowance (or would have been if not in hospital) at the time of death. A War Widow/Widower's Pension is also payable if the spouse was getting War Disablement Pension at the 80 per cent rate or higher and was receiving unemployability supplement at the time of death. War widows/widowers receive a standard rank-related rate, but a lower weekly rate is payable to war widows/widowers of personnel below the rank of Major who are under the age of 40, without children and capable of maintaining themselves. This is increased to the standard rate at age 40. Allowances are paid for children (in addition to child benefit) and adult dependants. An age allowance is automatically given when the widow/widower reaches 65 and increased at ages 70 and 80.

All War Pensions and War Widow/Widower's Pensions are tax-free and pensioners living overseas receive the same amount as those resident in the UK.

ARMED FORCES COMPENSATION SCHEME (AFCS)

The Armed Forces Compensation Scheme (AFCS) became effective on 6 April 2005 and replaced previous arrangements under the War Pensions Scheme. AFCS covers all regular (including Gurkhas) and reserve personnel whose injury, ill health or death is caused by service on or after 6 April 2005. Ex-members of the Armed Forces who served prior to this date or who are in receipt of a War Disablement Pension or War Widow's Pension will continue to receive their pension and any associated benefits in the normal way. The new scheme affects only those who served after 6 April 2005.

The AFCS provides compensation where service in the Armed Forces is the only or main cause of injury, illness or death. Compensation can also be paid in certain exceptional circumstances to off-duty personnel, for example, to victims of a terrorist attack targeted due to their position in the Armed Forces. Under the terms of the scheme a lump sum is payable to service or ex-service personnel based on a 15-level tariff, graduated according to the seriousness of the condition. A Guaranteed Income Payment (GIP), payable for life, is received by those who could be expected to experience a serious loss of earning capability. A GIP will also be paid to surviving partners (including unmarried and same sex partners). GIP is calculated by multiplying the pensionable age of the service person by a factor which depends on the age of the person's last birthday. The younger the person, the higher the factor, because there are more years to normal retirement age.

SUPPLEMENTARY ALLOWANCES

A number of supplementary allowances may be awarded to a war pensioner which are intended to meet various needs which may result from disablement or death and take account of its particular effect on the pensioner or spouse. The principal supplementary allowances are unemployability supplement, allowance for lowered standard of occupation and constant attendance allowance. Others include exceptionally severe disablement allowance, severe disablement occupational allowance, treatment allowance, mobility supplement, comforts allowance, clothing allowance, age allowance and widow/widower's age allowance. Rent and children's allowances are also available on War Widow/Widower's pensions.

DEPARTMENT FOR WORK AND PENSIONS BENEFITS

Most benefits are paid in addition to the basic War Disablement Pension, War Widow/Widower's Pension and those in receipt of payments under the AFCS, but may be affected by supplementary allowances in payment. Any State Pension for which a war widow/widower qualifies on their own NI contribution record can be paid in addition to War Widow/Widower's Pension.

CLAIMS AND QUESTIONS

For information on War Pensions, the Armed Forces Compensation Scheme and to find out where the nearest War Pensioners' Welfare Office is located, the Veteran's Agency can be contacted via a free telephone helpline:
T 0800-169 2277 or if living overseas, call
T (+44) (125) 386-6043
VETERANS AGENCY, Norcross, Blackpool FY5 3WP
E help@veteransagency.gsi.gov.uk
W www.veteransagency.mod.uk

THE WATER INDUSTRY

Water services in England and Wales are provided by private companies. In Scotland there is a single authority, Scottish Water, that is answerable to the Scottish Executive, and in Northern Ireland all services are provided by the Water Service, which remains in the public sector. In the UK, the water industry provides services to over 20 million properties and has an annual turnover of £7 billion. It also manages assets that include over 2,500 water and 9,000 sewerage treatment plants, 1,000 reservoirs and over 700,000 km of water mains and sewers.

ENGLAND AND WALES

The water industry supplies around 18,000 million litres of water every day. In 2002 water companies in England and Wales carried out around 2.9 million tests on drinking water samples of which 99.87 per cent met all British and European standards. In England and Wales the Secretary of State for Environment, Food and Rural Affairs and the National Assembly for Wales have overall responsibility for water policy and oversee environmental standards for the water industry.

Water UK is the industry association that represents all UK water and wastewater service suppliers at national and European level and is funded directly by its members who are the service suppliers for England, Scotland, Wales and Northern Ireland; every member has a seat on the Water UK Council.

WATER UK, 1 Queen Anne's Gate, London SW1H 9BT
T 020-7344 1844 W www.water.org.uk
Chief Executive, Pamela Taylor

WATER SERVICE COMPANIES (members of Water UK)

ANGLIAN WATER SERVICES LTD, Customer Services, PO Box 770, Lincoln LN5 7WX T 08457-919155
W www.anglianwater.co.uk

BOURNEMOUTH & WEST HAMPSHIRE WATER PLC, George Jessel House, Francis Avenue, Bournemouth, Dorset BH11 8NB T 01202-590059 W www.bwhwater.co.uk

BRISTOL WATER PLC, PO Box 218, Bridgwater Road, Bristol BS99 7AU T 0117-966 5881
W www.bristolwater.co.uk

CAMBRIDGE WATER PLC, 41 Rustat Road, Cambridge CB1 3QS T 01223-706050
W www.cambridge-water.co.uk

CHOLDERTON & DISTRICT WATER COMPANY, Estate Office, Cholderton, Salisbury, Wiltshire SP4 0DR
T 01980-629203

DEE VALLEY WATER PLC, Packsaddle, Wrexham Road, Rhostyllen, Wrexham LL14 4EH T 01978-846946

DWR CYMRU CYFYNGEDIG (WELSH WATER), Pentwyn Road, Nelson, Treharris, Mid Glamorgan CF46 6LY
T 01443-452300
W www.dwrcymru.co.uk

ESSEX & SUFFOLK WATER PLC (subsidiary of Northumbrian Water Ltd), Hall Street, Chelmsford, Essex CM2 0HH T 0800 919155
W www.eswater.co.uk

FOLKSTONE & DOVER WATER SERVICES LTD, Cherry Garden Lane, Folkestone, Kent CT19 4QB
T 01303-298800

MID KENT WATER PLC, Snodland, Kent ME6 5AH
T 0845-8508060 W www.midkentwater.co.uk

NORTHUMBRIAN WATER LTD, Abbey Road, Pity Me, Durham DH1 5FJ T 0191-383 2222 W www.nwl.co.uk

PORTSMOUTH WATER PLC, PO Box 8, West Street, Havant, Hampshire PO9 1LG T 02392-499888
W www.portsmouthwater.co.uk

SEVERN TRENT PLC, Sherbourne House, St Martin's Road, Finham, Coventry CV3 6SD
T 08457-500500
W www.severn-trent.com

SOUTH EAST WATER PLC, 3 Church Road, Haywards Heath, West Sussex RH16 3NY T 0845 3010845
W www.southeastwater.co.uk

SOUTH STAFFORDSHIRE WATER PLC, PO Box 63, Walsall WS2 7PJ T 0845-6070456 W www.south-staffs-water.co.uk

SOUTH WEST WATER LTD, Peninsula House, Rydon Lane, Exeter EX2 7HR T 01392-446688
W www.swwater.co.uk

SOUTHERN WATER, Southern House, Yeoman Road, Worthing, W. Sussex BN13 3NX T 0845-2780845
W www.southernwater.co.uk

SUTTON AND EAST SURREY WATER PLC, London Road, Redhill, Surrey RH1 1LY T 01737-764444
W www.waterplc.com

TENDRING HUNDRED WATER SERVICES LTD, Mill Hill, Manningtree, Essex CO11 2AZ T 01206-399333
W www.thws.co.uk

THAMES WATER UTILITIES LTD, PO Box 286, Swindon SN38 2RA T 0845-92000 888 W www.thameswater.com

THREE VALLEYS WATER PLC, PO Box 48, Bishops Rise, Hatfield, Hertfordshire AL10 9HL
T 01707-268111
W www.3valleys.co.uk

UNITED UTILITIES WATER PLC, PO Box 50, Warrington WA55 1AQ T 0845-7462222
W www.unitedutilities.com

WESSEX WATER SERVICES LTD, Claverton Down, Bath BA2 7WW T 01225-526000 W wessexwater.co.uk

YORKSHIRE WATER SERVICES LTD, Western House, Western Way, Halifax Road, Bradford BD6 2LZ
T 01274-600111
W www.yorkshirewater.com

ISLAND WATER AUTHORITIES (not members of Water UK)

COUNCIL OF THE ISLES OF SCILLY, Town Hall, St Mary's, Isles of Scilly TR21 0LW
T 01720-422902

ISLE OF MAN WATER AUTHORITY, Drill House, Tromode Road, Isle of Man IM2 5PA T 01624-624414

JERSEY NEW WATERWORKS COMPANY LTD, Mulcaster House, Westmount Road, St Helier, Jersey JE1 1DG
T 01534-509999

STATES OF GUERNSEY WATER BOARD, PO Box 30, South Esplanade, St Peter Port, Guernsey GY1 3AS
T 01481-724552 W www.gov.gg

WATER SUPPLY AND CONSUMPTION 2003–4

	Supply		Consumption			
	Supply from Treatment Works (Ml/day)	Total Leakage (Ml/day)	Household (l/head/day) Unmetered	Metered	Non-household (l/prop/day) Unmetered	Metered
WATER AND SEWERAGE COMPANIES						
Anglian	1,174	216	163	127	226	3,005
Dwr Cymru	876	231	153	122	657	2,314
Northumbrian	732	160	150	146	817	4,039
Severn Trent	1,967	512	137	135	531	2,149
South West	459	84	171	142	976	1,659
Southern	599	92	166	149	545	2,545
Thames	2,874	946	164	154	943	3,419
United Utilities	1,984	479	150	132	763	2,641
Wessex	379	75	157	135	2,987	2,461
Yorkshire	1,297	295	149	138	124	2,830
Total	12,823	3,160	—	—	—	—
Average	—	—	154	138	736	2,688
WATER ONLY COMPANIES						
Total	2,835	489	—	—	—	—
Average	—	—	158	141	894	2,793

Source: Office of Water Services

REGULATORY BODIES

The Office of Water Services (Ofwat) was set up under the Water Act 1989 and is the independent economic regulator of the water and sewerage companies in England and Wales. Overall responsibility for water policy and overseeing environmental standards for the water industry lies with the Department for Environment, Food and Rural Affairs and the Welsh Assembly. Ofwat's main duty is to ensure that the companies can finance and carry out their statutory functions and to protect the interests of water customers. Ofwat is a non-ministerial government department headed by the Director-General of Water Services.

Under the Competition Act 1998, from 1 March 2000 the Competition Appeal Tribunal has heard appeals against the regulator's decisions regarding anti-competitive agreements and abuse of a dominant position in the marketplace. The 2003 Water Bill placed a new duty on Ofwat to have regard to sustainable development.

The Environment Agency was set up by the 1995 Environment Act as a non-departmental public body and is sponsored largely by the Department for Environment, Food and Rural Affairs and the Welsh Assembly. The Environment Agency has statutory duties and powers in relation to water resources, pollution control, flood defence, fisheries, recreation, conservation and navigation in England and Wales. They are also responsible for issuing permits, licences, consents and registrations such as industrial licences to abstract water and fishing licences.

The Drinking Water Inspectorate (DWI) is the drinking water quality regulator for England and Wales, responsible for assessing the quality of the drinking water supplied by the water companies and investigating any incidents affecting drinking water quality, initiating prosecution where necessary. The DWI also provides scientific advice on drinking water policy issues to the Department of the Environment, Food and Rural Affairs and the Welsh Assembly.

OFWAT, Centre City Tower, 7 Hill Street, Birmingham, B5 4UA
T 0121-625 1300 E enquiries@ofwat.gsi.gov.uk
W www.ofwat.gov.uk
Director-General, Philip Fletcher

METHODS OF CHARGING

In England and Wales, most domestic customers still pay for domestic water supply and sewerage services through charges based on the old rateable value of their property. It is expected that by March 2006 about 28 per cent of householders will be charged according to consumption, which is recorded by meter. Industrial and most commercial customers are charged according to consumption.

Under the Water Industry Act 1999, water companies can continue basing their charges on the old rateable value of property. Domestic customers can continue paying on an unmeasured basis unless they choose to pay according to consumption. After having a meter installed (which is free of charge), a customer can revert to unmeasured charging within 12 months. Domestic, school and hospital customers cannot be disconnected for non-payment.

Price limits for the period 2005–10 were set by Ofwat in December 2004.

AVERAGE HOUSEHOLD WATER BILLS 2005–6

	Unmetered (£)	Metered (£)
Water	140	116
Sewerage	149	132
Combined	289	249

SCOTLAND

Overall responsibility for national water policy in Scotland rested with the Secretary of State for Scotland until July 1999 when it was devolved to the Scottish Ministers. Until The Local Government (Scotland) Act 1994, water supply and sewerage services were local authority responsibilities. The Central Scotland Water Development Board had the function of developing new sources of water supply for the purpose of providing water in bulk to water authorities whose limits of supply were within the Board's area. Under the Act, three new public water authorities, covering the north, east and west of Scotland respectively, took over the provision of water and sewerage services from April 1996. The Central Scotland Water Development Board was then abolished. The Act also established the Scottish Water and Sewerage Customers Council representing consumer interests. It monitored the performance of the authorities; approved charges schemes; investigated complaints; and advised the Secretary of State. The Water Industry Act 1999, whose Scottish provisions were accepted by the Scottish Executive, abolished the Scottish Water and Sewerage Customers Council and replaced it in November 1999 by a Water Industry Commissioner.

The Water Industry (Scotland) Act 2002 resulted from the Scottish Executive's proposal that a single authority was better placed than three separate authorities to harmonise changes across the Scottish water industry. In 2002 the three existing water authorities, East of Scotland Water, North of Scotland Water and West of Scotland Water merged to form Scottish Water. Scottish Water is a public sector company, structured and managed like a private company, but remains answerable to the Scottish Parliament. Scottish Water is regulated by the Water Industry Commissioner for Scotland, the Scottish Environment Protection Agency (SEPA), and the Drinking Water Quality Regulator for Scotland. The Water Industry Commissioner is responsible for regulating all aspects of economic and customer service performance, including water and sewerage charges and SEPA is responsible for environmental issues, including controlling pollution and promoting the cleanliness of Scotland's rivers, lochs and coastal waters.

SCOTTISH WATER, 26 Castle Drive, Carnegie Campus, Dunfermline KY11 8GG T 01383-848200
  W www.scottishwater.co.uk
SCOTTISH ENVIRONMENT PROTECTION AGENCY, Erskine Court, Castle Business Park, Stirling FK9 4TR
  T 01786-457700 W www.sepa.org.uk
WATER INDUSTRY COMMISSIONER FOR SCOTLAND, Ochil House, Springkerse Business Park, Stirling FK7 7XE
  T 01786-430200 W www.watercommissioner.co.uk

METHODS OF CHARGING
Scottish Water sets charges for domestic and non-domestic water and sewerage provision through charges schemes which are regulated by the Water Industries Commissioner for Scotland. In February 2004 the harmonisation of all household charges across the country was completed following the merger of the separate authorities under Scottish Water.

NORTHERN IRELAND

In Northern Ireland ministerial responsibility for water services lies with the minister of the Department for Regional Development. The Water Service, which is an executive agency of the Department for Regional Development, is responsible for policy and co-ordination with regard to supply, distribution and cleanliness of water, and the provision and maintenance of sewerage services.

The Water Service comprises four divisions, Eastern, Northern, Western and Southern. The main divisional offices are based in Belfast, Ballymena, Londonderry and Craigavon.

METHODS OF CHARGING
The Water service is currently funded from public funds and direct charges. The department's policy is to meter all properties that are not exclusively domestic. They are, however, granted an allowance of 200 cubic metres per annum to reflect domestic usage – this is known as the domestic usage allowance. Customers are charged only for water used in excess of the domestic usage allowance together with a standing charge, which is intended to cover the costs of meter provision, maintenance, reading and billing. This allowance is not granted if rates are not paid on the property. Traders operating from de-rated, rate exempt or rate rebated premises are required to pay for the treatment and disposal of trade effluent which they discharge into the public sewer.

In December 2002, the Northern Ireland Office announced that water and sewerage services would become self-financed by 2006. Domestic customers would be charged directly for water and sewerage services, currently a proportion of the rates paid on domestic properties. Following a major public consultation on *The Reform of the Water and Sewerage Services In Northern Ireland* the initial conclusions from the Department for Regional Development was that the new domestic charge would included a fixed element and a variable element, the latter determined by property value or consumption.

NORTHERN IRELAND WATER SERVICE, Northland House, 3 Frederick Street, Belfast BT1 2NR T 028-90 244711
  W www.waterni.gov.uk

ENERGY

The main primary sources of energy in Britain are oil, natural gas, coal, nuclear power and water power. The main secondary sources (e.g. sources derived from the primary sources) are electricity, coke and smokeless fuels and petroleum products. The Department for the Environment, Food and Rural Affairs (DEFRA) is responsible for promoting energy efficiency.

INDIGENOUS PRODUCTION OF PRIMARY FUELS
Million tonnes of oil equivalent

	2004
Coal	17.5
Petroleum	104.6
Natural gas	97.2
Primary electricity	18.6
Nuclear	18.1
Natural flow hydro	0.5
Total	256.5

Source: Department of Trade and Industry

INLAND ENERGY CONSUMPTION BY PRIMARY FUEL
Million tonnes of oil equivalent, seasonally adjusted

	2004
Coal	42.1
Petroleum	75.9
Natural gas	100.7
Primary electricity	19.2
Nuclear	18.1
Natural flow hydro	0.5
Net Imports	0.6
Total	257.1

Source: Department of Trade and Industry

TRADE IN FUELS AND RELATED MATERIALS 2004

	Quantity*	Value†
Imports		
Coal and other solid fuel	25.4	1,482
Crude petroleum	61.4	8,496
Petroleum products	28.9	5,195
Natural gas	11.4	670
Electricity	0.8	347
Total	127.9	16,190
Exports		
Coal and other solid fuel	0.6	60
Crude petroleum	66.2	9,348
Petroleum products	39.6	6,599
Natural gas	9.8	651
Electricity	0	151
Total	116.2	16,809

* Million tonnes of oil equivalent
† £ million
Source: HM Customs & Excise

OIL

Until the 1960s Britain imported almost all its oil supplies. In 1969 oil was discovered in the Arbroath field of the UK Continental Shelf (UKCS). The first oilfield to be brought into production was the Argyll field in 1975, and since the mid-1970s Britain has been a major producer of crude oil.

Licences for exploration and production are granted to companies by the Department of Trade and Industry; the leading British oil companies are BP and Shell. At the end of 2004, 565 Seaward Production Licences and 101 onshore Petroleum Exploration and Development Licences had been awarded, and there were a total of 264 offshore oil and gas fields in production. In 2003 there were 9 oil refineries and three smaller refining units processing crude and process oils. There are estimated to be reserves of 1,267 million tonnes of oil remaining in the UKCS. Royalties are payable on fields approved before April 1982 and petroleum revenue tax is levied on fields approved between 1975 and March 1993.

DRILLING ACTIVITY 2004

Number of wells started	Offshore	Onshore
Exploration and appraisal	63	3
Exploration	29	3
Appraisal	34	0
Development	166	14

Source: Department of Trade and Industry

VALUE OF UKCS OIL AND GAS PRODUCTION AND INVESTMENT
£ million

	2002	2003
Total income	24,118	23,562
Operating costs	4,596	4,496
Gross trading profits*	19,475	19,058
Percentage contribution to GVA	2.2	2.1
Exploration expenditure	389	334
Other capital investment	3,598	3,412
Percentage contribution to industrial investment	16	16

* Net of stock appreciation
Source: Department of Trade and Industry

INDIGENOUS PRODUCTION AND REFINERY RECEIPTS

	2003	2004
Indigenous production *(thousand tonnes)*	106,073	95,443
Crude oil	97,835	87,585
NGLs*	8,238	7,858
Refinery receipts *(thousand tonnes)*		
Indigenous	30,829	27,596
Other†	1,652	839
Net foreign imports	51,806	58,348

* Natural Gas Liquids: condensates and petroleum gases derived at onshore treatment plants
† Mainly recycled products
Source: Department of Trade and Industry

DELIVERIES OF PETROLEUM PRODUCTS FOR INLAND CONSUMPTION BY ENERGY USE

Thousand tonnes

	2003	2004
Industry	6,700	7,577
Transport	49,995	51,646
Domestic	3,093	2,723
Other	1,197	991
Total	60,985	62,937

Source: Department of Trade and Industry

COAL

Coal has been mined in Britain for centuries and the availability of coal was crucial to the industrial revolution of the 18th- and 19th-centuries. Mines were in private ownership until 1947 when they were nationalised and came under the management of the National Coal Board, later the British Coal Corporation. In addition to producing coal at its own deep-mine and opencast sites, of which there were 850 in 1955, British Coal was responsible for licensing private operators.

Under the Coal Industry Act 1994, the Coal Authority was established to take over ownership of coal reserves and to issue licences to private mining companies as part of the privatisation of British Coal. The Coal Authority also deals with the physical legacy of mining, eg subsidence damage claims, and is responsible for holding and making available all existing records. The mines were sold as five separate businesses in 1994 and coal production in the UK is now undertaken entirely in the private sector.

The main UK customer for coal is the electricity supply industry. A review of energy policy was undertaken on 1998 and the government announced measures in its October 1998 Energy White Paper which included a freeze on new applications to build gas-fired power stations in order to increase opportunities for coal-fired power stations. The moratorium on new gas-fired power stations was lifted in 2000 in the light of two measures to improve the competitiveness of coal-fired generation. Firstly, the government reached an agreement with the European Commission to make available temporary state aid for the coal industry. The second measure was the reform of the electricity wholesale market and the replacement of the Electricity Pool with the New Electricity Trading Arrangement (NETA) which took effect from 27 March 2001. In 2003 the government launched Coal Investment Aid with a budget of up to £60 million to be allocated between 2003–5 to coal producers for projects that maintain access to coal reserves. An Energy White Paper, published on 24 February 2003, stated that coal generation still provides around a third of the UK's power output, but recognised that for a low-carbon economy the development of cleaner coal technologies is required. By 2020 coal generation's contribution to the UK's power output is likely to be significantly lower than today.

COAL PRODUCTION AND FOREIGN TRADE

Thousand tonnes

	2003	2004p
Total production	28,258	25,097
Deep-mined	15,635	12,545
Opencast	12,126	11,993
Imports*	31,891	36,153
Exports†	543	620

* Includes an estimate for slurry
† As recorded in the Overseas Trade Statistics of the United Kingdom, although these are based on estimates from extra-EC trade until monthly statistics for intra-EC trade become available from HM Customs and Excise
p provisional
Source: Department of Trade and Industry

INLAND COAL USE

Thousand tonnes

	2003	2004p
Fuel producers		
Collieries	5	7
Electricity generators	53,087	50,480
Heat generation*	608	604
Coke ovens and blast furnaces	6,613	6,379
Other conversion industries†	396	326
Final users		
Industry‡	687	1,508
Domestic	944	1,195
Public administration, commerce and agriculture	29	113
Total	62,370	60,611

* Generation of heat for sale under the provision of a contract
† Low temperature carbonisation and patent fuel plants
‡ Includes estimates of imports
p provisional
Source: Department of Trade and Industry

GAS

From the late 18th-century gas in Britain was produced from coal. In the 1960s town gas began to be produced from oil-based feedstocks using imported oil. In 1965 gas was discovered in the North Sea in the West Sole field, which became the first gasfield in production in 1967, and from the late 1960s natural gas began to replace town gas. Britain is now the world's fourth largest producer of gas and in 1998 only 1.5 per cent of gas available for consumption in the UK was imported. From October 1998 Britain was connected to the continental European gas system via a pipeline from Bacton, Norfolk to Zeebrugge, Belgium. There are 275,000 km of mains pipeline including 6,400 km of high pressure gas pipelines owned and operated in the UK by National Grid Transco.

The gas industry in Britain was nationalised in 1949 and operated as the Gas Council. The Gas Council was replaced by the British Gas Corporation in 1972 and the industry became more centralised. The British Gas Corporation was privatised in 1986 as British Gas plc.

In 1993 the Monopolies and Mergers Commission found that British Gas's integrated business in Great Britain as a gas trader and the owner of the gas transportation system could operate against the public interest. In February 1997, British Gas demerged its trading arm to become two separate companies, BG plc and Centrica plc. BG Group, as the company is now known, is an international natural gas company whose principal business is finding and developing gas reserves and building gas markets. Its core operations are located in the UK, South America, Egypt, Trinidad & Tobago, Kazakhstan and India. Centrica runs the trading and services operations under the British Gas brand name in Great Britain. In October 2000 BG demerged its pipeline business, Transco, which became part of Lattice Group, finally merging with the National Grid Group in 2002 to become National Grid Transco plc.

Competition was gradually introduced into the industrial gas market from 1986. Supply of gas to the domestic market was opened to companies other than British Gas, starting in April 1996 with a pilot project in the West Country and Wales. From early 1997 competition was progressively introduced throughout the rest of Britain in stages which were completed in May 1998.

BG GROUP PLC, 100 Thames Valley Park Drive, Reading RG6 1PT T 0118-935 3222 W www.bg-group.com
Chairman, Sir Robert Wilson
Chief Executive, Frank Chapman

CENTRICA PLC, Millstream, Maidenhead Road, Windsor, Berkshire SL4 5GD T 01753-494000 W www.centrica.co.uk
Chairman, Roger Carr
Chief Executive, Sir Roy Gardner

NATIONAL GRID TRANSCO PLC, 1–3 Strand, London WC2N 5EH T 020-7004 3000 W www.ngtgroup.com
Chairman, Sir John Parker
Group Chief Executive, Roger Urwin

UK NATURAL GAS PRODUCTION
GWh

	2002	2003
Power stations	329,629	324,075
Petroleum Refineries	3,350	2,157
Nuclear fuel production	402	219
Production and distribution of other energy	709	893
Total final producers	334,090	327,344

Source: The Stationery Office: *Annual Abstract of Statistics 2005* (Crown copyright)

UK GAS CONSUMPTION *by industry*
GWh

	2002	2003
Iron and steel industry	19,522	19,121
Other industries	10,916	11,475
Domestic	376,372	385,985
Public administration	42,694	43,646
Agriculture	2,346	1,494
Miscellaneous	55,371	56,685
Total final users	507,221	518,406

Source: The Stationery Office: *Annual Abstract of Statistics 2005* (Crown copyright)

ELECTRICITY

The first power station in Britain generating electricity for public supply began operating in 1882. In the 1930s a national transmission grid was developed and it was reconstructed and extended in the 1950s and 1960s. Power stations were operated by the Central Electricity Generating Board.

Under the Electricity Act 1989, 12 regional electricity companies (RECs), which were responsible for the distribution of electricity from the national grid to consumers, were formed from the former area electricity boards in England and Wales. Four companies were formed from the Central Electricity Generating Board: three generating companies (National Power plc, Nuclear Electric plc and PowerGen plc) and the National Grid

Company plc, which owned and operated the transmission system. National Power and PowerGen were floated on the stock market in 1991. National Power was demerged in October 2000 to form two separate companies: International Power plc and Innogy plc, which manages the bulk of National Power's UK assets. Nuclear Electric was split into two parts in 1996: British Energy (*see* Nuclear Energy) and Magnox Electric, which owns the magnox nuclear reactors, remained in the public sector. Magnox was integrated into British Nuclear Fuels (BNFL) in 1998. The National Grid Company was floated on the stock market in 1995 and formed a new holding company, National Grid Group. National Grid Group completed a merger with Lattice in 2002 to form National Grid Transco, a public limited company.

NATIONAL GRID TRANSCO PLC, 1–3 Strand, London, WC2N 5EH T 020-7004 3000
W www.ngtgroup.com

Generators and suppliers participate in a competitive wholesale trading market known as NETA (New Electricity Trading Arrangements) which began in March 2001, replacing the Electricity Pool. The introduction of competition into the domestic electricity market was completed in May 1999. With the gas market also open, most suppliers now offer their customers both gas and electricity.

In Scotland, three new companies were formed under the Electricity Act 1989: Scottish Power plc and Scottish Hydro-Electric plc, which are responsible for generation, transmission, distribution and supply; and Scottish Nuclear Ltd, Scottish Power and Scottish Hydro-Electric were floated on the stock market in 1991. Scottish Hydro-Electric merged with Southern Electric in 1998 to become Scottish and Southern Energy plc. Scottish Nuclear was incorporated into British Energy in 1996.

In Northern Ireland, Northern Ireland Electricity plc was set up in 1993 under a 1991 Order in Council. In 1993 it was floated on the stock market and in 1998 it became part of the Viridian Group and is responsible for distribution and supply.

On 30 September 2003 the Electricity Association, the industry's main trade association, was replaced with three separate trade bodies:

ASSOCIATION OF ELECTRICITY PRODUCERS (AEP), First Floor, 17 Waterloo Place, London, SW1Y 4AR
T 020-7930 9390 W www.aepuk.com
Promotes the interests of members who generate electricity
ENERGY NETWORKS ASSOCIATION (ENA), 18 Stanhope Place, London, W2 2HH T 020-7706 5100
W www.energynetworks.org
Represents UK gas and electricity transmission and distribution licence holders
ENERGY RETAIL ASSOCIATION, 2nd Floor, 17 Waterloo Place, London, SW1Y 4AR T 020-7747 2932
W www.energy-retail.org.uk
Represents all the main suppliers operating in the UK energy market

ELECTRICITY GENERATION, SUPPLY AND
CONSUMPTION
GWh

	2002	2003
Electricity generated		
Major power producers: total	353,994	362,600
Conventional thermal and other*	126,694	146,382
Combined cycle gas turbine stations	132,016	121,076
Nuclear stations	87,848	88,686
Hydro-electric stations		
Natural flow	3,927	2,568
Pumped storage	2,652	2,734
Renewables other than hydro	856	1,154
Other generators: total	33,513	36,019
Electricity used on works: total	16,051	17,776
Major generating companies	10,577	10,759
Other generators	860	660
Electricity supplied (gross)		
Major power producers: total	338,248	345,854
Conventional thermal and other*	120,495	139,137
Combined cycle gas turbine stations	129,384	118,546
Nuclear stations	81,090	81,911
Hydro-electric stations		
Natural flow	3,914	2,559
Pumped storage	2,562	2,641
Renewables other than hydro	802	1,059
Other generators: total	32,087	34,528
Electricity used in pumping		
Major power producers	3,463	3,546
Electricity supplied (net): total	366,871	376,836
Major power producers	334,785	342,308
Other generators	32,087	34,528
Net imports	8,414	2,160
Electricity available	375,286	378,996
Losses in transmission	31,029	30,822
Electricity consumption: total	344,257	348,174
Fuel industries	10,027	9,629
Final users: total	334,229	338,546
Industrial sector	113,442	115,028
Domestic sector	114,534	115,761
Other sectors	106,253	107,757

* Includes electricity supplied by gas turbines, oil engines and plants producing electricity from renewable resources other than hydro.

Source: The Stationery Office – *Annual Abstract of Statistics 2005* (Crown copyright)

GAS AND ELECTRICITY SUPPLIERS

With both the gas and electricity markets open, most suppliers now offer their customers both gas and electricity. The majority of gas/electricity companies have become part of larger multi-utility companies, often operating internationally. The following list comprises a selection of some of the suppliers offering gas and electricity. Organisations in italics are subsidiaries of the companies listed in capital letters directly above.

ENGLAND, SCOTLAND AND WALES

CE ELECTRIC UK, W www.ce-electricuk.com
Northern Electric Distribution Ltd (NEDL), Manor House, Station Road, New Penshaw, Houghton-le-Spring DH4 7LA T 0845-070 7172
Yorkshire Electricity Distribution (YEDL), 161 Gelderd Road, Leeds LS1 1QZ T 0845-602 4454
CENTRICA PLC, Millstream, Maidenhead Road, Windsor, Berkshire SL4 5GD T 01753-494000 W www.centrica.com
British Gas/Scottish Gas, T 0845-070 9010 W www.house.co.uk
EDF ENERGY, 40 Grosvenor Place, Victoria, London SW1X 4EN T 020-7242 9050 W www.edfenergy.com
London Energy, 40 Grosvenor Place, Victoria, London SW1X 4EN T 0800-096 9000 W www.london-energy.com
Seeboard Energy, 40 Grosvenor Place, Victoria, London SW17 4EN T 0800-096 9696 W www.seeboard-energy.com
SWEB Energy, Osprey Road, Exeter EX2 7HZ T 0800-365000 W www.sweb-energy.com
Virgin Home Energy, Freepost LON14908, Exeter EX2 7BF T 0800-028 8269 W www.virginhome.co.uk
NPOWER, PO Box 93, Tyne House, Birchwood Drive, Peterlee SR8 2XX T 0800-389 2388 W www.npower.com
POWERGEN, PO Box 7750, Nottingham NG1 6WR T 0800-015 2029 W www.powergen.co.uk
SCOTTISH AND SOUTHERN ENERGY PLC, Inveralmond House, 200 Dunkeld Road, Perth PH1 3AQ W www.scottish-southern.co.uk
Scottish Hydro Electric, PO Box 7506, Perth PH1 3QR T 0845-300 2141 W www.hydro.co.uk
Southern Electric, PO Box 7506, Perth PH1 3QR T 0845-744 4555 W www.southern-electric.co.uk
SWALEC, PO Box 7506, Perth PH1 3QR T 0800-052 5252 W www.swalec.co.uk
SCOTTISHPOWER, Cathcart House, Cathcart Business Park, Spean Street, Glasgow G44 4BE T 0845-2700 700 W www.scottishpower.co.uk

NORTHERN IRELAND

VIRIDIAN GROUP PLC, 120 Malone Road, Belfast BT9 5HT T 028-9066 8416 W www.viridiangroup.co.uk
Energia, Energia House, 62 Newforge Lane, Belfast BT9 5NF T 028-9068 5900 W www.viridianenergia.co.uk
Northern Ireland Electricity, 120 Malone Road, Belfast BT9 5HT T 028-9066 1100 W www.nie.co.uk

REGULATION OF THE GAS AND ELECTRICITY INDUSTRIES

The Office of the Gas and Electricity Markets (Ofgem) regulates the gas and electricity industries in Great Britain. It was formed in 1999 by the merger of the Office of Gas Supply and the Office of Electricity Regulation. Ofgem's overriding aim is to protect and promote the interests of all gas and electricity customers by promoting competition and regulating monopolies. It is governed by an authority and its powers are provided for under the Gas Act 1986, the Electricity Act 1989 and the Utilities Act 2000.

NUCLEAR POWER

Nuclear reactors began to supply electricity to the national grid in 1956. It is generated at six magnox reactors, seven advanced gas-cooled reactors (AGRs) and one pressurised water reactor (PWR), Sizewell 'B' in Suffolk. In 1989 nuclear stations were withdrawn from privatisation. In 1996 Nuclear Electric Ltd and Scottish

Nuclear Ltd became operating subsidiaries of British Energy and the magnox stations were transferred to Nuclear Electric which became Magnox Electric, later part of British Nuclear Fuels Ltd (BNFL). In September 2002 the Government stepped in to provide a loan facility to British Energy, which was facing insolvency, and a major financial restructuring package was announced in November 2002. In March 2003 British Energy received formal approvals for loan standstill agreements from its creditors and the Government agreed to extend the loan facility until September 2004.

The UK Atomic Energy Authority (UKAEA) is responsible for the decommissioning of nuclear reactors and other nuclear facilities used in research and development. UKAEA is a non-departmental public body, funded mainly by the Department of Trade and Industry. UK Nirex, which was set up by the nuclear generating companies with the agreement of the Government, is responsible for the disposal of intermediate and some low-level nuclear waste. The Nuclear Safety Directorate of the Health and Safety Executive is the nuclear industry's regulator.

RENEWABLE SOURCES

Renewable sources of energy principally include biofuels, hydro, wind and solar. Renewable sources accounted for 3.23 million tonnes of oil equivalent of primary energy use in 2003; of this, about 2.57 million tonnes was used to generate electricity and 0.66 million tonnes to generate heat.

The Non-Fossil Fuel Obligation (NFFO) Renewables Orders have been the government's principal mechanism for developing renewable energy sources. NFFO Renewables Orders require the regional electricity companies to buy specified amounts of electricity from specified non-fossil fuel sources.

In January 2000 the government announced a target for renewables to supply 10 per cent of UK electricity by 2010, which would require about 10,000 megawatts of renewables to be installed. A new renewables obligation was introduced in England and Wales in April 2002 to give incentives to generators to supply progressively higher levels of renewable energy over time. These measures included:

- the exemption of renewable electricity sources from the Climate Change Levy
- the creation of a renewables support programme worth £250 million from 2002–5
- the creation of a strategic framework for a major expansion of offshore wind generation
- the formation of a new organisation within the government (Renewables UK) to help the industry grow and compete internationally

In July 2003 the DTI announced that the world's biggest wind farms will be built in three sites of the English coast (the Thames Estuary, the Wash on the east coast and from Morecambe Bay to north Wales), providing enough power for one in six British homes.

RENEWABLE ENERGY SOURCES 2003

	Percentages
Biofuels and wastes	87.3
Landfill gas	33.7
Sewage gas	5.1
Wood combustion	14.5
Waste combustion	14.9
Other biofuels	19.1
Hydro	8.3
Large-scale	8
Small-scale	0.3
Wind and wave	3.4
Geothermal and active solar heating	0.7
Total	100
Source: Department of Trade and Industry	

TRANSPORT

CIVIL AVIATION

Since the privatisation of British Airways in 1987, UK airlines have been operated entirely by the private sector. In 2004, total capacity of British airlines amounted to 46 billion tonne km, of which 34 billion tonne km was on scheduled services. In 2004 British airlines carried 118 million passengers, 86 million on scheduled services and 32 million on charter flights. Overall, passenger traffic grew by eight per cent. Traffic at the five main London airports grew by seven per cent over 2004 and regional airlines saw a growth of nine per cent, largely due to the expansion of 'no-frills' airlines. Leading British airlines include British Airways, Britannia Airways, BMI British Midland, Air 2000, My Travel, Thomas Cook Airlines, Monarch, Virgin Atlantic and easyJet. Irish airline Ryanair also operates frequent flights from Britain.

There are around 140 licensed civil aerodromes in Britain, with Heathrow and Gatwick handling the highest volume of passengers. BAA plc owns and operates the seven major airports: Heathrow, Gatwick, Stansted, Southampton, Glasgow, Edinburgh and Aberdeen, which between them handle about 65 per cent of air passengers and a high percentage of air cargo traffic in Britain. Other airports are controlled by local authorities or private companies.

The Civil Aviation Authority (CAA), an independent statutory body, is responsible for the regulation of UK airlines. This includes economic and airspace regulation, air safety, consumer protection and environmental research and consultancy. All commercial airline companies must be granted an Air Operator's Certificate, which is issued by the CAA to operators meeting the required safety standards. The CAA issues airport safety licences, which must be obtained by any airport used for public transport and training flights. All British-registered aircraft must be granted an airworthiness certificate, and the CAA issues professional licences to pilots, flight crew, ground engineers and air traffic controllers. The CAA also manages the Air Travel Organiser's Licence (ATOL), the UK's principal travel protection scheme. The CAA's costs are met entirely from charges on those whom it regulates; there is no direct government funding of the CAA's work.

The Transport Act, passed by Parliament on 29 November 2000, separated the CAA from its subsidiary, National Air Traffic Services (NATS), which provides air traffic control services to aircraft flying in UK airspace and over the eastern part of the North Atlantic. In the 2004–5 financial year a total of 2,200,665 flights used UK airspace, an increase of 4.8 per cent on 2003–4. In March 2001 the Airline Group, a consortium of seven UK airlines (British Airways, BMI British Midland, Virgin Atlantic, Britannia, Monarch, easyJet and My Travel), was selected by the government as its strategic partner for NATS. Financial restructuring of NATS was completed in March 2003 with additional equity investment of £65 million each from BAA and the government. The new structure enabled NATS to begin a ten-year £1 billion investment programme, to increase its flight handling capability to three million flights per annum by 2010. NATS is a public private partnership between the Airline Group, which holds 42 per cent of the shares; NATS staff, who hold 5 per cent; BAA, which holds 4 per cent, and the government, which holds 49 per cent and a golden share.

AIR PASSENGERS 2004*

ALL UK AIRPORTS: TOTAL	215,681,000
Aberdeen (BAA)	2,634,000
Barra (HIAL)†	9,000
Barrow-in-Furness	–
Belfast City	2,091,000
Belfast International	4,403,000
Benbecula (HIAL)†	30,000
Biggin Hill	1,000
Birmingham	8,797,000
Blackpool	266,000
Bournemouth	493,000
Bristol	4,603,000
Cambridge	3,000
Campbeltown (HIAL)†	8,000
Cardiff	1,873,000
Carlisle	–
City of Derry (Eglinton)	234,000
Coventry	462,000
Dundee	51,000
Durham Tees Valley	787,000
Edinburgh (BAA)	7,992,000
Exeter	614,000
Gatwick (BAA)	31,391,000
Glasgow (BAA)	8,557,000
Gloucestershire	–
Hawarden	29,000
Heathrow (BAA)	67,109,000
Humberside	531,000
Inverness (HIAL)†	520,000
Islay (HIAL)†	21,000
Isle of Man	762,000
Isles of Scilly (St Mary's)	141,000
Isles of Scilly (Tresco)	43,000
Kent International	101,000
Kirkwall (HIAL)†	102,000
Lands End (St Just)	26,000
Leeds Bradford	2,368,000
Lerwick (Tingwall)	2,000
Liverpool	3,352,000
London City	1,675,000
Luton	7,520,000
Lydd	4,000
Manchester	20,969,000
Metro London Heliport	–
Newcastle	4,708,000
Newquay	253,000
Norwich	444,000
Nottingham East Midlands International	4,375,000
Penzance Heliport	129,000
Plymouth	106,000
Prestwick	2,159,000
Scatsta	229,000
Sheffield City	–
Shoreham	4,000

Southampton (BAA)	1,531,000
Southend	3,000
Stansted (BAA)	20,907,000
Stornoway (HIAL)†	111,000
Sumburgh (HIAL)†	108,000
Swansea	18,000
Tiree (HIAL)†	6,000
Unst	–
Wick (HIAL)†	16,000
CHANNEL ISLANDS AIRPORTS: TOTAL	2,455,000
Alderney	74,000
Guernsey	900,000
Jersey	1,481,000

*All figures are rounded up to the nearest thousand, for airports where passengers numbers are less than 500, no figure is given.
†Highlands and Islands Airports Ltd (HIAL)
Source: Civil Aviation Authority

CAA, CAA House, 45–59 Kingsway, London WC2B 6TE
    T 020-7379 7311 W www.caa.co.uk
BAA PLC, 130 Wilton Road, London SW1V 1LQ
    T 020-7834 9449 W www.baa.co.uk

Heathrow Airport	T 0870-000 0123
Gatwick Airport	T 0870-000 2468
Stansted Airport	T 0870-000 0303
Glasgow Airport	T 0870-040 0008
Edinburgh Airport	T 0870-040 0007
Aberdeen Airport	T 0870-040 0006
Southampton Airport	T 0870-040 0009

BMI BRITISH MIDLAND, Donington Hall, Castle Donington, Derby DE74 2SB T 01332-854000 W www.flybmi.com
BRITISH AIRWAYS, PO Box 5619, Sudbury, Suffolk CO10 2PG
    T 0870-850 9850 W www.britishairways.com
EASYJET, London Luton Airport LU2 9LS T 0871-244 2366
    W www.easyjet.com
FIRST CHOICE AIRWAYS, Commonwealth House, Chicago Avenue, Manchester Airport M90 3DP T 0870-850 3999
    W www.firstchoice.co.uk
MONARCH, Prospect House, Prospect Way, London Luton Airport LU2 9NU T 01582-400000
    W www.monarch-airlines.com
MY TRAVEL, Parkway One, Parkway Business Centre, 300 Princess Road, Manchester M14 7QU T 0870-238 7701
    W www.mytravel.com
THOMAS COOK AIRLINES, Thomas Cook Business Park, Coningsby Road, Peterborough PE3 8XP T 0870-750 5711
    W www.thomascook.com
THOMSONFLY, London Luton Airport, Luton LU2 9ND
    T 0870–1900 737 W www.thomsonfly.com
VIRGIN ATLANTIC, Crawley Business Quarter, Manor Royal, West Sussex RH10 9NU T 0870-574 7747
    W www.virgin-atlantic.com

RAILWAYS

The railway network in Britain was developed by private companies in the 19th century. In 1948 the main railway companies were nationalised and were run by a public authority, the British Transport Commission. The Commission was replaced by the British Railways Board in 1963, operating as British Rail. On 1 April 1994, responsibility for managing the track and railway infrastructure passed to a newly formed company, Railtrack plc. In October 2001 Railtrack was put into administration under the Railways Act 1993 and Ernst

and Young was appointed as administrator. In October 2002 Railtrack was taken out of administration and replaced by the not-for-profit company Network Rail. The British Railways Board continued as operator of all train services until 1996–7 when they were sold or franchised to the private sector.

The Strategic Rail Authority (SRA) was created to provide strategic leadership to the rail industry and formally came into being on 1 February 2001 following the passing of the Transport Act 2000. In January 2002 it published its first Strategic Plan, setting out the strategic priorities for Britain's railways over the next ten years. In addition to its coordinating role, the SRA was responsible for allocating government funding to the railways and awarding and monitoring the franchises for operating rail services.

On 15 July 2004 the Secretary of State for Transport announced a new structure for the rail industry in the white paper *The Future of Rail*. These proposals were implemented under the Railways Act 2005, which abolished the Strategic Rail Authority, passing most of its functions to the Department for Transport; established the Rail Passengers Council (RPC) as a single national body, dissolving the regional committees; and gave devolved governments in Scotland and Wales more say in decisions at a local level. In addition, responsibility for railway safety regulation was transferred to the Office of Rail Regulation from the Health and Safety Executive.

OFFICE OF RAIL REGULATION (ORR)
The Office of Rail Regulation (ORR) was established on 5 July 2004 by the Railways and Transport Safety Act 2003, replacing the Office of the Rail Regulator. As the railway industry's economic and safety regulator, the Office's principal function is to regulate Network Rail's stewardship of the national network. ORR also licenses operators of railway assets, approves agreements for access by operators to track, stations and light maintenance depots, and enforces domestic competition law. ORR is led by a board appointed by the Secretary of State for Transport, under the chairmanship of Chris Bolt. Mr Bolt also fulfils the role of International Rail Regulator (IRR), a statutory office separate from the ORR, which licenses the operation of certain international rail services in the European Economic Area and access to railway infrastructure in Great Britain for the purpose of operating international services.

SERVICES
For privatisation, under the Railways Act 1993, domestic passenger services were divided into 25 train operating units, which were franchised to private sector operators via a competitive tendering process. The train operators formed the Association of Train Operating Companies (ATOC) to act as the official voice of the passenger rail industry and provide its members with a range of services enabling them to comply with conditions imposed on them through their franchise agreements and operating licences.

As at June 2005 there were 27 train operating companies (TOCs): Arriva Trains Wales; c2c Rail; Central Trains; Chiltern Railways; Eurostar; First Great Western; First Great Western Link; Gatwick Express; Great North Eastern Railway (GNER); Heathrow Express; Hull Trains; Island Line (Isle of Wight); MerseyRail Electrics; Midland Mainline; Northern Rail; One Railway; One Stansted Express; ScotRail; Silverlink Trains; South Eastern Trains;

South West Trains; Southern; Thameslink; TransPennine Express; Virgin Trains; WAGN and Wessex Trains.

Network Rail publishes a national timetable which contains details of rail services operated over the network, coastal shipping information and connections with Ireland, the Isle of Man, the Isle of Wight, the Channel Islands and some European destinations.

The national rail enquiries service offers information about train times and fares for any part of the country:

NATIONAL RAIL ENQUIRIES T 08457-484950
  W www.nationalrail.co.uk
TRANSPORT FOR LONDON T 020-7941 4500
  W www.tfl.gov.uk
EUROSTAR T 08705-186186 W www.eurostar.com

RAIL PASSENGERS' COUNCIL (RPC)
Rail Users' Consultative Committees (RUCCs) were set up under the Railways Act 1993 to protect the interests of users of the services and facilities provided on Britain's rail network. The Transport Act 2000 changed their name to Rail Passenger Committees (RPCs) and brought the committees under the overall sponsorship of the Strategic Rail Authority. There were eight RPCs nationwide, one for each of the six English regions and one each for Scotland and Wales. Under the Railways Act 2005, the eight regional committees were disbanded in June 2005 and their functions and duties transferred to the Rail Passengers' Council (RPC), a single national consumer body for rail.

The London Transport Users' Committee, sponsored by the London Assembly, represents users of buses, the Underground and rail services in and around London, including Eurostar and Heathrow Express, Croydon Tramlink and the Docklands Light Railway. The interests of pedestrians, cyclists and motorists are also represented, as are those of taxi users.

FREIGHT
On privatisation, British Rail's bulk freight haulage companies and Rail Express Systems, which carried Royal Mail traffic, were sold to English, Welsh and Scottish Railways (EWS), which also purchased Railfreight Distribution (international freight) in 1997. In 2003–4 18.9 billion-tonne-kilometres of freight was transported by EWS and other freight operating companies.

NETWORK RAIL
Network Rail owns and maintains 33,800 km (21,000 miles) of track, owns and provides access to 2,500 stations and operates and maintains more than 9,000 level crossings and 40,000 bridges and tunnels. In addition to providing the timetables for the passenger and freight operators Network Rail is also responsible for all the signalling and electrical control equipment needed to operate the rail network.

Network Rail is run as a commercial business but has members instead of shareholders. The members have similar rights to those of shareholders in a public company except they do not receive dividends or share capital and thereby having no financial or economic interest in Network Rail. All of Network Rail's profits are reinvested into maintaining and upgrading the rail infrastructure.

ASSOCIATION OF TRAIN OPERATING COMPANIES (ATOC), 3rd Floor, 40 Bernard Street, London WC1N 1BY
  T 020-7841 8000 W www.atoc.org
OFFICE OF RAIL REGULATION, 1 Waterhouse Square, 138–142 Holborn, London EC1N 2TQ T 020-7282 2000
  W www.rail-reg.gov.uk
  Chairman/International Rail Regulator, Chris Bolt
NETWORK RAIL, 40 Melton Street, London NW1 2EE
  T 020-7557 8000 W www.networkrail.co.uk
RAIL PASSENGERS COUNCIL (RPC), Whittles House, 14 Pentonville Road, London N1 9HF T 020-7713 2700
  W www.railpassengers.org.uk

RAIL SAFETY
The Railways (Safety Case) Regulations 2000 came into force on 31 December 2000 and transferred responsibility for safety cases from Railtrack to HM Railway Inspectorate, part of the Health and Safety Executive (HSE). The regulations demand that rail operators such as Network Rail and London Underground, or the station and train operators, must prepare a comprehensive safety case and have it accepted by HSE before being allowed to operate their business. The Office of Rail Regulation will not grant a licence to a railway operator without an accepted safety case or an exemption being in place.

Amendments to railway safety case regulations were announced in March 2003 and came into force on 1 April 2003. The requirement for infrastructure controllers to obtain an independent assessment of safety cases in addition to the Health and Safety Executive's acceptance was removed and the requirement to obtain annual independent health and safety audits of train and station operations was transferred from HSE to individual operators. The Rail Safety and Standards Board (RSSB) was established on 1 April 2003 as a new industry body to provide health and safety leadership for the railway industry.

ACCIDENTS ON RAILWAYS

	2002–3	2003–4
Train accidents: total	1,421	1,259
Persons killed: total	10	10
Passengers	6	0
Railway employees	1	2
Others	3	8
Persons injured: total	166	54
Passengers	128	25
Railway staff	23	11
Others	15	18

ACCIDENTS THROUGH MOVEMENT OF RAILWAY VEHICLES

Persons killed	32	19
Persons injured	908	911

ACCIDENTS ON RAILWAY PREMISES

Persons killed	7	10
Passengers	3	6
Railway staff	3	3
Others	1	1
Persons injured	3,984	3,911

TRESPASSERS AND SUICIDES

Persons killed	256	246
Persons injured	137	132

Source: Health and Safety Executive – *Annual Report on Railway Safety 2003–4*

OTHER RAIL SYSTEMS

Responsibility for the London Underground passed from the government to the Mayor and Transport for London on 15 July 2003, with a public-private partnership already in place. Plans for a public-private partnership (PPP) for London Underground were pushed through by the government in February 2002 despite opposition from the Mayor of London and a range of transport organisations. Under the PPP, long-term contracts with private companies were estimated to enable around £16 billion to be invested in renewing and upgrading the Underground's infrastructure over 15 years. Responsibility for stations, trains, operations, signalling and safety remains in the public sector. In 2003–4 there were 948 million passenger journeys on the London Underground, an increase of 0.6 per cent on the previous year.

Britain has seven other light rail systems: Altram Manchester Metrolink, Croydon Tramlink, Docklands Light Railway (DLR), Nexus (Tyne and Wear Metro), Nottingham Express Transit (NET), Stagecoach Supertram (Sheffield) and West Midland Metro. Most recently opened was the Nottingham Express Transit in March 2004.

Light rail and metro systems in Great Britain contributed to the growth in public transport, with 142 million passenger journeys in 2003–4, an increase of 18 per cent on the 120 million passenger journeys made in 2000–1. The government's 10-year Transport Plan target is to double light rail use in England (measured by number of passenger journeys) by 2010 from 2000 levels.

THE CHANNEL TUNNEL

The earliest recorded scheme for a submarine transport connection between Britain and France was in 1802. Tunnelling began simultaneously on both sides of the Channel three times: in 1881, in the early 1970s, and on 1 December 1987, when construction workers bored the first of the three tunnels which form the Channel Tunnel. Engineers 'holed through' the first tunnel (the service tunnel) on 1 December 1990 and tunnelling was completed in June 1991. The tunnel was officially inaugurated by The Queen and President Mitterrand of France on 6 May 1994.

The submarine link comprises two rail tunnels, each carrying trains in one direction, which measure 7.6 m (24.93 ft) in diameter. Between them lies a smaller service tunnel, measuring 4.8 m (15.75 ft) in diameter. The service tunnel is linked to the rail tunnels by 130 cross-passages for maintenance and safety purposes. The tunnels are 50 km (31 miles) long, 38 km (24 miles) of which is under the seabed at an average depth of 40 m (132 ft). The rail terminals are situated at Folkestone and Calais, and the tunnels go underground at Shakespeare Cliff, Dover, and Sangatte, west of Calais.

Eurostar is the high-speed passenger train service connecting London with Paris in three hours and Brussels in two hours 40 minutes, via the Channel Tunnel. Some trains stop en route at Ashford (Kent) and Calais, Disneyland Paris and Lille in France.

RAIL LINKS

The route for the British Channel Tunnel Rail Link will run from Folkestone to a new terminal at St Pancras station, London, with new intermediate stations at Ebbsfleet, Kent, and Stratford, east London; at present services run into a terminal at Waterloo station, London.

Construction of the rail link is being financed by the private sector with a substantial government contribution.

A private sector consortium, London and Continental Railways Ltd (LCR), is responsible for the design, construction and ownership of the rail link, and comprises Union Railways and the UK operator of Eurostar. Construction was expected to be completed in 2003, but on 28 January 1998 LCR informed the government that it was unable to fulfil its obligations. On 3 June 1998 the government announced a new funding agreement with LCR. The rail link will be constructed in two phases: phase one, from the Channel Tunnel to Fawkham Junction, North Kent, began in October 1998 and opened to fare-paying passengers on 28 September 2003; phase two, from Southfleet Junction to St Pancras, is due to be completed in 2007. Infrastructure developments in France have been completed and high-speed trains run from Calais to Paris and from Lille to the south of France.

ROADS

HIGHWAY AUTHORITIES

The powers and responsibilities of highway authorities in England and Wales are set out in the Highways Act 1980; for Scotland there is separate legislation.

Responsibility for trunk road motorways and other trunk roads in Great Britain rests in England with the Secretary of State for Transport, in Scotland with the Scottish Executive, and in Wales with the Welsh Assembly. The costs of construction, improvement and maintenance are paid for by central government in England and by the Welsh Assembly in Wales. The highway authority for non-trunk roads in England, Wales and Scotland is, in general, the local authority in whose area the roads lie. With the establishment of the Greater London Authority in July 2000, Transport for London became the highway authority for roads in London.

In Northern Ireland the Department of Regional Development is the statutory road authority responsible for public roads and their maintenance and construction; the Roads Service executive agency carries out these functions on behalf of the Department.

FINANCE

In England all aspects of trunk road and motorway funding are provided directly by the government to the Highways Agency which operates, maintains and improves a network of motorways and trunk roads, 7,754 km (4,818 miles) long, on behalf of the Secretary of State. The length of the network that the Highways Agency is responsible for has been decreasing in recent years due to a policy of de-trunking, which returns responsibility for non-core roads to local authorities. For the financial year 2005–6 the Highways Agency planned expenditure is £2 billion, of this £885 million is for maintenance, £610 million is for major improvements, including revenue support for private investment, and £327 million for smaller improvements and traffic management technology.

Government support for local authority capital expenditure on roads and other transport infrastructure is provided through grant and credit approvals as part of the Local Transport Plan (LTP). Local Authorities bid for resources on the basis of a five-year programme built around delivering integrated transport strategies. As well as covering the structural maintenance of local roads and the construction of major new road schemes, LTP funding also includes smaller-scale safety and traffic management measures with associated improvements for public transport, cyclists and pedestrians.

For the financial year 2005–6, planned expenditure in the form of LTP funding for local authorities is £1.6 billion. This includes £552 million for small-scale integrated transport measures, £660 million for road maintenance and £407 million for new and existing major projects.

Total expenditure by the Welsh Assembly on trunk roads, motorways and transport services (including grants to local authorities) in 2004–5 was £300.4 million. Planned expenditure for 2005–6 is £369.9 million.

Until 1999 the Scottish Office received a block vote from Parliament and the Secretary of State for Scotland determined how much was spent on roads. Since 1 July 1999 all decisions on transport expenditure have been devolved to the Scottish Executive. Total planned expenditure on motorways and trunk roads in Scotland during 2004–5 including depreciation and cost of capital charge is £721 million. Planned expenditure for 2005–6 is £745.03 million.

In Northern Ireland total expenditure by the Roads Service on trunk roads and motorways for 2004–5 was £92.9 million and £65.1 million has been allocated for expenditure in 2005–6.

The Transport Act 2000 gave English and Welsh local authorities (outside London) powers to introduce road-user charging or workplace parking levy schemes. The Act requires that the net revenue raised is used to improve local transport services and facilities for at least ten years. The aim is to reduce congestion and encourage greater use of alternative modes of transport. Schemes developed by local authorities require government approval. The government's Ten Year Plan for Transport assumes that eight large road user charging schemes and 12 large workplace parking levy schemes will be developed by 2010. The UK's first toll road, the M6 Toll, opened in December 2003 and runs for 43.5 km (27 miles) around Birmingham from junction 3a to junction 11a on the M6.

Charging schemes in London are allowed under the 1999 Greater London Authority Act. The Central London Congestion Charge Scheme began on 17 February 2003.

TARGETED PROGRAMME OF IMPROVEMENTS

The Targeted Programme of Improvements (TPI) constitutes the Highway Agency's investment programme in the trunk road and motorway networks. The programme comprises a number of schemes, each costing more than £5 million, funded either conventionally or by public-private partnerships. When announced in 1998 as part of *A New Deal for Trunk Roads in England* it consisted of 37 schemes. Since then a further 41 schemes have been added, with one scheme becoming the responsibility of Transport for London, making a current total of 78 TPI schemes.

ROAD LENGTHS 2004
kilometres

	England	Wales	Scotland	Great Britain
Motorways	2,995	141	386	3,523
Rural major roads	22,508	3,631	9,392	35,530
Urban major roads	9,692	542	904	11,138
Rural minor roads	150,821	22,112	34,632	207,565
Urban minor roads	111,764	6,753	11,401	129,917
Total	297,779	33,179	56,715	387,674

Source: Department for Transport

ROAD USE

ROAD TRAFFIC BY TYPE OF VEHICLE (GREAT BRITAIN) 2004
Million vehicle kilometres

All motor vehicles	498,600
Cars and taxis	398,100
Two-wheeled motor vehicles	5,200
Buses and coaches	5,200
Light vans	60,800
Other goods vehicles	29,400
Pedal cycles	3,900

Source: Department for Transport

FREIGHT TRANSPORT BY ROAD (GREAT BRITAIN) 2003

GOODS MOVED
By vehicles over 3.5 tonnes (billion tonne kilometres)

All modes	151.7
Own account	37.4
Public haulage	114.3

By gross weight of vehicle (billion tonne kilometres)

All weights	151.7
Not over 25 tonnes	17.3
Over 25 tonnes	134.4

GOODS LIFTED
By vehicles over 3.5 tonnes (million tonnes)

All modes	1,643
Own account	590
Public haulage	1,053

By gross weight of vehicle (million tonnes)

All weights	1,643
Not over 25 tonnes	265
Over 25 tonnes	1,378

Source: Department for Transport

BUSES

Nearly all bus and coach services in Great Britain are provided by private sector companies. The Transport Act 2000 outlines a 10-year transport plan intended to promote bus use, through agreements between local authorities and bus operators, and to improve the standard and efficiency of services. The 10-year plan sets targets for bus patronage and reliability of services. There are a number of ways in which the government supports bus services:

– Bus Service Operators Grant (BSOG) is paid directly to bus operators and reimburses 80 per cent of fuel duty and 100 per cent of duty for some 'clean' fuels
– Local authorities outside London have a duty to secure socially necessary bus services not provided commercially. Services are tendered and let to commercial operators in return for payment from the local authority
– Rural Bus Challenge supports innovative and flexible rural transport solutions, such as taxi-bus services, and awarded £20 million to 42 projects in 2003
– Rural Bus subsidy grant was £48.5 million in 2003–4 and supported some 21,000 services
– Urban Bus Challenge aims to improve transport in deprived urban areas and awarded £19.6 million to 40 projects in 2003

Since June 2001 it has been a statutory minimum requirement for all local authorities to provide at least hal fares and a free bus pass to pensioners and disabled people in the area. Local authorities recompense operators for the reduced fare revenue.

In London, Transport for London (TfL) has overall responsibility for setting routes, service standards and fares for the bus network. Almost all routes are competitively tendered to commercial operators. TfL budget for buses in 2004–5 is £229 million, in addition London also benefits from a share of the funding schemes listed above.

In Northern Ireland, passenger transport services are provided by Ulsterbus Limited and Citybus Limited, two wholly owned subsidiaries of the Northern Ireland Transport Holding Company. Along with Northern Ireland Railways, Ulsterbus and Citybus operate under the brand name of Translink and are publicly owned. Ulsterbus is responsible for virtually all bus services in Northern Ireland except Belfast city services which are operated by Citybus.

BUSES AND COACHES (GREAT BRITAIN) 2002–3

Vehicle kilometres (millions)	4,049
Local bus services passenger journeys (millions)	4,452
England	3,897
Scotland	445
Wales	109
Passenger receipts (£ million)	4,800

Source: Department for Transport

TAXIS

A taxi is a public transport vehicle with fewer than nine passenger seats, which is licenced to 'ply for hire'. This distinguishes taxis from private hire vehicles which must be booked in advance through an operator.

In London, taxis and their drivers are licensed by the Public Carriage Office (PCO) which is part of Transport for London (TfL). At the end of December 2004 there were 20,750 licensed taxis in London.

HOUSEHOLD EXPENDITURE ON TRANSPORT 2002–3
£ per week

Motoring	
Cars, vans and motorcycle purchase	25.57
Repairs, servicing, spares and accessories	6.79
Motor vehicle insurance and taxation	10.78
Petrol, diesels and other oils	14.83
Other motoring costs	2.03
All motoring expenditure	60.00
Fares and other travel costs	
Rail and tube fares	1.57
Bus and coach fares	1.28
Taxi, air and other travel costs*	4.86
All fares and other travel costs†	8.81

*includes combined fares
†includes expenditure on bicycles and boats (purchases and repairs)

Source: ONS – *Social Trends 2005* (Crown copyright)

ROAD SAFETY

In March 2000, the government published a new road safety strategy, *Tomorrow's Roads – Safer for Everyone,* which set new casualty reduction targets for 2010. The new targets include a 40 per cent reduction in the overall number of people killed or seriously injured in road accidents, a 50 per cent reduction in the number of children killed or seriously injured and a 10 per cent reduction in the slight casualty rate, all compared with the average for 1994–8.

There were 280,840 reported casualties on roads in Great Britain in 2004, 3 per cent less than in 2003. Road traffic levels were estimated to be 1.7 per cent higher than in 2003. Child casualties fell by 3 per cent with 166 child fatalities, 3 per cent less than in 2003. Car user casualties decreased by 2 per cent on the 2003 level to 183,858 and fatalities were 6 per cent lower. Pedestrian casualties were 34,881 in 2004, 4 per cent less than 2003, while pedestrian deaths decreased by 13 per cent to 671. Compared to 2003, pedal cyclist casualties fell by 2 per cent to 16,648, although the number of pedal cyclists killed on British roads increased by 18 per cent from 114 to 134.

ROAD ACCIDENT CASUALTIES 2004

	Fatal	Serious	Slight	All Severities
England	2,714	27,057	218,991	248,762
Wales	201	1,336	12,150	13,687
Scotland	306	2,737	15,348	18,391
Great Britain	3,221	31,130	246,489	280,840

	Killed	Injured
1965	7,952	389,985
1970	7,499	355,869
1975	6,366	318,584
1980	6,010	323,000
1985	5,165	312,359
1990	5,217	335,924
1995	3,621	306,885
1996	3,598	316,704
1997	3,599	323,945
1998	3,421	321,791
1999	3,423	316,887
2000	3,409	316,872
2001	3,450	313,309
2002	3,431	302,605
2003	3,508	290,607
2004	3,221	280,840

Source: Department for Transport

DRIVING LICENCES

It is necessary to hold a valid full licence in order to drive unaccompanied on public roads in the UK. Learner drivers must obtain a provisional driving licence before starting to learn to drive and must then pass theory and practical tests to obtain a full driving licence.

There are separate tests for driving motorcycles, cars, passenger-carrying vehicles (PCVs) and large goods vehicles (LGVs). Drivers must hold full car entitlement before they can apply for PCV or LGV entitlements.

The Driver and Vehicle Licensing Agency (DVLA) ceased the issue of paper licences in March 2000, however, those currently in circulation will remain valid until they expire or the details on them change. The photocard driving licence was introduced to comply with the second EC directive on driving licences. This requires a photograph of the driver to be included on all UK licences issued from July 2001.

To apply for a first photocard driving licence, individuals are required to complete the forms *Application for a Driving Licence* (D1) and *Application for a Photocard*

Driving Licence (D750). Application forms are available from post offices.

The minimum age for driving motor cars, light goods vehicles up to 3.5 tonnes and motorcycles is 17 (moped, 16). Since June 1997, drivers who collect six or more penalty points within two years of qualifying lose their licence and are required to take another test. A leaflet, *What You Need to Know About Driving Licences* (form D100), is available from post offices.

The DVLA is responsible for issuing driving licences, registering and licensing vehicles, and collecting excise duty in Great Britain. In Northern Ireland the Driver and Vehicle Licensing Northern Ireland (DVLNI) has similar responsibilities.

DRIVING LICENCE FEES *as at 1 April 2005*

First provisional licence	
Car, motorcycle or moped	£38.00
Bus or lorry	Free
Changing a car, motorcycle or moped provisional licence to a full licence	
If first provisional licence issued before 1 March 2004	£9.00
If first provisional licence issued after 1 March 2004	Free
Changing a bus or lorry provisional licence to a full licence	Free
After disqualification until passing re-test	Free
Licence renewal	
At age 70 and over	Free
For medical reasons	Free
Bus or lorry	Free
After disqualification	£50.00
After disqualification for some drink driving offences*	£75.00
After revocation	£38.00
Replacing a lost or stolen licence	£19.00
Adding an entitlement to a full licence	Free
Removing expired endorsements	£19.00
Exchanging	
a paper licence for a photocard licence	£19.00
for a full Northern Ireland licence	Free
for a full EC/EEA or other foreign licence (including Channel Islands and Isle of Man)	£38.00
Change of name or address (existing licence must be surrendered)	Free

*For an alcohol-related offence where the DVLA needed to arrange medical enquiries.

DRIVING TESTS

The Driving Standards Agency is responsible for carrying out driving tests and approving driving instructors in Great Britain. In Northern Ireland the Driver and Vehicle Testing Agency (Northern Ireland) is responsible for testing drivers and vehicles.

DRIVING TESTS TAKEN/PERCENTAGE PASSED
April 2004–March 2005

Type of Test	Number Taken	Percentage Passed
Practical Tests		
Car	1,675,822	42
Motorcycle	78,241	64
Large goods vehicle	79,805	46
Passenger carrying vehicle	12,300	44

Theory Tests		
Car	1,269,698	64
Motorcycle	69,244	86
Large goods vehicle	46,611	70
Passenger carrying vehicle	11,219	63

The theory and practical driving tests can be booked by postal application, online at www.dsa.gov.uk or by telephoning 0870-010 1372.

DRIVING TEST FEES (WEEKDAY RATE/EVENING AND SATURDAY RATE)
effective from 8 December 2004

Theory test	£20.50
Practical tests:	
For cars	£42.00/£51.00
For motorcycles	£51.00/£60.00
For lorries, buses	£80.00/£98.00
Extended test for cars (after disqualification)	£84.00/£102.00
Extended test for motorcycles (after disqualification)	£102.00/£120.00

Further information is available on the DSA website: www.dsa.gov.uk

VEHICLE LICENCES

Registration and first licensing of vehicles is through local offices of the Driver and Vehicle Licensing Agency in Swansea. Local facilities for relicensing are available at any post office which deals with vehicle licensing. Applicants will need to take their vehicle registration document; if this is not available the applicant must complete form V62 which is held at post offices. Postal applications can be made to the post offices shown in the V100 booklet, available at any post office. This V100 also provides guidance on registering and licensing vehicles.

Details of the present duties chargeable on motor vehicles are available at post offices and Local Offices. The Vehicle Excise and Registration Act 1994 provides *inter alia* that any vehicle kept on a public road but not used on roads is chargeable to excise duty as if it were in use. All non-commercial vehicles constructed before 1 January 1973 are exempt from vehicle excise duty. Any vehicle licensed on or after 31 January 1998, not in use and not kept on public roads must be registered as SORN (Statutory Off Road Notification) to be exempted from vehicle excise duty. From 1 January 2004 the registered keeper of a vehicle remains responsible for licensing a vehicle or making a SORN declaration until that liability is formally transferred to a new keeper.

MOTOR VEHICLES CURRENTLY LICENSED BY BODY TYPE 2004 (GREAT BRITAIN)

Thousands	
All cars	27,028
Taxis (black cabs only)	41
Motorcycles	1,191
Three wheelers	18
Light goods vehicles	2,581
Goods vehicles	663
Buses and coaches	178
Agricultural vehicles	321
Other vehicles	238
Total	32,529

Source: Department for Transport

VEHICLE EXCISE DUTY RATES *from 1 March 2005*
PRIVATE/LIGHT GOOD VEHICLES REGISTERED
BEFORE 1 MARCH 2001

Cars, taxis, light vans (not over 3,500 kg), etc	Twelve Months £	Six Months £
Under 1,549 cc	110.00	60.50
Over 1,549 cc	170.00	93.50
Motorcycles (with or without sidecar)		
Not over 150 cc	15.00	–
151–400 cc	30.00	–
401–600 cc	45.00	–
All other motorcycles	60.00	33.00

	Twelve Months £	Six Months £
Tricycles		
Not over 150 cc	15.00	–
All others	60.00	33.00
Buses* (excluding driver)		
Seating 9–16 persons	165.00 (165.00)	90.75 (90.75)
Seating 17–35 persons	220.00 (165.00)	121.00 (90.75)
Seating 36–60 persons	330.00 (165.00)	181.50 (90.75)
Seating 61+ persons	500.00 (165.00)	275.00 (90.75)

* Figures in parentheses refer to reduced pollution vehicles.

PRIVATE VEHICLES REGISTERED ON OR AFTER 1 MARCH 2001

Band	CO_2 Emissions (g/km)	Diesel Car 12 month rate £	6 month rate £	Petrol Car 12 month rate £	6 month rate £	Alternative Fuel Car 12 month rate £	6 month rate £
A	Up to 100	75.00	41.25	65.00	35.75	55.00	30.25
B	101–120	85.00	46.75	75.00	41.25	65.00	35.75
C	121–150	115.00	63.25	105.00	57.75	95.00	52.25
D	151–165	135.00	74.25	125.00	68.75	115.00	63.25
E	166–185	160.00	88.00	150.00	82.50	140.00	77.00
F	Over 185	170.00	93.50	165.00	90.75	160.00	88.00

LIGHT GOODS VEHICLES (NOT OVER 3,500 KG)
REGISTERED ON OR AFTER 1 MARCH 2001

	12 month rate £	6 month rate £
All vehicles	165.00	90.75

MOT TESTING

Cars, motorcycles, motor caravans, light goods and dual-purpose vehicles more than three years old must be covered by a current MOT test certificate. However, some vehicles i.e. minibuses may require a certificate at one year old. All certificates must be renewed annually. The MOT testing scheme is administered by the Vehicle and Operator Services Agency (VOSA) on behalf of the Secretary of State for Transport.

A fee is payable to MOT testing stations, which must be authorised to carry out tests. The maximum fees, which are prescribed by regulations as at 1 August 2005, are:

For cars and light vans	£44.15	
For solo motorcycles	£23.80	
For motorcycle combinations	£30.40	
For three-wheeled vehicles	£30.40	
Motor caravans	£44.15	
Dual purpose vehicles	£44.15	
Public service vehicles (up to 8 seats)	£44.15	
Ambulances and taxis	£44.15	
Private passenger vehicles and ambulances with:		
9–12 passenger seats	£46.15	£51.55†
13–16 passenger seats	£47.95	£64.85†
over 16 passenger seats	£65.00	£100.40†
Light goods vehicles (3,000–3,500 kg)	£47.20	

† Including seatbelt installation check

SHIPPING AND PORTS

Since earliest times sea trade has played a central role in Britain's economy. By the 17th century Britain had built up a substantial merchant fleet and by the early 20th century it dominated the world shipping industry. Until the late 1990s the size and tonnage of the UK-registered trading fleet had been steadily declining. In December 1998 the government published *British Shipping: Charting a New Course*, which outlined strategies to promote the long-term interests of British shipping. By the end of 2004 the number of ships in the UK fleet had increased by 58 per cent whilst tonnage more than tripled; and the UK-flagged merchant fleet now constitutes over 1.5 per cent of the world fleet.

Freight is carried by liner and bulk services, almost all scheduled liner services being containerised. About 95 per cent by weight of Britain's overseas trade is carried by sea; this amounts to 75 per cent of its total value. Passengers and vehicles are carried by roll-on, roll-off ferries, hovercraft, hydrofoils and high-speed catamarans. There were about 50 million ferry passengers a year in 2003, of whom 27 million travelled internationally. The leading British operators of passenger services are P&O Ferries and Stena Line (which has a Swedish parent company).

Lloyd's of London provides the most comprehensive shipping intelligence service in the world. *Lloyd's Shipping Index*, published daily, lists some 25,000 ocean-going vessels and gives the latest known report of each.

PORTS

There are more than 650 ports in Great Britain for which statutory harbour powers have been granted. Of these about 100 are commercially significant ports. In 2004 the biggest ports in terms of tonnage of freight traffic were Grimsby and Immingham, Tees and Hartlepool, London, Milford Haven, Southampton, Forth, Liverpool, Sullom Voe, Felixstowe and Dover. Belfast is the principal freight port in Northern Ireland.

Broadly speaking, ports are owned and operated by private companies, local authorities or trusts. The largest operator is Associated British Ports which owns 21 ports. Total freight traffic through UK ports in 2003 amounted to 556 million tonnes, a decrease of 0.35 per cent on the previous year's figure of 558 million tonnes. Provisional total freight traffic for 2004 is 572 million tonnes, an increase of 3 per cent on 2003.

MARINE SAFETY

The Maritime and Coastguard Agency (MCA) is an executive agency of the Department for Transport. Working closely with the shipping industry and the public its aims are to:
– reduce accidents and accident related deaths within UK search and rescue waters and coastline
– reduce accidents and accident related deaths from UK registered merchant ships and fishing vessels
– reduce the number of incidents of pollution from shipping activities in the UK pollution control zone

HM Coastguard maintains a 24-hour search and rescue response and co-ordination capability for the whole of the UK coast and the internationally agreed search and rescue region. HM Coastguard is responsible for mobilising and organising resources in response to people in distress at sea, or at risk of injury or death on the UK's cliffs or shoreline. There are about 560 full-time Coastguard Officers and a further 3,100 Auxiliary Coastguards. Each year HM Coastguard responds to around 13,000 incidents, of which 7,500 are accidents where search and rescue resources are deployed.

Locations hazardous to shipping in coastal waters are marked by lighthouses and other lights and buoys. The lighthouse authorities are the Corporation of Trinity House (for England, Wales and the Channel Islands), the Northern Lighthouse Board (for Scotland and the Isle of Man), and the Commissioners of Irish Lights (for Northern Ireland and the Republic of Ireland). Trinity House maintains 71 lighthouses, 11 major floating aids to navigation, 412 buoys, 19 beacons and 7 DGPS (Differential Positioning System) beacons*. The Northern Lighthouse Board maintains 210 lighthouses and 144 buoys; and Irish Lights 2 light floats, 2 LANBYs (large navigational buoys), 80 lighthouses and 146 buoys.

Harbour authorities are responsible for pilotage within their harbour areas; and the Ports Act 1991 provides for the transfer of lights and buoys to harbour authorities where these are used for mainly local navigation.

*DGPS is a satellite-based navigation system

UK-OWNED VESSELS OF 100 GROSS TONS AND OVER
as at end 2003

Type of vessel	No.	Gross tonnage
Tankers	156	3,832,000
Bulk carriers	49	1,915,000
Specialised carriers	16	83,000
Fully cellular container	92	3,552,000
Ro-Ro (passenger & cargo)	162	1,603,000
Other general cargo	205	906,000
Passenger	53	1,101,000
Miscellaneous (fish processing and catching vessels, tugs, dredgers etc.)	1,209	1,830,000
Total	1,942	14,822,000

Source: Department for Transport

UK INTERNATIONAL PASSENGER MOVEMENTS BY SEA 2003*

All passenger movements	27,245,700
Short sea journeys – Irish Republic and European continent	26,523,000
Long sea journeys – USA, Canada, Australia, New Zealand, Africa, Caribbean and rest of the world†	24,700
Pleasure cruises†	698,000

* Passengers are included at both departure and arrival if their journeys begin and end at a UK seaport
† Provisional figures
Source: Department for Transport

MARINECALL WEATHER FORECAST SERVICE

Marinecall provides information for coastal, inshore and offshore UK sea areas by telephone. Forecasts include gale and strong wind warnings, the general situation, wind speed and direction, probability and strength of gusts, developing weather conditions, visibility and sea state and can vary in format from current observations to six-hour summaries, to 48-hour and five-day forecasts.

	By Phone 6-hour coastal location and 5-day outlook forecasts	By Fax 6-hour coastal location and 48-hour outlook forecasts
COASTAL/INSHORE AREA	09014-737 4+	09065-300 2+
National inshore waters (3–5 day outlook only)	60	–
Cape Wrath – Rattray Head	61	51
Rattray Head – Berwick	62	52
Berwick – Whitby	63	53
Whitby – The Wash	64	54
The Wash – North Foreland	65	55
North Foreland – Selsey Bill	66	56
Selsey Bill – Lyme Regis	67	57
Lyme Regis – Hartland Point	68	58
Hartland Point – St David's Head	69	59
St David's Head – Colwyn Bay	70	60
Colwyn Bay – Mull of Galloway	71	61
Mull of Galloway – Mull of Kintyre	72	62
Mull of Kintyre – Ardnamurchan	73	63
Ardnamurchan – Cape Wrath*	74	64
Lough Foyle – Carlingford Lough*	75	65
Channel Islands*	76	–
OFFSHORE AREA		
English Channel	41	70
Southern North Sea	42	71
Irish Sea	43	73
Biscay	44	74
North-west Scotland	45	75

* Localised 6-hour forecasts are unavailable for these areas.
Based upon calls from a BT landline. Marinecall by telephone is charged at 60p per minute. Marinecall by fax is charged at £1.50 per minute.

UK SHIPPING FORECAST AREAS

Weather bulletins for shipping are broadcast daily on BBC Radio 4 at the following times: 0048 and 0535 (long wave and FM), 1200 and 1755 (normally long wave only). The bulletins consist of a gale warning summary, general synopsis, sea-area forecasts and coastal station reports. In addition, gale warnings are broadcast at the first available programme break after receipt. If this does not coincide with a news bulletin, the warning is repeated after the next news bulletin.

Crown copyright

RELIGION IN THE UK

The 2001 census included a voluntary question on religion for the first time (although the question had been included in previous censuses in Northern Ireland); 92 per cent of people chose to answer the question. In the UK, 71.6 per cent of people in Britain identified themselves as Christian (42.1 million people). After Christianity, the next most prevalent faith was Islam with 2.7 per cent describing their religion as Muslim (1.6 million people). The next largest religious groups were Hindus (559,000), followed by Sikhs (336,000), Jews (267,000), Buddhists (152,000) and people from other religions (179,000). Together, these groups accounted for less than 3 per cent of the total UK population. People in Northern Ireland were most likely to say that they identified with a religion (86 per cent) compared with 77 per cent in England and Wales and 67 per cent in Scotland. About 16 per cent of the UK population stated that they had no religion. This category included those who identified themselves as agnostics, atheists, heathens and Jedi Knights.

CENSUS 2001 RESULTS – RELIGIONS IN THE UK
(thousands)

Christian	42,079	71.6%
Buddhist	152	0.3%
Hindu	559	1.0%
Jewish	267	0.5%
Muslim	1,591	2.7%
Sikh	336	0.6%
Other religion	179	0.3%
All religions	45,163	76.8%
No religion	9,104	15.5%
Not stated	4,289	7.3%
All no religion / not stated	13,626	23.2%
Total	58,789	100%

Source: Census 2001

ADHERENTS TO RELIGIONS IN THE UK
(millions)

	1975	1985	1995	2000
Christian (Trinitarian)	40.2	39.1	38.1	37.5
Non-Trinitarian	0.7	1.0	1.3	1.3
Hindu	0.3	0.4	0.4	0.5
Jew	0.4	0.3	0.3	0.3
Muslim	0.4	0.9	1.2	1.4
Sikh	0.2	0.3	0.6	0.6
Other	0.1	0.3	0.3	0.4
Total	42.3	42.3	42.2	42.0

Source: Christian Research – UK Christian Handbook Religious Trends No. 3 2002–3

INTER-CHURCH AND INTER-FAITH CO-OPERATION

The main umbrella body for the Christian churches in the UK is Churches Together in Britain and Ireland. There are also ecumenical bodies in each of the constituent countries of the UK: Churches Together in England, Action of Churches Together in Scotland, CYTUN (Churches Together in Wales), and the Irish Council of Churches. The Free Churches' Council comprises most of the Free Churches in England and Wales, and the Evangelical Alliance represents evangelical Christians.

The Inter-Faith Network for the United Kingdom promotes co-operation between faiths, and the Council of Christians and Jews works to improve relations between the two religions. Churches Together in Britain and Ireland also has a Commission on Inter-Faith Relations.

ACTION OF CHURCHES TOGETHER IN SCOTLAND, Scottish Churches House, Kirk Street, Dunblane, Perthshire FK15 0AJ T 01786-823588 F 01786- 825844 E ecumenical@acts-scotland.org W www.acts-scotland.org *General Secretary,* Revd Dr Kevin Franz

CHURCHES TOGETHER IN BRITAIN AND IRELAND, Bastille Court, 2 Paris Garden, London SE1 8ND T 020-7654 7211 F 020-7654 7254 E info@ctbi.org.uk W www.ctbi.org.uk *General Secretary,* Dr David Goodbourn

CHURCHES TOGETHER IN ENGLAND, 27 Tavistock Square, London WC1H 9HH T 020-7529 8141 F 020-7529 8134 W www.churches-together.org.uk *General Secretary,* Revd Bill Snelson

COUNCIL OF CHRISTIANS AND JEWS, 5th Floor, Camelford House, 87–89 Albert Embankment, London SE1 7TP T 020-7820 0090 F 020-7820 0504 E cjrelations@ccj.org.uk W www.ccj.org.uk *Director,* Sister Margaret Shepherd

CYTUN (CHURCHES TOGETHER IN WALES), 58 Richmond Road, Cardiff CF24 3UR T 029-2046 4204 F 029-2045 5427 E post@cytun.org.uk W www.cytun.org.uk *General Secretary,* Revd Gethin Abraham-Williams

EVANGELICAL ALLIANCE, Whitefield House, 186 Kennington Park Road, London SE11 4BT T 020-7207 2100 F 020-7207 2150 E london@eauk.org W www.eauk.org *General Director,* Revd Joel Edwards

INTER-FAITH NETWORK FOR THE UNITED KINGDOM, 8A Lower Grosvenor Place, London SW1W 0EN T 020-7931 7766 F 020-7931 7722 E ifnet@interfaith.org.uk W www.interfaith.org.uk *Director,* Brian Pearce, OBE

IRISH COUNCIL OF CHURCHES, Inter-Church Centre, 48 Elmwood Avenue, Belfast BT9 6AZ T 028-9066 3145 F 028-9066 4160 E icpep@email.com W www.irishchurches.org *General Secretary,* Michael Earle

CHRISTIANITY

Christianity is a monotheistic faith based on the person and teachings of Jesus Christ and all Christian denominations claim his authority. Central to its teaching is the concept of God and his son Jesus Christ, who was crucified and resurrected in order to enable mankind to attain salvation.

The Jewish scriptures predicted the coming of a *Messiah,* an 'anointed one', who would bring salvation. To Christians, Jesus of Nazareth, a Jewish rabbi (teacher), who was born in Palestine, was the promised Messiah. Jesus' birth, teachings, crucifixion and subsequent resurrection are recorded in the *Gospels,* which, together with other scriptures that summarise Christian belief, form the *New Testament.* This, together with the Hebrew scriptures, entitled the *Old Testament* by Christians, makes up the *Bible,* the sacred texts of Christianity.

BELIEFS

Christians believe that sin distanced mankind from God, and that Jesus was the Son of God, sent to redeem mankind from that sin by his death. In addition, many believe that Jesus will return again at some future date, triumph over evil and establish a kingdom on earth, thus inaugurating a new age. The Gospel assures Christians that those who believe in Jesus and obey his teachings will be forgiven their sins and will be resurrected from the dead.

PRACTICES

Christian practices vary widely between different Christian churches, but prayer is universal to all, as is charity, giving for the maintenance of the church buildings, for the work of the Church, and to the poor and needy. In addition, certain days of observance, i.e. the *Sabbath, Easter* and *Christmas,* are celebrated by most Christians. The Orthodox, Roman Catholic and Anglican churches celebrate many more days of observance, based on saints and significant events in the life of Jesus. The belief in sacraments, physical signs believed to have been ordained by Jesus Christ to symbolise and convey spiritual gifts, varies greatly between Christian denominations; *Baptism* and the *Eucharist* are practised by most Christians. Baptism, symbolising repentance and faith in Jesus, is an act marking entry into the Christian community; the Eucharist, the ritual re-enactment of the Last Supper, Jesus' final meal with his disciples, is also practised by most denominations. Other sacraments, such as anointing the sick, the laying on of hands to symbolise the passing on of the office of priesthood or to heal the sick, and speaking in tongues, where it is believed that the person is possessed by the Holy Spirit, the Spirit of God, are less common. In denominations where infant baptism is practised, confirmation is common, where the person repeats the commitments made for him or her at infancy. Matrimony and the ordination of priests are also widely believed to be sacraments. Many Protestants only view baptism and the Eucharist as sacraments; the Quakers and the Salvation Army reject the use of sacraments.

Most Christians believe that God actively guides the Church.

THE EARLY CHURCH

The Apostles were Jesus' first converts and are recognised by Christians as the founders of the Christian community. The new faith spread rapidly throughout the eastern provinces of the Roman Empire. Early Christianity was subject to great persecution until AD 313, when Emperor Constantine's Edict of Toleration confirmed its right to exist and it became established as the religion of the Roman Empire in AD 381.

The Christian faith was slowly formulated in the first millennium of the Christian era. Between AD 325 and 787 there were seven Oecumenical Councils at which bishops from the entire Christian world assembled to resolve various doctrinal disputes. The estrangement between East and West began after Constantine moved the centre of the Roman Empire from Rome to Constantinople, and it grew after the division of the Roman Empire into eastern and western halves. Linguistic and cultural differences between Greek East and Latin West served to encourage separate ecclesiastical developments which became pronounced in the tenth and early 11th centuries.

Administration of the Church was divided between five ancient patriarchates: Rome and all the West, Constantinople (the imperial city – the 'New Rome'), Jerusalem and all of Palestine, Antioch and all the East, and Alexandria and all of Africa. Of these, only Rome was in the Latin West and after the schism in 1054, Rome developed a structure of authority centralised on the Papacy, while the Orthodox East maintained the style of localised administration.

Papal authority over the doctrine and jurisdiction of the Church in western Europe was unrivalled after the split with the Eastern Orthodox Church until the Protestant Reformation in the 16th century.

CHRISTIANITY IN BRITAIN

An English Church already existed when Pope Gregory sent Augustine to evangelise the English in AD 596. Conflicts between Church and State during the Middle Ages culminated in the Act of Supremacy in 1534, which repudiated papal supremacy and declared King Henry VIII to be the supreme head of the Church in England. Since 1559 the English monarch has been termed the Supreme Governor of the Church of England.

In 1560 the jurisdiction of the Roman Catholic Church in Scotland was abolished and the first assembly of the Church of Scotland ratified the Confession of Faith, drawn up by a committee including John Knox. In 1592 Parliament passed an Act guaranteeing the liberties of the Church and its Presbyterian government. King James VI (James I of England) and later Stuart monarchs attempted to reintroduce episcopacy, but a Presbyterian Church was finally restored in 1690 and secured by the Act of Settlement (1690) and the Act of Union (1707).

PORVOO DECLARATION

The Porvoo Declaration was drawn up by representatives of the British and Irish Anglican churches and the Nordic and Baltic Lutheran churches and was approved by the General Synod of the Church of England in July 1995. Churches that approve the Declaration regard baptised members of each other's churches as members of their own, and allow free interchange of episcopally ordained ministers within the rules of each church.

NON-CHRISTIAN RELIGIONS AND BELIEFS

BAHA'I FAITH

Mirza Husayn-'Ali, known as *Bahá'u'lláh* (Glory of God) was born in Iran in 1817 and became a follower of the *Báb*, a religious reformer and prophet who was imprisoned for his beliefs and executed on the grounds of heresy in 1850. *Bahá'u'lláh* was himself imprisoned in 1852, and in 1853 he had a vision that he was the Promised One foretold by the *Báb*. He was exiled after his release from prison and eventually arrived in Acre, now in Israel, where he continued to compose the Bahá'í sacred scriptures. He died in 1892 and was succeeded by his son, Abdu'l-Bahá, as spiritual leader, under whose guidance the faith spread to Europe and North America. He was followed by Shoghi Effendi, his grandson, who translated many of *Bahá'u'lláh*'s works into English. Upon his death in 1957, a democratic system of leadership was brought into operation.

The Bahá'í faith recognises the unity and relativity of religious truth and teaches that there is only one God, whose will has been revealed to mankind by a series of messengers, such as Zoroaster, Abraham, Moses, Buddha, Krishna, Christ, Muhammad, the Báb and Bahá'u'lláh, who were seen as the founders of separate religions, but whose common purpose was to bring God's message to mankind. It teaches that all races and both sexes are equal and deserving of equal opportunities and treatment, that education is a fundamental right and encourages a fair distribution of wealth. In addition, mankind is exhorted to establish a world federal system to promote peace and tolerance.

A Feast is held every 19 days, which consists of prayer and readings of Bahá'í scriptures, consultation on community business, and social activities. Music, food and beverages usually accompany the proceedings. There is no clergy; each local community elects a local assembly, which co-ordinates community activities, enrols new members, counsels and assists members in need, and conducts Bahá'í marriages and funerals. A national assembly is elected annually by locally elected delegates, and every five years the national spiritual assemblies meet together to elect the Universal House of Justice, the supreme international governing body of the Bahá'í Faith. Worldwide there are over 13,000 local spiritual assemblies; there are around five million members residing in about 235 countries, of which 182 have national organisations.

THE BAHÁ'Í OFFICE OF PUBLIC INFORMATION, 27 Rutland Gate, London SW7 1PD T 020-7584 2566 F 020-7584 9402 E nsa@bahai.org.uk W www.bahai.org.uk *Secretary of the National UK Spiritual Assembly,* Dr Kishan Manocha

BUDDHISM

Buddhism originated in northern India, in the teachings of Siddharta Gautama, who was born near Kapilavastu about 560 BC and became the *Buddha* (Enlightened One).

Fundamental to Buddhism is the concept of rebirth. Each life carries with it the consequences of the conduct of earlier lives (known as the law of *karma*). This cycle of death and rebirth is broken only when the state of *nirvana* has been reached. Buddhism steers a middle path between belief in personal immortality and belief in death as the final end.

The Four Noble Truths of Buddhism (*dukkha,* suffering; *tanha,* a thirst or desire for continued existence which causes dukkha; *nirvana,* the final liberation from desire and ignorance; and *ariya,* the path to nirvana) are all held to be universal and to sum up the *dhamma* or true nature of life. Necessary qualities to promote spiritual development are *sila* (morality), *samadhi* (meditation) and *panna* (wisdom).

There are two main schools of Buddhism: *Theravada* Buddhism, the earliest extant school, which is more traditional, and *Mahayana* Buddhism, which began to develop about 500 years after the Buddha's death and is more liberal – it teaches that all people may attain Buddhahood. Important schools that have developed within Mahayana Buddhism are *Zen* Buddhism, *Nichiren* Buddhism and Pure Land Buddhism or *Amidism.* There are also distinctive Tibetan forms of Buddhism. Buddhism began to establish itself in the West in the early 20th century.

The scripture of Theravada Buddhism is the *Pali Canon,* which dates from the first century BC. Mahayana Buddhism uses a Sanskrit version of the Pali Canon but also has many other works of scripture.

There is no set time for Buddhist worship, which may take place in a temple or in the home. Worship centres around meditation, acts of devotion centring on the image of the Buddha, and, where possible, offerings to a relic of the Buddha. Buddhist festivals vary according to local traditions and within Theravada and Mahayana Buddhism. For religious purposes Buddhists use solar and lunar calendars, the New Year being celebrated in April. Other festivals mark events in the life of the Buddha.

There is no supreme governing authority in Buddhism. In the United Kingdom communities representing all schools of Buddhism have developed and operate independently. The Buddhist Society was established in 1924; it runs courses and lectures, and publishes books about Buddhism. It represents no single school of Buddhism.

There are estimated to be at least 300 million Buddhists worldwide, and more than 500 groups and centres and up to 20 temples or monasteries in the UK.

THE BUDDHIST SOCIETY, 58 Eccleston Square, London SW1V 1PH T 020-7834 5858 E info@thebuddhistsociety.org W www.thebuddhistsociety.org

FRIENDS OF THE WESTERN BUDDHIST ORDER, FWBO Communications Office, 51 Roman Road, London E2 0HU T 0845-458 4716 E info@lbc.org.uk W www.lbc.org.uk

THE NETWORK OF BUDDHIST ORGANISATIONS, 6 Tyne Road, Bishopston, Bristol BS7 8EE T 0845-345 8978 E secretary@nbo.org.uk W www.nbo.org.uk

TIBET HOUSE TRUST, Tibet House, 1 Culworth Street, London NW8 7AF T 020-7722 5378 E secretary@tibet-house-trust.co.uk W www.tibet-house-trust.co.uk

SOKA GAKKAI UK, Taplow Court, Berry Hill, Taplow, Maidenhead, Berkshire SL6 0ER T 01628-773163 W www.sgi-uk.org

HINDUISM

Hinduism has no historical founder but had become highly developed in India by about 1200 BC. Its adherents originally called themselves Aryans; Muslim invaders first called the Aryans 'Hindus' (derived from 'Sindhu', the name of the river Indus) in the eighth century.

Most Hindus hold that *satya* (truthfulness), *ahimsa* (non-violence), honesty, sincerity and devotion to God are essential for good living. They believe in one supreme spirit *(Brahman),* and in the transmigration of *atman* (the soul). Most Hindus accept the doctrine of *karma* (consequences of actions), the concept of *samsara* (successive lives) and the possibility of all atmans achieving *moksha* (liberation from samsara) through *jnana* (knowledge), *yoga* (meditation), *karma* (work or action) and *bhakti* (devotion).

Most Hindus offer worship to *murtis* (images of deities) representing different incarnations or aspects of Brahman, and follow their *dharma* (religious and social duty) according to the traditions of their *varna* (social class), *ashrama* (stage in life), *jati* (caste) and *kula* (family).

Hinduism's sacred texts are divided into *shruti* ('that which is heard'), including the *Vedas;* or *smriti* ('that which is remembered'), including the *Ramayana,* the *Mahabharata,* the *Puranas* (ancient myths), and the sacred law books. Most Hindus recognise the authority of the *Vedas,* the oldest holy books, and accept the philosophical teachings of the *Upanishads,* the *Vedanta Sutras* and the *Bhagavad-Gita.*

Brahman is omniscient, omnipotent, limitless and all-pervading, and is usually worshipped in his deity form. Brahma, Vishnu and Shiva are the most important gods worshipped by Hindus; their respective consorts are Saraswati, Lakshmi and Durga or Parvati, also known as Shakti. There are believed to have been ten *avatars* (incarnations) of Vishnu, of whom the most important are Rama and Krishna. Other popular gods are Ganesha, Hanuman and Subrahmanyam. All gods are seen as aspects of the supreme God, not as competing deities.

Orthodox Hindus revere all gods and goddesses equally, but there are many denominations, including the Hare-Krishna movement (ISKCon), the Arya Samaj, the Swami Narayan Hindu mission and the Satya Sai-Baba movement, in which worship is concentrated on one deity. The *guru* (spiritual teacher) is seen as the source of spiritual guidance.

Hinduism does not have a centrally trained and ordained priesthood. The pronouncements of the *shankaracharyas* (heads of monasteries) of Shringeri, Puri, Dwarka and Badrinath are heeded by the orthodox but may be ignored by the various sects.

The commonest form of worship is a *puja,* in which offerings of water, flowers, food, fruit, incense and light are made to a deity. Puja may be done either in a home shrine or a *mandir* (temple). Many British Hindus celebrate *samskars* (purification rites) to name a baby, the sacred thread (an initiation ceremony), marriage and cremation.

The largest communities of Hindus in Britain are in Leicester, London, Birmingham and Bradford, and developed as a result of immigration from India, eastern Africa and Sri Lanka.

There are an estimated 800 million Hindus world-wide; there are about 500,000 adherents, according to the 2001 UK census, and over 150 temples in the UK.

ARYA PRATINIDHI SABHA (UK) AND ARYA SAMAJ LONDON, 69A Argyle Road, London W13 0LY
T 020-8991 1732
BHARATIYA VIDYA BHAVAN, Institute of Indian Art and Culture, 4A Castletown Road, London W14 9HE
T 020-7381 3086 E info@bhavan.net W www.bhavan.net
Executive Director, Dr M. N. Nandakumara
INTERNATIONAL SOCIETY FOR KRISHNA CONSCIOUSNESS (ISKCON) , Bhaktivedanta Manor, Dharam Marg, Hilfield Lane, Aldenham, Watford, Herts WD2 8EZ T 01923-857244 W www.krishnatemple.com
Temple President, Gauri Das
SWAMINARAYAN HINDU MISSION (SHRI SWAMINARAYAN MANDIR), 105–119 Brentfield Road, London NW10 8LD T 020-8965 2651 F 020-8965 6313
E admin@mandir.org W www.mandir.org

HUMANISM

Humanism traces its roots back to ancient times, with Indian, Chinese, Greek and Roman philosophers expressing Humanist ideas some 2,500 years ago. Confucius, the Chinese philosopher who lived around 500 BC, believed that religious observances should be replaced with moral values as the basis of social and political order and that 'the true way' is based on reason and humanity. He also stressed the importance of benevolence, respect for others and believed that the individual situation should be considered rather than the global application of traditional rules. Humanists believe that there is no God or other supernatural beings and that humans have only one life within the material universe (Humanists do not believe in an afterlife or reincarnation). Humanists believe that humans can live ethical and fulfilling lives without religious beliefs through a moral code derived from the lessons of history, personal experience and thought. Particular emphasis is placed on science as the only reliable source of knowledge

of the universe. Humanists have a positive outlook on life believing that the world's problems can be solved through co-operation and mutual respect and that personal inspiration can be gained from life, especially art, culture and the natural world. There are no sacred Humanist texts. Humanists believe in ceremonies to mark important occasions in life and the British Humanist Association has a network of accredited Officiants and Celebrants who are qualified to conduct baby namings, weddings and funerals. The British Humanist Association campaigns for a secular society and an end to religious privilege, and provides educational resources for schools, students and parents.

BRITISH HUMANIST ASSOCIATION, 1 Gower Street, London WC1E 6HD T 020-7079 3580 F 020-7079 3588
E info@humanism.org.uk W www.humanism.org.uk
President, Linda Smith

ISLAM

Islam (which means 'peace arising from submission to the will of Allah' in Arabic) is a monotheistic religion which was taught in Arabia by the Prophet Muhammad, who was born in Mecca (Al-Makkah) in 570 CE. Islam spread to Egypt, North Africa, Spain and the borders of China in the century following the Prophet's death, and is now the predominant religion in Indonesia, the Near and Middle East, northern and parts of western Africa, Pakistan, Bangladesh, Malaysia and some of the former Soviet republics. There are also large Muslim communities in other countries.

For Muslims (adherents of Islam), there is one God (*Allah*), who holds absolute power. His commands were revealed to mankind through the prophets, who include Abraham, Moses and Jesus, but his message was gradually corrupted until revealed finally and in perfect form to Muhammad through the angel *Jibril* (Gabriel) over a period of 23 years. This last, incorruptible message has been recorded in the *Qur'an* (Koran), which contains 114 divisions called *surahs,* each made up of *ayahs,* and is held to be the essence of all previous scriptures. The *Ahadith* are the records of the Prophet Muhammad's deeds and sayings (the *Sunnah*) as recounted by his immediate followers. A culture and a system of law and theology gradually developed to form a distinctive Islamic civilisation. Islam makes no distinction between sacred and worldly affairs and provides rules for every aspect of human life. The *Shari'ah* is the sacred law of Islam based upon prescriptions derived from the *Qur'an* and the *Sunnah* of the Prophet.

The 'five pillars of Islam' are *shahadah* (a declaration of faith in the oneness and supremacy of Allah and the messengership of Muhammad); *salat* (formal prayer, to be performed five times a day facing the *Ka'bah* (sacred house in the holy city of Al-Makkah)); *zakat* (welfare due); *sawm* (fasting during the month of Ramadan); and *hajj* (pilgrimage to Al-Makkah). Some Muslims would add *jihad* (striving for the cause of good and resistance to evil).

Two main groups developed among Muslims. *Sunni* Muslims accept the legitimacy of Muhammad's first four *caliphs* (successors as head of the Muslim community) and of the authority of the Muslim community as a whole. About 90 per cent of Muslims are Sunni Muslims.

Shi'ites recognise only Muhammad's son-in-law Ali as his rightful successor and the *Imams* (descendants of Ali, not to be confused with *imams* (prayer leaders or religious teachers)) as the principal legitimate religious authority. The largest group within Shi'ism is *Twelver Shi'ism,* which has been the official school of law and theology in Iran since the 16th century; other subsects include the *Ismailis,* the *Druze* and the *Alawis,* the latter two differing considerably from the main body of Muslims. The *Ibadhis* of Oman are neither Sunni nor Shi'a, deriving from the strictly observant *Khariji* (Seceeders). There is no organised priesthood, but learned men such as *ulama, imams* and *ayatollahs* are accorded great respect. The *Sufis* are the mystics of Islam. Mosques are centres for worship and teaching and also for social and welfare activities.

Islam was first known in western Europe in the eighth century AD when 800 years of Muslim rule began in Spain. Later, Islam spread to eastern Europe. More recently, Muslims came to Europe from Africa, the Middle East and Asia in the late 19th century. Both the Sunni and Shi'a traditions are represented in Britain, but the majority of Muslims in Britain adhere to Sunni Islam. Efforts to establish a representative central organisation recognised by all Muslims in Britain are beginning to yield results with the emergence of the Muslim Council of Britain. In addition, there are many other Muslim organisations in Britain. There are about 1,000 million Muslims worldwide, with nearly two million adherents and about 1,200 mosques in Britain.

IMAMS AND MOSQUES COUNCIL, 20–22 Creffield Road, London W5 3RP T 020-8992 6636 E zbadawi@aol.com
Chairman of the Council and Principal of the Muslim College, Dr M. A. Z. Badawi
Executive Secretary, Moulana M. S. Raza
ISLAMIC CULTURAL CENTRE & THE LONDON CENTRAL MOSQUE, 146 Park Road, London NW8 7RG
T 020-7724 3363 F 020-7724 0493 E info@iccuk.org
W www.iccuk.org
Director, Dr Ahmad Al-Dubayan
MUSLIM COUNCIL OF BRITAIN, Boardman House, 64 Broadway, Stratford, London E15 1NT
T 020-8432 0585/0586 F 020-8432 0587
E admin@mcb.org.uk W www.mcb.org.uk
Secretary-General, Iqbal Sacranie, OBE
MUSLIM WORLD LEAGUE, 46 Goodge Street, London W1T 4LU T 020-7636 7568
UNION OF MUSLIM ORGANISATIONS OF THE UK AND EIRE, 109 Campden Hill Road, London W8 7TL
T 020-7221 6608 F 020-7792 2130
Secretary-General, Dr Syed A. Pasha

JAINISM

Jainism traces its history to Vardhamana Jnatriputra, known as *Tirthankara Mahavira* (The Great Hero) whose traditional dates were 599–527 BC. He was the last of a series of 24 *Jinas* (those who overcome all passions and desires) or *Tirthankaras* (those who show a way across the ocean of life) stretching back to remote antiquity. Born to a noble family in north-eastern India, he renounced the world for the life of a wandering ascetic and after 12 years of austerity and meditation he attained enlightenment. He then preached his message until, at the age of 72, he passed away and reached *moksha,* total liberation from the cycle of death and rebirth.

Jains deny the authority of the *Vedas,* the Hindu sacred scriptures. They recognise some of the minor deities of the Hindu pantheon, but the supreme objects of worship are the *Tirthankaras.* The pious Jain does not ask favours from the *Tirthankaras,* but seeks to emulate their example in his or her own life.

Jains believe that the universe is eternal and self-subsisting: there is no omnipotent creator God ruling it

and the destiny of the individual is in his or her own hands. *Karma,* the fruit of past actions, determines the place of every living being and rebirth may be in the heavens, on earth as a human, an animal or other lower being, or in the hells. The ultimate goal of existence is *moksha* or *nirvana,* a state of perfect knowledge and tranquility for each individual soul, which can be achieved only by gaining enlightenment.

The path to liberation is defined by the Three Jewels, *samyak darshana* (right thought), *samyak jnana* (right knowledge) and *samyak charitra* (right conduct). Of the five fundamental precepts of the Jains *Ahimsa* (non-injury to any form of being, in any mode) is the first and foremost and was popularised by Gandhi as *Ahimsa paramo dharma.*

There are about 25,000 Jains in Britain, sizeable communities in North America and East Africa and smaller groups in many other countries.

INSTITUTE OF JAINOLOGY, Unit 18, Silicon Business Centre, 28 Wadsworth Road, Perivale, Greenford, Middx UB6 7JZ T 020-8997 2300 W www.jainology.org
Chairman, Ratilal P. Chandaria
Hon. Secretary, Dr Harshad N. Sanghrajka

JUDAISM

Judaism is the oldest monotheistic faith. The primary authority of Judaism is the Hebrew Bible or *Tanakh,* which records how the descendants of Abraham were led by Moses out of their slavery in Egypt to Mount Sinai where God's law *(Torah)* was revealed to them as the chosen people. The *Talmud,* which consists of commentaries on the *Mishnah* (the first text of rabbinical Judaism), is also held to be authoritative, and may be divided into two main categories: the *halakah* (dealing with legal and ritual matters) and the *Aggadah* (dealing with theological and ethical matters not directly concerned with the regulation of conduct). The *Midrash* comprises rabbinic writings containing biblical interpretations in the spirit of the Aggadah. The *halakah* has become a source of division; Orthodox Jews regard Jewish law as derived from God and therefore unalterable; Reform and Liberal Jews seek to interpret it in the light of contemporary considerations; and Conservative Jews aim to maintain most of the traditional rituals but to allow changes in accordance with tradition. Reconstructionist Judaism, a 20th-century movement, regards Judaism as a culture rather than a theological system and accepts all forms of Jewish practice.

The family is the basic unit of Jewish ritual, with the synagogue playing an important role as the centre for public worship and religious study. A synagogue is led by a group of laymen who are elected to office. The Rabbi is primarily a teacher and spiritual guide. The Sabbath is the central religious observance. Most British Jews are descendants of either the *Ashkenazim* of central and eastern Europe or the *Sephardim* of Spain, Portugal and the Middle East.

The Chief Rabbi of the United Hebrew Congregations of the Commonwealth is appointed by a Chief Rabbinate Conference, and is the rabbinical authority of the mainstream Orthodox sector of the Ashkenazi Jewish community, the largest body of which is the United Synagogue. His formal ecclesiastical authority is not recognised by the Reform Synagogues of Great Britain (the largest progressive group), the Union of Liberal and Progressive Synagogues, the Sephardi community, or the Assembly of Masorti Synagogues. He is, however, generally recognised both outside the Jewish community and within it as the public religious representative of the totality of British Jewry. The Chief Rabbi is President of the London *Beth Din*. *Beth Din* (Court of Judgement) is a rabbinic court. The *Dayanim* (Assessors) adjudicate in disputes or on matters of Jewish law and tradition; they also oversee dietary law administration.

The Board of Deputies of British Jews, established in 1760, is the representative body of British Jewry. The basis of representation is mainly synagogal, but communal organisations are also represented. It watches over the interests of British Jewry, acts as the central voice of the community and seeks to counter anti-Jewish discrimination and anti-Semitic activities.

In November 1998 a Consultative Committee was established comprising representatives of the Assembly of Masorti Synagogues, Reform Synagogues of Great Britain, Union of Liberal and Progressive Synagogues and the United Synagogue. The Committee holds discussions to further communal harmony and development.

There are over 12.5 million Jews worldwide; in Great Britain and Ireland there are an estimated 285,000 adherents and about 365 synagogues. Of these, 191 congregations and about 175 rabbis and ministers are under the jurisdiction of the Chief Rabbi; 99 orthodox congregations have a more independent status; and 79 congregations are outside the jurisdiction of the Chief Rabbi.

CHIEF RABBINATE, Adler House, 735 High Road, London N12 0US T 020-8343 6301 F 020-8343 6310
  E info@chiefrabbi.org W www.chiefrabbi.org
  Chief Rabbi, Dr Jonathan Sacks
BETH DIN (COURT OF THE CHIEF RABBI), 735 High Road, London N12 0US T 020-8343 6270 F 020-8343 6257
  E info@bethdin.org.uk
  Registrar, D. Frei
  Dayanim, Rabbi Chanoch Ehrentreu; Ivan Binstock; Menachem Gelley; Yonason Abraham
BOARD OF DEPUTIES OF BRITISH JEWS, 6 Bloomsbury Square, London WC1A 2LP T 020-7543 5400
  F 020-7543 0010 E info@bod.org.uk W www.bod.org.uk
  President, Henry Grunwald, QC
ASSEMBLY OF MASORTI SYNAGOGUES, 1097 Finchley Road, London NW11 0PU T 020-8201 8772 F 020-8201 8917 E office@masorti.org.uk W www.masorti.org.uk
  Executive Director, Michael Gluckman
FEDERATION OF SYNAGOGUES, 65 Watford Way, London NW4 3AQ T 020-8202 2263 F 020-8203 0610
  E info@federationofsynagogues.com
  W www.federationofsynagogues.com
  Chief Executive, G. D. Coleman
LIBERAL JUDAISM, The Montagu Centre, 21 Maple Street, London W1T 4BE T 020-7580 1663 F 020-7631 9838
  E montagu@liberaljudaism.org W www.liberaljudaism.org
  Chief Executive, Rabbi Danny Rich
REFORM SYNAGOGUE OF GREAT BRITAIN, The Sternberg Centre for Judaism, 80 East End Road, London N3 2SY T 020-8349 5640 F 020-8349 5699
  E admin@reformjudaism.org.uk
  W www.reformjudaism.org.uk
  Chief Executive, Rabbi Tony Bayfield
SPANISH AND PORTUGUESE JEWS' CONGREGATION, 2 Ashworth Road, London W9 1JY T 020-7289 2573
  F 020-7289 2709 E howardmiller@spsyn.org.uk
  W www.sandp.org
  Chief Executive, Howard Miller

UNION OF ORTHODOX HEBREW CONGREGATIONS, 140 Stamford Hill, London N16 6QT T 020-8802 6226
  Principal Rabbinical Authority, Rabbi Ephraim Padwa
UNITED SYNAGOGUE HEAD OFFICE, Adler House, 735 High Road, London N12 0US T 020-8343 8989
  F 020-8343 6262 E info@unitedsynagogue.org.uk
  W www.unitedsynagogue.org.uk
  Chief Executive, Rabbi Saul Zneimer

PAGANISM

Paganism draws on the ideas of the Celtic people of pre-Roman Europe and is closely linked to Druidism. The first historical record of Druidry comes from classical Greek and Roman writers of the 3rd century BC, who noted the existence of Druids among a people called the Keltoi who inhabited central and southern Europe. The word druid may derive from the Indo-European 'dreo-vid', meaning 'one who knows the truth'. In practice it was probably understood to mean something like 'wise-one' or 'philosopher-priest'. Pagans place much emphasis on the natural world and the ongoing cycle of life and death is central to Pagan beliefs. Most Pagans are eco-friendly and seek to live in a way that minimises harm to the natural environment. Pagans worship many different forms. The most important and widely recognised of these are the God and Goddess whose annual cycle of procreation, birth and dying defines the Pagan year. Paganism strongly emphasises the equality of the sexes, with women playing a prominent role in the modern Pagan movement and Goddess worship featuring in most ceremonies. Paganism is not based on doctrine and many pagans follow the code 'if it harms none, do what you will'.

The Pagan Federation was founded in 1971 to provide information on Paganism and publishes a quarterly journal, *Pagan Dawn*, and other publications. It arranges members-only and public events and maintains personal contact by letter with individual members and the wider Pagan community. An annual conference is held at the end of each November and there are regional gatherings throughout the year. The aims of the Pagan Federation are to provide contact between national and international Pagan organisations.

THE PAGAN FEDERATION, BM Box 7097, London WC1N 3XX

SIKHISM

The Sikh religion dates from the birth of Guru Nanak in the Punjab in 1469. 'Guru' means teacher but in Sikh tradition has come to represent the divine presence of God giving inner spiritual guidance. Nanak's role as the human vessel of the divine guru was passed on to nine successors, the last of whom (Guru Gobind Singh) died in 1708. The immortal guru is now held to reside in the sacred scripture, *Guru Granth Sahib*, and so to be present in all Sikh gatherings.

Guru Nanak taught that there is one God and that different religions are like different roads leading to the same destination. He condemned religious conflict, ritualism and caste prejudices. The fifth Guru, Guru Arjan Dev, largely compiled the Sikh Holy Book, a collection of hymns *(gurbani)* known as the *Adi Granth*. It includes the writings of the first five Gurus and the ninth Guru, and selected writings of Hindu and Muslim saints whose views are in accord with the Gurus' teachings. Guru Arjan Dev also built the Golden Temple at Amritsar, the centre of Sikhism. The tenth Guru, Guru Gobind Singh, passed on the guruship to the sacred scripture, Guru Granth

Sahib. He also founded the *Khalsa,* an order intended to fight against tyranny and injustice. Male initiates to the order added 'Singh' to their given names and women added 'Kaur'. Guru Gobind Singh also made five symbols obligatory: *kaccha* (a special undergarment), *kara* (a steel bangle), *kirpan* (a small sword), *kesh* (long unshorn hair, and consequently the wearing of a turban), and *kangha* (a comb). These practices are still compulsory for those Sikhs who are initiated into the Khalsa (the *Amritdharis*). Those who do not seek initiation are known as *Sehajdharis.*

There are no professional priests in Sikhism; anyone with a reasonable proficiency in the Punjabi language can conduct a service. Worship can be offered individually or communally, and in a private house or a *gurdwara* (temple). Sikhs are forbidden to eat meat prepared by ritual slaughter; they are also asked to abstain from smoking, alcohol and other intoxicants. Such abstention is compulsory for the *Amritdharis.*

There are about 20 million Sikhs worldwide and about 500,000 adherents and 250 gurdwaras in Great Britain. Every gurdwara manages its own affairs and there is no central body in the UK. The Sikh Missionary Society provides an information service.

SIKH MISSIONARY SOCIETY UK, 8–10 Featherstone Road, Southall, Middx UB2 5AA T 020-8574 1902
F 020-8574 1912 E info@sikhmissionarysociety.org
W www.sikhmissionarysociety.org
Hon. General Secretary, Surinder Singh Purewal
THE SIKH COURIER INTERNATIONAL, 88 Mollison Way, Edgware, Middx HA8 5QW
Editor, Dr Sukhbir Singh

ZOROASTRIANISM

Zoroastrianism was founded by Zarathushtra (or Zoroaster in its hellenised form) in Persia. Linguistic analysis of the earliest extant Zoroastrian texts suggests that he lived around 1500 BC. Zarathushtra's words are recorded in five poems called the *Gathas,* which, together with other scriptures, forms the *Avesta.*

Zoroastrianism teaches that there is one God, *Ahura Mazda* (the Wise Lord), and that all creation stems ultimately from God; the Gathas teach that human beings have free will, are responsible for their own actions and can choose between good and evil. Choosing *Asha* (truth or righteousness), with the aid of *Vohu Manah* (good mind), leads to happiness for the individual and society, whereas choosing evil leads to unhappiness and conflict. The *Gathas* also encourage hard work, good deeds and charitable acts. Zoroastrians believe that after death, the immortal soul is judged by God, and is then sent to paradise or hell, where it will stay until the end of time. It will be resurrected for the final judgement.

In Zoroastrian places of worship, an urn containing fire is the central feature; the fire symbolises purity, light, and truth and is a visible symbol of the *Fravashi* or *Farohar,* the presence of *Ahura Mazda* in every human being.

Zoroastrians respect nature and much importance is attached to cultivating land and protecting the air, the earth and water. The practice of leaving corpses on mountain tops or towers developed to avoid pollution.

Zoroastrians were persecuted in Iran following the Arab invasion of Persia in the seventh century AD, which also brought Islam and a group migrated to India in the tenth century AD, who are known as Parsis, to avoid harassment and persecution; there are fewer than 150,000 Zoroastrians worldwide, of which 7,000 reside in Britain, mainly in London and the south east.

ZOROASTRIAN TRUST FUNDS OF EUROPE, Zoroastrian Centre, 440 Alexandra Avenue, Rayners Lane, Harrow, Middx HA2 9TL T 020-8866 0765 E secretary@ztfe.com
W www.ztfe.com
President, Dorab E. Mistry

CHURCHES

There are two established, i.e. state, churches in the United Kingdom: the Church of England and the Church of Scotland. There are no established churches in Wales or Northern Ireland, though the Church in Wales, the Scottish Episcopal Church and the Church of Ireland are members of the Anglican Communion.

CHURCH OF ENGLAND

The Church of England is the established (i.e. national) church in England and seeks to serve the nation through its dioceses and parishes. It traces its life back to the first coming of Christianity to England. Its position is defined by the ancient creeds of the Church and by the 39 Articles of Religion (1571), the Book of Common Prayer (1662) and the Ordinal. The Church of England is thus both catholic and reformed. It is the mother church of the Anglican Communion.

THE ANGLICAN COMMUNION
The Anglican Communion consists of 38 independent provincial or national Christian churches throughout the world, many of which are in Commonwealth countries and originated from missionary activity by the Church of England. Every ten years all the bishops in the Communion meet at the Lambeth Conference, convened by the Archbishop of Canterbury. The Conference has no policy-making authority but is an important forum for discussing and forming consensus around issues of common concern. The Anglican Consultative Council was set up in 1968 to liaise between the member churches and provinces of the Anglican Communion. It meets every three years. Meetings of the Anglican primates have taken place every two years since 1979.

There are about 70 million Anglicans organised into 500 dioceses and 64,000 individual congregations world-wide.

STRUCTURE
The Church of England is divided into the two provinces of Canterbury and York, each under an archbishop. The two provinces are subdivided into 44 dioceses.

Legislative provision for the Church of England is made by the General Synod, established in 1970. It also discusses and expresses opinion on any other matter of religious or public interest. The General Synod has 580 members in total, divided between three houses: the House of Bishops, the House of Clergy and the House of Laity. It is presided over jointly by the Archbishops of Canterbury and York and normally meets twice a year. The Synod has the power, delegated by Parliament, to frame statute law (known as a Measure) on any matter concerning the Church of England. A Measure must be laid before both Houses of Parliament, who may accept or reject it but cannot amend it. Once accepted the Measure is submitted for royal assent and then has the full force of law. In addition to the General Synod, there are Synods at diocesan level.

The Archbishops' Council was established in January 1999. Its creation was the result of changes to the Church of England's national structure proposed in 1995 and subsequently approved by the Synod and Parliament. The Council's purpose, set out in the National Institutions Measure 1998, is 'to co-ordinate, promote and further the work and mission of the Church of England'. It reports to the General Synod. The Archbishops' Council comprises the Archbishops of Canterbury and York, ex officio, the Prolocutors elected by the Convocations of Canterbury and York, the Chairman and Vice-Chairman of the House of Laity, elected by that House, two bishops, two clergy and two lay persons elected by their respective Houses of the General Synod, and up to six persons appointed jointly by the two Archbishops with the approval of the General Synod.

There are also a number of national Boards, Councils and other bodies working on matters such as social responsibility, mission, Christian unity and education which report to the General Synod through the Archbishops' Council.

GENERAL SYNOD OF THE CHURCH OF ENGLAND, Church House, Great Smith Street, London SW1P 3NZ T 020-7898 1000
    Joint Presidents, The Archbishops of Canterbury and York
HOUSE OF BISHOPS. *Chairman,* The Archbishop of Canterbury; *Vice-Chairman,* The Archbishop of York
HOUSE OF CLERGY: *Chairmen (alternating),* Canon Bob Baker; Canon Glyn Webster
HOUSE OF LAITY: *Chairman,* Dr Christina Baxter; *Vice-Chairman,* Brian McHenry
ARCHBISHOPS' COUNCIL, Church House, Great Smith Street, London SW1P 3NZ T 020-7898 1000
    Joint Presidents, The Archbishops of Canterbury and York; *Secretary-General,* William Fittall

THE ORDINATION OF WOMEN
The canon making it possible for women to be ordained to the priesthood was promulgated in the General Synod in February 1994 and the first 32 women priests were ordained on 12 March 1994.

MEMBERSHIP
In 2003, 144,000 people were baptised, the Church of England had an electoral roll membership of 1.2 million, and each week about 1.2 million people attended services. As at December 2003 there were over 16,000 churches and places of worship. At December 2004 there were 373 dignitaries (including bishops, archdeacons and cathedral clergy); 8,219 parochial stipendiary clergy; 260 non parochial stipendiary clergy; 1,238 chaplains etc; 381 lay workers and Church Army evangelists; 8,426 licensed readers and 2,177 readers with permission to officiate and active emeriti; and approximately 4,500 active retired ordained clergy.

	Full-time Diocesan Clergy 2004		Church Electoral Roll 2003
	Male	Female	Membership
Bath and Wells	181	39	38,600
Birmingham	145	28	18,500
Blackburn	210	19	34,700
Bradford	94	18	12,100

Bristol	121	20	17,200
Canterbury	143	18	21,400
Carlisle	122	24	21,900
Chelmsford	347	58	48,800
Chester	213	42	46,900
Chichester	304	13	55,800
Coventry	117	27	16,500
Derby	145	26	20,300
Durham	169	33	24,200
Ely	111	28	19,200
Europe	80	5	9,900
Exeter	215	27	31,100
Gloucester	114	27	23,500
Guildford	142	34	30,300
Hereford	79	23	18,200
Leicester	122	33	17,300
Lichfield	276	52	46,100
Lincoln	150	37	28,700
Liverpool	183	41	28,900
London	444	61	60,700
Manchester	225	41	35,400
Newcastle	121	27	16,800
Norwich	162	26	23,900
Oxford	317	83	56,600
Peterborough	129	26	18,200
Portsmouth	104	13	18,000
Ripon and Leeds	109	29	17,900
Rochester	191	32	30,300
St Albans	203	62	40,500
St Edmundsbury and Ipswich	126	20	24,500
Salisbury	187	43	42,900
Sheffield	150	31	19,000
Sodor and Man	16	2	2,700
Southwark	281	58	46,000
Southwell	136	35	18,800
Truro	103	19	16,800
Wakefield	134	30	21,000
Winchester	211	23	39,200
Worcester	116	28	20,400
York	203	40	35,400
Total	7,451	1,401	1,235,000

STIPENDS 2005–6

Archbishop of Canterbury	£63,210
Archbishop of York	£54,180
Bishop of London	£49,670
Other diocesan bishops	£34,310
Suffragan bishops	£27,990
Assistant bishops (full-time)	£27,090
Deans and provosts	£27,990
Archdeacons (recommended)	£27,090
Residentiary canons	£21,670*
Incumbents and clergy of similar status	£19,420*

*National Stipend Benchmark (adjusted regionally to reflect variations in the cost of living)

CANTERBURY
104TH ARCHBISHOP AND PRIMATE OF ALL ENGLAND
Most Revd and Rt. Hon. Rowan Williams, *cons.* 1992, *apptd* 2002; Lambeth Palace, London SE1 7JU
Signs Rowan Cantuar

BISHOPS SUFFRAGAN
Dover, Rt. Revd Stephen Venner, *cons.* 1994, *apptd* 1999; Upway, St Martin's Hill, Canterbury, Kent CT1 1PR
Maidstone, Rt. Revd Graham Cray, *cons.* 2001, *apptd* 2001, Bishop's House, Pett Lane, Charing, Ashford, Kent TN27 0DL
Ebbsfleet, Rt. Revd Andrew Burnham, *cons.* 2000, *apptd* 2000 (provincial episcopal visitor); Bishop's House, Dry Sandford, Oxon OX13 6JP
Richborough, Rt. Revd Keith Newton, *cons.* 2002, *apptd* 2002 (provincial episcopal visitor); 6 Mellis Gardens, Woodford Green, Essex IG8 0BH

DEAN
Very Revd Robert Willis, *apptd* 2001
Organist, D. Flood, FRCO, *apptd* 1988

ARCHDEACONS
Canterbury, Ven. Patrick Evans, *apptd* 2002
Maidstone, Ven. Philip Down, *apptd* 2002

Vicar-General of Province and Diocese, Chancellor Sheila Cameron, QC
Commissary-General, His Hon. Judge Walker
Joint Registrars of the Province, Canon John Rees; Stephen Slack
Diocesan Registrar and Legal Adviser, Richard Sturt
Diocesan Secretary, David Kemp, Diocesan House, Lady Wootton's Green, Canterbury CT1 1NQ T 01227-459401

YORK
97TH ARCHBISHOP AND PRIMATE OF ENGLAND
Most Revd and Rt. Hon. Dr John Sentamu, *cons.* 1996, *trans.* 2005; Bishopthorpe, York YO23 2GE
Signs John Ebor

BISHOPS SUFFRAGAN
Hull, Rt. Revd Richard M. C. Frith, *cons.* 1998, *apptd* 1998; Hullen House, Woodfield Lane, Hessle, Hull HU13 0ES
Selby, Rt. Revd Martin Wallace, *cons.* 2003, *apptd* 2003; Bishop's House, Barton le Street, Malton, York YO17 6PL
Whitby, Rt. Revd Robert S. Ladds, *cons.* 1999, *apptd* 1999; 60 West Green, Stokesley, Middlesbrough TS9 5BD
Beverley, Rt. Revd Martyn Jarrett, *cons.* 1994, *apptd* 2000 (provincial episcopal visitor); 3 North Lane, Roundhay, Leeds LS8 2QJ

DEAN
Very Revd Keith Jones, *apptd* 2004
Organist, Philip Moore, FRCO, *apptd* 1983

ARCHDEACONS
Cleveland, Ven. Paul Ferguson, *apptd* 2001
East Riding, Ven. Peter Harrison, *apptd* 1998
York, Ven. Richard Seed, *apptd* 1999

Official Principal and Auditor of the Chancery Court, Sir John Owen, QC
Chancellor of the Diocese, His Hon. Judge Coningsby, QC, *apptd* 1977
Vicar-General of the Province and Official Principal of the Consistory Court, His Hon. Judge Coningsby, QC
Registrar and Legal Secretary, Lionel Lennox
Diocesan Secretary, vacant, Diocesan House, Aviator Court, Clifton Moor, York YO30 4WJ T 01904-699500

LONDON *(Province of Canterbury)*
132nd BISHOP
Rt. Revd and Rt. Hon Richard J. C. Chartres, *cons.* 1992, *apptd.* 1995; The Old Deanery, Dean's Court, London EC4V 5AA
Signs Richard Londin

AREA BISHOPS
Edmonton, Rt. Revd Peter W. Wheatley, *cons.* 1999, *apptd* 1999; 27 Thurlow Road, London NW3 5PP
Kensington, Rt. Revd Michael J. Colclough, *cons.* 1996, *apptd* 1996; Dial House, Riverside, Twickenham, Middx TW1 3DT
Stepney, Rt. Revd Canon Stephen J. Oliver, *cons.* 2003, *apptd* 2003; 63 Coborn Road, London E3 2DB
Willesden, Rt. Revd Peter Broadbent, *cons.* 2001, *apptd* 2001; 173 Willesden Lane, London NW6 7YN

BISHOP SUFFRAGAN
Fulham, Rt. Revd John C. Broadhurst, *cons.* 1996, *apptd* 1996, 26 Canonbury Park South, London N1 2FN

DEAN OF ST PAUL'S
Very Revd John H. Moses, PHD, *apptd* 1996

Organist, Malcolm Archer, *apptd* 2004

ARCHDEACONS
Charing Cross, Ven. Dr William Jacob, *apptd* 1996
Hackney, Ven. Lyle Dennen, *apptd* 1999
Hampstead, Ven. Michael Lawson, *apptd* 1999
London, Ven. Peter Delaney, *apptd* 1999
Middlesex, vacant
Northolt, vacant

Chancellor, Nigel Seed, QC, *apptd* 2002
Registrar and Legal Secretary, Paul Morris
Diocesan Secretary, Keith Robinson, London Diocesan House, 36 Causton Street, London SW1P 4AU T 020-7932 1226

DURHAM *(Province of York)*
71st BISHOP
Rt. Revd Dr N. Thomas Wright, *cons.* 2003, *apptd* 2003; Auckland Castle, Bishop Auckland DL14 7NR
Signs Thomas Dunelm

BISHOP SUFFRAGAN
Jarrow, Rt. Revd John Pritchard, *cons.* 2002, *apptd* 2002; Bishop's House, Ivy Lane, Low Fell, Gateshead NE9 6QD

DEAN
Very Revd Michael Sadgrove, *apptd* 2003

Organist, James Lancelot, FRCO, *apptd* 1985

ARCHDEACONS
Auckland, Ven. Ian Jagger, *apptd* 2001
Durham, Ven. Stephen Conway, *apptd* 2002
Sunderland, Ven. Stuart Bain, *apptd* 2002

Chancellor, Revd Canon Rupert Bursell, QC, *apptd* 1989
Registrar and Legal Secretary, Hilary Monckton-Milnes
Diocesan Secretary, Ian Boothroyd, Diocesan Office, Auckland Castle, Bishop Auckland, Co. Durham DL14 7QJ T 01388-604515

WINCHESTER *(Canterbury)*
96th BISHOP
Rt. Revd Michael C. Scott-Joynt, *cons.* 1987, *trans.* 1995: Wolvesey, Winchester SO23 9ND
Signs Michael Winton

BISHOPS SUFFRAGAN
Basingstoke, Rt. Revd Trevor Willmott, *cons.* 2002, *apptd* 2002; Bishopswood End, Kingswood Rise, Four Marks, Alton, Hants GU34 5BD
Southampton, Rt. Revd Paul Butler, *cons.* 2004, *apptd* 2004; Ham House, The Crescent, Romsey SO51 7NG

DEAN
Very Revd James Atwell, *apptd* 2005
Dean of Jersey (A Peculiar), Very Revd John Seaford, *apptd* 1993
Dean of Guernsey (A Peculiar), Very Revd Paul Mellor, *apptd* 2003
Director of Music, Andrew Lumsden, *apptd* 2002

ARCHDEACONS
Bournemouth, Ven. Adrian Harbidge, *apptd* 1998
Winchester, Ven. John Guille, *apptd* 1998

Chancellor, Christopher Clark, *apptd* 1993
Registrar and Legal Secretary, Peter White
Diocesan Secretary, Andrew Howard, Church House, 9 The Close, Winchester, Hants SO23 9LS T 01962-624742

BATH AND WELLS *(Canterbury)*
78th BISHOP
Rt. Revd Peter Price, *cons.* 1997, *apptd* 2002; The Palace, Wells BA5 2PD
Signs Peter Bath & Wells

BISHOP SUFFRAGAN
Taunton, Rt. Revd Andrew John Radford, *cons.* 1998, *apptd* 1998; The Bishop's Lodge, Monkton Heights, West Monkton, Taunton, Somerset TA2 8LU

DEAN
Very Revd John Clarke *apptd* 2004

Organist, Matthew Owens, *apptd* 2005

ARCHDEACONS
Bath, Ven. Andrew Piggott, *apptd* 2005
Taunton, Ven. John Reed, *apptd* 1999
Wells, Ven. Peter Maurice, *apptd* 2003

Chancellor, Timothy Briden, *apptd* 1993
Registrar and Legal Secretary, Tim Berry
Diocesan Secretary, Nicholas Denison, The Old Deanery, Wells, Somerset BA5 2UG T 01749-670777

BIRMINGHAM *(Canterbury)*
8th BISHOP
Rt. Revd Dr John Sentamu (Archbishop of York elect, due to start duties 5 December 2005), *cons.* 1996, *apptd* 2002; Bishop's Croft, Harborne, Birmingham B17 0BG
Signs Sentamu Birmingham

BISHOP SUFFRAGAN
Aston, vacant

PROVOST
vacant

Organist, Marcus Huxley, FRCO, *apptd* 1986

ARCHDEACONS
Aston, vacant
Birmingham, Ven. Hayward Osborne, *apptd* 2001

Chancellor, Martin Cardinal, *apptd* 2005
Registrar and Legal Secretary, Hugh Carslake
Diocesan Secretary, Jim Drennan, 175 Harborne Park Road,
Harborne, Birmingham B17 0BH T 0121-426 0400

BLACKBURN *(York)*
8th BISHOP
Rt. Revd Nicholas Reade, *apptd* 2003, *cons.* March 2004;
Bishop's House, Ribchester Road, Blackburn BB1 9EF
Signs Nicholas Blackburn

BISHOPS SUFFRAGAN
Burnley, Rt. Revd John Goddard, *cons.* 2000, *apptd* 2000;
Dean House, 449 Padiham Road, Burnley BB12 6TE
Lancaster, Rt. Revd Stephen Pedley, *cons.* 1998, *apptd*
1998; Shireshead Vicarage, Whinneybrow, Forton, Preston
PR3 0AE

DEAN
Very Revd Christopher Armstrong, *apptd* 2001

Organist, Richard Tanner, *apptd* 1998

ARCHDEACONS
Blackburn, Ven. John Hawley, *apptd* 2002
Lancaster, Ven. Colin Williams, *apptd* 1999

Chancellor, John Bullimore, *apptd* 1990
Registrar and Legal Secretary, Thomas Hoyle
Diocesan Secretary, Graeme Pollard, Diocesan Office,
Cathedral Close, Blackburn BB1 5AA T 01254-54421

BRADFORD *(York)*
9th BISHOP
Rt. Revd David James, *apptd* 2002; Bishopscroft, Ashwell
Road, Heaton, Bradford BD9 4AU
Signs David Bradford

DEAN
Very Revd Dr David Ison, *apptd* 2005

Organist, Andrew Teague, FRCO, *apptd* 2003

ARCHDEACONS
Bradford, Ven. David Lee, *apptd* 2004
Craven, Ven. Paul Slater, *apptd* 2005

Chancellor, John de G. Walford, *apptd* 1999
Registrar and Legal Secretary, Peter Foskett
Diocesan Secretary, Malcolm Halliday, Kadugli House,
Elmsley Street, Steeton, Keighley BD20 6SE T 01535-650555

BRISTOL *(Canterbury)*
55th BISHOP
Rt. Revd Michael Hill, *cons.* 1998, *apptd* 2003; Wethered
House, 11 The Avenue, Clifton, Bristol BS8 3HG
Signs Michael Bristol

BISHOP SUFFRAGAN
Swindon, Rt. Revd Dr Lee Rayfield, *cons.* 2005, *apptd*
2005; Mark House, Field Rise, Swindon, Wiltshire SN1 4HP

DEAN
Very Revd Robert W. Grimley, *apptd* 1997

Organist, Mark Lee, *apptd* 1998

ARCHDEACONS
Bristol, Ven. Tim McClure, *apptd* 1999
Malmesbury, Ven. Alan Hawker, *apptd* 1998

Chancellor, Dr James Behrens, *apptd* 2005
Registrar and Legal Secretary, Tim Berry
Diocesan Secretary, Lesley Farrall, Diocesan Church House,
23 Great George Street, Bristol, Avon BS1 5QZ
T 0117-906 0100

CARLISLE *(York)*
66th BISHOP
Rt. Revd Graham Dow, *cons.* 1985, *apptd* 2000; Rose
Castle, Dalston, Carlisle CA5 7BZ
Signs Graham Carlisle

BISHOP SUFFRAGAN
Penrith, Rt. Revd James Newcome, *cons.* 2002, *apptd*
2002; Holm Croft, Castle Road, Kendal, Cumbria LA9 7AU

DEAN
Very Revd Mark Boyling, *apptd* 2004

Organist, Jeremy Suter, FRCO, *apptd* 1991

ARCHDEACONS
Carlisle, Ven. David Thomson, *apptd* 2002
West Cumberland, Ven. Colin Hill, *apptd* 2004
Westmorland and Furness, Ven. George Howe, *apptd* 2000

Chancellor, Geoffrey Tattersall, QC, *apptd* 2003
Registrar and Legal Secretary, vacant
Diocesan Secretary, Derek Hurton,Church House, West Walls,
Carlisle CA3 8UE T 01228-522573

CHELMSFORD *(Canterbury)*
9th BISHOP
Rt. Revd John Warren Gladwin, *cons.* 1994, *apptd* 2003,
trans. 2004; Bishopscourt, Margaretting, Ingatestone
CM4 0HD
Signs John Chelmsford

BISHOPS SUFFRAGAN
Barking, Rt. Revd David Hawkins, *apptd* 2003; Barking
Lodge, Verulam Avenue, London, E17 8ES
Bradwell, Rt. Revd Laurence Green, *cons.* 1993, *apptd*
1993; Bishop's House, Orsett Road, Horndon-on-the-Hill,
Stanford-le-Hope, Essex SS17 8NS
Colchester, Rt. Revd Christopher Morgan, *cons.* 2001,
apptd 2001; 1 Fitzwalter Road, Colchester, Essex CO3 3SS

DEAN
Very Revd Peter S. M. Judd, *apptd* 1997

Master of Music, Peter Nardone, *apptd* 2000

ARCHDEACONS
Colchester, Ven. Annette Cooper, *apptd* 2004
Harlow, Ven. Peter Taylor, *apptd* 1996
Southend, Ven. David Lowman, *apptd* 2001
West Ham, Ven. Michael Fox, *apptd* 1996

Chancellor, George Pulman, QC, *apptd* 2001
Registrar and Legal Secretary, Brian Hood
Diocesan Secretary, Steven Webb, 53 New Street, Chelmsford,
Essex CM1 1AT T 01245-294400

CHESTER *(York)*
40th BISHOP
Rt. Revd Peter R. Forster, PHD, *cons.* 1996, *apptd* 1996;
Bishop's House, Chester CH1 2JD
Signs Peter Cestr

BISHOPS SUFFRAGAN
Birkenhead, Rt. Revd David A. Urquhart, *cons.* 2000, *apptd* 2000; Bishop's Lodge, 67 Bidston Road, Oxton, Birkenhead CH43 6TR
Stockport, Rt. Revd Nigel Stock, *cons.* 2000, *apptd* 2000; Bishop's Lodge, Back Lane, Dunham Town, Altrincham, Cheshire WA14 4SG

DEAN
Very Revd Dr Gordon McPhate, *apptd* 2002

Organist and Director of Music, David Poulter, FRCO, *apptd* 1997

ARCHDEACONS
Chester, Ven. Donald Allister, *apptd* 2002
Macclesfield, Ven. Richard Gillings, *apptd* 1994

Chancellor, His Hon. Judge Turner, QC, *apptd* 1998
Registrar and Legal Secretary, Alan McAllester
Diocesan Secretary, Stephen P. A. Marriott, Church House, Lower Lane, Aldford, Chester CH3 6HP T 01244-620444

CHICHESTER *(Canterbury)*
102nd BISHOP
Rt. Revd John Hind, *cons.* 1991, *apptd* 2001; The Palace, Chichester PO19 1PY
Signs John Cicestr

BISHOPS SUFFRAGAN
Horsham, Rt. Revd Lindsay G. Urwin, *cons.* 1993, *apptd* 1993; Bishop's House, 21 Guildford Road, Horsham, W. Sussex RH12 1LU
Lewes, Rt. Revd Wallace P. Benn, *cons.* 1997, *apptd* 1997; Bishop's Lodge, 16A Prideaux Road, Eastbourne, E. Sussex BN21 2NB

DEAN
Very Revd Nicholas Frayling, *apptd* 2002

Organist, Alan Thurlow, FRCO, *apptd* 1980

ARCHDEACONS
Chichester, Ven. Douglas McKittrick, *apptd* 2002
Horsham, Ven. Roger Combes, *apptd* 2003
Lewes and Hastings, Ven. Philip Jones, *apptd* 2005

Chancellor, Mark Hill
Registrar and Legal Secretary, Tim Gleeson
Diocesan Secretary, Jonathan Prichard, Diocesan Church House, 211 New Church Road, Hove, E. Sussex BN3 4ED T 01273-421021

COVENTRY *(Canterbury)*
8th BISHOP
Rt. Revd Colin J. Bennetts, *cons.* 1994, *apptd* 1997; The Bishop's House, 23 Davenport Road, Coventry CV5 6PW
Signs Colin Coventry

BISHOP SUFFRAGAN
Warwick, Rt. Revd John Stroyan, *cons.* 2005, *apptd* 2005; Warwick House, 139 Kenilworth Road, Coventry CV4 7AP

DEAN
Very Revd John Irvine, *apptd* 2001

Director of Music, Rupert Jeffcoat, *apptd* 2005

ARCHDEACONS
Coventry, Ven. Mark Bryant, *apptd* 2001
Warwick, Ven. Michael Paget-Wilkes, *apptd* 1990

Chancellor, Sir William Gage, *apptd* 1980
Registrar and Legal Secretary, David Dumbleton
Diocesan Secretary, Simon Lloyd, Cathedral & Diocesan Offices, 1 Hilltop, Coventry CV1 5AB T 024-7652 1200

DERBY *(Canterbury)*
7th BISHOP
Rt. Revd Alastair Redfern, *cons.*1997, *apptd* 2005; Bishop's House, 6 King Street, Duffield, Belper, Derbyshire DE56 4EU
Signs Alastair Derby

BISHOP SUFFRAGAN
Repton, Rt. Revd David C. Hawtin, *cons.* 1999, *apptd* 1999; Repton House, Lea, Matlock, Derbys DE4 5JP

DEAN
Very Revd Martin Kitchen, PHD, *apptd* 2005

Organist, Peter Gould, *apptd* 1982

ARCHDEACONS
Chesterfield, Ven. David Garnett, *apptd* 1996
Derby, vacant

Chancellor, His Hon. Judge John Bullimore, *apptd* 1981
Registrar and Legal Secretary, Mrs Nadine Waldron
Diocesan Secretary, Bob Carey, Derby Church House, Full Street, Derby DE1 3DR T 01332-388650

ELY *(Canterbury)*
68th BISHOP
Rt. Revd Dr Anthony Russell, *cons.* 1988, *apptd* 2000; The Bishop's House, Ely, Cambs CB7 4DW
Signs Anthony Ely

BISHOP SUFFRAGAN
Huntingdon, Rt. Revd Dr John Inge, *cons.* 2003, *apptd* 2003; 14 Lynn Road, Ely, Cambs CB6 1DA

DEAN
Very Revd Dr Michael Chandler, *apptd* 2003

Organist, Paul Trepte, FRCO, *apptd* 1991

ARCHDEACONS
Ely, Ven. John Beer, *apptd* 2004
Huntingdon Wisbech, Ven. Hugh McCurdy, *apptd* 2005

Chancellor, The Hon. Mr Justice Gage, QC
Registrar, Peter Beesley
Diocesan Secretary, Dr Matthew Lavis, Bishop Woodford House, Barton Road, Ely, Cambs CB7 4DX T 01353-652701

EXETER *(Canterbury)*
70th BISHOP
Rt. Revd Michael Langrish, *cons.* 1993, *apptd* 2000; The Palace, Exeter EX1 1HY
Signs Michael Exon

BISHOPS SUFFRAGAN
Crediton, Rt. Revd Robert Evens, *cons.* 2004, *apptd* 2004; 32 The Avenue, Tiverton EX16 4HW
Plymouth, Rt. Revd John Garton, *cons.* 1996, *apptd* 1996; 31 Riverside Walk, Tamerton Foliot, Plymouth PL5 4AQ

DEAN
Very Revd Cyril Meyrick, *apptd* 2005

Director of Music, Andrew Millington, *apptd* 1999

ARCHDEACONS
Barnstaple, Ven. David Gunn-Johnson, *apptd* 2003
Exeter, Ven. Dr Paul Gardner, *apptd* 2003
Plymouth, Ven. Tony Wilds, *apptd* 2001
Totnes, Ven. Richard Gilpin, *apptd* 1996

Chancellor, vacant
Registrar and Legal Secretary, R. Wheeler
Diocesan Secretary, Mark Beedell, Diocesan House, Palace
    Gate, Exeter, Devon EX1 1HX T 01392-272686

GIBRALTAR IN EUROPE *(Canterbury)*
BISHOP
Rt. Revd Dr Geoffrey Rowell, *cons.* 1994, *apptd* 2001;
    Bishop's Lodge, Church Road, Worth, Crawley, West Sussex
    RH10 7RT

BISHOP SUFFRAGAN
In Europe, Rt. Revd David Hamid, *cons.* 2002, *apptd*
    2002; 14 Tufton Street, London SW1P 3QZ
Dean, Cathedral Church of the Holy Trinity, Gibraltar, Very
    Revd Alan Woods
Chancellor, Pro-Cathedral of St Paul, Valletta, Malta,
    Canon Thomas Mendel
Chancellor, Pro-Cathedral of the Holy Trinity, Brussels,
    Belgium, Canon Dr Robert Innes

ARCHDEACONS
Eastern, Ven. Patrick Curran
North-West Europe, Ven. Dirk Van Leeuwen
France, Ven. Anthony Wells
Gibraltar, Very Revd Alan Woods
Italy, Ven. Arthur Siddall
Scandinavia and Germany, Ven. Mark Oakley
Switzerland, Ven. John Williams

Chancellor, Mark Hill
Registrar and Legal Secretary, John Underwood
Diocesan Secretary, Adrian Mumford, 14 Tufton Street,
    London SW1P 3QZ T 020-7898 1155

GLOUCESTER *(Canterbury)*
40th BISHOP
Rt. Revd Michael Perham, *cons.* 2004, *apptd* 2004;
    Bishopscourt, Pitt Street, Gloucester GL1 2BQ
Signs Michael Gloucestr

BISHOP SUFFRAGAN
Tewkesbury, Rt. Revd John S. Went, *cons.* 1995, *apptd*
    1995; Bishop's House, Staverton, Cheltenham GL51 0TW

DEAN
Very Revd Nicholas Bury, *apptd* 1997

Director of Music, Andrew Nethsingha, *apptd* 2002

ARCHDEACONS
Cheltenham, Ven. Hedley Ringrose, *apptd* 1998
Gloucester, Ven. Geoffrey Sidaway, *apptd* 2000

Chancellor and Vicar-General, June Rodgers, *apptd* 1990
Registrar and Legal Secretary, Chris Peak
Diocesan Secretary, Michael Williams, Church House,
    College Green, Gloucester GL1 2LY T 01452-410022

GUILDFORD *(Canterbury)*
9th BISHOP
Rt. Revd Christopher Hill, *cons.* 1996, *apptd* 2004;
    Willow Grange, Woking Road, Guildford GU4 7QS

BISHOP SUFFRAGAN
Dorking, Rt. Revd Ian Brackley, *cons.* 1996, *apptd* 1995;
    Dayspring, 13 Pilgrims Way, Guildford GU4 8AD

DEAN
Very Revd Victor Stock, *apptd* 2002

Organist, Stephen Farr, FRCO, *apptd* 1999

ARCHDEACONS
Dorking, Ven. Julian Henderson, *apptd* 2005
Surrey, Ven. Stuart Beake, *apptd* 2005

Chancellor, Andrew Jordan
Registrar and Legal Secretary, Peter Beesley
Diocesan Secretary, Stephen Marriott

HEREFORD *(Canterbury)*
105th BISHOP
Rt. Revd Anthony Priddis, *cons.* 1996, *apptd* 2004; The
    Bishop's House, Hereford HR4 9BN

BISHOP SUFFRAGAN
Ludlow, Rt. Revd Michael Wrenford Hooper, *cons.* 2002,
    apptd 2002; Bishop's House, Corvedale Road, Craven
    Arms, Shropshire SY7 9BT

DEAN
Very Revd Michael Tavinor, *apptd* 2002

Organist, Geraint Bowen, FRCO, *apptd* 2001

ARCHDEACONS
Hereford, Ven. Malcom Colmer, *apptd* 2005
Ludlow, Rt. Revd Michael Hooper, *apptd* 2002

Chancellor, Roger Kaye, *apptd*
Joint Registrars and Legal Secretaries, Tom Jordan; Peter
    Beesley
Diocesan Secretary, John Clark, The Palace, Hereford HR4 9BL
    T 01432-373300

LEICESTER *(Canterbury)*
6th BISHOP
Rt. Revd Timothy J. Stevens, *cons.* 1995, *apptd* 1999;
    Bishop's Lodge, 10 Springfield Road, Leicester LE2 3BD
    Signs Timothy Leicester

DEAN
Very Revd Vivienne F. Faull, *apptd* 2000

Master of Music, Jonathan Gregory, *apptd* 1994

ARCHDEACONS
Leicester, Ven. Richard Atkinson, *apptd* 2002
Loughborough, Ven. Paul Huckwood, *apptd* 2005

Chancellor, Dr James Behrens
Registrar and Legal Secretary, Trevor Kirkman
Diocesan Secretary, Jane Easton, Church House, 3–5 St
    Martin's East, Leicester LE1 5FX T 0116-248 7400

LICHFIELD *(Canterbury)*
98th BISHOP
Rt. Revd Jonathan Gledhill cons. 1996, apptd 2003;
    Bishop's House, The Close, Lichfield WS13 7LG

BISHOPS SUFFRAGAN
Shrewsbury, Rt. Revd Alan Smith, *cons.* 2001, *apptd* 2002;
  68 London Road, Shrewsbury SY2 6PG
Stafford, Rt. Revd Alfred Mursell, *cons.* 2005, *apptd* 2005;
  Ash Garth, 6 Broughton Crescent, Barlaston, Stoke on Trent
  ST12 9DD
Wolverhampton, Rt. Revd Michael G. Bourke, *cons.* 1993,
  apptd 1993; 61 Richmond Road, Wolverhampton WV3 9JH

DEAN
vacant

Organist, Philip Scriven, *apptd* 2002

ARCHDEACONS
Lichfield, Ven. Christopher Liley, *apptd* 2001
Salop, Ven. John Hall, *apptd* 1998
Stoke-on-Trent, Ven. Godfrey Owen Stone *apptd* 2002
Walsall, Revd Robert Jackson, *apptd* 2004

Chancellor, His Hon. Judge John Shand
Joint Registrars and Legal Secretaries, J. P. Thorneycroft; N.
  Blackie
Diocesan Secretary, D. R. Taylor, St Mary's House, The Close,
  Lichfield, Staffs WS13 7LD **T** 01543-306030

LINCOLN *(Canterbury)*
71st BISHOP
Rt. Revd Dr John Saxbee, *cons.* 1994, *apptd* 2002;
  Bishop's House, Eastgate, Lincoln LN2 1QQ
  Signs John Lincoln

BISHOPS SUFFRAGAN
Grantham, vacant
Grimsby, Rt. Revd David D. J. Rossdale, *cons.* 2000, *apptd*
  2000; Bishop's House, Church Lane, Irby-upon-Humber,
  Grimsby DN37 7JR

DEAN
Very Revd Alexander Knight, *apptd* 1998

Director of Music, A. Prentice, *apptd* 2003

ARCHDEACONS
Lincoln, Ven. Arthur Hawes, *apptd* 1995
Lindsey and Stow, Ven. Dr Timothy Ellis, *apptd* 2001

Chancellor, Peter Collier, QC, *apptd* 1999
Registrar and Legal Secretary, Derek Wellman
Diocesan Secretary, Max Manin, The Old Palace, Lincoln
  LN2 1PU **T** 01522-529241

LIVERPOOL *(York)*
7th BISHOP
Rt. Revd James Jones, *cons.* 1994, *apptd* 1998; Bishop's
  Lodge, Woolton Park, Liverpool L25 6DT
  Signs James Liverpool

BISHOP SUFFRAGAN
Warrington, Rt. Revd David Jennings, *cons.* 2000, *apptd*
  2000; 34 Central Avenue, Eccleston Park, Prescot,
  Merseyside L34 2QP

DEAN
Rt. Revd Dean Dr Rupert W. N. Hoare, *apptd* 2000

Organist, Prof. Ian Tracey, *apptd* 1980

ARCHDEACONS
Liverpool, Ven Richard Panter, *apptd* 2002
Warrington, Ven. Peter Bradley, *apptd* 2001

Chancellor, Hon. Sir Mark Hedley
Registrar and Legal Secretary, Roger Arden
Diocesan Secretary, Mike Eastwood, Church House,
  1 Hanover Street, Liverpool L1 3DW **T** 0151-709 9722

MANCHESTER *(York)*
11th BISHOP
Rt. Revd Nigel McCulloch, *cons.* 1986, *apptd* 2002, *trans.*
  2002; Bishopscourt, Bury New Road, Manchester M7 4LE
  Signs Nigel Manchester

BISHOPS SUFFRAGAN
Bolton, Rt. Revd David K. Gillett, *cons.* 1999, *apptd* 1999;
  4 Bishop's Lodge, Bolton Road, Hawkshaw, Bury BL8 4JN
Hulme, Rt. Revd Stephen R. Lowe, *cons.* 1999, *apptd.*
  1999; 14 Moorgate Avenue, Withington, Manchester
  M20 1HE
Middleton, Rt. Revd Michael A. O. Lewis, *cons.* 1999,
  apptd 1999; The Hollies, Manchester Road, Rochdale
  OL11 3QY

DEAN
vacant

Organist, Christopher Stokes, *apptd* 1992

ARCHDEACONS
Bolton, John Applegate, *apptd* 2002
Manchester, vacant
Rochdale, Ven. Andrew Ballard, *apptd* 2000

Chancellor, G. F. Tattersall
Registrar and Legal Secretary, Michael Darlington
Diocesan Secretary, Nigel Spraggins, 1st Floor, Diocesan
  Church House, 90 Deansgate, Manchester M3 2GH
  T 0161-833 9521

NEWCASTLE *(York)*
11th BISHOP
Rt. Revd J. Martin Wharton, *cons.* 1992, *apptd* 1997;
  Bishop's House, 29 Moor Road South, Gosforth, Newcastle
  upon Tyne NE3 1PA
  Signs Martin Newcastle

ASSISTANT BISHOP
Rt. Revd Paul Richardson, *cons.* 1987, *apptd* 1999

DEAN
Very Revd Christopher C. Dalliston, *apptd* 2003

Director of Music, Scott Farrell, *apptd* 2002

ARCHDEACONS
Lindisfarne, Ven. Robert Langley, *apptd* 2001
Northumberland, Ven. Geoffrey Miller, *apptd* 2004

Chancellor, Prof. David McClean, *apptd* 1998
Registrar and Legal Secretary, Jane Lowdon
Diocesan Secretary, Philip Davies, Church House, St John's
  Terrace, North Shields NE29 6HS **T** 0191-270 4100

NORWICH *(Canterbury)*
71st BISHOP
Rt. Revd Graham R. James, *cons.* 1993, *apptd* 2000;
  Bishop's House, Norwich NR3 1SB
  Signs Graham Norvic

BISHOPS SUFFRAGAN
Lynn, Rt. Revd James Langstaff, *cons.* 2004, *apptd* 2004;
   The Old Vicarage, Castle Acre, King's Lynn PE32 2AA
Thetford, Rt. Revd David J. Atkinson, *cons.* 2001, *apptd*
   2001; The Red House, 53 Norwich Road, Stoke Holy Cross,
   Norwich NR14 8AB

DEAN
Very Revd Graham Smith, *apptd* 2004

Organist, David Dunnett, *apptd* 1996

ARCHDEACONS
Lynn, Ven. Martin Gray, *apptd* 1999
Norfolk, Ven. David Hayden, *apptd* 2002
Norwich, Ven. Clifford Offer, *apptd* 1994

Chancellor, The Hon. Mr Justice Blofeld, *apptd* 1998
Registrar and Legal Secretary, John Herring
Diocesan Secretary, Revd Canon Richard Bowett, Diocesan
   House, 109 Dereham Road, Easton, Norwich, Norfolk
   NR9 5ES T 01603-880853

OXFORD *(Canterbury)*
41st BISHOP
Rt. Revd Richard D. Harries, *cons.* 1987, *apptd* 1987;
   Diocesan Church House, North Hinksey Lane, Oxford
   OX2 0NB
Signs Richard Oxon

AREA BISHOPS
Buckingham, Rt. Revd Dr Alan Wilson *cons.* 2003, *apptd*
   2003; Sheridan, Grimms Hill, Great Missenden, Bucks
   HP16 9BD
Dorchester, Rt. Revd Colin Fletcher, *cons.* 2000, *apptd*
   2000; Arran House, Sandy Lane, Yarnton, Oxon OX5 1PB
Reading, Rt. Revd Stephen Cottrell, *cons.* 2004, *apptd*
   2004; Bishop's House, Tidmarsh Lane, Tidmarsh, Reading
   RG8 8HA

DEAN OF CHRIST CHURCH
Very Revd Dr Christopher Lewis, *apptd* 2003

Organist, Dr Stephen Darlington, FRCO, *apptd* 1985

ARCHDEACONS
Berkshire, Ven. Norman Russell, *apptd* 1998
Buckingham, Ven. Sheila Watson, *apptd* 2002
Oxford, Ven. Julian Hubbard, *apptd* 2005

Chancellor, Revd Dr Rupert Bursell, *apptd* 2001
Registrars and Legal Secretaries, Revd Dr F. E. Robson and
   Revd. Canon John Rees
Diocesan Secretary, Rosemary Pearce, Diocesan Church
   House, North Hinksey, Oxford OX2 0NB T 01865-208202

PETERBOROUGH *(Canterbury)*
37th BISHOP
Rt. Revd Ian P. M. Cundy, *cons.* 1992, *apptd* 1996;
   Bishop's Lodging, The Palace, Peterborough PE1 1YA
Signs Ian Petriburg

BISHOP SUFFRAGAN
Brixworth, Rt. Revd Frank White, *cons.* 2002, *apptd*
   2002; 4 The Avenue, Dallington, Northampton NN1 4RZ

DEAN
Very Revd Michael Bunker, *apptd* 1992

Organist, Andrew Reid, *apptd* 2004

ARCHDEACONS
Northampton, Ven. Christine Allsopp
Oakham, Ven. David Painter, *apptd* 2000

Chancellor, Thomas Coningsby, QC, *apptd* 1989
Registrar and Legal Secretary, Canon Raymond Hemingray
Diocesan Secretary, Richard Pestell, Diocesan Office, The
   Palace, Peterborough, Cambs PE1 1YB T 01733-887000

PORTSMOUTH *(Canterbury)*
8th BISHOP
Rt. Revd Dr Kenneth Stevenson, *cons.* 1995, *apptd* 1995;
   Bishopsgrove, 26 Osborn Road, Fareham, Hants PO16 7DQ
Signs Kenneth Portsmouth

DEAN
Very Revd David Brindley, *apptd* 2002

Organist, David Price, *apptd* 1996

ARCHDEACONS
Isle of Wight, Ven. Trevor Reader, *apptd* 2003
Portsdown, Ven. Christopher Lowson, *apptd* 1999
The Meon, Ven. Peter Hancock, *apptd* 1999

Chancellor, C. Clark, QC
Registrar and Legal Secretary, Hilary Tyler
Diocesan Secretary, Michael Jordan, Cathedral House, St
   Thomas's Street, Portsmouth, Hants PO1 2HA
   T 023-9282 5731

RIPON AND LEEDS *(York)*
12th BISHOP
Rt. Revd John Packer, *cons.* 1996, *apptd* 2000; Bishop
   Mount, Ripon HG4 5DP
Signs John Ripon and Leeds

BISHOP SUFFRAGAN
Knaresborough, Rt. Revd James Bell, *cons.* 2004, *apptd*
   2004; Thistledown, Main Street, Exelby, Bedale DL8 2HD

DEAN
Very Revd John Methuen, *apptd* 1995

Director of Music, Andrew Bryden, *apptd* 2003

ARCHDEACONS
Leeds, Ven. John Oliver, *apptd* 1992
Richmond, Ven. Kenneth Good, *apptd* 1993

Chancellor, His Hon. Judge Grenfell, *apptd* 1992
Registrars and Legal Secretaries, Christopher Tunnard;
   Nichola Harding
Diocesan Secretary, Philip Arundel, Diocesan Office, St
   Mary's Street, Leeds LS9 7DP T 0113-200 0540

ROCHESTER *(Canterbury)*
106th BISHOP
Rt. Revd Dr Michael Nazir-Ali, *cons.* 1984, *apptd* 1994;
   Bishopscourt, Rochester ME1 1TS
Signs Michael Roffen

BISHOP SUFFRAGAN
Tonbridge, Rt. Revd Dr Brian C. Castle, *cons.* 2002, *apptd*
   2002; Bishop's Lodge, 48 St Botolph's Road, Sevenoaks
   TN13 3AG

DEAN
Very Revd Adrian Newman, *apptd* 2004

Director of Music, Roger Sayer, FRCO, *apptd* 1995

ARCHDEACONS
Bromley, Ven. Paul Wright, *apptd* 2003
Rochester, Ven. Peter Lock, *apptd* 2000
Tonbridge, Ven. Clive Mansell, *apptd* 2002

Chancellor, vacant
Registrar and Legal Secretary, Owen Carew-Jones
Diocesan Secretary, Mrs Louise Gilbert, St Nicholas Church, Boley Hill, Rochester ME1 1SL **T** 01634-830333

ST ALBANS *(Canterbury)*
9th BISHOP
Rt. Revd Christopher W. Herbert, *cons.* 1995, *apptd* 1995; Abbey Gate House, St Albans AL3 4HD
Signs Christopher St Albans

BISHOPS SUFFRAGAN
Bedford, Rt. Revd Richard N. Inwood, *apptd* 2002
Hertford, Rt. Revd Christopher R. J. Foster, *cons.* 2001, *apptd* 2001; Hertford House, Abbey Mill Lane, St Albans AL3 4HF

DEAN
Very Revd Jeffrey John, *apptd* 2004

Organist, Andrew Lucas, *apptd* 1998

ARCHDEACONS
Bedford, Ven. Paul Hughes, *apptd* 2004
Hertford, Ven. Trevor Jones, *apptd* 1997
St Albans, Ven. Helen Cunliffe, *apptd* 2003

Chancellor, Roger Kaye, *apptd* 2002
Registrar and Legal Secretary, David Cheetham
Diocesan Secretary, Susan Pope, Holywell Lodge, 41 Holywell Hill, St Albans AL1 1HE **T** 01727-854532

ST EDMUNDSBURY AND IPSWICH *(Canterbury)*
9th BISHOP
Rt. Revd J. H. Richard Lewis, *cons.* 1992, *apptd* 1997; Bishop's House, 4 Park Road, Ipswich IP1 3ST
Signs Richard St Edmundsbury and Ipswich

BISHOP SUFFRAGAN
Dunwich, Rt. Revd Clive Young, *cons.* 1999, *apptd* 1999; 28 Westerfield Road, Ipswich IP4 2UJ

DEAN
vacant

Organist, James Thomas, *apptd* 1997

ARCHDEACONS
Ipswich, vacant
Sudbury, Ven. John Cox, *apptd* 1995
Suffolk, Ven. Geoffrey Arrand, *apptd* 1994

Chancellor, The Hon. Mr Justice Blofeld, *apptd* 1974
Registrar and Legal Secretary, James Hall
Diocesan Secretary, Nicholas Edgell, Diocesan Office, St Nicholas Centre, 4 Cutler Street, Ipswich IP1 1UQ **T** 01473-298500

SALISBURY *(Canterbury)*
77th BISHOP
Rt. Revd Dr David S. Stancliffe, *cons.* 1993, *apptd* 1993; South Canonry, The Close, Salisbury SP1 2ER
Signs David Sarum

BISHOPS SUFFRAGAN
Ramsbury, Rt. Revd Peter F. Hullah, *cons.* 1999, *apptd* 1999
Sherborne, Rt. Revd Timothy M. Thornton, *cons.* 2001, *apptd* 2001

DEAN
Very Revd. June Osborne, *apptd* 2004

Organist, David Halls, *apptd* 2005

ARCHDEACONS
Dorset, Ven. Alistair Magowan, *apptd* 2000
Sherborne, Ven. Paul Taylor, *apptd* 2004
Wilts, Ven. John Wraw, *apptd* 2004
Sarum, Ven. Alan Jeans, *apptd* 2003

Chancellor, His Hon. Judge Samuel Wiggs, *apptd* 1997
Registrar and Legal Secretary, Andrew Johnson
Diocesan Secretary, Lucinda Herklots, Church House, Crane Street, Salisbury SP1 2QB **T** 01722-411922

SHEFFIELD *(York)*
6TH BISHOP
Rt. Revd John (Jack) Nicholls, *cons.* 1990, *apptd* 1997; Bishopscroft, Snaithing Lane, Sheffield S10 3LG
Signs Jack Sheffield

BISHOP SUFFRAGAN
Doncaster, Rt. Revd Cyril Guy Ashton, *cons.* 2000, *apptd* 2000; Bishop's House, 3 Farrington Court, Wickersley, Rotherham S66 1JQ

DEAN
Very Revd Peter Bradley, *apptd* 2003

Master of Music, Neil Taylor, *apptd* 1997

ARCHDEACONS
Doncaster, Ven. Robert Fitzharris, *apptd* 2001
Sheffield and Rotherham, Ven. Richard Blackburn, *apptd* 1999

Chancellor, Prof. David McClean, *apptd* 1992
Registrar and Legal Secretary, Mrs Miranda Myers
Diocesan Secretary, Tony Beck, FCIS, Diocesan Church House, 95–99 Effingham Street, Rotherham S65 1BL **T** 01709-309100

SODOR AND MAN *(York)*
80th BISHOP
Rt. Revd Graeme Knowles, *cons.* 2003 *apptd* 2003; Bishop's House, The Falls, Tromode Road, Cronkbourne, Douglas, Isle of Man IM4 4PZ
Signs Graeme Sodor and Man

ARCHDEACON
Isle of Man, Ven. Brian Smith, *apptd* 2005

Vicar-General and Chancellor, Clare Faulds
Registrar and Legal Secretary, Christopher Callow
Diocesan Secretary, Christine Roberts, Holly Cottage, Ballaughton Meadows, Douglas, Isle of Man IM2 1JG **T** 01624-626994

SOUTHWARK *(Canterbury)*
9th BISHOP
Rt. Revd Dr Tom F. Butler, *cons.* 1985, *apptd* 1998; Bishop's House, 38 Tooting Bec Gardens, London SW16 1QZ
Signs Thomas Southwark

AREA BISHOPS
Croydon, Rt. Revd Nicholas Baines, *cons.* 2003, *apptd* 2003
Kingston upon Thames, Rt. Revd Richard Cheetham, *cons.* 2002, *apptd* 2002
Woolwich, Rt. Revd Christopher Chessun, *cons.* 2005, *apptd* 2005

DEAN
Very Revd Colin B. Slee, OBE, *apptd* 1994

Organist, Peter Wright, FRCO, *apptd* 1989

ARCHDEACONS
Croydon, Ven. Tony Davies, *apptd* 1994
Lambeth, Ven. Christopher Skilton, *apptd* 2003
Lewisham, Ven. Christine Hardman, *apptd* 2001
Reigate, Ven. Daniel Kajumba, *apptd* 2001
Southwark, Revd Dr Michael Ipgrave, *apptd* 2004
Wandsworth, Ven. Stephen Roberts, *apptd* 2005

Chancellor, Charles George, QC
Registrar and Legal Secretary, Paul Morris
Diocesan Secretary, Simon Parton, Trinity House, 4 Chapel Court, Borough High Street, London SE1 1HW T 020-7939 9400

SOUTHWELL *(York)*
10th BISHOP
Rt. Revd George H. Cassidy, *cons.* 1999, *apptd* 1999; Bishop's Manor, Southwell NG25 0JR
Signs George Southwell

BISHOP SUFFRAGAN
Sherwood, vacant

DEAN
Very Revd David Leaning, *apptd* 1991

Organist, Paul Hale, *apptd* 1989

ARCHDEACONS
Newark, Ven. Nigel Peyton, *apptd* 1999
Nottingham, Ven. Gordon Ogilvie, *apptd* 1996

Chancellor, Linda Box, *apptd* 2005
Registrar and Legal Secretary, Christopher Hodson
Diocesan Secretary, Dunham House, Westgate, Southwell, Notts NG25 0JL T 01636-817204

TRURO *(Canterbury)*
14th BISHOP
Rt. Revd William Ind, *cons.* 1987, *apptd* 1997; Lis Escop, Truro TR3 6QQ
Signs William Truro

BISHOP SUFFRAGAN
St Germans, Rt. Revd Royden Screech, *cons.* 2000, *apptd* 2000

DEAN
Very Revd Dr Christopher Hardwick, *apptd* 2005

Organist, Robert Sharpe, *apptd* 2002

ARCHDEACONS
Cornwall, Ven. Rodney Whiteman, *apptd* 2000
Bodmin, Ven. Clive Cohen, *apptd* 2000

Chancellor, Timothy Briden, *apptd* 1998
Registrar and Legal Secretary, Martin Follett
Diocesan Secretary, Sheri Sturgess, Diocesan House, Kenwyn, Truro TR1 1JQ T 01872-274351

WAKEFIELD *(York)*
12TH BISHOP
Rt. Revd Stephen Platten, *cons.* 2003, *apptd* 2003; Bishop's Lodge, Woodthorpe Lane, Wakefield WF2 6JL
Signs Stephen Wakefield

BISHOP SUFFRAGAN
Pontefract, Rt. Revd Anthony William Robinson, *cons.* 2003, *apptd* 2002; Pontefract House, 181A Manygates Lane, Wakefield WF2 7DR

DEAN
Very Revd George P. Nairn-Briggs, *apptd* 1997

Organist, Jonathan Bielby, FRCO, *apptd* 1972

ARCHDEACONS
Halifax, Ven. Robert Freeman, *apptd* 2003
Pontefract, Ven. Jonathan Greener, *apptd* 2003

Chancellor, Peter Collier, QC, *apptd* 1992
Registrar and Legal Secretaries, Julian Gill; Julia Wilding
Diocesan Secretary, Ashley Ellis, Church House, 1 South Parade, Wakefield WF1 1LP T 01924-371802

WORCESTER *(Canterbury)*
112th BISHOP
Rt. Revd Dr Peter S. M. Selby, *cons.* 1984, *apptd* 1997; The Bishop's House, Hartlebury Castle, Kidderminster DY11 7XX
Signs Peter Wigorn

SUFFRAGAN BISHOP
Dudley, Rt. Revd Dr David S. Walker, *cons.* 2000, *apptd* 2000; The Bishop's House, Bishop's Walk, Cradley Heath B64 7JF

DEAN
Very Revd Peter J. Marshall, *apptd* 1997

Organist, Adrian Lucas, *apptd* 1996

ARCHDEACONS
Dudley, Ven. Fred Trethewey, *apptd* 2001
Worcester, Ven. Dr Joy Tetley, *apptd* 1999

Chancellor, Charles Mynors, *apptd* 1999
Registrar and Legal Secretary, Michael Huskinson
Diocesan Secretary, Robert Higham, The Old Palace, Deansway, Worcester WR1 2JE T 01905-20537

ROYAL PECULIARS
WESTMINSTER
The Collegiate Church of St Peter

Dean, Very Revd Dr Wesley Carr, *apptd* 1997
Sub Dean and Archdeacon, David Hutt, *apptd* 1995
Chapter Clerk and Receiver-General, Maj.-Gen. David Burden, CB, CBE, Chapter Office, 20 Dean's Yard, London SW1P 3PA
Organist, James O'Donnell, *apptd* 1999
Registrar, Stuart Holmes, MVO
Legal Secretary, Christopher Vyse, *apptd* 2000

WINDSOR
The Queen's Free Chapel of St George within Her Castle of Windsor

Dean, Rt. Revd David Conner, *apptd* 1998
Chapter Clerk, Charlotte Manley, LVO, OBE, *apptd* 2003, Chapter Office, The Cloisters, Windsor Castle, Windsor, Berks SL4 1NJ
Director of Music, Timothy Byram-Wigfield, *apptd* 2004

OTHER ANGLICAN CHURCHES

THE CHURCH IN WALES

The Anglican Church was the established church in Wales from the 16th century until 1920, when the estrangement of the majority of Welsh people from Anglicanism resulted in disestablishment. Since then the Church in Wales has been an autonomous province consisting of six sees. The bishops are elected by an electoral college comprising elected lay and clerical members, who also elect one of the diocesan bishops as Archbishop of Wales.

The legislative body of the Church in Wales is the Governing Body, which has 350 members divided between the three orders of bishops, clergy and laity. Its President is the Archbishop of Wales and it meets twice annually. Its decisions are binding upon all members of the Church. The Church's property and finances are the responsibility of the Representative Body. There are about 78,000 members of the Church in Wales, with 607 stipendiary clergy and 1,001 parishes.

THE GOVERNING BODY OF THE CHURCH IN WALES, 39 Cathedral Road, Cardiff CF11 9XF T 029-2034 8200
Lay Secretary, John Shirley
12th ARCHBISHOP OF WALES, The Most Revd Dr Barry C. Morgan (Bishop of Llandaff), *elected* 2003
Signs Barry Cambrensis

BISHOPS

Bangor (80th), Rt. Revd Anthony Crockett, *b.* 1946, *cons.* 2004, *elected* 2004; Ty'r Esgob, Bangor, Gwynedd LL57 2SS
Signs Anthony Bangor. *Stipendiary clergy,* 71
Llandaff (102nd), The Most Revd Dr Barry C. Morgan (*also* Archbishop of Wales), *b.* 1947, *cons.* 1993, *trans.* 1999; Llys Esgob, The Cathedral Green, Llandaff, Cardiff CF5 2YE
Signs Barry Cambrensis. *Stipendiary clergy,* 146
Monmouth (9th), Rt. Revd Dominic Walker, *b.* 1948, *cons.* 1997, *elected* 2003; Bishopstow, Stow Hill, Newport NP20 4EA
Signs, Dominic Monmouth. *Stipendiary clergy,* 98
St Asaph (74th), Rt. Revd John S. Davies, *b.* 1943, *cons.* 1999, *elected* 1999; Esgobty, Upper Denbigh Road, St Asaph, Denbighshire LL17 0TW
Signs John St Asaph. *Stipendiary clergy,* 109
St David's (127th), Rt. Revd Carl N. Cooper, *b.* 1960, *cons.* 2002, *elected* 2002; Llys Esgob, Abergwili, Carmarthen SA31 2JG
Signs Carl St Davids. *Stipendiary clergy,* 126
Swansea and Brecon (8th), Rt. Revd Anthony E. Pierce, *b.* 1941, *cons.* 1999, *elected* 1999; Ely Tower, Brecon, Powys LD3 9DE
Signs Anthony Swansea & Brecon. *Stipendiary clergy,* 85

The stipend for a diocesan bishop of the Church in Wales is £32,805 a year for 2005–6.

SCOTTISH EPISCOPAL CHURCH

The Scottish Episcopal Church was founded after the Act of Settlement (1690) established the presbyterian nature of the Church of Scotland. The Scottish Episcopal Church is a member of the world-wide Anglican Communion. The governing authority is the General Synod, an elected body of approximately 140 members which meets once a year. The diocesan bishop who convenes and presides at meetings of the General Synod is called the Primus and is elected by his fellow bishops.

There are 43,193 members of the Scottish Episcopal Church, of whom 28,470 are communicants. There are seven bishops, approximately 482 serving clergy, and 313 churches and places of worship.

THE GENERAL SYNOD OF THE SCOTTISH EPISCOPAL CHURCH, 21 Grosvenor Crescent, Edinburgh EH12 5EE
T 0131-225 6357 W www.scottishepiscopal.com
Secretary-General, J. F. Stuart
PRIMUS OF THE SCOTTISH EPISCOPAL CHURCH, Most Revd A. Bruce Cameron (Bishop of Aberdeen and Orkney), *elected* 2000

BISHOPS

Aberdeen and Orkney, Bruce Cameron, *b.* 1941, *cons.* 1992, *elected* 1992. *Clergy,* 54
Argyll and the Isles, Martin Shaw, *b.* 1944, *cons.* 2004, *elected* 2004, *Clergy* 22
Brechin, John Mantle, *b.* 1946, *cons.* 2005, *elected* 2005. *Clergy,* 35
Edinburgh, Brian Smith, *b.* 1943, *cons.* 1993, *elected* 2001. *Clergy,* 162
Glasgow and Galloway, Idris Jones, *b.* 1943, *cons.* 1998, *elected* 1998. *Clergy,* 99
Moray, Ross and Caithness, John Crook, *b.* 1940, *cons.* 1999, *elected* 1999. *Clergy,* 31
St Andrews, Dunkeld and Dunblane, David Chillingworth, *b.* 1951, *cons.* 2005, *elected* 2004. *Clergy,* 86

The minimum stipend of a diocesan bishop of the Scottish Episcopal Church for 2005 is £29,130 (i.e. 1.5 times the minimum clergy stipend of £19,420)

CHURCH OF IRELAND

The Anglican Church was the established church in Ireland from the 16th century but never secured the allegiance of the majority and was disestablished in 1871. The Church of Ireland is divided into the provinces of Armagh and Dublin, each under an archbishop. The provinces are subdivided into 12 dioceses.

The legislative body is the General Synod, which has 660 members in total, divided between the House of Bishops and the House of Representatives. The Archbishop of Armagh is elected by the House of Bishops; other episcopal elections are made by an electoral college.

There are about 375,000 members of the Church of Ireland, with two archbishops, ten bishops, about 600 clergy and about 1,100 churches and places of worship.
CENTRAL OFFICE, Church of Ireland House, Church Avenue, Rathmines, Dublin 6 T (+353) (1) 4978422
Chief Officer and Secretary of the Representative Church Body, D. C. Reardon

PROVINCE OF ARMAGH
ARCHBISHOP OF ARMAGH, PRIMATE OF ALL IRELAND AND METROPOLITAN, Most Revd Robert H. A. Eames, PHD, *b.* 1937, *cons.* 1975, *trans.* 1986. *Clergy,* 55

BISHOPS

Clogher, Michael G. Jackson, PHD, DPHIL, *b.* 1956, *cons.* 2002, *apptd* 2002. *Clergy,* 32
Connor, Alan E. T. Harper, OBE, *b.* 1944, *cons.* 2002, *apptd* 2002. *Clergy,* 106
Derry and Raphoe, Kenneth R. Good, *b.* 1952, *cons.* 2002, *apptd* 2002. *Clergy,* 51
Down and Dromore, Harold C. Miller, *b.* 1950, *cons.* 1997, *apptd* 1997. *Clergy,* 116
Kilmore, Elphin and Ardagh, Kenneth H. Clarke, *b.* 1949, *cons* 2001, *apptd* 2001. *Clergy,* 21

Tuam, Killala and Achonry, Richard C. A. Henderson, DPHIL, *b.* 1957, *cons.* 1998, *apptd* 1998. *Clergy,* 13

PROVINCE OF DUBLIN

ARCHBISHOP OF DUBLIN, BISHOP OF GLENDALOUGH, PRIMATE OF IRELAND AND METROPOLITAN, Most Revd John R. W. Neill, *b.* 1945, *apptd* 2002. *Clergy,* 86

BISHOPS

Cashel and Ossory, Peter F. Barrett, *b.* 1956, *cons.* 2003, *apptd* 2003. *Clergy,* 42

Cork, Cloyne and Ross, W. Paul Colton, *b.* 1960, *cons.* 1999, *apptd* 1999. *Clergy,* 30

Limerick and Killaloe, Michael H. G. Mayes, *b.* 1941, *cons.* 1993, *trans.* 2000. *Clergy,* 19

Meath and Kildare, (Most Revd) Richard L. Clarke, PHD, *b.* 1949, *cons.* 1996, *apptd* 1996. *Clergy,* 26

OVERSEAS

PRIMATES

PRIMATE AND PRESIDING BISHOP OF AOTEAROA, NEW ZEALAND AND POLYNESIA, Most Revd Whakahuihui Vercoe

PRIMATE OF AUSTRALIA, Most Rt. Revd Phillip Aspinall

PRIMATE OF BRAZIL, Most Revd Orlando Santos de Oliveira

ARCHBISHOP OF THE PROVINCE OF BURUNDI, Most Revd Bernard Ntahoturi

ARCHBISHOP AND PRIMATE OF CANADA, Most Revd Andrew Sandford Hutchison

ARCHBISHOP OF THE PROVINCE OF CENTRAL AFRICA, Most Revd Bernard Amos Malango

PRIMATE OF THE CENTRAL REGION OF AMERICA, Most Revd Martin de Jesus Barahona

ARCHBISHOP OF THE PROVINCE OF CONGO, Most Revd Dr Dirokpa Balufuga Fidèle

PRIMATE OF THE PROVINCE OF HONG KONG SHENG KUNG HUI, Most Revd Peter Kwong

ARCHBISHOP OF THE PROVINCE OF THE INDIAN OCEAN, Most Revd Remi Rabenirina

PRIMATE OF JAPAN (NIPPON SEI KO KAI), Most Revd James Toru Uno

PRESIDENT-BISHOP OF JERUSALEM AND THE MIDDLE EAST, Most Revd George Handford

ARCHBISHOP OF THE PROVINCE OF KENYA, Most Revd Benjamin M. P. Nzimbi

ARCHBISHOP OF THE PROVINCE OF KOREA, Most Revd Dr Matthew Chul Bum Chung

ARCHBISHOP OF THE PROVINCE OF MELANESIA, Most Revd Sir Ellison L. Pogo, KBE

ARCHBISHOP OF MEXICO, Most Revd Carlos Touche-Porter

ARCHBISHOP OF THE PROVINCE OF MYANMAR, Most Revd Samuel Si Htay

ARCHBISHOP OF THE PROVINCE OF NIGERIA, Most Revd Peter Akinola

ARCHBISHOP OF PAPUA NEW GUINEA, Most Revd James Ayong

PRIME BISHOP OF THE PHILIPPINES, Most Revd Ignacio C. Soliba

ARCHBISHOP OF THE PROVINCE OF RWANDA, Most Revd Emmanuel Musaba Kolini

PRIMATE OF THE PROVINCE OF SOUTH EAST ASIA, Most Revd Datuk Yong Ping Chung

METROPOLITAN OF THE PROVINCE OF SOUTHERN AFRICA, Most Revd Njongonkulu W. H. Ndungane

PRESIDING BISHOP OF THE SOUTHERN CONE OF AMERICA, Most Revd Gregory James Venables

ARCHBISHOP OF THE PROVINCE OF THE SUDAN, Most Revd Joseph Marona

ARCHBISHOP OF THE PROVINCE OF TANZANIA, Most Revd Donald L. Mtetemela

ARCHBISHOP OF THE PROVINCE OF UGANDA, Most Revd Henry Luke Orombi

PRESIDING BISHOP AND PRIMATE OF THE USA, Most Revd Frank T. Griswold

ARCHBISHOP OF THE PROVINCE OF WEST AFRICA, Most Revd Justice Ofei Akrofi

ARCHBISHOP OF THE PROVINCE OF THE WEST INDIES, Most Revd Drexel Gomez

OTHER CHURCHES AND EXTRA-PROVINCIAL DIOCESES

ANGLICAN CHURCH OF BERMUDA, *extra-provincial to Canterbury*
  Bishop of Bermuda, Rt. Revd Ewen Ratteray

CHURCH OF CEYLON, *extra-provincial to Canterbury*
  Bishop of Colombo, Rt. Revd Duleep Kamil de Chickera
  Bishop of Kurunagala, Rt. Revd Kumara Illangasinghe

EPISCOPAL CHURCH OF CUBA, Rt. Revd Miguel Tamayo (interim)

ETHIOPIAN EPISCOPAL CHURCH, Rt. Revd Sigqibo Dwane

LUSITANIAN CHURCH (*Portuguese Episcopal Church*), *extra-provincial to Canterbury*
  Bishop of Lustanian Church, Rt. Revd Dr Fernando da Luz Soares

SPANISH REFORMED EPISCOPAL CHURCH, Rt. Revd Carlos López-Lozano

MODERATION OF CHURCHES IN FULL COMMUNION WITH THE ANGLICAN COMMUNION

CHURCH OF BANGLADESH, Rt. Revd Michael Baroi

CHURCH OF NORTH INDIA, Most Revd Zechariah J. Terom

CHURCH OF SOUTH INDIA, Most Revd Badda Peter Sugandhar

CHURCH OF PAKISTAN, Rt. Revd Dr Alexander John Malik

CHURCH OF SCOTLAND

The Church of Scotland is the established (i.e. national) church of Scotland. The Church is Reformed in doctrine, and presbyterian in constitution, i.e. based on a hierarchy of councils of ministers and elders and, since 1990, of members of a diaconate. At local level the Kirk Session consists of the parish minister and ruling elders. At district level the presbyteries, of which there are 44 in Britain, consist of all the ministers in the district, one ruling elder from each congregation, and those members of the diaconate who qualify for membership. The General Assembly is the supreme authority, and is presided over by a Moderator chosen annually by the Assembly. The Sovereign, if not present in person, is represented by a Lord High Commissioner who is appointed each year by the Crown.

The Church of Scotland has about 536,000 members, 1,100 ministers and 1,500 churches. There are about 100 ministers and other personnel working overseas.

Lord High Commissioner (2005), The Rt. Hon. Lord Mackay of Clashfern, KT, PC

Moderator of the General Assembly (2005), Revd Dr David Lacey
Principal Clerk, Very Revd Dr F. A. J. Macdonald
Depute Principal Clerk, Revd. Dr M. A. MacLean
Procurator, L. Dunlop
Law Agent and Solicitor of the Church, Mrs J. S. Wilson
Parliamentary Agent, I. McCulloch *(London)*
General Treasurer, I. Grimmond
Secretary, Church and Society Council, Revd Dr D. Sinclair
CHURCH OFFICE, 121 George Street, Edinburgh EH2 4YN
   T 0131-225 5722

PRESBYTERIES AND CLERKS
Edinburgh, Revd W. P. Graham
West Lothian, Revd D. Shaw

Lothian, J. D. McCulloch, DL
Melrose and Peebles, Jack Stewart
Duns, Peter Johnson
Jedburgh, Revd W. Frank Campbell

Annandale and Eskdale, Revd C. B. Haston
Dumfries and Kirkcudbright, Revd G. M. A. Savage
Wigtown and Stranraer, Revd D. W. Dutton
Ayr, Revd J. Crichton
Irvine and Kilmarnock, Revd C. G. G. Brockie
Ardrossan, Revd J. Mackay

Lanark, Revd M. Frew
Greenock and Paisley, Revd David Kay
Glasgow, Revd D. W. Lunan
Hamilton, Revd S. Paterson
Dumbarton, Revd C. Caskie

Argyll, I. MacLagan

Falkirk, Revd I. W. Black
Stirling, Revd M. MacCormick

Dunfermline, Revd W. E. Farquhar
Kirkcaldy, A. Moore
St Andrews, vacant
Dunkeld and Meigle, Revd J. Russell
Perth, Revd D. G. Lawson
Dundee, Revd J. Wilson
Angus, Revd M. I. G. Rooney

Aberdeen, Revd I. MacLean
Kincardine and Deeside, Revd J. Holt
Gordon, Revd E. Glen
Buchan, George Berstan
Moray, Revd Hugh Smith

Abernethy, Revd J. A. I. MacEwan
Inverness, Revd A. S. Younger
Lochaber, Revd D. M. Anderson

Ross, Revd T. M. McWilliam
Sutherland, Revd J. L. Goskirk
Caithness, Mrs M. Gillies, MBE
Lochcarron-Skye, Revd A. I. MacArthur
Uist, Revd M. Smith
Lewis, Revd T. S. Sinclair

Orkney, Revd T. G. Hunt
Shetland, Revd C. H. M.Greig
England, Revd W. A. Cairns
Europe, Revd J. A. Cowie

The stipends for ministers in the Church of Scotland in 2005 range from £20,492–£25,679, depending on length of service. In addition, congregations can make extra payments.

ROMAN CATHOLIC CHURCH

The Roman Catholic Church is one world-wide Christian Church acknowledging as its head the Bishop of Rome, known as the Pope (Father). He leads a communion of followers of Christ, who believe they continue his presence in the world as servants of faith, hope and love to all society. The Pope is held to be the successor of St Peter and thus invested with the power which was entrusted to St Peter by Jesus Christ. A direct line of succession is therefore claimed from the earliest Christian communities. With the fall of the Roman Empire the Pope also became an important political leader. His territory is now limited to the 43.3 hectares (107 acres) of the Vatican City State, created to provide some independence to the Pope from Italy and other nations.

The Pope exercises spiritual authority over the Church with the advice and assistance of the Sacred College of Cardinals, the supreme council of the Church. He is also advised by bishops in communion with him, by a group of officers which form the Roman Curia and by his ambassadors, called Apostolic Nuncios, who liaise with the Bishops' Conference in each country.

Those members of the College of Cardinals who are under the age of 80 elect a successor of the Pope following his death. The assembly of the Cardinals called to the Vatican for the election of a new Pope is known as the Conclave. In complete seclusion the Cardinals vote by a secret ballot; a two-thirds majority is necessary before the vote can be accepted as final. When a Cardinal receives the necessary number of votes, the Dean of the Sacred College formally asks him if he will accept election and the name by which he wishes to be known. On his acceptance of the office of Supreme Pontiff, the Conclave is dissolved and the first Cardinal Deacon announces the election to the assembled crowd in St Peter's Square.

The number of cardinals was fixed at 70 by Pope Sixtus V in 1586 but has been steadily increased since the pontificate of John XXIII and at the end of March 2005 stood at 183, plus one cardinal 'in pectore' (their name kept secret by the Pope for fear of persecution). At the end of March 2005, 117 of the 183 Cardinals were Cardinal electors, who took part in the election of Pope Benedict XVI, following the death of Pope John Paul II in April 2005.

The Pope has full legislative, judicial and administrative power over the whole church. He is aided in his administration by the Curia, which is made up of a number of departments. The Secretariat of State is the central office for carrying out the Pope's instructions and is presided over by the Cardinal Secretary of State. It maintains relations with the departments of the Curia, with the episcopate, with the representatives of the Holy See in various countries, governments and private persons. The congregations and pontifical councils are the Pope's ministries and include departments such as the Congregation for the Doctrine of Faith, whose field of competence concern faith and morals; the Congregation for the Clergy and the Congregation for the Evangelisation of Peoples, the Pontifical Council for the Family and the Pontifical Council for the Promotion of Christian Unity.

The Vatican State does not have diplomatic representatives. The Holy See, composed of the Pope and those who help him in his mission for the Church, is recognised by the Conventions of Vienna as an International Moral Body. The representatives of the Holy See are known as Apostolic Nuncios. Where representation is only to the local churches and not to the government of a country, the Papal representative is known as an apostolic delegate. The Roman Catholic Church has an estimated 840 million adherents under the care of some 2,500 diocesan bishops world-wide.

SOVEREIGN PONTIFF
His Holiness Pope Benedict XVI (Joseph Ratzinger), *born* Bavaria, Germany, 16 April 1927; *ordained priest* 1951; *appointed Archbishop* of Munich, March 1977; *created Cardinal* June 1977; *assumed pontificate* 19 April 2005

SECRETARIAT OF STATE
Secretary of State, HE Cardinal Angelo Sodano
First Section (General Affairs), Archbishop Leonardo
   Sandri (Titular Archbishop of Cittanova)
Second Section (Relations with other states), Most Revd
   Giovanni Lajolo (Titular Archbishop of Cesariana)

BISHOPS' CONFERENCE
The Roman Catholic Church in England and Wales consists of a total of 22 dioceses and is governed by the Bishops' Conference, membership of which includes the Diocesan Bishops, the Apostolic Exarch of the Ukrainians, the Bishop of the Forces and the Auxiliary Bishops. The Conference is headed by the President *(HE Cardinal Cormac Murphy-O'Connor, Archbishop of Westminster)* and Vice-President *(The Most Revd Patrick Kelly, Archbishop of Liverpool).* There are six departments, each with an episcopal chairman: the Department for Christian Life and Worship (the Bishop of Leeds), the Department for Dialogue and Unity (the Archbishop of Southwark), the Department for Catholic Education and Formation (the Archbishop of Birmingham), the Department for Christian Responsibility and Citizenship (the Archbishop of Cardiff), the Department for International Affairs (the Bishop of Portsmouth) and the Department for Evangelisation and Catechesis (the Bishop of Nottingham).

The Bishops' Standing Committee, made up of all the Archbishops and the chairman of each of the above departments, has general responsibility for continuity of policy between the plenary sessions of the Conference. It prepares the Conference agenda and implements its decisions. It is serviced by a General Secretariat. There are also agencies and consultative bodies affiliated to the Conference.

The Bishops' Conference of Scotland is the permanently constituted assembly of the Bishops of Scotland. The Conference is headed by the President *(HE Cardinal Keith Patrick O'Brien, Archbishop of St. Andrews and Edinburgh).* To promote its work, the Conference establishes various agencies which have an advisory function in relation to the Conference. The more important of these agencies are called Commissions and each one has a Bishop President who, with the other members of the Commissions, are appointed by the Conference.

The Irish Episcopal Conference has as its president Archbishop Brady of Armagh. Its membership comprises all the Archbishops and Bishops of Ireland and it appoints various Commissions to assist it in its work. There are

three types of Commissions: (a) those made up of lay and clerical members chosen for their skills and experience, and staffed by full-time expert secretariats; (b) Commissions whose members are selected from existing institutions and whose services are supplied on a part-time basis; and (c) Commissions of Bishops only.

The Roman Catholic Church in the UK has an estimated 1,631,449 members, 6,583 priests and 4,475 churches.

Bishops' Conferences secretariats:

ENGLAND AND WALES, 39 Eccleston Square, London
   SW1V 1BX T 020-7630 8220 F 020 7901 4821
   E secretariat@cbcew.org.uk W www.catholic-ew.org.uk
   General Secretary, Mgr Andrew Summersgill
SCOTLAND, 64 Aitken Street, Airdrie, Lanarkshire ML6 6LT
   T 01236-764061 E gensec@bpsconfscot.com
   General Secretary, Rt. Revd Mgr Henry Docherty
IRELAND, Columba Centre, Maynooth, County Kildare
   Secretary, The Most Revd William Lee (Bishop of
   Waterford and Lismore); *Executive Secretary,* Revd
   Aidan O'Boyle

GREAT BRITAIN
APOSTOLIC NUNCIO TO GREAT BRITAIN
The Most Revd Faustino Sainz Muñoz, 54 Parkside, London
   SW19 5NE T 020-8944 7189

ENGLAND AND WALES
THE MOST REVD ARCHBISHOPS
Westminster, HE Cardinal Cormac Murphy-O'Connor,
   cons. 1977, *apptd* 2000. *Auxiliaries,* George Stack, *cons.*
   2001; Bernard Longley *cons.* 2003; Alan Hopes *cons.*
   2003 *Clergy,* 779. *Archbishop's Residence,* Archbishop's
   House, Ambrosden Avenue, London SW1P 1QJ
   T 020-7798 9055
Birmingham, Vincent Nichols, *cons.* 1992, *apptd* 2000
   Auxiliaries, Philip Pargeter, *cons.* 1990 *Clergy,* 443.
   Diocesan Curia, Cathedral House, St Chad's Queensway,
   Birmingham B4 6EX T 0121-236 5535
Cardiff, Peter Smith, *cons.* 1995, *apptd* 2001 *Clergy,* 126.
   Diocesan Curia, Archbishop's House, 41–43 Cathedral
   Road, Cardiff CF11 9HD T 029-2022 0411
Liverpool, Patrick Kelly, *cons.* 1984, *apptd* 1996
   Auxiliaries, Vincent Malone, *cons.* 1989; Thomas
   Williams, *cons.* 2003 *Clergy,* 486. *Diocesan Curia,*
   Archdiocese of Liverpool, Centre for Evangelisation,
   Croxteth Drive, Sefton Park, Liverpool L17 1AA
   T 0151-522 1000
Southwark, Kevin McDonald, *cons.* 2001, *apptd* 2003
   Auxiliary, John Hine, *cons.* 2001 *Clergy,* 449. *Diocesan
   Curia,* Archbishop's House, 150 St George's Road, London
   SE1 6HX T 020-7928 5592

THE RT. REVD BISHOPS
Arundel and Brighton, Kieran Conry, *cons.* 2001, *apptd*
   2001. *Clergy,* 111. *Diocesan Curia,* Bishop's House, The
   Upper Drive, Hove, E. Sussex BN3 6NE T 01273-506387
Brentwood, Thomas McMahon, *cons.* 1980, *apptd* 1980.
   Clergy, 175. *Bishop's Office,* Cathedral House, Ingrave
   Road, Brentwood, Essex CM15 8AT T 01277-232266
Clifton, Declan Lang, *cons.* 2001, *apptd* 2001.
   Clergy, 251. *Bishop's House,* St Ambrose, North Road,
   Leigh Woods, Bristol BS8 3PW T 0117-973 3072
East Anglia, Michael Evans, *cons* 2003, *apptd* 2003. *Clergy,*
   129. *Diocesan Curia,* The White House, 21 Upgate,
   Poringland, Norwich NR14 7SH T 01508-492202

Hallam, John Rawsthorne, *cons.* 1981, *apptd* 1997.
Clergy, 75. *Bishop's House,* 75 Norfolk Road, Sheffield
S2 2SZ T 0114-278 7988

Hexham and Newcastle, Kevin Dunn, *cons.* 2004, *apptd*
2004. *Clergy,* 214. *Diocesan Curia,* Bishop's House, East
Denton Hall, 800 West Road, Newcastle upon Tyne NE5 2BJ
T 0191-228 0003

Lancaster, Patrick O'Donoghue, *cons.* 1993, *apptd* 2001.
Clergy, 248. *Bishop's Residence,* Bishop's Apartment,
Cathedral House, Balmoral Road, Lancaster LA1 3BT
T 01524-596050

Leeds, Arthur Roche, *cons.* 2001, *apptd* 2004. *Clergy,* 226.
Diocesan Curia, Hinsley Hall, 62 Headingley Lane, Leeds
LS6 1BX T 0113-261 8000

Menevia (Wales), Mark Jabalé, *cons.* 2001, *apptd* 2001.
Clergy, 60. *Diocesan Curia,* 27 Convent Street, Swansea
SA1 2BX T 01792-644017

Middlesbrough, John Crowley, *cons.* 1986, *apptd* 1992.
Clergy, 113. *Diocesan Curia,* 50a The Avenue, Linthorpe,
Middlesbrough, Cleveland TS5 6QT T 01642-850505

Northampton, Peter Doyle. *Clergy,* 159. *Diocesan Curia,*
Bishop's House, Marriott Street, Northampton NN2 6AW
T 01604-715635

Nottingham, Malcolm McMahon, *cons.* 2000, *apptd* 2000.
Clergy, 214. *Bishop's House,* 27 Cavendish Road East, The
Park, Nottingham NG7 1BB T 0115-947 4786

Plymouth, Christopher Budd, *cons.* 1986, *apptd* 1985.
Clergy, 125. *Diocesan Curia,* Bishop's House, 31
Wyndham Street West, Plymouth PL1 5RZ T 01752-224414

Portsmouth, Crispian Hollis, *cons.* 1987, *apptd* 1989.
Clergy, 282. *Bishop's Residence,* Bishop's House, Edinburgh
Road, Portsmouth, Hants PO1 3HG T 023-9282 0894

Salford, Terence Brain, *cons.* 1991, *apptd* 1997. *Clergy,*
346. *Diocesan Curia,* 5 Gerald Road, Pendleton, Salford
M6 6DL T 0161-736 1421

Shrewsbury, Brian Noble, *cons.* 1995, *apptd* 1995. *Clergy*
170. *Diocesan Curia,* 2 Park Road South, Prenton, Wirral
CH43 4UX T 0151-652 9855

Wrexham (Wales), Edwin Regan, *cons.*1994, *apptd* 1994.
Clergy, 83. *Diocesan Curia,* Bishop's House, Sontley Road,
Wrexham LL13 7EW T 01978-262726

SCOTLAND

THE MOST REVD ARCHBISHOPS

St Andrews and Edinburgh, HE Cardinal Keith Patrick
O'Brien, *cons.* 1985, *apptd* 1985, *elevated* 2003. *Clergy,*
173. *Diocesan Office,* 113 Whitehouse Loan, Edinburgh
EH9 1BB T 0131-452 8244

Glasgow, Mario Joseph Conti, *cons.* 1977, *apptd* 2002.
Clergy, 253. *Diocesan Curia,* 196 Clyde Street, Glasgow
G1 4JY T 0141-226 5898

THE RT. REVD BISHOPS

Aberdeen, Peter Moran, *cons.* 2003, *apptd* 2003. *Clergy,* 43.
Diocesan Curia, Bishop's House, 3 Queen's Cross,
Aberdeen AB15 4XU T 01224-319154

Argyll and the Isles, Ian Murray, *cons.* 1999, *apptd* 1999.
Clergy, 32. *Bishop's House,* Esplanade, Oban, Argyll
PA34 5AB T 01631-571395

Dunkeld, Vincent Logan, *cons.* 1981. *Clergy,* 42. *Diocesan
Curia,* 24–28 Lawside Road, Dundee DD3 6XY
T 01382-225453

Galloway, John Cunningham, *cons.* 2004, *apptd* 2004.
Clergy 56. *Diocesan Curia,* 8 Corsehill Road, Ayr KA7 2ST
T 01292-266750

Motherwell, Joseph Devine, *cons.* 1977, *apptd* 1983.
Clergy, 126. *Diocesan Curia,* Coursington Road,
Motherwell ML1 1PP T 01698-269114

Paisley, vacant. *Clergy,* 85. *Diocesan Curia,* Diocesan Centre,
Cathedral Precincts, Incle Street, Paisley PA1 1HR
T 0141-847 6130

BISHOPRIC OF THE FORCES

Rt. Revd Thomas Matthew Burns, *cons.* 2002, *apptd*
2002. *Administration,* Bishopric of the Forces, Middle Hill,
Aldershot, Hants GU11 1PP T 01252-349004

IRELAND

There is one hierarchy for the whole of Ireland. Several of
the dioceses have territory partly in the Republic of
Ireland and partly in Northern Ireland.

APOSTOLIC NUNCIO TO IRELAND

HE Most Revd Dr. Giuseppe Lazzarotto (Titular
Archbishop of Numana), 183 Navan Road, Dublin 7
T (+353) (1) 838 0577 F (+353) (1) 838 0276

THE MOST REVD ARCHBISHOPS

Armagh, Seán Brady (*also* Primate of all Ireland), *cons.*
1995, *apptd* 1996. *Archbishop Emeritus,* HE Cardinal
Cahal B. Daly, *cons.* 1967, *elevated* 1991. *Auxiliary
Bishop,* Most Revd Gerard Clifford, *cons.* 1991. *Clergy,*
183. *Diocesan Office,* Ara Coeli, Armagh BT61 7QY
T 028-3752 2045

Cashel and Emly, Dermot Clifford, *cons.* 1986, *apptd* 1988.
Clergy, 103. *Archbishop's Residence,* Archbishop's House,
Thurles, Co. Tipperary T (+353) (504) 21512

Dublin, Diarmuid Martin, *cons.* 1999, *apptd Coadjutor
Archbishop* 2003, *succeeded as Archbishop* 2004.
Emeritus Archbishop, HE Cardinal Desmond Connell,
cons. 1988, *elevated* 2001. *Auxiliaries,* Eamonn Walsh,
cons. 1990; Fiachra O'Ceallaigh, *cons* 1994; Raymond
Field, *cons.* 1997. *Clergy,* 994. *General Secretariat,*
Archbishop's House, Dublin 9 T (+353) (1) 8373732

Tuam, Michael Neary, *cons.* 1992, *apptd* 1995. *Clergy,* 141.
Archbishop's Residence, Archbishop's House, Tuam, Co.
Galway T (+353) (93) 24166

THE MOST REVD BISHOPS

Achonry, Thomas Flynn, *cons.* 1977, *apptd* 1976. *Clergy,*
62. *Bishop's Residence,* Bishop's House, Ballaghaderreen,
Co. Roscommon T (+353) (9498) 60021

Ardagh and Clonmacnois, Colm O'Reilly, *cons.* 1983, *apptd*
1983. *Clergy,* 64. *Bishop's Residence,* St Michael's,
Longford, Co. Longford T (+353) (43) 46432

Clogher, Joseph Duffy, *cons.* 1979, *apptd* 1979. *Clergy,*
108. *Bishop's Residence,* Bishop's House, Monaghan
T (+353) (47) 81019

Clonfert, John Kirby, *cons.* 1988. *Clergy,* 71. *Bishop's
Residence,* St Brendan's, Coorheen, Loughrea, Co. Galway
T (+353) (91) 841560

Cloyne, John Magee, *cons.* 1987, *apptd* 1987. *Clergy,* 153.
Diocesan Centre, Cobh, Co. Cork T (+353) (21) 4811430

Cork and Ross, John Buckley, *cons.* 1984, *apptd* 1998.
Clergy, 153. *Diocesan Office,* Cork and Ross Offices,
Redemption Road, Cork T (+353) (21) 4301717

Derry, Seamus Hegarty, *cons.* 1982, *apptd* 1994. *Clergy,*
138. *Bishop's Residence,* Bishop's House, St Eugene's
Cathedral, Derry BT48 9AP T 028-7126 2302
Auxiliary, Francis Lagan, *cons.* 1988

Down and Connor, Patrick Walsh, *cons.* 1983, *apptd* 1991.
Clergy, 240. *Bishop's Residence,* Lisbreen, 73 Somerton
Road, Belfast, Co. Antrim BT15 4DE T 028-9077 6185.
Auxiliaries, Anthony Farquhar, *cons.* 1983; Donal
McKeown, *cons.* 2001

Dromore, John McAreavey, *cons.* 1999, *apptd* 1999. *Clergy*, 78. *Bishop's Residence*, Bishop's House, 44 Armagh Road, Newry, Co. Down BT35 6PN T 028-3026 2444

Elphin, Christopher Jones, *cons.* 1994, *apptd* 1994. *Clergy*, 70. *Bishop's Residence*, St Mary's, Sligo T (+353) (71) 62670

Ferns, Éamonn Walsh, *cons.* 1990, *apptd* 2002. *Clergy*, 138. *Bishop's Residence*, Bishop's House, Summerhill, Wexford T (+353) (53) 22177

Galway and Kilmacduagh and Kilfenora, Martin Drennan, *cons.* 1997, *apptd* 2005. *Clergy*, 87. *Bishop's Residence*, Mount Saint Mary's, Taylor's Hill, Galway T (+353) (91) 563566

Kerry, William Murphy, *cons.* 1995, *apptd* 1995. *Clergy*, 126. *Bishop's Residence*, Bishop's House, Killarney, Co. Kerry T (+353) (64) 31168

Kildare and Leighlin, James Moriarty, *cons.* 1991, *apptd* 2002. *Clergy*, 113. *Bishop's Residence*, Bishop's House, Dublin Road, Carlow T (+353) (59) 917 6725

Killala, John Fleming, *cons.* 2002, *apptd* 2002. *Clergy*, 52. *Bishop's Residence*, Bishop's House, Ballina, Co. Mayo T (+353) (96) 21518

Killaloe, William Walsh, *cons.* 1994. *Clergy*, 149. *Bishop's Residence*, Westbourne, Ennis, Co. Clare T (+353) (65) 6828638

Kilmore, Leo O'Reilly, *cons.* 1997, *apptd* 1998. *Clergy*, 98. *Bishop's Residence*, Bishop's House, Cullies, Co. Cavan T (1353) (49) 4331496

Limerick, Donal Murray, *cons.* 1982, *apptd* 1996. *Clergy*, 110. *Bishop's Residence*, Kilmoyle, North Circular Road, Limerick T (+353) (61) 451433

Meath, Michael Smith, *cons.* 1984, *apptd* 1990. *Clergy*, 141. *Bishop's Residence*, Bishop's House, Dublin Road, Mullingar, Co. Westmeath T (+353) (44) 48841

Ossory, Laurence Forristal, *cons.* 1980, *apptd* 1981. *Clergy*, 91. *Bishop's Residence*, Sion House, Kilkenny T (+353) (56) 7762448

Raphoe, Philip Boyce, *cons.* 1995, *apptd* 1995. *Clergy*, 90. *Bishop's Residence*, Ard Adhamhnáin, Letterkenny, Co. Donegal T (+353) (74) 9121208

Waterford and Lismore, William Lee, *cons.* 1993, *apptd* 1993. *Clergy*, 114. *Bishop's Residence*, John's Hill, Waterford T (+353) (51) 874463

OTHER CHURCHES IN THE UK

AFRICAN AND AFRO-CARIBBEAN CHURCHES

There are more than 160 Christian churches or groups of African or Afro-Caribbean origin in the UK. These include the Apostolic Faith Church, the Cherubim and Seraphim Church, the New Testament Church Assembly, the New Testament Church of God, the Wesleyan Holiness Church and the Aladura Churches. The Afro-West Indian United Council of Churches and the Council of African and Afro-Caribbean Churches UK (which was initiated as the Council of African and Allied Churches in 1979 to give one voice to the various Christian churches of African origin in the UK) are the media through which the member churches can work jointly to provide services they cannot easily provide individually.

There are about 70,000 adherents of African and Afro-Caribbean churches in the UK, and over 1,000 congregations. The Council of African and Afro-Caribbean Churches UK has about 17,000 members, 250 ministers and 125 congregations.

COUNCIL OF AFRICAN AND AFRO-CARIBBEAN CHURCHES UK, 31 Norton House, Sidney Road, London SW9 0UJ T 020-7274 5589
Chairman, His Grace The Most Revd Father Olu A. Abiola, OBE

ASSOCIATED PRESBYTERIAN CHURCHES OF SCOTLAND

The Associated Presbyterian Churches came into being in 1989 as a result of a division within the Free Presbyterian Church of Scotland. Following two controversial disciplinary cases, the culmination of deepening differences within the Church, a presbytery was formed calling itself the Associated Presbyterian Churches (APC). The Associated Presbyterian Churches has about 900 members, 9 ministers and 16 churches.

Clerk of the Scottish Presbytery, Revd A. N. McPhail, Fernhill, Polvinster Road, Oban PA34 5TN T 01631-567076

BAPTIST CHURCH

Baptists trace their origins to John Smyth, who in 1609 in Amsterdam reinstituted the baptism of conscious believers as the basis of the fellowship of a gathered church. Members of Smyth's church established the first Baptist church in England in 1612. They came to be known as 'General' Baptists and their theology was Arminian, whereas a later group of Calvinists who adopted the baptism of believers came to be known as 'Particular' Baptists. The two sections of the Baptists were united into one body, the Baptist Union of Great Britain and Ireland, in 1891. In 1988 the title was changed to the Baptist Union of Great Britain.

Baptists emphasise the complete autonomy of the local church, although individual churches are linked in various kinds of associations. There are international bodies (such as the Baptist World Alliance) and national bodies, but some Baptist churches belong to neither. However, in Great Britain the majority of churches and associations belong to the Baptist Union of Great Britain. There are also Baptist Unions in Wales, Scotland and Ireland which are much smaller than the Baptist Union of Great Britain, and there is some overlap of membership.

There are currently some 150,000 members and 2,150 churches associated with the Baptist Union of Great Britain. The Baptist Union of Great Britain is one of the founder members of the European Baptist Federation (1948) and the Baptist World Alliance (1905) which represents nearly 150,000 churches and over 40 million members world-wide.

In the Baptist Union of Scotland there are 14,002 members, 120 pastors and 176 churches.

In the Baptist Union of Wales (Undeb Bedyddwyr Cymru) there are about 15,900 members, 94 pastors and 450 churches.

In the Association of Baptist Churches in Ireland (formerly the Baptist Union of Ireland) there are 8,251 members, 85 pastors and 111 churches.

President of the Baptist Union of Great Britain (2005–6), Revd Roy Searle

General Secretary, Revd David Coffey, Baptist House, PO Box 44, 129 Broadway, Didcot, Oxon OX11 8RT T 01235-517700 E info@baptist.org.uk
W www.baptist.org.uk

General Director of the Baptist Union of Scotland, Revd William Slack, 14 Aytoun Road, Glasgow G41 5RT T 0141-423 6169 F 0141-424 1422
E admin@scottishbaptist.org.uk

President of the English Assembly of the Baptist Union of Wales (2005–6), Revd Michael Collis

President of the Welsh Assembly of the Baptist Union of Wales (2005–6), Dclyth Davies

General Secretaries of the Baptist Union of Wales, Revd Peter Thomas, 94 Mansel Street, Swansea SA1 5TZ T 01792-655468

Secretary of the Association of Baptist Churches in Ireland, Revd W. Colville, The Baptist Centre, 19 Hillsborough Road, Moira BT67 0HG T 028-9261 9267 E abc@thebaptistcentre.org

CONGREGATIONAL FEDERATION

The Congregational Federation was founded by members of Congregational churches in England and Wales who did not join the United Reformed Church in 1972. There are also churches in Scotland and France affiliated to the Federation. The Federation exists to encourage congregations of believers to worship in free assembly, but it has no authority over them and emphasises their right to independence and self-government.

The Federation has 10,058 members, 62 accredited ministers and 292 churches in England, Wales and Scotland.

President of the Federation (2005–6), Revd John Nockels

General Secretary, Revd. M. Heaney, 8 Castle Gate, Nottingham NG1 7AS T 0115-911 1460 E admin@congregational.org.uk

FREE CHURCH OF ENGLAND

The Free Church of England is an independent episcopal Church, constituted according to the historic faith, tradition and practice of the Church of England. Its roots lie in the 18th century, but most of its growth took place from the 1840s onwards, as clergy and congregations joined it from the established Church in protest against the Oxford Movement. The historic episcopate was conferred on the English Church in 1876 through bishops of the Reformed Episcopal Church (itself a breakaway from the Protestant Episcopal Church in the USA in 1873). A branch of the Reformed Episcopal Church was founded in the UK and this merged with the Free Church of England in 1927 to create the present Church.

Worship is according to the Book of Common Prayer (with slight modifications) and some modern liturgy is permissable. Only men are ordained to the orders of deacon, presbyter and bishop.

The Free Church of England has 25 congregations, now mainly confined to England. It also has a few members in New Zealand and one congregation in St Petersburg, Russia.

General Secretary, Revd Paul Hunt, 329 Wolverhampton Road West, Willenhall WV13 2RL T 01902-607335

FREE CHURCH OF SCOTLAND

The Free Church of Scotland was formed in 1843 when over 400 ministers withdrew from the Church of Scotland as a result of interference in the internal affairs of the church by the civil authorities. In 1900, all but 26 ministers joined with others to form the United Free Church (most of which rejoined the Church of Scotland in 1929). In 1904 the remaining 26 ministers were recognised by the House of Lords as continuing the Free Church of Scotland.

The Church maintains strict adherence to the Westminster Confession of Faith (1648) and accepts the Bible as the sole rule of faith and conduct. Its General

Assembly meets annually. It also has links with Reformed Churches overseas. In January 2000, a division occurred within the church, the larger body retains the name of the Free Church of Scotland with the smaller body known as the Free Church of Scotland (Continuing) and has around 2,000 members. The Free Church of Scotland has about 11,500 members, 82 ministers and 162 churches.

Chief Administrative Officer, R. M. Morrison, The Mound, Edinburgh EH1 2LS T 0131-226 5286 E offices@freechurchofscotland.org.uk

FREE PRESBYTERIAN CHURCH OF SCOTLAND

The Free Presbyterian Church of Scotland was formed in 1893 by two ministers of the Free Church of Scotland who refused to accept a Declaratory Act passed by the Free Church General Assembly in 1892. The Free Presbyterian Church of Scotland is Calvinistic in doctrine and emphasises observance of the Sabbath. It adheres strictly to the Westminster Confession of Faith of 1648.

The Church has about 3,000 members in Scotland and about 4,000 in overseas congregations. It has 20 ministers and 50 churches in the UK.

Moderator, Revd N. M. Ross, Free Presbyterian Manse, 10 Achany Road, Dingwall, Ross-shire IV15 9JB

Clerk of Synod, Revd J. MacLeod, Free Presbyterian Manse, 6 Church Avenue, Sidcup, Kent DA14 6BU T 020-8309 1623

HOLY APOSTOLIC CATHOLIC ASSYRIAN CHURCH OF THE EAST

The Holy Apostolic Catholic Assyrian Church of the East traces its beginnings to the middle of the first century. It spread from Upper Mesopotamia throughout the territories of the Persian Empire. The Assyrian church of the East became theologically separated from the rest of the Christian community following the Council of Ephesus in 431. The Church is headed by the Catholicos Patriarch and is episcopal in government. The liturgical language is Syriac (Aramaic). The Assyrian Church of the East and the Roman Catholic Church agreed a common Christological declaration in 1994 and a process of dialogue between the Assyrian Church of the East and the Chaldean Catholic Church, which is in communion with Rome but shares the Syriac liturgy, was instituted in 1996.

The Church numbers about 400,000 members in the Middle East, India, Europe, North America and Australasia. There are around 600 members in the UK.

The Church in Great Britain forms part of the diocese of Europe under Mar Odisho Oraham.

Representative in Great Britain, Very Revd Younan Y. Younan, 66 Montague Road, London W7 3PQ T 020-8579 7259

INDEPENDENT METHODIST CHURCHES

The Independent Methodist Churches were formed in 1805 and remained independent when the Methodist Church in Great Britain was formed in 1932. They are mainly concentrated in the industrial areas of the north of England.

The churches are Methodist in doctrine but their organisation is congregational. All the churches are members of the Independent Methodist Connexion of Churches. The controlling body of the Connexion is the Annual Meeting, to which churches send delegates. The Connexional President is elected annually. Between annual meetings the affairs of the Connexion are handled by departmental committees. Ministers are appointed by the churches and trained through the Connexion. The ministry is open to both men and women and is unpaid.

There are 2,108 members, 90 ministers and 89 churches in Great Britain.

Connexional President (2005–7), A. Geoffrey Mort
General Secretary, W. C. Gabb, 66 Kirkstone Drive, Loughborough LE11 3RW T 01942-223526

LUTHERAN CHURCH

Lutheranism is based on the teachings of Martin Luther, the German leader of the Protestant Reformation. The authority of the scriptures is held to be supreme over Church tradition. The teachings of Lutheranism are explained in detail in 16th century confessional writings, particularly the Augsburg Confession. Lutheranism is one of the largest Protestant denominations and it is particularly strong in northern Europe and the USA. Some Lutheran churches are episcopal, while others have a synodal form of organisation; unity is based on doctrine rather than structure. Most Lutheran churches are members of the Lutheran World Federation, based in Geneva.

Lutheran services in Great Britain are held in 18 languages to serve members of different nationalities. Services usually follow ancient liturgies. English-language congregations are members either of the Lutheran Church in Great Britain, or of the Evangelical Lutheran Church of England. The Lutheran Church in Great Britain and other Lutheran churches in Britain are members of the Lutheran Council of Great Britain, which represents them and co-ordinates their common work.

There are over 70 million Lutherans world-wide; in Great Britain there are about 100,000 members, 50 clergy and 100 congregations.

General Secretary of the Lutheran Council of Great Britain,
Revd T. Bruch, 30 Thanet Street, London WC1H 9QH
T 020-7554 2900 F 020-7383 3081
E enquiries@lutheran.org.uk W www.lutheran.org.uk

METHODIST CHURCH

The Methodist movement started in England in 1729 when the Revd John Wesley, an Anglican priest, and his brother Charles met with others in Oxford and resolved to conduct their lives and study by 'rule and method'. In 1739 the Wesleys began evangelistic preaching and the first Methodist chapel was founded in Bristol in the same year. In 1744 the first annual conference was held, at which the Articles of Religion were drawn up. Doctrinal emphases included repentance, faith, the assurance of salvation, social concern and the priesthood of all believers. After John Wesley's death in 1791 the Methodists withdrew from the established Church to form the Methodist Church. Methodists gradually drifted into many groups, but in 1932 the Wesleyan Methodist Church, the United Methodist Church and the Primitive Methodist Church united to form the Methodist Church in Great Britain as it now exists.

The governing body of the Methodist Church is the Conference, the Conference is held in June each year and consists of three parts: the Diaconal, Ministerial and Representative Sessions. In addition, there are also 33 district synods whose purpose is to decide policy for the district and be the link between the Conference and the Circuits. The Circuit is the basic structure of the Methodist Church and is usually formed from the local churches in a defined area; a number of Circuits make up each District. There are over 60 million Methodists world-wide; in Great Britain in 2004 there were 293,661 members, 3,584 Ministers and 228 Deacons.

President of the Conference in Great Britain (2005–6), Revd Tom Stuckey

Vice-President of the Conference (2005–6), John Bell
Secretary of the Conference, Revd David Deeks, Methodist Church House, 25 Marylebone Road, London NW1 5JR
T 020-7486 5502 W www.methodist.org.uk

THE METHODIST CHURCH IN IRELAND

The Methodist Church in Ireland is autonomous but has close links with British Methodism. It has a community roll of 53,990, 15,484 members, 203 ministers, 285 lay preachers and 220 churches.

President of the Methodist Church in Ireland (2004–5), Revd Desmond C. Bain, 71B, Rathgar, Dublin 6W
Secretary of the Methodist Church in Ireland, Revd W. Winston Graham, 1 Fountainville Avenue, Belfast BT9 6AN
T 028-9032 4554

EASTERN ORTHODOX CHURCH

The Eastern (or Byzantine) Orthodox Church is a communion of self-governing Christian churches recognising the honorary primacy of the Oecumenical Patriarch of Constantinople.

The position of Orthodox Christians is that the faith was fully defined during the period of the Oecumenical Councils. In doctrine it is strongly trinitarian, and stresses the mystery and importance of the sacraments. It is episcopal in government. The structure of the Orthodox Christian year differs from that of western Churches.

Orthodox Christians throughout the world are estimated to number about 300 million; there are an estimated 284,298 in the UK.

EASTERN ORTHODOX CHURCHES IN THE UK

THE PATRIARCHATE OF ANTIOCH

There are fifteen parishes in the UK. The Diocese of Western and Central Europe is lead by HE Metropolitan Gabriel, 22 Avenue Kleber, 75116 Paris, France T (+33) (145) 01 8356. In the UK the Patriarchate can be contacted through the Dean: Fr Michael Harper, 16 Pightle Close, Harston, Cambridge, CB2 5NN T 01223-872433
E fr.michael@antiochian.org.uk

THE GREEK ORTHODOX CHURCH (PATRIARCHATE OF CONSTANTINOPLE)

The presence of Greek Orthodox Christians in Britain dates back at least to 1677 when Archbishop Joseph Geogirenes of Samos fled from Turkish persecution and came to London. The present Greek cathedral in Moscow Road, Bayswater, was opened for public worship in 1879 and the Diocese of Thyateira and Great Britain was established in 1922. There are now 119 parishes and other communities (including monasteries) in the UK, served by five bishops, 109 clergy, nine cathedrals and about 93 churches.

In Great Britain the Patriarchate of Constantinople is represented by Archbishop Gregorios of Thyateira and Great Britain, Thyateira House, 5 Craven Hill, London W2 3EN
T 020-7723 4787 F 020-7224 9301

THE RUSSIAN ORTHODOX CHURCH (PATRIARCHATE OF MOSCOW) AND THE RUSSIAN ORTHODOX CHURCH OUTSIDE RUSSIA

The records of Russian Orthodox Church activities in Britain date from the visit to England of Tsar Peter I in the early 18th century. Clergy were sent from Russia to serve the chapel established to minister to the staff of the Imperial Russian Embassy in London.

In Great Britain the Patriarchate of Moscow is represented by Bishop Basil of Sergievo, 94a Banbury Road, Oxford OX2 6JT. He is assisted by one bishop and 30 clergy. There are 30 parishes and smaller communities.

The Russian Orthodox Church Outside Russia is represented by Archbishop Mark of Berlin, Germany and Great Britain, c/o *Dean of English-Language Parishes*, Very Revd Archimandrite Alexis, Saint Edward Brotherhood, St Cyprian's Avenue, Brookwood, Surrey GU24 0BL T 01483-487763

THE SERBIAN ORTHODOX CHURCH (PATRIARCHATE OF SERBIA)

There are 33 parishes and smaller communities in Great Britain served by 11 clergy. The Patriarchate of Serbia is represented by the Episcopal Vicar, the Very Revd Milenko Zebic, St. Tzar Lazar Church, 131 Cob Lane, Bournville, Birmingham B30 1QE T 0121-486 1220

OTHER NATIONALITIES

Most of the Ukrainian parishes in Britain have joined the Patriarchate of Constantinople, leaving a small number of Ukrainian parishes in Britain under the care of other patriarchates (not all of which are recognised by the other Orthodox Churches). The Latvian, Polish and some Belarusian parishes are also under the care of the Patriarchate of Constantinople. The Patriarchate of Romania has one parish served by two clergy. The Patriarchate of Bulgaria has one parish served by one priest. The Belarusian Autocephalous Orthodox Church has five parishes served by two priests.

ORIENTAL ORTHODOX CHURCHES

The term 'Oriental Orthodox Churches' is now generally used to describe a group of six ancient eastern churches which reject the Christological definition of the Council of Chalcedon (AD 451) and use Christological terms in different ways from the Eastern Orthodox Church. There are about 34 million members world-wide of the Oriental Orthodox Churches and about 22,020 in the UK.

ORIENTAL ORTHODOX CHURCHES IN THE UK
THE ARMENIAN ORTHODOX CHURCH (PATRIARCHATE OF ETCHMIADZIN)

The Armenian Orthodox Church is the longest-established Oriental Orthodox community in Great Britain. It is represented by the Rt. Revd Bishop Nathan Hovhannisian, Armenian Primate of Great Britain, Armenian Vicarage, Iverna Gardens, London W8 6TP T 020-7937 0152 E armchurchlondon@aol.com

THE COPTIC ORTHODOX CHURCH

The Coptic Orthodox Church is the largest Oriental Orthodox community in Great Britain.

Coptic Orthodox Church, HE Bishop Angaelos, Coptic Orthodox Church Centre, Shephalbury Manor, Broadhall Way, Stevenage, Herts SG2 8RH T 01438-745232
E info@CopticCentre.com
W www.CopticCentre.com

The British Orthodox Church is canonically part of the Coptic Orthodox Patriarchate of Alexandria. As it ministers to British people all its services are in English.

The British Orthodox Church, Metropolitan Seraphim,10 Heathwood Gardens, Charlton, London SE7 8EP T 020-8854 3090 E boc@nildram.co.uk W www.britishorthodox.org

THE ERITREAN ORTHODOX CHURCH

In Great Britain the Eritrean Orthodox Church is represented by Bishop Markos, 78 Edmund Street, Camberwell, London SE5 7NR

THE MALANKARA ORTHODOX SYRIAN CHURCH

The Malankara Orthodox Syrian Church is part of the Diocese of Europe, UK and Canada under Metropolitan Thomas Mar Makarios. The church in Great Britain can be contacted via Fr. Abraham Thomas, St Gregorios Indian Orthodox Church, Cranfield Road, Brockley, London SE4 1UF T 020-8691 9456 E vicar@indian-orthodox.co.uk
W www.indian-orthodox.co.uk

THE SYRIAN ORTHODOX CHURCH

The Syrian Orthodox Church in Great Britain comes under the Patriarch, whose representative is Fr Touma Hazim Dakkama, 5 Canning Road, Croydon CR0 6QA T 020-8654 7531

THE COUNCIL OF ORIENTAL ORTHODOX CHURCHES,
Secretary, Deacon Aziz M. A. Nour, 34 Chertsey Road, Church Square, Shepperton, Middlesex TW17 9LF
T 020-8368 8447
President, Rt. Revd Bishop Nathan Hovhannisian

PENTECOSTAL CHURCHES

Pentecostalism is inspired by the descent of the Holy Spirit upon the apostles at Pentecost. The movement began in Los Angeles, USA, in 1906 and is characterised by baptism with the Holy Spirit, divine healing, speaking in tongues (glossolalia), and a literal interpretation of the scriptures. The Pentecostal movement in Britain dates from 1907. Initially, groups of Pentecostalists were led by laymen and did not organise formally. However, in 1915 the Elim Foursquare Gospel Alliance (more usually called the Elim Pentecostal Church) was founded in Ireland by George Jeffreys and in 1924 about 70 independent assemblies formed a fellowship, the Assemblies of God in Great Britain and Ireland. The Apostolic Church grew out of the 1904–5 revivals in South Wales and was established in 1916, and the New Testament Church of God was established in England in 1953. In recent years many aspects of Pentecostalism have been adopted by the growing charismatic movement within the Roman Catholic, Protestant and Eastern Orthodox churches. There are about 105 million Pentecostalists world-wide, with about 280,260 adherents in Great Britain and Ireland.

THE APOSTOLIC CHURCH, International Administration Offices, PO Box 389, 24–27 St Helens Road, Swansea SA1 1ZH T 01792-473992
President, Warren Jones
The Apostolic Church has about 110 churches, 4,481 adherents and 77 ministers

THE ASSEMBLIES OF GOD INCORPORATED, PO Box 7634, Nottingham NG11 6ZY T 0115-921 7272 F 0115-921 7273 E info@aog.org.uk
General Superintendent, P. C. Weaver
The Assemblies of God has 640 churches, about 60,000 adherents (including children) and 1,039 accredited ministers

THE ELIM PENTECOSTAL CHURCH, PO Box 38, Cheltenham, Glos GL50 3HN T 01242-519904
E info@elimhq.net
General Superintendent, Revd J. J. Glass
The Elim Pentecostal Church has 600 churches, 68,500 adherents and 650 accredited ministers

THE NEW TESTAMENT CHURCH OF GOD, Main House,
Overstone Park, Overstone, Northampton NN6 0AD
T 01604-643311
Administrative Bishop, Bishop Eric Arthur Brown
The New Testament Church of God has about 115
congregations, about 21,540 members and more than
300 ministers

PLYMOUTH BRETHREN
The Brethren was founded in Dublin in 1827–28. It
rejected denominationalism and clericalism and based
itself on the structures and practices of the early Church.
Many groups sprang up and that at Plymouth became the
best known, which resulted in the designation by others
as Plymouth Brethren. Other groups are based in Ireland,
USA, Myanmar and Guyana.

Early worship had a prescribed form but quickly
assumed an unstructured, non-liturgical format. There
were services devoted to worship, usually involving the
breaking of bread, and separate preaching meetings.
There was no salaried ministry.

A theological dispute led in 1848 to schism between
the Open Brethren and the Closed or Exclusive Brethren,
each branch later suffering further divisions.

Open Brethren churches are completely independent,
but freely co-operate with each other. Churches are run by
appointed elders. Exclusive Brethren churches believe in a
universal fellowship between congregations. They do not
have elders, but appoint respected members of their
congregation to perform certain administrative functions.

The Brethren are established throughout the UK,
Ireland, Europe, India, Africa and Australasia. Total
membership in the UK is 80,210.
GOSPEL TRACT PUBLICATIONS, 411 Hillington Road,
Glasgow G52 4BL
CHAPTER TWO, Conduit Mews, London SE18 7AP
T 020-8316 5389 W www.chaptertwobooks.org.uk

PRESBYTERIAN CHURCH IN IRELAND
The Presbyterian Church in Ireland is reformed in
doctrine and presbyterian in constitution. Presbyterianism
was established in Ireland as a result of the Ulster
plantation in the early 17th century when English and
Scottish Protestants settled in the north of Ireland.

There are 21 presbyteries under the chief court known
as the General Assembly. The General Assembly meets
annually and is presided over by a Moderator who is
elected for one year. The ongoing work of the Church is
undertaken by 18 boards under which there are specialist
committees.

There are about 179,549 Presbyterians in Ireland,
mainly in the north, in 460 congregations and with 370
ministers.
Moderator (2005–6), Rt. Revd Dr Harry Uprichard
Clerk of Assembly and General Secretary, Revd Dr Donald
Watts, Church House, Belfast BT1 6DW T 028-9041 7301

PRESBYTERIAN CHURCH OF WALES
The Presbyterian Church of Wales or Calvinistic
Methodist Church of Wales is Calvinistic in doctrine and
presbyterian in constitution. It was formed in 1811 when
Welsh Calvinists severed the relationship with the
established church by ordaining their own ministers. It
secured its own confession of faith in 1823 and a
Constitutional Deed in 1826, and since 1864 the General
Assembly has met annually, presided over by a Moderator
elected for a year. The doctrine and constitutional

structure of the Presbyterian Church of Wales was
confirmed by Act of Parliament in 1931–2.

The Church has about 34,819 members, 89 ministers
and 765 churches.
Moderator (2005–6), Revd Robert Bebb
General Secretary, Revd Ifan Roberts, Tabernacle Chapel,
81 Merthyr Road, Whitchurch, Cardiff CF14 1DD
T 029-2062 7465

RELIGIOUS SOCIETY OF FRIENDS (QUAKERS)
Quakerism is a movement, not a church, which was
founded in the 17th century by George Fox and others in
an attempt to revive what they saw as 'primitive
Christianity'. The movement was based originally in the
Midlands, Yorkshire and north-west England, but there
are now Quakers in 36 countries around the world. The
colony of Pennsylvania, founded by William Penn, was
originally Quaker.

Emphasis is placed on the experience of God in daily
life rather than on sacraments or religious occasions.
There is no church calendar. Worship is largely silent and
there are no appointed ministers; the responsibility for
conducting a meeting is shared equally among those
present. Social reform and religious tolerance have always
been important to Quakers, together with a commitment
to non-violence in resolving disputes.

There are 338,000 Quakers world-wide, with over
15,500 in Great Britain and Ireland. There are about 500
meetings in Great Britain.
CENTRAL OFFICES: (GREAT BRITAIN) Friends House,
173–177 Euston Road, London NW1 2BJ T 020-7663 1000
F 020-7663 1001 W www.quaker.org.uk

SALVATION ARMY
The Salvation Army was founded by a Methodist minister,
William Booth, in the east end of London in 1865, and
has since become established in 108 countries world-
wide. In 1878 it adopted a quasi-military command
structure intended to inspire and regulate its endeavours
and to reflect its view that the Church was engaged in
spiritual warfare. Salvationists emphasise evangelism and
the provision of social welfare. In the UK there are 4,000
employees, 1,500 active officers (ministers) and 774 local
church centres and 107 social service centres.
International Leader, Gen. John Larsson
UK Territorial Commander, Commissioner Shaw Clifton
TERRITORIAL HEADQUARTERS, 101 Newington
Causeway, London SE1 6BN T 020-7367 4700
E thq@salvationarmy.org.uk W www.salvationarmy.org.uk

SEVENTH-DAY ADVENTIST CHURCH
The Seventh-day Adventist Church was founded in 1863
in the USA and the first church in the UK was established
in 1886. Its members look forward to the second coming
of Christ and observe the Sabbath (the seventh day) as a
day of rest, worship and ministry. The Church bases its
faith and practice wholly on the Bible and has developed
27 core beliefs. The World Church is divided into 13
divisions, each made up of unions of churches. The
Seventh-day Adventist Church in the British Isles is
known as the British Union Conference of Seventh-day
Adventists and is a member of the Trans-European
Division. In the British Isles the administrative
organisation of the church is arranged in three tiers: the
local churches; the regional conferences for south
England, north England, Wales, Scotland and Ireland; and
the national headquarters. There are over 12.9 million

members, 53,502 churches and 58,775 companies in 203 countries. In the UK and Ireland there are 24,502 members and 262 churches and companies.

President of the British Union Conference, Cecil Perry
BRITISH ISLES HEADQUARTERS, Stanborough Park,
Watford WD25 9JZ T 01923-672251

SWEDENBORGIAN NEW CHURCH
The New Church is based on the teachings of the 18th century Swedish scientist and theologian Emanuel Swedenborg (1688–1772), who believed that Jesus Christ appeared to him and instructed him to reveal the spiritual meaning of the Bible. He claimed to have visions of the spiritual world, including heaven and hell, and conversations with angels and spirits. He published several theological works, including descriptions of the spiritual world and a Bible commentary.

The Second Coming of Jesus Christ is believed to have already taken place and is still taking place, being not an actual physical reappearance of Christ, but rather His return in spirit. It is also believed that concurrent with our life on earth is life in a parallel spiritual world, of which we are usually unconscious until death. There are around 30,000 Swedenborgians world-wide, with 1,125 members, 24 Churches and 11 ministers in the UK.

THE GENERAL CONFERENCE OF THE NEW CHURCH,
Swedenborg House, 20 Bloomsbury Way, London
WC1A 2TH T 020-7229 9340

UNDEB YR ANNIBYNWYR CYMRAEG
Undeb Yr Annibynwyr Cymraeg, the Union of Welsh Independents, was formed in 1872 and is a voluntary association of Welsh Congregational Churches and personal members. It is mainly Welsh-speaking. Congregationalism in Wales dates back to 1639 when the first Welsh Congregational Church was opened in Gwent. Member churches are Calvinistic in doctrine, although a wide range of interpretations are permitted, and congregationalist in organisation. Each church has complete independence in the government and administration of its affairs.

The Union has 29,878 members, 209 ministers and 476 member churches.

President of the Union (2005–6), Revd Gareth Morgan-Jones
General Secretary, Revd D. Myrddin Hughes, 5 Axis Court,
Riverside Business Park, Swansea Vale, Swansea SA7 0AJ
T 01792-795888 F 01792-795376
E undeb@annibynwyr.org

UNITED REFORMED CHURCH
The United Reformed Church was first formed by the union of most of the Congregational churches in England and Wales with the Presbyterian Church of England in 1972. Congregationalism dates from the mid 16th century. It is Calvinistic in doctrine, and its followers form independent self-governing congregations bound under God by covenant, a principle laid down in the writings of Robert Browne (1550–1633). From the late 16th century the movement was driven underground by persecution, but the cause was defended at the Westminster Assembly in 1643 and the Savoy Declaration of 1658 laid down its principles. Congregational churches formed county associations for mutual support and in 1832 these associations merged to form the Congregational Union of England and Wales.

Presbyterianism in England also dates from the mid

16th century, and was Calvinistic and evangelical in its doctrine. It was governed by a hierarchy of courts.

In the 1960s there was close co-operation locally and nationally between Congregational and Presbyterian Churches. This led to union negotiations and a Scheme of Union, supported by Act of Parliament in 1972. In 1981 a further unification took place, with the Reformed Association of Churches of Christ becoming part of the URC. In 2000 a third union took place, with the Congregational Union of Scotland. In its basis the United Reformed Church reflects local church initiative and responsibility with a conciliar pattern of oversight. The General Assembly is the central body, and is made up of equal numbers of ministers and lay members.

The United Reformed Church is divided into 13 Synods, each with a Synod Moderator, and 78 Districts. There are 82,000 members, 628 full-time stipendiary ministers, 83 part-time stipendiary ministers, 138 non-stipendiary ministers, 18 active church related community workers and 1,691 local churches.

General Secretary, Revd Dr David C. Cornick, 86 Tavistock
Place, London WC1H 9RT T 020-7916 2020 F 7916 2021
E david.cornick@urc.org.uk

WESLEYAN REFORM UNION
The Wesleyan Reform Union was founded by Methodists who left or were expelled from Wesleyan Methodism in 1849 following a period of internal conflict. Its doctrine is conservative evangelical and its organisation is congregational, each church having complete independence in the government and administration of its affairs. The Union has 1,843 members, 15 ministers, 115 lay preachers and 108 churches.

President (2005–6), Revd C. Braithwaite
General Secretary, Revd A. J. Williams, Wesleyan Reform
Church House, 123 Queen Street, Sheffield S1 2DU
T 0114-272 1938

NON-TRINITARIAN CHURCHES

CHRISTADELPHIAN
Christadelphians believe that the Bible is the word of God and that it reveals both God's dealings with mankind in the past and his plans for the future. These plans centre on the work of Jesus Christ, who is believed shortly to return to earth to establish God's kingdom. Christadelphians have existed since the 1850s, beginning in the USA through the work of an Englishman, Dr John Thomas.

THE CHRISTADELPHIAN MAGAZINE AND PUBLISHING
ASSOCIATION, 404 Shaftmoor Lane, Birmingham B28 8SZ
T 0121-777 6324 F 0121-778 5024

THE CHURCH OF CHRIST, SCIENTIST
The Church of Christ, Scientist was founded by Mary Baker Eddy in the USA in 1879 to 'reinstate primitive Christianity and its lost element of healing'. Christian Science teaches the need for spiritual regeneration and salvation from sin, but is best known for its reliance on prayer alone in the healing of sickness. Adherents believe that such healing is a law, or Science, and is in direct line with that practised by Jesus Christ (revered, not as God, but as the Son of God) and by the early Christian Church.

The denomination consists of The First Church of Christ, Scientist, in Boston, Massachusetts, USA (the Mother Church) and its branch churches in over 80 countries world-wide. The Bible and Mary Baker Eddy's book, *Science and Health with Key to the Scriptures,* are used at services; there are no clergy. Those engaged in full-time healing are called practitioners, of whom there are 3,500 world-wide. The Church also publishes *The Christian Science Monitor.*

No membership figures are available, since Mary Baker Eddy felt that numbers are no measure of spiritual vitality and ruled that such statistics should not be published. There are almost 2,000 branch churches world-wide, including nearly 140 in the UK.

CHRISTIAN SCIENCE COMMITTEE ON PUBLICATION, Claridge House, 29 Barnes High Street, London SW13 9LW
T 020-8282 1645 F 020-8487 1566 E londoncs@csps.com
District Manager for the UK and the Republic of Ireland,
Tony Lobl

THE CHURCH OF JESUS CHRIST OF LATTER-DAY SAINTS

The Church (often referred to as 'the Mormons') was founded in New York State, USA, in 1830, and came to Britain in 1837. The oldest continuous branch in the world is to be found in Preston, Lancs. Mormons are Christians who claim to belong to the 'Restored Church' of Jesus Christ. They believe that true Christianity died when the last original apostle died, but that it was given back to the world by God and Christ through Joseph Smith, the Church's founder and first president. They accept and use the Bible as scripture, but believe in continuing revelation from God and use additional scriptures, including *The Book of Mormon: Another Testament of Jesus Christ.* The importance of the family is central to the Church's beliefs and practices. Church members set aside Monday evenings as Family Home Evenings when Christian family values are taught. Polygamy was formally discontinued in 1890. The Church has no paid ministry; local congregations are headed by a leader chosen from amongst their number. The world governing body, based in Utah, USA, is the three-man First Presidency, assisted by the Quorum of the Twelve Apostles. There are more than 11 million members world-wide, with 178,920 adherents and 371 congregations in the UK.

BRITISH HEADQUARTERS, Church Offices, 751 Warwick Road, Solihull, W. Midlands B91 3DQ T 0121-712 1207

JEHOVAH'S WITNESS

The movement now known as Jehovah's Witnesses grew from a Bible study group formed by Charles Taze Russell in 1872 in Pennsylvania, USA. In 1896 it adopted the name of the Watch Tower Bible and Tract Society, and in 1931 its members became known as Jehovah's Witnesses. Jehovah's (God's) Witnesses believe in the Bible as the word of God, and consider it to be inspired and historically accurate. They take the scriptures literally, except where there are obvious indications that they are figurative or symbolic, and reject the doctrine of the Trinity. Witnesses also believe that the earth will remain for ever and that all those approved of by Jehovah will have eternal life on a cleansed and beautified earth; only 144,000 will go to heaven to rule with Christ. They believe that the second coming of Christ began in 1914 and his thousand-year reign on earth is imminent, and that Armageddon (a final battle in which evil will be defeated) will precede Christ's rule of peace. They refuse to take part in military service, and do not accept blood transfusions. The 10-member world governing body is based in New York, USA. There is no paid ministry, but each congregation has elders assigned to look after various duties and every Witness is assigned homes to visit in their congregation. There are over 6 million Jehovah's Witnesses world-wide, with 130,000 Witnesses in the UK organised into 1,500 congregations.

BRITISH ISLES HEADQUARTERS, Watch Tower House, The Ridgeway, London NW7 1RN T 020-8906 2211
F 020-8371 0051 E opi@wtbts.org.uk
W www.watchtower.org

UNITARIAN AND FREE CHRISTIAN CHURCHES

Unitarianism has its historical roots in the Judaeo-Christian tradition but rejects the deity of Christ and the doctrine of the trinity. It allows the individual to embrace insights from all the world's faiths and philosophies, as there is no fixed creed. It is accepted that beliefs may evolve in the light of personal experience.

Unitarian communities first became established in Poland and Transylvania in the 16th century. The first avowedly Unitarian place of worship in the British Isles opened in London in 1774. The General Assembly of Unitarian and Free Christian Churches came into existence in 1928 as the result of the amalgamation of two earlier organisations.

There are about 4,400 Unitarians in Great Britain and Ireland and about 72 Unitarian ministers. Nearly 200 self-governing congregations and fellowship groups, including a small number overseas, are members of the General Assembly.

GENERAL ASSEMBLY OF UNITARIAN AND FREE CHRISTIAN CHURCHES, Essex Hall, 1–6 Essex Street, London WC2R 3HY T 020-7240 2384
E ga@unitarian.org.uk W www.unitarian.org.uk
President 2005–6, Brian Cockroft

COMMUNICATIONS

POSTAL SERVICES

The Royal Mail Group plc operates Parcelforce Worldwide, Post Office and Royal Mail, which handles around 84 million items of mail each day. The Postal Services Commission (Postcomm), an independent regulator accountable to Parliament, oversees postal operations in the UK and is responsible for the smooth introduction of competition into postal services; 1 January 2006 will see the removal of the final restrictions to competition, and the postal market will be fully open to alternative operators. Postwatch is the consumer organisation responsible for postal services and takes up complaints on behalf of consumers against any licensed provider of postal services.

POSTCOMM, Hercules House, Hercules Road, London SE1 7DB T 020-7593 2100 W www.postcomm.gov.uk
POSTWATCH, 28–30 Grosvenor Gardens, London SW1W 0TT T 08456-013265 W www.postwatch.co.uk
Below are details of a number of popular postal services along with prices correct as at August 2005. Note that 2006 will see the introduction by the Royal Mail of 'Pricing in Proportion', whereby the pricing of mail will depend upon its size as well as its weight. For further details please contact the relevant service provider, i.e. Royal Mail or Parcelforce.

INLAND POSTAL SERVICES AND REGULATIONS

INLAND POST RATES*

Maximum weight	First class	Second class†
60 g	£0.30	£0.21
100 g	£0.46	£0.35
150 g	£0.64	£0.47
200 g	£0.79	£0.58
250 g	£0.94	£0.71
300 g	£1.07	£0.83
350 g	£1.21	£0.94
400 g	£1.40	£1.14
450 g	£1.59	£1.30
500 g	£1.78	£1.48
600 g	£2.15	£1.75
700 g	£2.52	£2.00
750 g	£2.71	£2.12
800 g	£2.90	(not admissible
900 g	£3.27	over 750 g)
1000 g	£3.64	

First class items over 1 kg cost £3.64 plus 88p for every additional 250 g or part thereof.
* Includes postcards
† First class post is normally delivered the following day and second class within three days

UK PARCEL RATES

Maximum weight	Standard tariff*
1 kg	£3.60
1.5 kg	£4.63
2 kg	£4.97
4 kg	£7.20
6 kg	£8.17
8 kg	£9.32
10 kg	£10.00
20 kg	£11.65

* Standard parcels are normally delivered within three to five working days

OVERSEAS POSTAL SERVICES AND REGULATIONS

Royal Mail divides the world into three zones: **Europe** (Albania, Andorra, Armenia, Austria, Azerbaijan, Azores, Balearic Islands, Belarus, Belgium, Bosnia-Hercegovina, Bulgaria, Canary Islands, Corsica, Croatia, Cyprus, Czech Republic, Denmark, Estonia, Faeroe Islands, Finland, France, Georgia, Germany, Gibraltar, Greece, Greenland, Hungary, Iceland, Ireland, Italy, Kazakhstan, Kyrgyzstan, Latvia, Liechtenstein, Lithuania, Luxembourg, Macedonia, Madeira, Malta, Moldova, Monaco, Netherlands, Norway, Poland, Portugal, Romania, Russia, San Marino, Serbia and Montenegro, Slovakia, Slovenia, Spain, Spitzbergen, Sweden, Switzerland, Tajikistan, Turkey, Turkmenistan, Ukraine, Uzbekistan, Vatican City State); **Zone 1** (Africa, parts of Asia and the Indian sub-continent, most of southeast Asia, Canada, Hong Kong, the Middle East, South America and USA); **Zone 2** (American Samoa, Australia, China, East Timor, Fiji, French Southern and Antarctic Territories, French Polynesia, Guam, Japan, Kiribati, Korea, Marshall Islands, Micronesia, Mongolia, Nauru, New Caledonia, New Zealand and Territories, Norfolk Island, Northern Mariana Islands, Papua New Guinea, Philippines, Pitcairn Island, Solomon Islands, Taiwan, Tonga, Tuvalu, Vanuatu, Wake Island, Wallis and Futuna Island, Western Samoa).

OVERSEAS SURFACE MAIL RATES
(WORLD ZONES 1 & 2*)

Letters

Maximum weight		Maximum weight	
20 g†	£0.40	450 g	£3.62
60 g	£0.68	500 g	£4.00
100 g	£0.96	750 g	£5.90
150 g	£1.34	1,000 g	£7.80
200 g	£1.72	1,250 g	£9.70
250 g	£2.10	1,500 g	£11.60
300 g	£2.48	1,750 g	£13.50
350 g	£2.86	2,000 g	£15.40
400 g	£3.24		

* Letters and postcards to Europe are sent by Airmail
† Includes postcards

Small packets and printed papers

Maximum weight		Maximum weight	
100 g	£0.67	450 g	£2.28
150 g	£0.90	500 g	£2.51
200 g	£1.13	750 g	£3.66
250 g	£1.36	1,000 g	£4.81
300 g	£1.59	1,500 g	£7.11
350 g	£1.82	2,000 g*	£9.41
400 g	£2.05		

* Maximum weight. For printed papers only: up to maximum weight of 5 kg, add £0.23 for each additional 50 g

AIRMAIL LETTERS

Europe:

Maximum weight*		Maximum weight	
20 g*	£0.42	300 g	£2.88
40 g	£0.60	320 g	£3.05
60 g	£0.78	340 g	£3.22
80 g	£0.96	360 g	£3.39
100 g	£1.14	380 g	£3.56
120 g	£1.32	400 g	£3.73
140 g	£1.50	420 g	£3.90
160 g	£1.68	440 g	£4.07
180 g	£1.86	460 g	£4.24
200 g	£2.03	480 g	£4.41
220 g	£2.20	500 g	£4.58
240 g	£2.37	1,000 g	£8.83
260 g	£2.54	2,000 g†	£17.33
280 g	£2.71		

* Includes postcards

† Maximum weight. For printed papers only: up to maximum weight of 5 kg, add £0.09 for each additional 20 g

World Zones 1 and 2:

Maximum weight	Zone 1	Zone 2
Postcards	£0.47	£0.47
20 g	£0.68	£0.68
40 g	£1.05	£1.12
60 g	£1.42	£1.56
80 g	£1.79	£2.00
100 g	£2.16	£2.44
500 g	£9.56	£11.24
1,000 g	£18.81	£22.24
2,000 g*	£37.31	£44.24

* Maximum weight. For printed papers only: up to maximum weight of 5 kg, add £0.19 for each additional 20 g

SPECIAL DELIVERY SERVICES

SPECIAL DELIVERY NEXT DAY

A guaranteed next working day delivery service by 1 p.m. to 99 per cent of the UK for first class letters and packets (maximum item weight is 10 kg). Prices start at £3.85. There is also a service which guarantees delivery by 9 a.m. (maximum item weight is 2 kg). Prices start at £7.95.

INTERNATIONAL SIGNED FOR AND AIRSURE

Express airmail services. The fee for International Signed For is £3.30 plus airmail postage. The fee for Airsure is £4.00 plus airmail postage.

RECORDED SIGNED FOR

Provides a record of posting and delivery of letters and ensures a signature on delivery. This service is recommended for items of little or no monetary value. All packets must be handed to the post office and a receipt issued as proof of posting. Charge: 66p plus the standard first or second class postage.

OTHER SERVICES

BUSINESS SERVICES

A range of postal services are available to businesses including business collection, freepost, business reply services, business packaging for special deliveries and international bulk mailing options.

COMPENSATION

Compensation for loss or damage to an item sent varies according to the service used to send the item. Visit www.royalmail.com for more details.

PASSPORT APPLICATIONS

Around 2,000 post offices process passport applications. To find out your nearest office, and for further information, see contact details below.

TRACK AND TRACE

This online service, accessible from www.royalmail.com and www.postoffice.co.uk, enables customers to track the progress of items sent using the special delivery services listed above.

REDIRECTION

A printed form obtainable from the Post Office or from www.royalmail.com must be signed by the person to whom the letters are to be addressed. A fee is payable for each different surname on the application form. Charges: one month, £6.65 (abroad via airmail, £13.40); three months, £14.55 (£29.10); six months, £22.40 (£44.80); 12 months, £33.60 (£67.20).

KEEPSAFE

Mail is held for up to two months while the addressee is away and is delivered when the addressee returns. Prices start at £5.35. Perishable items are returned to the sender. Recorded items are held for a week and Special Delivery items are held for three weeks before being returned to the sender.

POST OFFICE BOX

A PO Box provides a short and memorable alternative address. Mail is held at a local delivery office until the addressee is ready to collect it. A PO Box costs £43.80 for six months or £54 for a year.

CONTACT DETAILS

Royal Mail general enquiries: 08457-740740
W www.royalmail.com
Royal Mail business enquiries: 08457-950950
Postcode enquiry line: 08457-111222 / 0906-302 1222
Parcelforce Worldwide: 08708-501150
W www.parcelforce.com
Post Office enquires: 08457-223344
W www.postoffice.co.uk

IDD CODES

INTERNATIONAL DIRECT DIALLING (IDD)
International dialling codes are composed of four elements which are dialled in sequence:

(i)   the international code
(ii)   the country code
(iii)   the area code
(iv)   the telephone number

Calls to Midway Island, Tristan da Cunha and Wake Island must be made by calling the international operator on 155.

*Varies depending on area and/or carrier

Country	IDD from UK	IDD to UK
Afghanistan	00 93	00 44
Albania	00 355	00 44
Algeria	00 213	00 44
Andorra	00 376	00 44
Angola	00 244	00 44
Anguilla	00 1 264	011 44
Antigua and Barbuda	00 1 268	011 44
Argentina	00 54	00 44
Armenia	00 374	00 44
Aruba	00 297	00 44
Ascension Island	00 247	00 44
Australia	00 61	00 11 44
Austria	00 43	00 44
Azerbaijan	00 994	810 44
Azores	00 351	00 44
Bahamas	00 1 242	011 44
Bahrain	00 973	00 44
Balearic Islands	00 34	00 44
Bangladesh	00 880	00 44
Barbados	00 1 246	011 44
Belarus	00 375	810 44
Belgium	00 32	00 44
Belize	00 501	00 44
Benin	00 229	00 44
Bermuda	00 1 441	011 44
Bhutan	00 975	00 44
Bolivia	00 591	0010 44*
		0011 44*
		0012 44*
		0013 44*
Bosnia-Hercegovina	00 387	00 44
Botswana	00 267	00 44
Brazil	00 55	0014 44*
		0015 44*
		0021 44*
		0023 44*
		0031 44*
British Virgin Islands	00 1 284	011 44
Brunei	00 673	00 44
Bulgaria	00 359	00 44
Burkina Faso	00 226	00 44
Burundi	00 257	00 44
Cambodia	00 855	001 44
Cameroon	00 237	00 44
Canada	00 1	011 44
Canary Islands	00 34	00 44
Cape Verde	00 238	0 44
Cayman Islands	00 1 345	011 44
Central African Republic	00 236	19 44
Chad	00 235	15 44
Chile	00 56	00 44
China	00 86	00 44
Colombia	00 57	009 44
Comoros	00 269	00 44
Congo, Dem. Rep. of	00 243	00 44
Congo, Republic of	00 242	00 44
Cook Islands	00 682	00 44
Costa Rica	00 506	00 44
Côte d'Ivoire	00 225	00 44
Croatia	00 385	00 44
Cuba	00 53	119 44
Cyprus	00 357	00 44
Czech Republic	00 420	00 44
Denmark	00 45	00 44
Djibouti	00 253	00 44
Dominica	00 1 767	011 44
Dominican Republic	00 1 809	011 44
East Timor	00 670	00 44
Ecuador	00 593	00 44
Egypt	00 20	00 44
El Salvador	00 503	00 44
Equatorial Guinea	00 240	00 44
Eritrea	00 291	00 44
Estonia	00 372	00 44
Ethiopia	00 251	00 44
Falkland Islands	00 500	00 44
Faeroe Islands	00 298	00 44
Fiji	00 679	00 44
Finland	00 358	00 44*
France	00 33	00 44
French Guiana	00 594	00 44
French Polynesia	00 689	00 44
Gabon	00 241	00 44
Gambia	00 220	00 44
Georgia	00 995	810 44
Germany	00 49	00 44
Ghana	00 233	00 44
Gibraltar	00 350	00 44
Greece	00 30	00 44
Greenland	00 299	00 44
Grenada	00 1 473	011 44
Guadeloupe	00 590	00 44
Guam	00 1 671	011 44
Guatemala	00 502	00 44
Guinea	00 224	00 44
Guinea-Bissau	00 245	00 44
Guyana	00 592	001 44
Haiti	00 509	00 44
Honduras	00 504	00 44
Hong Kong	00 852	001 44
Hungary	00 36	00 44
Iceland	00 354	00 44
India	00 91	00 44
Indonesia	00 62	001 44*
		008 44*
Iran	00 98	00 44
Iraq	00 964	00 44
Ireland, Republic of	00 353	00 44
Israel	00 972	00 44*
Italy	00 39	00 44
Jamaica	00 1 876	011 44
Japan	00 81	001 010 44*
		0033 010 44*
		0041 010 44*
		010 44*
Jordan	00 962	000 44*
Kazakhstan	00 7	810 44

Kenya	00 254	00 44	
Kiribati	00 686	00 44	
Korea, Dem. People's Rep. of	00 850	00 44	
Korea, Republic of	00 82	001 44* 002 44*	
Kuwait	00 965	00 44	
Kyrgyzstan	00 996	00 44	
Laos	00 856	00 44	
Latvia	00 371	00 44	
Lebanon	00 961	00 44	
Lesotho	00 266	00 44	
Liberia	00 231	00 44	
Libya	00 218	00 44	
Liechtenstein	00 423	00 44	
Lithuania	00 370	00 44	
Luxembourg	00 352	00 44	
Macao	00 853	00 44	
Macedonia	00 389	00 44	
Madagascar	00 261	00 44	
Madeira	00 351	00 44	
Malawi	00 265	00 44	
Malaysia	00 60	00 44	
Maldives	00 960	00 44	
Mali	00 223	00 44	
Malta	00 356	00 44	
Mariana Islands, Northern	00 1 670	011 44	
Marshall Islands	00 692	011 44	
Martinique	00 596	00 44	
Mauritania	00 222	00 44	
Mauritius	00 230	00 44	
Mayotte	00 269	10 44	
Mexico	00 52	00 44	
Micronesia, Federated States of	00 691	011 44	
Moldova	00 373	00 44	
Monaco	00 377	00 44	
Mongolia	00 976	001 44	
Montserrat	00 1 664	011 44	
Morocco	00 212	00 44	
Mozambique	00 258	00 44	
Myanmar	00 95	00 44	
Namibia	00 264	00 44	
Nauru	00 674	00 44	
Nepal	00 977	00 44	
Netherlands	00 31	00 44	
Netherlands Antilles	00 599	00 44	
New Caledonia	00 687	00 44	
New Zealand	00 64	00 44	
Nicaragua	00 505	00 44	
Niger	00 227	00 44	
Nigeria	00 234	009 44	
Niue	00 683	00 44	
Norfolk Island	00 672	00 44	
Norway	00 47	00 44	
Oman	00 968	00 44	
Pakistan	00 92	00 44	
Palau	00 680	011 44	
Panama	00 507	00 44	
Papua New Guinea	00 675	05 44	
Paraguay	00 595	002 44	
Peru	00 51	00 44	
Philippines	00 63	00 44	
Poland	00 48	00 44	
Portugal	00 351	00 44	
Puerto Rico	00 1 787	011 44	
Qatar	00 974	00 44	
Réunion	00 262	00 44	
Romania	00 40	00 44	
Russia	00 7	810 44	
Rwanda	00 250	00 44	
St Christopher and Nevis	00 1 869	011 44	
St Helena	00 290	00 44	
St Lucia	00 1 758	011 44	
St Pierre and Miquelon	00 508	00 44	
St Vincent and the Grenadines	00 1 784	011 44	
Samoa	00 685	0 44	
Samoa, American	00 1 684	00 44	
San Marino	00 378	00 44	
Sao Tomé and Principe	00 239	00 44	
Saudi Arabia	00 966	00 44	
Senegal	00 221	00 44	
Serbia and Montenegro	00 381	00 44	
Seychelles	00 248	00 44	
Sierra Leone	00 232	00 44	
Singapore	00 65	001 44	
Slovakia	00 421	00 44	
Slovenia	00 386	00 44	
Solomon Islands	00 677	00 44	
Somalia	00 252	00 44	
South Africa	00 27	09 44	
Spain	00 34	00 44	
Sri Lanka	00 94	00 44	
Sudan	00 249	00 44	
Suriname	00 597	00 44	
Swaziland	00 268	00 44	
Sweden	00 46	00 44	
Switzerland	00 41	00 44	
Syria	00 963	00 44	
Taiwan	00 886	002 44	
Tajikistan	00 992	810 44	
Tanzania	00 255	000 44	
Thailand	00 66	001 44	
Tibet	00 86	00 44	
Togo	00 228	00 44	
Tokelau	00 690	00 44	
Tonga	00 676	00 44	
Trinidad and Tobago	00 1 868	011 44	
Tunisia	00 216	00 44	
Turkey	00 90	00 44	
Turkmenistan	00 993	810 44	
Turks and Caicos Islands	00 1 649	011 44	
Tuvalu	00 688	00 44	
Uganda	00 256	000 44	
Ukraine	00 380	810 44	
United Arab Emirates	00 971	00 44	
Uruguay	00 598	00 44	
USA	00 1	011 44	
Uzbekistan	00 998	810 44	
Vanuatu	00 678	00 44	
Vatican City State	00 39	00 44	
Venezuela	00 58	00 44	
Vietnam	00 84	00 44	
Virgin Islands	00 1 340	011 44	
Yemen	00 967	00 44	
Zambia	00 260	00 44	
Zimbabwe	00 263	00 44	

MOBILE COMMUNICATIONS

CURRENT NETWORK OPERATOR MARKET SHARES (MILLIONS)

Last Quarter 2004	O2	Vodafone	T-Mobile	Orange	Hutchison
Current Subscriber Base	13.9	14.6	15.7	13.9	1.2 *(Aug. 2004)*

UK MOBILE PENETRATION

Date	Jan 1999	Jan 2000	Jan 2001	Jan 2002	Jan 2003	Jan 2004
Subscriber base	13,001,000	23,944,000	40,057,300	45,677,600	46,922,000	50,220,000
Penetration rate	22.3 %	41%	67.2%	76.6%	78.8%	84.4%

Source: Ofcom

Mobile penetration has grown rapidly in the UK, as illustrated in the table above, with estimates of over 54 million subscribers at the beginning of 2005. The UK mobile communications industry has been characterised by the introduction of new technologies with an increasing emphasis on expanding from voice-only to multi-media services, and the adoption of more expensive handset devices by consumers. The push towards new technology and enhanced service offerings is due to the near saturation of the mobile market as well as the need of network operators to increase average customer revenues through other means. The combination of very few new 'new' handset buyers entering the market, the heavy licence fee costs that the mobile network operators have incurred (the government sold the 3G operating licences at a great profit) and the costs associated with technology upgrades, has left network operators with vast financial gaps.

INDUSTRY PLAYERS

The mobile communications industry has a number of players: network operators who own the infrastructure and provide services; service providers and mobile virtual network operators (MVNOs) who do not own infrastructure but have commercial agreements with the network operators; and the telecommunications regulator, Ofcom, responsible for setting the controls of the mobile market, implementing EU-wide legislation and ensuring that industry players do not behave anti-competitively.

UK MOBILE NETWORK OPERATORS

Operator	Ownership	License	Launch
O2	Formerly BT Cellnet	Tacs-900	1985
	100% O2	GSM	1994
Vodafone	100% Vodafone	Tacs-900	1985
		GSM	1992
T-Mobile	Formerly One2One	GSM 1800	1993
	100% Deutsche Telekom		
Orange	100% France Telecom	GSM 1800	1994
Hutchison 3G	65% – Hutchison Whampoa	UMTS	2003
	20% – DoCoMo		
	15% – KPN Mobile		

NETWORK OPERATORS

Network operators are responsible for setting tariffs, billing, offering services and maintaining the network infrastructure. There are five licensed network operators in the UK.

ALTERNATIVE SERVICE PROVIDERS

Service providers were introduced into the UK market as a means to stimulate competition within the market. They buy airtime wholesale from the network operators and sell it on to end users. This agreement enables them to set their own tariff structures and to have a direct billing relationship with end users. The incumbent network operators (those who have been operating since the start), O2 and Vodafone, have an obligation under the terms of their licences to offer wholesale minutes of airtime to service providers. Orange and T-Mobile, as later entrants to the market, have not been subject to this condition. There are over 50 service providers operating in the UK market including One.Tel, Sainsbury's and Tesco Mobile. In order to maintain a viable business operation many of these service providers have diversified their products to other telecom or Internet-based services.

The newest players in the mobile market offering mobile services are MVNOs. Some of the network operators are obliged to open their networks to service providers, but none currently have to open their networks to MVNOs. That they choose to do so is purely a commercial agreement between the MVNO and network operator. The key difference between service providers and an MVNO is the degree of ownership over the equipment used. An MVNO has its own mobile network code, issues its own SIM cards (subscriber identity module card – the 'brain' of the handset), operates its own mobile switching centre and has a pricing structure fully independent from the network operator.

The best known MVNO and network operator agreement is that of Virgin Mobile and T-Mobile (formerly One 2 One), with Virgin Mobile operating its services on the back of the T-Mobile network. Virgin has been able to keep its costs low as it is not responsible for infrastructure maintenance. Other MVNOs in the UK include FT Mobile, a joint venture between the *Financial Times* and the Carphone Warehouse.

TYPES OF MOBILE SERVICE

Network operators, service providers and MVNOs offer two basic types of service: contract and pre-paid (also known as pay-as-you-go or PAYG). Contracts (generally paid on a monthly basis, though fixed to a minimum contract term) mean that the end user pays a fixed subscription fee each month that entitles them to a number of services. Initially this has been for more basic services, for example voicemail or SMS (short messaging service), but increasingly this has moved towards more comprehensive packages of limited multimedia services (for example, downloadable games, access to news and other information updates), which gives mobile subscribers a certain amount of complimentary airtime and access to services each month.

Pre-paid subscribers have access to the same services but pay in advance and simply 'top up' their account when credit is running low. The introduction of pre-paid services has allowed industry players to target additional consumer segments, in particular the youth market and those customers without an acceptable credit rating for a contract service. Pre-paid has proven to be a very popular option as it allows customers to control their spending. Throughout 2004-05 the split between pre-paid and contract customers in the UK remained fairly constant at around 68:32.

Stelios Haji-Ioannou, the entrepeneur behind the easyGroup companies, has recently entered the pre-paid market by launching easyMobile PAYG with half-price calls and texts. Carphone Warehouse quickly followed suit (through its PAYG service, Fresh) and Tesco Mobile has announced its intention to do the same. Consumers should still be wary of hidden costs in each offer, such as easyMobile's charge to top-up credit.

NETWORK TECHNOLOGY

Network technology has improved dramatically since the launch in 1985 of the first generation 900 MHz analogue GSM service, known as TACS, which offered little or no data capability. In 1992 Vodafone launched a new digital GSM network, usually referred to as 2G or second generation. BT Cellnet (now O_2) and two more entrants launched GSM services in the following two years, making the UK one of Europe's most competitive markets.

The latest development has been the introduction of 3G technology, or UMTS (universal mobile telecommunications system). UMTS differs from GPRS through its ability to offer increased data transmission speeds, therefore allowing expanded data facilities and Internet access. Additional advantages over GSM/GPRS include international roaming; at present, despite GSM's widespread presence, mobile technologies used in other parts of the world are incompatible with GSM handsets, for instance in parts of Asia and the USA.

Since 3G (or UMTS) technology is an entirely new network, network operators must hold a licence to deploy it. The UK was the third European country to license 3G operators, after Finland and Spain, and the first to auction its licences. Auctions are not new to the European communications industry – many of the second and third entrants to Europe's communications markets had to bid for their licences – but what was spectacular about the UK's 3G auction was the size of the bids. While industry observers had speculated that the auction might reach £4 billion, in the event a total of £22 billion was raised from the sale of the spectrum.

UK 3G LICENCE WINNERS AND TOTAL COST

Hutchison 3G UK	Licence A	2×15MHz paired €7 billion 5MHz unpaired
Vodafone	Licence B	2×15MHz paired €9.6 billion
BT Cellnet	Licence C	2×10MHz paired €6.5 billion 5MHz unpaired
One2One	Licence D	2×10MHz paired €6.5 billion 5MHz unpaired
Orange	Licence E	2×10MHz paired €6.6 billion 5MHz unpaired
TOTAL		€36.1 billion

DATA SERVICES

The upgrade to GSM from analogue brought clearer voice quality, while the upgrade from GSM through GPRS to UMTS also brings improved voice quality as well as new services (primarily data-based), as seen in the table below.

DATA SERVICES MIGRATION PATH

Mobile infrastructure	Data services available
GSM (2G) Speed: 10kb/sec	Phone calls Voicemail Receipt of simple email messages
GPRS (2.5G) Speed: 64–144kb/sec	Phone calls/fax Voicemail Receipt and transmission of large emails Web browsing Navigation/maps (cellular location accurate to 1km)
UMTS (3G) Speed: 144kb–2mb/sec	Phone calls/fax Global roaming Receipt and transmission of large emails High-speed web (broadband) Navigation/maps (cellular location accurate to 250m) Video streaming and downloads Video calling

The provision of improved and new data services is crucially important for the industry as it reaches saturation point. In order to maintain revenues, network operators have had to re-focus from customer acquisition strategies to increasing customer service usage levels, as well as encouraging more frequent handset renewal.

2G and 2.5G DATA SERVICES

To date, the most popular and readily available data service has been SMS. SMS, or 'text messaging', allows consumers to send and receive text messages of up to 160 characters on their mobile phones. Due to its simplicity and popularity, particularly among young users, the number of SMS messages being sent has been increasing dramatically (*see* table below). In the last few years SMS has helped boost revenues for network operators through integrated use with interactive TV – for example, in the voting for TV programme *Big Brother* last year, over 10 million SMS messages were sent during its 12-week run.

WAP (wireless application protocol) is a software language that allows Internet-style data to be downloaded and viewed on a mobile phone. WAP was billed as 'mobile Internet'; consumers could access content from mobile portals that, like traditional Internet portals, aggregate and display mobile Internet content in an accessible manner. WAP has been generally used by consumers to obtain travel information, sports headlines, financial news and emails. Mobile operators such as Vodafone, Orange, T-Mobile and O_2 all launched pan-European portals that allowed customers to have very similar – if not the same – services around their different countries of operations. However, WAP mobile portals have been characterised by poor usability and the limited online experience offered to end users. Many factors were to blame: unreliable early handsets, limited content, slow connections and poor portal navigation.

TOTAL NUMBER OF SMS SENT IN THE UK (PER MONTH)

Date	December '99	December '00	December '01	December '02	December '03
Number of messages	271 million	756 million	1.3 billion	1.6 billion	1.75 billion
*Includes volume of picture messages					

Some of the issues that made WAP so cumbersome have been largely solved by improved handsets, better content and high-speed infrastructure. Portal navigation remains a problem, with users routinely expected to make 20–25 'clicks' on their handset in order to pinpoint content, thus greatly limiting their ability to easily locate, and benefit from, wireless content.

With increased consumer familiarity and accessibility of SMS technology, network operators have repositioned their offerings to other new services – sending logos, basic pictures and downloading personal ringtones – that have proved to be very popular. These types of services are referred to as EMS (enhanced messaging services).

3G DATA SERVICES
The key advantages of 3G networks include increased bandwidth for data transfer, greater capacity for voice calls and improved accuracy in location-based services. From the user's viewpoint these advantages, coupled with the availability of more sophisticated 3G handsets, have provided more advanced, more interactive and more timely content services.

Hutchison 3G became the first operator in the UK to offer a UMTS service when, in March 2003, it launched the heavily advertised '3' service, which included video calling, content browsing, interactive games and location-based services. To date, the uptake of '3' has been relatively slow – in the second quarter of 2004 Hutchison 3G spent an average of £186 to attract each new customer and has had to offer cheap phone calls and text messages to see a significant take-up of its services. Compared to its initial target of 1 million customers, by March 2004 (one year after its launch), '3' had only 361,000 subscribers. The initial uptake and launch of 3G has also been exacerbated by delays in handset availability (leading to high handset prices), poor handset image – they are often seen as too large and impractical – as well as network teething problems, such as reports of 'lost' calls and low population coverage.

Despite the slow adoption of 3G services by consumers in the past year, other operators have followed Hutchison 3G's example. Vodafone officially launched its 3G mobile data card to business users in the UK in February 2004, followed by the global launch of Vodafone 'Live'. Orange, T-Mobile and O$_2$ have also launched their 3G offerings.

REGULATION

Until July 2003, the industry was regulated by two government bodies: Oftel, a government department independent of ministerial control, headed by the Director General of Telecommunications; and the Radiocommunications Agency, which was the part of the Department of Trade and Industry (DTI). The policies adopted and enforced were largely driven by the European Commission. This follows the European Court of Justice's ruling (in 1985) allowing the European Commission to apply the competition rules of the Treaty of Rome to telecommunications. In general, European policy has been aimed at providing access to networks and public services, and guaranteeing harmonised, objective, transparent and non-discriminatory conditions based on the so-called 'open network provision' (ONP) principles.

In July 2003, the regulation of the mobile industry changed significantly, with the passing of a communications bill in the UK and the implementation of a new EU framework for the regulation of electronic communications networks and service providers. The aim of the EU framework is to set out a technology-neutral regime for the regulation of communications companies across the EU. This technology-neutral regime is based on EU directives that cover interconnections and access, data protection, universal services, authorisation of electronic communications networks and services, and a common regulatory framework.

The Communications Bill in the UK took forward four of the directives and, following its enactment, has changed the UK's regulatory structure by creating a new regulatory body for the whole communications industry. Ofcom has replaced the existing communications and broadcasting regulators, including Oftel and the Radiocommunications Agency, and is funded by the levy of administration charges.

HEALTH
The possible health implications of mobile phone use have received a great deal of media coverage. A report produced by the National Radiological Protection Board (NRPB) in 2004 identified a possible danger concerning mobiles with a high SAR (specific energy absorption rate) – a measure of the energy absorbed by the user's head while he/she is talking. Different phones have different SAR values, but the SAR also depends on other factors, for example the proximity of a user to a mobile phone mast and the length of time the handset is in use. Presently, the long-term effects are unknown. The NRPB's report concluded that while 'there is as yet no hard evidence of adverse health effects on the general public', the discussion about SAR and mobile phone safety is ongoing.

CONTACTS

DEPARTMENT OF TRADE AND INDUSTRY (DTI)
General Enquiries
1 Victoria Street, London SW1H 0ET T 020 7215 5000
Mobile Communication Operators Enquiries
T 020 7215 1783 W www.dti.gov.uk

OFCOM
Riverside House, 2A Southwark Bridge Road, London SE1 9HA
T 020 7981 3000 W www.ofcom.org.uk

WEB DOMAIN NAMES BY COUNTRY

ad	Andorra	gi	Gibraltar	ni	Nicaragua
ae	United Arab Emirates	gm	Gambia	nl	The Netherlands
af	Afghanistan	gn	Guinea	no	Norway
ag	Antigua and Barbuda	gq	Equatorial Guinea	np	Nepal
al	Albania	gr	Greece	nz	New Zealand
am	Armenia	gt	Guatemala	om	Oman
ao	Angola	gw	Guinea-Bissau	pa	Panama
ar	Argentina	gy	Guyana	pe	Peru
at	Austria	hn	Honduras	pg	Papua New Guinea
au	Australia	hr	Croatia	ph	The Philippines
az	Azerbaijan	ht	Haiti	pk	Pakistan
ba	Bosnia-Hercegovina	hu	Hungary	pl	Poland
bb	Barbados	id	Indonesia	pt	Portugal
bd	Bangladesh	ie	Ireland	pw	Palau
be	Belgium	il	Israel	py	Paraguay
bf	Burkina Faso	in	India	qa	Qatar
bg	Bulgaria	iq	Iraq	ro	Romania
bh	Bahrain	ir	Iran	ru	Russian Federation
bi	Burundi	is	Iceland	rw	Rwanda
bj	Benin	it	Italy	sa	Saudi Arabia
bn	Brunei	jm	Jamaica	sb	Solomon Islands
bo	Bolivia	jo	Jordan	sc	Seychelles
br	Brazil	jp	Japan	sd	Sudan
bt	Bhutan	ke	Kenya	se	Sweden
bw	Botswana	kg	Kyrgyzstan	sg	Singapore
by	Belarus	kh	Cambodia	si	Slovenia
bz	Belize	ki	Kiribati	sk	Slovakia
ca	Canada	km	The Comoros	sl	Sierra Leone
cd	Dem. Republic of Congo	kn	St Christopher and Nevis	sn	Senegal
cf	Central African Republic	kp	Dem. People's Rep. of Korea	so	Somalia
cg	Republic of Congo	kr	Republic of Korea	sr	Suriname
ch	Switzerland	kw	Kuwait	st	São Tomé and Príncipe
ci	Côte d'Ivoire	kz	Kazakhstan	sv	El Salvador
cl	Chile	la	Laos	sy	Syria
cm	Cameroon	lb	Lebanon	sz	Swaziland
cn	China	li	Liechtenstein	td	Chad
co	Colombia	lk	Sri Lanka	tg	Togo
cr	Costa Rica	lr	Liberia	th	Thailand
cs	Serbia and Montenegro	ls	Lesotho	tj	Tajikistan
cu	Cuba	lt	Lithuania	tl	East Timor
cv	Cape Verde	lu	Luxembourg	tm	Turkmenistan
cy	Cyprus	lv	Latvia	tn	Tunisia
cz	Czech Republic	ly	Libya	to	Tonga
de	Germany	ma	Morocco	tp	East Timor
dj	Djibouti	mc	Monaco	tr	Turkey
dk	Denmark	md	Moldova	tt	Trinidad and Tobago
dm	Dominica	mg	Madagascar	tv	Tuvalu
do	Dominican Republic	mh	Marshall Islands	tw	Taiwan
dz	Algeria	mk	Macedonia	tz	Tanzania
ec	Ecuador	ml	Mali	ua	Ukraine
ee	Estonia	mm	Myanmar	ug	Uganda
eg	Egypt	mn	Mongolia	uy	Uruguay
er	Eritrea	mr	Mauritania	uz	Uzbekistan
es	Spain	mt	Malta	va	Vatican City State (Holy See)
et	Ethiopia	mu	Mauritius	vc	St Vincent and the Grenadines
fi	Finland	mv	Maldives	ve	Venezuela
fj	Fiji	mw	Malawi	vn	Vietnam
fm	Federated States of Micronesia	mx	Mexico	vu	Vanuatu
fr	France	my	Malaysia	ws	Samoa
ga	Gabon	mz	Mozambique	ye	Yemen
gd	Grenada	na	Namibia	za	South Africa
ge	Georgia	ne	Niger	zm	Zambia
gh	Ghana	ng	Nigeria	zw	Zimbabwe

INFORMATION TECHNOLOGY

ANCESTRY AND DEVELOPMENT

The ancestors of the modern computer are the Difference Engine and the Analytical Engine devised by mathematician Charles Babbage. Babbage abandoned construction of his mechanical, clockwork-like Difference Engine, designed to compute mathematical tables, in the 1840s for personal and financial reasons. In 1834 he began work on his Analytical Engine. Unlike the Difference Engine, the Analytical Engine was designed as a general-purpose tool with a store to hold information.

Babbage's work relied heavily on mechanics and physical machinery. It was not until the twentieth century invention of the electrical vacuum tube, and then the transistor, that computers became a feasible means of solving problems.

FIRST GENERATION

War has been a significant factor in the development of the computer. In 1943, during World War II, the British and Americans developed electro-mechanical computers. Colossus, a British effort, was specifically developed to crack German coding ciphers, whilst the US machine, Harvard Mark I, was developed as a more general-purpose electro-mechanical programmable computer (partly for atom bomb research). Regarded as early first generation computers, these machines primarily comprised wired circuits and vacuum tubes. Punched cards and paper tape were largely employed as the input, output and main storage systems. ENIAC (Electronic Numerical Integrator and Computer) was completed in 1946 at the University of Pennsylvania, USA. Capable of carrying out 100,000 calculations a second, it was remarkable for its day despite weighing 30 tons.

SECOND GENERATION

Similar to light bulbs, vacuum tubes (more commonly known as 'valves') were prone to failure, requiring tedious checks to resolve problems (ENIAC alone contained 18,000 vacuum valves). In 1947, the transistor was invented, initially to replace vacuum tubes used in amplifiers. Performing the same role as a vacuum tube but less prone to failure, smaller and more efficient, the transistor allowed smaller 'second generation' computers to be developed throughout the 1950s and early 1960s.

THIRD GENERATION

In 1958 Jack St Claire Kilby, of Texas Instruments, invented the first integrated circuit (or 'microchip'). Six months later Robert Noyce of Fairchild Semiconductors independently produced a similar integrated circuit. A microchip is comprised of a large number of transistors and other components fabricated from a wafer ('chip') of silicon, interconnected by a surface film of conductive material rather than by wires. By reducing distance between components, savings are made in both size and electricity. In 1963 the first 'third generation' computers based on microchip technology appeared.

FOURTH GENERATION

In 1971 Intel produced the first 'microprocessor', heralding a 'fourth generation' of computers. The Intel 4004 (capable of 60,000 instructions per second) grouped much of the processing functions onto a single microchip. Around the same time, Intel invented the RAM (random access memory) chip, which grouped significant amounts of memory onto a single chip. Supercomputers and mainframes, utilising scores of microprocessors, had terrific power in the order of 150 million instructions per second. Developments such as multi-layer circuits, and the use of copper instead of gold in microchips, yielded improvements in size and performance through miniaturisation. The size of the transistor was scaled down from thumb size to far smaller than the thickness of a human hair, allowing for greater density and thus exponentially increasing the total power of the computer.

NEXT GENERATION

Most modern computers are still regarded as 'fourth generation' as they use essentially the same technology, albeit highly miniaturised. Gordon Moore, co-founder of Intel, observed in 1965 that the number of transistors per square inch had doubled every 12 months since the inception of the integrated circuit. The pace of development has slowed somewhat. The widely recognised current definition of the so-called 'Moore's Law' is that the number of transistors on a microprocessor doubles every 18 months and is likely to do so for the next few decades.

There are many technological paradigms that are currently in research that could shape the next generation of computers. The future of computer technology could be dependent on the physics of light. Already used extensively in the computer industry for high-speed communications, light offers future possibilities for both calculation and storage. Another strong candidate is the use of quantum computing, where data is not held in bits (0s and 1s) but 'qubits' that, when combined, can hold a greater magnitude of information. Next generation computers may also utilise technology such as neural interfaces, joining the human central nervous system to a computer input and output system. Nanotechnology, a new manufacturing technology working on a molecular level, is fast becoming a major subject of research. Continuing miniaturisation in computer architecture will undoubtedly benefit from the ability to build at molecular level. Nanotechnology has a great deal of scope to advance many areas of science, such as medicine, robotics and materials. Theorised applications in medicine include the ability to produce cell-like structures that combat certain diseases or even destroy cancerous cells. Nanorobotics also presents the ability to construct devices that can regenerate when damaged, particularly useful in space exploration. With the current high investment into research, nanotechnology seems likely to become one of the next technological revolutions.

PROGRAMMING LANGUAGES

Numerous programming languages have been adopted with the common purpose of devising a program of instructions for computers to follow to achieve a task. The languages are categorised by generation:

1GL or first-generation language is the machine language that the processor chips execute in raw binary form (strings of zeros and ones).

2GL or second-generation language is a human-understandable language insofar as it uses names as well as numbers. An assembler program takes assembly language and turns it into a machine code program. Very common in early systems where resources (speed, storage) were at a premium, it is typically only used today as an output from 3GL and higher systems.

3GL or third-generation language is a 'high-level' programming language typically more readable and concise than assembly language. In the mid 1950s IBM devised FORTRAN (FORmula TRANslation), the first 3GL computer language. LISP (LISt Processing) was developed soon after and has survived until modern day programming. Although less common today, LISP has influenced the design of many languages and maintains a very high standing in academic circles.

4GL or fourth-generation language is designed to be closer to natural language than a 3GL language.

5GL or fifth-generation programming uses graphical development environments to create source language to be compiled with a 3GL or 4GL language compiler. Often a mix of generations is used, with a high level language (4 or 5GL) used to produce interface elements and a lower level language used to provide the processing power.

OPERATING SYSTEMS

An operating system (OS) is a set of utility programs that acts as the liaison between the computer user, the hardware (processor unit, memory), its peripherals (disk, mouse, display, printer, network, etc.) and the program that the user is running (e.g. a word processor). The first computers had no operating system, and each program had to directly control the hardware on its own, adding greatly to the burden of programming. Early operating systems were hardware and manufacturer-specific with assembly language or machine code as the programming language. Each computer model or series tended to have its own specific operating system. UNIX was one of the first operating systems that could be ported (converted) to a variety of system hardware. This ability was enabled largely through the use of the 'C' programming language. Since its development in the 1970s, UNIX has been a popular operating system for mainframes and other computers used as servers for large multi-user applications.

In 1991, Linus Torvalds started developing Linux, a small, open-source (see Glossary) free operating system that was based on a variant of UNIX. Originally a small hobby project, its open-source nature has facilitated its exponential development. It has been refined and evolved with the aid of users all over the world. Linux is increasingly popular for business enterprise applications: being highly scalable, it can be modified for anything from desktop systems to servers, supercomputers, DVD players, satellites and many other electronic devices. Linux's increasing use worldwide is making it a serious competitor to Microsoft Windows.

PERSONAL COMPUTER OPERATING SYSTEMS

Since the 1990s, the personal computer world has been dominated by the Microsoft Corporation. Although not a significant manufacturer of computer equipment, the Microsoft Corporation has built on its market share secured in the 1980s with MS-DOS (Microsoft Disk Operating System) to become the market leading operating system provider. Microsoft's Windows operating systems are installed on more computers than any other commercial operating system. Microsoft also continues to develop Windows for use in servers and

mainframes. One of Microsoft's rivals is Apple. Established in the 1970s, Apple became highly successful with its Apple I, II and III range of personal computers, and is one of the few personal computer companies from that time that has continued to manufacture both its own hardware and operating system to run upon it. It is now also known for its design innovation in the iMac, iBook and iPod.

THE INTERNET

Prior to the Internet ('the Net' or 'the Web' as it is known colloquially), computers tended to be connected together by hardware and protocols that were specific to each particular connection. Typically, links were point-to-point (a link had to be directly and physically established between the two computers). In 1969 ARPANET was formed by the US Department of Defence to establish a way for the computer capability of the military to be dispersed so that no one centre was critical to the operation of the network as a whole. This was achieved by interconnecting computers both directly and by way of other intermediary computers; thus if one computer was destroyed, other pathways of communication could be established. The interconnections, when drawn appeared as a mesh, or net or web. ARPANET was extended to non-military users such as universities early in the 1970s, with initial international links appearing in 1972.

The introduction of domain names (e.g. www.whitakersalmanack.com) in 1984 offered an easier means of using the Web. Prior to domain names one had to remember IP addresses (e.g.192.168.1.100) for accessing destination computers. However, before 1989 the Internet was still primarily limited to government agencies, the military, academic and research organisation and some big businesses.

In 1989, what most people perceive as 'the Net' was born. It was effectively invented at CERN (the European Particle Physics Laboratory) by Tim Berners-Lee as a way for scientists to share information by placing it in a prescribed format on a server. Initially text only, development of computer capability allowed inclusion of images.

The Internet is effectively a very large network of computers, connected through various telecommunications links. Millions of routers (see Glossary) around the world link together massive networks of computers to form a backbone to the Internet. Most home and business users will connect up to an ISP (Internet Service Provider) via a phone line or digital line. ISPs have their own routers, which all the lines connect to. The Internet 'traffic' is then routed to another (often larger) telecommunications company, which is also connected by fibre optic lines to other such companies across the globe. Websites are stored on servers that are designed for hosting, running a special program that 'serves' up the content.

As use of technology has increased, the downloading of music, pictures and video from the Internet has become faster and more practical. Because the Internet is computer-based system, all data is (at the lowest level) collection of 1s and 0s (on and off pulses). Analogue media, such as music stored on a tape, or a painting, lose quality in reproduction. Digital media on the other hand can be copied flawlessly between computers, as it is the simple process of replicating a string of 1s and 0s. In addition the Internet provides a large network over which the copied material can be easily transferred in a short space of time.

The Data Protection Act 1984 (revised 1998) was introduced to ensure the correct and proper handling of personal and sensitive data held on computer databases. During the 1980s computer hacking was still not illegal, but the number of serious computer attacks was rapidly increasing. Failed attempts to prosecute these hackers spurred on the Computer Misuse Act, passed in 1990 to protect computer systems from unauthorised access. Copyright law has also been amended to encompass the concept of 'digital property' and include criminal sanctions for breach of copyright with music, video, books, software and copyrighted website material.

INTERNET STATISTICS

• 9% of households had access to the Internet in 1998 compared with 52% of households in 2004.
• In October 2004, 34% of adults had never used the Internet. 43% of them did not wish to use it or had no interest in using it, 42% had no Internet connection and 37% felt they lacked knowledge or confidence to use it.
• 31% of UK businesses reported having a website at the end of 2003.
• One in four businesses used broadband as the primary method of Internet connection at the end of 2003, up from one in seven in 2002.

Sources: National Statistics Omnibus Survey; Office for National Statistics Expenditure and Food Survey

COUNTRIES WITH THE HIGHEST NUMBER OF BROADBAND SUBSCRIBERS *(as at 30 September 2004)*

Country	Broadband Subscribers
1. China	13,700,000
2. Japan	12,739,564
3. USA	12,594,346
4. South Korea	6,717,251
5. Germany	5,950,000
6. France	5,253,000
7. Italy	3,680,000
8. UK	3,335,000
9. Taiwan	2,900,000
10. Canada	2,568,351

Source: www.dslforum.org

GLOSSARY OF TERMS

The following is a selected list of modern computing terms. It is by no means exhaustive but is intended to cover those that the average computer user might encounter.

3G: Third Generation wireless – a populist term commonly used to describe high bandwidth (2 Mbps) wireless technologies for mobile phones. 3G is still in its infancy but when fully deployed 3G technology will offer high speed and capacity transmission of sound, vision and data to and from wireless devices and networks. European operator licences for 3G services were sold in Europe early this century for billions of euros; however, few comprehensive networks have been completed and consumer uptake has been slow. It's thought pornography will become a major driving force in 3G uptake.

AIRPORT: Apple, the first single manufacturer to popularise Wi-Fi technology, markets its Wi-Fi technology under this trade mark. *See* Wi-Fi.

ADSL: Asymmetric Digital Subscriber Line – high speed internet connection, four or more times faster than a modem, but using the same standard cables as a regular telephone. Faster at downloading than uploading.

ANIMATED GIF: A multi-layered GIF file that allows simple animations to be created by transitions between the layers. Banner advertising on the Internet tends to utilise animated GIFs. *See also* GIF.

ASCII: American Standard Code for Information Interchange – a widely used character encoding system, expressing letters, numbers and other symbols as binary numbers. It employs a string of eight binary digits or bits to represent 128 characters, enough for all the letters of the Roman alphabet and various permutations of every number between 0 and 9.

BLOG: A blog (short for weblog) is an online personal journal that is frequently updated and intended to be read by the public. Blogs generally represent the personality of the author and may include philosophy, commentary on Internet and other social issues, and links to favourite websites. Blogs are kept by 'bloggers'.

BLUETOOTH: Standard for short-range (10 metre) wireless connectivity between devices such as laptops, cell phones and printers to interact without cables. Bluetooth can presently operate at speeds of up to 2Mbps.

BROADBAND: Generic term to describe high speed Internet-using technologies such as ISDN, ADSL etc as opposed to narrowband connections via modem.

BROWSER: Typically referring to a 'web browser' program that allows a computer user to view web page content on their computer, e.g. Microsoft Explorer, Netscape Navigator, AOL, Safari, etc.

BURN: To 'burn' a file or files to a CD-ROM or similar media means to copy the files to the media from hard disk (or other source). Derived from the fact that CD-ROMs are burnt by a laser during the process of writing to the disk.

C: A 3GL programming language developed in the late 1960s in parallel with the UNIX operating system. Primarily limited to UNIX until the mid-1980s when standards such as POSIX emerged, allowing C to be widely adopted on many operating systems. UNIX used C as its core programming language.

C++: A variant of C that utilises object-orientated programming where 'objects' can be programmed to inherit behaviour and attributes from parent objects.

CAT-5: An electrical performance and cable quality standard prescribed to support high-speed Ethernet networks. There are higher category and capability specifications denoted by higher numbers but Cat-5 is the most commonly installed today.

CD: Compact Disc – a digital disk format capable of storing 650 megabytes of information per side. A laser head detects pits etched into the substrate of the spinning disk and interprets them as information. Widely used in an audio format for storing recorded music. The computer format CD-ROM is likely to be superseded by the higher capacity DVD in the next few years. CD-RAM/CD-RW and CD-R are modifiable versions that use lasers to alter the disk substrate to make the pits interpreted later as information. See also DVD.

DNS: Domain Name Server – a server that translates domain names into the IP addresses used by programs to directly access computers on the Internet. Each server has an IP address and a name. DNS is analogous to the telephone directory enquiry service, providing a means of looking up and locating a computer connected to the Internet.

DOMAIN: A set of words, numbers and letters separated

by dots used to identify an Internet server or group of servers, e.g. www.whitakersalmanack.co.uk, where 'www' denotes a web (http) server, 'whitakersalmanack' denotes the organisation name, 'co' denotes that the organisation is a company and 'uk' denotes United Kingdom (there are alternatives for every country but 'us' is typically omitted for the United States).

DVD: Digital Versatile Disc – DVD-ROM is a high capacity (read only) disk format that has the same form factor as CD-ROM but can store several gigabytes of information on each surface and can have four readable surfaces (through laser focusing technology). DVD-RAM is a modifiable version. Various formats are available, the most common being that used to store high-quality digital video, an alternative to the laser disk or videotape. *See also* CD.

EMAIL: Electronic mail – an email message is a document that is addressed to one or more persons from an individual address. Usually containing a message, it can also include other documents. It has superseded the telex, telegram, postcard and letter for rapidly exchanging information. The advent of the Internet has seen an explosion in the use of email in modern life. Without encryption or digital signature, an Internet email is not secure.

ETHERNET: Utilising simple, standard and relatively cheap cable and connectors, Ethernet has become the standard for local area networks. Ethernet employs a system whereby each computer listens for information addressed to its own unique address. Before transmitting, each computer waits for silence on the line; if multiple computers start transmitting simultaneously, they each detect the 'collision' and wait a random period of time before trying again, thus allowing communications to proceed politely.

EXTRANET: An extranet is a secure and private subset of the Internet, protected by security protocols and typically used for exchanging information and services between a specific group.

FILE SERVER: A computer on a network that stores computer files that users can access from other computers on the network. Popular modern systems include Microsoft Windows, UNIX, Novell NetWare, and MacOS Server.

FIREWALL: Computer or device to protect a network from security risks posed by the Internet. Just as a firewall protects parts of a building from a fire raging on the other side, a network firewall stops risks posed by the Internet from egressing into a private network.

FIREWIRE: Apple Computer's implementation of IEEE 1394. See also IEEE 1394.

FTP: File Transfer Protocol – an Internet protocol whereby an FTP client program can exchange files with a remote server.

GBPS: Giga bits per second – denoting 1,000 million bits transmitted per second.

GIF: Graphics Interchange Format – compressed graphic format suitable for logos and non-photographic images. Invented by Unisys to allow images to be sent electronically in an efficient manner.

GPRS: General Packet Radio Services – a service for continuous wireless communication over the Internet from mobile phones and computers. Presently available in data rates of between 56 and 114K Bps, GPRS tends to be charged by volume of information transferred rather than by time, which allows a more economic continuous connection compared with direct dial over a modem.

GZIP: Compression – a common mechanism on UNIX and Linux operating systems to compress information in order to save resources.

HTML: HyperText Mark-up Language – a small programming language used to denote or mark-up how an Internet page should be presented to a user from an HTTP server via a web browser. HTTP is an evolving standard that has grown greatly from its first version to accommodate new types of web content and features provided by the different web browsers (e.g. Netscape and Internet Explorer).

HTTP: HyperText Transfer Protocol – an Internet protocol whereby a web server sends web pages, images and files to a web browser. HTTP is an evolving protocol.

IEEE 1394: High-speed serial (400 Mbps) connection standard for hard disks, digital video cameras and other multimedia devices. Popularised as iLink (Sony) and FireWire (Apple).

iLINK: Sony's implementation of IEEE 1394. *See also* IEEE 1394.

IMAP: Internet Mail Access Protocol – an Internet protocol IMAP allows a user to review, manipulate and store email on a central server from one or more workstations without necessitating message removal from the server.

INTERNET: An abstract concept applied to describe the global network of INTER-connected computer NET-works of computers. *See* body of article.

INTRANET: Subset of the Internet, using Internet protocols over a local area network, common today for publishing information and services within an organisation.

IRC: Internet Relay Chat – protocol that allows users to 'chat' online with other users using their keyboards. Under IRC a user can log into various chat rooms under their own name or an alias and have a text 'conversation' in real time with other users.

ISDN: Integrated Services Digital Network – widely adopted in the United Kingdom and Europe but not North America, ISDN allows both digital computer data and voice telephony to exist simultaneously on the same cable circuits. Data can be digitally exchanged at 64 Kbps per circuit. Typically used for point-to-point file transfer of large documents when it was first introduced, more recently it has been used for 'dial-up' Internet.

JAVA: a high-level, object-orientated computer language developed by Sun Microsystems, especially designed for use via the web.

JPEG: Joint Photographic Experts Group – compressed graphic format suitable for compression of photographic images in a manner that simplifies the image, losing definition in the process. As the level of compression increases so too does the image degradation.

KBPS: Kilo bits per second – measure of transmission speed, denoting 1,000 bits transmitted per second.

LINUX: A UNIX-like operating system first developed as a free or low cost system for personal computers. Linux was first developed by Linus Torvalds, however large portions of its source code are now in the public domain and there are many distributions (versions) available. *See also* UNIX.

MACOS: Operating system developed by Apple Computer for use on their own Macintosh computers.

MBPS: Mega bits per second – denoting 1 million bits transmitted per second.

MODEM: Modulator-Demodulator – a device that modulates digital signals from a computer into analogue signals for transmission over a standard telephone line and demodulates an incoming analogue signal and converts it to a digital signal for the computer.

MP3: A popular format for compressing audio information for transmission over the Internet for later playback on personal computers, music players and other devices.

MPEG: Motion Picture Encoding Group – popular format standard for compressing video and audio information for transmission over the Internet for later playback on personal computers and on hand-held devices.

MS-DOS: Microsoft Corporation's Disk Operating System – an early OS commercially developed, but not invented, by Microsoft for use on early Intel-based personal computers. *See also* Operating System.

NNTP: Network News Transfer Protocol – an Internet protocol that implements a bulletin board on a global scale. Using an NNTP browser one can subscribe and contribute to one or more news groups covering a large variety of topics.

OPEN-SOURCE: a computer program that has its source-code (the instructions that make up a program) freely available for viewing and modification is said to be open-source.

OPERATING SYSTEM (OS): Computer software developed to provide computer programs with standard facilities to interact with users and with computer hardware (via drivers). *See also* MS-DOS, UNIX, MacOS.

PNG: An improved royalty-free graphics file replacement for GIF.

POP3: Post Office Protocol 3 – an Internet protocol whereby a workstation can collect email from a personal mailbox on an email server and move it to a user's own machine.

PRINT SERVER: A computer or device on a network that manages the sharing of one or more printers between multiple computers over a network. Many modern printers have a print server built in.

RAM: Random Access Memory – the main memory that is used by a computer to store temporary data (while accessing or altering individual storage locations) that is lost when the computer is turned off.

ROUTER: Where multiple networks are joined together, a router acts like a fast sorting office, examining the destination address of each information packet and passing or routing it to the appropriate network. Routers can select the most efficient route for packets.

SERVER: A node on a network that provides service to the terminals on the network. These computers have higher hardware specifications, i.e. more resources and greater speed, in order to handle large amounts of data.

SMTP: Simple Mail Transfer Protocol – an Internet protocol whereby a workstation can send email to a server or whereby two servers can exchange email.

SNMP: Simple Network Management Protocol – widely used protocol for remotely monitoring and managing network device status and function.

SPAM: A term used for unsolicited, generally junk, email. To spam someone is to send them (multiple) junk emails. Junk email is becoming a major internet issue with some estimates suggesting that spam is becoming more prevalent than legitimate email. Most spam contains offers of pornography, get-rich schemes, prescription drugs, low cost finance or discount goods or services. Many legislatures around the globe are taking steps to ban or regulate spam.

STUFFIT: Popular Apple Macintosh mechanism to compress to compress information in order to save resources. Stuffit is a proprietary brand name of Aladdin Systems. *See also* Zip.

TAR: Compression – a common mechanism on UNIX and Linux operating systems to archive information.

TCP/IP: Transmission Control Protocol/Internet Protocol – a protocol which is the lifeblood of the Internet, TCP/IP defines how information and requests generated by all other protocols are transmitted over the Internet. Information on the Internet is chopped up into small chunks or packets which are addressed with a destination and origination address. It sometimes happens that a packet gets lost and TCP/IP dictates how such a loss is handled.

UNIX: *See* body of article. Modern versions include Linux, MacOS X, Solaris, FreeBSD.

USB: Universal Serial Bus – standard for connecting serial devices such as scanners, mice, keyboards, modems and printers to computers. With USB, speeds of 10 Mbps and higher are possible.

USB 2: Universal Serial Bus 2 – a revised, higher performance version of USB.

URL: Uniform Resource Locator – address of an Internet file accessible on the Internet, e.g. http:/www. whitakersalmanack.co.uk.

VIRUS: A computer program or script written for the express purpose of replicating itself onto as many machines as possible (much like its biological namesake) often with negative side effects to the host computer and computer network. Such effects vary from harmless screen messages to corruption of document integrity, network overload or compromising data security or privacy. Historically transmitted slowly by floppy disk and over networks within offices, the prevalence of email means viruses can spread globally within minutes.

WAP: Wireless Application Protocol – a set of standards to define how portable devices connected via radio waves (such as cell phones) can access Internet services.

WARCHALKING: To 'warchalk' is to mark an open or security-exposed Wi-Fi or other wireless network by writing symbols on or outside the relevant buildings in chalk. The idea of warchalking derives from the early days of computer networks, when curious hackers would engage in wardialling expeditions. These involved telephoning a lot of numbers to see which of them answered with a data, rather than a dial tone. *See* Wi-Fi.

WARDRIVING: The activity of locating and exploiting security exposed Wi-Fi and other wireless networks to gain access to the network resource or information on or accessible to that network. *See* Wi-Fi.

WI-FI: Industry brand name for the increasingly popular high frequency wireless local area Ethernet networking technology specification IEEE 802.11. Most prevalent is the 802.11b specification offering speeds of up to 11 Mps.

WLAN: Wireless local area network where information is transferred by radio frequency rather than wires between computers and base stations. As radio waves can pass through objects such as walls, it is becoming increasingly important for WLANs to be secured by encryption against unauthorised access.

XML: Extensible Mark-up Language – similar to HTML but more powerful, XML allows information to be encoded or tagged in a manner that is both human and computer readable. The advent of XML has greatly simplified the exchange of information between many formerly incompatible systems.

ZIP: Compression – a popular mechanism on PCs to compress to compress information in order to save resources. *See also* Stuffit.

THE ENVIRONMENT

A Eurobarometer survey, carried out in November 2004, showed that almost 90 per cent of Europeans believe that environmental concerns should be taken into account when decisions are made in areas such as employment and the economy. The five environmental problems people worried about most were water pollution, man-made disasters (oil spills, industrial accidents etc.), climate change, air pollution and chemicals. There were differences between the new and old European Union (EU) member states: a significantly higher proportion of people in the 15 older member states are anxious about climate change, while in the ten countries that recently joined the EU, air and water pollution and waste management cause most concern.

The state of the environment in Europe has improved in several respects over the last decade; however, according to the European Environment Agency, further progress is needed to manage the environmental impacts of agriculture, transport and energy. Emissions from transport are a growing concern throughout the EU. In the new member states, carbon dioxide emissions from transport decreased by 12 per cent between 1990 and 1993 but subsequently rose and in 2002 were 9 per cent higher than the 1990 levels. In the 15 older member states transport emissions increased by nearly 22 per cent from 1990–2002.

Environmental policies are developed at several levels: international conventions and protocols (of which there are over 50), European directives (of which there are over 300), and national legislation and strategies.

EUROPEAN UNION MEASURES

The EU is developing an interlinked set of policies – the Sixth Environment Action Programme, the Cardiff Process (which aims to integrate environmental concerns into other policies) and the EU Sustainable Development Strategy – which form the framework for more detailed strategies. The European Commission (EC) is also diversifying the methods it uses, in particular to include market-based instruments such as environmental taxes and voluntary measures.

The Environment Action Programme began in the 1970s. The Sixth Environment Action Programme, *Environment 2010: Our Future, Our Choice*, was adopted in January 2001. It proposes five priority areas: improving the implementation of existing legislation; integration of environmental concerns into other policies; working more closely with the market; empowering private citizens and helping them to change behaviour; and taking account of the environment in land-use planning and management decisions. The programme focuses on four topics: climate change, nature and biodiversity, environment and health, and natural resources and waste.

Much EU environmental legislation is based around the principle that the polluter pays. The Environmental Liability Directive, agreed in February 2004, will be used to hold polluters financially liable for damage they cause. It is due to come into force in 2007. The new member states (Cyprus, the Czech Republic, Estonia, Hungary, Latvia, Lithuania, Malta, Poland, Slovenia and Slovakia) have been granted transition measures, in particular for investment-heavy sectors such as wastewater treatment.

These measures vary from country to country and include extensions for meeting the targets and legally-binding intermediate targets. It is estimated that to achieve full implementation the new member states will have to spend on average 2–3 per cent of GDP on the environment in the coming years, but expenditure has generally been well below this level. Financial assistance was given through a variety of EU programmes.

In general, most countries are on schedule to implement legislation, in particular horizontal legislation such as on air quality, waste management and water quality. However, some have significant work to do in waste management and industrial pollution. This is coupled with worrying recent trends, such as a decline in rail transport for freight, and a 73 per cent increase in car ownership.

SUSTAINABLE DEVELOPMENT AND LOCAL AGENDA 21

The environmental agenda has become part of a wider move to address sustainability that incorporates social, environmental and economic development. During the World Summit on Sustainable Development, held in Johannesburg in 2002, governments agreed on a series of commitments in five priority areas: water and sanitation, energy, health, agriculture and biodiversity. Targets and timetables approved include halving the number of people who lack access to clean water or proper sanitation by 2015, and reducing biodiversity loss by 2010. Following the summit, the United Nations Commission on Sustainable Development agreed its programme for the next 15 years. In addition, 2005–15 has been named as the 'Water for Life' decade.

The EU's sustainable development strategy, adopted in May 2001, sets out long-term objectives, such as limiting major threats to public health and breaking the link between economic growth and transport growth. In February 2005 the EC set out its plans to review the strategy. It expected to publish a proposed updated sustainable development strategy in the second half of 2005, in order to take into account findings from a public consultation run in late 2004.

In March 2005 the government published *Securing the Future*, its revised sustainable development strategy alongside a new Framework for Sustainable Development across the UK – shared between the government, the devolved administrations and the Northern Ireland Office. The key aspects of the UK's strategy include: new task force on sustainable public procurement that will draw up a national action plan; a scheme to enable government departments to offset the carbon impacts of their air travel by April 2006; and *Community Action 2020 – Together We Can*, which was to launch in autumn 2005 to enable local groups to help influence local authorities' sustainability strategies and development plans.

The Scottish Executive's vision, priorities and indicators for sustainable development were set out in *Meeting the Needs* in April 2002. A Scottish sustainable development strategy was to be developed during 2005. The Welsh National Assembly published sustainability schemes in November 2000 and March 2004. Its programme for putting the new scheme into effect is set out in its *Sustainable Development Action Plan*, published in

October 2004. Northern Ireland is aiming to launch a strategy and supporting indicator set in 2005.

Local authorities also have a role to play in sustainable development. Under Local Agenda 21, which came out of the United Nations (UN) Conference on Environment and Development in Rio, Brazil, in 1992, local authorities have an obligation to draw up sustainable development strategies for their areas. Regional Development Agencies take Local Agenda 21 strategies into account in sustainable development frameworks for each English region. At the World Summit, the UK government committed itself to taking further actions towards the implementation of Agenda 21 and achieving the Millennium Development Goals that have grown out of agreements and declarations at UN conferences.

Many businesses are also working towards sustainable development and some are assessing and reporting their own progress, enabled by initiatives such as the Global Reporting Initiative.

WASTE

Waste policy in the UK follows a number of principles: the waste hierarchy of reduce, re-use, recycle, dispose; the proximity principle of disposing of waste close to its generation; and national self-sufficiency. EU directives are playing an increasingly important role in driving UK policy, particularly regarding commercial and industrial waste. For instance, in response to the Landfill Directive, adopted in July 1999, the government has established a landfill allowance trading scheme, under which authorities have been set limits on the amount of biodegradable municipal waste they can dispose of in landfill sites. These 'landfill allowances' are tradable and authorities can buy, sell or save surplus allowances.

The proposed European Integrated Products Policy aims to internalise the environmental costs of products throughout their life cycle using market forces, by focusing on eco-design and incentives to ensure increased demand for greener products. The policy will culminate in 2007 with the identification of a first set of products with the greatest potential for environmental improvement.

The EU is already addressing greater responsibility for end-of-life products. Producer responsibility directives, which had to be enacted in member states by August 2004, include: the Directive for Packaging Waste; the End-of-Life Vehicle Directive; and the Directives on Waste from Electrical and Electronic Equipment (and on the restriction of the use of certain hazardous substances in such equipment). The Directive on Batteries has also been adopted, requiring all batteries on the EU market to be collected and recycled. In addition to meeting EU directives, the UK also has its own targets. To meet these the public and local authorities will have to increase their current recycling rates. The proportion of household waste recycled (including composting) has been steadily increasing, from 14.5 per cent in 2002–3 to 17.7 per cent in 2003–4. The amount of household waste collected for recycling has increased by 20.5 per cent, from 3.7 million tonnes in 2002–3 to 4.5 million tonnes in 2003–4.

CLIMATE CHANGE AND AIR POLLUTION

The UK's response to climate change is driven by the UN Framework Convention on Climate Change. This is a binding agreement that was ratified in the UK in December 1993 and came into force in March 1994. It aims to reduce the risks of global warming by limiting 'greenhouse' gas emissions.

Progress towards the convention's targets are assessed at regular conferences. At Kyoto in 1997, a protocol (the Kyoto Protocol) to the convention was adopted. It covers the six main greenhouse gases – carbon dioxide, methane, nitrous oxide, hydrofluorocarbons (HFCs), perfluorocarbons (PFCs) and sulphur hexafluoride. Under the protocol, industrialised countries agreed to legally-binding targets for cutting emissions of greenhouse gases by 5.2 per cent below 1990 levels by 2008–12. EU members agreed to an 8 per cent reduction and the UK's target is 12.5 per cent. The new EU member states have all ratified the Kyoto Protocol and have their own targets of between 6 and 8 per cent. The EU's 8 per cent target now only refers to the 15 older member states. The Protocol entered into force in February after it was ratified by Russia. The USA has stated that it will not ratify the treaty.

The latest data from the European Environment Agency, published in December 2004, shows that greenhouse gas emissions in the older member states in 2002 were 2.9 per cent below 1990 levels. From 1990 to 2002 their greenhouse gas emissions decreased in most sectors (energy supply, industry, agriculture, waste management); however emissions from transport increased by nearly 22 per cent. The older member states could cut their total emissions to 7.7 per cent below 1990 levels by 2010 with existing domestic policies and measures already being implemented, alongside additional policies and measures currently planned. However, this relies on several member states cutting emissions by more than is required to meet their national targets, which cannot be taken for granted. Plans by member states to use credits from emissions-saving projects in third world countries through the Kyoto Protocol's flexible mechanisms would contribute a further reduction of around 1.1 per cent, taking the total to 8.8 per cent, sufficient to achieve the Kyoto target.

In the new member states, emissions have declined substantially. In 2002 emissions were 33 per cent below 1990 levels, mainly due to the restructuring or closure of heavily polluting and energy-intensive industries. With existing domestic policies and measures, all new member states, except Slovenia, are on track to meet their Kyoto targets. However, in most countries emissions will increase between 2002 and 2010. Slovenia expects to meet its target with additional policies, and measures including carbon dioxide removals from land-use change and forestry.

In November 2000, a UK climate change programme was published that set out how the UK intends to meet its Kyoto target and progress towards its domestic goal of a 20 per cent cut in carbon dioxide emissions by 2010. The UK is currently on course to meet its Kyoto target. Consultation has so far highlighted areas where it can further reduce carbon emissions through emissions trading; energy efficiency; increasing biomass production; transport; and encouraging biofuels and cleaner vehicle technologies. The UK also has a voluntary greenhouse gas emissions trading scheme that started in April 2002. The scheme allows businesses to buy an emission allowance to meet emission targets or to sell surplus emission allowances.

The EC also set up a European Climate Change Programme in 2000 to identify measures to meet the Kyoto target, and introduced a mandatory emissions trading scheme at company level for carbon dioxide in the European Union in January 2005. The companies covered by the scheme account for almost half of the EU's total carbon dioxide emissions. The EU has also indicated its willingness to link the scheme to trading schemes in other countries that have ratified the Kyoto Protocol. The scheme will be reviewed next year and the EC will consider extending it to other sectors such as chemicals, aluminium and transport, as well as to other greenhouse gases.

The EC is considering plans for beyond 2012 when the Kyoto Protocol ends. These include broadening international participation in reducing emissions; including more sectors, notably aviation, maritime transport and forestry; a push for innovation in the EU to ensure the development and uptake of new climate-friendly technologies; and continued use of flexible market-based instruments for reducing emissions in the EU and globally. The EU's National Emission Ceilings Directive sets upper limits for each member state for the total emissions in 2010 of the four pollutants responsible for acidification, eutrophication and ground-level ozone pollution (sulphur dioxide, nitrogen oxides, volatile organic compounds and ammonia), but leaves it largely to the member states to decide which measures to take in order to comply. The EC plans to revise this, and a new proposal is expected in mid-2006.

The EC is also revisiting all of its air quality legislation under its *Clean Air for Europe* (CAFE) programme. CAFE brings together information on the likely development of air quality in Europe, taking into account both the full effect of all emission control legislation currently in the pipeline and future economic development. The European Integrated Pollution Prevention and Control (IPPC) Directive regulates emissions to any environmental medium from certain industrial sources and includes returning sites to a satisfactory state on closure, using energy efficiently and noise and vibration regulation. IPPC has been implemented in the UK through the Pollution Prevention and Control Regulations 2000.

The UK's National Air Quality Strategy sets air quality objectives for the main pollutants (benzene, butadiene, carbon monoxide, lead, nitrogen dioxide, sulphur dioxide, ozone, and particulates) to be met by 2003–8. Under the strategy, all district and unitary authorities have a duty to review air quality, including likely future air quality, in their areas. If authorities find that any part of their area breaches the objectives, an air quality management area must be declared and an action plan drawn up for improvements.

WATER

Water quality targets are set at both EU and UK level for drinking water sources, wastewater discharges, rivers, coastal water and bathing water. The EU's Water Framework Directive, which entered into force in December 2000, aims to achieve 'good water status' throughout the EU by 2015. In response to the requirements of the directive, in September 2003 the EC adopted a proposal for a new directive to protect groundwater from pollution, obliging member states to monitor and assess groundwater quality on the basis of common criteria, and to identify and reverse trends in groundwater pollution.

Under the UK Water Act, published in November 2003, a new Water Services Regulatory Authority will replace Ofwat in April 2006. The Water Environment and Water Services Bill for Scotland also completed its passage through the Scottish Parliament in 2003. It established, for the first time, a source-to-sea planning framework for river basin management.

In October 2002, the EC adopted a proposal for a new bathing water directive setting a tighter bathing water quality standard than the previous directive. From a total of 413 English coastal and freshwater bathing areas, 406 (98 per cent) have passed the main mandatory water quality standards. The 2004 results compare with a mandatory compliance rate of 83 per cent in 1994 and 90 per cent in 1999. Meanwhile, 69 per cent met the tougher guideline standards in 2004, compared with 29 per cent in 1994.

The Environment Agency sets river quality objectives for each stretch of river. Water quality is currently protected through licensing abstraction and regulating discharges. Discharge consents are based on the river quality objectives and relevant EU directives, and specify the concentration and quantity permitted. In 2003, 95 per cent of rivers were of good or fair biological quality (an indicator of overall river health), compared to 90 per cent in 1990. Between 1990 and 2003, some 31 per cent of rivers improved in biological quality. Most of this improvement occurred in the first five years and since then has been more gradual. In some places, for example in Wales, biological quality has deteriorated since 1995.

The European Urban Waste Water Treatment Directive sets minimum standards for sewage treatment before discharge into coastal waters, with the levels of treatment needed depending on the sensitivity of the receiving water. In 1999 the government set more stringent UK targets for all significant coastal discharges to have a minimum of secondary treatment by the end of 2005.

ENERGY

Energy used in the home is responsible for 25 per cent of the UK's carbon dioxide emissions. In February 2003, the UK government published a white paper, *Our Energy Future – Creating a Low Carbon Economy*, setting out a long-term strategy for UK energy policy to 2050 combining environmental, security of supply, competitiveness and social goals. It built on the Performance and Innovation Unit's (now the Prime Minister's Strategy Unit) Energy Review, published a year earlier. An energy bill was also introduced in November 2003.

In April 2004, the UK government published its first annual report on the implementation of the white paper. A total of 112 milestones were set as a first step towards achieving the long-term commitments; 56 had been met. Also in April, the government published *Energy Efficiency. The Government's Plan for Action*, which sets out how the energy efficiency strategy in the white paper will be delivered. The package of policies and measures aim to lead to a reduction of more than 12 million tonnes per year in carbon emissions by 2010.

In October 2004, building on the 2003 white paper, the government launched its *UK International Priorities – The Energy Strategy*, which sets out how it plans to meet the international energy challenge over the next five to ten years. The UK has a target to increase the contribution of renewables to 10 per cent of electricity by 2010, with an aspiration to reach 20 per cent by 2020.

The EC expects renewables' share of electricity production to reach only 18–19 per cent by 2010 on the basis of existing policies and measures carried out by the member states, while renewables' share of overall energy consumption will reach, at best, 10 per cent on the basis of legislation adopted so far. The European Parliament and various stakeholders have proposed that the enlarged EU should set a 20 per cent target for renewables' share of overall energy consumption for 2020. Environment ministers went beyond the EC's proposals by setting ambitious reduction targets: 15–30 per cent reduction of greenhouse gas emissions by 2020 and 60–80 per cent by 2050. The ministers also made it clear that a global approach is needed, including co-operation with large industrialised countries that have opted out of Kyoto and with emerging economic powers such as China and India.

ENVIRONMENT AND HEALTH

In October 2003, the EC put forward a proposal for a new chemicals policy under which industry will have to provide information on the effects of chemicals on human health and the environment, as well as on safe ways of handling them. The proposal has been met with stiff opposition and still has a long way to go before it is implemented. An amended proposal was to be put to the European Council for a political debate in June 2005.

The EC has also launched a strategy that will tackle environmental risks for human health in a broader sense. The strategy on science, children, awareness, legislation and evaluation, known as SCALE, was launched in June 2003. Apart from aiming to reduce diseases caused by environmental factors in Europe, it aims to strengthen the EU's capacity for policy-making in the area. The first cycle of the strategy, running from 2004 to 2010, will focus on four health effects – childhood respiratory diseases; asthma and allergies; neurodevelopment disorders; childhood cancer; and endocrine-disrupting effects. The EC launched an action plan in June 2004.

SELECTED UK TARGETS

AIR QUALITY AND ATMOSPHERE
- Reduce greenhouse gas emissions to 12.5 per cent below 1990 levels by 2010
- Reduce carbon dioxide emissions to 20 per cent below 1990 levels by 2010, and by 60 per cent by 2050
- Reduce emissions of volatile organic compounds by 40 per cent based on 1990 levels by 2010
- 15–30 per cent reduction of greenhouse gas emissions by 2020 and 60–80 per cent by 2050

FRESH WATER AND SEA
- 97 per cent of bathing waters to meet European directive standards consistently by 2005
- Provide secondary treatment for all significant coastal discharges by the end of 2005
- All inland and coastal water to reach good status (ecological, chemical and quantitative) by 2015

WASTE
- Recycle 50–75 per cent of waste electrical and electronic equipment by 2006
- Recover value from 70–80 per cent of waste electrical and electronic equipment by 2006
- Reduce industrial and commercial waste going to landfill by 85 per cent of 1998 levels by 2005
- Recover 40 per cent of municipal waste by 2005, 45 per cent by 2010 and 67 per cent by 2015
- Recycle or compost 25 per cent of household waste by 2005–6, 30 per cent by 2010 and 33 per cent by 2015
- Reduce biodegradable municipal waste sent to landfill to 75 per cent of 1995 levels by 2010, 50 per cent by 2013 and 35 per cent by 2020
- Recycle 55–80 per cent of packaging waste and recover a minimum of 60 per cent by the end of 2006
- 2008 EU packaging waste recycling targets: glass 60 per cent, paper — 60, metals — 50, plastics — 22.5, wood — 15

- Recover or recycle 70 per cent of packaging waste by 2008 in Scotland
- Proposed re-use and recovery of 85 per cent of the mass of end-of-life vehicles with a minimum of 80 per cent re-use and recycling by 2006, 95 and 85 per cent by 2015
- Reduce biodegradeable municipal waste going to landfill to 75 per cent of 1995 levels by 2010, 50 per cent by 2013 and 30 per cent by 2020
- 25 per cent recycling of municipal waste in Scotland by 2006 and 55 per cent by 2020 (35 per cent recycling and 20 composting)
- Collect 4kg of household waste electrical and electronic equipment per head of population per year by 31 December 2006
- Provide segregated kerbside waste collection to over 90 per cent of households in Scotland by 2020
- Stop the growth in municipal waste in Scotland by 2010

ENERGY
- Provide 10 per cent of electricity from renewable sources by 2010 in UK and Scotland
- Achieve at least 10,000 MW of installed good quality combined heat and power capacity by 2010
- Provide 20 per cent of electricity from renewable sources by 2020 in UK
- Secure annual carbon savings of 4.2 million tonnes by 2010 from the household sector in the UK

CONTACTS

DEPARTMENT OF ENVIRONMENT, FOOD AND RURAL AFFAIRS
Ergon House, 17 Smith Square, London SW1P 3JR
T 020-7238 6951 W www.defra.gov.uk

DEPARTMENT OF THE ENVIRONMENT, NORTHERN IRELAND
Clarence Court, 10–18 Adelaide Street, Belfast BT2 8GB
T 028-9054 0540 W www.doeni.gov.uk

ENVIRONMENT AGENCY
Rio House, Almondsbury, Bristol BS32 4UD T 01709-389201
W www.environment-agency.gov.uk

ENVIRONMENT AND HERITAGE SERVICE FOR NORTHERN IRELAND
Calvert House, 23 Castle Place, Belfast BT1 1FY
T 028-9025 6424 W www.ehsni.gov.uk

ENVIROWISE, THE ENVIRONMENT AND ENERGY HELPLINE
T 0800-585794 W www.envirowise.gov.uk

EUROPEAN ENVIRONMENT AGENCY
Kongens Nytorv 6, DK-1050 Copenhagen K, Denmark
W www.eea.eu.int

ROYAL COMMISSION ON ENVIRONMENTAL POLLUTION
Third Floor, The Sanctuary, London SW1P 3JS
T 020-7799 8970 W www.rcep.org.uk

SCOTTISH EXECUTIVE, ENVIRONMENT AND RURAL AFFAIRS DEPARTMENT
Pentland House, 47 Robb's Loan, Edinburgh EH14 1TY
T 0131-556 8400 W www.scotland.gov.uk

CONSERVATION AND HERITAGE

NATIONAL PARKS

ENGLAND AND WALES

Following the designation of the New Forest as a National Park on 1 March 2005 there are now 11 National Parks in England and Wales. In addition, the Norfolk and Suffolk Broads are considered to have equivalent status to a National Park. Under the provisions of the National Parks and Access to the Countryside Act 1949, areas designated as National Parks have a statutory requirement to conserve and protect scenic landscapes from inappropriate development and to provide access to the land for public enjoyment.

The Countryside Agency (established on 1 April 1999 from the merger of the Countryside Commission and the Rural Development Commission) is the statutory body which has the power to designate National Parks in England, and the Countryside Council for Wales is responsible for National Parks in Wales. Designations in England are confirmed by the Secretary of State for Environment, Food and Rural Affairs and those in Wales by the National Assembly for Wales. The designation of a National Park does not affect the ownership of the land or remove the rights of the local community. The majority of the land in the National Parks is owned by private landowners (74 per cent) or by bodies such as the National Trust (7 per cent) and the Forestry Commission (7 per cent). The National Park Authorities own only 2.3 per cent of the land.

The Environment Act 1995 replaced the existing National Park boards and committees with free-standing National Park Authorities (NPAs). NPAs are the sole local planning authorities for their areas and as such influence land use and development, and deal with planning applications. Their duties include conserving and enhancing the natural beauty, wildlife and cultural heritage of the National Parks; promoting opportunities for public understanding and enjoyment of the National Parks; and fostering the economic and social well-being of the communities within National Parks. The NPAs publish management plans as statements of their policies and appoint their own officers and staff.

The Broads Authority was established under the Norfolk and Suffolk Broads Act 1998 and meets the requirement for the Authority to have a navigation function in addition to a regard for the needs of agriculture, forestry and the economic and social interests of those who live or work in the Broads.

The New Forest NPA was established on 1 April 2005 with a limited range of staturory powers and functions, it is to become fully operational on 1 April 2006.

MEMBERSHIP

In England, those local authorities that have land in the Parks appoint one half plus one of the members of the National Parks Authorities. Of the remaining members, one half minus one are parish representatives who are elected through a process of local democracy while the rest are appointed by the Secretary of State to represent the national interest. The Secretary of State appoints nine of the 35 members of the Broads Authority, of which at least three are appointed after consulting boating interests and two following a consultation of farming and landowning interests. The remainder are appointed by the local authorities and the Countryside Agency.

In Wales two-thirds of NPA members are appointed by the constituent local authorities and one-third by the National Assembly for Wales, advised by the Countryside Council for Wales.

FUNDING

The English NPAs and the Broads Authority are funded by central government. In the financial year 2005–6 a grant totalling £42.13 million was allocated between the authorities. In Wales, National Parks are funded via a grant from the National Assembly and levies raised from constituent local authorities. In addition, all NPAs and the Broads Authority can take advantage of grants from other bodies including lottery and European grants.

The National Parks (with date designation confirmed) are:

BRECON BEACONS (1957), Powys (66 per cent)/ Carmarthenshire/Rhondda, Cynon and Taff/Merthyr Tydfil/Blaenau Gwent/Monmouthshire, 1,349sq. km/519 sq. miles – The park is centred on the Beacons, Pen y Fan, Corn Du and Cribyn, but also includes the valley of the Usk, the Black Mountains to the east and the Black Mountain to the west. There are information centres at the National Park visitor centre near Libanus, Abergavenny, Llandovery and Craig-y-nos Country Park.
National Park Authority, Plas y Ffynnon, Cambrian Way, Brecon, Powys LD3 7HP T 01874-624437
E enquiries@breconbeacons.org
Chief Executive Officer, Christopher Gledhill

BROADS (1989), Norfolk/Suffolk, 303 sq. km/117 sq. miles – The Broads is located between Norwich and Great Yarmouth on the flood plains of the six rivers flowing through the area to the sea. The area is one of fens, winding waterways, woodland and marsh. The 40 or so broads are man-made, and are connected to the rivers by dykes, providing over 200 km of navigable waterways. There are information centres at Beccles, Hoveton, Potter Heigham, Ranworth and Toad Hole Cottage at How Hill.
Broads Authority, 18 Colegate, Norwich NR3 1BQ
T 01603 610734 E broads@broads-authority.gov.uk
Chief Executive, Dr John Packman

DARTMOOR (1951), Devon, 954 sq. km/368 sq. miles – The park consists of moorland and rocky granite tors, and is rich in prehistoric remains. There are information centres at Haytor, Newbridge, Princetown (main visitor centre) and Postbridge.
National Park Authority, Parke, Bovey Tracey, Devon
TQ13 9JQ T 01626-832093 E hq@dartmoor-npa.gov.uk
Chief Executive, Dr Nick Atkinson

EXMOOR (1954), Somerset (71 per cent)/Devon, 693 sq. km/267 sq. miles – Exmoor is a moorland plateau inhabited by wild ponies and red deer. There are many ancient remains and burial mounds. There are National Park centres at Blackmoor Gate, County Gate, Dunster, Dulverton and Combe Martin.

National Park Authority, Exmoor House, Dulverton,
Somerset TA21 9HL T 01398-323665
E info@exmoor-nationalpark.gov.uk
National Park Officer, Dr Nigel Stone
LAKE DISTRICT (1951), Cumbria, 2,292 sq. km/885 sq.
miles – The Lake District includes England's highest
mountains (Scafell Pike, Helvellyn and Skiddaw) but it
is most famous for its glaciated lakes. There are
National Park information centres at Broughton,
Keswick, Waterhead, Hawkshead, Seatoller, Bowness,
Grasmere, Coniston, Glenridding and Pooley Bridge
and a visitor centre at Brockhole, Windermere.
National Park Authority, Murley Moss, Oxenholme Road,
Kendal, Cumbria, LA9 7RL T 01539-724555
E hq@lake-district.gov.uk
National Park Officer, Paul Tiplady
NEW FOREST (2005), Hampshire, 571 sq. km/221 sq.
miles – The forest has been protected since 1079 when
it was declared a royal hunting forest. The area consists
of forest, ancient woodland and heathland. Much of
the Forest is managed by the Forestry Commission,
which provides several campsites. The main villages are
Brockenhurst, Burley and Lyndhurst, which has a
visitor centre.
National Park Authority, The Queen's House, 4 High
Street, Lyndhurst SO43 7BD T 023-8028 4144
E enquiries@newforestnpa.gov.uk
Interim Chief Executive, Susan Carter
NORTH YORK MOORS (1952), North Yorkshire (96 per
cent)/Redcar and Cleveland, 1,432 sq. km/554 sq.
miles – The park consists of woodland and moorland,
and includes the Hambleton Hills and the Cleveland
Way. There are information centres at Danby, Sutton
Bank and at The Old Coastguard Station in Robin
Hood's Bay.
National Park Authority, The Old Vicarage, Bondgate,
Helmsley, York YO6 5BP T 01439-770657
E general@northyorkmoors-npa.gov.uk
National Park Officer, Andrew Wilson
NORTHUMBERLAND (1956), Northumberland,
1,049 sq. km/405 sq. miles – The park is an area of
hill country stretching from Hadrian's Wall to the
Scottish Border. There are information centres at
Ingram, Once Brewed and Rothbury.
National Park Authority, Eastburn, South Park, Hexham,
Northumberland NE46 1BS T 01434-605555
E admin@nnpa.org.uk
National Park Officer, Graham Taylor
PEAK DISTRICT (1951), Derbyshire (64 per cent)/
Staffordshire/South Yorkshire/Cheshire/West
Yorkshire/Greater Manchester, 1,438 sq. km/555 sq.
miles – The Peak District includes the gritstone moors
of the 'Dark Peak' and the limestone dales of the
'White Peak'. There are information centres at
Bakewell, Edale, Castleton and Upper Derwent.
National Park Authority, Aldern House, Baslow Road,
Bakewell, Derbyshire DE45 1AE T 01629-816200
E aldern@peakdistrict-npa.gov.uk
Chief Executive, Jim Dixon
PEMBROKESHIRE COAST (1952 and 1995),
Pembrokeshire, 620 sq. km/240 sq. miles – The park
includes cliffs, moorland and a number of islands,
including Skomer. There are information centres at St
David's and Newport.
National Park Authority, Llanion Park, Pembroke Dock,
Pembrokeshire SA72 6DY T 0845-345 7275
E pcnp@pembrokeshirecoast.org.uk
National Park Officer, Nic Wheeler

SNOWDONIA/ERYRI (1951), Gwynedd/Conwy,
2,171 sq. km/835 sq. miles – Snowdonia is an area of
deep valleys and rugged mountains. There are
information centres at Aberdyfi, Beddgelert, Betws y
Coed, Blaenau Ffestiniog, Conwy, Dolgellau and
Harlech.
National Park Authority, Penrhyndeudraeth, Gwynedd
LL48 6LF T 01766-770274 E parc@eryri-npa.gov.uk
Chief Executive, Aneurin Phillips
YORKSHIRE DALES (1954), North Yorkshire (88 per
cent)/Cumbria, 1,762 sq. km/683 sq. miles – The
Yorkshire Dales are composed primarily of limestone
overlaid in places by millstone grit. The three peaks of
Ingleborough, Whernside and Pen-y-Ghent are within
the park. There are information centres at Grassington,
Hawes, Aysgarth Falls, Malham and Reeth.
National Park Authority, Yorebridge House, Bainbridge,
Leyburn, N. Yorks DL8 3EE T 0870-1666333
E info@yorkshiredales.org.uk
Chief Executive, David Butterworth

In 1999 the Countryside Agency began the process of
designating the South Downs (within the Sussex Downs
and East Hampshire 'Areas of Outstanding Natural
Beauty') as a National Park. A Designation Order for a
South Downs National Park was submitted by the
Countryside Agency to the Secretary of State on 27
January 2003 and the planning inspector's decision is
expected to be announced at the end of 2005.

THE SOUTH DOWNS, West Sussex/Hampshire,1,637 sq.
km/632 sq. miles – The South Downs contains a
diversity of natural habitats, including flower-studded
chalk grassland, ancient woodland, flood meadow,
lowland heath and rare chalk heathland.
Sussex Downs Conservation Board, Victorian Barn,
Victorian Business Centre, Ford Lane, Ford, Arundel,
West Sussex, BN18 0EF T 01234-558700
E info@southdowns-aonb.gov.uk
Chief Officer, Martin Beaton

SCOTLAND
On 9 August 2000 The National Parks (Scotland) Bill
received Royal Assent, providing the Parliament with the
ability to create National Parks in Scotland. The first two
Scottish National Parks, *Loch Lomond and the Trossachs*
and the *Cairngorms*, became operational in 2002 and
2003 respectively. The Act gives Scottish Parks wider
powers than in England and Wales, including statutory
responsibilities for the economy and rural communities.
Membership of the two NPAs in Scotland consists of 20
per cent directly elected members. The remaining 80 per
cent are chosen by the Secretary of State, 40 per cent of
which are nominated by the constituent Local Authorities.
In Scotland, the National Parks are central government
bodies and wholly funded by the Scottish Executive.
Funding for 2005–6 totals £10.9 million; £6.6 million
allocated to Loch Lomond and the Trossachs and £4.3
million to the Cairngorms.

CAIRNGORMS (2003), Morayshire, 3,800 sq. km/1,461
sq. miles – The Cairngorms National Park is the largest
in the UK. It displays a vast collection of landforms and
includes four of Scotland's highest mountains.
National Park Authority, 14 The Square,
Grantown-on-Spey, Morayshire, PH26 3HG
T 01479-873535 E enquiries@cairngorms.co.uk
Chief Executive, Jane Hope

LOCH LOMOND AND THE TROSSACHS (2002), Argyll and Bute/Stirling/West Dunbartonshire, 1,865 sq. km/720 sq. miles – The park boundaries encompass lochs, rivers, forests, 20 mountains above 3,000 ft including Ben Moore and a further 20 mountains between 2,500 ft and 3,000 ft.
National Park Authority, The Old Station, Balloch Road, Balloch G83 8BF T 01389-722600
E info@lochlomond-trossachs.org
Chief Executive, Bill Dalrymple

NORTHERN IRELAND

There is power to designate National Parks in Northern Ireland under the Amenity Lands Act 1965 and the Nature Conservation and Amenity Lands Order (Northern Ireland) 1985.

AREAS OF OUTSTANDING NATURAL BEAUTY

ENGLAND AND WALES

Under the National Parks and Access to the Countryside Act 1949, provision was made for the designation of Areas of Outstanding Natural Beauty (AONBs) by the National Parks Commission, which later became the Countryside Commission. The Countryside Agency is now responsible for AONBs in England and since April 1991 the Countryside Council for Wales has been responsible for the Welsh AONBs. Designations in England are confirmed by the Secretary of State for Environment, Food and Rural Affairs and those in Wales by the National Assembly for Wales. The Countryside and Rights of Way (CROW) Act 2000 placed greater responsibility on local authorities to protect AONBs and made it a statutory duty for relevant authorities to produce a management plan for their AONB area. The CROW Act also provided for the creation of conservation boards for larger and more complex AONBs. Conservation boards for the Cotswolds and Chilterns AONBs were established on 8 July 2004 following confirmation by the Secretary of State.

The primary objective of the AONB designation is to conserve and enhance the natural beauty of the area. Where an AONB has a conservation board, it has the additional purpose of increasing public understanding and enjoyment of the special qualities of the area, with the first purpose having greater weight, if there should be a conflict of interests between the two. In addition to the above, the board is also required to foster the economic and social well-being of the local communities but without incurring significant expenditure in doing so. Overall responsibility for AONBs lies with the relevant local authorities or conservation board. To co-ordinate planning and management responsibilities between local authorities in whose area they fall, AONBs are overseen by a Joint Advisory Committee (or similar body) which includes representatives from the local authorities, landowners, farmers, residents and conservation and recreation groups. In addition, an AONB officer is appointed to oversee matters. Since April 2002, up to 75 per cent of core funding for AONBs has been provided by central government through the Countryside Agency and Countryside Council for Wales.

The 40* Areas of Outstanding Natural Beauty (with date designation confirmed) are:

ANGLESEY (1967), Anglesey, 221 sq. km/85 sq. miles
ARNSIDE AND SILVERDALE (1972), Cumbria/ Lancashire, 75 sq. km/29 sq. miles

BLACKDOWN HILLS (1991), Devon/Somerset, 370 sq. km/143 sq. miles
CANNOCK CHASE (1958), Staffordshire, 68 sq. km/26 sq. miles
CHICHESTER HARBOUR (1964), Hampshire/West Sussex, 74 sq. km/29 sq. miles
CHILTERNS (1965; extended 1990), Bedfordshire/ Buckinghamshire/Herefordshire/Oxfordshire, 833 sq. km/322 sq. miles
CLWYDIAN RANGE (1985), Denbighshire/Flintshire, 157 sq. km/60 sq. miles
CORNWALL (1959; Camel estuary 1983), 958 sq. km/ 370 sq. miles
COTSWOLDS (1966; extended 1990), Gloucestershire/ Oxfordshire/Wiltshire/Warwickshire/ Worcestershire, 2,038 sq. km/787 sq. miles
CRANBORNE CHASE AND WEST WILTSHIRE DOWNS (1983), Dorset/Hampshire/Somerset/Wiltshire, 983 sq. km/379 sq. miles
DEDHAM VALE (1970; extended 1978, 1991), Essex/ Suffolk, 90 sq. km/35 sq. miles
DORSET (1959), 1,129 sq. km/436 sq. miles
EAST DEVON (1963), 268 sq. km/103 sq. miles
EAST HAMPSHIRE (1962), 383 sq. km/148 sq. miles
FOREST OF BOWLAND (1964), Lancashire/North Yorkshire, 802 sq. km/310 sq. miles
GOWER (1956), Swansea, 188 sq. km/73 sq. miles
HIGH WEALD (1983), Kent/East Sussex/Surrey/West Sussex, 1,460 sq. km/564 sq. miles
HOWARDIAN HILLS (1987), North Yorkshire, 204 sq. km/79 sq. miles
ISLE OF WIGHT (1963), 189 sq. km/73 sq. miles
ISLES OF SCILLY (1976), 16 sq. km/6 sq. miles
KENT DOWNS (1968), 878 sq. km/339 sq. miles
LINCOLNSHIRE WOLDS (1973), 558 sq. km/215 sq. miles
LLEYN (1957), Gwynedd, 161 sq. km/62 sq. miles
MALVERN HILLS (1959), Gloucestershire/Worcestershire, 150 sq. km/58 sq. miles
MENDIP HILLS (1972; extended 1989), Somerset, 198 sq. km/76 sq. miles
NIDDERDALE (1994), North Yorkshire, 603 sq. km/233 sq. miles
NORFOLK COAST (1968), 451 sq. km/174 sq. miles
NORTH DEVON (1960), 171 sq. km/66 sq. miles
NORTH PENNINES (1988), Cumbria/Durham/ Northumberland, 1,983 sq. km/766 sq. miles
NORTH WESSEX DOWNS (1972), Hampshire/ Oxfordshire/Wiltshire, 1,730 sq. km/668 sq. miles
NORTHUMBERLAND COAST (1958), 135 sq. km/52 sq. miles
QUANTOCK HILLS (1957), Somerset, 99 sq. km/38 sq. miles
SHROPSHIRE HILLS (1959), 804 sq. km/310 sq. miles
SOLWAY COAST (1964), Cumbria, 115 sq. km/44 sq. miles
SOUTH DEVON (1960), 337 sq. km/130 sq. miles
SUFFOLK COAST AND HEATHS (1970), 403 sq. km/156 sq. miles
SURREY HILLS (1958), 419 sq. km/162 sq. miles
SUSSEX DOWNS (1966), 983 sq. km/379 sq. miles
TAMAR VALLEY (1995), Cornwall/Devon, 195 sq. km/ 115 sq. miles
WYE VALLEY (1971), Gloucestershire/Herefordshire/ Monmouthshire, 326 sq. km/126 sq. miles

* The South Hampshire Coast AONB was de-designated in March 2005 as the majority of it now lies within the New Forest National Park.

NORTHERN IRELAND

The Department of the Environment for Northern Ireland, with advice from the Council for Nature Conservation and the Countryside, designates Areas of Outstanding Natural Beauty in Northern Ireland. At present there are nine and these cover a total area of approximately 284,948 hectares (704,103 acres). Dates given are those of designation.

ANTRIM COAST AND GLENS (1988), Co. Antrim, 70,600 ha/174,452 acres

CAUSEWAY COAST (1989), Co. Antrim, 4,200 ha/10,378 acres

LAGAN VALLEY (1965), Co. Down, 2,072 ha/5,119 acres

LECALE COAST (1967), Co. Down, 3,108 ha/7,679 acres

MOURNE (1986), Co. Down, 57,012 ha/140,876 acres

NORTH DERRY (1966), Co. Londonderry, 12,950 ha/31,999 acres

RING OF GULLION (1991), Co. Armagh, 15,353 ha/37,938 acres

SPERRIN (1968), Co. Tyrone/Co. Londonderry, 101,006 ha/249,585 acres

STRANGFORD LOUGH (1972), Co. Down, 18,647 ha/46,077 acres

NATIONAL SCENIC AREAS

In Scotland, National Scenic Areas have a broadly equivalent status to AONBs. Scottish Natural Heritage recognises areas of national scenic significance. At the end of June 2004 there were 40, covering a total area of 1,001,800 hectares (2,475,448 acres).

Development within National Scenic Areas is dealt with by local authorities, who are required to consult Scottish Natural Heritage concerning certain categories of development. Disagreements between Scottish Natural Heritage and local authorities are referred to the Scottish Executive. Land management uses can also be modified in the interest of scenic conservation.

ASSYNT-COIGACH, Highland, 90,200 ha/222,884 acres

BEN NEVIS AND GLEN COE, Highland, 101,600 ha/251,053 acres

CAIRNGORM MOUNTAINS, Highland/Aberdeenshire/Moray, 67,200 ha/166,051 acres

CUILLIN HILLS, Highland, 21,900 ha/54,115 acres

DEESIDE AND LOCHNAGAR, Aberdeenshire, 40,000 ha/98,840 acres

DORNOCH FIRTH, Highland, 7,500 ha/18,532 acres

EAST STEWARTRY COAST, Dumfries and Galloway, 4,500 ha/11,119 acres

EILDON AND LEADERFOOT, The Borders, 3,600 ha/8,896 acres

FLEET VALLEY, Dumfries and Galloway, 5,300 ha/13,096 acres

GLEN AFFRIC, Highland, 19,300 ha/47,690 acres

GLEN STRATHFARRAR, Highland, 3,800 ha/9,390 acres

HOY AND WEST MAINLAND, Orkney Islands, 14,800 ha/36,571 acres

JURA, Argyll and Bute, 21,800 ha/53,868 acres

KINTAIL, Highland, 15,500 ha/38,300 acres

KNAPDALE, Argyll and Bute, 19,800 ha/48,926 acres

KNOYDART, Highland, 39,500 ha/97,604 acres

KYLE OF TONGUE, Highland, 18,500 ha/45,713 acres

KYLES OF BUTE, Argyll and Bute, 4,400 ha/10,872 acres

LOCH NA KEAL, MULL, Argyll and Bute, 12,700 ha/31,382 acres

LOCH LOMOND, Argyll and Bute, 27,400 ha/67,705 acres

LOCH RANNOCH AND GLEN LYON, Perthshire and Kinross, 48,400 ha/119,596 acres

LOCH SHIEL, Highland, 13,400 ha/33,111 acres

LOCH TUMMEL, Perthshire and Kinross, 9,200 ha/22,733 acres

LYNN OF LORN, Argyll and Bute, 4,800 ha/11,861 acres

MORAR, MOIDART AND ARDNAMURCHAN, Highland, 13,500 ha/33,358 acres

NORTH-WEST SUTHERLAND, Highland, 20,500 ha/50,655 acres

NITH ESTUARY, Dumfries and Galloway, 9,300 ha/22,980 acres

NORTH ARRAN, North Ayrshire, 23,800 ha/58,810 acres

RIVER EARN, Perthshire and Kinross, 3,000 ha/7,413 acres

RIVER TAY, Perthshire and Kinross, 5,600 ha/13,838 acres

ST KILDA, Western Isles, 900 ha/2,224 acres

SCARBA, LUNGA AND THE GARVELLACHS, Argyll and Bute, 1,900 ha/4,695 acres

SHETLAND, Shetland Isles, 11,600 ha/28,664 acres

SMALL ISLANDS, Highland, 15,500 ha/38,300 acres

SOUTH LEWIS, HARRIS AND NORTH UIST, Western Isles, 109,600 ha/270,822 acres

SOUTH UIST MACHAIR, Western Isles, 6,100 ha/15,073 acres

THE TROSSACHS, Stirling, 4,600 ha/11,367 acres

TROTTERNISH, Highland, 5,000 ha/12,355 acres

UPPER TWEEDDALE, The Borders, 10,500 ha/25,945 acres

WESTER ROSS, Highland, 145,300 ha/359,036 acres

THE NATIONAL FOREST

The National Forest is being planted across 200 square miles of Derbyshire, Leicestershire and Staffordshire. Nearly six million trees, of mixed species but mainly broadleaved, have been planted, with the aim being to eventually cover about one-third of the designated area. The project is funded by the Department for Environment, Food and Rural Affairs. It was developed in 1992–5 by the Countryside Commission and is now run by the National Forest Company, which was established in April 1995. Under the National Forest Tender Scheme, anybody wishing to undertake a woodland creation project can submit a competitive bid to the National Forest Company.

NATIONAL FOREST COMPANY, Enterprise Glade, Bath Lane, Moira, Swadlincote, Derbyshire DE12 6BD
T 01283-551211 E enquiries@nationalforest.org
W www.nationalforest.org
Chief Executive, Susan Bell, OBE

SITES OF SPECIAL SCIENTIFIC INTEREST

Site of Special Scientific Interest (SSSI) is a legal notification applied to land in England, Scotland or Wales which English Nature (EN), Scottish Natural Heritage (SNH) or the Countryside Council for Wales (CCW) identifies as being of special interest because of its flora, fauna, geological, geomorphological or physiographical features. In some cases, SSSIs are managed as nature reserves.

EN, SNH and CCW must notify the designation of an SSSI to the local planning authority, every owner/occupier of the land, and the Secretary of State for Environment, Food and Rural Affairs, the Scottish Ministers or the National Assembly for Wales. Forestry and agricultural departments and a number of other interested parties are also formally notified.

Objections to the notification of an SSSI can be made and ultimately considered at a full meeting of the Council of EN or CCW. In Scotland an objection will be dealt with by the appropriate area board or the main board of SNH, depending on the nature of the objection. Unresolved objections on scientific grounds from those with a legal interest in the land must be referred to the Advisory Committee on SSSI.

The protection of these sites depends on the co-operation of individual landowners and occupiers. Owner/occupiers must consult EN, SNH or CCW and gain written consent before they can undertake certain listed activities on the site. Funds are available through management agreements and grants to assist owners and occupiers in conserving sites' interests. As a last resort a site can be purchased.

The number and area of SSSIs in Britain as at May 2005 was:

	No.	Hectares	Acres
England	4,117	1,072,538	2,650,299
Scotland	1,451	1,005,157	2,482,725
Wales	1,019	263,991	652,322

NORTHERN IRELAND
In Northern Ireland 218 Areas of Special Scientific Interest (ASSIs) have been declared by the Department of the Environment for Northern Ireland.

NATIONAL NATURE RESERVES

National Nature Reserves are defined in the National Parks and Access to the Countryside Act 1949 as land designated for the study and preservation of flora and fauna, or of geological or physiographical features.

English Nature (EN), Scottish Natural Heritage (SNH) or the Countryside Council for Wales (CCW) can designate as a National Nature Reserve land which is being managed as a nature reserve under an agreement with one of the statutory nature conservation agencies; land held and managed by EN, SNH or CCW; or land held and managed as a nature reserve by another approved body. EN, SNH or CCW can make by-laws to protect reserves from undesirable activities; these are subject to confirmation by the Secretary of State for Environment, Food and Rural Affairs, the National Assembly for Wales or the Scottish Ministers in Scotland.

The number and area of National Nature Reserves in Britain as at May 2005 was:

	No.	Hectares	Acres
England	218	87,716	216,746
Scotland	66	117,228	289,612
Wales	67	24,123	59,584

NORTHERN IRELAND
Nature Reserves are established and managed by the Department of the Environment for Northern Ireland, with advice from the Council for Nature Conservation and the Countryside. Nature reserves are declared under the Nature Conservation and Amenity Lands (Northern Ireland) order 1985; to date, 47 nature reserves have been declared.

LOCAL NATURE RESERVES

Local Nature Reserves are defined in the National Parks and Access to the Countryside Act 1949 as land designated for the study and preservation of flora and fauna, or of geological or physiographical features. The Act gives local authorities in England, Scotland and Wales the power to acquire, declare and manage local nature reserves in consultation with English Nature, Scottish Natural Heritage and the Countryside Council for Wales. Other organisations, including wildlife trusts, may manage local nature reserves, providing that a local authority has a legal interest in the land.

The number and area of designated Local Nature Reserves in Britain as at May 2005 was:

	No.	Hectares	Acres
England	1,158	34,810	86,016
Scotland	37	9,431	23,304
Wales	50	4,676	11,554

FOREST NATURE RESERVES

The Forestry Commission is the government department responsible for forestry policy throughout Great Britain. Forestry is a devolved matter, with the separate Forestry Commissions for England, Scotland and Wales reporting directly to their appropriate minister. The Forestry Commission in each country is lead by a director who is also a member of the GB Board of Commissioners. As at March 2004 total Forestry Commission managed woodland amounted to 780,000 hectares; 205,000 hectares in England, 110,000 hectares in Wales and 465,000 hectares in Scotland.

NORTHERN IRELAND
There are 34 Forest Nature Reserves in Northern Ireland, covering 1,512 hectares (3,736 acres). They are designated and administered by the Forest Service, an agency of the Department of Agriculture and Rural Development for Northern Ireland. There are also 16 National Nature Reserves on Forest Service-owned property.

MARINE NATURE RESERVES

The Secretary of State for Environment, Food and Rural Affairs, the National Assembly for Wales and the Scottish Executive have the power to designate Marine Nature Reserves. English Nature, Scottish Natural Heritage and the Countryside Council for Wales select and manage these reserves. Marine Nature Reserves may be established in Northern Ireland under a 1985 Order.

Marine Nature Reserves provide protection for marine flora and fauna, and geological and physiographical features on land covered by tidal waters or parts of the sea in or adjacent to the UK. Reserves also provide opportunities for study and research.

The three statutory Marine Nature Reserves are:

LUNDY (1986), Bristol Channel
SKOMER (1990), Dyfed
STRANGFORD LOUGH (1995), Northern Ireland

WORLD HERITAGE SITES

The Convention Concerning the Protection of the World Cultural and Natural Heritage was adopted by the United Nations Educational Scientific and Cultural Organisation (UNESCO) in 1972 and ratified by the UK in 1984. As at 1 June 2005 the convention had been ratified by 180 states. The convention provides for the identification, protection and conservation of cultural and natural sites of outstanding universal value.

Cultural sites may be:
– monuments
– groups of buildings
– sites of historic, aesthetic, archaeological, scientific, ethnologic or anthropologic value
– historic areas of towns
– 'cultural landscapes', i.e. sites whose characteristics are marked by significant interactions between human populations and their natural environment
Natural sites may be:
– those with remarkable physical, biological or geological formations
– those with outstanding universal value from the point of view of science, conservation or natural beauty
– the habitat of threatened species and plants

Governments which are party to the convention nominate sites in their country for inclusion in the World Cultural and Natural Heritage List. Nominations are considered by the World Heritage Committee, an intergovernmental committee composed of 21 representatives of the parties to the convention. The committee is advised by the International Council on Monuments and Sites (ICOMOS), the International Centre for the Study of the Preservation and Restoration of Cultural Property (ICCROM) and the World Conservation Union (IUCN). ICOMOS evaluates and reports on proposed cultural sites, ICCROM provides expert advice and training on how to conserve the listed sites and IUCN advises on proposed natural sites. The Department for Culture, Media and Sport represents the UK government in matters relating to the convention.

A prerequisite for inclusion in the World Cultural and Natural Heritage List is the existence of an effective legal protection system in the country in which the site is situated (eg listing, conservation areas and planning controls in the United Kingdom) and a detailed management plan to ensure the conservation of the site. Inclusion in the list does not confer any greater degree of protection on the site than that offered by the national protection framework.

If a site is considered to be in serious danger of decay or damage, the committee may add it to a complementary list, the World Heritage in Danger List. Sites on this list may benefit from particular attention or emergency measures.

Financial support for the conservation of sites on the World Cultural and Natural Heritage List is provided by the World Heritage Fund. This is administered by the World Heritage Committee, which determines the financial and technical aid to be allocated. The fund's income is derived from contributions of the parties to the convention, voluntary contributions from other states, other United Nations and intergovernmental organisations, public or private bodies and individuals, through interest due on the fund and from events organised for the benefit of the fund.

DESIGNATED SITES

As at 18 July 2005, following the 29th session of the World Heritage Committee, 812 sites in 137 countries were inscribed on the World Cultural and Natural Heritage List. Of these, 23 are in the United Kingdom and three in British overseas territories; 20 are listed for their cultural significance (†), five for their natural significance (*) and one for both cutural and natural significance. The year in which sites were designated appears in parentheses. Hadrian's Wall, a World Heritage Site in its own right since 1987, was joined by the upper German-Raetian Limes to form the first section of a transnational world heritage site, *Frontiers of the Roman Empire*, created at the 29th session of the World Heritage Committee in 2005.

UNITED KINGDOM
†Bath – the city (1987)
†Blaenarvon, Wales (2000)
†Blenheim Palace and Park, Oxfordshire (1987)
†Canterbury Cathedral, St Augustine's Abbey, St Martin's Church, Kent (1988)
†Castle and town walls of King Edward I, north Wales – Beaumaris, Anglesey, Caernarfon Castle, Conwy Castle, Harlech Castle (1986)
†Derwent Valley Mills, Derbyshire (2001)
*Dorset and East Devon Coast (2001)
†Durham Cathedral and Castle (1986)
†Edinburgh Old and New Towns (1995)
†Frontiers of the Roman Empire, Hadrian's Wall, northern England (1987, 2005)
*Giant's Causeway and Causeway coast, Co. Antrim (1986)
†Greenwich, London – maritime Greenwich, including the Royal Naval College, Old Royal Observatory, Queen's House, town centre (1997)
†Heart of Neolithic Orkney (1999)
†Ironbridge Gorge, Shropshire – the world's first iron bridge and other early industrial sites (1986)
†Liverpool – six areas of the Maritime Mercantile City (2004)
†New Lanark, South Lanarkshire, Scotland (2001)
†Royal Botanic Gardens, Kew (2003)
†*St Kilda, Western Isles (1986)
†Saltaire, West Yorkshire (2001)
†Stonehenge, Avebury and related megalithic sites, Wiltshire (1986)
†Studley Royal Park, Fountains Abbey, St Mary's Church, N. Yorkshire (1986)
†Tower of London (1988)
†Westminster Abbey, Palace of Westminster, St Margaret's Church, London (1987)

BRITISH OVERSEAS TERRITORIES
*Henderson Island, Pitcairn Islands, South Pacific Ocean (1988)
*Gough Island wildlife reserve (part of Tristan da Cunha), South Atlantic Ocean (1995)
*St George town and related fortifications, Bermuda (2000)

WORLD HERITAGE CENTRE, UNESCO, 7 Place de Fontenoy, 75352 Paris 07 SP, France W www.unesco.org

CONSERVATION OF WILDLIFE AND HABITATS

The UK is party to a number of international conventions.

RAMSAR CONVENTION

The 1971 Ramsar Convention on Wetlands of International Importance especially as Waterfowl Habitat, entered into force in the UK in May 1976. As at June 2005, 146 countries were party to the convention.

The aim of the convention is the conservation and wise use of wetlands and their flora and fauna. Governments that are party to the convention must designate wetlands and include wetland conservation considerations in their land-use planning. A total of 1,456 wetland sites, totalling 125 million hectares have been designated for inclusion in the List of Wetlands of International Importance. The UK currently has 162 designated sites covering 864,652 hectares. The member countries meet every three years to assess the progress of the convention and the next meeting was scheduled for November 2005.

The UK has set targets under the Ramsar Strategic Plan, 2003–8. Progress towards these is monitored by the UK Ramsar Committee, known as the Joint Working Party. The UK and the Republic of Ireland have established a formal protocol to ensure common monitoring standards for waterbirds in the two countries.

RAMSAR CONVENTION BUREAU, Rue Mauverney 28, CH-1196 Gland, Switzerland **T** (+ 41) (22) 999 0170 **W** www.ramsar.org

BIODIVERSITY

There is much synergy between the Ramsar Convention and the 1992 Convention on Biological Diversity. In 1996 the Ramsar Secretariat became a lead partner in implementing activities under the Convention on Biological Diversity with joint work plans. The UK ratified the Convention on Biological Diversity in June 1994. As at May 2004 there were 188 parties to the convention.

The objectives are the conservation of biological diversity, the sustainable use of its components and the fair and equitable sharing of the benefits arising out of the use of genetic resources. There are thematic work programmes addressing marine and coastal, forest, inland waters, dry land and sub-humid land. The Conference of the Parties to the Convention on Biological Diversity adopted a supplementary agreement to the Convention known as the *Cartagena Protocol on Biosafety* on 29 January 2000. The protocol seeks to protect biological diversity from potential risks that may be posed by introducing modified living organisms, resulting from modern biotechnology, into the environment. As at June 2005, 123 countries were party to the protocol. The UK became party to the protocol on 17 February 2004.

The UK published its own Biodiversity Action Plan in 1994. A report from the UK Biodiversity Steering Group, published in 1995, proposed monitoring a list of 1,252 species to check on biodiversity within the UK.

A report, *Sustaining the Variety of Life: 5 years of the UK Biodiversity Action Plan*, was published in March 2001 and made a number of recommendations including to support actions for the conservation of species and habitats at UK, county and local levels. There are four country groups: England Biodiversity Group, Scotland Biodiversity Forum, Northern Ireland Biodiversity Group and Wales Biodiversity Partnership. These are involved in implementing the action plans at national level. In October 2002, the England Biodiversity Group, DEFRA and the Biodiversity Policy Unit jointly launched a *Biodiversity Strategy for England* as part of the UK Biodiversity Action Plan.

BIODIVERSITY POLICY UNIT, Zone 1/10D, Temple Quay House, 2 The Square, Temple Quay, Bristol BS1 6EB **T** 0117-372 6276 **E** biodiversity@defra.gsi.gov.uk **W** www.ukbap.org.uk

CITES

The 1973 Convention on International Trade in Endangered Species of Wild Fauna and Flora (CITES) came into force in the UK in July 1975. Currently 167 countries are members. The countries party to the convention ban commercial international trade in an agreed list of endangered species and regulate and monitor trade in others species that might become endangered. The convention covers approximately 30,000 species of animals and plants and accords them protection whether they are traded as live specimens or as products derived from them, such as fur coats and dried herbs.

The Conference of the Parties to CITES meets every two to three years to review the convention's implementation. The Global Wildlife Division at the Department for Environment, Food and Rural Affairs carries out the government's responsibilities under CITES .

CITES SECRETARIAT, International Environment House, Chemin des Anémones, CH-1219 Châtelaine, Geneva, Switzerland **T** (+ 41) (22) 917 8139/8140 **E** cites@unep.ch **W** www.cites.org

BONN CONVENTION

The 1979 Convention on Conservation of Migratory Species of Wild Animals came into force in the UK in October 1979. As at 1 June 2005, 90 countries were party to the convention.

It requires the protection of listed endangered migratory species and encourages international agreements covering these and other threatened species. International agreements can range from legally binding treaties to less formal memoranda of understanding.

Six agreements have been concluded to date under the convention. They aim to conserve: seals in the Wadden Sea; bat populations in Europe; small cetaceans of the Baltic and North Seas; African-Eurasian migratory waterbirds; cetaceans of the Mediterranean Sea, Black Sea and contiguous Atlantic area; and albatrosses and petrels. A further seven memorandums of understanding have been agreed for the Siberian Crane, Slender-billed Curlew, marine turtles of the Atlantic coast of Africa, Indian Ocean and South-East Asia, the middle-European population of the Great Bustard, Bukhara Deer and the Aquatic Warbler.

UNEP/CMS SECRETARIAT, Martin-Luther-King-Str. 8, D-53175, Bonn, Germany **T** (+ 49) (228) 815 2401/2 **E** secretariat@cms.int **W** www.cms.int

BERN CONVENTION

The 1979 Bern Convention on the Conservation of European Wildlife and Natural Habitats came into force in the UK in June 1982. Currently there are 45 Contracting Parties and a number of other states attend meetings as observers.

The aims are to conserve wild flora and fauna and their natural habitats, especially where this requires the co-operation of several countries, and to promote such co-operation. The convention gives particular emphasis to endangered and vulnerable species.

All parties to the convention must promote national conservation policies and take account of the conservation of wild flora and fauna when setting planning and development policies. Reports on contracting parties' conservation policies must be submitted to the Standing Committee every four years.

SECRETARIAT OF THE BERN CONVENTION STANDING COMMITTEE, Council of Europe, 67075 Strasbourg-Cedex, France T (+ 33) (3) 8841 2000 W www.coe.int

EUROPEAN WILDLIFE TRADE REGULATION

The Council (EC) Regulation on the Protection of Species of Wild Fauna and Flora by Regulating Trade Therein came into force in the UK on 1 June 1997. It is intended to standardise wildlife trade regulations across Europe and to improve the application of CITES.

UK LEGISLATION

The Wildlife and Countryside Act 1981 gives legal protection to a wide range of wild animals and plants. Subject to parliamentary approval, the Secretary of State for Environment, Food and Rural Affairs may vary the animals and plants given legal protection. The most recent variation of Schedules 5 and 8 came into effect in March and April 1998. The fourth quinquennial review of species listed in Schedules 5 and 8 is ongoing, but it is not expected that any legislative changes will be made to the Schedules until early 2006.

Under Section 9 of the Act it is an offence to kill, injure, take, possess or sell (whether alive or dead) any wild animal included in Schedule 5 of the Act and to disturb its place of shelter and protection or to destroy that place.

Under Section 13 of the Act it is illegal without a licence to pick, uproot, sell or destroy plants listed in Schedule 8. Since January 2001, under the Countryside and Rights of Way Act 2000, persons found guilty of an offence under part 1 of the Wildlife and Countryside Act 1981 face a maximun penalty of up to £5,000 and/or up to six months custodial sentence per specimen.

The Act lays down a close season for wild birds (other than game birds) from 1 February to 31 August inclusive, each year. Exceptions to these dates are made for:

Capercaillie and (except Scotland) Woodcock – 1 February to 30 September

Snipe – 1 February to 11 August

Birds listed on Schedule 2, part 1 (below high water mark) (see below) – 21 February to 31 August

Birds listed on Schedule 2, Part 1, which may be killed or taken outside the close season (except on Sundays and on Christmas Day in Scotland, and on Sundays in prescribed areas of England and Wales) are capercaille, coot, certain wild duck (gadwall, goldeneye, mallard, pintail, pochard, shoveler, teal, tufted duck, wigeon), certain wild geese (Canada, greylag, pink-footed, white-fronted (in England and Wales only)), moorhen, golden plover and woodcock. Section 16 of the 1981 Act allows licences to be issued on either an individual or general basis, to allow the killing, taking and sale of certain birds for specified reasons such as public health and safety. All other British birds are fully protected by law throughout the year.

ANIMALS PROTECTED BY SCHEDULE 5

Adder *(Vipera berus)*
Allis shad *(Alosa alosa)*
Atlantic Stream Crayfish *(Austropotomobius pallipes)*
Anemone, Ivell's Sea *(Edwardsia ivelli)*
Anemone, Starlet Sea *(Nematosella vectensis)*
Bat, Horseshoe *(Rhinolophidae, all species)*
Bat, Typical *(Vespertilionidae, all species)*
Beetle *(Hypebaeus flavipes)*
Beetle, Lesser Silver Water *(Hydrochara caraboides)*
Beetle, Mire Pill *(Curimopsis nigrita)*
Beetle, Rainbow Leaf *(Chrysolina cerealis)*
Beetle, Stag *(Lucanus cervus)*
Beetle, Spangled Water *(Graphoderus zonatus)*
Beetle, Violet Click *(Limoniscus violaceus)*
Beetle, Water *(Paracymus aeneus)*
Burbot *(Lota lota)*
Butterfly, Adonis Blue *(Lysandra bellargus)*
Butterfly, Black Hairstreak *(Strymonidia pruni)*
Butterfly, Brown Hairstreak *(Thecla betulae)*
Butterfly, Chalkhill Blue *(Lysandra coridon)*
Butterfly, Chequered Skipper *(Carterocephalus palaemon)*
Butterfly, Duke of Burgundy Fritillary *(Hamearis lucina)*
Butterfly, Glanville Fritillary *(Melitaea cinxia)*
Butterfly, Heath Fritillary *(Mellicta athalia* (or *Melitaea athalia))*
Butterfly, High Brown Fritillary *(Argynnis adippe)*
Butterfly, Large Blue *(Maculinea arion)*
Butterfly, Large Copper *(Lycaena dispar)*
Butterfly, Large Heath *(Coenonympha tullia)*
Butterfly, Large Tortoiseshell *(Nymphalis polychloros)*
Butterfly, Lulworth Skipper *(Thymelicus acteon)*
Butterfly, Marsh Fritillary *(Eurodryas aurinia)*
Butterfly, Mountain Ringlet *(Erebia epiphron)*
Butterfly, Northern Brown Argus *(Aricia artaxerxes)*
Butterfly, Pearl-bordered Fritillary *(Boloria euphrosyne)*
Butterfly, Purple Emperor *(Apatura iris)*
Butterfly, Silver Spotted Skipper *(Hesperia comma)*
Butterfly, Silver-studded Blue *(Plebejus argus)*
Butterfly, Small Blue *(Cupido minimus)*
Butterfly, Swallowtail *(Papilio machaon)*
Butterfly, White Letter Hairstreak *(Stymonida w-album)*
Butterfly, Wood White *(Leptidea sinapis)*
Cat, Wild *(Felis silvestris)*
Cicada, New Forest *(Cicadetta montana)*
Cricket, Field *(Gryllus campestris)*
Cricket, Mole *(Gryllotalpa gryllotalpa)*
Cricket, Wart-biter *(Decticus verrucivorus)*
Damselfly, Southern *(Coenagrion mercuriale)*
Dolphin *(Cetacea)*
Dormouse *(Muscardinus avellanarius)*
Dragonfly, Norfolk Aeshna *(Aeshna isosceles)*
Frog, Common *(Rana temporaria)*
Goby, Couch's *(Gobius couchii)*
Goby, Giant *(Gobius cobitis)*
Hatchet Shell, Northern *(Thyasira gouldi)*
Hydroid, Marine *(Clavopsella navis)*
Lagoon Snail *(Paludinella littorina)*
Lagoon Snail, De Folin's *(Caecum armoricum)*

Lagoon Worm, Tentacled *(Alkmaria romijni)*
Leech, Medicinal *(Hirudo medicinalis)*
Lizard, Sand *(Lacerta agilis)*
Lizard, Viviparous *(Lacerta vivipara)*
Marten, Pine *(Martes martes)*
Moth, Barberry Carpet *(Pareulype berberata)*
Moth, Black-veined *(Siona lineata* (or *Idaea lineata))*
Moth, Essex Emerald *(Thetidia smaragdaria)*
Moth, Fiery clearwing *(Bembecia chrysidiformis)*
Moth, Fisher's estuarine *(Gortyna borelii)*
Moth, New Forest Burnet *(Zygaena viciae)*
Moth, Reddish Buff *(Acosmetia caliginosa)*
Moth, Sussex Emerald *(Thalera fimbrialis)*
Mussel, Fan *(Atrina fragilis)*
Mussel, Pearl *(Margaritifera margaritifera)*
Newt, Great Crested (or Warty) *(Triturus cristatus)*
Newt, Palmate *(Triturus helveticus)*
Newt, Smooth *(Triturus vulgaris)*
Otter, Common *(Lutra lutra)*
Porpoise *(Cetacea)*
Sandworm, Lagoon *(Armandia cirrhosa)*
Sea Fan, Pink *(Eunicella verrucosa)*
Sea Slug, Lagoon *(Tenellia adspersa)*
Sea-mat, Trembling *(Victorella pavida)*
Shad, Twaite *(Alosa fallax)*
Shark, Basking *(Cetorhinus maximus)*
Shrimp, Apus *(Triops cancriformis)*
Shrimp, Fairy *(Chirocephalus diaphanus)*
Shrimp, Lagoon Sand *(Gammarus insensibilis)*
Slow-worm *(Anguis fragilis)*
Snail, Glutinous *(Myxas glutinosa)*
Snail, Sandbowl *(Catinella arenaria)*
Snake, Grass *(Natrix natrix (Natrix helvetica))*
Snake, Smooth *(Coronella austriaca)*
Spider, Fen Raft *(Dolomedes plantarius)*
Spider, Ladybird *(Eresus niger)*
Squirrel, Red *(Sciurus vulgaris)*
Sturgeon *(Acipenser sturio)*
Toad, Common *(Bufo bufo)*
Toad, Natterjack *(Bufo calamita)*
Turtle, Marine *(Dermochelyidae* and *Cheloniidae,* all species*)*
Vendace *(Coregonus albula)*
Vole, Water *(Arvicola terrestris)*
Walrus *(Odobenus rosmarus)*
Whale *(Cetacea)*
Whitefish *(Coregonus lavaretus)*

PLANTS PROTECTED BY SCHEDULE 8

Adder's tongue, Least *(Ophioglossum lusitanicum)*
Alison, Small *(Alyssum alyssoides)*
Anomodon, Long leaved *(Anomodon longifolius)*
Beech-lichen, New Forest *(Enterographa elaborata)*
Blackwort *(Southbya nigrella)*
Bluebell *(Hyacinthoides non-scripta)*
Bolete, Royal *(Boletus regius)*
Broomrape, Bedstraw *(Orobanche caryophyllacea)*
Broomrape, Oxtongue *(Orobanche loricata)*
Broomrape, Thistle *(Orobanche reticulata)*
Cabbage, Lundy *(Rhynchosinapis wrightii)*
Calamint, Wood *(Calamintha sylvatica)*
Caloplaca, Snow *(Caloplaca nivalis)*
Catapyrenium, Tree *(Catapyrenium psoromoides)*
Catchfly, Alpine *(Lychnis alpina)*
Catillaria, Laurer's *(Catellaria laureri)*
Centaury, Slender *(Centaurium tenuiflorum)*
Cinquefoil, Rock *(Potentilla rupestris)*
Cladonia, Convoluted *(Cladonia convoluta)*
Cladonia, Upright Mountain *(Cladonia stricta)*

Clary, Meadow *(Salvia pratensis)*
Club-rush, Triangular *(Scirpus triquetrus)*
Colt's-foot, Purple *(Homogyne alpina)*
Cotoneaster, Wild *(Cotoneaster integerrimus)*
Cottongrass, Slender *(Eriophorum gracile)*
Cow-wheat, Field *(Melampyrum arvense)*
Crocus, Sand *(Romulea columnae)*
Crystalwort, Lizard *(Riccia bifurca)*
Cudweed, Broad-leaved *(Filago pyramidata)*
Cudweed, Jersey *(Gnaphalium luteoalbum)*
Cudweed, Red-tipped *(Filago lutescens)*
Cut-grass *(Leersia oryzoides)*
Diapensia *(Diapensia lapponica)*
Dock, Shore *(Rumex rupestris)*
Earwort, Marsh *(Jamesoniella undulifolia)*
Eryngo, Field *(Eryngium campestre)*
Fern, Dickie's bladder *(Cystopteris dickieana)*
Fern, Killarney *(Trichomanes speciosum)*
Flapwort, Norfolk *(Leiocolea rutheana)*
Fleabane, Alpine *(Erigeron borealis)*
Fleabane, Small *(Pulicaria vulgaris)*
Fleawort, South stack*(Tephroseris integrifolia (ssp maritima))*
Frostwort, Pointed *(Gymnomitrion apiculatum)*
Fungus, Hedgehog *(Hericium erinaceum)*
Galingale, Brown *(Cyperus fuscus)*
Gentian, Alpine *(Gentiana nivalis)*
Gentian, Dune *(Gentianella uliginosa)*
Gentian, Early *(Gentianella anglica)*
Gentian, Fringed *(Gentianella ciliata)*
Gentian, Spring *(Gentiana verna)*
Germander, Cut-leaved *(Teucrium botrys)*
Germander, Water *(Teucrium scordium)*
Gladiolus, Wild *(Gladiolus illyricus)*
Goblin Lights *(Catolechia wahlenbergii)*
Goosefoot, Stinking *(Chenopodium vulvaria)*
Grass-poly *(Lythrum hyssopifolia)*
Grimmia, Blunt-leaved *(Grimmia unicolor)*
Gyalecta, Elm *(Gyalecta ulmi)*
Hare's-ear, Sickle-leaved *(Bupleurum falcatum)*
Hare's-ear, Small *(Bupleurum baldense)*
Hawk's-beard, Stinking *(Crepis foetida)*
Hawkweed, Northroe *(Hieracium northroense)*
Hawkweed, Shetland *(Hieracium zetlandicum)*
Hawkweed, Weak-leaved *(Hieracium attenuatifolium)*
Heath, Blue *(Phyllodoce caerulea)*
Helleborine, Red *(Cephalanthera rubra)*
Helleborine, Young's *(Epipactis youngiana)*
Horsetail, Branched *(Equisetum ramosissimum)*
Hound's-tongue, Green *(Cynoglossum germanicum)*
Knawel, Perennial *(Scleranthus perennis)*
Knotgrass, Sea *(Polygonum maritimum)*
Lady's-slipper *(Cypripedium calceolus)*
Lecanactis, Churchyard *(Lecanactis hemisphaerica)*
Lecanora, Tarn *(Lecanora archariana)*
Lecidea, Copper *(Lecidea inops)*
Leek, Round-headed *(Allium sphaerocephalon)*
Lettuce, Least *(Lactuca saligna)*
Lichen, Arctic kidney *(Nephroma arcticum)*
Lichen, Ciliate strap *(Heterodermia leucomelos)*
Lichen, Coralloid rosette *(Heterodermia propagulifera)*
Lichen, Ear-lobed dog *(Peltigera lepidophora)*
Lichen, Forked hair *(Bryoria furcellata)*
Lichen, Golden hair *(Teloschistes flavicans)*
Lichen, Orange fruited Elm *(Caloplaca luteoalba)*
Lichen, River jelly *(Collema dichotomum)*
Lichen, Scaly breck *(Squamarina lentigera)*
Lichen, Stary breck *(Buellia asterella)*

HISTORIC BUILDINGS AND MONUMENTS

Under the Planning (Listed Buildings and Conservation Areas) Act 1990, the Secretary of State for Culture, Media and Sport has a statutory duty to compile lists of buildings or groups of buildings in England which are of special architectural or historic interest. Under the Ancient Monuments and Archaeological Areas Act 1979 as amended by the National Heritage Act 1983, the Secretary of State is also responsible for compiling a schedule of ancient monuments. Decisions are taken on the advice of English Heritage. On 1 April 2005 responsibility for the administration of the listing system was transferred from the Secretary of State to English Heritage. This marked the start of a programme of changes designed to make the listing process more straightforward and more accountable.

Listed buildings are classified into Grade I, Grade II* and Grade II. There are currently about 370,000 individual listed buildings in England, of which about 92 per cent are Grade II listed. Almost all pre-1700 buildings are listed, and most buildings of 1700 to 1840. English Heritage carries out thematic surveys of particular types of buildings with a view to making recommendations for listing, and members of the public may propose a building for consideration. The main purpose of listing is to ensure that care is taken in deciding the future of a building. No changes which affect the architectural or historic character of a listed building can be made without listed building consent (in addition to planning permission where relevant). Applications for listed building consent are normally dealt with by the local planning authority, although English Heritage is always consulted about proposals affecting Grade I and Grade II* properties. It is a criminal offence to demolish a listed building, or alter it in such a way as to affect its character, without consent.

There are currently about 18,300 scheduled monuments in England. English Heritage is carrying out a Monuments Protection Programme assessing archaeological sites with a view to making recommendations for scheduling, and members of the public may propose a monument for consideration. All monuments proposed for scheduling are considered to be of national importance. Where buildings are both scheduled and listed, ancient monuments legislation takes precedence. The main purpose of scheduling a monument is to preserve it for the future and to protect it from damage, destruction or any unnecessary interference. Once a monument has been scheduled, scheduled monument consent is required before any works can be carried out. The scope of the control is more extensive and more detailed than that applied to listed buildings, but certain minor works, as detailed in the Ancient Monuments (Class Consents) Order 1994, may be carried out without consent. It is a criminal offence to carry out unauthorised work to scheduled monuments.

Under the Planning (Listed Buildings and Conservation Areas) Act 1990 and the Ancient Monuments and Archaeological Areas Act 1979, the Secretary of State for Wales is responsible for listing buildings and scheduling monuments in Wales on the advice of Cadw, the Historic Buildings Council for Wales and the Royal Commission on the Ancient and Historical Monuments of Wales. The criteria for evaluating buildings are similar to those in England and the same listing system is used. There are approximately 26,400 listed buildings and approximately 3,500 scheduled monuments in Wales.

Under the Planning (Listed Buildings and Conservation Areas) (Scotland) Act 1997 and the Ancient Monuments and Archaeological Areas Act 1979, Scottish Ministers are responsible for listing buildings and scheduling monuments in Scotland on the advice of Historic Scotland, the Historic Buildings Council for Scotland and the Royal Commission on the Ancient and Historical Monuments of Scotland. The criteria for evaluating buildings are similar to those in England but an A, B, C categorisation is used. There are approximately 46,000 listed buildings and 6,500 scheduled monuments in Scotland.

Under the Planning (Northern Ireland) Order 1991 and the Historic Monuments and Archaeological Objects (Northern Ireland) Order 1995, the Department of the Environment of the Northern Ireland Executive is responsible for listing buildings and scheduling monuments in Northern Ireland on the advice of the Historic Buildings Council for Northern Ireland and the Historic Monuments Council for Northern Ireland. The criteria for evaluating buildings are similar to those in England but no statutory grading system is used. There are approximately 8,500 listed buildings and 1,500 scheduled monuments in Northern Ireland.

OPENING TO THE PUBLIC
The following is a selection of the many historic buildings and monuments open to the public. Many properties are closed in winter (usually November–March) and some are also closed in the mornings. Most properties are closed on Christmas Eve, Christmas Day, Boxing Day and New Year's Day, and many are closed on Good Friday. During the winter season, many English Heritage monuments are closed on Mondays and Tuesdays and monuments in the care of Cadw are closed on Sunday mornings. In Northern Ireland many monuments are closed on Mondays except on bank holidays. Information about a specific property should be checked by telephone or online.

ENGLAND

For more information on any of the English Heritage properties listed below, the official website is:
www.english-heritage.org.uk
For more information on any of the National Trust properties listed below, the official website is:
www.nationaltrust.org.uk
(EH) English Heritage property
(NT) National Trust property

A LA RONDE (NT), Exmouth, Devon EX8 5BD
  T 01395-265514
  Unique 16-sided house completed c.1796
ALNWICK CASTLE, Alnwick, Northumberland NE66 1NQ
  T 01665-510777 W www.alnwick.com
  Seat of the Dukes of Northumberland since 1309; Italian Renaissance-style interior; gardens with spectacular water features

ALTHORP, Northants NN7 4HQ T 01604-770107
W www.althorp.com
Spencer family seat. Diana, Princess of Wales
memorabilia

ANGLESEY ABBEY (NT), Lode, Cambs CB5 9EJ
T 01223-810080
House built c.1600. Houses many paintings and a
unique clock collection. Gardens and Lode Mill

APSLEY HOUSE (EH), London W1J 7NT T 020-7499 5676
Built by Robert Adam 1771–8, home of the Dukes of
Wellington since 1817 and known as 'No. 1 London';
collection of fine and decorative arts

ARUNDEL CASTLE, Arundel, W. Sussex BN18 9AB
T 01903-882173 W www.arundelcastle.org
Castle dating from the Norman Conquest; seat of the
Dukes of Norfolk

AVEBURY (NT), Wilts SN8 1RF T 01672-539250
Remains of stone circles constructed 4,000 years ago
surrounding the later village of Avebury

BANQUETING HOUSE, Whitehall, London SW1A 2ER
T 0870-751 5178 W www.hrp.org.uk
Designed by Inigo Jones; ceiling paintings by Rubens;
site of the execution of Charles I

BASILDON PARK (NT), Reading, Berks RG8 9NR
T 0118-984 3040
Palladian house built in 1776–83 by John Carr

BATTLE ABBEY (EH), Battle, E. Sussex T 01424-773792
Remains of the abbey founded by William the
Conqueror on the site of the Battle of Hastings

BEAULIEU, Brockenhurst, Hants SO42 7ZN T 01590-612345
W www.beaulieu.co.uk
House and gardens; Beaulieu Abbey and exhibition of
monastic life; National Motor Museum

BEESTON CASTLE (EH), Cheshire CW6 9TX
T 01829-260464
13th-century inner ward with gatehouse and towers,
and remains of outer ward built by Ranulf sixth Earl of
Chester

BELTON HOUSE (NT), Grantham, Lincs NG32 2LS
T 01476-566116
17th-century house; formal gardens in landscaped park

BELVOIR CASTLE, Grantham, Lincs NG32 1PD
T 01476-871002 W www.belvoircastle.com
Seat of the Dukes of Rutland; 19th-century Gothic-
style castle

BERKELEY CASTLE, Glos GL13 9BQ T 01453-810332
W www.berkeley-castle.com
Completed 1153; site of the murder of Edward II
(1327)

BLENHEIM PALACE, Woodstock, Oxon OX20 1PX
T 01993-811091 W www.blenheimpalace.com
Seat of the Dukes of Marlborough and Winston
Churchill's birthplace; designed by Vanbrugh

BLICKLING HALL (NT), Blickling, Norfolk NR11 6NF
T 01263-738030
Jacobean house with state rooms; temple and 18th-
century orangery

BODIAM CASTLE (NT), Bodiam, E. Sussex TN32 5UA
T 01580-830436
Well-preserved medieval moated castle built in 1385

BOLSOVER CASTLE (EH), Bolsover, Derbys T 01246-822844
17th-century buildings on site of medieval castle

BOSCOBEL HOUSE (EH), Bishops Wood, Shrops ST19 9AR
T 01902-850244
Timber-framed 17th-century hunting lodge, refuge of
fugitive Charles II

BOUGHTON HOUSE, Kettering, Northants NN14 1BJ
T 01536-515731 W www.boughtonhouse.org.uk
A 17th-century house with French-style additions;
home of the Dukes of Buccleuch and Queensbury

BOWOOD HOUSE, Calne, Wilts SN11 9PQ T 01249-812102
W www.bowood-house.co.uk
An 18th-century house in Capability Brown park, with
lake, temple and arboretum

BROADLANDS, Romsey, Hants SO51 9ZD T 01794-505010
W www.broadlands.net
Palladian mansion in Capability Brown park;
Mountbatten exhibition

BRONTË PARSONAGE, Haworth, W. Yorks BD22 8DR
T 01535-642323 W www.bronte.org.uk
Home of the Brontë sisters; museum and memorabilia

BUCKFAST ABBEY, Buckfastleigh, Devon TQ11 0EE
T 01364-645500 W www.buckfast.org.uk
Benedictine monastery on medieval foundations

BUCKINGHAM PALACE, London SW1A 1AA T 020-7839
1377 W www.royal.gov.uk
Purchased by George III in 1761, and the Sovereign's
official London residence since 1837; 18 state rooms,
including the Throne Room, and Picture Gallery

BUCKLAND ABBEY (NT), Yelverton, Devon PL20 6EY
T 01822-853607
13th-century Cistercian monastery; home of Sir
Francis Drake

BURGHLEY HOUSE, Stamford, Lincs PE9 3JY
T 01780-752451 W www.burghley.co.uk
Late Elizabethan house built by William Cecil, first
Lord Burghley

CALKE ABBEY (NT), Ticknall, Derbys DE73 1LE
T 01332-863822
Baroque 18th-century mansion

CARISBROOKE CASTLE (EH), Newport, Isle of Wight
PO30 1XY T 01983-522107
W www.carisbrookecastlemuseum.org.uk
Norman castle; prison of Charles I 1647–8

CARLISLE CASTLE (EH), Carlisle, Cumbria CA3 8UR
T 01228-606000
Medieval castle; prison of Mary Queen of Scots

CARLYLE'S HOUSE (NT), Cheyne Row, London SW3 5HL
T 020-7352 7087
Home of Thomas Carlyle

CASTLE ACRE PRIORY (EH), Swaffham, Norfolk PE32 2AJ
T 01760-755394
Remains include 12th-century church and prior's
lodgings

CASTLE DROGO (NT), Drewsteignton, Devon EX6 6PB
T 01647-433306
Granite castle designed by Lutyens

CASTLE HOWARD, N. Yorks YO60 7DA T 01653-648444
W www.castlehoward.co.uk
Designed by Vanbrugh 1699–1726; mausoleum
designed by Hawksmoor

CASTLE RISING CASTLE (EH), King's Lynn, Norfolk
PE31 6AH T 01553-631330
12th-century keep in a massive earthwork with
gatehouse and bridge

CHARTWELL (NT), Westerham, Kent TN16 1PS
T 01732-868381
Home of Sir Winston Churchill

CHATSWORTH, Bakewell, Derbys DE45 1PP T 01246-565300
W www.chatsworth-house.co.uk
Tudor mansion in magnificent parkland

CHESTERS ROMAN FORT (EH), Chollerford,
Northumberland NE46 4EP T 01434-681379
Roman cavalry fort

CHYSAUSTER ANCIENT VILLAGE (EH), Penzance,
Cornwall T 07831-757934

Remains of Celtic settlement; eight stone-walled homesteads

CLIFFORD'S TOWER (EH), York T 01904-646940

13th-century tower built on a mound

CLIVEDEN (NT), Maidenhead, Berks SL6 0JA
T 01628-605069

Former home of the Astors, now a hotel set in garden and woodland

CORBRIDGE ROMAN SITE (EH), Corbridge, Northumberland NE45 5NT T 01434-632349

Excavated central area of a Roman town and successive military bases

CORFE CASTLE (NT), Wareham, Dorset BH20 5EZ
T 01929-481294

Ruined former royal castle dating from the 11th-century

CROFT CASTLE (NT), Herefordshire HR6 9PW
T 01568-780246

Pre-Conquest border castle with Georgian-Gothic interior

DEAL CASTLE (EH), Deal, Kent CT14 7BA T 01304-372762

Largest of the coastal defence forts built by Henry VIII

DICKENS HOUSE, Doughty Street, London WC1 2LF
T 020-7405 2127 W www.dickensmuseum.com

House occupied by Dickens 1837–9; manuscripts, furniture and portraits

DOVE COTTAGE, Grasmere, Cumbria LA22 9SH
T 01539-435544 W www.wordsworth.org.uk

Wordsworth's home 1799–1808; museum

DOVER CASTLE (EH), Dover, Kent CT16 1HU
T 01304-211067

Castle with Roman, Saxon and Norman features; wartime operations rooms

DR JOHNSON'S HOUSE, Gough Square, London EC4A 3DE
T 020-7353 3745 W www.drjh.dircon.co.uk

Home of Samuel Johnson

DUNSTANBURGH CASTLE (EH), Alnwick, Northumberland
T 01665-576231

A 14th-century castle on a cliff, with a substantial gatehouse-keep

ELTHAM PALACE (EH), Eltham, London SE9 5QE
T 020-8294 2548

Combines an Art Deco country house and remains of medieval palace set in moated gardens

FARLEIGH HUNGERFORD CASTLE (EH), Somerset
BA2 7RS T 01225-754026

Late 14th-century castle with two courts; chapel with tomb of Sir Thomas Hungerford

FARNHAM CASTLE KEEP (EH), Farnham, Surrey GU9 0AG
T 01252-713393

Large 12th-century Motte and Bailey

FOUNTAINS ABBEY (NT), nr Ripon, N. Yorks HG4 3DY
T 01765-608888 W www.fountainsabbey.org.uk

Deer park, visitor centre and St Mary's Church; ruined Cistercian monastery; 18th-century landscaped gardens of Studley Royal estate

FRAMLINGHAM CASTLE (EH), Woodbridge, Suffolk
IP13 9BP T 01728-724189

Castle (c.1200) with high curtain walls enclosing an almshouse (1639)

FURNESS ABBEY (EH), Barrow-in-Furness, Cumbria LH13 0TJ
T 01229-823420

Remains of church and conventual buildings founded in 1123

GLASTONBURY ABBEY, Glastonbury, Somerset BA6 9EL
T 01458-832267 W www.glastonburyabbey.com

Ruins of a 12th-century abbey rebuilt after fire; site of an early Christian settlement

GOODRICH CASTLE (EH), Ross-on-Wye, Herefordshire
HR9 6HY T 01600-890538

Remains of 13th- and 14th-century castle with 12th-century keep

GREENWICH, London SE10 T 020-8858 4422
W www.rog.nmm.ac.uk

Former Royal Observatory (founded 1675) housing the time ball and zero meridian of longitude; the Queen's House, designed for Queen Anne, wife of James I, by Inigo Jones; Painted Hall and Chapel (Royal Naval College)

GRIMES GRAVES (EH), Brandon, Norfolk
T 01842-810656

Neolithic flint mines. One shaft can be descended

GUILDHALL, London EC2P 2EJ T 020-7332 1313

Centre of civic government of the City; built c.1441; facade built 1788–9

HADDON HALL, Bakewell, Derbys DE45 1LA
T 01629-812855 W www.haddonhall.co.uk

Well-preserved 12th-century manor house

HAILES ABBEY (EH), Cheltenham, Glos GL54 5PB
T 01242-602398

Ruins of a 13th-century Cistercian monastery

HAM HOUSE (NT), Richmond-upon-Thames, Surrey
TW10 7RS T 020-8940 1950

Stuart house with lavish interiors and formal gardens

HAMPTON COURT PALACE, East Molesey, Surrey
KT8 9AU T 0870-752 7777 W www.hrp.org.uk

16th-century palace with additions by Wren; gardens with maze; Tudor tennis court (summer only)

HARDWICK HALL (NT), Chesterfield, Derbys S44 5QJ
T 01246-850430

Built 1591–7 for Bess of Hardwick; notable furnishings

HARDY'S COTTAGE (NT), Higher Bockhampton, Dorset
DT2 8QJ T 01305-262366

Birthplace and home of Thomas Hardy

HAREWOOD HOUSE, Harewood, W. Yorks LS17 9LQ
T 0113-218 1010 W www.harewood.org

18th-century house designed by John Carr and Robert Adam; park by Capability Brown

HATFIELD HOUSE, Hatfield, Herts AL9 5NQ
T 01707-287000 W www.hatfield-house.co.uk

Jacobean house built by Robert Cecil; surviving wing of Royal Palace of Hatfield (c.1485)

HELMSLEY CASTLE (EH), Helmsley, N. Yorks YO62 5AB
T 01439-770442

12th-century keep and curtain wall with 16th-century buildings; spectacular earthwork defences

HEVER CASTLE, nr Edenbridge, Kent TN8 7NG
T 01732-865224 W www.hevercastle.co.uk

13th-century double-moated castle; childhood home of Anne Boleyn

HOLKER HALL, Cumbria LA11 7PL
T 01539-558328 W www.holker-hall.co.uk

Former home of the Dukes of Devonshire; award-winning gardens

HOLKHAM HALL, Wells-next-the-Sea, Norfolk NR23 1AB
T 01328-710227 W www.holkham.co.uk

Palladian mansion; notable fine art collection

HOUSESTEADS ROMAN FORT (EH), Hexham, Northumberland NE47 6NN T 01434-344363

Excavated infantry fort on Hadrian's Wall with extra-mural civilian settlement

HUGHENDEN MANOR (NT), High Wycombe, Bucks
HP14 4LA T 01494-755573

Home of Disraeli; small formal garden

JANE AUSTEN'S HOUSE, Chawton, Hants GU34 1SD
T 01420-83262
W www.jane-austens-house-museum.org.uk
Jane Austen's home from 1809-17

KEDLESTON HALL (NT), Derbys DE22 5JH T 01332-842191
Classical Palladian mansion built 1759–65; complete Robert Adam interiors

KELMSCOTT MANOR, nr Lechlade, Glos GL7 3HJ
T 01367-252486 W www.kelmscottmanor.co.uk
Summer home of William Morris, with products of Morris and Co.

KENILWORTH CASTLE (EH), Kenilworth, Warks CV8 1NE
T 01926-852078
Largest castle ruin in England

KENSINGTON PALACE, Kensington Gardens, London
W8 4PX T 0870-751 5170 W www.hrp.org.uk
Built in 1605 and enlarged by Wren; bought by William and Mary in 1689; birthplace of Queen Victoria; Royal Ceremonial Dress Collection

KENWOOD HOUSE (EH), Hampstead Lane, London
NW3 7JR T 020-8348 1286
Adam villa housing the Iveagh bequest of paintings and furniture

KEW PALACE, Richmond-upon-Thames, Surrey TW9 3AB
T 020-8332 5655 W www.rbgkew.org.uk
Queen Charlotte's Cottage, used by King George III and family as a summerhouse

KINGSTON LACY (NT), Wimborne Minster, Dorset BH21 4EA
T 01202-883402
17th-century house with 19th-century alterations; important art collection

KNEBWORTH HOUSE, Knebworth, Herts SG3 6PY
T 01438-812661 W www.knebworthhouse.com
Tudor manor house concealed by 19th-century Gothic decoration; Lutyens gardens

KNOLE (NT), Sevenoaks, Kent TN15 0RP T 01732-462100
House dating from 1456 set in parkland; fine art treasures

LAMBETH PALACE, London SE1 7JU T 020-7898 1200
W www.archbishopofcanterbury.org
Official residence of the Archbishop of Canterbury; 19th-century house with parts dating from the 12th-century

LANERCOST PRIORY (EH), Brampton, Cumbria CA8 2HQ
T 01697 73030
The nave of the Augustinian priory church, c.1166, is still used; remains of other claustral buildings

LANHYDROCK (NT), Bodmin, Cornwall PL30 5AD
T 01208-265950
House dating from the 17th-century; 45 rooms, including kitchen and nursery

LEEDS CASTLE, nr Maidstone, Kent ME17 1PL
T 01622-765400 W www.leeds-castle.com
Castle dating from 9th-century, on two islands in lake

LEVENS HALL, Kendal, Cumbria LA8 0PD T 01539-560321
W www.levenshall.co.uk
Elizabethan house with unique topiary garden (1694); steam engine collection

LINCOLN CASTLE, Lincoln, Lincs LN1 3AA
T 01522-511068
Built by William the Conqueror in 1068

LINDISFARNE PRIORY (EH), Holy Island, Northumberland
T 01289-389200
Founded in AD 635; re-established in the 12th-century as a Benedictine priory, now ruined

LITTLE MORETON HALL (NT), Congleton, Cheshire
CW12 4SD T 01260-272018
Timber-framed moated manor house with knot garden

LONGLEAT HOUSE, Warminster, Wilts BA12 7NW
T 01985-844400 W www.longleat.co.uk
Elizabethan house in Italian Renaissance style

LULLINGSTONE ROMAN VILLA (EH), Eynsford, Kent
DA4 0JA T 01322-863467
Large villa occupied for much of the Roman period; fine mosaics

MANSION HOUSE, London EC4N 8BH
W www.cityoflondon.gov.uk
The official residence of the Lord Mayor of London

MARBLE HILL HOUSE (EH), Twickenham, Middx TW1 2NL
T 020-8892 5115
English Palladian villa with Georgian paintings and furniture

MICHELHAM PRIORY, Hailsham, E. Sussex BN27 3QS
T 01323-844224 W www.sussexpast.co.uk
Tudor house built onto an Augustinian priory

MIDDLEHAM CASTLE (EH), Leyburn, N. Yorks DL8 4QR
T 01969-623899
12th-century keep within later fortifications; childhood home of Richard III

MONTACUTE HOUSE (NT), Montacute, Somerset TA15 6XP
T 01935-823289
Elizabethan house with National Portrait Gallery collection of portraits from the period

MOUNT GRACE PRIORY (EH), Northallerton, N. Yorks
DL6 3JG T 01609-883494
Carthusian priory with remains of monastic buildings

NETLEY ABBEY (EH), Hants T 02392-581059
Remains of Cistercian abbey, used as house in Tudor period

OLD SARUM (EH), Salisbury, Wilts SP1 3SD T 01722-335398
Earthworks enclosing remains of the castle and the 11th-century cathedral

ORFORD CASTLE (EH), Orford, Suffolk T 01394-450472
Circular keep of c.1170 and remains of coastal defence castle built by Henry II

OSBORNE HOUSE (EH), East Cowes, Isle of Wight
PO32 6JY T 01983-200022
Queen Victoria's seaside residence

OSTERLEY PARK (NT), Isleworth, Middx TW7 4RB
T 020-8232 5050 W www.osterleypark.org.uk
Elizabethan mansion set in parkland

PENDENNIS CASTLE (EH), Falmouth, Cornwall TR11 4LP
T 01326-316594
Well-preserved 16th-century coastal defence castle

PENSHURST PLACE, Penshurst, Kent TN11 8DG
T 01892-870307 W www.penshurstplace.com
House with medieval Baron's Hall and 14th-century gardens

PETWORTH HOUSE (NT), Petworth, W. Sussex GU28 0AE
T 01798-342270
Late 17th-century house set in Capability Brown landscaped park

PEVENSEY CASTLE (EH), Pevensey, E. Sussex BN24 5LE
T 01323-762604
Walls of a 4th-century Roman fort; remains of an 11th-century castle

PEVERIL CASTLE (EH), Castleton, Derbys S33 8WQ
T 01433-620613
12th-century castle defended on two sides by precipitous rocks

POLESDEN LACEY (NT), nr Dorking, Surrey RH5 6BD
T 01372-452048
Regency villa remodelled in the Edwardian era; fine paintings and furnishings

PORTCHESTER CASTLE (EH), Portchester, Hants PO16 9QW
T 02392-378291

Baronial-style castle built for Victoria and Albert; The Queen's private residence

BLACKHOUSE, ARNOL (HS), Lewis, Western Isles
T 01851-710395
Traditional Lewis thatched house

BLAIR CASTLE, Blair Atholl, Perthshire PH18 5TL
T 01796-481207 W www.blair-castle.co.uk
Mid 18th-century mansion with 13th-century tower; seat of the Dukes and Earls of Atholl

BONAWE IRON FURNACE (HS), Taynuilt, Argyll PA35 1HE
T 01866-822432
Charcoal-fuelled ironworks founded in 1753

BOWHILL, Selkirkshire TD7 5ET T 01750-22204
Seat of the Dukes of Buccleuch and Queensberry; fine collection of paintings, including portrait miniatures

BROUGH OF BIRSAY (HS), Orkney
Remains of Norse church and village on the tidal island of Birsay

CAERLAVEROCK CASTLE (HS), nr Dumfries DG1 4RU
T 01387-770244
Triangular 13th-century castle with classical Renaissance additions

CAIRNPAPPLE HILL (HS), Torphichen, West Lothian
T 01506 634622
Neolithic and Bronze Age burial chambers and henge

CALANAIS STANDING STONES (HS), Lewis, Western Isles
HS2 9DY T 01851-621422
Standing stones in a cross-shaped setting, dating from 2900–2600 BC

CATERTHUNS (BROWN AND WHITE) (HS), nr Brechin, Angus
Two large Iron Age hill forts

CAWDOR CASTLE, Nairn, Moray IV12 5RD T 01667-404401
W www.cawdorcastle.com
14th-century keep with 15th- and 17th-century additions

CLAVA CAIRNS (HS), nr Inverness, Inverness-shire
T 01667-460232
Late Neolithic or early Bronze Age cairns

CRATHES CASTLE (NTS), nr Banchory, Aberdeenshire
AB31 5QJ T 01330-844525
16th-century baronial castle in woodland, fields and gardens

CULZEAN CASTLE (NTS), Maybole, Ayrshire KA19 8LE
T 01655-884455
18th-century Adam castle with oval staircase and circular saloon

DRYBURGH ABBEY (HS), nr Melrose, Roxburghshire
TD6 0RQ T 01835-822381
12th-century abbey containing tomb of Sir Walter Scott

DUNVEGAN CASTLE, Skye IV55 8WF T 01470-521206
W www.dunvegancastle.com
13th-century castle with later additions; home of the chiefs of the Clan MacLeod; trips to seal colony

EDINBURGH CASTLE (HS), EH1 2NG T 0131-225 9846
Includes the Scottish Crown Jewels, Scottish National War Memorial, Scottish United Services Museum and historic apartments

EDZELL CASTLE (HS), nr Brechin, Angus DD9 7UE
T 01356-648631
Medieval tower house; walled garden

EILEAN DONAN CASTLE, Dornie, Ross and Cromarty
IV40 8DX T 01599-555202
W www.eileandonancastle.com
13th-century castle with Jacobite relics

ELGIN CATHEDRAL (HS), Moray IV30 1EL T 01343-547171
13th-century cathedral and chapterhouse

FLOORS CASTLE, Kelso, Roxburghshire TD5 7SF
T 01573-223333 W www.floorscastle.com
Largest inhabited castle in Scotland; seat of the Dukes of Roxburghe; built 1721 by William Adam

FORT GEORGE (HS), Ardersier, Inverness-shire IV2 7TE
T 01667-462777
18th-century fort

GLAMIS CASTLE, Forfar, Angus DD8 1RJ T 01307-840393
W www.glamis-castle.co.uk
Seat of the Lyon family (later Earls of Strathmore and Kinghorne) since 1372

GLASGOW CATHEDRAL (HS), Lanarkshire G4 0RH
T 0141-552 8198 W www.glasgowcathedral.org.uk
Medieval cathedral with elaborately vaulted crypt

GLENELG BROCHS (HS), Shielbridge, Ross and Cromarty
T 01667-460232
Two broch towers with well-preserved structural features

HOPETOUN HOUSE, South Queensferry, W. Lothian
EH30 9SL T 0131-331 2451 W www.hopetounhouse.com
House designed by Sir William Bruce, enlarged by William Adam

HUNTLY CASTLE (HS), Aberdeenshire AB54 4SH
T 01466-793191
Ruin of a 16th- and 17th-century house

INVERARAY CASTLE, Argyll PA32 8XF T 01499-302203
W www.inveraray-castle.com
Gothic-style 18th-century castle; seat of the Dukes of Argyll

IONA ABBEY, Iona, Inner Hebrides PA76 6SJ
T 01681-700512
Monastery founded by St Columba in AD 563

JARLSHOF (HS), Sumburgh, Shetland ZE3 9JN
T 01950-460112
Prehistoric and Norse settlement

JEDBURGH ABBEY (HS), Roxburghshire TD8 6JQ
T 01835-863925
Romanesque and early Gothic church founded c.1138

KELSO ABBEY (HS), Kelso, Roxburghshire TD5 7JD
Remains of great abbey church founded 1128 by David I

KISIMUL CASTLE (HS), Castlebay, Barra, Western Isles
T 01871-810313
Medieval home of the Clan MacNeil

LINLITHGOW PALACE (HS), Kirkgate, W. Lothian
EH49 7AL T 01506-842896
Ruin of royal palace in park setting; birthplace of James V and Mary, Queen of Scots

MAES HOWE (HS), Stenness, Orkney KW16 3HA
T 01856-761606
Neolithic tomb

MEIGLE SCULPTURED STONES (HS), Meigle, Perthshire
PH12 8SB T 01828-640612
Twenty six Celtic Christian stones

MELROSE ABBEY (HS), Melrose, Roxburghshire
T 01896-822562
Ruin of Cistercian abbey founded c.1136 by David I

MOUSA BROCH (HS), Mousa, Shetland T 01466-793191
Finest surviving Iron Age broch tower

NEW ABBEY CORN MILL (HS), Dumfriesshire DG2 8BX
T 01387-850260
Working water-powered mill

PALACE OF HOLYROODHOUSE, Edinburgh EH8 8DX
T 0131-556 5100 W www.royal.gov.uk
The Queen's official Scottish residence; main part of the palace built 1671–9

RING O' BRODGAR (HS), nr Stromness, Orkney
T 01856-841815

Neolithic circle of upright stones with an enclosing ditch

ROSSLYN CHAPEL, Roslin, Midlothian FH25 9PH
T 0131 440 2159 W www.rosslynchapel.org.uk
Historic church with unique stone carvings

RUTHWELL CROSS (HS), Ruthwell, Dumfriesshire
T 01387-870249
Seventh-century Anglian cross

ST ANDREWS CASTLE AND CATHEDRAL (HS), Fife
KY16 9AR T 01334-477196 (castle); 01334-472563 (cathedral)
Ruins of 13th-century castle and remains of the largest cathedral in Scotland

SCONE PALACE, Perth, Perthshire PH2 6BD T 01738-552300
W www.scone-palace.co.uk
House built 1802–13 on the site of a medieval palace; home of the Earls of Mansfield

SKARA BRAE (HS), nr Stromness, Orkney
KW16 3LRT 01856-841815
Stone Age village with adjacent 17th-century house

SMAILHOLM TOWER (HS), Roxburghshire TD5 7PG
T 01573-460365
Well-preserved 15th-century tower-house

STIRLING CASTLE (HS), Stirlingshire FK8 1EJ
T 01786-450000
Great Hall and gatehouse of James IV, palace of James V, Chapel Royal remodelled by James VI

TANTALLON CASTLE (HS), North Berwick, E. Lothian
EH39 5PN T 01620-892727
Fortification with earthwork defences and a 14th-century curtain wall with towers

THREAVE CASTLE (HS), Castle Douglas, Kirkcudbrightshire
T 07711-223101
Late 14th-century tower on an island; accessible only by boat

URQUHART CASTLE (HS), Drumnadrochit, Inverness-shire
IV63 6XJ T 01456-450551
13th-century castle remains on the banks of Loch Ness

NORTHERN IRELAND

For more information on any of the National Trust properties listed below, the official website is:
www.nationaltrust.org.uk
For the Northern Ireland Environment and Heritage Service, the official website is: www.ehsni.gov.uk
(EHS) Property in the care of the Northern Ireland Environment and Heritage Service
(NT) National Trust property

CARRICKFERGUS CASTLE (EHS), Carrickfergus, Co. Antrim
BT38 7BG T 028-9335 1273
Castle begun in 1180 and garrisoned until 1928

CASTLE COOLE (NT), Enniskillen, Co. Fermanagh BT74 6JY
T 028-6632 2690
18th-century mansion by James Wyatt in parkland

CASTLE WARD (NT), Strangford, Co. Down BT30 7LS
T 028-4488 1204
18th-century house with Classical and Gothic facades

DEVENISH ISLAND (EHS), nr Enniskillen, Co. Fermanagh
T 028-6862 1588
Island monastery founded in the sixth-century by St Molaise

DOWNHILL CASTLE (NT), Castlerock, Co. Londonderry
T 028-7084 8728
Ruins of palatial house in landscaped estate including Mussenden Temple

DUNLUCE CASTLE (EHS), Bushmills, Co. Antrim BT57 8QG
T 028-2073 1938
Ruins of 16th-century stronghold of the MacDonnells

FLORENCE COURT (NT), Enniskillen, Co. Fermanagh
BT92 1DB T 028-6634 8249
Mid-18th-century house with rococo decoration

GREY ABBEY (EHS), Greyabbey, Co. Down T 028-9054 6552
Substantial remains of a Cistercian abbey founded in 1193

HILLSBOROUGH FORT (EHS), Hillsborough, Co. Down
BT26 6AG T 028-9268 3285
Square keep built in 1650

MOUNT STEWART (NT), Newtownards, Co. Down
BT22 2AD T 028-4278 8387
18th-century house, childhood home of Lord Castlereagh

NENDRUM MONASTERY (EHS), Mahee Island, Co. Down
T 028-9181 1491
Founded in the fifth-century by St Machaoi

TULLY CASTLE (EHS), Co. Fermanagh T 028-9054 6518
Fortified house and bawn built in 1613

WHITE ISLAND (EHS), Co. Fermanagh
Tenth-century monastery; 12th-century church featuring stone figures dating from the sixth-century

MUSEUMS AND GALLERIES

There are approximately 2,500 museums and galleries in the United Kingdom. Around 1,800 are registered with the Museums, Libraries and Archives Council (MLA), which indicates that they have an appropriate constitution, are soundly financed, have adequate collection management standards and public services, and have access to professional curatorial advice. Museums must achieve full or provisional registration status in order to be eligible for grants from MLA and from Area Museums Councils. Many registered museums are run by a local authority.

The national museums and galleries receive direct government grant-in-aid. These are: British Museum; Imperial War Museum; National Army Museum; National Galleries of Scotland; National Gallery; National Maritime Museum; National Museums and Galleries on Merseyside; National Museum of Wales; National Museums of Scotland; National Portrait Gallery; Natural History Museum; RAF Museum; Royal Armouries; Science Museum; Tate Gallery; Ulster Folk and Transport Museum; Ulster Museum; Victoria and Albert Museum; Wallace Collection. An online art museum (www.24hourmuseum.org.uk) has also been awarded national collection status.

The following is a selection of the museums and art galleries in the United Kingdom. Opening hours and admission charges vary. For further information about museums and galleries in the UK, including local authority status and whether a collection is designated pre-eminent, contact the Museums Association on 020-7426 6970.

ENGLAND

BARNARD CASTLE, Co. Durham – *The Bowes Museum*, Westwick Road DL12 8NP T 01833-690606
  W www.bowesmuseum.org.uk
  European art from the late medieval period to the 19th-century; music and costume galleries; English period rooms from Elizabeth I to Victoria; local archaeology
BATH – *American Museum*, Claverton Manor BA2 7BD
  T 01225-460503 W www.americanmuseum.org
  American decorative arts from the 17th- to 19th-century
Museum of Costume, Bennett Street BA1 2QH T 01225-477789
  W www.museumofcostume.co.uk
  Fashion from the 16th-century to the present day
Roman Baths Museum, Pump Room, Stall Street BA1 1LZ
  T 01225-477785 W www.romanbaths.co.uk
  Museum adjoins the remains of a Roman baths and temple complex
Victoria Art Gallery, Bridge Street BA2 4AT T 01225-477232
  W www.victoriagal.org.uk
  European Old Masters and British art since the 18th-century
BEAMISH, Co. Durham – *Beamish, The North of England Open Air Museum*, DH9 0RG T 0191-370 4000
  W www.beamish.org.uk
  Recreated northern town c.1900, with rebuilt and furnished local buildings, colliery village, farm, railway station, tramway, Pockerley Manor and horse-yard (set c.1800)

BEAULIEU, Hants – *National Motor Museum*, SO42 7ZN
  T 01590-612345 W www.beaulieu.co.uk
  Displays of over 250 vehicles dating from 1895 to the present day
BIRMINGHAM – *Aston Hall*, Trinity Road, B6 6JD
  T 0121-327 0062 W www.bmag.org.uk/aston_hall
  Jacobean House containing paintings, furniture and tapestries from the 17th- to 19th-century
Barber Institute of Fine Arts, off Edgbaston Park Road, B15 2TS
  T 0121-414 7333 W www.barber.org.uk
  Fine arts, including Old Masters
Birmingham Museum and Art Gallery, Chamberlain Square B3 3DH T 0121-303 2834
  W www.bmag.org.uk/museum_and_art_gallery
  Includes notable collection of Pre-Raphaelite art
Birmingham Nature Centre, Pershore Road, Edgbaston, B5 7RL
  T 0121-472 7775
  Indoor and outdoor enclosures displaying wildlife, especially British and European
Museum of the Jewellery Quarter, Vyse Street, Hockley B18 6HA
  T 0121-554 3598 W www.bmag.org.uk/jewellery_quarter
  Built around a real jewellery workshop
BOVINGTON, Dorset – *Tank Museum*, BH20 6JG
  T 01929-405096 W www.tankmuseum.co.uk
  Collection of 300 tanks from the earliest days of tank warfare to the present
BRADFORD – *Cartwright Hall Art Gallery*, Lister Park BD9 4NS
  T 01274-431212 W www.bradfordmuseums.org
  British 19th- and 20th-century fine art
Bradford Industrial Museum and Horses at Work, Moorside Road, Eccleshill BD2 3HP T 01274-435900
  W www.bradfordmuseums.org
  Engineering, textiles, transport and social history exhibits, including recreated back-to-back cottages, shire horses and horse tram-rides
National Museum of Photography, Film and Television, Bradford BD1 1NQ T 0870-7010200
  W www.nmpft.org.uk
  Photography, film and television interactive exhibits; features the UK's first IMAX cinema and the only public Cinerama screen in the world
BRIGHTON – *Booth Museum of Natural History*, Dyke Road BN1 5AA T 01273-292777
  W www.booth.virtualmuseum.info
  Zoology, botany and geology collections; British birds in recreated habitats
Brighton Museum and Art Gallery, Royal Pavilion Gardens, BN1 1EE
  T 01273-290900 W www.brighton.virtualmuseum.info
  Includes fine art and design, fashion, non-Western art, Brighton history
BRISTOL – *Arnolfini*, Narrow Quay BS1 4QA
  T 0117-917 2300 W www.arnolfini.org.uk
  Contemporary visual arts, dance, performance, music, talks and workshops
Blaise Castle House Museum, Henbury BS10 7QS
  T 0117-903 9818 W www.bristol-city.gov.uk/museums
  Agricultural and social history collections in an 18th-century mansion
Bristol Industrial Museum, Princes Wharf BS1 4RN
  T 0117-925 1470 W www.bristol-city.gov.uk/museums
  Industrial, maritime and transport collections

City Museum and Art Gallery, Queen's Road BS8 1RL
  T 0117-922 3571 W www.bristol-city.gov.uk/museums
  Includes fine and decorative art, oriental art,
  Egyptology and Bristol ceramics and paintings
CAMBRIDGE – *Fitzwilliam Museum*, Trumpington Street
  CB2 1RB T 01223-332900 W www.fitzmuseum.cam.ac.uk
  Antiquities, fine and applied arts, clocks, ceramics,
  manuscripts, furniture, sculpture, coins and medals
Imperial War Museum Duxford, Duxford CB2 4QR
  T 01223-835000 W duxford.iwm.org.uk
  Displays of military and civil aircraft, tanks, guns and
  naval exhibits
Sedgwick Museum of Earth Sciences, Downing Street, CB2 3EQ
  T 01223-333456 W www.sedgwickmuseum.org
  Extensive geological collection
University Museum of Archaeology and Anthropology, Downing
  Street CB2 3DZ T 01223-333516
  W museum.archanth.cam.ac.uk
  Archaeology and anthropology from all parts of the
  world
University Museum of Zoology, Downing Street CB2 3EJ
  T 01223-336650 W www.zoo.cam.ac.uk
  Extensive zoological collection
Whipple Museum of the History of Science, Free School Lane
  CB2 3RH T 01223-330906 W www.hps.cam.ac.uk/whipple
  Scientific instruments from the 14th-century to the
  present
CARLISLE – *Tullie House Museum and Art Gallery*, Castle
  Street CA3 8TP T 01228-534781 W www.tulliehouse.co.uk
  Prehistoric archaeology, Hadrian's Wall, Viking and
  medieval Cumbria, and the social history of Carlisle;
  also British 19th- and 20th-century art and English
  porcelain
CHATHAM – *The Historic Dockyard*, ME4 4TZ
  T 01634-823800 W www.chdt.org.uk
  Maritime attractions including HMS *Cavalier*, the UK's
  last World War II destroyer
Royal Engineers Museum of Military Engineering, Brompton
  Barracks ME4 4UG T 01634-822839
  W www.re-museum.co.uk/
  Regimental history, ethnography, decorative art and
  photography
CHELTENHAM – *Art Gallery and Museum*, Clarence Street
  GL50 3JT T 01242-237431
  W www.cheltenhammuseum.org.uk
  Paintings, arts and crafts
CHESTER – *Grosvenor Museum*, Grosvenor Street CH1 2DD
  T 01244-402008
  Roman collections, natural history, art, Chester silver,
  local history and costume
CHICHESTER – *Weald and Downland Open Air Museum*,
  Singleton PO18 0EU T 01243-811363
  W www.wealddown.co.uk
  Rebuilt vernacular buildings from south-east England;
  includes medieval houses, agricultural and rural craft
  buildings and a working watermill
COLCHESTER – *Colchester Castle Museum*, Castle Park
  CO1 1TJ T 01206-282939
  W www.colchestermuseums.org.uk
  Largest Norman keep in Europe standing on
  foundations of the Roman Temple of Claudius; tours of
  the Roman vaults, castle walls and chapel with
  medieval and prison displays
COVENTRY – *Coventry Transport Museum*, Hales Street
  CV1 1PN T 024-7683 2425 W www.transport-museum.com
  Hundreds of motor vehicles and bicycles
Herbert Art Gallery and Museum, Jordan Well CV1 5QP
  T 024-7683 2381 W www.coventrymuseum.org.uk

Local history, archaeology and industry, and fine and
  decorative art
DERBY – *Derby Industrial Museum*, Full Street DE1 3AF
  T 01332-255308 W www.derby.gov.uk/museums
  Rolls-Royce aero engine collection and railway
  engineering gallery
Derby Museum and Art Gallery, The Strand DE1 1BS
  T 01332-716659 W www.derby.gov.uk/museums
  Includes paintings by Joseph Wright of Derby and
  Derby porcelain
Pickford's House Museum, Friar Gate DE1 1DA T 01332-255363
  W www.derby.gov.uk/museums
  Georgian town house by architect Joseph Pickford;
  reconstructed period rooms and garden
DEVIZES – *Wiltshire Heritage Museum*,Long Street SN10 1NS
  T 01380-727369 W www.wiltshireheritage.org.uk
  Natural and local history, art gallery, archaeological
  finds from Bronze Age, Iron Age, Roman and Saxon sites
DORCHESTER – *Dorset County Museum*, High West Street,
  DT1 1XA T 01305-262735
  W www.dorsetcountymuseum.org
  Includes a collection of Thomas Hardy's manuscripts,
  books, notebooks and drawings
DOVER – *Dover Museum*, Market Square CT16 1PB
  T 01304-201066 W www.dovermuseum.co.uk
  Contains Dover Bronze Age Boat Gallery and
  archaeological finds from the Bronze Age, Roman and
  Saxon sites
EXETER – *Royal Albert Memorial Museum and Art Gallery*,
  Queen Street EX4 3RX T 01392-665858
  W www.exeter.gov.uk/museums
  Natural history, archaeology, worldwide fine and
  decorative art including Exeter silver
GATESHEAD – *Baltic Centre for Contemporary Art*, South
  Shore Road NE8 3BA T 0191-478 1810
  W www.balticmill.com
  Contemporary art exhibitions and events
Shipley Art Gallery, Prince Consort Road NE8 4JB T 0191-477 1495
  W www.twmuseums.org.uk/shipley
  Contemporary crafts
GAYDON, Warks – *Heritage Motor Centre*, Banbury Road
  CV35 0BJ T 01926-641188
  W www.heritage-motor-centre.co.uk
  History of British motor industry from 1895 to
  present; classic vehicles; engineering gallery; Corgi and
  Lucas collections
GLOUCESTER – *National Waterways Museum*, Gloucester
  Docks GL1 2EH T 01452-318200 W www.nwm.org.uk
  Two-hundred-year history of Britain's canals and
  inland waterways
GOSPORT, Hants – *Royal Navy Submarine Museum*, Haslar
  Jetty Road PO12 2AS T 023-9252 9217
  W www.rnsubmus.co.uk
  Underwater warfare, including the submarine *Alliance*;
  historical and nuclear galleries; first Royal Navy
  submarine
GRASMERE, Cumbria – *Dove Cottage* and the *Wordsworth
  Museum*, LA22 9SH T 01539-435544
  W www.wordsworth.org.uk
  William Wordsworth's home and garden
HULL – *Ferens Art Gallery*, Queen Victoria Square HU1 3RA
  T 01482-613902 W www.hullcc.gov.uk/museums
  European art, especially Dutch 17th-century paintings,
  British portraits from 17th- to 20th-century, and
  marine paintings
Hull Maritime Museum, Queen Victoria Square HU1 3DX
  T 01482-613902 W www.hullcc.gov.uk/museums
  Whaling, fishing and navigation exhibits

HUNTINGDON – *The Cromwell Museum*, Grammar School
Walk PE29 3LF T 01480-375830
W www.cambridgeshire.gov.uk/cromwell
Portraits and memorabilia relating to Oliver Cromwell

IPSWICH – *Christchurch Mansion* and *Wolsey Art Gallery*,
Christchurch Park IP4 2BE T 01473-433554
Tudor house with paintings by Gainsborough,
Constable and other Suffolk artists; furniture and
18th-century ceramics; temporary exhibitions

LEEDS – *Leeds City Art Gallery*, The Headrow LS1 3AA
T 0113-247 8248 W www.leeds.gov.uk/artgallery
British and European paintings including English
watercolours; modern sculpture; Henry Moore gallery;
print room

Leeds Industrial Museum at Armley Mills, Canal Road, Armley
LS12 2QF T 0113-263 7861 W www.leeds.gov.uk/armleymills
World's largest woollen mill

Lotherton Hall, Aberford LS25 3EB T 0113-281 3259
W www.leeds.gov.uk/lothertonhall
Costume and oriental collections in furnished
Edwardian house; deer park and bird garden

Royal Armouries Museum, Armouries Drive LS10 1LT
T 0113-220-1916 W www.royalarmouries.org
National collection of arms and armour from BC to
present; demonstrations of foot combat in museum's
five galleries; falconry and mounted combat in the
tiltyard

Temple Newsam, LS15 0AD T 0113-264 7321
W www.leeds.gov.uk/templenewsam
Old Masters and 17th- and 18th-century decorative art
in furnished Jacobean/Tudor house

LEICESTER – *Jewry Wall Museum*, St Nicholas Circle LE1 4LB
T 0116-225 4971 W www.leicestermuseums.ac.uk
Archaeology; Roman Jewry Wall and baths; mosaics

New Walk Museum and Art Gallery, New Walk LE1 7EA
T 0116-255 4900 W www.leicestermuseums.ac.uk
Natural history and geology; ancient Egypt gallery;
European art and decorative arts

LINCOLN – *Museum of Lincolnshire Life*, Burton Road
LN1 3LY T 01522-528448
Social history and agricultural collection

Usher Gallery, Lindum Road LN2 1NN T 01522-527980
Watches, miniatures, porcelain, silver; collection of
Peter de Wint works; Lincolnshire topography; Royal
Lincs Regiment memorabilia

LIVERPOOL – *Lady Lever Art Gallery*, Wirral CH62 5EQ
T 0151-478 4136 W www.ladyleverartgallery.org.uk
Paintings, furniture and porcelain

Liverpool Museum, William Brown Street L3 8EN T 0151-478 4399
W www.liverpoolmuseums.org.uk/livmus
Includes Egyptian mummies, weapons and classical
sculpture; planetarium, aquarium, vivarium and natural
history centre

Merseyside Maritime Museum, Albert Dock L3 4AQ
T 0151-478 4499 W www.liverpoolmuseums.org.uk/maritime
Floating exhibits, working displays and craft
demonstrations; incorporates *HM Customs and Excise
National Museum*

Sudley House, Mossley Hill Road L18 8BX T 0151-724 3245
W www.liverpoolmuseums.org.uk/sudley
Late 18th- and 19th-century British paintings in
former shipowner's home. Closed for refurbishment
until spring 2006

Tate Liverpool, Albert Dock L3 4BB T 0151-702 7400
W www.tate.org.uk/liverpool
Twentieth-century painting and sculpture

The Walker, William Brown Street L3 8EL T 0151-478 4199
W www.liverpoolmuseums.org.uk/walker
Paintings from the 14th- to 20th-century

LONDON: GALLERIES – *Barbican Art Gallery*, Barbican
Centre, Silk Street EC2Y 8DS T 020-7638 8891
W www.barbican.org.uk
Temporary exhibitions

Courtauld Institute of Art Gallery, Somerset House, Strand
WC2R 0RN T 020-7848 2526 W www.courtauld.ac.uk
The University of London galleries

Dulwich Picture Gallery, Gallery Road, Dulwich Village SE21 7AD
T 020-8693 5254 W www.dulwichpicturegallery.org.uk
England's first public art gallery; built by Sir John
Soane to house 17th- and 18th-century paintings

Hayward Gallery, Belvedere Road SE1 8XZ T 020-7960 5226
W www.hayward.org.uk
Temporary exhibitions

National Gallery, Trafalgar Square WC2N 5DN T 020-7747 2885
W www.nationalgallery.org.uk
Western painting from the 13th- to 20th-century; early
Renaissance collection in the Sainsbury wing

National Portrait Gallery, St Martin's Place WC2H 0HE
T 020-7306 0055 W www.npg.org.uk
Portraits of eminent people in British history

Percival David Foundation of Chinese Art, Gordon Square
WC1H 0PD T 020-7387 3909 W www.pdfmuseum.org.uk
Chinese ceramics from the 10th- to 18th-century

Photographers' Gallery, Great Newport Street WC2H 7HY
T 020-7831 1772 W www.photonet.org.uk
Temporary exhibitions

The Queen's Gallery, Buckingham Palace SW1A 1AA
T 020-7766 7301 W www.royal.org.uk
Art from the Royal Collection

Royal Academy of Arts, Piccadilly W1J 0BD
T 020-7300 8000 W www.royalacademy.org.uk
British art since 1750 and temporary exhibitions;
annual Summer Exhibition

Saatchi Gallery, County Hall, South Bank SE1 7PB
T 020-7928 8195 W www.saatchi-gallery.co.uk
Contemporary art including paintings, photographs,
sculpture and installations

Serpentine Gallery, Kensington Gardens W2 3XA
T 020-7402 6075 W www.serpentinegallery.org
Temporary exhibitions of British and international
contemporary art

Tate Britain, Millbank SW1P 4RG T 020-7887 8000
W www.tate.org.uk/britain
British painting and 20th-century painting and
sculpture

Tate Modern, Bankside SE1 9TG T 020-7887 8000
W www.tate.org.uk/modern
International modern art from 1900 to the present

Wallace Collection, Manchester Square W1U 3BN
T 020-7563 9500 W www.wallacecollection.org
Paintings and drawings, French 18th-century furniture,
armour, porcelain, clocks and sculpture

Whitechapel Art Gallery, Whitechapel High Street E1 7QX
T 020-7522 7888 W www.whitechapel.org
Temporary exhibitions of modern art

LONDON: MUSEUMS – *Bank of England Museum*,
Threadneedle Street EC2R 8AH (entrance on
Bartholomew Lane) T 020-7601 5545
W www.bankofengland.co.uk/museum
History of the Bank since 1694

British Museum, Great Russell Street WC1B 3DG
T 020-7323 8000
W www.thebritishmuseum.ac.uk
Antiquities, coins, medals, prints and drawings

Cabinet War Rooms, King Charles Street SW1A 2AQ
T 020-7930 6961 W www.cwr.iwm.org.uk

Underground rooms used by Churchill and the Government during the Second World War

Cutty Sark, Greenwich SE10 9HT **T** 020-8858 3445
  W www.cuttysark.org.uk
  Restored and re-rigged tea clipper with exhibits on board

Design Museum, Shad Thames SE1 2YD **T** 0870-833 9955
  W www.designmuseum.org
  The development of design and the mass-production of consumer objects

Firepower, the Royal Artillery Museum, Royal Arsenal, Woolwich SE18 6ST **T** 020-8855 7755 **W** www.firepower.org.uk
  The history and development of artillery over the last 700 years including the collections of the Royal Regiment of Artillery

Geffrye Museum, Kingsland Road E2 8EA **T** 020-7739 9893
  W www.geffrye-museum.org.uk
  English urban domestic interiors from 1600 to present day; also paintings, furniture, decorative arts, walled herb garden and period garden rooms

Gilbert Collection, Strand WC2R 1LA **T** 020-7420 9400
  W www.gilbert-collection.org.uk
  Collection comprising some 800 works of art including European silver, gold snuff boxes and Italian mosaics

HMS Belfast, Morgan's Lane, Tooley Street SE1 2JH **T** 020-7940 6300 **W** hmsbelfast.iwm.org.uk
  Life on a Second World War cruiser

Horniman Museum, London Road SE23 3PQ **T** 020-8699 1872
  W www.horniman.ac.uk
  Museum of ethnography, musical instruments and natural history; aquarium; reference library; sunken, water and flower gardens

Imperial War Museum, Lambeth Road SE1 6HZ **T** 020-7416 5320
  W london.iwm.org.uk
  All aspects of the two world wars and other military operations involving Britain and the Commonwealth since 1914

Jewish Museum, Camden Town, Albert Street NW1 7NB
  T 020-7284 1997 **W** www.jewishmuseum.org.uk
  Jewish life, history and religion

London's Transport Museum, Covent Garden Piazza WC2E 7BB
  T 020-7379 6344 **W** www.ltmuseum.co.uk
  Vehicles, photographs and graphic art relating to the history of transport in London

MCC Museum, Lord's, St John's Wood NW8 8QN
  T 020-7616 8656 **W** www.lords.org
  Cricket museum; conducted tours by appointment

Museum in Docklands, West India Quay, Hertsmere Road E14 4AL
  T 0870-444 3857 **W** www.museumindocklands.org.uk
  Explores the story of London's river, port and people over 2,000 years, from Roman times through to the recent regeneration of London's Docklands

Museum of Childhood at Bethnal Green, Cambridge Heath Road E2 9PA **T** 020-8980 2415
  W www.museumofchildhood.org.uk
  Toys, games and exhibits relating to the social history of childhood

Museum of Garden History, Lambeth Palace Road SE1 7LB
  T 020-7401 8865 **W** www.museumgardenhistory.org
  History and development of gardens and gardening; re-created 17th-century garden

Museum of London, London Wall, EC2Y 5HN **T** 020-7600 3699
  W www.museumoflondon.org.uk
  History of London from prehistoric times to present day

National Army Museum, Royal Hospital Road SW3 4HT
  T 020-7730 0717 **W** www.national-army-museum.ac.uk
  Five-hundred-year history of the British soldier; exhibits include model of the Battle of Waterloo and recreated First World War trench

National Maritime Museum, Greenwich SE10 9NF
  T 020-8858 4422 **W** www.nmm.ac.uk
  Maritime history of Britain; collections include globes, clocks, telescopes and paintings; comprises the main building, the Royal Observatory and the Queen's House

Natural History Museum, Cromwell Road SW7 5BD
  T 020-7942 5000 **W** www.nhm.ac.uk
  Natural history collections

Petrie Museum of Egyptian Archaeology, University College London, Malet Place WC1E 6BT **T** 020-7679 2884
  W www.petrie.ucl.ac.uk
  Egyptian archaeology collection

Royal Air Force Museum, Hendon NW9 5LL **T** 020-8205 2266
  W www.rafmuseum.org.uk
  Aviation from before the Wright brothers to the present-day RAF; features more than 70 full-size aircraft

Royal Mews, Buckingham Palace SW1A 1AA **T** 020-7766 7302
  W www.royal.gov.uk
  State vehicles, including The Queen's Gold State Coach; home to The Queen's horses

Science Museum, Exhibition Road, SW7 2DD **T** 0870 870 4868
  W www.sciencemuseum.org.uk
  Science, technology, industry and medicine collections

Shakespeare's Globe Theatre Tour and Exhibition, Bankside SE1 9DT **T** 020-7902 1400 **W** www.shakespeares-globe.org
  Recreation of Elizabethan theatre using 16th-century techniques

Sherlock Holmes Museum, Baker Street NW1 6XE
  T 020-7935 8866 **W** www.sherlock-holmes.co.uk
  Recreated rooms of the fictional detective

Sir John Soane's Museum, Lincoln's Inn Fields WC2A 3BP
  T 020-7405 2107 **W** www.soane.org
  Art and antiques

Theatre Museum, Russell Street WC2E 7PR **T** 020-7943 4700
  W www.theatremuseum.org.uk
  History of the performing arts

Tower Bridge Experience, SE1 2UP **T** 020-7403 3761
  W www.towerbridge.org.uk
  History of the bridge and display of Victorian steam machinery; panoramic views from walkways

Victoria and Albert Museum, Cromwell Road SW7 2RL
  T 020-7942 2000 **W** www.vam.ac.uk
  Includes National Art Library and Print Room; fine and applied art and design; furniture, glass, textiles and dress collections

Wimbledon Lawn Tennis Museum, Church Road SW19 5AE
  T 020-8946 6131 **W** www.wimbledon.org/museum
  Tennis trophies, fashion and memorabilia; view of Centre Court

MALTON, N. Yorks – *Eden Camp*, YO17 6RT **T** 01653 697777
  W www.edencamp.co.uk
  Restored POW camp and Second World War memorabilia

MANCHESTER – *Gallery of Costume*, Platt Hall, Rusholme M14 5LL **T** 0161-224 5217 **W** www.manchestergalleries.org
  Exhibits from the 16th- to 20th-century

Imperial War Museum North, Trafford Wharf Road, Trafford Park M17 1TZ **T** 0161-836 4000 **W** north.iwm.org.uk

Manchester Art Gallery, Mosley Street M2 3JL **T** 0161-235 8888
  W www.manchestergalleries.org
  Six centuries of European fine and decorative art

Manchester Museum, Oxford Road M13 9PL **T** 0161-275 2634
  W www.museum.man.ac.uk

Collections include archaeology, decorative arts Egyptology, natural history and zoology

Museum of Science and Industry, Liverpool Road, Castlefield M3 4FP **T** 0161-832 2244 **W** www.msim.org.uk

On site of world's oldest passenger railway station; galleries relating to space, energy, power, transport, aviation, textiles and social history; interactive science centre

People's History Museum, The Pump House, Bridge Street M3 3ER **T** 0161-839 6061 **W** www.peopleshistorymuseum.org.uk

Political and working life history

Whitworth Art Gallery, Oxford Road M15 6ER **T** 0161-275 7450 **W** www.whitworth.man.ac.uk

Watercolours, drawings, prints, textiles, wallpapers and 20th-century British art

MILTON KEYNES – *Bletchley Park National Codes Centre*, Bucks, MK3 6EB **T** 01908 640404 **W** www.bletchleypark.org.uk

Home of British codebreaking during the Second World War; Enigma machine; computer museum; wartime toys and memorabilia

MONKWEARMOUTH, Sunderland – *Monkwearmouth Station Museum*, North Bridge Street SR5 1AP **T** 0191-567 7075 **W** www.twmuseums.org.uk/monkwearmouth

Victorian train station

NEWCASTLE UPON TYNE – *Discovery Museum*, Blandford Square NE1 4JA **T** 0191-232 6789 **W** www.twmuseums.org.uk/discovery

Science and industry, local history, fashion; Tyneside's maritime history; *Turbinia* (first steam-driven vessel) gallery

Hancock Museum, Barras Bridge NE2 4PT **T** 0191-222 6765 **W** www.twmuseums.org.uk/hancock

Natural history; Egyptology

Laing Art Gallery, New Bridge Street NE1 8AG **T** 0191-232 7734 **W** www.twmuseums.org.uk/laing

British and European art, ceramics, glass, silver, textiles and costume; *Art on Tyneside* display

NEWMARKET – *National Horseracing Museum*, High Street CB8 8JL **T** 01638-667333 **W** www.nhrm.co.uk

Horseracing simulator, temporary exhibitions and tours of local trainers' yards and studs

NORTHAMPTON – *Northampton Museum and Art Gallery*, Guildhall Road NN1 1DP **T** 01604-838111 **W** www.northampton.gov.uk/museums

Boot and shoe collection

NORTH SHIELDS – *Stephenson Railway Museum*, Middle Engine Lane NE29 8DX **T** 0191-200 7146 **W** www.twmuseums.org.uk/stephenson

Locomotive engines and rolling stock

NOTTINGHAM – *Brewhouse Yard Museum*, Castle Boulevard NG7 1FB **T** 0115-915 3600

Daily life from the 17th- to 20th-century

Castle Museum and Art Gallery, NG1 6EL **T** 0115-915 3700

Paintings, ceramics, silver and glass; history of Nottingham

Industrial Museum, Wollaton NG8 2AE **T** 0115-915 3900

Lacemaking machinery, steam engines and transport exhibits

Natural History Museum, Wollaton NG8 2AE **T** 0115-915 3900

Local natural history and wildlife dioramas

OXFORD – *Ashmolean Museum*, Beaumont Street OX1 2PH **T** 01865-278000 **W** www.ashmol.ox.ac.uk

European and Oriental fine and applied arts, archaeology, Egyptology and numismatics

Museum of Modern Art, Pembroke Street OX1 1BP **T** 01865-722733 **W** www.modernartoxford.org.uk

Temporary exhibitions

Museum of the History of Science, Broad Street OX1 3AZ **T** 01865-277280 **W** www.mhs.ox.ac.uk

Displays include early scientific instruments, chemical apparatus, clocks and watches

Oxford University Museum of Natural History, Parks Road OX1 3PW **T** 01865-272950 **W** www.oum.ox.ac.uk

Entomology, geology, mineralogy and zoology

Pitt Rivers Museum, South Parks Road OX1 3PP **T** 01865-270927 **W** www.prm.ox.ac.uk

Ethnographic and archaeological artefacts

PLYMOUTH – *City Museum and Art Gallery*, Drake Circus PL4 8AJ **T** 01752-304774 **W** www.plymouthmuseum.gov.uk

Local and natural history; ceramics; silver; Old Masters; temporary exhibitions

Plymouth Dome, Hoe Road PL1 2NZ **T** 01752-60300

Maritime history museum

PORTSMOUTH – *Charles Dickens Birthplace*, Old Commercial Road PO1 4QL **T** 023-9282 7261 **W** www.charlesdickensbirthplace.co.uk

Dickens memorabilia

D-Day Museum, Clarence Esplanade, Southsea PO5 3NT **T** 023-9282 7261 **W** www.ddaymuseum.co.uk

Includes the Overlord Embroidery

Portsmouth Historic Dockyard, HM Naval Base PO1 3LJ **T** 023-9286 1533 **W** www.historicdockyard.co.uk

Incorporates the *Royal Naval Museum* (PO1 3NH **T** 023-9272 7562 **W** www.royalnavalmuseum.org), HMS *Victory* (PO1 3NH **T** 023-9286 1533 **W** www.hms-victory.com), HMS *Warrior* (PO1 3QX **T** 023-9277 8600 **W** www.hmswarrior.org), the *Mary Rose* (PO1 3LX **T** 023-9281 2931 **W** www.maryrose.org) and *Action Stations* (PO1 3LJ **T** 023-9289 3316 **W** www.actionstations.org)

History of the Royal Navy and of the dockyard; warships and technology spanning 500 years of British naval history

PRESTON – *Harris Museum and Art Gallery*, Market Square PR1 2PP **T** 01772-258248

British art since the 18th-century; ceramics, glass, costume and local history; contemporary exhibitions

National Football Museum, Deepdale PR1 6RU **T** 01772 908442 **W** www.nationalfootballmuseum.com

Home to the FIFA museum collection; FA, Football League and Wembley collections on long-term loan

ST ALBANS – *Verulamium Museum*, St Michael's Street AL3 4SW **T** 01727-751810 **W** www.stalbansmuseums.org.uk

Remains of Iron Age settlement and the third-largest city in Roman Britain; exhibits include Roman wall plasters, jewellery, mosaics and room reconstructions

ST IVES, Cornwall – *Tate Gallery St Ives*, Porthmeor Beach TR26 1TG **T** 01736-796226 **W** www.tate.org.uk/stives

Modern art, much by artists associated with St Ives. Includes the Barbara Hepworth Museum and Sculpture Garden

SALISBURY – *Salisbury and South Wiltshire Museum*, The Close SP1 2EN **T** 01722-332151 **W** www.salisburymuseum.org.uk

Archaeology collection

SHEFFIELD – *City Museum* and *Mappin Art Gallery*, Weston Park S10 2TP **T** 0114-278 2600 **W** www.sheffieldgalleries.org.uk

Currently undergoing refurbishment; set to re-open in spring 2006 as the Weston Park Museum

Graves Art Gallery, Surrey Street S1 1XZ **T** 0114-278 2600
W www.sheffieldgalleries.org.uk
Twentieth-century British art, Grice Collection of Chinese ivories
Kelham Island Museum, Alma Street S3 8RY **T** 0114-272 2106
W www.simt.co.uk
Local industrial and social history
Ruskin Gallery and *Ruskin Craft Gallery*, Arundel Gate S1 2PP
T 0114-278 2600 **W** www.sheffieldgalleries.org.uk
John Ruskin's collection of paintings, drawings, books and medieval manuscripts
SOUTHAMPTON – *City Art Gallery*, Commercial Road SO14 7LP **T** 023-8083 2277
W www.southampton.gov.uk/art
Fine art, especially 20th-century British
Maritime Museum, Town Quay Road SO14 2AR **T** 023-8022 3941
W www.southampton.gov.uk
Southampton maritime history
Museum of Archaeology, Town Quay SO14 2NY
T 023-8063 5904
Roman, Saxon and medieval archaeology
Tudor House Museum and Garden, Bugle Street SO14 2AD
T 023-8063 5904
Restored 16th-century garden; social history exhibitions. Closed for refurbishment until late 2006; guided tours available by appointment
SOUTH SHIELDS – *Arbeia Roman Fort*, Baring Street NE33 2BB **T** 0191-456 1369
W www.twmuseums.org.uk/arbeia
Excavated ruins
South Shields Museum and Art Gallery, Ocean Road NE33 2JA
T 0191-456 8740
South Tyneside history, including reconstructed street
STOKE-ON-TRENT – *Etruria Industrial Museum*, Etruria ST4 7AF **T** 01782-233144
Britain's sole surviving steam-powered potter's mill
Gladstone Pottery Museum, Longton ST3 1PQ **T** 01782-319232
A working Victorian pottery
Potteries Museum and Art Gallery, Hanley ST1 3DW
T 01782-232323
Pottery, china and porcelain collections and a Mark XVI Spitfire
STYAL, Cheshire – *Quarry Bank Mill*, SK9 4LA
T 01625-527468 **W** www.quarrybankmill.org.uk
Working mill illustrating history of cotton industry; costumed guides at restored Apprentice House
SUNDERLAND – *Sunderland Museum and Winter Gardens*, Burdon Road SR1 1PP **T** 0191-553 2323
W www.twmuseums.org.uk/sunderland
Fine and decorative art, local history and gardens
TELFORD – *Ironbridge Gorge Museums*, TF8 7DQ
T 01952-884391 **W** www.ironbridge.org.uk
World's first iron bridge; Blists Hill (late Victorian working town); Museum of Iron; Jackfield Tile Museum; Coalport China Museum; Tar Tunnel; Broseley Pipeworks
WAKEFIELD – *Yorkshire Sculpture Park*, West Bretton WF4 4LG **T** 01924-832631 **W** www.ysp.co.uk
Open-air sculpture gallery including works by Moore, Hepworth, Frink and others in 300 acres of parkland
WEYBRIDGE – *Brooklands Museum* KT13 0QN
T 01932-857381 **W** www.brooklandsmuseum.com
Birthplace of British Motorsport; world's first purpose-built motor racing circuit
WORCESTER – *City Museum and Art Gallery*, Foregate Street WR1 1DT **T** 01905-25371

W www.worcestercitymuseums.org.uk
Includes a military museum, 19th-century chemist shop and changing art exhibitions
Museum of Worcester Porcelain, Severn Street WR1 2NE
T 01905 746000 **W** www.worcesterporcelainmuseum.org.uk
Worcester Porcelain from 1751 to the present day. Also the *Royal Worcester Visitor Centre*
(**W** www.royal-worcester.co.uk)
WROUGHTON, nr Swindon, Wilts – *Science Museum*, Wroughton Airfield SN4 9NS **T** 01793-846200
W www.sciencemuseum.org.uk/wroughton
Aircraft displays and some of the Science Museum's transport and agricultural collection
YEOVIL, Somerset – *Fleet Air Arm Museum*, Royal Naval Air Station, Yeovilton BA22 8HT **T** 01935-840565
W www.fleetairarm.com
History of naval aviation; historic aircraft, including Concorde 002
YORK – *Beningbrough Hall*, Beningbrough YO30 1DD
T 01904-470666
Portraits from the National Portrait Gallery
Jorvik – The Viking City, Coppergate YO1 9WT **T** 01904-543403
W www.jorvik-viking-centre.co.uk
Reconstruction of Viking York
National Railway Museum, Leeman Road YO26 4XJ
T 01904-621261 **W** www.nrm.org.uk
Includes locomotives, rolling stock and carriages
York Castle Museum, Eye of York YO1 9RY **T** 01904-687687
W www.yorkcastlemuseum.org.uk
Reconstructed streets; costume and military collections
York Art Gallery, Exhibition Square YO1 7EW **T** 01904-687687
W www.yorkartgallery.org.uk
European and British painting spanning seven centuries; modern pottery
Yorkshire Museum and Gardens, Museum Gardens YO1 7FR
T 01904-687687 **W** www.yorkshiremuseum.org.uk
Yorkshire life from Roman to medieval times; geology gallery

WALES

BLAENAFON, Torfaen – *Big Pit National Mining Museum*, NP4 9XP **T** 01495-790311 **W** www.nmgw.ac.uk
Colliery with underground tour
BODELWYDDAN, Denbighshire – *Bodelwyddan Castle*, LL18 5YA **T** 01745-584060
W www.bodelwyddan-castle.co.uk
Portraits from the National Portrait Gallery; furniture from the Victoria and Albert Museum; sculptures from the Royal Academy
CAERLEON – *Roman Legionary Museum*, NP18 1AE
T 01633-423134 **W** www.nmgw.ac.uk
Material from the site of the Roman fortress of Isca and its suburbs
CARDIFF – *National Museum and Gallery Cardiff*, Cathays Park CF10 3NP **T** 029-2039 7951 **W** www.nmgw.ac.uk
Includes natural sciences, archaeology and Impressionist paintings
Museum of Welsh Life, St Fagans CF5 6XB **T** 029-2057 3500
W www.nmgw.ac.uk
Open-air museum with re-erected buildings, agricultural equipment and costume
DRE-FACH FELINDRE, nr Llandysul – *National Woollen Museum*, SA44 5UP **T** 01559-370929
W www.nmgw.ac.uk
Exhibitions, a working woollen mill and craft workshops
LLANBERIS, nr Caernarfon – *Welsh Slate Museum*, LL55 4TY
T 01286-870630 **W** www.nmgw.ac.uk

Former slate quarry with original machinery and plant; slate crafts demonstrations

LLANDRINDOD WELLS — *National Cycle Collection*, Automobile Palace, Temple Street LD1 5DL T 01597-825531
W www.cyclemuseum.org.uk
Over 200 bicycles on display, from 1818 to the present day

SWANSEA — *Glynn Vivian Art Gallery and Museum*, Alexandra Road SA1 5DZ T 01792-516900
W www.swansea.gov.uk/glynnvivian
Paintings, ceramics, Swansea pottery and porcelain, clocks, glass and Welsh art

Swansea Museum, Victoria Road SA1 1SN
T 01792-653763
Archaeology, social history, Swansea pottery

SCOTLAND

ABERDEEN — *Aberdeen Art Gallery*, Schoolhill AB10 1FQ
T 01224-523700 W www.aagm.co.uk
Art from the 18th- to 20th-century

Aberdeen Maritime Museum, Shiprow AB11 5BY T 01224-337700
W www.aagm.co.uk
Maritime history, including shipbuilding and North Sea oil

EDINBURGH — *Britannia*, Leith EH6 6JJ T 0131-555 5566
W www.royalyachtbritannia.co.uk
Former royal yacht with royal barge and royal family picture gallery

City Art Centre, Market Street EH1 1DE T 0131-529 3993
W www.cac.org.uk
Late 19th- and 20th-century art and temporary exhibitions

Museum of Childhood, High Street EH1 1TG T 0131-529 4142
W www.cac.org.uk
Toys, games, clothes and exhibits relating to the social history of childhood

Museum of Edinburgh, Canongate EH8 8DD T 0131-529 4143
W www.cac.org.uk
Local history, silver, glass and Scottish pottery

Museum of Flight, East Fortune Airfield, East Lothian EH39 5LF
T 01620-880308 W www.nms.ac.uk/flight
Display of aircraft

Museum of Scotland, Chambers Street EH1 1JF T 0131-247 4422
W www.nms.ac.uk/scotland
Scottish history from prehistoric times to the present

National Gallery of Scotland, The Mound EH2 2EL T 0131-624 6200 W www.nationalgalleries.org
Paintings, drawings and prints from the 16th- to 20th-century; the national collection of Scottish art

National War Museum of Scotland, Edinburgh Castle EH1 2NG
T 0131-225 7534 W www.nms.ac.uk/war
History of Scottish military and conflicts

Royal Museum of Scotland, Chambers Street EH1 1JF
T 0131-247 4219 W www.nms.ac.uk/royal
Scottish and international collections from prehistoric times to the present

Scottish National Gallery of Modern Art, Belford Road EH4 3DR
T 0131-624 6200 W www.nationalgalleries.org
20th-century painting, sculpture and graphic art

Scottish National Portrait Gallery, Queen Street EH2 1JD
T 0131-624 6200 W www.nationalgalleries.org
Portraits of eminent people in Scottish history; the national collection of photography

The Writers' Museum, Lawnmarket EH1 2PA T 0131-529 4901
W www.cac.org.uk
Robert Louis Stevenson, Walter Scott and Robert Burns exhibits

FORT WILLIAM — *West Highland Museum*, Cameron Square PH33 6AJ T 01397-702169
W www.westhighlandmuseum.org.uk
Includes tartan collections and exhibits relating to 1745 uprising

GLASGOW — *Burrell Collection*, Pollokshaws Road G43 1AT
T 0141-287 2550 W www.glasgowmuseums.com
Paintings, textiles, furniture, ceramics, stained glass and silver from classical times to the 19th-century

Gallery of Modern Art, Royal Exchange Square G1 3AH
T 0141-229 1996 W www.glasgowmuseums.com
Collection of contemporary Scottish and world art

Hunterian Museum and Art Gallery, Hillhead Street G12 8QQ
T 0141-330 4221 W www.hunterian.gla.ac.uk
Rennie Mackintosh and Whistler collections; Old Masters; Scottish paintings; modern paintings; sculpture; prints

Kelvingrove Art Gallery and Museum, Kelvingrove G3 8AG
T 0141 287 2699 W www.glasgowmuseums.com
Includes Old Masters, 19th-century French paintings and armour collection. Closed until summer 2006 for refurbishment

McLellan Galleries, Sauchiehall Street G2 3EH
T 0141-565 4137
W www.glasgowmuseums.com
Temporary exhibitions

Museum of Scottish Country Life, East Kilbride G76 9HR
T 0131-247 4377 W www.nms.ac.uk/countrylife
History of rural life and work

Museum of Transport, Bunhouse Road G3 8DP T 0141-287 2720
W www.glasgowmuseums.com
Includes a reproduction of a 1938 Glasgow street, cars since the 1930s, trams and a Glasgow subway station

People's Palace and Winter Gardens, Glasgow Green G40 1AT
T 0141-271 2951 W www.glasgowmuseums.com
History of Glasgow since 1175

St Mungo Museum of Religious Life and Art, Castle Street G4 0RH
T 0141-553 2557 W www.glasgowmuseums.com
Explores universal themes through objects from all the main world religions

ST ANDREWS — *The British Golf Museum*, Bruce Embankment KY16 9AB T 01334-460046
W www.britishgolfmuseum.co.uk
History of golf

NORTHERN IRELAND

BELFAST — *Ulster Museum*, Botanic Gardens BT9 5AB
T 028-9038 3000 W www.ulstermuseum.org.uk
Irish antiquities; natural and local history; fine and applied arts

HOLYWOOD, Co. Down — *Ulster Folk and Transport Museum*, Cultra BT18 0EU T 028-9042 8428 W www.uftm.org.uk
Open-air museum with original buildings from Ulster town and rural life c.1900; indoor galleries including Irish rail and road transport and *Titanic* exhibitions

LONDONDERRY — *The Tower Museum*, Union Hall Place BT48 6LU T 028-7137 2411
Tells the story of Ireland through the history of Londonderry

OMAGH, Co. Tyrone — *Ulster American Folk Park*, Castletown BT78 5QY T 028-8224 3292 W www.folkpark.com
Open-air museum telling the story of Ulster's emigrants to America; restored or recreated dwellings and workshops; ship and dockside gallery

SIGHTS OF LONDON

For historic buildings, museums and galleries in London, *see* the Historic Buildings and Monuments and Museums and Galleries sections.

BRIDGES

The bridges over the Thames (from east to west) are:
The Queen Elizabeth II Bridge, opened 1991, from Dartford to Thurrock
Tower Bridge, opened 1894
London Bridge, opened after rebuilding by Rennie, 1831; the new London Bridge opened 1973
Alexandra Bridge (also known as Cannon Street Railway Bridge), built 1863–6; renovated 1979–82
Southwark Bridge (Rennie), built 1814–19; rebuilt 1912–21
Millennium Bridge, opened June 2000; reopened after modification February 2002
Blackfriars Railway Bridge, completed 1864; rebuilt 1886
Blackfriars Bridge, built 1760–9; rebuilt 1860–9; widened 1907–10
Waterloo Bridge (Rennie), opened 1817; rebuilt 1937–42
Hungerford Footbridge, opened 2002
Hungerford Railway Bridge (Brunel), suspension bridge built 1841–5; replaced by present railway and footbridge 1863
Westminster Bridge, opened 1750; rebuilt 1854–62
Lambeth Bridge, built 1862; rebuilt 1929–32
Vauxhall Bridge, built 1811–16; rebuilt 1895–1906
Grosvenor Bridge (railway bridge), built 1859–60; rebuilt 1963–7
Chelsea Bridge, built 1851–8; rebuilt 1934; widened 1937
Albert Bridge, opened 1873; restructured (Bazalgette) 1884; strengthened 1971–3
Battersea Bridge (Holland), opened 1772; rebuilt (Bazalgette) 1890
Battersea Railway Bridge, opened 1863
Wandsworth Bridge, opened 1873; rebuilt 1940
Putney Railway Bridge, opened 1889
Putney Bridge, built 1727–9; rebuilt (Bazalgette) 1882–6; starting point of Oxford and Cambridge Boat Race
Hammersmith Bridge, built 1824–7; rebuilt (Bazalgette) 1883–7; closed 1997–9 for safety work
Barnes Railway Bridge (also pedestrian), built 1846–9; restructured 1893
Chiswick Bridge, opened 1933
Kew Railway Bridge, opened 1869
Kew Bridge, built 1758–9; rebuilt and renamed King Edward VII Bridge 1903
Richmond Lock, lock, weir and footbridge opened 1894
Twickenham Bridge, opened 1933
Richmond Railway Bridge, opened 1848; restructured 1906–8
Richmond Bridge, built 1774–7; widened 1937–39
Teddington Lock, footbridge opened 1889; marks the end of the tidal reach of the Thames
Kingston Bridge, built 1825–8; widened 1914
Hampton Court Bridge, built 1753; replaced by iron bridge 1865; present bridge built 1933

CEMETERIES

Abney Park, Stamford Hill, N16 (35 acres), tomb of General Booth, founder of the Salvation Army, and memorials to many Nonconformist divines. *Brompton*, Old Brompton Road, SW10 (40 acres), graves of Sir Henry Cole, Emmeline Pankhurst, John Wisden. *Bunhill Fields*, City Road, EC1 (4 acres), graves of William Blake, John Bunyan and Daniel Defoe. *City of London Cemetery and Crematorium*, Aldersbrook Road, E12 (200 acres). *Golders Green Crematorium*, Hoop Lane, NW11 (12 acres), with Garden of Rest and numerous memorials. *Hampstead*, Fortune Green Road, NW6 (36 acres), graves of Kate Greenaway, Lord Lister, Marie Lloyd. *Highgate*, Swains Lane, N6 (38 acres), tombs of George Eliot, Faraday and Karl Marx; guided tours only, west side. *Kensal Green*, Harrow Road, W10 (70 acres), tombs of Thackeray, Trollope, Sydney Smith, Wilkie Collins, Tom Hood, George Cruikshank, Leigh Hunt, Isambard Kingdom Brunel and Charles Kemble. Churchyard of the former *Marylebone Chapel*, Marylebone High Street, W1, chapel demolished in 1949, now Garden of Rest. *Nunhead*, Linden Grove, SE15 (26 acres), closed in 1969, subsequently restored and opened for burials. *West Norwood Cemetery and Crematorium*, Norwood High Street, SE27 (42 acres), tombs of Sir Henry Bessemer, Mrs Beeton, Sir Henry Tate and Joseph Whitaker *(Whitaker's Almanack)*.

MARKETS

The London markets are mostly administered by the Corporation of London. *Billingsgate* (fish), a market site for over 1,000 years, with the Lower Thames Street site dating from 1876; moved to the Isle of Dogs (Trafalgar Way, E14) in 1982. *Borough*, Southwark Street, SE1 (vegetables, fruit, flowers, etc.), established on present site in 1756; privately owned and run. *Columbia Road*, E2 (flowers), dates from 19th-century; became dedicated flower market in the 20th-century. *Covent Garden* (vegetables, fruit, flowers, etc.), established in 1670 under a charter of Charles II; moved in 1974 to Nine Elms, SW8. *Leadenhall*, Leadenhall Street, EC3 (meat, poultry, fish, etc.), site of market since 14th-century; present hall built 1881. *Petticoat Lane*, Middlesex Street, E1, a market has existed on the site for over 500 years, now a Sunday morning market selling almost anything. *Portobello Road*, W11, originally for herbs and horse-trading from 1870; became famous for antiques after the closure of the Caledonian Market in 1948. *Smithfield*, EC1 (meat, poultry) built 1866–68, refurbished 1993–4; the site of St Bartholomew's Fair from the 12th- to 19th-century. *New Spitalfields*, E10 (vegetables, fruit, etc.), established 1682, modernised 1928, moved out of the City to Leyton in 1991. *Old Spitalfields*, E1, continues to trade on the original Spitalfields site on Commercial Street, selling arts, crafts, books, clothes, organic food and antiques on Sundays.

MONUMENTS

CENOTAPH, Whitehall, London SW1. The word 'cenotaph' means 'empty tomb'. The monument, erected to 'The Glorious Dead', is a memorial to all ranks of the sea, land and air forces who gave their lives in the service of the Empire during the First World War. Designed by Sir Edwin Lutyens and erected as a temporary memorial in 1919, it was replaced by a permanent structure unveiled by George V on Armistice Day 1920. An additional inscription was made after the Second World War to commemorate those who gave their lives in that conflict.

LONDON MONUMENT (commonly called The Monument), Monument Street, EC3. Built from designs of Wren, 1671–7, to commemorate the Great Fire of London, which broke out in Pudding Lane on 2 September 1666. The fluted Doric column is 120 ft high, the moulded cylinder above the balcony supporting a flaming vase of gilt bronze is an additional 42 ft and the column is based on a square plinth 40 ft high (with fine carvings on the west face), making a total height of 202 ft. Splendid views of London from a gallery at the top of the column (311 steps).

OTHER MONUMENTS, (sculptor's name in parenthesis). *Albert Memorial* (Scott), Kensington Gore; *Royal Air Force* (Blomfield), Victoria Embankment; *Viscount Alanbrooke* (Roberts-Jones), Whitehall; *Beatty* (Wheeler), Trafalgar Square; *Belgian Gratitude* (setting by Blomfield, statue by Rousseau), Victoria Embankment; *Boadicea* (or *Boudicca*), Queen of the Iceni (Thornycroft), Westminster Bridge; *Brunel* (Marochetti), Victoria Embankment; *Burghers of Calais* (Rodin), Victoria Tower Gardens, Westminster; *Burns* (Steell), Embankment Gardens; *Canada Memorial* (Granche), Green Park; *Carlyle* (Boehm), Chelsea Embankment; *Cavalry* (Jones), Hyde Park; *Edith Cavell* (Frampton), St Martin's Place; *Charles I* (Le Sueur), Trafalgar Square; *Charles II* (Gibbons), Royal Hospital, Chelsea; *Churchill* (Roberts-Jones), Parliament Square; *Cleopatra's Needle* (68.5 ft high, c.1500BC, erected in 1878; the sphinxes are Victorian), Thames Embankment; *Clive* (Tweed), King Charles Street; *Captain Cook* (Brock), The Mall; *Oliver Cromwell* (Thornycroft), outside Westminster Hall; *Cunningham* (Belsky), Trafalgar Square; *Gen. Charles de Gaulle* (Conner), Carlton Gardens; *Disraeli, Earl of Beaconsfield* (Raggi), Parliament Square; *Lord Dowding* (Winter), Strand; *Duke of Cambridge* (Jones), Whitehall; *Duke of York* (124 ft column, with statue by Westmacott), Carlton House Terrace; *Edward VII* (Mackennal), Waterloo Place; *Elizabeth I* (Kerwin, 1586, oldest outdoor statue in London; from Ludgate), Fleet Street; *Eros* (Shaftesbury Memorial) (Gilbert), Piccadilly Circus; *Marechal/Marshall Foch* (Mallisard, copy of one in Cassel, France), Grosvenor Gardens; *Charles James Fox* (Westmacott), Bloomsbury Square; *George III* (Cotes Wyatt), Cockspur Street; *George IV* (Chantrey), Trafalgar Square; *George V* (Reid Dick and Scott), Old Palace Yard; *George VI* (Macmillan), Carlton Gardens; *Gladstone* (Thornycroft), Strand; *Guards'* (Crimea) (Bell), Waterloo Place; *(Great War)* (Ledward, figures, Bradshaw, cenotaph), Horse Guards' Parade; *Haig* (Hardiman), Whitehall; *Sir Arthur (Bomber) Harris* (Winter), Strand; *Irving* (Brock), north side of National Portrait Gallery; *James II* (Gibbons), Trafalgar Square; *Jellicoe* (Macmillan), Trafalgar Square; *Samuel Johnson* (Fitzgerald), opposite St Clement Danes; *Kitchener* (Tweed), Horse Guards' Parade; *Abraham Lincoln* (Saint-Gaudens, copy of one in Chicago), Parliament Square; *Milton* (Montford), St Giles, Cripplegate; *Mountbatten* (Belsky), Foreign Office Green; *Nelson* (170 ft 2 in, Railton), Trafalgar Square, with Landseer's lions (cast from guns recovered from the wreck of the *Royal George*); *Florence Nightingale* (Walker), Waterloo Place; *Palmerston* (Woolner), Parliament Square; *Peel* (Noble), Parliament Square; *Pitt* (Chantrey), Hanover Square; *Portal* (Nemon), Embankment Gardens; *Prince Albert* (Bacon), Holborn Circus; *Queen Elizabeth Gate* (Lund and Wynne),

Hyde Park Corner; *Raleigh* (Macmillan), Greenwich; *Richard I (Coeur de Lion)* (Marochetti), Old Palace Yard; *Roberts* (Bates), Horse Guards' Parade; *Franklin D. Roosevelt* (Reid Dick), Grosvenor Square; *Royal Artillery* (South Africa) (Colton), The Mall; *(Great War)* (Jagger and Pearson), Hyde Park Corner; *Captain Scott* (Lady Scott), Waterloo Place; *Shackleton* (Jagger), Kensington Gore; *Shakespeare* (Fontana, copy of one by Scheemakers in Westminster Abbey), Leicester Square; *Smuts* (Epstein), Parliament Square; *Sullivan* (Goscombe John), Victoria Embankment; *Trenchard* (Macmillan), Victoria Embankment; *Victoria Memorial* (Webb and Brock), in front of Buckingham Palace; *Raoul Wallenberg* (Jackson), Great Cumberland Place; *George Washington* (Houdon copy), Trafalgar Square; *Wellington* (Boehm), Hyde Park Corner, (Chantrey), outside Royal Exchange; *John Wesley* (Adams Acton), City Road; *Westminster School Crimean* (Scott), Broad Sanctuary; *William III* (Bacon), St James's Square; *Wolseley* (Goscombe John), Horse Guards' Parade.

PARKS, GARDENS AND OPEN SPACES

CORPORATION OF LONDON OPEN SPACES

Ashtead Common (500 acres), Surrey

Burnham Beeches and *Fleet Wood* (540 acres), Bucks. Purchased by the Corporation for the benefit of the public in 1880, Fleet Wood (65 acres) being presented in 1921.

Coulsdon Common (133 acres), Surrey

Epping Forest (6,000 acres), Essex. Purchased by the Corporation and opened to the public in 1882. The present forest is 12 miles long by 1 to 2 miles wide, about one-tenth of its original area.

Farthing Downs (121 acres), Surrey

Hampstead Heath (789 acres), NW3 Including: Golders Hill (36 acres) and Parliament Hill (271 acres)

Highgate Wood (70 acres), N6/N10

Kenley Common (138 acres), Surrey

Queen's Park (30 acres), NW6

Riddlesdown (90 acres), Surrey

Spring Park (51 acres), Kent

West Ham Park (77 acres), E15

West Wickham Common (25 acres), Kent

Woodredon and Warlies Park Estate (740 acres), Waltham Abbey

Also smaller open spaces within the City of London, including *Finsbury Circus* and *St Dunstan-in-the-East*.

OTHER PARKS AND GARDENS

CHELSEA PHYSIC GARDEN, 66 Royal Hospital Road, SW3 4HS T 020-7352 5646 W www.chelseaphysicgarden.co.uk
A garden of general botanical research and education maintaining a wide range of rare and unusual plants established in 1673 by the Society of Apothecaries

ROYAL PARKS
W www.royalparks.gov.uk

Bushy Park (1,099 acres), Middx. Adjoins Hampton Court contains avenue of horse-chestnuts enclosed in a fourfold avenue of limes planted by William III.

Green Park (40 acres), W1 Between Piccadilly and St James's Park, with Constitution Hill leading to Hyde Park Corner

Greenwich Park (183 acres), SE10

Hyde Park (350 acres), W1/W2 From Park Lane to Kensington Gardens and incorporating the Serpentine lake, Apsley House, the Achilles Statue, Rotten Row and the Ladies' Mile; fine gateway at Hyde Park Corner. To the north-east is the Marble Arch, originally erected by George IV at the entrance to Buckingham Palace and re-erected in the present position in 1851.

Kensington Gardens (275 acres), W2/W8 From the western boundary of Hyde Park to Kensington Palace; contains the Albert Memorial, Serpentine Gallery and Peter Pan statue

Kew, Royal Botanic Gardens, Richmond, Surrey TW9 3AB T 020-8332 5655 W www.rbgkew.org.uk Officially inscribed on the UNESCO list of World Heritage Sites.

Regent's Park and *Primrose Hill* (487 acres), NW1 From Marylebone Road to Primrose Hill surrounded by the Outer Circle; divided by the Broad Walk leading to the Zoological Gardens

Richmond Park (2,500 acres), Surrey

St James's Park (93 acres), SW1 From Whitehall to Buckingham Palace; ornamental lake of 12 acres; the Mall leads from the Admiralty Arch to Buckingham Palace, Birdcage Walk from Storey's Gate to Buckingham Palace.

Hampton Court Park and Gardens (669 acres), Surrey

PLACES OF HISTORICAL AND CULTURAL INTEREST

1 CANADA SQUARE, Canary Wharf, E14 5DY Also known as 'Canary Wharf', the steel and glass skyscraper is the tallest structure in London and the tallest habitable building in the UK.

30 ST MARY AXE, EC3A 8EP T 020-7071 5034 W www.30stmaryaxe.com Completed in 2004 and commonly known as the 'Gherkin', it is the second-tallest building in the City of London.

ALEXANDRA PALACE, Alexandra Palace Way, Wood Green, N22 7AY T 020-8365 2121 W www.alexandrapalace.com The Victorian palace was severely damaged by fire in 1980 but was restored, and reopened in 1988. Alexandra Palace now provides modern facilities for exhibitions, conferences, banquets and leisure activities. There is an ice rink, a boating lake, the Phoenix Bar and a conservation area.

BARBICAN CENTRE, Silk Street, EC2Y 8DS T 020-7638 4141 W www.barbican.org.uk Owned, funded and managed by the Corporation of London, the Barbican Centre opened in 1982 and houses the Barbican Theatre, a studio theatre called The Pit and the Barbican Hall; it is also home to the London Symphony Orchestra. There are three cinemas, six conference rooms, two art galleries, a sculpture court, a lending library, trade and banqueting facilities, a conservatory, shops, restaurants, cafes and bars.

CENTRAL CRIMINAL COURT, Old Bailey, EC4M 7EH T 020-7248 3277 The highest criminal court in the UK, the 'Old Bailey' was built in 1907 on the site of the old Newgate Prison. Trials held there have included those of Oscar Wilde, Dr Crippen and the Yorkshire Ripper.

CHARTERHOUSE, Charterhouse Square, EC1M 6AN T 020-7253 9503 A Carthusian monastery from 1371 to 1537, purchased in 1611 by Thomas Sutton, who endowed it as a residence for aged men 'of gentle birth' and a school for poor scholars (removed to Godalming in 1872).

DOWNING STREET, SW1 Number 10 Downing Street is the official town residence of the Prime Minister, Number 11 to the Chancellor of the Exchequer and Number 12 is the office of the Government Whips. The street was named after Sir George Downing, Bt.,

soldier and diplomat, who was MP for Morpeth from 1660 to 1684.

GEORGE INN, Borough High Street, SE1 1NH T 020-7407 2056 The last galleried inn in London, built in 1677. Now owned by the National Trust and run as an ordinary public house.

GREENWICH, SE10 The Royal Naval College, T 020-8269 4747, was until 1873 the Greenwich Hospital. It was built by Charles II, largely from designs by John Webb, and by Queen Mary II and William III, from designs by Wren. It stands on the site of an ancient abbey, a royal house and Greenwich Palace which was constructed by Henry VII. Henry VIII, Mary I and Elizabeth I were born in the royal palace and Edward VI died there. *Greenwich Park* (183 acres), T 020-8858 2608, W www.royalparks.gov.uk, was enclosed by Humphrey, Duke of Gloucester, and laid out by Charles II from the designs of Le Nôtre. On a hill in Greenwich Park is the *Royal Observatory* (founded 1675). Its buildings are now managed by the *National Maritime Museum*, T 020-8858 4422 and the earliest building is named Flamsteed House, after John Flamsteed (1646–1719), the first Astronomer Royal. *The Cutty Sark*, T 020-8858 3445, W www.cuttysark.org.uk, the last of the famous tea clippers, was moved into a specially-constructed dry dock in 1954 and opened to the public in 1957. Sir Francis Chichester's round-the-world yacht, *Gipsy Moth IV*, can also be seen.

HORSE GUARDS, Whitehall, SW1 Archway and offices built about 1753. The changing of the guard takes place daily at 11 a.m. (10 a.m. on Sundays) and the dismounted inspection at 4 p.m. Only those with the Queen's permission may drive through the gates and archway into *Horse Guards' Parade*, where the Colour is 'trooped' on The Queen's official birthday.

HOUSE OF COMMONS, Westminster, London, SW1A 0AA T724;020-7219 4272 E hcinfo@parliament.uk W www.parliament.uk

HOUSE OF LORDS, Westminster, London, SW1A 0PW T 020-7219 3107 E hlinfo@parliament.uk W www.parliament.uk The royal palace of Westminster, originally built by Edward the Confessor, was the normal meeting place of Parliament from about 1340. St Stephen's Chapel was used from about 1550 for the meetings of the House of Commons, which had previously been held in the Chapter House or Refectory of Westminster Abbey. The House of Lords met in an apartment of the royal palace. The fire of 1834 destroyed much of the palace and the present Houses of Parliament were erected on the site from the designs of Sir Charles Barry and Augustus Welby Pugin between 1840 and 1867. The chamber of the House of Commons was destroyed by bombing in 1941 and a new Chamber designed by Sir Giles Gilbert Scott was used for the first time in 1950. *Westminster Hall and the Crypt Chapel* was the only part of the old palace of Westminster to survive the fire of 1834. It was built by William Rufus from 1097–9 and altered by Richard II between 1394–9. The hammerbeam roof of carved oak dates from 1396–8. The Hall was the scene of the trial of Charles I. *The Victoria Tower* of the House of Lords is 323 ft high, and when Parliament is sitting, the Union flag flies by day from its flagstaff. *The Clock Tower* of the House of Commons is 316 ft high and contains 'Big Ben', the hour bell said to be named after Sir Benjamin Hall, First Commissioner of Works when the original bell was cast in 1856. This bell, which weighed 16 tons 11 cwt, was found to be cracked in

1857. The present bell (13.5 tons) is a recasting of the original and was first brought into use in 1859. The dials of the clock are 23 ft in diameter, the hands being 9 ft and 14 ft long (including balance piece). A light is displayed from the Clock Tower at night when Parliament is sitting. During session, tours of the Houses of Parliament are only available to UK residents who have made advance arrangements through an MP or peer. Overseas visitors are no longer provided with permits to tour the Houses of Parliament during session, although they can tour during the summer opening and attend debates for both houses in the Strangers' Galleries. During the summer recess tickets for tours of the Houses of Parliament can be booked by telephone: T 0870-906 3773 or bought on site at the ticket office on Abingdon Green opposite Parliament and the Victoria Tower Gardens. The Strangers' Gallery of the House of Commons is open to the public when the house is sitting. To acquire tickets in advance UK residents should write to their local MP and overseas visitors should apply to their Embassy or High Commission in the UK for a permit. If none of these arrangements have been made, visitors should join the public queue outside St Stephen's Entrance, where there is also a queue for entry to the House of Lords Gallery.

INNS OF COURT The Inns of Court are ancient unincorporated bodies of lawyers which for more than five centuries have had the power to call to the Bar those of their members who have qualified for the rank or degree of Barrister-at-Law. There are four Inns of Court as well as many lesser inns.

Lincoln's Inn, Chancery Lane/Lincoln's Inn Fields, WC2A 3TL T 020-7405 1393 W www.lincolnsinn.org.uk The most ancient of the inns with records dating back to 1422. The hall and library buildings are of 1845, although the library is first mentioned in 1474; the old hall (late 15th-century) and the chapel were rebuilt c. 1619–23.

Inner Temple, King's Bench Walk, EC4Y 7HL T 020-7797 8250 W www.innertemple.org.uk

Middle Temple, Middle Temple Lane, EC4Y 9AT T 020-7427 4800 W www.middletemple.org.uk Records for the Middle and Inner temple date back to the beginning of the 16th century. The site was originally occupied by the Order of Knights Templars c. 1160–1312. The two inns have separate halls thought to have been formed c. 1350. The division between the two societies was formalised in 1732 with Temple Church and the Masters house remaining in common. The Inner Temple Garden is normally open to the public on weekdays between 12.30 p.m. and 3 p.m.

Temple Church, EC4Y 7BB T 020-7353 3470 W www.templechurch.com The nave forms one of five remaining round churches in England.

Gray's Inn, South Square, WC1R 5ET T 020-7458 7800 W www.graysinn.org.uk Founded early 14th-century; Hall 1556–8 No other 'Inns' are active, but there are remains of *Staple Inn*, a gabled front on Holborn (opposite Gray's Inn Road). *Clement's Inn* (near St Clement Danes Church), *Clifford's Inn*, Fleet Street, and *Thavies Inn*, Holborn Circus, are all rebuilt. *Serjeants' Inn*, Fleet Street, and another (demolished 1910) of the same name in Chancery Lane, were composed of Serjeants-at-Law, the last of whom died in 1922.

INSTITUTE OF CONTEMPORARY ARTS, The Mall, SW1Y 5AH T 020-7930 3647 W www.ica.org.uk Exhibitions of modern art in the fields of film, theatre, new media and the visual arts.

LLOYD'S, Lime Street, EC3M 7HA T 020-7327 1000 W www.lloydsoflondon.com International insurance market which evolved during the 17th-century from Lloyd's Coffee House. The present building was opened for business in May 1986, and houses the Lutine Bell. Underwriting is on three floors with a total area of 114,000 sq. ft. The Lloyd's building is not open to the general public.

LONDON CENTRAL MOSQUE AND THE ISLAMIC CULTURAL CENTRE, Park Road, NW8 7RG T 020-7724 3363 W www.iccuk.org The focus for London's Muslims; established in 1944 but not completed until 1977, the mosque can accommodate about 5,000 worshippers; guided tours are available.

LONDON EYE, South Bank, SE1 1GZ 0870-500 0600 W www.londoneye.com Opened in February 2000 as London's millennium landmark, this 450ft observation wheel is the capital's fourth largest structure. The wheel provides a 30 minute ride offering panoramic views of the capital.

LONDON ZOO, Regent's Park, NW1 4RY T 020-7722 3333 W www.londonzoo.org

MADAME TUSSAUD'S AND THE LONDON PLANETARIUM, Marylebone Road, NW1 5LR T 0870-400 3000 W www.madame-tussauds.co.uk Waxwork exhibition and interactive star show

MARLBOROUGH HOUSE, Pall Mall, SW1Y 5HX T 020-7747 6491 Built by Wren for the first Duke of Marlborough and completed in 1711, the house reverted to the Crown in 1835. In 1863 it became the London house of the Prince of Wales and was the London home of Queen Mary until her death in 1953. In 1959 Marlborough House was given by The Queen as the headquarters for the Commonwealth Secretariat and it was opened as such in 1965. The Queen's Chapel, Marlborough Gate was begun in 1623 from the designs of Inigo Jones for the Infanta Maria of Spain, and completed for Queen Henrietta Maria. Marlborough House is not open to the public.

PORT OF LONDON, Port of London Authority, Bakers' Hall, 7 Harp Lane, EC3R 6LB T 020-7743 7900 W www.portoflondon.co.uk The Port of London covers the tidal section of the River Thames from Teddington to the seaward limit (the outer Tongue buoy and the Sunk light vessel), a distance of 150km. The governing body is the Port of London Authority (PLA). Cargo is handled at privately operated riverside terminals between Fulham and Canvey Island, including the enclosed dock at Tilbury, 40km below London Bridge. Passenger vessels and cruise liners can be handled at moorings at Greenwich, Tower Bridge and Tilbury.

ROMAN REMAINS, The city wall of Roman *Londinium* was largely rebuilt during the medieval period but sections may be seen near the White Tower in the Tower of London; at Tower Hill; at Coopers' Row; at All Hallows, London Wall, its vestry being built on the remains of a semi-circular Roman bastion; at St Alphage, London Wall, showing a succession of building repairs from the Roman until the late medieval period; and at St Giles, Cripplegate. Sections of the great forum and basilica, more than 165m², have been encountered during excavations in the area of Leadenhall, Gracechurch Street and Lombard Street. Traces of Roman activity along the river include a massive riverside wall built in the late Roman period, and a succession of Roman timber quays along Lower and Upper Thames Street. Finds from these sites can be seen at the Museum of London.

Other major buildings are the amphitheatre at Guildhall, remains of bath-buildings in Upper and Lower Thames Street, and the temple of Mithras in Walbrook.

ROYAL ALBERT HALL, Kensington Gore, SW7 2AP T 020-7589 8212 W www.royalalberthall.com The elliptical hall, one of the largest in the world, was completed in 1871; since 1941 it has been the venue each summer for the Promenade Concerts founded in 1895 by Sir Henry Wood. Other events include pop and classical music concerts, dance, opera, sporting events, conferences and banquets.

ROYAL COURTS OF JUSTICE, Strand, WC2A 2LL T 020-7947 6000 Victorian Gothic building that is home to the High Court. Visitors are free to watch proceedings.

ROYAL HOSPITAL, CHELSEA, Royal Hospital Road, SW3 4SR T 020-7881 5204 W www.chelsea-pensioners.co.uk Founded by Charles II in 1682, and built by Wren; opened in 1692 for old and disabled soldiers. The extensive grounds include the former Ranelagh Gardens and are the venue for the Chelsea Flower Show each May.

ROYAL OPERA HOUSE, Covent Garden, WC2E 9DD T 020-7240 1200 W www.royalopera.org Home of The Royal Ballet (1931) and The Royal Opera (1946). The Royal Opera House is the third theatre to be built on the site, opening 1858; the first was opened in 1732.

ST JAMES'S PALACE, Pall Mall, SW1A 1BQ T 020-7930 4872 W www.royal.gov.uk Built by Henry VIII, only the Gatehouse and Presence Chamber remain; later alterations were made by Wren and Kent. Representatives of foreign powers are still accredited 'to the Court of St James's'. *Clarence House* (1825), the official London residence of the Prince of Wales and his sons, stands within the St James's Palace environs.

ST PAUL'S CATHEDRAL, St Paul's Churchyard, EC4M 8AD T 020-7236 4128 E chapter@stpaulscathedral.org.uk W www.stpauls.co.uk Built 1675–1710. The cross on the dome is 365 ft above the ground level, the inner cupola 218 ft above the floor. 'Great Paul' in the south-west tower weighs nearly 17 tons. The organ by Father Smith (enlarged by Willis and rebuilt by Mander) is in a case carved by Grinling Gibbons, who also carved the choir stalls.

SOMERSET HOUSE, Strand, WC2R 1LA T 020 7845 4600 W www.somerset-house.org.uk The river façade (600 ft long) was built in 1776–1801 from the designs of Sir William Chambers; the eastern extension, which houses part of King's College, was built by Smirke in 1829–35. Somerset House was the property of Lord Protector Somerset, at whose attainder in 1552 the palace passed to the Crown, and it was a royal residence until 1692. Somerset House has recently undergone extensive renovation and is home to the Gilbert Collection, Hermitage Rooms and the Courtauld Institute Gallery. Open-air concerts and ice-skating (Dec–Jan) are held in the courtyard.

SOUTH BANK, SE1 Arts complex on the south bank of the River Thames which consists of the *Royal Festival Hall* T 020-7921 0600 W www.rfh.org.uk (opened in 1951 for the Festival of Britain), the adjacent 917-seat *Queen Elizabeth Hall*, the *Purcell Room*, and the *Voice Box*.

The *National Film Theatre* (opened 1952) T 020-7928 3232 W www.bfi.org.uk, administered by the British Film Institute, has three auditoria showing over 2,000 films a year. The London Film Festival is held here every November. There is also an IMAX cinema with 477 seats.

The *Royal National Theatre*, T 020-7452 3000 W www.nationaltheatre.org.uk, opened in 1976 and stages classical, modern, new and neglected plays in its three auditoria: the Olivier, the Lyttelton and the Cottesloe theatres.

SOUTHWARK CATHEDRAL, London Bridge, SE1 9DA T 020-7367 6700 E cathedral@southwark.anglican.org W www.dswark.org Mainly 13th-century, but the nave is largely rebuilt. The tomb of John Gower (1330–1408) is between the Bunyan and Chaucer memorial windows in the north aisle; Shakespeare's effigy, backed by a view of Southwark and the Globe Theatre, is in the south aisle; the tomb of Bishop Andrewes (died 1626) is near the screen. The lady chapel was the scene of the consistory courts of the reign of Mary (Gardiner and Bonner) and is still used as a consistory court. John Harvard, after whom Harvard University is named, was baptised here in 1607, and the chapel by the north choir aisle is his memorial chapel.

THAMES EMBANKMENTS The *Victoria Embankment*, on the north side from Westminster to Blackfriars, was constructed by Sir Joseph Bazalgette (1819–91) for the Metropolitan Board of Works, 1864–70; the seats, of which the supports of some are a kneeling camel, laden with spicery, and of others a winged sphinx, were presented by the Grocers' Company and by W. H. Smith, MP, in 1874; the *Albert Embankment*, on the south side from Westminster Bridge to Vauxhall, 1866–9; the *Chelsea Embankment*, 1871–4. The total cost exceeded £2,000,000. Bazalgette also inaugurated the London main drainage system, 1858–65. A medallion *(Flumini vincula posuit)* has been placed on a pier of the *Victoria Embankment* to commemorate the engineer.

THAMES FLOOD BARRIER Officially opened in May 1984, though first used in February 1983, the barrier consists of ten rising sector gates which span approximately 570 yards from bank to bank of the Thames at Woolwich Reach. When not in use the gates lie horizontally, allowing shipping to navigate the river normally; when the barrier is closed, the gates turn through 90 degrees to stand vertically more than 50 feet above the river bed. The barrier took eight years to complete and can be raised within about 30 minutes.

WESTMINSTER ABBEY, Broad Sanctuary, SW1P 3PA T 0207-222 5152 E info@westminster-abbey.org W www.westminster-abbey.org Founded as a Benedictine monastery over 1,000 years ago, the Church was rebuilt by Edward the Confessor in 1065 and again by Henry III in the 13th-century. The Abbey is the resting place for monarchs including Edward I, Henry III, Henry V, Henry VII, Elizabeth I, Mary I and Mary Queen of Scots, and has been the setting of coronations since that of William the Conqueror in 1066. In Poets' Corner there are memorials to many literary figures, and many scientists and musicians are also remembered here. The grave of the Unknown Warrior is to be found in the nave.

WESTMINSTER CATHEDRAL, Francis Street, SW1P 1QW T 020-7798 9090 W www.westminstercathedral.org.uk Roman Catholic cathedral built 1895–1903 from the designs of J. F. Bentley. The campanile is 284 feet high.

LONDON THEATRES

ADELPHI THEATRE, Strand, WC2E 7NA T 020-7344 0055 ⊖ Charing Cross

ALBERY THEATRE, St Martin's Lane, WC2N 4AH T 020-7369 1740 ⊖ Leicester Square

ALDWYCH THEATRE, Aldwych, WC2B 4DF T 020-7379 3367 ⊖ Covent Garden/Holborn

ALMEIDA THEATRE, Almeida Street, N1 1TA T 020-7359 4404 ⊖ Angel/Highbury & Islington

APOLLO THEATRE, Shaftesbury Avenue, W1V 7HD T 020-7494 5070 ⊖ Piccadilly Circus

APOLLO VICTORIA THEATRE, Wilton Road, SW1V 1LL T 0870-400 0650 ⊖ Victoria

ARCOLA THEATRE, Arcola Street, E8 2DJ T 020-7503 1646 ⊖ Highbury & Islington

ARTS THEATRE, Great Newport Street, WC2H 7JB T 020-7836 3334 ⊖ Covent Garden/Leicester Sq

BARBICAN THEATRE, Barbican Centre, EC2Y 8BQ T 020-7638 8891 ⊖ Barbican/Moorgate

BATTERSEA ARTS CENTRE, Lavender Hill, SW11 5TN T 020-7223 6557 ⊖ Clapham Common

BRIDEWELL THEATRE, Bride Lane EC4Y 8EQ T 020-7353 0259 ⊖ Blackfriars

CAMBRIDGE THEATRE, Earlham Street, WC2 9HU T 020-7494 5080 ⊖ Covent Garden/Leicester Square

CHELSEA THEATRE, World's End Place, SW10 0DR T 020-7352 1967 ⊖ Sloane Square

CHICKEN SHED THEATRE, Chase Side, N14 4PE T 020-8351 6161 ⊖ Cockfosters

COMEDY THEATRE, Panton Street, SW1Y 4DN T 020-7369 1731 ⊖ Leicester Square/Piccadilly Circus

CRITERION THEATRE, Piccadilly Circus, W1V 9LB T 020-7413 1437 ⊖ Piccadilly Circus

DOMINION THEATRE, Tottenham Court Road, W1T 7AQ T 0870-607 7400 ⊖ Tottenham Court Road

DONMAR WAREHOUSE, Earlham Street, WC2H 9LX T 020-7240 4882 ⊖ Covent Garden

DUCHESS THEATRE, Catherine Street, WC2B 5LA T 020-7494 5075 ⊖ Covent Garden

DUKE OF YORK'S THEATRE, St Martin's Lane, WC2N 4BG T 020-7854 7000 ⊖ Leicester Square/Piccadilly Circus

FORTUNE THEATRE, Russell Street, WC2B 5HH T 020-7369 1737 ⊖ Covent Garden

GARRICK THEATRE, Charing Cross Road, WC2H 0HH T 020-7494 5085 ⊖ Charing Cross/Leicester Square

GIELGUD THEATRE, Shaftesbury Avenue, W1V 8AR T 020-7494 5065 ⊖ Piccadilly Circus

GLOBE THEATRE, New Globe Walk, SE1 9DT T 020-7401 9199 ⊖ Mansion House

GREENWICH THEATRE, Crooms Hill, SE10 8ES T 020-8858 4447 ⊖ Greenwich (Docklands Light Railway)

HACKNEY EMPIRE, Mare Street, E8 1EJ T 020-8510 4500 ⊖ Bethnal Green

HAMPSTEAD THEATRE, Eton Avenue, NW3 3EU T 020-7449 4200 ⊖ Swiss Cottage

JERMYN STREET THEATRE, Jermyn Street, SW1Y 6ST T 020-7287 2875 ⊖ Piccadilly Circus

LONDON COLISEUM, St Martin's Lane, WC2N 4ES T 020-7836 0111 ⊖ Charing Cross

LONDON PALLADIUM, Argyll Street, W1F 7TA T 020-7494 5020 ⊖ Oxford Circus 020

LYCEUM THEATRE, Wellington Street, WC2E 7RQ T 0870-243 9000 ⊖ Covent Garden

LYRIC THEATRE SHAFTESBURY, Shaftesbury Avenue, W1D 7ES T 020-7494 5045 ⊖ Piccadilly Circus

LYRIC THEATRE, Hammersmith, King Street, W6 0QA T 020-8741 2311 ⊖ Hammersmith

NATIONAL THEATRE, South Bank, SE1 9PX T 020-7452 3000 ⊖ Waterloo

NEW AMBASSADORS THEATRE, West Street, WC2H 9ND T 020-7369 1761 ⊖ Leicester Square

NEW LONDON THEATRE, Drury Lane, WC2B 5PW T 0870-890 0141 ⊖ Holborn

OLD VIC THEATRE, Waterloo Road, SE1 8NB T 020-7369 1722 ⊖ Waterloo

OPEN AIR THEATRE, Regent's Park NW1 4NR T 020-7935 5756 ⊖ Regent's Park

PALACE THEATRE, Shaftesbury Avenue, W1V 8AY T 020-7434 0909 ⊖ Leicester Square/Piccadilly Circus

PHOENIX THEATRE, Charing Cross Road, WC2H 0JP T 020-7369 1733 ⊖ Tottenham Court Road

PICCADILLY THEATRE, Denman Street, W1D 7DY T 020-7478 8800 ⊖ Piccadilly Circus

PLAYHOUSE THEATRE, Northumberland Avenue, WC2N 5DE T 020-7839 4292 ⊖ Embankment

PRINCE OF WALES THEATRE, Coventry Street, W1D 6AS T 020-7839 5972 ⊖ Piccadilly Circus

QUEEN'S THEATRE, Shaftesbury Avenue, W1V 8BA T 020-7494 5040 ⊖ Piccadilly Circus

ROYAL ALBERT HALL, Kensington Gore, SW7 2AP T 020-7589 8212 ⊖ South Kensington

ROYAL COURT THEATRE, Sloane Square, SW1W 8AS T 020-7565 5000 ⊖ Sloane Square

ROYAL FESTIVAL HALL, South Bank SE1 8XX T 020-7921 0600 ⊖ Waterloo

SADLER'S WELLS, Rosebery Avenue, EC1R 4TN T 020-7863 8000 ⊖ Angel

ST MARTIN'S THEATRE, West Street, WC2H 9NH T 020-7836 1443 ⊖ Leicester Square

SAVOY THEATRE, Strand, WC2R 0ET T 020-7836 8888 ⊖ Charing Cross

SHAFTESBURY THEATRE, Shaftesbury Avenue, WC2H 8DP T 020-7379 5399 ⊖ Holborn/Tottenham Court Road

SOHO THEATRE, Dean Street, W1D 3NE T 020-7287 5060 ⊖ Tottenham Court Road

SOUTHWARK PLAYHOUSE, Southwark Bridge Road, SE1 0AT T 020 7652 2224 ⊖ Southwark

STRAND THEATRE, Aldwych, WC2B 5LD T 020-7836 4144 ⊖ Charing Cross

THEATRE ROYAL DRURY LANE, Catherine Street, WC2B 5JF T 020-7494 5000 ⊖ Covent Garden

THEATRE ROYAL HAYMARKET, Haymarket, SW1Y 4HT T 020-7930 8890 ⊖ Piccadilly Circus

TRICYCLE THEATRE, Kilburn High Road, NW6 7JR T 020-7328 1000 ⊖ Kilburn

VAUDEVILLE THEATRE, Strand, WC2R 0NH T 0870-890 0511 ⊖ Charing Cross

VICTORIA PALACE THEATRE, Victoria Street, SW1E 5EA T 020-7834 1317 ⊖ Victoria

WYNDHAM'S THEATRE, Charing Cross Road, WC2H 0DA T 020-7369 1736 ⊖ Leicester Square

YOUNG VIC, The Cut, SE1 8LZ T 020-7928 6363 ⊖ Waterloo

HALLMARKS

Hallmarks are the symbols stamped on gold, silver or platinum articles to indicate that they have been tested at an official Assay Office and that they conform to one of the legal standards. With certain exceptions, all gold, silver or platinum articles are required by law to be hallmarked before they are offered for sale. Hallmarking was instituted in England in 1300 under a statute of Edward I.

MODERN HALLMARKS

Since 1 January 1999, UK hallmarks have consisted of three compulsory symbols – the sponsor's mark, the fineness (purity) mark and the assay office mark. Traditional marks such as the year date letter, the Britannia for 958 silver, the lion passant for 925 silver (lion rampant in Scotland) and the orb for 950 platinum may be added voluntarily. The distinction between UK and foreign articles has been removed, and more finenesses are now legal, reflecting the more common finenesses elsewhere in Europe.

SPONSOR'S MARK
Instituted in England in 1363, the sponsor's mark was originally a device such as a bird or fleur-de-lis. Now it consists of the initial letters of the name or names of the manufacturer or firm. Where two or more sponsors have the same initials, there is a variation in the surrounding shield or style of letters.

FINENESS (PURITY) MARK
The fineness (purity) mark indicates that the content of the precious metal in the alloy from which the article is made, is not less than the legal standard. The legal standard is the minimum content of precious metal by weight in parts per thousand, and the standards are:

Gold	999	
	990	
	916.6	(22 carat)
	750	(18 carat)
	585	(14 carat)
	375	(9 carat)
Silver	999	
	958.4	(Britannia)
	925	(sterling)
	800	
Platinum	999	
	950	
	900	
	850	

ASSAY OFFICE MARK
This mark identifies the particular assay office at which the article was tested and marked. The British assay offices are:

LONDON, Goldsmiths' Hall, Gutter Lane, London EC2V 8AQ
T 020-7606 8971 W www.thegoldsmiths.co.uk

BIRMINGHAM, PO Box 151, Newhall Street, Birmingham
B3 1SB T 0121-236 6951 W www.theassayoffice.co.uk

SHEFFIELD, Guardian's Hall, 137 Portobello Street, Sheffield
S1 4DS T 0114-275 5111 W www.assayoffice.co.uk

EDINBURGH, Goldsmiths' Hall, 24a Broughton Street,
Edinburgh EH1 3RH T 0131-556 1144
W www.assayofficescotland.com

Assay offices formerly existed in other towns, e.g. Chester, Exeter, Glasgow, Newcastle, Norwich and York, each having its own distinguishing mark.

DATE LETTER
The date letter shows the year in which an article was assayed and hallmarked. Each alphabetical cycle has a distinctive style of lettering or shape of shield. The date letters were different at the various assay offices and the particular office must be established from the assay office mark before reference is made to tables of date letters. Date letter marks became voluntary from 1 January 1999.

The table which follows shows specimen shields and letters used by the London Assay Office on silver articles in each period from 1498. The same letters are found on gold articles but the surrounding shield may differ. Since 1 January 1975, each office has used the same style of date letter and shield for all articles.

LONDON (GOLDSMITHS' HALL) DATE

LETTERS FROM 1498

1498–9	1517–8	
1518–9	1537–8	
1538–9	1557–8	
1558–9	1577–8	
1578–9	1597–8	
1598–9	1617–8	
1618–9	1637–8	
1638–9	1657–8	
1658–9	1677–8	
1678–9	1696–7	
1697	1715–6	
1716–7	1735–6	
1736–7	1738–9	

1739–40	1755–6
1756–7	1775–6
1776–7	1795–6
1796–7	1815–6
1816–7	1835–6
1836–7	1855–6
1856–7	1875–6
1876–7	1895–6
1896–7	1915–6
1916–7	1935–6
1936–7	1955–6
1956–7	1974

A 1975	B 1976	C 1977	D 1978
E 1979	F 1980	G 1981	H 1982
I 1983	K 1984	L 1985	M 1986
N 1987	O 1988	P 1989	Q 1990
R 1991	S 1992	T 1993	U 1994
V 1995	W 1996	X 1997	Y 1998
Z 1999	a 2000	b 2001	C 2002
d 2003	e 2004	f 2005	g 2006

OTHER MARKS

FOREIGN GOODS

Foreign goods imported into the UK are required to be hallmarked before sale, unless they already bear a convention mark (*see* below) or a hallmark struck by an independent assay office in the European Economic Area which is deemed to be equivalent to a UK hallmark.

The following are the assay office marks used for gold until the end of 1998. For silver and platinum the symbols remain the same but the shields differ in shape.

 London   *Sheffield*

 Birmingham   *Edinburgh*

CONVENTION HALLMARKS

Special marks at authorised assay offices of the signatory countries of the International Convention on Hallmarking (Austria, the Czech Republic, Denmark, Finland, Ireland, the Netherlands, Norway, Portugal, Sweden, Switzerland and the UK) are legally recognised in the United Kingdom as approved hallmarks. These consist of a sponsor's mark, a common control mark, a fineness mark (arabic numerals showing the standard in parts per thousand), and an assay office mark. There is no date letter.

The common control marks are:

GOLD	SILVER	PLATINUM

COMMEMORATIVE MARKS

There are three other marks to commemorate special events: the silver jubilee of King George V and Queen Mary in 1935, the coronation of Queen Elizabeth II in 1953, and her silver jubilee in 1977. During 1999 and 2000 there was a voluntary additional Millennium Mark. A mark to commemorate the golden jubilee of Queen Elizabeth II was available during 2002.

BRITISH CURRENCY

The unit of currency is the pound sterling (£) of 100 pence. The decimal system was introduced on 15 February 1971.

COIN

Gold Coins	‡*Bi-colour Coins*
*One hundred pounds £100	Two pounds £2
*Fifty pounds £50	*Nickel-Brass Coins*
*Twenty-five pounds £25	§Two pounds £2 (pre-1997)
*Ten pounds £10	One pound £1
Five pounds £5	
Two pounds £2	*Cupro-Nickel Coins*
Sovereign £1	Crown £5 (since 1990)
Half-Sovereign 50p	50 pence 50p
	Crown 25p (pre-1990)
Silver Coins	20 pence 20p
(*Britannia coins*)	10 pence 10p
Two pounds £2	5 pence 5p
One pound £1	
50 pence 50p	*Bronze Coins*
Twenty pence 20p	2 pence 2p
	1 penny 1p
†*Maundy Money*	
Fourpence 4p	¶*Copper-plated Steel Coins*
Threepence 3p	2 pence 2p
Twopence 2p	1 penny 1p
Penny 1p	

*Britannia coins: gold bullion coins introduced 1987; silver coins introduced 1997
†Gifts of special money distributed by the Sovereign annually on Maundy Thursday to the number of aged poor men and women corresponding to the Sovereign's own age
‡Cupro-nickel centre and nickel-brass outer ring
§Commemorative coins; not intended for general circulation
¶Since September 1992, although in 1998 the 2p was struck in both copper-plated steel and bronze

GOLD COIN

Gold ceased to circulate during the First World War. Since then controls on buying, selling and holding gold coin have been imposed at various times but have subsequently been revoked. Under the Exchange Control (Gold Coins Exemption) Order 1979, gold coins may now be imported and exported without restriction, except gold coins which are more than 50 years old and valued at a sum in excess of £8,000; these cannot be exported without specific authorisation from the Department of Trade and Industry.

Value Added Taxation on the sale of gold coins was revoked in 2000.

SILVER COIN

Prior to 1920 silver coins were struck from sterling silver, an alloy of which 925 parts in 1,000 were silver. In 1920 the proportion of silver was reduced to 500 parts. From 1 January 1947 all 'silver' coins, except Maundy money, have been struck from cupro-nickel, an alloy of copper 75 parts and nickel 25 parts, except for the 20p, composed of copper 84 parts, nickel 16 parts. Maundy coins continue to be struck from sterling silver.

BRONZE COIN

Bronze, introduced in 1860 to replace copper, is an alloy of copper 97 parts, zinc 2.5 parts and tin 0.5 part. Bronze was replaced by copper-plated steel in September 1992 with the exception of 1998 when the 2p was made in both copper-plated steel and bronze.

LEGAL TENDER

Gold (dated 1838 onwards, if not below least current weight)	to any amount
£5 (Crown since 1990)	to any amount
£2	to any amount
£1	to any amount
50p	up to £10
25p (Crown pre-1990)	up to £10
20p	up to £10
10p	up to £5
5p	up to £5
2p	up to 20p
1p	up to 20p

The £1 coin was introduced in 1983 to replace the £1 note. The following coins have ceased to be legal tender:

Farthing	31 December 1960
Halfpenny (½ d)	1 July 1969
Half-crown	1 January 1970
Threepence	31 August 1971
Penny (1d)	31 August 1971
Sixpence	30 June 1980
Halfpenny (½ p)	31 December 1984
old 5 pence	31 December 1990
old 10 pence	30 June 1993
old 50 pence	28 February 1998

The Channel Islands and the Isle of Man issue their own coinage, which are legal tender only in the island of issue.

	Metal	Standard weight (g)	Standard diameter (mm)
Penny	bronze	3.564	20.3
Penny	copper-plated steel	3.564	20.3
2 pence	bronze	7.128	25.9
2 pence	copper-plated steel	7.128	25.9
5p	cupro-nickel	3.25	18.0
10p	cupro-nickel	6.5	24.5
20p	cupro-nickel	5.0	21.4
25p Crown	cupro-nickel	28.28	38.6
50p	cupro-nickel	8.00	27.3
£1	nickel-brass	9.5	22.5
£2	nickel-brass	15.98	28.4
£2	cupro-nickel, nickel-brass	12.00	28.4
£5 Crown	cupro-nickel	28.28	38.6

The 'remedy' is the amount of variation from standard permitted in weight and fineness of coins when first issued from the Mint.

THE TRIAL OF THE PYX

The Trial of the Pyx is the examination by a jury to ascertain that coins made by the Royal Mint, which have been set aside in the pyx (or box), are of the proper weight, diameter and composition required by law. The trial is held annually, presided over by the Queen's Remembrancer (the Senior Master of the Supreme Court), with a jury of freemen of the Company of Goldsmiths.

BANKNOTES

Bank of England notes are currently issued in denominations of £5, £10, £20 and £50 for the amount of the fiduciary note issue, and are legal tender in England and Wales. No £1 notes have been issued since 1984 and in March 1998 the outstanding notes were written off in accordance with the provision of the Currency Act 1983.

The current E series of notes was introduced from June 1990, replacing the D series (*see* below). The historical figures portrayed in this series are:

£5	May 2002–date	Elizabeth Fry
£5	June 1990–2003	George Stephenson*
£10	November 2000–date	Charles Darwin†
£20	June 1991–2001	Michael Faraday‡
£20	June 1999–date	Sir Edward Elgar
£50	April 1994–date	Sir John Houblon

* Ceased to be legal tender on 21 November 2003
†The version of the Bank of England £10 banknote issued in April 1992, bearing a portrait of Charles Dickens, ceased to be legal tender on 31 July 2003
‡ Withdrawn from circulation on 28 February 2001

NOTE CIRCULATION

Note circulation is highest at the two peak spending periods of the year, around Christmas and during the summer holiday period.

The value of notes in circulation at the end of February 2002 and 2003 was:

	2004	2005
£5	£1,024m	£1,054m
£10	£5,714m	£5,670m
£20	£20,070m	£21,649m
£50	£5,742m	£6,083m
Other notes*	£3,465m	£960m
Total	£36,015m	£35,416m

* Includes higher value notes used internally in the Bank of England, e.g. as cover for the note issues of banks in Scotland and Northern Ireland in excess of their permitted issue.

LEGAL TENDER

Banknotes which are no longer legal tender are payable when presented at the head office of the Bank of England in London.

The white notes for £10, £20, £50, £100, £500 and £1,000, which were issued until April 1943, ceased to be legal tender in May 1945, and the white £5 note in March 1946.

The white £5 note issued between October 1945 and September 1956, the £5 notes issued between 1957 and 1963 (bearing a portrait of Britannia) and the first series to bear a portrait of The Queen, issued between 1963 and 1971, ceased to be legal tender in March 1961, June 1967 and September 1973 respectively.

The series of £1 notes issued during the years 1928 to 1960 and the 10 shilling notes issued from 1928 to 1961 (those without the royal portrait) ceased to be legal tender in May and October 1962 respectively. The £1 note first issued in March 1960 (bearing on the back a representation of Britannia) and the £10 note first issued in February 1964 (bearing a lion on the back), both bearing a portrait of The Queen on the front, ceased to be legal tender in June 1979. The £1 note first issued in 1978 ceased to be legal tender on 11 March 1988. The 10 shilling note was replaced by the 50p coin in October 1969, and ceased to be legal tender on 21 November 1970.

The D series of banknotes was introduced from 1970 and ceased to be legal tender from the dates shown below. The predominant identifying feature of each note was the portrayal on the back of a prominent figure from British history:

£1	Feb. 1978–March 1988	Sir Isaac Newton
£5	Nov. 1971–Nov. 1991	The Duke of Wellington
£10	Feb. 1975–May 1994	Florence Nightingale
£20	July 1970–March 1993	William Shakespeare
£50	March 1981–Sept. 1996	Sir Christopher Wren

The £1 coin was introduced on 21 April 1983 to replace the £1 note.

OTHER BANKNOTES

SCOTLAND – Banknotes are issued by three Scottish banks. The Royal Bank of Scotland issues notes for £1, £5, £10, £20 and £100. Bank of Scotland and the Clydesdale Bank issue notes for £5, £10, £20, £50 and £100. Scottish notes are not legal tender in Scotland but they are an authorised currency.

NORTHERN IRELAND – Banknotes are issued by four banks in Northern Ireland. The Bank of Ireland, the Northern Bank and the Ulster Bank issue notes for £5, £10, £20, £50 and £100. The First Trust Bank issues notes for £10, £20, £50 and £100. Northern Ireland notes are not legal tender in Northern Ireland but they circulate widely and enjoy a status comparable to that of Bank of England notes.

CHANNEL ISLANDS – The States of Guernsey issues its own currency notes and coinage. The notes are for £1, £5, £10, £20 and £50, and the coins are for 1p, 2p, 5p, 10p, 20p, 50p, £1, £2 and £5. The States of Jersey issues its own currency notes and coinage. The notes are for £1, £5, £10, £20 and £50, and the coins are for 1p, 2p, 5p, 10p, 20p, 50p, £1 and £2.

THE ISLE OF MAN – The Isle of Man Government issues notes for £1, £5, £10, £20 and £50. Although these notes are only legal tender in the Isle of Man, they are accepted at face value in branches of the clearing banks in the UK. The Isle of Man issues coins for 1p, 2p, 5p, 10p, 20p, 50p, £1, £2 and £5.

Although none of the series of notes specified above is legal tender in the UK, they are generally accepted by banks irrespective of their place of issue. At one time banks made a commission charge for handling Scottish and Irish notes but this was abolished some years ago.

BANKING AND PERSONAL FINANCE

There are two main types of deposit-taking institutions: banks and building societies, although National Savings and Investments also provides savings products. Banks and building societies are supervised by the Financial Services Authority and National Savings and Investments is accountable to the Treasury. As a result of the conversion of several building societies into banks in the 1990s, the size of the banking sector, which was already substantially greater than the non-bank deposit-taking sector, increased further.

The main institutions within the British banking system are the Bank of England (the central bank), retail banks, investment banks and overseas banks. In its role as the central bank, the Bank of England acts as banker to the government and as a note-issuing authority; it also oversees the efficient functioning of payment and settlement systems.

Since May 1997, the Bank of England has had operational responsibility for monetary policy. At monthly meetings of its monetary policy committee the Bank sets the interest rate at which it will lend to the money markets.

OFFICIAL INTEREST RATES 2001–5

5 April 2001	5.50%
10 May 2001	5.25%
2 August 2001	5.00%
18 September 2001	4.75%
4 October 2001	4.50%
8 November 2001	4.00%
6 February 2003	3.75%
10 July 2003	3.50%
6 November 2003	3.75%
5 February 2004	4.00%
6 May 2004	4.25%
10 June 2004	4.50%
5 August 2004	4.75%
4 August 2005	4.50%

RETAIL BANKING

Retail banks offer a wide variety of financial services to individuals and companies, including current and deposit accounts, loan and overdraft facilities, automated teller (cash dispenser) machines, cheque guarantee cards, credit and debit cards, investment services, pensions, insurance and mortgages. All banks offer telephone and internet banking facilities in addition to traditional branch services.

The Financial Ombudsman Service provides independent and impartial arbitration in disputes between banks and their customers (*see* Financial Services Regulation).

PAYMENT CLEARINGS

The Association for Payment Clearing Services (APACS) is the UK trade association for payments and for those institutions that deliver payment services to customers. It is also the banking industry voice on payment issues regarding plastic cards, card fraud, cheques, electronic payments and cash. Membership of APACS is open to any member of a payment scheme which is widely used or significant in the UK. As at May 2005 APACS had 31 members, comprising the major banks, one building society and Royal Mail Group.

There are three separate companies which manage the majority of payment clearings in the UK (and which are contactable through APACS):
– BACS Payment Schemes Ltd manages the schemes under which bulk electronic payments are made; processing direct debits, direct credits and standing orders
– CHAPS Ltd provides electronic same-day value clearing for sterling and euro payments
– Cheque and Credit Clearing Company Ltd oversees the clearing of cheques and paper credits

APACS, Mercury House, Triton Court, 14 Finsbury Square, London EC2A 1LQ T 020-7711 6200 W www.apacs.org.uk

MAJOR RETAIL BANKS' FINANCIAL RESULTS 2004

Bank Group	Profit/(loss) before taxation £m	Profit/(loss) after taxation £m	Total assets £m
Abbey	273	129	169,741
Alliance and Leicester	320	230	50,163
Barclays	4,603	3,314	522,089
HBOS (Halifax/Bank of Scotland)	4,592	3,282	442,881
HSBC	2,592	1,826	289,975
Lloyds TSB	3,493	2,489	279,843
Northern Rock	431	306	42,790
RBS Group (Royal Bank of Scotland including NatWest)	6,917	4,762	583,467

GLOSSARY OF FINANCIAL TERMS

AER (ANNUAL EQUIVALENT RATE) – A notional rate quoted on savings and investment products which demonstrates the return on interest, when compounded and paid annually

APR (ANNUAL PERCENTAGE RATE) – Calculates the total amount of interest payable over the whole term of a product (such as investment or loan), allowing consumers to compare rival products on a like-for-like basis. Companies offering loans, credit cards, mortgages or overdrafts are required by law to provide the APR rate. Where typical APR is shown, it refers to the company's typical borrower and so is given as a best example; rate and costs may vary depending on individual circumstances.

ANNUITY – A type of insurance policy that provides regular income in exchange for a lump sum. Everyone who has a pension and has built-up a lump sum with their provider must buy an annuity by the time they reach 75. The annuity can be bought from a company other than the existing pension provider.

ASU – Accident, sickness and unemployment insurance taken out by a borrower to protect against being unable to work for these reasons. The policy will usually pay a percentage of the normal monthly mortgage repayment if the borrow is unable to work.

ATM (AUTOMATED TELLER MACHINES) – Commonly referred to as cash machines. Users can access their bank accounts using a card for simple transactions such as withdrawing and depositing cash. Some banks and independent ATM deployers charge for transactions.

BANKER'S DRAFT – A cheque drawn on a bank against a cash deposit. Considered to be a secure way of receiving money in instances where a cheque could 'bounce' or where not desirable to receive cash.

BASE RATE – The minimum rate at which banks are prepared to lend money. This acts as a benchmark for all other interest rates.

BASIS POINT – Unit of measure (usually one-hundredth of a percentage point) used to express movements in interest rates, foreign rates or bond yields.

BUY-TO-LET – The purchase of a residential property for the sole purpose of letting to a tenant. Not all lenders provide mortgage finance for this purpose. Buy-to-let mortgages typically require at least a 15–25 per cent deposit and the loan agreed is based on a combination of the borrower's income in addition to the rental value of the property. Because of the higher risks involved in letting property, buy-to-let mortgages are more expensive.

CAPITAL GAIN/LOSS – Increase/decrease in the value of a capital asset when it is sold or transferred compared to its initial worth.

CAPPED RATE MORTGAGES – The interest rate applied to a loan is guaranteed not to rise above a certain rate for a set period of time; the rate can therefore fall but will not rise above the capped rate. The level at which the cap is fixed is usually higher than for a fixed rate mortgage for a comparable period of time. The lender normally imposes early redemption penalties within the first few years.

CASH CARD – Issued by banks and building societies for withdrawing cash from ATMs.

CHARGE CARD – Charge cards, e.g. American Express and Diners Club, can be used in a similar way to credit cards but the debt must be settled in full each month.

CHIP AND PIN CARD – A credit/debit card which incorporates an embedded chip containing unique owner details. When used with a PIN number, such cards offer greater security as they are less prone to fraud.

CREDIT CARD – Normally issued with a credit limit, credit cards can be used for purchases until the limit is reached. There is normally an interest-free period on the outstanding balance of up to 56 days. Charges can be avoided if the balance is paid off in full within the interest-free period. Alternatively part of the balance can be paid and in most cases there is a minimum amount set by the issuer (normally a percentage of the outstanding balance) which must be paid on a monthly basis. Some card issuers charge an annual fee and most issuers belong to a least one major credit card network, e.g. Mastercard or Visa.

CREDIT RATING – Overall credit worthiness of a borrower based on information from a credit reference agency, such as Experian or Equifax, which holds details of credit agreements, payment records, county court judgements etc for all adults in the UK. This information is supplied to lenders who use it in their credit scoring or underwriting systems to calculate the risk of granting a loan to an individual and the probability that it will be repaid. Each lender sets their own criteria for credit worthiness and may accept or reject a credit application based on an individual's credit rating.

CRITICAL ILLNESS COVER – Insurance covering borrowers against critical illnesses such as stroke, heart attack or cancer and is designed to protect mortgage or other loan payments.

DEBIT CARD – Debit cards were introduced on a large scale in the UK in the mid-1980s, replacing cash and cheques to purchase goods and services. They can be used to withdraw cash from ATMs in the UK and abroad and may also function as a cheque guarantee card. Funds are automatically withdrawn from an individual's bank account after making a purchase and no interest is charged.

DISCOUNTED MORTGAGE – Discounted mortgages guarantee an interest rate set at a margin below the standard variable rate for a period of time. The discounted rate will move up or down with the standard variable rate, but the payment rate will retain the agreed differential below the standard variable rate. The lender normally imposes early redemption penalties within the first few years.

EARLY REDEMPTION PENALTY – see Redemption Penalty

ENDOWMENT MORTGAGE – Only the interest on a property loan is paid back to the lender each month as long as an endowment life insurance policy is taken out for an agreed amount of time, typically 25 years. When the policy matures the lender will take repayment of the money owed on the property loan and any surplus goes to the policyholder. If the endowment policy shows a shortfall on projected returns, the policy holder must make further provision to pay off the mortgage.

EQUITY – When applied to real estate, equity is the difference between the value of a property and the amount outstanding on any loan secured against it. Negative equity occurs when the loan is greater than the market value of the property.

FIXED RATE MORTGAGE – A repayment mortgage where

the interest on the loan is fixed rate for a set amount of time, normally a period of between one and ten years. The interest rate does not vary with changes to the base rate resulting in the monthly mortgage payment remaining the same for the duration of the fixed period. The lender normally imposes early redemption penalties within the first few years.

INTEREST ONLY MORTGAGE – Only interest is paid by the borrower and capital remains constant for the term of the loan. The onus is on the borrower to make provision to repay the capital at the end of the term. This is usually achieved through an investment vehicle such as an endowment policy or pension.

ISA – The individual savings account is a means by which investors can save and invest without paying any tax on the proceeds. Money can be invested across three investment elements: cash, stocks and shares and life insurance products. There are limits to the amount invested during any given tax year.

LOAN TO VALUE – This is the ratio between the size of a mortgage loan sought and the mortgage lender's valuation. On a loan of £55,000, for example, on a property valued at £100,000 the loan to value is 55 per cent. This means that there is sufficient equity in the property for the lender to be reassured that if interest/capital repayments were stopped, it could sell property and recoup the money owed. Fewer options are available to borrowers requiring high LTV.

MIG (MORTGAGE INDEMNITY GUARANTEE) – An insurance policy designed to protect the lender against loss in the event of the borrower defaulting or ceasing to repay a mortgage. It offers no protection to the borrower. Not all lenders charge MIG premiums.

ONLINE BANKING – Also known as internet or e-banking where a range of banking transactions from paying bills, transferring funds to arranging overdrafts can be carried out online.

PERSONAL PENSION PLAN (PPP) – Designed for pension-planning for the self-employed or those in non-pensionable employment. Contributions made to a PPP are exempt from tax and the retirement age may be selected at any time from age 50 to 75. Up to 25 per cent of the pension fund may be taken as a tax-free cash sum on retirement.

PIN (PERSONAL IDENTIFICATION NUMBER) – A PIN is issued alongside a cash card to allow the user to access a bank account via an ATM. PINs are also issued with Smart, Credit and Debit Cards and are often requested in shops and restaurants as a further security measure when making a purchase.

PORTABLE MORTGAGE – A mortgage product that can be transferred to a different property in the event of a house move. Preferable where early redemption penalties are charged.

REDEMPTION PENALTY – A charge made for paying off a loan, debt balance or mortgage before a date agreed with the lender.

REPAYMENT MORTAGE – In contrast to the interest only mortgage, the monthly repayment includes an element of the capital sum borrowed in addition to the interest charged.

SELF-CERTIFICATION – several lenders allow borrowers to self-certify their income. This type of scheme is useful to the self-employed who may not have accounts available or any other person who has difficulty proving their regular income.

SHARE – A share is a divided-up unit of the value of a company. If a company is worth £100 million, and there are 50 million shares in issue, then each share is worth £2 (usually listed as pence). As the overall value of the company fluctuates so does the share price.

SMART CARDS – A new generation of a cashless payment system. They carry more information than debit cards including mortgage and health details and a fixed number of units of real money. The card is used in conjunction with a PIN and once the money on the card is spent, it must be loaded again by transferring money to it from a bank account via an ATM or telephone.

TELEPHONE BANKING – Banking facilities which can be accessed via the telephone.

UNIT TRUST – A 'pooled' fund of assets, usually shares, owned by a number of individuals. Managed by professional, authorised fund-management groups, unit trusts have traditionally delivered better returns than average cash deposits, but do rise and fall in value as their underlying investment varies in value.

WITH-PROFITS – Usually applies to pensions, endowments, savings schemes or bonds. The concept is to smooth out the rises and falls in the stock market for the benefit of the investor. Actuaries working for the insurance company, or fund managers, hold back some profits in good years in order to make up the difference in years when shares perform badly.

VARIABLE RATE MORTGAGE – Repayment mortgages where the interest rate set by the lender increases or decreases in relation to the base interest rate which can result in fluctuating monthly repayments.

FINANCIAL SERVICES REGULATION

FINANCIAL SERVICES AUTHORITY

The FSA has been the single regulator for financial services in the UK since 1 December 2001, when the Financial Services and Markets Act 2000 (FSMA) came into force. The FSA's aim is to promote efficient, orderly and fair financial markets and help retail consumers get a fair deal.

The FSA is required to pursue four statutory objectives:
- maintaining market confidence
- raising public awareness
- protecting consumers
- reducing financial crime

The legislation also requires the FSA to carry out its general functions, while having regard to:
- using its resources in an economic and efficient way
- the responsibilities of regulated firms' own management
- being proportionate in imposing burdens or restrictions on the industry
- facilitating innovation
- the international character of financial services and the competitive position of the United Kingdom
- not impeding or distorting competition unnecessarily

ORGANISATION AND STRUCTURE

The FSA is a company limited by guarantee, financed by levies on the industry. It receives no funds from the public purse. It is accountable to Treasury ministers and, through them, to Parliament. The FSA must report annually on the achievement of its statutory objectives to the Treasury, which is required to lay the report before Parliament.

The FSA's budgeted costs for 2005–6 are £266.6 million.

FSA REGISTER OF AUTHORISED FIRMS AND PERSONS

The FSA maintains a register of all firms that are authorised to carry out regulated activities. The entry for each firm gives its name, address and telephone number; a reference number; its authorisation status (outlining exactly what financial services the firm is authorised to provide), stating which organisation regulates it, and whether it can handle client money. In addition the FSA keeps a list of approved persons in the industry who are authorised to carry out functions regulated by the FSA. Each entry includes a list of controlled functions an individual is authorised to perform and for which firms.

On 31 October 2004, mortgage lending, sales and administration and on 14 January 2005, general insurance sales and administration became FSA regulated activities. It is now a statutory requirement that all companies carrying out these activities are authorised by the FSA, or exempt.

FINANCIAL SERVICES AUTHORITY
  25 the North Colonade, Canary Wharf, London E14 5HS
  T 020-7066 1000 Helpline 0845-606 1234
  W www.fsa.gov.uk
  Chairman, Callum McCarthy
  Chief Executive, John Tiner

COMPENSATION

FINANCIAL SERVICES COMPENSATION SCHEME

The Financial Services Compensation Scheme (FSCS) is an independent statutory body created under the FSMA. It provides compensation if a firm authorised by the FSA is unable or likely to be unable to pay claims against it. This is usually when a firm becomes insolvent. The FSCS covers deposits, insurance policies and investment business. From 31 October 2004, the scheme has also provided protection to customers of firms that give mortgage advice and arrange mortgages and from 14 January 2005 to customers of firms that give advice on, and arrange, general insurance policies. The FSCS is independent from the FSA, with separate staff and premises. However, the FSA appoints the board of the FSCS and sets its guidelines. The FSCS is funded by levies on authorised firms.

FINANCIAL SERVICES COMPENSATION SCHEME
  7th Floor, Lloyds Chambers, Portsoken Street, E1 8BN
  T 020-7892 7300 E enquiries@fscs.org.uk
  W www.fscs.org.uk
  Chairman, Nigel Hamilton
  Chief Executive, Loretta Minghella

PENSION PROTECTION FUND

The Pension Protection Fund (PPF) is a statutory fund established under the Pensions Act 2004 and became operational on 6 April 2005. The Fund was set-up to pay compensation to members of eligible defined benefit pension schemes, where there is a qualifying insolvency event in relation to the employer, and where there are insufficient assets in the pension scheme to cover PPF levels of compensation. Compulsory annual levies are charged on all eligible schemes to help fund the PPF, in addition to investment of PPF assets.

PENSION PROTECTION FUND
  Knollys House, 17 Addiscombe Road, Croydon, Surrey, CR0
  6SR T 0845-600 2541 E information@ppf.gsi.gov.uk
  W www.pensionprotectionfund.org.uk
  Chairman, Lawrence Churchill
  Chief Executive, Myra Kinghorn

DESIGNATED PROFESSIONAL BODIES

Professional firms are exempt from requiring direct regulation by the FSA if they carry out only certain restricted activities that arise out of, or are complementary to the provision of professional services, such as arranging the sale of shares on the instructions of executors or trustees or providing services to small, private companies. These firms are, however, supervised by designated professional bodies (DPBs). There are a number of safeguards to protect consumers dealing with firms that do not require direct regulation. These arrangements include:
- the FSA's power to ban a specific firm from taking advantage of the exemption and to restrict the regulated activities permitted to the firms
- rules which require professional firms to ensure that

their clients are aware that they are not authorised persons
- a requirement for the DPBs to supervise and regulate the firms and inform the FSA on how the professional firms carry on their regulated activities

Please *see* Professional Education section for the contact details of the following DPBs:

INSTITUTE OF CHARTERED ACCOUNTANTS IN
    ENGLAND AND WALES
INSTITUTE OF CHARTERED ACCOUNTANTS OF
    SCOTLAND
INSTITUTE OF CHARTERED ACCOUNTANTS IN
    IRELAND
ASSOCIATION OF CHARTERED CERTIFIED
    ACCOUNTANTS
INSTITUTE OF ACTUARIES
THE LAW SOCIETY OF ENGLAND AND WALES
LAW SOCIETY OF NORTHERN IRELAND
LAW SOCIETY OF SCOTLAND

RECOGNISED INVESTMENT EXCHANGES

The FSA supervises six recognised investment exchanges (RIEs). These are organised markets on which member firms can trade investments such as equities and derivatives. As a regulator the FSA must also focus on the impact of changes brought about by the continued growth in electronic trading by exchanges and other organisations. Issues such as how these changes affect market quality, reliability and access are important and the FSA works with the exchanges to ensure that new systems meet regulatory requirements. The RIEs are listed with their year of recognition in parenthesis:

EUROPEAN DERIVATIVES EXCHANGE (EDX) (2003),
    10 Paternoster Square, London EC4M 7LS T 020-7797 1000
    W www.londonstockexchange.com/edx (*see also* London
    Stock Exchange)

INTERNATIONAL PETROLEUM EXCHANGE (IPE) (2001),
    International House, 1 St Katharine's Way, London E1W
    1UY T 020-7481 0643 W www.theipe.uk.com

LONDON INTERNATIONAL FINANCIAL FUTURES
    EXCHANGE (LIFFE) (2001), Cannon Bridge House,
    1 Cousin Lane, London EC4R 3XX T 020-7623 0444
    W www.liffe.com

LONDON METAL EXCHANGE (LME) (2001), 56 Leadenhall
    Street, London EC3A 2BJ T 020-7264 5555
    W www.lme.co.uk

LONDON STOCK EXCHANGE (LSE) (2001), 10 Paternoster
    Square, London EC4M 7LS T 020-7797 1000
    W www.londonstockexchange.com

VIRT-X EXCHANGE (2001), 34th Floor, One Canada Square,
    Canary Wharf, London E14 5AA T 020-7864 4310
    W www.virt-x.com

RECOGNISED CLEARING HOUSES

The FSA is also responsible for recognising and supervising recognised clearing houses (RCH). These are bodies which organise the settlement of transactions on recognised investment exchanges. There are two RCHs:

CREST CO LTD (2001), Watling House, 33 Cannon Street,
    London EC4M 5SB T 020-7849 0000 E info@crestco.co.uk
    W www.crestco.co.uk

LONDON CLEARING HOUSE CLEARNET LTD
    (LCH.CLEARNET) (2001), Aldgate House, 33 Aldgate High
    Street, London EC3N 1EA T 020-7426 7000
    W www.lchclearnet.com

OMBUDSMAN SCHEMES

The Financial Ombudsman Service was set up by the Financial Services and Markets Act 2000 to provide consumers with a free, independent service for resolving disputes with financial firms. It brought together eight complaints-handling schemes within the financial sector including the Banking Ombudsman, the Insurance Ombudsman, the Investment Ombudsman and the Personal Investment Authority Ombudsman. It can make binding awards up to £100,000. The Financial Ombudsman Service can help with most financial complaints about: banking services; credit cards issued by banks and building societies; endowment policies; financial and investment advice; health and loan protection insurance; household and buildings insurance; investment portfolio management; life assurance; mortgages; motor insurance; personal pension plans; private medical insurance; saving plans and accounts; stocks and shares; travel insurance; unit trusts and income bonds.

Complainants must first complain to the firm involved. They do not have to accept the ombudsman's decision and are free to go to court if they wish.

The Pensions Ombudsman is appointed and operates under the Pension Schemes Act 1993 as amended by the Pensions Act 1995; he is responsible to Parliament. He investigates and decides complaints and disputes concerning occupational and personal pension schemes, primarily alleged maladministration by the persons responsible for managing pension schemes.

FINANCIAL OMBUDSMAN SERVICE, South Quay Plaza,
    183 Marsh Wall, London, E14 9SR
    T 0845-080 1800 (helpline); 020-7964 1000
    E complaint.info@financial-ombudsman.org.uk
    W www.financial-ombudsman.org.uk
    Chief Ombudsman: Walter Merricks
    Principal Ombudsmen: Tony Boorman; David Thomas

PENSIONS OMBUDSMAN, 6th Floor, 11 Belgrave Road,
    London SW1V 1RB T 020-7834 9144
    Pensions Ombudsman, D. Laverick

TAKEOVER PANEL

The Takeover Panel was set up in 1968 in response to concern about practices unfair to shareholders in takeover bids for public and certain private companies. Its principal objective is to ensure equality of treatment and opportunity for all shareholders in takeover bids. It is a non-statutory body that operates the City code on take-overs and mergers.

The chairman, deputy chairmen and three lay members of the panel are appointed by the Bank of England. The remainder are representatives of the banking, insurance, investment, pension fund and accountancy professional bodies and the CBI.

PANEL ON TAKEOVERS AND MERGERS, 10 Paternoster
    Square, London EC4M 7DY T 020-7382 9026
    W www.takeoverpanel.org.uk
    Chairman, Peter Scott, QC

NATIONAL SAVINGS AND INVESTMENTS

National Savings and Investments (formerly National Savings) is one of the largest savings organisations in the UK, and is a government department and executive agency of HM Treasury. Savings and investment products are offered to personal savers and investors and the money is used to manage the national debt more effectively. When people invest in National Savings and Investments they are lending money to the government which pays them interest in return.

TAX-FREE PRODUCTS

NATIONAL SAVINGS AND INVESTMENT CERTIFICATES

INDEX-LINKED SAVING CERTIFICATES
Index-linked saving certificates are fixed rate investments that pay tax-free returns guaranteed to be above inflation. They are available in three and five-year terms and are sold in issues. The minimum investment for each issue is £100 and the maximum £15,000.

FIXED INTEREST CERTIFICATES
Fixed interest certificates are fixed rate investments that pay tax-free returns. They are available in two and five-year terms and are sold in issues for which the minimum investment is £100 and the maximum £15,000. The certificates are repaid in full with all interest gained at the end of the term.

PREMIUM BONDS
Premium bonds are a government security which were first introduced in 1956. Premium bonds enable savers to enter a regular draw for tax-free prizes, while retaining the right to get their money back. A sum equivalent to interest on each bond is put into a prize fund and distributed by monthly prize draws. The prizes are drawn by ERNIE (electronic random number indicator equipment) and are free of all UK income tax and capital gains tax. The top prize is £1 million.

Bonds are in units of £1, with a minimum purchase of £100; above this, purchases must be in multiples of £10, up to a maximum holding limit of £30,000 per person. The scheme offers a facility to reinvest prize wins automatically. Upon completion of an automatic prize reinvestment mandate, holders receive new bonds which are immediately eligible for future prize draws. Bonds can only be held in the name of an individual and not by organisations.

Bonds become eligible for prizes once they have been held for one clear calendar month following the month of purchase. Each £1 unit can win only one prize per draw, but it will be awarded the highest for which it is drawn. Bonds remain eligible for prizes until they are repaid. When a holder dies, bonds remain eligible for prizes up to and including the twelfth monthly draw after the month in which the holder dies.

Since the first prize draw in 1957, over 121 million prizes totalling £7.75 billion have been distributed.

CHILDREN'S BONUS BONDS
Children's bonus bonds were introduced in 1991. They can be bought for any child under 16 and will go on growing in value until he or she is 21. The bonds are sold in five-year issues at multiples of £25. For each issue the minimum holding is £25 and the maximum holding is £3,000 per child. Bonds for children under 16 must be held by a parent or guardian. All returns are totally exempt from UK income tax and a bonus is payable if the bond is held for the full five years.

OTHER PRODUCTS

GUARANTEED EQUITY BONDS
Guaranteed equity bonds are five-year investments where the returns are linked to the performance of the FTSE-100 index with a guarantee that the original capital invested will be returned even if the FTSE-100 index fell over the five years. They are sold in limited issues with a minimum investment of £1,000 and a maximum of £1 million. The returns are subject to income tax on maturity.

SAVINGS AND INVESTMENT ACCOUNTS
The easy access savings account was launched in January 2004 replacing the ordinary account (also known as the Post Office savings account) which was closed on 31 July 2004. The easy access savings account, offers access to savings via Post Office counters, an ATM card, telephone and the internet; it can be opened with a minimum balance of £100 and has a maximum limit of £2 million (£4 million jointly). The interest is paid without deduction of tax at source. Holders of the ordinary account can no longer undertake transactions except for closing the account or transferring the funds to an easy access savings account or the investment account.

The investment account is a passbook account and requires one-month notice for withdrawals. Repayments can be made without notice but incur a penalty equivalent to the previous days' interest on the amount withdrawn.

Since April 1999 individual savings accounts (ISAs) have been offered by National Savings and Investments. A cash mini ISA can be opened with £10. Interest is calculated daily and is free of tax. The same regulations apply for ISAs offered by all companies.

INCOME BONDS
National Savings and Investments Income Bonds were introduced in 1982. They are suitable for those who want to receive regular monthly payments of interest while preserving the full cash value of their capital. The bonds are sold in multiples of £500. The minimum holding is £500 and the maximum £1 million (sole or joint holding). Interest is calculated on a day-to-day basis and paid monthly. Interest is taxable but is paid without deduction of tax at source.

PENSIONERS GUARANTEED INCOME BONDS
Pensioners guaranteed income bonds were introduced in January 1994 and are designed for people aged 60 and over who wish to receive regular monthly payments with a rate of interest that is fixed for a period whilst preserving the full cash value of their investment. Five-, two- and

one-year terms are available and are sold in issues. The minimum limit for each issue is £500. The maximum holding is £1,000,000 (sole or joint holding) with the rate of interest fixed and guaranteed for each bond purchased. Interest is taxable but is paid without deduction of tax at source. The original capital investment is repaid in full at the end of the term.

FIXED RATE SAVINGS BOND

Fixed rate savings bonds are investments that earn fixed rates of interest. Five-, three- and one-year terms are available and are sold in issues. The minimum investment is £500 and the maximum £1 million. Interest, from which basic rate tax is deducted at source, can be paid out or reinvested into the bond monthly, annually or at the end of the term. Holders can also choose where the interest is paid. The original capital investment is repaid in full at the end of the term.

CAPITAL BONDS

National Savings and Investments capital bonds were introduced in 1989. Five-year capital bonds are sold in issues. The interest is taxable each year (for those who pay income tax) but is not deducted at source. For each issue, the minimum investment is £100 and the maximum £1 million. Capital bonds are repaid in full with all interest gained at the end of five years.

TREASURER'S ACCOUNT

The Treasurer's account, introduced in September 1996, offers attractive rates and security to non-profit making organisations such as charities, friendly societies, clubs, etc. The minimum holding is £10,000 and the maximum is £2 million.

FURTHER INFORMATION

For the latest information on National Savings and Investments' products and interest rates call T 0845-964 5000 or visit W www.nsandi.com or a Post Office branch. To buy National Savings and Investments' products T 0500-500 000 or visit W www.nsandi.com or a Post Office branch.

THE LONDON STOCK EXCHANGE

The London Stock Exchange serves the needs of industry and investors by providing facilities for raising capital and a central market-place for securities trading. This market-place covers government stocks (called gilts), UK and overseas company shares (called equities and fixed interest stocks), and other instruments such as covered warrants and exchange traded funds (EFTs).

PRIMARY MARKETS

The Exchange enables companies to raise capital for development and growth through the issue of securities. For a company entering the market for the first time there is a choice of Exchange markets, depending upon the size, history and requirements of the company. The first is the main market. A company's securities are admitted to the official list by the UK Listing Authority (UKLA), a division of the Financial Services Authority, and also admitted to trading by the Exchange.

The alternative investment market (AIM) was established in June 1995. It enables small, young and growing companies to raise capital, widen their investor base and have their shares traded on a regulated market without the expense of a full Exchange listing. Many companies use AIM as a stepping-stone to a full listing.

Once admitted to the AIM, all companies are obliged to keep their shareholders informed of their progress, making announcements of a price-sensitive nature through a primary information provider. At 31 December 2004 there were 2,486 UK companies listed on the London Stock Exchange; their equity capital had a total market value of £1,492.5 billion. In addition, 351 international companies were listed, with a total equity market value of £1,971.6 billion. By the end of 2004 AIM had attracted 1,021 companies, with a total market value of £31.8 billion.

UK equity turnover in 2004 was £2,316.2 billion with a total number 53.9 million equity bargains. International equity turnover in 2004 totalled £2,403.4 billion with a total number of 12.4 million equity bargains.

'BIG BANG'

During 1986 the London Stock Exchange went through the greatest period of change in its 200-year history. In March 1986 it opened its doors for the first time to overseas and corporate membership, allowing banks, insurance companies and overseas securities houses to become members of the Exchange and to buy existing member firms. On 27 October 1986, three major reforms took place and became known as 'Big Bang':
- the abolition of scales of minimum commissions, allowing clients to negotiate freely with their brokers about the charge for their services
- the abolition of the separation of member firms into brokers and jobbers: firms are now broker/dealers, able to act as agents on behalf of clients; to act as principals buying and selling shares for their own account; and to become registered market makers, making continuous buying and selling prices in specific securities

- the introduction of the Stock Exchange automated quotations system (SEAQ)

Since the introduction of SEAQ in 1986, dealing in stocks and shares has taken place by telephone in the firms' own dealing rooms, rather than face to face on the floor of the Exchange. The Stock Exchange electronic trading service (SETS), launched in 1997, introduced order-driven trading in which deals are executed electronically on an electronic order book. SETS runs alongside SEAQ and allows remote access to the Exchange. The new systems also provide increased investor protection. All deals taking place via the Exchange systems are recorded on a database which can be used to resolve disputes or to carry out investigations.

Firms trading on the London Stock Exchange buy and sell shares on behalf of the public, as well as institutions such as pension funds or insurance companies. In return for transacting the deal, the broker will charge a commission, which is usually based upon the value of the transaction. The market makers, or wholesalers, in each security do not charge a commission for their services, but will quote the broker two prices, a price at which they will buy and a price at which they will sell. It is the middle of these two prices which is published in lists of share prices in newspapers.

REGULATION

The Financial Services Authority has overall responsibility for regulating the UK's financial industry under the provisions of the Financial Services and Markets Act 2000. The Act compels business to be conducted through a recognised investment exchange (RIE). The London Stock Exchange is an RIE, regulating three main markets: UK equities, international equities and gilts.

DEVELOPMENTS

On 15 March 2000, the 298 members voted to become shareholders in a demutualised London Stock Exchange, making possible the further commercialisation of the company.

At the end of May 2001 the exchange announced its intention to list on its own main market. The exchange was listed on 20 July following an annual general meeting on 19 July 2001. The full listing is intended to enable the Exchange to exploit business opportunities with greater flexibility.

In 2003 the London Stock Exchange created EDX London (European derivatives exchange), a recognised investment exchange for international equity derivatives.

LONDON STOCK EXCHANGE, 10 Paternoster Square, London EC4M 7LS T 020-7797 1000
W www.londonstockexchange.com
Chairman, Chris Gibson-Smith
Chief Executive, Clara Furse

INSURANCE

AUTHORISATION AND REGULATION OF INSURANCE COMPANIES

Since 1 December 2001 the Financial Services Authority (FSA) has been the authorising, enforcement, supervisory and rule-making body of insurers. Since 14 January 2005 this also includes insurance brokers.

The FSA's powers are primarily conferred by the Financial Services and Markets Act 2000. This unified the previous sectoral arrangements and regulators.

FINANCIAL SERVICES AUTHORITY, 25 The North Colonnade, London E14 5HS **T** 020-7066 1000 **W** www.fsa.gov.uk

AUTHORISATION

As far as authorisation is concerned, the FSA's role is to ensure that firms to which it grants authorisation satisfy the necessary financial criteria, that the senior management of the company are 'fit and proper persons' and that unauthorised firms are not permitted to trade. This part of the FSA's role was previously undertaken by HM Treasury under the Insurance Companies Act 1982, which was repealed when the Financial Services and Markets Act came fully into force. At the end of 2004 there were nearly 800 insurance organisations and friendly societies with authorisation from the FSA to transact one or more classes of insurance business in the UK. However, the single European insurance market, established in 1994, gave insurers authorised in any other European Union country automatic UK authorisation without further formality. This means a potential market of over 5,000 insurance companies.

REGULATION

All life insurers, general insurers, reinsurers and composite firms are statutorily regulated. This is achieved by the formulation (after consultation) by the FSA of rules and guidance for regulated organisations. The FSA is also responsible for consumer education and the reduction of financial crime, particularly money laundering.

COMPLAINTS

Disputes between policyholders and insurers can be referred to another sector of the FSA's operations – the Financial Ombudsman Service. Policyholders with a complaint against their financial services provider must firstly take the matter to the highest level within the company. Thereafter, if it remains unresolved, they can refer their problem, free of charge to the Ombudsman who examines the facts of a complaint and delivers a decision which is binding on the insurer (but not the policyholder). Small businesses with a turnover of up to £1m also have access to the scheme. The Financial Ombudsman Service also covers other areas of the financial services industry including banks, building societies and investment firms.

FINANCIAL SERVICES OMBUDSMAN SERVICE, South Quay Plaza, 183 Marsh Wall, London E14 9SR **T** 020-7964 1000 **F** 020-7964 1002 **W** www.financial-ombudsman.org.uk
Ombudsman: Walter Merricks

ASSOCIATION OF BRITISH INSURERS

Over 96 per cent of the domestic business of UK insurance companies is transacted by the 390 members of the Association of British Insurers (ABI). ABI is a trade association which protects and promotes the interests of life and general insurers. Only insurers authorised in the UK or any EU country are eligible for membership. Brokers, intermediaries and claims handlers may not join ABI but may have their own trade associations.

ASSOCIATION OF BRITISH INSURERS (ABI), 51 Gresham Street, London EC2V 7HQ **W** www.abi.org.uk
Chair: Keith Satchell
Director-General: Stephen Haddrill

BALANCE OF PAYMENTS

The financial services industry contributes 5.3 per cent to the UK's Gross Domestic Product (GDP). In 2003 insurance companies generated net exports of £6.4bn.

TAKEOVERS AND MERGERS

Falling stock market returns continued to make insurance companies unattractive takeover targets in 2004. The result was a continuation of the very quiet period for takeovers and mergers.

GENERAL INSURANCE

In late 2003 the EU Commission published its draft Directive on gender discrimination, one of the effects of which would have been to ban insurers from taking gender-based information into account when deciding premiums and terms. The insurance industry launched a major campaign to combat this proposal as it would have had the effect of increasing premiums. In motor insurance it was argued, for example, that the accident rate and claims costs for women are lower and this was reflected in premiums charged and discounts offered. The proposal would have the effect of outlawing these discounts. As 2004 progressed the EU recognised the strength of the industry's view. By the middle of the year the Commission was seeking a compromise position and in October failed to reach a final agreement. By the end of the year it had been agreed that each country would make its own decision on whether to permit the use of gender-related data by insurers.

Flooding and climate change were also issues on the agenda throughout 2004. The government agreed to maintain spending on flood defences and the water regulator agreed to include higher provision for sewer repairs and improvements in his pricing decisions. The spectacular scenes from Boscastle in Cornwall, of serious flooding causing major damage to cars and property, in August, served to underline flooding risks and the need for adequate insurance cover. Insurers remained committed to offering flood cover for the majority of homes in the UK in return for the government's continued commitment to maintain or increase spending on flood defences and the inclusion of a consideration of flooding risk in new property planning applications.

After an initial delay, August saw the publication of the Greenway Report. This called for stiffer penalties for driving while uninsured and called on motor insurers to use databases more effectively and in conjunction with police authorities, to catch road tax and motor insurance evaders. Sensational headlines suggesting that offenders might have their cars forcibly scrapped and crushed served to draw attention to the issue, although the much predicted windscreen disc was dismissed as unworkable.

Claims results in 2004 continued to improve with fire, theft and weather damage all being at their lowest levels since the turn of the century. Business Interruption claims bucked the trend and recorded a year-on-year rise. Claims also continued to rise in respect of liability claims. Long tail employers' liability claims remain a cause for concern. During the year insurers met with employers and government bodies to discuss the possibility of a new fund to provide compensation for diseases like asbestosis outside the insurance market.

Rises in public liability claims also fuelled the existing suggestion that the UK is becoming an increasingly litigious society, partly driven by the activities accident claim and legal services firms.

During 2004 the final elements of the new regulatory framework for general insurance were formulated. This came into effect in January 2005 and means that all but a small number of insurance contracts are now statutorily regulated.

LONDON INSURANCE MARKET

The London Insurance Market is a unique wholesale marketplace and a distinct, separate sector of the UK insurance and reinsurance industry. It is the world's leading market for internationally traded insurance and reinsurance, its business comprising mainly overseas non-life large and high-exposure risks. The market is centred on the City of London, which provides the required financial, banking, legal and other support services. Currently 52 per cent of London Market business is transacted at Lloyd's, 45 per cent through insurance companies and 3 per cent through Protection and Indemnity Clubs. In 2003 the market had a written gross premium income of over £25,000 million. Around 160 Lloyd's brokers service the market.

The trade association for the international insurers and reinsurers writing primarily non-marine insurance and all classes of reinsurance business in the London Market is the International Underwriting Association (IUA).

INTERNATIONAL UNDERWRITING ASSOCIATION, London Underwriting Centre, 3 Mincing Lane, London EC3R 7DD
W www.iua.co.uk

BRITISH INSURANCE COMPANIES

The following insurance company figures refer to members and certain non-members of the ABI.

	2000	2001	2002	2003	2004
Theft	740	728	773	630	509
Fire	855	1,049	1,040	1,016	812
Weather	1,298	932	1,258	610	424
Domestic Subsidence	350	265	183	390	199
Business Interruption	202	97	236	92	108
Total	3,445	3,071	3,490	2,738	2,052

NET PREMIUM INCOME BY TERRITORY 2003 (£ millions)

	UK	Overseas
Motor	9,522	3,965
Non-motor	18,484	5,907
Marine, aviation and transport	560	161
Reinsurance	1,305	194
Total general business	29,871	10,227
Ordinary long-term	89,821	22,579
Industrial long-term	447	–
Total long-term business	90,268	22,579

WORLDWIDE GENERAL BUSINESS TRADING RESULTS (£ millions)

	2002	2003
Net written premiums	40,144	40,246
Underwriting results	(1,062)	(905)
Investment income	3,696	3,805
Overall trading profit	2,634	2,900
Profit as percentage of premium income	6.6	7.2

WORLDWIDE GENERAL BUSINESS UNDERWRITING RESULTS (£ millions)

	2002			2003		
	UK	Overseas	Total	UK	Overseas	Total
Motor						
Premiums (£m)	9,500	4,240	13,740	9,522	3,695	13,487
Profit (loss) (£m)	(74)	(222)	(296)	(5)	(56)	(61)
Percentage of premiums	0.7	5.2	2.2	0.1	1.5	0.5
Non-motor						
Premiums (£m)	17,036	6,880	23,916	18,484	5,907	24,391
Profit (loss) (£m)	10	(657)	(647)	675	(562)	113
Percentage of premiums	0.1	9.5	2.7	3.7	9.5	0.5

LLOYD'S OF LONDON

Lloyd's of London is an international market for almost all types of general insurance. Lloyd's currently has a capacity to accept insurance premiums of around £14,900 million. Much of this business comes from outside Great Britain and makes a valuable contribution to the balance of payments.

A policy is underwritten at Lloyd's by a mixture of private and corporate members, corporate members having been admitted for the first time in 1992. Specialist underwriters accept insurance risks at Lloyd's on behalf of members (referred to as 'Names') grouped in syndicates. There are currently 69 syndicates of varying sizes, each managed by an underwriting agent approved by the Council of Lloyd's.

Individual members are still in the majority at Lloyd's with a total of 1,625 individuals as opposed to 705 corporate members. In 2004 the market capacity of the corporate sector was £12,277 million while individuals represented £1,445 million of capacity.

Lloyd's is incorporated by an Act of Parliament (Lloyd's Acts 1971 onwards) and is governed by an 18-person Council of Lloyd's. The structure immediately below this changed when, in September 2002, Lloyd's Members voted at an Extraordinary General Meeting to implement a new franchise system for the market with the aim of improving profitability. The first move was the introduction of a new governance structure, replacing the Lloyd's Market Board and the Lloyd's Regulatory Board with a new 11-person Lloyd's Franchise Board. Four main committees report to this new Board.

The Corporation is a non-profitmaking body chiefly financed by its members' subscriptions. It provides the premises, administrative staff and services enabling Lloyd's underwriting syndicates to conduct their business. It does not, however, assume corporate liability for the risks accepted by its members. Individual members are responsible to the full extent of their personal means for their underwriting affairs.

At present, Lloyd's syndicates have no direct contact with the public. All business is transacted through insurance brokers accredited by the Corporation of Lloyd's. In addition, non-Lloyd's brokers in the UK, when guaranteed by Lloyd's brokers, are able to deal directly with Lloyd's motor syndicates, a facility which has made the Lloyd's market more accessible to the insuring public.

The FSA has ultimate responsibility for the regulation of the Lloyd's market. However, in situations where Lloyd's internal regulatory and compensation arrangements are more far-reaching, as for example with the Lloyd's Central Fund, which safeguards claim payments to policyholders, the regulatory role is delegated to the Council of Lloyd's.

Lloyd's also provides the most comprehensive shipping intelligence service in the world. The shipping and other information received from Lloyd's agents, shipowners, news agencies and other sources throughout the world is collated and distributed to the media as well as to the maritime and commercial sectors in general. *Lloyd's List* is London's oldest daily newspaper and contains news of general commercial interest as well as shipping information. *Lloyd's Shipping Index*, also published daily, lists some 25,000 ocean-going vessels in alphabetical order and gives the latest known report of each.

DEVELOPMENTS IN 2004

2004 produced another good result for Lloyd's with profits recorded at £1,357 million. This was the third successive year where annually accounted profits had been reported. But it was not all success, as the result was not as high as the previous year, reflecting continued long-tail liability claims and the heavy storm season which weather experts had predicted. The USA and Caribbean were hit by four major hurricanes (Charley, Frances, Ivan and Jeanne) costing $25,000 million with Lloyd's share estimated to be in the region of $2,300 million. There were also a record number of typhoons recorded in Japan. These weather incidents occurred at a time of softening of the market which has the effect of making underwriters more reluctant to increase premiums than in the previous year.

Like all insurers, Lloyd's have found in the recent period of lower investment returns that they have need to rely more on the skill of underwriters and loss prevention measures to maintain profitability. Nevertheless, Lloyd's remains cautiously optimistic for the future.

LLOYD'S OF LONDON, One Lime Street, London EC3M 7HA
T 020-7327 1000 W www.lloydsoflondon.co.uk
Chair: Lord Levene of Portsoken
Chief Executive: Nick Prettejohn

LLOYD'S GLOBAL ACCOUNTS

	2001 and prior years of account £m	2002 pure year result £m
Gross premiums written (net of brokerage)	11,085	11,319
Outward reinsurance premiums	4,293	3,783
Net premiums	6,792	7,536
Reinsurance to close premiums received from earlier years of account	6,023	—
Amounts retained to meet all known and unknown outstanding liabilities brought forward	2,792	—
	15,607	7,536
Gross claims paid	11,196	3,340
Reinsurers' share	5,096	726
Net claims	6,100	2,614
Reinsurance premiums paid to close the year of account	6,661	2,178
Amounts retained to meet all known and unknown outstanding liabilities carried forward	4,822	304
	17,583	5,096
Underwriting result	(1,976)	2,440
Profit/(loss) on exchange	30	69
Syndicate operating expenses	(658)	(667)
Balance on technical account	(2,604)	1,597
Investment income	600	529
Investment expenses and charges	(18)	(13)
Investment gains less losses	(60)	(88)
Result before personal expenses	(2,082)	(2,025)
Personal expenses	(296)	(532)
Result after personal expenses	(2,378)	(1,493)

LLOYD'S SEGMENTAL RESULTS 2004

	Accident and health	Motor (third party)	Motor (other classes)	MAT	Fire and other damage to property	Third party liability	Life	Other	Total direct
	£m	£m	£m	£m	£m	£m	£m	£m	£m
Gross premiums written	465	129	885	2,219	3,008	3,331	85	251	10,373
Gross premiums earned	460	127	911	2,273	3,079	3,557	40	289	10,736
Gross claims incurred	331	93	644	1,222	1,862	2,678	20	420	7,270
Gross operating expenses	137	31	207	574	840	898	15	79	2,781
Gross technical result	(8)	3	60	477	377	(19)	5	(210)	685
Reinsurance balance	(15)	8	(6)	(185)	(241)	(136)	(4)	66	(513)
Net technical result	(23)	11	54	292	136	(155)	1	(144)	172

WORLDWIDE LONG-TERM PREMIUM INCOME 1999–2003 *(£ millions)*

	1999	2000	2001	2002	2003
UK Life Insurance					
Regular Premium	13,085	13,041	12,226	12,015	11,629
Single Premium	23,384	25,727	25,340	23,731	17,010
Total	36,469	38,768	37,566	35,746	28,639
Individual Pensions					
Regular Premium	8,042	8,046	7,821	8,547	7,744
Single Premium	10,874	13,442	17,702	19,443	13,883
Total	18,916	21,488	25,523	27,990	21,627
Other Pensions					
Regular Premium	4,604	4,143	3,563	3,744	4,353
Single Premium	26,371	49,798	24,981	26,682	29,400
Total	30,975	53,941	28,544	30,426	33,753
Other (e.g. Income protection, Annuities)	1,208	1,641	1,806	1,922	5,802
Total UK Premium Income	87,568	115,838	93,439	96,084	89,821
Overseas Premium Income					
Regular Premium	5,118	6,583	6,933	7,436	7,921
Single Premium	12,943	13,893	17,069	17,833	14,658
Total	18,061	20,476	24,002	25,269	22,579
Total Worldwide Premium Income	105,629	136,314	117,441	121,353	112,400

LLOYD'S MEMBERSHIP

	2002	2003	2004
Individual	2,466	2,048	1,625
Corporate	837	752	705

TOTAL MARKET CAPACITY

	2002	2003	2004
	£m	£m	£m
Individual	1,766	1,869	1,445
Corporate	11,473	13,092	12,277
Total	13,239	14,961	13,722

LIFE AND LONG-TERM INSURANCE AND PENSIONS

The themes that began 2004 uppermost in Life and Pension companies' minds were the same ones that had been dogging them for some time. At the end of 2003 the Treasury Select Committee launched an inquiry into the life insurance and savings industry, and although the Committee's attitude appeared to mellow as the year went on, it was not before a number of insurers, the regulators and trade association staff had received a thorough grilling from the Committee on pension transfers and the problems of endowment policies not providing sufficient funds to pay off mortgages. These concerns led the Financial Services Authority to launch a major initiative called 'Treating Customers Fairly' – a recurring theme throughout the year.

The problem of endowment policy shortfalls was estimated at £20 billion in present-day terms, during the year. The savings industry tried to put a figure into some perspective by arguing that over the period that interest rates have been low policyholders have saved nearly £30,000 million in interest payments. However it was the shortfall that continued to get the attention from the media.

The image of the life insurance industry also came under close scrutiny in the spring with the publication of the Penrose Report into the well publicised problems of Equitable Life Assurance and its policyholders. Having received the report the government concluded that the company's problems were unique and that the fault lay largely with the company's directors. The conundrum that faced policyholders who had suffered financially was that any demands for compensation and financial penalties had to be measured against the fact that the payment of these penalties would almost certainly force the company into insolvency. If that occurred the Financial Services Compensation Scheme would have to bale the company out, which would penalise the policyholders of all other life insurers.

These issues and low investment returns must be major contributors to the falls in new business figures for both regular and single premium life and individual pensions. The endowment mortgage problems have also meant the demand for new policies of this type has all but dried up.

The poor new business figures did nothing to help alleviate the savings gap – the figure calculated as the difference between the amount currently being saved and the amount required for the working population to retain their current standard of living after retirement. It was estimated that the figure suggested for the shortfall in pension provision may be considerably more than the £27,000 million previously calculated. A survey also found that less than half of under-30-year-olds were

saving for a pension compared to a figure of 70 per cent during the 1960s. The issue of encouraging everyone to save more is one being carefully examined by the government, the financial services industry and the regulators alike, but to date no agreement has been reached on the best way of tackling the problem.

PAYMENTS TO POLICYHOLDERS

	2002 £m	2003 £m
Payments to UK policyholders	90,203	96,778
Payments to overseas policyholders	14,719	13,191
Total	104,922	109,969

PRIVATE MEDICAL INSURANCE 1999–2003

	1999	2000	2001	2002	2003
Number of policy holders (000s)					
Corporate	2,207	2,325	2,506	2,587	2,603
Personal	1,193	1,145	1,129	1,124	1,111
Total	3,400	3,470	3,635	3,711	3,714
Number of people covered (000s)					
Corporate	4,237	4,517	4,704	4,840	4,812
Personal	1,892	1,949	1,885	1,887	1,873
Total	6,129	6,466	6,589	6,727	6,685
Gross Earned Premiums, £m					
Corporate	1,027	1,092	1,253	1,363	1,418
Personal	1,039	1,146	1,256	1,369	1,422
Total	2,066	2,238	2,509	2,732	2,840
Gross Claims Incurred, £m	1,708	1,788	1,946	2,152	2,228

INVESTMENT OF INSURANCE COMPANIES 2003

Investment of funds	Long-term business £m	General business £m
Index-linked British Government securities	24,398	1,018
Non-index-linked British Government securities	116,762	15,843
Other UK public sector debt securities	14,968	1,859
Overseas government, provincial and municipal securities	46,096	11,696
Debentures, loan shares, preference and guaranteed stocks and shares		
UK	137,857	7,078
Overseas	74,564	9,422
Ordinary stocks and shares UK	268,575	8,319
Overseas	109,304	2,972
Unit trusts		
Equities	70,962	1,038
Fixed interest	9,261	417
Loans secured on property	17,054	1,045
Real property and ground rents	62,015	3,457
Other invested assets	80,692	42,303
Total invested assets	1,032,508	106,467
Net investment income	43,457	3,805

NEW BUSINESS

	New Individual Regular Premiums				New Individual Single Premiums					Group Business	
	Life	Pensions	Collective Investment Schemes	Total Regular	Life	Pensions	Pension Annuities & Income Drawdown	Collective Investment Schemes	Total Single	Regular	Single
1999	1,683	1,474	570	3,727	23,505	6,999	7,569	8,587	46,660	978	4,723
2000	1,334	1,593	626	3,553	25,109	7,329	7,911	8,718	49,067	940	3,539
2001	1,221	2,415	473	4,109	25,129	8,768	8,545	7,582	50,024	1,139	4,349
2002	1,311	2,233	417	3,961	23,886	11,201	9,577	7,314	51,978	1,075	5,146
2003	1,288	1,875	369	3,532	17,635	9,931	9,203	7,757	44,526	1,097	5,248

MUTUAL SOCIETIES

The term 'mutual societies' covers member-based organisations registered under the Building Societies Acts, the Friendly Societies Acts and the Industrial and Provident Societies Acts, and many are familiar long-established names, such as the Nationwide, the Co-op, and Liverpool Victoria.

Until 30 November 2001 the various statutory responsibilities for the supervision and registration of mutual societies rested with the Chief Registrar of Friendly Societies (CR), the Building Societies Commission (BSC) and the Friendly Societies Commission (FSC). The office of CR and the government department of the Registry of Friendly Societies (RFS), from which the BSC and FSC were supported, dated back to 1875. However, the existence in one form or another of an office for the registration of friendly societies and a registrar dated back to 1829, when its function was initially seen as bringing regulation and social control over a potentially revolutionary popular movement.

In 1997 the new Labour government announced the creation of a single financial regulatory authority for the UK, which became the Financial Services Authority (FSA). The FSA initially supported the functions of the CR, BSC and FSC under contract. On the full entry into force of the Financial Services and Markets Act 2000 on 1 December 2001, the responsibilities and powers of the BSC, FSC and CR passed to the FSA. The numbers of mutual societies registered with the FSA as at March 2005 were:

Industrial and Provident Societies*	8,373
Societies registered under the Friendly Societies Acts 1974 and 1992**	2,356
Credit Unions†	577
Building Societies‡	63

* Registered under the Industrial and Provident Societies Act 1965
** Includes friendly societies, working men's clubs, benevolent societies and specially authorised societies
† Registered as credit unions under the Industrial and Provident Societies Act 1965
‡ Registered under the Building Societies Act 1986

Detailed registration statistics for the various categories of society (*see* below) within each main registration act are no longer published by the FSA. However, printed lists of the names of all societies registered under a particular act can be obtained from the FSA on payment of a (sometimes substantial) fee. A more economical option may be to obtain electronic copies of all the lists. In addition, any public documents submitted by societies, such as annual returns and accounts, society rules, certificates of registration and details of directors may be inspected on the public files of individual societies and copies of the documents obtained, again on payment of the appropriate fees. Further details are available from the FSA website www.fsa.gov.uk or by telephoning the Mutual Societies Search and Copy Helpline on 020-7066 4916.

FRIENDLY SOCIETIES IN BRITAIN

Four different types of society are registered in Great Britain under the Friendly Societies Act 1974: friendly societies, benevolent societies, working men's clubs and specially authorised societies.

Friendly societies are voluntary mutual organisations, where the main purposes are assisting members during sickness, unemployment or retirement, and the provision of life assurance. Many of the older traditional societies complement their business activities by social activity and a general care for individual members in ways normally outside the scope of a purely commercial organisation. There are three main categories of friendly societies: societies with separately registered branches, commonly called orders; centralised societies, which conduct business directly with members (having no separately registered branches); and collecting societies which have traditionally conducted home service assurance.

The Friendly Societies Act 1992 created a new legislative framework for friendly societies, enabling them to provide a wider range of services to their members and allowing them to compete on more equal terms with other financial institutions. At the same time it provided for more flexible prudential supervision to safeguard members. The Act enabled friendly societies to incorporate and establish subsidiaries to provide various financial and other services to their members and the public. The activities which subsidiaries are able to conduct include those to establish and manage unit trust schemes and personal equity plans; to arrange for the provision of credit, whether as agents or providers; to carry on long-term or general insurance business; to provide insurance intermediary services; to provide fund management services for trustees of pension funds; to administer estates and execute trusts of wills; and to establish and manage sheltered housing, residential homes for the elderly, hospitals and nursing homes. This legislation also established a new framework to oversee friendly societies, including a Friendly Societies Commission, now superseded by the FSA, whose principal functions are to regulate the activities of friendly societies, promote their financial stability and protect members' funds. All friendly societies carrying on insurance or non-insurance business require authorisation by the FSA, which has a broad range of supervisory powers.

The Association of Friendly Societies is the official representative body for UK friendly societies. It produces a free brochure called *Friends For Life* which gives a brief history of the friendly society movement, what it is and what products are offered. Copies may be obtained by post from the Association at 51 Gresham Street, London EC2V 7HQ or by telephone at 020-7216 7436. Further news and information including member lists and research areas can be found at the Association's website www.afs.org.uk.

Of the other types of societies registered under the 1974 Act, benevolent societies are established for any charitable or benevolent purpose, to provide the same type of benefits as would be permissible for a friendly society, but in contrast the benefits must be for persons who are not members instead of, or in addition to, members. Working men's clubs provide social and recreational facilities for members. Specially authorised societies are registered for any purpose authorised by the Treasury as a purpose to which some or all of the provisions of the 1974 Act ought to be extended. Examples are societies for the promotion of science, literature and the fine arts, or to enable members to pursue an interest in sports and games.

INDUSTRIAL AND PROVIDENT SOCIETIES IN BRITAIN

Under this rather archaic-sounding category of mutual societies are grouped a broad range of co-operative enterprises and organisations that operate for the benefit of the community. They include the well-known high street 'Co-op' shops and stores, housing associations, agricultural and fishing co-operatives, social and recreational clubs and credit unions – almost 9,000 bodies in total.

The Industrial and Provident Societies Act 1965 provides for the registration of societies and lays down the broad framework within which they must operate. Internal relations of societies are governed by their registered rules. Registration under the Act confers upon a society corporate status by its registered name with perpetual succession and a common seal, and limited liability. A society qualifies for registration if it is carrying on an industry, business or trade, and it satisfies the FSA either (a) that it is a bona fide co-operative society, or (b) that in view of the fact that its business is being, or is intended to be, conducted for the benefit of the community, there are special reasons why it should be registered under the Act rather than as a company under the Companies Act.

Information about the process of registration of societies, including forms to download, can be found on the FSA website www.fsa.gov.uk. Also available from the FSA is a full list of names and contact details of representative and sponsoring bodies, covering between them the various types of societies that may be registered. These bodies provide model rules and some assistance with the registration process, thus attracting reduced FSA registration fees. They may also be able to provide information and assistance to aid research into their groups of societies.

The Credit Unions Act 1979 added a new class of society registrable under the 1965 Act. It also made provision for the supervision of these mutual savings and loan bodies. Unlike other classes, where the role of the FSA remains solely that of a registration authority, for Credit Unions (CUs) it is also the financial supervisor. For further information see the FSA website (*see* above).

BUILDING SOCIETIES IN THE UK

Building societies are probably the best known, with the most readily understood purpose, of all the mutual societies. There are 63 building societies in the UK with total assets approaching £250 billion. Nearly 21 million investing members have building society savings accounts and about 2.75 million borrowers are currently buying their own homes with the help of building society loans. This impact on so many people in the UK continues despite the fact that some of the best known names have ceased to be mutual building societies over a period of ten

years on takeover by or conversion to companies, effectively becoming banks. The list includes some of the biggest names:
Abbey National – floated July 1989
Cheltenham & Gloucester – taken over by Lloyds Bank, August 1995
National & Provincial – taken over by Abbey National plc, August 1996
Alliance & Leicester – floated April 1997
Halifax – floated June 1997
Woolwich – floated July 1997, taken over by Barclays Bank, October 2000
Bristol & West – taken over by Bank of Ireland, July 1997
Northern Rock – floated October 1997
Birmingham Midshires – taken over by Halifax plc, April 1999
Bradford & Bingley – floated December 2000
Against this trend, Britannia – currently the UK's second biggest building society – announced in June 2005 that it is to buy the Bristol & West savings business and branch network from Bank of Ireland (*see* above). Bristol & West's 850,000 customers will become members of Britannia in a move claimed to be the first re-mutualisation of a former building society. The Building Societies Association is the official representative body for UK building societies and further information on industry developments, as well as useful guidance on matters such as tracing dormant accounts, can be found on its website www.bsa.org.uk.

BUILDING SOCIETIES LEGISLATION
The Building Societies Act 1986 gave building societies a completely new legal framework for the first time since the initial comprehensive building society legislation in 1874. It set out detailed provisions in relation to their constitution; their powers in relation to raising funds, advances, loans, other assets and the provision of services; the powers of control of the Building Societies Commission (now superseded by the FSA); protection of investors, complaints and disputes; management of building societies; accounts and audit; and mergers and transfers of business.

The Act was prescriptive in respect of building societies' powers and the way in which they were exercised. However, it gave numerous powers to the Building Societies Commission and the Treasury to make statutory instruments which, subject to parliamentary approval, could amend, extend and supplement the provisions of the Act. Since it came into force on 1 January 1987 the Act had been amended and extended considerably, especially in respect of building societies' powers.

The Building Societies Act 1997 made substantive amendments to, but did not replace, the Building Societies Act 1986. It liberalised the statutory regime for building societies to enable them to compete on more level terms with other financial institutions, without having to forego their mutual status. It replaced the prescribed powers with a permissive regime, subject to appropriately revised balance-sheet 'nature limits'. This increased the commercial freedom of societies whilst allowing greater competition and wider choice for customers; enhanced the powers of control of the Building Societies Commission (now superseded by the FSA); introduced a package of measures to enhance the accountability of building societies' boards to their members; and made changes to the provisions covering the transfer of a building society's business to a company.

Under the 1997 Act a building society may pursue any activities set out in its memorandum, but its purpose or principal purpose must be that of making loans which are secured on residential properties and are funded substantially by its members. At least 75 per cent of its business assets must be loans fully secured on residential property and at least 50 per cent of its funds must be raised in the form of shares held by individual members. Further, subject to certain exceptions, it must not act as a market maker in securities, commodities or currencies; trade in commodities or currencies; enter into transactions involving derivatives, except in relation to hedging; nor create a floating charge over its assets. Most importantly, it must comply with the criteria of prudential management.

FACTS AND STATISTICS
At the end of the 2004 accounting year there were 63 building societies, exactly the same number as at the end of the previous year. The number has in fact fallen by only two over the last four years, despite the expectations by some financial commentators of widespread merger activity The 63 societies and their subsidiaries employed 43,942 full- and part-time staff, operated 2,074 branches and ran 559 estate agency offices.

Nearly 21 million investing members have building society savings accounts, a figure which has remained constant over the last three years. A number of these investors will, of course, have accounts with more than one society and so the number of building society investors will be below this figure. At the end of 2004, building society investors had 53 per cent of their funds in instant access accounts, 26 per cent in notice accounts, 19 per cent in term accounts, and 2 per cent in other savings. At the same time building societies had about 2.75 million borrowers and during the year made 811,000 loans, with the total amounting to over £59 billion compared to £50 billion in the previous year.

Mortgage arrears remained broadly stable during 2004. At the end of December mortgages with arrears equivalent to between 2.5 per cent and 5 per cent of the individual mortgage balance accounted for just 0.26 per cent of all mortgage balances. Mortgages with arrears of 5 per cent or more of the balance amounted to 0.12 per cent of all mortgage balances outstanding.

Comparative figures for building societies over the last five years are given below.

BUILDING SOCIETIES 2000–4

SERVICE ACTIVITY

| | | | Estate Agency Offices | Staff | | | | | Advances During Year | |
| | Societies | | | | | | | | | |
Year	Authorised	Branches		Full-time	Part-time	Shareholders 000s	Depositors 000s	Borrowers 000s	Number 000s	Amount £m
2000	67	2,361	607	32,334	10,823	22,237	740	3,107	548	31,514
2001	65	2,126	241	28,200	9,150	20,310	568	2,750	509	31,845
2002	65	2,103	229	28,982	9,257	20,724	511	2,688	558	37,303
2003	63	2,081	556	32,502	11,440	20,897	520	2,679	736	49,628
2004	63	2,074	559	33,155	11,571	20,734	525	2,749	811	59,283

LIABILITIES £million

| | | Funding | | | | Capital | | | Total liabilities |
| | | Deposits from | | Taxation and other | | | Life fund | and |
Year	Shares	individuals	Wholesale	liabilities	Reserves	Other	liabilities	capital
2000	119,295.5	5,531.0	38,047.5	2,033.6	9,577.0	1,861.7	1,397.8	177,747.1
2001	119,815.2	4,385.1	33,600.1	1,532.0	9,152.2	1,391.7	1,498.7	171,375.0
2002	132,373.0	4,191.2	33,459.6	1,401.1	9,932.8	1,684.8	1,410.3	184,452.8
2003	142,456.9	4,289.9	44,914.5	1,498.8	10,592.8	2,510.3	1,471.7	207,734.9
2004	153,844.0	4,648.1	59,194.4	1,761.5	11,385.6	3,574.8	1,782.9	236,146.3

ASSETS

Loans fully secured on land to:

| | Individuals on residential | | Other loans and | | Office | Other | Life fund | Total |
Year	properties	Others	investments	Liquidity	premises	assets	assets	assets
2000	125,555.9	8,544.2	1,230.0	37,900.8	1,044 7	2,073.7	1,397.8	177,747.1
2001	119,515.7	8,805.9	1,551.1	37,158.1	1,007.9	1,837.6	1,498.7	171,375.0
2002	129,001.3	9,882.7	1,877.1	39,201.8	1,050.6	2,029.0	1,410.3	184,452.8
2003	145,648.6	10,747.5	2,333.2	44,500.4	1,115.0	1,918.5	1,471.7	207,734.9
2004	168,501.4	11,671.0	2,870.4	47,810.8	1,202.7	2,307.7	1,782.9	236,146.3

BUILDING SOCIETIES AND TOTAL ASSETS
AT AUGUST 2005

Barnsley (Assets £329m), Regent St, Barnsley S70 2EH
T 01226-733999 W www.barnsley-bs.co.uk

Bath (£137m), 18–21 Charles St, Bath BA1 1HY
T 01225-423271 W www.bibs.co.uk

Beverley (£95m), 57 Market Place, Beverley HU17 8AA
T 01482-881510 W www.beverleybs.co.uk

Britannia (£23,298m), Cheadle Rd, Leek ST13 5RA
T 01538-399399 W www.britannia.co.uk

Buckinghamshire (£125m), High St, Chalfont St Giles HP8
4QB T 01494-873064 W www.bucksbuildingsociety.co.uk

Cambridge (£701m), PO Box 232, 51 Newmarket Road,
Cambridge CB5 8FF T 01223-727727
W www.cambridge-building-society.co.uk

Catholic (£37m), 7 Strutton Ground, London SW1P 2HY
T 020-7222 6736 W www.catholicbs.co.uk

Century (£20m), 21–23 Albany St, Edinburgh EH1 3QW
T 0131-556 1711 W www.century-building-society.co.uk

Chelsea (£8,868m), Thirlestaine Rd, Cheltenham GL53 7AL
T 01242-271271 W www.thechelsea.co.uk

Chesham (£188m), 12 Market Sq, Chesham HP5 1ER
T 01494-782575 W www.cheshambsoc.co.uk

Cheshire (£4,377m), Castle St, Macclesfield SK11 6AF
T 01625-613612 W www.thecheshire.co.uk

Chorley and District (£136m), Foxhole Rd, Chorley
PR7 1NZ T 01257-419110 W www.chorleybs.co.uk

City of Derry (£28m), 43 Carlisle Rd, Londonderry BT48 6JJ
T 028-7137 0037 W www.cityofderrybs.co.uk

Coventry (£9,443m), PO Box 9, High St, Coventry CV1 5QN
T 02476 555255 W www.coventrybuildingsociety.co.uk

Cumberland (£1,095m), Castle St, Carlisle CA3 8RX
T 01228-541341 W www.cumberland.co.uk

Darlington (£534m), Lingfield Way, Darlington DL1 4PR
T 01325-366366 W www.darlington.co.uk

Derbyshire (£4,407m), Duffield Hall, Duffield, Derby
DE56 1AG T 01332-841000 W www.thederbyshire.co.uk

Dudley (£184m), Stone St, Dudley DY1 1NP
T 01334-231414 W www.dudleybuildingsociety.co.uk

Dunfermline (£2,046m), Carnegie Avenue, Dunfermline
KY11 5PJ T 01383-627727 W www.dunfermline-bs.co.uk

Earl Shilton (£85m), 22 The Hollow, Earl Shilton, Leicester
LE9 7NB T 01455-844422 W www.esbs.co.uk

Ecology (£55m), 7 Belton Rd, Silsden, Keighley BD20 0EE
T 01535-650770 W www.ecology.co.uk

Furness (£739m), 51–55 Duke St, Barrow-in-Furness
LA14 1RT T 01229-824560 W www.furnessbs.co.uk

Hanley Economic (£281m), Festival Park, Hanley, Stoke-on-
Trent ST1 5TB T 01782-255161 W www.thehanley.co.uk

Harpenden (£117m), 14–16 Station Rd, Harpenden AL5 4SE
T 01582-765411 W www.harpendenbs.co.uk

Hinckley and Rugby (£635m), 81 Upper Bond St, Hinckley
LE10 1DG T 01455-251234 W www.hrbs.co.uk

Holmesdale (£130m), 43 Church St, Reigate RH2 0AE
T 01737-245716 W www.holmesdale.org.uk

Ipswich (£341m), PO Box 547, Freehold House, The Havens,
Ipswich IP3 9WZ T 0845-230 8686 W www.ipswich-bs.co.uk

Kent Reliance (£1,031m), Sun Pier, Chatham ME4 4ET
T 01634-848944 W www.krbs.co.uk

Lambeth (£1,082m), 118–120 Westminster Bridge Rd,
London SE1 7XE T 020-7928 1331 W www.lambeth.co.uk

Leeds and Holbeck (£6,129m), 105 Albion St, Leeds LS1
5 AS T 0113-225 2000 W www.leeds-holbeck.co.uk

Leek United (£620m), 50 St Edward St, Leek ST13 5DH
T 01538-384151 W www.leekunited.co.uk

Loughborough (£203m), 6 High St, Loughborough
LE11 2QB T 01509-610707 W www.theloughborough.co.uk

Manchester (£476m), Queens Court, 24 Queen St,
Manchester M2 5AH T 0161-833 8888
W www.themanchester.co.uk

Mansfield (£198m), Regent St, Mansfield NG18 1SS
T 01623-676300 W www.mansfieldbs.co.uk

Market Harborough (£351m), The Square, Market
Harborough LE16 7PD T 01858-463244 W www.mhbs.co.uk

Marsden (£333m), 6–20 Russell St, Nelson BB9 7NJ
T 01282-440500 W www.marsdenbs.co.uk

Melton Mowbray (£354m), 39 Nottingham St, Melton
Mowbray LE13 1NR T 01664-563937 W www.mmbs.co.uk

Mercantile (£233m), The Silverlink Business Park, Wallsend
NE28 9NY T 01912-959500 W www.mercantile-bs.co.uk

Monmouthshire (£401m), John Frost Square, Newport
NP20 1PX T 01633-844444 W www.monbsoc.co.uk

National Counties (£844m), 30 Church St, Epsom
KT17 4NL T 01372-742211 W www.ncbs.co.uk

Nationwide (£111,592m), Pipers Way, Swindon SN38 1NW
T 01793-513513 W www.nationwide.co.uk

Newbury (£509m), 17 Bartholomew St, Newbury RG14 5LY
T 01635-555700 W www.newbury.co.uk

Newcastle (£3,273m), New Bridge St, Newcastle upon Tyne
NE1 8AL T 0191-244 2000 W www.newcastle.co.uk

Norwich and Peterborough (£3,258m), Peterborough
Business Park, Lynch Wood, Peterborough PE2 6WZ
T 01733-372372 W www.npbs.co.uk

Nottingham (£2,190), 5–13 Upper Parliament St,
Nottingham NG1 2BX T 0115-948 1444
W www.thenottingham.com

Penrith (£72m), 7 King St, Penrith CA11 7AR
T 01768-863675 W www.penrithbuildingsociety.co.uk

Portman (£15,505m), Richmond Hill, Bournemouth BH2 6EP
T 01202-292444 W www.portman.co.uk

Principality (£4,052m), PO Box 89, Queen St, Cardiff
CF1 1UA T 029-2038 2000 W www.principality.co.uk

Progressive (£1,142m), 33–37 Wellington Place, Belfast
BT1 6HH T 01232-244926 W www.theprogressive.com

Saffron Walden Herts & Essex (£481m), 1A Market St,
Saffron Walden CB10 1HX T 01799-522211
W www.swhebs.co.uk

Scarborough (£1,438m), Prospect House, PO Box 6,
Scarborough YO12 6EQ T 01723-368155
W www.scarboroughbs.co.uk

Scottish (£203m), 23 Manor Place, Edinburgh EH3 7XE
T 0131-220 1111 W www.scottishbldgsoc.co.uk

Shepshed (£78m), Bull Ring, Shepshed, Loughborough
LE12 9QD T 01509-822000 W www.theshepshed.co.uk

Skipton (£8,137m), The Bailey, Skipton BD23 1DN
T 01756-705000 W www.skipton.co.uk

Stafford Railway (£107m), 4 Market Square, Stafford
ST16 2JH T 01785-223212 W www.srbs.co.uk

Stroud and Swindon (£2,306m), Rowcroft, Stroud GL5 3BG
T 01453-757011 W www.stroudandswindon.co.uk

Swansea (£385m), 11 Cradock St, Swansea SA1 3EW
T 01792-483700 W www.swansea-bs.co.uk

Teachers (£234m), Hanham Rd, Wimborne BH21 1AG
T 01202-843500 W www.teachersbs.co.uk

Tipton and Coseley (£262m), 70 Owen St, Tipton DY4 8HG
T 0121-557 2551 W www.tipton-coseley.co.uk

Universal (£534m), Kings Manor, Neacsle upon Tyne NE1
6PA T 0191-232 0973 W www.theuniversal.co.uk

Vernon (£203m), 19 St Petersgate, Stockport SK1 1HF
T 0845-1297100 W www.thevernon.co.uk

West Bromwich (£5,044m), 374 High St, West Bromwich
B70 8LR T 0121-525 7070 W www.westbrom.co.uk

Yorkshire (£15,034m), Yorkshire Drive, Bradford BD5 8LJ
T 0845-120 0100 W www.ybs.co.uk

ECONOMIC STATISTICS

THE BUDGET 2005

GOVERNMENT RECEIPTS   £ billion

	Outturn 2003–4	Outturn Estimate 2004–5	Projection 2005–6
Inland Revenue			
Income tax (gross of tax credits)	118.4	126.8	138.1
Income tax credits	−4.5	−4.1	−3.9
National Insurance Contributions	72.5	77.9	82.6
Corporation tax[1]	28.6	34.1	43.7
Tax credits[2]	−0.5	−0.5	−0.5
Petroleum revenue tax	1.2	1.3	1.5
Capital gains tax	2.2	2.3	3.0
Inheritance tax	2.5	2.9	3.4
Stamp duties	7.5	8.9	9.7
TOTAL INLAND REVENUE (NET OF TAX CREDITS)	228.0	249.6	277.5
Customs and Excise			
Value added tax	69.1	72.3	76.3
Fuel duties	22.8	23.5	24.6
Tobacco duties	8.1	8.1	8.4
Spirits duties	2.4	2.4	2.5
Wine duties	2.0	2.2	2.3
Beer and cider duties	3.2	3.3	3.4
Betting and gaming duties	1.3	1.4	1.4
Air passenger duty	0.8	0.9	1.0
Insurance premium tax	2.3	2.4	2.6
Landfill tax	0.6	0.7	0.7
Climate change levy	0.8	0.8	0.8
Aggregates levy	0.3	0.3	0.3
Customs duties and levies	1.9	2.2	2.2
TOTAL CUSTOMS AND EXCISE	115.7	120.4	126.5
Vehicle excise duties	4.8	4.8	5.1
Oil royalties	0.0	0.0	0.0
Business rates[3]	18.3	19.0	19.4
Council tax[4]	18.8	19.8	20.9
Other taxes and royalties[5]	11.2	12.0	12.4
NET TAXES AND NATIONAL INSURANCE CONTRIBUTIONS[6]	396.8	425.6	461.9
Accruals adjustments on taxes	3.2	2.3	0.9
Less own resources contribution to EC budget	−4.6	−4.0	−3.9
Less PC corporation tax payments	−0.1	−0.1	−0.1
Tax credits adjustment[7]	0.5	0.6	0.6
Interest and dividends	4.4	5.0	4.9
Other receipts[8]	18.5	20.2	22.4
CURRENT RECEIPTS	418.9	449.7	486.7
North Sea revenues[9]	4.3	5.2	7.1

[1] National accounts measure: gross of enhanced and payable tax credits

[2] Includes enhanced company tax credits

[3] Includes district council rates in Northern Ireland paid by business

[4] Cash numbers. The increase in accrued council tax in 2005–6 is based on the latest available estimates released by the Chartered Institute for Public Finance and Accountancy (CIPFA) and the increases for later years on the increases in council tax from 1993–94 onwards

[5] Includes VAT refunds and money paid into the National Lottery Distribution Fund

[6] Includes VAT and 'traditional own resources' contributions to EC budget

[7] Tax credits which are scored as negative tax in the calculation of net taxes and National Insurance Contributions but expenditure in the national accounts

[8] Includes gross operating surplus and rent; net of oil royalties and business rate payments by Local Authorities

[9] Consists of North Sea corporation tax, petroleum revenue tax and royalties

Source: HM Treasury – Budget 2005 (Crown copyright)

GOVERNMENT EXPENDITURE

The Economic and Fiscal Strategy Report in June 1998 introduced changes to the public expenditure control regime. Three-year departmental expenditure limits (DELs) now apply to most government departments. Spending which cannot easily be subject to three-year planning is reviewed annually in the Budget as annually managed expenditure (AME). Current and capital expenditure are treated separately.

DEPARTMENTAL EXPENDITURE LIMITS

RESOURCE AND CAPITAL BUDGETS			£ billion
	Outturn 2003–4	Outturn Estimate 2004–5	Plans 2005–6
Resource Budget			
Education and Skills	23.1	24.6	26.3
Health	62.7	69.1	75.1
– (of which NHS)	60.9	66.9	72.8
Transport	7.8	8.3	8.8
Office of the Deputy Prime Minister	6.0	6.2	6.4
Local Government	40.9	43.4	46.2
Home Office	11.7	12.3	12.8
Departments for Constitutional Affairs	3.2	3.4	3.7
Attorney General's Departments	0.6	0.7	0.7
Defence	31.3	32.6	32.7
Foreign and Commonwealth Office	1.6	1.8	1.8
International Development	3.8	3.9	4.5
Trade and Industry	4.4	5.3	5.9
Environment, Food and Rural Affairs	2.7	3.2	3.1
Culture, Media and Sport	1.3	1.5	1.5
Work and Pensions	8.3	8.4	8.4
Scotland[1]	18.8	20.0	21.4
Wales[1]	9.8	10.7	11.3

Northern Ireland			
Executive[1]	6.4	7.0	7.3
Northern Ireland Office	1.0	1.2	1.2
Chancellor's			
Departments	4.5	5.0	5.2
Cabinet Office	1.9	2.0	2.0
Invest to Save Budget	0.0	0.0	0.0
Reserve	0.0	0.0	0.4
Unallocated special			
reserve[2]	0.0	0.0	0.3
Allowance for shortfall[3]	0.0	−1.8	0.0
TOTAL RESOURCE			
BUDGET DEL	251.9	268.7	286.9
Capital Budget			
Education and Skills	3.2	3.7	4.4
Health	2.5	3.1	3.8
– (of which NHS)	2.5	3.0	3.7
Transport	3.0	3.3	3.3
Office of the Deputy			
Prime Minister	2.6	2.9	3.0
Local Government	0.2	0.3	0.3
Home Office	0.9	1.1	1.2
Departments for			
Constitutional Affairs	0.1	0.2	0.1
Attorney General's			
Departments	0.0	0.0	0.0
Defence	6.1	6.6	6.9
Foreign and			
Commonwealth			
Office	0.0	0.1	0.1
International			
Development	0.0	0.0	0.0
Trade and Industry	0.6	0.2	0.3
Environment, Food and			
Rural Affairs	0.4	0.3	0.3
Culture, Media and Sport	0.1	0.2	0.1
Work and Pensions	0.2	0.3	0.3
Scotland[1]	1.4	2.0	1.9
Wales[1]	0.8	0.9	0.9
Northern Ireland			
Executive[1]	0.4	0.4	0.4
Northern Ireland Office	0.1	0.1	0.1
Chancellor's			
Departments	0.3	0.4	0.3
Cabinet Office	0.5	0.3	0.2
Invest to Save Budget	0.0	0.0	0.0
Reserve	0.0	0.0	0.5
Allowance for shortfall[3]	0.0	−2.6	0.0
TOTAL CAPITAL			
BUDGET DEL	23.5	23.8	28.8
Depreciation	−9.4	−11.3	−11.8
TOTAL DEPARTMENTAL			
EXPENDITURE			
LIMITS	266.0	281.2	303.9

[1]For Scotland, Wales and Northern Ireland, the split between current and capital budgets is indicative and reflects the consequentials of the application of the Barnett formula to planned changes in UK departments spending

[2]This represents provision for the costs of the military conflict in Iraq and other international obligations. The figure for 2003–4 is after the further addition of £340 million announced in the Budget

[3]The allowance for shortfall reflect likely underspends in departmental forecasts

Source: HM Treasury – *Budget 2005* (Crown copyright)

ANNUALLY MANAGED EXPENDITURE			£ billion
	Outturn 2003–4	Outturn Estimate 2004–5	Projection 2005–6
Social security benefits[1]	112.7	121.4	127.3
Tax credits[1]	14.8	15.2	14.6
Common Agricultural			
Policy	2.9	3.2	3.3
Net public service			
pensions[2]	2.0	1.0	0.7
National Lottery	1.9	1.8	1.7
Non-cash items in AME	5.2	3.4	2.2
Other departmental			
expenditure	1.5	4.2	5.2
Net payment to EU			
institutions[3]	2.4	3.7	3.1
Locally-financed			
expenditure	21.2	24.3	25.4
Central government gross			
debt interest	22.2	23.8	25.6
Public corporations' own-			
financed capital			
expenditure	2.5	2.2	2.3
AME margin	0.0	0.0	1.0
Accounting adjustments[4]	−0.9	−1.2	2.3
ANNUALLY MANAGED			
EXPENDITURE	188.4	202.9	214.7

[1] All child allowances in Income Support and Jobseekers' Allowance which from 2003–4 are paid as part of the Child Tax Credit, have been included in the tax credits line and excluded from the social security benefits line. This is in order to give figures a consistent definition over the forecast period

[2] Reported on a national accounts basis

[3] Excludes contributions to the cost of EU aid to non-Member States , which is attributed to the aid programme. Total UK estimated net payments to the EU budget for 2004–5 are £4.3 billion, with projected spending for 2005–6 at £3.8 billion

[4] Excludes depreciation

Source: HM Treasury – *Budget 2005* (Crown copyright)

PUBLIC SECTOR FINANCES   *£ billion*

PUBLIC SECTOR CAPITAL EXPENDITURE			
	Outturn 2003–4	Outturn Estimate 2004–5	Projection 2005–6
Capital Budget DEL	23.5	23.8	28.8
Locally-financed			
expenditure	−0.6	2.1	2.2
National Lottery	1.2	0.9	0.9
Public corporations' own-			
financed capital			
expenditure	2.5	2.2	2.3
Other capital spending in			
AME	2.5	3.9	7.5
AME margin	0.0	0.0	0.1
PUBLIC SECTOR GROSS			
INVESTMENT[1]	29.0	33.0	41.7
Less depreciation	14.0	14.6	15.5
PUBLIC SECTOR NET			
INVESTMENT	15.0	18.3	26.2
Proceeds from the sale of			
fixed assets[2]	6.7	5.8	5.2

[1]This and previous lines are all net of sales of fixed assets

[2]Projections of total receipts from the sale of fixed assets by public sector

Source: HM Treasury – *Budget 2005* (Crown copyright).

SIZE OF ECONOMY

GDP	US$1,566,283 (2002)
GDP, annual percentage growth	1.8 (2001–2)
GNI	US$1,510.8 billion (2002)
GNI, per capita	US$25,510 (2002)

Source: The World Bank – *World Development Indicators 2004*

EMPLOYMENT

DISTRIBUTION OF THE UK WORKFORCE 2004

Claimant count	849,000
Workforce jobs	30,440,000
HM Forces	206,000
Self-employment jobs	3,860,000
Employees jobs	26,264,000
Government-supported trainees	109,000

Source: ONS – *Annual Abstract of Statistics 2005* (Crown copyright)

UK EMPLOYMENT BY AGE AND GENDER

Thousands

	2003		2004	
Age	*Male*	*Female*	*Male*	*Female*
16–17	322	336	310	333
18–24	1,779	1,606	1,854	1,655
25–34	3,495	2,894	3,422	2,867
35–49	5,641	4,924	5,715	4,955
50–64(m)/59(f)*	3,684	2,545	3,714	2,562
65+(m)/60+(f)*	336	597	335	660
All aged 16+	15,257	12,901	15,351	13,032

Source: ONS – *Annual Abstract of Statistics 2005* (Crown copyright)
* m = male, f = female

UK UNEMPLOYMENT BY AGE AND GENDER

Thousands

	2003		2004	
Age	*Male*	*Female*	*Male*	*Female*
16–17	100	76	101	72
18–24	246	161	216	177
25–34	188	123	–	–
35–49	211	152	–	–
50–64(m)/59(f)	149	62	–	–
65+(m)/60+(f)	–	10	–	–
All aged 16+	901	588	829	610

Source: ONS – *Annual Abstract of Statistics 2005* (Crown copyright)

DURATION OF UNEMPLOYMENT IN THE UK 2004

	Thousands
All unemployed	1,438
Duration of unemployment	
– Less than 6 months	915
– 6 months–1 year	232
– 1 year +	291
– *1 year + as percentage of total*	20.2

Source: ONS – *Annual Abstract of Statistics 2005* (Crown copyright)

AVERAGE EARNINGS AND HOURS OF FULL-TIME EMPLOYEES BY GENDER 2004 (UK)

	All	*Male*	*Female*
Average weekly earnings (£)	504.9	556.8	420.2
Average hours	39.6	40.8	37.5
Average hourly earnings (£)			
– Including overtime	12.75	13.63	11.19
– Excluding overtime	12.80	13.73	11.21

Source: ONS – *Annual Abstract of Statistics 2005* (Crown copyright)

NUMBER OF INDUSTRIAL STOPPAGES BY DURATION 2003 (UK)

0–5 days	113,000
5–10 days	10,000
11–20 days	5,000
21–30 days	1,000
31–50 days	1,000
50+ days	3,000
Total number of stoppages	133,000

Source: ONS – *Annual Abstract of Statistics 2005* (Crown copyright)

NUMBER OF INDUSTRIAL STOPPAGES BY INDUSTRY 2003 (UK)

Mining, quarrying, electricity, gas and water	1,000
Manufacturing	43,000
Construction	4,000
Transport, storage and communications	45,000
Public administration and defence	12,000
Education	15,000
Health and social work	7,000
Other community, social and personal services	9,000
All other industries and services	4,000

Source: ONS – *Annual Abstract of Statistics 2005* (Crown copyright)

NUMBER AND MEMBERSHIP OF TRADE UNIONS (UK)

Year	*No. of unions at end of year*	*Total membership at end of year (thousands)*
1992	315	9,171
1993	302	8,848
1994	281	8,297
1995	271	8,111
1996	261	7,982
1997	257	7,841
1998	243	7,894
1999	241	7,940
2000	230	7,823
2001	220	7,796
2002	218	7,783

Source: ONS – *Annual Abstract of Statistics 2005* (Crown copyright)

UK TRADE

UK TRADE IN GOODS ON A BALANCE OF PAYMENTS
BASIS   £ million

	Exports	Imports	
1993	122,229	135,295	−13,066
1994	135,143	146,269	−11,126
1995	153,577	165,600	−12,023
1996	167,196	180,918	−13,722
1997	171,923	184,265	−12,342
1998	164,056	185,869	−21,813
1999	166,166	195,217	−29,051
2000	187,936	220,912	−32,976
2001	190,055	230,703	−40,648
2002	186,517	233,192	−46,675
2003	187,846	235,136	−47,290

Source: ONS – Annual Abstract of Statistics 2005 (Crown
copyright)

BALANCE OF PAYMENTS 2003   £ million
CURRENT ACCOUNT
Trade in goods and services
− Trade in goods   −47,290
− Trade in services   14,617
Total trade in goods and services   −32,673
Income
− Compensation of employees   59
− Investment income   22,038
Total income   22,097
Current transfers
− Central government   −6,740
− Other sectors   −3,114
Total current transfers   −9,854
TOTAL (CURRENT BALANCE)   −20,430

Source: ONS – Annual Abstract of Statistics 2005 (Crown
copyright)

VALUE OF UK EXPORTS AND IMPORTS BY AREA 2003
                                               £ million

	Exports	Imports
European Union	109,807	135,362
Other Western Europe	6,609	13,187
North America	33,246	27,432
Other OECD countries	7,823	12,927
Oil exporting countries	7,626	3,942
Rest of the World	22,735	42,286

Source: ONS – Annual Abstract of Statistics 2005 (Crown
copyright)

HOUSEHOLD INCOME AND EXPENDITURE

AVERAGE INCOME OF UK HOUSEHOLDS BEFORE AND
AFTER TAXES AND BENEFITS 2002–3
Number of households in the UK population   24,346,000
Original annual income   £25,271
Disposable annual income   £23,483
Post-tax annual income   £19,002
Source: ONS – Annual Abstract of Statistics 2005 (Crown
copyright)

AVERAGE WEEKLY UK HOUSEHOLD INCOME BY
SOURCE 2002–3

	£	As % of total
Wages and salaries	373.90	68
Self-employment	44.50	8
Investments	18.80	3
Annuities and pensions (other than social security benefits)	39.90	7
Social security benefits	68.50	12
Other sources	6.70	1
Total	552.30	100

Source: ONS – Annual Abstract of Statistics 2005 (Crown
copyright)

AVERAGE WEEKLY UK HOUSEHOLD EXPENDITURE BY SOCIO-ECONOMIC CLASSIFICATION[1] 2002–3   £ per week

| | Occupations | | | | |
--	Managerial and Professional	Intermediate	Routine and Manual	Never worked[2] and long-term unemployed	All households[3]
Food and non-alcoholic drink	52.60	44.90	43.40	30.90	42.70
Alcohol and tobacco	13.50	11.60	13.80	9.00	11.40
Clothing and footwear	33.60	25.30	24.10	24.50	22.30
Housing, fuel and power[4]	47.00	39.40	38.30	67.20	36.90
Household goods and services	49.50	29.70	26.80	13.90	30.20
Health	7.30	4.50	3.10	2.00	4.80
Transport	98.40	72.10	57.70	37.80	59.20
Communication	13.80	12.40	11.40	17.10	10.60
Recreation and culture	86.30	59.20	57.20	44.00	56.40
Education	13.20	5.10	2.10	14.80	5.20
Restaurants and hotels	58.90	38.10	35.50	42.90	35.40
Miscellaneous goods and services	53.30	35.40	30.10	18.20	33.10
Other expenditure items	109.70	69.80	52.70	17.70	58.30
All household expenditure	637.00	447.50	396.10	340.00	406.60
Average household size (number of people)	2.7	2.6	2.7	2.5	2.4

[1] Of the household reference person
[2] Includes households where the reference person is a student
[3] Includes retired households and others that are not classified
[4] Excludes mortgage interest payments, water charges, council tax and Northern Ireland domestic rates. These are included in 'Other
expenditure items'
Source: ONS – Social Trends 2005 (Crown copyright)

AVAILABILITY IN UK HOUSEHOLDS OF CERTAIN DURABLE GOODS 2002–3

	% of households
Car	74
– One	44
– Two	25
– Three or more	6
Central heating, full or partial	93
Washing machine	94
Fridge/freezer or deep freezer	96
Dishwasher	29
Telephone	94
Home computer	55
Internet access	45
Video recorder	90

Source: ONS – *Annual Abstract of Statistics 2005* (Crown copyright)

MONEY SPENT ON GAMBLING 2003–4 (UK)

	£ millions
National Lottery – Total	4,614
– Online	3,225
– Instants	641
– Thunderball	351
– Lottery Extra	78
– Hot Picks	244
– Christmas draw	15
– Euromillions	15
– Daily Play	45
Other Lotteries	127
Bingo clubs	1,381
Football pools	112
Off-course betting	32,265

Source: ONS – *Annual Abstract of Statistics 2005* (Crown copyright)

SAVINGS

CREDIT AND DEBIT CARD USAGE

UK DEBIT AND CREDIT CARD SPENDING* 2003
£ billions

	Debit cards	Credit cards
Food and drink	33.7	13.2
Motoring	17.2	12.2
Household	10.0	12.7
Mixed business	7.6	8.0
Clothing	7.5	5.2
Travel	6.8	12.9
Entertainment	5.6	6.5
Financial	1.7	1.0
Hotels	1.3	4.3
Other services	17.9	15.7
Other retail	13.0	16.8
Total	122.3	108.3

* By principal business activity of where the purchase was made. Excludes spending outside the UK by UK cardholders
Source: ONS – *Social Trends 2005* (Crown copyright)

AVERAGE DWELLING PRICES BY REGION 2003

	£ sterling
UK	155,485
England	165,834
– North East	94,950
– North West	108,956
– Yorkshire & the Humber	107,325
– East Midlands	133,215
– West Midlands	132,898
– East	181,494
– London	236,476
– South East	213,115
– South West	170,560
Wales	104,140
Scotland	92,006
Northern Ireland	102,348

Source: ONS – *Social Trends 2005* (Crown copyright)

UK HOUSEHOLD SAVINGS BY ETHNIC GROUP OF HOUSEHOLD REFERENCE PERSON 2002–3					*Percentages**
	No savings	Less than £1,500	£1,500–£10,000	£10,000–£20,000	£20,000+
White	32	21	26	9	13
Mixed	46	25	–	–	–
Asian/Asian British	60	15	16	5	5
Black/Black British	63	18	15	–	–
Chinese/Other ethnic group	50	18	19	–	–
All Households	33	20	25	8	13

Source: ONS – *Social Trends 2005* (Crown copyright)
*Note: where available percentages are rounded up to the nearest whole number

COST OF LIVING AND INFLATION RATES

The first cost of living index to be calculated took July 1914 as 100 and was based on the pattern of expenditure of working-class families in 1914. The cost of living index was superseded in 1947 by the general index of retail prices (RPI), although the older term is still popularly applied.

The Harmonised Index of Consumer Prices (HICP) was introduced in 1997 to enable comparisons within the European Union using an agreed methodology. In 2003 the National Statistician renamed the HICP as the Consumer Prices Index (CPI) to reflect its role as the main target measure of inflation for macroeconomic purposes. The RPI and indices based on it will continue to be published alongside the CPI. The CPI does not replace the RPI as the most general purpose measure of inflation for UK domestic use. Pensions and benefits and index-linked gilts continue to be calculated with reference to RPI or its derivatives.

CONSUMER AND RETAIL PRICES INDICES

The RPI and CPI measure the changes month by month in the average level of prices of goods and services purchased by households in the UK. The indices are compiled using a selection of around 650 goods and services, and the prices charged for these items are collected at regular intervals in about 150 locations throughout the country. The Office for National Statistics reviews the components of the indices once every year to reflect changes in consumer preferences and the establishment of new products.

CPI excludes a number of items that are included in RPI, mainly related to housing such as council tax and a range of owner-occupier housing costs. The CPI covers all private households, whereas RPI excludes the top four per cent by income and some pensioner households. The two indices use different methodologies to combine the prices of goods and services, which means that since 1996 the CPI inflation measure is on average 0.5 per cent less than the RPI inflation measure.

INFLATION RATE

The twelve-monthly percentage change in the 'all items' index of the RPI or CPI is referred to as the rate of inflation. As the most familiar measure of inflation, RPI is often referred to as the 'headline rate of inflation'. CPI is the main measure of inflation for macroeconomic purposes and forms the basis for the Government's inflation target, which is currently 2 per cent. The percentage change in prices between any two months/years can be obtained using the following formula:

$$\frac{\text{Later date RPI/CPI} - \text{Earlier date RPI/CPI}}{\text{Earlier date RPI/CPI}} \times 100$$

e.g. to find the RPI rate of inflation for 2001, using the annual averages for 2000 and 2001:

$$\frac{173.3 - 170.3}{170.3} \times 100 = 1.76$$

PURCHASING POWER OF THE POUND

Changes in the internal purchasing power of the pound may be defined as the 'inverse' of changes in the level of prices: when prices go up, the amount which can be purchased with a given sum of money goes down. To find the purchasing power of the pound in one month or year, given that it was 100p in a previous month or year, the calculation would be:

$$100p \times \frac{\text{Earlier month/year RPI}}{\text{Later month/year RPI}}$$

Thus, if the purchasing power of the pound is taken to be 100p in 1975, the comparable purchasing power in 2002 would be: $100p \times \dfrac{34.2}{176.2} = 19.4p$

For longer term comparisons, it has been the practice to use an index which has been constructed by linking together the RPI for the period 1962 to date; an index derived from the consumers expenditure deflator for the period from 1938 to 1962; and the prewar 'cost of living' index for the period 1914 to 1938. This long-term index enables the internal purchasing power of the pound to be calculated for any year from 1914 onwards. It should be noted that these figures can only be approximate.

	Annual average RPI (1987 = 100)	Purchasing power of £ (1998 = 1.00)	Rate of inflation (RPI/CPI)
1914	2.8	58.18	
1915	3.5	46.54	
1920	7.0	23.27	
1925	5.0	32.58	
1930	4.5	36.20	
1935	4.0	40.72	
1938	4.4	37.02	
There are no official figures for 1939–45			
1946	7.4	22.01	
1950	9.0	18.10	
1955	11.2	14.54	
1960	12.6	12.93	
1965	14.8	11.00	
1970	18.5	8.80	
1975	34.2	4.76	
1980	66.8	2.44	18.0
1985	94.6	1.72	6.1
1990	126.1	1.29	9.5/7.0
1995	149.1	1.09	3.5/2.6
1998	162.9	1.00	3.4/1.6
2000	170.3	0.96	3.0/0.8
2001	173.3	0.94	1.8/1.2
2002	176.2	0.92	1.7/1.2
2003	181.3	0.90	2.9/1.4
2004	186.7	0.87	3.0/1.3

The RPI figures are published by the Office for National Statistics on either the second or third Tuesday of each month in an Indices bulletin and electronically on the National Statistics website www.statistics.gov.uk. They are also available as a recorded message which can be heard by telephoning 020-7533 5866.

TAXATION

INCOME TAX

Income tax is charged on the taxable income of individuals for a year of assessment commencing on 6 April and ending on the following 5 April. Many changes have been introduced during recent years which affect both the calculation of income chargeable to tax and the rate or rates at which the amount of tax due must be determined. The following information is confined to the year of assessment 2005–6 ending on 5 April 2006 and has only limited application to earlier years. Changes which are to come into operation at a later date are briefly mentioned where information is available.

An individual's liability to satisfy income tax for 2005–6 is determined by establishing the level of taxable income for the year. This income must then be allocated between three different headings, namely: (a) all income excluding that arising from savings and dividends; (b) income from savings; (c) company dividends, including distributions.

Once this allocation has been completed the first calculation must be limited to taxable income excluding that arising from both savings and dividends. This income will be reduced by an individual's personal allowance and any other available allowances. The first £2,090 of taxable income remaining is assessed to income tax at the starting rate of 10 per cent. The next £30,310 is taxable at the basic rate of 22 per cent. Should any excess over £32,400 (£2,090 plus £32,400) remain, this will be taxable at the higher rate of 40 per cent.

The second calculation is limited to income from savings, if any. Liability may arise at the starting rate of 10 per cent, the lower rate of 20 per cent or the higher rate of 40 per cent. There is no liability to income tax at the basic rate of 22 per cent. The appropriate rate which must be used is determined by adding income from savings to other taxable income, excluding dividends. To the extent that the addition does not increase taxable income above £2,090, income from savings is taxed at the starting rate of 10 per cent. Should this level be exceeded but total income does not reach £32,400 any excess remains taxable at the lower rate of 20 per cent. Where the addition of income from savings extends total income above £32,400 the excess is taxed at the higher rate of 40 per cent.

Finally, any company dividends are taxed at either the ordinary rate of 10 per cent or the upper rate of 32.5 per cent. The amount of dividends (with the addition of any tax credit) must be added to taxable income comprising general income together with income from savings. If this addition does not increase total taxable income above £32,400 dividends remain taxable at the ordinary rate of 10 per cent only. However, if or to the extent that the addition discloses dividends exceeding the £32,400 level the excess is taxed at the upper rate of 32.5 per cent.

Trustees administering settled property and personal representatives dealing with the estate of a deceased person are chargeable to income tax at the basic rate of 22 per cent. Where trustees retain discretionary powers or income from settled property is accumulated, liability may be increased to 40 per cent. Lower rates apply where income is received in the form of dividends. Under changes introduced to modernise and simplify the taxation system for trusts, from 2005–6 the first £500 of trust income is taxed at the basic rate, in substitution for 40 per cent.

Companies residing in the UK are not liable to income tax but suffer corporation tax on income, profits and gains. Income arising overseas will often incur liability to foreign taxation. If that income is also chargeable to UK income tax, excessive liability could arise. The UK has concluded double taxation agreements with the governments of many overseas territories and these ensure that the same slice of income is not doubly taxed.

HUSBAND AND WIFE

A husband and wife are separately taxed, with each entitled to his or her personal allowance. A married man 'living with' his wife can only obtain a married couple's allowance if one party to the marriage was over the age of 64 years before 6 April 2000. In the absence of any claim, this allowance must be used by the husband but where any balance remains the surplus may be transferred to the wife. It is possible for a married woman to claim half the basic married couple's allowance as of right. The entire basic allowance may be claimed by the wife, if her husband so agrees. Each spouse may obtain other allowances and reliefs where the required conditions are satisfied. Income must be accurately allocated between the couple by reference to the individual beneficially entitled to that income. Where income arises from jointly-held assets, this must be apportioned equally between husband and wife. However, where the assets comprise shares in closely controlled companies, the allocation of dividends and other distributions are based on the beneficial interests of each spouse. In other cases where the beneficial interests in jointly-held assets are not equal, a special declaration can be made to apportion income by reference to the actual interests in that income.

SELF-ASSESSMENT

Self-assessment for income tax purposes affects individuals, trustees and personal representatives. Central to self-assessment is the requirement to deliver a completed tax return. This must normally be submitted by 31 January following the end of the year of assessment (the previous 5 April) to which the return relates. The taxpayer must also calculate the amount of income tax due. If a taxpayer wishes the HM Revenue & Customs to calculate the tax due, the return must be forwarded to it not later than the previous 30 September.

It is the responsibility of the taxpayer to submit payments of income tax on time. There are three different dates on which payments may fall due:
(a) an interim payment due on 31 January in the year of assessment itself
(b) a second interim payment due on the following 31 July
(c) a balancing payment, or possibly a repayment, on the following 31 January
The two interim payments will be based on tax payable for the previous year of assessment but liability may be

reduced where income has fallen or avoided entirely where the amounts are not substantial.

The impact of self-assessment is largely restricted to some nine million persons receiving tax returns. These comprise self-employed individuals, those receiving income from the exploitation of land in the UK, company directors, others with investment income liable to higher rate income tax, trustees and personal representatives. Elderly persons receiving small amounts of untaxed income may be excluded from the need to complete a tax return. Others having relatively straightforward affairs may complete a shortened version of the normal return form.

It is a fundamental part of the self-assessment system that responsibility lies with the tax payer to file returns and pay the right amount of tax at the right time. Tax payers must not wait for HM Revenue & Customs to ask. Failure to submit completed tax returns by 31 January or to discharge payments of income tax on time will incur a liability to interest, surcharges and penalties.

INCOME TAXABLE

For many years income tax was assessed using a range of different schedules, with each applying to determine both the extent of liability and the amount to be included in taxable income. But the use of these schedules is now largely obsolete as a result of income tax legislation being re-written and simplified. However, the replacement of these schedules with new legislation does not affect future liability to income tax on matters previously dealt with under each schedule. Of the previous main schedules: Schedule A related to income tax on property; Schedule D to income tax on trade profits; Schedule E to income tax on employment, pension and social security income; and Schedule F to income tax on investment income.

INCOME FROM PROPERTY

Annual profits or gains arising from a business carried on for the exploitation of land in the UK are liable to income tax. Taxable profits include rents and other income from the exploitation of land offset by outgoings incurred wholly and exclusively for the purposes of the business.

Individuals who let furnished rooms in their only or main home can receive up to £4,250 of gross rental income a year free of income tax under the government's Rent a Room scheme. Income arising from the provision of certain furnished holiday accommodation also attracts a number of tax advantages.

TRADE PROFITS

Income tax is payable on profits arising from trades, professions and vocations, including farming and market gardening. Profits must be calculated on an accounting basis which provides 'a true and fair view' of business results. When calculating taxable profits, only sums laid out 'wholly and exclusively' for the purposes of a business may be deducted from receipts.

Capital expenditure incurred on assets used for business purposes will often produce an entitlement to capital allowances which reduce the profits chargeable. These profits may also be reduced by claims for loss relief and other matters.

EMPLOYMENT INCOME

Net taxable earnings arising in a year of assessment ending on 5 April are chargeable to income tax as employment income. This charge reflects taxable earnings remaining after subtracting the total of allowable deductions.

Taxable earnings will include all salaries, wages, director's fees and other money sums. In addition, the value of a wide range of benefits must be added. These benefits include the provision of living accommodation on advantageous terms and advantages arising from the use of vouchers.

Further taxable benefits accrue to directors and employees who are not classed as 'lower paid'. These exempt individuals receive annual earnings of no more than £8,500 calculated by including potentially taxable benefits. Such taxable benefits include the reimbursement of expenses, the availability of motor cars for private motoring, the provision of fuel for private motoring, interest free loans and other benefits provided at the employer's expense. The cost of providing a limited range of childcare facilities and a works bus for the transportation of employees may be ignored. Mileage allowances paid to employees who provide their own motor vehicles or cycles for business travel may also be excluded, unless they exceed stated limits.

All taxable earnings received by an individual who is resident, ordinarily resident and domiciled in the UK are chargeable to income tax. However, limitations may apply where there is some foreign element.

A 'receipts basis' applies for determining the year of assessment to which taxable earnings must be allocated. In general, the date of receipt will comprise the earlier of the date of payment or the date entitlement arises. In the case of company directors it is the earlier of these two dates, with the addition of the following three, which establishes the time of receipt: the date earnings are credited in the company's books; where earnings for a period are determined after the end of that period, the date of determination; where earnings for a period are determined in that period, the last day of that period.

In arriving at the amount of net taxable earnings all expenses incurred wholly, exclusively and necessarily in the performance of the duties, together with the cost of business travel, may be deducted. Fees and subscriptions paid to certain professional bodies and learned societies may also be deducted. In addition, fees paid to managers by entertainers, actors and others in respect of taxable earnings may be deducted, up to a maximum of 17.5 per cent.

Compensation for loss of office and other sums received on the termination of an employment are assessable to income tax. However, the first £30,000 may be excluded with only the balance remaining chargeable, unless the compensatory payment is linked with the retirement of the recipient or the performance of their duties.

A range of other matters loosely linked to an employment may also create employment income. Rules similar to those outlined above apply also to the holder of an office.

PENSION INCOME

Pensions received from various sources, including an occupational pension scheme, personal pension scheme, retirement annuity scheme and from other types of arrangement are treated as pension income chargeable to income tax. Liability is based on the amounts received in a year of assessment. However, where the pension is attributable to certain payments made overseas, only 90 per cent is taxable.

SOCIAL SECURITY INCOME

Many social security benefits are not liable to income tax. However, benefits which are taxable as social security income include the state retirement pension, widow's pension, widowed mother's allowance and jobseeker's allowance. Short-term sick pay and maternity pay payable by an employer are also chargeable to tax. Incapacity benefit remains taxable but no liability arises on most short-term benefit.

PAY AS YOU EARN

The Pay as You Earn (PAYE) system is not an independent form of taxation but is designed to collect income tax by deduction from most taxable earnings. When paying taxable earnings to employees an employer is usually required to deduct income tax and to account for that tax to the HM Revenue and Customs. In many cases this deduction procedure will fully exhaust the individual's liability to income tax, unless there is other income. The date of 'receipt' used to establish the time employment income arises also identifies the date of 'payment' when establishing liability to PAYE.

The PAYE system is used to collect tax on certain payments made 'in kind'. The system is also applied when collecting tax on many pensions, jobseeker's benefits, some incapacity benefits and maternity pay.

INCOME FROM SAVINGS

Many payments of interest made by building societies and banks are received after the deduction of income tax at the lower rate of 20 per cent. However, investors not liable to income tax may arrange to receive interest gross with no tax being deducted on payment.

Interest of this nature represents 'income from savings'; an expression which also extends to interest on government securities, interest on a restricted range of National Savings and Investments products and the income element of purchased life annuities. In addition, 'income from savings' may extend to other income of a similar nature arising outside the United Kingdom. Not all forms of investment income are included in the list, notable exceptions comprising income from letting property and company dividends.

A great deal of interest arising from sources in the United Kingdom will be received after deduction of income tax at the lower rate of 20 per cent. Although this interest is not taxable at the basic rate it remains chargeable at the starting rate of 10 per cent, the lower rate of 20 per cent or the higher rate of 40 per cent. Where such interest, when added to other income, excluding dividends, falls within the starting rate band tax will be due at 10 per cent. As tax will have been suffered by deduction at the lower rate of 20 per cent a repayment of the excess may well be obtained from the HM Revenue and Customs. To the extent that interest from savings when added to other income exceeds £2,090 but does not exceed £32,400, liability arises at the lower rate of 20 per cent. In those situations where income from savings when added to other income produces a combined total exceeding £32,400, liability arises at the higher rate of 40 per cent. As income tax will usually have been deducted at source at the rate of 20 per cent, higher rate liability arises at a further 20 per cent (40 per cent less 20 per cent).

Income from savings	Tax rate (2005–6) applied after personal allowances have been deducted
Most investment income	20%
Income from dividends up to the basic rate limit (£32,400)	10%
Income from dividends over the basic rate limit (£32,400)	32.5%

DIVIDENDS

Dividends and other distributions paid by a UK resident company have a tax credit attached equal to one-ninth of the sum received in 2005–6. Therefore, a recipient shareholder also residing in the UK who receives a cash dividend of £90 will have a tax credit of £10. The gross dividend or distribution (sum received plus tax credit) is regarded as having suffered income tax, equal to the tax credit, at the rate of 10 per cent. Where the shareholder is not liable, or not fully liable, to income tax it is not possible to claim a repayment of the tax credit. However, for 2005–6 dividends are taxed at the ordinary rate of 10 per cent or the upper rate of 32.5 per cent. Where the total income of an individual is not unduly substantial the amount of the tax credit, namely 10 per cent, will be offset against the ordinary rate of income tax, which is also 10 per cent, leaving no further liability. Should the gross amount of dividends or distributions when added to other taxable income exceed £32,400 the excess is chargeable at the upper rate of 32.5 per cent. The amount of the tax credit will then reduce tax otherwise payable at the upper rate. Although the rates of 10 per cent and 32.5 per cent apply primarily to dividends and distributions from United Kingdom companies, they also extend to income of a similar nature arising outside the UK.

INCOME NOT TAXABLE

Income which is not taxable in 2005–6 includes interest on National Savings and Investments saving certificates, most scholarship income, bounty payments to members of the armed services and annuities payable to the holders of certain awards. Dividend income arising from qualifying investments in personal equity plans (PEPs) and venture capital trusts is exempt from tax. Tax credits on dividends from such trusts cannot be recovered, nor has is it been possible for PEP managers to obtain repayment of credits since 5 April 2004. Payments made to an individual for the adoption of a child, together with income received under maintenance agreements and court orders made following separation or divorce will not be liable to tax. Nor will payments made under many deeds of covenant be recognised for tax purposes, unless the recipient is a charity. Interest arising on a tax exempt special savings account (TESSA) opened with a building society or bank will be exempt from tax if the account is maintained throughout a five-year period.

A popular investment, the individual savings account (ISA), is available to United Kingdom residents aged 18 years and over (16 and over for cash ISAs only). The ISA may have three components, namely cash, stocks and shares and life assurance. Interest on the cash component, usually comprising bank or building society deposits, is exempt from income tax. Dividends on most quoted holdings in the stocks and shares component are also immune from liability to income tax, with tax credits being repaid only for years up to and including that ending on 5 April 2004. Income and gains accruing to the provider of the life assurance component will be free of all liability to taxation.

A maximum subscription of £7,000 can be made by an individual to an ISA during 2005–6. Of this sum no more than £3,000 can be allocated to the cash component and £1,000 to the life assurance component. Potential investors are provided with the choice of whether to invest in a maxi-ISA or in mini-ISAs. Should a maxi-ISA be selected, the entire £7,000 can be invested in stocks and shares, but the use of a mini-ISA limits such an investment to £3,000 with the balance of £4,000 capable of being used to invest in the cash and life assurance components. The maximum permitted subscription of £7,000 per tax year was extended in the 2005 Budget until 2010.

Although new TESSA accounts can no longer be opened, where an existing TESSA matures at the end of a five-year period the capital (but not the income) proceeds can be separately invested in the cash component of an ISA. This is in addition to the normal limits governing investment in an ISA.

FOSTER CARERS

Profits arising to an individual from the provision of foster care are chargeable to income tax. Previously, the calculation of these taxable profits produced a great deal of uncertainty but a new arrangement was introduced for 2003–4 and future years. When determining the application of this arrangement for 2005–6, an individual must calculate two factors, namely:

(a) a fixed amount of £10,000 for a given residence in a year. Where the residence is shared by two or more individuals providing foster care the amount of £10,000 must be apportioned. Should the period of review fall short of a full twelve-month period, £10,000 must be suitably reduced.

(b) an amount per week for each foster child, comprising £200 per week for a child aged under 11 years and £250 per week for a child aged 11 or above.

Should the total receipts of an individual from the provision of foster care fall below the aggregate of (a) and (b) no liability to income tax will arise. However, should the receipts exceed the aggregate of (a) and (b) the individual is provided with a choice, namely:

(i)   to calculate profits in the normal way on total receipts less actual expenses and capital allowances, or

(ii) to treat as taxable profits the amount by which total receipts from the provision of foster care exceed the aggregate of (a) and (b), without any separate relief for expenses or capital allowances.

ALLOWANCES

Allowances which can be obtained for 2005–6 are shown below.

Personal allowance

Basic personal allowance	£4,895
Those over 64 on 5 April 2005	£7,090
Those over 74 on 5 April 2005	£7,220

The increased allowance for older individuals is available for those who died during the year of assessment but who would otherwise have achieved the appropriate age not later than 5 April 2006. The amount of the increased personal allowance for older taxpayers will be reduced by one-half of total income in excess of £19,500. This reduction in the allowance will continue until it has been reduced to the basic personal allowance of £4,895. The personal allowance is given as a deduction in calculating taxable income and may therefore produce relief at the rate of 10, 22 or 40 per cent, as appropriate.

Married couple's allowance

A married man who was 'living with' his wife at any time in the year ending on 5 April 2006 will be entitled to a married couple's allowance if at least one party to the marriage reached the age of 65 years before 6 April 2000. The allowance, which therefore applies only to those born before 6 April 1935, cannot be obtained where a husband or wife reaches 65 on some future date.

The allowance is £5,905. It may be increased to £5,975 where either party to the marriage was 75 or over on 5 April 2006. Where an individual would otherwise have reached the age of 75 by 5 April 2006 but who died earlier in the year, the increased allowance is given. The amount of the married couple's allowance will be reduced where the income of the husband (excluding the income of the wife) exceeds £19,500. In this situation the amount to be deducted from the allowance will comprise:

(a) one-half of the husband's total income in excess of £19,500, less

(b) the amount of any reduction made when calculating the husband's increased personal allowance.

This reduction in the married couple's allowance cannot reduce that allowance below a basic allowance of £2,280.

If husband and wife were married during 2005–6 the married couple's allowance must be reduced by one-twelfth for each complete month commencing on 6 April 2005 and preceding the date of marriage.

Unlike the personal allowance, the married couple's allowance does not reduce taxable income. Relief is granted by reducing the tax otherwise payable by 10 per cent of the allowance. For example, where the basic allowance of £2,280 is available, the amount of tax payable may be reduced by £228. Should the amount of the reduction exceed tax otherwise payable, no tax will be due, nor will any repayment arise.

In the absence of any further action, the married couple's allowance will be given to the husband. If he is unable to utilise all or any part of that allowance due to an absence of income, the husband may transfer the unused portion to his wife. The decision whether or not to transfer remains at the discretion of the husband. However, a wife may file an election to obtain one-half of the basic married couple's allowance of £2,280 as of right, leaving the husband with the balance of that allowance. Alternatively, the couple may jointly elect that the entire basic allowance should be allocated to the wife only. Should either spouse be unable to utilise his or her share of the total married couple's allowance the unused part may be transferred to the other spouse.

Blind person's allowance

An allowance of £1,610 is available to an individual if at any time during the year ending on 5 April 2006, he or she was registered as blind. If the individual is 'living with' a wife or husband, any unused part of the blind person's allowance can be transferred to the other spouse. The allowance reduces taxable income and may therefore give rise to relief at the taxpayer's highest rate of income tax suffered.

MAINTENANCE PAYMENTS

Relief for maintenance payments made in 2005–6 to a separated spouse or a divorced former spouse is limited to £2,200 or the amount of the payment, whichever is smaller. A further requirement before relief can be obtained is that at least one of the parties to the transaction had reached his/her 65th birthday before 6 April 2000. No relief is available to younger parties. Relief is given at the rate of 10 per cent and subtracted from the amount of tax otherwise due by the payer. The maintenance payment is exempt from liability to income tax in the hands of the recipient.

INTEREST

In some instances, interest paid by a business proprietor may be included when calculating trade profits chargeable to income tax. In addition, relief for interest paid on a loan applied to acquire or develop land and buildings for letting may be obtained by including the outlay in the calculation of income chargeable to tax. However, many private individuals cannot obtain relief in this manner and must satisfy stringent requirements before relief will be forthcoming. In general terms it is a requirement that before interest can qualify for relief it must be paid for a qualifying purpose. Relief will not be available to the extent that interest exceeds a reasonable commercial rate and no relief is forthcoming for interest on an overdraft.

Interest paid in 2005–6 which can be treated as laid out for a qualifying purpose will include the following payments:

(a) Interest on a loan used to acquire an interest in a close company or in a partnership, or to advance money to such a person or body

(b) Interest on a loan to a member of a partnership to acquire machinery or plant for use in the partnership business

(c) Interest on a loan to an employed person to acquire machinery or plant for the purposes of his or her employment

(d) Interest on a loan made for the purpose of contributing capital to an industrial co-operative

(e) Interest on a loan applied for investment in an employee-controlled company

(f) Interest on a loan to personal representatives to provide funds for the payment of inheritance tax

(g) Interest on a loan made to elderly persons for the purchase of an annuity where the loan is secured on land. If the loan exceeds £30,000, relief is limited to interest on this amount. This relief is restricted to income tax at the basic rate of 22 per cent. Whilst the relief remains for some borrowers, it cannot be obtained for interest only new loans taken out after 8 March 1999.

Relief under headings (a) to (f) is given by deducting interest from taxable income. This enables the taxpayer to obtain relief at his or her top rate of tax suffered.

CHARITABLE DONATIONS

A number of charitable donations qualify for tax relief and may involve donations of money or transferable assets. A popular arrangement is the Gift Aid scheme which requires the making of a money payment to a recognised charity. Providing that the donor receives little or no benefit in return, and certain formalities are complied with, the donation is then treated as a net sum paid after deducting income tax at the basic rate of 22 per cent. On the assumption that the donor suffers a sufficient amount of income tax at that rate, no additional income tax will be payable. However, if the donor suffers liability at the higher rate of 40 per cent, he or she may obtain relief for the outlay at the difference between the basic rate of 22 per cent and the higher rate of 40 per cent – 18 per cent – on the grossed up amount of the donation.

OTHER OUTGOINGS

Many employees pay contributions to an approved occupational pension scheme. The amount of their contributions may be deducted when calculating net taxable earnings treated as employment income. Relief should also be available for any additional voluntary contributions paid. Self-employed individuals and those receiving earnings not covered by an occupational pension scheme may contribute under personal pension scheme arrangements or under stakeholder schemes. Individuals may also pay premiums under retirement annuity schemes if the arrangements were concluded before 1 July 1988. Contributions paid under all headings and which do not exceed upper limits may obtain income tax relief by deduction from taxable income. Revised arrangements governing relief for pension contributions and the treatment of pension schemes are to be introduced on 6 April 2006.

MAXIMUM CONTRIBUTIONS TO A PERSONAL PENSION SCHEME (2005–6)

Age at start of tax year	Maximum percentage of net relevant earnings*
35 or less	17.5%
36–45	20%
46–50	25%
51–55	30%
56–60	35%
61–74	40%

*taxable income up to a maximum of £105,600 from employment or self-employment

MAXIMUM CONTRIBUTIONS TO AN OCCUPATIONAL PENSION SCHEME (2005–6)

Up to 15% of total employment remuneration up to a limit of £105,600

Subject to a maximum of £200,000 in 2005–6, the cost of subscribing for shares in an unquoted trading company or companies may qualify for relief under the Enterprise Investment Scheme. Many requirements must be satisfied before this relief can be obtained, but a husband and wife may each take advantage of the £200,000 maximum. Relief is given by reducing tax payable at the rate of 20 per cent of the share subscription cost. Further relief on an outlay up to a maximum of £200,000 annually is given at the increased rate of 40 per cent for a subscription of shares in a venture capital trust company. This increased rate applies only where shares are issued by such trusts after 5 April 2004 and not later than 5 April 2006 although the maximum investment limit continues beyond the latter date.

TAX CREDITS

Child tax credits and working tax credits are payable to qualifying individuals. Although the title of both credits incorporates the word 'tax', neither affects the amount of income tax payable or repayable. Both take the form of social security benefits.

CAPITAL GAINS TAX

An individual is potentially chargeable to capital gains tax on chargeable gains that accrue from disposals made by him/her during a year of assessment. The following information is largely confined to the year of assessment 2005–6, ending on 5 April 2006.

Liability extends to individuals who are either resident or ordinarily resident for the year but special rules apply where a person permanently leaves the UK or comes to this territory for the purpose of acquiring residence. Non-residents are not usually liable to CGT unless they carry on a business in the UK through a branch or agency. However, individuals who left the UK after 16 March 1998 and who have been resident or ordinarily resident in at least four of the seven years preceding departure may remain liable to CGT unless they reside overseas throughout a period of five complete tax years. Exceptions from this may apply where there is a disposal of assets acquired in the period of absence.

Trustees residing in the UK, together with personal representatives administering the estate of the deceased person, are chargeable to CGT at the flat rate of 40 per cent but chargeable gains accruing to companies are assessable to corporation tax.

In earlier years, CGT was chargeable on the net chargeable gains accruing to a person in a year of assessment after subtracting the annual exemption for that year. Net chargeable gains represented capital gains less capital losses arising from disposals carried out during the year. Unused losses brought forward from an earlier year could be offset against current net chargeable gains, but in the case of individuals were not to reduce the net gains below the annual exemption limit. It was possible to utilise trading losses against chargeable gains where those losses had not been offset against income.

TAPER RELIEF

However, the calculation of net gains chargeable to CGT is now governed by the availability of taper relief. The purpose of this relief, which replaced the former indexation allowance, is to require that only a percentage of gains become chargeable to CGT. Taper relief draws a distinction between business assets and non-business assets. The expression 'business asset' broadly identifies an asset used for business purposes in addition to some holdings of shares in both trading and non-trading companies. Where the nature of an asset has changed during the period of ownership from a business asset to a non-business asset, or vice versa, the asset must be effectively broken down into two parts. This may be particularly relevant where the period overlaps 5 April 2000, 5 April 2002 or 5 April 2003 when, on each occasion, some previously non-business assets were reclassified as business assets.

The percentage which must be used to calculate taper relief is governed by the number of complete years of ownership falling after 5 April 1998. Initially an additional 'bonus year' could be added for most assets acquired before 17 March 1998. This 'bonus year' continues to apply to non-business assets but has been withdrawn where the disposal of a business asset takes place after 5 April 2000.

The maximum percentage attributable to business assets was initially achieved after an ownership period extending throughout ten years but this period was reduced to one of four years only where the disposal occurred after 5 April 2000 and before 6 April 2002.

Finally, where the disposal of business assets takes place on and after 6 April 2002 the ownership period has been further reduced. Once that period exceeds one year only 50 per cent of the gain will be chargeable, falling to 25 per cent where two whole years are exceeded. No corresponding changes have been made to the ownership period of non-business assets, which has remained unchanged since the introduction of taper relief on 6 April 1998. The percentages of gains remaining chargeable for disposals taking place on and after 6 April 2003 are shown in the following table:

No. of whole years of ownership	Percentage of gain chargeable	
	Business assets	Non-Business assets
	%	%
1	50	100
2	25	100
3	25	95
4	25	90
5	25	85
6	25	80
7	25	75
8	25	70
9	25	65
10	25	60

If only chargeable gains arise from disposals carried out in 2005–6 the taper relief, if any, must be calculated by reference to each disposal. The aggregate sum of taper relief will then be subtracted from the total chargeable gains to produce the net gains for the year. Where disposals made in 2005–6 give rise to both gains and losses, the losses must be subtracted from the gains and taper relief calculated on the net sum remaining. It is necessary to allocate the losses between the gains where there are two or more disposals producing gains. Losses brought forward from an earlier year must also be subtracted when calculating the net gains qualifying for taper relief. However, the losses brought forward are not to reduce the net gains below the annual exemption limit of £8,500 which applies for 2005–6.

ANNUAL EXEMPTION

The initial slice of net gains arising in a tax year is exempt from liability to CGT. This slice, comprising the annual exemption, is £8,200 for 2004–5. Should any part of the exemption remain unused, this cannot be carried forward to a future year. A smaller exemption limit applies to most trusts.

RATES OF TAX

The net gains remaining, if any, calculated after subtracting the annual exemption, incur liability to capital gains tax for 2005–6. Although income tax rates are used for this purpose, liability arises only at the starting rate of 10 per cent, the lower rate of 20 per cent, the higher rate of 40 per cent, or a combination of the three rates. Unlike some income tax commitments, there is no liability at the basic rate of 22 per cent.

The first step is to calculate the amount of taxable income chargeable to income tax. This will include income from savings, company dividends and all other forms of taxable income. The second step is to add the amount of net chargeable gains to the taxable income chargeable to income tax. To the extent that this does not increase the aggregate total above £2,090, capital gains tax will be charged at the rate of 10 per cent. If the aggregate total exceeds £2,090 but does not exceed £32,400 any balance needed to reach £2,090 is chargeable at 10 per cent and the excess at 20 per cent. If, or to the extent that, any part of the chargeable gains exceed the limit of £32,400 the excess is chargeable at 40 per cent. Although some income tax rates are used, CGT remains an entirely separate tax. CGT for 2005–6 falls due for payment in full on 31 January 2007. If payment is delayed, interest or surcharges may be imposed.

HUSBAND AND WIFE
Independent taxation requires that a husband and wife 'living together' are separately assessed to CGT. Each spouse must independently calculate his or her gains and losses, with each entitled to the benefit of taper relief, if any, and the annual exemption of £8,500 for 2005–6. No liability to capital gains tax arises from the transfer of assets between husband and wife 'living together'.

DISPOSAL OF ASSETS
Before chargeable gains potentially liable to CGT can arise, a disposal or deemed disposal of an asset must take place. This occurs not only where assets are sold or exchanged but applies on the making of a gift. There is also a disposal of assets where any capital sum is derived from assets, e.g. where compensation is received for loss or damage to an asset. The date on which a disposal must be treated as having taken place will determine the year of assessment into which the chargeable gain or allowable loss falls. In those cases where a disposal is made under an unconditional contract, the time of disposal will be that when the contract was entered into and not the subsequent date of conveyance or transfer. A disposal under a conditional contract or option is treated as taking place when the contract becomes unconditional or the option is exercised. Disposals by way of gift are undertaken when the gift becomes effective.

VALUATION OF ASSETS
The amount received as consideration for the disposal of an asset will be the sum from which very limited outgoings must be deducted for the purpose of establishing the gain or loss. In cases where the consideration does not accurately reflect the value of the asset, a different basis must be used. This applies, in particular, where an asset is transferred by way of gift or otherwise than by a bargain made at arm's length. Such transactions are deemed to take place for a consideration representing market value, which will determine both the disposal proceeds accruing to the transferor and the cost of acquisition to the transferee.

Market value represents the price which an asset might reasonably be expected to fetch on a sale in the open market. In the case of unquoted shares or securities, it is to be assumed that the hypothetical purchaser in the open market would have available all the information which a prudent prospective purchaser of shares or securities might reasonably require if that person were proposing to purchase them from a willing vendor by private treaty and at arm's length. The market value of unquoted shares or securities will often be established following negotiations with the HM Revenue & Customs Shares Valuation Division. The valuation of land and interests in land in the UK will be dealt with by the District Valuer. Special rules apply to determine the market value of shares quoted on the Stock Exchange.

DEDUCTIONS FOR OUTGOINGS
Once the actual or notional disposal proceeds have been determined, it only remains to subtract eligible outgoings for the purpose of computing the gain or loss. There is the general rule that any outgoings deducted, or which are available to be deducted, when calculating income tax liability must be ignored. Subject to this, deductions will usually be limited to:
(a) the cost of acquiring the asset, together with incidental costs wholly and exclusively incurred in connection with the acquisition
(b) expenditure incurred wholly and exclusively on the asset in enhancing its value, being expenditure reflected in the state or nature of the asset at the time of the disposal, and any other expenditure wholly and exclusively incurred in establishing, preserving or defending title to, or a right over, the asset
(c) the incidental costs of making the disposal
Where the disposal concerns a leasehold interest having less than 50 years to run, any expenditure falling under (a) and (b) must be written off throughout the duration of the lease using a 'curved line' approach.

INDEXATION ALLOWANCE
For many years an indexation allowance could be inserted when calculating a gain on the disposal of an asset. The allowance was based on percentage increases in the retail prices index between the month of March 1982, or the month in which expenditure was incurred if later, and the month of disposal.

Taper relief has largely replaced the indexation allowance for disposals made after 5 April 1998. However, where an asset was acquired before this date, the indexation allowance will be calculated to the month of April 1998 and frozen. The frozen allowance then enters into the calculation of chargeable gain, if any, when the asset is disposed of at some later date. The adjustment for the indexation allowance must be made before calculating taper relief on the net sum remaining.

EXEMPTION
There is a general exemption from liability to CGT where the net gains of an individual for 2005–6 do not exceed £8,500. This general exemption applies separately to a husband and wife whether or not the parties are 'living together'. The disposal of many assets will not give rise to chargeable gains or allowable losses and these assets include:
(a) private motor cars
(b) government securities
(c) loan stock and other securities (but not shares)
(d) options and contracts relating to securities within (b) and (c)
(e) National Savings and Investments Certificates, Premium Bonds, Defence Bonds and National Development Bonds
(f) currency of any description acquired for personal expenditure outside the UK
(g) decorations awarded for valour
(h) betting wins and pools, lottery or games prizes
(i) compensation or damages for any wrong or injury suffered by an individual in his or her person, profession or vocation
(j) life assurance and deferred annuity contracts where the person making the disposal is the original beneficial owner
(k) dwelling-houses and land enjoyed with the residence which is an individual's only or main residence

(l)   tangible movable property, the consideration for the disposal of which does not exceed £6,000
(m)   certain tangible movable property which is a wasting asset having a life not exceeding 50 years
(n)   assets transferred to charities and other bodies
(o)   works of art, historic buildings and similar assets
(p)   assets used to provide maintenance funds for historic buildings
(q)   assets transferred to trustees for the benefit of employees
(r)   assets held in a Personal Equity Plan or Individual Savings Account

DWELLING HOUSE

Exemption from CGT will usually be available for any gain which accrues to an individual from the disposal of, or of an interest in, a dwelling-house or part of a dwelling-house which has been his or her only or main residence. The exemption extends to land which has been occupied and enjoyed with the residence as its garden or grounds. Some restriction may be necessary where the land exceeds half a hectare.

The gain will not be chargeable to CGT if the dwelling-house, or part, has been the individual's only or main residence throughout the period of ownership, or throughout the entire period except for all or any part of the final three years. A proportionate part of the gain will be exempt in other cases if the dwelling-house has been the individual's only or main residence for part only of the period of ownership. In the case of property acquired before 31 March 1982, the period of ownership is treated as commencing on this date. Where part of the dwelling-house has been used exclusively for business purposes, that part of the gain attributable to business use will not be exempt. In those cases where part of a qualifying dwelling-house has been used to provide rented residential accommodation, this non-personal use may frequently be ignored when calculating exemption from CGT, unless relatively substantial sums are involved. Dwellings occupied by dependent relatives, separated spouses or divorced former spouses, may also qualify for the exemption, but only where occupation commenced before 6 April 1988.

ROLL-OVER RELIEF

Persons carrying on business will often undertake the disposal of an asset and use the proceeds to finance the acquisition of a replacement asset. Where this situation arises, a claim for roll-over relief may be available. The broad effect of such a claim is that all or part of the gain arising on the disposal of the old asset may be disregarded. The gain or part is then subtracted from the cost of acquiring the replacement asset. As this cost is reduced, any gain arising from the future disposal of the replacement asset will be correspondingly increased, unless a further roll-over situation then develops.

It remains a requirement that both the old and the replacement asset must be used for the purpose of the taxpayer's business or for the purpose of business carried out by a company in which the taxpayer retains an interest. Relief will only be available if the acquisition of the replacement asset takes place within a period commencing twelve months before, and ending three years after, the disposal of the old asset, although the HM Revenue & Customs retains a discretion to extend this period where the circumstances were such that it was impossible for the taxpayer to acquire the replacement asset before the expiration of the normal time limit.

Whilst many business assets qualify for roll-over relief there are exceptions.

Roll-over relief may also be available where a gain arises on the disposal of land or buildings to an authority capable of exercising compulsory purchase powers. Similar relief may be forthcoming where shares in a company are transferred to trustees administering an employees' share incentive plan for the benefit of persons employed by that company or group of companies of which the company is a member.

DEFERRAL RELIEF

A form of roll-over relief, known as 'deferral relief' enables gains arising on the disposal of an asset to be matched, in whole or in part, with a subscription for shares in a restricted range of unquoted trading companies, including certain companies whose shares are dealt in on the Alternative Investment Market. Where matching can be achieved any part of the gain arising on disposal, not exceeding the cost of the qualifying share subscription, may become the subject of a claim. Unlike the usual form of roll-over relief, this claim for deferral relief does not eliminate or reduce the chargeable gain. It has the effect of deferring that gain until the time of some future event, which will usually be identified by the disposal of the newly acquired shares or the loss of UK residential status by the shareholder.

HOLD-OVER RELIEF — GIFTS

The gift of an asset is treated as a disposal made for a consideration equal to market value, with a corresponding acquisition by the transferee at an identical value. In the case of gifts made by individuals and a limited range of trustees to a transferee resident in the UK, a form of hold-over relief may be available. Relief, which must be claimed, is limited to the transfer of certain assets, including the following:

(a)   assets used for the purposes of a trade or similar activity carried on by the transferor or his/her personal company
(b)   shares or securities of a trading company which is not listed on a stock exchange
(c)   shares or securities of a trading company which is listed but which is the transferor's personal company
(d)   many interests in agricultural property qualifying for agricultural property relief for inheritance tax purposes
(e)   assets involved in transactions which are lifetime transfers for inheritance tax purposes, other than potentially exempt transfers

The transfer of shares or securities to a company is now precluded from obtaining relief. Restrictions may also arise where, after 10 December 2003, an individual transfers assets to trustees administering a trust in which the individual retains an interest or the assets transferred comprise a dwelling-house. Subject to these exceptions, the effect of a valid claim for hold-over relief is similar to that following a claim for roll-over relief on the disposal of business assets. However, adjustments may be necessary where some consideration is given for the transfer, or the asset has not been used for business purposes throughout the period of ownership, or not all assets of a company are used for business purposes.

DEATH

No CGT is chargeable on the value of assets retained by an individual at the time of death. However, the personal representatives administering the deceased's estate are deemed to acquire those assets for a consideration representing market value on death. This ensures that any increase in value occurring before the date of death will not be chargeable to CGT. If a legatee or other person acquires an asset under a will or intestacy no chargeable gain will accrue to the personal representatives, and the person taking the asset will also be treated as having acquired it at the time of death for its then market value.

INHERITANCE TAX

Liability to inheritance tax (IHT) may arise on a limited range of lifetime gifts and other dispositions and also on the value of assets retained, or deemed to be retained, at the time of death. An individual's domicile at the time of any gift or on death is an important matter. Domicile will generally be determined by applying normal rules, although special considerations may be necessary where an individual was previously domiciled in the UK but subsequently acquired a domicile of choice overseas. In addition, individuals who have been resident in the UK for at least 17 of the previous 20 years at the time of an event are treated as domiciled in the UK for this purpose. Where a person was domiciled, or treated as domiciled, in the UK at the time of a disposition or on death the location of assets is immaterial and full liability to IHT arises. Individuals domiciled outside the UK are, however, chargeable to IHT only on transactions or events affecting assets located in the UK. The assets of husband and wife are not merged for IHT purposes. Each spouse is treated as a separate individual entitled to receive the benefit of his or her exemptions, reliefs and rates of tax. Where husband and wife retain similar assets, e.g. shares in the same family company, special 'related property' provisions may require the merger of those assets for valuation purposes only.

LIFETIME GIFTS AND DISPOSITIONS

Gifts and dispositions made during lifetime fall under four broad headings, namely:
(a) dispositions which are not transfers of value
(b) exempt transfers
(c) potentially exempt transfers
(d) chargeable transfers

Dispositions which are not transfers of value
Several lifetime transactions are not treated as transfers of value and may be entirely disregarded for IHT purposes. These include transactions not intended to confer gratuitous benefit, the provision of family maintenance, the waiver of the right to receive remuneration or dividends, and the grant of agricultural tenancies for full consideration.

Exempt transfers
The main exempt transfers are:
Transfers between spouses – Transfers between husband and wife are usually exempt. However, if the transferor is, but the transferee spouse is not, domiciled in the UK, transfers will be exempt only to the extent that the total does not exceed £55,000. Unlike the requirement used for income tax and CGT purposes, it is immaterial whether husband and wife are living together.
Annual exemption – The first £3,000 of gifts and other dispositions made in a year ending on 5 April is exempt. If the exemption is not used, or not wholly used, in any year the balance may be carried forward to

the following year only. The annual exemption will only be available for a potentially exempt transfer if that transfer becomes chargeable by reason of the donor's subsequent death.
Small gifts – Outright gifts of £250 or less to any person in one year ending on 5 April are exempt.
Normal expenditure – A transfer made during lifetime and comprising normal expenditure is exempt. To obtain this exemption it must be shown that:
(a) the transfer was made as part of the normal expenditure of the transferer or;
(b) taking one year with another, the transfer was made out of income; and
(c) after allowing for all transfers of value forming part of normal expenditure the transferor was left with sufficient income to maintain his or her usual standard of living
Gifts in consideration of marriage – These are exempt if they satisfy certain requirements. The amount allowed will be governed by the relationship between the donor and a party to the marriage. The allowable amounts comprise:
(a) gifts by a parent, £5,000
(b) gifts by a grandparent, £2,500
(c) gifts by a party to the marriage, £2,500
(d) gifts by other persons, £1,000
Gifts to charities – These are exempt from liability.
Gifts to political parties – Gifts which satisfy certain requirements are generally exempt.
Gifts for national purposes – Gifts made to certain bodies are exempt from liability. These bodies include, among others, the National Gallery, the British Museum, the National Trust, the National Art Collections Fund, the National Heritage Memorial Fund, the Historic Buildings and Monuments Commission for England (English Heritage), any local authority, and any university or university college in the UK.
A number of other gifts made for the public benefit are also exempt.

Potentially exempt transfers
Lifetime gifts and dispositions which are neither to be ignored nor comprise exempt transfers incur possible liability to IHT. However, relief is available for a range of potentially exempt transfers. These comprise gifts made by an individual to:
(a) a second individual
(b) trustees administering an accumulation and maintenance trust
(c) trustees administering a disabled person's trust
The accumulation and maintenance trust mentioned in (b) must provide that on reaching a specified age, not exceeding 25 years, a beneficiary will become absolutely entitled to trust assets or obtain an interest in possession in the income from those assets. Additions to the above list affect settled property administered by trustees where an individual, or individuals, retain an interest in possession. The transfer of assets to, the removal of assets from, or the rearrangement of interests in such property comprise potentially exempt transfers if the person transferring an interest and the person benefiting from the transfer are both individuals.
No immediate liability to IHT will arise on the making of a potentially exempt transfer. Should the donor survive for a period of seven years, immunity from liability will be confirmed. However, the donor's death within the seven-year *inter vivos* period produces liability if the amounts involved are sufficiently substantial (*see* below).

Chargeable transfers

Any remaining lifetime gifts or dispositions which are neither to be ignored nor represent exempt transfers or potentially exempt transfers, incur liability to IHT.

GIFTS WITH RESERVATION

A lifetime gift of assets made at any time after 17 March 1986 may incur additional liability to IHT if the donor retains some interest in the subject matter of the gift. This may arise, for example, where a parent transfers a dwelling-house to a son or daughter and continues to occupy the property or to enjoy some benefit from that property. The retention of a benefit may be ignored where it is enjoyed in return for full consideration, perhaps a commercial rent, or where the benefit arises from changed circumstances which could not have been foreseen at the time of the original gift. The gift with reservation provisions will not usually apply to most exempt transfers.

There are three possibilities which may arise where the donor reserves or enjoys some benefit from the subject matter of a previous gift and subsequently dies, namely:

(a) if no benefit is enjoyed within a period of seven years before death there can be no further liability

(b) if the benefit ceased to be enjoyed within a period of seven years before the date of death, the original donor is deemed to have made a potentially exempt transfer representing the value of the asset at the time of cessation

(c) if the benefit is enjoyed at the time of death, the value of the asset must be included when arriving at the value of the deceased's estate on death

It must be emphasised that the existence of a benefit enjoyed at any time within a period of seven years before death will establish liability to tax on gifts with reservation, notwithstanding that the gift may have been made many years earlier, providing it was undertaken after 17 March 1986.

DEATH

Immediately before the time of death an individual is deemed to make a transfer of value. This transfer will comprise the value of assets forming part of the deceased's estate after subtracting most liabilities. Any exempt transfers may, however, be excluded. These include transfers for the benefit of a surviving spouse, a charity and a qualifying political party, together with bequests to approved bodies and for national purposes.

Death may also trigger three additional liabilities:

(a) A potentially exempt transfer made within the period of seven years ending on death loses its potential status and becomes chargeable to IHT

(b) The value of gifts made with reservation may incur liability if any benefit was enjoyed within a period of seven years preceding death

(c) Additional tax may become payable for chargeable lifetime transfers made within seven years before death

VALUATIONS

The valuation of assets establishes the value transferred for lifetime dispositions and also the value of a person's estate at the time of death. The value of property will represent the price which might reasonably be expected from a sale in the open market.

In some cases it may be necessary to incorporate the value of 'related property'. This will include property comprised in the estate of the transferor's spouse and certain property previously transferred to charities. The purpose of the related property valuation rules is not to add the value of the property to the estate of the transferor. Related property must be merged to establish the aggregate value of the respective interests and this value is then apportioned, usually on a *pro rata* basis, to the separate interests.

The value of shares and securities listed on the Stock Exchange will be determined by extracting figures from the daily list of official prices.

Where quoted shares and securities are sold or the quotation is suspended within a period of 12 months following the date of death, a claim may be made to substitute the proceeds or subsequent value for the value on death. This claim will only be beneficial if the gross proceeds realised are lower or the value has fallen below market value at the time of death. A similar claim may be available for interests in land sold within a period of four years following death.

RELIEF FOR SELECTED ASSETS

Special relief is made available for certain assets as follows:

Woodlands

Where woodlands pass on death the value will usually be included in the deceased's estate. However, an election may be made in respect of land in the UK on which trees or underwood is growing to delete the value of those assets. Relief is confined to the value of trees or underwood and does not extend to the land on which they are growing. Liability to IHT will arise if and when the trees or underwood are subsequently sold.

Agricultural property

Relief is available for the agricultural value of agricultural property. Such property must be occupied and used for agricultural purposes and relief is confined to the agricultural value only.

The value transferred, either on a lifetime gift or on death, must be determined. This value may then be reduced by a percentage. For events taking place after 9 March 1992, a 100 per cent deduction will be available if the transferor retained vacant possession or could have obtained that possession within a period of 12 months following the transfer. In other cases, notably including land let to tenants, a lower deduction of 50 per cent is usually available. However, this lower deduction may be increased to 100 per cent if the letting was made after 31 August 1995.

It remains a requirement that the agricultural property was either occupied by the transferor for the purposes of agriculture throughout a two-year period ending on the date of the transfer, or was owned by him or her throughout a period of seven years ending on that date and also occupied for agricultural purposes.

Business property

Where the value transferred is attributable to relevant business property, that value may be reduced by a percentage. The reduction in value applies to:

(a) property consisting of a business or an interest in a business (i.e. a partnership)

(b) securities of an unquoted company which, together with any unquoted shares in the same company provided the transferor with control

(c) other unquoted shares in a company

(d) shares or securities of a quoted company which provided the transferor with control

(e) any land, building, machinery or plant which, immediately before the transfer, was used wholly or mainly for the purposes of a business carried on by a company of which the transferor had control

(f) any land, building, machinery or plant which, immediately before the transfer, was used wholly or mainly for the purposes of a business carried on by a partnership of which the transferor was a partner

(g) any land, building, machinery or plant which, immediately before the transfer, was used wholly or mainly for the purposes of a business carried on by the transferor and was then settled property in which he/she retained an interest in possession

The percentage deduction has changed from time to time but for events occurring after 5 April 1996, a deduction of 100 per cent is available for assets falling within (a), (b) and (c). A deduction of 50 per cent remains for assets within (d) to (g).

It is a general requirement that the property must have been retained for a period of two years before the transfer or death and restrictions may be necessary if the property has not been used wholly for business purposes. The same property cannot obtain both business property relief and the relief available for agricultural property.

CALCULATION OF TAX PAYABLE

The calculation of IHT payable adopts the use of a cumulative total. Each chargeable lifetime transfer is added to the total with a final addition made on death. The top slice added to the total for the current event determines the rate at which IHT must be paid. However, the cumulative total will only include transfers made within a period of seven years before the current event and those undertaken outside this period must be excluded.

Lifetime chargeable transfers

The value transferred by the limited range of lifetime chargeable transfers must be added to the seven-year cumulative total to calculate whether any IHT is due. Should the nil rate band be exceeded, tax will be imposed on the excess at the rate of 20 per cent. However, if the donor dies within a period of seven years from the date of the chargeable lifetime transfer, additional tax may be due. This is calculated by applying tax at the full rate or 40 per cent in substitution for the rate of 20 per cent previously used. The amount of tax is then reduced to a percentage by applying tapering relief. This percentage is governed by the number of years from the date of the lifetime gift to the date of death, as follows:

Period of years before death

Not more than 3	100%
More than 3 but not more than 4	80%
More than 4 but not more than 5	60%
More than 5 but not more than 6	40%
More than 6 but not more than 7	20%

Should this exercise produce liability greater than that previously paid at the 20 per cent rate on the lifetime transfer, additional tax, representing the difference, must be discharged. Where the calculation shows an amount falling below tax paid on the lifetime transfer, no additional liability can arise nor will the shortfall become repayable.

Tapering relief will, of course, only be available if the calculation discloses a liability to IHT. There can be no liability to the extent that the lifetime transfer falls within the nil rate band.

Potentially exempt transfers

Where a potentially exempt transfer loses immunity from liability due to the donor's death within the seven-year *inter vivos* period, the value transferred by that transfer enters into the cumulative total. Any liability to IHT will be calculated by applying the full rate of 40 per cent, reduced to the percentage governed by tapering relief if the original transfer occurred more than three years before death. Liability can only arise to the extent, if any, that the nil rate band is exceeded.

Death

The final addition to the seven-year cumulative total will comprise the value of an estate on death. IHT will be calculated by applying the full rate of 40 per cent to the extent the nil rate band is exceeded. No tapering relief can be obtained.

RATES OF TAX

In earlier times there were several rates of IHT which progressively increased as the value transferred grew in size. However, since 1988 there have been only three rates, namely:

(a) a nil rate

(b) a lifetime rate of 20 per cent

(c) a full rate of 40 per cent

The nil rate band usually changes on an annual basis and for events taking place after 5 April 2005 applies to the first £275,000. Any excess over this level is taxable at 20 per cent or 40 per cent as the case may be. The IHT threshold will be increased to £285,000 for 2006–7 and to £300,000 for 2007–8.

PAYMENT OF TAX

IHT usually falls due for payment six months after the end of the month in which the chargeable transaction takes place. Where a transfer other than that made on death occurs after 5 April and before the following 1 October, tax falls due on the following 30 April, although there are some exceptions to this. IHT attributable to the transfer of certain land, controlling shareholding interests, unquoted shares, businesses and interests in businesses, together with agricultural property, may usually be satisfied by instalments spread over ten years. Except in the case of non-agricultural land, where interest is charged on outstanding instalments, no liability to interest arises where tax is paid on the due date. In all cases, delay in the payment of tax may incur a liability to discharge interest.

SETTLED PROPERTY

Complex rules apply to establish IHT liability on settled property. Where a person is beneficially entitled to an interest in possession, that person is effectively deemed to own the property in which the interest subsists. It follows that where the interest comes to an end during the beneficiary's lifetime and some other person becomes entitled to the property or interest, the beneficiary is treated as having made a transfer of value. However, this will usually comprise a potentially exempt transfer incurring no immediate liability. In addition, no liability will arise where the property vests in the absolute ownership of the beneficiary retaining the interest in possession. The death of a person entitled to an interest in possession will require the value of the underlying property to be added to the value of the deceased's estate.

In the case of other settled property where there is no interest in possession (e.g. discretionary trusts), liability to tax will arise on each ten-year anniversary of the trust. There will also be liability if property ceases to be held on discretionary trusts before the first ten-year anniversary date is reached or between anniversaries. The rate of tax suffered will be governed by several considerations, including previous dispositions made by the settlor of the trust, transactions concluded by the trustees, and the period throughout which property has been held in trust.

Accumulation and maintenance settlements which require assets to be distributed, or interests in income to be created, not later than a beneficiary's 25th birthday may be exempt from any liability to IHT.

CORPORATION TAX

Profits, gains and income accruing to companies resident in the UK incur liability to corporation tax. Non-resident companies are immune from this tax unless they carry on a trade in the UK through a permanent establishment, branch or office. Companies residing outside the UK may be liable to income tax at the basic rate on other income arising in the UK, perhaps from letting property. The following comments are confined to companies resident in the UK. Liability to corporation tax is governed by the profits, gains or income for an accounting period. This is usually the period for which financial accounts are made up, and in the case of companies preparing accounts to the same accounting date annually will comprise successive periods of 12 months.

RATE OF TAX
The amount of profits or income for an accounting period must be determined on normal taxation principles. The special rules which apply to individuals where a source of income is acquired or discontinued are ignored and consideration is confined to the actual profits or income for an accounting period.

The rate of corporation tax is fixed for a financial year ending on 31 March. Where the accounting period of a company overlaps this date and there is a change in the rate of corporation tax, profits and income must be apportioned.

The main rate of corporation tax for each of the five financial years ending on the 31 March 2000 to 31 March 2007 inclusive is 30 per cent. This may be reduced to a lower level where profits fall within the small companies' rate or companies' starting rate bands. Although the main rate of tax for the year ending on 31 March 2007 is known in advance, the small companies rate and the starting rate for the same year will not be announced until a later date.

SMALL COMPANIES' RATE
Where the profits of a company do not exceed stated limits, corporation tax becomes payable at the small companies' rate. This may be replaced by a lower starting rate where profits are very small, as discussed later. It is the amount of profits and not the size of the company which governs the application of both the small companies' rate and the starting rate.

For each of the three financial years ending on 31 March 2000, 31 March 2001 and 31 March 2002 the small companies' rate remained at 20 per cent. It was then reduced to 19 per cent for ensuing years and remains so for the year ending 31 March 2006.

The level of profits which a company may derive without losing the benefit of the small companies' rate is £300,000. However, if profits exceed £300,000 but fall below £1,500,000, marginal small companies' rate relief applies. The effect of marginal relief is that the average rate of corporation tax imposed on all profits steadily increases from the lower small companies' rate of 19 per cent (or previously 20 per cent) to the main rate of 30 per cent, with tax being imposed on profits in the margin at an increased rate. Where a change in the rate of tax is introduced and the accounting period of a company overlaps 31 March, profits must be apportioned to establish the appropriate rate for each part of those profits.

The lower limit of £300,000 and the upper limit of £1,500,000 apply to a period of 12 months and must be proportionately reduced for shorter periods. Some restriction in the small companies' rate and the marginal rate may be necessary if there are two or more associated companies, namely companies under common control.

The small companies' rate is not available for close investment holding companies.

COMPANIES' STARTING RATE
A companies' starting rate of zero is available where profits of a twelve-month period do not exceed £10,000, with marginal relief where profits exceed this figure but are not in excess of £50,000. The effect of marginal relief is to increase the average rate of tax suffered until it reaches the small companies' rate for the same financial year. The profits limits may be reduced for a company which is part of a group or has associated companies. The starting rate and marginal relief does not apply to close investment holding companies.

PAYMENT OF TAX
Corporation tax charged on profits for an accounting period usually falls due for payment in a single lump sum nine months after the end of that period. Most companies discharge corporation tax on this basis but other arrangements concern large companies for accounting periods ending on or after 1 July 1999. These companies must discharge their liability by four instalments. The receipt of annual profits amounting to £1,500,000 or more is sufficient to identify a large company. Where a company is a member of a group the profits of the entire group must be merged to establish whether the company is large.

CAPITAL GAINS
Chargeable gains arising to a company are calculated in a manner similar to that used for individuals. However, the withdrawal of the indexation allowance after April 1998, and the introduction of taper relief from the same date, have no application to companies. Nor are companies entitled to the annual exemption of £8,500. However, many gains arising to companies from the disposal of substantial shareholdings after 31 March 2002 are exempt from tax. Companies do not suffer CGT on chargeable gains but incur liability to corporation tax. Tax is due on the full chargeable gain of an accounting period after subtracting relief for losses, if any.

DISTRIBUTIONS
Dividends and other qualifying distributions made by a UK resident company on or after 6 April 1999 are not satisfied after deduction of income tax. Similar outgoings made by a company previously required the payment of advance corporation tax but this obligation no longer applies. The only effect which the payment of a dividend or the making of a distribution now has on a company is

that the outlay cannot form an ingredient in the calculation of profits.

INTEREST

On making many payments of interest a company is required to deduct income tax at the lower rate of 20 per cent and account for the tax deducted to the HM Revenue and Customs. The gross amount of interest paid will usually be included in the calculation of profits on which corporation tax becomes payable. The requirement to deduct tax will not usually apply where payments are being made to a second company.

GROUPS OF COMPANIES

Each company within a group is separately charged to corporation tax on profits, gains and income. However, where one group member realises a loss for which special rules apply, other than a capital loss, a claim may be made to offset the deficiency against profits of some other member of the same group.

The transfer of capital assets from one member of a group to a fellow member will usually incur no liability to tax on chargeable gains.

SPORTS CLUBS

Corporation tax is payable by 'companies', an expression which includes unincorporated associations. It follows that most clubs must be treated as companies potentially liable to corporation tax. However, a substantial exemption from liability is available to qualifying registered community amateur sports clubs. Since April 2002 registered clubs have been exempt from liability to corporation tax on:

(a) trading profits if turnover does not exceed £15,000 in a twelve-month period;
(b) bank and building society interest;
(c) income from property where gross rental income does not exceed £10,000 in a twelve-month period; and
(d) chargeable gains

The limit in (a) was doubled to £30,000 and that in (c) to £20,000 from 1 April 2004.

Among other advantages available to registered clubs is that donations may be received under the Gift Aid arrangements. Charities are also generally exempt from corporation tax where they operate through a company structure.

COMPLIANCE

For several years a 'pay and file' system affected all companies. A feature of this system required that tax should be payable nine months following the end of the accounting period involved, with accounts and returns being submitted three months later. This system was replaced following the introduction of self-assessment which extends to all companies for accounting periods ending after 30 June 1999.

Self-assessment requires that the corporation tax return should normally be submitted not later than 12 months following the end of the accounting period to which it relates. In addition, a copy of the financial accounts must be included. Failure to file the return within the appropriate time limit will incur a liability to penalties.

VALUE ADDED TAX

Value added tax (VAT) is charged on the value of the supplies made by a registered trader and extends to both the supply of goods and the supply of services. Throughout it has been administered by Customs and Excise which merged with the Inland Revenue on 1 September 2004 to form HM Revenue & Customs. Liability to account for VAT also arises on the value of goods imported into the UK from sources outside the European Community. In contrast goods imported by a trader from a second trader in a member state of the European Community attract no VAT on importation. Instead there is an acquisition tax whereby a trader who acquires goods must include the acquisition in his normal VAT return and account for the tax due. A UK trader who exports goods to a member state will not be required to account for VAT on the supply, if that trader observes the requirements laid down by regulations.

REGISTRATION

All traders, including professional persons and companies, making taxable supplies of a value exceeding stated limits are required to register for VAT purposes. Taxable supplies represent the supply of goods and services potentially chargeable with VAT. The limits which govern mandatory registration are amended periodically, and from 1 April 2005 an unregistered trader must register:

(a) at any time, if there are reasonable grounds for believing that the value of taxable supplies in the next 30 days will exceed £60,000
(b) at the end of any month if the value of taxable supplies in the 12 months then ending has exceeded £60,000.

Where the limits governing mandatory registration have been exceeded, the trader must notify HM Revenue & Customs. In the event of failure to provide prompt notification, the person concerned will be required to account for VAT from the proper registration date. A trader whose taxable supplies do not reach the mandatory registration limits may apply for voluntary registration. This step may be thought advisable to recover input tax or to compete with other registered traders.

A registered trader may submit an application for deregistration if the value of taxable supplies subsequently falls. From 1 April 2005, an application for deregistration can be made if the value of taxable supplies for the year beginning on the application date is not expected to exceed £58,000.

INPUT TAX

A registered trader will both suffer tax (input tax) when obtaining goods or services for the purposes of his business and also become liable to account for tax (output tax) on the value of goods and services which he or she supplies. Relief can usually be obtained for input tax suffered, either by setting that tax against output tax due or by repayment. Most items of input tax can be relieved in this manner. Where a registered trader makes both exempt supplies and taxable supplies to his customers or clients, there may be some restriction in the amount of input tax which can be recovered.

OUTPUT TAX

When making a taxable supply of goods or services, a registered trader must account for output tax, if any, on the value of the supply. Usually the price charged by the registered trader will be increased by adding VAT but failure to make the required addition will not remove liability to account for output tax. The liability to account for output tax, and also relief for input tax, may be affected where a trader is using a special second-hand goods scheme.

EXEMPT SUPPLIES

No VAT is chargeable on the supply of goods or services which are treated as exempt supplies. These include the provision of burial and cremation facilities, insurance, finance and education. The granting of a lease to occupy land or the sale of land will usually comprise an exempt supply, but there are numerous exceptions. In particular, the sale of new non-domestic buildings or certain buildings used by charities cannot be treated as exempt supplies. A taxable person may elect to tax rents and other supplies relating to buildings and agricultural land not used for residential or charitable purposes. Exempt supplies do not enter into the calculation of taxable supplies which governs liability to mandatory registration. Such supplies made by a registered trader may, however, limit the amount of input tax which can be relieved. It is for this reason that the election may be useful.

RATES OF TAX

Two main rates of VAT have applied for many years, namely:
(a)   a zero, or nil, rate
(b)   a standard rate of 17.5 per cent
In addition, a special reduced rate of 5 per cent applies to a limited range of supplies including domestic fuels, installation of energy saving materials in domestic premises and children's car seats.

ZERO-RATING

A large number of supplies are zero-rated. The following list is not exhaustive but indicates the wide range of supplies which may be included under this heading:
(a)   the supply of many items of food and drink. This does not include ice creams, chocolates, sweets, potato crisps and alcoholic drinks. Nor does it extend to supplies made in the course of catering or to items supplied for consumption in a restaurant or café. Whilst the supply of cold items, e.g. sandwiches for consumption away from the supplier's premises, is zero-rated, the supply of hot food, e.g. fish and chips, is not
(b)   animal feeding stuffs
(c)   sewerage and water, unless for industrial purposes
(d)   books, brochures, pamphlets, leaflets, newspapers, maps and charts
(e)   talking books for the blind and handicapped, and wireless sets for the blind
(f)   supplies of services, other than professional services, when constructing a new domestic building or a building to be used by a charity. The supply of materials for such a building is zero-rated, together with the sale or the grant of a long lease. Alterations to some protected buildings are zero-rated
(g)   the transportation of persons in a vehicle, ship or aircraft designed to carry not less than 10 persons
(h)   supplies of drugs, medicines and other aids for the handicapped
(i)   supplies of children's clothing and footwear
(j)   supplies of pedal cycle helmets
(k)   exports
Although no tax is due on a zero-rated supply, this does comprise a taxable supply which must be included in the calculation governing liability to register.

COLLECTION OF TAX

Registered traders submit VAT returns for accounting periods usually of three months in duration but arrangements can be made to submit returns on a monthly basis. Very large traders must account for tax on a monthly basis but this does not affect the three-monthly return. The return will show both the output tax due for supplies made by the trader in the accounting period and also the input tax for which relief is claimed. If the output tax exceeds input tax the balance must be remitted with the VAT return. Where input tax suffered exceeds the output tax due the registered trader may claim recovery of the excess from HM Revenue & Customs.

This basis for collecting tax explains the structure of VAT. Where supplies are made between registered traders the supplier will account for an amount of tax which will usually be identical to the tax recovered by the person to whom the supply is made. However, where the supply is made to a person who is not a registered trader there can be no recovery of input tax and it is on this person that the final burden of VAT eventually falls.

Where goods are acquired by a UK trader from a supplier within a member state of the European Community, the trader must also account for the tax due on acquisition.

An optional annual accounting scheme is available for registered traders having an annual turnover of taxable supplies not exceeding £660,000. Traders joining the scheme may render returns annually. Nine interim payments of VAT will be made on account with a final balancing payment accompanying submission of the return. The number of interim payments may be reduced if turnover is small. Once a trader has joined the annual accounting scheme membership may continue until the annual taxable turnover reaches £825,000.

A further optional scheme, the flat rate scheme, is available to small businesses having an annual taxable turnover not exceeding £150,000 and whose total turnover including both exempt and other non-taxable income does not exceed £187,500 annually. Businesses able to satisfy these requirements may discharge VAT calculating a flat rate percentage of their total turnover. The rate used is governed by the trade sector into which the business falls. The scheme can no longer be used once turnover exceeds £225,000.

BAD DEBTS

Many retailers operate special retail schemes for calculating the amount of VAT due. These schemes are based on the volume of consideration received in an accounting period. Should a customer fail to pay for goods or services supplied, there will be no consideration on which to calculate VAT.

To avoid the problem of bad debts incurred by traders not operating a special retail scheme, an optional system of cash accounting is available. This scheme, confined to traders with annual taxable supplies not exceeding £660,000, enables returns to be made on a cash basis, in substitution for the normal supply basis. Traders using such a scheme will not include bad debts in the calculation of cash receipts. Use of the scheme will be discontinued once annual taxable turnover reaches £825,000.

Where neither the cash accounting arrangements nor a special retail scheme applies, output tax falls due on the value of the supply and liability is not affected by failure to receive consideration. However, where a debt is more than six months old, relief for bad debts will be forthcoming. The calculation of the six-month period commences from the date on which payment for the supply falls due. In those cases where a supplier obtains relief for a bad debt, the person to whom the supply has been made must refund any input tax relief which may have been granted.

OTHER SPECIAL SCHEMES

In addition to the schemes for retailers, there are several special schemes applied to calculate the amount of VAT due and which also limit the ability to recover input tax. These include, for example, a special flat rate scheme for farmers who fulfil certain conditions.

STAMP DUTY

For the majority of people, contact with stamp duty arises when they purchase a property. Stamp duty is payable by the buyer as a way of raising revenue for the government based on the purchase price of a property, stocks and shares. This section aims to provide a broad overview of stamp duty as it may affect the average person. For comprehensive information, please consult a specialist publication or contact HM Revenue & Customs.

STAMP DUTY LAND TAX

Stamp duty land tax was introduced on 1 December 2003 and covers the purchase of houses, flats and other land, buildings and certain leases in the UK. The law was changed primarily to reduce tax avoidance in high-value commercial transactions while at the same time reducing the burden on small businesses and modernising the administration of tax for individuals. Under the new system, stamp duty on transactions involving property other than land, shares and interests in partnerships is abolished, removing many transactions from a tax burden.

Before 1 December 2003, purchasers of property had to submit documents providing all details of the purchase to the Stamp Office for 'stamping'. The purchaser's solicitor or licensed conveyancer would then send the stamped documentation to the appropriate land registry to register ownership of the property. Under stamp duty land tax, purchasers do not have to send documents for stamping – instead, a land transaction return form (SDLT1), which contains all information regarding the purchase that is relevant to HM Revenue & Customs, is signed by the purchaser. Buyers of property are responsible for completing the land transaction return and payment of stamp duty. It is generally the case, however, that a solicitor or licensed conveyancer acting for a buyer in a land transaction will complete the relevant paperwork.

Once the HM Revenue & Customs has received the completed land transaction return and the payment of any stamp duty due, a certificate will be issued which enables a solicitor or licensed conveyancer to register the property in the new owner's name at the Land Registry.

RATES OF STAMP DUTY LAND TAX

The stamp duty rates for buying a residential property (freehold or leasehold) are the same as under the pre-1 December 2003 system. The following table shows the rates of stamp duty land tax that apply on a purchase price. The most startling change for 2005, welcomed by many first-time buyers, was the doubling of the threshold from £60,000 to £120,000 below which no stamp duty is payable on residential property purchases. The new threshold took effect from 17 March 2005.

Purchase Price	Rate of Tax (% of purchase price)
£120,000 or less*	0%
£120,001 to £250,000	1%
£250,001 to £500,000	3%
£500,001 or more	4%

*For transactions of non-residential land and property, the zero per cent rate applies for purchases of up to £150,000. A 1 per cent rate is payable for transactions of £150,001–£250,000; thereafter, rates are as per residential property transactions. The zero per cent band for residential property transactions in certain Designated Disadvantaged Areas remains at £150,000, but a previous exemption for non-residential transactions in Designated Disadvantaged Areas ended on 16 March 2005.

When assessing how much stamp duty is payable, the entire purchase price must be taken into account. For example, on a property bought for £300,000, 3 per cent of the total price – £9,000 – is payable.

There are special rates for the rental element of leases. Since 1 December 2003, the charges have followed modern commercial practice in valuing the rent payable over the term of the lease at its net present value (NPV). There is a single rate of tax of 1 per cent of the amount by which the NPV of rental payments exceeds the threshold of £120,000 (residential property) or £150,000 (non-residential property). Where the NPV of a property is less than £120,000 (residential) or £150,000 (non-residential), no stamp duty is payable on the rental element.

FIXTURES AND CHATTELS

As well as buying property a purchaser may buy things inside the property. Some of these are, in law, part of the land. They are called 'fixtures'. Examples are fitted kitchen units and bathroom suites. Because these fixtures are part of the land, any price paid on them must be taken into account for stamp duty purposes. Other things inside a property are not part of the land, eg free-standing cookers, curtains and fitted carpets. These are called 'chattels' and are not chargeable to stamp duty. However, where both a property and chattels are purchased, the amount shown on the land transaction return form as the purchase price must be a 'just and reasonable' apportionment of the total amount paid. As with other entries on the form the purchaser is responsible for the accuracy of this information.

STAMP DUTY RESERVE TAX

Stamp duty or stamp duty reserve tax (SDRT) is paid at the rate of 0.5 per cent when shares are purchased. Stamp duty is payable when the shares are transferred using a stock transfer form, whereas SDRT is payable on 'paperless' share transactions (where the shares are transferred electronically without using a stock transfer form. Most share transactions nowadays and settled by stock brokers through CREST (the electronic settlement and registration system). CREST automatically deducts the SDRT and sends it to the HM Revenue and Customs. The buyer's stock broker will settle up with CREST for the cost of the shares and the SDRT and the bill the buyer for these and the broker's fees. SDRT therefore now accounts for the majority of taxation collected on share transactions effected through the London Stock Exchange.

The flat rate of 0.5 is based on the amount paid for the shares, not what they are worth. If they have been transferred for free, no SDRT is payable, whatever the value of the shares. A higher 1.5 per cent rate is paid if the shares are transferred into a 'depositary receipt scheme' or a 'clearance service'. These are special arrangements where the shares are held by a third party and can be traded free of stamp duty or SDRT.

If the shares are not bought through CREST, it is the buyer's responsibility to pay the stamp duty to HM Revenue and Customs. UK stamp duty is not payable on foreign shares, but there may be foreign taxes to pay.

SDRT is already accounted for in the price of units in unit trusts or shares in open-ended investment companies.

HELP AND INFORMATION

For further information on stamp duty land tax contact the taxes enquiry line on 0845-603 0135 or visit the HM Revenue and Customs website at www.hmrc.gov.uk, where a stamp duty calculator for both shares and land and property can be found. For information on SDRT contact HM Revenue and Customs on 01903-509 469/471/961. For buyers wishing to undertake their own conveyancing, copies of the land transaction return (SDLT1) and guidance notes (SDLT6) can be obtained by contacting 0845-302 1472.

LEGAL NOTES

These notes outline certain aspects of the law as they might affect the average person. They are intended only as a broad guideline and are by no means definitive. The law is constantly changing so expert advice should always be taken. In some cases, sources of further information are given in these notes.

It is always advisable to consult a solicitor without delay; timely advice will set your mind at rest but sitting on your rights can mean that you lose them. Anyone who does not have a solicitor already can contact the following for assistance in finding one: Citizens Advice Bureau (W www.nacab.org.uk), the Community Legal Service (W www.legalservices.gov.uk), the Law Society of England and Wales (113 Chancery Lane, London WC2A 1PL T 020-7242 1222 W www.lawsociety.co.uk), or the Law Society of Scotland (26 Drumsheugh Gardens, Edinburgh EH3 7YR T 0131-226 7411 W www.lawscot.org.uk).

The community legal service fund and legal aid and assistance schemes exist to make the help of a lawyer available to those who would not otherwise be able to afford one. Entitlement depends on an individual's means but a solicitor or Citizens Advice Bureau will be able to advise about entitlement.

ABORTION

Under the provisions of the Abortion Act 1967, a legally induced abortion must be:
- performed by a registered medical practitioner
- carried out in an NHS hospital or other approved premises
- certified by two registered medical practitioners as justified on one or more of the following grounds:

(a) that the pregnancy has not exceeded its twenty-fourth week and that the continuance of the pregnancy would involve risk, greater than if the pregnancy were terminated, of injury to the physical or mental health of the pregnant woman or any existing children of her family

(b) that the termination is necessary to prevent grave permanent injury to the physical or mental health of the pregnant woman

(c) that the continuance of the pregnancy would involve risk to the life of the pregnant woman, greater than if the pregnancy were terminated

(d) that there is a substantial risk that if the child were born it would suffer from such physical or mental abnormalities as to be seriously handicapped

In determining whether the continuance of a pregnancy would involve such risk of injury to health as is mentioned in grounds (a) or (b), account may be taken of the pregnant woman's actual or reasonably foreseeable environment.

The requirements relating to the opinion of two registered medical practitioners and to the performance of the abortion at an NHS hospital or other approved place cease to apply in circumstances where a registered medical practitioner is of the opinion, formed in good faith, that a termination is immediately necessary to save the life, or to prevent grave permanent injury to the physical or mental health, of the pregnant woman.

Further information and advice can be obtained from:

FAMILY PLANNING ASSOCIATION (UK)
2–12 Pentonville Road, London N1 9FP T 0845-310 1334

FAMILY PLANNING ASSOCIATION (SCOTLAND)
Unit 10, Firhill Business Centre, 76 Firhill Road, Glasgow G20 7BA T 0141-576 5088

BRITISH PREGNANCY ADVISORY SERVICE (BPAS)
T 08457-304030 W www.bpas.org

ADOPTION OF CHILDREN

The Adoption and Children Act 2002 (in this section, the Act) reforms the framework for domestic and intercountry adoption in England and Wales and some parts of it extend to Scotland and Northern Ireland. This section deals with the Act which, at the time of writing (5 July 2005), is only partially in force.

WHO MAY APPLY FOR AN ADOPTION ORDER
A couple (whether married or two people living as partners in an enduring family relationship) may apply for an adoption order where both of them are over 21 or where one is only 18 but the natural parent and the other is 21. An adoption order may be made for one applicant where that person is 21 and: a) the court is satisfied that person is the partner of a parent of the person to be adopted; or b) they are not married; or c) married but their spouse is either unable to be found, is incapable by reason of ill-health of making an application or is separated from that person, living apart and the separation is likely to be permanent. There are certain qualifying conditions an applicant must meet e.g. residency in the British Isles.

ARRANGING AN ADOPTION
There are nine steps that may only be taken by an adoption agency (local authorities or adoption societies registered with them) or a person acting in pursuance of an order of the High Court. These steps relate to arranging an adoption, receiving a child for adoption or causing another to carry out one of the steps. If a person or an adoption society act contrary to this provision they (the manager, in the event of an adoption society) may commit an offence. There may be a defence to some steps taken where the proposed adopter is a parent (or partner to that parent), relative or guardian of the child.

ADOPTION ORDER
Once an adoption has been arranged, a court order is necessary to make it legal; this may be obtained from the High Court, county court or magistrates court (including family proceedings court). An adoption order may not be given unless the court is either satisfied that the consent of the child's natural parents (or guardians) has correctly been given or that consent should be dispensed with e.g. where the parent or guardian cannot be found or is incapable of giving consent or where the welfare of the child so demands.

An adoption order has the effect of extinguishing the parental responsibility that a person other than the adopters (or adopter) has for the child, although where an order is made on the application of the partner of the parent, that parent keeps parental responsibility. This means that once adopted the child has the same status as a child born to the adoptive parents and will be treated as such for the purposes of intestate succession, National Insurance, child benefit etc. In addition the child may lose rights to the estates of those losing their parental responsibility.

REGISTRATION AND CERTIFICATES

All adoption orders made in England and Wales are required to be registered in the Adopted Children Register which also contains particulars of children adopted under registrable foreign adoptions. The General Register Office keeps this register from which certificates may be obtained in a similar way to birth certificates. The General Register Office also has equivalents in Scotland and Northern Ireland.

TRACING NATURAL PARENTS OR CHILDREN WHO HAVE BEEN ADOPTED

An adult adopted person may apply to the Registrar-General to obtain a certified copy of his/her birth certificate. For those adopted before 12 November 1975 it is obligatory to receive counselling services before this information is given; for those adopted after that date counselling services are optional. There is an Adoption Contact Register, created after the 1989 Children Act, which provides a safe and confidential way for birth parents and other relatives to assure an adopted person that contact would be welcome. The BAAF (see below) can provide addresses of organisations which offer advice, information and counselling to adopted people, adoptive parents and people who have had their children adopted. Further information can be obtained from:

BRITISH ASSOCIATION FOR ADOPTION AND
FOSTERING (BAAF)
Skyline House, 200 Union Street, London SE1 0LX
T 020-7593 2000 W www.baaf.org.uk

SCOTLAND

The relevant legislation is the Adoption (Scotland) Act 1978 (as amended by the Children Act 1995) and the provisions are similar to those described above. In Scotland, petitions for adoption are made to the Sheriff Court or the Court of Session.

Further information can be obtained from:

BRITISH ASSOCIATION FOR ADOPTION AND
FOSTERING (BAAF)
BAAF Scottish Centre, 40 Shandwick Place, Edinburgh EH2 4RT
T 0131-220 4749

SCOTTISH ADOPTION ADVICE SERVICE
Suite 5/3, Skypark SP5, 45 Finnieston Street, Glasgow G3 8JU
T 0141-248 7530

BIRTHS (REGISTRATION)

It is the duty of the parents of a child born in England or Wales to register the birth within 42 days of the date of birth at the register office in the district in which the baby was born. If it is inconvenient to go to the district where the birth took place, the information for the registration may be given to a registrar in another district. Failure to register the birth within 42 days without reasonable cause

may leave the parents liable to a penalty. If a birth has not been registered within 12 months of its occurrence it is possible for the late registration of the birth to be authorised by the Registrar-General, provided certain requirements can be met.

If the parents of the child were married to each other at the time of the birth (or conception), either the mother or the father may register the birth. If the parents were not married to each other at the time of the child's birth (or conception), the father's particulars may be entered in the register only where he attends the register office with the mother and they sign the birth register together. Where an unmarried parent is unable to attend the register office either parent may submit to the registrar a statutory declaration acknowledging the father's paternity (this form may be obtained from any registrar in England or Wales); alternatively a parental responsibility agreement or appropriate court order may be produced to the registrar.

If the parents do not register the birth of their child the following people may do so:
- the occupier of the house or hospital where the child was born
- a person who was present at the birth
- a person who is responsible for the child
Upon registration of the birth a short certificate is issued.

BIRTHS ABROAD

There are certain countries where birth registrations may be made for British subjects overseas. The British Consul or High Commission may register the births and issue certificates which are then sent to the General Register Office. If a birth is registered by the British Consul or High Commission, the registration would show the person's claim to British citizenship, British Dependent Territories citizenship or British Overseas citizenship.

SCOTLAND

In Scotland the birth of a child must be registered within 21 days at the register office of either the district in which the baby was born or the district in which the mother was resident at the time of the birth.

If the child is born, either in or out of Scotland, on a ship, aircraft or land vehicle that ends its journey at any place in Scotland, the child, in most cases, will be registered as if born in that place.

CERTIFICATES OF BIRTHS, DEATHS OR MARRIAGES

Certificates of births, deaths or marriages that have taken place in England and Wales since 1837 can be obtained from the Office for National Statistics (General Register Office) or the Family Records Centre.

Certificates of births, marriages and deaths may be obtained in any of the following ways:
- by a personal visit to the Family Records Centre
- by post, telephone, fax or online (details of which may be obtained by calling T +44 0870-243 7788 or visiting W www.statistics.gov.uk)
- locally from the register office where the event was originally registered
Marriage or death certificates may be obtained from the minister of the church in which the marriage or funeral took place. Any register office can advise about the best way to obtain certificates.

The fees for certificates are:

From the Family Records Centre, London, by personal application:

Full certificate of birth, marriage, death or adoption, £7.00

Short certificate of birth, £7.00

Short certificate of adoption, £5.50

By postal application:

Full certificate of birth, marriage, death or adoption, £11.50

Full certificate of birth, marriage, death or adoption with GRO index supplied, £8.50

Short certificate of birth, £11.50

Short certificate of adoption, £10.00

Extra copies of the same birth, marriage or death certificate issued at the same time, £7.00

A priority service is also available with certificates despatched on the working day following receipt of your application at an additional cost.

Visit W www.statistics.gov.uk or call T 0870-243 7788 for further information.

Indexes prepared from the registers are available for searching by the public at the Family Records Centre in London or at a Superintendent Registrar's Office; indexes at the latter relate only to births, deaths and marriages which occurred in that registration district. There is no charge for searching the indexes in the Public Search Room at the Family Records Centre but a general search fee is charged for searches at a Superintendent Registrar's Office. A fee is charged for verifying index references against the records.

The Society of Genealogists has many records of baptisms, marriages and deaths prior to 1837.

SCOTLAND

Certificates of births, deaths or marriages that have taken place in Scotland since 1855 can be obtained from the General Register Office for Scotland or from the appropriate local registrar. The General Register Office for Scotland also keeps the Register of Divorces (including decrees of declaration of nullity of marriage), and holds parish registers dating from before 1855.

Fees for certificates are:

Certificates (full or abbreviated) of birth, death, marriage or adoption:

Personal application: £11.00

Postal or telephone ordering: £13.00

Internet ordering: £16.00

A priority service for a response within 24 hours is available for an additional fee of £10.00

General search in the indexes to the statutory registers and parochial registers, per day or part thereof:

Full day (i.e. 9 a.m. to 4.30 p.m.) search, £17.00

Afternoon (i.e. 1 p.m. to 4.30 p.m.) search £10.00

Discounted full day (i.e. 9 a.m. to 4.30 p.m.) search with payment being made not less than 14 days in advance, £13.00 (only available for the period December 2005 to January 2006)

One-week search, £65.00

Four-week search, £220.00

One-quarter search, £500.00

One-year search, £1,500.00

Online searching is also available. For more information, visit W www.scotlandspeople.gov.uk

Further information can be obtained from:

THE GENERAL REGISTER OFFICE
Office for National Statistics, Smedley Hydro, Trafalgar Road, Southport, Merseyside PR8 2HH T 0870-243 7788

FAMILY RECORDS CENTRE
1 Myddelton Street, London EC1R 1UW

THE GENERAL REGISTER OFFICE FOR SCOTLAND
New Register House, 3 West Register Street, Edinburgh EH1 3YT
T 0131-314 4452 W www.gro-scotland.gov.uk

THE SOCIETY OF GENEALOGISTS
14 Charterhouse Buildings, Goswell Road, London EC1M 7BA
T 020-7251 8799

BRITISH CITIZENSHIP

Almost everyone who was a citizen of the UK and colonies and had a right of abode in the UK prior to the British Nationality Act 1981 became a British citizen when the Act came into force. British citizens have the right to live permanently in the UK and are free to leave and re-enter the UK at any time.

A person born on or after 1 January 1983 in the UK (including, for this purpose, the Channel Islands and the Isle of Man) is entitled to British citizenship if he/she falls into one of the following categories:

– he/she has a parent who is a British citizen
– he/she has a parent who is settled in the UK
– he/she is a newborn infant found abandoned in the UK
– his/her parents subsequently settle in the UK
– he/she lives in the UK for the first ten years of his/her life and is not absent for more than 90 days in each of those years
– he/she is adopted in the UK and one of the adopters is a British citizen.

A person born outside the UK may acquire British citizenship if he/she falls into one of the following categories:

– he/she has a parent who is a British citizen otherwise than by descent, e.g. a parent who was born in the UK
– he/she has a parent who is a British citizen serving the Crown overseas
– the Home Secretary consents to his/her registration while he/she is a minor
– he/she is a British Dependent Territories citizen, a British Overseas citizen, a British subject or a British protected person and has been lawfully resident in the UK for five years
– he/she is a British Dependent Territories citizen who acquired that citizenship from a connection with Gibraltar
– he/she is adopted or naturalised

Where parents are married, the status of either may confer citizenship on their child. If a child is illegitimate, the status of the mother determines the child's citizenship.

Under the 1981 Act, Commonwealth citizens and citizens of the Republic of Ireland were entitled to registration as British citizens before 1 January 1988. In 1985, citizens of the Falkland Islands were granted British citizenship.

Renunciation of British citizenship must be registered with the Home Secretary and will be revoked if no new citizenship or nationality is acquired within six months. If the renunciation was required in order to retain or acquire another citizenship or nationality, the citizenship may be reacquired once. The Secretary of State may deprive a person of a citizenship status if he or she is satisfied that the person has done anything seriously prejudicial to the vital interests of the United Kingdom, or a British overseas territory, unless making the order would have the effect of rendering a person stateless. A person may also be deprived of a citizenship status which results from his registration or naturalisation if the Secretary of State is satisfied that the registration or naturalisation was obtained by means of fraud, false representation or concealment of a material fact.

BRITISH DEPENDENT TERRITORIES CITIZENSHIP

Under the 1981 Act, this type of citizenship was conferred on citizens of the UK and colonies by birth, naturalisation or registration in British Dependent Territories. British Dependent Territories citizens may be entitled to registration as British citizens on completion of five years' legal residence in the UK.

On 1 July 1997 citizens of Hong Kong who did not qualify to register as British citizens under the British Nationality (Hong Kong) Act 1990 lost their British Dependent Territories citizenship on the handover of sovereignty to China; they may, however, have applied to register as British Nationals (Overseas).

BRITISH OVERSEAS CITIZENSHIP

Under the 1981 Act, as amended by the British Overseas Territories Act 2002, this type of citizenship was conferred on any UK and colonies citizens who did not qualify for British citizenship or citizenship of the British Dependent Territories. British Overseas citizenship may be acquired by the wife and minor children of a British Overseas citizen in certain circumstances. British Overseas citizens may be entitled to registration as British citizens on completion of five years' legal residence in the UK.

RESIDUAL CATEGORIES

British subjects, British protected persons and British Nationals (Overseas) may be entitled to registration as British citizens on completion of five years' legal residence in the UK.

Citizens of the Republic of Ireland who were also British subjects before 1 January 1949 can retain that status if they fulfil certain conditions.

EUROPEAN UNION CITIZENSHIP

British citizens (including Gibraltarians who are registered as such) are also EU citizens and are entitled to travel freely to other EU countries to work, study, reside and set up a business. EU citizens have the same rights with respect to the United Kingdom.

NATURALISATION

Naturalisation is granted at the discretion of the Home Secretary. The basic requirements are five years' residence (three years if the applicant is married to a British citizen), good character, adequate knowledge of the English, Welsh or Scottish Gaelic language, sufficient knowledge about life in the UK and an intention to reside permanently in the UK.

STATUS OF ALIENS

Aliens may not hold public office or vote in Britain and they may not own a British ship or aircraft. Citizens of the Republic of Ireland are not deemed to be aliens. Certain provisions of the Immigration and Asylum Act 1999 make provision about immigration and asylum and about procedures in connection with marriage by superintendent registrar's certificate.

CONSUMER LAW

SALE OF GOODS

A sale of goods contract is the most common type of contract. It is governed by the Sale of Goods Act 1979 (as amended by the Sale and Supply of Goods Act 1994). The Act provides protection for buyers by implying terms into every sale of goods contract. These terms include:

- an implied term that the seller will pass good title to the buyer (unless the seller agrees to transfer only such title as he has)
- where the seller sells goods by reference to a description, an implied term that the goods will match that description and, where the sale is by sample and description, it will not be sufficient that the bulk of the goods corresponds with the sample if the goods do not also correspond with the description
- where goods are sold by a business seller, an implied term that the goods will be of satisfactory quality if they meet the standard that a reasonable person would regard as satisfactory, taking into account any description of the goods, the price, and all other relevant circumstances. The quality of the goods includes their state and condition, relevant aspects being whether they are fit for the purposes for which such goods are commonly supplied, their appearance and finish, freedom from minor defects and their safety and durability. This term will not be implied, however, if a buyer has examined the goods and should have noticed the defect or if the seller specifically drew the buyer's attention to the defect
- where goods are sold by a business seller, an implied term that the goods are reasonably fit for any purpose made known to the seller by the buyer (either expressly or by implication), unless it is shown that the buyer does not rely on the seller's judgement, or it is not reasonable for him/her to do so
- where goods are sold by sample, implied terms that the bulk of the sample will correspond with the sample in quality, and that the goods are free from any defect rendering them unsatisfactory which would have been apparent on a reasonable examination of the sample

Some of the above terms can be excluded from contracts by the seller. The seller's right to do this is, however, restricted by the Unfair Contract Terms Act 1977. The Act offers more protection to a buyer who 'deals as a consumer' (that is where the seller is selling in the course of a business, the goods are of a type ordinarily bought for private use and the goods are bought by a buyer who is not a business buyer, though not allowing any liability for breach of the implied terms described above to be excluded). In a sale by auction or competitive tender, a buyer never deals as consumer. Also, a seller can never exclude the implied term as to title mentioned above.

HIRE-PURCHASE AGREEMENTS

Terms similar to those implied in contracts of sales of goods are implied into contracts of hire purchase, under the Supply of Goods (Implied Terms) Act 1973. The 1977 Act limits the exclusion of these implied terms as before.

SUPPLY OF GOODS AND SERVICES

Under the Supply of Goods and Services Act 1982, similar terms are also implied in other types of contract under which ownership of goods passes, e.g. a contract for

'work and materials' such as supplying new parts while servicing a car, and contracts for the hire of goods (though not hire-purchase agreements). These types of contracts have additional implied terms:
- that the supplier will use reasonable care and skill in carrying out the service
- that the supplier will carry out the service in a reasonable time (unless the time has been agreed)
- that the supplier will make a reasonable charge (unless the charge has already been agreed)

The 1977 Act limits the exclusion of these implied terms in a similar manner as before.

UNFAIR TERMS

The Unfair Terms in Consumer Contracts Regulations 1999 apply to contracts between business sellers (or suppliers of goods and services) and consumers. Where the terms have not been individually negotiated, i.e. where the terms were drafted in advance so that the consumer was unable to influence those terms, there will be an unfair term where a term operates to the detriment of the consumer (i.e. carries a significant imbalance in the parties' rights and obligations arising under the contract). An unfair term does not bind the consumer but the contract will continue to bind the parties if it is capable of existing without the unfair term. The regulations contain a non-exhaustive list of terms which are regarded as unfair. Whether a term is regarded as fair or not will depend on many factors, including the nature of the goods or services, the surrounding circumstances (such as the bargaining strength of both parties) and the other terms in the contract.

TRADE DESCRIPTIONS

It is a criminal offence under the Trade Descriptions Act 1968 for a business seller to apply a false trade description of goods or to supply or offer to supply any goods to which a false description has been applied. A 'trade description' includes descriptions of quality, size, composition, fitness for purpose, performance, method of manufacture, and place and date of manufacture of the goods.

FAIR TRADING

The Fair Trading Act 1973 is designed to protect the consumer. It provides for the appointment of a Director-General of Fair Trading, one of whose duties is to review commercial activities in the UK relating to the supply of goods and services to consumers. An example of a practice which has been prohibited by a reference made under this Act is that of business sellers posing in advertisements as private sellers.

CONSUMER PROTECTION

Under the Consumer Protection Act 1987, producers of goods are liable for any injury or for any damage exceeding £275 caused by a defect in their product (subject to certain defences).

The Consumer Protection (Cancellation of Contracts Concluded Away from Business Premises) Regulations 1987 allow consumers a seven-day period in which to cancel contracts for the supply of goods and services, where the contracts were made during an unsolicited visit by a trader to the consumer's home or workplace. A contract will not be enforceable at all in this situation unless the trader has written to the consumer to notify them of the right to cancel within seven days.

Consumers are also afforded protection under the Consumer Protection (Distance Selling) Regulations 2000 in relation to e.g. cancellation periods.

CONSUMER CREDIT

In matters relating to the provision of credit (or the supply of goods on hire or hire-purchase), consumers are also protected by the Consumer Credit Act 1974. Under this Act a licence, issued by the Director-General of Fair Trading, is required to conduct a consumer credit or consumer hire business or an ancillary credit business. Any 'fit' person as defined within the Act may apply to the Director General of Fair Trading for a licence, which is normally renewable after five years. A licence is not necessary if only exempt agreements are involved. The provisions of the Act only apply to 'regulated' agreements, i.e. those that are with individuals or partnerships, those that are not exempt (certain local authority and building society loans will be exempt), and those where the total credit does not exceed £25,000. Provisions include:
- the terms of the regulated agreement can be altered by the creditor, provided the agreement gives him/her the right to do so; in such cases the debtor must be given proper notice of this
- in order for a creditor to enforce a regulated agreement, the agreement must comply with certain formalities and must be properly executed. The debtor must also be given specified information by the creditor or his/her broker or agent during the negotiations which take place before the signing of the agreement. The agreement must state certain information such as the amount of credit, the annual interest rate, and the amount and timing of repayments
- if an agreement is signed other than at the creditor's (or credit broker's or negotiator's) place of business and oral representations were made in the debtor's presence during discussions pre-agreement, the debtor has a right to cancel the agreement. Time for cancellation expires five clear days after the debtor receives a second copy of the agreement. The agreement must inform the debtor of his right to cancel and how to cancel
- if the debtor is in arrears (or otherwise in breach of the agreement), the creditor must serve a default notice before taking any action such as repossessing the goods
- if the agreement is a hire-purchase or conditional sale agreement, the creditor cannot repossess the goods without a court order if the debtor has paid one-third of the total price of the goods
- in agreements where the debtor is required to make grossly exorbitant payments or where the agreement grossly contravenes the ordinary principles of fair trading, the debtor may request that the court alter or set aside some of the terms of the agreement. The agreement can also be reopened during enforcement proceedings by the court itself

Where a credit reference agency has been used to check the debtor's financial standing, the creditor must give the agency's name to the debtor, who is entitled to see the agency's file on him. A fee of £1 is payable to the agency.

SCOTLAND

The legislation governing the sale and supply of goods applies to Scotland as follows:
- the Sale of Goods Act 1979 applies with some modifications and it has been amended by the Sale and Supply of Goods Act 1994
- the Supply of Goods (Implied Terms) Act 1973 applies
- the Supply of Goods and Services Act 1982 does not extend to Scotland but some of its provisions were

introduced by the Sale and Supply of Goods Act 1994
- only Parts II and III of the Unfair Contract Terms Act 1977 apply
- the Trade Descriptions Act 1968 applies with minor modifications
- the Consumer Credit Act 1974 applies
- the Consumer Protection Act 1987 applies
- the General Product Safety Regulations 1994 apply
- the Unfair Terms in Consumer Contracts Regulations 1999 apply
- the Unfair Terms in Consumer Contracts (Amendment) Regulations 2001 apply
- the Consumer Protection (Distance Selling) Regulations 2000 apply the Sale and Supply of Goods to Consumers Regulations 2002 apply

PROCEEDINGS AGAINST THE CROWN

Until 1947, proceedings against the Crown were generally possible only by a procedure known as a petition of right, which put the litigant at a considerable disadvantage. The Crown Proceedings Act 1947 placed the Crown (not the Sovereign in his/her private capacity, but as the embodiment of the State) largely in the same position as a private individual. The Act did not however, extinguish or limit the Crown's prerogative or statutory powers, and it granted immunity to HM ships and aircraft. It also left certain Crown privileges unaffected. The Act largely abolished the special procedures which previously applied to civil proceedings by and against the Crown. Civil proceedings may be instituted against the appropriate government department or if there is doubt regarding which is the appropriate department, then against the Attorney General.

In Scotland proceedings against the Crown founded on breach of contract could be taken before the 1947 Act and no special procedures applied. The Crown could, however, claim certain special pleas. The 1947 Act applies in part to Scotland and brings the practice of the two countries as closely together as the different legal systems permit. As a result of the Scotland Act 1998 actions against government departments should be raised against the Lord Advocate or the Advocate-General. Actions should be raised against the Lord Advocate where the department involved administers a devolved matter. Devolved matters include agriculture, education, housing, local government, health and justice. Actions should be raised against the Advocate-General where the department is dealing with a reserved matter. Reserved matters include defence, foreign affairs and social security.

DEATHS

WHEN A DEATH OCCURS
If the death (including stillbirth) was expected, the doctor who attended the deceased during their final illness should be contacted. If the death was sudden or unexpected, the family doctor (if known) and police should be contacted. If the cause of death is quite clear the doctor will provide:
- a medical certificate that shows the cause of death
- a formal notice that states that the doctor has signed the medical certificate and that explains how to get the death registered

If the death was known to be caused by a natural illness but the doctor wishes to know more about the cause of death, he/she may ask the relatives for permission to carry out a post-mortem examination.

In England and Wales a coroner is responsible for investigating deaths occurring in the following circumstances:
- where there is no doctor who can issue a medical certificate of cause of death
- when no doctor has treated the deceased during his or her last illness or when the doctor attending the patient did not see him or her within 14 days before death, or after death
- when the death occurred during an operation or before recovery from the effect of an anaesthetic
- when the death was sudden and unexplained or attended by suspicious circumstances
- when the death might be due to an industrial injury or disease, or to accident, violence, neglect or abortion, attended by suspicious circumstances
- the death occurred in prison or in police custody

The doctor will write on the formal notice that the death has been referred to the coroner; if the post mortem shows that death was due to natural causes, the coroner may issue a notification which gives the cause of death so that the death can be registered. If the cause of death was violent or unnatural, the coroner is obliged to hold an inquest.

In Scotland the office of coroner does not exist. The local procurator fiscal inquires into sudden or suspicious deaths. A fatal accident inquiry will be held before the sheriff where the death has resulted from an accident during the course of the employment of the person who has died, or where the person who has died was in legal custody, or where the Lord Advocate deems it in the public interest that an inquiry be held.

REGISTERING A DEATH
In England and Wales the death must be registered by the registrar of births and deaths for the district in which it occurred; details can be obtained from the doctor or local council, or at a post office or police station. From April 1997, information concerning a death can be given before any registrar of births and deaths in England and Wales. The registrar will pass the relevant details to the registrar for the district where the death occurred, who will then register the death.

In England and Wales the death must normally be registered within five days; in Scotland it must be registered within eight days. If the death has been referred to the coroner/local procurator fiscal it cannot be registered until the registrar has received authority from the coroner/local procurator fiscal to do so. Failure to register a death involves a penalty in England and Wales and may lead to a court decree being granted by a sheriff in Scotland.

If the death occurred at a house or hospital, the death may be registered by:
- any relative of the deceased
- any person present at the death
- the occupier or any inmate of the house or hospital if he/she knew of the occurrence of the death
- any person making the funeral arrangements
- in Scotland, the deceased's executor or legal representative

For deaths that took place elsewhere, the death may be registered by:
- any relative of the deceased
- someone present at the death
- someone who found the body

– a person in charge of the body
– any person making the funeral arrangements
The majority of deaths are registered by a relative of the deceased. The registrar would normally allow one of the other listed persons to register the death only if there were no relatives available.

The person registering the death should take the medical certificate of the cause of death with them; it is also useful, though not essential, to take the deceased's birth and marriage certificates, NHS medical card (if possible), pension documents and life assurance details. The details given to the registrar must be absolutely correct, otherwise it may be difficult to change them later. The person registering the death should check the entry very carefully before it is signed. The registrar will issue a certificate for burial or cremation and a certificate of registration of death; both are free of charge. A death certificate is a certified copy of the entry in the death register; these can be provided on payment of a fee and may be required for the following purposes:

– the will
– bank and building society accounts
– savings bank certificates and premium bonds
– insurance policies
– pension claims
– certificate for applicable Social Security Benefits

If the death occurred abroad or on a foreign ship or aircraft, the death should be registered according to the local regulations of the relevant country and a death certificate should be obtained. The death can also be registered with the British Consul in that country and a record will be kept at the General Register Office. This avoids the expense of bringing the body back.

After 12 months (three months in Scotland) of death or the finding of a dead body, no death can be registered without the consent of the Registrar-General.

BURIAL AND CREMATION

In most circumstances in England and Wales a certificate for burial or cremation must be obtained from the registrar before the burial or cremation can take place. If the death has been referred to the coroner, an order for burial or a certificate for cremation must be obtained. In Scotland a body may be buried (but not cremated) before the death is registered.

Funeral costs can normally be repaid out of the deceased's estate and will be given priority over any other claims. If the deceased has left a will it may contain directions concerning the funeral; however, these directions need not be followed by the executor.

The deceased's papers should also indicate whether a grave space had already been arranged. This information will be contained in a document known as a 'Deed of Grant'. Most town churchyards and many suburban churchyards are no longer open for burial because they are full. Most cemeteries are non-denominational and may be owned by local authorities or private companies; fees vary.

If the body is to be cremated, an application form, two cremation certificates (for which there is a charge) or a certificate for cremation if the death was referred to the coroner, and a certificate signed by the medical referee must be completed in addition to the certificate for burial or cremation (the form is not required if the coroner has issued a certificate for cremation). All the forms are available from the funeral director or crematorium. Most crematoria are run by local authorities; the fees usually include the medical referee's fee and the use of the chapel.

Ashes may be scattered, buried in a churchyard or cemetery, or kept.

The registrar must be notified of the date, place and means of disposal of the body within 96 hours (England and Wales) or three days (Scotland).

If the death occurred abroad or on a foreign ship or aircraft, a local burial or cremation may be arranged. If the body is to be brought back to England or Wales, a death certificate from the relevant country or an authorisation for the removal of the body from the country of death from the coroner or relevant authority will be required. To arrange a funeral in England or Wales, an authenticated translation of a foreign death certificate or a death certificate issued in Scotland or Northern Ireland which must show the cause of death, is needed, together with a certificate of no liability to register from the registrar in England and Wales in whose sub-district it is intended to bury or cremate the body. If it is intended to cremate the body, a cremation order will be required from the Home Office or a certificate for cremation.

Further information can be obtained from:

THE GENERAL REGISTER OFFICE
Office for National Statistics, Smedley Hydro, Trafalgar Road,
Southport, Merseyside PR8 2HH **T** 0870-243 7788
E www.direct.gov.uk

THE GENERAL REGISTER OFFICE FOR SCOTLAND
New Register House, 3 West Register Street, Edinburgh EH1 3YT
T 0131-314 4452

DIVORCE AND RELATED MATTERS

There are three types of matrimonial suit: those seeking the annulment of marriage, judicial separation and divorce. To obtain an annulment, judicial separation or divorce in England and Wales: if a European Union court (except Denmark) has jurisdiction, and the one commencing the proceedings (the petitioner) and the one defending the proceedings (the respondent) must be habitually resident in England and Wales; or the petitioner and the respondent must have last been habitually resident in England and Wales and one of them must continue to reside there; or the respondent must be habitually resident in England and Wales; or the petitioner must have been habitually resident in England and Wales throughout the period of at least one year ending with the start of proceedings; or the petitioner must be domiciled in England and Wales and must have been habitually resident in England and Wales throughout the period of at least six months, ending with the start of the proceedings; or both parties must have been domiciled in England and Wales; or if no European Union court (except Denmark) has jurisdiction, one or both of them must be domiciled in England and Wales. All cases are commenced in a divorce county court or in the Principal Registry in London. If a suit is defended, it may be transferred to the High Court.

NULLITY OF MARRIAGE

Various circumstances will render a marriage invalid including if: there has been wilful non-consummation of the marriage; one partner has a venereal disease at the time of the marriage and the other did not know about it; the female partner was pregnant at the time of the marriage with another person's child and the male partner did not know of the pregnancy; the parties were within prohibited degrees of consanguinity, affinity or adoption;

the parties were not male and female; either of the parties was already married; either of the parties was under the age of 16; the formalities of the marriage were defective, eg the marriage did not take place in an authorised building and both parties knew of the defect.

SEPARATION

A couple may enter into a private agreement to separate by consent but for the agreement to be valid it must be followed by an immediate separation; a solicitor should be contacted.

Judicial separation does not dissolve a marriage and it is not necessary to prove that the marriage has irretrievably broken down. Either party can petition for a judicial separation at any time; the grounds listed below as grounds for divorce are also grounds for judicial separation. To petition for judicial separation, the parties do not have to prove that they have been married for twelve months or more.

A financial settlement between spouses in a separation agreement or which accompanies a judicial separation will not necessarily bind the court after instigation of divorce proceedings.

DIVORCE

Neither party can petition for divorce until at least one year after the date of the marriage. The sole ground for divorce is the irretrievable breakdown of the marriage; this must be proved on one or more of the following grounds:
- the respondent has committed adultery and the petitioner finds it intolerable to live with him/her; however, the petitioner cannot rely on an act of adultery by the respondent if they have lived together for more than six months after the discovery of the adultery
- the respondent has behaved in such a way that the petitioner cannot reasonably be expected to continue living with him/her
- the respondent has deserted the petitioner for two years immediately before the petition
- the petitioner and the respondent have lived separately for two years immediately before the petition and the respondent consents to the divorce
- the petitioner and the respondent have lived separately for five years immediately before the petition

A total period of less than six months during which the parties have resumed living together is disregarded in determining whether the prescribed period of separation or desertion has been continuous (but may not be included as part of the period of separation).

The Matrimonial Causes Act 1973 requires the solicitor for the petitioner to certify whether the possibility of a reconciliation has been discussed with the petitioner.

THE DECREE NISI

A decree nisi does not dissolve or annul the marriage, but must be obtained before a divorce or annulment can take place.

Where the suit is undefended, the evidence normally takes the form of a sworn written statement made by the petitioner which is considered by a district judge. If the judge is satisfied that the petitioner has proved the contents of the petition, a date will be set for the pronouncement of the decree nisi in open court: neither party need attend.

If the judge is not satisfied that the petitioner has proved the contents of the petition or if the suit is defended, the petition will be heard in open court with parties giving oral evidence.

THE DECREE ABSOLUTE

The decree nisi is made absolute on the application of the petitioner after six weeks. If the petitioner does not apply, the respondent must wait for a further three months before application may be made. If the judge thinks it may be necessary to exercise a judge's powers under the Children Act 1989 in exceptional circumstances the granting of the decree absolute may be delayed. The decree absolute dissolves or annuls the marriage. Where the couple were married in accordance with Jewish or other religious usages, the court may require them to produce a declaration that they have taken such steps as are required to dissolve the marriage in accordance with those usages before the decree absolute is issued.

MAINTENANCE

Either party may be liable to pay maintenance to a spouse or former spouse. If there were any children of the marriage, both parties have a legal responsibility to support them financially if they can afford to do so.

The courts are responsible for assessing maintenance for a spouse or former spouse, taking into account each party's income and essential outgoings and other aspects of the case. The court also deals with any maintenance for a child that has been treated by the spouses as a child of the family, such as a step-child, and any property settlements.

The Child Support Agency (CSA) is responsible for assessing the maintenance that absent parents shall pay for their natural or adopted children (whether or not a marriage has taken place). The CSA accepts applications only when all the people involved are habitually resident in the UK; the courts will continue to deal with cases where one of the individuals lives abroad. The CSA deals with all new cases unless it is agreed by the spouses that the court may grant an Order for child support (but even in agreed jurisdiction cases one parent may give the other 14 months' notice to have the case dealt with by the CSA).

A formula is used to work out how much child maintenance is payable under CSA jurisdiction. The formula requires the absent parent to pay 15 per cent net of post-tax, National Insurance and pension contributions for one child, 20 per cent for two and 25 per cent for more than two. An earnings cap of £104,000 net a year applies. The parent with care's income is not taken into account. Deductions are applied for staying contact for further children in the absent parent's household. In court jurisdiction cases, the CSA formula is adopted as a guideline only.

Some cases involving unusual circumstances are treated as special cases and the assessment is modified, and in some cases the court retains jurisdiction (for educational costs and high income cases, for example). Where there is financial need (eg because of disability or continual education) maintenance may be ordered by the court for children even beyond the age of 18.

CSA maintenance is reviewed automatically every two years. Either parent can report a change of circumstances and request a review at any time. An independent complaints examiner for the CSA has been appointed.

If the absent parent does not pay CSA maintenance, the CSA may make an order for payments to be deducted directly from his/her salary; if all other methods fail, the CSA may take court action to enforce payment.

OTHER FINANCIAL RELIEF

The approach of the court has changed dramatically since the House of Lords decision of *White v White* in October 2000. Now, after allowing the claimant's reasonable needs in terms of housing and a fund to provide income for life, the court has to measure that provisional award against the yardstick of equal division. The approach is therefore now much more based on percentage division and reasons being advanced for departure from it. It has become more so with the 2002 case of *Lambert v Lambert*. Ongoing spousal maintenance cases referred to above can justify a departure. The court has a duty to consider making a once and for all capital award, such as a payment and/or property or pension transfer if this can be afforded. This is known as a clean break. Alternatively the court will make a capital award and an ongoing spousal maintenance award if a clean break cannot be afforded. Maintenance is often payable during joint lives or until the recipient's remarriage, subject to the ability to vary or terminate in the meantime.

There is no concept of separate or marital property in England and Wales: all assets however derived are potentially vulnerable on divorce. This includes inherited wealth, gifted wealth and pre-marriage acquired wealth.

The court must consider the following factors when making financial orders, after giving first consideration to the welfare of any minor children of the family: the income, earning capacity, property and other financial resources which each of the parties to the marriage has or is likely to have in the foreseeable future, including in the case of earning capacity, any increase in that capacity which it would, in the opinion of the court, be reasonable to expect a party to the marriage to take steps to acquire; the financial needs, obligations and responsibilities which each of the parties to the marriage has or is likely to have in the foreseeable future; the standard of living enjoyed by the family before the breakdown of the marriage; the age of each party to the marriage and the duration of the marriage; any physical or mental disability of either of the parties to the marriage; the contribution which each of the parties has made or is likely in the foreseeable future to make to the welfare of the family, including any contribution by looking after the home or caring for the family; the conduct of each of the parties, if that conduct is such that it would, in the opinion of the court, be inequitable to disregard it; and in the case of proceedings for divorce or nullity of marriage, the value to each of the parties to the marriage of any benefit (for example a pension) which by reason of the dissolution of the marriage that party will lose the chance of acquiring.

The court has the power to award in addition to maintenance a lump sum order, a property transfer order and a pension sharing order as the main forms of financial relief.

COHABITING COUPLES

Rights of unmarried couples are not the same as for married couples. Agreements, whether express or inferred by conduct, often determine interests in money and property. Reliance upon inferences is problematic. By virtue of this, it is worth considering entering into a contract which establishes how money and property should be divided in the event of a relationship breakdown. These contracts are commonly known as 'separation deeds' or 'cohabitation contracts'.

CIVIL PARNERSHIP

When the Civil Partnership Act 2004 comes into force on 5 December 2005, same-sex couples, by registering as civil partners, will gain legal recognition of their relationship and thereby obtain rights and obligations broadly equivalent to those of married couples. These rights and responsibilities include a duty to provide reasonable maintenance for your civil partner and any children of the family, equitable treatment in respect of life assurance and pension benefits, recognition under intestacy rules and domestic violence protection. In addition, inheritance tax will be waived as with married couples and there will be a right of succession for tenancy.

DOMESTIC VIOLENCE

If one spouse has been subjected to violence at the hands of the other, it is possible to obtain a court order very quickly to restrain further violence and if necessary to have the other spouse excluded from the home. Such orders may also relate to unmarried couples and to a range of other relationships including parents and children.

SCOTLAND

Although the provisions are in most respects the same as those for England and Wales, there is separate legislation for Scotland covering nullity of marriage, judicial separation, divorce and ancillary matters. Also at the date of writing (August 2005), the Family Law (Scotland) Bill was progressing through Scottish Parliament. The bill aims to reform various aspects of Scottish family law, including giving financial and property rights to cohabiting couples. The following is confined to major points on which the law in Scotland differs from that of England and Wales.

An action for judicial separation or divorce may be raised in the Court of Session; it may also be raised in the Sheriff Court if either party was resident in the sheriffdom for 40 days immediately before the date of the action or for 40 days ending not more than 40 days before the date of the action. The fee for starting a divorce petition in the Sheriff Court is £81.

A simplified procedure for 'do-it-yourself divorce' was introduced in 1983 for certain divorces. If the action is based on two or five years' separation and will not be opposed, and if there are no children under 16 and no financial claims, and there is no sign that the applicant's spouse is unable to manage his or her affairs through mental illness or handicap, the applicant can write directly to the local Sheriff Court or to the Court of Session for the appropriate forms to enable him or her to proceed. The fee is £62, unless the applicant receives income support, family credit or legal advice and assistance, in which case there is no fee.

When adultery is cited as proof that the marriage has broken down irretrievably, it is not necessary in Scotland to prove also that it is intolerable for the pursuer to live with the defender. In the case of desertion, irretrievable breakdown is not established if, after the two-year desertion period has expired, the parties resume living together at any time after the end of three months from the date when they first resume living together. It is proposed in the Family Law (Scotland) Bill to reduce the period of separation required to establish irretrievable breakdown of the marriage, to one year's separation if the defender consents to the divorce, and two years' separation if the defendant does not consent. It is also proposed that the ground of desertion be abolished.

In relation to financial provision on divorce, there are

five principles to guide the court in making an award. The first, and most important, principle is fair sharing of the matrimonial property, which is property acquired by the parties from the date of the marriage to the date of separation. A house and furnishings purchased prior to the marriage for use by the parties as a family home constitutes matrimonial property. Inheritances, gifts, and any other assets acquired pre-marriage (with the exception of the family home) are not matrimonial property, and do not therefore fall to be shared.

Where a divorce action has been raised, it may be sisted or put on hold for a variety of reasons.

If the parties do cohabit during such postponement, no account is taken of the cohabitation if the action later proceeds.

In actions for divorce and separation, the court has the power to award a residence order in respect of any children of the marriage. The welfare of the children is of paramount importance, and the fact that a spouse has caused the breakdown of the marriage does not in itself preclude him/her from being awarded residence.

An extract decree, which brings the marriage to an end, will be made available 14 days after the divorce has been granted.

An action for 'declaration of nullity' can be brought only in the Court of Session. Where a spouse is capable of sexual intercourse but refuses to consummate the marriage, this is not a ground for nullity in Scots law, though it could be a ground for divorce. Where a spouse was suffering from venereal disease at the time of marriage and the other spouse did not know, this is not a ground for nullity in Scots law, neither is the fact that a wife was pregnant by another man at the time of marriage without the knowledge of her husband.

Further information can be obtained from:

THE PRINCIPAL REGISTRY
First Avenue House, 42–49 High Holborn, London WC2V 6NP

THE COURT OF SESSION
Parliament House, Parliament Square, Edinburgh EH1 1RQ
T 0131-225 2595

THE CHILD SUPPORT AGENCY
National Enquiry Line 08457-133133 W www.csa.gov.uk

EMPLOYMENT LAW

PAY AND CONDITIONS
The Employment Rights Act 1996 consolidates the statutory provisions relating to employees' rights. Employers must give each employee employed for one month or more a written statement containing the following information:
- names of employer and employee
- date when employment began and the date on which the employee's period of *continuous* employment began (taking into account any employment with a previous employer which counts towards that period)
- remuneration and intervals at which it will be paid
- job title or description of job
- hours and place(s) of work
- holiday entitlement and holiday pay
- provisions concerning incapacity for work due to sickness and injury, including provisions for sick pay
- details of pension scheme(s)
- length of notice period that employer and employee need to give to terminate employment

- if the employment is not intended to be permanent, the period for which it is expected to continue or, if it is for a fixed term, the end date of the contract
- details of any collective agreement which affects the terms of employment
- details of disciplinary and grievance procedures
- if the employee is to work outside the UK for more than one month, the period of such work and the currency in which payment is made

This must be given to the employee within two months of the start of their employment. The Working Time Regulations 1998, the National Minimum Wage Act 1998 and the Employment Relations Act 1999 now supplement the 1996 Act. If the employer does not provide the written statement within two months then the employee can complain to an employment tribunal, which can specify the information that the employer should have given. The Employment Act 2002 introduced a new provision which allows the tribunal to award compensation of between two to four weeks' pay when, in the context of an employee's successful tribunal claim, the employer is also found to have been in breach of the duty to provide the written statement at the time proceedings were commenced.

FLEXIBLE WORKING
The Employment Act 2002 gives employees the right to apply for a flexible working pattern for the purpose of caring for a child and is intended to cover anyone who has responsibility for the upbringing of a child. If an application under the Act is rejected, it is open to the employee to complain to an employment tribunal.

SICK PAY
Employees absent from work through illness or injury are entitled to receive Statutory Sick Pay (SSP) from the employer for a maximum period of 28 weeks in any three-year period. This applies to all employees, both men and women, up to the age of 65. If your average earnings before deductions such as tax and National Insurance are £82 a week or more, the standard rate of SSP is £68.20 per week.

MATERNITY AND PARENTAL RIGHTS
Under the Employment Relations Act 1999, the Employment Act 2002 and the Maternity and Parental Leave (Amendment) Regulations 2002, both men and women are entitled to take leave where they become a parent. Women are protected from discrimination, detriment or dismissal by reason of their pregnancy. Men are protected from suffering a detriment or dismissal for taking paternity or parental leave.

Women are entitled to 26 weeks' Ordinary Maternity Leave. There is no qualifying period of employment. Any woman who is absent from work during her Ordinary Maternity Leave period has the right to return to the job in which she was employed before her absence. An employee may take Additional Maternity Leave of up to 26 weeks if she has been continuously employed for not less than 26 weeks at the beginning of the 14th week before the expected week of childbirth. Women who qualify for Additional Maternity Leave will also qualify for Statutory Maternity Pay (SMP), which is payable for 26 weeks and generally starts when the employee stops work. The first six weeks of SMP are paid at 90 per cent of the employee's average weekly earnings, and the remaining 20 weeks are paid at the rate of £106.00 per week, or 90 per cent of weekly earnings, whichever is lower.

Employees are entitled to Paternity Leave for the purpose of caring for a child or supporting the child's mother on the birth or adoption of a child. The qualifying period of employment for this right is the same as for Additional Maternity Leave (that is, the employee must have been continuously employed for not less than 26 weeks at the beginning of the 14th week before the expected week of childbirth). The employee may take either one week's leave, or two consecutive weeks' leave. This leave may be taken from the date of the child's birth to 56 days later. During their Paternity Leave, most employees will be entitled to Statutory Paternity Pay, which is paid at the same rate as Statutory Maternity Pay.

Employees are entitled to Ordinary Adoption Leave, Additional Adoption Leave and Adoption Pay subject to fulfilment of criteria similar to those in relation to Maternity Leave and Pay. Where a couple is adopting a child, one may take Adoption Leave, and the adopter's spouse or partner may take Paternity Leave.

Any employee with one year's service who has, or expects to have, responsibility for a child may take parental leave. Each parent is entitled to a total of 13 weeks' parental leave for each of their children but this leave must be taken before the child's fifth birthday (or eighteenth birthday if the child is disabled).

SUNDAY TRADING
The Sunday Trading Act 1994 gives shop workers the right not to be dismissed, selected for redundancy or to suffer any detriment (such as the denial of overtime, promotion or training) if they refuse to work on Sundays. This does not apply to those who, under their contracts, are employed to work on Sundays.

TERMINATION OF EMPLOYMENT
An employee may be dismissed without notice if guilty of gross misconduct but in other cases a period of notice must be given by the employer. The minimum periods of notice specified in the Employment Rights Act 1996 are:
- one week if the employee has been continuously employed for one month or more but for less than two years
- two weeks if the employee has been continuously employed for at least two years
- a week is added for every complete year of continuous employment up to 12 years, up to a maximum of 12 weeks
- longer periods apply if these are specified in the contract of employment

If an employee is dismissed with less notice than he/she is entitled to by statute, or under their contract if longer, the employer is generally liable to pay the employee in lieu of notice (or for the period of the contract for those on fixed-term contracts). Generally, no notice needs to be given of the expiry of a fixed-term contract. If the employer does not give the employee pay in lieu of notice then the employer becomes liable to pay the employee damages for wrongful dismissal. This claim for wrongful dismissal can be brought by the employee either in the court system or the employment tribunal, but if brought in the tribunal the maximum amount that can be awarded is £25,000. This claim can also be brought by an employee whose fixed-term contract has been terminated prematurely, and without justification, by the employer.

REDUNDANCY
An employee dismissed because of redundancy may be entitled to redundancy pay. This applies if:
- the employee has at least two years' continuous service
- the employee is actually dismissed by the employer (even in cases of voluntary redundancy)
- dismissal is due to redundancy. Redundancy can mean closure of the entire business, closure of a particular site of the business, overmanning (surplus employees) or reduction in work of a particular kind

An employee may not be entitled to a redundancy payment if offered a suitable alternative job by the same employer. The amount of payment depends on the length of service, the age of the employee, and their earnings, subject to a weekly maximum of (currently) £280. The maximum award that can be made is £8,400. The redundancy payment is guaranteed by the State in cases where the employer becomes insolvent (subject to the conditions above).

UNFAIR DISMISSAL
Complaints of unfair dismissal are dealt with by an employment tribunal. Any employee with one year's continuous service (subject to exceptions) regardless of their hours of work, can make a complaint to the tribunal. At the tribunal, the employee must prove that he or she was dismissed, but it is for the employer to prove that the dismissal was due to one or more of the following acceptable reasons:
- the employee's capability or qualifications for the job he/she was employed to do
- the employee's conduct
- redundancy
- a legal restriction preventing the continuation of the employee's contract
- some other substantial reason

If the employer succeeds in showing this, the tribunal must then decide whether the employer acted reasonably in dismissing the employee for that reason. If the employee is found to have been unfairly dismissed, the tribunal can order that he/she be reinstated, re-engaged or compensated. Any person believing that they may have been unfairly dismissed should contact their local Citizens Advice Bureau or seek legal advice. A claim must be brought within three months of the date of termination of employment.

The maximum award for unfair dismissal is £56,800 which relates to dismissals occurring on or after 1 February 2005. Where an employer has failed to follow the statutory dismissal procedures which came into force on 1 October 2004, the tribunal must increase an award by between 10–50 per cent.

DISCRIMINATION
Discrimination in employment on the grounds of sex, sexual orientation, race, colour, nationality, ethnic or national origins, religion or belief, married status or (subject to wide exceptions) disability is unlawful. Discrimination legislation also covers sexual harassment and gender reassignment. Discrimination on the grounds of age will become unlawful when age discrimination legislation comes into force on 1 October 2006, although it is not currently unlawful. The following legislation applies to those employed in Great Britain but not to employees in Northern Ireland or (subject to EC exceptions) to those who work mainly abroad:
- The Equal Pay Act 1970 (as amended) entitles men and women to equality in matters related to their contracts

of employment. Those doing like work for the same employer are entitled to the same pay and conditions regardless of their sex
- The Sex Discrimination Act 1975 (as amended by the Sex Discrimination Act 1986 and by the Employment Equality (Sex Discrimination) Regulations 2005) makes it unlawful to discriminate on grounds of sex or marital status (although, under the Act it is only unlawful to discriminate against people because they are married, not because they are single). This covers all aspects of employment, including advertising for recruits, terms offered, opportunities for promotion and training, and dismissal procedures
- The Race Relations Act 1976 gives individuals the right not to be discriminated against on the grounds of race, colour, nationality, or ethnic or national origins. It applies to all aspects of employment
- The Disability Discrimination Act 1995 makes discrimination against a disabled person in all aspects of employment unlawful. An employer may show that the less favourable treatment is justified. The Act also imposes a duty on employers to make 'reasonable adjustments' to the arrangements and physical features of the workplace if these place disabled people at a substantial disadvantage compared with those who are not disabled. The Disability Discrimination Act 1995 is due to be amended by the Disability Discrimination Act 2005 which is due to come into force in stages between December 2005 and December 2006. The Act will extend protection to people diagnosed with HIV, cancer and multiple sclerosis and will also introduce a new positive duty on public bodies to promote equality of opportunity for disabled people

The Employment Equality (Religion or Belief) Regulations 2003, which implement an EC Directive, make discrimination against a person on the grounds of religion or belief, in all aspects of employment, unlawful.

The Employment Equality (Sexual Orientation) Regulations 2003, which implement another aspect of the same EC directive, make discrimination against an individual on the grounds of sexual orientation, in all aspects of employment, unlawful.

The Equal Opportunities Commission, the Commission for Racial Equality and the Disability Rights Commission have, as part of their roles, the function of eliminating such discrimination in the workplace, and can provide further information and assistance.

In Northern Ireland similar provisions exist but are contained in separate legislation (although the Disability Discrimination Act does extend to Northern Ireland).

In Northern Ireland there is one combined body working towards equality and eliminating discrimination, the Equality Commission for Northern Ireland.

The Employment Relations Act 1999 made a number of important changes to the existing law:
- a right of accompaniment. A worker attending a serious disciplinary or grievance hearing has the right to be accompanied by a trade union representative or co-worker of their choice
- a new scheme of compulsory trade union recognition following a workplace ballot
- greater protection from dismissal for striking employees

HUMAN RIGHTS

On 2 October 2000 the Human Rights Act 1998 came into force. This Act incorporates the European Convention on Human Rights into the law of the United Kingdom.

The main principles of the Act are as follows:
- all legislation must be interpreted and given effect by the courts as compatible with the Convention so far as it is possible to do so. Before the second reading of a new Bill the minister responsible for the Bill must provide a statement regarding the compatibility of the Bill with the Human Rights Act
- subordinate legislation (e.g. statutory instruments) which are incompatible with the Convention can be struck down by the courts
- primary legislation (e.g. Acts of Parliament) which is incompatible with the Convention cannot be struck down by a court, but the higher courts can make a declaration of incompatibility which is a signal to Parliament to change the law
- all public authorities (including courts and tribunals) must not act in a way which is incompatible with the Convention
- individuals whose Convention rights have been infringed by a public authority may bring proceedings against that authority, but the Act is not intended to create new rights as between individuals

The main human rights protected by the Convention are the right to life (article 2); protection from torture and inhuman or degrading treatment (article 3); protection from slavery or forced labour (article 4); the right to liberty and security of the person (article 5); the right to a fair trial (article 6); the right not to be subject to retrospective criminal offences (article 7); the right to respect for private and family life (article 8); freedom of thought, conscience and religion (article 9); freedom of expression (article 10); freedom of peaceful association and assembly (article 11); the right to marry and found a family (article 12); protection from discrimination (article 14); the right to property (article 1 Protocol No.1); the right to free election (article 3 Protocol No.1); and the right to education (article 2 Protocol No.1). Most of the Convention rights are subject to limitations which deem the breach of the right acceptable on the basis it is 'necessary in a democratic society'.

ILLEGITIMACY AND LEGITIMATION

The Children Act 1989 gives the mother parental responsibility for the child. An unmarried father does not automatically acquire parental responsibility but can do so either by agreement with the mother (in prescribed form) or by applying to the court. The Adoption and Children Act 2002 (not yet fully in force) also makes provision for a father who is not married to the child's mother to acquire parental responsibility for the child if he becomes registered as the child's father. If an illegitimate child is to be adopted, the father's consent is required only where he has been awarded parental rights by the court.

Every child born to a married woman during marriage is presumed to be legitimate, unless the couple are separated under court order when the child is conceived, in which case the child is presumed not to be the husband's child. It is possible to challenge the presumption of legitimacy or illegitimacy through civil proceedings.

In Scotland, the relevant legislation is the Children (Scotland) Act 1995, which also gives the mother parental responsibility for her child whether or not she is married to the child's father. The father currently has automatic parental rights only if married to the mother. An unmarried father has no automatic parental rights but can acquire parental rights and responsibilities by applying to the court or by acquiring them under a parental responsibilities an agreement made with the mother. The Family Law (Scotland) Bill proposes to give automatic parental rights and responsibilities to an unmarried father if he registers the child's birth along with the mother. The father of any child, regardless of parental rights, has a duty to aliment that child until he/she is 18 (25 if he/she is still in full-time education).

LEGITIMATION

Under the Legitimacy Act 1976, an illegitimate person automatically becomes legitimate when his/her parents marry. This applies even where one of the parents was married to a third person at the time of the birth. In such cases it is necessary to re-register the birth of the child. In Scotland, the relevant legislation is the Legitimation (Scotland) Act 1968, the Adoption (Scotland) Act 1978 and the Law Reform (Parent and Child) Scotland Act 1986 which gives illegitimate and legitimate persons equal status.

JURY SERVICE

In England and Wales a person charged with more serious criminal offences and more complex civil cases is entitled to be tried by jury. No such right exists in Scotland, although more serious offences are heard before a jury. In England and Wales there are 12 members of a jury in a criminal case and eight members in a civil case. In Scotland there are 12 members of a jury in a civil case in the Court of Session (the civil jury being confined to the Court of Session and a restricted number of actions), and 15 in a criminal trial. Jurors are normally asked to serve for ten working days, although jurors selected for longer cases are expected to sit for the duration of the trial.

Every 'registered' parliamentary or local government elector between the ages of 18 and 70 who has lived in the UK (including, for this purpose, the Channel Islands and the Isle of Man) for any period of at least five years since reaching the age of 13 is qualified to serve on a jury unless he/she is ineligible or disqualified.

Those ineligible for jury service include:
- those who have at any time been judges, tribunal chairmen, registrars, magistrates or senior court officials
- those who have within the previous ten years been concerned with the administration of justice
- priests and ministers of any religion and vowed members of religious communities
- certain sufferers from mental illness

Those disqualified from jury service include:
- those who have at any time been sentenced by a court in the UK (including, for this purpose, the Channel Islands and the Isle of Man) to a term of imprisonment or youth custody of five years or more
- those who have within the previous ten years served any part of a sentence of imprisonment, youth custody or detention, been detained in a young offenders' institution, received a suspended sentence of imprisonment or order for detention, or received a community service order
- those who have within the previous five years been placed on probation
- those who are on bail in criminal proceedings

Those who may be excused as of right from jury service include:
- persons over the age of 65
- members and officers of the Houses of Parliament
- members of the National Assembly for Wales
- representatives to the European Parliament
- full-time serving members of the armed forces
- registered and practising members of the medical, dental, nursing, veterinary and pharmaceutical professions
- those who have served on a jury in the previous two years
- peers and officers of the House of Lords
- practising members of religious societies or orders whose beliefs are incompatible with jury service

The court has the discretion to excuse a juror from service, or defer the date of service, if the juror can show there is good reason why he should be excused from attending or good reason why his attendance should be deferred. If a person serves on a jury knowing himself/herself to be ineligible or disqualified, he/she is liable to be fined up to £5,000 if disqualified and up to £1,000 for all other offences. The defendant can object to any juror if he/she can show cause.

A juror may claim travelling expenses, a subsistence allowance and an allowance for other financial loss (e.g. loss of earnings or benefits, fees paid to carers or child-minders) up to a stated limit. It is an offence for a juror to disclose what happened in the jury room even after the trial is over. A jury's verdict need not be unanimous. In criminal proceedings the agreement of ten jurors will suffice. In civil proceedings the agreement of seven jurors will suffice. However the court must be satisfied that the jury had reasonable time to consider its verdict based on the nature and complexity of the case. In criminal proceedings this must be no less than two hours.

SCOTLAND

Qualification criteria for jury service in Scotland are similar to those in England and Wales, except that the maximum age for a juror is 65, members of the judiciary are ineligible for ten years after ceasing to hold their post, and others concerned with the administration of justice are only eligible for service five years after ceasing to hold office. Certain persons who have the right to be excused include full-time members of the medical, dental, nursing, veterinary and pharmaceutical professions, full-time members of the armed forces, ministers of religion, persons who have served on a jury within the previous five years, members of the Scottish Parliament, members of the Scottish Executive and junior Scottish Ministers. Those convicted of a serious crime are automatically disqualified. Those who are incapable by reason of a mental disorder may also be excused. The maximum fine for a person serving on a jury knowing himself/herself to be ineligible is £1,000. The maximum fine for failing to attend without good cause is also £1,000. Further information can be obtained from:

THE COURT SERVICE
Southside, 105 Victoria Street, London SW1E 6QT
T 020-7210 2266

THE CLERK OF JUSTICIARY
High Court of Justiciary, Lawnmarket, Edinburgh EH2 2NS
T 0131-225 2595

LANDLORD AND TENANT

RESIDENTIAL LETTINGS

The provisions outlined here apply only where the tenant lives in a separate dwelling from the landlord and where the dwelling is the tenant's only or main home. It does not apply to licensees such as lodgers, guests or service occupiers.

The 1996 Housing Act radically changed certain aspects of the legislation referred to below; in particular, the grant of assured and assured shorthold tenancies under the Housing Act 1988.

ASSURED SHORTHOLD TENANCIES

If a tenancy was granted on or after 15 January 1989 and before 28 February 1997, the tenant would have an assured tenancy unless the landlord served notice under section 20 in the prescribed form prior to the commencement of the tenancy, stating that the tenancy is to be an assured shorthold tenancy and the tenancy is for a minimum fixed term period of six months (*see* below). An assured tenancy gives that tenant greater rights of security. The tenant could, for example, stay in possession of the dwelling for as long as the tenant observed the terms of the tenancy. The landlord cannot obtain possession from such a tenant unless the landlord can establish a specific ground for possession (set out in the Housing Act 1988) and obtains a court order. The rent payable is that agreed with the landlord at the start of the tenancy. The landlord has the right to increase the rent annually by serving a notice. If that happens the tenant can apply to have the rent fixed by the rent assessment committee of the local authority. The tenant or the landlord may request that the committee sets the rent in line with open market rents for that type of property.

Under the Housing Act 1996, all new lettings entered into on or after 28 February 1997 (for whatever term) will be assured shorthold tenancies unless the landlord serves a notice stating that the tenancy is not to be an assured shorthold tenancy. This means that the landlord is entitled to possession at the end of the tenancy provided he serves a notice under section 21 Housing Act 1988 and commences the proceedings in accordance with the correct procedure. The landlord must obtain a court order, however, to obtain possession if the tenant refuses to vacate at the end of the tenancy. If the tenancy is an assured shorthold tenancy, the court must grant the order. For both assured and assured shorthold tenancies, if the tenant is more than eight weeks in arrears, the landlord can serve notice and, if the tenant is still in arrears at the date of the hearing, the court must make an order for possession.

REGULATED TENANCIES

Before the Housing Act 1988 came into force (15 January 1989) there were regulated tenancies; some are still in existence and are protected by the Rent Act 1977. Under this Act it is possible for the landlord or the tenant to apply to the local rent officer to have a 'fair' rent registered. The fair rent is then the maximum rent payable.

SECURE TENANCIES

Secure tenancies are generally given to tenants of local authorities, housing associations (before 15 January 1989) and certain other bodies. This gives the tenant security of tenure unless the terms of the agreement are broken by the tenant and it is reasonable to make an order for possession. Those with secure tenancies may have the right to buy their property. In practice this right is generally only available to council tenants.

AGRICULTURAL PROPERTY

Tenancies in agricultural properties are governed by the Agricultural Holdings Act 1986 and the Rent (Agricultural) Act 1976, which give similar protections to those described above, e.g. security of tenure, right to compensation for disturbance, etc. The Agricultural Holdings (Scotland) Act 1991 applies similar provisions to Scotland.

EVICTION

The Protection from Eviction Act 1977 (as amended by the Housing Act 1988) sets out the procedure a landlord must follow in order to obtain possession of property. It is unlawful for a landlord to evict a tenant otherwise than in accordance with the law. For common law tenancies and for Rent Act tenants a Notice to Quit in the prescribed form giving 28 days is required. For secure and assured tenancies a Notice Seeking Possession must be served. It is unlawful for the landlord to evict a person by putting their belongings onto the street, by changing the locks and so on. It is also unlawful for a landlord to harass a tenant in any way in order to persuade him/her to give up the tenancy. The tenant may be able to obtain an injunction to restrain the actions of the landlord and get back into the property and be awarded damages.

LANDLORD RESPONSIBILITIES

Under the Landlord and Tenant Act 1985, where the term of the lease is less than seven years, the landlord is responsible for maintaining the structure and exterior of the property, for sanitation, for heating and hot water, and all installations for the supply of water, gas and electricity.

LEASEHOLDERS

Legally leaseholders have bought a long lease rather than a property and in certain limited circumstances the landlord can end the tenancy. Under the Leasehold Reform Act 1967 (as amended by the Housing Acts 1969, 1974 and 1980), leaseholders of houses may have the right to buy the freehold or to take an extended lease for a term of 50 years. This applies to leases where the term of the lease is over 21 years and where the leaseholder has occupied the house as his/her main residence for the last three years, or for a total of three years over the last ten.

The Leasehold Reform, Housing and Urban Development Act came into force in 1993 and allows the leaseholders of flats in certain circumstances to buy the freehold of the building in which they live.

Responsibility for maintenance of the structure, exterior and interior of the building should be set out in the lease. Usually the upkeep of the interior of his/her part of the property is the responsibility of the leaseholder, and responsibility for the structure, exterior and common interior areas is shared between the freeholder and the leaseholder(s).

If leaseholders are in any way dissatisfied with treatment from their landlord or with charges made in respect of lease extensions, they are entitled to have their situation evaluated by the Leasehold Valuation Tribunal.

The Commonhold and Leasehold Reform Act 2002 makes provision for the freehold estate in land to be registered as commonhold land and for the legal interest in the land to be vested in a 'commonhold association' i.e. a private limited company.

BUSINESS LETTINGS

The Landlord and Tenant Acts 1927 and 1954 (as amended) give security of tenure to the tenants of most business premises. The landlord can only evict the tenant on one of the grounds laid down in the 1954 Act, and in some cases where the landlord repossesses the property the tenant may be entitled to compensation.

SCOTLAND

In Scotland assured and short assured tenancies exist for lettings after 2 January 1989 and are similar to assured tenancies in England and Wales. The relevant legislation is the Housing (Scotland) Act 1988.

Most tenancies created before 2 January 1989 were regulated tenancies and the Rent (Scotland) Act 1984 still applies where these exist. The Act defines, among other things, the circumstances in which a landlord can increase the rent when improvements are made to the property. The provisions of the Rent Act do not apply to tenancies where the landlord is the Crown, a local authority, the development corporation of a new town or a housing corporation.

The Housing (Scotland) Act 1987 and its provisions relate to local authority responsibilities for housing, the right to buy, and local authority secured tenancies. The provisions are broadly similar to England and Wales.

In Scotland, business premises are not controlled by statute to the same extent as in England and Wales, although the Tenancy of Shops (Scotland) Act 1949 gives some security to tenants of shops. Tenants of shops can apply to the sheriff, within 21 days of being served a notice to quit, for a renewal of tenancy if threatened with eviction. This application may be dismissed on various grounds including where the landlord has offered to sell the property to the tenant at an agreed price or, in the absence of agreement as to price, at a price fixed by a single arbiter appointed by the parties or the sheriff. The Act extends to properties where the Crown or government departments are the landlords or the tenants.

Under the Leases Act 1449 the landlord's successors (either purchasers or creditors) are bound by the agreement made with any tenants so long as the following conditions are met:
- the lease, if for more than one year, must be in writing
- there must be a rent
- there must be a term of expiry
- the tenant must have entered into possession
- the subjects of the lease must be land
- the landlord, if owner, must be infeft i.e. the title deeds are recorded in the Register of Sasines or the Land Register.

LEGAL AID

The Access to Justice Act 1999 has transformed what used to be known as the Legal Aid system. The Legal Aid Board has been abolished and replaced from 1 April 2000 with the Legal Services Commission (85 Gray's Inn Road, London WC1X 8TX T 020-7759 0000 W www.legalservices.gov.uk). The Legal Services Commission is responsible for the development and administration of two legal funding schemes in England and Wales, namely the Criminal Defence Service (which replaced the old system of criminal legal aid) and the Community Legal Service fund (which replaced the old civil scheme of legal aid). The Community Legal Service is designed to increase access to legal information and advice by involving a much wider network of funders and providers in giving publicly funded legal services. In Scotland, provision of legal aid is governed by the Legal Aid (Scotland) Act 1986.

CIVIL LEGAL AID

From 1 January 2000, only organisations (solicitors or Citizens Advice Bureaux) with a contract with the Legal Services Commission have been able to give initial help in any civil matter. Moreover, from that date decisions about funding were devolved from the Legal Services Commission to contracted organisations in relation to any level of publicly funded service in family and immigration cases. For other types of case, applications for public funding are made through a solicitor (or other contracted legal services providers) in much the same way as the former Legal Aid. On 1 April 2001 the so-called civil contracting scheme was extended to cover all levels of service for all types of cases.

Under the new civil funding scheme there are broadly seven levels of service available:
- legal help
- help at court (the first two types of service are limited to advice and assistance with preparing a case, but do not include representation)
- approved family help – either general family help or help with mediation (special levels of service for family cases)
- legal representation – either investigative help or full representation (this covers assistance with representation in court)
- support funding – either investigative support or litigation support (this is a new type of assistance which allows the costs of a privately funded case to be topped up from public funds. It is only available for personal injury claims (excluding clinical negligence) and some multi-party action)
- family mediation
- such other services as are specifically authorised by the Lord Chancellor

In general, public funding is not available for the following types of cases:
- personal injury (except for the availability of support funding and clinical negligence claims)
- allegations of negligent damage to property
- conveyancing
- boundary disputes
- the making of wills
- matters of trust law
- defamation proceedings
- partnership disputes and company law
- other matters arising out of the carrying on of a business

ELIGIBILITY

Eligibility for funding from the Community Legal Service depends broadly on five factors:
- the level of service sought (see above)
- whether the applicant qualifies financially
- the merits of the applicant's case
- a costs-benefits analysis (if the costs are likely to outweigh any benefit that might be gained from the proceedings, funding may be refused)
- whether there is any public interest in the case being litigated (i.e. whether the case has a wider public interest beyond that of the parties involved – for example, a human rights case)

The limits on capital and income above which a person is

not entitled to public funding vary with the type of service sought.

CONTRIBUTIONS

Some of those who qualify for Community Legal Service funding will have to contribute towards their legal costs. Contributions must be paid by anyone who has a disposable income or disposable capital exceeding a prescribed amount. The rules relating to applicable contributions are complex and detailed information can be obtained from the Legal Services Commission.

STATUTORY CHARGE

A statutory charge is made if a person receives money or property in a case for which they have received legal aid. This means that the amount paid by the Community Legal Service fund on their behalf is deducted from the amount that the person receives. This does not apply if the court has ordered that the costs be paid by the other party (unless the amount paid by the other party does not cover all of the costs) or if the payments are for maintenance;

- or to the first £2,500 of any money or property the applicant gains or keeps in divorce cases and most other family proceedings
- where the solicitor is advising the applicant whilst they attend family mediation under a 'help with mediation' certificate
- where advice is given only under the 'legal help' scheme in any matter other than family or personal injury after 1 April 2000

CONTINGENCY OR CONDITIONAL FEES

This system was introduced by the Courts and Legal Services Act 1990. It offers legal representation on a 'no win, no fee' basis. It provides an alternative form of assistance, especially for those cases which are ineligible for funding by the Community Legal Service. The main area for such work is in the field of personal injuries, which claims are now largely exempt from public funding (except for clinical negligence claims).

Not all solicitors offer such a scheme and different solicitors may well have different terms. The effect of the agreement is that solicitors will not make any charges until the case is concluded successfully. If a case is won then the losing party will usually have to pay towards costs, with the winning party contributing around one-third.

SCOTLAND

Civil legal aid is available for cases in the following:
- the House of Lords
- the Court of Session
- the Lands Valuation Appeal Court
- the Scottish Land Court
- sheriff courts
- the Lands Tribunal for Scotland
- the Employment Appeal Tribunals
- the Restrictive Practices Court

Civil legal aid is not available for defamation actions, small claims or simplified divorce procedures.

Eligibility for civil legal aid is assessed in a similar way to that in England and Wales, though the financial limits differ in some respects and are as follows:
- a person is eligible and will not have to pay a contribution if his yearly disposable income is £2,931 or less and disposable capital is £6,465 or less
- if disposable income exceeds £9,570, the person is not eligible for legal aid

- if disposable income is between £2,931 and £9,570, contributions are payable
- if disposable capital exceeds £10,779, the person is not eligible for legal aid
- if disposable capital is between £6,465 and £10,779, contributions are payable
- those receiving income support or income-related job seeker's allowance qualify automatically

CRIMINAL LEGAL AID

The courts will grant criminal legal aid for representation if it is desirable in the interests of justice (e.g. if there are important questions of law to be argued or the case is so serious that if found guilty the person may go to prison) and the person needs help to pay their legal costs.

Criminal legal aid covers the cost of preparing a case and legal representation (including the cost of a barrister) in criminal proceedings. It is also available for appeals against verdicts or sentences in magistrates' courts, the Crown Court or the Court of Appeal. It is not available for bringing a private prosecution in a criminal court.

If granted criminal legal aid, either the person may choose their own solicitor or the court will assign one. Contributions to the legal costs must be paid by anyone who has a disposable income or disposable capital which exceeds a prescribed amount. The rules relating to applicable contributions are complex and detailed information can be obtained from the Legal Services Commission.

DUTY SOLICITORS

The Legal Aid Act 1988 also provides free advice and assistance to anyone questioned by the police (whether under arrest or helping the police with their enquiries). No means test or contributions are required for this.

SCOTLAND

Legal advice and assistance operates in a similar way in Scotland. A person is eligible:
- if disposable income does not exceed £203 a week. If disposable income is between £86 and £203 a week, contributions are payable
- if disposable capital does not exceed £1,412 (if the person has dependent relatives, the savings allowance is higher)
- if receiving income support or income-related job seeker's allowance they qualify automatically provided they have no savings over the limit.

The procedure for application for criminal legal aid depends on the circumstances of each case. In solemn cases (more serious cases, such as murder) heard before a jury, a person is automatically entitled to criminal legal aid until they are given bail or placed in custody. Thereafter, it is for the court to decide whether to grant legal aid. The court will do this if the person accused cannot meet the expenses of the case without undue hardship on him or his dependants. In less serious cases the procedure depends on whether the person is in custody:
- anyone taken into custody has the right to free legal aid from the duty solicitor up to and including the first court appearance
- if the person is not in custody and wishes to plead guilty, they are not entitled to criminal legal aid but may be entitled to legal advice and assistance, including assistance by way of representation
- if the person is not in custody and wishes to plead not guilty, they can apply for criminal legal aid. This must

be done within 14 days of the first court appearance at which they made the plea

The criteria used to assess whether or not criminal legal aid should be granted is similar to the criteria for England and Wales. When meeting with your solicitor, take evidence of your financial position such as details of savings, bank statements, pay slips, pension book or benefits book.

Further information can be obtained from:

THE SCOTTISH LEGAL AID BOARD
44 Drumsheugh Gardens, Edinburgh EH3 7SW
T 0131-226 7061

MARRIAGE

Any two persons may marry provided that:
- they are at least 16-years-old on the day of the marriage (in England and Wales persons under the age of 18 must generally obtain the consent of their parents; if consent is refused an appeal may be made to the High Court, the county court or a court of summary jurisdiction)
- they are not related to one another in a way which would prevent their marrying
- they are unmarried (a person who has already been married must produce documentary evidence that the previous marriage has been ended by death, divorce or annulment)
- they are not of the same sex
- they are capable of understanding the nature of a marriage ceremony and of consenting to marriage
- the marriage may be valid in England and Wales and void by the law of the domicile of both or either of the parties. The parties should check the marriage will be recognised as valid in their home country

DEGREES OF RELATIONSHIP

A marriage between persons within the prohibited degrees of consanguinity, affinity or adoption is void.

A man may not marry his mother, daughter, grandmother, granddaughter, sister, aunt, niece, great-grandmother, great-granddaughter, adoptive mother, former adoptive mother, adopted daughter or former adopted daughter. In some circumstances he may now be allowed to marry his former wife's daughter, former wife's granddaughter, father's former wife or grandfather's former wife.

A woman may not marry her father, son, grandfather, grandson, brother, uncle, nephew, great-grandfather, great-grandson, adoptive father, former adoptive father, adopted son or former adopted son. In some circumstances she may now be allowed to marry her former husband's son, former husband's grandson, mother's former husband or grandmother's former husband.

ENGLAND AND WALES

TYPES OF MARRIAGE CEREMONY

It is possible to marry by either religious or civil ceremony. A religious ceremony can take place at a church or chapel of the Church of England or the Church in Wales, or at any other place of worship which has been formally registered by the Registrar-General.

A civil ceremony can take place at a register office, a registered building or any other premises approved by the local authority.

An application for an approved premises licence must be made by the owners or trustees of the building concerned; it cannot be made by the prospective marriage couple. Approved premises must be regularly open to the public so that the marriage can be witnessed; the venue must be deemed to be a permanent and immovable structure. Open-air ceremonies are prohibited.

Non-Anglican marriages may also be solemnised following the issue of a Registrar-General's licence in unregistered premises where one of the parties is seriously ill, is not expected to recover, and cannot be moved to registered premises. Detained and housebound persons may be married at their place of residence.

MARRIAGE IN THE CHURCH OF ENGLAND OR THE CHURCH IN WALES

Marriage by banns

The marriage must take place in a parish in which one of the parties lives, or in a church in another parish if it is the usual place of worship of either or both of the parties. The banns must be called in the parish in which the marriage is to take place on three Sundays before the day of the ceremony; if either or both of the parties lives in a different parish the banns must also be called there. After three months the banns are no longer valid. The minister will not perform the marriage unless he or she is satisfied that the banns have been properly called.

Marriage by common licence

The vicar who is to conduct the marriage will arrange for a common licence to be issued by the diocesan bishop; this dispenses with the necessity for banns. One of the parties must have lived in the parish for 15 days immediately before the issuing of the licence or must usually worship at the church. At least one of the parties must be baptised. The licence is valid for three months.

Marriage by special licence

A special licence is granted by the Archbishop of Canterbury in special circumstances for the marriage to take place at any place, with or without previous residence in the parish, or at any time. Application must be made to the registrar of the Faculty Office, 1 The Sanctuary, London SW1P 3JT T 020-7222 5381.

Marriage by certificate

The marriage can be conducted on the authority of the superintendent registrar's certificate, provided that the vicar's consent is obtained. One of the parties must live in the parish or must usually worship at the church.

MARRIAGE BY OTHER RELIGIOUS CEREMONY

One of the parties must normally live in the registration district where the marriage is to take place. In addition to giving notice to the superintendent registrar it may also be necessary to book a registrar to be present at the ceremony.

CIVIL MARRIAGE

A marriage may be solemnised at any register office, registered building or approved premises in England and Wales. The superintendent registrar of the district should be contacted, and, if the marriage is to take place at approved premises, the necessary arrangements at the venue must also be made.

NOTICE OF MARRIAGE

Unless it is to take place by banns or under common or special licence in the Church of England or the Church in Wales, a notice of the marriage must be given in person to

the superintendent registrar. Notice of marriage may be given in the following ways:
– by certificate. Both parties must have lived in a registration district in England or Wales for at least seven days immediately before giving notice at the local register office. If they live in different registration districts, notice must be given in both districts. The marriage can take place in any register office or other approved premises in England and Wales no sooner than 16 days after notice has been given, when the superintendent registrar issues a certificate.
– by licence (often known as 'special licence'). One of the parties must have lived in a registration district in England or Wales for at least 15 days before giving notice at the register office; the other party need only be a resident of, or be physically in, England and Wales on the day notice is given. The marriage can take place one clear day (other than a Sunday, Christmas Day or Good Friday) after notice has been given.

A notice of marriage is valid for 12 months, unless it is to take place in the Church of England or Church of Wales, when it will usually only be accepted within three months of publication. It should be possible to make an advance (provisional) booking 12 months before the ceremony. In this case it is still necessary to give formal notice three months before the marriage. When giving notice of the marriage it is necessary to produce official proof, if relevant, that any previous marriage has ended in divorce or death by producing a decree absolute or death certificate; it is also useful, but not necessary, to take birth certificates or passports as proof of age and identity.

SOLEMNISATION OF THE MARRIAGE

On the day of the wedding there must be at least two other people present who are prepared to act as witnesses and sign the marriage register. A registrar of marriages must be present at a marriage in a register office or at approved premises, but an authorised person may act in the capacity of registrar in a registered building.

If the marriage takes place at approved premises, the room must be separate from any other activity on the premises at the time of the ceremony, and no food or drink can be sold or consumed in the room during the ceremony or for one hour beforehand.

The marriage must be solemnised between 8 a.m. and 6 p.m., with open doors. At some time during the ceremony the parties must make a declaration that they know of no legal impediment to the marriage and they must also say the contracting words; the declaratory and contracting words may vary according to the form of service. A civil marriage cannot contain any religious aspects, but it may be possible for non-religious music and/or poetry readings to be included. It may also be possible to embellish the marriage vows taken by the couple.

CIVIL FEES

Marriage at a Register Office
By superintendent registrar's certificate, £94.00
    This includes a fee of £34.00 for the registrar's attendance on the day of the wedding.

Marriage on Approved Premises
By superintendent registrar's certificate, £60.00
    An additional fee will also be payable for the superintendent registrar's and registrar's attendance at the marriage. This is set locally by the local authority responsible. A further charge is likely to be made by the owners of the building for the use of the premises. For

marriages taking place in a religious building other than the Church of England or Church of Wales, an additional fee of £40.00 is payable for the registrar's attendance at the marriage unless an 'Authorised Person' appointed by the trustees of the building has agreed to register the marriage. Additional fees may be charged by the trustees of the building for the wedding and by the person who performs the ceremony.

ECCLESIASTICAL FEES

(Church of England and Church in Wales*)
Marriage by banns
For publication of banns, £18.00
For certificate of banns issued at time of publication, £12.00
For marriage service, £198.00
Marriage by common licence
Fee for licence, £66.00
Marriage by special licence
Fee for licence, £133.00
* Some of these fees may not apply to the Church in Wales

SCOTLAND

REGULAR MARRIAGES

A regular marriage is one which is celebrated by a minister of religion or authorised registrar or other celebrant. Each of the parties must complete a marriage notice form and return it to the district registrar for the area in which they are to be married, irrespective of where they live, at least 15 days before the ceremony is due to take place. The district registrar must then enter the date of receipt and certain details in a marriage book kept for this purpose, and must also enter the names of the parties and the proposed date of marriage in a list which is displayed in a conspicuous place at the registration office until the date of the marriage has passed. All persons wishing to enter into a regular marriage in Scotland must follow the same preliminary procedure regardless of whether they intend to have a religious or civil ceremony. Before the marriage ceremony takes place any person may submit an objection in writing to the district registrar.

A marriage schedule, which is prepared by the registrar, will be issued to one or both of the parties in person up to seven days before a religious marriage; for a civil marriage the schedule will be available at the ceremony. The schedule must be handed to the celebrant before the ceremony starts; it must be signed immediately after the wedding and the marriage must be registered within three days.

The authority to conduct a religious marriage is deemed to be vested in the authorised celebrant rather than the building in which it takes place; open-air religious ceremonies are therefore permissible in Scotland.

From 10 June 2002 it has been possible, under the Marriage (Scotland) Act 2002, for venues or couples to apply to the local council for a licence to allow a civil ceremony to take place at a venue other than a registration office. To obtain further information, a venue or couple should contact the district registrar in the area they wish to marry. A list of licensed venues is also available on the General Registers of Scotland website at
W www.gro-scotland.gov.uk.

MARRIAGE BY COHABITATION WITH HABIT AND REPUTE

If two people live together constantly as husband and wife and are generally held to be such by the neighbourhood and among their friends and relations, there may arise a presumption from which marriage can be inferred. Before such a marriage can be registered, however, a decree of declarator of marriage must be obtained from the Court of Session.

CIVIL FEES

The fee for a religious marriage is £93.50, comprising a fee of £20.00 per person for the statutory notice of an intention to marry, a £45 fee for the solemnisation of the marriage in a register office and an £8.50 fee for a copy of the marriage certificate. The cost of marrying in a registration office or under a local authority licence can vary.

Further information can be obtained from:

THE GENERAL REGISTER OFFICE
Office for National Statistics, Smedley Hydro, Trafalgar Road, Southport, Merseyside PR8 2HH

THE GENERAL REGISTER OFFICE FOR SCOTLAND
New Register House, 3 West Register Street, Edinburgh EH1 3YT

TOWN AND COUNTRY PLANNING

The planning system is important in helping to protect the environment, as well as assisting individuals in assessing their land rights. There are a number of Acts governing the development of land and buildings in England and Wales and advice should always be sought from a Citizens Advice Bureau or local planning authority before undertaking building works on any land or to property. If development takes place which requires planning permission without permission being given, enforcement action may take place and the situation may need to be rectified.

PLANNING PERMISSION

Planning permission is needed if the work involves:
- making a material change in use, such as dividing off part of the house so that it can be used as a separate home or dividing off part of the house for commercial use, e.g. for a workshop
- going against the terms of the original planning permission, e.g. there may be a restriction on fences in front gardens on an open-plan estate
- building, engineering for mining, except for the permissions below
- new or wider access to a main road
- additions or extensions to flats or maisonettes

Planning permission is not needed to carry out internal alterations or work which does not affect the external appearance of the building, and are not works for making good damage or works begun after 5 December 1968 for the alteration of a building by providing additional space in it underground.

There are certain types of development for which the Secretary of State for the Environment, Food and Rural Affairs has granted general permissions (permitted development rights). These include:
- house extensions and additions (including conservatories, loft conversions, garages and dormer windows). Up to 10 per cent or up to 50 cubic metres (whichever is the greater) can be added to the original house for terraced houses or houses on land designated as an area of outstanding natural beauty or in a conservation area. Up to 15 per cent or 70 cubic metres (whichever is the greater) to other kinds of houses. The maximum that can be added to any house is 115 cubic metres
- buildings such as garden sheds and greenhouses so long as they are no more than 3 metres high (or 4 metres if the roof is ridged), are no nearer to a highway than the house or 20 metres (whichever is nearer), and at least half the ground around the house remains uncovered by buildings
- adding a porch with a ground area of less than 3 square metres and that is less than 3 metres in height and not within 2 metres of any boundary of the curtilage of the dwelling house with a highway
- putting up fences, walls and gates of under 1 metre in height if next to a road and under 2 metres elsewhere
- laying patios, paths or driveways for domestic use.

However, before carrying out any of the above permitted developments you should contact your local authority to find out whether the general permission has been modified in your area.

OTHER RESTRICTIONS

It may be necessary to obtain other types of permissions before carrying out any development. These permissions are separate from planning permission and apply regardless of whether or not planning permission is needed, e.g.:
- building regulations will probably apply if a new building is to be erected, if an existing one is to be altered or extended, or if the work involves building over a drain or sewer. The building control department of the local authority will advise on this
- any alterations to a listed building or the grounds of a listed building must be approved by the local authority. Listing will include not only the main building but everything in the curtilage of the building
- local authority approval is necessary if a building (or, in some circumstances, gates, walls, fences or railings) in a conservation area is to be demolished; each local authority keeps a register of all local buildings that are in conservation areas
- many trees are protected by tree preservation orders and must not be pruned or taken down without local authority consent
- bats and other species are protected and English Nature, the Countryside Council for Wales or Scottish Natural Heritage must be notified before any work is carried out that will affect the habitat of protected species, e.g. timber treatment, renovation or extensions of lofts
- any development in areas designated as a National Park, an Area of Outstanding National Beauty, a National Scenic Area or in the Norfolk or Suffolk Broads is subject to greater restrictions. The local planning authority will advise or refer enquirers to the relevant authority

If you think you require planning permission, contact your local authority. There may also be restriction on development contained in the title to the property which should be considered when works are planned.

VOTERS' QUALIFICATIONS

Those entitled to vote at parliamentary, European Union (EU) and local government elections are those who are:
- on the electoral roll. Local authorities administer the roll and non-registration can lead to a fine of up to £1,000
- over 18-years-old

– Commonwealth (which includes British) citizens or citizens of the Republic of Ireland
– In Northern Ireland electors must have been resident in Northern Ireland during the whole of the three-month period prior to the relevant date

British citizens resident abroad are entitled to vote, for 15 years after leaving Britain, as overseas electors in parliamentary and EU elections in the constituency in which they were last resident. Members of the armed forces, Crown servants and employees of the British Council who are overseas and their spouses are entitled to vote regardless of how long they have been abroad. British citizens who had never been registered as an elector in the UK are not eligible to register as an overseas voter unless they left the UK before they were 18, providing they left the country no more than 15 years ago.

European Union citizens resident in the UK may vote in EU and local government elections. The main categories of people who are not entitled to vote are:
– sitting peers in the House of Lords (although members of the House of Lords can vote at elections to local authorities, devolved legislatures and European Parliament)
– patients detained under mental health legislation who have criminal convictions
– those serving prison sentences
– those convicted within the previous five years of corrupt or illegal election practices

Under the Representation of the Peoples Act 2000, several new groups of people are permitted to vote for the first time. These include: people who live on barges; unconvicted or remand prisoners; people in mental health hospitals (other than those with criminal convictions) and homeless people who have made a 'declaration of local connection'.

REGISTERING TO VOTE

Voters must be entered on an electoral register. The Electoral Registration Officer (ERO) for each council area is responsible for preparing and publishing the register for his area by 1 December each year. Names may be added to the register to reflect changes in people's circumstances as they occur and each month during December to August, the ERO publishes a list of alterations to the published register.

A registration form is sent to all households in the autumn of each year and the householder is required to provide details of all occupants who are eligible to vote, including ones who will reach their 18th birthday in the year covered by the register. Anyone failing to supply information to the ERO when requested, or supplying false information, may be fined. Application forms and more information are available from the Electoral Commission on W www.electoralcommision.gov.uk.

VOTING

Voting is not compulsory in the UK. Those who wish to vote generally vote in person at the allotted polling station. Postal votes are now available to anyone on request and no reasons are required to be given. Those who will be away at the time of the election, those who will not be able to attend in person due to physical incapacity or the nature of their occupation, and those who have changed address during the period for which the register is valid, may apply for a postal vote or nominate a proxy to vote for them. Overseas electors who wish to vote must do so by proxy.

Further information can be obtained from the local authority's ERO in England and Wales or the electoral registration office in Scotland, or the Chief Electoral Officer in Northern Ireland.

WILLS

In a will a person leaves instructions as to the disposal of their property after they die. A will is also used to appoint executors (who will administer the estate), give directions as to the disposal of the body, appoint guardians for children and, for larger estates, can operate to reduce the level of inheritance tax. It is best to have a will drawn up by a solicitor but if a solicitor is not employed, the following points must be taken into account:
– if possible the will must not be prepared on behalf of another person by someone who is to benefit from it or who is a close relative of a major beneficiary
– the language used must be clear and unambiguous and it is better to avoid the use of legal terms where the same thing can be expressed in plain language
– it is better to rewrite the whole document if a mistake is made. If necessary, alterations can be made by striking through the words with a pen, and the signature or initials of the testator and the witnesses must be put in the margin opposite the alteration. No alteration of any kind should be made after the will has been executed
– if the person later wishes to change the will or part of it, it is better to write a new will revoking the old. The use of codicils (documents written as supplements or containing modifications to the will) should be left to a solicitor
– the will should be typed or printed, or if handwritten be legible and preferably in ink. Commercial will forms can be obtained from some stationers

The form of a will varies to suit different cases – a solicitor will be able to advise as to wording, however, 'DIY' will-writing kits can be purchased from good stationery shops and many banks offer a will-writing service.

LAPSED LEGATEES

If a person who has been left property in a will dies before the person who made the will, the gift fails and will pass to the person entitled to everything not otherwise disposed of (the residuary estate).

If the person left the residuary estate dies before the person who made the will, their share will generally pass to the closest relative(s) of the person who made the will (as in intestacy), unless the will names a beneficiary such as a charity who will take as a 'long stop' if this gift is unable to take effect for any reason. It is always better to draw up a new will if a beneficiary predeceases the person who made the will.

EXECUTORS

It is usual to appoint two executors, although one is sufficient. No more than four persons can deal with the estate of the person who has died. The name and address of each executor should be given in full (the addresses are not essential but including them adds clarity to the document). Executors should be 18 years of age or over. An executor may be a beneficiary of the will.

WITNESSES

A person who is a beneficiary of a will, or the spouse of a beneficiary at the time the will is signed, must not act as a witness or else he/she will be unable to take his/her gift. Husband and wife can both act as witnesses provided neither benefits from the will.

It is better that a person does not act as an executor and as a witness, as he/she can take no benefit under a will to which he/she is witness. The identity of the witnesses should be made as explicit as possible.

EXECUTION OF A WILL
The person making the will should sign his/her name at the foot of the document, in the presence of the two witnesses. The witnesses must then sign their names while the person making the will looks on. If this procedure is not adhered to, the will be considered invalid. There are certain exceptional circumstances where these rules are relaxed, e.g. where the person may be too ill to sign.

CAPACITY TO MAKE A WILL
Anyone aged 18 or over can make a will. However, if there is any suspicion that the person making the will is not, through reasons of infirmity or age, fully in command of his/her faculties, it is advisable to arrange for a medical practitioner to examine the person making the will at the time it is to be executed (to verify his/her mental capacity and to record that medical opinion in writing), and to ask the examining practitioner to act as a witness. If a person is not mentally able to make a will, the Court may do this for him/her by virtue of the Mental Health Act 1983.

REVOCATION
A will may be revoked or cancelled in a number of ways:
- a later will revokes an earlier one if it says so; otherwise the earlier will is impliedly revoked by the later one to the extent that it contradicts or repeats the earlier one
- a will is also revoked if the physical document on which it is written is destroyed by the person whose will it is. There must be an intention to revoke the will. It may not be sufficient to obliterate the will with a pen
- a will is revoked when the person marries, unless it is clear from the will that the person intended the will to stand after the marriage
- where a marriage ends in divorce or is annulled or declared void, gifts to the spouse and the appointment of the spouse as executor fail unless the will says that this is not to happen. A former spouse is treated as having predeceased the testator. A separation does not change the effect of a married person's will.

PROBATE AND LETTERS OF ADMINISTRATION
Probate is granted to the executors named in a will and once granted, the executors are obliged to carry out the instructions of the will. Letters of administration are granted where no executor is named in a will or is willing or able to act or where there is no will or no valid will; this gives a person, often the next of kin, similar powers and duties to those of an executor.

Applications for probate or for letters of administration can be made to the Principal Registry of the Family Division, to a district probate registry or to a probate sub-registry. Applicants will need the following documents: the original will (if any); a certificate of death; oath for executors or administrators; particulars of all property and assets left by the deceased and a list of debts and funeral expenses. Certain property, up to the value of £5,000, may be disposed of without a grant of probate or letters of administration.

WHERE TO FIND A PROVED WILL
Since 1858 wills which have been proved, that is wills on which probate or letters of administration have been granted, must have been proved at the Principal Registry of the Family Division or at a district probate registry. The Lord Chancellor has power to direct where the original documents are kept but most are filed where they were proved and may be inspected there and a copy obtained. The Principal Registry also holds copies of all wills proved at district probate registries and these may be inspected at First Avenue House, High Holborn. An index of all grants, both of probate and of letters of administration, is compiled by the Principal Registry and may be seen either at the Principal Registry or at a district probate registry.

It is also possible to discover when a grant of probate or letters of administration is issued by requesting a standing search. In response to a request and for a small fee, a district probate registry will supply the names and addresses of executors or administrators and the registry in which the grant was made, of any grant in the estate of a specified person made in the previous 12 months or following six months. This is useful for applicants who may be beneficiaries to a will but who have lost contact with the deceased and for creditors of the deceased.

SCOTLAND
In Scotland any person over 12 and of sound mind can make a will. The person making the will can only freely dispose of the heritage and what is known as the 'dead's part' of the estate because:
- the spouse has the right to inherit one-third of the moveable estate if there are children or other descendants, and one-half of it if there are not
- children are entitled to one-third of the moveable estate if there is a surviving spouse, and one-half of it if there is not

The remaining portion is the dead's part, and legacies and bequests are payable from this. Debts are payable out of the whole estate before any division.

From August 1995, wills no longer needed to be 'holographed' and it is now only necessary to have one witness. The person making the will still needs to sign each page. It is better that the will is not witnessed by a beneficiary although the attestation would still be sound and the beneficiary would not have to relinquish the gift.

Subsequent marriage does not revoke a will but the birth of a child who is not provided for may do so. A will may be revoked by a subsequent will, either expressly or by implication, but in so far as the two can be read together both have effect. If a subsequent will is revoked, the earlier will is revived.

Wills may be registered in the sheriff court Books of the Sheriffdom in which the deceased lived or in the Books of Council and Session at the Registers of Scotland.

CONFIRMATION
Confirmation (the Scottish equivalent of probate) is obtained in the sheriff court of the sheriffdom in which the deceased was resident at the time of death. Executives are either 'nominate' (named by the deceased in the will) or 'dative' (appointed by the court in cases where no executor is named in a will or in cases of intestacy). Applicants for confirmation must first provide an inventory of the deceased's estate and a schedule of debts, with an affidavit. In estates under £25,000 gross, confirmation can be obtained under a simplified procedure at reduced fees, with no need for a solicitor. The local sheriff clerk's office can provide assistance.

Further information can be obtained from:

PRINCIPAL REGISTRY (FAMILY DIVISION)
First Avenue House, 42-49 High Holborn, London WC2V 6NP
T 020-7947 6980

REGISTERS OF SCOTLAND
Meadowbank House, 153 London Road, Edinburgh EH8 7AU
T 0131-659 6111

INTESTACY

Intestacy occurs when someone dies without leaving a will or leaves a will which is invalid or which does not take effect for some reason. Intestacy can be partial, for instance, if there is a will which disposes of some but not all of the testator's property. In such cases the person's estate (property, possessions, other assets following the payment of debts) passes to certain members of the family. The relevant legislation is the Administration of Estates Act 1925, as amended by various legislation including the Intestates Estates Act 1952, the Law Reform (Succession) Act 1995, and the Trusts of Land and Appointment of Trustees Act 1996 and Orders made there under. Some of the provisions of this legislation are described below. If a will has been written that disposes of only part of a person's property, these rules apply to the part which is undisposed of.

If the person (intestate) leaves a spouse who survives for 28 days and children (legitimate, illegitimate and adopted children and other descendants), the estate is divided as follows:
- the spouse takes the 'personal chattels' (household articles, including cars, but nothing used for business purposes), £125,000 free of tax (with interest payable at six per cent from the time of the death until payment) and a life interest in half of the rest of the estate (which can be capitalised by the spouse if he/she wishes)
- the rest of the estate goes to the children*

If the person leaves a spouse who survives for 28 days but no children:
- the spouse takes the personal chattels, £200,000 free of tax (interest payable as before) and full ownership of half of the rest of the estate
- the other half of the rest of the estate goes to the parents (equally, if both alive) or, if none, to the brothers and sisters of the whole blood*
- if there are no parents or brothers or sisters of the whole blood or their children, the spouse takes the whole estate

If there is no surviving spouse, the estate is distributed among those who survive the intestate as follows:
- to surviving children*, but if none to
- parents (equally, if both alive), but if none to
- brothers and sisters of the whole blood* (including issues of deceased ones), but if none to
- brothers and sisters of the half blood* (including issues of deceased ones), but if none to
- grandparents (equally, if more than one), but if none to
- aunts and uncles of the whole blood*, but if none to
- aunts and uncles of the half blood*, but if none to
- the Crown, Duchy of Lancaster or the Duke of Cornwall (bona vacantia)

* To inherit, a member of these groups must survive the intestate and attain the age of 18, or marry under that age. If they die under the age of 18 (unless married under that age), their share goes to others, if any, in the same group. If any member of these groups predeceases the intestate leaving children, their share is divided equally among their children.

In England and Wales the provisions of the Inheritance (Provision for Family and Dependants) Act 1975 may allow other people to claim provision from the deceased's assets. This Act also applies to cases where a will has been made and allows a person to apply to the Court if they feel that the will or rules of intestacy or both do not make adequate provision for them. The Court can order payment from the deceased's assets or the transfer of property from them if the applicant's claim is accepted. The application must be made within six months of the grant of probate or letters of administration and the following people can make an application:
- the spouse
- a former spouse who has not remarried
- a child of the deceased
- someone treated as a child of the deceased's family
- someone maintained by the deceased
- someone who has cohabited for two years before the death in the same household as the deceased and as the husband or wife of the deceased

SCOTLAND

The rules of distribution are contained in the Succession (Scotland) Act 1964.

A surviving spouse is entitled to 'prior rights'. This means that the spouse has the right to inherit:
- the matrimonial home up to a value of £300,000, or one matrimonial home if there is more than one, or, in certain circumstances, the value of the matrimonial home
- the furnishings and contents of that home, up to the value of £24,000
- a cash sum of £42,000 if the deceased left children or other descendants, or £75,000 if not

These figures are increased from time to time by regulations.

Once prior rights have been satisfied jus relicti(ae) and legitim are settled. Legal rights are:

Jus relicti(ae) – the right of a surviving spouse to one-half of the net moveable estate, after satisfaction of prior rights, if there are no surviving children; if there are surviving children, the spouse is entitled to one-third of the net moveable estate

Legitim – the right of surviving children to one-half of the net moveable estate if there is no surviving spouse; if there is a surviving spouse, the children are entitled to one-third of the net moveable estate after the satisfaction of prior rights

Where there are no surviving spouse or children, half of the estate is taken by the parents and half by the brothers and sisters. Failing that, the lines of succession, in general, are:
- to descendants
- if no descendants, then to collaterals (i.e. brothers and sisters) and parents
- surviving spouse
- if no collaterals or parents or spouse, then to ascendants collaterals (i.e. aunts and uncles), and so on in an ascending scale
- if all lines of succession fail, the estate passes to the Crown. Relatives of the whole blood are preferred to relatives of the half blood. The right of representation, i.e. the right of the issue of a person who would have succeeded if he/she had survived the intestate, also applies

INTELLECTUAL PROPERTY

COPYRIGHT

Copyright protects all original literary, dramatic, musical and artistic works (including photographs, maps and plans), published editions of works, computer programs, sound recordings, films (including video and DVD) and broadcasts (including cable, radio, satellite broadcasts, and transmissions on the internet). Under copyright the creators of these works can control the various ways in which their material may be exploited, the rights broadly covering copying, adapting, issuing (including renting and lending) copies to the public, performing in public, and broadcasting the material. The transfer of copyright works to formats accessible to visually impaired persons without infringement of copyright was enacted in 2002.

Copyright protection in the United Kingdom is automatic and there is no official registration system. Steps can be taken by the work's creator to provide evidence that he/she had the work at a particular time (eg by depositing a copy with a bank or solicitor). The main legislation is the Copyright, Designs and Patents Act 1988, which has been amended by other Acts and by Statutory Instrument to take account of EU Directives. As a result of an EU directive effective from January 1996, the term of copyright protection for literary, dramatic, musical and artistic works lasts for 70 years after the death of the author, and for film lasts for 70 years after the death of the last to survive the director, authors of the screenplay and dialogue, or the composer of any music specially created for the film. Sound recordings are protected for 50 years after their publication, and broadcasts for 50 years from the end of the year in which the first broadcast/transmission was made. Published editions remain under copyright protection for 25 years from the end of the year in which the edition was published.

The main international treaties protecting copyright are the Bern Convention for the Protection of Literary and Artistic Works (administered by the World Intellectual Property Organisation (WIPO)), the Rome Convention for the Protection of Performers, Producers of Phonograms and Broadcasting Organisations (administered jointly by UNESCO and the International Labour Organisation), and the Universal Copyright Convention (UNESCO); the UK is a signatory to these conventions. Copyright material created by UK nationals or residents is protected in each country which is a member of the conventions by the national law of that country. A list of participating countries may be obtained from the Patent Office.

Two treaties which strengthen and update international standards of protection, particularly in relation to new technologies, were agreed in December 1996: the WIPO Copyright Treaty, and the WIPO Performance and Phonograms Treaty. In May 2001 the European Union passed a new directive, which in 2003 became law in the UK, aimed at harmonising copyright law throughout the EU to take account of the internet and other technologies. Further information can be found on:

W www.intellectual-property.gov.uk

LICENSING

Use of copyright material without seeking permission in each instance may be permitted under 'blanket' licences available from copyright licensing agencies. The International Federation of Reproduction Rights Organisations facilitates agreements between its member licensing agencies and on behalf of its members with organisations such as the WIPO, UNESCO, the European Union and the Council of Europe.

PATENTS

A patent is a document issued by the Patent Office relating to an invention and giving the proprietor the right for a limited period to stop others from making, using or selling the invention without the inventor's permission. In return the patentee pays a fee to cover the costs of processing the patent and publicly discloses details of the invention.

To qualify for a patent an invention must be new, must exhibit an inventive step, and must be capable of industrial application. The patent is valid for a maximum of 20 years from the date on which the application was filed, subject to payment of annual fees from the end of the fourth year.

The Patent Office, established in 1852, is responsible for ensuring that all stages of an application comply with the Patents Act 1977, and that the invention meets the criteria for a patent.

The WIPO is responsible for administering many of the international conventions on intellectual property. The Patent Co-operation Treaty allows inventors to file a single application for patent rights in some or all of the contracting states. This application is searched by an International Searching Authority and published by the International Bureau of WIPO. It may also be the subject of an (optional) international preliminary examination. Applicants must then deal directly with the patent offices in the countries where they are seeking patent rights. The European Patent Convention allows inventors to obtain patent rights in all the contracting states by filing a single application with the European Patent Office. For further information visit W www.patent.gov.uk.

RESEARCH DISCLOSURES

Research Disclosures are publicly disclosed details of an innovation. Once published, the innovation is considered no longer new and becomes prior art. Publishing a disclosure is significantly cheaper than applying for a patent, however unlike a patent, it does not entitle the author to exclusive rights to use or license the innovation. Instead Research Disclosures are primarily published to ensure the inventor freedom to use the innovation. This is because publishing legally prevents other parties from patenting the disclosed innovation and in the UK, patent law dictates that by disclosing, even the inventor relinquishes his/her right to a patent.

Legally, publishing details of an innovation anywhere is enough to make a research disclosure. However to be effective a Research Disclosure needs to be placed in an archive which Patent Examiners are guaranteed to include in their prior art searches. To ensure global legal precedent it must be included in a publication with a recognised date stamp and made publicly available across the world.

The Research Disclosure Journal established in 1960, published by KMP Ltd is the primary publisher of Research Disclosures. It is the only independent disclosure archive recognised by the Patent Co-operation Treaty as a mandatory search resource which must be consulted before the grant of a PCT patent. More information can be found at W www.researchdisclosure.com.

TRADE MARKS

Trade marks are a means of identification, whether a word or device or a combination of both, a logo, or the shape of goods or their packaging, which enable traders to make their goods or services readily distinguishable from those supplied by other traders. Registration prevents other traders using the same or similar trade marks for similar products or services for which the mark is registered.

In the UK trade marks are registered at the Trade Marks Registry in the Patent Office. In order to qualify for registration a mark must be capable of distinguishing its proprietor's goods or services from those of other undertakings; it should be non-deceptive, should not be contrary to law or morality and should not be similar or identical to any earlier marks for the same or similar goods or services. The relevant current legislation is the Trade Marks Act 1994.

It is possible to obtain an international trade mark registration, effective in 76 countries, under the Madrid Agreement or the Madrid Protocol, to which the UK is party. British companies can obtain international trade mark registration through a single application to the WIPO in those countries party to the protocol.

EC trade mark regulation is now in force and is administered by the Office for Harmonisation in the Internal Market (Trade Marks and Designs) in Alicante, Spain. The office registers EC trade marks, which are valid throughout the European Union. The national registration of trade marks in member states continues in parallel with EC trade mark standards.

DOMAIN NAMES
A domain name is a name by which a company or organisation is known on the internet and is a short-hand way of identifying a company's website. A domain name has to be registered separately from a trade mark. Although there are many registrars prepared to register domain names, each country has a central registry to store unique names and addresses used on the internet. A list of accredited registrars can be found on W www.icann.org.

DESIGN PROTECTION

Design protection covers the outward appearance of an article and takes two forms in the UK, registered design and design right, which are not mutually exclusive. Registered design protects the aesthetic appearance of an article, including shape, configuration, pattern or ornament, although artistic works such as sculptures are excluded, being generally protected by copyright. In order to qualify for protection, a design must be new and materially different from earlier UK published designs.

The owner of the design must apply to the Designs Registry at the Patent Office. Initial registration lasts for five years and can be extended in five-year increments to a maximum of 25 years. The current legislation, the Registered Designs Act 1949 is currently under review with the aim of making it easier for small to mid size companies to apply for and hold Registered Designs.

UK applicants wishing to protect their designs in the EU can do so by applying for a Registered Community Design with the Office of Harmonisation in the Internal Market. Outside the EU separate applications must be made in each country in which protection is sought.

Design right is an automatic right which applies to the shape or configuration of articles and does not require registration. Unlike registered design, two-dimensional designs do not qualify for protection but designs of semiconductor chips (topographies) are protected by design right. Designs must be original and non-commonplace. The term of design right is ten years from first marketing of the design and the right is effective only in the UK. The current legislation is Part 3 of the Copyright, Designs and Patents Act 1988, amended on 9 December 2001 to incorporate the European Designs Directive.

LEGAL DEPOSIT

Publishers are legally obliged to send one copy of every new printed publication distributed in the United Kingdom or Republic of Ireland to the legal deposit libraries within one month of publication. This is based on the Copyright Act of 1911 and the Irish Copyright Act 1963, replaced by similar provisions in the Copyright and Related Rights Act 2000. All printed publications come within the scope of legal deposit. A code of practice exists in the UK for the deposit of non-printed publications, including microform and electronic media. The Legal Deposit Libraries Act 2003, which is not yet in force, extends legal deposit legislation to automatically include non-print publications.

The aim of legal deposit is to keep a complete national archive of published works as a current reference and information source. The legal deposit libraries are the British Library, the Bodleian Library in Oxford, Cambridge University Library, the National Library of Scotland, the National Library of Wales, and Trinity College Library in Dublin.

INTELLECTUAL PROPERTY ORGANISATIONS

COPYRIGHT LIBRARIES AGENCY, 100 Euston Street, London NW1 2HQ T 020-7388 5061
COPYRIGHT LICENSING AGENCY LTD, 90 Tottenham Court Road, London W1T 0LP T 020-7631 5555 W www.cla.co.uk
EUROPEAN PATENT OFFICE, Headquarters, Erhardtstrasse 27, D-8000, Munich 2, Germany T (+49) 892 3990 W www.european-patent-office.org
THE PATENT OFFICE, Cardiff Road, Newport NP10 8QQ T 0845-950 0505 W www.patent.gov.uk
WORLD INTELLECTUAL PROPERTY ORGANISATION (WIPO), 34 chemin des Colombettes, CH-1211 Geneva 20, Switzerland T (+41) 22 338 9111 W www.wipo.int

THE MEDIA

CROSS-MEDIA OWNERSHIP

The Communications Act, which received Royal Assent on 17 July 2003, has overhauled the rules surrounding cross-media ownership. Some of them have been simplified and relaxed to encourage dispersion of ownership and new market entry while preventing the most influential media in any community being controlled by too narrow a range of interests. However, transfers and mergers will not be solely subject to examination on competition grounds by the competition authorities. The Secretary of State has a wide discretion to intervene and decide if a transaction is permissible on public interest grounds (relating both to newspapers and cross-media criteria, if broadcasting interests are also involved). The Office of Communications (Ofcom) has an advisory role. Government and Parliamentary assurances were given that any intervention into local newspaper transfers would be rare and exceptional.

Cross-media regulation has been reduced to three core rules:

- No-one controlling more than 20 per cent of the national newspaper market may hold any licence for ITV or hold a stake in any of its services. A company may not own more than a 20 per cent share in such a service if more than 20 per cent of its stock is in turn owned by a national newspaper proprietor with more than 20 per cent of the market
- No-one owning a regional ITV licence may own more than 20 per cent of the local/regional newspaper market in the same region
- There will also be a scheme to uphold the plurality of ownership that exists in local media. There should be at least three local commercial radio operators, and at least three local or regional commercial media voices (in TV, radio and newspapers), in most local communities

REGULATION

Ofcom is the regulator for the communication industries in the UK and has responsibility for television, radio, telecommunications and wireless communications services. It replaces the Broadcasting Standards Commission, the Independent Television Commission, the Radio Authority, the Radio Communications Agency and Oftel. Ofcom is required to report annually to Parliament and exists to further the interests of consumers by: balancing choice and competition with the duty to foster plurality, protect viewers and listeners and promote cultural diversity in the media; and ensuring full and fair competition between communications providers.

OFFICE OF COMMUNICATIONS (OFCOM)
Riverside House, 2A Southwark Bridge Road, London SE1 9HA
T 020-7981 3000
E enq@ofcom.org.uk
W www.ofcom.org.uk
Chief Executive, Stephen Carter

BROADCASTERS

The public service television broadcasters in the UK are: the British Broadcasting Corporation (BBC), a public corporation funded mainly by the television licence fee; Channel 4, a public corporation self-funded by advertising revenues; S4C, a public corporation broadcasting the fourth channel in Wales and funded by grant-in-aid from the government and advertising revenues; and ITV, Five and Teletext, commercial television companies funded by advertising revenues. The government sets the licence fee and awards grants to support the BBC and S4C.

On 1 May 1996 a new royal charter came into force that established the framework for the BBC's activities until 2006. Within the framework provided by the charter, the BBC Governors are responsible for ensuring that the BBC meets all its statutory obligations. However, the Secretary of State for the Department for Culture, Media and Sport has the power to approve and review the operation of new licence fee-funded public services. The BBC's regulator is Ofcom, although the Governors have some exclusive responsibilities, such as ensuring the editorial independence of the BBC. The S4C Authority regulates S4C, subject to the regulatory powers vested in Ofcom by the Communications Act 2003. Ofcom also monitors and licenses Channel 3, Channel 4 and Channel 5. All three commercial stations have to fulfil programming obligations.

COMPLAINTS

Under the Communications Act 2003 Ofcom's licensees are obliged to adhere to the provisions of Ofcom codes (including advertising, programme standards, fairness, privacy and sponsorship). Ofcom also inherited the Broadcasting Standards Commission's Standards Code and is transitionally applying it in respect of BBC/S4C programmes. Complainants should contact the broadcaster in the first instance (details can be found on Ofcom's website), however, if the complainant wishes the complaint to be considered by Ofcom, it will do so. Complaints should be made within a reasonable time as broadcasters are only required to keep recordings for the following periods of time: radio, 42 days; television, 90 days; and cable and satellite, 60 days.

TELEVISION

All terrestrial channels are broadcast in colour on 625 lines UHF from a network of transmitting stations. Transmissions are available to 99.4 per cent of the population. Signals of acceptable quality cannot be obtained where the line of sight path between transmitters and consumers is obstructed by hills, buildings or even local atmospheric conditions. The Department for Culture, Media and Sport is responsible for the policy on the allocation of frequencies for television and radio broadcasting together with reception matters and liaising with Ofcom, which has overall control for the management of frequencies.

The Broadcasting Act 1990 made the BBC responsible for licence administration, and TV Licensing is the trading name used by the agents who collect the licence fee on behalf of the BBC. In 2004–5 the total number of television licences in force in the UK was 24.7 million of which around 99.8 per cent were for colour televisions. Annual television licence fees from 1 April 2005 are: black and white, £42.00; colour, £126.50.

DIGITAL TELEVISION

Digital broadcasting has dramatically increased the number and reception quality of television channels. Sound and pictures are converted into a digital format and compressed, using as few bits as possible to convey the information on a digital signal. This technique enables several television channels to be carried in the space used by the current analogue signals to carry one channel. Digital signals can be received by standard aerials, satellite dishes or via cable, but have to be decoded and turned back into sound and pictures by using a separate set-top box, or a decoder built into the television set (an integrated digital TV set/iDTV). A basic package of channels is available without charge and services are also offered by cable and satellite companies.

The Broadcasting Act 1996 provided for the licensing of 20 or more digital terrestrial television channels (on six frequency channels or 'multiplexes'). The first digital services went on air in autumn 1998. Analogue broadcasting will eventually be discontinued, with the frequencies sold to mobile telephone companies.

In June 2002, following the collapse of the ITV Digital terrestrial service, a consortium made up of the BBC, BSkyB and Crown Castle, the transmitter company, was awarded the DTT (Digital Terrestrial Television) licence by the Independent Television Commission. Freeview, a new digital network, was launched on 30 October 2002. By 31 March 2005 digital penetration had reached just under 62 per cent of UK households.

ESTIMATED AUDIENCE SHARE

	Percentage of all homes	
	2003–4	2004–5
BBC One	25.2	24.4
BBC Two	10.9	9.6
ITV1	23.7	22.3
Channel 4	9.7	9.8
five	6.5	6.5
BBC Three	0.3	0.5
BBC Four	0.1	0.2
BBC News 24	0.4	0.4
ITV2	1.0	1.2
ITV3*	–	0.7
E4	0.6	0.6
Sky One	1.5	1.5
Sky News	0.5	0.4
All BBC channels (total)	37.8	36.2
All Sky channels (total)	6.3	6.5
Cable, satellite and digital channels (total)	24.0	27.3

*Commenced broadcasting on 1 November 2004

Source : BARB

THE BRITISH BROADCASTING CORPORATION

BBC TELEVISION

The BBC's experiments in television broadcasting started in 1929 and in 1936 it began the world's first public service of high-definition television from Alexandra Palace. The BBC broadcasts two UK-wide terrestrial television services, BBC One and BBC Two; outside England these services are designated BBC Scotland on One, BBC Scotland on Two, BBC One Northern Ireland, BBC Two Northern Ireland, BBC Wales on One and BBC Wales on Two. The BBC's digital services comprise BBC One, BBC Two, BBC Three, BBC Four, BBC News 24, BBC Parliament and two children's channels, CBeebies and CBBC. The services are funded by the licence fee.

Television Centre, Wood Lane, London W12 7RJ

T 020-8743 8000

W www.bbc.co.uk

BBC WORLDWIDE LTD

BBC Worldwide Limited is the commercial arm, and a wholly-owned subsidiary, of the British Broadcasting Corporation. The company was formed in 1994 and exists in order to maximise the value of the BBC's programme and publishing assets for the benefit of the licence payer, re-investing profit in public service programming. BBC Worldwide's businesses include international programming distribution, television channels, magazines, books, videos, spoken word, music, DVDs, licensed product, CD-ROMs, English language teaching, videos for education and training, interactive telephony, co-production, library footage sales, exhibitions, live events, film and media monitoring.

Woodlands, 80 Wood Lane, London W12 0TT

T 020-8433 2000

W www.bbcworldwide.com

INDEPENDENT TELEVISION NETWORK

The ITV network comprises 15 independent regional television licensees and one licensee providing the national breakfast-time service. Their licences were awarded by competitive tender for a minimum of ten years and commenced in January 1993; all 15 have since been renewed. In addition to the terrestrial channel ITV1, ITV has launched the following digital channels: ITV2, ITV3, ITV News and CiTV.

Channel 4 and S4C (the fourth channel in Wales) are also funded through advertising and were set up to provide programmes with a distinctive character that appeal to interests not catered for by ITV. Five began broadcasting on the fifth channel in 1997 and now reaches about 80 per cent of the population.

ITV NETWORK CENTRE/ITV ASSOCIATION

The ITV Network Centre is wholly owned by the ITV companies and undertakes commissioning and scheduling of programmes shown across the ITV network and, as with the BBC, 25 per cent of programmes must come from independent producers. There are over 1,500 independent production companies in the UK which generate over £1bn of programming.

200 Gray's Inn Road, London WC1X 8HF

T 020-7843 8000

W www.itv.com

Chair, Sir Peter Burt

INDEPENDENT TELEVISION NETWORK REGIONS AND COMPANIES

ANGLIA *(eastern England)*, Anglia House, Rose Lane, Norwich NR1 3JG **T** 01603-615151
 W www.angliatv.co.uk

BORDER *(Borders and the Isle of Man)*, The Television Centre, Carlisle CA1 3NT **T** 01228-525101
 W www.border-tv.com

CENTRAL *(east, west and south Midlands)*, Gas Street, Birmingham B1 2JT **T** 0870-6006766
 W www.itvregions.com/central

CHANNEL *(Channel Islands)*, The Television Centre, La Pouquelaye, St Helier, Jersey JE1 3ZD **T** 01534-816816
 W www.channeltv.co.uk

GRAMPIAN *(northern Scotland)*, Television Centre, Craigshaw Business Park, West Tullos, Aberdeen AB12 3QH **T** 01224-848848 **W** www.grampiantv.co.uk

GRANADA *(north-west England)*, Quay Street, Manchester M60 9EA **T** 0161-832 7211 **W** www.granadatv.com

LONDON *(London)*, London Television Centre, Upper Ground, London SE1 9LT **T** 020-7261 8163
 W www.lwt.co.uk

MERIDIAN *(south and south-east England)*, Solent Business Park, Whiteley, Hants PO15 7PA **T** 01489 442000
 W www.meridiantv.com

SCOTTISH *(central Scotland)*, 200 Renfield Street, Glasgow G2 3PR **T** 0141-300 3000
 W www.scottishtv.co.uk

TYNE TEES *(north-east England)*, City Road, Newcastle-upon-Tyne NE1 2AL **T** 0191-261 0181
 W www.tynetees.tv

ULSTER *(Northern Ireland)*, Havelock House, Belfast BT7 1EB **T** 02890-328122 **W** www.u.tv

WALES, The Television Centre, Culverhouse Cross, Cardiff CF5 6XJ **T** 029-2059 0590
 W www.itvregions.com/wales

WEST, Television Centre, Bath Road, Bristol BS4 3HG **T** 0117-972 2722
 W www.itvregions.com/west

WESTCOUNTRY *(south-west England)*, Langage Science Park, Western Wood Way, Plymouth PL7 5BQ **T** 01752-333333 **W** www.itvregions.com/westcountry

YORKSHIRE *(Yorkshire)*, 96–104 Kirkstall Road, Leeds LS3 1JS **T** 0113-243 8283
 W www.yorkshiretv.com

OTHER TELEVISION COMPANIES

CHANNEL FOUR TELEVISION, 124 Horseferry Road, London SW1P 2TX **T** 020-7396 4444 **W** www.channel4.com

FIVE BROADCASTING LTD, 22 Long Acre, London WC2E 9LY **T** 020-7550 5555 **W** www.five.tv

GMTV, The London Television Centre, Upper Ground, London SE1 9TT **T** 020 7827 7000 **W** www.gm.tv Owned by ITV and Disney, with 75 per cent and 25 per cent respectively, GMTV provides breakfast television and sells its own advertising.

INDEPENDENT TELEVISION NEWS, 200 Gray's Inn Road, London WC1X 8XZ **T** 020-7833 3000 **W** www.itn.co.uk

TELETEXT LTD, Building 10, Chiswick Park, 566 Chiswick High Road London W4 5TS **T** 0870-731 3000 Provides teletext services for the ITV companies and Channel 4

WELSH FOURTH CHANNEL AUTHORITY (Sianel Pedwar Cymru/Channel Four Wales), Parc Ty Glas, Llanishen, Cardiff CF14 5DU **T** 029-2074 7444 S4C schedules Welsh language and most Channel 4 programmes.

DIRECT BROADCASTING BY SATELLITE TELEVISION

British Sky Broadcasting is a direct broadcast satellite service operating in the UK and Ireland. Launched in February 1989, it was originally a four channel service, broadcast on a satellite owned by a Luxembourg-based consortium. The failure of rival company British Satellite Broadcasting lead to a merger in 1990 and the formation of British Sky Broadcasting.

Sky Digital, launched on 1 October 1998, offers almost 400 300 channels, pay-per-view services and interactive entertainment, including email, and on-screen shopping. BSkyB has more than 17 million viewers in 7 million households. BSkyB's own channels such as Sky News, Sky One and Sky Sports are available in a further 5.4 million homes receiving cable services in the UK and Ireland. BSkyB is listed on the London and New York Stock Exchanges.

BRITISH SKY BROADCASTING GROUP
Grant Way, Isleworth, Middx TW7 5QD
T 020-7705 3000 **W** www.sky.com

RADIO

UK domestic radio services are broadcast across three wavebands: FM (or VHF), medium wave and long wave (used by BBC Radio 4). In the UK the FM waveband extends in frequency from 87.5 MHz to 108 MHz and the medium wave band extends from 531 kHz to 1602 kHz. Older radios are calibrated in wavelengths rather than frequency. To convert frequency to wavelength, divide 300,000 by the frequency in kHz. A number of radio stations are now being broadcast in both analogue and digital as well as a growing number in digital alone.

DIGITAL RADIO

DAB (Digital Audio Broadcasting) allows more services to be broadcast to a higher technical quality and provides the data facility for text and pictures. It improves the robustness of high fidelity radio services, especially compared with current FM and AM radio transmissions. It was developed in a collaborative research project under the pan-European Eureka 147 initiative and has been adopted as a world standard for new digital radio systems. The frequencies allocated for terrestrial digital radio in the UK are 217.5 to 230 MHz. Plans are underway for developing a framework for frequencies in the 1.5 GHz (or L-Band) range.

The Broadcasting Act 1996 provided for the licensing of digital radio services (on 'multiplexes', where a number of stations share one frequency to transmit their services). The BBC has been allocated a multiplex capable of broadcasting six to eight national stereo services; BBC digital broadcasts began in the London area in September 1995. A national digital multiplex has also been made available to the three independent national radio stations, and local and regional services (BBC and commercial) will use the remaining five multiplexes. Ofcom is responsible for awarding licences for capacity on the non-BBC multiplexes. The first national independent radio digital licence was awarded to Digital One, which began broadcasting in November 1999. The first local multiplex licence was awarded in May 1999 (to CE Digital, for Birmingham) and commenced broadcasting in May 2000.

It is necessary to possess a digital radio set in order to receive digital radio broadcasts. Several types of sets are available including portable radios, hi-fi stacks, car radios and PC cards. Newer DAB radios allow the listener to rewind, pause and record broadcasts.

ESTIMATED AUDIENCE SHARE

| | Percentage | |
	Apr–Jun 2004	Apr–Jun 2005
BBC Radio 1	8.3	9.2
BBC Radio 2	16.2	16.0
BBC Radio 3	1.1	1.1
BBC Radio 4	11.0	11.2
BBC Radio 5 Live	4.5	4.4
BBC Local/Regional	10.9	10.9
BBC World Service	0.6	0.5
All BBC	53.1	54.0
All commercial	45.0	44.0
All national commercial	10.1	10.2
All local commercial	34.9	33.8
Other	1.9	2.0
Source: RAJAR/IPSOS-RSL		

BBC RADIO
BBC Radio broadcasts network services to the UK, Isle of Man and the Channel Islands. There is also a tier of national services in Wales, Scotland and Northern Ireland and 40 local radio stations in England and the Channel Islands. In Wales and Scotland there are also dedicated language services in Welsh and Gaelic respectively. The frequency allocated for digital BBC broadcasts is 225.648 MHZ.
Broadcasting House, Portland Place, London W1A 1AA
T 020-7580 4468

BBC NETWORK RADIO SERVICES
RADIO 1 (contemporary pop music and entertainment news) – 24 hours a day, frequencies: 97.6–99.8 FM, coverage 99%
RADIO 2 (popular music, entertainment, comedy and the arts) – 24 hours a day, frequencies: 88–90.2 FM, coverage 99%
RADIO 3 (classical music, classic drama, documentaries and features) – 24 hours a day, frequencies: 90.2–92.4 FM, coverage 99%
RADIO 4 (news, documentaries, drama, entertainment and cricket on long wave in season) – 5.30 a.m.–1 a.m. daily, with BBC World Service overnight, frequencies: 92.4–94.6 FM and 198 LW, coverage 99%
RADIO 5 LIVE (news and sport) – 24 hours a day, frequencies: 693 and 909 MW
RADIO 6 (digital only) (contemporary and classic pop and rock music) – 24 hours a day
RADIO 7 (digital only) (comedy and drama) – 7 a.m. to 1 a.m.
Asian Network (digital only) (news, music and sport for British Asians) – 5 a.m.–12.30 p.m. Monday–Saturday, 5 a.m.–12 p.m. Sunday, with BBC World Service overnight
1Xtra (digital only) (new black music) – 24 hours a day

BBC NATIONAL RADIO SERVICES
RADIO CYMRU (Welsh-language), frequencies: 92.4–94.6 FM, 95.7 FM (Llanfyllin), 96.1 FM (Llandinam), 96.8 FM and 103.5–105 FM, coverage 97%
RADIO FOYLE, frequencies: 792 AM and 93.1 MW

RADIO NAN GAIDHEAL (Gaelic service), frequencies: 103.5–105 FM plus 990 MW (Aberdeen), coverage 90%
RADIO SCOTLAND, frequencies: 810 MW plus two local fillers and 92.4–94.7 FM, coverage 99%. Local programmes for: Highlands and Islands; North East; Borders; South West (also 585 MW); Orkney; and Shetland
RADIO ULSTER, frequencies: 1341 MW (873 MW Enniskillen), plus two local fillers and 92.4–95.4 FM, coverage 96%. Local programmes on Radio Foyle
RADIO WALES, frequencies: 882 MW plus two local fillers; 95.1 FM, 95.9 FM (Gwent), 103.9 FM (Cardiff), 95.4 FM (Wrexham), coverage 97%

BBC LOCAL RADIO STATIONS
There are 40 local stations serving England and the Channel Islands:
BERKSHIRE, PO Box 1044, Reading RG4 8FH T 08459-001041
    Frequencies: 94.6/95.4/104.1/104.4 FM
BRISTOL, PO Box 194, Bristol BS99 7QT T 0117-974 1111
    Frequencies: 94.9/95.5 FM 1548 MW
CAMBRIDGESHIRE, 104 Hills Road, Cambridge CB2 1LD
    T 01223-259696
    Frequencies: 95.7/96.0 FM
CLEVELAND, Broadcasting House, Newport Road, Middlesbrough TS1 5DG T 01642-225211
    Frequency: 95.0 FM
CORNWALL, Phoenix Wharf, Truro TR1 1UA T 01872-275421
    Frequencies: 95.2/96.0/103.9 FM
CUMBRIA, Annetwell Street, Carlisle CA3 8BB
    T 01228-592444
    Frequencies: 95.2/95.6/96.1/104.1/104.2 FM, 756/837/1458 MW
DERBY, PO Box 1045, Derby DE1 3HL T 01332-361111
    Frequencies: 95.3/96.0/104.5 FM, 1116 MW
DEVON, PO Box 5, Plymouth PL1 1XT T 01752-260323
    Frequencies: 94.8/95.7/95.8/96.0/103.4/104.3 FM, 801/855/990/1458 MW
ESSEX, PO Box 765, Chelmsford CM2 9XB T 01245-616000
    Frequencies: 95.3/103.5 FM, 729/765/1530 MW
GLOUCESTERSHIRE, London Road, Gloucester GL1 1SW
    T 01452-308585
    Frequencies: 95.0/95.8/104.7 FM, 1413 MW
GMR (GREATER MANCHESTER RADIO), PO Box 951, Oxford Road, Manchester M60 1SD
    T 0161-200 2000
    Frequencies: 95.1/104.6 FM
GUERNSEY, Broadcasting House, Bulwer Avenue, St Sampson's GY2 4LA T 01481-200600
    Frequencies: 93.2 FM, 1116 AM
HEREFORD AND WORCESTER, Hylton Road, Worcester WR2 5WW T 01905-748485
    Frequencies: 94.7/104.0/104.6 FM, 738/1584 MW
HUMBERSIDE, Queen's Court, Hull HU1 3RH
    T 01482-323232
    Frequencies: 95.9 FM, 1485 MW
JERSEY, 18 Parade Road, St Helier JE2 3PL T 01534-870000
    Frequencies: 88.8 FM, 1026 MW
KENT, The Great Hall, Mount Pleasant, Tunbridge Wells TN1 1QQ T 01892-670000
    Frequencies: 96.7/97.6/104.2 FM, 774/1602 MW
LANCASHIRE, 20–26 Darwen Street, Blackburn BB2 2EA
    T 01254-262411
    Frequencies: 95.5/103.9/104.5 FM, 855/1557 MW
LEEDS, 2 St Peter's Square, Leeds LS9 8AH T 0113-244 2131
    Frequencies: 92.4 FM, 774 MW

LEICESTER, 9 St Nicholas Place, Leicester LE1 5LB
T 0116-251 6688
Frequency: 104.9 FM

LINCOLNSHIRE, PO Box 219, Lincoln LN1 3XY
T 01522-511411
Frequencies: 94.9/104.7 FM, 1368 MW

LONDON, PO Box 949, Marylebone High Street, London
W1A 6FL T 020-7224 2424
Frequency: 94.9 FM

MERSEYSIDE, 55 Paradise Street, Liverpool L1 3BP
T 0151-708 5500
Frequencies: 95.8 FM, 1485 MW

NEWCASTLE, Broadcasting Centre, Barrack Road, Newcastle
upon Tyne NE99 1RN T 08453-010954
Frequencies: 95.4/96.0/103.7/104.4 FM, 1458 MW

NORFOLK, The Forum, Millennium Plain, Norwich NR2 1BH
T 01603-617411
Frequencies: 95.1/104.4 FM, 855/873 MW

NORTHAMPTON, Broadcasting House, Abington Street,
Northampton NN1 2BH T 01604-239100
Frequencies: 103.6/104.2 FM

NOTTINGHAM, London Road, Nottingham NG2 4UU
T 0115-955 0500
Frequencies: 95.5/103.8 FM

OXFORD, 269 Banbury Road, Oxford OX2 7DW
T 01865-889077
Frequency: 95.2 FM

SHEFFIELD, 54 Shoreham Street, Sheffield S1 4RS
T 0114-273 1177
Frequencies: 88.6/94.7/104.1 FM

SHROPSHIRE, 2–4 Boscobel Drive, Harlescott, Shrewsbury
SY1 3TT T 01743-248484
Frequencies: 90.0/95.0/96.0/104.1 FM

SOLENT, Havelock Road, Southampton SO14 7PW
T 023-8063 2811
Frequencies: 96.1/103.8 FM, 999/1359 MW

SOMERSET SOUND, Broadcasting House, Park Street,
Taunton TA1 4DA T 01823-323956
Frequency: 1566 MW

SOUTHERN COUNTIES, Broadcasting Centre, Guildford
GU2 7AP T 01483-306306
Frequencies: 95–95.3/104–104.8 FM

STOKE, Cheapside, Hanley, Stoke-on-Trent ST1 1JJ
T 01782-208080
Frequencies: 94.6/104.1 FM, 1503 MW

SUFFOLK, Broadcasting House, St Matthew's Street, Ipswich
IP1 3EP T 01473-250000
Frequencies: 95.5/95.9/103.9/104.6 FM

SWINDON, PO Box 1234, Swindon T 01793-513626
Frequency: 103.6 FM

THREE COUNTIES, 1 Hastings Street, Luton LU1 5XL
T 01582-637400
Frequencies: 94.7/95.5/98.0/103.8/104.5 FM, 630/1161 MW

WILTSHIRE, PO Box 1234, Trowbridge and Salisbury
T 01793-513626
Frequencies: 103.5/104.3/104.9 FM, 1332/1368 MW

WM (COVENTRY AND WARWICKSHIRE), Holt Court, 1
Greyfriars Road, Coventry CV1 2WR T 024-7686 0086
Frequencies: 94.8/103.7/104.0 FM

WM (WEST MIDLANDS), The Mailbox, Birmingham B1 1RF
T 08453-009956
Frequency: 95.6 FM

YORK, 20 Bootham Row, York YO30 7BR T 01904-641351
Frequencies: 95.5/103.7/104.3 FM, 666/1260 MW

BBC WORLD SERVICE

The BBC World Service broadcasts over 1,280 hours of programmes a week, to an estimated weekly audience of 146 million worldwide, in 43 languages including English. It no longer broadcasts in Dutch, French for Europe, German, Hebrew, Italian, Japanese or Malay because it was found that most speakers of these languages preferred to listen to the English broadcasts. Many services are now available by satellite and on the Internet. *UK frequencies:* 648 MW in Southern England and on BBC Radio 4, BBC Radio Ulster, BBC Radio Wales or the Asian Network at night.

Regions and their languages (in addition to English):

AFRICA – Arabic, French, Hausa, Kinyarwanda, Kirundi, Portuguese, Somali, Swahili

AMERICAS – Portuguese, Spanish

ASIA PACIFIC – Burmese, Cantonese, Indonesian, Mandarin, Thai, Vietnamese

CENTRAL ASIA – Azeri, Kazakh, Kyrgyz, Uzbek

EUROPE – Albanian, Bulgarian, Croatian, Czech, Greek, Hungarian, Macedonian, Polish, Romanian, Russian, Slovak, Slovene, Turkish, Ukrainian

MIDDLE EAST – Arabic, Pashto, Persian, Turkish

SOUTH ASIA – Bengali, Hindi, Nepali, Sinhala, Tamil, Urdu

BBC ENGLISH teaches English world-wide through radio, television and a wide range of published and online courses

BBC AUDIENCE AND MARKET RESEARCH carries out audience research and sells printed publications and data

BBC MONITORING supplies news and information from the output of overseas radio and television stations and news agency sources

BBC WORLD SERVICE TRAINING runs journalism, management and skills training courses for overseas broadcasters

BBC WORLD SERVICE TRUST is a registered charity established in 1999 by BBC World Service. It promotes development through the innovative use of the media in the developing world. The trust presently works in over 30 countries worldwide, tackling health, education and good governance

Bush House, Strand, London WC2B 4PH T 020-7240 3456

INDEPENDENT RADIO

The UK's first commercial radio stations, known as Independent Local Radio stations, commenced broadcasting in 1973, when the Independent Broadcasting Authority (IBA) granted the London Broadcasting Company (LBC) the franchise to provide London's news and information service; LBC was followed by Capital Radio, which would provide the city's entertainment service, Radio Clyde in Glasgow and BRMB in Birmingham.

The IBA was dissolved when the Broadcasting Act of 1990 de-regulated broadcasting, to be succeeded by the less rigid Radio Authority (RA). The RA began advertising new licences for the development of independent radio in January 1991. It awarded national and local radio licences (including regional licences), satellite and cable services licences, and long-term restricted service licences for stations serving non-commercial establishments such as hospitals and universities. The first national commercial digital multiplex licence was awarded in October 1998 and a number of local digital multiplex licences followed. At the end of 2003 the RA was replaced by Ofcom, which now carries out the licensing administration. Ofcom's main priorities for commercial radio in 2005–6 are the further expansion of digital radio and how best to ensure the character of local commercial stations.

The Commercial Radio Companies Association (CRCA) is the trade body for commercial radio companies in the United Kingdom. It is a voluntary, non-profit making body, funded by the subscriptions of its member radio companies (who share the cost of CRCA in proportion to their shares of the industry's broadcasting revenue), and was formed by the first radio companies in 1973.

COMMERCIAL RADIO COMPANIES ASSOCIATION, 77 Shaftesbury Avenue, London W1D 5DU **T** 020-7306 2603 **W** www.crca.co.uk *Chief Executive,* Paul Brown, CBE

INDEPENDENT NATIONAL RADIO STATIONS
CLASSIC FM, 7 Swallow Place, London W1B 2AG
T 020-7343 9000 – 24 hours a day,
frequencies: 99.9–101.9 FM
TALK SPORT, 18 Hatfields, London SE1 8DJ **T** 020-7959 7800
– 24 hours a day, *frequencies:* 1053–1089 AM
VIRGIN 1215, 1 Golden Square, London W1F 9DJ
T 020-7434 1215 – 24 hours a day,
frequencies: 1215/1197/1233/1242/1260 AM

INDEPENDENT LOCAL RADIO STATIONS
England
2BR, Lomeshaye Business Village, Nelson, Lancs BB9 7DR
T 01282-690000 *Frequency:* 99.8 FM
2CR FM, 5–7 Southcote Road, Bournemouth BH1 3LR
T 01202-234900 *Frequency:* 102.3 FM
2-TEN FM, PO Box 2020, Reading, Berks RG31 7FG
T 0118-945 4400 *Frequencies:* 97.0/102.9/103.4 FM
3FM, 45 Victoria Street, Douglas, IOM IM1 3RS
T 01624-616333 *Frequencies:* 104–106 FM
3TR FM, Riverside Studios, Warminster, Wilts BA12 9HQ
T 01985-211111 *Frequency:* 107.5 FM
95.8 CAPITAL FM, 30 Leicester Square, London WC2H 7LA
T 020-7766 6000 *Frequency:* 95.8 FM
96 TRENT FM, 29–31 Castle Gate, Nottingham NG1 7AP
T 0115-952 7000 *Frequencies:* 96.2/96.5 FM
96.2 THE REVOLUTION, Sarah Moor Studios, Henshaw Street, Oldham OL1 3JF **T** 0161-621 6500
Frequency: 96.2 FM
96.3 RADIO AIRE, 51 Burley Road, Leeds LS3 1LR
T 0113-283 5500 *Frequency:* 96.3 FM
96.4 FM BRMB, Nine Brindleyplace, 4 Oozells Square, Birmingham B1 2DJ **T** 0121-245 5000
Frequency: 96.4 FM
96.4 THE EAGLE, Dolphin House, North Street, Guildford, Surrey GU1 4AA **T** 01483-300964 *Frequency:* 96.4 FM
96.9 CHILTERN FM, 55 Goldington Road, Bedford MK40 3LT
T 01234-235010 *Frequency:* 96.9 FM
96.9 VIKING FM, The Boathouse, Commercial Road, Hull, E. Yorks HU1 2SG **T** 01482-325141
Frequency: 96.9 FM
97 FM PLYMOUTH SOUND, Earl's Acre, Plymouth PL3 4HX
T 01752-275600 *Frequencies:* 96.6/97 FM
97.2 STRAY FM, The Hamlet, Hornbeam Park Avenue, Harrogate HG2 8RE **T** 01423-522972 *Frequency:* 97.2 FM
97.4 ROCK FM, PO Box 974, St. Paul's Square, Preston, Lancs PR1 1YE **T** 01772-477700 *Frequency:* 97.4 FM
97.6 CHILTERN FM, Chiltern Road, Dunstable LU6 1HQ
T 01582-676200 *Frequency:* 97.6 FM

100–102 CENTURY FM, Century House, PO Box 100, Gateshead NE8 2YY **T** 0191-477 6666
Frequencies: 96.2/96.4/100.7/101.8 FM
100.4 SMOOTH FM, 8 Exchange Quay, Manchester M5 3EJ
T 0845-050 1004 *Frequency:* 100.4 FM
100.7 HEART FM, 1 The Square, 111 Broad Street, Birmingham B15 1AS **T** 0121-695 0000 *Frequency:* 100.7 FM
102.2 SMOOTH FM, 26–27 Castlereagh Street, London W1H 5DL **T** 020-7706 4100 *Frequency:* 102.2 FM
102.4 WISH FM, Orrell Lodge, Orrell Road, Wigan, Lancs WN5 8HJ **T** 01942-761024 *Frequency:* 102.4 FM
102.7 HEREWARD FM, PO Box 225, Queensgate Centre, Peterborough PE1 1XJ **T** 01733-460600 *Frequency:* 102.7 FM
102.7 MERCURY FM, 9 The Stanley Centre, Kelvin Way, Crawley, W. Sussex RH10 9SE **T** 01293-519161
Frequencies: 97.5/102.7 FM
103.2 ALPHA FM, Radio House, 11 Woodland Road, Darlington, Co Durham DL3 7BJ **T** 01325-255552
Frequency: 103.2 FM
103.2 POWER FM, Radio House, Whittle Avenue, Segensworth West, Fareham, Hants PO15 5SH
T 01489-589911 *Frequency:* 103.2 FM
103.4 SUN FM, PO Box 1034, Sunderland, Tyne and Wear SR5 2YL **T** 0191-548 1034 *Frequency:* 103.4 FM
105.4 CENTURY FM, Laser House, Waterfront Quays, Manchester M5 2XW **T** 0161-400 0105
Frequency: 105.4 FM
106.9 SILK FM, Radio House, Bridge Street, Macclesfield, Cheshire SK11 6DJ **T** 01625-268000 *Frequency:* 106.9 FM
107.2 WIN FM, The Brooks, Winchester, Hants SO23 8FT
T 01962-841071 *Frequency:* 107.2 FM
107.4 THE QUAY, Flagship Studios, PO Box 1074, Portsmouth PO2 8YG **T** 023-9236 4141 *Frequency:* 107.4 FM
107.5 SOVEREIGN RADIO, 14 St Mary's Walk, Hailsham, E. Sussex BN27 1AF **T** 01323-442700
Frequency: 107.5 FM
107.7 SPLASH FM, The Guildbourne Centre, Worthing, W. Sussex BN11 1LZ **T** 01903-233005 *Frequency:* 107.7 FM
107.7 THE WOLF, 10th Floor, Mander House, Wolverhampton WV1 3NB **T** 01902-571070 *Frequency:* 107.7 FM
107.8 ARROW FM, Priory Meadow Centre, Hastings, E. Sussex TN34 1PJ **T** 01424-461177 *Frequency:* 107.8 FM
107.8 RADIO JACKIE, 110–112 Tolworth Broadway, Surbiton, Surrey KT6 7JD **T** 020-8288 1300
Frequency: 107.8 FM
107.9 DUNE FM, The Power Station, Victoria Way, Southport, Merseyside PR8 1RR **T** 01704-502500
Frequency: 107.9 FM
107.9 HOME FM, The Old Stable Block, Lockwood Park, Huddersfield HD1 3UR **T** 01484-321107
Frequency: 107.9 FM
1548 AM CAPITAL GOLD, 30 Leicester Square, London WC2H 7LA **T** 020-7766 6000 *Frequency:* 1548 AM
ASIAN SOUND RADIO, Globe House, Southall Street, Manchester M3 1LG **T** 0161-288 1000
Frequencies: 963/1377 AM
ATLANTIC FM, 4 Beachfield Avenue, Newquay, Cornwall TR7 1DR **T** 01840-211012 *Frequencies:* 105.1/107.0 FM
BATH FM, Station House, Ashley Avenue, Lower Weston, Bath BA1 3DS **T** 01225-471571 *Frequency:* 107.9 FM
THE BAY, PO Box 969, St George's Quay, Lancaster LA1 3LD
T 01524-848747 *Frequencies:* 96.9/102.3/103.2 FM
THE BEACH, PO Box 103.4, Lowestoft, Suffolk NR32 2TL
T 0845-345 1035 *Frequencies:* 97.4/103.4 FM
BEACON FM, 267 Tettenhall Road, Wolverhampton WV6 0DE
T 01902-461300 *Frequencies:* 97.2/103.1 FM

THE BEAR 102, The Guard House Studios, Banbury Road, Stratford-upon-Avon, Warks CV37 7HX T 01789-262636 *Frequency:* 102.0 FM

BRIDGWATER'S 107.4 BCR FM, Royal Clarence House, York Buildings, High Street, Bridgwater, Somerset TA6 3AT T 01278-727701 *Frequency:* 107.4 FM

BRIGHT 106.4, 11A The Market Place Shopping Centre, Burgess Hill, W. Sussex RH15 9NP T 01444-248127 *Frequency:* 106.4 FM

BRIGHTON'S JUICE 107.2, 170 North Street, Brighton BN1 1EA T 01273-386107 *Frequency:* 107.2 FM

BROADLAND 102, St George's Plain, 47–49 Colegate, Norwich NR3 1DB T 01603-630621 *Frequency:* 102.4 FM

CAPITAL GOLD (1152), Nine Brindleyplace, 4 Oozells Square, Birmingham B1 2DJ T 0121-245 5000 *Frequency:* 1152 AM

CAPITAL GOLD (1242/603), Radio House, John Wilson Business Park, Whitstable, Kent CT5 3QX T 01227-772004 *Frequencies:* 603/1242 AM

CAPITAL GOLD (1323/945), Radio House, PO Box 2000, Brighton BN41 2SS T 01273-430111 *Frequencies:* 945/1323 AM

CAPITAL 1458 AM, Laser House, Waterfront Quays, Manchester M5 2XW T 0161-400 0105 *Frequency:* 1458 AM

CAPITAL GOLD (1557/1170), Radio House, Whittle Avenue, Segensworth West, Farnham, Hants PO15 5SH T 01489-589911 *Frequencies:* 1170/1557 AM

CENTRE FM, 5–6 Aldergate, Tamworth, Staffs B79 7DJ T 01827-318000 *Frequencies:* 101.6/102.4 FM

CFM (CARLISLE AND WEST CUMBRIA), PO Box 964, Carlisle, Cumbria CA1 3NG T 01228-818964 *Frequencies:* 96.4/102.5 FM (Carlisle); 102.2/103.4 FM (west Cumbria)

CHOICE 107.1 FM, PO Box 969, London WC2H 7BB T 020-7766 6810 *Frequency:* 107.1 FM

CHOICE FM LONDON, PO Box 969, London WC2H 7BB T 020-7766 6810 *Frequency:* 96.9 FM

CLASSIC GOLD (666/954), Hawthorn House, Exeter Business Park, Exeter EX1 3QS T 01392-444444 *Frequencies:* 666/954 AM

CLASSIC GOLD (774), Bridge Studios, Eastgate Centre, Gloucester GL1 1SS T 01452-572400 *Frequency:* 774 AM

CLASSIC GOLD (828), 5–7 Southcote Road, Bournemouth, Dorset BH1 3LR T 01202-234900 *Frequency:* 828 AM

CLASSIC GOLD (828/792), Chiltern Road, Dunstable, Beds LU6 1HQ T 01582-676200 *Frequencies:* 792/828 AM

CLASSIC GOLD (936/1161), 1st Floor, Chiseldon House, Stonehill Green, Westlea, Swindon, Wilts SN5 7HB T 01793-663000 *Frequencies:* 936/1161 AM

CLASSIC GOLD (1152), Earl's Acre, Plymouth PL3 4HX T 01752 275600 *Frequency:* 1152 AM

CLASSIC GOLD (1260), PO Box 2000, One Passage Street, Bristol BS99 7SN T 0117-984 3200 *Frequency:* 1260 AM

CLASSIC GOLD (1332), PO Box 225, Queensgate Centre, Peterborough PE1 1XJ T 01733-460460 *Frequency:* 1332 AM

CLASSIC GOLD (1359), Hertford Place, Coventry CV1 3TT T 024-7686 8200 *Frequency:* 1359 AM

CLASSIC GOLD (1431/1485), The Chase, Calcot, Reading, Berks RG3 7FG T 0118-945 4400 *Frequencies:* 1431/1485 AM

CLASSIC GOLD (1521), 9 The Stanley Centre, Kelvin Way, Crawley, W. Sussex RH10 9SE T 01293-519161 *Frequency:* 1521 AM

CLASSIC GOLD (1557), 19–21 St Edmunds Road, Northampton NN1 5DY T 01604-795600 *Frequency:* 1557 AM

CLASSIC GOLD AMBER (NORFOLK), St George's Plain, 47–49 Colegate, Norwich NR3 1DB T 01603-630621 *Frequency:* 1152 AM

CLASSIC GOLD AMBER (SUFFOLK), Alpha Business Park, 6–12 White House Road, Ipswich IP1 5LT T 01473-461000 *Frequency:* 1170/1251 AM

CLASSIC GOLD BREEZE, 31 Glebe Road, Chelmsford, Essex CM1 1QG T 01245-524549 *Frequencies:* 1359/1431 AM

CLASSIC GOLD GEM, 29–31 Castle Gate, Nottingham NG1 7AP T 0115-952 7000 *Frequencies:* 945/999 AM

CLASSIC GOLD WABC, 267 Tettenhall Road, Wolverhampton WV6 0DQ T 01902-461200 *Frequencies:* 990/1017 AM

CLASSIC HITS (954/1530), PO Box 262, Worcester WR6 5ZE T 01905-740600 *Frequencies:* 954/1530 AM

CLUB ASIA 963 & 972 AM, Asia House, 227–247 Gascoigne Road, Barking, Essex IG11 7LN T 020-8594 6662 *Frequencies:* 936/972 AM

COMPASS FM, 26A Wellowgate, Grimsby, Lincs DN32 0RA T 01472-346666 *Frequency:* 96.4 FM

CONNECT 97.2 & 107.4, Unit 1, Centre 2000, Robinson Close, Telford Way Industrial Estate, Kettering, Northants NN16 8PU T 01536-412413 *Frequencies:* 97.2/107.4 FM

COUNTY SOUND RADIO 1566 AM, Dolphin House, North Street, Guildford, Surrey GU1 4AA T 01483-300964 *Frequency:* 1566 AM

CTR FM, 6–8 Mill Street, Maidstone, Kent ME15 6XH T 01622-662500 *Frequency:* 105.6 FM

DEARNE FM, Unit 7, Network Centre, Zenith Park, Whaley Road, Barnsley S75 1HT T 01226-321733 *Frequencies:* 97.1/102.0 FM

DEE 106.3, 2 Chantry Court, Chester CH1 4QN T 01244-391000 *Frequency:* 106.3 FM

DELTA FM, 65 Weyhill, Haslemere, Surrey GU27 1HN T 01428-651971 *Frequencies:* 97.1/101.6/101.8/102.0 FM

DREAM 100 FM, Northgate House, St Peter's Street, Colchester, Essex CO1 1HT T 01206-764466 *Frequency:* 100.2 FM

DREAM 107.7 FM, 6th Floor, Cater House, High Street, Chelmsford, Essex CM1 1AL T 01245-259400 *Frequency:* 107.7 FM

ENERGY FM, 100 Market Street, Douglas, IOM IM1 2PH T 01624-611936 *Frequencies:* 91.2 FM (Laxey); 93.4 FM (north Isle of Man); 98.4 FM (Ramsey); 98.6 FM (Douglas and south); 105.2 FM (north-east coast)

ESSEX FM, 19–20 Clifftown Road, Southend-on-Sea, Essex SS1 1SX T 01702-323206 *Frequencies:* 96.3/97.5/102.6 FM

FM 103 HORIZON, The Broadcast Centre, 14 Vincent Avenue, Crownhill, Milton Keynes MK8 0AB T 01908-269111 *Frequency:* 103.3 FM

FEN RADIO 107.55, Church Mews, Wisbech, Cambs PE13 1HL T 01945-467107 *Frequency:* 107.5 FM

FIRE 107.6 FM, Quadrant Studios, Old Christchurch Road, Bournemouth BH1 2AD T 01202-318100 *Frequency:* 107.6 FM

FOSSEWAY RADIO, Suite 1, 1 Castle Street, Hinckley, Leics LE10 1DA T 01455-614151 *Frequency:* 107.9 FM

FOX FM, Brush House, Pony Road, Oxford OX4 2XR T 01865-871000 *Frequencies:* 97.4/102.6 FM

FRESH RADIO, Firth Mill, Firth Street, Skipton, N. Yorks BD23 2PT T 01756-799991 *Frequencies:* 936/1413/1431 AM

GALAXY 102, 5th Floor, The Triangle, Hanging Ditch, Manchester M4 3TR T 0161-279 0300 *Frequency:* 102.0 FM

GALAXY 102.2, 1 The Square, 111 Broad Street, Birmingham B15 1AS T 0121-695 0000 *Frequency:* 102.2 FM

GALAXY 105, Joseph's Well, Westgate, Leeds LS3 1AB T 0113-213 0105 *Frequencies:* 105.1/105.6/105.8 FM

GALAXY 105–106, Kingfisher Way, Silverlink Business Park, Tyne and Wear NE28 9NX T 0191-206 8000 *Frequencies:* 105.3/105.6/106.4 FM

GEMINI FM, Hawthorn House, Exeter Business Park, Exeter EX1 3QS T 01392-444444 *Frequencies:* 96.4/97.0/103.0 FM

GWR FM (BRISTOL AND BATH), PO Box 2000, One Passage Street, Bristol BS99 7SN T 0117-984 3200
Frequencies: 96.3/103.0 FM

GWR FM (SWINDON AND WEST WILTSHIRE), Chiseldon House, Stonehill Green, Westlea, Swindon, Wilts SN5 7HB T 01793-663000
Frequencies: 96.5/97.2/102.2 FM

HALLAM FM, Radio House, 900 Herries Road, Sheffield S6 1RH T 0114-209 1000 *Frequencies:* 97.4/102.9/103.4 FM

HEART 106, City Link, Nottingham, NG2 4NG
T 0115-9106100
Frequency: 106 FM

HEART 106.2, The Chrysalis Building, Bramley Road, London W10 6SP T 020-7468 1062 *Frequency:* 106.2 FM

HERTBEAT FM, The Pump House, Knebworth Park, Herts SG3 6HQ T 01438-810900 *Frequencies:* 106.7/106.9 FM

HERTFORDSHIRE'S MERCURY 96.6, Unit 5, The Metro Centre, Dwight Road, Watford WD18 9UP T 01932-205470
Frequency: 96.6 FM

HIGH PEAK RADIO, The Studios, Smithbrook Close, Chapel-en-le-Frith, High Peak, Derbys SK23 0QD
T 01298-813144 *Frequencies:* 103.3/106.4 FM

IMAGINE FM, Regent House, Heaton Lane, Stockport SK4 1BX T 0161-609 1400 *Frequency:* 104.9 FM

INVICTA FM, Radio House, John Wilson Business Park, Whitstable, Kent CT5 3QX T 01227-772004
Frequencies: 95.9/96.1/97.0/102.8/103.1 FM

ISLE OF WIGHT RADIO, Dodnor Park, Newport, IOW PO30 5XE T 01983-822557 *Frequencies:* 102.0/107.0 FM

IVEL FM, The Studios, Middle Street, Yeovil, Somerset BA20 1DJ T 01935-848488 *Frequency:* 105.6/106.6 FM

KERRANG! 105.2 FM, Kerrang House, 20 Lionel Street, Birmingham B3 1AQ T 0845-053 1052
Frequency: 105.2 FM

KESTREL FM, 2nd Floor, Paddington House, Festival Place, Basingstoke, Hants RG21 7LJ T 01256-694000
Frequency: 107.6 FM

KEY 103, Castle Quay, Castlefield, Manchester M15 4PR
T 0161-288 5000 *Frequency:* 103.0 FM

KICK FM, The Studios, 42 Bone Lane, Newbury, Berks RG14 5SD T 01635-841600
Frequencies: 105.6/107.4 FM

KISMAT RADIO, Radio House, Merrick Road, Southall, Middx UB2 4AU T 020-8813 8900 *Frequency:* 1035 AM

KISS 100 FM, Mappin House, 4 Winsley Street, London W1W 8HF T 020-7975 8100 *Frequency:* 100.0 FM

KIX 96.2 FM, Watch Close, Spon Street, Coventry CV1 3LN
T 024-7652 5656 *Frequency:* 96.2 FM

KL.FM 96.7, 18 Blackfriars Street, King's Lynn, Norfolk PE30 1NN T 01553-772777 *Frequency:* 96.7 FM

KMFM FOR ASHFORD, Express House, 34–36 North Street, Ashford, Kent TN24 8JR T 01233-623232
Frequency: 107.6 FM

KMFM FOR CANTERBURY, 9 St Georges Place, Canterbury, Kent CT1 1UU T 01227-475950
Frequency: 106.0 FM

KMFM FOR MEDWAY, Medway House, Ginsbury Close, Sir Thomas Longley Road, Medway City Estate, Strood, Rochester, Kent ME2 4DU T 01634-711079
Frequencies: 100.4/107.9 FM

KMFM FOR SHEPWAY AND WHITE CLIFFS COUNTRY, 93–95 Sandgate Road, Folkstone, Kent CT20 2BQ
T 01303-220303 *Frequencies:* 96.4/106.8 FM

KMFM FOR THANET, Imperial House, 2–14 High Street, Margate, Kent CT9 1DH T 01843-220222
Frequency: 107.2 FM

KMFM FOR WEST KENT, 1 East Street, Tonbridge, Kent TN9 1AR T 01732-369200 *Frequencies:* 96.2/101.6 FM

LAKELAND RADIO, Lakeland Food Park, Plumgarths, Crook Road, Kendal, Cumbria LA8 8QJ T 01539-737380
Frequencies: 100.1/100.8 FM

LANTERN FM, Unit 2B, Lauder Lane, Roundswell Business Park, Barnstaple EX31 3TA T 01271-366350
Frequencies: 96.2/97.3 FM

LBC 97.3 FM, The Chrysalis Building, 13 Bramley Road, London W10 6SP T 020-7314 7300 *Frequency:* 97.3 FM

LBC NEWS 1152 AM, The Chrysalis Building, 13 Bramley Road, London W10 6SP T 020-7221 2213
Frequency: 1152 AM

LEICESTER SOUND, 6 Dominus Way, Meridian Business Park, Leicester LE19 1RP T 0116-256 1300
Frequency: 105.4 FM

LINCS FM, Witham Park, Waterside South, Lincoln LN5 7JN
T 01522-549900 *Frequencies:* 96.7/102.2/97.6 FM

LITE FM, 2nd Floor, 5 Church Street, Peterborough PE1 1XB
T 01733-898106 *Frequency:* 106.8 FM

LONDON GREEK RADIO, LGR House, 437 High Road, London N12 0AP T 020-8349 6950 *Frequency:* 103.3 FM

LONDON TURKISH RADIO, 185B High Road, Wood Green, London N22 6BA T 020-8881 0606
Frequency: 1584 AM

MAGIC 105.4 FM, Mappin House, 4 Winsley Street, London W1W 8HF T 020-7955 1054 *Frequency:* 105.4 FM

MAGIC 828, 51 Burley Road, Leeds LS3 1LR T 0113-283 5500
Frequency: 828 AM

MAGIC 999, St Paul's Square, Preston, Lancs PR1 1YE
T 01772-477700 *Frequency:* 999 AM

MAGIC 1152 (TYNE AND WEAR), Radio House, Newcastle upon Tyne NE99 1BB T 0191-420 3040
Frequency: 1152 AM

MAGIC 1161 AM, Commercial Road, Hull, E. Yorks HU1 2SG
T 01482-325141 *Frequency:* 1161 AM

MAGIC 1170, Radio House, Yales Crescent, Thornaby, Stockton-on-Tees, Cleveland TS17 6AA T 01642-888222
Frequency: 1170 AM

MAGIC 1548 AM, St John's Beacon, 1 Houghton Street, Liverpool L1 1RL T 0151-472 6800
Frequency: 1548 AM

MAGIC AM, Radio House, 900 Herries Road, Sheffield S6 1RH
T 0114-209 1000 *Frequencies:* 990/1305/1548 AM

MANCHESTER'S MAGIC 1152, Castle Quay, Castlefield, Manchester M1 4AW T 0161-288 5000
Frequency: 1152 AM

MANSFIELD 103.2 FM, The Media Suite, Brunts Business Centre, Samuel Brunts Way, Mansfield, Notts NG18 2AH
T 01623-646666 *Frequency:* 103.2 FM

MANX RADIO, PO Box 1368, Broadcasting House, Douglas, IOM IM99 1SW T 01624-682600
Frequencies: 89.0/97.2/103.7 FM, 1368 AM

MERCIA FM, Hertford Place, Coventry CV1 3TT T 024-7686 8200 *Frequencies:* 97.0/102.9 FM

MERSEYSIDE'S 106.7 THE ROCKET, The Studios, Cables Retail Park, Prescot, Merseyside L34 5SW T 0151-290 1501
Frequency: 106.7 FM

METRO RADIO, Radio House, Newcastle upon Tyne NE99 1BB T 0191-420 0971
Frequencies: 97.1/102.6/103.0/103.2 FM

MINSTER FM, PO Box 123, Dunnington, York YO19 5ZX
T 01904-488888 *Frequencies:* 102.3/104.7 FM

MIX 96, Friars Square Studios, 11 Bourbon Street, Aylesbury, Bucks HP20 2PZ T 01296-399396 *Frequency:* 96.2 FM

MIX 107, 11 Duke Street, High Wycombe, Bucks HP13 6EE
T 01494-446611 *Frequencies:* 107.4/107.7 FM

NORTH NORFOLK RADIO, The Studio, Breck Farm, Stody, Norfolk NR24 2ER T 01263-860808
Frequencies: 96.2/103.2 FM

NORTHANTS 96, 19–21 St Edmunds Road, Northampton
NN1 5DX T 01604 795600 *Frequency:* 96.6 FM

OAK 107, 7 Waldron Court, Prince William Road,
Loughborough, Leics LE11 5GD T 01509-211711
Frequency: 107.0 FM

OCEAN FM, Radio House, Whittle Avenue, Segensworth
West, Fareham, Hants PO15 5SH T 01489-589911
Frequencies: 96.7/97.5 FM

ORCHARD FM, Haygrove House, Shoreditch Road, Taunton,
Somerset TA3 7BT T 01823-338448
Frequencies: 96.5/97.1/102.6 FM

PASSION 107.9, 270 Woodstock Road, Oxford OX2 7NW
T 01865-315980 *Frequency:* 107.9 FM

PEAK 107 FM, Radio House, Foxwood Road, Chesterfield,
Derbys S41 9RF T 01246-269107
Frequencies: 102.0/107.4 FM

PIRATE FM, Carn Brea Studios, Wilson Way, Redruth,
Cornwall TR15 3XX T 01209-314400
Frequencies: 102.2/102.8 FM

PREMIER CHRISTIAN RADIO, 22 Chapter Street, London
SW1P 4NP T 020-7316 1300
Frequencies: 1305/1332/1413 AM

THE PULSE OF WEST YORKSHIRE, Pennine House, Forster
Square, Bradford, W. Yorks BD1 5NE T 01274-203040
Frequencies: 97.5/102.5 FM

PULSE CLASSIC GOLD, Forster Square, Bradford, W. Yorks
BD1 5NE T 01274-203040 *Frequencies* 1278/1530 AM

Q103 FM, Enterprise House, The Vision Park, Chivers Way,
Histon, Cambridge CB4 9WW T 01223-235255
Frequencies: 97.4/103.0 FM

QUAYWEST RADIO, Harbour Studios, The Esplanade,
Watchet, Somerset TA23 0AJ T 01984-634900
Frequencies: 100.8/102.4 FM

RADIO CITY 96.7, St John's Beacon, 1 Houghton Street,
Liverpool L1 1RL T 0151-472 6800
Frequency: 96.7 FM

RADIO WAVE 96.5 FM, 965 Mowbray Drive, Blackpool, Lancs
FY3 7JR T 01253-304965 *Frequency:* 96.5 FM

RADIO XL 1296 AM, KMS House, Bradford Street,
Birmingham B12 0JD T 0121-753 5353
Frequency: 1296 AM

RAM FM, 35/36 Irongate, Derby DE1 3GA T 01332-324000
Frequency: 102.8 FM

READING 107 FM, Radio House, Madejski Stadium, Reading,
Berks RG2 0FN T 0118-986 2555 *Frequency:* 107.0 FM

REAL RADIO (YORKSHIRE), 1 Sterling Court, Capitol Park,
Leeds WF3 1EL T 0113-238 1114
Frequencies: 106.2/107.6/107.7 FM

RIDINGS FM, 2 Thornes Office Park, Monckton Road,
Wakefield WF2 7AN T 01924-367177 *Frequency:* 106.8 FM

RUGBY FM, Suites 4–6, Dunsmore Business Centre, Spring
Street, Rugby, Warks CV21 3HH T 01788-541100
Frequency: 107.1 FM

RUTLAND RADIO, 40 Melton Road, Oakham, Rutland, Leics
LE15 6AY T 01572-757868 *Frequencies:* 97.4/107.2 FM

SABRAS RADIO, Radio House, 63 Melton Road, Leicester
LE4 6PN T 0116-261 0666 *Frequency:* 1260 AM

SAGA 105.7 FM, 3rd floor, Crown House, Beaufort Court,
123 Hagley Road, Birmingham B16 8LD T 0121-452 1057
Frequency: 105.7 FM

SAGA 106.6 FM, Saga Radio House, Unit 2, Alder Court,
Rennie Hogg Road, Riverside Retail Park, Nottingham
NG2 1RX T 0115-986 1066 *Frequencies:* 101.4/106.6 FM

THE SAINT, Saints Radio Ltd., The Friends Provident, St.
Mary's Stadium, Britannia Road, Southampton SO14 5FP
T 023-8033 0300 *Frequency:* 107.8 FM

SEVERN SOUND, Bridge Studios, Eastgate Centre, Gloucester
GL1 1SS T 01452-572400 *Frequencies:* 102.4/103.0 FM

SGR COLCHESTER, Abbeygate Two, 9 Whitewell Road,
Colchester, Essex CO2 7DE T 01206-575859
Frequency: 96.1 FM

SGR-FM, Alpha Business Park, 6–12 White House Road,
Ipswich, Suffolk IP1 5LT T 01473-461000
Frequencies: 96.4/97.1 FM

SIGNAL 1, Stoke Road, Stoke-on-Trent ST4 2SR
T 01782-441300 *Frequencies:* 96.4/96.9/102.6 FM

SIGNAL 2, Stoke Road, Stoke-on-Trent ST4 2SR
T 01782-441300 *Frequency:* 1170 AM

SOUTH HAMS RADIO, Unit 1G, South Hams Business Park,
Churchstow, Kingsbridge, Devon TQ7 3QH T 01548-854595
Frequency: 100.5/100.8/101.2/101.9 FM

SOUTHERN FM, Franklin Road, PO Box 2000, Brighton
BN41 2SS T 01273-430111
Frequencies: 96.9/102.0/102.4/103.5 FM

SPECTRUM RADIO, 4 Ingate Place, Battersea, London
SW8 3NS T 020-7627 4433 *Frequency:* 558 AM

SPIRE FM, City Hall Studios, Malthouse Lane, Salisbury, Wilts
SP2 7QQ T 01722-416644 *Frequency:* 102.0 FM

SPIRIT FM, 9/10 Dukes Court, Bognor Road, Chichester,
W. Sussex PO19 8FX T 01243-773600
Frequencies: 96.6/102.3/106.6 FM

STAR 106.6, The Observatory, Slough, Berks SL1 1LH
T 01753-551066 *Frequency:* 106.6 FM

STAR 107, 20 Mercers Row, Cambridge CB5 8HY
T 01223-305107 *Frequencies:* 107.1/107.9 FM

STAR 107.2, Bristol Evening Post Building, Temple Way, Bristol
BS99 7HD T 0117-910 6600 *Frequency:* 107.2 FM

STAR 107.5, Cheltenham Film Studios, 1st Floor, West Suite,
Arle Court, Cheltenham, Glos GL51 6PN T 01242-699555
Frequency: 107.5 FM

STAR 107.7, 11 Beaconsfield Road, Weston-super-Mare
BS23 1YE T 01934-624455 *Frequency:* 107.7 FM

STAR 107.9, Brunel Mall, London Road, Stroud GL5 2BP
T 01453-767369 *Frequencies:* 107.3/107.9 FM

SUNRISE FM, Sunrise House, 30 Chapel Street, Little
Germany, Bradford BD1 5DN T 01274-735043
Frequency: 103.2 FM

SUNRISE RADIO (LONDON), Radio House, Merrick Road,
Southall, Middx UB2 4AU T 020-8574 6666
Frequency: 1458 AM

SUNSHINE 855, Unit 11, Burway Trading Estate, Ludlow,
Shropshire SY8 1EN T 01584-873795 *Frequency:* 855 AM

TELFORD FM, c/o The Shropshire Star, Waterloo Road, Ketley
TF1 5HU T 01952-280011 *Frequency:* 107.4 FM

TEN 17, Latton Bush Centre, Southern Way, Harlow, Essex
CM18 7BB T 01279-431017 *Frequency:* 101.7 FM

TFM, Radio House, Yale Crescent, Thornaby, Stockton-on-Tees
TS17 6AA T 01642-888222 *Frequency:* 96.6 FM

TIME 106.8, 2–6 Basildon Road, Abbey Wood, London
SE2 0EW T 020-8311 3112 *Frequency:* 106.8 FM

TIME 107.3, 2–6 Basildon Road, Abbey Wood, London
SE2 0EW T 020-8311 3112 *Frequency:* 107.3 FM

TIME 107.5, 7th Floor, Lambourne House, 7 Western Road,
Romford, Essex RM1 3LD T 01708-731 643
Frequency: 107.5 FM

TOWER FM, The Mill, Brownlow Way, Bolton BL1 2RA
T 01204-387000 *Frequency:* 107.4 FM

TRAX FM (BASSETLAW), White Hart Yard, Bridge Street,
Worksop, Notts S80 1HR T 01909-500611
Frequency: 107.9 FM

TRAX FM (DONCASTER), 5 Sidings Court, White Rose Way,
Doncaster DN4 5SE T 01302-341166 *Frequency:* 107.1 FM

VALE FM, Longmead Studios, Shaftesbury, Dorset SP7 8QQ
T 01747-855711 *Frequencies:* 96.6/97.4 FM

VIBE FM 101, 26 Baldwin Street, Bristol BS1 1SE
T 0117-901 0101 *Frequencies:* 97.2/101 FM

VIBE FM 105–108, Reflection House, The Anderson Centre, Olding Road, Bury St Edmunds IP33 3TA T 01284-715300 *Frequencies:* 105.6/106.1/106.4/107.7 FM

VIRGIN RADIO 105.8 FM, 1 Golden Square, London W1F 9DJ T 020-7434 1215 *Frequency:* 105.8 FM

WAVE 105 FM, 5 Manor Court, Barnes Wallis Road, Segensworth East, Fareham, Hampshire PO15 5TH T 01489-481050 *Frequencies:* 105.2/105.8 FM

WESSEX FM, Radio House, Trinity Street, Dorchester, Dorset DT1 1DJ T 01305-250333 *Frequencies:* 96.0/97.2 FM

WIRE FM, Warrington Business Park, Long Lane, Warrington WA2 8TX T 01925-445545 *Frequency:* 107.2 FM

WIRRAL'S BUZZ 97.1, PO Box 971, Birkenhead CH41 6EY T 0151-650 1700 *Frequency:* 97.1 FM

WYVERN FM, 5–6 Barbourne Terrace, Worcester WR1 3JZ T 01905-545500 *Frequencies:* 96.7/97.6/102.8 FM

XFM, 30 Leicester Square, London WC2H 7LA T 020-7766 6000 *Frequency:* 104.9 FM

YORKSHIRE COAST RADIO (BRIDLINGTON), The Old Harbour Master's Office, Harbour Road, Bridlington, E. Yorks YO15 2NR T 01262-404400 *Frequency:* 102.4 FM

YORKSHIRE COAST RADIO (SCARBOROUGH), Unit 2B, Newchase Business Centre, Hopper Hill Road, Scarborough, N. Yorks YO11 3YS T 01723-581700 *Frequencies:* 96.2/103.1 FM

Wales

96.4 FM THE WAVE, PO Box 964, Victoria Road, Gowerton, Swansea SA4 3AB T 01792-511964 *Frequency:* 96.4 FM

97.1 RADIO CARMARTHENSHIRE, Unit 14, The Old School Estate, Station Road, Narberth, Pembrokeshire SA67 7DU T 0845-355 0570 *Frequencies:* 97.1/97.5 FM

97.5 SCARLET FM, The Foothold Centre, Stebonheath Terrace, Llanelli SA15 1NE T 0845-355 0570 *Frequency:* 97.5 FM

106.3 BRIDGE FM, PO Box 1063, Bridgend CF31 1WF T 01656-647777 *Frequency:* 106.3 FM

102.5 RADIO PEMBROKESHIRE, Unit 14, The Old School Estate, Station Road, Narberth, Pembrokeshire SA67 7DU T 01834-869384 *Frequencies:* 102.5/107.5 FM

CAPITAL GOLD (1359 & 1305), Atlantic Wharf, Cardiff CF10 4DJ T 029-2066 2066 *Frequencies:* 1305/1359 AM

CHAMPION FM 103, Llys-Y-Dderwen, Parc Menai, Bangor, Gwynedd LL55 4BN T 01248-673400 *Frequency:* 103.0 FM

CLASSIC GOLD MARCHER (1260), The Studios, Mold Road, Wrexham LL11 4AF T 01978-752202 *Frequency:* 1260 AM

COAST FM 96.3, PO Box 963, Bangor LL57 4ZR T 01248-673401 *Frequency:* 96.3 FM

MFM 103.4, The Studios, Mold Road, Gwersyllt, Wrexham LL11 4AF T 01978 752202 *Frequency:* 103.4 FM

RADIO CEREDIGION, Yr Hen Ysgol Gymraeg, Aberystwyth SY23 1LF T 01970-627999 *Frequencies:* 96.6/97.4/103.3/FM

RADIO MALDWYN, The Studios, The Park, Newtown, Powys SY16 2NZ T 01686-623555 *Frequency:* 756 AM

REAL RADIO, Unit 1, Ty-Nant Court, Ty-Nant Road, Morganstown, Cardiff CF15 8LW T 029-2031 5100 *Frequencies:* 105.2/105.4/105.7/105.9/106/106.2 FM

RED DRAGON FM, Atlantic Wharf, Cardiff CF10 4DJ T 029-2066 2066 *Frequencies:* 97.4/103.2 FM

SWANSEA SOUND, Victoria Road, Gowerton, Swansea SA4 3AB T 01792-511170 *Frequency:* 1170 AM

VALLEYS RADIO, PO Box 1116, Ebbw Vale, Gwent NP23 8XW T 01495-301116 *Frequencies:* 999/1116 AM

Scotland

107 THE EDGE, Radio House, Rowantree Avenue, Newhouse Industrial Estate, Newhouse, Lanarkshire ML1 5RX T 01698-733107 *Frequencies:* 107.5/107.9 FM

ARGYLL FM, 27–29 Longrow, Campbeltown, Argyll PA28 8ER T 01586-551800 *Frequencies:* 106.5/107.1/107.7 FM

BEAT 106, Four Winds Pavilion, Pacific Quay, Glasgow G51 1EB T 0141-566 6106 *Frequencies:* 105.7/106.1 FM

CENTRAL 103.1 FM, 201–203 High Street, Falkirk FK1 1DU T 01324-611164 *Frequency:* 103.1 FM

CLYDE 1, Clydebank Business Park, Clydebank, Glasgow G81 2RX T 0141-565 2200 *Frequencies:* 97/102.5/103.3 FM

CLYDE 2, Clydebank Business Park, Glasgow G81 2RX T 0141-565 2200 *Frequency:* 1152 AM

CUILLIN FM, Stormyhill Road, Portree, Isle of Skye IV51 9DY T 01478-611234 *Frequency:* 106.2 FM

FORTH ONE, Forth House, Forth Street, Edinburgh EH1 3LE T 0131-556 9255 *Frequencies:* 97.3/97.6/102.2 FM

FORTH 2, Forth House, Forth Street, Edinburgh EH1 3LE T 0131-556 9255 *Frequency:* 1548 AM

HEARTLAND FM, Atholl Curling Rink, Lower Oakfield, Pitlochry, Perthshire PH16 5HQ T 01796-474040 *Frequency:* 97.5 FM

ISLES FM, PO Box 333, Stornoway, Isle of Lewis HS1 2RE T 01851-703333 *Frequency:* 103.0 FM

KINGDOM FM, Haig House, Haig Business Park, Balgonie Road, Markinch, Fife KY7 6AQ T 01592-753753 *Frequencies:* 95.2/96.1/96.6/105.4/106.3 FM

LOCHBROOM FM, Radio House, Mill Street, Ullapool, Ross-shire IV26 2UN T 01854-613131 *Frequencies:* 96.8/102.2 FM

MORAY FIRTH RADIO (MFR), Scorguie Place, Inverness IV3 8UJ T 01463-224433 *Frequencies:* 97.4 FM, 1107 AM; *local opt-outs:* MFR Speysound 96.6 FM; MFR Keith Community Radio 102.8 FM; MFR Kinnaird Radio 96.7 FM; MFR Caithness 102.5 FM

NECR, The Shed, School Road, Kintore, Iveruie, Aberdeenshire AB51 0US T 01467-632909 *Frequencies:* 97.1/101.9/102.1/102.6/103.2/106.4 FM

NEVIS RADIO, Ben Nevis Estate, Claggan, Fort William PH33 6PR T 01397-700007 *Frequencies:* 96.6/97.0/102.3/102.4 FM

NORTHSOUND ONE, Abbotswell Road, West Tullos, Aberdeen AB12 3AJ T 01224-337000 *Frequencies:* 96.9/97.6/103.0 FM

NORTHSOUND TWO, Abbotswell Road, West Tullos, Aberdeen AB12 3AJ T 01224-337000 *Frequency:* 1035 AM

OBAN FM, 132 George Street, Oban, Argyll PA34 5NT T 01631-570057 *Frequency:* 103.3 FM

Q96, 65 Sussex Street, Kinning Park, Glasgow G41 1XD T 0141-429 9430 *Frequency:* 96.3 FM

RADIO BORDERS, Tweedside Park, Galashiels TD1 3TD T 01896-759444 *Frequencies:* 96.8/97.5/103.1/103.4 FM

REAL RADIO (SCOTLAND), Parkway Court, Glasgow Business Park, Glasgow G69 6GA T 0141-781 1011 *Frequencies:* 100.3/101.1 FM

RIVER FM, Stadium House, Alderstone Road, Livingston EH54 7DN T 01506-410411 *Frequency:* 103.4/107.7 FM

RNA FM, Radio North Angus Ltd., Rosemount Road, Arbroath, Angus DD11 2AT T 01241-879660 *Frequency:* 96.6 FM

SAGA 105.2FM, City Park, Alexandra Parade, Glasgow G31 3AU T 0141-551 1052 *Frequency:* 105.2 FM

SIBC, Market Street, Lerwick, Shetland ZE1 0JN T 01595-695299 *Frequencies:* 96.2/102.2 FM

SOUTH WEST SOUND, Unit 40, The Loreburne Centre, High St, Dumfries DG1 2BD T 01387-250999 *Frequencies:* 96.5/97.0/103.0 FM

TAY AM, 6 North Isla Street, Dundee DD3 7JQ
  T 01382-200800 *Frequencies:* 1161/1584 AM
TWO LOCHS RADIO, Gairloch, Ross-shire IV21 2LR
  T 0870-741 4657 *Frequencies:* 106.0/106.6 FM
UCA, University Campus Ayr, Beech Grove, Ayr, S. Ayrshire
  KA8 0SR T 01292-886385 *Frequency:* 87.7 FM
WAVE 102, 8 South Tay Street, Dundee DD1 1PA
  T 01382-901000 *Frequency:* 102.0 FM
WAVES RADIO, 7 Blackhouse Circle, Blackhouse Industrial
  Estate, Peterhead, Aberdeenshire AB42 1BW
  T 01779-491012 *Frequency:* 101.2 FM
WEST FM, Radio House, 54A Holmston Road, Ayr KA7 3BE
  T 01292-283662 *Frequencies:* 96.7/97.5 FM
WEST SOUND AM, Radio House, 54A Holmston Road,
  Ayr KA7 3BE T 01292-283662
  Frequency: 1035 AM

Northern Ireland
CITY BEAT 96.7FM, 48 Stranmillis Embankment, Belfast
  BT9 5FN T 028-9020 5967 *Frequency:* 96.7 FM
COOL FM, PO Box 974, Belfast BT1 1RT T 028-9181 7181
  Frequency: 97.4 FM
DOWNTOWN RADIO, Newtownards, Co. Down BT23 4ES
  T 028-9181 5555 *Frequencies:* 96.4 FM (Limavady); 96.6 FM
  (Enniskillen); 97.1 FM (Larne); 102.3 FM (Ballymena); 102.4 FM
  (Londonderry); 103.1 FM (Newry); 103.4 FM (Newcastle); 1026
  AM (Belfast)
MID FM, 2C Park Avenue, Cookstown, Co. Tyrone BT80 5AH
  T 028-8675 8696 *Frequencies:* 106.0/107.2 FM
Q97.2 FM, 24 Cloyfin Road, Coleraine, Co. Londonderry
  BT52 2NU T 028-7035 9100 *Frequency:* 97.2 FM
Q101.2 WEST FM, 42A Market Street, Omagh, Co. Tyrone
  BT78 1EH and 1A Belmore Mews, Enniskillen BT74 6AA
  T 028-8224 5777 *Frequency:* 101.2 FM
Q102.9 FM, The Riverview Suite, 87 Rossdowney Road,
  Waterside, Londonderry BT47 5SU T 028-7134 4449
  Frequency: 102.9 FM

Channel Islands
CHANNEL 103 FM, 6 Tunnell Street, St Helier, Jersey JE2 4LU
  T 01534-888103 *Frequency:* 103.7 FM
ISLAND FM, 12 Westerbrook, St Sampsons, Guernsey
  GY2 4QQ T 01481-242000 *Frequencies:* 93.7/104.7 FM

DIGITAL MULTIPLEXES
The information contained in this section is correct at
the time of writing (August 2005), however it is
advisable to check with the multiplex operator for
accurate listings.
CAPITAL RADIO DIGITAL LTD, 30 Leicester Square, London
  WC2H 7LA T 020-7766 6000
  Cardiff and Newport, *Frequency:* 11C
  Kent, *Frequency:* 11C
  South Hampshire, *Frequency:* 11C
  Sussex coast, *Frequency:* 11B
CE DIGITAL LTD, 30 Leicester Square, London WC2H 7LA
  T 020-7766 6000
  Birmingham, *Frequency:* 11C
  Greater London 1, *Frequency:* 12C
  Manchester, *Frequency:* 11C
DIGITAL ONE, 7 Swallow Place, London W1B 2AG
  T 020-7288 4600 W www.ukdigitalradio.com
  England and Wales, *Frequency:* 11D
  Scotland, *Frequency:* 12A

THE DIGITAL RADIO GROUP, 7 Swallow Place, London
  W1B 2AG T 0117-900 5301
  W www.thedigitalradiogroup.com
  Greater London 3,
  Frequency: 11B (operated by Now Digital Ltd)
EMAP DIGITAL RADIO LTD, Mappin House, 4 Winsley
  Street, London W1W 8HF T 020-7436 1515
  W www.emapdigitalradio.com
  Central Lancashire, *Frequency:* 12A
  Humberside, *Frequency:* 11B
  Leeds, *Frequency:* 12D
  Liverpool, *Frequency:* 11B
  South Yorkshire, *Frequency:* 11C
  Teesside, *Frequency:* 11B
  Tyne and Wear, *Frequency:* 11C
MXR, The Chrysalis Building, 13 Bramley Road, London
  W10 6SP T 020-7470 2213
  North-east England, *Frequency:* 12C
  North-west England, *Frequency:* 12C
  South Wales/Severn Estuary, *Frequency:* 12C
  West Midlands, *Frequency:* 12A
  Yorkshire, *Frequency:* 12A
NOW DIGITAL LTD, PO Box 2000, Bristol BS99 7SN
  T 0117-900 5301 W www.now-digital.com
  Bournemouth, *Frequency:* 11B
  Bristol and Bath, *Frequency:* 11B
  Cambridge, *Frequency:* 11C
  Coventry, *Frequency:* 12D
  Exeter and Torbay, *Frequency:* 11C
  Greater London 3, *Frequency:* 11B (owned by The Digital
  Radio Group)
  Leicester, *Frequency:* 11B
  Norwich, *Frequency:* 11B
  Nottingham, *Frequency:* 12C
  Peterborough, *Frequency:* 12D
  Reading and Basingstoke, *Frequency:* 12D
  Southend and Chelmsford, *Frequency:* 12D
  Swindon, *Frequency:* 11C
  West Wiltshire and Bath, *Frequency:* 12D
  Wolverhampton, Shrewsbury and Telford, *Frequency:* 11B
SCORE DIGITAL LTD, 3 South Avenue, Clydebank Business
  Park, Glasgow G81 2RX T 0141-565 2347
  W www.scoredigital.co.uk
  Ayr, *Frequency:* 11B
  Dundee and Perth, *Frequency:* 11B
  Edinburgh, *Frequency:* 12D
  Glasgow, *Frequency:* 11C
  Inverness, *Frequency:* 11B
  Northern Ireland, *Frequency:* 12D
SOUTH WEST DIGITAL RADIO LTD, c/o Now Digital Ltd,
  PO Box 2000, Bristol BS99 7SN T 0117-900 5301
  W www.now-digital.com
  Cornwall, *Frequency:* 11B
  Plymouth, *Frequency:* 12A
SWITCHDIGITAL LTD, 18 Hatfields, London SE1 8DJ T 020-
  7959 7800 W www.switchdigital.com
  Aberdeen, *Frequency:* 11C
  Central Scotland, *Frequency:* 11D
  Greater London 2, *Frequency:* 12A
TWG–EMAP DIGITAL (B & H) LTD, 18 Hatfields, London
  SE1 8DJ T 020-7959 7800
  Bradford and Huddersfield, *Frequency:* 11B
  Stoke-on-Trent, *Frequency:* 12D
  Swansea, *Frequency:* 12A

THE PRESS

The newspaper and periodical press in the UK is large and diverse, catering for a wide variety of views and interests. There is no state control or censorship of the press; however, it is subject to the laws on publication, and the Press Complaints Commission was set up by the industry as a means of self-regulation.

The press is not state-subsidised and receives few tax concessions. The income of most newspapers and periodicals is derived largely from sales and from advertising; the press is the largest advertising medium in Britain.

SELF-REGULATION

The Press Complaints Commission was founded by the newspaper and magazine industry in January 1991 to replace the Press Council (established in 1953). It is a voluntary, non-statutory body set up to operate the press' self-regulation system following the Calcutt report in 1990 on privacy and related matters, when the industry feared that failure to regulate itself might lead to statutory regulation of the press. The performance of the Press Complaints Commission was reviewed after 18 months of operation (the *Calcutt Review of Press Self-Regulation*, presented to Parliament in January 1993) to determine whether statutory measures were required. No proposals for replacing the self-regulation system have been made to date. The Commission is funded by the industry through the Press Standards Board of Finance.

COMPLAINTS

The Press Complaints Commission's aims are to consider, adjudicate, conciliate, and resolve complaints of unfair treatment by the press; and to ensure that the press maintains the highest professional standards with respect for generally recognised freedoms, including freedom of expression, the public's right to know, and the right of the press to operate free from improper pressure. The Commission judges newspaper and magazine conduct by a code of practice drafted by editors, agreed by the industry and ratified by the Commission.

Seven of the Commission's members are editors of national, regional and local newspapers and magazines, and ten, including the chairman, are drawn from other fields. The PCC received 3,618 complaints in 2004.

PRESS COMPLAINTS COMMISSION
1 Salisbury Square, London EC4Y 8JB
T 020-7353 1248 F 020-7353 8355
E complaints@pcc.org.uk
W www.pcc.org.uk
Chairman, Sir Christopher Meyer, KCMG

NEWSPAPERS

Newspapers are mostly financially independent of any political party, though most adopt a political stance in their editorial comments, usually reflecting proprietorial influence. Ownership of the national and regional daily newspapers is concentrated in the hands of large corporations whose interests cover publishing and communications. The rules on cross-media ownership, as amended by the Broadcasting Act 1996, which limited the extent to which newspaper organisations may become involved in broadcasting, have been relaxed by the Communications Act 2003: newspapers with over 20 per cent share of national circulation may own national and/or local radio licences.

There are about 12 daily and 12 Sunday national papers and several hundred local papers that are published weekly or twice-weekly. Scotland, Wales and Northern Ireland all have at least one daily and one Sunday national paper.

Newspapers are usually published in either broadsheet or smaller, tabloid format. The 'quality' daily papers, i.e. those providing detailed coverage of a wide range of public matters, have traditionally used a broadsheet format, while the tabloid papers typically take a more populist approach and are more illustrated. In 2004 this direct correspondence of format to content was abandoned when two traditionally broadsheet newspapers, *The Times* and *The Independent,* switched to tabloid-sized editions, while *The Guardian* launched a new 'Berliner' format in September 2005.

CIRCULATION *(Net average for July 2005)*
National Daily Newspapers

The Sun	3,343,486
Daily Mail	2,420,601
Daily Mirror	1,752,948
The Daily Telegraph	912,319
Daily Star	889,860
Daily Express	835,937
The Times	698,043
Daily Record	464,064
Financial Times	410,306
The Guardian	358,345
The Independent	255,603
Racing Post	81,269
The Herald	73,963
The Scotsman	66,053

National Sunday Newspapers

News of the World	3,701,988
The Mail on Sunday	2,261,511
Sunday Mirror	1,548,851
The Sunday Times	1,338,616
The People	976,194
Sunday Express	887,401
The Sunday Telegraph	682,900
Sunday Mail	553,054
The Observer	445,738
Daily Star Sunday	432,600
The Independent on Sunday	206,689
The Business	192,160
Sunday Sport	159,144
Scotland on Sunday	75,183
Sunday Herald	53,295

Source: Audit Bureau of Circulations Ltd. For further information please see www.abc.org.uk

NATIONAL DAILY NEWSPAPERS

DAILY EXPRESS
Northern & Shell Building, 10 Lower Thames Street, London
EC4R 6EN **T** 0871-434 1010 **W** www.express.co.uk
Editor, Peter Hill

DAILY MAIL
Northcliffe House, 2 Derry Street, London W8 5TT
T 020-7938 6000 **W** www.dailymail.co.uk
Editor, Paul Dacre

DAILY MIRROR
1 Canada Square, Canary Wharf, London E14 5AP
T 020-7293 3000 **W** www.mirror.co.uk
Editor, Richard Wallace

DAILY RECORD
1 Central Quay, Glasgow G3 8DA **T** 0141-309 3000
W www.dailyrecord.co.uk
Editor, Bruce Waddell

DAILY SPORT
19 Great Ancoats Street, Manchester M60 4BT
T 0161-236 4466 **W** www.dailysport.co.uk
Editor, David Beevers; *Editor-in-Chief,* Tony Livesey

DAILY STAR
Ludgate House, 245 Blackfriars Road, London SE1 9UX
T 020-7928 8000 **W** www.dailystar.co.uk
Editor, Dawn Neesom

THE DAILY TELEGRAPH
1 Canada Square, Canary Wharf, London E14 5DT
T 020-7538 5000 **W** www.telegraph.co.uk
Editor, Martin Newland

FINANCIAL TIMES
1 Southwark Bridge, London SE1 9HL **T** 020-7873 3000
W www.ft.com
Editor, Andrew Gowers

THE GUARDIAN
119 Farringdon Road, London EC1R 3ER **T** 020-7278 2332
W www.guardian.co.uk
Editor, Alan Rusbridger

THE HERALD
Newsquest Ltd, 200 Renfield Street, Glasgow G2 3PR
T 0141-302 7000 **W** www.theherald.co.uk
Editor, Mark Douglas-Home

THE INDEPENDENT
Independent House, 191 Marsh Wall, London E14 9RS
T 020-7005 2000 **W** www.independent.co.uk
Editor-in-Chief, Simon Kelner

MORNING STAR
People's Press Printing Society Ltd, William Rust House,
52 Beachy Road, London E3 2NS **T** 020-8510 0815
W www.morningstaronline.co.uk
Editor, John Haylett

RACING POST
Trinity Mirror, Floor 23, One Canada Square, Canary Wharf,
London E14 5AP **T** 020-7293 3291
W www.racingpost.co.uk
Editor, Chris Smith

THE SCOTSMAN
Barclay House, 108 Holyrood Road, Edinburgh EH8 8AS
T 0131-620 8620 **W** www.scotsman.com
Editor, John McGurk

THE SUN
News Group Newspapers Ltd, Virginia Street, London E1 9XP
T 020-7782 4000 **W** www.the-sun.co.uk
Editor, Rebekah Wade

THE TIMES
1 Pennington Street, London E98 1TT **T** 020-7782 5000
W www.timesonline.co.uk
Editor, Robert Thomson

WEEKLY NEWSPAPERS

THE BUSINESS
292 Vauxhall Bridge Road, London SW1V 1DE
T 020-7961 0000 **W** www.thebusinessonline.com

DAILY STAR SUNDAY
Express Newspapers, Ludgate House, 245 Blackfriars Road,
London SE1 9UX **T** 020-7928 8000 **W** www.megastar.co.uk
Editor, Gareth Morgan

THE INDEPENDENT ON SUNDAY
Independent House, 191 Marsh Wall, London E14 9RS
T 020-7005 2000 **W** www.independent.co.uk
Editor, Tristan Davies; *Editor-at-Large,* Janet Street-
Porter

THE MAIL ON SUNDAY
Northcliffe House, 2 Derry Street, London W8 5TS
T 020-7938 6000 **W** www.mailonsunday.co.uk
Editor, Peter Wright

NEWS OF THE WORLD
1 Virginia Street, London E98 1NW **T** 020-7782 1000
W www.newsoftheworld.co.uk
Editor, Andy Coulson

THE OBSERVER
3–7 Herbal Hill, London EC1R 5EJ **T** 020-7278 2332
W www.observer.co.uk
Editor, Roger Alton

THE PEOPLE
1 Canada Square, Canary Wharf, London E14 5AP
T 020-7293 3000 **W** www.people.co.uk
Editor, Mark Thomas

SCOTLAND ON SUNDAY
108 Holyrood Road, Edinburgh EH8 8AS **T** 0131-620 8620
W www.scotlandonsunday.co.uk
Editor, Iain Martin

SUNDAY EXPRESS
Northern & Shell Building, 10 Lower Thames Street, London
EC4R 6EN **T** 0871-434 1010 **W** www.express.co.uk
Editor, Martin Townsend

SUNDAY HERALD
200 Renfield Street, Glasgow G2 3QB **T** 0141-302 7800
W www.sundayherald.com
Editor, Richard Walker

SUNDAY MAIL
1 Central Quay, Glasgow G3 8DA **T** 0141-309 3000
W www.sundaymail.com
Editor, Allan Rennie

SUNDAY MIRROR
1 Canada Square, Canary Wharf, London E14 5AP
T 020-7293 3000 **W** www.sundaymirror.co.uk
Editor, Tina Weaver

THE SUNDAY POST
D. C. Thomson & Co. Ltd, 144 Port Dundas Road, Glasgow
G4 0HZ **T** 0141-332 9933 **W** www.sundaypost.com
Editor, David Pollington

SUNDAY SPORT
840 Melton Road, Thurmaston, Leicester LE4 8BE
T 0116-269 4892 **W** www.sundaysport.com
Editor, Mark Harris

THE SUNDAY TELEGRAPH
1 Canada Square, Canary Wharf, London E14 5DT
T 020-7538 5000 **W** www.telegraph.co.uk
Editor, Sarah Sands

THE SUNDAY TIMES
1 Virginia Street, London E1 9BD **T** 020-7782 4000
W www.timesonline.co.uk
Editor, John Whiterow

THE SUNDAY TIMES SCOTLAND
Times Newspapers Ltd, 124 Portman Street, Kinning Park,
Glasgow G41 1EJ T 0141-420 5100
W www.timesonline.co.uk
Editor, Les Snowdon
WALES ON SUNDAY
Thomson House, Havelock Street, Cardiff CF10 1XR
T 029-2058 3583 W www.icwales.co.uk
Editor, Tim Gordon

REGIONAL DAILY NEWSPAPERS

EAST ANGLIA
CAMBRIDGE EVENING NEWS
Winship Road, Milton, Cambs CB4 6PP T 01223-434437
W www.cambridge-news.co.uk
Editor, Murray Morse
EAST ANGLIAN DAILY TIMES
30 Lower Brook Street, Ipswich, Suffolk IP4 1AN
T 01473-230023 W www.eadt.co.uk
Editor, Terry Hunt
EASTERN DAILY PRESS
Prospect House, Rouen Road, Norwich NR1 1RE
T 01603-628311 W www.edp24.co.uk
Editor, Peter Franzen, OBE
EVENING GAZETTE
43 North Hill, Colchester, Essex CO1 1TZ T 01206 506000
W www.thisisessex.co.uk
Editor, Irene Kettle
EVENING STAR
30 Lower Brook Street, Ipswich, Suffolk IP4 1AN
T 01473-230023 W www.eveningstar.co.uk
Editor, Nigel Pickover
THE EVENING TELEGRAPH
57 Priestgate, Peterborough, Cambs PE1 1JW
T 01733-555111 W www.peterboroughtoday.co.uk
Editor, Rebecca Stephens
NORWICH EVENING NEWS
Prospect House, Rouen Road, Norwich NR1 1RE
T 01603-628311 W www.eveningnews24.co.uk
Editor, David Bourn

EAST MIDLANDS
BURTON MAIL
65–68 High Street, Burton upon Trent DE14 1LE
T 01283-512345 W www.burtonmail.co.uk
Editor, Paul Hazeldine
DERBY EVENING TELEGRAPH
Northcliffe House, Meadow Road, Derby DE1 2DW
T 01332-291111 W www.thisisderbyshire.co.uk
Editor, Mike Norton
LEICESTER MERCURY
St George Street, Leicester LE1 9FQ T 0116-251 2512
W www.leicestermercury.co.uk
Editor, Nick Carter
LINCOLNSHIRE ECHO
Brayford Wharf East, Lincoln LN5 7AT T 01522-820000
W www.thisislincolnshire.co.uk
Editor, Michael Sassi
NORTHAMPTON CHRONICLE & ECHO
Northamptonshire Newspapers Ltd, Upper Mounts,
Northampton NN1 3HR T 01604-467000
Editor, Mark Edwards
NOTTINGHAM EVENING POST
Castle Wharf House, Nottingham NG1 7EU
T 0115-948 2000 W www.thisisnottingham.co.uk
Editor, Graham Glen

LONDON
EVENING STANDARD
Northcliffe House, 2 Derry Street, London W8 5EE
T 020-7938 6000 W www.thisislondon.com
Editor, Veronica Wadley

NORTH EAST
EVENING CHRONICLE
Groat Market, Newcastle upon Tyne NE1 1ED
T 0191-232 7500 W www.icnewcastle.co.uk
Editor, Paul Robertson
EVENING GAZETTE
Gazette Media Company Ltd, Borough Road, Middlesbrough
TS1 3AZ T 01642-245401 W www.tees.net
Editor, Darren Thwaites
HARTLEPOOL MAIL
Northeast Press Ltd, New Clarence House, Wesley Square,
Hartlepool TS24 8BX T 01429-239333
W www.hartlepooltoday.co.uk
Editor, Paul Napier
THE JOURNAL
Groat Market, Newcastle upon Tyne NE1 1ED
T 0191-232 7500 W www.icnewcastle.co.uk
Editor, Brian Aitken
THE NORTHERN ECHO
Priestgate, Darlington, Co. Durham DL1 1NF
T 01325-381313 W www.thisisthenortheast.co.uk
Editor, Peter Barron
SUNDERLAND ECHO
Echo House, Pennywell, Sunderland, Tyne and Wear SR4 9ER
T 0191-501 5800 W www.sunderlandtoday.co.uk
Editor, Rob Lawson

NORTH WEST
BOLTON EVENING NEWS
Newspaper House, Churchgate, Bolton, Lancs BL1 1DE
T 01204-522345 W www.thisisbolton.co.uk
Editor-in-Chief, Steve Hughes
THE GAZETTE
Avroe House, Avroe Crescent, Blackpool Business Park,
Squires Gate, Blackpool FY4 2DP T 01253-400888
W www.blackpooltoday.co.uk
Editor, David Helliwell
LANCASHIRE & WIGAN EVENING POST
Unit 4, Fulwood Buiness Park, Caxton Road, Fulwood,
Preston, Lancs PR2 9NZ T 01772-254841 W www.lep.co.uk
Editor, Simon Reynolds
LANCASHIRE EVENING TELEGRAPH
Newspaper House, High Street, Blackburn, Lancs BB1 1HT
T 01254-678678 W www.thisislancashire.co.uk
Editor, Kevin Young
LIVERPOOL DAILY POST
PO Box 48, Old Hall Street, Liverpool L69 3EB
T 0151-227 2000 W www.liverpool.com
Editor, Jane Wolstenholme
LIVERPOOL ECHO
PO Box 48, Old Hall Street, Liverpool L69 3EB
T 0151-227 2000 W www.liverpool.com
Editor, Mark Dickinson
MANCHESTER EVENING NEWS
164 Deansgate, Manchester M60 2RD T 0161-832 7200
W www.manchesteronline.co.uk
Editor, Paul Horrocks
NEWS & STAR
Newspaper House, Dalston Road, Carlisle, Cumbria CA2 5UA
T 01228-612612 W www.newsandstar.co.uk
Editor, Keith Sutton

NORTH-WEST EVENING MAIL
Newspaper House, Abbey Road, Barrow-in-Furness, Cumbria LA14 5QS **T** 01229-840150 **W** www.nwemail.co.uk
Editor, Steve Brauner

OLDHAM CHRONICLE
PO Box 47, Union Street, Oldham, Lancs OL1 1EQ
T 0161-633 2121 **W** www.oldham-chronicle.co.uk
Editor, Jim Williams

SOUTH

THE ARGUS
Argus House, Crowhurst Road, Hollingbury, Brighton BN1 8AR **T** 01273-544544 **W** www.theargus.co.uk
Editor, Michael Beard

EVENING ECHO
Newspaper House, Chester Hall Lane, Basildon, Essex SS14 3BL **T** 01268-522792 **W** www.thisisessex.co.uk
Editor, Martin McNeill

MEDWAY MESSENGER
Medway House, Ginsbury Close, Sir Thomas Longley Road, Medway City Estate, Strood, Kent ME2 2DU
T 01634-227800 **W** www.kentonline.co.uk

THE NEWS
The News Centre, Hilsea, Portsmouth PO2 9SX
T 023-9266 4488 **W** www.thenews.co.uk
Editor, Mike Gilson

OXFORD MAIL
Newspaper House, Osney Mead, Oxford OX2 0EJ
T 01765-425262 **W** www.thisisoxfordshire.co.uk
Editor, Simon O'Neill

READING EVENING POST
8 Tessa Road, Reading, Berks RG1 8NS **T** 0118-918 3000
W www.getreading.co.uk
Editor, Andy Murrill

THE SOUTHERN DAILY ECHO
Newspaper House, Test Lane, Redbridge, Southampton SO16 9JX **T** 023-8042 4777 **W** www.thisishampshire.net
Editor, Ian Murray

SWINDON EVENING ADVERTISER
100 Victoria Road, Old Town, Swindon SN1 3BE
T 01793-528144 **W** www.thisiswiltshire.co.uk
Editor, Simon O'Neill

SOUTH WEST

THE BATH CHRONICLE
Bath Newspapers, Windsor House, Windsor Bridge, Bath BA2 3AU **T** 01225-322322 **W** www.bathchronicle.co.uk
Editor, John McCready

THE CITIZEN
Gloucestershire Newspapers Ltd, St John's Lane, Gloucester GL1 2AY **T** 01452-424442
W www.thisisgloucestershire.co.uk
Editor, Ian Mean

DAILY ECHO
Richmond Hill, Bournemouth BH2 6HH **T** 01202-554601
W www.thisisdorset.net
Editor, Neal Butterworth

DORSET ECHO
Newscom, Fleet House, Hampshire Road, Weymouth, Dorset DT4 9XD **T** 01305-830930 **W** www.thisisdorset.net
Editor, David Murdock

EVENING HERALD
17 Brest Road, Derriford Business Park, Plymouth, Devon PL6 5AA **T** 01752-765529 **W** www.thisisplymouth.co.uk
Editor, Alan Qualtrough

EVENING POST
Temple Way, Bristol BS99 7HD **T** 0117-934 3000
W www.thisisbristol.com
Editor-in-Chief, Mike Norton

EXPRESS & ECHO
Express & Echo Publications Ltd, Heron Road, Sowton, Exeter EX2 7NF **T** 01392-442211 **W** www.thisisexeter.co.uk
Editor, Steve Hall

GLOUCESTERSHIRE ECHO
1 Clarence Parade, Cheltenham, Glos GL50 3NY
T 01242-271900 **W** www.thisisgloucestershire.co.uk
Editor, Anita Syvret

HERALD EXPRESS
Harmsworth House, Barton Hill Road, Torquay, Devon TQ2 8JN **T** 01803-676000 **W** www.thisissouthdevon.co.uk
Editor, Brendon Hanrahan

WESTERN DAILY PRESS
Bristol Evening Post and Press Ltd, Temple Way, Bristol BS99 7HD **T** 0117-934 3000 **W** www.westpress.co.uk
Editor, Terry Manners

WESTERN MORNING NEWS
17 Brest Road, Derriford, Plymouth PL6 5AA
T 01752-765500 **W** www.westernmorningnews.co.uk
Editor-in-Chief, Alan Qualtrough

WEST MIDLANDS

BIRMINGHAM EVENING MAIL
Weaman Street, Birmingham B4 6AY **T** 0121-236 3366
W www.icbirmingham.co.uk
Editor, Steve Dyson

THE BIRMINGHAM POST
Weaman Street, Birmingham B4 6AT **T** 0121-236 3366
W www.icbirmingham.co.uk
Editor, Fiona Alexander

COVENTRY EVENING TELEGRAPH
Corporation Street, Coventry CV1 1FP **T** 024-7663 3633
W www.iccoventry.co.uk
Editor, Alan Kirby

EXPRESS & STAR
Queen Street, Wolverhampton WV1 1ES **T** 01902-313131
W www.expressandstar.com
Editor, Adrian Faber

THE SENTINEL
Sentinel House, Etruria, Stoke-on-Trent ST1 5SS
T 01782-602525 **W** www.thisisstaffordshire.co.uk
Editor, Sean Dooley

SHROPSHIRE STAR
Ketley, Telford TF1 5HU **T** 01952-242424
W www.shropshirestar.com
Editor, Sarah Jane Smith

WORCESTER NEWS
Berrows House, Hylton Road, Worcester WR2 5JX
T 01905-742277 **W** www.thisisworcester.co.uk
Editor, Stewart Gilbert

YORKSHIRE AND HUMBERSIDE

EVENING COURIER
PO Box 19, King Cross Street, Halifax HX1 2SF
T 01422-260200 **W** www.halifaxcourier.co.uk
Editor, John Furbisher

EVENING PRESS
PO Box 29, 76–86 Walmgate, York YO1 9YN
T 01904-653051 **W** www.thisisyork.co.uk
Editor, Kevin Booth

GRIMSBY TELEGRAPH
80 Cleethorpe Road, Grimsby, Lincs DN31 3EH
T 01472-360360 W www.thisisgrimsby.co.uk
Editor, Michelle Lalor
THE HUDDERSFIELD DAILY EXAMINER
PO Box A26, Queen Street South, Huddersfield HD1 2TD
T 01484-430000 W www.ichuddersfield.co.uk
Editor, Roy Wright
HULL DAILY MAIL
Blundell Corner, Beverley Road, Hull HU3 1XS
T 01482-327111 W www.thisishull.co.uk
Editor, John Meehan
SCARBOROUGH EVENING NEWS
17–23 Aberdeen Walk, Scarborough, N. Yorks YO11 1BB
T 01723-363636 W www.scarborougheveningnews.co.uk
Editor, Ed Asquith
THE STAR
York Street, Sheffield S1 1PU T 0114-276 7676
W www.sheffieldtoday.net
Editor, Alan Powell
TELEGRAPH & ARGUS
Hall Ings, Bradford, W. Yorks BD1 1JR T 01274-729511
W www.thisisbradford.co.uk
Editor, Perry Austin-Clarke
YORKSHIRE EVENING POST
PO Box 168, Wellington Street, Leeds LS1 1RF
T 0113-2432701 W www.yorkshire-evening-post.co.uk
Editor, Neil Hodgkinson
YORKSHIRE POST
Wellington Street, Leeds LS1 1RF T 0113-243 2701
W www.yorkshireposttoday.co.uk
Editor, Peter Charlton

SCOTLAND
THE COURIER
D.C. Thomson & Co. Ltd, 80 Kingsway East, Dundee DD4 8SL
T 01382-223131 W www.thecourier.co.uk
EDINBURGH EVENING NEWS
108 Holyrood Road, Edinburgh EH8 8AS T 0131-620 8620
W www.edinburghnews.scotsman.com
Editor, John McLellan
EVENING EXPRESS
Aberdeen Journals Ltd, Lang Stracht, Mastrick, Aberdeen
AB15 6DF T 01224-690222 W www.eveningexpress.co.uk
Editor, Donald Martin
EVENING TELEGRAPH AND POST
D.C. Thomson & Co. Ltd, 80 Kingsway East, Dundee DD4 8SL
T 01382-223131 W www.eveningtelegraph.co.uk
EVENING TIMES
200 Renfield Street, Glasgow G2 3PR T 0141-302 7000
W www.eveningtimes.co.uk
Editor, Charles McGhee
THE INVERNESS COURIER
New Century House, Stadium Road, Inverness IV1 1FF
T 01463-732222 W www.inverness-courier.co.uk
Editor, Jim Love
PAISLEY DAILY EXPRESS
Scottish and Universal Newspapers Ltd, 14 New Street,
Paisley, Renfrewshire PA1 1YA T 0141-887 7911
W www.icrenfrewshire.co.uk
Editor, Gordon Bury
THE PRESS AND JOURNAL
Aberdeen Journals Ltd, Lang Stracht, Aberdeen AB15 6DF
T 01224-690222 W www.pressandjournal.co.uk
Editor, Derek Tucker

WALES
SOUTH WALES ARGUS
South Wales Argus, Cardiff Road, Maesglas, Newport, Gwent
NP20 3QN T 01633-777219 W www.southwalesargus.co.uk
Editor, Gerry Keighley
SOUTH WALES ECHO
Thomson House, Havelock Street, Cardiff CF10 1XR
T 029-2022 3333 W www.icwales.co.uk
Editor, Richard Williams
SOUTH WALES EVENING POST
Adelaide Street, Swansea SA1 1QT T 01792-510 000
W www.thisissouthwales.co.uk
Editor, Spencer Feeney
WESTERN MAIL
Thomson House, Havelock Street, Cardiff CF10 1XR
T 029-2022 3333 W www.icwales.co.uk
Editor, Alan Edmunds

NORTHERN IRELAND
THE BELFAST TELEGRAPH
124–144 Royal Avenue, Belfast BT1 1EB T 028-9026 4000
W www.belfasttelegraph.co.uk
Editor, Edmund Curran
THE IRISH NEWS
113–117 Donegall Street, Belfast BT1 2GE T 028-9032 2226
W www.irishnews.com
Editor, Noel Doran
NEWS LETTER
46–56 Boucher Crescent, Boucher Road, Belfast BT12 6QY
T 028-9068 0000 W www.newsletter.co.uk
Editor, Austin Hunter

CHANNEL ISLANDS
THE GUERNSEY PRESS AND STAR
PO Box 57, Braye Road, Vale, Guernsey GY1 3BW
T 01481-240240 W www.guernsey-press.com
Editor, Richard Digard
JERSEY EVENING POST
PO Box 582, Jersey JE4 8XQ T 01534-611611
W www.jerseyeveningpost.com
Editor, Chris Bright

PERIODICALS

ACCOUNTANCY AGE
VNU Business Publications, VNU House, 32–34 Broadwick
Street, London W1A 2HG T 020-7316 9236
W www.accountancyage.com
Editor, Damian Wild
ACE TENNIS MAGAZINE
Tennis GB, 9–11 North End Road, London W14 8ST
T 020-7605 8000 E nigel.billen@acemag.co.uk
Editor, Nigel Billen
AEROPLANE MONTHLY
IPC Media Ltd, King's Reach Tower, Stamford Street, London
SE1 9LS T 020-7261 5849 W www.aeroplanemonthly.com
Editor, Michael Oakey
AFRICAN BUSINESS
IC Publications Ltd, 7 Coldbath Square, London EC1R 4LQ
T 020-7713 7711 E icpubs@africasia.com
Editor, Anver Versi
AMATEUR PHOTOGRAPHER
IPC Magazines Ltd, King's Reach Tower, Stamford Street,
London SE1 9LS T 020-7261 5100
E amateurphotographer@ipcmedia.com
Editor, Garry Coward-Williams

ANGLING TIMES
EMAP Active, Bushfield House, Orton Centre, Peterborough
PE2 5UW T 01733-232600 E richard.lee@emap.com
Editor, Richard Lee

ANTIQUES AND COLLECTABLES
Merricks Media Ltd, 3–4 Riverside Court, Lower Bristol
Road, Bath BA2 3DZ T 01225-786800
W www.antiques-collectables.co.uk
Editor (acting), Rachel Harrison

THE ARCHITECTS' JOURNAL
EMAP Business Communications, 151 Rosebery Avenue,
London EC1R 4GB T 020-7505 6700
Editor, Isabel Allen

ARCHITECTURE TODAY
161 Rosebery Avenue, London EC1R 4QX T 020-7837 0143
Editors, Ian Latham; Mark Swenarton

ARENA
EMAP East, Endeavour House, 189 Shaftesbury Avenue,
London WC2H 8JG T 020-7437 9011
E arenamag@emap.com
Editor, Anthony Noguera

ART MONTHLY
4th Floor, 28 Charing Cross Road, London WC2H 0DB
T 020-7240 0389 W www.artmonthly.co.uk
Editor, Patricia Bickers

THE ART NEWSPAPER
70 South Lambeth Road, London SW8 1RL T 020-7735 3331
W www.theartnewspaper.com
Editor, Christina Ruiz

ART REVIEW
Art Review Ltd, Hereford House, 23–24 Smithfield Street,
London EC1A 9LB T 020-7236 4880 W www.art-review.com
Editor, Ossian Ward

ASIAN TIMES
Ethnic Media Group, Unit 2.01, Technology Centre, 65
Whitechapel Road, London E1 1DU T 020-7650 2000
E asiantimes@ethnicmedia.com
Editor, Isaac Ham

ATTITUDE
Northern & Shell Tower, City Harbour, London E14 9GL
T 020-7308 5090 E attitude@nasnet.co.uk
Editor, Adam Mattera

AUTO EXPRESS
Dennis Publishing Ltd, 30 Cleveland Street, London W1T 4JD
T 020-7907 6200 W www.autoexpress.co.uk
Editor, David Johns

B
Hachette Filipacchi, 64 North Row, London W1K 7LL
T 020-7150 7020 W www.bmagazine.co.uk
Editor, Nina Ahmad

THE BANKER
Tabernacle Court, 16–28 Tabernacle Court, London EC2 4DD
T 020-7382 8000 E stephen.timewell@ft.com
Editor, Brian Caplen

THE BEANO
D.C. Thomson & Co. Ltd, Albert Square, Dundee DD1 9QJ
T 01382-223131
Editor, Euan Kerr

BELLA
H. Bauer Publishing, Academic House, 24–28 Oval Road,
London NW1 7DT T 020-7241 8000
Editor, Jayne Marsden

BEST
ACP-NatMag Ltd, 33 Broadwick Street, London W1F 0DQ
T 020-7339 4500
Editor, Louise Court

THE BIG ISSUE
1–5 Wandsworth Road, London SW8 2LN T 020-7526 3200
Editor, Matt Ford

BIKE
EMAP Automotive Ltd, Media House, Lynchwood,
Peterborough PE2 6EA T 01733-468000 E bike@emap.com
Editor, John Westlake

BIZARRE
Dennis Publishing, 30 Cleveland Street, London W1T 4JD
T 020-7687 7000 W www.bizarremag.com
Editor, Alex Godfrey

BLISS
EMAP Consumer Media, Endeavour House, 189 Shaftesbury
Avenue, London WC2H 8JG T 020-7437 9011
W www.blissmag.co.uk
Editor, Lisa Smosarski

THE BOOKSELLER
VNU Entertainment Media Ltd, 5th Floor, Endeavour
House, 189 Shaftesbury Avenue, London WC2H 8TJ
T 020-7420 6006 W www.thebookseller.com
Editor-in-Chief, Neill Denny

THE BRITISH JOURNAL OF PHOTOGRAPHY
Incisive Photographics Ltd, Incisive Media, Haymarket House,
28–29 Haymarket, London SW1Y 4RX T 020-7484 9700
W www.bjp-online.com
Editor, Simon Bainbridge

BRITISH MEDICAL JOURNAL
BMA House, Tavistock Square, London WC1H 9JR
T 020-7387 4499 W www.bmj.com
Editor, Dr Fiona Godlee

BROADCAST
EMAP Media, 33–39 Bowling Green Lane, London EC1R 0DA
T 020-7505 8014
Editor, Conor Dignam

BUSINESS TRAVELLER
Perry Publications Ltd, Nestor House, Playhouse Yard, London
EC4V 5EX T 020-7778 0000 W www.btonline.co.uk
Editor, Tom Otley

CAMPAIGN
Haymarket Business Publications Ltd, 174 Hammersmith
Road, London W6 7JP T 020-8943 5000
W www.brandrepublic.com
Editor, Claire Beale

CAR
EMAP Automotive Ltd, 3rd Floor, Media House, Lynchwood,
Peterborough PE2 6EA T 01733-468000 E car@emap.com
Editor, Greg Fountain

CARIBBEAN TIMES
Ethnic Media Group, Technology Centre, 65 Whitehchapel
Road, London E1 1DU T 020-7650 2000
W www.ethnicmedia.co.uk
Editor, Ron Shillingford

CATERER & HOTELKEEPER
Reed Business Information Ltd, Quadrant House, The
Quadrant, Sutton, Surrey SM2 5AS T 020-8652 3221
Editor, Mark Lewis

THE CATHOLIC HERALD
Herald House, Lambs Passage, Bunhill Row, London
EC1Y 8TQ T 020-7448 3603 W www.catholicherald.co.uk
Editor, Luke Coppen

CHAT
IPC Connect Ltd, King's Reach Tower, Stamford Street,
London SE1 9LS T 020-7261 6565 W www.ipcmedia.com
Editor, Gilly Sinclair

CLASSIC CARS
EMAP Automotive Ltd, Media House, Lynchwood,
Peterborough Business Park, Peterborough PE2 6EA
T 01733-468219 W www.classiccarsmagazine.co.uk
Editor, Martyn Moore

COMPANY
National Magazine House, 72 Broadwick Street, London
W1V 2BP T 020-7439 5000 E company.mail@natmags.co.uk
Editor, Victoria White

CONDÉ NAST TRAVELLER
Vogue House, Hanover Square, London W1S 1JU T 020-7499
9080 W www.cntraveller.com
Editor, Sarah Miller

COSMOGIRL
National Magazine House, 72 Broadwick Street, London
W1F 9EP T 020-7439 5081 W www.cosmogirl.co.uk
Editor, Celia Duncan

COSMOPOLITAN
National Magazine House, 72 Broadwick Street, London
W1F 9EP T 020-7439 5000
Editor-in-Chief, Sam Baker

COUNTRY HOMES AND INTERIORS
IPC Magazines Ltd, King's Reach Tower, Stamford Street,
London SE1 9LS T 020-7261 6451
Editor, Rhoda Parry

COUNTRY LIFE
IPC Media Ltd, King's Reach Tower, Stamford Street, London
SE1 9LS T 020-7261 6400 W www.countrylife.co.uk
Editor, Clive Aslet

COUNTRY LIVING
National Magazine House, 72 Broadwick Street, London
W1F 9EP T 020-7439 5000 W www.countryliving.co.uk
Editor, Susy Smith

THE DANDY
D.C. Thomson & Co. Ltd, Albert Square, Dundee DD1 9QJ
T 01382-223131

DARTS WORLD
World Magazines Ltd, 28 Arrol Road, Beckenham, Kent
BR3 4PA T 020-8650 6580
Editor, Tony Wood

DECANTER
IPC Country & Leisure Media Ltd, 1st Floor, Broadway House,
2–6 Fulham Broadway, London SW6 1AA T 020-7610 3929
W www.decanter.com
Editor, Amy Wislocki

DIRECTOR
116 Pall Mall, London SW1Y 5ED T 020-7766 8950
Editor, Joanna Higgins

DISABILITY NOW
6 Market Road, London N7 9PW T 020-7619 7323
W www.disabilitynow.org.uk
Editor, Mary Wilkinson

DOGS TODAY
Pet Subjects Ltd, Town Mill, Bagshot Road, Chobham, Surrey
GU24 8BZ T 01276-858880 E dogs.today@btconnect.com
Editor, Beverley Cuddy

EASTERN ART REPORT
Eastern Art Publishing Group, PO Box 13666, 27 Wallorton
Gardens, London SW14 8WF T 020-8392 1122
E ear@eapgroup.com
Executive Editor, Shirley Rizvi

EASTERN EYE
Ethnic Media Group, Unit 2, 65 Whitechapel Road, London
E1 1DU T 020-7650 2000 W www.ethnicmedia.co.uk
Editor, Amar Singh

THE ECOLOGIST
Unit 18, Chelsea Wharf, 15 Lots Road, London SW10 0QJ
T 020-7351 3578 E kim@theecologist.org
Editor, Zac Goldsmith

THE ECONOMIST
25 St James's Street, London SW1A 1HG T 020-7830 7000
W www.economist.com
Editor, Bill Emmott

EDINBURGH REVIEW
22A Buccleugh Place, Edinburgh EH8 9LN T 0131-651 1415
W www.edinburghreview.org.uk
Editor, Ronald Turnbull

ELECTRICAL TIMES
Media House, Azalea Drive, Swanley, Kent BR8 8HH
T 01322-660070 W www.electricaltimes.co.uk
Editor, Boris Sedacca

ELLE
Hachette Filipacchi, 64 North Row, London W1K 7LL
T 020-7150 7000
Editor, Lorraine Candy

EMBROIDERY
The Embroiderers' Guild, PO Box 42B, East Molesey, Surrey
KT8 9BB W www.embroiderersguild.com/embroidery
Editor, Joanne Hall

EMPIRE
Mappin House, 4 Winsley Street, London W1W 8HF
T 020-7436 1515 W www.empireonline.co.uk
Editor, Colin Kennedy

THE ENGINEER
Centaur Communications Ltd, St Giles House, 50 Poland
Street, London W1F 7AX T 020-7970 4000
W www.e4engineering.com
Editor, Andrew Lee

THE ENGLISH GARDEN
Romsey Publishing Ltd, Jubilee House, 2 Jubilee Place,
London SW3 3TQ T 020-7751 4800
E theenglishgarden@romseypublishing.com
Editor, Janine Wookey

THE EROTIC REVIEW
30 Cleveland Street, London W1T 4JD T 020-7907 6404
W www.theeroticreview.co.uk
Editor, Rowan Pelling

ESQUIRE
National Magazine House, 72 Broadwick Street, London
W1F 9EP T 020-7439 5000
Editor, Simon Tiffin

ESSENTIALS
IPC Media, King's Reach Tower, Stamford Street, London
SE1 9LS T 020-7261 6970
Editor, Julie Barton-Breck

EVENTING
IPC Media, Room 2005, King's Reach Tower, Stamford Street,
London SE1 9LS T 020-7261 5388
Editor, Amanda Gee

EXECUTIVE PA
11 Southwark Street, London SE1 1RQ T 020-7089 5880
E michael@executivepa.net
Editor, Sara Evans

FAMILY CIRCLE
IPC Media, King's Reach Tower, Stamford Street, London
SE1 9LS T 0870-444 5000 W www.familycircle.co.uk
Editor, Karen Livermore

FAMILY LAW
21 St Thomas Street, Bristol BS1 6JS T 0117-923 0600
W www.familylaw.co.uk
Editor, Elizabeth Walsh

FARMERS WEEKLY
Reed Business Information, Quadrant House, The Quadrant, Sutton, Surrey SM2 5AS **T** 020-8652 4911 **W** www.fwi.co.uk
Editor, Stephen Howe

FHM (FOR HIM MAGAZINE)
EMAP Élan Network, Mappin House, 4 Winsley Street, London W1W 8HF **T** 020-7436 1515 **W** www.fhm.com
Editor, Ross Brown

THE FIELD
IPC Media Ltd, King's Reach Tower, Stamford Street, London SE1 9LS **T** 020-7261 5198 **W** www.thefield.co.uk
Editor, Jonathan Young

FILM REVIEW
Visual Imagination Ltd, 9 Blades Court, Deodar Road, London SW15 2NU **T** 020-8875 1520 **E** filmreview@visimag.com
Editor, Grant Hempstan

FINANCIAL ADVISER
FT Finance Ltd, Maple House, 16–28 Tabernacle Court Street, London EC2A 4DD **T** 020-7382 8000
Editor, Hal Austin

FISHING NEWS
4th Floor, Albert House, 1–4 Singer Street, London EC2A 4BQ **T** 020-7017 4531 **E** tim.oliver@informa.com
Editor, Tim Oliver

FLIGHT INTERNATIONAL
Reed Business Information Ltd, Quadrant House, The Quadrant, Sutton, Surrey SM2 5AS **T** 020-8652 3842 **W** www.flightinternational.com
Editor, Murdo Morrison

FLY-FISHING & FLY-TYING
Rolling River Publications, Aberfeldy Road, Kenmore, Perthshire PH15 2HF **T** 01887-830526 **W** www.flyfishing-and-flytying.co.uk
Editor, Mark Bowler

FOCUS
Origin Publishing, 14th Floor, Tower House, Fairfax Street, Bristol BS1 3BN **T** 0117-927 9009
Editor, Paul Parsons

FOLIO
64–65 North Road, St Andrews, Bristol BS6 5AQ **T** 0117-942 8491 **W** www.venue.co.uk
Editor, Dave Higgitt

FOOTBALL FIRST
20–26 Brunswick Place, London N1 6DZ **T** 020-7417 5802 **W** www.sportfirst.com
Editor, Chris Wiltshire

FORTEAN TIMES
Box 2409, London NW5 4NP **T** 020-7907 6235 **W** www.forteantimes.com
Editor, David Sutton

FOURFOURTWO
Haymarket Leisure Publications Ltd, 38–42 Hampton Road, Teddington TW11 0JE **T** 020-8267 5337
Editor, Hugh Sleight

THE FRIEND
173 Euston Road, London NW1 2BJ **T** 020-7663 1010 **W** www.thefriend.org
Editor, Judy Kirby

THE GARDEN
4th Floor, Churchgate, New Road, Peterborough PE1 1TT **T** 01733-775775 **E** thegarden@rhs.org.uk
Editor, Ian Hodgson

GARDEN NEWS
EMAP Active Ltd, Bretton Court, Bretton Centre, Peterborough PE3 8DZ **T** 01733-264666 **E** sarah.page@ecm.emap.com
Editor, Sarah Page

GARDENLIFE MAGAZINE
Seven Publishing Ltd, 20 Upper Ground, London SE1 9PD **T** 020-7775 7727 **W** www.gardenlifemagazine.co.uk
Editor, Tiffany Daneff

GAY TIMES
Spectrum House, 32–34 Gordon House Road, London NW5 1LP **T** 020-7424 7400 **W** www.gaytimes.co.uk
Editor, Vicky Powell

GEOGRAPHICAL
Campion Interactive Publishing Ltd, Unit 11, Pall Mall Deposit, 124–8 Barlby Road, London W10 6BL **T** 020-8960 6400 **W** www.geographical.co.uk
Editor, Nick Smith

GIBBONS STAMP MONTHLY
Stanley Gibbons Ltd, 7 Parkside, Ringwood, Hants BH24 3SH **T** 01425-472363 **E** hjefferies@stanleygibbons.co.uk
Editor, Hugh Jefferies

GIRL ABOUT TOWN MAGAZINE
Independent Magazines, Independent House, 191 Marsh Wall, London E14 9RS **T** 020-7005 5000
Editor-in-Chief, Bill Williamson

GLAMOUR
The Condé Nast Publications Ltd, 6–8 Old Bond Street, London W1S 4PH **T** 020-7499 9080 **W** www.glamour.com
Editor, Jo Elvin

GOLF MONTHLY
IPC Magazines Ltd, King's Reach Tower, Stamford Street, London SE1 9LS **T** 020-7261 7237 **E** golfmonthly@ipcmedia.com
Editor, Jane Carter

GOLF WORLD
EMAP Active Ltd, Bushfield House, Orton Centre, Peterborough PE2 5UW **T** 01733-237111
Publishing Editor-in-Chief, Greg Sharp

GOOD HOUSEKEEPING
National Magazine House, 72 Broadwick Street, London W1F 9EP **T** 020-7439 5000 **W** www.natmags.co.uk
Editor-in-Chief, Lindsay Nicholson

GQ
Condé Nast Publications, Vogue House, Hanover Square, London W1S 1JU **T** 020-7499 9080 **W** www.gq-magazine.co.uk
Editor, Dylan Jones

GRANTA
2–3 Hanover Yard, Noel Road, London N1 8BE **T** 020-7704 9776 **W** www.granta.com
Editor, Ian Jack

GREEN FUTURES
Overseas House, 19–23 Ironmonger Row, London EC1V 3QN **W** www.greenfutures.org.uk
Editor, Martin Wright

THE GROCER
William Reed Publishing Ltd, Broadfield Park, Crawley, West Sussex RH11 9RT **T** 01293-613400 **W** www.thegrocer.co.uk
Editor, Julian Hunt

GUITARIST
Future Publishing UK, 30 Monmouth Street, Bath BA1 2BW **T** 01225-442244 **W** www.futurenet.co.uk
Editor, Michael Leonard

HAIRFLAIR
Hairflair Magazines Ltd, Freebournes House, Freebournes Road, Witham, Essex CM8 3US **T** 01376-534557
Editor, Ruth Page

HARPERS & QUEEN
National Magazine House, 72 Broadwick Street, London W1F 9EP **T** 020-7439 5000
Editor, Lucy Yeomans

HEALTH & FITNESS
Future Publishing Ltd, 30 Monmouth Street, Bath BA1 2BW
T 01225-442244 **W** www.hfonline.co.uk
Editor, Mary Comber

HEAT
Emap PLC, Endeavour House, 189 Shaftesbury Avenue,
London WC2H 8JG **T** 020-7437 9011 **E** heat@emap.com
Editor, Mark Frith

HELLO!
Wellington House, 69–71 Upper Ground, London SE1 9PQ
T 020-7667 8700
Editor, Ronnie Whelan

HERE'S HEALTH
EMAP Esprit, Greater London House, Hampstead Road,
London NW1 7EJ **T** 020-7347 1893
Editor, Sarah Wilson

HI-FI NEWS
IPC Country & Leisure Media Ltd, Focus House, Dingwall
Avenue, Croydon CR9 2TA **T** 020-8774 0846
E hi-finews@ipcmedia.com
Editor, Steve Harris

HISTORY TODAY
20 Old Compton Street, London W1D 4TW
T 020-7534 8000 **W** www.historytoday.com
Editor, Peter Furtado

HOMES AND GARDENS
IPC Magazines Ltd, King's Reach Tower, Stamford Street,
London SE1 9LS **T** 020-7261 5000
Editor, Deborah Barker

HORSE & HOUND
IPC Media Ltd, King's Reach Tower, Stamford Street, London
SE1 9LS **T** 020-7261 6315 **W** www.horseandhound.co.uk
Editor, Lucy Higginson

HORSE AND RIDER
Headley House, Headley Road, Grayshott, Surrey GU26 6TU
T 01428-601020 **W** www.horseandridermagazine.co.uk
Editor, Alison Bridge

HORTICULTURE WEEK
Haymarket Magazines Ltd, 174 Hammersmith Road, London
W6 7JP **T** 020-8267 4977
Editor, Graham Clarke

HOSPITAL DOCTOR
Reed Healthcare Publishing, Quadrant House, The Quadrant,
Sutton, Surrey SM2 5AS **T** 020-8652 8745
E hospital.doctor@rbi.co.uk
Editor, Mike Broad

HOTDOG
Paragon House, St Peter's Road, Bournemouth BH1 2JS
T 01202-299900 **W** www.hotdog-magazine.co.uk
Editor, Andy McDermott

HOUSE & GARDEN
Vogue House, Hanover Square, London W1S 1JU
T 020-7499 9080
Editor, Susan Crewe

HOUSE BEAUTIFUL
National Magazine House, 72 Broadwick Street, London
W1F 9EP **T** 020-7439 5000 **W** www.housebeautiful.co.uk
Editor, Kerryn Harper

HOUSEBUILDER
Byron House, 7–9 St James's Street, London SW1A 1DW
T 020-7960 1630 **W** www.house-builder.co.uk
Editor, Ben Roskrow

I-D MAGAZINE
124 Tabernacle Street, London EC2A 4SA **T** 020-7490 9710
E editor@i-Dmagazine.co.uk
Editor, Glen Waldron

IDEAL HOME
IPC Media Ltd, King's Reach Tower, Stamford Street, London
SE1 9LS **T** 020-7261 5000
Editor, Susan Rose

INSTYLE
Time Life International Inc., 5th Floor, Brettenham House,
Lancaster Place, London WC2E 7TL **T** 020-7322 1510
Editor, Dee Nolan

INSURANCE AGE
Informa House, 30–32 Mortimer Street, London W1W 7RE
T 020-7017 4129 **W** www.insuranceage.com
Editor, Jon Guy

INSURANCE BROKERS' MONTHLY
7 Stourbridge Road, Lye, Stourbridge, West Midlands
DY9 7DG **T** 01384-895228 **W** www.brokersmonthly.co.uk
Editor, Andrew Newman

INTERMEDIA
International Institute of Communications, 35 Portland Place,
London W1B 1AE **T** 020-7323 9622 **E** martin@iicom.org
Editor, Martin Sims

INTERNATIONAL AFFAIRS
Royal Institute of International Affairs, Chatham House,
10 St James's Square, London SW1Y 4LE **T** 020-7957 5700
W www.chathamhouse.org.uk
Editor, Caroline Soper

INVESTORS CHRONICLE
Tabernacle Court, 16–28 Tabernacle Street, London
EC2A 4DD **W** www.investorschronicle.co.uk
Editor, Matthew Vincent

JANE'S DEFENCE WEEKLY
Sentinel House, 163 Brighton Road, Coulsdon, Surrey
CR5 2YH **T** 020-8700 3700 **W** jdw.janes.com
Editor, Peter Felstead

JAZZ JOURNAL INTERNATIONAL
3 & 3a Forest Road, Loughton, Essex IG10 1DR
T 020-8532 0456
Publisher / Editorial Consultant, Eddie Cook

THE JEWISH QUARTERLY
PO Box 37645, London NW7 1WB **T** 020-8343 4675
W www.jewishquarterly.org
Editor, Matthew Reisz

JEWISH TELEGRAPH
Telegraph House, 11 Park Hill, Bury Old Road, Prestwich,
Manchester M25 0HH **T** 0161-740 9321
W www.jewishtelegraph.com
Editor, Paul Harris

JUNIOR EDUCATION
Scholastic Ltd, Villiers House, Clarendon Avenue, Leamington
Spa, Warks CV32 5PR **T** 01926-887799
W www.scholastic.co.uk
Editor, Alex Albrighton

JUNIOR MAGAZINE
Beach Magazines & Publishing Ltd, 4 Cromwell Place, London
SW7 2JE **T** 020-7761 8900 **W** www.juniormagazine.co.uk
Editor, Catherine O'Dolan

KERRANG!
EMAP Performance 2001, PO Box 2930, London W1A 6DZ
T 020-7436 1515 **W** www.kerrang.com
Editor, Paul Brannigan

KITCHEN GARDEN
12 Orchard Lane, Woodnewton, Peterborough PE8 5EE
T 01780-470097 **W** www.kitchengarden.co.uk
Editor, Andrew Blackford

KOI, PONDS & GARDENS
Origin Publishing, Tower House, Fairfax Street, Bristol
BS1 3BN **T** 0117-927 9009 **W** www.koimag.co.uk
Editor, Hilary Clapham

THE LADY
39–40 Bedford Street, London WC2E 9ER T 020-7379 4717
W www.lady.co.uk
Editor, Arline Usden

LANCET
32 Jamestown Road, London NW1 7BY T 020-7424 4910
W www.thelancet.com
Editor, Dr Richard Horton

THE LAWYER
Centaur Communications Group, 50 Poland Street, London
W1V 4AX T 020-7970 4614 W www.thelawyer.com
Editor, Catrin Griffiths

LEGAL WEEK
Global Professional Media Ltd, 99 Charterhouse Street,
London EC1M 6HR T 020-7566 5600 W www.legalweek.net
Editor, Caroline Pearce

THE LINGUIST
The Institute of Linguists, Saxon House, 48 Southwark Street,
London SE1 1UN T 020-7226 2822
W www.linguistonline.co.uk
Editor, Pat Treasure

THE LIST
14 High Street, Edinburgh EH1 1TE
T 0131-550 3050 E editor@list.co.uk
Editor, Nick Barley

THE LITERARY REVIEW
44 Lexington Street, London W1F 0LW T 020-7437 9392
Editor, Nancy Sladek

LOADED
IPC Media Ltd, King's Reach Tower, Stamford Street, London
SE1 9LS T 020-7261 5000 W www.uploaded.com
Editor, Martin Daubney

LONDON REVIEW OF BOOKS
28 Little Russell Street, London WC1A 2HN T 020-7209 1101
E edit@lrb.co.uk
Editor, Mary-Kay Wilmers

MACUSER
Dennis Publishing Ltd, 30 Cleveland Street, London W1T 4JD
T 020-7907 6000 W www.macuser.co.uk
Editor, Nik Rawlinson

MACWORLD
IDG Communications, 99 Gray's Inn Road, London
WC1X 8TY T 020-7831 9252 W www.macworld.co.uk
Editor, Simon Jary

MAKING MUSIC
VViP Highgate Studios, 53–79 Highgate Road, London
NW5 1TW T 020-7331 1170 W www.makingmusic.co.uk
Editor, Paul Fowler

MANAGEMENT TODAY
174 Hammersmith Road, London W6 7JP T 020-8267 4610
Editor, Matthew Gwyther

MARIE CLAIRE
European Magazines Ltd, 13th Floor, King's Reach Tower,
Stamford Street, London SE1 9LS T 020-7261 5240
E marieclaire@ipcmedia.com
Editor, Marie O'Riordan

MARKETER
c/o The Chartered Institute of Marketing, Moor Hall,
Cookham, Maidenhead, Berks SL6 9QH
W www.cim.co.uk/themarketer
Editor, Anna Ronay

MARKETING WEEK
St Giles House, 50 Poland Street, London W1F 7AX
T 020-7970 4000 W www.marketing-week.co.uk
Editor, Stuart Smith

MAXIM
Dennis Publishing Ltd, 30 Cleveland Street, London W1T 4JD
T 020-7907 6410 W www.maxim-magazine.co.uk
Editor, Greg Gutfield

MEDIA WEEK
Haymarket Publishing Ltd, 174 Hammersmith Road, London
W6 7JP T 020-8267 8026 E mweeked@mediaweek.co.uk
Editor, Philip Smith

MEN'S HEALTH
Rodale Press Ltd, 7–10 Chandos Street, London W1M 0AD
T 020-7291 6000 W www.menshealth.co.uk
Editor, Morgan Rees

METHODIST RECORDER
122 Golden Lane, London EC1Y 0TL T 020-7251 8414
W www.methodistrecorder.co.uk
Managing Editor, Moira Sleight

MILITARY MODELLING
Highbury Leisure Publishing Ltd, Berwick House, 8–10 Knoll
Rise, Orpington, Kent BR8 0PS T 01689-899200
Editor, Ken Jones

MIXMAG
EMAP Plc, Mappin House, 4 Winsley Street, London
W1N 8HF T 020-7436 1515 W www.mixmag.net
Editor, Pauline Haldane

MODEL BOATS
Highbury Leisure Publishing Services Ltd, Berwick House,
8–10 Knoll Rise, Orpington, Kent BR6 0PS T 01689-899200
Editor, John L. Cundell

MODERN PAINTERS
3rd Floor, 52 Bermondsey Street, London SE1 3UD
T 020-7407 9246 W www.modernpainters.co.uk
Editor, Karen Wright

MOJO
EMAP Metro, Mappin House, 4 Winsley Street, London
W1W 8HF T 020-7436 1515 W www.mojo4music.com
Editor, Phil Alexander

MONEYMARKETING
Centaur Communications, St Giles House, 50 Poland Street,
London W1T 3QN T 020-7970 4000
Editor, John Lappin

MONEYWISE
69 Old Broad Street, London EC2M 1QS T 020-7715 8465
W www.moneywise.co.uk
Editor, Ben Livesey

MORE
EMAP Élan, Endeavour House, 189 Shaftesbury Avenue,
London WC2H 8JG T 020-7208 3165
Editor, Donna Armstrong

MOTHER & BABY
EMAP Esprit, Greater London House, Hampstead Road,
London NW1 7EJ T 020-7347 1869
W www.motherandbabymagazine.com
Editor, Elena Dalrymple

MOTOR BOAT AND YACHTING
IPC Media Ltd, Room 2309, King's Reach Tower, Stamford
Street, London SE1 9LS T 020-7261 5333 W www.mby.com
Editor, Tom Isitt

MOTOR CYCLE NEWS
EMAP Active Ltd, Media House, Peterborough Business Park,
Lynchwood, Peterborough PE2 6EA T 01733-468000
W www.motorcyclenews.com
Editor, Marc Potter

MUSCLE & FITNESS
Weider Publishing, 10 Windsor Court, Clarence Drive,
Harrogate, North Yorkshire HG1 2PE T 01423-504516
W www.muscle-fitness-europe.com
Editor, Geoff Evans

MUSICAL TIMES
22 Gibson Square, London N1 0RD
Editor, Antony Bye
MUSIC WEEK
CMPi, 7th Floor, Ludgate House, 245 Blackfriars Road,
London SE1 9UR **T** 020-7921 8348
W www.musicweek.com
Editor, Martin Talbot
MY WEEKLY
D.C. Thomson & Co. Ltd, 80 Kingsway East, Dundee DD4 8SL
T 01382-223131 **E** myweekly@dcthomson.co.uk
THE NATIONAL TRUST MAGAZINE
The National Trust, 36 Queen Anne's Gate, London
SW1H 9AS **T** 020-7222 9251 **W** www.nationaltrust.org.uk
Editor, Gaynor Aaltonen
NATURAL WORLD
EMAP Active Ltd, Bushfield House, Orton Centre,
Peterborough PE2 5UW **T** 01733-237111
Editor, Trevor Lawson
NATURE
Macmillan Magazines Ltd, The Macmillan Building, 4 Crinan
Street, London N1 9XW **T** 020-7833 4000
W www.nature.com/nature
Editor, Philip Campbell
NAUTICAL MAGAZINE
Brown, Son & Ferguson Ltd, 4–10 Darnley Street, Glasgow
G41 2SD **T** 0141-429 1234 **W** www.skipper.co.uk
Editor, L. Ingram-Brown
NET THE INTERNET MAGAZINE
Future Publishing Ltd, Beaufort Court, 30 Monmouth Street,
Bath BA1 2BW **T** 01225-442244 **W** www.netmag.co.uk
Editor, Lisa Jones
NEW HUMANIST
1 Gower Street, London WC1E 6HD **T** 020-7436 1151
W www.newhumanist.org.uk
Editor, Frank Jordans
NME
IPC Magazines Ltd, 25th Floor, King's Reach Tower, Stamford
Street, London SE1 9LS **T** 020-7261 5000
Editor, Conor McNicholas
NEW SCIENTIST
RBI Ltd, 151 Wardour Street, London W1F 8WE
T 020-8652 3500 **W** www.newscientist.com
Editor, Jeremy Webb
NEW STATESMAN
3rd Floor, 52 Grosvenor Gardens, London SW1W 0AU
T 020-7730 3444 **E** info@newstatesman.co.uk
Editor, John Kampfner
NEW WOMAN
EMAP élan, Endeavour House, 189 Shaftesbury Avenue,
London WC2H 8JG **T** 020-7437 9011
W www.newwoman.co.uk
Editor, Margi Conklin
NOW
IPC Media Ltd, King's Reach Tower, Stamford Street, London
SE1 9LS **T** 020-7261 7366
Editor, Jane Ennis
NURSING TIMES
EMAP Healthcare, Greater London House, Hampstead Road,
London NW1 7EJ **T** 020-7874 0500
Editor, Rachel Downey
OK
Northern & Shell Plc, Ludgate House, 245 Blackfriars Road,
London SE1 9UX **T** 020-7928 8000
Editor, Nic McCarthy

THE OLDIE
65 Newman Street, London W1T 3EG **T** 020-7436 8801
W www.theoldie.co.uk
Editor, Richard Ingrams
OPERA
36 Black Lion Lane, London W6 9BE **T** 020-8563 8893
W www.opera.co.uk
Editor, John Allison
OXFORD POETRY
Magdalen College, Oxford OX1 4AU
W www.oxfordpoetry.co.uk
Editors, Kelly Grovier; Carmen Bogan
PC ADVISOR
IDG Communications Ltd, 5th Floor, 85 Tottenham Court
Road, London W1T 4TQ **T** 020-7291 5920
W www.pcadvisor.co.uk
Editor, Andrew Charlesworth
PENSIONS WORLD
LexisNexis Butterworths, Tolley House, 2 Addiscombe Road,
Croydon CR9 5AF **T** 020-8686 9141
W www.pensionsworld.co.uk
Editor, Stephanie Hawthorne
PERIOD LIVING & TRADITIONAL HOMES
EMAP East, Mappin House, 4 Winsley Street, London
W1W 8HF **T** 020-7343 8775 **E** period.living@emap.com
Editor, Sharon Parsons
PERSONAL COMPUTER WORLD
VNU House, 32–34 Broadwick Street, London W1A 2HG
T 020-7316 9000 **W** www.pcw.co.uk
Editor, Dylan Armbrust
THE PHOTOGRAPHER
The British Institute of Professional Photography, Fox Talbot
House, 2 Amwell End, Ware, Herts SG12 9HN
T 01920-487268 **W** www.bipp.com
Editor, Steve Bavister
THE PINK PAPER
Millivres Prowler Group, Spectrum House, 32–34 Gordon
House Road, London NW5 1LP **T** 020-7424 7400
W www.pinkpaper.com
Editor, Tris Reid-Smith
POETRY LONDON
1A Jewel Road, London E17 4QU **T** 020-8521 0776
W www.poetrylondon.co.uk
Editors, Pascale Petit; Scott Verner; Martha Kapos
POETRY REVIEW
22 Betterton Street, London WC2H 9BX **T** 020-7420 9880
W www.poetrysociety.org.uk
Editors, Robert Potts; David Herd
PR WEEK
Haymarket Marketing Publications, 174 Hammersmith Road,
London W6 7JP **T** 020-8267 4520
Editor, Daniel Rogers
PRACTICAL FISHKEEPING
EMAP Active Ltd, Bretton Court, Bretton, Peterborough
PE3 8DZ **T** 01733-264666
W www.practicalfishkeeping.co.uk
Editor, Karen Youngs
PRACTICAL PHOTOGRAPHY
EMAP Active Ltd, Bretton Court, Bretton, Peterborough
PE3 8DZ **T** 01733-264666
E practical.photography@emap.com
Editor, Andrew James
PRIMA
National Magazine Company, 72 Broadwick Street, London
W1F 9EP **T** 020-7439 5000
Editor, Maire Fahey

PRIVATE EYE
6 Carlisle Street, London W1D 3BN **T** 020-7437 4017
W www.private-eye.co.uk
Editor, Ian Hislop

PROFESSIONAL NURSE
EMAP Healthcare Ltd, Greater London House, Hampstead Road, London NW1 7EJ **T** 020-7874 0384
W www.professionalnurse.net
Editor, Carolyn Scott

PROSPECT
Prospect Publishing Ltd, 2 Bloomsbury Place, London WC1A 2QA **T** 020-7255 1281
W www.prospect-magazine.co.uk
Editor, David Goodhart

PUBLISHING NEWS
7 John Street, London WC1N 2ES **T** 0870-870 2345
W www.publishingnews.co.uk
Editor, Liz Thomson

Q MAGAZINE
EMAP Performance, Mappin House, 4 Winsley Street, London W1W 8HF **T** 020-7182 8000 **W** www.q4music.com
Editor, Paul Rees

RA MAGAZINE
Royal Academy of Arts, Burlington House, Piccadilly, London W1J 0BD **T** 020-7300 5820 **W** www.royalacademy.org.uk
Editor, Sarah Greenberg

RADIO TIMES
BBC Worldwide Ltd, 80 Wood Lane, London W12 0TT
T 020-8433 3400 **W** www.radiotimes.com
Editor, Gill Hudson

RAILWAY GAZETTE INTERNATIONAL
Reed Business Information, Quadrant House, The Quadrant, Sutton, Surrey SM2 5AS **T** 020-8652 8608
W www.railwaygazette.com
Editor, Murray Hughes

READER'S DIGEST
11 Westferry Circus, Canary Wharf, London E14 4HE
T 020-7715 8000 **W** www.readersdigest.co.uk
Editor-in-Chief, Katherine Walker

RECORD COLLECTOR
Unit 101, Wales Farm Road, London W3 6UG
T 0870-732 8080 **W** www.recordcollectormag.com
Editor, Alan Lewis

RED
Hachette Filipacchi, 64 North Row, London W1K 7LL
T 020-7150 7000 **W** www.redmagazine.co.uk
Editor, Trish Halpin

SAGA MAGAZINE
The Saga Building, Enbrook Park, Folkestone, Kent CT20 3SE **T** 01303-771523
Editor, Emma Soames

SCOTTISH HOME AND COUNTRY
42 Heriot Row, Edinburgh EH3 6ES **T** 0131-225 1724
W www.swri.org.uk
Editor, Liz Ferguson

SCREEN INTERNATIONAL
EMAP Media, 33–39 Bowling Green Lane, London EC1R 0DA
T 020-7505 8080 **W** www.screendaily.com
Editor, Michael Gubbins

SHE
National Magazine House, 72 Broadwick Street, London W1F 9EP **T** 020-7439 5000
Editor, Terry Tavner

SHOOTING TIMES AND COUNTRY MAGAZINE
IPC Magazines Ltd, King's Reach Tower, Stamford Street, London SE1 9LS **T** 020-7261 6180
W www.shootingtimes.co.uk
Editor, Camilla Collinson

SIGHT AND SOUND
British Film Institute, 21 Stephen Street, London W1T 1LN
T 020-7255 1444
Editor, Nick James

SKI AND BOARD
The Ski Club of Great Britain, The White House, 57–63 Church Road, London SW19 5SB **T** 0845-4580780
W www.skiclub.co.uk
Editor, Arnie Wilson

SMASH HITS
EMAP Performance, Mappin House, 4 Winsley Street, London W1W 8HF **T** 020-7182 8718 **E** letters@smashhits.net
Editor (acting), Lara Palamoudian

SNOOKER SCENE
Cavalier House, 202 Hagley Road, Edgbaston, Birmingham B16 9PQ **T** 0121-454 2931 **W** www.snookerscene.com
Editor, Clive Everton

THE SPECTATOR
56 Doughty Street, London WC1N 2LL **T** 020-7405 1706
W www.thespectator.co.uk
Editor, Boris Johnson

THE STAGE
Stage House, 47 Bermondsey Street, London SE1 3XT
T 020-7403 1818 **W** www.thestage.co.uk
Editor, Brian Attwood

STAMP MAGAZINE
IPC Media Ltd, Leon House, 233 High Street, Croydon CR9 1HZ **T** 020-8726 8241
Editor, Steve Fairclough

THE TABLET
1 King Street Cloisters, Clifton Walk, London W6 0QZ
T 020-8748 8484 **W** www.thetablet.co.uk
Editor, Catherine Pepinster

TAKE A BREAK
H. Bauer Publishing Ltd, Academic House, 24–28 Oval Road, London NW1 7DT **T** 020-7241 8000 **W** www.bauer.com
Editor, John Dale

TATLER
Vogue House, Hanover Square, London W1S 1JU
T 020-7499 9080 **W** www.tatler.co.uk
Editor, Geordie Greig

TAXATION
2 Addiscombe Road, Croydon, Surrey CR9 5AF
T 020-8686 9141 **W** www.taxation.co.uk
Editor, Mike Truman

THAT'S LIFE!
H. Bauer Publishing Ltd, Academic House, 24–28 Oval Road, London NW1 7DT **T** 020-7241 8000
Editor, Jo Checkley

TIME OUT
Time Out Group Ltd, Universal House, 251 Tottenham Court Road, London W1T 7AB **T** 020-7813 3000
W www.timeout.com
Editor, Gordon Thomson

THE TIMES EDUCATIONAL SUPPLEMENT
Admiral House, 66–68 East Smithfield, London E1W 1BX
T 020-7782 3000 **W** www.tes.co.uk
Editor, Judith Judd

TIMES EDUCATIONAL SUPPLEMENT SCOTLAND
Scott House, 10 South St Andrew Street, Edinburgh EH2 2AZ
T 0131-557 1133
Editor, Neil Munro

TIMES HIGHER EDUCATION SUPPLEMENT
Admiral House, 66–68 East Smithfield, London E1W 1BX
T 020-7782 3000
Editor, John O'Leary

THE TIMES LITERARY SUPPLEMENT
Admiral House, 66–68 East Smithfield, London E1W 1BX
T 020-7782 3000
Editor, Peter Stothard

TOP SANTÉ HEALTH & BEAUTY
EMAP Elán, Endeavour House, 189 Shaftesbury Avenue,
London WC2H 8JG T 020-7437 9011
Editor, Lauren Libbert

TOTAL FILM
99 Baker Street, London W1U 6FP T 020-7317 2600
E totalfilm@futurenet.co.uk
Editor-at-Large, Matt Mueller

TRAVELLER
Wexas Ltd, 45 Brompton Road, London SW3 1DE
T 020-7589 0500 W www.traveller.org.uk
Editor, Jonathan Lorie

TVTIMES MAGAZINE
IPC Media Ltd, 10th Floor, King's Reach Tower, Stamford
Street, London SE1 9LS T 020-7261 7000
Editor, Mike Hollingsworth

VANITY FAIR
Vogue House, Hanover Square, London W1S 1JU
T 020-7499 9080 W www.vanityfair.co.uk
London Editor, Henry Porter

THE VEGAN
The Vegan Society, Donald Watson House, 7 Battle Road,
St Leonards-on-Sea, East Sussex TN37 7AA
T 01424-448829 W www.vegansociety.com
Editor, Catriona Toms

VIZ
Dennis Publishing, 30 Cleveland Street, London W1T 4JD
T 020-7687 7000 W www.viz.co.uk
Editor, Simon Donald

VOGUE
Vogue House, Hanover Square, London W1S 1JU
T 020-7499 9080 W www.vogue.co.uk
Editor, Alexandra Shulman

THE VOICE
Blue Star House, 8th Floor, 234–244 Stockwell Road,
London SW9 9UG T 020-7737 7377
W www.voice-online.co.uk
Editor-in-Chief, Deidre Forbes

WALLPAPER
IPC Media, Brettenham House, Lancaster Place, London
WC2E 7TL T 020-7322 1177 W www.wallpaper.com
Editor-in-Chief, Jeremy Langmead

WANDERLUST
PO Box 1832, Windsor SL4 1YT T 01753-620426
W www.wanderlust.co.uk
Editor, Lyn Hughes

WHAT CAR?
Haymarket Motoring Magazines Ltd, 60 Waldegrave Road,
Teddington, Middlesex TW11 8LG T 020-8267 5688
W www.whatcar.com
Editor, David Motton

WINE
Quest Magazines Ltd, Wilmington Publishing,
6–8 Underwood Street, London N1 7JQ
T 020-7549 2571 W www.wineint.com
Editor, Catharine Lowe

THE WISDEN CRICKETER
1–4 Shepherds Building, Charecroft Way, London W14 0EE
T 020-7471 6900
Editor, John Stern

WOMAN'S OWN
IPC Connect Ltd, King's Reach Tower, Stamford Street,
London SE1 9LS T 020-7261 5000
Editor, Elsa McAlonan

THE WORLD OF INTERIORS
Vogue House, Hanover Square, London W1S 1JU
T 020-7499 9080 W www.worldofinteriors.co.uk
Editor, Rupert Thomas

WORLD SOCCER
IPC Media Ltd, King's Reach Tower, Stamford Street, London
SE1 9LS T 020-7261 5737
Editor, Gavin Hamilton

WRITING MAGAZINE
1st Floor, Victoria House, 143–145 The Headrow, Leeds
LS1 5RL T 0113-200 2929 W www.writersnews.co.uk
Publishing Editor, Derek Hudson

YACHTING WORLD
IPC Media Ltd, Room 2332, King's Reach Tower, Stamford
Street, London SE1 9LS T 020-7261 6800
W www.yachtingworld.com
Editor, Andrew Bray

YOGA & HEALTH
PO Box 16969, London E1W 1FY T 020-7480 5456
W www.yogaandhealthmag.com
Editor, Jane Sill

ZEST
National Magazine House, 72 Broadwick Street, London
W1F 9EP T 020-7439 5000 E zest.mail@natmags.co.uk
Editor, Alison Pylkkanen

BOOK PUBLISHERS

There are over 40,000 active publishers in the UK, but many of these are subsidiaries of larger publishing houses. The following list comprises a selection of publishers, their contact details and a letter code indicating the type of books published by them.

A	Fiction
B	Education
C	Religious
D	Technical and scientific
E	Legal and parliamentary
F	Medical
G	Commercial and professional
H	Naval and military
I	Dictionaries
J	Reference books
K	Maps and atlases
L	Directories and guides
M	Music and dance
N	Poetry, film and drama
O	Illustrated and photography
P	Art, architecture
Q	History, archaeology and biography
R	Politics, sociology and political economy
S	Philosophy
T	Other academic
U	Children's books
V	Sports, hobbies and interests
W	Foreign language
X	General literature, e.g. travel, essays, humour
Y	Audiobooks

AA PUBLISHING
Automobile Association and Business Services, Fanum House, Basingstoke, Hants RG21 4EA T 01256-491538
W www.theaa.com K, L
ABC-CLIO
26 Beaumont Street, Oxford OX1 2NP T 01865-517222
W www.abc-clio.com B, J, Q, R, T, V
ABSOLUTE PRESS
Scarborough House, 29 James Street West, Bath BA1 2BT
T 01225-316013 W www.absolutepress.co.uk V, X
IAN ALLAN PUBLISHING LTD
Riverdene Business Park, Molesey Road, Hersham, Surrey KT12 4RG T 01932-266600 W www.ianallanpublishing.com
H, J, V
J. A. ALLEN
Clerkenwell House, 45–47 Clerkenwell Green, London EC1R 0HT T 020-7251 2661 W www.halebooks.com V
ALLISON & BUSBY LTD
Bon Marché Centre, 241–251 Ferndale Road, London SW9 8BJ T 020-7738 7888 W www.allisonandbusby.com A, L, Q
AMBER LANE PRESS LTD
Church Street, Charlbury, Oxon OX7 3PR T 01608-810024
W www.amberlanepress.co.uk M, N
ANDERSEN PRESS LTD
20 Vauxhall Bridge Road, London SW1V 2SA T 020-7840 8703 W www.andersenpress.co.uk A, U
ANNESS PUBLISHING
88–89 Blackfriars Road, London SE1 8HA T 020-7401 2077
W www.annesspublishing.com O, U, V

ANVIL PRESS POETRY
Neptune House, 70 Royal Hill, London SE10 8RF
T 020-8469 3033 W www.anvilpresspoetry.com N
APPLETREE PRESS LTD
14 Howard Street South, Belfast BT7 1AP T 028-9024 3074
W www.appletree.ie L, O, Q, V, X
ARCADIA BOOKS LTD
15–16 Nassau Street, London W1W 7AB T 020-7436 9898
W www.arcadiabooks.co.uk A, Q, T, X
ASHGATE PUBLISHING LTD
Gower House, Croft Road, Aldershot, Hants GU11 3HR
T 01252-331551 W www.ashgate.com O, P, R, T
ATLANTIC BOOKS
Ormond House, 26–27 Boswell Street, London WC1N 3JZ
T 020-7269 1610 W www.groveatlantic.co.uk A, J, Q, R
AUREUS PUBLISHING LTD
Castle Court, Castle-upon-Alun, St Bride's Major, Vale of Glamorgan CF32 0TN T 01656-880033
W www.aureus.co.uk C, M, Q, V
AURUM PRESS LTD
25 Bedford Avenue, London WC1B 3AT T 020-7637 3225
W www.aurumpress.co.uk H, N, O, Q, V, X
DUNCAN BAIRD PUBLISHERS
6th Floor, Castle House, 75–76 Wells Street, London W1T 3QH T 020-7323 2229 W www.dbponline.co.uk J, O
BAREFOOT BOOKS LTD
124 Walcot Street, Bath BA1 5BG T 01225-322400
W www.barefootbooks.co.uk O, U, Y
BBC AUDIOBOOKS LTD
St James House, The Square, Lower Bristol Road, Bath BA2 3BH T 01225-878000 W www.bbcaudiobooks.com Y
BFI PUBLISHING
British Film Institute, 21 Stephen Street, London W1P 2LN
T 020-7255 1444 W www.bfi.org.uk J, N
BIRLINN LTD
West Newington House, 10 Newington Road, Edinburgh EH9 1QS T 0131-668 4371 W www.birlinn.co.uk H, L, P, Q, V, X
BLACK & WHITE PUBLISHING LTD
99 Giles Street, Edinburgh EH6 6BZ T 0131-625 4500
W www.blackandwhitepublishing.com A, Q, V, X
A&C BLACK PUBLISHERS LTD
38 Soho Square, London W1D 3QZ T 020-7758 0200
W www.acblack.com B, I, J, L, M, N, O, P, U, V
BLACK ACE BOOKS
PO Box 6557, Forfar DD8 2YS T 01307-465096
W www.blackacebooks.com A, Q, S
BLACKAMBER BOOKS LTD
3 Queen Square, London WC1N 3AU T 020-7278 2488
W www.blackamber.com A
BLACKSTAFF PRESS LTD
4C Heron Wharf, Sydenham Business Park, Belfast BT3 9LE
T 028-9045 5006 W www.blackstaffpress.com A, N, Q, R, V, X
BLACKWELL PUBLISHING LTD
9600 Garsington Road, Oxford OX4 2DQ T 01865-776868
W www.blackwellpublishing.com D, F, G, Q, R, T
BLOOMSBURY PUBLISHING PLC
36 Soho Square, London W1D 3HB T 020-7494 2111
W www.bloomsbury.com A, J, O, Q, U, X
MARION BOYARS PUBLISHERS LTD
24 Lacy Road, London SW15 1NL T 020-8788 9522
W www.marionboyars.co.uk A, M, N, X

BREEDON BOOKS PUBLISHING CO. LTD
Breedon House, 3 The Parker Centre, Mansfield Road, Derby
DE21 4SZ T 01332-384235 W www.breedonbooks.co.uk
J, O, Q, V

BRITISH LIBRARY PUBLICATIONS
Publishing Office, The British Library, 96 Euston Road,
London NW1 2DB T 020-7412 7469 W www.bl.uk K, L, M,
Q

CADOGAN GUIDES
2nd Floor, 233 High Holborn, London WC1V 7DN
T 020-7611 4660 W www.cadoganguides.com L, X

CALDER PUBLICATIONS UK LTD
51 The Cut, London SE1 8LF T 020-7633 0599
W www.calderpublications.com A, L, M, N, P, Q, W

CAMBRIDGE UNIVERSITY PRESS
The Edinburgh Building, Shaftesbury Road, Cambridge
CB2 2RU T 01223-325892 W www.cambridge.org B, C, D,
E, F, G, I, P, Q, R, S, T, W

CAMERON & HOLLIS
PO Box 1, Moffat, Dumfriesshire DG10 9SU T 01683-220808
W www.cameronbooks.co.uk N, P

CANONGATE BOOKS LTD
14 High Street, Edinburgh EH1 1TE T 0131-557 5111
W www.canongate.net A, M, Q, V, X

CARCANET PRESS LTD
4th Floor, Alliance House, 28–34 Cross Street, Manchester
M2 7AQ T 0161-834 8730 W www.carcanet.co.uk N

CAVENDISH PUBLISHING LTD
The Glass House, Wharton Street, London WC1X 9PX
T 020-7278 8000 W www.cavendishpublishing.com E, F

CHAMBERS HARRAP PUBLISHERS LTD
7 Hopetoun Crescent, Edinburgh EH7 4AY T 0131-556 5929
W www.chambersharrap.co.uk I, J, W

THE CHICKEN HOUSE
2 Palmer Street, Frome, Somerset BA11 1DS
T 01373-454488 W www.doublecluck.com U

CHRYSALIS BOOKS GROUP
The Chrysalis Building, Bramley Road, London W10 6SP
T 020-7314 1400 W www.chrysalisbooks.co.uk A, H, O, P,
Q, U, V, X

JAMES CLARKE & CO. LTD
PO Box 60, Cambridge CB1 2NT T 01223-350865
W www.lutterworth.com C, J, T

COLOURPOINT BOOKS
Colourpoint House, Jubilee Business Park, 21 Jubilee Road,
Newtownards, Co. Down, Northern Ireland BT23 4YH
T 028-9182 0505 W www.colourpoint.co.uk B, C, V

CONSTABLE & ROBINSON LTD
3 The Lanchesters, 162 Fulham Palace Road, London W6 9ER
T 020-8741 3663 E enquiries@constablerobinson.com
W www.constablerobinson.com A, H, Q, R, X

**THE CONTINUUM INTERNATIONAL
PUBLISHING GROUP LTD**
The Tower Building, 11 York Road, London SE1 7NX
T 020-7922 0880 W www.continuumbooks.com B, C, G, J,
N, Q, R, X

CRESCENT MOON PUBLISHING
PO Box 393, Maidstone, Kent ME14 5XU T 01622-729593
W www.crescentmoon.org.uk A, N, P, R

THE CROWOOD PRESS
The Stable Block, Ramsbury, Marlborough, Wilts SN8 2HR
T 01672-520320 W www.crowood.com H, J, V

DEDALUS LTD
24 St Judith's Lane, Sawtry, Cambs PE28 5XE
T 01487-832382 W www.dedalusbooks.com A

DORLING KINDERSLEY
80 Strand, London WC2R 0RL T 020-7010 3000
W www.dk.com J, K, L, O, U, V, X, Y

GERALD DUCKWORTH & CO. LTD
First Floor, 90–93 Cowcross Street, London EC1M 6BF
T 020-7434 4242 W www.ducknet.co.uk A, B, J, M, N, Q,
R, S, T, W, X

EDINBURGH UNIVERSITY PRESS
22 George Square, Edinburgh EH8 9LF T 0131-650 4218 E,
Q, R, S, X

EGMONT BOOKS
239 Kensington High Street, London W8 6SA
T 020-7761 3500 W www.egmont.co.uk O, U

ELLIOTT & THOMPSON
27 John Street, London WC1N 2BX T 020-7831 5013
W www.elliottthompson.com A, Q, X

ELSEVIER LTD
The Boulevard, Langford Lane, Kidlington, Oxford OX5 1GB
T 01865-843000 W www.elsevier.com B, D, F, G

ENCYCLOPAEDIA BRITANNICA UK LTD
Second Floor, Unity Wharf, 13 Mill Street, London SE1 2BH
T 020-7500 7800 W www.britannica.co.uk J

EVANS BROTHERS LTD
2A Portman Mansions, Chiltern Street, London W1V 6NR
T 020-7487 0920 W www.evansbooks.co.uk B

EVERYMAN'S LIBRARY
Northburgh House, 10 Northburgh Street, London EC1V 0AT
T 020-7566 6350 A, K, L, N, U, V, X

EXLEY PUBLICATIONS LTD
16 Chalk Hill, Watford, Herts WD19 4BG T 01923-250505
O, X

FABER & FABER LTD
3 Queen Square, London WC1N 3AU T 020-7465 0045
W www.faber.co.uk A, M, N, U

FLAME TREE PUBLISHING
Crabtree Hall, Crabtree Lane, London SW6 6TY
T 020-7386 4700 W www.flametreepublishing.com B, J, M,
P, V

FOLENS PUBLISHERS
Apex Business Centre, Boscombe Road, Dunstable, Beds
LU5 4RL T 0870-609 1237 W www.folens.com B

W. FOULSHAM & CO. LTD
The Publishing House, Bennetts Close, Slough, Berks SL1 5AP
T 01753-526769 V, X

SAMUEL FRENCH LTD
52 Fitzroy Street, London W1T 5JR T 020-7387 9373
W www.samuelfrench-london.co.uk N

DAVID FULTON PUBLISHERS LTD
Chiswick Centre, 414 Chiswick High Road, London W4 5TF
T 020-8996 3611 W www.fultonpublishers.co.uk B

THE GALLERY PRESS
Loughcrew, Oldcastle, Co. Meath, Republic of Ireland
T 049-8541779 W www.gallerypress.com A, N

GARNET PUBLISHING LTD
8 Southern Court, South Street, Reading RG1 4QS
T 01189-597847 W www.garnetpublishing.co.uk A, B, O,
P, X

GRANTA PUBLICATIONS
2–3 Hanover Yard, Noel Road, London N1 8BE
T 020-7704 9776 W www.granta.com A, Q, R, X

GRESHAM BOOKS LTD
46 Victoria Road, Oxford OX2 7QD T 01865-513582
W www.gresham-books.co.uk C

GUINNESS WORLD RECORDS
338 Euston Road, London NW1 3BD T 020-7891 4567 J

HACHETTE CHILDREN'S BOOKS
338 Euston Road, London NW1 3BH T 020-7873 6000 U

HARCOURT EDUCATION LTD
Halley Court, Jordan Hill, Oxford OX2 8EJ T 01865-310533
W www.harcourteducation.co.uk B

HARLEQUIN MILLS & BOON LTD
Eton House, 18–24 Paradise Road, Richmond, Surrey
TW9 1SR **T** 020-8288 2800 **W** www.millsandboon.co.uk **A**

HARPERCOLLINS PUBLISHERS
77–85 Fulham Palace Road, London W6 8JB **T** 020-8741
7070 **W** www.harpercollins.co.uk **A, I, J, K, L, Q, R, U, V,**
X, W, Y

HAYNES PUBLISHING
Sparkford, Yeovil, Somerset BA22 7JJ **T** 01963-440635
W www.haynes.co.uk **D, J, L, V**

HODDER HEADLINE LTD
338 Euston Road, London NW1 3BH **T** 020-7873 6000
W www.hodderheadline.co.uk **A, B, C, Q, U, V, X**

ICON BOOKS LTD
The Old Dairy, Brook Road, Thriplow, Cambridge SG8 7RG
T 01763-208008 **W** www.iconbooks.co.uk **C, D, M, N, Q,**
R, X

ILEX
The Old Candlemakers, West Street, Lewes, E. Sussex
BN7 2NZ **T** 01273-487440 **W** www.ilex-press.com **O, V**

INSIGHT GUIDES/BERLITZ PUBLISHING
58 Borough High Street, London SE1 1XF **T** 020-7403 0284
W www.insightguides.com **I, L, X**

IRISH ACADEMIC PRESS LTD
44 Northumberland Road, Ballsbridge, Dublin 4, Republic of
Ireland **T** 016-688244 **W** www.iap.ie **Q, T**

THE IVY PRESS LTD
The Old Candlemakers, West Street, Lewes, E. Sussex
BN7 2NZ **T** 01273-487440 **W** www.ivypress.com **O, P, V**

JANE'S INFORMATION GROUP
163 Brighton Road, Coulsdon, Surrey CR5 2YH **T** 020-8700
3700 **W** www.janes.com **H, J**

THE KENILWORTH PRESS LTD
Addington, Buckingham MK18 2JR **T** 01296-715101
W www.kenilworthpress.co.uk **V**

LAURENCE KING PUBLISHING LTD
71 Great Russell Street, London WC1B 3BP **T** 020-7430 8850
W www.laurenceking.co.uk **N, O, P**

KINGFISHER PUBLICATIONS PLC
New Penderel House, 283–288 High Holborn, London
WC1V 7HZ **T** 020-7903 9999 **W** www.kingfisher.com **J, U**

LAWRENCE & WISHART LTD
99A Wallis Road, London E9 5LN **T** 020-8533 2506
W www.lwbooks.co.uk **Q, R, S**

LETTS EDUCATIONAL
Chiswick Centre, 414 Chiswick High Road, London W4 5TF
T 020-8996 3333 **W** www.lettsed.co.uk **B, D, G, U**

LEXISNEXIS UK
Halsbury House, 35 Chancery Lane, London WC2A 1EL
T 020-7400 2500 **W** www.lexisnexis.co.uk **E, G**

FRANCES LINCOLN LTD
4 Torriano Mews, Torriano Avenue, London NW5 2RZ
T 020-7284 4009 **W** www.frances-lincoln.com **O, P, U, V**

LIVERPOOL UNIVERSITY PRESS
4 Cambridge Street, Liverpool L69 7ZU **T** 0151-794 2233
W www.liverpool-unipress.co.uk **Q, R, T, X**

LONELY PLANET PUBLICATIONS
72–82 Rosebery Avenue, London EC1R 4RW
T 020-7841 9000 **W** www.lonelyplanet.com **K, L, O, X**

MCGRAW-HILL EDUCATION
McGraw-Hill House, Shoppenhangers Road, Maidenhead,
Berks SL6 2QL **T** 01628-502500 **W** www.mcgraw-hill.co.uk
B, D, F, G, J, R, T

MACMILLAN PUBLISHERS LTD
The Macmillan Building, 4 Crinan Street, London N1 9XW
T 020-7833 4000 **W** www.macmillan.co.uk **A, B, G, J, M, N,**
Q, R, S, V, X, Y

MANCHESTER UNIVERSITY PRESS
Oxford Road, Manchester M13 9NR **T** 0161-275 2310
W www.manchesteruniversitypress.co.uk **B, E, P, Q, R, W,**
X

MERRELL PUBLISHERS LTD
81 Southwark Street, London SE1 0HX **T** 020-7928 8880
W www.merrellpublishers.com **O, P, V**

METHUEN PUBLISHING LTD
215 Vauxhall Bridge Road, London SW1V 1EJ
T 020-7798 1600 **W** www.methuen.co.uk **A, N, Q, V, X**

MICHELIN TRAVEL PUBLICATIONS
Hannay House, 39 Clarendon Road, Watford, Herts
WD17 1JA **T** 01923-205240 **W** www.viamichelin.com **K, L**

JOHN MURRAY PUBLISHERS LTD
338 Euston Road, London NW1 3BH **T** 020-7873 6000
W www.johnmurray.co.uk **A, Q, X**

NELSON THORNES LTD
Delta Place, 27 Bath Road, Cheltenham, Glos GL53 7TH
T 01242-267100 **W** www.nelsonthornes.com **B, G**

NEW HOLLAND PUBLISHERS UK LTD
Garfield House, 86 Edgware Road, London W2 2EA
T 020-7724 7773 **W** www.newhollandpublishers.com **J, K,**
L, V, X

W. W. NORTON & COMPANY
Castle House, 75–76 Wells Street, London W1T 3QT
T 020-7323 1579 **W** www.wwnorton.co.uk **A, D, M, T**

OBERON BOOKS
521 Caledonian Road, London N7 9RH **T** 020-7607 3637
W www.oberonbooks.com **N**

THE OCTAGON PRESS LTD
PO Box 227, London N6 4EW **T** 020-8348 9392
W www.octagonpress.com **Q, S, X**

ONEWORLD PUBLICATIONS
185 Banbury Road, Oxford OX2 7AR **T** 01865-310597
W www.oneworld-publications.com **C, Q, S**

THE ORION PUBLISHING GROUP LTD
Orion House, 5 Upper St Martin's Lane, London WC2H 9EA
T 020-7240 3444 **W** www.orionbooks.co.uk **A, J, U, Y**

PETER OWEN LTD
73 Kenway Road, London SW5 0RE **T** 020-7373 5628
W www.peterowen.com **A, N, P, Q**

OXFORD UNIVERSITY PRESS
Great Clarendon Street, Oxford OX2 6DP **T** 01865-556767
W www.oup.com **B, C, D, E, F, H, I, J, K, M, P, Q, R, S, T,**
U, W, X

PEARSON EDUCATION
Edinburgh Gate, Harlow, Essex CM20 2JE **T** 01279-623623
W www.pearsoned.co.uk **B**

PEN & SWORD BOOKS LTD
47 Church Street, Barnsley, S. Yorks S70 2AS
T 01226-734222 **W** www.pen-and-sword.co.uk **H, Q**

PENGUIN GROUP (UK)
80 Strand, London WC2R 0RL **T** 020-7010 3000
W www.penguin.co.uk **A, I, J, N, Q, R, U, V, X, Y**

PHAIDON PRESS LTD
Regent's Wharf, All Saints Street, London N1 9PA
T 020-7843 1000 **W** www.phaidon.com **M, N, O, P**

PIATKUS BOOKS
5 Windmill Street, London W1T 2JA **T** 020-7631 0710
W www.piatkus.co.uk **B, G, Q, v, X**

PLEXUS PUBLISHING LTD
55A Clapham Common Southside, London SW4 9BX
T 020-7622 2440 **W** www.plexusbooks.com **M, N, Q**

PLUTO PRESS
345 Archway Road, London N6 5AA **T** 020-8348 2724
W www.plutobooks.com **Q, R, T**

POLITY PRESS
65 Bridge Street, Cambridge CB2 1UR **T** 01223-324315
W www.polity.co.uk **Q, R, S, T**

POOLBEG PRESS LTD
123 Grange Hill, Baldoyle, Dublin 13, Republic of Ireland
T 018-321477 **W** www.poolbeg.com **A, R, U**

PRINCETON UNIVERSITY PRESS – EUROPE
3 Market Place, Woodstock, Oxon OX20 1SY
T 01993-814500 **W** http://pup.princeton.edu **D, G, R, S**

PROFILE BOOKS LTD
3A Exmouth House, Pine Street, London EC1R 0JH
T 020-7404 3001 **W** www.profilebooks.co.uk **G, Q, R, T**

PSYCHOLOGY PRESS LTD
27 Church Road, Hove, E. Sussex BN3 2FA **T** 01273-207411
W www.psypress.co.uk **T**

QUADRILLE PUBLISHING
Fifth Floor, Alhambra House, 27–31 Charing Cross Road,
London WC2H 0LS **T** 020-7839 7117
W www.quadrille.co.uk **O, V**

QUARTET BOOKS LTD
27 Goodge Street, London W1T 2LD **T** 020-7636 3992 **A, M,
Q**

RANDOM HOUSE GROUP LTD
20 Vauxhall Bridge Road, London SW1V 2SA **T** 020-7840
8400 **W** www.randomhouse.co.uk **A, G, M, N, P, Q, R, S,
V, X, Y**

THE READER'S DIGEST ASSOCIATION LTD
11 Westferry Circus, Canary Wharf, London E14 4HE
T 020-7715 8000 **A, I, J, K, L, M, V**

REAKTION BOOKS
77–79 Farringdon Road, London EC1M 3JU **T** 020-7404
9930 **W** www.reaktionbooks.co.uk **O, P, Q, T, X**

REYNOLDS & HEARN LTD
61A Priory Road, Kew, Richmond, Surrey TW9 3DH
T 020-8940 5198 **W** www.rhbooks.com **M, N**

RIVERS ORAM PRESS
144 Hemingford Road, London N1 1DE **T** 020-7607 0823 **O,
R, T**

RYLAND PETERS & SMALL
20–21 Jockey's Fields, London WC1R 4BW **T** 020-7025 2200
W www.rylandpeters.com **O, V**

SAGE PUBLICATIONS LTD
1 Oliver's Yard, 55 City Road, London EC1Y 1SP
T 020-7324 8500 **W** www.sagepub.co.uk **B, D, T**

ST PAULS
St Pauls Publishing, 187 Battersea Bridge Road, London
SW11 3AS **T** 020-7978 4300 **B, C, Q**

SALARIYA BOOK COMPANY LTD
Book House, 25 Marlborough Place, Brighton BN1 1UB
T 01273-603306 **W** www.salariya.com **U**

SCALA PUBLISHERS
Northburgh House, Northburgh Street, London EC1V 0AT
T 020-7490 9900 **W** www.scalapublishers.com **L, P**

SCHOFIELD & SIMS LTD
Dogley Mill, Fenay Bridge, Huddersfield, W. Yorks HD8 0NQ
T 01484-607080 **W** www.schofieldandsims.co.uk **B**

SCHOLASTIC LTD
Villiers House, Clarendon Avenue, Leamington Spa, Warks
CV32 5PR **T** 01926-887799 **W** www.scholastic.co.uk **B, U**

SCRIPTURE UNION
207–209 Queensway, Bletchley, Milton Keynes, Bucks
MK2 2EB **T** 01908-856000 **W** www.scriptureunion.org.uk **B,
C, U**

SERPENT'S TAIL
4 Blackstock Mews, London N4 2BT **T** 020-7354 1949
W www.serpentstail.com **A, M, X**

SEVERN HOUSE PUBLISHERS
9–15 High Street, Sutton, Surrey SM1 1DF **T** 020-8770 3930
W www.severnhouse.com **A**

SHELDRAKE PRESS
188 Cavendish Road, London SW12 0DA **T** 020-8675 1767
W www.sheldrakepress.demon.co.uk **M, P, Q, V, X**

SHEPHEARD-WALWYN (PUBLISHERS) LTD
Suite 604, 50 Westminster Bridge Road, London SE1 7QY
T 020-7721 7666 **W** www.shepheard-walwyn.co.uk **Q, R, S**

SHORT BOOKS LTD
15 Highbury Terrace, London N5 1UP **T** 020-7226 1607
W www.shortbooks.co.uk **Q, X**

SIGMA PRESS
5 Alton Road, Wilmslow, Cheshire SK9 5DY **T** 01625-531035
W www.sigmapress.co.uk **Q, V**

SIMON & SCHUSTER
Africa House, 64–78 Kingsway, London WC2B 6AH
T 020-7316 1900 **W** www.simonsays.co.uk **A, Q, R, U**

SOUVENIR PRESS LTD
43 Great Russell Street, London WC1B 3PD **T** 020-7580 9307
B, D, F, O, Q, V, X

SPORTSBOOKS LTD
PO Box 422, Cheltenham, Glos GL50 2YN **T** 01242-256755
W www.sportsbooks.ltd.uk **V**

SPRINGER-VERLAG LONDON LTD
Ashbourne House, The Guild Way, Old Portsmouth Road,
Guildford, Surrey GU3 1LX **T** 01483-734433
W www.springeronline.com **D, F**

SPRINGER
Suite 52, Alpha House, 100 Borough High Street, London
SE1 1LB **T** 020-7863 3318 **W** www.springer-sbm.com **B, D,
G, R**

STENLAKE PUBLISHING LTD
54–58 Mill Square, Catrine Ayrshire KA5 6RD
T 01290-552233 **W** www.stenlake.co.uk **V**

STRIDE PUBLICATIONS
11 Sylvan Road, Exeter, Devon EX4 6EW
W www.stridebooks.co.uk **M, N, P, X**

SUSSEX ACADEMIC PRESS
PO Box 2950, Brighton BN2 5SP **T** 01273-699533
W www.sussex-academic.co.uk **C, Q**

SUTTON PUBLISHING LTD
Phoenix Mill, Thrupp, Stroud, Glos GL5 2BU **T** 01453-731114
W www.suttonpublishing.co.uk **H, O, Q**

SWEET & MAXWELL
100 Avenue Road, London NW3 3PF **T** 020-7393 7000
W www.sweetandmaxwell.co.uk **E**

TANGO BOOKS
PO Box 32595, London W4 5YD **T** 020-8996 9970
W www.tangobooks.co.uk **U**

TASCHEN UK LTD
Fifth Floor, 1 Heathcock Court, 415 Strand, London
WC2R 0NS **T** 020-7845 8580 **W** www.taschen.co.uk **M, N,
O, P**

TATE PUBLISHING
The Lodge, Millbank, London SW1P 4RG **T** 020-7887 8869
W www.tate.org.uk **O, P**

TAYLOR & FRANCIS BOOKS LTD
4 Park Road, Milton Park, Abingdon, Oxon OX14 4RN
T 01235-828600 **W** www.tandf.co.uk **B, D, E, F, G, J, P, Q,
R, S, T**

THAMES & HUDSON LTD
181A High Holborn, London WC1V 7QX **T** 020-7845 5000
W www.thamesandhudson.com **C, O, P, Q, T, V**

TIME WARNER BOOK GROUP UK
Brettenham House, Lancaster Place, London WC2E 7EN
T 020-7911 8000 **W** www.twbg.co.uk **A, C, D, E, J, L, M,
O, P, Q, R, U, V, W, X, Y**

TITAN BOOKS
144 Southwark Street, London SE1 0UP **T** 020-7620 0200
W www.titanbooks.com A, N, O

TRANSWORLD PUBLISHERS
61–63 Uxbridge Road, London W5 5SA **T** 020-8579 2652
W www.booksattransworld.co.uk A, C, D, M, P, Q, V, X

TSO (THE STATIONERY OFFICE)
St Crispins, Duke Street, Norwich NR3 1PD **T** 0870-6005522
W www.tso.co.uk B, F, J, L

ULRIC PUBLISHING
PO Box 55, Church Stretton, Shrops SY6 6WR
T 01694-781354 **W** www.ulric-publishing.com H, Q, V

MERLIN UNWIN BOOKS
Palmers House, 7 Corve Street, Ludlow, Shrops SY8 1DB
T 01584-877456 **W** www.countrybooksdirect.com V

USBORNE PUBLISHING LTD
Usborne House, 83–85 Saffron Hill, London EC1N 8RT
T 020-7430 2800 **W** www.usborne.com U

V&A PUBLICATIONS
160 Brompton Road, London SW3 1HW **T** 020-7942 2966
W www.vandashop.co.uk/books O, P, V

VERSO LTD
6 Meard Street, London W1F 0EG **T** 020-7437 3546 Q, R, S, T

VIRGIN BOOKS LTD
Thames Wharf Studios, Rainville Road, London W6 9HA
T 020-7386 3300 **W** www.virginbooks.com G, J, M, N, V

VIRTUE BOOKS LTD
Edward House, Tenter Street, Rotherham S60 1LB
T 01709-365005 **W** www.virtue.co.uk G, V

UNIVERSITY OF WALES PRESS
10 Columbus Walk, Brigantine Place, Cardiff CF10 4UP
T 029-2049 6899 **W** www.wales.ac.uk/press B, Q, W

WALKER BOOKS LTD
87 Vauxhall Walk, London SE11 5HJ **T** 020-7793 0909
W www.walkerbooks.co.uk U, Y

WARD LOCK EDUCATIONAL CO. LTD
BIC Ling Kee House, 1 Christopher Road, East Grinstead,
West Sussex RH19 3BT **T** 01342-318980
W www.wardlockeducational.com B

THE WATTS PUBLISHING GROUP LTD
96 Leonard Street, London EC2A 4XD **T** 020-7873 6000
W www.wattspublishing.co.uk U

WEBSTERS INTERNATIONAL PUBLISHERS LTD
Second Floor, Axe & Bottle Court, 70 Newcomen Street,
London SE1 1YT **T** 020-7940 4700 **W** www.websters.co.uk
V, X

WEIDENFELD & NICOLSON
Orion House, 5 Upper St Martin's Lane, London WC2H 9EA
T 020-7240 3444 A, H, Q, R, X

WHICH? LTD
2 Marylebone Road, London NW1 4DF **T** 020-7770 7000
W http://bookshop.which.co.uk L, V

WHITTET BOOKS LTD
Hill Farm, Stonham Road, Cotton, Stowmarket, Suffolk
IP14 4RQ **T** 01449-781877 **W** www.whittetbooks.com V

WILEY EUROPE LTD
The Atrium, Southern Gate, Chichester, W. Sussex PO19 8SQ
T 01243-779777 **W** www.wiley.com B, D, E, F, G, P, T

PHILIP WILSON PUBLISHERS LTD
7 Deane House, 27 Greenwood Place, London NW5 1LB
T 020-7284 3088 **W** www.philip-wilson.co.uk P

THE WOMEN'S PRESS
Top Floor, 27 Goodge Street, London W1P 2LD
T 020-7580 7806 **W** www.the-womens-press.com A, Q, R,
V, T

WOODHEAD PUBLISHING LTD
Abington Hall, Abington, Cambridge CB1 6AH
T 01223-891358 **W** www.woodhead-publishing.com D

YALE UNIVERSITY PRESS LONDON
47 Bedford Square, London WC1B 3DP **T** 020-7079 4900
W www.yalebooks.co.uk C, M, P, Q, R, S

ZED BOOKS LTD
7 Cynthia Street, London N1 9JF **T** 020-7837 4014
W www.zedbooks.co.uk R, T

ZOË BOOKS LTD
15 Worthy Lane, Winchester, Hants SO23 7AB
T 01962-851318 **W** www.zoebooks.co.uk B, U

EMPLOYERS' AND TRADE ASSOCIATIONS

Most national employers' associations are members of the Confederation of British Industry (CBI).

CBI

Centre Point, 103 New Oxford Street, London WC1A 1DU
T 020-7379 7400

The CBI was founded in 1965 and is an independent non-party political body financed by industry and commerce. It exists primarily to ensure that the Government understands the intentions, needs and problems of British business. It is the recognised spokesman for the business viewpoint and is consulted as such by the Government.

The CBI speaks for some 240,000 businesses that together employ approximately one-third of the private sector workforce. Member companies, which decide all policy positions, include 80 of the FTSE 100 index, some 200,000 small and medium-size firms, more than 20,000 manufacturers and over 150 sectoral associations.

The governing body of the CBI is the Chairmen's Committee, which meets four times a year in London under the chairmanship of the president. It is assisted by 16 expert standing committees which advise on the main aspects of policy. There are 12 regional councils and offices, covering the administrative regions of England, Wales, Scotland and Northern Ireland. There is also an office in Brussels and one in Washington.

President, John Sunderland
Director-General, Sir Digby Jones
WALES: 2 Caspian Point, Caspian Way, Cardiff Bay, Cardiff, CF10 4DQ T 029-2045 3710
  Regional Director, David Rosser
SCOTLAND: 16 Robertson Street, Glasgow G2 8DS
  T 0141-222 2184
  Regional Director, Ian McMillan
NORTHERN IRELAND: Scottish Amicable Building, 11 Donegall Square, Belfast BT1 5SE T 028-9032 6658
  Regional Director, Nigel Smyth

ASSOCIATIONS

ADVERTISING ASSOCIATION, Abford House, 15 Wilton Road, London SW1V 1NJ T 020-7828 2771
E aa@adassoc.org.uk W www.adassoc.org.uk
Director-General, Andrew Brown
ASSOCIATION OF BRITISH INSURERS, 51 Gresham Street, London EC2V 7HQ T 020-7600 3333 E info@abi.org.uk
W www.abi.org.uk
Director-General, Stephen Haddrill
ASSOCIATION OF PRIVATE MARKET OPERATORS, 4 Worrygoose Lane, Rotherham S60 4AD T 01709-700072
E marketsman2@aol.com
W www.apmomarkets.co.uk
General Secretary, David J. Glasby
BLC LEATHER TECHNOLOGY CENTRE LTD, Leather Trade House, Kings Park Road, Moulton Park, Northampton NN3 6JD T 01604-679999 E info@blcleathertech.com
W www.blcleathertech.com
Managing Director, Michael W. Parsons

BOSS FEDERATION, 12 Corporation Street, High Wycombe HP13 6TQ T 0845-450 1565
E info@bossfederation.co.uk
W www.bossfederation.co.uk
Chief Executive, Keith Davies
BRITISH APPAREL AND TEXTILE CONFEDERATION, 5 Portland Place, London W1B 1PW T 020-7636 7788
E batc@dial.pipex.com
Director-General, John Wilson, OBE
BRITISH BANKERS' ASSOCIATION, Pinners Hall, 105–108 Old Broad Street, London EC2N 1EX T 020-7216 8800
E info@bba.org.uk W www.bba.org.uk
Chief Executive, Ian Mullen
BRITISH BEER AND PUB ASSOCIATION, Market Towers, 1 Nine Elms Lane, London SW8 5NQ T 020-7627 9191
E web@beerandpub.com W www.beerandpub.com
Chief Executive Officer, Rob Hayward, OBE
BRITISH CLOTHING INDUSTRY ASSOCIATION LTD, 5 Portland Place, London W1B 1PW T 020-7636 7788
E bcia@dial.pipex.com
Director, John Wilson, OBE
BRITISH ELECTROTECHNICAL AND ALLIED MANUFACTURERS' ASSOCIATION (BEAMA), Westminster Tower, 3 Albert Embankment, London SE1 7SL T 020-7793 3000 E info@beama.org.uk
W www.beama.org.uk
Chief Executive Officer, David Dossett
BRITISH MARINE FEDERATION, Marine House, Thorpe Lea Road, Egham TW20 8BF T 01784-473377
E info@britishmarine.co.uk W www.britishmarine.co.uk
Chief Executive, John Clarke, CBE, LVO
BRITISH PLASTICS FEDERATION, 6 Bath Place, Rivington Street, London EC2A 3JE T 020-7457 5000 E bpf@bpf.co.uk
W www.bpf.co.uk
Director-General, Peter Davis, OBE
BRITISH PORTS ASSOCIATION, Africa House, 64–78 Kingsway, London WC2B 6AH T 020-7242 1200
E info@britishports.org.uk W www.britishports.org.uk
Director, David Whitehead
BRITISH PRINTING INDUSTRIES FEDERATION, Farringdon Point, 29–35 Farringdon Road, London EC1M 3JF T 0870-2404085 E info@bpif.org.uk
W www.britishprint.com
Chief Executive, Michael Johnson
BRITISH PROPERTY FEDERATION, 7th Floor, 1 Warwick Row, London SW1E 5ER T 020-7828 0111
E info@bpf.org.uk W www.bpf.org.uk
Chief Executive, Liz Peace
BRITISH RETAIL CONSORTIUM, 2nd Floor, 21 Dartmouth Street, London SW1H 9BP T 020-7854 8900
E info@brc.org.uk W www.brc.org.uk
Director-General, Kevin Hawkins
BRITISH RUBBER MANUFACTURERS' ASSOCIATION LTD, 6 Bath Place, Rivington Street, London EC2A 3JE
T 020-7457 5040 E mail@brma.co.uk W www.brma.co.uk
Director, John Dorken
CHAMBER OF SHIPPING LTD, Carthusian Court, 12 Carthusian Street, London EC1M 6EZ T 020-7417 2800
E postmaster@british-shipping.org
W www.british-shipping.org
Director-General, Mark Brownrigg

CHEMICAL INDUSTRIES ASSOCIATION, Kings Buildings, Smith Square, London SW1P 3JJ T 020-7834 3399
E enquiries@cia.org.uk W www.cia.org.uk
Director-General, Mrs Judith Hackitt

COMMERCIAL RADIO COMPANIES ASSOCIATION (CRCA), The Radiocentre, 77 Shaftesbury Avenue, London W1D 5DU T 020-7306 2603 E info@crca.co.uk
W www.crca.co.uk
Chief Executive, Paul Brown, CBE

CONFEDERATION OF PAPER INDUSTRIES, 1 Rivenhall Road, Swindon SN5 7BD T 01793-889600
E cpi@paper.org.uk W www.paper.org.uk
Director-General, Dr Martin Oldman

CONFEDERATION OF PASSENGER TRANSPORT UK, Imperial House, 15–19 Kingsway, London WC2B 6UN
T 020-7240 3131 E admin@cpt-uk.org W www.cpt-uk.org/
Director-General, Brian Nimick

CONSTRUCTION CONFEDERATION, 55 Tufton Street, London SW1P 3QL T 020-7227 4500
E enquiries@thecc.org.uk W www.thecc.org.uk
Chief Executive, Stephen Ratcliffe

CONSTRUCTION PRODUCTS ASSOCIATION, 26 Store Street, London WC1E 7BT T 020-7323 3770
E enquiries@constprod.org.uk W www.constprod.org.uk
Chief Executive, Michael Ankers, FRSA

DAIRY UK, 93 Baker Street, London W1U 6QQ
T 020-7486 7244 E info@dairyuk.org W www.dairyuk.org
Director-General, J. Begg

ENGINEERING EMPLOYERS' FEDERATION (EEF), Broadway House, Tothill Street, London SW1H 9NQ
T 020-7222 7777 E enquiries@eef-fed.org.uk
W www.eef.org.uk
Director-General, Martin Temple

FEDERATION OF BAKERS, 6 Catherine Street, London WC2B 5JW T 020-7420 7190
W www.bakersfederation.org.uk

FEDERATION OF MASTER BUILDERS, Gordon Fisher House, 14–15 Great James Street, London WC1N 3DP
T 020-7242 7583 W www.fmb.org.uk
Director-General, I. Davis

FINANCE AND LEASING ASSOCIATION, 2nd Floor, Imperial House, 15–19 Kingsway, London WC2B 6UN
T 020-7836 6511 E info@fla.org.uk W www.fla.org.uk
Director-General, Martin Hall, MVO

FOOD AND DRINK FEDERATION, 6 Catherine Street, London WC2B 5JJ T 020-7836 2460
E generalenquiries@fdf.org.uk W www.fdf.org.uk
Director-General, Sylvia Jay

FREIGHT TRANSPORT ASSOCIATION LTD, Hermes House, St John's Road, Tunbridge Wells TN4 9UZ T 01892-526171
E enquiries@fta.org.uk W www.fta.org.uk
Chief Executive, Richard Turner

INSTITUTE OF CHARTERED FORESTERS, 7A St Colme Street, Edinburgh EH3 6AA T 0131-225 2705
E icf@charteredforesters.org W www.charteredforesters.org
Executive Director, Peter H. Wilson

KNITTING INDUSTRIES' FEDERATION LTD, 12 Beaumanor Road, Leicester LE4 5QA T 0116-266 3332
E directorate@knitfed.co.uk
Director, Anne Carvell

LEATHER PRODUCERS' ASSOCIATION, 8 Queensberry Road, Kettering NN15 7HL T 01536-483668
National Secretary, Jack Purvis

MANAGEMENT CONSULTANCIES ASSOCIATION, 49 Whitehall, London SW1A 2BX T 020-7321 3990
W www.mca.org.uk
Executive Director, Bruce Petter

NATIONAL FARMERS' UNION (NFU), Agriculture House, 164 Shaftesbury Avenue, London WC2H 8HL
T 020-7331 7200 E nfu@nfuonline.com
W www.nfu.org.uk
Director-General, Richard Macdonald

NATIONAL FEDERATION OF RETAIL NEWSAGENTS, Yeoman House, Sekford Street, London EC1R 0HF T 020-7253 4225 E info@nfrn.org.uk
Director of Operations, Adrian Holmes

NATIONAL MARKET TRADERS' FEDERATION, Hampton House, Hawshaw Lane, Hoyland, Barnsley S74 0HA
T 01226-749021 E enquiries@nmtf.co.uk
W www.nmtf.co.uk
General Secretary, D. E. Feeny

NEWSPAPER PUBLISHERS ASSOCIATION LTD, 34 Southwark Bridge Road, London SE1 9EU
T 020-7207 2200
Director, Steve Oram

NEWSPAPER SOCIETY, Bloomsbury House, 74–77 Great Russell Street, London WC1B 3DA T 020-7636 7014
E directorate@newspapersoc.org.uk
W www.newspapersoc.org.uk
Director, D. Newell

THE PUBLISHERS ASSOCIATION, 29B Montague Street, London WC1B 5BW T 020-7691 9191
E mail@publishers.org.uk W www.publishers.org.uk
Chief Executive, A. R. Williams, OBE

ROAD HAULAGE ASSOCIATION LTD, Roadway House, 35 Monument Hill, Weybridge KT13 8RN
T 01932-841515 E weybridge@rha.net
W www.rha.net
Chief Executive, Roger King

SOCIETY OF BRITISH AEROSPACE COMPANIES LTD, Duxbury House, 60 Petty France, London SW1H 9EU
T 020-7227 1000 E post@sbac.co.uk W www.sbac.co.uk
Director-General, Sally Howes

SOCIETY OF MOTOR MANUFACTURERS AND TRADERS LTD, Forbes House, Halkin Street, London SW1X 7DS
T 020-7235 7000 E membership@smmt.co.uk
W www.smmt.co.uk
Chief Executive, Christopher Macgowan

SPORT INDUSTRIES FEDERATION, Federation House, Stoneleigh Park, Kenilworth CV8 2RF T 024-7641 4999
E admin@sportslife.org.uk W www.thesportslife.com
Operations Director, David Pomfret

TIMBER TRADE FEDERATION, Clareville House, 26–27 Oxendon Street, London SW1Y 4EL T 020-7839 1891
E ttf@ttf.co.uk W www.ttf.co.uk
Director-General, John White

TRADE MARKS, PATENTS & DESIGNS FEDERATION, 5th Floor, 63–66 Hatton Garden, London EC1 8LE
W www.tmpdf.org.uk
President, Dr Michael Jewess

UK OFFSHORE OPERATORS ASSOCIATION LTD, Second Floor, 232–242 Vauxhall Bridge Road, London SW1V 1AY
T 020-7802 2400 E info@ukooa.co.uk
Chief Executive, Malcolm Webb

UK PETROLEUM INDUSTRY ASSOCIATION LTD, 9 Kingsway, London WC2B 6XF T 020-7240 0289
E info@ukpia.com W www.ukpia.com
Director-General, Chris Hunt

ULSTER FARMERS' UNION, 475 Antrim Road, Belfast BT15 3DA T 028-9037 0222 E info@ufuhq.com
W www.ufuni.org
Chief Executive, Clarke Black

TRADE UNIONS

CENTRAL ARBITRATION COMMITTEE

PO Box 51547, London SE1 1ZG T 020-7904 2300
F 020-7904 2301 W www.cac.gov.uk

The Central Arbitration Committee deals with the following employment relations issues: arbitration in trade disputes; adjudication of complaints that an employer has failed to disclose information for collective bargaining purposes; determining claims for statutory recognition and derecognition; deciding on issues relating to the implementation of European Works Councils and the European Company Statute; and resolving complaints under the Information and Consultation Regulations.
Chairman, Sir Michael Burton
Secretary and Chief Executive, Graeme Charles

TRADES UNION CONGRESS (TUC)

Congress House, 23–28 Great Russell Street, London
WC1B 3LS T 020-7636 4030 E info@tuc.org.uk
W www.tuc.org.uk

The Trades Union Congress, founded in 1868, is an independent association of trade unions. The TUC promotes the rights and welfare of those in work and helps the unemployed. It helps its member unions promote membership in new areas and industries, and campaigns for rights at work for all employees, including part-time and temporary workers, whether union members or not. TUC representatives sit on many public bodies at national and international level such as government, political parties, employers and the European Union.

The governing body of the TUC is the annual Congress. Between Congresses, business is conducted by a General Council, which meets five times a year, and an Executive Committee, which meets monthly. The full-time staff is headed by the General Secretary who is elected by Congress and is a permanent member of the General Council.

There are some 70 affiliated unions, with a total membership of nearly 7,000,000.
President (2004–5), Gloria Mills
General Secretary, Brendan Barber, elected 2002

SCOTTISH TRADES UNION CONGRESS

333 Woodlands Road, Glasgow G3 6NG T 0141-337 8100
E info@stuc.org.uk W www.stuc.org.uk

The Congress was formed in 1897 and acts as a national centre for the trade union movement in Scotland. The STUC promotes the rights to welfare of those in work and helps the unemployed. It helps its member unions to promote membership in new areas and industries, and campaigns for rights at work for all employees, including part-time temporary workers, whether union members or not. It makes representations to government and employers. In March 2005 it consisted of 46 unions with a total membership of 630,000 and 32 directly affiliated Trades Councils.

The Annual Congress in April elects a 39-member General Council on the basis of six industrial sections.
Chairperson, John Keenan
General Secretary, Bill Speirs

WALES TUC

1 Cathedral Road, Cardiff, CF11 9SD T 029 2034 7010
E wtuc@tuc.org.uk W www.wtuc.org.uk

The Wales TUC was established in 1974 to ensure that the role of the TUC was effectively undertaken in Wales. Its structure reflects the four economic regions of Wales and matches the regional committee areas of the National Assembly of Wales. The regional committees oversee the delivery of Wales TUC policy and campaigns in each region and liaise with local government, training organisations and regional economic development bodies. The Wales TUC seeks to reduce unemployment, increase the levels of skill and pay, and eliminate discrimination.

The governing body of Wales TUC is the Conference, which meets annually in the spring and elects a 50-person General Council which oversees the work of the TUC throughout the year.

There are 50 affiliated unions, with a total membership of around 500,000.
President, Margaret Hazell
General Secretary, Felicity Williams

AFFILIATED UNIONS

As at April 2004
ABBEY NATIONAL GROUP UNION (ANGU), 2nd Floor, 16–17 High Street, Tring HP23 5AH T 01442-891122 E info@angu.org.uk W www.angu.org.uk
   General Secretary, Linda Rolph *Membership*: 8,900
ACCORD, Simmons House, 46 Old Bath Road, Charvil RG10 9QR T 0118-934 1808 E info@accordhq.org W www.accord-myunion.org
   General Secretary, Ged Nichols *Membership*: 25,000
ALLIANCE AND LEICESTER GROUP UNION OF STAFF (ALGUS), 22 Upper King Street, Leicester LE1 6XE T 0116-285 6585 E terrialgus@aol.com W www.algus.org.uk
   General Secretary, Debbie Cort *Membership*: 2,838
AMICUS (FORMERLY AEEU AND MSF), 35 King Street, London WC2E 8JG T 020-7420 8900 W www.amicustheunion.org
   General Secretary, Derek Simpson
   Membership: 1,200,000
ASSOCIATED SOCIETY OF LOCOMOTIVE ENGINEERS AND FIREMEN (ASLEF), 9 Arkwright Road, London NW3 6AB T 020-7317 8600 E info@aslef.org.uk W www.aslef.org.uk
   General Secretary (acting), Keith Norman
   Membership: 17,000
ASSOCIATION FOR COLLEGE MANAGEMENT (ACM), 10 De Montfort Street, Leicester LE1 7GG T 0116-275 5076 E admin@acm.uk.com W www.acm.uk.com
   General Secretary, Peter Pendle *Membership*: 4,000
ASSOCIATION OF EDUCATIONAL PSYCHOLOGISTS (AEP), 26 The Avenue, Durham DH1 4ED T 0191-384 9512 E sao@aep.org.uk W www.aep.org.uk
   General Secretary, B. Harrison-Jennings
   Membership: 2,834

ASSOCIATION OF FIRST DIVISION CIVIL SERVANTS (FDA), 2 Caxton Street, London SW1H 0QH **T** 020-7343 1111 **E** head-office@fda.org.uk **W** www.fda.org.uk
General Secretary, Jonathan Baume *Membership*: 10,883

ASSOCIATION OF FLIGHT ATTENDANTS (AFA), United Airlines Cargo Centre, AFA Council 07, Shoreham Road East, Heathrow Airport TW6 3UA **T** 020-8276 6723 **E** afa@afalhr.org.uk **W** www.afalhr.org.uk
President, Kevin Creighan *Membership*: 632

ASSOCIATION OF MAGISTERIAL OFFICERS (AMO), 1 Fellmongers Path, 176 Tower Bridge Road, London SE1 3LY **T** 020-7403 2244 **E** hq@amo.org.uk **W** www.amo-online.org.uk
General Secretary, Rosie Eagleson *Membership*: 7,357

ASSOCIATION OF TEACHERS AND LECTURERS (ATL), 7 Northumberland Street, London WC2N 5RD **T** 020-7930 6441 **E** info@atl.org.uk **W** www.askatl.org.uk
General Secretary, Dr Mary Bousted *Membership*: 160,000

ASSOCIATION OF UNIVERSITY TEACHERS (AUT), Egmont House, 25–31 Tavistock Place, London WC1H 9UT **T** 020-7670 9700 **E** hq@aut.org.uk **W** www.aut.org.uk
General Secretary, Sally Hunt *Membership*: 48,000

BAKERS, FOOD AND ALLIED WORKERS' UNION (BFAWU), Stanborough House, Great North Road, Stanborough, Welwyn Garden City AL8 7TA **T** 01707-260150 **E** bfawuho@aol.com **W** www.bfawu.org
General Secretary, Joe Marino *Membership*: 28,168

BRITANNIA STAFF UNION (BSU), Court Lodge, Leonard Street, Leek ST13 5JP **T** 01538-399627 **E** bsu@themail.co.uk **W** www.britanniasu.org.uk
General Secretary, David O'Dowd *Membership*: 2,352

BRITISH AIR LINE PILOTS ASSOCIATION (BALPA), 81 New Road, Harlington, Hayes UB3 5BG **T** 020-8476 4000 **E** balpa@balpa.org **W** www.balpa.org
Chair, Capt Mervyn Granshaw *Membership*: 8,000

BRITISH AND IRISH ORTHOPTIC SOCIETY, Tavistock House North, Tavistock Square, London WC1H 9HX **T** 020-7387 7992 **E** bios@orthoptics.org.uk **W** www.orthoptics.org.uk
Executive Officer, Judith Dand *Membership*: 1,400

BRITISH ASSOCIATION OF COLLIERY MANAGEMENT-TECHNICAL, ENERGY AND ADMINISTRATIVE MANAGEMENT (BACM-TEAM), 17 South Parade, Doncaster DN1 2DR **T** 01302-815551 **E** enquiries@bacmteam.org.uk **W** www.bacmteam.org.uk
General Secretary, Patrick Carragher *Membership*: 3,580

BRITISH DIETETIC ASSOCIATION (BDA), 5th Floor, Charles House, 148–149 Great Charles Street, Queensway, Birmingham B3 3HT **T** 0121-200 8010 **E** info@bda.uk.com **W** www.bda.uk.com
President, Dame Barbara Clayton *Membership*: 5,076

BROADCASTING, ENTERTAINMENT, CINEMATOGRAPH AND THEATRE UNION (BECTU), 373–377 Clapham Road, London SW9 9BT **T** 020-7346 0900 **E** info@bectu.org.uk **W** www.bectu.org.uk
General Secretary, Roger Bolton *Membership*: 26,285

CARD SETTING MACHINE TENTERS' SOCIETY (CSMTS), 48 Scar End Lane, Staincliffe, Dewsbury WF13 4NY **T** 01924-400206
General Secretary, Anthony John Moorhouse *Membership*: 88

CERAMIC AND ALLIED TRADES UNION (CATU), Hillcrest House, Garth Street, Hanley, Stoke-on-Trent ST1 2AB **T** 01782-272755 **W** www.catu.org.uk
General Secretary, G. Bagnall *Membership*: 12,497

CHARTERED SOCIETY OF PHYSIOTHERAPY (CSP), 14 Bedford Row, London WC1R 4ED **T** 020-7306 6666 **W** www.csp.org.uk
Director of Employment Relations, Richard Griffin *Membership*: 34,857

COMMUNICATION WORKERS UNION (CWU), 150 The Broadway, Wimbledon, London SW19 1RX **T** 020-8971 7200 **E** info@cwu.org **W** www.cwu.org
General Secretary, B. Hayes *Membership*: 266,067

COMMUNITY, Swinton House, 324 Gray's Inn Road, London WC1X 8DD **T** 020-7239 1200 **E** info@community-tu.org **W** www.community-tu.org
General Secretary, Michael Leahy *Membership*: 70,059

COMMUNITY AND DISTRICT NURSING ASSOCIATION (CDNA), Walpole House, 18–22 Bond Street, Ealing, London W5 5AA **T** 020-8231 0180 **E** cdna@tvu.ac.uk **W** www.cdna.tvu.ac.uk
Chair, Rowena Smith *Membership*: 3,984

COMMUNITY AND SOUTH WORKERS UNION (CYWU), 302, The Argent Centre, 60 Frederick Street, Birmingham B1 3HS **T** 0121-244 3344 **E** kerry@cywu.org.uk **W** www.cywu.org.uk
General Secretary, Doug Nicholls *Membership*: 4,800

CONNECT, THE UNION FOR PROFESSIONALS IN COMMUNICATIONS, 30 St George's Road, London SW19 4BD **T** 020-8971 6000 **E** union@connectuk.org **W** www.connectuk.org
General Secretary, A. Askew *Membership*: 19,731

DERBYSHIRE GROUP STAFF UNION, The Lodge, Duffield Hall, DE56 1AG **T** 01332-844396 **E** dsmith@dbssa.co.uk
Chair, Deidre Smith *Membership*: 476

DIAGEO STAFF ASSOCIATION (DSA), Sun Works Cottage, Park Royal Brewery, London NW10 7RR **T** 020-8978 6069 **E** elizabeth.jude@diageo.com
Chair, David Orton *Membership*: 550

EDUCATIONAL INSTITUTE OF SCOTLAND (EIS), 46 Moray Place, Edinburgh EH3 6BH **T** 0131-225 6244 **E** enquiries@eis.org.uk **W** www.eis.org.uk
General Secretary, Ronald A. Smith *Membership*: 55,536

EQUITY, Guild House, Upper St Martin's Lane, London WC2H 9EG **T** 020-7379 6000 **E** info@equity.org.uk **W** www.equity.org.uk
General Secretary, Ian McGarry *Membership*: 35,610

FIRE BRIGADES UNION, THE (FBU), Bradley House, 68 Coombe Road, Kingston upon Thames KT2 7AE **T** 020-8541 1765 **E** office@fbu.org.uk **W** www.fbu.org.uk
General Secretary, Andy Gilchrist *Membership*: 50,000

GENERAL UNION OF LOOM OVERLOOKERS (GULO), 9 Wellington Street, St John's, Blackburn BB1 8AF **T** 01254-51760
General Secretary, Don Rishton *Membership*: 265

GMB, 22–24 Worple Road, London SW19 4DD **T** 020-8947 3131 **E** info@gmb.org.uk **W** www.gmb.org.uk
General Secretary (acting), Paul Kenny *Membership*: 615,000

HOSPITAL CONSULTANTS AND SPECIALISTS ASSOCIATION (HCSA), 1 Kingsclere Road, Overton, Basingstoke RG25 3JA **T** 01256-771777 **E** conspec@hcsa.com **W** www.hcsa.com
Chief Executive, Stephen Campion *Membership*: 2,850

MUSICIANS' UNION (MU), 60–62 Clapham Road, London SW9 0JJ **T** 020-7582 5566 **E** info@musiciansunion.org.uk **W** www.musiciansunion.org.uk
General Secretary, John F. Smith *Membership*: 31,312

NASUWT (NATIONAL ASSOCIATION OF SCHOOLMASTERS/UNION OF WOMEN TEACHERS), Hillscourt Education Centre, Rose Hill, Rednal, Birmingham B45 8RS **T** 0121-453 6150 **E** nasuwt@mail.nasuwt.org.uk **W** www.teachersunion.org.uk
General Secretary, Chris Keates *Membership:* 223,000

NATFHE (THE UNIVERSITY AND COLLEGE LECTURERS' UNION), 27 Britannia Street, London WC1X 9JP **T** 020-7837 3636 **E** hq@natfhe.org.uk **W** www.natfhe.org.uk
General Secretary, P. Mackney *Membership:* 68,000

NATIONAL ASSOCIATION OF COLLIERY OVERMEN, DEPUTIES AND SHOTFIRERS (NACODS), Deputy House, 37 Church Street, Barnsley S70 2AR **T** 01226-203743 **E** natnacods@aol.com **W** www.nacods.co.uk
General Secretary, Ian Parker *Membership:* 610

NATIONAL ASSOCIATION OF CO-OPERATIVE OFFICIALS (NACO), 6A Clarendon Place, Hyde, Cheshire, SK14 2QZ **T** 0161-351 7900 **E** lwe@nacoco-op.org
General Secretary, L. W. Ewing *Membership:* 2,477

NATIONAL ASSOCIATION OF EDUCATIONAL INSPECTORS, ADVISERS AND CONSULTANTS, Woolley Hall, Woolley WF4 2JR **T** 01226-383420 **E** naeiac@naeiac.org **W** www.naeiac.org
General Secretary, J. Chowcat *Membership:* 3,500

NATIONAL UNION OF DOMESTIC APPLIANCES AND GENERAL OPERATIVES (NUDAGO), 1st Floor, 7–8 Imperial Buildings, Corporation Street, Rotherham S60 1PB **T** 01709-382820 **E** nudago@btconnect.com
General Secretary, A. McCarthy *Membership:* 1,850

NATIONAL UNION OF JOURNALISTS (NUJ), Headland House, 308–312 Gray's Inn Road, London WC1X 8DP **T** 020-7278 7916 **E** info@nuj.org.uk **W** www.nuj.org.uk
General Secretary, Jeremy Dear *Membership:* 36,000

NATIONAL UNION OF MARINE, AVIATION AND SHIPPING TRANSPORT OFFICERS (NUMAST), Oceanair House, 750–760 High Road, London E11 3BB **T** 020-8989 6677 **E** enquiries@numast.org **W** www.numast.org
General Secretary, Brian Orrell *Membership:* 19,133

NATIONAL UNION OF MINEWORKERS (NUM), Miners' Offices, 2 Huddersfield Road, Barnsley S70 2LS **T** 01226-215555 **E** steve.kemp@nationalunionofmineworkers.com
National Secretary, Steve Kemp *Membership:* 3,042

NATIONAL UNION OF RAIL, MARITIME AND TRANSPORT WORKERS (RMT), Unity House, 39 Chalton Street, London NW1 1JD **T** 020-7387 4771 **E** info@rmt.org.uk **W** www.rmt.org.uk
General Secretary, Bob Crow *Membership:* 70,000

NATIONAL UNION OF TEACHERS (NUT), Hamilton House, Mabledon Place, London WC1H 9BD **T** 020-7388 6191 **W** www.teachers.org.uk
General Secretary, Steve Sinnott *Membership:* 267,471

NATIONWIDE GROUP STAFF UNION (NGSU), Middleton Farmhouse, 37 Main Road, Middleton Cheney, Banbury OX17 2QT **T** 01295-710767 **E** ngsu@ngsu.org.uk **W** www.ngsu.org.uk
General Secretary, Tim Poil *Membership:* 11,940

PRISON OFFICERS' ASSOCIATION (POA), Cronin House, 245 Church Street, London N9 9HW **T** 020-8803 0255 **W** www.poauk.org.uk
General Secretary, Brian Caton *Membership:* 34,119

PROFESSIONAL FOOTBALLERS' ASSOCIATION (PFA), 20 Oxford Court, Bishopsgate, Manchester M2 3WQ **T** 0161-236 0575 **E** info@thepfa.co.uk **W** www.thepfa.co.uk
Chief Executive, Gordon Taylor *Membership:* 2,485

PROSPECT, Prospect House, 75–79 York Road, London SE1 7AQ **T** 020-7902 6600 **E** enquiries@prospect.org.uk **W** www.prospect.org.uk
General Secretary, Paul Noon *Membership:* 105,480

PUBLIC AND COMMERCIAL SERVICES UNION (PCS), 160 Falcon Road, London SW11 2LN **T** 020-7924 2727 **E** ben@pcs.org.uk **W** www.pcs.org.uk
General Secretary, Mark Serwotka *Membership:* 325,000

SHEFFIELD WOOL SHEAR WORKERS' UNION (SWSWU), 129 Roughwood Road, Rotherham S61 3AA **T** 01709-560894
Secretary, B. Whomersley *Membership:* 9

SOCIETY OF CHIROPODISTS AND PODIATRISTS (SCP), 1 Fellmonger's Path, Tower Bridge Road, London SE1 3LY **T** 020-7234 8620 **E** enq@scpod.org **W** www.feetforlife.org
Chief Executive, Joanna Brown *Membership:* 10,000

SOCIETY OF RADIOGRAPHERS, THE (SOR), 207 Providence Square, Mill Street, London SE1 2EW **T** 020-7740 7200 **E** info@sor.org **W** www.sor.org
Chief Executive, Richard Evans *Membership:* 21,570

TRADE UNION AND PROFESSIONAL ASSOCIATION FOR FAMILY COURT AND PROBATION STAFF (NAPO), 4 Chivalry Road, London SW11 1HT **T** 020-7223 4887 **E** info@napo.org.uk **W** www.napo.org.uk
General Secretary, Judy McKnight *Membership:* 7,500

TRANSPORT AND GENERAL WORKERS' UNION (T&G), Transport House, 128 Theobalds Road, London WC1X 8TN **T** 020-7611 2500 **E** tgwu@tgwu.org.uk **W** www.tgwu.org.uk
General Secretary, Tony Woodley *Membership:* 806,000

TRANSPORT SALARIED STAFFS' ASSOCIATION (TSSA), Walkden House, 10 Melton Street, London NW1 2EJ **T** 020-7387 2101 **E** enquiries@tssa.org.uk **W** www.tssa.org.uk
General Secretary, Gerry Doherty *Membership:* 33,000

UBAC (UNION FOR BRADFORD AND BINGLEY STAFF AND STAFF IN ASSOCIATED COMPANIES), 18D Market Place, Malton YO17 7LX **T** 01653-697634 **E** ubac@btconnect.com
General Secretary, David Matthews *Membership:* 2,690

UNDEB CENEDLAETHOL ATHRAWON CYMRU (NATIONAL UNION OF THE TEACHERS OF WALES), Pen Roc, Rhodfa'r Môr, Aberystwyth SY23 2AZ **T** 01970-639950 **E** ucac@athrawon.com **W** www.athrawon.com
General Secretary, Moelwen Gwyndaf *Membership:* 4,000

UNION OF CONSTRUCTION, ALLIED TRADES AND TECHNICIANS (UCATT), UCATT House, 177 Abbeville Road, London SW4 9RL **T** 020-7622 2442 **E** info@ucatt.org.uk **W** www.ucatt.org.uk
General Secretary, Alan Ritchie *Membership:* 120,000

UNION OF SHOP, DISTRIBUTIVE AND ALLIED WORKERS (USDAW), 188 Wilmslow Road, Manchester M14 6LJ **T** 0161-224 2804 **E** enquiries@usdaw.org.uk **W** www.usdaw.org.uk
General Secretary, John Hannett *Membership:* 340,000

UNISON, 1 Mabledon Place, London WC1H 9AJ **T** 0845-355 0845 **W** www.unison.org.uk
General Secretary, Dave Prentis *Membership:* 1,301,000

WRITERS' GUILD OF GREAT BRITAIN (WGGB), 15 Britannia Street, London WC1X 9JN **T** 020-7833 0777 **E** admin@writersguild.org.uk **W** www.writersguild.org.uk
General Secretary, Bernie Corbett *Membership:* 2,200

YORKSHIRE INDEPENDENT STAFF ASSOCIATION (YISA), c/o Yorkshire Building Society, Yorkshire House, Yorkshire Drive, Rooley Lane, Bradford BD5 8LJ **T** 01274-472453 **E** kmwatson@ybs.co.uk
Chair, Karen Watson *Membership:* 1,436

NON-AFFILIATED UNIONS

As at April 2004

BRITISH RENTAL ASSOCIATION, 64 Wimpole Street, London W1G 8YS **T** 020-7935 0875 **E** enquiries@bda.org **W** www.bda.org
President, Anthony Kravitz *Membership:* 18,000

CHARTERED INSTITUTE OF JOURNALISTS, 2 Dock Offices, Surrey Quays Road, London SE16 2XU **T** 020-7252 1187 **E** memberservices@ioj.co.uk **W** www.ioj.co.uk
General Secretary, Dominic Cooper

NATIONAL ASSOCIATION OF HEAD TEACHERS (NAHT), 1 Heath Square, Boltro Road, Haywards Heath RH16 1BL **T** 01444-472472 **E** info@naht.org.uk **W** www.naht.org.uk
General Secretary, David Hart, OBE

NATIONAL SOCIETY FOR EDUCATION IN ART AND DESIGN, The Gatehouse, Corsham Court, Corsham SN13 0BZ **T** 01249-714825 **E** bookshop@nsead.org **W** www.nsead.org
General Secretary, Dr J. M. Steers

PRISON GOVERNORS ASSOCIATION, Room 405, Horseferry House, Dean Ryle Street, London SW1P 2AW **T** 020-7217 8591 **W** www.prisongovernors.org.uk
General Secretary, C. Bushell

RETAIL BOOK, STATIONERY AND ALLIED TRADES EMPLOYEES' ASSOCIATION, 8–9 Commercial Road, Swindon SN1 5NF **T** 01793-615811 **E** info@the-rba.org
President, David Pickles

ROYAL COLLEGE OF MIDWIVES, 15 Mansfield Street, London W1G 9NH **T** 020-7312 3535 **E** info@rcm.org.uk **W** www.rcm.org.uk
General Secretary, Dame Karlene Davis, DBE

SCOTTISH SECONDARY TEACHERS' ASSOCIATION (SSTA), 15 Dundas Street, Edinburgh EH3 6QG **T** 0131-556 5919 **E** info@ssta.org.uk **W** www.ssta.org.uk
General Secretary, David Eaglesham

SECONDARY HEADS ASSOCIATION, 130 Regent Road, Leicester LE1 7PG **T** 0116-299 1122 **E** info@sha.org.uk **W** www.sha.org.uk
General Secretary, Dr J. E. Dunford, OBE
Membership: 11,950

SOCIETY OF AUTHORS, 84 Drayton Gardens, London SW10 9SB **T** 020-7373 6642 **E** info@societyofauthors.org **W** www.societyofauthors.org
General Secretary, M. Le Fanu, OBE *Membership:* 7,800

UNITED ROAD TRANSPORT UNION, 76 High Lane, Chorlton-cum-Hardy, Manchester M21 9EF **T** 0800-526639 **E** info@urtu.com **W** www.urtu.com
General Secretary, Robert Monks *Membership:* 16,000

SPORTS BODIES

SPORTS COUNCILS

CENTRAL COUNCIL OF PHYSICAL RECREATION, Francis House, Francis Street, London SW1P 1DE **T** 020-7854 8500 **E** admin@ccpr.org.uk **W** www.ccpr.org.uk
Chief Executive, Margaret Talbot, OBE, PHD

SPORT ENGLAND, 3rd Floor, Victoria House, Bloomsbury Square, London WC1B 4SE **T** 0845-850 8508 **E** info@sportengland.org **W** www.sportengland.org
Chief Executive, Roger Draper

SPORT SCOTLAND, Caledonia House, South Gyle, Edinburgh EH12 9DQ **T** 0131-317 7200 **E** library@sportscotland.org.uk **W** www.sportscotland.org.uk
Chief Executive, Ian Taylor

SPORTS COUNCIL FOR NORTHERN IRELAND, House of Sport, Upper Malone Road, Belfast BT9 5LA **T** 028-9038 1222 **E** info@sportni.net **W** www.sportni.net
Chief Executive, Eamonn McCartan

SPORTS COUNCIL FOR WALES, Sophia Gardens, Cardiff CF11 9SW **T** 029-2030 0500 **E** publicity@scw.co.uk **W** www.sports-council-wales.co.uk
Chief Executive, Dr H. Jones

UK SPORT, 40 Bernard Street, London WC1N 1ST **T** 020-7211 5100 **E** info@uksport.gov.uk **W** www.uksport.gov.uk
Chief Executive, Liz Nicholl

ANGLING

NATIONAL FEDERATION OF ANGLERS, Halliday House, Egginton Junction, DE65 6GU **T** 01283-734735 **E** nfa.office@nfadirect.com **W** www.nfadirect.com
Chief Executive, Paul Baggaley

ARCHERY

GRAND NATIONAL ARCHERY SOCIETY, Lilleshall National Sports Centre, Newport TF10 9AT **T** 01952-677888 **E** enquiries@gnas.org **W** www.gnas.org
Chief Executive, D. Sherratt

ASSOCIATION FOOTBALL

FOOTBALL ASSOCIATION, 25 Soho Square, London W1D 4FA **T** 020-7745 4545 **W** www.thefa.com
Chief Executive, Brian Barwick

FOOTBALL ASSOCIATION OF WALES, Plymouth Chambers, 3 Westgate Street, Cardiff CF10 1DP **T** 029-2037 2325 **E** info@faw.org.uk **W** www.faw.org.uk
Secretary-General, D. G. Collins

FOOTBALL LEAGUE, 11 Connaught Place, London W2 2ET **T** 0870-4420 1888 **E** fl@football-league.co.uk **W** www.football-league.co.uk
Director of Operations, Andy Willliamson

IRISH FOOTBALL ASSOCIATION, 20 Windsor Avenue, Belfast BT9 6EE **T** 028-9066 9458 **E** enquiries@irishfa.com **W** www.irishfa.com
Chief Executive, H. Wells

IRISH FOOTBALL LEAGUE, 96 University Street, Belfast BT7 1HE **T** 028-9024 2888 **E** mail@irishpremierleague.com **W** www.irishpremierleague.com
Secretary, Harry Wallace

SCOTTISH FOOTBALL ASSOCIATION, Hampden Park, Glasgow G42 9AY **T** 0141-616 6000
E info@scottishfa.co.uk **W** www.scottishfa.co.uk
Chief Executive, D. Taylor

SCOTTISH FOOTBALL LEAGUE, The National Stadium, Hampden Park, Glasgow G42 9EB **T** 0141-620 4160 **E** info@scottishfootballleague.com **W** www.scottishfootballleague.com
Secretary, Peter Donald

ATHLETICS

ATHLETICS ASSOCIATION OF WALES, The Manor, Coldra Woods, Newport NP18 1WA **T** 01633-416633 **E** office@welshathletics.org **W** www.welshathletics.org
President, John Collins

NORTHERN IRELAND ATHLETIC FEDERATION, Athletics House, Old Coach Road, Belfast BT9 5PR **T** 028-9060 2707 **E** info@niathletics.org **W** www.niathletics.org
Hon. Secretary, John Allen
President, E. H. Wilson

SCOTTISH ATHLETICS, 9a South Gyle Crescent, Edinburgh EH12 9EB **T** 0131-539 7320 **E** admin@scottishathletics.org.uk **W** www.scottishathletics.org.uk
Chief Executive, Geoff Wightman

UK ATHLETICS, Athletics House, 10 Harborne Road, Edgbaston, Birmingham B15 3AA **T** 0870-998 6800 **E** information@ukathletics.org.uk **W** www.ukathletics.net
Chief Executive, D. Moorcroft OBE

BADMINTON

BADMINTON ASSOCIATION OF ENGLAND, National Badminton Centre, Bradwell Road, Loughton Lodge, Milton Keynes MK8 9LA **T** 01908-268400 **E** enquiries@baofe.co.uk **W** www.baofe.co.uk
Chief Executive, Eric Brown (*acting*)

SCOTTISH BADMINTON UNION, Cockburn Centre, 40 Bogmoor Place, Glasgow G51 4QT **T** 0141-445 1218 **E** name@badmintonscotland.org.uk **W** www.badmintonscotland.org.uk
Chief Executive, Miss A. Smillie

WELSH BADMINTON UNION, 4th Floor, Plymouth Chambers, 3 Westgate Street, Cardiff CF10 1DP **T** 029-2022 2082 **E** wbu@welshbadminton.net **W** www.welshbadminton.net
Executive Director, Lyndon Williams

BASEBALL

BASEBALLSOFTBALL UK, Ariel House, 74A Charlotte Street, London W1T 4QJ **T** 020-7453 7055 **E** info@baseballsoftballuk.com **W** www.baseballsoftballuk.com
Chief Operations Officer, John Boyd

BASKETBALL

BASKETBALL SCOTLAND, Caledonia House, Redheughs Rigg, South Gyle, Edinburgh EH12 9DQ **T** 0870-950 1033 **E** enquiries@basketball-scotland.com **W** www.basketball-scotland.com
Chief Executive, Kevin Pringle

ENGLISH BASKETBALL ASSOCIATION, EIS Sheffield,
Coleridge Road, Sheffield S9 5DA T 0870-7744225
E info@englandbasketball.co.uk
W www.englandbasketball.co.uk
Chief Executive, Keith Mair

BILLIARDS AND SNOOKER

WORLD LADIES BILLIARDS AND SNOOKER
ASSOCIATION, Richmand Lodge, 231 Ramnoth Road,
Wisbech PE13 2SN T 01945-588598
Chair, Mandy Fisher

WORLD PROFESSIONAL BILLIARDS AND SNOOKER
ASSOCIATION, Ground Floor, Albert House, 111–117
Victoria Street, Bristol BS1 6AX T 0117-317 8200
E enq@worldsnooker.com W www.worldsnooker.com
Chairman, Sir Rodney Walker

BOBSLEIGH AND LUGE

BRITISH BOB SKELETON ASSOCIATION, Department of
Sports Development and Recreation, University of Bath,
Claverton Down, Bath BA2 7AY T 01225-323696
E bba@dial.pipex.com W www.icetrack.org.uk
Hon. Secretary, Mike Callan

BRITISH BOBSLEIGH ASSOCIATION, Department of Sports
Development and Recreation, University of Bath, Claverton
Down, Bath BA2 7AY T 01225-386802
E bbaoffice@british-bobsleigh.com
W www.british-bobsleigh.com
Chairman, Bruce Ropner

GREAT BRITAIN LUGE ASSOCIATION, 61 West Malvern
Road, Malvern, Worcs WR14 4NF T 01684-576604
E markaluge@hotmail.com W www.gbla.org.uk
Chief Executive, Lt-Col Mark Armstrong

BOWLS

BRITISH ISLES BOWLS COUNCIL, 23 Leysland Avenue,
Countesthorpe LE8 5XX T 0116-277 3234
Hon. Secretary, M. Swatland

BRITISH ISLES WOMEN'S INDOOR BOWLS
COUNCIL, 101 Skyline Drive, Lambeg BT27 4HW
Hon. Secretary, Mrs Doreen Miskelly

ENGLISH BOWLING ASSOCIATION, Lyndhurst Road,
Worthing BN11 2AZ T 01903-820222
E ebaqueries@bowlsengland.com
W www.bowlsengland.com
Chief Executive, A. Allcock MBE

ENGLISH INDOOR BOWLING ASSOCIATION, David
Cornwell House, Bowling Green, Leicester Road, Melton
Mowbray LE13 0FA T 01664-481900
E enquiries@eiba.co.uk W www.eiba.co.uk
Secretary, Stephen Rodwell

ENGLISH WOMEN'S BOWLING ASSOCIATION, EWBA
Office, Victoria Park, Archery Road, Royal Leamington Spa
CV31 3PT T 01926-430686
E office@englishwomensbowling.net
W www.englishwomensbowling.net
Chief Executive, Mrs P. A. Biddlecombe

ENGLISH WOMEN'S INDOOR BOWLING
ASSOCIATION, 3 Moulton Business Park, Scirocco Close,
Northampton NN3 6AP T 01604-494163
E ewiba@btconnect.com W www.ewiba.com
Secretary, Mrs T. Thomas

BOXING

AMATEUR BOXING ASSOCIATION ENGLAND, Jubilee
Stand, Crystal Palace, National Sports Centre, London
SE19 2BB T 020-8778 0251 E hq@abae.org.uk
W www.abae.co.uk
Chairman, Jim Smart

BRITISH AMATEUR BOXING ASSOCIATION, 96 High
Street, Lochee, Dundee DD2 3AY T 01382-508261
E frankhendry@accnet.zzn.com
Chief Executive, Frank Hendry

BRITISH BOXING BOARD OF CONTROL, The Old Library,
Trinity Street, Cardiff CF10 1BH
T 029-2036 7000 E info@bbbofc.com
W www.bbbofc.com
General Secretary, Simon Block
Chairman, Lord Brooks of Tremorfa, DL

CANOEING

BRITISH CANOE UNION, John Dudderidge House, Adbolton
Lane, West Bridgford, Nottingham NG2 5AS
T 0115-982 1100 E info@bcu.org.uk W www.bcu.org.uk
Chief Executive, P. Owen

CHESS

BRITISH CHESS FEDERATION, The Watch Oak, Chain Lane,
Battle TN33 0YD T 01424-775222 E office@bcf.org.uk
W www.bcf.org.uk
President, Gerry Walsh

CRICKET

ENGLAND AND WALES CRICKET BOARD, Lord's Cricket
Ground, London NW8 8QN T 020-7432 1200
W www.ecb.co.uk
Chief Executive, D. Collier

MCC, Lord's Cricket Ground, St John's Wood, London
NW8 8QN T 020-7616 8500
E communications@mcc.org.uk W www.lords.org
Secretary and Chief Executive, R. D. V. Knight

CROQUET

CROQUET ASSOCIATION, c/o Cheltenham Croquet Club,
Old Bath Road, Cheltenham GL53 7DF T 01242-242318
E caoffice@croquet.org.uk W www.croquet.org.uk
Secretary, Klim Seabright

CURLING

BRITISH CURLING ASSOCIATION, Langhill, Lockerbie,
Dumfriesshire DG11 2QT T 01576-202635
E john@jmbroons.freeserve.co.uk
W www.britishcurlingassociation.org.uk
Chairman, John Brown

ROYAL CALEDONIAN CURLING CLUB, Cairnie House,
Avenue K, Ingliston Showground, Newbridge EH28 8NB
T 0131-333 3003 E office@royalcaledoniancurlingclub.org
W www.royalcaledoniancurlingclub.org
Chief Executive, Colin Grahamslaw

CYCLING

BRITISH CYCLING FEDERATION, National Cycling
Centre, Stuart Street, Manchester M11 4DQ
T 0870-871 2000 E info@britishcycling.org.uk
W www.britishcycling.org.uk
Chief Executive, P. King

CYCLING TIME TRIALS, 77 Arlington Drive, Pennington
Leigh WN7 3QP T 01942-603976
E nationalsecretary@rttchq.freeserve.co.uk
W www.ctt.org.uk
National Secretary, Phil Heaton

DARTS

BRITISH DARTS ORGANISATION, 2 Pages Lane, Muswell
Hill, London N10 1PS T 020-8883 5544
E britishdartsorg@btconnect.com W www.bdodarts.com
Managing Director, Olly Croft

EQUESTRIANISM

BRITISH EQUESTRIAN FEDERATION, National Agricultural Centre, Stoneleigh Park, Kenilworth CV8 2RH
T 024-7669 8871 E info@bef.co.uk W www.bef.co.uk
Chief Executive, Andrew Finding
BRITISH EVENTING, National Agricultural Centre, Stoneleigh Park, Kenilworth CV8 2RN T 024-7669 8856
E info@britisheventing.com W www.britisheventing.com
Chief Executive, P. Durrant

ETON FIVES

ETON FIVES ASSOCIATION, 3 Bourchier Close, Sevenoaks TN13 1PD T 01732-458775 E efa@etonfives.co.uk
W www.etonfives.co.uk
Secretary, M. R. Fenn

FENCING

BRITISH FENCING ASSOCIATION, 1 Baron's Gate, 33–35 Rothschild Road, London W4 5HT T 020-8742 3032
E british_fencing@compuserve.com
W www.britishfencing.com
President, Keith A. Smith

GLIDING

BRITISH GLIDING ASSOCIATION, Kimberley House, Vaughan Way, Leicester LE1 4SE T 0116-253 1051
E bga@gliding.co.uk W www.gliding.co.uk
Chairman, David Roberts

GOLF

LADIES' GOLF UNION, The Scores, St Andrews KY16 9AT
T 01334-475811 E info@lgu.org W www.lgu.org
Secretary/CEO, Andy Salmon
THE ROYAL AND ANCIENT GOLF CLUB OF ST ANDREWS, Golf Place, St Andrews KY16 9JD
T 01334-460000 E thesecretary@randagc.org
W www.randa.org
Secretary, P. Dawson

GREYHOUND RACING

NATIONAL GREYHOUND RACING CLUB, Twyman House, 16 Bonny Street, London NW1 9QD T 020-7267 9256
E mail@ngrc.org.uk W www.ngrc.org.uk
Chief Executive, F. Melville

GYMNASTICS

BRITISH GYMNASTICS, Ford Hall, Lilleshall National Sports Centre, Newport TF10 9NB T 0845-129 7129
E information@british-gymnastics.org
W www.british-gymnastics.org
Chief Executive, Alan Sommerville

HANDBALL

BRITISH HANDBALL ASSOCIATION, 40 Newchurch Road, Rawtenstall, Rossendale BB4 7QX T 01706-229354
E office@englandhandball.com
W www.englandhandball.com
Chairman, Stephen Neilson

HOCKEY

ENGLAND HOCKEY, The National Hockey Stadium, Silbury Boulevard, Milton Keynes MK9 1HA T 01908-544644
E info@englandhockey.org W www.hockeyonline.co.uk
Executive Chairman, Philip Kimberley
SCOTTISH HOCKEY UNION, 589 Lanark Road, Edinburgh EH14 5DA T 0131-453 9070 E info@scottish-hockey.org.uk
W www.scottish-hockey.org.uk
Chief Executive, John Gunn

WELSH HOCKEY UNION, Severn House, Station Terrace, Ely Cardiff CF5 4AA T 029-2057 3940
E info@welsh-hockey.co.uk W www.welsh-hockey.co.uk
Chief Executive, Mike Boll

HORSE RACING

BRITISH HORSERACING BOARD, 151 Shaftesbury Avenue, London WC2H 8AL T 020-7152 0000
E info@britishhorseracing.com
W www.britishhorseracing.com
Chief Executive, Greg Nichols
THE JOCKEY CLUB, 151 Shaftesbury Avenue, London WC2H 8AL T 020-7189 3800 E info@thejockeyclub.co.uk
W www.thejockeyclub.co.uk
Senior Steward, Julian Richmond-Watson

ICE HOCKEY

ICE HOCKEY UK, 47 Westminster Buildings, Theatre Square, Nottingham NG1 6LG T 0115-924 1441
E hockey@icehockeyuk.co.uk W www.icehockeyuk.co.uk
Chairman, Neville Moralee

ICE SKATING

NATIONAL ICE SKATING ASSOCIATION OF THE UK, National Ice Centre, Lower Parliament Street, Nottingham NG1 1LA T 0870-758 0278
E nisa@iceskating.org.uk W www.iceskating.org.uk
Chief Executive, Keith Horton

LACROSSE

ENGLISH LACROSSE ASSOCIATION, 26 Wood Street, Manchester M3 3EF T 0161-834 4582
E info@englishlacrosse.co.uk W www.englishlacrosse.co.uk
Chief Executive Officer, David Shuttleworth

LAWN TENNIS

LAWN TENNIS ASSOCIATION, The Queen's Club, Palliser Road, London W14 9EG T 020-7381 7000 E info@lta.org.uk
W www.lta.org.uk
Secretary, J. C. U. James

MARTIAL ARTS

BRITISH JUDO ASSOCIATION, Suite B, Loughborough Technology Centre, Epinal Way, Loughborough LE11 3GE
T 01509-631670 E bja@britishjudo.org.uk
W www.britishjudo.org.uk
Chairman, Densign White
BRITISH TAEKWONDO COUNCIL, Yiewsley Leisure Centre, Otterfield Road, West Drayton, Middx UB7 8PE
T 0117-955 1046 W www.britishtaekwondocouncil.org
Secretary General, Trevor Nicholls
MARTIAL ARTS DEVELOPMENT COMMISSION, PO Box 416, Wembley HA0 3WD T 0870-770 0461
E office@madec.org W www.madec.org
Chairman, R. Thomas

MODERN PENTATHLON

MODERN PENTATHLON ASSOCIATION OF GREAT BRITAIN, Norwood House, University of Bath, Bath BA2 7AY T 01225-386808 E enquiries@mpagb.org.uk
W www.mpagb.org.uk
Chief Executive, Peter Hart

MOTOR SPORTS

BRITISH SUPERBIKES RACE ORGANISATION, MCRCB, PO Box 6450, Woodford Halse, Daventry NN11 3ZD
T 01327-264010 E dougbarnfield@mcrcb.fslife.co.uk
Manager, D. R. Barnfield

MOTORCYCLE GREAT BRITAIN, Auto-Cycle Union, ACU House, Wood Street, Rugby CV21 2YX
T 01788-566400 E admin@acu.org.uk
W www.motorcyclinggb.com
General Secretary, Gary Thompson, MBE, BEM

SCOTTISH AUTO CYCLE UNION, 28 West Main Street, Uphall EH52 5DW T 01506-858354 E office@sacu.co.uk
W www.sacu.co.uk
Office Manager, Eric Jones

THE MOTOR SPORTS ASSOCIATION, Motor Sports House, Riverside Park, Colnbrook SL3 0HG
T 01753-765000 W www.msauk.org
Chief Executive, Colin Hilton

MOUNTAINEERING

BRITISH MOUNTAINEERING COUNCIL, 177–179 Burton Road, West Didsbury, Manchester M20 2BB
T 0870-010 4878 E office@thebmc.co.uk
W www.thebmc.co.uk
Chief Officer, D. Turnbull

MULTI-SPORTS BODIES

BRITISH OLYMPIC ASSOCIATION, 1 Wandsworth Plain, London SW18 1EH T 020-8871 2677
E firstname.surname@boa.org.uk W www.olympics.org.uk
Chief Executive, S. Clegg

BRITISH UNIVERSITIES SPORTS ASSOCIATION, 8 Union Street, London SE1 1SZ T 020-7357 8555
E office@busa.org.uk W www.busa.org.uk
Chief Executive, G. Gregory-Jones

COMMONWEALTH GAMES COUNCIL FOR ENGLAND, PO Box 36288, London SE19 2YY
T 020-8676 3543 E info@cgce.co.uk W www.cgce.co.uk
Chief Executive, Ann Hogbin

COMMONWEALTH GAMES FEDERATION, 2nd Floor, 138 Piccadilly, London W1J 7NR T 020-7491 8801
E info@thecgf.com
W www.thecgf.com
Chief Executive Officer, Michael Hooper

NETBALL

ALL ENGLAND NETBALL ASSOCIATION, Netball House, 9 Paynes Park, Hitchin SG5 1EH T 01462-442344
E info@englandnetball.co.uk
W www.england-netball.co.uk
Chief Executive, Pauline Harrison

NETBALL NORTHERN IRELAND, House of Sport, Upper Malone Road, Belfast BT9 5LA T 028-9038 1222
E netballni@houseofsportni.net
Secretary, Ms P. Dougherty

NETBALL SCOTLAND, Suite 196, 2nd Floor, Central Chambers, 93 Hope Street, Glasgow G2 6LD
T 0141-572 0114
E tellus@netballscotland.com
W www.netballscotland.com
Chief Executive, Moira Ord

WELSH NETBALL ASSOCIATION, 2nd Floor, 33–35 Cathedral Rd, Cardiff CF11 9HB
T 029-2023 7048
E welshnetball@welshnetball.com
W www.welshnetball.co.uk
Chief Executive Officer, Mrs S. J. Holvey

ORIENTEERING

BRITISH ORIENTEERING FEDERATION, Riversdale Dale Road North, Darley Dale, Matlock DE4 2HX
T 01629-734042 E bof@britishorienteering.org.uk
W www.britishorienteering.org.uk
Chief Executive, Robin Field

POLO

THE HURLINGHAM POLO ASSOCIATION, Manor Farm, Little Coxwell, Faringdon SN7 7LW T 01367-242828
E enquiries@hpa-polo.co.uk W www.hpa-polo.co.uk
Chief Executive, D. J. B. Woodd

RACKETS AND REAL TENNIS

TENNIS AND RACKETS ASSOCIATION, c/o The Queen's Club, Palliser Road, London W14 9EQ T 020-7386 3447/8
E james.wyatt@tennis-rackets.net W www.rackets.co.uk
Chief Executive and Secretary, James D. Wyatt

ROWING

AMATEUR ROWING ASSOCIATION, The Priory, 6 Lower Mall, London W6 9DJ T 0870-060 7100
E info@ara-rowing.org W www.ara-rowing.org
National Manager, Rosemary Napp

HENLEY ROYAL REGATTA, Regatta Headquarters, Henley-on-Thames RG9 2LY T 01491-572153 W www.hrr.co.uk
Secretary, R. S. Goddard

RUGBY FIVES

THE RUGBY FIVES ASSOCIATION, 32 Ashbourne Grove, East Dulwich, London SE22 8RL T 020-8693 0488
W www.rfa.org.uk
General Secretary, Ian Fuller

RUGBY LEAGUE

BRITISH AMATEUR RUGBY LEAGUE ASSOCIATION, West Yorkshire House, 4 New North Parade, Huddersfield HD1 5JP
T 01484-544131 E info@barla.org.uk W www.barla.org.uk
Chairman, Maurice Oldroyd

THE RUGBY FOOTBALL LEAGUE, Red Hall, Red Hall Lane, Leeds LS17 8NB T 0113-232 9111 E rfl@rfl.uk.com
W www.rfl.uk.com
Executive Chairman, Richard Lewis

RUGBY UNION

IRISH RUGBY FOOTBALL UNION, 62 Lansdowne Road, Ballsbridge, Dublin 4 T 00 353-1-647 3800
E info@irishrugby.ie W www.irishrugby.ie
Chief Executive, P. R. Browne

RUGBY FOOTBALL UNION, Rugby House, Rugby Road, Twickenham TW1 1DS T 020-8892 2000
E reception@rfu.com W www.rfu.com
Chief Executive, F. Baron

RUGBY FOOTBALL UNION FOR WOMEN, Rugby House, Rugby Road, Twickenham TW1 1DS T 020-8831 7996
E rfuw@therfu.com W www.rfu.com/rfuw.htm
Managing Director, Rosie Williams

SCOTTISH RUGBY UNION, Murrayfield, Roseburn Street, Edinburgh EH12 5PJ T 0131-346 5000
E feedback@sru.org.uk W www.scottishrugby.org
Chairman, Fred McLeod

SCOTTISH WOMEN'S RUGBY UNION, Scottish Rugby Union, Roseburn Terrace, Murrayfield, Edinburgh EH12 5PJ
T 0131-346 5163 E barbara.wilson@sru.org.uk
W www.scottishrugby.org
Chair, Sandra Kinnear

WELSH RUGBY UNION, 1st Floor, Golate House, 101 St Mary Street, Cardiff CF10 1GE T 0870-013 8600
E info@wru.co.uk W www.wru.co.uk
Group Chief Executive, David Moffett

SHOOTING

CLAY PIGEON SHOOTING ASSOCIATION, Edmonton House, Bisley Camp, Brookwood, Woking GU24 0NP
T 01483-485400 E info@cpsa.co.uk W www.cpsa.co.uk
Chief Executive, P. J. Boakes

GREAT BRITAIN TARGET SHOOTING FEDERATION,
Lord Roberts Centre, PO Box 122, Brookwood, Woking
GU24 0YW **T** 07775-640960 **E** pd@gbtsf-worldclass.co.uk
W www.gbtsf-worldclass.co.uk
Chairman, Lt-Col J. D. Hoare
NATIONAL RIFLE ASSOCIATION, Bisley Camp, Brookwood,
Woking GU24 0PB **T** 01483-797777 **E** info@nra.org.uk
W www.nra.org.uk
Chairman, John Jackman
NATIONAL SMALL-BORE RIFLE ASSOCIATION, Lord
Robert's Centre, Bisley Camp, Brookwood, Woking
GU24 0NP **T** 0845-130 6772 **E** info@nsra.co.uk
W www.nsra.co.uk
Secretary, Lt.-Col. J. D. Hoare

SKIING AND SNOWBOARDING

SNOWSPORT GB, Hillend, Biggar Road, Midlothian EH10 7EF
T 0131-445 7676 **E** info@snowsportgb.com
W www.snowsportgb.com
Chief Executive, J. Cockburn
SNOWSPORT SCOTLAND, Hillend, Biggar Road, Midlothian
EH10 7EF **T** 0131-445 4151 **E** info@snowsportscotland.org
W www.snowsportscotland.org
Chief Executive, Bruce Crawford

SPEEDWAY

SPEEDWAY CONTROL BOARD, ACU House, Wood Street,
Rugby CV21 2YX **T** 01788-565603
E office@scbureau.plus.com
Chairman, E. Bartlett

SQUASH RACKETS

ENGLAND SQUASH, National Squash Centre, Rowsley Street,
Manchester M11 3FF **T** 0161-438 4312
E enquires@englandsquash.com
W www.englandsquash.com
Chief Executive, Nick Rider
SCOTTISH SQUASH, Caledonia House, 1 Redheughs Rigg,
South Gyle, Edinburgh EH12 9DQ **T** 0131-317 7343
E info@scottishsquash.org **W** www.scottishsquash.org
Chief Operating Officer, Kim Atkinson
SQUASH WALES, St Mellons Country Club, St Mellons, Cardiff
CF3 2XR **T** 01633-682108
E squashwales@squashwales.co.uk
W www.squashwales.co.uk
Chairman, Phil Brailey

SUB-AQUA

BRITISH SUB-AQUA CLUB, Telford's Quay, South Pier Road,
Ellesmere Port CH65 4FL **T** 0151-350 6200
E postmaster@bsac.com **W** www.bsac.com
Chairman, P. Harrison

SWIMMING

AMATEUR SWIMMING ASSOCIATION, Harold Fern House,
Derby Square, Loughborough LE11 5AL **T** 01509-618700
E customerservices@swimming.org
W www.britishswimming.org
Chief Executive, D. Sparkes
SCOTTISH SWIMMING, National Swimming Academy,
University of Stirling, Stirling FK9 4LA **T** 01786-466520
E info@scottishswimming.com
W www.scottishswimming.com
Chief Executive, Ashley Howard
WELSH AMATEUR SWIMMING ASSOCIATION, Wales
National Pool, Sketty Lane, Swansea SA2 8QG
T 01792-513636 **E** julie.tyler@welshasa.co.uk
W www.welshasa.co.uk
Chief Executive, Robert James

TABLE TENNIS

ENGLISH TABLE TENNIS ASSOCIATION, Queensbury
House, Havelock Road, Hastings TN34 1HF **T** 01424-722525
E admin@englishtabletennis.org.uk
W www.englishtabletennis.org.uk
Chief Executive, R. Yule
SCOTTISH TABLE TENNIS ASSOCIATION, Caledonia
House, South Gyle, Edinburgh EH12 9DQ **T** 0131-317 8077
E ralph@tabletennisscotland.com
W www.tabletennisscotland.com
Chairman, Willie Wilson
TABLE TENNIS ASSOCIATION OF WALES, 8 Orchard Close,
Port Eynon, Swansea SA3 1NZ **T** 01792-391465
E ttaw@btinternet.com **W** www.ttaw.co.uk
Chairman, Phil Avery

VOLLEYBALL

ENGLISH VOLLEYBALL ASSOCIATION, Suite B,
Loughborough Technology Centre, Epinal Way,
Loughborough LE11 3GE **T** 01509-631699
E general@eng-volleyball.demon.co.uk
W www.volleyballengland.org
Hon. President, Don Anthony
NORTHERN IRELAND VOLLEYBALL
ASSOCIATION, House of Sport, Upper Malone Road,
Belfast BT9 5LA **T** 07966-056137 **E** nick@nivb.co.uk
W www.nivb.co.uk
General Secretary, Nick Wright
SCOTTISH VOLLEYBALL ASSOCIATION, 48 The Pleasance,
Edinburgh EH8 9TJ **T** 0131-556 4633
E info@scottishvolleyball.org **W** www.scottishvolleyball.org
Chief Executive, Kenny Barton

WALKING

RACE WALKING ASSOCIATION, Hufflers, Heard's Lane,
Shenfield, Brentwood CM15 0SF **T** 01277-220687
E racewalkingassociation@btinternet.com
W www.racewalkingassociation.btinternet.co.uk
Hon. General Secretary, P. J. Cassidy

WATER SKIING

BRITISH WATER SKI FEDERATION, The Tower, Thorpe
Road, Chertsey KT16 8PH **T** 01932-570885
E info@bwsf.co.uk **W** www.britishwaterski.org.uk
Executive Officer, Gavin Kelly

WEIGHTLIFTING

BRITISH WEIGHTLIFTERS ASSOCIATION (BWLA), Lillehall
National Sports Centre, Newport TF10 9AT **T** 01952-604201
E lorraine.fleming@uklifting.demon.co.uk
W www.bawla.com
Chief Executive, Steve Cannon

WRESTLING

BRITISH WRESTLING ASSOCIATION, 12 Westwood Lane,
Brimington, Chesterfield S43 1PA **T** 01246-236443
E admin@britishwrestling.org **W** www.britishwrestling.org
Chairman, M. Morley

YACHTING

ROYAL YACHTING ASSOCIATION, RYA House, Ensign Way,
Hamble, Southampton SO31 4YA **T** 0845-3450400
E info@rya.org.uk **W** www.rya.org.uk
Chief Executive, Rod Carr

CLUBS

LONDON CLUBS

ALPINE CLUB (1857) 55–56 Charlotte Road, London
EC2A 3QF T 020-7613 0755 E admin@alpine-club.org.uk
W www.alpine-club.org.uk
Hon. Secretary, R. M. Scott

AMERICAN WOMEN'S CLUB (1899) 68 Old Brompton
Road, London SW7 3LQ T 020-7589 8292
E awc@awclondon.org W www.awclondon.org
President, G. Goings (Women only)

ANGLO-BELGIAN CLUB (1955) 60 Knightsbridge, London
SW1X 7LF T 020-7235 2121 E secretary@ra-bc.com
Chairman, Alistair Voaden, FRICS

ARMY AND NAVY CLUB (1837) 36 Pall Mall, London
SW1Y 5JN T 020-7930 9721 E secretary@therag.co.uk
W www.armynavyclub.co.uk
Chief Executive and Secretary, Cdr. J. A. Holt, MBE, RN

ARTS CLUB (1863) 40 Dover Street, London W1S 4NP
T 020-7499 8581 E secretary@artclub.fsnet.co.uk
W www.theartsclub.co.uk
Secretary, Tony Derrett

ATHENAEUM (1824) 107 Pall Mall, London SW1Y 5ER
T 020-7930 4843 E library@hellenist.org.uk
Secretary, J. H. Ford

AUTHORS' CLUB (1892) 40 Dover Street, London W1S 4NP
T 020-7408 5092
Club Secretary, Miss Lucy Tetlow

BEEFSTEAK CLUB (1876) 9 Irving Street, London
WC2H 7AH T 020-7930 5722 E beefsteakclub@tiscali.co.uk
Secretary, Sir John Lucas-Tooth, BT (Men only)

BOODLE'S (1762) 28 St James's Street, London SW1A 1HJ
T 020-7930 7166
Secretary, Andrew Phillips secretary@boodles.org

BROOKS'S (1764) St James's Street, London SW1A 1LN
T 020-7493 4411 E secretary@brooksclub.org
Secretary, G. Snell (Men only)

BUCK'S CLUB (1919) 18 Clifford Street, London W1S 3RF
T 020-7734 2337 E secretary@bucksclub.co.uk
Secretary, Mrs G. Thomson (Men only)

CALEDONIAN CLUB (1891) 9 Halkin Street, London
SW1X 7DR T 020-7235 5162 E admin@caledonianclub.com
W www.caledonianclub.com
Secretary, P. J. Varney

CANNING CLUB (1910) 4 St James's Square, London
SW1Y 4JU T 020-7827 5757
E canningclub@compuserve.com
Secretary, T. M. Harrington

CARLTON CLUB (1832) 69 St James's Street, London
SW1A 1PJ T 020-7493 1164
E secretary@carltonclub.co.uk
W www.carltonclub.co.uk
Secretary, A. E. Telfer

CAVALRY AND GUARDS CLUB (1893) 127 Piccadilly,
London W1J 7PX T 020-7499 1261
E secretary@cavgds.co.uk W www.cavgds.co.uk
Secretary (acting), P. Vigors, FCA

CHELSEA ARTS CLUB (1891) 143 Old Church Street,
London SW3 6EB T 020-7376 3311
E secretary@chelseaartsclub.com W chelseaartsclub.com
Secretary, D. Winterbottom

CITY LIVERY CLUB (1914) 38 St. Mary Axe, London
EC3A 8EX T 020-7369 1672 E postbox@cityliveryclub.com
W www.cityliveryclub.com
Hon. Secretary, P. Herbage

CITY OF LONDON CLUB (1832) 19 Old Broad Street,
London EC2N 1DS T 020-7588 7991
E secretary@cityoflondonclub.com W www.cityclub.uk.com
Club Secretary, Ian Faul (Men only)

CITY UNIVERSITY CLUB (1895) 50 Cornhill, London
EC3V 3PD T 020-7626 8571
E secretary@cityuniversityclub.co.uk
W www.cityuniversityclub.co.uk
Secretary, Miss R. C. Graham

DEN NORSKE KLUB LTD (1887), In & Out, 4 St James's
Square, London SW1Y 4JU T 020-7839 6242
W www.dennorskeklub.co.uk
Secretary, Bjorg Tangen

EAST INDIA CLUB (1849) 16 St James's Square, London
SW1A 2EL T 020-7930 3577 E secretary@eastindiaclub.com
Secretary, M. Howell (Men only)

FARMERS CLUB (1842) 3 Whitehall Court, London
SW1A 2EL T 020-7930 3751 W www.thefarmersclub.com
Secretary, Gp Capt. G. P. Carson

FLYFISHERS' CLUB (1884) 69 Brook Street, London
W1K 4ER T 020-7629 5958
Secretary, Cdr. T. H. Boycott, OBE, RN (Men only)

GARRICK CLUB (1831) 15 Garrick Street, London
WC2E 9AY T 020-7379 6478 W www.garrickclub.co.uk
Secretary, M. J. Harvey (Men only)

GROUCHO CLUB (1985) 45 Dean Street, London W1V 5AP
T 020-7439 4685
Chief Executive, Joel Cadbury

HURLINGHAM CLUB (1869) Ranelagh Gardens, London
SW6 3PR T 020-736 8411
E membership@hurlinghamclub.org.uk
Chief Executive, Paul H. Covell

KENNEL CLUB (1873) 1–5 Clarges Street, London W1J 8AB
T 0870-606 6750 E info@the-kennel-club.org.uk
W www.the-kennel-club.org.uk
Chief Executive, Rosemary Smart

LANSDOWNE CLUB (1934) 9 Fitzmaurice Place, London
W1J 5JD T 020-7629 7200 E info@lansdowneclub.com
W www.lansdowneclub.com
Chief Executive and Secretary, Mark Anderson

LONDON ROWING CLUB (1856) Embankment, Putney,
London SW15 1LB T 020-8788 1400
E londonrc@lineone.net W www.londonrc.org.uk
Hon. Secretary, J. R. R. Ebsworth

MCC (MARYLEBONE CRICKET CLUB) (1787), Lord's
Cricket Ground, London NW8 8QN T 020-7289 1611
W www.lords.org
Secretary & Chief Executive, R. D. V. Knight

NATIONAL CLUB (1845), c/o Carlton Club, 69 St James's
Street, London SW1A 1PJ T 020-8579 0874
E ivorsowton@tiscali.co.uk
Hon. Secretary (acting), I. A. Sowton (Men only)

NATIONAL LIBERAL CLUB (1882) Whitehall Place, London
SW1A 2HE T 020-7930 9871 E secretary@nlc.org.uk
W www.nlc.org.uk
Secretary, S. J. Roberts

NAVAL AND MILITARY CLUB (1862) 4 St James's Square,
London SW1Y 4JU T 020-7827 5757
E club@navalandmilitaryclub.co.uk
W www.navalandmilitaryclub.co.uk
Club Secretary, John Andrew, MBE
NAVAL CLUB (1946) 38 Hill Street, London W1J 5NS
T 020-7493 7672 E reservations@navalclub.co.uk
W www.navalclub.co.uk
Chief Executive, Cdr J. L. L. Prichard
NEW CAVENDISH CLUB (1920) 44 Great Cumberland
Place, London W1H 7BS T 020-7723 0391
E jeanpaulncc@aol.com
W www.newcavendishclub.co.uk
General Manager, J. P. Dauvergne
ORIENTAL CLUB (1824), Stratford House, Stratford Place,
London W1C 1ES T 020-7629 5126
E sec@orientalclub.org.uk
Secretary, S. C. Doble
OXFORD AND CAMBRIDGE CLUB (1972) 71 Pall Mall,
London SW1Y 5HD T 020-7930 5151
E club@oandc.uk.com
W www.oxfordandcambridgeclub.co.uk
Secretary, G. R. Buchanan
PORTLAND CLUB (1816) 69 Brook Street, London W1Y 4ER
T 020-7499 1523
Secretary, J. Burns, CBE
PRATT'S CLUB (1841) 14 Park Place, London SW1A 1LP
T 020-7493 0397 E secretary@prattsclub.org
Secretary, Graham Snell (Men only)
QUEEN'S CLUB (1886) Palliser Road, London W14 9EQ
T 020-7385 3421 E admin@queensclub.co.uk
W www.queensclub.co.uk
Chief Executive, P. D. Elviss
REFORM CLUB (1836) 104–105 Pall Mall, London
SW1Y 5EW T 020-7930 9374
E generaloffice@reformclub.com
W www.reformclub.com
Secretary, M. D. B. McKerchan
ROEHAMPTON CLUB (1901) Roehampton Lane, London
SW15 5LR T 020-8480 4205
E admin@roehamptonclub.co.uk
W www.roehamptonclub.co.uk
Chief Executive, Mark Wilson
ROYAL AIR FORCE CLUB (1918) 128 Piccadilly,
London W1J 7PY T 020-7399 1000
E admin@rafclub.org.uk W www.rafclub.org.uk
Secretary, P. N. Owen
ROYAL AUTOMOBILE CLUB (1897), Pall Mall Clubhouse,
89 Pall Mall, London SW1Y 5HS T 020-7930 2345
E secretary@royalautomobileclub.co.uk
W www.royalautomobileclub.co.uk
Secretary, A. I. G. Kennedy
ROYAL OCEAN RACING CLUB (1925) 20 St James's Place,
London SW1A 1NN T 020-7493 2248 E info@rorc.org
W www.rorc.org
General Manager, P. C. Wykeham-Martin
ROYAL OVER-SEAS LEAGUE (1910), Over-Seas House,
Park Place, St James's Street, London SW1A 1LR
T 020-7408 0214 E info@rosl.org.uk W www.rosl.org.uk
Director-General, R. F. Newell, LVO
SAVAGE CLUB (1857) 1 Whitehall Place, London SW1A 2HD
T 020-7930 8118 E info@savageclub.com
W www.savageclub.com
Hon. Secretary, The Ven. B. H. Lucas, CB (Men only)
SAVILE CLUB (1868) 69 Brook Street, London W1K 4ER
T 020-7629 5462 E secretariat@savileclub.co.uk
W www.savileclub.co.uk
Secretary, Julian Malone-Lee (Men only)

SKI CLUB OF GREAT BRITAIN (1903), The White House,
57–63 Church Road, Wimbledon SW19 5DQ
T 020-8410 2000 E skiers@skiclub.co.uk
W www.skiclub.co.uk
Managing Director, Caroline Stuart-Taylor
ST STEPHEN'S CLUB (1870) 34 Queen Anne's Gate, London
SW1H 9AB T 020-7222 1382 E info@ststephensclub.co.uk
W www.ststephensclub.co.uk
Chief Executive, James M. Wilson
THAMES ROWING CLUB (1860) Putney Embankment,
London SW15 1LB T 020-8788 0798
E secretary@thamesrc.co.uk W www.thamesrc.demon.co.uk
Hon. Secretary, Rachael Dickie
TRAVELLERS CLUB (1819) 106 Pall Mall, London SW1Y 5EP
T 020-7930 8688 E secretary@thetravellersclub.org.uk
W www.csma.org.uk
Secretary, M. S. Allcock (Men only)
TURF CLUB (1868) 5 Carlton House Terrace, London
SW1Y 5AQ T 020-7930 8555 E mail@turfclub.co.uk
Secretary, Lt.-Col. O. R. StJ. Breakwell, MBE
UNIVERSITY WOMEN'S CLUB (1886) 2 Audley Square,
London W1K 1DB T 020-7499 2268
E uwc@uwc-london.com
W www.universitywomensclub.com
Acting Club Secretary, Ms S. McCrue (Women only)
VICTORY SERVICES CLUB (1907) 63–79 Seymour Street,
London W2 2HF T 020-7723 4474 E res@vsc.co.uk
W www.vsc.co.uk
Chief Executive, Brig. R. N. Lennox, CBE
WHITE'S (1693) 37–38 St James's Street, London SW1A 1JG
T 020-7493 6671
Secretary, D. A. Anderson (Men only)

CLUBS OUTSIDE LONDON AND YACHT CLUBS

ATHENAEUM (1797) Church Alley, Liverpool L1 3DD
T 0151-709 7770 E info@theathenaeum.org.uk
W www.theathenaeum.org.uk
Honorary Secretary, H. Thompson
BATH AND COUNTY CLUB (1858) Queen's Parade, Bath
BA1 2NJ T 01225-423732
E secretary@bathandcountyclub.com
W www.bathandcountyclub.com
President, Sir Alec Morris, KBE, CB
BEMBRIDGE SAILING CLUB (1886) Embankment Road,
Bembridge PO35 5NRN T 01983-872237
E sec@bembridgesailingclub.org
W www.bembridgesailingclub.org
Secretary, Lt.-Col. M. J. Samuelson, RM
BRISTOL CORINTHIAN YACHT CLUB, Cheddar Road,
Axminster BS26 2DL T 01934-843401
W www.bcyc.org.uk
Hon. Secretary, A. Sherlock
CARDIFF AND COUNTY CLUB (1866) Westgate Street,
Cardiff CF10 1DA T 029-2022 0846 E mail@countyclub.org
W www.countyclub.org
Hon. Secretary, Cdr J. E. Payn, RD (Men only)
CHICHESTER YACHT CLUB (1967) Chichester Marina,
Birdham, Chichester PO20 7EJ T 01243-512918
E secretary@cyc.co.uk W www.cyc.co.uk
Secretary, I. M. Clarke
CLIFTON CLUB (1882) 22 The Mall, Clifton, Bristol BS8 4DS
T 0117-974 5039 E thesecretary@thecliftonclub.co.uk
Secretary, R. B. Annesley (Men only)
CONISTON SAILING CLUB (1967), Coniston Old Hall,
Haws Bank, Coniston LA21 8AS T 01539-441580
W www.conistonsailingclub.co.uk
Hon. Secretary, Judy Leese

COUNTY CLUB, 158 High Street, Guildford GU1 3HJ
T 01483-575370 E office@thecountyclub.co.uk
W www.countyclubguildford.co.uk
Hon. Secretary, R. H. Middlehurst

CRUISING ASSOCIATION (1908), CA House, 1 Northey
Street, Limehouse Basin, London E14 8BT T 020-7537 2828
E office@cruising.org.uk W www.cruising.org.uk
Chairman, Robin Guilleret

DISTRICT AND UNION CLUB (1849), Northwood,
1 West Park Road, Blackburn BB2 6DE T 01254-51474
Hon. Secretary, A. Breckell (Men only)

DURHAM COUNTY CLUB (1890) 52 Old Elvet, Durham
DH1 3HJ T 0191-384 8156
Secretary, S. Smith

FREWEN CLUB (1869) 98 St Aldate's, Oxford OX1 1BT
T 01865-243816
Hon. Secretary, M. J. Dean (Men only)

GRAVESEND SAILING CLUB (1884) Promenade East,
Gravesend DA12 2RN T 01474-533974
E secretary@gravesendsc.org.uk
W www.gravesendsc.org.uk
Hon. Secretary, Ms. K. Lilley

ISLE OF MAN YACHT CLUB (1910) Lime Street, Port St.
Mary IM9 5ED T 01624-832088 E mail@iomyc.com
W www.iomyc.com
Hon. Secretary, David Fraser

JOCKEY CLUB (1752) 101 High Street, Newmarket CB8 8JL
T 01638 664151 E enquires@jockey-club-estates.co.uk
W www.jockey-club-estates.co.uk
Chairman, George Paul

KINGSWAY CLUB (1868), Lightfoot Institute, Kingsway,
Bishop Auckland DL14 7JN T 01388-603219
President, P. E. Cooke (Men only)

LEAMINGTON TENNIS COURT CLUB (1846) 50 Bedford
Street, Leamington Spa CV32 5DT T 01926-424977
Chairman, O. D. R. Dixon

LEANDER CLUB (1818) Henley-on-Thames RG9 2LP
T 01491-575782 E info@leander.co.uk
W www.leander.co.uk
Hon. Secretary, D. C. F. Latham

LEEDS CLUB (1849) 3 Albion Place, Leeds LS1 6JL
T 0113-242 1591 E info@leedsclub.org.uk
W www.leedsclub.org.uk
General Manager, Jonathon M. Blackburn

LIVERPOOL SAILING CLUB (1958), Liverpool Northern
Airfield, Liverpool T 01695-732333
E lscsecretary@hotmail.com
W www.liverpoolsailingclub.org
Hon. Secretary, Phil Gambrill

NEW CLUB (1874) 2 Atherstone Lawn, Montpellier Parade,
Cheltenham GL50 1UD T 01242-541121
E secretary@newclub.org.uk W www.newclub.org.uk
Secretary, Ian Dunbar

NORFOLK CLUB (1770) 17 Upper King Street, Norwich
NR3 1RB T 01603-626767 E thenorfolkclub@btconnect.com
Secretary, G. G. Hardaker

NORTH BAILEY CLUB (1842) 24 North Bailey, Durham
DH1 3EW T 0191-384 3724 E Union.Society@durham.ac.uk
W www.dus.org.uk
Permanent Secretary, Mrs M. C. Cleaver

NORTHERN CONSTITUTIONAL CLUB (1882) 37 Pilgrim
Street, Newcastle upon Tyne NE1 6QE T 0191-232 0884
Hon. Secretary, D. Blake

NOTTINGHAM CLUB (1920), Newdigate House, Castle
Gate, Nottingham NG1 6AF T 0115-912 6220
E secretary@nottinghamclub.com
W www.nottinghamclub.com
Chairman, A. Trease

OLD BOYS' AND PARK GREEN CLUB (1771) 7 Churchside,
Macclesfield SK10 1HG T 01625-423292
Hon. Secretary, G. S. Heatherington (Men only)

PAIGNTON CLUB (1882) The Esplanade, Paignton TQ4 6ED
T 01803-559682 E psa3grafton@blueyonder.co.uk
Hon. Secretary, P. Grafton

PARKSTONE YACHT CLUB (1895) Pearce Avenue, Poole
BH14 8EH T 01202-738824 E office@parkstoneyc.co.uk
W www.parkstoneyc.co.uk
General Manager, M. Simms

PENARTH YACHT CLUB (1880) The Esplanade, Penarth
CF64 3AU T 029-2070 8196 W www.penarthyachtclub.com
Hon. Secretary, R. S. McGregor

PHYLLIS COURT CLUB (1906) Marlow Road,
Henley-on-Thames RG9 2HT T 01491-570500
E enquiries@phylliscourt.co.uk W www.phylliscourt.co.uk
General Manager, L. Petas

POOLE HARBOUR YACHT CLUB (1949) 40 Salterns Way,
Lilliput, Poole BH14 8JR T 01202-709971
E marina@salterns.co.uk W www.salterns.co.uk
Managing Director, J. N. J. Smith

POOLE YACHT CLUB (1865) New Harbour Road West,
Hamworthy, Poole BH15 4AQ T 01202-672687
E secretary@pooleyc.co.uk W www.pooleyc.co.uk
Hon. Treasurer, R. Cooper

ROYAL AIR FORCE YACHT CLUB (1932), Riverside
House, Rope Walk, Hamble, Southampton SO31 4HD
T 023-8045 2208 E office@rafyc.co.uk W www.rafyc.co.uk
Hon. Secretary, A. Rose

ROYAL ANGLESEY YACHT CLUB (1802) 6–7 Green Edge,
Beaumaris LL58 8BY T 01248-810295
E info@royalangleseyyc.org.uk
W www.royalangleseyyc.org.uk
Hon. Secretary, K. Dobinson

ROYAL CHANNEL ISLANDS YACHT CLUB (1862), Le
Mont du Boulevard, St Brelade, Jersey JE3 8AD
T 01534-745783 E rciyc@localdial.com
W www.rciyc.org
Hon. Secretary, B. Murray

ROYAL CINQUE PORTS YACHT CLUB (1872) 5 Waterloo
Crescent, Dover CT16 1LA T 01304-206262
Hon. Secretary, Mrs L. Grant

ROYAL CORINTHIAN YACHT CLUB (1872) The Quay,
Burnham-on-Crouch CM0 8AX T 01621-782105
E info@royalcorinthian.co.uk W www.royalcorinthian.co.uk
Hon. Secretary, Sarah Sullivan

ROYAL DART YACHT CLUB (1866), Priory Street,
Kingswear TQ6 0AB T 01803-752496
E office@royaldart.uk W www.royaldart.co.uk
Hon. Secretary, Mrs V. Fairhurst

ROYAL DORSET YACHT CLUB (1875) 11 Custom House
Quay, Weymouth DT4 8BG T 01305-786258
E rdyc@weymouthharbour.fsnet.co.uk
W www.rdyc.freeuk.com
Secretary, Mrs M. Tye

ROYAL FOWEY YACHT CLUB (1881), Whitford Yard,
Fowey PL23 1BH T 01726-833573
E honsec@rfyc-fowey.org.uk
W www.rfyc.fowey.org.uk
Commodore, A. G. Williams

ROYAL HARWICH YACHT CLUB (1843) Woolverstone,
Ipswich IP9 1AT T 01473-780319
E secretary@rhyc.demon.co.uk W www.rhyc.demon.co.uk
Hon. Secretary, Colin Burrows

ROYAL LYMINGTON YACHT CLUB (1922) Bath Road,
Lymington SO41 3SE T 01590-672677 E sail@rlymyc.org.uk
W www.rlymyc.org.uk
Secretary, I. Gawn

ROYAL MERSEY YACHT CLUB (1844) Bedford Road East, Rock Ferry, Birkenhead CH42 1LS **T** 0151-645 3204 **W** www.royalmersey.co.uk
Hon. Secretary, P. A. Bastow

ROYAL NAVAL CLUB AND ROYAL ALBERT YACHT CLUB (1867) 17 Pembroke Road, Portsmouth PO1 2NT **T** 023-9282 5924 **E** secretary@rnc-raye.co.uk **W** www.mc-rayc.co.uk
Secretary, Cdr. P. Bolas, RN

ROYAL NORFOLK AND SUFFOLK YACHT CLUB (1859) Royal Plain, Lowestoft NR33 0AQ **T** 01502-566726 **E** rnsyc@ctc-net.co.uk **W** www.rnsyc.co.uk
Commodore, C. N. Faulkner

ROYAL PLYMOUTH CORINTHIAN YACHT CLUB (1877) Madeira Road, Plymouth PL1 2NY **T** 01752-664327 **E** admin@rpcyc.com **W** www.rpcyc.com
Hon. Secretary, A. L. Cooper

ROYAL SOLENT YACHT CLUB (1878), The Square, Yarmouth PO41 0NS **T** 01983-760256 **E** royal_solentyc@compuserve.com **W** www.royalsolentyc.org.uk
Secretary, Mrs J. White

ROYAL SOUTHAMPTON YACHT CLUB (1875) 1 Channel Way, Ocean Village, Southampton SO14 3QF **T** 023-8022 3352 **E** rsyc@rsyc.org.uk **W** www.rsyc.org.uk
Secretary, A. M. Paterson

ROYAL SOUTHERN YACHT CLUB (1837) Rope Walk, Hamble, Southampton SO31 4HB **T** 023-8045 0300 **E** sailing@royal-southern.co.uk **W** www.royal-southern.co.uk
Secretary, G. H. Robinson

ROYAL TEMPLE YACHT CLUB (1857) 6 Westcliff Mansions, Ramsgate CT11 9HY **T** 01843-591766 **E** info@rtyc.com **W** www.rtyc.com
Hon. Secretary, Mrs J. Beale

ROYAL THAMES YACHT CLUB (1775) 60 Knightsbridge, London SW1X 7LF **T** 020-7235 2121 **E** club@royalthames.com **W** www.royalthames.com
Secretary, Capt. D. A. K. Freeman, RN

ROYAL TORBAY YACHT CLUB (1863) 12 Beacon Terrace, Torquay TQ1 2BH **T** 01803-292006 **E** admin@royaltorbayyc.org.uk **W** www.royaltorbayyc.org.uk
Secretary, R. M. Porteous

ROYAL WELSH YACHT CLUB (1847) Porth-Yr-Aur, Caernarfon LL55 1SN **T** 01286-672599 **W** www.rwyc.net
Hon. Secretary, Dylan I. R. Kalis

ROYAL WESTERN YACHT CLUB OF ENGLAND (1827), Queen Anne's Battery, Plymouth PL4 0TW **T** 01752-660077 **E** admin@rwyc.org **W** www.rwyc.org
Club Secretary, Robert Gateshill

ROYAL WINDERMERE YACHT CLUB (1860) Fallbarrow Road, Bowness-on-Windermere, Windermere LA23 3DJ **T** 01539-443106 **E** contact@rwyc.co.uk
Hon. Secretary, Mrs M. A. Kirk

ROYAL YACHT SQUADRON (1815), The Castle, Cowes PO31 7QT **T** 01983-292191 **E** mail@royalyachtsquadron.org **W** www.rys.org.uk
Secretary, Mrs P. Lewington

ROYAL YORKSHIRE YACHT CLUB (1847) 1 Windsor Crescent, Bridlington YO15 3HX **T** 01262-672041 **E** sec@ryyc.org.uk **W** www.ryyc.org.uk
Secretary, Kate Mercer

SCOTTISH ARTS CLUB (1872) 24 Rutland Square, Edinburgh EH1 2BW **T** 0131-229 8157 **E** info@scottishartsclub.co.uk **W** www.scottishartsclub.o.uk

STOURBRIDGE OLD EDWARDIAN CLUB (1898) Drury Lane, Stourbridge DY8 1BL **T** 01384-395635
Hon. Secretary, C. M. Bowen-Davies (Men only)

THAMES ESTUARY YACHT CLUB (1895) 3 The Leas, Westcliff-on-Sea SS0 7ST **T** 01702-345967 **E** pbowden@operamail.com **W** homepages.rya-online.net/teyc/
Hon. Secretary, L. S. Skinner

ULSTER REFORM CLUB (1885) 4 Royal Avenue, Belfast BT1 1DA **T** 028-9032 3411 **E** info@ulsterreformclub.com **W** www.ulsterreformclub.com
General Manager, A. W. Graham

UNITED CLUB (1870) Pier Steps, St Peter Port, Guernsey GY1 2LF **T** 01481-725722
President, R. H. Marquis (Men only)

VICTORIA CLUB (1853) Beresford Street, St Helier, Jersey JE2 4WN **T** 01534-723381 **E** victoriaclub@jerseymail.co.uk
Hon. Secretary, Alan Blair

SOCIETIES AND INSTITUTIONS

ABBEYFIELD SOCIETY (1956), Abbeyfield House, 53
Victoria Street, St Albans AL1 3UW **T** 01727-857536
E post@abbeyfield.com **W** www.abbeyfield.com
Chief Executive, B. House

ACE STUDY TOURS (1958), Babraham, Cambridge
CB2 4AP **T** 01223-835055 **E** ace@study-tours.org
W www.study-tours.org
General Secretary, Paul Barnes

ACTION FOR BLIND PEOPLE (1857), 14–16 Verney
Road, London SE16 3DZ **T** 020-7635 4800 **E** info@afbp.org
W www.afbp.org
Chief Executive, Stephen Remington

ACTION MEDICAL RESEARCH (1952), Vincent House,
Horsham RH12 2DP **T** 01403-210406 **E** info@action.org.uk
W www.action.org.uk
Chief Executive, Simon Moore

ACTORS' BENEVOLENT FUND (1882), 6 Adam Street,
London WC2N 6AD **T** 020-7836 6378 **E** office@abf.org.uk
W www.actorsbenevolentfund.co.uk
General Secretary, Willie Bicket

ACTORS' CHARITABLE TRUST (1896), 255–256 Africa
House, 64–78 Kingsway, London WC2B 6BD
T 020-7242 0111 **E** robert@tactactors.org
W www.tactactors.org
General Secretary, Robert Ashby

ADAM SMITH INSTITUTE (1977), 23 Great Smith Street,
London SW1P 3BL **T** 020-7222 4995 **E** info@adamsmith.org
W www.adamsmith.org
President, Dr M. Pirie

ADVERTISING STANDARDS AUTHORITY (1962),
Mid City Place, 71 High Holborn, London WC1V 6QT
T 020-7492 2222 **E** enquiries@asa.org.uk
W www.asa.org.uk
Director-General, Christopher Graham

AGE CONCERN (1940), Astral House, 1268 London Road,
London SW16 4ER **T** 020-8765 7200
W www.ageconcern.org.uk
Director-General, Gordon Lishman, OBE

AGE CONCERN CYMRU, 4th Floor, 1 Cathedral Road,
Cardiff CF11 9SD **T** 029-2043 1555
E enquiries@accymru.org.uk **W** www.accymru.org.uk
Director, R. W. Taylor

AGRICULTURAL ENGINEERS ASSOCIATION (1875),
Samuelson House, Paxton Road, Orton Centre,
Peterborough PE2 5LT **T** 01733-362925 **E** dg@aea.uk.com
W www.aea.uk.com
Director-General, Jake Vowles

ALCOHOLICS ANONYMOUS (1947), PO Box 1,
Stonebow House, Stonebow, York YO1 7NJ
T 01904-644026 **W** www.alcoholics-anonymous.org.uk
General Secretary, Ann Napier

ALEXANDRA ROSE DAY (1912), 5 Mead Lane, Farnham,
Surrey GU9 7DY **T** 0870-770 0275
E enquiries@alexandraroseday.org.uk
W www.alexandraroseday.org.uk
Operations Director, Garry Shelford

ALZHEIMER'S SOCIETY (1979), Gordon House, 10
Greencoat Place, London SW1P 1PH
T 020-7306 0606. Helpline 0845-300 0336
E info@alzheimers.org.uk **W** www.alzheimers.org.uk
Chief Executive, N. Hunt

AMNESTY INTERNATIONAL UNITED KINGDOM
(1961), The Human Rights Action Centre, 17–25 New Inn
Yard, London EC2A 3EA **T** 020-7033 1500
E information@amnesty.org.uk **W** www.amnesty.org.uk
UK Director, Kate Allen

AMREF UK (1961), Kensington Charity Centre, 4th Floor,
Charles House, 375 Kensington High Street, London
W14 8QH **T** 020-7471 6755 **E** amref.uk@amrefuk.org
W www.amref.org
Director, A. Heroys

ANCIENT MONUMENTS SOCIETY (1924), St Ann's
Vestry Hall, 2 Church Entry, London EC4V 5HB
T 020-7236 3934
E office@ancientmonumentssociety.org.uk
W www.ancientmonumentssociety.org.uk
Secretary, M. J. Saunders, MBE

ANGLO-BELGIAN SOCIETY (1982), 5 Hartley Close,
Bickley BR1 2TP **T** 020-8467 8442
Hon. Secretary, P. R. Bresnan

ANGLO-DANISH SOCIETY (1924), 6 Keats Avenue,
Littleover, Derby DE23 4ED **T** 01332-517160
E info@anglo-danishsociety.org.uk
W www.anglo-danishsociety.org.uk
Chair, Simon Freeman

ANGLO-NORSE SOCIETY (1918), 25 Belgrave Square,
London SW1X 8QD **T** 020-7235 9529
E igarland115@compuserve.com **E** anglonorse@yahoo.co.uk
W www.norway.org.uk
Chair, Sir Richard Dales, KCMG

ANIMAL CONCERN (1876), PO Box 5178, Dumbarton
G82 5YJ **T** 01389-841639 **E** animals@jfrobins.force9.co.uk
W www.animalconcern.com

ANIMAL HEALTH TRUST (1942), Lanwades Park,
Kentford, Newmarket CB8 7UU **T** 08700-502424
E info@aht.org.uk **W** www.aht.org.uk
Executive Chair, E. A. Chandler

ANTHROPOSOPHICAL SOCIETY IN GREAT
BRITAIN (1923), Rudolf Steiner House, 35 Park Road,
London NW1 6XT **T** 020-7723 4400
E rsh-office@anth.org.uk **W** www.anth.org.uk/rsh
General Secretary, N. C. Thomas

ANTI-SLAVERY INTERNATIONAL (1839), Thomas
Clarkson House, The Stableyard, Broomgrove Road, London
SW9 9TL **T** 020-7501 8920 **E** antislavery@antislavery.org
W www.antislavery.org
Director, M. Cunneen

ARCHITECTS BENEVOLENT SOCIETY (1850),
43 Portland Place, London W1B 1QH **T** 020-7580 2823
E help@absnet.org.uk **W** www.absnet.org.uk
Company Secretary, Keith Robinson

ARLIS/UK AND IRELAND (1969), The Courtauld
Institute of Art, Somerset House, The Strand, London
WC2R 0RN **T** 020-7848 2703 **E** arlis@courtauld.ac.uk
W www.arlis.org.uk
Chair, Sue Price

ARTHRITIS CARE (1949), 18 Stephenson Way, London
NW1 2HD **T** 020-7380 6500 **W** www.arthritiscare.org.uk
Chief Executive, Neil Betteridge

ASSOCIATION FOR LANGUAGE LEARNING (1990),
150 Railway Terrace, Rugby CV21 3HN **T** 01788-546443
E langlearn@all-languages.org.uk
W www.all-languages.co.uk
President, B. Jones

ASSOCIATION OF ACCOUNTING TECHNICIANS
(1980), 154 Clerkenwell Road, London EC1R 5AD
T 020-7837 8600 **E** aat@aat.org.uk **W** www.aat.org.uk
Chief Executive, Jane Scott Paul

ASSOCIATION OF ANAESTHETISTS OF GREAT
BRITAIN AND IRELAND (1932), 21 Portland Place,
London W1B 1PY **T** 020-7631 1650 **E** info@aagbi.org
W www.aagbi.org
President, Prof. Mike Harmer

ASSOCIATION OF BRITISH DISPENSING
OPTICIANS (1925), 199 Gloucester Terrace, London
W2 6LD **T** 020-7298 5100 **E** general@abdo.org.uk
W www.abdo.org.uk
General Secretary, Sir Anthony Garrett, CBE

ASSOCIATION OF BRITISH INSURERS (1985),
51 Gresham Street, London EC2V 7HQ
T 020-7600 3333 **E** info@abi.org.uk
W www.abi.org.uk
Director-General, Stephen Haddrill

ASSOCIATION OF BUILDING ENGINEERS (1925),
Lutyens House, Billing Brook Road, Weston Favell,
Northampton NN3 8NW **T** 01604-404121
E building.engineers@abe.org.uk **W** www.abe.org.uk
Chief Executive, D. Gibson

ASSOCIATION OF BUSINESS RECOVERY
PROFESSIONALS (1990), 8th Floor, 120 Aldersgate
Street, London EC1A 4JQ **T** 020-7566 4200
E association@r3.org.uk **W** www.r3.org.uk
Chief Operating Officer, Graham Rumney

ASSOCIATION OF CONSULTING ENGINEERS,
Alliance House, 12 Caxton Street, London SW1H 0QL
T 020-7222 6557 **E** consult@acenet.co.uk
W www.acenet.co.uk
Chief Executive, Nelson Ogunshakin

ASSOCIATION OF CONSULTING SCIENTISTS
(1958), PO Box 4040, Thorpe-le-Soken, Clacton-on-Sea
CO16 0EL **T** 01206-571261
E secretary@consultingscientists.co.uk
W www.consultingscientists.co.uk
Secretary, Dr Diana Simpson

ASSOCIATION OF CONVENIENCE STORES LTD
(1995), Federation House, 17 Farnborough Street,
Farnborough GU14 8AG **T** 01252-515001 **E** acs@acs.org.uk
W www.thelocalshop.com
Chief Executive, David Rae

ASSOCIATION OF CORPORATE TREASURERS
(1979), Ocean House, 10–12 Little Trinity Lane, London
EC4V 2DJ **T** 020-7213 9728 **E** enquiries@treasurers.co.uk
W www.treasurers.org
Chief Executive, Richard Raeburn

ASSOCIATION OF COUNTY CHIEF EXECUTIVES
(1974), Chief Executive's Office, County Hall, Trowbridge,
BA14 8JF **T** 01225-713101 **E** jeanpotter@wiltshire.gov.uk
Hon. Secretary, Dr K. Robinson

ASSOCIATION OF DRAINAGE AUTHORITIES
(1937), The Mews, 3 Royal Oak Passage, Huntingdon
PE29 3EA **T** 01480-411123 **E** admin@ada.org.uk
W www.ada.org.uk
Chief Executive, David Noble, OBE

ASSOCIATION OF GENEALOGISTS AND
RESEARCHERS IN ARCHIVES (1968), 29 Badgers
Close, Horsham RH12 5RU **E** agra@agra.org.uk
W www.agra.org.uk
Company Secretary, David R. Young

ASSOCIATION OF HIGH SHERIFFS OF ENGLAND &
WALES (1971), PO Box 198, Letchworth SG6 3ZQ
T 01462-620356 **E** secretary@highsheriffs.com
W www.highsheriffs.com
Chair, Gloria Oates, OBE

ASSOCIATION OF LONDON GOVERNMENT (2000),
59½ Southwark Street, London SE1 0AL **T** 020-7934 9999
E info@alg.gov.uk
Chief Executive, Martin Pilgrim

ASSOCIATION OF ROYAL NAVY OFFICERS (1920),
70 Porchester Terrace, London W2 3TP **T** 020-7402 5231
E arno@eurosurf.com **W** www.eurosurf.com/arno
Secretary, Lt.-Cdr. A. Littleboy

ASSOCIATION OF SPEAKERS CLUBS (1971),
36 Pemberton Road, Winstanley, Wigan WN3 6DA
T 01942-222815 **E** connoki@planet-talk.co.uk
W www.the-asc.org.uk
National President, Neil McLeod

ASTHMA UK (1990), Providence House, Providence Place,
London N1 0NT **T** 020-7226 2260 **W** www.asthma.org.uk
Chief Executive, Donna Covey

AUDIT BUREAU OF CIRCULATIONS LTD (1931),
Saxon House, 211 High Street, Berkhamsted HP4 1AD
T 01442-870800 **E** marketing@abc.org.uk
W www.abc.org.uk
Chief Executive, C. Boyd

AUTOMOBILE ASSOCIATION (1905), Southwood East, Apollo Rise, Farnborough GU14 0JW T 08705-500600 E customer.services@theaa.com W www.theaa.com
Managing Director, Tim Parker

BALTIC AIR CHARTER ASSOCIATION (1949), The Baltic Exchange, 38 St Mary Axe, London EC3R 8BH T 020-7623 5501 W www.baca.org.uk
Chair, Steve Wells

BALTIC EXCHANGE (1744), 38 St Mary Axe, London EC3A 8BH T 020-7623 5501
E enquiries@balticexchange.com
W www.balticexchange.com
Chief Executive, Jeremy Penn

BAR ASSOCIATION FOR LOCAL GOVERNMENT AND THE PUBLIC SERVICE (1945), c/o Birmingham City Council, Ingleby House, 11–14 Cannon Street, Birmingham B2 5EN T 0121-303 9991
E chairman@balgps.org.uk W www.balgps.org.uk
Chair, M. F. N. Ahmad

BARNARDO'S (1866), Tanners Lane, Barkingside, Ilford IG6 1QG T 020-8550 8822 E information@barnardos.org.uk
W www.barnardos.org.uk
Chief Executive, R. Singleton

BARRISTERS' BENEVOLENT ASSOCIATION (1873), 14 Gray's Inn Square, London WC1R 5JP T 020-7242 4761 E enquiries@the-bba.com W www.the-bba.com
Secretary, Janet South

BCCB (1965), One Westminster Palace Gardens, 1–7 Artillery Row, London SW1P 1RJ T 020-7222 3651
E mail@bccb.org.uk W www.bccb.org.uk
Chief Executive, G. Hand

BEVIN BOYS ASSOCIATION (1989), School Cottage, 49a Hogshill Street, Beaminster, DT8 3AG T 01308-861488
Vice-President and Public Relations, Warwick H. Taylor, MBE

BIBLIOGRAPHICAL SOCIETY (1892), c/o University of London, Institute of English Studies, Room 304, Senate House, Malet Street, London WC1E 7HU T 020-7862 8679 E secretary@bibsoc.org.uk W www.bibsoc.org.uk
Hon. Secretary, M. L. Ford

BIRMINGHAM AND WARWICKSHIRE ARCHAEOLOGICAL SOCIETY (1870), c/o Birmingham and Midland Institute, Margaret Street, Birmingham B3 3BS W www.bwas.org.uk
Hon. Secretary, Chris Jones

BLUE CROSS (1897), Shilton Road, Burford OX18 4PF T 01993-822651 E info@bluecross.org.uk
W www.bluecross.org.uk
Chief Executive, John Rutter

BOOK AID INTERNATIONAL (1954), 39–41 Coldharbour Lane, London SE5 9NR T 020-7733 3577 E info@bookaid.org W www.bookaid.org
Director, Sara Harrity, MBE

BOOKSELLERS ASSOCIATION OF THE UK & IRELAND LTD (1895), Minster House, 272 Vauxhall Bridge Road, London SW1V 1BA T 020-7802 0802 E mail@booksellers.org.uk W www.booksellers.org.uk
Chief Executive, T. E. Godfray

BOOKTRUST (1926), Book House, 45 East Hill, London SW18 2QZ T 020-8516 2977 E info@booktrust.org.uk
W www.booktrust.org.uk
Executive Director, C. Meade

BOTANICAL SOCIETY OF SCOTLAND (1836), c/o Royal Botanic Garden Edinburgh, 20A Inverleith Row, Edinburgh EH3 5LR T 0131-552 7171
W www.diatom.free-online.co.uk
Hon. General Secretary, Dr P. Cochrane

BOTANICAL SOCIETY OF THE BRITISH ISLES (1836), c/o Department of Botany, The Natural History Museum, Cromwell Road, London SW7 5BD T 020-7942 5002 E dpearman4@aol.com
W www.bsbi.org.uk
Hon. General Secretary, D. Pearman

BOYS' BRIGADE (1883), Felden Lodge, Hemel Hempstead HP3 0BL T 01442-231681 E enquiries@boys-brigade.org.uk
W www.boys-brigade.org.uk
President, John Neil, OBE

BRISTOL AND GLOUCESTERSHIRE ARCHAEOLOGICAL SOCIETY (1876), 22 Beaumont Road, Gloucester GL2 0EJ T 01452-302610
W www.bgas.org.uk
Hon. Secretary, D. J. H. Smith, FSA

BRITISH AND FOREIGN BIBLE SOCIETY (1804), Stonehill Green, Westlea, Swindon SN5 7DG T 01793-418100 E contactus@biblesociety.org.uk
W www.biblesociety.org.uk
Chief Executive, James Catford

BRITISH ANTIQUE DEALERS' ASSOCIATION (1918), 20 Rutland Gate, London SW7 1BD T 020-7589 4128 E info@bada.org W www.bada.org
Secretary-General, Mrs E. J. Dean

BRITISH ASSOCIATION FOR EARLY CHILDHOOD EDUCATION (1923), 136 Cavell Street, London E1 2JA T 020-7539 5400 E office@early-education.org.uk
W www.early-education.org.uk
Director, Anne Nelson

BRITISH ASSOCIATION FOR LOCAL HISTORY PO Box 6549, Somersal Herbert DE6 5WH T 01283-585947 E mail@balh.co.uk W www.balh.co.uk

BRITISH ASSOCIATION OF COMMUNICATORS IN BUSINESS (1949), Suite A, First Floor, The Auriga Building, Davy Avenue, Knowlhill, Milton Keynes MK5 8ND T 0870-121 7606 E enquiries@cib.uk.com
W www.cib.uk.com
Secretary-General, Kathie Jones

BRITISH ASSOCIATION OF SOCIAL WORKERS (1970), 16 Kent Street, Birmingham B5 6RD T 0121-622 3911 W www.basw.co.uk
Director, I. Johnston

BRITISH ASTRONOMICAL ASSOCIATION (1890),
Burlington House, Piccadilly, London W1J 0DU
T 020-7734 4145 E office@britastro.com
W www.britastro.org
President, Dr Richard Miles

BRITISH BEE-KEEPERS' ASSOCIATION (1874),
National Beekeeping Centre, Stoneleigh Park, Kenilworth
CV8 2LG T 0247-669 6679 E bbka@britishbeekeepers.com
W www.britishbeekeepers.com
Chair, Dr Ivor Davis

BRITISH BOARD OF FILM CLASSIFICATION (1912),
3 Soho Square, London W1D 3HD T 020-7440 1570
E contact_the_bbfc@bbfc.co.uk W www.bbfc.co.uk
Director, David Cooke

BRITISH CATTLE BREEDERS' CLUB LTD (1946), Lake
Villa, Bradworthy, Holsworthy, Devon EX22 7SQ
T 01409-241579 E lesley.lewin@cattlebreeders.org.uk
W www.cattlebreeders.org.uk
Secretary, Mrs L. Lewin

BRITISH CHAMBERS OF COMMERCE, 1st Floor,
65 Petty France, St James Park, London SW1H 9EU
T 020-7654 5800 E info@britishchambers.org.uk
W www.chamberonline.co.uk
Director-General, David Frost

BRITISH CHESS FEDERATION (1904), The Watch Oak,
Chain Lane, Battle TN33 0YD T 01424-775222
E office@bcf.org.uk W www.bcf.org.uk
President, Gerry Walsh

BRITISH COMMONWEALTH EX-SERVICES LEAGUE
(1921), 48 Pall Mall, London SW1Y 5JG T 020-7973 7263
W www.commonwealthveterans.org.uk

BRITISH COPYRIGHT COUNCIL (1965), 29–33
Berners Street, London W1T 3AB T 01986-788122
E secretary@britishcopyright.org E www.britishcopyright.org
Secretary, Janet Ibbotson

BRITISH DEAF ASSOCIATION (1890), 1–3 Worship
Street, London EC2A 2AB T 020-7588 3520
E helpline@bda.org.uk W www.bda.org.uk
Executive Chair, Doug Alker

BRITISH DRIVING SOCIETY LTD (1957), 83 New
Road, Helmingham, Stowmarket IP14 6EA T 01473-892001
E email@britishdrivingsociety.co.uk
W www.britishdrivingsociety.co.uk
Secretary, Mrs T. K. Styles

BRITISH FALSE MEMORY SOCIETY (1993), Bradford
on Avon BA15 1NF T 01225-868682 E bfms@bfms.org.uk
W www.bfms.org.uk
Director, M. Greenhalgh

BRITISH FEDERATION OF WOMEN GRADUATES
(1907), 4 Mandeville Courtyard, 142 Battersea Park Road,
London SW11 4NB T 020-7498 8037
E bfwg@bfwg.demon.co.uk W www.bfwg.org.uk
Secretary, Mrs A. B. Stein

BRITISH HEART FOUNDATION (1961), 14
Fitzhardinge Street, London W1H 6DH T 020-7935 0185
E internet@bhf.org.uk W www.bhf.org.uk
Director-General, Peter Hollins

BRITISH HEDGEHOG PRESERVATION SOCIETY
(1982), Hedgehog House, Dhustone, Ludlow SY8 3PL
T 01584-890801 E bhps@dhustone.fsbusiness.co.uk
W www.software-technics.com/bhps
Chief Executive, Fay Vass

BRITISH HERPETOLOGICAL SOCIETY (1947),
c/o The Zoological Society of London, Regent's Park,
London NW1 4RY W www.thebhs.org
President, Dr H. Robert Bustard

BRITISH HOROLOGICAL INSTITUTE (1858), Upton
Hall, Upton, Newark NG23 5TE T 01636-813795
E info@bhi.co.uk W www.bhi.co.uk
General Manager, Martin Taylor

BRITISH HORSE SOCIETY (1947), Stoneleigh Deer Park,
Stareton Lane, Kenilworth CV8 2XZ T 08701-202244
E enquiry@bhs.org.uk W www.bhs.org.uk
Chief Executive, Graham Cory

BRITISH HOSPITALITY ASSOCIATION (1907),
Queens House, 55–56 Lincoln's Inn Fields, London
WC2A 3BH T 0845-880 7744 E info@bha.org.uk
W www.bha.org.uk
Chief Executive, Robert Cotton, OBE

BRITISH HUMANIST ASSOCIATION (1896), 1 Gower
Street, London WC1E 6HD T 020-7079 3580
E info@humanism.org.uk W www.humanism.org.uk
Executive Director, Hanne Stinson

BRITISH INSTITUTE IN EASTERN AFRICA (1959),
10 Carlton House Terrace, London SW1Y 5AH
T 020-7969 5201 E biea@britac.ac.uk
W www.britac.ac.uk/institutes/eafrica
President, Prof. David W. Phillipson

BRITISH INSTITUTE OF GRAPHOLOGISTS (1983),
PO Box 3060, Gerrards Cross, SL9 9XP T 01753-891241
E contact@britishgraphology.org
W www.britishgraphology.org
Chair, John Beck

BRITISH INSTITUTE OF PROFESSIONAL
PHOTOGRAPHY (1901), Fox Talbot House, Amwell
End, Ware SG12 9HN T 01920-464011 E info@bipp.com
W www.bipp.com
Executive Officer, M. Berry

BRITISH INSURANCE BROKERS' ASSOCIATION
(1978), 14 Bevis Marks, London EC3A 7NT
T Helpline: 0870-950 1790 E enquiries@biba.org.uk
W www.biba.org.uk
Chief Executive, Eric Galbraith

BRITISH INTERPLANETARY SOCIETY (1933), 27–29
South Lambeth Road, London SW8 1SZ T 020-7735 3160
E mail@bis-spaceflight.com W www.bis-spaceflight.com
Executive Secretary, Suszann Parry

BRITISH ISRAEL WORLD FEDERATION (1919),
121 Low Etherley, Bishop Auckland, Co Durham DL14 0HA
T 01388-834395 E admin@britishisrael.co.uk
W www.britishisrael.co.uk
Hon. Secretary, M. A. Clark

BRITISH LUNG FOUNDATION (1985), 73–75 Goswell
Road, London EC1V 7ER T 020-7688 5555
E enquiries@blf-uk.org W www.lunguk.org
Chief Executive, Dame Helena Shovelton, DBE

BRITISH MANAGEMANT DATA FOUNDATION
(1979), Highfield, Longbridge, Sheepscombe,
Stroud GL6 7QU T 01452-812837 W www.bmdf.co.uk
Director, Antony Cowgill, MBE

BRITISH MEDICAL ASSOCIATION (1832),
BMA House, Tavistock Square, London WC1H 9JP
T 020-7387 4499 E info.web@bma.org.uk
W www.bma.org.uk
Chief Executive, T. Bourne

BRITISH MENSA LTD (1946), St John's House, St John's
Square, Wolverhampton WV2 4AH T 01902-772771
E enquiries@mensa.org.uk W www.mensa.org.uk
Chief Executive and Company Secretary, John Stevenage

BRITISH MUSIC HALL SOCIETY, 'Meander', 361
Watford Road, Chiswell Green, St Albans AL2 3DB
T 01727-768878 W www.music-hall-society.com
Hon. Secretary, Daphne Masterton

BRITISH MUSIC INFORMATION CENTRE (1967),
10 Stratford Place, London W1C 1BA T 020-7928 1902
E info@bmic.co.uk W www.bmic.co.uk
Director, M. Greenall

BRITISH NATURALISTS' ASSOCIATION (1905),
1 Bracken Mews, London E4 7UT W www.bna-naturalists.org
Hon. Membership Secretary, Mrs Y. H. Griffiths

BRITISH NUCLEAR ENERGY SOCIETY (1962),
1 Great George Street, London SW1P 3AA T 020-7665 2241
E ian.andrews@ice.org.uk W www.bnes.org.uk
Executive Secretary, Ian M. Andrews, FRSA

BRITISH NUTRITION FOUNDATION (1967), High
Holborn House, 52–54 High Holborn, London WC1V 6RQ
T 020-7404 6504 E postbox@nutrition.org.uk
W www.nutrition.org.uk
Director-General, Prof. R. S. Pickard, PHD, CBIOL

BRITISH PHARMACOLOGICAL SOCIETY (1931),
16 Angel Gate, City Road, London EC1V 2SG
T 020-7417 0110 E yn@bps.ac.uk W www.bps.ac.uk
President, Prof. J. C. Buckingham

BRITISH PIG ASSOCIATION (1884), Trumpington
Mews, 40B High Street, Trumpington, Cambridge CB2 2LS
T 01223-845100 E bpa@britishpigs.org
W www.britishpigs.org.uk
Chief Executive, Marcus Bates

BRITISH POLIO FELLOWSHIP (1939), Eagle Office
Centre, The Runway, South Ruislip HA4 6SE
T 0800-018 0586 E info@britishpolio.org.uk
W www.britishpolio.org.uk
Chair, Sir Bryan Askew

BRITISH PSYCHOLOGICAL SOCIETY (1901), St
Andrews House, 48 Princess Road East, Leicester LE1 7DR
T 0116-254 9568 E mail@bps.org.uk W www.bps.org.uk
Chief Executive, Tim Cornford

BRITISH RED CROSS (1870), 44 Moorfields, London
EC2Y 9AL T 0870-170 7000 E information@redcross.org.uk
W www.redcross.org.uk
Chief Executive, Sir Nicholas Young

BRITISH TRUST FOR ORNITHOLOGY (1933),
The Nunnery, Thetford IP24 2PU T 01842-750050
E info@bto.org W www.bto.org
Director, Prof. Jeremy Greenwood

BRITISH UNION FOR THE ABOLITION OF
VIVISECTION (1898), 16A Crane Grove, London
N7 8NN T 020-7700 4888 E info@buav.org
W www.buav.org
Chief Executive, Adolfo Sansolini

BRITISH VETERINARY ASSOCIATION (1883),
7 Mansfield Street, London W1G 9NQ T 020 7636 6541
E bvahq@bva.co.uk W www.bva.co.uk
Chair, Brian D. Hoskin

BRITISH WOOD PRESERVING AND DAMP-
PROOFING ASSOCIATION (1930), 1 Gleneagles
House, Vernon Gate, Derby DE1 1UP T 01332-225100
E info@bwpda.co.uk W www.bwpda.co.uk
Director, Dr C. R. Coggins

BTBS THE BOOK TRADE CHARITY (1837), The Foyle
Centre, The Retreat, Kings Langley WD4 8LT
T 01923-263128 E btbs@booktradecharity.demon.co.uk
W www.booktradecharity.demon.co.uk
Chief Executive, David Hicks

BUCKINGHAMSHIRE ARCHAEOLOGICAL
SOCIETY (1847), County Museum, Church Street,
Aylesbury HP20 2QP T 01296-678114
Hon. Secretary, Mrs M. E. A. Brown

BUDGERIGAR SOCIETY (1925), Spring Gardens,
Northampton NN1 1DR T 01604-624549
W www.budgerigarsociety.com
General Secretary, D. Whittaker

BUILDING SOCIETIES ASSOCIATION (1869), 3 Savile
Row, London W1S 3PB T 020-7437 0655
E information@bsa.org.uk W www.bsa.org.uk
Director-General, A. Coles

BUSINESS AND PROFESSIONAL WOMEN UK LTD
(1938), PO Box 214, 24 Knifesmithgate, Chesterfield
S40 1XW T 01246-211988 E hq@bpwuk.co.uk
W www.bpwuk.co.uk
President, Ann Wiseall

CAFOD (CATHOLIC FUND FOR OVERSEAS
DEVELOPMENT) (1962), Romero Close, Stockwell
Road, London SW9 9TY T 020-7733 7900
E hq@cafod.org.uk W www.cafod.org.uk
Director, C. Bain

CALOUSTE GULBENKIAN FOUNDATION (1956), 98
Portland Place, London W1B 1ET T 020-7636 5313
E info@gulbenkian.org.uk W www.gulbenkian.org.uk
Director, Ms P. Ridley

CAMBRIAN ARCHAEOLOGICAL ASSOCIATION (1847), Halfway House, Pont y Pandy, Bangor LL57 3DG T 01248-364865 E f.m.lynch@btopenworld.com *General Secretary,* P. Llewellyn

CAMBRIDGE ANTIQUARIAN SOCIETY (1840), 21 High Street, West Wickham, Cambridge CB1 6RY E jmmorris@jmmorris.plus.com W www.camantsoc.org *Hon. Secretary,* Janet Morris

CAMERON FUND (1970), Tavistock House North, Tavistock Square, London WC1H 9HR T 020-7388 0796 E secretary@cameronfund.org.uk W www.cameronfund.org.uk *Secretary,* Mrs L. Dluska-Miziura

CAMPAIGN FOR NUCLEAR DISARMAMENT (CND) (1958), 162 Holloway Road, London N7 8DQ T 020-7700 2393 E enquiries@cnduk.org W www.cnduk.org *Chair,* Kate Hudson

CANADA-UNITED KINGDOM CHAMBER OF COMMERCE (1921), 38 Grosvenor Street, London W1K 4DP T 020-7258 6576 E info@canada-uk.org W www.canada-uk.org *Services Director,* R. Wormell

CANCER RESEARCH UK (2002), PO Box 123, Lincoln's Inn Fields, London WC2A 3PX T 020-7242 0200 W www.cancerresearchuk.org *Chief Executive,* Prof. Alex Markham

CARERS UK (1988), Ruth Pitter House, 20–25 Glasshouse Yard, London EC1A 4JT T 020-7490 8818 E info@carersuk.org W www.carersuk.org *Chief Executive,* Ms I. Redmond

CARNEGIE UNITED KINGDOM TRUST (1913), Comely Park House, Dunfermline KY12 7EJ T 01383-721445 W www.carnegieuktrust.org.uk *Chief Executive,* C. McConnell

CATHEDRALS FABRIC COMMISSION FOR ENGLAND (1991), Church House, Great Smith Street, London SW1P 3NZ T 020-7898 1863 E enquiries@cfce.c-of-e.org.uk *Secretary,* Ms Paula Griffiths

CATHOLIC TRUTH SOCIETY (1868), 40–46 Harleyford Road, London SE11 5AY T 020-7640 0042 E info@cts-online.org.uk W www.cts-online.org.uk *General Secretary,* Fergal Martin

CATHOLIC UNION OF GREAT BRITAIN (1872), St Maxmilian Kolbe House, 63 Jeddo Road, London W12 9EE T 020-8749 1321 E phiggs@cathunion.fsnet.co.uk W www.catholicunion.org *Secretary,* P. H. Higgs

CENTRAL AND CECIL HOUSING TRUST (1927), 266 Waterloo Road, London, Richmond SE1 8RQ T 020-7922 5300 E enquiries@ccht.org.uk W www.ccht.org.uk *Chief Executive,* Dorry McLaughlin

CENTRAL COUNCIL OF CHURCH BELL RINGERS (1891), The Cottage, School Hill, Warnham, Horsham RH12 3QN T 01403-269743 W www.cccbr.org.uk *Hon. Secretary,* Ian H. Oram

CENTREPOINT (1969), Neil House, 7 Whitechapel Road, London E1 1DU T 020-7426 5300 W www.centrepoint.org.uk *Chief Executive,* Anthony Lawton

CEREDIGION HISTORICAL SOCIETY, Abermagwr, Aberystwyth, SY23 4AR *Hon. Secretary,* Mrs. E. Baskerville

CHARITIES AID FOUNDATION (1924), Kings Hill, West Malling ME19 4TA T 01732-520000 E enquiries@cafonline.org W www.cafonline.org *Chief Executive,* Stephen Ainger

CHARTERED INSTITUTE OF ARBITRATORS (1915), 12 Bloomsbury Square, London WC1A 2LP T 020-7421 7444 E info@arbitrators.org W www.arbitrators.org *Secretary-General,* Dair Farrar-Hockley, MC

CHARTERED INSTITUTE OF ENVIRONMENTAL HEALTH (1883), Chadwick Court, 15 Hatfields, London SE1 8DJ T 020-7928 6006 E information@cieh.org W www.cieh.org.uk *Chief Executive,* G. Jukes

CHARTERED INSTITUTE OF JOURNALISTS (1884), 2 Dock Offices, Surrey Quays Road, London SE16 2XU T 020-7252 1187 E memberservices@ioj.co.uk W www.ioj.co.uk *General Secretary,* D. Cooper

CHARTERED MANAGEMENT INSTITUTE (1947), Management House, Cottingham Road, Corby NN17 1TT T 01536-204222 E enquiries@managers.org.uk W www.managers.org.uk *Chief Executive,* Ms M. Chapman

CHATHAM HOUSE (1920), Chatham House, 10 St James's Square, London SW1Y 4LE T 020-7957 5700 E contact@chathamhouse.org.uk W www.chathamhouse.org.uk *Director,* Prof. Victor Bulmer-Thomas

CHILDREN 1ST (1884), 83 Whitehouse Loan, Edinburgh EH9 1AT T 0131-446 2300 E info@children1st.org.uk W www.children1st.org.uk *Chief Executive,* Margaret McKay

CHILDREN'S SOCIETY (1881), Edward Rudolf House, Margery Street, London WC1X 0JL T 020-7841 4000 E supporteraction@childrenssociety.org.uk W www.childrenssociety.org.uk *Chief Executive,* Bob Reitermeier

CHRISTIAN AID SCOTLAND, 41 George IV Bridge, Edinburgh EH1 1EL T 0131-220 1254 E edinburgh@christian-aid.org W www.christian-aid.org.uk *National Secretary,* Revd J. Wylie

CHRISTIAN EDUCATION (1965), 1020 Bristol Road, Selly Oak, Birmingham B29 6LB T 0121-472 4242 E admin@christianeducation.org.uk W www.christianeducation.org.uk *Chief Executive*, Peter Fishpool

CHURCHILL SOCIETY - LONDON (1990), c/o 18 Grove Lane, Ipswich IP4 1NR T 01473-413533 E secretary@churchill-society-london.org.uk W www.churchill-society-london.org.uk/index.htm *General Secretary*, N. H. Rogers

CHURCH LADS' AND CHURCH GIRLS' BRIGADE (1891), 2 Barnsley Road, Wath-upon-Dearne, Rotherham S63 6PY T 01709-876535 E generalsecretary@clcgb.org.uk W www.clcgb.org.uk *General Secretary*, A. J. Reed Screen, OBE

CHURCH MISSION SOCIETY, Partnership House, 157 Waterloo Road, London SE1 8UU T 020-7928 8681 E info@cms-uk.org W www.cms-uk.org *General Secretary*, Revd Canon T. Dakin

CHURCH MONUMENTS SOCIETY (1979), 34 Bridge Street, Shepshed, LE12 9AD T 01837-851483 E churchmonuments@aol.com W www.churchmonumentssociety.org *President*, Dr Julian Litten

CHURCH UNION (1859), Faith House, 7 Tufton Street, London SW1P 3QN T 020-7222 6952 E churchunion@care4free.net W www.churchunion.care4free.net *Chair*, David Llewelyn-Morgan

CITIZENS ADVICE (1939), Myddelton House, 115–123 Pentonville Road, London N1 9LZ T 020-7833 2181 W www.citizensadvice.org.uk *Chief Executive*, D. Harker

CITY BUSINESS LIBRARY (1970), Corporation of London, 1 Brewers' Hall Garden, London EC2V 5BX T 020-7332 1812 E cbl@corpoflondon.gov.uk W www.cityoflondon.gov.uk/citybusinesslibrary *Librarian*, Diana Moulding

CITY OF COVENTRY FREEMEN'S GUILD (1946), 47 Brownshill Green Road, Coventry CV6 2AP T 024-7627 4321 W www.coventryfreemensguild.co.uk *Hon. Clerk*, K. Talbot

CITY OF STOKE-ON-TRENT MUSEUM ARCHAEOLOGICAL SOCIETY (1959), The Potteries Museum and Art Gallery, Hanley, Stoke-on-Trent ST1 3DW T 01782-232323 W www.stoke.gov.uk/museums/pmag/archaeology/archsoc.htm *Chair*, E. E. Royle, MBE

CIVIC TRUST (1957), Essex Hall, 1–6 Essex Street, London WC2R 3HU T 020-7539 7900 E info@civictrust.org.uk W www.civictrust.org.uk *Chair*, Nigel Burton

CLASSICAL ASSOCIATION (1903), Senate House, Malet Street, London WC1E 7HU T 020-7862 8706 E office@classicalassociation.org W www.classicalassociation.org *Secretary*, C. L. Roberts

COLLEGE OF OPTOMETRISTS (1980), 42 Craven Street, London WC2N 5NG T 020-7839 6000 E optometry@college-optometrists.org W www.college-optometrists.org *Chief Executive*, Mrs Bryony Pawinska

COLLEGE OF TEACHERS (1849), Institute of Education, 57 Gordon Square, London WC1H 0NU T 020-7947 9536 E enquiries@cot.ac.uk W www.collegeofteachers.ac.uk *Chief Executive Officer*, Prof. Ray Page

COMMONWEALTH SOCIETY FOR THE DEAF 'SOUND SEEKERS' (1959), 34 Buckingham Palace Road, London SW1W 0RE T 020-7233 5700 E sound.seekers@btinternet.com W www.sound-seekers.org.uk *Chief Executive*, Gary Williams

CONFED (2002), Humanities Building, University of Manchester, Oxford Road, Manchester M13 9PL T 0161-275 8810 W www.confed.org.uk *Executive Director*, Chris Waterman

CONTEMPORARY APPLIED ARTS (1948), 2 Percy Street, London W1T 1DD T 020-7436 2344 W www.caa.org.uk *Director*, Ms Tass Mavrogordato

CO-OPERATIVE GROUP (CWS) LTD. (1863), PO Box 53, New Century House, Manchester M60 4ES T 0161-834 1212 W www.co-op.co.uk *Chief Executive*, Martin Beaumont

CO-OPERATIVE PARTY (1917), 77 Weston Street, London SE1 3SD T 020-7357 0230 W www.party.coop *National Secretary*, Peter Hunt

CO-OPERATIVES UK, Holyoake House, Hanover Street, Manchester M60 0AS T 0161-246 2900 W www.co-opunion.coop *Chief Executive*, Dame Pauline Green

CORAM FAMILY (1739), 49 Mecklenburgh Square, London WC1N 2QA T 020-7520 0300 E reception@coram.org.uk W www.coram.org.uk *Chief Executive*, Honor Rhodes

CORONERS' SOCIETY OF ENGLAND AND WALES (1846), The Court House, Bewdley Road, Stourport on Severn, Worcestershire DY13 8XE T 01562-887795 E honsec.corsoc@btinternet.com W www.coroner.org *Hon. Secretary*, Victor Felix Round

CORPORATION OF CHURCH HOUSE (1888), Church House, Great Smith Street, London SW1P 3AZ T 020-7898 1000 *Secretary*, Colin D. L. Menzies

COUNCIL FOR BRITISH ARCHAEOLOGY (1944), St Mary's House, 66 Bootham, York YO30 7BZ T 01904-671417 E info@britarch.ac.uk W www.britarch.ac.uk *Director*, Dr M. Heyworth

COUNCIL FOR THE CARE OF CHURCHES (1921), Church House, Great Smith Street, London SW1P 3NZ T 020-7898 1866 E enquiries@ccc.c-of-e.org.uk *Secretary*, Paula Griffiths

COUNCIL FOR WORLD MISSION (1977), Ipalo House,
32–34 Great Peter Street, London SW1P 2DB
T 020-7222 4214 E council@cwmission.org.uk
W www.cwmission.org.uk
General Secretary, Revd Dr D. van der Water

COUNCIL OF CHRISTIANS AND JEWS (1942), 1st
Floor, Camelford House, 89 Albert Embankment, London
SE1 7TP T 020-7820 0090 E cjrelations@ccj.org.uk
W www.ccj.org.uk
Director, Sr Margaret Shepherd

COUNCIL OF UNIVERSITY CLASSICAL
DEPARTMENTS (1972), Institute of Classical Studies,
Senate House, Malet Street, London WC1E 7HU
T 0116-252 2775 E gjs@leicester.ac.uk
W www.rhul.ac.uk/classics/cucd
Chair, Prof D. G. J. Shipley, FSA

COUNSEL AND CARE (1954), Twyman House, 16 Bonny
Street, London NW1 9PG T 020-7241 8555
E advice@counselandcare.org.uk
W www.counselandcare.org.uk
Chief Executive, Stephen Burke

COUNTRY HOUSES ASSOCIATION (1955), Bloxham
Mill, Barford Road, Bloxham, Banbury OX15 4FF
T 01869-812800 E hq@cha.org.uk W www.cha.org.uk
Chief Executive, Amanda Witherall, CBE

COUNTRY LAND & BUSINESS ASSOCIATION
(1907), 16 Belgrave Square, London SW1X 8PQ
T 020-7235 0511 E mail@cla.org.uk W www.cla.org.uk
President, Mark Hudson

COUNTRYSIDE ALLIANCE (1998), Old Town Hall, 367
Kennington Road, London SE11 4PT T 020-7840 9200
E info@countryside-alliance.org
W www.countryside-alliance.org
Chair, J. Jackson

CPRE (CAMPAIGN TO PROTECT RURAL ENGLAND)
(1926), 128 Southwark Street, London SE1 0SW
T 020-7981 2800 E info@cpre.org.uk W www.cpre.org.uk
Director, Mr Shaun Spiers

CRAFTS COUNCIL, 44A Pentonville Road, London N1 9BY
T 020-7278 7700 W www.craftscouncil.org.uk
Director, Dr Louise Taylor

CRISIS UK (1967), 64 Commercial Street, London E1 6LT
T 0870-011 3335 E enquiries@crisis.org.uk
W www.crisis.org.uk
Chief Executive, S. Ghosh

CRUSE BEREAVEMENT CARE (1959), Cruse House,
126 Sheen Road, Richmond TW9 1UR
T 020-8939 9530 Helpline 0870-167 1677
E info@crusebereavementcare.org.uk
W www.crusebereavementcare.org.uk
Chief Executive, Anne Viney

CTC (THE UK'S NATIONAL CYCLISTS'
ORGANISATION) (1878), 69 Meadrow, Godalming
GU7 3HS T 0870-873 0060 E cycling@ctc.org.uk
W www.ctc.org.uk
Director, K. Mayne

CUMBERLAND AND WESTMORLAND
ANTIQUARIAN AND ARCHAEOLOGICAL
SOCIETY (1866), Brantbeck, Windy Hall Road,
Bowness-on-Windermere LA23 3HX T 01539-445276
E info@cwaas.org.uk W www.cwaas.org.uk
Hon. Secretary, Eric A. Jones

CYSTIC FIBROSIS TRUST (1964), 11 London Road,
Bromley BR1 1BY T 020-8464 7211
E enquiries@cftrust.org.uk W www.cftrust.org.uk
Chief Executive, Rosie Barnes

DESIGN AND INDUSTRIES ASSOCIATION (1915),
Studio 412–413, Custard Factory 2, Gibb Street,
Birmingham B9 4AA T 0121-772 4242 E info@dia.org.uk
W www.dia.org.uk

DEVON ARCHAEOLOGICAL SOCIETY (1929), Royal
Albert Memorial Museum, Queen Street, Exeter EX4 3RX
E dasonline@wanadoo.co.uk W www.ex.ac.uk/das
Hon. Secretary, Lorinda Legge

DIANA, PRINCESS OF WALES MEMORIAL FUND
(1997), County Hall, Westminster Bridge Road, London
SE1 7PB T 020-7902 5500
E memorial.fund@memfund.org.uk
W www.theworkcontinues.org
Chief Executive, Andrew Purkis, OBE

DIRECTORY & DATABASE PUBLISHERS
ASSOCIATION (1970), PO Box 23034, London W6 0RJ
T 020-7405 0836 E christine.scott@dpassoc.org
W www.directory-publisher.co.uk
Head, Christine Scott

DITCHLEY FOUNDATION (1958), Ditchley Park,
Enstone, Chipping Norton OX7 4ER T 01608-677346
E mail@ditchley.co.uk W www.ditchley.co.uk
Director, Sir Jeremy Greenstock, GCMG

DOWN'S SYNDROME ASSOCIATION (1970), The
Langdon Down Centre, 2a Langdon Park, Teddington
TW11 9PS T 0845-230 0372
E info@downs-syndrome.org.uk
W www.downs-syndrome.org.uk
Chief Executive Officer, Ms C. Boys

DUKE OF EDINBURGH'S AWARD (1956), Gulliver
House, Madeira Walk, Windsor SL4 1EU T 01753-727400
E info@theaward.org W www.theaward.org
Operations Director, Steve Sharp

DYSLEXIA INSTITUTE (1972), Park House, Wick
Road, Egham TW20 0HH T 01784-222300
E info@dyslexia-inst.org.uk W www.dyslexia-inst.org.uk
Chief Executive, Shirley Cramer

EAST HERTFORDSHIRE ARCHAEOLOGICAL
SOCIETY (1898), 11 St Leonard's Close, Bengeo,
Hertford SG14 3LL
Hon. Secretary, Mrs G. R. Pollard

EAST OF ENGLAND AGRICULTURAL SOCIETY
(1797), East of England Showground, Peterborough
PE2 6XE T 01733-234451 E info@eastofengland.org.uk
W www.eastofengland.org.uk
Chief Executive, Andrew Mercer

EATING DISORDERS ASSOCIATION, First Floor, Wensum House, 103 Prince of Wales Road, Norwich NR1 1DW **T** 0870-770 3256 **Helpline** 0845-634 1414 **E** info@edauk.com **W** www.edauk.com
Chief Executive, Mrs Susan Ringwood

ECCLESIOLOGICAL SOCIETY (1839), c/o Society of Antiquaries of London, Burlington House, London W1V 0HS **T** 020-7738 2965 **E** info@ecclsoc.org **W** www.ecclsoc.org
Hon. Secretary, Dr James F. Johnston

EDINBURGH CHAMBER OF COMMERCE (1786), 27 Melville Street, Edinburgh EH3 7JF **T** 0131-477 7000 **E** information@ecce.org **W** www.ecce.org
Chief Executive, Ron Hewitt

EGYPT EXPLORATION SOCIETY (1882), 3 Doughty Mews, London WC1N 2PG **T** 020-7242 1880 **E** enquiries@ees.ac.uk **W** www.ees.ac.uk
Secretary-General, Dr P. A. Spencer

ELECTORAL REFORM SOCIETY (1884), 6 Chancel Street, London SE1 0UU **T** 020-7928 1622 **E** ers@reform.demon.co.uk **W** www.electoral-reform.org.uk
Chief Executive, Ken Ritchie

ELGAR FOUNDATION (1935), The Elgar Birthplace Museum, Lower Broadheath, Worcester WR2 6RH **T** 01905-333224 **E** birthplace@elgarmuseum.org **W** www.elgarmuseum.org
Museum Director, Catherine Sloan

ELGAR SOCIETY (1951), c/o 29 Van Diemens Close, Chinnor OX39 4QE **T** 01844-354096 **E** elgar@music.com **W** www.elgar.org
Hon. Secretary, Wendy Hillary

EMERGENCY PLANNING SOCIETY (1993), The Media Centre, Culverhouse Cross, Cardiff CF6 6XJ **T** 0845-600 9587 **W** www.the-eps.org

ENABLE (1954), 7 Buchanan Street, Glasgow G1 3HL **T** 0141-226 4541 **E** enable@enable.org.uk **W** www.enable.org.uk
Director, N. Dunning

ENERGY INSTITUTE (2003), 61 New Cavendish Street, London W1G 7AR **T** 020-7467 7100 **E** info@energyinst.org.uk **W** www.energyinst.org.uk
Chief Executive, Louise Kingham

ENERGYWATCH (2000), 4th Floor, Artillery House, Artillery Row, London SW1P 1RT **T** 0845-906 0708 **E** enquiries@energywatch.org.uk **W** www.energywatch.org.uk
Chief Executive, Allan Asher

ENGINEERING COUNCIL (UK) (2002), 10 Maltravers Street, London WC2R 3ER **T** 020-7240 7891 **E** info@engc.org.uk **W** www.engc.org.uk
Executive Director, Andrew Ramsay

ENGLISH ASSOCIATION (1906), University of Leicester, University Road, Leicester LE1 7RH **T** 0116-252 3982 **E** engassoc@le.ac.uk **W** www.le.ac.uk/engassoc/
Chief Executive, Ms H. Lucas

ENGLISH FOLK DANCE AND SONG SOCIETY (1932), Cecil Sharp House, 2 Regent's Park Road, London NW1 7AY **T** 020-7485 2206 **W** www.efdss.org.com
Chief Executive, H. Miller

ENGLISH-SPEAKING UNION OF THE COMMONWEALTH (1918), Dartmouth House, 37 Charles Street, London W1J 5ED **T** 020-7529 1550 **E** esu@esu.org **W** www.esu.org
Director-General, Mrs V. Mitchell, OBE

ENVIRONMENT COUNCIL (1970), 212 High Holborn, London WC1V 7BF **T** 020-7836 2626 **E** info@envcouncil.org.uk **W** www.the-environment-council.org.uk
Chair, Malcolm Aickin

EPILEPSY ACTION (1950), New Anstey House, Gate Way Drive, Yeadon, Leeds LS19 7XY **T** 0113-210 8800 **Helpline** 0808-800 5050 **E** epilepsy@epilepsy.org.uk **W** www.epilepsy.org.uk
Chief Executive, P. Lee

ESPERANTO ASSOCIATION OF BRITAIN, Esperanto House, Barlaston, Stoke-on-Trent ST12 9DG **T** 01782-372141 **E** eab@esperanto-gb.org **W** www.esperanto-gb.org
President, Prof. J. Wells

EVANGELICAL LIBRARY, 78A Chiltern Street, London W1U 5HB **T** 020-7935 6997 **E** stlibrary@btinternet.com **W** www.elib.org.uk
Librarian, S. J. Taylor

EX-SERVICES MENTAL WELFARE SOCIETY (1919), Hollybush House, Hollybush, nr Ayr KA6 7EA **T** 01292-560214 **E** contactus@combatstress.org.uk **W** www.combatstress.com
Clinical Manager, Mrs F. Robertson

FABIAN SOCIETY (1884), 11 Dartmouth Street, London SW1H 9BN **T** 020-7227 4900 **E** info@fabian-society.org.uk **W** www.fabian-society.org.uk
General Secretary, S. Katwala

FACULTY OF ACTUARIES IN SCOTLAND (1856), 18 Dublin Street, Edinburgh EH1 3PP **T** 0131-240 1300 **E** faculty@actuaries.org.uk **W** www.actuaries.org.uk
Secretary, Richard Maconachie

FAIR ISLE BIRD OBSERVATORY TRUST (1948), Fair Isle Bird Observatory, Fair Isle ZE2 9JU **T** 01595-760258 **E** fairisle.birdobs@zetnet.co.uk **W** www.fairislebirdobs.co.uk
Administrator, H. Shaw

FAITH AND THOUGHT (1865), 15 The Drive, Harlow, CM20 3QD **T** 020-8303 0465 **E** brianht.weller@btinternet.com **W** www.faithandthought.org.uk
Hon. Secretary, Brian Weller

FAMILY WELFARE ASSOCIATION (1869), 501–505 Kingsland Road, London E8 4AU **T** 020-7254 6251 **E** fwa.headoffice@fwa.org.uk **W** www.fwa.org.uk
Chief Executive, Helen Dent

FAUNA AND FLORA INTERNATIONAL (1903), Great Eastern House, Tenison Road, Cambridge CB1 2TT
T 01223-571000 E info@fauna-flora.org
W www.fauna-flora.org
Chief Executive Officer, Mark Rose

FEDERATION OF BRITISH ARTISTS (1961),
17 Carlton House Terrace, London SW1Y 5BD
T 020-7930 6844 E info@mallgalleries.com
W www.mallgalleries.org.uk
Chair, J. R. S. Boas

FEDERATION OF FAMILY HISTORY SOCIETIES
(1974), PO Box 2425, Coventry, CV5 6YX T 07041-492032
E info@ffhs.org.uk W www.ffhs.org.uk
Administrator, Maggie Loughran

FEDERATION OF SMALL BUSINESSES (1974),
2 Catherine Place, London SW1E 6HF T 020-7592 8100
E london@fsb.org.uk W www.fsb.org.uk
Head of Parliamentary Affairs, Stephen Alambritis

FIELD STUDIES COUNCIL (1943), Preston Montford, Montford Bridge, Shrewsbury SY4 1HW T 01743-852100
E headoffice@field-studies-council.org W www.field-studies-council.org
Chief Executive, A. D. Thomas

FIRE SERVICES NATIONAL BENEVOLENT FUND
(1943), Second Floor, Copenhagen Court, 32 New Street, Basingstoke RG21 7DT T 01256-366566
E administration@fsnbf.org.uk W www.fsnbf.org.uk
Chief Executive, Roy Lawrenson

FLEET AIR ARM OFFICERS' ASSOCIATION (1957),
4 St James's Square, London SW1Y 4JU T 020-7930 7722
E faaoa@fleetairarmoa.org W www.fleetairarmoa.org
Chair, Rear-Adm. S. Lidbetter

FOOD FROM BRITAIN, 4th Floor, Manning House,
22 Carlisle Place, London SW1P 1JA T 020-7233 5111
E info@foodfrombritain.co.uk W www.foodfrombritain.com
Chief Executive, D. McNair

FOREIGN PRESS ASSOCIATION IN LONDON
(1888), 11 Carlton House Terrace, London SW1Y 5AJ
T 020-7930 0445 E secretariat@foreign-press.org.uk
W www.foreign-press.org.uk
General Manager, B. Jenner

FORENSIC SCIENCE SOCIETY (1959), Clarke House,
18A Mount Parade, Harrogate HG1 1BX T 01423-506068
W www.forensic-science-society.org.uk
President, Jim Fraser

FOUNDATION FOR SPORT AND THE ARTS (1991),
PO Box 20, Liverpool L13 1HB T 0151-259 5505
E contact@thefsa.net W www.thefsa.net
Secretary, R. Boardley

FOUNDATION FOR THE STUDY OF INFANT
DEATHS (1971), Artillery House, 11–19 Artillery Row,
London SW1P 1RT
T 0870-787 0885 Helpline: 0870-787 0554
E fsid@sids.org.uk W www.sids.org.uk/fsid/
Director, Mrs J. Epstein

FPA (1930), 2–12 Pentonville Road, London N1 9FP
T 020-7837 5432 W www.fpa.org.uk
Chief Executive, Ms A. Weyman

FRANCO-BRITISH SOCIETY (1904), Room 227, Linen Hall, 162–168 Regent Street, London W1R 5TB
T 020-7734 0815 E execsec@francobritishsociety.org.uk
W www.francobritishsociety.org.uk
Executive Secretary, Mrs K. Brayn

FRIENDS OF CATHEDRAL MUSIC (1956), 21 Bradford Road, Trowbridge BA14 9AL E info@fcm.org.uk
W www.fcm.org.uk
Secretary, Roger Bishton

FRIENDS OF FRIENDLESS CHURCHES (1957),
St Ann's Vestry Hall, 2 Church Entry, London EC4V 5HB
T 020-7236 3934
E office@friendsoffriendlesschurches.org.uk
W www.friendsoffriendlesschurches.org.uk
Hon. Director, M. Saunders, MBE

FRIENDS OF THE BODLEIAN (1925), Bodleian Library, Oxford OX1 3BG T 01865-277022/277234
E fob@bodley.ox.ac.uk W www.bodley.ox.ac.uk/friends
Secretary, Geoffrey Groom

FRIENDS OF THE EARTH SCOTLAND (1978), Lamb's House, Burgess Street, Edinburgh EH6 6RD
T 0131-554 9977 E info@foe-scotland.org.uk
W www.foe-scotland.org.uk
Chief Executive, Duncan McLaren

FRIENDS OF THE NATIONAL LIBRARIES (1931),
c/o Department of Manuscripts, The British Library,
96 Euston Road, London NW1 2DB T 020-7412 7559
W www.friendsofnationallibraries.org.uk
Chair, Lord Egremont

FURNITURE HISTORY SOCIETY (1964), 1 Mercedes Cottages, St John's Road, Haywards Heath RH16 4EH
T 01444-413845 E furniturehistorysociety@hotmail.com
W www.furniturehistorysociety.com
Membership Secretary, Dr Brian Austen

GALLIPOLI ASSOCIATION (1969), Earleydene Orchard, Earleydene, Ascot SL5 9JY T 01344-626523
E webmaster@gallipoli-association.org
W www.gallipoli-association.org
Hon. Secretary, J. C. Watson Smith

GAME CONSERVANCY TRUST (1969), Fordingbridge SP6 1EF T 01425-652381 E admin@gct.org.uk
W www.gct.org.uk
Chief Executive, Teresa Dent

GARDEN HISTORY SOCIETY (1965), 70 Cowcross Street, London EC1M 6EJ T 020-7608 2409
E enquiries@gardenhistorysociety.org
W www.gardenhistorysociety.org
Chair, Dominic Cole

GEMMOLOGICAL ASSOCIATION AND GEM
TESTING LABORATORY OF GREAT BRITAIN
(1931), 27 Greville Street, (Saffron Hill entrance), London
EC1N 8TN T 020-7404 3334 E information@gem-a.info
W www.gem-a.info
Chief Executive Officer, Dr Jack Ogden

GENERAL DENTAL COUNCIL (1956), 37 Wimpole Street, London W1G 8DQ T 020-7887 3800
E information@gdc-uk.org W www.gdc-uk.org
Chief Executive & Registrar, Antony Townsend

GENERAL MEDICAL COUNCIL (1858), 178 Great Portland Street, London W1W 5JE T 020-7580 7642
E gmc@gmc-uk.org W www.gmc-uk.org
President, Sir Graeme Catto

GENERAL OPTICAL COUNCIL (1959), 41 Harley Street, London W1G 8DJ T 020-7580 3898 E goc@optical.org
W www.optical.org
Chief Executive and Registrar, P. C. Coe

GENERAL OSTEOPATHIC COUNCIL (1993), Osteopathy House, 176 Tower Bridge Road, London SE1 3LU T 020-7357 6655 E info@osteopathy.org.uk
W www.osteopathy.org.uk
Chief Executive & Registrar, M. J. Craggs

GEOGRAPHICAL ASSOCIATION (1893), 160 Solly Street, Sheffield S1 4BF T 0114-296 0088
E ga@geography.org.uk W www.geography.org.uk
Chief Executive, David Lambert

GEOLOGICAL SOCIETY OF LONDON (1807), Burlington House, Piccadilly, London W1J 0BG
T 020-7434 9944 E enquiries@geolsoc.org.uk
W www.geolsoc.org.uk
Executive Secretary, E. Nickless

GEOLOGISTS' ASSOCIATION (1858), Burlington House, Piccadilly, London W1J 0DU T 020-7434 9298
E geol.assoc@btinternet.com
W www.geologist.demon.co.uk
Executive Secretary, Sarah Stafford

GEORGIAN GROUP, 6 Fitzroy Square, London, W1T 5DX
T 020-7529 8920 E info@georgiangroup.org.uk
W www.georgiangroup.org.uk/
Secretary, Robert Bargery

GIRLGUIDING UK (1910), 17–19 Buckingham Palace Road, London SW1W 0PT T 020-7834 6242
E chq@girlguiding.org.uk W www.girlguiding.org.uk
Chief Guide, Mrs Jenny Leach

GIRLS' BRIGADE ENGLAND AND WALES, PO Box 196, 129 The Broadway, Didcot OX11 8XN T 01235-510425
E admin@girlsbrigadeew.org.uk
W www.girlsbrigadeew.org.uk
National Director, Ruth Gilson

GIRLS' VENTURE CORPS AIR CADETS (1964), Phoenix House, 3 Handley Square, Finningley Airport, Doncaster DN9 3GH T 01302-775019
E gvcachq1@btopenworld.com W www.gvcac.org.uk
Chair, Yvonne McCarthy

GLASGOW CHAMBER OF COMMERCE (1783), 30 George Square, Glasgow G2 1EQ T 0141-204 2121
E chamber@glasgowchamber.org
W www.glasgowchamber.org
Chief Executive, Dr Lesley Sawers

GREEK INSTITUTE (1969), 34 Bush Hill Road, London N21 2DS T 020-8360 7968 E info@greekinstitute.co.uk
W www.greekinstitute.co.uk
Director, Dr K. Tofallis

GREENPEACE UK, Canonbury Villas, London N1 2PN
T 020-7865 8100 E info@uk.greenpeace.org
W www.greenpeace.org.uk
Executive Director, Stephen Tindale

GUIDE DOGS FOR THE BLIND ASSOCIATION (1934), Hillfields, Burghfield Common, Reading RG7 3YG
T 0118-983 5555 E guidedogs@guidedogs.org.uk
W www.gdba.org.uk
Chief Executive, Bridget Warr

GUILD OF AID FOR GENTLEPEOPLE (1904), 10 St Christopher's Place, London W1U 1HZ T 020-7935 0641
E admin@pcac.org.uk
Secretary, N. E. Inkson

GUILD OF FREEMEN OF THE CITY OF LONDON (1908), 4 Dowgate Hill, London EC4R 2SH
T 020-8541 1435 E clerk@guild-freemen-london.co.uk
W www.guild-freemen-london.co.uk
Clerk to the Guild, Brigadier M. I. Keun

GUILD OF GLASS ENGRAVERS (1975), 87 Nether Street, Finchley, London N12 7NP T 020-8446 4050
E enquiries@gge.org.uk W www.gge.org.uk
Secretary, Christine Reyland

GUILD OF PASTORAL PSYCHOLOGY (1937), Flat 5, 17 Hatton Street, London NW8 8PL
W www.guildofpastoralpsychology.org.uk
Chair, Mary Jo Radcliffe

GURKHA WELFARE TRUST (1969), PO Box 18215, 2nd Floor, 1 Old Street, London EC1V 9XB T 020-7251 5234
E secretary@gwt.org.uk W www.gwt.org.uk
Director, Col. William Shuttlewood

HAEMOPHILIA SOCIETY (1950), First Floor, Petersham House, 57A Hatton Garden, London EC1N 8JG
T 020-7831 1020 Helpline 0800-018 6068
E info@haemophilia.org.uk W www.haemophilia.org.uk
Chief Executive, G. Whitehead

HAIG HOMES (1929), Alban Dobson House, Green Lane, Morden SM4 5NS T 020-8685 5777
E haig@haighomes.org.uk W www.haighomes.org.uk
Major-General, P. V. R. Besgrove, CBE

HAKLUYT SOCIETY (1846), c/o Map Library, The British Library, 96 Euston Road, London NW1 2DB
T 01428-641850 E office@hakluyt.com
W www.hakluyt.com
President, Prof. R. C. Bridges

HALIFAX ANTIQUARIAN SOCIETY (1900), 66 Drub Lane, Gomersal, Cleckheaton BD19 4BU T 01274-865418
W www.halifaxhistory.org.uk
Hon. Secretary, J. H. Patchett

HANSARD SOCIETY FOR PARLIAMENTARY
GOVERNMENT (1944), St Philips Building North,
Sheffield Street, London WC2A 2EX T 020-7395 4000
E hansard@hansard.lse.ac.uk W www.hansardsociety.org.uk
Director, Clare Ettinghausen

HARVEIAN SOCIETY OF LONDON (1831), Lettsom
House, 11 Chandos Street, London W1G 9EB
T 020-7580 1043
Executive Secretary, Col. R. Kinsella-Bevan

HAWICK ARCHAEOLOGICAL SOCIETY (1856),
Orrock House, Stirches Road, Hawick TD9 7HF
T 01450-375546
Hon. Secretary, I. W. Landles

HEALTH PROFESSIONS WALES (2002), 2nd Floor,
Golate House, 101 St Mary Street, Cardiff CF10 1DX
T 029-2026 1400 E info@hpw.org.uk W www.hpw.org.uk
Chief Executive, Hilary Neagle

HEARING CONCERN (1947), 4th Floor, 275–281 King
Street, Hammersmith, London W6 9LZ
T 020-8233 2929 Helpline 0845-0744600
E info@hearingconcern.org.uk
W www.hearingconcern.org.uk
Director, Damian Barry

HELP THE AGED (1961), 207–221 Pentonville Road,
London N1 9UZ T 020-7278 1114
E info@helptheaged.org.uk W www.helptheaged.org.uk
Director-General, C. M. Lake, CBE

HERALDRY SOCIETY (1947), PO Box 772, Guildford
GU3 3ZX T 01483-237373
E memsec@theheraldrysociety.com
W www.theheraldrysociety.com
Secretary, Melvyn Jeremiah

HISPANIC AND LUSO BRAZILIAN COUNCIL (1943),
Canning House, 2 Belgrave Square, London SW1X 8PJ
T 020-7235 2303 E enquiries@canninghouse.com
W www.canninghouse.com
Director, Michael Valdes Scott

HISTORICAL ASSOCIATION (1906), 59A Kennington
Park Road, London SE11 4JH T 020-7735 3901
E enquiry@history.org.uk W www.history.org.uk
Chief Executive, Madeline Stiles

HISTORIC HOUSES ASSOCIATION (1973), 2 Chester
Street, London SW1X 7BB T 020-7259 5688
E info@hha.org.uk W www.hha.org.uk
Director-General, R. C. Wilkin, LVO, MBE

HONG KONG ASSOCIATION, Swire House, 59
Buckingham Gate, London SW1E 6AJ T 020-7963 9445/47
E info@hkas.rog.uk W www.hkas.org.uk
Executive Director, R. L. Guy

HONOURABLE SOCIETY OF CYMMRODORION
(1751), 30 Eastcastle Street, London W1W 8DJ
T 020-7631 0502 E aelodau1751we@yahoo.co.uk
W www.cymmrodorion1751.org.uk
Hon. Secretary, John Samuel

HOSPITAL SATURDAY FUND (1873), 24 Upper Ground,
London SE1 9PD T 020-7928 6662 E ukinfo@hsf.eu.com
W www.hsf.eu.com
Chief Executive, Keith Bradley

HOSPITAL SAVING ASSOCIATION (1922), Hambleden
House, Andover SP10 1LQ T 08702-425454
W www.hsa.co.uk
Chief Executive, Des Benjamin

HOSTELLING INTERNATIONAL NORTHERN
IRELAND (1931), 22–32 Donegall Road, Belfast BT12 5JN
T 028-9032 4733 E info@hini.org.uk W www.hini.org.uk
Hon. Secretary, Kevin Butler

HOUSING JUSTICE (1956), 209 Old Marylebone Road,
London NW1 5QT T 020-7723 7273
E info@housingjustice.org.uk W www.housingjustice.org.uk
Chief Executive, Ms R. Rafferty

HR SOCIETY LTD (1970), Bridge House, Church Road,
Burnham-on-Crouch CM0 8BZ T 01621-781035
E hrsoc@netcomuk.co.uk W www.hrsociety.co.uk
President, Dr Clive Purkis

HUGUENOT SOCIETY OF GREAT BRITAIN AND
IRELAND (1885), The Huguenot Library, University
College, Gower Street, London WC1E 6BT T 020-7679 5199
E library@huguenotsociety.org.uk
W www.huguenotsociety.org.uk
Hon. Secretary, Mrs B. Julien

HUMANE RESEARCH TRUST (1962), Brook House,
29 Bramhall Lane South, Bramhall, Stockport SK7 2DN
T 0161-439 8041 E info@humaneresearch.org.uk
W www.humaneresearch.org.uk
Chair, K. Cholerton

HYMN SOCIETY OF GREAT BRITAIN AND
IRELAND (1936), 99 Barton Road, Lancaster LA1 4EN
T 01524-66740 E robcanham@haystacks.fsnet.co.uk
W www.hymnsocgbi.org
Hon. Secretary, Revd Robert A. Canham

I CAN (1888), 4 Dyers Buildings, Holborn, London EC1N 2QP
T 0845-225 4071 E info@ican.org.uk W www.ican.org.uk
Chief Executive, Ms G. Edelman

ICIA (LONDON COURT OF INTERNATIONAL
ARBITRATION) (1892), 70 Fleet Street, London
EC4Y 1EU T 020-7936 7007 E lcia@lcia-arbitration.com
W www.lcia-arbitration.com
Director-General and Registrar, Adrian Winstanley

IMMIGRATION ADVISORY SERVICE (1970), 3rd Floor,
County House, 190 Great Dover Street, London SE1 4YB
T 020-7967 1200 E advice@iasuk.org W www.iasuk.org
Chief Executive, Keith Best

INCORPORATED COUNCIL OF LAW REPORTING
FOR ENGLAND AND WALES (1865), Megarry House,
119 Chancery Lane, London WC2A 1PP T 020-7242 6471
E postmaster@iclr.co.uk W www.lawreports.co.uk
Secretary, J. Cobbett

INCORPORATED SOCIETY OF MUSICIANS (1882), 10 Stratford Place, London W1C 1AA T 020-7629 4413 E membership@ism.org W www.ism.org
Chief Executive, N. Hoyle

INDEPENDENT AGE (1863), 6 Avonmore Road, London W14 8RL T 020-7605 4200 E charity@independentage.org.uk W www.independentage.org.uk
Chief Executive, Jonathan Powell

INDEPENDENT SCHOOLS' BURSARS ASSOCIATION (1932), Unit 11–12, Manor Farm, Cliddesden, RG25 2JB T 01256-330369 E office@theisba.org.uk W www.theisba.org.uk
General Secretary, Jonathan Cook

INDEPENDENT SCHOOLS CAREERS ORGANISATION (1972), 12A Princess Way, Camberley GU15 3SP T 01276-21188 E admin@isco.org.uk W www.isco.org.uk
National Director, John Stuart

INDEPENDENT SCHOOLS COUNCIL (1998), St Vincent House, 30 Orange Street, London WC2H 7HH T 020-7766 7070 E office@isc.co.uk W www.isc.co.uk
General Secretary, Jonathan Shephard

INDUSTRY AND PARLIAMENT TRUST (1977), Suite 101, 3 Whitehall Court, London SW1A 2EL T 020-7839 9400 E admin@ipt.org.uk W www.ipt.org.uk
Director and Chief Executive, Sally Muggeridge

INSTITUTE OF ACOUSTICS (1974), 77A St Peter's Street, St Albans AL1 3BN T 01727-848195 E ioa@ioa.org.uk W www.ioa.org.uk
Chief Executive, Roy D. Bratby

INSTITUTE OF ACTUARIES (1848), Staple Inn Hall, High Holborn, London WC1V 7QJ T 020-7632 2100 E institute@actuaries.org.uk W www.actuaries.org.uk
President, Michael Alan Pomery

INSTITUTE OF BIOLOGY (1950), 20–22 Queensberry Place, London SW7 2DZ T 020-7581 8333 E info@iob.org W www.iob.org
Chief Executive, Prof. A. D. B. Malcolm

INSTITUTE OF BREWING AND DISTILLING (1886), 33 Clarges Street, London W1J 7EE T 020-7499 8144 E enquiries@ibd.org.uk W www.ibd.org.uk
Chief Executive, B. E. A. Pegnall

INSTITUTE OF CANCER RESEARCH (1909), 123 Old Brompton Road, London SW7 3RP T 020-7352 8133 W www.icr.ac.uk
Chief Executive, Prof. Peter Rigby

INSTITUTE OF CAST METAL ENGINEERS (1904), National Metalforming Centre, 47 Birmingham Road, West Bromwich B70 6PY T 0121-601 6979 E info@icme.org.uk W www.icme.org.uk
Operations Manager, Marian Holland

INSTITUTE OF CHARTERED ACCOUNTANTS IN ENGLAND AND WALES (1880), Chartered Accountants' Hall, PO Box 433, Moorgate Place, London EC2P 2BJ T 020-7920 8100 W www.icaew.co.uk
Chief Executive, Eric Anstee

INSTITUTE OF CHARTERED SECRETARIES AND ADMINISTRATORS (1891), 16 Park Crescent, London W1B 1AH T 020-7580 4741 E info@icsa.co.uk W www.icsa.org.uk
Chief Executive, M. J. Ainsworth

INSTITUTE OF COMPLEMENTARY MEDICINE (1982), PO Box 194, London SE16 7QZ T 020-7237 5165 E info@i-c-m.org.uk W www.i-c-m.org.uk
Director, Michael Endacott

INSTITUTE OF DIRECTORS (1903), 116 Pall Mall, London SW1Y 5ED T 020-7839 1233 E enquiries@iod.com W www.iod.com
Chief Operating Officer, A. Main Wilson

INSTITUTE OF ECONOMIC AFFAIRS (1955), 2 Lord North Street, Westminster, London SW1P 3LB T 020-7799 8900 E iea@iea.org.uk W www.iea.org.uk
Director-General, John Blundell

INSTITUTE OF EXPORT (1935), Export House, Minerva Business Park, Lynch Wood, Peterborough PE2 6FT T 01733-404400 E institute@export.org.uk W www.export.org.uk
Director-General, Maria McCaffery, MBE

INSTITUTE OF FIELD ARCHAEOLOGISTS, School of Human and Environmental Science, Whiteknights, University of Reading, PO BOX 227 RG6 6AU T 0118-378 6446 E admin@archaeologists.net W www.archaeologists.net
Director, Peter Hinton

INSTITUTE OF FINANCIAL ACCOUNTANTS (1916), Burford House, 44 London Road, Sevenoaks TN13 1AS T 01732-458080 E mail@ifa.org.uk W www.ifa.org.uk
Chief Executive, J. M. Dean

INSTITUTE OF FOOD SCIENCE AND TECHNOLOGY (1964), 5 Cambridge Court, 210 Shepherd's Bush Road, London W6 7NJ T 020-7603 6316 E info@ifst.org W www.ifst.org
President, Jack Pearce

INSTITUTE OF HEALTH PROMOTION AND EDUCATION, Department of Oral Health and Development, University Dental Hospital, Higher Cambridge Street, Manchester M15 6FH T 0161-275 6610 W www.ihpe.org.uk
Hon. Secretary, Prof. A. S. Blinkhorn

INSTITUTE OF HERALDIC AND GENEALOGICAL STUDIES (1961), 79–82 Northgate, Canterbury CT1 1BA T 01227-768664 E ihgs@ihgs.ac.uk W www.ihgs.ac.uk
Principal, C. R. Humphery-Smith

INSTITUTE OF LINGUISTS (1910), Saxon House, 48 Southwark Street, London SE1 1UN T 020-7940 3100 E info@iol.org.uk W www.iol.org.uk
Chief Executive, Henry Pavlovich

INSTITUTE OF MANAGEMENT SERVICES (1941), Stowe House, Netherstowe, Lichfield WS13 6TJ E admin@ims-stowe-fsnet.co.uk W www.ims-productivity.com

INSTITUTE OF MARINE ENGINEERING, SCIENCE AND TECHNOLOGY (1889), 80 Coleman Street, London EC2R 5BJ T 020-7382 2600 E info@imarest.org W www.imarest.org
Director-General, Keith Read, CBE

INSTITUTE OF MASTERS OF WINE (1953), Five Kings House, 1 Queen Street Place, London EC4R 1QS T 020-7236 4427 E enquiries@masters-of-wine.org W www.masters-of-wine.org
Executive Director, Siobhan Turner

INSTITUTE OF MATERIALS, MINERALS AND MINING (2002), 1 Carlton House Terrace, London SW1Y 5DB T 020-7451 7300 E admin@iom3.org W www.iom3.org
Chief Executive, Dr Bernie Rickinson

INSTITUTE OF MATHEMATICS AND ITS APPLICATIONS (1964), Catherine Richards House, 16 Nelson Street, Southend-on-Sea SS1 1EF T 01702-354020 E post@ima.org.uk W www.ima.org.uk
Executive Director, David Youdan

INSTITUTE OF MEASUREMENT AND CONTROL (1944), 87 Gower Street, London WC1E 6AF T 020-7387 4949 W www.instmc.org.uk
President, Peter Payne

INSTITUTE OF PHYSICS AND ENGINEERING IN MEDICINE, Fairmount House, 230 Tadcaster Road, York YO24 1ES T 01904-610821 E office@ipem.org.uk W www.ipem.org.uk
General Secretary, R. W. Neilson

INSTITUTE OF QUALITY ASSURANCE (1919), 12 Grosvenor Crescent, London SW1X 7EE T 020-7245 6722 E iqa@iqa.org W www.iqa.org
Director-General, F. R. Steer, MBE

INSTITUTE OF QUARRYING (1917), 7 Regent Street, Nottingham NG1 5BS T 0115-945 3880 E mail@quarrying.org W www.quarrying.org
Executive Director, Jack Berridge

INSTITUTE OF ROAD SAFETY OFFICERS (1971), Pin Point, 1–2 Rosslyn Crescent, Harrow HA1 2SB T 0870-010 4442 E irso@dbda.co.uk W www.irso.org.uk
Chair, Anne James

INSTITUTE OF THE MOTOR INDUSTRY (IMI) (1920), Fanshaws, Brickendon, Hertford SG13 8PQ T 01992-511521 E imi@motor.org.uk W www.motor.org.uk
Chief Executive, Sarah Sillars

INSTITUTION OF CHEMICAL ENGINEERS (1922), Davis Building, 165–189 Railway Terrace, Rugby CV21 3HQ T 01788-578214 E icheme@icheme.org.uk W www.icheme.org
Chief Executive, Dr T. J. Evans

INSTITUTION OF ENGINEERING DESIGNERS (1945), Courtleigh, Westbury Leigh, Westbury BA13 3TA T 01373-822801 E ied@ied.org.uk W www.ied.org.uk
Chair, M. H. Lovell

INSTITUTION OF FIRE ENGINEERS (1918), London Road, Moreton-in-Marsh GL56 0RH T 01608-812580 E info@ife.org.uk W www.ife.org.uk
Chief Executive Officer, Ellen Jessett

INSTITUTION OF GAS ENGINEERS & MANAGERS (1863), Charnwood Wing, Holywell Park, Ashby Road, Loughborough LE11 3GH T 01509-282728 E general@igem.org.uk W www.igem.org.uk
Chief Executive, J. Williams

INSTITUTION OF MECHANICAL ENGINEERS (1847), 1 Birdcage Walk, London SW1H 9JJ T 020-7222 7899 W www.imeche.org.uk
Chief Executive, Sir Michael Moore, KBE, LVO

INSTITUTION OF OCCUPATIONAL SAFETY AND HEALTH (IOSH) (1945), The Grange, Highfield Drive, Wigston LE18 1NN T 0116-257 3100 E techinfo@iosh.co.uk W www.iosh.co.uk
Chief Executive, R. W. H. Strange

INSTITUTION OF ROYAL ENGINEERS (1875), Brompton Barracks, Chatham ME4 4UG T 01634-842669 E corps.secretary@inst-royal-engrs.co.uk W www.inst-royal-engrs.co.uk
Secretary, Lt.-Col. D. N. Hamilton, MBE

INTERCONTINENTAL CHURCH SOCIETY (1823), 1 Athena Drive, Tachbrook Park CV34 6NL T 01926-430347 E enquiries@ics-uk.org W www.ics-uk.org
Chief Executive, The Revd Canon Ian Watson

INTERNATIONAL AFRICAN INSTITUTE (1926), SOAS, Thornhaugh Street, Russell Square, London WC1H 0XG T 020-7898 4420 E iai@soas.ac.uk W www.iaionthe.net
Hon. Director, Prof. Philip Burnham

INTERNATIONAL CHURCHILL SOCIETY (1968), PO Box 1257, Melksham, Wilts SN12 6GQ T 01380-828609 W www.winstonchurchill.org
Chair, N. B. Knocker

INTERNATIONAL FEDERATION OF HYDROGRAPHIC SOCIETIES (1972), PO Box 103, Plymouth PL4 7YP T 01752-223512 E helen@hydrographicsociety.org W www.hydrographicsociety.org

INTERNATIONAL INSTITUTE FOR CONSERVATION OF HISTORIC AND ARTISTIC WORKS (1950), 6 Buckingham Street, London WC2N 6BA T 020-7839 5975 W www.iiconservation.org
Secretary-General, J. Ashley-Smith

INTERNATIONAL PEN (1921), 9–10 Charterhouse Buildings, Goswell Road, London EC1M 7AT T 020-7253 4308 E info@internationalpen.org.uk W www.internationalpen.org.uk
International Secretary, Joanne Leedom-Ackerman

INTERNATIONAL POLICE ASSOCIATION (BRITISH SECTION) (1950), 1 Fox Road, West Bridgford, Nottingham NG2 6AJ T 0115-981 3638 E mail@ipa-uk.org W www.ipa-uk.org
Executive Officer, Elizabeth Jones

INTERNATIONAL STUDENTS HOUSE (1962), 1 Park Crescent, London W1B 1SH T 020-7631 8300 E general@ish.org.uk W www.ish.org.uk
Executive Director, Peter Anwyl

INTERNATIONAL TREE FOUNDATION (1924), Sandy Lane, Crawley Down RH10 4HS T 0870-774 4269 E info@internationaltreefoundation.org W www.internationaltreefoundation.org
Company Secretary, Lynne Witheyman

INTERSERVE (1852), 325 Kennington Road, London SE11 4QH T 020-7735 8227 E enquiries@isewi.org W www.interserveonline.org.uk
National Director, Richard Clark

IRAN SOCIETY (1935), 2 Belgrave Square, London SW1X 8PJ T 020-7235 5122 E iransoc@rsaa.org.uk W www.iransoc.dircon.co.uk
Chair, M. Noël-Clarke

ISLE OF WIGHT NATURAL HISTORY AND ARCHAEOLOGICAL SOCIETY (1919), Salisbury Gardens, Dudley Road, Ventnor, PO38 1EJ T 01983-855385
President, Dr C. Pope

JACQUELINE DU PRÉ MUSIC BUILDING LTD (1995), St Hilda's College, Oxford OX4 1DY T 01865-276821 E jdp@st-hildas.ox.ac.uk W www.st-hildas.ox.ac.uk/jdp
Manager, Ms M. A. Frappat

JAPAN SOCIETY (1891), Swire House, 59 Buckingham Gate, London SW1E 6AJ T 020-7828 6330 E info@japansociety.org.uk W www.japansociety.org.uk
Executive Director, Capt. Robert Guy

JERUSALEM AND THE MIDDLE EAST CHURCH ASSOCIATION, 1 Hart House, The Hart, Farnham GU9 7HJ T 01252-726994 E secretary@jmeca.eclipse.co.uk W www.jmeca.org.uk
Secretary, Mrs V. Wells

JUSTICE (1957), 59 Carter Lane, London EC4V 5AQ T 020-7329 5100 E admin@justice.org.uk W www.justice.org.uk
Director, Roger Smith

JUSTICES' CLERKS' SOCIETY, 2nd Floor, Port of Liverpool Building, Pier Head, Liverpool L3 1BY T 0151-255 0790 E secretariat@jc-society.co.uk W www.jc-society.co.uk
Chief Executive, Sid Brighton

KENT ARCHAEOLOGICAL SOCIETY (1857), Three Elms, Woodlands Lane, Shorne, Gravesend DA12 3HH T 01474-822280 E secretary@kentarchaeology.org.uk W www.kentarchaeology.org.uk
Hon. General Secretary, A. I. Moffat

KING'S FUND (1897), 11–13 Cavendish Square, London W1G 0AN T 020-7307 2400 E sales&infopoint@kingsfund.org.uk W www.kingsfund.org.uk
Chief Executive, Niall Dickson

KIPLING SOCIETY (1927), 6 Clifton Road, London W9 1SS T 020-7286 0194 E jane@keskar.fsworld.co.uk W www.kipling.org.uk
Hon. Secretary, Jane Keskar

LEAGUE OF THE HELPING HAND (1908), PO Box 2548, Henfield, BN5 9WS T 01273-493551 E secretary@lhh.org.uk W www.lhh.org.uk
Secretary, Moira Parrott

LEPROSY MISSION (ENGLAND AND WALES) (1874), Goldhay Way, Orton Goldhay, Peterborough PE2 5GZ T 01733-370505 E post@tlmew.org.uk W www.leprosymission.org.uk
National Director, Warren Lancaster

LEUKAEMIA RESEARCH FUND (1960), 43 Great Ormond Street, London WC1N 3JJ T 020-7405 0101 E info@lrf.org.uk W www.lrf.org.uk
Chief Executive, D. L. Osborne

LINNEAN SOCIETY OF LONDON (1788), Burlington House, Piccadilly, London W1J 0BF T 020-7434 4479 W www.linnean.org
President, Prof. G. McG. Reid

LIONS CLUBS INTERNATIONAL (BRITISH ISLES AND IRELAND) (1950), 257 Alcester Road South, Kings Heath, Birmingham B14 6DT T 0121-441 4544 E lionsmd105@lineone.net W www.lions.org.uk
Office Manager, Mrs J. Davis

LISTENING BOOKS (1959), 12 Lant Street, London SE1 1QH T 020-7407 9417 E info@listening-books.org.uk W www.listening-books.org.uk
Director, Bill Dee

LLOYD'S OF LONDON, One Lime Street, London EC3M 7HA T 020-7327 6930 E maureen.clarke@lloyds.com W www.lloyds.com
Chief Executive Officer, N. E. T. Prettejohn

LOCAL GOVERNMENT ASSOCIATION (1997), Local Government House, Smith Square, London SW1P 3HZ T 020-7664 3131 E info@lga.gov.uk W www.lga.gov.uk
Chief Executive, Sir Brian Briscoe

LONDON AND MIDDLESEX ARCHAEOLOGICAL SOCIETY (1855), c/o Museum of London, 150 London Wall, London EC2Y 5HN E lamas@owlpost.plus.com W www.lamas.org.uk
Hon. Secretary, Jackie Keily

LONDON CATALYST (1873), 45 Westminster Bridge Road, London SE1 7JB T 020-7021 4204 E ruth@peabody.org.uk W www.londoncatalyst.org.uk
Chair, Timothy Cook, OBE

LONDON CITY MISSION (1835), 175 Tower Bridge Road, London SE1 2AH T 020-7407 7585 E enquiries@lcm.org.uk W www.lcm.org.uk
Chief Executive, Revd Dr John Nicholls

LONDON COLLEGE OF OSTEOPATHIC MEDICINE, 8–10 Boston Place, London NW1 6QH T 020-7262 1128
Clinic Manager, Anne Dalby

LONDON FLOTILLA (1937), 40 Endlesham Road, London SW12 8JL T 020-8673 1879 E richardupton@ntlworld.com *Hon. Membership Recruitment Secretary,* Lt.-Cdr. H. C. R. Upton, RD

LONDON LIBRARY (1841), 14 St James's Square, London SW1Y 4LG T 020-7930 7705 E membership@londonlibrary.co.uk W www.londonlibrary.co.uk *Librarian,* Inez T. P. A. Lynn

LONDON PLAYING FIELDS SOCIETY (1890), 21/22 Grosvenor Street, London W1K 4QJ T 020-7491 4992 E enquiries@lpfs.org.uk W www.lpfs.org.uk *Chief Executive,* Dr Charles Goodson-Wickes

LONDON SOCIETY (1912), Mortimer Wheeler House, 46 Eagle Wharf Road, London N1 7ED T 020-7253 9400 E info@londonsociety.org.uk W www.londonsociety.org.uk *Hon. Secretary,* John D. Hill

LORD'S DAY OBSERVANCE SOCIETY (1831), Units 7 & 8, Southern Avenue Industrial Estate, Leominster HR6 0XB T 01568-613740 E info@lordsday.co.uk W www.lordsday.co.uk *General Secretary,* John Roberts

MACA (THE MENTAL AFTER CARE ASSOCIATION) (1879), 1st Floor, Lincoln House, 296–302 High Holborn, London WC1V 7JH T 020-7061 3400 E maca-bs@maca.org.uk *Chief Executive,* Gil Hitchon

MACMILLAN CANCER RELIEF (1911), 89 Albert Embankment, London SE1 7UQ T 020-7840 7840 E cancerline@macmillan.org.uk W www.macmillan.org.uk *Chief Executive,* Peter Cardy

MAIL USERS' ASSOCIATION, 70 Main Road, Emsworth, PO10 8AX T 01243-370840 W www.mailusers.co.uk *Chair,* John Ivers

MAKING MUSIC, THE NATIONAL FEDERATION OF MUSIC SOCIETIES (1935), 7–15 Rosebery Avenue, London EC1R 4SP T 0870-903 3780 E info@makingmusic.org.uk W www.makingmusic.org.uk *Chief Executive,* R. Osterley

MANORIAL SOCIETY OF GREAT BRITAIN (1906), 104 Kennington Road, London SE11 6RE T 020-7735 6633 W www.msgb.co.uk *Executive Chairman,* Robert Smith

MARIE CURIE CANCER CARE (1948), 89 Albert Embankment, London SE1 7TP T 020-7599 7777 W www.mariecurie.org.uk *Chief Executive,* Tom Hughes-Hallett

MARINE BIOLOGICAL ASSOCIATION OF THE UK (1884), Citadel Hill, Plymouth PL1 2PB T 01752-633207 E sec@mba.ac.uk W www.mba.ac.uk *Director,* Prof. S. J. Hawkins

MARRIAGE CARE (1946), 1 Blythe Mews, Blythe Road, London W14 0NW T 020-7371 1341 E info@marriagecare.org.uk W www.marriagecare.org.uk *Chief Executive,* Terry Prendergast

THE MATERNITY ALLIANCE, Third Floor West, 2–6 Northburgh Street, London EC1V 0AY T 020-7490 7639 E office@maternityalliance.org.uk W www.maternityalliance.org.uk *Director,* Nancy Platts

MATHEMATICAL ASSOCIATION, 259 London Road, Leicester LE2 3BE T 0116-221 0013 E office@m-a.org.uk W www.m-a.org.uk *President,* Dr Sue Singer

MCPS-PRS ALLIANCE, 29–33 Berners Street, London W1T 3AB T 020-7580 5544 W www.mcps-prs-alliance.co.uk *Chief Executive Officer,* Adam Singer

MDF THE BIPOLAR ORGANISATION (1983), Castle Works, 21 St George's Road, London SE1 6ES T 020-7793 2600 E mdf@mdf.org.uk W www.mdf.org.uk *Chief Executive,* Michelle Rowett

ME ASSOCIATION (1976), 4 Top Angel, Buckingham Industrial Park, Buckingham MK18 1TH T 0870-444 8233 W www.meassociation.org.uk *Chair,* Christine Llewellyn

MEDIAWATCH-UK (1965), 3 Willow House, Kennington Road, Ashford TN24 0NR T 01233-633936 E info@mediawatchuk.org W www.mediawatchuk.org *Director,* John C. Beyer

MEDICAL WOMEN'S FEDERATION (1917), Tavistock House North, Tavistock Square, London WC1H 9HX T 020-7387 7765 E mwf@btconnect.com W www.medicalwomensfederation.org.uk *President,* Prof. Bhu Sandhu

MENCAP (ROYAL MENCAP SOCIETY) (1946), 123 Golden Lane, London EC1Y 0RT T 020-7454 0454 E information@mencap.org.uk W www.mencap.org.uk *Chief Executive,* Jo Williams, CBE

MENTAL HEALTH FOUNDATION, 20 Upper Ground, London SE1 9QB T 020-7803 1100 E mhf@mhf.org.uk W www.mentalhealth.org.uk *Chief Executive,* Andrew McCulloch

MERCHANT NAVY WELFARE BOARD (1948), 30 Palmerston Road, Southampton SO14 1LL T 023-8033 7799 E enquiries@mnwb.org.uk W www.mnwb.org *General Secretary,* Capt. D. A. Parsons

MIDDLE EAST ASSOCIATION (1961), Bury House, 33 Bury Street, London SW1Y 6AX T 020-7839 2137 E mail@the-mea.co.uk W www.the-mea.co.uk *Director-General,* James Lawday

MIGRAINE ACTION ASSOCIATION (1958), Unit 6, Oakley Hay Lodge Business Park, Great Folds Road, Great Oakley NN18 9AS T 01536-461333 W www.migraine.org.uk *Director,* Ann Turner

MIND (NATIONAL ASSOCIATION FOR MENTAL HEALTH) (1946), 15–19 Broadway, London E15 4BQ T 020-8519 2122 E contact@mind.org.uk W www.mind.org.uk *Chief Executive,* Richard Brook

MINERALOGICAL SOCIETY (1876), 41 Queen's Gate, London SW7 5HR T 020-7584 7516 E info@minersoc.org W www.minersoc.org
President, Prof. David Price

MISSION TO SEAFARERS (1856), St Michael Paternoster Royal, College Hill, London EC4R 2RL T 020-7248 5202 E general@missiontoseafarers.org W www.missiontoseafarers.org
Secretary-General, Revd Canon Bill Christianson

MULTIPLE SCLEROSIS SOCIETY (1953), MS National Centre, 372 Edgware Road, Staples Corner, London NW2 6ND T 020-8438 0700 E info@mssociety.org.uk W www.mssociety.org.uk
Chief Executive, Mike O'Donovan

MUSEUMS ASSOCIATION (1889), 24 Calvin Street, London E1 6NW T 020-7426 6970 E info@museumassociation.org W www.museumsassociation.org
Director, Mark Taylor

MUSICIANS BENEVOLENT FUND (1921), 16 Ogle Street, London W1W 6JA T 020-7636 4481 E info@mbf.org.uk W www.mbf.org.uk
Chief Executive, Ms R. Preston

NABS, 32 Wigmore Street, London W1U 2RP T 020-7292 7330 E nabs@nabs.org.uk W www.nabs.org.uk
Chair, Grant Duncan

NACRO, THE CRIME REDUCTION CHARITY (1966), 169 Clapham Road, London SW9 0PU T 020-7582 6500 E ceo@nacro.org.uk W www.nacro.org.uk
Chief Executive, Paul Cavadino

NATIONAL ADULT SCHOOL ORGANISATION (1899), Riverton, 370 Humberstone Road, Leicester LE5 0SA T 0116-253 8333 E gensec@naso.org.uk W www.naso.org.uk
Chair, Frances Sowden

NATIONAL ART COLLECTIONS FUND (1903), Millais House, 7 Cromwell Place, London SW7 2JN T 020-7225 4800 E info@artfund.org W www.artfund.org
Director, David Barrie

NATIONAL ASSOCIATION FOR COLITIS AND CROHN'S DISEASE , 4 Beaumont House, Sutton Road, St Albans AL1 5HH T 01727-830038 E nacc@nacc.org.uk W www.nacc.org.uk
Director, Richard Driscoll

NATIONAL ASSOCIATION FOR GIFTED CHILDREN (1967), Suite 14, Challenge House, Bletchley, Milton Keynes MK3 6DP T 0845-450 0221 E amazingchildren@nagcbritain.org.uk W www.nagcbritain.org.uk
Director, Dr S. Tommis

NATIONAL ASSOCIATION OF ALMSHOUSES (1951), Billingbear Lodge, Carter's Hill, Workingham RG40 5RU T 01344-452922 E naa@almshouses.org W www.almshouses.org
Director, A. P. de Ritter

NATIONAL ASSOCIATION OF BRITISH MARKET AUTHORITIES (1919), 13 Moor Road, Orrell Post, Wigan WN5 8ND T 01924-781073 E gwilsonconsultant@blueyonder.co.uk W www.nabma.com
Chief Executive, G. Wilson

NATIONAL ASSOCIATION OF CLUBS FOR YOUNG PEOPLE, 371 Kennington Lane, London SE11 5QY T 020-7793 0787 E office@clubsforyoungpeople.org.uk W www.clubsforyoungpeople.org.uk
Chief Executive, Simon Antrobus

NATIONAL ASSOCIATION OF PRISON VISITORS (1924), 32 Newnham Avenue, Bedford ME41 9PT E info@naopv.com W www.naopv.com
General Secretary, Mrs A. G. McKenna

NATIONAL BENEVOLENT INSTITUTION (1812), Peter Herve House, The Chipping, Tetbury GL8 8ET T 01666-505500 E nbi@btinternet.com W www.nbicharity.com
Chief Executive, Christopher Hill

NATIONAL CAMPAIGN FOR THE ARTS LTD (1985), Pegasus House, 37–43 Sackville Street, London W1S 3EH T 020-7333 0375 E nca@artscampaign.org.uk W www.artscampaign.org.uk
Director, Victoria Todd

NATIONAL CATTLE ASSOCIATION (DAIRY) (1998), Brick House, Risbury, Leominster, HR6 0NQ T 01568-760632 E timbrigstocke@hotmail.com
Executive Secretary, Tim Brigstocke

NATIONAL COUNCIL OF WOMEN OF GREAT BRITAIN, 72 Victoria Road, Darlington DL1 5JG T 01325-367375 E ncwgb@danburystreet.freeserve.co.uk W www.ncwgb.org
President, Amy Gibbs

NATIONAL EXTENSION COLLEGE (1963), Michael Young Centre, Purbeck Road, Cambridge CB2 2HN T 01223-400200 E info@nec.ac.uk W www.nec.ac.uk
Chief Executive, Alison West

NATIONAL FAMILY MEDIATION (1981), Alexander House, Telephone Avenue, Bristol BS1 4BS T 0117-904 2825 E general@nfm.org.uk W www.nfm.u-net.com
Chief Executive, Jane Robey

NATIONAL FOUNDATION FOR EDUCATIONAL RESEARCH IN ENGLAND AND WALES (1946), The Mere, Upton Park, Slough SL1 2DQ T 01753-574123 E enquiries@nfer.ac.uk W www.nfer.ac.uk
Director, Dr S. Hegarty

NATIONAL GARDENS SCHEME CHARITABLE TRUST (1927), Hatchlands Park, East Clandon, Guildford GU4 7RT T 01483-211535 E ngs@ngs.org.uk W www.ngs.org.uk
Chief Executive, Julia Grant

NATIONAL LIBRARY FOR THE BLIND (1828), Far Cromwell Road, Bredbury, Stockport SK6 2SG T 0161-355 2000 E enquiries@nlbuk.org W www.nlb-online.org
Chief Executive, Helen Brazier

NATIONAL MISSING PERSONS HELPLINE (1992),
Roebuck House, 284–286 Upper Richmond Road West,
London SW14 7JE T 020-8392 4590; Helpline 0500-700700
E admin@missingpersons.org W www.missingpersons.org
Co-Founders, Mrs M. Asprey, OBE; Mrs J. Newman,
OBE

NATIONAL OSTEOPOROSIS SOCIETY (1986),
Camerton, Bath BA2 0PJ T 01761-471771
E info@nos.org.uk W www.nos.org.uk
Communications Manager, Trevor Reid

NATIONAL PLAYING FIELDS ASSOCIATION (1925),
Stanley House, St Chad's Place, London WC1X 9HH
T 020-7833 5360 E npfa@npfa.co.uk
W www.playing-fields.com
Director, Alison Moore-Gwyn

NATIONAL SECULAR SOCIETY (1866), 25 Red Lion
Square, London WC1R 4RL T 020-7404 3126
E enquiries@secularism.org.uk W www.secularism.org.uk
Executive Director, K. P. Wood

NATIONAL SOCIETY FOR EPILEPSY (1892), Chesham
Lane, Chalfont St Peter, SL9 0RJ T 01494-601300
W www.epilepsynse.org.uk
Chief Executive, Graham Faulkner

NATIONAL SOCIETY FOR PROMOTING
RELIGIOUS EDUCATION (1811), Church House,
Great Smith Street, London SW1P 3NZ T 020-7898 1518
E info@natsoc.c-of-e.org.uk W www.natsoc.org.uk
General Secretary, Canon John Hall

NATIONAL TRUST (1895), 36 Queen Anne's Gate,
London SW1H 9AS T 0870-609 5380
E enquiries@thenationaltrust.org.uk
W www.nationaltrust.org.uk
Director-General, Fiona Reynolds

NATIONAL UNION OF STUDENTS (1922), Nelson
Mandela House, 461 Holloway Road, London N7 6LZ
T 020-7272 8900 E nusuk@nus.org.uk
W www.nusonline.co.uk

NATIONAL WOMEN'S REGISTER (1966), 3A Vulcan
House, Vulcan Road North, Norwich NR6 6AQ
T 01603-406767 E office@nwr.org W www.nwr.org
Membership Co-ordinator, Eilis Thorn

NAVY RECORDS SOCIETY (1893), c/o Department of
War Studies, King's College, The Strand, London WC2R 2LS
W www.navyrecordssociety.com
Hon. Secretary, Prof Andrew Lambert

NCH (1869), 85 Highbury Park, London N5 1UD
T 020-7704 7000 W www.nch.org.uk
Chief Executive, Clare Tickell

NEWCOMEN SOCIETY (1920), The Science Museum,
London SW7 2DD T 020-7371 4445
E office@newcomen.com W www.newcomen.com
Executive Secretary, Dick Swann

NEWSPAPER PRESS FUND (1864), Dickens House, 35
Wathen Road, Dorking RH4 1JY T 01306-887511
E enquiries@pressfund.org.uk
Director, David Ilott

NHS CONFEDERATION (1997), 29 Bressenden Place,
London SW1E 5DD T 020-7074 3200
W www.nhsconfed.net
Chief Executive, Dame Gill Morgan

NORFOLK AND NORWICH ARCHAEOLOGICAL
SOCIETY (1846), 30 Brettingham Avenue, Norwich
NR4 6XG T 01603-455913 W www.nnas.info
Secretary, Roger Bellinger

NORTHERN IRELAND TOURIST BOARD, St Anne's
Court, 59 North Street, Belfast BT1 1NB T 028-9023 1221
E info@nitb.com W www.nitb.com
Chief Executive, A. Clarke

NORTH OF ENGLAND ZOOLOGICAL SOCIETY
(1934), Chester Zoo, Upton, Chester CH2 1LH
T 01244-380280 E reception@chesterzoo.co.uk
W www.chesterzoo.co.uk
Zoo Director, Prof. G. McGregor Reid

NOTARIES SOCIETY (1882), 23 New Street, Woodbridge
IP12 1DN T 01394-380436
E admin@thenotariessociety.org.uk
W www.thenotariessociety.org.uk
Secretary, C. J. Vaughan

NSPCC (NATIONAL SOCIETY FOR THE
PREVENTION OF CRUELTY TO CHILDREN)
(1884), Weston House, 42 Curtain Road, London
EC2A 3NH T 020-7825 2500 W www.nspcc.org.uk
Director and Chief Executive, Mary Marsh

NUFFIELD FOUNDATION (1943), 28 Bedford Square,
London WC1B 3JS T 020-7631 0566
W www.nuffieldfoundation.org
Director, A. Tomei

NUFFIELD TRUST (1940), 59 New Cavendish Street,
London W1G 7LP T 020-7631 8450
E mail@nuffieldtrust.org.uk W www.nuffieldtrust.org.uk
Secretary, J. Wyn Owen, CB

NURSE AID (1919), Hollyhocks, 17 Tanners Street,
Faversham ME13 7JP T 01795-537787
E natnurses.fund@virgin.net W www.nurseaid.org.uk
Administrator, Ann Marie Barnard

NURSING AND MIDWIFERY COUNCIL (2002), 23
Portland Place, London W1B 1PZ T 020-7637 7181
W www.nmc-uk.org
Chief Executive, Sarah Thewlis

NUTRITION SOCIETY (1941), 10 Cambridge Court, 210
Shepherds Bush Road, London W6 7NJ T 020-7602 0228
E office@nutsoc.org.uk W www.nutsoc.org.uk
Executive Secretary, Frederick Wentworth-Bowyer

OFFICERS' ASSOCIATION (1919), 48 Pall Mall, London
SW1Y 5JY W www.officersassociation.com
General Secretary, Maj.-Gen. J. C. B. Sutherell, CBE

OMBUDSMAN FOR ESTATE AGENTS (1998), Beckett
House, 4 Bridge Street, Salisbury SP1 2LX T 01722-333306
E admin@oea.co.uk W www.oea.co.uk
Chair and Chief Operating Officer, Bill McClintock

OPEN-AIR MISSION (1853), 4 Harrier Court, Woodside Road, Slip End, Luton LU1 4DQ T 01582-841141 E info@oamission.com W www.oamission.com
General Secretary, Andy Banton

OPEN SPACES SOCIETY (1865), 25A Bell Street, Henley-on-Thames RG9 2BA T 01491-573535 E hq@oss.org.uk W www.oss.org.uk
General Secretary, Kate Ashbrook

OPSIS (1992), c/o Queen Alexandra College, Court Oak Road, Birmingham B17 9TG T 0121-428 5037 E opsis@dircon.co.uk W www.opsis.org.uk
Chief Executive, Mike Brace

ORDERS AND MEDALS RESEARCH SOCIETY (1942), PO Box 1904, Southam CV47 2ZX T 01295-690009 E generalsecretary@omrs.org W www.omrs.org.uk
General Secretary, P. M. R. Helmore

OVERSEAS DEVELOPMENT INSTITUTE, 111 Westminster Bridge Road, London SE1 7JD T 020-7922 0300 E odi@odi.org.uk W www.odi.org.uk
Director, S. Maxwell

OVERSEAS SERVICE PENSIONERS' ASSOCIATION (1960), 138 High Street, Tonbridge TN9 1AX T 01732-363836 E mail@ospa.org.uk W www.ospa.org.uk
Secretary, D. F. B. Le Breton, CBE

OXFAM GREAT BRITAIN (1942), Oxfam House, 274 Banbury Road, Oxford OX2 7DZ T 01865-311311 E enquiries@oxfam.org.uk W www.oxfam.org.uk
Director, B. Stocking, CBE

OXFORD PRESERVATION TRUST (1927), 10 Turn Again Lane, St Ebbes, Oxford OX1 1QL T 01865-242918 W www.oxfordpreservation.org.uk
Director, Debbie Dance

OXFORDSHIRE ARCHITECTURAL AND HISTORICAL SOCIETY (1839), 53 Radley Road, Abingdon OX14 3PN T 01235-525960 E tony@oahs.org.uk W www.oahs.org.uk
Hon. Secretary, Dr A. J. Dodd

OXFORD UNIVERSITY SOCIETY, Oxenford House, Magdalen Street, Oxford OX1 3AB T 01865-288088 E enquiries@ousoc.ox.ac.uk W www.alumni.ox.ac.uk
Secretary, Lady Nancy Kenny

PALAEONTOLOGICAL ASSOCIATION (1957), c/o Department of Geological Sciences, The University, South Road, Durham DH1 3LE T 0121-414 4173 E h.a.armstrong@durham.ac.uk W www.palass.org
Secretary, Dr H. A. Armstrong

PARLIAMENTARY AND SCIENTIFIC COMMITTEE (1939), 3 Birdcage Walk, Westminster, London SW1H 9JJ T 020-7222 7085 W www.scienceinparliament.org.uk
Administrative Secretary, Annabel Lloyd

PATIENTS ASSOCIATION (1963), PO Box 935, Harrow HA1 3YJ T 020-8423 9111 Helpline 0845-608 4455 E mailbox@patients-association.com W www.patients-association.com
Chair, Michael Summers

PENSIONS ADVISORY SERVICE (1983), 11 Belgrave Road, London SW1V 1RB T 0845-601 2923 E enquiries@pensionsadvisoryservice.org.uk W www.pensionsadvisoryservice.org.uk
Chief Executive, M. McLean, OBE

PERENNIAL (1839), Bridge House, 139 Kingston Road, Leatherhead KT22 7NT T 0845-230 1839 E info@perennial.org.uk W www.perennial.org.uk
Chief Executive, Ian Flanagan

PHILOLOGICAL SOCIETY (1842), Department of the Languages and Cultures of South East Asia and the Islands, School of Oriental and African Studies, Thornhaugh Street, London WC1H 0XG W secretary@philsoc.org.uk W www.philsoc.org.uk
Hon. Secretary, Dr J. Watkins

PHYSIOLOGICAL SOCIETY (1876), PO Box 11319, London WC1X 8WQ T 020-7269 5710 E admin@physoc.org W www.physoc.org
Executive Secretary, David Sewell

PILGRIMS OF GREAT BRITAIN (1902), Allington Castle, Maidstone ME16 0NB T 01622-606404 E sec@pilgrimsociety.org
Chair, Sir Robert Worcester, KBE

PILGRIM TRUST, THE (1930), Cowley House, 9 Little College Street, London SW1P 3SH T 020-7222 4723 W www.thepilgrimtrust.org.uk
Director, Georgina Nayler

PLAIN ENGLISH CAMPAIGN (1979), PO Box 3, New Mills, High Peak SK22 4QP T 01663-744409 E info@plainenglish.co.uk W www.plainenglish.co.uk
Director, Ms C. Maher

POLITE SOCIETY AND CAMPAIGN FOR COURTESY (1986), 16 Grice Road, Hartshill, Stoke-on-Trent ST4 7PJ T 01782-614407 *Secretary,* The Revd Ian Gregory

POSTWATCH (2001), 28–30 Grosvenor Gardens, London SW1W 0TT T 08456-013265 E info@postwatch.co.uk W www.postwatch.co.uk
Chief Executive, Gregor McGregor

POWYSLAND CLUB (1867), Llgyad y Dyffryn, Llanidloes SY18 6JD T 01686-412277 W www.powyslandclub.co.uk
Hon. Secretary, Miss P. M. Davies

PRE-SCHOOL LEARNING ALLIANCE (1961), 69 Kings Cross Road, London WC1X 9LL T 020-7833 0991 E pla@pre-school.org.uk W www.pre-school.org.uk
Chief Executive, Steve Alexander

PRINCESS ROYAL TRUST FOR CARERS, THE (1991), 142 Minories, London EC3N 1LB T 020-7480 7788 E info@carers.org W www.carers.org
Chief Executive, Ms S. Nicholas

PRINCE'S TRUST (1976), 18 Park Square East, London NW1 4LH T 0800-842842 E info@princes-trust.org.uk W www.princes-trust.org.uk
Chief-Executive, M. Milburn

PRISONERS ABROAD (1978), 89–93 Fonthill Road, London N4 3JH T 020-7561 6820
E info@prisonersabroad.org.uk
W www.prisonersabroad.org.uk
Chief Executive, Pauline Crowe

PRIVATE LIBRARIES ASSOCIATION (1956), Ravelston, South View Road, Pinner HA5 3YD E dchambers@aol.com
W www.the-old-school.demon.co.uk/pla.htm
Hon. Secretary, James Brown

PROFESSIONAL FOOTBALLERS' ASSOCIATION (1907), 20 Oxford Court, Bishopsgate, Manchester M2 3WQ T 0161-236 0575 E info@thepfa.co.uk
W www.givemefootball.com
Chief Executive, Gordon Taylor

PROSTATE RESEARCH CAMPAIGN UK (1994), 10 Northfields Prospect, Putney Bridge Road, London SW18 1PE T 020-8877 5840
W www.prostate-research.org.uk
President, Anthony Kilmister, OBE

PSORIASIS ASSOCIATION (1968), 7 Milton Street, Northampton NN2 7JG T 0845-676 0076
E mail@psoriasis.demon.co.uk
W www.psoriasis-association.org.uk
Chief Executive, Gladys Edwards

QUAKER PEACE AND SOCIAL WITNESS, Friends House, 173–177 Euston Road, London NW1 2BJ
T 020-7663 1000 E qpsw@quaker.org.uk
W www.quaker.org.uk
General Secretary, Linda Craig

QUEEN ELIZABETH'S FOUNDATION FOR DISABLED PEOPLE (1934), Leatherhead Court, Leatherhead KT22 0BN T 01372-841100
W www.qef.org.uk
Chief Executive, Cynthia Robinson

QUEEN'S ENGLISH SOCIETY (1973), The Clergy House, Hide Place, London SW1P 4NJ T 020-7630 1819
E enquiries@queens-english-society.com
W www.queens-english-society.com
Hon. Secretary, G. J. Hardwick

QUEEN'S NURSING INSTITUTE (1887), 3 Albemarle Way, London EC1V 4RQ T 020-7490 4227
E mail@qni.org.uk W www.qni.org.uk
Director, Rosemary Cook

QUEEN VICTORIA CLERGY FUND (1897), Church House, Great Smith Street, London SW1P 3AZ
T 020-7898 1000
Secretary, Colin Menzies

QUEEN VICTORIA SCHOOL (1908), Dunblane FK15 0JY T 01786-822288
E enquiries@qvs.org.uk
W www.qvs.org.uk
Head, Brian Raine

QUIT (1926), Ground Floor, 211 Old Street, London EC1V 9NR T 020-7251 1551 E info@quit.org.uk
W www.quit.org.uk
Chief Executive, Steve Crone

RADAR (ROYAL ASSOCIATION FOR DISABILITY AND REHABILITATION) (1977), 12 City Forum, 250 City Road, London EC1V 8AF T 020-7250 3222
E radar@radar.org.uk W www.radar.org.uk
Chief Executive, Kate Nash

RAILWAY AND CANAL HISTORICAL SOCIETY (1954), 3 West Court, West Street, Oxford OX2 0NP
T 01865-240514 E ms@bodley.ox.ac.uk
W www.bodley.ox.ac.uk/external/rchs/index.html
Hon. Secretary, M. Searle

RAILWAY BENEVOLENT INSTITUTION (1858), Electra Way, Crewe Business Park, Crewe CW1 6HS
T 01270-251316
Director, B. R. Whitnall

RAMBLERS' ASSOCIATION (1935), 2nd Floor, Camelford House, 87–90 Albert Embankment, London SE1 7TW T 020-7339 8500
E ramblers@london.ramblers.org.uk
W www.ramblers.org.uk
Chief Executive, Nick Barrett

RARE BREEDS SURVIVAL TRUST (1973), National Agricultural Centre, Stoneleigh Park, Kenilworth CV8 2LG
T 024-7669 6551 E enquiries@rbst.org.uk
W www.rbst.org.uk
Executive Director, Robert Terry

REFUGEE COUNCIL (1981), 240–250 Ferndale Road, London SW9 8BB T 020-7346 6700
E info@refugeecouncil.org.uk
W www.refugeecouncil.org.uk
Chief Executive, Maeve Sherlock

REGIONAL STUDIES ASSOCIATION (1965), PO Box 2058, Seaford BN25 4QU T 01323-899698
E rsa@mailbox.ulcc.ac.uk
W www.regional-studies-assoc.ac.uk
Chief Executive, Sally Hardy

RELATE (1938), Herbert Gray College, Little Church Street, Rugby CV21 3AP T 01788-573241
E enquiries@relate.org.uk W www.relate.org.uk
Chief Executive, Angela Sibson

RESEARCH DEFENCE SOCIETY (RDS) (1908), 25 Shaftesbury Avenue, London W1D 7EG
T 020-7287 2818 E info@rds-net.org.uk
W www.rds-net.org.uk
Executive Director, Dr S. Festing

RETHINK (1972), 30 Tabernacle Street, EC2A 4DD
T 0845-456 0455 E info@rethink.org W www.rethink.org
Chief Executive, Cliff Prior

RETIRED NURSES' NATIONAL HOME (1934), Riverside Avenue, Bournemouth BH7 7EE T 01202-396418
E anything@rnnh.co.uk W www.rnnh.co.uk
Chair, Mrs J. Kelleway

RICHARD III SOCIETY (1924), 4 Oakley Street, London SW3 5NN T 01689-823569 E neil_trump@rich ardiii.net
W www.richardiii.net
Secretary, Miss E. M. Nokes

RNIB (ROYAL NATIONAL INSTITUTE OF THE BLIND) (1868), 105 Judd Street, London WC1H 9NE
T 0845-669999 E helpline@rnib.org.uk
W www.rnib.org.uk
Director-General, Lesley Anne Alexander

RNID, 19–23 Featherstone Street, London EC1Y 8SL
T 020-7296 8000 E informationonline@rnid.org.uk
W www.rnid.org.uk
Chief Executive, Dr John Low

ROADS AND ROAD TRANSPORT HISTORY ASSOCIATION (1992), 124 Shenstone Avenue, Norton, Stourbridge Worcs DY8 3EJ T 01384-394832
Chair, Garry Turvey, CBE

ROTARY INTERNATIONAL IN GREAT BRITAIN AND IRELAND (1922), Kinwarton Road, Alcester B49 6PB T 01789-765411 E secretary@ribi.org
W www.rotary-ribi.org
Secretary, Robin Freeman

ROYAL AGRICULTURAL SOCIETY OF THE COMMONWEALTH (1957), 2 Grosvenor Gardens, London SW1W 0DH T 020-7259 9678
E rasc@commagshow.org W www.commagshow.org
Hon. Secretary, C. Runge

ROYAL AIR FORCE BENEVOLENT FUND (1919), 67 Portland Place, London W1B 1AR T 020-7580 8343
E info@rafbf.org.uk W www.rafbf.org.uk
Controller, Air Chief Marshal Sir David Cousins, KCB, AFC, BA

ROYAL ASIATIC SOCIETY (1823), 60 Queens Gardens, London W2 3AF T 020-7724 4741
E info@royalasiaticsociety.org
W www.royalasiaticsociety.org
Executive Officer, Catherine Melia

ROYAL ASSOCIATION FOR DEAF PEOPLE (1841), Centre for Deaf People, Walsingham Road, Colchester CO2 7BP T 01206-509509 Text: 01206 711260
E info@royaldeaf.org.uk W www.royaldeaf.org.uk
Chief Executive, Tom Fenton

ROYAL ASSOCIATION OF BRITISH DAIRY FARMERS (1879), Dairy House, 60 Kenilworth Road, Leamington Spa CV32 6JX T 01926-887477
E office@rabdf.co.uk
Chief Executive, N. Everington

ROYAL BIRMINGHAM SOCIETY OF ARTISTS (1814), 4 Brook Street, Birmingham B3 1SA T 0121-236 4353
E secretary@rbsa.org.uk W www.rbsa.org.uk
Gallery Director, Marie Considine

ROYAL BRITISH LEGION (1921), 48 Pall Mall, London SW1Y 5JY T 020-7973 7200 E info@britishlegion.org.uk
W www.britishlegion.org.uk
Secretary-General, Brig. Ian Townsend

ROYAL CAMBRIAN ACADEMY (1882), Crown Lane, Conwy LL32 8AN T 01492-593413 E rca@rcaconwy.org
W www.rcaconwy.org
President, Sir Kyffin Williams

ROYAL CELTIC SOCIETY (1820), 23 Rutland Street, Edinburgh EH1 2RN T 0131-228 6449
E gcameron@stuartandstuart.co.uk
Secretary, J. Gordon Cameron, WS

ROYAL CHORAL SOCIETY (1872), Studio 9, 92 Lots Road, London SW10 0QD T 020-7376 3718
E helenbody@royalchoralsociety.co.uk
W www.royalchoralsociety.co.uk
Administrator, Helen Body

ROYAL COLLEGE OF OBSTETRICIANS AND GYNAECOLOGISTS (1929), 27 Sussex Place, Regent's Park, London NW1 4RG T 020-7772 6200
W www.rcog.org.uk
Chief Executive, Helen Moffatt

ROYAL COLLEGE OF PAEDIATRICS AND CHILD HEALTH, 50 Hallam Street, London W1W 6DE
T 020-7307 5600 W www.rcpch.ac.uk
President, Prof. Alan Craft

ROYAL COLLEGE OF PATHOLOGISTS (1962), 2 Carlton House Terrace, London SW1Y 5AF
T 020-7451 6700 E info@rcpath.org W www.rcpath.org
President, Sir James Underwood

ROYAL COLLEGE OF PHYSICIANS (1518), 11 St Andrews Place, Regent's Park, London NW1 4LE
T 020-7935 1174 E info@rcplondon.ac.uk
W www.rcplondon.ac.uk
Chief Executive, A. P. Masterton-Smith

ROYAL COLLEGE OF RADIOLOGISTS (1975), 38 Portland Place, London W1B 1JQ T 020-7636 4432
E enquiries@rcr.ac.uk W www.rcr.ac.uk
Chief Executive, A. Hall

ROYAL COLLEGE OF SURGEONS OF ENGLAND (1800), 35–43 Lincoln's Inn Fields, London WC2A 3PE
T 020-7405 3474 W www.rcseng.ac.uk
Chief Executive, Craig Duncan

ROYAL ENGINEERS ASSOCIATION (1869), RHQ Royal Engineers, Brompton Barracks, Chatham ME4 4UG
T 01634-847005 W www.reahq.org.uk
Controller, Lt.-Col. John McLennan (retd)

ROYAL FACULTY OF PROCURATORS IN GLASGOW, 12 Nelson Mandela Place, Glasgow G2 1BT T 0141-331 0533 E i.c.pearson@rfpg.org W www.rfpg.org
General Manager, Iain C. Pearson

ROYAL GEOGRAPHICAL SOCIETY (WITH THE INSTITUTE OF BRITISH GEOGRAPHERS) (1830), 1 Kensington Gore, London SW7 2AR T 020-7591 3000
E info@rgs.org W www.rgs.org
Director, Dr R. Gardner, CBE

ROYAL HISTORICAL SOCIETY (1868), University College London, Gower Street, London WC1E 6BT
T 020-7387 7532 E royalhistsoc@ucl.ac.uk
W www.rhs.ac.uk
Executive Secretary, Jane Boland

ROYAL HORTICULTURAL SOCIETY (1804), 80 Vincent Square, London SW1P 2PE
T 020-7834 4333 E info@rhs.org.uk W www.rhs.org.uk
Director-General, Dr A. Colquhoun

ROYAL HOSPITAL FOR NEURO-DISABILITY (1854),
West Hill, Putney, London SW15 3SW T 020-8780 4500
E info@rhn.org.uk W www.rhn.org.uk
Chief Executive, Peter Franklyn

ROYAL INSTITUTE OF BRITISH ARCHITECTS
(1837), 66 Portland Place, London W1B 1AD
T 020-7580 5533. Information 0906-302 0400
E info@inst.riba.org W www.architecture.com
Chief Executive, Richard Hastilow, CBE

ROYAL INSTITUTE OF NAVIGATION (1947),
1 Kensington Gore, London SW7 2AT
T 020-7591 3130 E info@rin.org.uk
W www.rin.org.uk
Director, Gp Capt. D. W. Broughton, MBE

ROYAL INSTITUTE OF OIL PAINTERS (1882),
17 Carlton House Terrace, London SW1Y 5BD
T 020-7930 6844 E info@mallgalleries.com
W www.mallgalleries.org.uk
President, Dennis Syrett

ROYAL INSTITUTE OF PAINTERS IN WATER
COLOURS (1831), 17 Carlton House Terrace, London
SW1Y 5BD T 020-7930 6844 E info@mallgalleries.com
W www.mallgalleries.org.uk
President, Ronald Maddox

ROYAL INSTITUTE OF PHILOSOPHY (1925),
14 Gordon Square, London WC1H 0AG
T 020-7387 4130 W www.royalinstitutephilosophy.org
President, The Lord Quinton

ROYAL INSTITUTION OF CHARTERED
SURVEYORS (1868), 12 Great George Street, Parliament
Square, London SW1P 3AD T 020-7222 7000
E contactrics@rics.org W www.rics.org
Chief Executive, J. H. A. J. Armstrong

ROYAL INSTITUTION OF GREAT BRITAIN (1799),
21 Albemarle Street, London W1S 4BS T 020-7409 2992
E ri@ri.ac.uk W www.rigb.org
Director, Baroness Greenfield, CBE

ROYAL INSTITUTION OF NAVAL ARCHITECTS
(1860), 10 Upper Belgrave Street, London SW1X 8BQ
T 020-7235 4622 E hq@rina.org.uk W www.rina.org.uk
Chief Executive, T. Blakeley

THE ROYAL LIFE SAVING SOCIETY UK (1891), River
House, High Street, Broom B50 4HN T 01789-773994
E lifesavers@rlss.org.uk W www.lifesavers.org.uk
Chief Executive, D. Standley

ROYAL LONDON SOCIETY FOR THE BLIND (1838),
Dorton House, Seal, Sevenoaks TN15 0ED T 01732-592500
E ceosoffice@rlsb.org.uk W www.rlsb.org.uk
Chief Executive, Brian J. Cooney

ROYAL MASONIC BENEVOLENT INSTITUTION
(1842), 20 Great Queen Street, London WC2B 5BG
T 020-7596 2400 E enquiries@rmbi.org.uk
W www.rmbi.org.uk
Chief Executive, Peter J. Gray

ROYAL MASONIC TRUST FOR GIRLS AND BOYS
(1982), 31 Great Queen Street, London WC2B 5AG
W www.rmtgb.org
President, A. J. F. Stebbings

ROYAL MEDICAL BENEVOLENT FUND (1836),
24 Kings Road, London SW19 8QN T 020-8540 9194
E info@rmbf.org W www.rmbf.org
Chief Executive, Michael Baber

ROYAL MICROSCOPICAL SOCIETY (1839),
37–38 St Clements, Oxford OX4 1AJ T 01865-248768
E info@rms.org.uk W www.rms.org.uk
Executive Director, R. Flavin

ROYAL NATIONAL COLLEGE FOR THE BLIND
(1872), College Road, Hereford HR1 1EB T 01432-265725
E info@rncb.ac.uk W www.rncb.ac.uk
Principal, Mrs R. Burge

ROYAL NATIONAL LIFEBOAT INSTITUTION (1824),
West Quay Road, Poole BT15 1HZ T 0845-122 6999
E info@rnli.org.uk W www.rnli.org.uk
Chief Executive, A. Freemantle, MBE

ROYAL NAVAL BENEVOLENT SOCIETY FOR
OFFICERS (1739), 70 Porchester Terrace, London
W2 3TP T 020-7402 5231 E rnbso@lineone.net
Secretary, Cdr. W. K. Ridley, OBE, RN

ROYAL NAVAL BENEVOLENT TRUST (1922),
Castaway House, 311 Twyford Avenue, Portsmouth
PO2 8RN T 023-9269 0112/9266 0296 E rnbt@rnbt.org.uk
W www.rnbt.org.uk
Chief Executive, Cdr. J. Owens, RN

ROYAL PHARMACEUTICAL SOCIETY OF GREAT
BRITAIN (1841), 1 Lambeth High Street, London SE1 7JN
T 020-7735 9141 E enquiries@rpsgb.org W www.rpsgb.org
Secretary and Registrar, Ann Lewis

ROYAL PHILATELIC SOCIETY LONDON (1869),
41 Devonshire Place, London W1G 6JY T 020-7486 1044
E secretary@rpsl.org.uk W www.rpsl.org.uk
Hon. Secretary, K. B. Fitton

ROYAL PHILHARMONIC SOCIETY (1813),
10 Stratford Place, London W1C 1BA T 020-7491 8110
E admin@royalphilharmonicsociety.org
W www.royalphilharmonicsociety.org.uk
Chair, Tony Fell

ROYAL PHOTOGRAPHIC SOCIETY (1853), The
Octagon, Milsom Street, Bath BA1 1DN T 01225-325733
E rps@rps.org W www.rps.org
President, R. Reynolds

ROYAL SCHOOL OF CHURCH MUSIC (1927),
Cleveland Lodge, Westhumble, Dorking RH5 6BW
T 01306-872800 E enquiries@rscm.com W www.rscm.com
Director-General, Prof. J. Harper

ROYAL SCHOOL OF NEEDLEWORK (1872),
Apartment 12A, Hampton Court Palace, KT8 9AU
T 020-8943 1432 E enquiries@royal-needlework.co.uk
W www.royal-needlework.co.uk
Principal, Mrs E. Elvin

ROYAL SOCIETY (1660), 6–9 Carlton House Terrace, London SW1Y 5AG T 020-7451 2500 E info@royalsoc.ac.uk W www.royalsoc.ac.uk
Executive Secretary, Stephen Cox, CVO

ROYAL SOCIETY FOR ASIAN AFFAIRS (1901), 2 Belgrave Square, London SW1X 8PJ T 020-7235 5122 E sec@rsaa.org.uk W www.rsaa.org.uk
Chair, Sir Harold Walker, KCMG

ROYAL SOCIETY FOR THE ENCOURAGEMENT OF ARTS, MANUFACTURES AND COMMERCE (RSA) (1754), 8 John Adam Street, London WC2N 6EZ T 020-7930 5115 E general@rsa.org.uk W www.thersa.org
Executive Director, Penny Egan

ROYAL SOCIETY FOR THE PREVENTION OF ACCIDENTS (1917), ROSPA House, Edgbaston Park, 353 Bristol Road, Birmingham B5 7ST T 0121-248 2000 E help@rospa.com W www.rospa.com
Chief Executive, John Howard, OBE

ROYAL SOCIETY FOR THE PREVENTION OF CRUELTY TO ANIMALS (1824), Wilberforce Way, Horsham RH13 9RS T 0870-010 1181 W www.rspca.org.uk
Director-General, Jackie Ballard

ROYAL SOCIETY OF LITERATURE (1820), Somerset House, Strand, London WC2R 1LA T 020-7845 4676 E info@rslit.org W www.rslit.org
Chair, Maggie Gee, FRSL

ROYAL SOCIETY OF MARINE ARTISTS (1945), 17 Carlton House Terrace, London SW1Y 5BD T 020-7930 6844 E info@mallgalleries.com W www.mallgalleries.org.uk
President, G. Hunt

ROYAL SOCIETY OF MEDICINE (1805), 1 Wimpole Street, London W1G 0AE T 020-7290 2900 E membership@rsm.ac.uk W www.rsm.ac.uk
Executive Director, Dr A. Grocock

ROYAL SOCIETY OF MINIATURE PAINTERS, SCULPTORS AND GRAVERS (1895), 1 Knapp Cottages, Wyke, Gillingham SP8 4NQ T 01747-825718 E pamhenderson@dsl.pipex.com W www.royal-miniature-society.org.uk
Executive Secretary, Pam Henderson

ROYAL SOCIETY OF MUSICIANS OF GREAT BRITAIN (1738), 10 Stratford Place, London W1C 1BA T 020-7629 6137
Secretary, Mrs M. Gibb

ROYAL SOCIETY OF PORTRAIT PAINTERS (1891), 17 Carlton House Terrace, London SW1Y 5BD T 020-7930 6844 E info@mallgalleries.com W www.mallgalleries.org.uk
President, Andrew Festing

ROYAL SOCIETY OF ST GEORGE (1894), 127 Sandgate Road, Folkstone CT20 2BH T 01303-241795 E info@rssg.u-net.com W www.royalsocietyofstgeorge.com
Chair, J. C. Clemence, QPM

ROYAL SOCIETY OF TROPICAL MEDICINE AND HYGIENE (1907), 50 Bedford Square, London WC1B 3DP T 020-7580 2127 E mail@rstmh.org W www.rstmh.org
Hon. Secretaries, Prof. G. Pasvol and Dr J. R. Stothard

ROYAL STAR AND GARTER HOME FOR DISABLED EX-SERVICE MEN AND WOMEN (1916), Richmond Hill, Richmond TW10 6RR T 020-8439 8000 E generalenquiries@starandgarter.org W www.starandgarter.org
Chief Executive, Lynn McDougall

ROYAL ULSTER AGRICULTURAL SOCIETY (1896), The King's Hall, Balmoral, Belfast BT9 6GW T 028-9066 5225 E general@kingshall.co.uk W www.balmoralshow.co.uk
Chief Executive, Michael Guest

ROYAL UNITED SERVICES INSTITUTE FOR DEFENCE AND SECURITY STUDIES (1831), Whitehall, London SW1A 2ET T 020-7930 5854 W www.rusi.org
Director, Rear-Adm. Richard Cobbold

ROYAL WATERCOLOUR SOCIETY (1804), Bankside Gallery, 48 Hopton Street, London SE1 9JH T 020-7928 7521 E info@banksidegallery.com W www.royalwatercoloursociety.com
President, Trevor Frankland

RURAL SCOTLAND (1926), 3rd Floor, Gladstone's Land, 483 Lawnmarket, Edinburgh EH1 2NT T 0131-225 7012 E info@ruralscotland.org W www.ruralscotland.org
Director, Bill Wright

ST ALBANS AND HERTFORDSHIRE ARCHITECTURAL AND ARCHAEOLOGICAL SOCIETY (1845), 24 Monks Horton Way, St Albans AL1 4HA T 01727-851734 W www.stalbanshistory.org
Hon. Secretary, B. R. Hanlon

ST DEINIOL'S RESIDENTIAL LIBRARY (1894), Hawarden, Deeside CH5 3DF T 01244-532350 E deiniol.visitors@btconnect.com W www.st-deiniols.org
Warden and Chief Librarian, Revd Peter Francis

ST DUNSTAN'S (1915), 12–14 Harcourt Street, London W1H 4HD T 020-7723 5021 E enquiries@st-dunstans.org.uk W www.st-dunstans.org.uk
Chief Executive, Robert Leader

SALTIRE SOCIETY (1936), 9 Fountain Close, 22 High Street, Edinburgh EH1 1TF T 0131-556 1836 E saltire@saltiresociety.org.uk W www.saltiresociety.org.uk
Administrator, Mrs K. Munro

SANE (1986), 1st Floor, Cityside House, 40 Adler Street, London E1 1EE T 020-7375 1002 Helpline: 0845-767 8000 E info@sane.org.uk W www.sane.org.uk
Chief Executive, Ms M. Wallace, MBE

SAVE BRITAIN'S HERITAGE (1975), 70 Cowcross Street, London EC1M 6EJ T 020-7253 3500 E save@btinternet.com W www.savebritainsheritage.org
President, Marcus Binney, OBE

SCHOOL OF PUBLIC POLICY (1996), University College London, 29 Tavistock Square, London WC1H 9QU T 020-7679 4999 E spp@ucl.ac.uk W www.ucl.ac.uk/spp/ *Director,* Professor Stephen Smith

SCOTTISH ASSOCIATION FOR MENTAL HEALTH (1923), Cumbrae House, 15 Carlton Court, Glasgow G5 9JP T 0141-568 7000 E enquire@samh.org.uk W www.samh.org.uk *Chief Executive,* Ms S. M. Neil

SCOTTISH CHAMBERS OF COMMERCE (1948), 30 George Square, Glasgow G2 1EQ T 0141-204 8316 E admin@scottishchambers.org.uk W www.scottishchambers.org.uk *Director,* Liz Cameron

SCOTTISH COUNCIL FOR VOLUNTARY ORGANISATIONS, Mansfield Traquair Centre, 15 Mansfield Place, Edinburgh EH3 6BB T 0131-556 3882 E enquiries@scvo.org.uk W www.scvo.org.uk *Chief Executive,* M. Sime

SCOTTISH GENEALOGY SOCIETY (1953), Library and Family History Centre, 15 Victoria Terrace, Edinburgh EH1 2JL T 0131-220 3677 E info@scotsgenealogy.com W www.scotsgenealogy.com *Hon. Secretary,* Kenneth A. M. Nisbet

SCOTTISH NATIONAL WAR MEMORIAL (1927), The Castle, Edinburgh EH1 2YT T 0131-226 7393 W www.snwm.org *Secretary to the Trustees,* Lt.-Col. I. Shepherd

SCOTTISH NATURAL HISTORY LIBRARY (1970), Foremount House, Kilbarchan, PA10 2EZ T 01505-702419 *Director,* Dr J. A. Gibson

SCOTTISH RURAL PROPERTY AND BUSINESS ASSOCIATION (SRPBA), Stuart House, Eskmills Business Park, Musselburgh EH21 7PB T 0131-653 5400 E info@srpba.com W www.srpba.com *Director-General,* Dr M. S. Hankey

SCOTTISH SOCIETY FOR THE PREVENTION OF CRUELTY TO ANIMALS (1839), Braehead Mains, 603 Queensferry Road, Edinburgh EH4 6EA T 0131-339 0222 E enquiries@scottishspca.org W www.scottishspca.org *Chief Executive,* Mrs K. Driver

SCOTTISH SOCIETY FOR THE PROTECTION OF WILD BIRDS (1927), Foremount House, Kilbarchan PA10 2EZ T 01505-702419 *Secretary,* Dr J. A. Gibson

SCOTTISH WILDLIFE TRUST (1964), Cramond House, Cramond Glebe Road, Edinburgh EH4 6NS T 0131-312 7765 E enquiries@swt.org.uk W www.swt.org.uk *Chief Executive,* Simon Milne

SCOUT ASSOCIATION (1907), Gilwell Park, Chingford, London E4 7QW T 020-8443 7100 E info.centre@scout.org.uk W www.scoutbase.org.uk/ *Chief Executive,* D. M. Twine

SEA CADET ASSOCIATION, 202 Lambeth Road, London SE1 7JF T 020-7928 8978 E schq@sea-cadets.org W www.sea-cadets.org *Chief Executive,* Michael J. Cornish

SEEABILITY (1799), SeeAbility House, Hook Road, Epsom, KT19 8SQ T 01372-755000 E reception@seeability.org W www.seeability.org *Chief Executive,* D. Scott-Ralphs

SELDEN SOCIETY (1887), Faculty of Laws, Queen Mary and Westfield College, Mile End Road, London E1 4NS T 020-7882 5136 E selden-society@qmw.ac.uk W www.selden-society.qmw.ac.uk *Secretary,* V. Tunkel

SHAFTESBURY SOCIETY (1844), 16 Kingston Road, London SW19 1JZ T 020-8239 5555 E info@shaftesburysoc.org.uk W www.shaftesburysociety.org *Chief Executive,* Mrs Mary Bishop

SHELLFISH ASSOCIATION OF GREAT BRITAIN (1903), Fishmongers' Hall, London Bridge, London EC4R 9EL T 020-7283 8305 E sagb@shellfish.org.uk W www.shellfish.org.uk *Director,* Dr P. Hunt

SHELTER (NATIONAL CAMPAIGN FOR HOMELESS PEOPLE), 88 Old Street, London EC1V 9HU T 020-7505 4699 SHELTERLINE: 0808-800 4444 E info@shelter.org.uk W www.shelter.org.uk *Director,* Adam Sampson

SHIRE HORSE SOCIETY (1878), East of England Showground, Peterborough PE2 6XE T 01733-234451 E info@shire-horse.org.uk W www.shire-horse.org.uk *Chief Executive Officer,* Andrew Mercer

SHROPSHIRE ARCHAEOLOGICAL AND HISTORICAL SOCIETY (1877), Lower Wallop Farm, Westbury SY5 9RT T 01743-891215 E walloparch@farming.co.uk *Chair,* J. B. Lawson

SIGHT SAVERS INTERNATIONAL (ROYAL COMMONWEALTH SOCIETY FOR THE BLIND) (1950), Grosvenor Hall, Bolnore Road, Haywards Heath RH16 4BX T 01444-446600 E generalinformation@sightsavers.org W www.sightsavers.org.uk *Chief Executive,* Dr Caroline Harper

SIMPLIFIED SPELLING SOCIETY (1908), 4 Valetta Way, Wellesbourne, Warwick CV35 9TB E membership@spellingsociety.org W www.spellingsociety.org *Membership Secretary,* John Gledhill

SIR OSWALD STOLL FOUNDATION (1916), 446 Fulham Road, London SW6 1DT T 020-7385 2110 E info@oswaldstoll.org.uk W www.oswaldstoll.org.uk *Chief Executive,* R. C. Brunwin

SOCIALIST PARTY OF GREAT BRITAIN (1904), 52 Clapham High Street, London SW4 7UN T 020-7622 3811 E spgb@worldsocialism.org W www.worldsocialism.org *General Secretary,* John Bissett

SOCIÉTÉ JERSIAISE, ARCHAEOLOGICAL SECTION (1873), 7 Pier Road, St Helier, JE2 4XW T 01534-758314
E societe@societe-jersiaise.org W www.societe-jersiaise.org
Executive Director, Mrs P. Syvret

SOCIETY FOR PROMOTING CHRISTIAN
KNOWLEDGE (SPCK) (1698), 36 Causton Street,
London SW1P 4ST T 020-7592 3900 E spck@spck.org.uk
W www.spck.org.uk
General Secretary, G. C. King

SOCIETY FOR PSYCHICAL RESEARCH (1882), 49
Marloes Road, London W8 6LA T 020-7937 8984
W www.spr.ac.uk

SOCIETY FOR THE PROMOTION OF HELLENIC
STUDIES (1879), Senate House, Malet Street, London
WC1E 7HU T 020-7862 8730
E office@hellenicsociety.org.uk
W www.hellenicsociety.org.uk/
President, Prof. Robin Osborne

SOCIETY FOR THE PROMOTION OF ROMAN
STUDIES (1910), Senate House, Malet Street, London
WC1E 7HU T 020-7862 8727 E office@romansociety.org
W www.romansociety.org
Secretary, Dr Helen Cockle

SOCIETY FOR THE PROTECTION OF ANCIENT
BUILDINGS (1877), 37 Spital Square, London E1 6DY
T 020-7377 1644 E info@spab.org.uk W www.spab.org.uk
Chair, John Bailey

SOCIETY FOR THE PROTECTION OF UNBORN
CHILDREN (1967), 5–6 St Matthew Street, London
SW1P 2JT T 020-7222 5845 E information@spuc.org.uk
W www.spuc.org.uk
National Director, John Smeaton

SOCIETY OF ANTIQUARIES OF LONDON (1707),
Burlington House, Piccadilly, London W1J 0BE
E admin@sal.org.uk W www.sal.org.uk
General-Secretary, David Gaimster, PHD, FSA

SOCIETY OF ANTIQUARIES OF NEWCASTLE UPON
TYNE (1813), Black Gate, Castle Garth, Newcastle
upon Tyne NE1 1RQ T 0191-261 5390
E admin@newcastle-antiquaries.org.uk
W www.newcastle-antiquaries.org.uk
Secretary, N. Hodgson

SOCIETY OF ANTIQUARIES OF SCOTLAND (1780),
Royal Museum, Chambers Street, Edinburgh EH1 1JF
T 0131-247 4115/4133 E director@socantscot.org
W www.socantscot.org
Director, A. Smith, FSA

SOCIETY OF APOTHECARIES OF LONDON (1617),
Black Friars Lane, London EC4V 6EJ T 020-7236 1189
E clerk@apothecaries.org W www.apothecaries.org
Clerk, A. M. Wallington-Smith

SOCIETY OF ARCHIVISTS (1947), Prioryfield House,
20 Canon Street, Taunton TA1 1SW T 01823-327030
E societyofarchivists@archives.org.uk
W www.archives.org.uk
Executive Secretary, P. S. Cleary

SOCIETY OF AUTHORS (1884), 84 Drayton Gardens,
London SW10 9SB T 020-7373 6642
E info@societyofauthors.org W www.societyofauthors.org
General Secretary, Mark Le Fanu, OBE

SOCIETY OF BOTANICAL ARTS (1985), 1 Knapp
Cottages, Wyke, Gillingham SP8 4NQ T 01747-825718
E pam@soc-botanical-artists.org
W www.soc-botanical-artists.org
Executive Secretary, Pam Henderson

SOCIETY OF COUNTY TREASURERS, Surrey County
Council, PO Box 5, County Hall, Kingston-upon-Thames KT1
2EA T 020-8541 9200 E mjtaylor@surreycc.gov.uk
W www.sctnet.org.uk
Hon. Secretary, Mike Taylor

SOCIETY OF EDITORS (1999), University Centre, Granta
Place, Cambridge CB2 1RU T 01223-304080
E info@societyofeditors.org W www.societyofeditors.org
Executive Director, Bob Satchwell

SOCIETY OF GENEALOGISTS (1911 and 1999),
14 Charterhouse Buildings, Goswell Road, London
EC1M 7BA T 020-7251 8799 E info@sog.org.uk
W www.sog.org.uk
Director (acting), June Perrin

SOCIETY OF GLASS TECHNOLOGY, Don Valley House,
Savile Street East, Sheffield S4 7UQ T 0114-263 4455
E info@sgt.org W www.sgt.org
Managing Editor, D. Moore

SOCIETY OF INDEXERS (1957), Blades Enterprise
Centre, John Street, Sheffield S2 4SU T 0114-292 2350
E admin@indexers.org.uk W www.indexers.org.uk
Secretary, Ann Kingdom

SOCIETY OF LEGAL SCHOLARS (1908), School of Law,
Southampton University, Southampton SO17 1BJ
T 023-8059 3416 E njw@soton.ac.uk
W www.legalscholars.ac.uk
Hon. Secretary, Prof. N. J. Wikeley

SOCIETY OF LOCAL AUTHORITY CHIEF
EXECUTIVES AND SENIOR MANAGERS (1972),
Hope House, 45 Great Peter Street, London SW1P 3LT
T 0845-601 0649 E hope.house@solace.org.uk
W www.solace.org.uk
Director-General, David Clark

SOCIETY OF NAUTICAL RESEARCH (1910),
c/o National Maritime Museum, Park Row, Greenwich,
London SE10 9NF T 020-8312 6502 W www.snr.org
Chair, Prof. Richard Harding

SOCIETY OF SCHOOLMASTERS AND
SCHOOLMISTRESSES (1798), c/o L. I. Baggott, SGBI
Office, Queen Mary House, Manor Park Road, Chistlehurst
BR7 5PY T 020-8468 7997 E sgbi@sgbi.freeserve.co.uk
Secretary (acting), Laurence Baggott, FCA

SOCIETY OF SCRIBES AND ILLUMINATORS (1921),
6 Queen Square, London WC1N 3AT T 01524-251534
E scribe@calligraphyonline.org
W www.calligraphyonline.org
Chair, Tony Curtis

SOCIETY OF SOLICITORS IN THE SUPREME
COURT OF SCOTLAND (1784), SSC Library,
Parliament House, 11 Parliament Square, Edinburgh EH1 1RF
T 0131-225 6268 E enquiries@ssclibrary.co.uk
W www.ssclibrary.co.uk
Secretary, I. L. S. Balfour

SOCIETY OF WOMEN ARTISTS (1855), 1 Knapp
Cottages, Wyke, Gillingham SP8 4NQ T 01747-825718
E pamhenderson@dsl.pipex.com
W www.society-women-artists.org.uk
Executive Secretary, Pam Henderson

SOCIETY OF WRITERS TO HM SIGNET (1594),
Signet Library, Parliament Square, Edinburgh EH1 1RF
T 0131-220 3426 E enquiries@wssociety.co.uk
W www.signetlibrary.co.uk
General Manager, M. R. McVittie

SOIL ASSOCIATION (1946), Bristol House, 40–56 Victoria
Street, Bristol BS1 6BY T 0117-314 5000
E info@soilassociation.org W www.soilassociation.org
Director, P. Holden

SOMERSET ARCHAEOLOGICAL AND NATURAL
HISTORY SOCIETY (1849), Taunton Castle, Taunton
TA1 4AA T 01823-272429
E secretary@sanhs.freeserve.co.uk W www.sanhs.org
Chair, Pat Hill-Cottingham

SOUTH AMERICAN MISSION SOCIETY (1844), Allen
Gardiner Cottage, Pembury Road, Tunbridge Wells TN2 3QU
T 01892-538647 E gensec@samsgb.org
W www.samsgb.org
General Secretary, Revd. Canon J. W. Sutton

SOUTH WALES INSTITUTE OF ENGINEERS (1857),
2nd Floor, Empire House, Mount Stuart Square, Cardiff
CF10 5FN T 029-2048 1726 E info@swie.org.uk
W www.swie.org.uk
Hon. Secretary, D. M. Morgan

SPORT HORSE BREEDING OF GREAT BRITAIN
(1886), 96 High Street, Edenbridge TN8 5AR
T 01732-866277 E office@sporthorsegb.co.uk
W www.sporthorsegb.co.uk
General Secretary, Miss C. G. Burdock

SPURGEON'S CHILD CARE (1867), 74 Wellingborough
Road, Rushden NN10 9TY T 01933-412412
E scc@spurgeons.org W www.spurgeonschildcare.org
Chief Executive, D. C. Culwick

STANDING COUNCIL OF SCOTTISH CHIEFS,
Hope Chambers, 52 Leith Walk, Edinburgh EH6 5HW
T 0131-553 2232 E bevkel@btinternet.com
General Secretary, Romilly Squire of Rubislaw

STANDING COUNCIL OF THE BARONETAGE
(1903), 3 Eastcroft Road, West Ewell, Epsom KT19 9TX
T 020-8393 6620 E secretary@baronetage.org
W www.baronetage.org
Chair, Sir Geoffrey Errington, BT, OBE

SUFFOLK INSTITUTE OF ARCHAEOLOGY AND
HISTORY (1848), Roots, Church Lane, Playford IP6 9DS
W www.suffolkarch.org.uk
Hon. Secretary, B. J. Seward

SUNDERLAND ANTIQUARIAN SOCIETY (1900), c/o
Southwark Community School, Ryhope Road, Sunderland
SR2 7TF T 0191-522 0517
President, D. W. Smith

SURREY ARCHAEOLOGICAL SOCIETY (1854), Castle
Arch, Guildford GU1 3SX T 01483-532454
E info@surreyarchaeology.org.uk
Hon. Secretary, P. E. Youngs

SUSSEX ARCHAEOLOGICAL SOCIETY (1846), Bull
House, 92 High Street, Lewes BN7 1XH T 01273-486260
E admin@sussexpast.co.uk W www.sussexpast.co.uk
Chief Executive, J. Manley

SUZY LAMPLUGH TRUST (1986), 14 East Sheen Avenue,
London SW14 8AS T 020-8876 0305
E info@suzylamplugh.org W www.suzylamplugh.org
Chief Executive, Julie Bentley

SWEDENBORG SOCIETY (1810), 20/21 Bloomsbury
Way, London WC1A 2TH T 020-7405 7986
E swed.soc@netmatters.co.uk W www.swedenborg.org.uk
Secretary, Richard Lines

THEATRES TRUST (1976), 22 Charing Cross Road,
London WC2H 0QL T 020-7836 8591
E info@theatrestrust.org.uk W www.theatrestrust.org.uk
Director, P. Longman

THORESBY SOCIETY (1889), Claremont, 23 Clarendon
Road, Leeds LS2 9NZ T 0113-245 7910
W www.thoresby.org.uk
President, C. J. Morgan

TREE COUNCIL (1974), 71 Newcomen Street, London
SE1 1YT T 020-7407 9992 E info@treecouncil.org.uk
W www.treecouncil.org.uk
Director-General, Pauline Buchanan Black

TURNER SOCIETY (1975), BCM Box Turner, London
WC1N 3XX W www.turnersociety.org.uk
Chair, Eric Shanes

UK YOUTH (1911), 2nd Floor, Kirby House, 20–24 Kirby
Street, London EC1N 8TS T 020-7242 4045
E info@ukyouth.org.uk W www.ukyouth.org.uk
Chief Executive, J. Bateman, OBE

UNITED GRAND LODGE OF ENGLAND (1717),
Freemasons' Hall, Great Queen Street, London WC2B 5AZ
T 020-7831 9811 E ugle@ugle.org.uk W www.ugle.org.uk
Grand Master, HRH The Duke of Kent,
KG, GCMG, GCVO

UNITED KINGDOM RESERVE FORCES
ASSOCIATION (1972), Holderness House, 51–61 Clifton
Street, London EC2A 4EY T 020-7426 8361
E rfa@rfcacouncil.org.uk
President, Air Vice-Marshal B. H. Newton,
CB, CVO, OBE

UNITED NATIONS ASSOCIATION OF GREAT
BRITAIN AND NORTHERN IRELAND (1945),
3 Whitehall Court, London SW1A 2EL T 020-7766 3444
E info@UNA-UK.org W www.una-uk.org
Director, Sam Daws

UNITED REFORMED CHURCH HISTORY SOCIETY (1972), Westminster College, Madingley Road, Cambridge CB3 0AA T 01223-741300 E mt212@cam.ac.uk
Hon. Secretary, Revd E. J. Brown

UNIVERSITIES UK, 2000, Woburn House, 20 Tavistock Square, London WC1H 9HQ T 020-7419 4111
E info@universitiesuk.ac.uk W www.universitiesuk.ac.uk
Chief Executive, Baroness Warwick

VEGAN SOCIETY (1944), Donald Watson House, 7 Battle Road, St Leonards-on-Sea TN37 7AA T 0845-458 8244
E info@vegansociety.com W www.vegansociety.com
Chief Executive, Kostana Azmi

VEGETARIAN SOCIETY OF THE UNITED KINGDOM LTD (1847), Parkdale, Dunham Road, Altrincham, Cheshire WA14 4QG T 0161-925 2000
E info@vegsoc.org W www.vegsoc.org
Chief Executive, Ms T. Fox

VERNACULAR ARCHITECTURE GROUP (1952), 'Ashley', Willows Green, Chelmsford CM3 1QD
T 01245-361408 W www.vag.org.uk
Hon. Secretary, Mrs B. A. Watkin

VICTIM SUPPORT (NATIONAL ASSOCIATION OF VICTIMS SUPPORT SCHEMES) (1979), National Office, Cranmer House, 39 Brixton Road, London SW9 6DZ
T 020-7735 9166.Victim Support Line: 0845-3030 900
E contact@victimsupport.org.uk W www.victimsupport.org
Chief Executive, Dame Helen Reeves, DBE

VICTORIA CROSS AND GEORGE CROSS ASSOCIATION (1956), Horse Guards, Whitehall, London SW1A 2AX T 020-7930 3506
Secretary, Mrs D. Grahame, MVO

VICTORIAN SOCIETY (1958), 1 Priory Gardens, Bedford Park, London W4 1TT T 0870-774 3698 E admin@victorian-society.org.uk W www.victorian-society.org.uk
Director, Dr Ian Dungavell

VIKING SOCIETY FOR NORTHERN RESEARCH (1892), Department of Scandinavian Studies, University College, Gower Street, London WC1E 6BT T 020-7679 7176
E vsnr@ucl.ac.uk
Hon. Secretaries, Prof. M. P. Barnes and Prof. J. Jesh

VISITSCOTLAND (1969), 23 Ravelston Terrace, Edinburgh EH4 3TP T 0131-332 2433 E info@visitscotland.com
W www.visitscotland.com; www.scotexchange.net
Chief Executive, Philip Riddle

WELLBEING - HEALTH RESEARCH CHARITY FOR WOMEN AND BABIES (1965), 27 Sussex Place, Regent's Park, London NW1 4SP T 020-7772 6400
E wellbeingofwomen@rcog.org.uk
W www.wellbeingofwomen.org.uk
Director, Ms S. Farmer

WESLEY HISTORICAL SOCIETY (1893), 34 Spiceland Road, Northfield, Birmingham B31 1NJ T 0121-475 4914
E edgraham@tesco.net
W www.wesleyhistoricalsociety.org.uk
General Secretary, Dr E. D. Graham

WESTMINSTER FOUNDATION FOR DEMOCRACY (1992), 2nd Floor, 125 Pall Mall, London SW1Y 5EA
T 020-7930 0408 E wfd@wfd.org W www.wfd.org
Chief Executive, David French

WILDFOWL AND WETLANDS TRUST (1946), Slimbridge GL2 7BT T 0870-334 4000
E enquiries@wwt.org.uk W www.wwt.org.uk
Managing Director, M. Spray

WILLIAM MORRIS SOCIETY AND KELMSCOTT FELLOWSHIP (1955), Kelmscott House, 26 Upper Mall, London W6 9TA T 020-8741 3735
E williammorris@care4free.net W www.morrissociety.org
Hon. Secretary, P. Faulkner

WILTSHIRE ARCHAEOLOGICAL AND NATURAL HISTORY SOCIETY (1853), Wiltshire Heritage Museum, 41 Long Street, Devizes SN10 1NS
T 01380-727369 E wanhs@wiltshireheritage.org.uk
W www.wiltshireheritage.org.uk
Curator, Dr P. H. Robinson

WINE AND SPIRIT ASSOCIATION (1824), Five Kings House, 1 Queen Street Place, London EC4R 1XX
T 020-7248 5377 E wsa@wsa.org.uk W www.wsa.org.uk
Director, Q. Rappoport

WOMEN'S ENGINEERING SOCIETY (1919), 22 Old Queen Street, London SW1H 9HW T 020-7233 1974
E info@wes.org.uk W www.wes.org.uk
President, Pamela Wain

WOMEN'S ROYAL NAVAL SERVICE BENEVOLENT TRUST (1941), 311 Twyford Avenue, Portsmouth PO2 8RN T 023-9265 5301 E wrnsbt@care4free.net
General Secretary, Mrs S. Tarabella

WOODLAND TRUST (1972), Autumn Park, Dysart Road, Grantham NG31 6LL T 01476-581111
E enquiries@woodland-trust.org.uk
W www.woodland-trust.org.uk
Chief Executive, Sue Holden

WORCESTERSHIRE ARCHAEOLOGICAL SOCIETY (1854), 26 Albert Park Road, Malvern WR14 1HN
T 01299-250416 E museum@worcestershire.gov.uk
Hon. Secretary, Dr J. W. Dunleavey

WORK FOUNDATION, Peter Runge House, 3 Carlton House Terrace, London SW1Y 5DG T 0870-165 6700
E contactcentre@theworkfoundation.com
W www.theworkfoundation.com
Chief Executive, Will Hutton

WORKING FAMILIES, 1–3 Berry Street, London EC1V 0AA
T 020-7253 7243 E office@workingfamilies.org.uk
W www.workingfamilies.org.uk
Chief Executive, Sarah Jackson

WORLD SHIP SOCIETY LTD (1947), 101 The Everglades, Hempstead, Gillingham ME7 3PZ
T 01634-372015 E jimmy.poole@worldshipsociety.org
W www.worldshipsociety.org
Secretary, Jimmy Poole

WRVS (1938), Garden House, Milton Hill, Abingdon
OX13 6AD **T** 01235-442900 **E** enquiries@wrvs.org.uk
W www.wrvs.org.uk
Chair, Ms T. Tietjen

YORKSHIRE ARCHAEOLOGICAL SOCIETY (1863),
Claremont, 23 Clarendon Road, Leeds LS2 9NZ
T 0113-245 7910 **E** secretary@yas.org.uk
W www.yas.org.uk
Hon. Secretary, Ms J. Heron

YOUTH HOSTELS ASSOCIATION (ENGLAND &
WALES) (1930), Trevelyan House, Dimple Road, Matlock,
DE4 3YH **T** 01629-592600 **E** customerservices@yha.org.uk
W www.yha.org.uk
National Secretary, Terry Rollinson

YWCA ENGLAND & WALES (1855), Clarendon House,
52 Cornmarket Street, Oxford OX1 3EJ **T** 01865-304200
E info@ywca.org.uk **W** www.ywca.org.uk
Chief Executive, Gill Tishler

ZOOLOGICAL SOCIETY OF LONDON (1826),
Regent's Park, London NW1 4RY **T** 020-7722 3333
W www.zsl.org
Director-General, Ralph Armond

THE WORLD

THE WORLD IN FIGURES

THE EARTH

The shape of the Earth is that of an oblate spheroid or solid of revolution whose meridian sections are ellipses, whilst the sections at right angles are circles.

DIMENSIONS

Equatorial diameter = 12,756.27 km (7,926.38 miles)
Polar diameter = 12,713.50 km (7,899.80 miles)
Equatorial circumference = 40,075.01 km (24,901.46 miles)
Polar circumference = 40,007.86 km (24,859.73 miles)
Mass = 5,974,000,000,000,000,000,000 tonnes (5.879×10^{21} tons)

The equatorial circumference is divided into 360 degrees of longitude, which is measured in degrees, minutes and seconds east or west of the Greenwich meridian (0°) to 180°, the meridian 180° E. coinciding with 180° W. This dateline was internationally ratified on 13 October 1884.

Distance north and south of the Equator is measured in degrees, minutes and seconds of latitude. The Equator is 0°, the North Pole is 90° N. and the South Pole is 90° S. The Tropics lie at 23° 27′ N. (Tropic of Cancer) and 23° 27′ S. (Tropic of Capricorn). The Arctic Circle lies at 66° 33′ N. and the Antarctic Circle at 66° 33′ S. (NB The Tropics and the Arctic and Antarctic circles are affected by the slow decrease in obliquity of the ecliptic, of about 0.47 arcseconds per year. The effect of this is that the Arctic and Antarctic circles are currently moving towards their respective poles by about 14 metres per annum, while the Tropics move towards the Equator by the same amount.)

AREA, ETC

The surface area of the Earth is 510,069,120 km² (196,938,800 miles²), of which the water area is 70.92 per cent and the land area is 29.08 per cent.

The radial velocity on the Earth's surface at the Equator is 1,669.79 km per hour (1,037.56 mph). The Earth's mean velocity in its orbit around the Sun is 107,229 km per hour (66,629 mph). The Earth's mean distance from the Sun is 149,597,870 km (92,955,807 miles).

OCEANS

AREA

	km²	miles²
Pacific	155,557,000	59,270,000
Atlantic	76,762,000	29,638,000
Indian	68,556,000	26,467,000
Southern	20,327,000	7,848,300
Arctic	14,056,000	5,427,000

The Equator divides the Pacific into the North and South Pacific and the Atlantic into the North and South Atlantic. In 2000 the International Hydrographic Organisation approved the description of the 20,327,000 km² (7,848,300 miles²) of circum-Antarctic waters up to 60° S. as the Southern Ocean – a seventh ocean.

GREATEST OCEAN DEPTHS

Greatest depth	Location	metres	feet
Mariana Trench*	Pacific	10,924	35,840
Puerto Rico Trench	Atlantic	8,605	28,232
South Sandwich Trench	Southern	7,235	23,737
Java (Sunda) Trench	Indian	7,125	23,376
Molloy Deep	Arctic	5,680	18,400

*On 23 January 1960 Don Walsh (USA) and Jacques Piccard (Switzerland) attained a depth of 10,916 m (35,814 ft) in the bathyscaphe *Trieste*. A depth of 11,034 m (36,201 ft) recorded by the Soviet *Vityaz* is not internationally accepted.

SEAS

AREAS

	km²	miles²
South China	2,974,600	1,148,500
Caribbean	2,515,900	971,400
Mediterranean	2,509,900	969,100
Bering	2,261,000	873,000
Gulf of Mexico	1,507,600	582,100
Okhotsk	1,392,000	537,500
Japan	1,012,900	391,100
Hudson Bay	730,100	281,900
East China	664,600	256,600
Andaman	564,880	218,100
Black Sea	507,900	196,100
Red Sea	453,000	174,900
North Sea	427,100	164,900
Baltic Sea	382,000	147,500
Yellow Sea	294,000	113,500
Persian/Arabian Gulf	230,000	88,800

GREATEST DEPTHS OF SEAS LISTED ABOVE

	metres	feet
Caribbean	8,605	28,232
East China (Ryu Kyu Trench)	7,507	24,629
South China	7,258	23,812
Mediterranean (Ionian Basin)	5,150	16,896
Andaman	4,267	14,000
Bering	3,936	12,913
Gulf of Mexico	3,504	11,496
Okhotsk	3,365	11,040
Japan	3,053	10,016
Red Sea	2,266	7,434
Black Sea	2,212	7,257
North Sea	439	1,440
Hudson Bay	111	364
Baltic Sea	90	295
Persian Gulf	73	240
Yellow Sea	58	190

THE CONTINENTS

There are six geographic continents, although America is often divided politically into North and Central America, and South America, so making seven.

AFRICA is surrounded by sea except for the narrow isthmus of Suez in the north-east, through which was cut the Suez Canal (opened 17 November 1869). Its extreme longitudes are 17° 20′ W. at Cape Verde, Senegal, and 51° 24′ E. at Raas Xaafuun, Somalia. The extreme latitudes are 37° 20′ N. at Cape Blanc, Tunisia, and 34° 50′ S. at Cape Agulhas, South Africa, about 7,081 km (4,400 miles) apart. The Equator passes across Gabon, Republic of the Congo Uganda, Kenya and Somalia in the middle of the continent.

NORTH AMERICA, including Mexico, is surrounded by ocean except in the south, where the isthmian states of CENTRAL AMERICA link North America with South America. Its extreme longitudes are 168° 5′ W. at Cape Prince of Wales, Alaska, and 55° 40′ W. at Cape Charles, Newfoundland. The extreme continental latitudes are the tip of the Boothia peninsula, NW Territories, Canada (71° 51′ N.) and 14° 22′ N. in southern Mexico near La Victoria, Guatemala.

SOUTH AMERICA lies mostly in the southern hemisphere; the Equator passing across Ecuador, Colombia and Brazil in the north of the continent. It is surrounded by ocean except where it is joined to Central America in the north by the narrow isthmus through which was cut the Panama Canal (opened 15 August 1914). Its extreme longitudes are 34° 47′ W. at Cape Branco in Brazil and 81° 20′ W. at Punta Pariña, Peru. The extreme continental latitudes are 12° 25′ N. at Punta Gallinas, Colombia, and 53° 54′ S. at the southernmost tip of Peninsula de Brunswick, Chile. Cape Horn, on Cape Island, Chile, lies in 55° 59′ S.

ANTARCTICA lies almost entirely within the Antarctic Circle (66° 33′ S.) and is the largest of the world's glaciated areas. Ninety-eight per cent of the continent is permanently covered in ice. The ice amounts to some 30 million km³ (7.2 million miles³) and represents more than 70 per cent of the world's fresh water. The environment is too hostile for unsupported human habitation.

ASIA is the largest continent and occupies 29.6 per cent of the world's land surface. The extreme longitudes are 26° 05′ E. at Baba Buran, Turkey, and 169° 40′ W. at Mys Dezhneva (East Cape), Russia, a distance of about 9,656 km (6,000 miles). Its extreme northern latitude is 77° 45′ N. at Mys Chelyuskin, Russia, and it extends over 8,046 km (5,000 miles) south to Tanjong Piai, Malaysia.

AUSTRALIA is the smallest of the continents and lies in the southern hemisphere. It is entirely surrounded by ocean. Its extreme longitudes are 113° 11′ E. at Steep Point, Western Australia, and 153° 11′ E. at Cape Byron, New South Wales. The extreme latitudes are 10° 42′ S. at Cape York, Queensland, and 39° S. at South East Point, Tasmania. Australia, together with New Zealand (Australasia), Papua New Guinea and the Pacific Islands, comprises Oceania.

EUROPE, including European Russia, is the smallest continent in the northern hemisphere. Its extreme latitudes are 71° 11′ N. at Nord Kapp in Norway, and 36° 23′ N. at Akra Tainaron (Matapas) in southern Greece, a distance of about 3,862 km (2,400 miles). Its breadth from Cabo Carvoeiro in Portugal (9° 34′ W.) in the west to the Kara River, north of the Urals (66° 30′ E.) in the east is about 5,310 km (3,300 miles). The division between Europe and Asia is generally regarded as the watershed of the Ural Mountains; down the Ural river to Guryev, Kazakhstan; across the Caspian Sea to

Apsheronskiy Poluostrov, near Baku; along the watershed of the Caucasus Mountains to Anapa and then across the Black Sea to the Bosporus in Turkey; across the Sea of Marmara to Çanakkale Bogazi (Dardanelles).

Continent	Area	
	km²	miles²
Asia	43,998,000	16,988,000
America*	41,918,000	16,185,000
Africa	29,800,000	11,506,000
Antarctica	13,209,000	5,100,000
Europe†	9,699,000	3,745,000
Australia	7,618,493	2,941,526

*North and Central America has an area of 24,255,000 km² (9,365,000 miles²)
†Includes 5,571,000 km² (2,151,000 miles²) of former USSR territory, including the Baltic states, Belarus, Moldova, Ukraine and the part of Russia west of the Ural Mountains and Kazakhstan west of the Ural river. European Turkey (24,378 km²/9,412 miles²) comprises territory to the west and north of the Bosporus and the Dardanelles

GLACIATED AREAS

It is estimated that 15,915,000 km² (6,145,000 miles²) or 10.73 per cent of the world's land surface is permanently covered with ice. The largest glacier is the 515 km (320 mile)-long Lambert-Fisher Ice Passage, Mac Robertson Land, Eastern Antarctica.

Location	Area	
	km²	miles²
South Polar regions	13,830,000	5,340,000
North Polar regions (incl. Greenland or Kalaallit Nunaat)	1,965,000	758,500
Alaska-Canada	58,800	22,700
Asia	37,800	14,600
South America	11,900	4,600
Europe	10,700	4,128
New Zealand	1,015	391
Africa	238	92

PENINSULAS

Peninsula	Area	
	km²	miles²
Arabian	3,250,000	1,250,000
Southern Indian	2,072,000	800,000
Alaskan	1,500,000	580,000
Labradorian	1,300,000	500,000
Scandinavian	800,300	309,000
Iberian	584,000	225,500

LARGEST ISLANDS

Island and ocean	Area	
	km²	miles²
Greenland (Kalaallit Nunaat), Arctic	2,175,500	840,000
New Guinea, Pacific	792,500	306,000
Borneo, Pacific	725,450	280,100
Madagascar, Indian	587,041	226,674
Baffin Island, Arctic	507,451	195,928
Sumatra, Indian	427,350	165,000
Honshu, Pacific	227,413	87,805
Great Britain, Atlantic*	218,077	84,200
Victoria Island, Arctic	217,292	83,897

Ellesmere Island, Arctic	196,236	75,767
Sulawesi (Celebes), Indian	189,036	72,987
South Island, NZ, Pacific	151,213	58,384
Java (Jawa), Indian	126,650	48,900
North Island, NZ, Pacific	114,487	44,204
Cuba, Atlantic	110,862	42,804
Newfoundland, Atlantic	108,855	42,030
Luzon, Pacific	105,360	40,680
Iceland, Atlantic	102,820	39,700
Mindanao, Pacific	95,247	36,775
Ireland, Atlantic	82,462	31,839

*Mainland only

LARGEST DESERTS

Desert and location	Area (approx)	
	km²	miles²
The Sahara, N. Africa	9,000,000	3,500,000
The Gobi, Mongolia/China	1,300,000	500,000
Australian Desert		
(Great Sandy, Gibson, Simpson		
and Great Victoria)	1,120,000	460,000
Arabian (Eastern) Desert, Egypt	1,000,000	385,000
Kalahari Desert, Botswana/		
Namibia/S. Africa	570,000	220,000
Taklimakan Shamo, Mongolia/		
China	320,000	125,000
Kara Kum, Turkmenistan*	310,000	120,000
Thar Desert, India/Pakistan	260,000	100,000
Somali Desert, Somalia	260,000	100,000
Atacama Desert, Chile	180,000	70,000
Sonoran Desert, USA/Mexico	180,000	70,000
Namib, Namibia	135,000	52,000
Dasht-e Lut, Iran	52,000	20,000
Mojave Desert, USA	38,850	15,000

*Together with the Kyzyl Kum 259,000 km² (100,000 miles²) known as the Turkestan Desert
Antarctica is described as a Polar Desert since precipitation is less than 5 cm (2 in) per annum

DEEPEST DEPRESSIONS

Depression and location	Maximum depth below sea level	
	metres	feet
Dead Sea, Jordan/Israel	408	1,338
Lake Assal, Djibouti	156	511
Turfan Depression, Sinkiang, China	153	505
Qattara Depression, Egypt	132	436
Mangyshlak peninsula, Kazakhstan	131	433
Danakil Depression, Ethiopia	116	383
Death Valley, California, USA	86	282
Salton Sink, California, USA	71	235
W. of Ustyurt plateau, Kazakhstan	70	230
Prikaspiyskaya Nizmennost', Russia/		
Kazakhstan	67	220
Lake Sarykamysh, Uzbekistan/		
Turkmenistan	45	148
El Faiyum, Egypt	44	147
Peninsula Valdes, Chubut, Argentina	40	131
Lake Eyre, South Australia	16	52

The world's largest exposed depression is the Prikaspiyskaya Nizmennost' covering the hinterland of the northern third of the Caspian Sea, which is itself 28 m (92 ft) below sea level.

Western Antarctica and Central Greenland largely comprise crypto-depressions under ice burdens. The Antarctic Bentley subglacial trench has a bedrock 2,538 m (8,326 ft) below sea-level. In Greenland (lat. 73° N., long. 39° W.) the bedrock is 365 m (1,197 ft) below sea-level.

Nearly one quarter of the area of The Netherlands lies marginally below sea-level, an area of more than 10,000 km² (3,860 miles²).

No part of the Maldives is higher than 2.4 m (8 ft) and nowhere in Lesotho is lower than 1,381 m (4,531 ft).

LONGEST MOUNTAIN RANGES

Range and location	Length	
	km	miles
Cordillera de Los Andes,		
W. South America	7,200	4,500
Rocky Mountains,		
W. North America	4,800	3,000
Himalaya-Karakoram-Hindu Kush,		
S. Central Asia	3,850	2,400
Great Dividing Range,		
E. Australia	3,620	2,250
Trans-Antarctic Mts,		
Antarctica	3,540	2,200
Atlantic Coast Range,		
E. Brazil	3,050	1,900
West Sumatran-Javan Range,		
Indonesia	2,900	1,800
Aleutian Range, Alaska and NW		
Pacific	2,650	1,650
Tien Shan,		
S. Central Asia	2,250	1,400
Central New Guinea Range,		
Irian Jaya/Papua New Guinea	2,010	1,250

HIGHEST MOUNTAINS

Mountain	Height	
	metres	feet
Mt Everest* (Qomolangma)	8,850	29,035
K2 (Qogir)†	8,611	28,251
Kangchenjunga	8,597	28,208
Lhotse I	8,510	27,923
Makalu I	8,480	27,824
Lhotse Shar (II)	8,400	27,560
Dhaulagiri I	8,171	26,810
Manaslu I (Kutang I)	8,156	26,760
Cho Oyu	8,153	26,750
Nanga Parbat (Diamir)	8,125	26,660
Annapurna I	8,078	26,504
Gasherbrum I (Hidden Peak)	8,068	26,470
Broad Peak I	8,046	26,400
Shisham Pangma (Gosainthan)	8,012	26,287
Gasherbrum II	8,034	26,360
Makalu South-East	8,010	26,280
Broad Peak Central	8,000	26,246

*Named after Sir George Everest (1790–1866), Surveyor-General of India 1830–43, in 1863. He pronounced his name Eve-rest

†Formerly named after Col. Henry Haversham Godwin-Austen (1834–1923), who worked on the Trigonometrical Survey of India, which established the heights of the Himalayan peaks, including Everest

The world's twelve 8,000-m (26,247 ft) mountains (*with five subsidiary peaks*) are all in the Himalaya-Karakoram-Hindu Kush ranges.

The culminating summits in the other major mountain ranges are:

Mountain, by range or country	Height metres	feet
Pik Pobedy, Tien Shan	7,439	24,406
Cerro Aconcagua, Cordillera de Los Andes	6,960	22,834
Mt McKinley (S. Peak), Alaska Range	6,194	20,320
Kilimanjaro (Kibo), Tanzania	5,894	19,340
Hkakabo Razi, Myanmar	5,881	19,296
El'brus, (W. Peak), Caucasus	5,642	18,510
Citlaltépetl (Orizaba), Sierra Madre Oriental, Mexico	5,655	18,555
Vinson Massif, E. Antarctica	4,897	16,066
Puncak Jaya, Central New Guinea Range	4,884	16,023
Mt Blanc, Alps	4,807	15,771
Klyuchevskaya Sopka, Kamchatka peninsula, Russia	4,750	15,584

HIGHEST ACTIVE VOLCANOES

Volcano and location	Height metres	feet
Volcan Llullaillaco, Andes, Argentina/Chile	6,723	22,057
Volcan Guallatiri, Andes, Chile	6,069	19,882
Cotopaxi, Andes, Ecuador	5,897	19,347
Tupungatito, Andes, Chile	5,640	18,504
Lascar, Andes, Chile	5,591	18,346
Popocatepetl, Mexico	5,465	17,930
Nevado del Ruiz, Colombia	5,321	17,457
Sangay, Andes, Ecuador	5,188	17,021
Irraputuncu, Chile	5,163	16,939
Klyuchevskaya Sopka, Kamchatka peninsula, Russia	4,835	15,863
Guagua Pichincha, Andes, Ecuador	4,784	15,696
Purace, Colombia	4,756	15,601
Wrangell, Alaska, USA	4,316	14,163
Shasta, California, USA	4,316	14,163
Galeras, Colombia	4,275	14,028
Mauna Loa, Hawaii Is.	4,170	13,680
Cameroon, Cameroon	4,095	13,435

Although it displays fumarolic activity, emitting steam and gas, no major eruption has ever been observed of the world's highest volcano and second highest peak in the western hemisphere, the 6,893 m (22,615 ft) Ojos del Salado, in the Andes on the Argentina/Chile border.

LAKES

LARGEST LAKES

The areas of some of the lakes listed are subject to seasonal variation.

Lake and location	Area km²	miles²	Length km	miles
Caspian Sea, Iran/ Azerbaijan/Russia/ Turkmenistan/ Kazakhstan	371,000	143,000	1,171	728
Michigan–Huron, USA/ Canada*	117,610	45,300	1,010	627
Superior, Canada/USA	82,100	31,700	563	350
Victoria, Uganda/ Tanzania/Kenya	69,500	26,828	362	225
Tanganyika, Dem. Rep. of Congo/Tanzania/ Zambia/Burundi	32,900	12,665	725	450
Great Bear, Canada	31,328	12,096	309	192
Aral Sea, Kazakhstan/ Uzbekistan†	30,700	11,850	320	200
Baykal (Baikal), Russia‡	30,500	11,776	620	385
Malawi (Nyasa), Tanzania/Malawi/ Mozambique	28,900	11,150	580	360
Great Slave, Canada	28,570	11,031	480	298
Erie, Canada/USA	25,670	9,910	388	241
Winnipeg, Canada	24,390	9,417	428	266
Ontario, Canada/USA	19,010	7,340	310	193
Balkhash, Kazakhstan	18,427	7,115	605	376
Ladozhskoye (Ladoga), Russia	17,700	6,835	193	120

*Lakes Michigan and Huron may be regarded as lobes of the same lake. The Michigan lobe has an area of 57,750 km² (22,300 miles²) and the Huron lobe an area of 59,570 km² (23,000 miles²)

†Northern part (Little Aral Sea) dammed off in 1997

‡World's deepest lake (1,940 m/6,365 ft)

UNITED KINGDOM (BY COUNTRY)

Lough Neagh, Northern Ireland	381.73	147.39	28.90	18.00
Loch Lomond, Scotland	71.12	27.46	36.44	22.64
Windermere, England	14.74	5.69	16.90	10.50
Lake Vyrnwy, Wales (artificial)	4.53	1.75	7.56	4.70
Llyn Tegid (Bala), Wales (natural)	4.38	1.69	5.80	3.65

The most voluminous lakes are the Caspian Sea (saline) with 78,700 km³ (18, 880 miles³) and Baikal (fresh water) with 23,000 km³ (5,518 miles³).

LARGEST MANMADE LAKES

Dam/lake*	Location	Year completed	Volume km³	m³
Owen Falls	Uganda	1954	204.80	49.13
Kariba	Zimbabwe/ Zambia	1959	204.80	49.13
Bratsk	Russia	1964	169.27	40.61
High Aswan	Egypt	1970	168.90	40.52
Akosombo	Ghana	1965	148.00	35.51
Daniel Johnson	Canada	1968	141.85	34.03
Guri (Raul Leoni)	Venezuela	1986	138.00	33.11
Krasnoyarsk	Russia	1967	73.30	17.58
W.A.C. Bennett	Canada	1967	70.31	16.87
Zeya	Russia	1978	68.40	16.41

*Formed as a result of dam construction

DEEPEST LAKES

Lake	Location	Greatest Depth metres	feet
Baikal	Russia	1,637	5,371
Tanganyika	Burundi/Tanzania/ Dem. Rep. of Congo/Zambia	1,470	4,825
Caspian Sea	Azerbaijan/Iran/ Kazakhstan/ Russia/ Turkmenistan	1,025	3,363
Malawi	Malawi/Mozam- bique/Tanzania	706	2,316

Issyk Kul	Kyrgyzstan	702	2,303
Great Slave	Canada	614	2,015
Danau Toba	Indonesia	590	1,936
Hornindalsvastnet	Norway	514	1,686
Sarezskoye Ozero	Tajikistan	505	1,657
Tahoe	California/Nevada, USA	501	1,645
Lago Argentina	Argentina	500	1,640
Lac Kivu	Rwanda/Dem. Rep. of Congo	480	1,574
Quesnel	Canada	475	1,558

All these lakes would be sufficiently deep to submerge the Empire State Building – in the case of Lake Baikal, more than four times over.

LONGEST RIVERS

River, source and outflow	Length	
	km	miles
Nile (Bahr-el-Nil), R. Luvironza, Burundi–E. Mediterranean Sea	6,725	4,180
Amazon (Amazonas), Lago Villafro, Peru–S. Atlantic Ocean	6,448	4,007
Yangtze-Kiang (Chang Jiang), Kunlun Mts, W. China–Yellow Sea	6,380	3,964
Mississippi-Missouri-Red Rock, Montana–Gulf of Mexico	5,970	3,710
Yenisey-Angara, W. Mongolia–Kara Sea	5,536	3,440
Huang He (Yellow River), Bayan Har Shan range, Central China–Yellow Sea	5,463	3,395
Ob'-Irtysh, W. Mongolia–Kara Sea	5,410	3,362
Zaire (Congo), R. Lualaba, Dem. Rep. of Congo-Zambia–S. Atlantic Ocean	4,665	2,900
Amur-Argun, R. Argun, Khingan Mts, N. China–Sea of Okhotsk	4,416	2,744
Lena-Kirenga, R. Kirenga, W. of Lake Baykal–Laptev Sea, Arctic Ocean	4,400	2,734
Mekong, Lants'ang, Tibet–South China Sea	4,345	2,700
Mackenzie-Peace, Tatlatui Lake, British Columbia–Beaufort Sea	4,240	2,635
Paraná-Río de la Plata, R. Paranáiba, Central Brazil–S. Atlantic Ocean	4,240	2,635
Niger, Loma Mts, Guinea–Gulf of Guinea, E. Atlantic Ocean	4,170	2,590
Murray-Darling, SE Queensland–Lake Alexandrina, S. Australia	3,717	2,310
Volga, Valdai plateau–Caspian Sea	3,685	2,290

BRITISH ISLES

Shannon, Co. Cavan, Rep. of Ireland–Atlantic Ocean	386	240
Severn, Powys, Wales–Bristol Channel	354	220
Thames, Gloucestershire, England–North Sea	346	215
Tay, Perthshire, Scotland–North Sea	188	117
Clyde, Lanarkshire, Scotland–Firth of Clyde	158	98.5
Tweed, Scottish Borders–North Sea	155	96.5
Bann (Upper and Lower), Co. Down, N. Ireland–Atlantic Ocean	122	76

GREATEST WATERFALLS — BY HEIGHT

Waterfall, river and location	Total drop		Greatest single leap	
	metres	feet	metres	feet
Salto Angel, Carrao Auyan Tepui, Venezuela	979	3,212	807	2,648
Tugela, Tugela, Natal, S. Africa (5 leaps)	948	3,110	410	1,350
Utigard, Jostedal Glacier, Norway	800	2,625	600	1,970
Mongefossen, Monge, Norway	774	2,540	—	—
Yosemite, Yosemite Creek, USA	739	2,425	435	1,430
Ostre Mardola Foss, Mardals, Norway*	655	2,149	296	974
Tyssestrengene, Tysso, Norway*	646	2,120	289	948
Cuquenan, Arabopo, Venezuela	610	2,000	—	—
Sutherland, Arthur, NZ	580	1,904	248	815

*Volume much affected by hydroelectric harnessing

BRITISH ISLES, BY COUNTRY

Waterfall, river and location	Total drop	
	metres	feet
Eas a' Chual Aluinn, Glas Bheinn, Sutherland, Scotland	200	656
Powerscourt Falls, Dargle, Co. Wicklow, Rep. of Ireland	121	398
Pistyll-y-Llyn, Powys/Dyfed border, Wales	91	300 (cascades)
Pistyll Rhyadr, Clwyd/Powys border, Wales	71.5	235 (single leap)
Caldron Snout, R. Tees, Cumbria/Durham, England	61	200 (cascades)

GREATEST WATERFALLS — BY VOLUME

Waterfall, river and location	Mean annual flow m³/sec
Inga, Congo, Dem. Rep. of Congo	42,476
Livingstone Falls, Congo, Dem. Rep. of Congo	43,000
Boyoma (Stanley), Lualaba, Dem. Rep. of Congo	16,990
Khone, Mekong, Laos	11,610
Niagara (Horseshoe), R. Niagara/Lake Erie–Lake Ontario	6,009
Para, Caura, Venezuela	3,540
Paulo Afonso, Sao Francisco, Brazil	2,832
Cataratas del Iguaçu, Iguaçu, Brazil/Argentina	1,746
Patos e Maribondo, Grande, Brazil	1,500
Victoria (Mosi-oa-tunya), Zambezi, Zambia/Zimbabwe	1,000

DAMS

TALLEST DAMS

	metres	feet
Rogun, R. Vakhsh, Tajikistan	335	1,098
Nurek, R. Vakhsh, Tajikistan	300	984
Grande Dixence, Switzerland	285	935
Longtan, R. Hangshui, China	285	935
Inguri, Georgia	272	892
Borucu, Costa Rica	267	876
Vaiont, Italy	262	859
Manuel M. Torres, Chicoasén, Mexico	261	856
Tehri, R. Bhagivathi, India	261	856

GREATEST VOLUME* DAMS

Dam and location	Completed	Volume 000s m³	000s yd³
Syncrude Tailings, Canada	1992	540,000	706,293
Chapeton, Argentina	UC	296,200	387,415
Pati, Argentina	1990	230,180	301,064
New Cornelia Tailings, USA	1973	209,500	274,016
Tarbela, Pakistan	1976	121,720	159,204
Kambaratinsk, Kyrgyzstan	UC	112,200	146,752
Fort Peck, USA	1937	96,050	125,629
Lower Usuma, Nigeria	1990	93,049	121,703
Cipasang, Indonesia	UC	90,000	117,716
Ataturk, Turkey	1990	84,500	110,522

* Of material used in construction (earth, rocks, concrete, etc)
UC = under construction

TALLEST ...

INHABITED BUILDINGS

Building and location	Height metres	feet
Taipei 101, Taipei, Taiwan (2003) (101 storeys)	509	1,671
Petronas Towers I and II, Kuala Lumpur, Malaysia (1998) (88 storeys)	451.9	1,482
Sears Tower, Chicago* (1974) (110 storeys)	443	1,454
Jin Mao, Shanghai, China (1998) (86 storeys)	420	1,378
International Finance Centre, Hong Kong (2003)	412	1,352
CITIC Plaza, Guangzhou, China (1996)	391	1,283
Shun Hing Square, Shenzhen, China (1996)	384	1,260
Empire State Building, New York, USA† (1931)	381	1,250
Central Plaza, Hong Kong, China (1992)	373	1,227
Bank of China Tower, Hong Kong, China (1989)	368	1,209
Emirates Tower One, Dubai, UAE (2000)	355	1,165
The Centre, Hong Kong, China (1998)	350	1,148
Tuntex & Chein-Tai Tower, Kaohsiung, Taiwan (1998)	347	1,140
Aon Centre, Chicago, USA (1973)	346	1,136
Kingdom Centre, Riyadh, Saudi Arabia (2001)	345	1,132
John Hancock Centre, Chicago, USA (1969)	343	1,127
Baurj al Arab Hotel, Dubai, UAE (1999)	321	1,053
Chrysler Building, New York, USA (1930)	318	1,046

*With TV antennae, 520 m (1,707 ft)
†With TV tower (added 1950–1), 430.9 m (1,414 ft)
Note: The two World Trade Centre towers, One (1972) 110 storeys, 415 m (1,368 ft) or 521 m (1,716ft) with TV antennae; and Two (1973) 110 storeys, 415 m (1,362 ft), were destroyed by two terrorist-hijacked aircraft on 11 September 2001

STRUCTURES

Structure and location	Height metres	feet
Warszawa Radio Mast, Konstantynow, Poland (1974)*	646	2,120
KVLY (formerly KTHI)-TV Mast, Blanchard, North Dakota (guyed) (1963)	629	2,063
Indosat Telkom Tower, Jakarta, Indonesia	558	1,831
CN Tower, Metro Centre, Toronto, Canada (1975)	555	1,822
Ostankino Tower, Moscow (1967)	540	1,772

*Collapsed during renovation, August 1991. New structure planned on site at Solkajawski. The USA has eight other guyed TV towers above 555 m (1,822 ft)

TWIN TOWERS

Structure and location	Year	Storeys	Height metres	feet
Petronas Towers, Malaysia	1997	96	452	1,482
Al Fattan Towers, UAE	2006*	60	245	802
Grand Gateway, China	2005*	52	225	738
Atlantic Richfield Tower, USA	1972	52	213	699
Huaxia Finance Square, China	2005*	42	202	670
Parque Central Offinicas, Venezuela	1986	56	200	656
Murjan/Mesk Towers, UAE	2003	40	185	607
Collins Place, Australia	1981	50	185	607
101 California Plaza, USA	1986	48	183	600
Exchange Square, Hong Kong	1982	52	182	597
Destroyed				
World Trade Center One, USA	1972	110	417	1,368
World Trade Center Two, USA	1973	110	415	1,362

*Under construction; scheduled completion date

CHURCHES

Structure and location	Year	Height metres	feet
Sagrada Família, Barcelona, Spain	2020	170	558

Ulm Cathedral, Ulm, Germany	1890	162	530
Notre-Dame Cathedral, Rouen, France	1876	158	518
Cologne Cathedral, Cologne, Germany	1880	157	516
Our Lady of Peace Basilica, Yamoussoukro, Côte d'Ivoire	1990	149	489
St Nicholas Church, Hamburg, Germany	1847	147	482
Notre-Dame Cathedral, Strasbourg, France	1439	144	472
Queen of Peace Shrine and Basilica, Lichen, Poland	2002	140	459
Basilica of St Peter, Rome, Italy	1626	138	452
St Stephen's Cathedral, Vienna, Austria	1570	137	448

The Chicago Methodist Temple, Chicago, USA (completed 1924) is 173 m (568 ft) high, but is sited atop a 25-storey, 100 m (328 ft) building. Salisbury Cathedral (1521), at 123 m (404 ft), is the UK's tallest religious building. St Paul's Cathedral, London, and Liverpool Anglican Cathedral are the only others in the UK over 100 m (328 ft) tall.

TALLEST STRUCTURES: A CHRONOLOGY

Structure and location	Year	Height	
		m	ft
Djoser's Step Pyramid, Saqqara, Egypt	c.2650 BC	61	200
Pyramid of Meidum, Egypt	c.2600 BC	92	302
Snefru's Bent Pyramid, Dahshur, Egypt	c.2600 BC	102	336
Red Pyramid, Dahshur, Egypt	c.2590 BC	105	345
Great Pyramid, Giza, Egypt*	c.2580 BC	146	479
Liuhe (Six Harmonies) Pagoda, Hangzhou, China†	AD 970	150	492
Lincoln Cathedral, Lincoln, England‡	1311–1400	160	525
St Paul's Cathedral, London, England§€	1315	149	489
St Olaf's Church, Tallinn, Estonia**	1438–1519	159	522
Notre-Dame, Strasbourg, France§	1439	143	469
St Nicholas Church, Hamburg, Germany§	1847	147	482
Rouen Cathedral, Rouen, France	1876	148	485
Cologne Cathedral, Cologne, Germany	1880	157	515
Washington Monument, Washington DC, USA	1884	169	555
Eiffel Tower, Paris, France	1889	300	984
Chrysler Building, New York, USA	1930	319	1,046
Empire State Building, New York, USA	1930	381	1,250
KWTV Mast, Oklahoma City, USA	1954	479	1,572
KOBR-TV Tower, Caprock, USA	1960	490	1,608
KFVS TV Mast, Egypt Mills, USA	1960	511	1,677
Nexstar Broadcasting Tower Vivian, Vivian, USA	1961	534	1,752
KVLY (formerly KTHI)-TV Mast, Blanchard, USA§	1963	628	2,063
Warszawa Radio Mast, Konstantynow, Poland††	1974	645	2,118

*Later reduced through loss of topstone to 137m (449 ft)
†Destroyed in 1121
‡Destroyed in 1549
§The collapse of taller structures enabled these runners-up to gain or re-gain the status of 'world's tallest'
€Destroyed in 1561
**Spire burned down in 1625; renovated in 1931 to present height of 123 m (403 ft)
††Collapsed in 1991 during renovation

BRIDGES

The longest stretch of bridgings of any kind is that carrying the Interstate 55 and Interstate 10 highways at Manchac, Louisiana (1979), on twin concrete trestles over 55.21 km (34.31 miles). The 'floating' bridging at Evergreen Point, Seattle, Washington, USA (1963), is 3,839 m (12,596 ft) long, of which 2,310 m (7,578 ft) floats.

Bridge and location	Length	
	metres	feet
LONGEST SUSPENSION SPANS		
Akashi-Kaikyo, Shikoku, Japan (1998)	1,990	6,529
Storebaelt East Bridge, Denmark (1998)	1,624	5,328
Humber Estuary, Humberside, England (1981)	1,410	4,626
Jiangyin (Yangtze), China (1999)	1,385	4,544
Tsing Ma, Hong Kong, China (1997)	1,377	4,518
Verrazano Narrows, Brooklyn–Staten I, New York, USA (1964)	1,298	4,260
Golden Gate, San Francisco Bay, USA (1937)	1,280	4,200
Hoga Kusten, Sweden (1997)	1,210	3,970
Chesapeake Bay No.2, Virginia, USA (1999)	1,158	3,800
Mackinac Straits, Michigan, USA (1957)	1,158	3,800
Minami Bisan-Seto, Japan (1988)	1,100	3,609
Bosporus II Fatih Sultan Mehmet, Istanbul, Turkey (1992)	1,090	3,576
Bosporus I, Istanbul, Turkey (1973)	1,074	3,524
George Washington, Hudson River, New York City, USA (1931)	1,067	3,500
Kurushima III, Japan (1999)	1,030	3,379
Kurushima II, Japan (1999)	1,020	3,346
Ponte 25 de Abril (Tagus), Lisbon, Portugal (1966) (road and rail)	1,013	3,323
Firth of Forth (road), nr Edinburgh, Scotland (1964)	1,006	3,300
Kita Bisan-Seto, Japan (1988)	990	3,248
Severn River, Severn Estuary, England (1966)*	988	3,240

*The main span of the 5.15 km (3.2 mile) long Second Severn bridging, opened in 1996, is 456 m (1,496 ft).

LONGEST CANTILEVER SPANS		
Pont de Québec (rail-road), St Lawrence, Canada (1917)	548.6	1,800
Ravenswood, W. Virginia, USA (1981)	525.1	1,723
Firth of Forth (rail), nr Edinburgh, Scotland (two spans of 1,710 ft each) (1890)	521.2	1,710

Minato (Nanko), Osaka, Japan (1974)	510.0	1,673
Commodore Barry, Chester, Pennsylvania, Bridgeport, New Jersey USA (1974)	494.3	1,622
Greater New Orleans, Louisiana, USA (I 1958, II 1988)	480.0	1,575
Howrah (rail-road), Calcutta, India (1936–43)	457.2	1,500

LONGEST STEEL ARCH SPANS

Lupu, Shanghai, China (2003)	550.0	1,804
New River Gorge, Fayetteville, W. Virginia, USA (1977)	518.0	1,700
Bayonne (Kill van Kull), Bayonne, NJ–Staten I. NY, USA (1931)	510.5	1,675
Sydney Harbour, Sydney, Australia (1932)	502.9	1,650

TALLEST BRIDGE TOWERS

The UK's tallest bridge towers are those of the Forth Road Bridge, Queensferry, Scotland (completed 1964) at 156 m (512 ft).

LONGEST VEHICULAR TUNNELS

Tunnel and location	Length	
	km	miles
*Seikan (rail), Tsugaru Channel, Japan (1988)	53.85	33.46
*Channel Tunnel, (rail) Cheriton, Kent, UK–Sangatte, Calais, France (1994)	50.45	31.35
Moscow metro, Belyaevo–Bittsevsky, Moscow, Russia (1979)	37.90	23.50
Northern Line tube, East Finchley–Morden, London (1939)	27.84	17.30
Iwate (rail), Japan (2002)	25.81	16.03
Laerdal–Aurland Road Link, Norway (2000)	24.51	15.22
*Oshimizu (rail), Honshu, Japan (1982)	22.17	13.78
Simplon II (rail), Brigue, Switzerland–Iselle, Italy (1922)	19.82	12.31
Simplon I (rail), Brigue, Switzerland–Iselle, Italy (1906)	19.80	12.30
Vereina, Switzerland (1999)	19.06	11.84
*Shin-Kanmon (rail), Kanmon Strait, Japan (1975)	18.68	11.61
Appennino (rail), Vernio, Italy (1934)	18.50	11.50
St Gotthard (road), Göschenen–Airolo, Switzerland (1980, re-opened 2001)	16.91	10.51
*Sub-aqueous		

St Gotthard (rail) tunnel (2010) will be 57.07 km (35.46 miles).

The longest non-vehicular tunnelling in the world is the Delaware Aqueduct in New York State, USA, constructed in 1937–44 to a length of 168.9 km (105 miles).

BRITISH RAIL TUNNELS

	miles	yards
Severn, Bristol–Newport	4	484
Totley, Manchester–Sheffield	3	950
Standedge, Manchester–Huddersfield	3	66
Sodbury, Swindon–Bristol	2	924
Strood, Medway, Kent	2	426
Disley, Stockport–Sheffield	2	346
Ffestiniog, Llandudno–Blaenau Ffestiniog	2	338
Bramhope, Leeds–Harrogate	2	241
Cowburn, Manchester–Sheffield	2	182

The longest road tunnel in Britain is the Mersey Queensway Tunnel (1934), 3.42 km (2 miles 228 yards) long. The longest canal tunnel, at Standedge, W. Yorks, is 5.12 km/3 miles 417 yards long; it was completed in 1811, closed in 1944 and reopened in 2001.

LONGEST SHIP CANALS

Canal (opening date)	Length		Min. depth	
	km	miles	metres	feet
White Sea-Baltic (formerly Stalin) (1933), of which Canalised river 51.5 km (32 miles)	235	146.02	5.0	16.5
*Suez (1869) Links Red and Mediterranean Seas	162	100.60	12.9	42.3
V. I. Lenin Volga-Don (1952) Links Black and Caspian Seas	100	62.20	n/a	n/a
Kiel (or North Sea) (1895) Links North and Baltic Seas	98	60.90	13.7	45.0
*Houston (1940) Links inland city with sea	91	56.70	10.4	34.0
Alphonse XIII (1926) Gives Seville access to sea	85	53.00	7.6	25.0
Panama (1914) Links Pacific Ocean and Caribbean Sea; lake chain, 78.9 km (49 miles) dug	82	50.71	12.5	41.0
Manchester Ship (1894) Links city with Irish Channel	64	39.70	8.5	28.0
Welland (1932) Circumvents Niagara Falls and Rapids	43.5	27.00	8.8	29.0
Brussels (Rupel Sea) (1922) Renders Brussels an inland port	32	19.80	6.4	21.0

*Has no locks

The first section of China's Grand Canal, running 1,782 km (1,107 miles) from Beijing to Hangzhou, was opened in AD 610 and completed in 1283. Today it is limited to 2,000-tonne vessels.

The St Lawrence Seaway comprises the Beauharnois, Welland and Welland Bypass and Seaway 54-59 canals, and allows access to Duluth, Minnesota, USA via the Great Lakes from the Atlantic end of Canada's Gulf of St Lawrence, a distance of 3,769 km (2,342 miles). The St Lawrence Canal, completed in 1959, is 293 km (182 miles) long.

DISTANCES FROM LONDON BY AIR

This list details the distances in miles from London, Heathrow, to various cities (airports) abroad. Airport codes are given in brackets.

To	Miles
Abidjan (ABJ)	3,197
Abu Dhabi (AUH)	3,425
Addis Ababa (Bole, ADD)	3,675
Adelaide (ADL)	10,111
Aden (ADE)	3,670
Algiers (ALG)	1,035
Amman (Queen Alia, AMM)	2,287
Amsterdam (Schiphol, AMS)	230
Ankara (Esenboga, ESB)	1,770
Athens (ATH)	1,500
Atlanta (ATL)	4,198
Auckland (AKL)	11,404
Baghdad (SDA)	2,551
Bahrain (BAH)	3,163
Baku (Heydar Aliyev, BAK)	2,485
Bangkok (BKK)	5,928
Barcelona (BCN)	712
Basel-Mulhouse (BSL)	447
Beijing (Capital, PEK)	5,063
Beirut (BEY)	2,161
Belfast (BFS)	325
Belgrade (BEG)	1,056
Berlin (Tegel, TXL)	588
Bermuda (BDA)	3,428
Bern-Belp (BRN)	476
Bogotá (El Dorado, BOG)	5,262
Bombay/Mumbai (BOM)	4,478
Boston (Logan, BOS)	3,255
Brasília (BSB)	5,452
Bratislava (BTS)	817
Bridgetown (BGI)	4,193
Brisbane (BNE)	10,273
Brussels (BRU)	217
Bucharest (Otopeni, OTP)	1,307
Budapest (Ferihegy, BUD)	923
Buenos Aires (Ezeiza, AEP)	6,915
Cairo (CAI)	2,194
Calcutta/Kolkata (CCU)	4,958
Calgary (YYC)	4,357
Canberra (CBR)	10,563
Cape Town (CPT)	6,011
Caracas (Simón Bolívar, CCS)	4,639
Casablanca (CMN)	1,300
Chennai/Madras (MAA)	5,113
Chicago (O'Hare, ORD)	3,941
Cologne/Bonn (CGN)	331
Colombo (CMB)	5,411
Copenhagen (CPH)	608
Dakar (DKR)	2,706
Dallas (Fort Worth, DFW)	4,736
Dallas (Love Field, DAL)	4,732
Damascus (DAM)	2,223
Dar-es-Salaam (DAR)	4,662
Darwin (DRW)	8,613
Denver (DEN)	4,655

To	Miles
Detroit (DTW)	3,754
Dhahran (DHA)	3,143
Dhaka (Zia, DAC)	4,976
Doha (DOH)	3,253
Dubai (DXB)	3,414
Dublin (DUB)	279
Durban (DUR)	5,937
Düsseldorf (DUS)	310
Entebbe (EBB)	4,033
Frankfurt (Main, FRA)	406
Freetown (Lunghi, FNA)	3,046
Geneva (GVA)	468
Gibraltar (GIB)	1,084
Gothenburg (GOT)	664
Hamburg (HAM)	463
Harare (HRE)	5,156
Havana (José Martí, HAV)	4,647
Helsinki (Vantaa, HEL)	1,148
Hobart (HBA)	10,826
Ho Chi Minh City (SGN)	6,345
Hong Kong (HKG)	5,990
Honolulu (HNL)	7,220
Houston (George Bush Intercontinental, IAH)	4,821
Islamabad (ISB)	3,767
Istanbul (Atatürk, IST)	1,560
Jakarta (HLP)	7,295
Jeddah (King Abdulaziz, JED)	2,947
Johannesburg (GCJ)	5,634
Kabul (Khwaja Rawash, KBL)	3,558
Karachi (Jinnah, KHI)	3,935
Kathmandu (Tribhuvan, KTM)	4,570
Khartoum (KRT)	3,071
Kyiv (Borispol, KBP)	1,357
Kingston, Jamaica (KIN)	4,668
Kuala Lumpur (KUL)	6,557
Kuwait (KWI)	2,903
Lagos (LOS)	3,107
Larnaca (LCA)	2,036
Lima-Callao (LIM)	6,303
Lisbon (LIS)	972
Lomé (LFW)	3,129
Los Angeles (LAX)	5,439
Madrid (Barajas, MAD)	773
Malta (MLA)	1,305
Manila (MNL)	6,685
Marseille (Provence, MRS)	614
Mauritius (MRU)	6,075
Melbourne (Tullamarine, MEL)	10,499
Mexico City (MEX)	5,529
Miami (MIA)	4,414
Milan (Linate, LIN)	609
Minsk (National, MSQ)	1,176
Montego Bay (MBJ)	4,687
Montevideo (MVD)	6,841
Montréal (YUL)	3,241
Moscow (SVO)	1,557

To	Miles
Munich (MUC)	584
Muscat (Seeb, MCT)	3,621
Nairobi (NBO)	4,248
Naples (NAP)	1,011
Nassau (NAS)	4,333
New Delhi (DEL)	4,180
New York (JFK)	3,440
Nice (Côte d'Azur, NCE)	645
Oporto (OPO)	806
Oslo (OSL)	722
Ottawa (YOW)	3,321
Palma de Mallorca (PMI)	836
Paris (CDG)	215
Paris (Orly, ORY)	227
Perth, Australia (PER)	9,008
Port of Spain (Piarco, POS)	4,404
Prague (Ruzyne, PRG)	649
Pretoria (PRY)	5,602
Rangoon/Yangon (RGN)	5,582
Reykjavík (Domestic, RKV)	1,167
Reykjavík (Keflavík, KEF)	1,177
Rhodes (Diagoras, RHO)	1,743
Rio de Janeiro (GIG)	5,745
Riyadh (King Khaled, RUH)	3,067
Rome (Fiumicino, FCO)	895
St John's, Newfoundland (YYT)	2,308
St Petersburg (Pulkovo, LED)	1,314
Salzburg (W. A. Mozart, SZG)	651
San Francisco (SFO)	5,351
São Paulo (Guarulhos, GRU)	5,892
Sarajevo (SJJ)	1,017
Seoul (Gimpo, SEL)	5,507
Shanghai (SHA)	5,725
Shannon (SNN)	369
Singapore (Changi, SIN)	6,756
Sofia (SOF)	1,266
Stockholm (Arlanda, ARN)	908
Suva (Nausori, SUV)	10,119
Sydney (SYD)	10,568
Tangier (Boukhalef, TNG)	1,120
Tehran (Mehrabad, THR)	2,741
Tel Aviv (Ben Gurion, TLV)	2,227
Tokyo (Narita, NRT)	5,956
Toronto (YYZ)	3,544
Tripoli (TIP)	1,468
Tunis-Carthage (TUN)	1,137
Turin (TRN)	570
Ulaanbaatar (ULN)	4,340
Valencia (VLC)	826
Vancouver (YVR)	4,707
Venice (Marco Polo, VCE)	715
Vienna (VIE)	790
Vladivostok (VVO)	5,298
Warsaw (WAW)	912
Washington (Dulles, IAD)	3,665
Wellington (WLG)	11,692
Yokohama (YOK)	5,647
Zagreb (ZAG)	848
Zürich (ZRH)	490

TIME ZONES

Standard time differences from the Greenwich meridian

+ hours ahead of GMT
− hours behind GMT
* may vary from standard time at some part of the year (Summer Time or Daylight Saving Time)
‡ some areas may keep another time zone
h hours
m minutes

	h	m
Afghanistan	+ 4	30
*Albania	+ 1	
Algeria	+ 1	
*Andorra	+ 1	
Angola	+ 1	
Anguilla	− 4	
Antigua and Barbuda	− 4	
Argentina	− 3	
Armenia	+ 4	
Aruba	− 4	
Ascension Island	0	
*Australia		
*ACT, NSW (except Broken Hill area) Tas, Vic, Whitsunday Islands	+10	
Northern Territory	+ 9	30
Queensland	+10	
*South Australia	+ 9	30
Western Australia	+ 8	
*Austria	+ 1	
Azerbaijan	+ 4	
*Bahamas	− 5	
Bahrain	+ 3	
Bangladesh	+ 6	
Barbados	− 4	
*Belarus	+ 2	
*Belgium	+ 1	
Belize	− 6	
Benin	+ 1	
*Bermuda	− 4	
Bhutan	+ 6	
Bolivia	− 4	
*Bosnia-Hercegovina	+ 1	
Botswana	+ 2	
*Brazil		
western states	− 5	
central states	− 4	
N. and N.E coastal states	− 2	
*S. and E. coastal states, including Brasilia	− 3	
Fernando de Noronha Island	− 2	
British Antarctic Territory	− 3	
British Indian Ocean Territory	+ 5	
British Virgin Islands	− 4	
Brunei	+ 8	
*Bulgaria	+ 2	
Burkina Faso	0	
Burundi	+ 3	
Cambodia	+ 7	
Cameroon	+ 1	
*Canada		
*Alberta	− 7	
*‡British Columbia	− 8	
*Manitoba	− 6	
*New Brunswick	− 4	
*Newfoundland	− 3	30
*Northwest Territories	− 5	
*Nova Scotia	− 4	
*Nunavut	− 7	
central	− 6	
eastern	− 5	
mountain	− 7	
Ontario		
*east of 90° W.	− 5	
*west of 90° W.	− 6	
*Prince Edward Island	− 4	
*Québec		
east of 63° W.	− 4	
*west of 63° W.	− 5	
‡Saskatchewan	− 7	
*Yukon	− 8	
Cape Verde	− 1	
Cayman Islands	− 5	
Central African Republic	+ 1	
Chad	+ 1	
*Chatham Islands	+12	45
*Chile	− 4	
China (inc. Hong Kong and Macao)	+ 8	
Christmas Island (Indian Ocean)	+ 7	
Cocos (Keeling) Islands	+ 6	30
Colombia	− 5	
Comoros	+ 3	
Congo (Dem. Rep.)		
Haut-Zaïre, Kasai, Kivu, Shaba	+ 2	
Kinshasa, Mbandaka	+ 1	
Congo (Rep. of)	+ 1	
Costa Rica	− 6	
Côte d'Ivoire	0	
*Croatia	+ 1	
*Cuba	− 5	
*Cyprus	+ 2	
*Czech Republic	+ 1	
*Denmark	+ 1	
*Faeroe Islands	0	
*Greenland	− 3	
Danmarkshavn, Mesters Vig	0	
*Scoresby Sound	− 1	
*Thule area	− 4	
Djibouti	+ 3	
Dominica	− 4	
Dominican Republic	− 4	
East Timor	+ 9	
Ecuador	− 5	
Galápagos Islands	− 6	
*Egypt	+ 2	
El Salvador	− 6	
Equatorial Guinea	+ 1	
Eritrea	+ 3	
*Estonia	+ 2	
Ethiopia	+ 3	
*Falkland Islands	− 4	
Fiji	+12	
*Finland	+ 2	
*France	+ 1	
French Guiana	− 3	
French Polynesia	−10	
Guadeloupe	− 4	
Martinique	− 4	
Marquesas Islands	− 9	30
Wallis and Futuna	+12	
Réunion	+ 4	
Gabon	+ 1	
Gambia	0	
Georgia	+ 4	
*Germany	+ 1	
Ghana	0	
*Gibraltar	+ 1	
*Greece	+ 2	
Grenada	− 4	
Guam	+10	
Guatemala	− 6	
Guinea	0	
Guinea-Bissau	0	
Guyana	− 4	
Haiti	− 5	
Honduras	− 6	
*Hungary	+ 1	
Iceland	0	
India	+ 5	30
Indonesia		
Java, Kalimantan (west and central), Madura, Sumatra	+ 7	
Bali, Flores, Kalimantan (south and east), Lombok, Sulawesi, Sumbawa, West Timor	+ 8	
Irian Jaya, Maluku,	+ 9	
*Iran	+ 3	30
*Iraq	+ 3	
*Ireland, Republic of	0	
*Israel	+ 2	
*Italy	+ 1	
Jamaica	− 5	
Japan	+ 9	
*Jordan	+ 2	
Kazakhstan		
western	+ 4	
central	+ 5	
eastern	+ 6	
Kenya	+ 3	
Kiribati	+12	
Line Islands	+14	
Phoenix Islands	+13	
Korea, North	+ 9	
Korea, South	+ 9	

	h	m		h	m		h	m
Kuwait	+ 3		Puerto Rico	− 4		Aleutian Islands, east		
Kyrgyzstan	+ 5		Qatar	+ 3		of 169° 30′ W.	− 9	
Laos	+ 7		Réunion	+ 4		Aleutian Islands, west		
Latvia	+ 2		*Romania	+ 2		of 169° 30′ W.	−10	
Lebanon	+ 2		*Russia			*central time	− 6	
Lesotho	+ 3		Zone 1	+ 2		*eastern time	− 5	
Liberia	0		Zone 2	+ 3		Hawaii	−10	
Libya	+ 2		Zone 3	+ 4		*mountain time	− 7	
Liechtenstein	+ 1		Zone 4	+ 5		*Pacific time	− 8	
Lithuania	+ 2		Zone 5	+ 6		*Uruguay	− 3	
Luxembourg	+ 1		Zone 6	+ 7		Uzbekistan	+ 5	
*Macedonia	+ 1		Zone 7	+ 8		Vanuatu	+11	
Madagascar	+ 3		Zone 8	+ 9		*Vatican City State	+ 1	
Malawi	+ 2		Zone 9	+10		Venezuela	− 4	
Malaysia	+ 8		Zone 10	+11		Vietnam	+ 7	
Maldives	+ 5		Zone 11	+12		Virgin Islands (US)	− 4	
Mali	0		Rwanda	+ 2		Yemen	+ 3	
*Malta	+ 1		St Christopher and Nevis	− 4		Zambia	+ 2	
Marshall Islands	+12		St Helena	0		Zimbabwe	+ 2	
Mauritania	0		St Lucia	− 4				
Mauritius	+ 4		*St Pierre and Miquelon	− 3				
*Mexico	− 6		St Vincent and the					
*Nayarit, Sinaloa,			Grenadines	− 4				
S. Baja California	− 7		Samoa	−11				
*N. Baja California	− 8		Samoa, American	−11				
Sonora	− 7		*San Marino	+ 1				
Micronesia			São Tomé and Princípe	0				
Chuuk, Jap	+12		Saudi Arabia	+ 3				
Kosrae, Pingelap,			Senegal	0				
Pohnpei	+11		*Serbia and Montenegro	+ 1				
*Moldova	+ 2		Seychelles	+ 4				
*Monaco	+ 1		Sierra Leone	0				
Mongolia	+ 8		Singapore	+ 8				
Montserrat	− 4		*Slovakia	+ 1				
Morocco	0		*Slovenia	+ 1				
Mozambique	+ 2		Solomon Islands	+11				
Myanmar	+ 6	30	Somalia	+ 3				
*Namibia	+ 1		South Africa	+ 2				
Nauru	+12		South Georgia	− 2				
Nepal	+ 5	45	*Spain	+ 1				
*Netherlands	+ 1		*Canary Islands	0				
Netherlands Antilles	− 4		Sri Lanka	+ 6				
New Caledonia	+11		Sudan	+ 3				
*New Zealand	+12		Suriname	− 3				
Cook Islands	−10		Swaziland	+ 4				
Tokelau Island	−10		*Sweden	+ 1				
*Nicaragua	− 6		*Switzerland	+ 1				
Niger	+ 1		*Syria	+ 2				
Nigeria	+ 1		Taiwan	+ 8				
Niue	−11		Tajikistan	+ 5				
Norfolk Island	+11	30	Tanzania	+ 3				
Northern Mariana Islands	+10		Thailand	+ 7				
*Norway	+ 1		Togo	0				
Svalbard and Jan Mayen	+ 1		Tonga	+13				
Oman	+ 4		Trinidad and Tobago	− 4				
Pakistan	+ 5		Tristan da Cunha	0				
Palau	+ 9		*Tunisia	+ 1				
Panama	− 5		*Turkey	+ 2				
Papua New Guinea	+10		Turkmenistan	+ 5				
*Paraguay	− 4		*Turks and Caicos Islands	− 5				
Peru	− 5		Tuvalu	+12				
Philippines	+ 8		Uganda	+ 3				
Pitcairn Island	+ 8		*Ukraine	+ 2				
*Poland	+ 1		United Arab Emirates	+ 4				
*Portugal	0		*United Kingdom	0				
*Azores	− 1		*United States of America					
*Madeira	0		*Alaska	− 9				

CURRENCIES AND EXCHANGE RATES

AGAINST £ STERLING

COUNTRY/TERRITORY	AVERAGE RATE TO £1	27 AUGUST 2004	12 AUGUST 2005
Afghanistan	Afghani (Af) of 100 puls	Af 77.16	Af 77.75
Albania	Lek (Lk) of 100 qindraka	Lk 186.10	Lk 177.21
Algeria	Algerian dinar (DA) of 100 centimes	DA 129.69	DA 131.81
American Samoa	Currency is that of the USA	US$1.79	US$1.81
Andorra	Euro (€) of 100 cents	€1.48	€1.45
Angola	Readjusted kwanza (Krzl) of 100 lwei	Kzrl 145.95	Kzrl 161.29
Anguilla	East Caribbean dollar (EC$) of 100 cents	EC$4.84	EC$4.88
Antigua and Barbuda	East Caribbean dollar (EC$) of 100 cents	EC$4.84	EC$4.88
Argentina	Peso of 10,000 australes	Pesos 5.37	Pesos 5.21
Armenia	Dram of 100 louma	Dram 926.93	Dram 813.71
Aruba	Aruban florin	Florins 3.21	Florins 3.24
Ascension Island	Currency is that of St Helena	at parity with £ sterling	
Australia	Australian dollar ($A) of 100 cents	$A2.55	$A2.34
Austria	Euro (€) of 100 cents	€1.48	€1.45
Azerbaijan	Manat of 100 gopik	Manat 8813.53	Manat 8458.99
The Bahamas	Bahamian dollar (B$) of 100 cents	B$1.79	B$1.81
Bahrain	Bahraini dinar (BD) of 1,000 fils	BD 0.67	BD 0.68
Bangladesh	Taka (Tk) of 100 poisha	Tk 106.486	Tk 118.40
Barbados	Barbados dollar (BD$) of 100 cents	BD$3.58	BD$3.62
Belarus	Belarusian rouble of 100 kopeks	BYR 3883.62	BYR 3892.26
Belgium	Euro (€) of 100 cents	€1.48	€1.45
Belize	Belize dollar (BZ$) of 100 cents	BZ$3.55	BZ$3.56
Benin	Franc FCA	Francs 973.63	Francs 953.44
Bermuda	Bermuda dollar of 100 cents	$1.79	$1.81
Bhutan	Ngultrum of 100 chetrum (Indian currency is also legal tender)	Ngultrum 83.09	Ngultrum 78.74
Bolivia	Boliviano ($b) of 100 centavos	$b14.27	$b14.60
Bosnia-Hercegovina	Convertible marka	Marka 2.83	Marka 2.84
Botswana	Pula (P) of 100 thebe	P 8.64	P 9.72
Brazil	Real of 100 centavos	Real 5.29	Real 4.18
Brunei	Brunei dollar (B$) of 100 sen (fully interchangeable with Singapore currency)	B$3.07	B$2.98
Bulgaria	Lev of 100 stotinki	Leva 2.90	Leva 2.84
Burkina Faso	Franc CFA	Francs 973.63	Francs 953.44
Burundi	Burundi franc of 100 centimes	Francs 1902.34	Francs 1961.92
Cambodia	Riel of 100 sen	Riel 6900.43	Riel 7513.28
Cameroon	Franc CFA	Francs 973.63	Francs 953.44
Canada	Canadian dollar (C$) 100 cents	C$2.35	C$2.17
Cape Verde	Escudo Caboverdiano of 100 centavos	Esc 164.56	Esc 161.30
Cayman Islands	Cayman Islands dollar (CI$) of 100 cents	CI$1.48	CI$1.50
Central African Republic	Franc CFA	Francs 973.63	Francs 953.44
Chad	Franc CFA	Francs 973.63	Francs 953.44
Chile	Chilean peso of 100 centavos	Pesos 1126.95	Pesos 975.55
China	Renminbi Yuan of 10 jiao or 100 fen	Yuan 14.85	Yuan 14.65
Colombia	Colombian peso of 100 centavos	Pesos 4611.76	Pesos 4184.20
Comoros	Comorian franc (KMF) of 100 centimes	Francs 730.221	Francs 715.08
Congo, Rep. of	Franc CFA	Francs 973.63	Francs 953.44
Congo, Dem. Rep. of	Congolese franc	CFr 698.5	CFr 896.90
Cook Islands	Currency is that of New Zealand	NZ$2.75	NZ$2.56
Costa Rica	Costa Rican colón (C) of 100 céntimos	C797.05	C872.21
Côte d'Ivoire	Franc CFA	Francs 973.63	Francs 953.44
Croatia	Kuna of 100 lipa	Kuna 10.97	Kuna 10.70
Cuba	Cuban peso of 100 centavos	Pesos 37.56	Pesos 1.81
Cyprus	Cyprus pound (C£) of 100 cents	C£0.85	C£0.83
Czech Republic	Koruna (Kcs) of 100 haléru	Kcs 47.35	Kcs 42.79
Denmark	Danish krone of 100 øre	Kroner 11.03	Kroner 10.85
Dijibouti	Dijibouti franc of 100 centimes	Francs 305.53	Francs 314.64
Dominica	East Caribbean dollar (EC$) of 100 cents	EC$4.84	EC$4.88
Dominican Republic	Dominican Republic peso (RD$) of 100 centavos	RD$69.09	RD$51.99
East Timor	Currency is that of the USA	US$1.79	US$1.81

Ecuador	Currency is that of the USA (formerly sucre of 100 centavos)	US$1.79	US$1.81
Egypt	Egyptian pound (£E) of 100 piastres or 1,000 millièmes	£E11.12	£E10.44
El Salvador	Currency is that of USA	US$1.79	US$1.81
Equatorial Guinea	Franc CFA	Francs 973.63	Francs 953.44
Eritrea	Nakfa	Nafka 24.22	24.41
Estonia	Kroon of 100 sents	Kroons 23.22	Kroons 22.74
Ethiopia	Ethiopian birr (EB) of 100 cents	EB 15.43	EB 15.75
Faeroe Islands	Currency is that of Denmark	Kroner 11.03	Kroner 10.84
Falkland Islands	Falkland pound of 100 pence	at parity with £ sterling	
Fiji	Fiji dollar (F$) of 100 cents	F$ 3.19	F$3.06
Finland	Euro (€) of 100 cents	€1.48	€1.45
France	Euro (€) of 100 cents	€1.48	€1.45
French Guiana	Euro (€) of 100 cents	€1.48	€1.45
French Polynesia	Franc CFP	Francs 177.00	Francs 173.33
Gabon	Franc CFA	Francs 973.63	Francs 953.44
Gambia	Dalasi (D) of 100 butut	D 52.04	D 50.08
Georgia	Laria of 100 tetri	Laria 3.91	Laria 3.25
Germany	Euro (€) of 100 cents	€1.48	€1.45
Ghana	Cedi of 100 pesewas	Cedi 16196.7	Cedi 16446.0
Gibraltar	Gibraltar pound of 100 pence	at parity with £ sterling	
Greece	Euro (€) of 100 cents	€1.48	€1.45
Greenland	Currency is that of Denmark	Kroner 11.30	Kroner 10.85
Grenada	East Caribbean dollar (EC$) of 100 cents	EC$4.84	EC$4.88
Guadeloupe	Euro (€) of 100 cents	€1.48	€1.45
Guam	Currency is that of the USA	US$1.79	US$1.81
Guatemala	Quetzal (Q) of 100 centavos	Q 14.18	Q 13.73
Guinea	Guinea franc of 100 centimes	Francs 4585.33	Francs 6799.26
Guinea-Bissau	Franc CFA	Francs 973.63	Francs 953.44
Guyana	Guyana dollar (G$) of 100 cents	G$321.24	G$343.57
Haiti	Gourde of 100 centimes	Gourdes 61.1	Gourdes 75.31
Honduras	Lempira of 100 centavos	Lempiras 32.94	Lempiras 34.10
Hong Kong	Hong Kong (HK$) of 100 cents	HK$13.99	HK$14.05
Hungary	Forint of 100 fillér	Forints 370.58	Forints 353.77
Iceland	Icelandic króna (Kr) of 100 aurar	Kr 129.215	Kr 115.37
India	Indian rupee (Rs) of 100 paisa	Rs 83.09	Rs 78.74
Indonesia	Rupiah (Rp) of 100 sen	Rp 16699.2	Rp 17742.6
Iran	Rial	Rials 15663.7	Rials 16270.6
Iraq	New Iraqi dinar (NID)	—	NID 2657.40
Ireland, Republic of	Euro (€) of 100 cents	€1.48	€1.45
Israel	Shekel of 100 agora	Shekels 8.15	Shekels 8.18
Italy	Euro (€) of 100 cents	€1.48	€1.45
Jamaica	Jamaican dollar (J$) of 100 cents	J$109.72	J$111.95
Japan	Yen	Yen 196.64	Yen 198.79
Jordan	Jordanian dinar (JD) of 1,000 fils	JD 1.27	JD 1.28
Kazakhstan	Tenge	Tenge 245.13	Tenge 244.63
Kenya	Kenya shilling (Ksh) of 100 cents	Ksh 145.54	Ksh 136.98
Kiribati	Australian dollar ($A) of 100 cents	$A2.55	$A2.34
Korea, Dem. People's Rep. of	Won of 100 chon	Won 1615.18	1627.42
Korea, Republic of	Won	Won 2070.13	Won 1836.28
Kuwait	Kuwaiti dinar (KD) of 1,000 fils	KD 0.52	KD 0.53
Kyrgyzstan	Som	Som 75.67	Som 74.05
Laos	Kip (K) of 100 at	K 14071.8	K 18805.8
Latvia	Lats of 100 santims	Lats 0.97	Lats 1.01
Lebanon	Lebanese pound (L£) of of 100 piastres	L£2718.00	L£2716.90
Lesotho	Loti (M) of 100 lisente	M 11.84	M 11.46
Liberia	Liberian dollar (L$) of 100 cents	L$1.50	L$101.26
Libya	Libyan dinar (LD) of 1,000 dirhams	LD 2.35	LD 2.38
Liechtenstein	Swiss franc of 100 rappen (or centimes)	Francs 2.28	Francs 2.26
Lithuania	Litas of 100 centas	Litas 5.12	Litas 5.02
Luxembourg	Euro (€) of 100 cents	€1.48	€1.45
Macao	Pataca of 100 avos	Pataca 14.41	Pataca 14.47
Macedonia	Denar of 100 deni	Den 90.28	Den 89.51
Madagascar	Franc malgache (FMG) of 100 centimes	FMG 18260.6	FMG 3643.63
Malawi	Kwacha (K) of 100 tambala	MK 195.25	MK 223.67
Malaysia	Malaysian dollar (ringgit) (M$) of 100 sen	M$6.81	M$6.78

Maldives	Rufiyaa of 100 laaris	Rufiyaa 22.97	Rufiyaa 23.15
Mali	Franc CFA	Francs 973.63	Francs 953.44
Malta	Maltese lira (LM) of 100 cents of 1,000 mils	LM 0.63	LM 0.62
Marshall Islands	Currency is that of the USA	US$1.79	US$1.81
Martinique	Currency is that of France	€1.48	€1.45
Mauritania	Ouguiya (UM) of 5 khoums	UM 477.37	UM 484.92
Mauritius	Mauritius rupee of 100 cents	Rs 50.96	Rs 53.29
Mayotte	Euro (€) of 100 cents	€1.48	€1.45
Mexico	Peso of 100 centavos	Pesos 20.40	Pesos 19.13
Micronesia, Federated States of	Currency is that of the USA	US$1.79	US$1.81
Moldova	Moldovan leu of 100 bani	MDL 21.57	MDL 22.58
Monaco	Euro (€) of 100 cents	€1.48	€1.45
Mongolia	Tugrik of 100 möngö	Tugriks 2141.2	Tugriks 2166.28
Montserrat	East Caribbean dollar (EC$) of 100 cents	EC$4.84	EC$4.88
Morocco	Dirham (DH) of 100 centimes	DH 16.28	DH 16.03
Mozambique	Metical (MT) of 100 centavos	MT 39502.8	MT 44117.7
Myanmar	Kyat (K) of 100 pyas	K 11.52	K 11.61
Namibia	Namibian dollar of 100 cents	at parity with SA Rand	
Nauru	Australian dollar ($A) of 100 cents	$A2.55	$A2.34
Nepal	Nepalese rupee of 100 paisa	Rs 132.94	Rs 125.98
The Netherlands	Euro (€) of 100 cents	€1.48	€1.45
Netherlands Antilles	Netherlands Antilles guilder of 100 cents	Guilders 3.21	Guilders 3.24
New Caledonia	Franc CFP	Francs 191.04	Francs 173.33
New Zealand	New Zealand dollar (NZ$) of 100 cents	NZ$2.75	NZ$2.57
Nicaragua	Córdoba (C$) of 100 centavos	C$28.60	C$29.60
Niger	Franc CFA	Francs 973.63	Francs 953.44
Nigeria	Naira (N) of 100 kobo	N 239.22	N 249.54
Niue	Currency is that of New Zealand	NZ$2.75	NZ$2.56
Norfolk Island	Currency is that of Australia	$A2.55	$A2.33
Northern Mariana Islands	Currency is that of the USA	US$1.79	US$1.81
Norway	Krone of 100 øre	Kroner 12.37	Kroner 11.46
Oman	Rial Omani (OR) of 1,000 baisas	OR 0.69	OR 0.70
Pakistan	Pakistan rupee of 100 paisa	Rs 105.301	Rs 107.91
Palau	Currency is that of the USA	US$1.79	US$1.81
Panama	Balboa of 100 centésimos (US notes are in circulation)	Balboa 1.79	Balboa 1.81
Papua New Guinea	Kina (K) of 100 toea	K 5.48	K 5.48
Paraguay	Guarani (Gs) of 100 céntimos	Gs 10615.4	Gs 10817.9
Peru	New Sol of 100 cénts	New Sol 6.05	New Sol 5.88
The Philippines	Philippine peso (P) of 100 centavos	P 100.55	P 100.73
Pitcairn Islands	Currency is that of New Zealand	NZ$2.75	NZ$2.57
Poland	Zloty of 100 groszy	Zlotych 6.66	Zlotych 5.85
Portugal	Euro (€) of 100 cents	€1.48	€1.45
Puerto Rico	Currency is that of the USA	US$1.79	US$1.81
Qatar	Qatar riyal of 100 dirhams	Riyals 6.53	Riyals 6.58
Réunion	Euro (€) of 100 cents	€1.48	€1.45
Romania	Lei of 100 bani	Lei 60900.3	Lei 5.03
Russia	Rouble of 100 kopeks	Rbl 52.43	Rbl 51.24
Rwanda	Rwanda franc of 100 centimes	Francs 1012.00	Francs 980.52
St Christopher and Nevis	East Caribbean dollar (EC$) of 100 cents	EC$4.84	EC$4.88
St Helena	St Helena pound (£) of 100 pence	at parity with £ sterling	
St Lucia	East Caribbean dollar (EC$) of 100 cents	EC$4.84	EC$4.88
St Pierre and Miquelon	Euro (€) of 100 cents	€1.48	€1.45
St Vincent and the Grenadines	East Caribbean dollar (EC$) of 100 cents	EC$4.84	EC$4.88
Samoa	Tala (S$) of 100 sene	S$5.70	S$4.66
San Marino	Euro (€) of 100 cents	€1.48	€1.45
São Tomé and Príncipe	Dobra of 100 centavos	Dobra 15818.0	Dobra 14692.0
Saudi Arabia	Saudi riyal (SR) of 20 qursh or 100 halala	SR 6.73	SR 6.78
Senegal	Franc CFA	Francs 973.63	Francs 953.44
Serbia and Montenegro	New dinar of 100 paras	New Dinars 99.00	New Dinars 122.48
Seychelles	Seychelles rupee of 100 cents	Rs 9.90	Rs 9.98
Sierra Leone	Leone (Le) of 100 cents	Le 4405.89	Le 5231.35
Singapore	Singapore dollar (S$) of 100 cents	S$3.07	S$2.98
Slovakia	Koruna (Sk) of 100 halierov	Kčs 59.75	Kčs 58.89

Slovenia	Tolar (SIT) of 100 stotin	Tolars 356.19	Tolars 348.11
Solomon Islands	Solomon Islands dollar (SI$) of 100 cents	SI$13.34	SI$13.13
Somalia	Somali shilling of 100 cents	Shillings 4886.83	Shillings 4421.17
South Africa	Rand (R) of 100 cents	R 11.84	R 11.46
Spain	Euro (€) of 100 cents	€1.48	€1.45
Sri Lanka	Sri Lankan rupee of 100 cents	Rs 184.84	Rs 182.27
Sudan	Sudanese dinar (SD) of 100 piastres	SD 464.85	SD 439.00
Suriname	Surinam dollar of 100 cents	—	Dollar 4.95
Swaziland	Lilangeni (E) of 100 cents (South African currency is also in circulation)	at parity with SA Rand	
Sweden	Swedish krona of 100 öre	Kronor 13.55	Kronor 13.52
Switzerland	Swiss franc of 100 rappen (or centimes)	Francs 2.28 0	Francs 2.26
Syria	Syrian pound (S£) of 100 piastres	S£92.71	S£94.41
Taiwan	New Taiwan dollar (NT$) of 100 cents	NT$60.88	NT$57.69
Tajikistan	Somoni (TJS) of 100 dirams	—	—
Tanzania	Tanzanian shilling of 100 cents	Shillings 1948.99	Shillings 2018.01
Thailand	Baht of 100 satang	Baht 74.75	Baht 73.86
Togo	Franc CFA	Francs 973.63	Francs 953.44
Tokelau	Currency is that of New Zealand	NZ$2.75	NZ$2.57
Tonga	Pa'anga (T$) of 100 seniti	T$3.57	T$3.50
Trinidad and Tobago	Trinidad and Tobago dollar (TT$) of 100 cents	TT$11.17	TT$11.31
Tristan da Cunha	Currency is that of the UK	—	—
Tunisia	Tunisian dinar of 1,000 millimes	Dinars 2.27	Dinars 2.35
Turkey	New Turkish lira (TL) of 100 kurus	TL 2711717	TL 2.41
Turkmenistan	Manat of 100 tenge	—	Manat 9308.87
Turks and Caicos Islands	US dollar (US$)	US$1.79	US$1.81
Tuvalu	Australian dollar ($A) of 100 cents	$A2.55	$A2.33
Uganda	Uganda shilling of 100 cents	Shillings 3073.34	Shillings 3276.55
Ukraine	Hryvna of 100 kopiykas	UAH 9.55	UAH 9.01
United Arab Emirates	UAE dirham (Dh) of 100 fils	Dirham 6.59	Dirham 6.64
United States of America	US dollar (US$) of 100 cents	US$1.79	US$1.81
Uruguay	Uruguayan peso of 100 centésimos	Pesos 52.10	Pesos 44.17
Uzbekistan	Sum of 100 tiyin	Sum 1849.53	Sum 2037.95
Vanuatu	Vatu of 100 centimes	Vatu 206.04	Vatu 201.26
Vatican City State	Euro (€) of 100 cents y	€1.48	€1.45
Venezuela	Bolívar (Bs) of 100 céntimos	Bs 4711.75	Bs 4868.37
Vietnam	Dông of 10 hào or 100 xu	Dông 28309.7	Dông 28700.5
Virgin Islands, British	US dollar (US$) (£ sterling and EC$ also circulate)	US$1.79	US$1.81
Virgin Islands, US	Currency is that of the USA	US$1.79	US$1.81
Wallis and Futuna Islands	Franc CFP	Francs 191.04	Francs 167.95
Yemen	Riyal of 100 fils	Riyals 331.68	Riyals 347.93
Zambia	Kwacha (K) of 100 ngwee	K 8524.60	K 7956.31
Zimbabwe	Zimbabwe dollar (Z$) of 100 cents	Z$10068.8	Z$32548.6

Source: WM/Reuters Closing Spot Rates

TRAVEL OVERSEAS

PASSPORT REGULATIONS

Application forms for United Kingdom passports can be obtained from the UK Passport Service's general telephone enquiry line or website, regional passport offices, or from main post offices and WorldChoice travel agents.

T 0870-521 0410 W www.ukpa.gov.uk

BELFAST
Passport Office, Hampton House, 47–53 High Street, Belfast BT1 2QS

DURHAM
Passport Office, Millburngate House, Durham DH97 1PA

GLASGOW
Passport Office, 3 Northgate, 96 Milton Street, Cowcaddens, Glasgow G4 0BT

LONDON
Passport Office, Globe House, 89 Eccleston Square, London SW1V 1PN

LIVERPOOL
Passport Office, 101 Old Hall Street, Liverpool L3 9BP

NEWPORT
Passport Office, Olympia House, Upper Dock Street, Newport, Gwent NP20 1XA

PETERBOROUGH
Passport Office, Aragon Court, Northminster Road, Peterborough PE1 1QG

The passport offices are open Monday–Saturday on an appointment-only basis (appointments should be arranged by calling the central telephone number listed above). For an additional fee, passport offices provide either a guaranteed same-day service (for renewals, extensions or amendments only) or a one-week fast-track service (all types of applications).

Standard postal applications are processed within three weeks. The completed application form should be posted, with the appropriate supporting documents and fee, to the regional passport office indicated on the addressed envelope which is provided with each application form. Accompanying cheques and postal orders should be crossed and made payable to 'UK Passport Service'.

Applications can also be submitted through selected main post offices and WorldChoice travel agents ('partners'), who, in exchange for a small handling charge, will forward the application form to the relevant regional passport office after having checked that it has been completed correctly and has the appropriate documents attached. Applications through partners take a minimum of two weeks.

A passport cannot be issued or extended on behalf of a person already abroad; such persons should apply to the nearest British High Commission or Consulate.

UK passports are granted to:
- British citizens
- British Dependent Territories citizens
- British Nationals (Overseas)
- British Overseas Territories citizens
- British Subjects
- British Protected Persons

UK passports are generally available for travel to all countries. The possession of a passport does not, however, exempt the holder from compliance with any immigration regulations in force in British or foreign countries, or from the necessity of obtaining a visa where required.

Biometric passports are due to be introduced during 2006. The new design and security features, including a chip containing the facial image and biographical data of the holder, will render the passport more secure against forgery and aid border controls.

ADULTS
A passport granted to a person over 16 will normally be valid for ten years. Thereafter, or if at any time the passport contains no further space for visas, a new passport must be obtained.

The issue of passports including details of the holder's spouse has been discontinued, but existing family passports may be used until expiry. A spouse who is included in a family passport cannot travel on the passport without the holder.

British nationals born on or before 2 September 1929 are eligible for a free standard passport.

CHILDREN
Since 5 October 1998 all children under the age of 16 are required to have their own passport. This is primarily to help prevent child abductions. The passports are initially valid for five years, but can be renewed for a further five years at the end of this period. This replaced the system whereby children under the age of 16 could either have their own passport or be added to their parents' passports.

A passport granted to a child prior to this date was still valid for five years. On expiry, a new application must be made. Children included in their parents' passports when the new regulations came into force are not affected and can continue to travel on them until they reach the age of 16 or the passport expires or is amended.

COUNTERSIGNATURES
A countersignature is only needed if the application is for a first passport or to replace a lost, stolen or missing passport. The following is a list of acceptable countersignatories: MP; justice of the peace; minister of religion; a professionally qualified person (e.g. doctor, engineer, lawyer, teacher); bank officer; military officer; established civil servant; police officer; or a person of similar standing who has known the applicant for at least two years, and who is either a British citizen, British Dependent Territories citizen, British National (Overseas), British Overseas Territories citizen, British Subject or a citizen of a Commonwealth country. A relative or partner must not countersign the application.

If the application is for a child under the age of 16, the countersignature should be by someone of relevant standing who has known the parent or person with parental responsibility who signs the declaration of consent, rather than the child.

PHOTOGRAPHS
Two identical, unmounted, recent photographs of the applicant must be sent. These photographs should measure 45mm by 35mm, be printed on normal thin photographic paper and should be taken full face against a white background. The photo must show the applicant's full face, looking straight at the camera, with a neutral expression and with their mouth closed. The person who countersigns the application form should certify one photograph as a true likeness of the applicant.

DOCUMENTATION
The applicant's birth certificate or previous British passport, and other documents in support of the statements made in the application, must be produced at the time of applying. Details of which documents are required are set out in the notes accompanying the application form.

If the applicant for a passport is a British national by naturalisation or registration, the certificate proving this must be produced with the application, unless the applicant holds a previous UK passport issued after registration or naturalisation.

48-PAGE PASSPORTS
The 48-page passport is intended to meet the needs of frequent travellers who fill standard passports well before the validity has expired. It is valid for ten years but is not available for children.

PASSPORT FEES*
from September 2005

New adult passport	£42
New child passport	£25
Renewal or amendment of passport	£42
Renewal or amendment of child passport	£25
48-page passport	£54.50

* Standard postal applications only. A charge is added for applications made in person at a partner office in the UK, currently £7 at a post office and £6 at a WorldChoice travel agent.

HEALTH ADVICE

Health Advice for Travellers, published by the Department of Health, contains information on health precautions, reciprocal health agreements with other countries, and immunisation. It is available online, from some travel agents, local post offices or the Department of Health, Richmond House, 79 Whitehall, London SW1A 2NL. T 020-7210 4850 E dhmail@dh.gsi.gov.uk W www.dh.gov.uk

IMMUNISATION
In very general terms immunisation against typhoid, polio and hepatitis A should be considered for all countries where standards of hygiene and sanitation may be less than ideal. Protection against malaria, in the form of tablets, as well as measures to avoid mosquito bites, is advised for visits to malarious areas.

Immunisation against yellow fever is compulsory for entry into some countries, either for all travellers or for those arriving from a yellow fever-infected area, and is recommended for all travellers to infected areas.

A doctor should be consulted, preferably at least eight weeks before departure, and will advise travellers and arrange vaccinations. Most doctors will charge a fee for a course of vaccinations. If children will be travelling outside Europe, North America, Australia and New Zealand, the doctor should be informed, especially if they have not completed their full course of childhood immunisation. As a precaution, it is also recommended that all travellers be up to date with their polio and tetanus inoculations.

Country-by-country guidance is set out in *Health Advice for Travellers*. Healthcare professionals can obtain information about immunisation recommendations from the Department of Health publication *Health Information for Overseas Travel* or from:

ENGLAND AND WALES
HEALTH PROTECTION AGENCY, 7th Floor, Holborn Gate, 330 High Holborn, London WC1V 7PP
T 020-7759 2700 E webteam@hpa.org.uk W www.hpa.org.uk

SCOTLAND
SCOTTISH EXECUTIVE HEALTH DEPARTMENT, St Andrew's House, Edinburgh EH1 3DG
T 0131-556 8400 W www.scotland.gov.uk

HEALTH PROTECTION SCOTLAND, Clifton House, Clifton Place, Glasgow G3 7LN
T 0141-300 1100 E hpsenquiries@hps.scot.nhs.uk
W www.hps.scot.nhs.uk

NORTHERN IRELAND
DHSSPS, Castle Buildings, Stormont, Belfast BT4 3SJ
T 028-9052 0500 E webmaster@dhsspsni.gov.uk
W www.dhsspsni.gov.uk

MEDICAL TREATMENT ABROAD
Details of free or reduced cost emergency medical treatment when visiting European countries, and countries with which the UK has reciprocal health arrangements, are set out in *Health Advice for Travellers*. It also contains guidance on applying for the European Health Insurance Card (EHIC), which was introduced in September 2005 as a replacement for the E111 form (valid until 31 December 2005) and entitles people to urgent medical treatment in the European Economic Area (EEA) and Switzerland. The booklet also explains changes to entitlement and the claims process.

For countries where the UK has no health care agreements, including Canada, the USA, India, the Far East, and the whole of Africa and Latin America, it is advisable to take out medical insurance. A certain amount of insurance is also needed in countries with which the UK has healthcare agreements.

THE ANTARCTIC

The Antarctic is generally defined as the area lying within the Antarctic Convergence, the zone where cold northward-flowing Antarctic sea water sinks below warmer southward-flowing water. This zone is approximately at latitude 50° S. in the Atlantic Ocean and latitude 55°– 62° S. in the Pacific Ocean. The continent itself lies almost entirely within the Antarctic Circle, an area of around 13,660,000 million sq. km, 99.67 per cent of which is permanently ice-covered. The average thickness of the ice is 2,450 m but in places exceeds 4,500 m. The ice amounts to some 30 million cubic km and represents more than 70 per cent of the world's fresh water and 90 per cent of the world's ice. Much of the sea freezes in winter, forming fast ice which breaks up in summer and drifts north as pack ice.

CLIMATE AND TERRAIN

Antarctica is the highest, coldest and driest continent on Earth with average coastal temperatures ranging from just above freezing in the summer (December–February) to −20°C (−4°F) in the winter. Conditions on the interior plateau are more severe, with gravity winds and frequent cyclonic storms pushing average winter temperatures down to −65°C (−85°F). Vostok research station holds the current record for the lowest surface temperature ever recorded on earth at −89.5°C (−129°F).

Elevation extremes range from 4,897 m (Vinson Massif) at the highest point to −2,540 m (Bentley Subglacial Trench) at the lowest. The most conspicuous physical features of the Antarctic are the high inland plateau (much of which is 3,000 m above sea level), the Transantarctic Mountains, the Antarctic Peninsula and off-lying islands that extend north towards South America.

FLORA AND FAUNA

The only land animals to survive on the Antarctic continent are tiny insects and mites, with nematodes, rotifers and tardigrades in the mosses. Large numbers of seals, penguins and other sea-birds go ashore to breed in the summer; the emperor penguin is the only species that breeds ashore throughout the winter. By contrast, the Antarctic seas abound with life: a variety of invertebrates (including krill) and fish provide food for the seals, penguins and a residual population of whales (including Humpback and Blue whales). The Commission for the Conservation of Antarctic Marine Living Resources facilitates research into the potential environmental impact of fishing.

With almost all of the Antarctic continent permanently covered in ice, only a small number of flowering plants, ferns and clubmosses survive. Most of these are found on the sub-Antarctic islands while only two species (a grass and a pearlwort) extend south of 60° S. Antarctic vegetation is dominated by lichens and mosses, with a few liverworts, algae and fungi surviving in the cracks and pore spaces of sandstone and granite rocks.

ANTARCTIC LAW AND TREATY

The co-operative 12 nations (Argentina, Australia, Belgium, Chile, France, Japan, New Zealand, Norway, South Africa, the Soviet Union, the UK and the USA) pledged themselves to promote scientific and technical co-operation unhampered by politics, and the Antarctic Treaty was signed by the 12 states on 1st December 1959. The signatories agreed to establish free use of the Antarctic continent for peaceful scientific purposes; to freeze all territorial claims and disputes in the Antarctic; to ban all military activities in the area; and to prohibit nuclear explosions and the disposal of radioactive waste. The Antarctic Treaty was defined as covering areas south of latitude 60° S., excluding the high seas but including the ice shelves, and came into force in 1961. The treaty provides that any member of the United Nations can accede to it. It has since been signed by a further 31 states, 14 of which are active in the Antarctic and have therefore been accorded consultative status, bringing the number of consultative parties to 28. In 1998 an extension to the treaty came into effect, placing a 50-year ban on mining, oil exploration and mineral extraction in Antarctica. Furthermore, all tourists, explorers and expeditions will now need permission to enter the Antarctic.

TERRITORIAL CLAIMS

Under the provisions of the Antarctic Treaty all territorial claims and disputes were frozen. The US and Soviet governments also made it clear that although they had not made any specific territorial claims, they had not relinquished the right to make such claims.

Seven states have made claims in the Antarctic: Argentina claims the part of Antarctica between 74° W. and 25° W.; Chile—the part between 90° W. and 53° W.; Britain claims the British Antarctic Territory, an area of 1,709,340 sq. km (660,000 sq. miles) between 20° and 80° W. longitude; France claims Terre Adélie, 432,000 sq. km (166,800 sq. miles) between 136° and 142° E.; Australia claims the Australian Antarctic Territory, 6,120,000 sq. km (2,320,000 sq. miles) between 160° and 45° E. longitude excluding Terre Adélie; Norway claims Queen Maud Land between 20° W. and 45° E.; and New Zealand claims the Ross Dependency, 450,000 sq. km (175,000 sq. miles) between 160° E. and 150° W. longitude. The Argentinian, British and Chilean claims overlap, and the part of the continent between 90° W. and 150° W. is unclaimed by any state.

SCIENTIFIC RESEARCH AND POPULATION

There are some 26 nations with permanent research stations in Antarctica: Argentina (14), Australia (7), Brazil (1), Bulgaria (1), Chile (9), China (2), Ecuador (1), Finland (1), France (5), Germany (3), India (1), Italy (2), Japan (4), New Zealand (1), Norway (2), Peru (1), Poland (1), Republic of Korea (1), Russia (8), South Africa (4), Spain (2), Sweden (1), UK (5), Ukraine (1), Uruguay (1) and USA (3).

While there are no indigenous inhabitants, during the summer (December–February) the population reaches around 3,500 people, mostly comprising of tourists, scientists and seasonal research workers.

THE BRITISH ANTARCTIC SURVEY

The British Antarctic Survey (BAS) is part of the Natural Environment Research Council and carries out the majority of Britain's scientific research in Antarctica. Over 400 staff are employed by BAS and the organisation supports five research stations: Rothera, Halley and Signy in the Antarctic and King Edward Point and Bird Island on South Georgia.

W www.bas.ac.uk

THE EUROPEAN UNION

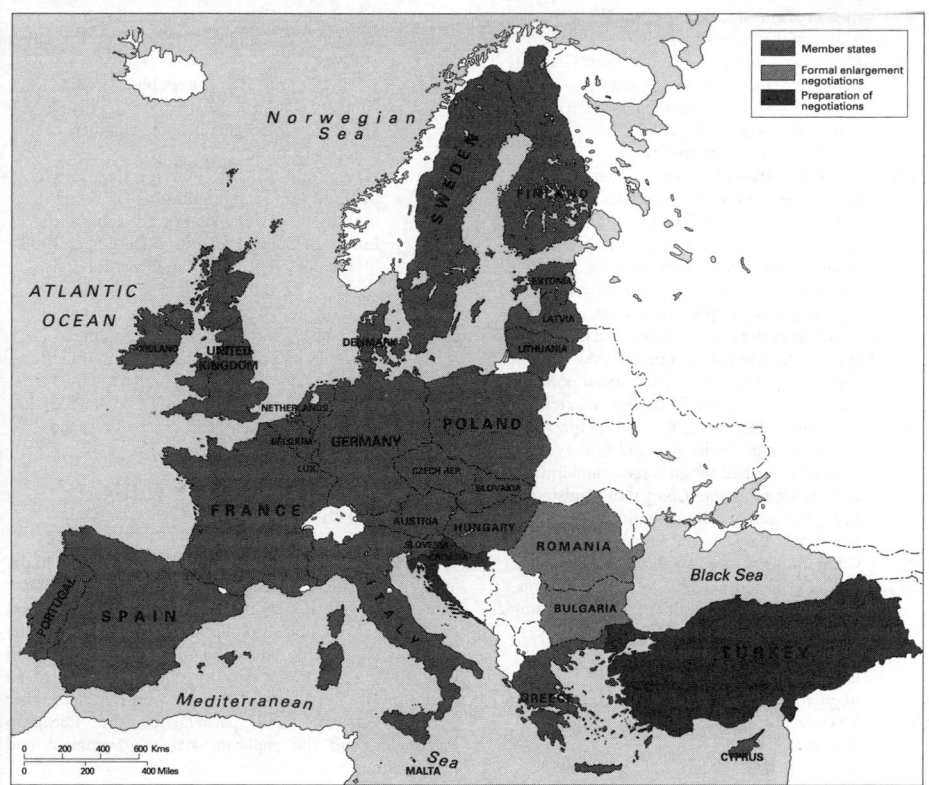

Note: At the time of going to press, Turkey was due to begin formal enlargement negotiations on 3 October 2005

MEMBER STATE	ACCESSION DATE	POPULATION (APPROX) (2004)	COUNCIL VOTES	EP SEATS
Austria	1 January 1995	8,140,100	10	18
Belgium	1 January 1958	10,396,400	12	24
Cyprus	1 May 2004	730,400	4	6
Czech Republic	1 May 2004	10,211,500	12	24
Denmark	1 January 1973	5,397,600	7	14
Estonia	1 May 2004	1,351,000	4	6
Finland	1 January 1995	5,219,700	7	14
France	1 January 1958	59,900,700	29	78
Germany	1 January 1958	82,531,700	29	99
Greece	1 January 1981	11,041,100	12	24
Hungary	1 May 2004	10,116,700	12	24
Ireland	1 January 1973	4,027,700	7	13
Italy	1 January 1958	57,888,200	29	78
Latvia	1 May 2004	2,319,200	4	9
Lithuania	1 May 2004	3,445,900	7	13
Luxembourg	1 January 1958	451,600	4	6
Malta	1 May 2004	399,900	3	5
The Netherlands	1 January 1958	16,258,000	13	27
Poland	1 May 2004	38,190,600	27	54
Portugal	1 January 1986	10,474,700	12	24
Slovakia	1 May 2004	5,380,100	7	14
Slovenia	1 May 2004	1,996,400	4	7
Spain	1 January 1986	42,345,300	27	54
Sweden	1 January 1995	8,975,700	10	19
UK	1 January 1973	59,673,100	29	78

Source: Eurostat

DEVELOPMENT

1950	Robert Schuman (French foreign minister) proposes that France and West Germany pool their coal and steel industries under a supranational authority (Schuman Plan)
1951	Paris Treaty, signed by France, West Germany, Belgium, Italy, Luxembourg and the Netherlands, establishes the European Coal and Steel Community (ECSC)
1952	ECSC Treaty enters into force
1957	25 March: Treaty of Rome, signed by the six ECSC member countries, establishes the European Economic Community (EEC) and the European Atomic Energy Authority (EURATOM). Treaty aims to create a customs union; remove obstacles to free movement of capital, goods, people and services; establish common external trade policy and common agricultural and fisheries policies; co-ordinate economic policies; harmonise social policies; promote co-operation in nuclear research
1958	1 January: EEC and EURATOM begin operation. Joint Parliament and Court of Justice established for all three communities, and the Commission, Council of Ministers, Economic and Social Committee and Investment Bank for the EEC established
1962	Common Agricultural Policy (CAP) agreed
1967	EEC, ECSC and EURATOM merge to form the European Communities (EC), with a single Council of Ministers and Commission
1968	EEC customs union completed Implementation of CAP completed
1974	Regular heads of governments summits begin
1975	'Own resources' funding of EC budget introduced UK renegotiates its terms of accession European Regional Development Fund created
1979	European Monetary System (EMS) comes into operation First direct elections to European Parliament (June)
1984	Fontainebleau summit settles UK annual budget rebate and agrees first major CAP reform
1986	Single European Act (SEA) signed European Political Co-operation (EPC) established
1988	Second major CAP reform
1991	Maastricht Treaty agreed
1992	31 December: Single internal market programme completed
1993	September: the exchange rate mechanism (ERM) of the EMS effectively suspended 1 November: The Maastricht Treaty enters into force, establishing the European Union (EU)
1994	1 January: European Economic Area (EEA) agreement comes into operation Norway rejects EU membership in referendum
1997	Amsterdam Treaty agreed
1998	11 states chosen to enter first round of European Monetary Union (EMU) European Central Bank replaces European Monetary Institute
1999	1 January: Euro launched 1 May: The Amsterdam Treaty enters into force
2000	9 December: Treaty of Nice agreed
2001	7 June: Ireland rejects Treaty of Nice in referendum
2002	1 January: Euro coins and banknotes enter circulation 23 July: ECSC Treaty expires following transfer of coal and steel sectors to the Treaty of Rome
2004	1 May: Cyprus, Czech Republic, Estonia, Hungary, Latvia, Lithuania, Malta, Poland, Slovakia and Slovenia become members of the European Union May: A draft EU constitution is discussed by the European foreign ministers following the breakdown of discussion on the topic at the European Council summit in December 2003 29 October: The European Constitution is signed in Rome. Before it can be adopted it must be ratified by all 25 EU member states
2005	September: At the time of going to press, 12 countries had approved the Constitution (Austria, Cyprus, Greece, Hungary, Italy, Latvia, Lithuania, Luxembourg, Malta, Slovakia, Slovenia and Spain), and two had rejected it (France and the Netherlands)

ENLARGEMENT AND EXTERNAL RELATIONS

The procedure for accession to the EU is laid down in the Treaty of Rome; states must be stable European democracies governed by the rule of law with free market economies. A membership application is studied by the Commission, which produces an Opinion. If the Opinion is positive, negotiations may be opened leading to an Accession Treaty that must be approved by all member state governments and parliaments, the European Parliament, and the applicant state's government and parliament.

Applicants: Morocco (applied 1987/rejected 1987), Turkey (applied 1987/negative Opinion 1989/offered accession partnership 1999), Cyprus (applied 1990/negotiations begun 1998), Malta (applied 1990/reapplied following a change of government 1998/negotiations begun 2000), Switzerland (applied 1992/application put on hold 1994), Hungary (applied 1994/negotiations begun 1998), Poland (applied 1994/negotiations begun 1998), Bulgaria (applied 1995/offered partnership 1998/negotiations begun 2000), Estonia (applied 1995/negotiations begun 1998), Latvia (applied 1995/offered partnership 1998/negotiations begun 2000), Lithuania (applied 1995/offered partnership 1998/negotiations begun 2000), Romania (applied 1995/offered partnership 1998/negotiations begun 2000), Slovakia (applied 1995/offered partnership 1998/negotiations begun 2000), the Czech Republic (applied 1996/negotiations begun 1998), Slovenia (applied 1996/negotiations begun 1998), Croatia (applied 2003), Macedonia (applied 2004).

Apart from the EEA Agreement, the EU has three types of agreements with other European and CIS states. 'Europe' agreements commit the EU and signatory states to long-term political and economic integration, a free trade zone (apart from agriculture and labour movement) and eventual EU membership. Government representatives from the signatory states are entitled to attend one summit and two finance and foreign council meetings a year. Agreements have been signed with Bulgaria (1993) and Romania (1993). Association agreements include a commitment to EU financial aid and to eventual membership; an agreement has been signed with Turkey (1963). Partnership and co-operation agreements (PCAs) are legal frameworks, based on the respect of democratic principles and human rights, setting out the political, economic and trade relationship between the EU and its partner countries. Each PCA is a ten-year bilateral treaty signed and ratified by the EU and the individual state. Agreements have been implemented with Mongolia (1993) Russia (1997), Ukraine and Moldova (1998) and Armenia, Azerbaijan, Georgia, Kazakhstan, Kyrgyzstan and Uzbekistan (1999). Agreements have been signed with Belarus (1995) and Turkmenistan (1998) but are not yet in force. At the PCA Council's St Petersburg summit in May 2003, it was decided to strengthen the existing co-operation council between Russia and the EU, to a Permanent Partnership Council (PPC). At the Council's first meeting on 27 April 2004 a protocol to the Partnership and Co-operation Agreement between the EU and the Russian Federation was signed, extending the agreement to the 10 new member states of the EU.

Agenda 2000, a document issued by the Commission in 1997, addressed both the challenges posed by further enlargement of the Union, the institutional reforms that would be required to enable the Union to function effectively with additional members, and also evaluated each applicant in relation to the accession criteria, establishing a new financial framework for the period 2000–6.

In March 1998, formal accession negotiations were begun with Hungary, Poland, Estonia, the Czech Republic, Slovenia and Cyprus; they were begun with Bulgaria, Romania, Latvia, Lithuania, Malta and Slovakia in 2000, following the Helsinki summit in December 1999, when it was also agreed that an accession partnership should be offered to Turkey.

The Göteborg summit in June 2001 agreed on a timetable for accession for the first group of countries to complete negotiations. At the Copenhagen summit in December 2002, Cyprus, the Czech Republic, Estonia, Hungary, Latvia, Lithuania, Malta, Poland, Slovakia and Slovenia were invited to join the EU. The ten states signed the Treaty of Accession in Athens on 16 April 2003 and became full members of the EU on 1 May 2004.

Following the findings of the European Commission's 2002 Regular Reports, accession plans for Bulgaria and Romania, which set 2007 as the target date for accession, were proposed. These plans were endorsed by the Copenhagen European Council in December 2002. A common Accession Treaty for the two countries was signed on 25 April 2005 in Luxembourg.

At the European Council meeting in Copenhagen in December 2002, the decision was made to recall the offer of an accession partnership to Turkey, following the Commission's conclusion that Turkey did not yet fully meet the required political criteria. However the European Council at its December 2004 meeting in Brussels decided that Turkey sufficiently met the Copenhagen political criteria and accession negotiations were due to begin on 3 October 2005, provided that Turkey continued with political and economic reforms and signed a customs accord extending to all EU members, including Cyprus, by that date.

Macedonia's application for EU membership is currently being examined by the European Commission, while accession talks with Croatia – due to begin on 17 March 2005 – were postponed due to the country's lack of co-operation with the UN war crimes tribunal.

LEGISLATIVE PROCESS

The core of the EU policy-making process is a dialogue between the Commission, which initiates and implements policy, and the Council of Ministers, which takes policy decisions. An increasing degree of democratic control is exercised by the European Parliament.

The original legislative process is known as the consultative procedure. The Commission drafts a proposal which it submits to the Council and to the Parliament. The Council then consults the Economic and Social Committee (ESC), the Parliament and the Committee of the Regions; the Parliament may request that amendments are made. With or without these amendments, the proposal is then adopted by the Council and becomes law. Under the Single European Act (SEA), the role of the Parliament was strengthened by the introduction of the co-operation procedure. The Parliament now has a second reading of proposals in some fields, and after the second reading its rejection of a proposal can only be overturned by a unanimous decision of the Council. The Maastricht Treaty extended the scope of the co-operation procedure, which was applied to Single Market laws and harmonisation, trans-European networks, development policy, the social fund, and some aspects of transport, environment, research, social policy and competition policy.

The SEA introduced the assent procedure, whereby an absolute majority of the Parliament must vote to approve laws in certain fields before they are passed. Issues covered by the assent procedure include foreign treaties, accession treaties, international agreements with budgetary implications, citizenship, residence rights, the CAP, and regional and structural funds.

The Maastricht Treaty introduced the co-decision procedure; if, after the Parliament's second reading of a proposal, the Council and Parliament fail to agree, a conciliation committee of the two will reach a compromise. If a compromise is not reached, the Parliament can reject the legislation by the vote of an absolute majority of its members. The Amsterdam Treaty extended the co-decision procedure to all areas covered by qualified majority voting, with the exception of measures related to European Monetary Union (EMU).

The Council issues the following legislation:
- Regulations, which are binding in their entirety and directly applicable to all member states; they do not need to be incorporated into national law to come into effect
- Directives, which are less specific, binding as to the result to be achieved but leaving the method of implementation open to member states; a directive thus has no force until it is incorporated into national law
- Decisions, which are also binding but are addressed solely to one or more member states or individuals in a member state
- Recommendations
- Opinions, which are merely persuasive

The Council also has certain budgetary powers, including the power to reject the budget as a whole and to increase expenditure or redistribute money within sectors. However, the final decision on whether the budget should be adopted or rejected lies with the Parliament.

The Council may delegate legislative powers to the Commission. These consist of implementing powers and technical updating of existing legislation.

The European Central Bank has legislative powers within its field of competence. The Commission also has limited legislative powers, where it has been delegated the power to implement or revise legislation by the Council.

The European Constitution, which can only come into force once it has been ratified by the 25 member states (either through a referendum or by vote in the national parliament), reorganises and codifies EU decision-making as well as replacing the main existing Treaties with a single text designed to suit the needs of an expanding European Union. The Constitution defines the relationships and functions of the European Parliament, the European Commission, the European Court of Justice and the Council of the European Union. It repeats existing EU agreements concerning the legal supremacy of EU law, economic co-operation and EU citizens' freedom of movement. It also introduces new legislation to establish the EU as a separate body in law; extend the powers of the European Parliament; remove member states' right of veto currently applicable in over 30 areas; and to incorporate the Charter of Fundamental Rights into the Constitution itself.

COMMUNITY BUDGET

The principles of funding the European Community budget were established by the Treaty of Rome and remain with modifications to this day. There is a legally binding limit on the overall level of resources (known as 'own resources') that the Community can raise from its member states; this limit is defined as a percentage of gross national product (GNP). Budget revenue and expenditure must balance and there is therefore no deficit financing. The 'own resources' decision, which came into effect in 1975 and has been regularly updated, states that there are four sources of Community funding under which each member state makes contributions: levies charged on agricultural imports into the Community from non-member states; customs duties on imports from non-member states; contributions based on member states' shares of a notional Community harmonised VAT base; and contributions based on member states' shares of Community GNP. The latter is the budget-balancing item and covers the difference between total expenditure and the revenue from the other three sources. Since 1984 the UK has had an annual rebate equivalent to 66 per cent of the difference between what the UK contributes to the budget and what it receives. This was introduced to compensate the UK for disproportionate contributions caused by its high proportion of agricultural and non-agricultural imports from non-member states and its relatively small receipts from the Common Agricultural Policy, the most important portion of Community expenditure.

BUDGET 2005 (FIGURES TO NEAREST BILLION)

	Billion euro*
Agriculture	49.7
Structural Operations	42.4
External Action	5.2
Pre-accession Strategy	2.1
Internal policies	9.1
Administration	6.4
Compensation	1.3
Reserves	0.5
TOTAL	116.6

Source: General Budget of the European Union for the Financial Year 2005

* 1 euro = £0.69 as at 1 June 2005

Under the Edinburgh summit agreement (December 1992) the EC budget rose to a maximum of 1.27 per cent of the EU's GNP in 1999. The agreed budget for 2000–6 will keep the 1.27 per cent ceiling, but resources devoted to the existing member states will fall to 0.98 per cent, with the remaining resources devoted to enlargement.

COMMON AGRICULTURAL POLICY

The Common Agricultural Policy (CAP) was established to increase agricultural production, provide a fair standard of living for farmers and ensure the availability of food at reasonable prices. This aim was achieved by a number of mechanisms:
- import levies
- intervention purchase
- export subsidies

These measures stimulated production but also placed increasing demands on the EC budget which were exacerbated by the increase in EC members and yields enlarged by technological innovation; CAP now accounts for over 40 per cent of EC expenditure. To surmount these problems reforms were agreed in 1984, 1988, 1992, 1997, 1999 and 2003.

REFORMS

The 1984 reforms created the system of co-responsibility levies: farm payments to the EC by volume of product sold. This system was supplemented by national quotas for particular products, such as milk. The 1988 reforms emphasised 'set-aside', whereby farmers are given direct grants to take land out of production as a means of reducing surpluses. The set-aside reforms were extended in 1993 for another five years and to every farm in the EC. The 1999 reforms further reduced surpluses of cereals, beef and milk by cutting the intervention prices by up to 20 per cent and compensating producers by making area payments. Under the reforms, CAP rules were also simplified, eliminating inconsistencies between policies.

Under the Uruguay round agreement of GATT concluded in 1993, the EU was required, over a six-year period from 1 January 1995, to reduce its import levies by 36 per cent, reduce its domestic subsidies by 20 per cent, reduce its export subsidies by 36 per cent in value, and reduce its subsidised exports by 21 per cent in volume. Agenda 2000, the programme to overhaul the policies of the EU and prepare it for the accession of new member states, will temporarily increase the cost of the CAP by €1 billion a year in compensation payments, but leave it broadly stable by the end of the current planning period in 2006.

On 26 June 2003, EU farm ministers adopted a fundamental reform of the CAP, which include the following provisions:
- a single farm payment for EU farmers, independent from production
- payment to be linked to the respect of environmental, food safety, animal and plant health and animal welfare standards, and the requirement to keep all farmland in good condition
- a strengthened rural development policy with more EU money to help farmers meet EU production standards starting in 2005
- a reduction in direct payments for bigger farms
- a mechanism for financial discipline to ensure that the farm budget fixed until 2013 is not exceeded

The single farm payment entered into force in 2005,

however, if a member state needs a transitional period due to its specific agricultural conditions, it may apply the single farm payment from 2007 at the latest. The ten new EU members were also given access to a special €5.8 billion three-year funding package.

SINGLE MARKET

Even after the removal of tariffs and quotas between member states in the 1970s and 1980s, the EC was still separated into a number of national markets by a series of non-tariff barriers. It was to overcome these internal barriers to trade that the concept of the Single Market was developed. The measures to be undertaken were codified in the Commission's 1985 White Paper on completing the internal market.

The White Paper included articles removing obstacles that distorted the internal market: the elimination of frontier controls; the mutual recognition of professional qualifications; the harmonisation of product specifications, largely by the mutual recognition of national standards; open tendering for public procurement contracts; the free movement of capital; the harmonisation of VAT and excise duties; and the reduction of state aid to particular industries. The Single European Act aided the completion of the Single Market by changing the legislative process within the EC, particularly with the introduction of qualified majority voting in the Council of Ministers for some policy areas, and the introduction of the assent procedure in the European Parliament. The SEA also extends EC competence into the fields of technology, the environment, regional policy, monetary policy and external policy. The Single Market came into effect on 1 January 1993. The full implementation of the elimination of frontier controls and the harmonisation of taxes have, however, been repeatedly delayed.

EUROPEAN ECONOMIC AREA

The EC Single Market programme spurred European non-member states to open negotiations with the EC on preferential access for their goods, services, labour and capital to the Single Market. Principal among these states were European Free Trade Association (EFTA) members who opened negotiations on extending the Single Market to EFTA by the formation of the European Economic Area (EEA), encompassing all 19 EC and EFTA states. Agreement was reached in May 1992 but the operation of the EEA was delayed by its rejection in a Swiss referendum, necessitating an additional protocol agreed by the remaining 18 states. The EEA came into effect on 1 January 1994 after ratification by 17 member states (Liechtenstein joined on 1 May 1995 after adapting its customs union with Switzerland).

Austria, Finland and Sweden joined the EU itself on 1 January 1995, leaving only Norway, Iceland and Liechtenstein as the non-EU EEA members. Under the EEA agreement, the three states are to adopt the EU's *acquis communautaire*, apart from in the fields of agriculture, fisheries, and coal and steel.

The EEA is controlled by regular ministerial meetings and by a joint EU-EFTA committee which extends relevant EU legislation to EEA states. Apart from single market measures, there is co-operation in education, research and development, consumer policy and tourism. An EFTA Court of Justice has been established in Luxembourg and an EFTA Surveillance Authority in Brussels to supervise the implementation of the EEA Agreement.

The EEA Enlargement Agreement came into force on 1 May 2004, which allowed the simultaneous expansion of both the EU and the EEA without disruption of the internal market.

EUROPEAN MONETARY SYSTEM AND THE SINGLE CURRENCY

The European monetary system (EMS) began operation in March 1979 with three main purposes. The first was to establish monetary stability in Europe, initially in exchange rates between EC member state currencies through the exchange rate mechanism (ERM), and in the longer term to be part of a wider stabilisation process, overcoming inflation and budget and trade deficits. The second purpose was to overcome the constraints resulting from the interdependence of EC economies, and the third was to aid the long-term process of European monetary integration.

The Maastricht Treaty set in motion timetables for achieving economic and monetary union (EMU) and a single currency (the euro). At the Brussels summit in May 1998, 11 member states were judged to fulfil or be close to fulfilling the necessary convergence criteria for participation in the first stage of EMU: Austria, Belgium, Finland, France, Germany, Ireland, Italy, Luxembourg, the Netherlands, Portugal and Spain.

The criteria were that:
- the budget deficit should be 3 per cent or less of gross domestic product (GDP)
- total national debt must not exceed 60 per cent of GDP
- inflation should be no more than 1.5 per cent above the average rate of the three best performing economies in the EU
- long-term interest rates should be no more than 2 per cent above the average of the three best performing economies in the EU in the previous 12 months
- applicants must have been members of the ERM for two years without having realigned or devalued their currency

Under the terms of a stability and growth pact agreed in Dublin in December 1996, penalties may be imposed on EMU members with high budget deficits. Governments with deficits exceeding 3 per cent of GDP will receive a warning and will be obliged to pay up to 0.5 per cent of their GDP into a fund after ten months. This will become a fine if the budget deficit is not rectified within two years. A member state with negative growth will be allowed to apply for an exemption from the fine in 'exceptional circumstances', e.g. a recession whereby GDP had fallen by 0.75 per cent or more during one year.

On 1 January 1999, the qualifying member states adopted the euro at irrevocably fixed exchange rates, the European Central Bank (ECB) took charge of the single monetary policy, and the euro replaced the ECU on a one-for-one basis.

On 19 June 2000, Greece was judged to have fulfilled the criteria for participation and adopted the euro on 1 January 2001. A referendum on the adoption of the euro was held in Denmark on 28 September 2000, but participation was rejected by the electorate.

The euro is now the legal currency in the participating states. Euro notes and coins were introduced on 1 January 2002 and circulated alongside national currencies for a period of up to two months, after which time national notes and coins ceased to be legal tender. The Swedish government held a referendum on adoption of the euro on

14 September 2003, in which 56 per cent voted against adopting the euro. On 10 June 2003 Britain announced that the euro would not be adopted at present on the grounds that the country was not economically ready to join the single currency. A future joining of the euro-zone was not ruled out. The 10 new EU member states are expected to adopt the euro when the necessary economic conditions have been met.

The ECB meets twice a month to set interest rates for the countries participating in the euro. Its governing council has 18 members, being the six members of the ECB's executive board and the 12 governors of the national central banks of the participating states.

With the advent of EMU, the ERM was revised and Denmark became a member of ERM II, which requires it to maintain its currencies within set margins of the euro. Membership of ERM II is voluntary, although all member states outside the euro zone are encouraged to take part. Sweden and the UK are currently not members.

MAASTRICHT TREATY

The Treaty on European Union was agreed at a meeting of the European Council in Maastricht, the Netherlands, in December 1991. It came into effect in November 1993 following ratification by the member states.

Three 'pillars' formed the basis of the new treaty:
- the European Community with its established institutions and decision-making processes
- a Common Foreign and Security Policy (see below) with the Western European Union as the potential defence component of the EU
- co-operation in justice and home affairs, with the Council of Ministers to co-ordinate policies on asylum, immigration, conditions of entry, cross-border crime, drug trafficking and terrorism

The Treaty established a common European citizenship for nationals of all member states and introduced the principle of subsidiarity whereby decisions are taken at the most appropriate level: national, regional or local. It extended EC competency into the areas of environmental and industrial policies, consumer affairs, health, and education and training, and extended qualified majority voting in the Council of Ministers to some areas which had previously required a unanimous vote. The powers of the European Parliament over the budget and over the Commission were also enhanced and a co-decision procedure enabled the Parliament to override decisions made by the Council of Ministers in certain policy areas. A separate protocol to the Maastricht Treaty on social policy was agreed by 11 states and was incorporated into the Amsterdam Treaty in 1997 following adoption by the UK.

COMMON FOREIGN AND SECURITY POLICY

The Common Foreign and Security Policy (CFSP) was created as a pillar of the EU by the Maastricht Treaty (see above). It adopted the machinery of the European Political Co-operation (EPC) framework, which it replaced, and was charged with providing a forum for member states and EU institutions to consult on foreign affairs.

The CFSP system is headed by the Council of the European Union, which provides general lines of policy. Specific policy decisions are taken by the Council of Foreign Ministers, which meets at least four times a year

to determine areas for joint action. The High Representative of the CFSP initiates action, manages the CFSP and represents it abroad. The Council of Ministers is supported by the Political Committee, which meets monthly, or within 48 hours if there is a crisis, to prepare for ministerial discussions. A group of correspondents, designated diplomats in each member's foreign ministry, provides day-to-day contact.

The Amsterdam Treaty introduced qualified majority voting for foreign affairs and created a high representative on CFSP to act as a spokesperson. It also established a new policy planning an early warning unit to monitor international developments. The unit consists of specialists from the member states, the Council and the Commission, as well as from the Western European Union (WEU).

The member states agreed at the Helsinki summit in December 1999 to establish a capability for military crisis-management operations, known as the rapid reaction force, which would be able to undertake peacemaking missions independently of NATO. The force was declared operational at the Laeken summit on 14–15 December 2001.

AMSTERDAM TREATY

The treaties of Rome and Maastricht were again amended through the Treaty of Amsterdam, which was signed in October 1997 and which came into effect on 1 May 1999. It extends the scope of qualified majority voting and the powers of the European Parliament. It also includes a formal commitment to fundamental human rights, gives additional powers to the European Court of Justice and provides for the appointment of a High Representative for EU Common Foreign and Security Policy.

SCHENGEN AGREEMENT

The Schengen Agreement was signed by France, Germany, Belgium, Luxembourg and the Netherlands in 1985. The Agreement committed the five states to abolishing internal border controls, erecting external frontiers against illegal immigrants, drug traffickers, terrorists and organised crime, and implementing the Schengen Information System to enable police stations and consular agents from Schengen member states to access data on specific individuals or vehicles and objects which are lost or stolen.

Subsequently signed by Spain and Portugal, the Agreement was ratified by the seven signatory states and entered into force in March 1995 with the removal of internal frontier, passport, customs and immigration controls. Italy and Austria became full members in April 1998 and Greece achieved full membership on 1 January 2000. Provisional agreement was reached in June 1995 between the signatory states and the Nordic Union on a merger of the two frontier-free zones – Denmark, Finland and Sweden joined in December 1996 and in March 2001 it was decided that the Schengen arrangements would also apply to Iceland and Norway. The 10 member states who became members of the EU on 1 May 2004 do not yet form part of the Schengen zone but are scheduled to become full members of the zone by 2006. The UK and the Republic of Ireland have not signed the Agreement, but have expressed their intention to join in some aspects of its work.

The Schengen Agreement originated as an

intergovernmental agreement but became part of the EU following the signing of the Amsterdam Treaty. A second generation Schengen Information System (SIS II), which will cater for the 10 new member states, is under development.

TREATY OF NICE

The Treaty of Nice was signed in February 2001 and came into effect on 1 February 2003. It aims to enable the EU to accommodate up to 13 new member states. It extends qualified majority voting to 30 further articles of the treaties that previously required unanimity. The weighting of votes in the EU Council was altered from 1 January 2005 in preparation for the new member states, whose numbers of votes have been set. To obtain a qualified majority, a decision will require a specified number of votes (to be reviewed following each accession); the decision will have to be approved by a majority of member states and represent at least 62 per cent of the total population of the EU. The Treaty also sets the number of MEPs that both existing and new member states will have following enlargement.

The Treaty of Maastricht established the right of groups of member states to work together without requiring the participation of all members (enhanced co-operation); the Treaty of Nice removes the right of individual member states to veto the launch of enhanced co-operation and establishes a minimum number of eight member states for enhanced co-operation in the field of common foreign and security policy (CFSP).

The European Commission has been limited to one member per member state since 2005, with a maximum of 27 commissioners; a rotation system is to be introduced once EU membership exceeds 27 states.

The Treaty also adds to the powers of the President of the Commission and amends the rules of the operation of the Court of Justice.

The Treaty was rejected by 54 per cent of voters in a referendum in Ireland, the only country to put the issue to its electorate.

LAEKEN SUMMIT

At the European Council held in Laeken, Belgium, on 14–15 December 2001, a declaration was agreed that established a convention to prepare for treaty reforms at the intergovernmental conference, which was held on 17–18 July 2004. The convention, composed of representatives of national governments (15 members), national parliaments (30), the European Parliament (16), the European Commission (2) and the applicant states (39), started work on 28 February 2002, under the chairmanship of former French president Valérie Giscard d'Estaing.

At the intergovernmental conference in July 2004, the Council produced a provisional consolidated version of the draft treaty establishing a constitution for Europe. The treaty will replace the existing EU and EC treaties. It was signed by the heads of state on 29 October 2004 at a ceremony in Rome. The European Constitution will only enter into force once it has been ratified by all of the member states.

The Laeken European Council also agreed a common definition of terrorism, decided to institute an EU-wide arrest warrant, creating a single security area and thereby making it no longer necessary to extradite those accused of serious crimes, and established Eurojust to co-ordinate cross-border co-operation in crime investigation.

COUNCIL OF THE EUROPEAN UNION
Wetstraat 175, B-1048 Brussels, Belgium

The Council of the European Union (Council of Ministers) formally comprises the foreign ministers of the member states but in practice the ministers attending depend on the subject under discussion. Council decisions are taken by qualified majority vote (in which members' votes are weighted), by a simple majority, or by unanimity. The Council is assisted by a General Secretariat, whose head has since 1999 been the High Representative for the Common Foreign and Security Policy.

Unanimity votes are taken on sensitive issues such as taxation and constitutional matters; in preparation for an expanded Union, the Amsterdam Treaty extended areas where qualified majority votes may be taken, to areas such as Single Market laws and harmonisation, environment policy, health and safety, transport policy, overseas aid, research and development, culture, consumer protection, education and training, the development of a single currency and some aspects of social policy. Member states have weighted votes in the Council loosely proportional to their relative population sizes (see introductory table), with a total of 321 votes. The acts of the Council can take the form of regulations, directives, decisions, common actions or common positions, recommendations or opinions. The Council can also adopt conclusions, declarations or resolutions. The number of votes each member state can cast is set by Treaties. The Treaties also define cases in which a simple majority, qualified majority or unanimity are required. From 1 November 2004, a qualified majority will be reached if the following two conditions are met:

– if a majority of member states approve (in some cases a two-thirds majority)
– a minimum of 232 votes is cast in favour of the proposal, i.e. 72.3 per cent of the total (roughly the same share as under the previous system)

In addition, a member state may ask for confirmation that the votes in favour represent at least 62 per cent of the total population of the Union. If this is found not to be the case, the decision will not be adopted.

The Treaty of Nice, which was agreed on 7–9 December 2000 and signed on 26 February 2001, agreed amendments to the treaties in relation to the size and composition of the European Commission, the weighting of votes and the extension of qualified majority voting in the Council of Ministers and other issues relating to the Treaty of Amsterdam. The extension of qualified majority voting to external border controls, the EU budget, the composition of the European Courts and certain committees, visa rules and, by 2007, structural funds, was also agreed.

The European Council, comprising the heads of state or government of the member states and the President of the European Commission, meets twice a year to provide overall policy direction. The presidency of the EC is held in rotation for six-month periods, setting the agenda for and chairing all Council meetings. The European Council holds a summit in the country holding the presidency at the end of its period in office. The holders of the presidency for the years 2004–5 are:
2005 January–June, Luxembourg
2005 July–December, UK
2006 January–June, Austria
2006 July–December, Finland

GENERAL SECRETARIAT OF THE COUNCIL OF THE
EUROPEAN UNION
Wetstraat 175, B-1048 Brussels, Belgium
E public.info@consilium.eu.int
Secretary-General of the Council of the European Union and
High Representative for the Common Foreign and Security
Policy, Javier Solana Madariaga (Spain)
Deputy Secretary-General of the Council of the European
Union, Pierre de Boissieu (France)

OFFICE OF THE UNITED KINGDOM PERMANENT
REPRESENTATIVE TO THE EUROPEAN UNION
Ave d'Auderghem 10, B-1040 Brussels, Belgium
Ambassador and UK Permanent Representative, Sir John
Grant, KCMG, *apptd* 2000

EUROPEAN COMMISSION
Wetstraat 200, B-1049 Brussels, Belgium
The Commission consists of 25 Commissioners, one per
member state. The members of the Commission are
appointed for five-year renewable terms by the agreement
of the member states; the terms run concurrently with the
terms of the European Parliament. The President and the
other Commissioners are nominated by the governments
of the member states, and, under the terms of the Nice
Treaty, the appointments are approved by the European
Parliament. The Commissioners pledge sole allegiance to
the EC. The Commission initiates and implements EC
legislation and is the guardian of the EC treaties. It is the
exponent of Community-wide interests rather than the
national preoccupations of the Council. Each
Commissioner is supported by advisers and oversees the
departments assigned to them, known as Directorates-
General Services (DGS). Each Directorate-General is
headed by a Director-General.

President José Durão Barroso was nominated by the
governments of the member states on 28 June 2004 and
the European Parliament confirmed his appointment with
a secret ballot vote on 22 July 2004. He announced the
finalised Commission on 4 November 2004, which
officially took office on 22 November.

The Commission has a total staff of around 17,000
permanent civil servants.

COMMISSIONERS *as at May 2005*
President, José Manuel Barroso (Portugal)
Vice-President, Administrative Affairs, Audit and Anti-
Fraud, Siim Kallas (Estonia)
Vice-President, Enterprise and Industry, Günter Verheugen
(Germany)
Vice-President, Institutional Relations and Communication
Strategy, Margot Wallström (Sweden)
Vice-President, Justice, Freedom and Security, Franco Frattini
(Italy)
Vice-President, Transport, Jacques Barrot (France)
Agriculture and Rural Development, Marian Fischer Boel
(Denmark)
Competition, Neelie Kroes (Netherlands)
Development and Humanitarian Aid, Louis Michel
(Belgium)
Economic and Monetary Affairs, Joaquin Almunia (Spain)
Education, Training, Culture and Multilingualism, Ján Figel
(Slovakia)
Employment, Social Affairs and Equal Opportunities,
Vladimir Spidla (Czech Republic)
Energy, Andris Piebalgs (Latvia)
Enlargement, Olli Rehn (Finland)
Environment, Stavros Dimas (Greece)

External Relations and European Neighbourhood Policy,
Benita Ferrero-Waldner (Austria)
Financial Programming and Budget, Dalia Grybauskaite
(Lithuania)
Fisheries and Maritime Affairs, Joe Borg (Malta)
Health and Consumer Protection, Markos Kyprianou
(Cyprus)
Information Society and Media, Viviane Reding
(Luxembourg)
Internal Market and Services, Charlie McCreevy (Ireland)
Regional Policy, Danuta Hübner (Poland)
Science and Research, Janez Potocnik (Slovenia)
Taxation and Customs Union, László Kovács (Hungary)
Trade, Peter Mandelson (UK)

EUROPEAN PARLIAMENT
E civis@europarl.eu.int W www.europarl.eu.int
The European Parliament (EP) originated as the Common
Assembly of the ECSC; it acquired its present name in
1962. Members (MEPs) were initially appointed from the
membership of national parliaments; direct elections to
the Parliament were first held in 1979 and take place at
five-year intervals. Elections to the Parliament are held on
differing bases throughout the EC; in June 1999, British
MEPs were elected for the first time by a 'regional list'
system of proportional representation. The Parliament
comprises 732 seats. The most recent elections were held
in June 2004 and the next elections are to be held in June
2009. MEPs serve on committees which scrutinise draft
EC legislation and the activities of the Commission. A
minimum of 12 plenary sessions a year are held in
Strasbourg and six additional shorter plenary sessions a
year are held in Brussels, committees meet in Brussels, and
the Secretariat's headquarters is in Luxembourg.

The EP has gradually expanded its influence within the
EU through the Single European Act, which introduced
the co-operation procedure, the Maastricht Treaty, which
extended the co-operation procedure and introduced the
co-decision procedure (*see* Legislative Process), and the
Amsterdam Treaty, which effectively extended co-
decision to all areas except economic and monetary
union. It has general powers of supervision over the
Commission, and consultation and co-decision with the
Council; it votes to approve a newly appointed
Commission and can dismiss it at any time by a two-thirds
majority (as it threatened to do in January 1999). Under
the Maastricht Treaty it has the right to be consulted on
the appointment of the new Commission and can veto its
appointment. It can reject the EU budget as a whole, alter
non-compulsory expenditure not specified in the EU
primary legislation, and can question the Commission's
management of the budget and call in the Court of
Auditors. Although the EP cannot directly initiate
legislation, its reports can spur the Commission into
action. In accordance with the Maastricht Treaty the EP
appointed an ombudsman in October 1995, to provide
citizens with redress against maladministration by EU
institutions.

The Parliament's organisation is deliberately biased in
favour of multinational political groupings, recognition of
a political grouping in the parliament entitling it to
offices, funding, representation on committees and
influence in debates and legislation. A political group
must comprise MEPs elected in at least one-fifth of the
member states. The minimum number of MEPs required
to form a political group is 19.
PARLIAMENT, Palais de l'Europe, Allée du Printemps,
BP 1024/F, F-67070 Strasbourg Cedex, France.

T (+33) (3) 8817 4001 F (+33) (3) 8825 6501 Wiertzstraat,
Postbus 1047, B-1047 Brussels, Belgium.
T (+32) (2) 284 2111 F (+32) (2) 284 6974
SECRETARIAT, Centre Européen, Plateau du Kirchberg,
BP 1601, L-2929 Luxembourg. T (+352) 43001
F (+352) 4300 29393/29292
President, Josep Borrell Fontelles (Spain)
OMBUDSMAN, Nikiforos Diamandouros (Greece),
 1 avenue du Président Robert Schuman, BP 403,
 F-67001, Strasbourg Cedex, France.
 E euro-ombudsman@europarl.eu.int
 W www.euro-ombudsman.eu.int

COMMITTEE OF THE REGIONS

Rue Belliard101, B-1040 Brussels, Belgium E INFO@COR.EU.INT
W WWW.COR.EU.INT
The Committee of the Regions (CoR) is the political
assembly which provides local and regional authorities
with a voice within the European Union. The EU Treaties
oblige the European Commission and Council of
Ministers to consult the Committee of the Regions
whenever new proposals are made in areas which have
repercussions at regional or local level. The CoR issues
opinions on proposals for EU laws, which directly affect
local and regional authorities. It can also draw up
opinions on its own initiative, which enables it to put
issues on the EU agenda.

The Committee has 317 full members and the same
number of alternate members. They are proposed by the
Member States to the Council of Ministers, which
appoints them for a four-year renewable term of office.
Members must hold a regional or local authority electoral
mandate or be politically accountable to an elected
assembly. They participate in the work of six specialist
commissions which are responsible for drafting the CoR's
opinions, for example on economic and social cohesion,
trans-European infrastructure networks, social policy, the
environment and vocational training.
President, Peter Straub
Secretary-General, Gerhard Stahl

COURT OF JUSTICE OF THE EUROPEAN COMMUNITIES

Palais de la Cour de justice, Boulevard Konrad Adenauer,
Kirchberg, L-2925 Luxembourg
E info@curia.eu.int W www.curia.eu.int
The Court of Justice is common to the two European
Communities. It exists to safeguard the law in the
interpretation and application of the Community treaties,
to decide on the legality of decisions of the Council of
Ministers or the Commission, and to determine
infringements of the treaties. Cases may be brought to it
by the member states, the Community institutions, firms
or individuals. Its decisions are directly binding on the
member countries, and the Maastricht Treaty enhanced
the Court's powers by permitting it to impose fines on
member states. The 25 judges and eight advocates-general
of the Court are appointed for renewable six-year terms
by the member governments in concert. During 2004,
531 new cases were lodged at the court and 665 cases
were concluded.
President, V. Skouris
First Advocate-General, A. Tizzano

COURT OF FIRST INSTANCE

Palais de la Cour de justice, Boulevard Konrad Adenauer,
Kirchberg, L-2925 Luxembourg
Established under powers conferred by the Single
European Act, the Court of First Instance has jurisdiction
to hear and determine all actions brought by natural or
legal persons. It is composed of 25 judges, appointed for
renewable six-year terms by the governments of the
member states. During 2004, 536 new cases were lodged
at the court and 361 cases were concluded.
President, Bo Vesterdorf

EUROPEAN ECONOMIC AND SOCIAL COMMITTEE

Rue Belliard 97/113, B-1000 Brussels, Belgium
W www.esc.eu.int
The European Economic and Social Committee (EESC) is
an advisory and consultative body, which has 317
members appointed by the governments of the 25
member states for a four-year renewable term. It is divided
into three groups: employers, workers, and other interest
groups such as consumers, farmers and the self-employed.
It issues opinions on draft EC legislation and can bring
matters to the attention of the Commission, Council and
Parliament. The EESC's competencies have increased as a
result of revisions to the Treaty of Rome, and the Treaty
Nice formally recognised the importance of the opinions
of the EU's economic and social partners.
President, Anne-Marie Sigmund (Austria)

EUROPEAN CENTRAL BANK

29 Kaiserstrasse, D-60311 Frankfurt-am-Main, Germany
E info@ecb.int W www.ecb.int
The European Central Bank (ECB), which superseded the
European Monetary Institute, was established on 1 July
1998. Its governing bodies are the Executive Board, the
Governing Council and the General Council. The
Executive Board consists of the President, the Vice-
President and four other members, who are appointed by
the governments of the states participating in the single
currency, at the level of Heads of State and Government.
The Governing Council comprises the six members of the
Executive Board and the governors of the national central
banks of the participating states; the General Council
comprises the President and Vice-President and the 25
governors of the national central banks, the other
members of the Executive Board being entitled to
participate but not to vote. The ECB is independent of
national governments and of all other EU institutions. It
became fully operational on 1 January 1999, and defines
and implements the single monetary policy necessary for
EMU. It operates as part of the European System of
Central Banks (ESCB), which consists of the ECB and the
national central banks of the EU member states.
President, Jean-Claude Trichet (France)
Vice-President, Lucas Papademos (Greece)

EUROPEAN COURT OF AUDITORS

12 rue Alcide De Gasperi, L-1615 Luxembourg
E euraud@eca.eu.int W www.eca.eu.int
The European Court of Auditors, established in 1977,
examines the accounts of all revenue and expenditure of
the European Communities and Community bodies and
evaluates whether all revenue has been received and all
expenditure incurred in a lawful and regular manner and
in accordance with the principles of sound financial
management. The Court issues an annual report and a
statement of assurance as to the reliability of the accounts
and the legality and regularity of the underlying
transactions. It also publishes special reports on specific
topics and delivers opinions on financial matters. The
Court has one member from each member state appointed

for a six-year term by the Council of Ministers following consultation with the European Parliament.
President, Hubert Weber (Austria)

EUROPEAN ENVIRONMENT AGENCY
Kongens Nytorv 6, DK-1050 Copenhagen K, Denmark
T (+45) 3336 7100 F (+45) 3336 7199
E eea@eea.eu.int W org.eea.eu.int
The European Environment Agency (EEA) aims to support sustainable development and to help achieve significant and measurable improvement in Europe's environment, through the provision of information to policy-making agents and the public. The EEA has been operational since 1994, and now has 31 members drawn from the 25 member states. It is a European Union body but is open to non-EU countries that share its objectives.
Executive Director, Prof. Jacqueline McGlade

EUROPEAN INVESTMENT BANK
100 boulevard Konrad Adenauer, L-2950 Luxembourg
E info@eib.org W www.eib.org
The European Investment Bank (EIB) was set up in 1958 under the terms of the Treaty of Rome to finance capital investment projects promoting the balanced development of the European Community by providing loans for capital investment projects furthering EU policy objectives, in fields such as regional development, transport and communications, security of energy supplies, the environment, international competitiveness, support for small and medium-sized enterprises, health and education investment, and investment to encourage a knowledge-based economy.

Outside the EU, the EIB participates in the implementation of the EU's development policy, through long-term loans from its own resources or subordinated loans and risk capital from EU or member states' budgetary funds, in some 130 non-EU countries: in pre-accession countries and, under the terms of different association or co-operation agreements, with countries in the Mediterranean region, in the Balkans, in Latin America, Asia and South Africa, in Africa, the Caribbean and the Pacific.

The Bank's total financing operations in 2004 amounted to €43.2 billion, of which €39.7 billion was for investment within the EU.

The shareholders of the EIB are the 25 member states of the EU, who have all subscribed to the Bank's capital of €163.7 billion. The bulk of the funds required by the Bank to carry out its tasks are borrowed on the capital markets of the EU and non-member countries, and on the international market.

As it operates on a non-profit-making basis, the interest rates charged by the EIB reflect the cost of the Bank's borrowings and closely follow conditions in world capital markets.

The Board of Governors of the EIB consists of one government minister nominated by each of the member countries, usually the finance, economic affairs or treasury minister, who lay down general directives on the credit policy of the Bank and appoint members to the Board of Directors (25 nominated by the member states, one by the European Commission), which takes decisions on the granting and raising of loans and the fixing of interest rates. A Management Committee, composed of the Bank's President and eight Vice-Presidents, also appointed by the Board of Governors, is responsible for the day-to-day operations of the Bank. The President and Vice-

Presidents also preside as Chairmen and Vice-Chairmen at meetings of the Board of Directors.
President, Philippe Maystadt (Belgium)

EUROPEAN POLICE OFFICE
PO Box 90850, NL-2509 LW The Hague, The Netherlands
E info@europol.eu.int W www.europol.eu.int
The European Police Office (Europol) came into being on 1 October 1998 and assumed its full powers on 1 July 1999. It superseded the Europol Drugs Unit and exists to improve police co-operation between member states and to combat terrorism, illicit traffic in drugs and other serious forms of international crime. It is ultimately responsible to the Council. Each member state has set up a national unit to liaise with Europol, and the units send at least one liaison officer to represent its interests at Europol headquarters. Europol maintains a computerised information system, designed to facilitate the exchange of information between member states; the system is maintained by the national units and may be consulted by Europol agents. The computerised database may contain both personal and non-personal data; individuals are entitled to request access to data concerning themselves. Europol has a Management Board comprising one senior police representative from each member state. All Europol activities are monitored by an independent joint supervisory body to ensure the rights of the individual are upheld.
Director, Max-Peter Ratzel (Germany)

EUROPEAN COMMUNITY INFORMATION

EUROPEAN COMMISSION REPRESENTATION OFFICES
ENGLAND, 8 Storey's Gate, London SW1P 3AT
   T 020-7973 1992
WALES, 2 Caspian Point, Caspian Way, Cardiff CF10 4QQ
   T 029-208 95020
SCOTLAND, 9 Alva Street, Edinburgh EH2 4PH
   T 0131-225 2058
NORTHERN IRELAND, Windsor House, 9–15 Bedford Street, Belfast BT2 7EG T 028-9024 0708
REPUBLIC OF IRELAND, 18 Dawson Street, Dublin 2

EUROPEAN COMMISSION DELEGATIONS
AUSTRALIA, 18 Arkana Street, Yarralumla, ACT 2600, Canberra
CANADA, 45 O'Connor Street, Suite 1900, Ottawa, Ontario K1P 1A4
USA, 2300 M Street, NW Washington DC 20037
UK OFFICE OF THE EUROPEAN PARLIAMENT, 2 Queen Anne's Gate, London SW1H 9AA T 020-7227 4300

EUROPEAN PARLIAMENT

POLITICAL GROUPINGS *as at April 2005*

	EPP-ED	PES	ALDE	EUL/NGL	Green/EFA	UEN	Ind-Dem	Others	Total
Austria	6	7	–		2	–	–	3	18
Belgium	6	7	6	–	2	–	–	3	24
Cyprus	3	–	1	2	–	–	–	–	6
Czech Republic	14	2	–	6	–	–	1	1	24
Denmark	1	5	4	1	1	1	1	–	14
Estonia	1	3	2	–	–	–	–	–	6
Finland	4	3	5	1	1	–	–	–	14
France	17	31	11	3	6	–	3	7	78
Germany	49	23	7	7	13	–	–	–	99
Greece	11	8	–	4	–	–	1	–	24
Hungary	13	9	2	–	–	–	–	–	24
Ireland	5	1	1	1	–	4	1	–	13
Italy	24	16	12	7	2	9	4	4	78
Latvia	3	–	1	–	1	4	–	–	9
Lithuania	2	2	7	–	–	2	–	–	13
Luxembourg	3	1	1	–	1	–	–	–	6
Malta	2	3	–	–	–	–	–	–	5
Netherlands	7	7	5	2	4	–	2	–	27
Poland	19	10	4	–	–	7	10	4	54
Portugal	9	12	–	3	–	–	–	–	24
Slovakia	8	3	–	–	–	–	–	3	14
Slovenia	4	1	2	–	–	–	–	–	7
Spain	24	24	2	1	3	–	–	–	54
Sweden	5	5	3	2	1	–	3	–	19
UK	28	19	12	1	5	–	10	3	78
Total	268	202	88	41	42	27	36	28	732

PES   Party of European Socialists (including the British, Irish and Dutch Labour Parties, Northern Ireland Social Democratic and Labour Party, Austrian, Danish, Finnish, German, Italian and Swedish Social Democrats, Belgian, French, Greek, Portuguese, and Spanish Socialists, Italian Democratic Left Party, Luxembourg Socialist Workers' Party, Cyprus KISOS Party, Czech Social Democrats (CSSD), Malta's Partit Laburista Party, Estonian, Latvian, Lithuanian, Polish, Slovakian, Slovenian and Hungarian Social Democrat Parties), Socialist, Social Democratic and Labour parties

EPP-ED   European People's Party and European Democrats (including British and Danish Conservative Parties, Spanish Popular Party, French Nouvelle UDF, RPR and DL, Irish Fine Gael, Swedish Moderate Party, Finnish National Coalition Party, Austrian People's Party, Greek New Democracy, Belgian Christian Socialists, Czech, Cypriot, Estonian, Hungarian, Italian , Latvian, Polish, Slovak and Slovenian Christian Democrats, Pensioners' Party and People's Party, Luxembourg Christian Socialists, Portuguese Social Democrats), Christian Democrats, Christian Socialists and Conservatives

UEN   Union for a Europe of Nations (including French, Italian, Irish, Portuguese, Danish, Polish, Estonian, Latvian and Slovak national parties

ALDE   Alliance of Liberals and Democrats for Europe (including British Liberal Democrats, Danish Left and Radical Left Parties, Dutch Democrats '66 and People's Party for Freedom and Democracy, Belgian Liberals, Italian and Luxembourg Democrats, Swedish Liberal People's Party, Finnish Swedish People's Party and Centre Party, Estonian Reform Party, Latvia's Way Party, Lithuanian Liberal Centre Union, Polish Liberal Party, Hungarian Alliance of Free Democrats, the Czech Democratic Alliance, Slovenian Liberals, and United Democrats Cyprus), centre and liberal parties

EUL/NGL   Confederal Group of the European United Left/Nordic Green Left (French, Greek, Italian, Czech, Slovak and Portuguese Communist Parties, Italian Refounded Communist Party, Cypriot Progressive Party of Working People, Danish, Dutch, Swedish, Finnish, Greek, Latvian and Spanish Socialist/Left parties)

Green/EFA   Greens/European Free Alliance Group (Austrian, British, Cypriot, Czech, Danish, Estonian, Finnish, French, German, Greek, Hungarian, Irish, Italian, Latvian, Luxembourgish, Maltese, Portuguese, Slovak, Spanish and Swedish Green Parties, Dutch Green Left Party, Belgian Ecological Parties, Plaid Cymru and Scottish National Parties), green and nationalist parties

Ind-Dem   Independence and Democracy Group (French Hunting, Fishing, Nature and Traditions, Dutch Calvinists and Christians, UK Independence Party, Danish June Movement and Movement Against the EU), anti-EU, anti-federalist and religious parties

Others   (Austrian Freedom Party, Belgian Flemish Block, French National Front, Italian National Alliance, Northern Ireland Democratic Unionist Party, Polish Self-Defence Party)

INTERNATIONAL ORGANISATIONS

ANDEAN COMMUNITY

General Secretariat, Paseo de la Republica 3895, esq. Aramburs, San Isidro, Lima 27, Peru T (+51) (1) 411 1400
E contacto@comunidadandina.org
W www.comunidadandina.org

The Andean Community came into being on 1 August 1997. It comprises five member states (Bolivia, Colombia, Ecuador, Peru and Venezuela) as well as the bodies of the Andean Integrated System (AIS). The Andean Community facilitates the development of the member countries through economic and social integration and co-operation, acceleration of the economic growth of the Andean countries, the promotion of job creation, furthering the aim of creating a Latin American common market, strengthening the position of the member states in the international economic context, and reducing the differences in development that exist between the member states.

It aims to achieve its objectives by a programme of complete trade liberalisation, a common external tariff, the reduction of border controls, the progressive harmonisation of economic and social policies, the co-ordination of national legislation in relevant fields, promoting industrialisation and agricultural development, and supporting technological development programmes.

The General Secretariat of the Andean Community is the executive body, which is responsible for administration, ensuring that member states comply with their obligations and resolving disputes. The General Secretariat operates under the direction of the secretary-general, who is elected by the Andean Council of Foreign Ministers (ACFM). The General Secretariat can propose decisions or suggestions to the ACFM and to the Commission. It also manages the integration process, ensures that Community commitments are fulfilled, and maintains relations with the member countries and the executive bodies of other international organisations.

The Andean Presidential Council is the highest-level body of the AIS and comprises the presidents of the member states; it meets at least once a year and decides on new policies, evaluates the integration process and makes decisions on reports and suggestions from other bodies. The chairmanship is rotated among the members of the council on a calendar year basis. The ACFM co-ordinates the positions of the member states in international issues, signs international agreements on behalf of its member states and can issue decisions that are legally binding in the member states. The Commission of the Andean Community is composed of a plenipotentiary representative from each member state and makes, implements and evaluates policies in the field of trade and investment in the region. The Court of Justice of the Andean Community comprises one judge from each member state. It ensures the uniform implementation of decisions and settles disputes. The Andean Development Corporation aims to support the sustainable development of the member states by promoting trade and investment. The Andean parliament became directly elected in 2003.
Secretary-General, Allan Wagner Tizon

ARAB MAGHREB UNION

14 Rue Zalagh, Agdal, Rabat, Morocco T (+212) (376) 71274
E sg.uma@maghrebarabe.org W www.maghrebarabe.org

The treaty establishing the Arab Maghreb Union (AMU) was signed on 17 February 1989 by the heads of state of the five member states: Algeria, Libya, Mauritania, Morocco and Tunisia. The AMU aims to strengthen ties between the member states, who share strong historical, cultural and linguistic affinities, by developing agriculture and commerce, introducing the free circulation of goods and services, and establishing joint projects and economic co-operation programmes.

Decisions are made by the Council of Heads of State, which meets annually, and must be unanimous. A Council of Foreign Affairs Ministers meets regularly to prepare for the sessions of the Council of Heads of State. The secretariat is based in Rabat and there is a consultative assembly, which consists of 30 representatives from each member state, based in Algiers, and a Court of Justice, with two judges from each country, based in Nouakchott, Mauritania.
Secretary-General, Habib Boulares (Tunisia)

ARCTIC COUNCIL

Ministry of Foreign Affairs of Russia, 32/34 Smolenskaya-Sennaya pl. 119200, Moscow G-200, Russia T (+95) 244 1239
W www.arctic-council.org

The Arctic Council was founded in 1996 in Ottowa, Canada, and is a regional forum for socio-economic development and scientific research within the Arctic region. An inter-governmental forum, the Arctic Council comprises eight states including Canada, the USA, Denmark (including Greenland and The Faroe Islands), Finland, Norway, Sweden, Iceland and Russia. A further six organisations representing indigenous peoples are granted permanent participatory status and include the Saami Council, Inuit Circumpolar Conference and the Arctic Athabaskan Council. The six states with observer status are France, Germany, the Netherlands, Poland and the United Kingdom.

Decisions within the Arctic Council are taken at biennial ministerial meetings attended by foreign ministers or designates of the member states. The chairmanship of the Council and secretariat rotates among member states, also on a biennial basis. Between these meetings, the operation of the Council is administered by the Committee of Senior Arctic Officials.

The main scientific work of the Arctic Council is carried out in five working groups, each focusing on specific issues such as monitoring, assessment and prevention of pollution, climate change, biodiversity and public health.
Executive-Secretary, Vitaly Churkin (Russia)

ASIAN DEVELOPMENT BANK

PO Box 789, 0980 Manilla, Philippines T (+63) (632) 632 4444
E information@adb.org W www.adb.org

The Asian Development Bank (ADB) was founded in 1966 and is a multilateral financial institution dedicated to reducing poverty in Asia and the Pacific. The ADB extends loans, equity investments and technical assistance to governments and public and private enterprises in its developing member countries, promotes the investment of public and private capital for development and assists in the co-ordination of development policies and plans in the developing member countries. The bank's projects and programmes prioritise economic growth, human development, gender and development, good governance, environmental protection, private sector development and regional co-operation.

The ADB raises funds through members' contributions and bond issues on the world's capital markets. In 2003, the ADB provided loans totalling US$6,100 million and technical assistance costing US$177 million. There are 63 member countries in the Asian and Pacific region and in Western Europe and North America. The ADB's headquarters is in the Philippines and there are 27 offices around the world.

President, Haruhiko Kuroda (Japan)

ASIA-PACIFIC ECONOMIC CO-OPERATION

35 Heng Mui Keng Terrace, Singapore 119616
T (+65) 6775 6012 **E** info@apec.org **W** www.apecsec.org.sg

Asia-Pacific Economic Co-operation (APEC) was founded in 1989 in response to the growing interdependence among Asia-Pacific economies. The 1994 Declaration of Common Resolve envisaged a free trade zone, to be established by 2010 in industrialised countries and by 2020 in developing member states. There are three pillars of APEC activities: trade and investment liberalisation, business facilitation, and economic and technical co-operation. Members define and fund work programmes for APEC's four committees, 11 working groups and other APEC fora.

The members are: Australia, Brunei, Canada, Chile, China (People's Republic), China (Hong Kong), Indonesia, Japan, Republic of Korea, Malaysia, Mexico, New Zealand, Papua New Guinea, Peru, the Philippines, Russia, Singapore, Chinese Taipei, Thailand, the USA and Vietnam.

The APEC chairman is responsible for hosting the annual ministerial meeting of foreign and economic ministers. The chairmanship rotates annually among member states. Senior officials of the organisation make recommendations to the ministers and carry out their decisions. They oversee and co-ordinate budgets and work programmes. In addition, there are many advisory groups.

There is a permanent secretariat based in Singapore.

Executive-Director, HE Choi Seok Young

ASSOCIATION OF SOUTHEAST ASIAN NATIONS

Jalan Sisingamangaraja 70a, Jakarta 12110, Indonesia
T (+62) (21) 724 3372 **E** public@asean.org **W** www.aseansec.org

The Association of Southeast Asian Nations (ASEAN) was formed in 1967 with the aims of accelerating economic growth, social progress and cultural development, and ensuring regional stability. The founding members are Indonesia, Malaysia, the Philippines, Singapore and Thailand. Brunei and Vietnam joined in 1984 and 1995 respectively. Laos and Myanmar were admitted in July 1997. Cambodia was admitted on 30 April 1999.

The ASEAN Summit, a meeting of the heads of government who convene every year, is ASEAN's highest authority. The ASEAN Ministerial Meeting (AMM) is an annual meeting of ASEAN foreign ministers and is responsible for the formulation of policy guidelines and the co-ordination of activities, although other relevant ministers are included in the AMM depending on the subject under discussion. The ASEAN Economic Ministers (AEM) meet annually to co-ordinate economic policy. The AMM and AEM usually hold a joint ministerial meeting before an ASEAN summit.

The 1992 Summit agreed to set up the ASEAN Free Trade Area (AFTA), which was fully implemented in 2003. A common preferential tariff was introduced in 1993. At the ASEAN summit in 1995, a South East Asia nuclear weapon-free zone (SEANFZ) was declared.

The secretary-general of ASEAN is appointed on merit by the heads of government and can initiate, advise, co-ordinate and implement ASEAN activities. In addition to the ASEAN secretariat based in Jakarta, each member state has a national secretariat in its foreign ministry which organises and implements activities at national level.

Secretary-General, Ong Keng Yong

BALTIC ASSEMBLY

Tornu 4, Kazarmas III, Section C, Room 301, Riga, LV1050, Latvia
T (+371) 7225 178 **E** baltasam@parks.lv **W** www.baltasam.org

Established in November 1991, the Baltic Assembly (BA) is an international organisation for co-operation between the parliaments of Estonia, Latvia and Lithuania. The legislature of each member state appoints 20 parliamentarians to the Assembly, including a head and deputy head of the national delegation. The Assembly holds two sessions per year in each of the member states in rotation. In addition, there are permanent and *ad hoc* committees.

The Baltic Assembly meets once a year with the Baltic Council of Ministers, which comprises the heads of government and ministers of the Baltic states and promotes intergovernmental and regional co-operation between the Baltic states; the joint sessions are known as the Baltic Council.

President, Andres Taimla (Estonia)

BANK FOR INTERNATIONAL SETTLEMENTS

Centralbahnplatz 2 & Aeschenplatz 1, CH-4002 Basel, Switzerland **T** (+41) (61) 280 8080 **E** email@bis.org **W** www.bis.org

The Bank for International Settlements (BIS), which was founded in 1930, fosters international monetary and financial co-operation by acting as a forum to promote discussion and facilitate decision-making processes among central banks and within the international financial community. It also acts as a centre for economic and monetary research and an agent in connection with international financial operations.

The statutory organs of the BIS are the General Meeting and the Board of Directors. There are 55 member central banks. At present, around 130 central banks and international financial institutions place deposits with the BIS. Total currency deposits placed with the BIS amounted to approximately US$133.2 billion at the end of March 2004, representing around 6 per cent of world foreign exchange reserves. Administrative control is vested in the Board of Directors which comprises 17 members, including the governor of the Bank of England.

Chairman of the Board of Directors and President of the Bank for International Settlements, Nout Wellink (Netherlands)

CAB INTERNATIONAL
Wallingford, Oxon OX10 8DE **T** 01491-832111
E corporate@cabi.org **W** www.cabi.org

CAB International (CABI) (formerly the Commonwealth Agricultural Bureau) was founded in 1929. It generates, disseminates and applies scientific knowledge in support of sustainable development, with an emphasis on agriculture, forestry and natural resources and the needs of developing countries. The organisation is owned and governed by its 44 member countries, each represented on an executive council. A governing board provides guidance on policy issues.

CABI has two divisions: bioscience and publishing. These undertake research and consultancy aimed at raising agricultural productivity, conserving biological resources, protecting the environment and controlling disease. The organisation publishes books, journals and newsletters and produces bibliographic databases on agriculture, health and allied disciplines. It also undertakes contracted scientific research and provides consultancy services and information support to developing countries. Any country is eligible to apply for membership. Applications are by invitation from existing members and are authorised by a head of state or delegated authority.
Director-General, Dr Denis Blight (Australia)

CARIBBEAN COMMUNITY AND COMMON MARKET
PO Box 10827, Georgetown, Guyana **T** (+592) 226 9281/9
E carisec3@caricom.org **W** www.caricom.org

The Caribbean Community and Common Market (CARICOM) was established in 1973 with the signing of the Treaty of Chaguaramas, which was revised in 2001. The objectives of CARICOM are to improve working and living standards, to aim for full employment, to promote economic development and convergence, to expand economic relations with third states, to enhance economic competitiveness and productivity, to co-ordinate member states' foreign and economic policies and enhance functional co-operation in the delivery of common services, including the promotion of activities in the fields of health, education, transport and telecommunications.

The supreme organ is the Conference of Heads of Government, which determines policy, takes strategic decisions and is responsible for resolving conflicts and all matters relating to the founding treaty. The Community Council of Ministers consists of ministers of government responsible for CARICOM affairs and any other ministers designated by member states, and is responsible for strategic planning in the areas of economic integration, functional co-operation and external relations. The principal administrative arm is the Secretariat, based in Guyana. The Bureau of the Conference of Heads of Government is the executive body. It comprises the chairman of the Conference, the outgoing chairman and the secretary-general, who are authorised to initiate proposals and to secure the implementation of CARICOM decisions. In addition, there are four ministerial councils dealing with trade and economic development, foreign and community relations, human and social development, and finance and planning.

The 15 member states are Antigua and Barbuda, the Bahamas (which is not a member of the Common Market), Barbados, Belize, Dominica, Grenada, Guyana, Haiti, Jamaica, Montserrat, St Christopher and Nevis, St Lucia, St Vincent and the Grenadines, Suriname and Trinidad and Tobago. Anguilla, Bermuda, the British Virgin Islands, the Cayman Islands and the Turks and Caicos Islands are associate members. Aruba, Colombia, the Dominican Republic, Mexico, the Netherlands' Antilles, Puerto Rico and Venezuela have observer status.
Secretary-General, Edwin W. Carrington

COMMISSION OF THE AFRICAN UNION
PO Box 3243, Addis Ababa, Ethiopia **T** (+251) (1) 517700
E webmaster@africa-union.org **W** www.africa-union.org

The Organisation of African Unity (OAU) was established in 1963 and has 53 members; Morocco suspended its participation in 1985 in protest at the Polisario-proclaimed Saharan Arab Democratic Republic (SADR), representing Western Sahara, being admitted as a member. The OAU aims to further African unity and solidarity, to co-ordinate political, economic, social and defence policies, and to eliminate colonialism in Africa.

The chief organs are the Assembly of heads of state or government, which is the supreme organ of the OAU and meets once a year to consider matters of common African concern and to co-ordinate the Organisation's policies; the Council of Foreign Ministers, which is the Organisation's executive body responsible for the implementation of the Assembly's policies, and which meets twice a year; and the Commission of Mediation, Conciliation and Arbitration which promotes the peaceful settlement of disputes between member countries. The main administrative body is the General Secretariat, based in Addis Ababa, headed by a secretary-general who is elected by the Assembly for a four-year term.

Substantial budgetary arrears due to delays in the payment of national contributions has meant that the OAU continually faces difficulties in furthering its aims. In June 1991 the Assembly adopted an African Economic Community Treaty which envisages establishment of the economic community after ratification by two-thirds of the OAU's membership. In June 1993 a mechanism was created for conflict prevention, management and resolution, and a peace fund was established.

Following an initiative put forward by Libyan leader Col. Muammar al-Gadhafi in September 1999, the creation of the African Union was declared at a summit meeting in Sirte on 1–2 March 2001, and it legally began operations on 26 May 2001. The first meeting of the African Union took place in 2002.
Secretary-General, H. E. Alpha Oumar Konare (Mali)

THE COMMONWEALTH
The Commonwealth is a voluntary association of 53 sovereign independent states together with their associated states and dependencies. All of the states were formerly parts of the British Empire or League of Nations (later the UN) mandated territories, except for Mozambique which was admitted as a unique case because of its history of co-operation with neighbouring Commonwealth nations.

The status and relationship of member nations were first defined by the Inter-Imperial Relations Committee of the 1926 Imperial Conference, when the six existing dominions (Australia, Canada, the Irish Free State, Newfoundland, New Zealand and South Africa) were described as 'autonomous Communities within the British

Empire, equal in status, in no way subordinate one to another in any aspect of their domestic or external affairs, though united by a common allegiance to the Crown and freely associated as Members of the British Commonwealth of Nations'. This formula was given legal substance by the Statute of Westminster 1931.

This concept of a group of countries owing allegiance to a single Crown changed in 1949 when India decided to become a republic. Her continued membership of the Commonwealth was agreed by the other members on the basis of her 'acceptance of the monarch as the symbol of the free association of its independent member nations and as such the Head of the Commonwealth'. This paved the way for other republics to join the association in due course. Member nations agreed at the time of the accession of Queen Elizabeth II to recognise Her Majesty as the new Head of the Commonwealth. However, the position is not vested in the British Crown.

THE MODERN COMMONWEALTH

As the UK's former colonies joined, initially with India and Pakistan in 1947, the Commonwealth was transformed from a grouping of all-white dominions into a multiracial association of equal, sovereign nations. It increasingly focused on promoting development and racial equality. South Africa withdrew in 1961 when it became clear that its reapplication for membership on becoming a republic would be rejected over its policy of apartheid.

The new goals of advocating democracy, the rule of law, good government and social justice were enshrined in the Harare Commonwealth Declaration (1991), which formed the basis of new membership guidelines agreed in Cyprus in 1993. Following the adoption of measures at the New Zealand summit in 1995 against serious or persistent violations of these principles, Nigeria was suspended in 1995 and Sierra Leone was suspended in 1997 for anti-democratic behaviour. Sierra Leone's suspension was revoked in March 1998 when the legitimate government was returned to power. Similarly, Nigeria's suspension was lifted on 29 May 1999, the day a newly elected civilian president took office. The heads of government meeting in Edinburgh in 1997 established a set of economic principles for the Commonwealth, promoting economic growth whilst protecting smaller member states from the negative effects of globalisation. Zimbabwe was suspended from the councils of the Commonwealth in March 2002 and, in December 2003, the Zimbabwe government officially confirmed that it was leaving the Commonwealth.

MEMBERSHIP

Membership of the Commonwealth involves acceptance of the association's basic principles and is subject to the approval of existing members. There are 53 members at present. (The date of joining the Commonwealth is shown in parenthesis.)

*Antigua and Barbuda (1981)
*Australia (1931)
*The Bahamas (1973)
Bangladesh (1972)
*Barbados (1966)
*Belize (1981)
Botswana (1966)
Brunei (1984)
Cameroon (1995)
*Canada (1931)
Namibia (1990)
Nauru (1968)
*New Zealand (1931)
Nigeria (1960)
†Pakistan (1947)
*Papua New Guinea (1975)
*St Christopher and Nevis (1983)
*St Lucia (1979)

Cyprus (1961)
Dominica (1978)
Fiji (1970, 1997, 2001)
The Gambia (1965)
Ghana (1957)
*Grenada (1974)
Guyana (1966)
India (1947)
*Jamaica (1962)
Kenya (1963)
Kiribati (1979)
Lesotho (1966)
Malawi (1964)
Malaysia (1957)
The Maldives (1982)
Malta (1964)
Mauritius (1968)
Mozambique (1995)
*St Vincent and the Grenadines (1979)
Samoa (1970)
Seychelles (1976)
Sierra Leone (1961)
Singapore (1965)
*Solomon Islands (1978)
South Africa (1931)
Sri Lanka (1948)
Swaziland (1968)
Tanzania (1961)
Tonga (1970)
Trinidad and Tobago (1962)
§Tuvalu (1978)
Uganda (1962)
*United Kingdom
Vanuatu (1980)
Zambia (1964)

* Realms of Queen Elizabeth II
† Suspended 18 October 1999
§ Originally a Special Member due to its small size, small economy and limited involvement in international affairs, Tuvalu became a full member on 1 September 2000.

COUNTRIES WHICH HAVE LEFT THE COMMONWEALTH

Fiji (1987, rejoined 1997, suspended 2000, readmitted 21 December 2001)
Republic of Ireland (1949)
Pakistan (1972, rejoined 1989, suspended 1999)
South Africa (1961, rejoined 1994)
Zimbabwe (2003)

Of the 53 member states, 16 have Queen Elizabeth II as head of state, 32 are republics, and five have national monarchies.

In each of the realms where Queen Elizabeth II is head of state (except for the UK), she is personally represented by a governor-general, who holds in all essential respects the same position in relation to the administration of public affairs in the realm as is held by Her Majesty in Britain. The governor-general is appointed by The Queen on the advice of the government of the state concerned.

INTERGOVERNMENTAL AND OTHER LINKS

The main forum for consultation is the Commonwealth heads of government meetings held biennially to discuss international developments and to consider co-operation among members. Decisions are reached by consensus, and the views of the meeting are set out in a communiqué. There are also annual meetings of finance ministers and frequent meetings of ministers and officials in other fields, such as education, health, women's affairs, agriculture and science. Intergovernmental links are complemented by the activities of some 300 Commonwealth non-governmental organisations linking professionals, sportsmen and sportswomen, and interest groups, forming a 'people's Commonwealth'. The Commonwealth Games take place every four years.

Assistance to other Commonwealth countries normally has priority in the bilateral aid programmes of the association's developed members (Australia, Britain, Canada and New Zealand), who direct about 30 per cent of their aid to other member countries. Developing Commonwealth nations also assist their poorer partners, and many Commonwealth voluntary organisations promote development.

COMMONWEALTH SECRETARIAT

The Commonwealth has a secretariat, established in 1965 in London, which is funded by all member governments. This is the main agency for multilateral communication between member governments on issues relating to the Commonwealth as a whole. It promotes consultation and co-operation, disseminates information on matters of common concern, organises meetings including the biennial summits, co-ordinates Commonwealth activities, and provides technical assistance for economic and social development through the Commonwealth Fund for Technical Co-operation.

The Commonwealth Foundation was established by Commonwealth governments in 1966 as an autonomous body with a board of governors representing Commonwealth governments that fund the Foundation. It promotes and funds exchanges and other activities aimed at strengthening the skills and effectiveness of professionals and non-governmental organisations. It also promotes culture, rural development, social welfare and the role of women.

COMMONWEALTH SECRETARIAT, Marlborough House, Pall Mall, London SW1Y 5HX T 020-7747 6500
E info@commonwealth.int W www.thecommonwealth.org
Secretary-General, Rt. Hon. Don McKinnon (New Zealand)
COMMONWEALTH FOUNDATION, Marlborough House, Pall Mall, London SW1Y 5HY T 020-7930 3783
E geninfo@commonwealth.int
W www.commonwealthfoundation.com
Chairman, Prof. Guido de Marco
COMMONWEALTH INSTITUTE, Kensington High Street, London W8 6NQ T 020-7603 4535
E information@commonwealth.org.uk
W www.commonwealth.org.uk
Finance Director and Secretary, Judy Curry

COMMONWEALTH OF INDEPENDENT STATES

Ul. Kirova 17, Minsk, Belarus T (+375) (17) 222 3517
E webmaster@www.cis.minsk.by W www.cis.minsk.by

The Commonwealth of Independent States (CIS) is a multilateral grouping of 12 sovereign states that were formerly constituent republics of the USSR (Armenia, Azerbaijan, Belarus, Georgia, Kazakhstan, Kyrgyzstan, Moldova, Russia, Tajikistan, Turkmenistan, Ukraine and Uzbekistan). It was formed in 1991. Georgia joined in 1993. The CIS charter, signed in 1993 by seven states (Armenia, Belarus, Kazakhstan, Kyrgyzstan, Russia, Tajikistan, Uzbekistan) and open for signing by the other states, formally established the functions of the organisation and the obligations of its member states.

The CIS acts as a co-ordinating mechanism for foreign, defence and economic policies and is a forum for addressing problems which have arisen from the break-up of the USSR. These matters are addressed in more than 70 inter-state, intergovernmental co-ordinating and consultative statutory bodies. However, member states have criticised the CIS for operating ineffectively and for failing to carry through decisions made by CIS organs.

STRUCTURE

The two supreme CIS bodies are the Council of Heads of State and the Council of Heads of Government. The Council of Heads of State is the highest organ of the CIS and there are various ministerial, parliamentary, banking, economic and security councils. The Executive Committee, based in Minsk and Moscow, provides administrative support.

DEFENCE CO-OPERATION

On becoming members of the CIS, the member states agreed to recognise their existing borders, respect one another's territorial integrity and reject the use of military force or other forms of coercion to settle disputes between them.

A Treaty on Collective Security was signed in 1992 by six states and a joint peacemaking force, to intervene in CIS conflicts, was agreed upon by nine states. Russia concluded bilateral and multilateral agreements with other CIS states under the supervision of the Council of Heads of Collective Security (established 1993). These were gradually upgraded into CIS agreements under the umbrella of the Treaty on Collective Security, enabling Russia to station troops in eight of the other 11 CIS states (not Moldova, Turkmenistan or Ukraine), and giving Russian forces *de facto* control of virtually all of the former USSR's external borders. Only Ukraine and Moldova remained outside the defence co-operation framework and did not sign the Treaty on Collective Security, from which Azerbaijan, Georgia and Uzbekistan withdrew in 1999, forming a new defensive grouping with Moldova and Ukraine. Russian border guards were also withdrawn from Georgia, Kyrgyzstan and Turkmenistan in 1999.

ECONOMIC CO-OPERATION

In 1991, 11 republics signed a treaty forming an economic community. The principles of the treaty were embodied within the CIS and formed the basis of its economic co-operation. Members agreed to refrain from economic actions that would damage each other and to co-ordinate economic and monetary policies. A co-ordinating consultative committee, an economic arbitration court and an inter-state bank were established. A single monetary unit, the rouble, was originally agreed upon by all member states, and the members recognised that the basis of recovery for their economies was private ownership, free enterprise and competition.

The 11 CIS members who signed the Treaty on the Establishment of an Economic Union in September 1993 (Ukraine is an associate member of the economic union) committed themselves to a common economic space with free movement of goods, services, capital and labour. Belarus, Kazakhstan, Kyrgyzstan and Russia signed the Treaty on the Establishment of a Customs Union in March 1996; the treaty was later signed by Tajikistan and on 10 October 2000, the presidents of the five countries approved a treaty establishing the Eurasian Economic Community. In 2003, Russia, Ukraine, Belarus and Kazakhstan proposed the formation of a united economic zone.

Executive Secretary, Vladimir Rushailo

CO-OPERATION COUNCIL FOR THE ARAB STATES OF THE GULF

PO Box 7153, Riyadh 11-462, Saudi Arabia
T (+966) (01) 482 7777 W www.gcc-sg.org

The Co-operation Council for the Arab States of the Gulf, or Gulf Co-operation Council (GCC), as it is informally known, was established on 25 May 1981 with the objectives of increasing co-ordination and integration between its member states, harmonising economic, commercial, educational and social policies and promoting scientific and technical innovation in key economic areas. The GCC has six members: Bahrain, Kuwait, Oman, Qatar, Saudi Arabia and the United Arab Emirates.

The highest authority of the GCC is the Supreme Council, whose presidency rotates among members' heads of states based on the (Arabic) alphabetical order of their names. It holds one regular session every year, but extraordinary sessions may be convened if necessary. The meeting of the Supreme Council is considered valid if attended by two-thirds of the member states.

The Ministerial Council, which ordinarily meets every three months, consists of the foreign ministers of the member states or other delegated ministers. The presidency of the Ministerial Council is held by the state which last presided over the Supreme Council or, if necessary, the state which is next to preside over the Supreme Council.

Secretary-General, Abdul-Rahman bin Hamad Al-Attiyah (Qatar)

COUNCIL OF THE BALTIC SEA STATES

Secretariat, Stromsberg, PO Box 2010, S-103 11 Stockholm, Sweden T (+46) (8) 440 1920 E cbss@cbss.st W www.cbss.st

The Council of the Baltic Sea States (CBSS) was founded in March 1992 with the aim of creating a regional forum to increase co-operation and co-ordination among the states which border on the Baltic Sea in assisting new democratic institutions, economic and technical development, humanitarian aid and health, energy and environmental issues, cultural programmes, education, tourism, transportation and communication.

There are 12 members: Denmark, Estonia, Finland, Germany, Iceland, Latvia, Lithuania, Norway, Poland, Russia, Sweden and the European Commission. The Council consists of the foreign ministers of each member state and a member of the European Commission. Chairmanship of the Council rotates on an annual basis, and the annual session is held in the country currently in the chair. The foreign minister of the presiding country is responsible for co-ordinating activities between the sessions.

Chairmanship, 2005-6, Iceland

COUNCIL OF EUROPE

F-67075 Strasbourg, France T (+33) (3) 8841 2033
E infopoint@coe.int W www.coe.int

The Council of Europe was founded in 1949. Its aim is to achieve greater unity between its members, to safeguard their European heritage and to facilitate their progress in economic, social, cultural, educational, scientific, legal and administrative matters, and in the furtherance of pluralist democracy, human rights and fundamental freedoms.

There are 46 members. The organs are the Committee of Ministers, consisting of the foreign ministers of member countries, who meet twice yearly, and the Parliamentary Assembly of 313 members (and 313 substitutes), elected or chosen by the national parliaments of member countries in proportion to the relative strength of political parties. There is also a Joint Committee of Ministers and Representatives of the Parliamentary Assembly.

The Committee of Ministers is the executive organ. The majority of its conclusions take the form of international agreements (known as European Conventions) or recommendations to governments. Decisions of the

Ministers may also be embodied in partial agreements to which a limited number of member governments are party. Member governments accredit permanent representatives to the Council in Strasbourg, who are also the Ministers' deputies. The Committee of Deputies meets every month to transact business and to take decisions on behalf of Ministers.

The Parliamentary Assembly holds three week-long sessions a year. Its 13 permanent committees meet once or twice between each public plenary session of the Assembly. The Congress of Local and Regional Authorities of Europe each year brings together mayors and municipal councillors in the same numbers as the members of the Parliamentary Assembly.

One of the principal achievements of the Council of Europe is the European Convention on Human Rights (1950) under which was established the European Commission and the European Court of Human Rights, which were merged in 1993. The reorganised European Court of Human Rights sits in chambers of seven judges or exceptionally as a grand chamber of 17 judges. Litigants must exhaust legal processes in their own country before bringing cases before the court.

Among other conventions and agreements are the European Social Charter, the European Cultural Convention, the European Code of Social Security, the European Convention on the Protection of National Minorities, and conventions on extradition, the legal status of migrant workers, torture prevention, conservation and the transfer of sentenced prisoners. Most recently, the specialised bodies of the Venice Commission and Demosthenes have been set up to assist in developing legislative, administrative and constitutional reforms in central and eastern Europe.

Non-member states take part in certain Council of Europe activities on a regular or *ad hoc* basis; thus the Holy See participates in all the educational, cultural and sports activities. The European Youth Centre is an educational residential centre for young people. The European Youth Foundation provides youth organisations with funds for their international activities. The Council's ordinary budget for 2005 totalled €186,012,700.

Secretary-General, Terry Davies (UK)
Permanent UK Representative, HE Stephen Howarth, *apptd* 2003

ECONOMIC COMMUNITY OF WEST AFRICAN STATES

Secretariat Building, 60 Yakubu Gowon Crescent, PMB 401, Abuja, Nigeria T (+234) (9) 31 47 6479 E info@ecowas.int
W www.ecowas.int

The Economic Community of West African States (ECOWAS) was founded in 1975 and came into operation in 1977. It aims to promote the cultural, economic and social development of West Africa through mutual co-operation. A revised ECOWAS Treaty was signed in 1993 and came into effect in July 1995. It makes the prevention and control of regional conflicts an aim of ECOWAS and provides for the imposition of a community tax and for the establishment of a regional parliament, an economic and social council and a court of justice.

The supreme authority of ECOWAS is vested in the annual summit of heads of government of all 15 member states. A Council of Ministers, two from each member state, meets biannually to monitor the organisation and make recommendations to the summit. ECOWAS operates through a secretariat, headed by the executive secretary. In addition there are four deputy executive secretaries. The ECOWAS parliament was inaugurated in November 2000 and justices for the Court of Justice were sworn in January 2001.

The Fund for Co-operation, Compensation and Development, situated at Lomé, Togo, has been restructured into three funds: the ECOWAS Regional Development Fund, the ECOWAS Bank for Investment and Development and the ECOWAS Regional Investment Bank. The funds finance development projects and provide compensation to member states that have suffered losses as a result of ECOWAS's policies, particularly trade liberalisation.

The members of ECOWAS are: Benin, Burkina Faso, Cape Verde, Cote d'Ivoire, Gambia, Ghana, Guinea, Guinea-Bissau, Liberia, Mali, Niger, Nigeria, Senegal, Sierra Leone and Togo.

An ECOWAS Monitoring Group (ECOMOG) peacekeeping force has been involved in attempts to restore peace in Liberia (1990–6), in Guinea-Bissau (1998–9) and in Sierra Leone (1997-9).

Executive Secretary, Dr Mohamed ibn Chambas (Ghana)

EUROPEAN BANK FOR RECONSTRUCTION AND DEVELOPMENT

One Exchange Square, London EC2A 2JN T 020-7338 6000 W www.ebrd.com

The European Bank for Reconstruction and Development (EBRD), established in 1991, is an international institution with 62 members (60 countries, the European Community and the European Investment Bank).

The aim of the EBRD is to build market economies and democracies in 27 countries in central and eastern Europe and Central Asia. The EBRD finances projects in both the private and public sectors, providing direct funding for financial institutions, infrastructure and other key sectors. The main forms of the EBRD financing are loans, equity investments and guarantees. No more than 40 per cent of the EBRD's investment can be made in state-owned concerns. The EBRD is the largest foreign investor in the region's private sector and in addition to its own lending, facilitates significant foreign direct investment. The EBRD pays particular attention to strengthening the financial sector and to promoting small and medium-sized enterprises. It works in co-operation with national governments, private companies, and international organisations such as the OECD, the IMF, the World Bank and the UN specialised agencies.

The EBRD has a subscribed capital of €20 billion. The EBRD is also able to borrow on world capital markets. Its major subscribers are the USA, 10 per cent; Britain, France, Germany, Italy and Japan, 8.5 per cent each. As at the end of 2004, the EBRD had committed €4,133,000 million to 129 new projects. Net profit in 2004 reached €297,700 million.

The highest authority is the Board of Governors; each member appoints one governor and one alternate. The governors delegate most powers to a 23-member Board of Directors; the directors are responsible for the EBRD's operations and budget, and are elected by the governors for three-year terms. The governors also elect the president of the Board of Directors, who acts as the Bank's president for a four-year term.

President of the Board of Directors, Jean Lemierre (France)

EUROPEAN FREE TRADE ASSOCIATION

Headquarters: 9–11 rue de Varembé, CH-1211 Geneva 20, Switzerland T (+41) (22) 749 1111 W www.efta.int
EEA matters: Rue Josef II, 12-16, B-1000, Brussels, Belgium T (+32) (2) 286 1711 E mail.bx1@efta.int

The European Free Trade Association (EFTA) was established in 1960 by Austria, Denmark, Norway, Portugal, Sweden, Switzerland and the UK, and was subsequently joined by Finland (associate member 1961, full member 1986), Iceland (1970) and Liechtenstein (1991). Six members have left to join the European Union: Denmark and the UK (1972), Portugal (1985), Austria, Finland and Sweden (1995). The existing members are Iceland, Liechtenstein, Norway and Switzerland.

The first objective of EFTA was to establish free trade in industrial products between members; this was achieved in 1966. Its second objective was the creation of a single market in western Europe and in 1972 EFTA signed free trade agreements with the EC covering trade in industrial goods; the remaining tariffs on industrial products were abolished in 1977 and the Luxembourg Declaration on broader co-operation between EFTA and the European Community was signed in 1984.

An agreement on the creation of the European Economic Area (EEA), an extension of the EC single market to the EFTA states, was signed in 1992 and entered into force on 1 January 1994. Switzerland rejected EEA membership in a referendum in 1992 and Liechtenstein joined on 1 May 1995 after adapting its customs union with Switzerland. The implementation of the agreement is supervised by the EEA Council, composed of EFTA and EU ministers, and the EFTA Surveillance Authority. The three EFTA EEA members also participate in a wide range of other EC programmes including research and development, environmental matters, and education and training.

In June 2002, a free trade agreement between the EFTA states and Singapore was signed in Egilsstagir (Iceland). In March 2003, EFTA initialled a free trade agreement with Chile in Geneva (Switzerland). The agreement with Chile is the second free trade agreement that the EFTA states have concluded with a country in the Americas, after the agreement concluded with Mexico in 2000. In March 2004, an initial Free Trade Agreement was reached with Lebanon. With these agreements the EFTA states will have concluded free trade agreements with 21 states and territories, representing a population of 344 million, in addition to the free trade relations with the European Union, comprising a population of 375 million. Negotiations on free trade agreements with Lebanon, South Africa, Tunisia and Egypt continued during 2004.

The EFTA Council is the principal organ of the Association. It meets regularly at the level of ambassadors to the EFTA Secretariat in Geneva.

Secretary-General, William Rossier (Switzerland)
Deputy Secretary-General (Geneva), Pétur G. Thorsteinsson (Iceland)
Deputy Secretary-General (Brussels), Oystein Hovdkinn (Norway)

EUROPEAN ORGANISATION FOR NUCLEAR RESEARCH (CERN)

CH-1211 Geneva 23, Switzerland T (+41) (22) 767 6111 W www.cern.ch

The Convention establishing the European Organisation

for Nuclear Research (CERN) came into force in 1954. CERN promotes European collaboration in high energy physics of a scientific, rather than a military nature.

The member countries are Austria, Belgium, Bulgaria, the Czech Republic, Denmark, Finland, France, Germany, Greece, Hungary, Italy, the Netherlands, Norway, Poland, Portugal, Slovakia, Spain, Sweden, Switzerland and the UK. India, Israel, Japan, Russia, Turkey, the USA, the EU Commission and UNESCO have observer status.

The Council, which is the highest policy-making body, comprises two delegates from each member state and is chaired by the President who is elected by the Council in Session. The Council also elects a director-general, who is responsible for the internal organisation of CERN. The director-general heads a workforce of approximately 2,500, including physicists, craftsmen, technicians and administrative staff. At present over 6,500 physicists use CERN's facilities.

The member countries contribute to the budget in proportion to their net national revenue (budget 2005 Sfr 1,340 million).

President of the Council, Enzo Iarocci (Italy)
Director-General (2004–8), Dr Robert Aymar (France)

EUROPEAN SPACE AGENCY

8–10 rue Mario Nikis, F-75738 Paris Cedex 15, France
T (+33) (1) 5369 7654 W www.esa.int

The European Space Agency (ESA) was created in 1975 by the merger of the European Space Research Organisation (ESRO) and the European Launcher Development Organisation (ELDO). Its aims include the advancement of space research and technology and the implementation of a long-term European space policy.

The member countries are Austria, Belgium, Denmark, Finland, France, Germany, Greece, Ireland, Italy, the Netherlands, Norway, Portugal, Spain, Sweden, Switzerland and the UK. Luxembourg was due to officially join ESA at the end of 2005. Canada and Hungary and the Czech Republic are co-operating states. ESA's mandatory activities are funded by contributions from all the member states, calculated in accordance with each country's gross national income (GNI). In 2005, ESA's budget was €2,977 million.

The agency is directed by a council composed of the representatives of the member states; its chief officer is the director-general who is elected by the council every four years. ESA has liaison offices in Belgium, the United States of America and Russia while a launch base is stationed in French Guiana.

Director-General, Jean-Jacques Dordain, *apptd* 2003

FOOD AND AGRICULTURE ORGANISATION OF THE UNITED NATIONS

Viale delle Terme di Caracalla, 00100 Rome, Italy
T (+39) (06) 57051 E fao-hq@fao.org W www.fao.org

The Food and Agriculture Organisation (FAO) is a specialised UN agency, established in 1945. It assists rural populations by raising levels of nutrition and living standards, and by encouraging greater efficiency in food production and distribution. It analyses and disseminates information on agriculture and natural resources. The FAO also advises governments on national agricultural policy and planning; its Investment Centre, together with the World Bank and other financial institutions, helps to prepare development projects. The FAO's field programme covers a range of activities, including strengthening crop production, rural and livestock development, and conservation.

The FAO's top priorities are sustainable agriculture, rural development and food security. The Organisation attempts to ensure the availability of adequate food supplies, stability in the flow of supplies and the securing of access to food by the poor. The FAO monitors potential famine areas. The Emergency Operations and Rehabilitation Division channels emergency aid from governments and other agencies, and assists in rehabilitation. The Technical Co-operation Programme responds to urgent or unforeseen requests for technical assistance.

The FAO has 188 members (187 states plus the EU). It is governed by a biennial conference of its members which sets a programme and budget. The budget for 2004–5 was US$749.1 million, funded by member countries in proportion to their gross national income. The FAO is also funded by the UN Development Programme, donor governments and other institutions.

The Conference elects a director-general and a 49-member council which governs between conferences. The Regular and Field Programmes are administered by a secretariat, headed by the director-general. Five regional, five sub-regional and over 78 national offices help administer the Field Programme.

Director-General, Jacques Diouf (Senegal)

INTERNATIONAL ATOMIC ENERGY AGENCY

Vienna International Centre, Wagramer Strasse 5, PO Box 100, A-1400 Vienna, Austria T (+43) (1) 26000
E official.mail@iaea.org W www.iaea.org

The International Atomic Energy Agency (IAEA) was established in 1957. It is an intergovernmental organisation that reports to, but is not a specialised agency of, the UN.

The IAEA aims to enhance the contribution of atomic energy to peace, health and prosperity and to ensure that any assistance that it provides is not used for military purposes. It establishes atomic energy safety standards and offers services to its member states for the safe operation of their nuclear facilities and for radiation protection. It is the focal point for international conventions on the early notification of a nuclear accident, assistance in the case of such an accident, civil liability for nuclear damage, physical protection of nuclear material, nuclear safety and the safety of spent fuel and radioactive waste management. The IAEA also encourages research and training in nuclear power. It is additionally charged with drawing up safeguards and verifying their use in accordance with the Nuclear Non-Proliferation Treaty (NPT) 1968, the Treaty for the Prohibition of Nuclear Weapons in Latin America (Tlatelolco Treaty) 1968, the Treaty on a South Pacific Nuclear Free Zone (Rarotonga Treaty), the South East Asia Nuclear Weapon-Free Zone Treaty (Bangkok Treaty) and the African Nuclear Weapon-Free Zone Treaty (Pelindaba Treaty) 1996.

The IAEA has 138 members that meet annually in a General Conference. The Conference decides policy, a programme and a budget (2005, US$270 million), as well as electing a director-general and a 35-member board of governors. The board meets four times a year to formulate policy which is implemented by the secretariat under a director-general.

Director-General, Mohamed El Baradei (Egypt)

INTERNATIONAL CIVIL AVIATION ORGANISATION

999 University Street, Montréal, Québec, Canada H3C 5H7
T (+1) (514) 954 8219 E icaohq@icao.int W www.icao.int

The International Civil Aviation Organisation (ICAO) was founded with the signing of the Chicago Convention on International Civil Aviation in 1944 and became a specialised agency of the United Nations in 1947. It sets international technical standards and recommends practices for all areas of civil aviation, including airworthiness, air navigation, air traffic control and pilot licensing. It encourages uniformity and simplicity in ground regulations and operations at international airports, including immigration and customs control. The ICAO also promotes regional air navigation, plans for ground facilities and collects and distributes air transport statistics world-wide. It is dedicated to improving safety and to the orderly development of civil aviation throughout the world.

The ICAO has 188 members and is governed by an assembly which meets at least once every three years. A council of 52 members is elected, which represents leading air transport nations as well as less developed countries. The council elects the president, appoints the secretary-general and supervises the organisation through subsidiary committees, serviced by a secretariat.

President of the Council, Dr Assad Kotaite (Lebanon)
Secretary-General, Dr Taieb Cherif (Algeria)
UK Representative, N. Denton

INTERNATIONAL CONFEDERATION OF FREE TRADE UNIONS

Koning Albert II laan 5, Bus 1, B-1210 Brussels, Belgium
T (+32) (2) 224 0211 E press@icftu.org W www.icftu.org

The International Confederation of Free Trade Unions (ICFTU) was created in 1949. It aims to establish, maintain and promote free trade unions, and to promote peace with economic security and social justice.

In December 2004, the ICFTU had 145 million members in 233 affiliated organisations in 154 countries and territories.

The Congress, the supreme authority of the ICFTU, convenes at least every four years. It is composed of delegates from the affiliated trade union organisations. The Congress elects an executive board of 53 members, including five nominated by the women's committee and one by the youth committee, which meets not less than once a year. The board establishes the budget and receives suggestions and proposals from affiliates as well as acting on behalf of the Confederation. The Congress also elects the general secretary.

General Secretary, Guy Ryder (UK)
UK Affiliate, TUC, Congress House, 23–28 Great Russell Street, London WC1B 3LS T 020-7636 4030

INTERNATIONAL CRIMINAL POLICE (INTERPOL)

200 Quai Charles de Gaulle, F-69006 Lyon, France
E compr@interpol.int W www.interpol.int

Interpol was set up in 1923 to establish an international criminal records office and to harmonise extradition procedures. As at May, the organisation comprised 182 member states. Interpol's aims are to promote co-operation between criminal police authorities, and to support government agencies concerned with combating crime, whilst respecting national sovereignty. It is financed by annual contributions from the governments of member states.

Interpol's policy is decided by the General Assembly which meets annually; it is composed of delegates appointed by the member states. The 13-member executive committee is elected by the General Assembly from among the member states' delegates, and is chaired by the president, who has a four-year term of office. The permanent administrative organ is the general secretariat, headed by the secretary-general, who is appointed by the General Assembly.

Secretary-General, Ronald Noble (USA)

INTERNATIONAL ENERGY AGENCY

9 rue de la Fédération, F-75739 Paris Cedex 15, France
T (+33) (1) 4057 6551 E info@iea.org W www.iea.org

The International Energy Agency (IEA), founded in 1974, is an autonomous agency within the framework of the Organisation for Economic Co-operation and Development (OECD). The IEA's objectives include improvement of energy co-operation world-wide, increased efficiency, development of alternative energy sources and the promotion of relations between oil producing and oil consuming countries. The IEA also maintains an emergency system to alleviate the effects of severe oil supply disruptions.

The main decision-making body is the Governing Board, composed of senior energy officials from member countries. Various standing groups and special committees exist to facilitate the work of the Board. The IEA secretariat, with a staff of energy experts, carries out the work of the Governing Board and its subordinate bodies. The executive director is appointed by the Board. The IEA has 26 member states.

Executive Director, Claude Mandil (France)

INTERNATIONAL FRANCOPHONE ORGANISATION

Cabinet du Secretaire general, 28 rue de Bourgogne, F-75007 Paris, France T (+33) (1) 441112 50 E oif@francophonie.org
W www.francophonie.org

The International Francophone Organisation (known as La Francophonie) is an intergovernmental organisation founded in 1970 by 21 French-speaking countries. It aims to prevent conflict and promote development and co-operation between the Francophone countries, to represent its member states internationally and to promote French culture and the use of the French language.

The Conference of Heads of State and Heads of Government of Countries Using French as a Common Language, also known as the Francophone Summit, takes place biennially. Other institutions include the Ministerial Conference of La Francophonie, the Permanent Council of La Francophonie and the Secretariat.

The Ministerial Conference of La Francophonie, which consists of the foreign minister or the minister responsible for Francophone affairs of each member state, implements decisions made at the summits and makes preparations for the following summit. It also puts forward prospective new members.

The Permanent Council of La Francophonie, which is chaired by the secretary-general and consists of representatives of the member states, oversees the execution of decisions made by the Ministerial

Conference, allocates funds, and reviews and approves projects.

La Francophonie has a current membership of 49 member states, 4 associate member states and 10 observers.

Secretary-General, Abdou Diouf

INTERNATIONAL FUND FOR AGRICULTURAL DEVELOPMENT

107 Via del Serafico, I-00142 Rome, Italy T (+39) (06) 54591
E ifad@ifad.org W www.ifad.org

The establishment of the International Fund for Agricultural Development (IFAD) was proposed by the 1974 World Food Conference and IFAD began operations as a UN specialised agency in 1977. Its purpose is to mobilise additional funds for agricultural and rural development projects in developing countries, provide employment and additional income for poor farmers, reduce malnutrition and improve food security systems.

IFAD has 164 members and membership is divided into three lists: List A (OECD countries), List B (OPEC countries), and List C (developing countries) which is subdivided into C1 (Africa), C2 (Europe, Asia and the Pacific) and C3 (Latin America and the Caribbean). All powers are vested in a Governing Council of all member countries. It elects an 18-member executive board (with 18 alternate members) responsible for IFAD's operations. The Council meets annually and elects a president who is also chairman of the board. The president serves a four-year term that is renewable once and is assisted by a vice-president and three assistant presidents.

Since its establishment, IFAD has committed a total of US$8,100 million in loans and US$35,400 million in grants for 653 approved projects in 115 countries and territories. IFAD's current annual commitment level is approximately $450 million.

President, Lennart Båge (Sweden), *apptd* 2001

INTERNATIONAL HYDROGRAPHIC ORGANISATION

International Hydrographic Bureau, 4 Quai Antoine 1ev, B.P. 445, MC98011, Monaco Cedex T (+377) 9310 8100
E info@ihb.mc W www.iho.shom.fr

The International Hydrographic Bureau (IHB) began its activity in 1921 with 19 member states and, at the invitation of H.S.H. Prince Albert 1st, was provided with headquarters in the Principality of Monaco. In 1970, an intergovernmental convention entered into force which changed the name and legal status of the IHB to the International Hydrographic Organisation (IHO).The IHO is an intergovernmental organisation that works in a purely consultative role and aims to support safety in international navigation and set policy for marine conservation. The IHO has a membership of 74 states that meet at five-yearly conferences to set policy, approve budget, review progress and adopt programmes of work to be pursued in the ensuing five-year period. Each member is represented at these conferences by their most senior hydrographer, usually the head of the hydrographic office for each particular country. All member states have an opportunity to initiate new proposals for IHO consideration and, during this time, a directing committee of three senior hydrographers is also elected. Outside of its membership, the IHO acts to promote hydrography and facilitate the exchange of technology with developing countries as well as working towards a standardisation of nautical products, services and survey practices.

President, Vice-Admiral Alexandros Maratos (Greece)

INTERNATIONAL LABOUR ORGANISATION

4 route des Morillons, CH-1211 Geneva 22, Switzerland T (+41) (22) 799 6111 W www.ilo.org

The International Labour Organisation (ILO) was established in 1919 as an autonomous body of the League of Nations and became the UN's first specialised agency in 1946. The ILO aims to increase employment, improve working conditions, raise living standards and encourage democratic development. It sets minimum international labour standards through the drafting of international conventions. Member countries are obliged to submit these to their domestic authorities for ratification, and thus undertake to bring their domestic legislation in line with the conventions. Members must report to the ILO periodically on how these regulations are being implemented. The ILO plays a major role in helping developing countries achieve economic stability and job expansion through its wide-ranging programme of technical co-operation. The ILO is also the world's principal resource centre for information, analysis and guidance on labour and employment. The organisation aims to improve working and living conditions throughout the world and to support the transition to democracy and market economies under way in many states.

The ILO has 178 members and is composed of the International Labour Conference, the Governing Body and the International Labour Office. The Conference of members meets annually, and is attended by national delegations comprising two government delegates, one worker delegate and one employer delegate. It formulates international labour conventions and recommendations, provides a forum for discussion of world employment and social issues, and approves the ILO's programme and budget. The programme and budget set out four strategic objectives for the ILO: the promotion of fundamental principles and rights at work; the creation of greater employment and earning opportunities; the enhancement of social protection; and the strengthening of social dialogue.

The 56-member Governing Body, composed of 28 government, 14 worker and 14 employer members, acts as the ILO's executive council. Ten governments, including the UK, hold permanent seats on the Governing Body because of their industrial importance. There are also various regional conferences and advisory committees. The ILO acts as a secretariat and as a centre for operations, publishing and research.

Director-General, Juan Somavia (Chile)
UK OFFICE, Millbank Tower, 21–24 Millbank, London SW1P 4QP T 020-7828 6401 E london@ilo-london.org.uk

INTERNATIONAL MARITIME ORGANISATION

4 Albert Embankment, London SE1 7SR T 020-7735 7611
E media@imo.org W www.imo.org

The International Maritime Organisation (IMO) was established as a UN specialised agency in 1948. Owing to delays in treaty ratification it did not commence operations until 1958. Originally it was called the Inter-Governmental Maritime Consultative Organisation (IMCO) but changed its name in 1982.

The IMO fosters intergovernmental co-operation in technical matters relating to international shipping, especially with regard to safety and security at sea, efficiency in navigation and protecting the marine environment by preventing and controlling marine pollution caused by shipping. The IMO is responsible for convening maritime conferences and drafting marine conventions. It also provides technical aid to countries wishing to develop their activities at sea.

The IMO had 164 members and three associate members as at March 2005. It is governed by an Assembly comprising delegates of all its members. It meets biennially to formulate policy, set a budget (2004–5, £46.2 million), vote on specific recommendations on pollution and maritime safety and security and elect the Council. The Council, which meets twice a year, fulfils the functions of the Assembly between sessions and appoints a secretary-general. It consists of 40 members: ten from the world's largest shipping nations, ten from the nations most dependent on seaborne trade, and 20 other members to ensure a fair geographical representation. The Maritime Safety, Marine Environment Protection, Legal, Technical Co-operation and Facilitation Committees make reports and recommendations to the Council and the Assembly. There are a number of other specialist subsidiary committees. The IMO acts as the secretariat for the London Convention (1972) which regulates the disposal of land-generated waste at sea.

Secretary-General, Efthimios E. Mitropoulos (Greece)

INTERNATIONAL MONETARY FUND

700 19th Street NW, Washington DC 20431, USA T (+1) (202) 623 7300 E publicaffairs@imf.org W www.imf.org

The International Monetary Fund (IMF) was established in 1944, at the UN Monetary and Financial Conference held at Bretton Woods, New Hampshire. Its Articles of Agreement entered into force in 1945 and it began operations in 1947.

The IMF exists to promote international monetary co-operation, the expansion of world trade, and exchange stability. It advises members on their economic and financial policies; promotes policy co-ordination among the major industrial countries; and gives technical assistance in central banking, balance of payments accounting, taxation, and other financial matters. The IMF serves as a forum for members to discuss important financial and monetary issues and seeks the balanced growth of international trade and, through this, high levels of employment, income and productive capacity. As at June 2005 the IMF had 184 members.

Upon joining the IMF, a member is assigned a 'quota', based on the member's relative standing in the world economy and its balance of payments position, that determines its capital subscription to the Fund, its access to IMF resources, its voting power, and its share in the allocation of special drawing rights (SDRs). Quotas are reviewed every five years and adjusted accordingly. The SDR, an international reserve asset issued by the IMF, is calculated daily on a basket of usable currencies and is the IMF's unit of account; on 30 May 2004, 1 SDR equalled US$1.45412. SDRs are allocated at intervals to supplement members' reserves and thereby improve international financial liquidity.

IMF financial resources derive primarily from members' capital subscriptions, which are equivalent to their quotas. In addition, the IMF is authorised to borrow from official lenders. It may also draw on a line of credit of SDR 18.5 billion from various countries under the so-called general arrangements to borrow (GAB). Periodic charges are also levied on financial assistance. At the end of February 2005, total outstanding IMF credits amounted to US$90 billion.

The IMF is not a bank and does not lend money; it provides temporary financial assistance by selling a member's SDRs or other members' currencies in exchange for the member's own currency. The member can then use the purchased currency to alleviate its balance of payments difficulties. The IMF's credit under its regular facilities is made available to members in tranches or segments of 25 per cent of quota. For first credit tranche purchases, members are required to demonstrate reasonable efforts to overcome their balance of payments difficulties. There are no performance criteria. Upper credit tranche purchases are normally associated with stand-by arrangements and are aimed at overcoming balance of payment difficulties and are required to meet certain performance criteria. Repurchases are made in three and a quarter to five years.

The IMF supports long-term efforts at economic reform and transformation as well as medium-term programmes under the extended Fund facility, which runs for three to four years and is aimed at overcoming balance of payments difficulties stemming from macroeconomic and structural problems. Members experiencing a temporary balance of payments shortfall have access to the compensatory and contingency financing facility.

The IMF is headed by a board of governors, comprising representatives of all members, which meets annually. The governors delegate powers to 24 executive directors, who are appointed or elected by member countries. The executive directors operate the Fund on a daily basis under a managing director, whom they elect.

Managing Director, Rodrigo de Rato y Figaredo (Spain)
UK Executive Director, Tom Scholar, Room 11-120, IMF, 700 19th Street NW, Washington DC 20431, USA

INTERNATIONAL ORGANISATION FOR MIGRATION

17, Route des Morillons, CH-1211 Geneva 19, Switzerland T (+41) 22717 9111 E info@iom.int W www.iom.int

The International Organisation for Migration (IOM) was founded in 1951 as an organisation to resettle European displaced persons and refugees. During the 1960s and 1970s the IOM developed links with the United Nations High Commissioner for Refugees (UNHCR) and began a programme of assistance and reintegration outside of the European region. There are currently 109 member states and 24 observers (including governmental and non-governmental organisations). Internally, the IOM is led by a director-general who is elected for a five-year term. The director-general's office has the constitutional authority to manage the organisation, carry out the activities within its mandate and develop current policies, procedures and strategies. The office of the inspector-general (OIG) incorporates the functions of evaluation, internal audit and assessment of projects for oversight purposes. The OIG is also involved in investigations within the formal complaints procedure.

The role of the IOM has recently expanded to cover migration health services, counter-trafficking measures, emergency and post-crises management and assisted voluntary returns. The estimated budget for 2005 was US$800 million.

Director-General, Brunson McKinley (USA)

INTERNATIONAL RED CROSS AND RED CRESCENT MOVEMENT

19 avenue de la Paix, CH-1202 Geneva, Switzerland T (+41) 22734-6001 W www.icrc.org

The International Red Cross and Red Crescent Movement is composed of three elements – the International Committee of the Red Cross, the International Federation of Red Cross and Red Crescent Societies and the national Red Cross and Red Crescent societies.

The International Committee of the Red Cross (ICRC), the organisation's founding body, was formed in 1863. It aims to negotiate between warring factions and to protect and assist victims of armed conflict. It also seeks to ensure the application of the Geneva Conventions with regard to prisoners of war and detainees.

The International Federation of Red Cross and Red Crescent Societies was founded in 1919 to contribute to the development of the humanitarian activities of national societies, to co-ordinate their relief operations for victims of natural disasters, and to care for refugees outside areas of conflict. There are Red Cross and Red Crescent societies in 175 countries, with a total membership of 250 million.

The International Conference of the Red Cross and Red Crescent meets every four years, bringing together delegates of the ICRC, the International Federation and the national societies, as well as representatives of nations bound by the Geneva Conventions.

President of the ICRC, Jakob Kellenberger

BRITISH RED CROSS SOCIETY, 44 Moorfields, London, EC2Y 9AL T 020-7877 7000
E information@redcross.org.uk
W www.redcross.org.uk
Chief Executive, Sir Nicholas Young

INTERNATIONAL TELECOMMUNICATION UNION

Place des Nations, CH-1211 Geneva 20, Switzerland
T (+41) (22) 730 5111 E itumail@itu.int W www.itu.int

The International Telecommunication Union (ITU) was founded in Paris in 1865 as the International Telegraph Union and became a UN specialised agency in 1947.

ITU is an intergovernmental organisation for the development of telecommunications and the harmonisation of national telecommunication policies. ITU comprises 189 member states and some 700 members who represent public and private organisations involved in telecommunications. ITU's mission is to promote the development of telecommunications and information and communication technologies; to promote and offer technical assistance to developing countries; and to promote at international level the adoption of a broader approach to the issues of telecommunications.

ITU fulfils its mission through initiatives aimed at promoting the growth and expansion of electronic commerce; a programme of strategic workshops; the adoption of international regulations and treaties governing uses of the frequency spectrum; the adoption of technical standards that foster global interconnectivity and interoperability and the provision of policy advice and technical assistance to developing countries.

ITU also organises world-wide and regional exhibitions and forums to exchange ideas, knowledge and technology.

Secretary-General, Yoshio Utsumi (Japan)

LEAGUE OF ARAB STATES

Maidane Al-Tahrir, Cairo, Egypt T (+20) (2) 575 0511
W www.arableagueonline.org

The purpose of the League of Arab States, founded in 1945, is to ensure co-operation among member states and protect their independence and sovereignty, to supervise the affairs and interests of Arab countries, to control the execution of agreements concluded among the member states, and to promote the process of integration among them. The League considers itself a regional organisation and has observer status at the United Nations.

Member states are Algeria, Bahrain, the Comoros, Djibouti, Egypt, Iraq, Jordan, Kuwait, Lebanon, Libya, Mauritania, Morocco, Oman, Palestine, Qatar, Saudi Arabia, Somalia, Sudan, Syria, Tunisia, the UAE and Yemen.

Member states participate in various specialised agencies of the League whose role is to develop specific areas of co-operation between Arab states. These include: the Arab Organisation for Mineral Resources; the Arab Monetary Fund; the Arab Satellite Communications Organisation; the Arab Academy of Maritime Transport; the Arab Bank for Economic Development in Africa; the Arab League Educational, Cultural and Scientific Organisation and the Council of Arab Economic Unity.

Secretary-General, Amre Moussa (Egypt)

UK OFFICE, 52 Green Street, London W1K 6RS
T 020-7629 0044

MERCOSUR

Luis Piera 1992, piso 1, 11200-Montevideo, Uruguay T (+598) (2) 402 9024 E secretaria@mercosur.org.uk
W www.mercosur.org.uy

Brazil and Argentina signed a Treaty for Integration, Co-operation and Development in 1988 which aimed to create a common market between the two countries within ten years, with the elimination of all tariff barriers and harmonisation of macroeconomic policies; the agreement was to be open to other Latin American countries. Paraguay and Uruguay expressed their interest and MERCOSUR (the Southern Common Market) was created by the Treaty of Asunción, which was signed by the four countries on 26 March 1991. Chile became an associate member in 1996 and Bolivia in 1997.

The Common Market Council (CMC) is the highest-level agency of MERCOSUR, with authority to conduct its policy, and responsibility for compliance with the objects and time frames set forth in the Asunción Treaty. It comprises the ministers of foreign affairs and the economy of the member states. Each country presides over the council for a period of six months, in rotating alphabetical order. The CMC meets at least once a year. The presidents of the member states can take part whenever possible.

The Common Market Group (CMG) is the executive body of MERCOSUR and is co-ordinated by the foreign ministries of the member states. Its function is to ensure compliance with the Asunción Treaty and to implement decisions made by the CMC, and where necessary, to help resolve disputes. It can establish subgroups to work on particular issues. It is composed of four permanent members and four substitutes from each country. It normally meets at least four times a year.

Other bodies include a joint parliamentary committee, a trade commission and a socio-economic advisory forum.

NON-ALIGNED MOVEMENT
Permanent Representative to the UN, New York 10016, USA
T (+1) (212) 213 5583 W www.nam.gov.za

The Non-Aligned Movement (NAM) was created following a conference of non-aligned states held in Belgrade, Yugoslavia in September 1961. Members must be committed to the coexistence of states with different political and social systems, they must not be members of multinational military alliances allied to the great powers, and they should support national liberation movements.

NAM was set up to campaign for an end to colonialism, neo-colonialism, racism and occupation, the dissolution of military blocs, national self-determination for all countries and non-interference in internal affairs, north-south dialogue and political-economic co-operation in the third world (south-south relations) and a new world economic mechanism involving military disarmament and the use of the thereby freed means for development projects.

There are 117 members and 14 observers and about 28 further countries have guest status.

The chairmanship of NAM is held by the head of state of the country due to hold the following summit. The chairman is responsible for the promotion of the principles and activities of the movement and the country's ambassador to the UN represents the organisation at UN level.

NORDIC COUNCIL
The Nordic Council was established in March 1952 as an advisory body on economic and social co-operation, comprising parliamentary delegates from Denmark, Iceland, Norway and Sweden. It was subsequently joined by Finland (1956), and representatives from the Faroes (1970), the Aland Islands (1970), and Greenland (1984).

Co-operation is regulated by the Treaty of Helsinki signed in 1962. This was amended in 1971 to create the Nordic Council of Ministers, which discusses all matters except defence and foreign affairs. Matters are given preparatory consideration by a Committee of Co-operation Ministers' Deputies and joint committees of officials. Decisions of the Council of Ministers, which are taken by consensus, are binding, although if ratification by member parliaments is required, decisions only become effective following parliamentary approval. The Council of Ministers is advised by the Nordic Council, to which it reports annually. There are Ministers for Nordic Co-operation in every member government.

The Nordic Council, comprising 87 voting delegates nominated from member parliaments and about 80 non-voting government representatives, meets at least once a year in plenary sessions. The full Council chooses a 13-member praesidium, which conducts business between sessions. A secretariat, headed by a secretary-general, liaises with the Council of Ministers and provides administrative support. The Council of Ministers has a separate secretariat. The presidency and chairmanship of the Nordic Council rotate between the five countries but the same country never holds the presidency and chair of both organisations for the same year.

President of the Nordic Council, Rannveig Gudmundsdottir (Iceland)
SECRETARIAT OF THE NORDIC COUNCIL, Store Strandstræde 18, DK-1255 Copenhagen K, Denmark
T (+45) 3396 0400 E nordisk-rad@norden.org
W www.norden.org
SECRETARIAT OF THE NORDIC COUNCIL OF

MINISTERS, Store Strandstræde 18, DK-1255 Copenhagen K, Denmark T (+45) 3396 0200
W www.norden.org
Secretary-General, Per Unckel (Sweden)

NORTH AMERICAN FREE TRADE AGREEMENT
NAFTA Secretariat, Canadian Section, 90 Sparks Street, Suite 705, Ottawa, Ontario K1P 5B4, Canada T (+1) (613) 992 9388
E canada@nafta-sec-alena.org
NAFTA Secretariat, Mexican Section, Blvd. Adolfo López Mateos 3025, 2° Piso, Col. Héroes de Padierna, C.P. 10700, Mexico, D.F. T (+52) (55) 629 9630
E mexico@nafta-sec-alena.org
NAFTA Secretariat, US Section, Room 2061, 4th Street and Constitution Avenue, NW, Washington DC, 20230, USA T (+1) (202) 482 5438 E usa@nafta-sec-alena.org
W www.nafta-sec-alena.org

The leaders of Canada, Mexico and the USA signed the North American Free Trade Agreement (NAFTA) on 17 December 1992 in their respective capitals; it came into force on 1 January 1994 after being ratified by the legislatures of the three member states.

NAFTA aims to eliminate barriers to trade in goods and services, promote fair competition within the free trade area, protect and enforce intellectual property rights and create a framework for further co-operation. To achieve these aims, import tariffs and quotas are being removed, with the aim of achieving a free trade zone by 2008 at the latest.

The NAFTA secretariat is composed of Canadian, Mexican and US sections. It is responsible for the administration of the dispute settlement provisions of the agreement, provides assistance to the Free Trade Commission and support for various committees and working groups, and facilitates the operation of the agreement.

NORTH ATLANTIC TREATY ORGANISATION
Leopold III laan, Brussels B-1110, Belgium T (+32) (2) 707 4111
E natodoc@hq.nato.int W www.nato.int

The North Atlantic Treaty (Treaty of Washington) was signed in 1949 by Belgium, Canada, Denmark, France, Iceland, Italy, Luxembourg, the Netherlands, Norway, Portugal, the UK and the USA. Greece and Turkey acceded to the Treaty in 1952, the Federal Republic of Germany in 1955 (the reunited Germany acceded in October 1990), Spain in 1982, and the Czech Republic, Hungary and Poland in 1999. Bulgaria, Estonia, Latvia, Lithuania, Romania, Slovakia and Slovenia signed membership protocols on 26 March 2003 and officially joined the North Atlantic Treaty Organisation (NATO) on 29 March 2004.

NATO is the structural framework for a political and military alliance designed to provide common security for its members through co-operation and consultation in political, military and economic as well as scientific and other non-military fields.

STRUCTURE
The North Atlantic Council (NAC), chaired by the secretary-general, is the highest authority of the Alliance and is composed of permanent representatives of the 26 member countries. It meets at ministerial level (foreign and/or defence ministers) at least twice a year. The

permanent representatives (ambassadors) head national delegations of advisers and experts. The Defence Planning Committee (DPC) and the Nuclear Planning Group (NPG) are composed of representatives of all member countries except France (which does not participate in NATO's integrated military structure). Both the DPC and the NPG also meet at ministerial level (defence ministers) at least twice a year. The NATO secretary-general chairs the Council, the DPC and the NPG.

The senior military authority in NATO, under the Council and DPC, is the Military Committee composed of the chief of defence staffs of each member country except Iceland, which has no military forces and is represented by a civilian. The Military Committee, which is assisted by an integrated international military staff, also meets in permanent session with permanent military representatives and is responsible for making recommendations to the Council and DPC on measures considered necessary for the common defence of the NATO area and for supplying guidance on military matters to the NATO strategic commanders. The chairman of the Military Committee, elected for a period of two to three years, represents the committee on the Council.

The Alliance's military command structure, formerly divided on strategic and regional lines for the purposes of military planning for the defence of the North Atlantic area, is now divided between two functional strategic commands. The strategic commanders have responsibility for all NATO military operations (Allied Command Operations or ACO) and for the further transformation of the Alliance's military forces and capabilities (Allied Command Transformation or ACT). There is also a Regional Planning Group for Canada and the USA. The headquarters of ACO is at Mons, Belgium, and comes under the command of the Supreme Allied Commander Europe (SACEUR). The headquarters of ACT is at Norfolk, Virginia, USA, and is under the command of the Supreme Allied Commander, Transformation.

POST COLD-WAR DEVELOPMENTS

The Euro-Atlantic Partnership Council (EAPC) was established in 1997 to develop closer security links with Eastern European and former Soviet states. Replacing the North Atlantic Co-operation Council (NACC) as the first institutional framework for co-operation between NATO member countries and former adversaries from Central and Eastern Europe, the EAPC focuses on defence planning, defence industry conversion, defence management and force structuring, and the democratic concepts of civilian-military relations. Its membership comprises the 26 NATO members and Albania, Armenia, Austria, Azerbaijan, Belarus, Croatia, Finland, Georgia, Ireland, Kazakhstan, Kyrgyzstan, Macedonia, Moldova, Russia, Sweden, Switzerland, Tajikistan, Turkmenistan, Ukraine and Uzbekistan. Its membership may in future be expanded to include Bosnia and Hercegovina and Serbia and Montenegro, once these countries have fulfilled the conditions for membership. The EAPC provides the multilateral, political framework for the partnership for peace programme (PFP) in which each of its member countries participates. The PFP is the basis for practical, bilateral security co-operation between NATO and individual partner countries in the fields of defence planning and budgeting, military exercises and civil emergency operations. It also works to improve interoperability between the forces of partner and member countries to enable them to undertake joint operations and has provided the context for co-operation by many of the partner countries in NATO-led peacekeeping and peace-support operations in Bosnia and Hercegovina, Kosovo and, more recently, in Afghanistan.

NATO and Russia committed themselves to help build a stable, secure and undivided continent on the basis of partnership and mutual interest, when they signed the 1997 Founding Act on Mutual Relations, Co-operation and Security, which provided for the creation of a NATO-Russia permanent joint council (PJC) consisting of the 26 member countries of NATO and Russia. In May 2002 agreement was reached on the establishment of the NATO-Russia council (NRC), replacing the PJC and providing a new co-operative framework bringing together the 27 participating countries for consultation and practical co-operation in fields of common interest and endeavour on the basis of equality. The NRC meets every month at ambassadorial level and twice each year at ministerial level to address issues of common concern such as the fight against terrorism as well as bilateral programmes in other areas of security including defence reform, search and rescue, and civil emergency planning. NATO and Ukraine pursue an annual programme of co-operation and consultation following the signing of a NATO-Ukraine Charter in 1997. NATO's Mediterranean Dialogue, launched in 1994, aims to improve trust and understanding of NATO's goals and objectives among the countries of the southern Mediterranean area and to establish a basis for co-operation in promoting security and stability in the Mediterranean region. The Dialogue brings together seven Mediterranean countries and NATO in the context of individual, bilateral co-operation and participation in NATO training programmes and other activities of interest to the participating countries, namely Algeria, Egypt, Israel, Jordan, Mauritania, Morocco and Tunisia.

At its summit meeting in June 2004, the Alliance launched the Istanbul Co-operation Initiative, inviting contacts and co-operation with interested countries in the broader Middle East region.

The development of a European Security and Defence Identity (ESDI), which would strengthen NATO's European pillar, was agreed at the 1999 NATO summit meeting in Washington. Since then further developments have served to strengthen co-operation between NATO and the European Union and to establish a strategic partnership between them. This has led *inter alia* to the transfer of responsibility from NATO to the European Union, for continuing peace-support operations in the former Yugoslav Republic of Macedonia and in Bosnia and Hercegovina, in accordance with special arrangements providing for NATO support for EU-led military operations of this kind.

At the Washington summit a Defence Capabilities Initiative (DCI) was also launched. It aims to improve defence capabilities and interoperability among Alliance forces to ensure the effectiveness of future multinational operations. At the 2002 Prague summit, further measures to improve capabilities were taken on the basis of a new Capabilities Commitment, in which member countries agreed to specific targets and time frames for improvements. A military concept for defence against terrorism was also agreed in Prague, and additional initiatives taken in the area of nuclear, biological and chemical weapons defence, and defence against cyber attacks. A missile defence feasibility study was also initiated.

NATO AND THE FORMER YUGOSLAVIA

In December 1995, based on a mandate from the United Nations, NATO deployed an Implementation Force (IFOR) to carry out the military aspects of the Dayton Peace accords, bringing to an end the prolonged conflict in Bosnia-Hercegovina. After one year IFOR was replaced by a Stabilisation Force (SFOR) which continued until the end of 2004, when responsibility for this task passed to the EU, drawing on NATO's military capabilities and assets. NATO maintains a smaller military presence in the country to assist with matters such as defence reform and the apprehension of persons indicted as war criminals by the International Criminal Tribunal for the former Yugoslavia (ICTY).

11 SEPTEMBER 2001

Following the terrorist attacks on the USA on 11 September 2001, the NATO members immediately declared their solidarity with the USA and on 12 September formally invoked Article 5 of the Washington Treaty (which stipulates that an armed attack against one or more NATO members is to be considered an attack against all), declaring that the terrorist attack on the USA was an attack on the NATO alliance.

AFGHANISTAN

From January 2001, following the establishment of the Afghan Transitional Authority, an International Security Assistance Force (ISAF) was created on the basis of a United Nations mandate to provide the security needed to allow the rebuilding of the country and the establishment of democratic government through the election process. A number of NATO member countries took on responsibility on a six-monthly rotational basis for the leadership of the force. In 2002, NATO began providing support for ISAF at the request of the lead nations and in August 2004, NATO assumed full responsibility for the leadership of ISAF. In accordance with decisions taken by Alliance leaders at the Istanbul summit meeting in June 2004, and at the request of the President Karzai, ISAF has subsequently enhanced its support and is assisting the government to extend its authority to outside the capital, Kabul, to the country as a whole.

IRAQ WAR

On 19 February 2003, following a request by Turkey for defensive assistance in the event of a US-led war with Iraq, NATO's Defence Planning Committee authorised deployment of surveillance aircraft and missile defences to help protect the country in the event of an attack on its territory or population. The deployment began on 20 February and was concluded on 16 April; the last elements of NATO forces deployed to Turkey left the country on 3 May 2003. In May 2003, NATO agreed to provide support for Poland's role in assuming responsibility for a sector in Iraq in the framework of the multinational stabilisation force deployed to Iraq in the aftermath of the war; and in autumn 2004, NATO undertook responsibility for the establishment of a NATO-Iraq training mission to assist the interim government in training and equipping its own national security forces.

Secretary-General and Chairman of the North Atlantic Council, of the DPC and of the NPG, Japp de Hoop Scheffer (Netherlands)

UK Permanent Representative on the North Atlantic Council, Sir Peter Ricketts

Chairman of the Military Committee, Gen. Harald Kujat (Germany)

ORGANISATION FOR ECONOMIC CO-OPERATION AND DEVELOPMENT

2 rue André-Pascal, F-75775 Paris Cedex 16
T (+33)(1)45248200 E webmaster@oecd.org W www.oecd.org

The Organisation for Economic Co-operation and Development (OECD) was formed in 1961 to replace the Organisation for European Economic Co-operation. It is the instrument for international co-operation among industrialised member countries on economic and social policies. Its objectives are to assist its member governments in the formulation and co-ordination of policies designed to achieve high, sustained economic growth while maintaining financial stability, to contribute to world trade on a multilateral basis and to stimulate members' aid to developing countries.

The members are Australia, Austria, Belgium, Canada, Czech Republic, Denmark, Finland, France, Germany, Greece, Hungary, Iceland, Republic of Ireland, Italy, Japan, Republic of Korea, Luxembourg, Mexico, the Netherlands, New Zealand, Norway, Poland, Portugal, Slovakia, Spain, Sweden, Switzerland, Turkey, the UK, the USA and the European Union.

The Council is the supreme body of the organisation. It is composed of one representative for each member country and meets at permanent representative level under the chairmanship of the secretary-general, and at ministerial level (usually once a year) under the chairmanship of a minister elected annually. Decisions and recommendations are adopted by the unanimous agreement of all members. Most of the OECD's work is undertaken in over 150 specialised committees and working parties. Seven autonomous or semi-autonomous bodies are associated in varying degrees to the Organisation: the Nuclear Energy Agency, the International Energy Agency, the Development Centre, the Centre for Educational Research and Innovation, and the European Conference of Ministers of Transport, the Sahel and West Africa Club, and Support for Improvement in Governance and Management in Central and Eastern European Countries. These bodies, the committees and the Council are serviced by an international secretariat headed by the secretary-general.

Secretary-General, Donald J. Johnston (Canada)
UK Permanent Representative, David Lyscom

ORGANISATION FOR SECURITY AND CO-OPERATION IN EUROPE

Kärntner Ring 5–7, A-1010 Vienna, Austria
T (+43) (1) 514 36 180 E info@osce.org W www.osce.org

The Organisation for Security and Co-operation in Europe (OSCE) was launched in 1975 (as the Conference on Security and Co-operation in Europe (CSCE) under the Helsinki Final Act. This established agreements between NATO members, Warsaw Pact members, and neutral and non-aligned European countries covering security, co-operation and human rights.

The Charter of Paris for a New Europe, signed on 21 November 1990, committed members to support multiparty democracy, free-market economics, the rule of law, and human rights. The signatories also agreed to regular meetings of heads of government, ministers and officials. The first institutionalised heads of state and government summit was held in Helsinki in December 1992, at which the Helsinki Document was adopted. This declared the CSCE to be a regional organisation and defined the structures of the organisation. The summit also appointed a High Commissioner on National Minorities. In 1994 the CSCE was renamed the Organisation for Security and Co-operation in Europe.

Three structures have been established: the Ministerial Council, which comprises the foreign ministers of participating states and is the central decision-making and governing body, and which meets at least once a year; the Senior Council, which prepares work for the Ministerial Council, carries out its decisions and is responsible for the overview, management and co-ordination of OSCE activities and meets at least three times a year; and the Permanent Council, which is responsible for the day-to-day operational tasks of the OSCE and is the regular body for political consultation, meeting weekly. The chairmanship of the OSCE rotates annually and the post of chairman-in-office is held by the foreign minister of a participating state. The chairman-in-office is assisted by the previous and succeeding chairmen. The Senior Council meets in Prague and the Permanent Council in Vienna.

The OSCE is also underpinned by four permanent institutions: a secretariat (Vienna); an Office for Democratic Institutions and Human Rights (Warsaw), which is charged with furthering human rights, democracy and the rule of law; an office of the High Commissioner on National Minorities (The Hague), which identifies ethnic tensions that might endanger peace and promotes their resolution; and a Representative on Freedom of the Media (Vienna), which is responsible for assisting governments in the furthering of free, independent and pluralistic media. There is also a documentation and conference centre in Prague, an OSCE parliamentary assembly with a secretariat based in Copenhagen, and a Court of Conciliation and Arbitration in Geneva.

The OSCE has monitoring missions in 16 OSCE countries. The OSCE supervised all elections in Bosnia-Hercegovina between 1996 and 2000 and in Kosovo since 2000. A Joint Consultative Group of the OSCE promotes the objectives and implementation of the Conventional Armed Forces in Europe (CFE) Treaty (1990) which limits conventional ground and air forces. In November 1999, the Charter on European Security committed the OSCE to co-operate with other organisations and institutions concerned with the promotion of security within the OSCE area. The OSCE has 55 participating states and in 2004 its budget was €172 million.

Chair of the OSCE, Slovenia (2005); Belgium (2006)
Chairman-in-Office, Dmitrij Rupel (Slovenia)

ORGANISATION OF AMERICAN STATES

17th Street and Constitution Avenue NW, Washington DC 20006, USA **T** (+1) (202) 458 3000 **E** pi@oas.org **W** www.oas.org

Originally founded in 1890 for largely commercial purposes, the Organisation of American States (OAS) adopted its present name and charter in 1948. The charter entered into force in 1951 and was amended in 1967, 1985 and 1996; the 1992 Protocol of Washington, which gives the OAS the right to suspend a member state whose democratically elected government is overturned by force, was ratified in 1997.

The OAS aims to strengthen the peace and security of the continent; to promote and consolidate representative democracy with due respect for the principle of non-intervention; to prevent possible causes of difficulties and to ensure the peaceful resolution of disputes arising among its member states; to provide for common action on the part of those states in the event of aggression; to seek the resolution of political, judicial and economic problems that may arise among them; to promote, by co-operative action, their economic, social and cultural development; and to achieve an effective limitation of conventional weapons so that resources can be devoted to economic and social development.

The Declaration of Principles and the Plan of Action resulting from the 1994 Miami summit and signed by all the members except Cuba, envisage the establishment of a free trade area, in which barriers to trade and investment will be progressively eliminated.

Policy is determined by the annual General Assembly, which is the supreme authority and elects the secretary-general for a five-year term. The Meeting of Consultation of ministers of foreign affairs considers urgent problems on an *ad hoc* basis. The Permanent Council, comprising one representative from each member state, promotes friendly inter-state relations, acts as an intermediary in case of disputes arising between states and oversees the General Secretariat, the main administrative body. The Inter-American Council for Integral Development was created in 1996 by the ratification of the Protocol of Managua to promote sustainable development.

The 35 member states are Antigua and Barbuda, Argentina, the Bahamas, Barbados, Belize, Bolivia, Brazil, Canada, Chile, Colombia, Costa Rica, Cuba, Dominica, Dominican Republic, Ecuador, El Salvador, Grenada, Guatemala, Guyana, Haiti, Honduras, Jamaica, Mexico, Nicaragua, Panama, Paraguay, Peru, St. Christopher (St. Kitts) and Nevis, St Lucia, St Vincent and the Grenadines, Suriname, Trinidad and Tobago, Uruguay, the USA and Venezuela. The European Union and 59 non-American states have permanent observer status.

Secretary-General, Jose Miguel Insulza (Chile)

ORGANISATION OF ARAB PETROLEUM EXPORTING COUNTRIES

PO Box 20501, Safat 13066, Kuwait **T** (+965) 484 4500 **E** oapec@qualitynet.net **W** www.oapecorg.org

The Organisation of Arab Petroleum Exporting Countries (OAPEC) was founded in 1968. Its objectives are to promote co-operation in economic activities, to safeguard members' interests, to unite efforts to ensure the flow of oil to consumer markets, and to create a favourable climate for the investment of capital and expertise.

The Ministerial Council is composed of oil ministers from the member countries and meets twice a year to determine policy and to approve the budgets and accounts of the General Secretariat and the Judicial Tribunal. The Judicial Tribunal is composed of seven part-time judges who rule on disputes between member countries and disputes between countries and oil companies. The executive organ of OAPEC is the General Secretariat.

The members are Algeria, Bahrain, Egypt, Iraq, Kuwait, Libya, Qatar, Saudi Arabia, Syria and the United Arab Emirates. Tunisia's membership has been inactive since 1987.

Secretary-General, Abdulaziz A. Al-Turki

ORGANISATION OF THE BLACK SEA ECONOMIC CO-OPERATION

Permanent International Secretariat, Istinye Caddesi, Müsir Fuad Pasa Yalisi, Eski Tersane, 80860 Istinye-Istanbul, Turkey
T (+90) (212) 229 6330/6335 E bsec@tnn.net
W www.bsec-organization.org

The Black Sea Economic Co-operation (BSEC) resulted from the Istanbul Summit Declaration and the adoption of the Bosporus Statement on 25 June 1992. BSEC acquired a permanent secretariat in 1994. Following the Yalta Summit of the Heads of State or Government in June 1998, a charter was drawn up to found the Organisation of the Black Sea Economic Co-operation, which was inaugurated on 1 May 1999.

The organisation aims to promote closer political and economic co-operation in the context of the European integration process between the countries in the Black Sea region and to foster security, regional initiatives, social justice, economic liberty and respect for human rights.

The Council of the Ministers of Foreign Affairs, the highest decision-making authority, meets twice yearly. The meetings rotate among the member states and the chairman is the foreign minister of the state in which the meeting is held. There is also a Committee of Senior Officials and 15 working groups, which deal with specific areas of co-operation.

There are 12 member states: Albania, Armenia, Azerbaijan, Bulgaria, Georgia, Greece, Moldova, Romania, Russia, Serbia and Montenegro, Turkey and Ukraine.
Secretary-General, Tedo Japaridze, (Georgia)

ORGANISATION OF THE ISLAMIC CONFERENCE

PO Box 178, Jeddah 21411, Saudi Arabia T (+966) (2) 690 0001
E oiccabinet@oic-un.org W www.oic-oci.org

The Organisation of the Islamic Conference (OIC) was established in 1969 with the purpose of promoting solidarity and co-operation between Islamic countries. It also has the specific aims of co-ordinating efforts to safeguard the Muslim holy places, supporting the formation of a Palestinian state, assisting member states to maintain their independence, co-ordinating the views of member states in international forums such as the UN, and improving co-operation in the economic, cultural and scientific fields.

The OIC has three central organs, supreme among them the Conference of the Heads of State which meets once every three years to discuss issues of importance to Islamic states. The Conference of Foreign Ministers meets annually to prepare reports for the Conference of Heads of State. The General Secretariat carries out administrative tasks. It is headed by a secretary-general who is elected by the Conference of Foreign Ministers for a four-year term.

In addition to this structure, the OIC has several subsidiary bodies, specialised institutions, affiliated bodies and standing committees. These include the Islamic Solidarity Fund, to aid Islamic institutions in member countries; the Islamic Development Bank, to finance development projects in poorer member states and the Islamic Educational, Scientific and Cultural Organisation.

The achievement of the OIC's aims has often been prevented by political rivalry and conflicts between member states, such as the Iran-Iraq war and the Iraqi invasion of Kuwait. Egypt's membership was suspended from 1979 to 1984 because of its peace treaty with Israel. Saudi Arabia, the main source of funding, exercises great influence within the OIC. Since 1991 the OIC has become more united and has spoken out against violence against Muslims in India, the Occupied Territories and Bosnia-Hercegovina. From 1993 to 1995 the OIC co-ordinated the offering of troops to the UN by Muslim states to protect Muslim areas of Bosnia-Hercegovina.

The Organisation has 57 members (56 sovereign Muslim states in Africa, the Middle East, central and south-east Asia and Europe, plus the Palestine Liberation Organisation) and two observers, the Central African Republic and the Turkish Republic of Northern Cyprus. The OIC has an annual budget of US$11 million.
Secretary-General, Prof. Ekmeleddin Ihsanoglu

ORGANISATION OF THE PETROLEUM EXPORTING COUNTRIES

Obere Donaustrasse 93, A-1020 Vienna, Austria
T (+43) (1) 21112 279 E prid@opec.org W www.opec.org

The Organisation of the Petroleum Exporting Countries (OPEC) was created in 1960 as a permanent intergovernmental organisation with the principal aims of unifying and co-ordinating the petroleum policies of its members, determining ways of protecting their interests individually and collectively, and ensuring the stabilisation of prices in international oil markets with a view to eliminating unnecessary fluctuations. Since 1982 OPEC has attempted (only partially successfully) to impose overall production limits and production quotas in an attempt to maintain stable oil prices.

The supreme authority is the Conference of Ministers of oil, mines and energy of member countries, which meets at least twice a year to formulate policy. The Board of Governors, nominated by member countries, directs the management of OPEC and implements conference resolutions. The Secretariat carries out executive functions under the direction of the Board of Governors.

The member states are Algeria, Indonesia, Iran, Iraq, Kuwait, Libya, Nigeria, Qatar, Saudi Arabia, the UAE and Venezuela. Ecuador withdrew in 1992 and Gabon in 1995.

OPEC member countries account for about 42 per cent of global crude oil production and 49 per cent of internationally traded crude oil, and have 80 per cent of the world's proven oil reserves. The value of OPEC oil exports in 2003 was US$258 billion and their proven crude oil reserves were 891,116 million barrels.
Secretary-General, Sheik Ahmad Fahad Al-Ahmad Al-Sabah (Kuwait)

PACIFIC ISLANDS FORUM

Secretariat, Private Mail Bag, Suva, Fiji T (+679) 331 2600
E info@forumsec.org.fj W www.forumsec.org.fj

The Pacific Islands Forum (PIF) was established in 1971 and represents heads of governments of all the independent and self-governing Pacific Island countries. It aims to foster co-operation between its governments and to represent the interests of the region in international organisations. The PIF meets annually, following which a dialogue is conducted at ministerial level with the Forum dialogue partners (Canada, China, the European Union, France, India, Indonesia, Japan, Korea, Malaysia, the Philippines, the UK and the USA).

The members of the PIF are Australia, the Cook Islands, Micronesia, Fiji, Kiribati, Nauru, New Zealand, Niue, Palau, Papua New Guinea, the Marshall Islands, Samoa, the Solomon Islands, Tonga, Tuvalu and Vanuatu.

The PIF secretariat comprises divisions dealing with development and economic policy, trade and investment, political and international affairs, and corporate services.
Secretary General, Gregory Lawrence Urwin (Australia)

SECRETARIAT OF THE PACIFIC COMMUNITY

BP D5, 98848 Nouméa Cedex, 95 Promenade Roger Laroque, New Caledonia T (+687) 262000 E spc@spc.int W www.spc.int

The Secretariat of the Pacific Community (formerly the South Pacific Commission) was established in 1947 by Australia, France, the Netherlands, New Zealand, the UK and the USA with the aim of promoting the economic and social stability of the islands in the region. The Community now numbers 26 member states and territories: the four remaining founder states (the Netherlands and the UK have withdrawn), in which no programmes are run, and the other 22 states and territories of Melanesia, Micronesia and Polynesia.

The Secretariat of the Pacific Community (SPC) is a technical assistance agency with programmes in marine resources (coastal and oceanic fisheries; maritime programme), land resources (agriculture, animal health and plant protection; forestry) and social resources (community health; socio-economic and statistical services; community education services). The governing body is the Conference of the Pacific Community, which meets every two years.
Director-General, Lourdes Pangelinan (Guam)

SOUTH ASIAN ASSOCIATION FOR REGIONAL CO-OPERATION

PO Box 4222, Tridevi Marg, Kathmandu, Nepal
T (+977) (1) 4221794/4221785 E saarc@saarc-sec.org
W www.saarc-sec.org

The South Asian Association for Regional Co-operation (SAARC) was established in 1985 by Bangladesh, Bhutan, India, the Maldives, Nepal, Pakistan and Sri Lanka. Its primary objective is the acceleration of the process of economic and social development in member states through collective action in agreed areas of co-operation. These include agriculture and rural development, human resource development, environment, meteorology and forestry, science and technology, transport and communications, energy, and social development.

A SAARC Preferential Trading Arrangement (SAPTA), which is designed to reduce tariffs on trade between SAARC member states, was signed in 1993 and entered into force in December 1995. A committee of experts was established in 1998 to draft a comprehensive treaty to create a South Asian Free Trade Area (SAFTA). Agreement was reached in January 2002 to work towards the establishment of a South Asian economic union.

The highest authority rests with the heads of state or government of each member state. The Council of Ministers, which meets twice a year, is made up of the foreign ministers of the member states; it is responsible for formulating policy and considering new projects. The Standing Committee is composed of the foreign secretaries of the member states and monitors and co-ordinates SAARC programmes; it meets twice a year. Technical committees are responsible for individual areas of SAARC's activities. Its secretariat co-ordinates, monitors, facilitates and promotes SAARC's activities and serves as a channel of communication between the association and other regional and intergovernmental institutions.
Secretary-General, HE Chenkyab Dorji (Bhutan)

SOUTHERN AFRICAN DEVELOPMENT COMMUNITY

Private Bag 0095, Gaborone, Botswana T (+267) 351 863
E sadcsec@sadc.int W www.sadc.int

The Southern African Development Community (SADC) was formed in August 1992 by the members of its predecessor, the Southern African Development Co-ordination Conference, founded in 1980 to harmonise economic development among the countries in Southern Africa and reduce their dependence on South Africa. The SADC now comprises 13 countries, including South Africa, and works on a regional basis to increase economic integration and regional security.

It aims to evolve common political values, systems and institutions, to promote development and economic growth, regional security, self-sustaining development and the interdependence of member states, and to maximise production and strengthen and consolidate the historical, social and cultural links among the peoples of the region.

The headquarters of the SADC is in Gaborone, Botswana, but member states each have a responsibility for an area of economic activity.
Executive Secretary, Dr Prega Ramsamy
Chair, Paul Raymond Berenger (Mauritius)

UNITED NATIONS

UN Plaza, New York, NY 10017, USA T (+1) (212) 963 1234
W www.un.org

The United Nations (UN) is an intergovernmental organisation of member states, dedicated through signature of the UN Charter to the maintenance of international peace and security and the solution of economic, social and political problems through international co-operation.

The UN was founded as a successor to the League of Nations and inherited many of its procedures and institutions. The name 'United Nations' was first used in the Washington Declaration 1942 to describe the 26 states that had allied to fight the Axis powers. The UN Charter developed from discussions at the Moscow Conference of the foreign ministers of China, the UK, the USA and the Soviet Union in 1943. Further progress was made at Dumbarton Oaks, Washington, in 1944 during talks involving the same states. The role of the Security Council was formulated at the Yalta Conference in 1945. The Charter was formally drawn up by 50 allied nations at the San Francisco Conference between April and 26 June 1945, when it was signed. Following ratification the UN came into effect on 24 October 1945, which is celebrated annually as United Nations Day. The UN flag is light blue with the UN emblem centred in white.

The principal organs of the UN are the General Assembly, the Security Council, the Economic and Social Council, the Trusteeship Council, the Secretariat and the International Court of Justice. The Economic and Social Council and the Trusteeship Council are auxiliaries, charged with assisting and advising the General Assembly and Security Council. The official languages used are Arabic, Chinese, English, French, Russian and Spanish. Deliberations at the International Court of Justice are in English and French only.

A Millennium summit was held in New York on 6–8 September 2000 at which the reform of the UN was debated and an attempt was made to redefine its role.

MEMBERSHIP

Membership is open to all countries which accept the Charter and its principle of peaceful co-existence. New members are admitted by the General Assembly on the recommendation of the Security Council. The original membership of 51 states has grown to 191.

Afghanistan; Albania; Algeria; Andorra; Angola; Antigua and Barbuda; Argentina*; Armenia; Australia*; Austria; Azerbaijan; Bahamas; Bahrain; Bangladesh; Barbados; Belarus*; Belgium*; Belize; Benin; Bhutan; Bolivia*; Bosnia-Hercegovina; Botswana; Brazil*; Brunei Darussalam; Bulgaria; Burkina Faso; Burundi; Cambodia; Cameroon; Canada*; Cape Verde; Central African Republic; Chad; Chile*; China*; Colombia*; Comoros; Congo; Costa Rica*; Côte d'Ivoire; Croatia; Cuba*; Cyprus; Czech Republic; Democratic Republic of the Congo; Denmark*; Djibouti; Dominica; Dominican Republic*; East Timor; Ecuador*; Egypt*; El Salvador*; Equatorial Guinea; Eritrea; Estonia; Ethiopia*; Fiji; Finland; France*; Gabon; Gambia; Georgia; Germany; Ghana; Greece*; Grenada; Guatemala*; Guinea; Guinea-Bissau; Guyana; Haiti*; Honduras*; Hungary; Iceland; India*; Indonesia; Iran*; Iraq*; Ireland; Israel; Italy; Jamaica; Japan; Jordan; Kazakhstan; Kenya; Kiribati; Korea, Democratic People's Republic of; Korea, Republic of; Kuwait; Kyrgyzstan; Laos; Latvia; Lebanon*; Lesotho; Liberia*; Libya; Liechtenstein; Lithuania; Luxembourg*; Macedonia; Madagascar; Malawi; Malaysia; Maldives; Mali; Malta; Marshall Islands; Mauritania; Mauritius; Mexico*; Micronesia (Federated States of); Moldova; Monaco; Mongolia; Morocco; Mozambique; Myanmar; Namibia; Nauru; Nepal; Netherlands*; New Zealand*; Nicaragua*; Niger; Nigeria; Norway*; Oman; Pakistan; Palau; Panama*; Papua New Guinea; Paraguay*; Peru*; Philippines*; Poland*; Portugal; Qatar; Romania; Russia*; Rwanda; St Christopher and Nevis; St Lucia; St Vincent and the Grenadines; Samoa; San Marino; São Tomé and Príncipe; Saudi Arabia*; Senegal; Serbia and Montenegro; Seychelles; Sierra Leone; Singapore; Slovakia; Slovenia; Solomon Islands; Somalia; South Africa*; Spain; Sri Lanka; Sudan; Suriname; Swaziland; Sweden; Switzerland; Syrian Arab Republic*;Tajikistan; Tanzania; Thailand; Togo; Tonga; Trinidad and Tobago; Tunisia; Turkey*; Turkmenistan; Tuvalu; Uganda; Ukraine*; United Arab Emirates; United Kingdom*; United States of America*; Uruguay*; Uzbekistan; Vanuatu; Venezuela*; Vietnam; Yemen; Zambia; Zimbabwe.

*Original member (i.e. from 1945). Czechoslovakia, Yugoslavia and the USSR were all original members until their dissolution.

OBSERVERS

Permanent observer status is held by the Holy See. The Palestine Liberation Organisation has special observer status.

THE GENERAL ASSEMBLY

UN Plaza, New York, NY 10017, USA

The General Assembly is the main deliberative organ of the UN. It consists of all members, each entitled to five representatives but having only one vote. The annual session begins on the third Tuesday of September, when the President is elected, and usually continues until mid-December. Special sessions are held on specific issues and emergency special sessions can be called within 24 hours.

The Assembly is empowered to discuss any matter within the scope of the Charter, except when it is under consideration by the Security Council, and to make recommendations. Under the 'uniting for peace' resolution, adopted in 1950, the Assembly may also take action to maintain international peace and security when the Security Council fails to do so because of a lack of unanimity of its permanent members. Important decisions, such as those on peace and security, the election of officers, the budget, etc., need a two-thirds majority. Others need a simple majority. The Assembly has effective power only over the internal operations of the UN itself; external recommendations are not legally binding.

The work of the General Assembly is divided among six main committees, on each of which every member has the right to be represented: disarmament and international security; economic and financial; social, humanitarian and cultural; special political issues and decolonisation (including non-self governing territories); administrative and budgetary; and legal. In addition, the General Assembly appoints ad hoc committees to consider special issues, such as human rights, peacekeeping, disarmament and international law. All committees consider items referred to them by the Assembly and recommend draft resolutions to its plenary meeting.

The Assembly is assisted by a number of functional committees. The General Committee co-ordinates its proceedings and operations, while the Credentials Committee verifies the credentials of representatives. There are also two standing committees, the Advisory Committee on Administration and Budgetary Questions and the Committee on Contributions, which suggests the scale of members' payments to the UN.

President of the General Assembly (2005-6), HE Jean Ping (Gabon)

The Assembly has created a large number of specialised bodies over the years, which are supervised jointly with the Economic and Social Council. They are supported by UN and voluntary contributions from governments, non-governmental organisations and individuals. These organisations include:

CONFERENCE ON DISARMAMENT

Palais des Nations, CH-1211 Geneva 10, Switzerland

The Conference on Disarmament (CD) was established in 1979 as the single multilateral disarmament negotiating forum of the international community. Originally comprising 40 member states, the CD has expanded to 66 members. The Treaty on the Non-Proliferation of Nuclear Weapons entered into force on 5 March 1970 and has so far been ratified by 188 states. A Chemical Weapons Convention was agreed in Paris in 1993 and came into force in April 1997 after being ratified by 87 countries. It bans the use, production, stockpiling and transfer of all chemical weapons. All US and Russian weapons must be destroyed within 15 years of the Convention entering into force and all other states' weapons must be destroyed within ten years.

THE UNITED NATIONS CHILDREN'S FUND (UNICEF)

3 UN Plaza, New York, NY 10017, USA

Established in 1947 to assist children and mothers in the immediate post-war period, UNICEF now concentrates on developing countries. It provides primary healthcare and health education. In particular, UNICEF conducts programmes in oral hydration, immunisation against leading diseases, child growth monitoring and the encouragement of breast-feeding. Its operations are often conducted in co-operation with the World Health Organisation (WHO).

THE UNITED NATIONS DEVELOPMENT PROGRAMME (UNDP)
1 UN Plaza, New York, NY 10017, USA

Established in 1966 from the merger of the UN Expanded Programme of Technical Assistance and the UN Special Fund, UNDP is the central funding agency for economic and social development projects around the world. Much of its annual expenditure is channelled through UN specialised agencies, governments and non-governmental organisations.

THE UNITED NATIONS HIGH COMMISSIONER FOR REFUGEES (UNHCR)
Case Postale 2500, CH-1211 Geneve 2 Depot, Switzerland
T (+41) 22 739 8111

Established in 1951 to protect the rights and interests of refugees, UNHCR organises emergency relief and longer-term solutions, such as voluntary repatriation, local integration or resettlement.

THE UN RELIEF AND WORKS AGENCY FOR PALESTINE REFUGEES IN THE NEAR EAST (UNRWA)
HQ Gaza PO Box 140157, Amman 11814, Jordan
T (+972 8) 677 7333

Established in 1949 to bring relief to the Palestinians displaced by the Arab-Israeli conflict. The UN General Assembly voted to extend the mandate of the UNRWA until 2008.

THE UNITED NATIONS HIGH COMMISSIONER FOR HUMAN RIGHTS
Established in 1993 to secure resepct for, and prevent violations of human rights by engaging in dialogue with governments and international organisations. Responsible for the co-ordination of all UN human rights activities.

THE SECURITY COUNCIL
UN Plaza, New York, NY 10017, USA

The Security Council is the senior arm of the UN and has the primary responsibility for maintaining world peace and security. It consists of 15 members, each with one representative and one vote. There are five permanent members, China, France, Russia, the UK and the USA, and ten non-permanent members. Each of the non-permanent members is elected for a two-year term by a two-thirds majority of the General Assembly and is ineligible for immediate re-election. Five of the elective seats are allocated to Africa and Asia, one to eastern Europe, two to Latin America and two to western Europe and remaining countries. Procedural questions are determined by a majority vote. Other matters require a majority inclusive of the votes of the permanent members; they thus have a right of veto. The abstention of a permanent member does not constitute a veto. The presidency rotates each month by state in (English) alphabetical order. Parties to a dispute, other non-members and individuals can be invited to participate in Security Council debates but are not permitted to vote.

The Security Council is empowered to settle or adjudicate in disputes or situations which threaten international peace and security. It can adopt political, economic and military measures to achieve this end. Any matter considered to be a threat to or breach of the peace or an act of aggression can be brought to the Security Council's attention by any member state or by the Secretary-General. The Charter envisaged members placing at the disposal of the Security Council armed forces and other facilities which would be co-ordinated by the Military Staff Committee, composed of military representatives of the five permanent members. The Security Council is also supported by a Committee of Experts, to advise on procedural and technical matters, and a Committee on Admission of New Members.

Owing to superpower disunity, the Security Council rarely played the decisive role set out in the Charter; the Military Staff Committee was effectively suspended from 1948 until 1990, when a meeting was convened during the Gulf Crisis on the formation and control of UN-supervised armed forces. However, at an extraordinary meeting of the Security Council in January 1992, heads of government laid plans to transform the UN in light of the changed post-Cold War world. The Secretary-General was asked to draw up a report on enhancing the UN's preventive diplomacy, peacemaking and peacekeeping ability. The report, *An Agenda for Peace*, was produced in June 1992 and centred on the establishment of a UN army composed of national contingents on permanent standby, as envisaged at the time of the UN's formation.

PEACEKEEPING FORCES
The Security Council has established a number of peacekeeping forces since its foundation, comprising contingents provided mainly by neutral and non-aligned UN members. Current operations include: the UN Truce Supervision Organisation (UNTSO), Israel, 1948; the UN Military Observer Group in India and Pakistan (UNMOGIP), 1949; the UN Peacekeeping Force in Cyprus (UNFICYP), 1964; the UN Disengagement Observer Force (UNDOF), Golan Heights, Syria, 1974; the UN Interim Force in Lebanon (UNIFIL), 1978; the UN Mission for the Referendum in Western Sahara (MINURSO), 1991; the UN Observer Mission in Georgia (UNOMIG), 1993; the United Nations Interim Administration Mission in Kosovo (UNMIK), 1999; the United Nations Mission in Sierra Leone (UNAMISIL), 1999; the United Nations Organisation Mission in the Democratic Republic of the Congo (MONUC), 1999; the United Nations Mission in Ethiopia and Eritrea (UNMEE), 2000; the United Nations Mission in Cote d'Ivoire (MINUCI), 2003 (replaced by the United Nations Operations in Cote d'Ivoire (UNOCI) in April 2004).

THE ECONOMIC AND SOCIAL COUNCIL
UN Plaza, New York, NY 10017, USA

The Economic and Social Council is responsible under the General Assembly for the economic and social work of the UN and for the co-ordination of the activities of the 14 specialised agencies and other UN bodies. It makes reports and recommendations on economic, social, cultural, educational, health and related matters, often in consultation with non-governmental organisations, passing the reports to the General Assembly and other UN bodies. It also drafts conventions for submission to the Assembly and calls conferences on matters within its remit.

The Council consists of 54 members, 18 of whom are elected annually by the General Assembly for a three-year term. Each has one vote and can be immediately re-elected on retirement. A President is elected annually and is also eligible for re-election. One substantive session is held annually and decisions are reached by simple majority vote of those present.

The Council has established a number of standing committees on particular issues and several commissions. Commissions include: Statistical, Human Rights, Social Development, Sustainable Development, Status of Women, Crime Prevention and Criminal Justice, Narcotic Drugs, Science and Technology for Development and Population; and Regional Economic Commissions for Europe, Asia and the Pacific, Western Asia, Latin America and Africa.

THE TRUSTEESHIP COUNCIL
UN Plaza, New York, NY10017, USA

With the independence of the Republic of Palau in October 1994, all 11 trusteeships have now progressed to independence or merged with neighbouring states and the Trusteeship Council suspended its operations on 1 November 1994.

THE SECRETARIAT
UN Plaza, New York, NY 10017, USA

The Secretariat services the other UN organs and is headed by a Secretary-General elected by a majority vote of the General Assembly on the recommendation of the Security Council. He is assisted by an international staff, chosen to represent the international character of the organisation. The Secretary-General is charged with bringing to the attention of the Security Council any matter which he considers poses a threat to international peace and security. He may also bring other matters to the attention of the General Assembly and other UN bodies and may be entrusted by them with additional duties. As chief administrator to the UN, the Secretary-General is present in person or via representatives at all meetings of the other five main organs of the UN. He may also act as an impartial mediator in disputes between member states.

The power and influence of the Secretary-General has been determined largely by the character of the office-holder and by the state of relations between the superpowers. The thaw in these relations since the mid-1980s has increased the effectiveness of the UN, particularly in its attempts to intervene in international disputes. It helped to end the Iran-Iraq war and sponsored peace in Central America. Following Iraq's invasion of Kuwait in 1990 the UN took its first collective security action since the Korean War. Conflicts in Cyprus, East Timor, Libya, Nigeria and Western Sahara have been successfully prevented from escalating or spreading during Kofi Annan's time in office. In addition to maintenance of international security, ending poverty and inequality, improving education, reducing HIV/AIDS and safeguarding the environment were some of the issues outlined in the UN Millennium Report.

Secretary-General, Kofi Annan, apptd 1996 (Ghana)
Deputy Secretary-General, Louise Frechette (Canada)

FORMER SECRETARIES-GENERAL

1946–53	Trygve Lie (Norway)
1953–61	Dag Hammarskjöld (Sweden)
1961–71	U Thant (Burma)
1971–81	Kurt Waldheim (Austria)
1981–91	Javier Pérez de Cuéllar (Peru)
1991–96	Boutros Boutros-Ghali (Egypt)

INTERNATIONAL COURT OF JUSTICE
The Peace Palace, NL-2517 KJ The Hague, The Netherlands

The International Court of Justice is the principal judicial organ of the UN. The Statute of the Court is an integral part of the Charter and all members of the UN are *ipso facto* parties to it. The Court is composed of 15 judges, elected by both the General Assembly and the Security Council for nine-year terms which are renewable. Judges may deliberate over cases in which their country is involved. If no judge on the bench is from a country which is a party to a dispute under consideration, that party may designate a judge to participate *ad hoc* in that particular deliberation. If any party to a case fails to adhere to the judgment of the Court, the other party may have recourse to the Security Council.

President, Shi Jiuyong (China)
Vice-President, Raymond Ranjeva (Madagascar)
Judges, Rosalyn Higgins (UK); Pieter H. Kooijmans (Netherlands); Abdul G. Koroma (Sierra Leone); Gonzalo Parra-Aranguren (Venezuela); José Francisco Rezek (Brazil); Vladlen S. Vereshchetin (Russia); Awn Shawkat Al-Khasawneh (Jordan); Thomas Buergenthal (USA); Ronny Abraham (France); Nabil Elaraby (Egypt); Hisashi Owada (Japan); Bruno Simma (Germany); Peter Tomka (Slovakia)

INTERNATIONAL CRIMINAL TRIBUNAL FOR THE FORMER YUGOSLAVIA
Churchill Plein 1, PO Box 13888, NL-2501 EW The Hague, The Netherlands

In February 1993, the Security Council voted to establish a war crimes tribunal for the former Yugoslavia to hear cases covering grave breaches of the Geneva Conventions and crimes against humanity. The Court was inaugurated in November 1993 in The Hague with 11 judges elected by the UN General Assembly from 11 states, divided into two trial chambers of three judges each and an appeal chamber of five judges. The court is unable to force suspects to stand trial but is empowered to pass verdicts in the absence of suspects and can put suspects under an 'act of accusation' which prevents them from leaving their own country.

In October 1995, the tribunal formally charged the Bosnian Serb leaders Radovan Karadzic and Gen. Ratko Mladic, the Croatian Serb President Milan Martic and 21 others with genocide and crimes against humanity. By January 1997 only one of the 75 suspected war criminals to be indicted had been imprisoned. In May 1999, the tribunal formally charged the Yugoslav President Slobodan Milosevic, the Serbian President Milan Milutinovic, two other Serb politicians and the Yugoslav armed forces chief of staff Dragoljub Ojdanic.

For up to date information regarding indictments and judgments of the Tribunal, visit www.un.org/icty.

President, Theodor Meron (United States)

INTERNATIONAL CRIMININAL TRIBUNAL FOR RWANDA

Following serious violations of humanitarian law in Rwanda, the United Nations Security Council created the International Criminal Tribunal for Rwanda (ICTR) on 8 November 1994. The purpose of this measure was to contribute to the process of national reconciliation in Rwanda and to the maintenance of peace in the region. The tribunal was established for the prosecution of persons responsible for genocide and other serious violations of international humanitarian law committed in the territory of Rwanda between 1 January 1994 and 31 December 1994. It may also deal with the prosecution of Rwandan citizens responsible for genocide and other such violations of international law committed in the territory of neighbouring states during the same period.

President, Judge Erik Mose (Norway)

UNITED NATIONS MONITORING, VERIFICATION AND INSPECTION COMMISSION

ALCOA Building, 866 United Nations Plaza, Room A-610, 48th St., New York, NY, 10017 USA T (+1) (212) 963 3022
E info@unmovic.org W www.unmovic.org

The United Nations Monitoring, Verification and Inspection Commission (UNMOVIC), was created by UN Security Council Resolution 1284, adopted in December 1999.

UNMOVIC is mandated to verify Iraq's compliance with its obligation not to possess or acquire weapons of mass destruction (biological or chemical weapons of mass destruction, together with ballistic missiles with a target distance of more than 150 km), to destroy all research, development and production facilities and to desist from the future development or acquisition of such weapons and operate a monitoring and verification programme to ensure that prohibited items and programmes are not reactivated.

In January 2003, three months after UN weapons inspectors were re-admitted, Dr Blix stated that Iraq had failed to disarm, greatly strengthening the American and British case for war. He insisted, however, that the weapons inspectors be given more time. US President George Bush presented the deadline of 17 March 2003 for Iraq to disarm and the UN removed all their staff from the region. A second UN resolution was not granted and on 19 March 2003 air strikes led by the USA began against Baghdad without UN backing. In the thirteenth quarterly report of UNMOVIC, covering March to May 2003, Hans Blix stated that the Commission had at no point during the inspections in Iraq found evidence of the continuation or resumption of programmes of weapons of mass destruction or significant quantity of proscribed items – whether pre-1991 or after. He stressed that this did not mean that such items could not exist as there remained long lists of unaccounted items.

In resolution 1483 (May 2003) lifting Iraqi economic sanctions, the Security Council declared its intention to revisit the mandate of UNMOVIC, which remains ready to resume its work in Iraq.

Executive Chairman (acting), Demetrius Perricos (Greece)

UK MISSION TO THE UN

1 Dag Hammarskjöld Plaza, 885 Second Avenue, New York, NY 10017, USA T (+1) (212) 745 9200 E uk@un.int
W www.ukun.org
Permanent Representative to the United Nations and

Representative on the Security Council, Sir Emyr Jones Parry, KCMG, apptd 2003
Deputy Permanent Representative, Adam Thomson

UK MISSION TO THE OFFICE OF THE UN AND OTHER INTERNATIONAL ORGANISATIONS IN GENEVA

37–39 rue de Vermont, CH-1211 Geneva 20, Switzerland
T (+41) (22) 918 2300 E mission.uk@ties.itu.int
Permanent UK Representative, Nicholas Thorne, CMG, apptd 2003
Deputy Permanent Representative, Julian Metcalfe

UK MISSION TO THE UN IN VIENNA

Jaurčsgasse 12, A-1030 Vienna, Austria
UK Permanent Representative, P. R Jenkins, apptd 2001
Deputy Permanent Representative, T. J. Andrews

REGIONAL UN INFORMATION CENTRE

Block C, Level 5, Residence Palace, 155 Rue de la Loi, Wetstraat 155, Brussels 1040, Belgium
T (+32) 2287-4019 F (+32) 2502-4061
E info@runic-europe.org W www.runic-europe.org

UNITED NATIONS EDUCATIONS, SCIENTIFIC AND CULTURAL ORGANISATION

7 place de Fontenoy, F-75352 Paris 07 SP, France
T (+33) (1) 4568 1000 E spokesperson@unesco.org
W www.unesco.orq

The United Nations Educational, Scientific and Cultural Organisation (UNESCO) was established in 1946. It promotes collaboration among its member states in education, science, culture and communication. It aims to further a universal respect for human rights, justice and the rule of law, without distinction of race, sex, language or religion, in accordance with the UN Charter.

UNESCO runs a number of programmes to improve education and extend access to it. It provides assistance to ensure the free flow of information and its wider and better balanced dissemination without any obstacle to freedom of expression, and to maintain cultural heritage in the face of development. It fosters research and study in all areas of the social and environmental sciences.

UNESCO had 191 member states and six associate members as at June 2005. The General Conference, consisting of representatives of all the members, meets biennially to decide the programme and the budget. It elects the 58-member executive board, which supervises operations, and appoints a director-general, who heads a secretariat responsible for carrying out the organisation's programmes. In most member states national commissions liaise with UNESCO to execute its programme. The UK withdrew from UNESCO in 1985; it rejoined on 1 July 1997.

Director-General, Koichiro Matsuura (Japan)

UNITED NATIONS INDUSTRIAL DEVELOPMENT ORGANISATION

Vienna International Centre, Wagramerstrasse 5, PO Box 300, A-1400 Vienna, Austria T (+43) (1) 260 260 E unido@unido.org
W www.unido.org

The United Nations Industrial Development Organisation (UNIDO) was established in 1966 by the UN General Assembly to act as the central co-ordinating body for industrial activities within the UN. It became a UN specialised agency in 1985. UNIDO aims to help developing countries and those with economies in transition to develop sustainable industrialisation by concentrating on economic competitiveness, environmental awareness and employment issues both in the public and private sectors. UNIDO designs and implements programmes to support industrial development in individual member states and offers specialised support for programme development.

UNIDO had 171 members as at June 2005. It is funded by regular and operational budgets, together with contributions for technical co-operation activities. The regular budget is derived from member states' contributions. Technical co-operation is funded mainly through voluntary contributions from donor countries and institutions and by intergovernmental and non-governmental organisations. A General Conference of all the members meets biennially to discuss strategy and policy, approve the budget (2004–5, regular budget €144 million) and elect the director-general. The Industrial Development Board is composed of members from 53 member states and reviews the work programme and the budget, which is prepared by the Programme and Budget Committee of 27 member states.

Director-General, Carlos Magarinos (Argentina)
Permanent UK Representative, Peter Jenkins, British
   Embassy, Vienna

UNIVERSAL POSTAL UNION

Weltpoststrasse 4, CH-3000 Bern 15, Switzerland
T (+41) (31) 350 3111 E info@upu.int W www.upu.int

The Universal Postal Union (UPU) was established by the Treaty of Bern 1874, taking effect from 1875, and became a UN specialised agency in 1948. The UPU is an intergovernmental organisation that exists to form and regulate a single postal territory of all member countries for the reciprocal exchange of correspondence without discrimination. With a total of 190 members, it also assists and advises on the improvement of postal services.

A Universal Postal Congress is the UPU's supreme authority and meets every five years. A Council of Administration composed of 41 members meets annually to ensure continuity between congresses, study regulatory developments and broad policies, approve the budget and examine proposed Treaty changes. A Postal Operations Council, composed of 40 members elected by the Congress, meets annually to deal with specific technical and operational issues. A new body, the Consultative Committee, was created in 2004. It represents the interests of the wider international postal sector and provides a forum for dialogue between postal industry stakeholders. The Consultative Committee consists of non-governmental organisations representing customers, worker's organisations and suppliers of goods and services as well as international mailers and printers. The three UPU bodies are served by the International Bureau, a secretariat headed by a director-general.

Funding is provided by members according to a scale of contributions drawn up by the Congress. The Council of Administration sets the budget which amounts to approximately SFr 35,000,000 per year.

Director-General, Edouard Dayan (France)

UNREPRESENTED NATIONS AND PEOPLES ORGANISATION

PO Box 85878, 2508 CN The Hague, The Netherlands
T (+31) (70) 364 6504 E unpo@unpo.org W www.unpo.org

The Unrepresented Nations and Peoples Organisation (UNPO) was founded in 1991 to offer an international forum for occupied nations, indigenous peoples and national minorities who are not represented in other international organisations.

UNPO does not aim to represent these nations and peoples, but rather to assist and empower them to represent themselves more effectively, and provides professional services and facilities as well as education and training in the fields of diplomacy, international and human rights law, democratic processes, institution building, conflict management and resolution, and environmental protection.

Participation is open to all nations and peoples who are inadequately represented at the United Nations and who declare allegiance to five principles relating to the right of self-determination of all peoples, human rights, democracy, non-violence and the rejection of terrorism, and protection of the natural environment. Applicants must show that they constitute a 'nation or people' and that the organisation applying for membership is representative of that nation or people.

As at June 2005, there were 61 full members and five former members, who have achieved full independence.

Director-General, Marino Busdachin (Croatia)

WESTERN EUROPEAN UNION

Rue de l'Association 15, 1000 Brussels, Belgium
T (+32) (2) 500 4412
E secretariatgeneral@weu.int W www.weu.int

Western European Union (WEU) originated as the Brussels Treaty Organisation (BTO) established under the Treaty of Brussels, signed in 1948 by Belgium, France, Luxembourg, the Netherlands and the UK, to provide collective self-defence and economic and social collaboration amongst its signatories. The BTO was modified to become WEU in 1954 with the admission of West Germany and Italy.

From the late 1970s onwards efforts were made to add a security dimension to the EC's European Political Co-operation. Opposition to these efforts from Denmark, Greece and Ireland led the remaining EC countries, all WEU members, to decide to reactivate the Union in 1984. Members committed themselves to harmonising their views on defence and security and developing a European security identity, while bearing in mind the importance of transatlantic relations. Portugal and Spain joined WEU in 1988, and Greece became a full member in 1995.

In 1991, the EU Maastricht Treaty committed the European Community to the establishment of a Common Foreign and Security Policy (CFSP). WEU was designated as the future defence component of the European Union and member states of the EU who were not already members of WEU were invited to join or become observers. In November 1992 WEU's role as the common security dimension of the EU was enhanced when WEU ministers signed a declaration with remaining European NATO members to give them various forms of WEU membership. Iceland, Norway and Turkey became associate members; the Republic of Ireland, Denmark, Austria, Finland and Sweden became observers. In 1994 WEU reached agreements with Estonia, Latvia, Lithuania, Poland, the Czech Republic, Slovakia, Hungary, Romania and Bulgaria, under which they all became associate partners; Slovenia became an associate partner in 1996. The Czech Republic, Hungary and Poland, who had been associate partners, became associate members in 1999, following their accession to NATO.

WEU has worked in close co-operation with the Atlantic Alliance, and relations between WEU and NATO were developed on the basis of transparency and complementarity. The 1993 Luxembourg Declaration states that WEU is ready to participate in the future work of the NATO Alliance as its European pillar, and at the Atlantic Alliance summit in January 1994, NATO expressed its readiness to make Alliance assets and capabilities available for WEU operations. In June 1996, NATO foreign and defence ministers approved the Combined Joint Task Force (CJTF) concept and the elaboration of multinational European command arrangements for WEU-led operations.

A Council of Ministers (foreign and defence) has met biannually in the presiding country; the presidency rotates biannually, and from 1999 the sequence of WEU presidencies has been harmonised with those of the EU Council of Ministers. A Permanent Council of the member states' permanent representatives meets in Brussels. The Permanent Council is chaired by the secretary-general and serviced by the secretariat.

In 1999, NATO and the EU decided to establish a direct relationship; the EU committed itself to ensuring that it was able to take decisions on conflict prevention and crisis management and NATO agreed to give the EU access to its collective assets and capabilities for operations in which NATO as a whole was not engaged. WEU's crisis management functions were transferred to the EU in July 2001. The necessary WEU functions and structures remain in place to enable member states to fulfil commitments arising from the modified Brussels Treaty including those relating to collective defence and the institutional relationship with WEU parliamentary assembly.

The Assembly of WEU is composed of 115 parliamentarians of member states and meets twice annually in Paris to debate matters within the scope of the revised Brussels Treaty.

Presidency Luxembourg, United Kingdom (2005); Belgium, United Kingdom (2006)

Secretary-General, Javier Solana Madariaga (Spain)

UK Representative on the Permanent Council, Julian King

ASSEMBLY, 43 avenue du Président Wilson, F-75775 Paris Cedex 16, France

WORLD BANK GROUP

1818 H Street NW, Washington DC 20433, USA
T (+1) (202) 473 1000 E feedback@worldbank.org
W www.worldbank.org

The World Bank Group was founded in 1944 and is one of the world's largest sources of development assistance. The Bank has 184 members. Originally directed towards post-war reconstruction in Europe, the Bank subsequently turned towards assisting less-developed countries and is currently working in more than 100 developing countries. The Bank works with government agencies, non-governmental organisations and the private sector to formulate assistance strategies. Its local offices implement the Bank's programme in each country. It has offices in more than 100 countries.

The Bank is owned by the governments of member countries and its capital is subscribed by its members. It finances its lending primarily from borrowing in world capital markets, and derives a substantial contribution to its resources from its retained earnings and the repayment of loans. The interest rate on its loans is calculated in relation to its cost of borrowing. Loans generally have a grace period of five years and are repayable within 20 years.

The World Bank Group consists of five institutions. The International Bank for Reconstruction and Development (IBRD) has 184 members and provides loans and development assistance to middle-income countries and creditworthy poorer countries (total loans for 2004 US$11 billion. The International Finance Corporation (IFC) has 176 members and promotes private sector investment in developing member countries by mobilising domestic and foreign capital (total loans for 2004 US$4.8 billion). The International Development Association (IDA) has 165 members and performs the same function as the World Bank but primarily to less-developed countries and on terms that bear less heavily on their balance of payments than IBRD loans (total loans for 2004 US$9 billion). The Multilateral Investment Guarantee Agency (MIGA) has 164 members and promotes foreign direct investment in developing states by providing guarantees to potential investors and advisory services to developing member countries (total guarantees issued in 2004 were US$1.1 billion). The International Centre for Settlement of Investment Disputes (ICSID) has 140 members and provides facilities for the settlement by conciliation or arbitration of investment disputes between foreign investors and their host countries.

The IBRD and its affiliates are financially and legally distinct but share headquarters. The IBRD is headed by a board of governors, consisting of one governor and one alternate governor appointed by each member country. Twenty-four executive directors exercise all powers of the Bank except those reserved to the board of governors. The president, elected by the executive directors, conducts the business of the Bank, assisted by an international staff. Membership in both the IFC and the IDA is open to all IBRD countries. The IDA is administered by the same staff as the Bank; the IFC has its own personnel but draws on the IBRD for administrative and other support. All share the same president.

President, Paul Wolfowitz (USA)

UK OFFICE, New Zealand House, 15th Floor, Haymarket, London SW1Y 4TE T 020-7930 8511

WORLD CUSTOMS ORGANISATION

Rue de Marche 30, B-1210, Brussels, Belgium
T (+32) 2209 9211
E information@wcoomd.org W www.wcoomd.org

The World Customs Organisation (WCO) is an independent body that works to enhance the effectiveness and efficiency of customs administrations world-wide. By developing the Harmonised Commodity Description and Coding System, the WCO introduced a universal goods classification and revenue collection method. The WCO also administers the World Trade Organisation Valuation Agreement.

With 165 member governments that process more than 95 per cent of international trade, the WCO is organised into a forum where each member has one representative and one vote. The WCO is directed by a council and a policy commission. Locally recruited staff are used to provide secretarial, translation, interpretation and general support services.

Secretary-General, Michel Danet (France)

WORLD HEALTH ORGANISATION

20 Avenue Appia, CH-1211 Geneva 27, Switzerland
T (+41) (22) 791 2111 E info@who.intch W www.who.ch

The UN International Health Conference, held in 1946,

established the World Health Organisation (WHO) as a UN specialised agency, with effect from 1948. It is dedicated to attaining the highest possible level of health for all. It collaborates with member governments, UN agencies and other bodies to improve health standards, control communicable diseases and promote all aspects of family and environmental health. It seeks to raise the standards of health teaching and training, and promotes research through collaborating research centres worldwide.

WHO has 192 members and is governed by the annual World Health Assembly of members which meets to set policy, approve the budget, appoint a director-general, and adopt health conventions and regulations. It also elects 32 members who designate one expert to serve on the executive board. The board effects the programme, suggests initiatives and is empowered to deal with emergencies. A secretariat, headed by the director-general, supervises the activities of six regional offices.

Director-General, Dr Jong-Wook Lee (Republic of Korea)

WORLD INTELLECTUAL PROPERTY ORGANISATION

34 chemin des Colombettes, Geneva, Switzerland
T (+41) (22) 338 8181 / 9111 E information.centre@wipo.int
W www.wipo.int

The World Intellectual Property Organisation (WIPO) was established in 1967 by the Stockholm Convention, which entered into force in 1970. In addition to that Convention, WIPO administers 23 treaties, the principal ones being the Paris Convention for the Protection of Industrial Property and the Bern Convention for the Protection of Literary and Artistic Works. WIPO became a UN specialised agency in 1974.

WIPO promotes the protection of intellectual property throughout the world through co-operation among states, and the administration of various 'Unions', each founded on a multilateral treaty and dealing with the legal and administrative aspects of intellectual property.

Intellectual property comprises two main branches: industrial property (inventions, trademarks, industrial designs and appellations of origin); and copyright (literary, musical, photographic, audiovisual and artistic works, etc.). WIPO also assists creative intellectual activity and facilitates technology transfer, particularly to developing countries.

WIPO had 182 members as at June 2005. The biennial session of all its governing bodies sets policy, a programme and a budget. A separate International Union for the Protection of New Varieties of Plants (UPOV), established by convention in 1961, is linked to WIPO. It has 58 members.

Director-General, Dr Kamil Idris (Sudan)

WORLD METEOROLOGICAL ORGANISATION

7 bis, avenue de la Paix, PO Box 2300, CH-1211 Geneva 2, Switzerland T (+41) (22) 730 8111 E wmo@gateway.wmo.ch
W www.wmo.int

The World Meteorological Organisation (WMO) was established in 1950 and became a UN specialised agency in 1951, succeeding the International Meteorological Organisation founded in 1873. It facilitates co-operation in the establishment of networks for making meteorological, climatological, hydrological and geophysical observations, as well as their exchange, processing and standardisation, and assists technology transfer, training and research. It also fosters collaboration between meteorological and hydrological services, and furthers the application of meteorology to aviation, shipping, environment, water problems, agriculture and the mitigation of natural disasters.

The WMO had 187 member states and six member territories as at June 2005. Six regional associations are responsible for the co-ordination of activities within their own regions. There are also eight technical commissions, which study meteorological and hydrological problems, establish methodology and procedures, and make recommendations to the executive council and the congress. The supreme authority is the World Meteorological Congress of member states and member territories, which meets every four years to determine general policy, make recommendations and set a budget (SFr 253.8 million for 2004–7). It also elects 27 members of the 37-member executive council, the other members being the president and three vice-presidents of the WMO, and the presidents of the six regional associations, who are ex-officio members. The council supervises the implementation of congress decisions, initiates studies and makes recommendations on matters needing international action. The secretariat is headed by a secretary-general, appointed by the congress.

Secretary-General, Michel Jarraud (France)

WORLD TOURISM ORGANISATION

T (+34) 91567 8100 E omt@world-tourism.org
W www.world-tourism.org

Originally formed in 1925 as the International Congress of Official Tour Associations, the World Tourism Organisation (WTO) was officially launched in 1975 as an intergovernmental body that acts as an executing agency of the United Nations Development Programme (UNDP). Primarily concerned with developing public and private sector partnerships, the WTO also promotes the Global Code of Ethics for Tourism, a framework of policy aimed at tour operators, governments, labour organisations and travellers. There are 145 member states, seven associate member states and two states with observer status.

The General Assembly is the principal gathering of the WTO and meets every two years in order to approve policy and budget. Every four years the Assembly will elect a secretary-general. The executive council is WTO's governing board and meets twice a year to ensure the Organisation adheres to policy and budget. It is composed of 27 members of the General Assembly in a ratio of one to five full members. As host country of WTO's headquarters, Spain has a permanent seat on the executive council.

Secretary-General, Francesco Frangialli (France)

WORLD TRADE ORGANISATION

Centre William Rappard, 154 rue de Lausanne,
1211 CH-Geneva 21, Switzerland T (+41) 22 739 5111
E enquiries@wto.org W www.wto.org

The World Trade Organisation was established on 1 January 1995 as the successor to the General Agreement on Tariffs and Trade (GATT). GATT was established in 1948 as an interim agreement until the charter of a new international trade organisation could be drafted by a committee of the UN Economic and Social Council and ratified by member states. The charter was never ratified and GATT became the only regime for the regulation of world trade, evolving its own rules and procedures.

GATT was dedicated to the expansion of non-discriminatory international trade and progressively extended free trade via 'rounds' of multilateral negotiations. Eight rounds were concluded: Geneva (1947), Annecy (1948), Torquay (1950), Geneva (1956), Dillon (1960–1), Kennedy (1964–7), Tokyo (1973–9) and Uruguay (1986–94). The Final Act of the Uruguay Round was signed by trade ministers from the 128 GATT negotiating states and the EU in Marrakesh, Morocco, on 15 April 1994. It established the World Trade Organisation (WTO) to supersede GATT and implement the Uruguay Round agreements. The implementation of the Uruguay Round measures in 2002 resulted in a reduction on duties on manufactured goods from 40 per cent in the 1940s to 3 per cent. New talks on agriculture and services began in 2000 and were incorporated into a broader agenda launched at the 2001 Ministerial Conference in Doha, Qatar.

The WTO is the legal and institutional foundation of the multilateral trading system. It provides the contractual obligations determining how governments frame and implement trade policy and provides the forum for the debate, negotiation and adjudication of trade problems. The WTO's principal aims are to liberalise world trade and place it on a secure basis, and it seeks to achieve this partly by an agreed set of trade rules and market access agreements and partly through further trade liberalisation negotiations. The WTO also administers and implements a further 29 multilateral agreements in fields such as agriculture, textiles and clothing, services, government procurement, rules of origin and intellectual property.

The highest authority of the WTO is the Ministerial Conference composed of all members, which meets at least once every two years. The General Council meets as required and acts on behalf of the Ministerial Conference in regard to the regular working of the WTO. Composed of all members, the General Council also convenes in two particular forms: as the Dispute Settlement Body, dealing with disputes between members arising from the Uruguay Round Final Act; and as the Trade Policy Review Body, conducting regular reviews of the trade policies of members. A secretariat of 500 staff headed by a Director-General services WTO bodies and provides trade performance and trade policy analysis.

As at June 2005 there were 148 WTO members. The WTO budget for 2005 was US$137.8 million, with members' contributions calculated on the basis of their share of the total trade conducted by WTO members. The official languages of the WTO are English, French and Spanish.

Director-General, Pascal Lamy

Permanent UK Representative, Simon Fuller, 37–39 rue de Vermont, CH-1211 Geneva 20

COUNTRIES OF THE WORLD A–Z

Definitions and Abbreviations

est. = estimate

Ψ = seaport.

(m) = male; (f) = female.

LIFE EXPECTANCY figures are averages for males and females.

INFANT MORTALITY RATE = total number of deaths of male and female infants under one year old.

HIV / AIDS ADULT PREVALENCE = estimate of the percentage of the total adult population (aged 15–49) living with HIV / AIDS.

POPULATION BELOW POVERTY LINE – although strict definitions of poverty vary considerably between nations, this figure represents the percentage of the adult population whose income is less than US$1 per day.

GROSS ENROLMENT RATIO is the ratio of total enrolment, regardless of age, to the population of the age group that officially corresponds to the level of education shown.

Death Penalty:

No = abolished for all crimes (year in which death penalty was abolished in parenthesis). This also includes 'abolitionists in practice', i.e. countries that retain the death penalty but have not executed anybody in the last ten years.

Yes* = abolished but retained for exceptional circumstances (i.e. crimes committed under military law).

Yes = used as a legal form of punishment.

Paramilitaries are not included in the total military personnel figure for each country, where separated by a semicolon.

Sources: Amnesty International; *CIA World Factbook 2005*; *IMF International Financial Statistics Yearbook 2005*; *World Development Indicators 2004* (World Bank); www.peopleinpower.com; *The Military Balance 2004-5*; *The Diplomatic Service List 2005*

AFGHANISTAN

Afğānistān (Pushtu) / *Afqânestân (Dari) Islamic Republic of Afghanistan*

AREA – 647,497 sq. km. Neighbours: Iran (west), Pakistan (east and south), Tajikistan, Uzbekistan and Turkmenistan (north), China (north-east)

POPULATION – 28,513,677 (2004 est.): Pushtuns (44 per cent) predominate in the south and west; Tajiks (25 per cent); Hazaras (10 per cent) in the centre; Uzbeks (8 per cent) in the north; Aimaqs (4 per cent); Baluchis (0.5 per cent). The principal languages are Dari (a form of Persian) and Pushtu

CAPITAL – Kabul (population, 2,678,000, 2002 est.)

MAJOR CITIES – Herat; Jalalabad; Kandahar; Mazar-e-Sharif

CURRENCY – Afghani (Af) of 100 puls

NATIONAL DAY – 19 August

NATIONAL FLAG – Three vertical stripes of black, red and green with the royal arms and Arabic device 'There is no God but Allah and Muhammad is His Messenger' in the centre

MORTALITY RATE (per 1,000 population) – 21.12 (2004 est.)

HIV / AIDS ADULT PREVALENCE – 0.01 (2001 est.)

DEATH PENALTY – Yes

POPULATION GROWTH RATE – 4.92 per cent (2004 est.)

CLIMATE AND TERRAIN

Mountains, chief among which are the Hindu Kush, cover three-quarters of the landlocked country, with plains in the north and south-west. Elevation extremes range from 5,143 m at the highest point (in the Hindu Kush) to 258 m at the lowest (Nowshak). There are three great river basins, the Amu Dar'ya (Oxus), Helmand, and Kabul. Natural hazards are flooding, drought and earthquakes. The climate is arid to semi-arid, with extreme temperatures. Summers are hot and dry and the winters cold with heavy snowfalls, particularly in the northern mountains. Annual rainfall varies between 101 mm and 406 mm per year. The temperatures in Kabul range between −22°C in January to 39°C in June.

HISTORY AND POLITICS

Afghanistan first became a nation in 1747 under Ahmad Shah Durrani. Britain and Russia vied to bring the country into their sphere of influence in the 19th and early 20th centuries, but it remained independent and the feudal monarchy survived until after the Second World War, when the constitution became more liberal. The king was deposed in 1973 and a republic was formed. After a coup in 1978 a communist government took power, and Muslim guerrilla (mujahidin) resistance began. The government was overthrown in a further coup in 1979 that prompted an invasion by the Soviet Union, which installed a pro-Soviet government. The mujahidin, with US backing, fought against Soviet forces, which withdrew in 1989, and against Afghan government forces until the government collapsed in 1992. Mujahidin forces overran Kabul and declared an Islamic state. However, factionalism led to continued fighting until the rise from 1994 of the Taliban (armed Islamic students), which extended its power across more than 90 per cent of the country by 1998 and imposed strict Shari'ah law.

The Taliban allowed al-Qa'eda to base terrorist training camps in Afghanistan, and its refusal to hand over Osama bin Laden and other al-Qa'eda leaders after the 11 September 2001 terrorist attacks on the USA led to the regime's overthrow in 2001 by a US-led international coalition, supported by the Northern Alliance, an alliance of the four main mujahidin factions. A multi-ethnic interim government under Hamid Karzai was installed in December 2001. Karzai was elected transitional president by a *Loya Jirga* (tribal council) in June 2002 and appointed a transitional government, which held office until October 2004. Karzai was elected president for a five-year term, with 55.4 per cent of the vote, in a direct presidential election on 9 October 2004 that was marred by allegations of vote-rigging. He appointed a new government on 23 December 2004.

Attempts to locate and capture Osama bin Laden and Mullah Omar, the Taliban leader, were unsuccessful and pockets of al-Qa'eda and Taliban forces remain at large. The government does not control the whole of the country because of factionalism and Taliban-inspired violence, despite the presence of a 5,000-strong UN peacekeeping force, the International Security Assistance Force (ISAF), and other foreign troops.

POLITICAL SYSTEM
Power has been exercised since December 2001 by the executive, headed by Hamid Karzai. A Loya Jirga approved the draft constitution in January 2004; this Loya Jirga had 500 members, 450 elected by the 15,000 electors registered to vote at the 2002 Loya Jirga, and 50 appointed by the president. The former legislature was abolished in 1992; a new legislature is to be established following legislative elections held on 18 September 2005.

HEAD OF STATE
President, Hamid Karzai, *elected* 9 October 2004, *sworn in* 7 December 2004
Vice-Presidents, Ahmed Zia Massood; Karim Khalili

SELECTED GOVERNMENT MEMBERS *as at July 2005*
Defence, Gen. Abdurrahim Wardak
Foreign Affairs, Abdullah Abdullah
Finance, Anwar-ul Haq Ahadi

EMBASSY OF THE ISLAMIC REPUBLIC OF AFGHANISTAN
31 Princes Gate, London SW7 1QQ
T 020-7589 8891
E info@afghanembassy.co.uk
Ambassador Extraordinary and Plenipotentiary, HE Ahmad Wali Masud

BRITISH EMBASSY
15th Street Roundabout Wazir Akbar Khan
PO Box 334, Kabul T (+93) (0) (70) 102250
E britishembassy.kabul.gov.uk
Ambassador Extraordinary and Plenipotentiary, HE Rosalind Marsden

ECONOMY AND TRADE
The economy has been devastated by the political upheavals of the last 30 years. During this period, up to one-third of the population fled the country, with Pakistan and Iraq sheltering a combined peak of 4–6 million refugees. Afghanistan's problems were compounded by three successive years of drought, and by the end of 2000 one million people were thought to be close to starvation. However, by October 2002 1.7 million refugees had returned to the country.

While the traditional industries of agriculture, sheep rearing and the manufacture of silk, woollen hair cloths and carpets have diminished, the narcotics trade has grown. Opium production, banned under the Taliban, rose from 185 tonnes in 2001 to 2,700 tonnes in 2002. It is currently estimated that 80–90 per cent of heroin consumed in Europe comes from Afghan opium. Salt, silver, copper, coal, iron, lead, rubies, lapis lazuli, gold, chrome, barite, uranium and talc can be found in the region.

International efforts to rebuild Afghanistan were addressed at the Tokyo Donors Conference for Afghan Reconstruction in January 2002, when US$4,500 million was pledged. Further World Bank and other aid was given in 2003. The eradication of the illegal opium trade and the search for oil and gas resources in the northern region are two major long-term objectives.

In the past, exports have been Persian lambskins (Karakul), dried fruits, nuts, cotton, raw wool, carpets, spice and natural gas. Imports are chiefly oil, cotton yarn and piece goods, tea, sugar, machinery and transport equipment.

GDP – US$19,000 million (2002); US$700 per capita (2002)
ANNUAL AVERAGE GROWTH OF GDP – 7.5 per cent (2004 est.)
INFLATION RATE – 5.2 per cent (2003 est.)
IMPORTS – US$1,300 million (2001)
EXPORTS – US$1,200 million (2001)

Trade with UK	2003	2004
Imports from UK	£9,871,000	£14,191
Exports to UK	467,000	2,219

TRANSPORT INFRASTRUCTURE
Main roads run from Kabul to Kandahar, Herat, Maimana via Mazar-e Sharif and Faizabad. Roads cross the border with Pakistan at Chaman and via the Khyber Pass, and there are roads from Herat to the borders of Turkmenistan and Iran. Much of the country's road system has been damaged during the fighting, although reconstruction work began in 2002. There are two international airports, at Kabul and Kandahar, and about 1,200 km of inland waterways.

EDUCATION
Education is free and nominally compulsory, elementary schools having been established in most centres; there are secondary schools in large urban areas and four universities, in Kabul, Jalalabad, Balkh and Herat. In March 2002, schools reopened to 1.5 million children, many of whom had not received schooling for six years under the Taliban.

ILLITERACY RATE – (m) 48.1 per cent; (f) 78.1 per cent (2000)
GROSS ENROLMENT RATIO (percentage of relevant age group) – primary 23 per cent (2002); secondary 12 per cent (2002)

MEDIA AND CULTURE
Afghanistan's media was seriously restricted under Taliban rule. However, in late 2001 Radio Afghanistan returned to the air in Kabul after the Taliban deserted the capital, and within days Kabul TV also began broadcasting. Relays of foreign radio stations are available in Kabul, including the BBC, Radio France Internationale, the German-run Voice of Freedom, US-funded broadcasts from Radio Free Afghanistan and the Voice of America, and Radio Azadi run by the International Security Assistance Force (ISAF). Local radio stations include Radio Afghanistan, Erat Radio Khilid Kabul (RKK) and Arman FM. Television services are mainly provided by the state-run TV Afghanistan, but ownership of television sets is very limited (100,000 in 1999). Afghanistan's press now enjoys considerable freedom of expression, although print runs are small. Titles include *Hewad*, *Anis* and the Northern Alliance organ *Payam-e Mojahed*.

Due to prolonged armed conflicts, much of the outstanding cultural heritage has been destroyed. During the civil war the Kabul Museum was looted, and treasures such as the Kunduz Hoard (silver Greek-style coins) were stolen. This was followed during the Taliban regime by systematic ideological destruction. Most notably the giant Bamiyan Buddhas, carved by Buddhist monks in the fourth to sixth centuries, were demolished in March 2001, and Kabul's remaining collections of statues destroyed, including many stored within the Ministry of Information and Culture.

ALBANIA

Republika e Shqipërisë – Republic of Albania

AREA – 28,748 sq. km. Neighbours: Serbia and Montenegro (north), Kosovo and Macedonia (east), Greece (south)
POPULATION – 3,544,808. Muslim (70 per cent), Greek Orthodox (20 per cent), Roman Catholic (10 per cent). The language is Albanian
CAPITAL – Tirana (population, 353,400, 2003)
CURRENCY – Lek (Lk) of 100 qindarka
NATIONAL ANTHEM – Rreth flamurit të për bashkuar [The flag that united us in the struggle]
NATIONAL DAY – 28 November
NATIONAL FLAG – Black two-headed eagle on a red field
MORTALITY RATE (per 1,000 population) – 5.02 (2003 est.)
DEATH PENALTY – Yes*
POPULATION BELOW POVERTY LINE – 30 per cent (2001 est.)
POPULATION GROWTH RATE – 0.51 per cent (2004 est.)
POPULATION DENSITY – 108 per sq. km (1999)
ILLITERACY RATE – (m) 7.7 per cent; (f) 20.5 per cent (2003 est.)
GROSS ENROLMENT RATIO (percentage of relevant age group) – primary 107 (2002); secondary 78 per cent (2002); tertiary 15 per cent (2002)

CLIMATE AND TERRAIN
Much of the country is mountainous, with the highest point at 2,753 m (Maja e Korabit), and nearly half is covered by forest. The lowest point of elevation is 0 m (Adriatic Sea). The climate is Mediterranean with frequent thunderstorms. The average daily temperature ranges from 8°C in January to 25°C in July.

HISTORY AND POLITICS
Albania was under Turkish suzerainty from 1468 until 1912, when independence was declared. After a period of unrest, a republic was declared in 1925 and in 1928 a monarchy. The king went into exile in 1939 when the country was occupied by the Italians; Albania was liberated in November 1944. Elections in 1945 resulted in a Communist-controlled assembly; the king was deposed *in absentia* and a republic declared in January 1946.

From 1946 to 1990 Albania was a one-party, communist state, and isolated from outside influence, particularly after breaking with the USSR in 1961 and China in 1978. Gradual moves towards democratic reform and westernisation began in the late 1980s, and between 1990 and 1992 democratic elections took place, the communists losing power in 1992. Economic decline and food shortages led to rioting in the early 1990s, and rioting broke out again in 1997 following the collapse of several investment schemes, with anti-government protests nationwide.

In 1999, Serbia expelled thousands of ethnic Albanians

from Kosovo and over 400,000 fled to Albania. In April, Albania granted NATO unrestricted access to its transport and military infrastructure to enable it to deal with the crisis. By the end of 1999, nearly all of the refugees had left Albania, and the number of NATO troops currently stationed in the country has fallen to 1,000.

In the July 2005 general election, the Democratic Alliance (DAP) won with 44.1 per cent of the vote and 54 seats in parliament.

POLITICAL SYSTEM
The current constitution was adopted in 1998. There is a single-chamber legislature, the People's Assembly, with 140 members directly elected for a four-year term. The president is indirectly elected by the People's Assembly for a five-year term, with a maximum of two successive terms. The president appoints the prime minister, who must be approved by the People's Assembly. The Assembly elects the Council of Ministers.

HEAD OF STATE
President, Gen. Alfred Moisiu (ret'd), *elected by the People's Assembly* 24 June 2002, *took office* 24 July 2002

SELECTED GOVERNMENT MEMBERS *as at July 2005*
Prime Minister, Sali Berisha
Foreign Affairs, Besnik Mustafaj
Defence, Fatmir Mediu
Finance, Ridvan Bode

EMBASSY OF THE REPUBLIC OF ALBANIA
2nd Floor, 24 Buckingham Gate, London SW1E 6LB
T 020-7828 8897
Ambassador Extraordinary and Plenipotentiary, HE Kastriot Robo, apptd 2002

BRITISH EMBASSY
Rruga Skenderbeg 12, Tirana T (+ 355) (42) 34973/4/5
Ambassador Extraordinary and Plenipotentiary, HE Richard
Jones

BRITISH COUNCIL
Rr. 'Ded Gjo Luli' 3/1, Tirana T (+355) (4) 240856/7
E info@britishcouncil.org.al
Director, Joan Barry

DEFENCE
The Army has 373 main battle tanks and 86 armoured
personnel carriers. The Navy has 20 patrol and coastal
combatant vessels at two bases. The Air Force has 26
combat aircraft.
MILITARY EXPENDITURE – 1.2 per cent of GDP (2003)
MILITARY PERSONNEL – 21,500: Army 16,000, Navy
2,000, Air Force 3,500

ECONOMY AND TRADE
Albania is one of the poorest countries in Europe – a
legacy of Communist rule and a sign of Albania's uneasy
relationship with the post-Communist free-market
economy.
Agriculture accounts for 40 per cent of economic
output although only 20 per cent of this is exported. The
main crops are wheat, maize, sugar beet, potatoes and
fruit. Production is frequently restricted by droughts and
the use of outdated equipment. The principal industries
are agricultural product processing, textiles, oil products
and cement.
Since April 1992, the government has imposed
austerity measures in an attempt to reduce the budget
deficit and to cut inflation. Albania receives annual
remittances from overseas workers (mainly in Greece and
Turkey), of US$400–600 million.
Exports include crude oil, minerals (bitumen, chrome,
nickel, copper), tobacco, fruit and vegetables. Large
chromium deposits are found in the region.
GNI – US$4,600 million (2002); US$1,450 per capita
(2002)
ANNUAL AVERAGE GROWTH OF GDP – 5.6 per cent
(2004 est.)
INFLATION RATE – 6 per cent (2002)
TOTAL EXTERNAL DEBT – US$800 million (2002)
IMPORTS – US$1,900 million (2003)
EXPORTS – US$500 million (2003)

BALANCE OF PAYMENTS
Trade – US$1,336 million deficit (2003)
Current account – US$407 million deficit (2003)

	2003	2004
Trade with UK		
Imports from UK	£9,884,000	£11,460,000
Exports to UK	3,927,000	1,677,000

MEDIA AND CULTURE
The public broadcaster is Albanian Radio and TV (RTSh).
There are around 75 private television channels and
approximately 30 private radio stations. Political parties,
trade unions, religious groups and state bodies are
prohibited from owning private television and radio
stations but can own newspapers.
Albanian culture is influenced by its geographical
location (midway between Rome and Istanbul), its recent
Russian-dominated political past, and its religions (Sunni
Muslim, Roman Catholic and Greek Orthodox). These
influences can be discerned in the work of Albanian
writers, who have gained prominence since 1909, when
written Albanian was standardised. One of the country's
most famous writers and literary critics is Fan Noli
(1882–1965). Albania's most prominent contemporary
writer is Ismail Kadare (b.1936), who won the Man
Booker International Prize in 2005.

ALGERIA

*Al-Jumhūriyya   al-Jazā'iriyya   ad-Dimuqratiyya   ash-
Sha'biyya – People's Democratic Republic of Algeria*

AREA – 2,460,500 sq. km. Neighbours: Morocco and
Western Sahara (west), Mauritania and Mali (south-
west), Niger (south-east), Libya and Tunisia (east)
POPULATION – 32,129,324 (2004 est.). Arabic and
Berber are the official languages although French is
also spoken. The state religion is Sunni Islam
CAPITAL – ΨAlgiers (El Djazair, Al-Jaza'ir) (population,
1,507,241, 1987). It is one of the principal ports of the
Mediterranean
MAJOR CITIES – ΨAnnaba; ΨBejaia; Blida (El Boulaida);
Constantine (Qacentina); ΨMostaganem; ΨOran
(Wahran); Setif; Sidi-Bel-Abbes; ΨSkikda; Tizi Ouzou;
Tlemcen
CURRENCY – Algerian dinar (DA) of 100 centimes
NATIONAL ANTHEM – Qassaman bin nazilat il-mahiqat
[We swear by the lightning that destroys]
NATIONAL DAY – 1 November
NATIONAL FLAG – Divided vertically green and white
with a red crescent and star over all in the centre
LIFE EXPECTANCY (years) – 72.74 (2004 est.)
MORTALITY RATE (per 1,000 population) – 4.61
(2004 est.)
INFANT MORTALITY (per 1,000 live births) – 32.16
(2004 est.)
HIV / AIDS ADULT PREVALENCE – 0.1 per cent
(2001 est.)
DEATH PENALTY – Yes
POPULATION BELOW POVERTY LINE – 23 per cent
(1999)
POPULATION GROWTH RATE – 1.28 per cent
(2004 est.)
POPULATION DENSITY – 13 per sq. km (2001)
ILLITERACY RATE – (m) 21.8 per cent; (f) 39 per cent
(2003)

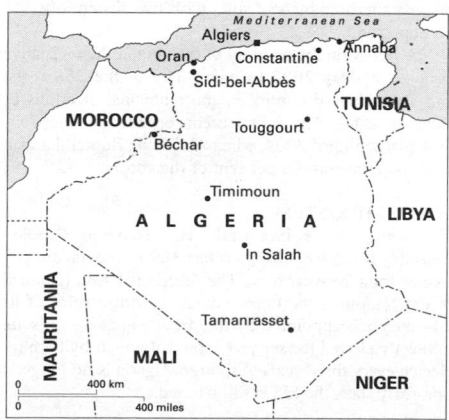

GROSS ENROLMENT RATIO (percentage of relevant age group) – primary 108 per cent (2002); secondary 72 per cent (2002)

CLIMATE AND TERRAIN

Algeria, the second largest country in Africa after Sudan, is dominated by the Sahara Desert, which covers 80 per cent of its territory. The eastern part of the Atlas mountain range crosses the north of the country, separating the coastal plain, where the majority of the population lives, from the desert plateaux of the interior. The mountains are subject to earthquakes, flooding and mudslides during the rainy season (November to March). The highest point of elevation is 2,918 m (Tahat) and the lowest is −40 m (Chott Melrhir). Algeria has mild, wet winters and hot, dry summers. The climate is drier along the coastline, while the high plateaux experience cold winters.

HISTORY AND POLITICS

Algeria was a Roman province, came under Arabic and Islamic influence from the eighth century, and was part of the Ottoman Empire from the 16th century until annexed by France in 1830. It gained its independence in 1962 following an eight-year guerrilla war by the socialist Front de Libération Nationale (FLN). Ben Bella was elected president in 1963, but was deposed in 1965 by Col. Houari Boumedine, who was formally elected president in 1976, when the FLN became the only permitted political party. Boumedine died in 1978 and was succeeded by Chadli Bendjedid.

A new constitution agreed by referendum in 1988 moved Algeria towards pluralism. However, the 1991 legislative elections were abandoned in anticipation of the success of the opposition Islamic Salvation Front (FIS), which had campaigned on a radical Islamist platform. The FIS was banned in 1991, triggering civil unrest and an armed campaign between Islamic groups (the FIS-backed Islamic Salvation Army and the more extreme Armed Islamic Group) and the military. A state of emergency was declared in 1992 and the country was wracked in the 1990s by a civil conflict that claimed an estimated 100,000 lives. The level of violence has fallen since 1999, when the newly elected president Abdelaziz Bouteflika initiated a policy of reconciliation with the Islamists, although there was a resurgence in 2003. Rioting broke out in the Berber-populated Kabyle region in 2001 resulting in about 80 deaths. A session of the National People's Assembly backed reform to give the Berber language, Tamazight, equal status with Arabic. The reform bill was approved by 482 votes with two abstentions and no opposition.

The FLN won the majority of the vote in the legislative elections of May 2002 (winning 199 of the 388 seats) and also achieved control in the municipal elections of October 2002. The most recent presidential elections took place in April 2004, when Abdelaziz Bouteflika won a second term with 85 per cent of the vote.

POLITICAL SYSTEM

The legislature is bicameral. The National People's Assembly (the lower chamber) has 389 members, directly elected for a five-year term. The Majlis al-Umma (Council of the Nation) is the upper chamber, with a third of its 144 members appointed by the president; two-thirds are indirectly elected for six-year terms, of which half are re-elected every three years. Although Algeria is no longer a one-party state, the FIS is still banned.

HEAD OF STATE
President, Defence, Abdelaziz Bouteflika, re-elected April 2004

SELECTED GOVERMENT MEMBERS as at July 2005
Prime Minister, Ahmed Ouyahia
Finance, Mourad Medelci
Ministers of State, Mohammed Bedjaoui (Foreign Affairs); Noureddine Yazid Zerhouni (Interior and Local Authorities)

ALGERIAN EMBASSY
54 Holland Park, London W11 3RS T 020-7221 7800
Ambassador Extraordinary and Plenipotentiary, HE Ahmed Attaf, apptd 2001

BRITISH EMBASSY
7th floor, Hotel Hilton International Algiers, Pins Maritimes, Palais des Expositions, El Mohammadia, Algiers
T (+1) (213) (21) 230068
Ambassador Extraordinary and Plenipotentiary, HE Brian Stewart, apptd 2004

BRITISH COUNCIL
c/o The British Embassy E rachida.benyahia@fco.gov.uk
Office Manager, Rachida Benyahia

DEFENCE

The Army has 1,000 main battle tanks, 989 armoured infantry fighting vehicles and 630 armoured personnel carriers. The Navy has two submarines, three frigates and 25 patrol and coastal vessels. The Air Force has 175 combat aircraft and 91 armed helicopters.
MILITARY EXPENDITURE – 3.4 per cent of GDP (2003)
MILITARY PERSONNEL – 127,500: Army 110,000, Navy 7,500, Air Force 10,000; Paramilitaries 181,200
CONSCRIPTION DURATION – 18 months

ECONOMY AND TRADE

The main industry is hydrocarbons, which accounted for 60 per cent of budget revenues and 30 per cent of GDP in 2003. Services provided 32 per cent of GDP and agriculture 8 per cent of GDP in 2003. Oil and natural gas are pumped from the Sahara to terminals on the coast before being exported; the gas is first liquefied at liquefaction plants at Skikda and Arzew, although pipelines serve Libya and Italy direct. In November 1996 a 1,200-km gas pipeline to Spain was opened, enabling Algeria to double its gas exports to Morocco, Spain, Germany and France.

Other major industries include steel, motor vehicles, building materials, paper making, chemical products and metal manufactures. Most major industrial enterprises are still under state control.

Prior to 1989 the economy was centrally planned and state-controlled in most sectors. In 1994 the government accepted full economic reform and liberalisation under a programme agreed with the IMF. The government reduced the budget deficit, devalued the currency and freed price controls. Algeria's foreign debt fell from 71.9 per cent of GDP in 1996 to 40.7 per cent in 2001. An extensive privatisation programme began in 1997. During 2000–3 the country's finances improved due to increased trade surpluses, record foreign exchange reserves and continued reductions to foreign debt.

Export earnings come mainly from crude oil and liquefied natural gas sales (97 per cent in 2003). Algeria's main trading partners are Italy, France, Spain, the USA and Brazil. Dates and wine are among the main food imports.

GNI – US$53,800 million (2002); US$1,720 per capita (2002)
ANNUAL AVERAGE GROWTH OF GDP – 6.1 per cent (2004 est.)
INFLATION RATE – 5.3 per cent (2002)
UNEMPLOYMENT – 25.4 per cent (2004 est.)
TOTAL EXTERNAL DEBT – US$25,002 million (2000)
IMPORTS – US$10,791 million (2002)
EXPORTS – US$18,635 million (2002)
FOREIGN DIRECT INVESTMENT – US$29 million (1997–2000)

Trade with UK	2003	2004
Imports from UK	£190,142,000	£167,524,000
Exports to UK	261,837,000	376,082,000

MEDIA

The state controls the television (Entreprise Nationale de Television) and radio stations (Radio-Télévision Algérienne) but domestic satellite dishes are used by the general population to receive French and European channels, some of which actively target Algerian viewers. There are five main daily newspapers, all of them published in French.

ANDORRA

Principat d'Andorra – Principality of Andorra

AREA – 468 sq. km. Neighbours: Spain and France
POPULATION – 69,865 (2004 est.); less than one-quarter of the population is Andorran. The official language is Catalan, but French and Spanish (Castilian) are also spoken. The established religion is Roman Catholicism
CAPITAL – Andorra la Vella (population, 20,724, 2002)
CURRENCY – Euro (€) of 100 cents
NATIONAL ANTHEM – El gran Carlemany, mon pare [Great Charlemagne, my father]
NATIONAL DAY – 8 September
NATIONAL FLAG – Three vertical bands, blue, yellow, red; Andorran coat of arms frequently imposed on central (yellow) band but not essential
LIFE EXPECTANCY (years) – 83 (2004 est.)
MORTALITY RATE (per 1,000 population) – 5.9 (2004 est.)
INFANT MORTALITY (per 1,000 births) – 4 (2004 est.)
DEATH PENALTY – No (abolished 1993)
POPULATION GROWTH RATE – 1 per cent (2004 est.)
POPULATION DENSITY – 194 per sq. km (2001)

CLIMATE AND TERRAIN

Located between the French and Spanish borders, Andorra is a country of dramatic mountains intersected with narrow valleys. A third of the country is classified as forest. The highest point of elevation is 2,946 m (Coma Pedrosa) while the lowest is 840 m (Riu Runer). The climate is alpine, with heavy snowfall in winter and warm summers. The average annual temperature ranges from 2°C in January to 19°C in July.

HISTORY AND POLITICS

Liberated from Muslim rule by Charlemagne in 803, Andorra is a small, neutral principality formed by a treaty in 1278. Formerly a feudal state owing dual allegiance to two co-princes, the Spanish Bishop of Urgel and the President of the French Republic, it became an independent democratic parliamentary co-principality in 1993. The first elections under the new constitution were held in 1993, and on 20 January 1994 the first sovereign government of Andorra took office. Andorra has subsequently formalised its links with the EU and joined the United Nations and the Council of Europe. Legislative elections were held in April 2005 and were won by the Liberal Party of Andorra (PLA) with 41.2 per cent of the vote and 14 seat in the General Council of the Valleys. Albert Pintat Santolaria of the PLA was nominated as president of the executive council and confirmed in office on 27 May 2005.

POLITICAL SYSTEM

Under the 1993 constitution, Andorra's sovereignty is vested in the people rather than in the two co-princes. The constitution enables Andorra to establish an independent judiciary and to conduct its own foreign policy, whilst its people may now join political parties and trade unions. The two co-princes remain heads of state, represented in Andorra by the Permanent Delegates (the Spanish Vicar-General of the diocese of Urgel and the French Prefect of the Pyrénées Orientales department at Perpignan), but now only have the power to veto treaties with France and Spain that affect the state's borders and security.

Andorra has a unicameral legislature of 28 members known as the *Consell General de las Valls d'Andorra* (Valleys of Andorra General Council), elected for a four-year term. Fourteen members are elected on a national list basis and 14 in seven dual-member constituencies based on Andorra's seven parishes. The Council appoints the head of the executive government, who designates government members.

Permanent French Delegate, Philippe Massoni
Permanent Episcopal Delegate, Nemesi Marqués Oste

SELECTED GOVERNMENT MEMBERS *as at July 2005*
President of the Executive Council, Albert Pintat Santolaria
Finance, Ferran Mirapeix
Foreign Affairs, Juli Minoves Triquell
Justice and Interior, Jordi Visent Guitart

ANDORRAN EMBASSY
63 Westover Road, London SW18 2RF T 020-8874 4806
Chargé d'affaires, Maria Rosa Picart de Francis

BRITISH AMBASSADOR
HE Stephen Wright, resident at Madrid, apptd 2003

ECONOMY AND TRADE

The economy is largely based on tourism (80 per cent of GDP, with nine million visitors annually), banking and commerce (due in part to the principality's tax-free status), tobacco, construction and forestry. Andorra has negotiated a customs union with the European Union which came into force in 1991.

GNI – US$18,000 per capita (2001)
ANNUAL AVERAGE GROWTH OF GDP – 2 per cent (2003 est.)

Trade with UK	2003	2004
Imports from UK	£9,333,000	£9,156,000
Exports to UK	314,000	338,000

TRANSPORT INFRASTRUCTURE

There are a total of 269 km of roads but no railways, airports, waterways or harbours. A road into Andorra from Spain is open all year round, and that from France is closed only occasionally in winter.

MEDIA AND CULTURE

The Andorran media is heavily influenced by France and Spain. There are two radio stations in Andorra, one privately owned and Radio Andorra, operated by the government, as well as a state-owned television station and two major daily newspapers (Diari d'Andorra and El Periodic).

The capital, Andorra la Vella, is over 1,100 years old and retains some of its ancient architecture and atmosphere in the Old Quarter (Barri Antic). The photographer Valenti Claverol (1902–2000) is particularly noted for his documentation of day-to-day life in Andorra and his work is considered a major example of vernacular photography.

ANGOLA

República de Angola – Republic of Angola

AREA – 1,245,790 sq. km. Neighbours: Democratic Republic of Congo (north and east), Zambia (east), Namibia (south). The enclave of Cabinda is separated from the rest of Angola by the Democratic Republic of Congo and also borders on the Republic of Congo
POPULATION – 10,978,552 (2004 est.). Main ethnic groups are Ovimbundu (37 per cent); Kimbundu (25 per cent); Bakongo (13 per cent). The official language is Portuguese
CAPITAL – ΨLuanda (population, 1,822,407, 1993)
CURRENCY – Readjusted kwanza (Kzrl) of 100 lwei
NATIONAL ANTHEM – Angola avante [Advance Angola]
NATIONAL DAY – 11 November (Independence Day)
NATIONAL FLAG – Red and black with a yellow star, machete and cog-wheel
LIFE EXPECTANCY (years) – 36.79 (2004 est.)
MORTALITY RATE (per 1,000 population) – 25.86 (2004 est.)
INFANT MORTALITY (per 1,000 births) – 192.5 (2004 est.)
HIV / AIDS ADULT PREVALENCE – 3.9 per cent (2004)
DEATH PENALTY – No (abolished 1992)
POPULATION GROWTH RATE – 1.93 per cent (2004 est.)
POPULATION DENSITY – 11 per sq. km (2001)
ILLITERACY RATE – (m) 44 per cent; (f) 72 per cent (1998 est.)
GROSS ENROLMENT RATIO (percentage of relevant age group) – secondary 19 per cent (2002); tertiary 1 per cent (2002)

CLIMATE AND TERRAIN

Angola's land rises from a narrow coastal plain to a large interior plateau. On the plateau rise the Cunene, Cubango and Cuanza rivers and the headwaters of tributaries of the Zambezi and Congo rivers, although some of these are dry except in the rainy season, when flooding may occur. The south is desert. The highest point of elevation is 2,620 m (Morro de Moco) and the lowest is 0 m (Atlantic Ocean). Angola's climate is tropical in the north, with a cool, dry season from May to October and a hot, rainy season from November to April, and sub-tropical in the south and along the coast to Luanda.

HISTORY AND POLITICS

A Portuguese colony became established in the region in the 15th century and its territory expanded over the centuries, the current boundaries being defined in the 19th century. An anti-colonial war began in 1961, and Angola became independent on 11 November 1975. Shortly afterwards, civil war broke out between the Popular Movement for the Liberation of Angola (MPLA) government and two factions, the National Union for the Total Independence of Angola (UNITA) led by Jonas Savimbi, and the Front for the Liberation of Angola (FNLA). The FNLA ceased operations in the 1980s and foreign support for the MPLA and UNITA was withdrawn after 1988, but the civil war between the government and UNITA continued. A peace agreement in 1991 was followed by multiparty elections in 1992 but UNITA refused to accept the results and fighting resumed. Another peace agreement (the Lusaka Protocol) was signed in 1994 but UNITA appeared not to comply with its provisions and UN peacekeeping forces were sent to Angola.

In April 1997 a government of national reconciliation was formed under the power-sharing provisions of the Lusaka Protocol, but despite its nominal participation in this UNITA refused to allow central state administration to be restored in key areas. In spite of intervention by the UN Security Council, fighting continued until 2002, when, following the death of Jonas Savimbi in February 2002, UNITA and the government signed a formal cease-fire agreement on 4 April 2002 and pledged to adhere to the 1994 peace agreement. In addition, provision was made for the demobilisation of around 100,000 UNITA fighters, to be monitored by the UN, and the provision of state aid for some 300,000 family members of these soldiers. In December 2002 the UN Security Council lifted all remaining economic and financial sanctions imposed on UNITA. Isaias Samakuva was elected leader of UNITA on 27 June 2003.

SECESSION

In the northern enclave of Cabinda, the Front for the Liberation of the Cabinda Enclave (FLEC) fought a 20-year war of independence until the signing of a cease-fire with the government in 1995, which was followed by the initialling of a peace agreement in 1996.

POLITICAL SYSTEM

The MPLA, formerly a Marxist-Leninist party, was the sole legal party until early 1991 when a multiparty system was adopted. The constitution declares Angola to be a democratic state and provides for an executive president directly elected for a five-year term. The president appoints a Council of Ministers to assist him. The 220-member National Assembly is directly elected for a four-year term. Neither presidential nor legislative elections have been held since 1992; in 1996, and again in 2000, the National Assembly adopted a constitutional amendment extending its own mandate. In 2004 the government announced a timetable of voter registration in preparation for elections in September 2006.

HEAD OF STATE

President, José Eduardo dos Santos, *re-elected* 30 September 1992

SELECTED GOVERNMENT MEMBERS *as at July 2005*
Prime Minister, Interior, Fernando da Piedade Dias dos Santos 'Nando'
Deputy Prime Minister, Aguinaldo Jaime
Defence, Kundi Paihama
Finance, José Pedro de Morais
Foreign Affairs, João Bernardo de Miranda
Interior, Osvaldo de Jesus Serra Van-Dúnem

EMBASSY OF THE REPUBLIC OF ANGOLA
22 Dorset Street, London W1U 3QY T 020-7299 9850
Ambassador Extraordinary and Plenipotentiary, HE António DaCosta Fernandes, apptd 1993

BRITISH EMBASSY
Rua Diogo Cao 4 (Caixa Postal 1244), Luanda
T (+244) (2) 334582
Ambassador Extraordinary and Plenipotentiary, HE John Thompson, MBE, apptd 2002

DEFENCE

The Army has an estimated 300 main battle tanks, 250 armoured infantry fighting vehicles and 170 armoured personnel carriers. The Navy has seven patrol vessels. The Air Force has 90 combat aircraft and 16 armed helicopters.

MILITARY EXPENDITURE – 5.7 per cent of GDP (2003)
MILITARY PERSONNEL – 108,400: Army 100,000, Navy 2,400, Air Force 6,000; Paramilitaries 10,000

ECONOMY AND TRADE

Angola is Africa's second-largest exporter of oil (after Nigeria), and in 2002 oil accounted for 45 per cent of GDP and 90 per cent of foreign exchange earnings and government revenue. The government plans to double oil production by 2010. Angola is also rich in diamond deposits but much of the trade in these gems is unregulated. Principal agricultural crops are cassava, maize, bananas, coffee, palm oil and kernels, cotton and sisal. Coffee, sisal, maize and palm oil are exported; exports also include mahogany and other hardwoods from the tropical rain forests in the north of the country.

The government is attempting to restructure the socialist economy by free market reforms but is making little progress, with high inflation and a fragile economy.

The government raised fuel prices by 1,600 per cent in February 2000 in response to IMF demands to remove state subsidies on petroleum products.

GNI – US$9,300 million (2002); US$710 per capita (2002)
ANNUAL AVERAGE GROWTH OF GDP – 11.7 per cent (2004 est.)
INFLATION RATE – 95.0 per cent (2002)
TOTAL EXTERNAL DEBT – US$9,900 million (2002)
FOREIGN DIRECT INVESTMENT – US$ 4,879 million (1997–2000)

Trade with UK	2003	2004
Imports from UK	£103,728,000	£119,285,000
Exports to UK	9,751,000	9,941,000

TRANSPORT INFRASTRUCTURE

There are 51,429 km of roads, 46,080 km of which are unsurfaced. The majority of roads are in very poor condition and most road travel is by convoy because of security problems. There are many uncleared landmines in Angola, especially on roads in remote areas. There are 2,761 km of railway. Most internal travel takes place by air between the country's 244 airports (32 of which have surfaced runways). The main ports are Luanda, Lobito and Benguela.

MEDIA AND CULTURE

Angola's only news agency, Angop, the country's biggest broadcaster, Televisao Popular de Angola (TPA), and the country's only daily newspaper, *Jornal de Angola*, are all government-owned. There are several commercial radio stations, one private television station, and some subscription services (operated by Multichoice Angola) that include Brazilian and Portuguese channels.

Up until relatively recently Angolan art was strictly controlled by the Ministry of Culture but since it released control in the late 1980s, art has become a significant industry. This liberalisation of the arts has affected many aspects of Angola's cultural life, creating, for example, a thriving traditional and contemporary music scene.

ANTIGUA AND BARBUDA

State of Antigua and Barbuda

AREA – 443 sq. km; Antigua 279 sq. km; Barbuda 160 sq. km; Redonda 1.2 sq. km
POPULATION – 65,000 (2001). The official language is English
CAPITAL – ΨSt John's (population, 24,226, 2000)
MAJOR TOWNS – Barbuda's main town is Codrington
CURRENCY – East Caribbean dollar (EC$) of 100 cents
NATIONAL ANTHEM – Fair Antigua and Barbuda
NATIONAL DAY – 1 November (Independence Day)
NATIONAL FLAG – Red with an inverted triangle divided black over blue over white, with a rising gold sun on the white band
LIFE EXPECTANCY (years) – 71 (2004 est.)
MORTALITY RATE (per 1,000 population) – 5.55 (2004)
INFANT MORTALITY (per 1,000 births) – 12 (2001 est.)
DEATH PENALTY – Yes
POPULATION GROWTH RATE – 0.6 per cent (2004 est.)
POPULATION DENSITY – 147 per sq. km (2001)
URBAN POPULATION – 37 per cent (2001)
ILLITERACY RATE – (m) 5 per cent; (f) 5 per cent (2001 est.)
MILITARY EXPENDITURE – 0.6 per cent of GDP (2003)
MILITARY PERSONNEL – 170: Army 125, Navy 45

CLIMATE AND TERRAIN

The subtropical island of Antigua is part of the Leeward Islands in the eastern Caribbean. It is distinguished from the rest of the Leeward Islands by an absence of high hills and forest, and has a drier climate than most of the West Indies. The elevation extremes range from 402 m at the highest point (Boggy Peak) to 0 m sea level (Caribbean Sea).

Barbuda is 48 km away from Antigua. It is a very flat coral island with a large lagoon. Both of the islands lie within the hurricane belt and are subject to tropical storms and hurricanes between June and November.

HISTORY AND POLITICS

Antigua was discovered by Columbus in 1493; colonised by the English in 1632, it was granted to Lord Willoughby by Charles II. Barbuda was colonised from Antigua in 1661. Administered as part of the Leeward Islands Federation from 1871 to 1956, it became internally self-governing in 1967 and fully independent on 1 November 1981.

The United Progressive Party won the elections of March 2004 with a landslide victory (4 of 12 seats to the Antigua Labour Party's (ALP) with one tied) that removed the ALP from power for the first time in three decades.

POLITICAL SYSTEM

Antigua and Barbuda is a constitutional monarchy with Queen Elizabeth II as head of state, represented by the Governor-General. There is a Senate of 17 appointed members and a House of Representatives of 19 members, 17 of whom are elected every five years. The Attorney-General may be appointed.

Governor-General, HE Sir James Carlisle, GCMG

SELECTED GOVERNMENT MEMBERS *as at July 2005*
Prime Minister, Foreign Affairs and Foreign Trade, National Security, Barbuda Affairs, Ecclesiastical Affairs, Baldwin Spencer
Deputy Prime Minister, Public Works, Transport, Energy and Environment, Wilmoth Daniel
Minister of Finance, Economic Development and Planning, Leon Errol Cort
Attorney General, Minister of Legal Affairs, Justin Simon

HIGH COMMISSION FOR ANTIGUA AND BARBUDA
15 Thayer Street, London W1M 5LD
T 020-7486 7073
High Commissioner, vacant

BRITISH HIGH COMMISSION
PO Box 483, 11 Old Parham Road, St John's
T (+1 268) 462 0008/9
High Commissioner, HE John White, apptd 2001, resident at Bridgetown, Barbados

ECONOMY AND TRADE

Antigua is now one of the Caribbean's most prosperous nations. The economy is largely based on tourism and related services (75 per cent of the workforce are employed in this sector), and offshore financial services. Agricultural production includes livestock, sea island cotton, mixed market gardening and fishing.
GNI – US$630 million (2001); US$9,150 per capita (2001)
ANNUAL AVERAGE GROWTH OF GDP – 3 per cent (2002)
INFLATION RATE – 1.0 per cent (2002)
IMPORTS – US$414 million (1999)
EXPORTS – US$38 million (1999)

BALANCE OF PAYMENTS
Trade – US$283 million deficit (2001)
Current Account – US$47 million deficit (2001)

Trade with UK	2003	2004
Imports from UK	£17,698,000	£11,414,000
Exports to UK	9,657,000	31,632,000

MEDIA AND CULTURE

Many of Antigua and Barbuda's television and radio stations are owned or controlled by the Antigua Labour Party. Antigua's first independent radio station began broadcasting in 2001.

The islands are rich in British naval history (Lord Nelson built Nelson's Dockyard on Antigua in 1784) and perfectly preserved colonial architecture (in English Harbourtown), but support a vibrant and colourful Afro-Caribbean culture.

ARGENTINA

República Argentina – Argentine Republic

AREA – 2,780,092 sq. km. Neighbours: Bolivia (north), Paraguay, Brazil and Uruguay (north-east), Chile (west) from which it is separated by the Cordillera de los Andes
POPULATION – 39,144,753 (2004 est.). The language is Spanish
CAPITAL – ΨBuenos Aires (population, 11,453,725, 2001; metropolitan area 2,768,772)
MAJOR CITIES – Córdoba; ΨLa Plata; ΨMar del Plata; Mendoza; ΨRosario; San Miguel de Tucumán
CURRENCY – Peso of 10,000 australes
NATIONAL ANTHEM – Oid mortales! [Hear, oh mortals!]
NATIONAL DAY – 25 May
NATIONAL FLAG – Horizontal bands of blue, white, blue; gold sun in centre of white band
LIFE EXPECTANCY (years) – 75.7 (2004 est.)
MORTALITY RATE (per 1,000 population) – 7.57 (2004 est.)
INFANT MORTALITY (per 1,000 births) – 15.66 (2004 est.)
HIV / AIDS ADULT PREVALENCE – 0.7 per cent (2004 est.)
DEATH PENALTY – Yes*
POPULATION BELOW POVERTY LINE – 37 per cent (2001 est.)
POPULATION GROWTH RATE – 1.02 per cent (2004 est.)
POPULATION DENSITY – 14 per sq. km (2001)
URBAN POPULATION – 88 per cent (2001)

CLIMATE AND TERRAIN

The Andes mountain range runs the full length of Argentina, a dramatic spine to the country's western border with Chile. Parts of the Andes are prone to earthquakes. In the east of the Andes, the north is mostly subtropical forest and savanna, the east is rich, grassy pampas, and the southern Patagonian plateau has an arid, desert-like terrain. The highest point of elevation is 6,960 m (Cerro Aconcagua) and the lowest is −105 m (Laguna del Carbon). Temperatures range from subtropical to subantarctic, with an average annual temperature of 16°C.

HISTORY AND POLITICS

The estuary of La Plata was discovered in 1515 by Juan Díaz de Solís and the region was subsequently colonised by the Spanish. Spain ruled the territory from the 16th century until 1810. In 1816, after a long campaign of liberation conducted by General José de San Martín, independence was declared by the Congress of Tucumán. The country's constitution was adopted in 1853 followed by a period of national organisation.

A 1943 coup introduced a period of military rule before Juan Domingo Perón became president in 1946. His overthrow in 1955 was followed by 18 years of political instability until 1973, when he was recalled from exile. Perón died within a year and was succeeded by his widow, Vice-President Mara Estela Martínez de Perón. A coup led to the establishment of a military junta in 1976, and conducted a 'dirty war' in which over 8,000 people 'disappeared' until civilian rule was restored in 1983 following the discrediting of the junta by the defeat of Argentina's attempt to annex the Falkland Islands/Malvinas in 1982.

President Fernando de la Rúa, elected in 1999, resigned in 2001 in the face of serious unrest caused by the collapsing economy. Following a series of interim presidents, Eduardo Alberto Duhalde was appointed president by Congress on 1 January 2002, to serve for the rest of de la Rúa's term. He resigned before the first round of presidential elections, held in April 2003, in which Carlos Menem (president 1989–99) gained 24.4 per cent of the vote and Néstor Kirchner 22 per cent. Menem withdrew from the second round and Néstor Kirchner became president-elect by default and was sworn in as president on 25 May.

POLITICAL SYSTEM

The 1853 constitution was amended in 1994. Power is vested in the president who appoints the cabinet and is directly elected for a once-renewable four-year term. A presidential candidate must win at least 45 per cent of the vote, or 40 per cent with a 10 per cent lead over the nearest challenger, to gain victory in the first round of voting; if no candidate meets these criteria, a second round must be held. The legislature consists of a 72-member (three for each province and three for Buenos Aires) Senate and a 257-member Chamber of Deputies. Half of the Chamber of Deputies is elected every two years, and deputies serve for a four-year term. Senators used to serve for a nine-year term, but the terms of all sitting senators ended in 2001, and since October 2001 the Senate has been directly elected by the provinces for a six-year term, with one-third renewable every two years.

HEAD OF STATE

President, Néstor Kirchner, *sworn* in 25 May 2003
Vice-President, Daniel Scioli

SELECTED GOVERNMENT MEMBERS *as at July 2005*
Cabinet Chief, Alberto Fernández
Defence, José Pampuro
Economy, Production, Roberto Lavagna
Foreign Relations, International Trade and Worship, Rafael Bielsa
Interior, Anibal Fernández

EMBASSY OF THE ARGENTINE REPUBLIC
65 Brook Street, London W1K 4AH T 020-7318 1300
Ambassador Extraordinary and Plenipotentiary, HE Frederico Mirré

BRITISH EMBASSY
Dr Luis Agote 2412, 1425 Buenos Aires
T (+54) (11) 4808 2200
Ambassador Extraordinary and Plenipotentiary, HE Dr John Hughes, apptd 2004

BRITISH COUNCIL
Marcelo T. de Alvear 590, C1058AAF Buenos Aires
T (+54) (11) 4311/9814/7519 E info@britishcouncil.org.ar
Director, Martin Fryer

FEDERAL STRUCTURE

The republic is divided into 23 provinces, each with an elected governor and legislature, and one federal district (Buenos Aires), with an elected mayor and autonomous government.

DEFENCE

The Army has 200 main battle tanks, 105 armoured infantry fighting vehicles and 422 armoured personnel carriers. The Navy has three submarines, five destroyers, eight frigates, 14 patrol and coastal vessels, 20 combat aircraft and 21 armed helicopters. The Air Force has 99 combat aircraft and 28 armed helicopters.

MILITARY EXPENDITURE – 1.5 per cent of GDP (2003)
MILITARY PERSONNEL – 71,400: Army 41,400, Navy 17,500, Air Force 12,500; Paramilitaries 31,240

ECONOMY AND TRADE

Since late 1998 Argentina has been in a recession. In 2001, measures to reassure international investors that the country would not default on its debt repayments were introduced. In November 2001, the president announced several economy-boosting measures but in December 2001 the government defaulted on part of its large public debt. A wave of protests took place across the country in the wake of continued economic instability. In 2003 the IMF made available an eight-month standby credit of approximately US$1,580 million to cover Argentina's payment obligations to the IMF. It was also agreed that US$2,000 million in repayments to the IMF would be postponed by one year, enabling Argentina to clear its arrears with the World Bank and the Inter-American Development Bank.

The main crops are wheat, maize, oats, barley, rye, linseed, sunflower seed, alfalfa, sugar, fruit and cotton. Argentina is pre-eminent in the production of beef, mutton and wool. There is an oil refinery in San Lorenzo (Santa Fé province). Natural gas is also produced. Coal, lead, zinc, tungsten, iron ore, sulphur, mica and salt are the other chief minerals being exploited. There are small worked deposits of beryllium, manganese, bismuth, uranium, antimony, copper, kaolin, arsenate, gold, silver and tin. Coal is produced at the Río Turbio mine in the province of Santa Cruz.

Meat-packing is one of the principal industries; flour-milling, sugar-refining, and the wine industry are also important. In recent years progress has been made by the textile, plastic and machine tool industries and engineering, especially in the production of motor vehicles and steel manufactures. Argentina's main trading partners are Brazil and the USA.

GNI – US$154 million (2002); US$4,220 per capita (2002)
ANNUAL AVERAGE GROWTH OF GDP – 8.3 per cent (2004 est.)
INFLATION RATE – 0.9 per cent (2000)
UNEMPLOYMENT – 14.8 per cent (2004 est.)
TOTAL EXTERNAL DEBT – US$146,172 million (2000)
IMPORTS – US$14,000 million (2003)
EXPORTS – US$29,000 million (2003)
FOREIGN DIRECT INVESTMENT – US$48,389 million (1997–2000)

BALANCE OF PAYMENTS
Trade – US$16,447 million surplus (2003)
Current Account – US$7,838 million surplus (2003)

Trade with UK	2003	2004
Imports from UK	£135,968,000	£178,678,000
Exports to UK	257,579,000	272,175,000

TRANSPORT INFRASTRUCTURE

The road and rail networks are extensive in the north and centre of the country; in Patagonia, roads are fewer and there are no railways. The 34,463 km of railway is state owned. The combined national and provincial road network totals approximately 215,471 km, of which 63,348 km are surfaced. A US$20,000 million programme of road-building and upgrading of existing road, rail and air infrastructure began in 2000. The main airports are at Buenos Aires, Cordoba, Salta and Rio Gallegos. Buenos Aires, Ensenada (La Plata) and Bahia Blanca are the main ports.

EDUCATION

Education is compulsory and free from the age of six to 15. The total number of universities is over 50 with 24 national, 25 private and a small number of provincial universities.

ILLITERACY RATE – (m) 2.9 per cent; (f) 2.9 per cent (2003)

GROSS ENROLMENT RATIO (percentage of relevant age group) – primary 120 per cent (2002); secondary 100 per cent (2002); tertiary 57 per cent (2002)

MEDIA AND CULTURE

Argentina's media is well developed, with over 150 daily newspapers (published in both English and Spanish), including seven major dailies published in Buenos Aires. There are more than a thousand commercial radio stations (many unlicensed), over 40 television stations and widespread access to cable television.

Culturally, Argentina enjoys a blend of pre-colonial and European influences. The arts and literature of Spain still form the bedrock of Argentinean education, while the character of the 'gaucho' (cowboy) remains a powerful and archetypal cultural presence. Despite these often disparate influences, Argentina has produced some of the 20th century's most important writers including Jorge Luis Borges (1899–1986) and Julio Cortazar (1914–1984). Dance, architecture, sport and cinema are all central to cultural life in Argentina.

ARMENIA

Hayastani Hanrapetut'yun – Republic of Armenia

AREA – 29,800 sq. km. Neighbours: Azerbaijan (east and south-west), Georgia (north), Iran (south), Turkey (west)

POPULATION – 2,991,360 (2004 est.). Armenians 93.8 per cent, Kurds 1.7 per cent and Russians 1.6 per cent. Azeris formed 2.6 per cent of the population, but most fled or were expelled after the outbreak of war with Azerbaijan. There are also Ukrainians, Greeks and Assyrians. The Armenian diaspora numbers some 5,300,000. Armenian is the official language, though Russian is widely spoken and understood. The main religion is Armenian Orthodox Christian (Armenian Church centred in Etchmiadzin). Armenia adopted Christianity as its official religion in AD 301, the first state in the world to do so

CAPITAL – Yerevan (population, 1,254,400, 1996 est.)

CURRENCY – Dram of 100 louma

NATIONAL ANTHEM – Mer hayrenik azat, ankakh [Land of our fathers]

NATIONAL DAY – 21 September (Independence Day)

NATIONAL FLAG – Three horizontal stripes of red, blue and orange

LIFE EXPECTANCY (YEARS) – 71.23 (2004)

MORTALITY RATE (per 1,000 population) – 8.12 (2004 est.)

HIV / AIDS ADULT PREVALENCE – 0.1 per cent (2003 est.)

DEATH PENALTY – Yes*

POPULATION BELOW POVERTY LINE – 50 per cent (2002)

POPULATION GROWTH RATE – –0.32 per cent (2004 est.)

POPULATION DENSITY – 127 per sq. km (1999)

CLIMATE AND TERRAIN

Armenia lies between the Black and Caspian Seas, occupying the south-western part of the Caucasus region of the former Soviet Union. It is very mountainous, consisting of several vast tablelands surrounded by ridges. The elevation extremes range from 4,090 m at the highest point (Aragats Lerrnagagat) to 400 m at the lowest (Debed River). The climate is continental, dry and cold, but the Ararat valley has a long, hot and dry summer. Armenia is in an active seismic zone, and the north of the country suffered an earthquake in 1988 that left an estimated 50,000 people dead.

HISTORY AND POLITICS

Armenia was first unified in 95 BC but was divided between the Persian and Byzantine empires in AD 387 and then conquered in the 11th century by the Seljuk Turks and the Mongols. In the 16th century most of Armenia was incorporated into the Ottoman Empire. In 1639 the country was divided again, the most easterly areas, now the Republic of Armenia, becoming part of the Persian Empire. In 1828 eastern Armenia became part of the Russian Empire while western Armenia remained under Ottoman rule. The Ottomans launched pogroms against the Armenians from 1894 onwards, and from 1915 to 1918 deported or killed over 1,500,000 Armenians.

Armenia declared its independence on 28 May 1918, but was crushed and divided between Turkish and Soviet forces in 1920, with the area under Soviet control proclaimed a Soviet Socialist Republic in November 1920. The Soviet government was overthrown by a nationalist revolt in 1921 but reinstated by the Red Army a few months later. In early 1922 Armenia acceded to the USSR.

An Armenian nationalist movement gained power in national elections in mid-1990. In a referendum in 1991, 99 per cent of the electorate voted for independence, which was declared on 21 September 1991. In 1992 a state of emergency was declared as a result of a worsening economic situation and the dispute with Azerbaijan over Nagorny-Karabakh. Prime Minister Vazgen Sarkissian and six other politicians were shot dead in the National Assembly during an attempted coup on 27 October 1999.

Presidential elections took place in February 2003. Robert Kocharian was re-elected president following the second round of voting in which he gained over 65 per cent of the vote. In the general election held in May 2004 the Republican Party of Armenia (HHK) became the dominant political party.

FOREIGN RELATIONS

The longstanding dispute with Azerbaijan over the predominantly Armenian-populated Azeri enclave of Nagorny-Karabakh escalated in May 1992 into war, when ethnic Armenian Nagorno-Karabakh forces, supported by Armenia, breached Azerbaijan's defences to form a land bridge to Armenia. By the end of summer 1992 all of Nagorny-Karabakh was under Armenian control, and by the end of 1993 all Azeri territory that separated Nagorny-Karabakh from Armenia and all mountainous Azeri territory around Nagorny-Karabakh was under the control of Nagorno-Karabakh Armenians. Armenia claims this territory as historically Armenian land arbitrarily given to Azerbaijan by Stalin in 1921–2. A cease-fire agreement between Armenia, Azerbaijan and Nagorny-Karabakh was reached in 1994, and talks mediated by the Organisation for Security and Co-operation in Europe (OSCE) continue to seek a peaceful resolution to the dispute.

POLITICAL SYSTEM
A new constitution was approved by referendum in 1995. There is a 131-member unicameral National Assembly *(Azgayin Joghov)*, directly elected every four years.

HEAD OF STATE
President, Robert Kocharian, *elected* 30 March 1998, *re-elected* 5 March 2003

SELECTED GOVERNMENT MEMBERS *as at July 2005*
Prime Minister, Andranik Markarian
Defence, Serge Sarkissian
Finance and Economy, Vardan Khachaturian
Foreign Affairs, Vardan Oskanian

EMBASSY OF THE REPUBLIC OF ARMENIA
25a Cheniston Gardens, London W8 6TG
T 020-7938 5435
Ambassador Extraordinary and Plenipotentiary, HE Dr Vahe Gabrielian, apptd 2003

BRITISH EMBASSY
28 Charents Street, Yerevan 375010 T (+374) (1) 264 301
Ambassador Extraordinary and Plenipotentiary, HE Thorda Abbott-Watt

BRITISH COUNCIL
c/o The British Embassy T (+374) (56) 99 23/24
E info@britishcouncil.am
Director, Roger Budd

DEFENCE
The Army has 110 main battle tanks, 104 armoured infantry fighting vehicles and 36 armoured personnel carriers. The Air Force has six combat aircraft and 8 armed helicopters.

Russia maintains 3,500 army personnel in Armenia. An agreement on military co-operation with Russia was signed in 1996 which paved the way for joint military exercises. A protocol was also signed on the establishment of coalition troops in Transcaucasia and the planned use of Russian and Armenian armed forces as part of coalition troops in cases of mutual interest. On 19 December 2001, Russian President Vladimir Putin signed a federal law relating to an agreement between the Russian Federation and the Republic of Armenia on the joint planning of the use of troops (forces) in the interests of joint security provision. This stipulates measures to prevent the use by third countries of the territory of Armenia for purposes that may inflict damage on Russian national interests.

MILITARY EXPENDITURE – 6.4 per cent of GDP (2003)
MILITARY PERSONNEL – 44,874: Army 41,714, Air Force 3,160; Paramilitaries 1,000
CONSCRIPTION DURATION – Two years

ECONOMY AND TRADE
The break-up of the USSR led to a severe economic decline in the Armenian economy in the early 1990s, which exacerbated the difficulties already being experienced as a result of the severe 1988 earthquake and the Azeri and Turkish economic embargoes that have been in place since 1988. Armenia has a strong agricultural sector in low-lying areas, where industrial and fruit crops are grown. Grain is produced in the hills and the country is also noted for its wine and brandy. There are large mineral deposits including copper ore and molybdenum. Armenia's chemicals, industrial vehicles and textiles industries were developed under Soviet rule.

The government introduced a programme of economic reforms in 1994 with IMF support, including the liberalisation of prices, stabilisation of the currency and privatisation, and growth rates over the past eight years have been positive. Armenia joined the World Trade Organisation (WTO) in 2003.

In 2003, the Russian Federation assumed the management of Armenia's only nuclear power station, and main electricity producer, in exchange for US$40 million in fuel debts.

GNI – US$2,400 million (2002); US$790 per capita (2002)
ANNUAL AVERAGE GROWTH OF GDP – 9 per cent (2004 est.)
INFLATION RATE – 3.0 per cent (2002)
UNEMPLOYMENT – 30 per cent (2003 est.)
TOTAL EXTERNAL DEBT – US$898 million (2000)
IMPORTS – US$1,270 million (2003)
EXPORTS – US$680 million (2003)

BALANCE OF PAYMENTS
Trade – US$440 million deficit (2003)
Current Account – US$186 million deficit (2003)

Trade with UK	2003	2004
Imports from UK	£5,575,000	£5,604,000
Exports to UK	64,069,000	632,000

EDUCATION
State education is free and compulsory for all children aged seven to 14. Children attend primary school for three years, until the age of nine, then progress on to secondary school for five years, until the age of 14. At the end of intermediate school a Certificate of Basic Education is awarded. Senior secondary school may be attended for two years from the ages of 14 to 16. There are 25 institutions of higher education in Armenia (including seven colleges).
ILLITERACY RATE – (m) 0.6 per cent; (f) 2 per cent
GROSS ENROLMENT RATIO (percentage of relevant age group) – primary 96 per cent (2002); secondary 87 per cent (2002); tertiary 26 per cent (2002)

MEDIA AND CULTURE
Television and radio in Armenia are controlled by the state. All print and broadcast media are obliged to register with the Ministry of Justice.

Armenia is Middle Eastern in character and atmosphere but with Christianity, not Islam, as the dominant religion – there are more than 40,000 churches and monuments throughout the country. Major cultural figures include the poets Nahapet Kuchak (16th century) and Sayat-Nova (18th century), the composer Aram Khachaturian (1903–78), and the film director Sergo Parajanov (1924–90).

AUSTRALIA

Commonwealth of Australia

AREA – 7,682,300 sq. km
POPULATION – 19,913,144 (2004 est.): 458,520 of
   Aboriginal and Torres Strait Islander origin (2001 est.).
   The language is English
CAPITAL – Canberra, in the Australian Capital Territory
   (population, 322,500, 2003 estimate). It has been the
   seat of government since 1927
MAJOR CITIES – ΨAdelaide; ΨBrisbane; ΨHobart;
   ΨMelbourne; ΨPerth, including Fremantle; ΨSydney
CURRENCY – Australian dollar ($A) of 100 cents
NATIONAL ANTHEM – Advance Australia fair
NATIONAL DAY – 26 January (Australia Day)
NATIONAL FLAG – The British Blue Ensign with five stars
   of the Southern Cross in the fly and the white
   Commonwealth Star of seven points beneath the Union
   Flag
LIFE EXPECTANCY (years) – 80 (2004 est.)
MORTALITY RATE (per 1,000 population) – 7.38
   (2004 est.)
INFANT MORTALITY (per 1,000 live births) – 4.76
   (2004 est.)
HIV / AIDS ADULT PREVALENCE – 0.1 per cent
DEATH PENALTY – No (abolished 1985)
POPULATION GROWTH RATE – 0.9 per cent (2004 est.)
POPULATION DENSITY – 3 per sq. km (2003)
URBAN POPULATION – 87 per cent (2001)

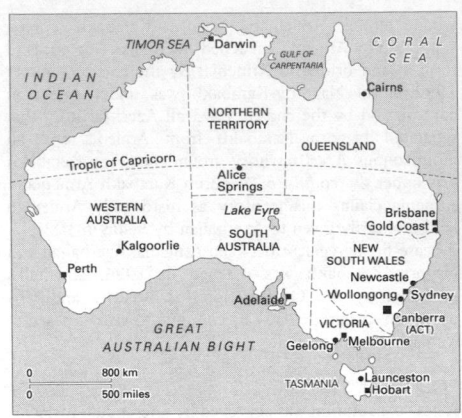

CLIMATE AND TERRAIN

Australia is a continent, the world's sixth-largest country and home to a wide variety of landscapes and weather conditions. The interior is dominated by hot deserts and is only thinly populated. The eastern and south-eastern coastlines are the most densely populated areas and feature mountains, flat golden beaches and primary rain forests. The highest point of elevation is 2,230 m (Mount Kosciuszko) and the lowest is −15 m (Lake Eyre). The summer begins in December, the winter in June, the spring in September and the autumn in March. Average annual temperatures range from zero to 34°C.

HISTORY AND POLITICS

The Aboriginals are thought to have arrived in Australia from south-east Asia *c*.40,000 years ago. Europeans first discovered Australia in the 17th century. Its eastern coast was claimed by Capt. James Cook on behalf of Britain in 1770 and became a penal colony; Tasmania, Western Australia, South Australia, Victoria and Queensland were established as colonies between 1825 and 1859. The individual colonies became self-governing from the 1850s onwards and were federated as the Commonwealth of Australia on 1 January 1901, at which time Australia gained dominion status within the British Empire. Australia became independent within the British Commonwealth by the 1931 Statute of Westminster. Following a referendum in 1967, the Aboriginal population was granted full political rights. In 1986, the Australia Act was passed, which abolished the remaining legislative, executive and judicial links to the UK, while

retaining the British monarch as head of state. In 1998, the Constitutional Convention voted to sever constitutional links with the British monarchy, but a national referendum in 1999 on the proposal to make Australia a republic was defeated, with 45.3 per cent voting in favour and 54.7 per cent against.

The general election of 9 October 2004 was won by the ruling Liberal Party/National Party coalition with 46.4 per cent of the vote and a total of 87 seats in the House of Representatives.

POLITICAL SYSTEM

The government is a federal commonwealth within the Commonwealth of Nations, the executive power being vested in the sovereign (through the Governor-General) assisted by a federal government. Under the constitution the powers of the federal government are defined, and residuary legislative power remains with the states. The right of a state to legislate on any matter is not abrogated except in connection with matters exclusively under federal control, but where a state law is inconsistent with a law of the Commonwealth, the latter prevails to the extent of the inconsistency.

Parliament consists of Queen Elizabeth II, the Senate and the House of Representatives. The constitution provides that the number of members of the House of Representatives shall be, as nearly as practicable, twice the number of senators. Members of the Senate are elected for six years by universal suffrage, half the members retiring every third year, except in the Australian Capital Territory and the Northern Territory, where members are elected for a three-year term. Each of the six states returns 12 senators, and the Australian Capital Territory and the Northern Territory two each. The House of Representatives, similarly elected for a maximum of three years, contains members proportionate to the population, with a minimum of five members for each state. There are now 150 members in the House of Representatives, including two members for the Northern Territory and two for the Australian Capital Territory.

Each state has its own judicature of supreme, superior and minor courts for criminal and civil cases. The federal courts are the Federal Court of Australia, which has jurisdiction mainly in areas of civil law and as a court of appeal from state and territory courts in some cases, and the High Court of Australia, which has jurisdiction mainly in areas of constitutional law, inter-state cases and external relations, and hears appeals from the Federal Court and from the Supreme Courts of states and territories.

Governor-General, Maj. Gen. Michael Jeffery AC, CVO, MC, *assumed office* 11 August 2003

SELECTED GOVERNMENT MEMBERS *as at July 2005*
Prime Minister, John Howard
Deputy Prime Minister, Transport and Regional Services, John Anderson
Defence, Robert Hill
Foreign Affairs, Alexander Downer
Treasurer, Peter Costello

AUSTRALIAN HIGH COMMISSION
Australia House, Strand, London WC2B 4LA T 020-7379 4334
High Commissioner, HE Michael L'Estrange, apptd 2000

NEW SOUTH WALES GOVERNMENT OFFICE,
Australia Centre, Strand, London WC2B 4LG
T 020-7887 5871
Director, Leanne Grogan
AGENT-GENERAL FOR QUEENSLAND, 392 Strand,
London WC2R 0LZ T 020-7836 1333
Agent-General, John Dawson
AGENT-GENERAL FOR SOUTH AUSTRALIA, Australia
Centre, Strand, London WC2B 4LG T 020-7836 3455
Agent-General, Maurice de Rohan
AGENT-GENERAL FOR VICTORIA, Australia Centre,
Strand, London WC2B 4LG T 020-7836 2656
Agent-General, David Buckingham
AGENT-GENERAL FOR WESTERN AUSTRALIA, Australia
Centre, Strand, London WC2B 4LG T 020-7240 2881
Agent-General, Robert Fisher

BRITISH HIGH COMMISSION
Commonwealth Avenue, Yarralumla, Canberra, ACT 2600
T (+61) (2) 6270 6666
High Commissioner, HE Sir Alastair Goodlad, KCMG,
apptd 1999
E bhc.canberra@mail.uk.emb.gov.au
Consuls-General, D. H. Cairns *(Brisbane)*; A. D. Sprake
(Melbourne); H. Dunnachie *(Perth)*; P. Beckingham
(Sydney)

BRITISH COUNCIL
PO BOX 88, Edgecliff, Sydney, NSW 2027
T (+61) (2) 9326 2022
E enquiries@britishcouncil.org.au
Director, Simon Gammell

FEDERAL STRUCTURE
In the states, executive authority is vested in a Governor (appointed by the Crown), assisted by a Council of Ministers or Executive Council. Each state has a legislature comprising a Legislative Council and a Legislative Assembly or House of Assembly which are elected for four-year terms, except Queensland, which has a Legislative Assembly only.

The Northern Territory and Australian Capital Territory have a Legislative Assembly only.

DEFENCE
The Army has 71 main battle tanks, 364 armoured personnel carriers and 255 light armoured vehicles.. The Navy has six submarines, 10 frigates, 15 patrol and coastal vessels and 16 armed helicopters. There are bases at Sydney, Stirling, Cairns, Darwin, Flinders, Jervis Bay and Noura. The Air Force has 152 combat aircraft.
MILITARY EXPENDITURE – 2.3 per cent of GDP (2003)
MILITARY PERSONNEL – 51,800: Army 25,300, Navy 12,850, Air Force 13,650

ECONOMY AND TRADE
The wide range of climatic and soil conditions has resulted in a diversity of crops. Generally, cereal crops (excluding rice and sorghum) are widely grown, while other crops are confined to specific locations in a few states. However, scant or erratic rainfall, limited potential for irrigation and unsuitable soils or topography have restricted intensive agriculture.

Cattle and sheep ranching is widespread and produces significant agricultural products including meat, meat derivatives, wool and dairy products.

Significant mineral resources include bauxite, coal, copper, crude petroleum, gems, gold, ilmenite, iron ore, lead, limestone, manganese, nickel, rutile, salt, silver, tin, tungsten, uranium, zinc and zircon. In 2003 349,470,000 tonnes of coal, 212,881,000 tonnes of iron ore, 2,006,000 tonnes of titanium minerals, 688,888 tonnes of lead, and 282,000 kilogrammes (metal content) of gold were produced.

In 2002–3 the main exports were coal, not agglomerated (10.3 per cent); petroleum and related products (5.1 per cent); gold (4.8 per cent); iron ore and concentrates (4.6 per cent); aluminium (3.5 per cent). The major imports were motor vehicles, excluding public transport (7.7 per cent); petroleum and related products (5.9 per cent); aircraft and associated equipment (4.1 per cent); computer technology (3.7 per cent); medicaments

STATES AND TERRITORIES

	Area (sq. km)	Resident population 30 September 2003	Capital	Governor 2004
Australian Capital Territory (ACT)	2,349	322,600	Canberra	–
New South Wales (NSW)	801,349	6,699,300	Sydney	HE Prof. Marie Bashir, AC
Northern Territory (NT)	1,352,158	198,600	Darwin*	John Anictomatis, OAM†
Queensland (QLD)	1,734,157	3,817,000	Brisbane	HE Quentin Bryce, AC
South Australia (SA)	985,335	1,529,400	Adelaide	Marjorie Jackson-Nelson, AC, MBE
Tasmania (TAS.)	67,914	478,400	Hobart	HE Richard W. Butler, AC
Victoria (VIC.)	227,594	4,933,600	Melbourne	HE John Landy, AC, MBE
Western Australia (WA)	2,534,483	1,959,700	Perth	HE Lt.-Gen. John M. Sanderson, AC

* Seat of administration † Administrator

(3.2 per cent); and telecommunications equipment (3.2 per cent)

Australia's main trading partners are Japan, the USA, New Zealand, China, Korea, Germany, Taiwan, Indonesia and the UK.

GNI – US$384,100 million (2002); US$19,530 per capita (2002)
ANNUAL AVERAGE GROWTH OF GDP – 3.5 per cent (2004 est.)
INFLATION RATE – 2.8 per cent (2003)
UNEMPLOYMENT – 5.8 per cent (2004)
FOREIGN DIRECT INVESTMENT – US$32,493 million (1997–2000)
IMPORTS – US$89,000 million (2003)
EXPORTS – US$72,000 million (2003)

BALANCE OF PAYMENTS
Trade – US$15,254 million deficit (2003)
Current Account - US$30,554 million deficit (2003)

Trade with UK	2003	2004
Imports from UK	£2,300,935,000	£2,405,247,000
Exports to UK	1,825,400,000	1,897,159,000

TRANSPORT INFRASTRUCTURE

Most long-distance internal travel is by air or road. Road and rail networks are concentrated in the more densely populated areas of the east and south, and around Perth in the west. Elsewhere, roads are more usual than railways, and both skirt the deserts of the interior, apart from a few transcontinental routes. There are six government-owned railway systems, and in 2002 there was a total of 41,286 km of railway track. Most heavy freight is moved by road trains, trucks hauling two or three trailers, which measure up to 45 metres in length and have a net capacity of about 100 tonnes. There are 811,603 km of highways. The state capitals are all major ports, and there are private mining ports at Gove and Groote Eylandt in the Northern Territory.

EDUCATION

Education is administered by the state governments and is compulsory between the ages of six and 15 (16 in Tasmania). It is available at government schools controlled by the state education department and at private or independent schools, some of which are denominational. Tertiary education is available through universities and technical and further education colleges. There are 41 universities in Australia; the Australian Capital Territory has three universities, New South Wales 13, Queensland nine, Northern Territory one, South Australia three, Tasmania one, Victoria nine and Western Australia five.

GROSS ENROLMENT RATIO (percentage of relevant age group) – primary 102 per cent (2002); secondary 154 per cent (2002); tertiary 65 per cent (2002)

MEDIA

Australia's leading newspapers are *The Sydney Morning Herald, Herald Sun, The Australian, The Daily Telegraph, The Age, The West Australian, The Australian Financial Review*, and *The Advertiser*. There is an established tradition of public service broadcasting (via the Australian Broadcasting Corporation and the Special Broadcasting Service) and of commercial television (Seven Network, Nine Network, Ten Network). Australian media tycoon Rupert Murdoch owns News Corporation and a considerable subscription-based television empire.

The Australian film industry is small but highly regarded and well funded. In 2004 there were 5.2 million internet users.

CULTURE

The roots of Australian Aboriginal art date back 30,000 years and, modern Aboriginal artists use traditional forms in contemporary ways. Australian theatre excels in established formats but is also known for its experimental edge. The Australian literary scene is internationally acclaimed with authors such as Patrick White (1912–90) winning the Nobel Prize in 1973 and Peter Carey (b. 1943) and Thomas Keneally (b. 1935) winning the Booker Prize.

EXTERNAL TERRITORIES

ASHMORE AND CARTIER ISLANDS

Ashmore Islands (known as Middle, East and West Islands) and Cartier Island are situated in the Indian Ocean 850 km and 790 km west of Darwin respectively. The uninhabited islands are a nature reserve and a marine reserve. The islands became an Australian territory in 1933, and are administered through the Department of Transport and Regional Services.

THE AUSTRALIAN ANTARCTIC TERRITORY

The Australian Antarctic Territory was established in 1933 and comprises all the islands and territories, other than Adélie Land, which are situated south of latitude 60° S. and lying between 160° E. longitude and 45° E. longitude. The territory is administered by the Antarctic Division of the Department of the Environment and Heritage.

CHRISTMAS ISLAND
AREA – 135 sq. km
POPULATION – 1,928 (2001)

Christmas Island is situated in the Indian Ocean about 1,408 km north-west of North West Cape in Western Australia. The island was annexed by Britain in 1888, sovereignty was transferred to Australia in 1958 and the island is administered through the Department of Transport and Regional Services. The Shire of Christmas Island (SOCI), which has nine elected members, is responsible for municipal functions and services on the island. The main industry is phosphate mining. A satellite launching facility is currently being built on the island for the Asia Pacific Space Centre.

COCOS (KEELING) ISLANDS
AREA – 14 sq. km
POPULATION – 600 (2001)

The Cocos (Keeling) Islands are two separate atolls (North Keeling Island and, 24 km to the south, the main atoll) comprising some 27 small coral islands, situated in the Indian Ocean, about 2,950 km north-west of Perth. The main islands of the southern atoll are West Island (about 9 km in length); Home Island, where 80 per cent of the population lives, including most of the Cocos Malay community; Direction Island, Horsburgh and South Island.

The islands were declared a British possession in 1857, and became an Australian territory in 1955. All land in the islands was granted to George Clunies-Ross and his heirs by Queen Victoria in 1886. The Australian government purchased most of the Clunies-Ross land and property in 1978, and the remainder in 1984 and 1993. The land is held in trust for the residents, with the local government body, the Shire of the Cocos (Keeling) Islands, as trustee. In 1984 the Cocos community, in a UN-supervised Act of Self-Determination, voted to integrate with Australia. The islands are administered by the Australian government through the Department of Transport and Regional Services.

CORAL SEA ISLANDS TERRITORY

The Coral Sea Islands Territory lies east of Queensland between the Great Barrier Reef and longitude 156° 06′ E., and between latitudes 12° and 24° S. It comprises scattered islands, spread over a sea area of 780,000 sq. km. The islands are formed mainly of coral and sand, and most are extremely small. There is a manned meteorological station on Willis Island but the remaining islands are uninhabited. The Territory was established in 1969 and is administered through the Department of Transport and Regional Services.

HEARD ISLAND AND MCDONALD ISLANDS

The Territory of the Heard and McDonald Islands, about 4,100 km south-west of Perth, comprises all the islands and rocks lying between 52° 30′ and 53° 30′ S. latitude and 72° and 74° 30′ E. longitude. The subantarctic islands were discovered in the 1850s; they are now administered by the Antarctic Division of the Department of the Environment and Heritage.

NORFOLK ISLAND

AREA – 34.5 sq. km
POPULATION – 2,037 (2001)
SEAT OF GOVERNMENT – Kingston

Norfolk Island is situated in the South Pacific Ocean, about 1,600 km north-east of Sydney. It is about 8 km long by 5 km wide. The climate is mild and subtropical.

Discovered by Captain Cook in 1774, the island served as a penal colony from 1788 to 1814 and from 1825 to 1855. In 1856, 194 descendants of the *Bounty* mutineers accepted an invitation to leave Pitcairn and settle on Norfolk Island.

The island has had a substantial degree of internal self-government since 1979, when the nine-member Legislative Assembly was established. The Administrator represents the federal government and is responsible to the Australian Minister for Regional Services, Territories and Local Government.

AUSTRIA

Republik Österreich – Republic of Austria

AREA – 83,854 sq. km. Neighbours: Czech Republic and Slovakia (north), Italy and Slovenia (south), Hungary (east), Germany (north-west), Switzerland and Liechtenstein (west)
POPULATION – 8,174,762 (2004 est.). The language is German, but the rights of the Slovene, Croat, Hungarian, Czech, Slovak, Roma and Sinti minorities are protected. The predominant religion is Roman Catholicism

CAPITAL – Vienna, on the Danube (population, 1,550,123, 2001 census)
MAJOR CITIES – Graz; Innsbruck; Klagenfurt; Linz; Salzburg
CURRENCY – Euro (€) of 100 cents
NATIONAL ANTHEM – Land der Berge, Land am Strome [Land of mountains, land on the river]
NATIONAL DAY – 26 October
NATIONAL FLAG – Three equal horizontal stripes of red, white, red
LIFE EXPECTANCY (years) – 78.87 (2004 est.)
MORTALITY RATE (per 1,000 population) – 9.56 (2004 est.)
HIV / AIDS ADULT PREVALENCE – 0.3 per cent (2003 est.)
DEATH PENALTY – No (abolished 1968)
INFANT MORTALITY (per 1,000 births) – 4.68 (2004 est.)
POPULATION GROWTH RATE – 0.14 per cent (2004 est.)
POPULATION DENSITY – 97 per sq. km (2002)

CLIMATE AND TERRAIN

The north and east of the landlocked country feature rolling hills, while the west and south contain the Austrian Alps, famous as a winter sports destination. The highest point of elevation is 3,798 m (Grossglockner) and the lowest is 115 m (Neusiedler See). There is a temperate climate, with temperature averages ranging from 2°C in January to 20°C in July.

HISTORY AND POLITICS

The Austrian state dates back to the eighth century AD when Emperor Charlemagne conquered the territory and founded the *Ostmark*, the eastern march of the Holy Roman Empire, which had been settled from the sixth century onwards by Germanic tribes. It became a duchy and in 1282 passed to the Habsburg dynasty, which established an empire that united much of central Europe, including present-day Austria and Hungary, and established hegemony over the other German states. Hegemony was lost to Prussia in the 19th century, when growing Hungarian nationalism also led to the establishment of the dual monarchy of Austria-Hungary. The assassination of the heir to the throne in 1914 triggered the First World War, towards the end of which the Austro-Hungarian Empire collapsed, and most of the German-speaking lands became the Republic of Austria in November 1918. In March 1938 Austria was incorporated into Nazi Germany (the *Anschluss*) under the name *Ostmark*. After the Second World War, the Republic of Austria was reconstituted within its 1937 frontiers and a freely elected government took office in December 1945. The country was divided into four zones occupied respectively by the UK, USA, USSR and France, while Vienna was jointly occupied by the four powers.

In 1955 the occupying powers withdrew, recognizing Austria as a sovereign, independent and democratic state, with the same frontiers as on 1 January 1938, under terms of the Austrian State Treaty. Austria joined the European Union in 1995. The national assembly ratified the EU constitution in May 2005. After the Social Democrats and the Austrian People's Party (ÖVP) failed to form a coalition following the general election of 1999, a coalition government comprising the ÖVP and the far-right Austrian Freedom Party (FPÖ) (led by Jörg Haider, who had expressed support for some aspects of the wartime Nazi regime) was sworn in on 5 February 2000 after both parties signed a document expressing their commitment to the European Union and aversion to discrimination and intolerance. International opposition to the inclusion of the FP in the government resulted in the suspension of bilateral relations between the governments of the other EU members and Austria. In May, Jörg Haider resigned as leader of the FPÖ in an attempt to calm the situation. The suspension of relations between the EU members and Austria was lifted in September 2000 following an investigation into the Austrian government which cleared it of any wrongdoing. The ÖVP won the legislative elections of November 2002 with 42.3 per cent of the vote. But the Party did not gain enough votes to form a government on its own. After coalition talks with the Social Democrats and Greens failed, ÖVP leader Wolfgang Schüssel announced in February 2003 that he had re-formed his previous coalition with the FPÖ and a new cabinet was appointed.

POLITICAL SYSTEM

There is a bicameral national assembly; the lower house *(Nationalrat)* has 183 directly elected members and the upper house *(Bundesrat)* has 64 representatives of the nine provinces (dependent on population). There is a four per cent qualification for parliamentary representation.

HEAD OF STATE

President of the Republic of Austria, Heinz Fischer, *took office* 8 July 2004

SELECTED GOVERNMENT MEMBERS *as at July 2005*
Chancellor, Wolfgang Schüssel
Vice-Chancellor, Minister for Infrastructure, Hubert Gorbach
Defence, Günther Platter
Finance, Karl-Heinz Grasser
Foreign Affairs, Ursula Plassnik
Interior, Liese Prokop

AUSTRIAN EMBASSY

18 Belgrave Mews West, London SW1 8HU
T 020-7235 3731
Ambassador Extraordinary and Plenipotentiary, HE Alexander Christiani, apptd 2000

BRITISH EMBASSY

Jaurèsgasse 12, 1030 Vienna T (+43) (1) 716130
Ambassador Extraordinary and Plenipotentiary, HE John MacGregor, CVO, apptd 2003

BRITISH COUNCIL

Siebensterngasse 21, 1070 Vienna T (+43) (1) 533 2616
E bc.vienna@britishcouncil.at
Director, Ruth Sinclair-Jones

FEDERAL STRUCTURE

There are nine provinces (population figures for 2001): Burgenland (277,569); Carinthia (559,404); Lower Austria (1,545,804); Salzburg (515,327); Styria (1,183,303); Tirol (673,504); Upper Austria (1,376,797); Vienna (1,550,123); Vorarlberg (351,095).

DEFENCE

The Army has 114 main battle tanks and 645 armoured personnel carriers. The Air Force has 63 combat aircraft and 11 armed helicopters.

MILITARY EXPENDITURE – 1.0 per cent of GDP (2003)
MILITARY PERSONNEL – Army 35,000, of which Air Force 6,000
CONSCRIPTION DURATION – Eight months, or seven months plus refresher training

ECONOMY AND TRADE

Major industries include iron and steel production, chemicals, electrical goods, mechanical engineering, textiles and paper production. Agricultural products include wheat, rye, barley, oats, maize, potatoes, sugar beet and turnips. Timber forms a valuable source of Austria's indigenous wealth with approximately 47 per cent of the total land area consisting of forest areas. However, strict regulations have preserved Austria's environment from over-production. Foreign exchange receipts from tourism are a major contribution to the balance of payments. Austria suffered low economic growth in 2001 and 2002.

Main exports are processed goods (iron and steel, other metal goods, textiles, paper and cardboard products), machinery and transport equipment, other finished goods (including clothing), raw materials, chemical products and foodstuffs. Main imports are machinery and transport equipment, processed goods, chemical products, foodstuffs, fuel and energy. Austria's main trading partners are Germany, Italy, France and Switzerland.

GNI – US$192,100 million (2002); US$23,860 per capita (2002)
ANNUAL AVERAGE GROWTH OF GDP – 1.9 per cent (2004 est.)
INFLATION RATE – 2.4 per cent (2000)
UNEMPLOYMENT – 4.4 per cent (2004)
FOREIGN DIRECT INVESTMENT – US$20,400 (1997–2000)
IMPORTS – US$88,300 million (2003)
EXPORTS – US$87,600 million (2003)

BALANCE OF PAYMENTS
Trade – US$1,932 million surplus (2003)
Current Account – US$2,392 deficit (2003)

Trade with UK	2003	2004
Imports from UK	£924,572,000	£1,072,849,000
Exports to UK	1,869,438,000	2,289,888,000

TRANSPORT INFRASTRUCTURE

There are 200,000 km of roads and a network of 1,613 km of *Autobahn* between major cities that also link up with German and Italian networks. The railways are state-owned and comprised 6,123 km of track in 2002, which includes 3,523 km of electrified track. Of the 425 km of waterways, 351 km are navigable and there is considerable trade through the Danube ports by both local and foreign shipping. There are six commercial airports.

EDUCATION

Education is free and compulsory between the ages of six and 15 and there are good facilities for secondary, technical and professional education. There are 14 public, six private and six art universities.

GROSS ENROLMENT RATIO (percentage of relevant age group) – primary 103 per cent (2002); secondary 99 per cent (2002); tertiary 57 per cent (2002)

MEDIA

The public broadcaster Österreichischer Rundfunk (ORF) dominated Austrian television and radio for many years, but the number of private broadcasters is now increasing. By contrast, Austria's print media is largely privately owned. There are approximately six main daily titles including *Der Standard* and *Neue Kronenzeitung*. In 2004 there were approximately 3.7 million internet users.

CULTURE

During the 18th, 19th and 20th centuries Vienna was one of Europe's most culturally important cities, attracting musicians (Wolfgang Amadeus Mozart (1756–91), Ludwig van Beethoven (1770–1827), Johann Strauss Jr. (1825–99), Arnold Schoenberg (1874–1951), and Alban Berg (1885–1935)), philosophers (Ludwig Wittgenstein (1889–1951)), artists (Gustav Klimt (1862–1918)), physicists (Ludwig Boltzmann (1844–1906) and Erwin Schrödinger (1887–1961)) and alternative thinkers (psychoanalyst Sigmund Freud (1856–1939)).

AZERBAIJAN

Azerbaycan Respublıkası – Republic of Azerbaijan

AREA – 86,600 sq. km. Neighbours: Iran (south), Armenia (west), Georgia and the Russian Federation (north)

POPULATION – 7,868,385 (2004 est.): 83 per cent Azeri, 6 per cent Russian and 6 per cent Armenian. There are also Kurds, Jews, Georgians and Turks. There are more Azeris in Iran than in Azerbaijan. The population is predominantly Shia Muslim although it was heavily secularised during the Soviet era. The language is Azeri

CAPITAL – ΨBaki (Baku), population, 1,817,900, 2001 estimate

MAJOR CITIES – Gäncä; Sumqayit

CURRENCY – Manat of 100 gopik

NATIONAL ANTHEM – Azerbaijan! Azerbaijan!

NATIONAL DAY – 28 May (Independence Day)

NATIONAL FLAG – Three horizontal stripes of blue, red and green with a white crescent and eight-pointed star in the centre

LIFE EXPECTANCY – 63.25 (2004 est.)

INFANT MORTALITY – 82.07 (2004 est.)

MORTALITY RATE (per 1,000 population) – 9.76 (2004 est.)

HIV / AIDS ADULT PREVALENCE – 0.1 per cent (2001 est.)

DEATH PENALTY – No (abolished 1998)

POPULATION BELOW POVERTY LINE – 49 per cent (2002)

POPULATION GROWTH RATE – 0.52 per cent (2004 est.)

POPULATION DENSITY – 92 per sq. km (1999)

CLIMATE AND TERRAIN

Azerbaijan occupies the eastern part of the Caucasus region of the former Soviet Union, on the western shore of the Caspian Sea. The highest point of elevation is 4,485 m (Bazarduzu Dagi) while the lowest is −28 m (Caspian Sea). The north-eastern part of the republic is taken up by the south-eastern end of the main Caucasus ridge, its south-western part by the smaller Caucasus hills and its south-eastern corner by the spurs of the Talysh Ridge. Central Azerbaijan is formed by a depression

irrigated by the River Kura and the lower reaches of its tributary the Araks. Azerbaijan has a continental climate.

HISTORY AND POLITICS

The Turkic Azeri people formed an independent state in the first century BC. By the seventh century, this precarious civilisation was invaded by Muslim Arabs who introduced Islam and secured the region as a province of the Muslim caliphate. Azerbaijan was again invaded by Persia in the 16th century. The country was divided during the Russo-Persian wars of the early 19th century, the northern portion (present-day Azerbaijan) becoming part of the Russian Empire and the southern portion remaining Persian and subsequently Iranian.

In 1918 the Azerbaijan Democratic Republic was established. It was overthrown by Communists and Azerbaijan acceded to the USSR in 1922.

In January 1990, the Azeri Popular Front took power from the local Communist Party and declared independence from the Soviet Union. Soviet troops overthrew the Popular Front and restored the Communist regime, which declared Azerbaijan's independence in August 1991. President Elchibey, elected in 1992, was overthrown in a coup and replaced by Heydar Aliyev, the former Communist Party leader, who retained power despite a number of coup attempts in the mid-1990s. President Aliyev won the presidential election in 1998, with 76.1 per cent of the vote. However, the elections were criticised by the Organisation for Security and Co-operation in Europe (OSCE) and other international monitoring groups. A general election was held in 2000. The New Azerbaijan Party, founded by Aliyev, won 62.5 per cent of the vote (78 seats). The election was boycotted by several parties, who alleged that electoral fraud had been committed; their claims were supported by OSCE observers. Repeat elections were held in January 2001 in 11 districts and Aliyev's party again won the vote. In October 2003 Aliyev withdrew from the presidential race due to health problems (he died in December 2003) and endorsed the campaign of his son, Ilham, who was elected.

SECESSION

In 1988 fighting broke out in the predominantly Armenian-populated region of Nagorny-Karabakh between Soviet Azeri forces and ethnic Armenians demanding unification with Armenia. In late 1993 Nagorno-Karabakh forces captured all of the region, together with all Azeri territory separating the region from Armenia (20 per cent of Azeri territory). Azeri forces pushed back the Nagorno-Karabakh forces in early 1994 before a cease-fire agreement was signed in May 1994. The fighting briefly flared up again along the Azeri-Armenian border in April and May 1997. Peace talks, held under the auspices of the OSCE, have yet to yield any significant results, although both sides reaffirmed their commitment to finding a peaceful solution at a meeting in October 1997, in which both sides rejected the idea of full independence for Nagorny-Karabakh as 'unrealistic'. Further talks in 2001 failed to reach an agreement.

POLITICAL SYSTEM

A new constitution was approved by a referendum in 1995 which created a republic with executive power to be exercised by the president and with legislative power vested in the unicameral *Milli Majlis* (National Assembly). The *Milli Majlis* has 125 seats, of which 100 are directly elected and 25 are allocated by proportional representation. The president appoints the prime minister and the cabinet. Both the president and the National Assembly are directly elected for five-year terms.

HEAD OF STATE
President, Ilham Aliyev, *assumed office* 31 October 2003

SELECTED GOVERNMENT MEMBERS *as at July 2005*
Prime Minister, Artur Rasizade
First Deputy Prime Ministers, Yakub Abdulla Eyyubov; Abbas Abbasov
Deputy Prime Ministers, Abid Sarifov; Ali Hasanov *(Chair of State Refugee Committee)*; Elchin Efendiyev
Defence, Lt.-Gen. Safar Abiyev
Finance, Avaz Alakbarov
Foreign Affairs, Elmar Mamedyarov
Interior, Col.-Gen. Ramil Usubov

EMBASSY OF THE REPUBLIC OF AZERBAIJAN
4 Kensington Court, London W8 5DL T 020-7938 5482
Ambassador Extraordinary and Plenipotentiary, HE Rafael Ibrahimov, apptd 2001

BRITISH EMBASSY
45 Khagani Street, Baku AZ1010 T (+994) (12) 975188/89/90
E office@britemb.baku.az
Ambassador Extraordinary and Plenipotentiary, HE Dr Laurie Bristow

BRITISH COUNCIL
1 Vali Mammadov Street, Icheri Sheher, Baku AZ1000
T (+994) (12) 497 1593 / 497 2013
E enquiries@britishcouncil.az
Director, Andy Williams

DEFENCE
The Army has 220 main battle tanks, 135 armoured infantry fighting vehicles and 468 armoured personnel carriers. The Navy is based at Baku, with a share of the former Soviet Caspian Fleet Flotilla, comprising six patrol and coastal vessels. The Air Force has 47 combat aircraft and 15 attack helicopters.
MILITARY EXPENDITURE – 3.2 per cent of GDP (2003)
MILITARY PERSONNEL – 66,490: Army 56,840, Navy 1,750, Air Force 7,900; Paramilitaries 15,000
CONSCRIPTION DURATION – 17 months but can be extended for ground forces

ECONOMY AND TRADE
Industry is dominated by oil and natural gas extraction and related industries centred in Baku and Sumgait. The oil deposits in the Caspian Sea are estimated to be more than 6,000 million barrels, and natural gas reserves are estimated to be more than 1,200,000 million cubic metres. Oil pipelines (1,631 km) link the Azeri oilfields to Black Sea ports in the Russian Federation and Georgia and a Mediterranean Sea port in Turkey.

The republic is also rich in mineral resources, with iron, copper, aluminium, lead and zinc, and is important as cotton-growing and silkworm-breeding areas.

Around 90 per cent of agricultural land has been privatised. Grapes, cereals (primarily wheat, barley, maize and rice), cotton, vegetables and fruit are the major agricultural products.
GNI – US$5,800 million (2002); US$710 per capita (2002)

ANNUAL AVERAGE GROWTH OF GDP – 9.8 per cent (2004 est.)
INFLATION RATE – 1.8 per cent (2000)
UNEMPLOYMENT – 1.2 per cent (2004)
TOTAL EXTERNAL DEBT – US$1,184 million (2000)
IMPORTS – US$1,036 million (1999)
EXPORTS – US$929 million (1999)

BALANCE OF PAYMENTS
Trade – US$98 million deficit (2003)
Current Account – US$2,021 million deficit (2003)

Trade with UK	2003	2004
Imports from UK	£139,681,000	£263,624,000
Exports to UK	16,385,000	15,525,000

TRANSPORT INFRASTRUCTURE
There are 2,200 km of railway track, much of it electrified, and over 25,000 km of roads. Moscow has agreed to provide US$300 million for the construction of the Azeri section of the north-south highway between northern and central Europe and the Gulf states. There are 72 airports. There are ferry links to Turkmenistan.

EDUCATION
Education up to university level is free. There are several universities and colleges of higher education.
ILLITERACY RATE – (m) 1 per cent; (f) 4 per cent (2000)
GROSS ENROLMENT RATIO (percentage of relevant age group) – primary 93 per cent (2002); secondary 80 per cent (2002); tertiary 23 per cent (2002)

MEDIA AND CULTURE
The state runs press, television and radio in Azerbaijan but there is an increasingly successful private sector, boosted by the issue of five new regional television licences in 2002.

Azerbaijan reflects both European (mainly Russian) and Islamic (mainly Turkish) cultures and has ancient and distinguished literary and musical traditions. The country is famous for its textiles – colourfully embroidered carpets, veils, towels and shawls featuring geometric patterns, sometimes worked with real gold or silver. Azerbaijan was the birthplace of the prophet Zoroaster, who founded one of the first monotheistic religions in the world (sixth century BC).

THE BAHAMAS

Commonwealth of the Bahamas

AREA – 13,939 sq. km
POPULATION – 299,697 (2004 est.). The language is English
CAPITAL – ΨNassau (population, 172,196, 1996 estimate)
CURRENCY – Bahamian dollar (B$) of 100 cents
NATIONAL ANTHEM – March on, Bahamaland
NATIONAL DAY – 10 July (Independence Day)
NATIONAL FLAG – Horizontal stripes of aquamarine, gold and aquamarine, with a black equilateral triangle on the hoist
LIFE EXPECTANCY (years) – 65.63 (2004 est.)
MORTALITY RATES (per 1,000 population) – 8.82 (2004 est.)

INFANT MORTALITY (per 1,000 births) – 25.7
(2004 est.)
HIV / AIDS ADULT PREVALENCE – 3 per cent (2003 est.)
DEATH PENALTY – Yes
POPULATION GROWTH RATE – 0.72 per cent
(2004 est.)
POPULATION DENSITY – 22 per sq. km (2001)
MILITARY EXPENDITURE – 0.6 per cent GDP (2003)
MILITARY PERSONNEL – 860

CLIMATE AND TERRAIN

The Bahamas extend in a chain running from the coast of
Florida in the north-west almost to Hispaniola in the
south-east. The group consists of more than 700 islands
and 2,400 cays, all low-lying; the highest point is 63 m at
Mount Alvernia, Cat Island. The principal islands include:
Abaco, Acklins, Andros, Berry Islands, Bimini, Cat Island,
Crooked Island, Eleuthera, Exuma, Grand Bahama,
Harbour Island, Inagua, Long Island, Mayaguana, New
Providence (on which the capital, Nassau, is located),
Ragged Island, Rum Cay, San Salvador and Spanish Wells.
The 14 major islands are inhabited, as are a few of the
smaller islands. The climate is semitropical. The hurricane
season is June to November.

HISTORY AND POLITICS

The Bahamas were discovered by Columbus in 1492,
settled by the British in the 17th century and became a
Crown colony in 1717. Taken over in 1782 by the
Spanish, the Treaty of Versailles in 1783 restored them to
the British. The Bahamas became self-governing in 1964
and gained their independence on 10 July 1973. The
Progressive Liberal Party held power for 25 years until
the Free National movement won an absolute majority in
the 1992 general election. A general election held in
2002 was won by the Progressive Liberal Party (PLP),
which defeated the Free National Movement Party
(FNM). The PLP holds 28 seats in the House of Assembly,
the FNM eight seats and Independents four seats.

POLITICAL SYSTEM
The head of state is Queen Elizabeth II who is represented
in the islands by a Governor-General. There is a Senate of
16 appointed members and a House of Assembly of 40
members elected by universal suffrage for a five-year term.
Governor-General, Dame Ivy Dumont, DCMG

SELECTED GOVERNMENT MEMBERS *as at July 2005*
Prime Minister, Finance, Perry Christie
Deputy Prime Minister, National Security, Cynthia Pratt
Minister of State for Finance, James Smith
Foreign Affairs, Public Service, Fred Mitchell

BAHAMAS HIGH COMMISSION
10 Chesterfield Street, London W1J 5JL
T 020-7408 4488
High Commissioner, HE Basil O'Brien, CMG, apptd 1999

BRITISH HIGH COMMISSION
Ansbacher House (3rd Floor), East Street
PO Box N-7516, Nassau
T (+1 242) 325 7471
High Commissioner, HE Roderick Gemmell, OBE apptd
2003

ECONOMY AND TRADE

The Bahamas enjoy low inflation and have enjoyed
sustained economic growth – making it the third
wealthiest independent nation in the Americas.

Tourism (90 per cent of which originates from North
America) employs about 40 per cent of the labour force
and provides about half of the country's GDP.
International banking and finance are also important,
accounting for about 15 per cent of GDP. The absence of
direct taxation coupled with internal stability have
enabled the country to become one of the world's leading
offshore financial centres. A securities exchange was
opened in May 2000.

Manufacturing and agriculture account for less than 10
per cent of GDP. The most established industries are
seafood, rum and salt. Agricultural production is mainly
of fresh vegetables, fruit, meat and eggs. Reserves of
aragonite and limestone are commercially exploited.
Freeport is the country's leading industrial centre, with a
pharmaceutical and chemicals plant, an oil trans-shipment
and storage terminal, and port and bunkering facilities.
There are also a brewery and a rum distillery on New
Providence.

The imports are chiefly vehicles, manufactured articles,
chemicals and petroleum. The chief exports are machinery
and transport equipment, foodstuffs and livestock, raw
materials, chemicals, manufactured goods, and beverages
and tobacco.

GNI – US$20,100 per capita (2001)
INFLATION RATE – 1.3 per cent (2004)
UNEMPLOYMENT – 10.2 per cent (2004 est.)
IMPORTS – US$1,800 million (2003)
EXPORTS – US$400 million (2003)

BALANCE OF PAYMENTS
Trade – US$1,151 million deficit (2001)
Current Account – US$348 million deficit (2001)

Trade with UK	2003	2004
Imports from UK	£27,561,000	£38,827,000
Exports to UK	5,210,000	4,790,000

TRANSPORT INFRASTRUCTURE

The main ports are Nassau (New Providence), Freeport
(Grand Bahama) and Matthew Town (Inagua).
International air services are operated from Abaco, Bimini,
Eleuthera, Exuma, Grand Bahama and New Providence.
More than 60 smaller airports and landing strips facilitate
services between the islands, the services being mainly
provided by Bahamasair, the national carrier. The
Bahamas have some 2,693 km of roads, 1,546 km of
which are paved. There are no railways.

EDUCATION

Education is compulsory between the ages of five and 16.
More than 66,000 students are enrolled in Ministry of
Education and independent schools in New Providence
and the Family Islands.
ILLITERACY RATE – (m) 5.0 per cent; (f) 3.6 per cent
(2000)

BAHRAIN

Dawlat al-Bahrayn – The Kingdom of Bahrain

AREA – 694 sq. km
POPULATION – 677,866 (2004 est.); about 70 per cent
are Bahraini; about 40 per cent of the Bahrainis are
Sunni Muslims, the remaining 60 per cent being Shias;
the ruling family and many of the most prominent
merchants are Sunnis. The official language is Arabic;

English is often used for business, and Farsi, Hindi and Urdu are also spoken

CAPITAL – ΨManama (Al-Manamah) (population, 140,401, 1991 census)

CURRENCY – Bahraini dinar (BD) of 1,000 fils

NATIONAL ANTHEM – Bahrayn ona, baladolaman [Our Bahrain, secure]

NATIONAL DAY – 16 December

NATIONAL FLAG – Red, with vertical serrated white bar next to staff

LIFE EXPECTANCY (years) – 74 (2004 est.)

MORTALITY RATE (per 1,000 population) – 4.03 (2004)

HIV / AIDS ADULT PREVALENCE – 0.3 per cent (2001 est.)

INFANT MORTALITY (per 1,000 births) – 17.91 (2004 est.)

DEATH PENALTY – Yes

POPULATION GROWTH RATE – 1.56 per cent (2004 est.)

POPULATION DENSITY – 939 per sq. km (2001)

ILLITERACY RATE – (m) 8.1 per cent; (f) 15 per cent (2003 est.)

CLIMATE AND TERRAIN

Bahrain consists of a group of 33 low-lying islands situated approximately half-way down the Gulf, some 32 km off the east coast of Saudi Arabia. The largest of these, Bahrain Island, is about 48 km long and 16 km wide at its broadest, with the capital, Manama, situated on the north shore. The elevation extremes range from 122 m at the highest point (Jabal ad Dukhan) to 0 m at the lowest (Persian Gulf). The climate is hot and humid (with average annual temperatures ranging from 20°C to 40°C) with little rainfall.

HISTORY AND POLITICS

Bahrain was ruled by Persia (Iran) from 1602 until the Persian rulers were ousted in 1783 by the al-Khalifa family, who still rule. It was under British political control from 1820 until 1971, when it became fully independent. In 1975 the National Assembly was suspended and the amir assumed virtually absolute power after clashes between the Sunni and Shi'ite Muslim communities. Moves to return to democratic rule were made only in response to civil agitation from the 1990s, and a 40-member Consultative Council, the *Majlis al-Shura*, was appointed in 1996; this was an advisory body with no legislative powers. A new constitution was introduced in 2002; it established Bahrain as a kingdom and a constitutional monarchy and legalized elections and political parties.

The first legislative elections since 1973 were held on 24 October 2002 when 174 candidates, including eight women, stood for 37 seats in the newly created House of Representatives. Moderate Sunni Islamists and Independents won 21 of the 40 seats. However, the country's main Shia opposition groups boycotted the poll, citing a proposed legislative right of veto by the Shura Council.

POLITICAL SYSTEM

Under the 2002 constitution, the amir declared himself 'King', and the country became a constitutional hereditary monarchy with the king as head of state. The king appoints the cabinet. There is a bicameral legislature consisting of a lower house, the Chamber of Deputies *(Majlis al-Nuwab)*, and an upper house, the Consultative Council *(Majlis al-Shura)*. The Chamber of Deputies has 40 members directly elected for a four-year term. The members of the Consultative Council are appointed by the king for a four-year term. The 2002 constitution granted women the vote for the first time.

HEAD OF STATE

HH The King of Bahrain, C.-in -C., Bahrain Defence Force, Shaikh Hamad bin Isa al-Khalifa, KCMG *succeeded* 6 March 1999, *proclaimed king* 14 Feburary 2002

Crown Prince, Chair of the National Economic Development Council, Shaikh Salman bin Hamad al-Khalifa

SELECTED GOVERNMENT MEMBERS *as at July 2005*

Prime Minister, HH Shaikh Khalifa bin Sulman al-Khalifa

Deputy Prime Minister, Foreign Affairs, Shaikh Mohammed bin Mubarak al-Khalifa

Deputy Prime Minister, Islamic Affairs, Shaikh Abdullah bin Khalid al-Khalifa

Defence, Maj.-Gen. Shaikh Khalifa bin Ahmed al-Khalifa

Finance and National Economy, Shaikh Ahmed bin Mohammed al-Khalifa

Interior, Maj.-Gen. Shaikh Rashid bin Abdulla bin Ahmed al-Khalifa

EMBASSY OF THE KINGDOM OF BAHRAIN
Belgrave Square, London SW1X 8QB
T 020-7201 9170
Ambassador Extraordinary and Plenipotentiary, HE Shaikh Khalid bin Ahmed al-Khalifa, apptd 2001

BRITISH EMBASSY
21 Government Avenue, Manama 306, PO Box 114
T (+973) 17574100
Ambassador Extraordinary and Plenipotentiary, HE Robin Lamb, apptd 2003

BRITISH COUNCIL
146 Shaikh Salman Highway, Manama 356, PO Box 452
T (+973) 261555 E bc.enquiries@britishcouncil.org.bh
Director, Sandra Hamrouni

DEFENCE

The Army has 180 main battle tanks and 235 armoured personnel carriers. The Navy, based at Mina Salman, has one frigate and 10 patrol and coastal vessels. The Air Force has 33 combat aircraft and 40 armed helicopters.

MILITARY EXPENDITURE – 5.6 per cent of GDP (2003)

MILITARY PERSONNEL – 11,200: Army 8,500, Navy 1,200, Air Force 1,500; Paramilitaries 10,160

ECONOMY AND TRADE

Oil was discovered in Bahrain in the 1930s, and the largest sources of revenue are oil production and refining. The Bahrain field is wholly owned by the Bahrain National Oil Company, and Bahrain also has a half share with Saudi Arabia in the profits of the offshore Abu Sa'afa field. A reservoir of natural gas has recently been developed on Bahrain Island. The Sitra refinery derives about 70 per cent of its crude oil by submarine pipeline from Saudi Arabia. Petroleum accounted for 60 per cent of total export value in 2002. There is some heavy industry on the islands, including a ship-repairing industry and a number of small to medium-sized industrial units. Bahrain has continued to develop as a financial centre and as a tourist destination. Apart from several commercial banks, many international banks have been licensed as offshore units; there are also money brokers and merchant banks. Services accounted for 64 per cent of GDP in 2002.

GNI – US$7,250 million (2001); US$11,130 per capita (2001)

ANNUAL AVERAGE GROWTH OF GDP – 4.9 per cent (2003)

INFLATION RATE – –0.2 per cent (2003)

IMPORTS – US$5,100 million (2003)

EXPORTS – US$6,400 million (2003)

BALANCE OF PAYMENTS

Trade – US$1,611 million surplus (2003)

Current Account – US$68 million deficit (2003)

Trade with UK	2003	2004
Imports from UK	£154,770,000	£157,765,000
Exports to UK	80,552,000	71,459,000

TRANSPORT INFRASTRUCTURE

Bahrain International airport is one of the main air traffic centres of the Gulf; it is the headquarters of Gulf Air, and a stopping point on routes between Europe and Australia and the Far East for other airlines. A 25-km causeway links Bahrain to Saudi Arabia. Of the 3,261 km of road, over three quarters (2,531 km) is paved. There are no railways.

MEDIA AND CULTURE

Domestic television and radio is run by the state-controlled Bahrain Radio and Television Corporation (BRTC). Bahrain has a free press but self-censorship is widely practised. There are four main daily newspapers, two of which are published in English. In 2002 there were 140,000 internet users.

Bahrain is one of the most liberal Gulf States. The capital, Manama, is typically modern but a slower, more traditional pace and way of life can still be found in the surrounding villages and islands.

BANGLADESH

Gaṇ Prajātantrī Bamlādeś – People's Republic of Bangladesh

AREA –143,998 sq. km. Neighbours: India (west, north and east), Myanmar (south-east)

POPULATION – 141,340,476 (2004). The state language is Bengali. Use of Bengali is compulsory in all government departments. English is understood and is used widely as an unofficial second language. The faith of 88 per cent of the population is Islam and of 10.5 per cent Hinduism. Islam has been declared the state religion

CAPITAL – Dhaka (population, 9,912,908, 2001 census)

CURRENCY – Taka (Tk) of 100 paisa

NATIONAL ANTHEM – Amar sonar Bangla [My golden Bengal]

NATIONAL DAY – 26 March (Independence Day)

NATIONAL FLAG – Red circle on a bottle-green ground

LIFE EXPECTANCY (years) – 61.71 (2004 est.)

MORTALITY RATE (per 1,000 population) – 8.52 (2004 est.)

HIV / AIDS ADULT PREVALENCE – 0.1 per cent (2001 est.)

INFANT MORTALITY (per 1,000 births) – 64.32 (2004 est.)

DEATH PENALTY – Yes

POPULATION LIVING BELOW POVERTY LINE – 33.7 per cent (2000)

POPULATION GROWTH RATE – 2.08 per cent (2004 est.)

POPULATION DENSITY – 1,042 per sq. km (2002)

URBAN POPULATION – 26 per cent (2001)

CLIMATE AND TERRAIN

Although hilly in the south-east and north-east, over 75 per cent of the country is less than 3 m above sea-level; the highest elevation is 1,230 m (Keokradong). The south-west forms the delta of the Ganges (Padma) and Brahmaputra (Jamuna) on the Bay of Bengal, the largest estuarine delta in the world, and, with annual rainfall of over 2,500 mm, about one third of the country floods each year during the monsoon season. The climate is tropical: hot, wet and extremely humid during the summer, and mild and dry during the winter.

HISTORY AND POLITICS

Bangladesh was the region of East Bengal and the Sylhet district of Assam in British India. On independence in 1947, these territories acceded to Pakistan, forming East Pakistan. Tensions between West and East Pakistan (separated by over 1,600 km) caused East Pakistan to seek autonomy; this led to fighting in 1970, which developed into civil war in 1971. After several months of war, and with the support of India, Bangladesh achieved its independence from Pakistan on 16 December 1971.

The late 1970s and 1980s were marked by political instability, with a number of coups and attempted coups, the assassination of President Mujibar Rahman in 1975 and President Zia in 1981, and long periods of government under martial law (1975–8, 1982–6) or a state of emergency (1987–8). Mass anti-government protests forced the resignation in 1990 of Gen. Ershad (assumed power in 1982, elected president in 1986); and the Bangladesh Nationalist Party (BNP) won the subsequent parliamentary elections. In 1991 a constitutional amendment returned Bangladesh to parliamentary government.

Parliamentary government has remained in place since 1991, despite boycotts of parliament in 1994–5 over alleged fraud by the BNP-led coalition and in 1997 over alleged repression by the successor Awami League government, which provoked public disorder. The governments have been formed, or coalitions have been led, by one of the two main parties: the BNP, led by Khaleda Zia (widow of President Zia), in 1991–6 and since 2001; and the Awami League, led by Sheikh Hasina Wajed (daughter of President Mujibar Rahman), in 1996–2001.

In the elections of 2001, held under a caretaker government, the BNP-led four-party alliance won more than two-thirds of the seats in parliament, and in October, Khaleda Zia was sworn in as prime minister for a fourth time. President Badruddoza Chowdhury resigned in June 2002 and was replaced by Iajuddin Ahmed, who was elected president in September 2002.

POLITICAL SYSTEM

The head of state is the president, elected by parliament for a five-year term. There is a unicameral parliament *(Jatiya Sangsad)* of 300 members directly elected for a five-year term; they can amend the constitution by a two-thirds majority. The president appoints the prime minister and the cabinet, on the advice of the prime minister.

HEAD OF STATE
President, Iajuddin Ahmed, *elected by Parliament* 5
September 2002

SELECTED GOVERNMENT MEMBERS *as at July 2005*
*Prime Minister, Armed Forces Division, Cabinet Division,
Defence, Establishment, Energy and Minerals, Hill Tracts
Affairs, Primary and Mass Education*, Khaleda Zia
Finance and Planning, Saifur Rahman
Foreign Affairs, Morshed Khan
Minister of Law, Justice and Parliamentary Affairs, Moudad
Ahmed

BANGLADESH HIGH COMMISSION
28 Queen's Gate, London SW7 5JA T 020-7584 0081
High Commissioner, HE A. H. Mofazzal Karim

BRITISH HIGH COMMISSION
United Nations Road, Baridhara, PO Box 6079, Dhaka-1212
T (+880) (2) 882 2705
High Commissioner, HE Anwar Chowdry

BRITISH COUNCIL
5 Fuller Road, PO Box 161, Dhaka 1000
T (+880) (2) 861 8905/7
E dhaka.enquiries@bd.britishcouncil.org
Director, Dr June Rollinson

DEFENCE
The Army has 180 main battle tanks and 180 armoured
personnel carriers. The Navy has five frigates and 33
patrol and coastal vessels. The Air Force has 83 combat
aircraft.
MILITARY EXPENDITURE – 1.2 per cent of GDP (2003)
MILITARY PERSONNEL – 125,500: Army 110,000, Navy
9,000, Air Force 6,500; Paramilitaries 63,200

ECONOMY AND TRADE
Bangladesh remains reliant on food production through
agriculture, a primary occupation of over 70 per cent of
the population. Products include rice, wheat, tobacco, tea,
oil seeds, pulses and sugar cane. The chief industries are
jute, cotton, tea, leather, pharmaceuticals, fertiliser, sugar,
prawn fishing and natural gas. Garment manufacturing is
the main export providing 73 per cent of export earnings
(2003). Remittances sent home by Bangladeshis abroad
are of considerable significance to the economy.
International financial institutions agreed in 2000 to
provide around US$2,000 million in additional aid over a
20-year period dependent on the introduction of free-
market reforms.
GNI – US$51,100 million (2002); US$380 per capita
(2002)
ANNUAL AVERAGE GROWTH OF GDP – 5.3 per cent
(2001)
INFLATION RATE – 2.3 per cent (2000)
TOTAL EXTERNAL DEBT – US$16,500 million (2002)
FOREIGN DIRECT INVESTMENT – US$902 million
(1997–2000)
IMPORTS – US$9,500 million (2003)
EXPORTS – US$5,300 million (2003)

BALANCE OF PAYMENTS
Trade – US$1,678 million deficit (2002)
Current Account – US$739 million surplus (2002)

Trade with UK	2003	2004
Imports from UK	£56,001,000	£68,036,000
Exports to UK	570,802,000	635,599,000

TRANSPORT INFRASTRUCTURE
The principal seaports are Chittagong and Khulna. The
Bangladesh Shipping Corporation was set up by the
government to operate the Bangladesh merchant fleet.
The principal airports are Dhaka (Zia International) and
Chittagong. The international airline, Bangladesh Biman,
serves Europe, the Middle East, south and south-east Asia,
and an internal network. There are 2,706 km of railways
internally, and rail links with India. The country's
207,486-km road network has only 19,773 km of paved
roads.

EDUCATION
Primary education is compulsory and free. There are 16
public universities, 29 private universities and more than
600 colleges.
ILLITERACY RATE – (m) 46.1 per cent; (f) 68.2 per cent
(2003)
GROSS ENROLMENT RATIO (percentage of relevant age
group) – primary 98 per cent (2002); secondary 47 per
cent (2002); tertiary 6 per cent (2002)

MEDIA AND CULTURE
The main broadcast medium (Bangladesh Television or
BTV) is subject to censorship and is state-owned. The
main commercial stations are ATN Bangla TV and
Channel i. The four main newspapers are *The Daily Star,
Dainik Ittefaq, Daily Prothom Alo* and *The New Nation*.
Bangladesh has a rich and ancient culture. Religious,
theatre and folk traditions have Buddhist, Hindu and
Muslim roots. Literature is dominated by the reputation of
the great Bengali poet Rabindranath Tagore (1861–
1941).

BARBADOS

AREA – 431 sq. km
POPULATION – 278,289 (2004 est.). The official
language is English
CAPITAL – ΨBridgetown in the parish of St Michael
(population, 108,000, 1990)
MAJOR TOWNS – Holetown in St James, Oistins in Christ
Church and Speightstown in St Peter
CURRENCY – Barbados dollar (BD$) of 100 cents
NATIONAL ANTHEM – In plenty and in time of need
NATIONAL DAY– 30 November (Independence Day)
NATIONAL FLAG – Three vertical stripes, aquamarine,
gold and aquamarine, with a trident head on gold
stripe
LIFE EXPECTANCY (years) – 71.64 (2001 est.)
MORTALITY RATE (per 1,000 population) – 9.08
(2004 est.)
INFANT MORTALITY (per 1,000 births) – 12.61
(2004 est.)
HIV / AIDS ADULT PREVALENCE RATE – 1.5 per cent
(2003 est.)
DEATH PENALTY – Yes
POPULATION GROWTH RATE – 0.36 per cent
(2004 est.)
POPULATION DENSITY – 622 per sq. km (2001)
URBAN POPULATION – 51 per cent (2001)
MILITARY EXPENDITURE – 0.5 per cent of GDP (2003)
MILITARY PERSONNEL – 610: Army 500, Navy 110

CLIMATE AND TERRAIN
Barbados is the most easterly of the Caribbean islands.
The land rises in a series of terraced tablelands, and

elevation extremes range from 336 m (Mt Hillaby) at the highest point to 0 m (Atlantic Ocean) at the lowest. The climate is tropical (the wet season is June to October) and the island is subject to occasional hurricanes.

HISTORY AND POLITICS

The first inhabitants of Barbados were Arawak Indians, but the island was uninhabited when settled by the British in 1627. It was a Crown Colony from 1652, achieved self-government in 1961, and became an independent state within the Commonwealth on 30 November 1966. Since independence, power has alternated between the two main political parties, the Barbados Labour Party (BLP) and the Democratic Labour Party (DLP). In the general election of 2003 the governing BLP won 23 seats in the 30-seat House of Assembly and the DLP won seven seats.

POLITICAL SYSTEM
The head of state is the British sovereign, represented by the Governor-General. The legislature consists of a Senate and a House of Assembly. The Senate comprises 21 senators appointed by the Governor-General for a five-year term, of whom 12 are appointed on the advice of the prime minister, two on the advice of the leader of the opposition and seven by the Governor-General at his/her discretion to represent religious, economic or social interests. The House of Assembly comprises 30 members elected every five years by adult suffrage.

There are 11 administrative areas (parishes): St Michael, Christ Church, St Andrew, St George, St James, St John, St Joseph, St Lucy, St Peter, St Philip and St Thomas.
Governor-General, HE Sir Clifford Husbands, GCMG, KA, apptd June 1996

SELECTED GOVERNMENT MEMBERS *as at July 2005*
Prime Minister, Defence and Security, Finance and Economic Affairs, Owen Arthur
Deputy Prime Minister, Attorney-General, Home Affairs, Mia Mottley
Commerce, Consumer Affairs and Business Development, Lynette Eastmond
Foreign Affairs, Foreign Trade, Billie Miller
Minister of State, Foreign Affairs and Foreign Trade, Kerrie Symmonds

BARBADOS HIGH COMMISSION
1 Great Russell Street, London WC1B 3ND T 020-7631 4975
High Commissioner, HE Edwin Pollard

BRITISH HIGH COMMISSION
Lower Collymore Rock, PO Box 676, Bridgetown
T (+1 246) 430 7800
E britishhc@sunbeach.net
High Commissioner, HE C. John White, apptd 2001

ECONOMY AND TRADE

Historically, Barbados' chief products were sugar, rum and molasses. Since independence, tourism and other service industries have become of greater significance, and the economy has suffered as a result of the downturn in tourism in recent years, but offshore finance and information services remain a valuable source of foreign exchange earnings. Chief exports are sugar, chemicals, electronic components and clothing.
GNI – US$2,610 million (2001); US$9,750 per capita (2001)

ANNUAL AVERAGE GROWTH OF GDP – 2.5 per cent (1999)
INFLATION RATE – 2.4 per cent (2000)
UNEMPLOYMENT – 10.7 per cent (2003)
TOTAL EXTERNAL DEBT – US$589 million (1999)
IMPORTS – US$1,130 million (2003)
EXPORTS – US$210 million (2003)

BALANCE OF PAYMENTS
Trade – US$702 million deficit (2002)
Current Account – US$172 million deficit (2002)

Trade with UK	2003	2004
Imports from UK	£52,347,000	£42,231,000
Exports to UK	20,921,000	19,993,000

TRANSPORT INFRASTRUCTURE

Barbados has some 1,793 km of roads, of which only 74 km are not surfaced. The Grantley Adams International airport is situated at Seawell, 19 km from Bridgetown. Bridgetown, the only port of entry, has a deep-water harbour with berths for eight ships; oil is pumped ashore at Spring Garden and at an Esso installation on the west coast.

EDUCATION

Education is free in government schools at primary (ages four to 11) and secondary (ages 11 to 18) levels. There are 74 government primary schools, 30 private primary schools, 23 government secondary schools and ten private secondary schools. Tertiary education is provided by a teachers college, a polytechnic, a community college and one of the three campuses of the University of the West Indies (the other two are on Trinidad and Jamaica).
ILLITERACY RATE – (m) 2 per cent; (f) 3.2 per cent (2003)

BELARUS

Respublika Belarus – Republic of Belarus

AREA – 207,500 sq. km. Neighbours: Latvia and Lithuania (north), Russia (east), Ukraine (south), Poland (west)
POPULATION – 10,310,520 (2004 est.): 78 per cent Belarusian, 13 per cent Russian, 4 per cent Polish and 3 per cent Ukrainian, with smaller numbers of Jews and Lithuanians. Belarusian and Russian have equal official language status. Most of the population are Belarusian Orthodox with a minority of Roman Catholics
CAPITAL – Minsk (population, 1,725,100); the administrative centre of the Commonwealth of Independent States
MAJOR CITIES – Brest; Homyel; Hrodna; Mahilyow; Vitsyebsk
CURRENCY – Belarusian rouble
NATIONAL ANTHEM – The former Soviet national anthem but with the words omitted
NATIONAL DAY – 3 July (Independence Day)
NATIONAL FLAG – Red with a green strip along the lower edge, and in the hoist a vertical red and white ornamental pattern
LIFE EXPECTANCY (years) – 68.57 (2004 est.)
MORTALITY RATE (per 1,000 population) – 14.1 (2004 est.)

HIV / AIDS ADULT PREVALENCE – 0.3 per cent
(2003 est.)
DEATH PENALTY – Yes
INFANT MORTALITY (per 1,000 births) – 13.62 (2004)
POPULATION BELOW POVERTY LINE – 22 per cent
(1995)
POPULATION GROWTH RATE – 0.11 per cent
(2004 est.)
POPULATION DENSITY – 49 per sq. km (2001)
URBAN POPULATION – 70 per cent (2001)

CLIMATE AND TERRAIN

Belarus is a landlocked country situated in the western part of the European area of the former USSR. The main rivers are the upper reaches of the Dnieper, of the Nyoman and of the Western Dvina. Much of the land is a plain, with many lakes, forests, swamps and marshy areas. The climate is continental with mild, humid winters and relatively cool and rainy summers. Elevation extremes range from 346 m (Dzyarzhynskaya Hara) at the highest point to 90 m (Nyoman River) at the lowest.

HISTORY AND POLITICS

The area was absorbed into Lithuania in the 13th century, and came under Polish rule from the 1570s, but following the partitions of Poland in the late 18th century it came under the control of the steadily expanding Russian Empire. It was the site of fierce fighting during the First World War, but its brief period of independence ended with a war over the territory and partition between Poland and the Soviet Union. The Polish territory was largely regained after the Second World War, which devastated Belarus; 25 per cent of the population was killed and thousands deported.

Belarus declared its independence from the Soviet Union after the failed coup in Moscow in August 1991. Stanislav Shuskevich became Belarusian leader at the head of a coalition of communists and democrats, but he was forced to resign in January 1994 and was replaced by Gen. Mecheslav Grib who pursued closer political, economic and trade relations with Russia. The presidential election in June 1994 was won by Alexander Lukashenko.

President Lukashenko resisted privatisation and economic liberalisation in the late 1990s, precipitating economic collapse and public unrest. An attempt to impeach him in 1996 was countered by the suspension of parliament, and his regime has become increasingly repressive, with many allegations of human rights abuses, particularly concerning the imprisonment or disappearance of opposition leaders and the violent suppression of public demonstrations. The 2000 legislative election and the 2001 presidential election were condemned as neither free nor fair by opposition groups and international observers. In the latest legislative election in October 2004, opposition parties failed to win any seats; this election was also condemned by observers. The EU and the USA have imposed travel restrictions and other sanctions several times in recent years because of the poor human rights record and the regime's obstructiveness towards Organisation for Security and Co-operation in Europe (OSCE) election observers.

FOREIGN RELATIONS

Belarus was a founder member of the Commonwealth of Independent States (CIS) in 1991. President Lukashenko, who opposed the break-up of the Soviet Union, has sought closer relations with Russia. In 1997 a treaty was signed with Russia providing for closer political and economic integration, and in 1999, the two countries signed the Treaty on the Creation of a Union State, which committed them to eventually becoming a confederal state. However, there has been little real progress towards integration, and Russia has increasingly condemned Belarus' poor economic development.

POLITICAL SYSTEM

Under the constitution, the president's term of office is five years. The president has the authority to appoint half the members of the constitutional court and the electoral commission. The legislature is the bicameral National Assembly, comprising a 110-member House of Representatives (lower chamber) and a 64-member Council of the Republic (upper chamber). Eight members of the upper chamber are appointed by the president, the rest being indirectly elected by members of the local soviets (councils) in each region.

President Lukashenko's term of office was extended by two years and his powers increased at the expense of parliament by a referendum in 1996. Another referendum in held in October 2005 approved amendments removing the limit on the number of terms a president could serve, opening the way for Alexander Lukashenko to become president for life.

HEAD OF STATE
President, Alexander Lukashenko, *elected* 10 July 1994, *re-elected* 9 September 2001

SELECTED GOVERNMENT MEMBERS *as at July 2005*
Prime Minister, Sergei Sidorsky
First Deputy Prime Minister, Vladimir I. Semashko
Deputy Prime Ministers, Ivan Bambiza*(Agroindustrial Complex)*; Andrei Kobyakov *(Economics, Trade and International Co-operation)*; Vasil Gapeev; Vladimir Drazhin *(Labour and Social Security, Social Affairs, Science)*
Defence, Col.-Gen. Leonid Maltsev
Finance, Nikolai Korbut
Foreign Affairs, Sergei Martynov
Internal Affairs, Maj.-Gen. Vladimir Naumov

EMBASSY OF THE REPUBLIC OF BELARUS
6 Kensington Court, London W8 5DL
l 020-7937 3288
Ambassador Extraordinary and Plenipotentiary, HE Dr Alyaksei Mazhukhou, apptd 2002

BRITISH EMBASSY
37 Karl Marx Street, 220030 Minsk
T (+375) (172) 105920 E pia@bepost.belpak.minsk.by
Ambassador Extraordinary and Plenipotentiary, HE Brian Bennett, apptd 2002

DEFENCE

The Army has 1,586 main battle tanks, 1,588 armoured infantry fighting vehicles and 916 armoured personnel carriers. The Air Force has 210 combat aircraft and 50 armed helicopters.
MILITARY EXPENDITURE – 4 per cent of GDP (2003)
MILITARY PERSONNEL – 72,940: Army 29,600, Central Units 25,170, Air Force and Air Defence Forces 18,170; Paramilitaries 110,000
CONSCRIPTION DURATION – Nine to 12 months

ECONOMY AND TRADE

Unlike the other former Soviet republics, there has been little privatisation of state enterprises or economic liberalisation in Belarus, and the period since independence has been one of dramatic economic decline, causing the World Bank and the IMF to suspend loans in 1995. A customs union agreement with Russia took effect in 1995, and in 1996 agreement was reached with Kazakhstan, Kyrgyzstan and Russia to establish a single customs territory. In 2000 the National Bank of Belarus (NBB) took action to liberalise the exchange market, but it continues to struggle to maintain a stable exchange rate. Industrial output increased 2.5 per cent in 2002. Arable farmland covers 27.3 per cent of the country and principal exports include chemical yarn, potash, fertilizers, textile and consumer goods. There were 1,694,000 tonnes of crude steel produced in 2003.

GNI – US$13,500 million (2002); US$1,360 per capita (2002)
AVERAGE ANNUAL GROWTH OF GDP – 4.7 per cent (2002)
INFLATION RATE – 168.6 per cent (2000)
UNEMPLOYMENT – 2 per cent (2004)
TOTAL EXTERNAL DEBT – US$851 million (2000)
FOREIGN DIRECT INVESTMENT – US$664 million (1997–2000)
IMPORTS – US$12,000 million (2003)
EXPORTS – US$10,000 million (2003)

BALANCE OF PAYMENTS
Trade – US$1,234 million deficit (2003)
Current Account – US$505 million deficit (2003)

Trade with UK	2003	2004
Imports from UK	£39,182,000	£53,385,000
Exports to UK	22,672,000	74,682,000

TRANSPORT INFRASTRUCTURE

Belarus has 5,523 km of railways and an extensive canal and river system. Of the 74,385 km of roads only 8,182 km are unsurfaced but many are in bad repair. Of the 124 airports, 28 have paved runways.

EDUCATION

The national education system comprises pre-school, general secondary, out-of-school, vocational training and trade schools, secondary specialised and higher education. General secondary education begins at the age of six.

ILLITERACY RATE – (m) 0.2 per cent; (f) 0.5 per cent (2003)
GROSS ENROLMENT RATIO (percentage of relevant age group) – primary 110 per cent (2002); secondary 84 per cent (2002); tertiary 62 per cent (2002)

MEDIA AND CULTURE

A Soviet-era attitude to press freedom remains as government controls media content and the appointment of senior editors in the print and broadcast media. State-run newspapers and television channels receive large subsidies and support government policies. The most popular privately owned newspaper is *Belorusskaya Delovaya Gazeta*. The Belarusian National State Teleradio Company operates domestic radio and TV channels. Radio Baltic Waves (Baltijos Bangos) is a private broadcaster that targets Belarusian audiences but operates from Vilnius in Lithuania. In 2002 there were 808,700 internet users.

Belarus has a strong musical tradition in the form of Orthodox hymns and sermons as well as secular folk music – both ancient and modern. With the appearance of written language in Belarus in the tenth century came some of the masterpieces of ancient Eastern Slavonic literature, including the autobiographical local chronicles centred around the cities of Polotsk and Smolensk. In 1517–19 Frantsisk Skorina, Belarusain humanist, writer and founder of East Slavic book printing, translated the Bible and printed the first book in the old-Belarusian language. From this point Belarusian literature flourished, developing roughly within the framework of dominant West European trends.

BELGIUM

Koninkrijk België/Royaume de Belgique/Königreich Belgien – Kingdom of Belgium

AREA – 30,200 sq. km. Neighbours: the Netherlands (north), France (south), Germany and Luxembourg (east)
POPULATION – 10,348,276 (2004 est.). Greater Brussels 978,384; Flanders 5,972,781; Wallonia 3,358,560. Roman Catholicism is the religion of 86 per cent of the population. The official languages are Flemish, French and German
CAPITAL – Brussels (population, 978,384, 2002)
MAJOR CITIES – ΨAntwerp, the chief port; Bruges; Charleroi; ΨGhent; Liège; Leuven; Mons; Namur
CURRENCY – Euro (€) of 100 cents
NATIONAL ANTHEM – O vaderland, o edel land der Belgen [Oh fatherland, oh noble land of the Belgians]
NATIONAL DAY – 21 July (Accession of King Leopold I, 1831)
NATIONAL FLAG – Three vertical bands, black, yellow, red
LIFE EXPECTANCY (years) – 78.44 (2004 est.)
MORTALITY RATE (per 1,000 population) – 10.2 (2004 est.)
HIV / AIDS ADULT PREVALENCE RATE – 0.2 per cent (2003 est.)
INFANT MORTALITY (per 1,000 births) – 4.76 (2004 est.)
DEATH PENALTY – No (abolished 1996)
POPULATION GROWTH RATE – 0.16 per cent (2004 est.)
POPULATION DENSITY – 340 per sq. km (2001)
URBAN POPULATION – 97 per cent (2001)

CLIMATE AND TERRAIN

Belgium is divided into two distinct and contrasting regions. The west of the country is generally low-lying and fertile, while the eastern region, the tableland of the Ardennes, is more rugged with poorer soil. Elevation extremes range from sea level on the North Sea coast to 694 m at the highest point (Signal de Botrange). The polders near the coast, which are protected by dykes against floods, cover an area of 499 sq. km. The principal rivers are the Schelde and the Meuse (Maas). Average temperatures range from 2°C in January to 18°C in July.

HISTORY AND POLITICS

Part of the Roman Empire until the 2nd century, after invasion by Germanic tribes it became part of the

Frankish Empire until much of the area was absorbed by the duchy of Burgundy from 1385. Under the rule of the Spanish Habsburgs from 1477 until 1713 and the Austrian Habsburgs until 1794, the area was conquered and held by Revolutionary France until the collapse of the Napoleonic regime in 1815, when it united with the kingdom of the Netherlands. The Belgian Revolution in 1830 led to the declaration of independence on 14 October 1830, and in 1831 the country became a constitutional monarchy. In the 20th century Belgium was invaded and occupied by Germany in both World Wars; Eupen and Malmédy were ceded to Belgium by Germany under the Versailles Treaty of 1919.

Tensions between the Flemings (Flemish speakers in the north of the country) and the Walloons (French speakers in the south) led to some political instability in the post-war period, and several governments collapsed. Inter-communal disputes led in 1980 to the establishment of regional assemblies, and in 1989 the country adopted a federal constitution.

A coalition government of Liberals and Socialists led by Guy Verhofstadt won the 2003 general election, securing a total of 62 seats in the federal parliament. Verhofstadt was sworn in as prime minister on 12 July 2003.

POLITICAL SYSTEM

Belgium is a constitutional representative and hereditary monarchy with a bicameral legislature, consisting of the king, the Senate and the Chamber of Deputies. The parliamentary term is four years. Amendments to the constitution since 1968 have devolved power to the regions. The national government retains competence only in foreign and defence policies, the national budget and monetary policy, social security, and the judicial, legal and penal systems. The Senate has 71 seats, of which 40 are directly elected, 21 indirectly elected and ten co-opted by the Flemish and Francophone communities. The Chamber of Deputies has 150 seats.

HEAD OF STATE

HM The King of the Belgians, King Albert II, *born* 6 June 1934; *acceded* 9 August 1993

Heir, HRH Prince Philippe Léopold Louis Marie, *born* 15 April 1960

SELECTED GOVERNMENT MEMBERS *as at July 2005*

Prime Minister, Guy Verhofstadt

Deputy Prime Minister and Minister for Budget and Private Enterprise, Johan Vande Lanotte

Deputy Prime Minister and Minister for Foreign Affairs, Louis Michel

Deputy Prime Minister for Interior, Patrick Dewael

Deputy Prime Minister and Minister of Justice, Laurette Onkelinx

Defence, André Flahaut

Finance, Didier Reynders

BELGIAN EMBASSY

103 Eaton Square, London SW1W 9AB T 020-7470 3700

Ambassador Extraordinary and Plenipotentiary, HE Thierry de Grüben, apptd 2002

BRITISH EMBASSY

Rue d'Arlon 85 Aarlenstraat, B-1040 Brussels

T (+32) (2) 287 6211

Ambassador Extraordinary and Plenipotentiary, HE Richard Kinchen

BRITISH COUNCIL

Leopold Plaza, Rue de Trône 108 Troonstraat, 1050 Brussels

T (+32) (2) 227 0840 E enquiries@britishcouncil.be

Director, Dr Ray Thomas

FEDERAL STRUCTURE

There are three communities: Flemish, Francophone, Germanophone. Each community has its own assembly, which elects the community government. At this level, Flanders is covered by the Flemish Community Assembly; most of Wallonia is covered by the Francophone Community Assembly, and the areas of Wallonia in the German-speaking communities of Eupen and Malmédy are covered by the Germanophone Community Assembly; Brussels is covered by a Joint Community Commission of the Flemish and Francophone Community Assemblies.

At regional level, Belgium is divided into the three regions of Wallonia, Brussels and Flanders. Each region has its own assembly and government.

The ten provinces of Belgium are (with 2002 population): Antwerp (1,652,450); East Flanders (1,366,652); Flemish Brabant (1,022,821); Limburg (798,583); West Flanders (1,132,275); Hainaut (1,281,042); Liège (1,024,130); Luxembourg (250,406); Namur (447,775); Walloon Brabant (355,207). In addition, Belgium has 589 communes as the lowest level of local government.

Minister-President of the Flemish Community and Flemish Region, Patrick Dewael

Minister-President of the Walloon Region, Jean-Claude Van Cauwenberghe

Minister-President of the French Community, Hervé Hasquin

Minister-President of the German-Speaking Community, Karl-Heinz Lambertz

Minister-President of the Brussels Capital Government, Jacques Simonet

DEFENCE

The Army has 143 main battle tanks, 332 armoured personnel carriers, 236 armoured infantry fighting vehicles. The Navy is based at Ostend and Zeebrugge and has three frigates. The Air Force has 90 combat aircraft.

The headquarters of NATO, Supreme Headquarters Allied Powers Europe, and the Western European Union Military Planning Cell are in Belgium; 1,390 US personnel are stationed in the country.

MILITARY EXPENDITURE – 1.3 per cent of GDP (2003)

MILITARY PERSONNEL – 37,500: Army 24,800, Navy 2,450, Air Force 10,250

ECONOMY AND TRADE

The establishment of the European Commission and other EU institutions in Belgium in the 1950s brought multinational companies to the country and promoted the service sector which accounts for over two-thirds of Belgium's GDP. With no natural resources except coal, production of which has now ceased, industry is based largely on the processing of imported raw materials for export. Principal industries are steel and metal products, chemicals and petrochemicals, textiles, glass and foodstuffs. Industry accounts for 24.4 per cent of GDP and services for 74.3 per cent (2001) – significantly lower than in previous years. In 2002 public debt was 100 per cent of GDP.

Belgium adopted the euro as its unit of currency on 1 January 2001.

External trade figures relate to Luxembourg as well as

Belgium since the two countries formed an economic union in 1921. The main trading partners are Germany, France, the Netherlands and the UK. Around 75 per cent of Belgium's trade is with other European Union countries.

GNI – US$237,100 million (2002); US$22,940 per capita (2002)

ANNUAL AVERAGE GROWTH OF GDP – 4.0 per cent (2000)

INFLATION RATE – 2.5 per cent (2000)

UNEMPLOYMENT – 12 per cent (2004)

IMPORTS – US$235,000 million (2003)

EXPORTS – US$255 million (2003)

BALANCE OF PAYMENTS

Trade – US$9,532 million surplus (2003)

Current Account – US$11,623 million surplus (2003)

Trade with UK	2003	2004
Imports from UK	£8,091,023,000	£10,114,441,000
Exports to UK	8,841,482,000	12,607,395,000

TRANSPORT INFRASTRUCTURE

The rail system is run by Belgian National Railways and at 3,471 km the network is one of the densest in the world. Major ports include Antwerp (the third largest port in Europe), Zeebrugge and Ostend. There are 1,570 km of inland waterways; ship canals link Ostend and Zeebrugge with Bruges and Ghent, Ghent with Terneuzen in the Netherlands, Brussels with Charleroi and Willebroek Rupel, and Liège with Antwerp. The rivers Meuse (Maas), Sambre and Schelde form an integral part of the network. There are nearly 148,216 km of roads, including 1,727 km of motorways.

EDUCATION

Nursery schools provide free education for children from two-and-a-half to six years. There are over 4,000 primary schools (six to 12 years), more than 1,000 secondary schools offering a general academic education, slightly over half of which are free institutions (predominantly Roman Catholic and subsidised by the state) and the remainder official institutions. The official school-leaving age is 18.

GROSS ENROLMENT RATIO (percentage of relevant age group) – primary 105 per cent (2002); secondary 154 per cent (2002); tertiary 58 per cent (2002)

MEDIA

The Belgian media reflects the multilingual population. There are two broadcasting authorities with programming priorities in radio, TV and external broadcasting. RTBF is the French-language broadcaster. VRT is the Flemish broadcaster. There are also French and Flemish commercial television channels and Belgischer Rundfunk (BRF), a German-language radio broadcaster. Cable television is very popular with 95 per cent of the population subscribing to domestic and foreign channels. A small number of media groups own and run the main news publications. In 2002 there were 3.76 million internet users.

CULTURE

Belgium is defined by language. The country is divided between those who speak Flemish (the Flemings) and those who speak French (the Walloons). Flemish is recognised as the official language in the northern areas and French in the southern (Walloon) area. Brussels is

officially bilingual. There is a small German-speaking area (Eupen and Malmédy) along the German border, east of Liège. Famous Belgian writers include Georges Simenon (1903–89) and Jean Ray (1887–1964) while artists include René Magritte (1898–1967). Bruges, Belgium's top tourist destination, is a beautifully preserved 13th-century town and is home to several art collections.

BELIZE

AREA – 22,800 sq. km. Neighbours: Mexico (north and north-west), Guatemala (west and south)

POPULATION – 272,945 (2004 est.): 44 per cent Mestizo (Maya-Spanish); 26 per cent Creole; 11 per cent Maya; plus a number of East Indian and Spanish descent. The races are now inter-mixed. The majority of the population is Christian, about 58 per cent Catholic and 34 per cent Protestant. The official language and language of instruction is English. Spanish is also widely spoken and English Creole is the vernacular. There are also Garifuna and Maya speakers

CAPITAL – Belmopan (population, 8,130, 2000 census)

MAJOR CITIES – ΨBelize City, the former capital; Corozal; Dangriga; Orange Walk; San Ignacio

CURRENCY – Belize dollar (BZ$) of 100 cents. The Belize dollar is tied to the US dollar

NATIONAL ANTHEM – Land of the free

NATIONAL DAY – 21 September (Independence Day)

NATIONAL FLAG – Blue ground with red band along top and bottom edges, and in the centre a white disc containing the coat of arms surrounded by a green garland

LIFE EXPECTANCY (years) – 67.43 (2004 est.)

MORTALITY RATE (per 1,000 population) – 6.04 (2004 est.)

INFANT MORTALITY (per 1,000 births) – 26.37 (2004 est.)

HIV / AIDS ADULT PREVALENCE RATE – 2.4 per cent (2003 est.)

DEATH PENALTY – Yes

POPULATION BELOW POVERTY LINE – 33 per cent (1999)

POPULATION GROWTH RATE – 2.39 per cent (2004 est.)

POPULATION DENSITY – 10 per sq. km (2001)

URBAN POPULATION – 48 per cent (2001)

MILITARY EXPENDITURE – 2.4 per cent of GDP (2003)

MILITARY PERSONNEL – Army 1,050

CLIMATE AND TERRAIN

Belize comprises a large coastal plain, swamps (in the north), fertile land (in the south) and the Maya Mountains. The highest point of elevation is 1,160 m (Victoria Peak), the lowest is at 0 m (Caribbean Sea). The climate is subtropical but is cooled by trade winds. There are frequent hurricanes (the hurricane season is June to November). Belize's inner coastal waters are protected by the world's second-largest barrier reef.

HISTORY AND POLITICS

Numerous ruins in the area indicate that Belize was heavily populated by the Maya Indians. The first British settlement was established in 1638 but was subject to repeated attacks by the Spanish, who claimed sovereignty until defeated by the British Royal Navy and settlers in 1798. In 1862 the area was recognised by Britain as a colony and called British Honduras. The colony became self-governing in 1964, with the UK retaining control of foreign policy, internal security and defence. In 1973 the colony was renamed Belize, and was granted independence on 21 September 1981. Since independence, power has alternated between the two main politicial parties, the People's United Party (PUP) and the United Democratic Party (UDP).

The general election held in 2003 was won by the ruling People's United Party who took 22 of the 29 seats in the House of Representatives.

FOREIGN RELATIONS
There has been a longstanding territorial dispute with Guatemala, which claims half of the territory of Belize. In 2002 Belize and Guatemala agreed on a draft settlement to the dispute but in 2003 Guatemala informed the Organisation of American States (OAS), the brokers of the agreement, that it could not accept the terms of the settlement. The OAS continues to work with Guatemala and Belize to resolve the dispute.

POLITICAL SYSTEM
The head of state is the British sovereign, represented in Belize by a Governor-General. There is a bicameral National Assembly, comprising a House of Representatives (29 members directly elected for a five-year term) and a Senate (13 members appointed by the Governor-General, including seven on the advice of the prime minister, three on the advice of the opposition leader, and one each from the National Trade Union Congress of Civil Society, the Belize Council of Churches and the Belize Chamber of Commerce). Executive power is vested in the cabinet, which is responsible to the National Assembly.
Governor-General, HE Sir Colville Norbert Young, GCMG, apptd 17 November 1993

SELECTED GOVERNMENT MEMBERS *as at July 2005*
Prime Minister, Finance, Defence, Said Musa
Deputy Prime Minister, Natural Resources, Environment, Commerce and Industry, John Briceo
Foreign Affairs and National Emergency Management, Godfrey Smith
Home Affairs and Investment, Ralph Fonseca

BELIZE HIGH COMMISSION
22 Harcourt House, 19 Cavendish Square, London W1G 0PL
T 020-7499 9728
High Commissioner, HE Alexis Rosado, apptd 2002

BRITISH HIGH COMMISSION
PO Box 91, Belmopan T (+501) 8222146 E brithicom@btl.net
High Commissioner, HE Alan Jones, apptd 2004

ECONOMY AND TRADE
About 27 per cent of the population is engaged in agriculture, which along with fishing accounted for more than 60 per cent of export revenue in 2002. The country is more or less self-sufficient in fresh beef, pork and poultry, but processed meat and dairy products are imported. About 25 per cent of timber production (mostly mahogany) is exported and there is a large US market for lobster, conch and scale fish. The main export items are sugar, citrus fruits and juice, bananas and marine products. The UK and the USA account for over 90 per cent of export revenue. Tourism is the second largest foreign exchange earner after agriculture, providing over 20 per cent of GDP in 2001.
GNI – US$730 million (2001); US$2,940 per capita (2001)
ANNUAL AVERAGE GROWTH OF GDP – 3.5 per cent (2004)
INFLATION RATE – 0.6 per cent (2000)
TOTAL EXTERNAL DEBT – US$499 million (2000)
IMPORTS – US$550 million (2003)
EXPORTS – US$200 million (2003)

BALANCE OF PAYMENTS
Trade – US$190 million deficit (2002)
Current Account – US$163 million deficit (2002)

Trade with UK	2003	2004
Imports from UK	£17,405,000	£8,982,000
Exports to UK	42,000,000	44,748,000

TRANSPORT INFRASTRUCTURE
The principal airport is at Belize City, and various airlines operate international flights to the USA and other Central American states. The main port is also Belize City, which has deep water quays. Several inland waterways are navigable. There are 2,984 km of roads, including four main highways, but there is no railway system.

EDUCATION
Education is free and compulsory from six to 14 years of age. There are 280 government and government-aided primary schools, 30 secondary schools and 11 tertiary institutions. The government maintains some schools but most are run by churches. The government administers and funds a school for mentally handicapped children and another for children with physical disabilities. Belize's first university, University College of Belize, opened in 1986.
ILLITERACY RATE – (m) 6.7 per cent; (f) 6.8 per cent (2000)

MEDIA
The government-operated radio service was privatised in 1998 and there are now a variety of commercial radio stations. There are no daily newspapers but there are a number of privately owned weekly news publications. There are three main television stations (Channels 5, 7 and 9), all of which are commercial. An automatic telephone service, operated by Belize Telecommunications Ltd, covers the whole country.

BENIN

République du Bénin – Republic of Benin

AREA – 112,622 sq. km. Neighbours: Togo (west), Burkina Faso and Niger (north), Nigeria (east)
POPULATION – 7,250,033 (2004 est.). The official language is French
CAPITAL – ΨPorto Novo (population, 232,756, 2000)
MAJOR TOWNS – ΨCotonou is the principal commercial town and port
CURRENCY – Franc CFA of 100 centimes
NATIONAL ANTHEM – L'aube nouvelle [The new dawn]
NATIONAL DAY – 30 November
NATIONAL FLAG – Two horizontal stripes of yellow over red with a vertical green band in the hoist

LIFE EXPECTANCY – 50.81 (2004 est.)
MORTALITY RATE (per 1,000 population) – 13.69
  (2004 est.)
INFANT MORTALITY (per 1,000 births) – 85.88
  (2004 est.)
HIV / AIDS ADULT PREVALENCE – 1.9 per cent
  (2003 est.)
DEATH PENALTY – Yes
POPULATION BELOW POVERTY LINE – 37 per cent
  (2001 est.)
POPULATION GROWTH RATE – 2.89 per cent
  (2004 est.)
POPULATION DENSITY – 54 per sq. km (1999)
MILITARY EXPENDITURE – 1.6 per cent of GDP (2003)
MILITARY PERSONNEL – 4,550: Army 4,300, Navy 100,
  Air Force 150; Paramilitaries 2,500
CONSCRIPTION DURATION – 18 months (selective)
ILLITERACY RATE – (m) 43.1 per cent; (f) 75.3 per cent
  (2000)
GROSS ENROLMENT RATIO (percentage of relevant age
  group) – primary 104 per cent (2002); secondary 26
  per cent (2002); tertiary 4 per cent (2002)

CLIMATE AND TERRAIN
Benin has a short coastline of 124 km on the Gulf of
Guinea but extends northwards inland for 699 km. The
coast is a sandbar backed by lagoons that are fed by rivers.
Elevation extremes range from 658 m (Mont Sokbara) at
the highest point to 0 m (Atlantic Ocean) at the lowest.
Benin has a tropical climate.

HISTORY AND POLITICS
Very little is known of Benin's pre-colonial origins.
Dahomey, on the site of modern-day Benin, was a West
African kingdom founded in the 11th and 12th centuries
that rose to prominence during the 15th and 16th
centuries. The first Europeans to visit the country were the
Portuguese in 1472. Slavery became the region's primary
commodity, hence the area's historical name of the Slave
Coast.

After a war between the French and the Dahomey
kingdom in 1892–4, the French established a protectorate
and this was incorporated into the federation of French
West Africa in 1899. Dahomey became an independent
republic within the French Community in 1958; full
independence outside the Community was proclaimed on
1 August 1960. Between 1960 and 1972 there was acute
political instability, with frequent switches from civilian to
military rule and regional ethnic conflicts, until a coup
d'état in 1972 brought to power a Marxist-Leninist
military government headed by Lt.-Col. Mathieu
Kérékou. The name of the country was changed to Benin
in 1975.

The country became more stable and moved gradually
towards democratic government: civilian rule was restored
in 1977 (though Kérékou remained president); Marxist-
Leninism was abandoned in 1989 and economic
liberalisation was adopted; and a pluralistic constitution
was adopted in 1990 and legislative and presidential
elections were held in 1991. Nicéphore Soglo was sworn
in as president and appointed a Benin Renaissance Party
(PRB)-dominated provisional government. He was
defeated by Gen. Kérékou (by then a civilian politician) in
the presidential election of 1996. In legislative elections
held in 2003, the Presidential Movement won an overall
parliamentary majority, winning 52 of the 83 seats in the
National Assembly.

POLITICAL SYSTEM
The president is head of government as well as head of
state, and is directly elected for a five-year term. The
president appoints and presides over the Council of
Ministers. The National Assembly has 83 members,
directly elected by proportional representation for a four-
year term.

HEAD OF STATE
President and Head of the Armed Forces, HE Gen. Mathieu
  Kérékou, *elected* 1996, *re-elected* 22 March 2001, *sworn
  in* 3 April 2001

SELECTED GOVERNMENT MEMBERS *as at June 2005*
Finance and Economy, Cosme Selhin
Foreign Affairs and African Integration, Rogatien Biaou
Interior, Security and Territorial Administration, Gen.
  Seydon Mama Sika
Minister of State for National Defence, Pierre Osho

EMBASSY OF THE REPUBLIC OF BENIN
87 Avenue Victor Hugo, F-75116 Paris, France
T (+33) (1) 4500 9882
Ambassador Extraordinary and Plenipotentiary, HE Edgar-
  Yves Monnou

BRITISH AMBASSADOR
HE Philip Gozney, apptd 2004, resident at Abuja, Nigeria

ECONOMY AND TRADE
The principal exports are cotton (accounting for 80 per
cent of official exports and 40 per cent of GDP), palm
products, groundnuts, shea-nuts, and coffee. Agriculture
employs an estimated 55 per cent of the workforce. Small
deposits of gold, iron and chrome have been found. Oil
production started in 1983. Industries have been steadily
privatised since 2001.

In 2000 the IMF and the International Development
Association agreed to a US$460 million debt reduction
package for Benin. In March 2003 the IMF announced
that Benin had taken the necessary steps to reach its
completion point under the enhanced Heavily Indebted
Poor Countries initiative.
GNI – US$2,500 million (2002); US$380 per capita
  (2002)
ANNUAL AVERAGE GROWTH OF GDP – 5 per cent
  (2004)
INFLATION RATE – 4.2 per cent (2000)
TOTAL EXTERNAL DEBT – US$1,599 million (2000)
IMPORTS – US$760 million (2003)
EXPORTS – US$540 million (2003)

BALANCE OF PAYMENTS
Trade – US$180 million deficit (2001)
Current Account – US$160 million deficit (2001)

Trade with UK	2003	2004
Imports from UK	£46,563,000	£35,822,000
Exports to UK	2,989,000	5,587,000

CULTURE
Benin's population is ethnically varied but the main
cultural divide is between the northern and southern
regions. Benin's largest group, the Fon, live in the south,
as do the Yoruba. The largest group in the north is the
Bariba.

Pre-colonial Benin encouraged diverse artistic traditions, some of which (such as the bronze heads of the Ife) have now disappeared and others of which such as the appliqué tapestries, now form the basis of an internationally notable contemporary arts scene.

BHUTAN

Druk Gyal Khab – Kingdom of Bhutan

AREA – 46,600 sq. km. Neighbours: Tibet (north), India (west, south and east)
POPULATION – 2,139,549 (2003 est.): about 80 per cent are Buddhists, the remainder (mostly the Nepali Bhutanese) are Hindu. The official language, for administrative and religious purposes, is Dzongkha, a variant of Tibetan, which functions as a lingua franca amongst a variety of languages and dialects. Nepali is a recognised language and English remains the medium of instruction and the working language of the administration
CAPITAL – Thimphu (population, 30,340, 1993 estimate)
CURRENCY – Ngultrum of 100 chetrum (Indian currency is also legal tender)
NATIONAL ANTHEM – Druk tsendhen koipi gyelknap na [In the thunder dragon kingdom]
NATIONAL DAY – 17 December
NATIONAL FLAG – Saffron yellow and orange-red divided diagonally, with dragon device in centre
MORTALITY RATE (per 1,000 population) – 13.2 (2004 est.)
INFANT MORTALITY RATE (per 1,000 births) – 102.56 (2004 est.)
HIV / AIDS ADULT PREVALENCE – 0.1 per cent (2001 est.)
DEATH PENALTY – No (abolished 2004)
POPULATION GROWTH RATE – 2.12 per cent (2004 est.)
POPULATION DENSITY – 44 per sq. km (1999)
MILITARY EXPENDITURE – 3.3 per cent of GDP (2001)
ILLITERACY RATE – (m) 38.9 per cent; (f) 66.4 per cent (2000)

CLIMATE AND TERRAIN

Bhutan is a landlocked country between China and India. There is a mountainous northern region which is infertile and sparsely populated, a central zone of upland valleys, where most of the population and cultivated land is found, and in the south the densely forested foothills of the Himalayas, which are mainly inhabited by Nepalese settlers and indigenous tribespeople. Extremes of elevation range from 7,553 m (K'ula Shan) at the highest point to 97 m (Drangme Chhu) at the lowest. The climate is dependent on altitude and average temperatures range from 4°C in January to 17°C in July. There is heavy annual rainfall of around 1,000 mm in the central valleys and 5,000 mm in the south.

HISTORY AND POLITICS

British relations with Bhutan date from the signing of a treaty of co-operation in 1774. In 1865 Britain and Bhutan signed a trade treaty after Britain had annexed the south of the country. A 1910 treaty placed foreign relations under the guidance of the British government in India, and in 1949 Bhutan signed a similar treaty with India under which it is guided by India in its external relations. It has its own diplomatic representatives and is a

member of the UN. Since the 1950s Bhutan has been moving towards the establishment of more formal political institutions. An elected legislature was established in 1953, and in 1969 the absolute monarchy was replaced by a form of democratic monarchy with the king as head of a cabinet. However, popular agitation in the 1990s for greater democracy led the king to transfer some of his powers to the National Assembly, and democratisation was taken further with the drafting of a written constitution, published in March 2005. The most recent legislative election was in June 2003 and all six cabinet ministers were re-elected.

In 1989 the king introduced a code of national etiquette designed to protect the national culture and language from Nepali encroachment. These measures, together with the granting of citizenship only to Nepalis settled in Bhutan before 1958, led to an exodus of ethnic Nepalis to Nepal. In 2001 Bhutan and Nepal began an agreed process of assessing which refugees were entitled to return to Bhutan. However, a number of Nepalese refugees went on hunger strike in early 2003 in protest at their conditions and the slow progress of the verification and repatriation process.

POLITICAL SYSTEM

Bhutan has no formal constitution at present, but a written constitution has been drafted and was published in March 2005. The head of state is the hereditary monarch, who has in the past defined the limits of the powers of political institutions. The unicameral legislature, the *Tshogdu Chhenmo* (National Assembly), has 155 members, 105 directly elected for a three-year term, 37 members nominated by the government, and 12 members representing religious bodies. The ten-member Royal Advisory Council, nominated by the king and the National Assembly, acts as a consultative body when the National Assembly is not in session. The *Lhengyal Shungtshog* (cabinet), which is responsible to the National Assembly, is headed by an annually rotating chairman. Ministers are elected for a five-year term, after which time they must face a vote of confidence. There are no political parties.

In 1998 the king introduced reforms giving the legislature the right to dismiss the king (dependent on a two-thirds majority) and to nominate the members of the cabinet, although the king retains the right to assign their portfolios.

HEAD OF STATE

HM The King of Bhutan, Jigme Singye Wangchuck, *born* 11 November 1955; *succeeded his father* July 1972; *crowned* 2 June 1974
Heir, Crown Prince Jigme Gesar Namgyal Wangchuck, *designated* 31 October 1988

SELECTED GOVERNMENT MEMBERS *as at July 2005*
Chairman of the Cabinet, Home and Cultural Affairs, Jigme Thinley
Finance, Wangdi Norbu
Foreign Affairs, Khandu Wangchuk

ECONOMY

The economy is based on industry (37 per cent of GDP in 2002), and agriculture (34 per cent of GDP). Agriculture and animal husbandry engage around 85 per cent of the workforce in what is largely a self-sufficient rural society. Services accounted for 29 per cent of GDP in 2002. The principal food crops are rice, wheat, maize and barley.

Vegetables and fruit are also produced. Bhutan is the world's largest producer of cardamom, which forms its principal export to countries other than India. Agriculture is, however, limited by the country's mountainous topography and 60 per cent forest cover.

The mountains contain rich deposits of limestone, gypsum, dolomite and graphite and small amounts of coal, which are exported to India. There are cement, chemicals and food-processing plants and a distillery; a forestry industries complex is being expanded. Tourism and postage stamps are increasingly important sources of foreign exchange. Principal exports are electricity, calcium carbide and timber; main imports are rice, machinery and diesel oil.

GNI – US$479 million (2000); US$640 per capita (2001)
ANNUAL AVERAGE GROWTH OF GDP – 7.0 per cent (2001)
TOTAL EXTERNAL DEBT – US$198 million (2000)
IMPORTS – US$200 million (2002)
EXPORTS – US$100 million (2002)

Trade with UK	2003	2004
Imports from UK	£2,060,000	£3,739,000
Exports to UK	347,000	3,155,000

BOLIVIA

República de Bolivia – Republic of Bolivia

AREA – 1,098,580 sq. km. Neighbours: Brazil (north and east), Paraguay and Argentina (south), Chile and Peru (west)
POPULATION – 8,724,156 (2004 est.): 12 per cent are of white European descent, 30 per cent Mestizo (mixed European-Indian), 25 per cent Quechua Indian and 17 per cent Aymará Indian. The official language is Spanish; Quechua and Aymará are also spoken. Roman Catholicism was the state religion until disestablishment in 1961
CAPITAL – La Paz, the seat of government (population, 739,453, 1998 estimate)
MAJOR CITIES – Cochabamba; El Alto; Oruro; Potosí; Santa Cruz; Sucre, the legal capital and seat of the judiciary
CURRENCY – Boliviano ($b) of 100 centavos
NATIONAL ANTHEM – Bolivianos, el hado propicio [Oh Bolivia, our long-felt desires]
NATIONAL DAY – 6 August (Independence Day)
NATIONAL FLAG – Three horizontal bands, red, yellow, green
LIFE EXPECTANCY (years) – 65.14 (2004 est.)
MORTALITY RATE (per 1,000 population) – 7.77 (2004 est.)
INFANT MORTALITY (per 1,000 births) – 54.58 (2004 est.)
HIV / AIDS ADULT PREVALENCE RATE – 0.1 per cent (2003 est.)
DEATH PENALTY – Yes*
POPULATION BELOW POVERTY LINE – 70 per cent (1999)
POPULATION GROWTH RATE – 1.56 per cent (2004 est.)
POPULATION DENSITY – 8 per sq. km (2001)
URBAN POPULATION – 63 per cent (2001)

CLIMATE AND TERRAIN

A landlocked country, Bolivia's chief topographical feature is its great central plateau. Over 800 km in length, at an average altitude of 3,750 m above sea level, this plateau lies between the two great chains of the Andes, which traverse the country from south to north. Elevation extremes range from 6,520 m (Nevado Sajama) at the highest point to 90 m (Rio Paraguay) at the lowest. The land falls from the Andean ridges in the west through forested foothills to the plains of the north and east. These are drained by the principal rivers, the Itenez, Beni, Mamore and Madre de Dios. The wet season is November to March. There is an average temperature of 26°C in most of the country but the south is prone to droughts and temperatures become subpolar at an altitude of 500 m.

HISTORY AND POLITICS

The area of present-day Bolivia was assimilated into the Inca Empire in 1450. The Inca Empire was conquered by the Spanish in 1525. Bolivia won its independence from Spain in 1825 after a war of liberation led by Simón Bolívar (1783–1830), from whom the country derives its name. Much territory was lost after wars with neighbouring countries, including a devastating defeat in the Chaco War (1932–5) against Paraguay.

Bolivia was ruled by military juntas from 1936 to 1952 and from 1964 to 1982, when civilian rule was restored amid worsening economic conditions as the tin market collapsed and inflation rose dramatically. Austerity measures introduced in 1983 succeeded over the next decade in curbing inflation and attracting foreign investment, but widened social divisions and created great social unrest.

Many former tinworkers and poor farmers turned to growing coca, the basis of cocaine, and crop-eradication programmes, essential to attract overseas aid, contributed to the economic hardship that led in 2000 to a wave of protests and strikes, which ended after the government made concessions and promised investment in coca-producing areas; in 2001 the protestors claimed that the government had failed to deliver the promised concessions and recommenced the campaign of demonstrations and strikes. A further source of tension are plans to exploit and export Bolivia's natural gas resources, which are opposed particularly by indigenous groups. Extensive civil unrest over these issues in 2002 caused President Gonzalo Sánchez de Lozada, elected by Congress in August 2002 after the presidential election in June was inconclusive, to resign in October. Vice-president Carlos D. Mesa Gisbert was sworn in as president on 17 October 2003. He has faced conflicting demands from the business sector, the unions, the coca growers and indigenous groups, and unrest has continued. In March 2005 he offered his resignation but this was rejected by Congress. However after further protests, clashes between riot police and demonstrators and the blockade of the capital La Paz, Congress finally accepted President Gisbert's resignation. Eduardo Rodriguez was appointed as interim president, and parliament announced that a presidential election would be held in December 2005.

POLITICAL SYSTEM

The constitution provides for a directly elected executive president who appoints the cabinet. The legislature (Congress) consists of a 27-member Senate and a 130-

member Chamber of Deputies. Both chambers and the president are elected for five-year terms.

HEAD OF STATE
Interim President, Eduardo Rodriguez, *sworn in* 10 June 2005

SELECTED GOVERNMENT MEMBERS *as at June 2005*
Defence, Gonzalo Mendez Gutierrez
Finance, Luis Carlos Jemio Mollinedo
Foreign Affairs, Armando Loayza Mariaca
Interior, Gustavo Avila Bustamante

BOLIVIAN EMBASSY
106 Eaton Square, London SW1W 9AD T 020-7235 4248
Ambassador Extraordinary and Plenipotentiary, HE
  Gonzalo Montenegro

BRITISH EMBASSY
Avenida Arce 2732, Casilla (PO Box) 694 La Paz
T (+591) (2) 2433424 E ppa@megalink.com
Ambassador Extraordinary and Plenipotentiary, HE William
  Sinton, OBE, apptd 2001

BRITISH COUNCIL
Avenida Arce 2708 (esq. Campos), Casilla 15047, La Paz
T (+591) (2) 2431240 E information@britishcouncil.org.bo
Director, Eric Lawrie

DEFENCE
The Army has 77 armoured personnel carriers and 36 light tanks. The Navy has 78 patrol vessels. The Air Force has 37 combat aircraft and 16 armed helicopters.
MILITARY EXPENDITURE – 1.7 per cent of GDP (2003)
MILITARY PERSONNEL – 31,500: Army 25,000, Navy 3,500, Air Force 3,000; Paramilitaries 37,100
CONSCRIPTION DURATION – 12 months (selective)

ECONOMY AND TRADE
Mining, natural gas, petroleum and agriculture are the principal industries. The ancient silver mines of Potosí are now worked chiefly for tin, but gold is obtained on the Eastern Cordillera of the Andes. Following a decline in the price of tin, many workers started growing coca, which has become a significant export. Small quantities of oil are produced for internal consumption and gas (currently providing about a quarter of export income) is piped to Argentina; in 1997 the World Bank approved financing for the 3,150-km Bolivia–Brazil gas pipeline, which is now in operation. Bolivia's natural gas production in 2003 was 7,398 million m³.

In 1996 the government signed an agreement with the South American Common Market (Mercosur) to create a free trade zone within 18 years.

Bolivia's principal exports are natural gas, tin, zinc, silver, gold, coffee and soya beans. The USA and UK are Bolivia's largest export trading partners. The country's low level of industrialisation makes Bolivia highly dependent on imports, mainly wheat and flour, iron and steel products, machinery, vehicles and textiles. In 2004 President Mesa Gisbert announced an economic plan designed to revive the economy and bring debt under control.
GNI – US$7,900 million (2002); US$900 per capita (2002)
INFLATION RATE – 4.6 per cent (2000)
TOTAL EXTERNAL DEBT – US$5,762 million (2000)

FOREIGN DIRECT INVESTMENT – US$3,222 million (1997–2000)
IMPORTS – US$1,600 million (2003)
EXPORTS – US$1,600 million (2003)

BALANCE OF PAYMENTS
Trade – US$54 million surplus (2003)
Current Account – US$19 million surplus (2003)

Trade with UK	2003	2004
Imports from UK	£6,386,000	£4,933,000
Exports to UK	10,540,00	10,878,000

TRANSPORT INFRASTRUCTURE
There are 3,519 km of railways in operation, but they are in a state of decay. There are about 53,790 km of roads, of which about 5 per cent are paved. Bolivia has 1,081 airports, but only 12 have surfaced runways. In 1993 Bolivia and Peru signed an agreement granting Bolivia a concession of 162 hectares at the southern Peruvian port of Ilo for 98 years to construct a free trade zone.

EDUCATION
Elementary education is compulsory and free from the ages of six to 11. There are secondary schools in urban centres but only about a third of children of secondary school age attend. There are 22 universities, four of which are private.
ILLITERACY RATE – (m) 6.9 per cent; (f) 18.4 per cent (2002)
GROSS ENROLMENT RATIO (percentage of relevant age group) – primary 114 per cent (2002); secondary 84 per cent (2002); tertiary 39 per cent (2002)

MEDIA AND CULTURE
Radio is the most important news medium in Bolivia due to low literacy levels (particularly in rural areas). The media is largely privately owned and run. Journalists practise self-censorship. There are six daily newspapers. Television is mostly commercial with only one government-run channel.

Due in part to its relative cultural isolation from the rest of Latin America, the literature of Bolivia has only recently risen to prominence. Carlos Medinaceli (1899-1949) is considered the chief exponent of the influential *novela de cholos* genre, a style of writing that centres on the experience of the urban Mestizo (mixed race) population.

BOSNIA-HERCEGOVINA

Republika Bosna i Hercegovina – Republic of Bosnia and Hercegovina

AREA – 51,129 sq. km. Neighbours: Serbia and Montenegro (east), Croatia (north and west)
POPULATION – 3,784,000; 4.4 million (2001 census): 44 per cent Bosniacs, 33 per cent Serbs and 17 per cent Croats. The languages are Bosnian (spoken by Bosniacs and written in the Latin script), Serbian (spoken by Serbs and written in the Cyrillic alphabet) and Croatian (spoken by Croats and written in the Latin script)
CAPITAL – Sarajevo (population, 529,021, 2001 est.)
MAJOR CITIES – Banja Luka; Mostar; Tuzla; Zenica
CURRENCY – Convertible marka
NATIONAL ANTHEM – Jedna si jedina [You are unique]
NATIONAL DAY – 1 March (anniversary of 1992 declaration of independence)

NATIONAL FLAG – Blue, bearing a yellow triangle above a line of white stars

MORTALITY RATE (per 1,000 population) – 8.33 (2004 est.)

HIV / AIDS ADULT PREVALENCE RATE – 0.1 per cent (2001 est.)

DEATH PENALTY – No (abolished 2001)

POPULATION GROWTH RATE – 0.45 per cent (2004 est.)

POPULATION DENSITY – 75 per sq. km (1999)

MILITARY EXPENDITURE – 2.2 per cent of GDP (2003)

MILITARY PERSONNEL – Bosniac Army (VF-B): 5,576; Croat Defence Council (VF-H): 2,424; Bosnian Serb Army (VRS): 8,200

CLIMATE AND TERRAIN

Lying in the Balkan peninsula, the country includes the Dinaric Alps in the west. The mountainous centre is split by gorges, while the north is lower-lying, falling to the valley of the River Sava, which forms the northern border with Croatia. There is 20 km of Adriatic coastline. The highest point of elevation is 2,226 m (Maglic), the lowest point is 0 m (Adriatic Sea).

HISTORY AND POLITICS

The country was settled by Slavs in the seventh century and conquered by the Ottoman Turks in 1463. Ruled by the Turks for over 400 years, the country came under Austro-Hungarian control in 1878. The assassination of the heir to the Austro-Hungarian throne in Sarajevo by an ethnic Serb precipitated the First World War, after which Bosnia-Hercegovina became part of the 'Kingdom of Serbs, Croats and Slovenes' (renamed Yugoslavia in 1929). It was occupied by German and Axis forces between 1941 and 1945. At the end of the war Bosnia-Hercegovina became part of the Socialist Federal Republic of Yugoslavia, which eventually collapsed with the secession of Slovenia and Croatia in 1991.

The Bosnia-Hercegovina government issued a declaration of sovereignty in October 1991 against the wishes of the ethnic Serb Democratic Party. Independence was declared on 1 March 1992 following a referendum which was boycotted by the Bosnian Serbs. Bosnia-Hercegovina was recognised as an independent state by the EU and USA in April 1992 and was admitted to UN membership in May 1992.

THE WAR

Fighting broke out in March 1992 between the pro-independence Muslims and Bosnian Serbs who wanted to merge with the Serbian republic to form a Greater Serbia. The Bosnian Serbs, assisted by the Federal Yugoslav Army (JNA), gained control of 70 per cent of Bosnia and in August 1992 declared their own 'Republika Srpska' with its capital at Pale.

The Bosnian government (Muslim) forces formed an alliance with Bosnian Croat and Croat forces in early 1992 which collapsed in 1993. The Muslims then came under attack by both Bosnian Serb and Bosnian Croat forces. In August 1993 the Bosnian Croats declared a 'Republic of Herceg-Bosna', with its capital in Mostar, and following a cease-fire in February 1994 joined the government forces in a Muslim-Croat Federation.

NATO galvanised the USA, Britain, France, Germany and Russia to form the Contact Group (CG) to co-ordinate peace efforts. The CG brought about a cease-fire in June 1994 and presented a peace plan, which was rejected by the Bosnian Serbs. The fighting intensified in 1995, climaxing in a land-grab during the final months of the war. Bosnian Serb forces overran the UN safe areas of Zepa and Srebrenica in July, allegedly massacring thousands of fleeing Muslims, and then laid siege to the Bihać 'safe area' together with Croatian Serbs and rebel Muslims. Bosnian government and Croatian forces lifted the siege of Bihać in August, enabling a joint attack on Serb-held central Bosnia.

The foreign ministers of Bosnia, Croatia and Serbia (rump Yugoslavia) met in Geneva in September 1995 and agreed to a US-sponsored peace accord. A cease-fire agreement was signed on 5 October and observed from 22 October, delayed by a Federation advance in the west and north-west, and Bosnian Serbs overrunning Tuzla.

Several Serb politicians and military commanders, including former Yugoslav president Slobodan Milosevic, have been tried or are currently on trial for war crimes by the International Criminal Tribunal for the Former Yugoslavia in The Hague.

THE PEACE AGREEMENT

The Dayton Peace Accord was signed in Paris on 14 December 1995. It was agreed to preserve Bosnia as a single state with a 51:49 division of territory between the Federation of Bosnia-Hercegovina (Bosniac/Croat) and the Republika Srpska (Bosnian Serbs). A republican (national) government, presidency and democratically elected institutions, based in Federation-controlled Sarajevo, were provided for. The Dayton agreement also established the Office of the High Representative, who decides cases where the authorities are unable to agree; the High Representative since 2002 has been Lord (Paddy) Ashdown of Norton-sub-Hamdon. The Dayton agreement provided for the deployment of a NATO-led Peace Implementation Force (IFOR) which took over from UNPROFOR in December 1995 and was mandated until December 1996. IFOR (60,000 troops) was replaced by a NATO-led Stabilisation Force (SFOR) (12,000 troops, reduced to 7,000 troops in May 2004), which was replaced by an EU-led force (EUFOR) in 2005.

POLITICAL SYSTEM

Under the Dayton Peace Accord, the Bosnian republican (national) government is responsible for foreign affairs, currency, citizenship and immigration. Executive authority is vested in a democratically elected rotating presidential triumvirate comprising a representative from each community.

Legislative authority is vested in a bicameral parliament, the Assembly of Bosnia-Hercegovina, comprising a House of Peoples and a House of Representatives. Both houses have two-year terms. The House of Peoples has 15 members, ten from the Federation and five from the Republika Srpska, who are selected by the House of Representatives. The House of Representatives has 42 members who are directly elected to the two constituent chambers, the Chamber of Deputies of the Federation, which has 28 members, and the Chamber of Deputies of the Republika Srpska, which has 14 members. Within the Federation there is a 140-member House of Representatives and ten cantonal assemblies; in the Republika Srpska there is an 83-member People's Assembly.

Legislative elections and elections for the collective presidency and the presidency of the Republika Srpska were held in 2002. The winning parties were: the

Bosniac Party of Democratic Action (SDA); the Serb Democratic Party (SDS) and the Croatian Democratic Community (HDZ). Dragan Cavić was elected President of the Republika Srpska and sworn in on 28 November. In January 2003, the all-Bosnian legislature approved the coalition government of Adnan Terzic of the SDA. Mirko Sarović, who was inaugurated as the first chair of the collective presidency in October 2002, resigned in April 2003. Borislav Paravac was elected to replace him and took office on 10 April. The chair of the presidency rotates among its three members every eight months.

HEADS OF STATE (FOR ALL BOSNIA-HERCEGOVINA)
Presidency Members, Sulejman Tihic, Borislav Paravac, Ivo Miro Jovic

HEAD OF THE FEDERATION
President, Niko Lozancić
Vice-Presidents, Sahbaz Dzikanovic; Desnica Radivojevic

HEAD OF REPUBLIKA SRPSKA
President, Dragan Cavić
Vice-Presidents, Adil Osmanović; Ivan Tomljenovic

SELECTED GOVERNMENT MEMBERS (FOR ALL BOSNIA-HERCEGOVINA) *as at July 2005*
Prime Minister, European Integration, Adnan Terzić
Finance and Treasury, Ljerka Marić
Foreign Affairs, Ana Trisic-Babic
Defence, Nikola Radovanovic

SELECTED GOVERNMENT MEMBERS OF FEDERATION CABINET *as at July 2005*
Prime Minister, Ahmet Hadzipasić
Deputy Prime Minister, Culture and Sport, Gavrilo Grahovac
Deputy Prime Minister, Finance, Dragan Vrankić
Defence, Miroslav Nikolić
Interior, Mevludin Halilović

SELECTED GOVERNMENT MEMBERS OF REPUBLIKA SRPSKA *as at July 2005*
Prime Minister, Pero Bukejlovic
Defence, Milovan Stanković
Finance, Svetlana Cenic
Interior, Darko Matijasevic

EMBASSY OF BOSNIA-HERCEGOVINA
5–7 Lexham Gardens, London W8 5JJ T 020-7373 0867
Ambassador Extraordinary and Plenipotentiary, HE Elvira Begovic, apptd 2001

BRITISH EMBASSY
8 Tina Ujevica, Sarajevo T (+387) (33) 444429
E britemb@bih.net.ba
Ambassador Extraordinary and Plenipotentiary, HE Matthew Rycroft, CBE, apptd 2005

BRITISH COUNCIL
Ljubljanska 9, 71000 Sarajevo T (+387) (33) 250220
E british.council@britishcouncil.ba
Director, Chris Rawlings

ECONOMY AND TRADE
The economy is still recovering from the devastation of the civil war. Progress has been made in repairing war-damaged infrastructure and economic growth and foreign investment are good, but unemployment is still high. Wheat, maize, potatoes and cabbage are among the major crops; crude steel and lignite are among the principal mineral products.

GNI – US$5,400 million (2002); US$1,310 per capita (2002)
TOTAL EXTERNAL DEBT – US$2,828 million (2000)

Trade with UK	2003	2004
Imports from UK	£12,531,00	£15,219,000
Exports to UK	4,048,000	3,698,000

TRANSPORT INFRASTRUCTURE
There are 1,021 km of railways and 21,846 km of roads, 11,424 km of which are paved. Many waterways are still being repaired. There are five heliports and 27 airports, eight of which are surfaced. Although the country has 20 km of coastline on the Adriatic Sea, there are no harbours.

MEDIA AND CULTURE
During the war all branches of the media were used by political factions to further their own propaganda aims. Since the 1995 Dayton Peace Accord, efforts have been made to reintroduce a more balanced press that crosses ethnic divides. These efforts have not been entirely successful and there is only limited press freedom. The Office of the High Representative is overseeing the development of a national broadcasting service. There are more than 200 commercial television and radio stations.

Modern-day Bosnia-Hercegovina is still dealing with the wounds left by three years of inter-ethnic war and people now divide geographically along religious lines – the Serb Republic is almost totally Christian and the Federation is mostly Muslim. The country's most well-known novelist is Ivo Andric (1892–1975), winner of the Nobel Prize for Literature in 1961.

BOTSWANA

Republic of Botswana

AREA – 581,730 sq. km. Neighbours: South Africa (south and east), Zimbabwe (north and north-east), Namibia (west), Zambia (north)
POPULATION – 1,561,973 (2004 est.): Batswana (95 per cent); the remainder are Bakalanga, Basarwa, Bakgalagadi, Basubya, Baherero, Bayei, Bambukushu and Europeans. The national language is Setswana and the official language is English
CAPITAL – Gaborone (population, 186,007, 2001 census)
MAJOR CITIES – Francistown; Molepolole; Selebi-Phikwe
CURRENCY – Pula (P) of 100 thebe
NATIONAL ANTHEM – Fatshe la rona [Blessed be this noble land]
NATIONAL DAY – 30 September
NATIONAL FLAG – Light blue with a horizontal black stripe fimbriated in white across the centre
LIFE EXPECTANCY (years) – 30.76 (2004 est.)
MORTALITY RATE (per 1,000 population) – 33.3 (2004 est.)
INFANT MORTALITY (per 1,000 births) – 69.98 (2004 est.)
HIV / AIDS ADULT PREVALENCE – 37.3 per cent (2003 est.)
DEATH PENALTY – Yes

POPULATION BELOW POVERTY LINE – 47 per cent (2001 est.)
POPULATION GROWTH RATE – –0.89 per cent (2004 est.)
POPULATION DENSITY – 3 per sq. km (2001)
URBAN POPULATION – 49 per cent (2001)
MILITARY EXPENDITURE – 3.8 per cent GDP (2003)
MILITARY PERSONNEL – 9,000: Army 8,500, Air Force 500; Paramilitary 1,500

CLIMATE AND TERRAIN
A landlocked country in southern Africa, Botswana is divided into two main topographical regions by a plateau with an average height of around 1,200 m. To the east of the plateau, streams run into the Marico, Notwani and Limpopo rivers; to the west lies a flat region comprising the Bakgalagadi Desert, the Okavango Swamps and the Northern State Lands area. Elevation extremes range from 1,375 m (Tsodilo Hills) at the highest point to 513 m (junction of the Limpopo and Shashe rivers) at the lowest. The climate is subtropical in the north (Okavango Delta, including the Central Kalahari Game Reserve), arid in the south and west (Kalahari Desert), and temperate in the east (arable farming land). Average annual temperatures range from 26°C in January to 13°C in July.

HISTORY AND POLITICS
The Tswana people were dominant in the area from the 17th century. In 1885, at the request of indigenous chiefs fearing invasion by the Boers, Britain formally took control of Bechuanaland, and the northern part of the territory was declared the Bechuanaland Protectorate, while land to the south of the Molopo River became British Bechuanaland, which was later incorporated into the Cape Colony. In 1964 the British Protectorate of Bechuanaland became self-governing, and on 30 September 1966 it became a republic within the Commonwealth under the name Botswana. Since independence, Botswana has been stable and relatively prosperous owing to the diamond mining industry, but it is now facing serious demographic and social problems because of the high level of HIV/AIDS among the population. The general election of October 2004 was won by the Botswana Democratic Party, with 51.7 per cent of the vote. In the presidential election the following day, Festus Mogae was re-elected for a second term.

POLITICAL SYSTEM
The president is head of state and is elected by the National Assembly for a five-year term, renewable only once. He appoints the vice-president and the cabinet. The National Assembly consists of the president, 57 members directly elected for a five-year term, plus a variable number of co-opted members (currently four), and the Attorney-General (non-voting). There is also a 15-member House of Chiefs which advises on tribal matters and constitutional changes.

HEAD OF STATE
President, C.-in-C. of the Armed Forces, HE Festus Mogae, *sworn in* 2 April 1998, *re-elected* 1 November 2004
Vice-President, Lt.-Gen. Ian Khama

SELECTED GOVERNMENT MEMBERS *as at July 2005*
Finance and Development Planning, Baledzi Gaolathe
Foreign Affairs, Lt.-Gen. Mompati Merafhe
Labour and Home Affairs, Gen. Moeng Pheto
Health, Sheila Tlou

BOTSWANA HIGH COMMISSION
6 Stratford Place, London W1C 1AY

T 020-7499 0031
High Commissioner, HE Roy Blackbeard, apptd 1998

BRITISH HIGH COMMISSION
Private Bag 0023, Gaborone
T (+ 267) 3952841
E bhc@botsnet.bw
High Commissioner, HE David Merry, CMG, apptd 2001

BRITISH COUNCIL
British High Commission Building, Queen's Road, The Mall, PO Box 439, Gaborone
T (+267) 3953602
E general.enquiries@british council.org.bw
Director, David Knox

ECONOMY AND TRADE
Botswana, relatively prosperous since independence because of its mining industry, is one of the few countries in Africa that invests in, rather than borrows from, the World Bank. However, economic problems are expected as the demographic profile changes because of the high levels of HIV/AIDS among the workforce.

Agriculture is predominantly pastoral and accounts for around 3 per cent of GDP. Cattle-rearing accounts for about 85 per cent of agricultural output.

Mineral extraction and processing is the major source of income; there are large mines for diamonds (30,412,000 carats were produced in 2003), copper and nickel. Large deposits of coal have been discovered and 822,780 tonnes were mined in 2003. Service industries account for nearly half of GDP. Tourism is the third largest industry, generating about 7 per cent of GDP. Main imports are motor vehicles, machinery and electrical equipment and foodstuffs; main exports are diamonds, motor vehicles, cupro-nickel and beef.

GNI – US$5,100 million (2002); US$3,010 per capita (2002)
ANNUAL AVERAGE GROWTH OF GDP – 4.2 per cent (2002)
INFLATION RATE – 8.6 per cent (2000)
TOTAL EXTERNAL DEBT – US$360 million (2002)
FOREIGN DIRECT INVESTMENT – US$262 million (2001)
IMPORTS – US$1,810 million (2001)
EXPORTS – US$1,950 million (1998)

BALANCE OF PAYMENTS
Trade – US$675 million surplus (1999)
Current Account – US$517 million surplus (1999)

Trade with UK	2003	2004
Imports from UK	£13,194,000	£15,742,000
Exports to UK	1,106,814,000	1,156,963,000

TRANSPORT INFRASTRUCTURE
The railway from Cape Town to Zimbabwe passes through eastern Botswana. The major road is the 595 km Trans-Kalahari Highway, completed in 1998, which connects the capital of Namibia with Gaborone. There are a total of 10,217 km of roads. The principal airport is Gaborone.

EDUCATION

Botswana does not have a compulsory education policy. Many children undergo ten years of education but the government announced in June 2004 that efforts would be made to increase this to 12 years (seven years of primary education, three years of junior secondary, and two years of senior secondary). There are 800 primary schools, 206 community junior secondary schools, 23 government and government-aided senior secondary schools and one university.

ILLITERACY RATE – (m) 23.1 per cent; (f) 17.6 per cent (2003)

GROSS ENROLMENT RATIO (percentage of relevant age group) – primary 103 per cent (2002); secondary 73 per cent (2002); tertiary 5 per cent (2002)

MEDIA

Newspapers are mostly found in cities and towns. In rural areas radio is the most important news medium (there are state-run and private commercial stations, and programmes are broadcast in both English and Setswana). State-run television (Botswana Television) was established in 2000.

BRAZIL

República Federativa do Brasil – Federative Republic of Brazil

AREA – 8,456,500 sq. km. Neighbours: Guyana, Suriname, French Guiana, Colombia and Venezuela (north), Peru, Bolivia, Paraguay and Argentina (west), Uruguay (south)

POPULATION – 184,101,109 (2004 est.). Portuguese is the national language. Spanish and English are widely spoken

CAPITAL – Brasília (population, 1,737,813, 2000 census)

MAJOR CITIES – Belo Horizonte; ΨFortaleza; ΨPorto Alegre; ΨRecife; ΨRio de Janeiro, the former capital; ΨSalvador; São Paulo

CURRENCY – Real of 100 centavos

NATIONAL ANTHEM – Ouviram do Ipiranga as margens plácidas [From peaceful Ypiranga's banks]

NATIONAL DAY – 7 September (Independence Day)

NATIONAL FLAG – Green with a yellow lozenge containing a blue sphere studded with white stars, and crossed by a white band with the motto *Ordem e Progresso*

LIFE EXPECTANCY (years) – 71.41 (2004 est.)

MORTALITY RATE (per 1,000 population) – 6.13 (2003 est.)

INFANT MORTALITY (per 1,000 births) – 30.66 (2004 est.)

HIV / AIDS ADULT PREVALENCE – 0.7 per cent (2003 est.)

DEATH PENALTY – Yes*

POPULATION GROWTH RATE – 1.11 per cent (2004 est.)

POPULATION DENSITY – 20 per sq. km (2001)

URBAN POPULATION – 82 per cent (2001)

CLIMATE AND TERRAIN

Brazil is South America's biggest country, taking up almost half of the continent. There are five distinct topographical areas: the Amazon Basin (north and west, taking up nearly a third of the country), the River Plate Basin (south), the Guyanan Highlands (north of the Amazon), the Brazilian Highlands (south of the Amazon), and the coastal strip. Brazil is mostly tropical with the equator passing through the north and the Tropic of Capricorn through the south-east. It is home to the world's biggest rainforest. The Amazon Basin sees annual rainfall of up to 2,000 mm a year and there is no dry season (average temperature 17°C). The north-east is the driest area of the country and can experience long periods of drought (average temperature 40°C). The southern states have a seasonal temperate climate (the average temperature is between 17°C and 19°C). Elevation extremes range from 3,014 m (Pico da Neblina) at the highest point to 0 m (Atlantic Ocean) at the lowest.

HISTORY AND POLITICS

Brazil was claimed by the Portuguese navigator Pedro Alvares Cabral in 1500 and colonised by Portugal in the early 16th century, becoming a viceroyalty in 1572. During the Napoleonic Wars the Portuguese court transferred to Brazil. In 1822 it became an independent monarchy under Dom Pedro I, son of King João VI of Portugal. In 1889, King Dom Pedro II was dethroned in a coup, and a republic was proclaimed in 1891. Brazil was a dictatorship from 1930 to 1945 and under military rule from 1964 to 1985, when civilian rule was restored after several years of gradual democratisation. Governments since then have faced difficult economic conditions, and planned development of the Amazon Basin has attracted controversy because it threatens the environmentally important rainforest.

In the first round of the presidential election held in 2002 Luis Inácio 'Lula' da Silva of the Workers' Party (PT) gained 46.4 per cent of the vote. In the second round of the election da Silva was elected president with 61.3 per cent of the vote. In the legislative election the same year, the Workers' Party became the largest party in the Chamber of Deputies, winning 91 of the 513 seats. The PT formed a coalition government with 11 other parties, giving it control of 381 seats in the Chamber of Deputies and 53 seats in the Senate.

POLITICAL SYSTEM

Under the 1988 constitution the president, who heads the executive, is directly elected for a four-year term; in June 1997 the constitution was amended to allow the president to stand for a second term. The Congress consists of an 81-member Senate (three senators per state, elected for an eight-year term) and a 513-member Chamber of Deputies which is elected every four years; the number of deputies per state depends upon the state's population. Each state has a governor and a Legislative Assembly with a four-year term.

HEAD OF STATE

President, Luis Inácio 'Lula' da Silva, *sworn in* 1 January 2003

Vice-President; Defence, José Alencar Gomes da Silva

SELECTED GOVERNMENT MEMBERS *as at July 2005*

Foreign Affairs, Celso Amorim

Finance, Antonio Palocci

Health, Humberto Costa

Development, Industry and Foreign Trade, Luis Fernando Furlan

BRAZILIAN EMBASSY

32 Green Street, London W1K 7AT T 020-7040 8900

Ambassador Extraordinary and Plenipotentiary, HE José Maurício Bustani, apptd 2003

BRITISH EMBASSY
Setor de Embaixadas Sul, Quadra 801, Conjunto K, 70408-900,
Brasilia DF T (+55) (61) 225 2710 E britemb@zaz.com.br
Ambassador Extraordinary and Plenipotentiary, HE Dr
Peter Collecot, CMG, apptd 2004

BRITISH COUNCIL
Edificio Centro Empresarial Varig, SCN Quadra 04, Bloco B, Torre
Oeste Conjunto 202, 70710-926 Brasília DF
T (+ 55) (61) 2106 7500 E brasilia@britishcouncil.org.br
Director, Dr David Cooke

FEDERAL STRUCTURE
The Federative Republic of Brazil is composed of the
federal district and 26 states (population 2000 census):
Distrito Federal (2,043,169); Goiás (4,996,439); Mato
Grosso (2,502,260); Mato Grosso do Sul (2,074,877);
Acre (557,226); Amapá (423,581); Amazonas
(2,813,085); Pará (6,189,550); Rondônia (1,337,792);
Roraima (324,152); Tocantins (1,155,913); Alagoas
(2,819,172); Bahia (13,066,910); Ceará (7,418,476);
Maranhão (5,642,960); Paraíba (3,439,344);
Pernambuco (7,911,937); Piauí (2,841,202); Rio Grande
de Norte (2,771,538); Sergipe (1,781,714); Paraná
(9,558,454); Rio Grande do Sul (10,181,749); Santa
Catarina (5,349,580); Espírito Santo (3,094,390); Minas
Gerais (17,866,402); Rio de Janeiro (14,367,083); São
Paulo (39,969,476).

DEFENCE
The Army has 178 main battle tanks, 803 armoured
personnel carriers and 15 armed helicopters. The Navy
has six bases and is equipped with four submarines, one
aircraft carrier, 15 frigates and 47 patrol and coastal
vessels. Naval aviation consists of 23 combat aircraft and
54 armed helicopters; the Marines have 45 armoured
personnel carriers and 17 light tanks. The Air Force has
254 combat aircraft.
MILITARY EXPENDITURE – 1.8 per cent of GDP (2003)
MILITARY PERSONNEL – 302,909: Army 189,000, Navy
48,600, Air Force 65,309; Paramilitaries 385,600
CONSCRIPTION DURATION – 12 months (can be
extended to 18)

ECONOMY AND TRADE
Reforms in the 1990s, including privatisation and the
removal of trade barriers, have brought some economic
stability following recent high inflation. There are large
mineral deposits including iron ore (hematite),
manganese, bauxite, beryllium, chrome, nickel, tungsten,
cassiterite, lead, monazite (containing rare earths and
thorium) and zirconium. In 2003 400,000 carats of
diamonds were produced as well as 40,438 kg of gold
(metal content). Brazil is the world's largest producer of
coffee; the other main agricultural products are cassava,
maize, soya, rice, wheat, sugar, potatoes, cotton, cocoa,
tobacco and peanuts. Tourism is a growing industry;
Brazil attracted 5.1 million visitors in 2000. Services
generated 72.9 per cent of GDP in 2002.
A new currency, the real, was introduced in 1994 to
help control inflation. Inflation rose, however, to 12.5 per
cent in 2002, the highest level for eight years.
Principal imports are machinery, fuel and lubricants,
mineral products, transport equipment and chemicals.
Principal exports are industrial goods, coffee, sugar cane,
iron ore, tobacco and soya.
GNI – US$494,500 million (2002); US$2,830 per capita
(2002)

ANNUAL AVERAGE GROWTH OF GDP – 5.1 per cent
(2004 est.)
INFLATION RATE – 7.6 per cent (2004 est.)
UNEMPLOYMENT – 11.5 per cent (2004 est.)
TOTAL EXTERNAL DEBT – US$237,953 million (2000)
FOREIGN DIRECT INVESTMENT – US$117,003 million
(1997–2000)
IMPORTS – US$51,000 million (2003)
EXPORTS – US$73,000 million (2003)

BALANCE OF PAYMENTS
Trade – US$24,825 million surplus (2003)
Current Account – US$4,063 million surplus (2003)

Trade with UK	2003	2004
Imports from UK	£828,586,000	£791,930,000
Exports to UK	1,512,283,000	1,581,103,000

TRANSPORT INFRASTRUCTURE
There are 1,670,148 km of roads, of which 161,503 km
are paved, and the route-length of railways is 30,129 km,
of which 2,150 km are electrified. There are ten
international airports and internal air services are highly
developed. There are 43,000 km of navigable inland
waterways. Rio de Janeiro and Santos are the two leading
ports but there are also another 14 fully equipped
harbours. A 3,415-km gas pipeline running from Santa
Cruz, Bolivia, to São Paolo, was opened in 2000.

EDUCATION
The education system includes both public and private
institutions. Public education is free at all levels. Brazil has
42 million students (2002) and 30.5 million of these are
enrolled in primary education.
ILLITERACY RATE – (m) 14.9 per cent; (f) 14.6 per cent
(2000)
GROSS ENROLMENT RATIO (percentage of relevant age
group) – primary 148 per cent (2002); secondary 108
per cent (2002); tertiary 18 per cent (2002)

MEDIA
Brazilian television is South America's biggest media
industry with Brazilian-made soap operas, game shows
and dramas exported all over the world. There are many
Brazilian radio stations and television channels. Globo,
Brazil's most successful broadcasting conglomerate,
dominates the market and owns television and radio
networks, newspapers and subscription television stations.
In 2002 there were 14.3 million internet users.

CULTURE
Brazil is a melting pot of races (European, African, Asian,
Arab and indigenous communities are all well
established), cultures, religious traditions, music and dance
(the samba, bossa nova and lambada are world-famous).
Literary development in Brazil can roughly be broken
down into the country's main historical periods: the
Colonial period (from 1500 until independence in 1822)
and the National period (since 1822). In the 20th century,
the emergence of the Modernist movement, with ideas of
avante-garde aestheticism, profoundly influenced not only
Brazil's literature, but also its painting, sculpture, music
and architecture. There are scores of noteworthy writers
over the centuries, but Luis de Camoes (1524–80) is
widely regarded as Brazil's national poet. Like many other
Latin American countries, one of Brazil's biggest cultural
exports is football. The national team has won the World
Cup a record five times.

BRUNEI

Negara Brunei Darussalam – State of Brunei Darussalam

AREA – 5,300 sq. km. Neighbour: Malaysia
POPULATION – 365,251 (2004 est.): 66.9 per cent
Malay, 15.2 per cent Chinese, 5.9 per cent indigenous
races and 12 per cent European, Indian and other races.
The majority are Sunni Muslims. The official language
is Malay; English and dialects of Chinese are also
spoken
CAPITAL – Bandar Seri Begawan (population, 46,000,
2001 estimate)
CURRENCY – Brunei dollar (B$) of 100 sen (fully
interchangeable with Singapore currency)
NATIONAL ANTHEM – Allah peliharakan Sultan [God
bless his Majesty]
NATIONAL DAY – 23 February
NATIONAL FLAG – Yellow with diagonal stripes of
white over black and the arms in red all over the
centre
LIFE EXPECTANCY (years) – 74.54 (2004 est.)
MORTALITY RATE (per 1,000 population) – 3.4
(2004 est.)
INFANT MORTALITY (per 1,000 births) – 13.05
(2004 est.)
HIV / AIDS ADULT PREVALENCE – 0.1 per cent
(2003 est.)
DEATH PENALTY – No (abolished 1957)
POPULATION GROWTH RATE – 1.95 per cent
(2004 est.)
POPULATION DENSITY – 63 per sq. km (2001)

CLIMATE AND TERRAIN

Lying in the north-east of the island of Borneo, the
country is divided into two sections by the Limbang River
valley in Sarawak. The terrain is mostly rainforest (75 per
cent), with extensive mangrove swamps along the coastal
plain. There are mountains on the border with Sarawak
(Malaysia). Elevation extremes range from 1,850 m (Bukit
Pagon) at the highest point to 0 m (South China Sea) at
the lowest. The climate is tropical, with high levels of
humidity and an average daily temperature of between
24°C and 30°C.

HISTORY AND POLITICS

Formerly a powerful Muslim sultanate that controlled
Borneo and parts of the Philippines, Brunei was reduced
to its present size by the mid-19th century and became a
British Protectorate in 1888. In 1959 the sultan
promulgated the first written constitution and on 1
January 1984 Brunei gained full independence from
Britain.

POLITICAL SYSTEM

Supreme executive authority rests with the sultan, who
presides over and is advised by the Privy Council, the
Religious Council and the Council of Ministers. The
sultan effectively rules by decree as a state of emergency
has been in effect since a revolt in 1962; there are no
political parties and no elections.

HEAD OF STATE

HM The Sultan of Brunei; Defence; Prime Minister; Finance,
HM Sultan Haji Hassanal Bolkiah Mu'izzaddin
Waddaullah, Sultan and Yang Di-Pertuan, GCB, *acceded*
1967, *crowned* 1 August 1968

*HM Crown Prince; Senior Minister in the Prime Minister's
Office,* Prince al-Muhtadee Billah

SELECTED GOVERNMENT MEMBERS *as at July 2005*
Foreign Affairs, Prince Mohamed Bolkiah
Energy, Yahya bin Begawan Mudim Bakar
Home Affairs, Pehin Dato Paduka Haji Adanan Yussof

BRUNEI DARUSSALAM HIGH COMMISSION
19–20 Belgrave Square, London SW1X 8PG
T 020-7581 0521
High Commissioner, HE Pengiran Haji Yunus, apptd 2001

BRITISH HIGH COMMISSION
PO Box 2197, Bandar Seri Begawan 8674
E brithc@brunet.bn
T (+673) (2) 222231
High Commissioner, John Saville, apptd 2005

BRITISH COUNCIL
Level 2, Block D, Yayasan Sultan Hj Hassanal Bolkiah, Jl Pretty,
Bandar Seri Begawan B58711 T (+673) (2) 237742
E all.enquiries@bn.britishcouncil.org
Director, Amanda Griffiths

DEFENCE

The Army has 20 light tanks and 39 armoured personnel
carriers. The Navy, based in Muara, has six patrol and
coastal vessels. The Air Force has five armed helicopters.
There are some 1,120 UK troops currently stationed in
Brunei.
MILITARY EXPENDITURE – 5.1 per cent of GDP (2003)
MILITARY PERSONNEL – 7,000: Army 4,900, Navy
1,000, Air Force 1,100; Paramilitaries 3,750

ECONOMY AND TRADE

Brunei is the fourth largest world producer of natural gas
and in 1999 this was the country's top export. The
economy is based on the production of this gas along
with oil and also on income from overseas investments
(which now exceed oil revenues). Royalties and taxes from
these operations form the bulk of government revenue
and have enabled the construction of free health,
education and welfare services.

In 2001 agriculture accounted for 5 per cent of GDP,
industry accounted for 45 per cent and services for 50 per
cent. Imports cover 80 per cent of domestic food
requirements.
GNI – US$24,630 (2001)
ANNUAL AVERAGE GROWTH OF GDP – 3.2 per cent
(2004 est.)

Trade with UK	2002	2003
Imports from UK	£61,263,000	£67,198,000
Exports to UK	36,442,000	67,185,000

TRANSPORT INFRASTRUCTURE

There are five ports, at Muara, Bandar Seri Begawan,
Seria, Tutong and Kuala Belait, and an international
airport at Bandar Seri Begawan. There are three
heliports and 209 km of waterways. There are 13 km of
privately owned railway. There is a road network of
2,525 km.

EDUCATION

All levels of education are free. Children undertake seven
years of primary education, three of lower secondary and
two years of upper secondary which can be in a secondary

school, a vocational school or technical college. There are 169 primary schools, 38 secondary schools, six technical and vocational colleges and two universities.

ILLITERACY RATE – (m) 1 per cent; (f) 1 per cent (2003)

MEDIA

The media is privately owned. The main publications are the *Borneo Bulletin* (English-language daily), *Brunei Direct* (online news service) and *Media Permata* (Malay-language daily). The only broadcast media organisation. Radio Television Brunei (RTB), is state-owned and controlled. It broadcasts television in Malay and English and radio in Malay, English, Mandarin Chinese and Gurkhali.

CULTURE

Brunei is famous for its traditional crafts of silverwork and weaving. The capital, Bandar Seri Begawan, is the only large town and is a mix of old (Kampung Ayer, an ancient area of 28 water villages built on stilts in the Brunei River) and new (ultra-modern public and government buildings set back from wide streets). Brunei is a Muslim country and Shari'ah law prevails in some areas.

BULGARIA

Republika Bălgarija – Republic of Bulgaria

AREA – 110,600 sq. km. Neighbours: Romania (north), Serbia and the Former Yugoslav Republic of Macedonia (west), Greece and Turkey (south)

POPULATION – 7,517,973 (2004 est.): 85.7 per cent Bulgarian, 9.4 per cent Turkish, 3.7 per cent Roma, 1.2 per cent others. The language is Bulgarian, a Southern Slavonic tongue closely allied to Serbo-Croat and Russian with local admixtures of modern Greek, Albanian and Turkish words. The alphabet is Cyrillic. The predominant religion is the Bulgarian Orthodox Church (85.7 per cent of the population); Islam is the second largest religion (13.1 per cent).

CAPITAL – Sofia (population, 1,096,389, 2001 census)

MAJOR CITIES – ΨBurgas; Plovdiv; ΨVarna

CURRENCY – Lev of 100 stotinki

NATIONAL ANTHEM – Gorda stara planina [Proud and ancient mountains]

NATIONAL DAY – 3 March

NATIONAL FLAG – Three horizontal bands, white, green, red

LIFE EXPECTANCY (years) – 71.75 (2004 est.)

MORTALITY RATE (per 1,000 population) – 14.25 (2004 est.)

INFANT MORTALITY (per 1,000 births) – 21.31 (2004 est.)

HIV / AIDS ADULT PREVALENCE – 0.1 per cent (2001 est.)

DEATH PENALTY – No (abolished 1998)

POPULATION BELOW POVERTY LINE – 12.6 per cent (2001 est.)

POPULATION GROWTH RATE – −0.92 per cent (2004 est.)

POPULATION DENSITY – 71 per sq. km (2001)

URBAN POPULATION – 68 per cent (2001)

CLIMATE AND TERRAIN

The Bulgarian landscape is dominated by mountains: the Balkan Mountains cross the country from west to east averaging 2,000 m in height; the Rhodope Mountains are found in the south-west, climbing to almost 3,000 m. Elevation extremes range from 2,925 m (Musala) at the highest point to 0 m (Black Sea) at the lowest. The lowland plains of the north and south-east are in the basins of the main rivers, the Danube in the north, which forms much of the border with Romania, and the Maritsa, which divides the Balkan from the Rhodope Mountains, and along the Black Sea coast.

HISTORY AND POLITICS

Bulgarians are descended from Slavs who came to the area of modern-day Bulgaria in the fifth century AD. The Bulgarian state can trace its foundation back to 680 AD. Bulgaria was part of the Ottoman Empire from 1390 until 1877 when this period of rule was brought to an end with the aid of Russia.

A principality of Bulgaria was created by the Treaty of Berlin in 1878, and in 1908 the country was declared an independent kingdom. It was allied with Germany in both World Wars and was occupied in 1944 by the Soviet Union. A coup d'état in September 1944 gave power to the Fatherland Front, a coalition of Communists, Agrarians and Social Democrats, which came to be dominated by the Communists. A referendum in September 1946 led to the abolition of the monarchy and the establishment of a republic dominated by the Communist Party (BCP), which in 1947 established a one-party state and centralised economy.

From the mid-1980s cautious reforms were introduced in line with the Soviet policies of *perestroika* and *glasnost*, and Bulgaria became a multiparty democracy in 1990. Political and economic liberalisation progressed slowly in the early 1990s, causing economic difficulties, and more radical economic reforms were introduced to stimulate the economy in 1996. In 2001 the Bulgarian Socialist Party's (BSP) candidate, Georgi Parvanov, was elected president. The general election that year was won by the National Movement for Simeon II (NDSV), a movement founded in April 2001 by the former king, which won 43.74 per cent of the vote. The June 2005 general election was won by the opposition Bulgarian Socialist Party with 31 per cent of the vote. However, this was not a clear enough majority and a coalition government was formed with the NDSV.

POLITICAL SYSTEM

Under the 1991 constitution, the head of state is the president who is directly elected for a five-year term, renewable once only. The head of government is the prime minister, who is appointed by the president, and is usually the leader of the largest party in the legislature. There is a unicameral National Assembly of 240 members who are directly elected by proportional representation for a four-year term.

HEAD OF STATE

President, Georgi Parvanov (BSP), *elected* 18 November 2001, *took office* 19 January 2002
Vice-President, Angel Marin (BSP)

SELECTED GOVERNMENT MEMBERS *as at August 2005*
Prime Minister, Sergei Stanishev
Deputy Prime Minister, Foreign Affairs, Ivaylo Kalfin
Defence, Vesselin Bliznakov
Finance, Plamen Oresharski
Internal Affairs, Rumen Petkov

EMBASSY OF THE REPUBLIC OF BULGARIA
186–188 Queen's Gate, London SW7 5HL
T 020-7584 9400/9433
E info@bulgarianembassy.org.uk
Ambassador Extraordinary and Plenipotentiary, HE
Valentin Dobrev, apptd 1998

BRITISH EMBASSY
9 Moskovska Street, Sofia T (+359) (2) 980 1220
E britembinf@mail.orbitel.bg
Ambassador Extraordinary and Plenipotentiary, HE Jeremy
Hill

BRITISH COUNCIL
7 Krakra Street, BG-1504 Sofia T (+359) (2) 942 4344
E bc.sofia@britishcouncil.bg
Director, Ian Stewart

DEFENCE
The Army has 1,474 main battle tanks, 214 armoured
infantry fighting vehicles and 1,643 armoured personnel
carriers. The Navy has one submarine, one frigate, 23
patrol and coastal vessels, and 10 armed helicopters. The
Air Force has 232 combat aircraft and 43 armed
helicopters. Bulgaria became a member of NATO in
March 2004.
MILITARY EXPENDITURE – 2.4 per cent of GDP (2003)
MILITARY PERSONNEL – 42,470: Army 25,000, Navy
4,370, Air Force 13,100; Paramilitaries 34,000
CONSCRIPTION DURATION – Nine months

ECONOMY AND TRADE
The government adopted a radical reform package in
1997, including pegging the lev to the Deutschemark to
stimulate the economy. A US$300 million agreement was
negotiated with the IMF at the end of 2001 to promote
economic growth. The principal crops are wheat, maize,
beet, tomatoes, tobacco, oleaginous seeds, fruit, vegetables
and cotton. Around 24 per cent of the population is
engaged in agriculture, which accounted for 12.5 per cent
of GDP in 2002. Cadmium, coal, copper, pig iron, kaolin,
lead, silver and zinc are produced. Industry accounted for
about 28 per cent of GDP in 2002.

Bulgaria is highly dependent on trade and has been a
member of the World Trade Organisation since 1996.
The principal exports are textiles and clothing, iron and
steel products, foodstuffs, beverages, industrial equipment,
telecommunications and sound recording equipment, oil
derivatives and non-ferrous metals.

Bulgaria is scheduled to join the European Union in
2007.
GNI – US$14,100 million (2002); US$1,770 per capita
(2002)
INFLATION RATE – 10.3 per cent (2000)
UNEMPLOYMENT – 12.7 per cent (2004 est.)
TOTAL EXTERNAL DEBT – US$10,026 million (2000)
FOREIGN DIRECT INVESTMENT – US$2,707 million
(1997–2000)
IMPORTS – US$11,000 million (2003)
EXPORTS – US$8,000 million (2003)

BALANCE OF PAYMENTS
Trade – US$2,474 million deficit (2003)
Current Account – US$1,666 million deficit (2003)

Trade with UK	2003	2004
Imports from UK	£153,709,000	£155,424,000
Exports to UK	125,978,000	150,340,000

EDUCATION
Education is free and compulsory for children from six to
16 years inclusive. There are three universities (at Sofia,
Plovdiv and Veliko Turnovo), an American University and
21 higher education establishments.
ILLITERACY RATE – (m) 0.9 per cent; (f) 1.8 per cent
(2003)
GROSS ENROLMENT RATIO (percentage of relevant age
group) – primary 99 per cent (2002); secondary 94 per
cent (2002); tertiary 40 per cent (2002)

TRANSPORT INFRASTRUCTURE
Bulgaria has a total of 4,294 km of railways, 37,286 km
of roads and 470 km of waterways. There are six harbours
(Burgas, Lom, Nesebur, Ruse, Varna and Vidin), the main
ports being Burgas and Varna; and there are 216 airports,
128 of which are surfaced, and one heliport.

MEDIA AND CULTURE
In 1996 Bulgaria gave national radio and television the
status of public services and granted them independence.
In 2003 BTV, the country's first national commercial
channel (part of the Rupert Murdoch News Corporation)
was launched. In 2003 Nova TV became the second
national commercial channel.

Bulgaria is still a country in transition from
Communism. Some rural areas are virtually unchanged
since the Communist era while urban centres are now
radically Western in character and outlook. Bulgaria's
Roman and Byzantine ruins are culturally significant, as
are its churches and monasteries. Notable Bulgarian
writers include Stoyan Mikhaylovski (1856–1927) and
Iordan Iovkov (1884–1938).

BURKINA FASO

*République Démocratique du Burkina Faso – Democratic
Republic of Burkina Faso*

AREA – 274,000 sq. km. Neighbours: Mali (west and
north), Niger (north-east), Benin (south-east), Togo,
Ghana and Côte d'Ivoire (south)
POPULATION – 13,574,820 (2004 est.) The official
language is French. Mossi, More, Dioula and
Gourmantché are indigenous languages
CAPITAL – Ouagadougou (population, 1,000,000, 2000
estimate)
MAJOR CITIES – Bobo-Dioulasso; Koudougou
CURRENCY – Franc CFA of 100 centimes
NATIONAL ANTHEM – Ditanyé [Hymn of victory]
NATIONAL DAY – 11 December
NATIONAL FLAG – Equal bands of red over green, with a
yellow star in centre
LIFE EXPECTANCY – 44.2 (2004 est.)
MORTALITY RATE (per 1,000 population) – 18.79
(2004 est.)
HIV / AIDS ADULT PREVALENCE – 4.2 per cent
(2004 est.)
DEATH PENALTY – No (abolished 1988)
POPULATION BELOW POVERTY LINE – 45 per cent
(2001 est.)
POPULATION GROWTH RATE – 2.57 per cent
(2004 est.)
POPULATION DENSITY – 42 per sq. km (1999)
MILITARY EXPENDITURE – 1.3 per cent of GDP
(2003)

MILITARY PERSONNEL – 10,800: Army 6,400, Air Force 200, Paramilitaries 4,200

ILLITERACY RATE – (m) 63.1 per cent, (f) 83.4 per cent (2003 est.)

GROS ENROLMENT RATIO (percentage of relevant age group) – primary 48 per cent (2003); secondary 10 per cent (2003)

CLIMATE AND TERRAIN

Burkina Faso is a landlocked state occupying a plateau in West Africa. There are wooded savannahs in the south and the north is semi-desert with elevation extremes ranging from 749 m (Tena Kourou) at the highest point to 200 m (Mouhoun River) at the lowest. The wet season runs from June to October and the dry season from December to May; there are recurring droughts. Average annual temperatures range from 24°C in January to 28°C in July.

HISTORY AND POLITICS

Burkina Faso (Upper Volta until 1983) was part of the Mossi Empire in the 18th and 19th centuries. It was annexed by France in 1896 and between 1932 and 1947 was administered as part of the Colony of the Ivory Coast. In 1947 its original borders were reconstituted, and in 1958 Upper Volta became autonomous within the French Community; full independence was achieved on 5 August 1960.

In the three decades after independence there were several military coups, the latest of which in 1987 brought to power Capt. Blaise Compaoré. Military power ended in 1991 when a new constitution was adopted, and multiparty elections were held in 1992. Presidential elections were held in November 1998 and won by Compaoré, the CDP candidate, in the face of a boycott by the opposition parties. A general election was held in May 2002 and won by the Congress for Democracy and Progress (CDP).

POLITICAL SYSTEM

Under the 1991 constitution, the president is directly elected; the presidential term was seven years but in 2000 was changed to five years, renewable once, with effect from 2005. The parliament (Parlement) has two chambers: the Assemblée Nationale (111 deputies elected for a five-year term) and the Chambre des Représentants (178 members appointed or indirectly elected for a three-year term).

HEAD OF STATE

President, Capt. Blaise Compaoré, *assumed office* October 1987, *elected* December 1991, *re-elected* November 1998

SELECTED GOVERNMENT MEMBERS *as at July 2005*
Prime Minister, Paramanga Ernest Yonli
Defence, Yero Boli
Finance and Budget, Jean-Baptiste Compaoré
Foreign Affairs and Regional Co-operation, Youssouf Ouédraogo

EMBASSY OF THE REPUBLIC OF BURKINA FASO
16 Place Guy d'Arezzo, 1180 Brussels, Belgium
T (+32) (2) 345 9912
Ambassador Extraordinary and Plenipotentiary, HE Kadré Désiré Ouédraogo, apptd 2001

BRITISH AMBASSADOR
HE David Coates, resident at Abidjan, Côte d'Ivoire

ECONOMY AND TRADE

The economy is fragile due to the high cost of services such as electricity, water and telephones, restricted access to healthcare and the limited nature of the export market. In June 2003 the IMF granted Burkina Faso a new three-year Poverty Reduction and Growth Facility worth around US$17 million. The majority of this money will be used for macroeconomic restructuring.

The principal industry is cattle and sheep rearing. Agriculture employs over 90 per cent of the workforce and contributes 33 per cent of GDP. The chief exports are cotton, livestock and animal feed, and gold. The chief imports are capital goods, foodstuffs and fuel oils.

GNI – US$2,900 million (2002); US$250 per capita (2002)

ANNUAL AVERAGE GROWTH OF GDP – 2.2 per cent (2000)

INFLATION RATE – 0.3 per cent (2000)

TOTAL EXTERNAL DEBT – US$1,332 million (2000)

IMPORTS – US$580 million (2002)

EXPORTS – US$166 million (2002)

BALANCE OF PAYMENTS
Trade – US$286 million deficit (2002)
Current Account – US$381 million deficit (2002)

Trade with UK	2003	2004
Imports from UK	£3,730,000	£3,247,000
Exports to UK	153,000	246,000

TRANSPORT INFRASTRUCTURE

There are 12,506 km of roads, of which 2,001 km are surfaced. An estimated 60 per cent of the country's villages are further than 3 km from a main road and paths are impassable during the wet season. There are 622 km of railway track in operation and two main airports.

MEDIA AND CULTURE

The Ministry of Communication and Culture regulates the media. There are several private radio stations and a private television channel.

The largest tribe is the Mossi (48 per cent) whose king, Moro Naba, still wields moral influence. There are over 60 other ethnic groups including Gurunsi, Sénufo, Lobi, Bobo, Mande and Fulani. Despite its poverty Burkina Faso is admired for its music, dance, theatre and film. The art of the Mossi, Bobo and Lobi is famous (Burkina Faso has Africa's largest crafts market). The country also plays host to the Pan-African Film Festival every two years.

BURUNDI

République du Burundi – Republic of Burundi

AREA – 27,834 sq. km. Neighbours: Rwanda (north), Tanzania (east and south), Democratic Republic of Congo (west)

POPULATION – 6,231,221: 83 per cent Hutu, 15 per cent Tutsi. The official languages are Kirundi, a Bantu language, and French. Kiswahili is also used

CAPITAL – Bujumbura (formerly Usumbura) (population, 235,440, 1990)

MAJOR CITIES – Kitega

CURRENCY – Burundi franc of 100 centimes

NATIONAL DAY – 1 July

NATIONAL FLAG – Divided diagonally by a white saltire into red and green triangles; on a white disc in the centre three red six-pointed stars edged in green

NATIONAL ANTHEM – Burundi Bwacu [Dear Burundi]

MORTALITY RATE (per 1,000 population) – 17.61 (2004 est.)

INFANT MORTALITY (per 1,000 births) – 70.4 (2004 est.)

LIFE EXPECTANCY – 44.2 (2004 est.)

HIV / AIDS ADULT PREVALENCE – 6 per cent (2003 est.)

DEATH PENALTY – Yes

POPULATION BELOW POVERTY LINE – 70 per cent (2002)

POPULATION GROWTH RATE – 2.2 per cent (2004 est.)

POPULATION DENSITY – 233 per sq. km (1999)

MILITARY EXPENDITURE – 7.2 per cent of GDP (2003)

MILITARY PERSONNEL – 50,500: Army 45,000, Paramilitaries 5,500

ILLITERACY RATE – (m) 42.5 per cent; (f) 54.8 per cent (2003 est.)

GROSS ENROLMENT RATIO (percentage of relevant age group) – primary 71 per cent (2002); secondary 11 per cent (2002); tertiary 2 per cent (2002)

CLIMATE AND TERRAIN

The landlocked country lies across the Nile-Congo watershed in central Africa. An interior plateau rises 1,500 m to the country's highest point at 2,685 m (Mt Karonje). The River Ruzizi forms part of the north-western border with the Democratic Republic of the Congo, along with Lake Tanganyika (at 780 m the lowest elevation in the country) in the south-west. The climate is equatorial. The dry season runs from June to September while the average daily temperature is 23°C.

HISTORY AND POLITICS

From the 16th century the area was ruled by Tutsi kings who dominated a predominantly Hutu population. Germany annexed the area in 1890 and included it in German East Africa, which after the First World War was administered by Belgium. In 1946 it was joined with Rwanda as a UN Trust Territory but broke the union when it became independent as a constitutional monarchy on 1 July 1962. The monarchy was overthrown in 1966 and the country became a republic and a one-party state.

The population remains mostly Hutu but since independence political and military power has tended to rest with the Tutsi minority, leading to intercommunal tensions that have often resulted in ethnic massacres. The first multiparty elections in 1993 ended Tutsi political dominance with the election of a Hutu president and a Hutu majority in the National Assembly. The president was killed shortly afterwards in a coup by the Tutsi-dominated army; although the coup was suppressed, inter-racial fighting left more than 100,000 dead. The following year the new (Hutu) president was killed when the plane in which he was travelling with the Rwandan president was shot down. These deaths sparked off fierce ethnic conflict which claimed over 200,000 lives between 1993 and 1995.

In July 1996 the Hutu president was ousted in another military coup, which installed Maj. Pierre Buyoya, a Tutsi, as head of state, and a multi-ethnic government was formed.

Talks between Burundi's 19 political parties began in 1998 and in July 2000 reached a peace accord at talks in Arusha (Tanzania) brokered by Nelson Mandela; the accord was ratified by the Transitional Assembly in November 2000, and in October 2001 the transitional constitution was adopted and transitional institutions were set up, with the intention of holding elections in 2004. However, the elections had to be postponed and the government's mandate was extended to mid-August 2005, when presidential and legislative elections took place. Pierre Nkurunziza was elected president by members of the National Assembly and Senate. Since 2000 the government has signed cease-fire agreements with most of the rebel groups, and only one group remains active. The UN is supervising the disarming of soldiers and former rebels, and the creation of a new national army.

POLITICAL SYSTEM

A transitional constitution introduced in 1998 provided for a political partnership between Hutus and Tutsis; it was superceded in 2001 by the transitional constitution agreed under the Arusha peace accord. A new constitution was approved by referendum in February 2005 and will come into effect following the August 2005 presidential and legislative elections.

A 117-member Transitional National Assembly was inaugurated in 1998; an additional 53 members were elected in January 2002, in accordance with the Arusha peace accord. A Transitional Senate with 51 co-opted members was inaugurated in February 2002. Under the Arusha peace accord, a three-year transitional government was inaugurated in October 2001, headed by President Buyoya, a Tutsi, with a Hutu as vice-president – the two switching roles midway through the three-year term, which was subsequently extended to August 2005.

HEAD OF STATE

President, Pierre Nkurunziza, *sworn in* 26 August 2005

Vice-President, Martin Nduwimana

SELECTED GOVERNMENT MEMBERS *as at July 2005*

Defence, Maj. Gen. Germain Niyoyankana

External Relations and Co-operation, Antoinette Batumubwira

Finance, Dieudonne Ngowembusa

Interior, Salvator Ntacombamaze

EMBASSY OF THE REPUBLIC OF BURUNDI

46 Sq. Marie Louise, 1000 Brussels, Belgium

T (+32) (2) 2304535

Ambassador Extraordinary and Plenipotentiary, HE Ferdinand Nyabenda, apptd 2003

BRITISH AMBASSADOR

HE Susan Hogwood, OBE, apptd 2001, resident at Kigali, Rwanda

ECONOMY AND TRADE

In October 2002 the IMF approved a credit of US$7.3 million in emergency post-conflict assistance to support the country's reconstruction and economic recovery programme. Agriculture accounted for 41 per cent of GDP and employed over 90 per cent of the workforce in 2002. The chief crop is coffee, accounting for around 50 per cent of export earnings in 2002. Tea, mineral, hide and skin exports are also important.

GNI – US$700 million (2002); US$100 per capita (2002)

INFLATION RATE – 24.3 per cent (2000)

TOTAL EXTERNAL DEBT – US$1,100 million (2000)

IMPORTS – US$160 million (2003)

EXPORTS – US$40 million (2003)

BALANCE OF PAYMENTS
Trade – US$73 million deficit (2002)
Current Account – US$3 million deficit (2002)

Trade with UK	2003	2004
Imports from UK	£1,940,000	£1,538,000
Exports to UK	617,000	245,000

TRANSPORT INFRASTRUCTURE
There are no railways in Burundi. There are 14,480 km of roads, but only 1,014 km of these are paved. There is one port, Bujumbura on Lake Tanganyika, and seven airports (one has a surfaced runway).

MEDIA
La Radiodiffusion et Télévision Nationale du Burundi (RTNB) is the main TV station and it is government controlled. Low literacy levels mean that the dominant news medium is radio. Radio Burundi (RTNB) broadcasts in Kirundi, Swahili, French and English and is state controlled. There are several newspapers but they are published sporadically due to government influence.

CAMBODIA

Preăh Réachéanachâkr Kâmpuchéa – Kingdom of Cambodia

AREA – 181,035 sq. km. Neighbours: Laos (north), Thailand (north and west), Vietnam (east and south)
POPULATION – 13,363,421 (2004 est.). The official language is Khmer. Chinese, Vietnamese and French are also spoken
CAPITAL – ΨPhnom Penh (population, 1,200,000, 2003 census)
CURRENCY – Riel of 100 sen
NATIONAL ANTHEM – Nokoreach
NATIONAL DAY – 9 November [Independence Day]
NATIONAL FLAG – Three horizontal stripes of blue, red, blue, with the blue of double width and containing a representation of the temple of Angkor in white
LIFE EXPECTANCY (years) – 58.41 (2004 est.)
HIV / AIDS ADULT PREVALENCE – 2.6 per cent (2003 est.)
DEATH PENALTY – No (abolished 1997)
POPULATION GROWTH RATE – 1.8 per cent (2004 est.)
POPULATION DENSITY – 60 per sq. km (1999)
GROSS ENROLMENT RATIO (percentage of relevant age group) – primary 123 per cent (2002); secondary 22 per cent (2002); tertiary 3 per cent (2002)

CLIMATE AND TERRAIN
Cambodia is a mostly flat country (with the exception of the Cardamom Mountains in the south-west and the uplands of the north-east). Dominated by the Mekong River, Cambodia is also home to Tonle Sap, the largest lake in south-east Asia. The highest point of elevation is at 1,810 m (Phnum Aoral) while the lowest is 0 m (Gulf of Thailand). The monsoon season is from May to November.

HISTORY AND POLITICS
Although the Khmer people have inhabited the region for almost 2,000 years, the Khmer kingdom was at its strongest during the 11th century, its territory covering modern-day Laos, Thailand and Vietnam. The kingdom lost power and territory from 1432 onwards.

Cambodia became a French protectorate in 1863 and part of Indochina in 1887. It became an Associate State within the French Union in 1949 and gained full independence in 1953 as the Kingdom of Cambodia. From the late 1960s there was growing guerrilla insurgency, led by the Khmer Rouge, and in 1970 Prince Norodom Sihanouk was overthrown in a right-wing coup and the country was renamed the Khmer Republic. Fighting throughout the country involved forces from North and South Vietnam and the USA. In 1975, Phnom Penh fell to the North Vietnamese-backed Khmer Rouge. During Khmer Rouge rule under Pol Pot (1975–8) extreme Marxist policies were brutally implemented and famine, disease and maltreatment caused the deaths of an estimated 2.5 million people. In 1978, Vietnamese troops invaded Cambodia and in 1979 established a government in Phnom Penh. Fighting continued between the Vietnamese-backed government and guerrilla resistance from the Khmer Rouge and Sihanouk's nationalist forces until the Vietnamese withdrawal in 1987–9.

A UN peace plan was agreed in 1991, and in 1992 the UN Transitional Authority for Cambodia (UNTAC) assumed authority from the government in the run-up to the multiparty elections, which were held in May 1993. In September 1993 a new constitution was adopted and Prince Sihanouk was elected king. There have been tensions within the political elite; in 1997 Hun Sen and armed supporters ousted Prince Ranariddh, the prime minister, and Hun Sen became prime minister in 1998 after an election whose validity was disputed. King Sihanouk abdicated on 6 October 2004 and was succeeded on 14 October by his son, Prince Norodom Sihamoni. The latest elections to the National Assembly were held on 27 July 2003. The incumbent Cambodian People's Party (CPP) won 73 of the 123 parliamentary seats.

INSURGENCIES
The Khmer Rouge was outlawed in 1994 but continued with guerrilla warfare until 1996, when it was weakened by internal divisions. Pol Pot was captured in June 1997 and died in captivity in April 1998. The remaining Khmer Rouge soldiers surrendered in February 1999. In 1997 negotiations began between the government and the UN to set up an international tribunal to prosecute former leaders of the Khmer Rouge regime for atrocities committed during its rule. In 2003 they signed an agreement allowing the majority of tribunal judges to be Cambodian but with a requirement for at least one foreign judge to support a tribunal ruling.

POLITICAL SYSTEM
A new constitution was adopted in 1993 under which Cambodia is a pluralist liberal democracy with a constitutional monarchy. Executive power rests with the government, with the king having the power only to make appointments and declare a state of emergency, in consultation with the government. Legislative power is vested in the National Assembly, which has 123 members elected for a five-year term, and the Senate, which has 61 appointed members and was formed on 25 March 1999 following an amendment to the constitution.

HEAD OF STATE
HM The King of Cambodia, Norodom Sihamoni, *elected by the Council of the Throne* 29 October 2004
Chair of the National Assembly, Prince Norodom Ranariddh

SELECTED GOVERNMENT MEMBERS *as at July 2005*
Prime Minister, Hun Sen
Deputy Prime Minister, Foreign Affairs and International Co-operation, Hor Namhong
Deputy Prime Minister, Co-Minister of Interior, Sar Kheng
Deputy Prime Minister, Minister in the Office of the Council of Ministers, Sok An
Deputy Prime Minister, Co-Minister of Interior, Yu Hokkri
Deputy Prime Minister, Co-Minister of National Defence, Gen. Tea Banh
Senior Minister, Economy and Finance, Keat Chhon

ROYAL EMBASSY OF CAMBODIA
28–32 Wellington Road, St John's Wood, London NW8 9SP
T 020 7483 9063
Ambassador Extraordinary and Plenipotentiary, HE Hor Nambora

BRITISH EMBASSY
27–29 Street 75, Phnom Penh
T (+855) (23) 427124
Ambassador Extraordinary and Plenipotentiary, HE Stephen Bridges, apptd 2001

DEFENCE
The Army has 150 main battle tanks and 190 armoured personnel carriers. The Navy has 4 patrol and coastal vessels. The Air Force has 24 combat aircraft.
MILITARY EXPENDITURE – 1.7 per cent of GDP (2003)
MILITARY PERSONNEL – 124,300: Army 75,000, Navy 2,800, Air Force 1,500, Provincial Forces 45,000; Paramilitaries 67,000

ECONOMY AND TRADE
The economy is largely based on agriculture, fishing and forestry. Agriculture employs over 75 per cent of the workforce and produced 30 per cent of GDP in 2003. In addition to rice, which is the staple crop, the major products are rubber, livestock, maize, timber, pepper, palm sugar, fresh and dried fish, kapok, beans, soya and tobacco. Textiles, leather goods, furnishings, timber and rubber are the main exports; the main imports are cigarettes, gold, diesel and oil. Tourism is the fastest-growing sector of the economy.
GNI – US$3,800 million (2002); US$300 per capita (2002)
ANNUAL AVERAGE GROWTH OF GDP – 4.5 per cent (2003)
INFLATION RATE – 3.5 per cent (2002)
TOTAL EXTERNAL DEBT – US$2,357 million (2000)
IMPORTS – US$2,000 million (2003)
EXPORTS – US$2,000 million (2003)

BALANCE OF PAYMENTS
Trade – US$563 million deficit (2002)
Current Account – US$64 million deficit (2002)

Trade with UK	2003	2004
Imports from UK	£3,572,000	£4,434,000
Exports to UK	100,887,000	107,529,000

TRANSPORT INFRASTRUCTURE
The country has about 34,100 km of roads, although most are in a state of disrepair. There are two railway lines, one from Phnom Penh to the Thai border, the other from Phnom Penh to Kampot and Sihanoukville (Kompong Som). The Mekong River is navigable, and ships of up to 2,500 tons can sail as far as Phnom Peng all year round. The deep-water port at Sihanoukville (Kompong Som) on the Gulf of Thailand can receive ships of up to 10,000 tons. The port is linked to Phnom Penh by a modern highway.

MEDIA AND CULTURE
Much of the Cambodian media is owned by political parties but the prime minister, Hun Sen, has been active in encouraging press freedom. The state broadcaster is National Television of Cambodia (TVK) and there are five other major commercial and privately owned channels. There are no restrictions on the ownership and use of private satellite dishes and foreign radio is also easily received and widely accessed.

Cambodia's Khmer culture can still be seen in the capital's many museums and temples. There are also vestiges of French colonial influence, most notably in the architecture and cuisine. The abandoned temples of Angkor Wat (9–13th centuries), a religious and administrative centre built by Khmer kings, are the country's most popular tourist destination.

CAMEROON

République du Cameroun – Republic of Cameroon

AREA – 465,400 sq. km. Neighbours: Nigeria (north and west), Chad and Central African Republic (east), Republic of Congo, Gabon and Equatorial Guinea (south)
POPULATION – 16,063,678 (2004 est.). French and English are both official languages and enjoy equal status
CAPITAL – Yaoundé (population, 653,670)
MAJOR CITIES – ΨDouala is the commercial centre
CURRENCY – Franc CFA of 100 centimes
NATIONAL ANTHEM – O Cameroun, berceau de nos ancêtres [O Cameroon, thou cradle of our forefathers]
NATIONAL DAY – 20 May
NATIONAL FLAG – Vertical stripes of green, red and yellow with single five-pointed yellow star in centre of red stripe
LIFE EXPECTANCY (years) – 47.95 (2004 est.)
MORTALITY RATE (per 1,000 population) – 15.34 (2004 est.)
INFANT MORTALITY (per 1,000 births) – 69.18 (2004 est.)
HIV / AIDS ADULT PREVALENCE – 6.9 per cent (2003 est.)
DEATH PENALTY – Yes
POPULATION BELOW POVERTY LINE – 48 per cent (2000)
POPULATION GROWTH RATE – 1.97 per cent (2004 est.)
POPULATION DENSITY – 33 per sq. km (2001)
MILITARY EXPENDITURE – 1.4 per cent of GDP (2003)
MILITARY PERSONNEL – 23,100: Army 12,500, Navy 1,300, Air Force 300, Paramilitaries 9,000
ILLITERACY RATE – (m) 16.3 per cent; (f) 26.6 per cent (2003 est.)
GROSS ENROLMENT RATIO (percentage of relevant age group) – primary 107 per cent (2002); secondary 33 per cent (2002); tertiary 5 per cent (2002)

CLIMATE AND TERRAIN

There are three main geographic zones: desert plains in the north (the Lake Chad basin), mountains and savannah plateau in the central region, and tropical rainforests in the south and east. Elevation extremes range from 4,070 m (Mt Cameroun) at the highest point to 0 m (Atlantic Ocean) at the lowest. The wet season runs from June to September in the north and from May to November in the south.

HISTORY AND POLITICS

The Bakas (Pygmies) and Bantu speakers of the Cameroonian highlands were probably the country's earliest peoples. Cameroon was explored by the Portuguese from 1472 and later by Spanish, Dutch and English traders. The Fulani people of the western Sahel conquered northern Cameroon from the 1770s to the early 1800s.

The German protectorate of Kamerun was established in 1884. After the First World War it divided into the League of Nations-mandated territories (later UN trusteeships) of East (French) and West (British) Cameroon. On 1 January 1960 East Cameroon became independent as the Republic of Cameroon. This was joined on 1 October 1961 by the southern part of West Cameroon after a plebiscite held under the auspices of the United Nations; the northern part voted to join Nigeria. Cameroon became a federal republic with separate East and West Cameroon state governments; the federal system was abolished in 1972. From 1972 to 1992, Cameroon was ruled by one party, the Cameroon People's Democratic Movement (RDPC), with Paul Biya as president since 1982.

Economic decline in 1990 provoked widespread civil unrest and political pluralism was restored. In the multiparty elections in 1992 the ruling RDPC won the legislative election, and Paul Biya won the presidential election, a result that was challenged by the opposition over alleged vote-rigging. In the 2002 legislative election the RDCP retained its overall majority in the National Assembly. Opposition groups alleged widespread fraud in the conduct of the elections. In the October 2004 presidential election, Paul Biya was returned to office with 70.8 per cent of the vote.

INTERNATIONAL RELATIONS

There have been armed clashes with Nigeria in a long-running dispute over the Bakassi peninsula, which is rich in oil. In 2002 the peninsula was awarded to Cameroon by the International Court of Justice, Nigeria was awarded a series of other strategically significant territories near the border, and a UN-led commission, the Cameroon-Nigeria Mixed Commission (CNMC), was established to defuse tension; negotiations continue. Cameroon joined the Commonwealth in 1995, the first country to do so that has never been fully under British rule at any point in its history.

POLITICAL SYSTEM

The president is directly elected for a seven-year term, and appoints the prime minister and cabinet. The National Assembly comprises 180 members, directly elected for a five-year term. Constitutional amendments in 1996 provided for the establishment of a Senate (100 seats, ten per province, with 70 members indirectly elected and 30 appointed by the president); this has not yet been implemented.

President and Commander-in-Chief of the Armed Forces, Paul Biya, *acceded* 6 November 1982, *elected* 14 January 1984, *re-elected* 24 April 1988, 10 October 1992, 12 October 1997, 25 October 2004

SELECTED GOVERNMENT MEMBERS *as at July 2005*
Prime Minister, Peter Mafany Musonge
Deputy Prime Minister, Justice, Keeper of the Seal, Ali Amaduo
Economy and Finance, Polycarpe Abah Abah
Foreign Affairs, Laurent Esso
Trade, Marafa Hamidou Yaya

HIGH COMMISSION FOR THE REPUBLIC OF CAMEROON
84 Holland Park, London W11 3SB T 020-7727 0771
Ambassador Extraordinary and Plenipotentiary, HE Samuel Libock-Mbei, apptd 1995

BRITISH HIGH COMMISSION
Avenue Winston Churchill, BP 547 Yaoundé
T (+237) (2) 220545
High Commissioner, HE Richard Wildash, LVO, apptd 2002

BRITISH COUNCIL
Avenue Charles de Gaulle, BP 818, Yaoundé
T (+237) (2) 211696/203172 E bc-yaounde@britishcouncil.cm
Director, Jenny Scott

ECONOMY AND TRADE

Principal products are cocoa, coffee, bananas, cotton, timber, groundnuts, aluminium, rubber and palm products. In 2003, Cameroon produced 3,500,000 tonnes of crude petroleum. Agriculture accounts for 46 per cent of GDP and employs 70 per cent of the workforce, services 33 per cent, and industry 21 per cent. In 2003 a new oil pipeline originating in Chad and passing through Cameroon opened; it is estimated that this could earn Cameroon revenue of US$500 million over the next 25 years. France, Italy, Spain, Belgium, the UK and Nigeria are Cameroon's main trading partners.

GNI – US$8,700 million (2002); US$550 per capita (2002)
ANNUAL AVERAGE GROWTH OF GDP – 5.3 per cent (2001)
INFLATION RATE – 1 per cent (2004 est.)
TOTAL EXTERNAL DEBT – US$8,600 million (2002)
FOREIGN DIRECT INVESTMENT – US$166 million (1997–2000)
IMPORTS – US$2,800 million (2002)
EXPORTS – US$2,300 million (2002)

Trade with UK	2003	2004
Imports from UK	£33,121,000	£26,986,000
Exports to UK	97,610,000	210,275,000

TRANSPORT INFRASTRUCTURE

The 34,300 km of roads include 4,288 km of paved roads linking the main population centres. A rail network of 1,008 km links the coast with the capital and the central highlands. The principal airports are at Yaoundé, Douala and Garoua. Douala is the main port.

MEDIA AND CULTURE

The government controls the media in Cameroon via the state-run Cameroon Radio-Television Corporation (CRTV) which operates national television and radio networks as well as provincial stations. Newspapers are also subject to government controls. There are two private television stations and numerous private radio stations.

Cameroon is characterised by geographical, cultural and linguistic diversity that is reflected in the work of Mongo Beti (1932–2001) and Ferdinand Oyono (b. 1929), two of Cameroon's most celebrated writers.

CANADA

AREA – 9,221,000 sq. km. Neighbours: USA (south), Alaska (USA) (west)

POPULATION – 32,507,874 (2004 est.). The languages are English and French

CAPITAL – Ottawa (population, 1,063,664, 2001 census).

MAJOR CITIES – Calgary; Edmonton; Hamilton; ΨMontréal; Québec; Toronto; ΨVancouver; Winnipeg

CURRENCY – Canadian dollar (C$) of 100 cents

NATIONAL ANTHEM – O Canada

NATIONAL DAY – 1 July [Canada Day]

NATIONAL FLAG – Red maple leaf with 11 points on white square, flanked by vertical red bars one-half the width of the square

LIFE EXPECTANCY (years) – 79.96 (2004 est.)

MORTALITY RATE (per 1,000 population) – 7.67 (2004 est.)

INFANT MORTALITY (per 1,000 births) – 4.82 (2004 est.)

HIV / AIDS ADULT PREVALENCE – 0.3 per cent (2003 est.)

DEATH PENALTY – No (abolished 1998)

POPULATION GROWTH RATE – 0.92 per cent (2004 est.)

POPULATION DENSITY – 3 per sq. km (2001)

URBAN POPULATION – 79 per cent (2001)

CLIMATE AND TERRAIN

Canada occupies the whole of the northern part of the North American continent, except for Alaska. In eastern Canada, the most southerly point is Middle Island in Lake Erie. The six main physiographic divisions are: the Appalachian-Acadian region, the Canadian shield, which comprises more than half the country, the St Lawrence-Great Lakes lowland, the interior plains, the Cordilleran region and the Arctic archipelago. Elevation extremes range from 5,959 m (Mt Logan) at the highest point to 0 m (Atlantic Ocean) at the lowest. The climate of the eastern and central portions presents greater extremes than in corresponding latitudes in Europe, but the climate is milder in the south-western portion of the prairie region and the southern portions of the Pacific slope. The tornado season is May to September, peaking in June and early July in southern Ontario, Alberta, south-eastern Québec and southern Saskatchewan and Manitoba through to Thunder Bay. The interior of British Columbia and western New Brunswick are also tornado zones.

HISTORY AND POLITICS

St John's, Newfoundland, was established as a shore base for English fisheries in 1504 and claimed for England in 1583. The French explored the St Lawrence Seaway from the 1530s, and founded Québec in 1608. The Hudson's Bay Company was founded in 1670 and was significant in exploring and opening up the interior. From the 17th century the territory was a pawn in the power struggles of the main colonial powers. Britain gained large areas of the country under the Treaty of Utrecht (1713), and after the Seven Years' War, during which Québec was captured by British forces under General Wolfe (1759), the Treaty of Paris (1763) awarded almost all of France's North American possessions to Britain. The American War of Independence caused many British loyalists to migrate to southern Canada, exacerbating existing tensions between British and French colonists, particularly over forms of government and legal codes. From the mid-19th century, Canadian territory still under Hudson's Bay Company control was brought under government rule.

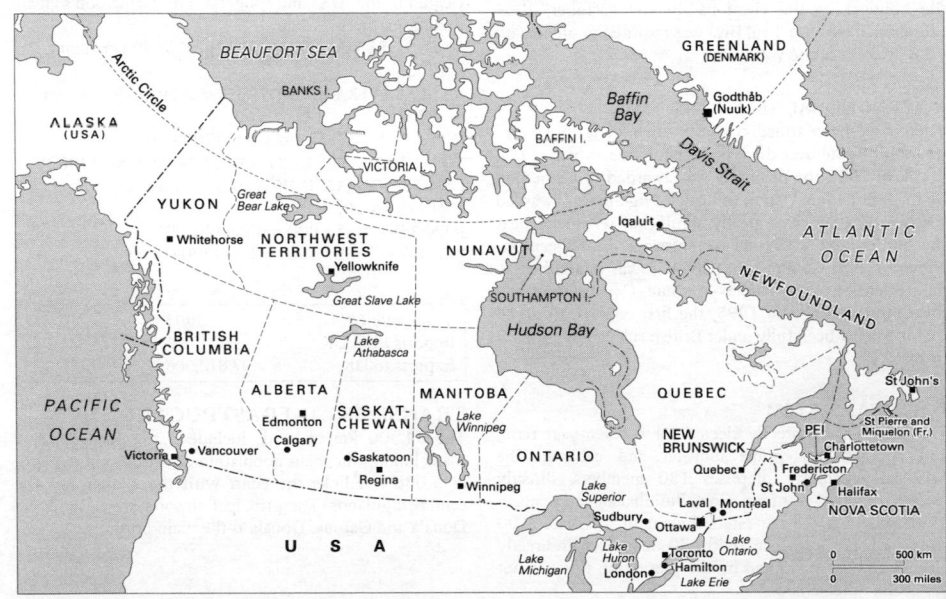

The British North America Act of 1867 formed the four provinces of Ontario, Québec, New Brunswick and Nova Scotia into a dominion under the name of Canada. To this confederation the other provinces and territories were subsequently added: Manitoba and Northwest Territories (1870), British Columbia (1871), Prince Edward Island (1873), Yukon Territory (1898), Alberta and Saskatchewan (1905) and Newfoundland (1949). In 1982, the constitution was patriated (severed from the British parliament) with the approval of all provinces except Québec. The Canada Act 1982 gave Canada full responsibility for its constitution.

In the second half of the 20th century there was recurring political tension arising from the French-Canadian separatist movement in Quebec and the desire for autonomy of the Native American and Inuit populations. The 1985 Meech Lake Accord between the federal and provincial governments provided for Québec to be recognised as a distinct society within Canada, but did not come into force as two provincial legislatures withheld approval. However, in 1997 the leaders of the other provinces and territories recognised Québec as having a 'unique character'. In Québec itself, a referendum in October 1995 which called for sovereignty and a new political and economic partnership was defeated, and support for independence has since declined.

A referendum in 1992 approved the creation of an autonomous territory for the Inuit people, Nunavut, created by partitioning the Northwest Territories, which was inaugurated on 1 April 1999. In the federal election of 28 June 2004 the Liberal Party won a fourth consecutive term of office. The state of parties in the House of Commons following the election was Liberals 135, Conservative Party of Canada 99, Bloc Québécois 54 and New Democratic Party 19.

POLITICAL SYSTEM

Under the 1982 constitution, executive power is vested in a Governor-General appointed by the British sovereign on the advice of the Canadian prime minister.

Parliament consists of a Senate and a House of Commons. The Senate consists of 104 members, nominated by the Governor-General on the advice of the prime minister, the seats being distributed between the various provinces. Senate members serve until the age of 75. The House of Commons has 301 members, directly elected for a five-year term. Representation is proportional to the population of each province. The judicature is administered by judges following the civil law in Québec province and common law in other provinces. Each province has a Court of Appeal. The highest federal court is the Supreme Court of Canada, which exercises general appellate jurisdiction throughout Canada in civil and criminal cases. There is one other federally constituted court, the Federal Court of Canada, which has jurisdiction on appeals from its trial division, from federal tribunals and reviews of decisions and references by federal boards.

GOVERNOR-GENERAL
Governor-General and Commander-in-Chief, HE Michaelle Jean

SELECTED GOVERNMENT MEMBERS *as at July 2005*
Prime Minister, Paul Martin
Deputy Prime Minister, Public Safety and Emergency Preparedness, Anne McLellan
Finance, Ralph Goodale
Foreign Affairs, Pierre Pettigrew
National Defence, William Graham

CANADIAN HIGH COMMISSION
Macdonald House, 1 Grosvenor Square, London W1K 4AB
T 020-7258 6600
High Commissioner, HE Mel Cappe, apptd 2002

BRITISH HIGH COMMISSION
80 Elgin Street, Ottawa K1P 5K7 T (+1) (613) 237 1530
High Commissioner, HE David Reddaway, apptd 2003

CONSULATES-GENERAL – Montréal, Toronto, Vancouver
CONSULATES – Halifax/Dartmouth, Québec City, St John's, Winnipeg

BRITISH COUNCIL
T (+1) (613) 237 1530
Director, Peter Chenery

DEFENCE
The Army (Land Forces) has 114 main battle tanks and 1,218 armoured personnel carriers. The Navy (Maritime Forces) has two submarines, four destroyers, 12 frigates

FEDERAL STRUCTURE

Provinces or Territories (with official contractions)	Population, 1 January 2001	Capital	Lieutenant-Governor	Premier
Alberta (AB)	3,022,861	Edmonton	Normie Kwon	Ralph Klein
British Columbia (BC)	4,077,369	Victoria	Iona Campagnolo	Gordon Campbell
Manitoba (MB)	1,149,220	Winnipeg	John Harvard	Gary Doer
New Brunswick (NB)	757,267	Fredericton	Hermenegilde Chiasson	Bernard Lord
Newfoundland and Labrador (NF)	537,797	St John's	Edward Roberts	Danny Williams
Northwest Territories (NT)	42,105	Yellowknife	†Tony Whitford	Joe Handley
Nova Scotia (NS)	942,322	Halifax	Myra Freeman	John Hamm
Nunavut (NT)§	27,978	Iqaluit	†Peter Irniq	Paul Okalik
Ontario (ON)	11,741,793	Toronto	James Bartleman	Dalton McGinley
Prince Edward Island (PE)	139,078	Charlottetown	J. Léonce Bernard	Patrick Binns
Québec (QC)	7,383,300	Québec	Lise Thibeault	Jean Charest
Saskatchewan (SK)	1,020,650	Regina	Lynda Haverstock	Lorne Calvert
Yukon Territory (YT)	30,194	Whitehorse	†Jack Cable	Dennis Fentie

Area figures include land and water area
† Commissioner
§ Nunavut was created in 1999 from the Northwest Territories

and 14 patrol and coastal vessels. The Air Force has 140 combat aircraft.

MILITARY EXPENDITURE – 1.2 per cent of GDP (2003)
MILITARY PERSONNEL – 41,800: Army 19,300, Navy 9,000, Air Force 13,500; Paramilitaries 9,350

ECONOMY AND TRADE

Canada had relatively high growth in GDP during 2002 at 3.3 per cent, and this allowed for an increase of 11.5 per cent in federal expenditure for 2003–4.

Around 7.3 per cent of the total land area (c.68 million hectares) is farmed. Over 60 per cent of this is under cultivation, the remainder being predominantly classified as unimproved pasture. More than 80 per cent of the cultivated land is in the prairie region of western Canada. The country is one of the world's leading food producers and in 2002 agriculture accounted for 2.1 per cent of GDP and employs about 3.7 per cent of the labour force.

Almost half of Canada's land area is forest, making it the world's largest exporter of timber, pulp and newsprint. The fishing industry employs 120,000 Canadians and contributes C$5,000 million a year to the economy, but Atlantic fish stocks are under restriction orders.

Canada is one of the world's largest exporters of minerals including potash, nickel, asbestos, cadmium, zinc, elemental sulphur and uranium (of which it is the world's largest single producer, meeting 28 per cent of world demand). The country is also rich in gold, copper, lead, molybdenum, platinum group metals, gypsum, cobalt, titanium concentrates, and aluminium. The total value of mineral production in 2003 was C$20,200 million.

Canada's second diamond mine opened in the Northwest Territories in 2003, bringing total production value to C$1,700 million. Canada ranks third in the world in terms of diamond production value.

The services sector contributed to 68.2 per cent of GDP in 2001, with finance and real estate generating the most revenue at 16.1 per cent.

There were 20 million foreign visitors in 2002 and four out of five tourists were from the USA.

The main exports are automotive products (including cars, trucks and parts), machinery and equipment, industrial products and raw materials, forestry products (including wood, wood pulp and paper products), agricultural products (chiefly wheat and meat products), fishery products, and energy products (including crude petroleum and natural gas).

Trade with the USA accounts for about 88 per cent of Canada's exports and 62 per cent of its imports.

GNI – US$702,000 million (2002); US$22,390 per capita (2002)
ANNUAL AVERAGE GROWTH OF GDP – 3.3 per cent (2002)
INFLATION RATE – 1.9 per cent (2004)
UNEMPLOYMENT – 7 per cent (2004)
FOREIGN DIRECT INVESTMENT – US$111,533 million (1997–2000)
IMPORTS – US$245,000 million (2003)
EXPORTS – US$273,000 million (2003)

BALANCE OF PAYMENTS
Trade – US$41,513 million surplus (2003)
Current Account – US$17,268 million surplus (2003)

Trade with UK	2003	2004
Imports from UK	£3,282,649,00	£3,335,176,000
Exports to UK	3,795,671,000	4,278,105,000

TRANSPORT INFRASTRUCTURE

In 2002 there were 1,408 million km of roads, of which 497,306 km were paved, including 16,900 km of national highways. The 7,300 km Trans-Canadian Highway links all ten provinces. There are about 50,000 km of railway track in operation.

The bulk of the 3,000 km of canal shipping in Canada is handled through the two sections of the St Lawrence Seaway, which provide access to the Great Lakes for ocean-going ships. There are 1,326 airports in Canada, 503 of which have surfaced runways.

EDUCATION

Education is under the control of the provincial governments, the cost of the publicly controlled schools being met by local taxation and aided by provincial grants. Education is compulsory between the ages of 6 and 15 or 7 and 16. There are 100 universities and 200 technical institutes and community colleges.

GROSS ENROLMENT RATIO (percentage of relevant age group) – primary 100 per cent (2002); secondary 106 per cent (2002); tertiary 59 per cent (2002)

MEDIA

The public broadcaster, the Canadian Broadcasting Corporation (CBC), was established in the 1930s and transmits programmes in English and French. Société Radio Canada is the French-language public broadcast service. There are several commercial TV channels. The CBC also operates four radio networks, and television channels and radio services for indigenous peoples in the north of the country. There are 2,000 licensed radio stations in Canada. The broadcasting regulator enforces quotas of Canadian material (30–35 per cent) on Canadian radio and television.

CULTURE

Canada is a multicultural society with British (28 per cent of people claim British descent), French (23 per cent claim French descent), aboriginal (2 per cent), Asian, German, Ukrainian, Dutch, Greek, Polish and Italian influences most dominant. Ninety per cent of the population lives within 200 km of the southern border with the USA.

Notable Canadians include the Nobel laureate Saul Bellow (1915–2005), the poet and novelist Margaret Atwood (b. 1939), the novelist Michael Ondaatje (b. 1943), the classical pianist Glenn Gould (1932–82) and the composer Howard Shore (b. 1946).

CAPE VERDE

República de Cabo Verde – Republic of Cape Verde

AREA – 4,033 sq. km. Comprising the Windward Islands (Santo Antão, São Vicente, Santa Luzia, São Nicolau, Bõa Vista and Sal) and Leeward Islands (Maio, São Tiago, Fogo and Brava)
POPULATION – 415,294 (2004 est.), the majority of whom are Roman Catholic. The official language is Portuguese; a creole is spoken by most of the population
CAPITAL – ΨPraia (population, 61,644, 1995 estimate)
CURRENCY – Escudo Caboverdiano of 100 centavos
NATIONAL ANTHEM – É patria amada [This is our beloved country]
NATIONAL DAY – 5 July (Independence Day)
NATIONAL FLAG – Blue with three horizontal stripes of

white, red, white near the bottom; over all on these near the hoist a ring of ten yellow stars
LIFE EXPECTANCY – 70.14 (2004 est.)
MORTALITY RATE (per 1,000 population) – 6.72 (2004 est.)
INFANT MORTALITY (per 1,000 population) – 49.14 (2004 est.)
HIV / AIDS ADULT PREVALENCE RATE – 0.04 per cent (2001 est.)
DEATH PENALTY – No (abolished 1981)
POPULATION LIVING BELOW POVERTY LINE – 30 per cent (2000 est.)
POPULATION GROWTH RATE – 0.73 per cent (2004 est.)
POPULATION DENSITY – 104 per sq. km (1999)
MILITARY EXPENDITURE – 1.5 per cent of GDP (2003)
MILITARY PERSONNEL – 1,200: Army 1,000, Air Force 100, Coast Guard 100
CONSCRIPTION DURATION – Selective conscription
ILLITERACY RATE – (m) 14.2 per cent; (f) 30.8 per cent (2003)

CLIMATE AND TERRAIN
The republic consists of a group of islands of volcanic origin lying 600 km off the West African coast. Elevation extremes range from 2,829 m (Mt Fogo) at the highest point to 0 m (Atlantic Ocean) at the lowest. The climate is hot and dry.

HISTORY AND POLITICS
The islands were uninhabited when they were first discovered and colonised c.1460 by Portugal. Administered with Portuguese Guinea until 1879, it became an overseas province of Portugal in 1951 and achieved independence on 5 July 1975 after a campaign by the African Party for the Independence of Guinea-Bissau and Cape Verde (PAIGC), a unified party with Guinea-Bissau. A federation of the islands with Guinea-Bissau was planned but this was dropped following the 1980 coup in Guinea-Bissau.

The republic was a one-party state under the African Party for the Independence of Cape Verde (PAICV) until the constitution was amended in 1990. Multiparty elections in 1991 were won by the opposition Movement for Democracy (MPD), and the MPD candidate António Mascarenhas Monteiro was elected president. The MPD was re-elected in the 1995 legislative elections with a landslide victory, and President Mascarenhas Monteiro was re-elected unopposed in 1996. The general election of 2001 returned the PAICV to power with 40 of the 72 seats in the National Assembly. The MPD won 30 seats and the Democratic Alliance for Change won two seats. Pedro Pires of the PAICV narrowly won the second round of the presidential election. The MPD candidate, Carlos Veiga, appealed to the Supreme Court, citing irregularities in the conduct of the elections; the court upheld some of the appeals, which reduced Pires' winning margin to just 12 votes.

POLITICAL SYSTEM
Under the 1992 constitution, the head of state is the president, who is directly elected for a five-year term. There is a unicameral National Assembly (Assembleia Naciona) with 72 members directly elected for a five-year term. The prime minister is nominated by the National Assembly and appointed by the president. The Council of Ministers (cabinet) is appointed by the president on the recommendation of the prime minister.

HEAD OF STATE
President, Pedro Pires, elected 25 February 2001, assumed office 22 March 2001

SELECTED GOVERNMENT MEMBERS as at July 2005
Prime Minister, José Maria Neves
Deputy Minister for Culture and Sports, Jorge Tolentino
Economy, Growth and Competitiveness, Avelino Bonifacio
Finance and Planning, Joao Serra
Foreign Affairs and Communities, Victor Borges
Interior Administration, Julio Correia
Parliamentary Affairs and Defence, Armindo Cipriano Mauricio

EMBASSY OF THE REPUBLIC OF CAPE VERDE
Burgemeester Patijnlaan 1930, 2585 CB, The Hague
T (+355) (36) 51/78
Ambassador Extraordinary and Plenipotentiary, vacant

BRITISH AMBASSADOR, HE Peter Newell, resident at Dakar, Senegal

ECONOMY AND TRADE
The islands have little rain and agriculture is mostly confined to irrigated inland valleys. The chief products are bananas and coffee (for export), maize, sugar cane and nuts. Fish and shellfish are important exports. Salt is obtained on Sal, Bõa Vista and Maio; volcanic rock is also mined for export.

The economy is heavily dependent on services, with tourism, commerce and public services accounting for 70 per cent of GDP.

Around 700,000 Cape Verdeans live outside the islands, particularly in the USA and Portugal, and remittances provide an important source of revenue and investment in the economy. Cape Verde has been a member of the Economic Community of West African States (ECOWAS) since 1977. The country is also a member of the Community of Portuguese-speaking Countries (CPLP).
GNI – US$587 million (2000); US$1,340 per capita (2001)
ANNUAL AVERAGE GROWTH OF GDP – 3.3 per cent (2001)
INFLATION RATE – 4.4 per cent (1998)
TOTAL EXTERNAL DEBT – US$325 million (2002)
IMPORTS – US$230 million (2001)
EXPORTS – US$10 million (2001)

BALANCE OF PAYMENTS
Trade – US$291 million deficit (2003)
Current Account – US$77 million deficit (2003)

Trade with UK	2003	2004
Imports from UK	£5,918,000	£3,229,000
Exports to UK	3,356,000	1,415,000

TRANSPORT INFRASTRUCTURE
The main ports are Praia, Mindelo and Tarrafal, and there is an international airport on Sal. There is a network of internal flights between the islands, with daily flights between Praia, Mindelo and Sal. Within the islands there are no railways or waterways. There are 1,100 km of road, 242 km of which are unpaved.

CULTURE

Cape Verdeans have more in common with Portuguese culture than with African culture. The islands are famed for their rich traditions of literature (in both Portuguese and Crioulo) and distinctive musical styles such as the *funana*, dance music and *morna*, a slow, atmospheric song style, accompanied by clarinet, accordion, violin and caraquinho, a Portuguese stringed instrument.

CENTRAL AFRICAN REPUBLIC

République Centrafricaine/Ködrö tî Bê-Afrîka – Central African Republic

AREA – 622,984 sq. km. Neighbours: Chad (north), Sudan (east), Democratic Republic of Congo and Republic of Congo (south), Cameroon (west)
POPULATION – 3,742,482 (2004 est.). French is the official language; the national language is Sangho
CAPITAL – Bangui (population, 560,000, 1994 estimate)
CURRENCY – Franc CFA of 100 centimes
NATIONAL ANTHEM – La renaissance [The revival]
NATIONAL DAY – 1 December
NATIONAL FLAG – Four horizontal stripes, blue, white, green, yellow, crossed by central vertical red stripe with a yellow five-pointed star in top left-hand corner
LIFE EXPECTANCY – 41.36 (2004 est.)
MORTALITY RATE (per 1,000 population) – 19.99 (2004 est.)
INFANT MORTALITY (per 1,000 births) – 92.15 (2004 est.)
HIV / AIDS ADULT PREVALENCE – 13.5 per cent (2003 est.)
DEATH PENALTY – No (abolished 1981)
POPULATION GROWTH RATE – 1.56 per cent (2004 est.)
POPULATION DENSITY – 6 per sq. km (1999)
MILITARY EXPENDITURE – 2.3 per cent of GDP (2003)
MILITARY PERSONNEL – 2,550: Army 1,400, Air Force 150, Paramilitaries 1,000
CONSCRIPTION DURATION – Two years (selective)
ILLITERACY RATE – (m) 36.9 per cent; (f) 59.9 per cent (2003 est.)
GROSS ENROLMENT RATIO (percentage of relevant age group) – primary 66 per cent (2002); tertiary 2 per cent (2002)

CLIMATE AND TERRAIN

This landlocked central African state is a plateau between the Chad and Congo river basins, with hills in the northeast and the west. The main river is the Oubangui and at 335 m it is the lowest point of elevation. The highest point of elevation is 1,420 m (Mount Ngaoui). The climate is tropical with a wet season in the north from June to September and from May to October in the south. The north can reach a temperature of 40°C between February and May and the humidity can be extreme. The south has a more equatorial climate.

HISTORY AND POLITICS

In December 1958 the French colony of Ubanghi Shari elected to remain within the French Community and adopted the title of the Central African Republic. It became fully independent on 17 August 1960. The first president, David Dacko, was overthrown in 1966 by the then Col. Bokassa, who in 1976 proclaimed himself emperor and renamed the country the Central African Empire. In 1979 Bokassa was deposed by Dacko in a bloodless coup and the country reverted to a republic. President Dacko surrendered power in 1981 to Gen. André Kolingba, who instituted military rule until 1985, when a civilian-dominated cabinet was appointed. In November 1986 a referendum was held which approved a new constitution and the establishment of a one-party state.

President Kolingba formed a coalition government in February 1993. Ange-Félix Patassé of the Central African People's Liberation Party (MLPC) won the presidential elections of 1993 and 1999. A multiparty coalition government was formed after the legislative elections of 1998.

A coup took place in March 2003, in which François Bozizé took power, declared himself president, suspended the constitution and dismissed the cabinet. A broad-based transitional government was formed on 31 March. In the presidential and legislative elections of May 2005, François Bozizé won 64 per cent of the vote to retain the presidency while the National Convergence party (Kwa Na Kwa) won 42 seats in the National Assembly.

POLITICAL SYSTEM

A new constitution was approved by referendum and promulgated in December 2004. Under this constitution, the president is elected for a five-year term, renewable only once. The prime minister is appointed by the president and appoints the ministers.

HEAD OF STATE
President, Minister of Defence, Gen. François Bozizé, *took power* 15 March 2003

SELECTED GOVERNMENT MEMBERS *as at July 2005*
Prime Minister, Elie Dote
Minister for Finance, Theodore Dabanger
Foreign Affairs, Regional Integration and Francophone Affairs, Jean-Paul Ngoupande
Interior and Territorial Administration, Lt.-Col. Michel Salle

EMBASSY OF THE CENTRAL AFRICAN REPUBLIC
30 rue des Perchamps, F-75016, Paris
T (+33) (1) 4224 4256
Ambassador Extraordinary and Plenipotentiary, vacant

BRITISH AMBASSADOR, HE Richard Wildash, LVO, resident at Yaoundé, Cameroon

ECONOMY AND TRADE

The country is largely undeveloped. The majority of the population is engaged in subsistence farming, and bananas, cassava, maize and yams are the main crops. Cotton, diamonds, coffee and timber are the major exports. Industrial goods, machinery and transport equipment, foodstuffs and fuels are the main imports. Major trading partners are the Benelux countries, France, Cameroon, Spain and China.
GNI – US$1,000 million (2002); US$250 per capita (2002)
INFLATION RATE – 1.5 per cent (1999)
TOTAL EXTERNAL DEBT – US$872 million (2000)
IMPORTS – US$120 million (2002)
EXPORTS – US$150 million (2002)

Trade with UK	2003	2004
Imports from UK	£902,000	£545,000
Exports to UK	1,224,000	304,000

TRANSPORT INFRASTRUCTURE

There are no railways. Most travel takes place on the 23,810 km of roads, of which only 643 km are paved. There are 50 airports, the principal one being at Bangui.

MEDIA

The most balanced media output is from the UN-sponsored radio broadcaster Radio Ndeke Luka. Central African Republic's other radio and television stations are operated by the state via Télévision Centrafricaine, (TVCA). There are a number of privately owned newspapers but relatively low literacy levels mean that they have little influence.

CHAD

République du Tchad – Republic of Chad

AREA – 1,284,000 sq. km. Neighbours: Niger, Nigeria and Cameroon (west), Libya (north), Sudan (east), Central African Republic (south)

POPULATION – 9,538,544 (2004 est.). French and Arabic are the official languages; there are more than 50 indigenous languages, of which the most widely spoken is Sara

CAPITAL – N'Djaména (population, 530,100, 1993 census)

CURRENCY – Franc CFA of 100 centimes

NATIONAL ANTHEM – Peuple Tchadien, debout et à l'ouvrage [People of Chad, arise and to work]

NATIONAL DAY – 1 December

NATIONAL FLAG – Vertical stripes, blue, yellow and red

LIFE EXPECTANCY– 48.24 (2004 est.)

MORTALITY RATE (per 1,000 population) – 16.38 (2004 est.)

INFANT MORTALITY RATE (per 1,000 live births) – 94.78 (2004 est.)

HIV / AIDS ADULT PREVALENCE – 4.8 per cent (2004 est.)

DEATH PENALTY – Yes

POPULATION LIVING BELOW POVERTY LINE – 80 per cent (2001)

POPULATION GROWTH RATE – 3 per cent (2004 est.)

POPULATION DENSITY – 6 per sq. km (1999)

MILITARY EXPENDITURE – 1.3 per cent of GDP (2003)

MILITARY PERSONNEL – 30,350: Army 25,000, Air Force 350, Republican Guard 5,000; Paramilitaries 4,500

ILLITERACY RATE – (m) 44 per cent; (f) 60.6 per cent (2003 est.)

GROSS ENROLMENT RATIO (percentage of relevant age group) – primary 73 per cent (2002); secondary 12 per cent (2002); tertiary 1 per cent (2002)

CLIMATE AND TERRAIN

The population of this landlocked country is concentrated in the fertile lowlands of the south, away from the arid central and northern desert areas. The highest point of elevation is 3,415 m (Emi Koussi) and the lowest is at 160 m (the Djourab Depression). The north is almost rainless, the south is tropical and the central plain is hot and dry with a wet season from June to September.

HISTORY AND POLITICS

Chad was colonised by France from the 1890s and became part of French Equatorial Africa. It became self-governing after the Second World War, and fully independent on 11 August 1960. Since independence the country has been politically unstable because of the tensions between the Muslim Arab north and the Christian and animist African south, different factions attracting support from Libya and France. After a number of coups in the 1960s and 1970s, factional fighting led to civil war. In 1982 French-supported rebels captured the capital and formed a government under Hissène Habré, but fighting with Libyan-backed factions continued until a cease-fire was agreed in 1987 by Chad, Libya and France. Habré was deposed in 1990 in a Libyan-backed coup led by Idriss Déby. Under Déby, there was gradual democratization and a new constitution, establishing a unified, democratic state, was introduced in 1996, but despite more stable government, unrest continues. Déby won the first multiparty presidential election in 1996 and was re-elected in 2001. The 2002 legislative election was won by Déby's Patriotic Salvation Movement (MPS).

INSURGENCIES

Three rebel movements, the Movement for Unity and the Republic (MUR), the Movement for Democracy and Justice in Chad (MDJT), and the Democratic Revolutionary Council (DRC), announced that they had formed an alliance in 2000. In 2002 the government signed a peace accord with the MDJT, and in 2003 an agreement was signed between the government and the National Resistance Army (ANR) which provided for an immediate cease-fire and a general amnesty. However, the agreement was rejected by at least one of the eight different movements within the ANR.

POLITICAL SYSTEM

The 1996 constitution makes provision for an executive president directly elected for a five-year term; following a 2004 amendment, there is no limit on re-election. The legislature is the Assemblée Nationale (National Assembly) of 155 members directly elected for a four-year term. The prime minister is appointed by the president.

HEAD OF STATE

President, Idriss Déby, *took power* December 1990, *elected* 3 July 1996, *re-elected* 20 May 2001

SELECTED GOVERNMENT MEMBERS *as at July 2005*
Prime Minister, Pascal Yoadimnadji
Finance and Economy, Ahmat Awat Sakine
Foreign Affairs and African Integration, Nagoum Yamassoum
National Defence, Veterans and Victims of War, Emmanuel Nadingar

EMBASSY OF THE REPUBLIC OF CHAD
52 Boulevard Lambermont 1030, Brussels, Belgium
T (+ 32) (2) 215 1975
Ambassador Extraordinary and Plenipotentiary, HE Abderahim Yacoub Ndiaye, apptd 2000

BRITISH AMBASSADOR, HE Richard Wildash, LVO, resident at Yaoundé, Cameroon

ECONOMY AND TRADE

About 90 per cent of the workforce is occupied in agriculture, fishing and forestry. Salt is mined around Lake Chad, but the most important activities are cotton growing and animal husbandry. Raw cotton (accounting for 40 per cent of total exports in 1999), meat and groundnuts are the main exports. Chad's main trading partners are France, Portugal, Germany, Thailand, Costa Rica, South Africa, Nigeria and Cameroon.

In July 2003 Chad began piping oil from the Doba basin in the south of the country. This oil is piped via Cameroon and on to international markets. It is estimated that this new industry could bring US$2,000 million into Chad over the next 25 years. The pipeline is expected to increase government revenues by 45–50 per cent during 2004–5.

In January 2000 the IMF approved a loan facility of around US$49.9 million to support the government's 1999–2002 economic programme. In October 2002 Chad's request for an extension of the commitment period under the Poverty Reduction and Growth Facility (PRGF) arrangement was approved by the IMF.

GNI – US$1,800 million (2002); US$210 per capita (2002)

INFLATION RATE – 3.8 per cent (2000)

TOTAL EXTERNAL DEBT – US$1,116 million (2000)

IMPORTS – US$1,650 million (2002)

EXPORTS – US$180 million (2002)

Trade with UK	2003	2004
Imports from UK	£3,383,000	£3,229,000
Exports to UK	1,144,000	163,000

TRANSPORT INFRASTRUCTURE

There are no railways in Chad. There are 33,400 km of roads, 267 km of which are paved. There are 2,000 km of waterways and 50 airports, seven of which have surfaced runways.

MEDIA AND CULTURE

Low levels of literacy make radio the most important news medium. Radiodiffusion Nationale Tchadienne is the state controlled radio station. There are private radio stations but they are closely monitored by the government. There is only one television station, Télétchad, and it is state-owned and controlled. Privately owned newspapers circulate in the capital.

Chad is made up of 200 ethnic groups, three major religious groupings (Islam, Christianity and traditional faiths), three different climatic zones and many differing lifestyles (from the urban to rural). For some peoples (the Maba) pre-Islamic social structures are still in place, while others (the Toubou) are nomadic, their territory defined by wells and oases.

CHILE

República de Chile – Republic of Chile

AREA – 748,800 sq. km. Neighbours: Peru (north), Bolivia and Argentina (east)

POPULATION – 15,823,957 (2004 est.). The main groups are: indigenous Araucanian Indians, Fuegians, Rapanui and Changos; Spanish settlers and their descendants; mixed Spanish Indians; and European immigrants. Because of extensive intermarriage only a few indigenous Indians are racially separate. The language is Spanish, with admixtures of local words of Indian origin. The main religion is Roman Catholicism

CAPITAL – Santiago (population, 4,690,684, 1998 UN estimate)

MAJOR CITIES – ΨAntofagasta; Concepción; Puente Alto; ΨValparaíso; ΨPunta Arenas, on the Straits of Magellan, is the southernmost city in the world

CURRENCY – Chilean peso of 100 centavos

NATIONAL ANTHEM – Canción nacional de Chile [National anthem of Chile]

NATIONAL DAY – 18 September (National Anniversary)

NATIONAL FLAG – Two horizontal bands, white, red; in top sixth a white star on blue square, next staff

LIFE EXPECTANCY (years) – 76.38 (2004 est.)

MORTALITY RATE (per 1,000 population) – 5.71 (2004 est.)

INFANT MORTALITY (per 1,000 births) – 9.05 (2004 est.)

HIV / AIDS ADULT PREVALENCE RATE – 0.3 per cent (2004 est.)

DEATH PENALTY – Yes*

POPULATION LIVING BELOW POVERTY LINE – 17 per cent (2001)

POPULATION GROWTH RATE – 1.01 per cent (2004 est.)

POPULATION DENSITY – 21 per sq. km (2001)

URBAN POPULATION – 86 per cent (2001)

CLIMATE AND TERRAIN

Chile lies between the Andes (1,524 m to 4,572 m above sea level) and the shores of the South Pacific, extending from the arid north around Arica to Cape Horn. The length of the country is about 4,480 km, with an average breadth, north of 41°, of 160 km. Elevation extremes range from 6,880 m (Nevado Ojos del Salado) at the highest point to 0 m sea level (Pacific Ocean) at the lowest. There are major vineyard areas in the central valley, clustered just south of the capital, Santiago.

HISTORY AND POLITICS

Chile was discovered by Spanish adventurers in the 16th century and remained under Spanish rule until 1810, when the first autonomous government was established. Full independence was consolidated in 1818 after a revolutionary war.

A Marxist, Salvador Allende, was elected president in 1970 as the candidate of the Popular Front Alliance, but was overthrown and killed in a military coup in 1973.

Gen. Pinochet, who led the coup, assumed the presidency until presidential and congressional elections were held in 1989, beginning the transition to full democracy.

Gen. Augusto Pinochet was arrested in London in October 1998 following a request by the Spanish government for his extradition, but extradition proceedings were dropped on the grounds of poor health in March 2000, and Pinochet was freed and allowed to return to Chile. The Chilean Supreme Court lifted his immunity from prosecution in August 2000, and in December he was put under house arrest pending trial on charges relating to the kidnapping and murder of more than 70 political opponents. The charges were dismissed by the Court of Appeal, but formally reinstated in January 2001 after it had been determined that Gen. Pinochet was fit to stand trial. In March the charges were reduced to conspiracy to conceal the actions of military death squads. In May 2004 a Chilean appeal court stripped Gen. Pinochet of his immunity, leading to speculation that he may soon stand trial for human rights atrocities committed during his time in office.

Ricardo Lagos Escobar of the Party for Democracy (PPD) won the presidential election of January 2000. In the legislative elections held in December 2001, the Coalition of Parties for Democracy (CPD) remained the largest group in the Chamber of Deputies but lost its majority in elections to the Senate.

POLITICAL SYSTEM
Executive power is held by the president who is advised by a cabinet of unelected ministers. Legislative power is exercised by a Congress which comprises a Senate of 48 senators (38 elected and ten appointed) and a Chamber of Deputies of 118 elected members. Senators serve eight-year terms and deputies serve four-year terms. The presidential term is six years with no possibility of re-election.

HEAD OF STATE
President of the Republic, Ricardo Lagos Escobar, *elected* 16 January 2000, *sworn in* 11 March 2000

SELECTED GOVERNMENT MEMBERS *as at July 2005*
Defence, Jaime Ravinet de la Fuente
Economy and Energy, Jorge Rodríguez Grossi
Finance, Nicolás Eyzaguirre Guzman
Foreign Affairs, Ignacio Walker Prieto
Interior, Francisco Vidal Salinas

EMBASSY OF CHILE
12 Devonshire Street, London W1G 7DS T 020-7580 6392
E embachile@embachile.co.uk
Ambassador Extraordinary and Plenipotentiary, HE Mariano Fernández, apptd 2002

BRITISH EMBASSY
Avenida El Bosque 0125, Casilla 72-D, Santiago
T (+56) (2) 370 4100 E chancery@santiago.mail.fsc.gov.uk
Ambassador Extraordinary and Plenipotentiary, HE Richard Wilkinson, apptd 2003

BRITISH COUNCIL
Eliodoro Yáñez 832, 750-0651 Providencia, Casilla 115 Correo 55, Santiago T (+56) (2) 410 6900
E info@britishcouncil.cl
Director, John Knagg, OBE

DEFENCE
The Army has 260 main battle tanks, 20 armoured infantry fighting vehicles, 908 armoured personnel carriers and 20 armed helicopters. The Navy has three submarines, two destroyers, four frigates, 24 patrol and coastal vessels, seven combat aircraft and six armed helicopters. The Air Force has 85 combat aircraft.
MILITARY EXPENDITURE – 3.9 per cent of GDP (2003)
MILITARY PERSONNEL – 77,700: Army 47,700, Navy 19,000, Air Force 11,000; Paramilitaries 38,000

ECONOMY AND TRADE
Economic reforms during the late 1970s and the 1980s, with large-scale privatisation and deregulation, have made Chile one of the most successful economies in Latin America. Cereals, vegetables, fruit, tobacco, hemp and vines are grown extensively, and livestock accounts for nearly 40 per cent of agricultural production. Sheep farming predominates in the extreme south. Agriculture employs about 12 per cent of the workforce. There are large timber tracts in the central and southern zones which produce timber, cellulose and wood for export. Fishing is also a major industry. Chile is currently the tenth largest wine producer in the world with 2.43 per cent of global vine plantations and about 2 per cent of the production in 2004. It is also the world's fifth largest wine exporter.

Chile is rich in copper ore (around 20 per cent of global reserves), iron ore and nitrates, and is the only commercial producer of nitrate of soda (Chile saltpetre) from natural resources in the world. There are large deposits of high-grade sulphur. Oil and natural gas are produced in the Magallanes area, but domestic production is now declining.

The principal exports are minerals, timber and metal products, fish products and vegetables. The principal imports are food products, industrial raw materials, machinery, and equipment and spares. The main trade partners are Japan, the USA, Argentina, the UK and Brazil; in 1996 Chile joined the Mercosur Free Trade Zone, and in 1998 signed an extension to a free trade agreement with Mexico. In January 2004, a free trade agreement was signed between the USA and Chile.
GNI – US$66,300 million (2002); US$4,250 per capita (2002)
ANNUAL AVERAGE GROWTH OF GDP – 5.8 per cent (2004 est.)
INFLATION RATE – 1.1 per cent (2003)
UNEMPLOYMENT – 8.5 per cent (2004 est.)
TOTAL EXTERNAL DEBT – US$40,956 million (2002)
FOREIGN DIRECT INVESTMENT – US$22,951 million (1997–2000)
IMPORTS – US$19,400 million (2003)
EXPORTS – US$21,000 million (2003)

BALANCE OF PAYMENTS
Trade – US$3,015 million surplus (2003)
Current Account – US$594 million deficit (2003)

Trade with UK	2003	2004
Imports from UK	£122,238,000	£135,315,000
Exports to UK	425,170,000	483,887,000

TRANSPORT INFRASTRUCTURE
With the improvement of the roads an increasing share of internal transportation is moving by road and rail, although shipping is still important. The road system is about 80,000 km in length, of which 15,484 km is paved.

There are 6,585 km of railway track. A railway line runs from Valparaíso through La Calera and Santiago to Puerto Montt. With the completion of a section of 696 km from Corumba, Brazil, to Santa Cruz, Bolivia, the Trans-Continental Line will link the Chilean Pacific port of Arica with Rio de Janeiro on the Atlantic. A line runs from Antofagasta to Salta (Argentina). The main ports are Valparaiso, Antofagasta, Arica, Iquique and Punta Arenas.

Domestic air traffic is carried by Línea Aérea Nacional (LAN) and LADECO, which also operate internationally, and smaller regional carriers.

EDUCATION
Elementary education is free and compulsory. There are 25 state universities and 45 private universities.
ILLITERACY RATE – (m) 4.1 per cent; (f) 4.5 per cent (2000)
GROSS ENROLMENT RATIO (percentage of relevant age group) – primary 103 per cent (2002); secondary 85 per cent (2002); tertiary 37 per cent (2002)

MEDIA AND CULTURE
Television is a combination of national and local, private and state-run, cable and terrestrial channels. Radio is the country's most important news medium with 800 stations

country-wide. In 2004 there were 3.5 million internet users.

Chile is the most 'European' of the Latin American countries with a vibrant arts culture. Chilean Nobel Prize-winners for Literature include the writers Gabriela Mistral (1889–1957), who won in 1945, and Pablo Neruda (1904–73), who won in 1971. There are numerous art galleries, museums and theatres, and Chilean art, architecture and music have considerable international influence.

Island possessions include the Juan Fernández group (three islands) about 576 km from Valparaíso; one of these islands is the reputed scene of Alexander Selkirk's (of *Robinson Crusoe* fame) shipwreck. Easter Island, about 3,200 km away in the South Pacific Ocean, contains hundreds of mysterious stone figures.

CHINA

Zhonghua Renmin Gongheguo – People's Republic of China

AREA – 9,597,400 sq. km. Neighbours: Russia and Mongolia (north), North Korea (east), Vietnam, Laos, Myanmar, India, Bhutan and Nepal (south), India, Pakistan, Afghanistan, Tajikistan, Kyrgyzstan and Kazakhstan (west)

POPULATION – 1,298,847,624 (2004 est.). Han Chinese make up 91.9 per cent of the population and the remainder of the population belongs to around 55 ethnic minorities. Among the largest are the Zhuang of Guangxi, the Hui of Ningxia, the Miao of southern China, the Manchu of Heilongjiang, the Uygurs and Kazakhs of Xinjiang, the Tibetans and the Mongols. The indigenous religions are Confucianism, Taoism and Buddhism. There are also Muslims (officially estimated at about 12 million) and Christians (unofficially estimated at about 50 million). The official language is Mandarin Chinese; of the many local dialects the largest are Cantonese, Fukienese, Xiamenhua and Hakka. The autonomous regions of Mongolia, Tibet and Xinjiang have their own languages

CAPITAL – Beijing (population, 7,362,426, 1990 estimate)

MAJOR CITIES – Chengdu; Chongqing; Dalian; Guangzhou (Canton); Harbin; Qingdo; ΨShanghai; Shenyang; Tianjin; Wuhan; Wuxi; Yantai; Zaozhuang

CURRENCY – Renminbi yuan of 10 jiao or 100 fen

NATIONAL ANTHEM – Yiyongjun jinxingqu [March of the volunteers]

NATIONAL DAY – 1 October (Founding of People's Republic)

NATIONAL FLAG – Red, with large gold five-point star and four small gold stars in crescent, all in upper quarter next staff

LIFE EXPECTANCY (years) – 71.96 (2004 est.)

MORTALITY RATE (per 1,000 population) – 6.92 (2004 est.)

INFANT MORTALITY (per 1,000 live births) – 25.28 (2004 est.)

HIV / AIDS ADULT PREVALENCE – 0.1 per cent (2003 est.)

DEATH PENALTY – Yes

POPULATION LIVING BELOW POVERTY LINE – 10 per cent (2001)

POPULATION GROWTH RATE – 0.57 per cent (2004 est.)

POPULATION DENSITY – 138 per sq. km (2001)

URBAN POPULATION – 37 per cent (2001)

CLIMATE AND TERRAIN

China is twice the size of western Europe and contains a vast range of landscapes and climates within its borders. Two-thirds of the country is hilly or mountainous. The highest mountains are on the Tibetan plateau, in the west of the country, where the highest elevation is 8,850 m (Mount Everest). To the north of the Tibetan plateau, the land drops to the arid, semi-desert steppes bisected by the Tian Shan mountains; the country's lowest elevation is −154 m at Aydingkon Hu, at the foot of the Tian Shan mountains. The southern plains and east coast have the most fertile land, irrigated by the rivers Huang He (Yellow), Chang Jiang (Yangtze) and Xi Jiang (West), and so are the most heavily populated areas. There are seven climate zones. The north-east has cold winters, fierce winds, hot and humid summers and erratic rainfall. The south-west has mild winters and warm summers. Inner Mongolia has cold winters and hot summers. Central China has hot and humid summers with the occasional tropical cyclone. South China is partly tropical with heavy rainfall. Xizang is a high plateau surrounded by mountains that is subject to harsh winters. Xinjiang and the west have a desert climate, cold winters and year-round rain.

HISTORY AND POLITICS

China was ruled by imperial dynasties from the second millennium BC. The last emperor of the Qing dynasty abdicated in 1912 after a revolution broke out in 1911. Central authority collapsed, leading to a period of chaos and regional warlord domination as neither the Guomindang, led by Sun Yat-sen nor the Chinese Communist Party (CCP), founded in 1921, were able to unify China, and the conflict between them hindered their individual and joint efforts to resist Japanese encroachment; Japan occupied Manchuria in 1932, and most northern and coastal areas of China by 1939. Japan's occupation was ended by its defeat by the allies in 1945. Despite allied support after 1941 for the Guomindang, now led by Chiang Kai-shek, the Communists established control over large areas of China in the early 1940s, seizing the territory abandoned by Japan in 1945. Following a civil war (1946–9) the successful CCP inaugurated the People's Republic of China (PRC), and the Guomindang went into exile in Taiwan. The USA continued to recognise the Chiang Kai-shek regime as the rightful government of China until 1971, when the PRC took over China's membership of the United Nations from Taiwan.

Under Mao Zedong China was ruled on the basis of four 'cardinal principles': Marxist-Leninist-Maoist thought, the Socialist Road, the dictatorship of the proletariat, and the leadership of the CCP. Mao's 'Great Leap Forward' (1958–61) was an attempt to industrialise rural areas which resulted in a famine in which 30–40 million people died. China was plunged into chaos during the Cultural Revolution (1966–70) when the Red Guards were used to rid the country of 'rightist elements'.

Following the death of Mao Zedong in 1976, the disgraced Deng Xiaoping was recalled and he became the dominant force within the party, eliminating leftist influence, rehabilitating fallen leaders and promoting an 'open door' policy of economic liberalisation. The Party Congresses of 1982 and 1987 reaffirmed Deng's policies, and in 1987 most of the revolutionary generation was replaced in the top posts by younger, more liberal supporters of reform.

Liberalisation suffered a setback in 1989, when student-led pro-democracy demonstrations in April and May, centred on Tiananmen Square in Beijing, were brutally repressed on 3–4 June by the army; over 2,000 protesters died. The events strengthened the position of hardliners within the leadership, who readopted policies of centralisation based on Marxist ideology. Deng retired from his last official post in November 1989 but retained effective control until late 1994.

At Deng's instigation, during 1992 the emphasis switched back to economic reform and the power of the hardliners waned. The 1992 Party Congress endorsed Deng's calls for faster, bolder economic reforms and his 'socialist market economy'. Following Deng's death in February 1997, Jiang Zemin became leader and continued the economic reforms. He also sought to improve China's standing in the international community. At the 16th Party Congress in 2002, Vice-President Hu Jintao was elected general secretary of the CCP. On 15 March 2003 Hu Jintao was elected by the National People's Congress as the new state president replacing Jiang Zemin who retained his position as head of the Central Military Commission.

INSURGENCIES

Separatists from the Uygur Muslim minority group in Xinjiang Autonomous Region have demonstrated against Han rule, and have claimed responsibility for bomb attacks in the provincial capital, Ürümqi, and in Beijing. Two Muslim separatists were executed in 1999 as part of an effort to tighten control of the region, and in 2001 the founder of an underground Islamic party was sentenced to death. In 1999 the government banned the Falun gong cult, which had claimed to have 70 million followers, after it was revealed that a large number of party officials and senior army officers had joined the cult. Tens of thousands of Falun gong members have been arrested since the ban.

POLITICAL SYSTEM

Under the 1982 constitution, the National People's Congress is the highest organ of state power. It is elected for a term of five years, has 2,979 members and is supposed to hold one session a year. It is empowered to amend the constitution, make laws, select the president and vice-president and other leading officials of the state, approve the national economic plan, the state budget and the final state accounts, and to decide on questions of war and peace. The State Council is the highest organ of the state administration. It is composed of the premier, the vice-premiers, the state councillors, heads of ministries and commissions, the Auditor-General and the Secretary-General. Command over the armed forces is vested in the Central Military Commission.

Deputies to Congresses at the primary level are 'directly elected' by the voters 'through a secret ballot after democratic consultation'. This is now extended to county level. These Congresses elect the deputies to the Congress at the next higher level. Deputies to the National People's Congress are elected by the People's Congresses of the provinces, autonomous regions and municipalities directly under the central government, and by the armed forces.

Local government is conducted through People's Governments at provincial, municipal and county levels.

Autonomous regions, prefectures and counties exist for national minorities and are described as self-governing.

HEAD OF STATE
President of the People's Republic of China, Hu Jintao, *elected* 15 March 2003
Vice-President, Zeng Qinghong

STATE COUNCIL *as at July 2005*
Premier, Wen Jiabao
Vice-Premiers, Huang Ju; Wu Yi *(Minister of Health)*; Zeng Peiyan; Hui Liangyu
State Councillors, Zhou Yongkang; Cao Gangchuan *(Minister for National Defence)*; Tang Jiaxuan; Hua Jianmin *(Secretary-General of the State Council)*; Chen Zhili

SELECTED GOVERNMENT MEMBERS *as at July 2005*
Civil Affairs, Li Xueju
Finance, Jin Renqing
Foreign Affairs, Li Zhaoxing
State Security, Xu Yongyue

EMBASSY OF THE PEOPLE'S REPUBLIC OF CHINA
49–51 Portland Place, London W1 1JL
T 020-7299 4049
Ambassador Extraordinary and Plenipotentiary, HE Zha Peixin, apptd 2002

BRITISH EMBASSY
11 Guang Hua Lu, Jian Guo Men Wai, Beijing 100600
T (+86) (10) 6532 1961
E beinfo@public.bta.net.cn
Ambassador, HE Christopher Hum, KCMG, apptd 2002

BRITISH CONSULATES-GENERAL
Chongqing, Shanghai and Guangzhou

BRITISH COUNCIL
Cultural and Education Section, British Embassy, 4th Floor Landmark Building Tower 1, 8 North Dongsanhuan Beilu, Beijing 100004
T (+86) (10) 6590 6903 E enquiry@britishcouncil.org.cn
Regional Director, Michael O'Sullivan

DEFENCE

All three military arms are parts of the People's Liberation Army (PLA). China has at least 30 intercontinental and 110 intermediate range land-based, and 13 submarine-launched nuclear ballistic missiles. The Army has some 7,580 main battle tanks and over 4,500 armoured personnel carriers and armoured infantry fighting vehicles.

The Navy has 69 submarines, 21 destroyers, 42 frigates, 331 patrol and coastal vessels, 700 shore-based combat aircraft and 45 armed helicopters. The Air Force has more than 1,900 combat aircraft and some armed helicopters.

MILITARY EXPENDITURE – 3.9 per cent of GDP (2003)
MILITARY PERSONNEL – 2,355,000: Army 1,600,000, Navy 255,000, Air Force 400,000, Strategic Missile Forces 100,000; Paramilitaries 1,500,000
CONSCRIPTION DURATION – 24 months (selective)

ECONOMY AND TRADE

Economic liberalisation in the early 1980s reduced central planning and broadened the role of the market, which led to an increase in manufacturing, concentrated in China's coastal regions. Foreign direct investment, especially from Hong Kong and Taiwan, enabled the construction of a significant industrial base and transport infrastructure. In the coastal regions the economy has become a free market in all but name, with several stock markets and Shanghai's emergence as a financial centre. Since 1980, special economic zones have been established in Guangdong, Fujian and Hainan provinces. In addition, there are free trade and development zones throughout the country, designed to stimulate both foreign trade and internal economic development. The reforms have enabled the economy to grow more than five-fold since 1980. China has become the third-largest beneficiary of foreign investment in the world, primarily into its export industries.

Agriculture remains of great importance, employing half the working population and accounting for about 15 per cent of GDP in 2002. Cereals, with peas and beans, are grown in the northern provinces, and rice, tea and sugar in the south. Cotton (mostly in valleys of the Yangtze and Yellow rivers), tea (in the west and south), with hemp, jute and flax, are the most important crops. Livestock is raised in large numbers. Sericulture is one of the oldest industries. Cottons, woollens and silks are manufactured in large quantities.

Coal, iron ore, tin, antimony, wolfram, bismuth and molybdenum are abundant. Oil is produced in several northern provinces, particularly in Heilongjiang and Shandong, but China desperately needs access to greater supplies of oil if economic expansion is to continue at the present rate (China has now overtaken Japan as the world's second-largest importer of oil after the USA). Plans for a 2,400-km oil pipeline from Russia's east Siberian reserves to Daqing in China were first announced in 2001, and in 2003 a co-operation pact was signed between Russia and China. The agreement has since run into difficulties as the Japanese government has offered Russia large financial incentives to construct an alternative pipeline that would bypass China and directly supply Japan. Economic analysts predict that this need for oil will lead to tensions within the region in the coming years and may have an effect on annual growth rates.

In June 2003 the sluice gates on the Three Gorges dam above the Yangtse River in central China were closed to allow the reservoir to fill up, and the first generator went into operation in July. The world's largest hydroelectric power project, it will supply electricity to central and eastern China. Its construction is controversial because of its environmental impact and the displacement of over 1 million people since construction began in 1993. The dam is due to be completed in 2009.

Overcapacity in some of the traditional industries is being tackled, with the closure of 26,000 coal mines and 2,500 steel smelters. There are long-term plans to privatise all corporations except those in sectors considered essential to national security.

Tourism has become a major industry, with over 91 million foreign visitors in 2003, although an outbreak of the Severe Acute Respiratory Syndrome (SARS) virus between November 2002 and June 2003 resulted in a decline in overseas visitors in early 2003. Foreign trade and external economic relations have grown enormously since 1978. In 1995, import tariffs were cut to an average 23 per cent in line with China's attempts to join the World Trade Organisation, to which China was formally admitted in 2001. China is the world's fifth largest exporter of goods which include clothing, electronics, machine plant, yarns and fabrics, chemicals,

footwear, travel goods, and iron and steel. The principal imports are machinery, electronics, raw materials, yarns and fabrics, plastics and motor vehicles. The main trading partners are the Japan, USA, Germany, South Korea and the UK.

GNI – US$1,234,200 million (2002); US$960 per capita (2002)
ANNUAL AVERAGE GROWTH OF GDP – 8.0 per cent (2000)
INFLATION RATE – 1.4 per cent (2001)
UNEMPLOYMENT – 9.8 per cent (urban areas) (2004 est.)
TOTAL EXTERNAL DEBT – US$149,800 million (2000)
FOREIGN DIRECT INVESTMENT – US$165,139 million (1997–2000)
IMPORTS – US$413,000 million (2003)
EXPORTS – US$224,000 (2003)

BALANCE OF PAYMENTS
Trade – US$44,167 million surplus (2002)
Current Account – US$35,422 million surplus (2002)

Trade with UK	2003	2004
Imports from UK	£1,933,271,000	£2,378,347,000
Exports to UK	8,554,222,000	10,628,493,000

TRANSPORT INFRASTRUCTURE
There are 70,058 km of railway lines, of which 18,668 km are electrified, and approximately 1,402,698 km of roads, of which 314,204 km are paved and 16,314 km are motorways. Internal civil aviation has been developed, with routes totalling more than 1,506,000 km. Thirty new airports were due for completion by 2005. In the past the principal means of communication east to west was by the rivers, the most important of which are the Huang He (Yellow), Chang Jiang (Yangtze) and Xi Jiang (West). These, together with the network of canals connecting them, are still much used but their overall importance has declined. Coastal port facilities are being improved and the merchant fleet expanded. The main ports are Tianjin (Tientsin), Shanghai, Qingdao (Tsingtao) and Guangzhou (Canton).

EDUCATION
Primary education lasts six years and secondary education six years (three years in junior middle school and three years in senior middle school). In 1998 there were 1,022 universities and colleges.
ILLITERACY RATE – (m) 8.3 per cent; (f) 23.7 per cent (2000)
GROSS ENROLMENT RATIO (percentage of relevant age group) – primary 114 per cent (2002); secondary 68 per cent (2002) tertiary 13 per cent (2002)

MEDIA
China's media industry is huge – it has 25,000 newspapers and magazines, 750,000 journalists and 12,000 radio and television stations. In 2002 Communist Party officials stated that China has a domestic television audience of 1,100 million. Subscription services are expected to have a market of 128 million by the year 2010. The Communist Party has always maintained a firm grip on the nation's news reporting but with the installation of a new president, Hu Jintao, a more liberal approach seems to have been adopted. Market reforms are also being introduced into the media with the closure in 2004 of hundreds of state-funded publications that relied on government departments for their readership. Despite these reforms journalists still exercise a

significant degree of self-censorship and the Communist Party still attempts to restrict access to foreign news media by blocking news websites and radio broadcasts and limiting the distribution of overseas newspapers. It is estimated that there were 68 million internet users in China as at mid-2003, the second highest in the world after the USA.

CULTURE

The Chinese language has many dialects, notably Cantonese, Hakka, Amoy, Foochow, Changsha, Nanchang, Wu (Shanghai) and the northern dialect. The Common Speech or *putonghua* (often referred to as Mandarin) is based on the northern dialect. The Communists have promoted it as the national language and it is taught throughout the country. As *putonghua* encourages the use of the spoken language in writing, the old literary style and ideographic form of writing has fallen into disuse. Since 1956 simplified characters have been introduced to make reading and writing easier. In 1958 the National People's Congress adopted a system of romanisation known as *pinyin*.

Chinese literature is one of the oldest in the world. Paper has been employed for writing and printing for nearly 2,000 years. The Confucian classics, which formed the basis of traditional Chinese culture, date from the Warring States period (fourth to third centuries BC), as do the earliest texts of Taoism. Histories, philosophical and scientific works, poetry, literary and art criticism, novels and romances survive from most periods.

TIBET

AREA – 1,199,164 sq. km
POPULATION – 2,610,000 (2001 estimate)
CAPITAL – Lhasa

Tibet is a plateau seldom lower than 3,000 m, in south-west China which forms the northern frontier with India (boundary imperfectly demarcated), from Kashmir to Myanmar, but is separated therefrom by the Himalayas. The Indus, Brahmaputra, Mekong and Yangtse rivers all rise on the Tibet plateau.

Tibet was under Mongol rule almost continuously from the 13th to the 17th century. Chinese control grew from the 18th century and direct rule began in 1910, but with the collapse of the Chinese Empire in 1911 Tibet declared its independence and the Dalai Lama ruled undisturbed until communist rule was established in China. In 1950 Chinese Communist forces invaded Tibet, and in 1951 the Tibetan authorities signed a treaty agreeing joint Chinese-Tibetan rule. A series of revolts against Chinese rule culminated in 1959 in a rising in the capital, which was crushed after several days of fighting and military rule was imposed. The Dalai Lama fled to India where he and his followers were granted political asylum and established a government in exile. Tibet became an Autonomous Region of China in 1965. Martial law was declared in Tibet in 1989, and sporadic outbursts of unrest continue.

The Panchen Lama remained in Lhasa after 1959; when he died in 1989, China rejected the Dalai Lama's choice of successor, who is believed to have been executed, and enthroned its own candidate. Subsequent appointments have increased tension between the Chinese authorities and the Tibetan government in exile. Although the 17th Karmapa Lama was the first lama to be recognised by both China and the Dalai Lama, he fled to India in 1999 and appealed for political asylum. The seventh Reting Lama was ordained in Tibet in 2000, but the Dalai Lama has refused to recognise him. Representatives of the Dalai Lama visited China in 2002 in an attempt to improve the situation but relations remain poor.

Another source of tension has been the number of Chinese migrants settling in Tibet. Since the 1980s large numbers of Chinese have been encouraged to move to Tibet, a development that the Tibetan government-in-exile regards as an attempt to eradicate the culture of the Tibetan people.

In 1997, the International Commission of Jurists issued a report declaring that Tibet was 'under alien subjugation' and called for a UN-managed referendum to decide its future status. China contested that the report failed to acknowledge its historical claims to the region.

In 2001 the Chinese government published details of a modernisation programme for Tibet which is intended to improve the low standard of living by promoting market reforms and extensive public construction projects.

SPECIAL ADMINISTRATIVE REGIONS

HONG KONG

AREA – 1,092 sq. km
POPULATION – 6,855,125 (2004 est.)
CURRENCY – Hong Kong dollar (HK$) of 100 cents
FLAG – Red, with a white bauhinia flower of five petals each containing a red star
LIFE EXPECTANCY (years) – 81.39 (2004 est.)
MORTALITY RATE (per 1,000 population) – 5.98 (2004 est.)
INFANT MORTALITY (per 1,000 births) – 2.97 (2004 est.)
HIV / AIDS ADULT PREVALENCE – 0.1 per cent (2003 est.)
POPULATION GROWTH RATE – 0.65 per cent (2004 est.)
POPULATION DENSITY – 6,158 per sq. km (2001)
URBAN POPULATION – 93.1 per cent (2000 estimate)

CLIMATE AND TERRAIN

Hong Kong consists of more than 230 islands and a portion of the mainland (Kowloon and the New Territories) on the south-east coast of China, situated on the eastern side of the mouth of the Pearl River. Hong Kong Island is about 18 km long and from three to eight km broad. It is separated from the mainland by a narrow strait. The highest point is Tai Mo Shan (958 m). The climate is subtropical, tending towards the temperate for nearly half the year. Mean monthly temperatures range from 16°C to 29°C. Tropical cyclones occur between May and November, and nearly 80 per cent of the average annual rainfall of 2,214 mm falls between May and September.

HISTORY AND POLITICS

Hong Kong Island was first occupied by Britain in 1841 and formally ceded to Britain under the Treaty of Nanking in 1842. Kowloon was acquired by the Beijing Convention (1860) and the New Territories, a peninsula in the southern part of Guangdong province and adjacent islands, by a 99-year lease signed in 1898.

In 1984 the UK and China agreed that China would resume sovereignty over Hong Kong on 1 July 1997. In the run-up to the handover, the Chinese government's insistence on a greater say in the running of the colony and the Governor's plan for an extension of democracy prompted acrimonious disputes. On 1 July 1997, Hong Kong became a Special Administrative Region (SAR) of the People's Republic of China.

The 1984 Joint Declaration, which took effect in May 1985, guarantees: the free movement of goods and capital; the retention of Hong Kong's free port status, separate customs territory and freely convertible currency; the protection of property rights and foreign investment; the right of free movement to and from Hong Kong; Hong Kong's autonomy in the conduct of its external commercial relations and its own monetary and financial policies; and judicial independence. Hong Kong's constitution is the Basic Law, which was passed by China's National People's Congress in 1990 and guarantees that the SAR's social and economic systems will remain unchanged for 50 years.

A Legislative Council election was held in 2000. The Democratic Party, a pro-democracy opposition party, remained the largest party, with 12 seats, and the pro-China Democratic Alliance for the Betterment of Hong Kong won 11 seats; 20 seats were won by independent candidates. Following pro-democracy demonstrations in 2003 against a proposed anti-subversion law, the government first announced public consultation on the bill and then shelved the bill indefinitely. Protestors also demanded the direct election of Hong Kong's chief executive and all members of the Legislative Council. Tung Chee-hwa resigned in March 2005 and in June Donald Tsang was voted in as chief-executive.

POLITICAL SYSTEM
Hong Kong is administered by the Hong Kong SAR Government, headed by the chief executive, who is appointed by a 400-strong selection committee and aided by an Executive Council and a Legislative Council. The Executive Council consists of 15 Principal Officials and five non-officials. The chief executive serves a five-year term.

The Legislative Council consists of 60 members, of whom 20 are directly elected. Thirty members are elected by functional constituencies composed of professional and business groups and ten are elected by an election committee composed of 800 representatives of the community.

Chief Executive, Donald Tsang, *sworn in* 24 June 2005

SELECTED GOVERNMENT MEMBERS *as at July 2005*
Chief Secretary for Administration (acting), Michael Suen
Economy and Finance, Henry Tang

CONSUL-GENERAL, Stephen Bradley
1 Supreme Court Road, Central (PO Box 528), Hong Kong
T (+852) 2901 3000 E consular@britishconsulate.org.hk

BRITISH COUNCIL
3 Supreme Court Road, Admiralty, Hong Kong
T (+852) 2913 5100 E info@britishcouncil.org.hk
Director, Ruth Gee

HONG KONG ECONOMIC AND TRADE OFFICE
6 Grafton Street, London W1S 4EQ T 020-7499 9821
Director-General, Andrew K. P. Leung, JP, apptd 2001

ECONOMY AND TRADE
The main economic sector is the services industry, especially financial services, insurance and real estate. It employed 19.5 per cent of the workforce and contributed 85 per cent of GDP in 2002. Principal exports are clothing, electrical machinery and apparatus, and textiles.

Diversification in terms of products and markets continues to be the main feature of recent industrial development, as are industrial partnerships with overseas companies. The economy is based on export rather than the domestic market.

Tourism is very important to the economy; 15.54 million people visited Hong Kong in 2003, although there was a 70 per cent drop in the number of visitors in April 2003 after the SARS virus spread to Hong Kong in March 2003, with a knock-on effect on the rest of the economy.

In 2003 imports totalled US$230,300 million and exports US$225,900 million. Hong Kong's principal customers for its domestic products, in order of value of trade, were China, USA and Japan. China was Hong Kong's principal supplier.

GNI – US$167,600 million (2002); US$24,690 per capita (2002)
ANNUAL AVERAGE GROWTH OF GDP – 10.5 per cent (2000)
INFLATION RATE – 3.7 per cent (2000)
IMPORTS – US$232 million (2003)
EXPORTS – US$224 million (2003)

Trade with UK	2003	2004
Imports from UK	£2,500,875,000	£2,641,881
Exports to UK	5,640,490,000	5,893,835,000

TRANSPORT INFRASTRUCTURE
Hong Kong has one of the world's finest natural harbours, and it is the busiest container port in the world, with eight terminals, as well as large modern cargo and liner terminals. Dockyard facilities include eight floating drydocks, the largest being capable of docking vessels up to 150,000 tonnes deadweight. There is one international airport.

EDUCATION
Education is free of charge and compulsory for children up to the age of 15. Post-secondary education is provided by six universities and one college. The Open Learning Institute of Hong Kong provides university education. There are also seven technical institutes and the Hong Kong Institute of Education.
ILLITERACY RATE – (m) 3.5 per cent; (f) 9.8 per cent (2000)
ENROLMENT (percentage of age group) – primary 98.7 per cent (2001); secondary 91 per cent (2001); tertiary 31.8 per cent (2001)

MACAO (AOMEN)
AREA – 24 sq. km
POPULATION – 460,000 (2001)
CURRENCY – Pataca of 100 avos
FLAG – Green, with a white lotus flower above a white stylised bridge and water, under a large gold five-point star and four gold stars in crescent

CLIMATE AND TERRAIN
Macao consists of a peninsula and the islands of Coloane and Taipa, situated at the mouth of the Pearl River. It is 64 km from Hong Kong. The highest point is Coloane Alto (172.4 m). The climate is subtropical.

HISTORY AND POLITICS

The first Portuguese ship arrived at Macao in 1513 and trade with China commenced in 1553. Macao became a Portuguese colony in 1557; China recognised Portugal's sovereignty over Macao by treaty in 1887. An agreement to transfer the administration of Macao to the Chinese authorities was signed on 13 April 1987, and Macao became the Macao Special Administrative Region (MSAR) of China on 19 December 1999. In April 1999 a 200-member committee of Macao residents was established to determine the composition of the first government of the Macao SAR, and it elected Edmund Ho Hao Wah as the first chief executive.

The Basic Law, approved in 1993, has served as Macao's constitution since 1999. The chief executive serves a five-year term of office; the election of the next chief executive must take place no more than 60 days before the incumbent office-holder's term expires. The chief executive is assisted in policy-making by the ten-member Executive Council. The Legislative Council has 23 members.

Chief Executive, Edmund Ho Hao Wah

SELECTED GOVERNMENT MEMBERS *as at July 2005*
Economy and Finance, Francis Tam Pak Yuen
Secretary for Administration and Justice, Florida Rosa Silver Chan

CONSUL-GENERAL
Stephen Bradley, resident at Hong Kong

ECONOMY AND TRADE

The service industries comprise the greatest part of the economy, providing 87 per cent of GDP in 2002. In 2003, gambling provided 40 per cent of GNI and there were 6.9 million foreign visitors. Gaming taxes accounted for about 70 per cent of government revenues in 2002. In 2002 imports totalled US$2,356 million and exports US$2,530 million.

The main trading partners are the EU, the USA, China, Hong Kong and Japan.

Trade with UK	2003	2004
Imports from UK	£14,332,000	£15,255,000
Exports to UK	42,343,000	39,451,000

COLOMBIA

República de Colombia – Republic of Colombia

AREA – 1,038,700 sq. km. Neighbours: Venezuela (north and east), Brazil (south-east), Peru (south), Ecuador (south-west), Panama (north-west)
POPULATION – 42,310,775 (2004 est.): 58 per cent mestizo, 20 per cent white, 14 per cent mulatto, 4 per cent black, 3 per cent mixed black-Amerindian, 1 per cent Amerindian. The language is Spanish. Roman Catholicism is the established religion
CAPITAL – Bogotá (population, 6,712,247, 2002 estimate)
MAJOR CITIES – ΨBarranquilla, the major port on the Caribbean; Bucaramanga; ΨBuenaventura, the major port on the Pacific; Cali; ΨCartagena; Medellín
CURRENCY – Colombian peso of 100 centavos
NATIONAL ANTHEM – Oh gloria inmarcesible [Oh glory unfading!]

NATIONAL DAY – 20 July (National Independence Day)
NATIONAL FLAG – Broad yellow band in upper half, surmounting equal bands of blue and red
LIFE EXPECTANCY (years) – 71.43 (2004 est.)
MORTALITY RATE (per 1,000 population) – 5.61 (2004 est.)
HIV / AIDS ADULT PREVALENCE RATE – 0.7 per cent (2003 est.)
INFANT MORTALITY (per 1,000 births) – 21.72 (2004 est.)
DEATH PENALTY – No (abolished 1910)
POPULATION BELOW POVERTY LINE – 55 per cent (2001 est.)
POPULATION GROWTH RATE – 1.53 per cent (2004 est.)
POPULATION DENSITY – 41 per sq. km (2001)
URBAN POPULATION – 76 per cent (2001)

CLIMATE AND TERRAIN

Colombia lies in the extreme north-west of South America, having a coastline on both the Caribbean Sea and Pacific Ocean. Elevation extremes range from 6,310 m (Chimborazo) at the highest point to 0 m (Pacific Ocean) at the lowest. The country is divided by the Cordillera de los Andes into a coastal region in the north and west and extensive plains in the east. The eastern range of the Colombian Andes is a series of vast tablelands. This temperate region is the most densely peopled portion of the country. The principal rivers are the Magdalena, Guaviare, Cauca, Caquetá, Putumayo and Patia. The climate is predominantly tropical but the Caribbean coastline is typically drier than the rest of the country.

HISTORY AND POLITICS

The Colombian coast was visited in 1502 by Columbus, and in 1536 a Spanish expedition penetrated the interior and established a government. The country remained under Spanish rule until 1819 when Simón Bolivar established the Republic of Gran Colombia, consisting of the territories now known as Colombia, Panama, Venezuela and Ecuador. In 1829–30 Venezuela and Ecuador withdrew, and in 1831 the remaining territories formed a separate state. The name of Colombia was adopted in 1866. After a civil war, Panama seceded in 1903.

In 1949 a civil war began. In 1957, hoping to end the violence, the Conservative and Liberal parties formed a 'National Front' government. This arrangement continued until 1974 and was revived in 1978 in an attempt to maintain the rule of law in the face of violence by drugs cartels, left-wing insurgency and counter-attacks by right-wing paramilitaries. Despite foreign assistance and increased military spending, drug trafficking continues to be widespread, although less of a threat to civil order than hitherto, but the government has been unable to suppress or reach a negotiated settlement with the insurgents.

In the 2002 legislative elections, the Liberal Party (PL) secured 54 seats in the House of Representatives, while the Social Conservative Party (PSC) won 21, leaving the balance of power in the hands of minor parties. In the Senate, the Liberal Party won 28 seats while some 38 minor parties collectively secured 49 seats. The 2002 presidential election was won by Álvaro Uribe Vélez.

INSURGENCIES
Colombia has been dogged by insurgency by left-wing guerrillas since the 1960s. The main guerrilla groups are

the Revolutionary Armed Forces of Colombia (FARC) and the National Liberation Army (ELN). FARC is known to be involved in drugs trafficking and other crime, and now acts to protect these sources of funding as much as to further its political aims. Talks between the government and guerrillas were held between 1998 and 2002, but were broken off by the government after further guerrilla attacks.

The main right-wing paramilitary group is the United Self-Defence Forces of Colombia (AUC), which is suspected of having links with the security forces. The AUC declared an indefinite cease-fire in 2002, and agreed in 2003 to start formal talks aimed at disarming all the paramilitary group's gunmen by the end of 2005.

POLITICAL SYSTEM

Under the 1991 constitution, the executive president is directly elected for a single four-year term; the Congress voted in 2004 to allow the current president to stand for a second term. The legislature, the Congress, is bicameral. The lower house (the House of Representatives) has 166 members directly elected for a four-year term. The upper house (the Senate) has 102 members directly elected for four years; two seats are reserved for representatives of indigenous people. The president appoints the cabinet.

HEAD OF STATE

President, Álvaro Uribe Vélez, *elected* 26 May 2002, *sworn in* 7 August 2003
Vice-President, Francisco Santos Calderon

SELECTED GOVERNMENT MEMBERS *as at July 2005*
Defence, Jorge Alberto Uribe Echavarria
Finance and Public Credit, Alberto Carrasquilla Barrera
Foreign Affairs, Carolina Barco
Interior and Justice, Sabas Pretelt de la Vega

EMBASSY OF COLOMBIA

Flat 3A, 3 Hans Crescent, London SW1X 0LN
T 020-7589 9177/5037 E mail@colombianembassy.co.uk
Ambassador Extraordinary and Plenipotentiary, HE Alfonso Lopez-Caballero, apptd 2002

BRITISH EMBASSY

Edificio ING Barings, Carrera 9, No 76–49, Piso 9, Bogotá
T (+57) (1) 317 6690/6310/6321 E britain@cable.net.co
Ambassador Extraordinary and Plenipotentiary, HE Tom Duggin, apptd 2001

BRITISH COUNCIL

Calle 87 No. 12–79, Bogotá T (+57) (1) 618 7680
E info@britishcouncil.org.co
Director, Charles Nuttal

DEFENCE

The Army has 12 light tanks and 192 armoured personnel carriers. The Navy has four submarines, four corvettes, 27 patrol and coastal vessels, seven aircraft and four helicopters at nine bases. The Air Force has 57 combat aircraft and 23 armed helicopters.
MILITARY EXPENDITURE – 4.2 per cent of GDP (2003)
MILITARY PERSONNEL – 200,000: Army 178,000, Navy 15,000, Air Force 7,000; Paramilitaries 121,000
CONSCRIPTION DURATION – 24 months

ECONOMY AND TRADE

Services account for around 56 per cent of GDP, industry 30 per cent and agriculture 14 per cent (2002). Coal, natural gas and hydroelectricity resources remain largely unexploited, although development of coal is now being given priority. The hydrocarbon sector accounts for over half of mining output, precious metals (gold, platinum and silver) and iron ore accounting for the remainder. Other mineral deposits include nickel, bauxite, copper, gypsum, limestone, phosphates, sulphur and uranium. Colombia is also the world's largest producer of emeralds. Mining generates 5 per cent of GDP.

Major cash crops are coffee, sugar, bananas, cut flowers and cotton. Cattle are raised in large numbers, and meat and cured skins and hides are also exported.

The government has encouraged diversification to reduce dependence on coffee as the major export and this has led to the growth of new export-orientated industries, particularly textiles, paper products and leather goods.

The IMF approved a two-year standby facility of US$2,100 million in 2003 to underpin government policies designed to reduce the fiscal deficit. Colombia also received a loan of US$3,300 million over three years from the World Bank for economic reform.

The principal trading partners are the USA, the EU and the rest of Latin America.

GNI – US$79,600 million (2002); US$1,820 per capita (2002)
ANNUAL AVERAGE GROWTH OF GDP – 3.6 per cent (2004 est.)
INFLATION RATE – 9.5 per cent (2000)
UNEMPLOYMENT – 13.6 per cent (2004 est.)
TOTAL EXTERNAL DEBT – US$34,081 million (2000)
DIRECT FOREIGN INVESTMENT – US$12,505 million (1997–2000)
IMPORTS – US$13,900 million (2003)
EXPORTS – US$12,700 million (2003)

BALANCE OF PAYMENTS
Trade – US$326 million surplus (2003)
Current Account – US$1,456 million deficit (2003)

Trade with UK	2003	2004
Imports from UK	£106,436,000	£116,669,000
Exports to UK	227,945,000	283,822,000

TRANSPORT INFRASTRUCTURE

The road network consists of more than 110,000 km of roads, of which around 26,000 km are surfaced. There are 3,304 km of railways and 18,140 km of waterways. The main road and rail networks do not extend east of the Andes, and much internal transport is by air. There are 1,052 airports, 96 of which have surfaced runways, and daily air services between Bogotá and all the principal towns, as well as frequent services to other countries. The main ports are Barranquilla, Cartagena and Buenaventura.

EDUCATION

Elementary education is free of charge and compulsory for five years. Most primary schools are run by the Roman Catholic church and courses in Roman Catholicism are compulsory. There are some Protestant church schools (mainly in the capital). The government finances secondary and university level education. There are 235 institutions of higher education in Colombia.
ILLITERACY RATE – (m) 8.2 per cent; (f) 8.2 per cent (2000)
GROSS ENROLMENT RATIO (percentage of relevant age group) – primary 110 per cent (2002); secondary 65 per cent (2002); tertiary 24 per cent (2004)

MEDIA AND CULTURE

There are state-owned television (Inravision) and radio stations (Radiodifusora Nacional de Colombia) as well as private commercial networks. There are five main daily newspapers including *El Espacio, La Republica* and *El Tiempo*.

Colombian literature and art remained relatively isolated from the rest of Latin America until the publication in 1967 of *One Hundred Years of Solitude* by Gabriel García Márquez (b. 1928, winner of the 1982 Nobel Prize for Literature).

THE COMOROS

L'Union des Comores – Union of the Comoros

AREA – 2,235 sq. km. The Comoros includes the islands of Njazidja (formerly Grande Comore), Anjouan (also known as Nzwani), Moheli (also known as Mwali) and certain islets in the Indian Ocean. The easternmost island of the archipelago, Mayotte, is a French dependency.

POPULATION – 651,901 (2004 est.), mostly Muslim. French and Arabic are the official languages; the majority of the population speak Comoran, a blend of Arabic and Swahili

CAPITAL – Moroni (population, 30,365, 1991 census), on Ngazidja

CURRENCY – Comorian franc (KMF) of 100 centimes. The Franc CFA of 100 centimes is also used

NATIONAL ANTHEM – Udzima wa ya masiwa [The union of the islands]

NATIONAL DAY – 6 July (Independence Day)

NATIONAL FLAG – Four horizontal stripes – gold, white, red, blue; a green triangle based on the hoist containing a white crescent and four white stars, horns towards the fly

MORTALITY RATE (per 1,000 population) – 8.63 (2004 est.)

HIV / AIDS ADULT PREVALENCE RATE – 0.12 per cent (2001 est.)

DEATH PENALTY – Yes

POPULATION BELOW POVERTY LINE – 60 per cent (2002 est.)

POPULATION DENSITY – 302 per sq. km (1999)

ILLITERACY RATE – (m) 36.3 per cent; (f) 50.6 per cent (2003 est.)

CLIMATE AND TERRAIN

Located in the Mozambique Channel between Africa and Madagascar, Njazidja, Anjouan and Moheli are volcanic islands in the Comoros archipelago. The highest point is Karthala (2,360 m) on Njazidja, an active volcano that last erupted in August 2003. There is a tropical climate with a dry season from May to October and a hot season from November to April. The average temperature ranges from 20°C to 28°C. Cyclones afflict the islands between January and April.

HISTORY AND POLITICS

The islands became a French protectorate in the late 19th century, and achieved internal self-government in 1961. In 1974 the islanders voted on independence from France and three main islands became independent on 6 July 1975; the island of Mayotte voted to remain part of France. The republic has been politically unstable since independence, with a number of coups between 1976 and 1999, some supported by European mercenaries, and demands for greater autonomy for the three main islands. In August 1997 separatists on the islands of Anjouan and Moheli demanded independence from the Comoros and a return to French rule, and in Ocotber 1997 the inhabitants of Anjouan voted overwhelmingly for independence. Talks mediated by the Organisation of African Unity (OAU) began in December 1997 and an agreement drawn up with OAU support was signed by Njazidja and Moheli, but was rejected by Anjouan. In April 1999 the president agreed to greater autonomy but was deposed in a military coup a week later, following which Col. Assoumani Azali became president. A return to civilian rule and the holding of elections was ruled out by Col. Azali until the separatist issue was settled. Talks produced a new constitution, which was approved by referendum in 2002 (though not initially in Njazidha), and a federal structure with greater autonomy for the individual islands was introduced. The elections of the Union president and the islands' presidents were held in March, April and May 2002; Col. Azali was elected President of the Union. Elections to the Union parliament and the islands' legislatures were held in March and April 2004; the Union government is a coalition.

POLITICAL SYSTEM

Under the 2002 constitution, the President of the Union is elected for a four-year term from each of the islands in turn. The president appoints the Union ministers. The Union legislature, the Assembly of the Union, has 33 members; five members are appointed by each of the three local parliaments and 18 are directly elected for a five-year term. Each island has its own president and legislative assembly, and each island president appoints the island's eight ministers. The islands' governments deal with local issues; foreign affairs, finance, defence, judicial and religious matters remain the responsibility of the Union government. There are still areas of dispute, principally over security, budget control and customs revenue.

HEAD OF STATE
President of the Union, Col. Assoumani Azali, *elected* 14 April 2002, *sworn in* 31 May 2002

SELECTED GOVERNMENT MEMBERS *as at July 2005*
Vice-President, Finance, Budget, Economy, External Trade, Investment and Privatisation, Caabi el-Yachroutu
Vice-President, Justice, Information, Religious Affairs, Human Rights, and Relations with the Houses of Parliament, Rachid Ben Massoundi
Foreign Relations and Co-operation, Souef Mohamed Elamine
Finance and Budget, Ahamadi Abdul Bastoi
Defence, Houmedi Msaidie

EMBASSY OF THE FEDERAL ISLAMIC REPUBLIC OF THE COMOROS
20 rue Marbeau, F-75016 Paris, France T (+33) (1) 4067 9054

BRITISH AMBASSADOR
HE Brian Donaldson, resident at Antananarivo, Madagascar

ECONOMY AND TRADE

Agriculture accounts for 40 per cent of GDP, service industries 56 per cent and the manufacturing industry 4 per cent. The Comoros are heavily dependent on foreign aid. The principal exports are vanilla, copra, cloves and essential oils; cacao, sisal and coffee are also cultivated. Njazidja is well forested and produces some timber. The islands have considerable potential for tourism but this has been undermined by the political instability of recent years.

GNI – US$213 million (2000); US$1,610 per capita (2001)

ANNUAL AVERAGE GROWTH OF GDP – 1.1 per cent (1998)

TOTAL EXTERNAL DEBT – US$177 million (2001)

Trade with UK	2003	2004
Imports from UK	£402,000	£1,251,000
Exports to UK	35,000	54,000

DEMOCRATIC REPUBLIC OF CONGO

République Démocratique du Congo – Democratic Republic of Congo

AREA – 2,344,858 sq. km. Neighbours: Central African Republic (north), Sudan (north-east), Uganda, Rwanda, Burundi and Tanzania (east), Zambia (south), Angola (south-west), Republic of Congo (north-west)

POPULATION – 58,317,930 (2004 est.). The population was 34,671,607 at the 1985 census, composed of Bantu, Hamitic, Nilotic, Sudanese and Pygmoid groups, divided into more than 200 semi-autonomous tribes. More than 400 languages are spoken. Swahili, a Bantu language with an admixture of Arabic, is the nearest approach to a common language in the east and south, while Lingala is the language of a large area along the river and in the north, and Kikongo of the region between Kinshasa and the sea. French is the language of administration. Roman Catholicism is the predominant religion; there are also Protestants, Muslims and Kimbanguists

CAPITAL – Kinshasa (population, 4,655,313, 1994 estimate)

MAJOR CITIES – Kananga; Kisangani; Likasi; Lubumbashi; ΨMatadi; Mbandaka

CURRENCY – Congolese franc

NATIONAL ANTHEM – Debout Congolais [Stand up, Congolese]

NATIONAL DAY – 30 June (Independence Day)

NATIONAL FLAG – Blue with a large yellow five-pointed star in the centre and five small yellow five-pointed stars in a vertical line down the hoist

MORTALITY RATE (per 1,000 population) – 14.64 (2004 est.)

HIV / AIDS ADULT PREVALENCE – 4.2 per cent (2003 est.)

DEATH PENALTY – Yes

POPULATION GROWTH RATE – 2.99 per cent (2004 est.)

POPULATION DENSITY – 21 per sq. km (1999)

MILITARY PERSONNEL – 64,800: Army 60,000, Navy 1,800, Air Force 3,000

ILLITERACY RATE – (m) 26.9 per cent; (f) 49.8 per cent (2000)

CLIMATE AND TERRAIN
The Democratic Republic of Congo is Africa's third largest state. Elevation extremes range from 5,110 m (Mount Ngaliema, also known as Mount Stanley) at the highest point to 0 m (Atlantic Ocean) at the lowest. The central region has an equatorial climate with high humidity and an average temperature of 26°C. The northern and southern regions have different climatic cycles with the dry season in the north taking place from December to February and the dry season in the south taking place from May to September.

HISTORY AND POLITICS
The state of the Congo, founded in 1885, became a Belgian colony in 1908 and gained its independence in 1960. Mobutu Sésé Seko came to power in a coup in 1965 and was elected president in 1970. Legislative power was vested in a unicameral National Legislative Council, with candidates proposed by the sole legal political party, Mouvement Populaire de la Révolution (MPR).

The government began moves towards a multiparty system from the end of the 1980s onwards, but progress was hindered by army revolts and political disagreements. In October 1996 fighting broke out between Zaïrean Tutsis *(Banyamulenge)* and the Zaïrean army in North and South Kivu provinces, which had received an influx of Hutu refugees from Rwanda. The pro-Hutu army attempted to expel the Tutsis from the region but found themselves outgunned by the rebels, under the leadership of Laurent Kabila, who were backed by the Rwandan and Ugandan governments. Kabila's Alliance of Democratic Forces for the Liberation of Congo-Zaïre (AFDL) captured Kinshasa in May 1997 and President Mobutu fled. Zaïre was renamed the Democratic Republic of Congo.

A rebellion against the government of Laurent Kabila began in Kivu in August 1998, and by the end of the month the rebels had seized large areas in the east and west of the country. Angola, Chad, Kenya, Namibia and Zimbabwe promised President Kabila military support. The Angolan army quickly recaptured several towns in the south-west, but the rebels maintained their grip on the eastern regions. The rebel movement, the Congolese Democratic Rally (RCD), was supported by Uganda and Rwanda. On 17 May 1999, Ernest Wamba dia Wamba, the RCD leader, was ousted, splitting the movement into two distinct factions, that led by Wamba dia Wamba being called the Congolese Democratic Rally-Liberation Movement (RCD-LM). A cease-fire signed on 31 August 1999 between the government and the two rebel groups has remained largely intact, although localised clashes have been frequent. The main rebel groups, the RCD, the RCD-LM and the Congolese Liberation Movement (MLC) reached agreement on 20 December 1999 to form an umbrella organisation to defeat the government. A new rebel group, the Congolese Democratic Rally-National (RCD-N), was founded in October 2000, and in January 2001 the RCD and the RCD-LM were reunited as the Congolese Liberation Front (FLC).

By December 2000, an agreement between the government and the rebel groups was signed to withdraw troops from the front line. All parties to the civil war had withdrawn their troops 15 km from their frontline positions by 26 March 2001.

President Laurent Désiré Kabila died on 18 January 2001, having been shot by his bodyguard. His son, Maj.-Gen. Joseph Kabila, was sworn in as president on 26 January. No elections have been held since.

UN-sponsored peace talks began in South Africa in February 2002, and on 16 December the government and the main rebel groups signed a power-sharing agreement. A transitional government including the political opposition as well as representatives of the RCD and FLC was to hold power for two years, after which elections would be held. On 16 March 2003 a draft constitution was agreed whereby incumbent president Joseph Kabila would be supported during the two-year transition period by four vice-presidents. On 7 April Joseph Kabila was sworn in as president of the transitional government and in July he named the transitional government cabinet. The four vice-presidents and most of the cabinet members were sworn in in July. However, the ministers representing the RCD and the FLC refused to take the oath of allegiance to President Kabila as head of the transitional government. The last Ugandan troops left eastern Congo in May 2003 but clashes between rival militias led to the deployment of French peacekeepers in Bunia as part of a UN rapid reaction force in June. By July 2004, there remained in the region over 10,000 UN troops from over 50 countries.

POLITICAL SYSTEM
A 300-member Transitional Constituent Assembly was established in August 2000. The members of the Assembly were appointed by former president Laurent Kabila.

There are 11 regions, each under a governor and provincial administration: Bas-Zaïre (provincial capital, Matadi); Bandundu (Bandundu); Equateur (Mbandaka); Haut-Zaïre (Kisangani); Kinshasa (Kinshasa); Maniema (Kindu); North Kivu (Goma); South Kivu (Bukavu); Shaba (Katanga) (Lubumbashi); East Kasai (Mbuji-Mayi); West Kasai (Kananga).

HEAD OF STATE
President, Maj.-Gen. Joseph Kabila, *sworn in* 26 January 2001, *sworn in as president of the transitional government* 7 April 2003
Vice-Presidents, Abdoulaye Yerodia *(government)*; Z'Ahidi Ngoma *(civilian opposition)*; Jean-Pierre Bemba (FLC); Azarias Ruberwa Manywa (RCD)

SELECTED GOVERNMENT MEMBERS *as at July 2005*
Defence, Adolphe Onusumba Yemba
Finance, Andre Philippe Futa *(Government)*
Foreign Affairs, Raymond Ramazani Baya *(MLC)*
Interior, Théophile Mbemba Fundu *(Government)*

EMBASSY OF THE DEMOCRATIC REPUBLIC OF CONGO
218 Gray's Inn Road, London WC1X 8QF T 020-87278 9825
Ambassador Extraordinary and Plenipotentiary, Henri N'Swana, apptd July 2003

BRITISH EMBASSY
83 Avenue du Roi Baudouin, Kinshasa
T (+243) 98 169 100/111/200
Ambassador Extraordinary and Plenipotentiary, HE Andrew Sparkes, apptd 2004

ECONOMY AND TRADE
Coffee, rubber, cocoa and timber are the most important agricultural exports but the production of cotton, pyrethrum and copal is steadily increasing. Copper is widely exploited, and industrial diamonds and cobalt are also produced. Oil deposits are exploited off the Zaïre estuary and reef-gold is mined in the north-east of the country.

The main industrial products are foodstuffs, beverages, tobacco, textiles, leather, wood products, cement and building materials, metallurgy, small river craft and bicycles. There are reserves of hydroelectric power and the Inga dam on the River Zaïre supplies electricity to Matadi, Kinshasa and Shaba.

Whilst the country has many natural resources, civil war has led to the collapse of the economy, with total debt amounting to more than twice the GNI.

In July 2003 the IMF announced that US$10,000 million of debt relief would be granted to the Democratic Republic of Congo under the Heavily Indebted Poor Countries (HIPC) initiative. In addition, the World Bank approved a US$120 million loan to boost investment and support public enterprises in key economic sectors.
GNI – US$5,000 million (2002); US$100 per capita (2002)
ANNUAL AVERAGE GROWTH OF GDP – 7.5 per cent (2004 est.)
INFLATION RATE – 14 per cent (2004 est.)
TOTAL EXTERNAL DEBT – US$11,645 million (2000)

Trade with UK	2003	2004
Imports from UK	£8,092,000	£6,555,000
Exports to UK	1,409,000	4,761,000

TRANSPORT INFRASTRUCTURE
There are approximately 157,000 km of roads, including 30 km of expressway. The expressway is surfaced and 20,500 km of roads are unsurfaced. There are 6,000 km of railways. The country has four international and 40 principal airports.

MEDIA
The state-controlled media (Radio-Télévision Nationale Congolaise (RTNC) and La Voix du Congo) has the greatest influence and broadcast reach. There are some eight other private and commercial television stations and ten radio stations (some run by the Catholic church, some by the UN). Around 15 newspapers are published regularly in Kinshasa.

REPUBLIC OF CONGO

République du Congo – Republic of Congo

AREA – 342,000 sq. km. Neighbours: Gabon (west), Cameroon and Central African Republic (north), Angola (Cabinda) (south-west), Democratic Republic of Congo (east and south)
POPULATION – 2,998,040 (2004 est.). The official language is French; Lingala, Monokutuba and Kikongo are widely spoken
CAPITAL – Brazzaville (population, 937,579, 1992 estimate)
MAJOR CITIES – ΨPointe Noire, the main commercial centre
CURRENCY – Franc CFA of 100 centimes
NATIONAL ANTHEM – La Congolaise
NATIONAL DAY – 15 August
NATIONAL FLAG – Divided diagonally into green, yellow and red bands
MORTALITY RATE (per 1,000 population) – 14.49 (2004 est.)
HIV / AIDS ADULT PREVALENCE – 4.9 per cent (2003 est.)
POPULATION GROWTH RATE – 1.42 per cent (2004 est.)
POPULATION DENSITY – 8 per sq. km (1999)
MILITARY EXPENDITURE – 3.1 per cent of GDP (2003)

MILITARY PERSONNEL – 10,000: Army 8,000, Navy 800, Air Force 1,200; Paramilitaries 2,000
ILLITERACY RATE – (m) 10.4 per cent; (f) 21.6 per cent (2003)
GROSS ENROLMENT RATIO (percentage of relevant age group) – primary 86 per cent (2002); secondary 32 per cent (2002); tertiary 4 per cent (2002)

CLIMATE AND TERRAIN

The republic is covered by grassland, mangrove and dense rainforest. The land rises from sea-level on the narrow Atlantic coastal plain to a central plateau, and then falls to the northern basin of the River Congo (Zaïre), which forms much of the border with the Democratic Republic of Congo. In the north, the main rivers are the Sangha and Alima. Elevation extremes range from 903 m (Mount Berongou) at the highest point to 0 m at the lowest (Atlantic Ocean). The climate is equatorial. The annual daily temperature in Brazzaville is between 28°C and 33°C. The dry season is June to September but the country is prone to flooding during the wet season (March to June).

HISTORY AND POLITICS

The first European visitors to the area were the Portuguese, who established slave trading in the 16th century. The French established a colonial presence in the area in the 1880s and, as Middle Congo, it was part of French Equatorial Africa from 1908. It became independent as the Republic of Congo on 17 August 1960. In 1968, a military coup created the first Marxist state in Africa, under the Parti Congolais du Travail (PCT). Marxism was renounced and, after popular pressure, the PCT abandoned its monopoly of power in 1990.

The results of elections in 1993 were disputed and fighting broke out between political factions. A cease-fire and the inclusion of some opposition members in the government helped to restore peace. In 1997, a civil war broke out and President Pascal Lissouba was overthrown and replaced by the former president (1979–92) Denis Sassou-Nguesso. A three-year transition to democracy was initiated but fighting between the new government and supporters of the deposed regime continued, despite peace talks, international mediation and settlements in 1999 and 2001, until 2003, when agreements were signed by the government and the rebels. Remnants of the rebel militias are still active in the south of the country, and many have turned to banditry.

In the 2002 presidential election, Denis Sassou-Nguesso was elected with nearly 90 per cent of the vote, although his victory was criticised after his candidature was unopposed owing to the barring of his main rivals. In the elections to the National Assembly in 2002, the Congolese Labour Party (PCT) won an overall majority. A prime minister was appointed in 2005, the first time the post had been filled since 1997.

POLITICAL SYSTEM

A new constitution was approved by referendum in 2002. Under this, the head of state is the president, directly elected for a seven-year term, who heads the government and appoints the cabinet. The parliament is bicameral. The Assemblé nationale (National Assembly) is the lower chamber, with 137 members directly elected for a five-year term. The upper house is the Sénat (Senate), with 66 members indirectly elected for a six-year term, one-third of members retiring every two years.

HEAD OF STATE
President, Defence, Denis Sassou-Nguesso, sworn in 25 October 1997, elected 10 March 2002

SELECTED GOVERNMENT MEMBERS as at July 2005
Prime Minister, Isidore Myouba
Economy, Finance and Budget, Pacifique Issoibeka
Foreign Affairs, Co-operation and Francophone Affairs, Rodolphe Adada
Minister in the President's Office in charge of State Control, Simon Mfoutou
Defence, Brig.-Gen. Jacques Yvon Ndolou

EMBASSY OF THE REPUBLIC OF CONGO BRAZZAVILLE
37 bis Rue Paul Valéry, 75116 Paris, France
T (+33) (1) 4500 6057
Ambassador Extraordinary and Plenipotentiary, HE Henri Marie Joseph Lopes, apptd 1999

BRITISH AMBASSADOR
HE Jim Atkinson, resident at Kinshasa, Democratic Republic of Congo

ECONOMY AND TRADE

In 2000 the government, the World Bank and the IMF agreed a Post-Conflict Assistance Programme which provided US$14 million for post-war reconstruction and economic development.

The republic has its own oil deposits, producing about nine million tonnes annually. These deposits make up over half of the Congo's economy. It also produces lead, zinc, gold and diamonds. Agriculture accounts for about 10 per cent of GDP. The principal agricultural products are timber, cassava and yams. Imports are mainly of machinery; 37 per cent of imports come from France, making it the Republic's biggest trading partner.

GNI – US$2,200 million (2002); US$610 per capita (2002)
INFLATION RATE – 0.9 per cent (2000)
TOTAL EXTERNAL DEBT – US$4,887 million (2000)
IMPORTS – US$460 million (2000)
EXPORTS – US$2,490 million (2000)

BALANCE OF PAYMENTS
Trade – US$1,598 surplus (2002)
Current Account – US$34 million deficit (2002)

Trade with UK	2003	2004
Imports from UK	£12,621,000	£17,476,000
Exports to UK	7,604,000	4,354,000

TRANSPORT INFRASTRUCTURE

Pointe Noire is the main port and is the centre of the offshore oil industry. It is linked to Brazzaville by rail and road. There are 894 km of railways and 12,800 km of roads, 1,242 km of which are surfaced. Four of the 31 airports have surfaced runways. There are 1,120 km of commercially navigable waterways on the Congo and Ubango rivers.

MEDIA

Brazzaville is at the centre of the print media industry with five privately owned newspapers regularly published there. TV Congo is the only television station and it is state-owned and controlled by Radiodiffusion Télévision Congolaise. Radio Congo is also state-controlled.

COSTA RICA

República de Costa Rica – Republic of Costa Rica

AREA – 51,022 sq. km. Neighbours: Nicaragua (north), Panama (south)
POPULATION – 3,956,507 (2004 est.), mainly of European origin. The language is Spanish
CAPITAL – San José (population, 1,982,339, 2000 census)
MAJOR CITIES – Alajuela; Cartago
CURRENCY – Costa Rican colón of 100 céntimos
NATIONAL ANTHEM – Noble patria, tu hermosa bandera [Noble fatherland, your beautiful flag]
NATIONAL DAY – 15 September
NATIONAL FLAG – Five horizontal bands, blue, white, red, white, blue (the red band twice the width of the others with emblem near staff)
LIFE EXPECTANCY (years) – 76.63 (2004 est.)
MORTALITY RATE (per 1,000 population) – 4.32 (2004 est.)
INFANT MORTALITY (per 1,000 births) – 10.26 (2004 est.)
HIV / AIDS ADULT PREVALENCE RATE – 0.6 per cent (2003 est.)
DEATH PENALTY – No (abolished 1877)
POPULATION BELOW POVERTY LINE – 20.6 per cent (1999)
POPULATION GROWTH RATE – 1.52 per cent (2004 est.)
POPULATION DENSITY – 77 per sq. km (2002)
URBAN POPULATION – 60 per cent (2001)
MILITARY EXPENDITURE – 0.6 per cent of GDP (2003)
MILITARY PERSONNEL – 8,400 Paramilitaries
ILLITERACY RATE – (m) 4.1 per cent; (f) 3.9 per cent (2003 est.)
GROSS ENROLMENT RATIO (percentage of relevant age group) – primary 108 per cent (2002); secondary 67 per cent (2002); tertiary 21 per cent (2002)

CLIMATE AND TERRAIN

The Cordillera de Guanacaste, (north-west), Cordillera Central, and Cordillera de Talamanca (south-east) form a chain of volcanic mountain ranges that traverse the country from north to south. Elevation extremes range from 3,837 m (Chirripó Grande) to 0 m (Pacific Ocean) at the lowest. The climate is tropical with an average annual temperature of 26°C to 28°C. The wet season runs from May to November. The area is subject to occasional earthquakes, hurricanes, flooding and landslides.

HISTORY AND POLITICS

Visited by Columbus in 1502, for nearly three centuries (1530–1821) Costa Rica was under Spanish rule. In 1821 the country gained its independence from Spain, and was a member of the United Provinces (Federation) of Central America from 1824 until its secession in 1839. Political unrest in the mid-20th century led to a brief civil war in 1948, after which the army was abolished and replaced with a national guard. President Arias Sanchez won the Nobel Peace Prize in 1987 for devising the Central American peace plan that ended the civil wars in Nicaragua and El Salvador. The main political parties are the Social Christian Unity Party (PUSC) and the National Liberation Party (PLN). In the 2002 legislative elections, the PUSC narrowly defeated the PLN. The 2002 presidential election was won in the second round by the PUSC candidate, Abel Pacheco.

POLITICAL SYSTEM

Executive power is vested in the president, who is head of state and government. The president is directly elected for a single four-year term. Legislative power is vested in the Legislative Assembly *(Asamblea Legislativa)*, which has 57 members directly elected for a single four-year term.

HEAD OF STATE
President, Abel Pacheco, *elected* 7 April 2002
First Vice-President, Co-ordinator of Social Policy, Planning, Lineth Saborio Chaverri

SELECTED GOVERNMENT MEMBERS *as at July 2005*
Finance, Frederico Carrillo
Foreign Affairs and Religion, Roberto Tovar Faja
Interior, Police and Public Security, Rogelio Ramos Martinez
Foreign Trade, Manuel Gonzalez

COSTA RICAN EMBASSY
Flat 1, 14 Lancaster Gate, London W2 3LH
T 020-7706 8844
Chargé d'affaires, Sylvia Uglade

BRITISH EMBASSY
Apartado 815–1007, Edificio Centro Colón (Eleventh Floor), San José T (+506) 258 2025 E britemb@racsa.co.cr
Ambassador Extraordinary and Plenipotentiary and Consul-General, Georgina Butler, apptd 2002

ECONOMY AND TRADE

The economy experienced serious problems in the 1990s as world prices for its main export commodities fell. This has largely been overcome by diversification. Tourism is the largest single industry, and with one third of the country designated as national parkland or nature reserve, 'ecotourism' is on the increase. In 2002, there were 1,113,359 tourists. The manufacturing industry accounts for around 30 per cent of GDP, the principal products being computer components, foodstuffs, textiles, plastic goods and pharmaceuticals. The principal agricultural products are coffee, bananas, sugar and cattle (for meat).

The chief exports are manufactured goods, bananas, coffee, fish and shellfish, machinery and tropical fruits. The chief imports are raw materials for industry, consumer goods, capital equipment, and fuel and mineral oils. The USA is Costa Rica's largest trading partner and accounts for around 36.7 per cent of imports and 31.5 per cent of exports. Other major trading partners are Japan, the UK, Mexico and the Netherlands.

GNI – US$16,100 million (2002); US$4,070 per capita (2002)
ANNUAL AVERAGE GROWTH OF GDP – 3.9 per cent (2004 est.)
INFLATION RATE – 11.0 per cent (2000)
UNEMPLOYMENT – 6.6 per cent (2004 est.)
TOTAL EXTERNAL DEBT – US$4,800 million (2002)
FOREIGN DIRECT INVESTMENT – US$1,694 million (1997–2000)
IMPORTS – US$7,700 million (2003)
EXPORTS – US$6,100 million (2003)

BALANCE OF PAYMENTS
Trade – US$1,170 million deficit (2003)
Current Account – US$967 million deficit (2003)

Trade with UK	2003	2004
Imports from UK	£40,466,000	£38,563,000
Exports to UK	437,198,000	586,876,000

TRANSPORT INFRASTRUCTURE

The chief ports are Limón on the Atlantic coast, through which passes most of the coffee exported, and Puntarenas on the Pacific coast. LACSA is the national airline, operating flights throughout Central and South America, the Caribbean and the USA, besides internal flights to over 100 local airports. There are 950 km of railways and 35,892 km of roads, 7,896 of which are surfaced. There are 151 airports, 30 of which have surfaced runways.

MEDIA AND CULTURE

Costa Rica has nine major newspapers, at least 18 television stations and over 35 radio stations. It is one of the most peaceful and prosperous countries in Central America.

The rise of Costa Rican literature came slowly and late compared to other South American countries. Its origins are usually placed in the colonial times, and until the 20th century the dominant forms of prose are considered to have been either *costumbrismo* (a colloquial narrative form that explores regional customs and dialects) or writing imitating European Symbolist and Modernist tendencies. Manuel Gonzalez Zeledon (Magon) (1864–1936) was the chief proponent of *costumbrismo* and began publishing sketches of Costa Rican life in 1885.

CÔTE D'IVOIRE

République de la Côte d'Ivoire – Republic of Côte d'Ivoire

AREA – 318,000 sq. km. Neighbours: Guinea and Liberia (west), Mali and Burkina Faso (north), Ghana (east)

POPULATION – 17,327,724 (2004 est.): 39 per cent Muslim, 28 per cent Christian (mainly Roman Catholic) and 17 per cent maintain traditional beliefs. The official language is French, but Agni, Baoulé, Dioula, Senoufo and Yacouba are spoken

CAPITAL – Yamoussoukro (population, 126,191), the political and administrative capital since 1983

MAJOR CITIES – ΨAbidjan, the economic and financial centre

CURRENCY – Franc CFA of 100 centimes

NATIONAL ANTHEM – L'Abidjanaise

NATIONAL DAY – 7 August

NATIONAL FLAG – Three vertical stripes, orange, white and green

LIFE EXPECTANCY (years) – 42.48 (2004 est.)

MORTALITY RATE (per 1,000 population) – 18.48 (2004 est.)

INFANT MORTALITY (per 1,000 births) – 97.1 (2004 est.)

HIV / AIDS ADULT PREVALENCE – 7 per cent (2003 est.)

DEATH PENALTY – No (abolished 2000)

POPULATION GROWTH RATE – 2.11 per cent (2004 est.)

POPULATION DENSITY – 52 per sq. km (2002)

MILITARY EXPENDITURE – 1.2 per cent of GDP (2003)

MILITARY PERSONNEL – 17,050: Army 6,500, Navy 900, Air Force 700, Paramilitaries 8,950

CONSCRIPTION DURATION – 18 months (selective)

ILLITERACY RATE – (m) 43.1 per cent; (f) 57.4 per cent (2003 est.)

GROSS ENROLMENT RATIO (percentage of relevant age group) – primary 80 per cent (2002); secondary 23 per cent (2002)

CLIMATE AND TERRAIN

The climate is equatorial in the southern and western rainforest areas; tropical in the central and eastern savannah regions, and dry and tropical in the north. Elevation extremes range from 1,752 m (Mount Nimba) at the highest point to 0 m (Gulf of Guinea) at the lowest. Average annual temperatures range from 24°C in August to 27°C in March.

HISTORY AND POLITICS

The first European visitors were Portuguese navigators in the 1460s, and Europeans established the ivory trade and some slave trading in the 16th century. The area came under French influence from 1842, Côte d'Ivoire became a protectorate in 1889 and a colony in 1893, although it was only finally pacified in 1912. It achieved self-government in 1958, and became independent on 7 August 1960 as a one-party state with Felix Houphouët-Boigny as president.

A multiparty system was introduced in 1990. President Houphouët-Boigny died in 1993 and was succeeded by Henri Konan-Bédié. The post-independence period of stability ended and President Konan-Bédié was deposed in 1999 in a military coup led by Gen. Robert Guëi, who became president. The religious and ethnic harmony of the post-independence period also broke down at this time as xenophobia was adopted as a political tool, opening divisions between the Muslim north and mainly Christian south and west of the country.

Violent protests broke out when President Guëi claimed victory in the 2000 presidential election. Guëi fled the country, and Laurent Gbagbo of the Ivorian Popular Front (FPI), believed to be the winning candidate, became president, but clashes occurred between his supporters and those of a northern presidential candidate. In 2002 a rebellion by recently demobilised troops in the north sparked off civil war, and the 2003 cease-fire left the country divided between the government-controlled south and the rebel-held north, with UN peacekeeping troops deployed in 2003 to maintain a buffer zone between the two. Despite the cease-fire, clashes have continued, drawing in UN peacekeepers in 2004, and the government has faced international allegations of human rights abuses over its suppression of political opposition. In late 2004 political reforms set out in the cease-fire agreement were implemented by parliament.

In legislative elections in December 2000 and January 2001, the FPI won 96 seats and the Democratic Party of Côte d'Ivoire (PDCI) won 94 seats. The election was boycotted by the Rally of Republicans (RDR), the strongest party in the north of the country. The next presidential election is due in October 2005 and the next legislative election in December 2005.

POLITICAL SYSTEM

A new constitution was approved by referendum in 2000. It provides for an executive president directly elected for a five-year term, renewable only once. The president appoints the prime minister. The legislature is the single-chamber National Assembly *(Assemblée nationale)* of 225 members, directly elected for a five-year term.

HEAD OF STATE

President, Laurent Gbagbo, *elected* 22 October 2000, *sworn in* 26 October 2000

SELECTED GOVERNMENT MEMBERS *as at July 2005*
Prime Minister, Planning and Development, Seydou Diarra
Defence, René Amani
Finance and Economy, Paul Bohoun Bouabre
Foreign Affairs and Ivorians Abroad, Bamba Mamadou

EMBASSY OF THE REPUBLIC OF CÔTE D'IVOIRE
2 Upper Belgrave Street, London SW1X 8BJ
T 020-7235 6991
Ambassador Extraordinary and Plenipotentiary, HE
   Youssoufou Bamba, apptd 2001

BRITISH EMBASSY
Immeuble Bank of Africa (3rd and 4th Floors), Angle Ave.,
Terrasson de Fougères et Rue Gourgas Abidjan-Plateau, BP 2581
T (+225) (20) 300800 E britemb.a@aviso.ci
Ambassador Extraordinary and Plenipotentiary, HE David
   Coates, apptd 2004

ECONOMY AND TRADE

In the late 1980s the economy contracted considerably.
Although reform programmes in 1989 and 1998
improved economic performance, the economy has since
had to deal with the impact of the civil war.

Agriculture accounts for 29 per cent of GDP, the
manufacturing industry for 22 per cent and the service
industries for 49 per cent. Agriculture employs around 68
per cent of the workforce. There are some deposits of
diamonds and minerals, including manganese and iron.
Oil and gas deposits have been exploited since 1995. The
principal exports are coffee, cocoa (Côte d'Ivoire is the
world's largest producer, supplying 40 per cent of global
demand), timber, palm oil, sugar, rubber, pineapples,
bananas and cotton. Côte d'Ivoire's main trading partner
is France.

GNI – US$10,200 million (2002); US$620 per capita
   (2002)
ANNUAL AVERAGE GROWTH OF GDP – –1 per cent
   (2004 est.)
INFLATION RATE – 2.5 per cent (2000)
TOTAL EXTERNAL DEBT – US$12,138 million (2000)
DIRECT FOREIGN INVESTMENT – US$1,218 million
   (1997–2000)
IMPORTS – US$3,300 million (2003)
EXPORTS – US$5,800 million (2003)

BALANCE OF PAYMENTS
Trade – US$2,524 million surplus (2003)
Current Account – US$353 million surplus (2003)

Trade	2003	2004
Imports from UK	£43,745,000	£67,886,000
Exports to UK	108,618,000	85,498,000

TRANSPORT INFRASTRUCTURE

Côte d'Ivoire has 660 km of railways and 50,400 km of
roads, 4,889 km of which are surfaced. There are 980 km
of navigable rivers and canals and the main ports are
Abidjan and San Pedro. There are 36 airports, seven of
which have surfaced runways.

MEDIA

The state broadcaster is Radiodiffusion Télévision
Ivoirienne (RTI). RTI operates two national radio stations
(La Chaîne Nationale and Frequence 2) and two television
channels (La Première and TV2). There are no private
terrestrial television stations although subscription

services are available. Radio is the most popular medium
for news, with around 30 non-commercial community
radio stations located throughout the country. The print
media is represented by two government-owned daily
newspapers and around 20 privately owned newspapers.

CROATIA

Republika Hrvatska – Republic of Croatia

AREA – 55,900 sq. km. Neighbours: Slovenia, Hungary
   (north), Serbia and Montenegro (east), Bosnia-
   Hercegovina (south, and east of Adriatic coastal strip)
POPULATION – 4,496,869 (2004 est.): 78 per cent
   Croat, 12 per cent Serb, 2 per cent Yugoslav; also
   Hungarians, Italians, Albanians, Czechs, Ukrainians
   and Jews. Roman Catholic 76.5 per cent, Eastern
   Orthodox 11.1 per cent, Protestant 1.4 per cent,
   Muslim 1.2 per cent. The language is Croatian in the
   Latin script
CAPITAL – Zagreb (population, 867,717, 2001 census)
MAJOR CITIES – Osijek; Rijeka; Split
CURRENCY – Kuna of 100 lipa
NATIONAL ANTHEM – Lijepa nasa domovina [Our
   beautiful homeland]
NATIONAL DAY – 30 May (Statehood Day)
NATIONAL FLAG – Three horizontal stripes of red, white,
   blue, with the national arms in the centre
LIFE EXPECTANCY (years) – 74.14 (2004 est.)
MORTALITY RATE (per 1,000 population) – 11.3
   (2004 est.)
INFANT MORTALITY (per 1,000 births) – 6.96
   (2004 est.)
HIV / AIDS ADULT PREVALENCE – 0.1 per cent
   (2001 est.)
DEATH PENALTY – No (abolished 1990)
POPULATION GROWTH RATE – –0.02 per cent
   (2004 est.)
POPULATION DENSITY – 80 per sq. km (2002)
ILLITERACY RATE – (m) 0.6 per cent; (f) 2.2 per cent
   (2003 est.)
GROSS ENROLMENT RATIO (percentage of relevant age
   group) – primary 96 per cent (2002); secondary 88 per
   cent (2002); tertiary 36 per cent (2002)

CLIMATE AND TERRAIN

Croatia is divided into three major geographic areas: the
Pannonian region in the north, the central mountain belt,
and the Adriatic coast region of Istria and Dalmatia,
which has 1,185 islands and islets and 1,778 km of
coastline. Elevation extremes range from 1,913 m
(Troglav) at the highest point to 0 m (Adriatic Sea) at the
lowest. The climate is continental in the Pannonian basin,
with average temperatures ranging from −1°C to 19°C.
The climate is Mediterranean on the Adriatic coast, with
average temperatures from 6°C (January) to 24°C (July).

HISTORY AND POLITICS

Croatia was ruled by the Habsburgs from 1526 to 1918.
With the collapse of the Austro-Hungarian Empire at the
end of the First World War, Croatia declared its
independence, on 29 October 1918, and soon after
joined with Slovenia, Bosnia-Hercegovina, Serbia and
Montenegro to form the 'Kingdom of Serbs, Croats and
Slovenes' (renamed Yugoslavia in 1929). From 1941 to
1945 Yugoslavia was occupied by the Axis powers; Italy

and Hungary annexed parts of Croatia and a pro-Nazi Croat puppet state was established in the remainder of Croatia and Bosnia-Hercegovina. The armed extremists of this state (the Ustae) engaged in fierce fighting with Serbian royalists, Communist partisans and pro-Allied Croat partisans.

At the end of the war Yugoslavia was re-established as a federal republic under Communist rule, but gradually disintegrated following the death of President Tito, the wartime partisan leader in 1980.

In 1991 Croatia declared its independence from the Yugoslav federation. The efforts of the Federal Yugoslav Army (JNA) and the ethnic Serbs in Croatia to prevent Croatia's secession from the federation led to civil war until January 1992, when a cease-fire was declared. Fighting restarted in 1993 as Croatian forces set out to retake the ethnic Serb areas of the country that had seceded; Krajina and Western Slavonia were recaptured in 1985, and Eastern Slavonia agreed in 1995 to eventual re-integration by 1998. From 1992 to 1995 Croatian forces were also involved in the war in Bosnia-Hercegovina, and Croatia signed the Dayton Accord in 1995.

Post-independence politics was dominated by the authoritarian President Franjo Tudjman, a former partisan first elected president in 1990, until his death in 1999. Since his death, Croatia has become more outward-looking, and plans to join the EU in 2007.

In the 2000 legislative election, the opposition coalition of the Social Democratic Party of Croatia (SPH) and the Croatian Social Liberal Party (HSLS) scored a decisive victory, winning a total of 68 seats. Stjepan Mesic was elected in presidential elections held in February 2000. In the presidential elections of January 2005, Stjepan Mesic was re-elected after winning 66 per cent of the vote in a second round run-off. Croatia submitted an application for EU membership in February 2003 which is currently under consideration.

FOREIGN RELATIONS
There has been a dispute with Serbia and Montenegro since independence over the Prevlaka peninsula, which lies within Croatian territory but controls access to Kotor Bay, Serbia and Montenegro's most important deep water port. A temporary protocol was signed between the two governments in 2002 which gave Croatia full sovereignty, although the area must remain demilitarised and have joint maritime police patrols.

POLITICAL SYSTEM
Executive power is vested in a president and government. The president is directly elected for a five-year term. Legislative power is vested in the 153-member Chamber of Representatives, whose members are directly elected for a four-year term.

The constitution was amended in November 2000 to reduce the powers of the presidency. A further amendment was agreed in March 2001, when the Chamber of Representatives voted to abolish the Chamber of Counties, the upper house of the legislature.

HEAD OF STATE
President, Stjepan Mesic, *elected* 7 February 2000, *re-elected* 17 January 2005

SELECTED GOVERNMENT MEMBERS *as at July 2005*
Prime Minister, Ivo Sanader
Deputy Prime Minister, Jadranker Kosor
Deputy Prime Minister, Damir Polancec

Defence, Berislav Roncevic
Finance, Ivan Suker
Foreign Affairs, Kolinda Grabar Kitarovic
Interior, Marijan Mlinaric

EMBASSY OF THE REPUBLIC OF CROATIA
21 Conway Street, London W1T 6BN
T 020-7387 2022
Ambassador Extraordinary and Plenipotentiary, HE Josip Paro, apptd 2002

BRITISH EMBASSY
Ivana Lucica 4, Zagreb T (+385) (1) 6009 100
E british.embassyzagreb@fco.gov.uk
Ambassador Extraordinary and Plenipotentiary, HE Sir John Ramsden, BT, apptd 2004

BRITISH COUNCIL
Illica 12, PO Box 55, 10001 Zagreb T (+385) (1) 4899 500
E zagreb.info@britishcouncil.hr
Director, Roy Cross

DEFENCE
The armed forces of Croatia are subject to an arms limitation regime established under the Dayton Peace Accord. The Army has 291 main battle tanks, 33 armoured personnel carriers and 104 armoured infantry fighting vehicles. The Air Force has 27 combat aircraft and 9 armed helicopters. The Navy has one submarine and seven patrol and coastal combatants at five bases.
MILITARY EXPENDITURE – 2.1 per cent of GDP (2003)
MILITARY PERSONNEL – 18,850: Army 14,050, Navy 2,500, Air Force 2,300; Paramilitaries 10,000
CONSCRIPTION DURATION – Six months

ECONOMY AND TRADE
During the conflict in 1991–5, there was an estimated US$27,000 million of damage to the infrastructure, large areas of farmland were destroyed, industrial production was severely hampered and the tourist industry, the source of one-third of total foreign exchange earnings in 1990, was decimated. Recovery has begun, and Croatia has seen a rise in tourism since 2000. The service industries account for 58 per cent of GDP, manufacturing industry for 33 per cent, and agriculture for 9 per cent. Shipbuilding and fishing are major industries on the Adriatic coast. Inland there is a light manufacturing sector, food-processing industries, bauxite deposits, thermal mineral springs and hydroelectric potential. The textile industry is one of the most important, employing more than 17 per cent of the population. Agriculture is based on production of grain, horticulture, livestock and tobacco. In 2003 the IMF approved a 14-month standby credit of around US$145.5 million to support Croatia's economic and financial programme.
GNI – US$20,300 million (2002); US$4,540 per capita (2002)
INFLATION RATE – 5.4 per cent (2000)
UNEMPLOYMENT – 13.8 per cent (2004 est.)
TOTAL EXTERNAL DEBT – US$12,120 million (2000)
FOREIGN DIRECT INVESTMENT – US$3,595 million (1997–2000)
IMPORTS – US$14,100 million (2003)
EXPORTS – US$6,200 million (2003)

BALANCE OF PAYMENTS
Trade – US$7,921 million deficit (2003)
Current Account – US$2,099 million deficit (2003)

Trade with UK	2003	2004
Imports from UK	£139,903,000	£126,169,000
Exports to UK	50,088,000	54,540,000

TRANSPORT INFRASTRUCTURE
There are 2,296 km of railways and 28,123 km of roads, 23,792 of which are surfaced. There are 59 airports, 16 of which are surfaced, and one heliport. The principal airports are at Zagreb and Split. The main ports are Rijeka (Fiume), Split, Zadar, Sibenik and Dubrovnik.

MEDIA
Croatia's constitution guarantees freedom of the press. Croatian Radio-Television (HRT) is the national state-owned broadcaster and is the main source of news. Nove TV is the country's first national private network. There are four main news publications: *Vecernji List* (daily), *Feral Tribune* (weekly), *Nacional* (weekly).

CUBA

República de Cuba – Republic of Cuba

AREA – 109,800 sq. km
POPULATION – 11,308,764 (2004 est.). The language is Spanish
CAPITAL – ΨHavana (population, 2,184,990, 1996 UN estimate)
MAJOR CITIES – Camagüey; Guantánamo; Holguín; Santa Clara; ΨSantiago
CURRENCY – Cuban peso of 100 centavos
NATIONAL ANTHEM – Al combate, corred Bayameses [To battle, men of Bayamo]
NATIONAL DAY – 1 January (Day of Liberation)
NATIONAL FLAG – Five horizontal bands, blue and white (blue at top and bottom) with red triangle, close to staff, charged with five-point star
LIFE EXPECTANCY (years) – 77.04 (2004 est.)
MORTALITY RATE (per 1,000 population) – 7.17 (2004 est.)
INFANT MORTALITY (per 1,000 births) – 6.45 (2004 est.)
HIV / AIDS ADULT PREVALENCE – 0.1 per cent (2003 est.)
DEATH PENALTY – Yes
POPULATION GROWTH RATE – 0.34 per cent (2004 est.)
POPULATION DENSITY – 103 per sq. km (2002)
URBAN POPULATION – 75 per cent (2001)

CLIMATE AND TERRAIN
Cuba, the largest island in the Caribbean, is part of an archipelago that also includes Isla de la Juventud and 1,600 other islets and cays. The island of Cuba itself has three mountainous ranges running from east to west. Elevation extremes range from 2,005 m (Pico Turquino) at the highest point to 0 m (Caribbean Sea) at the lowest. The climate is subtropical, with an average annual temperature of 25°C.

HISTORY AND POLITICS
The island was visited by Columbus in 1492. In the early 16th century the island was settled by the Spanish and remained under Spanish rule until 1898, when Spain ceded it to the USA after losing the Spanish-American War. Cuba became independent in 1902, with the USA retaining naval bases on the island. The dictatorship of Gen. Batista (1933–44, 1952–9) was overthrown in 1959 in a revolution led by Fidel Castro, and a communist state was established in 1961 which became allied with the Soviet Union. This alliance and the regime's policies on the one hand, and the USA's support of exiled Cuban opponents on the other, created great friction in US-Cuban relations, and the USA has maintained an economic and trade embargo on Cuba for over 30 years.

When the Soviet Union collapsed in 1991, Cuba lost the economic, commercial and military support it had enjoyed since 1960. Faced with severe economic deterioration, the government relaxed state controls on economic activity and has benefited from increased overseas investment and a growing tourist sector.

In 2003, the European Union imposed restrictions in its political and cultural contacts with Cuba over its poor human rights record. In the 2003 legislative election, all 609 unopposed candidates received the required 50 per cent of the vote; subsequently the National Assembly re-elected Fidel Castro as president.

POLITICAL SYSTEM
The Communist Party of Cuba (PCC), formed in 1965, is the only authorised political party. A new constitution came into force in 1976; it was amended in 1991, to allow direct election of the National Assembly by secret ballot, and in 2002 to enshrine socialism in the constitution. The president is indirectly elected by the National Assembly for five-year terms. The unicameral legislature is the National Assembly of the People's Power, with 609 members directly elected for a five-year term; all candidates are approved by the PCC and stand unopposed. Between its sessions, the National Assembly is represented by the Council of State, whose members are elected by the National Assembly.

HEAD OF STATE
President of Council of State and Council of Ministers, Dr Fidel Castro Ruz, since 1959, *appointed* 2 November 1976, *re-elected* 15 March 1993, 24 February 1998, 6 March 2003

COUNCIL OF STATE *as at July 2005*
President, Dr Fidel Castro Ruz
First Vice-President, Gen. Raúl Castro Ruz
Secretary, Jose Miyar Barrueco

SELECTED GOVERNMENT MEMBERS *as at July 2005*
President, Dr Fidel Castro Ruz
First Vice-President, Revolutionary Armed Forces, Gen. Raúl Castro Ruz
Finance, Georgina Barreiro Fajardo
Foreign Relations, Felipe Pérez Roque
Interior, Gen. Abelardo Colomé Ibarra

EMBASSY OF THE REPUBLIC OF CUBA
167 High Holborn, London WC1 6PA T 020-7240 2488
Ambassador Extraordinary and Plenipotentiary, HE Dr José Fernández de Cossío, apptd 2000

BRITISH EMBASSY
Calle 34 No. 702/4, Entre 7MA Avenida Y 17, Miramar, Havana
T (+53) (7) 204 1771
Ambassador Extraordinary and Plenipotentiary, HE John Dew, apptd 2001

BRITISH COUNCIL
7ma Avenida, e, Calle 34 y 36, Miramar, Havana
T (+53) (7) 204 1771/2 E information@cu.britishcouncil.org
Director, William Edmundson

Trade with UK	2003	2004
Imports from UK	£17,372,000	£11,480,000
Exports to UK	9,074,000	12,320,000

DEFENCE

The Army has about 900 main battle tanks and 700 armoured personnel carriers. The Navy has five patrol and coastal vessels at seven bases. The Air Force has 130 combat aircraft (of which only some 25 are operational) and 45 armed helicopters.

The last former Soviet combat personnel left Cuba in 1993, but 810 Russian military advisers remain to operate military intelligence facilities. In January 2002 Lourdes, Russia's last military base, closed down. The United States has 2,255 Joint Task Force personnel at Guantánamo Bay Naval Base, which has been leased since before the 1959 revolution.

MILITARY EXPENDITURE – 4 per cent of GDP (2003)
MILITARY PERSONNEL – 49,000: Army 38,000, Navy 3,000, Air Force 8,000; Paramilitaries 26,500
CONSCRIPTION DURATION – Two years

ECONOMY AND TRADE

After the revolution virtually all land and industrial and commercial enterprises were nationalised. With the collapse of communism in Europe in 1989–91, the economy deteriorated sharply, necessitating rationing of energy, food and consumer goods, and obliging the government to introduce reforms. Since 1993, the government has permitted private enterprise, cut subsidies to loss-making state industries, allowed prices for some goods and services to rise, and introduced income tax. State farms have been transformed into privately run co-operatives and are permitted to sell 20 per cent of their produce on the open market, but remain relatively unproductive. Lack of external finance has been a major obstacle to economic recovery, as has the long-standing US trade and economic embargo, which has attracted international criticism (although it was relaxed in 1998 to allow food and medicine into the country). However, British and Canadian companies have become involved in the oil and mining industries since 1995, when ownership of property and Cuban-based companies was opened to foreign investors. The economic reforms have also allowed tourism to grow, and in 2003, 1.9 million tourists visited Cuba.

Sugar is still one of the mainstays of the economy but is subject to fluctuating world prices. Sugar exports generated US$441 million in 2002 and the industry employs 327,000 workers. In 2002 the government announced the planned closure of 70 of its 156 sugar cane mills and the conversion of 14 of the remaining mills to the production of honey and/or into tourist attractions. Nickel production fell in 2002 but the world price rose to bring the economy an estimated US$512 million in revenue. Trade with the former Soviet bloc has declined since 1989, although Russia remains Cuba's second largest export partner (after the Netherlands at 18.5 per cent), taking 17.5 per cent of exports in 2002. Principal exports are sugar, nickel, seafood, citrus fruits, tobacco and rum.

GDP – US$23,901 million (1998); US$2,384 per capita (2000)
ANNUAL AVERAGE GROWTH OF GDP – 3 per cent (2004 est.)
UNEMPLOYMENT – 2.5 per cent (2004 est.)

TRANSPORT INFRASTRUCTURE

There are 3,442 km of railways, with an additional 7,742 km of track used exclusively by the sugar plantations. There are 60,858 km of roads, 29,820 km of which are surfaced and 638 km of which is motorway. In 1998 the ban on direct flights between Cuba and the USA was lifted, although the only air connection with the USA is a weekly charter service between Miami and Havana.

EDUCATION

Education is free of charge and compulsory at all levels. In some rural areas children attend boarding schools where agricultural tasks are compulsory in addition to schoolwork. After basic education students can choose to go to a pre-collegiate school or a technical school. The pre-collegiate school is free to graduates.

ILLITERACY RATE – (m) 2.8 per cent; (f) 3.1 per cent (2003)
GROSS ENROLMENT RATIO (percentage of relevant age group) – primary 100 per cent (2002); secondary 89 per cent (2002); tertiary 27 per cent (2002)

MEDIA AND CULTURE

Private ownership of electronic media is prohibited. The official Communist Party newspaper is *Granma*. The main television stations are Cubavision, Tele-Rebelde and CHTV, a subsidiary of Tele-Rebelde. The main radio stations are Radio Rebelde and Radio Reloj. Radio-TV Marti is a US government-backed station that targets Cuban listeners from its transmitting base in Florida.

Cubans are perhaps most famous for their music – a vibrant mix of Spanish traditional guitar melodies and African rhythms. Rumba, mambo, bolero, salsa and cha-cha-cha all evolved from *son*, a type of Cuban music that originated in the hills of Oriente at the turn of the 20th century. Cuba has produced writers of international standing such as José Martí (1853–95), Cirilo Villaverde y de la Paz (1812–94), Alejo Carpentier (1904–80), Nicolás Guillén (1902–89) and Guillermo Cabrera Infante (b. 1929).

CYPRUS

Kypriaki Dimokratía/Kıbrıs Çumhuriyeti – Republic of Cyprus

AREA – 9,200 sq. km
POPULATION – 775,927 (2004 est.): 85 per cent Greek, 12 per cent Turkish. Greek and Turkish are the official languages
CAPITAL – Nicosia (population 195,300, 2000 est.)
MAJOR CITIES – ΨFamagusta; ΨLarnaca; ΨLimassol; Paphos
CURRENCY – Cyprus pound (C£) of 100 cents
NATIONAL ANTHEM – Ymnos eis tin eleftherian [Ode to freedom]
NATIONAL DAY – 1 October [Independence Day]
NATIONAL FLAG – White with a gold map of Cyprus above crossed olive branches
LIFE EXPECTANCY (years) – 77.46 (2004 est.)
MORTALITY RATE (per 1,000 population) – 7.63 (2004 est.)

INFANT MORTALITY (per 1,000 births) – 7.36
(2004 est.)
HIV / AIDS ADULT PREVALENCE – 0.1 per cent
(2003 est.)
DEATH PENALTY – No (abolished 1962)
POPULATION GROWTH RATE – 0.55 per cent
(2004 est.)
POPULATION DENSITY – 86 per sq. km (2001)
URBAN POPULATION – 70 per cent (2001)
ILLITERACY RATE – (m) 1.1 per cent; (f) 3.6 per cent
(2003 est.)

CLIMATE AND TERRAIN

Cyprus is the third largest island in the Mediterranean. It has two mountain ranges, the Pentadaktylos range along the north coast, and the Troodos range (which includes Mount Olympus) in the central and western areas of the island. Elevation extremes range from 1,952 m (Mount Olympus) at the highest point to 0 m (Mediterranean Sea) at the lowest. The climate is Mediterranean.

HISTORY AND POLITICS

Cyprus has a recorded history of over 4,000 years, and its rulers have included the Greeks, Phoenicians, Ptolemaic Egyptians, Romans, Byzantines, Arabs, Franks, Venetians, Turks and British. Cyprus was ceded to Britain by Turkey in 1878, was formally annexed by Britain in 1914, and became a Crown colony in 1925. Greek Cypriot demands for union with Greece (*enosis*) led to guerrilla warfare against the British administration in the 1950s and a four-year state of emergency (1955–9). An agreement was signed in 1959 between Britain, Greece, Turkey and the Greek and Turkish Cypriots which stipulated that Cyprus would become an independent republic; the island became an independent republic on 16 August 1960, with Britain retaining sovereignty over the military bases as Akrotiri and Dhekelia.

The constitution provided for power-sharing between the Greek and Turkish Cypriots but this proved unworkable and led to intercommunal trouble throughout the 1960s and in 1971. The UN Peacekeeping Force in Cyprus (UNFICYP) was deployed in 1964. In 1974, a coup by mainland Greek officers in the Cypriot National Guard led Turkey, which feared *enosis*, to invade and occupy the northern third of the island, partitioning the island and displacing over 160,000 Greek Cypriots. Talks on reunification in the 1980s and 1990s were unsuccessful, and there were further, sporadic outbreaks of intercommunal violence, but the approach of Cyprus' admission to the EU gave added impetus to the search for a settlement. UN-sponsored talks from 1999 resulted in a reunification plan which was put to a referendum in April 2004. It was approved by Turkish Cypriots (64.9 per cent in favour) but rejected by Greek Cypriots (75.8 per cent against), and only the southern part of the island joined the EU in May 2004.

In the 2001 legislative election, the Progressive Party of the Working People (AKEL) became the largest party in the House of Representatives, winning 20 seats with the Democratic Coalition (DISI). Tassos Papadopoulos of the Democratic Party (DIKO) won the 2003 presidential election with 15.5 per cent of the vote.

HEAD OF STATE
President, Tassos Papadopoulos, *elected* 16 February 2003, *sworn in* 1 March 2003

SELECTED GOVERNMENT MEMBERS *as at July 2005*
Defence, Kiriakos Mavronikolas
Finance, Iakovos Keravnos
Foreign Affairs, Georgios Iakovou
Interior, Andreas Christou

CYPRUS HIGH COMMISSION
93 Park Street, London W1K 7ET T 020-7499 8272
High Commissioner, HE Petros Eftychiou, apptd 2004

BRITISH HIGH COMMISSION
Alexander Pallis Street (PO Box 21978), 1587 Nicosia
T (+357) (22) 861100
High Commissioner, HE Lyn Parker, apptd 2001

BRITISH COUNCIL
3 Museum Street (PO Box 25654), 1097 Nicosia
T (+357) 22585000 E enquiries@cy.britishcouncil.org
Director, Richard Walker

BRITISH SOVEREIGN BASE AREAS
The Sovereign Base Areas (SBAs) of Akrotiri and Dhekelia are those parts of the island which remained under British sovereignty and jurisdiction when Cyprus became independent in 1960. They have the status of a British Overseas Territory and are around 253 sq. km in size. There are approximately 15,700 people resident in the SBAs: 7,700 Cypriots, 3,900 service and UKBC personnel, of whom 3,600 live in the SBAs, and nearly 5,000 dependants, of whom over 4,400 live in the SBAs. There are also nearly 2,700 locally employed civilians.
Administrator of the British Sovereign Base Areas, Maj-Gen. P. T. C. Pearson, CBE

DEFENCE

The National Guard has 145 main battle tanks, 43 armoured infantry fighting vehicles and 310 armoured personnel carriers. Turkey has about 36,000 troops in northern Cyprus.

A military airfield in Paphos provides a base for Greek military aircraft, as Cyprus does not possess its own air force. There are some 3,275 UK service personnel at two Sovereign Base Areas.
MILITARY EXPENDITURE – 2.3 per cent of GDP (2003)
MILITARY PERSONNEL – National Guard 10,000,
Paramilitaries 750; Northern Cyprus Army 5,000,
Paramilitaries 150
CONSCRIPTION DURATION – 25 months

ECONOMY AND TRADE

In Greek Cyprus, the service industries accounted for 75.5 per cent of GDP in 2000; the manufacturing industry 13.1 per cent, construction 6.9 per cent and agriculture 4.5 per cent. In Turkish Cyprus, services accounted for about 74 per cent of GDP in 1998. Main products are citrus fruits, grapes and other vine products, meat, milk, potatoes and other vegetables. Manufacturing, construction, distribution and other service industries are additional major employers. Tourism is the main growth industry with around 2.5 million visitors every year. Tourism earns more than US$2,000 million annually and represents 20 per cent of GDP. Twenty per cent of the world's ships are Cypriot-registered. The accession of Greek Cyprus to the EU in 2004 is expected to have a detrimental effect upon the economic future of the Turkish community.

The UK was the main export market for Cyprus in 2003 with 28.2 per cent of all exports going to Britain.

Russia was the main import partner and provided 17.9 per cent of imported commodities.

GNI – US$9,370 million (2001); US$12,320 per capita (2001)

ANNUAL AVERAGE GROWTH OF GDP – 3.2 per cent (2004 est.)

INFLATION RATE – 4.1 per cent (2000)

UNEMPLOYMENT – 3.2 per cent (2004 est.)

IMPORTS – US$4,470 million (2003)

EXPORTS – US$920 million (2003)

Trade with UK	2003	2004
Imports from UK	£315,909,000	£111,541,000
Exports to UK	255,707,000	84,928,000

TRANSPORT

There are no railways. The road network (11,593 km in the Greek part of the island and 2,350 km in the Turkish part) serves the main population centres, although crossings between the Greek and Turkish parts of the island are closed or controlled. In the Greek area, the main airports are at Larnaca and Paphos, and the principal ports are Limassol, Larnaca and Paphos. In the Turkish area, the main ports are Famagusta and Kyrenia; there is an airport but flight connections are only with Turkey.

CULTURE

European and Middle Eastern cultures have been converging in Cyprus for over 9,000 years. Cyprus is a country of ancient castles (built during the crusades), Greek temples, monasteries (still inhabited by the Greek Orthodox monks of the south) and elaborate mosaics (left by the Romans). Osman Turkay (1927–2001), a Turkish Cypriot poet, was nominated for the Nobel Prize for Literature in 1988.

TURKISH REPUBLIC OF NORTHERN CYPRUS

In 1974, mainland Greek officers in the Cypriot National Guard, under instructions from the military junta in Athens, launched a coup and installed a former EOKA member, Nikos Sampson, as president. Turkey, fearing the coup was a precursor to the union of Cyprus with Greece, invaded northern Cyprus and occupied over a third of the island. In 1975 a 'Turkish Federated State of Cyprus' under Rauf Denktaş was declared in this area and in 1983 a 'Declaration of Statehood' was issued which purported to establish the 'Turkish Republic of Northern Cyprus'. The declaration was condemned by the UN Security Council and only Turkey has recognised the new 'state'. In 1985, Denktaş was elected president and a general election was held. Denktaş was re-elected in 1990, 1995 and 2000, retiring at the 2005 election. A UN plan for the re-unification of the island was approved by the Turkish Cypriot population in a referendum in 2004, but the plan's rejection by the Greek Cypriots has left the status of northern Cyprus unchanged. Recent confidence-building measures instituted by both governments have improved relations between the two communities.

The coalition government collapsed in late 2004. The legislative election in February 2005 was won by the party of the incumbent prime minister, Mehmet Ali Talat, and his allies. Talat won the presidential election in April 2005.

DE FACTO HEAD OF STATE
President, Mehmet Ali Talat, *sworn in* 24 April 2005
Prime Minister, Ferdi Sabit Soyer

CZECH REPUBLIC

Ceská Republika – Czech Republic

AREA – 77,300 sq. km. Neighbours: Poland (north-east), Germany (west and north-west), Austria (south), Slovakia (east)

POPULATION – 10,246,178 (2004 est.), 10,302,000 (1991 census): 95 per cent Czech, 3 per cent Slovak. Czech is the official language. The majority of the population is Roman Catholic, with a small Protestant minority

CAPITAL – Prague (Praha) on the Vltava (Moldau) (population, 1,178,576, 2001)

MAJOR CITIES – Brno (Brünn); Ostrava; Plzen (Pilsen)

CURRENCY – Koruna (Kcs) of 100 halérů

NATIONAL ANTHEM – Kde domov můj [Where is my motherland]

NATIONAL DAY – 28 October

NATIONAL FLAG – White over red horizontally with a blue triangle extending from the hoist to the centre of the flag

LIFE EXPECTANCY (years) – 75.78 (2004 est.)

MORTALITY RATE (per 1,000 population) – 10.54 (2004 est.)

INFANT MORTALITY (per 1,000 births) – 3.97 (2004 est.)

HIV / AIDS ADULT PREVALENCE – 0.1 per cent (2001 est.)

DEATH PENALTY – No (abolished 1990)

POPULATION GROWTH RATE – –0.05 per cent (2004 est.)

POPULATION DENSITY – 132 per sq. km (2002)

URBAN POPULATION – 75 per cent (2001)

CLIMATE AND TERRAIN

The landlocked republic is composed of Bohemia (the west and centre) and Moravia (the east). Bohemia is a fertile plain surrounded by mountain ranges, while Moravian land stretches to the Danubian basin. Roughly a third of the country is covered by forest. Elevation extremes range from 1,602 m (Snezka) at the highest point to 115 m (Elbe River) at the lowest. The climate is continental, with warm, humid summers and cold, dry winters. The average temperature in Prague ranges from 2°C in January to 19°C in July.

HISTORY AND POLITICS

The area came under the rule of the Habsburg dynasty in 1526 and remained part of the Austro-Hungarian Empire until 1918. The rise of Czech nationalism in the late 19th century led to Czechoslovakia's independence on 28 October 1918 following an amalgamation of Bohemia, Moravia, Slovakia and Ruthenia and was confirmed by the Versailles Peace Conference in 1919.

Czechoslovakia was forced to cede the ethnic German Sudetenland to Nazi Germany in 1938 after the Munich Agreement. German forces invaded the Czech Republic in 1939 and incorporated it into Germany while Slovakia became a puppet state. The Czech Republic was liberated by Soviet and American forces in 1945. The pre-war democratic Czechoslovak state was re-established in 1945, having ceded Ruthenia to the Soviet Union. The Communists took power in a coup in 1948 and remained in power until 1989.

In 1968 the Communist Party under Alexander Dubcek embarked on a political and economic reform programme (known as the Prague Spring). The reforms were suppressed following an invasion by Warsaw Pact troops on the night of 20 August 1968, and were abandoned when Gustav Husak became leader of the Communist Party in 1969.

Mass protests in November 1989 led to the resignation of the Communist Party Central Committee. The Party was forced to concede its monopoly of power and on 10 December a new government was appointed in which only half the ministers were Communists. Husak resigned as president and was replaced by the dissident writer Vaclav Havel. Free elections were held in June 1990 in which the Communist Party was defeated.

In late 1992 the leaders of the Czech and Slovak republics agreed to dissolve the federation and form two sovereign states, this took effect on 1 January 1993.

The general election of June 2002 produced no outright winner. Vladimir Spidla, leader of the Czech Social Democratic Party (CSSD) formed a coalition government on 15 July. The CSSD lost its majority in the Senate following elections held in October and November 2002. President Havel left office in February 2003 but parliament failed to elect a successor and Prime Minister Vladimir Spidla became acting president. On 28 February, Vaclav Klaus of the Civic Democrat Party (ODS) was elected president and took office in March.

The Czech Republic became a full member of the EU on 1 May 2004. Elections to the Senate in November 2004 saw the ODS win 18 of the contested seats.

POLITICAL SYSTEM
The 1992 constitution provided for the separation of the Czech Republic and Slovakia. The president is elected by parliament for a five-year term. The bicameral parliament comprises a 200-member Chamber of Deputies directly elected for a four-year term, and an 81-member Senate directly elected for a six-year term, one-third being renewed every two years. Executive power is held by the prime minister and Council of Ministers. The Council of Ministers is appointed by the president on the recommendation of the prime minister. The prime minister is appointed by the president. Federal laws remain in place unless superseded by Czech ones. A Constitutional Court has been established comprising 15 judges nominated by the president for ten-year terms with Senate approval.

HEAD OF STATE
President, Vaclav Klaus, elected by parliament 28 February 2003, sworn in 7 March 2003

SELECTED GOVERNMENT MEMBERS as at July 2005
Prime Minister, Jiri Paroubek
Minister of Vice-Premiers, Finance, Bohuslav Sabotka
Vice-Premier, Labour and Social Affairs, Zdenek Skromach
Vice-Premier, Economic Affairs, Martin Jahn
Vice-Premier, Justice, Pavel Nemec
Defence, Karel Kuhnl
Interior, Frantisek Bublan

EMBASSY OF THE CZECH REPUBLIC
26 Kensington Palace Gardens, London W8 4QY
T 020-7243 1115
Ambassador Extraordinary and Plenipotentiary, HE Ctefan Füle, apptd 2003

BRITISH EMBASSY
Thunovská 14, CZ-118 00 Prague 1 T (+ 420) 25740 2111
E info@britain.cz
Ambassador Extraordinary and Plenipotentiary, HE Linda Duffield, apptd 2004

BRITISH COUNCIL
Bredovsky dvur, Politickych veznu 13ý 110 00 Prague 1
T (+420) 221 991 111 E info.praha@britishcouncil.cz
Director, Mandy Johnson

DEFENCE
The Army has 541 main battle tanks, 879 armoured infantry fighting vehicles and 355 armoured personnel carriers. The Air Force has 54 combat aircraft and 34 attack helicopters. The Czech Republic became a member of NATO on 12 March 1999.
MILITARY EXPENDITURE – 2.2 per cent of GDP (2003)
MILITARY PERSONNEL – 43,300: Army 36,600, Air Force 6,700; Paramilitaries 5,600

ECONOMY AND TRADE
Under Communist rule industry and most agricultural land was state-owned. Economic reforms began in 1990 to produce a free-market economy. This has necessitated a restrictive monetary policy to stem inflation and a restructuring of industry to make it more competitive, and these were major reasons for the break with Slovakia. As a result, foreign investment (about US$8,500 million in 2002) and private enterprises have grown, over 90 per cent of the economy has been privatised, and reliance on trade with the former Soviet bloc countries has ended.

A customs union between the Czech and Slovak Republics is in place but separate currencies were introduced in 1993 following speculation. The koruna was made fully convertible in 1995. Services account for 55.2 per cent of GDP, industry for 41 per cent and agriculture for 3.8 per cent. The principal agricultural products are sugar beet, potatoes and cereal crops; the timber industry is also very important. Having been the major industrial area of the Austro-Hungarian empire, the country has long been industrialised, and machinery, industrial consumer goods and raw materials are major exports. The country's principal trading partner is Germany, which accounts for 40.2 per cent of exports and 39.1 per cent of imports.
GNI – US$56,000 million (2002); US$5,480 per capita (2002)
ANNUAL AVERAGE GROWTH OF GDP – 3.7 per cent (2004 est.)
INFLATION RATE – 4.1 per cent (2001)
UNEMPLOYMENT – 10.6 per cent (2004 est.)
TOTAL EXTERNAL DEBT – US$21,299 million (2000)
FOREIGN DIRECT INVESTMENT – US$13,516 million (1997–2000)
IMPORTS – US$43,000 million (2002)
EXPORTS – US$49,000 million (2002)

BALANCE OF PAYMENTS
Trade – US$2,240 million deficit (2002)
Current Account – US$4,485 million deficit (2002)

Trade with UK	2003	2004
Imports from UK	£999,393,000	£356,109,000
Exports to UK	1,434,385,000	559,551,000

TRANSPORT

There are extensive road (127,204 km) and rail (9,520 km) networks linking the main population centres. Navigable inland waterways include 664 km on the Elbe, Vltava and Oder Rivers. The principal airport is at Prague.

EDUCATION

Education is free of charge and compulsory for all children from the age of six to 15. Primary education lasts for nine years, divided into two stages of five and four years respectively. Secondary education comprises three main types of school: general schools, technical schools and vocational schools. There are nine universities of which the oldest and most famous is Charles University in Prague (founded 1348).

GROSS ENROLMENT RATIO (percentage of relevant age group) – primary 104 per cent (2002); secondary 95 per cent (2002); tertiary 30 per cent (2002)

MEDIA AND CULTURE

The public broadcaster is Ceska Televize (CT) and it runs two channels. There are several private television stations. Czech public radio, Cesky Rozhlas (CRo), operates three national networks and local services alongside over 70 private radio stations throughout the country.

Prague is famous for its Art Nouveau architecture, cobbled streets and squares and a thriving cultural life (particularly its contemporary jazz scene). Some of the most famous Czech composers are Antonin Dvorak (1841–1904), Bedrich Smetana (1824–84) and Leos Janacek (1854–1928). Important writers include Franz Kafka (1883–1924), Milan Kundera (b. 1929), Ivan Klima (b. 1931) and Vaclav Havel (b. 1936).

DENMARK

Kongeriget Danmark / Kingdom of Denmark

AREA – 43,000 sq. km. Neighbour: Germany (south)
POPULATION – 5,413,392 (2004). The majority of the population is Lutheran. The language is Danish
CAPITAL – ΨCopenhagen (population, 1,081,673, 2001)
MAJOR CITIES – ΨÅlborg; ΨÅrhus; ΨOdense
CURRENCY – Danish krone of 100 øre
NATIONAL ANTHEMS – Kong Kristian stod ved højen mast [King Christian stood by the lofty mast]; Det er et yndigt land [There is a lovely land]
NATIONAL DAY – 5 June (Constitution Day)
NATIONAL FLAG – Red, with white cross
LIFE EXPECTANCY (years) – 77.44 (2004 est.)
MORTALITY RATE (per 1,000 population) – 10.53 (2004 est.)
INFANT MORTALITY (per 1,000 births) – 4.63 (2004 est.)
HIV / AIDS ADULT PREVALENCE – 0.2 per cent (2001)
DEATH PENALTY – No (abolished 1978)
POPULATION GROWTH RATE – 0.35 per cent (2004 est.)
POPULATION DENSITY – 127 per sq. km (2002)

CLIMATE AND TERRAIN

Denmark consists of most of the Jutland peninsula and 406 islands, mostly in the Baltic Sea and part of the northern Frisian Islands in the North Sea. The largest islands are Sjælland (Zealand), Fyn, Lolland, Faister and Bornholm. It is a low-lying country, indented by fjords on its eastern coast and with lagoons and sand dunes along the west coast. Elevation extremes range from 173 m (Yding Skovhoej) at the highest point to −7 m (Lammefjord) at the lowest. There are cold winters and warm summers. Temperatures range from 0.5°C in January to 17°C in July.

HISTORY AND POLITICS

The Danes were at the forefront of Viking expansionism from the eighth century. Denmark was unified in the 10th century and was the centre of the empire, including also Norway and England, created by Cnut (Canute) in the 11th century. The Union of Kalmar (1397) brought Norway and Sweden (including Finland) under Danish rule. Danish power waned during the 16th century, enabling Sweden to re-establish its independence in 1523. In 1814 Norway was ceded to Sweden under the Treaty of Kiel, and in 1864 Schleswig and Holstein, which had been subsumed in 1460, were lost to Germany, although northern Schleswig was returned in 1919 after a plebiscite. Denmark was neutral during the First World War, but in the Second World War it was invaded and occupied by Germany.

Iceland declared its independence from Denmark in 1944 and the Faeroe Islands were granted home rule in 1948. Greenland, which had had the status of a colony, was integrated into Denmark in 1953 and granted home rule in 1979.

Social Democrat-led coalitions dominated the post-war era, creating a welfare state. They lost the 1982 election and a right-wing government was installed, but were in power again from 1993 to 2001.

Denmark joined the European Community in 1973. In a referendum in 2000, it rejected membership of the European single currency. A referendum on the EU constitution is scheduled for 27 September 2005. In the 2001 legislative election, the Liberal Party (Venstre – V) became the largest party in parliament, and formed a coalition government with the Conservative People's Party (KF). This coalition government retained power in the February 2005 general election, winning 94 of the 179 seats.

POLITICAL SYSTEM

The country is a constitutional monarchy, with the hereditary monarch as head of state. The head of government is the prime minister, who appoints the cabinet. The unicameral legislature, the *Folketing*, has 179 members, including two for the Faeroes and two for Greenland, who are elected for a four-year term. The voting age is 18 with an electoral system based on proportional representation and a 2 per cent threshold for parliamentary representation.

HEAD OF STATE
HM The Queen of Denmark, Queen Margrethe II, KG, *born* 16 April 1940, *acceded* 14 January 1972
Heir, HRH Crown Prince Frederik, *born* 26 May 1968

SELECTED GOVERNMENT MEMBERS *as at July 2005*
Prime Minister, Anders Fogh Rasmussen
Defence, Søren Gade Jensen
Finance, Thor Pedersen
Foreign Affairs, Per Stig Moeller
Interior and Health, Lars Loekke Rasmussen

ROYAL DANISH EMBASSY
55 Sloane Street, London SW1X 9SR T 020-7333 0200
Ambassador Extraordinary and Plenipotentiary, HE Tom Risdahl Jensen, apptd 2001

BRITISH EMBASSY
36–40 Kastelsvej, DK-2100 Copenhagen Ø
T (+45) 3544 5200 E info@britishembassy.dk
Ambassador Extraordinary and Plenipotentiary, HE Sir
  Nicholas Browne, apptd 2003

BRITISH COUNCIL
Gammel Mont 12.3, DK-1117 Copenhagen K
T (+45) (33) 369 400 E british.council@britishcouncil.dk
Director, Dr Michael Sorensen-Jones

DEFENCE

The Army has 231 main battle tanks, 310 armoured
personnel carriers and 12 attack helicopters. The Navy
has four submarines, three offshore patrol frigates and 27
patrol and coastal vessels at three bases. The Air Force has
60 combat aircraft.
MILITARY EXPENDITURE – 1.6 per cent of GDP (2003)
MILITARY PERSONNEL – 20,500: Army 12,500, Navy
  3,800, Air Force 4,200
CONSCRIPTION DURATION – Four months

ECONOMY AND TRADE

The largest sectors of employment are professional
services and administration (71 per cent of GDP);
manufacturing (26 per cent of GDP) and agriculture (3
per cent of GDP). The chief agricultural products are fish,
pigs, dairy products, poultry and eggs, seeds and cereals.
Denmark is self-sufficient in oil and natural gas and in
2000 became a net energy exporter through exports of
natural gas to Sweden.

The principal imports are industrial raw materials,
consumer goods, construction inputs, machinery, raw
materials, vehicles and textile products. The chief exports
are manufactured articles, windmills, chemicals, fish, ships
and agricultural and dairy products. Germany and Sweden
are Denmark's main trading partners.
GNI – US$162,600 million (2002); US$30,260 per
  capita (2002)
ANNUAL AVERAGE GROWTH OF GDP – 2.1 per cent
  (2004 est.)
INFLATION RATE – 2.4 per cent (2001)
UNEMPLOYMENT – 6.2 per cent (2004 est.)
DIRECT FOREIGN INVESTMENT – US$51,839 million
  (1997–2000)
IMPORTS – US$56,400 million (2003)
EXPORTS – US$65,700 million (2003)

BALANCE OF PAYMENTS
Trade – US$10,142 million surplus (2003)
Current Account – US$6,139 million surplus (2003)

Trade with UK	2003	2004
Imports from UK	£1,641,042,000	£1,992,204,000
Exports to UK	2,113,971,000	3,005,976,000

TRANSPORT INFRASTRUCTURE

In 2002, the Danish mercantile fleet numbered 282 ships
of more than 100 gross tonnage. The main ports are
Århus, Odense, Ålborg and Esbjerg. The principal airports
are at Copenhagen, Århus, Ålborg and near Vejle. There
are 3,164 km of railway, of which 595 km are electrified.
An additional network of 526 km is operated by private
companies. A rail tunnel and a bridge linking the islands
of Sjaelland (Zealand) and Fyn were opened in 1997, and
a road and rail tunnel and a bridge across the Öresund,

linking Copenhagen with Malmö (Sweden), were opened
in 2000. There are 71,591 km of roads, including 880
km of motorways.

EDUCATION

Education is free of charge and compulsory. Specialist
schools are numerous, with commercial, technical and
agricultural predominating. There are universities at
Copenhagen (founded in 1479), Århus (1928), Odense
(1966), Roskilde (1972) and Ålborg (1974).
GROSS ENROLMENT RATIO (percentage of relevant age
  group) – primary 102 per cent (2002); secondary 128
  per cent (2002); tertiary 59 per cent (2002)

MEDIA

The public broadcaster is Danmarks Radio (DR). DR
operates two television networks and national and
regional radio stations. Private television stations can be
obtained via satellite and cable. There are some 250 local
commercial and community radio stations in operation.
Some 38 newspapers are published in Denmark; eight
daily papers are published in Copenhagen.

CULTURE

Despite being a small country Denmark has made
significant contributions to the world of science. Nobel
laureates include atomic physicist Niels Bohr (1885–
1962) and medical researcher Niels Finsen (1860–1904).
Notable contributions have been made in music: Carl
Nielsen (1865–1931); design: Arne Jacobsen (1902–71),
Georg Jensen (1866–1935); and literature: Hans
Christian Andersen (1805–75), Karen Blixen (1885–
1962) and Peter Hoeg (b. 1957).

THE FAEROE ISLANDS

AREA – 1,399 sq. km
POPULATION – 47,000 (2001)
CAPITAL – Torshavn (population, 16,511, 2001)

The Faeroe (Sheep) Islands are a group of 22 islands (18
inhabited) in the North Atlantic Ocean, between the
Shetland Islands and Iceland. First settled in the ninth
century, the islands were a Norwegian province before
coming under Danish rule in the 18th century. Since
1948 the Faeroes have been self-governing. The islands
are not part of the EU.

The government *(Landsstryrid)* of three to six members
deals with internal Faeroes affairs. The parliament
(Løgting) has 27–32 members, elected for a four-year
term. The islands send two representatives to the *Folketing*
at Copenhagen. After the 2004 election to the *Løgting*,
the Social Democrats, Union Party and People's Party
formed a coalition government.
Prime Minister, Joannes Eidesgaard (Social Democrat)

Trade with UK	2001	2002
Imports from UK	£27,935,000	£6,715,000
Exports to UK	108,873,000	100,816,000

GREENLAND (KALAALLIT NUNAAT)

AREA – 2,175,600 sq. km
POPULATION – 56,676 (2003)
CAPITAL – Godthåb (Nuuk) (population 14,265 (2003))

Greenland, the world's largest island, lies between the
Atlantic and Arctic oceans, to the east of Canada and to
the west of Iceland. Most of Greenland is within the
Arctic Circle, with a permafrost covering almost 85 per

cent of the island. Elevation extremes range from 3,700 m (Gunnbjorn) at the highest point to 0 m (Atlantic Ocean) at the lowest. Natural resources include zinc, lead, iron ore, coal, molybdenum, gold, platinum and uranium. 90 per cent of all exports are derived from fish products.

Greenland was first discovered by small groups of hunters and nomadic groups who travelled from Canada c.500 BC. In the late 10th century Viking settlers began establishing settlements along the south-eastern coast and started subsistence farming and trading with northern Europe. These colonies came under Norwegian rule in 1261 and died out by the 16th century, though some Inuit settlements continued. Greenland became a Danish colony in the 18th century, and was granted internal autonomy in 1979. Greenland negotiated its withdrawal from the EU, without discontinuing relations with Denmark, and left in 1985. The USA has acquired the right to maintain air bases in Greenland.

The government (Landsstyret) deals with internal Greenland matters. The parliament (Landsting) has 31 members, elected for a four-year term. Greenland sends two representatives to the Folketing at Copenhagen. In the 2002 parliamentary election, the Forward (Siumut) party won ten seats and formed a coalition government with the Feeling of Community (Atassut) party.

Prime Minister, Hans Enoksen (Siumut)

Trade with UK	2003	2004
Imports from UK	£658,000	£1,265,000
Exports to UK	153,000	192,000

DJIBOUTI

Jumhūriyya Jībūtī/République du Djibouti – Republic of Djibouti

AREA – 23,200 sq. km. Neighbours: Eritrea (north), Ethiopia (west and south), Somalia (south-east)
POPULATION – 466,900 (2004 est.), mostly Afar or Issas. The official languages are Arabic and French; Afar and Somali are also spoken
CAPITAL – ΨDjibouti (population, 62,000, 1991)
CURRENCY – Djibouti franc of 100 centimes
NATIONAL ANTHEM – Hinjinne u sara kaca [Arise with strength]
NATIONAL DAY – 27 June (Independence Day)
NATIONAL FLAG – Blue over green with white triangle in the hoist containing a red star
LIFE EXPECTANCY – 43.12 (2004 est.)
MORTALITY RATE (per 1,000 population) – 19.42 (2004 est.)
INFANT MORTALITY (per 1,000 births) – 105.54 (2004 est.)
HIV / AIDS ADULT PREVALENCE – 2.9 per cent (2003 est.)
DEATH PENALTY – No (abolished 1995)
POPULATION BELOW POVERTY LINE – 50 per cent (2001)
POPULATION GROWTH RATE – 2.1 per cent (2004 est.)
POPULATION DENSITY – 27 per sq. km (1999)
MILITARY EXPENDITURE – 3.9 per cent of GDP (2003)
MILITARY PERSONNEL – 9,850: Army 8,000, Navy 200, Air Force 250, Gendarmerie 1,400; Paramilitaries 2,500
GNI – US$553 million (2000); US$880 per capita (2000)
TOTAL EXTERNAL DEBT – US$366 million (2002 est.)

ILLITERACY RATE – (m) 22 per cent; (f) 42.6 per cent (2003 est.)

CLIMATE AND TERRAIN
Djibouti is situated on the east coast of Africa, at the point where the Gulf of Aden and the Red Sea meet. Elevation extremes range from 2,028 m (Moussa Ali) at the highest point to −155 m (Lake Abbé) at the lowest. The country is prone to flash floods as well as cyclones, droughts and earthquakes. The climate is semi-arid with a hot season between May and September.

HISTORY AND POLITICS
Settled by the Afars (Ethiopian) and Issas (Somali) about 2,000 years ago, the area was annexed by the French in 1888 and became French Somaliland; in 1967 it was renamed the French Territory of the Afars and the Issas. The territory became independent as Djibouti on 27 June 1977, under President Hassan Gouled Aptidon (an Issa), the leader of the Rassemblement Populaire pour le Progrès (RPP) party, which became the only legal political party in 1981.

In 1991 Afar discontent with Issa domination of government under one-party rule led to civil war between the government and an alliance of rebel groups, the Front pour la Restauration de L'Unité et de la Democratie (FRUD). A multiparty constitution was introduced and multiparty elections were held in 1992, but fighting continued until power-sharing was agreed in 1994. The civil war ended with the signing of a peace accord in 1996, although a breakaway faction of the FRUD continued its armed opposition to the government until 2001.

In the 1997 election, in the first since the peace accord, the RPP and FRUD formed an alliance and won all 65 seats in the National Assembly. In the 1999 presidential election, Ismael Omar Guelleh, nephew of President Gouled Aptidon, was elected to replace his uncle as president. In the 2003 legislative election, for the first time since independence the number of parties allowed to contest an election was not limited. The Union for Presidential Majority (UMP), an alliance of the RPP, FRUD and two other parties supporting President Guelleh, won all 65 seats in the National Assembly. The presidential election in April 2005 was won by President Guelleh, who was the only candidate.

POLITICAL SYSTEM
Under the 1992 constitution, the president is directly elected for a six-year term. The single-chamber legislature, the National Assembly (Assemblée nationale) has 65 members, directly elected for a five-year term. The president appoints the Council of Ministers.

HEAD OF STATE
President, Ismael Omar Guelleh, elected 9 April 1999, re-elected 8 April 2005

SELECTED GOVERNMENT MEMBERS as at July 2005
Prime Minister, National and Regional Development, Dilleita Mohamed Dilleita
Defence, Ougoure Kifle Ahmed
Interior, Yacin Elmi Bouh
Economy, Finance and Privatisation, Ali Farah Assoweh
Foreign Affairs and International Co-operation, Muhammed Barkat Abdillahi

EMBASSY OF THE REPUBLIC OF DJIBOUTI
26 Rue Emile Ménier, F-75116 Paris, France
T (+33) (1) 4727 4922
Ambassador Extraordinary and Plenipotentiary, HE Richard
Farah, apptd 2004

BRITISH AMBASSADOR
HE Robert Dewar, apptd 2004, resident at Addis Ababa,
Ethiopia

ECONOMY AND TRADE
The economy depends mainly on the operation of the free
port, which accounts for 80 per cent of Djibouti's GDP.
Agriculture accounts for less than 4 per cent of GDP, but
employs three-quarters of the workforce. Industry
accounts for 15 per cent of GDP. The main imports are
foodstuffs, machinery, clothing, oil and oil derivatives.
The main exports are agricultural produce. Djibouti's
primary trading partners are Ethiopia, Somalia, Yemen
and France.

Trade with UK	2003	2004
Imports from UK	£22,152,000	£10,396,000
Exports to UK	797,000	1,866,000

TRANSPORT INFRASTRUCTURE
There is 100 km of railway (the Djibouti section of the
Addis Ababa–Djibouti railway, controlled by both
Djibouti and Ethiopia) and 2,890 km of roads, 364 km of
which are surfaced. Djibouti is the main port, important
both for trade and to the French and US military who are
stationed there. Three of the 13 airports have surfaced
runways, including the principal airport at Djibouti.

MEDIA
The government owns *La Nation*, the main newspaper in
Djibouti, as well as Radiodiffusion-Télévision de Djibouti
(RTD), the company which operates national radio and
television stations. There are a number of privately owned
newspapers including *Al Qarn*, *La République*, and *Le
Renouveau*. Independent newspapers are generally allowed
to circulate freely, but journalists exercise self-censorship.

DOMINICA

Commonwealth of Dominica

AREA – 750 sq. km
POPULATION – 69,278 (2004 est.). English is the official
language although Creole French is more commonly
used
CAPITAL – ΨRoseau (population, 16,243, 1991)
CURRENCY – East Caribbean dollar (EC$) of 100 cents
NATIONAL ANTHEM – Isle of beauty
NATIONAL DAY – 3 November (Independence Day)
NATIONAL FLAG – Green ground with a cross overall of
yellow, black and white stripes, and in the centre a red
disc charged with a Sisserou parrot in natural colours
within a ring of ten green stars
LIFE EXPECTANCY – 74.38 (2004 est.)
MORTALITY RATE (per 1,000 population) – 6.9
(2004 est.)
INFANT MORTALITY (per 1,000 births) – 14.75
(2004 est.)
DEATH PENALTY – Yes
POPULATION BELOW POVERTY LINE – 30 per cent
(2002 est.)

POPULATION DENSITY – 95 per sq. km (2001)
ILLITERACY RATE – (m) 6 per cent; (f) 6 per cent
(2003 est.)

CLIMATE AND TERRAIN
Dominica, in the Lesser Antilles, lies in the Windward
Islands group 95 miles south of Antigua. It is about 46
km long and 25 km wide, with a mountainous central
ridge. Elevation extremes range from 1,447 m (Morne
Diablotin) at the highest point to 0 m (Caribbean Sea) at
the lowest. The climate is tropical with average daily
temperatures ranging from 25°C to 32°C. The island is
located within a hurricane zone.

HISTORY AND POLITICS
Dominica was discovered by Columbus in 1493, when it
was a stronghold of the Caribs, the sole inhabitants of the
island until the French introduced settlements in the 18th
century. It was captured by the British in 1759 but passed
back and forth between France and Britain until 1805,
after which British possession was unchallenged. From
1871 to 1939 Dominica was part of the Leeward Islands
federation, then from 1940 part of the Windward Islands
federation, and from 1958 part of the West Indies
Federation. Internal self-government from 1967 was
followed on 3 November 1978 by independence as a
republic. In 1980 Eugenia Charles became prime minister,
the first woman prime minister in the Caribbean, at the
head of a Dominica Freedom Party (DFP) government,
and held office until 1995, when the United Workers'
Party (UWP) won the legislative election. The UWP lost
the 2000 election to the Dominica Labour Party (DLP),
which formed a coalition government with the DFP. The
DLP remained the largest party after the May 2005
election and continued in government in coalition with
the DFP.

POLITICAL SYSTEM
Under the 1978 constitution, executive authority is vested
in the president, who is elected by the House of Assembly
for a five-year term, which may not be renewed more than
once. The unicameral legislature, the House of Assembly,
has 21 members, directly elected for a five-year term, and
nine senators, five of appointed on the advice of the prime
minister and the other four on the advice of the leader of
the opposition, who sit for a five-year term.

HEAD OF STATE
President, Dr Nicholas Liverpool, *elected* 2 October 2003,
took office 6 October 2003

SELECTED GOVERNMENT MEMBERS *as at July 2005*
Prime Minister, Finance and Planning, Caribbean Affairs,
Roosevelt Skerrit
Foreign Affairs, Trade and Marketing, Charles Savarin

HIGH COMMISSION FOR THE COMMONWEALTH OF
DOMINICA
1 Collingham Gardens, London SW5 0HW
T 020-7370 5194/5
High Commissioner, Agnes Adonis

BRITISH HIGH COMMISSIONER
HE C. John White, resident at Bridgetown, Barbados

BRITISH CONSULATE
PO Box 2269, Roseau T (+1) (767) 448 7655
Honorary Consul, Simon Maynard

ECONOMY AND TRADE

In 2004 Dominica cut diplomatic relations with Taiwan after the Chinese government offered a $100 million aid package, equivalent to approximately $1500 per capita. Agriculture is the principal occupation, with tropical and citrus fruits the main crops. Products for export are bananas, fruit juices, lime oil, bay oil, copra and rum. However, Dominica is attempting to reduce its reliance on banana exports since the European Union phased out preferential treatment for producers from former colonies. Forestry, fisheries and agro-processing are being encouraged. The only commercially exploitable mineral is pumice, used chiefly for building purposes. Manufacturing consists largely of the processing of agricultural products although there have been attempts to diversify into light industry.

GNI – US$230 million (2001); US$3,200 per capita (2001)
ANNUAL AVERAGE GROWTH OF GDP – –1 per cent (2004 est.)
INFLATION RATE – 0.8 per cent (2000)
TOTAL EXTERNAL DEBT – US$108 million (2000)
IMPORTS – US$100 million (2003)
EXPORTS – US$100 million (2000)

BALANCE OF PAYMENTS
Trade – US$71 million deficit (2002)
Current Account – US$49 million deficit (2002)

Trade with UK	2003	2004
Imports from UK	£6,293,000	£7,982,000
Exports to UK	8,850,000	9,642,000

MEDIA AND CULTURE

While there is no national television service, a private cable network covers part of the island. There are no daily newspapers but there are weekly publications. Private and public radio stations are in operation throughout the country.

While the island has taken its political structure and love of football and cricket from the British, African, West Indian and French influences have combined to produce an unmistakable Creole culture with food, the local patois, customs and art all reflecting these multiple origins. The island's most famous writer is Jean Rhys (1890–1979), author of *Wide Sargasso Sea*.

DOMINICAN REPUBLIC

República Dominicana – Dominican Republic

AREA – 48,400 sq. km. Neighbour: Haiti (west)
POPULATION – 8,833,634 (2004 est.). The language is Spanish
CAPITAL – ΨSanto Domingo (population, 2,134,779, 1993)
MAJOR CITIES – Duarte; La Vega; Puerto Plata; San Cristóbal; San Juan; Santiago de los Caballeros
CURRENCY – Dominican Republic peso (RD$) of 100 centavos
NATIONAL FLAG – Divided into blue and red quarters by a white cross
NATIONAL ANTHEM – Quisqueyanos valientes, alcemos (Brave men of Quisqueya, let's raise our song)
NATIONAL DAY – 27 February (Independence Day 1844)
LIFE EXPECTANCY (years) – 67.63 (2004 est.)

MORTALITY RATE (per 1,000 population) – 7.1 (2004 est.)
INFANT MORTALITY (per 1,000 births) – 33.28 (2004 est.)
HIV / AIDS ADULT PREVALENCE – 1.7 per cent (2003 est.)
DEATH PENALTY – No (abolished 1966)
POPULATION BELOW POVERTY LINE – 25 per cent (2002)
POPULATION GROWTH RATE – 1.33 per cent (2004 est.)
POPULATION DENSITY – 178 per sq. km (2002)
URBAN POPULATION – 66 per cent (2001)
MILITARY EXPENDITURE – 1 per cent of GDP (2003)
MILITARY PERSONNEL – 24,500: Army 15,000, Navy 4,000, Air Force 5,500; Paramilitaries 15,000
ILLITERACY RATE – (m) 15.4 per cent; (f) 15.2 per cent (2003 est.)
GROSS ENROLMENT RATIO (percentage of relevant age group) – primary 126 per cent (2002); secondary 67 per cent (2002)

CLIMATE AND TERRAIN

The republic forms the eastern two-thirds of the island of Hispaniola (the remainder is Haiti) and is crossed from the north-west to the south-east by the Cordillera Central mountain range. Many of the mountains are over 3,000 m. Elevation extremes range from 3,175 m (Pico Duarte) at the highest point to −46 m (Lake Enriquillo) at the lowest. The climate is maritime tropical with average temperatures of between 23°C and 27°C.

HISTORY AND POLITICS

The island was discovered by Columbus in 1492, and became a Spanish colony. The eastern province of Santo Domingo remained Spanish after the partition of Hispaniola in 1697, but was ceded to France in 1795. It was restored to Spanish rule in 1809. Independence was declared in 1821, but in 1822 it was subjugated by the neighbouring Haitians who remained in control until 1844, when the Dominican Republic was proclaimed. Under Spanish occupation in 1861–5, a long dictatorship at the end of the 19th century was followed by revolution and bankruptcy, which led to occupation by US forces from 1916 until 1924. A military coup in 1930 established the dictatorship of Gen. Rafael Trujillo, who ruled until his assassination in 1961. After a period of political instability, a new constitution was adopted in 1966 and the Christian Social Reform Party (PRSC) came to power, with its candidate, Joaquin Balaguer, as president. In the 2002 legislative election the Dominican Revolutionary Party (PRD) retained its majority in both chambers of Congress, winning 73 seats in the Chamber of Deputies and 29 seats in the Senate. The 2004 presidential election was won by former president Leonel Fernandez of the Dominican Liberation Party (PLD), with 57.1 per cent of the vote.

POLITICAL SYSTEM

Under the 1966 constitution, executive power is vested in the president, who is directly elected for a four-year term, renewable once only, and appoints the cabinet. Legislative power is exercised by the bicameral Congress, both houses of which are directly elected for a four-year term. The lower chamber, the Chamber of Deputies, has 150 members, and the upper chamber, the Senate, has 30 members, one for each province and one for Santo Domingo.

HEAD OF STATE
President, Leonel Fernandez, *elected* May 2004, *sworn in* August 2004
Vice-President, Rafael Alberquerque

SELECTED GOVERNMENT MEMBERS *as at July 2005*
Foreign Affairs, Carlos Morales Troncoso
Defence, Sigfrido Pared Pérez
Finance, Vincente Bengoa
Interior and Police, Franklin Almeyda

EMBASSY OF THE DOMINICAN REPUBLIC
139 Inverness Terrace, London, W2 6JF T 020-7727 6285
Ambassador Extraordinary and Plenipotentiary, HE Anibal de Castro, apptd 2004

BRITISH EMBASSY
Edificio Corominas Pepín, Ave 27 de Febrero No 233, Santo Domingo T (+1 809) 472 7111
E brit.emb.sadom@codetel.net.do
Ambassador Extraordinary and Plenipotentiary, HE Andrew Ashcroft, apptd 2002

ECONOMY AND TRADE
Tourism is central to the economy with three million foreign visitors to the Dominican Republic in 2000 generating US$2,900 million. Services account for 55 per cent of GDP. Agriculture accounts for 11 per cent of GDP. The main crops are sugar, cocoa, coffee, bananas, rice and tobacco. Other products are maize, molasses, beans, tomatoes, cement, ferro-nickel, gold, silver and cattle. Light industry producing beer, tinned foodstuffs, glass products, textiles, soap, cigarettes, construction materials, plastic articles, paint, rum, matches and peanut oil accounts for 34 per cent of GDP.

The chief imports are fuel oils, foodstuffs, motor vehicles, pharmaceuticals and machinery components. The chief exports are minerals, sugar and sugar by-products, coffee and cocoa. The USA is the main trading partner with 85 per cent of exports going to the US market.

Remittances from Dominicans living in the USA are estimated to be worth US$1,500 million a year. Floods in June 2004 caused widespread damage to over 7,000 hectares of cultivated land.
GNI – US$19,000 million (2001); US$2,230 per capita (2001)
ANNUAL AVERAGE GROWTH OF GDP – 1.7 per cent (2004 est.)
TOTAL EXTERNAL DEBT – US$4,598 million (2000)
FOREIGN DIRECT INVESTMENT – US$3,387 (1997–2000)
IMPORTS – US$7,400 million (2000)
EXPORTS – US$1,040 million (2003)

BALANCE OF PAYMENTS
Trade – US$2,444 million deficit (2003)
Current Account – US$867 million deficit (2003)

Trade with UK	2003	2004
Imports from UK	£40,429,000	£30,679,000
Exports to UK	48,876,000	42,295,000

TRANSPORT INFRASTRUCTURE
There are over 12,600 km of roads, 6,224 km of which are surfaced, and a direct road from Santo Domingo to Port-au-Prince, the capital of Haiti, but that part of it in the border area has fallen into disuse. The frontier has been closed since 1967, except for a section that links the two capitals. The construction of a railway between the port of Haina and Santiago was expected to be completed by mid-2005. There are 30 airports, 13 of which have surfaced runways. The principle airport is at Santo Domingo.

MEDIA AND CULTURE
There are several terrestrial commercial broadcasting stations and 30 multi-channel cable TV operators. The government-owned channel is Radio Television Dominicana (Canal 4). There are more than 200 commercial radio stations as well as two government stations.

Rafael Trujillo founded the Escuela Nacional de Bellas Artes in 1942, instituting the country's fine painting tradition. Architecture is another important element of Dominican culture, from the well-preserved colonial Spanish buildings of Santo Domingo, to the brightly coloured farmhouses of the countryside. *Plena*, African-derived work songs, have fused with *decima*, a ten-line 17th-century Spanish verse form of song, to create a sophisticated Dominican tradition. The dance most associated with this fusion is called *merengue*. The poet and novelist Julia Álvarez (b. 1951) was raised in the Dominican Republic and her work often recalls life under the Trujillo dictatorship.

EAST TIMOR

República Democrática de Timor-Leste/Republik Demokratis Timor Leste/Repúblika Demokrátika Timór-Leste – Democratic Republic of East Timor (Timor-Lorosae)

AREA – 14,874 sq. km. Neighbour: Indonesia (west). The enclave of Oekussi is separated from the rest of East Timor by the Indonesian province of West Timor
POPULATION – 952,618 (2002 estimate): 78 per cent Timorese, 20 per cent Indonesian, 2 per cent Chinese. Tetum is the national language and is spoken by about 60 per cent of the population, although Mambai, Tokodede, Kemak, Galoli, Idate, Waima'a, Naueti, Bunak, Makasae and Fataluku are also spoken. Portuguese and Bahasa Indonesian are widely understood. The population is predominantly Roman Catholic
CAPITAL – ΨDili (population, 56,000, 2001 estimate)
MAJOR CITY – Lautem
CURRENCY – Currency is that of the USA
NATIONAL ANTHEM – Pátria, Pátria (Fatherland, Fatherland)
NATIONAL FLAG – Red with a yellow triangle based on the hoist and surmounted by a black triangle containing a white star
LIFE EXPECTANCY – 65.56 (2004 est.)
MORTALITY RATE (per 1,000 population) – 6.36 (2004 est.)
DEATH PENALTY – No (abolished 1999)
POPULATION BELOW POVERTY LINE – 42 per cent (2002)
POPULATION GROWTH RATE – 2.11 per cent (2004 est.)
POPULATION DENSITY – 59 per sq. km (1999)

CLIMATE AND TERRAIN
The republic comprises the eastern half of the island of Timor, plus the enclave of Oekussi on the northern coast.

The island, about 296 km long and 72 km wide, lies at the eastern end of the Indonesian archipelago. The interior is covered in forests and mountains. Elevation extremes range from 2,963 m (Mt Tatamailau) at the highest point to 0 m (Timor Sea) at the lowest. The climate is tropical.

HISTORY AND POLITICS

East Timor was a Portuguese colony from 1702 until 1975, when Portuguese rule was withdrawn following the 1974 coup in Portugal, but without a formal handover of power. The Revolutionary Front for an Independent East Timor (FRETLIN), which supported independence, emerged as the strongest party in the 1975 election, but oppositon by supporters of the integration of the territory into Indonesia led to civil war. Despite FRETLIN's success in suppressing opposition, Indonesia used the civil war as an excuse to invade in December 1975 and declared East Timor Indonesia's 27th province in July 1976. By 1979 most of East Timor was under Indonesia's control, although FRETLIN continued to engage in guerrilla warfare until the 1990s. The UN never recognised the annexation.

Following the fall of the Suharto regime in Indonesia, a plebiscite was held in August 1999 offering East Timor autonomy within Indonesia; in a turnout of 98.5 per cent, 78.5 per cent voted against autonomy within Indonesia; the Indonesian Consultative Assembly unanimously ratified the result in October. This result provoked violence and intimidation by pro-Indonesian militias and Indonesian troops, and Indonesia agreed to the deployment in September 1999 of UN peacekeeping troops. By early October, the UN's International Force for East Timor (INTERFET) had installed its forces on the border with West Timor, to prevent cross-border attacks by pro-Indonesia militias, and landed troops in the East Timorese enclave of Oekussi.

The UN Security Council set up a UN Transitional Administration in East Timor (UNTAET). The East Timor National Council (ETNC), which was established to make policy recommendations to UNTAET, held its first meeting in December. In the legislative election in August 2001 FRETLIN, with 55 seats, was the largest party but did not hold an overall majority. The presidential election in April 2002 was won by the former FRETLIN leader José Xanana Gusmão, who stood as an independent. East Timor became independent on 20 May 2002. UNTAET was succeeded by the UN Mission of Support in East Timor (UNMISET).

In 2000 two reports concluded that the Indonesian authorities and pro-Indonesian militias had co-operated in human rights abuses in East Timor. A UN-supported war crimes tribunal in East Timor has convicted over 700 suspects in the 1999 violence, but the tribunal is unable to extradite from Indonesia hundreds of other suspects. From 2002 to 2004, Indonesia tried 18 people over human rights abuses in 1999 but secured only one conviction.

Serious civil unrest, including the looting and burning of shops, offices and the prime minister's home in late 2002 and early 2003, led the UN Security Council to strengthen the 651-member police component of UNMISET in 2003; UNMISET's main force withdrew from peacekeeping duties in 2005, but a small police unit remained.

POLITICAL SYSTEM

The 2002 constitution established a parliamentary democracy. The president is directly elected for a five-year term, renewable only once. The legislature is the National Parliament, which took over from the Constituent Assembly in January 2002. It has 88 members, one from each of the 13 districts elected by a first-past-the-post system and 75 nationally elected by proportional representation; members serve a five-year term. The Council of Ministers is nominated by the prime minister; the post-independence government is a coalition of FRETLIN and Democratic Party members and independents.

HEAD OF STATE
President, José Xanana Gusmão, *elected* 14 April 2002,
    took office 20 May 2002

SELECTED GOVERNMENT MEMBERS *as at July 2005*
Prime Minister, Environment and Development, Mari bin
    Hamud Alkatiri
Interior, Rogerio Lobato
Foreign Affairs, José Ramos-Horta
Health, Rui Maria de Aravjo
Planning and Finance, Maria Madalena Brites Boavida

BRITISH EMBASSY
Pantai Kelapa (Avenida de Portugal), PO Box 194, Dili
T (+670) 331 2652 E herminia.freitas@fco.gov.uk
Ambassador Extraordinary and Plenipotentiary, HE Tina
    Redshaw, apptd 2004

ECONOMY AND TRADE

The economy has suffered as a result of the Indonesian withdrawal. One in three households lives below the poverty line (on an average of less than US$0.55 a day). The main commercial crops are timber, coffee, coconuts, cloves and cocoa. There are oil and gas reserves beneath the sea to the south of the island (Timor Sea oil) and the gasfield began production in 2004. Under a deal with Australia signed in 2001, East Timor should receive about 90 per cent of the revenues from exploiting these reserves.

Trade with UK	2003	2004
Imports from UK	£1,880,000	£199,000
Exports to UK	563,000	18,000

TRANSPORT INFRASTRUCTURE

There are no railways, waterways, ports or harbours. There is one major road, which links the main townships along the northern coast to the east of Dili. There are 3,800 km of roads in total, 428 km of which are surfaced. There are eight airports, three of which have surfaced runways, and one heliport.

MEDIA

East Timor's national public radio and television services began broadcasting in May 2002 but television broadcasts do not extend far beyond Dili.

ECUADOR

República del Ecuador – Republic of Ecuador

AREA – 276,800 sq. km. Neighbours: Colombia (north-east), Peru (east and south)
POPULATION – 13,212,742 (2004), descendants of the Spanish, Amerindians and mestizos. Spanish is the principal language but Quechua is also a recognised language and is spoken by most Indians

CAPITAL – Quito (population, 1,399,814, 2001 census)
MAJOR CITIES – Cuenca; ΨGuayaquil, the chief port
CURRENCY – Currency is that of the USA
NATIONAL ANTHEM – Salve, oh patria, mil veces, oh
patria [Hail, oh fatherland, a thousand times, oh
fatherland]
NATIONAL DAY – 10 August (Independence Day)
NATIONAL FLAG – Three horizontal bands, yellow, blue
and red (the yellow band twice the width of the
others); emblem in centre
LIFE EXPECTANCY (years) – 76.01 (2004 est.)
MORTALITY RATE (per 1,000 population) – 4.26
(2003)
INFANT MORTALITY (per 1,000 births) – 24.49
(2004 est.)
HIV / AIDS ADULT PREVALENCE RATE – 0.3 per cent
(2003 est.)
DEATH PENALTY – No (abolished 1906)
POPULATION BELOW POVERTY LINE – 70 per cent
(2001)
POPULATION GROWTH RATE – 1.03 per cent
(2004 est.)
POPULATION DENSITY – 46 per sq. km (2002)
URBAN POPULATION – 63 per cent (2001)
MILITARY EXPENDITURE – 2.4 per cent of GDP (2003)
MILITARY PERSONNEL – 46,500: Army 37,000, Navy
5,500, Air Force 4,000; Paramilitaries 270
CONSCRIPTION DURATION – 12 months (selective)

CLIMATE AND TERRAIN

Ecuador is an equatorial state lying on the north-west
coast of South America. Its territory includes the
Galápagos Islands in the Pacific Ocean. It has five
different climatic zones and is one of the most bio-diverse
countries on earth. The Andes run north to south through
the centre of the country, dividing the coastal plain in the
west from the low-lying rainforest in the east. Elevation
extremes range from 0 m (Pacific Ocean) at the lowest
point to 6,310 m (Chimborazo) at the highest. Other
Andean peaks include Cotopaxi (5,896 m) and Cayambe
(5,790 m) in the Eastern Cordillera. Ecuador is located in
an earthquake zone and has two active volcanoes
(Pichincha, only 12 km away from the capital, and
Tungurahua). The average annual temperature in Quito is
15°C.

HISTORY AND POLITICS

The former kingdom of Quito was conquered by the
Incas of Peru in the 15th century. In 1534 Francisco
Pizarro's (1475–1541) conquests led to the inclusion of
the present territory of Ecuador in the Spanish viceroyalty
of Quito. Independence was achieved in a revolutionary
war that culminated in the battle of Mount Pichincha
(1822). It then formed part of Gran Columbia with
Colombia, Panama and Venezuela but left this union to
become a fully independent state in 1830. Since
independence the country has experienced periods of
political instability interspersed with dictatorships or
military rule. In 1979, after seven years of military rule,
Ecuador returned to democracy.

The oil-generated economic and social transformation from the 1970s onwards also caused rapid
inflation and increased foreign debt, and the austerity
measures introduced by various governments in the 1980s
and 1990s caused widespread civil unrest. In recent years,
these problems have been exacerbated by economic
recession, and measures to improve the economy have
provoked strikes and demonstrations, particularly by

indigenous people, who have benefited least from the oil
boom but been hardest hit by the economic downturn.
Unrest over the economy and over corruption has forced
three presidents from office in eight years.

In legislative elections held in October 2002 the Social
Christian Party (PSC) became the largest party in the
National Congress, with 24 seats. Col. Lucio Gutiérrez,
the joint candidate of the Popular Socialist Party (SPS)
and the New Country–Pachakutik United Movement
(MUPP), was elected president in the second round of
voting in November and took office in January 2003.
Gutiérrez was voted out of office by Congress in April
2005 after violent popular protests at his replacement of
27 of the Supreme Court's 31 judges and the subsequent
dropping of corruption charges against two former
presidents. Vice-President Alfredo Palacio named as his
replacement.

FOREIGN RELATIONS

The border with Peru was demarcated by a 1942 treaty
that was partly revoked by Ecuador in 1960 in relation to
a disputed 80 km stretch. An inconclusive four-week
border war was fought with Peru in February 1995 until
a cease-fire was signed on 1 March 1995. An 86 km
demilitarised zone was agreed in July 1995. An
agreement was signed on 26 October 1998 by the
presidents of the two countries formally ending the
territorial dispute after mediation by Argentina, Brazil,
Chile and the USA.

POLITICAL SYSTEM

The 1998 constitution provides for a directly elected
president and vice-president, who serve for a single four-
year term. There is a unicameral National Congress which
has 121 members, 101 elected on a provincial basis and
20 elected on a national basis, all for a four-year term.
Voting is compulsory for all literate citizens and voluntary
for all illiterate citizens over the age of 18. The republic is
divided into 22 provinces.

HEAD OF STATE

President, Alfredo Palacio, *took office* 20 April 2005
Vice-President, Alejandro Serrano Aguilar

SELECTED GOVERNMENT MEMBERS *as at July 2005*
Finance and Economy, Rafael Correa Delgado
Health, Wellington Sandoval
Foreign Relations, Antonio Parra Gil
National Defence, Anibal Rigail

EMBASSY OF ECUADOR
Flat 3B, 3 Hans Crescent, London SW1X 0LS
T 020-7584 1367/2648/8084
Ambassador Extraordinary and Plenipotentiary, HE
Eduardo Cabezas, apptd 2003
Chargé d'Affaires Ricardo Falconi-Puig

BRITISH EMBASSY
Citiplaza Building, Av. Naciones Unidas and República de El
Salvador, 14th Floor, PO Box 17-17-830, Quito
T (+593) (2) 2970 800/1 E britembq@interactive.net.ec
Ambassador Extraordinary and Plenipotentiary, HE Richard
Lewington, LVO, apptd 2003

ECONOMY AND TRADE

The economy was transformed by the discovery in 1972
of major oil fields in the Oriente area, and oil is now a
principal export, accounting for approximately 50 per

cent of public sector revenue and export earnings. Although the oil revenues funded health and education programmes, the boom also brought soaring inflation and increased foreign debt. The sucre was replaced by the US dollar in 1999 in an attempt to stabilise the economy and reduce inflation.

After oil, agriculture is the most important sector of the economy. The main products for export are fish (shrimp), bananas (which provide a third of agricultural exports), cocoa and coffee. Other important crops are sugar, soya, rice, cotton, African palm, vegetables, fruit and timber. The main imports are manufactured goods and machinery.
GNI – US$19,100 million (2002); US$1,490 per capita (2002)
ANNUAL AVERAGE GROWTH OF GDP – 5.8 per cent (2004 est.)
INFLATION RATE – 96.1 per cent (2000)
UNEMPLOYMENT – 11.1 per cent (2004 est.)
TOTAL EXTERNAL DEBT – US$13,281 million (2000)
FOREIGN DIRECT INVESTMENT – US$2,808 million (1997–2000)
IMPORTS – US$6,500million (2003)
EXPORTS – US$6,000 million (2003)

BALANCE OF PAYMENTS
Trade – US$71 million deficit (2003)
Current Account – US$455 million deficit (2003)

Trade with UK	2003	2004
Imports from UK	£31,875,000	£31,113,000
Exports to UK	31,742,000	42,392,000

TRANSPORT INFRASTRUCTURE
There are 43,197 km of permanent roads, 8,164 of which are surfaced. There are 966 km of railways. Ten commercial airlines operate international flights and there are internal services between all major towns.

EDUCATION
Elementary education is free of charge and compulsory. There are ten universities (three at Quito, three at Guayaquil, and one each at Cuenca, Machala, Loja and Portoviejo), polytechnic schools at Quito and Guayaquil and eight technical colleges in other provincial capitals.
ILLITERACY RATE – (m) 6.9 per cent; (f) 10.5 per cent (2000)
GROSS ENROLMENT RATIO (percentage of relevant age group) – primary 117 per cent (2002); secondary 59 per cent (2002)

MEDIA AND CULTURE
Ecuadorian newspapers include *El Mercurio, El Universo* and *Dairio Hoy*. There are four commercial television stations including Ecuavision, Teleamazon, ETV Telerama and TC Television. Radio Nacional del Ecuador is the government-owned radio station.

Quito has been a UNESCO World Heritage Site since 1978 and the old town's colonial and traditional architecture and ancient churches have been preserved. South America's most famous market, which pre-dates Inca times, can be found in the small town of Otavalo. Ecuador's most celebrated writers include José de la Cuadra (1903–1941) and Jorge Icaza Coronel (1906–78), both of whom used social realism as a basis for their works.

GALÁPAGOS ISLANDS
The Galápagos (Giant Tortoise) Islands, forming the province of the Archipelago de Colón, were annexed by Ecuador in 1832. The archipelago lies in the Pacific, about 800 km from the mainland. There are 12 large and several hundred smaller islands with a total area of about 7,769 sq. km and an estimated population of 18,640. The capital is Puerto Barquerizo Moreno, on San Cristóbal Island. Although the archipelago lies on the equator, the temperature of the surrounding water is well below equatorial average owing to the Humboldt current. The province consists for the most part of National Park territory, where unique marine birds, iguanas, and the giant tortoises are conserved. There is some local subsistence farming; the main industry, apart from tourism, is tuna and lobster fishing.

EGYPT

Al-Jumhūriyya al-Miṣriyya al-'Arabiyya – Arab Republic of Egypt

AREA – 995,500 sq. km. Neighbours: Sudan (south), Libya (west), Gaza Strip and Israel (east)
POPULATION – 76,117,421 (2004 est.). The largest, or 'Egyptian' element, is a Hamito-Semite race. A second element is the Bedouin, or nomadic Arabs of the Western and Eastern deserts, who are now mainly semi-sedentary tent-dwellers. The third element is the Nubian of the Nile Valley of mixed Arab and Negro blood. Over 90 per cent of the population are Muslims of the Sunni denomination, and most of the rest are Coptic Christians. Arabic is the official language
CAPITAL – Cairo (population, 7,200,000, 1998 estimate) stands on the Nile about 14 miles from the head of the delta
MAJOR CITIES – ΨAlexandria, founded 332 BC by Alexander the Great, was the capital for over 1,000 years; Asyut; Faiyum; Ismailia; ΨPort Said; ΨSuez
CURRENCY – Egyptian pound (£E) of 100 piastres or 1,000 millièmes
NATIONAL ANTHEM – Biladi [My homeland]
NATIONAL DAY – 23 July (Anniversary of Revolution in 1952)
NATIONAL FLAG – Horizontal bands of red, white and black, with an eagle in the centre of the white band
LIFE EXPECTANCY (years) – 70.71 (2004 est.)
MORTALITY RATE (per 1,000 population) – 5.3 (2004 est.)
INFANT MORTALITY (per 1,000 births) – 33.9 (2004 est.)
HIV / AIDS ADULT PREVALENCE – 0.1 per cent (2001)
DEATH PENALTY – Yes
POPULATION BELOW POVERTY LINE – 22.9 per cent (2002)
POPULATION GROWTH RATE – 1.83 per cent (2004 est.)
POPULATION DENSITY – 69 per sq. km (2001)
URBAN POPULATION – 43 per cent (2001)
ILLITERACY RATE – (m) 31.7 per cent; (f) 53.1 per cent (2003 est.)
GROSS ENROLMENT RATIO (percentage of relevant age group) – primary 97 per cent (2002); secondary 85 per cent (2002)

CLIMATE AND TERRAIN
The country is mainly flat but there are mountainous areas in the south-west, along the Red Sea coast and in the south of the Sinai peninsula. Elevation extremes range from 2,629 m (Mount Catherina, Sinai) at the highest point to −133 m (Qattara Depression) at the lowest. Most of the land is desert and the Nile valley and delta were the only fertile areas until the opening of the Aswan Dam allowed areas of desert to be reclaimed. West of the Nile Valley is the Western Desert, containing some depressions whose springs irrigate oases. The Eastern Desert between the Nile and the mountains along the Red Sea coast is mostly plateaux dissected by wadis (dry watercourses). The average daily temperature ranges from 18°C to 30°C.

HISTORY AND POLITICS
The unification of the kingdoms of Lower Egypt and Upper Egypt c.3100 BC marked the establishment of the Egyptian state, with Memphis as its capital. Egypt was ruled for nearly 2,800 years by a succession of 31 Pharaonic dynasties which built the pyramids at Gizeh. Egypt's independence was lost to the Assyrians in 666 BC, and it was conquered by the Persians in 525 BC and by Alexander the Great in 332 BC. Subsequently ruled by Alexander's general Ptolemy and his descendants, it was conquered and ruled by Rome (30 BC to AD 324) and then by the Byzantine Empire. In AD 640 Egypt was subjugated by Arab Muslim invaders. In 1517 the country was incorporated into the Ottoman Empire, under which it remained until the early 19th century. Britain occupied Egypt in 1882, and a British Protectorate over Egypt lasted from 1914 to 1922, when Sultan Ahmed Fuad was proclaimed King of Egypt. Full independence was achieved in 1936. In 1953 the monarchy was deposed and Egypt became a republic.

In 1956 President Nasser seized the assets of the Suez Canal Company. Egyptian occupation of the Canal Zone was used as a pretext for military action by Britain and France in support of their Suez Canal Company interests. A cease-fire and Anglo-French withdrawal were negotiated by the UN.

Egypt was involved in the Arab-Israeli wars in 1948, 1967 and 1973. In the 1967 war (the June War/the Six Day War), the Sinai peninsula was lost to Israel. Sinai was returned to Egypt in 1982 under the 1979 treaty that resulted from the Camp David talks (1978–9) and formally terminated the 31-year-old state of war between the two countries. The treaty led to strained relations with other Arab nations until the mid-1980s.

President Hosni Mubarak, who took office after the assassination of President Sadat in 1981, played an active part in the Middle East peace process in the 1990s but was unable to suppress internal terrorism by Islamic fundamentalists. President Mubarak was re-elected for a fourth term in June 1999. A legislative election was held in three rounds in October and November 2000, in which the ruling National Democratic Party (NDP) won 388 of the 444 elective seats. In the September 2005 presidential election, Hosni Mubarak was re-elected with 88.6 per cent of the vote.

INSURGENCIES
Militant Islamic fundamentalists emerged in the 1980s. Their campaign against the government became increasingly violent from the early 1990s, and eventually was directed against foreign tourists as well as domestic targets. Although the largest fundamentalist organisation,

Gamaat-i-Islamiya, renounced violence in 1999, attacks continue, often aimed at foreign tourists.

POLITICAL SYSTEM
The 1971 constitution provides for an executive president who appoints the Council of Ministers and determines government policy. The president, who serves for six years, is nominated by the legislature and endorsed by national referendum; in May 2005, the constitution was changed to allow the president to be directly elected from a number of candidates. The legislature is the People's Assembly *(Majlis al-Sha'ab)* which has 454 members, 444 directly elected and ten nominated by the president, all for a five-year term. The Consultative Council *(Majlis al-Shura)* has 264 members, of whom 176 are directly elected and 88 presidential appointees.

HEAD OF STATE
President, Mohammed Hosni Mubarak, *elected* 1981, *re-elected* 1987, 1993, 2 June 1999, *confirmed by national referendum* 26 September 1999, *re-elected* 13 September 2005

SELECTED GOVERNMENT MEMBERS *as at July 2005*
Prime Minister, Economy, Ahmed Nazif
Defence and Military Production, Field Marshal Mohammad Hussein Tantawi
Finance, Yussef Boutros Ghali
Foreign Affairs, Ahmed Ali abu el-Ghait
Interior, Maj.-Gen. Habib al-Adli

EMBASSY OF THE ARAB REPUBLIC OF EGYPT
26 South Street, London W1K 1DW
T 020-7499 2401/3304
Ambassador Extraordinary and Plenipotentiary, HE Gehad Madi, apptd 2004

BRITISH EMBASSY
7 Ahmed Ragheb Street, Garden City, Cairo
T (+20) (2) 794 0850/2/8 E info@britishembassy.org.eg
Ambassador Extraordinary and Plenipotentiary, HE Sir Derek Plumbly, apptd 2003

BRITISH COUNCIL
192 El Nil Street, Agouza, Cairo
T (+20) (2) 303 1514 E british.council@britishcouncil.org.eg
Director, Dr John Grote, OBE

DEFENCE
The Army has 3,755 main battle tanks, 690 armoured infantry fighting vehicles and 4,300 armoured personnel carriers. The Navy has one destroyer, ten frigates, four submarines, 44 patrol and coastal vessels and 24 armed helicopters at eight bases. The Air Force has 571 combat aircraft and 121 armed helicopters.
MILITARY EXPENDITURE – 4 per cent of GDP (2003)
MILITARY PERSONNEL – 450,000: Army 320,000, Navy 20,000, Air Force 30,000, Air Defence Command 80,000; Paramilitaries 330,000
CONSCRIPTION DURATION – 12 months to three years (selective)

ECONOMY AND TRADE
Despite increasing industrialisation, agriculture remains the most important economic activity, employing 29 per cent of the labour force and producing 17 per cent of GDP in 2002–3. Egypt is still a net importer of foodstuffs, especially grain, and a food security

programme has been set up with the aim of achieving self-sufficiency. The main cash crop is cotton, of which Egypt is one of the world's main producers. Other important crops are maize, rice, sugar cane, wheat and potatoes. Other fruits and vegetables are also grown.

With its considerable reserves of petroleum and natural gas, and the hydroelectric power produced by the Aswan and High Dams, Egypt is self-sufficient in energy. Tourism is an important feature of the Egyptian economy as numbers of foreign visitors increased by 52 per cent between 1998 and 2003.

The government transferred control over exchange rates to the central bank in January 2001. In January 2003 the government allowed the Egyptian pound to free-float against the US dollar in an attempt to pre-empt the detrimental effect the imminent war with Iraq would be likely to have upon the economy.

The main imports are wheat, maize, chemicals and motor vehicles and parts. The main exports are crude petroleum, cotton, cotton yarn, oranges, rice and cotton textiles.

GNI – US$97,600 million (2002); US$1,470 per capita (2002)
ANNUAL AVERAGE GROWTH OF GDP – 4.5 per cent (2004 est.)
INFLATION RATE – 9.5 per cent (2004 est.)
UNEMPLOYMENT – 10.9 per cent (2004 est.)
TOTAL EXTERNAL DEBT – US$30,500 million (2002)
FOREIGN DIRECT INVESTMENT – US$4,267 million (1997–2000)
IMPORTS – US$11,100 million (2003)
EXPORTS – US$6,300 million (2003)

BALANCE OF PAYMENTS
Trade – US$4,201 million deficit (2003)
Current Account – US$3,743 million surplus (2003)

Trade with UK	2003	2004
Imports from UK	£462,052,000	£669,468,000
Exports to UK	442,035,000	509,467,000

TRANSPORT INFRASTRUCTURE

Egypt has 5,105 km of railways and 64,000 km of roads, 49,984 km of which are surfaced. There are international airports at Cairo and Luxor. Road and rail networks link the Nile valley and delta with the main development areas east and west of the river, but there are few routes in the interior. Egypt has 3,500 km of waterways, of which half are canals. The Suez Canal was re-opened in 1975 and a two-stage development project begun to widen and deepen the canal to allow the passage of larger shipping and to permit two-way traffic. Port Said and Suez have been reconstructed and the port of Alexandria is being improved.

MEDIA

The Egyptian media takes a central role in the Arab world and its newspapers are some of the most widely read and influential in the region. There are two state-run national television channels and six regional channels. Egypt has an important satellite television industry (Egypt was the first Arab country to have its own satellite, Nilesat 101) that is watched all over the Arab-speaking world. In 2001 Dream 1, Dream 2 and Al-Mihwar TV, the country's first private television stations, came on air. The state has a monopoly on all radio broadcasting. The government has actively encouraged foreign media to base themselves in Egypt by setting up a Free Media Zone in 2000 that offers economic incentives and access to its media infrastructure.

CULTURE

Egypt lies at the heart of the Arab world even though it is located on the African continent. It is most famous for the Pyramids of Gizeh and the art and architecture of its ancient civilisations (beginning in the fourth millennium BC and waning around 341 BC but the modern-day Egyptian state is also of great cultural, political and economic importance to the region.

The Egyptian author Naguib Mahfouz (b. 1911) won the Nobel Prize for Literature in 1988.

EL SALVADOR

República de El Salvador – Republic of El Salvador

AREA – 20,700 sq. km. Neighbours: Guatemala (north-west), Honduras (north-east and east)
POPULATION – 6,587,541 (2004 est.): 90 per cent mestizo, 1 per cent Amerindian, 9 per cent European. The language is Spanish
CAPITAL – San Salvador (population, 1,985,294, 2000 estimate)
MAJOR CITIES – San Miguel; Santa Ana
CURRENCY – US dollar (US$) of 100 cents
NATIONAL ANTHEM – Saludemos la patria orgullosos [Let us proudly hail the fatherland]
NATIONAL DAY – 15 September
NATIONAL FLAG – Three horizontal bands, sky blue, white, sky blue; coat of arms on white band
LIFE EXPECTANCY (years) – 70.92 (2004 est.)
MORTALITY RATE (per 1,000 population) – 5.93 (2004 est.)
INFANT MORTALITY (per 1,000 births) – 25.93 (2001 est.)
HIV / AIDS ADULT PREVALENCE – 0.7 per cent (2003 est.)
DEATH PENALTY – Yes*
POPULATION BELOW POVERTY LINE – 48 per cent (1999)
POPULATION GROWTH RATE – 1.78 per cent (2004 est.)
POPULATION DENSITY – 310 per sq. km (2002)
URBAN POPULATION – 61 per cent (2001)
MILITARY EXPENDITURE – 0.7 per cent of GDP (2003)
MILITARY PERSONNEL – 15,500: Army 13,850, Navy 700, Air Force 950; Paramilitaries 12,000
CONSCRIPTION DURATION – 12 months (selective)

CLIMATE AND TERRAIN

El Salvador extends along the Pacific coast of Central America for 307 km. The country is very mountainous (much of the interior has an average altitude of 600 m) and many of its peaks are extinct volcanoes. There are also numerous volcanic lakes. Elevation extremes range from 2,730 m (Cerro El Pital) at the highest point to 0 m (Pacific Ocean) at the lowest. Average temperatures vary with altitude with coastal areas tending to be hotter. The average annual temperature in San Salvador is 23°C. Earthquakes are common.

HISTORY AND POLITICS

El Salvador was part of the Aztec kingdom conquered in 1524 by Pedro de Alvarado, and formed part of the Spanish viceroyalty of Guatemala until 1821. It became part of the United Provinces of Central America in 1823 until the federation's dissolution, and became fully independent in 1841.

There was political unrest in the 1970s, and guerrilla activity by the left-wing Farabundo Martí National Liberation Front (FMLN), which intensified from 1977 amid reports of human rights abuses by government-backed militias. Decades of military rule ended in 1979, but elections in 1982 were boycotted by left-wing parties and the right-wing National Republican Alliance (ARENA) took office. The civil war between the FMLN and the US-backed government lasted throughout the 1980s, until a UN-sponsored peace agreement was signed in 1991. The FMLN was recognised as a political party, and it won a few seats in the 1994 election, which returned ARENA to power. Since then, the FMLN has increased its vote, often being the largest party in parliament, but it has never held office, as ARENA has always formed coalition governments with smaller right-wing parties.

In the 2003 legislative election, the FMLN won 31 seats; ARENA won 27 seats and the National Conciliation Party (PCN) won 16 seats; ARENA formed a coalition government with the PCN. In 2004, Elias Antonio Saca of the ARENA party won the presidential election with 57 per cent of the vote.

POLITICAL SYSTEM
Under the 1983 constitution, the executive president is directly elected for a five-year term. The Legislative Assembly has 84 members, who are directly elected for a three-year term. The country is divided into 14 Departments.

HEAD OF STATE
President, Elias Antonio Saca, *elected* 21 March 2004, *took office* 1 June 2004
Vice-President, Ana Vilma Albanez de Escobar

SELECTED GOVERNMENT MEMBERS *as at July 2005*
Defence, Gen. Otto Romero
Economy, Yolanda Mayora de Garida
Foreign Affairs, Francisco Lainez
Interior, Rene Figueroa

EMBASSY OF EL SALVADOR
Mayfair House, 39 Great Portland Street, London W1W 7JZ
T 020-7436 8282 E elsalvadorembassy@rree.gob.sv
Ambassador Extraordinary and Plenipotentiary, HE Eduardo Ernesto Vilanova, apptd 2002

BRITISH AMBASSADOR
HE Richard Lavers, apptd 2003, resident at Guatemala City

ECONOMY AND TRADE
In the 1990s, the country started to recover from the devastation of the civil war, only to be hit by a series of natural disasters, mostly significantly Hurricane Mitch in 1998 and several volcanic eruptions in 2001, which killed over 1,200 and left more than 1 million homeless. Although it is one of the most industrialised of Central American countries, the economy is heavily dependent on remittances from Salvadoreans working abroad. The US dollar was adopted in 2001 in place of the colón.

The principal agricultural products are coffee, cotton, sugar cane, maize, shrimps and balsam. In eastern areas,
sisal is produced and used in the manufacture of coffee and cereal bags.

Chief exports are coffee, cotton, sugar, shrimps, sisal, balsam, meat, cotton, hides and skins. The chief imports are chemicals, petroleum, manufactured goods, industrial and electronic machinery, pharmaceutical goods, vehicles and consumer goods. The USA is El Salvador's main trading partner; in 2004 the government ratified a free-trade agreement with the USA, Honduras, Nicaragua and Guatemala.

GNI – US$13,600 million (2002); US$2,110 per capita (2002)
ANNUAL AVERAGE GROWTH OF GDP – 1.8 per cent (2004 est.)
INFLATION RATE – 5.4 per cent (2004 est.)
UNEMPLOYMENT – 6.3 per cent (2004 est.)
TOTAL EXTERNAL DEBT – US$5,600 million (2001)
FOREIGN DIRECT INVESTMENT – US$439 million (1997–2000)
IMPORTS – US$4,400 million (2003)
EXPORTS – US$1,300 million (2003)

BALANCE OF PAYMENTS
Trade – US$2,274 million deficit (2002)
Current Account – US$734 million deficit (2003)

Trade with UK	2003	2004
Imports from UK	£17,395,000	£20,224,000
Exports to UK	49,411,000	7,270,000

TRANSPORT INFRASTRUCTURE
The principal ports are Cutuco, La Unión and Acajutla but ports in Honduras and Guatemala are also used. There are 10,029 km of roads of which 1,986 km are surfaced; there are 283 km of railways. The Pan-American Highway from the Guatemalan frontier passes through Santa Ana and San Salvador continuing to the Honduran frontier. Comalapa international airport has daily flights to other Central American capitals, Mexico and the USA.

EDUCATION
Primary education is state-run and is compulsory and free of charge. There are 2,400 primary schools and 240 secondary schools. There are 23 vocational and technical schools and three universities.

ILLITERACY RATE – (m) 18.3 per cent; (f) 23.8 per cent (2000)
GROSS ENROLMENT RATIO (percentage of relevant age group) – primary 112 per cent (2002); secondary 56 per cent (2002); tertiary 17 per cent (2002)

MEDIA
There are three major commercial television channels operating in El Salvador: Teledos, Canal Seis and TV Doce. There are hundreds of private radio stations (70 operate in San Salvador alone).

EQUATORIAL GUINEA

República de Guinea Ecuatorial – Republic of Equatorial Guinea

AREA – 28,051 sq. km. Neighbours: Cameroon (north), Gabon (east and south); comprises the mainland area (Río Muni) and several islands in the Gulf of Guinea, principally Bioko (40 km off the coast of Cameroon) and Annabón.

POPULATION – 523,051 (2004 est. estimate). The official languages are Spanish and French; Bubi, Fang, Ibo and English are also spoken

CAPITAL – ΨMalabo on Bioko Island (population, 30,418, 1983 estimate)

MAJOR TOWN – ΨBata is the principal town and port of Rio Muni

CURRENCY – Franc CFA of 100 centimes

NATIONAL ANTHEM – Caminemos pisando la senda de nuestra inmensa felicidad [Let's walk down the path of our immense happiness]

NATIONAL DAY – 12 October

NATIONAL FLAG – Three horizontal bands, green over white over red; blue triangle next staff; coat of arms in centre of white band

LIFE EXPECTANCY – 55.15 (2004 est.)

MORTALITY RATE (per 1,000 population) – 12.27 (2004 est.)

INFANT MORTALITY (per 1,000 births) – 87.08 (2004 est.)

HIV / AIDS ADULT PREVALENCE – 3.4 per cent (2001 est.)

DEATH PENALTY – Yes

POPULATION GROWTH RATE – 2.43 per cent (2004 est.)

POPULATION DENSITY – 16 per sq. km (1999)

MILITARY EXPENDITURE – 0.2 per cent of GDP (2003)

MILITARY PERSONNEL – 1,320: Army 1,100, Navy 120, Air Force 100

ILLITERACY RATE – (m) 6.7 per cent; (f) 21.6 per cent (2004)

CLIMATE AND TERRAIN

There are two provinces: Bioko Island and the mainland, where 80 per cent of the population lives. Bioko is of volcanic origin. The mainland rises from a narrow coastal plain to a mountainous interior plateau, and is covered in dense vegetation. The climate is tropical, with a rainy season from July to January on Bioko and from April to May and October to December on the mainland. Elevation extremes range from 3,008 m (Pico Basile) at the highest point to 0 m (Atlantic Ocean) at the lowest.

HISTORY AND POLITICS

The island of Fernando Po (Bioko) was claimed by the Portuguese in 1494 and held until 1778, when it was ceded to Spain. The mainland territory of Río Muni came under Spanish rule in 1885, and the whole colony became known as Spanish Guinea. Constituted as two provinces of Metropolitan Spain in 1959, the colony became autonomous in 1963, and fully independent in 1968 under its present name.

Francisco Macias Nguema won the first multiparty elections. In 1970 President Macias Nguema merged all the political parties into one, the Partido Unico Nacional de los Trabajadores (PUNT). Macias Nguema's regime was brutal and he was overthrown, tried and executed in 1979 in a military coup led by his nephew, Col. Obiang Nguema. A military regime was established after the coup and only presidential nominees could stand in the 1983 and 1988 elections, but constitutional amendments were introduced in 1992 to allow multiparty elections, and ten opposition parties were legalised, operating alongside the ruling Equatorial Guinea Democratic Party (PDGE). However, President Obiang Nguema and the PDGE have retained power since 1992, as most elections have been boycotted by the opposition parties because of election irregularities and intimidation. In 1997 the largest opposition party, the Progress Party (PPGE), was banned by the government, and in 1998 opposition party coalitions were deemed illegal. Some opposition party leaders were imprisoned in 2002 for allegedly taking part in an attempted coup, and an alleged coup by foreign nationals was suppressed in 2004, with arrests in Malabo and Harare, Zimbabwe. The regime has been accused of human rights abuses and suppressing political opposition, and in 2003 exiled opposition leaders set up a government-in-exile in Spain. Incumbent president Obiang Nguema won the 2002 presidential election unopposed, opposition candidates having withdrawn owing to alleged irregularities. In municipal and legislative elections in 2004, the PDGE took 98 out of 100 seats in parliament, and 237 out of 244 councillor seats.

POLITICAL SYSTEM

The 1991 constitution introduced a multiparty system. The president is directly elected for a seven-year term. The unicameral legislature, the House of Representatives of the People, has 100 members, who are directly elected for a five-year term.

HEAD OF STATE
President of the Supreme Military Council and Minister of Defence, Brig.-Gen. Teodoro Obiang Nguema Mbasogo, *took office* August 1979, *re-elected* June 1989, 25 February 1996, 15 December 2002

SELECTED GOVERNMENT MEMBERS *as at July 2005*
Prime Minister, Miguel Abia Biteo Borico
Deputy PM, Marcelino Oyono Ntutumu
Deputy PM, Ricardo Mangue Oboma Nfube
Economy and Trade, Jaime Ela Ndong
Foreign Affairs, International Co-operation and Francophone Affairs, Pastor Micha Ondo Bile
Interior and Local Corporations, Clemente Engonga Nguema Onguene

EMBASSY OF THE REPUBLIC OF EQUATORIAL GUINEA
29 Boulevard de Courcelles, 75008 Paris, France
T (+33) 15688 5454
Ambassador Extraordinary and Plenipotentiary, Eduardo Ndong Elo Nzang, apptd 2004

BRITISH AMBASSADOR
HE Richard Wildash, LVO, apptd 2002, resident at Yaoundé, Cameroon

ECONOMY AND TRADE

During the 1980s the chief products were cocoa, coffee and wood. Production has declined and except for cocoa there is now little commercial agriculture. The large oil and gas deposits discovered off Bioko in the 1990s have made the country one of the biggest oil producers in sub-Saharan Africa. A growth rate of 65 per cent was achieved in 2001, making Equatorial Guinea the fastest growing economy in Africa, but the economic boom has not benefited much of the population. Oil reserves are expected to run out in the next ten years. Over 90 per cent of exports come from the oil industry. However, the economy is still heavily dependent on outside aid, principally from Spain and the IMF.

GNI – US$327 million (2001); US$700 per capita (2001)
ANNUAL AVERAGE GROWTH OF GDP – 1.3 per cent (2001)
TOTAL EXTERNAL DEBT – US$248 million (2000)

IMPORTS – US$451 million (2000)
EXPORTS – US$1,100 million (2000)

Trade with UK	2003	2004
Imports from UK	£108,842,000	£34,295,00
Exports to UK	7,973,000	11,313,000

MEDIA

Television and radio broadcasts are state-controlled and the government owns Equatorial Guinea's only television station and radio station's, Television Nacional and Radio Nacional de Guinea Ecuatorial. There is a second radio station, Radio Asonga, which is owned by the president's son. The main newspaper, *Ebano*, is state-owned. A few privately owned publications appear sporadically.

ERITREA

Hagere Eretra/al-Dawla al-Iritra – State of Eritrea

AREA – 117,600 sq. km. Neighbours: Sudan (north and west), Ethiopia (south), Djibouti (south-east)
POPULATION – 4,447,307 (2004 est.), roughly half Coptic Christian (mainly highlanders) and half Muslim (mainly lowlanders). Arabic, Tigrinya and English are the main working languages. Italian is also widely spoken. There are nine indigenous language groups: Afar; Bilen; Hadareb; Kunama; Nara; Rashida; Saho; Tigre; Tigrinya
CAPITAL – Asmara (population, 450,000, 2001 estimate)
MAJOR TOWNS – ΨAssab; ΨMassawa
CURRENCY – Nakfa
NATIONAL DAY – 24 May (Independence Day)
NATIONAL FLAG – Divided into three triangles; the one based on the hoist is red and bears a gold olive wreath; the upper triangle is green and the lower one light blue
LIFE EXPECTANCY – 52.7 (2004 est.)
MORTALITY RATE (per 1,000 population) – 13.36 (2004 est.)
HIV / AIDS ADULT PREVALENCE – 2.7 per cent (2003 est.)
DEATH PENALTY – Yes
POPULATION GROWTH RATE – 2.57 per cent (2004 est.)
POPULATION DENSITY – 43 per sq. km (2002)
ILLITERACY RATE – (m) 30.1 per cent; (f) 52.4 per cent (2004 est.)
GROSS ENROLMENT RATIO (percentage of relevant age group) – primary 61 per cent (2002); secondary 20 per cent (2002); tertiary 2 per cent (2002)

CLIMATE AND TERRAIN

The northern end of the Ethiopian Highlands extends into central Eritrea, where the average altitude is over 2,000 m. The mountains fall in the west to a plateau, then rise to the hills on the Sudan border. To the east of the mountains, the land falls to the narrow coastal plain. The coastal strip extending to the Djibouti border is low-lying, the border with Ethiopia running along the edge of the Denakil Desert. Elevation extremes range from 3,018 m (Soira) at the highest point to –75 m (Denakil Depression) at the lowest. The climate changes with the country's varying altitudes (from 16°C in the mountains of the central highlands to 30°C on the coastal desert plain).

HISTORY AND POLITICS

From the mid-16th century, the area was under the control of the Ottoman Empire. It was occupied by Italy in the late 19th century and was the base for the 1936 Italian invasion of Abyssinia (now Ethiopia). After the Italian defeat in North Africa in 1941, Eritrea became a British protectorate until 15 September 1952, when a federation with Ethiopia was created by the UN. In 1962, Ethiopia annexed Eritrea.

The Eritrean Liberation Front (ELF) began a campaign for independence in 1961, fighting a guerrilla war from the 1960s until 1991 against first Emperor Haile Selassie's forces and from 1974 against the communist Mengistu regime. The Eritrean People's Liberation Front (a breakaway faction of the ELF) emerged as the dominant rebel group in the 1980s and joined with Ethiopian resistance groups, including the People's Front for Democracy and Justice (PFDJ), to help overthrow the Mengistu regime in 1991. The EPLF secured the whole of Eritrea and formed a provisional government. The new PFDJ-led government in Ethiopia agreed to an Eritrean referendum on independence, which was held in April 1993 and recorded a 99.89 per cent vote in favour. Independence was declared on 24 May 1993.

Following independence, a transitional government for a four-year period was formed under Issaias Afwerki, and the EPLF became the ruling political party, renaming itself the People's Front for Democracy and Justice (PFDJ) in 1994. The post-independence regime has become increasingly authoritarian; although a new constitution was introduced in 1997, no presidential election has taken place since independence, and legislative elections scheduled for 2001 did not take place and have not been rescheduled.

FOREIGN RELATIONS

Since independence, Eritrea has been involved in disputes with Yemen over the Hanish and Mohabaka Islands in the Red Sea (possession divided between Yemen and Eritrea by international arbitration), and with Djibouti over their common border.

There has been fighting with Ethiopia in disputes over border territory, especially in Tigray, since 1998. Though usually sporadic, fighting escalated into war in 1999–2000. Peace talks resulted in an agreement to set up regional military commissions to resolve local security issues. In 2002 the independent Eritrea-Ethiopia Boundary Commission (EEBC) defined the international border between the two countries. The Commission's 2003 ruling that the disputed town of Badme lay in Eritrea was rejected by the Ethiopian government, and relations between the two countries remain strained. The UN, which deployed peacekeeping troops in 2000, continues to patrol the disputed area.

POLITICAL SYSTEM

Under the 1997 constitution, the head of state is the president, elected for a five-year term by the legislature, and the 150-member unicameral National Assembly *(Hagerawi Baito)* is directly elected for a four-year term; however, presidential and legislative elections have yet to be held and the transitional president, State Council (cabinet) and legislature remain in place. The People's Front for Democracy and Justice (PFDJ) is the only legal political party.

HEAD OF STATE
President, Chairman of the National Assembly, Isaias
Afewerki, *elected by the National Assembly* 22 May 1993

SELECTED GOVERNMENT MEMBERS *as at July 2005*
Defence, Gen. Sebhat Ephrem
Finance and Development, Berhane Abrehe
Foreign Affairs, Ali Said Abdellah
Health, Saleh Meki

EMBASSY OF THE STATE OF ERITREA
96 White Lion Street, London N1 9PF **T** 020-7713 0096.
Ambassador Extraordinary and Plenipotentiary, HE Negassi
Sengal Ghebrezghi, apptd 2003

BRITISH EMBASSY
66–68 Mariam Ghimbi Street, PO Box 5584, Asmara
T (+291) (1) 120145 **E** asmara.enquiries@fco.gov.uk
Ambassador Extraordinary and Plenipotentiary, HE Michael
Murray, apptd 2002

BRITISH COUNCIL
Lorenzo Tazaz Street No 23, PO Box 997, Asmara
T (+291) (1) 123415/120529
E information@britishcouncil.org.er
Director, Dr Negusse Araya

DEFENCE
The Army has 150 main battle tanks and 40 armoured
infantry fighting vehicles and armoured personnel
carriers. The Navy has eight patrol and coastal
combatants. The Air Force has 18 combat aircraft.
MILITARY EXPENDITURE – 9.2 per cent of GDP (2003)
MILITARY PERSONNEL – 201,750: Army 200,000, Navy
1,400, Air Force 350
CONSCRIPTION DURATION – 16 months

ECONOMY AND TRADE
Over 30 years of conflict left the country's economy
devastated. The government hopes to base the rebuilding
of the economy on the return of well-educated exiles,
international aid and investment, the development of
tourism along the coast, and the diversification of the
economy away from subsistence agriculture, which
currently involves around 80 per cent of the population.
However, these aims are threatened by the frequent
droughts and the famines that can ensue; in 2005 the
World Food Programme extended its emergency
operations to cover over 800,000 people.

Mineral reserves include zinc, potash, gold, platinum,
and oil, but they are not fully exploited. Industries include
cement, construction, salt, paper, leather goods, textiles,
clothing and chemicals. Exports are skins, meat, live
animals and gum arabic. The major imports are food,
machinery, transportation equipment and manufactured
goods. Eritrea's largest source of foreign exchange is
remittances from overseas Eritreans, estimated to be
around US$250 million annually.
GNI – US$800 million (2003); US$190 per capita (2002)
ANNUAL AVERAGE GROWTH OF GDP – 2.5 per cent
(2004 est.)
TOTAL EXTERNAL DEBT – US$311 million (2000)

Trade with UK	2003	2004
Imports from UK	£7,521,000	£4,359,000
Exports to UK	165,000	270,000

TRANSPORT INFRASTRUCTURE
Since 1991 the government has attempted to rebuild the
transport infrastructure, which was devastated by over 30
years of war. The rebuilding programme has focused on
the ports of Massawa and Assab, the roads from the ports
to Ethiopia, and the railway from Massawa to Sudan via
Asmara. There are 306 km of railways and 4,010 km of
roads, of which 874 km are surfaced.

MEDIA
All privately owned news media organisations were closed
down by the government in 2001. Eri TV is the state-run
television station. There are no private networks or radio
stations.

ESTONIA

Eesti Vabariik – Republic of Estonia

AREA – 42,300 sq. km. Neighbours: Russia (east), Latvia
(south)
POPULATION – 1,341,664 (2004 est.): 65.3 per cent
Estonian, 28.1 per cent Russian, 1.5 per cent
Ukrainian, 0.9 per cent Belarusian, 0.9 per cent
Finnish. The majority religion is Lutheran, with
Russian Orthodox and Baptist minorities. Estonian is
the first language of 64.2 per cent and Russian of 28.7
per cent
CAPITAL – Tallinn (population, 404,000, 2000 census)
MAJOR TOWNS AND CITIES – Kohtla-Järve; Narva;
Pärnu; Tartu
CURRENCY – Kroon of 100 sents
NATIONAL ANTHEM – Mu isamaa, ja rõõm [My native
land, my joy, delight]
NATIONAL DAY – 24 February (Independence Day)
NATIONAL FLAG – Three horizontal stripes of blue, black,
white
LIFE EXPECTANCY (years) – 71.38 (2004 est.)
MORTALITY RATE (per 1,000 population) – 13.27
(2004 est.)
INFANT MORTALITY (per 1,000 births) – 8.08
(2004 est.)
HIV / AIDS ADULT PREVALENCE – 1 per cent (2001)
DEATH PENALTY – No (abolished 1998)
POPULATION GROWTH RATE – –0.66 per cent
(2004 est.)
POPULATION DENSITY – 32 per sq. km (2002)
URBAN POPULATION – 69 per cent (2001)
MILITARY EXPENDITURE – 2.0 per cent of GDP
(2003)
MILITARY PERSONNEL – 4,980: Army 4,450, Navy 335,
Air Force 195; Paramilitaries 2,600
CONSCRIPTION DURATION – Eight to 11 months

CLIMATE AND TERRAIN
The country is mostly a plain of lakes, marshes and
forests, with a low range of hills in the south-east.
Elevation extremes range from 318 m (Munamagi) at the
highest point to 0 m (Baltic Sea) at the lowest. Part of the
border with Russia runs through the large Lake Peipus.
The climate is mild, with average temperatures ranging
from −6°C in January to 17°C in July.

HISTORY AND POLITICS
Estonia came under Swedish control between 1561 and
1629, and was ceded in 1721 to the Russian Empire. An
Estonian nationalist movement developed in the late 19th

century, and fought against occupying German forces during the First World War. Estonia declared its independence in February 1918 and defended this against Soviet forces until 1920, when independence was recognised by the Soviet Union. However, the Soviet Union annexed Estonia in 1940, and the country was subsequently occupied by German forces when they invaded the Soviet Union in 1941. In 1944 the Soviet Union expelled the Germans and reannexed the country, beginning a process of 'Sovietisation'.

There was a resurgence of nationalist feeling in the 1980s, and in 1989 the Estonian Supreme Soviet declared the republic to be sovereign and its 1940 annexation by the Soviet Union to be illegal. In 1990 the Communist Party's monopoly of power was abolished and, following multiparty elections in which pro-independence candidates won the majority of seats, a period of transition to independence was inaugurated. Independence was declared on 20 August 1991. The last Russian troops were withdrawn in 1994. Since independence, Estonia has pursued pro-western policies. It joined NATO and the EU in 2004.

In 2001 Arnold Rüütel was elected president by an electoral assembly. In the 2003 legislative election, the left-wing Centrist Party (KP) and the right-wing Union for the Republic-Res Publica (RP) each won 28 seats in the parliament. A centre-right coalition government of the RP, the Reform Party (RE) and the People's Union (RL) was formed, with Juhan Parts (RP) as prime minister. Parts and his government resigned in March 2005 after a vote of no confidence and in April Andrus Ansip (RE) became prime minister at the head of a new coalition of the RE, KP and RL parties.

POLITICAL SYSTEM

Under the 1992 constitution, legislative power is exercised by the unicameral *Riigikogu* of 101 members, who are elected by proportional representation for a four-year term. The president is elected for a five-year term by the *Riigikogu* by a two-thirds majority or, if no candidate receives this majority after three rounds of voting, by an electoral assembly composed of the *Riigikogu* members and local government officials. Executive authority is vested in a prime minister, who is nominated by the president and who forms a government. Members of the government need not be members of the *Riigikogu*.

HEAD OF STATE

President, Arnold Rüütel, *elected by legislative assembly* 21 September 2001, *sworn in* 8 October 2001

SELECTED GOVERNMENT MEMBERS AS AT JULY 2005
Prime Minister, Andrus Ansip
Defence, Jaak Joeruut
Finance, Aivar Soerd
Foreign Affairs, Urmas Paet
Interior, Kalle Laanet

EMBASSY OF THE REPUBLIC OF ESTONIA
16 Hyde Park Gate, London SW7 5DG
T 020-7589 3428 E embassy.london@estonia.gov.uk
Ambassador Extraordinary and Plenipotentiary, HE Kaja Tael, apptd 2001

BRITISH EMBASSY
Wismari 6, Tallinn 10136
T (372) 667 4700 E information@britishembassy.ee
Ambassador Extraordinary and Plenipotentiary, HE Nigel Haywood, apptd 2003

BRITISH COUNCIL
Vana Posti 7, Tallinn 10146 T (+372) 625 7788
E british.council@britishcouncil.ee
Director, Kyllike Tohver

ECONOMY AND TRADE

Since 1992 the government has introduced free-market reforms, privatisation and restructuring.

Agriculture engages 11 per cent of the workforce and accounts for 6 per cent of GDP, the main products being rye, oats, barley, flax, potatoes, meat, milk, butter and eggs. Industry accounts for 20 per cent of employment and 28.6 per cent of GDP, concentrating on textiles, clothing and footwear, forestry, wood and paper products, and food and fish processing. Some heavy industry exists, mostly in the manufacture of chemicals and power equipment. Estonia's main trading partners are Finland, Sweden, Germany, Japan and Latvia. The main imports are machinery and equipment, chemicals, clothing and footwear, foodstuffs and vehicles. Estonia is still dependent on Russian natural gas supplies. Exports consist mainly of machinery and equipment, timber and wood products, textiles and clothing, foodstuffs, metals and furniture.

GNI – US$5,700 million (2002); US$4,190 per capita (2002)
ANNUAL AVERAGE GROWTH OF GDP – 6 per cent (2004 est.)
INFLATION RATE – 3 per cent (2004 est.)
UNEMPLOYMENT – 9.6 per cent (2004 est.)
TOTAL EXTERNAL DEBT – US$3,300 million (2001)
FOREIGN DIRECT INVESTMENT – US$1,539 million (1997–2001)
IMPORTS – US$6,500 million (2003)
EXPORTS – US$4,500 million (2003)

BALANCE OF PAYMENTS
Trade – US$1,580 million deficit (2003)
Current Account – US$1,199 million deficit (2003)

Trade with UK	2003	2004
Imports from UK	£92,067,000	£38,879,000
Exports to UK	268,149,000	218,490,000

EDUCATION

Estonia has a three-tier education system, consisting of primary level (four years), secondary level (six years) and university level (four to six years). Primary and secondary level education is compulsory from the age of seven to 17. There are ten universities: six public and four private. The country's most famous university is Tartu, founded in 1632.

GROSS ENROLMENT RATIO (percentage of relevant age group) – primary 103 per cent (2002); secondary 110 per cent (2002); tertiary 59 per cent (2002)

MEDIA AND CULTURE

Freedom of the press is guaranteed in the constitution, and the state monopoly on television and radio ended soon after independence. All newspapers have been privatised and broadcasting channels are in the process of being privatised (only one state owned channel remains).

Russian-language news and programmes are provided on Estonian Television.

The old town area of Tallinn is home to the country's parliament and national cathedral and is a UNESCO World Heritage Site. Estonia's cultural heritage is rich in traditional folk songs and poetry, both of which have influenced much contemporary writing, art and music. Estonia is particularly distinguished in the field of classical music and has produced many world-famous conductors, such as Neeme Järvi (b. 1937) and Tõnu Kaljuste (b. 1953), and composers Arvo Pärt (b. 1935), Veljo Tormis (b. 1930) and Erkki-Sven Tüür (b. 1959).

ETHIOPIA

Ya'Ityopya Federalawi Dimokrasyawi Repeblik – Federal Democratic Republic of Ethiopia

AREA – 1,127,130 sq. km. Neighbours: Sudan (west), Kenya (south), Somalia (east), Djibouti (north-east), Eritrea (north)

POPULATION – 67,851,281 (2004 est.). About one-third are of Semitic origin (Amharas and Tigreans) and the remainder mainly Oromos (40 per cent), Somalis (6 per cent) and Afar (4 per cent). Amharas, Tigreans and many Oromos are Ethiopian Orthodox Christians. The Afar people in the north and the Somalis in the south-east, as well as some Oromos, are Muslim. Amharic is the most widely used of the 70 indigenous languages

CAPITAL – Addis Ababa (population, 2,495,000, 2000 estimate)

MAJOR CITY – Dire Dawa

CURRENCY – Ethiopian birr (EB) of 100 cents

NATIONAL ANTHEM – Whedefit gesgeshi woude henate Ethiopia [March forward dear mother Ethiopia]

NATIONAL DAY – 28 May

NATIONAL FLAG – Three horizontal bands: green, yellow, red; in the centre a blue disc, containing a yellow pentagram

LIFE EXPECTANCY (years) – 40.88 (2004 est.)

MORTALITY RATE (per 1,000 population) – 20.36 (2004 est.)

INFANT MORTALITY (per 1,000 births) – 102.12 (2004 est.)

HIV / AIDS ADULT PREVALENCE – 4.4 per cent (2003 est.)

DEATH PENALTY – Yes

POPULATION BELOW POVERTY LINE – 45 per cent (2002)

POPULATION GROWTH RATE – 1.89 per cent (2004 est.)

POPULATION DENSITY – 67 per sq. km (2002)

URBAN POPULATION – 16 per cent (2001)

CLIMATE AND TERRAIN

Ethiopia is a landlocked country dominated by a central plateau, rising to the central mountains of the Ethiopian Highlands, which are divided by the Great Rift Valley. The western mountains are the source of the Blue Nile. The land drops to desert plains in the east (Ogaden) and north-east (Denakil Desert). Elevation extremes range from 4,620 m (Ras Dejen) at the highest point to −125 m (Denakil Depression) at the lowest. There is a tropical monsoon climate that varies according to altitude. The wet season is April to September.

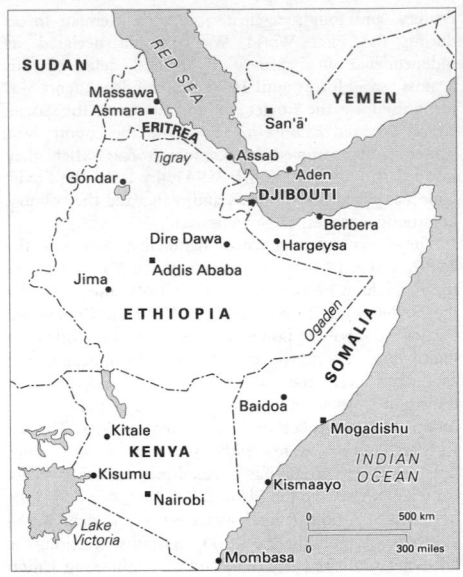

HISTORY AND POLITICS

The Hamitic culture was heavily influenced by Semitic immigration from Arabia at about the time of Christ, and Coptic Christianity was introduced in the fourth century. The empire attained its zenith in the sixth century under the Axum rulers but was checked by Islamic expansion from the east. The independent kingdom of Abyssinia emerged in the 11th century. Modern Ethiopia dates from 1855 when Theodros established supremacy over the various tribes. Menelik II repulsed an Italian invasion in 1896, but Italy conquered Abyssinia in 1936 and occupied the country until its liberation and the return of the emperor, Haile Selassie, in 1941. Ethiopia was federated with Eritrea in 1952 and annexed the area in 1962.

Following a severe famine in 1973–4, Emperor Haile Selassie was deposed in a military coup in 1974 and a military government was installed. By 1977 Lt.-Col. Mengistu Haile Mariam had become head of state and his single-party Marxist regime initiated reforms based on the Soviet model, brutally suppressing opposition. War with Somalia over the Ogaden (1977–8), internal conflict with Ethiopian resistence and Eritrean separatist forces, drought and severe famine (1984–5), and government mismanagement and corruption undermined the Mengistu regime. Under pressure from the Ethiopian People's Revolutionary Democratic Front (EPRDF) and the allied Eritrean People's Liberation Front (EPLF), the regime collapsed in 1991.

A transitional administration comprising the EPRDF and other opposition groups ruled until a new federal constitution was adopted in 1994. The Federal Democratic Republic of Ethiopia was proclaimed on 22 August 1995. The 2001 presidential election was won by Lt. Girma Wolde Giorgis, the EPRDF candidate. In the 2005 legislative election, the EPRDF retained its majority in parliament, though this was reduced; opposition parties accused the EPRDF of electoral fraud and there were violent protests in Addis Ababa in June 2005.

FOREIGN RELATIONS

There has been fighting with Eritrea in disputes over border territory, especially in Tigray, since 1998. Though usually sporadic, fighting escalated into war in 1999–2000. Peace talks resulted in an agreement to set up regional military commissions to resolve local security issues. In 2002 the independent Eritrea-Ethiopia Boundary Commission (EEBC) defined the international border between the two countries. The Commission's 2003 ruling that Badme lay in Eritrea was rejected by the Ethiopian government, and relations between the two countries remain strained. The UN, which deployed peacekeeping troops in 2000, continues to patrol the disputed area.

POLITICAL SYSTEM

The 1994 constitution provides for a federal government, responsible for foreign affairs, defence and economic policy, and nine ethnically based states. The president is elected by both houses of the legislature for a six-year term, renewable only once. The Federal Parliamentary Assembly *(Yememakirtoch Mekir Bet)* is bicameral. The lower house, the House of People's Representatives *(Yehizb Tewokayoch Mekir Bet)*, has 547 members, directly elected for a five-year term. The House of Federation *(Yefedereshn Mekir Bet)* has 108 members, indirectly elected for a five-year term by the government councils of the nine states in the federation. These regional administrations have considerable autonomy, and the right to secede.

HEAD OF STATE

President, Lt Girma Wolde Giorgis, *elected by parliament* 8 October 2001

SELECTED GOVERNMENT MEMBERS *as at July 2005*
Prime Minister, C.-in-C. of the National Armed Forces, Meles Zenawi
Deputy Prime Minister, Rural Development, Addisu Legesse
Finance and Economic Development, Sufian Ahmed
Foreign Affairs, Seyoum Mesfin
National Defence, Abbadula Gemeda

EMBASSY OF THE FEDERAL DEMOCRATIC REPUBLIC OF ETHIOPIA

17 Princes Gate, London SW7 1PZ **T** 020-7589 7212
E info@ethioembassy.org.uk
Ambassador Extraordinary and Plenipotentiary, HE Fisseha Adugna, apptd 2002

BRITISH EMBASSY

Fikre Mariam Abatechan Street (PO Box 858), Addis Ababa
T (+251) (1) 612354
E britishembassy.addisababa@fco.gov.uk
Ambassador Extraordinary and Plenipotentiary, HE Robert Dewar, apptd 2004

BRITISH COUNCIL

PO Box 1043, Artistic Building, Adwa Avenue, Addis Ababa
T (+251) (1) 550022
E bc.addisababa@et.britishcouncil.org
Director, Michael Moore, MBE

DEFENCE

The Army has 250 main battle tanks and 400 armoured infantry fighting vehicles and armoured personnel carriers. The Air Force has 48 combat aircraft and 25 armed helicopters.

MILITARY EXPENDITURE – 4.9 per cent of GDP (2003)
MILITARY PERSONNEL – 182,500: Army 180,000, Air Force 2,500

ECONOMY AND TRADE

Since 1993, the government has implemented a programme of free-market economic reform. The economy is highly dependent on agriculture, and therefore on the rains; recurring droughts led to famine conditions in 1984–5, 1992, 1997, 2000 and 2002, and much of the population is dependent on food aid. In 2004 a government resettlement programme began to move more than 2 million people away from the drought-stricken and overworked highlands in the east of the country; the government claimed this would be a long-term solution to food shortages.

Agriculture, hunting, forestry and fishing account for approximately 50 per cent of GDP, and around 85 per cent of the people are dependent upon the land for a living. The major food crops are teff, maize, barley, sorghum, wheat, pulses and oil seeds. Ethiopia's largely unexploited natural resources include gold, platinum, copper and potash. Traces of oil and natural gas have been found. The chief imports by value are machinery and transport equipment, manufactured goods and chemicals; the principal exports by value are coffee (which normally provides about 60 per cent of Ethiopia's foreign exchange earnings), oil seeds, hides and skins, and pulses. The country's main markets for exports are the UK, Djibouti, Germany, Italy, Japan, Saudi Arabia and the USA.

GNI – US$6,500 million (2002); US$100 per capita (2002)
ANNUAL AVERAGE GROWTH OF GDP – 11.6 per cent (2004 est.)
INFLATION RATE – 2.4 per cent (2004 est.)
TOTAL EXTERNAL DEBT – US$5,481 million (2000)
FOREIGN DIRECT INVESTMENT – $149 million (1997–2000)
IMPORTS – US$1,670 million (2002)
EXPORTS – US$480 million (2002)

BALANCE OF PAYMENTS
Trade – US$975 million deficit (2002)
Current Account – US$150 million deficit (2002)

Trade with UK	2003	2004
Imports from UK	£44,743,000	£35,435,000
Exports to UK	15,375,000	18,452,000

TRANSPORT INFRASTRUCTURE

A network of roads in rural areas links the major cities with each other, with the Sudanese and Kenyan borders and through Eritrea to the Red Sea coast. There are 31,571 km of roads, 3,789 km of which are surfaced. The only railway line, 681 km in length, links Addis Ababa to Djibouti city. Ethiopian Airlines maintains regular services throughout Africa and to Europe.

EDUCATION

Elementary and secondary education are provided by government schools in the main centres of population; there are also mission schools. The National University (founded 1961) co-ordinates the institutions of higher education. There are also universities at Alemaya (agricultural), Debub, Mekele, Bashir Dar and Jimma.
ILLITERACY RATE – (m) 56.4 per cent; (f) 66.8 per cent (2000)

GROSS ENROLMENT RATIO (percentage of relevant age group) – primary 62 per cent (2003); secondary 17 per cent (2003); tertiary 2 per cent (2003)

MEDIA AND CULTURE

There are over 50 privately owned newspapers in addition to the state-owned daily *Addis Zemen*. There is only one television station, the state-owned Ethiopian Television (ETV). Radio Ethiopia is state-owned but several private stations were given licences at the end of 2004.

Ethiopia is Africa's oldest independent country and, apart from five years of occupation by Italy, was never colonised. The country is also widely considered to be the spiritual home and birthplace of Rastafarianism and many Rastafari believe Haile Selassie to be God incarnate. Addis Ababa is home to the UN Economic Commission for Africa and to the National Museum, which holds the remains of 'Lucy', an *Australopithecus afarensis* skeleton found in Ethiopia in 1974 and estimated to be 3.18 million years old.

FIJI

Matanitu ko Viti – Republic of the Fiji Islands

AREA – 18,274 sq. km
POPULATION – 880,874 (2004 est.), 44 per cent Indians, 51 per cent Fijians, and 5 per cent other races. Since the 1987 coup many ethnic Indians have left, and by 1994 Melanesian Fijians formed the largest population group. The main languages are Fijian and Hindi
CAPITAL – ΨSuva (population, 77,366, 1996), on Viti Levu Island
CURRENCY – Fiji dollar (F$) of 100 cents
NATIONAL ANTHEM – God bless Fiji
NATIONAL DAY – 10 October (Fiji Day)
NATIONAL FLAG – Light blue ground with Union flag in top left quarter and the shield of Fiji in the fly
LIFE EXPECTANCY (years) – 69.2 (2004 est.)
MORTALITY RATE (per 1,000 population) – 5.68 (2004 est.)
INFANT MORTALITY (per 1,000 births) – 12.99 (2004 est.)
HIV / AIDS ADULT PREVALENCE – 0.1 per cent (2003 est.)
DEATH PENALTY – Yes*
POPULATION GROWTH RATE – 1.41 per cent (2004 est.)
POPULATION DENSITY – 44 per sq. km (1999)
MILITARY EXPENDITURE – 1.5 per cent of GDP (2003)
MILITARY PERSONNEL – 3,500: Army 3,200, Navy 300
ILLITERACY RATE – (m) 4.5 per cent; (f) 8.1 per cent (2003 est.)

CLIMATE AND TERRAIN

Fiji is a Melanesian island group of roughly 332 islands (about 100 permanently inhabited) and over 500 islets in the South Pacific, about 1,760 km north of New Zealand. The group extends 480 km from east to west and 480 km north to south. The International Date Line has been diverted to the east of the island group. The largest islands are Viti Levu and Vanua Levu. The terrain is mountainous and volcanic, with tropical rainforest and grassland, and most islands are surrounded by coral reefs. Elevation extremes range from 1,324 m (Tomaniivi, on Viti Levu) at the highest point to 0 m (Pacific Ocean) at the lowest. Fiji

has a tropical oceanic climate with high humidity and an average annual temperature of 27°C.

HISTORY AND POLITICS

The islands were visited by Tasman in 1643, and by Captain Cook in 1774. They became a British colony in 1874, and sugar plantations, employing more than 60,000 indentured Indian labourers, were established. Fiji became independent on 10 October 1970 as a constitutional monarchy within the Commonwealth.

Racial and political tension between the native Melanesians and the growing ethnic Indian population has caused considerable political instability since the 1980s. The Indian-dominated coalition government formed after the 1987 election was overthrown in military coups (May and September 1987) led by Lt.-Col. Sitveni Rabuka; his military government declared Fiji a republic. A new constitution was introduced in 1990 that guaranteed indigenous Fijians the most senior positions in government, but was attacked as racist by opposition parties and was revised in 1997 to remove the racial inequalities. The 1999 election brought to power a multiracial coalition government led by the country's first ethnic Indian prime minister. He and most of the cabinet were held hostage from May to July 2000 by indigenous Fijians; the army took power and revoked the 1997 constitutional revisions. An interim administration was set up in June by the military, which named an all-Fijian government intended to rule for two years and prepare for fresh elections. In July the Great Council of Chiefs appointed Vice-President Josefa Iliolo as president, to replace President Ratu Sir Kamisese Mara, who had resigned in May. The Fijian High Court in 2000 and the Court of Appeal in 2001 ruled that the 1997 constitutional amendments remained in force and that the interim government was not legitimate; these judgments were rejected by the Great Council of Chiefs, which reaffirmed its support for President Iloilo and the interim government.

Fiji withdrew from the Commonwealth from 1987 to 1997, and its membership was suspended from May 2000 until December 2001. In the 2001 legislative election, the Fijian People's Party (SDL) became the largest party in the House of Representatives with 31 seats, while the predominantly Indian Fijian Labour Party (FLP) won 27 seats. The SDL prime minister, Laisenia Qarase, formed a coalition government but failed to include any FLP members, in contravention of the constitution; in 2003 the Supreme Court ruled that ethnic Indian FLP members must be included in the government and posts were allocated, but in 2003 and 2004 the FLP declined cabinet seats in favour of forming the official opposition. In November 2004 Vice-President Ratu Jope Seniloii was convicted of treason for his part in the attempted 2000 coup and sentenced to four years in prison.

POLITICAL SYSTEM

The 1990 constitution was amended in 1997; its validity was confirmed by the courts in 2000 and 2001. The head of state is the president, appointed for a five-year term by the Great Council of Chiefs. The lower house of the bicameral parliament is the House of Representatives, which has 71 members directly elected for a five-year term. Of the 71 seats, 25 are open to all races, but elected in single member constituencies, while the other 46 are allocated for election by the country's various ethnic communities. The upper house, the Senate, has 32 members, who are appointed for a five-year term by the president on the recommendation of the political parties (in proportion to their representation in the lower house) and by the Great Council of Chiefs.

HEAD OF STATE
President, Ratu Josefa Iloilo, *appointed* 13 July 2000, *reappointed* 13 March 2001, *sworn in* 15 March 2001
Vice-President, Ratu Jope Naucabalavu Seniloii

SELECTED GOVERNMENT MEMBERS *as at July 2005*
Prime Minister, Minister for Fijian Affairs, Culture and Heritage, National Reconciliation and Unity, Laisenia Qarase
Finance and National Planning, Communications, Ratu Jone Kubuabola
Foreign Affairs and *External Trade*, Kaliopate Tavola
Home Affairs and Immigration, Yosef Vosanibola

HIGH COMMISSION OF THE REPUBLIC OF FIJI
34 Hyde Park Gate, London SW7 5DN
T 020-7584 3661
E fijirepuk@compuserve.com
High Commissioner, Emitai Lausiki Boladuadua, apptd 2002

BRITISH HIGH COMMISSION
Victoria House, 47 Gladstone Road, PO Box 1355, Suva
T (+679) 322 9100
E consularsuva@fco.gov.uk
High Commissioner, HE Charles Mochan, apptd 2002

ECONOMY AND TRADE
Agriculture accounts for 18 per cent of GDP and employed approximately 70 per cent of the workforce in 2001. The principal cash crop is sugar cane, which is the main export; in 2002 the government announced the privatisation of the industry, threatened with collapse by the withdrawal of EU subsidies. The other main cash crops are coconuts, ginger, fish, lumber, molasses and copra. A variety of other fruit, vegetables and root crops are also grown, and self-sufficiency in rice is a major objective. Forestry, fishing, beef production and light industry are being encouraged in order to diversify the economy. The processing of agricultural, marine and timber products are the main manufacturing industries, along with gold mining and textiles. Along with sugar, tourism is the mainstay of the economy and a major source of foreign exchange, with over 300,000 visitors annually. The chief imports are foodstuffs, machinery, mineral fuels, chemicals, beverages, tobacco and manufactured articles.
GNI – US$1,480 million (2000); US$2,150 per capita (2001)
ANNUAL AVERAGE GROWTH OF GDP – 3.6 per cent (2004 est.)
INFLATION RATE – 1.1 per cent (2000)
TOTAL EXTERNAL DEBT – US$136 million (2000)
IMPORTS – US$1,170 million (2003)
EXPORTS – US$680 million (2003)

BALANCE OF PAYMENTS
Trade – US$116 million deficit (1999)
Current Account – US$13 million surplus (1999)

Trade with UK	2003	2004
Imports from UK	£5,016,000	£6,345,000
Exports to UK	64,581,000	64,300,000

TRANSPORT INFRASTRUCTURE
Fiji is one of the main aerial crossroads in the Pacific, providing services to New Zealand, Australia, Tonga, Samoa, Vanuatu, the Solomon Islands, Kiribati, Tuvalu, New Caledonia and American Samoa. It has three ports of entry, at Suva, Lautoka and Levuka. There are 3,440 km of roads, 1,692 km of which are surfaced. There are 597 km of railways.

MEDIA
Fiji's privately owned newspapers are published in English, Fijian and Hindi. Government-owned newspapers are also multilingual. Radio (both public and private) is the main source of news, particularly on the more remote islands. There are two main television networks: Fiji 1, a national channel operated by Fiji Television Ltd, and Sky Fiji, a subscription channel, also operated by Fiji Television.

FINLAND

Suomen Tasavalta / Republiken Finland – Republic of Finland

AREA – 304,600 sq. km. Neighbours: Norway (north-west and north), Russia (east), Sweden (west)
POPULATION – 5,214,512 (2004 est.). Finnish and Swedish are both official languages, 93 per cent speaking Finnish as their first language and 5.6 per cent Swedish. Sami is spoken by 1,700 of the 6,500-strong Sami population who live in the far north. The population is predominantly Lutheran
CAPITAL – ΨHelsinki (Helsingfors) (population, 1,163,000, 2000 estimate)
MAJOR CITIES – Espoo (Esbo); ΨOulu (Uleåborg); Tampere (Tammerfors); ΨTurku (Åbo); Vantaa (Vanda)
CURRENCY – Euro (€) of 100 cents
NATIONAL ANTHEM – Maamme/Vårt land [Our land]
NATIONAL DAY – 6 December (Independence Day)
NATIONAL FLAG – White with blue cross
LIFE EXPECTANCY (years) – 78.24 (2004 est.)
MORTALITY RATE (per 1,000 population) – 9.69 (2004 est.)
INFANT MORTALITY (per 1,000 births) – 3.59 (2004 est.)
HIV / AIDS ADULT PREVALENCE – 0.1 per cent (2002)
DEATH PENALTY – No (abolished 1972)
POPULATION GROWTH RATE – 0.18 per cent (2004 est.)
POPULATION DENSITY – 17 per sq. km (2002)
URBAN POPULATION – 59 per cent (2001)

CLIMATE AND TERRAIN
Most of the country is a glaciated plain of forests (over 65 per cent of the land area) and over 60,000 lakes, with low hills along the eastern border with Russia and in the far north. Elevation extremes range from 1,328 m (Haltaitunturi) at the highest point to 0 m (Baltic Sea) at the lowest.

Owing to the isostatic uplift, a name given to the vertical movement of post-glaciated land masses since the last ice age, the surface area of Finland is growing by an estimated 7 sq. km. a year. A third of the country is north of the Arctic Circle and temperatures there can range from −20°C in January to 10°C in July. Temperatures in Helsinki range from −6°C in January to 17°C in July.

HEAD OF STATE
President, Tarja Kaarina Halonen, *elected* 6 February 2000, *inaugurated* 1 March 2000

SELECTED GOVERNMENT MEMBERS *as at July 2005*
Prime Minister, Matti Vanhanen
Deputy Prime Minister, Finance, Antti Kalliomäki
Defence, Seppo Kääriäinen
Foreign Affairs, Erkki Tuomioja
Interior, Kari Rajamäki

EMBASSY OF FINLAND
38 Chesham Place, London SW1X 8HW T 020-7838 6200
Ambassador Extraordinary and Plenipotentiary, HE Jaakko Laajava, apptd 2004

BRITISH EMBASSY
Itäinen Puistotie 17, FIN-00140 Helsinki
T (+358) (9) 2286 5100 E info@britishembassy.fi
Ambassador Extraordinary and Plenipotentiary, HE Matthew Kirk, apptd 2002

BRITISH COUNCIL
Hakaniemenkatu 2, FIN-00530 Helsinki
T (+358) (9) 7743 330 E office@britishcouncil.fi
Director, Tuija Talvitie

HISTORY AND POLITICS

Finland was part of the Swedish Empire from the Middle Ages until it was ceded to Russia in 1809 and became an autonomous grand duchy of the Russian Empire. After the Russian revolution in 1917, Finland declared its independence. An attempted coup by Finnish Bolsheviks led to a short civil war that ended in their defeat in 1918, and in 1919 a republic was set up. It resisted the 1939 invasion by the Soviet Union but was defeated in 1940 and forced to cede territory; in the hope of recovering this territory it joined Germany's attack on the USSR in 1941. After agreeing an armistice with the Soviet Union in 1944, Finland concluded a peace treaty in 1947 that conceded further territory to the Soviet Union and obliged it to pay reparations. A Soviet-Finnish co-operation treaty in 1948 forced Finland to demilitarise its Soviet border and to adopt a stance of neutrality; these terms lasted until the demise of the Soviet Union in 1991.

Since the mid-1960s the majority of Finnish governments have been coalitions of centre and moderate left-wing parties, with the Social Democratic Party (SDP) or the Centre Party (KESK) the leading parties in the coalitions. Finland joined the EU in 1995 and the European Monetary Union in 1998; a decision by its parliament on whether to ratify the EU constitution was scheduled for late 2005. The 2000 presidential election was won by Tarja Halonen of the SDP. The 2003 legislative election was narrowly won by KESK, with 55 seats in parliament. It formed a centre-left coalition government with the SDP and the Swedish People's Party (SFP), with Anneli Jaatteenmaki (KESK) as prime minister; she resigned a few months later and was replaced by Matti Vanhanen (KESK) but the rest of the government was virtually unchanged.

POLITICAL SYSTEM

Under the 2000 constitution, the executive president is directly elected for a six-year term. There is a unicameral legislature, the *Eduskunta*, with 200 members directly elected for a four-year term. The prime minister is elected by the *Eduskunta* and appointed by the president.

DEFENCE

The Army has 359 main battle tanks, 276 armoured infantry fighting vehicles and 1,101 armoured personnel carriers. The Navy has nine patrol and coastal vessels. The Air Force has 63 combat aircraft.
MILITARY EXPENDITURE – 1.4 per cent of GDP (2003)
MILITARY PERSONNEL – 27,000: Army 19,200, Navy 5,000, Air Force 2,800; Paramilitaries 3,100
CONSCRIPTION DURATION – Six to 12 months

ECONOMY AND TRADE

At the start of 2004 the World Economic Forum rated Finland at the top of its league for business competitiveness, despite economic difficulties in the early 1990s after the collapse of the Soviet Union. The economy is thriving as a result of the cutting-edge telecommunications industry, particularly the manufacture of mobile phones, as well as the traditional timber and metals industries. Other important industries include rubber, plastics, chemicals, pharmaceuticals, glass, ceramics, furniture, footwear, foodstuffs and shipbuilding. The main exports are electronic and electrical goods, paper and wood pulp, machinery and metal products. The principal imports are raw materials, machinery and manufactured goods. Trade with EU countries accounts for more than half of Finland's total trade.
GNI – US$124,200 million (2002); US$23,890 per capita (2002)
ANNUAL AVERAGE GROWTH OF GDP – 3 per cent (2004 est.)
INFLATION RATE – 0.7 per cent (2004 est.)
UNEMPLOYMENT – 8.9 per cent (2004 est.)
DIRECT FOREIGN INVESTMENT – US$28,036 million (1997–2000)
IMPORTS – US$41,600 million (2003)
EXPORTS – US$52,500 million (2003)

BALANCE OF PAYMENTS
Trade – US$13,390 million surplus (2003)
Current Account – US$9,295 million surplus (2003)

Trade with UK	2003	2004
Imports from UK	£1,291,666,000	£1,336,917,000
Exports to UK	1,950,476,000	2,289,888,000

TRANSPORT INFRASTRUCTURE

The road and rail networks are concentrated in the southern half of the country, where most of the population and industry are found. There are 77,943 km of roads, 50,305 km of which are surfaced. There are 5,850 km of railways; no lines run north of the Arctic Circle or to Sweden, though there are connections with Russia. The main ports are Turku and Oulu, and there are passenger services with Sweden, Estonia and Germany as well as countries outside the Baltic. The principal airports are at Helsinki, Turku and Oulu.

EDUCATION

Primary education is free of charge and compulsory for children from seven to 16 years. There are 4,300 schools ranging in size from ten pupils to 900. There are 20 institutes of higher education; ten universities, three technical colleges, three schools of economics and business administration and four art colleges.
GROSS ENROLMENT RATIO (percentage of relevant age group) – primary 102 per cent (2002); secondary 126 per cent (2002); tertiary 85 per cent (2002)

MEDIA AND CULTURE

Newspapers are privately owned and offer a wide spectrum of political views. There are both commercial and state-owned broadcasters; the state broadcaster is Yleisradio Oy (YLE). Newspapers, books, plays and films appear in both Finnish and Swedish.

The golden age of Finnish culture is considered to have begun in the late 19th century and went on well into the first decades of the 20th. For a small country Finland has produced a number of world famous composers and performers, including Jean Sibelius (1865–1957) and Esa-Pekka Salonen (b. 1958). The national author is Aleksis Kivi, who published his main work *The Seven Brothers* in 1870. F. E. Sillanpaa won the Nobel Price in Literature in 1939. Also well-known is the writer Tove Jansson (1914–2001), author of the Moomintroll books for children which were originally published in the 1940s and have been translated into over 30 languages.

FRANCE

République Française – French Republic

AREA – 550,100 sq. km. Neighbours: Belgium and Luxembourg (north-east), Germany, Switzerland and Italy (east), Monaco (south), Spain and Andorra (south-west)
POPULATION – 60,424,213 (2004 est.); 57,218,000 (Metropolitan France), and 58,745,000 including overseas departments (1992 official estimate): 72 per cent Catholic, 8 per cent Muslim, 2 per cent Jewish. The language is French; there are several regional languages including Basque, Breton, Catalan, Corsican, Flemish, German and Occitan
CAPITAL – Paris (population, 9,644,507, 1999 census)
MAJOR CITIES – ΨBordeaux; Grenoble; Lille; Lyon; ΨMarseille; Nantes; Nice; Strasbourg; Toulon; Toulouse. The chief towns of Corsica are ΨAjaccio and ΨBastia
CURRENCY – Euro (€) of 100 cents

NATIONAL ANTHEM – La Marseillaise
NATIONAL DAY – 14 July (Bastille Day 1789)
NATIONAL FLAG – The tricolour: three vertical bands, blue, white, red (blue next to flagstaff)
LIFE EXPECTANCY (years) – 79.44 (2004 est.)
MORTALITY RATE (per 1,000 population) – 9.06 (2004 est.)
INFANT MORTALITY (per 1,000 births) – 4.31 (2004 est.)
HIV / AIDS ADULT PREVALENCE – 0.4 per cent (2003 est.)
DEATH PENALTY – No (abolished 1981)
POPULATION GROWTH RATE – 0.39 per cent (2004 est.)
POPULATION DENSITY – 108 per sq. km (2002)

CLIMATE AND TERRAIN

The north and west are flat plains, especially in the basins of the Somme, Seine, Loire and Garonne rivers, with some low hills. The centre of the south is occupied by the Massif Central plateau, which is divided by the valley of the Rhone and Soane rivers from the French Alps and the Jura mountains on the eastern border with Switzerland. The Pyrenees range lies along the southern border with Spain. Elevation extremes range from 4,807 m (Mont Blanc, Alps) at the highest point to −2 m (Rhone river delta) at the lowest. The south of France has a Mediterranean climate with warm winters (average temperature 3°C) and hot, arid summers (average temperature 18°C). The east of France has a continental climate.

HISTORY AND POLITICS

The area that is now France was conquered by the Romans in the first century BC and, as the province of Gaul, remained part of the Roman Empire until the Frankish invasions of the fifth and sixth centuries. The Treaty of Verdun (AD 843) divided the Frankish Empire created by Charlemagne into three parts, of which the western part, *Francia Occidentalis*, became the basis for modern France. Weak central government allowed the great nobles to form virtually independent duchies, and the assertion of royal power over these nobles was not completed until the 16th century. France's attempts to establish itself as the supreme European power from the 16th century were hindered by civil and religious wars (1562–98), but by the early 18th century France was the

leading power in Europe and had a large overseas empire.

The ancien régime was overthrown in the French Revolution (1789), a republic was declared in 1792 and the king, Louis XVI, was executed. The republic was overthrown by Napoléon Bonaparte, who established the first French Empire (1804–14). The ensuing Congress of Vienna restored the monarchy, but in 1848 the Second Republic was declared, which lasted only until 1852, when the Second Empire was proclaimed under Napoléon III. He was forced to abdicate following the defeat of France in the Franco-Prussian war (1870–1), after which the Third Republic (1870–1940) was established.

France was one of the victors in the First World War, when German offensives in the north and east of the country were held and eventually defeated. However, the country was invaded during the Second World War and the north was occupied by Germany from 1940 until 1944, with a pro-German government in the south. The Fourth Republic was declared in 1946, but collapsed in 1958 because of the Algerian war; a new constitution was adopted and the Fifth Republic was proclaimed. France granted its colonies independence between 1954 and 1962.

Jacques Chirac, the candidate of the Rally for the Republic (RPR), was elected president in 1995. He was re-elected in 2002 after winning a second round run-off against the National Front leader Jean-Marie Le Pen. In the 2002 elections to the National Assembly, the Union for a Presidential Majority (UMP), an election coalition of the RPR and Liberal Democracy (DL), won an overall majority and a coalition of the UMP and the Union for French Democracy (UDF) formed a government. In September 2002 the RPR, DL and parts of the UDF merged to form the Union for a Popular Movement (UMP).

France was a founder member of the EEC in 1958, and joined the European Monetary Union in 1999. In a referendum in May 2005, the population rejected the EU constitution, prompting a political shake-up that included the dismissal of the prime minister, Jean-Pierre Raffarin; he was replaced by Dominique de Villepin, who appointed a new cabinet.

INSURGENCIES

A 25-year campaign of bombings and shootings by Corsican separatists began in the mid-1970s. In 2000 the Corsican regional parliament accepted the French government's proposals to combine the island's two departments and to give the regional parliament powers over cultural, educational, structural and planning affairs and limited legislative autonomy by 2004, in return for a permanent end to terrorism. The proposals, which were narrowly passed by the French National Assembly in 2001, suffered a setback in 2002 when the Constitutional Council rejected the legislation as unconstitutional. A referendum in 2003 voted narrowly against the establishment of a new unified assembly for Corsica with limited powers to raise and spend taxes.

POLITICAL SYSTEM

Under the 1958 constitution, the head of state is an executive president directly elected for a five-year term. The legislature, parlement, consists of the National Assembly and the Senate. The National Assembly has 577 deputies, 555 for metropolitan France and 22 for the overseas departments and territories. Members are directly elected for a five-year term. The Senate currently has 321 senators, 296 for metropolitan France, 13 for the overseas departments and territories, and 12 for French citizens abroad. Its members are elected by an electoral college to serve a nine-year term, with a third being elected every three years. By 2010, 25 new seats will be added to the Senate to make a total of 346 senators (326 for metropolitan France and the overseas departments, two for New Caledonia, two for Mayotte, one for St-Pierre and Miquelon, three for overseas territories and 12 for French nationals living abroad), and members will serve for a six-year term, with one half of the seats being renewed every three years.

The prime minister is nominated by the National Assembly and appointed by the president, as is the Council of Ministers. They are responsible to the legislature, but as the executive is constitutionally separate from the legislature, ministers may not sit in the legislature and must hand over their seats to a substitute.

A government plan for decentralisation of power from Paris was initiated in 2002, and constitutional amendments in 2003 paved the way for the devolution to the 22 regions and 96 departments of powers over economic development, transport, tourism, culture and further education.

HEAD OF STATE

President of the French Republic, Jacques René Chirac, elected 7 May 1995, re-elected 5 May 2002

SELECTED GOVERNMENT MEMBERS as at July 2005

Prime Minister, Dominique de Villepin
Minister of State; Interior and Regional Development, Nicolas Sarkozy
Defence, Michèle Alliot-Marie
Economy, Thierry Breton
Foreign Affairs, Philippe Douste-Blazy

FRENCH EMBASSY

58 Knightsbridge, London SW1X 7JT T 020-7073 1000
E consulat.londres-amba@diplomatie.fr
Ambassador Extraordinary and Plenipotentiary, HE Gérard Errera, apptd 2002

BRITISH EMBASSY

35 rue du Faubourg St Honoré, 75383 Paris Cedex 08
T (+33) (1) 4451 3100
Ambassador Extraordinary and Plenipotentiary, HE Sir John Eaton Holmes KBE, CVO, CMG, apptd 2001

BRITISH COUNCIL

9 rue de Constantine, 75340 Paris Cédex 07
T (+33) (1) 4955 7300 E information@britishcouncil.fr
Director, Paul de Quincey

DEFENCE

The Army has 614 main battle tanks, 3,700 armoured personnel carriers, 384 armoured infantry fighting vehicles and 418 helicopters.

The Navy has ten submarines including 4 strategic submarines, one aircraft carrier, one cruiser, 12 destroyers, 20 frigates and 35 patrol and coastal vessels, 58 combat aircraft and 30 armed helicopters. The Navy has four domestic and five overseas bases. The Air Force has 478 combat aircraft. There are currently two military satellites in service.

France deploys 34,303 armed forces personnel abroad; 3,200 in Germany (including members of Eurocorps); 15,900 in French Overseas Departments and Territories;

9,700 in former French colonies in Africa and 5,503 on UN and peacekeeping duties.
MILITARY EXPENDITURE – 2.6 per cent of GDP (2003)
MILITARY PERSONNEL 130,030: Army 137,000, Strategic Nuclear Forces 4,800, Navy 44,250, Air Force 64,000; Paramilitaries (Gendarmerie) 101,399

ECONOMY AND TRADE

The economy is not performing well and reform is necessary to stimulate growth and reduce government expenditure, but implementation has been difficult because of the constraints of euro zone membership. Also, the government's privatisation and labour, pension and welfare reform plans have been strongly resisted, particularly by the large public sector, provoking demonstrations and strikes. There have also been protests in recent years at reforms to the Common Agricultural Policy and other EU measures that impact on personal incomes.

Nearly 55 per cent of the land area of metropolitan France is utilised for agricultural production (there are around 45 million hectares of farmland) and a further quarter is accounted for by forests. Viniculture is extensive, regions famous for their wines including Bordeaux, Burgundy and Champagne, though France has lost market share to other countries in recent years. Production of wine in 2003 was 47.1 million hectolitres. Cognac, liqueurs and cider are also produced. Other important agricultural products include sugar beet, dairy products, cereals and oil seeds.

Oil is produced from fields in the Landes area, but France is a net importer of crude oil, for processing by its important oil-refining industry. Natural gas is produced in the foothills of the Pyrenees.

Heavy industries include the production of iron, steel and aluminium. In 2002 production of pig iron was 14 million tonnes and steel 20.3 million tonnes. Other important industries are in the construction and civil engineering sectors, chemicals, rubber and plastics, pharmaceutical industries, and vehicle production and telecommunications services. The principal imports are raw materials for the heavy and manufacturing industries (e.g. oil, minerals, chemicals), machinery and precision instruments, agricultural products, chemicals and vehicles. Agricultural products, chemicals, pharmaceuticals and vehicles are the principal exports. Most of France's trade is with other EU countries

GNI – US$1,362,100 million (2002); US$22,240 per capita (2002)
ANNUAL AVERAGE GROWTH OF GDP – 2.1 per cent (2004 est.)
INFLATION RATE – 2.3 per cent (2004 est.)
UNEMPLOYMENT – 10.1 per cent (2004 est.)
FOREIGN DIRECT INVESTMENT – US$133,044 (1997–2000)
IMPORTS – US$371,000 million (2003)
EXPORTS – US$366,000 million (2003)

BALANCE OF PAYMENTS
Trade – US$1,042 million surplus (2003)
Current Account – US$4,384 million surplus (2002)

Trade with UK	2003	2004
Imports from UK	£16,423,925,000	£18,281,709,000
Exports to UK	14,227,880,000	19,530,498,000

TRANSPORT INFRASTRUCTURE

There are extensive road and rail networks covering the whole country, with approximately 11,500 km of motorways, around 900,000 km of other roads, and about 32,682 km of railways. The world's tallest road bridge was opened at Millau in December 2004.

The principal ports are Marseille, Nice and Le Havre, and there are 14,932 km of navigable waterways inland. The French mercantile marine consisted in 2003 of 150 ships of 1,000 gross tonnage or over, 118 of which are registered overseas. There are two international airports serving Paris, and smaller airports at Lille, Le Havre, Rouen, Rennes, Brest, Nantes, Bordeaux, Toulouse, Lourdes, Perpignan, Montpellier, Marseille, Nice, Lyon, Clermont-Ferrand and Strasbourg.

EDUCATION

Education is compulsory, free of charge and secular from six to 16. Schools may be single-sex or co-educational. Primary education is given in nursery schools, primary schools and *collèges d'enseignement général* (four-year secondary modern course); secondary education in *collèges d'enseignement technique, collèges d'enseignement secondaire* and *lycées* (a seven-year course leading to one of the five *baccalauréats*). Specialist schools are numerous.

There are many *grandes écoles* in France which award diplomas in many subjects not taught at university, especially applied science and engineering. Most of these are state institutions but have a competitive system of entry, unlike universities. There are universities in 24 towns including 13 in Paris.
GROSS ENROLMENT RATIO (percentage of relevant age group) – primary 105 per cent (2002); secondary 108 per cent (2002); tertiary 54 per cent (2002)

MEDIA

There are over 100 daily newspapers in France. The main publications are: *Le Monde, Le Matin, Les Echos, Le Figaro, Libération, La Tribune,* and *Le Parisien.* The press is mostly privately owned. French state radio caters for both domestic (Radio France) and overseas (Radio France Internationale) audiences. Channel TV5 is an international French-language television channel co-financed by Belgium, Canada, France and Switzerland. The main domestic channel, TF1, was privatised in 1987. There are two digital satellite TV companies. In 2004 there were 23 million internet users.

OVERSEAS DEPARTMENTS

Greater powers of self-government were granted to French Guiana, Guadeloupe, Martinique and Réunion in 1982. These former colonies had enjoyed departmental status since 1946. Their directly elected Assemblies operate in parallel with the existing, indirectly constituted Regional Councils. The French government is represented by a Prefect in each.

FRENCH GUIANA
AREA – 83,534 sq. km
POPULATION – 185,000 (2001)
CAPITAL – ΨCayenne (50,675, 1999 census)

Situated on the north-eastern coast of South America, French Guiana is flanked by Surinam on the west and by Brazil on the south and east. Under the administration of French Guiana is the Îles du Salut group of islands (St Joseph, Île Royal and Île du Diable). The European Space Agency rocket launch site is situated at Kourou. The main

products are timber, shrimp and gold. Tourism is restricted by the lack of infrastructure.
Prefect, Ange Mancini

GUADELOUPE
AREA – 1,780 sq. km
POPULATION – 436,000 (2001)
CAPITAL – ΨBasse-Terre (12,410, 1999 census) on Guadeloupe

A number of islands in the Leeward Islands group of the West Indies, consisting of Guadeloupe (or Basse-Terre), Grande-Terre, Marie-Galante, La Désirade and the Îles des Saintes; under the administration of Guadeloupe are the islands of St-Barthélemy and the French part of St-Martin, which lie over 240 km to the north-west. The main towns are ΨLes Abymes; ΨSt-Martin; ΨPointe-à-Pitre (Grande-Terre) and ΨGrand Bourg (Marie-Galante). The main industries are sugar refining and rum distilling.
Prefect, Dominique Vian

MARTINIQUE
AREA – 1,128 sq. km
POPULATION – 390,000 (2001)
CAPITAL – ΨFort-de-France (94,778, 1999 census)

Martinique is an island situated in the Windward Islands group of the West Indies, between Dominica in the north and St Lucia in the south. Mount Pelée (1,397 m) is an active volcano that last erupted in 1902. Tourism is a major industry. The main products are bananas, rum and petroleum products.
Prefect, Yves Dassonville

RÉUNION
AREA – 2,547 sq. km
POPULATION – 745,000 (2001)
CAPITAL – St-Denis (158,139, 1999)

Réunion, which became a French possession in 1638, lies in the Indian Ocean, about 650 km east of Madagascar and 180 km south-west of Mauritius. The smaller, uninhabited islands of Bassas da India, Europa, les Glorieuses, Juan de Nova and Tromelin are administered from Réunion. The main industries are tourism, and sugar and rum production.
Prefect, Gonthier Friederici

TERRITORIAL COLLECTIVITIES

MAYOTTE
AREA – 372 sq. km
POPULATION – 170,879 (2002 estimate)
CAPITAL – Mamoudzou (32,733, 1997 census)

Part of the Comoros archipelago, Mayotte remained a French dependency when the other three islands became independent as the Comoros Republic in 1975. Since 1976 the island has been a *collectivité territoriale*, an intermediate status between Overseas Department and Overseas Territory. The main products are coffee, copra, vanilla and fish.
Prefect, Jean-Jacques Brot

Trade with UK	2003	2004
Imports from UK	£787,000	£288,000
Exports to UK	8,000	34,000

ST PIERRE AND MIQUELON
AREA – 242 sq. km
POPULATION – 6,954 (2002 estimate)
CAPITAL – ΨSt-Pierre (5,618, 1999)

These two small groups of eight islands off the south coast of Newfoundland became a *collectivité territoriale* in 1985. There is a French-appointed commissioner and an elected local council. The main industry is fishing.
Prefect, Claude Valleix

Trade with UK	2003	2004
Imports from UK	£64,000	£160,000
Exports to UK	—	—

OVERSEAS TERRITORIES

FRENCH POLYNESIA
AREA – 3,887 sq. km
POPULATION – 248,000 (2001)
CAPITAL – ΨPapeete (26,181), in Tahiti

French Polynesia consists of over 118 volcanic and coral islands and atolls in the South Pacific. There are five archipelagos: the Society Islands (Windward Islands group includes Tahiti, Moorea, Makatea, Mehetia, Tetiaroa, Tubuai Manu; Leeward Islands group includes Huahine, Raiatea, Tahaa, Bora-Bora, Maupiti), the Tuamotu Islands (Rangiroa, Hao, Turéia, etc.), the Gambier Islands (Mangareva, etc.), the Tubuai Islands (Rimatara, Rurutu, Tubuai, Raivavae, Rapa, etc.) and the Marquesas Islands (Nuku-Hiva, Hiva-Oa, Fatu-Hiva, Tahuata, Ua Huka, etc.). The territory has considerable autonomy, with its own parliament and president, as well as the French-appointed High Commissioner. An independence movement began in the 1970s. The main industries are tourism, pearl-fishing, and fish and coconut products.
High Commissioner, Michel Mathieu

Trade with UK	2003	2004
Imports from UK	£11,331,000	£8,117,000
Exports to UK	278,000	294,000

NEW CALEDONIA
AREA – 18,736 sq. km
POPULATION – 219,000 (2001)
CAPITAL – ΨNouméa (97,581)

New Caledonia is a large island in the western Pacific, 1,120 km off the eastern coast of Australia. Dependencies are the Isles of Pines, the Loyalty Islands (Mahé, Lifou, Urea, etc.), the Bélep Archipelago, the Chesterfield Islands, the Huon Islands and Walpole. A quarter of the world's nickel deposits are found in the territory, and nickel, chrome and iron are the main products.

New Caledonia was discovered in 1774 and annexed by France in 1853; from 1871 to 1896 it was a convict settlement. Tensions between indigenous Kanaks and the European population, particularly over independence, has caused sporadic violence from the 1980s until 1998, when the pro-independence and anti-independence parties and the French government agreed to hold a referendum on independence in 2014 and for greater autonomy for the territory in the intervening period. In 1995, the territory was divided into three provinces, each with a provincial assembly which combined to form the Territorial Assembly.
High Commissioner, Daniel Constantin

Trade with UK	2003	2004
Imports from UK	£8,289,000	£11,183,000
Exports to UK	78,000	809,000

SOUTHERN AND ANTARCTIC TERRITORIES
Created in 1955 from former Réunion dependencies, the territory comprises the islands of Amsterdam (64 sq. km) and St Paul (7 sq. km), the Kerguelen Islands (6,992 sq. km) and Crozet Islands (300 sq. km) archipelagos and Adélie Land (302,500 sq. km) in the Antarctic continent. The population consists only of members of staff of the scientific stations.
Administrator, François Garde

WALLIS AND FUTUNA ISLANDS
AREA – 200 sq. km
POPULATION – 15,585 (2002 estimate)
CAPITAL – ΨMata-Utu on Uvea, the main island of the Wallis group

The two groups of islands (the Wallis Archipelago and the Îles de Horne) lie in the South Pacific, north-east of Fiji. The main products are copra, yams and bananas.
Administrator, Christian Job

Trade with UK	2003	2004
Imports from UK	£53,000	£17,000
Exports to UK	—	—

THE FRENCH COMMUNITY
The constitution of the Fifth French Republic, promulgated in 1958, envisaged the establishment of a French Community of States. A number of the former French states in Africa have seceded from the Community but for all practical purposes continue to enjoy the same close links with France as those that remain formally members. Most former French African colonies are closely linked to France by financial, technical and economic agreements.

GABON

République Gabonaise – Gabonese Republic

AREA – 257,700 sq. km. Neighbours: Equatorial Guinea and Cameroon (north), Republic of Congo (east and south)
POPULATION – 1,355,246 (2004 est.). The official language is French; Fang is widely spoken
CAPITAL – ΨLibreville (population, 362,400, 1993)
CURRENCY – Franc CFA of 100 centimes
NATIONAL ANTHEM – La Concorde
NATIONAL DAY – 17 August
NATIONAL FLAG – Horizontal bands, green, yellow and blue
LIFE EXPECTANCY (years) – 56.46 (2004 est.)
MORTALITY RATE (per 1,000 population) – 11.43 (2004 est.)
INFANT MORTALITY (per 1,000 births) – 54.34 (2004 est.)
HIV / AIDS ADULT PREVALENCE – 8.1 per cent (2003 est.)
DEATH PENALTY – Yes
POPULATION GROWTH RATE – 2.5 per cent (2004 est.)

POPULATION DENSITY – 5 per sq. km (2002)
MILITARY EXPENDITURE – 0.2 per cent of GDP (2003)
MILITARY PERSONNEL – 4,700: Army 3,200, Navy 500, Air Force 1,000; Paramilitaries 2,000
ILLITERACY RATE – (m) 20.2 per cent; (f) 37.8 per cent (2000)
GROSS ENROLMENT RATIO (percentage of relevant age group) – primary 134 per cent (2002); secondary 51 per cent (2002)

CLIMATE AND TERRAIN
The terrain rises from a narrow coastal plain to a hilly interior; approximately 85 per cent of the land is rainforest, with savannah in the east and south. Elevation extremes range from 1,575 m (Mount Iboundji) at the highest point to 0 m (Atlantic Ocean) at the lowest. The climate is hot and humid with an average temperature of 27°C. There are two wet seasons each year, from February to May, and from October to December.

HISTORY AND POLITICS
The first Europeans to visit the region were the Portuguese in the 15th century and Dutch, French and English traders arrived soon after. Sovereignty was signed over to the French in 1839 by a local Mpongwe ruler. In 1849 a slave ship was captured by the French, and the freed slaves formed a settlement which they called Libreville, the current capital. The country was occupied by the French in 1885 and became part of French Equatorial Africa in 1910. Gabon became autonomous within the French Community in 1958 and gained full independence on 17 August 1960.

President Bongo came to power in 1967, and in 1968 a one-party state was established with the Parti Démocratique Gabonais (PDG) as the only party. By the late 1980s, the deteriorating economy was provoking unrest, and in 1991 a multiparty system was reintroduced.

Under the multiparty system, the PDG has remained in power, amid allegations of electoral fraud, although it has included opposition party members in coalition governments since 1994. President Bongo of the PDG was re-elected for a fifth term of office in 1998; the next presidential elections are scheduled for December 2005. The last elections to the National Assembly in 2001 were won by the PDG. The government is dominated by the PDG but includes opposition party members.

POLITICAL SYSTEM
The 1991 constitution, amended in 1995, 1997 and 2003, provides for an executive president, directly elected for a seven-year term; since 2003, there has been no limit on the number of terms a president may serve. The prime minister is appointed by the president, and then appoints the Council of Ministers in consultation with the president. There is a bicameral parliament, with a National Assembly of 120 members directly elected for a five-year term, and a Senate with 91 members elected for a six-year term by municipal and regional councillors.

HEAD OF STATE
President, El Hadj Omar Bongo, *assumed office* December 1967, *re-elected* 1973, 1979, 1986, 1993 and 6 December 1998
Vice-President, Didjob Divungi-di-Ndinge

SELECTED GOVERNMENT MEMBERS *as at July 2005*
Prime Minister, Jean-François Ntoutoume-Emane
Deputy Prime Minister, Human Rights, Paul Mba Abessole

Deputy Prime Minister, Town and Country Planning,
  Emmanuel Ondo Methogo
Deputy Prime Minister; Urban Affairs, Antoine de Padoue
  Mboumbou Miyakou
Defence, Ali Ben Bongo
Finance, Economy, Budget and Privatisation, Paul Toungui
Foreign Affairs, Co-operation and Francophone Affairs, Jean
  Ping
Interior, Public Security, Decentralisation, Clotaire Christian
  Irala

EMBASSY OF THE REPUBLIC OF GABON
27 Elvaston Place, London SW7 5NL T 020-7823 9986
Ambassador Extraordinary and Plenipotentiary, HE Alain
  Mensah-Zaguelet, apptd 2003

BRITISH AMBASSADOR
HE Richard Wildash, LVO, resident at Yaoundé,
Cameroon

ECONOMY AND TRADE
One of the most economically stable countries in Africa,
Gabon has the highest income per capita in the region.
The economy is heavily dependent on oil, which
contributes 50 per cent of GDP and is the leading export,
and, to a lesser extent, on other mineral resources,
including manganese and uranium. Gabon has
considerable timber reserves, with 85 per cent of the
country still forested, although production has stagnated
in recent years.

The government has begun investment in agriculture in
order to ease the country's dependence on oil revenue.
Agricultural products include cocoa, coffee, rubber, sugar
and pineapples.
GNI – US$4,000 million (2002); US$3,060 per capita
  (2002)
ANNUAL AVERAGE GROWTH OF GDP – 1.9 per cent
  (2004 est.)
INFLATION RATE – 1.5 per cent (2004 est.)
TOTAL EXTERNAL DEBT – US$3,800 million (2002)
FOREIGN DIRECT INVESTMENT – US$200 million
  (1997–2000)
IMPORTS – US$860 million (2001)
EXPORTS – US$2,600 million (2001)

Trade with UK	2003	2004
Imports from UK	£33,289,000	£47,260,000
Exports to UK	23,644,000	6,756,000

MEDIA AND CULTURE
The biggest broadcaster, Radiodiffusion-Télévision
Gabonaise, is state-controlled and operates two stations.
There are two other main channels: TéléAfrica, which is
privately owned; and TV Sat, a subscription operator.
There are several privately owned newspapers that usually
publish on a weekly basis. The only daily newspaper,
L'Union, is government run. Radio is an important news
medium because of rural illiteracy rates. Africa No1 is a
pan-African broadcaster based in Gabon which is partly
French-owned.

Due in part to the influx of oil money, the cities of
Gabon are some of the most modern in Africa. The
Gabonese are mainly of Bantu descent and subdivide into
about ten main ethnic groups, the largest of which is the
Fang. Historically, Gabon has been admired for its
woodcarving, and Fang masks are the most famous of all
the Gabonese woodcarving traditions.

THE GAMBIA

Republic of the Gambia

AREA – 11,295 sq. km. Neighbour: Senegal, which
  surrounds the Gambia except at the coast
POPULATION – 1,546,848 (July 2004), mainly Wollof,
  Mandinka and Fula peoples who originally migrated
  from the north and east. The official language is
  English; Fula, Jola, Mandinka, Serahule and Wollof are
  indigenous languages
CAPITAL – ΨBanjul (population, 42,407, 1993 census)
CURRENCY – Dalasi (D) of 100 butut
NATIONAL ANTHEM – For the Gambia, our homeland
NATIONAL DAY – 18 February (Independence Day)
NATIONAL FLAG – Horizontal stripes of red, blue and
  green, separated by narrow white stripes
MORTALITY RATE (per 1,000 population) – 12.08
  (2004 est.)
HIV / AIDS ADULT PREVALENCE – 1.2 per cent
  (2003 est.)
DEATH PENALTY – No (abolished 1981)
POPULATION GROWTH RATE – 2.98 per cent
  (2004 est.)
POPULATION DENSITY – 139 per sq. km (2002)
MILITARY EXPENDITURE – 0.6 per cent of GDP (2003)
MILITARY PERSONNEL – Army 800

CLIMATE AND TERRAIN
The Gambia consists of a narrow strip of land along the
Gambia River; the low-lying land is mostly a flood plain
flanked by hills. Elevation extremes range from 53 m at
the highest point to 0 m (Atlantic Ocean) at the lowest.
The climate is tropical with an average temperature of
between 23°C and 40°C. The wet season runs from June
to September.

HISTORY AND POLITICS
The Gambia River basin was part of a region dominated in
the 10th to 16th centuries by the Mali and Songhai
kingdoms. The Portuguese reached the Gambia River in
1447; English merchants began to trade along the river
from 1588. Merchants from France, Courland (now
Latvia) and the Netherlands also established trading posts
there. In 1816 the British stationed a garrison on an
island at the river mouth that became the capital of a small
British-administered colony, which became a Crown
colony in 1843. In 1889 France agreed that the British
rights along the upper river should extend to 10 km from
the river on either bank. The Gambia became
independent within the Commonwealth on 18 February
1965, and a republic on 24 April 1970.

The post-independence prime minister, Sir Dawda
Jawara, was president from 1970 until he was overthrown
in 1994, in a coup by junior army officers. The coup
leader, Lt. (later Capt.) Jammeh, assumed the presidency,
the constitution was suspended and a civilian-military
government was formed to rule in conjunction with the
Ruling Military Council. A referendum approved a new
constitution in August 1996, Jammeh was elected
president the following month and the Ruling Military
Council was dissolved. In the 2001 presidential election
Jammeh was re-elected with 56 per cent of the vote. The
2002 legislative election was won by President Jammeh's
party, the Alliance for Patriotic Reorientation and
Construction (APRC); the election was boycotted by
opposition parties and there was low voter turnout.

POLITICAL SYSTEM

Under the 1996 constitution, the president is directly elected for a five-year term; there is no limit on re-election. The unicameral legislature, the National Assembly, has 53 members, of whom 48 are directly elected and five are appointed by the president, for a five-year term.

HEAD OF STATE

President, Defence, Capt. Yahya A. J. J. Jammeh, *took power* 23 July 1994, *elected* 26 September 1996, *re-elected* 18 October 2001

Vice-President, Women and Social Affairs, Isatou Njie-Saidy

SELECTED GOVERNMENT MEMBERS *as at July 2005*
External Affairs, Bala Musa Gaye
Finance and Economic Affairs, Alieu Ngum
Interior, Samba D. Bah

GAMBIA HIGH COMMISSION

57 Kensington Court, London W8 5DG
T 020-7937 6316/7/8
High Commissioner, HE Gibril Sumen Joof, apptd 2000

BRITISH HIGH COMMISSION

48 Atlantic Road, Fajara (PO Box 507), Banjul
T (+220) 449 5133
E bhcbanjul@gamtel.gm
High Commissioner, HE Eric Jenkinson, apptd 2003

ECONOMY AND TRADE

Agriculture accounts for 75 per cent of employment and contributes 33 per cent of GDP. The chief product, groundnuts, forms over 80 per cent of exports, leaving the economy vulnerable to market fluctuations. Other crops are cotton, rice, millet, sorghum, sesame, palm kernels, corn, cassava and maize. Manufacturing is limited to groundnut processing, minor metal fabrications, paints, furniture, soap and bottling. Tourism is an important source of foreign revenue, as are remittances from Gambians working abroad.

Trade through the Gambia re-exporting imported goods to neighbouring countries was an important element in the economy but was damaged in 1999 when the government imposed preshipment inspection plans. The main exports are groundnuts, cotton, fish and fish products. The main imports are foodstuffs and live animals, industrial goods, machinery and transport equipment, and fuels.

In 2004 President Jammeh announced that large oil deposits had been discovered off the coast of the Gambia.
GNI – US$400 million (2002); US$270 per capita (2002)
ANNUAL AVERAGE GROWTH OF GDP – 6 per cent (2004 est.)
INFLATION RATE – 7 per cent (2004 est.)
TOTAL EXTERNAL DEBT – US$471 million (2000)
IMPORTS – US$150 million (2002)
EXPORTS – US$2 million (2002)

BALANCE OF PAYMENTS
Trade – US$87 million deficit (1997)
Current Account – US$24 million deficit (1997)

Trade with UK	2003	2004
Imports from UK	£18,958,000	£15,682,000
Exports to UK	2,766,000	3,380,000

EDUCATION

There are four types of school in the Gambia: primary school (ages four to 10); junior school (ages 11–14); secondary school (ages 14–15), and Islamic school. There are 15 secondary schools. Two high schools provide A-level education. The Gambia College provides post-secondary courses in education, agriculture, public health and nursing. There are seven vocational training institutions. There is one university, based in Serrekunda.
ILLITERACY RATE – (m) 56.0 per cent; (f) 70.6 per cent (2000)
GROSS ENROLMENT RATIO (percentage of relevant age group) – primary 79 per cent (2002); secondary 34 per cent (2002)

MEDIA AND CULTURE

Since 2002 private newspapers and radio stations have been regulated by a government-run commission that has the power to suspend publication or transmission licences and imprison journalists. The state operates the only national television station, Gambia Television. There is one private satellite channel, Premium TV Network. State-run Radio Gambia produces tightly controlled news broadcasts, which are relayed by private radio stations.

The Gambia has a rich musical and literary tradition that plays an important part in everyday life. *Griots*, or 'praise-singers', preserve and pass on the stories of families and clans. There is also a vibrant modern literary scene. Contemporary Gambian authors include Ebou Dibba (1943–2000), Lenrie Peters (b. 1932) and William Conton (1925–2003).

GEORGIA

Sak'art'velos Respublikis – Georgia

AREA – 69,700 sq. km. Neighbours: Russian Federation (north), Azerbaijan (east and south), Armenia (south), Turkey (south-west). It includes the autonomous republics of Abkhazia and Ajaria and the disputed region of South Ossetia (Tskhinvali)
POPULATION – 4,693,892 (July 2004): 70 per cent Georgian, 8 per cent Armenian, 6 per cent Russian, 6 per cent Azerbaijani, 3 per cent Ossetian and 2 per cent Abkhazian, with smaller groups of Greeks, Ukrainians, Jews and Kurds. Georgian is the sole official language, except in Abkhazia where Abkhazian is also officially recognised. Russian and Armenian are commonly spoken. About 65 per cent of the population are adherents of the Georgian Orthodox Church, 11 per cent are Muslims, 10 per cent are Russian Orthodox and 8 per cent are Armenian Orthodox
CAPITAL – Tbilisi (population, 1,253,100, 1997 est.)
MAJOR CITIES – Batumi; Kutaisi; Rustavi; Sukhumi (capital of Abkhazia)
CURRENCY – Lari of 100 tetri
NATIONAL ANTHEM – Tavisupleba [Freedom]
NATIONAL DAY – 26 May (Independence Day)
NATIONAL FLAG – Cherry red with a canton in the upper hoist divided black over white
LIFE EXPECTANCY (years) – 75.62 (2004 est.)
MORTALITY RATE (per 1,000 population) – 8.98 (2004 est.)
INFANT MORTALITY (per 1,000 births) – 19.34 (2004 est.)
HIV / AIDS ADULT PREVALENCE – 0.1 per cent (2001 est.)

DEATH PENALTY – No (abolished 1997)

POPULATION BELOW POVERTY LINE – 54 per cent (2001 est.)

POPULATION GROWTH RATE – –0.36 per cent (2004 est.)

POPULATION DENSITY – 74 per sq. km (2002)

URBAN POPULATION – 56 per cent (2001)

MILITARY EXPENDITURE – 2.7 per cent of GDP (2003)

MILITARY PERSONNEL – 11,970: Army 8,620, Navy 2,000, Air Force 1,350; Paramilitaries 11,700

CONSCRIPTION DURATION – 18 months

GROSS ENROLMENT RATIO (percentage of relevant age group) – primary 92 per cent (2002); secondary 79 per cent (2002); tertiary 36 per cent (2002)

CLIMATE AND TERRAIN

Georgia lies in the western part of the Caucasus region, with the Black Sea to the west. It is mountainous, with the Great Caucasus mountain range in the north and the Lesser Caucasus in the south, divided by the valleys of the Kura and Rioni rivers. Elevation extremes range from 5,201 m (Mt Shkhara) at the highest point to 0 m (Black Sea) at the lowest.

HISTORY AND POLITICS

The Georgians formed two states, Colchis and Iberia, on the edge of the Black Sea around 1000 BC. After several centuries of Arab rule, Georgia was liberated and entered its 'Golden Age' in the 12th century AD when trade, irrigation and communications were developed. Invasions by the Khazars and Mongols led to the division of Georgia into several states. These precarious states struggled against the Turkish and the Persian empires from the 16th to the 18th centuries, gradually turning to the Russian Empire for protection and support. Eastern Georgia signed a treaty of alliance with Russia which recognised Russian supremacy in 1783 and joined the Russian Empire in 1801, followed soon after by Western Georgia.

In the late 19th century, nationalist and Marxist movements competed for limited political influence under autocratic Russian rule. One of the most prominent Marxist activists was Iosif Dzhugashvili (Josef Stalin). After the Russian Revolution of 1917, an independent nationalist government came to power in Georgia supported by allied intervention forces. In 1921 Soviet forces occupied Tbilisi, and in 1922 Georgia joined the Soviet Union as part of the Transcaucasian Soviet Socialist Republic, becoming a separate republic in 1936.

In the 1980s there were growing demands for autonomy, and in 1990 the Communist Party's monopoly on power was abolished. In multiparty elections held in October and November 1990 the nationalist leader Zviad Gamsakhurdia was elected president. Georgia declared its independence from the Soviet Union in May 1991 and severed all relations.

Demonstrations against Gamsakhurdia's increasingly dictatorial government in 1991 developed into civil war that resulted in Gamsakhurdia's overthrow and replacement by Eduard Shevardnadze in 1992. The war continued until 1993, when, with most government forces engaged in Abkhazia, Georgia was forced to accept Russian armaments and troops to defeat the rebels and in return agreed to join the Commonwealth of Independent States (CIS). Georgia rescinded its participation in the CIS Collective Security treaty in 1999 and Russian troops, who had been guarding Georgia's frontier with Turkey, began to withdraw.

President Shevardnadze was re-elected in 2000, but resigned in November 2003 after mass demonstrations against alleged electoral fraud in the 2003 parliamentary elections. Mikhail Saakashvili, leader of the National Movement, was elected president in a landslide victory in January 2004. In the rerun elections in the disputed parliamentary seats in March 2004, the National Movement Democrats won 67 per cent of the vote. Prime minister Zurab Zhvania was killed by carbon monoxide poisoning in February 2005 and finance minister Zurab Noghaideli was appointed to replace him.

SECESSION

The growth of Georgian nationalism and demands for autonomy in the 1980s led the minority Ossetians and Abkhazians to demand secession. The Georgian government resisted these demands and there was conflict with both regions in the early 1990s.

The South Ossetians rebelled in late 1990 in an attempt to join North Ossetia, itself part of Russia, and declared itself independent in 1991, but the province's status remains unresolved. After fighting ended in June 1992, a joint Russian-Georgian-Ossetian peacekeeping force was deployed, but clashes have occurred since, most recently in summer 2004. The 2001 presidential election in South Ossetia was won by Eduard Kokoiti, a Russian citizen, but the 2004 parliamentary election was not recognised by Georgia. In January 2005, the Ossetian leadership rejected Georgia's proposal that the province should have autonomy within Georgia and demanded independence.

In the Autonomous Republic of Abkhazia, the parliament declared Abkhazia independent in July 1992, leading to fighting between Georgian forces and Abkhazian separatists supported by Russia; Georgian forces were defeated and were forced to withdraw in September 1993. After an Abkhaz-Georgian cease-fire was signed in May 1994, CIS peacekeepers and UN military observers were deployed on the Abkhaz-Georgian border; the peace is fragile and subsequent clashes in 2001 seemed on the point of triggering a wider conflict drawing in Russian and Chechnya. Although Abkhazia was granted autonomous republic status under Georgia's 1995 constitution, this was rejected by the Abkhazian parliament, which had again declared Abkhazia independent in 1994. The chaotic 2004 presidential election, rerun in January 2005 and won by Sergei Bagapsh, was not recognised by Georgia. Abkhazia's isolation has ruined its economy and brought it increasingly under Russian influence.

In 2004, relations between Georgia and Ajaria, a semi-autonomous region on the Black Sea coast bordering Turkey, rapidly deteriorated. Aslan Abashidze, Ajaria's leader since 1991, refused to recognise the authority of the newly elected Georgian president Mikhail Saakashvili, and in May 2004 accused Georgia of planning to invade Ajaria and ordered the destruction of bridges between Ajaria and Georgia. Public demonstrations against Abashidze followed and he was forced to resign. Abashidze's post was abolished by Georgia and an interim government (administered by Georgia) remained in control until parliamentary elections in June 2004, when President Saakashvili's party Saakashvili-Victorious Ajaria (SUA) won 28 of the 30 seats in the Ajarian parliament, which has powers over local affairs.

POLITICAL SYSTEM

The 1995 constitution provides for a federal republic with a unicameral legislature, to become bicameral 'following the creation of appropriate conditions'; and a directly elected president who serves a five-year term, renewable only once. The present parliament has 235 members, 85 elected in single-member constituencies and 150 from party lists by proportional representation, who serve for a four-year term.

HEAD OF STATE

President, Mikhail Saakashvili, *elected* 4 January 2004, *sworn in* 25 January 2004

SELECTED GOVERNMENT MEMBERS *as at July 2005*

Prime Minister, Zurab Noghaideli
Deputy Prime Minister, Minister for Justice, Kote Kemularia
*Deputy Prime Minister; State Minister for European and
    Euro-Atlantic Integration*, Giorgi Baramidze
Defence, Irakil Okruashvili
Finance and Tax Revenue, Valeri Chechelashvili
Foreign Affairs, Salome Zurabishvili-Kashia

EMBASSY OF GEORGIA

4 Russell Gardens, London W14 8EZ T 020-7603 7799
E geoemb@dircon.co.uk
Ambassador Extraordinary and Plenipotentiary, HE Amiran Kavadze, apptd 2004

BRITISH EMBASSY

Sheraton Metechi Palace Hotel, GE-380003 Tbilisi
T (+995) (32) 955497 E british.embassy@caucasus.net
Ambassador Extraordinary and Plenipotentiary, HE Donald MacLaren, apptd 2004

BRITISH COUNCIL

34 Rustaveli Avenue, Tbilisi, 380008 Tbilisi
T (+995) (32) 250407/ 988014 E office.bc@britishcouncil.org.ge
Director, Jo Bakowski

ECONOMY AND TRADE

The economy was brought to the brink of collapse by civil and secessionist wars and the ending of former Soviet trading relationships. In 2001 the IMF approved a three-year loan to Georgia amounting to some US$152 million, but this programme was halted in 2003 because the Georgian authorities failed to comply with the requirements set by the fund.

Although Georgia has deposits of coal, they have not been exploited and it is desperately short of energy supplies. In 2005, oil began to flow through the pipeline that runs from the Azeri oilfields through Georgia to Turkey, and Georgia should benefit from the revenues. The only productive sector of the economy is agriculture, which employs 30 per cent of the workforce and generates 21 per cent of GDP, with a concentration on viniculture, tea and tobacco growing, and citrus fruits. The main exports are iron alloys, wine, nuts, chemical fertilisers, and oil and oil products. The main imports are oil and oil products, gas, automobiles, pharmaceuticals and wheat.

GNI – US$3,400 million (2002); US$650 per capita (2002)
INFLATION RATE – 5.5 per cent (2004 est.)
UNEMPLOYMENT – 17 per cent (2004 est.)
TOTAL EXTERNAL DEBT – US$1,633 million (2000)
FOREIGN DIRECT INVESTMENT US$313 million (1997–2000)

IMPORTS – US$733 million (2002)
EXPORTS – US$349 million (2002)

BALANCE OF PAYMENTS
Trade – US$636 million deficit (2003)
Current Account – US$397 million deficit (2003)

Trade with UK	2003	2004
Imports from UK	£25,469,000	£46,977,000
Exports to UK	5,406,000	8,998,000

MEDIA

Georgia has a press of over 200 privately owned newspapers. *Sakartvelos Respublika* is the main state-owned newspaper. Georgian State TV is the state-owned broadcaster.

GERMANY

Bundesrepublik Deutschland – Federal Republic of Germany

AREA – 356,700 sq. km. Neighbours: Denmark (north), Poland and Czech Republic (east), Austria and Switzerland (south), France, Luxembourg, Belgium and the Netherlands (west)
POPULATION – 82,424,609 (2004 est.). Approximately 80 per cent of the population live in former West Germany. 34 per cent of the population are Protestant, 34 per cent Roman Catholic, 28 per cent unaffiliated or of other religions and 4 per cent Muslim. The language is German; there are Danish- and Frisian-speaking minorities in Schleswig-Holstein and a Sorbian-speaking minority in Saxony
CAPITAL – Berlin (population, 3,388,434, 2001 est.). The seat of government and parliament was transferred from Bonn to Berlin in 2000
MAJOR CITIES – Bremen; Cologne; Dortmund; Dresden; Duisburg; Düsseldorf; Essen; Frankfurt am Main; Hamburg; Hannover; Leipzig; Munich; Nuremberg; Stuttgart
CURRENCY – Euro (€) of 100 cents
NATIONAL ANTHEM – Einigkeit und Recht und Freiheit [Unity and right and freedom]
NATIONAL DAY – 3 October (Anniversary of 1990 Unification)
NATIONAL FLAG – Horizontal bars of black, red and gold
LIFE EXPECTANCY (years) – 78.54 (2004 est.)
MORTALITY RATE (per 1,000 population) – 10.44 (2004 est.)
INFANT MORTALITY (per 1,000 births) – 4.2 (2004 est.)
HIV / AIDS ADULT PREVALENCE – 0.1 per cent (2001 est.)
DEATH PENALTY – No (abolished 1949 in FRG and 1987 in GDR)
POPULATION GROWTH RATE – 0.02 per cent (2004 est.)
POPULATION DENSITY – 236 per sq. km (2002)
URBAN POPULATION – 88 per cent (2001)

CLIMATE AND TERRAIN

The north of the country is low-lying, rising in the central region to uplands, alpine foothills and then to the Bavarian Alps in the south. Elevation extremes range from 2,963 m (Zugspitze, Bavaria) at the highest point to −3.54 m (Neuendorf bei Wilster) at the lowest. The Rhine, Weser and Elbe rivers flow from the south to the North Sea, the Oder and Neisse rivers flow north to

the Baltic Sea, and the River Danube flows east from its source in the south of the country to the Austrian border. More than a third of the land is covered by forest. The climate is temperate, with average annual temperatures ranging from −5°C in January to 19°C in July.

HISTORY AND POLITICS

Charlemagne extended Frankish authority over the Germanic tribes in the eighth century, and took the title of Holy Roman Emperor. The Treaty of Verdun (AD 843) divided this empire into three, the eastern part, corresponding to modern Germany, comprising hundreds of small dukedoms and principalities that enjoyed virtual independence under the hegemony of a nominally elective Holy Roman Emperor. Although a succession of dynasties succeeded at times in centralising power between AD 962 and 1806, shifting allegiances and alliances enabled the states to challenge the authority of the emperor, which was never sufficient to overcome the fragmentation and achieve unification into a nation state.

The Empire was replaced in 1806 by a loose association of sovereign states known as the German Confederation, which was dissolved in 1866 and replaced by the Prussian-dominated North German Federation. The south German principalities united with the northern federation to form a second German empire in 1871 and the King of Prussia was proclaimed emperor.

Defeat in the First World War led to the abdication of the emperor, and the country became a republic. The Treaty of Versailles (1919) ceded Alsace-Lorraine to France, and large areas in the east were lost to Poland. The world economic crisis of 1929 contributed to the collapse of the Weimar Republic and the subsequent rise to power of the National Socialist movement of Adolf Hitler, who became chancellor in 1933.

After concluding a Treaty of Non-Aggression with the Soviet Union in August 1939, Germany invaded Poland (1 September 1939), precipitating the Second World War, which lasted until 1945. Hitler committed suicide on 30 April 1945. On 8 May 1945, Germany unconditionally surrendered.

Germany was divided into American, French, British and Soviet zones of occupation. The Federal Republic of Germany (FRG) was created out of the three western zones in 1949. A Communist government was established in the Soviet zone (henceforth the German Democratic Republic (GDR)). In 1961 the Soviet zone of Berlin was sealed off, and the Berlin Wall was built along the zonal boundary, partitioning the western sectors of the city from the eastern.

Soviet-initiated reform in eastern Europe during the late 1980s led to unrest in the GDR, culminating in the opening of the Berlin Wall in November 1989 and the collapse of the Communist government. The 'Treaty on the Final Settlement with Respect to Germany' concluded between the FRG, GDR and the four former occupying powers in September 1990, unified Germany with effect from 3 October 1990 as a fully sovereign state. Economic and monetary union preceded formal union on 1 July 1990. Unification is constitutionally the accession of Berlin and the five reformed Länder (states) of the GDR to the FRG, which remains in being. Berlin was declared to be the capital of the unified Germany and parliament and government departments were transferred from Bonn.

Germany was a founder member of the EEC in 1958, and joined the euro zone in 2000. Its parliament ratified the EU constitution in May 2005.

The distribution of seats following the 2002 election for the Bundestag was: Social Democratic Party (SPD) 250; Christian Democratic Union (CDU)/Christian Social Union (CSU) 248; Greens 55; Free Democratic Party (FDP) 47; Party of Democratic Socialism (PDS) 2. Gerhard Schröder of the SPD was re-elected as federal chancellor and formed a coalition government of the SPD and the Greens. Chancellor Schröder resigned as chairman of the SPD in February 2004 and was succeeded by Franz Muenterfering. After the SPD was defeated in a regional election in May 2005, Chancellor Schröder then lost a vote of no confidence. An early election was called for 18 September but provisional results gave no clear majority to either main party (SPO and CDU/CSU), both Chancellor Schröder and Angela Merkel (leader of the CDU/CSU) claimed victory. A presidential election was held in May 2004 and Professor Horst Koehler, a former director of the IMF, was elected president.

POLITICAL SYSTEM

The Basic Law (constitution) provides for a president, elected by a Federal Convention (electoral college) for a five-year term, and a bicameral legislature. The lower house *(Bundestag)* has 603 members directly elected for a four-year term. The upper house *(Bundesrat)* is composed of 69 members appointed by the governments of the states *(Länder)* in proportion to *Länder* populations, without a fixed term of office. German elections are governed by a system of proportional representation.

Judicial authority is exercised by the Federal Constitutional Court *(Bundesverfassungsgericht)*, the federal courts provided for in the Basic Law and the courts of the *Länder*.

HEAD OF STATE

Federal President, Horst Koehler, *elected* 23 May, *sworn in* 1 July 2004

EMBASSY OF THE FEDERAL REPUBLIC OF GERMANY
23 Belgrave Square/Chesham Place, London SW1X 8PZ
T 020-7824 1300 E mail@german-embassy.org.uk
Ambassador Extraordinary and Plenipotentiary, HE Thomas Matussek, apptd 2002

BRITISH EMBASSY
Wilhelmstrasse 70, D-10117 Berlin T (+49) (30) 204570
Ambassador Extraordinary and Plenipotentiary, HE Sir
   Peter Torry, KCMG, apptd 2003

BRITISH COUNCIL
Hackescher Markt 1, D-10178 Berlin
T (+49) (30) 311 0090 E bc.berlin@britishcouncil.de
Director, Kathryn Board, OBE

FEDERAL STRUCTURE

Germany is a federal republic composed of 16 states
(Länder) (ten from the former West, five from the former
East, and Berlin). Each *Land* has its own directly elected
legislature and government led by Minister-Presidents
(prime ministers) or equivalents. The 1949 Basic Law
vests executive power in the *Länder* governments except in
those areas reserved for the federal government.

State	Capital	Population (2001)
Baden-Württemberg	Stuttgart	10.6m
Bavaria	Munich	12.3m
Berlin	—	3.4m
Brandenburg	Potsdam	2.6m
Bremen	—	0.7m
Hamburg	—	1.7m
Hesse	Wiesbaden	6.1m
Lower Saxony	Hannover	8.0m
Mecklenburg-Western		
Pomerania	Schwerin	1.8m
North Rhine-		
Westphalia	Düsseldorf	18.0m
Rhineland-Palatinate	Mainz	4.0m
Saarland	Saarbrücken	1.1m
Saxony	Dresden	4.4m
Saxony-Anhalt	Magdeburg	2.6m
Schleswig-Holstein	Kiel	2.8m
Thuringia	Erfurt	2.4m

DEFENCE

The Army has 2,398 main battle tanks, 3,123 armoured
personnel carriers, 2,255 armoured infantry fighting
vehicles, and 199 attack helicopters. The Navy has 12
submarines, one destroyer, 12 frigates, 25 patrol and
coastal vessels, 65 combat aircraft and 22 armed
helicopters. The Air Force has 384 combat aircraft. There
remain 97,681 NATO personnel in Germany (USA
69,790; UK 22,000; France 3,200; Netherlands 2,600,
Italy 91). Major cuts were made in military procurement
in late 2002.

MILITARY EXPENDITURE – 1.5 per cent of GDP (2003)
MILITARY PERSONNEL – 284,500: Army 191,350, Navy
   25,650, Air Force 67,500.
CONSCRIPTION DURATION – Nine months

ECONOMY AND TRADE

Although Germany has the world's fifth largest economy,
recent years have seen stagnation with unemployment,
slow growth, and a budget deficit in excess of the 3 per
cent required by euro zone rules. These difficulties,
coming after decades of strong economic performance,
are largely an aftermath of reunification. After a mini-
boom generated by new East German demand in 1990
and 1991, Germany entered its most severe post-war
recession, induced by the costs of reunification. In 1993 a
'Solidarity Pact' was agreed, laying down the basis of
future funding transfers to the East based on a 5.5 per
cent rise in income taxes, wage restraint in the West, more

private investment in the East, and the distribution of the
funding burden between the federal and *Länder*
governments. The economy in the east remains
particularly weak, with unemployment double and
economic growth half that of the west.

The rate of economic growth increased in 1999 and
2000, but began to slow in 2001 and achieved less than
one per cent growth between 2001 and 2003.
Unemployment has risen to about 5 million. In 2003
Chancellor Schröder announced tax cuts and labour and
welfare reforms designed to reduce unemployment and
revive the economy.

Principal industries are coal mining, iron and steel
production, machine construction, the domestic electrical
industry, the manufacture of steel and metal products,
chemicals, automobile production, electronics, textiles and
the processing of foodstuffs. In 2000 the government
announced the closure over a 32-year period of all of
Germany's 19 nuclear power stations, which supply over
30 per cent of the energy generated in the country.

GNI – US$1,876,300 million (2002); US$22,740 per
   capita (2002)
ANNUAL AVERAGE GROWTH OF GDP – 1.7 per cent
   (2004 est.)
INFLATION RATE – 1.6 per cent (2004 est.)
UNEMPLOYMENT – 10.6 per cent (2004 est.)
FOREIGN DIRECT INVESTMENT – $259,778 million
   (1997–2000)
IMPORTS – US$602,000 million (2003)
EXPORTS – US$751,000 million (2003)

BALANCE OF PAYMENTS
Trade – US$149,367 million surplus (2003)
Current Account – US$53,513 million surplus (2003)

Trade with UK	2003	2004
Imports from UK	£15,057,073,000	£21,385,804,000
Exports to UK	24,070,953,000	34,327,740,000

TRANSPORT INFRASTRUCTURE

There is an extensive road network of around 230,735
km in 2000, including 11,515 km of highways. There are
45,514 km of railways. Around 20 per cent of domestic
freight is carried on the 7,500 km of inland waterways.
The main ports are Hamburg, Kiel, Bremerhaven and
Rostock. The principal airports are at Berlin, Frankfurt,
Munich, Bonn, Bremen, Dresden, Düsseldorf/Essen,
Hamburg, Hannover, Leipzig, Nuremberg and Stuttgart.

EDUCATION

Education is free of charge and compulsory between the
ages of six and 18 and comprises nine years of full-time
education at primary and main schools and three years of
vocational education on a part-time basis. The secondary
school leaving examination *(Abitur)* entitles the holder to
a place at a university or another institution of higher
education.

Children below the age of 18 who are not attending a
general secondary or a full-time vocational school have
compulsory day-release at a vocational school.

There are over 300 higher education institutes and the
largest universities are in Munich, Berlin, Hamburg, Bonn,
Frankfurt and Cologne. Germany's oldest university is
Heidelberg, founded in 1386.

GROSS ENROLMENT RATIO (percentage of relevant age
   group) – primary 103 per cent (2002); secondary 99
   per cent (2002)

MEDIA

Each of the country's 16 federal states operates its own television stations, both private and public. Germany is implementing digital radio and television and will cease analogue services in 2010. Over 90 per cent of German households receive cable or satellite television. Germany also has a considerable press industry and is home to many international media companies.

CULTURE

Modern German language has steadily developed from the time of the Reformation to the present day. Differences in dialect can be found in Austria, Alsace, Luxembourg, Liechtenstein and the German-speaking cantons of Switzerland. Great figures emerge from all areas of the cultural landscape, from literature (Goethe 1749–1832) and philosophy (Kant 1724–1804), to classical music (Beethoven 1770–1827) and physics (Einstein 1879–1955).

GHANA

Republic of Ghana

AREA – 227,500 sq. km. Neighbours: Burkina Faso (north), Côte d'Ivoire (west), Togo (east)
POPULATION – 20,757,032 (2004 est.). Most are black Sudanese, although Hamitic strains are common in the north. The official language is English. The principal indigenous language group is Akan, of which Twi and Fanti are the most commonly used. Ga, Ewe and languages of the Mole-Dagbani group are common in certain regions. Most Ghanaians are Christians, although there is a substantial Muslim minority in the north
CAPITAL – ΨAccra (population, 1,445,515, 1998), Greater Accra Region (including Tema) 2,909,643 (2000 census)
MAJOR CITIES – Koforidua; Kumasi; ΨTakoradi; Tamale
CURRENCY – Cedi of 100 pesewas
NATIONAL FLAG – Equal horizontal bands of red over gold over green; five-point black star on gold stripe
NATIONAL ANTHEM – God bless our homeland Ghana
NATIONAL DAY – 6 March (Independence Day)
LIFE EXPECTANCY (years) – 56.27 (2004 est.)
MORTALITY RATE (per 1,000 population) – 10.67 (2004 est.)
INFANT MORTALITY (per 1,000 births) – 52.22 (2004 est.)
HIV / AIDS ADULT PREVALENCE – 3.1 per cent (2003 est.)
DEATH PENALTY – Yes
POPULATION GROWTH RATE – 1.36 per cent (2004 est.)
POPULATION DENSITY – 89 per sq. km (2002)
MILITARY EXPENDITURE – 0.3 per cent of GDP (2003)
MILITARY PERSONNEL – 7,000: Army 5,000, Navy 1,000, Air Force 1,000

CLIMATE AND TERRAIN

Ghana consists mostly of tropical inland plains bisected by the Volta river basin and the great central Lake Volta, and rising to the Ashanti plateau in the west. Elevation extremes range from 880 m (Mount Afadjato) at the highest point to 0 m (Atlantic Ocean) at the lowest. The climate is tropical but there is also a warm and dry coastal area in the south-east. The average temperature in Accra is 30°C.

HISTORY AND POLITICS

First reached by Europeans in the 15th century, after which it became a centre for gold- and slave-trading, the constituent parts of Ghana came under British administration at various times, the original Gold Coast colony being constituted in 1874, and Ashanti and the Northern Territories Protectorate in 1901. Trans-Volta-Togoland, part of the former German colony of Togo, was mandated to Britain by the League of Nations after the First World War and was integrated with the Gold Coast colony in 1956 following a plebiscite. The colony became independent on 6 March 1957, and became a republic in 1960.

Since 1966, Ghana has experienced long periods of military rule interspersed with short-lived civilian governments. A coup in 1978 led to the formation of an Armed Forces Revolutionary Council chaired by Flt. Lt. Jerry Rawlings. Civilian rule was restored in 1979 but another coup in 1981 brought Rawlings back to power.

A referendum in 1992 approved a new multiparty constitution and the legalisation of political parties. The National Democratic Congress (NDC) was established as a political party from the ruling Provisional National Defence Council. The presidential and parliamentary elections in late 1992 were won by Rawlings and the NDC, but the 2000 legislative election brought to power the New Patriotic Party (NPP), which won 101 seats to the NDC's 92, and the presidential election was won by the NPP candidate, John Lufuor. In the 2004 elections, President Kufuor was re-elected with 52.75 per cent of the vote, and the NPP retained its majority in parliament, winning 129 seats.

Since the mid-1990s there have been intermittent clashes over land ownership between different ethnic groups in the Northern Region. A five-month state of emergency was imposed after the latest ethnic violence in 2002.

In 2002 President Kufuor inaugurated a reconciliation commission to investigate human rights violations during military rule. The commission made its final report to the government in August 2004.

POLITICAL SYSTEM

Under the 1993 constitution, the executive president is directly elected for a four-year term, renewable only once. The president nominates members of the Council of Ministers subject to approval by parliament. The unicameral legislature, the parliament, has 230 members, who are directly elected for a four-year term.

HEAD OF STATE

President, John Kufuor, *elected* 28 December 2000, *sworn in* 7 January 2001, *re-elected* 7 December 2004
Vice-President, Aliu Mahama

SELECTED GOVERNMENT MEMBERS *as at July 2005*
Defence, Kwame Addo-Kufuor
Finance and Economic Planning, Kwadwo Baah Wiredu
Foreign Affairs, Nana Akufo Addo
Interior, Papa Owusu-Ankomah

OFFICE OF THE HIGH COMMISSION OF GHANA
13 Belgrave Square, London SW1X 8PN T 020-7235 4142
High Commissioner, HE Isaac Osei, apptd 2001

BRITISH HIGH COMMISSION

Osu Link, off Gamel Abdul Nasser Avenue, PO Box 296, Accra
T (+233) (21) 221665/7010650
E high.commission.accra@fco.gov.uk
High Commissioner, Gordon Wetherell

BRITISH COUNCIL

Liberia Road, PO Box GP 771, Accra
T (+233) (21) 683068
E infoaccra@gh.britishcouncil.org
Director, John Payne

ECONOMY AND TRADE

Agriculture is the basis of the economy, generating 35 per cent of GDP. Crops include cocoa, rice, cassava, plantains, oranges and pineapples, groundnuts, corn, millet, oil palms, yams, maize and vegetables. Livestock is raised in uncultivated areas. Fishing is important in coastal areas and in the Volta lake and river system. Around 60 per cent of the workforce are employed in farming, forestry and fishing.

Manganese production ranks among the world's largest, with an average of 280,000 tonnes of ore being produced annually. Ghana is Africa's second largest gold producer after South Africa and gold is the main export, providing over 25 per cent of export revenue. Diamonds and bauxite are also produced. Other exports include pineapples, tuna, cocoa (which provides the largest single source of revenue, 25 per cent of export earnings), electricity, timber and prepared fish.

Principal imports are capital goods, semi-manufactures, consumables and petroleum.

Since 1966 the Volta Dams at Akosombo and Kpong have generated hydroelectric power for the processing of bauxite and fed a power transmission network for most of Ghana, Togo and Benin. There is considerable foreign investment in Ghana, and its economy has grown consistently. Since 2000 inflation and borrowing costs have been reduced.

GNI – US$5,500 million (2002); US$270 per capita (2002)
INFLATION RATE – 13 per cent (2004 est.)
TOTAL EXTERNAL DEBT – US$7,200 million (2002)
FOREIGN DIRECT INVESTMENT – $US313 million (1997–2000)
IMPORTS – US$3,000 million (2000)
EXPORTS – US$1,800 million (1998)

BALANCE OF PAYMENTS
Trade – US$692 million deficit (2002)
Current Account – US$33 million deficit (2002)

Trade with UK	2003	2004
Imports from UK	£152,219,000	£170,903,000
Exports to UK	143,323,000	136,986,000

EDUCATION

The government provides compulsory, free basic education for all children. In 2003, investment in education constituted 25 per cent of all government spending. Ghana has one of Africa's oldest universities, at Legon in Accra.

ILLITERACY RATE – (m) 19.7 per cent; (f) 37.1 per cent (2000)
GROSS ENROLMENT RATIO (percentage of relevant age group) – primary 81 per cent (2002); secondary 38 per cent (2002); tertiary 3 per cent (2002)

MEDIA

The Ghana Broadcasting Corporation (GBC) is the state-owned broadcaster. GBC operates a television network and various radio stations that transmit in English and Ghanaian dialects. TV3 is a private television channel, Multichoice is a cable television operator and Metro TV is jointly owned by the government and private backers. Ghana's private press and broadcasters operate without major restrictions.

GREECE

Elliniki Dimokratia – Hellenic Republic

AREA – 128,900 sq. km. Neighbours: Albania, Macedonia and Bulgaria (north), Turkey (east)
POPULATION – 10,647,529 (2004 est.): 98 per cent Greek Orthodox, 1 per cent Catholic, 1 per cent Muslim. The language is Greek
CAPITAL – Athens (population 3,072,922, 1991); including ΨPiraeus and suburbs, 3,096,775 (1991 census)
MAJOR CITIES – ΨIráklion (Heraklion); Lárisa; ΨPátrai (Patras); ΨThessaloníki (Salonika); ΨVólos
CURRENCY – Euro (€) of 100 cents
NATIONAL ANTHEM – Imnos eis tin eleftherian [Hymn to freedom]
NATIONAL DAY – 25 March (Independence Day)
NATIONAL FLAG – Blue and white stripes with a white cross on a blue field in the canton
LIFE EXPECTANCY (years) – 78.94 (2004 est.)
MORTALITY RATE (per 1,000 population) – 10.08 (2004 est.)
INFANT MORTALITY (per 1,000 births) – 5.63 (2004 est.)
HIV / AIDS ADULT PREVALENCE – 0.2 per cent (2001)
DEATH PENALTY – Yes*
POPULATION GROWTH RATE – 0.2 per cent (2004 est.)
POPULATION DENSITY – 82 per sq. km (2002)

CLIMATE AND TERRAIN

The main areas are: Macedonia, Thrace, Epirus, Thessaly, Continental Greece, the Peloponnese and the island of Crete. The main island groups are the Sporades, the Dodecanese or Southern Sporades, the Cyclades, and the Aegean islands (Chios, Lesbos, Limnos and Samos) in the

Aegean Sea, and the Ionian islands and Corfu in the Ionian Sea. Low-lying coastal areas rise to a hilly or mountainous interior on the mainland and the islands. The Pindos mountains form a spine down the centre of the mainland, continuing down the Peloponnese, which is divided from the mainland by the Gulf of Corinth, the largest of the gulfs and large bays indenting the coast. Elevation extremes range from 2,917 m (Mount Olympus) at the highest point to 0 m (Mediterranean Sea) at the lowest. The coastline and islands have a Mediterranean climate with hot, dry summers and mild, wet winters. The average annual temperature in Athens ranges from 9°C in January to 28°C in July.

HISTORY AND POLITICS

Successive civilizations flourished in ancient Greece from the second millennium BC until conquered by Philip II of Macedon in the fourth century BC and then the Romans in 146 BC. When the western Roman Empire fell, the eastern part continued as the Byzantine Empire until conquered by the Turks in the mid-15th century. Turkish rule began to be overthrown in a war of independence (1821–7) that led to the establishment of a Greek kingdom in the Peloponnese in 1829. The remainder of Greece gradually became independent until the Dodecanese were returned by Italy in 1947. After the German Nazi occupation of 1941–4, a civil war between monarchist and Communist groups lasted from 1946 to 1949, and although it resulted in the restoration of democracy, tension between right-wing and radical groups continued after 1949. In 1967 right-wing elements in the army seized power and established a military regime (the 'Greek Colonels'). The king went into voluntary exile in 1967. Unrest in Athens in 1973–4 intensified after the government was involved in the overthrow of President Makarios of Cyprus in July 1974, and led the Colonels to surrender power. Konstantinos Karamanlis (prime minister 1955–63) returned from exile to form a provisional government, and the first elections for ten years were held in 1974. The restoration of the monarchy was rejected by referendum in December 1974 and Greece became a republic. The restored democracy has proved stable, with political life dominated for the next two decades by Karamanlis, founder of the conservative New Democracy (ND) party, and Andreas Papandreou, who founded the left-wing Panhellenic Socialist Party (PASOK). Greece joined the European Community in 1981 and the euro zone in 2001. The parliament ratified the EU constitution in April 2005.

In the 2004 legislative election, ND won an overall majority in parliament, with 165 seats and PASOK, which had been in power since 1994, won 117 seats. The 2005 presidential election was won by Karolos Papoulias.

POLITICAL SYSTEM

The 1975 constitution was amended in 1986, when most of the president's remaining executive powers were transferred to the government. The head of state is the president, elected by parliament for a five-year term, renewable only once. The unicameral 300-member parliament *(Vouli)* is directly elected for a four-year term by proportional representation, with a 3 per cent threshold for parliamentary representation.

HEAD OF STATE
President of the Hellenic Republic, Karolos Papoulias, *elected by parliament* 2005

SELECTED GOVERNMENT MEMBERS *as at July 2005*
Prime Minister, Minister for Culture, Costas Karamanlis
Foreign Affairs, Petros Molyviatis
Interior, Public Administration and Decentralisation,
   Prokopis Pavlopoulos
National Defence, Spilios Spiliotopoulos
National Economy and Finance, Georgios Alogoskoufis

EMBASSY OF GREECE
1A Holland Park, London W11 3TP T 020-7229 3850
E consulategeneral@greekembassy.org.uk
Ambassador Extraordinary and Plenipotentiary, HE
   Anastase Scopelitis, apptd 2003

BRITISH EMBASSY
1 Ploutarchou Street, GR-106 75 Athens
T (+30) (210) 727 2600 E information.athens@fco.gov.uk
Ambassador Extraordinary and Plenipotentiary, HE Simon
   Gass, apptd 2004

BRITISH COUNCIL
17 Kolonaki Square, GR 106 73, Athens
T (+30) (210)369 2333 E general.enquiries@britishcouncil.gr
Director, Desmond Lauder

DEFENCE

The Army has 1,723 main battle tanks, 1,640 armoured personnel carriers, 501 armoured infantry fighting vehicles and 20 attack helicopters. The Navy has eight submarines, two destroyers, 12 frigates, 40 patrol and coastal vessels and 18 armed helicopters. The Air Force has a total of 389 combat aircraft.

Greece maintains 1,250 army personnel in Cyprus. There are 538 US military personnel stationed in Greece.
MILITARY EXPENDITURE – 4.1 per cent of GDP (2003)
MILITARY PERSONNEL – 159,200: Army 110,000, Navy
   19,000, Air Force 30,200; Paramilitaries 4,000
CONSCRIPTION DURATION – Up to 19 months

ECONOMY AND TRADE

Greece experienced rapid economic growth in the final quarter of the 20th century, partly through revenues from tourism and partly through membership of the EC. Tourism is a major industry, accounting for an estimated 15 per cent of annual GDP and contributing more than US$8,000 million every year in foreign exchange earnings.

The principal minerals are nickel, bauxite, iron ore, iron pyrites, manganese magnesite, chrome, lead, zinc and emery. The chief industries are textiles (cotton, wool and synthetics), chemicals, cement, glass, metallurgy, shipbuilding, domestic electrical equipment and footwear, the production of aluminium, nickel, iron and steel products, tyres, chemicals, fertilisers and sugar (from locally grown beet). Food processing and ancillary industries are also expanding.

In 2002 Greece and Turkey signed an agreement to build a gas pipeline which will supply Greece with gas from Turkey.

Though there has been substantial industrialisation, agriculture still employs a fifth of the working population and contributes 8.1 per cent of GDP. The most important agricultural products are tobacco, wheat, cotton, sugar, rice, fruit (olives, peaches, vines, oranges, lemons, figs, almonds and currant-vines). Exports of fresh fruit, currants and vegetables are an important contributor to the economy.

In 1998 the drachma was admitted to the ERM; Greece

became a member of EMU in 2001 since when it has participated in the European Single Currency. The euro replaced the drachma in 2002.

GNI – US$123,900 million (2002); US$11,660 per capita (2002)

ANNUAL AVERAGE GROWTH OF GDP – 3.7 per cent (2004)

INFLATION RATE – 2.9 per cent (2004 est.)

UNEMPLOYMENT – 10 per cent (2004 est.)

FOREIGN DIRECT INVESTMENT – US$3,051 million (1997–2000)

IMPORTS – US$44,400 million (2003)

EXPORTS – US$13,200 million (2003)

BALANCE OF PAYMENTS

Trade – US$25,606 million deficit (2003)

Current Account – US$11,225 million deficit (2003)

Trade with UK	2003	2004
Imports from UK	£885,063,000	£1,380,548,000
Exports to UK	463,517,000	649,000,000

TRANSPORT INFRASTRUCTURE

There are extensive rail and road networks. The railways are state-owned, with the exception of the Athens–Piraeus Electric Railway. There are 9,255 km of motorways and 29,350 km of provincial roads. The main ports are Piraeus, Thessaloniki and Pátrai on the mainland and Iraklion on Crete. An extensive ferry system connects the islands to one another and to the mainland. The main airports are at Athens, Thessaloniki, Iraklion (Crete) and Corfu town (Corfu), although several of the other islands have airports.

EDUCATION

Education is free of charge and compulsory from the age of six to 15, and is maintained by state grants. There are 18 universities and several other institutes of higher education.

ILLITERACY RATE – (m) 1.5 per cent; (f) 4.0 per cent (2000)

GROSS ENROLMENT RATIO (percentage of relevant age group) – primary 97 per cent (2002); secondary 96 per cent (2002); tertiary 61 per cent (2002)

MEDIA

Although the Greek media is considerably free from regulation, editors and publishers risk prosecution should their material be deemed offensive to religious beliefs or the president. A sizeable proportion of the country's 1,700 private radio and television stations are unlicensed. In 2004 there were an estimated 1.7 million internet users.

CULTURE

Greek civilisation emerged c.1300 BC and the poems of Homer, which were probably current c.800 BC, record the struggle between the Achaeans of Greece and the Phrygians of Troy (1194 to 1184 BC).

The spoken language of modern Greece is descended from the Common Greek of Alexander the Great's empire. *Katharevousa*, a conservative literary dialect evolved by Adamantios Korais (1748–1833), which was used for official and technical matters, has been phased out. Novels and poetry are mostly in *dimotiki*, a progressive literary dialect which owes much to Yannis Psycharis (1854–1929). The poets Dionysios Solomos (1798–1857), Constantine P. Cavafy (1863–1933) and Angelos

Sikelianos (1884–1951) have won a European reputation. Georgos Seferis (1900–71) and Odysseus Elytis (1911–96) both won the Nobel Prize for Literature, in 1963 and 1979 respectively.

GRENADA

State of Grenada

AREA – 345 sq: km

POPULATION – 89,357 (2004 est.), of which about 75 per cent are of African descent; there are minorities of Europeans and Indians. The language is English

CAPITAL – ΨSt George's (population, 4,788)

CURRENCY – East Caribbean dollar (EC$) of 100 cents

NATIONAL ANTHEM – Hail Grenada, land of ours

NATIONAL DAY – 7 February (Independence Day)

NATIONAL FLAG – Divided diagonally into yellow and green triangles within a red border containing six yellow stars, a yellow star on a red disc in the centre and a nutmeg on the green triangle in the hoist

LIFE EXPECTANCY (years) – 64.74 (2004 est.)

MORTALITY RATE (per 1,000 population) – 7.31 (2004 est.)

INFANT MORTALITY (per 1,000 births) – 14.62 (2004 est.)

DEATH PENALTY – No

POPULATION BELOW POVERTY LINE – 32 per cent (2000)

POPULATION GROWTH RATE – 0.14 per cent (2004 est.)

POPULATION DENSITY – 272 per sq. km (2001)

CLIMATE AND TERRAIN

The most southerly of the Windward Islands, Grenada comprises three islands – Grenada (the largest at 18 km in length and 34 km in width), Carriacou and Petite Martinique. Elevation extremes range from 840 m (Mount Saint Catherine) at the highest point to 0 m (Caribbean Sea) at the lowest. The climate is subtropical with a wet season running from June to December. Grenada is in a hurricane zone.

HISTORY AND POLITICS

Discovered by Columbus in 1498, and named Concepción, Grenada was originally colonised by France and was ceded to Great Britain in 1763. It became a Crown colony in 1877, an Associated State in 1967 and an independent nation within the Commonwealth on 7 February 1974.

The government was overthrown in 1979 by the New Jewel Movement led by Maurice Bishop, and a People's Revolutionary Government (PRG) was set up with Bishop as prime minister. In October 1983 disagreements within the PRG led to the deposition and execution of Bishop, whose government was replaced by a Revolutionary Military Council. These events prompted the intervention of Caribbean and US forces. The Governor-General installed an advisory council to act as an interim government until a general election was held in December 1984. A phased withdrawal of US forces was completed by June 1985. Since the restoration of democracy, power has alternated between the New National Party (NNP) and the National Democratic Congress (NDC).

In the 2003 general election, the New National Party (NNP), led by Keith Mitchell, was narrowly re-elected to a third successive term of office, winning eight seats.

POLITICAL SYSTEM

Queen Elizabeth II is head of state and is represented locally by a Governor-General. Legislative power is vested in a bicameral parliament consisting of a lower house, the House of Representatives, with 15 members directly elected for a five-year term, and a Senate with 13 members appointed by the Governor-General on the advice of the prime minister and the leader of the opposition.

Governor-General, HE Sir Daniel Williams, GCMG, QC, apptd 1996

SELECTED GOVERNMENT MEMBERS *as at July 2005*
Prime Minister, National Security and Information, Keith Mitchell
Deputy Prime Minister, National Security, Information, Gregory Bowen
Finance, Trade, Industry and Planning, Anthony Boatswain
Foreign Affairs and International Trade, Legal Affairs, Carriacou and Petit Martinique Affairs, Elvin Nimrod
Health, Ann-David Antoine

HIGH COMMISSION FOR GRENADA
5 Chandos Street, London W1G 9DG
T 020-7631 4277 E grenada@high-commission.demon.co.uk
High Commissioner, HE Joslyn Raphael Whiteman, apptd 2004

BRITISH HIGH COMMISSION
Netherlands Building, Grand Anse, St George's
T (+1 473) 440 3536/ 3222 E bhcgrenada@caribsurf.com
High Commissioner, C. John White, resident at Bridgetown, Barbados

ECONOMY AND TRADE

The service industries, such as tourism and financial services, account for 62 per cent of employment and 68.4 per cent of GDP. The economy was principally agrarian, but agriculture now employs only 24 per cent of the workforce and produces 7 per cent of GDP. Manufacturing consists of processing agricultural products and the production of textiles, concrete, aluminium and handicrafts. Tourism is the main foreign exchange earner; 123,351 tourists visited Grenada in 2001.

The most important exports are nutmeg and cocoa; Grenada is the world's second-largest producer of nutmeg, accounting for about a third of the world's annual supply. Imports include machinery and transport equipment, livestock, foodstuffs and beverages, manufactured goods, and fuels. The main trading partners are the USA, Germany, Bangladesh, the Netherlands, France, the UK and Trinidad and Tobago.
GNI – US$360 million (2001); US$3,610 per capita (2001)
ANNUAL AVERAGE GROWTH OF GDP – 2.5 per cent (2002 est.)
INFLATION RATE – 2.8 per cent (2001)
UNEMPLOYMENT – 12.5 per cent (2004 est.)
TOTAL EXTERNAL DEBT – US$207 million (2000)
IMPORTS – US$250 million (2000)
EXPORTS – US$30 million (1998)

BALANCE OF PAYMENTS
Trade – US$136 million deficit (2000)
Current Account – US$79 million deficit (2000)

Trade with UK	2003	2004
Imports from UK	£7,485,000	£6,559,000
Exports to UK	1,735,000	378,000

MEDIA

There are no daily newspapers but several weekly publications. There are two television stations: GBN TV, which is operated by the public broadcaster Grenada Broadcasting Network, and MTV which is owned by the US company Viacom. There are several radio stations jointly owned by the public and private sector.

GUATEMALA

República de Guatemala – Republic of Guatemala

AREA – 108,400 sq. km. Neighbours: Mexico (north and west), El Salvador, Honduras and Belize (east)
POPULATION – 14,280,596 (2004 est.): 56 per cent mestizo, 44 per cent Amerindian. The language is Spanish, but 40 per cent of the population speak an Indian language
CAPITAL – Guatemala City (population, 1,675,589, 1990 estimate)
MAJOR CITIES – Mazatenango; ΨPuerto Barrios; Quetzaltenango; Cobán; Escuintla
CURRENCY – Quetzal (Q) of 100 centavos
NATIONAL ANTHEM – Guatemala feliz [Guatemala be praised]
NATIONAL DAY – 15 September
NATIONAL FLAG – Three vertical bands, blue, white, blue; coat of arms on white stripe
LIFE EXPECTANCY (years) – 65.19 (2004 est.)
MORTALITY RATE (per 1,000 population) – 6.79 (2004 est.)
INFANT MORTALITY (per 1,000 births) – 36.91 (2004 est.)
HIV / AIDS ADULT PREVALENCE RATE – 1.1 per cent (2003 est.)
DEATH PENALTY – Yes
POPULATION BELOW POVERTY LINE – 75 per cent (2002 est.)
POPULATION GROWTH RATE – 2.61 per cent (2004 est.)
POPULATION DENSITY – 111 per sq. km (2002)
URBAN POPULATION – 40 per cent (2001)
MILITARY EXPENDITURE – 0.4 per cent of GDP (2003)
MILITARY PERSONNEL – 29,200: Army 27,000, Navy 1,500, Air Force 700; Paramilitaries 19,000
CONSCRIPTION DURATION – 30 months (selective)
ILLITERACY RATE – (m) 22 per cent; (f) 36.6 per cent (2003 est.)
GROSS ENROLMENT RATIO (percentage of relevant age group) – primary 103 per cent (2002); secondary 33 per cent (2002)

CLIMATE AND TERRAIN

Narrow plains on both the north (Caribbean) and south (Pacific) coasts rise to a mountainous interior in the centre and south. The mountains fall to the north to a plateau, which drops further to low-lying marshland. Elevation extremes range from 4,211 m (Volcan Tajumulco) at the highest point to 0 m (Pacific Ocean) at the lowest. There are 33 volcanoes. The climate is tropical but is cooler in the highlands. The wet season runs from May to October, when mudslides and hurricanes can occur. There are also frequent minor earth tremors and some earthquakes.

HISTORY AND POLITICS

Mayan civilization flourished in the area until the Spanish conquest in 1523, when the area became a Spanish colony. It gained its independence in 1821, and formed part of the United Provinces of Central America from 1823 to 1835. After independence, the country was ruled by a series of dictatorships and military regimes, interspersed with periods of democratic government. The latest restoration of civilian rule in 1984 has survived an attempted coup in 1989 and the mass protests and military intervention that ousted President Serrano in 1993 when he attempted to introduce rule by decree; he was replaced by Ramiro de León Carpio, who was elected president by the Congress to serve out Serrano's term.

Alvaro Alvarez, elected president in 1996, concluded a peace agreement with the left-wing Guatemalan Revolutionary National Unity guerrillas in 1996 that ended the 36-year civil war, in which over 200,000 died or disappeared, and began a reduction in the size and political influence of the army that has been continued by his successors. In 1999, an independent commission found that 93 per cent of human rights abuses during the war had been instigated by the security forces, and in 2000 and 2004 the state formally admitted guilt in several human rights crimes, paying damages to the victims. Only a small number of the military personnel found to be responsible for the atrocities have been prosecuted so far.

The 2003 legislative election was won by Gran Alianza Nacional (GANA) with 49 seats. The 2003 presidential election was won by Oscar Berger, the GANA candidate, with 54 per cent of the vote.

POLITICAL SYSTEM

Under the 1986 constitution, executive power is vested in the president, who is directly elected for a single four-year term. He appoints the cabinet. Legislative authority is vested in the unicameral Congress of the Republic, whose 158 members are directly elected for a four-year term.

HEAD OF STATE

President, Oscar Berger, *elected* December 2003, *sworn in* 14 January 2004
Vice-President, Eduardo Stein Barillas

SELECTED GOVERNMENT MEMBERS *as at July 2005*
Defence, Carlos Aldana Villanueva
Economy, Marcio Cuevas Quezada
Foreign Affairs, Jorge Briz Abularach
Interior, Carlos Vielman

EMBASSY OF GUATEMALA

13 Fawcett Street, London SW10 9HN T 020-7351 3042
Chargé d'affaires, Rodrigo Vielmann

BRITISH EMBASSY

Edificio Torre Internacional, Nivel 11, 16 Calle 0-55, Zona 10, Guatemala City T (+502) 367 5425/6/7/8/9
E embassy@intelnett.com
Ambassador Extraordinary and Plenipotentiary, Richard D. Lavers, apptd 2001

ECONOMY AND TRADE

Agriculture provides 22.5 per cent of GDP and employs half of the workforce. The principal export is coffee (approximately a third of exports), with other exports including manufactured goods, sugar, bananas (15 per cent of exports) and cardamom. The chief imports are raw materials and semi-manufactures, capital goods, consumer goods, and fuel oils. Guatemala has a free-trade agreement with El Salvador, Honduras and Mexico; the USA is also one of the country's main trading partners.

In 2002, the IMF announced that a one-year standby credit of US$67 million had been approved in order to underpin the government's economic policies and the implementation of the 1996 peace accords. In 2003 a further US$84 million of credit was made available until 2004.

GNI – US$21,000 million (2002); US$1,760 per capita (2002)
ANNUAL AVERAGE GROWTH OF GDP – 2.6 per cent (2004 est.)
INFLATION RATE – 7.2 per cent (2004 est.)
TOTAL EXTERNAL DEBT – US$4,622 million (2000)
FOREIGN DIRECT INVESTMENT – US$1,148 million (1997–2000)
IMPORTS – US$6,500 million (2003)
EXPORTS – US$2,500 million (2003)

BALANCE OF PAYMENTS
Trade – US$2,950 million deficit (2002)
Current Account – US$1,193 million deficit (2002)

Trade with UK	2003	2004
Imports from UK	£25,739,000	£33,444,000
Exports to UK	15,452,000	15,253,000

MEDIA AND CULTURE

Freedom of the press is enshrined in the constitution and there are four major daily newspapers, including *Prensa Libre* and *El Periodico*. Five privately run channels dominate Guatemalan television.

Guatemala enjoys a rich and varied cultural history. The ruins of the ancient Mayan civilisation (at its height between AD 600 and AD 900) dot the country while the influences of African culture are evident along the Caribbean coast. Guatemala has been home to many distinguished writers, including Miguel Angel Asturias (1899–1974), who won the Nobel Prize for Literature in 1967, and Luis Cardoza y Aragon (1901–92), who edited the influential periodical *Revista de Guatemala* after the 1944 revolution.

GUINEA

République de Guinée – Republic of Guinea

AREA – 245,857 sq. km. Neighbours: Guinea-Bissau (west), Senegal and Mali (north), Côte d'Ivoire (east), Liberia and Sierra Leone (south)
POPULATION – 9,246,462 (2004 est.). The official language is French; Fullah, Malinké and Soussou are the indigenous languages
CAPITAL – ΨConakry (population, 763,000)
MAJOR CITIES – Kankan; Kindia; Labé; Mamou; N'Zérékoré; Siguiri
CURRENCY – Guinea franc of 100 centimes
NATIONAL ANTHEM – Liberté [Liberty]
NATIONAL DAY – 2 October (Anniversary of the Proclamation of Independence)
NATIONAL FLAG – Three vertical stripes of red, yellow and green
LIFE EXPECTANCY – 49.7 (2004 est.)
MORTALITY RATE (per 1,000 population) – 15.53 (2004 est.)

INFANT MORTALITY – 91.82 (2004 est.)
HIV / AIDS ADULT PREVALENCE RATE – 3.2 per cent
(2003 est.)
DEATH PENALTY – Yes
POPULATION BELOW POVERTY LINE – 40 per cent
(2001 est.)
POPULATION DENSITY – 32 per sq. km (2002)
MILITARY EXPENDITURE – 1.9 per cent of GDP (2003)
MILITARY PERSONNEL – 9,700: Army 8,500, Navy 400,
Air Force 800; Paramilitaries 2,600
CONSCRIPTION DURATION – Two years
ILLITERACY RATE – (m) 44.9 per cent; (f) 73.0 per cent
(2000)
GROSS ENROLMENT RATIO (percentage of relevant age
group) – primary 77 per cent (2002)

CLIMATE AND TERRAIN

Guinea has a flat coastal plain that rises to a mountainous
interior, where the Senegal and Niger rivers rise. The
River Gambia rises on the Fouta Djallon plateau in the
north-west of the country. Elevation extremes range from
1,752 m (Mont Nimba) at the highest point to 0 m at the
lowest (Atlantic Ocean). The south-east is forested. There
is a wet season from June to November and the average
daily temperature is 27°C.

HISTORY AND POLITICS

Susi kingdoms were established in the area by the 13th
century, and in the 16th century the north-east of the
country was part of the Mali empire. The Portuguese
developed ivory and slave trading from the mid-15th
century. In 1849 the French established a protectorate
over the coastal areas, and the country was governed with
Senegal until the 1890s, when it was renamed French
Guinea, becoming part of French West Africa in 1904.
Guinea became independent on 2 October 1958 under
President Ahmed Sekou Touré, who established a one-
party state pursuing Marxist policies in the 1960s and
1970s. Decades of economic stagnation followed as
Sekou Touré attempted first to ally Guinea to the Soviet
Union, and then, when the relationship with the USSR
soured, imposed a series of socialist reforms. Touré died in
1984, shortly after making limited free-market reforms in
response to strong opposition to his policies, and his
death was followed by a military coup that brought to
power Lansana Conté. As president, Conté introduced
economic liberalisation and, following strikes and mass
protests in 1991, reintroduced a multiparty system.
President Conté narrowly won the presidential election in
1993, and was re-elected in 1998 with 54 per cent of the
vote, and in 2003 with 95 per cent of the vote after
several opposition parties boycotted the election.

The 2002 legislative election was won by President
Conté's Party of Unity and Progress (PUP), which gained
85 of the 114 National Assembly seats. In May 2004
Prime Minister François Fall resigned and went into exile
after just two months in the job, protesting that President
Conté was blocking his attempts at political and economic
reform. He was replaced in December by Cellou Dalein
Diallo.

The country has been badly affected since 2000 by the
civil wars in neighbouring Sierra Leone, Liberia and Côte
d'Ivoire. In addition to border incursions, the economy
has been badly affected by the influx of refugees,
exacerbating the poor conditions which have contributed
to the growing unpopularity of the government.

POLITICAL SYSTEM

Under the 1991 constitution, the executive president is
directly elected for a five-year term, renewable only once;
a referendum in 2001 approved an amendment to allow
the president a third term, for a longer period of seven
years, following the 2003 election. The unicameral
legislature, the National Assembly, has 114 members, who
are directly elected for a five-year term. The president
appoints the Council of Ministers.

HEAD OF STATE

President, Maj.-Gen. Lansana Conté, *took power* 3 April
1984, *elected* 19 December 1993, *re-elected* 14
December 1998 and 21 December 2003

SELECTED GOVERNMENT MEMBERS *as at July 2005*

Prime Minister, Cellou Dalein Diallo
Health, Amara Cisse
Economic Affairs, Finance, Mady Kaba Kamara
Foreign Affairs, Sidibe Fatoumata Kaba

EMBASSY OF THE REPUBLIC OF GUINEA

51 rue de la Faisanderie, F-75016 Paris, France
T (+33) (1) 4704 8148

Ambassador Extraordinary and Plenipotentiary, Lansana
Keita, apptd 2004

BRITISH CONSULATE GENERAL

BP 834 Conakry, Guinea T (+224) 455 807/456 020/452 959

BRITISH AMBASSADOR

HE John McManus, resident at Freetown, Sierra Leone

ECONOMY AND TRADE

Despite holding over 30 per cent of global bauxite
resources, Guinea's economic performance is poor owing
to decades of mismanagement. Guinea is the world's
second largest exporter of bauxite, and also exports
alumina (a by-product of bauxite), gold, diamonds, coffee,
fish and agricultural products. Rice, coffee, pineapples,
sweet potatoes and cassava all form part of Guinea's
agricultural produce.
GNI – US$3,200 million (2002); US$410 per capita
(2002)
ANNUAL AVERAGE GROWTH OF GDP – 1 per cent
(2004 est.)
TOTAL EXTERNAL DEBT – US$3,388 million (2000)

BALANCE OF PAYMENTS
Trade – US$218 million surplus (2002)
Current Account – US$46 million deficit (2002)

Trade with UK	2003	2004
Imports from UK	£26,180,000	£13,508,000
Exports to UK	1,393,000	2,616,000

TRANSPORT INFRASTRUCTURE

Guinea has over 1,000 km of railways, 30,000 km of
roads and 1,295 km of navigable waterways. The major
port is Conakry. Guinea has 15 airports, including five
with surfaced runways; the principal airport is at
Conakry.

MEDIA AND CULTURE

There are five national newspapers and a single state-run
television broadcaster. The varied musical tradition of
Guinea remains strong through the verse of the *griots*, a
social caste of professional musicians.

GUINEA-BISSAU

República da Guiné-Bissau – Republic of Guinea-Bissau

AREA – 36,125 sq, km Neighbours: Senegal (north), Guinea (east and south)

POPULATION – 1,388,363 (2004 est.). The main ethnic groups are the Balante, Malinké, Fulani, Mandjako and Pepel. The official language is Portuguese; most of the population speak Guinean Creole

CAPITAL – ΨBissau (population, 195,400, 1991)

CURRENCY – Franc CFA

NATIONAL ANTHEM – É patria amada [This is our beloved country]

NATIONAL DAY – 24 September (Independence Day)

NATIONAL FLAG – Horizontal bands of yellow over green with vertical red band in the hoist charged with a black star

MORTALITY RATE (per 1,000 population) – 16.57 (2004 est.)

INFANT MORTALITY (per 1,000 births) – 108.72 (2004 est.)

HIV / AIDS ADULT PREVALENCE – 10 per cent (2003 est.)

DEATH PENALTY – No (abolished 1993)

POPULATION GROWTH RATE – 1.99 per cent (2004 est.)

POPULATION DENSITY – 51 per sq. km (2002)

MILITARY EXPENDITURE – 4 per cent of GDP (2003)

MILITARY PERSONNEL – 9,250: Army 6,800, Navy 350, Air Force 100, Paramilitaries 2,000

CONSCRIPTION DURATION – Selective conscription

ILLITERACY RATE – (m) 41.9 per cent; (f) 72.6 per cent (2003 est.)

GROSS ENROLMENT RATIO (percentage of relevant age group) – primary 70 per cent (2002); secondary 18 per cent (2002)

CLIMATE AND TERRAIN

Guinea-Bissau has a low coastal plain that rises to savannah in the east. Elevation extremes range from 300 m at the highest point to 0 m (Atlantic Ocean) at the lowest. Average yearly temperatures range from 24°C in January to 27°C in October, with a wet season from June to November.

HISTORY AND POLITICS

A part of the ancient African empire of Mali, Guinea-Bissau was once the kingdom of Gabú, which became independent of the empire in 1546 and survived until 1867. In 1446 Portuguese traders discovered the coast and established slave trading, administering Guinea-Bissau with the Cape Verde islands. After becoming a separate colony in 1879, Guinea-Bissau achieved independence in 1974 after a guerrilla war led by the left-wing African Party for the Independence of Guinea and Cape Verde (PAIGCV).

Since independence, Guinea-Bissau has suffered severe political instability. From 1981 until 1994 the country was under military and one-party rule by the PAIGC. A multiparty system was introduced in 1991 after popular agitation. The first multiparty elections in 1994 were won by the PAIGC, and General Vieira was confirmed as president. In 1998 President Vieira was overthrown in a military coup which developed into a civil war until 1999, when a military junta appointed an interim president.

In 2000 Kumba Yala was elected president, but his increasingly erratic behaviour and fraught relations with his ministers and the military led to his overthrow in a military coup in 2003. ECOWAS persuaded the military to accept a form of constitutional government that included a large civilian element, and a civilian-led transitional government was set up with Henrique Rosa as interim president. In the legislative election of March 2004, the PAIGC won 45 seats, the Party for Social Renewal (PSR) won 35 seats and the United Social Democratic Party (USDP) won 27. The presidential election of July 2005 was won by Joao Bernardo Vieira.

POLITICAL SYSTEM

Under the 1999 constitution, the executive president is directly elected for a five-year term, which is renewable only once. The president appoints the Council of Ministers. There is a unicameral legislature, the Assembleia Nacional Popular (National People's Assembly), composed of 102 members who are directly elected for a four-year term.

HEAD OF STATE
President, Joao Bernardo Vieira, *elected* July 2005

SELECTED GOVERNMENT MEMBERS *as at July 2005*
Prime Minister, Carlos Gomez
Economy and Finance, Joao al Hadji Amadu Fadia
Foreign Affairs, Soares Sambu
Internal Administration, Joaquim Mumini Embalo
National Defence, Martin ho Ndufa Kabi

EMBASSY OF THE REPUBLIC OF GUINEA-BISSAU
94 rue St Lazare, Paris F-75009, France
T (+33) (1) 4526 1851
Chargé d'Affaires, Fali Embalo

BRITISH CONSULATE
Mavegro Int., CP100, Bissau T (+245) 201 224/201 216
British Ambassador, HE Peter Newell, resident at Dakar, Senegal

ECONOMY AND TRADE

The economy is in a poor state after decades of mismanagement and corruption and the devasting effects of the 1998–9 civil war. There is a massive foreign debt and the country is heavily dependent on foreign aid.

Although there is the possibility of offshore oil reserves, Guinea-Bissau has very few natural resources and the economy is based almost exclusively on agriculture and fishing. Exports include cashew nuts, fish, seafood, peanuts, palm kernels and timber.

GNI – US$200 million (2002); US$130 per capita (2002)
INFLATION RATE – 8.6 per cent (2000)
TOTAL EXTERNAL DEBT – US$942 million (2000)
IMPORTS – US$69 million (2003)
EXPORTS – US$69 million (2003)

BALANCE OF PAYMENTS
Trade – US$14 million deficit (1997)
Current Account – US$30 million deficit (1997)

Trade with UK	2003	2004
Imports from UK	£804,000	£731,000
Exports to UK	215,000	—

members elected for six years; one-third of the senators are elected every two years. The president appoints the prime minister, who must be approved by the National Assembly.

HEAD OF STATE
Interim President, Boniface Alexandre, *sworn in* 8 March 2004

SELECTED GOVERNMENT MEMBERS *as at July 2005*
Prime Minister, Gerard Latourte
Foreign and Religious Affairs, Herard Abraham
Finance and Economy, Henri Bazin
Interior, Paul Gustav Magloire

BRITISH AMBASSADOR
HE Andrew Ashcroft, apptd 2002, resident at Santo Domingo, Dominican Republic

BRITISH CONSULATE
Hotel Montana (PO Box 1302), Port-au-Prince
T (+509) 257 3969

ECONOMY AND TRADE
Around 70 per cent of the population depend on agriculture, predominantly small-scale subsistence farming. Massive inflation has only partly been alleviated by aid following the departure of former president Jean-Bertrand Aristide. Remittances from the estimated one in six Haitians living abroad, principally in the USA, are of importance. Leather goods, textiles, electronic components and sports equipment are manufactured, using imported raw materials, for re-export. Principal imports are foodstuffs, machinery and transport equipment and fuels. In July 2002 Haiti was accepted as the 15th member of the Caribbean Community (Caricom) trade bloc.

GNI – US$3,600 million (2002); US$440 per capita (2002)
ANNUAL AVERAGE GROWTH OF GDP – 1.1 per cent (2000)
INFLATION RATE – 13.7 per cent (2000)
TOTAL EXTERNAL DEBT – US$1,169 million (2000)
IMPORTS – US$1,188 million (2003)
EXPORTS – US$347 million (2003)

BALANCE OF PAYMENTS
Trade – US$341 million deficit (1998)
Current Account – US$38 million deficit (1998)

Trade with UK	2003	2004
Imports from UK	£15,480,000	£6,960,000
Exports to UK	381,000	496,000

TRANSPORT INFRASTRUCTURE
Haiti has approximately 40 km of railway. Nearly a quarter of the country's 4,160 km of highways are surfaced, and less than 100 km of waterways are navigable. Haiti has 12 airports of which only three have surfaced runways. Haitien and Port au Prince are the largest ports in Haiti.

MEDIA
There are more than 250 radio stations broadcasting in French and Creole. A single state broadcaster, Télévision Nationale d'Haiti, provides four television channels and these have been joined by two privately owned French-language stations.

HONDURAS

República de Honduras – Republic of Honduras

AREA – 112,088 sq. km. Neighbours: Guatemala (north-west), El Salvador (south-west), Nicaragua (south)
POPULATION – 6,823,568 (2004 est.) of mixed Spanish and Indian descent. The Garifunas in the north are of West Indian origin. The language is Spanish, although English is spoken on the Bay Islands
CAPITAL – Tegucigalpa (population, 850,445, 2001 census)
MAJOR CITIES – Choluteca; ΨLa Ceiba; ΨPuerto Cortés; San Pedro Sula; ΨTela (2001 census)
CURRENCY – Lempira of 100 centavos
NATIONAL ANTHEM – Tu bandera es un lampo de cielo [Your flag is a heavenly light]
NATIONAL DAY – 15 September
NATIONAL FLAG – Three horizontal bands, blue, white, blue (with five blue stars on the white band)
LIFE EXPECTANCY – 66.15 (2004 est.)
MORTALITY RATE (per 1,000 population) – 6.64 (2004 est.)
HIV / AIDS ADULT PREVALENCE – 1.8 per cent (2003 est.)
DEATH PENALTY – No (abolished 1956)
POPULATION GROWTH RATE – 2.24 per cent (2004 est.)
POPULATION DENSITY – 61 per sq. km (2002)
MILITARY EXPENDITURE – 0.8 per cent of GDP (2003)
MILITARY PERSONNEL – 12,000: Army 8,300, Navy 1,400, Air Force 2,300; Paramilitaries 8,000

CLIMATE AND TERRAIN
Honduras is the second largest country in central America. Elevation extremes range from 2,870 m (Cerro Las Minas) at the highest point to 0 m (Caribbean Sea) at the lowest. Average annual temperatures range from 19°C in January to 23°C in June.

HISTORY AND POLITICS
Honduras hosted an arm of the Mayan civilisation between the fifth and ninth centuries AD. Christopher Columbus first set foot on the American mainland at Trujillo in Honduras in 1502, but it was 20 years before Spanish conquistadors reached the country. The economic importance of Honduras declined in the 18th century. In 1824 Honduras joined all its neighbouring Central American provinces in declaring independence from Spain.

The Sandinista revolution in neighbouring Nicaragua in 1979 made Honduras a centre for US endeavours to back the anti-Sandinista Nicaraguan Contras. Honduras returned to civilian rule in 1981 with an executive presidency, a 128-seat unicameral congress, and a multiparty system. In October 1997, Congress approved a constitutional amendment reducing the legislature to 80 members. The ending of the civil wars in Nicaragua and El Salvador meant a reduction in the number of US troops in Honduras and a decline in the power of the army.

Legislative elections held on 25 November 2001 were won by the National Party (PNH) who gained 61 seats, with the Liberal Party (PLH) gaining 55 seats. The presidential election held on the same day was won by Ricardo Maduro of the PNH.

HEAD OF STATE
President of the Republic, C-in-C of the Armed Forces,
   Ricardo Maduro, *elected* 25 November 2001, *took office*
   27 January 2002
Vice-Presidents, Vicente Williams; Armida De Lopez;
   Alberto Diaz

SELECTED GOVERNMENT MEMBERS *as at July 2005*
Defence, Federico Breve Travieso
Finance, William Chong Wong
Foreign Relations, Leonidas Rosa Bautista
Interior and Justice, Jorge Ramón Hernández Alcerro

EMBASSY OF HONDURAS
115 Gloucester Place, London W1U 6JT T 020-7486 4880
Chargé d'Affaires, Irma Alejandrina Rosa

ECONOMY AND TRADE

Economic reliance in Honduras is on banana and coffee exports, but the markets for both of these crops have been in steady decline over recent years. Other chief exports include frozen meat, shrimps, lobsters and timber, the most important being pine, mahogany and cedar. The main imports are machinery and electrical equipment, industrial chemicals and lubricants.

A foreign debt of around 80 per cent of total GDP, and the devastation to the country's infrastructure caused by Hurricane Mitch in 1998, have caused considerable economic problems for Honduras. In 2003 President Ricardo Maduro joined the heads of Central American states to push for a Central American Free Trade Agreement with the USA. In 2004 Honduras signed agreements with the IMF which, if targets are met, will allow Honduras to be granted debt relief under the Heavily Indebted Poor Countries (HIPC) initiative.

GNI – US$6,300 million (2002); US$930 per capita
   (2002)
ANNUAL AVERAGE GROWTH OF GDP – 4.2 per cent
   (2004 est.)
INFLATION RATE – 7 per cent (2004 est.)
UNEMPLOYMENT – 28.5 per cent (2004 est.)
TOTAL EXTERNAL DEBT – US$5,487 million (2000)
IMPORTS – US$3,300 million (2003)
EXPORTS – US$1,300 million (2003)

BALANCE OF PAYMENTS
Trade – US$987 million deficit (2003)
Current Account – US$279 million deficit (2003)

Trade with UK	2003	2004
Imports from UK	£14,666,000	£10,747,000
Exports to UK	23,890,000	25,817,000

TRANSPORT INFRASTRUCTURE

Honduras has a number of ports and 465 km of waterways are navigable by small craft. There are 699 km of railway and 13,603 km of roads. The mountainous terrain has led to the development of a large number of airports, though only 12 of the 115 have surfaced runways.

EDUCATION

Primary and secondary education is free of charge, primary education is compulsory from the age of seven to 12, and the government has launched a campaign to eradicate illiteracy.

ILLITERACY RATE – (m) 25.6 per cent; (f) 25.2 per cent
   (2000)
GROSS ENROLMENT RATIO (percentage of relevant age
   group) – primary 106 per cent (2002); secondary 33
   per cent (1991); tertiary 141 per cent (2002)

MEDIA AND CULTURE

Honduras has a state owned radio station as well as several privately run broadcasters and newspapers. Televicentro operates several television channels.

The most historically important Mayan site in Honduras is located at Copán, and is famous for its stone carvings and temple complexes. The town of Santa Rosa de Copán is renowned for its fine colonial architecture. Two Honduran writers are considered central to the country's literary heritage: the poet and playwright José Reyes (1797–1855), who founded the National University of Honduras and Lucila Gamero de Medina (1873–1964) who published the first Honduran novel *Amalia Montiel* in 1893. Medina's most famous work is her 1903 novel *Blanca Olmedo,* which was controversial at the time of publication because of its critique of Catholicism and the clergy.

HUNGARY

Magyar Köztársaság – Republic of Hungary

AREA – 92,300 sq. km. Neighbours: Slovakia (north),
   Ukraine and Romania (east), Serbia and Montenegro
   and Croatia (south), Slovenia and Austria (west)
POPULATION – 10,032,375 (2004 est.). There are
   minorities of Romanies (4 per cent), ethnic Germans (3
   per cent), Serbs (2 per cent), Romanians (1 per cent)
   and Slovaks (1 per cent). About two-thirds of the
   population are Roman Catholic and the remainder
   mostly Calvinist. The language is Hungarian (Magyar)
CAPITAL – Budapest (population, 1,775,203, 2001
   census)
MAJOR CITIES – Debrecen; Miskolc; Pécs; Szeged
CURRENCY – Forint of 100 fillér
NATIONAL ANTHEM – Isten aldd meg a Magyart [God
   bless the Hungarians]
NATIONAL DAYS – 15 March, 20 August, 23 October
NATIONAL FLAG – Red, white, green (horizontally)
LIFE EXPECTANCY (years) – 72.25 (2004 est.)
MORTALITY RATE (per 1,000 population) – 13.16
   (2004 est.)
INFANT MORTALITY (per 1,000 births) – 8.68
   (2004 est.)
HIV / AIDS ADULT PREVALENCE – 0.1 per cent
   (2001 est.)
DEATH PENALTY – No (abolished 1990)
POPULATION GROWTH RATE – −0.25 per cent
   (2004 est.)
POPULATION DENSITY – 110 per sq. km (2002)
URBAN POPULATION – 65 per cent (2001)

CLIMATE AND TERRAIN

A landlocked state in central Europe, Hungary is mostly low-lying with a mountainous region in the north. Elevation extremes range from 1,014 m (Kekes) at the highest point to 78 m (Tisza River) at the lowest. Average annual temperatures range from −1°C in January to 21°C in July.

HISTORY AND POLITICS

Hungary became a Christian kingdom in the year AD 1,000, but had been settled by Magyar tribes (the ancestors of modern Hungarians) since 896. Between 1699 and 1867, Hungary was precariously ruled as a province of the Austrian Habsburg empire. Following years of Hungarian agitation, a Dual Monarchy was created giving Hungary control of internal affairs in return for the continued union of the Austrian and Hungarian crowns. The Austro-Hungarian Empire is remembered as a time of great cultural achievement and economic success. Nevertheless, the union took the country into the First World War on the side of Germany, resulting in defeat for the Hungarians and the destruction of the Habsburgs. An unstable republic after the war, Hungary suffered invasion from Romania and was reduced in size following the Treaty of Trianon. Hungary looked to the fascist regimes in Germany and Italy for aid in re-establishing its historic size, and so entered the Second World War on the side of the Axis powers. Hungary endured massive military defeat at the hands of the Soviets, and the destruction of its Jewish community at the hands of the Nazis.

The elections of 1947, which brought the communists to power, set the tone for subsequent communist rule. The communist leader János Kádár's attempts at national reconciliation led to reforms which developed Hungary's most wealthy and liberal regime.

The collapse of communist rule saw Hungary become the Republic of Hungary in 1989. Free and fair elections were not matched by economic success, and the early 1990s saw Hungary suffer a host of economic problems. In the legislative elections in April 2002, no one party won an overall majority. The Federation of Young Democrats-Hungarian Civic Party (Fidesz-MPP) won the largest number of seats but Péter Medgyessy of the Hungarian Socialist Party (MSzP) formed a coalition government with the Alliance of Free Democrats (SzDSz). The composition of the national assembly as at July 2005 was: Fidesz-MPP 188, MSzP 178, SzDSz 20.

POLITICAL SYSTEM

The unicameral 386-seat National Assembly is elected on a mixed first-past-the-post and proportional representation basis. The president, elected by the National Assembly, has a largely ceremonial role, but his powers include appointing the prime minister, who in turn selects the cabinet ministers and has the exclusive right to dismiss them.

HEAD OF STATE

President, Laszlo Solyom, *elected* June 2005, *sworn in* 5 August 2005

SELECTED GOVERNMENT MEMBERS *as at July 2005*
Prime Minister, Ferenc Gyurcsany
Defence, Ferenc Juhász
Finance, Janos Veres
Foreign Affairs, Ferenc Somogyi
Interior, Mónika Lamperth

EMBASSY OF THE REPUBLIC OF HUNGARY
35 Eaton Place, London SW1X 8BY
T 020-7235 5218
Ambassador Extraordinary and Plenipotentiary, HE Béla Szombati, apptd 2002

BRITISH EMBASSY
Harmincad Utca 6, H-1051 Budapest
T (+36) (1) 266 2888 E info@britemb.hu
Ambassador Extraordinary and Plenipotentiary, HE John Nichols, apptd 2003

BRITISH COUNCIL
Benczúr Utca 26, H-1068 Budapest
T (+36) (1) 478 4700
E information@britishcouncil.hu
Director, Jim McGrath

DEFENCE

The Army has 704 main battle tanks, 680 armoured infantry fighting vehicles and 798 armoured personnel carriers. The Air Force has 27 combat aircraft and 32 attack helicopters.
MILITARY EXPENDITURE – 1.9 per cent of GDP (2003)
MILITARY PERSONNEL – 31,510: Army 23,950, Army Maritime Wing 60, Air Force 7,500; Paramilitaries 14,000
CONSCRIPTION DURATION – Six months

ECONOMY AND TRADE

Hungary is one of the largest economies of the ten countries to enter the European Union in 2004. The private sector accounts for around 80 per cent of GDP and Hungary has attracted large amounts of foreign investment since the end of communist rule in 1989. Industry includes mining, metallurgy, construction materials, processed foods, textiles, chemicals (especially pharmaceuticals) and motor vehicles. Germany remains Hungary's largest trading partner.
GNI – US$53,700 million (2002); US$5,290 per capita (2002)
ANNUAL AVERAGE GROWTH OF GDP – 3.5 per cent (2003 est.)
INFLATION RATE – 4.7 per cent (2004 est.)
UNEMPLOYMENT – 5.5 per cent (2003 est.)
TOTAL EXTERNAL DEBT – US$29,415 million (2000)
FOREIGN DIRECT INVESTMENT – US$7,657 million (1997–2000)
IMPORTS – US$47,600 million (2003)
EXPORTS – US$42,500 million (2003)

BALANCE OF PAYMENTS
Trade – US$3,365 million deficit (2003)
Current Account – US$7,364 million deficit (2003)

Trade with UK	2003	2004
Imports from UK	£851,910,000	£924,547,000
Exports to UK	1,136,610,000	1,564,012,000

TRANSPORT INFRASTRUCTURE

Hungary has 188,203 km of highways, 7,875 km of railways (including a cross-border line to Austria, jointly managed by the two countries) and 1,373 km of permanently navigable waterways. Hungary maintains several major ports and harbours on the Danube River including the capital Budapest.

EDUCATION

Hungarians have 10 years of compulsory education, though a further two years at secondary level is optional.
ILLITERACY RATE – (m) 0.5 per cent; (f) 0.8 per cent (2000)

GROSS ENROLMENT RATIO (percentage of relevant age group) – primary 102 per cent (2002); secondary 98 per cent (2002); tertiary 40 per cent (2002)

MEDIA AND CULTURE

Hungary's state-run broadcaster (Magyar Televizio) competes with privately owned television and radio stations. Hungary has a wide range of weekly and daily newspapers, some of which are owned by foreign investors.

Hungary has an exceptional folk culture which has influenced a powerful musical tradition including the composers Franz Liszt (1811–86), Béla Bartók (1881–1945), Zoltan Kodaly (1882–1967) and Gyorgy Ligeti (b. 1923). Janos Arany (1817–82) and Endre Ady (1877–1919) are two of Hungary's finest poets. Hungary's best-known author is Imre Kertesz (b. 1929) who won the Nobel Prize for Literature in 2002.

ICELAND

Lýðveldið Ísland – Republic of Iceland

AREA – 103,000 sq. km
POPULATION – 293,966 (2004 est.). Some 86.5 per cent of the population are members of the (Lutheran) Church of Iceland. The language is Icelandic
CAPITAL – ΨReykjavík (population, 113,387, 2004)
MAJOR CITIES – Akranes; ΨAkureyri; Egilsstaðir; ΨHafnarfjörður; ΨIsafjörður; Kópavogur; Reykjanesbær; ΨSiglufjörður
CURRENCY – Icelandic króna (Kr) of 100 aurar
NATIONAL ANTHEM – O Gud vors lamds [God of our country]
NATIONAL DAY – 17 June
NATIONAL FLAG – Blue, with white-bordered red cross
LIFE EXPECTANCY (years) – 80.18 (2004 est.)
MORTALITY RATE (per 1,000 population) – 6.57 (2004 est.)
INFANT MORTALITY (per 1,000 births) – 3.31 (2004 est.)
HIV / AIDS ADULT PREVALENCE – 0.2 per cent (2001 est.)
DEATH PENALTY – No (abolished 1928)
POPULATION GROWTH RATE – 0.97 per cent (2004 est.)
POPULATION DENSITY – 3 per sq. km (2001)
URBAN POPULATION – 93 per cent (2001)
MILITARY PERSONNEL – Paramilitaries: 130
GROSS ENROLMENT RATIO (percentage of relevant age group) – primary 101 per cent (2002)

CLIMATE AND TERRAIN

Iceland is located in the North Atlantic Ocean, to the east of Greenland and to the west of Norway, and its northernmost coasts reach the Arctic Circle. Some coasts have narrow strips of low-lying land, others sheer cliffs. An inland plateau of glaciers, lakes and lava fields covers 79 per cent of the interior, with mountainous areas in the north and at the four glaciers in the centre and south. Elevation extremes range from 2,119 m (Hvannadalshnukur) at the highest point to 0 m (North Atlantic Ocean) at the lowest. There are geysers and hot springs owing to volcanic activity, which can create new islands, such as Surtsey in 1963; it is estimated that over the past 500 years, Iceland has emitted a third of the earth's total lava flow. Iceland's climate is influenced by the Gulf Stream and average annual temperatures ranging from −3°C in January to 11°C in July.

HISTORY AND POLITICS

The first major settlements occurred from about 870 onwards as turmoil in Scandinavia drove migrants to seek new homelands. Iceland hosted a flourishing Viking culture in the 9th and 10th centuries, becoming a fully Christian country in 999. Iceland recognised Norwegian sovereignty in 1263, and with Norway came under Danish rule in 1397. When Norway was ceded to Sweden in 1814, Iceland remained Danish territory, achieving autonomy in domestic affairs in 1874. Though it became an independent state with the same sovereign as Denmark in 1918, Copenhagen continued to control foreign policy and defence. The treaty of union with Denmark expired in 1943, while Denmark was under German occupation, and in a referendum Icelanders voted to become fully independent as a republic, which was proclaimed on 17 June 1944.

The country's dependence on the fishing industry has led occasionally to fraught foreign relations. The introduction and extensions of an exclusive fishing limit around Iceland in 1958, 1972 and 1975 caused the 'Cod War' disputes with the UK, with clashes between Icelandic patrol boats and British fishing trawlers and naval protection vessels. Subsequent restrictions on fishing in Icelandic waters in the 1990s were less controversial.

In the 2003 legislative election, the Conservative Independence Party (SSF) remained the largest party, with 22 seats. Incumbent prime minister David Oddsson of the SSF was sworn into office for a further term at the head of a coalition government formed with the Progressive Party (FSF). In September 2004, Oddsson exchanged positions with Halldór Ásgrímsson of the FSF, who had been foreign minister since 1995. In the 2004 presidential election, incumbent president Ólafur Grímsson was returned to office for a third term.

POLITICAL SYSTEM

Under the 1944 constitution, the head of state is the president, who is directly elected for a four-year term, which is renewable. The unicameral legislature, the *Althing*, has 63 members, who are directly elected for a four-year term. Founded in 930, the *Althing* is the world's oldest parliament.

HEAD OF STATE
President, Ólafur Ragnar Grímsson, *elected* 29 June 1996, *re-elected* 1 August 2000 and 26 June 2004

SELECTED GOVERNMENT MEMBERS *as at July 2005*
Prime Minister, Statistical Bureau of Iceland, Halldór Ásgrímsson
Finance, Geir Haarde
Foreign Affairs, David Oddsson
Social Affairs, Arni Magnusson

EMBASSY OF ICELAND
2A Hans Street, London SW1X 0JE
T 020-7259 3999
Ambassador Extraordinary and Plenipotentiary, HE Sverrir Haukur Gunnlaugsson, apptd 2003

BRITISH EMBASSY
Laufásvegur 31, IS-101 Reykjavík
T (+354) 550 5100 E britemb@centrum.is
Ambassador Extraordinary and Plenipotentiary and Consul-General, HE Alp Mehmet, MVO, apptd 2004

ECONOMY AND TRADE

The Icelandic economy is heavily reliant on the fishing industry and 70 per cent of its exports are marine products. Careful management of the industry, including the banning of direct foreign investment, has allowed stocks to recover from the over-fishing of the 1980s, when declining catches adversely affected the economy. Although only 5 per cent of land in Iceland is suitable for farming, the country is self-sufficient in meat and dairy products. Attempts to reduce the country's dependence on fishing have included the introduction of aluminium smelters, which can be run on Iceland's plentiful supply of clean geothermal fuel. The subterranean hot water supplies also provide most of the island's heating. Tourism is encouraged and is becoming increasingly significant, with over 40,000 tourists from the UK in 2000. The main export markets are the UK, Germany, the USA, the Netherlands, Spain, Norway, Denmark, Japan and Switzerland.

GNI – US$8,150 million (2001); US$28,910 per capita (2001)
ANNUAL AVERAGE GROWTH OF GDP – 4.0 per cent (2003 est.)
INFLATION RATE – 4.6 per cent (2002 est.)
UNEMPLOYMENT – 2.1 per cent (2002 est.)
IMPORTS – US$2,790 million (2003)
EXPORTS – US$2,390 million (2003)

BALANCE OF PAYMENTS
Trade – US$210 million deficit (2003)
Current Account – US$572 million deficit (2003)

Trade with UK	2003	2004
Imports from UK	£146,296,000	£172,145,000
Exports to UK	309,900,000	368,967,000

TRANSPORT INFRASTRUCTURE

Iceland has no railways and no navigable waterways. Although the country has almost 13,000 km of roads, the majority remain unsurfaced and in winter these are often blocked by snow. Consequently much internal travel is by air or sea. Iceland has 100 airports, the principal ones being at Keflavík, near Reykjavík, in the south and Akureyri in the north. There are nine major ports and the capital, Reykjavík, operates shipping services to the USA and Europe.

MEDIA AND CULTURE

The state provides a public service broadcaster for television and radio, the Icelandic National Broadcasting Service (RUV), which is joined by several commercial stations.

Iceland enjoys a rich literary tradition. The *Icelandic Sagas* are among the most important works of European medieval literature. Written anonymously between the 12th and 13th centuries, the Sagas relate the battles and triumphs of the original Icelanders who settled from Norway and Denmark. One of Iceland's most famous contemporary writers is Halldor Laxness (1902–98), winner of the Nobel Prize for Literature in 1955.

INDIA

The Republic of India/Bhāratīya Ganarājya

AREA – 2,973,200 sq. km. Neighbours: Pakistan (north-west), China, Tibet, Nepal and Bhutan (north), Myanmar and Bangladesh (east)
POPULATION – 1,065,070,607 (2004 est.): Hindu (81 per cent), the rest being Muslim (12 per cent), Christian (2.3 per cent), Sikh (1.9 per cent), Buddhist (0.8 per cent) and Jain (0.4 per cent). The official languages are Hindi in the Devanagari script and English, though 17 regional languages are also recognised for adoption as official state languages
CAPITAL – New Delhi (population, 9,817,439 including Delhi/Dilli, 2001)
MAJOR CITIES – Ahmedabad; Bangalore; ΨBombay/Mumbai; ΨCalcutta/Kolkata; Hyderabad; Kanpur; Lucknow; ΨMadras/Chennai; Pune
CURRENCY – Indian rupee (Rs) of 100 paise
NATIONAL ANTHEM – Jana-gana-mana [Thou art the ruler of the minds of all people]
NATIONAL DAY – 26 January (Republic Day)
NATIONAL FLAG – A horizontal tricolour with bands of deep saffron, white and dark green in equal proportions. In the centre of the white band appears an Asoka wheel in navy blue
LIFE EXPECTANCY (years) – 63.99 (2004 est.)
MORTALITY RATE (per 1,000 population) – 8.38 (2004 est.)
INFANT MORTALITY (per 1,000 births) – 57.92 (2004 est.)
HIV / AIDS ADULT PREVALENCE – 0.8 per cent (2001 est.)
DEATH PENALTY – Yes
POPULATION BELOW POVERTY LINE – 25 per cent (2002 est.)
POPULATION GROWTH RATE – 1.44 per cent (2004 est.)
POPULATION DENSITY – 353 per sq. km (2002)
URBAN POPULATION – 28 per cent (2001)

CLIMATE AND TERRAIN

India has three well-defined regions: the mountain range of the Himalayas, the Indo-Gangetic plain, and the southern peninsula. The Himalayas along the northern border reach 8,598 m (Kanchenjunga) at the highest point of elevation, then drop to the northern plains formed by the basins of the Indus, Ganges and Brahmaputra rivers and their tributaries before rising to low hills running east to west that mark the division with the southern, Deccan peninsula. The peninsula has narrow coastal plains rising to a central plateau, with the Western Ghats and Eastern Ghats ranges of hills lying along the west and east coasts respectively. The Thar Desert lies in the north-west. The average annual temperature in New Delhi ranges from 14°C in January to 34°C in June.

HISTORY AND POLITICS

The Indus civilisation emerged in the Indus river valley region *c.*2500 BC, and the beginnings of Hinduism date from this period. This civilisation was destroyed by Aryan tribes from central Asia between 1500 and 200 BC. Buddhism emerged in India from *c.*500 BC and was embraced by the Emperor Ashoka; it spread to the rest of eastern Asia via trade routes, but a Hindu revival from

AD 40 onwards pushed Buddhism into decline in the sub-continent.

The first Muslim advances into India occurred in the 10th and 11th centuries. Incursions swept across the north of the country, where large Muslim communities were established. India thus became a country with two great religious traditions: a Muslim-dominated north, and a largely Hindu south. Europeans arrived in India in the 15th century and had established territorial holdings by the 18th century, though it was not until 1803, when the British East India Company consolidated its influence, that a single power came to dominate the entire subcontinent. In 1857, rule passed to the British government. Opposition to British rule, led by the Indian National Congress (INC) under the leadership of Mahatma Gandhi, became a concerted nationwide movement, and India achieved its independence in 1947. Against a backdrop of violence, India's predominantly Muslim regions were partitioned and became the separate state of Pakistan; the eastern part of Pakistan seceded and became Bangladesh in 1971. India became a republic in 1950.

The INC was the dominant party in Indian politics in the decades after independence, holding power nearly continuously for four decades, with periods in opposition only in 1977–80, 1989–91 and 1996–2004. Jawaharlal Nehru's appointment as prime minister at independence began the rise of the Gandhi, India's great political family, which came to dominate the INC. Nehru was succeeded by his daughter, Indira Gandhi, who was succeeded after her assassination in 1984 by her son Rajiv until his assassination in 1991; Rajiv's widow Sonia became president of the party in 1998. The INC's dominance appeared to be over in the early 1990s when the Hindu nationalist Bharatiya Janata Party (BJP), on a Hindu nationalist platform, began to beat the INC at the polls and formed a series of coalition governments. The Gandhi dynasty returned to popularity with a surprise INC victory in the 2004 parliamentary election, winning 217 seats in the Lok Sabha (House of the People). Italian-born Sonia Gandhi was nominated as prime minister but declined the office, and Manmohan Singh became India's first Sikh prime minister at the head of a coalition government called the United Progressive Alliance; Sonia Gandhi remains the INC party leader.

COMMUNALISM

Tensions between India's Hindu majority and large Muslim minority have never been fully resolved. Violence between the two at the time of partition in 1947 is thought to have cost the lives of up to one million people. The rise of Hindu nationalism in the 1990s accompanied a rise in communal clashes. In 1992 a mosque in the town of Ayodhya was destroyed by Hindus who claimed it was built on the site of the Hindu god Rama's birth. Anti-Muslim mobs rampaged through many parts of India and the army was called upon to restore order. Intercommunal violence flared up again in 2002 when the massacre of pilgrims returning from Ayodhya prompted revenge killings.

Sikh separatist agitation for an independent Sikh state in the Punjab became increasingly violent in the 1980s. The suppression of militant Sikh separatism, and particularly the Indian army offensive at the Golden Temple at Amritsar, led to the assassination of Indira Gandhi by her Sikh bodyguards in 1984.

FOREIGN RELATIONS

Partition produced a bitter stand-off between India and Pakistan over the largely Muslim state of Kashmir and a short war in 1947–8 that resulted in the state being partitioned between the two countries; it is claimed in its entirety by both. This unresolved issue led to further outbreaks of war in 1965 and 1971, and, since 1985, low-level conflict at altitude for control of the Siachen glacier. Military exchanges increased in 1999–2002, with tensions heightened by the fact that both countries have nuclear weapons. Tension remained high in 2003, with frequent exchanges of fire across the demarcation line, until a cease-fire in November 2003. Diplomatic talks between the two countries began in 2004, and diplomatic missions and transport links have been reopened.

In the Sino-Indian war in 1962, India lost territory to China. In addition, China claims Arunachal Pradesh and does not recognise Indian sovereignty over Sikkim. Talks between India and China in 2003 resulted in India's formal recognition of the Tibetan Autonomous Region as a part of China and a cross-border trade agreement on Sikkim.

POLITICAL SYSTEM

Under the 1950 constitution, executive power is vested in the president, who is elected for a five-year term by an electoral college consisting of members of the upper and lower houses of the legislature. The president appoints the prime minister. The Council of Ministers is collectively responsible to the Lok Sabha (House of the People). The vice-president is ex-officio chairman of the Rajya Sabha (House of the States). Legislative power rests with the president and the two houses of parliament (Sansad). The upper house, the Rajya Sabha, has up to 250 members serving a six-year term, with one-third of seats contested every two years; up to 238 members are indirectly elected by the state legislative assemblies and 12 are nominated by the president. In the lower house, the Lok Sabha, there are 545 members; 543, representing the States and Union Territories, are directly elected for a five-year term, and two representatives of the Anglo-Indian community are nominated by the president.

HEAD OF STATE

President of the Republic of India, A. P. J. Abdul Kalam, *elected* 15 July 2002, *took office* 25 July 2002
Vice-President, Bhairon Singh Shekhawat

SELECTED GOVERNMENT MEMBERS *as at July 2005*
Prime Minister, Atomic Energy, Planning, Space, Statistics and Programme Implementation, Manmohan Singh
Defence, Pranab Mukherjee
Foreign Affairs, K. Natwar Singh
Finance, Palaniappan Chidambaram

INDIAN HIGH COMMISSION
India House, Aldwych, London WC2B 4NA
T 020-7836 8484
High Commissioner, HE Kamalesh Sharma, apptd 2005

BRITISH HIGH COMMISSION
Chanakyapuri, New Delhi 110021 T (+91) (11) 687 2161
High Commissioner, HE Sir Michael Arthur, apptd 2003

BRITISH COUNCIL
17 Kasturba Gandhi Marg, New Delhi 110 001
T (+91) (11) 2371 1401
E delhi.enquiry@inbritishcouncil.org
Minister, Edmund Marsden

FEDERAL STRUCTURE

There are 28 states and six union territories and the national capital territory. Each state is headed by a governor, who is appointed by the president and holds office for five years, and by a Council of Ministers. All states have a legislative assembly, and some also have a legislative council, elected directly by adult suffrage for a maximum period of five years. The union territories are administered, except where otherwise provided by parliament, by the president acting through an administrator or lieutenant-governor, or other authority appointed by him. The states have considerable autonomy, although the union government controls such matters as foreign policy, defence and external trade.

DEFENCE

The Army has 3,898 main battle tanks, 1,600 armoured infantry fighting vehicles, 162 helicopters and 317 armoured personnel carriers. The Navy has 16 submarines, one aircraft carrier, eight destroyers, 16 frigates, 42 patrol and coastal vessels, 35 combat aircraft and 32 armed helicopters. It has nine bases including one under construction. The Air Force has 679 combat aircraft and 40 armed helicopters.

India exploded its first nuclear weapon in 1974 and is since believed to have acquired a stockpile of nuclear arms. It conducted further nuclear tests in May 1998. In 1993–4 India successfully test-fired its intermediate-range 'Agni' and 'Prithvi' ballistic missiles, and the latter went into production in September 1997.

MILITARY EXPENDITURE – 2.6 per cent of GDP (2003)
MILITARY PERSONNEL – 1,325,000: Army 1,100,000, Navy 55,000, Air Force 170,000; Paramilitaries 1,089,700

ECONOMY AND TRADE

India remains largely agrarian with agriculture, forestry and fishing supporting approximately 75 per cent of the population and contributing 30 per cent of GDP. Food crops occupy three-quarters of the total cultivated area. The main food crops are rice, cereals (principally wheat) and pulses. The major cash crops include sugarcane, jute, cotton and tea. Other products include oil seeds, spices, groundnuts, soya beans, tobacco, rubber and coffee. Livestock is raised, principally for dairy purposes or for the hides. Agricultural development has been hampered by serious environmental issues. Deforestation, soil erosion, over-grazing and desertification threaten India's agriculture and forests.

Large numbers of graduates have driven the growth of knowledge-based sectors, such as information, communications and technology. Other industries, such as pharmaceuticals, are also experiencing growth. Tourism has become a major industry for the country. The economy has experienced an average growth rate of six per cent since 1990. Large-scale problems remain, with a public-sector budget deficit of 10 per cent of GDP.

India exports tea, coffee, fish, iron and steel, textile goods, gems and jewellery, engineering goods, chemicals and leather goods. Its main trading partners are the USA, Russia, the UK and Germany.

GNI – US$494,800 million (2002); US$470 per capita (2002)
ANNUAL AVERAGE GROWTH OF GDP – 6.2 per cent (2004 est.)
INFLATION RATE – 4.0 per cent (2000 est.)
TOTAL EXTERNAL DEBT – US$100,600 million (2001 est.)

FOREIGN DIRECT INVESTMENT – US$7,657 million (1997–2000)
IMPORTS – US$71,200 million (2003)
EXPORTS – US$57,100 million (2003)

BALANCE OF PAYMENTS
Trade – US$12,416 million deficit (2002)
Current Account – US$4,656 million surplus (2002)

Trade with UK	2003	2004
Imports from UK	£2,293,037,000	£2,340,322,000
Exports to UK	2,147,328,000	2,243,314,000

TRANSPORT INFRASTRUCTURE

India has over 63,518 km of railway, 3,319,644 km of roads and 3,631 km of navigable waterways. There are 333 airports, the principal ones being at Delhi, Bombay/Mumbai, Madras/Chennai and Calcutta/Kolkata. The chief seaports are Bombay/Mumbai, Calcutta/Kolkata, Haldia, Madras/Chennai, Cochin, Visakhapatnam, Mangalore and Tuticorin.

EDUCATION

Education is free of charge and compulsory up to the age of 14. There are 226 universities in India.

ILLITERACY RATE – (m) 31.6 per cent; (f) 54.6 per cent (2000)
GROSS ENROLMENT RATIO (percentage of relevant age group) – primary 99 per cent (2002); secondary 48 per cent (2002), tertiary 11 per cent (2002)

MEDIA AND CULTURE

The state's monopoly of television broadcasting ended in 1992, and India has seen an increase in the number of channels available. Doordarshan and Zee TV are major broadcasters. The private press is a thriving and diverse industry, often outspoken and critical of the government and in 2004 some 142 million newspapers were sold throughout the country. English language newspapers include the Times of India, Indian Express and Hindustan Times, while popular Hindi titles are Amar Ujala, Dainik Jagran, Dainik Bhaskar and NavBharat Times.

Successive empires and invaders have left distinctive traces on Indian art. The Hindu Mauryans, from the third century BC and the Muslim Mughals from the 16th century both instigated what are considered to be the 'Golden Ages' of Indian culture.

Contemporary Indian writers of international standing include Vikram Seth (b. 1952), Salman Rushdie (b. 1947), Arundhati Roy (b. 1961) and Shashi Deshpande (b. 1938). The Indian film industry, known as 'Bollywood', is perhaps the most successful in the world and there are an estimated 800 films made every year.

INDONESIA

Republik Indonesia – Republic of Indonesia

AREA – 1,811,600 sq. km. Indonesia shares borders with Malaysia (on Borneo), Papua New Guinea (on New Guinea) and East Timor (on Timor)
POPULATION – 238,452,952 (2004 est.): 87 per cent Muslim, with Christian, Buddhist, Hindu and Animist minorities. Bahasa Indonesian, a variant of Malay, is the national language, although more than 250 dialects are spoken

CAPITAL – ΨJakarta (population, 8,347,083, 2000 estimate)
MAJOR CITIES – (Java) Bandung, ΨSemarang, ΨSurabaya; (Kalimantan) Banjarmasin, ΨPontianak; (Maluku) Ambon, (Sulawesi) ΨUjung Pandang; (Sumatra) Medan, Palembang
CURRENCY – Rupiah (Rp) of 100 sen
NATIONAL ANTHEM – Indonesia raya [Great Indonesia]
NATIONAL DAY – 17 August (Anniversary of Proclamation of Independence)
NATIONAL FLAG – Equal bands of red over white
LIFE EXPECTANCY (years) – 69.26 (2004 est.)
MORTALITY RATE (per 1,000 population) – 6.26 (2004 est.)
INFANT MORTALITY (per 1,000 births) – 36.82 (2004 est.)
HIV / AIDS ADULT PREVALENCE – 0.1 per cent (2001 est.)
DEATH PENALTY – Yes
POPULATION GROWTH RATE – 1.49 per cent (2004 est.)
POPULATION DENSITY – 117 per sq. km (2002)
URBAN POPULATION – 42 per cent (2001)
ILLITERACY RATE – (m) 7.5 per cent; (f) 16.6 per cent (2004 est.)
GROSS ENROLMENT RATIO (percentage of relevant age group) – primary 111 per cent (2002); secondary 58 per cent (2002); tertiary 15 per cent (2002)

CLIMATE AND TERRAIN

Indonesia comprises over 13,000 islands, of which over 6,000 are inhabited. They include the islands of Java, Madura, Sumatra, the Riouw-Lingga archipelago, Bangka and Billiton, part of the island of Borneo (Kalimantan), Sulawesi (formerly Celebes), Maluku (formerly Moluccas), the islands of Bali, Lombok, Sumbawa, Sumba, Flores and others comprising the provinces of East and West Nusa Tenggara, and the western half of the islands of New Guinea (Irian Jaya) and Timor. Elevation extremes range from 5,030 m (Puncak Jaya, in Irian Jaya) at the highest point to 0 m (Indian Ocean) at the lowest. Many of the islands have narrow coastal plains with hilly or mountainous interiors, and over half of the country is covered by tropical rainforest. Average annual temperatures in Jakarta range from 23°C in January to 32°C in August.

HISTORY AND POLITICS

Hindu and Buddhist kingdoms existed in some parts of the Indonesia until the 14th century. Islam was introduced in the 13th century and spread over the next three centuries.Trading by the Portuguese began in the 16th century, but the Portuguese themselves were displaced by the Dutch who, lured by the rich spice trade, came to dominate the whole of Indonesia by the early 20th century. Opposition to Dutch rule grew in the 1920s and the Japanese occupation of Indonesia during the Second World War strengthened nationalism, leading to a declaration of independence after liberation in 1945. This was not recognised by the Dutch, who attempted to reassert control, but after four years of guerrilla warfare granted independence to the Netherlands Indies in 1949; Irian Jaya was ceded in 1963, and East Timor was invaded and annexed in 1975 but gained its independence in 2002.

Achmed Soekarno, the foremost proponent of self-rule since the 1920s, became president in 1949 but was deposed in 1966 in a military coup that brought to power General Soeharto. Soeharto remained in power until 1998 when, amidst economic and social upheaval, he was succeeded by his deputy B. J. Habibie. Habibie's cautious introduction of social and economic reforms led to him being ousted in the 1999 elections, the first democratically held elections for 44 years, in which Abdurrahman Wahid was elected president.

President Wahid was impeached for alleged financial corruption and in July 2001 the People's Consultative Assembly appointed Megawati Soekarnoputri (daughter of President Soekarno) to replace him.

In the April 2004 legislative elections, the greatest number of seats was won by Golkar, the former ruling party. The October 2004 presidential election was won by H. Susilo Yudhoyono of the Democratic Party, who defeated Megawati Soekarnoputri in the second round; he appointed a coalition government that included two Golkar ministers.

INSURGENCIES

Separatist movements of varying degrees of intensity developed in several parts of Indonesia after independence, including Maluku (which fought an unsuccessful separatist war in the 1950s and experienced further separatist-linked violence in 1999), Irian Jaya, East Timor after its annexation, Kalimantan and Aceh province in Sumatra. Several of these movements have become more vocal, encouraged by the granting of greater autonomy to Irian Jaya in 1999 and East Timor's independence in 2002. The Aceh separatist movement appeared to have won autonomy for the province in a 2002 peace accord but talks broke down and conflict resumed, although it was suspended in the aftermath of the December 2004 Indian Ocean earthquake.

POLITICAL SYSTEM

The legislature is bicameral. The lower house, the House of Representatives, has 550 directly-elected members while the upper house, the House of Representatives of the Regions, has 128 members – four per province. The People's Consultative Assembly is made up of all members of both houses and is the state's highest authority, having powers to alter or make decisions on the constitution. All three bodies have five-year terms of office. The president has a five-year term of office and is directly elected. The prime minister and cabinet are appointed by the president.

HEAD OF STATE
President, H. Susilo Yudhoyono, *sworn in* 20 October 2004
Vice-President, Muhammad Jusuf Kalla

SELECTED GOVERNMENT MEMBERS *as at July 2005*
Defence, Juwono Sudarsono
Economy, Aburizal Bakrie
Foreign Affairs, Hasan Wirayuda
Home Affairs, Lt.-Gen. Muhammad Ma'aruf

INDONESIAN EMBASSY
38 Grosvenor Square, London W1K 2HW T 020-7499 7661
Chargé d'affaires, Eddy Pratomo, apptd 2004

BRITISH EMBASSY
Jalan M. H. Thamrin 75, Jakarta 10310 T (+62) (21) 315 6264
Ambassador Extraordinary and Plenipotentiary, HE Charles Humfrey

BRITISH COUNCIL
S. Widjojo Centre, Jalan Jenderal Sudirman Kav 71,
Jakarta 12190 T (+62) (21) 252 4115
E information@britishcouncil.or.id
Director, Dr Patrick Brazier

DEFENCE

The Army has 356 armoured personnel carriers, 11 armoured infantry fighting vehicles and 11 aircraft. The Navy has two submarines, 16 frigates, 39 patrol and coastal vessels and 17 armed helicopters. There are five principal naval bases. The Air Force has 94 combat aircraft (of which 45 per cent are operational).
MILITARY EXPENDITURE – 3 per cent of GDP (2003)
MILITARY PERSONNEL – 302,000: Army 233,000, Navy 45,000, Air Force 24,000; Paramilitaries 280,000
CONSCRIPTION DURATION – 24 months (selective)

ECONOMY AND TRADE

Indonesia has a wide range of natural resources, including petroleum, tin, natural gas, nickel, timber, bauxite, copper, fertile soils, coal, gold and silver. The country has a large agricultural sector, with 45 per cent of the labour force engaged in agriculture.

Industries include the production of petroleum (of which it is the biggest producer in the Far East) and natural gas. It is also the world's biggest producer of tin. Timber is Indonesia's second largest foreign exchange earner after oil, while textiles, mining and chemicals are also important to the economy. Tourism had begun to recover after the 2002 Bali bombing but in parts of the country has been devastated by the 2004 tsunami. In 2003 Indonesia graduated from IMF support. Inflation and interest rates have both declined, the budget deficit has been reduced to 1.8 per cent of GDP and debt has fallen to 65 per cent of GDP. Its main trading partners are other Pacific Rim countries.
GNI – US$149,900 million (2002); US$710 per capita (2002)
ANNUAL AVERAGE GROWTH OF GDP – 4.9 per cent (2004 est.)
INFLATION RATE – 3.7 per cent (2000 est.)
UNEMPLOYMENT – 9.2 per cent (2004 est.)
TOTAL EXTERNAL DEBT – US$141,803 million (2000 est.)
FOREIGN DIRECT INVESTMENT – US$2,974 million (1997–2000)
IMPORTS – US$32,600 million (2003)
EXPORTS – US$61,100 million (2003)

BALANCE OF PAYMENTS
Trade – US$23,513 million surplus (2002)
Current Account – US$7,823 million surplus (2002)

Trade with UK	2003	2004
Imports from UK	£452,316,000	£398,521,000
Exports to UK	958,693,000	962,737,000

TRANSPORT INFRASTRUCTURE

Indonesia has 342,700 km of highways and 6,458 km of railways. An extensive network of ferry services links the islands. There are 661 airports and 21,579 km of navigable waterways.

MEDIA

A state-run television broadcaster, Televisi Republik Indonesia (TVRI), competes with several commercial stations. There are several nationwide newspapers and many radio stations. In 2003 more than 2,000 unlicensed radio and television stations were given the chance to apply for licences.

IRAN

Jomhûri-ye-Eslâmi-ye-Îrân – Islamic Republic of Iran

AREA – 1,622,000 sq. km. Neighbours: Armenia, Azerbaijan, Turkmenistan (north), Afghanistan and Pakistan (east), Iraq and Turkey (west)
POPULATION – 69,018,924 (2004 est.): 99 per cent Muslims (Shia 89 per cent and Sunni 10 per cent) with small minorities of Zoroastrians, Jews, and Armenian and Assyrian Christians. The official language is Persian (Farsi). Minority languages are Turkic (26 per cent), Kurdish (9 per cent), Luri (2 per cent), Arabic, Baluchi and Turkish (1 per cent each)
CAPITAL – Tehran (population 6,758,845, 1996 census)
MAJOR CITIES – Ahwaz; Esfahan; Mashhad; Qom; Shiraz; Tabriz
CURRENCY – Rial
NATIONAL ANTHEM – Sorûd-E Jomhûri-Ye Eslâmi [Anthem of the Islamic Republic of Iran]
NATIONAL DAY – 11 February
NATIONAL FLAG – Three horizontal stripes of green, white, red, with the slogan *Allahu Akbar* repeated 22 times along the edges of the green and red stripes, and the national emblem in the centre
LIFE EXPECTANCY (years) – 69.66 (2004 est.)
MORTALITY RATE (per 1,000 population) – 5.53 (2004 est.)
INFANT MORTALITY (per 1,000 births) – 42.86 (2004 est.)
HIV / AIDS ADULT PREVALENCE – 0.1 per cent (2001 est.)
DEATH PENALTY – Yes
POPULATION BELOW POVERTY LINE – 40 per cent (2002 est.)
POPULATION GROWTH RATE – 1.07 per cent (2004 est.)
POPULATION DENSITY – 40 per sq. km (2002)
URBAN POPULATION – 65 per cent (2001)

CLIMATE AND TERRAIN

Apart from narrow coastal strips at sea-level on the Gulf coasts and the shores of the Caspian Sea, the interior is plateau rising to mountains in the north, west and east. The western and eastern ranges are divided by the Dasht-e Kavir desert. Elevation extremes range from 5,671 m (Qolleh-ye Damavand) at the highest point to 0 m (Persian Gulf) at the lowest. Earthquakes are frequent. Average annual temperatures in Tehran are 3°C in January and 30°C in July.

HISTORY AND POLITICS

Iran is part of the Middle East's 'fertile crescent', an area associated with the development of sophisticated agriculture. In the sixth century BC the Achaemenian king Cyrus the Great developed his control over the area. His dynasty founded the Persian empire under the Zoroastrian religion. In the fourth century BC Persia was conquered by Alexander the Great. Alexander's death led to a period of economic turbulence, civil conflict and foreign invasion until the Sassanian Persian empire was founded in the second century AD. This was destroyed in AD 637 by Arab conquerors who, introduced Islam, converting the majority of the population and creating a cultural revolution. The area was ruled by the Arabs, Turks and Mongols until the Safavid dynasty, which ruled from the 16th to the 18th century, a time recognised as one of Iran's periods of great cultural production; it was followed by the Qajar dynasty in the 19th and 20th centuries.

The Qajar dynasty was overthrown in 1921 by Reza Khan, who became prime minister in 1923 and was crowned Shah in 1925. He was succeeded in 1941 by his son, Mohammad Reza Shah Pahlavi, who began a programme of economic modernisation, Westernisation and secularisation in the 1960s. Opposition to reform and popular protests against the Shah's regime in the 1970s led to a revolution in 1978. The Shah went into exile and in 1979 a non-party theocratic Islamic republic was proclaimed under Ayatollah Khomeini.

On Ayatollah Khomeini's death in 1989, a struggle for political dominance began between conservatives and more liberal reformers. The reformists have generally appeared to be in the ascendant since Khomeini's death, with the election as president of Hashemi Rafsanjani in 1989 and Ayatollah Mohammad Khatami, a moderate cleric, in 1997, with their supporters holding majorities in the *Majlis*. However, a counterweight to the reformists is the conservative judiciary, which also constitutes the membership of the Council of Guardians and so is able to block liberalising legislation. There is a vocal popular pro-democracy movement.

The Assembly of Experts was last elected in 1998. In the 2004 legislative election, conservative candidates won the majority of seats; over 2,500 reformist candidates were disqualified from standing by the Council of Guardians. The presidential election in June 2005 was won in the second round by a conservative, Mahmoud Ahmadinejad, with 61.6 per cent of the vote.

FOREIGN RELATIONS

Between 1980 and 1988, Iran was engaged in a bitter war with Iraq. Ostensibly a boundary dispute over the Shatt-al-Arab waterway, it arose from Iran's fear that Iraq was fomenting demands for autonomy by Arabs in its westernmost province. Fighting ended with a cease-fire in 1988 and a peace settlement in 1990. Iran remained neutral in the Gulf War (1991) and the Iraq War (2003).

Since the 1978 revolution, Iran's relations with the West, and especially the USA, have been strained. It has not co-operated with international efforts to achieve peace in the Middle East, and has long been suspected of sponsoring terrorism by Islamic fundamentalists; since 2003 it has been accused of subverting Western efforts at reconstruction in Iraq. In addition, there have been fears that it is developing nuclear weapons after it started to build a nuclear reactor in 2002, although an IAEA investigation in 2003 found no evidence of weapons development. In November 2004 Iran agreed with the EU to suspend most of its uranium enrichment programme.

POLITICAL SYSTEM

Under the 1979 constitution, overall authority rests with the spiritual leader of the republic, who is elected by the Assembly of Experts *(Majlis-e Khobregan)*; this consists of 83 clerics who are directly elected every eight years and decides religious and spiritual matters. The executive president is directly elected for a four-year term,

renewable only once. Ministers are nominated by the president but must be approved by the legislature. The unicameral legislature, the *Majlis al-Shoura* has 290 members who are directly elected for a four-year term on a non-party basis. Laws passed by the *Majlis* must be approved by the Council of Guardians of the Constitution, a 12-member judicial body which also has a supervisory role in elections. In 1997, the Committee for the Implementation and Supervision of the Constitution, a five-member body, was established to supervise the proper implementation of constitutional laws.

Spiritual Leader of the Islamic Republic and C.-in-C. of Armed Forces, Ayatollah Seyed Ali Khamenei, *appointed* June 1989

President, Mahmoud Ahmadinejad, *elected* 24 June 2005

First Vice-President, Mohammad Reza Aref

SELECTED GOVERNMENT MEMBERS *as at July 2005*

Defence and Logistics, Mostafa Najjar

Economic Affairs and Finance, Davoud Jafari

Foreign Affairs, Manouchehr Mottaki

Interior, Chair of State Security Council, Mostafa Pourmohammadi

EMBASSY OF THE ISLAMIC REPUBLIC OF IRAN

16 Prince's Gate, London SW7 1PT

T 020-7225 3000

Ambassador Extraordinary and Plenipotentiary, HE Mohammad Hoseyn Adeli, apptd 2005

BRITISH EMBASSY

143 Ferdowsi Avenue, PO Box 11365–4474, Tehran 11344

T (+98) (21) 670 5011

Ambassador Extraordinary and Plenipotentiary, HE Richard Dalton, CMG, apptd 2002

DEFENCE

The Army has around 1,613 main battle tanks, 640 armoured personnel carriers, 610 armoured infantry fighting vehicles and 20 attack helicopters. The Navy has three submarines, three frigates, 56 patrol and coastal vessels, five combat aircraft and 19 armed helicopters. There are seven naval bases. The Air Force has some 306 combat aircraft, of which about 60–80 per cent are serviceable.

MILITARY EXPENDITURE – 2.4 per cent of GDP (2003)

MILITARY PERSONNEL – 540,000: Army 350,000, Revolutionary Guard Corps 120,000, Navy 18,000, Air Force 52,000; Paramilitaries 40,000

CONSCRIPTION DURATION – 18 months

ECONOMY AND TRADE

The economy is heavily reliant on its state-run oil industry and has benefited from relatively high oil prices in recent years, enabling it to amass some US$15,000 million in foreign exchange reserves. Petroleum also accounts for 85 per cent of Iran's export commodities. Apart from petroleum and petrochemicals, Iran produces textiles, construction materials and armaments. Agricultural production includes wheat, rice, other grains, sugar beets, fruits, nuts, cotton, dairy products, wool and caviar.

Reserves of gas with an estimated value of US$16,500 million were found in 2000 in the Gavband region.

GNI – US$112,900 million (2002); US$1,720 per capita (2002)

ANNUAL AVERAGE GROWTH OF GDP – 6.3 per cent (2004 est.)

INFLATION RATE – 14.5 per cent (2000 est.)
TOTAL EXTERNAL DEBT – US$7,953 million (2000 est.)
FOREIGN DIRECT INVESTMENT – US$198 million
(1997–2000)
IMPORTS – US$21,000 million (2002)
EXPORTS – US$28,000 million (2002)

BALANCE OF PAYMENTS
Trade – US$13,138 million surplus (2000)
Current Account – US$12,645 million surplus (2000)

Trade with UK	2003	2004
Imports from UK	£476,882,000	£443,815,000
Exports to UK	30,608,000	43,779,000

TRANSPORT INFRASTRUCTURE
Iran has a number of ports on the Persian Gulf, though Abadan was largely destroyed during the 1980–8 war with Iraq. Iran has 904 km of waterways in total, the most important being the Shatt-al-Arab, which is navigable for 130 km. There are a total of 167,157 km of roads, of which 94,109 km are surfaced, and 7,201 km of railways. The principal airports are at Tehran and Mashhad.

EDUCATION
Since 1943 primary education has been compulsory and free of charge. There are 48 universities.
ILLITERACY RATE – (m) 16.5 per cent; (f) 30.1 per cent (2000)
GROSS ENROLMENT RATIO (percentage of relevant age group) – primary 92 per cent (2002); secondary 81 per cent (2002); tertiary 19 per cent (2002)

MEDIA AND CULTURE
President Khatami's reformist government has pushed for greater freedom in the Iranian media. Restrictions on satellite television have also been relaxed. The Islamic Republic of Iran Broadcasting (IRIB) is a state-run national television broadcaster which is supplemented by regional channels.

Iran is exceptionally rich in both Islamic and pre-Islamic architecture. Persepolis, constructed by Darius in the sixth century BC and the seat of the Achaemenian empire, lies at the foot of Kuh-i-Rahmat, in the plain of Marvdasht 400 miles south of the present capital city of Tehran.

Iranian cinema has recently emerged as one of the world's most respected film industries and the director Abbas Kiarostami (b. 1940), whose films include *Taste of Cherry* and *Ten*, has received much critical acclaim.

IRAQ

Al-Jumhuriyya al-Iraqiyya – Republic of Iraq

AREA – 437,400 sq. km. Neighbours: Iran (east), Saudi Arabia, Kuwait (south), Jordan and Syria (west), Turkey (north)
POPULATION – 25,374,691 (2004 est.). The official language is Arabic. Minority languages include Kurdish (about 15 per cent), Turkic and Aramaic
CAPITAL – Baghdad
MAJOR CITIES – ΨAl-Basra; Kirkuk; Al-Mawsil
CURRENCY – Iraqi dinar (ID) of 1,000 fils
NATIONAL ANTHEM – Land of two rivers
NATIONAL DAY – 9 April (Overthrow of Ba'ath regime of Saddam Hussein)

NATIONAL FLAG – Pale blue crescent on a white background, with a yellow strip between two blue lines at the bottom
LIFE EXPECTANCY (years) – 68.26 (2004 est.)
MORTALITY RATE (per 1,000 population) – 5.66 (2004 est.)
INFANT MORTALITY (per 1,000 births) – 52.71 (2004 est.)
HIV / AIDS ADULT PREVALENCE – 0.1 per cent (2001 est.)
POPULATION GROWTH RATE – 2.7 per cent (2004 est.)
POPULATION DENSITY – 55 per sq. km (2001 est.)
URBAN POPULATION – 68 per cent (2001)
ILLITERACY RATE – (m) 54.1 per cent; (f) 76.6 per cent (2003 est.)
GROSS ENROLMENT RATIO (percentage of relevant age group) – primary 99 per cent (2002); secondary 38 per cent (2002); tertiary 14 per cent (2002)

CLIMATE AND TERRAIN
Iraq is mostly desert with mountainous areas in the north. The wide valley of the Euphrates and Tigris rivers run across the country from north-west to south-east, discharging into the Persian Gulf. Elevation extremes range from 3,600 m (Haji Ibrahim) at the highest point to 0 m (Persian Gulf) at the lowest. Average temperatures in Baghdad range from 9°C in January to 35°C in July.

HISTORY AND POLITICS
The Sumerians, the world's oldest civilisation, were the first people to populate the areas around the Tigris and Euphrates rivers. They began to build city-states from around 3000 BC of which Ur, Lagash and Eridu are the earliest examples; the city-states were unified into an empire *c.*2350 BC. In the seventh century BC, the area became part of the Assyrian empire until this was destroyed by the Babylonians and the Medes. Apart from 150 years of Roman rule (114–266) Iraq was under Persian rule from the mid-sixth century BC until the Persian defeat and conquest by Arab Muslims in AD 637. The Battle of Karbala in AD 680 marked one of the decisive moments in Islamic history: a split between Sunnis and Shias was created when the Shi'ite leader Hussein was killed attempting to claim the Caliphate. In 1533 Iraq came under the control of the Ottoman empire until 1916 when the Ottomans, weakened by the First World War, ceded control to the British. A provisional government was set up in 1920, and in 1921 the Emir Faisal was elected King Faisal I of Iraq. King Faisal II was assassinated in 1958 in a military-led revolution, following which a left-wing military regime assumed power. Iraq came under the control of the socialist Ba'ath Party briefly after a coup in 1963 and then from 1968. In 1979 Saddam Hussein deposed President Bakr and became president.

Iraq fought a bitter war with Iran from 1980–8. Ostensibly a border dispute over the Shatt-al-Arab waterway, it arose from Iraq's fear that Iran was encouraging a Shi'ite majority uprising against its predominantly Sunni regime. Fighting ended with a cease-fire in 1988 and a peace settlement in 1990. In August 1990, Iraq invaded and annexed Kuwait, ignoring international and UN demands for it to withdraw. In January 1991 a US-led alliance of NATO and Middle East countries launched a military offensive against Iraq that liberated Kuwait in February. UN sanctions, imposed after Kuwait's annexation, remained in place owing to Iraq's obstruction of attempts to verify the destruction of its weapons of mass destruction. It was Iraq's failure to comply with the latest attempts at inspection in 2002 that led to the invasion in March 2003 by US-led military forces. Saddam Hussein was captured in December 2003 and is currently in prison, awaiting trial on charges of genocide.

Following the invasion and occupation in March–May 2003, a Coalition Provisional Authority (CPA) became the occupying authority in Iraq before handing over sovereignty in June 2004 to the Iraqi Interim Governing Council (IGC), despite deteriorating internal security.

Elections to the Transitional National Assembly took place amid tight security on 30 January 2005. The turnout was generally high, but low among Sunni Muslims. The Shia United Iraqi Alliance (UIA) won 48.2 per cent of the vote and 140 seats, followed by the Democratic Patriotic Alliance of Kurdistan, which won 25.7 per cent of the vote and 75 seats; groups led by the then prime minister Iyad Allawi came third. In April 2005, the Assembly elected a Sunni Muslim as Speaker, a Kurd as president, and one Sunni Muslim and one Shi'ite Muslim as vice-presidents. The government, many of whom have no party affiliation, includes Shias, Sunnis, a Christian, Kurds and Turkomen.

INSURGENCIES

There are about 4 million Kurds in north-east Iraq, in areas adjoining the predominantly Kurdish areas in Iran and Turkey. Iraq's Kurdish nationalists have demanded an autonomous homeland, Kurdistan, since the 1960s, and turned to militant tactics in the 1970s. Their demands were opposed by Saddam Hussein's regime with great brutality, including the use of chemical weapons in 1984–9, killing 25,000, and thousands were forcibly rehoused. An uprising after the Gulf War (1991) was suppressed by surviving Iraqi troops, prompting the creation of UN 'safe havens' in the north which enabled the Kurds to set up a semi-autonomous region in the north. An air exclusion zone was also set up but there were further attacks on the Kurds in 1996. In the Iraq War (2003), Kurdish fighters fought alongside US troops, taking control of northern cities and establishing relatively stable administration in the area. The Democratic Patriotic Alliance of Kurdistan is the second largest party in the Transitional National Assembly following the 2005 election.

The Shi'ites in southern Iraq also rebelled after the Gulf War and were brutally suppressed. The UN established an air exclusion zone over southern Iraq in 1992 to protect the population, retaliating against Iraqi incursions with air strikes, but persecution continued until the Iraq War.

Since the end of the Iraq War in May 2003, there has been insurgent activity throughout the country, though it is particularly marked in the Baghdad area and the 'Sunni triangle' of predominantly Sunni-populated towns in the centre of the country. Attacks, usually shootings and car and suicide bombings, are mainly aimed at foreign troops and Iraqi military and police personnel, although international agencies, such as the UN and Red Cross, and foreign aid and reconstruction workers have also been targets. The attacks are believed to be the work of Islamic militants, such as al-Qa'eda, remnants of the Ba'athist regime and members of the Sunni minority fearful for their future in a predominantly Shi'ite Iraq. Coalition forces remain in Iraq to assist with internal security.

POLITICAL SYSTEM

The system is still in transition and the transitional government is to draft a new constitution that will be put to a national referendum. The head of state during this period is the president, who, with two vice-presidents, was elected by the Transitional National Assembly *(Majlis Watani)* in April 2005. The president and vice-presidents make up the Presidency Council, which appoints the prime minister and government, who must be approved by the Assembly. The Transitional National Assembly has 275 members, directly elected in January 2005, who will serve until elections can be held under the new constitution.

HEAD OF STATE IN TRANSITIONAL GOVERNMENT

President, Jalal Talabani, *elected* 6 April 2005
Vice-President, Ghazi Mashal Ajil al-Yawer
Vice-President, Adil Abd al-Mahdi

SELECTED TRANSITIONAL GOVERNMENT MEMBERS *as at July 2005*

Prime Minister, Ibrahim al-Jaafari
Deputy Prime Minister, Ahmed Chalabi
Deputy Prime Minister, Ruz Nuri Shawis
Deputy Prime Minister, Abid Mutlak al-Jubouri
Foreign Affairs, Hoshyar al-Zebari
Finance, Ali Abdel Amir Allawi
Defence, Saadoun al-Dulaimi
Interior, Bagir Solagh

EMBASSY OF IRAQ

169 Knightsbridge, London SW7 1DW T 020-7581 2264
Ambassador Extraordinary and Plenipotentiary, Salah al-Shaikhly apptd 2004

BRITISH DIPLOMATIC REPRESENTATION

c/o Iraq Policy Unit, King Charles Street, London, SW1A 2AH
T 020 7008-1500
Ambassador Extraordinary and Plenipotentiary, HE Edward Chaplin, CMG, OBE, apptd 2004 (resident in Baghdad)

DEFENCE

On 23 May 2003, Iraq's armed forces were officially disbanded by the Coalition Provisional Authority (CPA). Since then, new Iraqi security forces have been recruited and trained by coalition troops. As at June 2004 the Iraqi armed forces consisted of 226,765 personnel and included: Navy, 410; Air Wing, 500; Border Enforcement, 18,208; National Guard 37,790; Facilities Protection Service, 74,069 and Paramilitaries, 86,944.

In June 2004, there was an estimated 121,600 US troops and 23,000 troops provided by other countries stationed in Iraq.

ECONOMY AND TRADE

Years of dictatorship, warfare and UN sanctions have devastated the economy and infrastructure of the country, reducing it to a pre-industrial state by 1991, according to the UN. Since May 2003, the reconstruction of the oil industry, the electricity and water supplies and other essential infrastructure has proceeded but has been hampered by continuing violence and instability. The UN and World Bank estimated the cost of reconstruction at US$55 billion, and US$33 billion of aid was pledged by international donors in October 2003.

The major industry is oil production, which was nationalised in 1972, and petroleum has traditionally accounted for about 95 per cent of Iraq's foreign exchange earnings. Other industries include the production of textiles, chemicals and construction materials. Free trade agreements have been signed with Egypt, Syria and Tunisia, and were to be put into effect when UN sanctions were lifted in 2003.

Trade with UK	2003	2004
Imports from UK	£129,593,000	£86,729,000
Exports to UK	145,000	775,000

TRANSPORT INFRASTRUCTURE

Iraq's transport infrastructure has been severely damaged during the 1991 and 2003 wars. There are 1,963 km of railways and 45,550 km of highways. The Shatt-al-Arab, Iraq's main waterway, is navigable for 130 km, and the Tigris and Euphrates rivers have navigable sections for shallow draft boats. The main port is Basra, and the principal airport is at Baghdad.

EDUCATION

Since May 2003 the country's education system has been reviewed, and over 2,500 schools have been refurbished and more than 70 million textbooks have been reprinted.

ILLITERACY RATE – (m) 34.4 per cent; (f) 54.1 per cent (2000)

GROSS ENROLMENT RATIO (percentage of relevant age group) – primary 99 per cent (2002); secondary 38 per cent (2002); tertiary 14 per cent (2002)

MEDIA AND CULTURE

Once strictly controlled, the media has begun to flourish since May 2003, although media workers have fallen victim to the insurgency. There are more than 200 newspapers and periodicals, many with an ethnic or religious affiliation, and private radio and television have also begun to thrive. The television and radio stations set up by the Coalition Provisional Authority (CPA) are being incorporated into a new publicly funded Iraqi Public Broadcasting Service. The Iraqi Media Network (IMN), which was set up by the CPA, operates the *Al-Iraqiya* television station and publishes the *Al-Sabah* newspaper. The *Al-Zaman* daily newspaper is based in London but printed in Baghdad and Basra.

Much of the rich cultural history of Iraq has been destroyed or irreparably damaged through years of war and state control. However, since May 2003, many former dissident writers and artists have returned to the country. Significant contemporary figures include the poet Fawzi Karim (b. 1945), the filmmaker Saad Salman (b. 1950) and the artist Ismail Fattah (1934–2004), who is best known for creating the *Martyr* sculpture in Baghdad.

IRELAND

Éire / Ireland

AREA – 68,900 sq. km. Neighbour: Northern Ireland (north)

POPULATION – 3,969,558 (2004 est.). In 2000 religious adherence as a percentage of the population was: Roman Catholic 87.2 per cent, Protestant 0.9 per cent, Anglican 3.7 per cent. Irish is the first official language; English is recognised as a second official language, but is more commonly used

CAPITAL – ΨDublin *(Baile Átha Cliath)* (population, 1,122,600, 2002 census)

MAJOR CITIES – ΨCork *(Corcaigh)*; ΨGalway *(Gaillimh)*; ΨLimerick *(Luimheach)*; ΨWaterford *(Port Láirge)*

CURRENCY – Euro (€) of 100 cents

NATIONAL ANTHEM – Amhrán na bhFiann [The soldier's song]

NATIONAL DAY – 17 March (St Patrick's Day)

NATIONAL FLAG – Equal vertical stripes of green, white and orange

LIFE EXPECTANCY (years) – 77.36 (2004 est.)

MORTALITY RATE (per 1,000 population) – 7.91 (2004 est.)

INFANT MORTALITY (per 1,000 births) – 5.5 (2004 est.)

HIV / AIDS ADULT PREVALENCE – 0.1 per cent (2001 est.)

DEATH PENALTY – No (abolished 1990)

POPULATION GROWTH RATE – 1.16 per cent (2004 est.)

POPULATION DENSITY – 57 per sq. km (2002)

URBAN POPULATION – 59 per cent (2001)

MILITARY EXPENDITURE – 0.5 per cent of GDP (2003)

MILITARY PERSONNEL – 10,460: Army 8,500, Navy 1,100, Air Force 860

CLIMATE AND TERRAIN

The greatest length of the island, from north-east to south-west (Torr Head to Mizen Head), is 486 km, and the greatest breadth, from east to west (Dundrum Bay to Annagh Head), is 280 km. On the north coast of Achill Island (Co. Mayo) are the highest cliffs in the British Isles, 609 m above sea level. Elevation extremes range from 1,040 m (Carrantuohill, Co. Kerry) at the highest point to 0 m (Irish Sea) at the lowest. There is a central plain surrounded by hills, including the Wicklow, Knockmealdown, Galty and Boggeragh Mountains, and drained by theprincipal river, the Shannon (386 km), which flows into the Atlantic Ocean. The other main rivers are the Slaney, the Liffey and the Boyne, flowing to the east coast, and the Lee, the Blackwater, the Suir, the Barrow and the Nore flowing to the south coast.

The chief hydrographic feature is the loughs; the Shannon chain of Allen, Boderg, Forbes, Ree and Derg; the upper part of the Erne chain, Gowna and Oughter; Melvin, Gill, Gara and Conn in the north-west; and Corrib and Mask (joined by a hidden channel) in the west.

HISTORY AND POLITICS

Settled by the Celts around 300 BC, Ireland developed a flourishing and distinct culture that remained largely intact until Christianity was introduced in the fifth century AD. The spread of Christianity is attributed in large part to St Patrick and, in the fifth and sixth centuries, Ireland established itself as a centre of learning and high culture, a place of intellectual thought and spiritual refuge. When Viking raiders began sustained attacks c.800 many of the Christian monks left Ireland, migrating to the Faroes and Iceland. In the 12th century Anglo-Norman barons invited to Ireland by one of the Gaelic kings, seeking allies, brought much of the south of the island under their own control, and Henry II of England, declared himself Lord of Ireland in 1171. The island was unified under English control under Elizabeth I. As English power became consolidated throughout Ireland, and the north-eastern kingdom of Ulster emerged as the final stronghold of Celtic power at the beginning of the 17th century, England began a programme of sending Protestant Scottish settlers to the area. This policy produced a long-standing rivalry, sometimes erupting into hostility, between the north's Protestant and Catholic populations.

In the mid-17th century there was widespread support in Ireland for the Royalist side in the English Civil War (largely because of the marriage of Charles I to a Roman Catholic), prompting bloody reprisals from Oliver Cromwell, who invaded Ireland and reasserted English control in 1649–50. Catholic Irish support for the deposed Catholic king James II was defeated by William III at the Battle of the Boyne (1690) and penal laws passed in 1695 suppressed Catholic wealth and power. Popular discontent in the late 18th century and a rebellion in 1798 led to the abolition of the Irish parliament by the Act of Union (1800), which united Britain and Ireland. Simultaneously, Catholic opposition to English rule became increasingly organised with the formation of the Catholic Association under the leadership of Daniel O'Connell, but agitation for home rule failed until 1912, when legislation was passed but did not come into effect because of World War I.

By 1916 demands in some quarters had shifted from home rule to independence from Britain, and a rebellion broke out in Dublin. Known as the Easter Uprising, it was eventually repressed by the British but inspired Irish nationalists to contest the 1918 elections and, on gaining a majority of the Irish seats, to declare Irish independence under the leadership of Eamon de Valera. The British response was an attempt at violent suppression of the nationalists. The ensuing Anglo-Irish War lasted from 1919 to 1921 when the two sides negotiated the Anglo-Irish Treaty, giving Ireland internal self-government as the Irish Free State, with dominion status within the Commonwealth, but leaving the six predominantly Protestant counties in the north part of the UK. This partition was not accepted by all nationalists, opposition developing into civil war in 1922–3. In 1937, the Irish Free State declared itself independent and sovereign, and in 1948 it left the Commonwealth and became a republic.

The status of Northern Ireland remained divisive, the partition unacknowledged by the Irish constitution of 1937. The Anglo-Irish Agreement in 1985 gave the Irish government a consultative role in the government of Northern Ireland, and in 1993 the Downing Street Declaration set out a joint Anglo-Irish peace proposal to end the 'Troubles' in the north. The Irish government helped in the negotiation of the 1998 Good Friday Agreement; its proposals, including Irish recognition of the partition and the right of the north to self-determination, were approved in a referendum by 94 per cent of voters in the Irish Republic.

Ireland joined the EEC in 1973 and the euro zone in 1999; it has yet to schedule a referendum on the EU constitution.

The 1997 presidential election was won by Mary McAleese, and she was confirmed in office unopposed in 2004. In the 2002 elections to the House of Representatives, Fianna Fáil (FF) remained the largest party but without an overall majority. The coalition government, led by Bertie Ahern of the FF, includes members of the Progressive Democrats (PD). The composition of the Dáil Éireann as at July 2005 was: FF 81; Fine Gael 31; Labour 21; PD 8; Green Party 6; Sinn Fein 5; Socialist Party 1; Independents 13.

POLITICAL SYSTEM

Under the 1937 constitution, the president (Uachtarán na Éireann) is directly elected for a term of seven years, and is eligible for a second term. The National Parliament (Oireachtas) consists of the House of Representatives (Dáil Éireann) and the Senate (Seanad Éireann). Dáil Éireann is composed of 166 members elected for a five-year term on a basis of proportional representation by means of the single transferable vote. Seanad Éireann is composed of 60 members who serve a five-year term; of these, 11 are nominated by the prime minister (Taoiseach) and 49 are elected, six by institutions of higher education and 43 from panels of candidates established on a sectoral basis.

Executive power is vested in the government, which is responsible to the Dáil Éireann. The Taoiseach is appointed by the president on the nomination of the Dáil Éireann, while other members of the government are appointed by the president on the nomination of the Taoiseach with the previous approval of the Dáil Éireann. The Taoiseach appoints a member of the government to be deputy prime minister (Tánaiste).

HEAD OF STATE
President, Mary McAleese, elected 30 October 1997, confirmed in office 1 October 2004, sworn in 11 November 2004

SELECTED GOVERNMENT MEMBERS as at July 2005
Taoiseach (Prime Minister), Bertie Ahern
Tánaiste (Deputy PM), Enterprise, Trade and Employment, Mary Harney
Defence, Willie O'Dea
Finance, Brian Cowen
Foreign Affairs, Dermot Ahern

IRISH EMBASSY
17 Grosvenor Place, London SW1X 7HR T 020-7235 2171
Ambassador Extraordinary and Plenipotentiary, HE Dáithí O'Ceallaigh, apptd 2001

BRITISH EMBASSY
29 Merrion Road, Ballsbridge, IE-Dublin 4
T (+353) (1) 205 3700 E bembassy@internet-ireland.ie
Ambassador Extraordinary and Plenipotentiary, HE Stewart Eldon, CMG, OBE, apptd 2003

BRITISH COUNCIL
Newmount House, 22/24 Lower Mount Street, IE-Dublin 2
T (+353) (1) 676 4088 E helen.jones@ie.britishcouncil.org
Director, Tony Reilly, MBE

ECONOMY AND TRADE

The economy boomed during the 1990s, largely thanks to investment from the EU. The major industries are computer software, information technology, food and drink production, pharmaceuticals and tourism, which have helped transform Ireland from a mainly rural economy. Agriculture has been entirely overtaken by light industry and the service industries, and now accounts for only 5 per cent of the economy. Growth between 1995 and 2002 was 8 per cent, however, this slowed to 2.1 per cent in 2003, which was attributed to the global slowdown in the information technology sector.

The Kinsale gas field off the south coast provided 28 per cent of Ireland's gas needs in 2000, with 72 per cent coming via an undersea pipeline from Moffat, Scotland. There are five government-funded power stations. Hydroelectric power from the Shannon barrage and other schemes are also important but Ireland still imports 47 per cent of oil and coal for power generation. Metal content of ores raised in 2003 included: lead (50,300 tonnes) and zinc (419,000 tonnes).

GNI – US$90,300 million (2002); US$23,030 per capita (2002)
ANNUAL AVERAGE GROWTH OF GDP – 5.1 per cent (2004 est.)
INFLATION RATE – 5.6 per cent (2000 est.)
UNEMPLOYMENT – 3.8 per cent (2001 est.)
FOREIGN DIRECT INVESTMENT – US$47,516 million (1997–2000)
IMPORTS – US$53,300 million (2003)
EXPORTS – US$92,400 million (2003)

BALANCE OF PAYMENTS
Trade – US$37,807 million surplus (2003)
Current Account – US$2,105 million deficit (2003)

Trade with UK	2003	2004
Imports from UK	£14,277,800,000	£13,774,073,000
Exports to UK	8,953,187,000	10,055,439,000

TRANSPORT INFRASTRUCTURE

Ireland has 92,500 km of highways and 3,312 km of railways. There are 700 km of waterways, though these are of limited use to commercial traffic. The main ports are Cork, Dun Laoghaire, Galway, Limerick and Waterford. The principal airport is at Dublin, with others at Shannon, Waterford, Cork, Killarney, Galway and Knock.

EDUCATION

Primary education is directed by the state, with the exception of 37 private primary schools. In 2005 there were 3,278 state primary schools, 406 state secondary schools, 90 community and comprehensive and 247 vocational schools.
GROSS ENROLMENT RATIO (percentage of relevant age group) – primary 119 per cent (2002); tertiary 47 per cent (2002)

MEDIA AND CULTURE

Irish broadcasting is regulated by a commission appointed by the Department of Communications. The main Irish broadcaster is the state-run Radio Telefis Eireann (RTE). The British satellite broadcaster BSkyB is widely available throughout Ireland. There are three national newspapers: the Irish Times, Irish Independent and Irish Examiner.

Ireland has a distinct and rich literary history and notable figures include George Bernard Shaw (1856–1950), winner of the Nobel Prize for Literature in 1925; W. B. Yeats (1865–1939), winner of the Nobel Prize for Literature in 1923; James Joyce (1882–1941); and Samuel Beckett (1906–89), Nobel Prize for Literature, 1969. Other notable figures include the musician Sir James Galway (b. 1939), the physicist Ernest Walton ((1903–95) joint winner of the Nobel Prize for Physics in 1951) and the scientist Sir Francis Beaufort (1774–1857).

ISRAEL

Medinat Yisra'el / Dawlat Isrā'īl – State of Israel

AREA – 20,600 sq. km. Neighbours: Lebanon (north), Syria (north-east), Jordan and the West Bank (east), the Gaza Strip and the Egyptian province of Sinai (south-west)
POPULATION – 6,199,008 (2004 est.): roughly 82 per cent Jewish, 14 per cent Arab Muslims, 2.5 per cent Christians, of whom 90 per cent are Arab and 2 per

cent Druze. Since independence Israel has had a policy of granting an immigration visa to every Jew who expresses a desire to settle in Israel. Between 1948 and 1992, 2.3 million immigrants had entered Israel from over 100 different countries. Hebrew and Arabic are the official languages. Arabs are entitled to transact all official business with government departments in Arabic
CAPITAL – Most of the government departments are in Jerusalem (population 758,000, 2001 estimate). A resolution proclaiming Jerusalem as the capital of Israel was adopted by the Knesset in 1950. It is not, however, recognised as the capital by the UN because East Jerusalem is part of the Occupied Territories captured in 1967. The UN and international law continues to reject the Israeli annexation of East Jerusalem and considers the pre-1950 capital Tel Aviv (population, 1,919,700) to be the capital.
MAJOR CITIES – Beersheba; ΨHaifa; Rishon Le'Zion
CURRENCY – Shekel of 100 agora
NATIONAL ANTHEM – Hatikvah [The hope]
NATIONAL FLAG – White, with two horizontal blue stripes, the Shield of David in the centre
LIFE EXPECTANCY (years) – 79.17 (2004 est.)
MORTALITY RATE (per 1,000 population) – 6.19 (2004 est.)
INFANT MORTALITY (per 1,000 births) – 7.21 (2004 est.)
HIV / AIDS ADULT PREVALENCE – 0.1 per cent (2001 est.)
DEATH PENALTY – Yes*
POPULATION BELOW POVERTY LINE – 18 per cent (2001 est.)
POPULATION GROWTH RATE – 1.29 per cent (2004 est.)
POPULATION DENSITY – 318 per sq. km (2002)
URBAN POPULATION – 92 per cent (2001)

CLIMATE AND TERRAIN

Israel comprises the hill country of Galilee and parts of Judea and Samaria, the coastal plain from the Gaza strip to north of Acre, including the plain of Esdraelon running from Haifa Bay to the south-east which divides the hill region; the Negev, a semi-desert triangular-shaped region, extending from a base south of Beersheba to an apex at the head of the Gulf of Aqaba, and parts of the Jordan valley, including the Hula region, Tiberias and the south-western extremity of the Dead Sea. Elevation extremes range from 2,000 m (Mount Hermon) at the highest point, to −408 m (Dead Sea) at the lowest, which is the Earth's deepest depression. Average temperatures in Tel Aviv range from 14°C in January to 27°C in August.

HISTORY AND POLITICS

Regarded by Jews as their homeland since the Israelite settlement in Old Testament times, Palestine was conquered by the Babylonians, the Greeks and the Romans between the sixth and first centuries BC, beginning the Diaspora. Conquered by Muslim Arabs in the seventh century AD, the area was contested between Muslims and Christians during the Crusades before becoming part of the Turkish Ottoman Empire in the 16th century. Zionist settlement in Palestine began in the 1880s and the British declared support for a Jewish homeland there in 1917 after capturing much of the Middle East from the Ottoman Empire during the First World War. Britain administered the area under a League of Nations mandate from 1918 to 1947, during which period Jewish immigration from Europe was encouraged, but this resulted in tension with the Arab population of Palestine, who had also been promised recognition for an Arab state from the British.

After the Second World War, the British mandate became increasingly untenable and in 1947 the British withdrew. The UN voted to partition Palestine, creating a Jewish and an Arab state, but the proposal was rejected by the Arabs, prompting the Jews to announce the creation of the independent State of Israel on 14 May 1948. This led to the first of a series of conflicts between Israel and neighbouring Arab states, creating a large number of Palestinian refugees. Further conflict occurred in 1956, when Israel attacked the Suez Canal zone; in 1967, when Israel gained control of the Gaza Strip, the Sinai peninsula, the West Bank and east Jerusalem, and the Golan Heights in Syria (the 'Occupied Territories'); 1973, when Egypt and Syria attempted to regain their lost territory; and in 1982, when Israel invaded Lebanon to drive PLO guerrillas out of Beirut, occupying a 'buffer zone' in the south until 2000. A peace agreement with Egypt was reached in 1979, as a result of which Israel withdrew from Sinai, and an peace agreement with Jordan was reached in 1994.

From the 1960s, the Palestine Liberation Organisation (PLO), under Yasser Arafat, fought a guerrilla war against Israeli occupation of the territories taken in 1967, and in 1974 the PLO was recognised by the Arab League as the official representative of the Palestinian people. Talks between Israel and the PLO resulted in the Oslo Accords (1993–5), which led to the establishment of the Palestinian Autonomous Areas in 1994. This appeared to end the popular Palestinian uprising (intifada) in the Gaza Strip and West Bank, which had begun in 1987, but the situation deteriorated from the mid-1990s, with further violence in the West Bank and suicide bombings in Israeli cities evoking an increasingly hard line from a new Israeli government already critical of the peace accords. Implementation of the Oslo Accords stalled and negotiations on outstanding issues became deadlocked. Palestinian frustration was inflamed by a remark about the status of Jerusalem by an Israeli politician in 2000, triggering a second intifada. In 2002, Israel began building a security wall between Israeli and Palestinian areas to prevent suicide bombings, despite international diplomatic and legal opposition to a de facto partitioning of the country.

In 2003, the USA, Russia, the EU and the UN proposed a 'road map' for peace which envisioned a two-state solution to the conflict. Progress stalled until the death of Arafat in 2005. The Israeli goverment's commitment on a key issue, the evacuation and dismantling of Jewish settlements in the Gaza Strip, was approved by the Knesset in October 2004. By August 2005 the last remaining Jewish settlers had been removed from Gaza.

President Ezer Weizman resigned from office in 2000, and Moshe Katsav was elected president. After the collapse of a Likud-led coalition government in October 2002, a general election was held in January 2003 that resulted in Likud winning the most seats in the Knesset but failing to achieve an overall majority. A Likud-dominated coalition government was appointed that controlled 68 of the 120 seats in the Knesset but by December 2004 the non-Likud members had withdrawn over the dismantling of Jewish settlements or budget issues, and a new coalition comprising Likud and Labor members was formed in January 2005.

POLITICAL SYSTEM

There is no written constitution; most constitutional provision is set out in the Basic Law on Government: this was amended in 2001 to end the system of separate prime ministerial elections. The unicameral legislature, the Knesset, has 120 members elected by proportional representation for a maximum term of four years, but a 'final settlement' has yet to be reached. The president is head of state and is elected by the Knesset to serve for a seven-year term which is not renewable. The prime minister is head of the executive and responsible to the Knesset, and is formally appointed by the president.

HEAD OF STATE

President of Israel, Moshe Katsav, elected 31 July 2000, sworn in 1 August 2000

SELECTED GOVERNMENT MEMBERS as at July 2005

Prime Minister, Communications and Religious Affairs, Ariel Sharon
Vice Prime Minister, Shimon Peres
Deputy Prime Minister; Foreign Affairs, Sylvan Shalom
Defence, Gen. Shaul Mofaz
Interior and Communications, Ophir Pines-Paz

EMBASSY OF ISRAEL

2 Palace Green, Kensington, London W8 4QB
T 020-7957 9500
Ambassador Extraordinary and Plenipotentiary, HE Zvi Haifetz, apptd 2004

BRITISH EMBASSY

192 Hayarkon Street, Tel Aviv 63405 T (+972) (3) 725 1222
Ambassador Extraordinary and Plenipotentiary, HE Simon McDonald, CMG, LVO, apptd 2003

BRITISH COUNCIL

Crystal House, 12 Hahilazon Street, Ramat Gan 52136 Tel Aviv
T (+972) (3) 611 3600 E bcta@britishcouncil.org.il
Director, Kevin Lewis

DEFENCE

Israel is believed to have a nuclear capacity of around 200 warheads which could be delivered by aircraft or Jericho I and II missiles. The Army has 3,090 main battle tanks and around 12,670 armoured personnel carriers. The Navy has three submarines and 54 patrol and coastal vessels at three bases. The Air Force has 399 combat aircraft and 95 armed helicopters.

MILITARY EXPENDITURE – 9.5 per cent of GDP (2003)
MILITARY PERSONNEL – 168,000: Army 125,000, Navy 8,000, Air Force 35,000; Paramilitaries 8,050
CONSCRIPTION DURATION – 24–48 months (Jews and Druze only; Christians, Circassians and Muslims may volunteer.)

ECONOMY AND TRADE

Israel exports diamonds, chemicals and agricultural products and has developed a respected technology sector, central to which are the electronics, biotechnology and software industries. As well as a strong technology sector, Israel is an important producer of citrus fruits, vegetables, cotton, beef, poultry and dairy products. Other important manufacturing industries include plastics, rubber, cement, glass, paper and oil refining. Industry accounted for 27 per cent and the service industries for 47 per cent of GDP in 2000.

In 2001 the country entered recession. The intifada and a downturn in the technology sector produced the country's longest recession since the 1960s. A recovery package was approved by the *Knesset* in 2003, and although the trade unions forced some reforms on the measures, which included cuts in public spending, in 2004 interest rates were reduced to 8 per cent and there were signs of rising business and consumer confidence as well as increased demand for exports.

Around half of Israel's debt is owed to the USA, which is Israel's main source of economic and military aid. The USA is also Israel's main trading partner, accounting for 40.3 per cent of exports in 2002.

GNI – US$105,200 million (2002); US$16,020 per capita (2002)

ANNUAL AVERAGE GROWTH OF GDP – 5.7 per cent (2000 est.)

INFLATION RATE – 1.1 per cent (2000 est.)

UNEMPLOYMENT – 8.8 per cent (2000 est.)

FOREIGN DIRECT INVESTMENT – US$11,311 million (1997–2000)

IMPORTS – US$36,300 million (2003)

EXPORTS – US$32,000 million (2003)

BALANCE OF PAYMENTS
Trade – US$2,177 million deficit (2003)
Current Account – US$665 million surplus (2003)

Trade with UK	2003	2004
Imports from UK	£1,377,010,000	£1,394,150,000
Exports to UK	881,639,000	943,156,000

TRANSPORT INFRASTRUCTURE

Israel State Railways serves Haifa, Tel Aviv, Jerusalem, Lod, Nahariya, Beersheba, Dimona, Ashdod and intermediate stations with a network of 647 km. There were 15,965 km of surfaced roads in 2000. A major road-building programme has been under way in the West Bank since 1992. The chief ports are Haifa and Ashdod on the Mediterranean, and Eilat on the Red Sea; Acre has an anchorage for small vessels. The chief international airport is Ben Gurion between Tel Aviv and Jerusalem.

EDUCATION

Education from five to 16 years is free of charge and compulsory. Youths aged 16–18, who are in work but have not completed their education, can be given time off to complete their studies. There are seven universities, including two engineering and technological institutes.

ILLITERACY RATE – (m) 2.1 per cent; (f) 5.8 per cent (2000)

GROSS ENROLMENT RATIO (percentage of relevant age group) – primary 114 per cent (2002); secondary 93 per cent (2002); tertiary 53 per cent (2002)

MEDIA AND CULTURE

The Israeli Broadcasting Authority (IBA) is a public broadcaster operating television and radio services funded largely by a licence fee. It competes with two main terrestrial commercial channels and a number of satellite and cable stations. The radio sector features a number of commercial stations, but there are also a large number of unlicensed radio stations. The press includes five national dailies including *Ha'aretz*, *Jerusalem Post*, *Ma'ariv* and *Yediot Aharonot*.

The Israel Museum in Jerusalem houses the Dead Sea Scrolls along with an extensive collection of Jewish religious and folk art. Jerusalem has a vast number of historic sites, including the Church of the Holy Sepulchre, sacred to Christians, and the al-Aqsa Mosque, which stands on the remains of Temple Mount.

Israel has absorbed large numbers of Jewish refugees

from Europe and so has strong traditions in European classical music. Shmuel Yosef Agnon (1888–1970) was the first Hebrew writer to win the Nobel Prize for Literature in 1966.

PALESTINIAN AUTONOMOUS AREAS

AREA – The total area is 6,231 sq. km. The area which is fully autonomous is 412 sq. km, of which the Gaza Strip is 352 sq. km and the Jericho enclave 60 sq. km.

POPULATION – 3,634,585 (2003 estimate), of whom 394,105 live in East Jerusalem. Some 90 per cent of Palestinians are Muslim (the vast majority Sunni) and 10 per cent are Christians

CAPITAL – Although Palestinians claim East Jerusalem as their capital, the administrative capital has been established in Gaza City (population 460,899)

MAJOR TOWNS – Khan Yunis, Rafah in the Gaza Strip; Nablus, Hebron, Jericho, Ramallah and Bethlehem on the West Bank

FLAG – Three horizontal stripes of black, white, green with a red triangle based on the hoist (the PLO flag)

NATIONAL ANTHEM – Fidai, fidai [Freedom fighter, freedom fighter]

HISTORY AND POLITICS

Since 1967, the West Bank and Gaza Strip have been under Israeli occupation and until 1994 were administered by the Israeli Ministry of Defence. Frustration at continued Israeli occupation led to the start of a popular Palestinian uprising, the *intifada*, in 1987. Negotiations between Israel and the Palestinian Liberation Organisation (PLO) led to the signing of the 'Declaration of Principles on Interim Self-Government Arrangements' (Oslo Accords) on 13 September 1993. The Declaration of Principles established self-government in the Palestinian areas and set a timetable for progress towards a final settlement; the 1993 provisions were intended to be for a five-year interim period during which the 'final status' of the West Bank, Gaza and Jerusalem was to be resolved.

The 'Oslo B' or Taba Accord was signed on 28 September 1995 and provided for Israeli withdrawal from six West Bank towns and 85 per cent of Hebron; the extension of self-rule to most of the West Bank by 1998; the release of 5,300 Palestinian prisoners; and the striking out of the demand for Israel's destruction from the PLO's charter. On 29 December 1995 an agreement was reached on the transfer of 17 areas of civilian power to the PNA in Hebron.

The first areas, the Gaza Strip and the town of Jericho on the West Bank, were handed over to the Palestinian National Authority in 1994, and the six West Bank towns in 1995. The final status talks opened in 1996, but stalled in the late 1990s and broke down in 2001. Efforts to restart negotiations were hindered by the election of Israeli governments critical of the peace accords and the outbreak of the second *intifada*.

In 2003, the USA, Russia, the EU and the UN proposed the 'road map' peace plan, a staged process leading to the establishment of an autonomous Palestinian state by 2005, which also sought political reforms in the Palestinian National Authority. The plan was endorsed by the Palestinian and Israeli prime ministers, while the three main groups responsible for violent attacks on Israelis, Hamas, Islamic *Jihad* and *Fatah*, announced a three-month truce, and Israeli forces withdrew from some key areas in the West Bank and the Gaza Strip. However, implementation of the peace plan made little progress because of the continuing *intifada*, the refusal of Israel and the USA to negotiate with Yasser Arafat, and the division among key players over the Iraq War. Arafat's clinging to power prevented Palestinian prime ministers, Mahmoud Abbas in 2003 and Ahmed Qurei from 2003, from taking matters forward and matters reached a stalemate that was broken only by the death of Yasser Arafat in November 2004. By August 2005 the last remaining Jewish settlers were removed from Gaza, but despite the handover to Palestinian control, a final settlement has yet to be reached.

The presidential election in January 2005 to elect Arafat's successor was won by the Fatah candidate Mahmoud Abbas, who secured 67.4 per cent of the vote. Since his election, Abbas has resumed peace talks with the Israeli prime minister Ariel Sharon and a new cease-fire was agreed in February 2005.

POLITICAL SYSTEM

The executive president is directly elected for a five-year term. Legislative authority is vested in the Palestinian Legislative Council, which has one seat for the president and 88 seats for members who are directly elected by means of a first past the post system. The president appoints the prime minister, who appoints the executive authority, or cabinet.

SELECTED GOVERNMENT MEMBERS *as at July 2005*
President, Mahmoud Abbas
Prime Minister, Ahmed Qurei
Economy and Trade, Salam Fayad
Foreign Affairs, Naser al-Qidweh
Interior, Hakam Balaawi

PALESTINIAN GENERAL DELEGATION
5 Galena Road, London W6 0LT T 020-8563 0008
General Delegate, Afif Safieh

BRITISH CONSULATE-GENERAL
19 Nashashibi Street, PO Box 19690, East Jerusalem 97200
T (+972) (2) 541 4100
Consul-General, John Jenkins, CMG, LVO, apptd 2003

BRITISH COUNCIL
31 Nablus Road, PO Box 19136, East Jerusalem
T (+972) (2) 628 2545 E british.council@ej.britishcouncil.org
Director, Sarah Ewans, OBE

ECONOMY AND TRADE

The major industries produce construction materials, textiles and metal goods, and are mainly run by small family businesses. The main export is citrus fruits, and the main trading partners are Israel and Jordan. The economy of the Palestinian areas has been severely affected by Israeli security restrictions and retaliations against the *intifada*. However, G8 leaders agreed a US$3 billion a year aid package for Palestine which would be focused on rebuilding infrastructure.
GNI – US$3,000 million (2002); US$930 per capita (2002)
ANNUAL AVERAGE GROWTH OF GDP – 19.1 per cent (2002 est.)
INFLATION RATE – 23.6 per cent (2002 est.)
POPULATION BELOW POVERTY LINE – 59 per cent (2002 est.)

Trade with UK	2003	2004
Imports from UK	£691,000	£1,611,000
Exports to UK	442,000	429,000

ITALY

Repubblica Italiana – Italian Republic

AREA – 294,100 sq. km. Neighbours: Switzerland and Austria (north), Slovenia (east), France (west)
POPULATION – 58,057,477 (2004 est.): 83 per cent Catholic. The language is Italian, a Romance language derived from Latin. There are several regional languages including Sardinian and Catalan in Sardinia, Friulian in Friuli, German and Ladin in the South Tyrol, French in the Valle d'Aosta, and Slovene in parts of Gorizia
CAPITAL – Rome (population, 2,459,776, 2001 census). The Eternal City was founded, according to legend, by Romulus in 753 BC. It was the centre of Latin civilisation and capital of the Roman Republic and Roman Empire
MAJOR CITIES – Bologna; Florence; ΨGenoa; Milan; ΨNaples; Turin; Sicily, ΨPalermo; Sardinia, ΨCagliari
CURRENCY – Euro (€) of 100 cents
NATIONAL ANTHEM – Inno di Mameli [Hymn of Mameli]
NATIONAL DAY – 2 June
NATIONAL FLAG – Vertical stripes of green, white and red
LIFE EXPECTANCY (years) – 79.54 (2004 est.)
MORTALITY RATE (per 1,000 population) – 10.12 (2004 est.)
INFANT MORTALITY (per 1,000 births) – 6.07 (2004 est.)
HIV / AIDS ADULT PREVALENCE – 0.4 per cent (2001 est.)
DEATH PENALTY – No (abolished 1994)
POPULATION GROWTH RATE – 0.09 per cent (2004 est.)
POPULATION DENSITY – 196 per sq. km (2002)
URBAN POPULATION – 67 per cent (2001)

CLIMATE AND TERRAIN

Italy consists of a peninsula, the islands of Sicily, Sardinia, Elba and about 70 other small islands. The peninsula is for the most part mountainous, but between the Apennines, which form its spine, and the eastern coastline are two large fertile plains: Emilia-Romagna in the north and Apulia in the south. Italy is divided from France and Switzerland by the Alps, and from Austria and Slovenia by the Alps and the Dolomites. Three volcanoes, Vesuvius, Etna and Stromboli, are still active. Elevation extremes range from 4,061 m (Gran Paradiso) at the highest point to 0 m (Mediterranean Sea) at the lowest. At the foot of the Alps lie the great lakes of Como, Maggiore and Garda. The chief rivers are the Po (651 km) and the Adige, flowing through the northern plain to the Adriatic Sea, and the Arno (Florentine plain) and the Tiber (flowing through Rome to Ostia), which flow to the west coast. The climate is Mediterranean, with warm dry summers and mild winters.

Sicily, Sardinia and many of the other islands are mountainous. The smaller islands include: Pantelleria Island, in the narrows between Sicily and Tunisia; the Pelagian islands (Lampedusa, Linosa and Lampione), off Sicily; the Eolian islands (including Stromboli and Lipari), north of Sicily; Capri, in the Bay of Naples; the Flegrean islands (including Ischia) and the Pontine archipelago (including Ponza) in the Tyrrhenian Sea; the Tremiti islands; and the Tuscan archipelago (including Elba).

HISTORY AND POLITICS

The Etruscans were the first people to control the Italian peninsula. Their empire flourished between the 12th and eighth centuries BC, but was eventually overtaken by the Romans. At the height of its power, the Roman Empire spread from Italy across Europe, Asia Minor and North Africa. Conquered and settled by a variety of invaders throughout the 'Dark Ages', Italy began to develop into a number of competing city states. These, with their powerful and wealthy merchant classes, became the locations (and provided the capital) for the Renaissance. Italian nationalists began to agitate for a unified Italy in the 19th century, culminating in the declaration of the Kingdom of Italy in 1861; unification was achieved by 1870. The major figures in Italian unification were Mazzini (1805–72), Garibaldi (1807–82) and Cavour (1810–61).

In 1923 the fascist leader Benito Mussolini, promising a firm rule to end the disruption, seized power. Mussolini tied Italy into an alliance with Adolf Hitler's Germany, and thus led Italy into the Second World War on the Axis side. The Allies invaded Sicily in 1943, which led to a coup to depose Mussolini, who was eventually captured and killed by partisans in April 1945. Italy became a republic after the war, the king abdicating when the country's new constitution came into force and the monarchy was abolished. A post-war economic boom lasted until the late 1970s, when high inflation and unemployment ensued. This was a time of serious civil unrest, with unions opposed to often corrupt governments, and extreme right- and left-wing groups conducting violent campaigns.

In the early 1990s there was a drive to reform the political establishment after links were exposed between the government and organised crime; many politicians were arrested. In 1993, the electoral system was changed from proportional representation to majority voting in 75 per cent of the seats, helping to remedy the political instability that had resulted in over 45 governments in 47 years. Although governments have continued to be coalitions, those of the past ten years have generally been longer-lived.

Italy was a founding member of the EEC in 1957 and of the euro zone in 1999. Its parliament ratified the EU constitution in April 2005.

The 2001 legislative election was won by the centre-right Freedom Alliance, led by Forza Italia and including the Christian Democratic Centre, the Christian Democratic Union, the National Alliance, the New Italian Socialist Party and the Northern League. Silvio Berlusconi, leader of Forza Italia, was sworn in as prime minister at the head of a coalition government; he stood trial on bribery charges, which were dismissed in 2004. His government, the longest in Italy's history, collapsed in April 2005 after a defeat in regional elections, but the president asked him to form a new government and a new coalition was formed.

POLITICAL SYSTEM

The 1948 constitution provides for a president as head of state, elected for a seven-year term by an electoral college which consists of both houses of the parliament and 58 regional representatives. The president, who must be over 50 years of age, has the right to dissolve one or both houses after consultation with the Speakers. The bicameral parliament *(Parlamento)* comprises the Chamber of Deputies and the Senate. Since 1993, 75 per cent (232) of the 315 elected seats in the Senate are elected for a five-year term on a first past the post basis and the remaining elected seats are filled by proportional representation; there is also a variable number of life senators, who are past presidents and senators appointed by incumbent presidents. In the Chamber of Deputies, 75 per cent (472) of seats are elected on a first past the post basis, and 25 per cent (158) by proportional representation, with a 4 per cent threshold for parliamentary representation; deputies serve for five years. A national referendum in 2001 approved greater autonomy for the 20 regions in tax, education and environment.

HEAD OF STATE
President, Carlo Azeglio Ciampi, *elected* 13 May 1999, took office 18 May 1999

SELECTED GOVERNMENT MEMBERS *as at July 2005*
Prime Minister, Silvio Berlusconi
Deputy Prime Minister; Foreign Affairs, Gianfranco Fini
Defence, Antonio Martino
Economy and Finance, Domenico Siniscalco
Interior, Giuseppe Pisanu

ITALIAN EMBASSY
14 Three Kings Yard, Davies Street, London W1K 4EH
T 020-7312 2200
Ambassador Extraordinary and Plenipotentiary, HE Giancarlo Aragona, apptd 2004

BRITISH EMBASSY
Via XX Settembre 80A, I-00187 Rome T (+39) (6) 4220 0001
Ambassador Extraordinary and Plenipotentiary, HE Sir Ivor Roberts, KCMG, apptd 2003

BRITISH COUNCIL
Via Quattro Fontane 20, I-00184 Rome
E studyandcultureuk@britishcouncil.it
Director, Paul Docherty

DEFENCE

The Army has 1,293 main battle tanks, 98 armoured infantry fighting vehicles and 3,290 armoured personnel carriers. The Navy has six submarines, one aircraft carrier, one cruiser, four destroyers, 12 frigates, 21 patrol and coastal vessels, 17 combat aircraft and 63 armed helicopters. There are four naval bases. The Air Force has 220 combat aircraft and six armed helicopters. Conscription ended in December 2004.
MILITARY EXPENDITURE – 1.9 per cent of GDP (2003)
MILITARY PERSONNEL – 198,000: Army 116,000, Navy 34,000, Air Force 48,000; Paramilitaries 254,300

ECONOMY AND TRADE

Italy is the world's fifth-largest industrial economy, and it has achieved this with few natural resources. It remains divided between a prosperous and industrially developed north and a largely agricultural south that has suffered high unemployment. Agricultural produce includes fruits, vegetables, grapes, potatoes, sugar beets, soy beans, grain, olives; beef, dairy products and fish.

Small and medium-sized family industries provide a large amount of economic output. Many of these are centred around manufactured goods. Major industries include motor vehicles, chemicals, pharmaceuticals, electrical goods, textiles, fashion, clothing and footwear. Tourism is a significant contributor in the services sector.

Trade with EU partners accounts for 54.4 per cent of trade, with Germany being Italy's main trading partner.
GNI – US$1,100,700 million (2002); US$19,080 per capita (2002)
ANNUAL AVERAGE GROWTH OF GDP – 2.9 per cent (2000 est.)
INFLATION RATE – 2.7 per cent (2003 est.)
UNEMPLOYMENT – 8.7 per cent (2004 est.)
FOREIGN DIRECT INVESTMENT – US$26,293 million (1997–2000)
IMPORTS – US$292 million (2003)
EXPORTS – US$294 million (2003)

BALANCE OF PAYMENTS
Trade – US$9,700 million surplus (2003)
Current Account – US$21,942 million deficit (2003)

Trade with UK	2003	2004
Imports from UK	£6,279,175,000	£8,277,256,000
Exports to UK	8,387,810,000	11,794,232,000

TRANSPORT INFRASTRUCTURE
The main railway system is state run by the *Ferrovia dello Stato*. There are 19,466 km of railways. A 9,500 km network of motorways *(autostrade)* covers the country but there are 305,881 km of roads in total. In 2001, Italy and France agreed plans to build a 52 km rail tunnel through the Alps as part of a high-speed rail link between Turin and Lyons; commissioning of the project is scheduled for 2012. Alitalia is the principal international and domestic airline. There are airports at Rome, Milan, Naples, Venice, Genoa, Turin, Florence, Livorno, Bari, Palermo and Catania (Sicily) and Cagliari (Sardinia). The main ports are Naples, Genoa, Bari, Trieste, Palermo and Catania.

EDUCATION
Education is free of charge and compulsory between the ages of six and 16. Pupils who obtain a middle school certificate may seek admission to any 'senior secondary school', which may be a lyceum with a classical or scientific or artistic bias, or an institute directed at technology, trade or industry, or teacher training. Courses at the lyceums and technical institutes usually last five years and success in the final examination qualifies for admission to university. There are 42 state and six private universities, three technical universities and 12 university institutes. The universities at Bologna, Modena, Parma and Padua are of ancient foundation and were started in the 12th century.
ILLITERACY RATE – (m) 1.1 per cent; (f) 2.0 per cent (2000)
GROSS ENROLMENT RATIO (percentage of relevant age group) – primary 101 per cent (2002); secondary 96 per cent (2002); tertiary 50 per cent (2002)

MEDIA
Rai is Italy's public broadcaster and competes with a number of private broadcasters, including Mediaset, part of Prime Minister Berlusconi's media empire. The press includes many regional publications, as well as five national dailies including *La Stampa* and *La Repubblica*. Italy has one of Europe's highest levels of internet use, with 28.61 million users in 2004.

CULTURE
Florence, the capital of Tuscany, was one of the greatest cities in Europe from the 11th to the 16th centuries, and the cradle of the Renaissance. Under the Medici family in the 15th century flourished many of the greatest names in Italian art, including Fra Filippo Lippi, Botticelli, Donatello and Brunelleschi and, in the 16th century, Michelangelo and Leonardo da Vinci. The world's oldest university is in Bologna.

Dante Alighieri (1265–1321) and Boccaccio (1313–75) were two of the earliest writers to compose works in vernacular languages. Notable contemporary Italian writers include Umberto Eco (b. 1932); Dario Fo (b. 1926), winner of the Nobel Prize for Literature in 1997; and Eugenio Montale (1896–1981), winner of the Nobel Prize for Literature in 1975.

In the 20th century, Italian cinema was distinguished as a powerful force by directors such as Luchino Visconti (1906–76) and Roberto Rossellini (1906–77).

JAMAICA

AREA – 10,800 sq. km
POPULATION – 2,713,130 (2004 est.). The official language is English; a local patois is also spoken
CAPITAL – ΨKingston (population, 524,638, 1991)
MAJOR CITIES – Mandeville; May Pen; ΨMontego Bay; Ocho Rios; Spanish Town
CURRENCY – Jamaican dollar (J$) of 100 cents
NATIONAL ANTHEM – Jamaica, land we love
NATIONAL DAY – 6 August (Independence Day)
NATIONAL FLAG – Gold diagonal cross forming triangles of green at top and bottom, triangles of black at hoist and in fly
LIFE EXPECTANCY (years) – 76.07 (2004 est.)
MORTALITY RATE (per 1,000 population) – 5.4 (2004 est.)
INFANT MORTALITY (per 1,000 births) – 12.81 (2004 est.)
HIV / AIDS ADULT PREVALENCE – 1.2 per cent (2003 est.)
DEATH PENALTY – Yes
POPULATION BELOW POVERTY LINE – 34.2 per cent (2002 est.)
POPULATION GROWTH RATE – 0.66 per cent (2004 est.)
POPULATION DENSITY – 242 per sq. km (2002)
URBAN POPULATION – 57 per cent (2001)
MILITARY EXPENDITURE – 0.7 per cent of GDP (2003)
MILITARY PERSONNEL – 2,830: Army 2,500, Coast Guard 190, Air Wing 140
ILLITERACY RATE – (m) 15.9 per cent; (f) 8.4 per cent (2003 est.)
GROSS ENROLMENT RATIO (percentage of relevant age group) – primary 101 per cent (2002); secondary 84 per cent (2002); tertiary 17 per cent (2002)

CLIMATE AND TERRAIN
An island in the Caribbean Sea, south of Cuba and west of Hispaniola, Jamaica is mountainous with tropical vegetation. Elevation extremes range from 2,256 m (Blue Mountain Peak) at the highest point to 0 m (Caribbean Sea) at the lowest. The climate is hot and humid, with average temperatures ranging from 25°C in January to 29°C in July.

HISTORY AND POLITICS

Jamaica was visited by Columbus in 1494 and settled by the Spanish from 1509. Captured by the British in 1655, it achieved autonomy in 1947 and became independent in 1962.

Post-independence politics has been dominated by the Jamaican Labour Party (JLP) and People's National Party (PNP). Relations between the two parties, often fraught, degenerated in the 1970s into violence that marred elections and political life for some years.

The People's National Party (PNP) has been in power since 1989. At the 2002 general election, the PNP retained an overall majority with 34 out of a total of 60 seats, securing a fourth term for the party and a third term as prime minister for Percival Patterson.

POLITICAL SYSTEM

Queen Elizabeth II is the head of state, represented locally by a governor-general. The bicameral legislature consists of a Senate of 21 nominated members and a House of Representatives consisting of 60 members directly elected for a five-year term. The prime minister is the leader of the majority party in the House of Representatives.
Governor-General, HE Sir Howard Felix Hanlon Cooke, GCMG, GCVO, apptd 1991

SELECTED GOVERNMENT MEMBERS *as at July 2005*
Prime Minister, Defence, Percival J. Patterson, QC
Finance and Planning, Omar Davies
Foreign Affairs and Foreign Trade, Keith Desmond Knight
National Security, Peter Phillips

JAMAICAN HIGH COMMISSION
1–2 Prince Consort Road, London SW7 2BZ T 020-7823 9911
High Commissioner, HE Gail Mathurin, apptd 2004

BRITISH HIGH COMMISSION
PO Box 575, Trafalgar Road, Kingston 10
T (+1 876) 510 0700 E bhckingston@cwjamaica.com
High Commissioner, HE Jeremy Cresswell, CVO, apptd 2005

BRITISH COUNCIL
28 Trafalgar Road, Kingston 10 T (+1 876) 929 7090
E bcjamaica@britishcouncil.org.jm
Manager, Nicola Johnson

ECONOMY AND TRADE

Sugarcane and bananas continue to play a major part in the economy, though it is now more reliant on the service industries, including tourism, which makes up 70 per cent of GDP; industry accounted for 24 per cent, and agriculture for 6 per cent in 2003. Natural resources include alumina and bauxite, which comprise the majority of exports. Remittances from Jamaicans living abroad are also of economic significance.

Tight fiscal and monetary policies have slowed inflation but the economy remains weak owing to high interest rates, increased foreign competition, unemployment and growing internal debt, and the devastation by Hurricane Ivan in 2004. Tourism, the main foreign exchange earner, is vulnerable because of the high levels of violent crime.

GNI – US$7,000 million (2002); US$2,690 per capita (2002)
ANNUAL AVERAGE GROWTH OF GDP – 1.9 per cent (2004 est.)
INFLATION RATE – 10.3 per cent (2003 est.)

UNEMPLOYMENT – 15.9 per cent (2004 est.)
TOTAL EXTERNAL DEBT – US$4,287 million (2000 est.)
FOREIGN DIRECT INVESTMENT – US$1,486 million (1997–2000)
IMPORTS – US$3,640 million (2003)
EXPORTS – US$1,180 million (2003)

BALANCE OF PAYMENTS
Trade – US$1,871 million deficit (2002)
Current Account – US$1,119 million deficit (2002)

Trade with UK	2003	2004
Imports from UK	£60,488,000	£53,560,000
Exports to UK	119,652,000	94,076,000

TRANSPORT INFRASTRUCTURE

There are several harbours, Kingston being the main port and the location of the principal airport. The island has 2,944 miles of main roads and 7,264 miles of subsidiary roads.

MEDIA AND CULTURE

The state broadcaster was privatised in 1997, and now operates Television Jamaica Limited (TVJ). It competes with a commercial and a religious broadcaster.

Jamaica's diverse cultural heritage includes a vibrant contemporary music scene (Kingston is widely regarded as the birthplace of reggae), as well as a strong literary tradition. Significant cultural figures include the poet Linton Kwesi Johnson (b. 1952), the musician Bob Marley (1945–81) and the politician and human rights activist Marcus Garvey (1887–1940).

JAPAN

Nihon-koku – State of Japan

AREA – 364,500 sq. km
POPULATION – 127,333,002 (2004 est.). The principal religions are Mahayana Buddhism and Shinto. About 1 per cent of Japanese are Christians. The language is Japanese
CAPITAL – Tokyo (population, 12,310,000, 2003 census)
MAJOR CITIES – ΨFukuoka; ΨKobe; Kyoto, the ancient capital; ΨNagoya; ΨOsaka; Sapporo; ΨYokohama
CURRENCY – Yen
NATIONAL ANTHEM – Kimigayo [His Majesty's reign]
NATIONAL FLAG – White, charged with sun (red)
LIFE EXPECTANCY (years) – 81.04 (2004 est.)
MORTALITY RATE (per 1,000 population) – 8.75 (2004 est.)
INFANT MORTALITY (per 1,000 births) – 3.28 (2004 est.)
DEATH PENALTY – Yes
POPULATION GROWTH RATE – 0.08 per cent (2004 est.)
POPULATION DENSITY – 349 per sq. km (2002)
URBAN POPULATION – 79 per cent (2001)

CLIMATE AND TERRAIN

Japan consists of four large islands: Honshu (or Mainland), 230,448 sq. km, Shikoku, 18,757 sq. km, Kyushu, 42,079 sq. km, Hokkaido, 78,508 sq. km, and many small islands (including Okinawa). The interior is very mountainous, and crossing the mainland from the Sea of Japan to the Pacific Ocean is a group of volcanoes, mainly extinct or dormant. Elevation extremes range from 3,776 m (Mount Fuji) at the highest point to −4 m (Hachiro gata) at the lowest. Average temperatures in Tokyo range from 3°C in January to 27°C in August.

HISTORY AND POLITICS

By the ninth century AD, a single empire had been established across what is now modern Japan. In the 12th century, the country was plunged into centuries of rivalry and aggression between different *samurai* (Japan's feudal warrior class) families, who were subdued and ruled by successive dynasties of *shoguns* (military overlords) nominally appointed by the emperor. Imperial domination was re-established in 1868 after long periods of civil warfare.

Contact with the West was severely restricted until the 19th century, when the visit of a US naval officer, Commodore Perry, led to the Japanese starting to receive foreign trade. Industrialisation followed and Japan adopted a western-style constitution in 1889. Policies became more outward-looking and, in the case of foreign policy, more aggressive, with successful wars against imperial China (1894–5) and Russia (1904–5), and the annexation of Korea in 1910.

Emperor Hirohito's accession in 1926 ushered in a period of intense nationalism, accompanied by a rise in militarism that led the country into an invasion of China in 1931 and a pact with Germany and Italy in 1940. Japan entered the Second World War with an attack on the US naval base at Pearl Harbor, Hawaii, in 1941 and occupied British, French and Dutch possessions in southeast Asia in 1941–2. Pushed back by allied forces in 1943–5, Japan surrendered after atomic bombs were dropped on Hiroshima and Nagasaki in 1945.

The Liberal Democrat Party (LDP) has dominated postwar politics, holding power continuously from 1955 until 1993. It returned to power in 1995, though usually as the main party in coalition governments. In the 2003 legislative election, the LDP won 237 seats in the House of Representatives, making it the largest party but it was without an overall majority until the New Conservative Party agreed to a merger in November 2003. The 2004 elections to the House of Councillors saw the LDP retain 114 seats. Prime Minister Koizumi announced an early general election would be held following the government's defeat in a vote on the reformation of Japan Post, the country's postal service. The election was held on 11 September and was won by the LDP coalition party with 327 seats in the country's parliament.

POLITICAL SYSTEM

The 1947 constitution established Japan as a constitutional monarchy with the emperor as head of state. Legislative authority rests with the bicameral Diet *(Kokkai)*, which comprises the House of Representatives *(Shugi-in)* and the House of Councillors *(Sangi-in)*. The House of Representatives has 480 members directly elected for a four-year term; 180 by proportional representation in 11 regional blocks and 300 in single-member, first-past-the-post constituencies. It elects the prime minister from among its ranks. The House of Councillors has 242 members, half elected every three years, to serve a six-year term. Unlike the lower house it cannot be dissolved by the prime minister. Executive authority is vested in the cabinet which is responsible to the legislature.

HEAD OF STATE

His Imperial Majesty The Emperor of Japan, Emperor Akihito, *born* 23 December 1933; *succeeded* 8 January 1989; *enthroned* 12 November 1990

Heir, HRH Crown Prince Naruhito Hironomiya, *born* 23 February 1960

SELECTED GOVERNMENT MEMBERS *as at July 2005*
Prime Minister, Junichiro Koizumi
Finance, Sadakazu Tanigaki
Foreign Affairs, Nobutaka Machimura
Internal Affairs and Communications, Taro Aso

EMBASSY OF JAPAN
101–104 Piccadilly, London W1J 7JT **T** 020-7465 6500
Ambassador Extraordinary and Plenipotentiary, HE Yoshiji Nogami, apptd 2005

BRITISH EMBASSY
No. 1 Ichiban-cho, Chiyoda-ku, Tokyo 102–8381
T (+81) (3) 5211-1100 **E** embassytokyo@fco.gov.uk
Ambassador Extraordinary and Plenipotentiary, HE Grahame Fry, apptd 2004

BRITISH COUNCIL
1–2 Kagurazaka, Shinjuku-ku, Tokyo 162–0825
T (+81) (3) 3235 8031 **E** enquires@britishcouncil.or.jp
Director, Alan Currey

DEFENCE

The constitution prohibits the maintenance of armed forces, although internal security forces were created in the 1950s and their mission was extended in 1954 to include the defence of Japan against aggression. In the 1990s legislation was passed permitting the armed forces limited participation in UN peacekeeping missions and allowing them to enter foreign conflicts in order to rescue Japanese nationals. A revision to the USA–Japan defence co-operation guidelines agreed in 1997 permits Japan to play a supporting role in US military operations in areas surrounding Japan. In 2003 the Japanese parliament passed legislation approving the deployment of Japanese troops in Iraq to assist with post-war reconstruction.

The Ground Self-Defence Force (GSDF) has some 980 main battle tanks, around 730 armoured personnel carriers, 70 armoured infantry fighting vehicles, 20 aircraft and 90 attack helicopters. The Maritime Self-Defence Force (MSDF) has 16 submarines, 45 destroyers, nine frigates, five patrol and coastal vessels, 80 combat aircraft and 102 armed helicopters at five bases. The Air Self-Defence Force (ASDF) has 280 combat aircraft.
MILITARY EXPENDITURE – 1 per cent of GDP (2003)
MILITARY PERSONNEL – 238,200: GSDF 148,200, MSDF 44,400, ASDF 45,600; Paramilitaries 12,250

ECONOMY AND TRADE

Japan is the third-largest economy in the world after the USA and China. Over-investment in the late 1980s slowed the economy in the 1990s and it was hard hit by the 1997 Asian economic crisis. Reforms introduced since 2001, particularly financial sector, public spending and private sector reforms, have improved economic growth, which averaged 4 per cent between 2003 and 2004. Service industries contribute 67.7 per cent of GDP, industry 30.9 per cent, and agriculture 1.9 per cent.

Owing to the mountainous terrain, less than 20 per cent of the land can be cultivated and only 14 per cent is used for agriculture; 67 per cent is wooded. The soil is only moderately fertile but intensive cultivation secures good crops. Tobacco, tea, potatoes, rice, maize, wheat and other cereals are all cultivated. Rice is the staple foodstuff.

Major industries include the production of motor vehicles, electronic equipment, machine tools, steel and non-ferrous metals, ships, chemicals, textiles and processed foods. Motor vehicles, semiconductors, office machinery and chemicals are the major exports. The USA is by far the largest trading partner, taking 28.8 per cent of exports. China is of increasing importance and takes 9.6 per cent.

GNI – US$4,323,900 million (2002); US$34,010 per capita (2002)
ANNUAL AVERAGE GROWTH OF GDP – 0.5 per cent (2000 est.)
INFLATION RATE – 0.1 per cent (2001 est.)
UNEMPLOYMENT – 5.0 per cent (2004 est.)
FOREIGN DIRECT INVESTMENT – US$27,003 million (1997–2000)
IMPORTS – US$383 million (2003)
EXPORTS – US$472 million (2003)

BALANCE OF PAYMENTS
Trade – US$106,395 million surplus (2003)
Current Account – US$136,215 million surplus (2003)

Trade with UK	2002	2003
Imports from UK	£3,739,070,000	£3,787,853,000
Exports to UK	8,247,215,000	8,236,588,000

TRANSPORT INFRASTRUCTURE
There are 23,654 km of railway track and 1,152,207 km of roads. *Shinkansen* (bullet train) tracks are currently being expanded. The Seikan rail tunnel and the Seto Ohashi rail bridge link the four major islands. There are six international airports. The main ports are Osaka, Nagoya, Yokohama, Kobe and Kawasaki.

EDUCATION
Elementary education is free of charge and compulsory at elementary level (six-year course) and lower secondary (three-year course). The upper secondary schools (three-year course) are attended by 96.7 per cent of the relevant age group. There are two- or three-year colleges and four-year universities.
GROSS ENROLMENT RATIO (percentage of relevant age group) – primary 101 per cent (2002); secondary 102 per cent (2002); tertiary 48 per cent (2002)

MEDIA AND CULTURE
A public broadcaster, NHK, competes with four national terrestrial television companies. NHK also runs national radio networks. Satellite and cable television is widespread and digital broadcasting is increasingly significant. Popular daily newspapers include *Asahi Shimbun*, *Nikkei Net* and the english language title *The Japan Times*.

Japanese is one of the Ural-Altaic group of languages and remained a spoken language until the fifth to seventh centuries AD, when Chinese characters came into use. Modern Japanese is written in a mixture of Chinese characters (about 1,800) and also the syllabary characters called Kana. Traditional arts include woodblock printing and the production of intricate silk hangings. Notable writers include Kawabata Yasunari (1899–1972), winner of the Nobel Prize for Literature in 1968, and Kazuo Ishiguro (b. 1954).

JORDAN

Al-Mamlaka al-Urdunniyya al-Hashimiyya – Hashemite Kingdom of Jordan

AREA – 88,900 sq. km. Neighbours: Syria (north), Israel and the West Bank (west), Saudi Arabia (south and east), Iraq (east)
POPULATION – 5,611,202 (2004 est.). The majority are Sunni Muslims and Islam is the religion of the state; however, freedom of belief is guaranteed by the constitution
CAPITAL – Amman (population, 1,270,000, 1997 estimate)
MAJOR CITIES – Irbid; Az-Zarqa
CURRENCY – Jordanian dinar (JD) of 1,000 fils
NATIONAL ANTHEM – Asha al Malik [Long live the King]
NATIONAL DAY – 25 May (Independence Day)
NATIONAL FLAG – Three horizontal stripes of black, white, green and a red triangle based on the hoist, containing a seven-pointed white star
LIFE EXPECTANCY (years) – 78.06 (2004 est.)
MORTALITY RATE (per 1,000 population) – 2.62 (2004 est.)
INFANT MORTALITY (per 1,000 births) – 18.11 (2004 est.)
HIV / AIDS ADULT PREVALENCE – 0.1 per cent (2001 est.)
DEATH PENALTY – Yes
POPULATION BELOW POVERTY LINE – 30 per cent (2002)
POPULATION GROWTH RATE – 2.67 per cent (2004 est.)
POPULATION DENSITY – 58 per sq. km (2002)
ILLITERACY RATE – (m) 4.1 per cent; (f) 3.6 per cent (2003)
GROSS ENROLMENT RATIO (percentage of relevant age group) – primary 99 per cent (2002); secondary 86 per cent (2002); tertiary 31 per cent (2002)

CLIMATE AND TERRAIN
Most of the country is a desert plateau, with a range of hills in the south along the edge of the Great Rift Valley and a hilly outcrop in the centre of the desert. The Great Rift Valley is an important topographical feature that separates the east and west banks of the River Jordan. Elevation extremes range from 1,734 m (Jabal Ram) at the highest point to –408 m (Dead Sea) at the lowest. Average temperatures in Amman range from 7°C in January to 26°C in August, although temperatures in the Jordan Valley have been known to reach 49°C.

HISTORY AND POLITICS
The area was part of the Roman Empire and subsequently of the Byzantine Empire. It came under Arab control in the seventh century, and in the 16th century became part of the Turkish Ottoman Empire. With the collapse of the empire in 1918, the state of Transjordan was created and administered by the British under a League of Nations mandate. Transjordan became independent in 1946 and changed its name to Jordan. During the first Arab–Israeli War of 1948, Jordan seized the West Bank and part of Jerusalem, but these areas were recaptured by Israel in the Six Day War of 1967, resulting in an influx of Palestinian refugees into Jordan; the descendents of these refugees now constitute the majority of the Jordanian population. Jordan attempted to expel Palestinian guerrillas from the

West Bank in 1970–1, causing a civil war until 1973. Jordan recognised the Palestinian Liberation Organisation (PLO) as the sole representative of the Palestinian people in the Occupied Territories in 1974, but severed links with the PLO and expelled its personnel in 1986. Jordan formally renounced sovereignty over the West Bank and East Jerusalem in 1999, having signed a peace agreement with Israel in 1994.

Jordan's economy declined in the 1980s and internal stability became increasingly precarious. Riots in 1989 forced the government to adopt a process of economic and political liberalisation. The country's first free elections under universal suffrage took place in December 1989. The ban on political parties was lifted in 1992; Islamist parties have gained increasing support, but the system favours people's tribal loyalties over their religious affiliation. Real power, however, effectively rests with the king, with parliament amending or approving legislation originating with the monarch.

In the 2003 legislative election, independent candidates loyal to King Abdullah won 62 of the seats in the House of Deputies. Candidates for the Islamic Action Front party were also elected. A quota for women resulted, for the first time in Jordan's history, in the election of six female candidates.

POLITICAL SYSTEM

The 1952 constitution provides a constitutional monarchy with the king as head of state. The bicameral legislature comprises the House of Deputies and the Senate. The House of Deputies has 110 members, directly elected for a four-year term; six seats are reserved for women. The Senate has 55 members, who are appointed by the king for a four-year term. The king appoints the members of the Council of Ministers.

HEAD OF STATE

His Majesty The King of the Jordan, Abdullah II, *born* 30 January 1962, *succeeded* 7 February 1999
Crown Prince, Hamzeh ibn al-Hussein, *born* 29 March 1982

SELECTED GOVERNMENT MEMBERS *as at July 2005*
Prime Minister, Defence, Adnan Badran
Deputy Prime Minister, Hesham al-Tal
Finance, Adel Qudah
Foreign Affairs, Farouq al-Qasrawi
Interior, Awni Yerfas

EMBASSY OF THE HASHEMITE KINGDOM OF JORDAN
6 Upper Phillimore Gardens, London W8 7HA
T 020-7937 3685
Ambassador Extraordinary and Plenipotentiary, HE Timoor Daghistani, GCVO, apptd 1999

BRITISH EMBASSY
Abdoun (PO Box 87), Amman T (+962) (6) 592 3100
Ambassador Extraordinary and Plenipotentiary, HE Christopher Prentice, apptd 2002

BRITISH COUNCIL
Rainbow Street, PO Box 634, Amman 11118
T (+962) (6) 463 6147 E bcamman@britishcouncil.org.jo
Director, Tim Gore

DEFENCE
The Army has 1,120 main battle tanks, 1,200 armoured personnel carriers and 226 armoured infantry fighting vehicles. The Navy has three patrol and coastal vessels at its base at Aqaba. The Air Force has 101 combat aircraft and 20 armed helicopters.
MILITARY EXPENDITURE – 8.7 per cent of GDP (2003)
MILITARY PERSONNEL – 100,500: Army 85,000, Navy 500, Air Force 15,000; Paramilitaries 10,000

ECONOMY AND TRADE
The economy is affected by several external factors, of which the most significant are the conflict between Israel and Palestine, which has restricted Jordan's trading capacity, and the impact of war, UN sanctions and extreme political instability on Iraq, which would normally represent a significant market for Jordanian goods.

King Abdullah has embarked on economic reforms, including a reduction of the public sector, privatisation and a commitment to trade liberalisation. The country has recently been rewarded with debt rescheduling and increased exports to the USA and EU.

Jordan has no oil reserves of its own and relied on supplies from Iraq, which were cut off by the 2003 invasion of Iraq. Several Gulf states have temporarily extended aid to Jordan in order to compensate for the loss. The Trans-Arabian oil pipeline (Tapline) runs through north Jordan from Saudi Arabia to the Lebanese port of Sidon. A branch pipeline, together with oil brought by road from Iraq, feeds a refinery at Zerqa, which meets most of Jordan's requirements for refined petroleum products. Sufficient reserves of natural gas have been discovered in the north-east to produce electricity for the national grid since 1989, and in 2001 Jordan, Syria and Egypt inaugurated an electricity link between their three national grids. Jordan has also begun joint ventures with Israel and Syria to guarantee water supplies.

Of the Jordanian labour force, 12.5 per cent are engaged in industry, which includes phosphate mining, pharmaceuticals, petroleum refining, cement, potash and light manufacturing. Of the remainder of the labour force, 82.5 per cent are engaged in the service industries, especially tourism, and only 5 per cent in agriculture. Jordan's agricultural products include wheat, barley, citrus, tomatoes, melons, olives; sheep, goats and poultry.
GNI – US$9,100 million (2002); US$1,760 per capita (2002)
ANNUAL AVERAGE GROWTH OF GDP – 5.1 per cent (2004 est.)
INFLATION RATE – 3.3 per cent (2002 est.)
TOTAL EXTERNAL DEBT – US$8,226 million (2000 est.)
FOREIGN DIRECT INVESTMENT – US$1,048 million (1997–2000)
IMPORTS – US$5,000 million (2002)
EXPORTS – US$2,770 million (2002)

BALANCE OF PAYMENTS
Trade – US$1,915 million deficit (2003)
Current Account – US$1,088 million surplus (2003)

Trade with UK	2003	2004
Imports from UK	£175,155,000	£160,673,000
Exports to UK	17,761,000	20,011,000

TRANSPORT INFRASTRUCTURE
Amman is linked to Aqaba, Damascus, Baghdad and Jiddah by roads which are of considerable importance in the overland trade of the Middle East. The former Hejaz Railway runs from Syria through Jordan, and is used mainly for freight between Amman and Damascus. The

Aqaba railway carries phosphate rock from the mines of al-Hasa and al-Abiad to Aqaba. Jordan has 7,245 km of highways, but no waterways. Its main port is Aqaba. The principal airport is at Amman.

MEDIA AND CULTURE

Jordan practices strict media censorship. Laws were tightened in 2001, and long prison sentences were introduced for anyone criticising the king or harming the country's reputation. Jordan Radio and Television is a state run broadcaster. It operates three terrestrial channels and a satellite channel. These broadcast a mixture of sport, films and general programming. There are radio services in Arabic, English and French. Radio Fann is an entertainment station run by the armed forces.

Jordan has a large Bedouin population and this ancient nomadic culture is reflected in its music and cuisine. Jordan is also home to one of the best-known works of Arab literature, *Alf Layla wa Layla* [A Thousand and One Nights].

KAZAKHSTAN

Qazaqstan Respublikasy – Republic of Kazakhstan

AREA – 2,699,700 sq. km. Neighbours: Russia (north and west), Turkmenistan, Uzbekistan and Kyrgyzstan (south), China (east)

POPULATION – 15,143,704 (2004 est.): Kazakhs (53 per cent), Russians (30 per cent), Ukrainians (4 per cent) and ethnic Germans (2 per cent), with smaller numbers of Tatars, Uzbeks, Koreans and Belarusians. The Russian population is concentrated in the north of the country, where it forms a significant majority, and in Almaty. The majority of ethnic Kazakhs are Sunni Muslims, and this is the main religion of the republic. Kazakh (one of the Turkic languages) became the official language in 1993; a law passed in 1997 decreed Kazakh as the language of state administration; Russian has a special status as the 'social language between peoples'. Otherwise each ethnic group uses its own language

CAPITAL – Astana (population, 320,000, 2000 estimate; previously known as Akmola and Tselinograd). The capital was moved from Alma-Ata (Almaty) in 1997

MAJOR CITIES – Almaty; Pavlodar; Karagandy; Shymkent

CURRENCY – Tenge

NATIONAL DAY – 25 October (Republic Day)

NATIONAL FLAG – Dark blue with a sun and a soaring eagle in the centre all in gold, and a red vertical ornamentation stripe near the hoist

LIFE EXPECTANCY (years) – 66.07 (2004 est.)

MORTALITY RATE (per 1,000 population) – 9.59 (2004 est.)

INFANT MORTALITY (per 1,000 births) – 30.54 (2004 est.)

HIV / AIDS ADULT PREVALENCE – 0.1 per cent (2001 est.)

POPULATION BELOW POVERTY LINE – 26 per cent (2001 est.)

POPULATION GROWTH RATE – 0.26 per cent (2004 est.)

POPULATION DENSITY – 6 per sq. km (2002)

URBAN POPULATION – 56 per cent (2001)

GROSS ENROLMENT RATIO (percentage of relevant age group) – primary 99 per cent (2002); secondary 89 per cent (2002); tertiary 39 per cent (2002)

CLIMATE AND TERRAIN

Kazakhstan stretches from the Volga and the Caspian Sea in the west to the Altai and Tien Shan mountains in the east. The terrain consists of arid steppes and semi-deserts, flat in the west, hilly in the east and mountainous in the south-east (Southern Altai and Tien Shan mountains). Elevation extremes range from 6,995 m (Khan Tangiri Shyngy) at the highest point to −132 m (Vpadina Kaundy) at the lowest. It includes the norther part of the Aral Sea in the west, and Lakes Balkash and Zaysan in the east. The climate is warm and dry in much of the country, but can be Siberian in the north. Average yearly temperatures in the capital Astana range from −16°C in January to 24°C in July.

HISTORY AND POLITICS

Kazakhstan was inhabited by nomadic tribes before being invaded by Ghenghis Khan and incorporated into his empire in 1218. After his empire disintegrated, feudal towns emerged based on large·oases and the nomadic tribes formed federations led by khans. The towns affiliated and established a Kazakh state in the late 15th century which engaged in almost continuous warfare with the marauding khanates on its southern border. After turning to Russia for protection in the 1730s, the Kazakh khanates formally acceded to the Russian empire. Russian control was gradually established in the country, tsarist rule replacing that of the khans in the early 19th century. A nationalist movement was violently suppressed in the early 20th century. The 1917 Bolshevik revolution in Russia was followed by civil war in Kazakhstan, which in 1920 became an autonomous republic in the Soviet Union and in 1936 a full union republic. Kazakhstan suffered bitterly under Stalin's twin policies of agricultural collectivisation and 'sedentarisation', which forced nomadic tribes to become farmers. The country lost around 1.5 million people to famine and disease. Later Soviet rule saw the country used as a testing ground for nuclear weapons.

Growing nationalism in the 1980s and a reformist leader led to economic and cultural reforms in 1989 and a declaration of sovereignty in 1990. Kazakhstan declared its independence in December 1991, and became a founding member of the Commonwealth of Independent States (CIS), formed in Almaty the same month. It entered an economic, social and military union with Kyrgyzstan and Uzbekistan in 1994, and an economic and military pact with Russia in 1995, when it achieved nuclear-free status. Privatisation and other economic reforms began in 1993, but despite these and considerable foreign investment, the country has serious economic, social and environmental problems, while its international standing is tarnished by political illiberalism and corruption.

Nursultan Nazarbayev, the reformist communist leader from 1989, became head of state in 1990 and was re-elected in 1991 and 1999, although his second election victory was achieved after the banning of his main rival. In 2000 he was granted special powers for life to address *Parlament* and advise future presidents. He has been criticised for concentrating power in the presidency and suppressing political and media criticism.

The September 2004 elections to the *Majlis* were won by the pro-Nazarbayev Fatherland Republican Party (Otan), which won a majority of seats in the first round of voting. Monitors from the Organisation for Security and Co-operation in Europe (OSCE) criticised the elections as flawed, and the Speaker of the *Majlis* resigned in protest at the conduct of voting. One of the main opposition parties, Democratic Choice, called for popular protests against the result, but in January 2005 a court ordered its dissolution for breaching state security. In March 2005 opposition parties joined together to form the For a Just Kazakhstan movement, led by Zharmakhan Tuyakbai, the former parliamentary Speaker.

POLITICAL SYSTEM
Under the 1995 constitution, executive power is vested in the president and government. The president is directly elected for a term that was extended in 1998 from five years to seven years. The bicameral legislature, the *Parlament*, is composed of a lower house, the *Majlis*, and the Senate. The *Majlis* has 77 members, 67 directly elected in single constituencies and 10 allocated proportionately on a regional basis; members serve a five-year term. The Senate has 39 members, of whom 32 are indirectly elected and seven are appointed, for a six-year term, with half elected every three years. The Constitutional Council is subject to presidential veto.

HEAD OF STATE
President, Commander-in-Chief of the Armed Forces,
   Nursultan Nazarbayev, *elected* 1 December 1991,
   confirmed in office by referendum 29 April 1995,
   re-elected 10 January 1999

SELECTED GOVERNMENT MEMBERS *as at July 2005*
Prime Minister, Daniyal Akhmetov
First Deputy Prime Minister, Akhmetzhan Yessimov
Deputy Prime Minister, Sauat Mynbayev
Defence, Gen. Mukhtar Altynbayev
Finance and State Revenues, Arman Dunaev
Foreign Affairs, Kasymzhomart Tokayev
Interior, Zautbek Turisbekov

EMBASSY OF THE REPUBLIC OF KAZAKHSTAN
33 Thurloe Square, London SW7 2SD
T 020-7581 4646
Ambassador Extraordinary and Plenipotentiary, Yerlan
   Idrissov, apptd 2002

BRITISH EMBASSY
ul Furmanova 173, Almaty
T (+ 7) (3272) 506191/2 E british-embassy@kaznet.kz
Ambassador Extraordinary and Plenipotentiary, HE Paul
   Brummell, apptd 2005

BRITISH COUNCIL
Republic Square 13, KZ-480013 Almaty
T (+ 7) (3272) 633339 E general@kz.britishcouncil.org
Director, James Kennedy

DEFENCE
An agreement signed with Russia in 1995 provides for eventual re-unification of the two states' armed forces. The CIS mutual defence treaty of 1993, to which Kazakhstan is a signatory, retains a common air defence force, while Kazakh forces also take part in the CIS peacekeeping force along the Tajikistan–Afghanistan border. By 1996, all nuclear warheads had been returned to Russia, although Kazakhstan retained 48 SS-18 intercontinental ballistic missiles. Kazakhstan participates in the NATO Partnership for Peace programme. The Army has 930 main battle tanks and 573 armoured infantry fighting vehicles. The Caspian Sea Flotilla, which Kazakhstan shares with Russia and Turkmenistan, operates under Russian command. The Air Force has 164 combat aircraft and 14 attack helicopters.

MILITARY EXPENDITURE – 1.5 per cent of GDP (2003)
MILITARY PERSONNEL – 65,800: Army 46,800, Air
   Force 19,000; Paramilitaries 34,500
CONSCRIPTION DURATION – 24 months

ECONOMY AND TRADE
As part of the Soviet Union, the Kazakh economy was dominated by the exploitation of its considerable mineral resources, producing phosphorus, chrome, lead, zinc and silver. The economy still relies on these resources, but principally on the exploitation of its vast oil and natural gas supplies; lack of adequate export pipelines limited the benefits of these until the Caspian Consortium pipeline opened in 2001, linking the Tengiz oilfield with Black Sea ports, but since 2001 there has been an oil-fuelled economic boom. Oil revenues, currently over 60 per cent of government revenues, will increase when the pipeline from the Caspian fields to the Chinese border, begun in 2004, is completed. As a result of the boom, the government has eliminated the budget deficit, but it is also trying to stimulate growth in other industries to reduce dependency on oil. A Stabilisation Fund was set up in 2001 to manage state finances and protect the economy from volatile oil prices.

About 30 per cent of the labour force is engaged in industry, 50 per cent in services and 20 per cent in agriculture. Agriculture, including stock-raising, is highly developed, particularly in the central and south-west of the republic, and accounts for 11 per cent of GDP. Grain is grown in the north and north-east, and cotton and wool produced in the south and south-east.

The main exports are oil and oil products, ferrous metals, chemical, machinery, grain, wool, meat and coal. Russian takes 30 per cent of exports.

GNI – US$22,600 million (2002); US$1,520 per capita
   (2002)
ANNUAL AVERAGE GROWTH OF GDP – 9.1 per cent
   (2004 est.)
INFLATION RATE – 6 per cent (2002 est.)
UNEMPLOYMENT – 8 per cent (2004 est.)
TOTAL EXTERNAL DEBT – US$6,664 million (2000 est.)
FOREIGN DIRECT INVESTMENT US$5,316 million
   (1997–2000)
IMPORTS – US$8,300 million (2003)
EXPORTS – US$12,900 million (2003)

BALANCE OF PAYMENTS
Trade – US$4,088 million surplus (2003)
Current Account – US$183 million deficit (2003)

Trade with UK	2003	2004
Imports from UK	£103,419,000	£137,687,000
Exports to UK	51,851,000	36,573,000

TRANSPORT INFRASTRUCTURE
Kazakhstan's size makes internal air travel essential, and the country has 392 airports. There are extensive rail and road networks (13,601 km of railways and 81,331 km of highways), although the roads are concentrated in the more populous east. There are important ports on the Caspian and Aral seas, and the Syr Darya and Irtysh rivers provide 3,900 km of navigable waterways.

MEDIA AND CULTURE
There are several public television broadcasters operating in Kazakhstan including Kazakh Television and Khabar

TV (which is broadcast in Russian). Popular newspapers include *Karavan, Kazakhstanskaya Pravda* and the English language title *Almaty Herald*. Although freedom of the press is protected by the constitution, opposition and privately owned media are subject to censorship.

In the 19th century Abai Kunanbaev (1845–1904) translated Russian works into Kazakh, and so founded Kazakhstan's literary culture, which until then had been chiefly oral. The former capital city Almaty is home to the celebrated Abai State Academic Theatre while the Kazakh Film Studio, founded in 1944, is noted for its contribution to world cinema.

KENYA

Jamhuri ya Kenya – Republic of Kenya

AREA – 569,100 sq. km. Neighbours: Somalia (east), Ethiopia (north), Sudan (north-west), Uganda (west), Tanzania (south)
POPULATION – 32,021,856 (2004 est.). The main tribal groups are the Kikuyu, Luhya, Luo, Kalenjin, Kamba and Masai. The official languages are Swahili, which is generally understood throughout Kenya, and English; numerous indigenous languages are also spoken
CAPITAL – Nairobi (population, 2,143,254, 1999)
MAJOR CITIES – ΨKisumu; ΨMombasa; Nakuru
CURRENCY – Kenya shilling (Ksh) of 100 cents
NATIONAL ANTHEM – Ee mungu nguvu yetu [Oh god of all creation]
NATIONAL DAY – 12 December (Independence Day)
NATIONAL FLAG – Horizontally black, red and green with the red fimbriated in white, and with a shield and crossed spears in the centre
LIFE EXPECTANCY (years) – 44.94 (2004 est.)
MORTALITY RATE (per 1,000 population) – 16.31 (2004 est.)
HIV / AIDS ADULT PREVALENCE – 6.7 per cent (2003 est.)
INFANT MORTALITY (per 1,000 births) – 62.62 (2004 est.)
DEATH PENALTY – Yes
POPULATION BELOW POVERTY LINE – 50 per cent (2001 est.)
POPULATION GROWTH RATE – 1.14 per cent (2004 est.)
POPULATION DENSITY – 55 per sq. km (2002 est.)
MILITARY EXPENDITURE – 1.8 per cent of GDP (2003)
MILITARY PERSONNEL – 24,120: Army 20,000, Navy 1,620, Air Force 2,500; Paramilitaries 5,000
ILLITERACY RATE – (m) 9.4 per cent; (f) 20.3 per cent (2003 est.)
GROSS ENROLMENT RATIO (percentage of relevant age group) – primary 96 per cent (2002); secondary 32 per cent (2002); 4 per cent (2002)

CLIMATE AND TERRAIN
The coastal plain in the south-east and semi-desert terrain in the east rise to an arid interior of highlands and mountains in the centre and west. Elevation extremes range from 5,199 m (Mount Kenya) at the highest point to 0 m (Indian Ocean) at the lowest. The country includes part of Lake Victoria in the south-west and Lake Turkana (Rudolph) in the north. As an equatorial country, the climate is tropical, with average temperatures reaching 27°C in February and 22°C in June.

HISTORY AND POLITICS
Fossils of early hominids found in the Lake Turkana region suggest that the area was inhabited some 2.6 million years ago. Arabs and Persians settled on the Kenyan coast from the eighth century AD. The Portuguese gained control of coastal areas in the 16th century but Arab overlordship was reasserted in the 18th century. European exploration of the interior began in the 19th century and in 1895, Kenya became part of Britain's East African Protectorate, becoming a colony in 1920. Demands for internal self-government by white settlers were rejected in 1923, but from 1944 the Kenya African Union (KAU) campaigned for African rights. The Mau Mau rebellion of 1952–6, intended to drive white settlers from African tribal lands, resulted in a state of emergency that lasted until 1960, when preparations for majority African rule began. Kenya became independent in 1963, with Jomo Kenyatta as prime minister; in 1964 it declared itself a republic and Kenyatta became president. On Kenyatta's death in 1978, Daniel T arap Moi became president, remaining in power (amid allegations of electoral fraud) until 2002, when he was barred from standing for re-election.

Kenya was a one-party state ruled by the Kenya African National Union (KANU) between 1964 (in effect, though not formally declared until 1982) and 1991. A multiparty system was reintroduced after violent agitation and international pressure in the early 1990s but KANU maintained its grip on power until the 2002 elections. The NARC government that came to power in 2002 has tried to tackle the serious problems of extreme poverty, high levels of crime and endemic official corruption but has made little headway. After decades of stability, intercommunal violence and conflict over land and water rights have become more frequent since the 1990s, exacerbated by a rural food crisis following drought and crop failures in 2004.

In the 2002 elections, the National Rainbow Coalition (NARC) gained control of the legislature, with 125 out of 210 seats. Mwai Kibaki of NARC won the simultaneous presidential election with 62.2 per cent of the vote.

POLITICAL SYSTEM
The 1963 constitution is still in effect, although a new constitution, drafted in 2002, is ready to be submitted to a referendum. The head of state is the president, directly elected for a five-year term, who is head of government and appoints the cabinet. The unicameral National Assembly, the *Bunge*, has 224 members, of whom 210 are directly elected for a five-year term, 12 are appointed by the president, and two, the Attorney-General and the Speaker, are *ex-officio* members.

HEAD OF STATE
President and C.-in-C. Armed Forces, Mwai Kibaki (NARC), *elected* 27 December 2002, *took office* 30 December 2002
Vice-President, Minister for Home Affairs and National Heritage, Moody Awori

SELECTED GOVERNMENT MEMBERS *as at July 2005*
Finance, David Mwiraria
Foreign Affairs and International Co-operation, Ali Chirau Mwakwere
Minister of State in the Vice-President's Office for Home Affairs, Linah Jebii Kilimo

KENYA HIGH COMMISSION
45 Portland Place, London W1B 1AS
T 020-7636 2371
High Commissioner, HE Joseph Kirugumi Muchemi

BRITISH HIGH COMMISSION
Upper Hill Road, PO Box 30465 Nairobi
T (+254) (2) 714699
E consular@nairobi.mail.fco.gov.uk
High Commissioner, HE Adam Wood, apptd 2004

BRITISH COUNCIL
ICEA Building, Kenyatta Avenue, PO Box 40751, Nairobi
T (+254) (2) 334 855/6
E information@britishcouncil.or.ke
Director, Peter Elborn

ECONOMY AND TRADE

Kenya is an overwhelmingly agricultural country, with up to 80 per cent of the population engaged in agricultural and horticultural production. The world's fourth largest producer of tea, it also grows coffee, maize, sugarcane and wheat. Its natural resources include gold, limestone, soda ash, salt, rubies, garnets, wildlife and hydropower.

There has been considerable industrial development over the last 15 years in new industries producing steel, textiles and tyres and processing of dehydrated vegetables. Smaller schemes have added to the country's manufacturing base in consumer goods. There is an oil refinery in Mombasa supplying both Kenya and Uganda, and a fuel pipeline connects Mombasa and Nairobi. Tourism generates some US$400 million per year but the industry has adversely affected since 2001 by fears of terrorist attacks.

International aid, suspended because of concerns over political corruption, resumed in 2003, when the IMF approved a three-year facility for poverty reduction and economic growth.

Principal exports are coffee and tea, which account for roughly one-third of total export earnings. Also exported are fruit, vegetables and agricultural products. Industrial machinery is the largest single import; other imports are transport equipment, petroleum and petroleum products, metals, pharmaceuticals and chemicals.

GNI – US$11,200 million (2002); US$360 per capita (2002)
ANNUAL AVERAGE GROWTH OF GDP – 1.1 per cent (2001 est.)
INFLATION RATE – 5.9 per cent (2000 est.)
TOTAL EXTERNAL DEBT – US$5,700 million (2002 est.)
FOREIGN DIRECT INVESTMENT – US$156 million (1997–2000)
IMPORTS – US$3,700 million (2003)
EXPORTS – US$2,400 million (2003)

BALANCE OF PAYMENTS
Trade – US$996 million deficit (2002)
Current Account – US$137 million deficit (2002)

Trade with UK	2003	2004
Imports from UK	£171,992,000	£186,960,000
Exports to UK	217,126,000	220,638,000

TRANSPORT INFRASTRUCTURE

The Kenya Railways Corporation has 2,778 km of railways. There are also 67,000 km of road, of which 8,900 km are surfaced. The principal port is Mombasa, operated by the Kenya Ports Authority. International air services operate from airports at Nairobi and Mombasa.

MEDIA

There are a number of television channels, including the state-administered Kenya Broadcasting Corporation (KBC). Radio is a popular medium outside urban areas. There are six national newspapers that report a range of political views including *The Daily Nation*, *The East African Standard* and *The East African*.

KIRIBATI

Ribaberikin Kiribati – Republic of Kiribati

AREA – 726 sq. km
POPULATION – 100,798 (2004 est.): predominantly Christian. The languages are I-Kiribati and English
CAPITAL – Tarawa (population, 36,717, 2000)
CURRENCY – Australian dollar ($A) of 100 cents
NATIONAL ANTHEM – Teirake kain Kiribati [Stand Kiribati]
NATIONAL DAY – 12 July (Independence Day)
NATIONAL FLAG – Red, with blue and white wavy lines in base, and in the centre a gold rising sun and a flying frigate bird
MORTALITY RATE (per 1,000 population) – 8.49 (2004 est.)
INFANT MORTALITY (per 1,000 births) – 49.9 (2004 est.)
DEATH PENALTY – No (abolished 1979)
POPULATION GROWTH RATE – 2.25 per cent (2004 est.)
POPULATION DENSITY – 113 per sq. km (1999)

CLIMATE AND TERRAIN

Kiribati (pronounced *kiribas*) comprises 36 islands, of which about 20 are inhabited: the Kiribati (Gilbert) group (17) including Banaba (formerly Ocean Island), the Rawaki (Phoenix) islands (8), and some of the Line Islands (11), including Kirimati (Christmas Island). They are situated in the southern central Pacific Ocean, crossed by the Equator; it was also crossed by the International Date Line until 1995, when the government unilaterally moved the date line eastwards so that the whole country shared the same day. The atolls are coral, and few are more than 800 m wide or more than 3 m high.

HISTORY AND POLITICS

The islands were settled by Austronesian-speaking peoples in the first millennium BC and Samoans, Fijians and Tongans migrated there in the 11th to 14th centuries. British seafarers visited the islands in the 18th century, and in 1892 the Gilbert (Kiribati) and Ellice (Tuvalu) Islands were proclaimed a British protectorate and in 1916 a British colony, which subsequently incorporated the Line Islands and Phoenix Islands. During the Second World War the islands were occupied by the Japanese and were the scene of fierce fighting between Japanese and US troops. Kiritimati (Christmas) Island became the site of British nuclear weapons tests in the 1950s and 1960s. In 1975 the territories separated and the Gilbert, Phoenix and Line Islands became independent as the Republic of Kiribati in 1979.

The republic faces a number of environmental problems. Open-cast phosphate mining left Banaba unfit for human habitation and the population was evacuated in

1945, now living on Rabi Island, Fiji; they have since been compensated for the environmental damage. The rise in the sea level owing to global warming threatens low-lying countries such as Kiribati, which reported in 1999 that two uninhabited atolls were completely submerged. In 2002, along with Tuvalu and the Maldives, Kiribati began legal action against the USA over its refusal to sign the Kyoto Protocol.

Teburoro Tito, first elected president in 1994, was re-elected for a third term in 2003 but resigned a month later after losing a parliamentary vote on the budget. In the subsequent legislative election in May 2003, the Maneaban Te Mauri (Protect the Maneaba) won 24 seats, an overall majority, and Boutokaan Te Koaua (BTK, Pillars of Truth) won 16 seats. The July 2003 presidential election was won by Anote Tong of the BTK, with 47.4 per cent of the vote.

POLITICAL SYSTEM

Under the 1979 constitution, the president is head of state and head of government, and is directly elected for a four-year term, with a maximum of three terms. The unicameral legislature, the House of Assembly, has 42 members (40 members directly elected for a four-year term, a representative of the Banaban community on Rabi Island, and the Attorney General). There are no formal political parties but some associations of politicians formed for elections have proved durable enough to be given names.

HEAD OF STATE
President, Foreign Affairs, Anote Tong, *elected* 4 July 2003, *sworn in* 6 July 2003
Vice-President, Minister for Education, Youth and Sport Development, Teima Onorio

SELECTED GOVERNMENT MEMBERS *as at July 2005*
Internal Affairs and Social Development, Amberoti Nikora
Finance and Economic Development, Nabuti Mwemwenikarawa

KIRIBATI HIGH COMMISSION
c/o Office of the President, PO Box 68, Bairiki, Tarawa
High Commissioner, Makurita Baaro

BRITISH HIGH COMMISSIONER
HE Charles Mochan, appthd 2002, resident at Suva, Fiji

ECONOMY AND TRADE

The once rich phosphate deposits on Banaba ran out in 1979 and mining ended. The economy is now dependent on coconut exports. Other sources of income are fishing, tourism, remittances from islanders working abroad (worth over $5 million a year) and revenues from the trust fund established with phosphate mining revenues. The principal imports are foodstuffs, consumer goods, machinery and transport equipment. The principal exports are copra and fish. In 2000, improved port facilities at Betio, funded by Japan, were opened.
GNI – US$880 per capita (2002)
ANNUAL AVERAGE GROWTH OF GDP – 1.5 per cent (2001 est.)

Trade with UK	2003	2004
Imports from UK	£32,000	£60,000
Exports to UK	1,000	11,000

TRANSPORT INFRASTRUCTURE

Air communication exists between most of the islands and is operated by Air Kiribati, a statutory corporation. Air Marshall Islands operates a weekly service between Majuro, Tarawa, Funafuti and Nadi, and Air Nauru between Tarawa, Nauru and Nadi. Inter-island shipping is operated by another statutory corporation, the Shipping Corporation of Kiribati. The main port is Betio, on Tarawa.

MEDIA

Kiribati has no domestic television, so radio forms the islands' main source of communication. There is one state-run and one private weekly newspaper.

KOREA

The Korean language is of the Ural-Altaic Group. Its script, Hangul, was invented in the 15th century; prior to this Chinese characters alone were used. Despite the great cultural influence of the Chinese, Koreans have developed and preserved their own cultural heritage.

HISTORY AND POLITICS

The independent kingdoms in the peninsula were united by the Buddhist Silla dynasty in AD 668, and a distinct culture developed. The Silla were succeeded by the Koryo dynasty in 935 and the Yi dynasty from 1395 to 1910, during which period Korea became a vassal of China and Confucianism replaced Buddhism. Contact with outside cultures was discouraged by successive Korean rulers until 1876, when Japan forced the country to open up to foreign trade. Subsequently, Japan, China and Russia competed for influence, with Japan emerging as the dominant state, formally annexing Korea in 1910. Japanese rule ended with its Second World War defeat in 1945, when Korea was divided along the 38th parallel by the occupying armies of liberation: US troops in the south and Soviet troops in the north. The Republic of Korea was founded in the south on 15 August 1948, following a general election and the adoption of a constitution. The Democratic People's Republic of Korea (DPRK) was established in the north on 9 September 1948, a Supreme People's Soviet was elected and a Soviety-style constitution was adopted.

UN plans to reunify the country after nationwide elections in 1950 were defied by North Korea. After elections in the south, South Korea declared its independence, which prompted its invasion by North Korea. A multinational UN force, with a large US contingent, intervened and pushed the North Korean troops back to the Chinese frontier. This brought China into the war in support of North Korea and their combined forces pushed back the UN troops, occupying Seoul. A UN counter-attack retook all territory south of the 28th parallel by the time an armistice was signed in 1953; a demilitarised border zone was established. The war devastated the entire peninsula, and particularly North Korea, and left over 2 million people dead.

Reunification talks between North and South Korea have taken place intermittently; they were broken off by North Korea in 1980 but further talks took place in 1990, 1997–9 and 2000. A non-aggression pact was signed in 1991 and an agreement on mutual inspection of nuclear facilities in 1992. The 2000 talks ended with a joint declaration under which both sides agreed to work independently for reunification and to recognise the common elements in each side's proposals for federation-confederation; since the declaration, meetings have become more frequent. However, tensions remain owing to North Korea's nuclear programme and its economic weakness, and the South's concern about the prospect of US troop withdrawals from the demilitarised zone.

DEMOCRATIC PEOPLE'S REPUBLIC OF KOREA

Chosun Minchu-chui Inmin Kongwa-guk – Democratic People's Republic of Korea

AREA – 120,400 sq. km. Neighbours: China, Russia (north), Republic of Korea (south)
POPULATION – 22,697,553 (2004 est.). The language is Korean
CAPITAL – Pyongyang (2,741,260)
CURRENCY – Won of 100 chon
NATIONAL ANTHEM – Aegug-ga [Patriotic hymn]
NATIONAL DAY – 16 February (Kim Jong-il's birthday)
NATIONAL FLAG – Red with white fimbriations and blue borders at top and bottom; a large red star on a white disc near the hoist
LIFE EXPECTANCY (years) – 71.08 (2004 est.)
MORTALITY RATE (per 1,000 population) – 6.99 (2004 est.)
INFANT MORTALITY (per 1,000 births) – 24.84 (2004 est.)
DEATH PENALTY – Yes
POPULATION GROWTH RATE – 0.98 per cent (2004 est.)
POPULATION DENSITY – 187 per sq. km (2002)
URBAN POPULATION – 61 per cent (2001)

CLIMATE AND TERRAIN
The republic occupies the northern half of the Korean peninsula. A wide coastal plain in the west rises to mountains divided by deep valleys in the interior. Elevation extremes range from 2,744 m (Paektu-san) at the highest point to 0 m (Sea of Japan) at the lowest. The climate is mild, although winters can be cold.

HISTORY AND POLITICS
After the Korean war ended in 1953, Kim Il-sung continued the process of Soviet-style reform begun with land reform and nationalisation in 1946. He also developed *Juche* (self-reliance), an ideology demanding total economic independence. North Korea pursued an isolationist foreign policy for several decades, signing a mutual assistance treaty with China only in 1961 and improving relations with the Soviet Union in 1985. It established diplomatic contacts with South Korea and Japan in 1990, raising hopes that it was abandoning its isolationism, but it remains a secretive, closed country under tight Communist Party control, rejecting outside influences.

This situation has had serious consequences domestically and internationally. The economy has suffered a long decline under communist rule, and a series of natural disasters in the 1990s caused severe famine, obliging the government to request international aid. It is estimated that 2 million people have died since the 1990s as a result of the acute food shortages, which continue despite international food and fuel aid.

There has been international concern since the 1990s over North Korea's covert development of nuclear weapons. In 1994, North Korea agreed to freeze its nuclear development programme in return for aid, but in 2002 it became clear that it had reactivated the programme, and it expelled international nuclear inspectors. In 2003 North Korea withdrew from the Treaty on the Non-Proliferation of Nuclear Weapons (NPT) and announced that it had enough material to produce nuclear weapons. Six-nation talks to resolve the nuclear issue began in 2003, but North Korea suspended its involvement indefinitely in February 2005.

Kim Il-sung died in 1994. His son, Kim Jong-il, became Chairman of the National Defence Commission, designated as the 'highest post of the state', and general secretary of the Korean Workers' Party in 1997. The most recent legislative elections were held in 2003.

POLITICAL SYSTEM
The (communist) Korean Workers' Party, which was founded in 1946 by Kim Il-sung, is the only permitted political party. However, political control and leadership is maintained by the cult of personality created by Kim Il-sung and continued by his son and successor Kim Jong-il.

The 1972 constitution was amended in 1998 to designate leading state posts; it made Kim Il-sung the 'Eternal President' and the chairmanship of the National Defence Commission, held by Kim Jong-il, the 'highest post in the state', while providing that the chairman of the Presidium of the Supreme People's Assembly would represent the state on formal occasions. There is a unicameral legislature, the Supreme People's Assembly, which has 687 deputies, directly elected from a single list of candidates for a five-year term. The Assembly elects a presidium and the premier, appointing the government on the recommendation of the premier. The Central People's Committee, which is also elected by the Assembly, directs the Administrative Council (government), which implements the policy formulated by the Committee.

HEAD OF STATE
Eternal President, Kim Il-sung (deceased)
Chair of the National Defence Commission, Kim Jong-il
Chair of the Presidium of the Supreme People's Assembly, Kim Yong-nam

SELECTED GOVERNMENT MEMBERS *as at July 2005*
Premier, Pak Pong-chu
Deputy Premier, Kwak Pon-ki,
Deputy Premier, Ro Tu-chol
Deputy Premier, Chon Sung-hun
Finance, Mun Il-bong
Foreign Affairs, Paek Nam-sun
People's Armed Forces, Vice-Marshall Kim Il-chol

EMBASSY OF THE DEMOCRATIC PEOPLE'S REPUBLIC OF KOREA
73 Gunnersbury Avenue, London, W5 4LP T 020-8992 4965
Ambassador Extraordinary and Plenipotentiary, HE Ri Yong-ho, apptd 2003

BRITISH EMBASSY
Munsu Dong, Pyongyang T (+850) 2381-7980
Ambassador Extraordinary and Plenipotentiary, HE David Slinn, apptd 2002

DEFENCE
The Army has about 3,500 main battle tanks and 2,500 armoured personnel carriers. The Navy has 26 submarines, three frigates and about 310 patrol and

coastal vessels at 15 bases. The Air Force has 584 combat aircraft and 24 armed helicopters.

MILITARY EXPENDITURE – 25 per cent of GDP (2003)
MILITARY PERSONNEL – 1,106,000: Army 950,000, Navy 46,000, Air Force 110,000; Paramilitaries 189,000
CONSCRIPTION DURATION – Three to 12 years

ECONOMY AND TRADE

Although North Korea is rich in natural resources, such as coal, iron ore, magnesite, graphite, copper, zinc, lead, and precious metals, and Japan developed heavy industry during its years of occupation at the beginning of the 20th century, the economy is in a disastrous state. Internal mismanagement, low export levels and increasing debt sent the economy into a long decline that was compounded by the collapse of Soviet communism in the 1990s.

Severe floods and a series of disastrous harvests in the 1990s brought famine, and the centrally planned economy has not been able to pull North Korea out of its desperate condition. Lack of arable land, collective farming, natural disasters and chronic shortages of fuel and fertizers have reduced food production. A relaxation of restrictions on farmers' markets since 2003 means that some people have been able to purchase extra food, but the majority continue to suffer acute shortages. Industrial output is centred on coal, steel, chemicals and machine tools, but antiquated machinery and fuel shortages have limited capacity to a fraction of pre-1989 levels.

The USA has provided food aid since the mid-1990s, increasing the amounts in 1999, but political tension since 2002 over North Korea's nuclear programme has led to a reduction in international food and fuel aid.

GNI – US$1,000 per capita (2001)
ANNUAL AVERAGE GROWTH OF GDP – 1 per cent (2004 est.)
IMPORTS – US$431 million (2002)
EXPORTS – US$298 million (2002)

BALANCE OF PAYMENTS
Trade – US$217 million deficit (2002)
Current Account – US$82 million deficit (2002)

Trade with UK	2003	2004
Imports from UK	£8,715,000	£1,327,000
Exports to UK	1,205,000	293,000

TRANSPORT INFRASTRUCTURE

North Korea has 5,214 km of railways and 31,200 km of highways. There are some 2,253 km of navigable waterways. The principal airport is at Pyongyang.

MEDIA

There is no independent media in North Korea. All televisions and radios are pre-tuned to government stations which broadcast state propaganda. There are five national papers in circulation that include the titles *Rodong Sinmun* and *Minju Choson*.

REPUBLIC OF KOREA

Taehan Min'guk – Republic of Korea

AREA – 98,700 sq. km. Neighbour: Democratic People's Republic of Korea (north)
POPULATION – 48,598,175 (2004 est.). The largest

religions are Buddhism (10.3 million) and Christianity (8.8 million Protestants, 2.9 million Roman Catholics). The language is Korean

CAPITAL – Seoul (population, 10,321,000, 1999 estimate)
MAJOR CITIES – ΨInchon; ΨPusan; Taegu
CURRENCY – Won
NATIONAL ANTHEM – Aegug-ga [Patriotic hymn]
NATIONAL DAY – 15 August (Liberation Day)
NATIONAL FLAG – White with a red and blue yin-yang symbol in the centre, surrounded by four black trigrams
LIFE EXPECTANCY (years) – 75.58 (2004 est.)
MORTALITY RATE (per 1,000 births) – 6.13 (2004 est.)
INFANT MORTALITY (per 1,000 births) – 7.18 (2004 est.)
DEATH PENALTY – Yes
POPULATION GROWTH RATE – 0.62 per cent (2004 est.)
POPULATION DENSITY – 483 per sq. km (2002)
URBAN POPULATION – 82 per cent (2001)

CLIMATE AND TERRAIN

The country occupies the southern part of the mountainous Korean peninsula, with highlands and mountains accounting for around 70 per cent of the land area. Elevation extremes range from 1,950 m (Halla-san) at the highest point to 0 m (Sea of Japan) at the lowest. The climate is mild. Average temperatures in Seoul range from –4°C in January to 29°C in August.

HISTORY

Since 1948, South Korea has experienced mostly authoritarian, often military, rule and great industrial development. Syngman Rhee, president since 1948, resigned in 1960 in the face of popular protests at corruption and electoral fraud. A military coup in 1961 brought General Park Chung-hee to power and he instigated a programme of industrial development; by 1979 Korea was a leading shipbuilding nation and producer of electronic goods. Park's repressive regime introduced military law in 1972, and he was assassinated in 1979. Following riots against the interim government, General Chun Do-hwan assumed power. Pro-democracy agitation in the mid-1980s led to constitutional changes in 1987 and the first multiparty elections in 1988, but despite the anti-corruption campaign of the new democratically elected president Roh Tae-woo, politics continued to be plagued by allegations of corruption and electoral fraud, and to be subject to military influence; the first civilian president and the first wholly civilian government since 1961 were appointed only in 1993. Kim Dae-jung's inauguration as president in 1998 saw the adoption of the 'sunshine policy' of engagement with North Korea.

Roh Moo-hyunwas elected president in 2002 and took office in February 2003. He was suspended from March until May 2004 after the legislature voted to impeach him over alleged electoral irregularities and for incompetence; the Constitutional Court rejected the move and he was reinstated. In the 2004 legislative election, the pro-presidential Uri party won an overall majority and formed a government.

POLITICAL SYSTEM

A new constitution was adopted when the Sixth Republic was inaugurated in 1988. Under this, the president, who is head of state, chief of the executive and commander-in-chief of the armed forces, is directly elected for a single five-year term. He appoints the prime minister with the consent of the National Assembly, and members of the State Council (cabinet) on the recommendation of the prime minister. The president is also empowered to take wide-ranging measures in an emergency, including the declaration of martial law, but must obtain the agreement of the National Assembly. The unicameral National Assembly *(Kuk Hoe)* has 299 members who are directly elected for a four-year term.

HEAD OF STATE
President, Roh Moo-hyun, *elected* 19 December 2002, *sworn in* 25 February 2003

SELECTED GOVERNMENT MEMBERS *as at July 2005*
Prime Minister, Lee Hae-chan
Deputy Prime Minister, Education and Human Resources, Kim Jin-pyo
Deputy Prime Minister, Finance and Economy, Han Duck-so
Defence, Yoon Kwang-woong
Foreign Affairs and Trade, Ban Ki-moon
Government Administration and Home Affairs, Oh Young-kyo

EMBASSY OF THE REPUBLIC OF KOREA
60 Buckingham Gate, London SW1E 6AJ
T 020-7227 5500/2
Ambassador Extraordinary and Plenipotentiary, HE Yoon Je-cho, apptd 2004

BRITISH EMBASSY
No. 4, Chung-dong, Chung-Ku, Seoul 100–120
T (+ 82) (2) 3210 5500 E bembassy@britain.or.kr
Ambassador Extraordinary and Plenipotentiary, HE Warwick Morris, apptd 2003

BRITISH COUNCIL
Joongwhoo Building, 61–21 Taepyungro1-Ka, Choong-ku, Seoul 100–101 E info@britishcouncil.or.kr
Director, Shoba Ponnappa

DEFENCE
The Army has 2,330 main battle tanks, 2,480 armoured personnel carriers and 117 armed helicopters. The Navy has 20 submarines, six destroyers, nine frigates, 84 patrol and coastal vessels, 16 combat aircraft, 43 armed helicopters and 60 main battle tanks. There are eight naval bases. The Air Force has 538 combat aircraft.

The USA maintains 34,500 personnel in the country.
MILITARY EXPENDITURE – 2.8 per cent of GDP (2003)
MILITARY PERSONNEL – 687,700: Army 560,000, Navy 63,000, Air Force 64,700; Paramilitaries 4,500
CONSCRIPTION DURATION – 26–30 months

ECONOMY AND TRADE
Industrialisation from the 1960s transformed South Korea from a predominantly agrarian country into one of the Asian 'miracle' economies by the 1980s. Initially based on shipbuilding and electrical goods, production shifted towards electronics and IT goods in the 1980s. By 1997 South Korea was the world's eleventh largest economy, with an annual GDP growth rate of 8 per cent. However, the effects of the Asian financial crisis began to be felt in 1997 when Hanbo Steel, a flagship company, collapsed. The country was forced to appeal to the IMF for assistance after the economy deteriorated further, but strict financial policies saw the country return to growth in 2000.

Major manufacturing industries include steel, automobiles, shipbuilding, electronics, textiles, clothing and leather goods and chemicals. Tourism is a growing industry, with 5,320,000 foreign visitors in 2000.

Electronic products, machinery, metal goods, passenger vehicles, chemical products and fabric and clothing are the main exports. Electronic products, petroleum, machinery and chemical products are the main imports. The USA, Japan, the EU and China are the main trading partners.
GNI – US$473,000 million (2002); US$9,930 per capita (2002)
ANNUAL AVERAGE GROWTH OF GDP – 4.6 per cent (2004 est.)
INFLATION RATE – 3.5 per cent (2003 est.)
UNEMPLOYMENT – 3.4 per cent (2003 est.)
TOTAL EXTERNAL DEBT – US$159,800 million (2003 est.)
IMPORTS – US$179 million (2003)
EXPORTS – US$194 million (2003)

BALANCE OF PAYMENTS
Trade – US$14,180 million surplus (2002)
Current Account – US$6,092 million surplus (2002)

Trade with UK	2003	2004
Imports from UK	£1,464,871,000	£1,450,552,000
Exports to UK	2,616,393,000	3,127,988,000

TRANSPORT INFRASTRUCTURE
In 2000, there were 3,124 km of railway in commercial operation, of which 661 km were electrified. A high-speed railway line is being constructed between Seoul and Pusan and there are plans to build high-speed rail links between Seoul and Mokp'o and Seoul and Kangnung. There were 88,775 km of roads, of which 2,131 km are motorways. There are international airports in Seoul (Kimpo), Kimhae (near Pusan), Taegu, Cheju city and Inch'on. Pusan and Inch'on are the major ports, although development and operation at Inch'on are hampered by tidal variations of 9–10 m.

EDUCATION
Primary education is free of charge and compulsory for six years from the age of six. Secondary and higher education is extensive, with the option of middle school to age 15 and high school to age 18.
ILLITERACY RATE – (m) 0.9 per cent; (f) 3.6 per cent (2000)
GROSS ENROLMENT RATIO (percentage of relevant age group) – primary 100 per cent (2002); secondary 94 per cent (2002); tertiary 82 per cent (2002)

MEDIA
Korea has a number of public broadcasters, such as Korea Broadcasting System (KBS), Munhwa Broadcasting Corporation (MBC) and Education Broadcasting System (EBS). RTV, South Korea's first public-access television channel, is run by the Citizen's Broadcast Foundation. Newspapers currently in circulation include *Hangyore Sinmun*, and the English language title *Korea Daily News*.

KUWAIT

Dawlat al-Kuwayt – State of Kuwait

AREA – 17,800 sq. km. Neighbours: Iraq (north and
west); Saudi Arabia (south and west)
POPULATION – 2,257,549 (2004 est.): 41.6 per cent are
Kuwaiti citizens, the remainder being other Arabs,
Iranians, Indians, Pakistanis and Westerners. Islam is
the official religion, though religious freedom is
constitutionally guaranteed. The official language is
Arabic, and English is widely spoken as a second
language
CAPITAL – ΨKuwait City (Al-Kuwayt) (population,
388,663, 1998)
CURRENCY – Kuwaiti dinar (KD) of 1,000 fils
NATIONAL ANTHEM – Al-Nashid Al-Watani (National
anthem)
NATIONAL DAY – 25 February
NATIONAL FLAG – Three horizontal stripes of green,
white and red, with black trapezoid next to staff
LIFE EXPECTANCY (years) – 76.84 (2004 est.)
MORTALITY RATE (per 1,000 population) – 2.44
(2004 est.)
INFANT MORTALITY (per 1,000 births) – 9 (2001 est.)
HIV / AIDS ADULT PREVALENCE – 0.12 per cent
(2001 est.)
DEATH PENALTY – Yes
POPULATION GROWTH RATE – 3.36 per cent
(2004 est.)
POPULATION DENSITY – 131 per sq. km (2002)

CLIMATE AND TERRAIN

Kuwait is an almost entirely flat and arid country with
elevation extremes ranging from 306 m (unnamed
location) at the highest point to 0 m (Persian Gulf) at the
lowest. Its territory includes the island of Bubiyan and
others at the head of the Persian Gulf. Average
temperatures range from 10°C in January to 37°C in July.

HISTORY AND POLITICS

The area was under the nominal control of the Ottoman
empire from the late 16th century, but in 1756 an
autonomous sheikdom was founded that has been ruled
by the al-Sabah family ever since. Kuwait entered into a
'Special Treaty of Friendship' with Britain in 1899, in
order to protect itself from Ottoman and Saudi
domination, and it became a British protectorate in 1914.
The borders with Saudi Arabia and Iraq were agreed
between 1922 and 1933. Full independence was
achieved in 1961, although Britain retained a military
presence in the country until 1971.

An attempted Iraqi invasion shortly after independence
in 1961 was discouraged by British troops in the Gulf.
However, in August 1990 Iraq invaded and occupied
Kuwait, proclaiming it a province of Iraq. In 1991 a short
military campaign by a US-led coalition force expelled
the Iraqi forces, although there were further Iraqi
incursions in 1993 before Iraq publicly renounced its
claim to Kuwait in 1994 and recognised the new UN-
demarcated border. Extensive damage was caused to the
country's infrastructure and environment during the Iraqi
occupation and the allied liberation campaign, and
reconstruction was a priority throughout the 1990s. In
2003 Kuwait was a base for the build-up of forces for the
Iraq War, and it remains an important transit route for
military and civilian traffic into and out of Iraq.

In recent years, there have been clashes between
security forces and militant Islamists, some of whom are
alleged to have links to al-Qa'eda.

Although Kuwait was the first Arab country in the Gulf
to have an elected parliament, the National Assembly was
suspended from 1977 to 1981 and again from 1986. The
Assembly was restored in 1992 and, despite a brief
suspension in 1999 because of a dispute between
members and the government, has sat regularly, with
regular democratic elections. In May 2005 women were
given full political rights following amendments to the
constitution.

Although liberal candidates did well in the 1992
election, they have had fluctuating fortunes since, while
support for Islamist candidates has grown. In the 2003
election, Islamists won 21 of the 50 seats, government
supporters won 14, independents won 12 and liberals
won three. In July 2003 the Amir appointed Shaikh
Sabah al-Ahmad al-Jaber al-Sabah as prime minister,
separating the post from the role of heir to the throne for
the first time since independence.

POLITICAL SYSTEM

Under the 1962 constitution, the head of state is the
Amir, chosen from among the ruling family. He exercises
executive power throught the Council of Ministers. The
unicameral legislature is the National Assembly, which has
50 members directly elected for a four-year term. The
electorate consists of all Kuwaiti male nationals over 21
whose families have lived in the emirate since before
1921; in 2005 the franchise was extended to women,
who are now allowed to vote and to stand for election.
There are no political parties. There are six governorates:
Capital, Hawalli, Ahmadi, Al-Jahrah, Al-Farwaniya and
Al-Asimah.

HEAD OF STATE

HH The Amir of Kuwait, Shaikh Jabir al-Ahmad al-Jabir
al-Sabah, *born* 1928, *acceded* 31 December 1977
Crown Prince, HH Shaikh Saad al-Abdullah al-Salim al-
Sabah

SELECTED GOVERNMENT MEMBERS *as at July 2005*
Prime Minister, Shaikh Sabah al-Ahmad al-Jaber al-Sabah
First Deputy Prime Minister; Interior, Shaikh Nawaf al-
Ahmad al-Jaber al-Sabah
*Deputy Prime Minister; Cabinet and National Assembly
Affairs*, Mohammed Dhaifallah Sharar
Deputy Prime Minister; Defence, Shaikh Jaber Mubarak al-
Hamad al-Sabah
Finance, Bader Nasser al Humaidi
Foreign Affairs, Shaikh Muhammad Sabah al-Salem al-
Sabah

EMBASSY OF THE STATE OF KUWAIT
2 Albert Gate, London SW1X 7JU T 020-7590 3400
Ambassador Extraordinary and Plenipotentiary, HE Khaled
al-Duwaisan, GCVO, apptd 1993

BRITISH EMBASSY
PO Box 2, Safat, 13001 Kuwait T (+ 965) 240 3334/5/6
Ambassador Extraordinary and Plenipotentiary, HE
Christopher Wilton, apptd 2002

BRITISH COUNCIL
2 Al Arabi Street, Block 2, PO Box 345, 13004 Safat,
Mansouriya, Kuwait City T (+ 965) 252 0067
E bc.kuwait@kw.britishcouncil.org
Director, John Pare *(acting)*

DEFENCE

The Army has 368 main battle tanks, 321 armoured personnel carriers and 450 armoured infantry fighting vehicles. The Navy has ten patrol and coastal vessels, based at Ras al-Qalaya. The Air Force has 80 combat aircraft and 16 armed helicopters. The USA has 25,250 service personnel stationed in Kuwait.

MILITARY EXPENDITURE – 9.4 per cent of GDP (2003)
MILITARY PERSONNEL – 15,500: Army 11,000, Navy 2,000, Air Force 2,500; Paramilitaries 6,600

ECONOMY AND TRADE

Oil was discovered in 1938 and exploitation after 1945 transformed the economy. Kuwait has around 9 per cent of the world's oil reserves and proven reserves of around 98 billion barrels. Petroleum accounts for 95 per cent of export revenues and 80 per cent of government income. Income from foreign reserves and investment is also high.

The country has a very large proportion of immigrant labour, which makes up about 80 per cent of the work force. Workers are mainly Pakistanis, Indians and Iranians, with a significant number of North Americans and Europeans.

Non-oil exports, mainly to Asian countries and the Indian sub-continent, include chemical fertilisers, ammonia and other chemicals, metal pipes and building materials. Re-exports to neighbouring states traditionally accounted for a major proportion of non-oil exports but were brought to a halt by the Iraqi invasion. Major trading partners are Japan, the USA, the UAE, Saudi Arabia and Western Europe.

GNI – US$38,000 million (2002); US$16,304 per capita (2002)
ANNUAL AVERAGE GROWTH OF GDP – 6.4 per cent (2004 est.)
INFLATION RATE – 1.8 per cent (2000 est.)
FOREIGN DIRECT INVESTMENT – US$163 million (1997–2000)
IMPORTS – US$10,800 million (2003)
EXPORTS – US$19,400 million (2003)

BALANCE OF PAYMENTS
Trade – US$11,261 million surplus (2003)
Current Account – US$7,567 million surplus (2003)

Trade with UK	2003	2004
Imports from UK	£381,128,000	£355,829,000
Exports to UK	341,679,000	418,235,000

TRANSPORT INFRASTRUCTURE

Kuwait has 4,450 km of highways but no waterways or railways. The main ports are Ash Shu'aybah, Ash Shuwaykh, Kuwait, Mina' 'Abd Allah, Mina' al Ahmadi and Mina' Su'ud.

EDUCATION

Education is free of charge and compulsory from six to 14 years. In 1999 there were 969 schools (608 government run, 322 private and 39 vocational) and one university.

ILLITERACY RATE – (m) 15.4 per cent; (f) 19.7 per cent (2000)
GROSS ENROLMENT RATIO (percentage of relevant age group) – primary 94 per cent (2002); secondary 85 per cent (2002)

MEDIA

Kuwaiti newspapers are far more outspoken in their coverage of politics than newspapers in neighbouring Arab nations. KUNA (Kuwait News Agency) is the official media agency; *Kuwait Times*, the English language daily newspaper and Radio Kuwait is the state radio broadcaster.

KYRGYZSTAN

Kyrgyz Respublikasy – Kyrgyz Republic

AREA – 199,900 sq. km. Neighbours: Kazakhstan (north), China (east), Tajikistan (south and west), Uzbekistan (west)
POPULATION – 5,081,429 (2004 est.): 64.9 per cent Kyrgyz (Turkic origin), 12.5 per cent Russian and 13.8 per cent Uzbek, with smaller numbers of Ukrainians, Germans, Tatars and Kazakhs. Islam is the main religion. Kyrgyz, the official language since independence, is a Turkic language, written in the Roman alphabet since 1992. Russian is also an official language having equal rights with Kyrgyz
CAPITAL – Bishkek (population, 589,400, 1997 estimate)
CURRENCY – Som of 100 tyin (introduced in 1993)
NATIONAL ANTHEM – Mamlekettik gimni [National anthem]
NATIONAL DAY – 31 August (Independence Day)
NATIONAL FLAG – Red with a rayed sun containing a representation of a yurt, all in gold
LIFE EXPECTANCY (years) – 67.84 (2004 est.)
MORTALITY RATE (per 1,000 population) – 7.19 (2003 est.)
INFANT MORTALITY RATE (per 1,000 births) – 36.81 (2004 est.)
HIV / AIDS ADULT PREVALENCE – 0.1 per cent (2001 est.)
DEATH PENALTY – Yes
POPULATION BELOW POVERTY LINE – 55 per cent (2001 est.)
POPULATION GROWTH RATE – 1.25 per cent (2004 est.)
POPULATION DENSITY – 26 per sq. km (1999)
URBAN POPULATION – 33.3 per cent (2000)
MILITARY EXPENDITURE – 2.6 per cent of GDP (2003)
MILITARY PERSONNEL – 12,500: Army 8,500, Air Force 4,000; Paramilitaries 5,000
CONSCRIPTION DURATION – 18 months
GROSS ENROLMENT RATIO (percentage of relevant age group) – primary 102 per cent (2002); secondary 85 per cent (2002); tertiary 44 per cent (2002).

CLIMATE AND TERRAIN

Kyrgyzstan (formerly Kyrgyzia) is a landlocked and mountainous country lying in the Tien Shan mountain range, with the Pamirs in the extreme south. Elevation extremes range from 7,439 m (Pik Pobedy) at the highest point to 132 m (Kara-Darya) at the lowest, though most of the country lies at over 1,000 m. The principal rivers are the Naryn and the Chu.

HISTORY AND POLITICS

After a long period under Turkic, Mongol and Chinese rule, the Kyrgyz became part of the Russian Empire in the 1860s and 1870s. After the October 1917 revolution in Russia, the area became part of the Turkestan autonomous republic with the Soviet Union until 1924, when the

Kirgiz Autonomous Region was formed; it became an autonomous republic in 1926 and a constituent republic of the Soviet Union in 1936. Soviet rule brought land reforms in the 1920s that resulted in the settlement of many of the nomadic Kyrgyz.

Reform in the Soviet Union in the 1980s provoked an upsurge in nationalism in Kyrgyzstan, and agitation for independence. Following the attempted coup in Moscow in August 1991, Kyrgyzstan became an independent republic and joined the Commonwealth of Independent States (CIS). Economic reforms were introduced from 1992; these caused considerable hardship, with inflation of over 700 per cent in 1993, high levels of unemployment and malnutrition. The privatisation of state assets was suspended between 1997 and 1998 because of fears that they were being sold too cheaply. Kyrgyzstan formed the Central Asian Union with Kazakhstan and Uzbekistan in 1994, agreeing to create a single economic market in 1996.

Since independence, there has been tension between Kyrgyz and ethnic Uzbeks, concentrated around Osh, and this has flared into intercommunal violence on occasions. There have also been clashes between security forces and militant Islamists, active near the border with Tajikistan. Both the USA and Russia have troops stationed in the country as part of the international fight against terrorism.

Askar Akayev, a pro-reform communist, was elected president in 1990 and re-elected 1991, 1995 and 2000, although the 2000 election was considered flawed. After growing unrest since 2002 over political and media suppression, persistent economic problems and corruption, Akayev was deposed in March 2005 in a popular uprising over alleged government interference in the 2005 legislative election. He was replaced as acting president by opposition leader Kurmanbek Bakiyev, who formed an interim government. A presidential election was held in July 2005 and was won by Bakiyev with 89 per cent of the vote.

POLITICAL SYSTEM
The 1994 constitution was amended in 2003 to make the legislature unicameral and to give the president the power of veto over a wide range of legislation. The head of state is the president, who is directly elected for a five-year term, renewable only once. The 2005 legislative election replaced the bicameral legislature with the unicameral Supreme Council, which has 75 members directly elected for a five-year term. The president nominates the prime minister, who must be approved by the Supreme Council, and the other members of the government. The Assembly of the People of Kyrgyzstan, which comprises the leaders of the republic's ethnic communities, was designated a consultative body in 1997.

HEAD OF STATE
President, Kurmanbek Bakiyev, *elected*, 10 July 2005

SELECTED GOVERNMENT MEMBERS *as at July 2005*
Prime Minister, Feliks Kulov
First Deputy Prime Minister, Medetbek Kerimkulov
Defence, Maj.-Gen. Ismail Isakov
Finance, Akylbek Jarapov
Foreign Affairs, Roza Otunbayeva
Interior, Pol. Lt.-Gen. Myktybek Abdyldayev

EMBASSY OF THE KYRGYZ REPUBLIC
Ascot House, 119 Crawford Street, London W1U 1BJ
T 020-7935 1462

Ambassador Extraordinary and Plenipotentiary, Urkaly Isaev, apptd 2004

BRITISH AMBASSADOR
HE Paul Brummell, apptd 2005, resident at Almaty, Kazakhstan

BRITISH COUNCIL
Director, James Kennedy, resident at Almaty, Kazakhstan

ECONOMY AND TRADE
Kyrgyzstan's economic reforms in the early 1990s caused soaring inflation. With assistance from the World Bank and the IMF since 1994, this was brought under control by the late 1990s and is now in single figures. However, the transition to a market economy has not been completed successfully and the economy is severely depressed, with high unemployment, particularly in the industrial sector, and a high level of government debt. Poverty has led to malnutrition.

The economy is highly agrarian and agriculture represents 40 per cent of GDP. Though the country does not enjoy vast natural resources, there are deposits of gold, iron ore and mercury.

GNI – US$1,400 million (2002); US$290 per capita (2002)
ANNUAL AVERAGE GROWTH OF GDP – 5.1 per cent (2003 est.)
INFLATION RATE – 2.4 per cent (2003 est.)
TOTAL EXTERNAL DEBT – US$1,500 million (2002 est.)
IMPORTS – US$700 million (2003)
EXPORTS – US$600 million (2001)

BALANCE OF PAYMENTS
Trade – US$54 million deficit (2002)
Current Account – US$85 million deficit (2002)

Trade with UK	2003	2004
Imports from UK	£1,880,000	£3,266,000
Exports to UK	131,000	671,000

TRANSPORT INFRASTRUCTURE
Kyrgyzstan has 18,500 km of highways and 420 km of railways. There are 600 km of waterways and 61 airports.

MEDIA
There is a large number of newspapers currently in circulation, several of which have affiliations to particular political parties. There are also a number of private and independent television and radio broadcasters. However, there have been attempts by the government in recent years to control the press and broadcasters. Publications by Islamist fundamentalists are banned in Kyrgyzstan.

LAOS

Satharanarath Pasathipatai Pasason Lao – Lao People's Democratic Republic

AREA – 236,800 sq. km. Neighbours: China (north), Vietnam (east), Cambodia (south), Thailand (west), Myanmar (north-west)
POPULATION – 6,068,117 (2004 est.): 68 per cent Lao Loum (lowland Lao), 22 per cent Lao Theung (upland Lao), 9 per cent Lao Soung (highland Lao, including Hmong and Yau). Lao is the official language; French and English are spoken

CAPITAL – Vientiane (population, 555,100, 1997 est.)
CURRENCY – Kip (K) of 100 at
NATIONAL ANTHEM – Pheng xat Lao [Hymn of the Lao people]
NATIONAL DAY – 2 December
NATIONAL FLAG – Blue background with a central white circle, framed by two horizontal red stripes
LIFE EXPECTANCY – 54.69 (2004 est.)
MORTALITY RATE (per 1,000 population) – 12.1 (2004 est.)
INFANT MORTALITY RATE (per 1,000 births) – 87.06 (2004 est.)
HIV / AIDS ADULT PREVALENCE – 0.1 per cent (2003 est.)
DEATH PENALTY – Yes
POPULATION BELOW POVERTY LINE – 40 per cent (2002 est.)
POPULATION GROWTH RATE – 2.44 per cent (2004 est.)
POPULATION DENSITY – 24 per sq. km (2002)
MILITARY EXPENDITURE – 2 per cent of GDP (2003)
MILITARY PERSONNEL – 29,100: Army 25,600 (of which Navy 600), Air Force 3,500; Paramilitaries 100,000
CONSCRIPTION DURATION – 18 months minimum
ILLITERACY RATE – (m) 22.6 per cent; (f) 44.5 per cent (2000)
ENROLMENT (percentage of age group) – primary 115 per cent (2002); secondary 41 per cent (2002); tertiary 4 per cent (2002)

CLIMATE AND TERRAIN

Laos is landlocked, the land rising from the Mekong river basin in the west to a range of hills in the east of the country and mountains in the north. Elevation extremes range from 2,817 m (Phon Bia) at the highest point to 70 m (Mekong River) at the lowest. Much of the land is covered by rainforest. The climate is tropical, with a wet season from May to November. Average annual temperatures in Vientiane range from 14°C in January to 34°C in July.

HISTORY AND POLITICS

From the ninth to 13th centuries, Laos was part of the Khmer empire centred on Angkor in Cambodia. Small principalities developed from the 12th century and were united in the 14th century into the kingdom of Lan Xang ('the Land of a Million Elephants'), which dominated until 1713, when it split into the separate kingdoms of Luang Prabang, Vientiane and Champassac, which became tributaries of Siam (Thailand) in the late 18th century and then a protectorate of France from 1893.

Japanese occupation during the Second World War inspired a Lao nationalist movement, which proclaimed independence in 1945, but the French regained control of the country in 1946. Independence as a constitutional monarchy was granted in 1953, but much of the following 20 years was spent in civil war between the communist Pathet Lao, backed first by China and then by North Vietnam, and royalists, who attracted US support from the early 1960s as the USA became embroiled in neighbouring Vietnam. A cease-fire in 1973 partitioned the country between the two sides, but in 1975 the Pathet Lao seized power and proclaimed a republic, introducing a one-party state and initiating socialist policies. Greater economic liberalisation was introduced from the mid-1980s, and the first elections to the National Assembly since 1975 were held in 1989.

The Hmong ethnic minority people have maintained a low-level insurgency against the communist regime since 1975. In 2000 and 2003 Laos suffered some serious civil disturbances, including bombings and armed attacks on buses. These were variously attributed to Hmong insurgents and anti-government groups based abroad.

In the 2002 election to the National Assembly, party candidates won 108 of 109 seats, and the remaining seat was won by an approved non-partisan candidate. The president, prime minister and Council of Ministers were subsequently confirmed in their posts by the National Assembly.

POLITICAL SYSTEM

Under the 1991 constitution, the head of state is a president elected by the National Assembly for a five-year term. The unicameral legislature, the National Assembly, was enlarged from 99 to 109 members at the 2002 election; members are party-approved candidates directly elected for a five-year term. The Lao People's Revolutionary Party (LPRP) is the only legal political party, although non-partisan candidates for the National Assembly have been approved by it. Party congresses are held every five years.

HEAD OF STATE
President, Gen. Khamtay Siphandone, *elected by the National Assembly* 24 February 1998, *re-elected* 9 April 2002
Vice-President, Choummaly Sayasone

SELECTED GOVERNMENT MEMBERS *as at July 2005*
Prime Minister, Bounnyang Vorachit
Deputy Prime Minister, Somsavat Lengsavad
Deputy Prime Minister; Foreign Affairs, Thongloun Sisoulit
Deputy Prime Minister; State Planning Committee, Maj-Gen. Asang Laoly
Finance, Chansy Phosikham
Interior, Maj.-Gen. Soutchay Thammasith
National Defence, Maj.-Gen. Douangchay Phichit

EMBASSY OF THE LAO PEOPLE'S DEMOCRATIC REPUBLIC
74 Avenue Raymond-Poincaré F-75116 Paris
T (+ 33) (1) 4553 0298
Ambassador Extraordinary and Plenipotentiary, HE Soutsakhone Pathammavong, apptd 2003

BRITISH EMBASSY
PO Box 6626, Vientiane T (+ 856) (21) 413606
Ambassador Extraordinary and Plenipotentiary, HE David Fall, apptd 2003, resident at Bangkok, Thailand

ECONOMY AND TRADE

A degree of economic liberalisation from the mid-1980s encouraged inward investment and a measure of private enterprise, promoting some economic growth, but the country is still very poor and was damaged by the collapse of the Soviet Union in 1991 and the Asian financial crisis in 1997.

The economy is heavily dependent on subsistence agriculture, principally rice, which accounts for half of GDP and 80 per cent of employment; agricultural development was made the principal economic goal by the LPRP's seventh congress in 2001. There is potential to increase revenues by exporting hydroelectric power to Thailand from a new dam on the Mekong, for which World Bank funding was received in April 2005. Some

deposits of coal, tin, iron ore, gold, bauxite and lignite are exploited, as is the abundance of timber in the rainforests.
GNI – US$1,700 million (2002); US$310 per capita (2002)
ANNUAL AVERAGE GROWTH OF GDP – 5.7 per cent (2000 est.)
INFLATION RATE – 25.1 per cent (2000 est.)
TOTAL EXTERNAL DEBT – US$2,499 million (2000 est.)
IMPORTS – US$500 million (2003)
EXPORTS – US$400 million (2003)

BALANCE OF PAYMENTS
Trade – US$217 million deficit (2001)
Current Account – US$82 million deficit (2001)

Trade with UK	2003	2004
Imports from UK	£3,391,000	£1,215,000
Exports to UK	9,446,000	16,111,000

TRANSPORT INFRASTRUCTURE

There are no railways and only a limited road network (21,916 km). The 'Friendship bridge' over the River Mekong connects Laos with Thailand, and links up the road routes from Singapore to China. There are around 4,587 km of navigable waterways on the River Mekong and other rivers. The principal airports are at Vientiane and Luang Prabang.

MEDIA

There are three state-run newspapers, although circulation is low and all media is strictly controlled by the government. There are also state-run television and radio broadcasters.

LATVIA

Latvijas Republika – Republic of Latvia

AREA – 62,100 sq. km. Neighbours: Estonia (north), Russia (east), Lithuania and Belarus (south)
POPULATION – 2,306,306 (2004 est.): 57.7 per cent Latvian, 29.6 per cent Russian, 4.1 per cent Belarusian, with small Ukrainian and Polish minorities. The main religions are Lutheran, Roman Catholic and Russian Orthodox. The official language is Latvian; Russian is also spoken. Education is in Latvian and Russian.
Public sector employees must pass language tests in Latvian to a level commensurate with the nature of their employment. The right of minorities to use their mother tongue has been acknowledged
CAPITAL – Ψ Riga (population, 747,157, 2002 estimate)
MAJOR CITIES – Daugavpils; Jelgava; Jurmala; Ψ Liepaja; Ψ Ventspils
CURRENCY – Lats of 100 santims
NATIONAL ANTHEM – Dievs, sveti Latviju [God bless Latvia]
NATIONAL DAY – 18 November (Independence Day 1918)
NATIONAL FLAG – Crimson, with a white horizontal stripe across the centre
LIFE EXPECTANCY (years) – 70.86 (2004 est.)
INFANT MORTALITY (per 1,000 births) – 9.67 (2004 est.)
MORTALITY RATE (per 1,000 population) – 13.73 (2004 est.)
HIV / AIDS ADULT PREVALENCE – 0.4 per cent (2001 est.)

POPULATION GROWTH RATE – −0.71 per cent (2004 est.)
POPULATION DENSITY – 38 per sq. km (2002)
URBAN POPULATION – 96 per cent (2001)

CLIMATE AND TERRAIN

Latvia is a flat, low-lying country that has its coast on the eastern shores of the Baltic Sea. Elevation extremes range from 312 m (Gaizinkalns) at the highest point to 0 m (Baltic Sea) at the lowest. Average annual temperatures in Riga range from −4°C in January to 18°C in July.

HISTORY AND POLITICS

Conquered and Christianised in the 13th century by the German Teutonic Knights, Latvia was successively ruled by Polish, Lithuanian and Swedish rule in the 16th and 17th centuries, until it was incorporated into the Russian empire in 1721. Under partial German occupation during the First World War, it declared its independence in 1918 and successfully defended this against the Bolsheviks in 1918–20. A dictatorship was established in 1934, following political instability and economic depression. The Soviet Union invaded and annexed Latvia in 1940, and regained control in 1944 after ousting the German forces that had invaded in 1941. Latvia suffered huge civilian losses during the Second World War, including the destruction of its large Jewish community. Many more Latvians died after the war in purges and deportations ordered by Stalin.

Agitation by nationalist groups grew from the mid-1980s and in 1990 talks on independence began with the Soviet Union. Following the failed coup in Moscow in August 1991, the Latvian parliament declared the country's independence and this was internationally recognised. The last Russian troops left in 1994 but a large Russian minority remains and there are intercommunal tensions. Since the first post-Soviet elections in 1993, there has been a succession of centre-right coalition governments.

Latvia joined the EU in 2004. Its parliament ratified the EU constitution in June 2005.

Vaira Vike-Freiberga was elected president in 1999, the first woman president in East Europe, and she was re-elected unopposed in 2003.

In the 2002 legislative election, the New Era party (JL) became the largest parliamentary party, winning 26 of the 100 seats. Its leader, Einars Repse, was nominated prime minister and formed a coalition government, but the coalition collapsed in February 2004 after the withdrawal of one of the coalition partners. A new coalition was formed by Indulis Emsis of the Farmers' Union (ZZS) but resigned in October 2004. Aigars Kalvitis of the People's Party (TP) then formed a coalition government that included the JL, ZZS and the First Party of Latvia (LPP); this was approved by parliament in December 2004.

POLITICAL SYSTEM

The 1922 constitution was restored in 1993. The head of state is a president, who is elected by the legislature for a four-year term which may be renewed only once. The president appoints the prime minister, who appoints the cabinet subject to approval by the legislature. The unicameral legislature, the *Saeima*, has 100 deputies who are elected for a four-year term by proportional representation, with a five per cent threshold for parliamentary representation.

HEAD OF STATE
President, Vaira Vike-Freiberga, *elected* 17 June 1999,
re-elected 20 June 2003, *sworn in* 8 July 2003

SELECTED GOVERNMENT MEMBERS *as at July 2005*
Prime Minister, Aigars Kalvitis
Minister of Transport, Ainars Slesers
Defence, Einars Repse
Finance, Oskars Spurdzins
Foreign Affairs, Artis Pabriks
Interior, Eriks Jekabsons

EMBASSY OF THE REPUBLIC OF LATVIA
45 Nottingham Place, London W1U 5LR **T** 020-7312 0040
Ambassador Extraordinary and Plenipotentiary, HE Indulis
   Berzins, apptd 2004

BRITISH EMBASSY
5, J. Alunana iela, Riga LV-1010
T (+ 371) 777 4700 **E** british.embassy@apollo.lv
Ambassador Extraordinary and Plenipotentiary, HE Ian
   Bond, apptd 2004

BRITISH COUNCIL
5a Blaumana iela, Riga LV-1011
T (+ 371) 728 1730 **E** mail@britishcouncil.lv
Director, Agita Kalvina

DEFENCE
The Army has three main battle tanks and 13 armoured
personnel carriers, the Navy has four patrol and coastal
combatants at three bases and the Air Force has 19 aircraft
and five helicopters. Latvia, Lithuania and Estonia operate
a joint naval unit BALTRON which located at five naval
bases: Liepaja, Riga, Ventspils, Tallinn and Klaipeda.
Latvia joined NATO in April 2004.
MILITARY EXPENDITURE – 1.9 per cent of GDP (2003)
MILITARY PERSONNEL – 4,870: Army 4,000, Navy 620,
   Air Force 250; Paramilitaries 3,200
CONSCRIPTION DURATION – 12 months

ECONOMY AND TRADE
Latvia planned to join the European Monetary Union in
2005 and to adopt the euro in 2008, though progress
could be hampered by its GDP per capita, which is the
lowest of the countries that joined the EU in 2004.
   Transit, services and banking are large sectors, with
services contributing 70.6 per cent of GDP in
2001. Important industries include the manufacture of
buses, vans, cars, synthetic fibres, agricultural machinery,
fertilisers, washing machines, radios, electronics,
pharmaceuticals, processed foods and textiles.
   Latvia is an agricultural exporter, specialising in cattle
and pig breeding, dairy farming and crops, including
sugar beet, flax, cereals and potatoes. In 2001, 13.5 per
cent of the population was employed in agriculture, which
accounted for 4.1 per cent of GDP. Natural resources
include limestone, gypsum, peat and timber.
   Western economic markets take approximately 60 per
cent of Latvian goods. The largest trading partners are
Germany, Sweden and the UK. Most of Latvia's timber
products are exported to the UK.
GNI – US$8,100 million (2002); US$3,480 per capita
   (2002)
ANNUAL AVERAGE GROWTH OF GDP – 7.6 per cent
   (2004 est.)
INFLATION RATE – 2.7 per cent (2000 est.)
UNEMPLOYMENT – 14.6 per cent (2000 est.)

TOTAL EXTERNAL DEBT – US$3,379 million (2000 est.)
FOREIGN DIRECT INVESTMENT – US$1,633 million
   (1997–2000)
IMPORTS – US$5,000 million (2003)
EXPORTS – US$3,000 million (2003)

BALANCE OF PAYMENTS
Trade – US$1,998 million deficit (2003)
Current Account – US$956 million deficit (2003)

Trade with UK	2003	2004
Imports from UK	£113,448,000	£39,152,000
Exports to UK	508,193,000	239,656,000

TRANSPORT INFRASTRUCTURE
Latvia has 2,413 km of railway track and some 20,400
km of roads. There are several warm-water ports, of which
three, Riga, Ventspils and Liepaja, are developed for
commercial transport. The main airport is at Riga.

EDUCATION
There are 27 higher education institutions, of which five
are universities.
ILLITERACY RATE – (m) 0.2 per cent; (f) 0.2 per cent
   (2003 est.)
GROSS ENROLMENT RATIO (percentage of relevant age
   group) – primary 99 per cent (2002); secondary 93 per
   cent (2002); tertiary 64 per cent (2002)

MEDIA
There are around 140 newspapers in circulation including
24 national dailies. The most popular include *Diena,*
Latvijas Avize and *Neatkariga RA.* Latvian Television is
a public service broadcaster that has two channels, and
Latvijas Neatkariga Televizija is the biggest private
broadcaster.

LEBANON

Al-Jumhūriyya al-Lubnāniyya – Republic of Lebanon

AREA – 10,200 sq. km. Neighbours: Syria (north and
   east), Israel (south)
POPULATION – 3,777,218 (2004 est.): 32 per cent
   Shi'ite Muslim; 21 per cent Sunni Muslim, 40 per cent
   Christian, 7 per cent Druze. Arabic is the official
   language, and French and English are also widely used
CAPITAL – ΨBeirut (Bayrut) (population, 1,100,000,
   1994)
MAJOR CITIES – ΨSayda (Sidon); ΨTarabulus (Tripoli);
   ΨSur (Tyre)
CURRENCY – Lebanese pound (L£) of 100 piastres
NATIONAL ANTHEM – Kulluna lil watan lil 'ula lil'alam
   [We all belong to the homeland]
NATIONAL DAY – 22 November
NATIONAL FLAG – Horizontal bands of red, white and
   red with a green cedar of Lebanon in the centre of the
   white band
LIFE EXPECTANCY (years) – 72.35 (2004 est.)
MORTALITY RATE (per 1,000 population) – 6.28
   (2004 est.)
INFANT MORTALITY (per 1,000 births) – 25.48
   (2004 est.)
HIV / AIDS ADULT PREVALENCE – 0.9 per cent
   (2001 est.)
DEATH PENALTY – Yes

POPULATION GROWTH RATE – 1.3 per cent (2004 est.)
POPULATION DENSITY – 434 per sq. km (2002)
URBAN POPULATION – 90 per cent (2001)

CLIMATE AND TERRAIN

There is a narrow plain on the Mediterranean Sea coast, and the fertile Bekaa valley runs from north to south between the Lebanon and Anti-Lebanon mountain ranges. Elevation extremes range from 3,088 m (Qurnat as Sawda') at the highest point to 0 m (Mediterranean Sea) at the lowest. The climate is Mediterranean, with average annual temperatures of 13°C in January and 29°C in August.

HISTORY AND POLITICS

Lebanon was part of the Phoenician empire from the fifth century BC until the first century AD, when it came under Roman rule and Christianity was introduced. Islam was introduced by Arabs in the seventh century AD, and the Druse faith was developed by local Muslims in the 11th century. The area was contested between Muslims and Christians during the Crusades before becoming part of the Turkish Ottoman Empire in the 16th century. Following the collapse of the Ottoman empire at the end of the First World War, Lebanon became a French-administered mandated territory, achieving independence in 1943 with a constitution that enshrined power-sharing by all the country's religions.

The complicated system of government established by the constitution created tensions between Christians and Muslims that in 1975 erupted into a civil war that pitted a coalition of Christian groups against Druze and Muslim militias. The Arab forces were supported by the Palestine Liberation Organisation (PLO), founded in Beirut in 1964. A cease-fire was agreed in 1976 and Arab troops, dominated by the Syrian contingent, deployed as a peace-keeping force.

Further fighting occurred when Israel invaded south Lebanon in 1978 in response to PLO guerrilla raids in Israel. A second Israeli offensive in 1982, when it laid siege to Palestinian and Syrian forces in Beirut, succeeded in forcing the PLO to withdraw from Lebanon, moving its headquarters to Tunis. However, Syrian abrogation of a 1983 agreement on Israeli and Syrian troop withdrawal sparked off renewed civil conflict, with intense fighting between Christian Phalangists and Muslim Druse militias. By 1985, most international peace-keeping troops had withdrawn, the country was in chaos and many foreigners were taken hostage. Rival political and religious factions sought to gain control and the country came close to partition. An Arab League-sponsored cease-fire came into effect in 1989 and a peace plan, the Ta'if Accord, proposed revisions to the constitution that would reduce Christian Maronite dominance. This was rejected by some Christian factions and fighting continued until this opposition was crushed by Syrian forces. A fragile peace was achieved in 1991, and elections in 1992 were peaceful, although they were boycotted by some Christian parties. In the 'security zones' established by Israel in south Lebanon in 1985, clashes continued between occupying Israeli troops, or the Israeli-backed South Lebanon Army (SLA), and Hezbollah guerrillas throughout the 1990s but the SLA collapsed after Israel withdrew its forces in 2000. The border has been continually breached since 2000 and the area remains very tense, with sporadic clashes.

Syria exerted a strong influence on Lebanese politics during and after the civil war; most Lebanese governments were pro-Syrian, and Syrian troops remained in the country. However, popular opposition to Syria's influence was inflamed by the assassination in February 2005 of former prime minister Rafik Hariri for which Syria was blamed. Huge rallies in Beirut brought down the pro-Syrian government and obliged Syria to withdraw its troops and intelligence agents, which it claimed to have completed in May 2005.

In the legislative elections held in May and June 2005, an alliance of anti-Syrian parties led by Saad Hariri won an overall majority of seats in the National Assembly (although pro-Syrian groups won the majority in south Lebanon), and the parliament appointed Fouad Siniora, an ally of Hariri, as prime minister. The new parliament has called on pro-Syrian President Emile Lahoud to resign; his six-year term of office, due to end in November 2004, was extended by a further three years in September 2004. However, the influential pro-Syrian parliamentary speaker Nabih Berri was re-elected for a fourth term of office.

POLITICAL SYSTEM

The constitution dates from 1926 but has been heavily amended, most significantly in 1943, when the National Covenant set out the division of power between the religious communities, and in 1989 to incorporate the provisions of the Ta'if Accord. By convention, the presidency is held by a Maronite Christian, the prime minister is a Sunni Muslim and the speaker is a Shia Muslim. The executive comprises the president, prime minister and Cabinet. The president is elected by the National Assembly for a six-year term, which is not renewable; the National Assembly voted to extend the current president's term by three years in September 2004. The unicameral National Assembly has 128 members, directly elected for a four-year term; seats are divided equally between Christians and Muslims. The prime minister is appointed by the president following consultation with the National Assembly.

HEAD OF STATE
President of the Republic of Lebanon, Gen. Émile Lahoud,
   elected 15 October 1998, *sworn in* 24 November 1998

SELECTED GOVERNMENT MEMBERS *as at July 2005*
Prime Minister, Fouad Siniora
Deputy Prime Minister; Defence, Elias Murr
Finance, Jihad Azour
Foreign Affairs, Fawzi Salloukh
Interior and Municipal Affairs, Hassan Sabaa

LEBANESE EMBASSY
15–21 Palace Gardens Mews, London W8 4QN
T 020-7229 7265/7727 6696
Ambassador Extraordinary and Plenipotentiary, HE Jihad
   Mortada, apptd 1999

BRITISH EMBASSY
Embassies Complex, Army Street, Zkak al-Blat, Serail Hill PO Box
11–471, Beirut
T (+ 961) (1) 990 400 E britemb@cyberia.net.lb
Ambassador Extraordinary and Plenipotentiary, HE James
   Watt, apptd 2003

BRITISH COUNCIL DIRECTOR
Sidani Street, Azar Building, Ras Beirut
T (+ 961) (1) 740 123
E general.enquiries@lb.britishcouncil.org
Director, Dr Ken Churchill, OBE

DEFENCE
The Army has 310 main battle tanks and 1,338 armoured personnel carriers. The Navy has seven patrol and coastal vessels at two bases. There is a 1,994-strong UN (UNIFIL) peacekeeping force and 150 Iranian Revolutionary Guards operating in Lebanon.

MILITARY EXPENDITURE – 2.8 per cent of GDP (2003)
MILITARY PERSONNEL – 72,100: Army 70,000, Navy 1,100, Air Force 1,000; Paramilitaries 13,000
CONSCRIPTION DURATION – 12 months

ECONOMY AND TRADE
In the aftermath of the civil war foreign exchange was provided by remittances from Lebanese working abroad, banking services, manufacturing and farm exports, and international aid. In 1993 the Lebanese government launched 'Horizon 2000', a US$20 billion reconstruction programme. The initiative raised GDP by 8 per cent in the following year, though this slowed to 3 per cent by 2003. The plan also succeeded in reducing inflation. The government borrowed heavily to fund reconstruction, and debt is now a serious problem. Receipts from donor nations stabilised government finances throughout 2002 and 2003. Agriculture is an important part of the Lebanese economy and provides much of the country's exports.

Principal exports include foodstuffs, chemical products, jewellery, machinery and electrical goods, textiles, metals and metal products, paper and paper products, and vehicles. Principal imports are foodstuffs, machinery and electrical equipment, vehicles, chemical products, mineral ores, and metals and metal products. There is a free-trade agreement with Syria.

GNI – US$17,700 million (2002); US$3,990 per capita (2002)
ANNUAL AVERAGE GROWTH OF GDP – 4 per cent (2004 est.)
TOTAL EXTERNAL DEBT – US$10,311 million (2000 est.)
FOREIGN DIRECT INVESTMENT – US$898 million (1997–2000)
IMPORTS – US$7,200 million (2003)
EXPORTS – US$1,500 million (2003)

Trade with UK	2003	2004
Imports from UK	£210,283,000	£210,482,000
Exports to UK	16,625,000	16,992,000

TRANSPORT INFRASTRUCTURE
There are 7,370 km of roads, of which 6,265 km are surfaced; there is 222 km of railway track. There is an international airport at Beirut and an internal service operates from Beirut to Tripoli. The principal ports are Tripoli, Tyre, Sidon and Jounieh.

EDUCATION
There is a good provision throughout the country of primary and secondary schools, among which are a great number of private schools. There are 16 universities and colleges of higher education, among them American and French universities, and the Lebanese National University, the Beirut University College, the Kaslik Saint Esprit University and the Arab University in Beirut, with the University of Balamand situated near Tripoli.

ILLITERACY RATE – (m) 7.9 per cent; (f) 19.6 per cent (2000)

GROSS ENROLMENT RATIO (percentage of relevant age group) – primary 103 per cent (2002); secondary 77 per cent (2002); tertiary 45 per cent (2002)

MEDIA
There are a number of daily newspapers in circulation, including French and English language publications. Tele-Liban is the state-run broadcaster that competes with several commercial stations, including the pro-Hezbollah al-Manar TV.

LESOTHO

Mmuso wa Lesotho – Kingdom of Lesotho

AREA – 30,355 sq. km. Neighbour: South Africa, which completely surrounds Lesotho
POPULATION – 1,865,040 (2004 est.). The languages are Sesotho and English
CAPITAL – Maseru
CURRENCY – Loti (M) of 100 lisente. The South African rand is also legal tender
NATIONAL ANTHEM – Pina ea sechaba
NATIONAL DAY – 4 October (Independence Day)
NATIONAL FLAG – Diagonally white over blue over green with the white of double width, and an assegai and knobkerrie on a Basotho shield in brown in the upper hoist
LIFE EXPECTANCY – 36.81 (2004 est.)
MORTALITY RATE (per 1,000 population) – 24.79 (2004 est.)
INFANT MORTALITY (per 1,000 births) – 85.22 (2004 est.)
HIV / AIDS ADULT PREVALENCE – 28.9 per cent (2003 est.)
DEATH PENALTY – Yes
POPULATION GROWTH RATE – 0.14 per cent (2004 est.)
POPULATION DENSITY – 59 per sq. km (2002)
MILITARY EXPENDITURE – 2.3 per cent of GDP (2003)
MILITARY PERSONNEL – Army 2,000

CLIMATE AND TERRAIN
Lethoso is a landlocked highland plateau region with hilly and mountainous areas. Elevation extremes range from 3,482 m (Thabana Ntlenyana) at the highest point to 1,400 m (the junction of the Orange and Makhaleng rivers) at the lowest. The climate is temperate.

HISTORY AND POLITICS
The area was organised into a single territory by Moshoeshoe the Great around 1820. Later in the 19th century the Sotho people came under pressure from both the expanding Zulu nation and Europeans (the Boers) to give up land. In 1868, after fighting two wars with the Europeans, pressure from the Boers forced the Sotho to seek protection from the British government, and Basutoland became a British territory in 1868, and a Crown colony in 1884.

The country gained independence in 1966 as the kingdom of Lesotho, under Moshoeshoe II and with Chief Lebua Jonathan as prime minister. The post-independence period has been one of political instability, with a number of coups and mutinies as rival political parties, army factions and the royal family competed for power. Chief Jonathan declared a state of emergency in 1970, fearing defeat in the elections. Although the constitution was restored in 1973, Jonathan was overthrown in a military coup in 1986, and another military coup in 1990 forced King Moshoeshoe II into exile, his son ruling as Letsie III. Military rule ended with multiparty elections in 1993, although serious civil unrest followed the ousting of the military rulers; democratic rule was restored in 1994 and King Moshoeshoe II was reinstated in 1995; he died in a car accident in 1996 and King Letsie III returned to the throne.

Lesotho continued to be troubled by civil violence, and the 1998 elections were followed by particularly severe disturbances, put down by an intervention force from neighbouring countries at the government's request. An Interim Political Authority set up to review the constitution introduced a more representative electoral system in time for the 2002 election. This election in May 2002 returned the Lesotho Congress for Democracy to power in a poll that was endorsed by foreign observers but which the opposition rejected as fraudulent. In 2004 the prime minister declared a state of emergency and requested food aid after three years of drought.

POLITICAL SYSTEM
In September 1999 it was announced that the first past the post electoral system would be replaced by a new system incorporating a degree of proportional representation and that the number of seats in the National Assembly would be increased by 40 to 120.

HEAD OF STATE
HM The King of Lesotho, King Letsie III, acceded February 1996, crowned 31 October 1997

SELECTED GOVERNMENT MEMBERS as at July 2005
Prime Minister; Defence, Public Service, Bethuel Pakalitha Mosisili
Deputy Prime Minister, Lesao Lehohla
Finance and Development Planning, Timothy Thahane
Foreign Affairs, Monyane Moleleki

HIGH COMMISSION FOR THE KINGDOM OF LESOTHO
7 Chesham Place, London SW1X 8HN
T 020-7235 5686 E lhclesotholondon.org.uk
Chargé d'affaires, Calvin Masenyetse

BRITISH HIGH COMMISSION
PO Box Ms 521, Maseru 100
T (+ 266) 2231 3961 E hcmaseru@lesoff.co.za
High Commissioner, HE Frank Martin, apptd 2002

ECONOMY AND TRADE
The country faces serious demographic, economic and social problems because of the high level of HIV/AIDS infection while life expectancy is among the lowest in the world. Lesotho's economy is closely linked to South Africa, to which it exports its primary natural resource, water. It is also dependent on the remittances from the large number of its male labour force, about 35 per cent, employed in South Africa's mines. Lesotho is self-sufficient in power from hydroelectricity facilities, but the industrial sector is still small, although the USA's African Growth and Opportunity Act programme has created 45,000 jobs in the garment industry and made Lesotho the second-largest exporter in sub-Saharan Africa of garments to the USA. Subsistence agriculture continues to be the largest sector of the economy, engaging 86 per cent of the resident population. Tourism is being developed, especially in the Highlands.

GNI – US$1,000 million (2002); US$550 per capita (2002)
ANNUAL AVERAGE GROWTH OF GDP – 3.3 per cent (2004 est.)
INFLATION RATE – 6.1 per cent (2000 est.)
TOTAL EXTERNAL DEBT – US$735 million (2002 est.)
IMPORTS – US$1,200 million (2003)
EXPORTS – US$194 million (1998)

BALANCE OF PAYMENTS
Trade – US$381 million deficit (2002)
Current Account – US$119 million deficit (2001)

Trade with UK	2003	2004
Imports from UK	£202,000	£190,000
Exports to UK	516,000	262,000

TRANSPORT INFRASTRUCTURE
A surfaced road links Maseru to several of the main lowland towns. The mountainous areas are linked by surfaced, gravelled and rough earth roads and tracks. Other roads link border towns in South Africa with the main towns in Lesotho. Maseru is also connected by rail with the main Bloemfontein–Natal line managed by South African Railways. There are a number of scheduled international air services in operation.

EDUCATION
There are over 1,200 primary and over 180 secondary schools, with emphasis being laid on agricultural and vocational education. The National University of Lesotho at Roma was established in 1975.
ILLITERACY RATE – (m) 27.6 per cent; (f) 6.4 per cent (2000)
GROSS ENROLMENT RATIO (percentage of relevant age group) – primary 124 per cent (2002); secondary 34 per cent (2002); tertiary 2 per cent (2002)

MEDIA
Lesotho has a mixture of state-run and private media. Radio is the most important medium and reforms established in 1998 prompted the growth of a number of commercial stations. State-run Radio Lesotho is the only national station. Lesotho's press publishes a range of weekly papers in both Sesotho and English.

LIBERIA

Republic of Liberia

AREA – 111,369 sq. km. Neighbours: Guinea (north), Côte d'Ivoire (east), Sierra Leone (north-west)
POPULATION – 3,390,635 (2004 est.). The official language is English. The main African languages are Bassa, Kpelle and Kru, though some 16 ethnic languages are spoken
CAPITAL – ΨMonrovia (population, 421,000, 2000 estimate)
MAJOR CITIES – ΨBuchanan (Grand Bassa); ΨGreenville (Sinoe); ΨHarper (Cape Palmas)
CURRENCY – Liberian dollar (L$) of 100 cents
NATIONAL ANTHEM – All hail, Liberia, hail
NATIONAL DAY – 26 July
NATIONAL FLAG – Alternate horizontal stripes (five white, six red), with a five-pointed white star on a blue field in the upper corner next to the flagstaff
LIFE EXPECTANCY (years) – 47.93 (2004 est.)

MORTALITY RATE (per 1,000 population) – 17.86 (2004 est.)
INFANT MORTALITY RATE (per 1,000 births) – 130.51 (2004 est.)
HIV / AIDS ADULT PREVALENCE – 5.9 per cent (2003 est.)
DEATH PENALTY – Yes
POPULATION BELOW POVERTY LINE – 38.6 per cent (2000 est.)
POPULATION GROWTH RATE – 2.7 per cent (2004 est.)
POPULATION DENSITY – 34 per sq. km (2002)
URBAN POPULATION – 44.9 per cent (2000)
MILITARY EXPENDITURE – 11.4 per cent of GDP (2003)
MILITARY PERSONNEL – 11–15,000 (including militias supporting government forces)
ILLITERACY RATE – (m) 26.6 per cent; (f) 58.4 per cent (2003 est.)

CLIMATE AND TERRAIN
Liberia sits just north of the equator, on the west African coast. There are forested highlands in the interior and swampy plains on the coast, where several rivers enter the ocean. Elevation extremes range from 1,380 m (Mount Wuteve) at the highest point to 0 m (Atlantic Sea) at the lowest. The climate is tropical and average annual temperatures are an almost constant 28°C.

HISTORY AND POLITICS
The land was purchased by the American Colonisation Society in 1821 and turned into a settlement for liberated black slaves from the USA, gaining recognition as an independent state in 1847; it is the only west African country never to be colonised. Much of the first century of statehood was dominated by the True Whig Party, but political stability ended in 1980 when a coup installed a military government under Samuel Doe. When civilian rule was restored in 1985, Doe became president but his regime's arbitrary and corrupt rule and an economic collapse led to a revolt in 1990 by National Patriotic Forces of Liberia (NPFL), led by Charles Taylor, and the Armed Forces of Liberia (AFL). This swiftly descended into a civil war that took on an ethnic character, the NPFL being dominated by the Gio and Mano peoples, and the AFL by the Krahn and Mandingo.

The Economic Community of West African States (ECOWAS) sent a peace-keeping force (ECOMOG) into the country in 1990, and attempted to broker a peace agreement. Despite a number of peace initiatives and cease-fires, the war continued until a peace agreement was signed in 1996 that led to an election being held in 1997. This were won by Charles Taylor with 80 per cent of the vote, most of the electorate fearing that he would restart the civil war if he lost the election. However, the outcome did not address the causes of the war, and rebel groups continued to destabilise the country in an attempt to depose Taylor. By mid-2003 the Movement of Democracy for Liberia (MODEL) controlled much of eastern Liberia and Liberians United for Reconciliation and Democracy (LURD) forces were close to capturing the capital. Taylor went into exile in Nigeria and, following mediation by a number of African and European countries, all factions in the conflict signed the Comprehensive Peace Agreement in September 2003. A UN peacekeeping force (UNMIL) was deployed in September 2003 and the disarming of militias started in April 2004.

The Comprehensive Peace Agreement created the National Transitional Government of Liberia (NTGL). Gyude Bryant, a former businessman, leads the government, which is made up of LURD, MODEL, Charles Taylor's forces and Liberian civil society. Elections are scheduled for 11 October 2005.

POLITICAL SYSTEM
Under the 1996 constitution, the head of state is the executive president, directly elected for a six-year term, and there is a bicameral legislature consisting of a 64-member lower chamber, the House of Representatives, which is directly elected for a six-year term, and a 26-member Senate, elected for a nine-year term. The 2003 Comprehensive Peace Agreement established a transitional government, whose chairman is the head of government, and a 76-member National Transitional Legislative Assembly (NTLA).

HEAD OF STATE
Chair of the National Transitional Government, Gyude Bryant, *sworn in* 14 October 2003

SELECTED GOVERNMENT MEMBERS, *as at July 2005*
Vice-Chair, Wesley Momo Johnson
Defence, Daniel Chea
Finance, Lusinee Kamara
Foreign Affairs, Thomas Yaya Nimely
Internal Affairs, Horatio Dan Morias

EMBASSY OF THE REPUBLIC OF LIBERIA
2 Pembridge Place, London W2 4XB T 020-7221 1036
Chargé d'affaires, Jeff Gongoer Dawana

BRITISH AMBASSADOR
HE David Gordon, apptd 2004, resident at Abidjan, Côte d'Ivoire

ECONOMY AND TRADE
The civil war of 1980–2003 has devastated the economy. Liberia is rich in timber, gold, diamonds and rubber, though the UN has imposed sanctions on the export of timber and diamonds. Agriculture centres around timber, rubber, coffee, cocoa, rice, cassava (tapioca), palm oil, sugarcane, bananas; sheep and goats. Much of the population has no mains electricity or running water. Since the signing of the Comprehensive Peace Agreement, over US$500m of foreign aid has been pledged to finance reconstruction.
GNI – US$500 million (2002); US$140 per capita (2002)
ANNUAL AVERAGE GROWTH OF GDP – 21.8 per cent (2004 est.)
TOTAL EXTERNAL DEBT – US$2,032 million (2000 est.)

Trade with UK	2003	2004
Imports from UK	£4,966,000	£8,603,000
Exports to UK	14,803,000	619,000

TRANSPORT INFRASTRUCTURE
The main ports are Monrovia, Buchanan and Greenville. There are 10,300 km of roads, of which 628 km are surfaced, and 490 km of railway track. Robertsfield International Airport and Spriggs Payne airfield are currently used for flights to other West African countries.

MEDIA
Radio is the main medium for news in Liberia. Many stations were shut down under President Taylor's rule, but there is now a growing number of them. Liberia has no television service.

LIBYA

Al-Jamāhīriyya Al-'Arabiyya Al-Lībiyya Ash-Sha'biyya Al-Ishtirākiyya – Great Socialist People's Libyan Arab Jamahiriya

AREA – 1,759,500 sq. km. Neighbours: Egypt and Sudan (east), Chad and Niger (south), Algeria and Tunisia (west)
POPULATION – 5,631,585 (2004 est.). The people of Libya are principally Arab with some Berbers in the west and some Tuareg tribesmen in the Fezzan. Islam is the official religion and the official language is Arabic
CAPITAL – ΨTripoli (Tarabulus) (population, 1,000,000, 1991 estimate)
MAJOR CITIES – ΨBangazi; ΨMisratah; Sirte
CURRENCY – Libyan dinar (LD) of 1,000 dirhams
NATIONAL ANTHEM – Allahu akbar [God is great]
NATIONAL DAY – 1 September
NATIONAL FLAG – Libya uses a plain emerald green flag
LIFE EXPECTANCY (years) – 76.28 (2004 est.)
MORTALITY RATE (per 1,000 population) – 3.48 (2004 est.)
INFANT MORTALITY (per 1,000 births) – 25.7 (2004 est.)
HIV / AIDS ADULT PREVALENCE – 0.2 per cent (2001 est.)
DEATH PENALTY – Yes
POPULATION GROWTH RATE – 2.37 per cent (2004 est.)
POPULATION DENSITY – 3 per sq. km (2002)

CLIMATE AND TERRAIN

Plains in the north rise to plateaus and depressions in the centre and south, with some hills on the north-west and north-east coasts and in the far south. The terrain is arid, and much of it is desert. Elevation extremes range from 2,267 m (Bikku Bitti) at the highest point to −47 m (Sabkhat Guzayyil) at the lowest. The climate is Mediterranean on the coast and hot and dry in the interior. Average temperatures in Tripoli range from 13°C in January to 31°C in August.

HISTORY AND POLITICS

Libya comprises the three ancient regions of Tripolitania, Cyrenaica and Phazzania (Fezzan). Tripolitania was settled by the Phoenicians in the seventh century BC and then became the eastern part of the kingdom of Carthage. Cyrenaica was colonised by the Greeks in the fourth century BC. All three regions became provinces of the Roman empire in the first century BC, and subsequently were under the control of the Byzantine empire until conquered by the Arabs in the seventh century AD, when Islam was introduced. Libya was part of the Turkish Ottoman empire from the mid-16th century until 1911, when the country was conquered by Italy despite fierce resistance, and made a colony. Libya suffered heavy fighting in the Second World War, and then came under British and French control until 24 December 1951, when it acheived independence as the Kingdom of Libya through a UN resolution.

The discovery of oil in 1959 made the country wealthy but created social problems. In 1969 the king was deposed in a military coup led by Colonel Muammar al-Gaddafi and a Revolutionary Command Council (RCC) was installed that proclaimed the country a republic. Economic activity, including the oil industry, was nationalised in the 1970s, but a degree of liberalisation was introduced in the late 1980s.

FOREIGN RELATIONS

After the 1969 revolution, Colonel Gaddafi developed a brand of Islamic socialism and sought to promote pan-Arab unity and Islam abroad. This led Libya to support militant and revolutionary groups and to become involved in international terrorism. Relationships with Western governments became increasingly strained and brought US military reprisals for terrorist activities in the 1980s. The worst of these terrorist attacks, the bombing of a Pan Am aircraft over Lockerbie, Scotland, in 1988, led to greater diplomatic isolation. UN sanctions were imposed in 1992 when Libya refused to extradite the two suspects in the case. Sanctions were suspended in 1999 after the suspects were handed over for trial under Scottish law at the International Court of Justice, and were lifted in 2003 after Libya admitted responsibility for the bombing and paid compensation.

Since the 2003 General People's Congress, Gaddafi has made further moves to end Libya's isolation, such as abandoning its development of weapons of mass destruction, and he promised in 2004 to allow UN nuclear weapons' inspections.

POLITICAL SYSTEM

Under the 1977 constitution, the head of state is the 'Leader of the Revolution', Col. Muammar al-Gaddafi. The legislature is the General People's Congress, which has 750 members appointed by local 'basic' and 'municipal' people's congresses for a three-year term, together with representatives from unions and other organisations. The General People's Congress is the highest policy-making body in the country. It appoints the General People's Committee, which exercises executive power; the Secretary-General of the General People's Committee is in effect the prime minister. The General People's Congress also has its own administrative secretariat. The Arab Socialist Union is the only legal political party.

Leader of the Revolution and Supreme Commander of the Armed Forces, Col. Muammar al-Gaddafi

SELECTED GOVERNMENT MEMBERS *as at July 2005*
Secretary-General (Prime Minister), Shukri Muhammad Ghanim
Assistant Secretary-General (Deputy Prime Minister), Al-Baghdadi Ali al-Mahmudi
Secretary, Economy and Trade, Abd-al-Qadir Umar Bilkhayr
Secretary, Finance, Mohamed Ali al-Houeiz
Secretary, Foreign Liaison and International Co-operation, Abdel Rahman Muhammad Shalgam

LIBYAN PEOPLE'S BUREAU
61–62 Ennismore Gardens, London SW7 1NH
T 020-7589 6120
Ambassador Extraordinary and Plenipotentiary, HE Muhammad Abu-al-Qasim al-Zawi, apptd 2001

BRITISH EMBASSY
Sharia Uahran 1, PO Box 4206, Tripoli
T (+ 218) (21) 340 3644/5
Ambassador Extraordinary and Plenipotentiary, HE Anthony Layden, apptd 2002

BRITISH COUNCIL
British Embassy, 24th Floor, Burj al Fatah, PO Box 4206, Tripoli
E info.libya@britishcouncil-ly.org
Director, Carl Reuter

DEFENCE

The Army has about 800 main battle tanks, 1,000 armoured infantry fighting vehicles and 945 armoured personnel carriers. The Navy has one submarine, one frigate, nine patrol and coastal vessels, and seven armed helicopters at seven bases. The Air Force has 400 combat aircraft and 41 armed helicopters.
MILITARY EXPENDITURE – 4.2 per cent of GDP (2003)
MILITARY PERSONNEL – 76,000: Army 45,000, Navy 8,000, Air Force 23,000
CONSCRIPTION DURATION – One to two years (selective)

ECONOMY AND TRADE

The economy is heavily dependent on the oil industry, which is state-controlled. Although the oil and gas sector is relatively undeveloped, in 2004 Libya signed an agreement with the Royal Dutch/Shell Group to development the country's gas resources. Oil accounts for 95 per cent of total exports, 30 per cent of GDP and 75 per cent of revenue; as Libya has a small population, this gives the country a comparatively high per capita GNI. However, attempts are being made to diversify the economy away from such reliance on oil. The manufacturing and construction sectors, which account for 20 per cent of GDP, have been expanded to include the production of petrochemicals, iron, steel and aluminium. The nature of the terrain means that Libya does not have a large agricultural sector and imports 75 per cent of its food.

Principal exports are oil, natural gas, wool, cattle, sheep and horses, olive oil, and hides and skins. Principal imports are machinery and transport equipment, foodstuffs, livestock, and most construction materials and consumer goods.

Italy is Libya's main trading partner; other trading partners include the UK, France and Germany.
GNI – US$6,700 per capita (2001)
ANNUAL AVERAGE GROWTH OF GDP – 21.8 per cent (2004 est.)
IMPORTS – US$4,400 (2002)
EXPORTS – US$8,000 (2002)

BALANCE OF PAYMENTS
Trade – US$2,974 million surplus (1999)
Current Account – US$2,136 million surplus (1999)

Trade with UK	2003	2004
Imports from UK	£241,056,000	£216,246,000
Exports to UK	202,093,000	196,047,000

TRANSPORT INFRASTRUCTURE

There are about 19,300 km of roads; the coastal road running from the Tunisian frontier through Tripoli, Benghazi and Tubruq to the Egyptian border, serves the main population centres. Main roads also link the provincial centres, and the oil-producing areas of the south with the coastal towns. Libya has had no railways in operation since 1965, though there are plans to reconstruct some systems. The main ports are Benghazi, Misurata and Tobruq.

EDUCATION

There are nine years of compulsory education. The Libyan education system allows for six years each at primary and secondary level.
ILLITERACY RATE – (m) 9.2 per cent; (f) 31.7 per cent (2000)
GROSS ENROLMENT RATIO (percentage of relevant age group) – primary 114 per cent (2002); secondary 105 per cent (2002); tertiary 58 per cent (2002)

MEDIA AND CULTURE

The state maintains strict control over the media. Great Jamahiriya TV is the state-run television broadcaster.

The Berber and Tuareg folk cultures have a strong influence in Libya. The rock paintings at Tadrart Acacus are believed to be at least 14,000 years old and in 1985 this area was designated a UNESCO World Heritage Site.

LIECHTENSTEIN

Fürstentum Liechtenstein – Principality of Liechtenstein

AREA – 160 sq. km. Neighbours: Austria, Switzerland
POPULATION – 33,436 (2004 est.). The language of the principality is Standard German. An Alemannic dialect is in general use. About 65.8 per cent of the population are Liechtensteiners, the remainder being mainly Swiss, Austrians and Germans. Roman Catholicism is the religion of 80.4 per cent of the population; there is a Protestant minority
CAPITAL – Vaduz (population, 5,038, 2002)
CURRENCY – Swiss franc of 100 rappen (or centimes)
NATIONAL ANTHEM – Oben am jungen Rhein [Up on the young Rhine]
NATIONAL DAY – 15 August
NATIONAL FLAG – Equal horizontal bands of blue over red; gold crown on blue band near staff
LIFE EXPECTANCY (years) – 79.4 (2004 est.)
MORTALITY RATE (per 1,000 population) – 6.94 (2004 est.)
INFANT MORTALITY (per 1,000 births) – 4.77 (2004 est.)
DEATH PENALTY – No (abolished 1987)
POPULATION GROWTH RATE – 0.86 per cent (2004 est.)
POPULATION DENSITY – 212 per sq. km (2001)

CLIMATE AND TERRAIN

Liechtenstein is a small landlocked principality in the Alps, with part of the Rhine river valley running through the west of the country. Elevation extremes range from 2,599 m (Grauspitz) at the highest point to 466 m (Ruggeller Riet) at the lowest. There is heavy snowfall in winter and average annual temperatures range from 0°C in January to 21°C in July.

HISTORY AND POLITICS

Although there was a sovereign state within the present boundaries from the 14th century, the present state of Liechtenstein was formed from the lordships of Schellenberg and Vaduz in 1719. Part of the Holy Roman Empire, the principality became a member of the Confederation of the Rhine that succeeded the Empire in 1806 during the Napoleonic occupation, and then of the German Confederation from 1815 until 1866. It was the only German principality to remain outside the German empire when it was formed in 1871. The country abolished its armed forces and declared permanent neutrality in 1868. The country's neutrality was not violated in either of the the World Wars.

Economic decline in the years following the First World War led Liechtenstein to adopt the Swiss currency in 1921 and to enter into a customs with Switzerland in 1923. The country became extremely prosperous as an international finance centre after the Second World War. However, it faced criticism in recent years about the laxness of its financial regulation, and in 2000 tightened its laws to prevent money laundering. Nevertheless, it was threatened with sanctions in 2002 for failing to meet international financial transparency and information exchange standards

Governments in the 20th century have been formed by the two main parties, each dominating at different periods: the northern-based Progressive Citizens' Party (FBP) from 1938 to 1970, and the southern-based Patriotic Union (VU) from 1970 to 2001, except for 1974–8. In the 2001 legislative election, the FBP returned to power for the first time since 1978, but although it remained the largest party after the February 2005 election, it did not have an overall majority and formed a coalition government with the VU. However, the government's power is limited by the role and power of the monarchy, which has resisted attempts at reform. Prince Hans Adam II threatened to step down as head of state when the government suggested a reducation in his powers in 1995, and a referendum in 2003 approved constitutional changes that give the monarchy greater powers over the government and judiciary. Prince Hans Adam remains head of state but in 2004 he handed over day-to-day responsibility for running the principality to his son and heir, Prince Alois.

POLITICAL SYSTEM
Under the 1921 constitution, Liechtenstein is a constitutional monarchy, with the hereditary prince as head of state. Constitutional reforms approved in 2003 increase the prince's power over the government and the judiciary, giving him the authority to dismiss the government. The unicameral legislature, the *Landtag*, has 25 members directly elected for a four-year term. There is a threshold of 8 per cent for parties to gain representation. The cabinet is appointed by the prince on the advice of the *Landtag* and consists of the head of government and four ministers.

HEAD OF STATE
HSH The Prince of Liechtenstein, Hans Adam II, *born* 14 February 1945; *succeeded* 13 November 1989
Heir, HSH Prince Alois, *born* 11 June 1968

SELECTED GOVERNMENT MEMBERS *as at July 2005*
Head of Government, Construction, Family Affairs and Equal Rights, Finance, General Government Affairs, Otmar Hasler
Deputy Head of Government, Economy, Justice, Sports, Klaus Tschutscher
Foreign Affairs, Culture, Family, Rita Kieber-Beck
Home Affairs, Public Health, Transport, Martin Meyer

BRITISH AMBASSADOR,
Basil Eastwood, CMG, resident at Bern, Switzerland

ECONOMY AND TRADE
Liechtenstein has a highly diversified economy with a strong financial services sector and a light industrial base.

In 1991 Liechtenstein became a member of the European Free Trade Association, and joined the European Economic Area in 1995.
GNI – US$40,000 per capita (2001)
ANNUAL AVERAGE GROWTH OF GDP – 11 per cent (1999)

Trade with UK	2003	2004
Imports from UK	£4,705,000	£7,866,000
Exports to UK	27,580,000	16,545,000

TRANSPORT INFRASTRUCTURE
Liechtenstein has no airports and only 250 km of highways and 18.5 km of railways.

MEDIA AND CULTURE
Liechtenstein relies on foreign broadcasters for television. Circulation for its two newspapers, *Liechtenstein News* and *Liechtensteiner Volksblatt*, is under 10,000. Due in part to its small size, Liechtenstein's cultural identity has been profoundly influenced by its neighbours. Joseph Rheinburger (1839–1901) is perhaps the country's most famous composer.

LITHUANIA

Lietuvos Respublika – Republic of Lithuania

AREA – 64,800 sq. km. Neighbours: Latvia (north), Belarus (east and south), Poland and the Kaliningrad region of the Russian Federation (south-west)
POPULATION – 3,607,899 (2004 est.): 80.6 per cent Lithuanian, 8.7 per cent Russian, 7 per cent Polish, 1.6 per cent Belarusian, 2.1 per cent other minority ethnic groups. The majority are Roman Catholic (79 per cent), with Russian Orthodox (4.1 per cent) and Lutheran minorities. Lithuanian is the state language
CAPITAL – Vilnius (population, 542,287, 2001 estimate)
MAJOR CITIES – Kaunas; Klaipeda
CURRENCY – Litas of 100 centas, pegged to the euro
NATIONAL ANTHEM – Tautiska giesme [The national song]
NATIONAL DAY – 16 February (Independence Day)
NATIONAL FLAG – Three horizontal stripes of yellow, green and red
LIFE EXPECTANCY (years) – 73.46 (2004 est.)
MORTALITY RATE (per 1,000 population) – 11.03 (2004 est.)
INFANT MORTALITY (per 1,000 births) – 7.13 (2004 est.)
HIV / AIDS ADULT PREVALENCE – 0.1 per cent (2001 est.)
DEATH PENALTY – No (abolished 1998)
POPULATION GROWTH RATE – –0.33 (2004 est.)
POPULATION DENSITY – 54 per sq. km (2002)
URBAN POPULATION – 69 per cent (2001)

CLIMATE AND TERRAIN
Lithuania is a low-lying country with low hills in the west and south-east. It contains over 2,800 lakes, many of which lie in the east of the country. Elevation extremes range from 292 m (Kalnas) at the highest point to 0 m (Baltic Sea) at the lowest. The climate is mainly continental and average annual temperatures range from −3°C in January to 17°C in July.

HISTORY AND POLITICS

Lithuania became a nation in the late 12th century. It remained pagan for far longer than any other European country and only became fully Christian in the 15th century, when the Samogitians and the Aukstaitiai, the two main ethnic groups in the region, were converted. In the 14th century a strong grand duchy was formed that stretched from the Baltic to the Black Sea and eastwards nearly to Moscow, and it confederated with Poland in the 16th century, before coming under Russian rule in 1795. The country joined Poland in rebelling against Russian domination twice in the 19th century.

Occupied by Germany during the First World War, in 1918 Lithuania declared its independence and successfully defended this against the Bolsheviks in 1918–19. However, the province and city of Vilnius were occupied by the newly independent Poland from 1920 until 1939. The Soviet Union invaded and annexed Lithuania in 1940, but Lithuania revolted in 1941 and briefly established its own government before being invaded and occupied by the Germans in their 1941 offensive against the Soviet Union; around 210,000 Lithuanians, mainly Jews, were killed during the German occupation. Soviet troops ousted the Germans in 1944 and re-established Soviet control, against which Lithuanians carried on a guerrilla war until 1952.

Growing nationalist sentiment led to the formation of the pro-democracy Sajudis (The Movement) in 1988 to campaign for greater autonomy. A unilateral declaration of independence in 1990 was blocked by the Soviet Union but following the failed August coup in Moscow, in 1991 Lithuania declared its independence, and this was internationally recognised. The last Russian troops left the country in 1993.

Lithuania joined the EU in 2004. Its parliament ratified the EU constitution in November 2004.

Rolandas Paksas was elected president in January 2003 but became embroiled in allegations of corruption and was impeached and dismissed in April 2004. Valdus Adamkus was elected president in June 2004. In the October legislative elections, the Labour Party became the largest party but without a majority, and in November the ruling coalition of the Social Democratic Party (SD) and New Union (Social Liberals) (NS(SL)) was widened to include the Labour Party and the Union of Farmers Democracy Party. Algirdas Brazauskas, the last communist-era leader, president 1993–8 and prime minister since 2001, remained in office as prime minister.

POLITICAL SYSTEM

Under the 1992 constitution, the head of state is a president, who is directly elected for a five-year term, renewable only once. Legislative power is exercised by the unicameral parliament, the *Seimas*, which has 141 members who are directly elected for a four-year term; 71 members are elected in first past the post constituencies and 70 by proportional representation, with a 5 per cent threshold for representation. Executive authority is vested in the prime minister, who is appointed by the president with the approval of the *Seimas*, and ministers, who are appointed upon the recommendation of the prime minister.

HEAD OF STATE

President, Valdas Adamkus, *sworn in* 12 July 2004

SELECTED GOVERNMENT MEMBERS *as at July 2005*

Prime Minister, Algirdas Brazauskas
Defence, Gediminas Kirkilas
Finance, Zigmantas Balcytis
Foreign Affairs, Antanas Valionis
Interior, Gintautas Furmanavicius

EMBASSY OF THE REPUBLIC OF LITHUANIA
84 Gloucester Place, London W1U 6AU T 020-7486 6401/2
E chancery@lithuanianembassy.co.uk
Ambassador Extraordinary and Plenipotentiary, HE
    Aurimas Taurantas, apptd 2002

BRITISH EMBASSY
2 Antakalnio, LT-2055 Vilnius T (+370) (2) 222 070/1
Ambassador Extraordinary and Plenipotentiary, HE Colin
    Roberts, apptd 2004

BRITISH COUNCIL
Business Centre 2000, Jogailos 4, LT 2001 Vilnius
T (+370) 5 264 4890/1 E lina.balenaite@britishcouncil.lt
Director, Lina Balenaite

DEFENCE

The Army has 177 armoured personnel carriers; the Navy has two frigates and five patrol and coastal vessels based at Klaipeda; the Air Force has eight helicopters.

Lithuania joined NATO in 2004.

MILITARY EXPENDITURE – 1.8 per cent of GDP (2003)
MILITARY PERSONNEL – 13,510: Army 11,600, Navy
    710, Air Force 1,200; Paramilitaries 14,600
CONSCRIPTION DURATION – 12 months

ECONOMY AND TRADE

Attempts to transform Lithuania into a free-market economy directly after the fall of communism pushed the country into deep recession. Recovery in the mid-1990s was hampered by the Russian financial crisis of 1998, when Lithuania lost 20 per cent of its export market. Recovery has come courtesy of exports to the European Union, though unemployment remains high. The EU now takes 50 per cent of Lithuania's exports and large-scale privatisation has led to Lithuania being confirmed as a functioning market economy by the European Commission. Lithuania joined the World Trade Organisation in 2001.

Lithuania has a diverse economy, and industries include the mining and cutting of amber, metal-cutting machine tools, electric motors, television sets, refrigerators and freezers, petroleum refining, shipbuilding, furniture making, textiles, food processing, fertilizers, agricultural machinery, optical equipment, electronic components and computers.

GNI – US$12,700 million (2002); US$3,670 per capita
    (2002)
ANNUAL AVERAGE GROWTH OF GDP – 5.9 per cent
    (2001 est.)
INFLATION RATE – 1.3 per cent (2001 est.)
UNEMPLOYMENT – 15.4 per cent (2000 est.)
TOTAL EXTERNAL DEBT – US$4,855 million (2000 est.)
FOREIGN DIRECT INVESTMENT – US$2,417 million
    (1997–2000)
IMPORTS – US$10,000 million (2003)
EXPORTS – US$7,000 million (2003)

BALANCE OF PAYMENTS
Trade – US$1,704 million deficit (2003)
Current Account – US$1,278 million deficit (2003)

Trade with UK	2003	2004
Imports from UK	£188,440,000	£68,704,000
Exports to UK	290,168,000	105,632,000

TRANSPORT INFRASTRUCTURE
There are 71,375 km of roads, and a relatively well-developed railway system of 2,898 km running east to west and north to south and linking the major towns with Vilnius and Klaipeda, the main port. Vilnius has an international airport.

EDUCATION
Lithuania re-established a national education system in 1990. Education is free of charge and compulsory from seven to 16 years, with the system comprising elementary schools (four years), nine-year schools (five years), and secondary schools (three years). The language of instruction is predominantly Lithuanian, but there are also Russian and Polish schools. There are 105 vocational schools and 65 colleges. Lithuania has eight universities and seven other institutes of higher education. Vilnius University, founded in 1579, is one of the oldest universities in eastern Europe.
ILLITERACY RATE – (m) 0.3 per cent; (f) 0.5 per cent (2000)
GROSS ENROLMENT RATIO (percentage of relevant age group) – primary 104 per cent (2002); secondary 98 per cent (2004); tertiary 59 per cent (2002)

MEDIA
The largest selling daily newspapers are *Lietuvos Rytas* and *Lietuvos Aidas*. A mix of public and private television broadcasters operate. BTV is the largest commercial company while LTV is the publicly run station.

LUXEMBOURG

Groussherzogtom Lëtzebuerg / Grand-Duché de Luxembourg / Großherzogtum Luxembourg – Grand Duchy of Luxembourg

AREA – 2,586 sq. km. Neighbours: Germany (east), Belgium (west and north), France (south)
POPULATION – 462,690 (2004 est.), nearly all Roman Catholic. The officially designated 'national language' is Lëtzebuergesch (Luxembourgish), a mainly spoken language. French and German are the official languages for written purposes, and French is the language of administration
CAPITAL – Luxembourg (population, 77,400, 1996)
CURRENCY – Euro (€) of 100 cents
NATIONAL ANTHEM – Ons hémécht [Our homeland]
NATIONAL DAY – 23 June
NATIONAL FLAG – Three horizontal bands, red, white and blue
LIFE EXPECTANCY (years) – 78.58 (2004 est.)
MORTALITY RATE (per 1,000 population) – 8.42 (2004 est.)
INFANT MORTALITY (per 1,000 births) – 4.88 (2004 est.)
HIV / AIDS ADULT PREVALENCE – 0.2 per cent (2001 est.)
DEATH PENALTY – No (abolished 1979)
POPULATION GROWTH RATE – 1.28 per cent (2004 est.)
POPULATION DENSITY – 171 per sq. km (2001)

CLIMATE AND TERRAIN
A landlocked principality, Luxembourg has the forested plateau of the Ardennes in the north, forming part of the Natural Germano-Luxembourg Park which extends east into Germany. The south of the country is mainly fertile farmland and in the east is the wine-growing region of the Moselle valley. Elevation extremes range from 559 m (Buurgplaatz) at the highest point to 133 m (Moselle River) at the lowest. The climate is mild and average temperatures range from 1°C in January to 22°C in July.

HISTORY AND POLITICS
The area was part of the Roman Empire and then became part of the Frankish Empire in the fifth century AD. It became autonomous within the Holy Roman Empire under Siegfried, Count of Ardennes and was given the status of a duchy in 1354. Controlled by a succession of European powers after 1437, when the House of Luxembourg died out, after the Napoleonic wars Luxembourg was made a grand duchy and passed to the Netherlands. Much of Luxembourg joined the Belgians in their revolt against the Netherlands in 1830; in 1838 the western, French-speaking region was assigned to Belgium, and the remainder of the grand duchy was granted autonomy. The Treaty of London in 1867 confirmed its independence and neutrality. Occupation by Germany in both World Wars prompted Luxembourg to give up its neutrality and it was a founding member of NATO in 1949.

Luxembourg entered into economic union with Belgium in 1921 and joined the Benelux economic union in 1948. It was a founder member of the European Economic Community in 1958 and joined the euro zone in 1999. A referendum in July 2005 approved ratification of the EU constitution.

In the 2004 legislative election, the Christian Social Party (CSV) won the largest number of seats but without an overall majority. It formed a new coalition goverment with the Luxembourg Socialist Workers' Party (LSWP), the second largest party, under the leadership of Jean-Claude Juncker, who has been prime minister since 1995.

POLITICAL SYSTEM
Under the 1868 constitution, the head of state is a hereditary grand duke. There is a unicameral legislature, the Chamber of Deputies, which has 60 members directly elected for a five-year term. There is also a Council of State, which has 21 members nominated by the grand duke; this acts as the supreme administrative tribunal and has some legislative functions. The prime minister is appointed by the grand duke on the basis of the election results and appoints the cabinet.

HEAD OF STATE
HRH The Grand Duke of Luxembourg, HRH Grand Duke Henri, *born* 16 April 1955, *succeeded* 7 October 2000
Heir, HRH Prince Guillaume, *born* 11 November 1981

SELECTED GOVERNMENT MEMBERS *as at July 2005*
Prime Minister, Finance, Jean-Claude Juncker
Foreign Affairs, Immigration, Jean Asselborn
Justice, Defence, Treasury and Budget, Luc Frieden
Economy and Foreign Trade, Jeannot Krecke
Home Affairs, Jean-Marie Halsdorf

EMBASSY OF LUXEMBOURG
27 Wilton Crescent, London SW1X 8SD T 020-7235 6961
Ambassador Extraordinary and Plenipotentiary, HE Jean-Louis Wolzfeld, apptd 2002

BRITISH EMBASSY
14 Boulevard Roosevelt, L-2450 Luxembourg
T (+352) 229861/5/6
Ambassador Extraordinary and Plenipotentiary, HE James
Clarke, apptd 2004

DEFENCE

For legal reasons, NATO's squadron of E-3A Sentry
airborne early warning aircraft is registered in
Luxembourg.
MILITARY EXPENDITURE – 0.9 per cent of GDP (2003)
MILITARY PERSONNEL – Army 900; Paramilitaries 612

ECONOMY AND TRADE

The economy was dominated by steel production, which
still comprises a quarter of the country's exports, but it has
diversified its industrial sector to include rubber and
chemicals. The financial sector now comprises 22 per cent
of the GDP. Strong growth, low inflation and low
unemployment mean that Luxembourg enjoys an
exceptionally high standard of living. The small
agricultural sector consists mainly of family-owned farms.
GNI – US$17,570 million (2001); US$39,840 per capita
(2001)
ANNUAL AVERAGE GROWTH OF GDP – 2.3 per cent
(2004 est.)
INFLATION RATE – 2 per cent (2003 est.)
UNEMPLOYMENT – 3.6 per cent (2003 est.)
IMPORTS – US$14,000 (2003)
EXPORTS – US$10,000 (2003)

BALANCE OF PAYMENTS
Trade – US$2,463 million deficit (2003)
Current Account – US$2,492 million surplus (2003)

Trade with UK	2003	2004
Imports from UK	£208,047,000	£255,524,000
Exports to UK	422,203,000	821,841,000

TRANSPORT INFRASTRUCTURE

Luxembourg has two airports, with 38,200 aircraft
departures each year. There are 5,189 km of highways
(including 114 km of motorways), and 274 km of
railways.

MEDIA

Media group RTL broadcasts to audiences in France,
Germany and the UK as well as serving the domestic
market. Luxembourg also hosts the Société Européenne
des Satellites (SES), which operates the Astra satellite fleet,
Europe's largest satellite operation. The two best-selling
daily newspapers in Luxembourg are *Luxembuger Wort*
and *Tageblatt*.

MACEDONIA

Republika Makedonija – Republic of Macedonia

AREA – 25,713 sq. km. Neighbours: Serbia (north),
Bulgaria (east), Greece (south), Albania (west)
POPULATION – 2,071,210 (2004 est.): 66.5 per cent
Macedonian, 22.9 per cent Albanian, 4.0 per cent
ethnic Turks, 2.3 per cent Romanies, 2.0 per cent Serbs
and 0.4 per cent Vlachs. The census results are disputed
by the ethnic Albanians and Serbs. Macedonian
Orthodox Christianity is the majority religion, with a

Muslim minority. The main language is Macedonian (a
south Slavic language), which is written in the Cyrillic
script
CAPITAL – Skopje (population, 429,964, 1994)
MAJOR CITIES – Bitola; Kumanovo; Prilep
CURRENCY – Denar of 100 deni
NATIONAL ANTHEM – Denes nad Makedonija se radja
novo sonce na slobodata [Today a new sun of liberty
appears over Macedonia]
NATIONAL FLAG – Red with an eight-rayed sun displayed
over the whole field
LIFE EXPECTANCY (years) – 74.73 (2004 est.)
MORTALITY RATE (per 1,000 population) – 7.83
(2004 est.)
INFANT MORTALITY RATE (per 1,000 births) – 11.74
(2004 est.)
HIV / AIDS ADULT PREVALENCE – 0.1 per cent
(2001 est.)
DEATH PENALTY – No (abolished 1991)
POPULATION BELOW POVERTY LINE – 24 per cent
(2001)
POPULATION GROWTH RATE – 0.39 per cent (2004
est.)
POPULATION DENSITY – 80 per sq. km (2002)
URBAN POPULATION – 62 per cent (2000)
MILITARY EXPENDITURE – 3.1 per cent of GDP (2003)
MILITARY PERSONNEL – Army 9,760; Paramilitaries
7,600
CONSCRIPTION DURATION – Six months
GROSS ENROLMENT RATIO (percentage of relevant age
group) – primary 99 per cent (2002); secondary 85 per
cent (2002); tertiary 24 per cent (2002)

CLIMATE AND TERRAIN

The landlocked country is a mountainous plateau divided
by the valleys of the rivers Struma and Vardar. Elevation
extremes range from 2,753 m (Golem Korab) at the
highest point to 50 m (Vardar River) at the lowest. Lakes
Ohrid and Prespa lie on the south-west border with
Albania. The climate is Mediterranean, average
temperatures ranging from 1°C in January to 23°C in July.

HISTORY AND POLITICS

The area of the former Yugoslav republic was part of the
ancient kingdom of Macedonia, which also included
northern Greece and south-west Bulgaria, in the fourth
century BC. Macedonia became a province of the Roman
empire in the second century BC, coming under the
control of the Byzantine empire from the fourth century
AD. Slav peoples settled the area in the seventh century
and mixed with the Greek, Illyrian, Thracian, Scythian
and Turkish peoples. From the ninth to the 14th centuries
it was under the rule successively of the Bulgars,
Byzantium and Serbs, and became part of the Islamic
Ottoman empire in the late 14th century. The Russo-
Turkish war of 1877–8 concluded with a treaty that gave
Macedonia to the newly independent Bulgaria, but the
other European powers, unhappy at the prospect of a
powerful Bulgaria allied to Russia, forced Bulgaria to
return Macedonia to Turkey. After this, a nationalist
movement emerged that campaigned for independence
but to little effect, and following the Balkan wars of 1912
and 1913 the country was partitioned between Bulgaria,
Serbia and Greece. The Serbian part was awarded to the
newly created state that became Yugoslavia after the First
World War. During the Second World War, this area was
occupied by Bulgaria from 1941 to 1944, and after

liberation became a republic within the communist Federal Republic of Yugoslavia.

Nationalist sentiment grew after the death of the Yugoslav leader Josip Tito in 1980, and Macedonia formally seceded from Yugoslavia in 1992 following a referendum in favour of independence in September 1991. International recognition was initially held up by Greece's objections to the republic's name (Greece claims that its region of Macedonia is the only one entitled to the name), but the country joined the UN in 1993 as the Former Yugoslav Republic of Macedonia; Greece recognised it under this name and lifted its trade blockade in 1995. UN and US peacekeeping troops arrived in 1992 and 1993 to prevent the conflict in Bosnia-Hercegovina spreading to Macedonia, but were withdrawn in 1998 after China vetoed the renewal of their mandate.

Throughout the 1990s there was tension and sporadic violence between the ethnic Albanians and Macedonians. Instability in neighbouring Kosovo spilled over into Macedonia in 2001, and in April 2001 there was an uprising by ethnic Albanian separatists aggrieved at their lack of civil rights. NATO negotiated a cease-fire in June and deployed peacekeeping troops in August 2001. Peace talks facilitated by international bodies resulted in the Ohrid Framework Agreement, giving Albanians greater recognition within Macedonia and making Albanian an official language. The insurgents were disarmed and most displaced persons returned to their homes. In 2003, NATO handed over peacekeeping duties to the EU. Since the peace agreement, over $500 million of aid has been pledged to aid reconstruction.

In the 2002 elections to the Assembly, the largest number of seats was won by Together for Macedonia (ZMZ), a coalition of the Social Democratic Alliance of Macedonia (SDSM) and the Liberal Democratic Party (LDP), with 59 of the 120 seats. The Internal Macedonian Revolutionary Organisation – Democratic Party for Macedonian National Unity (VMRO-DMPNE) won 34 seats. A multi-ethnic coalition government, including members of the SDSM, the LDP and the ethnic Albanian Democratic Union for Integration (BDI), took office in November.

President Trajkovski, elected in 1999, died in an air crash in February 2004. The prime minister Branko Crvenkovski was elected to replace him as president in April 2004. Hari Kostov was appointed prime minister in place of Crvenkovski but resigned in November 2004 following policy disputes in the coalition. Former defence minister Vlado Buckovski was named as the new prime minister on 26 November.

POLITICAL SYSTEM
The 1991 constitution was amended in 2001 to incorporate provisions relating to ethnic Albanian rights and in 2004 to give ethnic Albanians greater local autonomy in areas where they predominate. Under the constitution, the head of state is a president directly elected for a five-year term. The unicameral Assembly *(Sobranie)* has 120 members directly elected for a four year term. The prime minister is appointed by the president. Government ministers are elected by the Assembly but not members of it.

HEAD OF STATE
President, Branko Crvenkovski, *elected*, 28 April 2004,
sworn in, 12 May 2004

SELECTED GOVERNMENT MEMBERS *as at July 2005*
Prime Minister, Vlado Buckovski
Deputy Prime Ministers, Musa Xhaferi; Radmila
Sekerinska; Minco Jordanov; Jovan Manasievski
Foreign Affairs, Ilinka Mitreva
Interior, Ljubomir Mihajlovski
Finance, Nikola Popovski

EMBASSY OF THE REPUBLIC OF MACEDONIA
5th Floor, 25 James Street, London W1U 1DU
T 020 7935 2823
Ambassador Extraordinary and Plenipotentiary, HE Gjorgji
Spasov, apptd 2003

BRITISH EMBASSY
Dimitrija Chupovski 4/26, Skopje 1000 T (+389) (2) 3299 299
Ambassador Extraordinary and Plenipotentiary, HE Robert
Chatterton-Dickson, apptd 2004

BRITISH COUNCIL
Bulevar Goce Delcev 6, PO Box 562, MK-1000 Skopje
T (+389) (2) 135 035 E info@britishcouncil.org.mk
Director, Andrew Hadley

ECONOMY AND TRADE
Macedonia has attempted to transform its economy into a market-orientated one since 1992. Over half the economy has been privatised, but it suffered during the trade embargo by Greece (1993–5) and the country remains poor, with high unemployment. In March 2004, the government applied to join the EU, but Macedonia has a long way to go to rebuild the economy, and to fight crime and corruption, which are factors detering foreign investment. A 1999 economic co-operation agreement with Albania covers energy, mining and trade.

In 2000, 63 per cent of GDP was produced by the service industries, 25 per cent by industry, and 12 per cent by agriculture. The main exports are textiles, tobacco, wine, zinc, iron ore and iron products. The main imports are oil, energy, telecommunications equipment, metal goods, foodstuffs and pharmaceuticals.

GNI – US$3,500 million (2002); US$1,710 per capita
(2002)
ANNUAL AVERAGE GROWTH OF GDP – 1.3 per cent
(2004 est.)
INFLATION RATE – 1.1 per cent (2002 est.)
TOTAL EXTERNAL DEBT – US$1,465 million (2000 est.)
IMPORTS – US$2,200 million (2003)
EXPORTS – US$1,400 million (2003)

BALANCE OF PAYMENTS
Trade – US$768 million deficit (2002)
Current Account – US$325 million deficit (2002)

Trade with UK	2003	2004
Imports from UK	£18,590,000	£19,756,000
Exports to UK	24,496,000	28,520,000

TRANSPORT INFRASTRUCTURE
Macedonia has 8,216 km of roads, of which 4,900 km are surfaced. There are 699 km of railways, of which 233 km are electrified. A 53 km railway line from Beljakovci to the Bulgarian border was scheduled for completion in 2005 but remains under construction. The principal airport is at Skopje, and there are a further 17 around the country.

MEDIA

The three channels of the state-run television broadcaster compete with a growing number of commercial stations. There are 11 major daily and weekly press publications, reflecting a range of views. *Nova Makedonija* is the leading newspaper and is partially government-owned.

MADAGASCAR

Repoblikan'i Madagasikara / République de Madagascar – Republic of Madagascar

AREA – 587,041 sq. km

POPULATION – 17,501,871 (2004 est.). The people are of mixed Malayo-Polynesian, Arab and African origin. There are sizeable French, Chinese and Indian communities. The official languages are Malagasy and French

CAPITAL – Antananarivo (population, 2,000,000, 1998 estimate)

MAJOR CITIES – ΨAntsiranana; Fianarantsoa; ΨMahajanga; ΨToamasina, the chief port

CURRENCY – Franc malgache (FMG) of 100 centimes

NATIONAL ANTHEM – Ry tanindrazanay malala o [O, our beloved country]

NATIONAL DAY – 26 June (Independence Day)

NATIONAL FLAG – Equal horizontal bands of red (above) and green, with vertical white band by staff

LIFE EXPECTANCY (years) – 56.54 (2004 est.)

MORTALITY RATE (per 1,000 population) – 11.62 (2004 est.)

INFANT MORTALITY (per 1,000 births) – 78.52 (2004 est.)

HIV / AIDS ADULT PREVALENCE – 1.7 per cent (2003 est.)

DEATH PENALTY – No (abolished 1958)

POPULATION GROWTH RATE – 3.03 per cent (2004 est.)

POPULATION DENSITY – 28 per sq. km (2002)

MILITARY EXPENDITURE – 1.5 per cent of GDP (2003)

MILITARY PERSONNEL – 13,500: Army 12,500, Navy 500, Air Force 500; Paramilitaries 8,100

CONSCRIPTION DURATION – 18 months

CLIMATE AND TERRAIN

Madagascar, the fourth largest island in the world, lies 240 miles off the south-east coast of Africa, from which it is separated by the Mozambique Channel. Coastal plains rise to central highlands indented with river valleys. The terrain is arid in the south. Elevation extremes range from 2,876 m (Maromokotro) at the highest point to 0 m (Indian Ocean) at the lowest. Because of its isolation, most mammals and plants and half of its bird species are unique to the island. The climate is tropical along the coastline and temperate in the highlands. Average temperatures range from 9°C in July to 29°C in January. Madagascar is subject to tropical cyclones, which cause torrential rain and flooding.

HISTORY AND POLITICS

The island was settled by Indonesians from the first century AD and by African traders from the eighth century. Although first visited by Europeans c.1500, local kingdoms ruled until 1885, when the island became a French protectorate; it became a colony in 1895 after the last indigenous resistance was defeated. During the Second World War the British invaded to replace the pro-Vichy government with a Free French government. At the end of the war Madagascar was returned to France, which suppressed a nationalist uprising in 1947–8. Nationalist agitation continued throughout the 1950s and resulted in independence in 1960.

The military took control in 1972 following civil disturbances, and in 1975 martial law was imposed after a coup, and a Marxist one-party state was created with Lt.-Com. Didier Ratsiraka as president. Marxism was abandoned in 1980 and, following pro-democracy agitation throughout the 1980s and early 1990s, other political parties were legalised in 1990 and a new constitution, adopted in 1992, made Madagascar a parliamentary democracy.

Didier Ratsiraka was defeated in the 1993 presidential elections but returned to office in 1997 after winning the 1996 election. In the first round of voting in the December 2001 presidential election there were allegations of vote-rigging by both candidates and the ensuing civil unrest brought the country close to civil war. A recount of the votes in April 2002 showed that Marc Ravalomanana had won the election and he was sworn in as president in May. Ratsiraka refused to accept the result at first and violence continued until July, when Ratsiraka went into exile and his supporters surrendered.

The first elections to the Senate were held in March 2001; the majority of seats are held by the I Love Madagascar party (TIM), which supports President Ravalomanana. TIM also won the majority of seats in the December 2002 election to the National Assembly.

POLITICAL SYSTEM

The 1992 constitution was amended in 1998 to create an upper chamber in the parliament, increase the powers of the presidency and increase the autonomy of the six provinces. The president is directly elected and serves a five-year term. The legislature is bicameral. The National Assembly has 160 members directly elected for a five-year term. The Senate has 90 members, of whom two-thirds are elected by an electoral college and one-third are nominated by the president; they serve a six-year term. The prime minister is appointed by the president, and appoints the ministers.

HEAD OF STATE
President Marc Ravalomanana, *elected* 29 April 2002, *sworn in* 6 May 2002, *accepted* 5 July 2002.

SELECTED GOVERNMENT MEMBERS *as at July 2005*
Prime Minister, Jacques Sylla
Defence, Maj.-Gen. Petera Behajaina
Foreign Affairs, Gen. Marcel Ranjeva
Finance and Economy, Benjamin Andriamparany Radavidson

EMBASSY OF THE REPUBLIC OF MADAGASCAR
4 avenue Raphael, F- 75016 Paris, France
T (+ 33) (1) 4504 6211
Ambassador Plenipotentiary and Extraordinary, Guy Rakatomena, apptd 2004

BRITISH EMBASSY
Lot II, 164 Ter Alarobia Ambonilioa, BP 167, Antananarivo 101
T (+ 261) (20) 2249378/9
Ambassador Extraordinary and Plenipotentiary, HE Brian Donaldson, apptd 2002

HIV / AIDS ADULT PREVALENCE – 0.4 per cent (2003 est.)

DEATH PENALTY – Yes

POPULATION GROWTH RATE – 1.83 per cent (2004 est.)

POPULATION DENSITY – 74 per sq. km (2002)

URBAN POPULATION – 58 per cent (2001)

ILLITERACY RATE – (m) 8 per cent; (f) 14.6 per cent (2002 est.)

GROSS ENROLMENT RATIO (percentage of relevant age group) – primary 95 per cent (2002); secondary 70 per cent (2002); tertiary 26 per cent (2002)

CLIMATE AND TERRAIN

Malaysia comprises the 11 states of peninsular Malaya plus Sabah and Sarawak on the island of Borneo. Each is separated from the other by about 640 miles of the South China Sea. The Malay peninsula, which extends from the isthmus of Kra to the Singapore Strait, is a plain with two highland areas in the north. The Malaysian part of Borneo is mostly high plateau, rising to mountains in western Sabah and eastern Sarawak, while Sarawak also has lower-lying land along the coast and in the Rajang river valley. Elevation extremes range from 4,100 m (Gunung Kinabalu, Sabah) at the highest point to 0 m (Indian Ocean) at the lowest. There are monsoon seasons in the south-west of the country from April to October and from October to February in the north-east. Average temperatures in Kuala Lumpur range from 22°C in January to 31°C in September.

HISTORY AND POLITICS

Malaysia formed part of the Srivijaya empire in the ninth to 14th centuries. From the 16th century, the Portuguese, Dutch and British vied for control in the region. The British possessions of Singapore, Penang and Malacca were formed in 1826 into the Straits Settlement, which became a Crown colony in 1867. British protection was extended over four Malay states, which federated in 1896, and protection treaties were agreed with several other states between 1885 and 1930. Following occupation by the Japanese from 1941 to 1945, the United Malay National Organisation (UMNO) was founded in 1946 to oppose plans for centralisation. The nine peninsular states were federated as the Federation of Malaya in 1948.

An armed insurrection by communist guerrillas began in 1948 and was suppressed by British forces (the Malayan Emergency) by the mid-1950s, although formally it ended only in 1960. In 1957 the Federation of Malaya became independent, and in 1963 it combined with Singapore, Sarawak and Sabah to form the Federation of Malaysia; Singapore withdrew from the federation in 1965. From 1963 to 1966 guerrillas opposed to federation and supported by Indonesia, which claimed territory in eastern Malaysia, carried on an intermittent war.

UMNO has dominated post-independence political life, initially as the governing party and since 1971 as the dominant partner in the Barisan Nasional (National Front) coalition governments. Mahathir bin Muhammad became prime minister in 1981 and his 22-year tenure of office saw increasingly authoritarian rule, particularly as opposition to Malay dominance of political life grew in the 1980s and 1990s. There is considerable tension between the ethnic groups in Malaysia; Malay resentment of the large Chinese minority's economic dominance led to the adoption in 1971 of policies that favour ethnic Malays in education and employment, although the

Chinese remain the wealthiest section of society. In recent years there has been intercommunal violence between ethnic Indians, the poorest group, and Malays.

In the 2004 legislative election, the Barisan Nasional party retained its large majority in the House of Representatives, with 198 seats, and prime minister Abdullah Ahmed Badawi, appointed in 2003, formed a new coalition government.

POLITICAL SYSTEM

The 1957 constitution provides for a federal government and a degree of autonomy for the state governments. The head of state is the *Yang di-Pertuan Agong* (supreme head of state) who is elected by the rulers from among their number and serves a five-year term. The Malay rulers are either chosen or succeed to their position in accordance with the custom of their particular state; in other states of Malaysia, choice of the head of state is at the discretion of the Yang di-Pertuan Agong after consultation with the chief minister of the state.

The federal legislature has two houses, the House of Representatives and the Senate. The House of Representatives *(Dewan Rakyat)* is the lower house and has 219 members, directly elected for a five-year term. The Senate *(Dewan Negara)* has 70 members who serve a six-year term; the legislative assembly of each state elects two members to the Senate, and 44 are nominated by the head of state.

FEDERAL STRUCTURE

Each state has its own constitution, which may not be inconsistent with the federal constitution. The ruler or governor acts on the advice of an executive council appointed on the advice of the chief minister and a single-chamber legislative assembly. The legislative assemblies are elected on the same basis as the federal House of Representatives.

HEAD OF STATE

Supreme Head of State, HM Tuanku Syed Sirajuddin Putra Jamalullail *(Yang di-Pertuan Agong of Perlis), sworn in* 13 December 2001

SELECTED GOVERNMENT MEMBERS *as at July 2005*
Prime Minister, Finance, Abdullah Ahmed Badawi
Deputy Prime Minister, Defence, Najib Tun Razak
Foreign Affairs, Hamid bin Jaafer Albar
Home Affairs, Azmi bin Khalid

MALAYSIAN HIGH COMMISSION
45 Belgrave Square, London SW1X 8QT
T 020-7235 8033 E mwlondon@btinternet.com
High Commissioner, HE Abd Aziz bin Mohammed

BRITISH HIGH COMMISSION
185 Jalan Ampang 50450 Kuala Lumpur *or* PO Box 11030, 50732 Kuala Lumpur T (+ 60) (3) 2170 2200
High Commissioner, HE Bruce Cleghorn, CMG, apptd 2001

BRITISH COUNCIL
Ground Floor, West Block, Wisma Selangor Dredging 142 C Jalan Ampang 50450 Kuala Lumpur T (+ 60) (3) 2723 7900
E kualalumpur@britishcouncil.org.my
Director, Gerry Liston

DEFENCE

The Army has 1,020 armoured personnel carriers. The Navy has four frigates, 41 patrol and coastal vessels and six armed helicopters at four bases. The Air Force has 73 combat aircraft.

MILITARY EXPENDITURE – 2.3 per cent of GDP (2003)
MILITARY PERSONNEL – 110,000: Army 80,000, Navy 15,000, Air Force 15,000; Paramilitaries 20,100

ECONOMY AND TRADE

The economy grew vigorously in the 1980s, although growth slowed following the Asian financial crisis of 1997. Its highly developed industrial production includes rubber manufacturing, palm oil processing, electronics, tin mining and smelting, and logging and timber processing; petroleum is produced in Sabah and Sarawak, and refined in Sarawak, which also processes agricultural produce.

GNI – US$86,100 million (2002); US$3,540 per capita (2002)
ANNUAL AVERAGE GROWTH OF GDP – 7.1 per cent (2004 est.)
INFLATION RATE – 1.1 per cent (2002 est.)
UNEMPLOYMENT – 3.1 per cent (2000 est.)
TOTAL EXTERNAL DEBT – US$41,797 million (2000 est.)
FOREIGN DIRECT INVESTMENT – US$13,319 million (1997–2000)
IMPORTS – US$81,900 million (2003)
EXPORTS – US$99,400 million (2003)

BALANCE OF PAYMENTS
Trade – US$18,135 million surplus (2002)
Current Account – US$7,190 million surplus (2002)

Trade with UK	2003	2004
Imports from UK	£1,040,389,000	£996,065,000
Exports to UK	1,915,245,000	2,068,415,000

TRANSPORT INFRASTRUCTURE

There are six main ports in peninsular Malaysia plus Kita Kinabalu (Sabah) and Kuching (Sarawak), as well as 7,296 km of navigable waterways. There are 65,877 km of highways, and in peninsular Malaysia 2,418 km of railways. The main airports are at Kuala Lumpur, Kuala Terengganu, Penang, Langkawi and Kota Kinbalu, with over 110 smaller airports and airstrips around the country

MEDIA

The government operates extremely strict censorship of all media outlets and newspapers must renew their licences annually. The four main national daily newspapers are English-language and titles include *The Star*, *Business Times* and *The Malay Mail*. Radio Television Malaysia is the state-run broadcaster which competes with two main commercial broadcasters.

MALDIVES

Divehi Rājjē ge Jumhūriyyā – Republic of the Maldives

AREA – 298 sq. km
POPULATION – 339,330 (2004 est.). The people are Sunni Muslims and the Maldivian (Dhivehi) language is akin to Elu or old Sinhalese
CAPITAL – ΨMalé (population, 74,069, 2000)
CURRENCY – Rufiyaa of 100 laaris

NATIONAL ANTHEM – Gavmi mi ekuverikan mati tibegen kurime salam [In national unity we salute our nation]
NATIONAL DAY – 26 July
NATIONAL FLAG – Green field bearing a white crescent, with wide red border
LIFE EXPECTANCY (years) – 63.68 (2004 est.)
MORTALITY RATE (per 1,000 population) – 7.44 (2004 est.)
INFANT MORTALITY (per 1,000 population) – 58.32 (2004 est.)
HIV / AIDS ADULT PREVALENCE – 0.1 per cent (2001 est.)
DEATH PENALTY – No (abolished 1952)
POPULATION GROWTH RATE – 2.86 per cent (2004 est.)
MILITARY EXPENDITURE – 6.4 per cent of GDP (2003)
ILLITERACY RATE – (m) 3.7 per cent; (f) 3.6 per cent (2000)

CLIMATE AND TERRAIN

The republic is a chain of coral atolls in the Indian Ocean, 643 km to the south-west of Sri Lanka. There are about 1,196 coral islands grouped into 12 clusters of atolls, about 198 of which are inhabited. The islands are all flat and low-lying; none is more than eight feet above sea-level. There is a tropical climate and daily temperatures rarely drop below 28°C.

HISTORY AND POLITICS

The Maldives converted to Islam in 1153 and came under Portuguese rule in the 16th century. After becoming a dependency of Ceylon in 1645, the islands were under Dutch and then British rule until 1887, when they became an internally self-governing British protectorate. Full independence was achieved in 1968, when the Maldives became a republic under President Ibrahim Nasir. The autocratic Nasir retired in 1978 and was succeeded by Maumoon Abdul Gayoom. Despite attempted coups in the 1980s, his tenure has ensured political stability and allowed economic development, although he has been accused of authoritarianism and human rights abuses. Unprecedented violence during anti-government demonstrations in 2003 and 2004 has led to the introduction of constitutional reforms. The Indian Ocean tsunami in December 2004 devastated the islands, destroying many homes and tourist resorts; the number of dead and missing was low, but over 21,000 people were displaced.

In the 2003 presidential election, President Gayoom was re-elected for a sixth term with 90.3 per cent of the vote. In the legislative election in January 2005, all candidates for the elected seats ran as independents, although some were backed by the Maldivian Democratic Party, based in Sri Lanka. The government was unchanged after the election.

POLITICAL SYSTEM

The 1998 constitution was amended in June 2005 to legalise political parties. The executive president is elected by the legislature and confirmed by national referendum. The legislature is the unicameral People's Assembly *(Majlis)* which has 50 members, two elected from each of the 21 provinces and eight appointed by the president, to serve a five-year term.

and pro-US policies were adopted after the election of the Nationalist Party in 1987. Accession to the EU was approved in a referendum in 2003, and Malta became a member in 2004.

POLITICAL SYSTEM

Under the 1974 constitution, the president is elected by the House of Representatives for a five-year term, renewable only once. The unicameral legislature, the House of Representatives, has 65 members directly elected by proportional representation for a five-year term; if a party wins the majority of votes in a general election without winning a majority of seats, new seats are created until that party holds a majority of one seat. The prime minister is appointed by the president and nominates the other ministers.

HEAD OF STATE
President, Edward Fenech Adami, *took office*, 15 April 2004

SELECTED GOVERNMENT MEMBERS *as at July 2005*
Prime Minister, Finance, Lawrence Gonzi
Deputy Prime Minister, Social Policy, Justice and Home Affairs, Tonio Borg
Foreign Affairs, Michael Frendo

MALTA HIGH COMMISSION
Malta House, 36–38 Piccadilly, London W1J 0LE
T 020-7292 4800
High Commissioner, HE Michael Refalo, apptd 2004

BRITISH HIGH COMMISSION
Whitehall Mansions, Ta'Xbiex Seafront, Ta'Xbiex MSD 11, Malta GC T (+ 356) 2323 0000 E bhccomm@vol.net.mt
High Commissioner, HE Vincent Fean, apptd 2002

BRITISH COUNCIL
c/o British High Commission
E veronica.attard@britcouncil.org.mt
Director, Ronnie Micallef

ECONOMY AND TRADE

Malta has low unemployment, low inflation and consistent growth rates. The public sector accounts for a large proportion of revenue – 49 per cent of GDP. The country only produces 20 per cent of its own food, has limited access to fresh water (there is an increasing reliance on desalination) and has no domestic sources of energy. The mainstay of the economy for over a century was the dockyard, and ship-building and ship repairs remain significant industries, but the main source of income is now tourism, which brings in over one million tourists each year. The chief exports are processed food, electronics, textiles, and other manufactures. The principal imports are foodstuffs, fodder, beverages and tobacco, fuels, chemicals, textiles and machinery.
GNI – US$3,640 million (2001); US$9,210 per capita (2001)
ANNUAL AVERAGE GROWTH OF GDP – 0.8 per cent (2004 est.)
INFLATION RATE – 2.4 per cent (2000 est.)
UNEMPLOYMENT – 7 per cent (2004 est.)
IMPORTS – US$2,840 million (2002)
EXPORTS – US$2,230 million (2002)

BALANCE OF PAYMENTS
Trade – US$689 million deficit (2003)
Current Account – US$271 million deficit (2003)

Trade with UK	2003	2004
Imports from UK	£258,750,000	£92,930,000
Exports to UK	186,994,000	70,133,000

TRANSPORT AND MEDIA

The main ports are Marsaxlokk and Valletta. There are 2,254 km of highways, no internal waterways or railways, and one airport.

There are seven major daily and weekly news publications and include *Malta Independent* and *It-Torca*.

EDUCATION

Education is free at all levels and compulsory between the ages of five and 16. There are ten junior lyceums, 18 secondary schools and five centres catering for low achievers. The junior college prepares students specifically for a university course. Tertiary education is available at the University of Malta. The Malta College of Arts, Science and Technology provides technical and vocational courses at post-secondary level.
ILLITERACY RATE – (m) 8.6 per cent; (f) 7.2 per cent (2000)

MARSHALL ISLANDS

Republic of the Marshall Islands

AREA – 181 sq. km
POPULATION – 57,738 (2004 est.): 99 per cent are Micronesian. Almost half the population is under 15. About 60 per cent of the population is concentrated on the two atolls of Majuro and Kwajalein. The population is Christian, primarily Protestant, but with a substantial Catholic minority. Marshallese and English are the official languages.
CAPITAL – Dalap-Uliga-Darrit, on Majuro Atoll (population, 20,000)
MAJOR TOWN – Ebeye
CURRENCY – Currency is that of the USA
NATIONAL ANTHEM – Forever Marshall Islands
NATIONAL DAY – 1 May (Independence Day)
NATIONAL FLAG – Blue with a diagonal ray divided white over orange running from the lower hoist to the upper fly; in the canton a white sun
MORTALITY RATE (per 1,000 population) – 4.94 (2004 est.)
DEATH PENALTY – No (abolished 1986)
POPULATION GROWTH RATE – 2.29 per cent (2004 est.)

CLIMATE AND TERRAIN

The republic consists of an archipelago of 29 coral atolls, five islands and over 1,000 islets in the west Pacific Ocean. All the islands are low-lying and a 1989 UN report warned that a rise in sea level could submerge them all by 2030. There is a wet season from May to November and average temperatures range from 25°C in January to 31°C in August.

HISTORY AND POLITICS

The Marshall Islands were claimed by Spain in 1592 but were left undisturbed by the Spanish and in 1886 formally became a German protectorate. Japan took control of the islands in 1914 on behalf of the allied powers and administered them as a mandate from 1920 until 1944, when US forces seized the islands from the

Japanese after intense fighting. In 1947 the islands became part of the UN Trust Territory of the Pacific Islands, administered by the USA. Between 1946 and 1962, US nuclear weapon tests were held on Bikini and Enewetak atolls. Enewetak has been partially decontaminated but Bikini is uninhabitable; the USA paid compensation to the test victims in the 1980s but the government is seeking US$2.7 billion in further compensation to cover the medical care of radiation victims and rectify environmental damage.

The islands became internally self-governing in 1979, and the US-UN trusteeship administration came to an end in 1986, when a Compact of Free Association between the USA and the Republic of the Marshall Islands came into effect. By this compact, the USA recognised the Republic of the Marshall Islands as a fully sovereign and independent state but retains control of external security and defence as well as giving financial help; the USA controls the Kwajalein Atoll, where it has a military base and missile test site. UN Trust Territory status was terminated in 1990 and full independence was granted in December 1990. A renegotiated compact was negotiated in 2003.

The United Democratic Party (UDP) won the legislative elections in 1999 and 2003. The UDP supported the candidacy of Kessai Note, who was elected president in 2000 and re-elected in 2004.

POLITICAL SYSTEM
Under the 1979 constitution, the executive president is elected by the legislature from among its members to serve a four-year term. The unicameral legislature, the Nitijela, has 33 members, directly elected for a four-year term. There is also a 12-member Council of Chiefs, the Iroij who are traditional leaders with a consultative and advisory role.

HEAD OF STATE
President, Kessai Note, elected 3 January 2000, re-elected 14 January 2004

SELECTED GOVERNMENT MEMBERS as at July 2005
Finance, Brendan Wase
Foreign Affairs, Gerald Zackios
Internal Affairs and Welfare, Rien Morris

BRITISH AMBASSADOR
HE Ian Powell, resident at Suva, Fiji

ECONOMY AND TRADE
The economy is largely dependent on aid from the USA. It is thought that the Marshall Islands has great potential in marine resources and seabed mineral deposits, but at present the government is the largest employer and most islanders live by subsistence farming. Tourism is being encouraged, and the sales of fishing rights and ship registration fees also generate income.

Trade with UK	2003	2004
Imports from UK	£5,242,000	£334,000
Exports to UK	1,145,000	734,000

TRANSPORT AND MEDIA
Air Marshall Islands provides air services within the islands and to Hawaii. Continental Air Micronesia serves Majuro and Kwajalein with flights to Hawaii and Guam. Majuro also has shipping links to Hawaii, Australia, Japan and throughout the Pacific.

The Marshall Islands Journal is a private weekly newspaper and the Marshall Islands Gazette is a government monthly newspaper.

MAURITANIA

Al-Jumhūriyya al-Islāmiyya al-Mawrītāniyya – Islamic Republic of Mauritania

AREA – 1,025,520 sq. km. Neighbours: Senegal (south-west), Mali (east and south), Algeria and Western Sahara (north)
POPULATION – 2,998,563 (2004 est.). The official language is Arabic. Pulaar, Soninke, Wolof and French are also spoken
CAPITAL – ΨNouakchott (population, 850,000)
CURRENCY – Ouguiya (UM) of 5 khoums
NATIONAL DAY – 28 November
NATIONAL FLAG – Yellow star and crescent on green ground
LIFE EXPECTANCY (years) – 52.32 (2004 est.)
MORTALITY RATE (per 1,000 population) – 12.74 (2004 est.)
HIV / AIDS ADULT PREVALENCE – 0.6 per cent (2003 est.)
DEATH PENALTY – Yes
POPULATION BELOW POVERTY LINE – 50 per cent (2001 est.)
POPULATION GROWTH RATE – 2.91 (2004 est.)
POPULATION DENSITY – 3 per sq. km (2002)
MILITARY EXPENDITURE – 1.7 per cent of GDP (2003)
MILITARY PERSONNEL – 15,750: Army 15,000, Navy 500, Air Force 250; Paramilitaries 5,000
CONSCRIPTION DURATION – 24 months
ILLITERACY RATE – (m) 49.2 per cent; (f) 69.1 per cent (2003 est.)
GROSS ENROLMENT RATIO (percentage of relevant age group) – primary 86 per cent (2002); secondary 22 per cent (2002); tertiary 3 per cent (2002)

CLIMATE AND TERRAIN
The terrain is arid, apart from in the Senegal river valley, and flat, with some hilly regions in the centre of the country. Temperatures range from 16°C in January to 41°C in July.

HISTORY AND POLITICS
Eastern Mauritania was part of the Ghana empire and then the Mali and Songhai empires from the seventh to the 16th century. The area came under French influence in the 19th century, becaming a French protectorate in 1903 and a French colony in 1920. The country became independent as the Islamic Republic of Mauritania on 28 November 1960. There were military coups in 1978 and 1984, the latter bringing to power Col. Maaouya ould Sid Ahmed Taya. Civilian rule was restored after multiparty elections in 1992; the presidential election was won by Col. Taya.

When the Spanish withdrew from Western Sahara in 1976, Morocco and Mauritania divided it between them. Mauritania renounced all claims to the region in 1979 after several years of guerrilla warfare with the separatist Polisario Front. In 1989 race riots broke out because of a border dispute with Senegal; diplomatic relations were suspended until 1992.

In the 1990s and early 2000s, ethnic tension between the Arab north and African south and internal unrest by

MEXICO

Estados Unidos Mexicanos – United Mexican States

AREA – 1,908,700 sq. km. Neighbours: USA (north),
Guatemala and Belize (south-east)
POPULATION – 104,959,594 (2004 est.). Spanish is the
official language and is spoken by about 95 per cent of
the population. There are five main groups of Indian
languages (Náhuatl, Maya, Zapotec, Otomí, Mixtec)
and 59 dialects derived from them
CAPITAL – Mexico City (population, 8,591,309, 2000
census)
MAJOR CITIES – Ciudad Juárez; Ecatepec de Morelos;
Guadalajara; León; Monterrey; Nezahualcóyotl;
Puebla; Tijuana; Toluca; Torreón
CURRENCY – Peso of 100 centavos
NATIONAL ANTHEM – Mexicanos, al grito de guerra
[Mexicans, to the war cry]
NATIONAL DAY – 16 September (Proclamation of
Independence)
NATIONAL FLAG – Three vertical bands in green, white
and red, with the Mexican emblem (an eagle on a
cactus devouring a snake) in the centre
LIFE EXPECTANCY (years) – 74.94 (2004 est.)
MORTALITY RATE (per 1,000 population) – 4.73
(2004 est.)
INFANT MORTALITY (per 1,000 births) – 21.69
(2004 est.)
HIV / AIDS ADULT PREVALENCE RATE – 0.3 per cent
(2003 est.)
DEATH PENALTY – Yes*
POPULATION BELOW POVERTY LINE – 40 per cent
(2001 est.)
POPULATION GROWTH RATE – 1.18 per cent
(2004 est.)
POPULATION DENSITY – 53 per sq. km (2002)
URBAN POPULATION – 75 per cent (2001)

CLIMATE AND TERRAIN

Coastal plains rise to a central plateau and then to a spine
of high mountains, the Sierra Madre, running north-west
to south-east. The Yucatán peninsula in the south-east is
low-lying, and marshy on the coast. The narrow Lower
California peninsula, separated from the rest of the
country by the Gulf of California, has a range of hills
running along it. The mountains include volcanoes such
as Popocatepetl. Elevation extremes range from 5,700 m
(Volcan Pico de Orizaba) at the highest point to −10 m
(Laguna Salada) at the lowest. The Rio Grande forms the
eastern part of the northern border with the USA. Average
temperatures in Mexico City range from 23°C in October
to 30°C in July.

HISTORY AND POLITICS

Mexico was the centre of Mesoamerican civilisations for
over 2,500 years: the Olmecs (1200–600 BC), based on
the Mexican Gulf Coast; the Zapotecs (300 BC to 300
AD) in the Oaxaca valley; the Mayas (c.300–900 AD) in
southern Mexico and the Yucatán peninsula; the Mixtecs
(seventh–14th centuries) in the Oaxaca valley; and the
Toltecs (c.900–1170) in central Mexico and the Yucatán
peninsula. The Aztecs, who came to the region in the
13th century, subjugated these peoples and ruled until
their civilisation fell to the Spanish under Hernán Cortés
in 1519–21. As the Viceroyalty of New Spain, Mexico
remained under Spanish rule until the 19th century. In the
first century of Spanish occupation, the indigenous
population fell from about 21 million to about one
million, largely through lack of resistance to European
diseases.

After an unsuccessful revolt in 1810, independence was
declared in 1821 and a federal republic was instituted in
1824. Mexico suffered extreme instability, civil war and
invasion throughout much of the 19th century. War with
the USA in 1836 and 1846–8 led to the loss of about
one-third of its territory. There was civil war in 1858–61
between liberals and conservatives, and in 1862–7 war
with Britain, France and Spain after Mexico defaulted on
its foreign debt. Porfirio Díaz ruled as a dictator between
1876 and 1911. He can be credited with beginning the
industrialisation of Mexico, but his tenure was also
marked by terrible repression that led his overthrow in
1911. This revolution introduced radical land and labour
reforms but instability continued.

The National Revolutionary Party, founded in 1929,
came to dominate political life. Renamed the Institutional
Revolutionary Party (PRI) in 1946, it formed a succession
of authoritarian governments and, although unrest was
not eliminated under its regime, the 1960s saw rapid
industrialisation and the 1970s an oil-fuelled economic
boom. Falling oil prices led to a serious financial crisis in
1982 and Mexico defaulted on its debt. Economic
difficulties were eased in the 1990s with the introduction
of market reforms and privatisation, and membership of
the North American Free Trade Agreement (NAFTA) from
1994.

These reforms led to a degree of social upheaval.
Fearing for the status of the already marginalised
indigenous peoples, the Zapatista National Liberation
Front (EZLN) led revolts in the south of the country in
1994 and 1995. Although violence tailed off in the late
1990s, civil campaigning continued, culminating in a
mass march from Chiapas to Mexico City in 2001 in
support of a bill of indigenous rights. The bill was enacted
in May 2001 but the Zapatistas claimed its provisions had
been watered down and vowed to continue their
insurgency. The government also faces problems with
corruption and violent crime, often drug-related;
President Fox said in 2005 that drugs cartels were trying
to infiltrate state institutions.

The PRI's political dominance ended at the 1997
election, when it lost its absolute majority in the lower
house of the legislature. In the 2000 presidential and
legislative elections, Vicente Fox, the Partido de Accion
Nacional (PAN) candidate, was elected as president and
the PAN-led alliance won 224 seats in the 500 Chamber
of Deputies seats. However, in the 2003 legislative
elections the PRI regained its majority, winning 241 seats
to the PAN's 153 seats.

POLITICAL SYSTEM

Under the 1917 constitution, the federal republic consists
of 31 states and the federal capital. The head of state is an
executive president, directly elected for a six-year term
that may not be renewed. The bicameral legislature is the
Congress of the Union, the lower house of which is the
Chamber of Deputies and the upper house is the Senate.
The Chamber of Deputies *(Cámara de Diputados)* has 500
members, directly elected for a three-year term. The
Senate has 128 members, elected for a six-year term. The
president appoints the cabinet. The states are
administered by a governor, elected for a six-year term,
and a state Chamber of Deputies, elected for a three-year
term.

HEAD OF STATE
President, Vicente Fox, *elected* 2 July 2000, *sworn in* 1 December 2000

SELECTED GOVERNMENT MEMBERS *as at July 2005*
Defence, Gen. Gerardo Clemente Ricardo Vega
Economy, Fernando Canales Clariond
Foreign Affairs, Luis Ernesto Derbez
Interior, Santiago Creel Miranda

MEXICAN EMBASSY
42 Hertford Street, London W1J 7JR **T** 020-7499 8586
Ambassador Extraordinary and Plenipotentiary, HE Juan-José Bremer de Martino, *apptd* 2004

BRITISH EMBASSY
Calle Río Lerma 71, Colonia Cuauhtémoc, 06500 Mexico City
T (+ 52) (55) 5242 8500 **E** consular.mexico@fco.gov.uk
Ambassador Extraordinary and Plenipotentiary, HE Denise Holt, CMG, apptd 2002

BRITISH COUNCIL
Lope de Vega 316, Col. Chapultepec Morales, 11570 Mexico DF
T (+ 52) (55) 5263 1900 **E** bcmexico@britishcouncil.org.mx
Director, Clive Bruton

DEFENCE
The Army has 862 armoured personnel carriers. The Navy has three destroyers, eight frigates, 109 patrol and coastal vessels, and eight combat aircraft. There are 20 naval bases. The Air Force has 107 combat aircraft and 71 armed helicopters.
MILITARY EXPENDITURE – 0.5 per cent of GDP (2003)
MILITARY PERSONNEL – 192,770: Army 144,000, Navy 37,000, Air Force 11,770; Paramilitaries 11,000
CONSCRIPTION DURATION – 12 months (four hours per week) by lottery

ECONOMY AND TRADE
Despite its oil and natural gas reserves and mineral resources, Mexico is a poor country. A large proportion of the male population works overseas, most often in the USA, and remittances from these workers are a significant source of revenue. Agriculture is diverse and productive; major crops include corn, wheat, soy beans, rice, beans, cotton, coffee, fruit, tomatoes, beef, poultry and dairy products. Agriculture accounts for 4 per cent of GDP and 18 per cent of the labour force. Tobacco, chemicals, iron and steel, petroleum, mining, textiles, clothing, motor vehicles, and tourism are all major industries. The industrial sector has increased since Mexico joined NAFTA in 1994 as its cheap labour has led US companies to establish factories in the north to assemble goods for the US market.

Principal exports include oil, cars, auto engines, fruits and vegetables, shrimps, coffee, computers, cattle, glass, iron and steel pipes, and copper. Major imports include computers, auto assembly material, electrical parts, car and truck parts, powdered milk, corn and sorghum, vehicles, sound-recording and power-generating equipment, chemicals, industrial machinery, pharmaceuticals and specialised appliances. Membership of NAFTA has tripled Mexico's trade with the USA and Canada, and it is hoped that trade agreements with the EU in 2000 and Japan in 2004 will also boost trade.
GNI – US$597,000 million (2002); US$5,920 per capita (2002)

ANNUAL AVERAGE GROWTH OF GDP – 1.3 per cent (2003 est.)
INFLATION RATE – 3.8 per cent (2003 est.)
UNEMPLOYMENT – 3.3 per cent (2003 est.)
TOTAL EXTERNAL DEBT – US$159,400 million (2003 est.)
FOREIGN DIRECT INVESTMENT – US$47,787 million (1997–2000)
IMPORTS – US$179,000 million (2003)
EXPORTS – US$165,000 million (2003)

BALANCE OF PAYMENTS
Trade – US$5,624 million deficit (2003)
Current Account – US$9,247 million deficit (2003)

Trade with UK	2003	2004
Imports from UK	£693,248,000	£626,299,000
Exports to UK	509,161,000	420,452,000

TRANSPORT INFRASTRUCTURE
Veracruz, Tampico and Coatzacoalcos are the chief ports on the Atlantic coast, and Guaymas, Mazatlán, Puerto Lázaro Cárdenas and Salina Cruz on the Pacific. There are 19,510 km of railways; the rail network is currently undergoing reorganisation. There are 329,532 km of roads, of which 108,087 km are surfaced, and 2,900 km of navigable waterways and coastal canals. The principal airports are at Mexico City and Monterrey, with major airports at 13 other regional cities.

EDUCATION
Although Mexico allows for 10 years of free and compulsory education, on average Mexican adults have only completed 7.2 years. The country's largest university is the National Autonomous University of Mexico, situated in Mexico City.
ILLITERACY RATE – (m) 6.7 per cent; (f) 10.6 per cent (2000)
GROSS ENROLMENT RATIO (percentage of relevant age group) – primary 110 per cent (2002); secondary 73 per cent (2002); tertiary 20 per cent (2002)

MEDIA AND CULTURE
Televisa used to control all Mexican broadcasting but now competes with other channels and a multitude of independent radio stations. There are six national newspapers, including *La Jornada, Reforma* and *Excelsior.*

Pre-Columbian civilisation has significantly influenced contemporary Mexican culture. After the Spanish conquest, the intricate designs and bright colours used in native American arts were often mixed with European techniques and religious themes to create a hybrid and uniquely Mexican artistic style. Important cultural figures include the mural painters Diego Rivera (1886–1957) and José Clemente Orozco (1883–1949) and essayist and poet Octavio Paz (1914–98 (Nobel Prize for Literature 1990)).

FEDERATED STATES OF MICRONESIA

AREA – 702 sq. km
POPULATION – 108,155 (2004 est.). The population is Micronesian and predominantly Christian. English (official) and eight other languages are used in different parts of the Federated States: Yapese, Ulithian,

Woleaian, Pohnpeian, Nukuoran, Kapingamarangi,
Chuukese and Kosraean
FEDERAL CAPITAL – Palikir, on ΨKolonia (Pohnpei)
CURRENCY – Currency is the US dollar
NATIONAL ANTHEM – Patriots of Micronesia
NATIONAL FLAG – United Nations blue with four white
stars in the centre
LIFE EXPECTANCY (years) – 69.44 (2004 est.)
MORTALITY RATE (per 1,000 population) – 4.97
(2004 est.)
DEATH PENALTY – No (abolished 1986)
POPULATION BELOW POVERTY LINE – 26.7 per cent
(2001 est.)
POPULATION GROWTH RATE – −0.2 per cent
(2004 est.)
POPULATION DENSITY – 165 per sq. km (1999)

CLIMATE AND TERRAIN
The republic consists of more than 600 volcanic islands
extending 2,900 km across the archipelago of the
Caroline Islands in the western Pacific Ocean. Elevation
extremes range from 791 m (Totolom) at the highest point
to 0 m (Pacific Ocean) at the lowest. The islands lie to the
north of the Equator, and the climate is tropical with an
almost constant 30°C temperature.

HISTORY AND POLITICS
Inhabited since around 4000 BC by migrants from the
Philippines and Indonesia, Micronesia came into contact
with Europeans in the 1520s and the islands were
colonised by Spain from the 16th century. German
encroachment in the 1870s and 1880s was resisted but in
1899 Germany purchased the islands from Spain. The
islands were occupied by Japan on behalf of the allies
during the First World War, and administered as a League
of Nations mandated territory by Japan from 1920 until
the Japanese defeat in the Second World War. In 1947 the
islands became part of the UN Trust Territory of the
Pacific, administered by the USA.

A constitution was adopted in 1979 and the islands
became independent in 1986 under a Compact of Free
Association with the USA by which the USA retains
responsibility for defence and provides substantial
financial aid; a renegotiated compact was signed in 2003.
The UN trusteeship was formally terminated in 1990.

The republic is threatened by the effects of global
warming, particularly an increase in the frequency and
intensity of storms in the region. A typhoon in 2004
devastated Yap, destroying or badly damaging nearly all
the island's infrastructure.

POLITICAL SYSTEM
The 1979 constitution established a federal republic of
four states: Chuuk, Kosrae, Pohnpei and Yap. The federal
head of state is an executive president, who is elected by
the Congress for a four-year term. The unicameral
Congress has 14 members, ten senators directly elected
for a two-year term and four senators 'at large' (one from
each state) elected for a four-year term; the president and
vice-president must be selected from the senators 'at
large'. The federal cabinet is appointed by the president
and approved by the Congress. There are no political
parties. Each state has its own government and legislative
system.

HEAD OF STATE
President, Joseph J. Urusemal, *elected* 10 May 2003
Vice-President, Redley Killion

SELECTED GOVERNMENT MEMBERS *as at July 2005*
Economic Affairs, Akillino H. Susaia
Finance and Administration, Nick L. Andon
Foreign Affairs, Sebastion L. Anefal
Health, Nena S. Nena

BRITISH AMBASSADOR
HE Ian Powell, resident at Suva, Fiji

ECONOMY AND TRADE
Micronesia is highly dependent on aid from the USA. The
islands have few mineral resources apart from deposits of
phosphate. Subsistence farming and fishing are the
primary economic activities, and both are threatened by
climate change and over-fishing. The islands' extreme
isolation hampers the development of tourism. The 1986
compact with the USA provided for US$1.3 billion in
financial assistance over 15 years until 2001. Since then
assistance from the USA has been gradually reduced. In
2002 aid to Micronesia was US$100 million.

Exports include fish, black pepper, tropical fruits and
vegetables, coconuts, tapioca, betel nuts and sweet
potatoes.
GNI – US$250 million (2000); US$2,110 per capita
(2000)

Trade with UK	2003	2004
Imports from UK	£7,000	£27,000
Exports to UK	1,000	6,000

TRANSPORT INFRASTRUCTURE
The main ports are Colonia (Yap), Kolonia (Pohnpei), Lele
and Moen. There are 240 km of highways and no
railways.

MEDIA
There are four weekly news publications. One
government television channel competes with two
commercial channels and there are several radio stations.

MOLDOVA

Republica Moldova – Republic of Moldova
AREA – 33,851 sq. km. Neighbours: Ukraine (north, east
and south-east), Romania (west)
POPULATION – 4,446,455 (2004 est.): 65 per cent are
Moldovan, 14.2 per cent Ukrainian and 13 per cent
Russian, together with smaller numbers of Gagauz
(ethnic Turks), Jews and Bulgarians. Most of the
population are adherents of the Moldovan Orthodox
Church. Moldovan was made the official language
(written in the Latin script) in 1989 but the use of
Russian in official business is permitted
CAPITAL – Chisinau (population, 655,940, 1997
estimate)
CURRENCY – Moldovan leu of 100 bani (plural lei)
NATIONAL ANTHEM – Limba noastra [Our language]
NATIONAL DAY – 27 August (Independence Day)
NATIONAL FLAG – Vertical stripes of blue, yellow and
red, with the national arms in the centre
LIFE EXPECTANCY (years) – 65.03 (2004 est.)
MORTALITY RATE (per 1,000 population) – 12.76
(2004 est.)
INFANT MORTALITY (per 1,000 births) – 41 (2004 est.)
HIV / AIDS ADULT PREVALENCE – 0.2 per cent
(2001 est.)
DEATH PENALTY – No (abolished 1995)

World Physical

Modified Gall Projection
Equatorial Scale 1:166,000,000
© Oxford Cartographers
+44 (0) 1365 882 884
95602

ICELAND

Reykjavik

Arctic Circle

Norwegian Sea

Trondheim

0 100 200 300 400 Miles
0 100 200 300 400 500 600 Kms

Conical Orthomorphic Projection

© Oxford Cartographers
+44 (0) 1865 882 884

Faroe Is.
(Denmark)

Shetland Is.

Bergen

Oslo

Stavanger

Kristiansand

Värö

Örebro

Gothenburg

ATLANTIC

Hebrides

Orkney Is.

North Sea

Skagerrak

Ålborg

Århus

Helsingborg

DENMARK

Copenhagen

Odense

Malmö

Inverness

Aberdeen

Dundee

Glasgow

Edinburgh

UNITED

Belfast

Newcastle
upon Tyne

KINGDOM

Leeds

Kiel

Rostock

Londonderry

Galway

Dublin

REP. OF
IRELAND

Liverpool

Manchester

Sheffield

Hamburg

Bremen

Elbe

OCEAN

Cork

Stoke-
on-Trent

Birmingham

Nonwich

Osnabrück

Hanover

Berlin

Swansea

Cardiff

Bristol

Amsterdam

NETHERLANDS

Münster

Essen

Leipzig

Dresden

Plymouth

London

Rotterdam

Antwerp

Düsseldorf

Cologne

Chemnitz

Southampton

Brussels

GERMANY

English Channel

Lille

BELGIUM

Frankfurt

Plzeň

Pra

Cherbourg

Le Havre

Amiens

LUX.

Luxembourg

CZEC

Brest

Caen

Rouen

Reims

Metz

Mannheim

Nuremberg

Regensburg

Rennes

Seine

Paris

Strasbourg

Stuttgart

Nantes

Loire

Orléans

Nancy

Danube

Salzburg

Tours

Dijon

Munich

Innsbruck

AUST

Bay of

FRANCE

Zurich

Bern

LIECH.

Limoges

Mt. Blanc
4808

Geneva

SWITZERLAND

SLOV

Biscay

Bordeaux

Clermont-
Ferrand

Lyon

Grenoble

Trento

Ljubljana

Trieste

Verona

Venice

La Coruña

Gijón

Montpellier

Nîmes

Milan

Po

Turin

Parma

Vigo

Bilbao

San Sebastian

Toulouse

Genoa

Bologna

SAN
MARINO

Ancona

Oporto

Douro

León

Pamplona

Burgos

Pyrenees

Lérida

Nice

MONACO

Marseille

La Spezia

Livorno

Florence

Coimbra

Valladolid

Zaragoza

ANDORRA

Corsica
(Fr.)

Ajaccio

Rome

ITALY

Apennines

Pesca

Lisbon

PORTUGAL

Tagus

Salamanca

Madrid

Barcelona

Setúbal

Badajoz

SPAIN

Valencia

Balearic Is.
(Sp.)

Sardinia
(It.)

Sassari

Naples

Huelva

Córdoba

Murcia

Palma

Mallorca

Faro

Seville

Granada

Cartagena

Cadiz

Málaga

Almería

Cagliari

Palermo

Mas

Tangier

Gibraltar(U.K.)

Ceuta(Sp.)

Melilla(Sp.)

Oran

Algiers

Blida

Bejaia

Skikda

Annaba

Sicily

Mediterranea

Rabat

Tétouan

Casablanca

Fès

Meknès

Oujda

Sidi Bel Abbès

Constantine

Tunis

Valletta

MALT

MOROCCO

Mountains

ALGERIA

TUNISIA

Atlas

Sfax

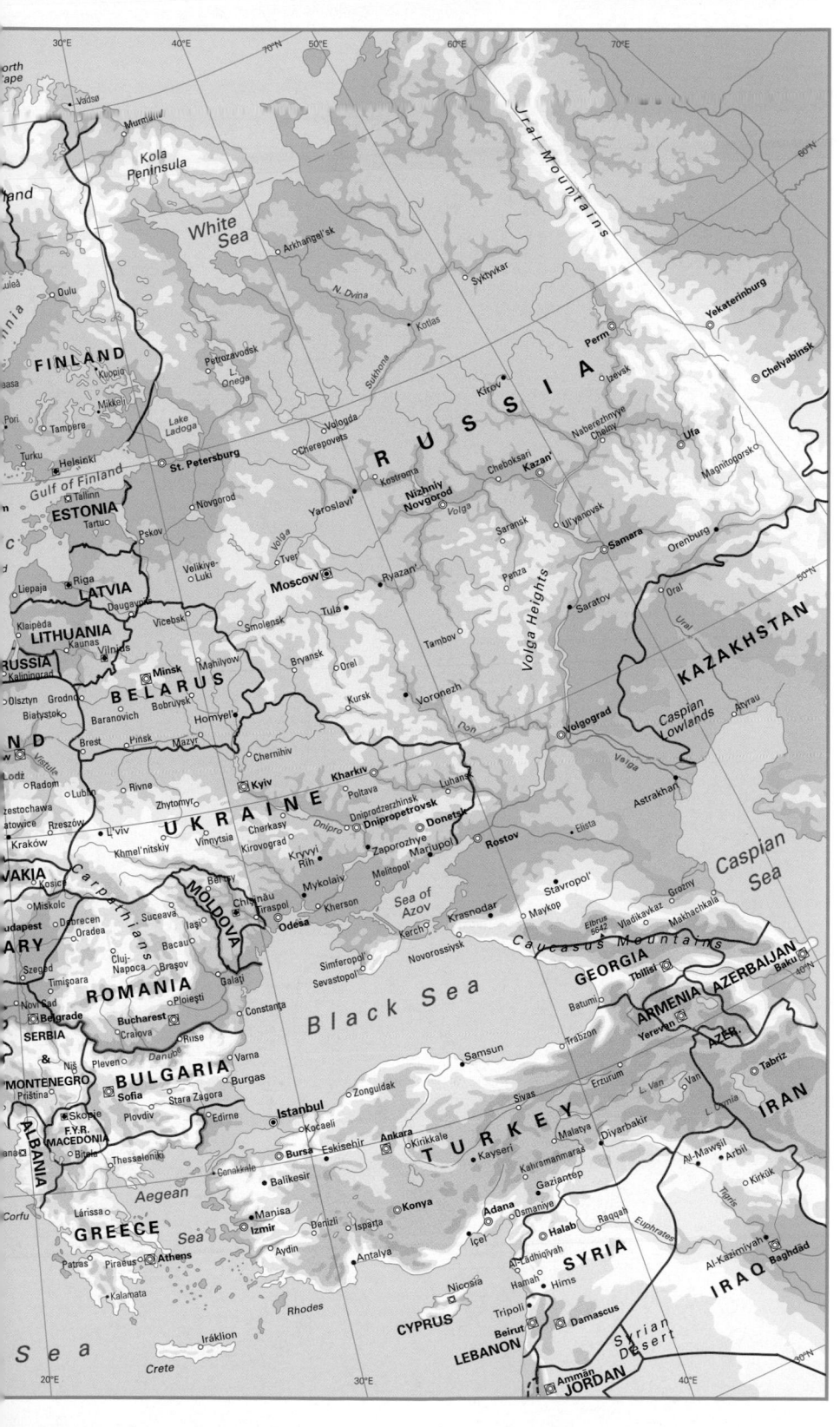

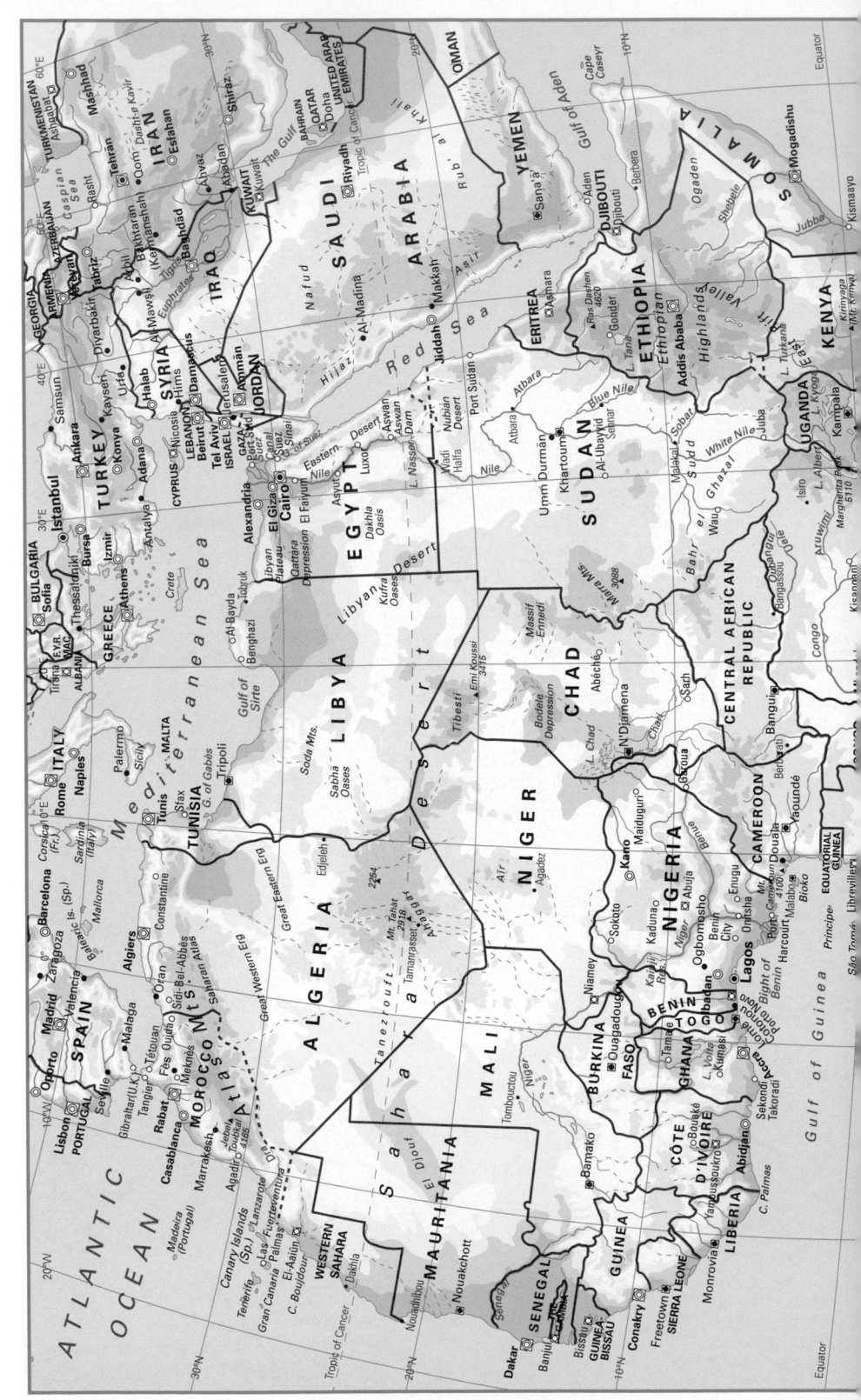

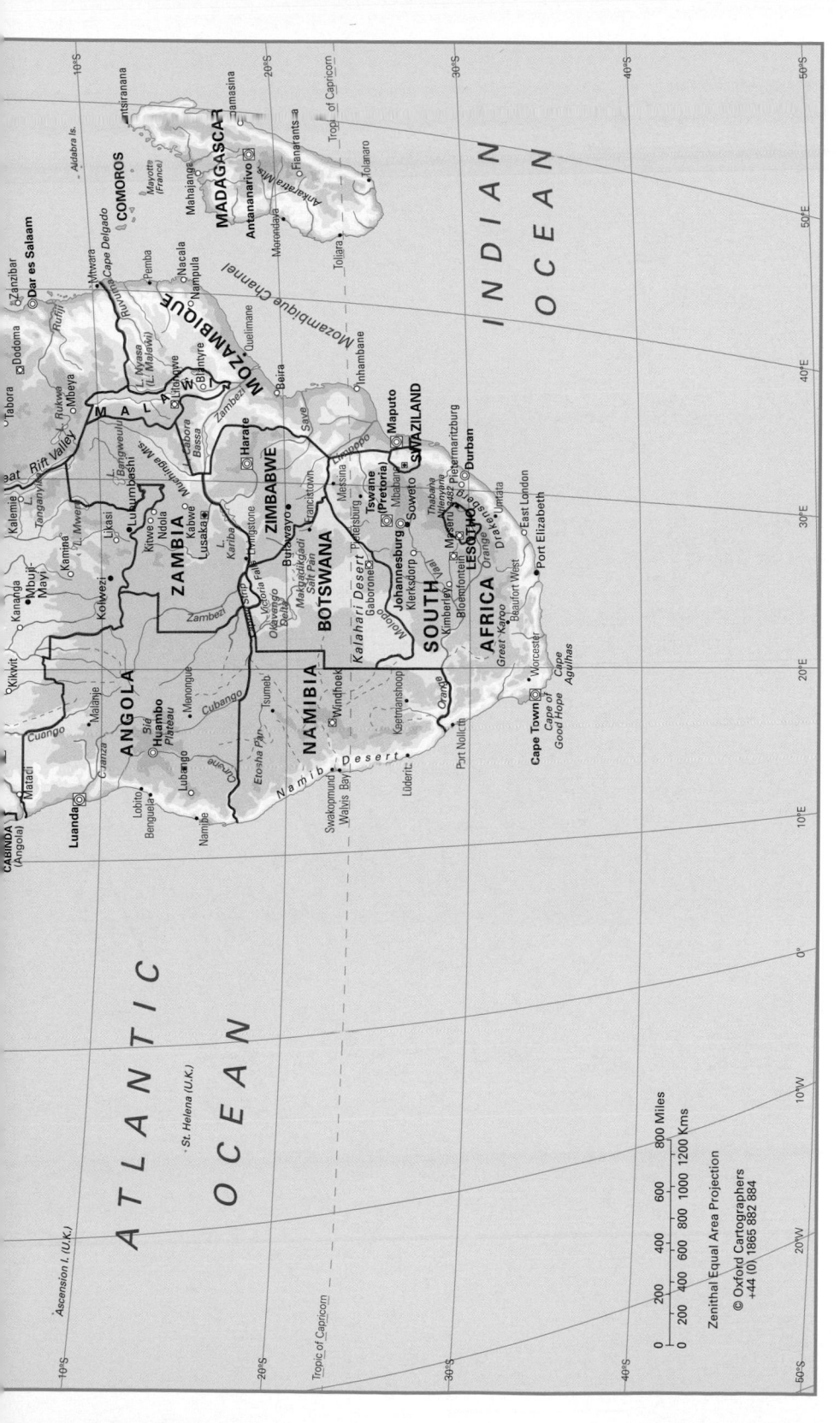

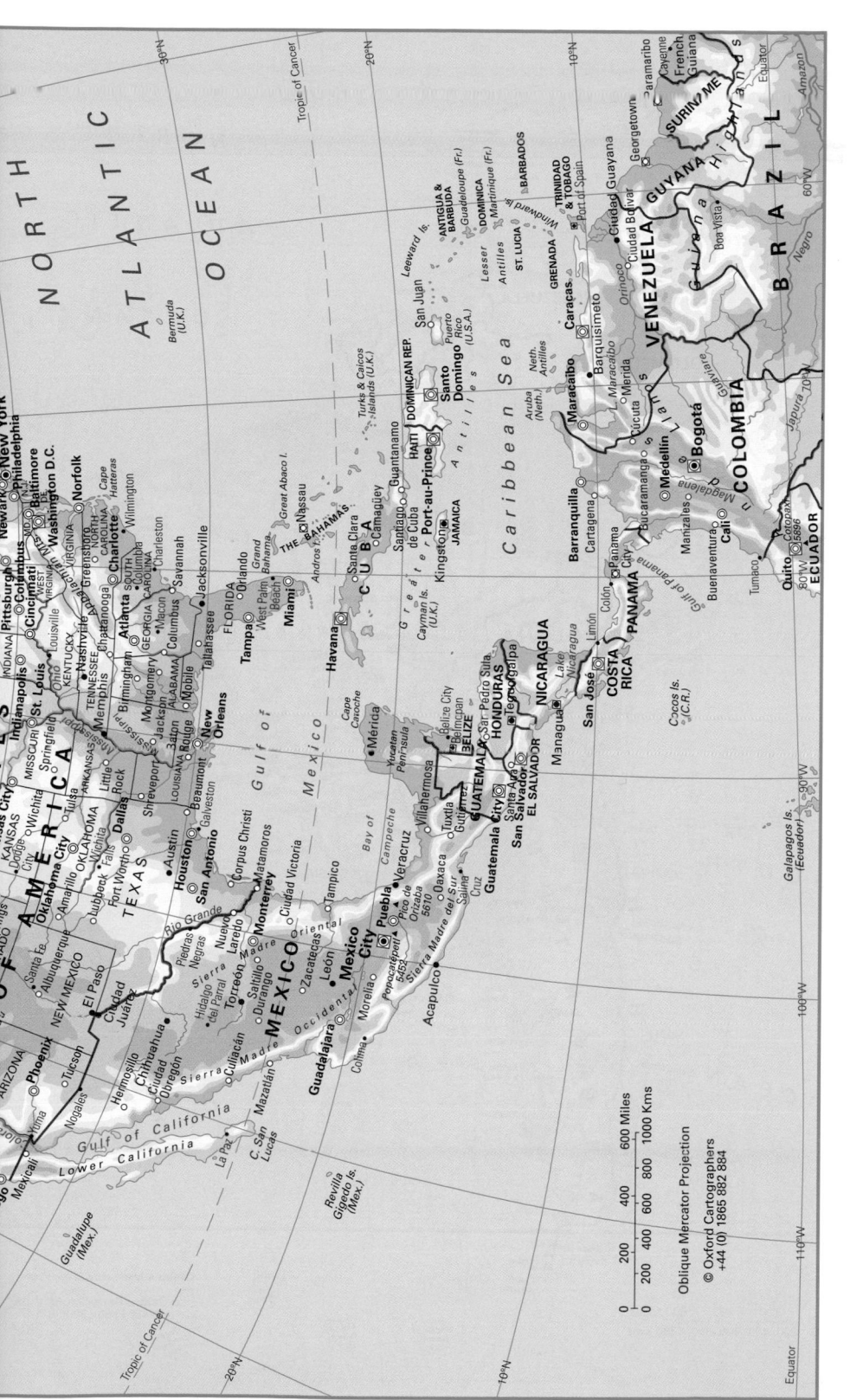

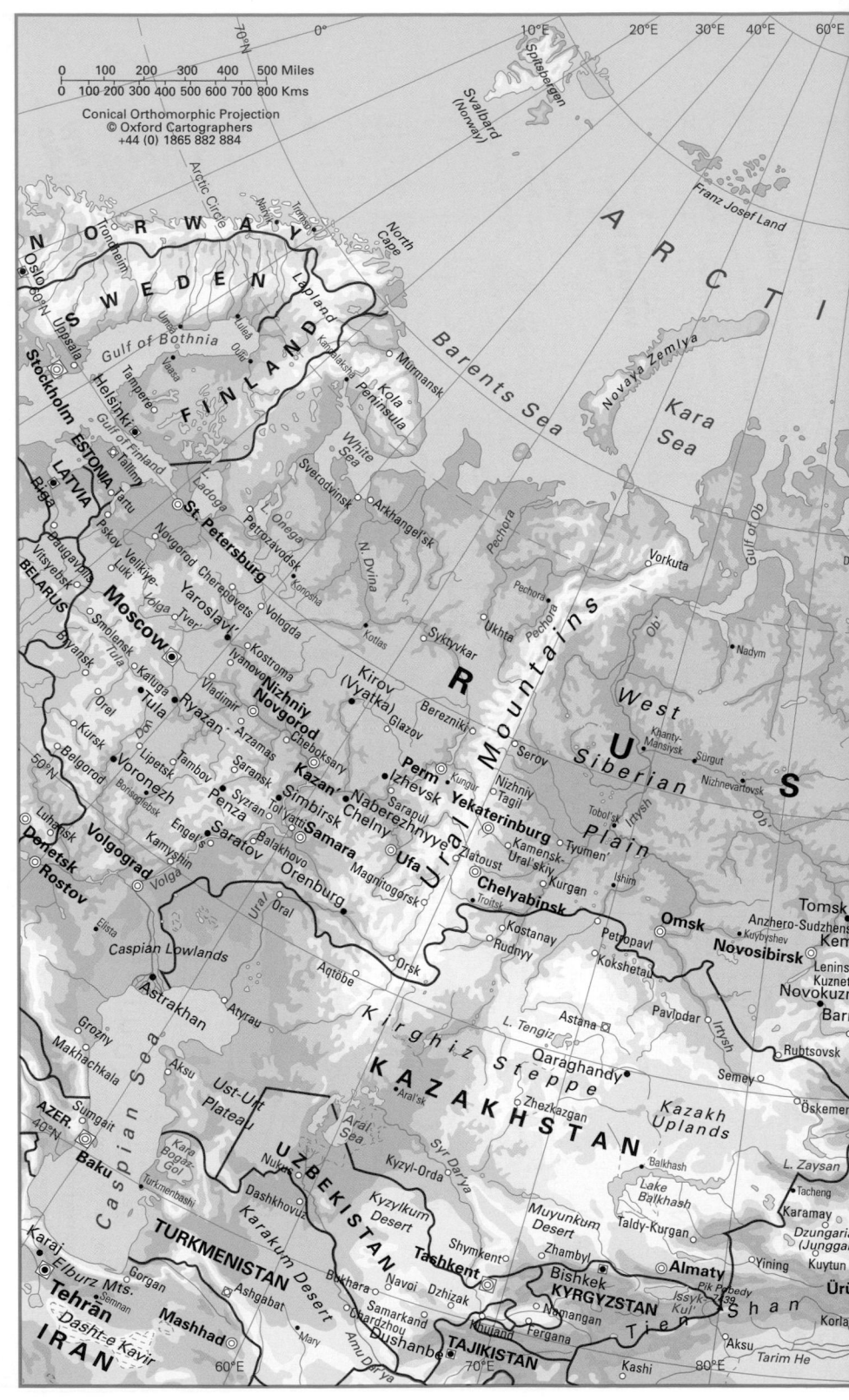

120°E 140°E 150°E 160°E 170°E 70°N 180° Anadyr Range

O C E A N

Severnaya
Zemlya

Taymyr Pen.

L. Taymyr

Tiksi

Laptev
Sea

New Siberia Is.

Lyakhov Is.

East Siberian Sea

Wrangel I.

Pevek

Koryak Range

Anadyr

Olenek

Central

Siberian

Plateau

Verkhoyansk Range

Cherskogo Range

Yana

Indigirka

Kolyma

Kolyma Mts.

60°N

Okhotsk

Magadan

Sea of
Okhotsk

Lena

Vilyuy

Yakutsk

Aldan

Dzhugdzhur Range

Sakhalin

S   A

guska

Lensk

Olekminsk

I

Komsomol'sk
na-Amure

Tunguska

Angara

Ust'
Ilimsk

Ust'-Kut

Stanovoy Mts.

Neryungri

Tynda

Skovorodino

50°N

Kansk Tayshek

hinsk

Krasnoyarsk

Bratsk

Tulun

Severobaikal'sk

Yablonovyy Mts.

Lake Baikal

Lena

Chita

Sretensk

Amur

Skovorodino

Belogorsk

Blagoveshchensk

Birobidzhan

Khabarovsk

Komsomol'sk
na-Amure

Amur

Da Hinggan Ling

Yichun

Hegang

Jiamusi

Shuangyashan
Qitaihe
Jixi

Mudanjiang

Ussuriysk

Yanji

Vladivostok

Chongjin

Sayan Mts.

Abakan

Kyzyl

Usol'ye-
Sibirskoye
Angarsk

Irkutsk

Hövsgöl
Nuur

Ulan-
Ude

Darhan

Manzhouli

Ulanhot

Hailar

Bei'an

Qiqihar

Daqing

Baicheng

Harbin

Jilin

Uvs Nuur

Hangayan Mts.

Hovd

Altay

Ulaanbaatar

Öndörhaan

Changchun

Tongliao

Siping

Liaoyuan

Fushun

Sea of
Okhotsk

hai Range

M O N G O L I A

Saynshand

I N N E R   M O N G O L I A

Chifeng

Shenyang

Fuxin
Jinzhou

Chengde

Anshan

Liaoyang

DEM. PEOPLE'S
REP. OF KOREA

Pyongyang

40°N

Gobi   Desert

Jining Zhang-
jiakou

Hohhot

Beijing
(Peking)

Tangshan

Korea
Bay

Dalian

Yantai

Seoul

Inchon

REP. OF
KOREA

Hami
Depression

Linhe

Baotou

Datong

C   H   I   N   A

Huang He (Yellow)

Baoding

Cangzhou

Tianjin

Bo Hai

Weihai

Lop Nur

Wuhai

Shizuishan

Taiyuan

Yuci

Shijiazhuang

Dezhou

Zibo

Jinan

Handan

Weifang

Qingdao

Yellow
Sea

100°E 110°E 120°E

Beaufort Sea

Banks Island

Melville Island

McClure Strait

Viscount Melville Sound

Somerset I.

Devon Island

Baffin Bay

Amundsen Gulf

Victoria Island

Gulf of Boothia

Baffin Island

Foxe Basin

Cumberland Sound

Trinity Bay

Arctic Circle

Range

aska
(SA)

Mt. McKinley 6194

Mt. Logan 5959

Anchorage

Range

Mackenzie Mts.

Great Bear Lake

Gr. Slave Lake

Caribou Mts.

L. Athabasca

Reindeer Lake

Hudson Strait

Ungava Peninsula

Ungava Bay

Gulf of Alaska

Coast Mountains

Queen Charlotte Islands

Rocky

Yukon

Peace

Lake Winnipeg

C A N A D A

Hudson Bay

James Bay

Labrador

H

Vancouver I.

Vancouver

Edmonton

Mt. Robson 3945

Calgary

Saskatoon

Manitoba

Regina

Thunder Bay

Lake Superior

Sudbury

Québec

Montréal

St. Lawrence

Nova Scotia

Gulf of St. Lawrence

Tacoma

Seattle

Portland

Mt. Rainier 4392

Boise

Minneapolis

St. Paul

Milwaukee

Lake Michigan

Lake Huron

Detroit

Toronto

L. Ontario

Ottawa

Buffalo

Boston

Halifax

C

Sacramento

San Francisco

San José

Salt Lake City

Mt. Whitney 4418

Colorado Plateau

Denver

U S A

Omaha

Kansas City

Chicago

Indianapolis

Cleveland

Pittsburgh

St. Louis

Cincinnati

New York

Philadelphia

Baltimore

Washington DC

A T L A N T I C

Las Vegas

Los Angeles

San Diego

Phoenix

Tucson

Albuquerque

Amarillo

Oklahoma City

Memphis

Raleigh

Norfolk

Bermuda I. (UK)

Ciudad Juárez

Hermosillo

Chihuahua

Fort Worth

Dallas

M E X I C O

Baton Rouge

Atlanta

Columbus

Tallahassee

O C E A N

Durango

Monterrey

Houston

New Orleans

Corpus Christi

St. Petersburg

Orlando

Tampa

Miami

B A H A M A S

Mazatlán

Ciudad Victoria

Tampico

Gulf of Mexico

Havana

Nassau

Tropic of Cancer

Guadalajara

Mexico City

Popocatépetl 5452

Veracruz

Bay of Campeche

Mérida

Campeche

Camagüey

CUBA

Port-au-Prince

DOMINICAN REPUBLIC

Santo Domingo

Revilla Gigedo Is. (Mex.)

Acápulco

GUATEMALA

BELIZE

Belmopan

HAITI

JAMAICA

Kingston

DOMINICA

Guatemala City

Tegucigalpa

HONDURAS

Greater Antilles

Caribbean Sea

TRINIDAD & TOBAGO

San Salvador

EL SALVADOR

NICARAGUA

Managua

Cartagena

Maracaibo

Caracas

COSTA RICA

San José

Panamá City

PANAMA

VENEZUELA

Medellín

Bogotá

Orinoco

Buenaventura

Cali

COLOMBIA

Galapagos Is. (Ecuador)

Quito

ECUADOR

Cuenca

Equator

Iquitos

Selvas

Amazon

Marquesas Is. (Fr.)

Piura

Chiclayo

Trujillo

P E R U

B R A Z I L

Lima

Society Islands (Fr.)

French Polynesia

Tuamotu Arch.

Gambier Is. (Fr.)

Pitcairn Is. (UK)

La Paz

Oruro

BOLIVIA

Sucre

Arica

Potosí

Gran Chaco

Antofagasta

Salta

Tropic of Capricorn

Easter I. (Chile)

Catamarca

Córdoba

O U T H   P A C I F I C

Juan Fernández Is. (Chile)

Valparaíso

Santiago

Aconcagua 6960

C H I L E

A R G E N T I N A

Concepción

Bahía Blanca

O C E A N

Puerto Montt

Comodoro Rivadavia

| 0 | 500 | 1000 | 1500 miles |
| 0 | 500 | 1000 | 1500 | 2000 | 2500 kms |

Miller Projection

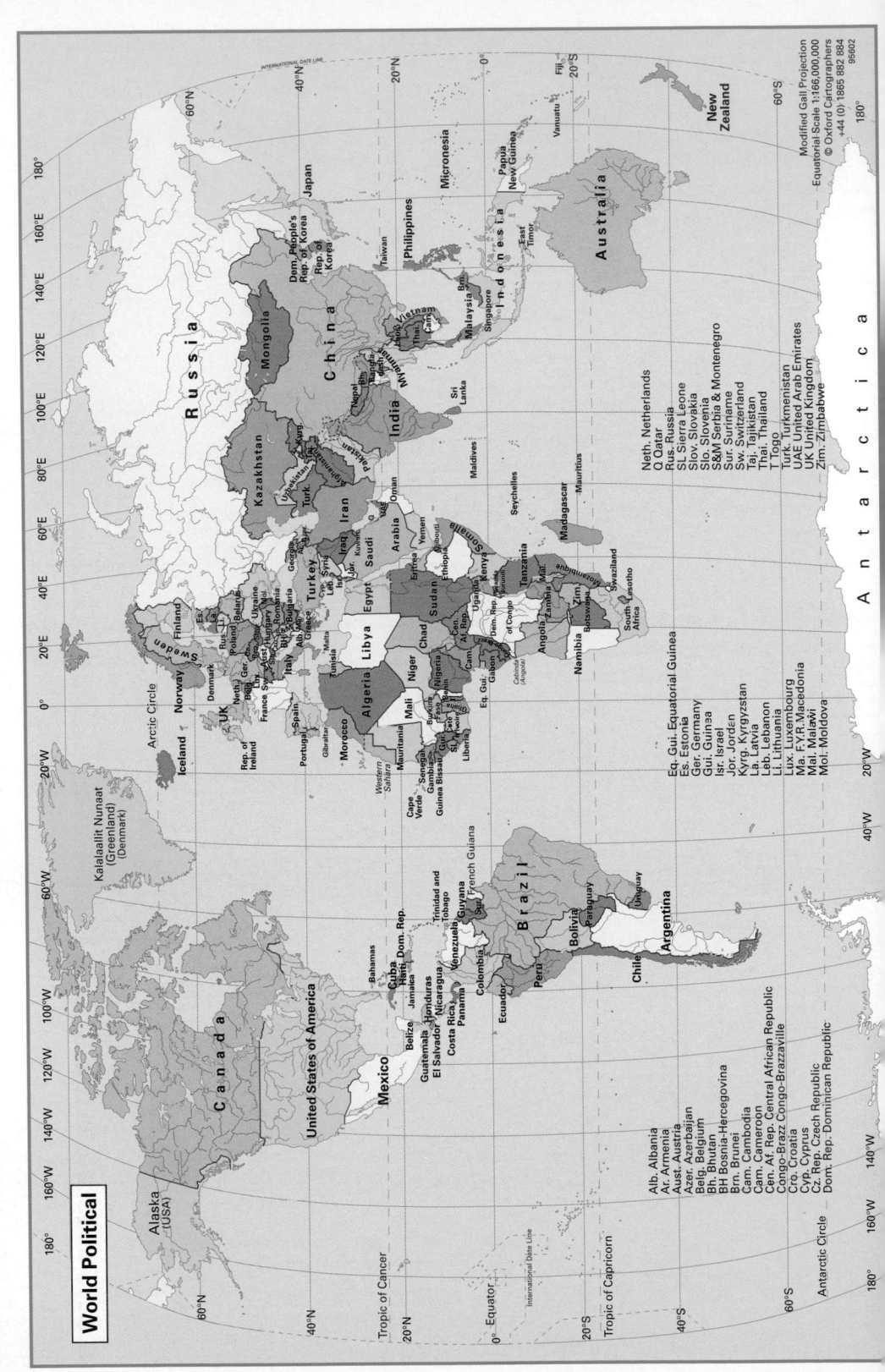

World Political

POPULATION BELOW POVERTY LINE – 80 per cent
(2001 est.)

POPULATION GROWTH RATE – 0.18 per cent
(2004 est.)

POPULATION DENSITY – 129 per sq. km (2002)

MILITARY EXPENDITURE – 2.4 per cent of GDP
(2003)

MILITARY PERSONNEL – 6,562: Army 5,512, Air
Force 1,050; Paramilitaries 3,279

CONSCRIPTION DURATION – 12 months

ILLITERACY RATE – (m) 0.4 per cent; (f) 1.3 per cent
(2003 est.)

GROSS ENROLMENT RATIO (percentage of relevant
age group) – primary 85 per cent (2002); secondary 72
per cent (2002); tertiary 29 per cent (2002)

CLIMATE AND TERRAIN

A landlocked country to the north-west of the Black Sea,
Moldova is a hilly plain lying mostly between the Prut
and Dneister rivers. Elevation extremes range from 430 m
(Dealul Bulanesti) at the highest point to 2 m (Dneister
River) at the lowest. The climate is continental and
average temperatures range from –4°C in January to 20°C
in August.

HISTORY AND POLITICS

Part of the Roman province of Dacia from AD 106,
Moldova saw centuries of invasion and occupation after
the fall of the Roman empire but formed part of an
independent Moldovan state from the mid-14th century.
The principality became a tributary state of the Ottoman
empire in the 16th century and then under Russian
protection in the 18th century. Partition saw the west
(Bukovina) lost to Austria in the 18th century and the east
(Bessarabia) to Russia in 1812. The remainder became
independent of Turkish overlordship in 1856 and in
1859 joined with Wallachia to form the principality of
Romania, which became fully independent in 1878. After
the Russian revolution in 1917, Bessarabia was seized and
incorporated into Romania in 1918, and the area east of
the River Dneister formed the Moldovan autonomous
republic in the Soviet Union from 1924. Romania was
forced to return Bessarabia to the Soviet Union in 1940
but, with its German allies, invaded and occupied the
Soviet republic of Moldova in 1941 until its reconquest
by Soviet forces in 1944.

Moldovan nationalism grew in the late 1980s as
President Gorbachev introduced reform in the Soviet
Union. The parliament declared political and economic
sovereignty in 1990, achieving independence and joining
the Commonwealth of Independent States (CIS) in 1991
after the failed August coup in Moscow caused the
collapse of the Soviet Union. Economic reforms,
including privatisation of state industry, were introduced
from 1993. Nationalist advocacy of unification with
Romania was defeated in a plebiscite in 1994.

The rise in Moldovan nationalism was matched by the
growing demands for autonomy by the republic's Russian
and Ukrainian ethnic minorities in the Transdnistria
region (east of the River Dneister) and the Gagauz in the
south-west. Both areas declared their independence in
1990, though this was not recognised. Both regions were
granted special autonomy status by the 1994 constitution,
and the Gagauz exercise a degree of autonomy over
political, economic and cultural affairs in 1994, but a
stalemate has developed over the status of Transdnistria.
Fighting between separatists and government forces in
1991 was followed by a fragile peace settlement in 1992

maintained by Russian peacekeeping troops. Talks
sponsored by the OSCE, EU, Russia and Ukraine
eventually led in 2003 to a draft proposal for a new
constitution for Moldova that would guarantee
Transdnistria federal status within the republic; the
question of the exact degree of autonomy that
Transdnistria would enjoy remains the major barrier to a
final agreement. In 2004 the government withdrew from
talks and imposed economic sanctions on the region, but
in June 2005 the parliament backed a Ukrainian
settlement proposal.

The governments in the first decade after independence
were made up of moderate reformists, but their
ineffectualness led to a resurgence in support for the
Communist Party of Moldova (PCM), which won the
majority of seats in the 1998 and March 2001 legislative
elections. In 2001, the new parliament elected the PCM
leader, Vladimir Voronin, as president and approved a new
government led by Vasile Tarlev, an independent member
of parliament. The PCM won the March 2005 legislative
election and, in April Vladimir Voronin was re-elected
president and Vasile Tarlev was reappointed prime
minister.

POLITICAL SYSTEM

The 1997 constitution was amended in 2000 to increase
the powers of the legislature and the executive. The head
of state is a president who (since 2000) is elected by the
legislature for a four-year term. The unicameral
legislature, *Parlamentul*, has 101 members, who are
directly elected for a four-year term. The prime minister
and government are nominated by the president.

HEAD OF STATE
President, Vladimir Voronin, *elected* 4 April 2001,
  re-elected 4 April 2005

SELECTED GOVERNMENT MEMBERS *as at July 2005*
Prime Minister, Vasile Tarlev
Deputy Prime Ministers, Valerian Cristea *(Without
  Portfolio)*; Andrei Stratan *(Foreign Affairs)*
Defence, Valeriu Lazar
Finance, Zinaida Greceanii
Foreign Affairs, Andrei Stratan
Interior, Col. Gheorghe Papuc

EMBASSY OF THE REPUBLIC OF MOLDOVA
Rue Tenbosch 54, Brussels 1050, Belgium
T (+ 32) 273 29659
Ambassador Extraordinary and Plenipotentiary, Mariana
  Durlesteanu, apptd 2004

BRITISH EMBASSY
ASITO Building Office 320, 57/1 Banulescu-Bodoni St,
Chisinau 2005 T (+ 373) 222 38991
Ambassador Extraordinary and Plenipotentiary, HE Bernard
  Whiteside, CVO, CMG, apptd 2002

ECONOMY AND TRADE

Moldova's moves towards a market economy have had
little success in achieving sustained economic growth and
it remains heavily dependent on the precarious Russian
economy, especially for energy supplies. Borrowing from
the World Bank and IMF was often interrupted
throughout the 1990s by Moldova's failure to meet the
conditions of its loans. This process was repeated in 2003
when the IMF announced it would not be continuing
with an aid package because Moldova had not met the

BRITISH EMBASSY
30 Enkh Taivny Gudamzh (PO Box 703), Ulaanbaatar 13.
T (+ 976) (11) 458133 E britemb@magicnet.mn
Ambassador Extraordinary and Plenipotentiary, HE Richard
Austen, apptd 2004

ECONOMY AND TRADE

The economy suffered after the withdrawal of Soviet
support and during the transition to a market economy,
though in recent years it has shown signs of growth. A
12.4 per cent increase in the price of copper (which, along
with cashmere, is Mongolia's main export commodity) in
2003 delivered an increase in exports. Ample mineral
deposits of gold, copper, tin, coal, uranium and tungsten
are being exploited and gold mining has increased
steadily since 1990. Mining, however, has played a part in
environmental degradation in the country and other
environmental problems such as desertification (caused in
part by the rapid conversion of virgin land to agriculture,
so accelerating soil erosion), over-grazing and
deforestation are increasing. This poses a threat to the
agrarian sector, which makes up 20.6 per cent of GDP.
The semi-desert areas of the Gobi region provide pasture
for sheep, goats, camels, horses and some cattle. In the
steppe areas to the north of the Gobi, pasturage is better
and livestock more abundant, although exceptionally
severe winter weather in 2000–1 decimated herds.

Mongolia joined the World Trade Organisation in
1997 and two years later the international donor
community pledged over US$300 million per year at the
Consultative Group Meeting held in Ulaanbaatar.
Mongolia has been successful in attracting foreign
investors and since 1990, 2,400 foreign companies have
invested more than US$800 million into mining,
agriculture processing and infrastructure.

GNI – US$1,100 million (2002); US$430 per capita
(2002)
ANNUAL AVERAGE GROWTH OF GDP – 5 per cent
(2003 est.)
INFLATION RATE – 1.5 per cent (2004 est.)
UNEMPLOYMENT – 4.6 per cent (2001 est.)
TOTAL EXTERNAL DEBT – US$859 million (2000 est.)
IMPORTS – US$600 million (2001)
EXPORTS – US$400 million (2001)

BALANCE OF PAYMENTS
Trade – US$156 million deficit (2002)
Current Account – US$158 million deficit (2002)

Trade with UK	2003	2004
Imports from UK	£2,641,000	£1,720,000
Exports to UK	1,840,000	2,331,000

TRANSPORT INFRASTRUCTURE

Mongolia has 1,815 km of railways and 49,250 km of
highways, though only about 20 per cent of the roads are
surfaced; many rural roads are rough tracks. The only
airport of any size is at Ulaanbaatar, though there are over
40 other airports and airstrips around the country. The
main rivers are navigable in the summer months but
remain ice-bound in winter.

MEDIA

There are five daily newspapers, including *Onoodor*,
which has the biggest circulation, and *Unen*, the organ of
the Mongolian People's Revolutionary Party and the
country's oldest publication. Television is a mixture of
state and privately owned broadcasters.

MOROCCO

Al-Mamlaka Al-Maghribiyya – Kingdom of Morocco

AREA – 446,300 sq. km. Neighbours: Algeria (east and
south-east), Western Sahara (south-west)
POPULATION – 32,209,101 (2004 est.). Standard Arabic
is the official language. Maghrebi Arabic and various
Berber languages (Tachelhit, Tamazight and Tarafit)
are the vernacular. French and Spanish are also spoken,
mainly in the towns. Islam is the state religion
CAPITAL – ΨRabat (population, 1,385,872, 1994
census)
MAJOR CITIES – ΨAgadir; ΨCasablanca (Ad-Dar-el-
Beida); Fez; Marrakesh; Meknès; Oujda
CURRENCY – Dirham (DH) of 100 centimes
NATIONAL ANTHEM – Hymne Cherifien
NATIONAL DAY – 30 July (Anniversary of the Throne)
NATIONAL FLAG – Red, with a green pentagram
LIFE EXPECTANCY (years) – 70.35 (2004 est.)
MORTALITY RATE (per 1,000 population) – 5.71
(2004 est.)
INFANT MORTALITY (per 1,000 births) – 43.25
(2004 est.)
HIV / AIDS ADULT PREVALENCE – 0.1 per cent
(2001 est.)
DEATH PENALTY – Yes
POPULATION GROWTH RATE – 1.61 per cent
(2004 est.)
POPULATION DENSITY – 66 per sq. km (2002)
URBAN POPULATION – 33 per cent (2001)

CLIMATE AND TERRAIN

Fertile coastal plains in the west rise to a mountainous
centre, with ranges, including the Atlas range, running
north-east to sourth-west. The Rif mountains lie along
the northern, Mediterranean coast. Elevation extremes
range from 4,165 m (Jbel Toubkal) at the highest point to
−55 m (Sebkha Tah) at the lowest. Average temperatures
in Rabat range from 7°C in January to 29°C in July,
although summer temperatures in the desert interior can
reach 41°C.

HISTORY AND POLITICS

From the tenth century BC, the northern coast was settled
by the Phoenicians, then in the first century AD became
part of the Roman empire until it was invaded by Vandals
and Visigoths in the fifth and sixth centuries. Arab
conquest of the area began in the seventh century and
Morocco was part of a succession of Arab empires, but
successfully resisted inclusion in the Turkish Ottoman
empire in the 16th century. The current Alawite dynasty
was founding in the mid-17th century and under its rule
Morocco remained independent but isolated until the
mid-19th century, when the country opened up to
European trade. The subsequent growth in Spanish and
French influence resulted in its partition into two
protectorates. In the Second World War, Morocco was a
base for the allied offensives that drove German forces out
of North Africa.

Nationalist campaigning for independence began in
the 1940s. French and Spanish forces withdrew in 1956,
leaving Morocco independent under Sultan Mohammed
V, who adopted the title of king in 1957; the coastal
towns of Ceuta and Melilla remain under Spanish control.
King Hassan II, who ruled from 1961 to 1999, annexed
the mineral-rich Western Sahara region in 1975.

Since the accession of King Mohammed VI in 1999,

Morocco has been moving away from absolute monarchy, increasing civil liberties and addressing human rights issues. The 2002 election to the House of Representatives was held to be the most democratic the country had ever witnessed. The Union Socialiste des Forces Populaires (USFP) and the Independence Party remained the two largest parties, and led the coalition government formed by prime minister Driss Jetou.

POLITICAL SYSTEM
The 1992 constitution was amended in 1996 to introduce a bicameral legislature. The head of state is a hereditary constitutional monarch. The king appoints the prime minister and, on the latter's recommendation, appoints the members of the Council of Ministers. There is a bicameral legislature. The lower house, the House of Representatives *(Majlis al-Nuwab)*, has 325 members who are directly elected for a five-year term. The Chamber of Councillors *(Majlis al-Mustashareen)* has 270 members, 60 per cent of whom are elected by local councils, 20 per cent by professional organisations and 20 per cent by trade unions. One-third of its members is elected every three years, to serve a nine-year term.

HEAD OF STATE
HM The King of Morocco, King Mohammed VI (Sidi Mohammed Ben Hassan), *born* 21 August 1963, *acceded* 23 July 1999
Heir, HRH Crown Prince Moulay Hassan, *born* 2003

SELECTED GOVERNMENT MEMBERS *as at July 2005*
Prime Minister, Driss Jetou
Finance and Privatisation, Fathallah Oualalou
Foreign Affairs and Co-operation, Mohamed Benaissa
Interior Affairs, Al Mustapha Sahel

EMBASSY OF THE KINGDOM OF MOROCCO
49 Queen's Gate Gardens, London SW7 5NE
T 020-7581 5001/4
Ambassador Extraordinary and Plenipotentiary, HE Mohammed Belmahi, apptd 1999

BRITISH EMBASSY
17 Boulevard de la Tour Hassan (BP 45), Rabat
T (+ 212) (0) 37 238600 E consular.rabat@fco.gov.uk
Ambassador Extraordinary and Plenipotentiary, HE Haydon Warren-Gash, apptd 2002

BRITISH COUNCIL
BP 427, 36 rue de Tanger, Rabat
E bc.morocco@britishcouncil.org.ma
Director, Steve McNulty

DEFENCE
The Army has 744 main battle tanks, 115 armoured infantry fighting vehicles, and 740 armoured personnel carriers. The Navy has two frigates and 27 patrol and coastal combatant vessels at five bases. The Air Force has 95 combat aircraft and 24 armed helicopters.
MILITARY EXPENDITURE – 4.2 per cent of GDP (2003)
MILITARY PERSONNEL – 196,300: Army 175,000, Navy 7,800, Air Force 13,500; Paramilitaries 50,000
CONSCRIPTION DURATION – 18 months

ECONOMY AND TRADE
Morocco's economy has been liberalised since the accession of King Mohammed VI, and this has attracted foreign investment. It remains a poor country, with large numbers of emigrant workers providing significant revenue in remittances. The large agrarian sector generates 20 per cent of GDP and 50 per cent of the labour force is engaged in agricultural production. There are a number of environmental issues connected with agriculture, such as desertification and soil erosion from farming. Cereal production is of high importance and the country produces 107,000 metric tonnes per year.

Morocco has some mineral reserves, mainly phosphate rock. Other industries include food processing, textiles and leather goods, while tourism is becoming increasingly important. The main imports are petroleum products, machinery, chemical products, iron and steel and grain and textiles. The EU, with which the country signed an association agreement in 1995, is Morocco's largest trading partner and in 1998 it awarded Morocco grants totalling US$98 million.
GNI – US$34,700 million (2002); US$1,170 per capita (2002)
ANNUAL AVERAGE GROWTH OF GDP – 6 per cent (2003 est.)
INFLATION RATE – 1.9 per cent (2000 est.)
UNEMPLOYMENT – 19 per cent (2003 est.)
TOTAL EXTERNAL DEBT – US$17,944 million (2000 est.)
FOREIGN DIRECT INVESTMENT – US$1,535 million (1997–2001)
IMPORTS – US$11,900 million (2002)
EXPORTS – US$7,900 million (2002)

BALANCE OF PAYMENTS
Trade – US$4,310 million deficit (2003)
Current Account – US$1,603 million surplus (2003)

Trade with UK	2003	2004
Imports from UK	£357,160,000	£340,000,000
Exports to UK	456,294,000	521,198,000

TRANSPORT INFRASTRUCTURE
There are 1,907 m of railways linking the major towns and 60,449 km of roads; an extensive network of 30,374 km of surfaced roads covers all the main towns. The main ports are Tangier, Casablanca and Agadir, all on the Atlantic coast. The principal airports are at Tangier and Casablanca; Royal Air Maroc is the national airline.

EDUCATION
Education is compulsory between the ages of seven and 16. There are government primary, secondary and technical schools. At Fez there is a theological university of great repute in the Muslim world. There is a secular university at Rabat. Schools for special denominations, Jewish and Catholic, are permitted and may receive government grants. American schools operate in Rabat and Casablanca. There is an English language university in Ifrane.
ILLITERACY RATE – (m) 38.1 per cent; (f) 63.9 per cent (2000)
GROSS ENROLMENT RATIO (percentage of relevant age group) – primary 107 per cent (2002); secondary 41 per cent (2002); tertiary 10 per cent (2002)

MEDIA
State control of the media has eased a little since the accession of King Mohammad VI, although its freedom to cover some topics is limited. There are three daily newspapers, one of which is state-owned. State-owned television and radio compete with a private broadcaster.

WESTERN SAHARA
Al-Jumhūriyya al-'Arabiyya as-Ṣahrāwiyya ad-Dimuqrāṭiyya – Sahrawi Arab Democratic Republic

AREA – 252,120 sq. km. Neighbours: Morocco (north), Algeria (north-east), Mauritania (east and south)
POPULATION – 244,943 (2000 estimate). Arabic is the official language. Hassaniya and Moroccan Arabic are the main spoken languages; Spanish is widely spoken in the towns. Almost all the population is Sunni Muslim
CAPITAL – El-Aaiūn (population, 139,000, 1990 estimate)
NATIONAL FLAG – Three horizontal stripes of black, white and green with a red crescent and a five-pointed star in the centre and a red triangle based on the hoist

Western Sahara came under Spanish rule in 1884, and became a province of Spain in 1934. Following Spain's withdrawal in 1975, the territory was divided between Morocco and Mauritania. The separatist Polisario Front began a guerrilla war to secure the Western Sahara's independence as the Sahrawi Arab Democratic Republic, setting up what they called a 'government in exile' in 1976. In 1979 Mauritania withdrew from its part of the territory, which was annexed by Morocco. Fighting between Polisario and Moroccan forces continued at varying levels of intensity until 1991, when a UN-brokered cease-fire came into effect. Around 180,000 Sahrawis were driven into exile, some to Algeria and some to Mauritania.

The 1991 cease-fire was established following both sides' agreement in 1988 to UN proposals for a peace settlement, which included the holding of a referendum on the future status of Western Sahara. Although both sides agreed to the proposals, the precise terms of the referendum have proved a sticking point and an impasse was reached that has still not been overcome despite further proposals in 2001–4; at these, Polisario agreed to a referendum offering the options of independence, semi-autonomy or integration, but Morocco is only prepared to accept semi-autonomy or integration for Western Sahara. The UN suspended the process of preparing for the referendum in 1996 because of disagreements over voter registration; the cease-fire remains in place.

MOZAMBIQUE

República de Moçambique – Republic of Mozambique

AREA – 784,100 sq. km. Neighbours: Swaziland (south), South Africa (south and west), Zimbabwe (west), Zambia and Malawi (north-west), Tanzania (north)
POPULATION – 18,811,731 (2004 est.). The official language is Portuguese but 16 other ethnic languages are spoken
CAPITAL – ΨMaputo (population, 1,039,700, 1998 census)
MAJOR CITIES – ΨBeira, ΨMatola; Nampula
CURRENCY – Metical (MT) of 100 centavos
NATIONAL ANTHEM – Hino nacional [National anthem]
NATIONAL DAY – 25 June (Independence Day)
NATIONAL FLAG – Horizontal green, black, yellow with white fimbriations; a red triangle based on the hoist containing the national emblem
LIFE EXPECTANCY (years) – 37.1 (2004 est.)
MORTALITY RATE (per 1,000 population) – 23.86 (2004 est.)

INFANT MORTALITY (per 1,000 births) – 137.8 (2004 est.)
HIV / AIDS ADULT PREVALENCE – 12.2 per cent (2003 est.)
DEATH PENALTY – No (abolished 1990)
POPULATION BELOW POVERTY LINE – 70 per cent (2001 est.)
POPULATION GROWTH RATE – 1.22 per cent (2004 est.)
POPULATION DENSITY – 24 per sq. km (2002)
MILITARY EXPENDITURE – 2.2 per cent of GDP (2003)
MILITARY PERSONNEL – 10,200–11,200: Army 9,000–10,000, Navy 200, Air Force 1,000
CONSCRIPTION DURATION – Two years
ILLITERACY RATE – (m) 36.5 per cent; (f) 67.3 per cent (2003 est.)
GROSS ENROLMENT RATIO (percentage of relevant age group) – primary 99 per cent (2002); secondary 13 per cent (2002); tertiary 1 per cent (2002)

CLIMATE AND TERRAIN
Coastal plains rise to plateaux in the centre and west, with mountains on the western borders. Elevation extremes range from 2,436 m (Monte Binga) at the highest point to 0 m (Indian Ocean) at the lowest. A number of the rivers run from the western highlands to the Indian Ocean coast, including the Zambezi, Limpopo, Sava and Ruvuma. The climate is tropical, with average temperatures in the capital ranging from 26°C in July to 30°C in January.

HISTORY AND POLITICS
Between the first and fourth centuries Mozambique was settled by Bantu peoples. Trade with India and the Arabian peninsula grew and migrants from both these regions settled in the coastal areas. The first European contact was with the Portuguese explorer Vasco de Gama, who arrived in 1498. Over the next three centuries the Portuguese exploited Mozambique for gold, ivory, spices and slaves. Proximity to the South African gold mines led to Mozambique's development as an important trading post from the late 19th century, and also as a source of cheap labour. It was administered as part of Portuguese India from 1751, becoming a separate colony in the late 19th century and an overseas province of Portugal in 1951. Concessions to private companies that had operated as de facto rulers over much of the country were ended in 1930.

The *Frente de Libertação de Moçambique* (Frelimo) was founded in 1962 to fight for independence and a ten-year guerrilla war against Portuguese forces began in 1964. Independence was achieved in 1975, when a one-party socialist republic was set up. Opposition to this was led from 1977 by the *Resistência Nacional de Moçambique* (Renamo) and a brutal civil war broke out that lasted until 1992, when a peace settlement was agreed and Renamo became a political party. Since the end of the civil war, the country has struggled to reconstruct its economy and infrastructure, hampered by devastating floods in 2000 and 2001 and severe drought in 2002 and 2003. An added problem is the large number of remaining landmines, and the resulting amputees, and the high level of HIV/AIDS infection.

In 1990 Frelimo abandoned Marxist-Leninism and ended one-party rule, introducing a multiparty system. The first elections under the new constitution were held in 1994 and won by Frelimo. Frelimo retained power in the 1999 and 2004 legislative and presidential elections, prompting allegations of vote-rigging by Renamo, though monitors believe that any irregularities were minor. In the December 2004 elections, the Frelimo candidate, Armando Guebuza, was elected president with 63.7 per cent of the vote, and Frelimo won 160 seats in the legislature, retaining its overall majority.

POLITICAL SYSTEM
Under the 2004 constitution, the executive president is directly elected and serves for a five-year term, which is renewable only once. The unicameral legislature, the Assembly of the Republic *(Assembleia da Republica)*, has 250 members, who are directly elected for a five-year term. The president appoints the prime minister and the Council of Ministers.

HEAD OF STATE
President, Armando Guebuza, *elected* 22 December 2004, *sworn in* 2 February 2005

SELECTED GOVERNMENT MEMBERS *as at July 2005*
Prime Minister, Minister of Planning and Finance, Luisa Diogo
Foreign Affairs and Co-operation, Alcinda Abreu
Industry and Commerce, Antonio Fernando
National Defence, Tobias Dai

HIGH COMMISSION FOR THE REPUBLIC OF MOZAMBIQUE
21 Fitzroy Square, London W1T 6EL T 020-7383 3800
High Commissioner, HE Antonio Gumende, apptd 2002

BRITISH HIGH COMMISSION
Av. Vladimir I Lenine 310, Box 55, Maputo
T (+ 258) (1) 320111/2/5/6/7 E bhc@virconn.com
High Commissioner, HE Howard Parkinson, apptd 2002

BRITISH COUNCIL
Rua John Issa 226, PO Box 4178, Maputo T (+ 258) (1) 310 921
E general.enquiries@britishcouncil.org.mz
Director, Simon Ingram-Hill

ECONOMY AND TRADE
Reconstruction of the economy and infrastructure after the civil war succeeded in achieving economic growth and attracting foreign investment. But development has been hampered by natural disasters, with devastating flooding in 2000 and 2001 and drought in 2002 and 2003 affecting the agricultural sector. This accounts for 26 per cent of GDP and employs 83 per cent of the labour force, and shellfish, cotton, cashew nuts, sugar and coconuts are important agricultural exports. There are considerable oil, gas, mineral and hydro-electric resources.
GNI – US$3,600 million (2002); US$200 per capita (2002)
ANNUAL AVERAGE GROWTH OF GDP – 13.9 per cent (2001 est.)
INFLATION RATE – 15.2 per cent (2002 est.)
TOTAL EXTERNAL DEBT – US$7,135 million (2000 est.)
FOREIGN DIRECT INVESTMENT – US$771 million (1997–2000)
IMPORTS – US$1,000 million (2000)
EXPORTS – US$364 million (2000)

BALANCE OF PAYMENTS
Trade – US$348 million deficit (2003)
Current Account – US$516 million deficit (2003)

Trade with UK	2003	2004
Imports from UK	£15,996,000	£10,536,000
Exports to UK	8,478,000	2,718,000

TRANSPORT INFRASTRUCTURE
The main ports are Maputo, Beira, Nacala and Quelimane; these handle trade also for landlocked countries such as Malawi and Zimbabwe, to which they are linked by rail. A new rail link to South Africa has been commissioned, and there are plans to develop rail and road links to Malawi and Zambia. There is currently a total of 3,123 km of railways. Of the 30,400 km of highways, only about one sixth is surfaced. The 460 km of navigable waterways are on Cahora Bassa Lake and the lower reaches of the Zambezi. The principal airports are at Maputo and Beira, with many more smaller airports and airstrips around the country.

MEDIA
Freedom of speech is guaranteed in the constitution and there are two daily newspapers and three weekly publications plus two television stations. Radio remains the main medium for the majority of the population, with UNESCO and the government funding around 40 stations.

MYANMAR

Pyidaungsu Myanmar Naingngandaw – Union of Myanmar

AREA – 676,578 sq. km. Neighbours: Bangladesh and India (west), China (north), Laos and Thailand (east)
POPULATION – 42,720,196 (2004 est.). The indigenous inhabitants are of similar racial types and speak languages of the Tibeto-Burman, Mon-Khmer and Thai groups. The three significant non-indigenous peoples are Indians, Chinese and Bangladeshis. Burmese is the official language, but minority languages include Bamar, Chin, Kachin, Kayah, Kayin (Karen), Mon, Rakhine and Shan. English is spoken in educated circles. Buddhism is the religion of 89.3 per cent of the people, with 5.6 per cent Christians, 3.8 per cent Muslims, 0.2 per cent Animists and 0.5 per cent Hindus
CAPITAL – ΨRangoon (Yangon)
MAJOR CITIES – Mandalay; ΨMawlamyine (Moulmein); ΨPathein (Bassein)
CURRENCY – Kyat (K) of 100 pyas
NATIONAL ANTHEM – Gba majay Myanmar [We shall love Myanmar for ever]
NATIONAL DAY – 4 January
NATIONAL FLAG – Red, with a canton of dark blue, inside which are a cogwheel and two rice ears surrounded by 14 white stars
LIFE EXPECTANCY (years) – 56.01 (2004 est.)
MORTALITY RATE (per 1,000 population) – 12.16 (2004 est.)
HIV / AIDS ADULT PREVALENCE – 1.2 per cent (2003 est.)
DEATH PENALTY – Yes
POPULATION GROWTH RATE – 0.47 per cent (2004 est.)

CLIMATE AND TERRAIN
Central lowlands are ringed by mountains in the west, north (part of the foothills of the Himalayas) and east, and running down the Kra isthmus that Myanmar shares with Thailand. Elevation extremes range from 5,881 m (Hkakabo Razi) at the highest point to 0 m (Andaman Sea) at the lowest. The lowlands are drained by the Irrawaddy river and its chief tributary, the Chindwin, and

the eastern mountains by the Salween. The climate is tropical, with a wet season from May until October. Average temperatures range from 16°C in January to 36°C in July, although interior summer temperatures can reach up to 43°C.

HISTORY AND POLITICS
Myanmar (previously known as Burma) was first unified in the 11th century by King Anawrahta, who adopted Theravada Buddhism. The Mongols under Kublai Khan invaded in 1287. The country was reunified in the 15th century but was weakened by internal dissension and wars with Siam (Thailand). King Alaunghpaya reunited the nation in the 18th century. Throughout the first half of the 19th century, border disputes with British India often spiralled into border clashes and eventually wars. Following the third Anglo-Burmese war, Burma was annexed as part of British India in 1885. Burma became a separate Crown colony in 1937, and was occupied by the Japanese during the Second World War. Following liberation by British troops and Burmese nationalists, the country gained its independence as the quasi-federal Union of Burma in 1948.

In 1962 a left-wing military coup led by General Ne Win led to the abolition of the federal system and the nationalisation of the economy. In 1974, a one-party socialist republic was formally established. Another coup in 1988 brought to power Gen. Saw Maung, who replaced all existing state institutions with the State Law and Order Council (SLORC), imposed martial law and changed the country's name to Myanmar; the SLORC was replaced by the State Peace and Development Council in 1997.

Pro-democracy forces, notably the National League for Democracy (NLD) under Aung San Suu Kyi, opposed military rule. In 1990 the NLD won a landslide victory in the first multiparty elections for 30 years. The military ignored the election results, prevented the Constituent Assembly from convening, and have continued to rule by diktat, suppressing and persecuting pro-democracy campaigners. Aung San Suu Kyi was under house arrest from 1989 to 1995 and almost continuously from 2000 to date. The NLD took part in UN-brokered talks with the government in 2000 but these stalled in 2003 and the NLD boycotted a constitutional convention that began in May 2004.

The constitutional convention was called by the then prime minister Khin Nyut, who was perceived to be a moderate; he was dismissed amid rumours of a power struggle in October 2004, and placed under house arrest on charges of corruption. Lt.-Gen. Soe Win was immediately named as his replacement. The constitutional convention resumed in February 2005, but without the participation of the leading opposition and ethnic groups.

INSURGENCIES
Since independence in 1948 the government has fought various insurgencies, mostly by ethnic groups. These have included the Kachin, Kayin (Karen), Karenni, Wa, Shan, Mon, Arakan and Chin ethnic minorities. Since 1992, 15 ethnic groups have signed cease-fire agreements following government offensives against them, although the Kayin (Karen) National Union (KNU) guerrillas and their allies in Karen state continue to fight. Many governments and non-governmental organisations believe that abuse of Myanmar's ethnic minorities continues. The UN Commission for Human Rights passed a resolution in 2004, co-sponsored by the EU, that expressed concern over human rights abuses.

POLITICAL SYSTEM
The constitution was effectively abrogated in 1988 when the executive and legislature were abolished and replaced by the State Law and Order Restoration Council (SLORC); the SLORC was replaced by the State Peace and Development Council (SPDC) in 1997. The *de facto* head of state is the chair of the SPDC. A unicameral 485-member Constituent Assembly was elected in 1990 but has not been allowed to convene. There are no permitted political parties.

STATE PEACE AND DEVELOPMENT COUNCIL *as at July 2005*
Chairman, Senior Gen. Than Shwe
Vice-Chairman, Gen. Maung Aye

SELECTED GOVERNMENT MEMBERS *as at July 2005*
Prime Minister, Lt.-Gen. Soe Win
Finance and Revenue, Maj.-Gen. Hla Tun
Foreign Affairs, Maj.-Gen. Nyan Win
Home Affairs, Maj.-Gen. Maung Oo

EMBASSY OF THE UNION OF MYANMAR
19A Charles Street, Berkeley Square, London W1J 5DX
T 020-7499 8841
Ambassador Extraordinary and Plenipotentiary, HE Dr Kyaw Win, apptd 1999

BRITISH EMBASSY
80 Strand Road (Box No. 638), Rangoon T (+ 95) (01) 256918
Ambassador Extraordinary and Plenipotentiary, HE Victoria Bowman, apptd 2002

BRITISH COUNCIL
78 Kanna Road, PO Box 638, Rangoon
T (+ 95) (01) 254658/256290
E enquiries@britishcouncil.org.mm
Director, Dr Marcus Milton

DEFENCE
The Army has some 150 main battle tanks and 325 armoured personnel carriers. The Navy has 75 patrol and coastal vessels at six bases. The Air Force has 125 combat aircraft and 29 armed helicopters.
MILITARY EXPENDITURE – 9.6 per cent of GDP (2003)
MILITARY PERSONNEL – 378,000: Army 350,000, Navy 13,000, Air Force 15,000; Paramilitaries 107,250

ECONOMY AND TRADE
Myanmar is extremely rich in natural resources such as timber (it is the world's largest exporter of teak) and precious gems (jade, pearls, rubies and sapphires). Fertile soil makes it an excellent environment for agriculture and it enjoys oil and gas deposits. However, the military junta controls all the major industries and the economy is characterised by corruption, mismanagement and widespread human rights abuses such as the use of forced labour. As a consequence, the country has become increasingly more poverty-stricken under military rule. The principal imports are capital goods, chiefly transport equipment, machinery and plant, consumer goods and semi-manufactures.

In 1997, Myanmar became a member of ASEAN. In 1997 the EU stripped Myanmar of trading privileges and the USA imposed economic sanctions; in 2003 the USA imposed further sanctions on the government.
ANNUAL AVERAGE GROWTH OF GDP – −1.3 per cent (2004 est.)
INFLATION RATE – 0.1 per cent (2000 est.)

TOTAL EXTERNAL DEBT – US$6,046 million (2000 est.)
IMPORTS – US$2,090 million (2003)
EXPORTS – US$2,480 million (2003)

BALANCE OF PAYMENTS
Trade – US$268 million deficit (2002)
Current Account – US$306 million deficit (2002)

Trade with UK	2003	2004
Imports from UK	£5,001,000	£2,164,000
Exports to UK	62,251,000	73,838,000

TRANSPORT INFRASTRUCTURE

The 12,800 km of navigable waterways includes the Irrawaddy and Chindwin rivers, the main stream of the Irrawaddy being navigable 900 miles from its mouth and carrying much traffic. The chief ports are Rangoon, Mawlamyine (Moulmein), Akyab (Sittwe), Pathein (Bassein), Pegu and Mandalay.

The railway network of 3,955 km covers most of the country. There are 2,452 miles of highways and 14,318 miles of other main roads. The main airports are at Rangoon, Mandalay and Tavoy.

EDUCATION

Most children attend primary school, and nearly five million are currently enrolled; in middle and high schools, enrolment is over two million. There are 16 universities, nine degree-awarding colleges and 87 other higher education institutions.

Vocational training is provided at 17 teacher training institutes and schools, 11 technical institutes, 17 technical high schools, 17 agricultural institutes and schools, and 41 vocational schools.

ILLITERACY RATE – (m) 11.0 per cent; (f) 19.4 per cent (2000)

GROSS ENROLMENT RATIO (percentage of relevant age group) – primary 90 per cent (2002); secondary 39 per cent (2002); tertiary 11 per cent (2002)

MEDIA

Nearly all the media outlets in Myanmar are controlled by the government. Four national publications and two television stations are all owned and controlled by the state. An opposition radio station, Democratic Voice of Myanmar, broadcasts on short-wave from Norway.

NAMIBIA

Republic of Namibia

AREA – 823,300 sq. km. Neighbours: Angola (north), South Africa (south), Botswana (east), Zambia and Zimbabwe (north-east)

POPULATION – 1,954,033 (2004 est.). The main population groups include: Ovambo (587,000), Kavango (110,000), Damara (89,000), Herero (89,000), whites (78,000), Nama (57,000), mixed race (48,000), Caprivians (44,000), Rehoboth Baster (29,000), Tswana (7,000). English is the official language, with Afrikaans, German and local languages also in use

CAPITAL – Windhoek (population, 147,056, 1995)

MAJOR TOWNS – Ondangwa; Oshakati; Rehoboth; Swakopmund; ΨWalvis Bay

CURRENCY – Namibian dollar of 100 cents, at parity to South African rand

NATIONAL ANTHEM – Namibia, land of the brave

NATIONAL DAY – 21 March (Independence Day)

NATIONAL FLAG – Divided diagonally blue, red and green with the red fimbriated in white; there is a gold twelve-rayed sun in the upper hoist

LIFE EXPECTANCY (years) – 40.53 (2004 est.)

MORTALITY RATE (per 1,000 population) – 21.02 (2004 est.)

INFANT MORTALITY (per 1,000 births) – 69.58 (2004 est.)

HIV / AIDS ADULT PREVALENCE – 21.3 per cent (2003 est.)

DEATH PENALTY – No (abolished 1990)

POPULATION BELOW POVERTY LINE – 50 per cent (2002 est.)

POPULATION GROWTH RATE – 1.25 (2004 est.)

POPULATION DENSITY – 2 per sq. km (2002)

MILITARY EXPENDITURE – 2.3 per cent of GDP (2003)

MILITARY PERSONNEL – 9,200: Army 9,000, Coast Guard 200; Paramilitaries 6,000

ILLITERACY RATE – (m) 15.6 per cent; (f) 6.3 per cent (2003 est.)

GROSS ENROLMENT RATIO (percentage of relevant age group) – primary 106 per cent (2002); secondary 61 per cent (2002); tertiary 7 per cent (2002)

CLIMATE AND TERRAIN

The Namib desert runs along the Atlantic coast and the Kalahari desert covers south-eastern Namibia, with veld in the north-east. The interior and coastal desert areas are divided by a line of hills and higher land. The terrain is almost completely arid and dry. Elevation extremes range from 2,606 m (Konigstein) at the highest point to 0 m (Atlantic Ocean) at the lowest. The only rivers not dependent on rains are the River Orange, which forms the southern border with South Africa, and the Zambezi, which is reached via the Caprivi Strip in the extreme north-east of the country. Average temperatures range from 21°C in July to 36°C in January.

HISTORY AND POLITICS

Pre-colonial Namibia was inhabited by Bantu tribes and San (Bushmen). It was annexed by Germany in 1884 and named South West Africa. From 1904 the Germans brutally suppressed indigenous uprisings, killing over half of some peoples and an estimated 80 per cent of the Herero. The territory was occupied by South Africa on behalf of the allies in 1914 and after the First World War it became a League of Nations mandated territory, administered by South Africa. After the Second World War, South Africa continued to administer South West Africa, but it started to treat the country as its sovereign territory, extending representation in South Africa's parliament to the white population in 1949, and extending its apartheid laws to South West Africa in 1966. These moves were despite the UN's refusal to permit the country's incorporation into South Africa in 1946 and the UN's vote to end the mandate in 1964, which South Africa ignored. In 1968 the UN General Assembly changed the country's name to Namibia, and the South West Africa People's Organisation (SWAPO), which had campaigned for racial equality and independence since the late 1950s, began a guerrilla war against South Africa. In 1978 South Africa accepted and then rescinded its acceptance of UN Security Council Resolution 435 for the granting of full independence to Namibia. South Africa's peace talks with Angola in 1998 led to agreement on independence for Namibia, and this was achieved on 21 March 1990; South Africa's Walvis Bay enclave was returned to Namibia in 1994.

The country has enjoyed stability since independence, apart from a brief period of secessionist violence in the Caprivi Strip in the late 1990s. In recent years there has been agitation for land reform, but although the government is committed to this policy, it has said that forced sales and illegal land occupation will not be allowed. The country's main problems arise from the demographic, economic and social impact of the high level of HIV/AIDS infection in the population.

SWAPO has been the dominant party since independence, holding the presidency and commanding a parliamentary majority without interruption. The 2004 presidential election was won by Hifikepunye Pohamba, who replaced Sam Nujoma, the president since independence. In the 2004 legislative elections, SWAPO retained its majority in both houses of parliament.

POLITICAL SYSTEM
Under the 1990 constitution, the executive president is directly elected for a five-year term, renewable only once (although in 1998, the constitution was amended to allow President Nujoma to stand for a third term in 1999). There is a bicameral legislature consisting of the 72-member National Assembly, directly elected for a five-year term, and the National Council, whose 26 members are indirectly elected by the regional councils from among their own members; the National Council is elected for a six-year term, and its main function is to review and consider legislation from the National Assembly. The president appoints the prime minister and the other ministers.

HEAD OF STATE
President, Hifikepunye Pohamba, *elected* 16 November 2004, *sworn in* 21 March 2005

SELECTED GOVERNMENT MEMBERS *as at July 2005*
Prime Minister, Nahas Angula
Deputy Prime Minister, Libertina Amathila
Defence, Maj.-Gen. Charles Namoloh
Finance, Saarah Kuugongelwa-Amathila
Foreign Affairs, Marco Hausiku
Home Affairs, Rosalind Nghidinwa

HIGH COMMISSION OF THE REPUBLIC OF NAMIBIA
6 Chandos Street, London W1G 9LU T 020-7636 6244
E namibia-highcomm@btconnect.com
High Commissioner, HE Ringo Aded, apptd 2004

BRITISH HIGH COMMISSION
116 Robert Mugabe Avenue, PO Box 22202, Windhoek
T (+ 264) (61) 274800 E bhc@mweb.com.na
High Commissioner, HE Alasdair MacDermott, apptd 2002

BRITISH COUNCIL
1–5 Fidel Castro Street, Windhoek T (+ 264) (61) 226 776
E general.enquiries@britishcouncil.org.na
British Council Officer, Patience Mahlalela

ECONOMY AND TRADE
The country has rich mineral deposits; diamonds account for 34 per cent and uranium for 10 per cent of exports. In total, minerals account for 54 per cent of exports. Agriculture and fisheries are also important. Some 55 per cent of Namibians are subsistence farmers. Tourism is

being developed as a way of diversifying the economy. The principal imports are machinery and transport equipment, foodstuffs, beverages, tobacco and mineral fuels.
GNI – US$3,500 million (2002); US$1,790 per capita (2002)
ANNUAL AVERAGE GROWTH OF GDP – 2.7 per cent (2001 est.)
INFLATION RATE – 8 per cent (2001 est.)
FOREIGN DIRECT INVESTMENT – US$187 million (1997–2000)
IMPORTS – US$1,550 (2001)
EXPORTS – US$1,180 (2001)

BALANCE OF PAYMENTS
Trade – US$179 million deficit (2002)
Current Account – US$97 million surplus (2002)

Trade with UK	2003	2004
Imports from UK	£10,070,000	£17,421,000
Exports to UK	103,947,000	220,892,000

TRANSPORT INFRASTRUCTURE
Namibia has 2,382 km of railways and 66,467 km of highways. In 2002, a road bridge across the Zambezi opened, linking Namibia with Zambia and raising hopes of an increase in regional trade. The main airports are at Windhoek and Odangwa, with over 130 smaller airports and airstrips around the country. The two main seaports are Luderitz and Walvis Bay.

MEDIA
There are six national newspapers including *The Namibian* and the Afrikkan language title *Die Republikein*. The state-administered Namibian Broadcasting Corporation runs alongside Desert TV, a private network based at Windhoek.

NAURU

The Republic of Nauru/Naoero

AREA – 21 sq. km
POPULATION – 12,809 (2004 est.). About 43 per cent of Nauruans are adherents of the Nauruan Protestant Church and there is a Roman Catholic mission on the island. The main languages are English and Nauruan
CAPITAL – ΨNauru
CURRENCY – Australian dollar ($A) of 100 cents
NATIONAL ANTHEM – Nauru bwiema (Nauru, our homeland)
NATIONAL DAY – 31 January (Independence Day)
NATIONAL FLAG – Twelve-point star (representing the 12 original Nauruan tribes) below a gold bar (representing the Equator), all on a blue background
LIFE EXPECTANCY (years) – 62.33 (2004 est.)
MORTALITY RATE (per 1,000 population) – 6.95 (2004 est.)
INFANT MORTALITY (per 1,000 births) – 10.14 (2004 est.)
DEATH PENALTY – No (abolished 1968)
POPULATION GROWTH RATE – 1.87 per cent (2004 est.)
POPULATION DENSITY – 609.9 per sq. km (2004 est.)

CLIMATE AND TERRAIN

Nauru is a low-lying coral island in the Pacific Ocean 42 km south of the Equator and 4,000 km north-east of Sydney, Australia. The climate is tropical, with average daily temperatures an almost consistent 29°C.

HISTORY AND POLITICS

Nauru was first settled by Polynesian and Melanesian groups. The first Europeans to visit the island were British whalers in 1798 and by 1888 Nauru was annexed by Germany. At the outbreak of the First World War Nauru was occupied by Australia, which continued to administer the island under a League of Nations mandate in 1920. During the Second World War, the island was occupied by the Japanese in 1942–3. UN trusteeship status superseded the mandate in 1947 by the UN and Nauru continued to be administered by Australia until it became independent on 31 January 1968.

The country's looming financial crisis led to rapid changes in president in 2003, with four presidents between January and May. Ludvig Scotty, elected president in May 2003, was dismissed following a vote of no confidence and replaced by Rene Harris in August 2003. However, Harris's government lost a vote of no confidence in June 2004 and Scotty returned to office. Scotty dismissed the parliament in September 2004 after it failed to pass a reform budget. In the ensuing general election in October, his supporters won a majority of seats and Scotty was re-elected president unopposed.

POLITICAL SYSTEM

Under the 1968 constitution, the executive president is elected by parliament from among its members for a three-year term. The unicameral parliament has 18 members, who are directly elected for a three-year term. The president appoints the cabinet, which comprises no fewer than five, nor more than six members including the president.

HEAD OF STATE
President, Ludvig Scotty, *elected*, 26 October 2004

SELECTED GOVERNMENT MEMBERS *as at July 2005*
Foreign Affairs, Finance and Internal Affairs, David Adeang
Health, Keiren Keke

HONORARY CONSULATE
Romshed Courtyard, Underriver, Sevenoaks, Kent TN15 0SD
T 01732-746061 E nauru@weald.co.uk
Honorary Consul, Martin Weston

BRITISH HIGH COMMISSIONER
HE Charles Mochan, resident at Suva, Fiji

ECONOMY AND TRADE

The economy is heavily dependent on phosphate extraction, but reserves are nearing exhaustion with only 112,900 tonnes mined in 2003 compared with 650,751 tonnes in 2000. Once revenue from mining ceases, the country will derive income from the Nauru Phosphate Royalties Trust set up using profits from mining and from compensation for environmental damage from Australia. However, the future is very uncertain as the phosphates were the island's only resource and all other goods, including food and water, have to be imported. The government currently faces severe financial problems after defaulting on loans and is dependent on international aid. Attempts at diversification include small-scale tourism and offshore banking, although the latter has attracted international criticism over alleged money-laundering. The country had started to default on its loan payments from April 2004, causing its assets in Australia to be seized, and in July 2004 Australian officials took charge of Nauru's state finances.

Trade with UK	2003	2004
Imports from UK	£402,000	£445,000
Exports to UK	211,000	252,000

EDUCATION AND MEDIA

Education is free of charge and compulsory between the ages of six and 17. There are 10 infant and primary, and two secondary schools on the island with a total enrolment of about 2,707 pupils.

Nauru has no daily press but three weekly or fortnightly publications. A domestic radio service is supplemented by Nauru Television (NTV), which broadcasts programmes from New Zealand.

NEPAL

Nepāl Adhirājya / Kingdom of Nepal

AREA – 147,181 sq. km. Neighbours: China (north), India (west, south and east)
POPULATION – 27,070,666 (2004 est.). The inhabitants are of mixed stock, with Tibetan characteristics prevailing in the north and Indian in the south. The official religion is Hinduism; 87 per cent of the population are Hindus, 8 per cent Buddhist and 3 per cent Muslim. The official language is Nepali
CAPITAL – Kathmandu (population, 535,000, 1993)
MAJOR CITIES – Lalitpur; Biratnagar; Bhaktapur
CURRENCY – Nepalese rupee of 100 paisa
NATIONAL ANTHEM – Sri Man Gumbhira Nepali Prachanda Pratapi Bhupati (May glory crown our illustrious Sovereign, the gallant Nepalese)
NATIONAL DAYS – 18 February (National Democracy Day); 28 December (The King's Birthday)
NATIONAL FLAG – Double pennant of crimson with blue border on peaks; white moon with rays in centre of top peak; white quarter sun, recumbent in centre of bottom peak
LIFE EXPECTANCY (years) – 59.4 (2004 est.)
MORTALITY RATE (per 1,000 population) – 9.66 (2004 est.)
HIV / AIDS ADULT PREVALENCE – 0.5 per cent (2003 est.)
DEATH PENALTY – No (abolished 1997)
POPULATION GROWTH RATE – 2.23 per cent (2004 est.)
POPULATION DENSITY – 169 per sq. km (2002)
MILITARY EXPENDITURE – 1.9 per cent of GDP (2003)
MILITARY PERSONNEL – Army 72,000; Paramilitaries 62,000
ILLITERACY RATE – (m) 37.3 per cent; (f) 72.4 per cent (2003 est.)
GROSS ENROLMENT RATIO (percentage of relevant age group) – primary 122 per cent (2002); secondary 44 per cent (2002); tertiary 5 per cent (2002)

CLIMATE AND TERRAIN

The north of landlocked Nepal lies in the Himalayas, with the snowline at about 4,880 m. The terrain descends from the mountains through a hilly central belt with fertile valleys to a southern region, the Terai, that lies in the valley of the River Ganges; the Terai forms approximately 23 per cent of the total land area. Elevation extremes range from 8,850 m (Mt Everest) at the highest point to 70 m (Kanchan Kalan) at the lowest. Average temperatures in Khatmandu range from 2°C in January to 28°C in July.

HISTORY AND POLITICS

Modern Nepal was formed from a number of hill states that were unified in the 18th century by the Gurkha ruler Prithvi Naryan Shah, who founded the current ruling dynasty. After war with the British in 1815–16, Nepal became a British-dependent buffer state; its independence was formally recognised by Britain in 1923.

Power was seized by Jung Bahdur in 1846. He assumed the title Rana and his family became hereditary chief ministers, reducing the monarchy to a purely ceremonial role and keeping the country isolated. In 1950–1 the Ranas were overthrown in a 'palace revolution' and the monarchy was restored to power. A parliamentary system of government was introduced in 1959 but was replaced in 1962 by a system of indirectly elected *panchyats* (village councils); political parties were proscribed. In 1980, elections to the National Assembly became direct, though parties remained banned. Major constitutional reform came in 1990 after violent pro-democracy demonstrations; the *panchyat* system was abolished, the monarchy's powers were restricted and a multiparty parliamentary system was reintroduced.

Since 1990, the factionalised nature of Nepali politics has led to frequent changes of government, causing social instability and doing little to remedy the extreme poverty of much of the population. This instability has been exacerbated since 1996 by a Maoist insurgency led by the Nepal Communist Party. The insurgency began in the remote west but has spread to most of the country. The government's often brutal attempts to suppress the insurgency have met with little success; both the insurgents and the army and police have been implicated in human rights abuses and atrocities. Cease-fires in 2001 and 2003 were shortlived.

In June 2001, King Birendra, Queen Aishwarya and seven other members of the royal family were murdered by Crown Prince Dipendra, who then shot himself. A few days later, King Birendra's brother, Prince Gyanendra, became king.

In the 1999 elections to the House of Representatives, an overall majority of seats was won by the Nepali Congress Party, which has dominated politics since the restoration of the monarchy in 1951. However, the largest party in the National Council after the 2001 election was the Nepal Communist Party – United Marxist Leninist (CPN-UML). In 2002 the king dissolved parliament at the prime minister's request but the elections that were supposed to follow have been repeatedly postponed. Attempts by politicians to reopen parliament have failed, although some 'special sessions' were held in June and July 2003 to debate restrictions on the king's powers. In February 2005, the king took direct control of government, appointing a new Council of Ministers with himself as the chair.

POLITICAL SYSTEM

Under the 1990 constitution, the head of state is a hereditary constitutional monarch. Executive power is vested in the king and the Council of Ministers; the prime minister is appointed by the king but must be able to command a parliamentary majority. The bicameral legislature consists of a 205-member House of Representatives, directly elected for a five-year term, and a 60-member National Council comprising ten royal nominees and 50 members indirectly elected for a six-year term, with one-third elected every two years. The House of Representatives was dissolved in 2002, and there has been no prime minister since the king took direct power in February 2005.

HEAD OF STATE
HM The King of Nepal, Chair of the Council of Ministers, Defence King Gyanendra Bir Bikram Shah Dev, *acceded* 4 June 2001
Heir, Crown Prince Paras Bir Bikram Shah Dev

SELECTED GOVERNMENT MEMBERS *as at July 2005*
Foreign Affairs, Ramesh Nath Pandey
Finance, Madhukar Shumsher Rana
Home Affairs, Dan Bahadur Shahi

ROYAL NEPALESE EMBASSY
12A Kensington Palace Gardens, London W8 4QU
T 020-7229 1594/6231 E rnelondon@btconnect.com
Ambassador Extraordinary and Plenipotentiary, Prabal Shumsher Jung Bahadur Rana

BRITISH EMBASSY
Lainchaur Kathmandu, PO Box 106
T (+977) (1) 4410583 E britemb@wlink.com.np
Ambassador Extraordinary and Plenipotentiary, HE Keith Bloomfield, apptd 2002

BRITISH COUNCIL
PO Box 640, Lainchaur, Kathmandu
T (+977) (1) 410798 E general.enquiry@britishcouncil.org.np
Director, Barbara Hewitt

ECONOMY AND TRADE

The country is very poor, and dependent on foreign aid and trade with India. About 90 per cent of Nepalese are employed in agricultural production, which centres around rice, corn, wheat, sugar cane and root crops. Manufacturing accounts for 9 per cent of GDP, with construction and the financial sector contributing 10 per cent each. Tourism's contribution to revenue is restricted by the violent insurgency in much of the country and development might compound Nepal's existing environmental problems, which include deforestation, destruction of animal habitats and vehicle pollution in Kathmandu.

GNI – US$5,500 million (2002); US$230 per capita (2002)
ANNUAL AVERAGE GROWTH OF GDP – 6.0 per cent (2000 est.)
INFLATION RATE – 1.5 per cent (2000 est.)
TOTAL EXTERNAL DEBT – US$2,823 million (2000 est.)
IMPORTS – US$1,750 million (2003)
EXPORTS – US$662 million (2003)

BALANCE OF PAYMENTS
Trade – US$765 million deficit (2001)
Current Account – US$339 million deficit (2001)

Trade with UK	2003	2004
Imports from UK	£6,944,000	£6,561,000
Exports to UK	10,179,000	10,407,000

TRANSPORT INFRASTRUCTURE

There is a total of 13,223 km of roads, of which 4,073 km are surfaced. A major highway runs the length of the country through the Terai, linking the main lowland centres and extending into the hills to Kathmandu and Pokhara. Major highways connect Kathmandu with India and Tibet. There are 155 km of railways. The principal airport is at Kathmandu, and there are over 40 smaller airports and airstrips around the country.

MEDIA

The two most widely circulated newspapers are the *Kathmandu Post* and *Rising Nepal*. The government-run Radio Nepal is the most influential media outlet in the country.

THE NETHERLANDS

Koninkrijk der Nederlanden – Kingdom of the Netherlands

AREA – 33,900 sq. km Neighbours: Belgium (south), Germany (east)
POPULATION – 16,318,199 (2004 est.): 36 per cent Catholic, 27 per cent Reformed Church, 8 per cent Muslim. The language is Dutch, a West Germanic language of Low Franconian origin closely akin to Old English and Low German. It is spoken in the Netherlands and the northern part of Belgium (Flanders). Frisian is spoken in Friesland. Dutch is the official language in the Netherlands Antilles and Aruba; Papiamento, a mixture of Dutch and Spanish, is the vernacular
CAPITAL – ΨAmsterdam (population, 736,538, 2001)
SEAT OF GOVERNMENT – The Hague (Den Haag or, in full, 's-Gravenhage), population 443,745 (2001)
MAJOR CITIES – Eindhoven; Groningen; Haarlem; ΨRotterdam; Tilburg; Utrecht
CURRENCY – Euro (€) of 100 cents
NATIONAL ANTHEM – Wilhelmus van Nassouwe (William of Nassau)
NATIONAL FLAG – Three horizontal bands of red, white and blue
LIFE EXPECTANCY (years) – 78.68 (2004 est.)
MORTALITY RATE (per 1,000 population) – 8.67 (2004 est.)
INFANT MORTALITY (per 1,000 births) – 5.11 (2001 est.)
HIV / AIDS ADULT PREVALENCE – 0.2 per cent (2001 est.)
DEATH PENALTY – No (abolished 1982)
POPULATION GROWTH RATE – 0.57 (2004 est.)
POPULATION DENSITY – 477 per sq. km (2002)
URBAN POPULATION – 90 per cent (2001)

CLIMATE AND TERRAIN

The Netherlands is a low-lying country, below sea level in many places, making it susceptible to flooding despite the coastal defences and network of dykes and canals. Its land area has been extended over the centuries by land reclamation (polders), found especially in the west around the huge freshwater lake of the IJsselmeer, created in the 1930s by damming the Zuider Zee. The country is crossed by three major European rivers, the Rhine, Mass and Scheldt, whose estuaries are in the south-west. Elevation extremes range from 322 m (Vaalserberg) at the highest point and −7 m (Zuidplaspolder) at the lowest

point. The climate is temperate with average temperatures ranging from 0°C in January to 23°C in July.

HISTORY AND POLITICS

The area was part of the Frankish empire by the eighth century and was subsequently part of the Holy Roman Empire. From the 12th century the mercantile towns of the Low Countries became virtually independent principalities. These came under the influence of the dukes of Burgundy in the 15th century and of the Habsburgs in 1477, passing to the Spanish branch of the Habsburgs in 1555. The northern provinces, led by William, Prince of Orange, rebelled against Spanish rule in 1568. The war of independence ended with the seven northern provinces forming the Union of Utrecht in 1579, and in 1581 independence was declared; the United Provinces were formally recognised as an independent republic in 1648.

The 17th century was a 'golden age' in which the Dutch led the world in trade, art and science, founding colonies in the East and West Indies. But commercial and colonial rivalries led to three wars with Britain in the late 17th century, and resisting French attempts at domination exhausted the country in the 18th century. In 1795 French revolutionary armies overran the country and it remained under French rule until 1814. In 1815 the northern and southern provinces were reunited into one kingdom, with the hereditary stadholder of the northern provinces becoming King William I of the Netherlands and grand duke of Luxembourg; the southern provinces seceded to form Belgium in 1830 and the Duchy of Luxembourg was made an independent state in 1867. The Netherlands was neutral during the First World War, but during the Second World War the country was invaded and occupied by Germany from 1940 until 1945.

The post-war period was marked by economic expansion and the construction of a liberal welfare state. The Netherlands formed the Benelux economic union with Belgium and Luxembourg in 1948, was a founder member of the EEC in 1958 and joined the euro zone in 1999. In a referendum in June 2005, its population rejected ratification of the EU constitution.

Although a stable democracy, one party has rarely commanded a sufficient majority to govern alone and post-war governments have usually been coalitions of two or more parties. After the 2003 legislative election, the Christian Democratic Appeal (CDA) remained the largest party, with 23 seats; the Partij van de Arbeid (PvdA) gained 19 seats. After four months of talks, a new coalition comprising members of the CDA, the Volkspartij voor Vrijheid en Democratie (VVD) and the Democrats 66, led by Jan Peter Balkenende, was sworn into office in May 2003.

POLITICAL SYSTEM

Under the 1983 constitution, the kingdom consists of three autonomous elements: the Netherlands, the Netherlands Antilles, and Aruba. The head of state is a hereditary constitutional monarch. The legislature, the States-General, consists of the First Chamber *(Eerste Kamer)* of 75 members, elected for four years by provincial councillors; and the Second Chamber *(Tweede Kamer)* of 150 members, directly elected for a four-year term. The head of government is the prime minister, who is responsible to the States-General.

HEAD OF STATE

HM The Queen of the Netherlands, Queen Beatrix
Wilhelmina Armgard, KG, GCVO, *born* 31 January
1938; *succeeded* 30 April 1980
Heir, HRH Prince Willem Alexander, *born* 27 April 1967

SELECTED GOVERNMENT MEMBERS *as at July 2005*
Prime Minister, General Affairs, Jan Peter Balkenende
Deputy Prime Ministers, Gerrit Zalm, Thom de Graf
Defence, Henrik Kamp
Economic Affairs, Laurens Jan Brinkhorst
Foreign Affairs, Bernard Bot
Interior, Johan Remkes

ROYAL NETHERLANDS EMBASSY
38 Hyde Park Gate, London SW7 5DP **T** 020-7590 3200
Ambassador Extraordinary and Plenipotentiary, HE Count
Jan Mark Vladimir Anton de Marchant et
d'Ansembourg, apptd 2003

BRITISH EMBASSY
Lange Voorhout 10, The Hague, NL-2514 ED
T (+ 31) (0) 70 4270 427
Ambassador Extraordinary and Plenipotentiary, HE Sir
Colin Budd, KCMG, apptd 2001

BRITISH COUNCIL
Weteringschans 85A, NL-1017 RZ Amsterdam
T (+ 31) (0) 20 550 6060 **E** david.alderdice@britcoun.nl
Director, David Alderdice

DEFENCE

The Army has 283 main battle tanks, 345 armoured
infantry fighting vehicles and 318 armoured personnel
carriers. The Navy has four submarines, six destroyers,
nine frigates, ten combat aircraft and 21 armed
helicopters. The Air Force has 137 combat aircraft and 30
armed helicopters.
MILITARY EXPENDITURE – 1.6 per cent of GDP (2003)
MILITARY PERSONNEL – 46,330: Army 23,150, Navy
12,130, Air Force 11,050; Paramilitaries 6,800

ECONOMY AND TRADE

After two decades of growth the economy started to falter
in 2000 with the slowdown in the global economy.
Unemployment has risen, as has the government budget
deficit. Public spending cuts and welfare reforms were
introduced in 2004, provoking demonstrations.

Despite employing a mere 4 per cent of the labour
force, agricultural exports such as fruit, flower bulbs and
cut flowers form a major part of economic activity and the
country is ranked third in the world for the scale of its
agricultural industries. Produce includes wheat, rye,
barley, sugar cane, cattle, poultry, pig farming and dairy
products; there is also an important fishing industry. The
industrial sector includes the manufacture of electrical
machinery and equipment, metal and engineering
products, chemicals, petroleum refining, construction and
micro-electronics. The service industries represent 70 per
cent of the economy. Eighty per cent of trade is with other
EU countries.
GNI – US$377,600 million (2002); US$23,390 per
capita (2002)
ANNUAL AVERAGE GROWTH OF GDP – –0.7 per cent
(2003 est.)
INFLATION RATE – 2.1 per cent (2003 est.)
UNEMPLOYMENT – 5.3 per cent (2003 est.)

FOREIGN DIRECT INVESTMENT – US$130,363 million
(1997–2000)
IMPORTS – US$232,000 million (2003)
EXPORTS – US$259,000 million (2003)

BALANCE OF PAYMENTS
Trade – US$26,570 million surplus (2003)
Current Account – US$16,467 million surplus (2003)

Trade with UK	2003	2004
Imports from UK	£10,076,160,000	£11,864,126,000
Exports to UK	11,066,270,000	17,778,667,000

TRANSPORT INFRASTRUCTURE

The major seaport is Rotterdam, although there are a
number of other ports on the river estuaries or linked to
the coast by the canals; 5,046 km on inland waterways,
including canals, is navigable by ships of up to 50 tons.
There are 58,133 km of interurban roads, of which 2,207
km are motorways. The total length of the railway system
is 2,808 km, of which 2,061 km are electrified. The
principal airports are at Amsterdam, Rotterdam and
Eindhoven, with a further 24 smaller airports and airstrips
around the country.

EDUCATION

Primary and secondary education is given in both
denominational and state schools and is compulsory. The
principal universities are at Leiden, Utrecht, Groningen,
Amsterdam (two), Nijmegen, Maastricht and Rotterdam,
and there are technical universities at Delft, Eindhoven,
Enschede and Wageningen (agriculture).
GROSS ENROLMENT RATIO (percentage of relevant age
group) – primary 108 per cent (2002); secondary 124
per cent (2002); tertiary 55 per cent (2002)

MEDIA AND CULTURE

There are five national daily papers and a competitive
television sector that includes Nederlandse Omroep
Stichting (NOS), which oversees the country's three
public networks and a large number of commercial
stations.

The Netherlands has produced many of the world's
major artists including Rembrandt (1606–69), Jan
Vermeer (1632–75) and Vincent van Gogh (1853–90).
The thinker Baruch Spinoza (1632–77), whose work
Ethics is considered foremost in rationalist philosophy, was
born in Amsterdam.

OVERSEAS TERRITORIES

ARUBA

AREA – 193 sq. km
POPULATION – 70,007 (2001 estimate)
CAPITAL – ΨOranjestad (population 25,000); and Sint
Nicolaas (17,000)
CURRENCY – Aruban florin

The Caribbean island became part of the Dutch West
Indies from 1828 and part of the Netherlands Antilles
from 1845. On 1 January 1986 it became a separate
territory, with full internal autonomy; plans to achieve
independence by 1996 were dropped in 1994. The
principal economic activities are tourism, petroleum
refining and offshore financial services.
Governor, Fredis Refunjol
Prime Minister, Nelson O. Oduber

NETHERLANDS ANTILLES

AREA – 800 sq. km
POPULATION – 255,000 (2001) Curaçao 143,307,
Bonaire 13,724, St Maarten 41,718, St Eustatius
2,249, Saba 1,704
CAPITAL – ΨWillemstad (on Curaçao) (pop. 50,000)
CURRENCY – Netherlands Antilles guilder of 100 cents

The Netherlands Antilles comprise the Caribbean islands of Curaçao, Bonaire, part of St Maarten, St Eustatius, and Saba. The islands were colonised by the Dutch in the 17th century and became a self-governing federation with a 22-member federal parliament in 1954. By April 2005, the islands had all held referendums on the future status of the federation; most backed dissolution of the federation but did not support independence. The principal economic activities are tourism, petroleum refining and offshore financial services.
Governor, Frits Goedgedrag
Prime Minister, Etienne Ys

NEW ZEALAND

AREA – 268,000 sq. km
POPULATION – 3,993,817 (2004 est.): 79 per cent European stock, 13 per cent Maori, 5 per cent other Pacific islanders. The main religion is Christianity. In 1991 the principal denominations were Anglican 22.1 per cent, Presbyterian 16.3 per cent, Roman Catholic 15 per cent, Methodist 4.2 per cent, Baptist 2.1 per cent. The official languages are English and Maori
CAPITAL – ΨWellington (population, 340,719, 2001 census)
MAJOR CITIES – ΨAuckland; ΨChristchurch; ΨDunedin; Hamilton; ΨNapier-Hastings
CURRENCY – New Zealand dollar (NZ$) of 100 cents
NATIONAL ANTHEM – God save the Queen/God defend New Zealand
NATIONAL DAY – 6 February (Waitangi Day)
NATIONAL FLAG – Blue ground, with Union Flag in top left quarter, four five-pointed red stars with white borders on the fly
LIFE EXPECTANCY (years) – 78.49 (2004 est.)
MORTALITY RATE (per 1,000 population) – 7.54 (2004 est.)
INFANT MORTALITY (per 1,000 births) – 5.96 (2004 est.)
HIV / AIDS ADULT PREVALENCE – 0.1 per cent (2003 est.)
DEATH PENALTY – No (abolished 1989)
POPULATION GROWTH RATE – 1.05 per cent (2004 est.)
POPULATION DENSITY – 15 per sq. km (2002)
URBAN POPULATION – 86 per cent (2001)

CLIMATE AND TERRAIN

New Zealand consists of a number of islands in the South Pacific Ocean, and also administers a number of territories and associated states in the region. The two larger islands, North Island and South Island, are separated by the relatively narrow Cook Strait. The remaining islands are much smaller and widely dispersed.

Much of the North and South Islands is mountainous. The North Island mountains include several volcanoes, three of which are active. The principal range is the Southern Alps, extending the entire length of the South Island to the west of the Canterbury Plains. There are geysers and hot springs in the Rotorua district and glaciers in the Southern Alps. Elevation extremes range from 3,764 m (Mt Cook) at the highest point to 0 m (Pacific Ocean) at the lowest. Average temperatures in Christchurch (South Island) range from 1°C in July to 24°C in January.

HISTORY AND POLITICS

Settled by Polynesian tribes since the ninth century, New Zealand was sighted by the the Dutch navigator Abel Tasman in 1642 but he did not land. The British explorer James Cook surveyed the coastline in 1769, the year in which the islands were claimed by the British. In 1840, under the Treaty of Waitangi, the Maoris accepted British sovereignty, with Maoris retaining some territorial rights. The Maoris attempted to resist the loss of their land in the 1840s and 1860s; their resistance was defeated but concessions such as parliamentary representation were won. New Zealand was administered as part of the New South Wales colony until 1841, when it became a separate colony. In 1907 it was granted dominion status; in 1931 the Statute of Westminster tacitly acknowledged its independence, which was formally confirmed in 1947.

New Zealand forces took part in the First and Second World Wars, the Korean War and the Vietnam War (1965–72). With Australia and the USA it formed the ANZUS Pacific security treaty in 1951, but its non-nuclear military policy led to disagreements with the USA (and France) in 1985, and in 1986 the USA suspended its ANZUS obligations towards New Zealand. The UK's entry into the EEC in 1973 forced New Zealand to form closer trade links with Australia; the two countries entered into a free-trade agreement in 1988. In the 1990s Maori demands for compensation for land lost to European settlers were settled either by compensation payments or grants of land.

Post-war politics has been dominated by the National Party and the Labour Party, forming governments on their own or in coalition with smaller parties. Following the 2002 legislative election, the state of the parties in the House of Representatives was: Labour Party 52 seats, National Party 27, New Zealand First 13, ACT New Zealand 9; Green Party 9; United Future 8; Jim Anderton's Progressive Coalition 2. The Labour Party and the Progressive Coalition formed a goverment, with support in the House from the United Future and Green parties. A general election was held on 17 September 2005 and was won by the ruling Labour Party with 50 seats in the Parliament and 41 per cent of the vote. Prime Minister Helen Clarke announced she would run a caretaker government until a coalition government could be formed.

POLITICAL SYSTEM

There is no written constitution. The head of state is the British sovereign, represented by the governor-general, who is appointed on the advice of the New Zealand government. The unicameral legislature, the House of Representatives, has 120 members, elected by proportional representation for a three-year term; there are 61 members from single-member constituencies, six from Maori constituencies and 53 allocated from party lists. A non-binding referendum in 1999 approved a reduction in the number of members to 100 in future parliaments. The prime minister and the cabinet are appointed by the governor-general on the advice of the House of Representatives.

GOVERNOR-GENERAL
Governor-General and Commander-in-Chief, HE Dame
Silvia Cartwright, *sworn in* April 2001

SELECTED GOVERNMENT MEMBERS *as at July 2005*
Prime Minister, Arts, Culture and Heritage, Helen Clark
Deputy Prime Minister, Finance and Revenue, Dr Michael
Cullen
Defence, Mark Burton
Economic Development, Industry and Regional Development,
Jim Anderton
Foreign Affairs and Trade, Justice, Pacific Island Affairs,
Phil Goff

NEW ZEALAND HIGH COMMISSION
New Zealand House, 80 The Haymarket, London SW1Y 4TQ
T 020-7930 8422
High Commissioner, HE Russell Marshall, apptd 2002

BRITISH HIGH COMMISSION
44 Hill Street (PO Box 1812), Wellington 1
T (+64) (4) 924 2888 E ppa.mailbox@fco.gov.uk
High Commissioner, HE Richard Fell, CVO, apptd 2001

BRITISH COUNCIL
44 Hill Street (PO Box 1812) Wellington 1
T (+64) (4) 495 0987 E enquiries@britishcouncil.org.nz
Director, Paul Atkins

DEFENCE

The Army has 41 armoured personnel carriers. The Navy
has three frigates, four patrol and coastal vessels and three
armed helicopters. The Air Force has 6 combat aircraft.
MILITARY EXPENDITURE – 1.5 per cent of GDP (2003)
MILITARY PERSONNEL – 8,610: Army 4,430, Navy
1,980, Air Force 2,200

ECONOMY AND TRADE

The economy is diverse and enjoys strong manufacturing
and service industries as well as a successful agricultural
sector. The major industries are food processing, wood
and paper products, wool, textiles, dairy products, iron
and steel. Non-metallic minerals such as coal, clay,
limestone and dolomite are heavily exploited while gold
and iron production is economically important. Natural
gas deposits in the offshore Taranaki Maui field and
onshore fields are used for electricity generation but a
significant amount of the country's energy is still derived
from sustainable sources such as hydropower. Tourism is a
steadily growing industry.

Some 32 per cent of total output is from the export of
goods and services. Between 70 and 80 per cent of
exports are agricultural products, mainly wheat, barley,
fruits, vegetables, dairy products and meat. Since 1973,
when the UK joined the EEC, New Zealand has
developed stronger trade links with Australia, the USA
and Asia, especially Japan.
GNI – US$52,000 million (2002); US$13,260 per capita
(2002)
ANNUAL AVERAGE GROWTH OF GDP – 3.5 per cent
(2003 est.)
INFLATION RATE – 1.8 per cent (2003 est.)
UNEMPLOYMENT – 4.7 per cent (2003 est.)
FOREIGN DIRECT INVESTMENT – US$4,887 million
(1997–2000)
IMPORTS – US$18,600 million (2003)
EXPORTS – US$16,500 million (2003)

BALANCE OF PAYMENTS
Trade – US$428 million deficit (2003)
Current Account – US$3,531 million deficit (2003)

Trade with UK	2003*	2004*
Imports from UK	£413,777,000	£418,415,000
Exports to UK	565,109,000	593,343,000

*Includes Niue, Tokelau and Cook Islands

TRANSPORT INFRASTRUCTURE

The national railway system is owned and operated by
Tranz Rail Ltd; there are 4,439 km of railway track. The
principal airports at Auckland, Wellington (North Island),
Christchurch and Dunedin (South Island); the
government holds a 83 per cent stake in Air New
Zealand. Auckland is the main seaport.

EDUCATION

Education is free of charge and compulsory between the
ages of six and 15. There are 2,226 state and 56 private
primary schools and 320 state and 23 private secondary
schools. There are seven universities and 25 polytechnics.
GROSS ENROLMENT RATIO (percentage of relevant age
group) – primary 99 per cent (2002); secondary 113
per cent (2002); tertiary 72 per cent (2002)

MEDIA AND CULTURE

The broadcasting sector was deregulated in 1988. Two
public networks, Television New Zealand and Maori TV,
compete with four main private networks. There are four
main national daily papers that include the titles *The Press*
and the *New Zealand Herald* and large number of radio
stations, including Ruai Mai, a Maori owned and operated
broadcaster.

New Zealand's cultural history is long and complex,
stretching back to the first Maori settlers who brought the
art form *Whakapapa,* a type of oral genealogy, to the
islands. Notable cultural figures include the writers
Katherine Mansfield (1888–1923) and Hone Tuwhare (b.
1922), the poet Sam Hunt (b. 1946) and the filmmakers
Jane Campion (b. 1954) and Peter Jackson (b. 1961).

TERRITORIES

TOKELAU

Tokelau is a group of three atolls, Fakaofo, Nukunonu and
Atafu. Formerly part of the Gilbert and Ellis Islands
colony, they were transferred to New Zealand
administration in 1926 and proclaimed part of New
Zealand in 1949. The Council of Faipule, composed of
one elected representative from each atoll, was established
in 1992 to govern Tokelau when the General Fono was
not in session. The position of *Ulu-o-Tokelau* (leader) is
rotated among the three Faipule members annually. The
General Fono has 48 seats and its numbers are chosen by
each atoll's Council of Elders *(Taupulega)* to serve a three-
year term. The Tokelau Amendment Act, passed by the
New Zealand Parliament in 1996, conferred legislative
power on the General Fono.
Administrator, Neil Walter, apptd 2002

THE ROSS DEPENDENCY

New Zealand has administrative responsibility for the
Ross Dependency. This is defined as all the Antarctic
islands and territories between 160° E. and 150° W.
longitude which are situated south of the 60° S. parallel,
including Edward VII Land and portions of Victoria Land.

ASSOCIATED STATES

COOK ISLANDS

The Cook Islands consist of the 15 volcanic islands and coral atolls of Rarotonga, Aitutaki, Mangaia, Atiu, Mauke, Mitiaro, Manuae, Takutea, Palmerston, Penrhyn or Tongareva, Manihiki, Rakahanga, Suwarrow, Pukapuka or Danger, and Nassau in the south Pacific Ocean. A former British protectorate, since 1965 the islands have been in free association with New Zealand and enjoy complete internal self-government. Queen Elizabeth II has a representative on the islands, and there is a New Zealand High Commissioner. There is a 25-member Legislative Assembly and executive power is exercised by a prime minister and a cabinet of five other ministers. The main economic activities are tourism and pearl-fishing.

HM Representative, Sir Frederick Goodwin
Prime Minister, Jim Marurai

NIUE

The island was part of the Cook Islands group but has been administered separately since 1903. Since 1974 Niue has been self-governing in free association with New Zealand. A New Zealand High Commissioner is stationed on the island. There is a 20-member legislative assembly, and executive power is exercised by a prime minister and a three-member cabinet drawn from the Assembly's members.

New Zealand High Commissioner, Sandra Lee

NICARAGUA

República de Nicaragua – Republic of Nicaragua

AREA – 130,000 sq. km. Neighbours: Honduras (north), Costa Rica (south)

POPULATION – 5,359,759 (2004 est.): three-quarters are of mixed stock, another 15 per cent are white, mostly of pure Spanish descent, and the remaining 10 per cent are West Indians or Indians. The latter group includes the Misquitos, who live on the Atlantic coast. The official language is Spanish and the majority are Roman Catholic, although the English language and the Moravian Church are widespread on the Atlantic coast

CAPITAL – Managua (population, 864,201, 1995 estimate)

MAJOR CITIES – Chinandega; Granada; León; Masaya

CURRENCY – Córdoba (C$) of 100 centavos

NATIONAL ANTHEM – Salve a tí Nicaragua [Hail, Nicaragua]

NATIONAL DAY – 15 September

NATIONAL FLAG – Horizontal stripes of blue, white and blue, with the Nicaraguan coat of arms in the centre of the white stripe

LIFE EXPECTANCY (years) – 70.02 (2004 est.)

MORTALITY RATE (per 1,000 population) – 4.54 (2004 est.)

HIV / AIDS ADULT PREVALENCE – 0.2 per cent (2003 est.)

DEATH PENALTY – No (abolished 1979)

POPULATION GROWTH RATE – 1.97 per cent (2004 est.)

POPULATION DENSITY – 44 per sq. km (2002)

ILLITERACY RATE – (m) 32.8 per cent; (f) 32.2 per cent (2003 est.)

GROSS ENROLMENT RATIO (percentage of relevant age group) primary 103 per cent (2002); secondary 57 per cent (2002)

CLIMATE AND TERRAIN

The narrow Pacific coastal plain is separated from the broad Atlantic coastal plain by volcanic mountains and lakes Managua and Nicaragua. Elevation extremes range from 2,438 m (Mogoton) at the highest point to 0 m (Pacific Ocean) at the lowest. The climate is generally tropical near the coast with average temperatures in Managua ranging from 20°C in January to 34°C in August. The country is subject to frequent earthquakes.

HISTORY AND POLITICS

The area was settled by Indians from Mexico and Mesoamerica from the tenth century AD. Spanish colonisation began in 1523 but in the 17th and 18th centuries the British were the dominant presence on the Caribbean coast, the Spanish controlling the Pacific plain. Independence from Spain was achieved in 1821 and the area was initially part of Mexico. In 1823 it became part of the United Provinces of Central America but seceded from the federation and became fully independent in 1838. British control of the Caribbean coast was ceded to Nicaragua in 1860. In 1893 José Santos Zelaya established a dictatorship that lasted until 1909, when he was overthrown by US marines. Anastasio Somoza established a dictatorship in 1938 and ruled until his assassination in 1956, when he was succeeded by first one son, Luis Somoza, and then in 1967 another. The family amassed a huge fortune in its 44 years in power, until overthrown in 1979 by a popular revolt led by the *Frente Sandinista de Liberacíon Nacional* (FSLN), popularly known as the Sandinistas.

The Sandinistas' socialist government redistributed land and promoted education and health services, but was opposed by US-backed right-wing guerrillas (the Contras). The civil war lasted until cease-fires and disarmament were agreed with different Contra factions in 1990 and 1994. The cease-fires were the result of the Sandinistas' unexpected defeat in the 1990 elections by a coalition of opposition parties. The country has struggled to recover from the effects of the civil war. Although some foreign debt has been cancelled, poverty is widespread and rises in fuel prices and the cost of living provoked protests, some violent, in 2005.

Since the civil war ended, governments have been Liberal or Liberal-dominated coalitions, keeping the FSLN from power even though it is often the largest party in the National Assembly. In the 2001 presidential and legislative elections, Enrique Bolaños Geyer of the Liberal Constitutionalist Party (PLC) was elected president and the PLC gained 47 seats in the National Assembly; the FSLN won 43 seats. The government is a PLC-led coalition. It has struggled in 2005 to maintain its control of the National Assembly against an alliance of the main opposition parties, causing a political crisis.

POLITICAL SYSTEM

The 1987 constitution was amended in 1995 to reduce the presidential term. The executive president is directly elected for a five-year term; a second term may be served, but terms may not be consecutive. There is a unicameral legislature, the National Assembly, with 90 members directly elected for a five-year term. The cabinet is appointed by the president.

HEAD OF STATE
President, Enrique Bolaños Geyer, *elected* 4 November
2001, *sworn in* 10 January 2002
Vice-President, José Rizo Castellon

SELECTED GOVERNMENT MEMBERS *as at July 2005*
Defence, José Adán Guerra
Finance and Public Credit, Eduardo Montealegre Rivas
Foreign Affairs, Norman Caldera Cardinal
Interior, Eduardo Urcuyo Llanes

EMBASSY OF NICARAGUA
Suite 31, Vicarage House, 58–60 Kensington Church Street,
London W8 4DP **T** 020-7938 2373
Chargé d'affaires, Andres Gomez

BRITISH EMBASSY
(all diplomatic affairs are currently handled by Costa
Rica)

DEFENCE
The Army has 127 main battle tanks and 166 armoured
personnel carriers. The Navy has five patrol and coastal
vessels at three bases. The Air Force has 15 armed
helicopters. Full military relations with the USA were
restored in 2000 after 21 years.
MILITARY EXPENDITURE – 1.2 per cent of GDP (2003)
MILITARY PERSONNEL – 14,000: Army 12,000, Navy
    800, Air Force 1,200
CONSCRIPTION DURATION – 18–36 months

ECONOMY AND TRADE
The economy and infrastructure were wrecked by the civil
war, and progress towards recovery was reversed in 1998
by Hurricane Mitch, which devastated the country, killed
3,000, and left 20 per cent of the population homeless.
Some financial relief was provided in 2004, when the
World Bank wrote off 80 per cent of the country's debt to
the institution, and Russia wrote off debts incurred during
the Soviet era.

There are few natural resources and agriculture is the
mainstay of the economy, but a drop in demand for its
agricultural exports meant that the economic growth
could not be sustained. The sector faces the additional
problems of deforestation, soil erosion and water
pollution. Agricultural production and food processing
includes coffee, sugar, bananas, sesame, cattle-rearing and
seafood fishing. Light industrial goods are also produced.
Considerable quantities of foodstuffs are imported as well
as cotton goods, jute, iron and steel, machinery and
petroleum products.
GNI – US$3,800 million (2002); US$710 per capita
    (2002)
ANNUAL AVERAGE GROWTH OF GDP – 4 per cent
    (2004 est.)
INFLATION RATE – 5.3 per cent (2003 est.)
UNEMPLOYMENT – 22 per cent (2003 est.)
TOTAL EXTERNAL DEBT – US$7,019 million (2000 est.)
IMPORTS – US$1,800 million (2002)
EXPORTS – US$600 million (2002)

BALANCE OF PAYMENTS
Trade – US$972 million deficit (2003)
Current Account – US$780 million deficit (2003)

Trade with UK	2003	2004
Imports from UK	£3,680,000	£3,661,000
Exports to UK	5,241,000	3,632,000

TRANSPORT INFRASTRUCTURE
The inter-American Highway runs between the Honduras
and the Costa Rican borders; the inter-Oceanic highway
runs from Corinto on the Pacific coast via Managua to
Rama, where there is a natural waterway to Bluefields on
the Atlantic; there are 15,478 km of roads and 252 miles
of railway. The main airport is at Managua. The chief
ports are Corinto (Pacific) and Puerto Cabezas and El
Bluff (Caribbean Sea).

MEDIA
There are three daily newspapers, including *El Nuevo
Diario*, a pro-Sandinista publication. Canal 6, the state-
owned broadcaster, competes with three commercial
networks to provide television services. There are a large
number of radio stations.

NIGER

République du Niger – Republic of Niger

AREA – 1,267,000 sq. km. Neighbours: Algeria and
    Libya (north), Chad (east), Nigeria and Benin (south),
    Mali and Burkina Faso (west).
POPULATION – 11,360,538 (2004 est.): Hausa (54 per
    cent) in the south, Songhai and Djerma in the south-
    west, Fulani, Beriberi-Manga, and nomadic Tuareg in
    the north. The main religion is Islam (95 per cent),
    with Christian and Animist minorities. The official
    language is French. Hausa, Djerma and Fulani are also
    spoken
CAPITAL – Niamey (population, 627,400, 1999 estimate)
CURRENCY – Franc CFA of 100 centimes
NATIONAL ANTHEM – Auprès du grand Niger puissant
    [By the banks of the mighty great Niger]
NATIONAL DAY – 18 December
NATIONAL FLAG – Three horizontal stripes, orange,
    white and green with an orange disc in the middle of
    the white stripe
LIFE EXPECTANCY (years) – 42.18 (2004 est.)
MORTALITY RATE (per 1,000 population) – 21.51
    (2004 est.)
INFANT MORTALITY (per 1,000 population) – 122.66
    (2004 est.)
HIV / AIDS ADULT PREVALENCE – 1.2 per cent
    (2003 est.)
DEATH PENALTY – No (abolished 1976)
POPULATION GROWTH RATE – 2.67 per cent
    (2004 est.)
POPULATION DENSITY – 9 per sq. km (2002)
MILITARY EXPENDITURE – 1 per cent of GDP (2003)
MILITARY PERSONNEL – 5,300: Army 5,200, Air Force
    100; Paramilitaries 5,400
CONSCRIPTION DURATION – Two years (selective)
ILLITERACY RATE – (m) 74.2 per cent; (f) 90.3 per cent
    (2003 est.)
GROSS ENROLMENT RATIO (percentage of relevant age
    group) – primary 40 per cent (2002); secondary 6 per
    cent (2002); tertiary 1 per cent (2002)

CLIMATE AND TERRAIN
A landlocked country, much of the country is desert, with
low hills in the north and savannah in the south. Elevation
extremes range from 1,944 m (Mt Greboun) at the highest
point to 200 m (River Niger) at the lowest. The Niger
valley in the south-west and the seasonal part of Lake
Chad in the south-east are the only well-watered areas.

Average temperatures range from 24°C in January to 34°C in May.

HISTORY AND POLITICS

Different areas of the country were part of a number of kingdoms formed by different tribes (Tuareg, Songhai, Hausa, Fulani) from the tenth to 19th centuries. French colonial expansion from the 1880s brought the whole area under French control in 1898 and in 1904 it became part of French West Africa. The country became autonomous in 1958 and achieved full independence in 1960. A coup in 1974 ushered in a military dictatorship. A civilian government was introduced in 1989 but under a one-party system until other parties were legalised in 1990 following civil unrest. In 1992 a multiparty constitution was introduced. Elections in 1993 produced a left-of-centre government that was overthrown in 1996 by the military under the leadership of Brig. Ibrahim Barre Mainassara. He was assassinated during a coup in 1999, and a new constitution was approved.

In presidential and legislative elections in November 1999, Mamadou Tandja of the National Movement for Society in Development (MNSD) was elected president and the MNSD won an overall majority in the National Assembly. In the 2004 elections, President Tandja was re-elected president, and the MNSD remained the largest party in the National Assembly but lost its overall majority.

POLITICAL SYSTEM
Under the 1999 constitution, the head of state is a president directly elected for a five-year term, which may be renewed. The unicameral legislature, the National Assembly, has 83 members, who are directly elected for a five-year term. The prime minister is appointed from the party with the parliamentary majority.

HEAD OF STATE
President, Mamadou Tandja, *elected* 24 November 1999, *sworn in* 22 December 1999, *re-elected* 4 December 2004

SELECTED GOVERNMENT MEMBERS *as at July 2005*
Prime Minister, Hama Amadou
Finance and Economy, Ali Lamine Zené
Foreign Affairs, Co-operation and African Integration, Aissatou Mindaoudou
Interior and De-centralisation, Albade Abouba
National Defence, Souley Hassane 'Bonto'

EMBASSY OF THE REPUBLIC OF NIGER
154 rue de Longchamp, F-75116, Paris
T (+33) (1) 4504 8060
Ambassador Extraordinary and Plenipotentiary, HE Adamou Seydou

BRITISH AMBASSADOR
HE David Coates, resident at Abidjan, Côte d'Ivoire

ECONOMY AND TRADE
There are large uranium deposits at Arlit and Akouta, and gold deposits north-west of Niamey. Uranium is the largest export, but its price is susceptible to fluctuations on the world market, and efforts are being made to expand gold mining. Exploration for oil is currently in progress. Agriculture employs 90 per cent of the labour force, though much production is at subsistence level. Groundnuts and livestock are the two main exports. Other agricultural products include millet, cassava and sugar cane. Production is threatened by desertification, overgrazing and drought. Drought and a swarm of locusts in 2004 caused that year's crops to fail and there are severe shortages of food and grazing areas in south Niger despite repeated requests for international aid. Other environmental problems include deforestation and the destruction of wildlife through poaching; a hunting ban was introduced in 2001 to protect wildlife.

The country has a high level of foreign debt, but qualified for debt relief in 2000.

GNI – US$2,000 million (2002); US$180 per capita (2002)
ANNUAL AVERAGE GROWTH OF GDP – 3.5 per cent (2003 est.)
INFLATION RATE – 2.9 per cent (2000 est.)
TOTAL EXTERNAL DEBT – US$1,638 million (2000 est.)
IMPORTS – US$460 million (2003)
EXPORTS – US$340 million (2003)

Trade with UK	2003	2004
Imports from UK	£6,150,000	£5,722,000
Exports to UK	2,844,000	287,000

TRANSPORT INFRASTRUCTURE
There are no railways. Of the 10,100 km of highways, less than 1,000 km are surfaced. The River Niger is navigable from the capital, Niamey, to the Benin frontier between December and March. The principal airport is at Niamey.

MEDIA
Radio, the most important form of communication in the country, is a growing sector and the state-owned broadcaster competes with a number of private stations. A single state-owned daily newspaper *Le Sahel* competes with a proliferating number of private publications.

NIGERIA

Federal Republic of Nigeria

AREA – 910,800 sq. km. Neighbours: Benin (west), Niger (north), Chad (north-east), Cameroon (east)
POPULATION – 137,253,133 (2004 est.). The main ethnic groups are Hausa/Fulani, Yoruba and Ibo and the principal languages are English, Hausa, Yoruba and Ibo. There are some 373 ethnic groups, who speak over 500 different languages. The main religions are Christianity (49 per cent, mainly in the south) and Islam (45 per cent, mainly in the north and west), the remainder being Animists
CAPITAL – Abuja (population, 378,671), declared the federal capital in 1991
MAJOR CITIES – Ibadan; Kaduna; Kano; Lagos, the former capital; Ogbomosho; ΨPort Harcourt
CURRENCY – Naira (N) of 100 kobo
NATIONAL ANTHEM – Arise, o compatriots
NATIONAL DAY – 1 October (Independence Day)
NATIONAL FLAG – Three equal vertical bands, green, white and green
LIFE EXPECTANCY (years) – 50.49 (2004 est.)
MORTALITY RATE (per 1,000 population) – 13.99 (2004 est.)
INFANT MORTALITY (per 1,000 births) – 70.49 (2004 est.)

governed for most of the period from 1945 to 1965, introducing economic planning and an extensive welfare state. Since 1965 it has continued to hold office for long periods, either on its own or in coalition with smaller parties.

In the 2001 legislative election, no party won an outright majority. The Labour Party (DNA) had the largest number of seats (43) but three parties, the Conservative Party (H), the Christian Democratic Party (KrF) and the Liberal Party (V), agreed to form a coalition government, and Kjell Magne Bondevik of the KrF was appointed Prime Minister. The September 2005 legislative election was won by the opposition Labour Party with 32.7 per cent of the vote. The out-going coalition government announced it would remain in office until parliament reconvened in October.

POLITICAL SYSTEM
Norway is a constitutional monarchy, with a hereditary monarch as head of state. Under the 1814 constitution, the unicameral legislature, the *Storting*, has 165 members who are directly elected for a four-year term. When legislative matters are under discussion, the Storting divides into two chambers. It elects one-quarter of its members to constitute the *Lagting* (Upper Chamber), the other three-quarters forming the *Odelsting* (Lower Chamber). The prime minister, who is responsible to the Storting, appoints the other ministers.

HEAD OF STATE
HM The King of Norway, King Harald V, KG, GCVO, *born* 21 February 1937; *succeeded* 17 January 1991
Heir, HRH Crown Prince Hakon Magnus, *born* 20 July 1973

SELECTED GOVERNMENT MEMBERS *as at July 2005*
Prime Minister, Kjell Magne Bondevik
Defence, Kristin Krohn Devold
Finance, Per-Kristian Foss
Foreign Affairs, Jan Petersen

ROYAL NORWEGIAN EMBASSY
25 Belgrave Square, London SW1X 8QD T 020-7591 5500
Ambassador Extraordinary and Plenipotentiary, HE Tarald Osnes Brautaset, apptd 2000

BRITISH EMBASSY
Thomas Heftyesgate 8, N-0244 Oslo T (+47) 2313 2700
Ambassador Extraordinary and Plenipotentiary, HE Mariot Leslie, apptd 2002

BRITISH COUNCIL
Fridtjof Nansens Plass 5, N-0160 Oslo T (+47) (22) 396 190
E british.council@britishcouncil.no
Director, Sarah Prosser

DEFENCE
The Army has 165 main battle tanks, 157 armoured infantry fighting vehicles and 189 armoured personnel carriers. The Navy has six submarines, three frigates and 15 patrol and coastal vessels at three bases. The Air Force has 61 combat aircraft.
MILITARY EXPENDITURE – 2 per cent of GDP (2003)
MILITARY PERSONNEL – 25,800: Army 14,700, Navy 6,100, Air Force 5,000
CONSCRIPTION DURATION – 12 months plus refresher training

ECONOMY AND TRADE
The economy relies primarily upon its oil and gas sectors and fisheries. The third largest oil exporter after Saudi Arabia and Russia, Norway's net exports of oil and petroleum products reached 3.1 million barrels per day in 2002. In 2001 oil and gas accounted for 36 per cent of all exports, but reserves in currently operating fields will be exhausted in the foreseeable future. Plans were announced in 2003 to explore for oil and gas in the Barents Sea, a move opposed by environmentalists. As a safeguard against the decline of oil and gas stocks, Norway has invested its budget surpluses into the Government Petroleum Fund, now worth about US$43,000 million.

Shipping freight services are also significant, with Norwegian companies controlling 10 per cent of the world's shipping fleet. The export of timber and aluminium is also important. The chief imports are motor vehicles, ships and machinery, clothing, foods and textiles.
GNI – US$175,800 million (2002); US$38,730 per capita (2002)
ANNUAL AVERAGE GROWTH OF GDP – 2.7 per cent (2000 est.)
INFLATION RATE – 1.3 per cent (2001 est.)
UNEMPLOYMENT – 3.4 per cent (2000 est.)
FOREIGN DIRECT INVESTMENT – US$16,621 million (1997–2000)
IMPORTS – US$39,500 million (2003)
EXPORTS – US$67,500 million (2003)

BALANCE OF PAYMENTS
Trade – US$28,109 million surplus (2003)
Current Account – US$28,643 million surplus (2003)

Trade with UK	2003	2004
Imports from UK	£1,948,815,000	£1,99,410,000
Exports to UK	6,591,022,000	8,805,724,000

TRANSPORT INFRASTRUCTURE
There are about 4,021 km of public railways and 90,880 km of public roads. The rail network stops at Bodo, a little way north of the Arctic Circle. A major form of transport to the north is by sea, and the state ferries between Bergen and Kirkenes carry freight, vehicles and passengers. The principal airports are at Oslo, Bergen, Stavanger, Trondheim, Bodo, Tromso and Kirkenes.

EDUCATION
Education from six to 16 is free of charge and compulsory in the 'basic schools', and free from 16 to 19 years. The majority of pupils receive post-compulsory schooling at 'upper secondary' schools, regional colleges, and 11 universities and specialist colleges.
GROSS ENROLMENT RATIO (percentage of relevant age group) – primary 101 per cent (2002); secondary 115 per cent (2002); tertiary 70 per cent (2002)

MEDIA AND CULTURE
Broadcasting is deregulated and there are a number of commercial channels, with satellite networks becoming increasingly popular. There are five national daily newspapers and a single national weekly newspaper *Morgenbladet*.

Influential cultural figures include the artist Edvard Munch (1863–1944), the writers Knut Hamsun (1859–1952) and Henrik Ibsen (1828–1906), the composer Edvard Grieg (1843–1907) and the ecological philosopher Arne Naess (b. 1912).

TERRITORIES

SVALBARD, area 62,923 sq. km; population 2,332 (2001 estimate). The Svalbard archipelago consists of Spitsbergen, the main island, North East Land, the Wiche Islands, Barents Island, Edge Island, Prince Charles Forcland, Hope Island and Bear Island. Under a 1925 treaty, Norway has sovereignty but allows free scientific and economic access to other nations. Around 60 per cent of the islands in the archipelago are covered by ice. Over half of the Svalbard archipelago has been designated as a national park, such is the diversity of it's wildlife. Polar bears, arctic foxes and reindeer are common on land while there are a number of sea mammals including walrus, ring seal, bearded seal, white-nosed dolphin and various whales in the surrounding arctic waters.

JAN MAYEN ISLAND was joined to Norway in 1930.

NORWEGIAN ANTARCTIC TERRITORIES

BOUVET ISLAND (since 1930)
PETER THE FIRST ISLAND (since 1931)
PRINCESS RAGNHILD LAND (since 1931)
QUEEN MAUD LAND (since 1939)

OMAN

Saltanat 'Umān – Sultanate of Oman

AREA – 300,00 sq. km. Neighbours: Yemen (south-west), Saudi Arabia (west) and the UAE (north-west)
POPULATION – 2,903,165 (2004 est.). The official language is Arabic. Islam is the official religion. The majority of the population are Ibadhi Muslims; there is a large Sunni and a small Shia minority. Other religions are tolerated
CAPITAL – ΨMuscat (Masqat) (population, 540,000 2001 estimate)
MAJOR CITIES – ΨBarka; ΨMutrah and Ruwi (the commercial centres); ΨSalalah (the main town of Dhofar); ΨSuhar; ΨSur
CURRENCY – Rial Omani (OR) of 1,000 baisas
NATIONAL ANTHEM – Ya Rabbana ifadh lana jalalat al Sultan [O Lord, protect for us his majesty the Sultan]
NATIONAL DAY – 18 November
NATIONAL FLAG – Red with a white panel in the upper fly and a green one in the lower fly; in the canton the national emblem in white
LIFE EXPECTANCY (years) – 72.85 (2004 est.)
MORTALITY RATE (per 1,000 population) – 3.91 (2004 est.)
INFANT MORTALITY (per 1,000 births) – 20.26 (2004 est.)
HIV / AIDS ADULT PREVALENCE – 0.1 per cent (2001 est.)
DEATH PENALTY – Yes
POPULATION GROWTH RATE – 3.35 per cent (2004 est.)
POPULATION DENSITY – 8 per sq. km (2002)

CLIMATE AND TERRAIN

Oman lies at the south-eastern corner of the Arabian peninsula. There are mountains in the north and the south-west of the country, divided by nearly 643 km of high desert plateau. This descends to a fertile plain on the Arabian Sea coast. Elevation extremes range from 2,980 m (Jabal Shams) at the highest point to 0 m (Arabian Sea) at the lowest. Average temperatures range from 12°C in January to 44°C in July.

HISTORY AND POLITICS

Oman began to build an empire in the Middle East from the eighth century AD and remained unchallenged until the arrival of the Portuguese in 1507; they were ousted in 1650. Following a civil war in the early 18th century, an independent sultanate was established in 1749 by the founder of the dynasty that stills rules the country. By the early 19th century Omani rule extended to the east African coast and parts of Persia and Baluchistan (in modern Pakistan). The kingdom came under British influence in the late 19th century, but control of the country was split between the sultan and the religious leaders of the Ibadhi sect in 1920 after internal dissension since 1913. Oman achieved full independence from Britain in 1951. Clashes between the sultan and religious leaders flared up again in the 1950s but by 1959 the sultan had established his control over the whole country. An insurrection in the south by left-wing rebels supported by South Yemen began in 1965 and was defeated with British military assistance in 1975. The discovery and subsequent exploitation of oil in the mid-1960s led to the steady economic transformation of Oman and, in 1970, Sultan Qaboos bin Said al-Said overthrew his father in a bloodless coup and initiated a modernisation programme.

A degree of political liberalisation has occurred in the past 20 years but the country is still essentially an absolute monarchy. Universal adult suffrage was introduced in 2002; the franchise was previously restricted to an electoral college of tribal leaders, intellectuals and businessmen, including some women from 1997. The first direct election to the Consultative Council was held in 2000 and the first by universal adult suffrage in 2003. The 2003 election produced little change in the composition of the Council; two women were elected, and a number of female ministers were appointed in 2004. Basic Law was adopted in 1996 and established a succession mechanism, codified the system of Government and developed political and legal systems. On 4 October 2003 elections for the Consultative Council were held, the first time all Omanis over the age of 21 (including women) had been allowed to vote. Two women were elected to the Council.

POLITICAL SYSTEM

In 1996 the sultan issued the Basic Statute of the State, which decreed Oman to be a hereditary absolute monarchy. There is no legislature; legislation is by decree of the sultan, and is implemented by the cabinet of ministers, which the sultan appoints. The sultan is advised by the Consultative Council *(Majlis al-Shura)* which has 83 members directly elected for a three-year term. The Council has the right to review legislation, question ministers and make policy proposals. In 1997 the sultan set up the Council of State *(Majlis al-Dawlah)*, which has 41 members appointed by him; it is intended to facilitate 'constructive co-operation' between the sultan and the people.

HEAD OF STATE

HM The Sultan of Oman, Sultan Qaboos bin Said al-Said,
succeeded on deposition of Sultan Said bin Taimur,
23 July 1970

SELECTED GOVERNMENT MEMBERS *as at July 2005*
Prime Minister, The Sultan
Deputy Prime Minister, Fahd bin Mamud al-Said
Defence, Badr bin Saud bin Hareb al-Busaidi
Foreign Affairs, Yusuf bin Alawi bin Abdullah
Interior, Saud bin Ibrahim al-Busaidi
National Economy, Ahmed bin Abdulnabi Makki

EMBASSY OF THE SULTANATE OF OMAN
167 Queen's Gate, London SW7 5HE T 020-7225 0001
Ambassador Extraordinary and Plenipotentiary, HE Hussain Ali Abdullatif, apptd 1995

BRITISH EMBASSY
PO Box 185, Mina Al Fahal, Muscat, Postal Code 116
T (+968) 609 000 E becomu@omantel.net.om
Ambassador Extraordinary and Plenipotentiary, HE Stuart Laing, apptd 2002

BRITISH COUNCIL
Road One, Madinat al Sultan, Qaboos West, PO Box 73, Muscat
T (+968) 600 548 E bc.muscat@om.britishcouncil.org
Director, Jim Scarth

DEFENCE
The Army has 117 main battle tanks and 204 armoured personnel carriers. The Navy has 13 patrol and coastal vessels at six bases. The Air Force has 40 combat aircraft.
MILITARY EXPENDITURE – 11.6 per cent of GDP (2003)
MILITARY PERSONNEL – 39,700: Army 25,000, Navy 4,200, Air Force 4,100, Royal Household 6,400; Paramilitaries 4,400

ECONOMY AND TRADE
The economy is primarily dependent on the export of oil and gas, although the agriculture and fishing sectors are also important. Oil production began in 1967 and accounts for 80 per cent of government revenue. The natural gas industry is being developed, as are tourism and communication technology industries. Agriculture, which accounts for only 2.1 per cent of GDP, produces dates, limes, bananas, alfalfa and vegetables.
Oman joined the World Trade Organisation (WTO) in 2000 and has since begun to privatise its utilities.
GNI – US$19,900 million (2002); US$7,830 per capita (2002)
ANNUAL AVERAGE GROWTH OF GDP – 1.2 per cent (2004 est.)
INFLATION RATE – –0.3 per cent (2003 est.)
TOTAL EXTERNAL DEBT – US$6,267 million (2000 est.)
FOREIGN DIRECT INVESTMENT – US$279 million (1997–2000)
IMPORTS – US$6,570 million (2003)
EXPORTS – US$11,700 million (2003)

BALANCE OF PAYMENTS
Trade – US$5,763 million surplus (2001)
Current Account – US$2,315 surplus (2001)

Trade with UK	2003	2004
Imports from UK	£265,068,000	£335,991,000
Exports to UK	87,893,000	111,883,000

TRANSPORT AND MEDIA
Port Qaboos at Mutrah has eight deep-water berths which have been constructed as part of the harbour facilities. There are some 34,000 km of roads, of which 9,000 km are surfaced. There are airports at Seeb, Salalah, Sur, Masirah, Khasab and Diba.
The only television broadcaster is the state-controlled Oman TV. Satellite television is popular. There are a large number of newspapers, including four national dailies.

EDUCATION
In 2000 there were 1,008 state schools. There is one state university and several private universities.
ILLITERACY RATE – (m) 19.8 per cent; (f) 38.4 per cent (2000)
GROSS ENROLMENT RATIO (percentage of relevant age group) – primary 83 per cent (2002); secondary 79 per cent (2002); tertiary 7 per cent (2002)

PAKISTAN

Islāmī Jamhūriya-e-Pākistān – Islamic Republic of Pakistan

AREA – 770,900 sq. km. Neighbours: Iran (west), Afghanistan (north and north-west), China (north-east), the disputed territory of Kashmir, India (east)
POPULATION – 159,196,336 (2004 est.); 95 per cent Muslim, 3.5 per cent Christian, about 1 per cent Hindu, and 0.5 per cent Buddhist. Urdu is the national language, but is only spoken by a small minority of the population. The most widely used language is Punjabi, followed by Sindi and Pushto. English is widely used in business, government and higher education
CAPITAL – Islamabad (population, 350,000, 1998 census)
MAJOR CITIES – Faisalabad; ΨKarachi; Lahore; Rawalpindi
CURRENCY – Pakistan rupee of 100 paisa
NATIONAL ANTHEM – Pak sarzmin shad bad [Blessed be the sacred land]
NATIONAL DAYS – 23 March (Pakistan Day), 14 August (Independence Day)
NATIONAL FLAG – Green with a white crescent and star, and a white vertical strip in the hoist
LIFE EXPECTANCY (years) – 62.61 (2004 est.)
MORTALITY RATE (per 1,000 population) – 8.67 (2004 est.)
INFANT MORTALITY (per 1,000 births) – 74.43 (2004 est.)
HIV / AIDS ADULT PREVALENCE – 0.1 per cent (2001 est.)
DEATH PENALTY – Yes
POPULATION BELOW POVERTY LINE – 35 per cent (2001 est.)
POPULATION GROWTH RATE – 1.98 (2004 est.)
POPULATION DENSITY – 188 per sq. km (2002)
URBAN POPULATION – 34 per cent (2001)

CLIMATE AND TERRAIN
The arid Thar desert in the east gives way to the fertile Indus valley in the centre of the country. The terrain then rises to the Makran, Kirthar and Sulaiman mountain ranges in the west and the Karakoram and Himalayan ranges in the north. Elevation extremes range from 8,611 m (K2) at the highest point to 0 m (Indian Ocean) at the lowest. The climate varies greatly. Average temperatures in Islamabad range from 2°C in January to 40°C in June.

HISTORY AND POLITICS

Islam was introduced to the area from the eighth century onwards. From the 12th century, the territory formed part of successive empires covering northern India, including the Delhi sultanate and the Mughal empire, and eventually came under British control by the mid-19th century, when it formed part of the the empire of British India. From 1940, Muslim leaders in British India campaigned for a separate state for Muslims and the predominantly Muslim areas were partitioned at independence in 1947, forming the state of Pakistan. This state comprised West Pakistan (now Pakistan) and East Pakistan, the Muslim areas of Bengal which became the independent state of Bangladesh in 1971 following a short civil war.

Pakistan became an Islamic republic in 1956. A coup in 1958 led to military rule until 1971, when Zulfiqar Ali Bhutto became head of a civilian government following Bangladesh's secession. He was overthrown in a military coup in 1977 that brought to power General Zia ul-Haq, whose government initiated an Islamisation programme. Following Zia's death in 1988, civilian government was again restored but proved unstable, with several rapid changes of government in the 1990s amid allegations of corruption. In 1999 the government was overthrown in a military coup led by General Pervez Musharraf, who became head of government and then, in 2001, also became president. A 2002 referendum confirmed his tenure of the presidency for a five-year term following an agreement, which he did not keep, to resign his army post at the end of 2004 and become a civilian president; a bill passed in October 2004 allowed General Musharraf to continue as president and in his army post until 2007.

Although his early policies included recognition of the Taleban regime in Afghanistan and support for Kashmiri insurgents, since 11 September 2001 President Musharraf has aligned Pakistan with the West in its war on terror, providing support to the allies in the Afghan War. This policy has angered militant factions, who are believed to be responsible for attacks on Westerners and Christians in Pakistan. Political opponents have used procedural disruption to prevent the National Assembly from functioning properly since the 2002 elections.

In the 2002 elections to the National Assembly, the Pakistan Muslim League (Qaid-i-Azam-PML-Q) won 77 seats, making it the largest single party but without an overall majority and a coalition government was formed. It also gained a majority in the Senate elections in February 2003.

INSURGENCIES

Since the early 1990s there has been civil disorder in the Sind province, especially in Karachi, where armed militants of the Mohajir Qaumi Movement (MQM), which represents Urdu-speaking Indian Muslims who fled India at partition and their descendants, are fighting for an autonomous Karachi province.

Factional violence between Shia and Sunni fundamentalists has been a problem in Baluchistan, Punjab and Sind provinces since the 1980s, and has led to thousands of deaths. The government has banned several of these groups.

FOREIGN RELATIONS

Partition produced a bitter stand-off between Pakistan and India over the largely Muslim state of Kashmir and a short war in 1947–8 resulted in the state being partitioned between the two countries; it is claimed in its entirety by both. This unresolved issue led to further outbreaks of war in 1965 and 1971, and, since 1985, low-level conflict at altitude for control of the Siachen glacier. Military exchanges increased in 1999–2002, with tensions heightened by the fact that both countries have nuclear weapons. Tension remained high in 2003, with frequent exchanges of fire across the demarcation line, until a cease-fire in November 2003. Diplomatic talks between the two countries began in 2004, and diplomatic missions and transport links have been reopened.

International concern was raised in 2004 by disclosures that Pakistan has sold its nuclear technology to other countries.

POLITICAL SYSTEM

Pakistan is a federal republic. The 1973 constitution was suspended following the 1999 coup and the political system operates under a Legal Framework Order promulgated unilaterally by President Musharraf in 2002. Under the constitution, the head of state is a president elected by parliament for a five-year term; the extension of President Musharraf's term as president for a further five years was approved by a national referendum in 2002 and confirmed by the parliament and provincial assemblies in 2004. The legislature was suspended following the 1999 coup but new elections took place under the Legal Framework Order in 2002 and 2003. Under the 1973 constitution, the National Assembly (*Majlis as-Shoora*) had 237 members; this total was increased to 342 members in 2002. Of these, 10 represent religious minorities and 60 are co-opted women. Members serve for a five-year term. The Senate has 100 members, 88 elected by provincial assemblies, eight chosen by tribal agencies and four elected by the National Assembly; they serve a six-year term. General Musharraf was 'chief executive' from 1999 until 2002, when a new prime minister was appointed to lead the cabinet.

There are six provinces: Baluchistan, North-West Frontier Province, Punjab and Sind each have a provincial assembly and government; the Federal Capital Territory and the Tribal Areas are federally administered.

HEAD OF STATE

President, Chief of Army Staff, Gen. Pervez Musharraf, *assumed office* 20 June 2001, *confirmed in office by referendum* 30 April 2002

SELECTED GOVERNMENT MEMBERS *as at July 2005*

Prime Minister, Minister of Finance, Shaukat Aziz
Senior Federal Minister, Defence, Rao Sikandar Iqbal
Foreign Affairs, Law, Justice and Human Rights, Mian Khursheed Mehmood Kasuri
Interior, Aftab Ahmad Khan Sherpao

HIGH COMMISSION FOR THE ISLAMIC REPUBLIC OF PAKISTAN

35–36 Lowndes Square, London SW1X 9JN
T 020-7664 9200
High Commissioner, HE Maleeha Lodhi

BRITISH HIGH COMMISSION

Diplomatic Enclave, Ramna 5, PO Box 1122, Islamabad
T (+92) (51) 2206071/5 E bhctrade@isb.comsats.net.pk
High Commissioner, HE Mark Lyall Grant, CMG, apptd 2003

BRITISH COUNCIL
PO Box 1135, Islamabad T (+92) (51) 111 424 424
E bc.islamabad@britishcouncil.org.pk
Director, Dr Tome Craig-Cameron

DEFENCE

The Army has some 2,461 main battle tanks, 1,266 armoured personnel carriers and 22 attack helicopters. The Navy has 11 submarines, seven frigates, nine patrol and coastal vessels, six combat aircraft and nine armed helicopters based at Karachi (two more bases are under construction at Gwadar and Ormara). The Air Force has 415 combat aircraft.

MILITARY EXPENDITURE – 4.5 per cent of GDP (2003)
MILITARY PERSONNEL – 569,000: Army 500,000,
    Navy 24,000, Air Force 45,000; Paramilitaries
    289,000–294,000

ECONOMY AND TRADE

Pakistan's massive military expenditure has restricted growth in the economy. A large number of its labour force has emigrated to the Middle East to work, providing valuable remittances, but also causing a growth in the use of child labour in Pakistan. Agriculture employs 44 per cent of the labour force, producing cotton, wheat, rice, sugar cane, fruits, vegetables, milk, beef and mutton. Significant manufacturing industries include cotton yarn, thread, and fabrics. Food processing, pharmaceuticals and construction materials are also important. Principal exports are cotton yarn and cloth, carpets, rice, petroleum products, textiles, leather and fish. Principal imports are petroleum products, machinery, fertilisers, transport equipment, edible oils, chemicals and ferrous metals.

GNI – US$60,900 million (2002); US$420 per capita
    (2002)
ANNUAL AVERAGE GROWTH OF GDP – 6.1 per cent
    (2004 est.)
INFLATION RATE – 4.8 per cent (2003 est.)
UNEMPLOYMENT – 8.3 per cent (2004 est.)
TOTAL EXTERNAL DEBT – US$32,091 million
    (2000 est.)
FOREIGN DIRECT INVESTMENT – US$2,051 million
    (1997–2000)
IMPORTS – US$13,000 million (2003)
EXPORTS – US$11,900 million (2003)

BALANCE OF PAYMENTS
Trade – US$100 million deficit (2003)
Current Account – US$3,597 million surplus (2003)

Trade with UK	2003	2004
Imports from UK	£293,989,000	£345,373,000
Exports to UK	532,456,000	565,380,000

TRANSPORT INFRASTRUCTURE

There are 86,597 km of roads and 7,344 km of railways. The main seaports are Karachi and Port Qasim. The principal airports are at Karachi, Islamabad, Lahore, Peshawar and Quetta. Pakistan International Airlines operates domestic air services between the principal cities as well as international services.

EDUCATION

Education is free of charge to upper secondary level. The system consists of five years of primary education (five to nine years), three years of middle or lower secondary (general or vocational), two years of upper secondary, two years of higher secondary (intermediate) and two to five years of higher education in colleges and universities.

ILLITERACY RATE – (m) 40.1 per cent; (f) 68.9 per cent
    (2000)
GROSS ENROLMENT RATIO (percentage of relevant age
    group) – primary 73 per cent (2002)

MEDIA AND CULTURE

There are eight national newspapers, and the state-owned broadcaster, Pakistan Television Corporation Ltd, competes with several private networks. In 2004, the government granted licences for a number of satellite television and radio stations.

Pakistan is rich in the remains of the earliest Buddhist and Hindu civilisations, as well as the distinct architecture of the Mughal period.

Important Pakistani writers include the poet Muhammad Iqbal (1877–1938) and the Urdu novelist Altaf Fatima (b. 1929).

PALAU

Belu'u era Belau – Republic of Palau

AREA – 458 sq. km
POPULATION – 20,016 (2004 est.); 13,900 live on Koror
    and Babelthaup. The population is Micronesian, and
    predominantly Roman Catholic with a Protestant
    minority. Palauan and English are the official languages
CAPITAL – Koror (population, 13,303, 2000)
CURRENCY – Currency is that of the USA
NATIONAL FLAG – Light blue with a yellow disc set near
    the hoist
LIFE EXPECTANCY (years) – 69.82 (2004 est.)
MORTALITY RATE (per 1,000 population) – 6.89
    (2004 est.)
INFANT MORTALITY (per 1,000 births) – 15.3
    (2004 est.)
DEATH PENALTY – No (abolished 1994)
POPULATION GROWTH RATE – 1.46 (2004 est.)
POPULATION DENSITY – 44 per sq. km (2001)

CLIMATE AND TERRAIN

The republic consists of 340 volcanic and coral islands and islets in the western Pacific Ocean, of which only eight are inhabited. The islands are mainly low-lying, with elevation extremes ranging from 242 m (Mt Ngerchelchauus) at the highest point to 0 m (Pacific Ocean) at the lowest. The climate is tropical, with a wet season from May to November. Average daily temperatures are an almost constant 27°C.

HISTORY AND POLITICS

Britain became Palau's main trading partner in the 18th century, but did not colonise the islands. Control of the islands passed from Spain to Germany in 1889, who exploited the country for its phosphate deposits and coconut plantations. Japan occupied the islands on behalf of the allies in 1914 and adminstered them after the First World War under a League of Nations mandate. Japanese forces were ousted by USA during the Second World War. In 1947 the islands became part of the UN Trust Territory of the Pacific, administered by the USA. After adopting a constitution, the islands became an autonomous republic in 1981. In 1982 a Compact of Free Association was signed with the USA under which the USA retained responsibility for defence and foreign policy in return for providing economic aid; the Compact was implemented in 1993. Palau became independent in 1994.

In the 2004 presidential and legislative elections, President Remengesau was re-elected president and Elias Camsek Chin was elected vice-president.

POLITICAL SYSTEM

Under the 1981 constitution, the executive president is directly elected for a four-year term, renewable only once. The president appoints the cabinet. There is a bicameral legislature *(Olbiil era Kelulau)* composed of the House of Delegates and the Senate. The lower house, the House of Delegates, has 16 members (one member from each of the 16 constituent states), who are directly elected for a four-year term. The Senate has 14 members elected for a four-year term. Members of both houses stand for election as independents. The council of indigenous chiefs, composed of the paramount chief from each of the 16 constituent states, acts as an advisory body to the president on matters concerning traditional law and customs. Each of the 16 component states has its own elected governor and legislature.

HEAD OF STATE
President, Tommy Remengesau, *elected* 7 November 2000, *took office* 19 January 2001, *re-elected* 2 November 2004
Vice-President, Health, Elias Camsek Chin

SELECTED GOVERNMENT MEMBERS *as at July 2005*
Commerce and Trade, Otoichi Besebes
Justice, Michael Rosenthal
Minister of State, Temmy Shmull

BRITISH AMBASSADOR
HE Ian Powell, resident at Suva, Fiji

ECONOMY AND TRADE

The economy is dependent on economic aid from the USA and on the growing tourist industry, which caters for around 50,000 tourists a year. Many other industries are influenced by tourism, such as the production of arts and crafts. The government is keen to reduce its dependence on economic aid but wants to limit tourism to protect the natural environment.

Agriculture is largely at subsistence level and production centres on crops such as coconuts, copra, cassava and sweet potatoes. Fishing plays a large part in the economy, and the republic also derives an income from the sale of licences to fishing fleets.

GNI – US$130 million (2001); US$6,780 per capita (2001)
ANNUAL AVERAGE GROWTH OF GDP – 1 per cent (2001 est.)

Trade with UK	2003	2004
Imports from UK	£16,000	£11,000
Exports to UK	–	–

TRANSPORT INFRASTRUCTURE

There are 61 km of roads in total and no railways or waterways. There are three airports, on Koror, Peleliu and Angaur, which have daily flights from Guam operated by Continental Micronesia.

MEDIA

Most Palauans rely on satellite and cable services from the USA. T8AA Eco Paradise is the government-run radio station. There are a further two commercial stations. Palau has three weekly news publications and titles include *Tia Belau* and *Palau Horizon.*

PANAMA

República de Panamá – Republic of Panama

AREA – 74,400 sq. km. Neighbours: Colombia (east), Costa Rica (west)
POPULATION – 3,000,463 (2004 est.): 70 per cent mestizo, 14 per cent mixed Amerindian and Black, 10 per cent European, 6 per cent Amerindian. Spanish is the official language
CAPITAL – ΨPanama City (population, 464,928, 2000 census)
CURRENCY – Balboa of 100 centésimos (the US dollar is in circulation)
NATIONAL ANTHEM – Alcanzamos por fin la victoria [Victory is ours at last]
NATIONAL DAY – 3 November
NATIONAL FLAG – Four quarters; white with blue star (top, next staff), red (in fly), blue (below, next staff) and white with red star
LIFE EXPECTANCY (years) – 72.14 (2004 est.)
MORTALITY RATE (per 1,000 population) – 6.39 (2004 est.)
INFANT MORTALITY (per 1,000 births) – 20.95 (2004 est.)
HIV / AIDS ADULT PREVALENCE – 0.9 per cent (2003 est.)
DEATH PENALTY – No (abolished 1903)
POPULATION GROWTH RATE – 1.31 per cent (2004 est.)
POPULATION DENSITY – 40 per sq. km (2002 est.)
URBAN POPULATION – 57 per cent (2001 est.)
MILITARY EXPENDITURE – 0.9 per cent of GDP (2003)
MILITARY PERSONNEL – Paramilitaries 11,800
ILLITERACY RATE – (m) 6.8 per cent; (f) 8.1 per cent (2003 est.)
GROSS ENROLMENT RATIO (percentage of relevant age group) – primary 110 per cent (2002); secondary 69 per cent (2002); tertiary 34 per cent (2002)

CLIMATE AND TERRAIN

Coastal plains on the Pacific and Atlantic coasts rise to a mountainous interior. There is rainforest in the north-west and the east. Elevation extremes range from 3,475 m (Volcan de Chiriqui) at the highest point to 0 m (Pacific Ocean) at the lowest. The climate is tropical, with a prolonged wet season from May to January. Average temperatures range from 20°C in January to 31°C in June.

HISTORY AND POLITICS

Panama was visited by Spanish explorers in 1502 and became part of the Viceroyalty of New Andalucia, later New Grenada. It became a strategically important centre of trade. When it gained its independence from Spain in 1821, Panama joined the confederacy of Gran Colombia (comprising Colombia, Venezuela, Ecuador, Peru and Bolivia). The confederacy split up in 1830 and Panama became part of Colombia until 1903, when it achieved its independence.

In the 1880s, France attempted to construct a canal across Panama to link the Atlantic and Pacific oceans. The attempt failed and in 1903 the USA bought the rights to build the canal and was given control of a 10-mile strip, the Canal Zone, in perpetuity. In 1979 Panama and the USA agreed that sovereignty over the Canal Zone would transfer to Panama from 2000, with the USA guaranteeing the zone's protection and providing an annual payment.

Panama was under the military rule of General Omar Torrijos Herrara from 1968 until 1981. In 1983, General Noriega seized power and instigated a period of military rule, supported by the USA until 1987, when the US authorities ordered his arrest for money laundering and drug trafficking. An internal coup to unseat Noriega was unsuccessful in 1988, but in 1989 US forces invaded and deposed him. Noriega surrendered in 1990 and was tried and sentenced in the USA in 1992. In 1991, Panama abolished its armed forces.

The 2004 presidential election was won by Martín Torrijos Espino of the Partido Revolucionario Democrática (PRD), who gained 47.4 per cent of the vote. In the 2004 legislative election, the PRD won 41 seats in the Legislative Assembly.

POLITICAL SYSTEM
The executive president is directly elected for a five-year term, which is not renewable. The unicameral Legislative Assembly has 78 members, who are directly elected for a five-year term. The president, who is responsible to the Legislative Assembly, appoints the cabinet.

HEAD OF STATE
President, Martín Torrijos Espino, *elected* 2 May 2004, *sworn in*, 14 September 2004
First Vice-President, Foreign Affairs, Samuel Lewis Navarro
Second Vice-President, Ruben Arosemena

SELECTED GOVERNMENT MEMBERS *as at July 2005*
Interior, Hector Aleman
Economy and Finance, Ricaurte Vasquez
Health, Camilo Alleyne

EMBASSY OF THE REPUBLIC OF PANAMA
40 Hertford Street, London W1J 7SH T 020-7493 4646
Ambassador Extraordinary and Plenipotentiary, HE Liliana Fernandes, apptd 2005

BRITISH EMBASSY
Swiss Tower, Calle 53 (Apartado 889) Zona 1, Panama City
T (+507) 269 0866 E britemb@cwpanama.net
Ambassador Extraordinary and Plenipotentiary, HE Jim Malcolm, OBE, apptd 2002

ECONOMY AND TRADE
Although traffic on the canal generates substantial revenue, in recent years international banking, manufacturing and shipping have developed and provide more jobs and revenue. Service industries account for 76 per cent of GDP. Other important industries include petroleum refining, the manufacture of construction materials and sugar refining. Agriculture, which employs 20.8 per cent of the labour force and accounts for 7 per cent of GDP, is centred on bananas, rice, coffee, corn and sugar cane.
GNI – US$11,800 million (2002); US$4,020 per capita (2002)

ANNUAL AVERAGE GROWTH OF GDP – 6 per cent (2004 est.)
INFLATION RATE – 2 per cent (2004 est.)
UNEMPLOYMENT – 12.6 per cent (2004 est.)
TOTAL EXTERNAL DEBT – US$7,000 million (2002 est.)
FOREIGN DIRECT INVESTMENT – US$2,861 million (1997–2000)
IMPORTS – US$3,090 million (2003)
EXPORTS – US$860 million (2003)

BALANCE OF PAYMENTS
Trade – US$1,092 million deficit (2003)
Current Account – US$408 million deficit (2003)

Trade with UK	2002	2003
Imports from UK	£86,515,000	£72,005,000
Exports to UK	5,9000,000	8,409,000

TRANSPORT INFRASTRUCTURE
The Panama Canal was built between 1903 and 1914 to connect the Pacific and Atlantic oceans, shortening sea journeys significantly. In 2000 the total number of transits by ocean-going commercial traffic was 12,303; canal net tons totalled 229,459,659; cargo tons totalled 193,714,277. Panama's chief ports are Colon and Bilboa, at either end of the canal. Apart from the 82 km of the canal, there are 822 km of navigable waterways. These are supplemented by 355 km of railways and 11,400 km of highways. The principal airport is at Panama City.

MEDIA
Five television and five radio networks – all commercial – join six daily newspapers to constitute the news media. *La Prensa*, *Panama News* and *El Siglo* are popular newspapers.

PAPUA NEW GUINEA

Gau Hedinarai ai Papua-Matamata Guinea – Independent State of Papua New Guinea

AREA – 452,900 sq. km. Neighbour: Indonesia (west, on New Guinea)
POPULATION – 5,420,280 (2004 est.). English is the official language; Hiri Motu and Neo-Melanesian are widely spoken
CAPITAL – ΨPort Moresby (population, 173,500, 2000 estimate)
MAJOR CITIES – Goroka; Lae; Madang; Mount Hagen; Rabaul; Wewak
CURRENCY – Kina (K) of 100 toea
NATIONAL ANTHEM – Arise all you sons
NATIONAL DAY – 16 September (Independence Day)
NATIONAL FLAG – Divided diagonally red (fly) and black (hoist); on the red is a soaring Bird of Paradise in yellow and on the black five white stars of the Southern Cross
LIFE EXPECTANCY (years) – 64.56 (2004 est.)
MORTALITY RATE (per 1,000 population) – 7.5 (2004 est.)
INFANT MORTALITY (per 1,000 births) – 53.15 (2004 est.)
HIV / AIDS ADULT PREVALENCE – 0.6 per cent (2003 est.)
DEATH PENALTY – No (abolished 1950)
POPULATION BELOW POVERTY LINE – 37 per cent (2002 est.)

POPULATION GROWTH RATE – 2.3 (2004 est.)
POPULATION DENSITY – 12 per sq. km (2002)
MILITARY EXPENDITURE – 0.5 per cent of GDP (2003)
MILITARY PERSONNEL – 3,100: Army 2,500, Navy 400, Air Force 200
ILLITERACY RATE – (m) 28.9 per cent; (f) 42.3 per cent (2003 est.)
GROSS ENROLMENT RATIO (percentage of relevant age group) – primary 77 per cent (2002); secondary 23 per cent (2002)

CLIMATE AND TERRAIN
Papua New Guinea lies in the south-west Pacific Ocean and consists of the eastern half of the island of New Guinea, the islands of Bougainville, New Britain and New Ireland, the Admiralty Islands, the D'Entrecasteaux Islands and the Louisiade archipelago. A range of densely forested mountains runs across the centre of the Papuan part of New Guinea, descending to coastal plains. Elevation extremes range from 4,509 m (Mt Wilhelm) at the highest point to 0 m (Pacific Ocean) at the lowest. The climate is tropical and average temperatures range from 28°C in August to 31°C in January.

HISTORY AND POLITICS
New Guinea was visited by the Portuguese and Spanish in the 16th century before being colonised by the British and Dutch in the late 19th century. The western part of the island (now Irian Jaya province, Indonesia) was incorporated into the Netherlands East Indies in 1828. In 1884 a British protectorate, British New Guinea, was proclaimed over south-eastern New Guinea (Papua) and the adjacent islands, which were annexed outright in 1888. The territory was placed under Australian administration in 1906. The north-east of the island was claimed by Germany in 1884 and became a colony in 1899. It was occupied by Australia in the First World War and both the British territory and the German mandated territory were administered by Australia from 1920 until 1942. The territories were occupied by Japan between 1942 and 1945. After the Second World War the territories were combined and administered by Australia before becoming independent on 16 September 1975.

In 1989 fighting began on Bougainville island between separatists led by the Bougainville Revolutionary Army (BRA) and government forces. A cease-fire came into effect in 1998 and further talks led to a peace agreement in 2001 which provided for autonomy for the island and guaranteed a referendum on independence in 10 to 15 years. The first elections for an autonomous government were held in May and June 2005.

Border areas are sometimes affected by the overspill from fighting between separatists and Indonesian forces in Irian Jaya. Thousands of refugees from this conflict live in camps on the border.

An Australian report in December 2004 warned that Papua New Guinea was in imminent danger of economic and social collapse because of its weak economy, high unemployment and high levels of crime.

Following the 2002 legislative election, the National Alliance Party (NAP) was the largest party in Parliament, and on 5 August 2002, the NAP leader Sir Michael Somare was elected prime minister for the third time and formed a coalition cabinet.

POLITICAL SYSTEM
The 1975 constitution was amended in 1998 as part of the moves towards autonomy for Bougainville. The head of state is the British sovereign, represented by a governor-general who is appointed by parliament for a six-year term. There is a unicameral legislature, the National Parliament, which has 109 elected members, 20 from regional electorates and the remainder from open electorates, who are directly elected for a five-year term. The prime minister is nominated by the National Parliament and appointed by the governor-general. Provincial governments were abolished in 1995, and replaced with councils combining local and national politicians and headed by an appointed governor.
Governor-General, Sir Paulias Matane, sworn in 29 June 2004

SELECTED GOVERNMENT MEMBERS *as at July 2005*
Prime Minister, Minster of Housing, Sir Michael Somare
Defence, Matthew Gubag
Finance and Treasury, Bart Philemon
Foreign Affairs and Immigration, Sir Rabbie Namaliu

PAPUA NEW GUINEA HIGH COMMISSION
3rd Floor, 14 Waterloo Place, London SW1R 4AR
T 020-7930 0922/7
High Commissioner, HE Jean L. Kekedo, OBE, apptd 2002

BRITISH HIGH COMMISSION
PO Box 212, Waigani NCD, Port Moresby
T (+ 675) 325 1677 E bhcpng@datec.net.pg
High Commissioner, HE David Gordon-Macleod, apptd 2003

ECONOMY AND TRADE
The country has extensive mineral deposits, including copper, gold, silver, nickel, bauxite and commercial deposits of oil and natural gas, but exploitation is hampered by the terrain and poor infrastructure. Foreign investment in its industries and infrastructure is also discouraged by corruption, political instability and unresolved land compensation issues. Over the last decade, public services have deteriorated and the advances made in public health in the years following independence have not been sustained. The government that came to power in 2002 has halted its predecessor's privatisation programme in order to evaluate state assets.

Only about 1 per cent of the land area is suitable for commercial crops; these include coffee and cocoa. Over 80 per cent of the population practices subsistence farming, including some tribes in the interior so isolated from the outside world that they live within a unmonetarised economy.
GNI – US$2,800 million (2002); US$530 per capita (2002)
ANNUAL AVERAGE GROWTH OF GDP – −0.5 per cent (2002 est.)
INFLATION RATE – 9.8 per cent (2002 est.)
TOTAL EXTERNAL DEBT – US$2,604 million (2000 est.)
FOREIGN DIRECT INVESTMENT – US$737 million (1997–2000)
IMPORTS – US$1,300 million (2003)
EXPORTS – US$2,200 million (2003)

BALANCE OF PAYMENTS
Trade – US$881 million surplus (2001)
Current Account – US$282 million surplus (2001)

Trade with UK	2003	2004
Imports from UK	£7,979,000	£5,290,000
Exports to UK	60,541,000	61,355,000

TRANSPORT INFRASTRUCTURE

There are 21,433 km of roads, the most important road being that linking Lae with the populous highlands. Air Niugini operates regular services to other countries in the region, as well as internal air services. Several shipping companies operate cargo services to Australia, Europe, the Far East and USA. The main seaports are Port Moresby on New Guinea and Rabaul on New Britain. There are very limited cargo and passenger services between the main ports, outports, plantations and missions.

MEDIA

EMTV is the country's sole television broadcaster. Radio is of vital importance due to Papua New Guinea's widely scattered population and low levels of literacy. The state-run National Broadcasting Corporation runs a radio network which competes with the commercial NAU FM. There are two daily newspapers and a number of weekly publications.

PARAGUAY

República del Paraguay – Republic of Paraguay

AREA – 397,300 sq. km. Neighbours: Bolivia (north-west), Brazil (north-east and east), Argentina (south)
POPULATION – 6,191,368 (2004 est.): 95 per cent mestizo. Spanish is the official language of the country but outside the larger towns Guaraní, the language of the largest single group of Amerindian inhabitants, is widely spoken, and is also an official language
CAPITAL – Asunción (population, 550,060 1997)
MAJOR CITIES – Ciudad del Este; San Lorenzo
CURRENCY – Guaraní (Gs) of 100 céntimos
NATIONAL ANTHEM – Paraguayos, república o muerte [Paraguayans, republic or death]
NATIONAL DAY – 15 May
NATIONAL FLAG – Three horizontal bands, red, white and blue with the National seal on the obverse white band and the Treasury seal on the reverse white band
LIFE EXPECTANCY (years) – 74.64 (2004 est.)
MORTALITY RATE (per 1,000 population) – 4.58 (2004 est.)
INFANT MORTALITY (per 1,000 births) – 26.67 (2004 est.)
HIV / AIDS ADULT PREVALENCE – 0.5 per cent (2003 est.)
DEATH PENALTY – No (abolished 1992)
POPULATION BELOW POVERTY LINE – 36 per cent (2001 est.)
POPULATION GROWTH RATE – 2.51 per cent (2004 est.)
POPULATION DENSITY – 14 per sq. km (2002)
MILITARY EXPENDITURE – 0.8 per cent of GDP (2003)
MILITARY PERSONNEL – 10,100: Army 7,600, Navy 1,400, Air Force 1,100; Paramilitaries 14,800
CONSCRIPTION DURATION – One to two years

CLIMATE AND TERRAIN

Landlocked Paraguay lies in the grassy and occasionally marshy plains of the River Paraguay, which divides the country, and the rivers Parana and Pilcomayo. Elevation extremes range from 875 m (Cerro Pero) at the highest point to 46 m (the junction of the River Paraguay and River Parana) at the lowest. Average temperatures in Asunción range from 23°C in June to 34°C in January.

HISTORY AND POLITICS

Spanish colonisation of Paraguay began in the early 16th century and Asunción was founded in 1537. Paraguay became independent from Spain in 1811, under the dictator José Gaspar Rodriguez de Francia, who ruled until his death in 1840. His successors instigated a period of reform and modernisation which ended in 1865–70 with the catastrophic War of the Triple Alliance against Brazil, Uruguay and Argentina over access to the sea. The war resulted in the loss of over half the population as well as 150,000 square km of territory, and initiated a period of political unstability that lasted until 1912. In the Chaco War of 1932–5, Paraguay gained territory in the west from Bolivia.

Political instability and conflict after the Second World War ended with a coup in 1954 in which General Alfredo Stroessner seized power. His rule was autocratic and increasingly repressive, marked by corruption and human right abuses. He was ousted in a coup in 1989 that paved the way for free multiparty elections to the presidency and legislature in 1993. These were won by the National Republican Association–Colorado Party (ANR-PC) and its presidential candidate. The ANR-PC has won the subsequent elections but splits in the party have contributed to the instability that has prevailed since the 1990s, with the assassination of a vice-president, an attempted coup, widespread corruption and the growth of organised crime.

In the 2003 presidential and legislative elections, the ANR-PC remained the largest party in Congress, winning 16 out of the 45 seats; its candidate, Nicanor Duarte Frutos, won the presidential election with 37.1 per cent of the vote.

POLITICAL SYSTEM

Under the 1992 constitution, the executive president is directly elected for a five-year term, which is not renewable. There is a bicameral legislature, the Congress, consisting of a 45-member Senate and an 80-member Chamber of Deputies, both directly elected for a five-year term. Deputies are elected on a regional basis, the number of seats allocated to each regional department being directly proportional to the department's population. Voting is compulsory for all citizens over 18. The president, who is responsible to Congress, appoints the Council of Ministers.

HEAD OF STATE

President, Nicanor Duarte Frutos, *elected* 27 April 2002, *sworn in* 15 August 2003
Vice-President, Luis Alberto Castiglioni Soria

SELECTED GOVERNMENT MEMBERS *as at July 2005*

Defence, Roberto Segoria
Finance and Economy, Ernst Schmidt
Foreign Affairs, Leila Rachid de Cowles
Interior, Rogelio Vargas

EMBASSY OF PARAGUAY
344 High Street Kensington, 3rd Floor, London W14 8NS
T 020-7610 4180
Chargé d'Affaires, Christina Alvarez

BRITISH EMBASSY
Avda Boggiani 5848, C/R I6 Boquerón, Asunción
T (+595) (21) 612611 E brembasu@rieder.net.py
Ambassador Extraordinary and Plenipotentiary, HE
   Anthony Cantor, apptd 2001

ECONOMY AND TRADE

After slow but steady growth in the 1990s, the economy has experienced serious difficulties since 2002, partly owing to the financial crisis in Argentina. The IMF has made emergency loans, conditional on economic reforms, but demonstrators demanded an end to free-market reforms in 2002 and in 2005 the Chamber of Deputies rejected government proposals to privatise public utilities. Other problems include a lack of infrastructure and environmental damage from deforestation and water pollution.

The country has few mineral resources and the economy is largely agricultural, much of it at subsistence level. Agricultural production, which accounts for 27 per cent of GDP, is centred on cassava, seed cotton, sugar cane, corn, wheat, root crops such as sweet potatoes, and fruits such as bananas and oranges. Livestock – cattle, horses, pigs and sheep – is an important aspect of the farming industry. The main industries are sugar refining, cement production and textiles.

GNI – US$6,400 million (2002); US$1,170 per capita (2002)
ANNUAL AVERAGE GROWTH OF GDP – 2.4 per cent (2004 est.)
INFLATION RATE – 5.1 per cent (2004 est.)
TOTAL EXTERNAL DEBT – US$3,091 million (2000 est.)
FOREIGN DIRECT INVESTMENT – US$660 million (1997–2000)
IMPORTS – US$2,000 million (2001)
EXPORTS – US$1,000 million (2001)

BALANCE OF PAYMENTS
Trade – US$260 million deficit (2003)
Current Account – US$146 million surplus (2003)

Trade with UK	2003	2004
Imports from UK	£14,802,000	£15,798,000
Exports to UK	1,325,000	948,000

TRANSPORT INFRASTRUCTURE

Although landlocked, Paraguay has 3,100 km of navigable waterways. Direct shipping services operate between Asunción and Europe and the USA, and river steamer services provide internal transport. There are 28,900 km of roads in Paraguay, connecting Asunción with São Paulo via the Bridge of Friendship and Foz de Yguazú, and with Buenos Aires via Puerto Pilcomayo. However, many of these roads are impassable in wet weather. Paraguay has 971 km of railways and the principal airport is at Asunción.

EDUCATION

Education is free of charge and compulsory. There are 11 universities and one institute of education.

ILLITERACY RATE – (m) 5.6 per cent; (f) 7.8 per cent (2000)
GROSS ENROLMENT RATIO (percentage of relevant age group) – primary 112 per cent (2002); secondary 64 per cent (2002); tertiary 18 per cent (2002)

MEDIA AND CULTURE

Paraguay has three daily newspapers, three commercial television channels and a range of radio broadcasters.

The Guarani, the original inhabitants of Paraguay, retain much of their traditional culture, with songs, dances and myths constituting a rich body of folklore. Paraguay enjoys a rich and diverse literary history that includes the writer Augusto Roa Bastos (1917–2005), the novelist Neida de Mendonca (b. 1933) and the poet Tadeo Zarratea (b. 1947), who wrote extensively in the Guarini idiom.

PERU

República del Perú – Republic of Peru

AREA – 1,280,000 sq. km. Neighbours: Ecuador and Colombia (north), Brazil and Bolivia (east), Chile (south)
POPULATION – 27,544,305 (2004 est.): 50 per cent Amerindian, 40 per cent mestizo, 7 per cent European, also Africans, Chinese and Japanese. The official languages are Spanish and Quechua. Aymara is also widely spoken
CAPITAL – Lima (including ΨCallao, population, 6,723,130, 2000 estimate)
MAJOR CITIES – Arequipa; Chiclayo; Chimbote; Trujillo
CURRENCY – New Sol of 100 cénts
NATIONAL ANTHEM – Somos libres, seámoslo siempre [We are free, let us remain so forever]
NATIONAL DAY – 28 July (Anniversary of Independence)
NATIONAL FLAG – Three vertical stripes of red, white and red
LIFE EXPECTANCY (years) – 69.22 (2004 est.)
MORTALITY RATE (per 1,000 population) – 6.29 (2004 est.)
INFANT MORTALITY (per 1,000 births) – 32.95 (2004 est.)
HIV / AIDS ADULT PREVALENCE – 0.5 per cent (2003 est.)
POPULATION BELOW POVERTY LINE – 50 per cent (2001 est.)
POPULATION GROWTH RATE – 1.39 per cent (2004 est.)
POPULATION DENSITY – 21 per sq. km (2002)
MILITARY EXPENDITURE – 1.4 per cent of GDP (2003)
MILITARY PERSONNEL – 80,000: Army 40,000, Navy 25,000, Air Force 15,000; Paramilitaries 77,000
CONSCRIPTION DURATION – Two years (selective)

CLIMATE AND TERRAIN

Peru has three main regions: the Costa, the coastal plain west of the Andes; the Sierra or mountain range of the Andes, which runs parallel to the Pacific coast and includes the Punas or mountainous wastes below the region of perpetual snow; and the Montaña or Selva, a vast area of jungle stretching from the eastern foothills of the Andes to the country's eastern and north-eastern borders. Elevation extremes range from 6,768 m (Nevado Huascaran) at the highest point to 0 m (Pacific Ocean) at the lowest. Average temperatures in Lima range from 16°C in July 26°C in January.

HISTORY AND POLITICS

The Inca empire centred on Cuzco had superceded earlier civilisations in Peru by the 15th century, when the empire reached its zenith before falling to Spanish conquistadores led by Franciso Pizarro in 1532–3. The territory formed the Viceroyalty of Peru and its gold and silver mines made Peru the principal source of wealth in Spain's American empire. After 1810, Peru became the centre for the Spanish government as its other colonies rebelled. Although it declared its independence in 1821, this was achieved only with the final defeat of Spanish forces in 1824. Peru entered into several border disputes with its neighbours in the 19th and 20th centuries, including the Pacific War (1879–83) in which it lost three southern coastal provinces to Chile. A border dispute with Ecuador was renewed in 1981, leading to a short, inconclusive war in 1995, but was resolved in 1998 following adjudication. A border dispute with Chile ended in 1999 with the implementation of accords first agreed in 1929.

Following independence, Peru alternated between military dictatorships and periods of democratic rule. The last military dictator was General Franciso Morales Bermundez, who guided the country to democracy in 1980. Civilian rule, however, has not brought political stability or greater economic and social equality. Two left-wing insurgencies, by the Maoist Sendero Luminoso (Shining Path) and the Movimento Revolucionario Tupac Amaru (MRTA), began in the 1980s. The activities of the Sendero Luminoso in particular destabilised the government and the economy, the conflict causing about 69,000 deaths and provoking human rights abuses by both the security forces and the guerrillas. By the late 1990s both insurgencies had been overcome, although a few Sendero Luminoso members remain active. However, the conflict has also left a legacy of criminal violence, much of it related to drug trafficking.

The economy deteriorated badly in the late 1980s and by 1990 inflation was running at 400 per cent. Alberto Fujimori was elected president in 1990 on a platform of economic reform. Within two years he had dismantled the existing order in Peru by dismissing Congress, sacking senior judges, imposing order through an 'Emergency National Reconstruction Government' and changing the constitution. He fled to Japan in 2000 to escape corruption charges, and was succeeded by Alejandro Toledo, the candidate of the Peru Possible (PP) party, who won the 2001 presidential election, becoming the country's first president of Quechan descent. In the 2001 legislative election, the Peru Possible (PP) party won 43 seats and the Peruvian Aprista Party (APRA) won 28 seats. Toledo's presidency has been dogged by frequent cabinet reshuffles (seven so far) and he narrowly escaped impeachment for electoral fraud in May 2005.

POLITICAL SYSTEM
Under the 1993 constitution, the executive president is directly elected for a five-year term, renewable only once. The unicameral legislature, the Congress of the Republic, has 120 members, directly elected for a five-year term. The president, who is responsible to the Congress, appoints the Council of Ministers.

HEAD OF STATE
President of the Republic, Alejandro Toledo Manrique, *elected* 3 June 2001, *sworn in* 28 July 2001
Second Vice-President, David Waisman

SELECTED GOVERNMENT MEMBERS *as at July 2005*
President of the Council of Ministers, Pedro Kuczynski
Defence, Marciano Rengifo Ruiz
Economy and Finance, Fernando Zavala

Foreign Affairs, Oscar de Romana
Interior, Romulo Pizarro

EMBASSY OF PERU
52 Sloane Street, London SW1X 9SP T 020-7235 1917
Ambassador Extraordinary and Plenipotentiary, Luis Solari Tuleda

BRITISH EMBASSY
Torre Parque Mar (Piso 22), Avenida José Larco 1301, Miraflores, Lima T (+51) (1) 617 3000
E consvisa.lima@fco.gov.uk
Ambassador Extraordinary and Plenipotentiary, HE Richard Ralph, CMG, CVO, apptd 2003

BRITISH COUNCIL
c/o British Embassy, Lima T (+51) (1) 617 3060
E bc.lima@britishcouncil.org.pe
Director, Frank Fitzpatrick

ECONOMY AND TRADE
Peru has significant mineral wealth (including gold, though much of this has been exhausted). In addition to this, important industries include petroleum, shipbuilding, textiles, food processing and metal fabrication. Agriculture is centred on coffee, cotton, sugar cane, rice, wheat, potatoes, corn, plantains and coca.

Since 1990 the government has launched a radical free-market restructuring programme which has rebuilt the foreign exchange reserves, reduced inflation, cut subsidies and import tariffs, freed interest rates and privatised most state companies. Foreign investment has been encouraged and has grown dramatically.

Peru faces a range of environmental challenges such as deforestation, soil erosion and desertification, all of which are on the increase and may affect the economy. Its substantial coastal fishing resources are threatened by pollution from mining wastes.

GNI – US$54,000 million (2002); US$2,020 per capita (2002)
ANNUAL AVERAGE GROWTH OF GDP – 4.2 per cent (2003 est.)
INFLATION RATE – 3.8 per cent (2000 est.)
UNEMPLOYMENT – 7.4 per cent (2000 est.)
TOTAL EXTERNAL DEBT – US$28,560 million (2000 est.)
FOREIGN DIRECT INVESTMENT – US$6,609 million (1997–2000)
IMPORTS – US$8,900 million (2000)
EXPORTS – US$9,000 million (2003)

BALANCE OF PAYMENTS
Trade – US$731 million deficit (2003)
Current Account – US$1,061 million deficit (2003)

Trade with UK	2003	2004
Imports from UK	£45,159,000	£42,031,000
Exports to UK	126,943,000	135,275,000

TRANSPORT INFRASTRUCTURE
There are 73,766 km of roads, of which 16,876 km are surfaced. A section of the Andean Highway, linking the Pacific Ocean through the Amazon basin with the Atlantic Ocean, runs through Peru. The Pan-American Highway runs along the Peruvian coast, connecting it with Ecuador and Chile.

The state-controlled railway has 1,992 km of track. There is also steam navigation on the Ucayali and

Huallaga rivers in the north and on Lake Titicaca in the south. Air services are maintained throughout Peru, and there is an international airport at Lima.

EDUCATION
Education is free of charge and compulsory between seven and 16. There are 51 universities.
ILLITERACY RATE – (m) 5.3 per cent; (f) 14.6 per cent (2000)
GROSS ENROLMENT RATIO (percentage of relevant age group) – primary 121 per cent (2002)

MEDIA AND CULTURE
Media freedom has greatly improved since the end of the Fujimori administration. Commercial television and radio receives a higher market share than the state networks. There are six national daily newspapers and a host of commercial radio broadcasters. The state-owned Television Nacional de Peru competes with three commercial broadcasters, including America TV and Panamericana.

Mestizo architecture and Cuzco painting are a fusion of Spanish and indigenous styles that have greatly influenced European art, notably Paul Gauguin. Peru's most famous novelist Mario Vargas Llosa (b. 1936), whose first novel was publicly burnt, ran for president in 1990. Other notable writers include José Maria Arguedas (1911–69), who used a first-hand knowledge of the Quechua language, and Ciro Alegria (1909–67).

THE PHILIPPINES

Repúblika ng Pilipinas – Republic of the Philippines

AREA – 298,200 sq. km
POPULATION – 86,241,697 (2004 est.). The inhabitants are of Malay stock, with admixtures of Spanish and Chinese blood in many localities. The Chinese minority is estimated at 500,000, with smaller numbers of Spanish, American and Indian. About 90 per cent are Christian, predominantly Roman Catholics. Most of the remainder are Muslims or indigenous animists. The official languages are Filipino and English. Filipino is based on Tagalog, one of the Malay-Polynesian languages. English, the language of government, is spoken by at least 44 per cent of the population. Spanish is now spoken by a very small minority
CAPITAL – ΨManila (population, 9,906,048, 2000 census)
MAJOR CITIES – Quezon; ΨCebu; ΨDavao; ΨIloilo; ΨZamboanga
CURRENCY – Philippine peso (P) of 100 centavos
NATIONAL ANTHEM – Lupang hinirang [Beloved land]
NATIONAL DAY – 12 June (Independence Day 1898)
NATIONAL FLAG – Equal horizontal bands of blue (above) and red; a gold sun with three stars on a white triangle next staff
LIFE EXPECTANCY (years) – 69.6 (2004 est.)
MORTALITY RATE (per 1,000 population) – 5.53 (2004 est.)
INFANT MORTALITY (per 1,000 births) – 24.24 (2004 est.)
HIV / AIDS ADULT PREVALENCE – 0.1 per cent (2003 est.)
DEATH PENALTY – Yes

POPULATION GROWTH RATE – 1.88 per cent (2004 est.)
POPULATION DENSITY – 268 per sq. km (2002)
URBAN POPULATION – 59 per cent (2001)

CLIMATE AND TERRAIN
The Philippines comprises over 7,000 islands in the western Pacific Ocean. The principal islands of the Philippines (area in sq. km) are: Luzon (104,688); Mindanao (94,630); Samar (13,080); Negros (12,710); Palawan (11,785); Panay (11,515); Mindoro (9,735); Leyte (7,214); Cebu (4,422); Bohol (3,865) and Masbate (3,269). Other groups are the Sulu islands (capital, Jolo); Babuyanes and Batanes; the Calamian islands; and Kalayaan Islands. The larger islands are traversed by volcanic mountain ranges; some volcanoes are still active. Elevation extremes range from 2,954 (Mt Apo) at the highest point to 0 m (Philippine Sea) at the lowest. The climate is tropical with average temperatures ranging from 23°C in January to 31°C in June.

HISTORY AND POLITICS
The Philippines were conquered by Spain in 1565 and colonial rule lasted until 1898, when Spain ceded the colony to the USA following the Spanish-American War. The country became internally self-governing in 1935, was occupied by Japan from 1942 to 1944, and achieved independence from the USA in 1946.

After a period of instability, Ferdinand Marcos seized power in 1965, imposing martial law in 1972. His regime became increasingly repressive, corrupt and violent, and was believed to be responsible for the assassination of opposition leader Benigno Aquino in 1983. Aquino's death provoked mass demonstrations against Marcos' rule and when Marcos falsifed election results in 1986 to prevent Aquino's widow Corazon from taking office as president, mass protests forced him to flee the country. Corazon Aquino survived political unrest and six attempted military coups to introduce a new constitution and plant democratic politics in the Philippines.

Fidel Ramos, Aquino's successor in 1992, built on her work by instigating peace talks with the communist and Muslim rebels involved in long-running insurgencies; a peace agreement with one Muslim group, the Moro National Liberation Front, was reached in 1996. Ramos was succeeded in 1998 by Joseph Estrada. Under his presidency the peace process with the communist insurgents and the main Muslim insurgent group, the Moro Islamic Liberation Front (MILF), began to stall. Popular dissatisfaction with Estrada grew and altough his impeachment on corruption and other charges was suspended, he was forced out of office by popular protests in January 2001. His term was completed by Vice-President Gloria Arroyo. She re-established peace talks with the MILF and the National Democratic Front (NDF), a front organisation for the communist insurgents. The talks with the MILF, though often interrupted by violence, achieved a cease-fire in 2003 and a breakthrough in talks in 2005. Progress with the NDF have proved more problematic and clashes have continued despite six months' of peace talks in 2004. Since the 11 September 2001 attacks, Abu Sayyaf, a Muslim group suspected of links with al-Qa'eda, has emerged on the island of Jolo, undertaking a spate of violent kidnappings.

In the 2004 presidential and legislative elections, Gloria Arroyo was re-elected president, and Lakas remained the largest party in the House of Representatives. Since the elections, President Arroyo's popularity has plummeted, her anti-corruption measures and economic reforms undermined by a series of corruption scandals, and she came under intense pressure to resign in July 2005 over accusations that she tried to influence the 2004 presidential election result. Arroyo requested the resignation of the entire cabinet in July 2005 in order to carry out an extensive reshuffle but on 25th July, opposition MPs launched an impeachment motion against the her.

POLITICAL SYSTEM

Under the 1987 constitution, the executive president is directly elected for a six-year term, which is not renewable. There is a bicameral Congress. The lower house, the House of Representatives, has 236 members, of whom 212 are directly elected and the rest are appointed from party and minority group lists by the president; all serve a three-year term. The Senate has 24 members directly elected for a six-year term, with half re-elected every three years. The president appoints the cabinet.

The Autonomous Region of Mindanao consists of four provinces: Sulu, Tawi-Tawi, Lanao del Sur and Maguinadanao. There is a 24-member regional assembly and a governor.

HEAD OF STATE

President, Gloria Macapagal Arroyo, *assumed office* 20 January 2001
Vice-President, Noli de Castro

SELECTED GOVERNMENT MEMBERS *as at July 2005*
Finance, Juanita Amatong
Interior and Local Government, Angelo Reyes
Defence, Avelino Cruz
Health, Manuel Dayrit

EMBASSY OF THE REPUBLIC OF THE PHILIPPINES
9A Palace Green, London W8 4QE T 020-7937 1600
Ambassador Extraordinary and Plenipotentiary, HE
Edgardo Espiritu, apptd 2003

BRITISH EMBASSY
Floors 15–17, LV Locsin Building, 6752 Ayala Avenue, Corner of Makati Avenue, 1226 Makati, Manila (PO Box 2927 MCPO)
T (+63) (2) 816 7116 E uk@info.com.ph
Ambassador Extraordinary and Plenipotentiary, HE Paul
Dimond, apptd 2002

BRITISH COUNCIL
10th Floor, Taipan Place, Emerald Avenue, Ortigas Centre, Pasig City 1605 T (+63) (2) 914 1011
E britishcouncil@britishcouncil.org.ph
Director, Gill Westaway

DEFENCE

The Army has 85 armoured infantry fighting vehicles and 370 armoured personnel carriers. The Navy has one frigate and 58 patrol and coastal vessels at three bases. The Air Force has 36 combat aircraft and 25 armed helicopters.
MILITARY EXPENDITURE – 1 per cent of GDP (2003)
MILITARY PERSONNEL – 106,000: Army 66,000, Navy 24,000, Air Force 16,000; Paramilitaries 44,000

ECONOMY AND TRADE

The economy was one of the best-performing in the region until the Asian economic crisis of 1997. It has experienced some growth in recent years, owing to growth in agricultural exports and the services industries, but is hampered by a high level of national debt and a large budget deficit. The government is attempting to introduce market reforms but investor confidence has suffered from recent political turmoil and insurgency. Remittances from the millions of Filipinos working abroad are vital to the economy.

Major industries include food processing and fishing, electronics assembly, textile manufacture, pharmaceuticals, chemical production and petroleum refining. The country still has a large agricultural sector, employing 45 per cent of the labour force and producing rice, coconuts, corn, sugar cane, bananas and pineapples. The agriculture and fishing industries face environmental problems from soil erosion, deforestation, and air and water pollution. Water pollution is a particular problem in the coastal mangrove swamps, which are important fish breeding grounds
GNI – US$82,400 million (2002); US$1,030 per capita (2002)
ANNUAL AVERAGE GROWTH OF GDP – 5.9 per cent (2004 est.)
INFLATION RATE – 5.5 per cent (2004 est.)
UNEMPLOYMENT – 11.7 per cent (2004 est.)
TOTAL EXTERNAL DEBT – US$50,063 million (2000 est.)
FOREIGN DIRECT INVESTMENT – US$5,537 million (1997–2000)
IMPORTS – US$39,500 million (2003)
EXPORTS – US$37,000 million (2003)

BALANCE OF PAYMENTS
Trade – US$1,253 million deficit (2003)
Current Account – US$3,347 million surplus (2003)

Trade with UK	2003	2004
Imports from UK	£384,757,000	£316,235,000
Exports to UK	730,553,000	671,349,000

TRANSPORT INFRASTRUCTURE

The road system covers about 187,000 km, and Philippine National Railway operates 429 km of railways. The main ports are Manila (Luzon), Cebu, Davao and Zamboanga (Mindanao), and there are over 400 smaller ports. There are 82 national airports and 137 privately operated airports. Philippine Airlines has regular flights throughout the Far East, to the USA and Europe, in addition to inter-island services.

EDUCATION

Secondary and higher education is extensive and there are 21 public and 53 private universities recognised by the government, including the Dominican University of Santo Tomás (founded in 1611). There are also 530 other institutions of higher education.
ILLITERACY RATE – (m) 4.5 per cent; (f) 4.8 per cent (2000)
GROSS ENROLMENT RATIO (percentage of relevant age group) – primary 112 per cent (2002); secondary 82 per cent (2002); tertiary 30 per cent (2002)

MEDIA

The government-owned IBC television network competes with two commercial broadcasters. There is a large number of radio stations and four main national press publications.

POLAND

Rzeczpospolita Polska – Republic of Poland

AREA – 304,400 sq. km. Neighbours: the Russian
Federation (Kaliningrad) (north), Germany (west), the
Czech Republic and Slovakia (south), Belarus and
Ukraine (east) and Lithuania (north-east)

POPULATION – 38,626,349 (2004 est.). Roman
Catholicism is the religion of 95 per cent of the
inhabitants. The language is Polish; there are German,
Ukrainian and Belarusian minorities

CAPITAL – Warsaw (population, 1,609,780, 2001
estimate), on the Vistula

MAJOR CITIES – Bydgoszcz; ΨGdansk (Danzig);
Katowice; Krakow; Lodz; Poznan; ΨSzczecin (Stettin);
ΨWroclaw (Breslau)

CURRENCY – Zloty of 100 groszy

NATIONAL ANTHEM – Jeszcze Polska nie zginela [Poland
has not yet perished]

NATIONAL DAY – 3 May

NATIONAL FLAG – Equal horizontal stripes of white
(above) and red

LIFE EXPECTANCY (years) – 74.16 (2004 est.)

MORTALITY RATE (per 1,000 population) – 9.97
(2004 est.)

INFANT MORTALITY (per 1,000 births) – 8.73
(2004 est.)

HIV / AIDS ADULT PREVALENCE – 0.1 per cent
(2001 est.)

DEATH PENALTY – No (abolished 1997)

POPULATION BELOW POVERTY LINE – 18.4 per cent
(2000 est.)

POPULATION GROWTH RATE – 0.02 per cent
(2004 est.)

POPULATION DENSITY – 127 per sq. km (2002)

URBAN POPULATION – 63 per cent (2001)

CLIMATE AND TERRAIN

Poland lies mostly in a great plain crossed by the Oder,
Neisse and Vistula rivers. The land rises to the Carpathian,
Tatra and Sudeten mountains along the southern border.
Elevation extremes range from 2,499 m (Rysy) at the
highest point to −2 m (Raczki Elblaskie) at the lowest.
The climate is continental and average temperatures in
Warsaw range from −5°C in January to 24° C in July.

HISTORY AND POLITICS

Poland emerged as an independent kingdom in the ninth
century. It formed a union with Lithuania in 1569 that
stretched from the Baltic to the Black Sea. This
commonwealth was weakened by attacks by its
neighbours and in 1772, 1793 and 1795 its territory was
partitioned between Russia, Prussia and Austria.
Following the Congress of Vienna in 1815, eastern
Poland became a semi-independent kingdom within the
Russian empire. After the First World War, Poland became
independent again with the signing of the Treaty of
Versailles. The Second World War began with the German
invasion of western Poland on 1 September 1939; on 17
September, Soviet forces invaded eastern Poland, and on
21 September Germany and the Soviet Union declared
that Poland had ceased to exist. After the Soviet Union
aligned with the Allies, the country was liberated by
Soviet forces in 1944–5, and after the war its boundaries
were redrawn; eastern Poland was ceded to the Soviet
Union but the country gained German territory in Silesia
along the Oder and Neisse rivers, effectively shifting the
state 240 km westwards.

The post-war coalition government was Soviet-
influenced and in 1947 a communist republic was
proclaimed. Nationalisation and agricultural collectivisation programmes were introduced and the Roman Catholic
Church was persecuted. By the 1970s attempts to boost
the economy had failed and the country had a large
foreign debt. Following riots against food price rises in
1970, labour organisation increased, backed by a
committed intelligentsia, with workers' delegations
convening under the Solidarity trade union banner, led by
Lech Walesa. In 1981, the demoralised communist
government declared martial law and interned Walesa and
other leaders, driving Solidarity underground. Economic
decline and continuing unrest in the 1980s eventually
resulted in round-table talks between Solidarity, the
government and the Roman Catholic Church in 1989. In
multiparty parliamentary elections later that year, the
communists lost power and Solidarity helped to form a
coalition government. In 1990 Walesa was elected
president. The communist party subsequently dissolved
and reformed as the Democratic Left Alliance (SLD).

The post-communist governments introduced
economic reforms from 1990 but the transition to a
market economy caused unemployment and a sharp drop
in living standards. Popular discontent and a fragmented
parliament led to a succession of short-lived governments.
In 1997 a new constitution was adopted that eradicated
all signs of the former communist system. Poland joined
NATO in 1999 and the EU in 2004. No date has yet been
set for a referendum on the EU constitution.

Aleksander Kwasniewski, the Democratic Left Alliance
(SLD) candidate, was elected president in 1995, narrowly
defeating Walesa, and was re-elected in 2000. In the
2001 elections, an electoral alliance of the SLD and the
Labour Union (UP) won 216 seats in the Diet and 75 in
the Senate, and formed a coalition government that also
included the Polish Peasant Party (PSL). The PSL left the
coalition in 2003 when it failed to support government tax
proposals, and the coalition continued as a minority
government. Legislative elections were scheduled for 25
September 2005 and a presidential election was expected
to be held in October *see* stop press.

POLITICAL SYSTEM

Under the 1997 constitution, the head of state is the
president, who is directly elected for a five-year term,
renewable only once. The president appoints the prime
minister and has the right to be consulted over the
appointment of the foreign, defence and interior
ministers. The National Assembly is the bicameral
legislature. The lower house, the Diet *(Sejm)*, has 460
members directly elected for a four-year term. The Senate
has 100 members elected on a provincial basis for a four-
year term.

HEAD OF STATE

President, Aleksander Kwasniewski, *elected* 19 November
1995, *sworn in* 23 December 1995, *re-elected* 8
October 2000

SELECTED GOVERNMENT MEMBERS *as at July 2005*

Prime Minister, Marek Belka

Deputy Prime Minister, Social Policy, Izabela Jaruga-
Nowacka

Internal Affairs and Administration, Ryszard Kalisz

Defence, Jerzy Szmajdzinski

Foreign Affairs, Adam Daniel Rotfeld

Treasury, Jacek Socha

EMBASSY OF THE REPUBLIC OF POLAND
47 Portland Place, London W1B 6JH **T** 0870-774 2700
Ambassador Extraordinary and Plenipotentiary, Zbigniew
Matuszewski, apptd 2005

BRITISH EMBASSY
Aleje Róz No. 1, PL00-556 Warsaw
T (+48) (22) 628 1001/5 **E** britemb@it.com.pl
Ambassador Extraordinary and Plenipotentiary, HE Charles
Crawford, apptd 2003

BRITISH COUNCIL
Al. Jerozolimskie 59, PL-00-697 Warsaw
E bc.warsaw@britishcouncil.pl
Director, Susan Maingay, OBE

DEFENCE
The Army has 947 main battle tanks, 1,281 armoured
infantry fighting vehicles, 33 armoured personnel carriers
and 65 attack helicopters. The Navy has four submarines,
one destroyer, three frigates, 23 patrol and coastal vessels,
26 combat aircraft and 12 armed helicopters at five bases.
The Air Force has 224 combat aircraft.
MILITARY EXPENDITURE – 2 per cent of GDP (2003)
MILITARY PERSONNEL – 133,300: Army 89,000, Navy
14,300, Air Force 30,000; Paramilitaries 21,400
CONSCRIPTION DURATION – 9 months

ECONOMY AND TRADE
The transition to a free market economy caused
unemployment to double between 1990 and 1995, and it
remains high. Industrial output has improved and the
growth rate of GDP has increased although inflation
remains high. A programme to modernise the large
agricultural sector and adapt it the EU's common
agricultrual policy has taken place but the sector remains
inefficient. Future EU subsidy levels are an area of
controversy, with corruption one of the main concerns.
   Poland has vast mineral resources. 102,873, 500
tonnes of bituminous coal were produced in 2003 while
sulphur, copper, zinc, lead, silver, natural gas and salt are
also produced.
   Major exports include machinery and vehicles, leather
and textiles, metal goods, livestock, foodstuffs, luxury
goods and chemical products. The major imports are
machinery and vehicles, manufactured goods, fuels and
lubricants. Germany is the main trading partner.
GNI – US$176,000 million (2002); US$4,570 per capita
(2002)
ANNUAL AVERAGE GROWTH OF GDP – 5.6 per cent
(2004 est.)
INFLATION RATE – 3.4 per cent (2004 est.)
UNEMPLOYMENT – 19.5 per cent (2004 est.)
TOTAL EXTERNAL DEBT – US$63,561 million
(2000 est.)
FOREIGN DIRECT INVESTMENT – US$5,537 million
(1997–2000)
IMPORTS – US$68,000 million (2003)
EXPORTS – US$54,000 million (2003)

BALANCE OF PAYMENTS
Trade – US$5,725 million deficit (2003)
Current Account – US$4,085 million deficit (2003)

Trade with UK	2003	2004
Imports from UK	£1,453,498,000	£490,311,00
Exports to UK	1,568,109,000	666,247,000

TRANSPORT INFRASTRUCTURE
The country has a total of 23,420 km of railways;
364,656 km of roads, and 3,812 km of navigable rivers
and canals. Around 122 airports are in use, and principal
ports and harbours include Gdansk, Gdynia, Gliwice,
Kolobrzeg, Szczecin, Swinoujscie, Ustka, Warsaw and
Wroclaw.

EDUCATION
Elementary education (ages seven to 15) is free of charge
and compulsory. Secondary education is also free, but
optional. There are 179 institutions of higher education,
including universities at Krakow, Warsaw, Poznan, Lodz,
Wroclaw, Lublin and Torun.
ILLITERACY RATE – (m) 0.3 per cent; (f) 0.3 per cent
(2000)
GROSS ENROLMENT RATIO (percentage of relevant age
group) – primary 100 per cent (2002); secondary 101
per cent (2002); tertiary 55 per cent (2002)

MEDIA AND CULTURE
Poland's broadcasting network is the largest in eastern
and central Europe, and there is freedom and diversity of
information in the media, although laws against criticism
of the political system are still in force. State-owned TV
(TVP) still has the largest share of the audience for its two
national channels. State-owned radio reaches just over
half the population and there are more than 200 other
commercial local and regional stations on air. Poland has
over 300 newspapers, most of them local or regional.
   Polish literature has a long and rich history that
stretches back to beyond the 14th century and the
country's writers have won many Nobel Prizes for
Literature. Major writers include Henryk Sienkiewicz
(1846–1916), Nobel Prize winner in 1905; Boleslaw
Prus (1847–1912); Wladyslaw Stanislaw Reymont
(1867–1925), Nobel Prize winner in 1924; Czeslaw
Milosz (b. 1911), Nobel Prize winner in 1980; and
Wislawa Szymborska (b. 1923), Nobel Prize winner in
1996.

PORTUGAL

República Portuguesa – Portuguese Republic

AREA – 91,500 sq. km. Neighbour: Spain (north and
east)
POPULATION – 10,524,145 (2004 est.); 9,833,014
(excluding the Azores and Madeira, 1995). 94 per cent
of the population are Catholic. The language is
Portuguese
CAPITAL – ΨLisbon (population, 1,878,006, 2000)
MAJOR CITIES – ΨOporto
CURRENCY – Euro (€) of 100 cents
NATIONAL ANTHEM – A Portuguesa
NATIONAL DAY – 10 June
NATIONAL FLAG – Divided vertically into unequal parts
of green and red with the national emblem over all on
the line of division
LIFE EXPECTANCY (years) – 77.35 (2004 est.)
MORTALITY RATE (per 1,000 population) – 10.37
(2004 est.)
INFANT MORTALITY (per 1,000 births) – 5.13
(2004 est.)
HIV / AIDS ADULT PREVALENCE – 0.5 per cent
(2001 est.)
DEATH PENALTY – No (abolished 1976)

POPULATION GROWTH RATE – 0.14 per cent
(2004 est.)
POPULATION DENSITY – 111 per sq. km (2002)
URBAN POPULATION – 66 per cent (2001)

CLIMATE AND TERRAIN
The terrain is mountainous north of the Tagus river, with rolling plains in the south. Elevation extremes range from 2,351 m (Ponta do Pico) at the highest point to 0 m (Atlantic Ocean) at the lowest. Forests of pine, cork and eucalyptus cover about 38 per cent of the country. The climate is mild, with average temperatures in Lisbon ranging from 8°C in January to 28°C in July.

HISTORY AND POLITICS
Part of the Roman empire from the second century BC, the country was overrun by Vandals and Visigoths in the fifth century AD. The Visigoths were ousted by Muslims from north Africa in the eighth century but Christian reconquest began in the tenth century and an independent Christian kingdom was established in the 12th century. Portuguese navigators led the 15th-century age of exploration, and in the 16th century Portugal was a major commercial and colonial power, its empire including Brazil and parts of China as well as vast areas of Africa. In 1807 Portugal was invaded by Napoleonic France, then became the base from which allied forces liberated Portugal and Spain in the Peninsular War. The 19th century was politically turbulent, with power struggles between conservative and liberal politicians and between different factions of the royal family. In 1910 armed uprising in Lisbon drove King Manuel II into exile and a republic was declared.

A period of political instability ensued until the military intervened in 1926. The constitution of 1933 gave formal expression to the authoritarian 'Estado Novo' (New State) introduced by Dr Antonio Salazar, prime minister from 1932 until 1968. Marcello Caetano succeeded Salazar in 1968 but the regime's failure to liberalise at home or to conclude the wars in the African colonies resulted in the government's overthrow by a military coup in 1974. Great political turmoil followed until July 1976, a period in which most of the colonies gained their independence, but with the failure of an attempted coup by the extreme left in November 1975 the situation stabilised. Full civilian government was restored in 1982. Portugal joined the EEC in 1986 and the euro zone in 1999. A referendum on the EU constitution was scheduled for December 2005.

In the 2001 presidential election, Jorge Sampaio of the Socialist Party was re-elected with 55.8 per cent of the total vote. The 2005 legislative election was won by the Socialist Party with 120 seats, giving them their first absolute majority in the Assembly since Portugal returned to democracy in 1974.

POLITICAL SYSTEM
Under the 1976 constitution, amended in 1982 and 1989, the head of state is a president who is elected for a five-year term, renewable only once. Legislative authority is vested in the unicameral 230-member Assembly of the Republic, which has 230 members directly elected by proportional representation for a four-year term. The prime minister, appointed by the president, is usually the leader of the largest party in the Assembly.

HEAD OF STATE
President of the Republic, Jorge Sampaio, elected 14 January 1996, inaugurated 9 March 1996, re-elected 14 January 2001

SELECTED GOVERNMENT MEMBERS as at July 2005
Prime Minister, Jose Socrates
Foreign Affairs, Diogo Freitas do Amaral
Interior, Antonio Costa
Finance, Fernando Teixeira dos Santos
Defence, Luis Amado

PORTUGUESE EMBASSY
11 Belgrave Square, London SW1X 8PP T 020-7235 5331
Ambassador Extraordinary and Plenipotentiary, HE
    Fernando Andresen Guimaraes, apptd 2003

BRITISH EMBASSY
Rua de São Bernardo 33, P-1249-082 Lisbon
T (+351) (21) 392 4000 E consular@lisbon.mail.fco.gov.uk
Ambassador Extraordinary and Plenipotentiary, HE John
    Buck apptd 2005

BRITISH COUNCIL
Rua Luís Fernandes, 1–3, P-1249-062 Lisbon.
T (+351) (21) 321 4500)
E lisbon.enquiries@pt.britishcouncil.org
Director, Rosemary Hilhorst, OBE

DEFENCE
The Army has 187 main battle tanks and 353 armoured personnel carriers. The Navy has two submarines, six frigates and 28 patrol and coastal vessels at four bases. The Air Force has 50 combat aircraft.

Lisbon is the base of the NATO Iberian Atlantic Command and the USA maintains 1,058 personnel in mainland Portugal and on the Azores.
MILITARY EXPENDITURE – 2.1 per cent of GDP (2003)
MILITARY PERSONNEL – 44,900: Army 26,700, Navy 10,950, Air Force 7,250; Paramilitaries 47,700
CONSCRIPTION DURATION – Four to 12 months

ECONOMY AND TRADE
Portugal has experienced rapid economic growth since joining the EU in 1986 and tourism continues to be a steady source of national income. However, in recent years Portugal has developed a large budget deficit and unemployment is rising.

Around 13 per cent of the workforce is engaged in agriculture, the highest percentage in the EU. The chief agricultural products are wine, dairy products, potatoes, tomatoes, maize, meat, fruit, olives, wheat, fish and rice. The principal mineral products are limestone, granite, marble, copper, coal, kaolin and wolframite.

The country is moderately industrialised. The principal manufactures are motor vehicle components, clothing and footwear, textiles, machinery, pulp and paper, pharmaceuticals, foodstuffs, chemicals, fertilisers, wood, cork, furniture, cement, glassware and pottery. There are a modern steelworks and large shipbuilding and repair yards at Lisbon and Setúbal, working mainly for foreign shipowners. There are several hydroelectric power stations and two thermal power stations.

The main exports are textiles, clothing and shoes, machinery, automobile parts, wood, pulp, paper, cork and minerals. Principal imports include machinery, vehicles, textiles, agricultural products, chemicals, oil and base metals.

GNI – US$109,100 million (2002); US$10,720 per capita (2002)

ANNUAL AVERAGE GROWTH OF GDP – 3.3 per cent (2000 est.)

INFLATION RATE – 2.9 per cent (2000 est.)

UNEMPLOYMENT – 4.0 per cent (2000 est.)

FOREIGN DIRECT INVESTMENT – US$10,835 million (1997–2000)

IMPORTS – US$40,800 million (2003)

EXPORTS – US$30,600 million (2003)

BALANCE OF PAYMENTS

Trade – US$12,444 million deficit (2003)

Current Account – US$7,549 million deficit (2003)

Trade with UK	2003	2004
Imports from UK	£2,158,673,000	£1,549,158,000
Exports to UK	1,399,300,000	1,898,583,000

TRANSPORT INFRASTRUCTURE

There are 2,850 km of railways, of which 623 km are electrified. There is a total of 68,732 km of roads. There are international airports at Lisbon, Oporto, Faro and Santa Maria, Lages (Azores) and Funchal (Madeira). The main ports are Oporto and Setúbal.

EDUCATION

Education is free of charge and compulsory for nine years from the age of six. Secondary education is mainly conducted in state general unified schools, lyceums, technical and professional schools and private schools. There are also military, naval, polytechnic and other specialist schools. There are 17 universities including those at Coimbra (founded in 1290), Oporto, Lisbon, Braga, Aveiro, Vila Real, Faro, Evora and in the Azores.

ILLITERACY RATE – (m) 5.2 per cent; (f) 10.0 per cent (2000)

GROSS ENROLMENT RATIO (percentage of relevant age group) – primary 121 per cent (2002); secondary 114 per cent (2002); tertiary 50 per cent (2002)

MEDIA AND CULTURE

Portugal's public broadcaster RTP enjoyed a monopoly until commercial TV was launched in 1992. Public radio networks are operated by RTP, while the Roman Catholic church owns Radio Renascenca. There are some 300 other local and regional commercial radio stations.

Principal national newspapers include the daily titles *Diario de Noticias, Publico, Correio da Manha* and *Jornal de Noticias.*

Portuguese culture dates back to prehistoric times and retains traces of Roman and Arab and later Flemish, French and Italian influences. A rich archaeological legacy includes the prehistoric cave paintings at Escoral, the Roman township of Conimbriga, the Temple of Diana in Évora, and the typical Arab-inspired architecture of such southern towns as Olhão and Tavira. Celebrated Portuguese writers include José Cardoso Pires (1925–98), Fernando Pessoa (1888–1935) and José Saramago (b. 1922), winner of the 1998 Nobel Prize for Literature.

AUTONOMOUS REGIONS

Madeira and the Azores are two administratively autonomous regions of Portugal, having locally elected assemblies and governments.

MADEIRA is a group of islands in the Atlantic Ocean about 520 miles south-west of Lisbon, and consists of Madeira, Porto, Santo and three uninhabited islands (Desertas). Total area is 779 sq. km; population, 253,482 (2001). ΨFunchal in Madeira, the largest island, is the capital (population 103,961)

THE AZORES are a group of nine islands (Flores, Corvo, Terceira, São Jorge, Pico, Faial, Graciosa, São Miguel and Santa Maria) in the Atlantic Ocean; area 2,330 sq. km; population, 243,895 (2001). ΨPonta Delgada, on São Miguel, is the capital (population, 137,700). Other ports are ΨAngra, in Terceira (55,900) and ΨHorta (16,300)

QATAR

Dawlat Qatar – State of Qatar

AREA – 11,000 sq. km. Neighbours: United Arab Emirates (south), Saudi Arabia (south-west)

POPULATION – 840,290 (2004 est.). Most of the population is concentrated in the urban district of Doha. Arabic is the official language. Islam is the religion of 95 per cent of the population

CAPITAL – ΨDoha (Ad-Dawhah) (population, 285,000 2001 estimate)

MAJOR CITIES – Ar-Rayyan; Dukhan; ΨMusay'id; Al-Wakrah

CURRENCY – Qatar riyal of 100 dirhams

NATIONAL DAY – 3 September

NATIONAL FLAG – White and maroon; white portion nearer the mast; vertical indented line comprising 17 angles divides the colours

LIFE EXPECTANCY (years) – 73.4 (2004 est.)

MORTALITY RATE (per 1,000 population) – 4.52 (2004 est.)

INFANT MORTALITY (per 1,000 births) – 19.32 (2004 est.)

HIV / AIDS ADULT PREVALENCE – 0.09 per cent (2001 est.)

DEATH PENALTY – Yes

POPULATION GROWTH RATE – 2.74 per cent (2004 est.)

POPULATION DENSITY – 52 per sq. km (2001)

MILITARY EXPENDITURE – 10 per cent of GDP (2003)

MILITARY PERSONNEL – 12,400: Army 8,500, Navy 1,800, Air Force 2,100

ILLITERACY RATE – (m) 18.6 per cent; (f) 15 per cent (2003 est.)

CLIMATE AND TERRAIN

The terrain is mostly flat desert, with salt flats in the south. Elevation extremes range from 103 m (Qurayn Abu al Bawl) at the highest point to 0 m (Persian Gulf) at the lowest. The country has a desert climate and average temperatures range from 23°C in January to 35°C in July. Humidity along the coast often reaches 90 per cent during the summer. Average annual rainfall is below 75 mm.

HISTORY AND POLITICS

Qatar developed into an important trading centre from the eighth century. It came under the rule of the al-Khalifa family, which in the 18th century moved its base to Bahrain island. A revolt against al-Khalifa rule in the 1860s was suppressed but Britain intervened in 1867, recognising Qatar as no longer a dependency of Bahrain, and the al-Thani family became rulers of Qatar. Nominally under the rule of the Ottoman empire from 1871 until the outbreak of the First World War, Qatar became a British protectorate in 1916. It became independent in 1971. In 1972 Shaikh Ahmad was overthrown by the Crown Prince and prime minister, Shaikh Khalifa. Shaik Khalifa was overthrown in 1995 by his son and heir, Shaikh Hamad, who introduced liberal reforms. Municipal elections, the first democratic polls since independence, were held in 1999. A referendum in 2003 approved a new constitution which would include a partially elected consultative council and allow female suffrage. Elections to this council were due to take place in late 2005.

POLITICAL SYSTEM
A new constitution was promulgated in 2004 and will replace the 1970 constitution. The head of state is a hereditary absolute monarch, the amir. There is no legislature at present, although the 2004 constitution provides for a *Shura* Council with 45 members, 30 directly elected and 15 appointed by the amir, and this will have legislative powers. There is an advisory council with 35 members appointed by the amir. Ministers are appointed by the amir. There are no political parties. Women were able to vote and stand for election in 1999, and the first female cabinet member was appointed in 2003.

HEAD OF STATE
HH Amir of Qatar, Minister of Defence and Commander-in-Chief of Armed Forces, Shaikh Hamad bin Khalifa al-Thani, KCMG, *assumed power* 27 June 1995
Crown Prince, HH Shaikh Tamim bin Hamad al-Thani

SELECTED GOVERNMENT MEMBERS *as at July 2005*
Prime Minister, HH Shaikh Abdulla bin Khalifa al-Thani
First Deputy Prime Minister, Foreign Affairs, Shaikh Hamad bin Jassem bin Jabr al-Thani
Internal Affairs, Shaikh Abdulla bin Khalid al-Thani
Finance, Yousef bin Hussain Kamal

EMBASSY OF THE STATE OF QATAR
1 South Audley Street, London W1K 1NB T 020-7493 2200
Ambassador Extraordinary and Plenipotentiary, HE Nasser bin Hamid M. Al-Khalifa, apptd 2000

BRITISH EMBASSY
PO Box 3, Doha T (+974) 4421991 E bembcomm@qatar.net.qa
Ambassador Extraordinary and Plenipotentiary, HE David MacLennan, apptd 2002

BRITISH COUNCIL
93 Al Sadd Street, PO Box 2992, Doha T (+974) 442 6193/4
Director, Tony Jones

ECONOMY AND TRADE
The economy is based largely on the production of oil, gas and petrochemicals. These account for more than 55 per cent of GDP, roughly 85 per cent of export earnings, and 70 per cent of government revenues. The state-owned Qatar General Petroleum Corporation controls the industry, and is responsible for oil production onshore and offshore. The large reserves of natural gas in the North Field came into production in 1991.

Other industries include a steel mill, a fertiliser plant, a cement factory, a petrochemical complex and two natural gas liquids plants. With the exception of the cement works at Umm Bab, all these industries are at Musay'id, about 30 miles south of Doha. Qatar is also expanding its infrastructure, including electrical generation and water

distillation, roads, houses, and government buildings. The chief imports are machinery and equipment, manufactures, foodstuffs, livestock and chemicals.
GNI – US$17,100 per capita (2001)
ANNUAL AVERAGE GROWTH OF GDP – 8.7 per cent (2004 est.)
INFLATION RATE – 2.3 per cent (2003 est.)
IMPORTS – US$4,050 million (2002)
EXPORTS – US$7,100 million (1999)

Trade with UK	2003	2004
Imports from UK	£316,552,000	£335,561,000
Exports to UK	54,931,000	86,101,000

TRANSPORT INFRASTRUCTURE
There are 1,210 km of roads, of which 1,089 km are surfaced. Doha is the chief port and also the location of the principal airport. Gulf Air and Qatar Airways provide regular international air services. Halul is the terminal for offshore oilfields.

MEDIA
Qatar officially lifted media censorship in 1995 and since then the press has been essentially free from government interference. The Qatari satellite station Al Jazeera, launched in 1997, has become one of the most important broadcasters in the Middle East. Radio is state-run by the Qatar Broadcasting Service (QBS), and the BBC World Service is available in Doha. The most popular newspapers are *Al-Watan* and the English-language *Gulf Times*.

ROMANIA

România – Romania

AREA – 230,300 sq. km. Neighbours: Ukraine (north and east), Moldova (east), Bulgaria (south), Serbia (south-west), Hungary (north-west)
POPULATION – 22,355,551 (2004 est.): 89.4 per cent Romanian, 7.1 per cent Hungarian, 1.7 per cent Roma, 0.5 per cent German, 0.3 per cent Ukrainian, 0.04 per cent Jews and other minorities. Religious affiliation: Orthodox 86.8 per cent, Roman Catholic 5 per cent, Reformed 3.5 per cent, Greek Catholic 1 per cent. Romanian is a Romance language with many archaic forms and admixtures from Slavonic, Turkish, Magyar and French
CAPITAL – Bucharest (population, 2,066,723, 2001 estimate)
MAJOR CITIES – ΨBraşov; Constanţa; Cluj-Napoca; Craiova; ΨGalaţi; Iaşi; Oradea; Ploieşti; Timişoara
CURRENCY – Leu (Lei) of 100 bani
NATIONAL ANTHEM – Deşteapta-te, Romane, din somnul cel de moarte [Awake ye, Romanians, from your deadly slumber]
NATIONAL DAY – 1 December
NATIONAL FLAG – Three vertical bands, blue, yellow and red
LIFE EXPECTANCY (years) – 71.12 (2004 est.)
MORTALITY RATE (per 1,000 population) – 11.69 (2004 est.)
INFANT MORTALITY (per 1,000 births) – 27.24 (2004 est.)
HIV / AIDS ADULT PREVALENCE – 0.1 per cent (2001 est.)
DEATH PENALTY – No (abolished 1989)

POPULATION BELOW POVERTY LINE – 44.56 per cent
(2000 est.)
POPULATION GROWTH RATE – –0.11 (2004 est.)
POPULATION DENSITY – 97 per sq. km (2002)
URBAN POPULATION – 55 per cent (2001)

CLIMATE AND TERRAIN

The Carpathian mountains in the east and the Transylvanian Alps in the centre enclose a plateau, while to the south and east lie the plains of the Danube and Siret rivers. The mountains are thickly forested. Elevation extremes range from 2,544 m (Moldoveanu) at the highest point to 0 m (Black Sea) at the lowest. The climate is continental, with average temperatures in Bucharest ranging from –2°C in January to 22°C in July.

HISTORY AND POLITICS

Romania was incorporated into the Roman empire in the early part of the second century AD but abandoned 200 years later when the power of Rome started to decline. After centuries of rule by invading and often disparate tribal forces, Romania was incorporated into the Ottoman Empire during the 15th century. The principalities of Moldavia and Wallachia were unified under a single native ruler in 1859, and independence was recognised by the Congress of Berlin in 1878. Romania joined the Allies in the First World War, and in the post-war peace settlement acquired Transylvania, Bukovina and Bessarabia.

In 1940 Romania was forced to cede territory to the Soviet Union and Hungary, and power was seized by the Romanian fascists, who took Romania into the Second World War on the Axis side. When its fascist leaders were overthrown in 1944, Romania changed sides. It was occupied in 1945 by Soviet forces and a communist-dominated government was installed. In 1947 King Michael abdicated, the monarchy was abolished and Romania became a communist republic. In 1965 Nicolae Ceauşescu became leader of the Romanian Communist Party and pursued a foreign policy increasingly independent of the Soviet Union, forming relationships with China and several Western countries. The brutality and corruption of Ceauşescu's regime provoked a popular uprising in December 1989 that deposed and executed the dictator and his wife. A provisional government led by Ion Iliescu abolished the leading role of the Communist Party and held elections in 1990. Although Romania became a multiparty democracy in 1991, governments continued to be dominated by former communists until 1996, when Emil Constantinescu was elected president in place of Ion Iliescu. Popular unrest and demonstrations have continued throughout the post-communist period, as most of the population has yet to benefit much from the transition to a market economy. Further economic (and constitutional) changes have been introduced to prepare for EU membership; Romania signed the EU accession treaty in April 2005 and could join in 2007 if reforms progress sufficiently. Romania became a member of NATO in 2004.

Presidential and legislative elections were held in November and December 2004. Traian Basescu, the candidate of a coalition of the Democratic and National Liberal parties won the presidential election with 51.2 per cent of the vote. In the legislative election, the Social Democratic Party of Romania (PSDR) remained the largest party in parliament, with 189 seats, but without an overall majority. It formed a coalition government with three other centre parties under Calin Tariceanu. In July 2005, Tariceanu announced the government's intention

to resign and call early elections after the constitutional court blocked judicial reforms demanded by the EU. Tariceanu later reversed this decision and agreed to remain as head of the government following a series of catastrophic floods in the east of the country.

POLITICAL SYSTEM

The 1991 constitution was amended in 2003 to bring it into line with other EU members. The head of state is a president who is directly elected for a five-year term, renewable only once. The bicameral parliament comprises the Chamber of Deputies with 345 seats, of which 18 are reserved for ethnic minorities, and the Senate with 140 seats. Both houses are elected for a four-year term. The prime minister is appointed by the president.

HEAD OF STATE
President of the Republic, Traian Basescu, *elected* 12
    December 2004

SELECTED GOVERNMENT MEMBERS *as at July 2005*
Prime Minister, Calin Tariceanu
Defence, Teodor Atanasiu
Economics, Gheorghe Copos
Foreign Affairs, Mihai Razvan Ungereanu
Interior, Vasile Blaga

EMBASSY OF ROMANIA
Arundel House, 4 Palace Green, London W8 4QD
T 020-7937 9666
Ambassador Extraordinary and Plenipotentiary, HE Dan
    Ghibernea, apptd 2002

BRITISH EMBASSY
24 Strada Jules Michelet, RO-70154 Bucharest
T (+40) (21) 201 7200
Ambassador Extraordinary and Plenipotentiary, HE
    Quinton Quayle, apptd 2002

BRITISH COUNCIL
Calea Dorobantilor 14, RO-71132 Bucharest
T (+40) (21) 307 9600 E bc.romania@britishcouncil.ro
Director, Stephen Roman

DEFENCE

The Army has 1,258 main battle tanks, 1,583 armoured personnel carriers and 177 armoured infantry fighting vehicles. The Navy has one frigate, 38 patrol and coastal vessels at four bases. The Air Force has 106 combat aircraft.

MILITARY EXPENDITURE – 2.3 per cent of GDP (2003)
MILITARY PERSONNEL – 97,200: Army 66,000, Navy
    7,200, Air Force 14,000; Paramilitaries 79,900
CONSCRIPTION DURATION – 12 months

ECONOMY AND TRADE

The transition to a market economy has been slow and the country still suffers from widespread poverty, while corruption and red tape hinder foreign investment. Further reforms are needed in order to join the EU, and the president and government elected in 2004 have pledged to accelerate these.

Agriculture employed 40.8 per cent of the workforce in 2000 and contributed 12.8 per cent of GDP. The principal crops are cereals, vegetables, flax and hemp. Vines and fruits are also grown, and extensive forests in the mountains support an important timber industry. There are plentiful supplies of natural gas, together with mineral deposits including coal, iron ore, bauxite, chromium and uranium.

Principal exports include textiles, metallurgical products, machinery components, minerals, chemicals, shoes and transport equipment. The main imports are machines and equipment, minerals, textiles, chemicals and metallurgical products. Italy, Germany, Russia, France and the UK are Romania's most important trading partners.
GNI – US$41,700 million (2002); US$1,870 per capita (2002)
ANNUAL AVERAGE GROWTH OF GDP – 5.3 per cent (2001 est.)
INFLATION RATE – 22.5 per cent (2002 est.)
UNEMPLOYMENT – 7.1 per cent (2000 est.)
TOTAL EXTERNAL DEBT – US$10,224 million (2000 est.)
FOREIGN DIRECT INVESTMENT – US$5,312 million (1997–2000)
IMPORTS – US$24,000 million (2003)
EXPORTS – US$17,600 million (2003)

BALANCE OF PAYMENTS
Trade – US$4,537 million deficit (2003)
Current Account – US$3,311 million deficit (2003)

Trade with UK	2003	2004
Imports from UK	£507,927,000	£606,735,000
Exports to UK	689,850,000	790,002,000

TRANSPORT INFRASTRUCTURE
There are 11,376 km of railways, over one-third of which are electrified. There are 153,358 km of roads, of which 78,213 km are surfaced and 113 km are motorway. The principal ports are Constanța and Mangalia (on the Black Sea), Sulina (on the Danube estuary), Galati, Braila, Giurgiu and Drobeta-Turnu Severin. The Danube and the Black Sea are linked by a canal. The main airports are at Bucharest and Timisoara.

EDUCATION
Primary and secondary education is free of charge and compulsory. There are state universities in seven cities, 66 private universities, six polytechnics, two commercial academies, and five agricultural colleges.
ILLITERACY RATE – (m) 1.0 per cent; (f) 2.8 per cent (2000)
GROSS ENROLMENT RATIO (percentage of relevant age group) – primary 99 per cent (2002); secondary 82 per cent (2002); tertiary 27 per cent (2002)

MEDIA
Romania has a dynamic media network with television audiences predominantly shared between the state-owned Romania 1 and the private commercial stations Pro TV and Antena 1. Most households in Bucharest have cable TV. There are more than 100 private radio stations. State-run Radio Romania operates four national networks and regional and local stations. There are four main daily newspapers: *Adevarul, Libertatea, Evenimentul Zillei* and *Romania Libera.*

RUSSIAN FEDERATION

Rossiiskaya Federatsiya – Russian Federation

AREA – 16,888,500 sq. km. Neighbours: Norway, Finland, Estonia, Latvia, Belarus and Ukraine (west), Georgia, Azerbaijan, Kazakhstan, China, Mongolia and North Korea (south). The Kaliningrad enclave borders Lithuania and Poland
POPULATION – 143,782,338 (2004 est.): 87.5 per cent Russian, 3.5 per cent Tatar, 2.7 per cent Ukrainian, 1.3 per cent ethnic German, 1.1 per cent Chuvash, 0.9 per cent Bashkir, 0.7 per cent Belarusian and 0.7 per cent Mordovian. There are another six minorities with populations of over half a million and more than 130 nationalities in total. The Russian Orthodox Church is the predominant religion, though the Tatars and many in the north Caucasus are Muslims and there are Jewish communities in Moscow and St Petersburg. The language is Russian
CAPITAL – Moscow (population, 10,101,500, 2002 estimate), founded about 1147, became the centre of the rising Moscow principality and in the 15th century the capital of the whole of Russia (Muscovy). In 1325 it became the seat of the Metropolitan of Russia. In 1703 Peter the Great transferred the capital to St Petersburg, but on 14 March 1918 Moscow was again designated as the capital
MAJOR CITIES – ΨSt Petersburg, from 1914 to 1924 Petrograd and from 1924 to 1991 Leningrad. Other cities: Chelyabinsk; Kazan; Nizhny-Novgorod/Gorky; Novosibirsk/Novonikolayevsk; Omsk; Perm/Molotov; Rostov-on-Don; Samara/Kuibyshev; Ufa; Yekaterinburg/Sverdlovsk
CURRENCY – Rouble of 100 kopeks
NATIONAL ANTHEM – Russia, sacred our empire (the former Soviet national anthem, with new lyrics)
NATIONAL DAY – 12 June (Independence Day)
NATIONAL FLAG – Three horizontal stripes of white, blue and red
LIFE EXPECTANCY (years) – 66.39 (2004 est.)
MORTALITY RATE (per 1,000 population) – 15.17 (2004 est.)
INFANT MORTALITY (per 1,000 births) – 16.96 (2004 est.)
HIV / AIDS ADULT PREVALENCE – 0.9 per cent (2001 est.)
DEATH PENALTY – No (abolished 1997)
POPULATION GROWTH RATE – −0.45 (2004 est.)
POPULATION DENSITY – 9 per sq. km (2002)
URBAN POPULATION – 73 per cent

Russia occupies three-quarters of the land area of the former Soviet Union.

The Russian Federation comprises 89 members: 49 regions *(oblast)* – Amur, Arkhangelsk, Astrakhan, Belgorod, Bryansk, Chelyabinsk, Chita, Irkutsk, Ivanovo, Kaliningrad, Kaluga, Kamchatka, Kemerovo, Kirov, Kostroma, Kurgan, Kursk, Leningrad, Lipetsk, Magadan, Moscow, Murmansk, Nizhny-Novgorod, Novgorod, Novosibirsk, Omsk, Orel, Orenburg, Penza, Perm, Pskov, Rostov, Ryazan, Sakhalin, Samara, Saratov, Smolensk, Sverdlovsk, Tambov, Tomsk, Tula, Tver, Tyumen, Ulyanovsk, Vladimir, Volgograd, Vologda, Voronezh, Yaroslavl; six autonomous territories *(krai)* – Altai, Khabarovsk, Krasnodar, Krasnoyarsk, Primorye, Stavropol; 21 republics *(respublika)* – Adygeia, Altai, Bashkortostan, Buryatia, Chechnya, Chuvashia, Daghestan,

Ingushetia, Kabardino-Balkaria, Kalmykia, Karachai-Cherkessia, Karelia, Khakassia, Komi, Mari-El, Mordovia, North Ossetia (Alania), Sakha, Tatarstan, Tyva, Udmurtia; ten autonomous areas *(okrug)* – Aga-Buryat, Chuckchi, Evenki, Khanty-Mansi, Komi-Permyak, Koryak, Nenets, Taimyr, Ust-Orda-Buryat, Yamal-Nenets; two cities of federal status – Moscow, St Petersburg; and one autonomous Jewish region, Birobijan.

CLIMATE AND TERRAIN
The Russian Federation includes the easternmost areas of Europe and the whole of northern Asia. There are three principal geographic areas: a low-lying flat western area stretching eastwards up to the Yenisei and divided in two by the Ural mountain range; the eastern area between the Yenisei and the Pacific, consisting of plateaux and mountain ranges; and a southern mountainous area. Elevation extremes range from 5,633 m (Mt El'brus, Caucusus) at the highest point to −28 m (Caspian Sea) at the lowest. The country has a very long coastline, including the longest Arctic coastline in the world (over 27,000 km).

The most important rivers are the Volga, the Northern Dvina and the Pechora, the Neva, the Don and the Kuban in the European part, and in the Asiatic part, the Ob, Irtysh, the Yenisei, the Lena and the Amur, and, further north, Khatanga, Olenek, Yana, Indigirka, Kolyma and Anadyr. Lake Baikal in eastern Siberia is the deepest lake in the world.

The climate varies dramatically, from the frozen tundra of the north Siberian plain, to the temperate regions of the far east. Throughout the country, winters are cold, while summers are hot in the south and relatively warm elsewhere. Rainfall is highest in the westerly mountain regions, which have an average annual precipitation of up to 2,000 mm. Average temperatures in Moscow range from −16°C in January to 23°C in July.

HISTORY AND POLITICS
Russia was settled by many ethnic groups, including Slavs, Turks and Bulgars in the third to seventh centuries AD, and in the 13th century came under the overlordship of the Mongols. In the 15th century the grand duke of Moscovy threw off Mongol overlordship and began a process of unification and territorial expansion continued by his successors. Internal disorder and war with neighbouring countries held back Russian development until the reign of Peter I (The Great) (1682–1725), who introduced Western ideas of government, modernised the army and founded the navy. Under Catherine II (The Great) (1762–96) Russia became a great power, extending its territory further. Russian expansion in Asia led to a war with Japan in 1904–5 that ended in an unexpected defeat for Russia. This provoked a revolution in 1905 which, though suppressed, forced the emperor to establish Russia's first parliament (Duma).

The Duma's powers were limited and it was unable to ameliorate the Tsarist regime's endemic misgovernment or the conditions of the increasingly militant urban working class. During the First World War, discontent caused by autocratic rule, the poor military conduct of the war and wartime privation led to a revolution which broke out in March 1917. The emperor abdicated. A power struggle ensued between the provisional government and the Bolshevik Party. This led to a second revolution in November 1917 in which the Bolsheviks, led by Lenin, seized power.

Civil war between 'red' Bolshevik forces and 'white'

monarchist and anti-communist forces, the latter supported by foreign powers, lasted until the end of 1922. During the civil war, Russia had been declared a Soviet Republic and other Soviet republics had been formed in Ukraine, Belorussia and Transcaucasia. These four republics merged to form the Union of Soviet Socialist Republics (USSR) on 30 December 1922.

During the 1930s Joseph Stalin introduced a policy of rapid industrialisation under a series of five-year plans, brought all sectors of industry under government control, abolished private ownership and enforced the collectivisation of agriculture. Many ethnic minority groups suffered under Stalin's regime and it is estimated that up to 1.5 million people were deported to the Gulags of Siberia and the central Asian republics.

Mikhail Gorbachev became Soviet leader in March 1985 and introduced the policies of *perestroika* (complete restructuring) and *glasnost* (openness) in order to revamp the economy, which had stagnated since the 1970s, to root out corruption and inefficiency, and to end the Cold War. The retreat from total control by the Communist Party unleashed ethnic and nationalist tensions.

Following the defeat of an attempted coup by hardline communists in August 1991, effective political power was in the hands of the republican leaders, especially Russian President Yeltsin, and the Soviet Union began to break up as the constituent republics declared their independence. Gorbachev resigned as Soviet president on 25 December 1991 and the following day the USSR formally ceased to exist. The Russian Federation took over the Soviet Union's seat at the UN in December 1991, recognised as an independent state by the EC and USA in January 1992, and joined the G7 group of industrialised countries in 1996.

A new Russian Federal Treaty was signed on 13 March 1992 between the central government and the autonomous republics within Russia. Tatarstan and Bashkortostan signed the treaty in 1994 after securing considerable legislative and economic autonomy.

Vladimir Putin was re-elected president in March 2004 with 71.2 per cent of the vote. His presidency has seen an increasing degree of centralisation, the partial renationalisation of the oil industry, and the re-assertion of state control over the media. In the 2003 legislative elections, the pro-Putin United Russia Party retained its majority in the Duma. In February 2004, President Putin dismissed Prime Minister Mikhail Kasyanov and the entire council of ministers. The president named Mikhail Fradkov as prime minister, who took office in March 2004 at the head of a smaller, restructured council of ministers.

INSURGENCIES
Chechnya's attempt to achieve independence has led to two wars with the Russian federal government, in 1994–6 and since 1999. The area is strategically important to Russia because routes from central Russia to the Black Sea and the Caspian Sea pass through it, and oil and gas pipelines from neighbouring countries.

The Chechen republic declared its independence in November 1991 and refused to sign the Russian Federal Treaty in 1992. Civil war began in early 1994 between the Chechen government and armed opposition forces tacitly supported by the Russian government. The Russian military invaded Chechnya in December 1994, meeting strong opposition from the Chechen army, guerrillas and civilians. The conflict became unpopular in Russia but the federal government was reluctant to withdraw for fear of encouraging other separatist movements in the Russian Federation. Peace negotiations in 1996 resulted in the signing of the Khasavyurt accords and Russian troops withdrew in January 1997.

The accords left the issue of Chechen independence unresolved and the uneasy peace broke down in September 1999 when Russian forces invaded Chechnya again. This followed bombings in Russia that were blamed on Chechen extremists and an incursion by Chechen forces into neighbouring Dagestan in August 1999. The Russians captured Grozny in February 2000. Refusing to negotiate with the Chechen government, President Putin imposed direct rule from Moscow in May 2000. Violent unrest has continued in Chechnya, leading to accusations of human rights violations by Russian troops, and Chechen separatists have carried out suicide bombings and other attacks in Russia, such as the Moscow theatre siege in 2002 and the Beslan school siege in 2004.

In a referendum in Chechnya in March 2003, the majority voted in favour of a new constitution promising autonomy for the republic but also stating that Chechnya was an integral part of the Russian Federation. The election of a Russian-backed candidate, Alu Alkhanov, as president of Chechnya in August 2004 (following the assassination of his predecessor in May) has helped reduce the level of violence in Chechnya. Violence has spilled over into other parts of the North Caucasus as Russian forces attempt to capture Chechen separatists based in the republics neighbouring Chechnya.

POLITICAL SYSTEM

The 1993 constitution introduced multiparty democracy and enshrines various human rights and civil liberties. The head of state is a president, who is directly elected for a a four-year term, renewable only once consecutively. Legislative power is vested in the Federal Assembly, comprising the Federation Council (upper house) of 178 members, two elected by each of the 89 members of the Russian Federation; and the State *Duma* (lower house) of 450 members, of which 225 are elected by constituencies on a first past the post basis and 225 by proportional representation, with a 5 per cent threshold for representation. The president appoints the chairman of the council of ministers (prime minister) but is also entitled to chair sessions of the council.

A Constitutional Court of 19 members appointed for a 12-year term protects and interprets the Constitution and decides if laws are compatible with it.

HEAD OF STATE
President, Vladimir Putin, *elected* 26 March 2000, *inaugurated* 7 May 2000, *re-elected*, 14 March 2004

SELECTED GOVERNMENT MEMBERS *as at July 2005*
Chair, Mikhail Fradkov
Defence, Sergei Ivanov
Finance, Alexei Kudrin
Foreign Affairs, Sergei Lavrov
Interior, Rashid Nurgaliyev

EMBASSY OF THE RUSSIAN FEDERATION
13 Kensington Palace Gardens, London W8 4QX
T 020-7229 2666/3628/6412
Ambassador Extraordinary and Plenipotentiary, HE Yury Fedotov, apptd 2005

BRITISH EMBASSY
Smolenskaya Naberezhnaya 10, 121099 Moscow
T (+7) (095) 956 7200 E moscow@britishembassy.ru
Ambassador Extraordinary and Plenipotentiary, HE Anthony Brenton, apptd 2005

BRITISH COUNCIL
Ulitsa Nikoloyamskaya 1, RUS-109189 Moscow
T (+7) (095) 782 0200 E bc.moscow@britishcouncil.ru
Director, Adrian Greer

DEFENCE

Since the demise of the Soviet Union the Russian Federation armed forces have been considerably reduced. In November 2000 it was announced that the armed forces would be reduced to 850,000 personnel by 2005. Major army reform is planned for the period 2004–10, including the transition from conscription to voluntary service.

A joint CIS air defence system covers Russia, Armenia, Belarus, Georgia, Kazakhstan, Kyrgyzstan, Tajikistan, Turkmenistan, Ukraine and Uzbekistan.

The Strategic Deterrent Forces have 14 nuclear-powered ballistic missile submarines with 216 missiles, 635 intercontinental ballistic missiles and 100 anti-ballistic missiles.

The Army has about 22,800 main battle tanks, 24,990 armoured personnel carriers and armoured infantry fighting vehicles, and 1,700 helicopters. The Navy has 51 submarines, one aircraft carrier, six cruisers, 14 destroyers, six frigates, 86 patrol and coastal vessels, 266 combat aircraft and 161 armed helicopters. The Air Force has 1,736 combat aircraft.

The Russian Federation deploys forces in Armenia (3,500), Georgia (3,000), Moldova (1,400) and Tajikistan (7,800) and remains the world's third largest contributor to peacekeeping operations. An agreement with Ukraine on the division on the Black Sea Fleet was signed in May 1997.

MILITARY EXPENDITURE – 4.9 per cent of GDP (2003)
MILITARY PERSONNEL – 848,600: Strategic Deterrent Forces 149,000, Army 360,000, Navy 155,000, Air Force 184,600; Paramilitaries 359,100
CONSCRIPTION DURATION – 18–36 months

ECONOMY AND TRADE

Under the Soviet regime, an essentially agrarian economy in 1917 was transformed by the early 1960s into the second strongest industrial power in the world. However, by the early 1970s the concentration of resources on the military-industrial complex was causing the civilian economy to stagnate. Economic reforms were introduced by President Gorbachev, including the legalisation of small private businesses, the reduction of state control over the economy, and denationalisation and privatisation. The first stage of mass privatisation of state industries began in October 1992 and the central distribution system was abolished with effect from January 1993. By February 1996, 80 per cent of the economy had been privatised.

The transition to a market economy caused a severe economic crisis in 1993 and again in 1998, when the country came close to defaulting on its foreign debts as the rouble collapsed. But following the devaluation of the rouble, the economy began to grow in 1999 and has sustained this growth in subsequent years. Foreign debt now stands at around 28 per cent of GDP, down from 90 per cent of GDP, inflation has been reduced, and under President

Putin the budget has balanced. Nevertheless, considerable problems remain to be overcome: the country's manufacturing base is dilapidated, its banking system is weak, and widespread corruption has led to a lack of trust in banking institutions. The economy is also heavily dependent on world oil prices.

The Russian Federation has some of the richest mineral deposits in the world. Coal is mined in the Kuznetsk area, in the Urals, south of Moscow, in the Donets basin and in the Pechora area in the north. Oil is produced in the northern Caucasus, between the Volga and the Urals, and in western Siberia, which also has large deposits of natural gas. A pipeline to bring Caspian oil into the Russian Federation via Daghestan and North Ossetia is under construction. Oil production in 2000 was 323.3 million tonnes. Coal and gas deposits in Siberia and the far east (especially Yakutia) are being developed. The Ural mountains contain many precious natural resources including high-quality iron ore, manganese, copper, aluminium, platinum, precious stones, salt, asbestos, pyrites, coal and oil. Iron ore is also mined near Kursk, Tula, Lipetsk, in several areas in Siberia and in the Kola Peninsula. Non-ferrous metals are found in the Altai, eastern Siberia, the northern Caucasus, the Kuznetsk basin, the far east and the far north. Some 190 tonnes of gold were produced in 2003.

The vast area and the great variety in climatic conditions are reflected in the structure of agriculture. In the far north reindeer breeding, hunting and fishing are predominant. Further south, the timber industry is combined with grain growing. In the southern half of the forest zone and in the adjacent forest-steppe zone, the acreage under grain crops is larger and the structure of agriculture more complex. Between the Volga and the Urals, cericulture is predominant (particularly summer wheat), followed by cattle breeding. Beyond the Urals is another important grain-growing and stock-breeding area in the southern part of the western Siberian plain. In 2001, 85 million tonnes of grain was harvested, an increase of 20 million tonnes on 2000. In the extreme south cotton is cultivated. Vine, tobacco and other southern crops are grown on the Black Sea shore of the Caucasus.

Moscow and St Petersburg are still the two largest industrial centres in the country, but new industrial areas have been developed in the Urals, the Kuznetsk basin, Siberia and the far east.

The Russian Federation's main trading partners are Germany, the USA, Italy, China and fellow members of the CIS.

GNI – US$306,600 million (2002); US$2,130 per capita (2002)

ANNUAL AVERAGE GROWTH OF GDP – 6.7 per cent (2004 est.)

INFLATION RATE – 13.7 per cent (2003 est.)

UNEMPLOYMENT – 8.3 per cent (2004 est.)

TOTAL EXTERNAL DEBT – US$160,300 million (2000 est.)

FOREIGN DIRECT INVESTMENT – US$15,028 million (1997–2000)

IMPORTS – US$82,000 million (2003)

EXPORTS – US$134,000 million (2003)

BALANCE OF PAYMENTS
Trade – US$60,493 million surplus (2003)
Current Account – US$35,845 million surplus (2003)

Trade with UK	2003	2004
Imports from UK	£1,416,739,000	£1,468,396,000
Exports to UK	2,481,230,000	3,545,501,000

TRANSPORT INFRASTRUCTURE

The European area of the Russian Federation is well served by railways, but there are still large areas, notably in the far north and Siberia, with few or no railways. In 2001 there were 149,000 km of railways, of which 86,000 km were used for passenger transport. The road system is similarly concentrated in the more densely populated European part of the country, and in the southernmost parts of Asian Russia. There are 537,289 km of roads, 362,133 km of which are paved.

The most important ports (Taganrog, Rostov and Novorossiisk) lie around the Black Sea and the Sea of Azov. The northern ports (St Petersburg, Murmansk and Arkhangelsk) are, with the exception of Murmansk, icebound during winter. Several ports have been built along the Arctic Sea route between Murmansk and Vladivostok and are in regular use every summer. The far eastern port of Vladivostok, the Pacific naval base of the Russian Federation, is kept open by icebreakers all the year round.

There are 95,900 km of waterways. The great rivers of European Russia flow outwards from the centre, linking all parts of the plain with the chief ports. They are supplemented by a system of canals which provide a through route between the White, Baltic, Black and Caspian Seas. The most notable are the White Sea–Baltic Canal, the Moscow–Volga Canal and the Volga–Don Canal linking the Baltic and the White Seas in the north to the Caspian Sea, the Black Sea and the Sea of Azov in the south.

Because of the vast distances, the terrain and the winter climate, air transport is the quickest form of long-distance internal travel. There are over 2,500 airports and airstrips, although only about 570 have paved runways; about 55 of these are capable of accepting the largest planes.

EDUCATION

There are 11 years of compulsory education, nine at basic school level and a further two at senior secondary level. Higher education is provided by public and private accredited Higher Education Institutions (HEIs). There are 609 public and 206 private HEIs and around 3000 non-university level educational institutions *(technikum)* or colleges.

ILLITERACY RATE – (m) 0.3 per cent; (f) 0.5 per cent (2003 est.)

GROSS ENROLMENT RATIO (percentage of relevant age group) – primary 114 per cent (2002); secondary 92 per cent (2002); tertiary 68 per cent (2002)

MEDIA

The country's main national TV networks, Channel One, Radio Broadcasting company (RTR) and NTV, are state-run. Many newspapers are privately owned and popular titles include *Kommersant*, *Izvestia* and the English language title *The Moscow Times*. The principal radio network is run by Russian State Television and RTR, alongside numerous regional and external services.

CULTURE

Russian is a branch of the Slavonic family of languages and is written in the Cyrillic script.

Before the westernisation of Russia under Peter the Great (1672–1725), Russian literature consisted mainly of folk ballads *(byliny)*, epic songs, chronicles and works of moral theology. The 18th and 19th centuries saw the development of poetry and fiction. Poetry reached its zenith with Alexander Pushkin (1799–1837), Mikhail Lermontov (1814–41), Alexander Blok (1880–1921), the 1958 Nobel Prize winner Boris Pasternak (1890–1960), Vladimir Mayakovsky (1893–1930) and Anna Akhmatova (1889–1966). Celebrated figures in philosophy and literary theory include Mikhail Bakhtin (1895–1975) and Viktor Shklovsky (1893–1984). Fiction is associated with the names of Nikolai Gogol (1809–52), Ivan Turgenev (1818–83), Fyodor Dostoyevsky (1821–81), Leo Tolstoy (1828–1910), Anton Chekhov (1860–1904), Maxim Gorky (1868–1936), Ivan Bunin (1870–1953), Mikhail Bulgakov (1891–1940), Mikhail Sholokhov (1905–84) and Alexander Solzhenitsyn (b. 1918), winner of the Nobel Prize for Literature in 1970.

Great names in music include Glinka (1804–57), Borodin (1833–87), Mussorgsky (1839–81), Rimsky-Korsakov (1844–1908), Tchaikovsky (1840–93), Rachmaninov (1873–1943), Skriabin (1872–1915), Prokofiev (1891–1953), Stravinsky (1882–1971), Shostakovich (1906–75), Gubaidulina (b. 1931) and Schnittke (1934–98).

Eisenstein (1898–1948), Andrei Tarkovsky (1932–86) and Nikita Mikhalkov (b. 1945) are celebrated figures in Russian cinema.

RWANDA

Republika y'u Rwanda / République Rwandaise – Republic of Rwanda

AREA – 26,338 sq. km. Neighbours: Burundi (south), Democratic Republic of Congo (west), Uganda (north), Tanzania (east)

POPULATION – 7,954,013 (2004 est.): Hutus 90 per cent, Tutsis 9 per cent, Twa (pygmy) 1 per cent. Kinyarwanda, French and English are the official languages. Swahili is also spoken

CAPITAL – Kigali (population, 608,141, 2002 census)

CURRENCY – Rwanda franc of 100 centimes

NATIONAL ANTHEM – Rwanda rwacu, Rwanda gihugu cyambyage [My Rwanda, Rwanda who gave me birth]

NATIONAL DAY – 1 July

NATIONAL FLAG – Broad blue band in upper half, with a sun next the fly surmounting equal bands of yellow and green

LIFE EXPECTANCY (years) – 39.18 (2004 est.)

MORTALITY RATE (per 1,000 population) – 21.86 (2004 est.)

INFANT MORTALITY RATE (per 1,000 births) – 101.68 (2004 est.)

HIV / AIDS ADULT PREVALENCE – 5.1 per cent (2003 est.)

DEATH PENALTY – Yes

POPULATION GROWTH RATE – 1.82 per cent (2004 est.)

POPULATION DENSITY – 331 per sq. km (2002)

MILITARY EXPENDITURE – 4.1 per cent of GDP (2002)

MILITARY PERSONNEL – 51,000: Army 40,000, Air Force 1,000, Paramilitaries 10,000

ILLITERACY RATE – (m) 23.7 per cent; (f) 35.3 per cent (2003 est.)

GROSS ENROLMENT RATIO (percentage of relevant age group) – primary 117 per cent (2002); secondary 14 per cent (2002); tertiary 2 per cent (2002)

CLIMATE AND TERRAIN

Landlocked Rwanda's terrain is mostly mountainous and includes the volcanic Virunga range in the north-west. Elevation extremes range from 4,519 m (Volcan Karisimbi) at the highest point to 950 m (Rusizi River) at the lowest. Rwanda's western border runs through Lake Kivu. The climate is tropical, with two wet seasons, from February to April and November to January. Average daily temperatures range from 15°C in January to 35°C in July.

HISTORY AND POLITICS

Rwanda was settled by Hutu peoples from the tenth century. From the 14th century, they came under the dominance of Tutsi peoples migrating to the area, who established a monarchy in the 15th century and a unified state in the late 19th century; the historic dominance of the majority Hutus by the minority Tutsis is the source of the conflict between the two ethnic groups that has dominated the country's history. The country became a German protectorate in the 1890s and was occupied by Belgium when the First World War broke out. After the war, it became a mandated territory administered by Belgium. In 1959, the Hutu population rebelled against Tutsi domination, causing the king and some 150,000 Tutsis to flee the country. Rwanda became a republic in 1961 and independence was achieved in July 1962 under a Hutu president. This president was overthrown in 1973 in a military coup led by Maj.-Gen. Juvenal Habyarimana, who became president. His National Revolutionary Development Movement (MRND) was the only legal party until 1991.

Armed Tutsi exiles repeatedly attempted to invade Rwanda in the 1960s and 1970s but were defeated by the predominantly Hutu army. Continued conflict left thousands dead over a period of 30 years. The exiles and opponents of the MRND regime eventually formed the Tutsi-led Rwandan Patriotic Front (FPR), and in October 1990 they again invaded the country, winning control of parts of the north. After the government reneged on a 1992 peace agreement, the RPF advanced on Kigali and forced the government to restart negotiations, which led to the Arusha peace accord in August 1993.

In April 1994, President Habyarimana, who had retained the interim presidency, died in a plane crash blamed variously on extremist sections of the Hutu army and the FPR. His death sparked off massacres of the Tutsi minority and moderate Hutus by the army and militia *(interahamwe)*; 800,000 people were massacred in three months and millions fled to neighbouring countries. The FPR campaign to counter this led to it establishing its control over the country, forcing the defeated government forces and millions more Hutus to flee. In July 1994 the FPR established a broad-based government of national unity in which moderate Hutus were given the presidency and premiership and the FPR took eight of the 22 seats. An International Criminal Tribunal for Rwanda was established in 1995 to bring to trial those directly responsible for the 1994 genocide. A government report in 2002 stated that 1,074,017 people, more than 93 per cent of them Tutsis, were killed between 1990 and 1994.

In spite of continuing attacks by extremist Hutu insurgents and Rwandan involvement in the civil war in the neighbouring Democratic Republic of the Congo from 1996 until 2002, reconciliation efforts and political reforms have been introduced since 1994 in an attempt to stabilise the country. Local elections were held in 1999, and presidential and legislative elections were held in 2003 following the approval of a new constitution. In the presidential election in August 2003, the FPR leader Paul Kagame was elected, with 95.1 per cent of the vote. In the legislative elections, the FPR won 40 of the 53 directly elected seats and formed a coalition government with the Social Democratic Party, the Christian Democratic Party, the Islamic Democratic Party, the Liberal Party and a number of independent members. The FPR is regarded as authoritarian, suppressing criticism of the government, but the country has achieved relative stability under its rule.

POLITICAL SYSTEM

Under the 2003 constitution, the head of state is a president directly elected for a seven-year term, renewable once only. The bicameral legislature consists of a National Assembly and a Senate. The National Assembly has 80 members, of whom 53 are directly elected, 24 are women members elected by the provinces, two represent youth organisations and one represents organisations of disabled people; all serve a five-year term. The upper house, the Senate, has 26 members indirectly elected for an eight-year term.

HEAD OF STATE

President, Maj.-Gen. Paul Kagame, *appointed* 17 April 2000, *sworn in* 22 April 2000, *elected* 25 August 2003

SELECTED GOVERNMENT MEMBERS *as at July 2005*
Prime Minister, Bernard Makusa
Defence and National Security, Maj.-Gen. Marcel Gatsinzi
Finance and Economic Planning, Donald Kaberuka
Foreign Affairs and Regional Co-operation, Charles Murigande
Internal Affairs, Christopher Bazivamo

EMBASSY OF THE REPUBLIC OF RWANDA
Uganda House, 58–59 Trafalgar Square, London WC2N 5DX
T 020-7930 2570
Ambassador Extraordinary and Plenipotentiary, HE Rosemary K. Museminali, apptd 2000

BRITISH EMBASSY
Parcelle No. 1131, Blvd de l'Umuganda, Kacyira-Sud, BP 576 Kigali T (+ 250) 84098/85771/85773
Ambassador Extraordinary and Plenipotentiary, HE Jeremy Macadie, apptd 2004

ECONOMY AND TRADE

Rwanda is the most densely populated country in Africa, with few natural resources and minimal industry. Around 90 per cent of the population is engaged in subsistence agriculture. Primary foreign exchange earners are coffee and tea, and tin, hides, quinine and pyrethrum are also exported, although the lack of adequate transport infrastructure is a handicap. Rwanda was given IMF-World Bank Heavily Indebted Poor Country (HIPC) status debt relief in late 2000.
GNI – US$1,800 million (2002); US$230 per capita (2002)
ANNUAL AVERAGE GROWTH OF GDP – 6.0 per cent (2000 est.)
INFLATION RATE – 4.3 per cent (2000 est.)
TOTAL EXTERNAL DEBT – US$1,271 million (2000 est.)
IMPORTS – US$250 million (2003)
EXPORTS – US$60 million (2003)

BALANCE OF TRADE
Trade – US$166 million deficit (2002)
Current Account – US$126 million deficit (2002)

Trade with UK	2003	2004
Imports from UK	£3,199,000	£4,391,000
Exports to UK	248,000	278,000

TRANSPORT INFRASTRUCTURE

Rwanda has 12,000 km of roads, of which around 996 km are surfaced, but landslides can occur during the wet season. There are no railways and Lake Kivu is navigable by shallow boats. The principal airport is at Kigali.

MEDIA

Rwanda's network media is mainly government-controlled. A privately run radio station began broadcasting in 2004. The BBC World Service, Voice of America and Deutsche Welle all broadcast in Kigali. There is a growing number of newspapers but they face government restrictions and generally exercise self-censorship.

ST CHRISTOPHER AND NEVIS

Federation of St Christopher and Nevis

AREA – 262 sq. km
POPULATION – 38,836 (2004 est.). The language is English
CAPITAL – ΨBasseterre (population, 12,200, 1994 estimate)
MAJOR TOWNS – ΨCharlestown, the chief town of Nevis
CURRENCY – East Caribbean dollar (EC$) of 100 cents
NATIONAL ANTHEM – Oh land of beauty
NATIONAL DAY – 19 September (Independence Day)
NATIONAL FLAG – Three diagonal bands, green, black and red; each colour separated by a stripe of yellow. Two white stars on the black band
MORTALITY RATE (per 1,000 population) – 8.65 (2004 est.)
LIFE EXPECTANCY (years) – 71.86 (2004 est.)
INFANT MORTALITY (per 1,000 births) – 14.94 (2004 est.)
POPULATION GROWTH RATE – 0.25 (2004 est.)
POPULATION DENSITY – 145 per sq. km (2001)

CLIMATE AND TERRAIN

The volcanic islands of St Christopher (St Kitts) (109.5 sq. km) and Nevis (58 sq. km) are part of the Leeward group in the eastern Caribbean Sea. The central area of St Christopher is forest-clad and mountainous, rising to 1,158 m (Mount Liamuiga) at the highest point. Nevis, separated from the southern tip of St Christopher by a strait two miles wide, is dominated by Nevis Peak, 985 m. The climate is tropical and influenced by north-east trade winds. The average annual rainfall, principally during May to September, is 1,375 mm, with average daily temperatures of 24°C.

HISTORY AND POLITICS

The islands were visited in 1493 by Christopher Columbus, who named St Christopher. It was settled by the British, becoming the first British colony in the West Indies in 1623; Nevis was settled from 1628. Control was disputed between the British and French in the 17th and 18th centuries, until France dropped its claims in 1783. The islands of St Christopher and Nevis were united in the late 19th century, and became a state in association with Britain in 1967 with internal self-government. Independence was achieved in September 1983.

A separatist movement was formed on Nevis in 1970, and in 1997 the Nevis government voted to secede. A referendum on the issue in 1998 resulted in a 61.8 per cent vote in favour of secession, which fell short of the two-thirds majority required.

In the 2004 legislative election, the Labour Party retained its overall majority and began its third consecutive term of office.

POLITICAL SYSTEM
Under the 1983 constitution, the head of state is the British monarch, represented in the islands by a governor-general appointed on the advice of the prime minister. The unicameral National Assembly has 15 members, 11 directly elected for a five-year term, a speaker, and three senators appointed by the governor-general on the advice of the prime minister and the leader of the opposition. The prime minister, who is responsible to the National Assembly, and the cabinet are appointed by the governor-general. Nevis is responsible for its own internal affairs, has an eight-member Nevis Island Assembly and is governed by the Nevis Island Administration, headed by the premier of Nevis.

Governor-General, HE Sir Cuthbert Montraville Sebastian, GCMG, OBE, apptd 1996

SELECTED GOVERNMENT MEMBERS *as at August 2005*
Prime Minister, Finance, National Security, Planning, Development, Denzil Douglas
Deputy Prime Minister, Labour, Social Security, International Trade and Caricom Affairs, Telecommunications and Technology, Sam Condor
Foreign Affairs, Education, Timothy Harris
National Security, Gerald Astaphan

HIGH COMMISSION FOR ST CHRISTOPHER AND NEVIS
2nd Floor, 10 Kensington Court, London W8 5DL
T 020-7460 6500
High Commissioner for St Christopher and Nevis, HE James Ernest Williams, apptd 2001

BRITISH HIGH COMMISSIONER
HE C. John White, resident at Bridgetown, Barbados

ECONOMY AND TRADE
The sugar industry was the mainstay of the economy for over 300 years but is now being phased out as it has become unviable; the government announced its closure in March 2005. Tourism (the chief source of foreign exchange), offshore financial services and light industry, concentrating on distilling, food processing, clothing and electronics, are now being developed. The economy of Nevis relies on farming, but a sea-island cotton industry is being developed for export.

The main exports are sugar, lobsters, beverages and electrical equipment. Foodstuffs, energy, machinery and transport equipment are the main imports.
GNI – US$299 million (2002); US$6,630 per capita (2002)
ANNUAL AVERAGE GROWTH OF GDP – −1.9 per cent (2002 est.)
INFLATION RATE – 1.7 per cent (2001 est.)

TOTAL EXTERNAL DEBT – US$140 million (2000)
IMPORTS – US$149 million (1999)
EXPORTS – US$22 million (1999)

Trade with UK	2003	2004
Imports from UK	£8,282,000	£9,646,000
Exports to UK	5,819,000	1,491,000

TRANSPORT INFRASTRUCTURE
The islands have a total of 320 km of roads, of which 136 km are surfaced, and 50 km of narrow-gauge railways on St Christopher that serve the sugar cane plantations. Basseterre is a port of registry and has deep-water harbour facilities. Robert Bradshaw international airport, on St Christopher, can take most large jet aircraft; Vance Amory international airport on Nevis can take small aircraft and has night-time landing facilities. The sea ferry route from Basseterre to Charlestown is 11 miles.

MEDIA
The government operates national television and radio stations; there are several private radio stations, and multi-channel cable TV offers a range of local and international TV stations.

ST LUCIA

AREA – 616 sq. km
POPULATION – 164,213 (2004 est.). The official language is English. French creole is spoken by most of the population
CAPITAL – ΨCastries (population, 62,967, 2000 estimate)
CURRENCY – East Caribbean dollar (EC$) of 100 cents
NATIONAL ANTHEM – Sons and daughters of Saint Lucia
NATIONAL DAY – 22 February (Independence Day)
NATIONAL FLAG – Blue, bearing in the centre a device of yellow over black over white triangles having a common base
LIFE EXPECTANCY (years) – 73.34 (2004 est.)
MORTALITY RATE (per 1,000 population) – 5.18 (2004 est.)
INFANT MORTALITY (per 1,000 births) – 13.95 (2004 est.)
DEATH PENALTY – Yes
POPULATION GROWTH RATE – 1.27 per cent (2004 est.)
POPULATION DENSITY – 242 per sq. km (2001)

CLIMATE AND TERRAIN
St Lucia, the second largest of the Windward group, is 43.5 km in length, with an extreme breadth of 22.5 km. The terrain is mountainous, with elevation extremes that range from 958 m (Mt Gimie) at the highest point to 0 m (Caribbean Sea) at the lowest. The volcanic peaks of Gros Piton and Petit Piton were declared a UNESCO World Heritage Site in 2004. The climate is tropical and there is a wet season from June to September. The average daily temperature is 25°C.

HISTORY AND POLITICS
Originally inhabited by Arawak Indians and then settled by Carib Indians from AD 800, the island was sighted by Columbus in 1502. French settlement began in 1635 but control was disputed with Britain from 1659 until 1814, when the island was ceded to Britain. It achieved internal

self-government in 1967 and became independent within the Commonwealth on 22 February 1979.

The St Lucia Labour Party maintained its majority in the House of Assembly in the 2001 general election, winning 14 seats.

POLITICAL SYSTEM

Under the 1979 constitution, the head of state is the British monarch, represented by a governor-general appointed on the advice of the prime minister. The bicameral parliament consists of the House of Assembly and the Senate. The Senate has 11 members, six appointed by the government, three by the opposition and two by the governor-general. The House of Assembly, which serves for a five-year term, has 17 elected members and an appointed speaker. The prime minister, who is responsible to parliament, and the cabinet are appointed by the governor-general.

Governor-General, HE Dame Pearlette Louisy, apptd 1997

SELECTED GOVERNMENT MEMBERS *as at August 2005*
Prime Minister, Finance, Economic Affairs, Information,
  International Financial Services, Kenny Anthony
Foreign Affairs, International Trade and Civil Aviation,
  Petrus Compton
Home Affairs and Internal Security, Calixte George

HIGH COMMISSION FOR ST LUCIA
1 Collingham Gardens, London SW5 0HW
T 020-7370 7123
High Commissioner for St Lucia, HE Emmanuel Cotter, MBE, apptd 1998

OFFICE OF THE BRITISH HIGH COMMISSION
Francis Compton Building, 2nd Floor (PO Box 227), Waterfront, Castries T (+1 758) 452 2484/5 E britishhc@candw.lc
High Commissioner, HE C. John White, resident at Bridgetown, Barbados

ECONOMY AND TRADE

The economy is mainly agrarian, with the manufacturing industry based on agricultural and food processing. The principal crops are bananas, coconuts, cocoa, mangoes, breadfruit, yam and citrus fruit. After sugar production was phased out in the 1960s, the economy became heavily dependent on bananas (which still account for about one third of export earnings), but production has diversified into other crops to compensate for the ending of preferential access to EU markets for West Indian bananas in 1999. Attempts are being made to increase industrialisation and to develop offshore financial services and tourism; tourism is now the main source of foreign exchange.

The principal exports are bananas, coconut products (copra, edible oils, soap), cardboard boxes, beer, and textiles. The chief imports are flour, meat, machinery, building materials, motor vehicles, manufactured goods, petroleum and fertilisers.

GNI – US$620 million (2001); US$3,950 per capita (2001)
ANNUAL AVERAGE GROWTH OF GDP – 3.3 per cent (2002 est.)
INFLATION RATE – 3 per cent (2002 est.)
TOTAL EXTERNAL DEBT – US$237 million (2000 est.)
IMPORTS – US$300 million (2002)
EXPORTS – US$100 million (1999)

BALANCE OF PAYMENTS
Trade – US$207 million deficit (2002)
Current Account – US$104 million deficit (2002)

Trade with UK	2003	2004
Imports from UK	£15,153,000	£16,161,000
Exports to UK	15,940,000	20,502,000

TRANSPORT INFRASTRUCTURE

St Lucia contains around 1,210 km of roads, of which 63 km are surfaced. The island has two airports: Hewanorra international airport in Vieux Fort, at the remote southern tip of the island, and Vigie airport in Castries, near the main tourist area. Castries also has a deep-water harbour.

MEDIA

St Lucia's television and radio outlets are mainly privately owned. The government operates a radio network, which broadcasts in English and Creole. The island has two main newspapers, *The Star* and *The Voice*, which are both published three times a week.

ST VINCENT AND THE GRENADINES

AREA – 388 sq. km
POPULATION – 117,714 (2004 est.). The language is English
CAPITAL – ΨKingstown (population, 13,857, 2000)
CURRENCY – East Caribbean dollar (EC$) of 100 cents
NATIONAL ANTHEM – St Vincent, land so beautiful
NATIONAL DAY – 27 October (Independence Day)
NATIONAL FLAG – Three vertical bands, of blue, yellow and green, with three green diamonds in the shape of a 'V' mounted on the yellow band
MORTALITY RATE (per 1,000 population) – 6.04 (2004 est.)
DEATH PENALTY – Yes
POPULATION GROWTH RATE – 0.31 per cent (2004 est.)
POPULATION DENSITY – 289 per sq. km (1999)

CLIMATE AND TERRAIN

The territory of St Vincent in the Windward group includes certain of the northern Grenadines, a chain of small islands stretching 40 miles across the eastern Caribbean Sea between Grenada and St Vincent; the larger of these include Bequia, Canouan, Mayreau, Mustique, Union Island, Petit St Vincent and Prune Island. St Vincent itself has volcanic mountains, which are densely forested. Elevation extremes range from 1,234 m (La Soufrière volcano) at the highest point to 0 m (Caribbean Sea) at the lowest. The climate is tropical with an average daily temperature of 28°C.

HISTORY AND POLITICS

St Vincent was discovered by Christopher Columbus in 1498. It was granted by Charles I to the Earl of Carlisle in 1627 but British settlement did not begin until 1762, and was resisted by the French and the native Caribs. It was recognised as a British colony by the French in 1783. A Carib uprising in 1795–7 resulted in thousands of Caribs being deported. It became internally self-governing in 1969 and achieved full independence as St Vincent and the Grenadines on 27 October 1979.

After elections in 1998 the New Democratic Party (NDP), which had been in power since 1984, retained the majority of seats. However, following its approval of increased benefits for members of the legislature, it was forced by the opposition United Labour Party (ULP) to hold an early general election. This took place in March 2001 and was decisively won by the ULP, which obtained 12 seats. The NDP won the remaining three seats.

POLITICAL SYSTEM

Under the 1979 constitution, the head of state is the British monarch, represented by a governor-general appointed on the advice of the prime minister. The unicameral House of Assembly has 21 members, directly elected for a five-year term and six senators appointed by the governor-general, four on the advice of the government and two on the advice of the opposition. The prime minister, who is responsible to the House of Assembly, and the cabinet are appointed by the governor-general.

Governor-General, Sir Frederic Ballantyne, GCMG, apptd 2002

SELECTED GOVERNMENT MEMBERS *as at August 2005*
Prime Minister, Finance, Planning, Economic Development, Labour, Information, Grenadine Affairs, Legal Affairs, Ralph Gonsalves
Deputy Prime Minister, Transport and International Trade, Louis Straker
National Security, Public Service, Airport Development, Vincent Beache
Foreign Affairs, Mike Browne

HIGH COMMISSION FOR ST VINCENT AND THE GRENADINES
10 Kensington Court, London W8 5DL
T 020-7565 2874 E svghighcom@clara.co.uk
High Commissioner for St Vincent and the Grenadines, HE Cenio E. Lewis, apptd 2001

BRITISH HIGH COMMISSION
Granby Street (PO Box 132), Kingstown
T (+1 784) 457 1701 E bhcsvg@caribsurf.com
High Commissioner, HE C. John White, resident at Bridgetown, Barbados

ECONOMY AND TRADE

The economy is based mainly on agriculture but the tourism and manufacturing industries have been expanding. The main products are bananas, arrowroot, coconuts, cocoa, spices and various other kinds of food crops, although these have suffered severely in some years from tropical storms. In common with other Windward Islands, the country has attempting to reduce its reliance on banana exports, following the ending of preferential access to EU markets for West Indies bananas in 1999; bananas accounted for 39 per cent of exports in 2002. Diversification has been partially successful, but the development of tourism is hampered by drug-related crime. The main imports are foodstuffs, textiles, lumber, chemicals, motor vehicles and fuel.
GNI – US$317 million (2001); US$2,740 per capita (2001)
ANNUAL AVERAGE GROWTH OF GDP – 0.7 per cent (2002 est.)
INFLATION RATE – 0.2 per cent (2000 est.)
TOTAL EXTERNAL DEBT – US$192 million (2000 est.)
IMPORTS – US$120 million (2003)
EXPORTS – US$40 million (2003)

BALANCE OF PAYMENTS
Trade – US$117 million deficit (2002)
Current Account – US$42 million deficit (2002)

Trade with UK	2003	2004
Imports from UK	£9,142,000	£8,512,000
Exports to UK	9,679,000	12,122,000

TRANSPORT INFRASTRUCTURE

The islands have around 1,040 km of roads, of which 320 km are surfaced. The main harbour is at Kingstown, and there are six airports, although none can accommodate international traffic.

MEDIA

The press is privately owned, and its freedom to criticise the government is guaranteed by the constitution. Most newspapers are published weekly. There are several private radio stations and a national radio service which is partly government-funded. Television broadcasting is operated by the St Vincent and the Grenadines Broadcasting Corporation.

SAMOA

Ole Malo Tutoatasi o Samoa / Independent State of Samoa

AREA – 2,831 sq. km
POPULATION – 177,714 (2004 est.); the largest numbers being on Upolu (114,980) and ΨSavai'i (43,150). The Samoans are a Polynesian people, though the population also includes other Pacific Islanders, Euronesians, Chinese and Europeans. The main languages are Samoan and English. The islanders are Christians of different denominations
CAPITAL – ΨApia (population, 38,836, 2001), on Upolu.
CURRENCY – Tala (S$) of 100 sene
NATIONAL ANTHEM – The banner of freedom
NATIONAL DAY – 1 June (Independence Day)
NATIONAL FLAG – Red with a blue canton bearing five white stars of the Southern Cross
LIFE EXPECTANCY (years) – 70.41 (2004 est.)
MORTALITY RATE (per 1,000 population) – 6.47 (2004 est.)
INFANT MORTALITY (per 1,000 births) – 28.27 (2004 est.)
DEATH PENALTY – No (abolished 2004)
POPULATION GROWTH RATE – –0.25 per cent (2004 est.)
ILLITERACY RATE – (m) 0.4 per cent; (f) 0.3 per cent (2003 est.)

CLIMATE AND TERRAIN

Samoa consists of the islands of Savai'i, Upolu, Apolima, Manono, Fanuatapu, Namua, Nuutele, Nuulua and Nuusafee in the south Pacific Ocean. All the islands are mountainous and volcanic, with elevation extremes ranging from 1,857 m (Mauga Silisili) at the highest point to 0 m (Pacific Ocean) at the lowest. The climate is tropical with a wet season from November to April. Average temperatures range between 22 and 30°C all year round.

HISTORY AND POLITICS

Inhabited since *c*.1000 BC, Samoa was visited by Dutch traders and French explorers in the 18th century. In 1889, Germany took control of the nine western islands

(Western Samoa) and the USA of the other Samoan islands (American Samoa). Western Samoa was occupied by New Zealand on the outbreak of the First World War and became a mandated territory administered by New Zealand from 1920. Internal self-government was established in 1959, and Western Samoa became fully independent on 1 June 1962. The state was treated as a member country of the Commonwealth until its formal admission in 1970. In 1997 the state changed its name to the Independent State of Samoa.

In the 2001 general election, the Human Rights Protection Party won 23 seats, the Samoan National Development Party won 13 seats, and 13 seats were won by independents.

POLITICAL SYSTEM

Under the 1962 constitution, the head of state is an elected monarch; initially two of the four paramount chiefs held the office jointly for life and when one died in April 1963, Susuga Malietoa Tanumafili II became head of state for life. In future, the monarch will be elected by the Legislative Assembly for a five-year term. The head of state's functions are analogous to those of a constitutional monarch. The unicameral Legislative Assembly *(Fono)* has 49 members elected for a five-year term. The prime minister is appointed by the monarch on the recommendation of the Legislative Assembly and appoints the cabinet. Universal adult suffrage was introduced in 1990.

HEAD OF STATE

Head of State for Life, HH Susuga Malietoa Tanumafili II, GCMG, CBE, *since* 15 April 1963

SELECTED GOVERNMENT MEMBERS *as at August 2005*
Prime Minister, Foreign Affairs, Foreign Trade, Tuilaepa Sailele Malielegaoi
Deputy Prime Minister, Finance, Misa Telefoni Retzlaff
Health, Mulitalo Saifausa Vui

HIGH COMMISSION FOR THE INDEPENDENT STATE OF SAMOA
123 Avenue Franklin D. Roosevelt Bte 14, 1050 Brussels
T (+32) (2) 660 8454
High Commissioner for the Independent State of Samoa, HE Tau'ili'ili'U'ili Meredith, apptd 1998

BRITISH HIGH COMMISSIONER
HE Richard Fell, CVO, apptd 2002, resident at Wellington, New Zealand

ECONOMY AND TRADE

Agriculture is the basis of the economy, employing about two-thirds of the labour force and supplying about 40 per cent of GDP and 90 per cent of exports. The principal cash crops (and exports) are coconuts (copra, oil and cream), cocoa and bananas. Efforts are being made to develop fishing on a commercial scale. Attempts at diversification are bearing fruit; manufacturing is branching out from small-scale processing of agricultural products into light manufacturing; and offshore financial services are being developed. Tourism has grown rapidly and now accounts for about 25 per cent of GDP. Remittances from Samoans working abroad are also a valuable contribution to the economy.
GNI – US$1,490 per capita (2001)
ANNUAL AVERAGE GROWTH OF GDP – 5 per cent (2002 est.)

INFLATION RATE – 4 per cent (2002 est.)
TOTAL EXTERNAL DEBT – US$197 million (2000 est.)
IMPORTS – US$137 million (2003)
EXPORTS – US$15 million (2003)

BALANCE OF PAYMENTS
Trade – US$98 million deficit (1999)
Current Account – US$19 million deficit (1999)

Trade with UK	2003	2004
Imports from UK	£431,000	£176,000
Exports to UK	347,000	558,000

TRANSPORT INFRASTRUCTURE

There are 790 km of roads, of which 332 km are surfaced. Upolu contains the harbours of Apia and Mulifanua, and Savai'i the harbour of Salelologa. Most international flights land at Faleolo Airport, 35 km west of Apia on Upolu.

MEDIA

There are two daily papers, one weekly and one fortnightly. The government operates the sole TV service, Televise Samoa, and there are three FM radio stations and one state-run commercial radio service.

SAN MARINO

Repubblica di San Marino – Republic of San Marino

AREA – 61 sq. km. Neighbour: Italy
POPULATION – 28,503 (2004 est.). The official language is Italian and the religion is Roman Catholic
CAPITAL – San Marino (population, 4,357, 1994), on the slope of Monte Titano
CURRENCY – Euro (€) of 100 cents
NATIONAL ANTHEM – Inno nazionale [National anthem]
NATIONAL DAY – 3 September
NATIONAL FLAG – Two horizontal bands, white and blue (with the coat of arms of the republic in centre)
LIFE EXPECTANCY (years) – 81.53 (2004 est.)
MORTALITY RATE (per 1,000 population) – 7.96 (2004 est.)
INFANT MORTALITY (per 1,000 births) – 5.85 (2004 est.)
DEATH PENALTY – No (abolished 1865)
POPULATION GROWTH RATE – 1.33 per cent (2004 est.)
POPULATION DENSITY – 426 per sq. km (1999)
URBAN POPULATION – 87 per cent (2001)

CLIMATE AND TERRAIN

A landlocked enclave in central Italy, the republic lies in the foothills of the Apennines, 20 km from the Adriatic Sea. Elevation extremes range from 755 m (Monte Titano) at the highest point to 55 m (Torrente Aussa) at the lowest. The climate is Mediterranean, characterised by cool winters and warm summers. Average annual rainfall is 762 mm, while average temperatures range between −6°C in January to 25°C in June.

HISTORY AND POLITICS

The republic is said to have been founded in the fourth century by a Christian stonecutter seeking refuge from religious persecution. By the 12th century a self-governing commune was established, and a parliamentary constitution was adopted in 1600. The republic resisted papal claims and those of neighbouring dukedoms during the 15th to 18th centuries, and the papacy recognised its independence in 1631. In 1862 it signed a treaty with the newly united kingdom of Italy which recognised its integrity and sovereignty and accorded it the protection of Italy. San Marino became a member of the UN in 1992.

Following the 2001 election to the Grand and General Council, the Christian Democratic Party (PDCS) held 25 seats, the Socialist Party (PSS) 15, the Progressive Democratic Party (PPDS) 12, and other parties eight seats. The PDCS and the PSS formed a coalition government, later joined by the Party of Democrats (PdD), but this collapsed in June 2002. A coalition of the PSS, PdD and Popular Democratic Alliance (APDS) collapsed in December 2002. The PSS and PDCS then formed a new coalition, which was joined by the PdD in December 2003.

POLITICAL SYSTEM
The 1600 constitution has been amended several times. The joint heads of state are two captains-regent who are elected at six-monthly intervals (March and September) by the Great and General Council, taking office the month after the election. Executive power is vested in the captains-regent and the Congress of State (cabinet), which is also elected by the Great and General Council. The unicameral legislature, the Great and General Council, has 60 members, directly elected for a five-year term. A Council of Twelve forms in certain cases a Supreme Court of Justice.

HEADS OF STATE *as at August 2005*
Captain-Regent, Cesare Antonio
Captain-Regent, Fausta Simona Morganti

SELECTED GOVERNMENT MEMBERS *as at August 2005*
Finance, Budget, Post and Telecommunications, Relations with the Philatelic and Numismatic State Corporations, Pier Marino Mularoni (PDCS)
Foreign and Political Affairs, Fabio Berardi (PSS)
Internal Affairs, Civil Protection, Rosa Zafferani (PDCS)

EMBASSY OF THE REPUBLIC OF SAN MARINO
c/o Consulate of the Republic of San Marino,
Flat 51, 162 Sloane Street, London SW1X 9BS
T 020-7823 4762
Ambassador Extraordinary and Plenipotentiary, HE Countess Marina Meneghetti de Camillo, apptd 2002, resident at Rome, Italy

BRITISH AMBASSADOR
HE Sir Ivor Roberts, KCMG, apptd 2003, Resident at Rome, Italy

BRITISH CONSULATE-GENERAL FOR SAN MARINO
Lungarno Corsini 2, I-50123 Florence, Italy
T (+39) (55) 284133
Consul-General, Moira Macfarlane

ECONOMY AND TRADE
Tourism is the basis of the economy, contributing over 50 per cent of GDP. Postage stamps and coins also generate significant revenue. The principal agrricultural products are wine, cereals and fruits, and the main manufacturing industries produce metal, machinery, textiles and foodstuffs. The island is in a customs union with the EU.
ANNUAL AVERAGE GROWTH OF GDP – 7.5 per cent (2001 est.)
UNEMPLOYMENT – 2.6 per cent (2001 est.)

Trade with UK	2003	2004
Imports from UK	£4,978,000	£7,648,000
Exports to UK	5,239,000	5,050,000

MEDIA
San Marino has one state-run radio and television station, and one private radio station. The two daily newspapers are *La Tribuna Sammarinese* and *San Marino Oggi*.

SÃO TOMÉ AND PRÍNCIPE

República Democrática de São Tomé e Príncipe – Democratic Republic of São Tomé and Príncipe

AREA – 964 sq. km
POPULATION – 181,565 (2004 est.). The official language is Portuguese
CAPITAL – ΨSão Tomé (population, 43,420, 1995 estimate)
CURRENCY – Dobra of 100 centavos
NATIONAL ANTHEM – Independência total (Total independence)
NATIONAL DAY – 12 July (Independence Day)
NATIONAL FLAG – Horizontal stripes of green, yellow and green, the yellow of double width and bearing two black stars; a red triangle in the hoist
LIFE EXPECTANCY (years) – 66.63 (2004 est.)
MORTALITY RATE (per 1,000 population) – 6.89 (2004 est.)
DEATH PENALTY – No (abolished 1990)
POPULATION GROWTH RATE – 3.18 per cent (2004 est.)
POPULATION DENSITY – 149 per sq. km (1999)

CLIMATE AND TERRAIN
The republic consists of the islands of São Tomé, Príncipe and several smaller islands in the Gulf of Guinea, off the west coast of Africa. All the islands are volcanic, thickly forested and fertile. Elevation extremes range from 2,024 m (Pico de São Tomé) at the highest point to 0 m (Atlantic Ocean) at the lowest. The climate is tropical with a wet season from October to May. Average daily temperatures are an almost constant 30°C.

HISTORY AND POLITICS
The uninhabited islands were discovered by the Portuguese between 1469 and 1472, and settlement began in 1493. Plantations were established that became important producers of sugar cane, cocoa and coffee in the 18th and 19th centuries. Resistance to Portuguese rule began in the 1950s. The islands gained independence from Portugal in July 1975 and became a one-party state under the rule of the Movement for the Liberation of São Tomé and Príncipe (MLSTP). The government nationalised the plantations and formed close links with the communist bloc. These were scaled down in the 1980s as the economy deteriorated and in 1990 the MLSTP abandoned Marxism and introduced a democratic constitution in 1990. The first multiparty elections were held in 1991.

The 2001 presidential election was won by Fradique

de Menezes of the Independent Democratic Alliance, with 56.31 per cent of the vote. In the 2002 legislative election, the Movement for the Liberation of São Tomé and Príncipe (MLSTP-PSD) won 24 seats, the Force for Change Democratic Movement-Democratic Convergence Party (MDFM-PCD) 23 seats and the Ue Kedadji coalition (UK) 8 seats. A government of national unity, comprising members of all three parties and independents, was formed in April 2002 but was dismissed by the president in September 2002. A new government was named on 7 October, led by Maria das Neves de Sousa.

The president was deposed briefly in July 2003 in a military coup that occurred while he was out of the country. He was reinstated a week later following negotiations and in September 2003 appointed a new prime minister and a government comprising members of the MLSTP-PSD and the MDFM-PCD. Disagreement over how to use the expected revenue from offshore oil reserves nearly toppled this government, but it was dismissed in September 2004 after a series of corruption scandals. The government that replaced it resigned in June 2005.

POLITICAL SYSTEM

Under the 1990 constitution, the head of state is the president, who is directly elected for a five-year term, renewable only once. The unicameral National Assembly *(Assembleia Nacional)* has 55 members, directly elected for a four-year term. The prime minister is appointed by the president and appoints the cabinet. Since 1995, Príncipe has been internally self-governing, with an eight-member regional council.

HEAD OF STATE
President and Commander-in-Chief of the Armed Forces,
Fradique de Menezes, *elected* 29 July 2001, *sworn in* 3 September 2001

SELECTED GOVERNMENT MEMBERS *as at August 2005*
Prime Minister, Finance and Planning, Maria do Carmo Silveira
Defence and Interior, Oscar Aguiar Sacramento Sousa
Foreign Affairs and Co-operation, Communities, Ovidio Manuel Barbosa Pequeno

EMBASSY OF THE DEMOCRATIC REPUBLIC OF SÃO TOMÉ AND PRÍNCIPE
Square Montgomery, 175 Avenue de Tervuren, B-1150 Brussels
T (+32) (2) 734 8966
Chargé d'Affaires, Antonio de Lima Viegas

BRITISH CONSULATE
Residencial Avenida, Av. Da Independencia CP 257, São Tomé
T (+239) (12) 21026/7
British Ambassador, HE John Thompson, MBE

ECONOMY AND TRADE

Economic mismanagement and over-dependency on cocoa contributed to a large foreign debt that stood at about US$270 million in 1998. A debt-reduction package worth about US$200 million was agreed with the IMF and World Bank in 2000, when the government also received IMF credit of US$8.7 million to support its 2000–2 economic programme. The government is encouraging diversification away from cocoa; tourism is being promoted. The exploitation of recently discovered offshore oil reserves in the Gulf of Guinea is expected to generate considerable revenue in a few years' time. The principal trading partners are Portugal, Spain, Netherlands and the UK.

GNI – US$43,000 (2002); US$280 per capita (2002)
ANNUAL AVERAGE GROWTH OF GDP – 7.5 per cent (2001 est.)
TOTAL EXTERNAL DEBT – US$316 million (2000 est.)
INFLATION RATE – US$3.3 per cent (2001 est.)
IMPORTS – US$16 million (1997)
EXPORTS – US$5 million (1997)

Trade with UK	2003	2004
Imports from UK	£459,000	£377,000
Exports to UK	314,000	136,000

TRANSPORT INFRASTRUCTURE

São Tomé and Príncipe has a total of 320 km of roads, 12 km of which are on Príncipe. The majority are surfaced, though most are in poor condition. There are ports at Santo Antonio and São Tomé, and two international airports.

MEDIA

Freedom of expression is guaranteed by the constitution. The islands' only radio and television stations are state-run. There are three privately owned newspapers and one which is published by the government.

SAUDI ARABIA

Al-Mamlaka al-'Arabiyya as-Sa'ūdiyya – Kingdom of Saudi Arabia

AREA – 2,149,700 sq. km. Neighbours: UAE and Qatar (east), Jordan, Iraq and Kuwait (north), Yemen and Oman (south)
POPULATION – 25,795,938 (2004 est.). Islam is the only permitted religion. The language is Arabic
CAPITAL – Riyadh (Ar-Riyad) (population, 4,761,000, 2001)
MAJOR CITIES – ΨJiddah (1.5 million); Buraydah; ΨAd-Dammam; Al-Hofuf; Al-Makkah (Mecca); Al-Madinah (Medina); Tabuk
CURRENCY – Saudi riyal (SR) of 20 qursh or 100 halala
NATIONAL ANTHEM – Ash Al-Malik [Long live our beloved King]
NATIONAL DAY – 23 September (proclamation and unification of the Kingdom, 1932)
NATIONAL FLAG – Green oblong, white Arabic device in centre: 'There is no God but God and Muhammad is the Prophet of God', and a white scimitar beneath the lettering
LIFE EXPECTANCY (years) – 75.23 (2004 est.)
MORTALITY RATE (per 1,000 population) – 2.66 (2004 est.)
INFANT MORTALITY (per 1,000 births) – 13.7 (2004 est.)
DEATH PENALTY – Yes
POPULATION GROWTH RATE – 2.44 per cent (2004 est.)
POPULATION DENSITY – 10 per sq. km (2002)

CLIMATE AND TERRAIN

Saudi Arabia comprises most of the Arabian peninsula. The Nejd ('plateau') extends over the centre, including the Nafud and Dahna deserts. The Hejaz ('the boundary') extends along the Red Sea coast to Asir and contains the holy towns of Al-Makkah (Mecca) and Al-Madinah (Medina). Asir (meaning inaccessible) is so named for its mountainous terrain, and, with the coastal plain of the Tihama, lies along the southern Red Sea coast from the Hejaz to the border with Yemen. The east and south-east of the country are low-lying and largely desert. Elevation extremes range from 3,133 m (Jabal Sawda) at the highest point to 0 m (Persian Gulf) at the lowest. The climate is hot and dry and average temperatures in Riyadh range from 21°C in January to 42°C in July.

HISTORY AND POLITICS

The Arabian peninsula was the birthplace of the Muslim faith in the seventh century, and the base from which the faith and a Muslim empire expanded, eventually stretching from India to Spain. When this empire declined in the 12th century, Arabia became isolated and internally divided. The rise of the al-Saud family began in the 18th century, when it united the Nejd in support of the Wahhabi religious movement. The modern state was formed in 1932 when the head of the dynasty, Abd-al Aziz al-Saud (often known as Ibn Saud), united the four tribal provinces of the Hejaz, Asir, Najd and Al Hasa; the Kingdom of Saudi Arabia was proclaimed on 23 September 1932.

The ruling family preserved stability for many years by suppressing dissent and resisting calls for greater democracy, some of its actions raising international concerns over human rights abuses. Internal tension grew in the 1990s because of the continuing presence of foreign, particularly US, troops in the country after the 1991 Gulf War, and troops and foreign nationals became terrorist targets. Despite the redeployment of the troops to Qatar in early 2003, the frequency of attacks increased following the start of the Iraq war and included Saudi as well as foreign victims. Some dissident groups are believed to have links with al-Qa'eda. From 2003 demand for political reform has grown, and become more militant. In February 2005, the first-ever nationwide municipal elections were held, with voting by universal male suffrage.

King Fahd died in July 2005 and was succeeded by his half-brother Abdullah, who had carried out many of the king's official functions after King Fahd suffered a debilitating stroke in 1996.

POLITICAL SYSTEM

Saudi Arabia is a hereditary monarchy. The line of succession passes from brother to brother in the al-Saud family according to age; all sons and grandsons of Abd-al Aziz al-Saud must be consulted before a new king accedes to the throne.

There is no written constitution; constitutional practice is provided for by Articles of Government based on the Koran (Qur'an) and the Sunnah (teachings and sayings of the Prophet Muhammad) and issued by royal decree. In 1992 the king announced a new 'Basic System of Government' based on Shari'ah law and including rules to protect personal freedoms. The king is head of government and appoints the Council of Ministers (established in 1953), whose term of office was fixed in 1993 at four years. There is no legislature; a Consultative Council (Majlis-al-Shura) was established in 1993. It debates policy in the areas of the budget, defence, foreign and social affairs, and makes recommendations to the king; in 2003 its powers were widened and it is now permitted to propose legislation without the king's permission. The Council's 150 members are appointed by

the king and serve a four-year term. Its decisions are taken by majority vote. There are no political parties.

In 1993 the country was reorganised into 13 provinces: Riyadh; Makkah; Al-Madinah; Al Qasim; Eastern; Asir; Tabuk; Ha'il; Northern Border; Jizan; Najran; Baha; Al-Jawf. Each province has a governor appointed by the king and a council of prominent local citizens to advise the governor on local government, budgetary and planning issues.

HEAD OF STATE
HM The King of Saudi Arabia, Custodian of the Two Holy Mosques, Prime Minister, Commander of the National Guard, King Abdullah ibn Abdul Aziz al-Saud, born 1923, ascended the throne 2 August 2005
HRH Crown Prince, Deputy Prime Minister, Defence and Civil Aviation, Prince Sultan ibn Abdul Aziz al-Saud

SELECTED GOVERNMENT MEMBERS as at August 2005
Interior, HRH Prince Nayef ibn Abdul Aziz al-Saud
Finance, Ibrahim ibn Abdel Aziz al-Assaf
Foreign Affairs, HRH Prince Saud al-Faisal ibn Abdul Aziz al-Saud
Health, Hamad ibn Abdallah al-Mani

ROYAL EMBASSY OF SAUDI ARABIA
30 Charles Street, London W1X 7PM T 020-7917 3000
Ambassador Extraordinary and Plenipotentiary, HRH Prince Turki Al-Faisal, apptd 2003

BRITISH EMBASSY
PO Box 94351, Riyadh 11693 T (+966) (1) 488 0077
Ambassador Extraordinary and Plenipotentiary, HE Sherard Cowper-Cole, apptd 2003

CONSULATE-GENERAL
PO Box 393, Jiddah 21411 T (+966) (2) 622 5550
Consul-General, A. Henderson

BRITISH COUNCIL
Tower B, 2nd Floor, Al-Mousa Centre, Olaya Street, PO Box 58012, Riyadh 11594
E enquiry.riyadh@sa.britishcouncil.org
Director, Alan Smart

DEFENCE

The Army has 1,055 main battle tanks, 3,190 armoured personnel carriers, 970 armoured infantry fighting vehicles and 12 attack helicopters. The Navy has seven frigates, 26 patrol and coastal vessels and 21 armed helicopters at six bases. The Air Force has 291 combat aircraft.

Saudi Arabia is the base of the Gulf Co-operational Council Peninsula Shield Force of 10,000 troops. In 2003 US troops, except for some training personnel, were redeployed to Qatar. Leaders of both countries stressed that co-operation would continue and they would remain allies.

MILITARY EXPENDITURE – 8.9 per cent of GDP (2003)
MILITARY PERSONNEL – 124,500: Army 75,000, Navy 15,500, Air Force 18,000, Air Defence Force 16,000; National Guard 75,000; Paramilitaries 15,500

ECONOMY AND TRADE

The principal industry is oil extraction and processing. Oil was first found in commercial quantities in 1938 and its extraction since the 1940s has brought great prosperity. Proven oil reserves of 259 billion barrels account for more than one-quarter of the world's reserves and recoverable gas reserves are estimated at over 220 trillion cubic feet. The oil and gas industry contributes around 35–40 per cent of GDP, depending on world prices. Exploitation of other minerals, including gold, silver and copper, has been developed.

The government, in a series of five-year development plans begun in 1970, has encouraged the establishment of manufacturing industries. Industries developed so far include the manufacture of construction materials, metal fabrication, simple machinery, electrical equipment and textiles, and the processing of foodstuffs, beverages, chemicals and plastics. Agriculture accounted for only 7 per cent of GDP in 1998, but the productivity of traditional dryland farming is supplemented by extensive irrigation, desalination and the use of aquifers.

The seventh development plan, covering 2000–5, aimed to eliminate the budget and current account deficits, promote economic growth and diversity, encourage the private sector (responsible for around 40 per cent of GDP) and introduce legislation to increase the proportion of Saudi Arabian citizens in the workforce.

The leading suppliers of imports are the USA, the UK, Germany and Japan. The chief export markets are in Japan, the USA, South Korea and Singapore. There is a total ban on the importation of alcohol, pork products, firearms, and items regarded as non-Islamic or pornographic.

GNI – US$186,800 million (2002); US$8,530 per capita (2002)
ANNUAL AVERAGE GROWTH OF GDP – 4.5 per cent (2000 est.)
INFLATION RATE – 0.8 per cent (2000 est.)
IMPORTS – US$37,000 million (2003)
EXPORTS – US$73,000 million (2002)

BALANCE OF PAYMENTS
Trade – US$61,456 million surplus (2003)
Current Account – US$29,701 million surplus (2003)

Trade with UK	2003	2004
Imports from UK	£1,841,629,000	£1,615,377,000
Exports to UK	780,591,000	1,216,463,000

TRANSPORT INFRASTRUCTURE
There are 1,392 km of railways, running between Riyadh and Ad-Dammam, which and is operated by the Saudi Government Railway Organisation. The service is being extended to the port of Al-Jubayl on the Gulf. In 2000 the road network totalled 152,044 km (of which 45,461 km were surfaced), including an expressway system, connecting all the cities and main towns. The 25 km-long King Fahd Causeway connects the Eastern Province to Bahrain and is the world's second longest causeway. Jiddah is the main cargo sea port on the Red Sea coast and Ad-Dammam on the Gulf coast. The main oil port (the world's largest) is Ras Tanura. There are three international airports, at Al-Makkah (Mecca), Riyadh and Az-Zahran, and 22 other commercial airports.

EDUCATION
With the exception of a few schools for expatriate children, all schools are supervised by the government and are segregated. There are universities in Jiddah, Al-Makkah (Mecca), Riyadh (branches in Abha and Qassim), Ad-Dammam (branch at Al-Hufuf) and Az-Zahran, and there are Islamic universities in Al-Madinah (Medina) and Riyadh together with 83 tertiary colleges. There is great emphasis on vocational training, provided at literacy and

artisan skill training centres and more advanced industrial, commercial and agricultural education institutes.
ILLITERACY RATE – (m) 15.9 per cent; (f) 32.8 per cent (2000)
GROSS ENROLMENT RATIO (percentage of relevant age group) – primary 67 per cent (2002); secondary 69 per cent (2002); tertiary 22 per cent (2002)

MEDIA AND CULTURE
Saudi Arabia has one of the most tightly controlled media environments in the Middle East. Criticism of the government and royal family and the questioning of religious tenets are not tolerated.

The state-run Broadcasting Service of the Kingdom of Saudi Arabia (BSKSA) is responsible for all broadcasting, operating four TV networks, including the news channel al-Ikhbariyya. Private radio and TV stations cannot operate from Saudi soil, but the country is a key market for pan-Arab satellite and subscription-based broadcasters. Saudi newspapers are created by royal decree. There are 10 dailies and many magazines. Pan-Arab newspapers, subject to censorship, are also available.

Saudi culture revolves almost entirely around Islam – two of Islam's holiest sites are in the country, and it considers itself the birthplace of the religion. Al-Makkah (Mecca) was the birthplace of the Prophet Muhammad, and contains the Great Mosque, within which is the Kaaba *(Ka'abah)* or sacred shrine of the Muslim religion. This is the focus of the annual *Hajj* (pilgrimage). Al-Madinah Al-Munawwarah (Medina, the City of Light), some 300 km north of Mecca, is celebrated as the first city to embrace Islam and as the burial place of the Prophet Muhammad.

SENEGAL

République du Sénégal – Republic of Senegal

AREA – 196,722 sq. km. Neighbours: Mauritania (north), Mali (east), Guinea-Bissau and Guinea (south), the Gambia (surrounded by Senegal)
POPULATION – 10,852,147 (2004 est.), 94 per cent Muslim, 4 per cent Christian, 1 per cent Animist. The official language is French; the principal local language is Wolof. Fulani, Serer, Mandinka, Jola and Sarakole are also spoken
CAPITAL – ΨDakar (population, 1,641,358, 1998 UN estimate)
MAJOR CITIES – Rufisque; Thiés; ΨZiguinchor
CURRENCY – Franc CFA of 100 centimes
NATIONAL ANTHEM – Pincez tous vos koras, frappez les balafons [All pluck your koras, strike the balafons]
NATIONAL DAY – 4 April
NATIONAL FLAG – Three vertical bands, green, yellow and red; a green star on the yellow band
LIFE EXPECTANCY (years) – 56.56 (2004 est.)
MORTALITY RATE (per 1,000 population) – 10.74 (2004 est.)
INFANT MORTALITY (per 1,000 births) – 56.53 (2004 est.)
HIV / AIDS ADULT PREVALENCE – 0.8 per cent (2003 est.)
DEATH PENALTY – No (abolished 1967)
POPULATION BELOW POVERTY LINE – 54 per cent (2001 est.)
POPULATION GROWTH RATE – 2.52 per cent (2004 est.)

POPULATION DENSITY – 52 per sq. km (2002)
MILITARY EXPENDITURE – 1.4 per cent of GDP (2003)
MILITARY PERSONNEL – 13,620: Army 11,900, Navy
    950, Air Force 770; Paramilitaries 5,000
CONSCRIPTION DURATION – Two years (selective)
ILLITERACY RATE – (m) 50 per cent; (f) 69.3 per cent
    (2003 est.)
GROSS ENROLMENT RATIO (percentage of relevant age
    group) – primary 75 per cent (2002); secondary 19 per
    cent (2002)

CLIMATE AND TERRAIN
The terrain is generally low and rolling, with plains rising
to foothills in the south-east. There is desert in the north
and tropical forest in the south. Elevation extremes range
from 581 m (Nepen Diakha) at the highest point to 0 m
(Atlantic Ocean) at the lowest. The River Senegal runs
close to the northern border and the River Gambia flows
through the south-east of the county. The climate is
tropical, with a wet season from June to September.
Average temperatures in Dakar range from 18°C in
January to 32°C in July.

HISTORY AND POLITICS
Senegal was part of the Mali empire in the 14th to 15th
centuries. The first European visitors were the Portuguese
in 1445. The French established a fort at Saint-Louis in
1659 and European traders established trades in slaves,
ivory, gold and other commodities in the 17th and 18th
centuries. The interior was occupied by the French in the
mid-19th century and the territory became part of French
West Africa in 1902. It became an autonomous state in
1958 and achieved independence as part of the
Federation of Mali in June 1960, seceding to form
the Republic of Senegal in September 1960. In 1966 the
country became a one-party state under the rule of the
Senegalese Progressive Union (UPS), which changed its
name to the Socialist Party (PS) in 1976. A three-party
system was introduced in 1978. Senegal joined with
Gambia to form the Confederation of Senegambia from
1982 to 1989.

The Social Party's 40 years of political domination
ended in March 2000 with the election as president of
Abdoulaye Wade, leader of the Senegalese Democratic
Party (PDS). The legislative election in April 2001 was
won by an alliance of 40 parties, the *Sopi* (Change)
coalition, led by the PDS; the PS retained only ten seats.
President Wade dismissed the government in 2002 and
appointed Idrissa Seck as prime minister, along with a
new Council of Ministers. Seck was dismissed by
President Wade in 2004 and replaced by Macky Sall,
formed a new government.

In the early 1980s a violent separatist insurgency
began in the southern Casamance region led by the
Movement of Democratic Forces of Casamance (MFDC).
A cease-fire in 1999 led to a peace agreement in March
2001, but this was not implemented because of splits and
leadership changes among the separatists. Violence in the
region increased during the 2001 election campaign, but
subsequently declined. In 2003 the MFDC leader said
that the secessionist war was over, and a peace agreement
with the government was signed in December 2004 after
two years of relative calm.

POLITICAL SYSTEM
Under the 2001 constitution, the executive president is
directly elected for a five-year term, renewable only once.
The Senate was abolished in 2001 and the legislature is
now unicameral; the National Assembly has 120
members, directly elected for a five-year term. The
president appoints the prime minister, who nominates the
other ministers.

HEAD OF STATE
President, Abdoulaye Wade, *elected* 19 March 2000, *sworn
in* 1 April 2000

SELECTED GOVERNMENT MEMBERS *as at August 2005*
Prime Minister, Macky Sall
Defence, Becaye Diop
Finance and Economy, Abdoulaye Diop
Interior, Chiekh Sadibou Fall
Minister of State for Foreign Affairs, Cheikh Tidiane Gadio

EMBASSY OF THE REPUBLIC OF SENEGAL
39 Marloes Road, London W8 6LA
T 020-7938 4048/7937 7237
Ambassador Extraordinary and Plenipotentiray, HE Gen.
    Mamadou Niang, apptd 2005

BRITISH EMBASSY
20 rue du Docteur Guillet (BP 6025), Dakar
T (+221) 823 7392/9971 E britemb@telecomplus.sn
Ambassador Extraordinary and Plenipotentiary, HE Peter
    Newall, apptd 2005

BRITISH COUNCIL
34–36 Blvd de la République, BP 6232, Dakar
T (+221) 822 2015/822 2048 E postmaster@britishcouncil.sn
Director, Andrew McNab

ECONOMY AND TRADE
Economic reform began in 1994, with the support of the
international donor community, and GDP has grown by
an average of 5 per cent a year as a result. Even so, the
country is poor, with high unemployment. Around 60 per
cent of the workforce are employed in the agricultural
industry. Tourism is of growing importance as a source of
revenue, with around half a million overseas visitors a
year. The principal exports are fish, groundnuts (raw and
processed) and phosphates. Principal imports are
foodstuffs, machinery, fuel oils and transport equipment.
GNI – US$4,600 million (2002); US$470 per capita
    (2002)
ANNUAL AVERAGE GROWTH OF GDP – 3.2 per cent
    (2004 est.)
INFLATION RATE – 0.7 per cent (2000 est.)
TOTAL EXTERNAL DEBT – US$3,372 million (2000 est.)
IMPORTS – US$2,030 million (2003)
EXPORTS – US$1,330 million (2003)

BALANCE OF PAYMENTS
Trade – US$537 million deficit (2002)
Current Account – US$317 miillion deficit (2002)

Trade with UK	2003	2004
Imports from UK	£52,829,000	£67,415,000
Exports to UK	7,906,000	7,127,000

TRANSPORT INFRASTRUCTURE
Senegal has a road network of some 14,576 km, of which
4,271 km are surfaced. There are also 906 km of railways,
and 897 km of navigable waterways on the Senegal and
Saloum rivers. Dakar is the main port and the location of
the principal airport.

MEDIA

The constitution guarantees freedom of the news media and there are three private television channels, many private radio stations, and subscription-based television is readily available. Publications must be registered as a formality, but foreign media circulate freely. There are at least five daily newspapers, of which one is state-owned.

SERBIA AND MONTENEGRO

Srbija I Crna Gora

AREA – 102,100 sq. km. Neighbours: Hungary (north), Romania and Bulgaria (east), the Former Yugoslav Republic of Macedonia and Albania (south), Bosnia-Hercegovina and Croatia (west)

POPULATION – 10,825,900 (2004 est.): 67.6 per cent Serb and Montenegrin, 16.5 per cent Albanian, 3.2 per cent Muslim Slavs, 3.3 per cent Hungarian, with smaller numbers of Romanies, Croats, Slovaks and Bulgarians. The majority religion is Serbian Orthodox, with significant Muslim and small Roman Catholic minorities. The main language is Serbian (74 per cent), with Albanian and Hungarian minorities. Serbian is a South Slav language usually written in the Cyrillic script

CAPITAL – ΨBelgrade (population, 1,574,050, 2002 census)

MAJOR CITIES – Kragujevac; Nis; ΨNovi Sad; Podgorica, the capital of Montenegro; Pristina; Subotica

CURRENCY – New dinar of 100 paras

NATIONAL ANTHEM – Hej, Sloveni, joste ivi rec nasih dedova [Oh! Slavs, our ancestors' words still live]

NATIONAL DAY – 27 April

NATIONAL FLAG – Three horizontal stripes of blue, white and red

LIFE EXPECTANCY (years) – 74.4 (2004 est.)

MORTALITY RATE (per 1,000 population) – 10.53 (2004 est.)

INFANT MORTALITY (per 1,000 births) – 13.43 (2004 est.)

HIV / AIDS ADULT PREVALENCE – 0.2 per cent (2001 est.)

DEATH PENALTY – No (abolished 2002)

POPULATION BELOW POVERTY LINE – 30 per cent (2001 est.)

POPULATION GROWTH RATE – 0.03 per cent (2004 est.)

POPULATION DENSITY – 103 per sq. km (2001)

MILITARY EXPENDITURE – 3 per cent of GDP (2003)

MILITARY PERSONNEL – 65,300: Army 55,000, Navy 3,800, Air Force 6,500; Paramilitaries 45,100

CONSCRIPTION DURATION – 12–15 months

GROSS ENROLMENT RATIO (percentage of relevant age group) – primary 99 per cent (2002); secondary 89 per cent (2002); tertiary 36 per cent (2002)

CLIMATE AND TERRAIN

Montenegro and southern Serbia are extremely mountainous, while the north is dominated by the low-lying plains of the Danube. Elevation extremes range from 2,656 m (Daravica) at the highest point to 0 m (Adriatic Sea) at the lowest. The major rivers are the Danube, the Sava, the Drina, the Tisa and the Morava. The climate inland is moderate and continental, while along the coast a Mediterranean-Adriatic climate prevails. Average temperatures in Belgrade range from 2°C in January to 18°C in July.

HISTORY AND POLITICS

The medieval kingdom of Serbia emerged from the rule of the Byzantine Empire in the 13th century to form a large and prosperous state in the Balkans. Defeat by the Turks in 1389 led to almost 500 years of Turkish rule. After gaining autonomy within the Ottoman Empire in 1815, Serbia became fully independent in 1878 and a kingdom in 1881. Montenegro was part of the Serbian state before it was conquered by the Turks in the 15th century; it became independent in 1878. At the end of the First World War Serbia and Montenegro joined the former Austro-Hungarian provinces of Slovenia, Croatia and Bosnia-Hercegovina to form the 'Kingdom of Serbs, Croats and Slovenes', which was renamed Yugoslavia in 1929. Yugoslavia was occupied by Axis forces in 1941 and reformed as a communist federal republic under the presidency of partisan leader Josip Tito in 1945.

Tito died in 1980 and was succeeded by a rotating federal presidency which was unable to contain the growing nationalist movements. Economic difficulties and the collapse of communism in the rest of Europe led to the introduction of multiparty systems in the republics in 1990. Elections in 1990 brought to power in four of the republics non-communist governments seeking looser federal ties. Efforts by the six republican presidents to negotiate a new federal or confederal structure for the country failed in 1991, and the federation disintegrated as the republics with non-communist governments declared their independence: Slovenia and Croatia on 25 June 1991, Macedonia on 18 September 1991, and Bosnia-Hercegovina on 1 March 1992. This left Serbia and Montenegro to form the new 'Federal Republic of Yugoslavia' (FRY), which was declared on 27 April 1992.

In Croatia the ethnic Serb minority refused to accept Croatia's independence and fighting began in July 1991 between Croat Defence Forces and Serbian guerrillas, backed by the Yugoslav National Army (JNA). By September 1991 this had escalated into war between Croatia and Yugoslavia. Fighting continued until January 1992 when the EU and the UN were able to bring about a cease-fire (*see* Croatia).

In Bosnia-Hercegovina, independence was supported by the Bosniacs (Muslims) and Croats but rejected by the ethnic Serbs, and fighting between Bosniacs and Serbs broke out in March 1992. The JNA intervened against the Bosniacs, but in May 1992 withdrew to Serbia and Montenegro (*see* Bosnia-Hercegovina).

Slobodan Milosevic, president of Serbia from 1989 until 1996, supported various military and militia efforts to unite ethnic Serbs in neighbouring republics into a 'Greater Serbia'. All these efforts were ultimately unsuccessful. Milosevic dominated Serbian and federal politics in the 1990s, becoming president of the Federal Republic in 1997. His corrupt and repressive regime was ended by the September 2000 federal elections, in which the Democratic Opposition of Serbia became the largest party in both chambers of the parliament and the Democratic Party of Serbia presidential candidate, Vojislav Kostunica, won the most votes. Milosevic's attempts to pervert the outcome of the presidential election and remain in power were met with mass demonstrations and strikes, forcing him to stand down in October 2000. He was arrested in April 2001 on corruption charges and extradited to the UN International Criminal Tribunal for the Former Yugoslavia, where his trial on charges of crimes against humanity, genocide and ethnic cleansing began in February 2002.

Montenegro's desire for independence led in March 2002 to an EU-brokered agreement between the leaders of Serbia, Montenegro and the Federal Republic of Yugoslavia to restructure the Federal Republic into a union of two semi-independent states; the union government remains responsible for defence and foreign policy and each republic is responsible for its own economy and other internal affairs. The union was renamed Serbia and Montenegro. The constitutional charter for the new union came into effect in March 2003 for a minimum of three years, after which the two republics can hold referenda on whether to retain or end the union. Svetozar Marovic was elected president of Serbia and Montenegro by the union parliament and a union government was approved in March 2003. Since the December 2003 elections to the Serbian parliament, the largest party in the union parliament has been the right-wing Serbian Radical Party.

POLITICAL SYSTEM
The president of Serbia-Montenegro is elected by the Serbia-Montenegro union parliament. The unicameral union legislature, the Assembly of Serbia and Montenegro *(Skupstina Srbije i Crne Gore)*, has 126 members elected by the republican assemblies, 91 from Serbia and 35 from Montenegro, for a four-year term. The union government consists of a council of three Serb and two Montenegrin ministers with the president as *ex officio* chair. The republics each have their own president, legislature and government.

HEAD OF STATE
President, Chair of the Council of Ministers, Svetozar Marovic, *elected* 3 March 2003

SELECTED GOVERNMENT MEMBERS *as at August 2005*
Foreign Affairs, Vuk Draskovic (Serbia) (DOS)
Human Rights and Minorities, Rasim Ljajic (Serbia) (DOS)

MONTENEGRO
AREA – 13,182 sq. km
POPULATION – 615,000: 62 per cent Montenegrin, 14.5 per cent Bosniac, 6.5 per cent Albanian and 3 per cent Serb

The Assembly of the Republic of Montenegro has 77 members, elected for a four-year term. The October 2002 legislative elections were won by the Democratic Party of Socialists (DPS) and Filip Vujanovic, prime minister since 1998, was nominated to form a government by early November. President Milo Djukanovic resigned on 25 November 2002 to become prime minister in place of Vujanovic, who became chair of the parliament and therefore acting president after the presidential election in December was invalidated by a low turnout. The minimum turnout rule was altered, and in a third round of voting in May 2003 Filip Vujanovic was elected president.

SELECTED GOVERNMENT MEMBERS *as at August 2005*
President, Filip Vujanovic, *elected* 11 May 2003
Prime Minister, Milo Djukanovic
Deputy Prime Ministers, Jusuf Kalamperovic; Dragan Djurovic *(Political System, Minister of the Interior)*; Branimir Gvozdenovic *(Economic Policy)*
Finance, Igor Luksic
Foreign Affairs, Miodraq Vlahovic

SERBIA
AREA – 88,538 sq. km
POPULATION – 9,300,000, of whom 66 per cent are Serbs

Serbia includes the formerly autonomous provinces of Kosovo (population 1.6 million), of great historic importance to Serbs, and Vojvodina (population 2 million). Kosovo, with its capital at Pristina, is predominantly Albanian (90 per cent). Vojvodina, with its capital at Novi Sad, has a large Hungarian minority (21 per cent).

The Serbian National Assembly has 250 members, elected for a four-year term. In the December 2003 election, the Serbian Radical Party won the most seats but without an overall majority. A four-party coalition government was formed in March 2004, led by Vojslav Kostunica of the Democratic of Serbia. The 2004 presidential election was invalidated owing to a low turnout and the chair of the parliament became acting president. In February 2004 the parliament voted to abolish the 50 per cent turnout needed to elect a president, and in June 2004 Boris Tadic, leader of the Democratic Party, was elected president with 53 per cent of the vote.

SELECTED GOVERNMENT MEMBERS *as at August 2005*
President, Boris Tadic, *elected* 27 June 2004, *took office* 11 July 2004
Prime Minister, Vojslav Kostunica
Deputy Prime Minister, Miroljub Labus
Finance, Mladjan Dinkic
Interior, Dragan Jocic

EMBASSY OF THE SERBIA AND MONTENEGRO
28 Belgrave Square, London SW1X 8QB T 020-7235 9049
Ambassador Extraordinary and Plenipotentiary, HE Dragisa Burzan, apptd 2005

BRITISH EMBASSY
Resavska 46, YU-11000 Belgrade T (+381) (11) 645055
Ambassador Extraordinary and Plenipotentiary, HE David Gowan, apptd 2003

BRITISH COUNCIL
Terazije 8/1, POB 248, YU-11001 Belgrade
T (+381) (11) 3023 800 E info@britcoun.org.yu
Director, Chris Gibson

INSURGENCIES
The provinces of Kosovo and Vojvodina were stripped of their autonomy in 1990 by President Milosevic of Serbia. Following the break-up of Yugoslavia, many Hungarians and Croats fled or were expelled from Vojvodina and their homes allocated to Serb refugees from Croatia.

In Kosovo the loss of autonomy resulted in the progressive exclusion of the Albanian majority from public life. The Kosovars' decisive vote in a 1991 referendum for independence from both Serbia and Yugoslavia was declared illegal by the Serbian government, which tightened its control. Fighting between Kosovar nationalists and Serb forces peaked in the late 1990s, the Serbs beginning a renewed crackdown in 1998 which by the following year had developed into a brutal and systematic process of ethnic cleansing. On the pretext of eliminating support for the Kosovo Liberation Army (KLA), Serb forces attacked villages, murdering or expelling the inhabitants and destroying buildings.

Despite international condemnation, the attacks continued until NATO commenced high-altitude bombing against military targets in Yugoslavia in March 1999. Over 1.3 million people fled or were forced to leave their homes; over 800,000 sought refuge in Albania, Macedonia or Montenegro (which, although part of the Yugoslav Federation, had refused to become involved in the fighting), and over 500,000 people were internally displaced.

In June 1999 Serbia accepted a peace plan agreed by NATO and Russia, and the Yugoslav army withdrew, to be replaced by NATO forces. Since the Yugoslav withdrawal, Kosovo has been under the administration of the UN's Interim Administration Mission in Kosovo (UNMIK), which has established the Kosovo Transitional Council, composed of four UN and four Kosovar representatives. The NATO-led Kosovo Force (KFOR) has facilitated the disarming of the KLA and the return of over 850,000 refugees, but at least 200,000 Kosovar Serbs have fled, fearing reprisal attacks, which have frequently occurred.

In May 2001, UNMIK announced that a legislative assembly for Kosovo would be established, with powers over health, education, environment and the economy, but with UNMIK retaining final authority. Elections to the 120-member assembly in November 2001 were won by the Democratic League of Kosovo (LDK), which gained 47 seats. A power-sharing government was agreed in February 2002 with Bajram Rexhepi of the Democratic Party of Kosovo (PDK) as its head. Ibrahim Rugova of the LDK was elected unopposed as president in March. In the 2004 elections, the LDK remained the largest party, though without an overall majority, and Rugova was re-elected president. His choice as prime minister, Ramush Haradinaj, resigned in March 2005 after being indicted for war crimes, and was replaced by Bajram Kosumi.

The ethnic Albanian Liberation Army of Precevo, Medvedja and Bujanovac (UCPMB) launched attacks on Serbs in Albanian-populated areas of southern Serbia in November 2000. The rebels wanted to annex these areas into Kosovo. A cease-fire was signed in March 2001 after NATO agreed to permit Yugoslav forces to enter the demilitarised buffer zone which had been established on the Serbian side of the border with Kosovo in 1999.

ECONOMY AND TRADE

Since 1991 the economy has been devastated by the wars in Croatia and Bosnia-Hercegovina, by the UN economic sanctions and trade embargo, and because of the lack of free-market reforms. NATO bombing in 1999 further damaged the already fragile infrastructure. However, the Democratic Opposition of Serbia (DOS) coalition government that took office in 2000 implemented aggressive remedial measures and began to reintegrate into the international community, renewing its membership in the IMF and rejoining the World Bank and the European Bank for Reconstruction and Development. Since then the country has received donor finance for economic restructuring and rescheduled a large proportion of its debts. Progress remains slow, and only the country's agricultural self-sufficiency has kept it afloat. Industrial production remains extremely low and there is high unemployment, estimated to be around 34.5 per cent in 2003. GDP in 2000 was roughly 40 per cent of 1989 levels.

GNI – US$11,600 million (2002); US$1,400 per capita (2002)

ANNUAL AVERAGE GROWTH OF GDP – 5.5 per cent (2001 est.)

INFLATION RATE – 19 per cent (2002 est.)
TOTAL EXTERNAL DEBT – US$11,960 million (2000 est.)

Trade with UK	2003	2004
Imports from UK	£65,613,000	£66,087,000
Exports to UK	34,410,000	40,462,000

TRANSPORT INFRASTRUCTURE

Serbia and Montenegro have some 49,805 km of roads, around 31,029 km of which are surfaced (including 560 km of expressways). There are also 4,059 km of railways, linking Belgrade directly to Athens, Bucharest, Budapest, Istanbul, Ljubljana, Munich, Skopje, Sofia, Thessaloniki, Vienna, and Zagreb. Principal ports include Bar and Kotor on the Adriatic coast, and Belgrade and Novi Sad on the Danube. The main international airport is at Belgrade.

MEDIA AND CULTURE

The end of the Milosevic era saw a huge proliferation of media outlets. There are many privately owned television stations and around 1,000 radio stations were thought to be operating by late 2003. The state-run national broadcaster, RTS, aims to develop into a public service, and private operators anticipate the formulation of regulatory and licensing procedures. Newspapers include Danas daily and a weekly publication Vreme and NIN.

In Kosovo, a Temporary Media Commission (TMC), set up by the UN, has set out a code of conduct for journalists which aims to prevent incitement to hatred in the media.

Serbia and Montenegro have a rich architectural and archaeological heritage that includes ornate Orthodox churches, mosques, monasteries and palaces dating from the Ottoman Empire. Notable cultural figures include the writer Ivo Andric (1892–1975) winner of the Nobel Prize for Literature in 1961, the playwright Marin Drzic (1508–67), the film producer Branko Lustig (b. 1932), the sculptor Ivan Mestrovic (1883–1962) and composers Jakov Gotovac (1895–1982) and Josip Stolcer-Slavenski (1896–1955).

SEYCHELLES

Republic of Seychelles / République des Seychelles / Repiblik Sesel

AREA – 455 sq. km
POPULATION – 80,832 (2004 est.). The languages are English, French and Créole
CAPITAL – ΨVictoria (population, 71,000, 1998 estimate), on Mahé
CURRENCY – Seychelles rupee of 100 cents
NATIONAL ANTHEM – Koste Seselwa [Seychellois unite]
NATIONAL DAY – 18 June
NATIONAL FLAG – Five rays extending from the lower hoist over the whole field, coloured blue, yellow, green, white and red
LIFE EXPECTANCY (years) – 71.53 (2004 est.)
MORTALITY RATE (per 1,000 population) – 6.41 (2004 est.)
INFANT MORTALITY (per 1,000 births) – 15.97 (2004 est.)
DEATH PENALTY – No (abolished 1993)
POPULATION GROWTH RATE – 0.45 per cent (2004 est.)
POPULATION DENSITY – 178 per sq. km (2001)
MILITARY EXPENDITURE – 1.6 per cent of GDP (2003)

MILITARY PERSONNEL – 450: Army 200, Paramilitaries 250

CLIMATE AND TERRAIN
The Seychelles consists of 115 islands spread over 643,737 sq. km of the south-west Indian Ocean, north of Madagascar. There is a relatively compact granitic group, 32 islands in all, with high hills and mountains, of which Mahé is the largest and most populated (90 per cent of the population live on Mahé); and the outlying coralline group, for the most part only a little above sea-level. Elevation extremes range from 905 m (Morne Seychellois) at the highest point to 0 m (Indian Ocean) at the lowest and the climate is tropical, with an average temperature of 26°C.

HISTORY AND POLITICS
The islands were first sighted by European navigators in the early 15th century and were proclaimed French territory in 1756. The Mahé group was settled as a dependency of Mauritius from 1770, but was captured by the British in 1794 and ceded to Britain in 1814. In 1903 these islands, together with the coralline group, were formed into a colony separate from Mauritius. On 29 June 1976, the islands became an independent republic within the Commonwealth. Following a coup d'état in 1977, when France-Albert René became president, Seychelles became a one-party state ruled by the Seychelles People's Progressive Front (SPPF) in 1979. Opposition parties were permitted from 1991 and in 1993 President René reintroduced a multiparty democratic system. Power has remained with the SPPF under the pluralist system, as it dominates the parliament and holds the presidency, although opposition parties are beginning to achieve a greater share of the vote.

In the 2001 presidential election, President René was re-elected with 54 per cent of the vote. He stepped down in April 2004 and the rest of his term is being served by the vice-president James Michel. In the 2002 legislative election, the SPPF retained its overall majority with 23 seats, and the Seychelles National Party won 11 seats.

POLITICAL SYSTEM
Under the 1993 constitution, the executive president is directly elected for a five-year term, with a maximum of three consecutive terms. The unicameral National Assembly has up to 34 members, 23 directly elected by constituencies and up to 11 allocated by proportional representation; members serve a five-year term. The council of ministers is appointed by the president.

HEAD OF STATE
President, Head of Government, Defence, Interior and Legal Affairs, James Michel, *assumed office*, 14 April 2004
Vice-President, Finance, Economic Planning, Information Technology and Communications, Joseph Belmont

SELECTED GOVERNMENT MEMBERS *as at August 2005*
Economic Planning and Development, Jacquelin Dugasse
Foreign Affairs, Patrick Pillay
Health and Social Affairs, Vincent Meriton

SEYCHELLES HIGH COMMISSION
2nd Floor, Eros House, 111 Baker Street, London W1N 6RR
T 020 7224-1660
High Commissioner, Callixte D'Offay

BRITISH HIGH COMMISSION
Oliaji Trade Centre, PO Box 161, Victoria, Mahé
T (+248) 283666 E bhcsey@seychelles.net
High Commissioner, HE Diana Skingle, apptd 2005

ECONOMY AND TRADE
The economy is based on tourism, fishing, agriculture and small-scale manufacturing industries, and the re-export of fuel for aircraft and ships. Deep-sea tuna fishing by foreign fleets under licence, improved port facilities at Victoria and exports from a tuna-canning factory attract growing revenues. The government is attempting to reduce the reliance on tourism, which generates the majority of foreign exchange earnings, by promoting offshore financial services. Principal exports are tuna, frozen prawns, fish and cinnamon bark. The principal imports are machinery and transport equipment, manufactures, foodstuffs, tobacco, fuel oils and chemicals.
GNI – US$538 million (2002); US$6,530 per capita (2002)
ANNUAL AVERAGE GROWTH OF GDP – 1.5 per cent (2004 est.)
INFLATION RATE – 6.3 per cent (2000 est.)
TOTAL EXTERNAL DEBT – US$163 million (2000 est.)
IMPORTS – US$430 million (2003)
EXPORTS – US$280 million (2003)

BALANCE OF PAYMENTS
Trade – US$140 million deficit (2002)
Current Account – US$131,000 million deficit (2002)

Trade with UK	2003	2004
Imports from UK	£13,207,000	£12,719,000
Exports to UK	53,802,000	60,955,000

TRANSPORT INFRASTRUCTURE
The Seychelles has around 373 km of roads, the majority of which are surfaced. The main port is Victoria, and ferries run regularly between Mahé, Praslin and la Digue. Some 15 airports, eight with surfaced runways, serve the islands.

MEDIA
The government controls much of the islands' media, and operates the only radio and TV stations and the sole daily newspaper. Freedom of speech has improved since one-party rule was abolished in 1993, although the opposition weekly newspaper, *Regar*, has regularly been sued for libel by the government, and expensive licensing fees have discouraged the development of privately owned broadcast media. The BBC World Service and Radio France Internationale broadcast in the area.

SIERRA LEONE

Republic of Sierra Leone

AREA – 71,740 sq. km. Neighbours: Guinea (north, north-east), Liberia (south-east)
POPULATION – 5,883,889 (2004 est.). The south is inhabited by peoples whose languages fall into the Mende group; the north by the Temne and smaller groups such as the Limba, Loko, Koranko and Susu
CAPITAL – ΨFreetown (population, 469,776, 1985)
CURRENCY – Leone (Le) of 100 cents
NATIONAL ANTHEM – High we exalt thee, realm of the free

NATIONAL DAY – 27 April (Independence Day)

NATIONAL FLAG – Three horizontal stripes of leaf-green, white and cobalt blue

LIFE EXPECTANCY (years) – 42.69 (2004 est.)

MORTALITY RATE (per 1,000 population) – 20.62 (2004 est.)

INFANT MORTALITY (per 1,000 births) – 145.24 (2004 est.)

HIV / AIDS ADULT PREVALENCE – 7 per cent (2001 est.)

DEATH PENALTY – Yes

POPULATION BELOW POVERTY LINE – 68 per cent (2001 est.)

POPULATION GROWTH RATE – 2.27 per cent (2004 est.)

POPULATION DENSITY – 73 per sq. km (2002)

MILITARY EXPENDITURE – 2.2 per cent of GDP (2003)

MILITARY PERSONNEL – Army 12–13,000, Navy 200

CLIMATE AND TERRAIN

The terrain rises from coastal mangrove swamps to wooded hill country, upland plateau and mountains in the east. Elevation extremes range from 1,948 m (Bintimani) at the highest point to 0 m (Atlantic Ocean) at the lowest. The climate is tropical, with a wet season from May to October. Average daily temperatures in Freetown are 30°C all year round.

HISTORY AND POLITICS

Coastal trading posts were established by the Portuguese in the 15th century and the British in the 17th century. In the late 18th century British philanthropists bought land to establish a settlement for liberated and escaped African slaves on the Freetown peninsula. In 1808 the settlement was declared a Crown colony and became the main base in West Africa for enforcing the 1807 Act outlawing the slave trade. Africans from North America and the West Indies, and Africans rescued from slave ships, also settled there. In 1896 a protectorate was declared over the hinterland. In 1951 the colony of Freetown and the protectorate were united and on 27 April 1961 Sierra Leone became a fully independent state within the Commonwealth.

The country became a republic in 1971 and a one-party state in 1978, but in September 1991 a new multiparty constitution was adopted and an interim government formed, which was overthrown by a military coup in April 1992. In 1996 the military head of state was deposed and the country returned to civilian rule following the election of a government headed by Ahmad Tejan Kabbah of the Sierra Leone People's Party (SLPP).

A military coup in May 1997 overthrew President Kabbah's government and set up a 20-member Armed Forces Revolutionary Council with Maj. Paul Koroma, the coup leader, as chairman and the Revolutionary United Front (RUF) leader Foday Sankoh as vice-chairman. However, in July 1997, a Nigerian-led ECOMOG force was sent to Sierra Leone to oust Koroma and restore the legitimate government. Under a peace agreement reached in October 1997, President Kabbah returned to Freetown in March 1998.

The transition to multiparty and civilian rule was complicated by the civil war with the Revolutionary United Front (RUF), which began in 1991. A cease-fire in May 1999 led to the signing in July 1999 of the Lomé peace accord, which created a power-sharing structure that brought the RUF into the government. However, violence continued and the cease-fire collapsed in May

2000 despite the deployment of the UN Mission to Sierra Leone (UNAMSIL), which had taken over peacekeeping duties from ECOMOG in April 2000. A cease-fire in November 2000 was not fully implemented but another cease-fire agreement in May 2001 proved more effective. The state of emergency imposed in 1998 was lifted in March 2002, and the disarmament of rebel forces was completed in 2004. A UN-supported war crimes tribunal was set up in March 2004 to try senior militia leaders from both sides in the civil war.

In the 2002 presidential election, President Kabbah was re-elected with 70 per cent of the vote. The simultaneous legislative election was won by the SLPP, with 83 seats. A new cabinet, composed of members of the SLPP and independents, was appointed.

POLITICAL SYSTEM

Under the 1991 constitution, the head of state is an executive president who is directly elected for a four-year term and who is responsible to parliament. The unicameral parliament has 124 members, 112 directly elected for a five-year term and 12 indirectly elected to represent the 12 provincial districts. The president appoints the cabinet.

HEAD OF STATE

President, Defence, Ahmad Tejan Kabbah, *elected* 15 March 1996, *re-elected* 14 May 2002

Vice-President, Solomon Berewa

SELECTED GOVERNMENT MEMBERS *as at August 2005*

Finance, John Benjamin

Foreign Affairs and International Co-operation, Momodu Koroma

Internal Affairs, Pascal Egbenda

SIERRA LEONE HIGH COMMISSION

1st and 3rd Floors, Oxford Circus House, 245 Oxford Street, London W1D 2LX T 020-7287 9884

High Commissioner, HE Sulaiman Tejan-Jalloh, apptd 2000

BRITISH HIGH COMMISSION

Spur Road, Freetown

T (+232) (22) 232961/362/563/565 E bhc@sierratel.sl

High Commissioner, HE John Mitchiner, apptd 2003

BRITISH COUNCIL

PO Box 124, Tower Hill, Freetown

T (+232) (22) 222 223 E info.enquiry@sl.britishcouncil.org

Director, Rajive Bendre

ECONOMY AND TRADE

The country has been devastated by a decade of civil war, and unemployment, already high, has increased with the demobilisation of former combatants. Between 60 and 70 per cent of government expenditure is financed by donor support.

The economy has always depended largely on exports of minerals, mainly diamonds, gold and bauxite, although production was disrupted by the war. Agriculture on the Freetown peninsula is largely confined to the production of cassava and crops such as maize and vegetables for local consumption. In the hinterland the principal agricultural product is rice, which is the staple food of the country, and cash crops such as cocoa, coffee, palm kernels and ginger. Cattle production is also important.

GNI – US$700 million (2002); US$140 per capita (2002 est.)
ANNUAL AVERAGE GROWTH OF GDP – 6 per cent (2004 est.)
INFLATION RATE – 1 per cent (2001 est.)
TOTAL EXTERNAL DEBT – US$1,273 million (2000 est.)
IMPORTS – US$300 million (2003)
EXPORTS – US$90 million (2003)

BALANCE OF PAYMENTS
Trade – US$195 million deficit (2002)
Current Account – US$73 million deficit (2002)

Trade with UK	2003	2004
Imports from UK	£32,352,000	£24,030,000
Exports to UK	4,206,000	2,076,000

TRANSPORT INFRASTRUCTURE
Since the phasing out of the railway system in 1974 the road network has been developed considerably; and there are now 11,200 km (7,000 miles) of roads in the country. A bridge has been constructed over the Mano River linking Sierra Leone and Liberia.

The Freetown international airport is situated at Lungi. The main port is Freetown, which has one of the largest natural harbours in the world. There are smaller ports at Pepel, Bonthe and Niti.

EDUCATION
Technical education is provided in the two government technical institutes, situated in Freetown and Kenema, in two trade centres and in the technical training establishments of the mining companies. Teacher training is carried out at the University of Sierra Leone, six colleges in the provinces and in the Milton Margai Training College near Freetown.
ILLITERACY RATE – (m) 49.3 per cent; (f) 77.4 per cent (2000)
GROSS ENROLMENT RATIO (percentage of relevant age group) – tertiary 76 per cent (2002); tertiary 2 per cent (2002)

MEDIA
The UN Mission in Sierra Leone (UNMASIL) operates a number of radio services, broadcasting news of UN activities and human rights information as well as music and news. BBC World Service and Radio France Internationale are broadcast from Freetown. Dozens of privately run newspapers are published in Freetown, despite low literacy levels.

SINGAPORE

Repablik Singapura / Xinjiapo Gongheguo / Singapur Kuṭiyaraśu / Republic of Singapore

AREA – 648 sq. km
POPULATION – 4,353,893 (2004 est.): Chinese 76.8 per cent, Malays 13.9 per cent, Indians (including those of Pakistani, Bangladeshi and Sri Lankan origin) 7.9 per cent and 1.4 per cent from other ethnic groups. Malay, Mandarin, Tamil and English are the official languages. At least eight Chinese dialects are used. Malay is the national language and English is the language of administration. The religions are Buddhism 42.5 per cent, Islam 14.9 per cent, Christianity 14.6 per cent, Taoism 8.5 per cent, Hinduism 4.0 per cent

CURRENCY – Singapore dollar (S$) of 100 cents
NATIONAL ANTHEM – Majullah Singapura [May Singapore progress]
NATIONAL DAY – 9 August
NATIONAL FLAG – Horizontal bands of red over white; crescent with five five-point stars on red band near staff
LIFE EXPECTANCY (years) – 81.53 (2004 est.)
MORTALITY RATE (per 1,000 population) – 4.05 (2004 est.)
INFANT MORTALITY (per 1,000 births) – 2.28 (2004 est.)
HIV / AIDS ADULT PREVALENCE – 0.2 per cent (2003 est.)
DEATH PENALTY – Yes
POPULATION GROWTH RATE – 1.71 per cent (2004 est.)
POPULATION DENSITY – 6,826 per sq. km (2002)
MILITARY EXPENDITURE – 5.2 per cent of GDP (2003)
MILITARY PERSONNEL – 72,500: Army 50,000, Navy 9,000, Air Force 13,500; Paramilitaries 96,300
CONSCRIPTION DURATION – 24–30 months
ILLITERACY RATE – (m) 3.3 per cent; (f) 11.4 per cent (2002)

CLIMATE AND TERRAIN
Singapore consists of the island of Singapore and 63 islets. Singapore island is 42 km long and 22.5 km wide and is situated just north of the Equator off the southern extremity of the Malay peninsula, from which it is separated by the Straits of Johore. A causeway crosses the 1.21 km to the mainland. Elevation extremes range from 166 m (Bukit Timah) at the highest point to 0 m (Singapore Strait) at the lowest. The average temperature is 29°C all year round. Average annual rainfall is 2,410 mm, and floods and violent wind squalls are common.

HISTORY AND POLITICS
Singapore, a trading site since the 12th century, was leased from the Sultan of Johore by the British East India Company in 1819. In 1826 it was incorporated with Penang and Malacca to form the Straits Settlements and they became a Crown colony in 1867. Singapore became the principal British military base in the Far East in the 1920s and during the Second World War fell to Japanese forces in 1942. Liberated in 1945, it became a separate colony in 1946. Internal self-government was introduced in 1959 and it became part of the Federation of Malaysia in 1963, before withdrawing to become an independent sovereign state within the Commonwealth on 9 August 1965.

Although Singapore is a multiparty state, the People's Action Party (PAP) has dominated politics since 1959; opposition candidates were elected to parliament for the first time only in 1984. The PAP leader, Lee Kuan Yew, was prime minister from 1959 until he retired in 1990. Sellapan Rama Nathan became president of Singapore in September 1999; no election was held as he was the sole candidate. After the 2001 general election, the PAP won 82 seats in parliament and opposition parties two. Goh Chok Tong, prime minister since 1990, resigned in August 2004 and was succeeded by Lee Hsien Loong, the son of Lee Kuan Yew. A presidential election was held in August 2005.

POLITICAL SYSTEM
The 1959 constitution was amended in 1965 to enable Singapore to become a republic, and in 1991 to make the presidency directly elective with increased responsibilites.

The head of state is the president, directly elected for a six-year term, who has the power to veto government decisions relating to internal security, the budget, financial reserves and the appointment of senior civil servants. The president appoints the prime minister and, on his advice, the members of the cabinet. There is a unicameral parliament with 84 members directly elected and up to six extra members from opposition parties (NCMPs), depending on their share of the vote; they serve a five-year term. Up to nine members can also be nominated by the government for a two-year term (NMPs). In the present parliament, there are two NCMPs and six NMPs.

HEAD OF STATE
President, Sellapan Rama Nathan, *took office* 1 September 1999, *re-elected* 17 August 2005

SELECTED GOVERNMENT MEMBERS *as at August 2005*
Prime Minister, Lee Hsien Loong
Senior Minister, Prime Minister's Office, Goh Chok Tong
Deputy Prime Minister, Tony Tan Kheng Yam
Foreign Affairs, George Yong Boon Yeo
Home Affairs, Wong Kan Seng

HIGH COMMISSION FOR THE REPUBLIC OF SINGAPORE
9 Wilton Crescent, London SW1X 8SP T 020-7235 8315
High Commissioner, HE Michael Eng Cheng Teo, apptd 2002

BRITISH HIGH COMMISSION
100 Tanglin Road, Singapore 247919
T (+65) 424 4200 E commercial.singapore@fco.gov.uk
High Commissioner, HE Alan Collins, CMG, apptd 2003

BRITISH COUNCIL
30 Napier Road, Singapore 258509
T (+65) 6473 111 E english@britishcouncil.org.sg
Director, Les Dangerfield

ECONOMY AND TRADE

Historically the economy was based on the sale and distribution of raw materials from surrounding countries and on entrepôt trade in finished products. An industrialisation programme launched in 1968 established a wide range of manufacturing industries, including shipbuilding, iron and steel, micro-electronics, electrical goods, telecommunications equipment, office machinery, scientific instruments and pharmaceuticals. Singapore has also become an important financial services centre with significant insurance and foreign exchange markets, a stock exchange, 149 commercial banks and 79 merchant banks and an oil-refining centre. In 1998 the government announced substantial liberalising reforms of the financial sector, aimed at allowing the country to compete more competitively with other financial sectors in the region. Singapore was not as badly affected as its neighbours by the 1997 economic crisis in south-east Asia or the 2003 SARS virus outbreak, due in part to currency reserves estimated at US$118 billion.

Singapore's major trading partners are the USA, Malaysia, the EU, Hong Kong and Japan.

GNI – US$86,100 million (2002); US$20,690 per capita (2002)
ANNUAL AVERAGE GROWTH OF GDP – 8.1 per cent (2004 est.)
INFLATION RATE – 0.5 per cent (2003 est.)
UNEMPLOYMENT – 4.4 per cent (2004 est.)

FOREIGN DIRECT INVESTMENT – US$29,223 million (1997–2000)
IMPORTS – US$128,000 million (2003)
EXPORTS – US$144,200 million (2003)

BALANCE OF PAYMENTS
Trade – US$18,549 million surplus (2002)
Current Account – US$18,704 million surplus (2002)

Trade with UK	2003	2004
Imports from UK	£1,588,585,000	£1,717,192,000
Exports to UK	2,738,956,000	3,456,659,000

TRANSPORT INFRASTRUCTURE

There are 25.8 km of railway, connected to the Malaysian rail system by the causeway across the Straits of Johore, and 3,122 km of roads. Singapore is one of the largest and busiest seaports in the world, with six terminals, deep-water wharves and ship-repairing facilities. The international airport is at Changi, in the east of the island, with 64 airlines operating flights to 50 countries.

MEDIA

There are 19 radio and four television channels operated by the Singapore Broadcasting Corporation, and three private broadcasting stations. Singapore Press Holdings, which has close links to the ruling party, has a virtual monopoly of the newspaper industry, and publish 15 newspapers and six periodicals.

SLOVAKIA

Slovenská Republika – Slovak Republic

AREA – 48,100 sq. km. Neighbours: Poland (north), Ukraine (east), Hungary (south), Austria (west), the Czech Republic (north-west)
POPULATION – 5,423,567 (2004 est.): 87.7 per cent are ethnic Slovaks, 10.6 per cent ethnic Hungarians, 1.4 per cent Romany, 1 per cent Czech, with smaller numbers of Ruthenians, Ukrainians and Germans. The population is mainly Christian, some 60 per cent Roman Catholic and 8 per cent Protestant. Slovak is the official language, while Hungarian and Czech are also spoken
CAPITAL – ΨBratislava (population, 428,672, 2001 census), on the Danube
MAJOR CITIES – Kosice (236,093), 2001 census
CURRENCY – Koruna (Sk) of 100 halierov
NATIONAL ANTHEM – Nad Tatrou sa Blýska [Storm over the Tatras]
NATIONAL DAYS – 1 January (Establishment of Slovak Republic); 5 July (Day of the Slav Missionaries); 29 August (Slovak National Uprising); 1 September (Constitution Day)
NATIONAL FLAG – Three horizontal stripes of white, blue and red with the arms all over near the hoist
LIFE EXPECTANCY (years) – 74.19 (2004 est.)
MORTALITY RATE (per 1,000 population) – 9.48 (2004 est.)
INFANT MORTALITY (per 1,000 births) – 7.62 (2004 est.)
HIV / AIDS ADULT PREVALENCE – 0.1 per cent (2001 est.)
DEATH PENALTY – No (abolished 1990)
POPULATION GROWTH RATE – 0.14 per cent (2004 est.)

POPULATION DENSITY – 112 per sq. km (2001)
URBAN POPULATION – 58 per cent (2001)
GROSS ENROLMENT RATIO (percentage of relevant age
  group) – primary 103 per cent (2002); secondary 83
  per cent (2002); tertiary 30 per cent (2002)

CLIMATE AND TERRAIN

The Danube river plain lies in the south-west. Elsewhere the terrain is mountainous, lying in the western Carpathian range, including the Tatra and Beskid mountains to the north. Elevation extremes range from 2,655 m (Gerlachorsky Stit) at the highest point to 94 m (Bodrock River) at the lowest. The climate is continental, with warm humid summers and cold dry winters. Average temperatures range from 1°C in January to 21°C in July.

HISTORY AND POLITICS

The area was part of the kingdom of Greater Moravia in the ninth century, became part of the Hungarian Magyar empire in the tenth century and came under Austrian Habsburg rule from the 16th century. Following the dissolution of the Austro-Hungarian Empire, Slovakia became part of Czechoslovakia on 28 October 1918. Following the German annexation of Czechoslovakia in 1939, Slovakia became a nominally independent state but was exploited as part of the German war effort. After an abortive uprising in 1944, Slovakia was liberated by Soviet forces in 1945 and returned to Czechoslovakia, where a communist regime assumed power in 1948. The formation of a federal republic between the Czech lands and Slovakia was the only Prague Spring reform to survive the Soviet invasion of 1968. Following the collapse of communist rule in 1989, Slovak separatist feeling increased and the Czech and Slovak republics negotiated the dissolution of the federation into two sovereign states in 1992. Dissolution took effect on 1 January 1993 and Slovakia joined the UN.

The Movement for a Democratic Slovakia (HZDS), led by the authoritarian Vladimir Meciar, dominated the coalition governments that held office in the 1990s, pursuing nationalist and populist policies. It was ousted at the 1998 election by an alliance of liberals, centrists, left-wingers and ethnic Hungarians, which formed a coalition government under Mikulas Dzurinda of the Slovak Democratic and Christian Union (SDKU). This government, which was re-elected in 2002, introduced the constitutional and economic reforms necessary to meet the requirements for membership of NATO and the EU. Slovakia joined NATO and the EU in 2004. Its parliament ratified the EU constitution in May 2005.

After the 2002 legislative election, the HZDS remained the largest party in the National Council, but Mikulas Dzurinda remained prime minister at the head of a four-party coalition led by the SDKU. The presidential election in April 2004 was won by Ivan Gasporovic, with 59.9 per cent of the vote; he was chair of the HZDS but resigned from this position after his election.

POLITICAL SYSTEM

The 1993 constitution has been amended a few times, most recently in 1999 to allow direct elections to the presidency. The head of state is the president, directly elected for a five-year term, renewable only once. The unicameral National Council of the Slovak Republic has 150 members, who are directly elected for a four-year term by proportional representation with a 5 per cent threshold for parliamentary representation. The prime minister, who is appointed by the president, nominates the cabinet.

HEAD OF STATE
President, Ivan Gasporovic, *elected* 17 April 2004, *sworn in* 15 June 2004

SELECTED GOVERNMENT MEMBERS AS AT JULY 2005
Prime Minister, Mikulas Dzurinda
Deputy Prime Ministers, Pal Csaky; Pavol Rusko
  (Economy); Ivan Miklos *(Finance)*; Daniel Lipsic
  (Justice)
Defence, Juraj Liska
Foreign Affairs, Eduard Kukan
Interior, Vladimir Palko

EMBASSY OF THE SLOVAK REPUBLIC
25 Kensington Palace Gardens, London W8 4QY
T 020-7313 6470
Ambassador Extraordinary and Plenipotentiary, HE
  Frantisek Dlhopolcek, apptd 2000

BRITISH EMBASSY
Panska 16, SK-811 01 Bratislava
T (+421) (2) 5998 2000 E bebra@internet.sk
Ambassador Extraordinary and Plenipotentiary, HE Judith
  Macgregor, apptd 2005

BRITISH COUNCIL
PO Box 68, Panska 17, SK-814 99 Bratislava
T (+421) (2) 5443 1074 / 5443 1185
E information.centre@britishcouncil.sk
Director, Huw Jones

DEFENCE

The Army has 271 main battle tanks, 120 armoured personnel carriers and 404 armoured infantry fighting vehicles. The Air Force has 71 combat aircraft and 19 attack helicopters.
MILITARY EXPENDITURE – 1.9 per cent of GDP (2003)
MILITARY PERSONNEL – 18,020: Army 12,860, Air
  Force 5,160; Paramilitaries 4,700
CONSCRIPTION DURATION – Six months

ECONOMY AND TRADE

From independence until mid-1994 Slovakia faced widespread economic difficulties that were caused, partially, by the structure of its centrally planned and inefficiently managed economy. The centre-right coalition in power since 1998 introduced economic reforms and good progress has been made in macroeconomic stabilisation and structural reform and privatisation. As a result, foreign investment has increased. The reforms have caused some hardship, although unemployment is falling from the 2003 peak of 20 per cent.

Natural resources include brown coal, natural gas, iron ore, antimony, lead and zinc. Major industries include foodstuffs, metal production, gas and oil, textiles, transport vehicles and rubber. The main trading partners include Germany, Austria, the Czech Republic and Italy.
GNI – US$21,300 million (2002); US$3,970 per capita
  (2002)
ANNUAL AVERAGE GROWTH OF GDP – 5.3 per cent
  (2004 est.)
INFLATION RATE – 8.6 per cent (2003 est.)
UNEMPLOYMENT – 20 per cent (2003 est.)
TOTAL EXTERNAL DEBT – US$9,462 million (2000 est.)

FOREIGN DIRECT INVESTMENT – US$3,133 million (1997–2000)

IMPORTS – US$24,000 million (2003)

EXPORTS – US$22,000 million (2003)

BALANCE OF PAYMENTS

Trade – US$895 million deficit (2000)

Current Account – US$694 million deficit (2000)

Trade with UK	2003	2004
Imports from UK	£236,419,000	£81,871,000
Exports to UK	261,664,000	98,294,000

TRANSPORT INFRASTRUCTURE

Slovakia has a total of 42,717 km of roads, of which 37,036 km are surfaced (including 296 km of expressways). There are 3,668 km of railways, and 172 km of navigable waterway on the Danube. The main Danube ports are Bratislava and Komarno, and the principal airport is at Bratislava.

MEDIA

The two main television providers are Slovak TV (public) and TV Markiza (private). All three major daily newspapers are privately owned and there are more than 20 private radio stations, in addition to the public broadcaster Slovak Radio, which operates five national networks and an external service.

SLOVENIA

Republika Slovenija – Republic of Slovenia

AREA – 20,100 sq. km. Neighbours: Austria (north), Hungary (north-east), Croatia (east and south), Italy (west)

POPULATION – 2,011,473 (2004 est.). The population is mostly Slovenian. There are small Hungarian (0.5 per cent) and Italian (0.1 per cent) minorities, together with a Romany population. The main religion is Roman Catholicism. Slovene is the official language, together with Hungarian and Italian in ethnically mixed regions

CAPITAL – Ljubljana (population, 257,338, 2002 census)

MAJOR CITIES – Maribor

CURRENCY – Tolar (SIT) of 100 stotin

NATIONAL ANTHEM – Zdravljica [A toast]

NATIONAL DAY – 25 June (Statehood Day)

NATIONAL FLAG – Three horizontal stripes of white, blue and red, with the arms in the upper hoist

LIFE EXPECTANCY (years) – 75.93 (2004 est.)

MORTALITY RATE (per 1,000 population) – 10.15 (2004 est.)

INFANT MORTALITY (per 1,000 births) – 4.5 (2004 est.)

HIV / AIDS ADULT PREVALENCE – 0.1 per cent (2001 est.)

DEATH PENALTY – No (abolished 1989)

POPULATION GROWTH RATE – –0.01 per cent (2004 est.)

POPULATION DENSITY – 98 per sq. km (2002)

URBAN POPULATION – 49 per cent (2001)

MILITARY EXPENDITURE – 1.4 per cent of GDP (2003)

MILITARY PERSONNEL – Army 6,550; Paramilitaries 4,500

CONSCRIPTION DURATION – Seven months

CLIMATE AND TERRAIN

The terrain is mountainous and elevation extremes range from 2,864 m (Triglav) at the highest point to 0 m (Adriatic Sea) at the lowest. The only low-lying areas are in the valleys of the rivers Sava and Drava, and on the short Adriatic coastline. Average temperatures in Ljubljana range from 0°C in January to 22°C in July.

HISTORY AND POLITICS

Settled by Slovenes in the sixth century, the area was later controlled by Slavs, Franks and Hungarians before coming under the control of the Austrian Habsburg empire in the 14th centuries. Following the collapse of the Austro-Hungarian Empire in 1918, Slovenia became part of the Kingdom of the Serbs, Croats and Slovenes (later Yugoslavia). German forces invaded Yugoslavia in 1941 and Slovenia was divided between Germany, Italy and Hungary. In 1945 it was reformed as a constituent republic of Yugoslavia, which became a communist state in 1946. After a dispute with Italy and nine years of international administration, the Adriatic coast and hinterland were returned to Slovenia in 1954, while Italy retained Trieste.

Slovenia's fears of Serbian dominance led the Slovene Assembly in 1989 to amend the republican constitution to allow secession. The first multiparty elections, held in April 1990, were won by the pro-independence 'Demos' coalition. In a referendum in December 1990, 88 per cent of the electorate voted for independence, which was declared on 25 June 1991. A ten-day war with the Yugoslav National Army followed before the army withdrew under the terms of an EU-brokered cease-fire. Slovenia joined the UN in 1992, and in 2004 became a member of NATO and the EU. The National Assembly ratified the EU constitution in February 2005.

The Liberal Democracy of Slovenia party (LDS) was the major party in every government, all coalitions, from 1991 to 2004. In the 2004 legislative election, the Slovenian Democratic Party became the largest party in the National Assembly and its leader, Janez Jansa, formed a four-party coalition government. Janez Drnovsek, the LDS candidate, was elected president in 2002, with 56.5 per cent of the vote.

POLITICAL SYSTEM

Under the 1991 constitution, the head of state is the president, directly elected for a five-year term. Executive power is vested in the prime minister and cabinet. The unicameral legislature, the National Assembly, has 90 members directly elected for a four-year term on a proportional representation basis, with one seat each reserved for the Italian and Hungarian minorities. The National Council, which has 40 members, has an advisory role.

HEAD OF STATE

President, Janez Drnovsek, *elected* 1 December 2002

SELECTED GOVERNMENT MEMBERS *as at August 2005*

President of the Executive Council (Prime Minister), Janez Jansa

Defence, Karl Erjavek

Finance, Andrej Bajuk

Foreign Affairs, Dimitrij Rupel

Internal Affairs, Dragutin Mate

EMBASSY OF THE REPUBLIC OF SLOVENIA
10 Little College Street, London SW1P 3SH
T 020 7222 5400
Ambassador Extraordinary and Plenipotentiary, HE Iztok
   Mirosic, apptd 2004

BRITISH EMBASSY
4th Floor, Trg Republike 3, SI-1000 Ljubljana
T (+386) (1) 200 3910 E info@british-embassy.si
Ambassador Extraordinary and Plenipotentiary, HE
   Timothy Simmons, apptd 2004

BRITISH COUNCIL
Cankarjevo nabrezje 27, SI-1000 Ljubljana
T (+386) (1) 200 0130 E info@britishcouncil.si
Director, Steve Green

ECONOMY AND TRADE

Always the most prosperous and the most politically
liberal republic of the former Yugoslavia, Slovenia's
transition to a market economy has been relatively
smooth. The privatisation process was completed in 1998
and it has successfully re-orientated its exports towards
Western markets. Its main trading partners are Germany,
Italy, France, Austria and Croatia. In 2002 agriculture
contributed 3.1 per cent to the total GDP, the
manufacturing industry 32.7 per cent and the service
industries 64.2 per cent. The main agricultural products
are potatoes, wheat, corn, sugar cane and grapes. The
major manufacturing sectors are metalworking,
electronics, textiles, automobiles and automotive parts,
chemicals, glass products and food-processing. The tourist
industry is a major earner, with 1,957,000 visitors in
2000.
GNI – US$20,400 million (2002); US$10,370 per capita
   (2002)
ANNUAL AVERAGE GROWTH OF GDP – 3.9 per cent
   (2004 est.)
INFLATION RATE – 7.4 per cent (2002 est.)
UNEMPLOYMENT – 6.4 per cent (2004 est.)
FOREIGN DIRECT INVESTMENT – US$843 million
   (1997–2000)
IMPORTS – US$14,000 million (2003)
EXPORTS – US$13,000 million (2003)

BALANCE OF PAYMENTS
Trade – US$624 million deficit (2003)
Current Account – US$15 million surplus (2003)

Trade with UK	2003	2004
Imports from UK	£158,931,000	£55,465,000
Exports to UK	171,807,000	63,948,000

TRANSPORT INFRASTRUCTURE

There are 20,128 km of roads and 1,201 km of railways,
of which 499 km are electrified. Important international
road and rail communications cross the country from west
to east and north to south. There are international airports
at Ljubljana, Maribor and Portoroz (Adriatic Coast).
Koper is the main port, receiving shipments from
landlocked countries such as Austria, Hungary, the Czech
Republic and Slovakia.

EDUCATION

Education is free of charge and compulsory between the
ages of six and 14. There are 44 colleges and two
universities (Ljubljana and Maribor).

ILLITERACY RATE – (m) 0.3 per cent; (f) 0.4 per cent
   (2000)
GROSS ENROLMENT RATIO (percentage of relevant age
   group) – primary 100 per cent (2002); secondary 106
   per cent (2002); tertiary 61 per cent (2002)

MEDIA

The main newspapers are privately owned, and the
broadcasting sector is a mix of public and private
ownership. The television market is mainly shared
between the public service RTV Slovenia and the private
stations Pop TV and Kanal A. About two-thirds of
households are connected to cable or satellite.

SOLOMON ISLANDS

AREA – 28,896 sq. km
POPULATION – 523,617 (2004 est.) English is the
   official language but there are over 80 local languages
CAPITAL – ΨHoniara (population, 49,107)
CURRENCY – Solomon Islands dollar (SI$) of 100 cents
NATIONAL ANTHEM – God bless our Solomon Islands
NATIONAL DAY – 7 July (Independence Day)
NATIONAL FLAG – Blue over green divided by a diagonal
   yellow band, with five white stars in the top left quarter
LIFE EXPECTANCY (years) – 72.38 (2004 est.)
MORTALITY RATE (per 1,000 population) – 4.04
   (2004 est.)
INFANT MORTALITY (per 1,000 births) – 22.09
   (2004 est.)
DEATH PENALTY – No (abolished 1966)
POPULATION GROWTH RATE – 2.76 per cent
   (2004 est.)
POPULATION DENSITY – 15 per sq. km (1999)

CLIMATE AND TERRAIN

Forming a scattered archipelago of mountainous islands
and low-lying coral atolls in the south-west Pacific
Ocean, the Solomon Islands stretches about 1,448 km in
a south-easterly direction from the Shortland Islands to
the Santa Cruz islands. The six biggest islands are
Choiseul, New Georgia, Santa Isabel, Guadalcanal,
Malaita and Makira (San Cristobal). They are
characterised by thickly forested mountain ranges
intersected by deep, narrow valleys. Elevation extremes
range from 2,447 m (Mt Makarakomburu) at the highest
point to 0 m (Pacific Ocean) at the lowest. The climate is
tropical and the average temperature in Honiara is 27°C.
The islands are occasionaly prone to earthquakes,
tsunamis and volcanic activity.

HISTORY AND POLITICS

The islands were discovered by the Spanish in 1568 and
visited by Europeans intermittently for about 300 years,
following the inauguration of sugar plantations in
Queensland and Fiji (which created a need for labour),
and the arrival of missionaries and traders. Britain
declared a protectorate in 1893 over the southern
Solomons, adding the Santa Cruz group in 1898 and
1899. The Shortland Islands were transferred from
Germany to Britain by treaty in 1900. The islands were
occupied by the Japanese in 1942, and recaptured by US
forces in 1943 after fierce fighting, especially on
Guadalcanal. Campaigning for self-government began
after the Second World War and was achieved in 1976,
and independence in July 1978.
   Ethnic tension on Guadalcanal between native people

and migrants from another island began in 1998 and descended into conflict between two rival militias. The government was unable to stem the violence, and in an attempted coup in June 2000, one militia held the prime minister hostage and forced him to resign. A fragile peace began with an agreement signed in October 2000, allowing elections to be held in 2001. But escalating economic and social problems in early 2002 led to growing lawlessness. Violence and disorder increased until, in June 2003, the government requested peace-keeping assistance from other countries in the region. An Australian-led peace-keeping force deployed in July 2003, restoring order and disarming the militias.

Threats by some islands to secede led a conference of provincial governmental heads in November 2000 to call for the introduction of a federal system of government. In the 2001 legislative election, the People's Alliance Party gained 20 seats in the National Parliament. The party's parliamentary leader, Sir Allan Kemakeza, was elected prime minister on 17 December and the new cabinet was sworn in on 19 December.

POLITICAL SYSTEM
Under the 1978 constitution, the Solomon Islands is a constitutional monarchy. The head of state is the British monarch, represented by a governor-general, who is chosen by the National Parliament. The unicameral National Parliament has 50 members who are directly elected for a four-year term. The prime minister is elected by the parliament from among the members, and nominates the cabinet, who are formally appointed by the governor-general.
Governor-General, Nathaniel Waena, apptd 2004

SELECTED GOVERNMENT MEMBERS *as at August 2005*
Prime Minister, Sir Allan Kemakesa
Deputy Prime Minister, Finance, Snyder Rini
Foreign Affairs and Trade Relations, Laurie Hok Si Chan
Home Affairs, Nelson Kile

HIGH COMMISSION OF THE SOLOMON ISLANDS
Avenue Edourd Lacomble 17, B-1040 Brussels
T (+32) (2) 2732 7085
E siembassy@compuserve.com
High Commissioner, HE Robert Sisilo, apptd 1996

BRITISH HIGH COMMISSION
Telekom House, Mendana Avenue, Honiara
T (+677) 21705/6 E bhc@solomon.com.sb
High Commissioner, HE Richard Lyne, apptd 2005

ECONOMY AND TRADE
The five years of conflict have left the economy virtually bankrupt, increasing the country's dependency on foreign aid, principally from Australia. The main export commodity is timber, which is subject to world price fluctuations. It is hoped that palm oil production and gold mining can be resumed. Principal exports are timber, fish, palm oil, copra and cocoa. The main imports are foodstuffs, consumer goods, machinery and transport materials.
GNI – US$253 million (2002); US$590 per capita (2002)
ANNUAL AVERAGE GROWTH OF GDP – 5.8 per cent (2003 est.)
INFLATION RATE – 1.8 per cent (2001 est.)
TOTAL EXTERNAL DEBT – US$137 million (2001 est.)
IMPORTS – US$48 million (2002)
EXPORTS – US$58 million (2002)

BALANCE OF PAYMENTS
Trade – US$55 million surplus (1999)
Current Account – US$21 million surplus (1999)

Trade with UK	2003	2004
Imports from UK	£94,000	£544,000
Exports to UK	42,000	73,000

TRANSPORT INFRASTRUCTURE
There are 1,360 km of roads, of which only 34 km are surfaced. The main ports are Honiara and Yandina. Solomon Airlines operates international services to other Pacific states and Australia. Air Niugini flies from Port Moresby to Honiara.

MEDIA
The Solomon Islands Broadcasting Corporation (SIBC) operates a public radio service. There are no television services on the islands, although external satellite services can be received.

SOMALIA

Jamhuuriyadda Dimoqraadiya Soomaaliya – Somali Democratic Republic

AREA – 637,657 sq. km. Neighbours: Djibouti (north-west), Ethiopia (west), Kenya (south-west)
POPULATION – 8,304,601 (2004 est.). Somali and Arabic are the official languages. English and Italian are also spoken
CAPITAL – ΨMogadishu (population, 525,000, 1995 estimate)
MAJOR CITIES – ΨBerbera; Boroma; Burao; Hargeysa; ΨKisimaayo
CURRENCY – Somali shilling of 100 cents
NATIONAL FLAG – Five-pointed white star on a blue ground
LIFE EXPECTANCY (years) – 47.71 (2004 est.)
MORTALITY RATE (per 1,000 population) – 17.3 (2004 est.)
INFANT MORTALITY (per 1,000 births) – 118.52 (2004 est.)
HIV / AIDS ADULT PREVALENCE – 1 per cent (2001 est.)
DEATH PENALTY – Yes
POPULATION GROWTH RATE – 3.41 per cent (2004 est.)
POPULATION DENSITY – 15 per sq. km (2002)

CLIMATE AND TERRAIN
The terrain is mostly arid, flat or undulating plateau, rising to hills in the north. Elevation extremes range from 2,416 m (Shimbiris) at the highest point to 0 m (Indian Ocean) at the lowest. The climate is tropical, influenced by the north-east and south-west monsoons. There are two wet seasons, from March to May and October to November. Average temperatures in Mogadishu are an almost constant 33°C.

HISTORY AND POLITICS
Arab settlement from the eighth century onwards introduced Islam and established coastal trading towns that developed into sultanates. European contact began in the early 16th century, Italian, French and British interest intensifying after the Suez Canal opened in 1869. Protectorates were established in the north by the British and in the centre (subsequently taking in the south) by the

Italians in the 1880s. Italian Somalia was returned to Italian administration as a UN Trust Territory in 1950. The two protectorates became independent and merged to form the United Republic of Somalia in July 1960.

In 1969, the armed forces seized power in a coup led by Maj.-Gen. Muhammad Siad Barre, and established a socialist Islamic regime which became a one-party state in 1979. Insurrection in the north began in 1978 and by the late 1980s opposition to the government had developed into a civil war which affected much of the country. The rebels captured Mogadishu in January 1991, forcing Siad Barre to flee. Attempts to establish a new central government failed as political and clan rivalries split the former rebels, and the situation degenerated into civil war between rival 'warlords'. Part of northern Somalia seceded in 1991, declaring independence as the Somaliland Republic under the Somali National Movement (SNM).

The fighting had devastated large areas of the south, exacerbating famine conditions in 1992. UN relief convoys were attacked and attempts by international peace-keeping forces to secure aid distribution routes met with limited success. All foreign troops were withdrawn in early 1995, after which the state effectively disintegrated amid clan-based factional conflict. The north-east of the country proclaimed its autonomy as the region of Puntland in 1998.

A peace plan proposed by Djibouti in 1999 led to the establishment of transitional institutions in August 2000, including a transitional national assembly, which appointed Abdulkiassim Salat Hassan as president. A prime minister and a government with members drawn from different clans were appointed in autumn 2000. The principal warlords were hostile to the transitional regime and in March 2001 held a reconciliation conference at which they named a rival council. The transitional government's attempts to assert its authority led to further fighting in the south of the country in 2001, and in April 2002 warlords in the south-west unilaterally declared the autonomy of six districts.

In October 2002 internationally backed peace talks began in Kenya and a cease-fire agreement was signed by 21 warring factions and the transitional national government, under which hostilities would end for the duration of the talks. The second phase of the peace talks began in Nairobi in February 2003 but was plagued by boycotts and disputes. In January 2004, all the parties signed an agreement to establish a federal government and a new transitional parliament, which would appoint the federal president and hold power until elections in 2007. In October 2004 the interim assembly elected Col. Abdullahi Yusuf Ahmed as president and an interim government had been formed by January 2005. Members of the transitional institutions started to return to Somalia from Kenya only in mid-2005 because of the security situation and internal disagreement over the location of the seat of government.

SECESSION

The northern-based Somali National Movement (SNM) took control of the north-west (the former British Somaliland protectorate) after Siad Barre's deposition and in May 1991 declared unilateral independence as the 'Somaliland Republic'. A referendum on a new constitution, which confirmed the independence of Somaliland, was held on 31 May 2001 and was approved by 97.09 per cent of the voters. The leaders of the regime have refused to take part in the peace process since 1999 and have not signed the 2004 peace agreement.

In July 1998, an autonomous administration was proclaimed in north-eastern Somalia, calling the region Puntland. Col. Abdullahi Yusuf Ahmed was named as 'president' of the region in 1998, and refused to relinquish the post after Jama Ali Jama was elected 'president' in November 2001. By May 2002 his supporters had taken control of the whole region and Abdullahi remained in power. The leaders of the Puntland regime have taken part in the peace process, signing the 2004 peace agreement. Abdullahi was elected national president in October 2004 and left Puntland for the south in July 2005.

HEAD OF STATE
President, Muhammad Abdi Yusuf, *sworn in* 10 October 2004

SELECTED GOVERNMENT MEMBERS *as at August 2005*
Prime Minister, Ali Muhammed Ghedi
Deputy Prime Minister, Mahamoud Mohamed
Deputy Prime Minister, Finance, Salim Aliow Ibrow
Deputy Prime Minister, Home Affairs, Hussein Mohammed Aideed
Defence, Abdirrahman Mahmud Ali
Foreign Affairs, Abdullahi Shaykh Isma'il

ECONOMY AND TRADE

Livestock-raising is the main occupation and there is a modest export trade in livestock, skins and hides. Italy, the Gulf states and Saudi Arabia import the bulk of the banana crop, the biggest export, which accounts for approximately 40 per cent of exports. The principal imports are machinery and transport equipment, industrial goods and foodstuffs.

Although the infrastructure, education and health services have suffered badly from the fighting and the years without a central government, lack of regulation has led to a thriving entrepreneurial economy in some sectors, such as telecommunications; the three main telecommunications companies are co-operating to fund the internet infrastructure. Businesses have also built small airstrips and use natural harbours to trade with overseas countries. The main factor inhibiting trade is the lack of a central bank.

ANNUAL AVERAGE GROWTH OF GDP – 2.8 per cent (2004 est.)

TOTAL EXTERNAL DEBT – US$2,562 million (2000 est.)

Trade with UK	2003	2004
Imports from UK	£3,597,000	£7,105,000
Exports to UK	76,000	32,000

TRANSPORT INFRASTRUCTURE

Somalia has a total of 22,100 km of roads, of which 2,608 km are surfaced. The main ports include Berbera, Kismaayo, Merca and Mogadishu, although these have all been damaged in the war. The principal airport is at Hargeisa, and there are five other airports with surfaced runways.

MEDIA

Many new print and broadcast outlets emerged after Siad Barre was ousted in 1991, but most were tied to one or another of the country's warring factions. Even though recent years have seen the emergence of stronger regional media, broadcasters and journalists operate in a dangerous environment, limiting their ability to report freely and objectively. Many Somalis rely on foreign broadcasts for their news: CNN and Al-Jazeera are available in some parts of the country.

SOUTH AFRICA

Republic of South Africa

AREA – 1,221,000 sq. km. Neighbours: Namibia (north-west), Botswana and Zimbabwe (north), Mozambique and Swaziland (north-east), Lesotho (surrounded by South Africa)

POPULATION – 47,718,530 (2004 est.); 78 per cent African, 10.1 per cent white, 8.6 per cent mixed race, 2.5 per cent Indian/Asian. The constitution designates 11 official languages: Afrikaans (spoken by 14.4 per cent as a first language); English (8.6 per cent); IsiNdebele (1.5 per cent); IsiXhosa (17.9 per cent); IsiZulu (22.9 per cent); Sepedi (9.2 per cent); Sosetho (7.7 per cent); SiSwati (2.5 per cent); Setswana (8.2 per cent); Tshivenda (2.2 per cent); Xitsonga (4.4 per cent). Afrikaans and English are to remain the languages of administration although any citizen may correspond official business in his own language. The majority (75 per cent) of the population is Christian. There are also Hindus (1.4 per cent), Muslims (1.4 per cent) and Jews (0.2 per cent), as well as native religions (21 per cent)

CAPITAL – The seat of the government is Tshwane (Pretoria (population 1,800,000, 1999 estimate)); the seat of the legislature is Cape Town (population, 3,088,028, 1999 estimate); the seat of the judiciary is Bloemfontein (467,400, 1999 estimate)

MAJOR CITIES – ΨDurban; ΨEast London; Johannesburg; Pietermaritzburg; ΨPort Elizabeth

CURRENCY – Rand (R) of 100 cents

NATIONAL ANTHEMS – Nkosi sikelel' iAfrika [God bless Africa]; Die stem van Suid-Afrika [The call of South Africa]

NATIONAL DAY – 27 April (Freedom Day)

NATIONAL FLAG – Divided red over blue by a horizontal white-fimbriated green Y; in the hoist is a black triangle fimbriated in yellow

LIFE EXPECTANCY (years) – 44.19 (2004 est.)

MORTALITY RATE (per 1,000 population) – 20.54 (2004 est.)

INFANT MORTALITY (per 1,000 births) – 62.18 (2004 est.)

HIV / AIDS ADULT PREVALENCE – 21.5 per cent (2004 est.)

DEATH PENALTY – No (abolished 1997)

POPULATION BELOW POVERTY LINE – 50 per cent (2000 est.)

POPULATION GROWTH RATE – –0.25 per cent (2004 est.)

POPULATION DENSITY – 37 per sq. km (2002)

URBAN POPULATION – 52.6 per cent (2002)

CLIMATE AND TERRAIN

South Africa occupies the southernmost part of the African continent from the courses of the Limpopo, Marico, Molopo, Nosop and Orange rivers to the Cape of Good Hope, with the exception of Lesotho, Swaziland and the extreme south of Mozambique. To the west, east and south lie the south Atlantic and southern Indian Oceans. Some 1,920 km to the south-east of Cape Town lie Prince Edward and Marion Islands, part of South Africa since 1947. The country lies on a high plateau

fringed by mountains, including the Drakensberg mountains, with lower-lying strips along the coast. Elevation extremes range from 3,408 m (Njesuthi) at the highest point to 0 m (Atlantic Ocean) at the lowest. The climate is temperate and is influenced by the warm Agulhas current from Mozambique. Average temperatures in Tshwane (Pretoria) range from 3°C in June to 29°C in January.

HISTORY AND POLITICS

Hunter-gatherers, the San (Bushmen) and Khoikhoi (Hottentots), inhabited southern Africa from c.8000 BC. By the eighth century AD, Bantu-speaking peoples had arrived from the north and settled. The Portuguese navigator Bartolomeu Días charted the coast in 1488 and the Dutch founded the colony of the Cape of Good Hope in 1652. The British arrived in 1795, occupying the Cape after Revolutionary France had conquered the Netherlands, and the colony was ceded to Britain in 1806. From 1836 the Boers (descendants of Dutch settlers) migrated north-east in the Great Trek to escape British rule, and founded the republic of Natal in 1839; the British annexed Natal in 1844, made it a colony in 1856 and added Zululand to it in 1897 after victory in the Zulu wars. The Boer republics of Transvaal (founded 1852) and Orange Free State (founded 1854) were recognised by Britain in 1853–4.

The discovery in the Boer republics of diamonds (1866) and gold (1886), and the Boers' need for British assistance in defeating the Zulus in the 1870s, led to disputes and political tension between them that eventually resulted in the Boer Wars of 1880–1 and 1899–1902. After the British victory in the Second Boer War, Transvaal and the Orange Free State became British colonies. The four self-governing colonies were united in 1910 to form the Union of South Africa, with dominion status. It became a sovereign state within the Commonwealth in 1931. South Africa left the Commonwealth and became a republic on 31 May 1961, largely as a result of international condemnation of the Sharpeville massacre.

The Afrikaner National Party came to power in 1948 and adopted a policy of apartheid ('separateness'), which it pursued until 1991. As a result, South Africa's social and political structure came to be based on racial segregation, with separate institutions and facilities for different racial groups. The African National Congress (ANC) and other opposition groups mounted a civil disobedience campaign that culminated in the Sharpeville massacre in 1960, following which most opposition groups were banned. Internal opposition continued, with strikes and violence in the 1980s leading to the declaration of a state of emergency in 1985. Internationally, the country became isolated as economic and cultural sanctions were imposed.

In 1984, a new constitution extended the franchise to mixed race and Asian people, but the progressive dismantling of apartheid began with the desegregation of public facilities in 1989. This was followed by the lifting of the bans on the ANC and other anti-apartheid groups and the release from prison of ANC leader Nelson Mandela (1990), and the effective abolition of the laws implementing apartheid in 1991. Negotiations between the government, the ANC and other political and civic groups reached agreement in 1991 on the establishment of an inter-racial administration and the formation of a five-year coalition government following multiracial elections. In 1993 the franchise was extended to all adults, and the first multiracial elections took place on 26–29 April 1994. The ANC won a majority in both houses of parliament, and Nelson Mandela was elected president. South Africa rejoined the Commonwealth and took its UN seat again in 1994.

The parliament passed two significant pieces of legislation to settle the legacy of the apartheid era. The first, in November 1994, restored the rights of those dispossessed of their land, and the second, in June 1995, established the Truth Commission, whose remit is to assess confessions, grant amnesties for political crimes and set compensation for victims.

In 2003, after years of denial of the problem, the government approved a programme to tackle the high levels of HIV/AIDS infection in the country. Other problems include the lawlessness, social disruption and lack of education that resulted from apartheid and opposition to it.

The ANC has won both the legislative elections held since 1994, increasing its majority each time. In the 2004 election, it won 279 seats in the National Assembly, and majorities in all the provincial assemblies. As a result, the ANC's candidate holds the presidency; Thabo Mbeki was elected to succeed Nelson Mandela in 1999 and was re-elected in 2004.

POLITICAL SYSTEM
Under the 1997 constitution, the executive president is elected by the National Assembly for a five-year term, renewable only once. The president, who is responsible to parliament, appoints the cabinet. The bicameral parliament consists of the National Assembly, the lower house, and the National Council of Provinces. The National Assembly has 400 members directly elected by proportional representation for a five-year term. The National Council of Provinces has 90 members, ten for each province, elected by the provincial legislatures for a five-year term.

South Africa is divided into nine provinces (Eastern Cape, Free State, KwaZulu/Natal, Gauteng, Limpopo, Mpumalanga, North-West, Northern Cape, Western Cape). Each province has its own premier, legislature and constitution.

HEAD OF STATE
President, Commander-in-Chief of the Armed Forces, Thabo Mbeki, *elected by parliament* 14 June 1999, *sworn in* 16 June 1999, *re-elected* 24 April 2004
Executive Deputy President, Phumzile Mlambo-Ngucka

SELECTED GOVERNMENT MEMBERS *as at August 2005*
Defence, Mosiua Lekota
Finance, Trevor Manuel
Foreign Affairs, Nkosazana Dlamini-Zuma
Home Affairs, Nosiriwe Mapisa-Ngakula

HIGH COMMISSION FOR THE REPUBLIC OF SOUTH AFRICA
South Africa House, Trafalgar Square, London WC2N 5DP
T 020-7451 7299
High Commissioner, HE Dr Lindiwe Mabuza, apptd 2001

BRITISH HIGH COMMISSION
255 Hill Street, Arcadia 0002 Pretoria
T (+27) (12) 421 7800
91 Parliament Street, Cape Town, 8001
T (+27) (21) 405 2400 E britain@icon.co.za
High Commissioner, HE Paul Boateng, apptd 2005

BRITISH COUNCIL
Ground Floor, Forum I, Braampark, 33 Hoofd Street, Braamfontein, Johannesburg 2001
T (+27) (11) 718 4300 E information@british council.org.za
Director, Rosemary Arnott

DEFENCE
The new South African National Defence Force (SANDF) was created from the merger of the South African Defence Forces (SADF), the Umkhonto we Sizwe (MK) armed wing of the ANC, the Azanian People's Liberation Army (APLA) of the Pan Africanist Congress of Azania, and the defence forces of the four former independent homelands.

The Army has 167 main battle tanks, 810 armoured personnel carriers and 1,200 armoured infantry fighting vehicles. The Navy has three submarines and eight patrol and coastal vessels at two bases. The Air Force has 50 combat aircraft and 12 armed helicopters.
MILITARY EXPENDITURE – 1.6 per cent of GDP (2003)
MILITARY PERSONNEL – 49,750: Army 36,000, Navy 4,500, Air Force 9,250

ECONOMY AND TRADE
South Africa is rich in natural resources and its well-developed industries and agriculture thrived despite the sanctions of the apartheid era. Mining is of great importance, employing more than 400,000 people in 2000 and providing the largest source of foreign exchange. The principal minerals produced are gold, coal, diamonds, copper, iron ore, manganese, lime and limestone, uranium, platinum, fluorspar, andalusite, zinc, zirconium, vanadium, titanium and chrome. South Africa is the world's largest producer of gold, platinum, diamonds, manganese, chrome and vanadium, and has the world's largest reserves of chrome ore, manganese, vanadium and andalusite.

Agriculture, forestry and fishing accounted for 3.2 per cent of GDP in 2000. Over 70 per cent of land is pasture so livestock farming is widespread. Principal crops are maize, sugar cane, fruits and vegetables, wheat, sorghum, sunflower seeds and groundnuts. Cotton is widely grown, and viticulture is also widespread.

The manufacturing industries, concentrated most heavily around Johannesburg, Pretoria and the major ports, process foodstuffs, metals and non-metallic mineral products, produce oil from coal, and also produce beverages and tobacco, motor vehicles, chemicals and chemical products, machinery, textiles and clothing, and paper and paper products. Industry contributed 30.9 per cent of GDP in 2000.

Energy production is based upon coal and natural gas and the production of synthetic liquid fuel from coal. One nuclear power station is in operation and others are planned. South Africa exports electricity through its electricity grid connections to all states in southern Africa.

The tourism industry accounts for 3.4 per cent of GDP. In 2000, 5.9 million foreign tourists visited South Africa.

Principal exports are gold, base metals and metal products, coal, diamonds, food (especially fruit) and wool. Principal imports are machinery, chemicals, motor vehicles, metals and metal products, food, inedible raw materials and textiles. The main trading partners are Germany, the USA, the UK, Italy and Japan.
GNI – US$113,400 million (2002); US$2,500 per capita (2002)
ANNUAL AVERAGE GROWTH OF GDP – 1.9 per cent (2003 est.)
INFLATION RATE – 5.8 per cent (2003 est.)

UNEMPLOYMENT – 31.2 per cent (2003 est.)
TOTAL EXTERNAL DEBT – US$36,097 million
(2003 est.)
FOREIGN DIRECT INVESTMENT – US$4,612 million
(1997–2000)
IMPORTS – US$41,000 million (2003)
EXPORTS – US$36,500 million (2003)

BALANCE OF PAYMENTS
Trade – US$3,701 million surplus (2003)
Current Account – US$1,456 million deficit (2003)

Trade with UK	2003	2004
Imports from UK	£1,757,340,000	£1,883,369,000
Exports to UK	3,026,357,701	3,348,687,000

TRANSPORT INFRASTRUCTURE

The country has 22,298 km of railways and 362,099 km
of roads, of which 73,506 km are surfaced (including
2,032 km of expressways). There are international
airports at Johannesburg, Durban and Cape Town. South
African Airways operates international services to Europe,
South America, the Far East, Africa, Australia and the
USA, and it is the principal operator of domestic flights.
Durban is the largest seaport. Other major ports are Cape
Town, Port Elizabeth, East London, Saldanha Mossel Bay
and Richards Bay.

EDUCATION

Higher education is provided at 21 universities and 15
other tertiary-level colleges.
ILLITERACY RATE – (m) 14.0 per cent; (f) 15.4 per cent
(2000)
GROSS ENROLMENT RATIO (percentage of relevant age
group) – primary 105 per cent (2002); secondary 86
per cent (2002); tertiary 15 per cent (2002)

MEDIA AND CULTURE

The South African Broadcasting Corporation (SABC) is a
major state-owned television and radio broadcaster while
Channel Africa (owned by SABC) is an external radio
service that reaches the entire continent. *The Star* is
Johannesburg's oldest daily newspaper, while the *Sunday
Times* is the longest running weekly title. *Beeld* is a
popular Afrikaans daily title.

South Africa is home to a diversity of cultures, and
black cultures – such as Zulu, Xhosa and Ndebele – are
reviving after suppression during the apartheid years.
Celebrated figures include the writers J. M. Coetzee (b.
1940), winner of the Nobel Prize for Literature in 2003,
and Nadine Gordimer (b. 1923), winner of the Nobel
Prize for Literature in 1991. Desmond Tutu (b. 1931) was
the winner of the Nobel Peace Prize in 1984.

SPAIN

Reino de España – Kingdom of Spain

AREA – 499,400 sq. km. Neighbours: Portugal (west),
France and Andorra (north-east)
POPULATION – 40,280,780 (2004 est.): 96 per cent
Catholic, 1 per cent Muslim. Castilian Spanish is the
official language, although Basque, Catalan, Galician
and Valencian, a dialect of Catalan, are spoken and
have official status in the autonomous regions where
they are spoken
CAPITAL – Madrid (population, 5,086,635, 2001)

MAJOR CITIES – ΨBarcelona; ΨValencia; ΨMálaga;
Sevilla; Zaragoza
CURRENCY – Euro (€) of 100 cents
NATIONAL ANTHEM – Marcha real Española [Spanish
royal march]
NATIONAL DAY – 12 October
NATIONAL FLAG – Three horizontal stripes of red, yellow
and red, with the yellow of double width
LIFE EXPECTANCY (years) – 79.37 (2004 est.)
MORTALITY RATE (per 1,000 population) – 9.55
(2004 est.)
INFANT MORTALITY (per 1,000 births) – 4.48
(2004 est.)
HIV / AIDS ADULT PREVALENCE – 0.5 per cent
(2001 est.)
DEATH PENALTY – No (abolished 1995)
POPULATION GROWTH RATE – 0.16 per cent
(2004 est.)
POPULATION DENSITY – 82 per sq. km (2002)
URBAN POPULATION – 78 per cent (2001)

CLIMATE AND TERRAIN

The interior of the Iberian peninsula consists of an
elevated tableland surrounded and traversed by mountain
ranges: the Pyrenees on the border with France, the
Cantabrian Mountains (north-west), the Sierra de
Guadarrama, Sierra Morena, Montes de Toledo (centre)
and the Sierra Nevada (south). The principal rivers are the
Duero, the Tajo (Tagus), the Guadiana, the Guadalquivir,
the Ebro and the Miño. Elevation extremes range from
3,718 m (Pico de Teide) at the highest point to 0 m
(Mediterranean Sea) at the lowest. The climate is
Mediterranean in the southern and eastern coastal areas,
and temperate further inland. Average temperatures in
Madrid range from 1°C in January to 31°C in July.

HISTORY AND POLITICS

The Romans conquered the Iberian peninsula in the
second century BC. It was overrun by Vandals and
Visigoths in the fifth century BC, and invaded and
occupied by Muslims from Africa in the eighth century.
Christians in the north formed small kingdoms which
reconquered the peninsula by 1492. Spain's modern form
derives from the dynastic union of the kingdoms of
Castile and Aragón in 1479. In the 16th century, Spain's
exploration and colonisation of the New World made it
one of the richest and most powerful nations in Europe,
with an empire that covered most of central and southern
America. However, a succession of costly wars and revolts
in the 17th and 18th centuries saw this empire go into
steady decline. Its central and southern American
possessions declared independence in the early 19th
century, and most other overseas possessions had been
lost by 1900.

The restoration of the Bourbon monarchy after the
Napoleonic occupation of 1808–14 initiated over a
century of political instability, with power struggles
between conservative and liberal factions in royal,
political and military circles. The dictatorship of Gen.
Primo de Rivera (1923–30) ended with the exiling of
King Alfonso XIII and the declaration of the Second
Republic in 1931. The success of moderate and religious
candidates in the 1933 elections provoked a socialist and
Catalan insurrection in 1934. A narrow victory by the
left-wing Popular Front (PF) in fresh elections in 1936 led
to an army revolt in military garrisons in Spanish
Morocco and this spread throughout Spain, led by Gen.
Francisco Franco. Civil war ensued until March 1939,

when the PF governments in Madrid and Barcelona surrendered to the Nationalists (as Gen. Franco's followers were then called). Gen. Franco became president and ruled the country until his death in 1975. His death was followed, according to his wishes, by the restoration of the monarchy, and Prince Juan Carlos of Bourbon (grandson of Alfonso XIII) became head of state as King Juan Carlos I. The first free election was held in June 1977, and a referendum in 1978 endorsed a democratic constitution.

Spain joined NATO in 1982 and the EEC in 1986, becoming a member of the euro zone in 1999. A referendum in February 2005 approved the ratification of the EU constitution.

There was strong opposition in Spain to its involvement in the 2003 Iraq war. Polling on 14 March 2004 was overshadowed by a series of explosions on commuter trains in Madrid on 11 March, which killed over 200 people. Responsibility for the attack was attributed to Islamic militants with links to al-Qa'eda. The election resulted in an unexpected victory for the Spanish Socialist Workers' Party (PSOE), with 164 seats in the Congress of Deputies and 81 seats in the Senate. José Luis Rodríguez Zapatero became prime minister and formed a minority PSOE government, which withdrew Spanish troops from Iraq by May 2004.

INSURGENCIES

The Basque separatist organisation ETA (*Euzkadi ta Azkatasuna* – Basque Nation and Liberty) has since its formation in 1959 carried out a terrorist campaign of bombings, shootings and kidnappings in an attempt to gain independence for the Basque country. ETA rejected regional autonomy for the Basque country in 1979 as insufficient and continued its campaign, but was greatly weakened in the early 1990s by increased co-operation between French and Spanish security forces. The banning of the Basque political party *Herri Batasuna*, regarded as ETA's political wing, was approved by the Supreme Court in 2003 because of its links with ETA. In May 2005, the PSOE government offered to hold peace talks with ETA if it would disarm.

POLITICAL SYSTEM

The 1978 constitution has been amended to devolve powers to the 19 autonomous regions. The head of state is a hereditary constitutional monarch. There is a bicameral general assembly *(Cortes Generales)* comprising a 350-member Congress of Deputies *(Congreso de los Diputados)* directly elected for a four-year term and a Senate *(Senado)* with 259 members, 208 directly elected and 51 appointed by the assemblies of the autonomous regions. There are 19 autonomous regions: Andalucía, Aragón, Asturias, Balearics, the Basque Country, Canary Islands, Cantabria, Castilla-La Mancha, Castilla y León, Catalonia, Ceuta, Extremadura, Galicia, Madrid, Melilla, Murcia, Navarra, La Rioja and Valencia. Each has its own legislature and government.

HEAD OF STATE

HM The King of Spain, King Juan Carlos I de Borbón, KG, GCVO, *born* 5 January 1938, *acceded to the throne* 22 November 1975

Heir, HRH The Prince of the Asturias (Príncipe Felipe Juan Pablo Alfonso y Todos los Santos), *born* 30 January 1968

SELECTED GOVERNMENT MEMBERS *as at August 2005*
Prime Minister, José Luis Rodríguez Zapatero
First Deputy Prime Minister, Cabinet Office, Government Spokesperson, Maria Teresa Fernandez de la Vega
Second Deputy Prime Minister, Economy, Pedro Solbes
Foreign Affairs, Miguel Ángel Moratinos
Interior, José Antonio Alonso

SPANISH EMBASSY
39 Chesham Place, London SW1X 8SB T 020-7235 5555
Ambassador Extraordinary and Plenipotentiary, Count Carlos Miranda

BRITISH EMBASSY
Calle de Fernando el Santo 16, E-28010 Madrid
T (+34) (91) 700 8200
Ambassador Extraordinary and Plenipotentiary, HE Stephen Wright, CMG, apptd 2003

BRITISH COUNCIL
Paseo del General Martínez, Campos 31, E-28010 Madrid
T (+34) (91) 337 3500 E madrid@britishcouncil.es
Director, Christine Melia *(acting)*

DEFENCE

The Army has 552 main battle tanks, 2,023 armoured personnel carriers and 28 attack helicopters. The Navy has six submarines, one aircraft carrier, 16 frigates, 37 patrol and coastal vessels, 17 combat aircraft and 37 armed helicopters at seven bases. The Air Force has 177 combat aircraft. The USA maintains 1,760 naval and 270 air force personnel in Spain.

MILITARY EXPENDITURE – 1.2 per cent of GDP (2003)
MILITARY PERSONNEL – 141,250: Army 95,600, Navy 22,900, Air Force 22,750; Paramilitaries 73,360

ECONOMY AND TRADE

The conservatism and international isolation of Franco's regime initially held back economic development in the mid-20th century, but the economy improved from the 1950s with industrialisation and the development of tourism. Tourism is a major industry and generated US$33,609 million in 2002, employing some 11 per cent of the population. 51,748 million tourists visited in 2002. The principal industrial goods are cars, steel, ships, manufactured goods, textiles, chemical products, footwear and other leather goods. The mineral resources of coal, iron, wolfram, copper, zinc, lead and iron ores are exploited. Since 1999, the government has withdrawn subsidies from uncompetitive industries and privatised the steel industry.

Agriculture is an important sector and the generally fertile country produces olives, oranges, lemons, almonds, pomegranates, bananas, apricots, tomatoes, peppers and cucumbers. Other agricultural products include wheat, barley, oats, rice, hemp and flax. The vine is cultivated widely; in the south-west, around Jerez, sherry and wine are produced. Spain has one of Europe's largest fishing industries.

The principal exports include manufactures, military hardware, vehicles, semi-manufactures, foodstuffs, consumer goods and energy. The principal imports are manufactures, military hardware, semi-manufactures, vehicles, consumer goods, foodstuffs and energy.

GNI – US$596,500 million (2002); US$14,580 per capita (2002)

ANNUAL AVERAGE GROWTH OF GDP – 2.6 per cent
(2004 est.)
INFLATION RATE – 3 per cent (2003 est.)
UNEMPLOYMENT – 10.4 per cent (2004 est.)
FOREIGN DIRECT INVESTMENT – US$62,292 million
(1997–2000)
IMPORTS – US$208,500 million (2003)
EXPORTS – US$156,000 million (2003)

BALANCE OF PAYMENTS
Trade – US$42,923 million deficit (2003)
Current Account – US$23,676 million deficit (2003)

Trade with UK	2003	2004
Imports from UK	£7,524,060,000	£8,963,306,000
Exports to UK	6,388,691,000	8,646,355,000

TRANSPORT INFRASTRUCTURE
Spain has a total of 663,795 km of roads, of which
657,157 km are surfaced (including 10,317 km of
expressways). Railways total 14,189 km. The main ports
are Barcelona, Bilbao, Cádiz, Cartagena, Málaga,
Santander, Valencia and Vigo, and there are 1,045 km of
navigable waterways. The principal airports are at Madrid,
Barcelona, Alicante, Málaga, Valencia, Bilbao, Gijón and
Santiago de Compostela, and there are over 80 other
small airports around the country.

EDUCATION
Education is free of charge from age six to 18, and
compulsory up to the age of 16. Private schools (30 per
cent of primary and 60 per cent of secondary schools)
have to fulfil certain criteria to receive government
maintenance grants. There are 73 universities, the oldest
of which, Salamanca, was founded in 1218. Other ancient
foundations are Valladolid (1346), Barcelona (1430),
Zaragoza (1474), Santiago (1495), Valencia (1500),
Seville (1505), Madrid (1508), Granada (1531), and
Oviedo (1604). Private universities are Deusto in Bilbao,
Navarra in Pamplona, Carlos III in Madrid and one in
Salamanca.
ILLITERACY RATE – (m) 1.4 per cent; (f) 3.2 per cent
(2000)
GROSS ENROLMENT RATIO (percentage of relevant age
group) – primary 107 per cent (2002); secondary 114
per cent (2002); tertiary 57 per cent (2002)

MEDIA AND CULTURE
Broadcasting has expanded in recent years and digital
services are increasingly popular. Public radio and TV
services are run by RadioTelevision Espanola (RTVE),
which is funded by advertising and state subsidies. Many
private radio and TV stations operate alongside, on both a
national and regional level. There are four Madrid-based
daily newspapers, and another two based in Barcelona.
Popular titles include El Mundo, ABC, La Razon and El
Periodico de Catalunya.
Spain's literature is one of the oldest and richest in the
world. The Poem of the Cid, the earliest of the heroic
songs of Spain, was written about 1140. The outstanding
writings of Spain's 'Golden Age' are those of Miguel de
Cervantes (1547–1616), Lope Felix de Vega
Carpio (1562–1635) and Pedro Calderón de la Barca
(1600–81). The Nobel Prize for Literature has been
awarded to five Spanish authors: J. Echegaray (1832–
1916), J. Benavente (1866–1954), Juan Ramón Jiménez
(1881–1958), Vicente Aleixandre (1898–1984) and

Camilo José Cela (1916–2002). Federico Garciá Lorca
(1898–1936) is the most significant modern dramatist.
Spain's long tradition in fine art includes the work of El
Greco (1541–1614), Velázquez (1599–1660), Goya
(1746–1828), Picasso (1881–1973), Miró (1893–1983)
and Dali (1904–89).

ISLANDS AND ENCLAVES
THE BALEARIC ISLES form an archipelago off the east
coast of Spain. There are four large islands (Majorca,
Minorca, Ibiza and Formentera), and seven smaller
(Aire, Aucanada, Botafoch, Cabrera, Dragonera, Pinto
and El Rey). Area 5,011 sq. km; population 841,669.
The archipelago forms a province of Spain, the capital
is ΨPalma in Majorca, population 432,113
THE CANARY ISLANDS are an archipelago in the Atlantic,
off the African coast, consisting of seven islands and six
islets. Area 7,270 sq. km; population 1,694,477. The
Canary Islands form two provinces of Spain: Las
Palmas, comprising Gran Canaria, Lanzarote (38,500),
Fuerteventura (19,500) and the islets of Alegranza,
Roque del Este, Roque del Oeste, Graciosa, Montaña
Clara and Lobos, with the seat of administration at
ΨLas Palmas (587,641) in Gran Canaria; and Santa
Cruz de Tenerife, comprising Tenerife, La Palma
(76,000), Gomera (31,829), and Hierro (10,000), with
the seat of administration at ΨSanta Cruz in Tenerife,
population estimate 399,104
ISLA DE FAISANES is an uninhabited Franco-Spanish
condominium, at the mouth of the Bidassoa in La
Higuera bay
ΨCEUTA is a fortified post on the Moroccan coast,
opposite Gibraltar. Area 13 sq. km; population 71,505
ΨMELILLA is a town on a rocky promontory of the
Moroccan coast, connected with the mainland by a
narrow isthmus. Population 66,411. Ceuta and Melilla
are autonomous regions of Spain

OVERSEAS TERRITORIES
The following territories, which are Spanish settlements
on the Morrocan seaboard, come under direct Spanish
administration.
PEÑÓN DE ALHUCEMAS is a bay including six islands;
population 366
PEÑÓN DE LA GOMERA (or Peñón de Velez) is a fortified
rocky islet; population 450
THE CHAFFARINAS (or Zaffarines) is a group of three
islands near the Algerian frontier; population 610

SRI LANKA

Śrī Laṅkā Prajātāntrika Samājavādi Janarajaya/Ilaṅkaiś
Śaṅanāyaka Śośaliśak Kuṭiyaraśa – Democratic Socialist
Republic of Sri Lanka

AREA – 64,600 sq. km
POPULATION – 19,905,165 (2004 est.): 74 per cent
Sinhalese, 12.6 per cent Sri Lankan Tamils, 5.6 per cent
Indian Tamils, 7.1 per cent Sri Lankan Moors, 0.7 per
cent Burghers, Malays and others. The religion of the
majority is Buddhism (69.3 per cent), then Hinduism
(15.5 per cent), Islam (7.6 per cent), and Christianity
(7.5 per cent). The national languages are Sinhala and
Tamil
CAPITAL – ΨColombo (population, 642,163, 2000)
MAJOR CITIES – ΨGalle; ΨJaffna; Kandy; ΨTrincomalee

CURRENCY – Sri Lankan rupee of 100 cents
NATIONAL ANTHEM – Namo namo matha [We all stand together]
NATIONAL DAY – 4 February (Independence Day)
NATIONAL FLAG – On a dark red field, within a golden border, a golden lion passant holding a sword in its right paw, and a representation of a *bo*-leaf, issuing from each corner; and to its right, two vertical stripes of saffron and green also placed within a golden border
LIFE EXPECTANCY (years) – 72.89 (2004 est.)
MORTALITY RATE (per 1,000 population) – 6.47 (2004 est.)
INFANT MORTALITY (per 1,000 births) – 14.78 (2004 est.)
HIV / AIDS ADULT PREVALENCE – 0.1 per cent (2001 est.)
DEATH PENALTY – No (abolished 1976)
POPULATION GROWTH RATE – 0.81 per cent (2004 est.)
POPULATION DENSITY – 293 per sq. km (2002)
ILLITERACY RATE – (m) 5.2 per cent; (f) 10 per cent (2003 est.)
GROSS ENROLMENT RATIO (percentage of relevant age group) – primary 110 per cent (2002); secondary 81 per cent (2002)

CLIMATE AND TERRAIN

Sri Lanka (formerly Ceylon) is an island in the Indian Ocean, off the southern tip of India and separated from it by the narrow Palk Strait. The land is low-lying in the north and around the coasts, with hills and mountains in the south and centre of the interior. Forests, jungle and scrub cover the greater part of the island. In areas over 600 m above sea level grasslands *(patanas* or *talawas)* are found. Elevation extremes range from 2,524 m (Pidurutalagala) at the highest point to 0 m (Indian Ocean) at the lowest. The climate is tropical with little seasonal variation in conditions and humidity, which is frequently around 90 per cent. The island experiences the south-west monsoon in May and the north-east monsoon in November. Average annual temperatures in Colombo are 29°C all year round.

HISTORY AND POLITICS

Modern Sri Lanka is a product of its long history of occupation, which began with the arrival of the Sinhalese late in the sixth century BC. They settled the north, but gradually moved southwards under pressure from Tamil invasions from southern India, which began in the third century BC. These Tamils settled in the northern and eastern coastal areas. The Portuguese landed in the early 16th century and established control over most of the island by 1618. These territories were conquered by the Dutch in 1658 and held until 1798, when they were ceded to the British, becoming a British Crown colony in 1802. With the annexation of the kingdom of Kandy in 1815, all Ceylon came under British rule. Another influx of Indian Tamils took place in the 19th and 20th centuries, to work on the plantations in the central highlands. Ceylon achieved independence with dominion status within the British Commonwealth on 4 February 1948. A republican constitution was adopted in 1972 and the country was renamed Sri Lanka (meaning 'Resplendent Island').

Tension between the Buddhist Sinhalese majority and the Hindu Tamil minority dates from the early 20th century, and policies discriminating against Tamils were introduced after independence. Separatist movements developed in the 1970s to campaign for an independent Tamil state in the north and east of the island, and in the early 1980s the Liberation Tigers of Tamil Eelam (LTTE) began a guerrilla war against government forces for control these areas. Although fighting has tended to be confined to the north, especially the Jaffna peninsula, bombings have occurred throughout the island and led to the state of emergency being extended nationwide in 1996. The LTTE control areas in the north and east, and succeeded in capturing the Elephant Pass, the only land link to the Jaffna peninsula, in 2000.

An Indian-brokered peace accord in 1987 had no impact on the violence, apart from provoking a short guerrilla campaign by extremist Sinhalese opponents of the accord. Various attempts at peace talks in the 1990s were unsuccessful, and LTTE cease-fires in 2000 and 2001 were not reciprocated by the government. In 2002, however, a cease-fire was arranged in January, peace talks began in May and the first formal direct negotiations in seven years began in September. Agreement was reached on a power-sharing arrangement providing for a federal system of government with substantial regional autonomy for the northern and eastern areas held by the LTTE. Talks stalled in 2003 amid a power struggle in the government over the concessions made to the Tamils, and an early election was called. A bombing in Colombo in July 2004 raised fears that violence might resume, but generally the cease-fire has held.

In the 1999 presidential election, President Kumaratunga was elected for a second term, gaining 51.37 per cent of the vote. In the April 2004 legislative election, the President Kumaratunga's United People's Freedom Alliance won 105 seats in the National Assembly, the United National Party won 82 and the Sri Lanka Tamil Government Party secured 22. Mahinda Rajapakse became prime minister and formed a coalition government. The government lost its parliamentary majority after one coalition partner withdrew in February 2005; the nationalist Sinhalese JVP withdrew from the coaliton in June 2005 over the inclusion of Tamil separatist organisations in the arrangements for distributing foreign aid to tsunami victims. The next presidential election was sheduled for December 2006. In August 2005, foreign minister Lakshman Kadirgamar was assassinated at his home in Colombo.

POLITICAL SYSTEM

The 1978 constitution was amended in 1983 to ban parties advocating separatism and in 1987 to create provincial councils. The president is head of state and government, and is directly elected for a six-year term which may be renewed; President Kumaratunga announced in 2004 that her term would run until December 2006. The unicameral Parliament has 225 members directly elected by proportional representation for a six-year term. The president appoints the cabinet.

Under the Indo-Sri Lankan peace accord in 1987, eight elected provincial councils were set up in an attempt to diffuse ethnic tensions. Since 1988 all provinces, except for the temporarily merged North-East province, have elected provincial councils.

HEAD OF STATE
President, Defence, Media, Welfare, Chandrika Bandaranaike Kumaratunga, *elected* 9 November 1994, *re-elected* 21 December 1999, *sworn in* 22 December 1999

SELECTED GOVERNMENT MEMBERS *as at July 2005*
Prime Minister, Highways, Mahinda Rajapakse
Finance, Sarath Amunugama
Home Affairs, Amarasiri Dodangoda
Foreign Affairs, Anura Bandaranaike

HIGH COMMISSION FOR THE DEMOCRATIC
SOCIALIST REPUBLIC OF SRI LANKA
13 Hyde Park Gardens, London W2 2LU
T 020-7262 1841/6 E mail@slhc.globalnet.co.uk
High Commissioner, HE Kshenuka Senewiratne, apptd
2005

BRITISH HIGH COMMISSION
190 Galle Road, Kollupitiya, PO Box 1433, Colombo 3
T (+94) (1) 437336/43 E bhc@eureka.lk
High Commissioner, HE Stephen Evans, OBE, apptd 2002

BRITISH COUNCIL
49 Alfred House Gardens, PO Box 753, Colombo 3
E enquiries@britishcouncil.lk
Director, Tony O'Brien

DEFENCE

The Army has 62 main battle tanks, 217 armoured
personnel carriers and 62 armoured infantry fighting
vehicles. The Navy has 61 patrol and coastal vessels at five
bases. The Air Force has 22 combat aircraft and 24 armed
helicopters.

MILITARY EXPENDITURE – 2.8 per cent of GDP (2003)
MILITARY PERSONNEL – 151,000: Army 118,000, Navy
15,000, Air Force 18,000; Paramilitaries 88,600

ECONOMY AND TRADE

The economy, already damaged by two decades of
violence, was devastated by the Indian Ocean earthquake
disaster in December 2004. The central highlands, the
centre of most cash crop production, were unscathed but
the damage to the coastal areas has wiped out cultivation
there and destroyed the subsidence fishing industry.
Tourism, an important source of revenue, with over
400,000 foreign visitors in 2000, has been badly affected
by the destruction of coastal resorts. The estimated total
cost of reconstruction is US$1.6 billion. Nearly US$3
billion has been received in aid and in June 2005, the
government and the LTTE agreed a deal to share the aid
among the Sinhalese, Tamils and Muslims.

The main crops are tea, rubber, copra and spices. There
has been an emphasis in recent years on producing food,
especially rice, for the home market, and plans for the
large-scale production of sugar cane, cotton and citrus
fruits. Gems are also mined.

The prinicpal exports are industrial goods, agricultural
products and oil derivatives. Principal imports are
manufactures, textiles and clothing, capital goods,
consumer goods and oil.

GNI – US$16,100 million (2002); US$850 per capita
(2002)
ANNUAL AVERAGE GROWTH OF GDP – 5.2 per cent
(2004 est.)
INFLATION RATE – 6.3 per cent (2003 est.)
UNEMPLOYMENT – 7.8 per cent (2004 est.)
TOTAL EXTERNAL DEBT – US$9,066 million (2000)
FOREIGN DIRECT INVESTMENT – US$973 million
(1997–2000)
IMPORTS – US$6,670 million (2003)
EXPORTS – US$5,103 million (2003)

BALANCE OF PAYMENTS
Trade – US$1,406 million deficit (2002)
Current Account – US$290 million deficit (2002)

Trade with UK	2003	2004
Imports from UK	£122,155,000	£138,836,000
Exports to UK	409,488,000	466,908,000

TRANSPORT INFRASTRUCTURE

There are 96,695 km of roads, of which 91,860 km are
surfaced. The rail network is government-run and there
are 1,459 km of railway. Colombo is the main port, and
the principal airport is to the north of Colombo.

MEDIA AND CULTURE

Many of Sri Lanka's main media outlets are government-
controlled, including two major TV stations and radio
networks operated by the Sri Lanka Broadcasting
Corporation (SLBC). There are also privately owned
broadcast media and newspapers. As part of the peace
process, in 2002 the government permitted the Tamil
Tiger to broadcast their Voice of Tigers radio station in
the north of the island.

Sri Lanka's classical architecture, sculpture and painting
is predominantly Buddhist. One of the highest peaks in
the central massif is Adam's Peak (2,243 m) and is a place
of pilgrimage for Buddhists, Hindus and Muslims. Most
notable are several enormous Buddha sculptures,
particularly at Aukana and Buduruvagala. Anuradhapura
and Polonnaruwa have an impressive archaelogical legacy,
but Kandy is the most thriving cultural centre today.

SUDAN

Al-Jumhūriyya as-Sūdān – Republic of Sudan

AREA – 2,376,000 sq. km. Neighbours: Egypt (north),
Eritrea and Ethiopia (east), Kenya, Uganda and the
Democratic Republic of Congo (south), Central African
Republic, Chad and Libya (west)
POPULATION – 39,148,162 (2004 est.). Arab and
Nubian peoples populate the north and centre, Nilotic
and black African peoples the south. Arabic is the
official language and Islam the state religion, although
the Nilotics of the Bahr el-Ghazal and Upper Nile
valleys are generally Animists or Christians
CAPITAL – Khartoum (Al-Khartum) (population,
947,483, 1993 census). The combined population of
Khartoum, Khartoum North and Umm Durman
(excluding refugees and displaced people) is estimated
at 3,000,000
MAJOR CITIES – Al-Ubayyid; Nyala; ΨPort Sudan (Bur
Sudan)
CURRENCY – Sudanese dinar (SD) of 100 piastres
NATIONAL ANTHEM – Nahnu Djundullah [We are the
army of God]
NATIONAL DAY – 1 January (Independence Day)
NATIONAL FLAG – Three horizontal stripes of red, white
and black with a green triangle next to the hoist
LIFE EXPECTANCY (years) – 58.13 (2004 est.)
MORTALITY RATE (per 1,000 population) – 9.37
(2004 est.)
INFANT MORTALITY (per 1,000 births) – 64.05
(2004 est.)
HIV / AIDS ADULT PREVALENCE – 2.6 per cent
(2001 est.)

DEATH PENALTY – Yes
POPULATION GROWTH RATE – 2.64 per cent
(2004 est.)
POPULATION DENSITY – 14 per sq. km (2002)
URBAN POPULATION – 37 per cent (2001)
MILITARY EXPENDITURE – 2.7 per cent of GDP (2003)
MILITARY PERSONNEL – 104,800: Army 100,000, Navy
1,800, Air Force 3,000; Paramilitaries 17,500
CONSCRIPTION DURATION – Two years

CLIMATE AND TERRAIN

Sudan is the largest country in Africa and is predominately desert, the Libyan desert in the west being separated from the high rocky Nubian desert in the east by the fertile valley of the River Nile and its tributaries. There are mountains in the west and along the Red Sea coast in the east. Elevation extremes range from 3,187 m (Kinyeti) at the highest point to 0 m (Red Sea) at the lowest. The climate is as varied as the terrain, with arid conditions in the desert, tropical conditions in the lower land, and cooler conditions in the highlands. There is a wet season from April to October. Average temperatures in Khartoum range from 15°C in January to 38°C in July.

HISTORY AND POLITICS

Parts of northern Sudan formed part of the Egyptian empire from 1900 BC, and of the Nubian empire from the sixth century BC. The country was converted to Coptic Christianity in the sixth century AD, and Islam was introduced in the seventh century by Arab invaders, but did not become widespread until the 15th century. From the eighth century onwards, northern Sudan was conquered and occupied by several Arab and Arab-African powers. The south remained independent. Egypt established its control over the north in the early 19th century but the Mahdi revolt in the 1880s led to a joint Anglo-Egyptian campaign to subdue the country. It was administered as an Anglo-Egyptian condominium from 1899. On 19 December 1995, the Sudan House of Representatives declared Sudan an independent sovereign state. A republic was proclaimed on 1 January 1956, and was recognised by Britain and Egypt.

Tension between the dominant Arab Muslim north and the black African Christian and animist south has dominated the entire post-independence history of the country. The first civil war in the south began in 1955 and ended in 1972 when the south was given greater autonomy. However, another civil war broke out in 1983, largely as a result of attempts to impose Shariah law over the whole country. A peace process began in September 2000 and a cease-fire was agreed in 2002. The parties to the peace process – the government, the Sudan People's Liberation Army (SPLA) and the southern opposition National Democratic Alliance – finalised a peace agreement in December 2004. Under this, a largely autonomous administration will govern in the south following national elections in late 2005, and a referendum on independence for the south will be held after six years. The war caused an estimated 1.5 million deaths, including over 300,000 in the 1988 and 1994 war-induced famines. Some three million people have been internally displaced or become refugees in neighbouring states. Large areas of the south are now desolate and uninhabitable.

The civil war caused years of political instability in the country as a whole, resulting in several coups, and Sudan spent much of the period from 1958 until 1996 under military rule. Although presidential and legislative elections were held in 1996 and 2000, the legislative election due in December 2004 was postponed owing to the peace process. Following the conclusion of the 2004 peace agreement, a new constitution was approved in July 2005. The president was sworn into office under this constitution and John Garang, the leader of the SPLM (the renamed SPLA), was sworn in as first vice-president; Garang was killed in a helicopter accident in late July and was succeeded as SPLM leader by Salva Kiir Mayardit. Presidential and legislative elections were scheduled for late 2005.

INSURGENCIES

The western region of Darfur has two main ethnic groupings, both Muslim: Arabs, who tend to be nomadic livestock herders; and black African peoples, who tend to be farmers. There has long been competition over resources, but prolonged drought and increasing desertification exacerbated tensions from the late 1990s, leading to increasing intercommunal violence. In 2003, rebels began to attack government targets, demanding more government resources for the region and an end to discrimination against the black African peoples. The government responded with severe reprisals, operating through Arab militia (*Janjaweed*) which carried out mass executions and forcible depopulation, leading to accusations of ethnic cleansing. Over two million people were displaced in 2003–5, fleeing to other parts of the country and across the border into Chad. Aid agencies have struggled to prevent starvation in the refugee camps inside Dafur, and in some cases to gain access to areas, because of continuing violence and government obstructiveness. A cease-fire brokered by the UN in April 2004 has been repeatedly violated. Although the government acceded to settlements brokered by the African Union and the UN in 2004, it has not acted upon them and continues to resist international pressure to disarm the militias. It has also resisted the extension of the very limited mandate and numbers of African Union peace-keeping troops deployed in Darfur. In March 2005 the UN Security Council imposed sanctions on those breaking the cease-fire and agreed to refer those accused of war crimes to the International Criminal Court.

POLITICAL SYSTEM

A new constitution was approved in July 2005 which shares power between the Islamic north and Christian and animist south. Elections under this constitution are due to be held in late 2005. The president, who is directly elected for a five-year term, is head of state and head of government. The unicameral National Assembly (*Majlis Watani*) has 400 members who are directly elected for a four-year term. The president appoints the cabinet.

HEAD OF STATE

President, Prime Minister, Lt.-Gen. Omar Hassan Ahmad
al-Bashir, *seized power* 1989, *elected* 1996, *re-elected*
2000, *sworn in under new constitution* 9 July 2005
Vice-President, Salva Kiir

SELECTED GOVERNMENT MEMBERS *as at August 2005*
Defence, Maj.-Gen. Bakri Hassan Salih
Finance and National Economy, Ahmad Hasan al-Zubayr
Foreign Affairs, Mustapha Osman Ismail
Foreign Trade, Abdel Hamid Mussa Kasha

EMBASSY OF THE REPUBLIC OF THE SUDAN
3 Cleveland Row, London SW1A 1DD T 020-7839 8080
Ambassador Extraordinary and Plenipotentiary, HE Dr
   Hasan Abdin, apptd 2000

BRITISH EMBASSY
PO Box 801, Khartoum East T (+ 249) (183) 777105
E information.khartoum@fco.gov.uk
Ambassador Extraordinary and Plenipotentiary, HE Ian
   Cliff, apptd 2005

BRITISH COUNCIL
14 Abu Sin Street (PO Box 1253), Khartoum
E british.council@sd.britishcouncil.org
Director, Paul Doubleday

ECONOMY AND TRADE
Agriculture provides employment for around 80 per cent
of the labour force and contributes nearly half of GDP.
The industry is based on large and medium-sized public
sector irrigation projects; mechanised and traditional
agriculture is practised in areas with sufficient rainfall.
The principal grain crops are *dura* (great millet) and
wheat, the staple food of the population. Sesame and
groundnuts are other important crops, which also yield an
exportable surplus, and a promising start has been made
with castor seed.

Since 1997 Sudan has been implementing IMF
economic reforms which, despite the country's political
instability and vulnerability to drought, have stabilised the
economy to a considerable degree. In 1999 Sudan began
exporting crude oil, and this sector contributed 6.1 per
cent to GDP growth in 2003.
GNI – US$12,200 million (2002); US$370 per capita
   (2001)
ANNUAL AVERAGE GROWTH OF GDP – 6.4 per cent
   (2004 est.)
INFLATION RATE – 9.2 per cent (2002 est.)
TOTAL EXTERNAL DEBT – US$15,741 million
   (2000 est.)
FOREIGN DIRECT INVESTMENT – US$1,134 million
   (1997–2000)
IMPORTS – US$1,600 million (2001)
EXPORTS – US$1,700 million (2001)

BALANCE OF PAYMENTS
Trade – US$297 million deficit (2003)
Current Account – US$727 million deficit (2003)

Trade with UK	2003	2004
Imports from UK	£88,774,000	£91,628,000
Exports to UK	6,257,000	14,222,000

TRANSPORT INFRASTRUCTURE
The railway network, adversely affected by the civil war,
is about 5,516 km in length. There are 11,610 km of
roads, of which 4,203 km are surfaced. The Nile is
navigable but river services between Khartoum and Juba
were interrupted by the civil war in the south. Port Sudan,
on the Red Sea, is the main seaport. The principal airports
are at Khartoum and Juba. Sudan Airways flies services
from Khartoum to other parts of Sudan and to other
African states, Europe and the Middle East.

EDUCATION
Education is free of charge for most children but not
compulsory. Six years of primary education, is followed
by three years of secondary education; there are three

types of secondary school: general, academic and
vocational. The language of instruction is Arabic.

In addition to 20 universities there are various technical
tertiary institutes as well as professional and vocational
training establishments.
ILLITERACY RATE – (m) 30.2 per cent; (f) 53.7 per cent
   (2000)
GROSS ENROLMENT RATIO (percentage of relevant age
   group) – primary 59 per cent (2002); secondary 32 per
   cent (2002)

MEDIA
Radio and television are controlled by the government,
and a permanent military censor ensures that the news
reflects official views. There are no privately owned TV
broadcasters, and private radio stations are not permitted.
Satellite dishes are becoming common in affluent areas
and pan-Arab TV stations are popular among viewers, as
are foreign radio stations such as the BBC World Service
and Paris-based Radio Monte Carlo, which broadcast in
Khartoum. There are several privately owned newspapers.

SURINAME

Republiek Suriname – Republic of Suriname

AREA – 163,265 sq. km. Neighbours: French Guiana
   (east), Brazil (south), Guyana (west)
POPULATION – 436,935 (2004 est.): 37 per cent
   Hindustani, 31 per cent Creole, 15 per cent Javanese,
   10 per cent African and small numbers of Amerindian,
   Chinese and Europeans. The official language is Dutch,
   the native language is Sranang Tongo, and other widely
   used languages are Hindustani and Javanese
CAPITAL – ΨParamaribo (population, 213,836, 2000)
CURRENCY – Suriname dollar of 100 cents
NATIONAL ANTHEM – God zij met ons Suriname [God
   be with our Suriname]
NATIONAL DAY – 25 November
NATIONAL FLAG – Horizontal stripes of green, white,
   red, white and green, with a five-pointed yellow star in
   the centre
LIFE EXPECTANCY (years) – 69.1 (2004 est.)
MORTALITY RATE (per 1,000 population) – 6.99
   (2004 est.)
INFANT MORTALITY(per 1,000 births) – 24.15
   (2004 est.)
HIV / AIDS ADULT PREVALENCE – 1.2 per cent (2001)
DEATH PENALTY – No (abolished 1982)
POPULATION BELOW POVERTY LINE – 70 per cent
   (2002)
POPULATION GROWTH RATE– 0.31 per cent (2004 est.)
POPULATION DENSITY – 3 per sq. km (1999)
MILITARY EXPENDITURE – 0.7 per cent of GDP (2003)
MILITARY PERSONNEL – 1,840: Army 1,400, Navy 240,
   Air Force 200
ILLITERACY RATE – (m) 4.1 per cent; (f) 7.4 per cent
   (2000)

CLIMATE AND TERRAIN
A narrow coastal plain rises to a hilly, forested interior.
Elevation extremes range from 1,230 m (Juliana Top) at
the highest point to −2 m (Atlantic coastal plain) at the
lowest. The climate is tropical, with high rainfall, high
humidity and hot temperatures which are modified by the
north-east trade winds. There are two wet seasons, from
April to August and November to February. Average

annual precipitation in Paramaribo is 2,200 mm and average temperatures are an almost constant 27°C.

HISTORY AND POLITICS

Although visited and claimed by Spanish explorers in 1593, the first European settlement was by the Dutch in 1602. A British colony was founded in 1651 but this was ceded to the Dutch in 1667. Dutch rule was interrupted by British occupation during the French Revolutionary and Napoleonic wars, but was restored in 1816. The colony, known as Dutch Guiana, remained part of the Netherlands West Indies until 25 November 1975, when it achieved independence as Suriname. At independence, about 40 per cent of the population emigrated to the Netherlands.

The early years of independence were politically unstable, with coups in 1980, 1982 and 1990. A guerrilla campaign for the restoration of democracy began in 1986. A peace accord with the guerrillas in 1989, following the return to civilian rule in 1988, was opposed by the military leader and former dictator Desi Bouterse, who engineered a coup in 1990 that deposed the president. Elections in 1991 were won by the New Front for Democracy and Development alliance, led by Ronald Venetiaan, who became president. President Venetiaan introduced an unpopular austerity programme, which improved the economy but lost him the 1996 election.

Suriname has a long-running dispute with its neighbour, Guyana, over the ownership of a potentially oil-rich offshore area. The matter was referred for settlement to a UN tribunal set up in June 2004.

In 2000 the legislative election was won by the New Front for Democracy, a four-party alliance, and Ronald Venetiaan was elected to a second term as president. The New Front for Democracy remained the largest bloc on the National Assembly after the May 2005 legislative election, but without an overall majority. Two rounds of voting in the July 2005 presidential election failed to produce the required majority and a third round of voting by a United People's Conference (UPC) was required to elect in August. The UPC voted in favour of Ronald Venetiaan who became president.

POLITICAL SYSTEM

Under the 1987 constitution, the president is head of state and head of government. The president is elected for a five-year term by a two-thirds majority in the National Assembly or, if the required majority cannot be achieved, by a specially convened United Peoples' Conference including district and local council representatives. The vice-president is elected in the same way. The unicameral legislature, the National Assembly, has 51 members, directly elected for a five-year term.

HEAD OF STATE
President, Ronald Venetiaan, *sworn in*, 12 August 2005
Vice-President, Prime Minister, Jules Ajodhia

SELECTED GOVERNMENT MEMBERS *as at August 2005*
Defence, Ivan Fernald
Finance, Humphrey Hildenberg
Foreign Affairs, Lygia Kraag-Keteldijk
Internal Affairs, Trade and Industry, Maurits Hassankhan

EMBASSY OF THE REPUBLIC OF SURINAME
Alexander Gogelweg 2, NL-2517 JH The Hague, The Netherlands T (+ 31) (070) 361 7445
Ambassador Extraordinary and Plenipotentiary, Edgar Amanh

BRITISH AMBASSADOR
HE Stephen Hiscock, apptd 2002, resident at Georgetown, Guyana

ECONOMY AND TRADE

Although an austerity programme in the mid-1990s achieved economic stability, this was undermined by the expansion of the public sector in the late 1990s. Since 2000, public spending cuts and other measures have stabilised the currency and contained inflation. The mining and refining of bauxite is the mainstay of the economy, making it vulnerable to world price fluctuations; and reserves are declining. Rice and sugar cane are the main crops, along with bananas. There are large timber reserves. The main exports are bauxite, alumina, aluminium, crude oil, timber, shrimp, rice and bananas. Principal trading partners are the Netherlands, the USA and Norway.

GNI – US$761 million (2002); US$1,810 per capita (2002)
ANNUAL AVERAGE GROWTH OF GDP – 5.9 per cent (2001 est.)
INFLATION RATE – 64.3 per cent (2000 est.)
IMPORTS – US$700 million (2003)
EXPORTS – US$640 million (2003)

BALANCE OF PAYMENTS
Trade – US$300 million surplus (2003)
Current Account – US$159 million deficit (2003)

Trade with UK	2003	2004
Imports from UK	£10,113,000	£9,828,000
Exports to UK	325,000	424,000

TRANSPORT INFRASTRUCTURE

There are 4,492 km of roads in total, of which approximately one-quarter is surfaced. There are no railways. The 1,200 km of waterways provide the most effective means of transport. The main seaports include Albina, New Nickerie and Paramaribo. The principal airport is at Paramaribo.

MEDIA

State broadcast media offer a range of views, and are on the air alongside commercial radio and TV stations. The country's two daily newspapers *De West* and *De Ware Tijd* are privately owned.

SWAZILAND

Umbuso we Swatini / Kingdom of Swaziland

AREA – 17,364 sq. km. Neighbours: South Africa (north, west and south), Mozambique (east)
POPULATION – 1,169,241 (2004 est.). The languages are English and Swazi
CAPITAL – Mbabane (population, 67,200, 2002 estimate)
MAJOR TOWNS – Manzini (73,000); Hlatikulu; Mhlume; Nhlangano; Pigg's Peak; Siteki
CURRENCY – Lilangeni (E) of 100 cents (South African currency is also in circulation). Swaziland is a member of the Common Monetary Area and its unit of currency *Emalangeni* (singular *Lilangeni*) has a par value with the South African rand
NATIONAL ANTHEM – Ingoma Yesive

NATIONAL DAY – 6 September (Independence Day)

NATIONAL FLAG – Blue with a wide crimson horizontal band bordered in yellow across the centre, bearing a shield and two spears horizontally

LIFE EXPECTANCY (years) – 37.54 (2004 est.)

MORTALITY RATE (per 1,000 population) – 23.06 (2004 est.)

INFANT MORTALITY (per 1,000 births) – 68.35 (2004 est.)

HIV / AIDS ADULT PREVALENCE – 38.8 per cent (2003 est.)

DEATH PENALTY – Yes

POPULATION GROWTH RATE – 0.55 per cent (2004 est.)

POPULATION DENSITY – 63 per sq. km (2002)

ILLITERACY RATE – (m) 17.4 per cent; (f) 19.2 per cent (2003 est.)

GROSS ENROLMENT RATIO – (percentage of relevant age group) – primary 100 per cent (2002); secondary 45 per cent (2002); tertiary 5 per cent (2002)

CLIMATE AND TERRAIN

The broken mountainous Highveld along the western border, with an average altitude of 1,219 m, is densely forested; the Middleveld, averaging about 609 m, is a mixed farming area; and the Lowveld in the east was mainly scrubland until the introduction of sugar cane plantations. Four rivers, the Komati, Usutu, Mbuluzi and Ngwavuma, flow from west to east. Elevation extremes range from 1,862 m (Emlembe) at the highest point to 21 m (Great Usutu River) at the lowest.

The climate varies from region to region. The Highveld is humid and temperate, the Middleveld and Lebombo range are subtropical and the Lowveld is tropical and semi-arid. Average annual temperatures in Mbabane range from 6°C in June to 25°C in January.

HISTORY AND POLITICS

The Swazi people are believed to have arrived in the area in the 16th century, and developed a strong kingdom which by the mid-19th century was three times the size of the present kingdom. It became a protectorate of the Transvaal in 1884, of the Transvaal and Britain jointly in 1894 and of Britain in 1903. The Kingdom of Swaziland became independent and a member of the Commonwealth on 6 September 1968. In 1973 King Sobhuza II suspended the constitution, banned political parties and assumed absolute power. The parliamentary system was replaced by traditional tribal communities (tinkhundla). Sobhuza II died in 1982; his son was under age and succeeded in 1986 at the age of 18 as King Mswati III. The regency between 1982 and 1986 led to power struggles within the royal family, but the real power passed to the Dlamini family, which dominates the government.

Demands for democratisation of the constitution have grown over the past 20 years, the campaigning of trade unions and political movements supported by popular demonstrations, general strikes and blockades of the border with South Africa.

Swaziland has one of the highest levels of HIV/AIDS infections in the world and faces severe demographic, economic and social problems as a consequence. Three years of erratic rainfall in recent years have compounded food shortages and led the prime minister to appeal for international aid in 2004 to avert a humanitarian crisis.

POLITICAL SYSTEM

A Constitutional Review Commission published findings in 2001 which suggested that most of the population wanted to extend the already wide powers of the king and maintain the ban on political parties. A new constitution introduced in 2003 retained the party ban and the extent of the king's powers, but offered more protection for human rights. Another new constitution was approved by parliament in June 2005 but the king rejected it in July 2005, asking for certain clauses to be reconsidered. The head of state is a hereditary king who is effectively an absolute monarch. There is a bicameral Parliament comprising a 30-member Senate and a 65-member House of Assembly. Each of the country's 55 administrative districts (tinkhundla) directly elects one member to the House of Assembly, and the king appoints ten members. The members of the House of Assembly elect ten of their own number to the Senate, and a further 20 senators are appointed by the king. The King can appoint commissions to assess public opinion, and there are also public gatherings where any citizen can express an opinion.

HEAD OF STATE

King of Swaziland, HM King Mswati III, *inaugurated* 25 April 1986

SELECTED GOVERNMENT MEMBERS *as at August 2005*

Prime Minister, Absalom Themba Dlamini

Deputy Prime Minister, Albert Shabangu

Finance, Majozi Sithole

Foreign Affairs and Trade, Mabili Dlamini

Home Affairs, Prince Gabheni Dlamini

KINGDOM OF SWAZILAND HIGH COMMISSION

20 Buckingham Gate, London SW1E 6LB

T 020-7630 6611

High Commissioner, Mary Kanya

BRITISH HIGH COMMISSION

2nd Floor, Lilunga House, Gilfillan Street, Mbabane

T (+268) 404 2581/2/3/4 E enquiries.mbabane@fco.gov.uk

High Commissioner, HE George Squires, apptd 2005

ECONOMY AND TRADE

The economy is heavily dependent on trade with South Africa, which takes about 60 per cent of Swaziland's exports and provides about 85 per cent of imports. GDP growth rates declined in the 1990s partly as a result of lower growth rates in South Africa. Manufacturing has replaced agriculture as the dominant sector, with timber, textiles and footwear the main products. Agricultural products include sugar cane and fruit.

GNI – US$1,400 million (2002); US$1,240 per capita (2002)

ANNUAL AVERAGE GROWTH OF GDP – 2.5 per cent (2004 est.)

INFLATION RATE – 11.8 per cent (2002 est.)

TOTAL EXTERNAL DEBT – US$262 million (2000 est.)

IMPORTS – US$980 million (2002)

EXPORTS – US$940 million (2002)

BALANCE OF PAYMENTS

Trade – US$79 million deficit (2002)

Current Account – US$46 million deficit (2002)

Trade with UK	2003	2004
Imports from UK	£1,951,000	£3,944,000
Exports to UK	32,320,000	33,439,000

TRANSPORT INFRASTRUCTURE

The railway network is 297 km long and connects with the Mozambique port of Maputo and the South African railway to Richards Bay. A rail line to the north-west border provides a link to Komatipoort. There are 3,800 km of roads, of which 1,064 km are surfaced. There is an international airport at Manzini. Royal Swazi National Airways provides scheduled air services to southern and eastern Africa.

MEDIA

State control of the media is strong; all radio and TV stations, with the exception of a Christian radio station, are under government control and the country's only private daily newspaper, *The Times of Swaziland*, is strictly monitored. Criticism of the monarchy is banned.

SWEDEN

Konungariket Sverige – Kingdom of Sweden

AREA – 411,600 sq. km. Neighbours: Norway (west), Finland (east)

POPULATION – 8,986,400 (2004 est.). The state religion is Lutheran Protestant, to which over 95 per cent officially adhere. The language is Swedish; in the north there are both Finnish- and Lapp-speaking communities

CAPITAL – ΨStockholm (population, 1,684,420, 2002 estimate)

MAJOR CITIES – ΨGothenburg (Göteborg); ΨMalmö; Uppsala

CURRENCY – Swedish krona of 100 öre

NATIONAL ANTHEM – Du gamla, du fria [Thou ancient, thou freeborn]

NATIONAL DAY – 6 June (Day of the Swedish Flag)

NATIONAL FLAG – Yellow cross on a blue ground

LIFE EXPECTANCY (years) – 80.3 (2004 est.)

MORTALITY RATE (per 1,000 population) – 10.38 (2004 est.)

INFANT MORTALITY (per 1,000 births) – 2.77 (2004 est.)

HIV / AIDS ADULT PREVALENCE – 0.1 per cent (2001 est.)

DEATH PENALTY – No (abolished 1972)

POPULATION GROWTH RATE – 0.18 per cent (2004 est.)

POPULATION DENSITY – 22 per sq. km (2002)

CLIMATE AND TERRAIN

The terrain is mostly flat or rolling lowlands in the south and along the east coast, with mountains in the west. Elevation extremes range from 2,111 m (Kebnekaise) at the highest point to 0 m (Baltic Sea) at the lowest. There are many lakes, including Vanern, Vattern, Malaren and Hjalmaren in the south, and over 20,000 off the coast near Stockholm. The climate is continental, with average temperatures in Stockholm ranging from −5°C in January to 22°C in July.

HISTORY AND POLITICS

Sweden takes its name from the Svear people who inhabited the region during the seventh century AD. The country was united *c*.1000, apart from the south and west, which remained under Danish rule until conquered in the 17th century. The Swedes participated in the Viking expansion during the ninth to 11th centuries and

established sovereignty over Finland in the 13th century. The Union of Kalmar (1397) brought Sweden and Norway under Danish rule. Sweden regained its independence following a rebellion by noblemen in 1521 which resulted in the election of Gustav I (of the House of Vasa) to the Swedish throne.

Sweden's power reached its zenith in the 17th century under Gustavus II. The Danes were driven out of southern Sweden, the Baltic coast of Russia was seized, and the Swedish army pushed into Germany after vanquishing the Catholic League. Swedish power waned in the late 17th and 18th centuries. Finland was lost to Russia in 1809; Norway was ceded to Sweden by the Congress of Vienna (1814–15) but seceded in 1905.

Sweden remained neutral during both World Wars. Post-war governments have been dominated by Social Democrat-led coalitions which established a mixed economy and a generous welfare state between 1946 and 1969. Right-wing and centrist parties held power from 1976–82 and 1991–4. Sweden joined the EU in 1995, but decided against membership of the euro zone in 1997, a decision confirmed in a 2003 national referendum. It has yet to ratify the EU constitution; a parliamentary vote was expected in December 2005.

After the 2002 general election, the Swedish Social Democratic Labour Party (SAP) remained the largest party in the legislature with 144 seats. Prime Minister Goran Persson was unable to conclude an agreement on a coalition, which resulted in a minority SAP government.

POLITICAL SYSTEM

Sweden is a constitutional hereditary monarchy, with the monarch retaining purely ceremonial functions as head of state. The constitution is based upon the Instrument of Government 1974, which removed from the monarch the roles of appointing the prime minister and signing parliamentary bills into law. A 1979 amendment vested the succession in the monarch's eldest child irrespective of sex.

There is a unicameral legislature *(Riksdag)* of 349 members directly elected by proportional representation (with a 4 per cent threshold for representation) for a four-year term. The prime minister appoints the council of ministers *(Statsrad)*; the cabinet is responsible to the *Riksdag*. Sweden is divided into 24 counties *(län)* and 288 municipalities *(kommun)*.

HEAD OF STATE
HM The King of Sweden, Carl XVI Gustaf, KG, *born* 30 April 1946, *succeeded* 15 September 1973
Heir, HRH Crown Princess Victoria Ingrid Alice Désirée, Duchess of Västergötland, *born* 14 July 1977

SELECTED GOVERNMENT MEMBERS *as at August 2005*
Prime Minister, Goeran Persson
Defence, Leni Bjoerklund
Finance, Paer Nuder
Foreign Affairs, Laila Freivalds

EMBASSY OF SWEDEN
11 Montagu Place, London W1H 2AL T 020-7917 6400
Ambassador Extraordinary and Plenipotentiary, HE Staffan Carlson, apptd 2005

BRITISH EMBASSY
Skarpögatan 6–8, Box 27819, S-115 93 Stockholm
T (+46) (8) 671 3000
Ambassador Extraordinary and Plenipotentiary, HE Anthony Cary, CMG, apptd 2003

BRITISH COUNCIL
PO Box 27819, S-115 93 Stockholm
T (+46) (8) 671 3110 E info@britishcouncil.se
Director, Jim Potts OBE

DEFENCE

The Army has 280 main battle tanks, 433 armoured personnel carriers and 1,328 armoured infantry fighting vehicles. The Navy has seven submarines and 36 patrol and coastal vessels at four bases. The Air Force has 207 combat aircraft.

Sweden has a policy of non-alignment in peace and neutrality in war and has declined to become a member of NATO. It maintains a 'total defence' which includes peacetime organisations for civil, economic and psychological defence.

MILITARY EXPENDITURE – 1.8 per cent of GDP (2003)
MILITARY PERSONNEL – 27,600: Army 13,800, Navy 7,900, Air Force 5,900; Paramilitaries 600
CONSCRIPTION DURATION – Seven to 15 months

ECONOMY AND TRADE

Sweden developed from an agricultural to an industrial economy in the early 20th century. The prosperity that had funded the generous welfare state after 1946 ended in the early 1990s, when Sweden experienced a deep recession. Austerity measures and free-market economy reforms enabled an economic recovery.

Industrial prosperity is based on natural resources: forests, mineral deposits and water power. The forests cover about half the total land surface and sustain the timber, finished wood products, pulp and paper milling industries. Mineral resources include iron ore, lead, zinc, sulphur, granite, marble, precious and heavy metals (the latter not exploited) and extensive deposits of low-grade uranium ore. Industries based on mining are important but it is the general engineering industry that provides 80 per cent of exports, especially specialised machinery and systems, motor vehicles, aircraft, electrical and electronic equipment, pharmaceuticals, plastics and chemical industries.

Hydroelectricity supplies 15 per cent of energy needs. Sweden has no significant indigenous resources of conventional hydrocarbon fuels and relies for 50 per cent of its energy needs upon imported oil and coal. Less than 10 per cent of the land area is farmland and less than 3 per cent of the labour force is employed in farming, although Sweden is more than 80 per cent self-sufficient in food.

About 45 per cent of industrial output is exported, mainly in the form of cars, trucks, machinery, and electrical and communications equipment. Sweden conducts 70 per cent of its trade with EFTA and the rest of the EU.

GNI – US$231,800 million (2001); US$25,970 per capita (2002)
ANNUAL AVERAGE GROWTH OF GDP – 3.6 per cent (2004 est.)
INFLATION RATE – 1.9 per cent (2003 est.)
UNEMPLOYMENT – 5.6 per cent (2004 est.)
FOREIGN DIRECT INVESTMENT – US$110,791 million (1997–2000)
IMPORTS – US$82,700 million (2003)
EXPORTS – US$101,200 million (2003)

BALANCE OF PAYMENTS
Trade – US$18,933 million surplus (2003)
Current Account – US$22,844 million surplus (2003)

Trade with UK	2003	2004
Imports from UK	£3,443,633,000	£4,284,723,000
Exports to UK	3,316,388,000	5,034,754,000

TRANSPORT INFRASTRUCTURE

The total length of the railway network is 12,821 km. There are approximately 210,000 km of roads, of which 166,500 km are surfaced (including 1,499 km of expressways). There are also 2,052 km of waterways, navigable to small steamers and barges. The main ports are Gothenburg, Helsingborg, Malmö and Stockholm. The principal airports are at Stockholm, Vasteras, Orebro, Gothenburg, Malmo, Kristianstad, Umea and Kiruna. Scandinavian Airlines System provides international and domestic flights, and domestic flights are also provided by Malmö Aviation. The Oresund Bridge connects Sweden to Denmark.

EDUCATION

The state education system provides nine years' free and compulsory schooling from the age of seven to 16 in the comprehensive elementary schools. Around 95 per cent continue into further education of two to four years' duration in the upper secondary schools and a unified higher education system administered in six regional areas containing one of the universities: Uppsala (founded 1477); Lund (1668); Stockholm (1878); Gothenburg (1887); Umeå (1963) and Linköping (1967). There are 40 institutions of higher education including three technical universities in Stockholm, Gothenburg and Lulea.

GROSS ENROLMENT RATIO (percentage of relevant age group) – primary 110 per cent (2002); secondary 149 per cent (2002); tertiary 70 per cent (2002)

MEDIA AND CULTURE

Public television is run by Sveriges Television (SVT). There are a number of commercial stations and around 66 per cent of households have cable or satellite television. Commercial radio began in 1993, and some of the main stations now have near-national networks, in competition with public broadcaster Sveriges Radio. The country is among the top consumers of newspapers in the world, and the government provides subsidies to newspapers regardless of their political affiliation. There are four Stockholm-based daily newspapers and one based in Gothenburg. Titles include *Aftonbladet*, *Expressen* and *Goteborgs Posten*.

Swedish belongs, with Danish and Norwegian, to the North Germanic language group. Swedish literature dates back to King Magnus Eriksson, who codified the old Swedish provincial laws in 1350. With his translation of the Bible, Olaus Petri (1493–1552) formed the basis for the modern Swedish language. Literature flourished during the reign of Gustavus III, who founded the Swedish Academy in 1786.

The Swedish scientist Alfred Nobel (1833–96) founded the Nobel Prizes for physics, chemistry, medicine, literature, and world peace. Notable Swedish writers include Almquist (1793–1866), Strindberg (1849–1912) and Lagerlof (1858–1940), winner of the Nobel Prize for Literature in 1909. Contemporary authors include Lagerquist (1891–1974), Nobel Laureate in 1951, and Martinson (1904–78) and Johnson (1900–76), joint winners of the Nobel Prize for Literature in 1974.

SWITZERLAND

Schweizerische Eidgenossenschaft/Confédération Suisse/
Confederazione Svizzera/Confederaziun Svizra – Swiss
Confederation

AREA – 39,600 sq. km. Neighbours: France (west and
north-west), Germany (north), Austria and
Liechtenstein (east), Italy (south)
POPULATION – 7,450,874 (2004 est.): 46.1 per cent
Roman Catholic, 40 per cent Protestant, 5 per cent
other religions and 8.9 per cent without religion. The
official languages are German (the first language of
63.7 per cent), French (19.2 per cent), Italian (7.6 per
cent) and Romansch (0.6 per cent). German is the
dominant language in 19 of the 26 cantons; French in
Fribourg, Jura, Geneva, Neuchatel, Valais and Vaud;
Italian in Ticino; and Romansch in parts of
Graubünden
CAPITAL – Bern (population, 317,367, 2001 estimate)
MAJOR CITIES – Basel; Geneva; Lausanne; Lucerne;
Winterthur; Zurich
CURRENCY – Swiss franc of 100 rappen (or centimes)
NATIONAL ANTHEM – Schweizerpsalm [Swiss psalm]
NATIONAL DAY – 1 August
NATIONAL FLAG – Square and red, bearing a couped
white cross
LIFE EXPECTANCY (years) – 80.31 (2004 est.)
MORTALITY RATE (per 1,000 population) – 8.44
(2004 est.)
INFANT MORTALITY (per 1,000 births) – 4.43
(2004 est.)
HIV / AIDS ADULT PREVALENCE – 0.5 per cent
(2001 est.)
DEATH PENALTY – No (abolished 1992)
POPULATION GROWTH RATE – 0.54 per cent
(2004 est.)
POPULATION DENSITY – 184 per sq. km (2002)
URBAN POPULATION – 67 per cent (2001)

CLIMATE AND TERRAIN

Landlocked Switzerland is the most mountainous country
in Europe. The Alps, nowhere lower than 1,700 m,
occupy the south and east, and include peaks such as
Dufourspitze, Matterhorn (4,478 m), Finsteraarhorn
(4,274 m), Aletschhorn (4,195 m) and Jungfrau (4,158
m). The Jura mountains lie in the north-west, and the area
between these and the Alps is a plateau of rolling hills,
flatland and lakes. Elevation extremes range from 4,634 m
(Dufourspitze) at the highest to 195 m (Lake Maggiore) at
the lowest. The climate is temperate, with conditions that
vary with altitude. Average temperatures in Zurich range
from −3°C in January to 24°C in July.

HISTORY AND POLITICS

The area was conquered by the Romans in 58 BC and
then overrun by Germanic tribes in the fourth century AD.
It was a province of the medieval Holy Roman Empire
from 1033. The Swiss confederation began in 1291 as an
alliance of three cantons to resist Habsburg control, and
expanded during the 14th century, when it became
independent of the Habsburgs. Its independence was
recognised under the Treaty of Westphalia in 1648.
French revolutionary forces seized Switzerland in 1789
and named it the Helvetic Republic. Independence was
restored in 1814, and the Congress of Vienna (1815)
joined Geneva, Neuchatel and Valais to the confederation
and recognised the country's perpetual neutrality in

international affairs. In 1847 a brief civil war between the
federal government and seven Roman Catholic cantons
over centralisation ended in the latter's defeat.

Many policy decisions are submitted to national
referenda. Although the federal government has pursued a
policy of gradual integration with the EU and applied for
membership in 1992, referenda have rejected
membership of the European Economic Area (1992),
approved bilateral trade agreements with the EU (2000),
and rejected EU membership (2001). A referendum in
2002 led to Switzerland joining the UN.

Proportional representation, introduced in 1919, has
resulted in coalition governments throughout the 20th
and into the 21st century. Since 1959 the federal
government has been a coalition of four parties: the Swiss
People's Party, the Social Democratic Party, the Christian
Democratic People's Party and the Radical Democratic
Party. Following the 2003 legislative election, the Swiss
People's Party was the largest party in the National
Council, with 55 seats.

POLITICAL SYSTEM

The 1998 constitution replaces that of 1874. The head of
state is a president elected annually (along with the vice-
president) for a one-year term by the Federal Assembly
from the members of the Federal Council. The federal
legislature, the Federal Assembly, has two chambers: the
National Council *(Nationalrat)* has 200 members, directly
elected for a four-year term; the States Council *(Ständerat)*
has 46 members (two from each canton and one from
each half-canton) directly elected within each canton for a
four-year term. Executive power is in the hands of a
Federal Council *(Bundesrat)* of seven members, elected for
a four-year term by the Federal Assembly after every
legislative election. The Federal Council is presided over
by the President of the Confederation. Not more than one
person from the same canton may be elected a member of
the Federal Council; however, there is a tradition that
Italian- and French-speaking areas should between them
be represented on the Federal Council by at least two
members.

Any citizen able to obtain 100,000 voters' signatures
in support of holding a referendum on a given issue can
initiate a national referendum.

SELECTED GOVERNMENT MEMBERS *as at August 2005*
President of the Swiss Confederation, Public Economy,
Samuel Schmid
Vice-President, Defence, Civil Protection and Sport,
Moritz Leuenberger
Federal Chancellor, Annemarie Huber-Hotz
Finance, Hans-Rudolf Merz
Foreign Affairs, Micheline Calmy-Rey

EMBASSY OF SWITZERLAND
16–18 Montagu Place, London W1H 2BQ T 020-7616 6000
Ambassador Extraordinary and Plenipotentiary, HE Alexis
Lautenburg, apptd 2005

BRITISH EMBASSY
Thunstrasse 50, CH-3005 Bern T (+41) (31) 359 7700
E info@britain-in-switzerland.ch
Ambassador Extraordinary and Plenipotentiary, HE Simon
Featherstone, apptd 2003

BRITISH COUNCIL
Sennweg 2, PO Box 532, CH-3000 Bern 9 T (+31) 301 1473
E britishcouncil@britishcouncil.ch
Director, Caroline Morrissey

CONFEDERAL STRUCTURE

There are 23 cantons, three of which are subdivided, making 20 cantons and six half-cantons, or 26 in all. Each canton and half-canton has its own government and a substantial degree of autonomy. The main language in 19 of the cantons is German; in the others it is French (*) or Italian (†).

(Population 2001 census): Aargau (549,500), Appenzell-Ausserrhoden (53,200), Appenzell-Innerrhoden (15,100), Basel-Country (262,300), Basel-Town (187,600), Bern (946,100), *Fribourg (239,200), *Geneva (413,800), Glarus (38,500), Graubünden/ Grischun (187,500), *Jura (68,900), Lucerne (349,600), *Neuchatel (166,600), Nidwalden (38,400), Obwalden (32,700), St Gallen (452,200), Schaffhausen (73,200), Schwyz (133,000), Solothurn (245,100), Thurgau (227,700), †Ticino (312,200), Uri (35,000), *Valais (277,600), *Vaud (625,000), Zug (101,000), Zurich (1,227,900)

DEFENCE

The Army has 355 main battle tanks, 1,034 armoured personnel carriers and 435 armoured infantry fighting vehicles. The Air Force has 111 combat aircraft.

MILITARY EXPENDITURE – 1.1 per cent of GDP (2003)

MILITARY PERSONNEL – 4,400 active (139,000 to be mobilised: Army 139,000, Air Force 30,600); Paramilitaries 280,000

CONSCRIPTION DURATION – 15 weeks, then ten refresher courses

ECONOMY AND TRADE

Switzerland has a prosperous and stable modern market economy with low inflation and a highly skilled labour force. Agriculture is followed chiefly in the valleys and the central plateau, where cereals, flax, hemp, wine and tobacco are produced, and fruits and vegetables are grown. Dairy farming and stock-raising are the principal industries; there are 293,949 hectares of open arable land, 115,933 hectares of cultivated grassland and 626,799 hectares of natural grassland and pasture. The forests cover about 30 per cent of the whole surface. The chief manufacturing industries comprise engineering and electrical engineering, metalworking, chemicals and pharmaceuticals, textiles, watchmaking, woodworking, foodstuffs and footwear. Banking, insurance and tourism are also major industries.

The principal imports are machinery, chemicals, vehicles, metals and textiles. The principal exports are machinery, chemicals, precision instruments, watches and jewellery, and metals.

GNI – US$263,700 million (2002); US$36,170 per capita (2002)

ANNUAL AVERAGE GROWTH OF GDP – 1.8 per cent (2004 est.)

INFLATION RATE – 0.6 per cent (2003 est.)

UNEMPLOYMENT – 3.4 per cent (2004 est.)

FOREIGN DIRECT INVESTMENT – US$33,334 million (1997–2000)

IMPORTS – US$92,000 million (2003)

EXPORTS – US$97,000 million (2003)

BALANCE OF PAYMENTS

Trade – US$6,432 million surplus (2002)

Current Account – US$26,011 million surplus (2002)

Trade with UK	2003	2004
Imports from UK	£2,904,499,000	£2,947,337,000
Exports to UK	3,924,072,000	3,573,968,000

TRANSPORT INFRASTRUCTURE

There are 71,086 km of roads, all of which are surfaced, including 1,613 km of national highways; a further 200 km of motorway construction is expected to be completed by 2010. Railway track totals 4,511 km, almost all of which is electrified. Transnational Alpine routes are served by all-weather road and rail tunnels. The Rhine carries heavy shipping traffic on the Basel-Rheinfelden and Schaffhausen-Bodensee stretches, and there are 12 navigable lakes. The principal airports are at Zurich, Basel, Bern and Geneva.

EDUCATION

Education is controlled by cantonal and communal authorities and is free and compulsory from age seven to 16. Special schools make a feature of commercial and technical instruction. Universities are Basel (founded 1460), Bern (1834), Fribourg (1889), Geneva (1873), Lausanne (1890), Zurich (1832), and Neuchatel (1909), the technical universities of Lausanne and Zurich and the economics university of St Gall.

GROSS ENROLMENT RATIO (percentage of relevant age group) – primary 107 per cent (2002); secondary 100 per cent (2002); tertiary 42 per cent (2002)

MEDIA AND CULTURE

Broadcasting is dominated by the public-service Swiss Broadcasting Corporation (SRG/SSR), which operates seven TV networks and 18 radio stations, mainly funded through licence fees. Private radio and TV stations operate at regional level, and television stations from France, Germany and Italy are widely available through multi-channel cable and satellite television. The press operates mainly along regional lines, reflecting linguistic divisions: there are two German-language dailies based in Zurich, two French-language dailies in Geneva, and an Italian-language daily in Lugano.

Important cultural figures include the writer and philosopher Jean-Jacques Rousseau (1712–78), the psychoanalyst Carl Gustav Jung (1875–1961), the poet Carl Spitteler (1845–1924), who won the Nobel Prize for Literature in 1919, and the writer and founder of modern structural linguistics Ferdinand de Saussure (1857–1913).

SYRIA

Al-Jumhūriyya Al-'Arabiyya as-Sūriyya – Syrian Arab Republic

AREA – 183,800 sq. km. Neighbours: Lebanon (west), Israel and Jordan (south-west), Iraq (east), Turkey (north)

POPULATION – 18,016,874 (2004 est.): mostly Muslim. Arabic is the principal language, but Kurdish, Turkish and Armenian are spoken among significant minorities and a few villages still speak Aramaic, the language believed to have been spoken by Christ and the Apostles. English has taken over from French as the main foreign language

CAPITAL – Damascus (Dimashq) (population, 1,549,000, 1994)

MAJOR CITIES – Halab (Aleppo); Hamah; Hims;
ΨAl-Ladhiqiyah, the principal port
CURRENCY   Syrian pound (S$) of 100 piastres
NATIONAL ANTHEM – Humata al-diyari alaykum salaam
[Defenders of the realm on you be peace]
NATIONAL DAY – 17 April
NATIONAL FLAG – Red over white over black horizontal
bands, with two green stars on central white band
LIFE EXPECTANCY (years) – 69.71 (2004 est.)
MORTALITY RATES (per 1,000 population) – 4.96
(2004 est.)
INFANT MORTALITY (per 1,000 births) – 30.6
(2004 est.)
DEATH PENALTY – Yes
POPULATION GROWTH RATE – 2.4 per cent (2004 est.)
POPULATION DENSITY – 92 per sq. km (2002)
URBAN POPULATION – 52 per cent (2001)

CLIMATE AND TERRAIN
The terrain is primarily semi-arid and desert plateaux in
the interior, with a narrow coastal plain and mountains in
the west, and in the east the fertile basin of the River
Euphrates. Elevation extremes range from 2,814 m
(Mount Hermon) at the highest point to −200 m (Lake
Tiberias) at the lowest. The climate varies; the coast has a
Mediterranean climate, the mountains have moderate
summers, the interior plateaux have very hot summers and
cold winters, and the Hamad region has a desert climate.
Average temperatures in Damascus range from 0°C in
January to 37°C in August.

HISTORY AND POLITICS
The country was part of the Phoenician, Persian, Roman
and Byzantine empires. It was conquered by Muslim
Arabs in the seventh century, and was subsequently ruled
by foreign dynasties before being conquered by the Turks
in the 11th century. The location of many battles during
the medieval Crusades, it became part of the Ottoman
empire in 1516. With the collapse of the empire after the
First World War, Syria became a mandated territory in
1920, administered by France with the mandated
territory of Lebanon as 'Greater Lebanon'. Syria's
declaration of independence in 1944 was resisted by the
French, but was effectively achieved in 1946 when French
forces withdrew. It formed part of the United Arab
Republic with Egypt from 1958 until 1961, when it
seceded. Syria was involved in the Arab-Israeli wars in
1948, 1967 and 1973, losing the Golan Heights to Israel
in 1967.

Syrian intervention in Lebanon began in 1976, its
military presence influencing politics there after the civil
war ended. Forces remained until 2005, when they were
withdrawn in response to massive protest rallies in
Lebanon and intense international pressure following the
assassination of a Lebanese politician. Syria's involvement
in the US-led coalition against Iraq in 1991 improved its
relations with the USA, but these deteriorated again after
2001 over Syria's alleged support for terrorism and
development of weapons of mass destruction.

The Arab Socialist Renaissance (Ba'ath) Party has been
the ruling party since 1963. Hafez al-Assad seized power
in a coup in 1970 and was elected president in 1971. He
remained president until his death in 2000, when he was
succeeded by his son, Bashar al-Assad, whose election as
president by parliament was confirmed by a national
referendum. In the 2003 legislative election, the Ba'ath
Party and its allies retained its 167 seats and independents
won 83 seats.

POLITICAL SYSTEM
The 1973 constitution declares that the Arab Socialist
Renaissance (Ba'ath) Party is the leading party in the state
and society. The president is head of state and head of
government. He is elected for a seven-year term by the
People's Council and confirmed in office by a national
referendum. The president appoints the Council of
Ministers. The unicameral legislature, the People's
Council (Majlis al-Sha'ab) has 250 members directly
elected for a four-year term. The only candidates
permitted to stand in elections are from parties allied with
the Ba'ath Party or independents.

HEAD OF STATE
President, Bashar al-Assad, elected by parliament 27 June
2000, approved by referendum 10 July 2000
Vice-Presidents, Abdel Halim Khaddam; Muhammed
Zuheir Mashariqa

SELECTED GOVERNMENT MEMBERS as at August 2005
Prime Minister, Mohammed Naji al-Otari
Deputy Prime Minister, Foreign Affairs, Farouk al-Shara
Defence, Lt.-Gen. Hassan Turkmani
Interior, Brig.-Gen. Ghazi Kanaan
Finance, Mohammad al-Husayn
Commerce, Economy and Foreign Trade, Ghassan al-Rifa'i

EMBASSY OF THE SYRIAN ARAB REPUBLIC
8 Belgrave Square, London SW1X 8PH T 020-7245 9012
Ambassador Extraordinary and Plenipotentiary, Sami
Kyami, apptd 2005

BRITISH EMBASSY
Kotob Building, 11 Mohammad Kurd Ali Street, Malki,
Damascus (PO Box 37) T (+963) (11) 373 9241/2/3/7
Ambassador Extraordinary and Plenipotentiary, HE Peter
Ford, apptd 2003

BRITISH COUNCIL
Maysaloun Street, Shalaan, PO Box 33105, Damascus
T (+963) (11) 331 0631
E general.enquiries@sy.britishcouncil.org
Director, Paul Doubleday

DEFENCE
The Army has 4,600 main battle tanks, 1,600 armoured
personnel carriers and 2,200 armoured infantry fighting
vehicles. The Navy has two frigates, 20 patrol and coastal
vessels and 16 armed helicopters at three bases. The Air
Force has 520 combat aircraft and 71 armed helicopters.
A small force of 1,029 UN troops (UNDOF) is deployed
on the Golan Heights.
MILITARY EXPENDITURE – 7 per cent of GDP (2003)
MILITARY PERSONNEL – 296,800: Army 200,000, Navy
7,600, Air Force 35,000, Air Defence Command
54,200; Paramilitaries 108,000
CONSCRIPTION DURATION – 30 months

ECONOMY AND TRADE
The economy is state-dominated. The principal resources
are oil, produced in the Deir ez Zor region, and gas. An
oil pipeline to Banias via Hims supplies the oil refineries
at those two towns. Syria also has deposits of phosphate
and rock salt, and produces asphalt. Its industrialisation
programme is developing steadily, producing leather
goods, wool and silk, textiles, vegetable oil, soap, sugar,
plastics and metal utensils.

The principal imports are manufactures, metals and

metal goods, machinery, foodstuffs and transport equipment. Principal exports include oil and oil derivatives, gas, agricultural products (chiefly fruit and vegetables, cotton and wheat) and textiles.

GNI – US$19,100 million (2002); US$1,130 per capita (2002)

ANNUAL AVERAGE GROWTH OF GDP – 2.3 per cent (2004 est.)

INFLATION RATE – 0.4 per cent (2000)

UNEMPLOYMENT RATE – 20 per cent (2002 est.)

TOTAL EXTERNAL DEBT – US$21,657 million (2000 est.)

FOREIGN DIRECT INVESTMENT – US$362 million (1997–2000)

IMPORTS – US$21,000 million (2002)

EXPORTS – US$28,100 million (2002)

BALANCE OF PAYMENTS

Trade – US$2,210 million surplus (2002)

Current Account – US$1,440 million surplus (2002)

Trade with UK	2003	2004
Imports from UK	£81,963,000	£88,694,000
Exports to UK	58,005,000	51,869,000

TRANSPORT INFRASTRUCTURE

There are 2,743 km of railways, which connect the major towns and cities, and link with the networks of neighbouring countries. The country has 43,381 km of roads, 10,021 km of which are surfaced. All the principal towns are connected by roads, which vary from modern dual carriageways to narrow country lanes. The principal airport is at Damascus; internal air services operate between all major towns. The main port is Latakia.

EDUCATION

Education is under state control. Elementary education is free at state schools and is compulsory from the age of seven. Secondary education is not compulsory and is free only at the state schools. There are universities at Damascus, Halab, Tishrin, Latakia and the Ba'ath University at Hims.

ILLITERACY RATE – (m) 11.7 per cent; (f) 39.5 per cent (2000)

GROSS ENROLMENT RATIO (percentage of relevant age group) – primary 112 per cent (2002); secondary 45 per cent (2002)

MEDIA AND CULTURE

There was a brief period of press freedom when Bashar al-Assad became president in 2000 and instigated the first licensing of private publications in almost 40 years, but restrictions have since been imposed. Most of Syria's print and broadcast media are owned by the government and the Ba'ath Party. There are three state-run television networks, but satellite receivers are permitted and many viewers consequently have access to foreign television broadcasts. Conditions were set out in 2002 for the licensing of private and commercial radio stations.

The region is rich in historical remains. Damascus is said to be the oldest continuously inhabited city in the world, having existed as a city for over 4,000 years. It contains the Omayed mosque and the tomb of Saladin. To the north-east is the Roman outpost of Dmeir and further east is Palmyra. On the Mediterranean coast at Amrit are ruins of the Phoenician town of Marath, and of Crusaders' fortresses at Margat, Sahyoun, and Krak des Chevaliers. One of the oldest alphabets in the world has been discovered at Ugarit (Ras Shamra), a Phoenician village near Latakia. Hittite cities dating from 2000 to 1500 BC have been explored on the west bank of the Euphrates at Jerablus and Kadesh.

TAIWAN

Chung-hua Min-kuo – Republic of China

AREA – 36,175 sq. km

POPULATION – 22,749,838 (2004 est.). Mandarin Chinese has been the official language since 1949. Now Taiwanese, spoken by 85 per cent of the population, is growing in importance

CAPITAL – ΨTaipei (population, 2,646,474, 2001 estimate)

MAJOR CITIES – ΨKaohsiung; ΨKeelung; Taichung; Tainan

CURRENCY – New Taiwan dollar (NT$) of 100 cents

NATIONAL ANTHEM – San min chu i [Our aim shall be to found a free land]

NATIONAL DAY – 10 October

NATIONAL FLAG – Red, with blue quarter at top next staff, bearing a 12-point white sun

LIFE EXPECTANCY (years) – 77.06 (2004 est.)

MORTALITY RATE (per 1,000 population) – 6.29 (2004 est.)

INFANT MORTALITY (per 1,000 births) – 6.52 (2004 est.)

DEATH PENALTY – Yes

POPULATION GROWTH RATE – 0.64 per cent (2004 est.)

POPULATION DENSITY – 618 per sq. km (2001)

CLIMATE AND TERRAIN

An island in the China Sea, Taiwan, formerly Formosa, lies 90 miles east of the Chinese mainland. The island is mountainous and forested in the east, with lowlands in the west. Elevation extremes range from 3,952 m (Yu Shan) at the highest point to 0 m (South China Sea) at the lowest.

Territories include the Penghu (Pescadores) islands (80.47 sq. km), some 56 km west of Taiwan, as well as Kinmen (Quemoy) (109 sq. km) and Matsu (7 sq. km), which are only a few kilometres from mainland China. The climate is tropical, influenced by the monsoons. Typhoons from the South China Sea bring heavy rains between July and September. Average temperatures in Taipei range from 12°C in January to 34°C in July.

HISTORY AND POLITICS

Settled for centuries by the Chinese, the island was annexed by China in the 17th century, and ceded to Japan in 1895 at the end of the Sino-Japanese War. It was returned to China after Japan's defeat in the Second World War. The Kuomintang (KMT) government, led by Gen. Chiang Kai-shek, withdrew to Taiwan in 1949 after being defeated by the communists in mainland China. The territory remained under Chiang Kai-shek's presidency until his death in 1975. He was succeeded as president by his son, Gen. Chiang Ching-kuo, who ruled until his death in 1988. Martial law was lifted in 1987 after 38 years. In 1991 the Taiwanese government declared an end to the state of war with China, officially recognising the People's Republic of China for the first time, and ended emergency measures that had frozen political life in Taiwan since 1949.

Demands for democratisation of the authoritarian one-party state in the late 1980s led the first multiparty elections in 1992. The 'Senior Parliamentarians' who had retained their seats since being elected on the mainland in 1948 were forcibly retired in 1991–2. From this point, power has shifted away from the mainlanders to the native Taiwanese, and 50 years of Kuomintang rule ended when the Democratic Progressive Party (DPP), which favours self-determination, won the presidency in 2000 and the 2001 legislative election.

President Chen Shui-bian of the DPP, first elected in 2000, was re-elected in 2004 with 51.1 per cent of the vote. After the 2001 legislative election, the DPP formed a coalition government with independents. In the December 2004 legislative election, the DPP won 89 seats, remaining the largest party in the Legislative Yuan. However, an alliance of opposition parties led by the KMT commands 114 seats. A National Assembly was convened in May 2005 to consider possible constitutional changes.

FOREIGN RELATIONS
Legally, most nations acknowledge the position of the Chinese government that Taiwan is a province of the People's Republic of China, and as a result Taiwan has formal diplomatic relations with only 26 countries and no seat at the UN. China has sanctioned the use of force to prevent Taiwan declaring itself independent.

Direct tourism, trade and communications links between mainland China and the Taiwanese islands of Kinmen and Matsu were inaugurated in 2001, the first direct links between Taiwan and China since 1949.

POLITICAL SYSTEM
The 1947 constitution (which originally applied to the whole of China) has been amended a number of times since 1991. The head of state is a president directly elected for a four-year term, renewable only once. The legislature is effectively unicameral; the Legislative Yuan has 225 members, 176 directly elected and 49 elected proportionately by party, and serves a three-year term. The National Assembly, formerly an elected upper chamber, voted in 2000 to transform itself into a largely ceremonial body. It is convened when necessary, to consider constitutional amendments, the impeachment of a president, or territorial changes. Members are appointed proportionally by the parties represented in Legislative Yuan.

HEAD OF STATE
President, Chen Shui-bian, *elected* 18 March 2000,
    re-elected 20 March 2004
Vice-President, Annette Lu

SELECTED GOVERNMENT MEMBERS *as at August 2005*
Prime Minister, Frank Chang-ting Hsieh
Finance, Lin Chuan
Foreign Affairs, Chen Tang-shan
Interior, Su Jia-chyuan
National Defence, Lee Jye

BRITISH COUNCIL
7-F-1, British Trade and Cultural Office, Education and Cultural Section, 99 Jen Ai Road, Section 2, Taipei 100
T (+886) (2) 2192 7000 E inquiries@britishcouncil.org.tw
Director, Gordon Slaven

DEFENCE
The Army has 926 main battle tanks, 950 armoured personnel carriers, 225 armoured infantry fighting vehicles and 20 aircraft. The Navy has four submarines, 11 destroyers, 21 frigates, 59 patrol and coastal vessels, 32 combat aircraft and 20 armed helicopters at four bases. The Air Force has 479 combat aircraft.
MILITARY EXPENDITURE– 2.4 per cent of GDP (2003)
MILITARY PERSONNEL – 290,000: Army 200,000, Navy
    45,000, Air Force 45,000; Paramilitaries 26,650
CONSCRIPTION DURATION – 20 months

ECONOMY AND TRADE
Since the 1950s, Taiwan has transformed itself from a mainly agricultural country to a highly developed industrial economy. The industrial base has expanded to include steel, shipbuilding, chemicals, cement, machinery, electrical equipment and textiles, and the island is now one of the world's top producers of computer technology. In 2002, agriculture contributed 2 per cent of GDP, industry 31 per cent and services 67 per cent.

The soil is very fertile, producing sugar, rice, sweet potatoes, tea, fruit and tobacco. Livestock provided a third of the value of Taiwan's agricultural produce in 1996. Taiwan produces one-tenth of its coal needs and some natural gas.

The principal exports are electronic goods, machinery, metal goods, textiles, plastic products, and toys and games. The main imports are oil, chemicals, machinery and natural resources. The main trading partners are China, the USA, Japan, Hong Kong, Germany, and the Republic of Korea.
GNI – US$14,188 million per capita (2001)
IMPORTS – US$112,800 million (2002)
EXPORTS – US$130,500 million (2002)

BALANCE OF PAYMENTS
Trade – US$24,899 million (2003)
Current Account – US$29,202 million (2003)

Trade with UK	2003	2004
Imports from UK	£903,977,000	£952,909,000
Exports to UK	2,254,791,000	2,395,505,000

TRANSPORT INFRASTRUCTURE
Taiwan has 1,108 km of railways and a total road network of 35,931 km, 31,583 km of which is surfaced (including 608 km of expressways). The main ports are Keelung and Kaohsiung, and there are international airports at Taoyuan (near Taipei) and Kaohsiung. There are internal flights between all the major cities.

MEDIA
The media is among the most liberal in Asia. There are some 350 newspapers, all privately owned and reflecting a wide range of views. There are two main Chinese-language dailies, and three published in English.

TAJIKISTAN

Çumhurii Toçikiston – Republic of Tajikistan

AREA – 143,100 sq. km. Neighbours: Uzbekistan (north
    and west), Kyrgyzstan (north), China (east),
    Afghanistan (south)
POPULATION – 7,011,556 (2004 est.): 62 per cent Tajik,
    23 per cent Uzbek and 8 per cent Russian, with smaller

numbers of Tatars, Kyrgyz, Germans and Ukrainians. The people are predominantly Sunni Muslim. The main languages are Tajik, Uzbek and Russian. Tajik is close to the Farsi spoken in Iran

CAPITAL – Dushanbe (population, 509,300 1998 estimate)

CURRENCY – Somoni of 100 dirams

NATIONAL DAY – 9 September (Independence Day)

NATIONAL FLAG – Three horizontal stripes of red, white and green with the white of double width and charged with a crown and seven stars, all in gold

LIFE EXPECTANCY (years) – 64.47 (2004 est.)

MORTALITY RATE (per 1,000 population) – 8.42 (2004 est.)

INFANT MORTALITY (per 1,000 births) – 112.1 (2004 est.)

HIV / AIDS ADULT PREVALENCE – 0.1 per cent (2001 est.)

DEATH PENALTY – Yes

POPULATION GROWTH RATE – 2.14 per cent (2004 est.)

POPULATION DENSITY – 45 per sq. km (2002)

MILITARY EXPENDITURE – 2.1 per cent of GDP (2003)

MILITARY PERSONNEL – Army 7,600; Paramilitaries 5,300

CONSCRIPTION DURATION – Two years

ILLITERACY RATE – (m) 0.4 per cent; (f) 0.9 per cent (2003 est.)

GROSS ENROLMENT RATIO (percentage of relevant age group) – primary 107 per cent (2002); secondary 82 per cent (2002); tertiary 15 per cent (2002)

CLIMATE AND TERRAIN

The landlocked country is mountainous, with the Pamir highlands in the east and the high ridges of the Pamir-Altai system in the centre. Plains are formed by wide stretches of the Syr-Darya valley in the north and of the Amu-Darya in the south. Elevation extremes range from 7,495 m (Pik Imeni Ismail Samani) at the highest point to 300 m (Syr-Darya) at the lowest. The climate is continental, with average temperatures ranging from –4°C in January to 18°C in July.

HISTORY AND POLITICS

The area that is now Tajikistan was conquered by Alexander the Great in the fourth century BC and remained under Greek and Greco-Persian rule for 200 years, until the kingdom of Kusha was established, based on Bacharia (Bukhara). Tajikistan was invaded by both the Arabs and the Samanid Persians between the seventh and ninth centuries AD. The cities of Bukhara and Samarkand were two of the most important cultural and educational centres in the Islamic world. The area became part of the Mongol empire in the 13th century, and remained under the control of various feudal emirates until the 19th century. In 1868, the northern part was subsumed within the Russian empire, while the south was annexed by the emirate of Bukhara. At the time of the Russian revolution in 1917 the central Asian emirates attempted to establish their independence. Bolshevik power was established in northern Tajikistan by 1 April 1918, when the Turkestan Soviet Socialist Republic was formed, and the Bukhara emirate was overthrown by Soviet forces in 1920. In 1924 the Tajikistan Autonomous Soviet Socialist Republic was formed as part of the Uzbek Republic, before Tajikistan was given full republican status within the Soviet Union in 1929.

Tajikistan declared its independence on 9 September

1991, and Rahmon Nabiyev, communist leader in 1982–5, was elected president. In 1992, anti-government demonstrations escalated into a civil war between pro-government forces and Islamic and pro-democracy groups. President Nabiyev was forced to resign and was replaced by Emomaly Rakhmonov. The government re-established control in 1993 and a cease-fire in 1994 allowed elections to take place but fighting resumed in 1995 and continued until December 1996. A four-part peace accord signed in 1997 was implemented by a National Reconciliation Commission by 2000. There have been several assassinations and bombings, targeted at government ministers and buildings since the end of the civil war. The war caused an estimated 20,000 deaths, displaced 600,000 people and devastated the economy.

The former communists have dominated the presidency and the governments since 1991. Some elections have been boycotted by opposition parties, and most have been deemed by international observers to fail to meet acceptable standards of fairness. A number of opposition leaders have been arrested on criminal charges, moves that their supporters claim are politically motivated.

President Rakhmonov was re-elected in 1999 for a second seven-year term. The legislative elections in February and March 2005 were won by the incumbent (former communist) People's Democratic Party of Tajikistan (HDKT), and the government continued in office after a cabinet reshuffle.

POLITICAL SYSTEM

The 1994 constitution was amended in 1999 and 2003, following referenda, to introduce changes to the presidential term of office and the legislative structure. Under the 1999 amendments, the executive president, who is directly elected, serves a single seven-year term; the 2003 amendment permits the current incumbent to stand for two further terms. The bicameral legislature consists of the Assembly of Representatives *(Majlisi Namoyandogan)*, which has 63 members directly elected for a five-year term, and the National Assembly *(Majlisi Milli)*, which has 33 members, 25 elected by five regional assemblies and eight appointed by the president, to serve a five-year term. Administratively Tajikistan is divided into two regions and the Gorno-Badakhstan autonomous region.

HEAD OF STATE

President, Emomaly Rakhmonov, *elected by Supreme Soviet* 19 November 1992, *elected* 6 November 1994, *re-elected* 6 November 1999

SELECTED GOVERNMENT MEMBERS *as at August 2005*

Prime Minister, Akil Akilov

First Deputy Prime Minister, Relations with CIS States, Haji Akbar Turajonzoda

Defence, Col.-Gen. Sherali Khayrulloyev

Finance, Safarali Najmiddinov

Foreign Affairs, Talbak Nazarov

Interior, Col.-Gen. Khumdin Sharipov

BRITISH EMBASSY

43 Lufti Street, Dushanbe 734017 T (+992) (91) 901 5079

Ambassador Extraordinary and Plenipotentiary, HE Graeme Loten, apptd 2004

ECONOMY AND TRADE

In spite of steady progress since the end of the civil war, Tajikistan's economy is fragile. A debt restructuring agreement was reached with Russia in 2002, and the country has received more than $60 million in aid from the USA. Although only around 5 per cent of the land is arable, agriculture is the major sector of the economy, concentrating on cotton-growing and cattle-breeding. Tajikistan also has rich mineral deposits of mercury, lead, zinc, oil, gold and uranium. Industry specialises in the production of clothing and textiles.

GNI – US$1,100 million (2002); US$180 per capita (2002)

ANNUAL AVERAGE GROWTH OF GDP – 10.5 per cent (2004 est.)

INFLATION RATE – 16.3 per cent (2003 est.)

TOTAL EXTERNAL DEBT – US$1,000 million (2002)

Trade with UK	2003	2004
Imports from UK	£2,320,000	£3,073,000
Exports to UK	1,417,000	185,000

TRANSPORT INFRASTRUCTURE

The country has 482 km of railways, and a total of 27,767 km of roads. Many roads, including the main highway from Dushanbe to Khujand, are only open in the summer months. About 200 km of the River Vakhsh is navigable. There are two major airports and over 50 other airports and airstrips around the country.

MEDIA

Broadcasting is dominated by state-run radio and television, alongside more than 30 local and regional private television stations and a few private radio stations. Tajikistan also has more than 200 registered newspapers, some government-owned and others linked to political parties and movements.

TANZANIA

Jamhuri ya Muungano wa Tanzania / United Republic of Tanzania

AREA – 883,600 sq. km. Neighbours: Kenya and Uganda (north), Mozambique (south), Malawi and Zambia (south-west), Rwanda, Burundi and the Democratic Republic of Congo (west)

POPULATION – 36,588,225 (2004 est.). Africans form a large majority, with European, Asian, and other non-African minorities. The African population consists mostly of tribes of mixed Bantu race. The official languages are Swahili and English

CAPITAL – Dodoma (population, 1,502,344, 1995)

MAJOR CITIES – ΨDar es Salaam, the economic and administrative centre; Mbeya; Mwanza; ΨTanga

CURRENCY – Tanzanian shilling of 100 cents

NATIONAL ANTHEM – Mungu ibariki Afrika [God bless Africa]

NATIONAL DAY – 26 April (Union Day)

NATIONAL FLAG – Green (above) and blue; divided by diagonal black stripe bordered by gold, running from bottom (next staff) to top (in fly)

LIFE EXPECTANCY (years) – 44.39 (2004 est.)

MORTALITY RATE (per 1,000 population) – 17.45 (2004 est.)

INFANT MORTALITY (per 1,000 births) – 102.13 (2004 est.)

HIV / AIDS ADULT PREVALENCE – 8.8 per cent (2003 est.)

DEATH PENALTY – Yes

POPULATION BELOW POVERTY LINE – 30 per cent (2002 est.)

POPULATION GROWTH RATE – 1.95 per cent (2004 est.)

POPULATION DENSITY – 40 per sq. km (2002)

MILITARY EXPENDITURE – 3.1 per cent of GDP (2003)

MILITARY PERSONNEL – 27,000: Army 23,000, Navy 1,000, Air Force 3,000; Paramilitaries 1,400

CONSCRIPTION DURATION – Two years

CLIMATE AND TERRAIN

Tanzania comprises the former Tanganyika, on the mainland of east Africa, and the islands of Zanzibar, Pemba and Mafia. Most of the country lies on the central African plateau, from which rise mountains that run across the centre of the country from north-east to south-west. Peaks include Mount Kilimanjaro (5,894 m), the highest point on the continent of Africa, and Mount Meru (4,564 m). The land falls to plains in the south-east and along the coast, and to swamps in the west. Large areas of lakes Victoria, Tanganyika and Nyasa lie on the northern and western borders, and there are smaller lakes in the north-east and south-west. The Serengeti National Park covers an area of 9,656 sq. km in the north of the country. The climate is tropical equatorial, modified by altitude. The north has two wet seasons, from March to May and from November to December, while the rest of the country has one wet season from November to May. The average temperature in Dar es Salaam is 29°C all year round.

HISTORY AND POLITICS

The area was settled by Bantu people from the fifth century AD, and city states developed along the coast from the eighth century, trading with Arab, Indian and Persian merchants. Portuguese explorers arrived in the 15th century, and in the 16th century the Portuguese conquered Zanzibar and exercised spasmodic control over the coastal states on the mainland. They were ousted from Zanzibar in 1699 by Arabs from Oman, and Oman exercised overlordship over the east African coast from Zanzibar until 1861, when the sultanates of Oman and Zanzibar were separated. The sultanate of Zanzibar became a British protectorate in 1890 and Germany established the colony of German East Africa on the mainland in the 1890s. After the First World War, Tanganyika became a mandated territory under British administration, and achieved its independence on 9 December 1961. It became a republic in 1962. Zanzibar, comprising the islands of Zanzibar, Pemba and Mafia, became independent as a constitutional monarchy on 10 December 1963. The sultan was overthrown in a revolution in 1964 and Zanzibar united with Tanganyika on 26 April 1964 to form the United Republic of Tanzania.

The sole legal political party from 1977 to 1992 was the Chama Cha Mapinduzi, the Revolutionary Party of Tanzania (CCM). The constitution was amended in 1992 to allow multiparty politics, with the stipulation that all parties must be active in both the mainland and in Zanzibar and that parties must not be formed on regional, religious, tribal or racial grounds. The first multiparty presidential and parliamentary elections were held in 1995 and were won by the CCM, which has continued to dominate politics.

In the 2000 presidential and legislative elections, President Mkapa was re-elected, winning 71.7 per cent of the vote, and the CCM won an overwhelming majority in

BRITISH COUNCIL
254 Chulalongkorn Soi 64, Siam Square, Phayathai Road,
Pathumwan, Bangkok 10330 T (+662) 652 5480
E info@britishcouncil.or.tz
Director, Peter Upton

DEFENCE

The Army has 333 main battle tanks, 950 armoured
personnel carriers and five attack helicopters. The Navy
has one aircraft carrier, 12 frigates, 115 patrol and coastal
vessels, 44 combat aircraft and eight armed helicopters at
five bases. The Air Force has 190 combat aircraft.

MILITARY EXPENDITURE – 1.3 per cent of GDP (2003)
MILITARY PERSONNEL – 306,600: Army 190,000, Navy
　70,600, Air Force 46,000; Paramilitaries 113,700

ECONOMY AND TRADE

The economic crisis in south-east Asia in 1997 caused
bankruptcies, recession and unemployment. The stock
and property markets fell and the currency was devalued
by 20 per cent, triggering a currency crisis throughout
south-east Asia. An IMF loan of US$16.7 billion was
announced in return for emergency financial reforms.
Once these were implemented, the economy started to
recover in 1999 and by 2002 was one of east Asia's best
performers; GDP growth was 6.3 per cent in 2003.

The agricultural sector employs around half of the
labour force. Rice remains the most important crop; other
main crops are sugar, maize, sorghum, cassava, rubber,
tobacco, kenaf and jute. In recent years fishing and
livestock production have also gained importance. There
are reserves of oil, natural gas and lignite; mineral
resources include tin, tungsten, lead and iron.

Important industrial sectors include textiles,
transportation vehicles and equipment, construction
materials, brewing, petroleum refining, electrical
appliances, plastics, computers and parts, and integrated
circuits. In 2002, industry contributed 42 per cent of
GDP. Tourism has been the main foreign exchange earner
since the early 1980s. However, the west coast of
Thailand, including outlying islands and the tourist resort
of Phuket, was severely damaged in the 2004 Indian
Ocean earthquake disaster and tourist numbers have
dropped sharply in this region.

The main exports are computers and parts, cars,
integrated circuit boards, precious stones, rice, maize,
canned seafood, fabrics, sugar and tin. Main imports are
crude oil, chemicals, electrical goods, industrial
machinery, iron, steel and transport equipment.

GNI – US$118,500 million (2001); US$1,940 per capita
　(2001)
ANNUAL AVERAGE GROWTH OF GDP – 6.1 per cent
　(2004 est.)
INFLATION RATE – 1.8 per cent (2003 est.)
UNEMPLOYMENT – 1.5 per cent (2004 est.)
TOTAL EXTERNAL DEBT – US$79,675 million
　(2000 est.)
FOREIGN DIRECT INVESTMENT – US$20,265 million
　(1997–2000)
IMPORTS – US$76,000 million (2003)
EXPORTS – US$81,000 million (2003)

BALANCE OF PAYMENTS
Trade – US$11,606 million surplus (2003)
Current Account – US$7,965 million surplus (2003)

Trade with UK	2003	2004
Imports from UK	£572,692,000	£639,133,000
Exports to UK	1,687,385,000	1,801,809,000

TRANSPORT INFRASTRUCTURE

There are 64,600 km of roads, almost all of which are
surfaced, and around 4,071 km of railways. Bangkok is
the international airport, though airports at Chiang Mai,
Phuket and Hat Yai also receive international flights. The
main ports are Bangkok and Sattahip, and there are 3,701
km of navigable waterways.

EDUCATION

Primary education is compulsory and free, and secondary
education in government schools is free. Private
universities and colleges are playing an increasing role in
higher education. There are 62 higher institutes of
learning.

ILLITERACY RATE – (m) 2.8 per cent; (f) 6.1 per cent
　(2000)
GROSS ENROLMENT RATIO (percentage of relevant age
　group) – primary 98 per cent (2002); secondary 83 per
　cent (2002); tertiary 37 per cent (2002)

MEDIA AND CULTURE

The government and military control nearly all the
national terrestrial television networks and operate many
of the country's radio networks. However, media reforms
are currently in progress, aimed at reducing military
interest and opening up more opportunities to the private
sector. The radio market, particularly in Bangkok, is
already fiercely competitive, with more than 60 stations in
and around the capital. Newspapers are largely privately
run, with popular titles including *Bangkok Post* and
Thairath.

The countryside is rich in Buddhist temples and
archaeological remains. Most notable is Ayuthaya, 85 km
north of Bangkok, the capital of the Siamese dynasties
from 1350, whose scattered temples and ruins have been
declared a UNESCO World Heritage Site. Nakhon
Pathom is the country's oldest city and is home to the
tallest Buddhist monument in the word – the 127 m
high Phra Pathom Chedi.

TOGO

République Togolaise – Togolese Republic

AREA – 56,785 sq. km. Neighbours: Ghana (west),
　Burkina Faso (north), Benin (east)
POPULATION – 5,556,812 (2004 est.). The official
　language is French; Ewe, Watchi and Kabiyé are the
　main indigenous languages
CAPITAL – ΨLomé (population, 700,000, 1997 estimate)
CURRENCY – Franc CFA of 100 centimes
NATIONAL ANTHEM – Écartons tous mauvais esprit qui
　gêne l'unité nationale [Let us discard all ill feelings
　which harm national unity]
NATIONAL DAY – 27 April
NATIONAL FLAG – Five alternating green and yellow
　horizontal stripes; a quarter in red at top next staff
　bearing a white star
LIFE EXPECTANCY (years) – 53.05 (2004 est.)
MORTALITY RATE (per 1,000 population) – 11.64
　(2004 est.)
INFANT MORTALITY (per 1,000 births) – 67.66
　(2004 est.)

HIV / AIDS ADULT PREVALENCE – 4.1 per cent (2003 est.)
DEATH PENALTY – Yes
POPULATION GROWTH RATE – 2.27 per cent (2004 est.)
POPULATION DENSITY – 88 per sq. km (2002)
MILITARY EXPENDITURE – 1.7 per cent of GDP (2003)
MILITARY PERSONNEL – 8,550: Army 8,100, Navy 200, Air Force 250; Paramilitaries 750
CONSCRIPTION DURATION– Two years (selective)
ILLITERACY RATE – (m) 24.6 per cent; (f) 53.1 per cent (2003 est.)
GROSS ENROLMENT RATIO (percentage of relevant age group) – primary 124 per cent (2002); secondary 36 per cent (2002); tertiary 4 per cent (2002)

CLIMATE AND TERRAIN

From hills in the centre of the country, the terrain flattens out to savannah in the north and a plateau leading to a marshy coastal plain in the south. Elevation extremes range from 986 m (Mount Agou) at the highest point to 0 m (Atlantic Ocean) at the lowest. The climate is tropical, with two wet seasons (March to July and September to November). The average temperature in Lome is 27°C all year round.

HISTORY AND POLITICS

Formerly part of the kingdom of Togoland, the territory became a German protectorate in 1884 but was occupied on the outbreak of the First World War by Britain and France. The country was divided between Britain and France as a League of Nations mandate after the war and the mandate was renewed by the UN in 1946. In 1957, following a plebiscite, British Togoland integrated with Ghana when it became independent. French Togoland achieved independence as the Republic of Togo in 1960.

There were military coups in 1963 and 1967, the latter bringing to power the army commander Lt.-Col. (later Gen.) Gnassingbé Eyadéma, who named himself president. Political parties were banned, and in 1969 the president's *Rassemblement du peuple togolais* (RPT) became the sole legal political party. Violent anti-government demonstrations in 1990 forced the government to legalise other political parties and introduce a multiparty constitution in 1992. Eyadéma and the RPT were returned to power in the first multiparty elections in 1993 and in both subsequent elections. President Eyadéma remained in power until his death in February 2005. His regime continued its brutal suppression of opposition, particularly before and after the 1998 elections, when an international inquiry concluded there was systematic abuse of human rights.

Following President Eyadéma's death, the army attempted to install his son, Faure Gnassingbé, as president but this attracted domestic and international condemnation. An interim president took office until a presidential election in April 2005, which was won by Faure Gnassingbé amid opposition accusations of electoral irregularities. In June 2005, the moderate opposition leader Edem Kojo was appointed prime minister and a new cabinet was approved.

POLITICAL SYSTEM

Under the 1993 constitution, the head of state is a president who is directly elected for a five-year term. The unicameral legislature, the National Assembly, has 81

members who are directly elected for a five-year term. The prime minister, who is appointed by the president, is head of government and appoints the cabinet in consultation with the president.

HEAD OF STATE

President, Faure Gnassingbé, *elected* 24 April 2005, *sworn in* 4 May 2005

SELECTED GOVERNMENT MEMBERS *as at August 2005*

Prime Minister, Edem Kojo
Economic Affairs, Finance and Privatisation, Payadowa Boukpessi
Foreign Affairs and African Integration, Zarifou Ayeva
National Defence and Veterans, Kpatcha Gnassingbe

EMBASSY OF THE REPUBLIC OF TOGO

8 rue Alfred-Roll, F-75017 Paris, France T (+33) (1) 4380 1213
Ambassador Extraordinary and Plenipotentiary, HE Sotou Bere, apptd 2003

BRITISH AMBASSADOR

HE Gordon Wetherell, resident at Accra, Ghana

ECONOMY AND TRADE

Although the economy remains largely agricultural, exports of phosphates have superseded agricultural products as the main source of export earnings. Other exports include palm kernels, copra and manioc.

In 1998 the EU announced that it would not resume developmental aid to Togo following irregularities in the country's election process.

GNI – US$1,300 million (2002); US$270 per capita (2002)
ANNUAL AVERAGE GROWTH OF GDP – 2.7 per cent (2001 est.)
INFLATION RATE – –1 per cent (2003 est.)
TOTAL EXTERNAL DEBT – US$1,435 million (2000 est.)
IMPORTS – US$840 million (2003)
EXPORTS – US$620 million (2003)

BALANCE OF PAYMENTS
Trade – US$159 million deficit (2001)
Current Account – US$169140 million deficit (2001)

Trade with UK	2003	2004
Imports from UK	£38,055,000	£27,274,000
Exports to UK	981,000	359,000

TRANSPORT INFRASTRUCTURE

Togo has about 7,500 km of roads, of which approximately one third is surfaced. There are about 500 km of railways. The chief waterway is the Mono river, and the main ports are Lomé and Kpeme. The principal airport is at Lomé.

MEDIA

Television Togolaise is the sole national television station, and is government-owned. The government owns the national radio station, Radiodiffusion Togolaise, and, in association with the ruling party RPT, some of the private stations. Togo's only daily newspaper, the *Togo-Presse*, is also government-owned.

TONGA

Pule'anga Tonga / Kingdom of Tonga

AREA – 650 sq. km
POPULATION – 110,237 (2004 est.). The languages are
Tongan and English
CAPITAL – ΨNuku'alofa (population, 34,000, 1990), on
Tongatapu
CURRENCY – Pa'anga (T$) of 100 seniti
NATIONAL ANTHEM – E, 'Otua Mafimafi [Oh, almighty
God above]
NATIONAL DAY – 4 June (Emancipation Day)
NATIONAL FLAG – Red with a white canton containing a
couped red cross
LIFE EXPECTANCY (years) – 69.2 (2004 est.)
MORTALITY RATE (per 1,000 population) – 5.45
(2004 est.)
INFANT MORTALITY (per 1,000 births) – 12.99
(2004 est.)
DEATH PENALTY – No (abolished 1982)
POPULATION GROWTH RATE – 1.94 per cent
(2004 est.)
POPULATION DENSITY – 151 per sq. km (1999)

CLIMATE AND TERRAIN

Tonga comprises three groups of islands, over 170 islands
in all, situated in the south Pacific Ocean some 724 km
east-south-east of Fiji. Most of the islands are of coral
formation, but some are volcanic (Tofua, Kao and
Niuafoou or 'Tin Can' Island). Elevation extremes range
from 1,033 m (unnamed location on Kao island) at the
highest point to 0 m (Pacific Ocean) at the lowest. The
climate is subtropical, influenced by prevailing south-west
trade winds with average temperatures 26°C all year
round.

HISTORY AND POLITICS

The islands were settled by Polynesians from c.1000 AD.
They were visited by Dutch explorers in 1643 and by
Capt. Cook in 1773. The country was reunited in 1845
after a civil war and a modern constitution adopted in
1875. Tonga became a British protectorate in 1900, and
gained its independence on 4 June 1970, remaining
within the Commonwealth.

A pro-democracy movement began in 1992 and
gathered momentum throughout the 1990s, with the first
political party being established in 1994. In the 2002
legislative election, the Human Rights and Democracy
Movement won seven of the popularly elected seats, and
the party won the same number of seats in the March
2005 election. Following the 2005 election, some
ministers were appointed from among the elected
representatives in the Legislative Assembly for the first
time.

POLITICAL SYSTEM

The Kingdom of Tonga is a constitutional monarchy, with
the hereditary monarch as head of state. The 1875
constitution was amended in 2003 to give the king
greater powers, limit judicial review of royal decisions and
increase state control of the media. The unicameral
Legislative Assembly *(Fale Alea)* consists of the king, the
11-member privy council, nine hereditary nobles elected
by their peers, and nine popularly elected representatives;
the elected representatives serve a three-year term. The
prime minister is head of government, and the appointed
privy council acts as a cabinet.

HEAD OF STATE

King of Tonga, HM King Taufa'ahau Tupou IV, GCMG,
GCVO, KBE, *born* 4 July 1918, *acceded* 16 December
1965
Heir, HRH Crown Prince Tupouto'a

SELECTED GOVERNMENT MEMBERS *as at August 2005*
*Prime Minister, Agriculture and Fisheries, Civil Aviation and
Communications,* HRH Prince 'Ulukalala Lavaka Ata
*Deputy Prime Minister, Works, Marines and Ports and
Environment, Interior,* James Cecil Cocker
Finance, Siosiua 'Utoikamanu
Governor of Ha'apai, Malupo
Governor of Vava'u, Akau'ola

TONGA HIGH COMMISSION
36 Molyneux Street, London W1H 5BQ T 020-7724 5828
High Commissioner, HE Viela Tupou, apptd 2004

BRITISH HIGH COMMISSION
PO Box 56, Nuku'alofa T (+676) 24285/24395
E britcomt@kalianet.to
High Commissioner, HE Paul Nessling, apptd 2002

ECONOMY AND TRADE

There are few natural resources and the economy is
dependent on agriculture, fishing and remittances from
Tongans working abroad. The main crops are coconuts,
vanilla, yams, taro, cassava, groundnuts, squash pumpkins
and other fruit. Fish is an important staple food, though
recent shortfalls have led to canned fish being imported.
Industry is based on the processing of agricultural
produce, and the manufacture of foodstuffs, clothing and
sports equipment. Tourism is developing, and is the
principal source of foreign earnings.

The principal exports are fish and vanilla. The principal
imports are manufactures, foodstuffs, machinery and
transport equipment and combustible fuels.

GNI – US$154 million (2000); US$1,530 per capita
(2000)
ANNUAL AVERAGE GROWTH OF GDP – 1.5 per cent
(2002 est.)
INFLATION RATE – 5.9 per cent (2000)
TOTAL EXTERNAL DEBT – US$58 million (2000)
IMPORTS – US$89 million (2002)
EXPORTS – US$14 million (2002)

Trade with UK	2003	2004
Imports from UK	£1,059,000	£465,000
Exports to UK	57,000	19,000

TRANSPORT INFRASTRUCTURE AND MEDIA

There are 680 km of roads in Tonga, 180 km of which are
surfaced. Its principal ports are Neiafu, Nuku'alofa, and
Pangai. There are about six airfields on the islands; one
has a surfaced runway.

The government-run broadcasters are Television Tonga
and A3Z Radio Tonga. The weekly newspaper is *Tonga
Chronicle,* which is also owned by the state.

TRINIDAD AND TOBAGO

Republic of Trinidad and Tobago

AREA – 5,100 sq. km
POPULATION – 1,096,585 (2004 est.). The language is
  English. The main religions are Roman Catholicism
  (29.4 per cent of the population), Hinduism (23.8 per
  cent), Anglicanism (10.9 per cent), Islam (5.8 per cent)
  and Presbyterianism (3.4 per cent)
CAPITAL – ΨPort of Spain (population, 49,031, 2000
  census)
MAJOR CITIES – San Fernando; ΨScarborough, the main
  town of Tobago
CURRENCY – Trinidad and Tobago dollar (TT$) of 100
  cents
NATIONAL ANTHEM – Forged from the love of liberty
NATIONAL DAY – 31 August (Independence Day)
NATIONAL FLAG – Black diagonal stripe bordered with
  white stripes, running from top by staff, all on a red
  field
LIFE EXPECTANCY (years) – 69.28 (2004 est.)
MORTALITY RATE (per 1,000 population) – 9.02
  (2004 est.)
INFANT MORTALITY (per 1,000 births) – 24.64
  (2004 est.)
HIV / AIDS ADULT PREVALENCE – 3.2 per cent
  (2003 est.)
DEATH PENALTY – Yes
POPULATION GROWTH RATE – −0.71 per cent
  (2004 est.)
POPULATION DENSITY – 254 per sq. km (2002)
MILITARY EXPENDITURE – 0.3 per cent of GDP (2003)
MILITARY PERSONNEL – 2,700: Army 2,000, Coast
  Guard 700

CLIMATE AND TERRAIN

Trinidad, the most southerly of the West Indian islands,
lies seven miles off the north coast of Venezuela. The
island is mostly flat, with low mountains, the Northern
Range, across almost its entire northern width and some
low hills in the centre. Elevation extremes range from 940
m (Mt Aripo) at the highest point to 0 m (Caribbean Sea)
at the lowest. Pitch Lake on the south-west coast, is one of
the world's largest natural sources of asphalt.

Tobago lies 30 km north-east of Trinidad. The island
has a range of hills, Main Ridge, running along its length;
the highest point is 565 m. Several islands, of which
Chacachacare, Huevos, Monos and Gaspar Grande are the
most important, lie west of Corozal Point, the north-west
extremity of Trinidad. There is a wet season from June to
December. The average temperature in the coastal regions
is 27°C all year round.

HISTORY AND POLITICS

Trinidad is assumed to be the oldest site of human
habitation in the Caribbean archipelago, with excavated
human remains dating back some 7,200 years. For much
of its history, the islands were home to a number of
indigenous peoples, including the Nepuyo, Yaio and
Carib peoples.

Trinidad and Tobago were discovered by Columbus in
1498. Trinidad was colonised in 1532 by Spain,
capitulated to the British in 1797, and was ceded to
Britain in 1802. Tobago was colonised by the Dutch from
1632 but subsequently changed hands numerous times
until it was ceded to Britain by France in 1814. The two
islands were amalgamated as a British colony in 1889.

The Territory of Trinidad and Tobago became
independent within the Commonwealth on 31 August
1962, and became a republic in 1976.

The republic has been politically stable since
independence, political power passing between the
People's National Movement (PNM), principally
supported by those of African descent, and the United
National Congress (UNC), most of whose supporters are
of Asian descent. The 2001 legislative election was
inconclusive, the two main parties each winning half the
seats. After political deadlock prevented the election of a
speaker for Parliament and of the president, fresh
elections were held in October 2002. These were won by
the PNM, with 20 seats and its leader, Patrick Manning,
became prime minister. The PNM also won the January
2005 election for the Tobago House of Assembly.

POLITICAL SYSTEM

Under the 1976 constitution, the head of state is a
president elected for a five-year term by an electoral
college consisting of all members of the parliament. The
bicameral parliament comprises the House of
Representatives, the lower house, and the Senate. The
House of Representatives has 36 members, directly
elected for a five-year term. The Senate has 31 members,
of whom 16 are appointed on the advice of the prime
minister, six on the advice of the leader of the opposition
and nine at the discretion of the president, to serve a five-
year term. Since 1980 Tobago has had internal self-
government through the Tobago House of Assembly,
which has 15 members, 12 directly elected and three
chosen by the House for a four-year term.

HEAD OF STATE
President, George Maxwell Richards, *elected* 14 February
  2003, *took office* 17 March 2003

SELECTED GOVERNMENT MEMBERS *as at August 2005*
Prime Minister, Finance, Patrick Manning
Foreign Affairs, Knowlson Gift
National Security, Martin Joseph

HIGH COMMISSION OF THE REPUBLIC OF TRINIDAD
AND TOBAGO
42 Belgrave Square, London SW1X 8NT T 020-7245 9351
High Commissioner, Glenda Patricia Morean, apptd 2003

BRITISH HIGH COMMISSION
19 St Clair Ave, St Clair, Port of Spain
T (+1 868) 622 2748/8960 E csbhc@opus.co.tt
High Commissioner, HE Ronald Nash, apptd 2004

ECONOMY AND TRADE

The republic's main sources of revenue are oil and natural
gas, of which it has considerable reserves; gas is expected
to overtake oil soon as its principal export. Fertilisers,
tyres, clothing, soap, furniture and foodstuffs are
manufactured locally, while motor vehicles, radios, TV
sets, and electro-domestic equipment are assembled from
parts, mainly from Japan. The main agricultural products
are sugar, cocoa, coffee, horticultural products and teak.
GNI – US$8,800 million (2002); US$6,750 per capita
  (2002)
ANNUAL AVERAGE GROWTH OF GDP – 5.7 per cent
  (2004 est.)
INFLATION RATE – 3.8 per cent (2003 est.)
UNEMPLOYMENT – 10.4 per cent (2004 est.)
TOTAL EXTERNAL DEBT – US$2,467 million (2000 est.)

FOREIGN DIRECT INVESTMENT – US$2,353 million (1997–2000)
IMPORTS – US$3,600 million (2002)
EXPORTS – US$3,900 million (2002)

BALANCE OF PAYMENTS
Trade – US$718 million deficit (2001)
Current Account – US$416 million deficit (2001)

Trade with UK	2003	2004
Imports from UK	£104,062,000	£96,746,000
Exports to UK	75,048,000	71,622,000

TRANSPORT INFRASTRUCTURE
The two islands have about 8,300 km of roads, of which about half are surfaced. There is no passenger-carrying railway service. The three main ports are Scarborough (Tobago), Port of Spain and Point Lisas where new industries powered by local natural gas are located. The international airport, Piarco, is at Port of Spain.

EDUCATION
Education is free at all state-owned and government-assisted denominational schools, and certain faculties at the University of the West Indies. Attendance is compulsory for children aged six to 12 years, after which attendance at free secondary schools is determined by success in the secondary school entrance examination at 11 years.
ILLITERACY RATE – (m) 1.1 per cent; (f) 2.4 per cent (2000)
GROSS ENROLMENT RATIO (percentage of relevant age group) – primary 105 per cent (2002); secondary 70 per cent (2002); tertiary 7 per cent (2002)

MEDIA
There are both private and state-run media organisations. Private television and radio stations predominate and the freedom of the press is constitutionally protected.

TUNISIA

Al-Jumhūriyya at-Tūnisiyya – Republic of Tunisia

AREA – 155,400 sq. km. Neighbours: Algeria (west), Libya (south)
POPULATION – 9,974,722 (2004 est.). Arabic is the official language
CAPITAL – ΨTunis (population, 929,500 2001 estimate)
MAJOR CITIES – ΨBizerte; ΨSfax; ΨSousse
CURRENCY – Tunisian dinar of 1,000 millimes
NATIONAL ANTHEM – Himat al hima [Defenders of the homeland]
NATIONAL DAY – 20 March
NATIONAL FLAG – Red with a white disc containing a red crescent and star
LIFE EXPECTANCY (years) – 74.66 (2004 est.)
MORTALITY RATE (per 1,000 population) – 5.05 (2004 est.)
INFANT MORTALITY (per 1,000 births) – 25.76 (2004 est.)
HIV / AIDS ADULT PREVALENCE – 0.1 per cent (2004 est.)
DEATH PENALTY – Yes
POPULATION BELOW POVERTY LINE – 6 per cent (2000 est.)

POPULATION GROWTH RATE – 1.01 per cent (2004 est.)
POPULATION DENSITY – 63 per sq. km (2002)
URBAN POPULATION – 66 per cent (2001)
MILITARY EXPENDITURE – 2 per cent of GDP (2003)
MILITARY PERSONNEL – 35,000: Army 27,000, Navy 4,500, Air Force 3,500; Paramilitaries 12,000
CONSCRIPTION DURATION – 12 months (selective)

CLIMATE AND TERRAIN
The north is mountainous with a central plateau that gives way to the semi-arid desert plains of the south. There are salt lakes in the west. Elevation extremes range from 1,544 m (Jebel ech Chambi) at the highest point to −17 m (Shatt al Gharsah) at the lowest. The climate varies considerably from north to south; average temperatures in Tunis range from 11°C in January to 34°C in June.

HISTORY AND POLITICS
The area was ruled successively by the Phoenicians, Carthaginians, Romans, Byzantines, Arabs, Turks and French before formally becoming a French protectorate in 1883. It was briefly occupied by Germany during the Second World War (1942–3), and became independent as a monarchy under the bey in 1956. In 1957 the bey was deposed and the country became a republic under one-party rule with Habib Bourguiba as president.

There was a growing demand throughout the 1970s for the legalisation of other political parties and the government's resistance to these led to serious unrest. Multiparty legislative elections were held in 1981, but the ruling party (now known as the Constitutional Democratic Rally (RCD)) has retained its grip on power over the past two decades. Although proclaimed president for life in 1975, President Bourguiba was deposed in 1987 on the grounds of senility by the prime minister Zine el-Abidine Ben Ali. Ben Ali was subsequently elected president in unopposed elections in 1989 and 1994, and in multiparty elections in 1999 and 2004.

President Ben Ali was elected for a fourth term of office in October 2004, gaining 94.5 per cent of the vote; the main opposition party pulled out of the poll beforehand, claiming that its participation would only legitimise a show of democracy. The simultaneous legislative election was won by the ruling RCD, again with an overwhelming majority of seats after capturing 87.7 per cent of the vote. The Chamber of Councillors was elected for the first time on 3 July 2005; membership is dominated by the RCD.

POLITICAL SYSTEM
The 1959 constitution has been amended a number of times, most recently in 2002 to allow the president to seek a fourth term and to establish a second parliamentary assembly. The president is head of state and head of government. He is directly elected for a five-year term. The legislature, the Chamber of Deputies *(Majlis al-Nuwaab)*, has 189 members directly elected for a five-year term. The Chamber of Councillors *(Majlis al-Mustasharin)* has 167 members, 126 indirectly elected by regions and professional organisations and 41 appointed by the president, who serve a six-year term.

HEAD OF STATE
President, Gen. Zine el-Abidine Ben Ali, *took office* 7 November 1987, *elected* 2 April 1989, *re-elected* 1994, 1999, 24 October 2004

SELECTED GOVERNMENT MEMBERS *as at August 2005*
Prime Minister, Mohammed Ghannouchi
Finance, Mohamed Rachid Kechiche
Foreign Affairs, Abdelbaki Hermassi
Interior, Rafik Belhaj Kacem
National Defence, Hedi M'henni

TUNISIAN EMBASSY
29 Prince's Gate, London SW7 1QG **T** 020-7584 8117
Ambassador Extraordinary and Plenipotentiary, HE
   Mohammed Ghariani, apptd 2004

BRITISH EMBASSY
Rue du Lac Windemere, 1053 Tunis
T (+216) (71) 108700 **E** british.emb@planet.tn
Ambassador Extraordinary and Plenipotentiary, HE Alan
   Goulty, CMGapptd 2004

ECONOMY AND TRADE

Agriculture and fisheries employed 22 per cent of the workforce in 1999 and accounted for 12 per cent of GDP in 2003. The valleys of the north support large amounts of livestock and contain rich agricultural areas in which cereal crops, citrus fruits, dates, melons, potatoes, peppers and tomatoes are grown. Vines and olives are extensively cultivated. Crude oil production in 2002 was 3.6 million tonnes. Gas has also been discovered off the east coast but is only exploited in small quantities. Tourism is the main foreign exchange earner.

The chief exports are manufactures, textiles and leather goods, phosphates, mechanical and electronic products, agricultural products and energy. The chief imports are manufactures, raw materials and semi-manufactures, consumer goods, capital goods, and foodstuffs. France remains the main trading partner. Tunisia became an associate of the EC in 1969. In 1995 a new EU-Tunisian partnership agreement was signed which aims to modernise Tunisia's economy and improve its competitiveness with a view to creating a free trade zone with the EU by 2008.

GNI – US$19,500 million (2002); US$1,990 per capita
   (2002)
ANNUAL AVERAGE GROWTH OF GDP – 5.1 per cent
   (2004 est.)
INFLATION RATE – 2.7 per cent (2003 est.)
UNEMPLOYMENT – 13.8 per cent (2004 est.)
TOTAL EXTERNAL DEBT – US$10,610 million
   (2000 est.)
FOREIGN DIRECT INVESTMENT – US$2,068 million
   (1997–2000)
IMPORTS – US$10,900 million (2003)
EXPORTS – US$8,000 million (2003)

BALANCE OF PAYMENTS
Trade – US$2,269 million deficit (2003)
Current Account – US$730 million deficit (2003)

Trade with UK	2003	2004
Imports from UK	£146,523,000	£151,648,000
Exports to UK	141,428,000	192,772,000

TRANSPORT INFRASTRUCTURE

Tunisia has 19,000 km of roads, over 12,000 km of which are surfaced. There are 2,100 km of railways. The main ports include Bizerte, Sfax, Sousse and Tunis. The principal airport is at Tunis.

EDUCATION

There are 111 centres of higher education, of which eight are universities.

ILLITERACY RATE – (m) 18.6 per cent; (f) 39.4 per cent
   (2000)
GROSS ENROLMENT RATIO (percentage of relevant age
   group) – primary 112 per cent (2002); secondary 79
   per cent (2002); tertiary 23 per cent (2002)

MEDIA AND CULTURE

Alongside the state-run radio and television stations, many satellite television channels are available. In addition, a private radio station has recently been founded, ending the state monopoly on radio broadcasting. An independent press exists in Tunisia but its coverage of local political issues is monitored by the government. Popular titles include *La Presse, Assabah* and *Le Quotidien.*

The country's archaeological remains are one of its biggest tourist attractions and include the famous ruins of Carthage and El-Jem and the ancient hot springs at Hamman Mellegue.

TURKEY

Türkiye çumhuriyeti – Republic of Turkey

AREA – 769,600 sq. km. Neighbours: Greece (west) and
   Bulgaria (north) in Europe; Georgia, Armenia,
   Azerbaijan and Iran (east), Syria and Iraq (south) in
   Asia
POPULATION – 68,893,918 (2004 est.); Islam ceased to
   be the state religion in 1928 but 98.99 per cent of the
   population are Muslim. The main religious minorities,
   which are concentrated in Istanbul and on the Syrian
   frontier, are Greek Orthodox, Armenian, Syrian
   Christian, and Jewish. The language is Turkish;
   Kurdish is widely spoken in the south-east of the
   country
CAPITAL – Ankara (Angora), in Asia (population,
   3,203,362, 2000 census). Ankara (or Ancyra as it was
   known during Roman times) was the capital of the
   Roman Province of *Galatia Prima*, and a marble temple
   (now in ruins), dedicated to Augustus, contains the
   Monumentum (Marmor) Ancyranum, inscribed with a
   record of the reign of Augustus Caesar
MAJOR CITIES – Adana; Bursa; Gaziantep; ΨIstanbul;
   ΨIzmir; Konya Istanbul, in Europe, is the former
   capital.
CURRENCY – New Turkish lira (TL) of 100 kurus
NATIONAL ANTHEM – Istiklal marşi [The independence
   march]
NATIONAL DAY – 29 October (Republic Day)
NATIONAL FLAG – Red, with white crescent and star
LIFE EXPECTANCY (years) – 72.08 (2004 est.)
MORTALITY RATE (per 1,000 population) – 5.95
   (2004 est.)
INFANT MORTALITY (per 1,000 births) – 42.62
   (2004 est.)
HIV / AIDS ADULT PREVALENCE – 0.1 per cent
   (2001 est.)
DEATH PENALTY – No (abolished 2004)
POPULATION GROWTH RATE – 1.13 per cent
   (2004 est.)
POPULATION DENSITY – 90 per sq. km (2002)
URBAN POPULATION – 66 per cent (2001)

NATIONAL ANTHEM – Garashciiz bitarap
Turkmenistaniin devlet gimni [Independent neutral
Turkmenistan state anthem]
NATIONAL DAY – 27–28 October (Independence Day)
NATIONAL FLAG – Green with a vertical carpet pattern
near the hoist in black, white, green and wine-red; and
in the lower part of the carpet design two laurel
branches; in the upper hoist a crescent and five stars, all
in white
LIFE EXPECTANCY (years) – 61.29 (2004 est.)
MORTALITY RATE (per 1,000 population) – 8.82
(2004 est.)
DEATH PENALTY – No (abolished 1999)
POPULATION BELOW POVERTY LINE – 34.4 per cent
(2001 est.)
POPULATION GROWTH RATE – 1.81 per cent
(2004 est.)
POPULATION DENSITY – 10 per sq. km (2002)
MILITARY EXPENDITURE – 1.2 per cent of GDP (2003)
MILITARY PERSONNEL – 26,000: Army 21,000, Navy
700, Air Force 4,300
CONSCRIPTION DURATION – 24 months

CLIMATE AND TERRAIN

Ninety per cent of the country is taken up by the Kara
Kum (Black Sands) desert. There are mountains in the
south, and areas below sea level along the edges of the
Caspian Sea. Elevation extremes range from 3,139 m
(Gora Ayribaba) at the highest point to –81 m (Vpadina
Akchanaya) at the lowest. Average temperatures in
Ashgabat range from 0°C in January to 29°C in June.

HISTORY AND POLITICS

Turkmenistan has been invaded and occupied by many
empires including the Persian, Greek (under Alexander
the Great), Parthian and Mongol. From the early 19th
century until 1886 Turkmenistan was gradually
incorporated into the Russian Empire. A Turkmen revolt
against Russian rule in 1916 brought a period of
autonomy until 1921, when Soviet control over
Turkmenistan was established and it became an
Autonomous Soviet Socialist Republic. Turkmenistan
became a full republic of the Soviet Union in 1925.
It declared its independence from the Soviet Union on
27 October 1991. It joined the Commonwealth of
Independent States (CIS) in 1991 and the UN in 1992.

Saparmurad Niyazov became leader of the Turkmen
Communist Party in 1985, and was elected president in
1990 and re-elected in 1992. After extending his term of
office to 2002 the legislature removed the limit on his
term of office altogether and elected him president for life
in 2004. The autocratic regime has, through harassment
and authoritarianism, prevented any effective political
opposition or free press developing since independence.
The leadership has rejected political pluralism and instead
a cult of personality has developed around President
Niyazov. The Democractic Party of Turkmenistan (DP),
the renamed Communist Party, is the only legal political
party, and held all seats in the parliament after the
elections of 1998 and 2004–5.

POLITICAL SYSTEM

The 1992 constitution was amended in 1999 to remove
restrictions on the number of terms a president can serve,
and in 2003 to alter the status, powers and composition
of the People's Council. The president is head of state and
head of government, directly elected to serve a five-year
term; the decision to extend the term of the present

incumbent and then to make him president for life means
that no presidential election has taken place since 1992.
The parliament *(Majlis)* has 50 members directly elected
for a five-year term. The People's Council *(Khalk
Maslakhaty)* is the supreme representative, legislative and
supervisory body. It has 2,507 members: the president
(who is chair for life), the Council of Ministers, the 50
members of the parliament, regional governors, appointed
members and ethnic and regional representatives.

The country is divided into five regions: Ashgabat,
Charjou, Krasnovodsk, Mary and Tashauz.

HEAD OF STATE
*President, Head of Government, Chair of the Council of
Ministers*, Saparmurad Niyazov, *elected* 27 October
1990, *re-elected* 21 June 1992, *term extended to 2002 by
referendum* 15 January 1994, *term extended indefinitely*
28 December 1999, *appointed president for life* 26
October 2004

SELECTED GOVERNMENT MEMBERS *as at August 2005*
Prime Minister, The President
Defence, Secretary of the State Security Council, Col.-Gen.
Agageldy Mamedgeldiyev
Deputy Chair, Economy and Finance, Amandurdy
Myratguliyev
Economy and Finance, Bibitac Vekilova
Foreign Affairs, Rashid Meredov
Interior, Akmammed Rakhmanov

EMBASSY OF TURKMENISTAN
2nd Floor South, St George's House, 14/17 Wells Street, London
W1P 3FP T 020-7255 1071
Ambassador Extraordinary and Plenipotentiary, HE
Yazmurad Seryayev, apptd 2003
Counsellor, Nurmurat Redjebov

BRITISH EMBASSY
301–308, Office Building, Four Points Ak Altin Hotel, Ashgabat
T (+993) (12) 363462/363463/363464
Ambassador Extraordinary and Plenipotentiary, HE Peter
Butcher, apptd 2005

ECONOMY AND TRADE

Turkmenistan has the world's fifth largest reserves of
natural gas (*c.*8,000,000 million cubic metres) and also
substantial oil reserves (*c.*700 million tonnes). Revenues
from gas sales make the country economically viable and
have enabled the government to maintain low prices for
basic commodities and utilities. Oil exploitation is held
back by a legal dispute with the other Caspian Sea states
over the status of the oil-yielding areas. Exports of gas are
restricted at present by the lack of export routes. However,
the pipeline to Ukraine and western Europe is to be
supplemented by new pipelines under the Caspian Sea
and through Azerbaijan and Georgia to supply gas to
Turkey. Russia is also about to become a major customer
for gas, following an agreement to purchase 60 billion
cubic metres annually from 2004.

The building of the Niyazov (formerly Kara Kum) canal
in the 1960s greatly expanded the amount of land
available for cultivation. The principal industries are gas
and oil production, cotton cultivation, stock-raising,
mineral extraction and the silk industry.
GNI – US$5,143 million (2001); US$950 per capita
(2001)
TOTAL EXTERNAL DEBT – US$2,259 million (2000)

BALANCE OF PAYMENTS
Trade – US$231 million deficit (1997)
Current – US$80 million deficit (1997)

Trade with UK	2003	2004
Imports from UK	£7,241,000	£11,271,000
Exports to UK	2,097,000	5,606,000

TRANSPORT INFRASTRUCTURE

Turkmenistan has 24,000 km of roads, nearly 20,000 km of which are paved. There are 2,440 km of railways. There are two important waterways, the Amudarya river in the north-east and the Niyazov (formerly Kara Kum) canal running across the Kara Kum desert from the Amudarya river to the Caspian Sea. The main port is Turkmenbashi, on the Caspian Sea.

MEDIA

The government's control of the media, both broadcast and print, is total. Newspapers are produced on government-owned presses, programmes from broadcasters other than the state channels are censored before airing in Turkmenistan, and internet access is controlled by the country's communication authorities. Newspapers include *Galkynys*, *Turkmen Dunyasi* and *Adalat*.

TUVALU

Fakavae Aliki-Moloi Tuvalu/Constitutional Monarchy of Tuvalu

AREA – 26 sq. km
POPULATION – 11,468 (2004 est.). About 1,500
 Tuvaluans work overseas, mostly in Nauru, or as
 seamen. The people are almost entirely Polynesian. The
 principal languages are Tuvaluan and English. A large
 majority of the population is Christian, predominantly
 Protestant
CAPITAL – ΨFunafuti (population, 3,856)
CURRENCY – The Australian dollar ($A) of 100 cents is
 legal tender. In addition there are Tuvalu dollar and
 cent coins in circulation
NATIONAL ANTHEM – Tuvalu mo te Atua [Tuvalu for the
 Almighty]
NATIONAL DAY – 1 October (Independence Day)
NATIONAL FLAG – Light blue ground with Union flag in
 top left quarter and nine five-pointed gold stars in the
 fly
LIFE EXPECTANCY (years) – 67.66 (2004 est)
MORTALITY RATE (per 1,000 population) – 7.24
 (2004 est.)
DEATH PENALTY – No (abolished 1978)
POPULATION GROWTH RATE – 1.44 per cent
 (2004 est.)
POPULATION DENSITY – 423 per sq. km (1999)

CLIMATE AND TERRAIN

Tuvalu comprises nine low-lying islands, five of them coral atolls, in the south-west Pacific Ocean. The highest elevation is 4.5 m. There are no streams or rivers. The climate is tropical, and the average temperature is 26°C all year round.

HISTORY AND POLITICS

The islands were discovered by Europeans in the 18th century and as the Ellice Islands came under the control of the British in 1877. They formed part of the Gilbert and Ellice Islands protectorate (later a colony) from 1892, but were granted separate status from the Gilbert Islands in 1975. Tuvalu became a fully independent state within the Commonwealth on 1 October 1978. It became a full member of the UN in 2000. Tuvalu is threatened by rising sea levels, and in 2002 it joined with Kiribati and the Maldives to begin legal action against the USA over its refusal to sign the Kyoto Protocol.

There are no political parties; allegiances are influenced by geography and personalities. Although politically stable as a democracy, there are frequent changes in government as support in parliament shifts. Following the 2002 legislative election, Saufatu Sopanga was elected prime minister by parliament in August 2002. He lost a vote of confidence in August 2004 and resigned; his deputy Maatia Toafa taking over as acting prime minister and was elected to the post in October 2004. Maatia Toafa announced plans for a referendum in 2005 on whether to replace the British monarch as head of state but, as at August 2005, no date had been set.

POLITICAL SYSTEM

Under the 1978 constitution, Tuvalu is a constitutional monarchy with the British monarch as head of state, represented by a governor-general who is appointed on the advice of the prime minister. The unicameral legislature, the Parliament of Tuvalu, has 15 members who are directly elected for a four-year term. The prime minister is elected by the legislature from among its members, and appoints the cabinet, who must be members of parliament. Local government services are provided by elected island councils.
Governor-General, Filoimea Telito

SELECTED GOVERNMENT MEMBERS *as at August 2005*
Prime Minister, Foreign Affairs, Maatia Toafa
*Deputy Prime Minister, Works, Communications and
 Transport*, Saufatu Sopoanga
Finance and Economic Planning, Industry, Bikenibeu
 Paeniu
Home Affairs and Rural Development, Leti Pelesale

HONORARY CONSULATE OF TUVALU
Tuvalu House, 230 Worple Road, London SW20 8RH
T 020-8879 0985
Honorary Consul, Iftikhar Ayaz

BRITISH HIGH COMMISSIONER
HE Charles Mochan, apptd 2002, resident at Suva, Fiji

ECONOMY AND TRADE

Tuvalu is dependent on direct foreign aid. It raises revenue also through the sale of tuna fishing licences, postage stamps, the leasing of its '900' telephone code and '.tv' internet suffix. The leasing arrangements generate several million dollars of revenue annually. Agriculture is at subsistence level and has started to be affected by the increasing salination of the soil as the sea level rises. The only cash crop is copra. The main imports are foodstuffs, semi-manufactures, machinery and transport equipment and fuels. The main exports are copra, fish and handicrafts.
ANNUAL AVERAGE GROWTH OF GDP – 3 per cent
 (2000 est.)

ILLITERACY RATE – (m) 0.2 per cent; (f) 0.4 per cent (2003 est.)

GROSS ENROLMENT RATIO (percentage of relevant age group) – primary 90 per cent (2002); secondary 97 per cent (2002); tertiary 57 per cent (2002)

CLIMATE AND TERRAIN

Much of the country lies in a plain, rising to steppes and then to the Carpathian mountains in the west, and the mountains in the south of the Crimean peninsula. Elevation extremes range from 2,061 m (Hora Hoverla) at the highest point to 0 m (Black Sea) at the lowest. The main rivers are the Dnieper, which runs through the centre of the country, the Southern Bug and the Northern Donets (a tributary of the Don). Average annual temperatures in Kiev range from −8°C in January to 28°C in June.

HISTORY AND POLITICS

The earliest Slavic state was formed in the middle reaches of the River Dnieper with its capital at Kiev in the ninth century AD. The area was invaded successively by the Goths, Huns and Khazars, and then by the Tatar-Mongols in the 13th century. It came under Lithuanian rule in the 14th to 15th centuries, Polish rule in the 16th century, and gradually became part of Russia in the 17th to 18th centuries.

Ukraine declared its independence in 1918, and a civil war ensued between Ukrainian nationalists, Bolsheviks, anarchists, Russian monarchists and the Poles which ended in 1921 with the partitioning of Ukraine between the Soviet Union and Poland. In 1922 Ukraine became a constituent republic of the Soviet Union. Germany invaded and occupied Ukraine from 1941 until forced to withdraw by the Red Army in 1944. Ukraine gained territory in the west in the aftermath of the Second World War, and in 1954 the Crimea was transferred from Russia to Ukraine.

In 1986 Ukraine was the scene of the world's worst nuclear disaster, when a reactor at the Chernobyl nuclear plant exploded. At least 10,000 people have died from radiation poisoning, the long-term health of millions more has been affected and a large area of the country is permanently contaminated.

Ukraine declared itself independent of the Soviet Union on 24 August 1991. Independence was confirmed by a referendum in December 1991 and Leonid Kravchuk was elected to the presidency. In the 1994 presidential election Leonid Kuchma defeated President Kravchuk and won a further term of office in the 1999 presidential election. His resignation was demanded in mass protests in late 2002 and early 2003 after the 2002 legislative election resulted in a hung parliament amid allegations of electoral fraud. The Our Ukraine bloc, an alliance of parties opposed to President Kuchma, was the largest party but a coalition government was formed by supporters of the president and a number of independents.

The 2004 presidential election illustrated Ukraine's divide between the Russian-influenced east and the pro-European west, with prime minister Viktor Yanukovych representing an authoritarianism associated with the Soviet era, while leader of the opposition Viktor Yushchenko promoted political and economic liberalisation and EU membership. After two rounds of voting in October and November 2004, the official result was a victory for Viktor Yanukovych, the Russian-backed prime minister, despite observers' reports of widespread vote-rigging. The announcement triggered mass demonstrations and civil disobedience by Yushchenko's supporters, with counter-demonstrations by Yanukovych's supporters. The Supreme Court annulled the result and ordered a rerun, which was held in December 2004 and won by Viktor Yushchenko, with 52 per cent of the vote. President Yushchenko appointed Yuliya Tymoshenko as prime minister in January 2005 and she formed a coalition government led by the Our Ukraine bloc including the Socialist Party and the Industrialists and Entrepreneurs party. However, in September 2005, Yushchenko sacked his entire government citing serious divisions between his party. He named Yuri Yekhanurov as acting prime minister on 8 September but as at the time of going to press, a new government had yet to be announced.

SECESSION

The Crimea was transferred from Russian to Ukrainian rule only in 1954. When the Soviet Union started to break up in 1991, a pro-Russian majority in the Crimean parliament voted to make Crimea an autonomous republic in September 1991, a vote that was accepted by the newly independent Ukraine. However, when the Crimean parliament voted in favour of independence in May 1992, Ukraine did not accept the decision and the parliament was suspended. In 1994, the parliament attempted to restore the declaration of sovereignty, leading eventually to Ukraine imposing direct presidential rule over Crimea that ended only after parliamentary elections in 1995 saw a dramatic drop in support for pro-Russian parties. Since January 1999 Crimea has had considerable autonomy. Crimean Tatars, exiled en masse by Stalin after the Second World War, returned to Crimea in large numbers in the early to mid 1990s.

FOREIGN RELATIONS

In the aftermath of the Soviet Union's disintegration in 1991, relations between Ukraine and Russia were strained by disputes over the status of the Black Sea fleet and the status of Crimea. Agreement over the division of the Black Sea Fleet was reached in 1997. In 1998, the two countries signed a treaty on economic co-operation intended to strengthen industrial and commercial links and to lead to the introduction of the free movement of goods, services, capital and labour. Relations were strained again briefly in 2003 by a border dispute in the Crimean region.

Ukraine signed a partnership and co-operation agreement with the EU in 1994, and EU membership is a declared long-term objective of the current president. Ukraine was involved in NATO's Partnership for Peace programme in the 1990s, and announced in 2002 that it was abandoning neutrality and applying for NATO membership. In April 2005 President Yushchenko visited the USA and addressed both houses of Congress, an indication of Ukraine's willingness to strengthen ties with the west.

POLITICAL SYSTEM

Under the 1996 constitution, the head of state is a president directly elected for a five-year term. The unicameral legislature, the Supreme Council, has 450 members, who are directly elected for a four-year term; half of the members are elected from single-seat constituencies by a simple majority, and the other 225 are filled by proportional representation from party lists, with a 4 per cent threshold for representation. A member may only be elected if the turnout in the electoral district is above 50 per cent.

The country is divided into 24 regions and the autonomous republic of Crimea.

HEAD OF STATE
President, Viktor Yushchenko, *elected* 26 December 2004, *sworn in* 23 January 2005

SELECTED GOVERNMENT MEMBERS *as at September 2005*
Prime Minister (acting), Yuri Yekhanurov

UKRAINIAN EMBASSY
60 Holland Park, London W11 3SJ T 020-7727 6312
Ambassador Extraordinary and Plenipotentiary, Ihor Mityukov, apptd 2002

BRITISH EMBASSY
UA-01025 Kyiv, Desyatinna 9 T (+380) (44) 462 0011/2/3/4
Ambassador Extraordinary and Plenipotentiary, HE Robert Brinkley, apptd 2002

BRITISH COUNCIL
4/12 Vul. Hryhoriya Skovorody, UA-04070 Kyiv
T (+380) (44) 490 5600 E enquiry@britishcouncil.org.ua
Director, Liliana Biglou

DEFENCE
The constitution bans the stationing of foreign troops on Ukrainian soil, but permits Russia to retain naval bases. The Army has 3,784 main battle tanks, 1,702 armoured personnel carriers, 3,043 armoured infantry fighting vehicles and 205 attack helicopters. The Navy has one submarine, three principal surface combat vessels and eight patrol and coastal vessels at six bases. The Air Force has 499 combat aircraft.
MILITARY EXPENDITURE – 2.1 per cent of GDP (2003)
MILITARY PERSONNEL – 187,600: Army 125,000, Navy 13,500, Air Force 49,100; Paramilitaries 108,400
CONSCRIPTION DURATION – 18 months to two years

ECONOMY AND TRADE
The first decade of independence was characterised by economic mismanagement and opposition to economic restructuring. Reform began in the late 1990s and brought economic growth, with rises in output and exports and a reduction in inflation. However, corruption was and remains a major problem, discouraging overseas investors.

Metal processing, the manufacture of machinery, and chemical and petrochemical industries are major contributors to Ukraine's GDP; mining and metallurgy account for more than 40 per cent of exports. There are coal-mining, iron and steel industries in the south, and ship-building, engineering and chemical industries on the Black Sea coast. Ukrainian agricultural production is good, with large areas under cultivation with wheat, cotton, flax and sugar beet; stock-raising is also important. There are large deposits of coal and salt, iron ore and manganese.

Russia is the main trading partner, accounting for 24 per cent of exports and 41.7 per cent of imports in 2000. Trade negotiations between Ukraine and Russia in 2002 included agreements on gas transits and oil pipelines. Turkey, Germany, the USA and Turkmenistan are also major trading partners.
GNI – US$37,900 million (2002); US$780 per capita (2002)

ANNUAL AVERAGE GROWTH OF GDP – 12 per cent (2004 est.)
INFLATION RATE – 5.2 per cent (2003 est.)
UNEMPLOYMENT – 3.5 per cent (2004 est.)
TOTAL EXTERNAL DEBT – US$12,166 million (2000 est.)
FOREIGN DIRECT INVESTMENT – US$2,457 million (1997–2000)
IMPORTS – US$23,000 million (2003)
EXPORTS – US$23,000 million (2003)

BALANCE OF PAYMENTS
Trade – US$269 million deficit (2003)
Current Account – US$2,891 million surplus (2003)

Trade with UK	2003	2004
Imports from UK	£245,680,000	£222,972,000
Exports to UK	96,087,000	111,060,000

TRANSPORT INFRASTRUCTURE
Ukraine has a total of 170,000 km of roads, 164,000 km of which are surfaced. It has 22,500 km of railways, and 4,500 km of waterways. Its main seaports are Mariupol on the Sea of Azov, and Kherson, Mykolayiv, Odessa and Sevastopol on the Black Sea. The principal airports are at Kiev and Odessa.

MEDIA AND CULTURE
There are several private and state-owned television and radio networks in operation. Ukraine has seven daily newspapers, many of which are mass-circulation publications; titles include *Silski Visti* and *Segodnya.*

Ukraine's folk music has an ancestry that can be traced back to the 16th century. In the 20th century, Ukrainian literature – which dates from the 12th century – became politically significant as authors became openly critical of the Soviet regime. Celebrated cultural figures include the poet Taras Shevchenko (1814–61) and the novelist Olha Kobylianska (1863–1942).

UNITED ARAB EMIRATES

Dawlat Al-Amārat Al-'Arabiyya Al-Muttahida – United Arab Emirates

AREA – 83,600 sq. km approximately. Neighbours: Oman (north-east and east), Saudi Arabia (south and west), Qatar (north-west)
POPULATION – 2,523,915 (2004 est.), of which 75 per cent are expatriates. The official language is Arabic, and English is widely spoken. The established religion is Islam
CAPITAL – ΨAbu Dhabi (population, 450,000)
CURRENCY – UAE dirham (Dh) of 100 fils
NATIONAL DAY – 2 December
NATIONAL FLAG – Horizontal stripes of green over white over black with vertical red stripe in the hoist
LIFE EXPECTANCY (years) – 74.99 (2004 est.)
MORTALITY RATE (per 1,000 population) – 4.14 (2004 est.)
INFANT MORTALITY (per 1,000 births) – 15.06 (2004 est.)
HIV / AIDS ADULT PREVALENCE – 0.18 per cent (2001 est.)
DEATH PENALTY – Yes
POPULATION GROWTH RATE – 1.57 per cent (2004 est.)
POPULATION DENSITY – 38 per sq. km (2002)

CLIMATE AND TERRAIN
The United Arab Emirates (UAE) is situated in the south-east of the Arabian peninsula. Six of the emirates lie on the shore of the Gulf, between the Musandam peninsula in the east and the Qatar peninsula in the west, while the seventh, Fujairah, lies on the Gulf of Oman. Much of the inland terrain is desert, leading to the flat coastal plain and there are mountains in the east. Elevation extremes range from 1,527 m (Jabal Yibir) at the highest point to 0 m (Persian Gulf) at the lowest. Average temperatures in Sharjah range between 12°C in January to 38°C in August.

HISTORY AND POLITICS
The United Arab Emirates (formerly the Trucial States) is composed of seven emirates. Six of these came together as an independent state on 2 December 1971 when they ended their individual special treaty relationships with the British government, and were joined by Ras al-Khaimah on 10 February 1972. On independence, the union government assumed full responsibility for all internal and external affairs apart from some internal matters that remained the prerogative of the individual emirates.

Sheikh Zayed of Abu Dhabi was president from independence until his death in 2004. He was succeeded as Sultan of Abu Dhabi by his son, Sheikh Khalifa, who was also elected president of the UAE.

POLITICAL SYSTEM
The provisional constitution in use since 1971 was finally approved in 1996. Overall authority lies with the Supreme Council of the seven hereditary rulers of the emirates, each of whom also governs in his own territory. The president and vice-president are elected every five years by the Supreme Council from among its members. The president appoints the Council of Ministers. A Federal National Council is a consultative body which considers draft legislation proposed by the Council of Minister. It has 40 members, eight members each from Abu Dhabi and Dubai, six each from Sharjah and Ras al-Khaimah and four each for Fujairah, Umm al-Qaiwain and Ajman, appointed for a two-year term by the rulers of each emirate.

FEDERAL STRUCTURE
Each emirate has its own government, court system and penal code. Abu Dhabi has an executive council chaired by the Crown Prince. The emirates are (population 2000 census): Abu Dhabi (1,186,000), Ajman (174,000), Dubai (913,000), Fujairah (98,000), Ras al-Khaimah (171,000), Sharjah (520,000), Umm al-Qaiwain (46,000).

HEAD OF STATE
President, HH Sheikh Khalifa bin Zayed al-Nahyan *(Abu Dhabi), elected* 3 November 2004
Vice-President, Prime Minister, HH Sheikh Maktoum bin Rashid al-Maktoum *(Dubai)*

SELECTED GOVERNMENT MEMBERS *as at August 2005*
Deputy Prime Minister, Sheikh Sultan bin Zayed al-Nahyan
Defence, HH Gen. Sheikh Mohammed bin Rashid al-Maktoum
Finance and Industry, HH Sheikh Hamdan bin Rashid al-Maktoum
Foreign Affairs, Rashid Abdullah al-Nuaimi
Interior, Lt.-Gen. Mohammed Saeed al-Badi

EMBASSY OF THE UNITED ARAB EMIRATES
30 Princes Gate, London SW7 1PT T 020-7581 1281
Ambassador Extraordinary and Plenipotentiary, HE Easa Saleh al-Gurg, CBE, apptd 1991

BRITISH EMBASSIES
PO Box 248, Abu Dhabi T (+971) (2) 610 1100
Ambassador Extraordinary and Plenipotentiary, HE Richard Makepeace, apptd 2003
PO Box 65, Dubai T (+971) (4) 309 4444

BRITISH COUNCIL
Villa no. 7, Al-Nasr Street, Khalidiya, PO Box 46523, Abu Dhabi
T (+971) (2) 665 9300
E information@ae.britishcouncil.org
Director, Peter Ellwood, OBE

DEFENCE
The Army has 469 main battle tanks, 860 armoured personnel carriers and 430 armoured infantry fighting vehicles. The Navy has two frigates and 16 patrol and coastal vessels. The Air Force has 106 combat aircraft and 59 armed helicopters.
MILITARY EXPENDITURE – 2.1 per cent of GDP (2003)
MILITARY PERSONNEL – 50,500: Army 44,000, Navy 2,500, Air Force 4,000

ECONOMY AND TRADE
Exploitation of the territories' oil reserves began in the 1960s and the UAE is the Gulf's third largest oil producer after Saudi Arabia and Iran; oil reserves are about 98,200 million barrels and gas reserves about 5,800 million cubic metres. Oil production in 2000 accounted for 33.9 per cent of GDP. Other important sectors of the economy are manufacturing (aluminium, cement, chemicals, fertilisers, pharmaceuticals, ship repair), government services, construction, transport, communications, financial services and tourism. Agricultural production has been increased through large-scale water desalination and irrigation projects. There is no personal or corporate taxation apart from on oil companies and foreign banks. There are several free zones, where overseas companies can trade tax-free.

Oil revenues over the past 30 years have enabled the government to invest heavily in education, health and social services, housing, transport and communications infrastructure, and agriculture.
GNI – US$49,205 million (1998); US$17,870 per capita (1998)
ANNUAL AVERAGE GROWTH OF GDP – 5.7 per cent (2004 est.)
INFLATION RATE – 3.2 per cent (2003 est.)

Trade with UK	2003	2004
Imports from UK	£1,084,002,000	£2,702,038,000
Exports to UK	2,080,595,000	1,110,687,000

TRANSPORT INFRASTRUCTURE
Roads total 1,088 km, all of which are surfaced, but the country has no railway system. There are 15 ports, of which Dubai is the most significant, and six international airports.

EDUCATION
In 2000 there were 747 government schools, where education is free; and 426 private schools. There are five universities.

ILLITERACY RATE – (m) 23.9 per cent; (f) 18.3 per cent (2003 est.)

GROSS ENROLMENT RATIO (percentage of relevant age group) – primary 92 per cent (2002); secondary 79 per cent (2002)

MEDIA

Dubai is an important media hub and is home to pan-Arab satellite television channels and other international media organisations. UAE residents can receive several local and pan-Arab television and radio stations. There are three national newspapers, *Al-Bayan*, *Gulf News* and *Khaleej Times*.

UNITED STATES OF AMERICA

AREA – 9,159,000 sq. km. Neighbours: Canada (north), Mexico (south)

POPULATION – 293,027,571 (2004 est.). The language is English. There is a significant Spanish-speaking minority

CAPITAL – Washington DC (population, 4,923,153, 2000 census). The area of the District of Columbia (with which the City of Washington is considered co-extensive) is 61 sq. miles, with a resident population (2000 census) of 572,059. The District of Columbia is governed by an elected mayor and City Council

MAJOR CITIES – ΨChicago; Dallas; ΨDetroit; ΨHouston; ΨLos Angeles; ΨNew York; ΨPhiladelphia; Phoenix; San Antonio; ΨSan Diego

CURRENCY – US dollar (US$) of 100 cents

NATIONAL ANTHEM – The star-spangled banner

NATIONAL DAY – 4 July (Independence Day)

NATIONAL FLAG – Thirteen horizontal stripes, alternately red and white, with blue canton in the hoist showing 50 white stars in nine horizontal rows of six and five alternately (known as the Star-Spangled Banner)

LIFE EXPECTANCY (years) – 77.43 (2004 est.)

MORTALITY RATE (per 1,000 population) – 8.34 (2004 est.)

INFANT MORTALITY (per 1,000 births) – 6.63 (2004 est.)

HIV / AIDS ADULT PREVALENCE – 0.6 per cent (2003 est.)

DEATH PENALTY – Yes

POPULATION BELOW POVERTY LINE – 12.7 per cent (2001 est.)

POPULATION GROWTH RATE – 0.92 per cent (2004 est.)

POPULATION DENSITY – 31 per sq. km (2002)

URBAN POPULATION – 77 per cent (2001)

CLIMATE AND TERRAIN

The coastline has a length of about 3,329 km on the Atlantic Ocean, 12,268 km on the Pacific, 1,705 km on the Arctic, and 2,624 km on the Gulf of Mexico. The principal river is the Mississippi-Missouri-Red (5,970 km long), traversing the whole country to its mouth in the Gulf of Mexico. The chain of the Rocky Mountains separates the western portion of the country from the remainder. West of these, bordering the Pacific coast, the Cascade Mountains and Sierra Nevada form the outer edge of a high tableland, consisting in part of stony and sandy desert and partly of grazing land and forested mountains, and including the Great Salt Lake, which extends to the Rocky Mountains. In the eastern states large forests still exist, the remnants of the forests which formerly extended over all the Atlantic slope. The highest point is Mount McKinley (6,193 m) in Alaska, and the lowest point of dry land is in Death Valley (Inyo, California), 85 m below sea level. Temperatures vary dramatically and average temperatures in Washington DC range from 6°C in January to 27°C in June.

Two states are detached: Alaska and Hawaii. Alaska occupies the north-western extremity of the North America, separated from the rest of the USA by the Canadian province of British Columbia. The terrain is arctic tundra with mountain ranges, and the climate is arctic. The state of Hawaii is a chain of about 20 volcanic islands in the north Pacific Ocean, of which the chief islands are Hawaii, Maui, Oahu, Kauai and Molokai. The climate is tropical.

HISTORY AND POLITICS

The area which is now the USA was first inhabited by nomadic hunters who probably arrived from Asia *c.*30,000 BC. The continent was explored by the Norse in the ninth century and the Spanish in the 16th century. European colonisation began in the 16th century, with Spanish settlements in the south, and British, Dutch, French, German and Swedish settlements in the east; Britain, France and Spain developed the strongest colonial presence. Many black Africans were introduced as slaves to work on the plantations. By 1733 there were 13 British colonies, composed largely of religious non-conformists who had left Britain to escape persecution. A rebellion broke out in these colonies in 1775, largely because of the colonists' objection to being taxed by, but having no representation in, the British Parliament. The forces of the British government were defeated with French, Spanish and Dutch assistance. The Declaration of Independence which inaugurated the United States of America was signed on 4 July 1776; Britain recognised American sovereignty in 1783. The first federal constitution was drawn up in 1787; ten amendments, termed the Bill of Rights, were added in 1791. The 13 original states of the Union ratified the constitution between 1787 and 1790. Vermont, Kentucky and Tennessee were admitted in the 1790s but most of the states acceded in the 19th century as the opening up of the centre and west led to the creation of new states and European or neighbouring countries ceded or sold their territories to the USA.

The Civil War (1861–5) was fought over the issue of slavery, which was integral to the economy of the southern states but was opposed by the northern states. The northern states defeated the Confederacy of 11 southern states (Virginia, North Carolina, South Carolina, Georgia, Alabama, Florida, Tennessee, Mississippi, Louisiana, Texas, Arkansas) after they seceded in 1860–1.

The USA industrialised rapidly in the late 19th century. It emerged as a world economic and military superpower in the 20th century and played a decisive role in the two world wars. Its economic and military (including nuclear) supremacy has given the USA a key role in shaping the post-war world. The 'Cold War' with the Soviet Union after the Second World War ended in 1990. Following terrorist attacks in New York and Washington DC on 11 September 2001, President George W Bush declared a 'war on terror'. As part of this, the USA led multi-national forces in wars on Afghanistan in 2001 (*see* Afghanistan) and Iraq in 2003 (*see* Iraq); US troops remain in both countries to help stabilise internal security. In response to the threat of terrorist attacks on US territory, the Department of Homeland Security was created in 2002.

The 2000 presidential election was won by the

Republican candidate, George W. Bush, with 47.9 per cent of the vote. On 31 October 2004, President Bush was re-elected, with 51 per cent of the vote. In the simultaneous legislative elections, the Republican Party retained its majorities in both houses of Congress, with 55 seats in the Senate and 232 seats in the House of Representatives.

POLITICAL SYSTEM

By the constitution of 17 September 1787 (to which amendments were added in 1791, 1798, 1804, 1865, 1868, 1870, 1913, 1920, 1933, 1951, 1961, 1964, 1967, 1971 and 1992), the government of the USA is entrusted to three separate authorities: the federal executive (the president and cabinet), the legislature (Congress) and the judicature. The president is indirectly elected by an electoral college to serve a four-year term and may serve a maximum of two terms. If a president dies in office, the vice-president serves the remainder of his term. The president appoints the cabinet officers and all the chief officials, subject to confirmation by the Senate. He makes recommendations of a general nature to Congress, and when laws are passed by Congress he may return them to Congress with a veto. But if a measure so vetoed is again passed by both houses of Congress by a two-thirds majority in each house, it becomes law, notwithstanding the objection of the president.

Each of the 50 states in the Union has its own executive, legislature and judiciary. In theory, they are sovereign, but in practice their autonomy is increasingly circumscribed.

PRESIDENTIAL ELECTIONS

Candidates for the presidency must be at least 35 years of age and a native citizen of the USA. The electoral college for each state is directly elected by universal adult suffrage in the November preceding the January in which the presidential term expires. The number of members of the electoral college is equal to the whole number of senators and representatives to which the state is entitled in the Congress. The electoral college for each state meets in its state in December and each member votes for a presidential candidate by ballot. The ballots are sent to Washington, and opened on 6 January by the President of the Senate in the presence of Congress. The candidate who has received a majority of the whole number of electoral votes cast is declared president for the ensuing term. If no one has a majority, then from the highest on the list (not exceeding three) the House of Representatives elects a president, the votes being taken by states, the representation from each state having one vote. A presidential term begins at noon on 20 January.

HEAD OF STATE

President of the United States, George Walker Bush, *born* 6 July 1946, *elected* 2000, *re-elected* 2 November 2004, *sworn in* 20 January 2005
Vice-President, Richard B. Cheney, *born* 30 January 1941

SELECTED GOVERNMENT MEMBERS *as at August 2005*

Secretary of State, Condoleezza Rice
Defence, Donald Rumsfeld
Interior, Gale Norton
Treasury, John Snow
Secretary for Homeland Security, Michael Chertoff
Attorney General, Alberto Gonzales
Education, Margaret Spellings
Health, Mike Leavitt
National Security Adviser, Stephen Hadley
Chief of Staff, Andrew Card

THE CONGRESS

Legislative power is vested in two houses, the Senate and the House of Representatives. The Senate has 100 members, two from each state, elected for a six-year term, with one-third elected every two years. The House of Representatives has 435 members directly elected in each state for a two-year term, a resident commissioner from Puerto Rico and a delegate each from American Samoa, the District of Columbia, Guam and the Virgin Islands, making a total of 440 members. Members of the 109th Congress were elected on 2 November 2004 and the next elections are scheduled for November 2006. The 109th Congress is constituted as follows:

Senate: Republicans 55; Democrats 44; Independent 1
House: Republicans 232; Democrats 202; Independent 1; total 435
President of the Senate, The Vice-President
Senate Majority Leader, Bill Frist *(R),* Tennessee
Speaker of the House of Representatives, J. Dennis Hastert *(R), Illinois*

THE JUDICATURE

The federal judiciary consists of three sets of federal courts: the Supreme Court at Washington DC, consisting of a Chief Justice and eight Associate Justices, the United States Courts of Appeals, consisting of 168 circuit judges within 13 regional circuits, and the 94 United States district courts served by 575 district court judges.

THE SUPREME COURT

US Supreme Court Building, Washington DC 20543
Chief Justice, John Roberts, apptd 2005

UNITED STATES EMBASSY

24 Grosvenor Square, London W1A 1AE T 020-7499 9000
Ambassador Extraordinary and Plenipotentiary, HE Robert H. Tuttle, apptd 2005

US CONSULATES

3 Regent Terrace, Edinburgh, EH7 5BW T 0131-556 8315
Danesfort House, 223 Stranmillis Road, Belfast BT9 5GR
T 028-9038 6100

BRITISH EMBASSY

3100 Massachusetts Avenue NW, Washington DC 20008.
T (+1) (202) 588 7800
Ambassador Extraordinary and Plenipotentiary, HE Sir David Manning, KCMG, apptd 2003

BRITISH COUNCIL

(Cultural Attaché), c/o The British Embassy, 3100 Massachusetts Avenue NW, Washington DC 20008–3600
T (+1) (202) 588 7838 E enquiries@us.britishcouncil.org
Director, Andy Mackay

THE STATES OF THE UNION

The United States of America is a federal republic consisting of 50 states and the federal District of Columbia and of organised territories. Of the present 50 states, 13 are original states, seven were admitted without previous organisation as territories, and 30 were admitted after such organisation.

	Area sq. km	Population (2003 est.)	Capital	Governor (end of term in office)
Alabama (AL) (1819, 22)	133,915	4,500,752	Montgomery	Robert Riley (R), Jan. 2007
Alaska (AK) (1959, 49)	1,530,694	648,818	Juneau	Frank Murkowski (R), Dec. 2006
Arizona (AZ) (1912, 48)	295,259	5,580,811	Phoenix	Janet Napolitano (D), Jan. 2007
Arkansas (AR) (1836, 25)	137,754	2,725,714	Little Rock	Mike Huckabee (R), Jan. 2007
California (CA) (1850, 31)	411,047	35,484,453	Sacramento	Arnold Schwarzenegger (R) Jan. 2007
Colorado (CO) (1876, 38)	269,595	4,550,688	Denver	Bill Owens (R), Jan. 2007
Connecticut (CT) § (1788, 5)	12,997	3,483,372	Hartford	M. J. Rell (R), Jan. 2007
Delaware (DE) § (1787, 1)	5,297	817,491	Dover	Ruth Ann Minner (D), Jan. 2009
Florida (FL) (1845, 27)	151,939	17,019,068	Tallahassee	Jeb Bush (R), Jan. 2007
Georgia (GA) § (1788, 4)	152,576	8,684,715	Atlanta	Sonny Perdue (R), Jan. 2007
Hawaii (HI) (1959, 50)	16,760	1,257,608	Honolulu	Linda Lingle (R), Dec. 2006
Idaho (ID) (1890, 43)	216,430	1,336,332	Boise	Dirk Kempthorne (R), Jan. 2007
Illinois (IL) (1818, 21)	145,933	12,653,544	Springfield	Rod Blagojevich (D), Jan. 2007
Indiana (IN) (1816, 19)	93,719	6,195,643	Indianapolis	Mitch Daniels (R), Jan. 2009
Iowa (IA) (1846, 29)	145,752	2,944,062	Des Moines	Tom Vilsack (D), Jan. 2007
Kansas (KS) (1861, 34)	213,097	2,723,507	Topeka	Kathleen Sebelius (D), Jan. 2007
Kentucky (KY) (1792, 15)	104,661	4,117,827	Frankfort	Ernie Fletcher (R), Dec. 2007
Louisiana (LA) (1812, 18)	123,677	4,496,334	Baton Rouge	Kathleen Blanco (D), Jan. 2008
Maine (ME) (1820, 23)	86,156	1,305,728	Augusta	John Baldacci (D), Jan. 2007
Maryland (MD) § (1788, 7)	27,091	5,508,909	Annapolis	Robert Ehrlich (R), Jan. 2007
Massachusetts (MA) § (1788, 6)	21,455	6,433,422	Boston	Mitt Romney (R), Jan. 2007
Michigan (MI) (1837, 26)	151,584	10,079,985	Lansing	Jennifer Granholm (D), Jan. 2007
Minnesota (MN) (1858, 32)	218,600	5,059,375	St Paul	Tim Pawlenty (R), Jan. 2007
Mississippi (MS) (1817, 20)	123,514	2,881,281	Jackson	Haley Barbour (R), Jan. 2008
Missouri (MO) (1821, 24)	180,514	5,704,484	Jefferson City	Matt Blunt (R), Jan. 2009
Montana (MT) (1889, 41)	380,848	917,621	Helena	Brian Schweitzer (D), Jan. 2009
Nebraska (NE) (1867, 37)	200,349	1,739,291	Lincoln	Dave Heineman (R), Jan. 2007
Nevada (NV) (1864, 36)	286,352	2,241,154	Carson City	Kenny Guinn (R), Jan. 2007
New Hampshire (NH) § (1788, 9)	24,033	1,287,687	Concord	John Lynch (D), Jan. 2007
New Jersey (NJ) § (1787, 3)	20,168	8,638,396	Trenton	Richard Codey (D), Jan. 2006
New Mexico (NM) (1912, 47)	314,925	1,874,614	Santa Fé	Bill Richardson (D), Jan. 2007
New York (NY) § (1788, 11)	127,189	19,190,115	Albany	George Pataki (R), Jan. 2007
North Carolina (NC) § (1789, 12)	136,412	8,407,248	Raleigh	Mike Easley (D), Jan. 2009
North Dakota (ND) (1889, 39)	183,117	633,837	Bismarck	John Hoeven (R), Jan. 2008
Ohio (OH) (1803, 17)	107,044	11,435,798	Columbus	Bob Taft (R), Jan. 2007
Oklahoma (OK) (1907, 46)	181,185	3,511,532	Oklahoma City	Brad Henry (D), Jan. 2007
Oregon (OR) (1859, 33)	251,418	3,559,596	Salem	Ted Kulongoski (D), Jan. 2007

Famous early novelists include Charles Brockden Brown (1771–1810), Nathaniel Hawthorne (1804–1864) and Mark Twain (1835–1910). Walt Whitman (1819–1892) and Emily Dickinson (1830–1886) are two of 19th-century America's finest poets. The early 20th century saw the emergence of the writers such as F. Scott Fitzgerald (1896–1940), William Faulkner (1897–1962), Ernest Hemingway (1899–1961) and John Steinbeck (1902–1968). Notable modern writers include Toni Morrison (b. 1931), John Irving (b. 1942) and Paul Auster (b. 1947).

The Hollywood film industry is the most wide-reaching in the world and celebrated names include Orson Welles (1915–85), Frank Capra (1897–1991), Stanley Kubrick (1928–99), Francis Ford Coppola (b. 1939), Martin Scorsese (b. 1942) and Steven Spielberg (b. 1946).

Modern art found a spiritual home on the east coast and the Guggenheim and Metropolitan Museums of art in New York both house vast collections of famous works. Renowned artists include Edward Hopper (1882–1967), Jackson Pollock (1912–56), Roy Lichtenstein (1923–97) and Andy Warhol (1928–87).

US TERRITORIES, ETC

Responsibility within the federal government for the US insular areas other than Puerto Rico and Kingman Reef lies with the US Department of the Interior: the Office of Insular Affairs deals with American Samoa, Guam, the Northern Mariana Islands, the US Virgin Islands, Navassa Island (7.8 sq. km), Palmyra Atoll (4 sq. km) and Wake Atoll (6.4 sq. km) (shared with the United States Army Space and Missile Defense Command); and the US Fish and Wildlife Service deals with Baker Island (1.5 sq. km), Howland Island (2.5 sq. km) and Jarvis Island (4.2 sq. km), Midway Atoll (5.2 sq. km) and Johnston Atoll (2.5 sq. km) (shared with the Defence Special Weapons Agency).

Four of the eight populated insular areas are represented in the US House of Representatives, Puerto Rico by a resident commissioner and American Samoa, Guam and the US Virgin Islands by one non-voting delegate each. Although represented in the US House of Representatives by a delegate, the District of Columbia was an incorporated territory for only three years (1871–4).

THE COMMONWEALTH OF PUERTO RICO

AREA – 9,104 sq. km

POPULATION – 3,834,000 (2001 est.). The majority of the inhabitants are of Spanish descent, and Spanish and English are the official languages

CAPITAL – ΨSan Juan, population of the municipality (2002 estimate), 433,412. Other major towns are: Bayamón; Carolina; ΨPonce

Puerto Rico (Rich Port) is an island of the Greater Antilles group in the West Indies and was discovered in 1493 by Columbus. It was a Spanish possession until 1898, when it was ceded to the USA after the Spanish–American War. The 1952 constitution establishes the Commonwealth of Puerto Rico with full powers of internal self-government. The bicameral Legislative Assembly consists of the 27-member Senate and the 51-member House of Representatives, who serve a four-year term; proposals to replace these bodies with a one-chamber legislature were approved by referendum in July 2005. The governor is

popularly elected for a term of four years. Residents of Puerto Rico are US citizens. Puerto Rico is represented in Congress by a resident commissioner, elected for a term of four years, who has a seat in the House of Representatives but not a vote, although he has a right to vote on those committees of which he is a member.

Governor, Anibal Acevedo Vila (PDP)

Trade with UK	2003	2004
Imports from UK	£321,846,000	£188,890,000
Exports to UK	486,244,000	430,673,000

GUAM

AREA – 545 sq. km

POPULATION – 160,000 (2001 est.): 43 per cent Chamorro stock mixed with Filipino and Spanish. The Chamorro language belongs to the Malayo-Polynesian family, but with considerable admixture of Spanish. Chamorro and English are the official languages; most Chamorro residents are bilingual

CAPITAL – Hagatna (also known as Agana). Port of entry, ΨApra

Guam is the largest of the Mariana Islands, in the north Pacific Ocean. A Spanish colony for centuries, it was ceded to the USA in 1898 after the Spanish–American War. Guam was occupied by the Japanese in 1941 but was recaptured by US forces in 1944. Under the Organic Act of Guam 1950, Guam has statutory powers of self-government, and any person born in Guam is a US citizen but cannot vote in a US presidential election. A 15-member unicameral legislature is popularly elected biennially. The governor and lieutenant-governor are popularly elected. There is also a District Court of Guam, with original jurisdiction in cases under federal law. Guam's two main sources of revenue are tourism (particularly from Japan) and US military spending.

Governor, Felix Perez Camacho (R)

AMERICAN SAMOA

AREA – 199 sq. km

POPULATION – 67,084 (2001 est.)

CAPITAL – ΨPago Pago (population, 3,519)

NATIONAL DAY – 17 April (Flag Day)

American Samoa consists of the islands of Tutuila, Aunu'u, Ofu, Olesega, Ta'u, Rose and Swains Islands. Those born in American Samoa are US non-citizen nationals, but some have acquired citizenship through service in the US armed forces or other naturalisation procedure. The 1966 constitution grants American Samoa a measure of self-government, with certain powers reserved to the US Secretary of the Interior. There is a bicameral legislature of 21 seats, 20 elected, one appointed, with popularly elected representatives and 18 traditionally elected senators, and a popularly elected governor.

Governor, Togiola Tulafono (D)

THE UNITED STATES VIRGIN ISLANDS

AREA – 363 sq. km

POPULATION – 123,000 (2001 est.)

CAPITAL – ΨCharlotte Amalie (population, 12,331, 1990), on St Thomas

The US Virgin Islands were purchased from Denmark and came under US sovereignty in 1917. There are three main islands, St Thomas, St Croix, St John and about 50 small islets or cays. Under the provisions of the Revised Organic Act of the Virgin Islands 1954, legislative power is vested in the unicameral Legislature, composed of 15 senators popularly elected for two-year terms. The governor is popularly elected. Those born in the US Virgin Islands are US nationals.

Governor, Charles Wesley Turnbull (D)

NORTHERN MARIANA ISLANDS
AREA – 477 sq. km
POPULATION – 77,000 (2001 est.)
SEAT OF GOVERNMENT – Saipan (population, 52,706, 1995 census)

The USA administered the Northern Mariana Islands, in the north-west Pacific Ocean, as part of a UN Trusteeship until the trusteeship agreement was terminated in 1986, bringing fully into effect a 1976 congressional law establishing the Northern Mariana Islands as a Commonwealth under US sovereignty. Most of the then residents became US citizens. Those born subsequently in the Northern Mariana Islands are US citizen nationals. There is a popularly elected bicameral legislature and a popularly elected governor.

Governor, Juan N. Babauta (R)

URUGUAY

República Oriental del Uruguay – Eastern Republic of Uruguay

AREA – 175,000 sq. km. Neighbours: Argentina (west), Brazil (north and east)
POPULATION – 3,399,237 (2004 est.): predominantly of Spanish and Italian descent. Spanish is the official language. Many Uruguayans are Roman Catholics. There is no established church
CAPITAL – ΨMontevideo (population, 1,303,182, 1996)
MAJOR CITIES – Canelones; Melo; Mercedes; Minas; ΨPaysandú; Punta del Este; Rivera; Salto
CURRENCY – Uruguayan peso of 100 centésimos
NATIONAL ANTHEM – Orientales, la patria o la tumba [Uruguayans, the fatherland or death]
NATIONAL DAY – 25 August (Declaration of Independence, 1825)
NATIONAL FLAG – Four blue and five white horizontal stripes surcharged with sun on a white ground in the top corner, next flagstaff
LIFE EXPECTANCY (years) – 75.92 (2004 est.)
MORTALITY RATE (per 1,000 population) – 9.07 (2004 est.)
INFANT MORTALITY (per 1,000 births) – 12.31 (2004 est.)
HIV / AIDS ADULT PREVALENCE – 0.3 per cent (2001 est.)
DEATH PENALTY – No (abolished 1907)
POPULATION GROWTH RATE – 0.51 per cent (2004 est.)
POPULATION DENSITY – 19 per sq. km (2002)
URBAN POPULATION – 92 per cent (2001)
MILITARY EXPENDITURE – 0.9 per cent of GDP (2003)
MILITARY PERSONNEL – 24,000: Army 15,200, Navy 5,700, Air Force 3,100; Paramilitaries 920

CLIMATE AND TERRAIN
The country consists mainly of undulating grassy plains, with low hills. Elevation extremes range from 514 m

(Cerro Catedral) at the highest point to 0 m (Atlantic Ocean) at the lowest. The principal river is the Rio Negro (with its tributary the Yi), flowing from north-east to south-west into the Rio Uruguay. Average temperatures in Montevideo range from 6°C in July and to 28°C in January.

HISTORY AND POLITICS
Originally populated by the Charras Amerindians, the Rio de la Plata was first visited by the Spanish in 1515 and, although initially colonised by the Portuguese, the *Banda Oriental*, as the territory lying on the eastern bank of the Uruguay River was then called, formed part of Spanish South America from 1726 to 1814. Briefly independent, it became a province of Brazil in 1820, throwing off Brazilian rule in 1825. Its independence was recognised in 1828, and a republic was inaugurated in 1830. In the mid-19th century there was a power struggle, descending into civil war, between the conservatives *(Blancos)* and liberals *(Colorados)* which ended when the latter took office in the 1860s and governed until 1958, interspersed with periods of military dictatorship.

The period from 1962 until 1973 saw unrest caused by the Marxist Tupamaros guerrillas. They were crushed by a military dictatorship that held power from 1973 until 1985, when a return to civilian rule was agreed after violent anti-government protests at the regime's repressive rule and the deteriorating economy. The presidential and general elections returned the Colorado Party to power and Julio Sanguinetti became president. The first fully free presidential and legislative elections since 1971 were held in 1989, and were won by the National *(Blanco)* Party.

The Colorado and National *(Blanco)* parties now both occupy the centre ground, and their dominance of politics has been eroded by left-wing parties such as New Space and coalitions such as the Progressive Encounter–Broad Front (EP-FA). The EP-FA won the most seats in both houses of the General Assembly in the 1999 elections but lacked an overall majority in either, and a coalition government was formed by the Colorado Party and the National Party. In the legislative election in October 2004, the EP-FA won outright majorities in both houses and formed the government. The presidential election in October 2004 was won by Tabaré Vázquez of the EP-FA, the first left-wing president to hold office.

POLITICAL SYSTEM
Under the 1997 constitution, the head of state is a president directly elected for a five-year term that may not immediately be renewed. The president, who is also head of government and appoints the Council of Ministers, is responsible to the General Assembly. The bicameral legislature, the General Assembly, consists of a Chamber of Representatives, the lower house, and a Chamber of Senators. The Chamber of Representatives has 99 members directly elected for a five-year term. The Chamber of Senators has 31 members, 30 directly elected for five years by proportional representation and the vice-president as an *ex officio* member. The republic is divided into 19 departments, each with an elected governor and legislature.

HEAD OF STATE
President, Tabaré Vázquez, *elected* October 2004, *took office* 1 March 2005
Vice-President, Rodolfo Nin Novoa

SELECTED GOVERNMENT MEMBERS *as at August 2005*
Economy and Finance, Danilo Astori
Foreign Relations, Reinaldo Gargano
Interior, Jose Diaz
Defence, Azucena Berruti

EMBASSY OF URUGUAY
2nd Floor, 140 Brompton Road, London SW3 1HY
T 020-7589 8835
Ambassador Extraordinary and Plenipotentiary, HE Ricardo
   Varela, apptd 2005

BRITISH EMBASSY
Calle Marco Bruto 1073, 11300 Montevideo (PO Box 16024).
T (+598) (2) 622 3650/3630 E bemonte@internet.com.uy
Ambassador Extraordinary and Plenipotentiary, HE John
   Everard, apptd 2001

ECONOMY AND TRADE

The economic problems of Brazil and Argentina,
Uruguay's main export markets and sources of tourists,
caused an economic crisis in 2002. Inflation,
unemployment and external debt all increasing
significantly. IMF loans and rescheduling of foreign debt
repayments, along with the government's emergency
measures, helped to achieve a fragile recovery. However,
the recession has left many living in poverty in what had
previously been a moderately prosperous society.

Ranching and livestock products (beef, mutton, wool)
have been the mainstay of the economy since the mid-
19th century, generating the prosperity that enabled
Uruguay to develop an extensive welfare system in the
early years of the 20th century. However, the dependence
on these products leaves the economy vulnerable to price
fluctuations, a cause of the recent recession. Other crops
include rice, wheat, barley, linseed and sunflower seed.
Other foodstuffs (citrus, wine, beer), fishing and textile
industries are also of importance. Textiles, tyres, sheet-
glass, three-ply wood, cement, leather-curing, beet-sugar,
plastics, household consumer goods and edible oils are
produced. Exploited minerals include clinker, dolomite,
marble and granite. In recent years, tourism and offshore
financial services have contributed substantially to
revenue.

The major exports are meat, meat by-products and
livestock, agricultural products and textiles. The principal
imports are machinery and transport equipment and
chemical products. Principal trading partners are Brazil,
Argentina, the USA and Germany.

GNI – US$14,600 million (2002); US$4,340 per capita
   (2002)
ANNUAL AVERAGE GROWTH OF GDP – 10.2 per cent
   (2004 est.)
INFLATION RATE – 19.4 per cent (2003 est.)
UNEMPLOYMENT – 13 per cent (2004 est.)
TOTAL EXTERNAL DEBT – US$8,196 million (2000 est.)
FOREIGN DIRECT INVESTMENT – US$851 million
   (1997–2000)
IMPORTS – US$2,200 million (2003)
EXPORTS – US$2,200 million (2003)

BALANCE OF PAYMENTS
Trade – US$182 million surplus (2003)
Current Account – US$52 million surplus (2003)

Trade with UK	2003	2004
Imports from UK	£31,723,000	£30,806,000
Exports to UK	44,265,000	43,931,000

TRANSPORT INFRASTRUCTURE

There are nearly 9,000 km of roads, 8,000 km of which
are surfaced, and over 2,000 km of railway in use. The
international airport of Carrasco lies 19 km outside
Montevideo. There are 1,600 km of navigable waterways,
mainly on the Uruguay and Negro rivers. A bridge across
the River Plate links Uruguay and Argentina. The main
ports are Montevideo and Colonia on the coast, and Fray
Bentos and Paysandú on the River Uruguay.

EDUCATION

Primary and secondary education is compulsory and free,
and technical and trade schools and evening courses for
adult education are state-controlled. The university at
Montevideo (founded in 1849) has ten faculties and a
new university has been built at Salto.
ILLITERACY RATE – (m) 2.6 per cent; (f) 1.8 per cent
   (2000)
GROSS ENROLMENT RATIO (percentage of relevant age
   group) – primary 108 per cent (2002); secondary 101
   per cent (2002); tertiary 38 per cent (2002)

MEDIA

The constitution enshrines freedom of expression. There
are more than 100 daily and weekly newspapers, all
privately owned, and more than 100 radio stations, as
well as 20 television channels. The government runs one
television and one radio station.

UZBEKISTAN

Ŭzbekiston Zumhurijati – Republic of Uzbekistan

AREA – 414,200 sq. km. Neighbours: Kazakhstan (north
   and west), Kyrgyzstan and Tajikistan (east),
   Afghanistan and Turkmenistan (south)
POPULATION – 26,410,416 (2004 est.): 72 per cent
   Uzbek, 8 per cent Russian, 5 per cent Tajik and 4 per
   cent Kazakh, with smaller numbers of Tatars, Kara-
   Kalpaks, Koreans, Ukrainians and Kyrgyz. The
   predominant religion is Sunni Muslim. Islam is
   tolerated within strict bounds; it is allowed to play no
   part in politics. The official language is Uzbek (72 per
   cent); Russian (8 per cent), Tajik (5 per cent) and
   Kazakh (4 per cent) are also spoken. Uzbek is one of
   the Turkic group of languages. In 1994 the
   government approved a six-year programme for the
   transfer of the Uzbek language to a Latin script
CAPITAL – Tashkent (population, 2,142,700, 1998
   estimate)
MAJOR CITIES – Samarkand, which contains the Gur-
   Emir (Tamerlane's Mausoleum); Bukhara, which
   contains the Samanid Mausoleum and the Ulughbek
   Madrassah
CURRENCY – Sum of 100 tiyin
NATIONAL DAY – 1 September (Independence Day)
NATIONAL FLAG – Three horizontal stripes of blue,
   white, green, with the white fimbriated in red; on the
   blue near the hoist a crescent and twelve stars, all in
   white
LIFE EXPECTANCY (years) – 64.09 (2004 est.)
MORTALITY RATE (per 1,000 population) – 7.95
   (2004 est.)
INFANT MORTALITY (per 1,000 births) – 71.3
   (2004 est.)
DEATH PENALTY – Yes

POPULATION GROWTH RATE – 1.65 per cent
(2004 est.)
POPULATION DENSITY – 61 per sq. km (2002)
URBAN POPULATION – 37 per cent (2001 est.)
MILITARY EXPENDITURE – 5 per cent of GDP (2004)
MILITARY PERSONNEL – 50,000–55,000: Army
40,000, Air Force 10,000–15,000; Paramilitaries
18,000–20,000
CONSCRIPTION DURATION – 12 months
ILLITERACY RATE – (m) 0.4 per cent; (f) 1 per cent
(2003 est.)
GROSS ENROLMENT RATIO (percentage of relevant age
group) – primary 103 per cent (2002); secondary 99
per cent (2002); tertiary 9 per cent (2002)

CLIMATE AND TERRAIN

The terrain of landlocked Uzbekistan falls from the high
Tien Shan mountains and the Pamir highlands in the east
and south-east to the desert lowlands in the west and
north-west, in the basin of the Amudarya river and the
southern part of the Aral Sea. Elevation extremes range
from 4,301 m (Adelunga Toghi) at the highest point to
−12 m (Sariqarnish Kuli) at the lowest. Average
temperatures in Tashkent range from −2°C in January to
33°C in June.

HISTORY AND POLITICS

Part of the Persian empire and then the empire of
Alexander the Great, Samarkand developed as an
important transit point on the ancient 'Silk Road' in the
first century BC. In the 13th century the area became part
of the Mongol empire, with Samarkand as its capital
during the reign of Amir Timur (Tamerlane). With the
decline of the Mongol empire, independent emirates and
khanates emerged. The three khanates in what is now
Uzbekistan, Khiva, Kokand and Bukhara, were annexed
by the Russian Empire in the second half of the 19th
century. In 1917 a Bolshevik revolution broke out in
Tashkent and by 1921 all of Uzbekistan had been
absorbed into the Soviet Union. Under Soviet rule a
massive land irrigation programme was implemented to
allow the cultivation of cotton, but led to the drying up of
the Aral Sea.

Uzbekistan declared its independence from the Soviet
Union on 1 September 1991. Post-independence,
political life is dominated by the former communists. The
main opposition parties, Erk (Freedom) and Birlik (Unity),
have been banned since 1992, other forms of opposition
are suppressed and the government has been accused of
human rights abuses, including the systematic use of
torture. The former communist leader Islam Karimov, who
came to power in 1990, was elected president in 1991
and has retained the presidency since in unopposed
elections or through the extension of his term of office in
referenda. All legislative elections since independence
have been won by the People's Democratic Party, the
former Communist Party, or its allies. Following the latest
legislative election in December 2004 and January 2005,
the largest party in the Legislative Chamber is the pro-
Karimov Liberal Democratic Party; opposition parties
were barred from contesting the election. Most elections
have been reported by observers to be neither free nor fair
and have attracted international criticism.

INSURGENCIES

The Islamic Movement of Uzbekistan (IMU), which seeks
to establish an Islamic state, was founded in 1996. Whilst
it has carried out car bombings in Tashkent, its activities
have centred on the Fergana valley, where it has clashed
with Kyrgyz armed forces. The government is suspected
of using the insurgency as a means of suppressing
opposition by non-IMU members.

POLITICAL SYSTEM

The 1992 constitution was amended in 2002 to create a
bicameral legislature and extend the president's term of
office. The president is directly elected; his term of office
was five years, renewable only once, but was extended in
2002 to seven years. The legislature, the Supreme
Assembly, became bicameral after the 2004/5 elections.
The lower house, the Legislative Assembly, has 120
members directly elected for a five-year term. The Senate
has 100 members, 16 appointed by the president and the
rest elected by regional deputies to represent the regions
and the capital, who serve a five-year term. The president
appoints the cabinet, which is chaired by the prime
minister.

The country is divided into the republic of
Karakalpakstan and 12 regions: Andijan, Bukhara, Jizak,
Fergana, Kashka-Darya, Khorezm, Namanghan, Navoi,
Samarkand, Surhan-Darya, Syr-Darya and Tashkent.

HEAD OF STATE
President, Islam Karimov, *elected* 29 December 1991,
elected by referendum for a five-year term 26 March 1995,
re-elected 9 January 2000

SELECTED GOVERNMENT MEMBERS *as at August 2005*
Prime Minister, Shavkat Mirziyaev
Defence, Bkadyr Ghulomov
Finance, Saidakhmoad Rakhimov
Foreign Affairs, Eler Ganiev
Interior, Zokirjon Almatov

EMBASSY OF THE REPUBLIC OF UZBEKISTAN
41 Holland Park, London W11 3RP T 020-7229 7679
Ambassador Extraordinary and Plenipotentiary, HE
Tukhtapulat Riskiev, apptd 2003

BRITISH EMBASSY
Ul. Gulyamova 67, UZ-700000 Tashkent T (+998) (71) 1206451
Ambassador Extraordinary and Plenipotentiary, HE David
Moran, apptd 2005

BRITISH COUNCIL
11 D. Kounaev Street, Tashkent T (+998) (71) 120 6752
E bc-tashkent@britishcouncil.uz
Director, Neville McBain

ECONOMY AND TRADE

The economy remains centrally planned and economic
growth and living standards are among the worst in the
former Soviet republics. Much foreign aid has been cut or
withdrawn in protest at the country's poor human rights
record. The economy is based on intensive agricultural
production. Cotton production is approximately 4 million
tonnes per year, made possible by extensive irrigation
schemes. Textile manufacture, silk production and leather
goods are also important while wheat, potatoes and rice
are widely grown. There are some agricultural and textile
machinery plants and several chemical combines.
Uzbekistan possesses a wide range of mineral deposits,
including copper, uranium, oil, gold and many other
metals; total gold reserves are estimated at more than
5,000 tons. In 1998 oil output was 8.0 million tons, and
gas production was 55 billion cubic metres. The principal

exports are cotton, gold, natural gas, mineral fertilisers, ferrous metals, textiles and motor vehicles.

GNI – US$7,800 million (2002); US$310 per capita (2002)

ANNUAL AVERAGE GROWTH OF GDP – 4.4 per cent (2004 est.)

TOTAL EXTERNAL DEBT – US$4,340 million (2000 est.)

FOREIGN DIRECT INVESTMENT – US$698 million (1997–2000)

Trade with UK	2003	2004
Imports from UK	£18,225,000	£20,475,000
Exports to UK	28,956,000	26,538,000

TRANSPORT INFRASTRUCTURE

Uzbekistan has 81,600 km of roads, 71,000 km of which are paved. It has nearly 4,000 km of railway, and 1,100 km of waterways. The principal airport is at Tashkent.

MEDIA

There is a mix of government-run and private television and radio stations in Uzbekistan. Almost all newspapers are produced by the state or by pro-government organisations. In both print and broadcast media, despite constitutional protection of free speech, the government strictly controls political content. *Khalq Sozi* is one of the major daily newspapers.

VANUATU

Ripablik blong Vanuatu / Republic of Vanuatu / République de Vanuatu

AREA – 12,189 sq. km

POPULATION – 202,609 (2004 est.). About 95 per cent are Melanesian, the rest being mostly Micronesian, Polynesian and European. The national language is Bislama, but English and French are also official languages

CAPITAL – ΨPort Vila (population, 29,356, 1999 census), on Efate

MAJOR TOWN – Luganville, on Espiritu Santo

CURRENCY – Vatu of 100 centimes

NATIONAL ANTHEM – Nasonal sing sing blong Vanuatu [National anthem of Vanuatu]

NATIONAL DAY – 30 July (Independence Day)

NATIONAL FLAG – Red over green with a black triangle in the hoist, the three parts being divided by fimbriations of black and yellow, and in the centre of the black triangle a boar's tusk overlaid by two crossed fern leaves

LIFE EXPECTANCY (years) – 62.1 (2004 est.)

MORTALITY RATE (per 1,000 population) – 8.02 (2004 est.)

INFANT MORTALITY (per 1,000 births) – 56.63 (2004 est.)

DEATH PENALTY – No (abolished 1980)

POPULATION GROWTH RATE – 1.57 per cent (2004 est.)

POPULATION DENSITY – 15 per sq. km (1999)

CLIMATE AND TERRAIN

Situated in the south Pacific Ocean, Vanuatu includes 13 large and some 70 small islands, of coral and volcanic origin, including the Banks and Torres Islands in the north. The principal islands are Vanua Lava, Espiritu Santo, Maewo, Pentecost, Ambae, Malekula, Ambrym, Epi, Efate, Erromango, Tanna and Aneityum. Most islands are mountainous and there are active volcanoes on several. Elevation extremes range from 1,877 m (Tabwemasana) at the highest point to 0 m (Pacific Ocean) at the lowest. The climate is tropical, and the average temperature is 29°C all year round.

HISTORY AND POLITICS

Some of the islands of Vanuatu have been inhabited for over 4,000 years. Europeans first visited in the early 17th century, and Captain Cook named the islands the New Hebrides in 1774. Settlers began to arrive in Vanuatu in the second half of the 19th century. The islands were settled in the 19th century by the British and the French, who established plantations, and from 1906 were jointly administered as the Condominium of the New Hebrides. This became independent as the Republic of Vanuatu in 1980.

In the July 2004 legislative elections, the National United Party (NUP) won 10 seats, becoming the largest party in parliament. On 29 July 2004, Serge Vohor of the Union of Moderate Parties (UMP) was elected prime minister and formed a six-party coalition government. Vohor lost a vote of confidence in December 2004 and was replaced by Ham Lini and formed a nine-party coalition government. Alfred Maseng was elected president in April 2004 but was removed from office on 10 May because he was ineligible to stand for election. His successor, Kalkot Matas Kelekele, was elected on 17 August 2004.

POLITICAL SYSTEM

Under the 1980 constitution, the head of state is a president who is elected for a five-year term by an electoral college consisting of the presidents of the six provincial governments and the members of parliament. The unicameral parliament has 52 members, directly elected for a four-year term. The executive is the prime minister, who is elected by parliament from among its members, and the council of ministers. A Council of Chiefs advises on matters of custom.

HEAD OF STATE
President, Kalkot Matas Kelekele, *elected* 17 August 2004

SELECTED GOVERNMENT MEMBERS *at August 2005*
Prime Minister, Public Services, Ham Lini
Deputy Prime Minister, Foreign Affairs, Sato Kilman
Finance and Economic Development, Moana Carcasses
Foreign Affairs, Barak Tame Sope
Internal Affairs, Georges Andre Wells

BRITISH HIGH COMMISSION
KPMG House, Rue Pasteur, PO Box 567, Port Vila
T (+678) 23100 E bhcvila@vanuatu.com.vu
High Commissioner, HE Michael Hill, OBE, apptd 2000

ECONOMY AND TRADE

Most of the population is employed on plantations or in subsistence agriculture. Subsistence crops include yams, taro, manioc, sweet potato and breadfruit; the principal cash crops are copra, cocoa and coffee. Cattle are kept on the plantations. There is a small light industrial sector. Eco-tourism is of growing importance, and the absence of direct taxation has led to growth in the finance and associated industries. The principal exports are copra, timber, beef and cocoa. The main trading partner is Japan.

GNI – US$212 million (2001); US$1,050 per capita (2001)

ANNUAL AVERAGE GROWTH OF GDP – 1.1 per cent (2003 est.)
INFLATION RATE – 2 per cent (2002 est.)
TOTAL EXTERNAL DEBT – US$69 million (2000 est.)
IMPORTS – US$105 million (2003)
EXPORTS – US$21 million (2003)

BALANCE OF PAYMENTS
Trade – US$58 million deficit (2001)
Current Account – US$15 million deficit (2001)

Trade with UK	2003	2004
Imports from UK	£121,000	£213,000
Exports to UK	219,000	343,000

TRANSPORT INFRASTRUCTURE
Vanuatu has just over 1,000 km of roads, of which about one quarter is surfaced. The islands have no waterways or railways. The main ports are Forari, Port Vila and Santo. There are about 30 airports and airstrips on the islands.

MEDIA
The majority of media in Vanuatu is state-owned. This includes one television station and one radio company. There are four newspapers, one of which, *Vanuatu Weekly*, is state-run.

VATICAN CITY STATE

Status Civitatis Vaticanae/Stato della Città del Vaticano – State of the Vatican City

AREA – 0.44 sq. km. Neighbour: Rome (Italy)
POPULATION – 911 (2003 est.). The languages are Latin and Italian
CAPITAL – Vatican City (population, 766, 1988)
CURRENCY – Euro (€) of 100 cents
NATIONAL ANTHEM – Inno e Marcia Pontificale (Hymn and Pontifical March)
NATIONAL DAY – 22 October (Inauguration of present Pontiff)
NATIONAL FLAG – Square flag; equal vertical bands of yellow (next staff), and white; crossed keys and triple crown device on white band
DEATH PENALTY – No (abolished 1969)
POPULATION DENSITY – 2,273 per sq. km (1997)
ANNUAL AVERAGE GROWTH OF GDP – 1.3 per cent (1998)

HISTORY
The Vatican City is surrounded on all sides by Rome. The head of the Roman Catholic Church became a temporal ruler in the eighth century. The Papal States were annexed in 1860 by the newly unified kingdom of Italy and Rome was captured by Italian troops in 1870–1, when the pope withdrew into the Vatican Palace. In the Lateran Treaties (1929), Italy recognised the pope's sovereignty over the city of the Vatican, and declared the state to be neutral and inviolable territory.

The head of state is the the Pope, the Sovereign Pontiff. He is elected for life by a conclave consisting of members of the Sacred College of Cardinals. Administration of the Vatican City State is carried out by the Pontifical Commission, which is appointed by the pope. All Vatican officials vacate their offices on the death of a pope. Pope Benedict XVI confirmed in office the president of the Pontifical Commission and the Secretariat of State in April 2005.

Sovereign Pontiff, His Holiness Pope Benedict XVI (Joseph Ratzinger), *born* at Bavaria 1927, *elected* in succession to Pope John Paul II, 19 April 2005, *inaugurated* 24 April 2005

SECRETARIAT OF STATE *as at August 2005*
Secretary of State, Cardinal Angelo Sodano, apptd 1990, re-apptd April 2005
Assistant Secretary of State, Archbishop Leonardo Sandri
Secretary for Relations with States, Giovanni Lajolo

PONTIFICAL COMMISSION
President, Cardinal Edmund Casimir Szoka

APOSTOLIC NUNCIATURE
54 Parkside, London SW19 5NE T 020-8944 7189
Apostolic Nuncio, HE Archbishop Faustino Sainz Munoz, apptd 2005

BRITISH EMBASSY TO THE HOLY SEE
91 Via dei Condotti, I-00187 Rome T (+39) (06) 6992 3561
Ambassador Extraordinary and Plenipotentiary, HE Kathryn Colvin, apptd 2002

MEDIA AND CULTURE
There is one official television channel in the Vatican City, and one official radio station (Vatican Radio), broadcasting seven channels. The Vatican Information Service is the state's official news service.

The city is a World Heritage Site. Its architectural masterpiece, St Peter's Basilica, is famed for its domed roof and the Sistine Chapel ceiling, respectively designed and painted by Michelangelo. Much of the state's wealth is in a vast art collection.

VENEZUELA

República Bolivariana de Venezuela – Bolivarian Republic of Venezuela

AREA – 882,100 sq. km. Neighbours: Colombia (west), Guyana (east), Brazil (south)
POPULATION – 25,017,387 (2004 est.): 67 per cent mestizo, 21 per cent white, 10 per cent black and 2 per cent Amerindian. The language is Spanish. 93 per cent of the population is Roman Catholic
CAPITAL – Ψ Caracas (population, 3,435,795, 2002 estimate)
MAJOR CITIES – Barquisimeto; ΨMaracaibo; Maracay; Valencia
CURRENCY – Bolívar (Bs) of 100 céntimos
NATIONAL ANTHEM – Gloria al bravo pueblo [Glory to the brave people]
NATIONAL DAY – 5 July
NATIONAL FLAG – Three horizontal stripes of yellow, blue, red with an arc of seven white stars on the blue stripe and a coat of arms on the upper hoist.
LIFE EXPECTANCY (years) – 74.06 (2004 est.)
MORTALITY RATE (per 1,000 population) – 4.9 (2004 est.)
INFANT MORTALITY (per 1,000 births) – 22.99 (2004 est.)
HIV / AIDS ADULT PREVALENCE – 0.5 per cent (2001 est.)
DEATH PENALTY – No (abolished 1863)

POPULATION GROWTH RATE – 1.44 per cent (2004 est.)
POPULATION DENSITY – 28 per sq. km (2002)
URBAN POPULATION – 87 per cent (2001)
ILLITERACY RATE – (m) 6.2 per cent; (f) 6.9 per cent
(2003 est.)
GROSS ENROLMENT RATIO (percentage of relevant age
group) – primary 106 per cent (2002); secondary 69
per cent (2002); tertiary 18 per cent (2002)

CLIMATE AND TERRAIN

The Andean mountains, of which the main range is the
Sierra Nevada de Mérida, run across the north-west of the
country, separating the northern coast from the central
plains (llanos). The Guiana Highlands occupy the south-
east of the country. Elevation extremes range from 5,007
m (Pico Bolivar) at the highest point to 0 m (Caribbean
Sea) at the lowest. The River Orinoco flows across the
centre of the country to its delta on the Atlantic coast. Its
upper waters are united with those of the Rio Negro (a
Brazilian tributary of the Amazon) by a natural river or
canal, known as the Brazo Casiquiare. The coastal regions
contain many lagoons and lakes, including Maracaibo
(area 13,351 sq. km), the largest lake in South America.
The wet season lasts from May to November. Average
temperatures in Caracas range from 16°C in January to
29°C in June.

HISTORY AND POLITICS

The first Spanish settlement was established at Cumaná in
1520 and Venezuela became part of the Viceroyalty of
New Granada in the early 18th century. There were
several revolts against Spanish colonial rule, and a
declaration of independence in 1811 was followed by
several years of struggle until troops led by Simón Bolivar
defeated the Spanish at the battle of Carabobo in 1821.
Venezuela became part of Gran Colombia (with
Colombia, Ecuador and Panama), and then an
independent republic in 1830 under the first of a series of
caudillos (military leaders). The first truly democratic
elections were held in 1947 but the government was
overthrown by the military within months. An enduring
civilian democracy was established in 1958 and
introduced a period of relative political stability.

Oil revenues supported a buoyant economy in the
1970s but economic difficulties since the mid-1980s, and
the austerity measures adopted since 1989 to address
these, have caused social unrest and a number of
attempted coups against President Carlos Andrés Pérez
and President Hugo Chávez, elected in 1998. President
Chávez's economic reforms and his authoritarian style
have provoked strikes and demonstrations, an attempted
military coup in 2002 and a recall referendum in 2004,
which he won.

In the 2000 legislative election, the president's
Patriotic Front movement retained power. The next
legislative election is scheduled for 4 December 2005.

POLITICAL SYSTEM

Under the 1999 constitution, the executive president is
directly elected for a six-year term, renewable only once.
The unicameral legislature, the National Assembly
(Asamblea Nacional), has 165 members, directly elected
for a five-year term. The president appoints the vice-
president and the Council of Ministers.

The country is divided into 22 states, two federal
territories, one federal district (around the capital) and 72
federal dependencies. The states have considerable

autonomy and each has its own legislature and elected
governor.

HEAD OF STATE

President, Hugo Chávez Frías, elected 6 December 1998,
sworn in 2 February 1999, re-elected 30 July 2000
Vice-President, José Vicente Rangel

SELECTED GOVERNMENT MEMBERS as at August 2005
Interior and Justice, Jesse Chacón
Defence, Orlando Manigilia
Finance, Nelson Morentes
Foreign Relations, Ali Rodriguez Arague

EMBASSY OF THE BOLIVARIAN REPUBLIC OF
VENEZUELA
1 Cromwell Road, London SW7 2HR T 020-7584 4206
Ambassador Extraordinary and Plenipotentiary, HE Alfredo
Toro-Hardy, apptd 2001

BRITISH EMBASSY
Edificio Torre Las Mercedes (Piso 3), Avenida La Estancia, Chuao
(Apartado 1246), Caracas 1061 T (+58) (212) 993 4111/4224
Ambassador Extraordinary and Plenipotentiary, HE Donald
Lamont apptd 2003

BRITISH COUNCIL
Piso 3, Torre Credicard, Av. Principal Fl Bosque, El Bosque,
Caracas T (+58) (212) 952 9965
E bc-venezuela@britishcouncil.org.ve
Director, Barbara Wickham

DEFENCE

The Army has 81 main battle tanks, 290 armoured
personnel carriers and seven attack helicopters. The Navy
has two submarines, six frigates, six patrol and coastal
vessels, three combat aircraft and nine armed helicopters
at nine bases. The Air Force has 125 combat aircraft and
31 armed helicopters.
MILITARY EXPENDITURE – 1.5 per cent of GDP (2003)
MILITARY PERSONNEL – 82,300: Army 34,000, Navy
18,300, Air Force 7,000, National Guard 23,000
CONSCRIPTION DURATION – 30 months (selective)

ECONOMY AND TRADE

The oil and gas industries are the mainstays of the
economy, accounting for 78 per cent of exports but
making the economy very vulnerable to price fluctuations.
Much of industry is state-owned and there is a large
public sector. Agriculture comprises large-scale
commercial farms and subsistence farming. Land
distribution is uneven, with 1 per cent of farms occupying
46 per cent of arable land and 250,000 smallholdings
occupying less than 2 per cent of arable land. Agricultural
products include corn, bananas, cocoa beans, coffee,
cotton, rice, maize, sugar, sesame, groundnuts, potatoes,
tomatoes, other vegetables, sisal and tobacco. There is an
extensive beef and dairy farming industry. Products of the
tropical forest region include orchids, wild rubber, timber,
mangrove bark, balata gum and tonka beans.

There are very large deposits of minerals, especially
coal, iron ore, bauxite and gold, which are being
exploited. Other industry includes a wide variety of
manufacturing and component assembly, principally
petrochemicals, gold, diamonds and foodstuffs.

The main exports are petroleum, bauxite, iron ore,
agricultural products and basic manufactures. The main
imports are machinery and transport equipment,

chemicals and foodstuffs. The USA and Colombia are the major trading partners.

GNI – US$102,300 million (2002); US$4,080 per capita (2002)

ANNUAL AVERAGE GROWTH OF GDP – 16.8 per cent (2004 est.)

INFLATION RATE – 22.4 per cent (2004 est.)

UNEMPLOYMENT – 17.1 per cent (2004 est.)

TOTAL EXTERNAL DEBT – US$38,196 million (2000 est.)

FOREIGN DIRECT INVESTMENT – US$17,173 million (1997–2000)

IMPORTS – US$9,000 million (2003)

EXPORTS – US$5,000 million (2003)

BALANCE OF PAYMENTS

Trade – US$15,043 million surplus (2003)

Current Account – US$9,624 million surplus (2003)

Trade with UK	2003	2004
Imports from UK	£143,961,000	£187,324,000
Exports to UK	115,360,000	212,680,000

TRANSPORT INFRASTRUCTURE

There are 96,155 km of roads, some 32,308 km of them surfaced. Road and river communications have made railways of negligible importance, except for carrying iron ore in the south-east, although the government is expanding the network and there are now some 682 km of railway lines. The Orinoco is navigable for ocean-going ships. The main ports are Maracaibo and Caracas, which are also the locations of the principal airports.

MEDIA

There are six daily newspapers, including *El Mundo* and *El Nacional*. Radio and television services are a mixture of state and private ownership.

VIETNAM

Công Hòa Xã Hôi Chu Nghĩa Viêt Nam – Socialist Republic of Vietnam

AREA – 325,500 sq. km. Neighbours: China (north), Laos and Cambodia (west)

POPULATION – 82,689,518 (2004 est.). The language is Vietnamese. French, English and Khmer are also spoken

CAPITAL – Hanoi (population, 1,073,760, 1992 estimate)

MAJOR CITIES – ΨHaiphong; ΨHo Chi Minh City

CURRENCY – Dông of 10 ho or 100 xu

NATIONAL ANTHEM – Tien quan ca [The troops are advancing]

NATIONAL DAY – 2 September

NATIONAL FLAG – Red, with yellow five-point star in centre

LIFE EXPECTANCY (years) – 70.35 (2004 est.)

MORTALITY RATE (per 1,000 population) – 6.14 (2004 est.)

INFANT MORTALITY (per 1,000 births) – 29.88 (2004 est.)

HIV / AIDS ADULT PREVALENCE – 0.4 per cent (2003 est.)

DEATH PENALTY – Yes

POPULATION GROWTH RATE – 1.3 per cent (2004 est.)

POPULATION DENSITY – 247 per sq. km (2002)

ILLITERACY RATE – (m) 6.1 per cent; (f) 13.1 per cent (2002 est.)

GROSS ENROLMENT RATIO (percentage of relevant age group) – primary 103 per cent (2002); secondary 70 per cent (2002); tertiary 10 per cent (2002)

CLIMATE AND TERRAIN

The terrain consists of flat river deltas, of the Hong (Red) in the north and of the Mekong in the south, divided by central highlands. The country is mountainous in the far north and north-west. Elevation extremes range from 3,144 m (Ngoc Linh) at the highest point to 0 m (South China Sea) at the lowest. The climate is tropical, dominated by a monsoon season that lasts from May to September in the north of the country, and from September to January in the south. Average temperatures in Hanoi range from 17°C in January to 29°C in June.

HISTORY AND POLITICS

Independent kingdoms in Vietnam were unified in the 15th century but power became decentralised until the early 19th century, when central power was reasserted with the assistance of France. From 1858 to 1884 France conquered Vietnam, establishing three protectorates which in 1887 became part of France's Indo-Chinese Union with Cambodia and Laos. Vietnam was under Japanese occupation from 1940 to 1945; Vietnamese communists fought a guerrilla war of resistance against the occupiers and, controlling most of the country when the Second World War ended, declared independence. France's attempts to reassert its control led to the Indo-China War (1946–54) and ended with France's withdrawal and an armistice dividing the country into communist North Vietnam and non-communist South Vietnam. In 1957 a communist insurgency began in South Vietnam, which was receiving support from the USA, and in 1964 the USA entered the conflict on the side of the south. A cease-fire and peace talks led to the withdrawal of US troops in 1973. North Vietnam violated the peace agreements to capture Saigon and took control of the south in 1975. North and South Vietnam were reunified in 1976 as the Socialist Republic of Vietnam. The national flag, anthem and capital of North Vietnam were adopted, and Saigon was renamed Ho Chi Minh City. In the mid- to late 1970s, nearly one million people attempted to leave the country as 'boat people' to find refuge in the West.

Vietnam intervened in Cambodia in 1979 to help overthrow the Khmer Rouge regime. This prompted a Chinese invasion of Vietnam and a 17-day war in which Vietnamese forces succeeded in repelling the invading forces. Relations with China remained poor until 1991 but have improved since. Relations with the USA have been normalised since the mid-1990s. A degree of economic liberalisation was introduced from 1986 and was enshrined in a new constitution in 1992 which approved many economic and political reforms, but power remains with the ruling Communist Party. In the 2002 legislative election, Communist Party candidates won 449 of the 500 seats.

POLITICAL SYSTEM

The head of state is a president elected by the National Assembly to serve a five-year term. The unicameral National Assembly *(Quoc-Hoi)* has 500 members, who are directly elected for a five-year term, and appoints the Council of Ministers. The head of government is the prime minister, who is responsible to the National

Assembly. However, effective power lies with the Vietnamese Communist Party (VCP). Its highest executive body is the Central Committee, elected by the national Party Congress held every five years. The Politburo and the Secretariat of the Central Committee exercise the real power.

HEAD OF STATE
President, Tran Duc Luong, *elected* 25 September 1997, *re-elected* 24 July 2002
Vice-President, Truong My Hoa

SELECTED GOVERNMENT MEMBERS *as at July 2005*
Prime Minister, Phan Van Khai
Deputy Prime Ministers, Nguyen Tan Dzung; Vu Khoan; Pham Gia Khiem
Finance, Nguyen Sinh Hung
Foreign Affairs, Nguyen Dy Nien
Internal Affairs, Do Quang Trung
National Defence, Gen. Pham Van Tra

EMBASSY OF THE SOCIALIST REPUBLIC OF VIETNAM
12–14 Victoria Road, London W8 5RD T 020–7937 1912
Ambassador Extraordinary and Plenipotentiary, HE Trinh Duc Du, apptd 2003

BRITISH EMBASSY
Central Building, 31 Hai Ba Trung, Hanoi
T (+84) (4) 936 0500 E behanoi@fpt.vn
Ambassador Extraordinary and Plenipotentiary, HE Robert Gordon, apptd 2003

BRITISH COUNCIL
40 Cat Linh Street, Dong Da, Hanoi
T (+84) (4) 843 6780 E bchanoi@britishcouncil.org.vn
Director, David Cordingley *(Cultural Attaché)*

DEFENCE
The Army has 1,315 main battle tanks, 1,380 armoured personnel carriers and 300 armoured infantry fighting vehicles. The Navy has two submarines, six frigates and 42 patrol and coastal vessels at seven principal bases. The Air Force has 195 combat aircraft and 26 armed helicopters.

MILITARY EXPENDITURE – 7.4 per cent of GDP (2003)
MILITARY PERSONNEL – 484,000: Army 412,000, Navy 42,000, Air Force 30,000; Paramilitaries 40,000
CONSCRIPTION DURATION – Two to three years

ECONOMY AND TRADE
Vietnam experienced economic difficulties following the imposition of socialist reforms in the south after 1975. However, economic liberalisation since 1986, accession to ASEAN in 1995 and the opening of a stock exchange in 2000 have been successful in improving economic performance and attracting foreign investment and international aid. The state's share of control has been greatly reduced in most sectors, leading to significant improvement in agricultural production, with Vietnam becoming a major rice exporter. Agriculture is still the main employer, of about two-thirds of the workforce, but the government has said that it wishes to turn Vietnam into an industrialised country by 2020. Industry now contributes around 37 per cent of GDP. Building materials, chemicals, machinery and foodstuffs are the main products. Oil production has increased and large

natural gas reserves have been found offshore, though these are also claimed by China.
GNI – US$34,800 million (2002); US$430 per capita (2002)
ANNUAL AVERAGE GROWTH OF GDP – 6.8 per cent (2001 est.)
TOTAL EXTERNAL DEBT – US$12,787 million (2000 est.)
FOREIGN DIRECT INVESTMENT – US$5,907 million (1997–2000)
IMPORTS – US$25 million (2003)
EXPORTS – US$20 million (2003)

BALANCE OF PAYMENTS
Trade – US$1,054 million surplus (2002)
Current Account – US$604 million deficit (2002)

Trade with UK	2003	2004
Imports from UK	£100,640,000	£105,226,000
Exports to UK	606,820,000	714,490,000

TRANSPORT INFRASTRUCTURE
Vietnam has 93,300 km of roads, nearly 70,000 km of which are unsurfaced. It has over 3,000 km of railway, and 17,700 km of navigable waterways. Chief ports include Da Nang, Haiphong, and Ho Chi Minh City. The principal airports are at Ho Chi Minh City, Hanoi, Da Nang and Nha Trang.

MEDIA
There are many local television stations and one national station; some satellite channels are also available, though these, like all other media, are closely controlled by the government. The state-run radio network operates several national stations. The Communist Party and the People's Army both publish a daily newspaper, and there are also newspapers published in English and French.

YEMEN

Al-Jumhūriyya Al-Yamaniyya – Republic of Yemen

AREA – 527,968 sq. km. Neighbours: Saudi Arabia (north), Oman (east)
POPULATION – 20,024,867 (2004 est.). The language is Arabic
CAPITAL – Sana'a (population, 1,590,624, 2001)
MAJOR CITIES – ΨAden ('Adan), the former capital of South Yemen; ΨAl-Hudaydah; Ta'izz
CURRENCY – Riyal of 100 fils
NATIONAL ANTHEM – Raddidi ayyatuha ad-dunya nashidi [Repeat, o world, my song]
NATIONAL DAY – 22 May
NATIONAL FLAG – Horizontal bands of red, white and black
LIFE EXPECTANCY (years) – 61.36 (2004 est.)
MORTALITY RATE (per 1,000 population) – 8.78 (2004 est.)
INFANT MORTALITY (per 1,000 births) – 63.26 (2004 est.)
HIV / AIDS ADULT PREVALENCE – 0.1 per cent (2001 est.)
DEATH PENALTY – Yes
POPULATION GROWTH RATE – 3.44 per cent (2004 est.)
POPULATION DENSITY – 35 per sq. km (2002)
ILLITERACY RATE – (m) 29.5 per cent; (f) 70 per cent (2003 est.)

GROSS ENROLMENT RATIO (percentage of relevant age group) – primary 81 per cent (2002); secondary 46 per cent (2002)

Included in the state of Yemen are the offshore islands of Perim and Kamaran in the Red Sea, and Suqutra in the Gulf of Aden. The border with Saudi Arabia, except for the north-west corner, is unclear and is being delineated following an agreement between the two countries signed on 12 June 2000.

CLIMATE AND TERRAIN

A mountainous region in the west and south divides the desert interior from the coastal regions. Elevation extremes range from 3,760 m (Jabal an Nabi Shu'ayb) at the highest point to 0 m (Arabian Sea) at the lowest. The coastal area has high humidity, but rainfall throughout the country is unpredictable, resulting in droughts and severe floods. Average temperatures in Aden range from 22°C in January to 37°C in June.

HISTORY AND POLITICS

The area of northern Yemen became part of the Ottoman empire in the early 16th century. Independence from the Ottoman Empire was initiated by the Zaydi dynasty in the 17th century. The Ottoman empire re-established control over northern Yemen in the 1870s and remained until the empire collapsed at the end of the First World War. In 1918 north Yemen became an independent kingdom under the rule of the Hamid al-Din dynasty. A revolution in 1962 overthrew the monarchy and the Yemen Arab Republic was declared. Fighting between royalists and republicans continued until 1967, when the republican regime was recognised.

Aden came under British rule in 1839, and a protectorate was gradually established over the sultanates of the southern hinterland in the second half of the 19th century. An armed rebellion against British rule began in 1963. After British troops withdrew in 1967, power was seized by the National Liberation Front, which established a repressive communist regime in the People's Republic of South Yemen (later renamed the People's Democratic Republic of Yemen).

There were border clashes between the two Yemeni states in 1971–2 and again in 1978, when a cease-fire agreement included a commitment to merging the two states. Negotiations began in 1979 and the two countries united as the Republic of Yemen on 22 May 1990. A power struggle between the former northern and southern elites led to a brief civil war in 1994 after southern Yemen attempted to secede in May; this was crushed by northern government forces in July. Tensions remain between the north and south, some southerners believing that the south is marginalised. Tourists have been kidnapped on several occasions by groups wanting to make demands of the government.

Lt.-Gen. Ali Abdullah Saleh, president of North Yemen from 1978, became president of the united country in 1990. He was elected president for a five-year term by the House of Representatives in 1994 and, following constitutional changes, re-elected for a seven-year term in the first direct presidential election in 1999. In the 2003 legislative election, the ruling General People's Congress (GPC) won 238 seats and formed a coalition goverment with the Yemeni Alliance for Reform (YAR or al-Islah) led by Abd al-Qadir Abd al-Rahman Bajammal.

POLITICAL SYSTEM

The 1991 constitution was amended following a referendum in 2001. The head of state is a president who is directly elected for a seven-year term, renewable once only. The unicameral legislature, the House of Representatives *(Majlis al-Nowab)*, has 301 members directly elected for a six-year term. In addition, there is an advisory Shura Council, whose 111 members are appointed by the president. The prime minister is appointed by the president.

HEAD OF STATE
President, Field Marshal Ali Abdullah Saleh, *took office* 22 May 1990, *elected* 1 October 1994, *re-elected* 23 September 1999
Vice-President, Gen. Abd Rabbah Mansur Hadi

SELECTED GOVERNMENT MEMBERS *as at August 2005*
Prime Minister, Abd al-Qadir Abd al-Rahman Bajammal
Deputy Prime Minister, Finance, Alawi Salih al-Salami
Deputy Prime Minister, Planning and International Co-operation, Ahmad Muhammad Abdallah al-Sufan
Defence, Maj.-Gen. Abdallah Ali Alywah
Foreign Affairs, Abu-Bakr Abdallah al-Qirdi
Interior, Rashad al-Alimi

EMBASSY OF THE REPUBLIC OF YEMEN
57 Cromwell Road, London SW/ 2ED **T** 020-7584 6607
Ambassador Extraordinary and Plenipotentiary, HE Dr Mutahar Abdullah Alsaeede, apptd 2001

BRITISH EMBASSY
129 Haddah Road, PO Box 1287, Sana'a'
T (+967) (1) 264 081/2/3/4
Ambassador Extraordinary and Plenipotentiary, HE Michael Gifford, apptd 2005

BRITISH COUNCIL
3rd Floor, Administrative Tower, Sana'a' Trade Centre, Algiers Street, PO Box 2157, Sana'a' **T** (+967) 1448 356/7
E britishcouncil@ye.britishcouncil.org
Director, Aziz al-Baar

DEFENCE

The Army has 790 main battle tanks, 710 armoured personnel carriers and 200 armoured infantry fighting vehicles. The Navy has 11 patrol and coastal vessels at two bases. The Air Force has 72 combat aircraft and eight attack helicopters.
MILITARY EXPENDITURE – 7 per cent of GDP (2003)
MILITARY PERSONNEL – 66,700: Army 60,000, Navy 1,700, Air Force 5,000; Paramilitaries 70,000
CONSCRIPTION DURATION – 24 months

ECONOMY AND TRADE

Oil is the basis of the economy, and in 1995 an agreement was signed with the French oil company Total for the exploitation of liquefied natural gas over a 25-year period and the construction of a gas liquefaction plant. Agriculture is the main occupation of the inhabitants. This is largely of a subsistence nature, although coffee and cotton are grown as cash crops. Exports include oil, cotton, coffee, fish, fruit, vegetables and hides. The principal imports are machinery and transport equipment, raw materials, and foodstuffs and livestock.
GNI – US$9,100 million (2002); US$490 per capita (2002)

ANNUAL AVERAGE GROWTH OF GDP – 3.1 per cent (2001 est.)
INFLATION RATE – 12.2 per cent (2004 est.)
TOTAL EXTERNAL DEBT – US$6,200 million (2002 est.)
IMPORTS – US$2,000 million (2001)
EXPORTS – US$3,000 million (2001)

BALANCE OF PAYMENTS
Trade – US$377 million surplus (2003)
Current Account – US$149 million surplus (2003)

Trade with UK	2003	2004
Imports from UK	£80,395,000	£66,916,000
Exports to UK	9,062,000	14,195,000

TRANSPORT INFRASTRUCTURE
Yemen has 67,000 km of roads, of which 7,700 km are surfaced. Its main ports are at Aden, Al-Hudaydah and Al Mukalla. The principal airport is at Sana'a.

MEDIA
All broadcasting is state-run. The government also funds some newspapers, and controls most of the printing. There are four newspapers: *Al-Thawrah*, *Yemen Times*, *Yemen Observer* and *Al-Ayyam*.

ZAMBIA

Republic of Zambia

AREA – 743,400 sq. km. Neighbours: Democratic Republic of Congo and Tanzania (north), Malawi (east), Mozambique, Zimbabwe and Namibia (south), Angola (west)
POPULATION – 10,462,436 (2004 est.). English is the official language; other languages spoken include Bemba, Kaonda, Lozi, Lunda, Luvale, Nyanja and Tonga
CAPITAL – Lusaka (population, 1,269,848, 1999)
MAJOR CITIES – Chingola; Kabwe; Kitwe; Luanshya; Mufulira; Ndola
CURRENCY – Kwacha (K) of 100 ngwee
NATIONAL ANTHEM – Stand and sing of Zambia, proud and free
NATIONAL DAY – 24 October (Independence Day)
NATIONAL FLAG – Green with three small vertical stripes, red, black and orange (next fly); eagle device on green above stripes
LIFE EXPECTANCY (years) – 35.18 (2004 est.)
MORTALITY RATE (per 1,000 population) – 24.35 (2004 est.)
INFANT MORTALITY (per 1,000 births) – 98.4 (2004 est.)
HIV / AIDS ADULT PREVALENCE – 16.5 per cent (2003 est.)
DEATH PENALTY – Yes
POPULATION GROWTH RATE – 1.47 per cent (2004 est.)
POPULATION DENSITY – 14 per sq. km (2002)
MILITARY EXPENDITURE – 0.6 per cent of GDP (2003)
MILITARY PERSONNEL – 18,100: Army 16,500, Air Force 1,600; Paramilitaries 1,400
ILLITERACY RATE – (m) 19.4 per cent; (f) 25.2 per cent (2004 est.)
GROSS ENROLMENT RATIO (percentage of relevant age group) – primary 79 per cent (2002); tertiary 2 per cent (2002)

CLIMATE AND TERRAIN
Landlocked Zambia in central Africa lies on a forested plateau cut through by river valleys and with higher land in the north and north-east. Elevation extremes range from 2,361 m (Mafinga Hills) at the highest point to 321 m (Zambezi River) at the lowest. Lake Bangweulu and parts of Lakes Tanganyika, Mweru and Kariba lie within its boundaries. The climate is tropical, with an average temperature of 28°C all year.

HISTORY AND POLITICS
Most of the ethnic groups in Zambia had migrated there between the 16th and the 18th centuries. Portuguese explorers arrived in the late 18th century and, with Arab traders, began slave-trading in the 19th century. The area came under British administration as Barotseland in 1889, was named Northern Rhodesia in 1911 and became a British protectorate in 1924. It was part of the Central African Federation with South Rhodesia (Zimbabwe) and Nyasaland (Malawi) from 1953 and 1963, when the federation was dissolved and Northern Rhodesia achieved internal self-government. It became an independent republic within the Commonwealth on 24 October 1964 under the name of Zambia. Kenneth Kaunda of the United National Independence Party (UNIP) became president at independence and remained in power until 1991.

Zambia was a one-party state ruled by the UNIP from 1972 until 1990, when pressure from opposition groups led to a new constitution, under which multiparty legislative and presidential elections were held in 1991. The Movement for Multiparty Democracy (MMD) won a majority of seats in the parliament, and the MMD candidate Frederick Chiluba defeated Kenneth Kaunda in the presidential election. President Chiluba was re-elected in 1996, surviving coup attempts in 1993 and 1997.

Serious food shortages have occurred in recent years owing to floods and drought, and in 2001 the government appealed for international food aid. The country also faces serious demographic, economic and social problems because of the high levels of HIV/AIDS infection.

The 2001 presidential election was won by MMD candidate Levy Mwanawasa with 28.7 per cent of the vote. In simultaneous legislative elections, the MMD won 69 seats, the United Party for National Development (UPND) won 49 seats, and other parties and independents won 32 seats. A new cabinet composed of the MMD was appointed in early 2002 after the inauguration of the new president.

POLITICAL SYSTEM
Under the 1991 constitution, the executive president is directly elected for a five-year term, renewable only once. The unicameral legislature, the National Assembly, has 150 directly elected members, up to eight appointed by the president and a speaker; all serve a five-year term. The president appoints the cabinet.

HEAD OF STATE
President, Minister of Defence, Levy Mwanawasa, *elected* 27 December 2001, *sworn in* 2 January 2002
Vice-President, Lupando Mwape

SELECTED GOVERNMENT MEMBERS *as at August 2005*
Home Affairs, Bates Namuyamba
Foreign Affairs, Lt.-Gen. Ronnie Shikapwasha
Finance, Peter Ng'andu Magande
Health, Sylvia Masebo

HIGH COMMISSION FOR THE REPUBLIC OF ZAMBIA
2 Palace Gate, London W8 5NG T 020-7589 6655
High Commissioner, HE Anderson Chibwa, apptd 2003

BRITISH HIGH COMMISSION
5210 Independence Avenue (PO Box 50050),
15101 Ridgeway, Lusaka
T (+ 260) (1) 251133 E brithc@zamnet.zm
High Commissioner, HE Timothy David, apptd 2002

BRITISH COUNCIL
Heroes Place, Cairo Road (PO Box 34571), Lusaka
T (+ 260) (1) 223 602/228 332 E info@britishcouncil.org.zm
Director, John Mitchell

ECONOMY AND TRADE

Since 1991, the economy has moved from a state-controlled to a free market system. Privatisation has improved productivity but the country is still very poor, with a large foreign debt. In April 2005, the World Bank approved a US$3.8 billion debt relief package that will write off more than 50 per cent of Zambia's foreign debt.

Copper mining has been the mainstay of the economy since the 1920s, and is still the main source of foreign earnings. The economy was devastated by a collapse in world prices in the mid-1970s but demand has increased since owing to the needs of electronics industries. Most of the workforce, about 85 per cent, are engaged in agriculture, which accounted for 14.9 per cent of GDP in 2001. Principal agricultural products are maize, sugar, groundnuts, cotton, livestock, vegetables and tobacco. The principal exports are copper and cobalt. The principal imports are industrial goods, machinery and transport equipment, fuel and foodstuffs.

GNI – US$3,500 million (2002); US$340 per capita (2002)
ANNUAL AVERAGE GROWTH OF GDP – 4.6 per cent (2004 est.)
INFLATION RATE – 18.3 per cent (2004 est.)
TOTAL EXTERNAL DEBT – US$5,730 million (2000 est.)
FOREIGN DIRECT INVESTMENT – US$505 million (1997–2000)
IMPORTS – US$1,100 million (2000)
EXPORTS – US$760 million (2000)

Trade with UK	2003	2004
Imports from UK	£21,465,000	£23,270,000
Exports to UK	15,983,000	16,553,000

MEDIA

The broadcast media is dominated by the government-run television and radio networks. There are private radio stations (in contrast to television, where the only service is the state-run channel Zambia National Broadcasting Association) but they do not provide much political content. Three of the four newspapers are state-owned.

ZIMBABWE

Republic of Zimbabwe

AREA – 386,900 sq. km. Neighbours: Zambia (north), Mozambique (north and east), South Africa (south), Botswana and Namibia (west)

POPULATION – 12,671,860 (2004 est.); 77 per cent Shona, 17 per cent Ndebele, 1.4 per cent Europeans. The official language is English, with Shona the largest indigenous language group
CAPITAL – Harare (population, 1,189,103, 1992)
MAJOR CITIES – Bulawayo, the largest town in Matabeleland; Chitungwiza
CURRENCY – Zimbabwe dollar (Z$) of 100 cents
NATIONAL ANTHEM – Ngaikomberarwe nyika ye Zimbabwe [Blessed be the country of Zimbabwe]
NATIONAL DAY – 18 April (Independence Day)
NATIONAL FLAG – Seven horizontal stripes of green, yellow, red, black, red, yellow, green; a white, black-bordered, triangle based on the hoist containing the national emblem
LIFE EXPECTANCY (years) – 37.82 (2004 est.)
MORTALITY RATE (per 1,000 population) – 23.3 (2004 est.)
INFANT MORTALITY (per 1,000 births) – 67.08 (2004 est.)
HIV / AIDS ADULT PREVALENCE – 33.7 per cent (2001 est.)
DEATH PENALTY – Yes
POPULATION BELOW POVERTY LINE – 70 per cent (2002 est.)
POPULATION GROWTH RATE – 0.68 per cent (2004 est.)
POPULATION DENSITY – 34 per sq. km (2002)
MILITARY EXPENDITURE – 1.7 per cent of GDP (2003)
MILITARY PERSONNEL – 29,000: Army 25,000, Air Force 4,000; Paramilitaries 21,800

CLIMATE AND TERRAIN

The terrain is mainly high plateau with a central high veld and mountains in the east. Elevation extremes range from 2,592 m (Inyangani) at the highest point to 162 m (Runde River) at the lowest. Average temperatures in Harare range from 7°C in May to 29°C in November.

HISTORY AND POLITICS

Organised settlement of the region began at least 20,000 years ago and culminated in the establishment of a powerful settlement at Great Zimbabwe in the 12th century AD. In the 19th century this was taken over by the Nbebele people and became the kingdom of Matabeleland, which was often in dispute with the people of Mashonaland to the north. The area came under British influence from the 1880s, when the British started to exploit the mineral resources. The British invaded Mashonaland in 1890 and seized Matabeleland in 1893. The two areas became a British protectorate as Southern Rhodesia in 1898, and South Rhodesia became a self-governing colony in 1923. It was part of the Central African Federation from 1953 until 1963, when Northern Rhodesia (Zambia) and Nyasaland (Malawi) became independent. Opposition to independence under black majority rule in Southern Rhodesia prompted a unilateral declaration of independence (UDI) by the white-dominated colonial government, led by Ian Smith, in 1965. Economic sanctions and guerrilla warfare by African nationalist groups forced the government to negotiate, and UDI was trminated in 1979. Power was transferred to the majority population, and the country became independent within the Commonwealth as the Republic of Zimbabwe on 18 April 1980.

Robert Mugabe became prime minister at independence and executive president in 1987. He was re-elected in 1990, 1996 and 2002, winning 56.2 per cent of the vote in 2002.

President Mugabe's regime has become increasingly autocratic, brutally suppressing opposition and dissent, and rejecting international criticism of human rights and other abuses; Zimbabwe left the Commonwealth in 2003 because its membership had been suspended indefinitely over the political situation. The appropriation of white-owned farms, which began in 2000, was accompanied by intimidation and violence, and the government defied Supreme Court rulings that the appropriations were illegal. The appropriations caused an agricultural collapse that, combined with a long drought, led to widespread food shortages in 2001, and a state of disaster was declared in 2002; international food aid sent to prevent famine has not always been distributed equitably. Mass anti-government protests, including a general strike in 2003, provoked a brutal crackdown by the authorities, which arrested hundreds. In May–July 2005, thousands of shanty dwellings and street markets in the cities were demolished as part of a government 'clean-up' programme; the UN estimated that the programme left 700,000 people homeless. The country also faces serious demographic, economic and social problems owing to the high levels of HIV/AIDS infection.

The 2002 election was criticised as seriously flawed by the opposition and international observers. The legislative election in March 2005 was won by President Mugabe's party, the Zimbabwe African National Union – Patriotic Front (ZANU-PF), which won 78 of the elective seats, giving it an overall majority. The results were disputed by the main opposition party, the Movement for Democratic Change, and many international observers, although observers from the Southern African Development Community said that the results reflected the will of the voters.

POLITICAL SYSTEM
The 1980 constitution was amended in 1987 to create an executive presidency and in 1990 to make the legislature unicameral and provide for direct elections to the presidency. The executive president is directly elected for a six-year term. The unicameral legislature, the parliament, has 150 members, 120 directly elected for a five-year term, 20 appointed by the president and ten traditional chiefs. The president appoints the cabinet.

The country is divided into eight provinces: Manicaland, Mashonaland Central, Mashonaland East, Mashonaland West, Masvingo, Matabeleland North, Matabeleland South and Midlands.

HEAD OF STATE
President, C.-in-C. of the Defence Forces, Transport and Energy, Robert Gabriel Mugabe, *elected* 30 December 1987, *re-elected* March 1990, March 1996, 11 March 2002
Vice-President, Joseph Msika

SELECTED GOVERNMENT MEMBERS *as at August 2005*
Defence, Sidney Tigere Sekeramayi
Finance and Economic Development, Herbert Murerwa
Foreign Affairs, Simbarashe Mumbengegwi
Home Affairs, Kembo Mohadi
National Security, Nicholas Goche

HIGH COMMISSION OF THE REPUBLIC OF ZIMBABWE
Zimbabwe House, 429 Strand, London WC2R 0JR
T 020-7836 7755
High Commissioner, HE Godfrey Magwenzi, apptd 2004

BRITISH HIGH COMMISSION
Corner House, Samora Machel Avenue/Leopold Takawira Street (PO Box 4490), Harare T (+263) (4) 772990/774700
High Commissioner, HE Roderick Pullen

BRITISH COUNCIL
Corner House, Samora Machel Avenue, PO Box 664, Harare
T (+263) (4) 775 313/4
E general.enquiries@britishcouncil.org.zw
Director, Dr Marcus Milton

ECONOMY AND TRADE
The economy remains highly regulated and weak, unemployment is high and huge rises in the prices of basic commodities and fuel, caused by rampant inflation, have resulted in widespread strike action and protests. Agriculture accounted for 28 per cent of GDP in 1998 and engaged two-thirds of the workforce, but the activities of squatters and the government land acquisition campaign have had a dramatic effect on productivity at commercial farms, many of which are no longer in production. Tobacco remains the most important crop in terms of export (Zimbabwe is the largest exporter in the world), and maize the most important for domestic consumption. Other crops include wheat, cotton, sugar, horticultural products, fruit and vegetables.

The manufacturing sector is very dependent on the agricultural sector for raw materials and on imports such as fuel oil, steel products and chemicals, as well as heavy machinery and items of transport. The mining sector, although contributing a relatively small portion to GDP, is important to the economy as a foreign exchange earner. Almost all mineral production is exported. Gold is the most important product; others are asbestos, diamonds, silver, nickel, copper, platinum, chrome ore, tin, iron ore and cobalt. There is a successful ferro-chrome industry and a substantial steel works which has been heavily subsidised by government. The main trading partners are South Africa and the UK.

GNI – US$6,200 million (2001); US$480 per capita (2001)
ANNUAL AVERAGE GROWTH OF GDP – −8.2 per cent (2004 est.)
INFLATION RATE – 133 per cent (2004 est.)
UNEMPLOYMENT – 70 per cent (2002 est.)
TOTAL EXTERNAL DEBT – US$4,002 million (2000 est.)
FOREIGN DIRECT INVESTMENT – US$284 million (1997–2000)
IMPORTS – US$1,740 million (2001)
EXPORTS – US$2,280 million (2001)

Trade with UK	2003	2004
Imports from UK	£29,294,000	£26,005,000
Exports to UK	58,295,000	47,782,000

TRANSPORT INFRASTRUCTURE
Zimbabwe has at least 18,000 km of roads, over 8,500 km of which are surfaced. There are also 3,000 km of railways. It relies on rail connections through Mozambique and South Africa for access to seaports. The main airports are at Harare and Bulawayo.

EDUCATION

Education is compulsory, and the language of instruction is English. Over 80 per cent of schools are government-aided. There are four universities; the University of Zimbabwe was founded in 1955.

ILLITERACY RATE – (m) 7.2 per cent; (f) 15.3 per cent (2000)

GROSS ENROLMENT RATIO (percentage of relevant age group) – primary 99 per cent (2002); secondary 43 per cent (2002); tertiary 4 per cent (2002)

MEDIA

The government exercises strict control over the print and broadcast media, and some foreign journalists are prevented from reporting from within the country. The only television and radio stations are government-controlled. There is one independent radio station that broadcasts in Zimbabwe. Two of the three daily newspapers, *The Herald* and *The Chronicle* are run by the government.

UK OVERSEAS TERRITORIES

ANGUILLA

AREA – 96 sq. km
POPULATION – 13,008 (2004 est.)
CAPITAL – The Valley (population, 2,400, 1994)
CURRENCY – East Caribbean dollar (EC$) of 100 cents
FLAG – British blue ensign with the coat of arms and three dolphins in the fly
POPULATION GROWTH RATE – 1.98 (2004 est.)
POPULATION DENSITY – 134 per sq. km (1999)

CLIMATE AND TERRAIN

Anguilla is a flat coralline island in the Caribbean, and is the most northerly of the Leeward islands. The climate is tropical, modified by north-east trade winds, with temperatures ranging from 24°C to 30°C throughout the year. Elevation extremes range from 65 m (Crocus Hill) at the highest point to 0 m (Caribbean Sea) at the lowest.

HISTORY AND POLITICS

Anguilla has been a British colony since 1650. For much of its history it was linked administratively with St Kitts, but three months after the Associated State of Saint Christopher (St Kitts)-Nevis-Anguilla came into being in 1967, the Anguillans repudiated government from St Kitts. A Commissioner was installed in 1969 and in 1976 Anguilla was given a new status and separate constitution. Final separation from St Kitts and Nevis was effected in December 1980 and Anguilla reverted to a British dependency.

A new constitution was introduced in 1982, providing for a Governor, an Executive Council comprising four elected Ministers and two ex-officio members (the Attorney-General and Deputy Governor), and a 12-member legislative House of Assembly, consisting of seven elected members, two nominated members, two *ex-officio* members (the Attorney-General and Deputy Governor) and presided over by a Speaker. The last general election was held in February 2005 and was won by the Anguilla United Front with 38.9 per cent of the vote.

Governor, HE Alan Huckle, *apptd* 2004
Deputy Governor, Roger Cousins, OBE, *apptd* 1997

ECONOMY

Low rainfall limits agricultural output and export earnings are mainly from sales of fish and lobsters. Tourism has developed rapidly in recent years and accounts for most of the island's economic activity.

BALANCE OF PAYMENTS
Trade – US$57 million deficit (2002)
Current Account – US$35 million deficit (2001)

Trade with UK	2003	2004
Imports from UK	£695,000	£2,869,000
Exports to UK	1,443,000	1,317,000

TRANSPORT INFRASTRUCTURE

Highways total 105 km, of which 65 km are paved (1997). Ports and harbours include Blowing Point and Road Bay, and there are three airports, though only one has a paved runway.

BERMUDA

AREA –52 sq. km
POPULATION – 64,935 (2004 est.)
CAPITAL – ΨHamilton (population, 2,277, 1994)
CURRENCY – Bermuda dollar of 100 cents
FLAG – British red ensign with the shield of arms in the fly
LIFE EXPECTANCY (years) – 77.6 (2004 est.)
POPULATION GROWTH RATE – 0.68 per cent (2004 est.)
POPULATION DENSITY – 1,231 per sq. km (2001)

CLIMATE AND TERRAIN

Bermuda is a group of over 100 small islands, of which about 20 are inhabited, in the North Atlantic Ocean. All the islands are volcanic in origin, with hilly interiors, surrounded by coral reefs. Elevation extremes range from 76 m (Town Hill) at the highest point to 0 m (Atlantic Ocean) at the lowest. The climate is subtropical, regulated by the Gulf Stream, with an average temperature of 23°C.

HISTORY AND POLITICS

Internal self-government was introduced in 1968. There is a Senate of 11 members and an elected House of Assembly of 40 members. The Governor retains responsibility for external affairs, defence, internal security and the police, although administrative matters for the police service have been delegated to the Minister of Labour, Home Affairs and Public Safety. Independence from the UK was rejected in a referendum in 1995. The last general election was held on 24 July 2003 when the Progressive Labour Party won 22 of the 40 seats.

Governor and Commander-in-Chief, HE Sir John Vereker, KCB, *apptd* 2002

ECONOMY

The islands' economic structure is based on tourism and international company business, attracted by the low level of taxation and sophisticated telecommunications system.

Locally manufactured concentrates, perfumes, cut flowers and pharmaceuticals are the islands' leading exports.

Trade with UK	2003	2004
Imports from UK	£41,983,000	£32,506,000
Exports to UK	67,991,000	55,612,000

EDUCATION

Free elementary education was introduced in 1949. Free secondary education was introduced in 1965 for those children in the aided and maintained schools who were below the upper limit of the statutory school age of 18.

TRANSPORT INFRASTRUCTURE AND MEDIA

There are 450 km of roads, all of which are paved, and one airport. Hamilton is the main port. One daily and two weekly newspapers are published in Bermuda. Three commercial companies operate radio and television services, including a cable-television system.

BRITISH ANTARCTIC TERRITORY

AREA - 1,709,340 sq. km
FLAG - British white ensign, without the cross of St George, with the coat of arms of the territory in the fly

CLIMATE AND TERRAIN

The British Antarctic Territory (BAT) consists of the areas south of 60°S. latitude and bounded by longitudes 20°W. and 80°W. The territory includes the South Orkney Islands, the South Shetland Islands, the mountainous Antarctic Peninsula (highest point 4,191 m above sea level, on Dyer Plateau) and all adjacent islands, and the land mass extending to the South Pole.

HISTORY AND POLITICS

Britain made its first territorial claim to part of the Antarctic in 1908. Since 1943, a permanent presence has been maintained which became the British Antarctic Survey (BAS) in 1962. In the same year, the BAT – originally administered as a Dependency of the Falkland Islands – became an Overseas Territory of the United Kingdom in its own right.

GOVERNMENT

The BAT is administered by the Foreign and Commonwealth Office (FCO), and has a full suite of laws, and legal and postal administrations. All activities are governed by the Antarctic Treaty of 1961, agreed with the objectives of keeping Antarctica demilitarised and to promote international scientific co-operation.

GOVERNMENT OF THE BRITISH ANTARCTIC TERRITORY
Polar Regions Unit, Overseas Territory Department, Foreign and Commonwealth Office, London SW1A 2AH T 020-7008 3543
Commissioner (non-resident), Anthony Campbell Crombie, *apptd* 2004

BRITISH INDIAN OCEAN TERRITORY

AREA – 60 sq. km
FLAG – Divided horizontally into blue and white wavy stripes, with the Union Flag in the canton and a crowned palm-tree over all in the fly

CLIMATE AND TERRAIN

The British Indian Ocean Territory (BIOT) comprises the Chagos Archipelago of 2,300 islands that covers some 54,400 sq. km of the Indian Ocean, about 1,900 km north-east of Mauritius. The islands have a land area of only 60 sq. km and 698 km of coastline.

HISTORY AND POLITICS

The British Indian Ocean Territory was established by an Order in Council in 1965 and included islands formerly administered from Mauritius and the Seychelles. The islands of Farquhar, Desroches and Aldabra became part of the Seychelles when it became independent in 1976; since then the Territory has consisted of the Chagos Archipelago only. Successive Mauritian governments have asserted a sovereignty claim to the islands, arguing that they were annexed illegally.

The Chagos Archipelago consists of six main groups of islands situated on the Great Chagos Bank. The largest and most southerly of the Chagos Islands is Diego Garcia, a sand cay with a land area of about 44 sq. km, used as a joint naval support facility by Britain and the USA. In 2003, Diego Garcia hosted around 3,000 UK and US military personnel and civilian contract employees.

The other main island groups of the archipelago, Peros Banhos (29 islands with a total land area of 6.5 sq. km) and Salomon (11 islands with a total land area of 3.2 sq. km) are uninhabited.

The islands' former inhabitants (the Ilois) were expelled between 1967 and 1973 to allow for the construction of the naval base, most being resettled in Mauritius. Following legal action by representatives of the Ilois, in November 2000 the High Court overturned the ordinance that had required the Ilois to seek permission to visit the territory, effectively granting them the right of return.
Commissioner, Tony Crombie, *apptd* 2004

BRITISH VIRGIN ISLANDS

AREA – 153 sq. km
POPULATION – 22,187 (2004 est.: Tortola 16,630; Virgin Gorda 3,063; Anegada 204; Jost Van Dyke 176; other islands 181)
CAPITAL – ΨRoad Town (population, 3,983, 2001 est.)
CURRENCY – US dollar (US$)
FLAG – British blue ensign with the shield of arms in the fly
LIFE EXPECTANCY (years) – 76.27 (2004 est.)
INFANT MORTALITY (per 1,000 births) – 18.05 (2004 est.)
POPULATION GROWTH RATE – 2.06 per cent (2004 est.)
POPULATION DENSITY – 134 per sq. km (2001)

CLIMATE AND TERRAIN

Part of the Virgin Islands archipelago, the northernmost of the Leeward Islands in the Caribbean Sea, the British Virgin Islands comprise Tortola, Virgin Gorda, Anegada, Jost Van Dyke and about 40 islets. Apart from Anegada, which is a flat coral island, the British Virgin Islands are hilly. The highest point of elevation is 1,780 m (Sage Mountain) while the lowest is 0 m (Caribbean Sea).

HISTORY AND POLITICS

Initially settled by the Arawak Indians from South America, the islands were named by Christopher Columbus on his second voyage to the New World. Under the 1977 constitution, the Governor, appointed by the Crown, remains responsible for defence and internal security, external affairs and the civil service but in other matters acts in accordance with the advice of the Executive Council. The Executive Council consists of the Governor as chairman, one ex-officio member (the Attorney-General), the Chief Minister and four other ministers. The Legislative Council consists of a Speaker chosen from outside the Council, one ex-officio member

(the Attorney-General), and 13 elected members returned from ten electoral districts.
Governor, HE Thomas Macan

ECONOMY
Tourism is the main industry but the offshore financial centre is gaining importance. Other industries include a rum distillery, three stone-crushing plants and factories manufacturing concrete blocks and paint. The major export items are fresh fish, gravel, sand, fruit and vegetables. Chief imports are building materials, machinery, cars and beverages.

Trade with UK	2003	2004
Imports from UK	£13,944,000	£5,221,000
Exports to UK	32,636,000	31,188,000

TRANSPORT INFRASTRUCTURE
The principal airport is on Beef Island, linked by bridge to Tortola, and an extended runway enables larger aircraft to call. There is a second airfield on Virgin Gorda and a third on Anegada. There are direct shipping services to the UK and the USA while fast passenger services connect the main islands by ferry.

CAYMAN ISLANDS

AREA – 264 sq. km
POPULATION – 43,103 (2004 est.)
CAPITAL – ΨGeorge Town (population, 20,626, 1999 census)
CURRENCY – Cayman Islands dollar (CI$) of 100 cents
FLAG – British blue ensign with the arms on a white disc in the fly
LIFE EXPECTANCY (years) – 79.81 (2004 est.)
INFANT MORTALITY (per 1,000 births) – 8.41 (2004 est.)
POPULATION GROWTH RATE – 2.7 per cent (2004 est.)
POPULATION DENSITY – 163 per sq. km (2002)
GNI – US$43,703 per capita (2002)
ANNUAL AVERAGE GROWTH OF GDP – 1.7 per cent (2002)

CLIMATE AND TERRAIN
The Cayman Islands comprise Grand Cayman, Cayman Brac, and Little Cayman. About 241 km south of Cuba, the low-lying islands are divided from Jamaica, 289 km to the south-east, by the Cayman Trench, the deepest part of the Caribbean Sea.

HISTORY AND POLITICS
The territory derives its name from the Carib word for the crocodile, 'caymanas', which appeared in the log of an early English visitor to the islands, Sir Francis Drake. Permanent settlers followed the first land grant by Britain in 1734 and the islands were placed under direct control of Jamaica in 1863. When Jamaica became independent in 1962, the islands opted to remain under the British Crown.

The constitution provides for a Governor, a Legislative Assembly and a Cabinet, and allows a large measure of self-government. Unless there are exceptional reasons, the Governor accepts the advice of the Cabinet, which comprises three appointed official members and five ministers elected from the 15 elected members of the Assembly. The official members also sit in the Assembly. The Governor has responsibility for the police, civil service, defence and external affairs. The normal life of the Assembly is four years; a general election took place in May 2005 and was won by the People's Progressive Movement who won nine seats in the Assembly.

A constitutional review, begun in 2001, resulted in the Executive Council being renamed the Cabinet and the official appointment (incorporated in the constitution for the first time) of a Leader of Government Business, Leader of the Opposition, and an Electoral Boundary Commission.
Governor, HE Bruce Dinwiddy, CMG, *apptd* 2002

CAYMAN ISLANDS GOVERNMENT OFFICE
6 Arlington Street, London SW1A 1RE T 020-7491 7772
Government Representative, Jennifer Dilbert

ECONOMY
With a complete absence of direct taxation, the Cayman Islands have become successful as an offshore financial centre. At the end of 2003 there were 474 banks and trust companies. In addition, there were 672 licensed insurance companies, 68,078 registered companies, 4,820 registered mutual funds, and 735 listings on the stock exchange. Tourism, with an emphasis on scuba diving, has also been developed successfully.

Import duties and fees have provided revenue enabling the government to undertake investment in education, health, social programmes and infrastructure.

Trade with UK	2003	2004
Imports from UK	£8,694,000	£10,460,000
Exports to UK	3,754,000	30,901,000

TRANSPORT INFRASTRUCTURE
There are two main airports on the Cayman Islands and one small airfield on the island of Little Cayman. Georgetown is the main port and there are 785 km of surfaced roads.

FALKLAND ISLANDS

AREA –12,173 sq. km
POPULATION – 2,967 (2004 est.)
CAPITAL – ΨStanley (population, 1,989,2001 census)
CURRENCY – Falkland pound of 100 pence
FLAG – British blue ensign with the arms on a white disc in the fly
POPULATION GROWTH RATE – 2.44 per cent (2004 est.)
URBAN POPULATION – 84.0 per cent (2001)

CLIMATE AND TERRAIN
The Falkland Islands consist of East Falkland (area 6,759 sq. km), West Falkland (5,413 sq. km) and over 700 small islands. Elevation extremes range from 705 m (Mt Usbourne) at the highest point to 0 m (Atlantic Ocean) at the lowest.

HISTORY AND POLITICS
The Falkland Islands have a long history of occupation by European countries including France, Spain and the UK, which established its first settlement in 1766.

After Argentina declared independence from Spain, the Argentine government in 1820 proclaimed its sovereignty over the Falklands and a settlement was founded in 1826 but was subsequently destroyed by the USA in 1831. In 1833 occupation was resumed by the British for the protection of the seal-fisheries, and the islands were permanently colonised. Argentina continued to claim sovereignty over the islands (known to them as *las Islas Malvinas*), and invaded the islands in April 1982. A naval and military task-force dispatched from the UK recaptured the islands some seven weeks later on 14 June 1982. A British naval and military garrison of 1,265 personnel remains in the area.

Under the 1985 constitution, the Governor is advised by an Executive Council consisting of three elected members of the Legislative Council and two *ex-officio* members, the Chief Executive and the Financial Secretary. The Legislative Council consists of eight elected members and the same two *ex-officio* members.

Governor and Chairman of the Executive Council, HE
 Howard Pearce, CVO, *apptd* 2002

FALKLAND ISLANDS GOVERNMENT OFFICE
Falkland House, 14 Broadway, London SW1H 0BH
T 020-7222 2542
Government Representative, Miss S. Cameron, MBE

ECONOMY

Since the establishment of a conservation and managed fishing zone around the islands in 1987 and the consequent introduction of a licensing regime for vessels fishing within the 321 km zone, the economy has diversified. Income from the associated fishing activities, mainly for illex squid, is now the largest source of revenue. The increase in government revenue from fishing licences has led to the establishment of a substantial health, education and welfare system. Chief imports are provisions, alcoholic beverages, timber, clothing and hardware. An EU-standard abattoir was opened in 2001, enabling the Falkland Islands to export meat to the European Union.

In 2002, a consortium of oil companies, led by Global Petroleum, were awarded 10 exploration licences by the Falkland Islands government. It is expected that substantial reserves of oil will be found within the next five years.

Trade with UK	2003	2004
Imports from UK	£27,345,000	£28,274,000
Exports to UK	8,979,000	6,867,000

TRANSPORT INFRASTRUCTURE

There is one international airport and the Falkland Islands Government Air Service (FIGAS) provides charter flights. There are some 440 km of roads, 50 km of which are paved. The main port is Stanley Harbour.

GIBRALTAR

AREA – 6 sq. km
POPULATION – 27,833 (2004 est.)
CAPITAL – ΨGibraltar
CURRENCY – Gibraltar pound of 100 pence
FLAG – White with a red stripe along the lower edge; over all a red castle with a key hanging from its gateway
POPULATION GROWTH RATE – 0.19 per cent (2004 est.)
POPULATION DENSITY – 4,338 per sq. km (2001)
GNI – US$5,000 per capita (2001)

CLIMATE AND TERRAIN

Gibraltar is a rocky promontory that juts southwards from the south-east coast of Spain, with which it is connected by a low isthmus. It is about 32 km (20 miles) from the opposite coast of Africa.

HISTORY AND POLITICS

Gibraltar was captured in 1704, during the War of the Spanish Succession, by a combined Dutch and English force, and was ceded to Great Britain by the Treaty of Utrecht (1713). This treaty stipulates that if Britain ever relinquishes colonial rights over Gibraltar the colony would return to Spain.

The 1969 constitution makes provision for certain domestic matters to devolve on a local government of ministers appointed from among elected members of the House of Assembly. The House of Assembly consists of an independent Speaker, 15 elected members, the Attorney-General and the Financial and Development Secretary. The Governor retains responsibility for external affairs, defence, internal security and financial security, while the local government is responsible for other domestic matters.

The last elections were held on 27 November 2003 and the Gibraltar Social Democrats won 51.5 per cent of the vote and secured 8 seats in the House of Assembly. A coalition of the Gibraltar Socialist Labour Party and the Liberal Party won 39.7 per cent and 7 seats in the Assembly.

Gibraltar is part of the EU (with the UK government responsible for enforcing EU directives affecting Gibraltar), but is not a full member and is exempt from the Common Customs Tariff and the Common Agricultural Policy. The Gibraltar government has recently been pressing for greater autonomy, especially in its relations with the EU, and this has led to tension with the UK and Spanish governments. Talks were taking place between the UK and Spain on the future of Gibraltar, but stalled after Gibraltar residents voted overwhelmingly by referendum in 2003 against a 'total shared sovereignty' arrangement.

Governor and Commander-in-Chief, HE Sir Francis
 Richards, KCMG, CVO, *apptd* 2003

GOVERNMENT OF GIBRALTAR
Arundel Great Court, 178–179 The Strand, London WC2R 1EL
T 020-7836 0777
Government Representative, A. Poggio

ECONOMY

Gibraltar has an extensive shipping trade and is a popular shopping centre and tourist resort. The chief sources of revenue are the port dues, the rent of the Crown estate in the town, and duties on consumer items (although valued added tax is not applied in the territory). A financial services industry is expanding, based on Gibraltar's status as an offshore financial centre.

Trade with UK	2003	2004
Imports from UK	£154,382,000	£158,569,000
Exports to UK	25,757,000	14,900,000

TRANSPORT INFRASTRUCTURE

Gibraltar has one international airport and about 29 km of roads. There is also a regular ferry service from the promonotory to Tangiers.

MONTSERRAT

AREA – 102 sq. km
POPULATION – 9,245 (2004 est.)
CAPITAL – ΨPlymouth
CURRENCY – East Caribbean dollar (EC$) of 100 cents
FLAG – British blue ensign with the shield of arms in the fly
POPULATION GROWTH RATE – 1.03 per cent (2004 est.)
POPULATION DENSITY – 108 per sq. km (1999)

CLIMATE AND TERRAIN
Montserrat is a mountainous volcanic island in the Leeward group in the Caribbean Sea, with elevation extremes ranging from 914 m (Chances Peak) at the highest point to 0 m (Caribbean Sea) at the lowest. The climate is tropical and the average temperature is 29°C.

HISTORY AND POLITICS
Discovered by Columbus in 1493, Montserrat became a British colony in 1632. The first settlers were predominantly Irish indentured servants from St Kitts. France and Britain fought over the island during the 17th and 18th centuries but Montserrat was finally assigned to Great Britain in 1783.

A ministerial system was introduced in Montserrat in 1960. The Executive Council is presided over by the Governor and is composed of four elected members (the Chief and three other Ministers) and two ex-officio members (the Attorney-General and the Financial Secretary). The four Ministers are appointed from the members of the political party or coalition holding the majority in the Legislative Council. The Legislative Council consists of the Speaker, two ex-officio members (the Attorney-General and the Financial Secretary) and nine elected members. Following elections in April 2001, New People's Liberation Movement held 7 seats and the National Progressive Party 2 seats.

The Soufrière Hills volcano became active again in 1995, and a particularly severe eruption in 1997 devastated much of the island, closing sea and air ports and leaving half the island uninhabitable. Two-thirds of the population fled the island, but some have started to return. However, reconstruction is hampered by lack of resources and the restriction of agriculture, industry and communications by continuing volcanic activity.
Governor, HE Deborah Barnes-Jones, *apptd* May 2004

BRITISH HIGH COMMISSION
Lower Collymore Rock (PO Box 676), Bridgetown, Barbados
T (+1) (246) 430 7800

Trade with UK	2003	2004
Imports from UK	£2,581,000	£1,164,000
Exports to UK	62,000	151,000

PITCAIRN ISLANDS

AREA – 4.5 sq. km
POPULATION – 46 (2004 est.). Since 1887 the islanders have generally been adherents of the Seventh-day Adventist Church. English and Pitkern are the official languages; the latter is a mixture of English and Tahitian and became an official language in 1997
CAPITAL – ΨAdamstown

CURRENCY – Currency is that of New Zealand
FLAG – British blue ensign with the arms in the fly

CLIMATE AND TERRAIN
Pitcairn is the chief of a group of islands situated about midway between New Zealand and Panama in the South Pacific Ocean. The other three islands of the group (Henderson, lying 168 km east-north-east of Pitcairn, Oeno, lying 120 km north-west, and Ducie, lying 470 km east) are all uninhabited. The climate is tropical, and the average temperature is 29°C.

HISTORY AND POLITICS
Pitcairn became a British settlement under the British Settlement Act 1887 and was administered by the Governor of Fiji from 1952 until 1970, when the administration was transferred to the British High Commission in New Zealand and the British High Commissioner was appointed Governor. The Local Government Ordinance of 1964 provides for a Council of ten members, of whom six are elected.
Governor of Pitcairn, Henderson, Ducie and Oeno Islands, HE Richard Fell, CVO *(British High Commissioner to New Zealand)*

ECONOMY
The islanders live by subsistence gardening and fishing. Apart from small fees charged for gun and driving licences there are no taxes and government revenue is derived almost solely from the sale of postage stamps and income from investments. Henderson Island, the largest of islands in the group, was declared a UNESCO World Heritage Site in 1988.

Trade with UK	2003	2004
Imports from UK	£97,000	£3,000
Exports to UK	133,000	3,000

TRANSPORT INFRASTRUCTURE
There are 6.4 km of roads on the islands, none of which are paved. Communication with the outside world is maintained by cargo vessels travelling between New Zealand and Panama which call at irregular intervals.

ST HELENA AND DEPENDENCIES

AREA – 122 sq. km
POPULATION – 7,415 (2004 est.)
CAPITAL – ΨJamestown (population, 884, 1998)
CURRENCY – St Helena pound (£) of 100 pence
FLAG – British blue ensign with the shield of arms in the fly
POPULATION GROWTH RATE – 0.62 (2004 est.)
POPULATION DENSITY – 40 per sq. km (1998)
URBAN POPULATION – 39.2 per cent (1998)

CLIMATE AND TERRAIN
St Helena is situated in the South Atlantic Ocean, 1,500 km south of the Equator and about 1,900 km west of Africa. The island is rugged and volcanic, with sheer cliffs rising to a central plateau. The climate is tropical but mild, tempered by trade winds, and the annual average temperature is 27°C.

HISTORY AND POLITICS

St Helena is believed to have been discovered by the Portuguese navigator João da Nova in 1502. It was used as a port of call for vessels of all nations trading to the East until it was annexed by the Dutch in 1633. It was never occupied by them, however, and the English East India Company seized it in 1659.

From 1815 to 1821 the island was lent to the British government as a place of exile for the Emperor Napoleon Bonaparte, who died in St Helena on 5 May 1821, and in 1834 it was annexed to the British Crown. The Zulu Chief, Dinizulu, was exiled to the island in 1890 and up to 6,000 Boer prisoners were held there between 1900 and 1903. Its importance as a port of call declined with the opening of the Suez Canal.

The government of St Helena is administered by a Governor, with the aid of a Legislative Council, consisting of a Speaker, three *ex-officio* members (Chief Secretary, Financial Secretary and Attorney-General) and 12 elected members. Five committees of the Legislative Council are responsible for the overseeing of the activities of the five biggest government departments, having a wide range of statutory and administrative functions. The Governor is assisted by an Executive Council of the three *ex-officio* members and the chairmen of the Council committees.
Governor, HE Michael Clancy, *apptd* 2004

ECONOMY AND TRADE

St Helena was intended as a maritime base, with an economy dedicated to the provision of supplies for shipping and the local garrison, rather than as a self-sufficient colony. St Helena still receives an annual grant from the UK, the only UK Overseas Territory to do so apart from Montserrat. The only significant export is canned and frozen fish.

Trade with UK	2003	2004
Imports from UK	£12,450,000	£7,886,000
Exports to UK	606,000	808,000

TRANSPORT INFRASTRUCTURE AND MEDIA

St Helena has 138 km of roads, most of which are single track. James's Bay, on the north-west of the island is the principal port.

Television programmes are received in St Helena via satellite and distributed by cable. The island also has one radio station.

ASCENSION ISLAND

AREA – 88 sq. km
POPULATION – 980 (2001 est.)
CAPITAL – ΨGeorgetown
CURRENCY – Currency is that of St Helena or the UK

CLIMATE AND TERRAIN

The small island of Ascension lies in the South Atlantic some 1,200 km north-west of St Helena. It is a rocky peak of purely volcanic origin. The highest point (Green Mountain), some 860 m, is covered with lush vegetation.

HISTORY AND POLITICS

Ascension is said to have been discovered by João da Nova in 1501 and two years later was visited on Ascension Day by Alphonse d'Albuquerque, who gave the island its present name. It was uninhabited until the arrival of Napoleon in St Helena in 1815 when a small British naval garrison was stationed on the island. As HMS *Ascension* it remained under the supervision of the Board of Admiralty until 1922, when it was made a dependency of St Helena.

The British Foreign Secretary appoints the Administrator, who is responsible to the Governor resident in St Helena. There is a small police force, bank and post office. In August 2002, a plebiscite was held to decide on a form of democratic self-government for the island, and an Island Council was formed as a result. A general election to appoint members to the Council took place in November. The Council consists of seven elected members plus the Director of Financial Services and the Attorney-General, and is chaired by the Governor, represented locally by the Administrator.
Administrator, Andrew Kettlewell, *apptd* 2002

ECONOMY AND TRANSPORT

A new fiscal regime was introduced in 2002, and finance for public and common services is raised through taxation. Healthcare and schooling are provided free of charge to local tax payers.

Ascension has 40 km of roads, and there is a monthly shipping service and a flight every five days by RAF aircraft which transit Ascension en route to the Falkland Islands. Georgetown is the port.

TRISTAN DA CUNHA

AREA – 98 sq. km
POPULATION – 277 (2003 est.)
CAPITAL – ΨEdinburgh of the Seven Seas
CURRENCY – Currency is that of the UK
FLAG – Tristan da Cunha's own flag was raised on 18 November 2002 and the coat of arms reads: 'Our Faith is our Strength'.

CLIMATE AND TERRAIN

Tristan da Cunha is the chief of a group of islands in the South Atlantic Ocean which lie some 2,333 km south-south-west of St Helena. All the islands are volcanic and steep-sided with cliffs or narrow beaches. The highest point of elevation is 2,060 m (Queen Mary's Peak) while the lowest is 0 m (Atlantic Ocean).

HISTORY AND POLITICS

Tristan da Cunha was discovered in 1506 by the Portuguese admiral Tristão da Cunha. In 1760 a British naval officer visited the islands and gave his name to Nightingale Island. In 1816 the group was annexed to the British Crown and a garrison was placed on Tristan da Cunha, but this force was withdrawn in 1817. Corporal William Glass remained at his own request with his wife and two children and this party, with two others, formed a settlement. In 1827 five women from St Helena, and afterwards others from Cape Colony, joined the party. Due to its position on a main sailing route the colony thrived, with an economy based on trading with whalers, sealers and other passing ships, until the late 19th century, when the replacement of sail by steam and the opening of the Suez Canal led to decline.

In October 1961 a volcano, believed to have been extinct for thousands of years, erupted and the danger of further volcanic activity led to the evacuation of inhabitants to the UK until 1963.

In 1938 Tristan da Cunha and the neighbouring islands of Inaccessible, Nightingale (both uninhabited) and Gough were made dependencies of St Helena. They are administered by the Governor of St Helena through a

resident Administrator, with headquarters at Edinburgh. Under a constitution introduced in 1985, the Administrator is advised by an Island Council of eight elected members, of whom one must be a woman, and three appointed members. Elections are held every three years.
Administrator, Mike Hentley, *apptd* 2004

ECONOMY

The island is almost financially self-sufficient; UK government aid finances training scholarships and a resident medical officer at the hospital. The main industries are crayfish fishing, fish-processing and agriculture.

TRANSPORT INFRASTRUCTURE

Tristan da Cunha has 20 km of roads. Scheduled visits to the island are restricted to about six calls a year by fishing vessels from Cape Town and annual calls of the RMS *St Helena* and the SA *Agulhas*, also from Cape Town, which carry passengers, cargo and mail to and from the island.

SOUTH GEORGIA AND THE SOUTH SANDWICH ISLANDS

AREA – 4,092 sq. km
POPULATION – No permanent population
CAPITAL – Ψ King Edward Point (Administrative Centre)
CURRENCY – Pound Sterling
FLAG – British blue ensign, with the shield of arms in the fly

CLIMATE AND TERRAIN

South Georgia is an island 1,390 km east-south-east of the Falkland Islands. More than half of the island is covered by permanent ice with many large glaciers reaching the sea at the head of fjords. The main mountain range is the Allardyce and elevation extremes range from 2,960 m (Mt Paget) at the highest point to 0 m (Atlantic Ocean) at the lowest. The South Sandwich Islands, lying some 750 km miles south-east of South Georgia, consist of a chain of 11 uninhabited volcanic islands some 350 km long. Some of these volcanoes are still active.

HISTORY AND POLITICS

Britain annexed South Georgia and the South Sandwich Islands in 1908 and since then they have been under continuous British occupation apart from a brief period during the Falklands war in 1982. Following the conflict, a small British Army garrison was maintained at King Edward Point on South Georgia, but this was withdrawn in March 2001. The population comprises the government's marine officer and the staff of the scientific research station operated by the British Antarctic Survey at King Edward Point, the curators of the museum at Grytviken and staff of the British Antarctic Survey at Bird Island, to the north-west of South Georgia.
The present constitution came into effect in 1985. It provides for a Commissioner who, for the time being, is the officer administering the government of the Falkland Islands.
Commissioner for South Georgia and the South Sandwich Islands, HE Howard Pearce, CVO, *apptd* 2002

ECONOMY

Some fishing takes place in adjacent waters, and there is a potential source of income from harvesting finfish and krill. In 1993 the UK government decreed an extension of Crown sovereignty and jurisdiction from 19 km to 321 km around South Georgia and the South Sandwich Islands in order to preserve marine stocks.
The islands receive income from postage stamps produced in the UK, sale of fishing licences, and harbour and landing fees from tourist vessels. Tourism from specialised cruise ships is increasing.

TURKS AND CAICOS ISLANDS

AREA – 497 sq. km
POPULATION – 19,956 (2004 est.)
CAPITAL – ΨGrand Turk (Cockburn Town; population, 3,691, 1994)
CURRENCY – US dollar (US$)
FLAG – British blue ensign with the shield of arms in the fly
POPULATION GROWTH RATE – 3.3 per cent (2004 est.)
POPULATION DENSITY – 37 per sq. km (2001)

CLIMATE AND TERRAIN

The Turks and Caicos Islands are about 80 km south-east of the Bahamas, of which they are geographically an extension. There are over 30 islands, of which eight are inhabited. The principal island and seat of government is Grand Turk. The climate is marine tropical, moderated by trade winds; the average annual temperature is 27°C.

HISTORY AND POLITICS

The islands were part of Jamaica until its independence in 1962, when they became a separate Crown colony and were administered from the Bahamas from 1965 to 1973. Since the Bahamas' independence in 1973, the territory has had its own governor.
A constitution introduced in 1988, and amended in 1993, provides for an Executive Council and a Legislative Council. The Executive Council is presided over by the Governor and comprises the Chief Minister and five elected Ministers, together with the *ex-officio* Chief Secretary and Attorney-General.
At the general election of 24 April 2003, the People's Democratic Movement won seven seats and the Progressive National Party six seats in the Legislative Council.
Governor, HE Jim Poston, *apptd* 2002

ECONOMY

The most important industries are fishing, tourism and offshore financial services. The islands were visited by 151,000 tourists in 2000, although tourism fell by 6 per cent in 2002.

Trade with UK	2003	2004
Imports from UK	£1,167,000	£1,858,000
Exports to UK	344,000	19,000

TRANSPORT INFRASTRUCTURE

The principal airports are on the islands of Grand Turk and Providenciales. Air services link Providenciales with the UK, USA and other Caribbean countries, and there are regular internal air services between the principal islands. There are direct shipping services to the USA (Miami). The islands also have a total of 121 km of roads, 24 km of which are surfaced.

THE YEAR 2004–5

EVENTS OF THE YEAR

BRITISH AFFAIRS

SEPTEMBER 2004

7. The new Scottish Parliament building, which cost £431 million, was officially opened. **8.** In a Cabinet reshuffle, the Prime Minister, Tony Blair, appointed Alan Milburn as Chancellor of the Duchy of Lancaster and Alan Johnson succeeded Andrew Smith as Work and Pensions Secretary. **13.** The Metropolitan Police Commissioner, Sir John Stevens, demanded a full report into a Buckingham Palace security breach after a 'Fathers 4 Justice' protester got over the perimeter wall of the palace and climbed up the front of the building. The Prime Minister addressed the Trades Union Congress in Brighton, seeking to reassure union members that he was focused on domestic issues despite the war in Iraq. **15.** The House of Commons voted in favour of a ban on hunting with dogs in England and Wales. A pro-hunting demonstration in Parliament Square ended in violent clashes between protesters and police. **16.** Following a security breach at the House of Commons by five pro-hunting protestors, the Leader of the Commons, Peter Hain, strongly criticised existing security arrangements. **19.** The Countryside and Rights of Way Act 2000 came into force and was marked with a walk through the Forest of Bowland, Lancashire. Rural Affairs Minister Alun Michael, who had planned to lead the walk, did not join ramblers following a statement from the Countryside Alliance that it would stage a pro-hunting demonstration should he attend. **20.** Fifty-three new Virgin Pendolino trains and 900 carriages entered service on the main West Coast line following the completion of the first stage of a £7.6 billion modernisation programme. The new trains have a special tilting mechanism that allows them to go round corners without slowing down, reducing non-stop journey times between London and Manchester by 35 minutes. **21.** The Department of Health announced that it had sent out 6,000 letters to people warning that they may have been exposed to CJD through transfusions of blood plasma products from Britain's supply of donated blood. **23.** The Ministry of Defence announced that a new test to screen for exposure to depleted uranium would be offered to military and civilian personnel who served in the Gulf area between 1 August 1990 and 31 July 1991 and also in Kosovo on or after 5 August 1994. **24.** The Department of Trade and Industry (DTI) informed its 10,200 staff that as part of government plans to streamline the civil service, 1,500 jobs would be cut, including 1,010 from its headquarters in London. **26.** The Labour Party's annual conference began in Brighton. Following a bomb scare, a plane bound for New York from Athens made an emergency landing at Stansted airport. **27.** The Chancellor of the Exchequer, Gordon Brown, addressed the Labour Party conference, urging delegates to support the prime minister over the conflict in Iraq, and stating that Britain's economic policies should form the centrepiece of the party's election campaign. A new five-in-one vaccine for babies combining diphtheria, tetanus, whooping cough, polio and Hib, became available nationwide through doctors' surgeries. **28.** The Prime Minister addressed the Labour Party conference in Brighton. In his speech he outlined the Labour manifesto for health and education, plans for financial help for first-time homebuyers, the introduction of identity cards, and an enhanced basic state pension. Mr Blair also apologised to his party and the country for using misleading security information regarding weapons of mass destruction as the basis to invade Iraq, but appealed to party members for their continued support over the conflict. **30.** Following media speculation, Downing Street announced that Tony Blair would serve a third term as prime minister if the Labour Party returned to power in the next general election.

OCTOBER 2004

1. The prime minister went into hospital for a routine procedure to correct an irregular heartbeat. **5.** Michael Howard addressed the Conservative Party conference for the first time as party leader. Mr Howard pledged that a Conservative government would renegotiate Britain's membership of the EU, cut wasteful government spending, freeze civil service recruitment, cut taxes where possible and set an annual limit on the number of immigrants allowed into the UK. **8.** Kenneth Bigley, the British civilian held hostage in Iraq for 22 days, was killed by his captors. **11.** London Underground announced plans to install a new 'driverless' system on the Jubilee, Northern and Piccadilly lines. **12.** A government-commissioned report by Adair Turner, chairman of the Pensions Commission, concluded that more than 12 million people are not saving enough for their old age; the report stated that unless the government increases taxes, compels workers to save or extends the official retirement age, the situation would reach crisis point in 30 years' time. **13.** A parliamentary joint committee on security agreed to a recommendation to appoint a new head of security in the Houses of Parliament, working with the Serjeant-at-Arms and Gentleman Usher of the Black Rod, who are responsible for security in the Commons and Lords respectively. **14.** Professor David Healy of the University of Wales told a Commons health select committee that as many as half the articles published by respected clinicians in medical journals were written by representatives of the pharmaceutical industry. **15.** The Ministry of Defence announced that it was considering a request from the USA for British soldiers to be redeployed to US-controlled areas of Iraq to free US forces for other operations. Boris Johnson, vice-chairman of the Conservative Party and editor of *The Spectator,* issued a formal apology for an article published in his magazine that suggested people from Liverpool 'enjoyed seeing themselves as victims' and claimed that 'drunken Liverpool fans' contributed to the 1989 Hillsborough disaster. The Tomlinson Committee published its report on reforms in education for 14–19-year-olds; it recommended the replacement of the GCSE and A-level system with a single diploma which would offer both vocational and academic qualifications. **19.** Margaret Hassan, British director of the Iraq branch of the international charity CARE, who had lived in Iraq for 30 years, was kidnapped in Baghdad. The Department for Culture, Media and Sport published the Gambling Bill, in which it proposed legislative changes permitting betting on Good Friday and Christmas Day as well as allowing casinos to remain open for 24-hour periods, advertise and to have unlimited jackpots. **21.** Following a US request for reinforcements, the Defence Secretary, Geoff Hoon, announced that 500 soldiers of the Black Watch battalion and 350 support personnel stationed in Basra, would be redeployed to a US-controlled area near Baghdad. With the Freedom of Information Act about to come into force in January 2005, the breakdown of all MPs' expenses was made available for the first time; the total MP expense claim for 2003–4 was £78 million. **22.** Video footage of Margaret Hassan, the charity worker held hostage in Iraq, was broadcast by the Arab television network Al-Jazeera. **26.** The House of Lords voted by a majority of 250 against an outright ban on fox-hunting, opting for a system allowing traditional fox-hunting to continue under a strict licensing arrangement. **27.** The Health Secretary John Reid announced that the first national screening programme for bowel cancer would be introduced throughout the country from April 2006. The UKIP MEP Robert Kilroy-Silk resigned from his posts in the party following a dispute over his refusal to abandon his attempt to become the party's national leader. The National Institute for Clinical Excellence published new guidelines for NHS dentists recommending that the frequency of dental check-ups should match a patient's need, instead of being at the present six-monthly intervals.

NOVEMBER 2004
1. Universities announced that they would set up mumps vaccination programmes following an outbreak among young people in their late teens and early twenties; official figures from the Health Protection Agency showed an increase of a third in the first six months of 2004 compared to the same period in 2003. **4.** The Armed Forces minister, Adam Ingram, confirmed that three soldiers of the Black Watch regiment and their Iraqi interpreter had been killed in Iraq. In an all-postal referendum in north-east England, 78 per cent of the 46 per cent turn-out voted against plans for a regional assembly. **6.** A First Great Western passenger train was derailed after striking a vehicle on a level crossing at Ufton Nervet, Berkshire; seven people were killed and 150 injured. **10.** Scottish ministers unanimously approved measures to ban smoking in public places in Scotland, planning for legislation to be in place by spring 2006. **14.** Shadow arts spokesman Boris Johnson was sacked by Conservative leader Michael Howard after revelations concerning an extramarital affair, previously denied by Mr Johnson, were published in a number of Sunday newspapers. Eurostar announced that it would not run some of its international services from Waterloo station when the Channel Tunnel link to St Pancras station opens in 2007. **15.** The government published a White Paper which proposed a ban on smoking at work, in restaurants and in public houses serving prepared food. Conservative and Liberal Democrat peers tabled an amendment to the Pensions Bill proposing that the compulsory purchase of an annuity at 75 should be scrapped provided a pensioner can demonstrate sufficient financial resources other than means-tested benefits; the amendment was defeated the following day. **16.** Arab television station Al-Jazeera screened video footage of British aid worker Margaret Hassan apparently being killed by her kidnappers. **17.** An independent inquiry chaired by Lord Lloyd of Berwick concluded that the government should publicly acknowledge that 6,000 British veterans were suffering from Gulf war syndrome. **18.** The Hunting Bill was passed by parliament, making it unlawful for hunting with dogs to take place in England

and Wales from 18 February 2005, after the invocation of the Parliament Act by the Speaker of the House of Commons. **22.** The Prime Minister refused to discuss reports claiming that the Home Secretary, David Blunkett, had requested a paternity test on the two-year old son and unborn baby of his former lover Kimberly Quinn, publisher of *The Spectator*. **23.** The Queen's Speech announced 32 new Bills for the next parliamentary session, many concerned with law and order, including measures to combat terrorism, serious crime, drugs and anti-social behaviour and plans to introduce a new identity card scheme. **28.** The Home Office announced there would be an independent review by Sir Alan Budd into allegations that David Blunkett had abused his position as Home Secretary to fast-track a visa application for a nanny employed by Kimberly Quinn. Mr Blunkett denied any attempt to influence the application process. **29.** The Prime Minister stated that he had no doubt that the Home Secretary would be exonerated by the inquiry.

DECEMBER 2004
2. The Chief Minister of the Isle of Man, Richard Corkhill, who had lead the government of the Crown dependency for three years, resigned from his post after allegations of corruption. **6.** The Work and Pensions Secretary, Alan Johnson, announced that in April 2005 most benefits based on the national insurance contribution would rise by 3.1 per cent in line with the retail prices index (RPI) and income-related benefits would rise by 1 per cent. **8.** Four crew from a Royal Navy helicopter were reported missing after their aircraft disappeared 15 miles south-east of the Lizard peninsula in Cornwall; their bodies were found the following day, close to the wreckage of the helicopter and a board of inquiry was set up to investigate the incident. **9.** The RAF began the first phase of its redundancy programme, announced by the government in July 2004, calling for 450 personnel to volunteer to leave the service by 2006. **10.** It was announced that the Millennium Dome would be used by the charity Crisis as its 2004 Christmas shelter for the homeless. **15.** The Foreign Secretary, Jack Straw, announced an overhaul of the British Diplomatic Service which would see diplomats withdrawn from consulates in continental Europe and redeployed to new embassies and consulates in central Asia and the Middle East. David Blunkett resigned after Sir Alan Budd's inquiry team found correspondence from Mr Blunkett's office regarding the visa application of Kimberley Quinn's nanny. Charles Clarke replaced Mr Blunkett as Home Secretary and Ruth Kelly became Education Secretary. **16.** The Defence Secretary announced details of plans to restructure the Army: existing infantry battalions are to be merged to create larger multi-battalion regiments. A panel of nine law lords ruled that the sections of the Anti-Terrorism, Crime and Security Act 2001 allowing terrorist suspects to be detained without trial contravened the European Convention on Human Rights. **21.** The official inquiry by Sir Alan Budd concluded that an intervention by the former Home Secretary's private office had been responsible for speeding up the visa application of the nanny of Mr Blunkett's former lover, but it remained indeterminable whether this related directly to orders issued by Mr Blunkett. **23.** The Department of Health announced that stocks of the painkilling drug diamorphine could reach critically low levels within weeks and asked doctors to prescribe alternatives where possible. **26.** The Foreign and Commonwealth Office set up a helpline number for families and friends of the

hundreds of Britons missing as a result of the Indian Ocean tsunami (see Asia). **27.** The Foreign and Commonwealth Office confirmed the deaths of 15 Britons in the tsunami but said the final toll was expected to be higher. **30.** The government announced that Britain would give £50 million to the tsunami disaster fund; donations from the public reached £25 million by the end of the day.

JANUARY 2005

1. The new Freedom of Information Act came into force; more than 100,000 public bodies, as well as family doctors, hospitals, local councils, schools and police forces are subject to the Act; security and intelligence agencies, courts and tribunals remain exempt, as does some information held by the Houses of Parliament. **6.** Chancellor Gordon Brown, speaking at the National Gallery of Scotland in Edinburgh, set out his proposals to reduce Africa's debt; he suggested that wealthier nations should waive historic loans to African states and meet the costs of writing off loans to international organisations such as the World Bank. The Chancellor's speech came ahead of his week-long tour of African states including Kenya, Tanzania, Mozambique and South Africa. **7.** The police casualty bureau disclosed that 2,000 Britons were still unaccounted for in the countries worst hit by the Indian Ocean tsunami. **8.** Gales and torrential rain in northern Britain caused flooding in Carlisle and other towns; five people died. **9.** After the gales, severe flood warnings remained in place for Carlisle and nearby Denton Holme. The commander of British Forces in Gibraltar was found dead in his swimming pool following a Ministry of Defence inquiry into allegations that he had downloaded child pornography from the internet. The court martial began at a British army base in Germany of the first of four soldiers from the Royal Regiment of Fusiliers accused of torturing and sexually abusing Iraqi prisoners while on duty in Iraq. **12.** A tabloid newspaper published a photograph showing Prince Harry wearing a Nazi Afrika Corps uniform and a swastika armband at a fancy dress party: the prince later issued an apology. **15.** The Conservative MP for Wantage, Robert Jackson, announced his defection to the Labour Party, declaring it to be in the country's best interest that Tony Blair forms the next government. **17.** In a speech to the Hansard Society, the chief inspector of schools, David Bell, cautioned that faith schools needed to be monitored to ensure that pupils attending them were taught an understanding of other faiths and the wider aspects of British society. **20.** The Foreign and Commonwealth Office announced that the usual seven-year wait before death can be certified when there is no body of the deceased would be suspended for families of victims missing in the Indian Ocean tsunami, allowing families of those presumed dead to settle their affairs. **21.** During a one-day visit to Beijing, the Foreign Secretary signed an agreement with the Chinese government lifting visa restrictions for Chinese people travelling to the UK with licensed tour agencies under the Approved Destination Status scheme. **24.** The government published its five-year plan for housing, which included allowing a further 300,000 local authority and housing association tenants the opportunity to purchase a stake in their homes. **25.** The last four British citizens held at the US military detention centre in Guantanamo Bay arrived back in the UK following their release without charge by the US authorities. On arrival they were arrested by British anti-terrorist police but were released without charge after 28 hours in custody. **26.** A four-year study into the 1998 Camelford water poisoning incident, when 20 tonnes of highly caustic aluminium sulphate contaminated the water supply of 20,000 people, was published; the report concluded that the failure to order thorough medical checks at the time had made it difficult to link symptoms reported by the victims directly to the incident. Ellington colliery in Northumberland, one of eight collieries left in Britain, was closed after its owner, UK Coal, said that flood waters had proved unstoppable; 340 miners were made redundant. **29.** Chris Smith, a Labour MP and former Culture Secretary, announced that he had been HIV-positive for 17 years.

FEBRUARY 2005

3. The Attorney-General, Lord Goldsmith, announced that seven members of the Parachute Regiment would be charged with the murder of an Iraqi civilian in southern Iraq on 11 May 2003. **8.** The Conservative MP for Mid-Bedfordshire, Jonathan Sayeed, was suspended from parliament for two weeks for his role in a company that arranged private tours of the House of Commons for American tourists. Statistics released by the DWP showed that only 63 per cent of those eligible for a minimum-income guarantee, a means-tested benefit for pensioners on low incomes, had applied for the benefit. **10.** The Prince of Wales announced his engagement to Mrs Camilla Parker Bowles; the marriage was to be a civil ceremony at Windsor Castle on 8 April. The midnight opening of a new Ikea store in Edmonton, north London, descended into chaos as security guards were overwhelmed by the 6,000 customers enticed by special offers; the shop was forced to close after 30 minutes and six people were kept in hospital overnight. **14.** At the 158th and last Waterloo Cup, the leading event in the hare-coursing calendar, blood-sports enthusiasts clashed with anti-hunt protestors. **16.** Greenpeace protesters were confronted by angry traders when they stormed the International Petroleum Exchange in London; the protest was timed to coincide with the Kyoto Protocol coming into force. At midnight the Hunting Act 2004 came into force, making hunting with dogs illegal in England and Wales. **17.** The Prince of Wales changed the venue for his forthcoming wedding to the Guildhall in Windsor after officials discovered that a licence permitting a civil ceremony at Windsor Castle would be valid for three years, allowing other couples to marry at the castle. **18.** The Food Standards Agency withdrew millions of food products from sale after traces of Sudan 1, a banned carcinogenic dye, was found in a batch of Crosse & Blackwell Worcester Sauce distributed to more than 200 caterers and food manufacturers. Its distributor, Premier Foods, traced the source of contamination to a consignment of red chilli powder imported from India in 2002. **22.** An Ofsted review of the literacy and numeracy strategies for primary education showed that 56 per cent of boys and 71 per cent of girls reached the expected standard in writing by the end of primary education. The government announced public sector pay levels for 2005: MPs, ministers, doctors, teachers and judges received salary increases of between 2.5 and 3.2 per cent, coupled with the introduction of performance-related payments for teachers and an extended bonus scheme for civil servants. Senior civil servants averaged a 4.2 per cent pay increase and the Prime Minister's salary increased by 2.8 per cent. **23.** MPs in the House of Commons voted 309 to 233 in favour of the Prevention of Terrorism Bill which proposed putting suspected terrorists under house arrest;

32 Labour MPs voted against the Bill and it faced strong opposition in the run-up to the next round of voting. **24.** A Heathrow-bound British Airways jet with 351 passengers on board was forced to make an emergency landing at Manchester airport after flying from Los Angeles with one failed engine. Figures published by the ONS showed that the number of deaths in which the MRSA superbug was recorded as a factor had nearly doubled in the five years to 2003. **25.** Data gathered for the Health Survey for England 2003 showed that 22.9 per cent of men and 23.5 per cent of women had a body mass index (BMI) rating of over 30, classifying them as obese. **27.** A study by the Patients Association found that hundreds of babies, many just a few days old, had been infected by the MRSA superbug while in hospital. **28.** Prior to the House of Commons debate on the Prevention of Terrorism Bill, Home Secretary Charles Clark conceded that judges rather than ministers should be responsible for issuing house-arrest control orders. The call for judges to approve all control orders, proposed by Labour backbencher Win Griffiths with cross-party support, was defeated by just 14 votes (267 to 253).

MARCH 2005

1. The Department of Health announced that it would buy 14.6 million courses of the antiviral drug Tamiflu as a measure against a national flu epidemic. Figures published by the Home Office showed a 5 per cent increase in drug-related offences in England and Wales in 2003, with Class A drug offences (relating to heroin, cocaine, LSD and Ecstasy-type drugs) rising by 6 per cent. **2.** The army was called in to help emergency services in south-east England after heavy snowfall brought road and rail traffic to a standstill. **7.** In a debate on the Prevention of Terrorism Bill, the House of Lords voted in favour of judges making the initial decision to impose any type of control order, not just those pertaining to house arrest. **8.** The House of Lords voted to insert a 'sunset clause' into the Prevention of Terrorism Bill, creating a time limit after which the legislation would expire, to ensure that better measures were prepared to replace the Bill. **10.** A report by the Commission for Africa concluded that the continent required at least an extra US$50 billion (£26 billion) a year in aid from the West and proposed the removal of trade restrictions and subsidies alongside the cancellation of the entire debt of poorer African states. **11.** The Prevention of Terrorism Bill received royal assent after Home Secretary Charles Clarke conceded that a counter-terrorism bill due to be introduced into the Commons in spring 2006 could be used to amend it. **12.** Mr Clarke used new powers under the Prevention of Terrorism Act 2005 to impose control orders on ten foreign terrorist suspects released on bail from prison two days earlier. **13.** The National Missing Persons Helpline charity announced that it faced bankruptcy and closure unless the Home Office provided immediate funding. **15.** The leader of the GMB union was suspended following claims that he tried to interfere with an investigation into alleged vote-rigging in merger talks with the Amicus and Transport and General Workers' unions. **17.** Official figures given in answer to an MP's question in parliament revealed that at the end of the 2003–4 financial year, nine hospital trusts had deficits of more than £10 million, 14 had deficits of more than £5 million and 39 of more than £1 million; overall almost one-third of all NHS trusts were in deficit, with the total debt standing at more than £350 million. Private Johnson Beharry was awarded the Victoria Cross for bravery during a tour of duty in Iraq; he

is the first recipient in 23 years. **24.** Howard Flight, the MP for Arundel and South Downs, was dismissed as Conservative Party deputy chairman and had his party membership withdrawn after he made comments to *The Times* suggesting that the party, if elected, planned extra spending cuts. It was reported that motorways and bridges across the West Country were in danger of crumbling because they were built from sub-standard cement after employees at the Lafarge Cement UK plant in Wiltshire falsified alkali-level test results for the concrete; the Highways Agency said they were monitoring structures and roads for signs of damage. **30.** The villages of Ferryside and Llansteffan in Carmarthenshire, Wales, had their analogue television signal permanently switched off and replaced with digital television services as part of a trial prior to analogue television being switched off nationally in 2008.

APRIL 2005

2. Pope John Paul II died at his private apartment in the Vatican City. **4.** The Prince of Wales' wedding was postponed by 24 hours to enable the prince, the Prime Minister and the Archbishop of Canterbury to attend the funeral of Pope John Paul II in Rome. **5.** The Prime Minister called a general election for 5 May. **4.** Six Labour councillors on Birmingham City Council were stripped of their office by the Election Commissioner, Sir Richard Mawrey, and banned from standing for election or voting for the next five years after being found guilty of rigging the June 2004 local election results. **6.** The Commons education and skills select committee stated that it was unacceptable that one in five children could not read properly by the age of 11, eight years after the National Literary Strategy was introduced in primary schools. **9.** The Prince of Wales married Mrs Camilla Parker Bowles in a civil ceremony at the Guildhall, Windsor, followed by a service of dedication at St George's Chapel, Windsor. **10.** The Ministry of Defence released figures showing that British troops had killed around 200 Iraqi insurgents since the Iraq war officially ended on 1 May 2003. **21.** On the advice of the Healthcare Commission, Health Secretary John Reid ordered special measures to be taken at a maternity unit at Northwick Park Hospital, London, following the deaths of ten mothers in three years. **24.** A report by the Royal College of Nursing showed that in 2004, 35,000 nurses in England left the profession, 20,000 nurses were newly registered and 12,700 nurses were recruited from abroad. **26.** West Yorkshire police announced an investigation into allegations of electoral fraud against Jamshed Khan, Conservative councillor in Bradford West, a key Labour-held marginal constituency, after 13 people were found to be registered for postal votes at his home in Bradford and a further 12 people at a second address in the constituency formerly owned by Mr Khan. Mr Khan resigned from the Conservative Party shortly before the investigation was announced. **27.** A Channel 4 programme disclosed that in a confidential document the Attorney-General, Lord Goldsmith, had warned the Prime Minister ten days before the invasion of Iraq in March 2003 that he could not be confident that a court would regard military action as lawful. The disclosure came as the latest *Populus* election poll showed that only a quarter of voters trusted Mr Blair. **30.** An emergency hotline was set up as concerns grew that the large number of postal votes requested for the general election on 5 May could result in postal ballot malpractice and fraud; returning officers were instructed to report to the police anyone bringing more than five postal ballot papers into a polling station.

MAY 2005

1. The Oxford tradition of jumping from Magdalen bridge into the River Cherwell at first light on May Day resulted in around 60 people being injured as the river was only 3 ft deep. **2.** The FSA ordered tests on all spices entering Britain, particularly chilli powder, paprika, cayenne pepper and turmeric, after the carcinogenic chemical dyes Sudan 1 and Para Red, whose use in foodstuffs is banned, were found in chilli powder and paprika on sale in Britain. **3.** A tornado caused devastation in the village of Hoghton, near Preston; most of the damage was confined to a small strip of the village, no wider than 100 m at any point, which was hit directly by the tornado. **5.** The Labour Party won the general election, securing Tony Blair's government a third term in office. The FSA named 35 product lines contaminated with the dye Para Red and ordered their immediate withdrawal from sale. **6.** Prime Minister Tony Blair appointed a new Cabinet, which included David Blunkett's return to a Cabinet post as Work and Pensions Secretary; Alan Johnson, formerly the Pensions Secretary, became the new Secretary of State for Productivity, Energy and Industry (formerly Trade and Industry); and John Reid became Defence Secretary. Michael Howard announced that he would resign as the leader of the Conservative Party in six months' time, allowing a new leadership selection process to be introduced before his successor was elected. **11.** Construction began of new wharves on the Grand Union Canal in west London as part of a British Waterways plan to increase the amount of freight carried on Britain's canals. **17.** In Washington, the British MP George Galloway appeared before a US Senate subcommittee to answer accusations that he received payment from the Iraqi government during Saddam Hussein's regime. US investigators for the subcommittee believed the money was received through his charity, the Mariam Appeal, originally set up to fund leukaemia treatment for a young Iraqi girl; Mr Galloway staunchly denied receiving any such payments. At the state opening of Parliament, the Queen outlined 45 bills and five draft bills to be passed during the next 18-month session. **23.** Around 10,000 BBC employees staged a one-day strike in protest at plans to cut 3,780 jobs at the corporation; programme scheduling was affected, with a number of live broadcasts, particularly news programmes, forced off the air. **25.** The Deputy Prime Minister, John Prescott, announced that 800 government sites, totalling 3,600 hectares in area and including disused railway stations, former NHS hospitals and MOD land, would be made available for the development of affordable housing. **26.** The Defence Secretary, John Reid, announced that as part of a forces changeover 400 British troops would be posted to Iraq, bringing UK military strength in Iraq to 8,500.

JUNE 2005

11. The G8 finance ministers agreed at a meeting in London to cancel the debts of the world's 18 poorest countries, immediately writing off US$40 billion of debt owed to the International Development Association, the International Monetary Fund and the African Development Bank. In the Queen's Birthday Honours List, Dame Judi Dench was made a Companion of Honour and actor David Jason was knighted. **13.** The Defence Secretary announced that Britain was to make a limited contribution to the peacekeeping mission in Darfur, Sudan. **15.** The Permanent Secretary at the Treasury, Sir Gus O'Donnell, was appointed Secretary to the Cabinet and Head of the Home Civil Service in succession to Sir Andrew Turnbull, who retired at the end of July. **16.** The Registrar-General for Scotland, Duncan Macniven, authorised 12 registered celebrants of the Humanist Society of Scotland to conduct legal marriages under section 12 of the Marriage (Scotland) Act 1977; this gave Humanists in Scotland a status similar to religious groups and civil registrars. **17.** It was announced that Lord Phillips of Worth Matravers would succeed Lord Woolf as Lord Chief Justice of England and Wales on 1 October 2005, and would be replaced as Master of the Rolls by Lord Justice Clarke. **19.** The Healthcare Commission, the main regulator for the health service and independent care, said that it would be carrying out unannounced assessments of the cleanliness of about 100 NHS and private hospitals following an increase in hospital-acquired infections. Southern England recorded the hottest June day since 1976, while the north of England and Scotland experienced storms and floods. **20.** A 20-mile stretch of North Yorkshire, between Thirsk and Helmsley, was hit by flash flooding and RAF helicopters were deployed to rescue people stranded by the flooding; hundreds of sheep and cattle drowned but no people were killed. **22.** With the introduction of two new Labour peers in the House of Lords, Labour achieved parity in the Lords with the Conservatives for the first time. **23.** *The Times* reported that Zimbabwean asylum-seekers had begun a hunger strike at three UK detention centres following the lifting of a two-year ban on enforced removals in November 2004, and a Home Office ruling that it was safe for failed asylum-seekers to be returned to Zimbabwe. Figures from the Department of Education and Skills showed school expulsions to be at their highest level for five years; violence and threats against other pupils and teachers accounted for almost half the 9,880 exclusions in 2004. **27.** The 48,000 former Railtrack shareholders who lost money in 2001 when Railtrack went into administration began their case for government compensation. Immigration officers were instructed to suspend all deportations of failed asylum-seekers to Zimbabwe, despite the Government's insistence that there would be no official suspension of deportation; the move came as the hunger strikes by Zimbabwean asylum-seekers continued. **30.** A 20-metre section of a new railway tunnel collapsed onto the tracks near Gerrards Cross, Buckinghamshire, minutes after one train had passed through it and just before another, which managed to stop in time.

JULY 2005

2. About 200,000 people attended a protest rally in Edinburgh organised by the Make Poverty History campaign in advance of the G8 summit in Scotland. Ten *Live 8* concerts calling for action against world poverty took place simultaneously in the G8 countries and South Africa; the UK hosted two concerts, in London and at the Eden Project, Cornwall. **6.** The three-day G8 conference and summit of heads of government began at the Gleneagles Hotel, Perthshire; the leaders considered issues such as climate change and the global economy, and concluded by pledging to increase aid to developing countries, including doubling aid to Africa by 2010. A rally took place in Edinburgh during the day and in the evening the final *Live 8* concert was held at Murrayfield, Edinburgh. London won its bid to host the 2012

Olympic Games, beating Paris in the final round of voting. **7.** Four suicide bombings in London killed 52 people and injured 700. The three bombs on London Underground trains exploded at 8.50 a.m. on a Piccadilly Line train between King's Cross and Russell Square stations and on two Circle Line trains, one between Liverpool Street and Aldgate stations, and the other between Edgware Road and Paddington stations. The fourth bomb exploded on a bus in Tavistock Square at 9.47 a.m. The transport system was suspended for several hours. A statement claiming responsibility was posted on an Islamist website by 'the Secret Organisation Group of Al-Qaeda of Jihad Organisation in Europe'. Recovery work to remove bodies and clear the tracks of wreckage took several days, especially on the Piccadilly Line, where emergency services were severely hampered by the depth and narrowness of the tunnel, temperatures of 60°C and the risk of the tunnel collapsing. **10.** An Identification Commission chaired by Paul Knapman, the coroner for Westminster, was set up to formally identify the victims of the bombings. **11.** The General Synod of the Church of England voted to initiate the legal processes that will eventually enable women to become bishops. **12.** Armed police raided six addresses in West Yorkshire, including the homes of three men suspected of being among the London suicide bombers, and found bombmaking equipment at one address; a house in Aylesbury, Buckinghamshire, was raided by police on 13 July. The area around Luton station was evacuated after police found explosives in a car parked near to the station. From evidence found at the scenes of the explosions and in the raids and CCTV footage, police were subsequently able to identify the suicide bombers as Hasib Hussain, aged 19, Shehzad Tanweer, aged 22, Mohammad Sidique Khan, aged 30, and Jamal (Germaine) Lindsay, aged 20, and to establish that the four travelled by car to Luton station and then travelled together by train to London. **14.** Former Transport Secretary Stephen Byers admitted in the High Court that he had not been entirely truthful in his evidence to the Commons Transport Select Committee in 2001 concerning his actions in the lead-up to the collapse of Railtrack; Railtrack shareholders have accused Mr Byers of misfeasance in public office (*see* 27 June). **21.** In a second terrorist attack on London, four bombs were detonated but did not explode properly; no-one was killed or injured in the attacks. The three bombs at London Underground stations exploded at Shepherd's Bush at 12.25 p.m., at Oval at 12.30 p.m. and at Warren Street at 12.45 p.m. A fourth explosion occurred on a bus in Hackney Road, Shoreditch, at 1.27 p.m.; the following day, the police released CCTV footage of the four men they believed to be responsible. **22.** Police officers shot dead a man they suspected of involvement in the London terrorist bombings on an Underground train at Stockwell station, south London. The following day, the police acknowledged that the man, who was shot several times at close range, had no connection to the terrorist attack; he was named as Jean Charles de Menezes, a 27-year-old electrician from Brazil who had been working legally in Britain for three years. **24.** The Queen won planning permission to build a hydro-electric power plant at Windsor Castle that will supply about a third of the castle's power requirements. **29.** Three men suspected of the 21 July bombings in London were arrested by police in raids in west London, and the fourth was arrested in Rome by Italian police acting on information from Scotland Yard.

AUGUST 2005
2. A report published by the Department of Health showed that the amount spent on alcohol to drink at home had increased by nearly 50 per cent to £40 billion a year in the decade to 2004. **4.** In London, the Piccadilly Underground line was fully operational for the first time since 7 July; large numbers of police officers, including more than 3,000 marksmen, remained on duty in the capital. The MP and former Foreign Secretary Robin Cook collapsed while walking with his wife in the Scottish Highlands and was airlifted to hospital in Inverness, where he was pronounced dead. **11.** Thousands of holidaymakers were stranded at Heathrow airport after British Airways workers staged a walk-out in sympathy with 800 staff sacked by the airline's catering supplier, Gate Gourmet; more than 100 flights were cancelled. **12.** British Airways resumed a limited service from Heathrow after BA workers ended their unofficial strike, but warned that flights would remain disrupted for several days. **17.** The postal regulator Postcomm approved plans by Royal Mail to base postal charges on the size and shape as well as the weight of items; the change is due to be introduced in September 2006. **18.** The national A-level results were published, with nearly a quarter of candidates receiving a grade A. The Universities and Colleges Admissions Service (UCAS) reported unprecedented demand for university places, with 90 per cent of places filled immediately, leaving around 100,000 applicants vying for 37,700 places through the clearing system. **24.** St Georges Hospital in Tooting, south-west London, became the first UK hospital to make death rates, across all specialities, available to the public.

NORTHERN IRELAND AFFAIRS

SEPTEMBER 2004
12. The Northern Ireland Secretary, Paul Murphy, announced that unless devolved government was restored, members of the Northern Ireland Assembly at Stormont would not continue to be paid a salary indefinitely. **13.** At Belfast Crown Court, Kenneth Barrett pleaded guilty to the murder of republican solicitor Patrick Finucane in February 1989; he was subsequently sentenced to life imprisonment. **14.** It was reported that a 'sophisticated listening device' had been discovered in the offices of Sinn Fein; the party's president, Gerry Adams, demanded to know from the Prime Minister, Tony Blair, who had authorised the planting of the bug. **16–18.** Talks at Leeds Castle between Tony Blair and the Irish prime minister, Bertie Ahern, on the rewording of the Good Friday Agreement, to ensure full decommissioning of IRA weapons, ended without an agreement being reached. **20.** Following a landmark ruling at Belfast High Court, properties worth £1.2 million were seized by the Assets Recovery Agency from the estate of deceased loyalist Jim 'Jonty' Johnston, who had been a member of the loyalist Red Hand Commando group. **21.** At Belfast Crown Court, Margaret Hewitt and her former lover Robert Anderson were jailed for 11 and 18 years respectively after they were found guilty of sexual and physical abuse of eight children in their care 25 years ago at a Barnardo's home near Belfast. **21–22.** The Northern Ireland Secretary and Irish Minister of State Tom Kitt met Northern Ireland's political parties at Stormont for talks intended to restore the Northern Ireland Assembly; negotiations broke down on 22 September. **23.** The British government ordered an inquiry into the death of

Patrick Finucane, who was shot dead by loyalists at his home in 1989, after allegations that British forces were involved. **26.** Northern Ireland police chiefs announced that a specialist unit would be set up to review some 1,800 unsolved murders during the three decades of the troubles in Northern Ireland.

NOVEMBER 2004

4. A report by the Independent Monitoring Commission claimed that the IRA was still recruiting volunteers and gathering intelligence. **7.** Martin Kaitcer, the son of murdered Jewish businessman Leonard Kaitcer, appealed to Sinn Fein chief negotiator Martin McGuinness for help in finding out why his father was shot dead in south Belfast in 1980; no one was charged or claimed responsibility for the murder. **12.** The Northern Ireland Secretary announced that an Ulster Defence Association (UDA) ceasefire had been officially recognised by the government. **23.** The Bloody Sunday inquiry ended after 434 days at a cost of £155 million. Lord Saville of Newdigate was expected to submit his report on the inquiry to the government in summer 2005.

DECEMBER 2004

6. The leader of the Democratic Unionist Party, Revd Ian Paisley, demanded that the IRA produce photographs of their final acts of weapons decommissioning. **7.** An agreement to restore devolved government in Northern Ireland collapsed hours before it was due to be signed after the Democratic Unionist Party insisted that photographs be produced of the IRA destroying weapons; the IRA refused to meet the demand and said such a condition was humiliating. **16.** At an appeal court hearing in Colombia, James Monaghan, Martin McCauley and Niall Connolly were found guilty of training members of a Colombian terrorist group in IRA terrorist techniques, and sentenced to 17-and-a-half years in prison; the men immediately disappeared, evaded capture by the Colombian police and subsequently escaped from Colombia. **21.** Armed robbers forced two executives of the Northern Bank in Belfast to open the bank vaults, and escaped with £26.5 million; police suspected dissident republicans were responsible. **25.** Police raided the homes of two suspected IRA members in connection with the robbery of the Northern Bank in Belfast.

JANUARY 2005

7. The Chief Constable of the Northern Ireland Police Service, Hugh Orde, announced that police believed the Provisional IRA was responsible for the Northern Bank robbery in December. **10.** The loyalist terrorist leader Johnny Adair was freed from Maghaberry prison, Belfast, and flown to Bolton, Lancashire, where his family were living after being forced to leave Belfast by threats to their safety. **15.** The head of MI5, Eliza Manningham-Buller, admitted that British intelligence agents had planted the listening device found at the head offices of Sinn Fein in September 2004. **18.** The IRA issued a statement denying involvement in the Northern Bank robbery. **21.** The Court of Criminal Appeal in Dublin found that police officers had fabricated evidence against Colm Murphy, who was serving a sentence in Portlaoise prison for the 1998 Omagh bombing, and ordered a retrial. **30.** A Roman Catholic man, Robert McCartney, was killed in Belfast by suspected members of the IRA after he stood up to a group of men in a minor disagreement.

FEBRUARY 2005

2. The IRA stated that it was withdrawing its agreement to decommission all its weapons after both the British and Irish governments stated publicly that they believed the IRA was responsible for the Northern Bank robbery. **9.** Anthony Joseph Donegan was charged with supplying the Real IRA with the stolen car used as a car bomb in Omagh in 1998, killing 29 people. **17.** Six men and one woman were arrested in Cork and Dublin in connection with the Northern Bank robbery after police discovered £2.6 million in banknotes. **18.** Phil Flynn, the chairman of the Bank of Scotland in Ireland, resigned from his post at the bank and stood down from his government adviser post after his home was searched by police investigating the Northern Bank robbery; Mr Flynn was a vice-president of Sinn Fein in the early 1980s. **23.** The Irish prime minister, Bertie Ahern, said that Sinn Fein had to prove its opposition to criminality by urging its supporters to offer information to the police about the IRA gang accused of killing Robert McCartney in January. **24.** The British government announced that MI5 would be given a key role in investigating organised crime by the IRA after it was reported that the organisation had become the largest organised crime gang in Europe. **25.** The IRA expelled three of its members over the murder of Robert McCartney, stating that it had conducted its own investigation into the murder of Mr McCartney.

MARCH 2005

2. The White House announced that no leaders from any of Northern Ireland's political parties would be invited to attend the 2005 St Patrick's Day celebrations in the USA; the decision was linked to the Northern Bank robbery. **3.** Sinn Fein president Gerry Adams announced that he had given the Police Ombudsman of Northern Ireland the names of seven republicans in connection with the murder of Robert McCartney. **8.** The Provisional IRA released a statement in which it offered to kill the men responsible for the murder of Robert McCartney. The statement also said that two of the four men responsible for the murder were IRA members. **9.** The US envoy to Northern Ireland, Mitchell Reiss, called on the IRA to disband and for Sinn Fein to accept the legitimacy of the Police Service of Northern Ireland. **10.** MPs at Westminster agreed to suspend the Commons allowances of the four Sinn Fein MPs for one year as a punishment for the party's alleged links to the IRA robbery of the Northern Bank. **13.** The US government banned Sinn Fein from fundraising during its traditional St Patrick's Day visit to the USA. **27.** The family of Robert McCartney announced that they were considering taking civil action against the IRA members who murdered him. **28.** Police in Belfast and Co. Down reported that they had found bombs in shopping centres and believed them to have been planted by dissident republicans. **30.** The Ulster Defence Association leader Jim Gray was sacked by the organisation.

APRIL 2005

6. Sinn Fein leader Gerry Adams urged the Provisional IRA to 'fully embrace and accept' an exclusively political route to a united Ireland and stated that armed struggle was no longer acceptable. **7.** The Provisional IRA issued a statement agreeing to give due consideration to Gerry Adams's appeal. **19.** A public inquiry opened at Craigavon Civic Centre, Co. Armagh, into the death of solicitor Rosemary Nelson, killed by a loyalist bomb under her car in 1999; no-one has ever been charged with

No 1 single. **17.** George Szirtes won the T. S. Eliot Prize for Poetry for his collection *Reel.* **19.** The International Federation of the Phonographic Industry reported a tenfold increase in legal internet and mobile phone downloads, with 5.7 million download tracks sold in 2004 compared with virtually no sales in 2003. **22.** A charity concert in aid of the Indian Ocean tsunami victims was held at the Millennium Stadium in Cardiff and raised over £1 million. **26.** A Canaletto painting of the Bacino di San Marco, which had been in England since it was painted in 1740, was sold for £2.8 million at Christie's in New York. **27.** Amma Asante won the Breakthrough Award at the *South Bank Show* Awards for her film *A Way of Life* about racism in urban Wales.

FEBRUARY 2005
1. The current London production of Mel Brooks's *The Producers* won the Best Musical award at the Critics Circle Theatre Awards. **4.** Thirteen-year-old Emma Maree Urquhart's first novel, *Dragon Tamers,* sold 50,000 copies in six weeks; a second print run was ordered and Miss Urquhart was said to be writing a sequel. **6.** Mike Leigh's film *Vera Drake* won the Best Film award at the *Evening Standard* British Film Awards and Imelda Staunton won Best Actress for her role in the film. **8.** A 'peace deal' was agreed between Scotland Yard and reggae artists after many were banned from performing in Britain because their lyrics were deemed to be homophobic and to incite violence; the reggae artists agreed to prevent record releases or live performances of songs which advocate violence against homosexuals. **9.** At the Brit Awards, Joss Stone won Best British Female Artist award, Mike Skinner of The Streets won Best British Male Artist award and Franz Ferdinand won the Best British Group award. **12.** The Bafta film awards gave the Best Film award to Martin Scorsese's *The Aviator,* the Best Actor award to Jamie Foxx for *Ray* and the Best Actress award to Imelda Staunton for *Vera Drake.* **13.** Ray Charles won six posthumous Grammy awards, including Best Album for *Genius Loves Company.* **14.** A statue of Baroness Thatcher by Neil Simmons was put back on display in the Guildhall Art Gallery, London, following its restoration after a protester vandalised the sculpture in 2002. **20.** A 1933 Clarice Cliff dish originally purchased for £1 at a car boot sale was sold at Christie's for £1,920. *The Producers* won Best New Musical, Best Actor and Best Performance in a Supporting Role awards at the Olivier Awards in London. **26.** Inventories of missing items released under the Freedom of Information Act showed that 8,000 books worth at least £250,000 had gone missing from the British Library since it moved to its new headquarters on Euston Road in 1997, the most expensive single theft being that of a first edition of the *Dennis the Menace* comic. **27.** An 1822 letter from the computer pioneer Charles Babbage to inventor Sir Humphry Davy sold for £20,200 at a Christie's auction in New York. At the Oscar film awards ceremony in Los Angeles, Jamie Foxx won the Best Actor award for *Ray,* Hilary Swank won the Best Actress award and Clint Eastwood won the Best Director award for *Million Dollar Baby,* which was also received the Best Picture award.

MARCH 2005
1. The Advertising Standards Authority upheld complaints about advertising for McVitie's Go Ahead! bars and cakes which claimed that they were a healthier option than other biscuits and cakes. **2.** The Culture Secretary, Tessa Jowell, announced that the BBC had

secured a ten-year extension of the television licence fee from 2007 until 2017. **4.** The British Phonographic Industry announced that it had ordered 23 people who downloaded music files from the internet in breach of copyright laws to pay £50,000 in compensation. **7.** *Bezhti,* the play cancelled by the Birmingham Repertory Theatre in December 2005, won a US$10,000 (£5,200) Anglo-American theatre prize and a staging in the USA. **9.** Ekow Eshum was appointed director of the Institute of Contemporary Arts, the first black person to hold the post. **10.** The BBC announced plans to make redundant 1,730 central support staff, nearly half the BBC's support staff. **11.** The biennial Comic Relief's Red Nose Day telethon took place; the event raised over £55 million for charity. **13.** Geraldine McCaughrean was chosen to write a sequel to *Peter Pan* after the descendants of J. M. Barrie gave their approval; all proceeds will be given to the Great Ormond Street Hospital. **15.** A lock of Charles Dickens's hair was sold for £3,120 at auction at Bonhams, London. A national tour of the musical *Jerry Springer – The Opera* was postponed after several regional theatres pulled out of the tour following a campaign by the Christian Voice organisation, which described the production as blasphemous. **16.** The British author Philip Pullman and the Japanese illustrator Ryoji Arai were joint winners of the Astrid Lindgren Memorial Award. **17.** Michael Holroyd was awarded the David Cohen Prize for Literature for his biographical works, which include books on Augustus John and George Bernard Shaw. **20.** The Roxy Music rock group, prominent in the 1970s and 80s, announced that it had reformed and was working on its first studio album in 23 years. **21.** Tate Britain paid £1.2 million for *French Coast with Fishermen,* an 1825 painting by Richard Parkes Bonington. **22.** The International Federation of the Phonographic Industry reported that Britons buy more CDs than any other nationality, each buying an average of 3.2 CDs a year. **24.** Peter Fincham was appointed controller of BBC1 and promised to make comedy programmes a priority. **25.** It was reported that a BBC special-effects team had set a record for British television by creating 800 digital special effects for the new BBC series of *Doctor Who.* **27.** Stroud District Council announced that it had paid £4,500 to the Royal Academy of Dramatic Art to teach its committee members how to speak and interview more effectively. **28.** McDonald's food chain offered hip hop artists money to mention the chain's Big Mac burger in their lyrics. **29.** *Maps for Lost Lovers,* a novel by Nadeem Aslam about an honour killing in a Pakistani community, won the Kiriyama Prize.

APRIL 2005
2. BBC Four screened a two-hour live production of the 1950s drama *The Quatermass Experiment.* **3.** Tickets for the Glastonbury Festival in June 2005 went on sale and all 112,000 sold out in two-and-a-half hours, the fastest sell-out in Glastonbury's history. **4.** The author Bill Bryson was appointed chancellor of Durham university to replace Peter Ustinov, who died in 2004. **14.** Katharine Davies won the Romantic Novel of the Year Award for *A Good Voyage.* **15.** David Tennant was confirmed as the BBC's new Doctor Who, after Christopher Eccleston declined to continue in the role in the second series of the revived show. **17.** It was reported that a new typeface called Read Regular had been designed to help dyslexics overcome reading difficulties; each letter is uniquely shaped and none can be inverted or mirrored to produce another. The performance artist Mark McGowan

scratched the paintwork of 47 cars with a key in Glasgow and London as part of the 'creative process', although he would have faced prosecution for criminal damage had any of the car-owners lodged a complaint. At the Bafta television awards, Matt Lucas and David Walliams won awards for the Best Comedy Series and Best Comedy Performance for their sketch show *Little Britain*. **20.** At the British Book Awards, Dan Brown's *The Da Vinci Code* won the Book of the Year Award, Sheila Hancock won the Author of the Year Award for *The Two of Us*, David Mitchell's *Cloud Atlas* won the Literary Fiction Award, and Sir John Mortimer won the Lifetime Achievement Award. **21.** Charles Saatchi sold Mark Quinn's *Self*, a cast of the artist's head made from his frozen blood, to a US collector for £1.5 million. **26.** Christina Mackie's sculptural installation won the Beck's Futures prize for art. **29.** Coldplay's *Speed of Sound* was the first single by a British group to debut inside the US top ten since the Beatles' *Hey Jude* in 1968; the single also became the world's fastest-selling track downloaded from the internet.

MAY 2005
5. The Man Booker Prize announced that its annual international fiction prize would include a new £15,000 translation award, in recognition of the work of translators in bringing foreign-language fiction to an English-speaking audience. **7.** The Rose d'Or international television festival in Lucerne, Switzerland, was dominated by British broadcasting, with *Little Britain*, *Nighty Night* and *Strictly Come Dancing* among the prize-winners. **9.** Christian O'Connell, a DJ on London-based radio station Xfm, won three awards at the Sony Radio Academy awards, and BBC Radio 2 won UK Station of the Year. **13.** A Kentucky Fried Chicken television advertisement showing people singing with their mouths full prompted a record number of complaints to the Advertising Standards Authority because it set a bad example to children. **16.** The BBC introduced three-dimensional computer graphics in weather forecasts, designed to be more precise, in place of the symbols for sun, rain and cloud used since 1936. The final instalment in the six-episode *Stars Wars* film saga premiered in Leicester Square, London. **21.** At the Cannes Film Festival, the Belgian brothers Jean-Pierre and Luc Dardenne won a second Palme d'Or award, for their film *L'Enfant*, and Jim Jarmusch won the Grand Prix prize for *Broken Flowers*, starring Bill Murray. **23.** Industrial action by BBC staff disrupted programmes and news coverage for 24 hours; the strike was in response to management plans to cut around 4,000 jobs. **26.** Novelist Jacqueline Wilson was named as the new Children's Laureate. The Big Pit National Mining Museum in Blaenafon, Wales, won the Gulbenkian Prize for Museum of the Year; the former coal mine was praised for bringing Britain's industrial past to life. **31.** Sir Bob Geldof announced that ten *Live 8* concerts would be held on 2 July in support of the Make Poverty History campaign to persuade the G8 summit in Scotland on 6–8 July to drop the debt of the world's poorest countries.

JUNE 2005
1. Readers of the monthly film magazine *Empire* voted Steven Spielberg the greatest cinema director of all time; Alfred Hitchcock and Martin Scorsese were placed second and third respectively. **2.** The first Man Booker International Prize was awarded to Ismail Kadare, an Albanian who lives in political exile in Paris; other contenders included Ian McEwan, Gabriel García Márquez, Margaret Atwood and Philip Roth. **5.** *Spamalot*, a musical loosely based on the film *Monty Python and the Holy Grail*, won the Best Musical award at the American Theatre Wing Tony Awards. **7.** A *Radio Times* poll of radio executives and presenters named Jonathan Ross as the most powerful person on the radio; the BBC Radio 2 presenter beat Terry Wogan and John Humphreys to the title. Lionel Shriver's *We Need to Talk About Kevin* won the Orange Prize for Fiction. **13.** The British artist Dean Marsh won the BP Portrait Award for an oil painting of his girlfriend; the prize also included a commission from the National Portrait Gallery. **14.** Jonathan Coe won the BBC Four Samuel Johnson Prize for Non-fiction for *Like a Fiery Elephant: The Story of B. S. Johnson*, a biography of the eponymous avant-garde novelist, who committed suicide in 1973. **15.** In response to criticisms that most performers taking part in the Live 8 concerts are white, an additional concert is announced featuring African performers, to be held at the Eden Project, Cornwall. The Archbishop of Canterbury, Dr Rowan Williams, attacked the UK's media, accusing it of encouraging cynicism and paranoia and of having a 'tribal identity'. **16.** The Royal Fine Art Commission Trust's Building of the Year award was won by the McLaren Technology Centre, the Woking base of the Formula One racing team, which was designed by Foster and Partners. **23.** The BBC published updated editorial guidelines that told its journalists to prioritise accuracy over speed. **24.** A poem by the Greek poet Sappho, written more than 2,600 years ago and pieced together from fragments of papyrus recovered from an Egyptian mummy and university archives in Cologne, was published for the first time in the *Times Literary Supplement*. Flash floods and electric storms brought chaos to the Glastonbury Festival, causing power failures and forcing campers to evacuate their tents when fields became submerged in water. **27.** John Carey, the critic and chairman of the judges of the first International Man Booker prize, warned that foreign writing was being neglected by the UK publishing industry. **30.** The National Gallery revealed that, through the use of an infrared camera, it had discovered an unknown work by Leonardo da Vinci beneath the layers of his painting *The Madonna of the Rocks*.

JULY 2005
2. Ten *Live 8* concerts were held world-wide to raise awareness of poverty in Africa; the venues included London, Paris, Berlin, Rome, Philadelphia, Barrie (Canada), Chiba, Moscow, Johannesburg and the Eden Project, Cornwall. **12.** Senior BBC executives were criticised by broadcasting unions for accepting bonuses worth up to 30 per cent of their salaries at a time when 4,000 BBC staff were to be made redundant. A 14th-century Yuan dynasty jar sold for around £15.5 million at Christie's in London, fetching 14 times its estimate and becoming the world's most expensive piece of Asian art. **13.** A public poll on BBC Radio 4's *In Our Time* programme voted Karl Marx the greatest philosopher of all time; David Hume and Wittgenstein came second and third respectively. The Committee of Advertising Practice found Channel Five guilty of raising the volume of commercial breaks during a broadcast of *Groundhog Day* in March so that they sound louder than the feature film. **16.** *Harry Potter and the Half-Blood Prince*, the sixth in J. K. Rowling's series of books about a young wizard, sold more than two million copies in the first 24 hours of release in the UK, and nearly seven million copies in the

USA. **17.** A survey in *The Observer* found that people in the Midlands had larger record collections and spent more of their time listening to music than those in other parts of the country. **18.** *The Guardian*'s annual list of the most powerful people in the media was topped by both Michael Grade, the BBC's chairman, and Mark Thompson, the BBC's director-general; Rupert Murdoch, managing director of News Corporation, was in third place. **20.** BBC data showed that Beethoven's symphonies, offered free on the corporation's website, were downloaded nearly 1.4 million times; the most popular, *Symphony No 6 (Pastoral)*, was accessed 220,000 times, ten times as much as the top pop music download, a version of *Sgt Pepper's Lonely Hearts Club Band* by Sir Paul McCartney and U2. **28.** The BBC removed a song by the children's television characters the Tweenies from their website after the British Dental Health Association accused it of encouraging children to eat sweets.

AUGUST 2005
1. The BBC apologised to listeners after Jonathan King, the pop music impresario imprisoned for the sexual abuse of boys, was allowed to protest his innocence on a Radio 5 Live phone-in show about paedophilia. **3.** Channel 4 faced criticism in the media and complaints from viewers after airing an episode of the reality television show *Big Brother* in which a contestant appeared to perform sex acts with a wine bottle. **7.** The Magic Numbers pop group walked out of their debut appearance on *Top of the Pops* after presenter Richard Bacon introduced them with an apparently derogatory remark about their weight. **10.** A survey in the lesbian magazine *Diva* named Manchester Metropolitan and Brighton universities as the best places to be a gay student. The opening episode of the US television drama *Lost* attracted more than 6.4 million viewers, becoming the most successful debut of a US import on Channel 4. **14.** Victoria Beckham, a former member of the Spice Girls, admitted in a Spanish magazine interview that she had never read a book, preferring fashion magazines and listening to music. **17.** Three rare engravings, believed to be 10,000 years old, were discovered in a Somerset cave by members of the University of Bristol Speleological Society. **19.** The management for the rap star Eminem revealed that he was addicted to sleeping pills; the dependency caused him to cancel his European tour, scheduled for September 2005. **21.** The ashes of the writer Hunter S. Thompson, who committed suicide in February 2005, were packed into fireworks and fired into the sky at his ranch in Colorado, USA. **26.** Lord Birt, the former director-general of the BBC, delivered a speech at the Media Guardian Edinburgh International Television Festival in which he attacked the media's 'desire to humiliate', as well as its superficial coverage of politics. **27.** Laura Solon won the Perrier Comedy Award, the second solo woman stand-up comic to do so in its 25-year history. **29.** The US punk rock group Green Day won seven awards at the MTV Video Music Awards, including Video of the Year and Best Group.

CRIMES AND LEGAL AFFAIRS

SEPTEMBER 2004
1. William Hofton, a priest at a London church, was sentenced at Middlesex Guildhall Crown Court to four years in prison for sex offences against two teenage brothers; he had previously pleaded guilty to seven counts of gross indecency with a child and nine counts of

indecent assault relating to the brothers. Five members of a teenage gang known as the 'lords of Stratford crew', were sentenced at Middlesex Guildhall Crown Court to five years' custody for attacking travellers on London trains and buses over a two-week period. **2.** A 50-year-old cyclist, Denis Finnegan, was stabbed to death in Richmond Park, London; a psychiatric patient, John Barrett, was arrested on suspicion of murder after he was found hiding in bushes by police. On 22 March 2005, Barrett was sentenced to life imprisonment for the murder. **3.** Home Office statistics showed that 14 men and women committed suicide in prisons in England and Wales in August 2004, the highest number of people to take their own lives in one month in the past 20 years. **6.** John Coffey was robbed and stabbed to death on the London-bound platform of Wood Street station in Walthamstow, London. **7.** The Attorney-General, Lord Goldsmith, overturned a decision by the Army that a soldier in the Royal Tank Regiment was innocent of the murder of an Iraqi lawyer in Basra, and charged the soldier with murder. **8.** Brian Blackwell, aged 18, was arrested and charged with the murder of his parents, Brian and Jackie Blackwell, who were found stabbed to death on 5 September at their home in Melling, Merseyside; on 29 June he was found guilty of manslaughter and sentenced to life imprisonment. **10.** At the Central Criminal Court, London, tennis coach Marc Lewis was jailed for four-and-a-half years for sex offences against a 15-year-old girl he was coaching. **13.** A 15-year-old boy was charged at the Inner London Youth Court with raping a female teacher at his school in Westminster. **16.** At Maidstone Crown Court, Elias Cecchetti, aged 16, was sentenced to life imprisonment for stabbing Monica Watts in Clissold Park, London, in December 2003 and to two-and-a-half years for stabbing a friend because he believed the friend had stolen his hat. At Leeds Crown Court, Nathan Eyre was jailed for eight years for grooming a young boy to be a prostitute; he then sold the boy to Raymond Hawthorne, the leader of a national paedophile ring, who was jailed for seven years for abduction, indecency with a child and conspiring to live off the earnings of a prostitute. Leslie Loram was also jailed for three-and-a-half years after he admitted two counts of buggery and one of indecent assault on the boy. **17.** Dr Roy Murray was sentenced at Liverpool Crown Court to six years in prison after he was convicted of 23 indecent assaults on separate patients; the court was told that he carried out sexual attacks on his patients for 14 years. **21.** Statistics compiled by *The Economist* showed that 48.3 per cent of 15-year-old girls in Britain consume alcohol on a weekly basis, the highest for that age group in the world; they ranked fourth highest in prevalence of obesity and third highest in cannabis use. **29.** Police searching for clues to the murder of PC Keith Blakelock in the Broadwater Farm estate riots in October 1985 recovered a rusty metal object believed to have been the blade of one of the weapons used in the murder. **30.** The Department for Transport's annual report on road casualties showed that 560 people died in drinking and driving accidents in 2003, the highest number in seven years.

OCTOBER 2004
4. William Goad was jailed for life at Plymouth Crown Court for sexually abusing thousands of young boys over a period of 30 years. He admitted 14 charges of gross indecency and two of indecent assault after the court was told that he was the most prolific paedophile to have been convicted in Britain. **6.** Stuart Mackenzie of the

Lancastrian and Cumbrian Volunteers Territorial Army unit was charged over faked photographs published in the *Daily Mirror* that appeared to show British soldiers abusing Iraqi prisoners. **7.** At the High Court in London, Mr Justice Hedley ruled that 11-month-old Charlotte Wyatt should not be artificially resuscitated the next time she stopped breathing; doctors at Portsmouth Hospitals NHS Trust had sought the court's ruling against her parents' wishes. **9.** Fourteen-year-old Danielle Beccan died after being shot in the stomach in the St Ann's area of Nottingham. **10.** It was announced that in future armed policemen would guard the entrance to the House of Commons chamber in addition to the House of Commons' own security staff, the Badge Messengers. **15.** Anthony Kesler, a disabled pensioner, was sentenced at Derby Crown Court to seven-and-a-half years in prison for possession of heroin with intent to supply. Richard Watson was jailed for life for shooting dead Amratlal Kanabar; he had pursued his victim's car on 7 October 2003 after Mr Kanabar left a casino in Nottingham. **17.** Brian Blackburn was charged with the murder of his terminally ill wife after calling an ambulance to their home in Guildford; it appeared that the couple had made a suicide pact, as Mrs Blackburn's wrists had been slashed and Mr Blackburn had lacerations on his wrists. **18.** Edith McAlinden was charged with the murder of David Gillespie, who was found dead with two other men at a flat in Glasgow on 17 October. **22.** Leslie Skinner was jailed for four-and-a-half years at Kingston Crown Court for five sexual assaults on male soldiers at Deepcut army barracks in Surrey. **28.** Paul Smith, aged 18, was jailed for life at Nottingham Crown Court for murdering 10-year-old Rosie Storrie at a family party on 28 December 2003. The *British Medical Journal* announced that suicides from overdoses of paracetamol and aspirin had dropped by almost a quarter in the three years since new laws, introduced in 1998, limited how many tablets could be sold in one pack. **29.** An inquest jury at St Pancras Coroner's Court ruled that Inspector Neil Sharman had unlawfully killed Harry Stanley after he shot him in the head on a London street in September 1999 believing the table leg Mr Stanley was carrying to be a sawn-off shotgun. **31.** New police powers came into force enabling police officers to issue on-the-spot fines of up to £80 for offences such as shoplifting, under-age drinking and dropping litter.

NOVEMBER 2004

4. Six teenagers were arrested in connection with the murder of David Morley, who was beaten to death in central London on 30 October. **5.** Fabio Pereira was jailed for life at Reading Crown Court for the murder of John Goodman on 8 April 2003. Mr Goodman was asphyxiated when he returned from work to find Mr Pereira had illegally moved into his home in Ealing, London. **9.** Margaret Smith was cleared of the murder of her four-month-old son Keith at a retrial at Newcastle Crown Court after being convicted on the basis of evidence provided by expert witness Professor Sir Roy Meadows in 2002. Professor Meadows' evidence was discredited, and he subsequently faced charges of professional misconduct for his role in the convictions of other mothers, including Trupti Patel, Angela Cannings and Sally Clark. **10.** A 24-year-old woman was shot in the chest as she walked past the Barbican Exhibition Centre, London, when a gun battle broke out between rival gangs at the Urban Music Awards; on 12 November, Tyrone Headley, Linton Ambursley and Fabian Augustus

Clarke were charged with attempted murder and firearms offences. **15.** An inquest jury at Trowbridge, Wiltshire, ruled that RAF engineer Ronald Maddison had been unlawfully killed on 6 May 1953 after the Ministry of Defence conducted sarin nerve gas tests on servicemen, who believed the experiments were to help find a cure for the common cold. The Domestic Violence, Crime and Victims Act received royal assent; the Act is designed to put victims at the forefront of the justice system with a statutory code of practice enshrining victims' rights, and also introduced a new offence of causing or allowing the death of a child or vulnerable adult. **18.** A bill to ban fox-hunting received royal assent after the Speaker of the House of Commons, Michael Martin, certified that the Hunting Bill should pass under the Parliament Act after it was rejected by the House of Lords. **19.** Daniel Alderson was sentenced at Portsmouth Crown Court to six years in prison after he was found guilty of two indecent assaults, carried out in 1992 and 1997; he was convicted after being traced through a relative's DNA. **22.** It was announced that police officers in Scotland would be given the power to arrest anyone believed to be carrying a knife or offensive weapon after the Scottish Executive reported that Scotland has the third-highest rate of stabbings in Europe. **24.** The Serious Organised Crime and Police Bill was published by the government; it outlined a new Serious Organised Crime Agency which would have powers to monitor convicted crime bosses for 20 years to try to dismantle the £20 billion-a-year underworld economy. **26.** The Disability Discrimination Bill came into force; it improves the rights of an estimated 18,000 disabled people, for example by allowing blind tenants to keep guide dogs in a property where the lease prohibits pets.

DECEMBER 2004

1. Police in Scotland seized £10 million worth of counterfeit CDs, DVDs and computer games and arrested 28 people in an operation targeting 20 homes and two public markets in Falkirk and Stirling. **2.** David Bieber was jailed for life at Newcastle Crown Court after he was convicted of killing PC Ian Broadhurst in Leeds on 26 December 2003; he was also convicted of the attempted murder of PC Neil Roper. **5.** It was announced that the Clean Neighbourhoods Bill would enable community support officers and council wardens to issue fixed-penalty fines of up to £50 for any person whose dog leaves excrement in public parks or on pavements. **7.** Peers in the House of Lords voted 229 to 206 in favour of the Lord Chancellor remaining a member of the House of Lords; the current Lord Chancellor, Lord Falconer of Thoroton, had put forward a proposal to allow members of the House of Commons to take up the post. **8.** Poplar Coroner's Court was told that the boy known as 'Adam', whose headless torso was found in the Thames in 2001, had died from neck wounds after he was paralysed by a potion he had ingested; a verdict of unlawful killing was recorded. **10.** Six men were arrested after Customs and Excise officers found £100 million worth of cocaine hidden in coconuts at Spitalfields market in London. **14.** Nick Griffin, the chairman of the British National Party, was arrested for alleged incitement to racial hatred after a BBC television documentary showed him calling Islam 'a vicious, wicked faith'. **15.** In a landmark ruling, Worcester Magistrates' Court banned Paul Orbell, a drug addict with convictions for shoplifting, from entering every store in Britain. **16.** The law lords voted 8–1 in favour of a motion that the new anti-terrorism laws, which allow the imprisonment of terrorist suspects indefinitely without charge, breach the human rights of the suspects. **22.** Police were given new powers to test any motorist they suspect of having taken drugs; refusal to take a test is an offence. **23.** After one man was stabbed to death and five other people were seriously wounded within two hours in Haringey and Enfield, Ismail Dogan was arrested in north London on suspicion and subsequently charged with the murder of Ernest Meads and the attempted murder of the other five victims. **26.** The Police Minister, Hazel Blears, announced that police officers would be given the power to issue on-the-spot fines of £40 to parents of children accused of antisocial behaviour.

JANUARY 2005

4. In an initiative by the Crown Prosecution Service, magistrates' courts began to hear domestic violence and homophobic hate cases for the first time. **6.** Hassan Jihad and two other teenagers were charged with the murder of Damilola Taylor on 27 November 2000 after the emergence of new DNA evidence. **7.** A nursing home was opened at Norwich prison to provide care for elderly inmates serving life sentences. **13.** Ian and Angela Gay were convicted at Worcester Crown Court of the manslaughter of their adoptive son, Christian Blewitt, and sentenced to five years in prison; they fed the three-year-old boy four teaspoons of salt and he died of brain damage as a result. **15.** Home Office figures showed that 4,000 people in Britain suffered shooting injuries between April 2002 and March 2003, with 81 being shot dead and more than 500 seriously wounded. **17.** The Independent Police Complaints Commission announced that the arrest of terror suspects would be filmed to guard against allegations of excessive force. **23.** The Law Society announced that nine men detained under anti-terror laws must be tried or released, as holding prisoners without trial or charge had been ruled unlawful by the law lords. **24.** The pub chain J. D. Wetherspoon announced that smoking would be banned in 60 of its city pubs from May 2005 and in the rest of the chain within a year. **25.** Four British citizens, Moazzam Begg, Martin Mubanga, Feroz Abbasi and Richard Belmar, were flown to London after their release from the US Guantanamo Bay detention camp in Cuba; they had been held there for three years without charge. **26.** The Home Office and the Foreign and Commonwealth Office jointly launched the Forced Marriages Unit to tackle forced and coerced marriages in Britain, especially where under-18-year-olds were involved. **28.** Gordon Park was jailed for life at Manchester Crown Court for murdering his wife, Carol Ann Park, in July 1976; her body was found by divers in August 1997 in Coniston Water in the Lake District. The Home Office announced that arrests for possession of cannabis had fallen by a third in the first year since the drug was reclassified as a Class C drug.

FEBRUARY 2005

1. A foreign terror suspect known as C, believed to be the leader of Egyptian Islamic Jihad in Britain, was released from Woodhill prison after being held without charge for three years. **6.** Martin Mubanga, one of the four British terrorist suspects held at Guantanamo Bay, announced that he would sue the British government for colluding in his detention. **8.** The government announced that Commonwealth citizens aged 17 to 30 who visit Britain on the Working Holidaymaker Scheme would only be able to work for a maximum of 12 months during a two-year stay. **11.** At the High Court in Edinburgh, Luke Mitchell was sentenced to a minimum of 20 years in prison for the murder of his 14-year-old girlfriend Jodi Jones. **15.** The European Court of Human Rights ruled that the human rights of Dave Morris and Helen Steel had been violated and that the British legal system breached their right to a fair trial and freedom of expression after they were forced into a 15-year libel battle by the fast-food chain McDonald's; Mr Morris and Ms Steel handed out leaflets in 1980 accusing the company of paying low wages, cruelty to animals and other malpractice and were obliged to justify every word of the allegations in the libel trial but were denied legal aid by the British legal system. **22.** The Home Secretary, Charles Clarke, announced that 10 terrorist suspects would be released from Belmarsh prison after being detained for two years without charge; the Home Secretary also postponed plans to introduce with immediate effect powers to place the suspects under house arrest after the law lords objected to the proposals. **24.** Maxine Carr was granted lifelong anonymity by a high court judge, replacing the temporary injunction she was granted following her release in May 2004 from Foston Hall women's prison; she had served half of a 42-month sentence for conspiring to pervert the course of justice and providing a false alibi for Ian Huntley, who murdered Holly Wells and Jessica Chapman in August 2002. It was reported that the number of times stop-and-search tactics were used by police fell by 15 per cent to 738,000 in 2003–4; the measure was used more frequently with black and Asian people, who were respectively 6.4 per cent and 1.9 per cent more likely to be stopped than white people.

MARCH 2005

3. The government announced that a new commission for equality and human rights would be set up in 2007 and would consider issues such as equality for women and the disabled as well as age and religion. **9.** The Commons select committee on home affairs reported that more than 75 per cent of crimes in England and Wales remain unsolved and that more needs to be done to bring criminals to justice. **11.** The government's Prevention of Terrorism Bill received royal assent after it was debated in the House of Commons in one of the longest-ever sittings in Parliament. A 12-year-old boy who raped his teacher at a special needs centre in Co. Durham was jailed for life at Teeside Crown Court. **16.** Shaban Maka, Ilir Barjami and Xhevahir Pisha were found guilty at Sheffield Crown Court of trafficking a teenage girl for sexual exploitation and were given sentences of 18, 15 and seven years respectively; the prosecution was the first under a new law designed to prevent the trafficking of women. **17.** Gloucestershire Fire Service announced that it would ban British National Party members from the force for fear of racial discrimination whilst carrying out their duties. **21.** Marcus Ellis, Michael Gregory, Nathan Martin and Rodrigo Simms were jailed for life at Leicester Crown Court for the murders of Charlene Ellis and Letisha Shakespeare on 2 January 2003. **22.** The Court of Appeal ruled that women prison officers who received less pay than their male counterparts had the right to equal pay and that the Home Office would have to justify paying female employees less. **29.** Moutaz Almallah Dabas appeared at Bow Street Magistrates' Court, London, accused of involvement in the March 2002 Madrid train bombings.

APRIL 2005

1. Damien Brutus, a 'community care' mental patient, was jailed for life at the Central Criminal Court for torturing to death Peter Greenfield, whom he mistakenly believed to be a paedophile. Research by York University showed that since the September 11 attacks on New York, 43 per cent of non-Muslim British teenagers admitted that they had become noticeably more anti-Islamic. **3.** Revd Geoffrey Morris called for the legalisation of euthanasia after a YouGov poll showed that 20 per cent of the population would be more likely to support an election candidate in favour of such a move. **5.** The Transport Minister, Tony McNulty, announced that the fine for rail passengers travelling without a ticket would double from £10 to £20. **6.** Nick Griffin, the leader of the British National Party, was charged with four offences of inciting racial hatred and ordered to appear at Leeds Magistrates' Court within 24 hours. **7.** In a landmark legal case, the Court of Appeal granted a lesbian woman the right to have contact with her former partner's biological children. The Ministry of Defence released figures showing that British troops had killed around 200 Iraqi insurgents since the Iraq war officially ended on 1 May 2003. **11.** The Court of Appeal quashed the murder conviction of Donna Anthony because it relied heavily on the evidence of Professor Roy Meadow; she had spent seven years in prison for the murder of her two children. **15.** Jennie Smith, aged 74, became the oldest person to be given an antisocial behaviour order after she plagued neighbours in Carnforth, Lancashire, for 20 years by playing classical music loudly at all hours, abusing passers-by and falsely accusing her neighbours of benefit fraud and other crimes. **20.** The Court of Appeal overturned a 35-year-old ban on judges giving any indication of sentence before a defendant enters a plea; more defendants are now expected to admit their crimes. **21.** Annual crime figures showed that although the number of incidents involving handguns fell by 13 per cent in 2004, the use of imitation guns rose by 66 per cent. The House of Lords ruled that parents cannot sue doctors and social workers who have wrongly accused them of abusing their children. **22.** The inquest into Harold Shipman's death concluded that the serial killer committed suicide partly to ensure that his wife would receive the widows' entitlement from his forfeited NHS pension. **27.** Hemant Lakhani, a British businessman, was found guilty by a court in New Jersey, USA, of trying to sell missiles to an FBI informant posing as a Somali terrorist. **28.** The law lords unanimously ruled that the Embryology and Fertilisation Authority had the power to license fertility treatment undertaken with the aim of saving a sibling's life. **30.** A mother from Greater Manchester was electronically tagged and given a curfew for failing to ensure that her two teenage daughters attended school regularly.

MAY 2005

4. In the UK's longest-running antisocial behaviour order to date, a 16- and a 17-year-old were banned from parts of Gloucester until they are 24-years-old. **11.** The Lord Chancellor, Lord Falconer of Thoroton, outlined reforms to the legal aid system designed to cut the length and cost of criminal trials. **12.** The High Court overturned an inquest's verdict that Chief Inspector Neil Sharman, a police inspector at the time, unlawfully killed Harry Stanley (*see* 29 October 2004). **15.** Wiltshire Police introduced roadside dexterity tests for motorists suspected of driving under the influence of drugs. **17.** A court in Ludlow, Shropshire, cleared a police officer of six charges of speeding and dangerous driving after hearing that PC Mark Milton had driven at speeds of up to 159 mph in order to familiarise himself with the car. **19.** Glaister Earl Butler, who suffers from paranoid schizophrenia, was convicted of manslaughter after stabbing a police officer to death; he was cleared of murder but will be held indefinitely in a secure hospital. The law lords ruled that jurors who believe that a defendant is the victim of a miscarriage of justice can inform the courts, a lawyer or an organisation such as the Citizens' Advice Bureau of their concerns. **25.** Home Office statistics showed that 40 per cent of offenders who serve short sentences and are released early under supervision return to prison after reoffending. **31.** A widow whose husband smoked 60 cigarettes a day and died from lung cancer in 1993 lost her legal battle for compensation from Imperial Tobacco.

JUNE 2005

2. Surrey Police arrested Chief Inspector Neil Sharman and Constable Kevin Fagan on suspicion of murder, manslaughter and conspiracy to pervert the course of justice in connection with the death of Harry Stanley (*see* 12 May), following the emergence of new forensic evidence. **3.** A 12-year-old girl was charged with attempting to pervert the course of justice and with inflicting grievous bodily harm on five-year-old Anthony Hinchliffe, who was found with bruises on his body and apparent ligature marks on his neck near his home in Dewsbury, West Yorkshire. **5.** The Metropolitan Police Commissioner, Sir Ian Blair, ordered an urgent review of how the force conducts rape investigations following a sharp decline in the number of successful prosecutions. **6.** A poll showed that 80 per cent of criminal barristers would be prepared to strike if rates of pay for legal aid work did not increase. **12.** A leaked government report proposed that children as young as three who display aggressive tendencies should be singled out by teachers as being most at risk of developing into criminals. **15.** A builder was given ten life sentences at St Albans Crown Court for six charges of rape and three of actual bodily harm between January 2003 and April 2004. **18.** The Metropolitan Police released figures showing that the number of hard drug dealers arrested in London had fallen by nearly 20 per cent in four years. **21.** The Attorney-General, Lord Goldsmith, announced that there would be a parliamentary vote on whether to hear complex fraud trials without a jury. **27.** Research showed that the prison population had increased by 15 per cent since 1999. An inquest found that the fatal shooting by police of a mentally ill man who aimed a replica gun at officers was lawful.

JULY 2005

11. A jury at the Central Criminal Court was unable to reach a verdict in the retrial of Siôn Jenkins for the murder of his foster daughter Billie-Jo in 1997; a third trial was ordered. **13.** The first of the Countryside Alliance's legal challenges to the ban on hunting with dogs opened in front of a panel of nine law lords; the alliance claims that the government's use of the Parliament Act to over-rule the House of Lords was invalid. **14.** A judge dismissed charges of manslaughter against the engineering group Balfour Beatty and five rail executives over the Hatfield rail disaster in 2000, in which four people died. **18.** A retrial at the Central Criminal Court found Faryadi Sarwar Zardad, an Afghan warlord who fled to Britain in 1998, guilty of torture and hostage-taking; the trial was a legal landmark because it tried a defendant who is not a British citizen and for crimes that were not committed in the UK. **19.** The Attorney-General announced that three British soldiers would stand trial under the International Criminal Court Act for war crimes against Iraqi detainees in Basra in 2003. **20.** A High Court judge ruled that it was illegal to forcibly remove children from curfew zones under the 2003 Anti-Social Behaviour Act; the Home Office said that it would contest the ruling. The Home Secretary told the House of Commons that a database would be compiled in order to identify Islamist militants in the UK and abroad whose language or behaviour is deemed inflammatory and likely to provoke terrorism. **21.** The British Crime Survey showed that overall crime fell by 7 per cent in 2004–5. **25.** An inquest opened at Southwark Crown Court into the death of Jean Charles de Menezes, a Brazilian man shot dead by police officers on 22 July (*see* British Affairs); the Independent Police Complaints Commission also began an inquiry into the shooting. **29.** Pro-hunting campaigners lost their second High Court challenge to the ban on hunting with dogs when two senior judges ruled that the ban did not breach the European convention on human rights; the campaigners will find out the result of their first challenge (now in the House of Lords after being thrown out by the High Court and the Court of Appeal – *see* 13 July) later in 2005. Anthony Walker, a black 18-year-old, was murdered with an axe in an unprovoked racist attack in Huyton, Liverpool.

AUGUST 2005
1. Richard Whelan was stabbed to death on a bus in London after confronting another passenger for throwing food at Mr Whelan's girlfriend; Anthony Joseph was arrested for the murder and on 8 July was remanded in custody until a further hearing in November. **5.** The Prime Minister announced new measures designed to counter terrorism, including the possible deportation of those involved in any bookshop, organisation or website listed by the government as extremist; the stripping of citizenship from those engaged in extremism; the closure of mosques preaching hatred; the extension of control orders for British citizens; and the deportation of those seen to be inciting terrorism; Mr Blair said that, if necessary, he would amend the Human Rights Act in order to enact the plan. Paul Taylor and Michael Barton were charged with the murder of Anthony Walker on 29 July. **8.** Three of the four men alleged to have attempted to bomb London's transport system on 21 July were remanded in custody to appear at the Central Criminal Court in November 2005. **12.** Two British women who had a same-sex wedding in Canada went to court in Britain to demand equal rights with heterosexual married couples under British law. The Home Secretary banned a radical Muslim cleric, Omar Bakri Mohammed, from ever returning to Britain on the grounds that his presence is 'not conducive to the public good'. **16.** Documents leaked to the media from a source within the Independent Police Complaints Commission contradicted the Metropolitan Police's version of the events leading to the shooting of Jean Charles de Menezes on 22 July; the documents showed that, contrary to reports, de Menezes did not jump over the ticket barriers, was not wearing a bulky jacket, and did not run away from the police. **17.** The families of 17 soldiers killed in Iraq launched a legal bid for an independent inquiry into the legality of the war. **18.** The Home Office launched the Violent and Sex Offenders Register (Visor), a national computer database containing photographs and personal details of Britain's

most dangerous criminals; the system is designed to allow police, probation officers and prison staff throughout the country to share intelligence about individuals more quickly. **25.** The parents of Charlotte Wyatt lost an appeal against the High Court's ruling in October 2004 that doctors should not resuscitate her in the event of respiratory failure; however, the appeal court judge ordered an urgent review of the baby's medical condition following a marked improvement. **26.** Hussein Osman, the man held in Rome in connection with the attempted London bombings on 21 July, launched an appeal against his extradition to Britain, arguing that he would not receive a fair trial. **27.** A gang that gatecrashed a christening in Peckham, London, shot dead a guest, Zainab Kalokoh, before snatching handbags and mobile phones from other guests.

BUSINESS AND ECONOMIC AFFAIRS

SEPTEMBER 2004
1. An investigation for Hollinger International, former owner of the Daily Telegraph Group, found that Lord Black of Crossharbour and his main business associates had transferred US$400 million to their own accounts over a seven-year period. Hollinger International had already begun legal proceedings to sue Lord Black and his associates for US$1.25 billion (£700 million) in damages and compensation for the alleged 'looting' of the company. **8.** British Airways agreed to sell its £425 million stake in the Australian airline Qantas, stating that revenue generated from the sale would be used to offset the airline's debt. **14.** The high street pharmacist Boots announced that it was to close all its laser eye-surgery clinics, dental and chiropody practices after losses of £3.8 million in the 2003–4 financial year. **17.** Jaguar announced that its Coventry headquarters was to close, with the loss of 600 jobs, in an effort to stem losses estimated at £30 million a month. The FTSE 100 index rose to 4,591, its highest level since July 2002. **18.** Annual results published by National Savings and Investments showed that sales of premium bonds increased by 57 per cent to £7.49 billion in 2003–4 compared with the previous year. **20.** Figures released by the British Bankers' Association (BBA) showed that mortgage-lending slowed to £25 billion in August 2004 from £28.9 billion in July 2004, suggesting that interest rate increases by the Bank of England had started to take effect. **22.** British Energy received approval from the European Commission for a restructuring package involving £3.4 billion of government aid. A report by the UN Conference on Trade and Development showed that direct foreign investment in Russia rose to US$6.7 billion in 2003, almost doubling from US$3.4 billion in 2002; China also emerged as a major recipient of foreign investment, with inward investment of US$53 billion in 2003. In comparison, inward investment in the UK dropped to US$14.5 billion in 2003 from US$27.8 billion in 2002. **28.** The price of US crude oil rose to US$50.35 a barrel and in the UK the Brent crude oil price rose to US$45.93. **29.** Capital Radio and GWR, which holds the licence for Classic FM and a number of local stations, announced details of their merger. The new group will own one national station, 55 local analogue stations, 93 digital stations and an interest in 28 digital multiplexes, making it the largest radio group in the country with a 36 per cent audience share.

OCTOBER 2004
1. The minimum wage increased from £4.50 to £4.85 per hour for workers aged 21 and over, from £3.80 to £4.10 per hour for workers aged between 18 and 21 years and a new rate of £3 per hour was introduced for 16- and 17-year-olds. **4.** The Association for Payment Clearing Services (APACS) announced that fraud on credit and debit cards rose by 18 per cent to £478.8 million in the 12 months to June 2004. **7.** The Standard Life Group announced that it could no longer keep its promise, made in 2000, to make up any shortfall on mortgage endowment polices that mature after the end of 2005; 600,000 customers were believed to be affected. The Group also introduced a deadline for claims of mis-selling, and warned of the possibility of bonus cuts. **13.** Lloyd's of London announced that it planned to raise £500 million through a 20-year sterling and euro bond offer, making an entry into the corporate debt market for the first time. Figures released by the Office of National Statistics (ONS) showed that 1.1 million people under 25 were unemployed and not in full-time education in the three months to August 2004; 5,000 more than in 1997. **21.** The £9 billion takeover of the British bank Abbey by the Spanish bank Banco Santander was approved by Santander's shareholders; Francisco Gómez-Roldán, Santander's chief financial officer, was appointed chief executive of Abbey. **26.** The Office of Fair Trading (OFT) announced that it was investigating whether 'late payment' charges imposed on credit card borrowers could be in breach of fair trading laws. **27.** Figures published by the BBA showed that the number of agreed mortgage loans fell to 59,905 in September 2004 compared to 85,626 in September 2003. **28.** The price of oil, metal and mining stocks fell on the London Stock Exchange after the Chinese central bank raised its interest rate by 0.27 per cent to 5.58 per cent, the first increase in nine years.

NOVEMBER 2004
5. DTI figures showed that there were 11,967 personal insolvencies in England and Wales between July and September 2004, an increase of 31 per cent compared to the same period in 2003. The US dollar fell to an all-time low of $1.2942 against the euro and closed at a three-month low of £1.8484 against the pound. **10.** The Governor of the Bank of England, Mervyn King, said that on average house prices had stopped rising over the past two months and a slowdown in the housing market was evident in virtually all the indicators used by the bank. In the USA, the Federal Reserve voted unanimously to increase US interest rates to 2 per cent. The OFT extended its inquiry into the alleged anti-competitive nature of credit-card handling fees to include Visa as well as Mastercard. The telecommunications group Cable and Wireless announced that it was making 600 redundancies, half of them in Britain, and closing its London headquarters to reduce costs. **13.** Norwich Union sent letters to all pension-holders who had previously opted out of the State Second Pension, previously known as the State Second Pension Scheme or SERPS, to strongly recommend that they rejoin the scheme. **14.** The Financial Secretary to the Treasury, Stephen Timms, announced that the government was working with the banking industry to try to reduce the number of households without access to a basic bank account; one in twelve UK households do not have a bank account of any kind. **15.** The Securities and Exchange Commission, the US financial regulator, charged Lord Black of

Crossharbour, the former chairman and chief executive of Hollinger International (HI) and David Radler, former president of HI, with fraud. **17.** The supermarket group J Sainsbury reported its first-ever half-year loss, of £39 million, for the six-month period ending 9 October. **26.** Network Rail reported a decrease in half-year pre-tax losses from £233 million to £34 million; this was mainly due to a £70 million cut in operating costs and the receipt of a £51 million performance incentive payment from the Strategic Rail Authority for service improvements across the network.

DECEMBER 2004
1. The pound reached a 12-year high of $1.93 against the US dollar. **2.** The Chancellor of the Exchequer, Gordon Brown, presented his pre-budget report, promising a number of family-orientated measures, including extending paid maternity leave from six to nine months, a £40-a-week bonus for one year for lone parents who return to work and an extra tax-free £50 a week towards childcare for those in employment. The water industry regulator Ofwat announced that consumers could expect an 18 per cent increase over the next five years to fund the modernisation of the UK's supply and sewerage network. **10.** Centrica, the owner of British Gas, revealed that 630,000 customers had switched to other gas suppliers following a 21 per cent energy price increase in September 2004. The nuclear power group British Energy, which was undergoing financial restructuring, reported half-year losses in the six months to 30 September 2004 of £234 million, compared with losses of £60 million in the half year to 31 March 2004. **14.** ONS figures for November 2004 showed that inflation measured on the retail price index (RPI) rose to 3.4 per cent, its highest level for more than four years; this was coupled with a sharp increase in domestic fuel costs, up 11 per cent since November 2003. **29.** The BBA announced that 47,095 new mortgages were agreed by its member banks in November 2004, the lowest monthly figure since January 2001.

JANUARY 2005
5. The consumer magazine *Which?* published research showing that credit card companies earn an estimated £400 million a year in interest and fees from customers who fail to pay their bills on time or exceed borrowing limits. **13.** The Bank of England left the bank base rate unchanged at 4.75 per cent for the fifth consecutive month. The European Central Bank (ECB) held rates at 2 per cent for the 19th consecutive month and indicated that the rates were likely to remain unchanged for most of 2005 because of slow economic growth in Germany and France. **14.** It became illegal for companies to sell insurance without being registered with the Financial Services Authority (FSA). Halifax Bank, Britain's largest mortgage lender, published figures for the fourth quarter of 2004 showing that the average house price for the UK overall increased by 0.1 per cent, mainly owing to a 6.4 per cent increase in Northern Ireland; however, most regions saw a fall in average prices, with Wales experiencing the sharpest decline. **19.** The European Commission announced an investigation into the methods of commercial property rate valuation used by the Valuation Office Agency for the UK telecommunications sector following a complaint from a telecoms service provider that BT and Hull-based Kingston Communications were favoured under the present system. ONS figures for the three months to November 2004

showed that the number of people in employment reached 28.49 million, the highest level since comparable records began in 1971. **21.** Halifax Bank's annual first-time buyer review showed that 361,000 people bought their first property in 2004, a decrease from 532,000 people in 2002; the review also showed that in 548 of 597 main postal towns, property was too expensive for the typical first-time buyer. Treasury figures were published showing that the national deficit stood at £3.9 billion in December 2004, a decrease from £6.4 billion in 2003. **26.** More than 2,000 business and political leaders arrived in Davos, Switzerland, for the World Economic Forum. The Council of Mortgage Lenders announced that the number of homeowners three to six months in arrears with their mortgage payments had increased from 49,700 in the first half of 2004 to 53,960 in the second half of 2004, the first rise in mortgage arrears since 1998. The 45-strong chain of Allders department and homewares stores went into administration after directors failed to find a buyer for the group, which had estimated debts of £150 million. **27.** BAE Systems, Britain's biggest defence contractor, announced that 1,400 jobs would be cut across 13 sites in the UK.

FEBRUARY 2005

7. The Land Registry released figures showing that the average house price in England and Wales fell by 2.7 per cent in the final quarter of 2004. **23.** After the telecommunications regulator Ofcom said that it had no plans to review the terms of BT's universal service obligations, BT asked the government to end its sole responsibility for the maintenance of telephone boxes nationwide. **26.** Insurers estimated that the withdrawal from sale of products contaminated with the banned carcinogenic dye Sudan 1 could cost the manufacturer Premier Foods an estimated £100 million and was unlikely to be covered by standard product recall insurance. Dr Mike Mitchell, director of FirstGroup, the UK-based international bus and rail operator, was appointed to a newly created post of director-general of railways at the Department for Transport. **28.** HSBC bank announced record pre-tax profits of £9.6 billion for 2004.

MARCH 2005

3. HBOS bank, one of the country's biggest lenders, revealed a 20 per cent increase in 2004 in the number of borrowers with debt payment arrears of three months or more, triggering a fall in the share prices of some of Britain's biggest banks. APACS released figures showing that credit and debit card fraud had reached a record £500 million in 2004 despite the introduction of chip-and-pin technology. **9.** Figures released by IMS Health, a New York-based consultancy, showed that global pharmaceutical sales reached US$550 billion in 2004, but the rate of sales growth slowed to 7 per cent, the lowest growth rate in the industry for seven years. **10.** The director-general of the BBC, Mark Thompson, announced that 980 employees would be made redundant over the next 18 months and a further 750 jobs would be outsourced to other companies; the cuts amounted to the loss of nearly half the BBC's support staff. The confectionery manufacturer Mars announced the loss of 700 jobs in the UK, including 500 in Slough. The Bank of England's Monetary Policy Committee voted to keep the base interest rate at 4.75 per cent for a seventh successive month. **16.** In his ninth Budget, the Chancellor announced, among other measures, that from April 2005

the stamp duty threshold would be raised from £60,000 to £100,000. **30.** ONS published figures showing that average household income had fallen for the first time since the mid-1990s. The Institute for Fiscal Studies said that the decrease was due to the 1 per cent increase in national insurance in 2002 and above-inflation increases in council tax. The car manufacturer MG Rover dismissed reports of problems with a partnership agreement with the Chinese state-owned car manufacturer Shanghai Automotive Industry Corporation and confirmed that negotiations were continuing. **21.** ONS published its annual list of the goods and services whose prices are monitored monthly as the basis for the Consumer Price Index, used to measure inflation; the list included an increased number of services, such as fees for private surgery, home deliveries and chiropractors, and also, for the first time, the cost of a small household pet. **31.** Paul Wolfowitz, the candidate nominated by US President Bush, was unanimously approved as the new president of the World Bank.

APRIL 2005

1. The government offered MG Rover a £100 million bridging loan to cover costs until a deal with the Chinese state-owned Shanghai Automotive Industry Corporation (SAIC) was secured; the loan was in addition to other government assistance, including the deferrment of VAT and national insurance payments worth around £50 million. **4.** The DTI announced that talks to broker a joint venture between MG Rover and SAIC had stalled, putting the future of the car manufacturer and up to 20,000 jobs in jeopardy. **5.** The Petrol Retailers Association announced that the price of diesel had risen above £4 a gallon for the first time. **6.** The Pension Protection Fund (PPF) officially opened; financed by a levy on companies with a final salary scheme, the fund was set up to help workers who lose their pension contributions when their employers become bankrupt. **7.** Trading on the floor of the International Petroleum Exchange ended; in future, all trading will be electronic. The Trade and Industry Secretary, Patricia Hewitt, announced that, despite government intervention, MG Rover had failed to secure a deal with SAIC and had gone into receivership. Treasury figures showed that the administrative cost of government in the financial year to April 2005 had risen by £1 billion, an increase of 7 per cent. **10.** A survey by the Department for Work and Pensions showed that in 2003–4, 45 per cent of working adults made no provision for retirement. **15.** About 5,000 car workers were officially made redundant from the MG Rover car plant in Longridge, West Midlands; the government announced £150 million in support of redundancy payments and retraining for the employees. **16.** The government ordered an independent inquiry, chaired by Sir Bryan Nicholson, into the finances of MG Rover. **21.** HM Revenue and Customs released figures showing that an estimated 500,000 more people would become liable for income tax in the 2005–6 tax year, after tax allowances were remained unchanged in the March Budget. **25.** HM Revenue and Customs published estimated figures which showed that stamp duty on property generated an extra £1.4 billion for the Treasury in 2004–5; inheritance tax revenues increased by £400 million, at 16.1 per cent the biggest rise for nearly 20 years, as an estimated 2.4 million estates became liable to the tax. **27.** The Department for Constitutional Affairs published figures showing that house repossessions rose by nearly 25 per cent, to 14,048, in the first quarter of 2005, compared with the same period in 2004; court actions by banks and building societies seeking repossession reached 25,869, the highest quarterly total since 1997.

MAY 2005

3. The Confederation of British Industry's (CBI) monthly survey of reported sales showed high street sales in April were at a 13-year low. Figures from the Chartered Institute of Purchasing and Supply (CIPS) revealed that manufacturing activity suffered its first decline in two years, with new orders for industry at their lowest since March 2003. **9.** Despite the drop in retail sales and manufacturing activity, the Bank of England kept interest rates at 4.75 per cent for the ninth successive month. **19.** The AA Motoring Trust reported that the annual cost of owning and running a petrol engine car rose by 6 per cent in 2004–5, while the costs for a diesel car increased by 5.3 per cent. **20.** A Halifax Bank survey showed that key workers, such as nurses, teachers and firefighters, were financially unable to buy a property in nine out of ten towns in Britain; only 13 per cent could afford to buy a property in their area in 2004, compared to 52 per cent in 2001. **23.** The London Metal Exchange, the only exchange still with trading on the floor of the exchange, began trading in plastics for the first time. **24.** An OFT report declared that the average time taken to transfer money electronically from one account to another by banks in Britain was unacceptable; it gave the banks six months to decide how they would speed up processes and a further two years to implement changes. **25.** The President of Azerbaijan opened the Baku-Tbilisi-Ceyhan (BTC) oil pipeline, a £2.1 billion project built by a BP-led consortium to transport oil 1,094 miles from the Caspian Sea to the Mediterranean. Abbey bank was fined £800,000 by the Financial Services Regulator for mishandling endowment complaints; the fine was the biggest levied by the regulator for endowment mishandling.

JUNE 2005

5. The Engineering Employers Federation (EEF) reported that output in manufacturing and engineering in the second quarter of 2005 was at its lowest level since the last quarter of 2003. **7.** Halifax bank reported that house prices had fallen by 0.6 per cent in May, the sharpest monthly fall since October 2004. **8.** ONS figures showed that average household spending continued to outstrip income in 2003–4; average weekly household income rose by 3 per cent while average weekly household spending increased by nearly 5 per cent. **11.** The chairman of Eurotunnel, Jacques Gounon, stated that the company was facing financial collapse unless it could reach an agreement with its creditors by October; it was estimated to owe about £6.4 billion. **21.** It was reported that public borrowing rose to a record monthly high of £8.7 billion in May, the highest monthly figure since records began in 1992. **26.** Italian prosecutors announced that Calisto Tanzi, founder and former chief executive of Parmalat, the Italian food and dairy multinational, would stand trial for his part in the collapse of the company in a €14.5 billion (£9.6 billion) fraud scandal discovered in December 2003. In addition, 15 executives and the Italian offices of Bank of America, auditors Deloitte and Touche and the former Italian affiliate of Grant Thornton were charged with market manipulation and falsifying accounts.

JULY 2005

5. A study by the Council of Mortgage Lenders showed that in 2003, despite higher levels of home ownership in the population as a whole, only 22 per cent of people had bought their first home by the time they were 25, compared with more than a third in 1985; the average age of a first-time buyer rose from 31 to 34 years. **7.** The FTSE-100 index dropped by 207.5 points during the day's trading as news of the terrorist attack on London reached the Stock Exchange; however, the market recovered slightly by the end of the day, closing 71.3 points lower at 5,158.3. **8.** Prices for Brent crude oil reached a new high in London of US$60.36 a barrel amid market fears over the impact of Hurricane Dennis on oil production in the Gulf of Mexico. **22.** ONS figures showed that GDP grew by only 0.4 per cent in the second quarter of 2005, the slowest rate of growth since the first quarter of 1993; the report also showed that manufacturing was technically in recession, as output declined by 0.9 per cent in the first quarter and 0.7 per cent in the second quarter of 2005. **27.** Home repossessions in the first half of 2005 rose at their fastest rate since the second half of 1991.

AUGUST 2005

2. Fraser Welford-Winton, a former managing director at MG Rover, announced that he would be working with China's Najing Automobile Corporation to restart manufacturing of the MG-TF sports car and a range of MG saloons at the former MG Rover plant in Longbridge. **4.** The Bank of England reduced the bank base rate by 0.25 per cent to 4.5 per cent, the first cut in interest rates since July 2003 and the first change in interest rates since August 2004. **5.** DTI figures showed that 15,000 people had declared themselves bankrupt in the three months to 30 June, the highest quarterly figure since official figures were first compiled 40 years ago and nearly 40 per cent more than in the same period in 2004; 80 per cent of the bankruptcies comprised debts amassed through personal borrowing. **11.** Prices for Brent crude oil rose to more than US$63 a barrel for the first time. **17.** Labour Force Survey statistics showed that the unemployment claimant count had risen for a sixth successive month, the longest run of increases since 1992; total claimant unemployment stood at 866,000 at the end of July 2005, a rise of 39,700 since January 2005. **29.** Lloyds TSB became the first bank in 130 years to open some of its branches on a bank holiday.

ENVIRONMENT AND SCIENCE

SEPTEMBER 2004

6. A study carried out by the British Association for Advancement of Science revealed that one in five Scottish children aged 11 to 14 has arterial flaws that could contribute to cardiovascular disease. **8.** A NASA probe carrying samples of particles from the Sun crashed in the Utah desert after two of its parachutes failed to open. **19.** Research led by Henrik Mouritsen at the University of Oldenburg in Germany suggested that some migratory bird species may be able to see the Earth's magnetic field and use it as a navigational tool after cryptochrome proteins, which are highly sensitive to magnetism, were found in the retinas of garden warblers. **22.** Two NASA studies published in *Geophysical Review Letters* showed that global warming could bring about a significant rise in sea level more quickly than previously thought; satellite images charting the flow of glaciers after the collapse of the Larsen B ice-shelf into the Weddell Sea in early 2002 were used in the studies. **24.** *The Times* reported that the fossilised skeleton of an ancient aquatic lizard, *Dinocephalosaurus orientalis*, had been discovered in Guizhou province, China; the creature measured 9 ft (2.7 m) in length, with a neck almost twice as long as its body, and is thought to have lived 230 million years ago. **25.** Police launched an investigation into the shooting, during the close season, of 12 grey seals found on the shore at Burwick Ferry, South Ronaldsay. **30.** The prescription painkiller Vioxx was withdrawn from circulation worldwide by its manufacturer, Merck, after it was found that taking the drug doubled the risk of heart attack and stroke.

OCTOBER 2004

6. A rare form of salmonella was reported to have caused at least 350 cases of food poisoning since the beginning of September. Investigations into the separate outbreaks indicated that the bacteria was carried on lettuce. **15.** The results of a trial for a new malaria vaccine, published in the *Lancet*, showed malaria attacks were cut by 30 per cent in a sample of 2,022 children in Mozambique. **18.** The International Council for the Exploration of the Sea called on the European Union to impose a total ban on cod fishing in the North Sea, Irish Sea and west of Scotland after its annual assessment showed there had been no recovery in cod stocks in these areas. **27.** A team of scientists from the Indonesian Research Centre for Archaeology discovered a near-complete 3ft-tall fossilised human female skeleton on the Indonesian island of Flores; the skeleton is about 18,000 years old and scientists believe that it represents a new species of human, given the name *Homo floresiensis*.

NOVEMBER 2004

5. It was announced that UK trials of a high-intensity focused ultrasound treatment for prostrate cancer would begin. The technique presents patients with a decreased risk of the side effects of incontinence and impotence compared with surgery or radiotherapy. **7.** An assessment published by Birdlife International showed that 226 species of birds, 43 per cent of those occurring regularly in Europe, were in decline; among those most affected were migratory birds wintering in sub-Saharan Africa, including the wood warbler, northern wheatear and the northern house martin. **10.** The Forestry Commission reported that a fungal disease similar to the one that causes 'sudden oak death' in the USA had been found on native oak trees in Cornwall. The first observations of the weather on Uranus, made with the Keck II telescope on Mauna Kea in Hawaii, were shown at a meeting of the American Astronomical Society. The telescope captured several Uranian weather oddities, including a large southern hemisphere storm moving backwards and forwards over five degrees of latitude for the course of several years and a narrow complex of 18,000 mile-long cloud. **22.** A new drug to treat osteoporosis, Protelos, was launched in Britain; research indicated that the drug can reduce the risk of spinal fractures in sufferers by half and the risk of hip fractures was reduced by a third after three years. **24.** The Health Protection Agency published figures showing that the number of new cases of HIV in Britain had more than doubled since 1999, with a total of 7,000 new cases diagnosed in 2003. In total 53,000 adults in Britain were living with HIV at the end of 2003.

DECEMBER 2004

12. It was announced that human trials for a vaccine to cure Type-1 diabetes would begin in August 2005; the vaccine was developed by scientists at Bristol University and King's College, London, following the successful inoculation of mice with a protein which stopped the destruction of insulin-producing cells. **15.** *The Times* reported that scientists stationed at the McMurdo research base in Antarctica faced being cut off from four ships carrying the January supplies for the base by the 3,000 square km (1,200 square miles) B15A iceberg, which was travelling in the path of the ships. The iceberg also threatened to cut off four colonies of Adélie penguins from their food source. The *New York Times* reported that NASA's Mars probe *Spirit* had detected a mineral known to form only in the presence of water, reinforcing evidence found by its sister probe in June that suggested water had been present on the planet several billion years ago. **17.** The journal *Science* considered the discovery of evidence of water on Mars by NASA's *Opportunity* and *Spirit* probes to be the most important scientific discovery of 2004. **22.** A University of Bristol study of more than 7,000 children showed a correlation between households with a high frequency of household chemical usage and the incidence of persistent wheezing in young children. **25.** The European Space Agency's *Huygens* probe was released from the Cassini spacecraft to begin the final 20-day stage of its seven-year journey to Titan, the largest of Saturn's moons.

JANUARY 2005

6. The online version of the *British Medical Journal* published a review of clinical trials showing that in women taking HRT the risk of ischaemic stroke was increased by almost a third (29 per cent) and the risk of fatal or disabling stroke by more than half (59 per cent). **10.** A study by John Moores University, Liverpool, of the effects of ageing on the cardiovascular system found that between the ages of 18 and 70 the power of the male heart falls by 20–25 per cent while no age-related decline is detected in the female heart. **11.** A report, *Mobile Phones and Health*, by Sir William Stewart, chairman of the National Radiological Protection Board, advised that children under the age of eight should not use mobile phones. The report concluded that, despite the health risk remaining unproven, four studies had linked heavy use to ear and brain tumours and any effects would be more pronounced in young people. **14.** The *Huygens* probe landed on Titan at about 10.28 GMT. The probe transmitted to mission control in Darmstadt, Germany, four-and-a-half hours of data, including images taken during its descent to the surface. **18.** The new Airbus A-380, a joint British, French, German and Spanish project, was unveiled in Toulouse, France; the two-decker super jumbo jet has a maximum take-off weight of 560 tonnes and a fuel capacity of 310,000 litres, and can carry up to 800 passengers. **21.** David Southwood, head of science at the European Space Agency, announced that initial analysis of data sent back by the *Huygens* probe revealed that the moon's surface was saturated with liquid methane. **25.** The Chinese Bureau of Surveying and Mapping announced that it would be recalculating the height of Everest's summit using radar and GPS equipment following suggestions that melting glaciers had reduced the height by about 4 ft. **27.** The 2005 Environmental Sustainability Index, compiled by researchers at Yale and Columbia universities using 21 indicators covering pollution levels, government policy and vulnerability to environmental damage, placed Britain 66 out of 146 countries; Finland was at the top of the index and North Korea at the bottom.

FEBRUARY 2005

1. Cancer Research UK announced that trials for two vaccines which prevent infection with strains of the human papilloma virus (HPV), responsible for 70 per cent of cervical cancers, had been highly successful. **3.** Figures from the Health Protection Agency showed that 3,504 suspected mumps cases were reported in the first three weeks of January 2005, a huge increase on the 248 cases reported over the same period in 2004. Two-thirds of those affected were in the 15–24 age bracket. **12.** Figures released by the British Heart Foundation showed an average £60 per capita was spent on healthcare for heart disease in 2003. **16.** The World Health Organisation warned of the risk of an avian flu pandemic; the announcement came as British scientists stated that cases were being misdiagnosed as diarrhoea and encephalitis, suggesting that the virus may be more common in humans than previously thought. A redating of two partial skeletons discovered near Kibish, Ethiopia, in 1967 aged them at 196,000 years, making them the oldest examples of *Homo sapiens* discovered to date.

MARCH 2005

3. The reconstruction of the brain of *Homo floresiensis,* the hominid skeleton found in October 2004, by a team of scientists led by Prof. Dean Falk from Florida State University, confirmed that the skeleton represented a new species and refuted suggestions that the skeleton belonged to a pygmy or a modern human with microcephaly. **8.** Doctors at King's College Hospital, London, announced that they had successfully reversed Type-1 diabetes in a patient by transplanting insulin-producing cells into the patient's liver, enabling the liver to take on the function of regulating blood sugar. **25.** The Environment Agency issued a warning that salmon could become extinct in the River Test and the River Itchen, stating that rises in water temperature caused by hot weather and reduced water levels, rather than direct human intervention, was responsible for the decline in stocks. **29.** The Royal Society announced that the Astronomer Royal, Sir Martin Rees, had been unanimously nominated to succeed Lord May of Oxford as president at the end of November 2005.

APRIL 2005

8. The European Space Agency confirmed its intention to attempt a second mission to Mars following the failure of *Beagle 2* in 2003; the new mission is scheduled to leave Earth in June 2011 and arrive at Mars in June 2013. **17.** A British entrepreneur won the backing of former South African president Nelson Mandela and the World Bank for his 'roundabout' water pump to be installed in villages across Africa; the invention utilises energy generated from the circular motion of a child's roundabout to pump water from a borehole into a tank, from which it can be drawn by means of a nearby tap. **18.** A study by the RAC Foundation reported that there are more than 30 million cars on the roads in Britain, and that households with two or more cars outnumber those with no car. **24.** Biologists were called to test water samples from a lake in Hamburg after an outbreak of exploding toads; the amphibians were reported to appear perfectly healthy in the day, but after nightfall they started to inflate to more than three times their normal size before exploding. **27.** The new

Airbus A-380, the world's biggest commercial passenger jet, made its four-hour maiden flight from Toulouse airport. **28.** A team of ophthalmologists at the Queen Victoria Hospital, East Grinstead, reported that they had successfully treated more than a dozen patients with impaired corneas, who had been blinded accidentally or because of a congenital disorder, by transplanting human stem cells onto the surface of the eye.

MAY 2005

3. A team of US scientists at the Duke Medical centre in North Carolina announced that they were a step closer to developing a vaccine for HIV after isolating naturally produced HIV antibodies from five people; the team discovered the human body is able to produce antibodies against HIV but because these have very similiar characteristics to autoantibodies, which damage normal tissues, they are mistakenly destroyed by the immune system. **19.** Scientists at Newcastle University became the first British scientists to clone human embryonic cells for use in therapeutic stem cell research, although they were unsuccessful in extracting any stem cells during this cloning attempt. **27.** The US Food and Drug Administration (FDA) announced that it was investigating 42 reports of blindness from optic neuropathy in connection with the use of anti-impotence drugs Viagra and Cialis.

JUNE 2005

2. It was reported that a new species of dinosaur had been discovered in the fossil-rich region near Cerro Condor in Argentina; the *Brachytrachelopan Mesai* dates from the late Jurassic period and is the first example of a short-necked sauropod, suggesting that sauropods may have had greater adaptive plasticity than previously thought. **7.** An American woman became the first successful ovary transplant patient to give birth; the ovary was donated by her identical twin in 2004. **9.** A trial of non-steroidal anti-inflammatory drugs, commonly used by sufferers of arthritis, indicated that regular use increased the risk of heart attack by at least 20 per cent. **16.** The Marine Conservation Society reported that there had been three times the average number of sightings of basking sharks in Scottish waters in May; scientists believe that the large plankton-eating mammals are gradually moving north as a result of global warming. **19.** A survey by the RSPB, British Trust for Ornithology, English Nature and the Forestry Commission showed that the nightjar, one of the country's most threatened birds, had a population of at least 4,500 males, an increase of more than a third since 1992. **20.** The world's first spacecraft powered by solar sails, *Cosmos 1,* was launched from a Russian nuclear submarine in the Barents Sea; the craft is powered by eight 14-metre-long sails, which unfurl in a windmill formation once the craft is in orbit. **22.** The British Medical Association stated that a million children under 16 are obese and are developing conditions normally associated with old age, such as diabetes, fatty liver disease, sleep apnoea, asthma and orthopaedic problems, due to their obesity.

JULY 2005

14. The journal *Science* published the genetic codes of the three parasites responsible for African sleeping sickness, Chagas disease and Leishmaniais, which kill 150,000 people a year; scientists hope that understanding the genetic make-up of the parasites will enable the development of new drugs and vaccines to treat these illnesses. **26.** NASA launched the space shuttle *Discovery,* the first launch since the space shuttle fleet was grounded in 2003 following the disintegration of the *Columbia* shuttle on re-entry, killing seven astronauts. During the launch, a large chunk of insulating foam broke off *Discovery*'s external fuel tank, causing NASA to ground the rest of the fleet the following day. **31.** NASA announced that *Discovery* would stay in orbit for a day longer than planned so that the crew could assist colleagues aboard the international space station with maintenance.

AUGUST 2005

2. An *Atlas 5* rocket carrying NASA's *Mars Reconnaissance Orbiter (MRO)* blasted off from Cape Canaveral, Florida, at 12.43 BST; the probe is due to arrive in orbit around Mars in 2006 and is equipped with three specialised cameras, ground-penetrating radar equipment and a spectrometer. **3.** Astronaut Steve Robinson carried out external repairs to the space shuttle, removing two pieces of ceramic that had come loose during launch to ensure that the shuttle's exterior surface remained smooth for re-entry into the Earth's atmosphere. **8.** Scientists at the University of California, Los Angeles, discovered that the loss of brain cells that occurs naturally in the ageing process makes people much more likely to stop breathing suddenly while asleep, which could help to explain why older people are more likely to die in their sleep. **9.** The *Discovery* space shuttle successfully re-entered the Earth's atmosphere and landed safely in California; its landing had been postponed for one day by bad weather on Earth. **21.** A Dutch student discovered a manuscript by Einstein entitled 'Quantum Theory of the Monatomic Ideal Gas' in the archives of the University of the Netherlands. **26.** The Agriculture Ministry of Finland announced that avian flu had been detected among sick and dead seagulls found in Oulu, 370 miles north of Helsinki. **27.** *The Times* reported that eight white-tailed or sea eagles, the rarest British bird of prey, had been successfully reared this year on the Isle of Mull.

SPORT

SEPTEMBER 2004

1. The champion jockey Kieren Fallon was among 16 people arrested following allegations of fraudulent gambling practices within the sport. **2.** Sir Clive Woodward resigned as the head coach of England's rugby union squad. **4.** Showjumper Caroline Pratt was killed at the Burghley Horse Trials after falling from her mount *Primitive Streak* at the 26th fence. **6.** British tennis player Tim Henman reached the quarter-finals of the US Open for the first time since Nicolas Kiefer (Germany) withdrew through injury when 0–3 down in the fifth set. **17.** The Paralympic Games opened in Athens with a record 136 nations competing. Pending a final review by the Canadian Centre for Ethics in Sport, the Canadian athlete Earle Connor was suspended from Canada's Paralympic team after testing positive for nandrolone and testosterone. **19.** The bowler Steve Harmison pulled out of the England cricket tour of Zimbabwe citing moral objections to President Mugabe's regime. In golf, Europe defeated the USA to win the Ryder Cup, its fourth win in five tournaments. **24.** The inaugural Chinese Grand Prix opened in Shanghai. **26.** Australian Benita Johnson won the BUPA Great North Run, completing the course in 67 min 55 sec, 32 seconds ahead of Edith Masai of Kenya. **29.** Former cricketer Tom Graveney took office as the

new president of the Marylebone Cricket Club (MCC). **30.** The International Cricket Council (ICC) abandoned its inquiry into racism in cricket in Zimbabwe after the Zimbabwe Cricket Union (ZCU) and the protesting white players failed to agree on preliminary conditions for the hearing; former captain Heath Streak and 14 other players demanded that three ZCU directors, accused of being the principal instigators of racism, should be excluded from the hearing when the players were called to appear.

OCTOBER 2004

1. The British Racing Drivers' Club, owner of Silverstone race track, failed to meet a deadline set by Formula One owner Bernie Ecclestone to agree a new contract securing the rights to stage the 2005 British Grand Prix. **6.** The British Horseracing Board launched the Order of Merit league, with points awarded to steeplechase horses based on their finishing positions for all pattern races between October and April, and a £250,000 prize for the leading horse. **8.** The International Equestrian Federation announced that *Waterford Crystal*, the horse with which Cian O'Connor of Ireland won the Olympic showjumping gold medal, had tested positive for a banned substance; O'Connor was stripped of his medal. **13.** A provisional date was set for the British Formula One Grand Prix in 2005 and approved by the FIA, the sport's world governing body, subject to the British Racing Drivers' Club agreeing a new contract with Bernie Ecclestone. **15.** In rugby union, Andy Robinson was appointed head coach of the England team in place of Sir Clive Woodward. **17.** The ICC cleared the Zimbabwe Cricket Union of a charge of racism brought by former captain Heath Streak and 14 other players. **18.** The England and Wales Cricket Board (ECB) suspended Graham Wagg from competitive cricket for 15 months and Warwickshire County Cricket Club terminated his contract, following Wagg's admission that he had taken cocaine. **21.** The Football Association ruled that there was insufficient evidence to charge England captain David Beckham with bringing the game into disrepute, despite Beckham's admission in a national broadsheet that he had deliberately fouled Ben Thatcher during the World Cup qualifying match against Wales on 9 October. **27.** The ECB declared that it was safe for the England cricket team to compete in a series of one-day matches in Zimbabwe. **28.** The City of London Police announced that it was extending to April 2005 the bail terms of 16 people arrested on 1 September on race-fixing charges, as more time was needed to investigate the alleged corruption; a further six people were arrested in connection with the case.

NOVEMBER 2004

7. In her first race since the Athens Olympics, Paula Radcliffe won the New York Marathon in 2 hr, 23 min, 10 sec. Andy Robinson named Jason Robinson as captain of the England rugby union team, in place of the injured Jonny Wilkinson, for the game against Canada at Twickenham on 13 November. **8.** The Football Association charged Arsenal manager Arsène Wenger with improper conduct for comments made about opposition players, following the Premiership game against Manchester United on 24 October when Arsenal's unbeaten run ended in a 2–0 defeat. **17.** During a friendly football match between England and Spain in Madrid, England's black players were subjected to a chorus of racist chants from Spanish fans. **19.** The candidature file for London's bid to host the 2012 Olympic Games was unveiled by the bid chairman Lord Coe. The Spanish Football Federation sent a letter to the Football Association apologising for the racist abuse of England players by home supporters on 17 November; FIFA announced that it had launched an inquiry into the incident, and on 21 December it fined the Spanish Football Association 100,000 Swiss francs. **23.** Thirteen of the 29 journalists who had applied for accreditation to report on England's cricket tour of Zimbabwe were told by the Zimbabwean Cricket Union that they would not be allowed access to the country. **24.** The ECB postponed the England team's flight from South Africa to Zimbabwe. Football supporter Jason Perryman was banned from all football stadiums in England and Wales for five years and fined £1,000 for racially aggravated disorderly behaviour, following his verbal abuse of black player Dwight Yorke during Blackburn Rovers' match against Birmingham City. **25.** The ECB announced that England's cricket tour of Zimbabwe would go ahead after Zimbabwe's Information Minister announced that the 13 journalists denied access to the country on 23 November had been cleared for accreditation by the official media commission. **28.** Yachtswoman Ellen MacArthur began a solo round-the-world record attempt.

DECEMBER 2004

9. The British Racing Drivers' Club announced that it had signed a five-year contract with Bernie Ecclestone, ensuring that the British Grand Prix would be held at Silverstone in July 2005. **12.** Double Olympic champion Kelly Holmes won the BBC Sports Personality of the Year award. **14.** The Jockey Club dropped charges of bringing racing into disrepute against jockeys Kieren Fallon and John Egan; Fallon remained the subject of a police inquiry into allegations of race fixing. **15.** The ECB announced that the satellite television operator BSkyB had been awarded exclusive broadcasting rights for all live home international and domestic cricket coverage in a four-year deal worth £220 million. **18.** The England batsman Andrew Strauss scored 120 runs against South Africa on the second day of the first Test match. **20.** The Brazilian footballer Ronaldinho was voted FIFA World Player of the Year. **21.** The multimillionaire businessman Steve Morgan withdrew his offer of a £70 million investment in Liverpool Football Club. **22.** The Greek sprinters Kostas Kenteris and Katerina Thanou and their coach Christos Tzekos were suspended by the International Association of Athletics Federations pending disciplinary hearings over their failure to report for testing on the eve of the Athens Olympics. **23.** Manchester City player Joey Barton was fined six weeks' wages (around £90,000) for violent conduct at the club's Christmas party. **29.** Manchester United player Wayne Rooney was charged by the Football Association with violent conduct following an incident involving Rooney and Tal Ben Haim of Bolton Wanderers; Rooney was given a three-match ban. **30.** Athlete Kelly Holmes, rower Matthew Pinsent and paralympian Tanni Grey-Thompson all received awards in the New Years Honours List. Ding Junhui, a 17-year-old snooker player from Shanghai, was granted a wildcard entry to the UK Masters in February.

JANUARY 2005

1. Former world rally champion Colin McRae took the overall lead in the Dakar Rally after winning the third stage in Spain. The Jockey Club stated that it would be unable to cede its control of the regulation of the sport to the Horse Racing Regulatory Authority as planned as funding and human resources issues had yet to be arranged. **3.** FIFA president Sepp Blatter stated that the 2005 Carling Cup final would be the first football match to utilise goal-line technology. **4.** The International Olympic Committee announced that it was pledging US$1 million to the relief effort following the Indian Ocean tsunami, and FIFA promised US$2 million to help rebuild the football infrastructure of the countries affected. **5.** The Women's Tennis Association Tour announced a £47 million sponsorship deal with Sony Ericsson. The Football Association stated that non-league clubs risk being barred from the FA Cup if they cannot guarantee the security and safety of spectators. Dame Kelly Holmes was voted European Female Athlete of the Year in a European Athletic Association poll. Colin McRae crashed out of the Dakar Rally when he lost control of his vehicle during the sixth stage. **6.** The Royal Bank of Scotland signed a three-year sponsorship deal, worth around £36 million, with the Williams Formula One racing team. **10.** A Spanish motorcyclist, José Perez, died of injuries sustained in a fall from his motorcycle during the Dakar Rally. **11.** Fabrizio Meoni of Italy became the second rider to die of injuries in the Dakar Rally. **12.** The 12th stage of the Dakar Rally motorcycle event was cancelled following the deaths of two riders in two days. **13.** In England's fourth Test match against South Africa, Andrew Strauss scored his fifth century in 11 Test matches. Sebastian Sainsbury announced that he was withdrawing his £25 million offer to buy Leeds United Football Club. A planned £15 million sale of Headingley cricket ground collapsed. **14.** Tim Henman announced his retirement from Davis Cup tennis. **15.** The England cricket captain Michael Vaughan was fined £5,500 for publicly criticising umpires during the fourth Test match against South Africa. **19.** The racing car manufacturers Ferrari announced that they would sign an extension to the Concorde Agreement and commit to Formula One until 2012. **21.** Ken Bates became the chairman of Leeds United FC after buying a 50 per cent share in the club. Land Rover announced that it would sponsor the Burghley Horse Trials in a £1 million deal. **24.** Eddie Jordan announced that he was selling his 51.1 per cent shareholding in the Jordan Formula One team. Martin Johnson announced that he would retire from international and domestic rugby in June. **25.** Football commentator Rodney Marsh was sacked by Sky Sports for making an on-air joke about the Indian Ocean tsunami. **26.** The European Union Court of First Instance ruled that FIFA was not breaking competition laws with its regulations on football agents and their practices. A report by the National Audit Office stated that UK Sport, the body behind the Great Britain Olympic team, had to take 'tough decisions' on which sports deserved national lottery funding in the future; it was estimated that the cost of each medal won by Great Britain in the Athens Olympics was £2.4 million.

FEBRUARY 2005

1. It was announced that Xchanging would be the new sponsor of the University boat race. **4.** In sailing, Britain's Mike Golding came third in the Vendee Globe round-the-world race despite his boat, *Ecover,* suffering from a broken keel. **5.** The Football Association announced that clubs will be liable for fines up to £250,000 if players verbally abuse match officials during games. **6.** The Football Premier League announced that it would hold an inquiry into allegations that officials from Chelsea

Football Club held illegal contract negotiations with Arsenal player Ashley Cole; Cole, Chelsea FC and its manager Jose Mourinho were charged with holding illegal contract negotiations on 23 March. Manchester United FC announced that it had received a takeover proposal from a shareholder, American billionaire businessman Malcolm Glazer. **7.** Ellen MacArthur circumnavigated the globe non-stop in the fastest time to date, clipping one day and 8 hours off the previous record. **8.** Fast Track, the promoter of athletics in Britain, announced that Dame Kelly Holmes would face a fine for missing the Norwich Union AAA Championships in Sheffield. **9.** Around 400 football fans gathered outside Old Trafford to protest against the proposed takeover of Manchester United FC by Malcolm Glazer. **10.** The DIY chain Wickes signed a three-year deal to co-sponsor the Coca-Cola Football Championship. Formula One promoter Bernie Ecclestone announced a deal that secured the continued involvement of the nine Formula One teams that had been threatening to form a breakaway championship. **11.** The executive board of Manchester United FC announced that the takeover offer from Malcolm Glazer was not in the best interests of the club. **12.** The Chelsea footballer Eidur Gudjohnsen was arrested for allegedly drinking and driving. **15.** International football players, including David Beckham and Ronaldinho, took part in a benefit match in Barcelona to raise money for victims of the Indian Ocean tsunami. **17.** Members of the International Olympic Committee began a three-day tour of London in order to asses the capital's potential to hold the 2012 games. **21.** The Football Association announced a review of early-evening kick-off times following serious crowd disturbances at three FA Cup fifth-round matches. **22.** The McLaren Formula One team announced a £15 million-a-year sponsorship deal with Johnnie Walker (whisky). Ladbrokes announced its three-year sponsorship of the St Leger horse race. **24.** The Northampton rugby union coach Budge Pountney was fined £2,000 and banned from match-day coaching for six weeks for verbally abusing a referee. **27.** The Chelsea football manager Jose Mourinho was banned from the touchline after making a rude gesture to opposition fans during the Carling Cup final. **28.** David Prutton, the Southampton footballer, was charged with improper conduct after manhandling referee Alan Wiley during a match against Arsenal; on 2 March, Prutton was given a ten-match ban.

MARCH 2005

1. The Manchester United player Roy Keane appeared before Manchester magistrates' court charged with assaulting a 16-year-old boy. **2.** Jermaine Pennant, the Arsenal player on loan to Birmingham City FC, was jailed for three months for drinking and driving. Sue Campbell was appointed chair of UK Sport. It was announced that the energy company Npower would extend its sponsorship of Test matches in the UK until the end of the 2007 season. The horse racing trainer Martin Pipe was fined £7,500 by the Jockey Club disciplinary panel after refusing to allow one of his horses to be drug tested. **3.** Two Manchester United footballers, Mads Timm and Callum Flanagan, were sentenced to detention in a young offenders' institute after being found guilty of dangerous driving. **8.** A lime tree was planted at the St Lawrence cricket ground, Canterbury, to replace a 200-year-old tree that was blown down in January. The Court of Appeal overturned a High Court ruling that had awarded the former Manchester City football manager Joe Royle more

than £500,000 in owed wages when the club dismissed him in 2001; Royle was ordered to pay back the sum. A freelance jockey, Gyles Parkin, was arrested at his home in connection with the police investigation into race-fixing. **9.** Ryan Hudson, the former Castleford and England A rugby league captain, received a two-year suspension after he was found guilty of taking Stanozolol, a banned anabolic agent. **10.** Kevin Keegan resigned as manager of Manchester City FC. **12.** An international football referee, Anders Frisk, resigned following death threats to his family. **15.** The Leicester prop Matt Hampson broke his neck in a training session with the England under-21 rugby union team. The chief executive of the Football Association, Gordon Taylor, called for players to be punished for swearing or verbally abusing referees during matches. **16.** The darts player Kevin Painter was fined £800 by the Darts Regulation Authority. **18.** Konstantinos Kenteris and Ekaterini Thanou, the two Greek sprinters accused of deliberately missing three drug tests, were cleared of all charges by the Greek Athletics Federation. **21.** UEFA officials announced that the Chelsea football manager Jose Mourinho, assistant manager Steve Clarke and security officer Les Miles would be charged with bringing the game into disrepute following Chelsea's Champions League match against Barcelona. The Tottenham Hotspur footballer Thimothee Atouba was charged with violent conduct after elbowing Manchester City's Joey Barton during a premiership match. **22.** A police investigation began into allegations that Manchester United footballer Wayne Rooney assaulted a man in a Manchester nightclub. The Football Association announced an investigation into an alleged fight between Aston Villa and Birmingham City players after a premiership match. **23.** Two outstanding cricket Test matches, first scheduled in 2004 between England and Zimbabwe, were finally cancelled and the English Cricket Board announced it had paid £133,900 compensation to the Zimbabwe cricket authorities; the Test series was disrupted when Zimbabwe's Test status was suspended last year. **29.** The Jockey Club announced that any horse racing trainer or jockey found guilty of misleading future investigations by the Jockey Club's security department would face an automatic ban from the sport. **31.** Chelsea FC and its manager Jose Mourinho were fined £33,000 and £9,000 respectively by UEFA after being found guilty of bringing the game into disrepute. Mourinho was also banned from the touchline for two European games.

APRIL 2005

4. Lee Bowyer was fined six weeks' wages (£200,000) and given a four-match ban by Newcastle United FC after fighting with teammate Kieron Dyer during a premiership match against Aston Villa; on 22 April, he was given a further three-match ban. Sir Bobby Robson, former manager of Newcastle United FC, reached a financial settlement with the club for about £2.1 million in lost earnings after being sacked before his contract expired. **5.** The managing director of Aintree race course announced that the Grand National start time would be moved back by 25 minutes to allow the BBC to broadcast the wedding of the Prince of Wales and Mrs Camilla Parker-Bowles. Guinness announced that it would sponsor the English rugby union premiership in 2006 in a £20 million deal. **7.** The Royal Ocean Racing Club announced the Admiral's Cup, which had been scheduled to take place at Cowes in July. **11.** The rugby league player Sean Penkywicz of Huddersfield Giants tested positive for the banned anabolic steroid Stanozolol and was subsequently banned for two years. **14.** Peter Moores was appointed director of the English Cricket Board's National Academy. **18.** It was announced that Sport England would provide £9.2 million of funding for golf over the next four years. **19.** The Football Association charged Blackburn Rovers captain Andy Todd with violent conduct after he appeared to elbow Arsenal player Robin van Persie during a premiership match. It was announced that Hampden Park, Glasgow, will host the UEFA cup final in 2007. Yorkshire County Cricket Club's proposed purchase of its Headingley ground collapsed after the county club failed to attract sufficient investment to raise the £15 million required. In Rugby Union, the England captain and Leicester player Martin Corry was banned for three weeks after elbowing Saracens flanker Richard Hill during a rugby union premiership match. **20.** Manchester United player Gary Neville was banned for three matches after kicking a football at a spectator during a premiership match against Everton. Dame Kelly Holmes announced that she would retire from athletics at the end of the 2005 season. A Football Association disciplinary commission fined Leeds United FC £3,000 over a 20-man brawl in a championship match against Gillingham. **22.** Ian Taylor resigned as chief executive of Sportscotland. **24.** The Chelsea defender John Terry was named PFA Player of the Year 2004–5, and Wayne Rooney of Manchester United was named PFA Young Footballer of the Year 2004–5. **25.** Arsenal striker Quincy Owusu-Abeyie was arrested following a fight outside a London hotel. Beverly Lewis was appointed captain of the Professional Golfer's Association, the first woman to hold the post. **28.** Shareholder Malcolm Glazer was given a deadline of 17 May 2005 to make a formal offer for Manchester United FC.

MAY 2005

1. The former world boxing champion Prince Naseem Hamed was involved in a multiple car crash. **5.** The BAR Formula One team was banned for two races and stripped of its points in the constructors' championship after a concealed fuel tank was discovered in one of its cars. **9.** The Warwickshire wicketkeeper Keith Piper was suspended after failing a drugs test; on 2 June his contract with the club was terminated. **12.** Malcom Glazer launched a formal takeover bid for Manchester United FC by purchasing a 70 per cent stake in the club. Ian Millward, the former St Helens rugby league coach, lost an appeal over his sacking for gross misconduct. **13.** Six British tennis players, including Arvind Parmar and Jamie Delgado, had to be escorted away from the Andijan Futures tournament in Uzbekistan by an armed guard following serious civil disturbances in the city. Athlete Mark Lewis-Francis was given a warning by UK Athletics after he tested positive for cannabis. **16.** Malcom Glazer secured a controlling 75.7 per cent stake in Manchester United FC. **17.** An auction held at Sotheby's raised almost £400,000 for various horse racing charities. It was announced that Sir Matthew Pinsent was to be awarded the Thomas Kellar medal, the highest honour in rowing. **19.** A rugby union disciplinary panel found England player Neil Back guilty of punching Wasps player Joe Worsley during the premiership final at Twickenham and was suspended for the first three Lions matches in New Zealand. The Rugby Football League announced plans to scrap automatic promotion and relegation to and from the Super League. Frank Lampard received the Football Writers' Association award for footballer of the year. **23.**

The Football Association charged the Newcastle United manager Graheme Souness with bringing the game into disrepute for criticising a referee after a premiership match. **25.** Liverpool FC won the Champions League final on a penalty shoot-out after overturning a 3–0 half-time deficit; however, UEFA announced that the team would not be able to compete in the 2006 competition as the allocation was already full. **26.** The jockey Johnny Murtagh lodged an appeal against a three-day riding ban for careless riding at Newmarket; on 1 June, his suspension was reduced to two days.

JUNE 2005

1. A Football Association disciplinary commission found Ashley Cole, Chelsea FC and its manager Jose Mourinho guilty of an illegal contract-negotiation meeting; Ashley Cole was fined £100,000, Jose Mourinho £200,000 and Chelsea FC £300,000 and the club was threatened with a three-point deduction at the beginning of the 2005–6 season. The European Commission opened a formal investigation into the British government's plans to sell the Tote, the state-owned bookmakers, to the racing industry. **2.** The jockey Frankie Dettori was banned for six days after being found guilty of careless riding at Haydock Park. **4.** The sporting director of Tottenham Hotspur FC, Frank Arnesen, was suspended after allegations of involvement in an illegal contract-negotiation meeting with Chelsea. **6.** Millwall FC was fined £25,000 for the racist behaviour of its supporters during a Carling Cup match against Liverpool. **8.** The Sports Minister, Richard Caborn, urged the Football Association to turn women's football professional after record attendance figures at the England ladies opening match in the European Cup. Newcastle United footballer Lee Bowyer was summoned to appear in court over his fight with teammate Keiron Dyer. **10.** UEFA announced that Liverpool FC would be allowed to compete in the 2005–6 Champions League despite finishing outside the qualification places. **14.** The Irish showjumper Cian O'Connor announced that he would not appeal against the ruling that stripped him of the Olympic gold medal after his horse failed a drug test. The Arsenal footballer Robin van Persie was arrested over an allegation of rape. The Jamaican athlete Asafa Powell set a new world record of 9.77 seconds for the 100 metres. **15.** Channel 4 announced that full coverage of horse racing would continue on the channel until the end of 2006. **17.** The Football Association banned three unnamed footballers for six months for using recreational drugs. The president of UEFA, Lennart Johansson, was forced to apologise after saying that sponsorship companies should exploit women's looks in their promotion of women's football. **21.** The employment tribunal of Faria Alam, a former personal assistant at the FA who left after a scandal over her alleged relationships with Mark Palios and the England football coach, Sven-Goran Eriksson, began. **26.** A rugby union player with the Lions team touring New Zealand, Danny Grewcock, was suspended for two months after being found guilty of biting the New Zealand hooker Keven Mealamu during a one-day international match in Christchurch. **29.** Up to 400 Manchester United fans protested outside Old Trafford as Joel, Bryan and Avi Glazer toured the ground after the club's £790 million takeover by their father, Malcolm Glazer.

JULY 2005

3. The jockey Tom Halliday was killed after falling from his horse at Market Rasen. **5.** The Prime Minister, Tony Blair, arrived in Singapore to support the British bid to stage the 2012 Olympic Games. **6.** The International Olympic Committee announced that London would be the host city for the 2012 Olympic Games. **7.** The British Olympic bid team announced that all celebration plans had been cancelled following the terrorist bombings in London. The ICC gave official status to a new series of cricket fixtures between countries from Africa and Asia. **13.** It was revealed that the proposed 2012 Olympic park in east London had formerly been the site of an experimental nuclear reactor. **14.** The ruling body of Formula One motor racing announced that the teams who boycotted the US grand prix in June would not be penalised. **18.** The Football Association found the Manchester United FC manager Alex Ferguson guilty of improper conduct after he publicly questioned officials' attitudes towards his team. **21.** The chairman of the Football League, Lord Mawhinney, called for a regulatory framework to be put in place to govern football agents after the Premier League announced that it had paid agents £7.8 million in the 2004–5 season. The Jockey Club suspended jockey Alan Munro for seven days after he brawled with a fellow jockey in the Newmarket weighing-in room. **23.** Bernie Ecclestone turned down a £570 million offer from a Hong Kong-based media conglomerate to buy Formula One motor racing. The chairman of Crystal Palace Football Club, Simon Jordan, threatened to sue the Italian club Internazionale after it cancelled a tour of England in light of the London bombings. **25.** The chairman of Newcastle United FC, Sir John Hall, revealed that he had been asked to sell his 28.5 per cent stake in the club. **26.** Millwall FC cancelled a proposed friendly with the Iranian national side following police advice that the match could attract right-wing extremist groups.

AUGUST 2005

2. The Horseracing Board won an appeal against an Office of Fair Trading ruling that racecourses infringed competition law by the joint selling of interactive betting rights to Attheraces in 2001. It was revealed that the Football Association had made plans to hold the 2006 FA Cup final at the Millennium Stadium in Cardiff in case the new Wembley Stadium was not finished in time. **2.** The International Association of Athletics Federations announced that plans to introduce life bans for drug-taking in athletics had been dropped. **4.** The International Rugby Board, the sport's governing body, announced a £30-million investment package intended to increase the competitiveness of the smaller rugby-playing countries. **9.** The London Development Agency criticised lawyers and other professional advisers involved in negotiating the sale and management of land needed for the London 2012 Olympics for inflating their fees. Sir Matthew Pinsent ruled himself out of the post of chairman of the British Olympic Association, preferring a media career. **10.** Following an appeal, the fine of Chelsea manager Jose Mourinho for making an illegal approach to Ashley Cole was reduced from £200,000 to £75,000. **11.** In the third Test match at Old Trafford, the England cricket captain Michael Vaughn scored 166 and Australia's Shane Warne took his 600th Test match wicket. The jockey Richard Quinn was stood down from riding at Salisbury after failing a random alcohol breath-test. **12.** The Burns Review of the management and executive structure of the

Football Association was published. **15.** David Morris, a director of Queen's Park Rangers FC, appeared before a London magistrate charged with conspiracy to commit blackmail after an alleged incident involving a fellow executive. **16.** It was announced that Arsenal FC had received planning permission to build an extra 154 flats on its Highbury site when redevelopment of the ground begins in 2006. Captain Mark Phillips was appointed as the course designer for the Burghley Horse Trials in September. **18.** It was revealed that the International Olympic Committee had contractually committed Locog (the London organising committee) to reschedule some major non-Olympic sporting events that are held in the UK before, during and after the 2012 Olympic Games. **19.** Talks between the Jockey's Association and Arena Leisure, the owner of Wolverhampton racecourse, failed to find a solution to the jockeys' proposed boycott of the venue over Arena Leisure's plans to use its own stalls handlers in place of those from RaceTech, the national handlers. **23.** Hilary Lister became the first quadriplegic to sail solo across the English Channel. **25.** The International Cricket Council announced that it would not bow to pressure from the governments of New Zealand, Australia and the UK to cancel forthcoming cricket matches in Zimbabwe. The Jockey Club announced that an investigation would be held after the horse *Mossman George* returned a positive drug test. **26.** Andy Murray became the youngest British male tennis player to qualify for the US Open.

INTERNATIONAL EVENTS

AFRICA

SEPTEMBER 2004

4. In Zimbabwe, President Robert Mugabe's Zanu-PF Party recaptured the Seke parliamentary seat after the opposition Movement for Democratic Change party boycotted a by-election in protest at alleged government repression. **9.** The US Secretary of State, Colin Powell, described the campaign by the Sudanese government and the Janjaweed militias in the Darfur region as 'genocide'. **10.** Simon Mann, a former British SAS officer, was jailed at a court in Harare for seven years for buying weapons to help in a coup to overthrow Equatorial Guinea's President Nguema. **16.** Amnesty International reported that around 500 people had been killed during clashes between rival gangs in the Nigerian city of Port Harcourt. **17.** An oil pipeline exploded near Lagos, Nigeria, killing around 50 people. **29.** In Nigeria, the Niger Delta People's Volunteer Force announced they would start 'an all-out war on the Nigerian state' unless multinational oil companies in the country shut down their installations and an agreement was reached on political autonomy and oil revenues. **7.** Three car bombs exploded in tourist resorts on the Red Sea coast of Egypt, killing around 30 people and injuring 100 more.

OCTOBER 2004

5. The UN Secretary-General, Kofi Annan, reported that the Sudanese government had failed to disarm the Arab militias who were estimated to have killed around 50,000 people since February 2003. **12.** Islamic courts in Nigeria sentenced a 29-year-old man and a 35-year-old woman to death by stoning for having sex out of wedlock. **15.** At the High Court in Zimbabwe, Morgan Tsvangirai, the leader of the opposition Movement for Democratic

Change party, was acquitted of treason after it was found that there was no evidence to show that he had plotted to kill President Mugabe. **17.** Chinua Achebe, the Nigerian author of the award-winning novel *Things Fall Apart*, rejected a national award by President Obasanjo because of the 'dangerous' state of affairs in the country. **25.** President Ben Ali of Tunisia was re-elected for a fourth term, claiming more than 94 per cent of the vote.

NOVEMBER 2004

2. President Mogae of Botswana was sworn in for a second term after his Botswana Democratic Party won the election. **6.** In Côte d'Ivoire, the Ivorian air force attacked a French-run UN peacekeeping camp based in Bouaké in the north of the country, killing nine French peacekeepers. French forces responded on the orders of French President Jacques Chirac, destroying the Ivorian air force and seizing control of the international airports at Abidjan and Yamoussoukro. **7.** Riots broke out in Abidjan after French forces destroyed the Ivorian air force. **12.** Several hundred Britons were flown out of Côte d'Ivoire by RAF transport aircraft as anti-European violence continued in the region. **18.** Friday Jumbe, the former finance minister of Malawi, was charged with the theft of £2.1 million while in office. **21.** Namibia's Lands Minister, Hifikepunye Pohamba, won more than 76 per cent of the vote in the presidential election. **26.** Kenya's High Court ruled that the former president, Daniel arap Moi, would have to appear at a commission investigating the theft of about £527 million in public money through bogus exports of gold and diamonds.

DECEMBER 2004

1. The Democratic Republic of Congo asked the United Nations to impose sanctions against Rwanda after 100 Rwandan troops entered eastern Congo in search of Hutu rebels believed to be sheltering there. **3.** In Mozambique, Armando Guebuza of the Frelimo party won the presidential election with 64 per cent of the vote. **9.** The Democratic Republic of Congo's Defence Minister announced that it had sent 10,000 troops to the east of the country after reports that Rwandan soldiers had entered the area to search for Hutu rebels. **19.** UN officials announced that over 100,000 people had been displaced since fighting broke out in eastern Congo. **21.** The UK-based charity Save the Children announced that its staff would withdraw from Darfur, western Sudan, owing to concerns about their safety. In Nigeria, the 2003 presidential election result was upheld by a court ruling, despite the judge admitting some results may have been manipulated; Olusegun Obasanjo won the election with 61.9 per cent of the vote. Ten men accused of attempting to overthrow the Sierra Leone government were found guilty of treason and sentenced to death. **23.** Twenty-six people were killed in an oil pipeline explosion in Nigeria. **26.** A gas explosion in a residential tower block killed 17 people in Algeria. **30.** The UN announced it was suspending food aid programmes in the Darfur region of Sudan following renewed violence in the region. Ugandan government officials announced that negotiations with rebel groups had concluded and a cease-fire agreement had been reached.

JANUARY 2005

2. In Somalia, police arrested a man wanted for the murder of British couple Richard and Enid Eyeington in 2003. Up to 50,000 people demonstrated in the

Ethiopian capital Addis Ababa following government attempts to reopen peace talks with Eritrea. **4.** In Zimbabwe, President Mugabe banned two of his cabinet ministers from standing in the forthcoming elections. **5.** In Malawi, three officials from the United Democratic Front, the country's ruling party, were charged with treason. **6.** Nelson Mandela, the former president of South Africa, revealed that his son Makgatho had died of Aids aged 54. Somali authorities stated that up to 300 people had died in the north of the country following the Indian Ocean tsunami. **7.** In Nigeria, two navy admirals were found guilty of stealing an oil tanker in 2003 and dismissed from the navy. **9.** Government officials in Sudan officially declared that a peace settlement had been reached with the Sudan People's Liberation Army rebels in the south. **13.** In South Africa, Sir Mark Thatcher received a four-year suspended jail sentence and a £265,000 fine when he pleaded guilty to involvement in an alleged coup attempt in Equatorial Guinea. **18.** Around 150 people died in the Democratic Republic of Congo when a boat capsized on the Kasai river. **19.** In Guinea, gunmen opened fire on President Lansana Conte's convoy, wounding a security guard. **20.** Up to 30 commuters died after two buses crashed in the Nigerian city of Lagos. **23.** In Kenya, 13 people were killed during clashes between the rival Kikuyu and Masai groups. South African government officials announced that 40 members of parliament, past and present, were to face corruption charges. **28.** Up to 100 people were killed in southern Darfur when a Sudanese military aircraft bombed villages outside the town of Shangil Tobaya. **31.** A UN Commission of Inquiry report stated that crimes under international law had been committed in Darfur.

FEBRUARY 2005

5. The president of Togo, Gnassingbé Eyadéma, died of a heart attack. **6.** Faure Gnassingbé, son of the former president, was sworn in as president of Togo. At the International Forest Conference in the Republic of Congo, African government leaders announced that 800,000 square miles of rainforest in the Congo basin would become a protected area. **9.** In the Somali capital Mogadishu, a lone gunman shot dead a BBC journalist, Kate Peyton. **10.** UN secretary-general Kofi Annan announced that an investigation would begin into the alleged abuse of under-age girls by UN peacekeeping soldiers in the Democratic Republic of Congo; six Moroccan peacekeepers were arrested on sexual assault charges on 13 February. **11.** Zimbabwe's government announced it was starting a drought relief programme for 1.5 million Zimbabweans it claimed faced starvation. **24.** A South African engineering company announced plans to build a £26.2 billion hydroelectric power plant in the Congo river basin. **25.** Togolese president Faure Gnassingbé announced he would resign ahead of the presidential election in April. Nine Bangladeshi UN peacekeepers were killed by militia fighters in Ituri province in the north-east of the Democratic Republic of Congo.

MARCH 2005

2. Up to 50 suspected militia fighters were killed by UN troops in the Ituri province of the Democratic Republic of Congo. **3.** In Nigeria, the government sent troops into the central town of Makurdi following riots and street-fighting. **7.** In South Africa, officials from the Pretoria metropolitan council voted to change the capital's name to Tshwane. **11.** More than 500 UN troops launched an offensive against militia fighters in the Ituri province of the Democratic Republic of Congo. **13.** Presidential and parliamentary elections were held in the Central African Republic. **14.** The presidential election in the Republic of Congo was won by incumbent leader Denis Sassou Nguesso with 90 per cent of the vote. **15.** A spokesman for the UN emergency relief co-ordinator announced that up to 10,000 people a month were dying from starvation in Dafur, Sudan. **16.** Around 30 people were killed when Somali militia raided a village near the Kenya-Somalia border. **18.** The Somali government agreed to allow peacekeeping forces into the country. Zimbabwe's supreme court announced that expatriate citizens would not be allowed to vote in the parliamentary election at the end of the month. **30.** The general election in Zimbabwe was won by the ruling Zanu-PF party with 78 seats and 59.59 per cent of the vote, while the opposition Movement for Democratic Change secured 41 seats and 39.52 per cent of the vote. **31.** A Rwandan Hutu rebel group, the Democratic Forces for the Liberation of Rwanda (FDLR), announced it would cease all offensive operations against the Rwandan government and offered an apology for its part in the 1994 genocide.

APRIL 2005
4. Up to 150 people were confirmed dead in an outbreak of Marburg virus in Angola. **5.** In Nigeria, the president of the senate, Aldolphus Wabara, was forced to resign over his alleged involvement in a bribery scandal. **6.** In South Africa, peace talks between Cote d'Ivoire government officials and rebel leaders concluded with the signing of an agreement to end the civil war. **9.** A presidential election in Djibouti was won by the incumbent president, Ismael Omar Guelleh, the only candidate. **12.** Libyan government officials announced that a trade and investment embargo would be imposed on Bulgaria after five Bulgarian nurses and a Palestinian doctor were accused of infecting some 400 children with the HIV virus at a hospital in Benghazi. **19.** Italy returned to Ethiopia a section of the 1,700-year-old Axum obelisk taken from the country in 1937 by Italian soldiers. **24.** The presidential election took place in Togo; Faure Gnassingbé was provisionally named as president after securing around 60 per cent of the vote, and was confirmed on 2 May. **26.** Opposition supporters in Togo staged protests in the capital at the results of the presidential election. **29.** The UK government cancelled £5 million of aid to Uganda. The UN admitted that some peacekeepers in Liberia had carried out sexual abuse against women. **30.** Eight people were killed in two separate terrorist attacks in Cairo, Egypt.

MAY 2005
1. Around 115 people were killed in flooding in eastern Ethiopia. **3.** In Somalia, a bomb attack at a political rally in Mogadishu killed around 10 people. **5.** The Ugandan parliament voted to hold a referendum on the possible re-establishment of multi-party government. **8.** The second round of parliamentary and presidential elections took place in the Central African Republic. **12.** Sixty-two suspected mercenaries, arrested over an alleged coup attempt against President Obiang of Equatorial Guinea, were discharged from a Zimbabwe jail. **15.** A parliamentary election in Ethiopia was won by the ruling Ethiopian People's Revolutionary Democratic Front (EPRDF). **16.** The South African government announced that the 62 suspected mercenaries accused of taking part in a coup attempt in Equatorial Guinea would be charged

with violating the Regulation of Foreign Military Assistance Act. **24.** In South Africa, the National Geographic Names Council voted unanimously to change the name of Pretoria to Tshwane.

JUNE 2005
1. A judge in South Africa announced there was overwhelming evidence to implicate vice-president Jacob Zuma in the corruption for which a prominent South African businessman, Schabir Shaik, was standing trial. **4.** A court in South Africa found Schabir Shaik guilty of corruption and fraud. **8.** In Ethiopia, around 20 protesters were killed when police clashed with students accusing the ruling party of fraud in the recent elections. **9.** President Mugabe of Zimbabwe defended in parliament his policy of destroying shanty towns in urban areas as an effort to crack down on illegal trading. **14.** President Mbeki of South Africa dismissed vice-president Jacob Zuma over his implication in the case of Schabir Shaik; Jacob Zuma was charged with corruption on 20 June. **19.** A presidential election was held in Guinea-Bissau. **22.** In South Africa, Phumzile Mlambo-Ngcuka was appointed as the new vice-president, the first woman to hold the post. **30.** A UN aid ship was hijacked off the coast of Somalia by gunmen demanding a US$500,000 ransom.

JULY 2005
3. A parliamentary election was held in Mauritius. **4.** A parliamentary election was held in Burundi. **7.** The Ugandan government announced plans to curb the numbers of tourists visiting mountain gorilla habitats. **8.** In Sudan, former rebel leader John Garang was sworn in as vice-president. **11.** A Ugandan minister announced that Owor Lakati, the leader of the Lord's Resistance Army (LRA) rebel group, had been killed by government forces. **12.** In Kenya, around 56 people, including children, were killed when members of the Borana tribe attacked a primary school in a neighbouring Gabra village. The International Court of Justice ruled that a small island at the centre of a dispute between Niger and Benin belongs to Niger. **20.** UN officials announced that 25 per cent of Niger's population were short of food and some 20 per cent of children were facing starvation following a prolonged drought. **22.** The Kenyan parliament approved a draft new constitution. **23.** In Uganda, a referendum was held on the introduction of multi-party democracy. **29.** The Rwandan government decided to free 36,000 jail inmates, many of whom confessed to a part in the 1994 genocide, because of overcrowding problems.

AUGUST 2005
1. In Sudan, vice-president John Garang was killed in a helicopter crash. The Zimbabwean government announced that all treason charges would be dropped against opposition leader Morgan Tsvangirai. **2.** Rioting broke out in the Sudanese capital Khartoum following the announcement of John Garang's death; Salva Kiir Mayardit replaced Garang as leader of the Sudan People's Liberation Party. President Taya of Mauritania was deposed in an army coup while he was out of the country; the military announced that a military council would rule for two years, after which elections would be held. President Taya of Mauritania, who was attending the funeral of King Fahd of Saudi Arabia, diverted his plane to Niger after the coup. **4.** In Mauritania, Colonel Ely Ould Mohammed Vall was named as leader by the ruling military council. The African Union voted to suspend

Mauritania following the military coup in the country. **6.** In Sudan, the funeral of John Garang was held in the southern town of Juba. Somali gunmen who had been holding a UN aid ship since June agreed to release the vessel and crew. **8.** In South Africa, 100,000 gold miners went on strike over pay and living conditions. **11.** Salva Kiir was sworn in as vice-president of Sudan. **18.** In Zimbabwe, a constitutional amendment was passed by the government that nationalised all agricultural land that has been listed for seizure since 2000. The amendment also denied landowners compensation or the right to contest eviction. In the Western Sahara, the Polisario Front announced that it would free some 404 prisoners held for the past 16 years.

THE AMERICAS

SEPTEMBER 2004

3. More than 2.5 million people were evacuated from their homes in Florida as Hurricane Frances approached the east coast of the USA. **6.** Former US president Bill Clinton underwent a successful quadruple heart bypass operation. **12.** Hurricane Ivan passed over the Cayman Islands, causing flash flooding and mudslides; across the Caribbean, 60 people were killed as a result of the storm. **14.** A court in Canada approved the country's first same-sex divorce, which was granted to a lesbian couple after the judge ruled that the definition in the Divorce Act of spouses as a man and a woman was unconstitutional. **16.** Hurricane Ivan flooded towns in Florida and Alabama, and killed 12 people. **19.** Flooding in Haiti in the wake of tropical storm Jeanne submerged the northern coastal city of Gonaives, killing at least 250 people; the storm caused floods and mudslides that killed around 1,000 people in total. **28.** A 15-year-old boy shot dead four students and wounded six at his school in Carmen de Patagones, Argentina.

OCTOBER 2004

14. The Bolivian Congress voted to put former president Gonzalo Sanchez de Lozada and 15 of his ministers on trial for the deaths of at least 56 people during street protests against his government in 2003.

NOVEMBER 2004

1. Tabaré Vázquez won just over 50 per cent of the vote in Uruguay's presidential election and his party Frente Amplio (Broad Front), an alliance of more than 40 socialist parties, won the legislative election. **3.** In the US presidential primary elections, President George W. Bush won a second term in office by gaining 279 electoral college seats to Senator John Kerry's 252 seats. **15.** Colin Powell resigned from his post as US Secretary of State. **16.** President Bush nominated Condoleezza Rice as the new US Secretary of State. **29.** Chile's President Lagos announced that 27,000 citizens who were tortured during General Pinochet's dictatorship would receive £100 monthly pension payments in compensation. **30.** Tom Ridge resigned from his position as the US Homeland Security Secretary; he had been the first person to hold the post, created in October 2001. The Cuban government freed the dissident poet and journalist Raúl Rivero from jail as a response to criticism by the European Union.

DECEMBER 2004

3. US President Bush nominated the former New York Police Commissioner Bernard Kerik as US Homeland Security Secretary. **9.** Canada's Supreme Court ruled that the government had the authority to legislate on marriage and that its proposed definition of marriage as 'the lawful union of two persons' did not violate the country's 1867 Constitution; the government planned to make homosexual marriage legal following the ruling. **10.** More than 1,000 members of the Colombian Catatumbo Bloc paramilitary group gathered in the north-east of the country to give up their weapons as part of a peace plan. **13.** In Chile, Judge Juan Guzmán formally charged General Augusto Pinochet with homicide and kidnapping and placed him under house arrest. **20.** US President Bush admitted for the first time that the insurgency in Iraq was having a detrimental effect on the January elections. **21.** A Chilean appeals court upheld the house arrest and indictment of Augusto Pinochet after the former president's legal team contested the charges. **30.** In the USA, Pentagon officials announced that one of its aircraft carriers would be decommissioned in the first phase of defence cuts. The USA announced the deployment of the aircraft carriers USS *Abraham Lincoln* and USS *Bonhomme Richard* and a strike force of cruisers and destroyers to aid the relief effort following the Indian Ocean tsunami. **31.** A fire in a Buenos Aires nightclub killed 175 people and injured 712. US President Bush pledged US$350 million in aid to the victims of the Indian Ocean tsunami. The FBI launched an investigation after seven passenger jet pilots reported that laser beams had been directed into their cockpits while flying over the USA.

JANUARY 2005

2. Four police officers were killed and 17 taken hostage when rebel army reservists stormed a police station in Andahuaylas, Peru. **3.** British businessman Hemant Lakhani went on trial in the USA charged with supplying missiles to terrorists. **4.** In the USA, the Roman Catholic diocese of Orange paid US$100 million compensation to 90 Californian victims of sexual abuse by priests. The Supreme Court of Chile upheld the indictment of Augusto Pinochet following a challenge by the former president's legal team. In Peru, rebel army reservists released their 17 hostages unharmed. **6.** The US defence department announced a new investigation into allegations of prisoner abuse at the Guantanamo Bay detention centre. **7.** Approximately 25 people were killed when three buses collided near La Paz, Bolivia. **12.** US navy officials announced that a nuclear submarine had crashed into an underwater mountain, killing one crewman and injuring 60. **13.** The Venezuelan ambassador to Colombia was recalled following allegations that Colombian police abducted a rebel Revolutionary Armed Forces of Colombia (FARC) leader on Venezuelan territory. Twenty US soldiers were killed in a helicopter crash in south-west Colombia. **15.** In the USA, Charles Graner, a US soldier found guilty of abusing Iraqi prisoners in Abu Ghraib prison, was sentenced to ten years in prison. **20.** George W. Bush was sworn in for his second term as president of the USA. **26.** In the USA, ten people were killed in Los Angeles when three commuter trains crashed. **31.** A US federal judge ruled that the special military tribunals held at Guantanamo Bay were unlawful.

FEBRUARY 2005

1. Members of the FARC rebel group attacked a marine post in Bogota, Colombia, killing 14 soldiers and injuring 25. **3.** The US Senate confirmed Albert Gonzales as the new Attorney General. **4.** In Bolivia, President Carlos

Mesa swore in 15 new ministers in a cabinet reshuffle. **10.** The president of Costa Rica, Abel Pacheco, was admitted to hospital after complaining of chest pains. **12.** In the USA, Howard Dean was named as the new chairman of the Democratic Party. In Costa Rica, President Pacheco was discharged from hospital with a clean bill of health. **15.** The US government withdrew its ambassador to Syria in response to the assassination of the former Lebanese prime minister Rafik Hariri. **17.** In the USA, President George W. Bush named John Negroponte as the first Director of National Intelligence. A sale of Kennedy family memorabilia made US$5.5 million at an auction in New York. **18.** Brazilian president Lula da Silva signed a decree creating two national reserves in Para state, following social unrest in the area. **21.** Venezuelan president Hugo Chavez accused the US President Bush of plotting to assassinate him. **23.** The Mexican supreme court ruled that former president Luis Echeverria could not be charged with genocide following the 1971 attack on student protesters in which 40 people died as too much time had elapsed since the atrocity.

MARCH 2005

1. The US Supreme Court abolished the death penalty for minors. **3.** In the USA, Steve Fossett landed in Salina, Kansas, becoming the first person to fly solo around the world without refuelling or stopping. **7.** US President Bush nominated John Bolton as the new US ambassador to the UN. Bolivian president Carlos Mesa offered his resignation to congress following a series of street protests by radical indigenous political groups. Around 133 prison inmates were killed in a prison fire in the Dominican Republic. **9.** FBI director Robert Mueller admitted to Congress that a project to upgrade the bureau's computer system, which had cost almost US$170 million, had been abandoned. **11.** The US government reached a US$25.5 million settlement with Hungarian survivors of the Holocaust over a trainload of gold and valuables stolen by the Nazis and subsequently seized by US forces after the Second World War. In Atlanta, USA, three people were killed in a shooting in a courthouse. **14.** A judge in San Francisco, USA, ruled that California's ban on same-sex marriages was unconstitutional. **15.** Bernard Ebbers, the former chief executive of US company WorldCom, was found guilty on nine counts of securities fraud. **16.** US President Bush nominated deputy defence secretary Paul Wolfowitz as head of the World Bank. The US Senate voted to begin oil exploration in the north-eastern region of Alaska. In Canada, two Sikh men were cleared of planning the bombing of an Air India jet in 1985. **20.** US President Bush signed an emergency bill to review the case of Terri Schiavo, who had previously been granted the right to die by a Florida court. **22.** A Florida federal judge rejected a request for Terri Schiavo to have her life-support systems reactivated. **23.** In Quito, Ecuador, riot police fired tear gas into the congress building after opposition politicians refused to leave the chamber following an aborted legislative referendum. **25.** The US Supreme Court refused to order Terry Schiavo's life-support systems to be reactivated. The Chilean supreme court announced that former leader General Pinochet would not be stripped of his immunity from prosecution for the assassination of his predecessor in 1974. **31.** Paul Wolfowitz was confirmed as the next president of the World Bank.

APRIL 2005

1. Sandy Berger, the national security adviser to President Clinton between 1997 and 2001, pleaded guilty to shredding documents relating to al-Qa'eda shortly before he was due to give evidence to the 9/11 commission. **20.** The president of Ecuador, Lucio Gutierrez, was dismissed by the country's senate after being accused of overstepping his constitutional authority; the deputy president, Alfredo Palacio, was sworn in as president. **21.** The Brazilian government granted asylum to Lucio Gutierrez. **22.** In the USA, Zacarias Moussaoui pleaded guilty to charges including terrorist conspiracy, air piracy and murder. **24.** Thousands of demonstrators protested in Mexico City over an alleged dirty tricks campaign by the government against the mayor of Mexico City and presidential candidate Andres Obrador. **26.** The USA's chief weapons inspector announced that the hunt for weapons of mass destruction in Iraq was over, and that no such weapons had been found. **29.** In the USA, a Washington military court found sergeant Hasan Akbar of the 101st Airborne Division guilty of murdering two fellow soldiers in Afghanistan. **30.** Lynndie England, a US soldier who served at the Abu Ghraib prison in Iraq, pleaded guilty to charges of maltreating prisoners of war, conspiracy and dereliction of duty at a special military court.

MAY 2005

2. José Miguel Insulza, formerly the interior minister of Chile, was elected secretary-general of the Organisation of American States (OAS). **5.** Two small bombs exploded outside the British consulate in New York, causing minor damage. In Washington, military commanders announced that a US marine, filmed shooting an apparently unarmed and injured Iraqi man in a Fallujah mosque, would not be punished for his actions. In Dominica, the Labour Party won the general election. **11.** The White House and US Capitol were evacuated after a two-seater plane flew into the three-mile air exclusion zone above central Washington. **19.** The Canadian prime minister Paul Martin narrowly survived a vote of no confidence. In Brazil, seven members of the Green Party withdrew from the ruling coalition government in protest at huge increases in deforestation announced by environment ministers; the ministers said that more than 10,000 square miles of rainforest were cleared in 2004, the second largest amount in one year since records began in 1988. **20.** In Peru, the congress voted against the impeachment of President Toledo for alleged fraud. **24.** The US House of Representatives approved a bill loosening restrictions on stem cell research. **25.** Legislative elections in Suriname were won by the ruling New Front for Democracy party (NF) with 41 per cent of the vote. **27.** In the USA, four Tennessee politicians were charged with taking bribes after a two-year undercover operation by the FBI.

JUNE 2005

1. In the USA, former FBI deputy head Mark Felt identified himself as 'Deep Throat', the codename of the informant who supplied the *Washington Post* newspaper with details of the 1973 Watergate scandal. **3.** In Bolivia, protestors shut down an estimated 60 per cent of the country's main roads after protests over alleged government corruption escalated into violent confrontation. The US government announced that it was withdrawing all non-essential diplomatic staff from Uzbekistan following warnings of attacks by Islamic militants. **4.** A US military inquiry revealed that there had been serious mishandling and abuse of the Koran by prison guards at the Guantanamo Bay detention camp. **7.** A court in Santiago stripped Augusto Pinochet of immunity from prosecution so that he could be tried on tax fraud charges. Bolivian president Carlos Mesa resigned after thousands of protesters marched through the capital city and fought running battles with riot police. **10.** Eduardo Rodriguez was appointed as interim president of Bolivia. **13.** In the USA, the singer Michael Jackson was found not guilty of child molestation and 11 other charges following a 14-week trial. In Philadelphia, USA, Edgar Ray Killen, a former Baptist lay preacher, went on trial for the murder of three civil rights workers in 1964; Killen was convicted of manslaughter on 21 June. **14.** The Argentine supreme court ruled that military officers who served under the military junta from 1976 to 1983 could be tried for human rights abuses. **15.** The Mexican supreme court overturned an earlier ruling that had protected the former president Luis Echeverria from genocide charges dating back to 1971. **17.** The US Peace Corps suspended operations in Haiti after increased violence around the capital Port-au-Prince. **26.** In Colombia, up to 25 soldiers were killed by FARC rebel fighters in the southern Putumayo region. **30.** In Venezuela, President Chavez announced that the country's oil would be sold to 13 Caribbean countries as part of a 'energy alliance' in the region.

JULY 2005
1. Sandra Day O'Connor resigned from the US Supreme Court. **4.** In Mexico, scientists announced they had discovered footprints dating back some 40,000 years, overturning the commonly held theory that settlers discovered the Americas some 15,000 years ago. **6.** In the USA, a *New York Times* journalist, Judith Miller, was jailed for refusing to co-operate with a panel investigating claims that the US government leaked the identity of a top undercover CIA official to the press. **8.** Twenty people were killed after Hurricane Dennis hit Cuba. **10.** Around 1.4 million people were evacuated from parts of Alabama and Florida as Hurricane Dennis reached the Gulf of Mexico. **13.** Bernard Ebbers, former head of telecommunications company WorldCom, was sentenced to 25 years in jail for nine counts of securities fraud. **25.** In Venezuela, a new satellite television channel aimed at central and south American audiences, *Telesur*, was launched. After several days' delay caused by technical faults, the space shuttle *Discovery* took off from the Kennedy Space Centre Florida. **27.** The Colombian government announced plans to hold talks with members of the FARC rebel group. **30.** Astronauts onboard the space shuttle *Discovery* conducted an examination of the craft after several heat-resistant tiles were damaged during its launch.

AUGUST 2005
1. John Bolton was installed as US ambassador to the UN. **3.** In Toronto, Canada, all the passengers and crew of an Air France airliner escaped without serious injury when the plane left the runway on landing and crashed into a nearby ravine. **4.** Canadian prime minister Paul Martin announced that former journalist and documentary film-maker Michaelle Jean would become the country's next governor-general. **5.** The US government announced plans to transfer some 70 per cent of detainees at Guantanamo Bay to jails in Saudi Arabia, Yemen and Afghanistan. **9.** The space shuttle *Discovery* landed safely

at Edwards air force base in California. In Argentina, Milan Lukic, a suspected war criminal wanted by the International Criminal Tribunal for the Former Yugoslavia, was arrested outside his apartment in Buenos Aires. **16.** A Columbian passenger jet crashed in the north-western Venezuelan state of Zulia, killing all 160 passengers and crew. **17.** An Ecuadorian-registered ship sank off the coast of Colombia, killing 104 people. **28.** US federal agents announced that the US home of Nigerian vice-president Atiku Abubakar had been searched as part of a corruption investigation. The mayor of New Orleans, Ray Nagin, ordered the evacuation of the city as Hurricane Katrina, a category five hurricane, approached; the hurricane subsequently passed over other parts of Louisiana, Mississippi and Alabama, causing widespread devastation. **29.** Breaches in the levees protecting low-lying New Orleans led to the flooding of 80 per cent of the city, leaving thousands of residents stranded for days without essential supplies. **30.** Mississippi, Louisiana and Alabama were all declared major disaster areas after Hurricane Katrina. The leader of Brazil's ruling Workers' Party resigned following a corruption scandal. **31.** The US government declared a public health emergency along the entire Gulf of Mexico coast; President Bush described the Hurricane Katrina disaster as one of the worst in the USA's history.

ASIA

SEPTEMBER 2004
2. The former deputy prime minister of Malaysia, Anwar Ibrahim, was released from prison after his conviction for sodomy was overturned by the Federal Court. **6.** Around 90 people died, 77 were missing and 450,000 were evacuated in south-west China after rainstorms caused landslides. **9.** A British couple was shot dead by an off-duty policeman in Thailand following an argument in a restaurant. **12.** It was reported that a large explosion causing a two-mile-wide mushroom cloud had occurred in North Korea, close to its border with China. Preliminary results for Hong Kong's elections showed that Democratic Party candidates won 18 directly elected seats in the legislative council while the pro-Beijing Party took 12 seats. **19.** The military chief of China, Jiang Zemin, resigned from his post and the President of China, Hu Jintao, was named the new military leader of the country. **20.** In the Indonesian presidential election, former security minister Susilo Bambang Yudhoyono defeated incumbent President Megawati Sukarnoputri. In India, 150,000 people were left homeless in west Bengal following flooding caused by eight days of monsoon rain. **27.** Security forces in Pakistan announced that they had shot dead Amjad Hussain Farooqi, a member of al Qa'eda wanted for the kidnapping and murder of American journalist Daniel Pearl and two failed assassination attempts against President Musharraf.

OCTOBER 2004
1. A suicide bomber detonated a device in a Shia mosque in the Pakistani city of Sialkot, killing around 30 people. **19.** Burma's state television reported that the moderate prime minister General Khin Nyunt had been allowed to retire 'for health reasons' and had been replaced by General Soe Win. **20.** Typhoon Tokage hit Japan, killing 21 people and injuring around 200. **21.** A gas explosion at a coal mine in Xinmi, in China's Henan province, killed around 60 people and left 88 missing. **23.** In the Niigata region of Japan, an earthquake measuring 6.8 on the

Richter scale killed 23 people and injured around 2,000. **25.** The interim president of Afghanistan, Hamid Karzai, was named as the winner of the country's first presidential election. **27.** In Thailand, 78 Muslim protesters died after they were taken into military custody and loaded onto overcrowded lorries. **29.** Norodom Sihamoni was crowned king of Cambodia.

NOVEMBER 2004

1. A British man, Anthony Flanaghan, was sentenced to death in Thailand after he was found guilty of drug possession with intent to sell. **12.** An earthquake measuring 6.0 on the Richter scale struck Alor island in eastern Indonesia, killing 17 and injuring 160 people. **17.** One thousand Indian troops were withdrawn from the disputed territory of Kashmir in a goodwill gesture timed to coincide with a visit to the region by Indian prime minister Dr Manmohan Singh. **21.** The Burmese military junta freed about 4,000 prisoners, including the dissident Min Ko Naing, who was jailed for 15 years after leading student pro-democracy protests. **20.** A typhoon struck the Philippines, causing flooding; a tropical storm on 23 November caused further flooding, in which around 65 people were killed and thousands were left homeless. **24.** In eastern China, the death sentence was carried out on Jia Qingyou, who was executed for injuring 25 schoolchildren with a kitchen knife. **26.** At least 17 people were killed, around 130 injured and 300 homes destroyed after an earthquake hit Indonesia's Papua province.

DECEMBER 2004

7. Hamid Karzai was sworn in as president of Afghanistan. **13.** In South Korea, Yoo Young Chul was sentenced to death for the murder of 20 pensioners and women between September 2003 and July 2004; he claimed to have eaten his victims' livers. **19.** Parliamentary elections were held in Turkmenistan. **20.** In China, 14 mine-workers were killed in an underground explosion at a coal mine in the province of Suchuan. In a reform of its legal system, Chinese officials announced that jury trials would be introduced in 2005. **21.** Police in Pakistan re-arrested Asif Ali Zardari, the husband of former Prime Minister Benazir Bhutto, after he failed to attend a hearing in a murder trial; he was released on 31 December. **23.** President Karzai of Afghanistan appointed a cabinet of 25 ministers, including three women. **26.** An underwater earthquake measuring nine on the Richter Scale created a tsunami in the Indian Ocean which struck the coasts of Indonesia, Thailand, Malaysia, India, Sri Lanka, Myanmar, the Maldives and eastern Africa, causing widespread devastation; the toll was eventually estimated at 175,000 dead, 107,000 missing and 1.75 million displaced.

JANUARY 2005

2. In the Quetta region of Pakistan, 35 people were killed in mudslides following heavy rainfall. A US soldier was killed in Afghanistan following a gunfight in the Shindand district. **3.** Pledges of international aid for the tsunami victims reached US$150 billion. **4.** The UN warned that it had received reports of child traffickers kidnapping orphaned children from areas affected by the tsunami. **8.** The Chinese government announced that the selective abortion of female foetuses would become illegal. **9.** Fourteen people died following riots in the northern Pakistan town of Gilgit. **13.** The Chinese government announced plans to build a 100-mile road link between

Taiwan and mainland China. **14.** The North Korean government announced that it would be prepared to resume six-party nuclear talks. **25.** Around 300 Hindu pilgrims were killed in a stampede at a religious festival in western India. **30.** An estimated 23 people were killed in a bus crash in southern Pakistan.

FEBRUARY 2005

1. In Nepal, King Gyanendra dismissed the government, declared a state of emergency and took control of the country. China's state oil company, the China National Petroleum Corporation, agreed to lend around US$6 billion to the Russian state oil company Rosneft. Nine survivors of the Indian Ocean tsunami were found in the Nicobar Islands. **3.** Around 52 people were killed in a train crash in the Indian province of Maharashtra. **6.** The Thai general election was won by the ruling Phak Thai Rak Thai party. **8.** A bus carrying five foreign journalists was attacked by gunmen in south Waziristan, Pakistan, and two journalists were killed. **10.** The North Korean government announced that it would not take part in six-nation talks aimed at ending North Korea's nuclear programme. **11.** A dam burst in Baluchistan, Pakistan, killing around 130 people. **14.** Around 200 mine-workers were killed in a gas explosion at a coal mine in north-east China. **17.** A car bomb in the southern Thai town of Sungai Kolok killed six people and injured 40. **20.** Seventy-nine people were confirmed dead and a further 120 feared drowned after a ferry accident near Dhakar, Bangladesh. **21.** Up to 40 people were killed following heavy rains and landslides in Bandung, western Java. **25.** Several independent newspapers and radio stations were closed by the Kyrgyz government in advance of elections. **27.** Parliamentary elections were held in Kyrgyzstan and Tajikistan. **28.** The Indian government announced that up to £3 billion of the government budget had been earmarked for poverty reduction schemes.

MARCH 2005

2. David Moran was appointed as the British ambassador to Uzbekistan; his predecessor resigned stating the Foreign Office's failure to condemn widespread human rights abuses in the country as his reason. **3.** In Indonesia, Abu Bakar Ba'asyir was sentenced to 30 months in jail for conspiring in the 2002 Bali bombing. **8.** The chief executive of Hong Kong, Tung Chee-hwa, resigned owing to ill health. **13.** Run-off elections to the Kyrgyz parliament were held in 40 constituencies. Donald Tsang became acting chief executive of Hong Kong; he was confirmed as the new chief executive on 12 June. **14.** The Japanese ambassador to South Korea was recalled following a diplomatic dispute between the two countries over a group of uninhabited islands in the Sea of Japan. China passed a law allowing Chinese military strikes on Taiwan if the island ever formally declared its independence. **15.** Thousands protested in the Kyrgyz capital, Bishkek, over alleged flaws in the recent elections, and demanded the president's resignation. Around 45 people were killed in a bomb attack on a Shia shrine in south-west Pakistan. **19.** Around 27 mine-workers were killed following a gas explosion at the Xishui colliery in Shouzhou, China. **21.** President Akayev of Kyrgyzstan ordered the Central Election Commission and the Supreme Court to investigate alleged election violations following further civil disturbances in the city of Osh. **23.** President Akayev sacked the Kyrgyz interior minister and the prosecutor general over their handling of the mass demonstrations. **25.** Protesters in Bishkek, Kyrgyzstan, stormed the presidential building, prompting the government to dissolve and President Akayev to flee the country; an opposition MP, Kurmanbek Bakiyev, was named by the outgoing government as acting president and prime minister of Kyrgyzstan. **28.** An earthquake, measuring up to 8.7 on the Richter Scale, struck off the coast of Indonesia, killing about 430 people. The king of Bhutan announced that a draft constitution establishing democratic multiparty rule had been approved.

APRIL 2005

3. Thousands of people took to the streets in Shenzhen, southern China, attacking Japanese-owned businesses and protesting at plans to offer Japan a permanent seat on the UN Security Council. The demonstrations were sparked by the publication of a controversial Japanese history textbook that allegedly played down events during Japan's occupation of China during the Second World War. **4.** President Akayev of Kyrgyzstan announced his resignation after the mass civil protests and dissolution of the government of Kyrgyzstan. **9.** Up to 200 workers were feared dead following an explosion at a garment factory in Dhaka, Bangladesh. **6.** A US military helicopter crashed in Afghanistan, killing all 16 service people on board. **10.** In China, protesters in Beijing demonstrated against Japan's attempt to gain a permanent seat on the UN Security Council. **11.** In central India, 53 Hindu pilgrims were killed when a dam was opened on the River Narmada. **27.** The Chinese parliament ruled that the term of the next Hong Kong chief executive would be cut from five years to two.

MAY 2005

3. In Lahore, Pakistan, a gas explosion at an industrial and residential complex killed 25 people. **11.** In Afghanistan, four protestors were shot dead by police during anti-US demonstrations in Jalalabad. **13.** Protestors clashed with police and soldiers in the eastern Uzbek city of Andijan; several hundred people are believed to have died. **14.** In the Taiwanese legislative election, the Democratic Progressive Party won the largest number of seats. **17.** UN investigators arrived in Jakarta, Indonesia, to inquire into alleged crimes against humanity that occurred during East Timor's move to independence. **22.** In Delhi, India, bombs exploded at two cinemas, killing one person and injuring 50. Over 4,000 people took part in a demonstration in Kathmandu, Nepal, demanding the restoration of the government. China closed nature reserves in the western Qinghai province following the discovery of the Asian avian flu virus in migrating geese. **23.** The Chinese prime minister, Wu Yi, cancelled a scheduled meeting with the Japanese prime minister Junichiro Koizumi in Tokyo. In Mongolia, Nambaryn Enkhbayar won the presidential election. **28.** Twenty-two people were killed when two bombs exploded in Tentena, Indonesia. **29.** In Pakistan, 24 people were killed and 100 injured by a suicide bomber at a mosque in Karachi. **31.** Six Kentucky Fried Chicken employees were killed when rioters set fire to their restaurant in Karachi, Pakistan.

JUNE 2005

1. Protesters in Bishkek, Kyrgyzstan, broke into the Supreme Court in an attempt to evict pro-opposition supporters who had occupied the building since April. **4.** The parliament of the Maldives voted unanimously for constitutional amendments to allow multiparty elections. **10.** The Kyrgyz MP Jyrgalbek Surabaldiyev was shot

dead in Bishkek. **12.** Around 87 children were killed when a flash flood hit a school in north-eastern China. **15.** In Sri Lanka, the People's Liberation Front (JVP) party left the ruling coalition government after President Chandika pledged to share tsunami relief aid with the Tamil rebels. **16.** A Canadian boy was shot dead during a six-hour siege at an international school in Siem Reap, Cambodia. **17.** In Kyrgyzstan, troops cleared the government headquarters after 2,000 people took over the building in protest at plans to bar a presidential candidate from standing in the forthcoming elections. **21.** The International Whaling Commission, meeting in Tokyo, rejected the reinstatement of commercial whaling by 29 votes to 23. **23.** Torrential rain in southern China killed 81 people and forced authorities to evacuate up to 900,000 more from their homes. **29.** In Afghanistan, 16 US soldiers were killed when their helicopter was shot down in Kunar province.

JULY 2005

2. Two US Navy SEAL troops were found dead in Afghanistan after going missing in action. **4.** In Afghanistan, 17 civilians were killed when US planes bombed a remote village in Kunar province. **5.** The Japanese parliament voted through six bills to privatise the country's postal system and its related customer services, insurance and savings businesses. In India, gunmen attacked security officers at the site of the Barbi mosque, which was destroyed by Hindu extremists in 1992. The Indian supreme court announced that Lal Krishna Advani, leader of the Bharatiya Janata party, would stand trial over the 1992 destruction of the Barbi mosque. **7.** President Arroyo of the Philippines refused to resign over allegations of vote-rigging in the 2004 presidential election. **10.** Voters in Kyrgyzstan elected former opposition leader Kurmanbek Bakiyev as president. Ten ministers resigned from the Philippine government and called on President Arroyo to resign. **11.** Four prisoners escaped from a US military prison at the Bagram air base, Afghanistan. **17.** The Indonesian government announced a peace accord with the Free Aceh Movement (Gam), including the withdrawal of Indonesian troops from the province and permitting Gam to form a political party. **18.** The Thai prime minister, Thaksin Shinawatra, was granted sweeping powers, such as the imposition of curfews and use of telephone tapping, to counter the growing insurgency in the south of Thailand. **19.** In Pakistan, armed police arrested 24 people suspected of having links with terrorist activities, including one man with alleged links to the London suicide bombers. **21.** China revalued the yuan. **25.** Top diplomats from the USA and North Korea met in Beijing, in advance of the expected resumption of six-party nuclear talks. In the Philippines, moves to impeach President Arroyo were initiated. **28.** Severe floods in western India killed around 800 people; the government announced on 4 August that 962 people had died and up to US$2.8 billion worth of damage had been caused in Mumbai. In China, protesters took control of the Communist Party headquarters in Qianjin after a series of land compensation disputes with the local government. **29.** The Uzbekistan government requested the withdrawal within six months of US personnel at the Karshi-Khanabad air base.

AUGUST 2005

2. In Thailand, Paul Chetwynd-Talbot, boyfriend of murdered British teacher Debra O'Hanlon, was arrested in connection with her death. **6.** Ceremonies were held in the Japanese city of Hiroshima to mark the 60th anniversary of the dropping of the first atomic bomb. **7.** Up to 102 miners were trapped after a coal mine in the southern Chinese province of Xingning was flooded. **8.** The Japanese prime minister called a snap general election for 11 September after the government's surprise loss of a key vote on the reformation of the country's postal service. **9.** Around 40 Nepalese soldiers were killed and 100 were reported missing after Maoist guerrillas assaulted an army camp in the remote north-western Kalikot district. **11.** Pakistan test-fired its first cruise missile at an undisclosed location. The Malaysian government declared a 'haze emergency' in several areas of Kuala Lumpur after pollution levels in the city rose. **12.** The Sri Lankan foreign minister Lakshman Kadirgamar was assassinated by a suspected sniper at his home in Colombo; on 14 August, the police announced that a dozen people had been arrested in connection with his assassination. **16.** In Afghanistan, 17 Spanish soldiers were killed in a helicopter crash near Herat. **22.** The Indonesian government announced that two battalions of combat troops had begun to withdraw from the province of Aceh, two weeks ahead of the planned pull-out. **26.** The supreme court of Sri Lanka ruled that President Kumaratunga would have to step down in December, dismissing her claims that a year left over from her first term entitled her to stay on as head of state until late 2006. The upper house of the Uzbekistan parliament approved legislation that would remove all US personnel from an air base in the south of the country. **30.** The Indonesian government granted amnesty to over 1,400 imprisoned members of the Free Aceh Movement, all of whom will be released from prison. India and Pakistan announced a joint agreement to release hundreds of civilians held in the jails of both countries and provide better consular access to all existing prisoners. **31.** In the Philippines, impeachment charges against President Arroyo were defeated in the country's legislature.

AUSTRALASIA AND THE PACIFIC

SEPTEMBER 2004
30. In a ceremony at the Museum of Ethnography in Stockholm, the bones of around 20 Australian Aborigines were returned to their descendants from the Kirrae Whurrung people in Victoria.

OCTOBER 2004
2. The Australian Justice Minister, Christopher Ellison, announced that 700 people were under investigation and 200 people had been arrested suspected of crimes including sexual abuse of minors, distributing pornography and child sex tourism. **10.** In the Australian general election, the Liberal-National Party coalition under prime minister John Howard won a fourth term of office. **15.** Ian Previte was jailed for life at Queensland's Supreme Court in Australia for the murder of the British backpacker Caroline Stuttle in 2002. **25.** Six men from Pitcairn Island in the Pacific were found guilty on 32 charges of sex crimes against children, including rape, sexual assault and indecent assault.

NOVEMBER 2004
Australia's Immigration Department published figures showing that the number of British immigrants into Australia had doubled in the past two years from 8,749 in 2002 to 18,272 in 2004. **26.** Around 300 Aborigines burnt down a police station in a riot on Palm Island, off

Australia's Queensland coast, after Cameron Doomadgee, a 35-year-old Aborigine, died a week earlier whilst in police custody.

DECEMBER 2004
9. The Civil Union Act, recognising the rights of unmarried partners, was passed by a vote of 65–55 by the New Zealand parliament.

JANUARY 2005
11. In Australia, eight people were killed in bush fires on the Eyre Peninsula, west of Adelaide. **18.** In Australia, the leader of the opposition Labor Party, Mark Latham, resigned from politics owing to ill health. **27.** Kim Beazley became leader of the Australian Labor Party.

MAY 2005
24. In Sidney, Australia, six Pitcairn Islanders were found guilty of sexually abusing young girls failed to have their convictions overturned.

JUNE 2005
1. The Indonesian embassy in Australia was closed after a package containing a suspected biological agent was discovered there. **4.** An Iraqi man was found guilty of people trafficking after a Brisbane court heard that he had smuggled 398 Iraqis into Australia.

JULY 2005
24. New Zealand prime minister Helen Clarke called a general election for 17 September.

AUGUST 2005
5. A gathering of scientific and political figures in Perth, Australia, were told that a tsunami early-warning system could be in place within a year if sufficient funding was made available. **25.** The Australian government announced that it would adopt a new national standard time based upon the atomic clock or Coordinated Universal Time (UTC), in place of Greenwich Mean Time. **29.** John Brogden, the leader of the Liberal Party in New South Wales, resigned after allegedly making sexist remarks at a dinner party about the Malaysian wife of a political rival; Mr Brogden was found unconscious at his office the following day and the police confirmed that he had tried to commit suicide.

EUROPE

SEPTEMBER 2004
1. Twenty Chechen terrorists took over 900 adults and children hostage in a school in Beslan, southern Russia, as the children returned after the summer holiday. The terrorists threatened to blow up the school if the Russian government did not withdraw its troops from Chechnya and release prisoners held after Chechen guerrilla attacks on the neighbouring region of Ingushetia. **2.** The siege of the school in Beslan continued; 15 children and 11 women were released following negotiations. **3.** The Beslan siege ended after two explosions followed by gunfire from within the school led Russian special forces to storm the building; official figures released the following day said that 323 people died during the siege and more than 600 were injured. **12.** The head of the Greek air force was dismissed following the death of Patriarch Petros VII of the African Orthodox Church and 16 others in a helicopter crash in northern Greece. **13.** In Russia, President Putin proposed that legislation should

be introduced by the end of 2004 to allow the Kremlin to nominate regional leaders, thereby abolishing regional elections, and to limit the number of parties in the Duma, the lower house of parliament. **15.** The Organisation of Petroleum Exporting Countries (OPEC) met in Vienna, Austria; delegates agreed to raise OPEC production by one million to 27 million barrels a day from 1 November 2004. In Iceland, Prime Minister David Oddsson, after 13 years in office, exchanged posts with the Foreign Minister, Halldor Asgrimsson, in accordance with a coalition deal made after the 2003 elections. **17.** In a statement posted on a website, Chechen rebel leader Shamil Basayev claimed responsibility for the Beslan school siege. **19.** In Germany, regional elections were held in Saxony and Brandenburg; in both states the ruling parties, the Christian Democrats and a Social and Christian Democrat coalition respectively, retained power but lost a percentage of the vote to far-right parties. **26.** In Turkey, the Grand National Assembly approved reforms to the Turkish penal code; a proposal to criminalise adultery was dropped after the European Commission threatened to postpone talks on Turkey's EU accession if the proposal received approval. **28.** Two female Italian aid workers, held hostage for three weeks in Iraq, arrived at Ciampino military airport in Rome. **29.** In Hungary, the National Assembly formally endorsed Ferenc Gyurcsany as prime minister in succession to Peter Medgyessy, who resigned on 25 August.

OCTOBER 2004

8. In France, the Court of Justice charged Charles Pasqua, the interior minister between 1993–5, with three offences of corruption during his time in office. **11.** In Russia, the Moscow Arbitration Court ruled that the Russian oil company Yukos must pay nearly all of a US$1.4 billion (£775 million) fine and penalties bill relating to unpaid taxes in 2001. **17.** In Belarus, a referendum was held in which 77.3 per cent of voters voted in favour of a constitutional change to the law restricting presidents to two terms in office. **22.** The Russian Federation became the 55th nation to ratify the Kyoto Protocol on global warming. **23.** In the UN-run Serbian province of Kosovo, just over half of Kosovo's 1.4 million voters participated in a general election resulting in victory for President Ibrahim Rugova of the moderate Albanian Democratic League of Kosovo (LDK) party. **31.** Ukraine's presidential election resulted in a near dead heat between the two major contenders, the incumbent prime minister Viktor Yanukovych and the leader of the main opposition party Our Ukraine, former prime minister Viktor Yushchenko.

NOVEMBER 2004

1. The Ukrainian electoral commission announced that as neither candidate in the presidential election had won more than 50 per cent of the vote, a second round of voting would take place. **9.** In Belgium, the high court banned the Vlaams Blok party, making it illegal for the party to receive funding of any kind, and forcing its disbandment. **15.** In the former Yugoslav republic of Macedonia, prime minister Hari Kostev resigned, claiming that ethnic Albanians in his coalition government were controlling the country's political agenda. **19.** In Russia, the Federal Property Fund announced that it would force the sale of Yugoskneftegaz, the main asset of oil company Yukos, at an auction on 19 December to reclaim some of Yukos's US$20 billion tax debt. **20.** Group Menatep, the largest shareholder in Yukos, filed a legal complaint against the

Russian state in an attempt to block the sale of the oil company's main asset. **21.** Following the second round of Ukraine's presidential election, supporters of both candidates claimed victory and riot police were deployed in Kiev and other cities as tensions rose between rival supporters in the streets. **24.** Demonstrations continued throughout Ukraine after the authorities declared Viktor Yanukovich the winner of the presidential election, despite the poll being widely condemned as flawed by western observers; thousands of opposition supporters called for Mr Yanukovich to accept electoral defeat and stand down in favour of Viktor Yushchenko. **27.** The supreme council of Ukraine ruled the presidential election invalid on the grounds of fraud and voted to appoint a new Central Electoral Commission. **28.** In France, former finance minister Nicolas Sarkozy took over from President Jacques Chirac as leader of the UMP party. The first round of Romania's presidential election took place. **30.** A half-day general strike took place in Italy in protest at government tax reforms announced in the 2005 Budget.

DECEMBER 2004

3. The Ukrainian Supreme Court ordered that a new presidential election be held on 26 December. Five small bombs planted by the ETA exploded on the outskirts of the Spanish capital Madrid; no one was injured. **8.** The Ukrainian parliament approved changes to electoral laws in preparation for the rerun presidential election. **10.** The Italian prime minister Silvio Berlusconi was acquitted by a Milan court of corruption charges relating to a corporate take-over involving his Fininvest company in the 1980s. **11.** Dr Michael Zimpfer, the director of a private clinic in Austria, claimed that the Ukrainian opposition leader Viktor Yushchenko was poisoned with dioxin during his election campaign; Mr Yushchenko was treated at the clinic in Vienna four days after falling ill on 6 September. **12.** In the second round of voting, Traian Basescu was elected president of Romania. **19.** In Russia, Yuganskneftegaz, the main asset of the oil company Yukos, was sold at auction to Baikal Finance Group for 260.75 billion roubles. **22.** Russia's state-owned oil company Rosneft bought the Baikal Finance Group, giving the government control of Yuganskneftegaz. **20.** Members of the Basque regional parliament voted in favour of proposals for greater autonomy from the Spanish government. **22.** Calin Tariceanu was appointed prime minister of Romania. **26.** In Ukraine, opposition leader Viktor Yushchenko claimed victory in the rerun presidential election. **27.** The Ukrainian election commission's preliminary results confirmed Viktor Yushchenko's victory, with 52.1 per cent of the vote to Viktor Yanukovych's 44.1 per cent; Mr Yanukovych contested the result, claiming irregularities. **30.** The Ukrainian Supreme Court and the Central Election Commission rejected calls from Viktor Yanukovych for the second-round election results to be investigated; Mr Yanukovych resigned as prime minister the following day. **31.** In Greece, a policeman was shot dead while guarding the home of Colonel Mark Blatherwick, Britain's military attaché.

JANUARY 2005

2. In the Croatian presidential election, incumbent Stjepan Mesic narrowly missed re-election with 49 per cent of the vote, one per cent off the 50 required for an outright victory. **3.** Djamel Beghal went on trial in France, accused of plotting a suicide bomb attack on the US embassy in Paris; he was found guilty on 15 March. **5.**

Former Ukraine prime minister Viktor Yanukovych asked the Supreme Court to annul the presidential election results due to fraud. In Chechnya, 14 Russian troops and three Chechen soldiers were killed in separate incidents. **7.** Thirteen people were killed in a train crash near Bologna, Italy. **10.** A ban on smoking in some public places came into effect throughout Italy. Viktor Yushchenko was officially declared winner of the Ukrainian presidential election. **12.** Eleven people were arrested following a series of raids on mosques throughout Germany. **13.** Jose Luis Zapatero, the Spanish prime minister, rejected calls to negotiate with the Basque regional premier Juan Jose Ibarretxe over planned autonomy for the Basque region. **14.** The trial of a former Argentine naval officer accused of genocide, torture and terrorism during Argentina's 'dirty war' of 1976–83, began in Spain following new laws allowing local prosecution for crimes committed in another country; he was found guilty and on 19 April was sentenced to 640 years in prison. **18.** In Toulouse, France, Airbus unveiled the A-380 passenger jet. **19.** The Supreme Court of Ukraine confirmed Viktor Yushchenko as the winner of the presidential election after rejecting Viktor Yanukovych's final appeal against the result. **23.** Viktor Yushchenko was sworn in as president of Ukraine. **24.** Yulia Tymoshenko was appointed prime minister of Ukraine. **27.** World leaders gathered at the site of Auschwitz to commemorate the 60th anniversary of the camp's liberation. Seven suspected Islamic militants were killed when Russian special forces stormed an apartment block in the Kabardino-Balkar region. **30.** One person was injured following a bomb blast in Denia, southern Spain. **31.** In France, 16 people appeared in court accused of manslaughter following the 1999 Mont Blanc tunnel fire. The UN war crimes tribunal at The Hague found former Yugoslav army general Pavle Strugar guilty of two charges and he was sentenced to eight years in prison.

FEBRUARY 2005
1. Pope John Paul II was admitted to hospital suffering from breathing difficulties. Four Moroccan citizens were arrested in Spain in connection with the Madrid train bombings in 2004. Three policemen were killed in Georgia in a bomb attack outside a police station. **2.** German government statistics showed that unemployment had reached its highest level since 1933, with 5 million people out of work. **3.** The prime minister of Georgia, Zurab Zhvania, was found dead in a flat in Tbilisi; his death was blamed on a carbon monoxide poisoning by a faulty appliance. **6.** Eighteen people were discovered dead from carbon monoxide poisoning in a holiday hostel near Todolella, eastern Spain. **7.** In Bern, Switzerland, a seven-hour siege by gunmen at the Spanish consulate ended when special forces troops stormed the building. **8.** The French government reformed its labour policy, allowing people to work longer than the established 35-hour week. The Danish general election was won by the incumbent Liberal Party. In Georgia, finance minister Zurab Nogaideli was appointed prime minister. **9.** The Hungarian prime minister Ferenc Gyurcsany was forced to apologise for remarks made during a private party in which he called members of the Saudi Arabian football team 'terrorists'. In Spain, 43 people were injured after a car bomb exploded in Madrid. **10.** Kristiina Ojuland, the Estonian foreign minister, was dismissed from government following allegations that over 90 confidential documents had disappeared from her office. **20.** In Portugal, the opposition Socialist Party was confirmed as the winner of

the general election. A general election in the 'Turkish Republic of Northern Cyprus' was won by the incumbent Republican Turkish Party with 44 per cent of the vote. US president George W. Bush arrived in Belgium at the start of a four-day visit to Europe. **23.** At a court martial at a British army base in Osnabrück, Germany, three British soldiers were found guilty of abuses against detainees and prisoners of war in Iraq. The Czech government announced that compensation would be paid to the victims of the 1968 Soviet-led invasion that defeated the Prague Spring reformist movement. **24.** Pope John Paul II was re-admitted to hospital and underwent minor surgery. **28.** Russian president Vladimir Putin dismissed six ministers. Serbia-Montenegro's foreign minister, Vuk Draskovic, was fined for refusing to testify against a group of security officials accused of attempting to kill him.

MARCH 2005
3. The trial began in France of 66 adults charged with sexually abusing 45 children over a three-year period; on 27 July, 65 of the defendants were convicted of running a paedophile ring. **4.** The former Ukrainian interior minister Yuri Kravchenko was found dead a few hours before prosecutors were due to question him about the murder of a journalist in 2000. **6.** Parliamentary elections were held in Moldova; the Party of Communists of the Republic of Moldova secured 46.1 per cent of the vote while the Electoral bloc won 28.41 per cent. Prince Rainier of Monaco was admitted to hospital with a severe lung infection. **8.** Aslan Maskhadov, the former Chechen president and one of Russia's most wanted men, was killed by Russian troops in the Chechen village of Tolstoy Yurt. Ramush Haradinaj resigned as prime minister of Kosovo after being indicted by the UN war crimes tribunal in The Hague. Spanish police arrested a Moroccan man in connection with the 2004 Madrid train bombings. **9.** In southern Italy, 40 houses were destroyed by landslides in the village of Cavallerizzo after severe storms and heavy rain. **10.** An unarmed group of Iranian protesters began a hunger strike aboard a Lufthansa jet at Brussels airport. In Paris, a French magistrate placed Continental Airlines under formal investigation over the Concorde crash at Charles de Gaulle airport in 2000. **13.** Two people were injured following a bomb attack on a church near Venice, Italy. **15.** The Kosovan president, Ibrahim Rugova, escaped injury when a bomb exploded as his convoy passed through the capital city, Pristina. The annual snow sculpture festival in Greenland was cancelled owing to an unprecedented heatwave. **18.** A Dutch businessman, Frans van Anraat, appeared before a Dutch court accused of international war crimes and complicity in genocide over his alleged involvement in the gassing of Iraqi Kurds in 1988. **20.** In Bosnia-Hercegovina, Vinko Pandurevic, a former Bosnian-Serb general, gave himself up to war crimes investigators. **22.** The French parliament adopted changes to the standard 35-hour working week, allowing employees to work longer hours. Estonian prime minister Juhan Parts announced that he would resign and dissolve his government following a parliamentary vote of no confidence in justice minister Ken-Marti Vaher. **23.** Police arrested José Segurola Querejeta, the suspected leader of the Basque separatist group ETA, in southern France. Bajram Kosumi was sworn in as the new interim prime minister of Kosovo. **29.** Dragan Covic, the Croat member of Bosnia's tripartite joint presidency, was dismissed by the chief international envoy Lord Ashdown after Covic was charged with serious corruption during his time as finance minister in 2000. **30.** Alexei Pichugin,

a former senior executive of the Russian oil company Yukos, was jailed for 20 years for murder and attempted murder. Spanish police arrested a man after discovering 755kg of dynamite and 750kg of ammonium nitrate in his garage in Catalonia. **31.** Prince Albert became regent of Monaco as Prince Rainier's condition deteriorated.

APRIL 2005

1. In Spain, 12 people were arrested in connection with the 2004 Madrid train bombings. **2.** Pope John Paul II died in his private apartment in the Vatican City. **3.** Police discovered 100kg of the plastic explosive Semtex hidden in a heavy goods vehicle 20 miles from Calais, France. **4.** Jorg Haider, the former leader of Austria's Freedom party, announced that he was forming a new political party, the Alliance for the Future of Austria. **5.** Prince Rainier of Monaco died. **7.** Dutch police arrested 18 people in Amsterdam in connection with human trafficking. **8.** The funeral of Pope John Paul II took place in St Peter's Square, Vatican City. **13.** The Ukrainian prime minister Yuliya Tymoshenko cancelled a diplomatic visit to Russia after the Russian prosecutor-general said that she was liable to be arrested there on charges of bribery. **14.** The German ambassador to Switzerland was sacked after publicly criticising foreign minister Joschka Fischer. **15.** The funeral of Prince Rainier of Monaco took place in Monte Carlo. Around 21 people were killed in a fire at a Paris hotel. In Italy, the Union of Christian Democrats and the New Italian Socialist Party resigned from the coalition government, accusing prime minister Silvio Berlusconi of ineffective leadership. **17.** Mehmet Ali Talat won the presidential election in the 'Turkish Republic of Northern Cyprus'. **18.** In the Vatican City, 115 cardinals gathered in conclave to elect the next Pope; on 19 April, Cardinal Joseph Ratzinger was elected pope and took the name Benedict XVI. In Russia, the Krasnoyarsk, Evenki and Taimyr regions voted to unite. **20.** In Italy, Silvio Berlusconi resigned as prime minister and dissolved the coalition government. **23.** Silvio Berlusconi's new centre-right coalition government was sworn into office. **24.** Pope Benedict XVI was inaugurated in a special mass at the Vatican City. Thousands demonstrated in the Ukrainian capital, Kiev, to demand more government compensation for the 1986 Chernobyl nuclear disaster. **25.** Stanislav Gross resigned as prime minister of the Czech Republic following a financial scandal; Jiri Paroubek was appointed prime minister. The Georgian government announced that 3,000 Russian troops stationed in the country would withdraw by 2008. The Kazakh government published a law effectively banning street rallies during and after elections. In Turkey, a memorial service was held to mark the 90th anniversary of the Gallipoli landings. **26.** Thirty demonstrators were arrested in the Belarusian capital, Minsk, during a rally to commemorate the 19th anniversary of the Chernobyl disaster. **27.** The maiden flight of the Airbus A-380 took place at Toulouse, France.

MAY 2005

8. World leaders gathered in Moscow's Red Square to commemorate the 60th anniversary of VE day. The Spanish government announced an amnesty for 700,000 illegal migrants, allowing them to apply for legal residency and work permits. **9.** In Belgium, two Rwandan citizens Etienne Nzabonimana and Samuel Ndashyikirwa, appeared before a Belgian court charged with genocide. **10.** US President Bush began a visit to Georgia. **12.** The Turkish government announced that it would order a retrial of the jailed Kurdish leader Abdullah Ocalan following a ruling by the European Court of Human Rights. The remains of 38 people, thought to be Bosnian Muslims murdered during the 1992–5 war, were found 50 miles north of Sarajevo. **17.** In Russia, Nurpashi Kulayev, the sole survivor of the militant group that carried out the Beslan school siege, went on trial accused of murder, banditry and terrorism. The Spanish parliament voted to open talks with the Basque separatist group ETA. **22.** The German chancellor Gerhard Schroder announced that he would seek to bring forward the date of the general election after a heavy defeat for his government in regional elections. **25.** In Spain, 52 people were injured when a car-bomb planted by ETA exploded in Madrid. In Slovenia, a former post-war communist leader and deputy chief of Slovenia's secret police was charged with ordering the murders of up to 234 people in the aftermath of the Second World War. Much of Moscow lost electricity after an explosion at the Shagino power plant. **26.** In Sarajevo, NATO troops raided the home of Radovan Karadzic's wife and children looking for information on his whereabouts. In Spain, Arnaldo Otegi, the leader of Batasuna, the outlawed political wing of ETA, was jailed for membership of the organisation. **30.** The French prime minister, Jean-Pierre Raffarin, resigned following the electorate's rejection in a referendum of the EU constitution treaty. The Russian government announced that Russian troops would be withdrawn from Russia's two remaining military bases in Georgia. **31.** Former interior minister Dominique de Villepin was appointed prime minister of France. In Russia, the former head of the Yukos oil company, Mikhail Khodorkovsky, was found guilty of fraud and tax evasion and sentenced to nine years in jail.

JUNE 2005

1. An Italian court jailed five members of the left-wing Red Brigades for the murder of a senior government adviser in 1999. **3.** In Russia, state-owned oil company Gazprom announced it was buying a 50 per cent controlling stake in the national daily newspaper *Izvestia*. **5.** Switzerland voted to join the Schengen agreement zone by 2007. Thousands of people marched in Madrid in protest at government plans to hold talks with ETA. **8.** In Denmark, a car belonging to immigration minister Rikke Hvilshoej was set alight at her home; the culprits were believed to be opponents of the government's immigration policies. **10.** A Basque separatist group attacked a civilian airport near Madrid with home-made mortars. **16.** In France, two men were jailed for assisting Richard Reid, the British man convicted of attempting to blow up a passenger jet with explosives hidden in his shoe. **18.** The Basque separatist group ETA announced that it was ceasing all operations against Spanish politicians in advance of proposed talks between itself and the Spanish government. **20.** Spanish police arrested 28 people in 11 cities along the Costa del Sol in an operation against organised crime. **25.** A general election was held in Bulgaria; the Bulgarian Socialist Party (BSP) won the most seats but failed to secure an overall majority and began negotiations to form a coalition government with other parties. **28.** The former German junior defence minister Ludwig-Holger Pfahls admitted to a Berlin court that he had accepted bribes over arms sales to Saudi Arabia in the 1990s; on 12 August he was jailed for two years and three months for bribery and tax evasion offences. **29.** A Belgian court convicted two Rwandan half-brothers of assisting acts of genocide in Rwanda in

1994. **30.** The Spanish parliament voted to approve a law allowing same-sex couples to marry and adopt children.

JULY 2005

2. The German parliament supported a motion of no confidence in Chancellor Gerhard Schroder, clearing the way for general elections. **3.** Parliamentary elections were held in Albania. **4.** Prince Albert of Monaco publicly acknowledged that he has a 22-month-old son, born out of wedlock. **5.** In Berlin, 19-year-old Sven Jaschan went on trial, accused of developing the Sasser and Netsky software viruses that infected almost 18 million computers worldwide. **10.** A bomb exploded in the Turkish resort of Cesme, injuring 20 people. **11.** A ceremony to commemorate the tenth anniversary of the Srebrenica massacre was held at the Potocari cemetery in Bosnia-Hercegovina. In Ukhta, Russia, 19 people were killed when a container of liquid gas was thrown through a shop window. **12.** Prince Albert II was installed as head of state in Monaco. **16.** Five people, including a British national, were killed in a suicide bomb attack at the Turkish resort of Kusadasi. **17.** Forest fires destroyed about 12,000 acres of woodland in the Guadalajara region of Spain; 14 people died in the fires. **18.** In Belgrade, eight aides of the former Yugoslav president Slobodan Milosevic were convicted of murdering former Serbian president Ivan Stambolic in 2000. **21.** The Russian energy minister announced that 40,000 tons of chemical weapons would be deactivated and destroyed by 2012. **25.** An Italian court issued arrest warrants for six alleged CIA agents said to be involved in the kidnapping of an Egyptian imam. **28.** Fires in the suburbs of Athens caused severe damage to homes and businesses. In Belarus, special forces troops and police took control of a Polish community building which the police claimed was being used for espionage; the Polish ambassador to Belarus was recalled following the incident. **29.** A man wanted in connection with attempted bomb attacks in London on 21 July was arrested in Rome.

AUGUST 2005

1. In Germany, police discovered the remains of nine unborn babies buried in a garden in Brieskow-Finkenheerd, a village near to the Polish border. **3.** In France, an investigation began after 351 foetuses and stillborn babies were found stored illegally at a Paris mortuary. **5.** Kurdish insurgents killed five soldiers in a rocket attack on a police station in south-east Turkey. **6.** A Tunisair passenger plane crashed into the sea off the Sicilian coast, killing 13 people. **7.** Seven Russian sailors who had been trapped in a submarine at the bottom of Berezovaya Bay were brought safely to the surface following a British-led rescue mission. **11.** The Polish ambassador to Russia delivered a letter to the Russian foreign ministry calling for greater security for embassy staff after two Polish diplomats were attacked outside the Polish Embassy in Moscow. **14.** A Cypriot passenger jet crashed 25 km north of Athens, killing all 121 people on board. **15.** In Bulgaria, the Bulgarian Socialist Party and the National Movement party agreed to form a coalition government, ending seven weeks of political stalemate since the general election. **17.** Brother Roger Shutz, the 90-year-old Swiss-born founder of the Taizé Christian ecumenical community in France, was stabbed to death at a prayer service by a Romanian woman. **18.** Pope Benedict XVI began a visit to his home country of Germany. **19.** After a year-long retrial, a German court found Mounir el Motassadeq, a friend of one of the 9/11

suicide bombers, guilty of belonging to a terrorist cell. **21.** The Portuguese government requested assistance in dealing with some 50 forest fires around the country. **23.** The jailed Russian businessman Mikhail Khodorkovsky announced that he was going on hunger strike after his business partner, Platon Lebedev, also in jail, was moved to solitary confinement. Torrential rain caused the worst flooding in central Europe for a century; over 40 people were killed, and in Austria and Germany hundreds were evacuated from their homes. **26.** Around 17 people, including 13 children, died in a fire at an apartment block in Paris used to house immigrants. **30.** President Chirac of France promised urgent measures to ease the housing crises for hundreds of immigrants after a fire at another apartment block in Paris killed seven immigrants. **31.** A French judge investigating the 2000 Concorde crash at Charles de Gaulle airport announced that he would summon seven aviation officials for questioning over the disaster.

EUROPEAN UNION

SEPTEMBER 2004

10–11. The EU Council of Economic and Finance Ministers, meeting in Scheveningen, Netherlands, agreed in principle on the need to reform the stability and growth pact governing participation in the single European currency. **23.** The Turkish prime minister, Recep Tayyip Erdogan, arrived in Belgium to meet the European Commission and make a case for Turkey's membership of the EU.

OCTOBER 2004

6. The European Commission voted in favour of beginning EU accession negotiations with Turkey after the country satisfied the democratic and human rights criteria set by the EC. The European Commission announced that Romania and Bulgaria were on track to join the European Union on 1 January 2007. **11.** All 25 EU foreign ministers agreed to lift an 18-year-old arms embargo on Libya. **27.** MEP Robert Kilroy-Silk resigned from UKIP following an internal dispute over his refusal to abandon his attempt to become the party's national leader. **29.** In Rome, heads of government and foreign ministers of the 25 EU member states signed a treaty providing for the introduction of an EU constitution.

NOVEMBER 2004

4. José Manuel Barroso, the incoming president of the European Commission, presented his new team of commissioners to the European Parliament. Franco Frattini, Italy's foreign minister, replaced Rocco Buttiglione as European Commissioner for Justice and Civil Liberties, and Andris Piebalgs replaced Latvian nominee Ingrida Udre, who was under investigation for electoral fraud. **11.** Lithuania ratified the EU constitution treaty. **18.** The European Parliament voted by 449 to 149, with 82 abstentions, to approve the new 24-member European Commission. **22.** The new European Commission began its five-year term of office.

DECEMBER 2004

2. The EU formally took over responsibility from NATO for peacekeeping operations in Bosnia. **8.** The EU announced that the 25 EU countries had agreed in principal to lift a 15-year-old embargo on arms exports to China, subject to a new code of conduct for arms sales. **17.** The 25 EU leaders agreed on conditions for the commencement of accession negotiations with Turkey. The conditions had to be fulfilled by Turkey prior to EU accession talks, scheduled to begin on 3 October 2005. **20.** Hungary ratified the EU constitution treaty. **21.** The European Commission began talks on national fishing quotas with national fisheries ministers.

JANUARY 2005

9. The European Commissioner for Trade, Peter Mandelson, was appointed as a communications strategist within the European Commission, becoming the only EU commissioner to sit on the board of four out of the five decision-making committees. **10.** Nicholas Burns, the US Ambassador to NATO, criticised the majority of EU countries for failing to increase defence budgets at a time when NATO is trying to expand its role. Opponents of the EU constitution from several countries announced that they had joined together to form the European No campaign, headed by Thomas Rupp from Germany and heavily financed by British businesses. **13.** Dalia Grybauskaite, the EU's Budget Commissioner, said that Britain must increase its EU contributions over the next seven years and give up its annual budget rebate in order to help Europe's poorest countries as Britain was now the second-richest country in the EU. **21.** The European Commission told Britain to phase out tax breaks for offshore companies based in Gibraltar because they flout EU competition rules. **26.** The British Foreign Secretary, Jack Straw, revealed that the question to be asked in a British referendum on the EU constitution would be 'Should the United Kingdom approve the treaty establishing a constitution for the European Union?'.

FEBRUARY 2005

1. Slovenia ratified the EU constitution treaty. **14.** The EU's Environment Commissioner, Stavros Dimas, threatened Britain with legal action after Margaret Beckett, the British Environment Secretary, set out new quotas for Britain's carbon dioxide emissions which would exceed the levels agreed with the EU in 2004. **16.** The European Commission announced plans to spend €8 million (£5.5 million) to inform citizens of some European member states about the proposed EU constitution. **20.** In a national referendum in Spain, 76.7 per cent of voters approved ratification of the EU constitution treaty; the treaty was ratified on 18 May following parliamentary approval. **24.** The European Parliament adopted legislation put forward by the Unfair Commercial Practices Directive to ban 28 different commercial practices, including advertising aimed at children, telephone prize-draw scams, pyramid marketing schemes and 'bait' advertising; the legislation was backed by the British government and will replace all existing national consumer protection laws in Britain when it comes into force in 2007.

MARCH 2005

1. The European Commissioner for Health, Markos Kyprianou, announced a €72 million (£49 million) campaign to encourage people in the EU to stop smoking. **8.** The House of Lords' select committee on the EU called for an urgent review of the EU budget, claiming that Britain was contributing too much money toward the budget and not receiving a proportionally fair amount of money from it in return. **15.** The European Court of Justice ruled that European students living in other EU member states should be eligible to maintenance loans from the country in which they are living if they attend

secondary school or university in that country. **16.** EU accession talks with Croatia were suspended because of Croatia's repeated failure to hand over a suspected war criminal, Ante Gotovina, to the war crimes tribunal. **30.** The EU supported Paul Wolfowitz's appointment as president of the World Bank.

APRIL 2005

6. Italy ratified the EU constitution treaty. **19.** Greece ratified the EU constitution treaty.

MAY 2005

11. The European Parliament voted to change working hours legislation to prevent employees working more than 48 hours per week. Slovakia ratified the EU constitution treaty. **24.** EU ministers announced a US$80 billion aid and development programme for Africa and countries in the developing world. **25.** Austria ratified the EU constitution treaty. **27.** Germany ratified the EU constitution treaty. **29.** In a national referendum in France, 54.68 per cent of voters rejected ratification of the EU constitution treaty.

JUNE 2005

1. In a national referendum in the Netherlands, 61.6 per cent of voters rejected ratification of the EU constitution treaty. **2.** Latvia ratified the EU constitution treaty. **6.** The UK government announced that it was suspending the parliamentary process for ratifying the EU constitution treaty. **17.** The European Council decided that, in light of the referendum results in France and the Netherlands, the original timetable for the introduction of the EU constitution was untenable and would need to be revised. **30.** Cyprus ratified the EU constitution treaty.

JULY 2005

1. The United Kingdom assumed the presidency of the European Union. **6.** Malta ratified the EU constitution treaty. The European parliament voted against a bill to allow the potential patenting of computer software. **10.** In a national referendum in Luxembourg, 57 per cent of voters approved ratification of the EU constitution treaty; final approval by parliament is required for ratification and the vote has yet to take place. **12.** The EU fined the French government £13.75 million for contravention of the EU fisheries law over a 20-year period. **18.** Following an air crash in Greece, the European Commission announced that it would publish a list of all airlines that fail to meets its safety standards.

MIDDLE EAST

SEPTEMBER 2004

1. Insurgents in Iraq released a video showing the killing of 12 Nepalese labourers kidnapped on 19 August 2004. In Israel, suicide bombers blew up two buses in Beersheba, killing 16 and injuring 91 others. **4.** In Iraq, US forces launched a raid on an alleged militant cell near Mosul. **6.** Israeli forces launched an air attack on a Hamas training camp in Gaza City, killing 13 Palestinians and wounding 45. **14.** Around 60 people died and more than 100 were wounded by a suicide car bomb in Baghdad. **18.** In Iraq, Tawhid wal Jihad insurgents released video footage of three hostages (a British engineer and two Americans), threatening to behead them if Iraqi women prisoners were not released within 48 hours. **20.** Tawhid wal Jihad released a video showing the beheading of one of the American hostages. **21.** Tawhid wal Jihad announced that the second American hostage had been killed. **22.** Tawhid wal Jihad released a video of the third hostage, Kenneth Bigley, in which he made a direct plea to the British prime minister to intervene. **26.** Izz el-Deen al-Sheikh Khalil, a leading figure of the Palestinian Hamas group, was killed in Damascus, Syria, by a bomb planted in his car. **30.** Around 34 children were killed in Baghdad by three suicide bombs, set off simultaneously as they played football and were given sweets by US soldiers.

OCTOBER 2004

3. US and Iraqi troops captured the Iraqi city of Samarra, killing 125 insurgents and capturing 88. **8.** It was reported that the British hostage Ken Bigley had been beheaded on 7 October. **13.** US and British investigators found nine mass graves near the Iraqi town of Hatra, containing the bodies of around 300 women and children. **19.** In Iraq, a charity worker with dual British and Iraqi nationality was kidnapped in west Baghdad by insurgents and later shown in a video broadcast on television. **20.** Lebanon's prime minister, Rafik Hariri, resigned. **21.** At a US court martial in Baghdad, Staff Sergeant Ivan Frederick was sentenced to eight years in prison for abusing and humiliating Iraqi detainees at the Abu Ghraib prison. **26.** The Knesset voted in favour of the Israeli government's plan to withdraw Jewish settlers from Jewish settlements in the Palestinian territory of Gaza.

NOVEMBER 2004

1. In Israel, a suicide bomber killed three and injured dozens in Tel Aviv. **3.** Sheikh Khalifa bin Zayed al-Nahyan was appointed president of the United Arab Emirates by its Supreme Council. **7.** The interim government in Iraq declared a 60-day state of emergency after insurgents killed 21 Iraqi police and carried out kidnappings, assassinations and car bombings throughout the predominantly Sunni centre of the country. **11.** Yasser Arafat, the Palestinian president, died in Paris after travelling to France for medical treatment. **15.** The NBC television network broadcast footage of a US marine shooting dead at point-blank range an Iraqi prisoner in a mosque in Fallujah. **16.** It was reported that Margaret Hassan, an aid worker for CARE International taken hostage several weeks earlier, had been shot dead by Iraqi insurgents. **21.** It was announced that 80 per cent of Iraq's foreign debt (about £25 billion) would be written off by creditor countries. Iraq's electoral commission announced that a general election would be held on 30 January 2005.

DECEMBER 2004

3. Insurgents killed over 30 people in two dawn attacks in Baghdad. **8.** An official cease-fire was agreed by the Palestinian and Israeli governments following talks in the Egyptian resort of Sharm al-Sheikh. **13.** A car bomb in Baghdad killed 13 people, including seven US servicemen. **16.** The Iraqi Deputy Communications Minister, Qassim Mehawi, was assassinated in Baghdad. **19.** In Iraq, three election officials were assassinated in Baghdad. Three bombs in the Iraqi holy cities of Najaf and Karbala killed 67 people and injured 200. **21.** The British prime minister, Tony Blair, visited Baghdad. Two French journalists kidnapped in Iraq in August were released unharmed. In Israel, the central committee of the opposition Labour party voted to join Ariel Sharon's Lukid party in a coalition government. **22.** Iran closed all its borders with Iraq and banned the movement of people

to or from the country as attacks against Iranian pilgrims in Iraq increased. **27.** A car bomb exploded outside the Baghdad headquarters of the Supreme Council for Islamic Revolution in Iraq, the main Shia political party. **29.** In Iraq, a bomb exploded inside a suspected insurgent safe house, killing 30 people, including six police officers. **30.** Two Syrian men were sentenced to death in Damascus for carrying out a car-bomb attack in April.

JANUARY 2005

2. A suicide car bomb in Iraq killed 18 national guardsmen. **4.** The Governor of Baghdad, Ali al-Haidari, was assassinated in Baghdad. **5.** The British Embassy in Yemen was closed after a specific terrorist threat was made. **6.** In Iraq, nine US soldiers were killed by a roadside bomb. **8.** A presidential election was held in the Palestinian Autonomous Areas; Mahmoud Abbas was elected president with 66.3 per cent of the vote. **10.** The deputy police chief of Baghdad, Amer Ali Nayef, was assassinated in Baghdad. **13.** Five Israeli civilians were killed and five wounded in a Palestinian attack on a Gaza border crossing; the following day the Israeli government announced that it was suspending contact with the Palestinian administration because of the attack. **17.** In Iraq, the Archbishop of Mosul, Basile Georges Casmoussa, was kidnapped; he was freed the following day. Eight Iraqi soldiers were killed at a military checkpoint in northern Baghdad. **19.** A number of bombings in Baghdad killed about 26 people. **21.** A suicide bomb attack on a mosque in Baghdad killed 15 people. Hundreds of Palestinian police and security guards were deployed in northern Gaza in an effort to stop militant rocket attacks on Jewish settlements. **26.** Thirty-one US soldiers were killed in a helicopter crash in northern Iraq. Four US marines were killed in combat in the Anbar province of Iraq and two US soldiers were killed in Baghdad. Fifteen Iraqi soldiers were killed and 30 wounded in a suicide bomb attack in the north-western town of Sinjar. **28.** Hamas won control of seven of the ten councils in elections in Gaza. **29.** Two US civilians were killed in a bomb attack on the US embassy in Baghdad **30.** In Iraq, elections to the Transitional National Assembly took place amid tight security; the turnout was generally high, but low among Sunni Muslims. Ten British service personnel were killed in a plane crash near Baghdad. **31.** Security forces in Kuwait killed four suspected Islamic militants.

FEBRUARY 2005

3. The Israeli government announced that it would free up to 900 Palestinian prisoners and move its security forces out of five West Bank towns. **4.** In Iraq, an Italian journalist, Giuliana Sgrena, was kidnapped in Baghdad. **6.** Twenty-two Iraqi policemen were killed in a gun battle with militants in Mahawil, south of Baghdad. **7.** Suicide attacks in the Iraqi towns of Baquaba and Mosul killed about 27 people. **8.** Twenty-one Iraqi army recruits were killed in a suicide bomb attack in Baghdad. **10.** Palestinian president Mahmoud Abbas dismissed three senior security commanders following a Hamas mortar attack on a Jewish settlement in Gaza. Elections were held in Saudi Arabia. **14.** The former Lebanese prime minister Rafik Hariri and 16 other people were killed in a car bomb attack in Beirut; Mr Hariri's death provoked a strong backlash against Syrian involvement in Lebanese political life and massive demonstrations against the Syrian military presence in the country. **17.** It was announced that Omri Sharon, the son of Israeli prime minister Ariel Sharon, was to be charged with perjury and fraud following a long-running investigation. **18.** Three separate suicide bombings in Baghdad killed more than 30 people. **20.** The Saudi Arabian ambassador to Hungary was recalled after the Hungarian prime minister described members of the Saudi national football team as terrorists. The Israeli government approved plans to withdraw settlers from parts of the Gaza Strip and the West Bank. **21.** Palestinian MPs rejected a list of proposed cabinet members put forward by prime minister Ahmed Qureia on the grounds there were too many closely associated with the former Arafat administration. As part of confidence-building measures between Israel and Palestine, 500 Palestinian prisoners were released from an Israeli jail. **22.** In Iraq, Ibrahim al-Jaafari was confirmed as first choice for the position of prime minister. An earthquake in Iran's Kerman province killed nearly 500 people. **24.** Palestinian MPs approved a new cabinet list submitted by prime minister Ahmed Qureia. The Lebanese government announced that Syria would begin redeploying troops to the eastern Bekka Valley region. **25.** In Iraq, three US troops were killed by a roadside bomb. Four Israelis were killed in a suicide bomb attack on a Tel Aviv nightclub. **27.** Sabawi Ibrahim al-Hassan, the half-brother of Saddam Hussein and one of the most wanted men in Iraq, was handed over to Iraqi security chiefs following his capture in Syria. **28.** The pro-Syrian Lebanese government resigned following a series of massive demonstrations. In Iraq, a suicide car bomb at a police recruitment centre in Hilla killed about 125 people and injured 130.

MARCH 2005

2. In Iraq, Barwez Mahmoud Marwani, a senior judge involved in the trial of Saddam Hussein, was assassinated in Baghdad. **3.** In Saudi Arabia, the country's first local elections were held. **5.** In Iraq, Giuliana Sgrena, the Italian journalist who was kidnapped on 4 March, was released by her captors; the car carrying Ms Sgrena to Baghdad airport was accidentally fired upon by US soldiers, killing Nicola Calipari, the secret service agent who helped secure her release. The Syrian president, Bashar al-Assad, announced that Syrian troops would begin to withdraw from Lebanon. **9.** Iraqi police found a mass grave containing 26 bodies in the town of Qaim. **10.** A suicide bomber at a Shia mosque in Mosul, Iraq, killed about 46 people. Omar Karami was reinstated as prime minister of Lebanon after he won the support of 78 MPs in the 128-seat parliament, and attempted to form a government. **11.** In Egypt, the opposition leader Ayman Nour was released from prison and announced that he would stand in the presidential election in September 2005. **13.** In the Gaza Strip, around 2,500 men stormed the parliament building in protest at high unemployment. **15.** Representatives from over 40 countries attended the opening of a new Holocaust memorial museum in Jerusalem. **16.** The Iraqi Transitional Nation Assembly was officially opened and the 275 deputies were sworn in. **17.** In Palestine, several Palestinian militant groups, including Hamas, agreed a conditional truce with Israel. **19.** A bomb attack at a Qatar theatre killed one person and injured 12. **21.** The Israeli government announced plans to build up to 3,500 homes in the West Bank. **23.** The Iranian government announced that it would hold talks on its nuclear programme with British, French and German officials. Iraqi soldiers, backed by US aircraft, attacked a suspected insurgent training camp in Baghdad. **28.** The Knesset rejected calls for a referendum on the

Israeli government's plans to withdraw from all Jewish settlements in the Gaza Strip.

APRIL 2005

2. Yemeni security forces attacked and killed about 36 insurgents in the northern province of Saada, in retaliation for an attack on a Yemeni army camp. **3.** In Iraq, insurgents attacked the Abu Ghraib prison, injuring 44 US soldiers and 12 prisoners. **5.** Jalal Talabani, a Kurdish politician, was named as president of Iraq. **7.** A bomb in Cairo's old city killed around 20 people. Ibrahim al-Jaafari, a Shia, was appointed as prime minister-designate of Iraq. **8.** The British embassy in Yemen was closed owing to the high risk of terrorist attack. **12.** The Iranian parliament voted to legalise abortion in cases where the mother's life is in danger or a child would be disabled. **13.** Omar Karami resigned as prime minister of Lebanon after failing to form a coalition government. **14.** A suicide bomb in Baghdad killed 15 people. **16.** President Lahoud of Lebanon appointed Najib Mikati prime minister pending elections in May. In Madaen, Iraq, Sunni extremists took around 60 people hostage. **19.** Iran closed down the Tehran office of the al-Jazeera television station, accusing it of promoting ethnic unrest in the country. **20.** In Jerusalem, the Israeli consul to The Hague, Uriel Yitzhaki, was arrested on suspicion of supplying 150 passports in return for money and perquisites. In Iraq, the bodies of 57 people were discovered in the River Tigris. **21.** In Baghdad, 11 civilian contract workers were killed after their helicopter was shot down by suspected insurgents. **22.** In Lebanon, two of the country's most senior security advisers resigned as the UN investigated the death of the former prime minister Rafik Hariri. **24.** In Iraq, two bombs exploded near a Shia mosque in Baghdad, killing around 15 people and wounding 60. **25.** Syrian forces completed their withdrawal from Lebanon after almost 30 years of occupation. **28.** The Iraqi assembly approved the new government of prime minister-designate Ibrahim al-Jaafari. **30.** Four US soldiers were killed in the Iraqi town of Tall Afar.

MAY 2005

2. In Israel, the minister for Jerusalem and diaspora affairs, Natan Sharansky, resigned in protest at the government's plan to withdraw Jewish settlers and troops from the Gaza Strip. **3.** The Iraqi government was sworn in. **4.** A suicide bomb in Arbil, Iraq, killed about 60 people. **6.** A car bomb in Baghdad killed 58 people. **10.** The governor of Iraq's western Anbar province, Raja al-Mahalawi, was kidnapped by gunmen. The lower house of the Egyptian parliament voted to allow more than one candidate to stand in the presidential election in September 2005. **11.** In Iraq, suicide bombings in Tikrit, Baghdad and Hawija killed 71 people. **16.** Kuwait's parliament passed a law allowing women to vote in elections and to stand as candidates. **23.** In Iran, Ayatollah Ali Khamenei ordered the council of guardians, a powerful religious watchdog, to reassess its decision to bar more than 1,000 prospective candidates in the forthcoming presidential election. A UN inspection team in Lebanon confirmed that all Syrian military personnel had left the country. **26.** The Iraqi government announced that an operation to counter insurgent bombings in Baghdad would begin with the deployment of up to 40,000 Iraqi security personnel. In a referendum in Egypt, 83 per cent of voters approved a proposal to allow more than one candidate to stand in presidential elections. **27.** King Fahd of Saudi Arabia was admitted to hospital with suspected pneumonia. **29.** In

Lebanon, the first round of voting took place in a four-stage parliamentary election. The Israeli government approved the release of 400 Palestinian prisoners.

JUNE 2005

4. US soldiers in Iraq discovered a network of underground bunkers used by insurgents. **7.** The Syrian deputy president Abdel Khaddam announced that he was stepping down to allow a younger person to assume the role. **12.** The first female minister, Massouma al-Mubarak, was appointed to the Kuwaiti government **13.** Douglas Wood, an Australian citizen captured by Iraqi insurgents and held for six weeks, was freed in a joint US-Iraqi military operation. **15.** A presidential election took place in Iran; no candidate won outright victory. **19.** The final round of elections took place in Lebanon; the election was won by the anti-Syrian opposition alliance led by Saad Hariri, son of former prime minister Rafik Hariri. A suicide bomber killed 23 people in a Baghdad restaurant. **22.** A US spy plane crashed in the United Arab Emirates. **24.** The second round of voting in the Iranian presidential election was won by Mahmoud Ahmadinejad. **27.** In Jerusalem, Taysir Hayb, an Israeli soldier, was convicted of the manslaughter of the British student and peace activist Tom Hurndall; on 11 August, Hayb was sentenced to eight years in jail. **30.** The Lebanese parliament chose Fouad Siniora as prime minister.

JULY 2005

2. The Egyptian ambassador to Iraq, Ihab al-Sherif, was kidnapped outside his Baghdad residence; on 7 July, a militant group claimed that it had killed the ambassador. **4.** The Palestinian militant group Hamas declined to join the cabinet of President Abbas after being offered seats in a proposed coalition government. **5.** In Iraq, insurgents attacked a diplomatic convoy. **12.** A suicide bomber killed two Israelis in the town of Netanya. A car bomb attack on the convoy of Lebanon's interim defence minister, Elias Murr, killed two people and injured the minister. **13.** A suicide bomb in Iraq killed 27 people, including one US soldier. **16.** A suicide bomber driving a hijacked petrol tanker killed 100 people and injured 160 in the Iraqi town of Musayyib. Three British soldiers were killed by a roadside bomb in Iraq. **19.** Two Iraqi legislators involved in drafting the country's new constitution were assassinated in Baghdad. Jewish settlers opposed to the withdrawal from the Gaza Strip clashed with Israeli security forces near the Gush Katif settlement. **21.** Two Algerian diplomats were kidnapped in Iraq; on 27 July an insurgent group claimed to have killed them. **23.** Three bombs exploded at the Egyptian resort of Sharm el-Sheikh, killing 88 people. **24.** A suicide bomb attack on a police station in Baghdad killed 40 people. **26.** In Lebanon, Samir Geagea, a former Christian militia leader who had served 11 years of a jail sentence for the 1987 assassination of prime minister Rashid Karami, was freed by a Lebanese court. **28.** President Mubarak of Egypt announced he would stand for re-election in the presidential election on 7 September.

AUGUST 2005

1. King Fahd of Saudi Arabia died, and was succeeded by his half-brother, Crown Prince Abdullah. Egyptian police shot dead one of the suspects in the Sharm el-Sheikh hotel bombings. **3.** In Iraq, 14 US marines and a civilian translator were killed by a roadside bomb near Haditha. In Iran, President Ahmadinejad was confirmed in office by Iran's supreme leader, Ayatollah Khamenei. King Abdullah of Saudi Arabia was invested at a ceremony in Riyadh. **4.** An Israeli soldier killed five Arabs on a bus in Shfaram. **7.** The Israeli finance minister, former prime minister Binyamin Netanyahu, resigned from the government in protest at the planned Israeli withdrawal from Gaza. **8.** Two UN aid workers and their driver were kidnapped by militants in Gaza, but were later freed by Palestinian security forces. The US government closed its diplomatic missions in Saudi Arabia following a security alert. The Iranian government announced that it had restarted its uranium conversion programme; the move prompted an emergency meeting of the International Atomic Energy Agency and raised the possibility of UN sanctions. **9.** The Palestinian president, Mahmoud Abbas, announced that a general election would be held in January 2006. **14.** President Ahmadinejad of Iran named his new cabinet. **15.** The deadline for completing the draft of the new Iraqi constitution was extended by a week after the main ethnic and sectarian groups failed to agree on its content. **16.** In Gaza, the Israeli government's deadline for the voluntary withdrawal of Jewish settlers passed with many still refusing to leave their homes; Israeli troops moved into the Gush Katif settlement in preparation for the clearing of the settlements. **16.** In Afghanistan, 17 Spanish soldiers were killed in a helicopter crash near Herat. **17.** Three simultaneous bomb explosions in Baghdad killed 43 people. **18.** Israeli police and troops clashed with Jewish settlers as they sought to evict them from the Kfar Darom settlement. In Saudi Arabia, police and security forces claimed to have killed an al-Qae'da leader, Salih al-Awfi, in a shoot-out in Medina. **19.** In Jordan, terrorists with links to al-Qae'da claimed responsibility for three simultaneous rocket attacks on a US warship and a military hospital. **22.** Iraqi government submitted a draft constitution to parliament but the vote on it was delayed after Sunni leaders objected to some points, fearing that federalism could lead to the break-up of Iraq. **23.** The Israeli government announced that settlers had been cleared from all the Jewish settlements in Gaza. **26.** In Iraq, the constitution committee announced that the extended deadline for the submission of a fully agreed constitution had passed without consensus. **28.** The Iraqi constitution was delivered to parliament amid protestations from minority Sunni politicians, who said they would try to defeat the constitution in the October referendum. **30.** In Lebanon, four men were arrested in connection with the murder of former prime minister Rafik Hariri. **31.** In Iraq, around 700 people died and more than 300 were injured in a stampede at a religious festival in Baghdad.

OBITUARIES

HRH PRINCESS ALICE, DUCHESS OF GLOUCESTER, GCB, CI, GCVO, GBE, Grand Cordon of Al Kamal
Princess Alice was born Lady Alice Christabel Montagu-Douglas-Scott on Christmas Day 1901, the third daughter of the 7th Duke of Buccleuch and Queensberry. Lady Alice married Prince Henry, Duke of Gloucester and third son of King George V on 6 November 1935. Both of her sons were born during the Second World War; the eldest, Prince William, was tragically killed in a flying accident on 28 August 1972.

Princess Alice took a great interest in the work of the Red Cross and the Order of St John and had close connections with the Women's Royal Voluntary Service and the Women's Royal Air Force, which she headed since 1940. In 1945 she moved with her family to Australia, where the Duke of Gloucester was Governor-General from 1945–7. There she became Commandant-in-Chief of the Australian Women's Land Army and of the three women's services. On her return to Britain Princess Alice increased her charitable commitments becoming president or patron of many organisations, including several hospitals.

Princess Alice became the oldest living member of the royal family, reaching the age of 102, before dying peacefully in her sleep at Kensington Palace on 29 October 2004.

Aberdare (4th), Lord, KBE, PC, politician, who as a hereditary peer was elected to remain in the House of Lords following the 1999 reforms; president of the Tennis and Rackets Association (1972–2004), aged 85 – d. 23 January 2005, b. 16 June 1919

Aiken, Air Chief Marshal Sir John, KCB, Commander British Forces Near East (1973–6); director-general of Intelligence, MOD (1978–81), aged 82 – d. 31 May 2005, b. 22 December 1922

Allen, Dave, comedian, aged 68 – d. 10 March 2005, b. 6 July 1936

Al-Nahyan, Sheikh Zayed bin Sultan, president of the United Arab Emirates (1971–2004), aged 86 – d. 2 November 2004, b. 1918

Al-Saud, King Fahd ibn Abdul Aziz, king and prime minister of Saudi Arabia (1982–2005), aged 82 – d. 1 August 2005, believed to have been born in 1923

Arafat, Yasser, Palestinian leader (1974–2004), aged 75 – d. 11 November 2004, b. 24 August 1929

Austin, Vice-Adm. Sir Peter, aged 84 – d. 13 May 2005, b. 16 April 1921

Avedon, Richard, photographer, aged 81 – d. 1 October 2004, b. 15 May 1923

Axelrod, Julius, American biochemist and joint winner of the 1970 Nobel Prize for Physiology, aged 92 – d. 29 December 2004, b. 30 May 1912

Bancroft, Anne, American actor, aged 73 – d. 6 June 2005, b. 17 September 1931

Bellow, Saul, American novelist, aged 89 – d. 5 April 2005, b. 10 June 1915

Benenson, Peter, British lawyer and founder of Amnesty International, aged 83 – d. 25 February 2005, b. 31 July 1921

Bethe, Hans, German-born physicist, winner of the 1967 Nobel Prize for his work on stellar and solar energy, aged 98 – d. 6 March 2005, b. 2 July 1906

Bishop, Sir Frederick, CB, CVO, civil servant and director of the National Trust (1971–5), aged 89 – d. 2 March 2005, b. 4 December 1915

Blacker, Gen. Sir Jeremy, KCB, CBE, Master-General of the Ordnance (1991–5), aged 65 – d. 17 March 2005, b. 6 May 1939

Blatch, Baroness, CBE, PC, politician, deputy leader of the Opposition in the House of Lords (2000–5), aged 67, d. 31 May 2005, b. 24 July 1937

Blumenfeld, Simon, author and journalist, aged 97 – d. 13 April 2005, b. 25 November 1907

Bolton, Michael, silversmith, aged 66 – d. 7 January 2005, b. 24 October 1938

Brown, Bill, footballer, aged 73 – d. 30 November 2004, b. 8 October 1931

Buller, John, composer, aged 77 – d. 12 September 2004, b. 7 February 1927

Britton, Sir Edward, CBE, general secretary of the National Union of Teachers (1970–5), aged 95 – d. 3 January 2005, b. 7 December 1909

Brown, Vice-Admiral Sir David, KCB, Flag Officer Plymouth (1982–5), aged 77 – d. 13 July 2005, b. 27 November 1927

Bruce of Donington, Lord, aged 92 – d. 18 April 2005, b. 3 October 1912

Bryson, Adm. Sir Lindsay, KCB, Controller of the Navy (1981–5), aged 80 – d. 24 March 2005, b. 22 January 1925

Callaghan of Cardiff, Lord, KG, PC, Labour prime minister (1976–9), aged 92 – d. 26 March 2005, b. 27 March 1912

Calton, Patsy, Liberal Democrat MP for Cheadle (2001–5), aged 56 – d. 29 May 2005, b. 19 September 1948

Campbell of Croy, Lord, MC and bar, PC, Conservative MP for Moray and Nairn (1959–74), Secretary of State for Scotland (1970–4); created a life peer in 1974, aged 83 – d. 26 April 2005, b. 8 June 1921

Carlisle of Bucklow, Lord, PC, QC, cabinet minister (1979–81), aged 76 – d. 14 July 2005, b. 8 July 1929

Carson, Johnny, American television presenter, aged 79 – d. 23 January 2005, b. 23 October 1925

Chapple, Lord, leader of the Electrical Trades Union (1966–) and chairman of the Trades Union Congress (1983–4); awarded a life peerage in 1985, aged 83 – d. 19 October 2004, b. 8 August 1921

Chisholm, Shirley, American politician, the first black woman elected to Congress (1968–83), aged 80 – d. 1 January 2005, b. 30 November 1924

Clark of Kempston, Lord, PC, Conservative MP, aged 86 – d. 4 October 2004, b. 18 October 1917

Clough, Brian, footballer and manager, aged 69 – d. 20 September 2004, b. 21 March 1935

Cook, Robin, PC, MP, Secretary of State for Foreign Affairs (1997–2001), leader of the Commons (2001–3) and MP for Livingston (1983–2005), aged 59 – d. 6 August 2005, b. 28 February 1946

Corfield, Sir Frederick, PC, QC, Conservative MP for South Gloucester (1955–74), aged 90 – d. 25 August 2005, b. 1 June 1915

Craig, Barbara, Principal of Somerville College, Oxford (1967–80), aged 89 – d. 25 January 2005, b. 22 October 1915

Crook, Arthur, editor of *The Times Literary Supplement* (1959–74), aged 93 – d. 15 July 2005, b. 16 February 1912

Crossley-Holland, Joan, MBE, potter and founder of the Oxford Gallery, aged 92 – d. 12 January 2005, b. 3 April 1912

Curtis, John, editor and publisher, aged 76 – d. 3 February 2005, b. 25 December 1928

Dacie, Sir John, FRS, haematologist and founder of the Leukaemia Research Fund (1960), aged 92 – d. 12 February 2005, b. 20 July 1912

Debreu, Gerard, French-born mathematician and economist, winner of the 1983 Nobel Prize for Economics, aged 83 – d. 31 December 2004, b. 4 July 1921

Derrida, Jacques, French philosopher and literary theorist, aged 74 – d. 8 October 2004, b. 15 July 1930

Doll, Sir Richard, CH, epidemiologist, aged 92 – d. 24 July 2005, b. 28 October 1912

Donaldson of Lymington, Lord, PC, Master of the Rolls (1982–92), aged 84 – d. 31 August 2005, b. 6 October 1920

Duisenberg, Wim, first president of the European Central Bank (1998–2003), aged 70 – 31 July 2005, b. 9 July 1935

Dworkin, Andrea, feminist author, aged 58 – d. 9 April 2005, b. 26 September 1946

Emery, Sir Peter, Conservative MP for Reading (1959–66), Honiton (1967–97) and Devon East (1997–2001), aged 78 – d. 9 December 2004, b. 27 February 1926

Evans, Gwynfor, president of Plaid Cymru (1945–81) and MP for Carmarthen (1966–70 and 1974–9), aged 92, d. 21 April 2005, b. 1 September 1912

Eyadema, Gnassingbe, president of Togo (1967–2005), aged 69 – d. 5 February 2005, b. 26 December 1937

Faulkner, Max, OBE, golfer, aged 88 – d. 26 February 2005, b. 29 July 1916

Fisher, Sir Henry, lawyer, banker and president of Wolfson College, Oxford (1975–85), aged 87 – d. 10 April 2005, b. 20 January 1918

Fitt, Lord, MP for Belfast West (1966–83) and former leader of the Social Democratic and Labour Party in Northern Ireland, aged 79 – d. 26 August 2005, b. 9 April 1926

FitzWalter (21st), Lord, aged 90 – d. 14 October 2004, b. 15 January 1914

Franklin, Gretchen, actor, aged 94 – d. 11 July 2005, b. 7 July 1911

Garang, John, vice-president of Sudan, aged 60 – d. 30 July 2005, b. 23 June 1945

Gibbs, Field Marshal Sir Roland, Chief of the General Staff (1976–9), aged 83 – d. 31 October 2004, b. 22 June 1921

Godwin, Fay, photographer, aged 74 – d. 27 May 2005, b. 17 February 1931

Hastings, Sir Stephen, MC, MP for Mid-Bedfordshire (1960–83), aged 83 – d. 9 January 2005, b. 4 May 1921

Hanson, Lord, Conservative peer and businessman, aged 82 – d. 1 November 2004, b. 20 January 1922

Heath, Sir Edward, KG, MBE, PC, Conservative Prime Minister (1970–4), aged 89 – d. 17 July 2005 b. 9 July 1916

Holland, Sir Kenneth, CBE, QFSM, fire-fighter, aged 86 – d. 3 June 2005, b. 20 September 1918

Hunter, Bob, Canadian environmental activist and co-founder of Greenpeace, aged 63 – d. 2 May 2005, b. 13 October 1941

Johnson, Derek, athlete and 800 m silver medallist at the 1956 Olympic Games in Melbourne, aged 71 – d. 30 August 2004, b. 5 January 1933

Kear, Janet, OBE, ornithologist, aged 71– d. 24 November 2004, b. 13 January 1933

Kilby, Jack, inventor of the microchip, winner of the Nobel Prize for Physics in 2000, aged 81 – d. 20 June 2005, b. 8 November 1923

King of Wartnaby, Lord, businessman, chairman of British Airways (1981–93), aged 87 – d. 12 July 2005, b. 29 August 1918

Kintore (13th), Earl of, chief of the Clan Keith, aged 65 – d. 30 October 2004, b. 22 February 1939

Kübler-Ross, Elisabeth, Swiss-born physician, author and pioneer of terminal care, aged 78 – d. 24 August 2004, b. 8 July 1926

Lane, Lord, PC, AFC, Lord Chief Justice of England (1980–92), aged 87 – d. 22 August 2005, b. 17 July 1918

Lloyd, Maude, ballerina (1927–40) and, jointly with her husband, ballet critic for *The Observer* under the pseudonym 'Alexander Bland' (1955–82), aged 96 – d. 27 November 2004, b. 16 August 1908

Leigh, Janet, American actor, aged 77 – d. 3 October 2004, b. 6 July 1927

Leinster (8th), The Duke of, aged 90 – d. 3 December 2004, b. 27 May 1914

Lothian (12th), Marquess of, aged 82 – d. 11 October 2004, b. 8 September 1922

Lympany, Dame Moura, DBE, concert pianist, aged 89 – d. 28 March 2005, b. 18 August 1916

Markova, Dame Alicia, DBE, ballerina, aged 94 – d. 2 December 2004, b. 1 December 1910

McGeown, Prof. Mollie, nephrologist whose work at Belfast City Hospital spearheaded the development of kidney transplantation, aged 81 – d. 21 November 2004, b. 19 July 1923

Meadows, Bernard, sculptor and Professor of sculpture, Royal College of Art (1960–80), aged 89, d. 12 January 2005, b. 19 February 1915

Merchant, Ismail, film producer, aged 68 – d. 25 May 2005, b. 25 December 1936

Meyer, Sir Anthony, Bt., Conservative MP for Eton and Slough (1964–6), West Flint (1970–83) and Clwyd North-East (1983–92), aged 84 – d. 24 December 2004, b. 27 October 1920

Miller, Arthur, American playwright, aged 89 – d. 10 February 2005, b. 17 October 1915

Mills, Sir John, CBE, actor, aged 97 – d. 23 April 2005, b. 28 February 1908

Mowlam, Dr Mo (Marjorie), PC, Labour politician, Secretary of State for Northern Ireland (1997–9), aged 55 – d. 19 August 2005, b. 18 September 1949

Murray, Dame Rosemary, DBE, vice-chancellor of the University of Cambridge (1975–7), aged 91– d. 8 October 2004, b. 28 July 1913

Nicholson, Bill, footballer and manager of Tottenham Hotspur Football Club (1958–74), aged 85 – d. 23 October 2004, b. 26 January 1919

Nicolson, Nigel, MBE, writer, politician and founder of Weidenfeld and Nicolson publishers, aged 87 – d. 23 September 2004, b. 3 May 1926

Ogilvy, Sir Angus, KCVO, PC, husband to HRH Princess Alexandra, The Hon. Lady Ogilvy, and second son of the 12th Duke of Airlie, aged 76 – d. 26 December 2004, b. 14 September 1928

Orme, Lord, Labour MP for Salford West (1964–83) and Salford East (1983–97), aged 82 – d. 28 April 2005, b. 5 April 1923

Pain, Lt.-Gen. Sir Rollo, KCB, MC, head of British Defence Staff, Washington (1975–8), aged 83 – d. 14 April 2005, b. 11 May 1921

Page, Sir Frederick, CBE, FRS, aero-engineer, aged 88 – d. 29 May 2005, b. 20 February 1917

Patriarch Petros VII of Alexandria, spiritual leader of Africa's Greek Orthodox community, aged 55 – d. 11 September 2004, b. 3 September 1949

Paolozzi, Sir Eduardo, CBE, artist, aged 81, d. 22 April 2005, b. 7 March 1924

Pope John Paul II, His Holiness (Karol Wojtyla), appointed Archbishop of Krakow, 1964, created Cardinal, 1967, assumed pontificate 16 October 1978, aged 84 – d. 2 April 2004 in Rome, b. 18 May 1920 in Poland

Peel, John, broadcaster and columnist, aged 65 – d. 25 October 2004, b. 31 August 1939

Pereira, Sir Charles, FRS, tropical agriculturist, aged 91 – d. 19 December 2004, b. 12 May 1913

Peyton, Kate, BBC producer and news reporter, killed on assignment in Somalia, aged 39 – d. 9 February 2005, b. 13 December 1965

Phillips, Hugh, FRCS, orthopaedic surgeon and president of the Royal College of Surgeons (2004–5), aged 65 – d. 24 June 2005, b. 19 March 1940

Polworth (10th), Lord, Minister of State, Scottish Office (1972–4), aged 88 – d. 4 January 2005, b. 17 November 1916

Pratt, Caroline, showjumper, aged 42 – d. 4 September 2004, b. 23 June 1962

Prince Rainier III of Monaco, aged 81 – d. 6 April 2005, b. 31 May 1923

Ratcliffe, Derek, conservationist, architect of the 1977 Nature Conservation Review, which identified important wildlife habitats in Britain, aged 75 – d. 23 May 2005, b. 29 July 1929

Ramone, Johnny (John Cummings), guitarist, aged 55 – d. 15 September 2004, b. 8 October 1948

Reeve, Christopher, US actor, aged 52 – d. 10 October 2004, b. 25 September 1952

Richards, Lt.-Gen. Sir John, KCB, KCVO, Commandant General Royal Marines (1977–81) and Marshal of the Diplomatic Corps (1982-92), aged 77 – d. 5 October 2004, b. 21 February 1927

Ridley, Dame Betty, DBE, Third Church Estates Commissioner (1972–81), aged 95 – d. 1 August 2005, b. 10 September 1909

Robin, Gordon, director of the Scott Polar Research Institute, Cambridge (1958–82), aged 83 – d. 21 September 2004, b. 17 January 1921 in Melbourne, Australia

Roll of Ipsden, Lord, KCMG, CB, aged 97 – d. 30 March 2005, b. 1 December 1907

Rotblat, Prof. Sir Joseph, FRS, recipient of the Nobel Prize for Peace (1995), aged 96 – d. 31 August 2005, b. 4 November 1908

Rothschild, Dame Miriam, DBE, FRS, naturalist, entomologist and conservationist, aged 96 – d. 20 January 2005, b. 5 August 1908

Rue, DBE, Dr Dame (Elsie) Rosemary, founder of the 'part-time training scheme for married women doctors' in the 1960s and president of the Women's Medical

Federation (1982–3), aged 76 – d. 24 December 2004, b. 14 June 1928

Russell (5th), Earl, Professor of British history, King's College, London (1990–2002) and Liberal Peer, aged 67 – d. 14 October 2004, b. 15 April 1937

Sadie, Stanley, CBE, musicologist, writer and editor of the 20-volume *The New Grove Dictionary of Music and Musicians,* aged 74 – d. 21 March 2005, b. 30 October 1930

Scarman, Lord, PC, OBE, Lord of Appeal in Ordinary and author of the report on the Brixton riots of April 1981, aged 93 – d. 8 December 2004, b. 29 July 1911

Scott, Sir Nicholas, KBE, Northern Ireland Minister (1986–7), Social Security Minister (1987–94) and Conservative MP for Paddington South (1966–74) and Chelsea (1974–97), aged 71 – d. 6 January 2005, b. 5 August 1933

Sams, Eric, linguist and musical and literary theorist, aged 78 – d. 13 September 2004, b. 3 May 1926

Saunders, Dame Cicely, OM, DBE, founder of the modern hospice movement, aged 87 – d. 14 July 2005, b. 22 June 1918

Shaw, Artie, American jazz clarinettist, aged 94 – d. 30 December 2004, b. 23 May 1910

Shearman, William, founder of Crisis, the charity for the homeless, aged 61 – d. 17 June 2005, b. 16 November 1937

Sheppard of Liverpool, Lord, English cricket captain (1954), Bishop of Liverpool (1975–97), aged 75 – d. 5 March 2005, b. 6 March 1929

Sontag, Susan, American writer, political activist and theorist, aged 71 – d. 28 December 2004, b. 16 January 1933

Smieton, Dame Mary, DBE, civil servant and Permanent Secretary at the Ministry of Education (1959–63), aged 102 – d. 23 January 2005, b. 5 December 1902

Spender, Humphrey, photographer, textile designer and painter, aged 94 – d. 11 March 2005, b. 19 April 1910

Tait, Adm. Sir Gordon, KCB, DSC, Second Sea Lord (1977–9), aged 83 – d. 29 May 2005, b. 30 October 1921

Thomas, Frank, Disney Studios animator (1934–1978) whose work included *Snow White and the Seven Dwarfs* (1937) and *Cinderella* (1950), aged 92 – d. 8 September 2004, b. 5 September 1912

Thompson, Sir Donald, Conservative MP for Sowerby (1979–83) and Calder Valley (1983–97), party whip and Lord Commissioner of the Treasury (1983–6) and Parliamentary Secretary to the Ministry of Agriculture, Fisheries and Food (1986–9), aged 73 – d. 14 March 2005, b. 13 November 1931

Thompson, Hunter S., American writer, aged 67 – d. 20 February 2005, b. 18 July 1937

Trintignant, Maurice, French racing driver, aged 87 – d. 12 February 2005, b. 30 October 1917

Trotman, Lord, chairman and chief executive of the Ford Motor Company (1993–8), created a life peer in 1999, aged 71 – d. 26 April 2005, b. 22 July 1933

Tyrrell, David, CBE, FRS, virologist and head of the Common Cold Research Unit (1982–90), aged 79 – d. 2 May 2005, b. 19 June 1925

Vandross, Luther, American soul singer, aged 54 – d. 1 July 2005, b. 20 April 1951

Vane, Sir John, FRS, pharmacologist, winner of the Nobel Prize for Medicine in 1982 for his discovery in 1976 of the blood-clotting inhibitor prostaglandin and his work on aspirin, aged 77 – *d.* 19 November 2004, *b.* 29 March 1927

Vasconcellos, Josefina de, MBE, sculptor, aged 100, *d.* 20 July 2005, *b.* 26 October 1904

Velthuijs, Max, Dutch children's author and illustrator whose work was translated into over 50 languages, aged 81 – *d.* 25 January 2005, *b.* 22 May 1923

Walker, Prof. George, FRS, volcanologist, aged 78 – *d.* 17 January 2005, *b.* 2 March 1926

Wardington (2nd), Lord, book collector, aged 91 – *d.* 6 July 2005, *b.* 22 January 1924

Whaddon, Lord, Labour MP for King's Lynn (1964–70), aged 78 – *d.* 16 August 2005, *b.* 14 August 1927

Whipple, Fred, astronomer, aged 97 – *d.* 30 August 2004, *b.* 5 November 1906

Whiteley, Richard, OBE, television presenter, aged 61 – *d.* 26 June 2005, *b.* 28 December 1943

Whyte, The Very Revd James, Moderator of the General Assembly of the Church of Scotland (1988–9), aged 85 – *d.* 17 June 2005, *b.* 28 January 1920

Wilkins, Maurice, CBE, FRS, biophysicist, winner of the 1962 Nobel Prize for Physiology or Medicine together with Crick and Watson, for discovering the structure of DNA, aged 87 – *d.* 5 October 2004, *b.* 16 December 1916

Williams, Clifford, theatre director, aged 78 – *d.* 20 August 2005, *b.* 30 December 1926

Williamson, Audley Bowdler, inventor of Swarfega, aged 88 – *d.* 21 November 2004, *b.* 28 February 1916

Winskill, Air Cdre Sir Archibald, KCVO, CBE, DFC and bar, AE, fighter pilot and former Captain of The Queen's Flight (1968–82), aged 88 – *d.* 9 August 2005, *b.* 24 January 1917

Wonfor, Andrea, OBE, television executive, aged 60 – *d.* 10 September 2004, *b.* 31 July 1944

Wood, Ivor, children's television animator who worked on *The Magic Roundabout* and *The Wombles,* aged 72 – *d.* 13 October 2004, *b.* 4 May 1932

Wright, Sir Denis, GCMG, ambassador to Iran (1963–71), aged 94, *d.* 18 May 2005, *b.* 23 March 1911

Wright, Sir Edward, mathematician and principal and vice-chancellor of University of Aberdeen (1962–76), aged 98 – *d.* 2 February 2005, 13 February 1906

Zhvania, Zurab, Prime Minister of Georgia (2004–5), aged 41 – *d.* 3 February 2005, *b.* 12 September 1963

Ziyang, Zhao, General Secretary of the Chinese Communist Party (1987–9), aged 85 – *d.* 17 January 2005, *b.* 17 October 1919

ARCHAEOLOGY

ROCK ART OF THE STONE AGE DWELLERS

Compared to the rich and varied cave paintings of Continental Europe, British upper Palaeolithic (Old Stone Age) caves appeared barren and devoid of art. Convention had it that Britain was so close to the ice sheets that the lives of hunters here were too fraught for any such indulgence. This soon changed when archaeologist Paul Bahn and a team that included cave art specialists from Spain decided to take a fresh look at the caves at Creswell Crags near Worksop on the Nottinghamshire-Derbyshire border. Amazingly, unseen by hordes of sightseers to the area over many years, they spotted not just one or two, but dozens of engravings.

In the cliffs of Creswell Crags there is a series of small caves, most of them inhabited at various times during the last Ice Age, particularly around 13,000 years ago. The region has given its name to the main stone tool industry in Britain at the time – 'Creswellian' – roughly equivalent to the late Magdalenian on the Continent.

Antiquarian investigators had excavated cave floors at Creswell in the 1870s and discovered a series of major occupation sites – Robin Hood's Cave, Pin Hole Cave, and Mother Grundy's Parlour, all on the south-facing Derbyshire side of the valley, and Church Hole, on the opposite, north-facing Nottinghamshire side. The excavators found bones of extinct animals like hyena, mammoth and bison, as well as stone and bone tools – but almost no art: just a couple of engravings on bone. These represented the only figurative art of the period known from Britain, and compared poorly even with discoveries in Belgium and Germany, let alone France or Spain, where the corpus runs to thousands of examples.

Perhaps it was this extreme paucity of portable art that caused Palaeolithic specialists to assume that Britain had no cave art. Yet why should this be so – given that much of Britain was occupied in the late Upper Palaeolithic? The problem could lie in the sheer difficulty of evidence-gathering. In cave art, engravings greatly outnumber paintings, but unlike paintings, they are often difficult to see. They usually need to be lit from the side, since that is how they were made, and if lit from the front may be invisible. So it takes a great deal of experience of decorated caves to be able to detect and decipher engraved figures, and to differentiate them from natural cracks and animal claw marks.

Paul Bahn and his team made their first significant discovery in Church Hole, which revealed a figurative panel of engravings, dubbed 'the bird panel', since most of the team believe it to show several birds. Then a second image was seen: a half-metre-long herbivore. Finally, with bright lights and scaffolding installed, more engravings appeared – of a bison, a small herbivore, a headless horse and two triangles, a dozen separate figures in all.

Later, searching the Church Hole entrance chamber, a bas-relief image of a bird with a long curved bill appeared, taking the form of an ibis or flamingo. This first image in the chamber gave the key to reading other parts of the ceiling, and several more bas-reliefs were detected, including what seemed to be a bison, a complete bear, and a large red-deer stag. The ceiling turned out to be decorated over its entire surface – all 14 square metres of it.

This small cave produced a total of up to 90 recognised figures, including engravings, bas-reliefs and paintings. Two of the caves on the opposite side of the gorge have also now revealed some interesting examples of rock art. The style is firmly of the Upper Palaeolithic Magdalenian period – a perfect fit with the radiocarbon dates from Creswellian occupation levels.

The meaning of such images is open to debate. Probably they were linked with the rituals of a hunting community, one concerned to ensure an abundance of prey and success in its pursuit and slaughter. Whatever the explanation, the Creswell discoveries have demonstrated that the need served by such images was general among Upper Palaeolithic peoples and Britain is not an exception in being without Ice Age art. Indeed, Church Hole is now a site of international importance, having produced the richest of all Upper Palaeolithic carved ceilings.

A BRONZE AGE MEGA AND SOME HOLY COWS

Most prehistoric settlements are small. Even when numerous structures are found, it often seems that only a few were actually contemporary. But at Corrstown near Portrush in County Derry, archaeologists working in advance of a proposed housing development unearthed a Middle Bronze Age village of 52 roundhouses.

The houses were closely and equally spaced. A large metalled roadway ran through part of the settlement, and an associated network of smaller tracks linked individual houses to one another and to the roadway. It was obviously a well-ordered settlement. The houses were solidly built and often paired, with one of the pair having an annex, a pattern that might represent the standard domestic unit. The houses seem to have been built close to one another, giving the impression of close communal living and a strong sense of group identity.

The archaeologists found numerous 'surplus' postholes implying many successive structures or rebuilds on the same plot. For this reason the excavators concluded that virtually all the houses were in use at the same time. Nineteen radiocarbon dates all fell approximately between 1500 and 1300 BC. Corrstown is therefore set to become one of the classic sites for studying the Middle Bronze Age.

Analysis of animal bones from the excavation of a Bronze Age barrow next to the River Great Ouse at Gayhurst in Buckinghamshire has provided an extraordinary window on a 4,000-year-old funeral. The barrow was huge – 34 m across – and the burials it contained were radiocarbon-dated to c. 2100–1900 BC, the Early Bronze Age, a period when rich grave-goods are common. Yet the central burial – an adult male in an oak-lined chamber – contained only the foreleg of a very small pig. Perhaps there were other ways of expressing rank in this period than through grave-goods. In fact, the original, inner ring-ditch around the barrow had been found carpeted with animal bones, and it was these that yielded the first clues.

Approximately a third of the total length of the inner ditch had been excavated, yielding 183 kg of bones, filling 50 storage boxes. A count of humeri (the upper bones of the front legs) produced a total of 102 bones from separate animals, which, given that about a third of the ditch had been excavated, implied a minimum of about 300 slaughtered animals.

At first sight the Gayhurst evidence appeared to represent the biggest Early Bronze Age funerary feast in the archaeological record. But further examination of the bone revealed more complex detail. The animals appeared to have been culled fairly indiscriminately, with no obvious preference for, say, prime steers or elderly cows. However, there was a deliberate selection of certain body parts for deposition on the barrow. The preference was for the major limb bones, those that would have held the prime meat, even though some had been filleted and presumably eaten. Other evidence implied that more than one herd was represented. This may indicate that many local groups – each subject in some way to the man buried in the oak-lined chamber – had contributed.

Evidence of human processing was sparse: only about 2 per cent of the bones bore recognisable cut-marks, and these were attributable to filleting. Only one conclusion was possible: though choice meat cuts were removed from some animals after slaughtering – and were no doubt cooked and eaten – the animals were not systematically skinned and dismembered further. Instead, it seems that the carcasses were left to rot and fall apart (known as excarnation). Strangely, only about 2 per cent of the bones show any recognisable trace of having been gnawed by dogs, so the rotting carcasses must have been protected in some way. Though the bone surfaces were slightly eroded and split, evidence of exposure to the elements for a time, the damage was not excessive and exposure was probably for a few months only. Then they must have been raked down into the ditch and quickly buried beneath the enlarged mound formed when a second, outer ditch was dug. The great ceremony was over. The burial was finally, definitively sealed.

But what kind of ceremony was this? Since few of the bones recovered bore human-made cut marks, are we witness to some ritual bonding of the living and the dead in an imaginary shared feast? While some of the meat – the choice cuts – might have been eaten at a first feast, perhaps this glut of cow bones represent a second ritual/imaginary feast at the end of a period of mourning, when the passage of the dead man to the Other Side was considered complete.

Rich grave-goods were clearly not the only way to display wealth in death in the Early Bronze Age. The 300-odd cattle slaughtered to celebrate the death of the great lord laid to rest under the Gayhurst barrow represented enormous wealth – in meat, milk, hide and bone. There may have been a huge funerary feast attended by hundreds, but the meat provided was far in excess of need. Symbolically, perhaps, this permitted the ancestors to join the feasting and have their share. Politically, no doubt, waste consumption on such a grand and conspicuous scale was an effective assertion of rank and authority. The slaughter of cattle was, it seems, part of the language of power in Early Bronze Age Britain.

BROTHELS, BARBED WIRE AND LOST ROMAN EMPERORS

The recovery of a military tombstone at Alchester, a Roman fort and small-town ten miles north of Oxford, by a team of research excavators led by Eberhard Sauer has changed the history of the Roman conquest of Britain. In under three weeks a total of 19 fragments were found, making possible a full reconstruction of the text. It reads: 'To the souls of the departed, Lucius Valerius Geminus,

the son of Lucius, of the Pollia voting tribe, from Forum Germanorum, veteran of the Second Augusta Legion, aged around 50, lies here. His heir had this set up in accordance with his will.'

The traditional story of the Roman invasion of Britain usually has Vespasian, later the Roman emperor, but at the time the commander of the Second Augusta Legion, conquering the West Country. But did he? The new legionary tombstone has rewritten the story by moving Vespasian to the Midlands.

Ancient sources record that Vespasian was in command when the legion was brought from Strasbourg to Britain; that he played a leading role in a bloody battle when an unnamed river was crossed on the army's march to the Lower Thames and Colchester; and that he fought 30 times with the enemy and subjugated two 'most powerful' (but unnamed) tribes, over 20 oppida (native forts or towns), and the Isle of Wight. Lucius Valerius Geminus is likely to have been personally involved in much or all of this. His commander was later, in AD 69, to be proclaimed emperor while in charge of the forces involved in crushing a Jewish revolt on the other side of the empire. He would reign for ten years until his death in AD 79.

It has been long accepted as a virtual certainty that Vespasian and the Second Augusta Legion were based somewhere south of the Thames. There is, in fact, no good evidence for this – while Dorchester (Dorset) and Silchester (Berkshire) have both been tentatively suggested as conquest-period army bases, neither of them has yielded any certain military structures at all.

The discovery of Valerius Geminus' tombstone therefore provides the best evidence so far that Vespasian's base was, most unexpectedly, at Alchester. According to current theory all legionary veterans who chose to stay in Britain settled at either the main base of their legion or at a colony (a special town formed of Roman citizens). Not a single tombstone of a legionary veteran has ever been found at another type of location in Britain. Alchester was not a colony. Therefore, unless the new tombstone represents the only known exception to the rule, we must assume that the town was the main base of Valerius Geminus' unit, the Second Augusta Legion, during the early years of Roman military occupation – moving Vespasian's principal theatre of operations in the mid AD 40s from the West Country to the Midlands.

New light on the Roman army has also come from excavations at the eastern end of Hadrian's Wall, at Byker and Throckley, part of the urban sprawl of Newcastle upon Tyne. Paul Bidwell's team discovered an entanglement of forked branches – the Roman equivalent of barbed wire – that may have run along the entire 73-mile length of the Wall.

No one knows for sure the purpose of Hadrian's Wall. Some argue it was an elaborate system of border control, enabling the Romans to police movement across the frontier, levy customs duties, and prevent small-scale raiding. Others emphasise its cultural significance, seeing it as a symbolic barrier, a way of marking the furthest limit of civilisation, of 'separating the barbarians from the Romans'. Few, by contrast, at least in recent discussions, have regarded it as primarily a military defence-work. Roman military doctrine in the early second century AD, when the Wall was built, was based on pre-emptive aggression. The new discoveries challenge that perception.

At Byker, on the berm between the wall itself and the military ditch to the north, three rows of pits were uncovered, 49 altogether, extending along the entire 32 m stretch of the defences exposed. The pits were roughly rectangular in shape, about 80 cm by 40 cm, had near vertical sides, flat bottoms, and an average depth of 46 cm. The pits were arranged in a quincunx pattern (one in which five objects are arranged such that four are at the corners of a square and the fifth is at its centre). Each pit appears to have contained two wooden uprights. Almost certainly these were dug to support a thicket of forked and sharpened branches – known in Latin as *cippi* – since these are described by Caesar in his *Gallic War* account of the siege of Alesia in 52 BC, and examples very similar to those at Byker have been revealed by excavation on the site itself. The branches may have been linked in some way to prevent them being pulled from the ground too easily – perhaps there were two per pit so they could be tied together underground.

But how typical are the Byker pits? Were they part of a local defence system, or did they extend the entire length of the wall? Excavations seven miles west of Byker, in a 2.2 km long contractor's pipe-trench at Throckley produced the decisive evidence: though the trench was very narrow and machine-gouged, no less than 145 Byker-style pits were identified at various points along it. Suddenly, every reconstruction of Hadrian's Wall looked wrong. In effect, the berm in front of the Wall had disappeared: instead of a flat expanse of grass a few metres wide between ditch and wall, there was now a dense thicket of spikes. And assuming the spacing at Byker was standard, there would have been approximately 3,500 pits and 7,000 uprights per mile – that is, a quarter of a million pits and half a million branches along the entire Wall. Evidence suggests, moreover, that the *cippi* were part of the original design of Hadrian's Wall as constructed in the AD 120s and 130s. Is it not time, therefore, to reassess our interpretations of the wall's purpose?

A third startling discovery in Romano-British archaeology has been that of a previously unknown emperor: Domitianus II has entered the historical record thanks to the discovery of a single Roman coin amid a hoard of 5,000 recovered from farmland in Oxfordshire by amateur archaeologist and metal-detectorist Brian Malin.

The hoard came up as a mass of fused coins within the fragmentary remains of a pottery container. Even before the coins were separated and cleaned in the conservation department at the British Museum, it was clear that they were 3rd century 'radiates' – one of the most common coin types of the ancient world – where the emperor on the obverse wears a spiky or radiate crown representing sun-rays. The hoard seemed unremarkable, and the real importance of the find did not emerge until the work of identifying the coins began much later.

Richard Abdy, curator of Roman coins at the British Museum, identified a single coin carrying the unexpected inscription *IMP C DOMITIANVS P F AVG*, representing the names and titles 'Emperor, Caesar, Domitianus, Dutiful, Fortunate, Augustus'. Nowhere is there any mention of a 3rd century emperor of the name Domitianus.

Political, economic and social decline characterise the 3rd century. All across the Roman world armies struggled to defend the empire against attack, and successful commanders were sometimes proclaimed emperor by their soldiers. In the 50 years after the death of the emperor Severus Alexander in AD 235, no fewer than 60 individuals were proclaimed emperor.

The name Domitianus appears only twice in the historical records of this period, and neither source names him as an emperor. Both, however, suggest there was a senior military officer of this name involved in the events of the mid 3rd century. The *Augustan Histories*, a notoriously unreliable and fanciful account, mentions a certain Domitianus as the general responsible for suppressing a revolt by Macrianus in AD 261. The second reference, in the pages of the 7th century Byzantine historian Zosimus, simply records that a Domitianus was punished for a revolt during the reign of the emperor Aurelian (AD 270–275). Is this the same person, and is he our man?

The coin itself provides further clues. Its style places Domitianus in the rebel 'Gallic Empire' – a secessionist state in existence from AD 259 to 273. At this time, portraits on coins bore little resemblance to the person they were meant to portray, being merely an updated version of the equally conventional image of the previous ruler. The portrait on the new Domitianus coin is strikingly similar to those of Victorinus and Tetricus I, two known 'Gallic' emperors. Furthermore, it can be most favourably compared to the very latest of the portraits of Victorinus and the earliest of Tetricus. On this basis, the reign of Domitianus should be placed immediately after the assassination of Victorinus and before the accession of Tetricus – that is, in the year AD 271.

We can do little more than speculate on Domitianus' reign. It may have lasted months, weeks or just days. He would have begun issuing coins immediately as a way of consolidating his authority; the fact they are so rare indicates a very short-lived regime. But it now seems likely that one Domitian II ruled as a Roman emperor in the north-western provinces in AD 271.

Yet more Roman news comes from London. An elaborate Roman bath house, the second largest ever discovered in London, with masonry still rising 1.75 m in places, was found beneath the site of the American-themed 'Babe Ruth' diner in Shadwell. But what was it doing here, well east of the Roman city, which extended no further than the present Tower of London?

One suggestion is that it represents a replacement port for London in late Roman times. The closure of London's first Roman port happened amid the chaos of the mid 3rd century AD, when the barbarians crossed the Rhine and ravaged the hitherto peaceful provinces of Gaul. London, like so many other cities in the empire at the time, erected new fortifications, building a wall along the waterfront that must have crippled the city's booming commerce. How did trade continue? Were new port facilities established east of the city?

The 'Babe Ruth' bath-house was built around AD 240, and continued in use until about AD 375. To the north of it, archaeologists also found what appeared to be an 'accommodation block'. It comprised a number of clay-and-timber buildings with reasonably well-appointed rooms (3 star accommodation by Roman London standards). Some of the rooms even had hearths, presumably for heating or cooking, and red painted walls. A number of spectacular small finds were found here, such as a stone palette for mixing cosmetics, 82 hair pins, jewellery including bronze finger rings, jet bracelets, a gold earring, part of a necklace, and 272 coins dating to between AD 260 and 285.

Red plaster, women's paraphernalia, money: was this a Roman brothel? We might expect one in a Roman port. But we might also, perhaps, expect one in a liminal zone beyond but close to the city walls, a place to which men could sneak away without attracting undue attention.

PRINCES AND PAUPERS IN ANGLO-SAXON ENGLAND

In October 2003, excavating at Prittlewell just outside Southend in Essex, archaeologists discovered the richest Anglo-Saxon burial since Sutton Hoo. It lay in a cemetery of at least 34 burials, many rich with grave-goods, including three females buried with jewellery such as a rock crystal and an amber necklace, and 19 males with weapons, including six with swords. The principal burial – dubbed 'the Prince of Prittlewell' – was placed in a wooden chamber 4 m square and 1.5 m high with numerous grave goods including metal and glass vessels, wooden tubs, drinking horns with decorated gold rims, a folding stool, a lyre and gaming pieces. The assemblage has been dated to *c.* AD 600–650, and is thought to be that of an Early Anglo-Saxon king, perhaps King Saeberht of Essex; laid to rest alongside the kinsmen and warriors of his retinue. Clearly we have evidence of a powerful aristocracy, but what of the people they ruled?

The answer came by chance, just a year after Prittlewell, a mere five miles away at Rayleigh where another Anglo-Saxon cemetery was excavated. But here, instead of jewels, swords, bronzes and a glitter of gold, there was little more than handmade pots, fragments of iron and a scatter of beads.

Essex County Council's Field Archaeology Unit was excavating beneath the playing fields of a former school. They found a cremation cemetery of 145 burials, most comprising a handmade pottery vessel filled with the burnt remains of the deceased and placed in a small burial pit. Some pots were plain, but around half were decorated with complex combinations of bosses, stamps and incised lines. Probably these designs made symbolic reference to lineages and kinship groupings.

Close examination of the contents of the cremation vessels produced melted glass beads – perhaps worn by the deceased when they were placed on the funeral pyre; and ironwork – the remains of buckles, knife blades, and chatelaines (belt-chains). The buckles and blades could have been used by either sex, the beads and chatelaines were probably worn by women. There was no evidence of shield bosses, swords or axes – generally only found in inhumation graves, implying a low-status agricultural community.

Since no Saxon settlement is known in the vicinity, perhaps the cemetery served a range of farmsteads and hamlets scattered across the surrounding rural landscape. The Rayleigh cemetery has been dated to *c.* AD 450–600. It is fairly typical of East Anglian cremation cemeteries at the time.

Compared to Prittlewell, Rayleigh is another world made up of ordinary farming folk who laboured in the fields and paid tribute to the warrior caste. While the elite had moved on from the simple Germanic culture of the past, importing luxury goods in Roman style – and the Christian religion – from the Continent and the Byzantine Empire; the common people of Rayleigh remained true to the Germanic style of the Anglo-Saxons – a style that was fast being displaced by new fashions at the top. The comparison between the near-contemporary cemeteries in Essex shows just how completely different traditions flourished side by side in Dark Age south-east England.

A CASTLE, A 'LOST' TOWN, AND A MEDIEVAL CAESAREAN

Wales has been in the forefront of recent developments in medieval archaeology, due partly to heightened interest in Welsh heritage since devolution. The principality is known mainly for its English castles, but one of the longest-running field projects in the British Isles has just been completed at the Welsh castle of Dolforwyn in Powys, and this has now been opened to the public.

Dolforwyn Castle occupies a prominent rectangular hilltop site on the north bank of the Severn. It was built by Prince Llywelyn ap Gruffudd, the last independent Welsh ruler, in 1273 as a frontier outpost facing an English royal castle at Montgomery, six miles to the west, and that of a rival Welsh ruler at Powys, ten miles to the north-east. The site was dug over 20 summer seasons by students and other volunteers under the leadership of Lawrence Butler. They revealed two main phases. The original Welsh castle was heavily defensive: a strong natural position was reinforced with a round tower and a square keep, both with massively thick walls, and a rectangular curtain wall which embraced the whole of the hilltop. But this phase was very brief. The castle was besieged and captured after ten days in 1277 and was then remodelled for English occupation, remaining in use until about 1380. The new features of the castle comprised various interior structures – represented by walls built of stronger grey shale with liberal use of lime mortar – including bakehouse, brewhouse, grand hall and a well.

The excavation was comprehensive: the whole of the interior was uncovered, and all walls and floors were exposed. The policy now, however, is to allow vegetation to return, and 'the ruins of Dolforwyn have been sympathetically preserved and sensitively displayed to become an eloquent testimony to the changing balance of power on a disputed medieval frontier.'

Another border site has also featured heavily in recent Welsh medieval archaeology. Trelech in Monmouthshire was founded by the de Clares, the Norman marcher lords of Glamorgan, and was one of the great English successes in building up a buffer zone of castles and walled towns on the frontier. Documentary evidence dated 1288 records no less than 378 burgages (separate building plots) in the town, when it may have been bigger than Cardiff. Then disaster struck when a hundred houses were burnt by Welsh rebels in 1296. The ruling de Clares' male line was destroyed at Bannockburn in 1314 and their holdings subsequently broken up. The Black Death struck in 1348. And then the native Welsh rose under Owain Glyndwr in 1404 – and Trelech, a vulnerable outpost of English feudal empire – disappeared.

But excavations beginning in the late 1980s have proved controversial. Two teams are working on the site, one led by Ray Howell of the University of Wales, the other by Steve Clarke of the Monmouth Archaeological Society. Howell believes the core of the medieval town lies within the existing village, where there is a parish church, a motte-and-bailey castle, and impressive remains of stone buildings from excavations in Church Field West, including a possible pilgrim inn. Clarke argues that the main settlement lies a quarter of a mile to the south. Numerous excavations at widely scattered sites within the existing village have yielded nothing, whereas the fields either side of the roads leading south have produced abundant evidence for medieval buildings, in some cases still visible on the surface. Howell, on the other hand, sees this as an industrial suburb. Industrial-scale iron production at Trelech supported the de Clares' operations across Glamorgan, making the town a veritable 'medieval Merthyr'. So while Clarke talks in terms of having rediscovered a 'lost town', Howell insists the town was

A secretarial space separates them from the public corridor on the inner courtyard side. Each MSP's office has an irregularly shaped projecting oriel window, which includes a built-in seat opposite a set of tall steps, and in some cases an external shading 'curtain' of the wavy timber poles seen elsewhere. The elevation is highly articulated, idiosyncratic and enjoyable to observe. The yellow window frames and timber poles provide a pleasing colour foil to the pale and dark greys of the cladding. The only unfortunate aspect is the domineering presence of the concrete blast wall lining the site perimeter that very effectively hides the building from the lowest parts of the close.

The east face of the MSP block is panelled, but not in any obviously co-ordinated way. The cladding comprises assorted panels of laminated oak louvres, pre-cast concrete louvres, solid infill panels of natural stone, stainless steel clad oak-framed windows and a bizarre system of rainwater drainage that looks as though it might have been designed by Escher. This has diagonal lengths of half round gutters discharging into sections of horizontal trough linked together by vertical box section stainless steel downpipes, that then discharge again into other diagonal sloping gutters until the water reaches ground level. The horizontal lengths of trough are co-ordinated with the location of deeply recessed horizontal slots that permit lighting and ventilation to reach the central core spaces, while the sloping diagonals are clearly expressed on the outside face. It is wacky and wilful detailing, arguably excessively complex, and has a disturbingly misaligned quality to its visual appearance that suggests it has been 'thrown up' – though this, of course, is the absolute reverse of the reality in that construction quality is of the highest order throughout.

Aside from the hugely impressive debating chamber, the most delightful feature of the building is unquestionably the Garden Foyer, a fantastic, vibrant and visually stimulating space reminiscent of the finest hotel foyers with its high quality stone flooring and ravishing roofscape of sagging trussed rooflights, echoing the shape of upturned hulls at differing angles and sizes, that allows dappled light to penetrate the deepest recesses. For its size it is an intimate space that can provide private nooks and crannies within a spectacular setting.

Much debate has already taken place concerning the lengthy delays to completion and the huge cost overruns, and the recent Fraser Report has attempted to identify the underlying reasons for these. Taken in the long term however it can be argued that Scotland has acquired a masterpiece of international architecture built to exacting quality standards, for which the price tag of some £430 million may in time seem on a par with equivalent buildings realised elsewhere over the ages. In taking its cue from the language of the Scottish landscape rather than traditional classical or vernacular sources, it is setting a new challenge and opening up new horizons for those seeking to define what it means to be Scottish, not least for the MSPs whose responsibility it is to define and order the future path of Scottish devolution.

THE BRINDLEY PERFORMING ARTS CENTRE, RUNCORN

Architect: John Miller & Partners

Despite having been given the status of a new town back in the 1960s, with all the development possibilities that might have generated, Runcorn is one of a number of Merseyside towns that have never really emerged from the shadow cast by their overpowering neighbour, Liverpool.

Having acquired its new shopping centre, and a heavily upgraded network, in anticipation of greater things to come, further development failed to materialise and with its industrial base in decline the town has subsequently suffered culturally, economically and socially. This new arts centre, partly funded by a grant of £2.5 million from the Arts Lottery Fund, is an ambitious attempt on the part of the local borough of Halton to revitalise the town centre and try to address some of these problem issues.

The selected site for the new building is in the town centre bordering the towpath of the Bridgewater Canal. The theatre building takes its name from the canal's original engineer, James Brindley, and the name of its principal auditorium, 'The Transporter', from a local Victorian transporter.

The key components of the building are the principal auditorium, expressed as a bold cylindrical form emerging from the tall rectangular block of the flytower, and a 'black box' studio theatre jutting out as an extension to one side, at right angles to the central axis of the main theatre. Wrapped around the keyhole plan form of the auditorium and stage are the supporting public facilities and back up spaces. This encircling wing of accommodation is separated from the main auditorium by a generous top-lit double height concourse atrium, rising to a glazed roof supported on a series of radiating beams, like the spokes of a wheel.

The composition is simple, bold and logical and gives rise to a clearly articulated external expression directly related to the functional elements within, and designed to be seen in the round as a piece of sculptural form-making. Even subsidiary elements in the plan, such as stair and lift towers and the dressing rooms, are handled as distinct expressive elements within the overall composition.

The building is entered from the north and town centre side, through a projecting double height porch, framed by the tall masonry elevations of the studio theatre. The porch opens into the broad sweeping double-height foyer, from which a grand flight of stairs climbs upwards and around to meet the main theatre. The staircase balustrade continues as a wall to the ground level, giving it a simplicity and grandeur of form set against the tall, enclosing drum of banded brickwork that defines the semicircular foyer atrium. At the upper level and beyond the bridge the staircase plane continues as a flat balcony, opening out into a south-facing café seating area that overlooks an external raised terrace fronting the canal through a curved full height glazed screen.

The banded brickwork features both internally, around the outer face of the concourse, and externally, with alternating bands three courses high of red and blue engineering facing brick, the red bands finishing above ground level on the lower entrance side to leave a substantial plinth band of blue brick. The treatment adds a most satisfying feeling of richness and visual stimulation to what are for the most part plain masonry walls, with occasional punched openings for windows.

The contrast between the surrounding walls and the drum of the auditorium is clear, this latter element being clad externally in copper-green copolymer-coated aluminium cladding panels (traditional copper sheeting having proved to be beyond the limited budget) with a pronounced vertical pattern of raised joints. Two stair towers, tucked in at either side of the line of the proscenium arch and framing the junction of the lower auditorium drum and the higher flytower, pursue a related theme, with pale coppery turquoise cladding panels,

never 'lost' since the existing settlement, though hugely contracted, still marks the spot.

Another medieval story arises from research on finds from the deserted medieval village of Wharram Percy near Malton in North Yorkshire. Analysis of the 687 skeletons recovered has revealed a raft of information about diet, health, and lifestyle in medieval England. Of all the graves excavated over the 40 years of the project, 15 per cent contained the remains of children under the age of one. This has helped to feed the notion that medieval people were used to death, particularly infant mortality.

However, a newly excavated burial of a mother and child rebuts this. The burial has signs of an attempted Caesarean operation. It seems that the foetus was cut free from the womb in a bid to save it. This suggests that life, including that of children, was regarded as precious, leading to drastic acts to preserve it.

Simon Mays, skeletal biologist at English Heritage's Centre for Archaeology, explains that the mother had probably died of TB, some 10 weeks short of full-term. The foetus was cut free from the dead woman's womb in the hope it might survive. Caesareans do not seem to have been carried out on living women at this time, no doubt because the procedure was far too dangerous.

ANOTHER BIG DIG

Two years ago, Channel Four's *Time Team* caused quite a rumpus in the archaeological world by organising its first 'Big Dig'. The idea was for ordinary people to dig 1 m by 1 m test-pits in their back gardens or on the village green to uncover and record what was there. During a glorious weekend in late June, a total of 1,337 test-pits were dug around the country, alongside some more formal flagship digs by larger teams, and the whole event was shown live on prime-time TV. But there was bitter hostility in some quarters: it was 'ludicrous', 'grotesque', 'cheating the public', 'devaluing professional standards', and 'wrong ethically because it tears up the principle that sites should only be excavated as a last resort'.

Time Team has now compounded the offence in the eyes of critics by organising the 'Big Roman Dig'. Running for a week in late June 2005, the main focus was on a variety of research digs, which involved large numbers of students and local volunteers, and a flagship *Time Team* dig at Dinnington Roman villa in Somerset, a large Late Roman courtyard villa with splendid mosaics. The aim was to sample the whole range of Romano-British archaeology and to use this to tell the story of Roman Britain and to look at different aspects of life within it. Viewing figures were consistently high and the project was judged a TV success.

Criticism was more mooted than before, mainly because amateur involvement was to be in the context of established professionally-run research digs. It was clear, however, that a substantial body of opinion remains within archaeology that is hostile to metal detecting, amateur excavation, and TV-driven archaeology. The dispute erupted in the letters pages of *Current Archaeology*, where Henrietta Quinnell, President of the Cornwall Archaeological Society, denounced the magazine editor, who had written in defence of the Big Roman Dig, as 'uncomprehending of the fundamental processes controlling archaeological field research'. No doubt the argument around TV archaeology will rage as long as the subject remains popular with broadcasters and the televisual services of its practitioners are in demand.

WHAT IS THE FUTURE OF ENGLISH HERITAGE?

Simon Thurley, Chief Executive of English Heritage (EH), the government body responsible for heritage matters in England, has announced plans for the future of EH. A desire to transform the image of conservation is at the top of Thurley's EH action-plan. He is mainly concerned with conservation of the built environment, and hopes to bring about a new code of 'constructive conservation' based on 'respect, understanding and consent'. This will be achieved partly through greater dialogue between EH and members of the public, particularly historic listed-building home-owning members of the public, who often find themselves burdened by EH's many regulations.

EH also announced its intention to combine Planning Policy Guidance numbers 15 (which deals with protecting the built environment) and PPG 16 (archaeology) by 2010. This will unite all elements of England's heritage, from historic buildings, to sites of historic interest, to archaeology into one PPG. EH also intends to extend the 'At Risk' register to include all buildings, monuments and landscapes at all grades that are at risk.

Then there is to be an overhaul of EH's own portfolio of heritage sites open to the public, of which there are currently 410. Thurley explained there is to be a major new funding programme for choice sites, including Kenilworth Castle in the Midlands, and a £10 million grant to Chiswick House in London. With a 20 per cent growth of membership in 2004, EH is currently Britain's third largest interest organisation. Investing money in sites to attract ever more members is clearly a key way of making more revenue.

ARCHITECTURE

THE SCOTTISH PARLIAMENT BUILDING, HOLYROOD, EDINBURGH

Architect: EMBT (Enrico Miralles Benedetta Tagliabue) *in association with* RMJM (Edinburgh)

The creation of a new national parliament building is a rare event, and one of especial significance for the population whose political aspirations and culture it is duty bound to try and express. Such projects understandably attract a disproportionate amount of public interest and criticism. There can be no doubt that the new Scottish Parliament has been the subject of long running and fervent controversy, not only about the management and communication shortcomings that led to huge cost and programme overruns, but also about the meaning and relevance of its architectural vocabulary.

Enrico Miralles, an internationally renowned architect based in Barcelona, won the international competition to design a new Scottish Parliament building in July 1998, working in association with the Scotland office of RMJM, a long established and highly respected firm of British architects. His concept for the building centred on expressing 'the land of Scotland'. The views from the chosen site – at the foot of the dramatic volcanic cliffs of the Salisbury Crags and Arthur's Seat, facing Holyrood Palace at the end of the Royal Mile – are skilfully exploited in the recurring theme throughout this complex composition of sculptured forms. The often sharp-edged forms have something of the craggy randomness of a rocky outcrop themselves. On the south and east sides away from the city the landscape flows into and around the component parts in a deliberate attempt to accentuate the building's close relationship with its natural surroundings.

Formerly the home of Scottish and Newcastle Breweries, the site effectively occupies a whole city block. It is not prominent topographically and it is interesting that from the majority of the city, the building is well nigh invisible, making no attempt to present an imposing or ordered civic facade in the traditional manner of such national icons. Proceeding down the Royal Mile from the Castle the casual visitor could almost miss it completely: the entrances are not obvious and there is no sense of arriving at a key space in front of the building. It is subtly integrated into the urban fabric of the old City, its walls hugging the pavement line and knitting into the old street pattern, and taking in the now restored 17th-century Grade A listed Queensberry House on Canongate.

Miralles' composition is a hectic agglomeration of all manner of volumes, surfaces and materials in a seemingly random and chaotic mess of forms. The plan at upper levels reveals a roughly U-shaped distribution of major building components placed around the perimeter, creating the impression of a harbour – a huddled mass of boat-shaped forms that might have been swept in by the tide and left high and dry on the harbour floor. Some of these boat shapes are developed upwards as office towers, providing back-up space for the huge number of support staff accommodated on the site, while the smaller ones, pointed at both ends and more delicate, leaf-like, turn out to be the glazed rooflights to the space that functions as the social and cultural heart of the whole complex, the Garden Foyer.

The Garden Foyer is the hub linking all the main routes through the building between the main entrance for members, the MSPs' offices, the debating chamber and committee rooms and the facilities of the retained Queensberry House. The main entrance for MSPs is tucked into an open slot in the north-east corner, approached under the shadow of an enormous overhanging pointed prow at the end of Canongate Wall. Set into the building are lumps of natural stone drawn from around Scotland, with carved quotations from Scottish literature and incised representations of the Edinburgh skyline and street architecture. At the north-east corner the solid wall retreats, and an amazing view opens up across the serried structural piers to the rear of the debating chamber, the sharp prows of the office towers, and the strange complexities of the courtyard elevation of the MSPs' offices at the rear.

Framing the entrance slot and leading the visitor around to the eastern frontage is the blunt end of the media tower, which contains offices with television and radio broadcast facilities. A curve in the outer wall indicates the location of the public entrance, recessed beneath a long colonnade of concrete columns. A canopy of wavy timber poles, more sunshade than canopy, lends a rather impromptu and informal Mediterranean feeling to the facade. The colonnade extends the vista along the elevation and out towards the Salisbury Crags, as the building form gradually modulates into a series of stepped landscaped terraces. At the upper levels, a second long sweeping curve of facade reveals the volume of the debating chamber, again boat-shaped on plan, its high level windows partially shaded by external 'curtains' of more wavy timber poles.

The floor of the debating chamber is laid out with a semi-circular seating pattern, focused on the central desk positions taken by the Lord Advocate, the Solicitor-General and the Presiding Officer. The seating layout is designed specifically to avoid the confrontational model exemplified by Westminster, and to allow party representations to expand and contract seamlessly. Around the rear of the tiered seating runs a broad semi-circular public gallery, accessed from the public foyer below the naturally lit chamber. Over the chamber sails an exuberant steel and timber trussed roof (the chamber is free of any internal columns), with laminated oak beams supported at ceiling level connected by stainless steel joints and tensioned stainless steel tie rods. Timber finishes predominate, with a strip finish to the walls and ceiling surfaces, and timber panelling to the balcony fronts.

The western boundary of the site is delineated by the six-storey-high wing of the MSPs' offices running almost the full length of the narrow close separating it from the adjacent city buildings. Its two major elevations, west, onto the public close, and east, onto the landscaped inner courtyard, are completely different in their architecture, and both highly original in design. The offices face outwards, towards the west, being spaced on a 3-metre office module, the MSPs' rooms being vaulted in section.

---

vertically proportioned, set into a dark gun metal coloured framing.

Constructed to a remarkably tight budget of approximately £6 million, £2.5million of which was provided by the Arts Lottery Fund, this is a lean, but very definitely not mean, building, with a solid no-nonsense quality achieved through the simplicity and formal clarity of its layout, robust but carefully detailed materials, and a serious and dignified tone to its architectural expression. The architects can be congratulated for having achieved such a substantial amount of high quality space and building for such a modest outlay. The Brindley seems set to transform the cultural life of Runcorn as part of a wider programme of regeneration, and has already proved a popular attraction with a successful and varied programme of events aimed at satisfying the needs and desires of the local population.

MAGGIE'S CENTRE, RAIGMORE HOSPITAL, INVERNESS, SCOTLAND

Architect: Page & Park

Landscape Design: Charles Jencks

The latest in an expanding corpus of friendly, domestically scaled and inspirational support centres for cancer sufferers has reached fruition on a rather less than inspirational site at the front of Inverness' Raigmore Hospital. Developed on a green open space separating the hospital building from a busy road and a nearby supermarket, the building has endeavoured to maintain the effect of a green breathing space. The building mirrors new carefully designed landscape features in both its plan layout and massing, and its elevational treatment and use of materials.

The Maggie's Centre programme owes its existence to the enlightened patronage of Charles Jencks, a designer and architectural critic and writer, and arose as a practical response and subsequent testimonial to the experiences of his wife, Maggie Keswick, whose death from the disease during the 1990s provoked a fundamental debate about the whole culture of cancer care as it was then practised. The Inverness project is the fourth in a continuing series of buildings designed by carefully selected and frequently high profile architectural practices. These aim to provide an environment in which cancer sufferers can seek advice and counselling, carry out their own research and fact-finding, and avoid the often pressurised and controlling ambience and interventionist culture of large clinical institutions. Where the previous project at Dundee was outward looking, the Inverness Centre is introspective, turning its back on the relative chaos of its surroundings to create an oasis of calm, and an ordered but friendly and sympathetic atmosphere.

The concept for this design was developed from the basis of a simple leitmotif, repeated and transformed throughout the various component elements. Taking its cue from the concept of cells and cell division, a subject crucial to the study and understanding of cancer, the design features the use of a symbolic cell shape, a pointed lens-shaped form that provides the driving geometric impulse for the building itself as well as two small sculpted hillocks occupying the majority of the surrounding landscaped area outside a separate enclosed garden integrated with the building.

Four such lens shapes make up the complete Centre, two of them landscaped mounds, one the enclosed garden and the fourth the building itself. The two small grass-covered mounds emerge out of a gravel-covered floor, and feature narrow gravel paths cut into the smooth contours of the mounds, following the outline of the lens shape as they wind their way up to small seating platforms at the top of each mound. Artfully contrived radiating segments of grass link the two mounds together and respond to the curving pathways like ripples across a pond. The surroundings being as they are, this setting is best enjoyed as a landscape seen at ground level, the views out tending to dispel the abiding feeling of a tranquil and enclosed world.

The plan of the building develops the cell motif, and when read in conjunction with the walls of the enclosed garden to which it is linked can be interpreted as two overlapping or separating cells, all the accommodation being housed within the smaller cell while the garden occupies the remainder of the larger cell. The curving walls both define and bisect the building and are canted outwards by about 10 degrees. The garden walls are clad with close-fixed vertical strips of timber, but when they enclose the building proper the outward leaning faces are clad in green patinated copper panels arranged as narrow overlapping horizontal bands, like ship-lap boarding. These follow the rising profile of the eaves line as it sweeps up around the upper levels of the central mezzanine. The building has something of a rowing boat-like quality as it emerges above the timber garden walls.

The gently curving dining/kitchen area is lit by a continuous roof-light that abuts and follows the profile of the upper storey. To emphasise the coiling nature of the wall surfaces the patinated copper cladding is brought inside as well, finishing at the soffit of the staircase enclosure. Other high-level windows maintain the feeling of light and airiness and help to make the three dimensional qualities of the structure more apparent. The feeling is that of a spacious modern house, with its warm timber finishes and comfortable, non-institutional furnishings. The interior feels much larger than its small plan area of 245 sq. metres, attributable principally to the use of outward leaning walls, aided by the incorporation of glazed walls at the ends of the principal rooms, leading the eye out into the landscaped garden areas.

Costing £850,000, this small but memorable building successfully continues a programme of friendly, caring and life-enhancing facilities in which the full potential of a creative architectural response can make an important contribution to the processes of healing. Its unusual integration of symbolic architectural and landscape forms has provided a distinctive and reassuring framework for the valuable support which the Maggie's Centre charity endeavours to provide for its users.

THE SAGE, MUSIC AND PERFORMANCE CENTRE, GATESHEAD, TYNESIDE

Architect: Foster & Partners

The banks of the River Tyne, most particularly where the river passes through the broad and deep ravine separating the conurbations of Newcastle-upon-Tyne and Gateshead, have in recent years witnessed a stunning renaissance of fortunes, built on the region's industrial heritage and culminating in a series of memorable architectural improvements. Not least of these is the extraordinary and distinctive new building, housing three new concert and performance auditoria; its bulbous form looming over the skyline in the shadow of the original and ultimate icon of the north-east, the Tyne Bridge. Following on from the successes of the Millennium Bridge and the Baltic Mills Art Gallery, it is fast assuming an iconic status all of its own as the newest Tyneside landmark.

The building's brief called for three very different performance spaces comprising a principal 1700-seat concert hall intended as a permanent home for the Northern Sinfonia; a 400-seat auditorium for performances 'in the round'; and a smaller rehearsal hall that can double up as a venue for chamber, solo and smaller group performances. The outward formal expression of the envelope completely separates the spatial and formal expression of these performance halls from the external skin, whose undulating and all-embracing shape makes passing reference to their relative size and disposition but otherwise follows entirely its own structural and aesthetic logic. Given the separation of the three halls internally, this development is almost a tale of four buildings rather than one.

The building sits at the top of a steep-sided landscaped bank that slopes down towards the river, with the three halls arranged in sequence along its ridge. These are connected by a broad sweep of public concourse that wraps around the front of each hall to form a common datum level and continues out into the landscaped terraces at either side. The two major halls are placed either side of the smaller rehearsal hall, known officially as the Northern Rock Foundation Hall, with deep slots of clear space rising up to the roof plane along each side. The smaller central hall is pushed back from the leading edge of its neighbours to create a swelling in the main concourse.

Four flights of stairs climb up through the lofty spaces from the concourse to landings, with short bridge links connecting to the balconies at the upper levels. The crisply detailed clean white lines of the upper curving balcony edges, stepping back as they rise through the space and enveloping the smooth, white plaster walls of the halls themselves, are reminiscent of the after decks of an ocean liner, and similarly afford panoramic views, here back over the concourse and out through glazed sections of the outer shell to the cityscape of Newcastle on the opposite bank of the river.

Each of the three performance halls has been designed to provide optimum acoustic characteristics for the size of venue and for the range of music or other events that they may stage, and to offer the flexibility to adapt successfully to different requirements. Hall One follows the classic 'shoe-box' form, rectangular in plan and approximately twice as long as it is wide. The concert platform is designed to accommodate a classical chamber orchestra as its primary function, but can be extended to house a full symphony orchestra if necessary. Seating balconies run right round the space on two upper levels, but for acoustic reasons those along the sides are very narrow, only one and two rows deep respectively, merging into a deeper balcony at the end opposite the stage. To help control the pattern of sound reflections through the space, the side walls are angled gently on plan and lined with vertical timber strips. Acoustic control is provided through adjustable suspended ceiling panels and by drawing curtains across up to 90 per cent of selected areas of the timber lining to the walls. An almost endless set of acoustic permutations is therefore available to suit everything from Mozart to the spoken word. The price paid for such perfection however would appear to be a certain lack of variety and interest in the arrangements of the seating areas and in the very restricted palette of materials, American white ash being predominant throughout.

Hall Two is much more intimate in scale and layout, with seats for 400 people, and is designed as a venue for chamber music, folk and jazz, and experimental forms of music including 3D and surround-sound formats. Audience and performers are in close proximity, with seating set around the perimeter of the ten-sided space on shallow balconies. Six out of the ten sides are given a bowed profile on plan to assist in deflecting sound, and the acoustic characteristics of the space can be altered by raising or lowering a series of sound-absorbent banners. The bright red colours of the seating and the balcony fronts, coupled with the angularity of the balcony shapes and dark wooden background, give the space the feel of a private club, and it certainly has a more vibrant atmosphere than the larger Hall One.

The third and smallest hall is designed as the primary rehearsal space for the Northern Sinfonia, but also to put on chamber music and solo recitals as well as concerts by the music school orchestra. The wood-lined space has no fixed seating and the acoustic ambience has been designed to match as closely as possible that experienced on the stage of Hall One, enabling the performers to transfer from rehearsal to performance without the need for drastic alterations of balance.

The oversailing roof structure is designed to totally envelop all three halls as an independent structural entity, ensuring acoustic isolation between them. The main structural supports comprise four primary steel arches, two located directly over the slots between the three halls, and one at each end. The arched beams span approximately 80 metres and are curved in a spiral form, the profile being achieved by connecting successive segments of increasing/decreasing radii. Tall, slender cigar-shaped columns set at raking angles prop the arched beams and permit the beam depth to be reduced to a visually slender proportion.

When viewed from various angles, particularly from the dramatic glass box viewing gallery at the top of the Baltic arts centre, there is a clear synergy between the organic curves of the Sage and the arched forms of the Millennium and Tyne bridges. But the Sage clings rather precariously to its site, lacking the firmly founded base of the others. Even the landscape treatment, which comprises a series of planted furrows stepping down the steep slope, seems to suggest that the whole edifice is slowly creeping over the edge and sliding into the river. The engineers will of course have ensured this will not happen, and the building is already being recognised as a successful contribution to the continuing regeneration of the Newcastle/Gateshead region. Whether or not it achieves number one icon status will ultimately be irrelevant if it continues to provide a wealth of cultural activity in state-of-the-art auditoria, a role it appears to have been performing very successfully since its acclaimed opening weekend prior to Christmas 2004.

THE JUBILEE LIBRARY, BRIGHTON, SUSSEX

Architect: Bennetts Associates, in conjunction with Lomax Cassidy & Edwards

Brighton's new Jubilee library is the centrepiece of a mixed-use urban regeneration scheme on a substantial city centre site, in close proximity to Brighton's other cultural landmarks: the Dome, the Theatre Royal and the Royal Pavilion. The development of the site has taken a long time to materialise and the present proposals for the regeneration of the area date from the reorganisation of the Local Authority structure in 1996. Following the creation of the Brighton and Hove Authority, Private Finance Initiative (PFI) bids were invited for the regeneration of the whole area, in a project comprising a mixture of retail, office, hotel, leisure and residential facilities as well as the new library. While the PFI procurement format has not generally been successful in establishing a reputation for achieving high quality design, in this case the library building has benefited from being bound up within a whole package of buildings, enabling a degree of cross-subsidisation.

The masterplan has endeavoured to ensure that a range of different building types is closely knitted into the urban fabric and surrounding street patterns, while also creating a new pedestrianised civic square at its heart linked to the surrounding area through narrow lanes and footpaths. The library building, and its adjoining café wing, form the north and east sides of the new square, which is dominated by the sheer glass facade of the central library hall, rising to a height of four storeys and surmounted by a horizontal projecting cornice of aluminium solar shading blades. The layout of the building is organised around a simple plan concept in which two lofty library hall spaces, each two storeys high and placed one above the other, are surrounded by wings of ancillary accommodation on three sides, the south-facing glazed wall of the library front occupying the fourth side. The concept has been transformed into a dramatic spatial experience by the simple expedient of physically separating the structure of the central library floors from that of the surrounding sides by the introduction of a generous clear gap, top-lit from glazed perimeter rooflights above.

The structure of the central spaces has a strong sculptural quality, with chunky circular columns supporting a series of trays whose underside is shaped into four thin tapering ribs cantilevering outwards to the corner of each structural bay like the fingers of a hand supporting a tray of drinks. Eight square bays, each with a central column and tree-like vaults, are arranged into four bays of two, and the whole construction is repeated on the upper level. The spreading vaults are constructed of in-situ concrete cast into pre-shaped fibreglass forms with a white paint finish, the original concept of pre-cast concrete having proved too expensive. On the upper level, at the centre of each group of four bays, a smaller square has been cut out of the floor slab to provide a void through which daylight can flow and views up and down be enjoyed, adding to the spatial inter-relationship and sense of openness of the central halls.

The walls surrounding the central halls are lined in beech-faced plywood panels providing a warm and friendly contrast to the cool structural finishes of the central floor plates. About 80 per cent of these panels have a ridged finish covering an absorbent material, to provide an appropriate degree of acoustic damping. These thick lining walls are punctuated by a series of large openings, affording views into the surrounding rooms, which are devoted to more specialised library uses, such as rare books and backup facilities and to the circulation spaces linking them together. These openings, clear except for a simple glazed balustrade, reinforce the sense of interconnection between the various functions of the library and enable the overriding presence of the central spaces to permeate throughout.

They also serve an important secondary function in the environmental strategy and performance of the design, which has been as much aimed at procuring an energy efficient and sustainable building as a piece of dramatic and inspiring architecture. The designers have been able to insulate, as it were, the special features of the library design against the potential inroads of the PFI and Design and Build procurement routes by making the most distinctive features of the design critical to the energy performance. Thus the exposed heavy concrete structure, the controlled use of daylight and solar energy through the facade, and the exploitation of the exposed nature of the site to sea breezes are all used to reduce the need for energy-consuming mechanical services to provide acceptable internal conditions.

The concrete structure provides a heat sink, storing heat through the day and releasing it at night. The perimeter wings of accommodation utilise a system of hollow concrete floor planks to provide a supply of cooled air which is drawn into the central library halls through the clear openings in the surrounding walls. In summer the air flow process is driven by three wind towers at roof level, one located over each of the central upper level voids, which vent stale air and work in conjunction with the perimeter rooflights to provide night time ventilation. In winter the wind towers are closed and air is extracted by fans, with a heat recovery system used to temper incoming fresh air. Solar gain is controlled by the use of fixed solar shading louvres, and excess heat is controlled by allowing hot air to dissipate up the perimeter void and out through openings at high level. Among a number of other environmental provisions, the consumption of fresh water is also reduced by collecting and re-using rainwater for the flushing of toilets.

The south-facing facade of the main spaces is a frameless double glazed skin, using high performance coated glass, each pane fixed to the paired metal column supports with stainless-steel structural bolts. During the day this presents a rather inscrutable reflective face to the public realm, but at night reveals the drama of the double height spaces behind to full effect. Above the glazed public entrance screen a two-storey aluminium framed window fronts the square and turns the corner onto the side elevation, facing onto Jubilee Street. The external cladding of both east and west side wings features the use of handmade square glazed tiles in a rich and subtly varied range of dark slate blue colours. The café block attached to the library and projecting at right angles from the eastern frontage continues the simple framed glazed skin for its upper levels. The simple palette of materials that is used throughout displays careful attention to detail and ensures that the elevations present an appropriately dignified face to the public realm.

This project reflects well on the skill and commitment of the designers and does demonstrate that, when carefully controlled and managed and in the right hands, from client through to provider and contractor, the PFI procurement option can deliver a high quality product. Regrettably this outcome remains the exception rather than the rule. In this context therefore Brighton's new Jubilee Library is a refreshing example of inspiring architectural design combined with effective sustainable environmental principles.

ART

FAIR CONDITIONS THROUGHOUT THE CAPITAL

The second Frieze Art Fair took place on 15–18 October 2004 in London's Regent's Park, establishing its position as arguably the most important event of the UK's international contemporary art diary, and a fair to rival Art Basel and New York's Armory Show. In marked contrast to what used to pass for the capital's contemporary art fair at the Business Design Centre in Islington – which had to cajole London's premier galleries into participating at all – there had been rampant competition to be selected for the 150 stands in Frieze's David Adjaye-designed marquee.

In a week coinciding with the opening of numerous shows and auctions throughout the city, London was awash with collectors, artists and curators from around the globe, relatively few of whom zipped through the rain in artist Pae White's specially commissioned VIP Rover courtesy cars. It was estimated that the fair attracted 42,000 visitors and shifted £26m worth of art, including a reported £450,000 for a sculpture by Jake and Dinos Chapman, the artists whose mutant Nazi atrocity diorama, *Hell* (2000), was a victim of the 24 May 2004 Momart warehouse fire.

Responding to the fact that several smaller London galleries were not included over big-hitting American dealers such as Sperone Westwater and Barbara Gladstone, a satellite fair by the name of Zoo showed 22 galleries in the captivating setting of nearby London Zoo. The future for the more modest London galleries in the light of the increasing presence of American and European behemoths in the capital remains to be seen.

PRIZES AND COMPETITIONS

The 2004 Turner Prize exhibition at Tate Britain (20 October–23 December) was sponsored for the first time by Gordon's Gin. The shortlisted artists were Kutlug Ataman, Jeremy Deller, Yinka Shonibare and Langlands & Bell. One of the film works by the latter duo, shot at the Supreme Court in Kabul, Afghanistan, in 2002, was withdrawn on legal advice on the grounds that it could have affected the trial of the Afghan warlord Faryadi Sarwar Zardad that was taking place at the Old Bailey. The winner of the prize was announced on 9 December as Jeremy Deller. Best known for his re-enactment artwork of a confrontation between police and pickets during the 1984 miners' strike, Deller's presentation included *Memory Bucket* (2003), which documented his explorations of Texas, including visits to President George W. Bush's hometown and the site of the 1993 Branch Davidian siege in Waco. The 2005 Turner Prize shortlist was announced as Darren Almond, Gillian Carnegie, Jim Lambie and Simon Starling.

Another corporately backed competition, the annual *Beck's Futures* prize exhibition, was exhibited at the ICA (18 March–15 May). The shortlisted artists were Lali Chetwynd, Luke Fowler, Ryan Gander, Christina Mackie, Daria Martin and Donald Urquhart, with three of the list – Chetwynd, Urquhart and Martin – represented by Herald Street (née Millers Terrace), London's hip new gallery of the year. Christina Mackie took the £26,666 cheque on 26 April.

August 2004 saw another incarnation of a cherry-picked artistic 'east' in the shape of the thriving annual *East International*, run by Norwich Gallery and the Norwich School of Art and Design (5 July–21 August). This year's selectors were the painter Neo Rauch and the gallerist Gerd Harry Lybke, both from Leipzig, and there was a clear East German slant to the selection. Of the 1,620 artists from 38 countries who applied to be in the show, 20 of the 30 artists selected were figurative painters, and 11 were German. Yet half of the artists selected also worked in the UK and the show made a persuasive case for the established and ongoing dialogue between German and British art.

BIENNALS

The pre-eminent contemporary art festival, the 51st Venice Biennale, opened in mid-June 2005 under the direction for the first time by women – Maria de Corral and Rosa Martínez. Gilbert and George – selected by the British Council some two decades too late some argued – filled the British Pavilion with new photographic works using imagery of ginkgo leaves. British artist highlights in the Arsenale venue's *Always a Little Further* included Runa Islam's film *Be The First To See What You See As You See It* (2004), and Tacita Dean's *Palast* (2004), a film of Berlin as reflected in the former GDR government building. Elsewhere in the city, Peter Finnemore, Laura Ford and Paul Granjon represented Wales, while Alex Pollard, Joanne Tatham & Tom O'Sullivan and Cathy Wilkes comprised the Scottish Pavilion.

In the UK, the Liverpool Biennial ran from 18 September to 28 November 2004. Among its various strands were *International 2004* at Tate Liverpool and other venues; the *John Moores 23* painting prize at The Walker Art Gallery and a series of new commissions under the umbrella *Open Eye*. The artists included important practitioners such as Yoko Ono and Cildo Meireles, and the events provided much-needed impetus for unofficial venues. This Biennial was always conceived as a blatant cultural makeover for the city, and questions as to whether this was to the benefit of the art generally led to a rather muted response from the critics.

Other international Biennial exhibitions in September 2004 included those in São Paulo, Shanghai, Gwangju and Busan.

COMINGS AND GOINGS

Whether the fact that London looked increasingly formidable as a city for new art raised the game a notch, or that the continuing investment in the art infrastructure of regional Britain encouraged circulation of personnel, summer 2004 to summer 2005 saw a surprising number of high profile job shuttles in the contemporary art world.

London's Institute of Contemporary Arts (ICA) announced on July 20 that its director, Philip Dodd, was to leave after seven years in the position to become co-founder and chairman of Made in China, an agency which develops cultural, educational and commercial projects between the UK and China. By March 2005, broadcaster and style writer Ekow Eshun was named as the ICA's new director.

In July 2004 Susan Ferleger Brades left the Hayward Gallery after 24 years, including eight years as director, and Professor Brendan Neiland, head of the Royal Academy Schools, Britain's oldest art college, was forced to resign following financial irregularities involving an undocumented £80,000.

In November 2004 the London outpost of Zurich-based gallery Hauser & Wirth appointed a new director, Gregor Muir. Muir had left the Tate where he had been the Kramlich Curator for two-and-a-half years, and this was to be his first commercial gallery position.

Also in November 2004, Stephen Snoddy resigned after a rocky year at the helm of the Baltic Arts Centre in Gateshead, which was opened in 2002 at a cost of £41.3m in lottery funding. It was not until April 2005 that a replacement was found in Peter Doroshenko, an American who was formerly director of the Stedelijk Museum voor Actuele Kunst in Ghent, Belgium, while Snoddy went on to the New Art Gallery in Walsall.

The spring saw further job shuffling as Eddie Berg, founder of Liverpool's Foundation for Art and Creative Technologies (FACT), left the organisation to become the artistic director of the National Centre for the Moving Image in London. FACT played an important role in Liverpool winning the bid to be the European Capital of Culture in 2008.

And after only a year at art publisher Phaidon, Kate Bush was on the move again in April as she took up the post as head of the galleries at the Barbican Centre, following the sudden death of Carol Brown. In the same month, there were two departures from Bush's former employers, the Photographers' Gallery, with director Paul Wombell and head of programming Charlotte Cotton both leaving within weeks of each other.

The spring of 2005 witnessed the deaths of two vital figures of British art that came to prominence in the 1960s, Mark Boyle (who worked collaboratively as Boyle Family) and Eduardo Paolozzi, one of the founders of the Pop Art movement in the UK. The latter's major exhibition, *Paolozzi at 80*, was shown in 2004 (29 May–31 October) at the Dean Gallery, National Galleries of Scotland, Edinburgh.

The groundbreaking Swiss curator Harald Szeemann, often referred to as the first independent or freelance exhibition maker, died on February 18 2005. Szeemann's landmark 1969 exhibition *When Attitudes Become Form* had championed the work of radical American and European artists, including Joseph Beuys.

EXHIBITIONS ROUND-UP: MUSEUMS AND MAJOR SPACES

Tate Modern unveiled the latest commission for its Unilever Series in the building's turbine hall in the week of the Frieze Art Fair – a multi-speaker sound work entitled *Raw Materials* (2004) by one of the giants of contemporary art, American Bruce Nauman (12 October–2 May). Overlapping with this was a major posthumous show of the work of Joseph Beuys (4 February–2 May). The presentation included many seminal works including *The Pack* (1969), *Show Your Wound* (1974–5) and *Economic Values* (1980). Later on, Tate's big summer shows tackled aesthetic sea changes in *Open Systems: Rethinking Art c. 1970* (1 June–29 August), and celebrated the career of Frida Kahlo (9 June–9 October). Tate Modern's visitor figures for 2004 were released around the same time: 2,069,000 had passed through its doors, a 113 per cent increase since 2001.

The ICA's newly appointed director of exhibitions Jens Hoffman kicked off his programme in the summer with the two-'act' *Artists' Favourites* (5 June–5 September), a show for which 40 artists were each asked to select a single artwork made since 1947, the year of the founding

of the institution. Hoffman's reflexive and theatrical approach to exhibition-making reinvigorated the central London venue this year after it had lost its way following the public spat with the then-chairman Ivan Massow two years ago. Later at the ICA, John Bock took a novel approach to making a solo show with *Klütterkammer* (24 September–7 November). Visitors found themselves negotiating a tangle of cardboard, plywood tunnels, ladders and hay bales to encounter artworks by many of the artist's influences – Cindy Sherman and Otto Muehl amongst them – as well as curiosities such as Rasputin's fingernail.

At the Saatchi Gallery, *The Triumph of Painting* (26 January–28 May 2005) marked the 20th anniversary of the gallery, and its first part was devoted to five artists: Peter Doig, Luc Tuymans, Marlene Dumas, Martin Kippenberger and Jörg Immendorff, to be followed by a show of younger painters. A walk along the South Bank saw *Africa Remix: Contemporary Art of a Continent,* the highest profile exhibition of *Africa 05*, at the Hayward Gallery (10 February–17 April), while later on the Barbican Art Gallery proposed an alternative visual history in *Colour after Klein* (26 May–11 September).

EXHIBITIONS ROUND-UP: WEST END

Zurich-based Hauser & Wirth showed the latest work by Martin Creed (8–30 October) at their London outpost during the Frieze Art Fair. Creed, a British artist most famous for his *Work No.227: The lights going on and off* (2000) at the Turner Prize exhibition in 2003, scattered the floor of the former bank on Piccadilly with hundreds of balls of all types, colours and sizes.

The artists' commissioning agency Artangel and the London-based Turkish artist Kutlug Ataman presented *Küba* in a disused former post-sorting office in London's New Oxford Street (22 March–4 June). Forty second-hand televisions and chairs were set up to broadcast footage of inhabitants of Istanbul relating their personal histories and reflecting on the hybrid identity of Küba, the mostly Kurdish sector of the city.

EXHIBITIONS ROUND-UP: EAST END

The Whitechapel Art Gallery presented its revamped open exhibition, rebranded – or rather, reverting to its original 1932 title – as the *East End Academy* (11 June–29 August), lending an institutional stamp of approval to the eastward shift in London's art geography over the last decade-and-a-half. The statistic that around 10,000 artists live in the East End of London lent some credence to the exhibition's claim that east London hosts the 'greatest concentration of artists in Europe'. The biggest exhibition at the Whitechapel Gallery this year was *Faces in the Crowd: Picturing Modern Life from Manet to Today* (3 December–6 March), which included work by around 100 artists. The gallery had also announced it was likely to close for several months in 2006 due to its imminent expansion into the neighbouring building, an 1892 public library.

Also in Whitechapel, Artangel revealed Gregor Schneider's terrifying *Die Familie Schneider* with two troubling identical neighbouring houses, inhabited by duplicate sets of actors who performed bleakly monotonous activities (12 October–23 December). Intrepid visitors individually explored each wretched and neglected interior in turn.

EXHIBITIONS ROUND-UP: REGIONAL

Winter exhibition highlights in Edinburgh included Ellen Gallagher's exhibition at the Fruitmarket Gallery (11 December–13 February) which included the painting *Double Natural* (2002), based on 400 advertisements for black beauty products. Also in Edinburgh, collaborative duo Beagles & Ramsay inadvertently kicked up their own tabloid storm as they planned to do a cooking performance on 12 February. The problem was that they were planning to fry black puddings – made from their own blood. Though the artists never intended the food sculptures for public consumption, the city council demanded that they be destroyed as hazardous waste.

During February one could have seen two major shows by senior Continental artists associated with *Arte Povera*, literally 'poor art': Jannis Kounellis at Modern Art Oxford (15 December–20 March) and *Giovanni Anselmo: Where the Stars Come a Span Closer* at Ikon Gallery, Birmingham (1 February–28 March). Both artists presented seminal works from the 1960s alongside new sculptures. Over on Merseyside, Tate Liverpool opened a major show of British artist Richard Wentworth (21 January–24 April). Included was *False Ceiling* (1995), a suspended ceiling of second-hand books.

Arrivals: New Art from the EU – a two-year rolling programme of exhibitions and projects by artists from each of the ten new member states of the European Union, organised by Modern Art Oxford and the to-be-built Turner Contemporary in Margate – kicked off with an exhibition in Oxford by Pawel Althamer and Artur Zmijewski (5 April–29 May). The show featured a documentary of Polish Catholics visiting holy sites in Jerusalem.

Elsewhere a retrospective of the work of William Turnbull (14 May–9 October) opened the Yorkshire Sculpture Park's £3.5m new gallery, built into the existing hillside and incorporating a grassed roof. Also in Yorkshire in the spring, *Situation* (16–19 May), a festival of 40 core events and interventions took place throughout the city of Leeds.

PUBLIC DONATIONS AND RECORD-BREAKING PRIVATE SALES

Tate launched its 'Building the Tate Collection' initiative at the end of October, by announcing that several established artists – including Anish Kapoor, Peter Blake, Chris Ofili, Lucian Freud, David Hockney, Antony Gormley and Damien Hirst – had been persuaded to donate works to the Collection. This strategy was framed in the context of the institution's chagrin at the government's declining grant in real terms. Figures were produced to show that Tate's annual attendance had risen sharply from 2.5m in 1999 to 6.2m, but the institution still only received £28m from the government. To remain internationally competitive and cope with the rapidly rising prices of the contemporary art market, director Sir Nicholas Serota argued that the Collection could not rely on the government and must take its own initiatives such as this public solicitation of gifts from high-profile artists. As Tate's 2004 audit showed it generated 59 per cent of its income from the private sector. The further challenge for the national collection of art is to avoid an American situation, where public collections are often largely driven by the tax incentives and market-tastes of extremely wealthy individuals.

In January 2005 rumours were confirmed that Charles Saatchi had sold Damien Hirst's infamous shark-in-formaldehyde sculpture, *The Physical Impossibility of Death in the Mind of Someone Living* (1991). Despite visible deterioration, it was bought by an American collector for a reported $12m, making Hirst the world's most expensive living artist with the exception of Jasper Johns, and making a handsome profit for Saatchi, who had originally commissioned the work for £50,000.

Further economic values were on display in the London auction houses Christie's and Sotheby's contemporary art sales in February. Buyers were doubtless mindful that from January 2006 sales will have to take into account *droit de suite*, a re-sale royalty to living artists and the heirs of those deceased in the last 70 years. The impact is expected to be felt by the UK auction market as major works will inevitably be sold elsewhere in the future to avoid this tax. Auction house legislation in its entirety, some of which remains unchanged since 1845, has been marked for imminent review. Despite – perhaps because of – these gathering storms, the February 2005 sales were record-breaking. Christie's evening sale on February 9 (£24.5m), for example, was the house's highest grossing contemporary art auction. Lucian Freud's *Red-Haired Man on a Chair* (1962) sold for the highest price for a living British artist at auction at £4.1m, while his bizarre portrait of model Kate Moss went for £3.9m. A now much sought-after work by Glenn Brown, a painter who had had his first and long overdue major public exhibition at the Serpentine Gallery in the autumn of 2004, sold for £198,400 at Sotheby's.

OLYMPIC ANTICIPATION

The July announcement that the Olympic Games are to come to London in 2012 will initiate a cultural as well as sporting programme – the bid included provision for four years of arts events in the build-up to the Games. Despite the fact that a sizeable chunk of the budget earmarked for culture will be blown just on the opening ceremony, a plethora of parallel initiatives and investments are already being considered for 2012. Tate Modern plans to complete a £135m development of the cavernous oil tank spaces to the south of the turbine hall by 2011 to give it 60 per cent more exhibition space and a new education and performance studio.

For art as for sport, capital investments have to be weighed up against regional concerns, and grass-roots support for emerging talent has to be sustained alongside a continuing awareness of the global marketplace. Although many people would trust that the values of culture and of sport have nothing whatsoever to do with each other (the proliferation of goal-oriented art prizes might suggest otherwise), the next seven years are set to define – at least by dint of funding priorities and government ministers' portfolios – the climate for both in the UK.

BROADCASTING

TELEVISION

Technological change, promoted by the growth and development of digital media, was a constant preoccupation for television and radio broadcasters throughout the period under review. As around two-thirds of British homes bought into digital TV, the growth of additional services such as interactive TV enabled, for instance, BBC audiences to take their pick from a choice of up to five viewing options during the coverage of the Athens Olympics. Around nine million people took advantage of this. Similar technology, meanwhile, gave subscribers to British Sky Broadcasting greater opportunity to bet via their remote controls and participate in quizzes where money changed hands. Meanwhile Four Docs, an all-documentary station delivered via broadband, was launched by Channel 4. In some cases, such as the emergence of TV channels on mobile phones, the new media was experiencing teething troubles that needed to be resolved before mass consumer take-up could begin.

The fact that the consumption of TV and radio was becoming more portable and, arguably, more tailored towards individual choice, provided audiences were prepared to pay, continued to encourage TV channels to go to ever greater lengths to retain their competitive edge. Reality shows like Channel 4's *Big Brother* and ITV1's *Celebrity Love Island* provoked intense controversy as their critics claimed they were plumbing new depths in coarsening and cheapening public taste. Ironically, while all the main TV channels continued to ride the reality bandwagon with shows as different as *The Apprentice* (BBC2) and *The Farm* (Five), or *Musicality* (Channel 4), two of the year's most successful programmes were revivals of ideas first created in a more culturally innocent age, *Dr Who* and *Strictly Come Dancing*, both Saturday night hits for BBC1. Meanwhile Five, once synonymous with downmarket shows, managed to build its business by steering a broadly up-market course. This was despite broadcasting a show that led to front-page headlines in the *Sun* when Rebecca Loos, famous for her association with David Beckham, masturbated a pig in *The Farm*.

BBC SHOWS HIT AS STAFF STAGE ONE-DAY STRIKE

It was another turbulent year for the BBC as it attempted to future-proof itself against the digital revolution that some maintained would lead to the end of traditional TV channels within a decade. In May staff staged a 24-hour strike in protest at part-privatisation and job cuts that threatened one in four BBC jobs. The industrial action wiped out the Corporation's news and current affairs programmes across TV and radio as shows such as Radio 4's *Today* and BBC2's *Newsnight* failed to appear. The BBC insisted that the radical reforms were necessary for the organisation to thrive and operate efficiently in an entirely digital age. Another walk-out, this time planned to last for 48 hours, was averted when management and unions reached a compromise – essentially the partial sell-off and job losses would go ahead but every effort would be made to avoid compulsory redundancies for the time being.

In March the government published its Green Paper on the Corporation's future. The document, launched by Culture Secretary Tessa Jowell, contained little to worry the BBC in the short term: the licence fee was effectively guaranteed until 2016 and although the Green Paper warned the BBC to avoid 'chasing ratings for ratings' sake', and to reduce repeats and the number of US imports, commentators expected no big changes in the BBC's programme policy. In any case, for some time the BBC had deliberately stressed its upmarket credentials in the run-up to the renewal of its Royal Charter in 2006. Possibly the most radical proposal was the Green Paper's idea to replace the BBC's existing board of governors with a trust. For many years critics had argued that the governors were an inherently compromised body because of their dual role as both regulator and cheerleader for the Corporation. In theory, the proposed trust would be more independent of the BBC. In any case under new chairman Michael Grade, the governors were attempting to become a more objective body.

Commercial rivals were disappointed that the licence fee looked safe for at least another 11 years. They argued that as the number of channels multiplied and the BBC's share of viewing fell, the argument for having a BBC funded by a compulsory licence fee levied on all TV viewers became difficult to sustain. However, Grade and the BBC's new director-general, Mark Thompson, stressed that the coming digital revolution increased the case for a BBC funded by an exclusive licence fee because the Corporation could offer a guarantee of high quality in a sea of digital mediocrity where programme budgets would be hit remorselessly. Sceptics, however, reminded the public that on occasion the BBC was as guilty as any private broadcaster as quality was compromised in the rush to remain in touch with an increasingly fickle audience. BBC2's disastrous revival of *Ask the Family*, presented by children's TV hosts Richard McCourt and Dominic Wood, was a case in point. As the BBC's Annual Report noted in July: 'It is becoming harder than ever to make an impact on viewers, particularly as television viewing becomes more fragmented.'

As the realities of the digital era began to sink in, the BBC's old rival, ITV, also had to readjust. On 1 November it launched another digital channel, ITV3, based on repeats of old shows such as *Inspector Morse* and Hollywood feature films. Ofcom, the new communications regulator, concluded its study into public service television during 2004–5. It argued that it was vital for the BBC to have public service competition, but reasoned that as competition for audiences made it harder for ITV to screen expensive non-entertainment programmes, especially non-news regional shows, religion, arts and children's TV, the commercial public service TV burden would increasingly need to be borne by Channel 4 and possibly by a newly created entity called a Public Service Publisher. Commentators wondered if Ofcom wasn't letting ITV off too easily – and questioned where the money for the Public Service Publisher would come from.

BIG BROTHER'S LANDMARK MOMENT OF DEPRAVITY

As far as programmes were concerned, throughout the period under review reality and entertainment TV remained the dominant genres, followed by factual shows Arguably drama, apart from the soaps, continued to be squeezed. Comedy too was erratic, despite some notable successes by the BBC and Channel 4. In the summer *Big Brother*, perhaps predictably, once again generated newspaper headlines over the sexual antics of one of the contestants who had been drinking excessively. Kinga Karolczak, a 20-year-old barmaid and market researcher from London, was seen simulating sex acts with a wine bottle and appearing topless with two of the male contestants. Ofcom received some 80 complaints. 'Clean-up TV' campaigner John Beyer from Mediawatch-UK told reporters: 'It is absolutely appalling although it was thoroughly predictable. From the outset Channel 4 has calculated that this kind of thing was going to happen. Channel 4 is a public service broadcaster that has high aspirations for quality and innovation, but this sort of indecent, pornographic behaviour shows *Big Brother* for what it really is, which is just to be controversial. The time has come for the plug to be pulled on this.' Beyer criticised Ofcom for failing to sanction programmes in the past and letting standards slip. 'The regulator is not fulfilling its role, it seems to me that in terms of after 9 p.m. they won't do anything.' Beyer found an unusual ally in the critic Mark Lawson who, writing in *The Guardian*, said that the incident in *Big Brother* represented 'a landmark moment of depravity . . . after six years of escalating excess, it may be time for this show to bottle out'. In the same newspaper a leading article struck a more despairing note by concluding: 'The message seems to be that after 9 p.m. on television, pretty much anything goes. Is that what society wants? It may not be, but that is what it has got.' Several weeks earlier Andy Duncan, the new head of Channel 4 and a practising Anglican on the church's evangelical wing, acknowledged that *Big Brother* was nothing more or less than an entertainment show – and of huge commercial value to the TV station.

Earlier in the summer ITV1 had launched *Celebrity Love Island*, an original format by Granada Television, designed to compete head-to-head with *Big Brother* and featuring a dozen so-called celebrities holed up in luxury on an island in the Pacific. The critics claimed it was one of the worst shows ITV had ever shown. In the *Sun* Ally Ross described it as 'the TV equivalent of a cricket test match with lots of rain'. The embarrassment for ITV was compounded by the fact that it followed two flops, *Celebrity Wrestling* and *Celebrity Stitch-Up*, and was broadcast as ITV began celebrating its 50th anniversary with a history of the network, *The Story of ITV, the People's Channel*, hosted by Melvyn Bragg. For many observers, the contrast between past glories and today's output was all too obvious. Eventually *Celebrity Love Island*'s ratings picked up and a second series was commissioned.

There was widespread praise, however, for a different type of reality series, *The Apprentice*, a BBC2 reality show presented by the entrepreneur Alan Sugar in which he put a group of young, aspiring businesspeople through a series of tests before selecting one of them to work for his company. Another reality programme shown on the same channel, *The Monastery*, featuring a group of men participating on a spiritual retreat, was welcomed for its sensitive handling of the situation, and received praise from members of the church.

DOCUMENTARIES CLIMB THE HEIGHTS

Overall, the year 2004–5 represented rich pickings for fans of documentary programmes. An undoubted highlight was Laurence Rees' latest history programme, BBC2's *Auschwitz: the Nazis and the Final History*. The series used dramatic reconstructions and computer-generated imagery to demonstrate the horrors of the camp. During January more people watched the series than *Celebrity Big Brother* as almost 4 million tuned in. BBC1's Michael Palin's apparently final TV travelogue, *Himalaya*, was popular with viewers and critics alike. One of the year's most original films, according to reviewers, was BBC2's *The Power of Nightmares*, Adam Curtis' trilogy examining the roots of the conflict between the US neo-conservatives and Islamic extremists. Curtis suggested that the Americans had exaggerated the terrorist threat from militant Islamic fundamentalists in order to exert political control. BBC2 also scored with the more mainstream documentary, *Soul Deep*, examining the history of American soul music. Critics praised the high quality of the archive material and the original interviews. Writing in *The Tablet* John Morrish said: 'The first programme was the usual blend of music, interviews and film clips, done with real intelligence. But it also looked at areas that few dare to discuss: race, sex and what happens when they collide.'

BBC2's *Who Do You Think You Are*, a family genealogy show in which celebrities traced their ancestors and gave audiences the tools to investigate their own family histories, was a surprise hit in the autumn. Further proof that TV didn't have to shock in order to make an impact came later in the year. The three-week long *Springwatch*, co-presented by Bill Oddie, Simon King and Kate Humble, won a loyal and large following. The *Daily Telegraph* remarked: 'The programme is successful because it has tapped into the British love of gardens and wildlife, and their apparently insatiable appetite to see both on their television screens.' Commentators noted that this programme that used hidden cameras to film the wildlife inhabiting an organic farm in north-west Devon and the wilds of Scotland was more popular than ITV1's much hyped *Celebrity Love Island*. An average audience of 3.3 million tuned in. It certainly provided a fresh perspective on a time-honoured TV genre – the natural history programme.

The year's most controversial programme, judged by the number of complaints it received, was a TV version of the West End stage hit, *Jerry Springer – The Opera*, shown on BBC2 in January. The show sought to satirise the US daytime chat show, *Jerry Springer*, by staging a mock version of the TV programme set in hell and featuring God and members of the holy family. A concerted campaign by a group of right-wing Christians, who claimed the play was blasphemous, led to some 47,000 complaints by email prior to transmission and another 8,000 following the broadcast. The BBC's director of television, Jana Bennett, told journalists: 'We are not running some kind of *Pop Idol* competition in which the greatest number of votes gets a programme pulled. Giving these activists power to restrict freedom of expression is a slippery slope.' Reports suggested that the man responsible for televising the programme, BBC2 controller Roly Keating, was the subject of death threats. This, however, was denied. The BBC's governors decided by a majority of four to one not to uphold complaints: 'The majority view of the committee was that the outstanding artistic significance of the programme outweighed the offence it caused to some viewers,' the BBC said. Ofcom also defended the programme.

MAKING A MEAL OF SCHOOL DINNERS

The role of television in influencing public policy is usually hard to pin down, but there can be no doubt that the Channel 4 documentary, *Jamie's School Dinners*, forced politicians to grapple with an issue that has worried many parents for years – the low nutritional standards of school meals. The series, watched by more than five million viewers, pointed out that schoolchildren were expected to be fed at a cost of just 37p a day. It showed how the quality of these meals could be improved by retraining dinner ladies as junk food was replaced by more healthy fare. *Jamie's School Dinners* prompted education secretary Ruth Kelly to promise headteachers a £280m boost to their budget. Aired during the general election campaign, Tony Blair seized on the series and invited Oliver to Downing Street. 'His programme [has] brought into focus what everyone in their heart of hearts knows – which is if you feed children decent food, you are more likely to get responsible children who are healthier and fitter,' declared the prime minister. Typically Oliver himself was rather more direct: 'We [have been] encouraging them to be fat, unhealthy bastards.' Sceptics hoped that the change in government policy would be a lasting benefit and not just a pre-election stunt. The show enhanced Oliver's reputation further as the culinary Bob Geldof.

Jamie's School Dinners provided Channel 4 with some welcome evidence that its public service output was alive and well and not only restricted to the universally acclaimed *Channel 4 News*, presented by Jon Snow. 'If you want ballsy, provocative, red-meat news these days you have to turn to *Channel 4 News*,' advised the *Sunday Telegraph*. Another exceptional Channel 4 documentary was *The Boy Whose Skin Fell Off*, winner of an international Emmy. The programme documented the last few months in the life of Johnny Kennedy, a 36-year-old sufferer from a rare skin condition, dystrophic epidermolysis bullosa. *The Times* said: 'The most extraordinary people and the greatest spirits often pass their lives in total obscurity ... we often think of television as a debased medium but it is unique in bringing such people into our homes.'

During the year under review, the station impressed reviewers by the high calibre of much of its drama. *Shameless*, created by Paul Abbott, returned for a Christmas special and a second series in 2005, and dominated TV awards ceremonies. Set on a Manchester sink estate, this semi-autobiographical drama, critics agreed, consistently matched the high standards of top American series such as *Six Feet Under* and *The Sopranos*. The *Sunday Telegraph* opined: '*Shameless* is very funny, extremely rude and brimming with inventiveness.' Other Channel 4 fiction that impressed reviewers during the year 2004–5 included the drama-documentary *Omagh*, the hard-edged *Sex Traffic* starring Anamaria Marinica and the Peter Cook biopic, *Not Only But Always*, featuring Rhys Ifans in the lead role. In generally a strong year for Channel 4, the death of one of its best-loved presenters, *Countdown*'s Richard Whiteley, was one of the few setbacks it suffered.

BBC1's big drama event of the year was the return of *Dr Who*, launched in March. Starring Christopher Eccleston and Billie Piper, the show was recreated by the scriptwriter Russell T. Davies. Critics were unanimous in their praise. Stephen Pile in the *Daily Telegraph* wrote: 'It's like watching a completely new programme but with enough references to the great tradition to make it authentic. It has the Tardis, the monsters, the female companion responsible for the sexual awakening of boy viewers everywhere, the sonic screwdriver and that critical balance between scariness and comedy. But no scarves.' Another stand-out BBC1 drama of the year was *Blackpool*, a contemporary saga starring David Morrissey as the owner of a Blackpool amusement arcade in trouble with the police. It may have been indebted to the late Dennis Potter by virtue of its impromptu song and dance routines, but reviewers nonetheless welcomed the high degree of originality. Meanwhile, there were signs that BBC2 was regaining its confidence in drama thanks to shows like *The Rotter's Club*, based on Jonathan Coe's novel, and the historical naval serial, *To the Ends of the Earth*, adapted from William Golding's *Rites of Passage*. There was praise too for BBC3 dramas, *Bodies*, another hospital series from writer Jed Mercurio, and the historical romp, *Casanova*.

ITV DRAMA IN A CLASS OF ITS OWN

ITV1 proved that it could still deliver big ratings for its drama. One of the most successful was *Ahead of the Class*, starring Julie Walters and based on the real-life story of Dame Marie Stubb turning around a London school following the murder of headmaster Philip Lawrence. More than 10 million viewers watched, a considerable achievement in the multi-channel world. David Jason too remained a draw for ITV1 albeit on a somewhat smaller scale than in the past: the Jason vehicle *Diamond Geezer* drew 9.9 million viewers. Now that ITV was effectively one united company, Granada and Carlton having merged the previous year, some producers worried that the lack of internal creative competition between regional ITV companies, combined with such a ruthlessly commercial marketplace, made it difficult for ITV to produce original, innovative drama that took creative risks. An exception was the award-winning *Dirty Filthy Love*, the story of a man whose life is devastated by obsessive compulsive disorder and Tourette's syndrome. But when *Coronation Street*, featuring a guest appearance from Sir Ian McKellen as author Mel Hutchwright in the spring, continued to win audiences in excess of 14 million, perhaps ITV's critic missed the point. On the other hand, no new ITV1 drama series could quite match the impact of the hottest new US dramas, *Desperate Housewives*, *Lost* (both screened by Channel 4) and *House*, starring Hugh Laurie as a doctor and shown on Five. Meanwhile, Channel 4's purchase of *The Simpsons* helped the station to secure high ratings when the animation made its debut on the channel in November; the station had poached *The Simpsons* from BBC2, whose audience figures suffered as a result.

Ant and Dec's Saturday Night Takeaway and *I'm a Celebrity ... Get Me Out of Here!* once again did great business for ITV1, but comedy was effectively a no-go area for the network. As ITV's programme director, Nigel Pickard, wryly acknowledged in the spring: 'The biggest joke about ITV comedy is there isn't any.' Fortunately for comedy fans, the BBC and Channel 4 put on a much better performance. *Little Britain* transferred successfully to BBC1 and secured its iconic status thanks to the powers of invention of its creators Matt Lucas and David Walliams; Ricky Gervais' keenly anticipated follow-up to *The Office*, *Extras*, did not disappoint, and Channel 4 lived up to its reputation for innovation thanks to the quirky hospital comedy, *Green Wing*, described by the *Sun* as 'bonkers but consistently brilliant'. *Max and Paddy's Road to Nowhere*, about a pair of two nightclub bouncers, also generated good notices for Channel 4, but Chris Morris' latest effort, the situation comedy *Nathan Barley*, represented a big disappointment for Channel 4 as audience levels went into freefall. By contrast, a new BBC4 comedy, *The Thick of It*, seen as a modern-day version of *Yes, Minister*, did well.

The year under review was a busy one for news as broadcasters had to respond to the Boxing Day tsunami, a general election, the death of Pope John Paul II, the trial of Michael Jackson and the London bombings in July. By and large Sky News, which had carried nightly reconstructions of the Jackson trial, was seen by industry experts as the news channel to beat.

RADIO

As the BBC's governors commented in the Corporation's Annual Report: 'The radio landscape in Britain continues to change very rapidly, driven by intensifying competition and the continual arrival of new technology, allowing people to listen in new ways.' During the period under review listening via the internet proved more popular than ever. In January it was reported that the number of listeners accessing BBC Radio programmes online had increased by 70 per cent year-on-year. The Corporation's online radio player, enabling audiences to tune in to their favourite shows up to a week following the original broadcast, was also gaining in popularity. In February listeners spent more than 4.4 million hours using the radio player – up from 2.5 million a year earlier. One of the new technologies that arrived during the year 2004–5 was podcasting – a term derived from the fashionable Apple MP3 player, the iPod. Podcasting allows listeners to transfer programmes from the internet onto their MP3 players and listen at their own convenience, perhaps while commuting or working out at the gym, or even lying on a beach in the Mediterranean.

The BBC noted 'the extraordinary levels of demand' as some 380,000 requests were received for Radio 4's weekly discussion on the history of ideas, *In Our Time*, one of the first BBC Radio shows to be made available to podcasters. However, music radio was driving podcasting take-up. Radio 1 controller Andy Parfitt explained: 'It is a shift from the old broadcasting model where you pushed content at people ... Now that technology allows listening on demand on downloading, we've got to be there to make sure our content and programmes are there for the audience to consume.' Virgin Radio was the first British radio station to make a daily show available as a podcast, with *Pete and Geoff's Breakfast Show*. The station claimed the programme was being downloaded 80,000 times a month.

AUDIENCE FALTERS FOR DIGITAL RADIO

As digital radio sets once again proved popular during the run-up to Christmas, the radio industry estimated there were now some 1.5 million digital receivers in British homes. This, argued industry leaders like GCap's executive chairman Ralph Bernard, was set to grow rapidly in the years ahead with a third of all sets predicted to be digital by 2008. However, audience figures, those that were big enough to be measured accurately, suggested that digital stations were performing indifferently. Some dissenting voices in the radio business, like independent producer Steve Ackerman, claimed that digital radio was failing to produce 'innovative, unusual programmes'. Figures published in August by RAJAR, the radio audience measurement body, showed that the BBC was

failing to persuade significantly greater numbers of people to listen to its five digital stations, despite investment to the tune of £70.7m in the current financial year. Earlier in the year a government appointed inquiry into the BBC's digital radio project suggested that each of the services needed to be 'redrafted to reflect more accurately the points of distinctiveness from their commercial counterparts'.

Overall, BBC Radio's lead over commercial radio reached record levels in the year under review; in the first quarter of 2005, the national broadcaster achieved a 54.2 per cent share of the market. Radio 1's new strategy began to pay off as the station finally rid itself of the ghost of its former star presenter Chris Evans. Following a period of decline, audience levels once again nudged upwards, passing the psychologically important 10 million-listener threshold during the summer. The improvement was due to a daily line-up anchored by Chris Moyles (replacing Sara Cox) at breakfast, Colin Murray and Edith Bowman in the afternoon and double Sony-award-winning Zane Lowe (seen in some quarters as the new John Peel) in the early evening. Moyles' audience of 6.25 million was up by almost a million on the 2004 figure.

Proof that age can be a state of mind, rather than a figure printed on a birth certificate, came as the veteran DJ Annie Nightingale, 63, continued to broadcast on Radio 1. At least one radio critic thought it was a mistake on the part of the *Radio Times* to exclude her from its peer poll of the most powerful people in British radio, published in June and headed by Jonathan Ross. 'Nightingale wasn't included, and yet she has been just as much a pioneer as John Peel – not only musically but for joining an all-male line-up at Radio 1, and somehow staying put through all the station's reinventions,' observed *The Guardian's* Elisabeth Mahoney.

TRIBUTES ARE PAID TO JOHN PEEL

Peel, aged 65, had died of a heart attack in October while holidaying in Peru. The sole broadcasting survivor of the original Radio 1, the premature death of this great broadcaster generated front-page headlines and genuine grief across the nation. 'Integrity, a kind heart, perfect manners and a gently questing intelligence were qualities that would have given John Peel a place of his own in any profession,' remarked Gillian Reynolds in the *Daily Telegraph*. Thousands of people attended his funeral held at St Edmundsbury Cathedral, Bury St Edmunds. In his tribute fellow broadcaster Paul Gambaccini said: 'You broke more artists than any broadcaster in the history of radio. Every artist once needed a John Peel – some of the people who paid tribute to you were Pink Floyd, Robert Plant, Led Zeppelin and Elton John.' Finding a permanent successor to Peel as the presenter of Radio 4's *Home Truths* proved difficult. As late as the following July the BBC was still wondering who to appoint. Tributes were also paid to another BBC broadcaster, Humphrey Carpenter, who died in January, aged 58. Radio 3 controller Roger Wright said: 'Humphrey Carpenter was a wonderfully engaging broadcaster, intelligent and hugely wide-ranging in his tastes and interests. He played a vital role in launching Radio 3's ongoing arts discussion programme *Night Waves* and was a regular presenter of other programmes on the network including our afternoon drive-time programme *In Tune*.'

Throughout 2004–5 Radio 2 continued its winning streak achieving its biggest-ever audience share of 16.5 per cent. Named Station of the Year at the Sony Radio Awards, there were also prizes at the Sony's for lunchtime host Jeremy Vine and afternoon presenter, Steve Wright.

The station's biggest new signing of the year was former enfant terrible, Chris Evans. In July he announced he was returning to work at the BBC and would front a new Saturday afternoon show. Typically the publicity-savvy Evans signed his new BBC contract, to run initially for seven months, on stage at the Radio Festival in Edinburgh before an audience composed almost entirely of radio industry executives.

Earlier in the year Evans had presented the UK Radio Aid show, staged to raise money for victims of the Asian tsunami. It was his first time on air since quitting Virgin Radio three years earlier. The Radio Aid initiative involved some 250 commercial stations and claimed to be the biggest ever radio event. The one-day special broadcast ran from 7 a.m. to 7 p.m. An estimated 26 million listeners heard a line-up that included the prime minister, Sting, and presenters Johnny Vaughan and Kate Thornton. Commentators agreed that Radio Aid was a brilliant example of what commercial radio could accomplish when it tried.

ARISE SIR TEL

Radio 2's flagship show, *Wake up to Wogan*, drew record audiences of more than eight million in the year under review. The broadcaster, who reportedly renewed his BBC contract for another two years, received a knighthood in The Queen's Birthday Honours in June, a move that led the *Daily Telegraph* to pen a leading article in his praise. The network won acclaim too for its music documentaries: there were series on Eric Clapton, to celebrate his 60th birthday, Crosby, Stills and Nash; *In Search of Nick Drake*, narrated by Brad Pitt, and Hugh Masekela's *Freedom Sounds*, examining the development of South African music. Another style of documentary, *Vietnam Notebook*, presented by veteran reporter Michael Nicholson to commemorate the 30th anniversary of the fall of Saigon, was also praised.

During the year Radio 4 came under the new management of Mark Damazer, a BBC veteran of some 23 years, appointed controller of the network in September. Still recovering from the fall-out following the Hutton report – prompted by a report by then defence correspondent Andrew Gilligan on Radio 4's flagship programme, *Today* – commentators were keen to know what impact Damazer would have on the chattering classes' best loved (and sometimes most reviled) radio station. In the *Daily Telegraph* veteran radio critic Gillian Reynolds thought that parts of Radio 4's schedule, especially Saturday mornings and Sunday afternoons, needed to be rethought. Jenny Abramsky, the BBC's director of radio, appeared to agree that the station could benefit from a facelift. Speaking in the autumn to a government inquiry on the BBC's future, Abramsky admitted: 'There have been times when some programming has not been good enough. Some of the quizzes on Radio 4 have been painful.' In his first interview since accepting the job Damazar indicated that Radio 4 intended to take a more inclusive approach. 'I think it would be desirable to find a voice that was British and Asian or British and black,' Damazar told *The Guardian* in February. 'Radio 4 needs to feel to anybody that experiences it as a light listener that it is open to anybody with an interest in intelligent speech. I would certainly like people all over the UK to feel that it was for them.'

Damazer's policy of broadening the network's appeal got off to a promising start. In the second quarter of 2005, Radio 4's audience increased by 200,000 on the previous

quarter. *Today* itself won 150,000 extra listeners as 6.3 million people tuned in. The late afternoon current affairs show, *PM*, also enjoyed improved listening figures. Its audience of 3.46 million was the highest for two years. Overall, however, Radio 4's audience was below the level it had been at its peak under the previous controller Helen Boaden – in excess of 11 million compared with the present 9.2 million.

THE ARCHERS – JUST ANOTHER BRAND

As ever, controversy stalked Radio 4's veteran soap, *The Archers*. The writer John Mortimer complained that too many of the serial's storylines concerned drugs. Others, like the *Daily Telegraph*'s Gillian Reynolds, thought *The Archers* had fallen victim to the 21st century's habit of turning all popular culture into a brand. '*The Archers* have become a BBC brand,' she wrote in May. 'True, they will never be as big as the *Tweenies* or *Dr Who*, but what used to be a secret pleasure for millions has turned into just another promotable soap.' There was, however, praise for a storyline dealing with Jack's deteriorating health, and Stephen Fry confessed delight when he was selected by an audience vote to take a guest role in an affectionate spoof Comic Relief episode, specially written by Victoria Wood. He enthused: 'As a child, as a barely divided embryo, I remember sitting at my mother's knee listening to *The Archers'* music. It's just stitched into the fabric of my being.' In December a storyline involving Owen raping Kathy Perks at the end of a rehearsal for the annual panto generated interest. Many commentators felt that dealing with rape in a fictional context might console real rape victims. Speaking to *The Guardian*, *Brookside* creator Phil Redmond said: 'It helps people break out of an island mentally – it makes them realise they're not alone.' In October veteran actor Graham Roberts, who had played *The Archers'* George Barford for 31 years, died.

Throughout the year finding a successor to Alistair Cooke's *Letter From America* proved a challenge for Radio 4. One of the candidates was the ex-*Weekend World* interviewer, Brian Walden, who wrote and presented a series of 15-minute talks on topical issues. His programmes met a mixed response. It subsequently emerged that the BBC intended to use Walden alongside other commentators, including former *Sunday Times* editor Harold Evans. The year witnessed the silencing of one of BBC Radio's best known voices, that of newsreader Peter Donaldson, who was due to retire on his 60th birthday in August. However, as he told *Today*'s John Humphrys, he hoped to return to the studio as a freelancer.

BEETHOVEN STRIKES A CHORD FOR NEW MEDIA

In August it emerged that Radio 3 had sunk to its lowest-ever audience figure, amidst more complaints that the arts and culture network had strayed too far from its classical music roots. More than 100,000 listeners had deserted Radio 3 during the year 2004–5 as 1.91 million listeners tuned in a week. Meanwhile Classic FM's audience was broadly stable – 6.31 million compared to 6.48 million a year earlier. The BBC denied there was a surfeit of jazz and world music on Radio 3. 'We have noted the desire of some listeners for more classical music,' commented the board of governors, 'but having examined the output . . . we feel that the current schedule offers an appropriate balance of musical genres.'

Radio 3's popularity may have waned during the year but in June the network was delighted by the response to *The Beethoven Experience*, six days of programmes covering the works of Beethoven in their entirety. In a technological first, the BBC offered free downloads of the complete Beethoven symphonies. Over a week in June the symphonies were downloaded 1.4 million times. This, according to Matthew Cosgrove, director of Warner Classics, was equivalent to upwards of five years' of CD sales. Radio 3 controller Roger Wright claimed the idea had started as 'just a little extra add-on to draw attention to the fact that the BBC Philharmonic was performing their first complete Beethoven cycle for 30 years'. The record industry was worried that the experiment amounted to unfair competition and could undermine its own market, already suffering from the revolution in music downloads. Listeners, however, were thrilled. Said one: 'This is a fantastic experiment in the democratisation of high culture, and shows exactly what direction BBC Radio should take.'

COMMERCIAL RADIO UNITES
In commercial radio, the year's biggest development was the £711m merger of GWR and Capital Radio to create GCap, owner of Classic FM, Capital, Choice and Xfm, plus four digital national stations. High on the group's list of ambitions was for national digital stations Core and Life to compete effectively against Radios 1 and 2 once digital sets become commonplace. Ralph Bernard, executive chairman of GCap, told *The Independent*: 'I believe we will have a majority of listeners in five years.' Some ten points behind the BBC, Bernard and co. have their work cut out.

The success of UK Radio Aid encouraged other collective initiatives by commercial radio, including UK Leaders Live (broadcast during the general election campaign on 1 May) and the united coverage of the international Live 8 concerts using presenters such as Johnny Vaughan, Liza Tarbuck, Richard Bacon and Jamie Theakston. Commentators thought these initiatives might pose a threat to the dominance of the BBC's coverage of events such as Glastonbury and even the Proms in the long term. It remains to be seen, however, if internal commercial rivalries between radio companies Chrysalis,

EMAP, GCap and Scottish Media Group can be put aside so that collaborative endeavours like Live 8 can be repeated.

In the intensely competitive London radio market, battling Capital Radio clawed back its lead over rival Heart 106.2 although Capital's audience fell below two million. In the battle of the breakfast presenters, Heart's Jamie Theakston lost audiences, despite a £2 million advertising campaign aimed at taking listeners away from Capital's Johnny Vaughan, who remained London's most popular early morning presenter. From June London station Jazz FM was renamed Smooth FM, following permission from regulator Ofcom allowing it to change its music policy. Owners Guardian Media Group said the change would allow the station to make a profit for the first time since launching in 1990, but critics suggested the licence should have been handed back in order to allow another company with more enthusiasm for jazz to make a go of Jazz FM.

A sister station in the North-West had already successfully relaunched as Smooth FM, according to the Guardian Media Group.

The award of a coveted Manchester radio licence in June by Ofcom generated considerable competition. The 12-year licence for the Manchester FM commercial contract was the most keenly contested in the history of British radio. The contest attracted 19 applications. One leading radio commentator, Paul Robinson, writing in *The Guardian*, argued that giving the prize to London music station Xfm could threaten Radio 1's popularity in Manchester. 'Of the 19 applications, three were Asian formats, one was speech-based, two were aimed at children or youth audiences, seven targeted older listeners, and six were rock,' wrote Robinson. 'If Xfm can deliver, the radio station will dramatically broaden choice in Manchester.' Xfm presenter Christian O'Connell collected three trophies at the Sony Awards. He also presents *Fighting Talk*, a knockabout Saturday morning talk show on Radio 5 Live. O'Connell was praised for his irreverence and is due to transfer to Virgin Radio early in 2006.

BUSINESS AND FINANCE

Prospects for the UK economy were dominated by a slowdown in consumer spending, which started in the autumn of 2004 and persisted well into 2005. Mortgage approvals and borrowing were restrained and new car registrations were well below the peaks seen in early 2004. The slump in high street spending was blamed in part on flat house prices, with consumers no longer counting on a surge in the price of their homes to finance a spending spree. Previously, home-owners had been happy to tap into remortgages or equity-release schemes to free up cash for new cars or electronic goods.

The price of oil created a cause for concern for everyone from motorists to manufacturers, to airlines. World oil prices hit a record $60 a barrel in New York in June 2005. Rising demand from the USA, China and India caught world producers and refiners off guard, leaving little spare capacity in the event of supply disruption. America and China were expected to account for more than 40 per cent of the 1.8 million barrel-a-day growth in world demand for oil in 2005. Airlines responded to the rising oil price by imposing a fuel surcharge on tickets.

The FTSE 100 index of leading shares finally emerged from the doldrums and surged nearly 5 per cent in the first half of 2005. The index broke through the 5,000 level in June 2005, its highest level in three years. Forecasts for the rest of the year were mixed, with some City analysts predicting that the FTSE 100 would hit 6,000 while others saw it slipping to 4,750.

Britain's financial powerhouse, the City of London, continued to strengthen, with City jobs forecast to average 320,000 in 2005, up just over 4,000 on 2004, according to the Centre for Economics and Business Research (CEBR). City employment was back to the level seen in 2000 at the peak of the dot-com boom.

International financial sector activity was expected to rise as mergers and acquisitions multiplied. Hirings picked up in the equities sector, while corporate finance was also expected to show growth. Fund management added jobs at a faster rate than any other part of the international financial sector in London. Some 40,000 people worked in fund management by mid-2005.

Much of the growth was driven by hedge funds – investment funds that 'hedge' against downturns in the markets being traded. Internationally, the number of hedge funds doubled between 2000 and 2005 to about 8,000. They grew to control about $1 billion in assets worldwide and account for up to half of the daily turnover of the London and New York stock markets. About 125 hedge fund companies opened in London in 2004 alone.

In June 2005, the Financial Services Authority, the chief UK regulator, began investigating the hedge fund industry amid concerns that some managers could be guilty of insider trading and market manipulation. The remuneration of the fund managers is heavily performance-related. In 2004, the US Securities and Exchange Commission voted to extend its oversight of hedge funds, including targeted inspections.

THE ACCOUNTING INDUSTRY

There was buoyant recruitment among the Big Four accountancy firms – PricewaterhouseCoopers, KPMG, Deloitte and Ernst & Young. America's Sarbanes-Oxley Act, named after two US senators, left UK companies with operations in America – effectively most big UK multinationals – with a requirement to prepare annual reports showing that they had assessed risk within their organisations. This resulted in many Big Four staff being poached for internal positions with companies. This in turn triggered a wave of inter-firm poaching, with rivals competing with each other for the best accounting staff.

The activity marked a welcome reversal on the years following the dot-com boom and bust, when a slump in dealmaking led to hiring freezes and saw many accountancy firms shed staff.

For directors of UK businesses with a presence in the US, Sarbanes-Oxley proved a challenge. Section 404 of the Act requires boards to report on the effectiveness of their internal controls. Companies were obliged to spend millions of pounds implementing and testing systems.

This added to the burden on UK company directors, who complained that more and more board time was taken up ensuring compliance with rules and regulations. Too little time was left free to debate key decisions around running the company. This, combined with ever-growing scrutiny from City analysts, shareholder activists and the media, encouraged a flow of talent from UK quoted companies to the venture capital sector. Directors of private equity vehicles stood to make far more money without the scrutiny and criticism that goes with life on the board of a publicly quoted company. Headhunters despaired that finding good non-executive directors – and deepening the pool of available boardroom talent – would become ever-more difficult.

Elsewhere, uncertainty continued to cloud prospects for the accounting profession. Under draft legislation published in 2005, auditors won the right to limit their liability, affording some protection against catastrophic lawsuits. The move to 'proportionate liability by contract' would allow auditors to agree with clients in advance that they would only be liable for their share of fraud or negligence if the company failed. Under 'joint and several liability' auditors could be sued for the entire cost of a company's collapse.

The same company law bill proposed prison sentences for auditors who 'knowingly and recklessly' give incorrect audit opinions. The profession argued that this could land innocent accountants in jail simply because they made a bad mistake.

Ernst & Young, the smallest of the Big Four, found itself at the centre of a landmark High Court action over its role as auditor of Equitable Life, the troubled life assurance company. Equitable sued Ernst & Young along with 15 former directors for a combined £3.75 billion, alleging that their negligence brought the company to the brink of liquidation.

More than a million Equitable policyholders had their pensions and savings cut after the House of Lords ruled in 2000 that the company must honour its pledges to those with guarantees built into their pensions. The judgment blew a £1.5 billion hole in Equitable's finances and forced it to close to new business. Equitable's clients included lawyers, doctors, accountants and other professionals.

The case opened in April 2005. Former Equitable directors in the firing line included Jennifer Page, one-time chief executive of the company behind the Millennium Dome in Greenwich, and Peter Davis, former director-general of the National Lottery.

One floor below, one of the world's most complex court cases rolled into its second year. Deloitte, liquidators of the Bank of Credit and Commerce International (BCCI), sued the Bank of England for 'misfeasance', alleging failings in the Bank's supervisory responsibilities. BCCI was domiciled in Luxembourg but run from London, and the Bank, it was alleged, should have taken full responsibility for supervising it. The Bank denied this. Unusually, the case, which opened in January 2004, was fought mainly through an examination of past memos and internal documents.

Opening speeches lasted 18 months. By the time the first witness was called in June 2005, fees on both sides had reached £70 million. The Bank of England's legal costs were running at £21 million a year. Fees for the liquidators were estimated at £10 million a year. The case looked set to last at least until the summer of 2006, at a cost of more than £100 million.

PENSIONS

Pensions, a dry subject at the best of times, came to dominate headlines for all the wrong reasons. Companies faced huge disruption to their balance sheets under international accounting standards, effective from January 2005. Under the new international accounting standard for employee benefits, IAS19, BT, the telecoms group, swung from a pensions asset of £1.1 billion to a liability of £5.1 billion. Overall, FTSE 100 index companies with final salary pension schemes had a combined pensions deficit of £50 billion. There were fears that shifts in company balance sheets would trigger sharp falls in share prices as City analysts struggled to absorb the implications.

April 2005 saw the introduction of a Pensions Regulator with new 'moral hazard' powers to ensure that company directors and shareholders, including private equity funds, did not abandon their pension obligations. There was a simultaneous debut for the new Pension Protection Fund (PPF), intended to guarantee pensions for members of schemes where companies go bust.

The PPF was set up to compensate workers who lose their retirement savings when their employer goes bankrupt with a pensions deficit. Each year, the fund expected to face a £300 million shortfall between the assets and liabilities of pension funds of companies that went bust. The £300 million was to be collected through an annual levy on companies with final salary pension schemes.

MG ROVER

MG Rover fell into administration just before the May 2005 General Election. The company employed just over 6,000 people at Longbridge, Birmingham, and supported at least another 12,000 jobs in components suppliers and the local economy. This made grim news for Labour given the number of marginal seats in the West Midlands.

MG Rover had been in rescue talks with Shanghai Automotive Industry Corporation, which was keen to make Rover cars in China. But the company's £40 million pension fund deficit proved a sticking point in negotiations.

The company had been struggling since 2000, when it was sold by BMW to a consortium led by John Towers, chief executive of Rover in the 1990s. The 'Phoenix Four' took over the company for a nominal £10, with the safety net of a £550 million long-term loan from Rover. The loss-making company burned through the money in less than five years.

Despite the heavy losses, the four Phoenix directors extracted generous sums from MG Rover. They drew more than £15 million in pay and benefits and channelled £13 million into a trust fund. The men argued that they had taken a huge risk in taking on MG Rover from the Germans, but won little sympathy. Questions were raised about whether MG Rover had been trading while insolvent, which would have severe consequences for its directors.

In July 2005, MG Rover was sold to Nanjing, China's oldest carmaker, for close to £60 million.

OUTSOURCING TRENDS

Another chapter in British manufacturing ended in April 2005 when C&J Clark, maker of Clarks shoes, closed its last major UK plant. About 70 jobs were lost at the factory near Ilminster in Somerset. In its heyday, Clarks exported millions of shoes from more than 20 UK factories. But it shifted production to China, Vietnam and other cheaper destinations. Clarks was set up by two Quaker brothers, Cyrus and James Clark, in 1825 and grew to become one of the UK's biggest privately owned companies.

Outsourcing of services continued to gather pace as banks, insurers and others saw the logic in shifting back office and call centre services to cheaper overseas destinations such as India. However, fears about the security of data in developing countries were heightened in June 2005 when an undercover reporter from a UK tabloid succeeded in buying personal information. The reporter paid a computer expert in New Delhi $5,000 in return for account numbers, bank card details, secret passwords and other personal details of 1,000 British bank customers.

In 2002, Accenture, the consultant, forecast that 65,000 jobs in Britain's insurance industry alone would move overseas within a decade. By 2005, 33 companies, among them Barclays, British Airways, Lloyds TSB and Reuters, had collectively outsourced 52,000 jobs. Amicus, the trade union, estimated that 200,000 British jobs could be lost to offshore outsourcing by 2010.

TAKEOVERS AND MERGERS

Another prominent UK private company cashed in in October 2004. Saga, the insurance and travel provider for the over-50s, was sold to Charterhouse, the private equity group, for £1.35 billion. The deal made a billionaire of Roger de Haan, the son of Sidney de Haan, who founded the company in 1949. After costs and debt, he cleared at least £1.1 billion from the sale.

The deal came a year after the death of Sidney de Haan, who was known in the travel industry as 'the man who turned silver hair into gold'. The son of a shoe factory foreman from London's East End, he started out offering all-inclusive holidays to pensioners at his hotel in Folkestone, Kent. The aim was to fill rooms during the lean winter months. Fifty years later, Saga had diversified into insurance and financial services. Charterhouse was attracted by its database of millions of names and addresses.

The London Stock Exchange (LSE) found itself at the centre of a takeover battle. In December 2004, Deutsche Borse, the German stock exchange, made an indicative offer for the LSE, valuing the exchange at £1.35 billion. Deutsche Borse's move triggered interest from Euronext, a Brussels-based exchange operator. Clara Furse, LSE chief executive, rejected the Deutsche Borse offer, but began holding talks with its chief executive Werner Seifert. The Borse forecast 'significant' tariff reductions as a result of the cost savings derived from putting the two exchanges together.

Discussions dragged on for five months before ending in failure, heaping humiliation on Herr Seifert. He resigned in May 2005. His departure was a sop to rebel Deutsche Borse shareholders who had opposed a takeover of the LSE. The rebels had proposed a vote of no-confidence in the Borse's supervisory board. Rolf Breuer, the Borse chairman, said he would step down by the end of the year.

THE HIGH STREET
The drama continued at Marks & Spencer (M&S), the nation's favourite high street store, which briefly in 2004 became a target of Philip Green, the Bhs billionaire. Green walked away from a £9 billion bid for M&S in July 2004, complaining that the management had refused to allow him access to key information. Stuart Rose, the M&S chief executive, acknowledged that, having seen off Mr Green at the cost of about £40 million, the store 'had to deliver' on its promises. Paul Myners, who was appointed acting chairman of M&S in May 2004 after the departure of Luc Vandevelde, found himself in the role for much longer than he anticipated. It took more than a year for the headhunters to secure Lord Burns, the former Treasury mandarin, as the new M&S chairman.

Elsewhere on the high street, the pain continued at J Sainsbury, the supermarket group. The company admitted that a £3 billion programme of investment – a legacy of Sir Peter Davis, who stepped down as chairman in July 2004 – had failed to generate any improvements. Sainsbury changed its distribution system, but problems with deliveries resulted in empty shelves and food that was close to its sell-by date. Sir Peter received a £2.5 million pay-off.

In further indications of tough trading on the high street, Allders, the department store group, went bust, and Dickins & Jones, the West End store, was closed by its owner, House of Fraser. Laura Ashley closed its flagship Oxford Street branch.

Figures from the Confederation of British Industry (CBI) and British Retail Consortium (BRC) charted a fall in both retail sales and in the number of people visiting stores. Consumer caution and a slowdown in the housing market continued to hit sales of big-ticket and household items. Sales of flat-screen televisions and digital cameras were hard hit.

Year-on-year, the drop in high street sales in June 2005 was the worst in 22 years, according to the CBI. UK consumer confidence was said to be at an all-time low, even before the terrorist bombings. The Bank of England faced repeated calls to reduce interest rates.

One of the most far-reaching public sector shake-ups in years was cemented in April 2005 when the Inland Revenue merged with Customs & Excise to form HM Revenue & Customs. The new tax super-department, headed by David Varney, former chief executive of BG Group, was set to cull 12,000 people from its workforce by 2008 as part of an efficiency drive. It was hoped that the merger would result in fewer points of contact for businesses on tax issues.

HIRING AND FIRING
A round of boardroom musical chairs guaranteed a busy time for Britain's headhunting community. Rod Eddington, the Australian who replaced Bob Ayling as chief executive of British Airways in 2000, stepped down in the summer of 2005. His successor, Willie Walsh, arrived from Aer Lingus. Eddington, who returned to Australia, was credited with steering BA through the worst crisis ever faced by the airline industry – the slump following the terrorist attacks of September 11 2001. He was rewarded with a knighthood in the 2005 Queen's birthday honours.

In a further reshuffle at BA, Lord Marshall of Knightsbridge stepped down as chairman in July 2004 in favour of Martin Broughton, veteran chairman of British American Tobacco. Mr Broughton became BA's third chairman since 1987 when the carrier was privatised.

Lord King, who led BA to privatisation, died in July 2005 aged 87.

Sir Christopher Hogg, long-serving chairman of GlaxoSmithKline (GSK), the pharmaceuticals group, and Reuters, the media company, took his leave of both roles. Sir Christopher Gent, the Vodafone chief executive, replaced him at GSK, while Niall FitzGerald, Unilever's co-chairman (and a 30 year company veteran), took the Reuters job.

Jonathan Bloomer was forced out as chief executive of the Prudential amid investor anger. After failing to find a buyer for the Pru's majority stake in Egg, the internet bank, saying it did not need the money, Mr Bloomer enraged shareholders by launching a £1 billion rights issue. He told City investors that the Pru needed the money to concentrate on growing market share in the UK, a market in which the insurer had been steadily decreasing its share for several years.

Nearly 50,000 private shareholders in Railtrack, the defunct rail operator, took the government to court, alleging that Stephen Byers, Transport Secretary at the time Railtrack was forced into administration in 2001, acted against their interests. Members of the Railtrack Private Shareholders Action Group accused Mr Byers of in effect renationalising Railtrack without having to pay them compensation. They were seeking nearly £160 million to compensate them for the collapse in value of Railtrack shares. The former Transport Secretary strongly denied impropriety and said he had acted in the best interests of the travelling public.

Bust-ups continued to rage at Eurotunnel, operator of the Channel Tunnel rail link. In the summer of 2004, shareholders, the majority of whom are French, sacked the entire board and installed dissidents to run the company. The new chairman, Jacques Maillot, resigned after less than a year amid boardroom feuding and fears over Eurotunnel's precarious financial situation. His successor, Jacques Gounon, gave warning that Eurotunnel would go bankrupt within two years unless creditors agreed to write off half the company's debt of £6 billion.

As negotiations with bankers continued, Eurotunnel disclosed a net 2004 loss of £570 million. It blamed a price war with cross-channel ferries and low-cost airlines. Interest payments were costing Eurotunnel £300 million a year. Eurotunnel's chief executive, Jean-Louis Raymond, resigned in June 2005 ahead of the shareholder annual meeting, but the chairman, Gounon, defeated calls that he too should resign.

CRIME AND PUNISHMENT
Martha Stewart, the television lifestyle personality, went on trial in New York accused of misleading government investors over dealings in the shares of ImClone, a biotech company owned by a friend, Sam Waksal. She was convicted in July 2004 and spent five months in a low-security prison in West Virginia. Following her release in March 2005, she spent a further five months under house arrest wearing an electronic ankle bracelet. Ironically, the publicity gave a boost to Stewart's career.

Another iconic US woman, Carly Fiorina, was ousted in February 2005 as chairman and chief executive of Hewlett-Packard (HP), the computer group. She departed after falling out with her fellow directors over HP's business strategy, collecting a $21 million (£11 million) pay-off. HP shares halved during Ms Fiorina's five-and-a-half-year reign. She pushed through HP's controversial $19 billion acquisition of Compaq in 2002 as part of an ambitious plan to transform HP into a computing and services giant to challenge IBM. The merger never delivered the promised results and Dell leapfrogged HP to become the leading seller of personal computers.

Other former Wall Street stockmarket stars suffered greater humiliation. In March 2005, Bernie Ebbers, former chief executive of WorldCom, was found guilty of orchestrating the biggest fraud in American corporate history. The nine counts of securities fraud, including making false statements to the Securities and Exchange Commission (SEC) and conspiracy to commit securities fraud, were laid by government prosecutors who claimed Ebbers was the mastermind behind the massive deception that brought about WorldCom's $11 billion bankruptcy in 2001. Ebbers, 63, was sentenced to 25 years in prison.

In June 2005, Dennis Kozlowski, the former chief executive of Tyco, and his former finance director, Mark Swartz, were found guilty of stealing more than $150 million (£80 million) from the company. They faced up to 30 years in prison after a New York jury found them guilty of 22 out of 23 charges including conspiracy, securities fraud and grand larceny. Kozlowski was found guilty of granting himself about $96 million of bonuses without board authorisation.

In his heyday, Kozlowski was synonymous with corporate excess. He spent $11 million of Tyco's money buying antiquities and furnishings, including a $6,000 shower curtain, a $19,000 bathroom scale and emerald-encrusted remote control. More Tyco money went on a $2.1 million Roman-themed birthday party for his wife.

Upcoming trials included that of Kenneth Lay and Jeff Skilling, former executives at Enron, the collapsed energy trader.

In the UK, complex fraud prosecutions came under attack with the collapse of a case involving contractors on London's Jubilee Line. The trial was abandoned in March 2005 after 21 months after the jury said they could go on no longer. The case cost £60 million, and the legal aid bill alone exceeded £13 million.

Weeks later a judge castigated prosecuting authorities for contemptuous and scandalous blunders as he threw out a multi-million-pound fraud trial involving two former employees of Prudential, the insurance group.

Elizabeth Forsyth, the only person to be jailed – and later freed on appeal – over the collapse of Polly Peck, the iconic 1980s conglomerate, was due to go on trial in 2005 charged with money laundering in a case brought by HM Revenue & Customs. The case, which involved more than a dozen defendants, was abandoned before it came to trial, costing the taxpayer an estimated £16 million. Preparations had dragged on for more than three years.

It was with these cases in mind that the government announced its intention to scrap juries in complex fraud trials. Judges would try such cases alone, aided occasionally by expert assessors. The plans, which would be debated in parliament, were condemned by civil libertarians and lawyers.

A prominent London stockbroker emerged at the centre of a legal action involving a former employee. Terry Smith, chief executive of Collins Stewart Tullett, faced a £3 million claim for wrongful dismissal from James Middleweek, a former analyst at the company. The claim was settled, but Mr Smith sued the *Financial Times* over its reporting of allegations of malpractice by Mr Middleweek. He claimed that several reports in the FT were unbalanced and malicious. The newspaper stood by its story and said the revelations were a matter of public interest. The case was due to come to court later in 2005.

Some 50,000 investors who suffered losses in the split capital investment trust scandal moved closer to winning compensation after many of the stockbrokers and fund managers which sold 'split caps' put up £144 million as a settlement. The Financial Services Authority had been investigating allegations that a 'magic circle' of brokers and trust managers colluded to buy each other's shares to prop up fees and prices.

Split caps are funds designed to pay either regular income or a one-off payment at the end of a set time. Investors lost more than £600 million after investing in the trusts. Many thought their investments were low-risk and had bought them to pay for school fees or to fund retirement.

Extradition arrangements between the UK and America came under the spotlight. US authorities requested the extradition of three City bankers, David Bermingham, Giles Darby and Gary Mulgrew. The Americans wanted to put them on trial in connection with the collapse of Enron, the energy trader. The men denied conspiring with two Enron executives to defraud Greenwich NatWest, a subsidiary of National Westminster Bank, of nearly £4 million. They allegedly persuaded Greenwich NatWest to sell its stake in a Cayman Islands company to Enron at a discount.

After deliberating for months, the UK government ruled in May 2005 that extradition should proceed. The men pledged to appeal the decision all the way to the European Court of Human Rights, if necessary, potentially delaying moves to extradite them for years. As British citizens working for a UK employer, they argued that their case should be heard in a British court. By mid-2005, 45 British citizens had been issued with extradition orders to the USA under new fast-track laws originally aimed at terrorists, but which were increasingly ensnaring alleged white-collar criminals.

CONSERVATION AND HERITAGE

THE NATURAL ENVIRONMENT

NATURE CONSERVATION SHAKE-UP

In March 2005 the Department for Environment, Food and Rural Affairs (DEFRA) launched its proposals for integrating nature conservation and sustainable farming in England. The new arrangements for farm subsidy, called Environmental Stewardship, will replace the old ESAs (Environmentally Sensitive Area) as well as the successful Countryside Stewardship and Organic Farming schemes. The streamlining of hitherto separate schemes was recommended by Lord Haskins, whose report criticised the previous system as confusing and inefficient. The new catch-all system will also supersede English Nature's Wildlife Enhancement Scheme for Sites of Special Scientific Interest (SSSIs).

For the first time the subsidy will be open to all farmers and land managers in England. In return for the whole-farm subsidy, paid on an acreage basis, the farmer is expected to offer a basic level of environmental management. The scheme has three levels, with a variable subsidy fixed to increasing levels of environmental protection. It is hoped that all farmers will eventually join at least the basic entry-level scheme, which has a flat-rate payment of £30 per hectare (£8 on the upland farms) per year over at least five years. The applicant has to complete a basic audit of 'environmental features' including areas of soil prone to erosion. At a higher level of subsidy are the Organic Entry Level Stewardship for organic farmers, and Higher Level Stewardship, which is tailored towards SSSIs and other environmentally important sites.

Among the manifold targets of the new scheme are reducing soil erosion and the pollution of watercourses, and protecting and enhancing wildlife and historical features. The Higher Level Stewardship will form a key part of the government's aim of getting 95 per cent of SSSIs into 'favourable condition' by 2010, as well as halting the loss of biodiversity (at the current rate of progress it must be said that the government has no chance at all of achieving it). Scotland and Wales are developing similar homegrown schemes. The Welsh whole-farm environmental subsidy, Tir Gofal, will be retained but its administration is to pass from the Countryside Council for Wales (CCW) to the direct control of the Welsh Assembly. Scotland has chosen a system of Land Management Contracts with three grades of subsidy.

Streamlining the environmental subsidy has required a wholesale shake-up of government environmental agencies. In line with Lord Haskins' recommendations, English Nature is to be merged with the Rural Development Service and the Countryside Agency to form a 'new, powerful and independent' body called Natural England. Its headquarters is to be in Sheffield. The new body will be responsible for nature conservation, environment-friendly agriculture, access and recreation, and will have an enlarged remit for coastal and maritime issues – a mass of potentially conflicting demands. Whether such a body will be able to improve the delivery of government policy and also meet government environmental targets remains to be seen. Meanwhile the Joint Nature Conservation Committee (JNCC), responsible since 1991 for science-based advice on wildlife and the environment, is to be made an independent body and, hopefully, renamed.

CHANGING NUMBERS OF MAMMALS AND BIRDS

The latest census of British mammals by the Mammal Society shows how much animal numbers can change in the decade since the last such survey. The most spectacular increase has been in deer numbers. While the native Red and Roe Deer have remained stable over the past ten years, numbers of the introduced Sika Deer have doubled to about 26,500 while those of Muntjac have increased from 40,000 to 128,000 (see below). The native Polecat is another winner, increasing from 15,000 to 63,000 and expanding its range eastwards from its stronghold in Wales. The Mink, on the other hand, has declined from 110,000 in 1995 to about 37,000. This has been linked to the recovery of the otter from 7,350 to about 19,000. Five species of bat, including the still common Pipistrelle and the two rare Horseshoe Bats, are showing a welcome upswing in numbers, the first since populations began to be monitored regularly in 1997. The Water Vole and the Dormouse, on the other hand, continue their downward path despite conservation measures.

There are also winners and losers among the birds. The disappearance of the House Sparrow in London gardens and parks is still a mystery, but a study by the British Trust for Ornithology suggested that the clearance of shrubbery in London parks (for 'human safety' reasons) may be partly responsible. Birds in serious decline include the migratory Spotted Flycatcher, Tree Pipit and Lesser Whitethroat and the resident Lesser-Spotted Woodpecker. A new survey of the uplands revealed big declines in Ring Ousel, Lapwing and Curlew. The summer drought of 2005 spelt breeding failure for many Lapwings, Redshanks and Snipe in south-east England. One of the most-declined species is the Turtle Dove, whose numbers have fallen by 70 per cent since 1965. It seems that fewer are attempting to nest, and this may be linked to changes in the bird's food supply, such as its favourite fumitory, an arable weed.

Winners include the Pink-Footed Goose. In December 2004, some 280,000 geese – about half of the world population – descended on Norfolk. The wintering grounds of the goose are shifting from the west coast to the east, where the main attraction is Norfolk's huge open fields of sugar beet. The discarded crowns and tails of beet make ideal high-energy food for this long-distance migrant. Other winners include the Buzzard and the introduced Red Kite, which continue to expand their ranges across England and are now familiar birds in many areas where they were absent in 1995. The Cormorant has increased inland to the point where it has become a nuisance to anglers (see below). The Dartford Warbler and the Woodlark continue to move northwards, helped by our recent run of warm winters.

INVASION OF THE HARLEQUIN LADYBIRD

A new and potentially invasive ladybird beetle arrived in

Britain in September 2004. The Harlequin Ladybird, *Harmonia oxyridis*, is so-named because it appears in many colours: red, yellow, black and, most commonly, orange. It is slightly larger than the common Seven-Spot Ladybird and has a distinctive 'M' shaped mark near the head. Like other ladybirds, the Harlequin is a predator of Greenfly and scale-insects, and as such has been used as a biological control agent. Unfortunately it will also eat any other insect of the right size, including butterfly eggs and caterpillars as well as other ladybirds.

The Harlequin Ladybird is a native of East Asia, and was introduced to North America and Europe in the 1980s to control greenfly. It soon became established in the wild, and is now the commonest ladybird over parts of the United States, easily noticed from its habit of entering outhouses and garden sheds to overwinter. It is also attracted to bright lights. In America the ladybird's numbers have multiplied to the point that its droppings are spoiling stored fruit, as well as wallpaper and fabrics. Yet despite the known dangers, the ladybird is still sold as a pest-control agent in Europe. Over the past ten years it has become established in the wild – first in Germany, then in France and the Low Countries. In 2004 it crossed the Channel. Most British records are from the south-east, often in gardens, especially where its favourite trees, lime and maple, are present. It was present in hundreds in Great Yarmouth.

Whether the Harlequin Ladybird can survive Britain's winters is unknown, but late summer invasions from across the Channel will probably continue. The beetle's progress is being monitored at Cambridge University but once established in the wild there is little that can be done to control it.

CORMORANT CULL

Cormorants are large fish-eating birds whose predations have made them unpopular with anglers. Around 3,500 pairs of Cormorants nest in the UK, but some 23,000 birds currently spend the winter here – a rise of 68 per cent since 1989. On the coast the Cormorant is tolerated, but it has been increasing inland by large rivers, gravel pits and reservoirs where they nest in colonies in waterside trees. There they feed on young Trout and coarse fish, which has brought them into conflict with anglers. The increase is attributed to immigration from the European mainland and to more birds surviving their first year. Officially the birds are a protected species, though the government grants licences to scare the birds away or even to shoot small numbers of them where significant damage to fish stocks can be demonstrated. One study claimed that up to half the sea-going young Salmon (smolts) were being eaten by Cormorants on some rivers.

The government succumbed to pressure from angling bodies in September 2004, dramatically increasing the cull licence to up to 3,000 birds per year wherever 'a threat to angling interests' can be proven. Licences to shoot up to 1,800 birds were issued between September 2004 and February 2005. The RSPB claim that the cull is based on flawed science and that it contravenes European law on species protection (a claim likely to be challenged in court). It says that licences are being granted unnecessarily and that there are ways of sustaining fish populations without killing Cormorants, for example by using 'fish refuges' such as netting, brushwood, or planted reeds.

WIND FARMS IN SCOTLAND

Wind energy is expected to provide a significant proportion of Britain's electricity in line with our commitments towards clean energy under the Kyoto agreement. In Scotland, 20 per cent of the country's energy needs are to be met by wind power by 2010. This would require an estimated 5,000 turbines. Applications for wind farms are multiplying, and, according to Scottish Natural Heritage, have already exceeded the target figure. However sensitively sited, the impact on the landscape will be considerable. Building the turbines in remote, windy areas requires considerable new infrastructure in the form of roads, quarries and construction sites, not to mention tall pylons transferring the energy across the Highlands to centres of population further south.

The most contentious development is on the Isle of Lewis in the Outer Hebrides, where an application to build 234 turbines was filed in November 2004. This would be the largest wind farm in the world to date. The developers, Lewis Wind Power Ltd, claim that it would meet the energy needs of 1.1 million people and reduce carbon dioxide emissions by 1.85 million tones per year. The construction and maintenance work would also provide about 300 jobs. With further applications on Lewis, Skye and elsewhere in the region, the promoters believe that 'the Western Isles can become the renewable energy capital of Europe'.

The application has had a mixed reception. The 2,000 formal objectors include Scottish Natural Heritage and the RSPB. The farm is situated inside a Special Protection Area (SPA) for birds, used by Golden Eagles and other rare species, and the developer's impact assessment failed to address their concerns. Furthermore the development requires transmission lines suspended by pylons 50 metres high – the height of the Statue of Liberty. The favoured route would pass through beautiful coastal and Highland scenery, including Drummochter Pass along the southern end of the Cairngorms National Park. Objectors organised as 'Highlands before Pylons' are lobbying for the less intrusive but even more expensive alternative of an underwater cable.

Apart from the impact on scenic beauty and the possible dangers to overflying birds, wind farms are open to the criticism of cost and inefficiency. If one includes the cost of infrastructure, including transmission lines and new roads, wind energy is an expensive way of generating energy compared with, say, solar power. In the meantime, the Scottish Executive has promised to review its remarkably liberal guidelines on new wind farms.

'KEEPERS OF TIME'

In June 2005 the Forestry Commission announced that the maintenance of ancient and native woodlands would henceforth be the cornerstone of its policy in England. Ancient woods are defined as those more than 400 years old, while native woods consist mainly of native broadleaved trees. Of 1.1 million hectares of woodland in England, 340,000 has come into these categories, although about one-third have been heavily planted with conifers. Most are privately owned, and some are nature reserves, owned by the Woodland Trust, the Wildlife Trusts and other conservation bodies. The Forestry Commission itself manages large blocks of ancient or native woodland in the New Forest, the Forest of Dean and elsewhere.

The Forestry Commission's new policy, called 'Keepers of Time', promises to remove 'millions' of planted conifers from the woods in its estate and replace them with native trees like oak, ash and beech, by natural regeneration wherever possible. In line with the changed public perception of old woodlands, the Commission now sees them as important sources of historic features and wildlife as well as recreational and educational assets. It recognises their role in flood defence and reducing carbon dioxide and other pollutants in the air. It also recognises the woods as areas of 'tranquility and inspiration as retreats from modern life'. Lord Clark, the Commission's Chairman, proclaimed: 'our ancient and semi-natural woodlands are the jewels in the crown of English forestry, and protecting and enhancing them will now be a high priority'.

This represents a remarkable turn around for a body which not long ago was devoting its activities to turning ancient woods into plantations, and later sold off as many of the smaller and now damaged woods as possible. The new policy will face formidable obstacles from the current large number of deer in English woodlands which make traditional activities like coppicing almost impossible without expensive fences. Moreover the modern forestry industry's reliance on heavy vehicles and machinery militate against sensitive management in ancient woods, especially on heavy clays. Yet without management, the woods become too shady, with the loss of much of their biodiversity. The Forestry Commission's new policy is essentially a statement of good intentions. Whether it results in better conservation remains to be seen.

TOO MANY DEER?
There are between 1.25 and 2.6 million wild deer in Britain, probably more than at any time during the past thousand years. They consist of our two native deer, Red and Roe, plus the introduced Fallow Deer, Muntjac, Sika Deer and Chinese Water Deer. There are also increasing numbers of hybrid deer, especially the Red Deer-Sika Deer cross. From most points of view, two million deer is too many. It is leading to reduced natural regeneration and fewer woodland wild flowers. Another problem is the transmission by the animals of bovine TB and human Lyme disease, which is spread by deer ticks. Car collisions have caused in excess of £11 million of damage since 2003. There are also increasing complaints from gardeners.

Nearly everyone agrees that the Scottish Highlands are over-stocked with Red Deer, but attempts to reduce their numbers have failed. More deer are surviving the generally milder winters of recent years. Deer control (under the fashionable soubriquet of 'sustainable management') in the Highlands is currently the responsibility of the Deer Commission for Scotland which operates through voluntary agreements with private landowners. However, estates depend on stalking for much of their income and have a vested interest in large numbers of deer. Only the stags are shot for sport. The hinds are controlled by culling, and such control is expensive. This has created tensions between the Deer Commission and Scottish Natural Heritage (SNH), which is under orders to bring 80 per cent of SSSIs into 'favourable condition' by 2008. It has already removed nature reserve status from several large Highland properties on the grounds that it can do nothing about over-grazing by deer. SNH now says that if it cannot make better progress over the next three years it will call for new legislation, including fines for landowners who fail to meet designated cull targets.

Meanwhile, in England the Forestry Commission made public its latest action plan on deer management in tandem with its new policy on ancient woodlands (qv). The plan boils down to changing the law to allow licensed shooting in the close season and at night, a move which would effectively change the status of wild deer from game to pests. It also wants to change the Game Laws to allow the sale of venison throughout the year, as

well as develop markets for the meat. However, Roe Deer and Muntjac are small, shy and hard to shoot. Even with better incentives, a sufficiently vigorous 'sustainable management' policy will be difficult to maintain.

GLOBAL WARMING STARTS TO BITE
We hear much about the predicted impact of global warming but less about its early effects in the field. There are in fact abundant signs of change. Ten out of the last 14 years have been hotter than any year preceding 1991. Insects seem to be the most sensitive indicators of a changing climate. Easily observed species like the Orange-Tip Butterfly have extended their range northwards, though there is as yet little sign of a complementary shrinkage in the distribution of northern and montane species (which, however, are less easily observed). Some migratory species, like the Red Admiral and the Hummingbird Hawkmoth are starting to survive the winter. New species, including several Dragonflies, are starting to colonise Britain from continental Europe. The UK Phenology Network, which runs the 'Springwatch' programme with the BBC, is reporting ever earlier first sightings of events like frog spawn, hawthorn flowering and the first Swallow. However there is variation between years, with 2005 being a later year than 2004 or 2003.

In the sea only small differences in temperature can have a dramatic effect. Sea temperatures around Britain have increased by an average of only 0.4°C since 1981, but locally the rise has been as much as 2°C. Fishermen have reported a large increase in warm-water squid in the North Sea, as well as Red Mullet, Pilchards, Sea Bass and other species previously confined to warmer waters. Sightings of Common and White-Beaked Dolphins are increasing in the North Sea, while in western Scotland there are more sightings of Striped Dolphins, which prefer warmer water. Cold water fish like Cod and Haddock seem to be retreating northwards; most of the Cod and Haddock on our shelves now come from Icelandic waters.

Climate change may be partly responsible for the near-total breeding failure of many seabirds in 2004, especially in the northern isles of Orkney, Shetland and Fair Isle. Birds like Kittiwake and Guillemot depend on sufficient stocks of Sand-Eel close inshore. The eels have been overfished, but more fundamental change may be taking place. One possibility is that warmer water has reduced the plankton on which the Sand-Eels feed. Another is that the recent recovery of Herring stocks may be changing the ecosystem to a more 'normal' balance, with fewer Sand-Eels, and therefore fewer seabirds. Seabirds are long-lived and one or two bad seasons do not spell catastrophe. However the recent changes may be the start of a long-term trend by which the survival of the large seabird colonies which attract many visitors to the northern isles would indeed be questionable. Rather late in the day the EU closed the Sand-Eel fishery to commercial fishing in 2005 to give stocks a chance to recover.

ENDANGERED WILD FLOWERS
In 2005, the JNCC published a new Red Data List for vascular plants (wild flowers, trees and ferns), the fourth revision since the first Red Data Book was published in the 1970s. It is based on data from the recently published New Atlas of the British and Irish Flora. Unlike previous lists, the new one is based on changes in plant distribution as well as rarity. This has produced some curious results. Since the degree of danger is based on the rate at which a species seems to be declining, the list includes plants that are not yet rare but which could theoretically become so if

decline continued at the same rate. On this basis, Field Gromwell, still locally common in cornfields, is classed as 'vulnerable', while the once familiar Corn Buttercup is seen as 'critically endangered'. Conversely, species like Western Clover are classed as 'least concern' because their populations appear stable, even though they are confined to a few square kilometres. A few Red-Listed species even show signs of increasing, perhaps with the help of a warming climate.

Among the most threatened groups of plants are upland flowers, victims of overgrazing by sheep and deer, and also vulnerable to climate change. It is said that we are good at preserving very rare species but bad at preventing the decline of once common ones. Perhaps most alarmingly, the latest Red List includes one in five of the entire British flora of native and long-introduced vascular plants – that is, 345 species out of 1,756. The list can be downloaded at www.jncc.gov.uk.

NEW AND RESTORED WILD PLANTS

The British flora is one of the most thoroughly recorded on the planet and few new species have been discovered in recent years. Two wild orchids, the Lindisfarne Helleborine, *Epipactis sancta*, and the Hebridean Marsh-orchid, *Dactylorhiza ebudensis*, have been added to the list on the basis of their distinctive DNA. In July 2004 a new and almost certainly native sedge was discovered in a remote part of Scotland. This is *Carex salina*, now called Saltmarsh Sedge, which was found growing along saltwater channels at the head of Loch Duich on the north-west coast. Though not a plant to attract notice from anyone except an expert botanist, it is interesting as a circumpolar arctic species, found along the northern shores of the world with Scotland representing one of its southernmost outposts. Now that people recognise and are looking for it, Saltmarsh Sedge will probably turn up in other suitable places in northern Scotland.

English Nature announced the successful re-establishment of a grass once believed to be extinct. Interrupted Brome, *Bromus interruptus*, so-named because of the gaps among its flower-heads, is found nowhere else in the world outside southern England. It is believed to have evolved recently by mutation and for a few decades in the last century became established as a weed in fields of clover and sanfoin grown as fodder for horses. With changing agricultural practices, including the use of herbicides and chemical fertiliser, it declined and was last seen in the wild in Cambridgeshire in 1972. Fortunately the late Philip Smith, a Cambridge-based botanist, had had the foresight to grow some in a pot. The grass was propagated at Kew and later sown along the edge of a field at Aston Rowant nature reserve in the Chilterns. Thousands of plants appeared there in summer 2005, and it is hoped that a self-sustaining population has been established. English Nature have plans to introduce Interrupted Brome to other sites.

'REWILDING'

Nature conservation in Britain has traditionally been based on designated sites such as nature reserves. Many have management plans which involve a surprising amount of farming to retain characteristics of value to wildlife such as hay meadows and coppiced woodland. Unfortunately many reserves are too small and isolated among intensive farmland to sustain their full biodiversity at a time of unprecedented change. For this reason there is growing interest in securing larger areas with more room for the interchange of species, and also for more 'natural'

management involving free-range 'wild-type' breeds of cattle and ponies.

In his book *Beyond Conservation*, published in August 2005, Peter Taylor, an environmental consultant, argued the case for a full-blooded 'rewilding' of remote areas. He advocates introducing large herbivores like wild cattle and Elk, and, more contentiously, of their predators – Lynx, Wolf and even Brown Bear. He identified three areas apparently suitable for such an experiment, the 1,500 sq. km wilderness around Glen Affric in Scotland, and, at a more modest level, in the Rhinogs of Snowdonia and Dartmoor. Taylor believes that this form of 'wildland' conservation would capture the public imagination and appeal to our suppressed longing for truly wild places. Glen Affric and places like it could become homegrown safari parks.

While the introduction of wolves and bears is not likely to happen in the foreseeable future, some landowning bodies are consciously pursuing a policy of 'rewilding'. The National Trust hopes to acquire land in Cambridgeshire sufficient to recreate part of the lost Fens, drained in the mid-19th century. Its sister, the National Trust for Scotland, is encouraging the natural regeneration of woodland at Mar Lodge in the Cairngorms and on its newly acquired estate at West Affric by reducing sheep stockage and culling Red Deer. The wildlife trusts are experimenting with animals such as Beaver, Water Buffalo and wild Konik Ponies on some wetland nature reserves in the belief that they produce more natural landscapes than domestic stock, and thus encourage more biodiversity. Quite how far we go along that road will depend on public opinion reflected in political debate.

GM CROPS CREATE A 'SUPERWEED'

Modified genes from a GM crop trial have spread into the wild despite assurances from government scientists that such an occurrence was impossible. Cross-fertilisation between GM Oilseed Rape and its distant wild relative, Charlock, was discovered when the latter plant showed no ill effects from a normally lethal herbicide. Similar resistance was shown by Wild Turnip, another weed growing nearby. The findings were submitted to the government but picked up by a Guardian journalist. As English Nature's advisor on GM technology remarked, 'you only need one such event in several million. As soon as it has taken place the new plant will have a huge selective advantage and will multiply rapidly.'

It is not clear whether the charlock plants contaminated with modified genes are fertile, but they have the appearance of normal healthy plants. If the GM trait is in the plant's pollen it will inevitably be carried to other plants in the area. Once seeds have been produced the 'superweed' will be impossible to eradicate, since charlock seeds can survive in the soil for up to 30 years. The findings mirror the experience of GM crop trials in Canada, where farmers had to resort to stronger, more environmentally damaging types of herbicide to combat the new resistant superweeds. GM crops are not grown commercially in Britain and the three-year period of trials ceased in 2003.

THE BUILT ENVIRONMENT

REFORMS

The overview of 2003 commenced with an assessment of the Heritage Protection Review that was launched in July of that year. Heralded as the biggest shake-up in the protection of what is now termed 'the historic environment' since the great Town and Country Planning Act of 1947 which first introduced listing, the government announced in late June 2004 how it hoped to carry out the reforms. The principal items were:

- The take over by English Heritage from the Secretary of State (at the Department for Culture, Media and Sport) of the administration of the listing regime. This came into force on 1 April 2005 with all applications to protect buildings, mainly by listing, going direct to English Heritage. Until the promised legislation the Secretary of State retains the power to list or to de-list. In the long term the Department's powers will be limited to the conduct of a formal appeal system, or 'review procedure' as it is be called.
- A review of the criteria for deciding which buildings should be protected. A consultation is expected in late 2005 or early in 2006.
- The inclusion as a matter of course in each new listing of 'an Assessment of Importance' setting out why the structure in question had been accorded protection.
- The provision of a public map showing the extent of the listing and in particular the confines of the curtilage.
- The beginning of consultations with owners and local planning authorities whenever an application is made to add a new building to the list.
- The production of an information pack for owners, over and above the brief description presently available.

And in the longer term:

- The introduction of a single unified 'Register of Historic Sites and Buildings of England' (at present the reforms do not embrace Scotland, Wales or Northern Ireland). This will bring together the current regimes of listing, scheduling, registration (of gardens) and will incorporate World Heritage Sites. In addition there will be a 'Local Section' which will contain a record of all conservation areas and local lists.
- At present there are three grades of listed buildings: Grade II, which encompasses some 94%; Grade II* which are especially important; and Grade I which are regarded as exceptional. Under the new regime there will be two grades: Grade I and Grade II, although Grade II will now be called G2. Grade II*, a category which currently holds some 25,000 buildings, would be abolished altogether. It is understood that there is likely to be a wholesale migration of those currently in Grade II* to Grade I with some selective demotion to G2 over time.
- The introduction of an interim protection order once a proposal to list is mooted, in order to ensure that there is no pre-emptive demolition or alteration.
- An increased stress on statutory Management Agreements although their use will be limited and mainly applicable to vast complexes such as hospitals, university campuses or local authority housing estates.
- The introduction over time of new 'integrated consent regimes' to be administered, as they are largely now, by the local authorities. English Heritage would do the listing, the Secretary of State would consider appeals, but fielding applications to demolish or alter would be the responsibility of a planning authority. The major difference would be the protection of scheduled monuments – mostly buried sites, ruins and monuments of the Industrial Revolution – where Scheduled Monument Consent will no longer be administered by the Secretary of State.
- The introduction of legislation to require local authorities to establish and maintain Historic

Environment Records, or at least have access to them. These used to be called Sites and Monuments Records, but have never hitherto been made mandatory. It is envisaged that in the given district each site of importance, whether archaeological or architectural, would be described in the Records.

How the new regime would be implemented is being honed by the findings of a number of pilot projects where a 'single heritage regime' seemed to offer the promise of a clearer, better understood system of protection. The projects covered included Arnos Vale Cemetery in Bristol, the bridges of Cornwall, the Godolphin Estate in Cornwall, the Holkham Estate in Norfolk, the Piccadilly Line of the London Underground, RAF Scampton in Lincolnshire, the Water Meadows at Eastleigh in Hampshire, and the city walls of York.

At some stage, probably early in 2006, a White Paper will spell out the further legal steps envisaged. However, the commitment of English Heritage to the new regime is already pronounced, even in the context of the constant harrying of their finances. The number of designations staff within English Heritage has increased from 49 to 56, and associated offices to receive and process listing applications are either open or planned in Bristol, York, London and Cambridge.

The Secretary of State, Tessa Jowell, at one stage had planned to extend the administrative changes further, with a proposal to consider the marrying together of English Heritage and the Heritage Lottery Fund, despite the fact that one receives its money from the tax payer, the other from the Lottery player. A management study showed the potential of some £16 million in savings but to offset that was the very real risk in fusing the distribution of two fundamentally different sources of public money – allowing an unscrupulous government to conceal cuts in money available from taxation. The idea now seems to have been quietly dropped. Just before the general election in 2005 Mrs Jowell, who enjoys a reputation for manifest indifference towards the heritage, surprised many with a personal essay on the history and built environment entitled 'Better Places to Live'. Although the press comments were limited to making easy fun of the rather naive suggestion that advances in digital photography and cinematography make it easy and affordable to create virtual moving images of buildings, to such an extent that the latter itself can then be demolished, the essay was thoughtful and strong on facts. She noted that the membership of the National Trust was easing its way towards 3.5 million people, with that of English Heritage over 500,000. She noted too the existence of 160,000 volunteers within the sector, whilst for her Heritage Open Days in September, which attracted 300,000 visits in 2004, is 'the largest single cultural event held annually in England'. She also offered reassurance on heritage as a Good Cause under the National Lottery, affirming her view that 'people want Lottery funding to support heritage in the widest sense...'.

NEW LEGISLATION AND COMPENSATION SCHEMES

Something of the sense that heritage was worthy of support was reflected by the Chancellor of the Exchequer in his decision in the Spending Review to replenish the resources of the National Heritage Memorial Fund from the present £5 million to £10 million over three years – and to extend the Listed Places of Worship Scheme. Under this he introduced a grant system which allowed churches to claim back all but 5 per cent of VAT they otherwise paid on repairs. In 2004 he extended the concession to cover all the 17.5 per cent, and in the Budget for 2005 the timetable for concessions was extended to March 2008 and further broadened to cover war memorials and lightning conductors. However within its own bailiwick, the Department for Culture, Media and Sport (DCMS) was widely reported in the press as continuing to undervalue the work of its principal quango, English Heritage. In the Spending Review announced at the end of 2004 English Heritage suffered a further round of cuts of 4.6 per cent. These were accompanied by the allocation of several million pounds to allow English Heritage to acquire the great Northamptonshire house of Apethorpe on which a compulsory purchase order had been confirmed in 2004, and a further £9 million for 'improvements' to properties actually owned by English Heritage. And yet the Review was trumpeted by the government as being its most harsh in its impact on the heritage responsibilities of the DCMS. Guided by the 2003 and 2004 annual reports of the Department, the comparative five-year growth between 2000–1 and 2005–6 has been a mere 3 per cent for English Heritage, which compares with 36 per cent for Museums, Galleries and Libraries, 53.4 per cent for the Arts Council, and 98 per cent for Sport England. The figures excluded earlier allocations for time limited schemes which, in English Heritage's case, includes millions of pounds to improve the presentation of Stonehenge.

And there was some compensation in other areas. The government confirmed in 2004 that it was to extend the Aggregate Levy Sustainability Fund (ALSF) Grant Scheme beyond its successful two-year pilot. This would bring English Heritage more than £3 million to distribute to new projects in 2004–5, of which at least £600,000 has been ring fenced to fund maritime related projects. The ALSF was introduced in 2002 to provide funds to tackle a wide range of problems in areas affected by the extraction of aggregates, and in the last two years the grants have helped to finance ambitious environmental, heritage and access projects.

Finally, in the context of a broad strategic framework, the Planning and Compulsory Purchase Act received the royal assent in 2004. Its principal novelties were the abolition of Structure and Local Plans to be replaced by Regional Spatial Strategies and Local Development Frameworks, but it also provided for the final abolition of Crown Exemption from heritage controls and the reduction in the life of planning permissions and listed building consents from five years to three.

In Wales there was also a review of the Ecclesiastical Exemption of churches in use from listed building consent and conservation area consent regimes. The review, conducted by Peter Howell on behalf of Cadw and the Welsh Assembly, generally found in favour of the continuation of the Exemption but advocated a large number of administrative reforms.

GRANTS AND REPAIRS

Protecting historic buildings and sites is one thing, offering money to save them is another. English Heritage had some £30 million to spend on such projects in the 12 months under review and the proportionate budgets of organisations like Historic Scotland did permit single grants of substantial size – £764,000 in the case of that offered to Donaldsons College in Edinburgh where work was completed in 2004. But by far the greatest distribution came from the coffers of the Heritage Lottery Fund (HLF), administering one of the Good Causes under the National Lottery. In 2004–5 it had some £330 million to distribute to a huge variety of heritage projects, from public parks to works of art, to museums, historic townscapes, churches, research and education projects, nature conservation and the land, and archives. £4 million also went on a training bursary scheme 'to keep alive essential heritage skills such as harling, pargeting, flint knapping, heather thatching, dry stone walling, stone masonry, gold leaf and hedge laying'. Major grants in the year under review included the Darnley Mausoleum at Cobham in Kent (£4.98 million); the Ashmolean Museum in Oxford (£15 million); Benjamin Franklin's house in Craven Street, Charing Cross (£984,500); the Cotswold Canal (just short of £11 million); Fulham Palace (£2.56 million); the Musical Museum at Brentford, Middlesex (£1.8 million); Northumbria National Park Authority (£989,000) to run a 5-year traditional skills project to restore the dry stone boundaries of the Park; The Museum of Childhood at Bethnal Green in London (£3.5 million); the Cutty Sark (£11.7 million); the John Murray Archive (£17.7 million); to allow the purchase of 150,000 manuscripts, papers and correspondence of people as various and influential as David Livingstone, Charles Darwin, Jane Austen, Walter Scott, Thomas Carlyle, Benjamin Disraeli, Michael Faraday and Gladstone to allow its rehousing in the National Library of Scotland; a new Riverside Museum in Glasgow (£15 million); the Great North Museum in Newcastle (£8.7 million); the Royal Albert Museum in Exeter (£8.4 million); Gordon Square and Woburn Square in Bloomsbury, London (£998,500); The Royal Hall, Harrogate (£6 million); the Walks at Kings Lynn in Norfolk (£3.75 million); the creation of a National Database of Historic Parks and Gardens and Landscapes in Wales (just short of £1 million); The Victoria County History (£3.374 million) to increase access to the resources of the Local History Research Centre of the VCH; the purchase of the Sir Basil Spence Archive by the Royal Commission on the Ancient and Historical Monuments of Scotland (£975,000); and Dinefwr Park and Castle, Llandeilo in Wales (£1.2 million) to allow the National Trust to conserve the broader estate, including the only ancient herd of white cattle in Wales. And beside these show stoppers were hundreds of smaller grants to collect memories, write guides, repair village ponds and commons and arrange exhibitions.

And many more grants fed through to projects were now completed and open. Projects completed in 2004–5 included the repair of Christ Church, Spitalfields, Hawksmoor's great masterpiece in East London; the reopening of the Theatre Royal in Richmond, North Yorkshire; the re-siting of the greatest collection of architectural drawings in the world, those held by the Royal Institute of British Architects (RIBA), in its new premises in the Henry Cole Wing of the Victoria & Albert Museum which opened in November 2004; the reopening of the Cambridge and County Folk Museum; the Foundling Hospital in Bloomsbury, including the collection of 150 pictures painted by England's leading artists given to the hospital between 1740 and 1770; the reopening of the huge covered stables at Buxton in Derbyshire, latterly the Hounds Hospital, as the new campus for the University of Derby; the Swansea Maritime and Industrial Museum; 78 Derngate, Northampton, the only work south of the Border by Charles Rennie Mackintosh which is now open for public inspection; and the Playfair Project, Edinburgh, the £30 million scheme to repair, and to connect underground, the Royal Scottish Academy and the National Gallery of Scotland.

Not all attractions of course are funded by the HLF and among newcomers not needing to rely on the National Lottery was Danson Park in Bexley which reopened in March 2005. The house was for many years a byword for systematic neglect, initially at the hands of the local authority. In 1995 English Heritage bravely stepped in and embarked on a £4 million rescue campaign and the conveyance of the building to a specially established trust. This quintessential late Palladian villa designed by Sir Robert Taylor, instead of standing derelict at the heart of a public park, is now immaculate and open to the public. In the City of London Temple Bar, expelled to Hertfordshire in 1878 as the result of a road widening scheme, has been re-erected on a site next to St Paul's Cathedral. The former House of Correction at Little Dean in Gloucestershire, one of four in the county erected in the 18th century by a leading prison reformer, has now been handed over as a new tourist attraction for the Forest of Dean. Netherby Hall, Cumbria, the home of the Graham clan built in the early 16th century, is open for the first time having been repaired after some 16 years of dereliction. Norfolk Record Office has secured the extraordinarily important archive of the King Studio in Norwich, the leading firm of glaziers involved in repair campaigns at most of the surviving medieval windows in the country.

And there have been institutional innovations too. In 2004 a new institution called Jewish Heritage UK was launched to study and protect not just synagogues but many of the other Jewish building types. The government itself established a National Historic Ships Unit, whilst the search for craftsmen was made easier by the establishment of the new website at www.conservationregister.com – some compensation for the recent effective death of 'Heritage Information', launched on the web with such optimism but now de facto dormant. Also freshly available from the RIBA is its Conservation Review which includes the first published and illustrated inventory of architects accredited in conservation.

DEMOLITIONS

Two listed buildings are still threatened with application to demolish every week, the total number of applications in England and Wales in 2004 being 120. Buildings so threatened included Commerce House, Market Street, Haverfordwest in Pembrokeshire (application refused); the roofless Modernist South Side and Linstead, student housing in Princes Gardens, London SW7 of 1960 by Sheppard Robson (permission given); the former Governor's House at Brixton Prison of 1819 of an intriguing octagonal form (application refused); the Theatre Royal, Chatham in Kent of 1899 (application refused); and the Libanus Chapel at Treherbert in Glamorgan of 1858 where permission to demolish is likely, given the extent of structural failure. Fire is always a threat and several very important buildings were lost or damaged in 2004–5 including the Grade I listed Quaker Meeting House at Jordans in Buckinghamshire where the roof was destroyed; Hafodunos House, one of the few domestic designs of Sir Gilbert Scott, where the roof and interior were virtually obliterated; and Stoke Rochford Hall in Lincolnshire, latterly the conference centre of a teachers' union where the damage was severe. One of the few manufacturers of terracotta, Hathernware in Leicestershire, founded in 1874, closed its doors for the last time with the loss of 28 jobs. This left only one domestic supplier of the material which provides the external face of Harrods, the Natural History Museum and many an office of the Prudential Assurance Company.

Sometimes the reaction to a threat is direct acquisition. English Heritage stepped in to buy the great Flax Mill at Ditherington in Shrewsbury of 1796, acknowledged as 'the earliest multi-storeyed iron-framed building ever erected'. A number of important redundant churches passed to the Churches Conservation Trust, including Imber in Wiltshire and Redgrave in Suffolk. The Friends of Friendless Churches, having taken Henry Wilson's great church of Brithdir in Gwynedd, also acquired the impressive medieval church at Rhoscrowther in Pembrokeshire. The Historic Chapels Trust completed the programme of repairs at St George's German Lutheran Church in Alie Street on the borders of the City of London and Tower Hamlets and moved its offices there. The Landmark Trust, which saves idiosyncratic structures and puts them to use as holiday accommodation, has added to its portfolio the Grade II* listed Freston Tower near Ipswich in Suffolk built in 1578, and received help from the Heritage Lottery Fund to save Clavells Tower at Kimmeridge Bay in Dorset which threatened to tumble down a cliff face.

PUBLICATIONS AND VETERAN TREES

The list of publications in 2004–5 which advanced the frontiers of scholarship is headed by Dr Giles Worsley's major study of the stable, Sheila Kirk's biography of Philip Webb, and Dr Terry Friedman's history of the Georgian church. There were new Buildings of England volumes in the Pevsner series on the East End of London, Lancashire, Manchester and the South-East, with city volumes on Liverpool, Sheffield, Bristol and Birmingham. Considered English Heritage advice on disabled access to historic buildings and their protection from flooding were issued, as were guidelines on how to prevent clutter in 'Save our Streets'. English Heritage's 'Heritage Counts', the bringing together of key facts and perspectives looks set to become an annual event. So is its updated Buildings at Risk List, the latest of which came out in June 2005. Historic Scotland's excellent Technical Guidance continued with books on mortars in historic buildings, the maintenance and repair of carved stone structures, the care and conservation of 17th century plasterwork, early medieval sculpture, chemical consolidants and water repellents on sandstone.

And, finally, the major new campaign of the year was one launched by the Woodlands Trust to protect ancient or, as they termed it, veteran trees from destruction. The Trust has compiled a list of 100 ancient trees at 50 sites, including Windsor Great Park, spurred on by the recent loss of an ancient yew tree at Lullingstone in Kent. Its researches suggest that Britain's oldest tree is a Yew at Ashbrittle Church in Somerset which is credited as being 3,800 years old.

DANCE

Sir Frederick Ashton, the founder choreographer of the Royal Ballet, was born in Ecuador in 1904, and the Royal Ballet's 2004–5 season was dedicated to paying homage to him and celebrating the centenary of his birth. Ashton spent his early years in Peru, and there he saw Pavlova dance. It was an experience that stayed with him for the rest of his life and inspired a romantic, idealised image of the ballerina that he later sought to create – or find – in his dancers. After moving to England, he pursued his career first as a dancer and then as a choreographer. His first ballet was *A Tragedy of Fashion,* created in 1926 with the encouragement of Marie Rambert for the 'Riverside Nights' revue in London; he went on to create more works for Rambert, and then for de Valois and her new young company, the Vic-Wells (later Royal) Ballet. In 1935 he joined de Valois as both dancer and choreographer, and the works he created over the subsequent half-century defined the 'English' style of ballet, and gave the Royal Ballet and its dancers a gift beyond measure. Technically demanding, his style combines fast footwork with a deeply pliant upper body, speed with lyricism, and musicality with an innate romanticism. His work ranges from the quiet, plotless beauty of *Symphonic Variations,* created in 1946 to mark the end of the Second World War, to the witty humour of *A Wedding Bouquet* (1937) and the dramatic skill of such works as *The Dream* (1964), *Enigma Variations* (1968) and *A Month in the Country* (1976). He created the first full-length ballet for a British company when he made *Cinderella* in 1948. He was inspired by his dancers, especially by Margot Fonteyn, but he also moulded them and influenced their development so that they could give life to his vision. The company paid tribute to his lasting influence in a season that displayed an impressive range of his works, and also acknowledged his period as director of the company (from 1963 to 1970) with a revival of Nijinska's great work *Les Noces,* acquired by him for the Royal Ballet in 1966. This was teamed on the opening bill of the season with *A Wedding Bouquet* and MacMillan's moving *Requiem,* to the gentle and uplifting setting by Fauré. The season continued with a well-chosen selection of full-length and one-act works from Ashton's oeuvre, including *Cinderella, La fille mal gardée, Ondine,* a successful revival of *Sylvia* (not seen in its entirety since 1965), *Scènes de Ballet, Rhapsody* and *A Month in the Country.* The shorter works were complemented by ballets by MacMillan, Balanchine and Nijinska. However, the only creation of the season, *Three Songs, Two Voices* by Christopher Bruce, was unremarkable and served to underline the serious problem faced not only by the Royal Ballet but by classical companies throughout the world.

The Royal Ballet has an unmatched repertoire, superb dancers, and a competent director in Monica Mason, but it has no resident choreographer, and the supply of talented classical choreographers has dwindled alarmingly in recent years. Christopher Wheeldon, who trained at the Royal Ballet School but has spent most of his career to date in New York, was scheduled to create a work for the Royal Ballet during the season, but this had to be cancelled when he fell ill and could not finish the work. The creative talents of Ashton and MacMillan (and his

contemporary, John Cranko) have influenced later generations of British choreographers, but have not yet been matched, and without great new works an art form is in danger of atrophying. Ashton's work, at least, should be safeguarded by the setting up of an Ashton Trust, which was announced in October 2004 and should help to ensure the coherent preservation of his legacy.

The ballerina Alicia Markova, one of Ashton's first muses and a crucial influence on both the development of his choreographic talent and the development of ballet in the 20th century, died at the age of 94 on 2 December 2004. She was born Lilian Alicia Marks in London in 1910, and after taking up ballet as a child to combat various health problems she blossomed into a dancer of great technical ability and expressive musicality. She joined Diaghilev's *Ballets Russes* in 1925 and caught the interest of a new generation of choreographers, including George Balanchine, who were struck by the new possibilities suggested by her androgynous young body and her strong technique. When Diaghilev died in 1929 she returned to England and put her gifts to the service of the fledgling companies run by Rambert and de Valois, becoming the first ballerina of the Vic-Wells Ballet. She was particularly renowned for her portrayal of *Giselle,* but she also created roles for Ashton and helped to establish the high technical standards aimed at by the company ever since. In 1935 she left to set up her own company with Anton Dolin, and toured widely throughout Britain, sowing the seeds that would later flourish as a result of the wartime touring of the Vic-Wells Ballet. In 1938 she left Britain to join the Ballet Russe de Monte Carlo, and there followed more than a decade of touring throughout the world with various companies, helping to popularise ballet in many countries and coming to embody the image of a darkly glamorous, fragile ballerina while nevertheless dancing with enormous strength and artistry. On her eventual return to Britain, she founded the London Festival Ballet with Dolin in 1950 as a touring company that would take ballet all over the country and ensure that as wide as possible an audience could see the art form at its best. She then resumed her peripatetic career, travelling widely and guesting with many companies (including the Royal Ballet). She retired from dancing in 1962 but continued to work as a director, coach, teacher and producer until shortly before her death.

Another of Ashton ballerinas, Pamela May, died on 6 June 2005 at the age of 88. She joined the Vic-Wells Ballet in 1934 and created a series of important roles for both Ashton and de Valois, including the Red Queen in de Valois' *Checkmate,* one of the roles in Ashton's *Symphonic Variations,* and the Fairy Godmother in his *Cinderella.* She epitomised the English classical style, and went on to teach and to coach for the rest of her life. Maude Lloyd, who inspired Ashton, Antony Tudor and Andrée Howard to create roles for her in the 1930s and whose career was centred on Ballet Rambert (now Rambert Dance Company) died on 26 November 2004 at the age of 96.

Markova's Festival Ballet, now English National Ballet, survives with much the same aim as that with which she founded it. It has battled on through a series of financial crises, and has used the security built up from long runs of the classics – especially *The Nutcracker* – to fund the performance and creation of more modern works. This season, however, after a financially disastrous run at Christmas 2003 in London at the Apollo Hammersmith while the London Coliseum, its usual London base, was refurbished, the company found itself having to rely entirely on a small repertoire of popular full-length works, including two productions of *Romeo and Juliet,* to keep itself afloat. After four years in charge, its artistic director, Matz Skoog, announced that he would be leaving the company in October 2005 after overseeing the European première of MacMillan's *The Sleeping Beauty.* Skoog maintained a high standard of dancing in the company, but was frustrated in his wish to perform a varied repertoire including new works. The company will be left in a fragile position on his departure and needs to find a new director who can work with the board to strengthen the company both artistically and financially.

Maude Lloyd's home company, Rambert Dance Company, continues to flourish under the directorship of Mark Baldwin. During the season he created his first work for the company since taking over as director in 2003; *Constant Speed* (referring to the constant speed of light) was commissioned by the Institute of Physics to mark 'Einstein Year' in 2005, celebrating the centenary of the publication of Albert Einstein's major theories, including the theory of relativity. The work premièred at Sadler's Wells in May 2005 and was a joyous and attractive piece set to Franz Lehár waltzes. Baldwin also revived Michael Clark's influential 1986 work *Swamp* during the season, and reiterated the company's commitment to developing new choreographers from within the company when he used Mikaela Polley's promising work *Momenta,* created during a workshop season in January 2005, in the company's main repertoire for its spring 2005 tour.

Scottish Ballet, unlike Rambert, is in the process of forging a new identity. Under the directorship of Ashley Page the company had an encouraging season during which the standard of dancing improved markedly and the repertoire began to develop. Page has already mounted a new production of *The Nutcracker,* and plans to follow this with *Cinderella* in 2005; at the same time, he is creating works for the company in his own edgy, contemporary style and is acquiring works from other choreographers that will stretch and challenge both dancers and audience. In early 2005 the company secured lottery funding to enable it to develop plans to move into a state-of-the-art dance centre as part of the Tramway complex in Glasgow. The Edinburgh International Festival presented the company for the first time in nearly 20 years in the summer of 2005.

Ashley Page's former Royal Ballet colleague, David Bintley, continues to direct Birmingham Royal Ballet and to consolidate its reputation as a top-quality touring company. It presented a bill during the season entitled 'Stravinsky! a Celebration', which was the first part of a plan by the company, the Royal Ballet Sinfonia and the City of Birmingham Symphony Orchestra to perform the entire works of Stravinsky. The performances formed part of Birmingham's 'Urban Fusion' celebrations, and included the first performances by a UK company of Nijinsky's *The Rite of Spring* as reconstructed by Millicent Hodson. A number of new works were created during the season, including an attractive piece by Michael Kopinksi

to Stravinsky's *Dumbarton Oaks* and an enjoyable interpretation of Vivaldi's *The Four Seasons,* choreographed by Oliver Hindle around the successful 'Summer' section premièred in 1998. Bintley's own fine choreographic talent has become less reliable as his career has progressed, hampered perhaps by the demands of running a large company. His new work, *The Orpheus Suite,* a reworking of the Orpheus myth based on Duke Ellington, fell into the same trap as several of Bintley's other recent works by getting bogged down in its own complexity.

The smaller-scale touring company Northern Ballet Theatre has a distinctive style that has been maintained and developed by its artistic director, David Nixon, and continues to attract audiences. It mounted a successful new production of *Peter Pan* during the year, and gave the first UK performances of Veronica Paeper's *La Traviata,* created in 1990 for Cape Town City Ballet in South Africa. It also presented Nixon's spirited *Dangerous Liaisons,* to Vivaldi and with excellent designs by Nixon himself, in September 2004.

Another production of the same work, *Les Liaisons Dangereuses,* received rather more critical attention and public acclaim. This was a version co-directed by Adam Cooper and the designer Lez Brotherston and created in Japan in January 2005; it was shown at Sadler's Wells Theatre in July of the same year. Starring Cooper himself and his wife, the former Royal Ballet dancer Sarah Wildor, the work was conceived as a 'gritty drama told through dance'. It proved to be an intelligent, beautifully designed and strongly danced production, to an effective score by Philip Feeney.

Cooper's erstwhile collaborator, Matthew Bourne, for whom Cooper danced his unforgettable Swan in the so-called 'all-male' *Swan Lake* a decade ago, celebrated the 10th anniversary of that ground-breaking show by staging performances of it at Sadler's Wells in December 2004. Two other former Royal Ballet dancers who have forged successful careers away from the company are Michael Nunn and William Trevitt (aka The Ballet Boyz), whose company George Piper Dances presented a much-trailed new work, *Naked,* choreographed by the Boyz themselves, at Sadler's Wells in June 2005. *Naked* was, as always with this company, skilfully danced, but it was choreographically weak and unfocused. Nunn and Trevitt, in spite of their strongly classical training, have positioned themselves nearer the contemporary end of the dance spectrum. Britain's foremost contemporary choreographers, Richard Alston and Siobhan Davies, both produced new works during the season. Alston was celebrating the tenth anniversary of the formation of his company, and his two new works, *Gypsy Mixture* and *Such Longing,* expressed a range of moods from carefree high spirits to a melancholy romanticism. Davies' beautiful new work, *Birdsong,* was set to a score by Andy Pink built around the call of the Australian pied butcher bird.

The great American, Merce Cunningham, still avant-garde after all these years and still working with huge energy and creativity, mounted his first ever tour of the UK as part of Dance Umbrella 2004, as well as producing six 'Events' at the Barbican Centre in London in June 2005. The development of contemporary dance in the UK has been heavily influenced both by Cunningham and by Martha Graham, and it was an American, Robert Cohan, who came to London to run the newly-established London School of Contemporary Dance in 1967. Cohan celebrated his 80th birthday in 2005, and his unique contribution to the development of dance in the UK was marked by a gala at Sadler's Wells in his honour in May 2005.

A younger generation of contemporary choreographers also showed new works during the year. Akram Khan presented *Ma*, an interesting but somewhat disjointed work, in November 2004; he also collaborated with Sidi Larbi Cherkaoui in the remarkable *Zero Degrees*, to a score by Nitin Sawhney and with designs by the sculptor Antony Gormley, at Sadler's Wells in July 2005. Shobana Jeyasingh presented a double bill of new works, *Flicker* and *Transtep*, at the Queen Elizabeth Hall in March 2005, and Jasmin Vardimon's *Park*, staged at Sadler's Wells in May 2005, was an ambitious work set in an inner city playground, continuing her exploration of dance as physical theatre.

Merce Cunningham was not the only significant visitor from across the Atlantic during the year. Mark Morris brought his company to Sadler's Wells in November 2004 to show his take on *The Nutcracker*, entitled *The Hard Nut*, which was a huge hit when created in 1991 but now seems surprisingly dated. San Francisco Ballet performed at Sadler's Wells once more in September 2004, and Trisha Brown brought her brand of choreographic minimalism to the same theatre in June 2005. A group of principals and soloists of New York City Ballet also gave performances at Sadler's Wells, in October 2004, under the banner *Danses Concertantes*.

Other visitors included the Royal Danish Ballet, who performed Bournonville extracts at Sadler's Wells in June 2005; Pina Bausch and her company, who presented *Nelken* and *Palermo Palermo* there in February 2005, and the Australian Ballet, which brought Graeme Murphy's reinterpretation of *Swan Lake*, reputedly inspired by the Charles/Diana/Camilla love triangle, to the London Coliseum in July 2005. The Kirov Ballet also gave another major season at the Royal Opera House in July 2005.

In September 2004 the government produced its response to the *Culture, Media and Sport Select Committee Report on Arts Development: Dance* published in July 2004. The response outlined a range of schemes to promote positive experiences of dance in schools, and a new national grants scheme to enable talented children to undertake specialist training. It also described the Department for Culture, Media and Sport's priorities for dance, covering participation, access, buildings, professional dancers and the dance infrastructure.

The year saw the opening of a number of high-profile and successful musicals which incorporated dance as an essential element of their appeal. Richard Eyre's *Mary Poppins* was choreographed by Matthew Bourne and Stephen Mear, and achieved both popular and critical acclaim. Productions of *On the Town* and *Grand Hotel* were followed by a hugely successful transfer of the film *Billy Elliot* to the musical stage in a production directed by Stephen Daldry and choreographed by Peter Darling.

The most surprising dance hit of the year, however, came courtesy of the small screen. Ballroom dancing, an apparently outdated and anachronistic activity that was once an essential social skill for both men and women, suddenly waltzed back into favour in 2004 with the unlikely success of the television programme *Strictly Come Dancing*, in which teams of celebrities and professional dancers competed for glory, inspiring thousands of people to take up the pastime themselves. This in its turn spawned several programmes in which amateur dancers competed in a range of styles before deliberately (and self-consciously) exacting judges. The energy and enthusiasm of the participants was infectious, and the ratings for the shows indicate an untapped potential for a wider audience for dance in the UK than has so far been achieved.

PRODUCTIONS

ROYAL BALLET
Founded 1931 as the Vic-Wells Ballet
Royal Opera House, Covent Garden, London WC2E 9DD

WORLD PREMIÈRE: *Three Songs, Two Voices* (Christopher Bruce), 12 May 2005. A one-act work. Music, Nigel Kennedy based on Jimi Hendrix; design, Marian Bruce. Cast led by Deirdre Chapman, Tamara Rojo and Zenaida Yanowsky

FULL-LENGTH WORKS FROM THE REPERTOIRE: *Sylvia* (Ashton, 1952 recreated by Christopher Newton, *Cinderella* (Ashton, 1948), *Swan Lake* (Petipa/Ivanov, prod. Dowell 1987), *La fille mal gardée* (Ashton, 1960), *Manon* (MacMillan, 1974), *Ondine* (Ashton, 1958).

ONE-ACT WORKS FROM THE REPERTOIRE: *A Wedding Bouquet* (Ashton, 1937), *Requiem* (MacMillan, 1976 redesigned by Yolanda Sonnabend 1983), *Les Noces* (Nijinska, 1923), *Scènes de Ballet* (Ashton, 1948), *Divertissements* by Ashton *(Awakening pas de deux* from *The Sleeping Beauty, Five Brahms Waltzes in the Manner of Isadora Duncan, Voices of Spring, Thaïs pas de deux* and extracts from *Devil's Holiday), Daphnis and Chloë* (Ashton, 1951), *Rhapsody* (Ashton, 1980), *Symphony in C* (Balanchine, 1947), *Marguerite and Armand* (Ashton, 1963), *Tombeaux* (Bintley, 1993), *Enigma Variations* (Ashton, 1968), *The Rite of Spring* (MacMillan, 1962), *The Dream* (Ashton, 1964), *Les Biches* (Nijinska, 1924), *Symphonic Variations* (Ashton, 1946), *A Month in the Country* (Ashton, 1976), *Duo Concertant* (Balanchine, 1972), *Pavane pour une infante défunte* (Wheeldon, 1996).

Dancers from the company performed in a programme of new and recent works in the Linbury Studio Theatre in June 2005 under the banner 'Inspired by Ashton'. The works were created by Antony Dowson, Kim Brandstrup, Peter Quanz, Wayne McGregor and Will Tuckett.

The company toured the Far East in June and July 2005, performing *Manon*, *Swan Lake* and *Cinderella* in Singapore, Korea and Japan.

BIRMINGHAM ROYAL BALLET
Founded 1946 as the Sadler's Wells Opera Ballet
Birmingham Hippodrome, Thorp Street, Birmingham B5 4AU

WORLD PREMIÈRES: *The Orpheus Suite* (David Bintley), 6 October 2004. A one-act work. Score, Colin Towns; sets, Steve Scott; costumes, Kandis Cook. Cast led by Robert Parker, Elisha Willis, Tiit Helimets and Iain Mackay

The Four Seasons (Oliver Hindle), 9 March 2005. A one-act work including the 'Summer' section already created by Hindle in 1998. Music, Vivaldi; design, Conor Murphy. Cast included Ambra Vallo, Elisha Willis, Molly Smolen and Tiit Helimets

Dumbarton Oaks (Michael Kopinski), 19 April 2005. A one-act work. Music, Stravinsky; costumes, Michael Kopinski. Cast led by Robert Parker and Elisha Willis

Into the Ferment (Jonathan Payn), 15 June 2005. A one-act work. Music, James MacMillan; design, Mark Simmonds. Cast led by Rory Mackay, James Grundy, Tyrone Singleton and Virginia de Gersigny

The Planets (a collaborative one-act work created by BRB dancers), 15 June 2005. Music, Holst; design, Mark Simmonds

COMPANY PREMIÈRES: *Duo Concertant* (Balanchine, 1972), 19 April 2005. A *pas de deux*. Music, Stravinsky. Dancers, Iain Mackay and Asta Bazeviciute

Les Petits Riens (Bintley, 1991), 19 April 2005. Music, Mozart; costumes, Claire Leadbeater. Cast led by Molly Smolen and Tiit Helimets

The Rite of Spring (Nijinsky, 1913, reconstructed and staged by Millicent Hodson), 8 June 2005. Music, Stravinsky; design, after Nicholas Roerich, reconstructed and supervised by Kenneth Archer. Cast led by Molly Smolen

FULL-LENGTH WORKS FROM THE REPERTOIRE: *The Two Pigeons* (Ashton, 1961), *The Nutcracker* (Ivanov, prod. Wright, additional choreography by Redmon, 1990), *Romeo and Juliet* (MacMillan, 1965).

ONE-ACT WORKS FROM THE REPERTOIRE: *The Nutcracker Sweeties* (Bintley, 1996), *Concerto Barocco* (Balanchine, 1941), *Enigma Variations* (Ashton, 1968), *Western Symphony* (Balanchine, 1954), *The Shakespeare Suite* (Bintley, 1999), *Prodigal Son* (Balanchine, 1929), *In the Upper Room* (Tharp, 1986), *Elite Syncopations* (MacMillan, 1974), *Scènes de Ballet* (Ashton, 1948), *Brouillards* (Cranko, 1970), *Monotones II* (Ashton, 1966), *Five Tangos* (Van Manen, 1977), *Allegri Diversi* (Bintley, 1987).

In addition to performances at the Birmingham Hippodrome, the full company toured to London (Sadler's Wells Theatre), Plymouth, Salford, Sunderland and Bradford.

In April 2005 the company split into two sections, with half performing *Les Petits Riens, Brouillards* and *Elite Syncopations* in Bath, Exeter, Yeovil and Truro, and half performing *Dumbarton Oaks, Duo Concertant, Monotones II* and *Five Tangos* in Hull, York, Durham and Middlesbrough.

ENGLISH NATIONAL BALLET
Founded 1950 as London Festival Ballet
Markova House, 39 Jay Mews, London SW7 2ES

FULL-LENGTH WORKS FROM THE REPERTOIRE: *Romeo and Juliet* (Nureyev, 1977), *The Nutcracker* (Hampson, 2002), *Giselle* (Coralli and Perrot revised by Petipa, prod. Skeaping 1971), *Romeo and Juliet* (Deane, 1998).

The full company toured to Manchester, Liverpool, Bristol, Southampton and London (the Coliseum and the Royal Albert Hall).

It also toured to Biarritz in September 2004 and to Dubai in October 2004, performing *Perpetuum Mobile* (Hampson, 1997), *Side Show* (MacMillan, 1972), the *Grand Pas* from *Raymonda,* and *pas de deux* from *Swan Lake Act II* and *Don Quixote.*

RAMBERT DANCE COMPANY
Founded 1926 as the Marie Rambert Dancers
94 Chiswick High Road, London W4 1SH

WORLD PREMIÈRES: *Songs of a Wayfarer* (Kim Brandstrup), 2 September 2004 at the Edinburgh International Festival. Music, Mahler; design, Steven Scott

Momenta (Mikaela Polley), 27 April 2005 (first performed at the Rambert workshop season in January 2005). Score, Patrick Nunn; costumes, Sasha Keir from original designs by Sarah Jobling and Gemma Bates

Constant Speed (Mark Baldwin), 24 May 2005. Music, Franz Lehár; design, Michael Howells

COMPANY PREMIÈRES: *Five Rückert Songs* (Peter Darrell, 1978), 2 September 2004 at the Edinburgh International Festival. Music, Mahler; design, Yolanda Sonnabend. Cast led by Angela Towler

Irony of Fate (Rafael Bonachela, 2004), 2 November 2004. Score, Vytautas Barkauskas; design, Robert Cary-Williams

WORKS FROM THE REPERTOIRE: *Dark Elegies* (Tudor, 1937), *Swamp* (Clark, 1986), *PreSentient* (McGregor, 2002), *Five Brahms Waltzes in the Manner of Isadora Duncan* (Ashton, 1976), *A Tragedy of Fashion* (Spink, 2004), *Elsa Canasta* (de Frutos, 2003), *Linear Remains* (Bonachela, 2001), *Judgment of Paris* (Tudor, 1938).

RICHARD ALSTON DANCE COMPANY
Founded 1994
The Place, 17 Duke's Road, London WC1H 9AB

WORLD PREMIÈRES: *Gipsy Mixture* (Richard Alston), 19 October 2004. Music, Electric Gypsyland; design, Peter Todd

Charge (Martin Lawrance), 9 November 2004. Music, Steve Reich; design, Peter Todd

Such Longing (Richard Alston), 11 February 2005. Music, Chopin; design, Peter Todd

WORKS FROM THE REPERTOIRE: *Brisk Singing* (Alston, 1997), *Shimmer* (Alston, 2004), *Fever* (Alston, 2001).

The company performed in Milton Keynes, High Wycombe, Snape, Malvern, Brecon, Edinburgh, Sheffield, Canterbury, London (Sadler's Wells Theatre), Liverpool, Norwich, Salford, Oxford and Bath.

SCOTTISH BALLET
Founded 1956 as the Western Theatre Ballet
261 West Princes Street, Glasgow G4 9EE

WORLD PREMIÈRES: *Nightswimming into Day* (Ashley Page), 15 September 2004. A one-act work. Music, John Adams, Brian Eno and J. Peter Schwalm; design, Jon Morrell

The Pump Room (Ashley Page), 13 April 2005. A short work for four dancers. Music, Aphex Twin and Nine Inch Nails; design, Ashley Page. Cast, Jarkko Lehmus, Paul Liburd, Diana Loosmore and Sophie Martin

COMPANY PREMIÈRES: *Two Pieces for HET* (Hans van Manen, 1998), 15 September 2004. A *pas de deux*. Music, Arvo Pärt and Erkki-Sven Tüür. Dancers, Claire Robertson and Erik Cavallari

Twilight (Hans van Manen, 1972), 15 September 2004. A *pas de deux*. Music, John Cage; design, Jean Paul Vroom. Dancers, Tatiana Loginova and Cristo Vivancos

Suite From Artifact (William Forsythe, reworked from his 1984 work *Artifact IV*), 15 September 2004. Music, Bach and Eva Crossman-Hecht; design, William Forsythe. Cast led by Tatiana Loginova, Robert Docherty, Sohpie Martin, Cristo Vivancos and Diane Loosmore

Walking in the Heat (Ashley Page, 1992), 13 April 2005. A *pas de deux* extracted from his 1992 work *Touch Your Coolness to my Fevered Brow.* Music, Orlando Gough; design, Antony McDonald. Dancers, Soon Ja Lee and Oliver Rydout

Façade (Ashton, 1931). A one-act work. Music, Walton; design, John Armstrong

FULL-LENGTH WORK FROM THE REPERTOIRE: *The Nutcracker* (Page, 2003).

ONE-ACT WORKS FROM THE REPERTOIRE: *The Four Temperaments* (Balanchine, 1946), *32 Cryptograms* (Page, 2004).

FILM

If there was anything new in 2005, cinematically speaking, it was a preoccupation with the old. This year more than ever the movies seemed at a loss for new ideas, stuck in a rut of remakes, sequels and spin-offs. The winner for Best Picture at the Academy Awards – 74-year-old director Clint Eastwood's *Million Dollar Baby* – was an old fashioned boxing melodrama which, minus its gender switch and controversial ending, might have been made in the 1930s; the sort of picture that might have been produced by Howard Hughes in fact, whose life story inspired the year's other serious Oscar contender, Martin Scorsese's *The Aviator*. Even critics' darling *Sideways* was a rather conservative comedy about middle-aged white men: a throwback, if not to the 1930s, then at least to the 1970s.

In many of the year's more interesting films the theme of familial inheritance kept cropping up, with sons (mostly sons) in search of their fathers or vice versa (*Broken Flowers; The Life Aquatic with Steve Zissou; Don't Come Knocking;* and the Dardenne Brothers' Palme d'Or winner *The Child*). 'Can the son escape his father's shadow?' wondered Bill Condon in his biopic *Kinsey* and Ira Sachs in the Sundance winner *40 Shades of Blue*. 'Can he redeem the father?' asked George Lucas in his climactic *Star Wars Episode III – Revenge of the Sith*. 'Can he live up to his father's memory?' posed Christopher Nolan in *Batman Begins*.

Across these films there seems to be a searching response to the rootlessness of the times, an attempt to recover the ethical certitude which, by implication, has been forfeited along the way. While our politicians preach the moral high ground in stridently bellicose rhetoric, film artists seem far more tentative in their diagnosis.

Hollywood of course was forced to concede defeat with the re-election of President George W. Bush in November 2004, despite the strenuous efforts of Michael Moore and the overwhelmingly liberal filmmaking community (late entries in the campaign war included the documentary *Going Upriver: The Long War of John Kerry* and John Sayles' pointed mystery thriller *Silver City*, with Chris Cooper lampooning a clueless Republican senator, Dickie Pilager).

THE POWER OF NIGHTMARES

You can be sure the re-election will do nothing to stem the flow of political documentaries, including *Enron: The Smartest Guys in the Room, Mondovino, The Yes Men* and *The Take*. The first of these delineated the rise and fall of the Enron corporation, once upon a time a company dealing in natural gas, but latterly a trader in smoke and mirrors, gambling billions on stock prices, backed only by their own, purely hypothetical, share value. This story might serve as the working definition of the word 'scandal'.

Enron executives perpetrated a massive fraud with the collusion of the most prestigious banks, law firms and accountants on Wall Street. Not only did they become fantastically rich, they became stars in the financial world, even role models for the new market economy. George W. Bush liked to call Enron's chairman by his pet name, 'Kenny Boy'. But when they ran short of reserves, they instituted rolling power blackouts across deregulated California. When push came to shove, the company went bust in a matter of weeks, putting tens of thousands of employees out of work, their pensions worthless. Only the executives had the foreknowledge to stash away their millions.

The film is dismaying in many ways, not least because it holds out no hope that lessons have been learned. The smart guys don't even recognise they did anything wrong.

Then there was Eugene Jarecki's *Why We Fight*, actually a BBC Storyville production, and a more coherent, closely argued deconstruction of the reasons Bush went to war in Iraq than *Fahrenheit 9/11*. It kicks off with President Eisenhower's farewell address from the White House in 1960, when the former Second World War general issued a grave warning about the unchecked power of what he dubbed the 'military-industrial complex'.

Jarecki (who made *The Trials of Henry Kissinger* and whose brother directed *Capturing the Friedmans*) dissects the way war drives America's economy, and the weapons industry has put politicians on the payroll; how economic colonialism is the prevailing doctrine in Washington think-tanks (a phrase that takes on a whole new resonance if you lay the stress on the second word).

Interviewing a New York cop who lost his son in the World Trade Centre and a Pentagon staffer who resigned in disgust at the way intelligence reports were twisted to justify the attack on Saddam Hussein, Jarecki subverts the title of Frank Capra's Second World War propaganda series. *Why We Fight* is no longer a call to arms, although it ends with a plea for men and women of good conscience to object to the wars fought in our name.

Another BBC-backed documentary, Adam Curtis' *The Power of Nightmares* was even more radical, linking the philosophies of Islamic fundamentalists and the neo-conservative right, and arguing that al-Qa'eda scarcely exists. Broadcast on the BBC as a three-part series, it was picked up and showcased in feature form at the Cannes film festival and consequently bought for theatrical distribution in the USA – although the London bombings of July 2005 probably undermined the film's impact.

Strangely enough, one of the year's biggest studio blockbusters sounded echoes of the Curtis thesis. *Batman Begins* is a film much exercised with fear and the manipulation thereof.

Eschewing Tim Burton's fairytale vision and giving a properly wide berth to the terminal camp to which the franchise succumbed under Joel Schumacher, cowriter-director Christopher Nolan devotes the first hour to establishing Batman's bona fides in an exotic but naturalistic setting, painstakingly explaining where he comes from, how he can do what he does, and why.

Grounded, adult, psychological, it's the opposite approach to the one adverts director Pitof took with *Catwoman* for the same studio (Warner Bros). Maybe they're learning from their mistakes, because there was little reason to suppose the 'machine' could still produce a blockbuster as good as this one. Crucially, Nolan is a filmmaker interested in telling stories, not just another trumped up window-dresser. The difference is most evident in the characterisation of Batman himself: where

Michael Keaton, George Clooney and Val Kilmer were so many interchangeable chins, Christian Bale always plays the man underneath the mask. The strategy has the happy side-effect of restoring vulnerability, threat and violence – in a word, excitement – to a superhero who seemed inured to all of the above.

Nolan, who made *Memento,* is no slouch when it comes to dovetailing flashbacks, so his ambitious prologue is as compelling as it is well-founded. In a round-about way, it's the young Bruce Wayne's fear of bats which leads to his parents' death at the hands of a mugger and it's the guilt and anger from that experience which leads him to a prison in outer Mongolia, and into the hands of Henri Ducard (Liam Neeson) and the League of Shadows. 'You must confront your fear, and master it, to turn fear against those who prey on the fearful,' Ducard teaches him. 'You must become a terrible thought. An idea. A legend.'

Batman Begins lays a lot of store in establishing this logic of the legend. Terrorised by a crime syndicate, Gotham City has become corrupted from top to bottom. Can Batman renew hope by putting the frighteners on the fear-mongers? Or perhaps the whole sorry state is too decadent to salvage, as Ducard decides. He would push the panic button and precipitate mass self-destruction.

Gotham has always been a double for New York, and in this earnestly post 9/11 movie Nolan suggests the very American ideal hangs in the balance, perched precariously like Batman himself between the vigilante impulse for vengeance, and the infinitely more elusive quest for justice.

THE END OF THE SAGA
There are similar resonances to be found in the last installment of the *Star Wars* saga (which is, oddly enough, episode three of six).

Star Wars Episode III – Revenge of the Sith is not just in a different league from its two immediate predecessors, it's on a par with *The Empire Strikes Back,* the strongest in the original trilogy. It's no coincidence that these are the darkest films in the series, both dominated by the looming shadow of Darth Vader. Now that we can see the whole six movie cycle, it's clear that *Star Wars* is Vader's story, from birth to death, from Jedi to Sith. Which is to say it is the story of Lucifer, the brightest angel who fell from grace and went over to the Dark Side. *Revenge of the Sith* explains that defection. It is the most probing and harrowing chapter in Anakin Skywalker's life.

How does a man stray from hero to villain? It's a central question in American cinema. Look at the lost hopes and broken promises of *Citizen Kane,* Ethan Edwards in *The Searchers,* Michael Corleone in *The Godfather.* When Anakin (Hayden Christensen) loses his way it's through an entirely credible mixture of fear, love, ambition and greed. Rebuffed by the same Jedi council who have singled him out as the chosen one, he is seduced by the promises of power and immorality held out by Chancellor Palpatine (Ian McDiarmid), who is after all the elected leader of the Republic they're all striving to defend.

Lucas has been mapping out this scenario for decades, but it's hard to miss the contemporary political resonance in a movie which dares to suggest that a democracy can lose its way just as easily as any man. For the Empire, read the USA. For Palpatine, read President Bush. 'If you're not with me, then you're my enemy' declares Anakin, echoing Bush's notorious soundbite for the War on Terror, 'You're either with us or against us.' 'This is how liberty dies,' observes a dismayed Padme (Natalie Portman) after the

Senate has voted to extend unilateral emergency powers to the Chancellor, 'to thunderous applause'. Under the guise of safety and security, a new evil Empire is born.

The movie is certainly not flawless. When it comes to dialogue Lucas is rarely more than pedestrian. Sometimes whole scenes seem to be constructed around the principle of 'connect-the-cliché'. Good actors like Ewan McGregor (Obi Wan Kenobi), Samuel L. Jackson (Mace Windu) and Ian McDiarmid do their best to inject some life into proceedings, but the movie demands more of Hayden Christensen than he can muster. The boy can glower, but he seems petty and peevish when Lucas is hunting for tragic hubris. In fact it's telling that the most consistent scene-stealers are Yoda, General Grievous, and our old friend R2-D2... Somehow Lucas seems most comfortable with robots and alien lifeforms; the closer his characters get to humanity, the more dull they become.

Lucas is not all that inventive with action scenes either. By the nth staging of a light sabre duel on the edge of an unscientifically gravitational precipice it's hard to suppress a guilty yawn. Nevertheless, it's a shock how far he goes in a climactic fight between Obi-Wan and Anakin against a sea of surging lava. Graphic and brutal, this scene is more than enough to merit the film's 12A certificate. Much more adult in tone than Episodes I and II, *Revenge of the Sith* satisfies the generation who grew up with the saga but might alienate their kids. It's just a pity that Mr Lucas' merchandising empire sees fit to pitch toys and action figures to an age group who probably shouldn't be seeing this film.

Movies such as these (and others: Spielberg's *War of the Worlds;* Ridley Scott's surprisingly emancipatory crusades epic *Kingdom of Heaven*) suggest that whatever its limitations as a narrative form – they tend to be unwieldy and bombastic – the blockbuster can resonate with the zeitgeist in more interesting ways than is often appreciated. Indeed you could make the argument that these popular fables are more politically engaged than many eminently respectable bourgeois art films. What's more, these films have enormous global reach. *Kingdom of Heaven* opened on the same day in North America and across Europe, but a week earlier it had been released in Kuwait, the United Arab Emirates, Lebanon, Singapore, Indonesia, Egypt and Israel.

BOX OFFICE FEELS THE STRAIN
Despite these blanket releases, in show business reporting the summer of 2005 was dominated by coverage of the box office slump. For 19 straight weeks the US box office figures were down on 2004 levels. (After a one week rally in mid July, the slump continued into August.)

Admittedly, the figures are less clear-cut than the media often implies. In fact, dollar for dollar, the studios have actually made more money this year than last – when the box office was dominated by two independent, non-studio pictures, *The Passion of The Christ* and *Fahrenheit 9/11.* Indies or (this year) no indies, an overall box office decline of seven per cent has to be cause for concern.

Even the big hits underperformed against expectations. Case in point: the final installment of *Star Wars* is a massive hit, no question (at a little under $800 million it surpassed the figures for *The Passion of the Christ*), but as the culmination of such an epoch-making saga, it still feels anti-climactic. Two weekends after its massive 3,600 screen US opening it wasn't even topping the chart anymore, adding a paltry $25 million to Lucasfilm's coffers.

Similarly *Batman Begins* has effectively relaunched a moribund franchise and looks set to become a bigger money-earner than any of its predecessor, but it's lagging way behind the kind of business *Spider Man 2* managed a couple of years back. And these are the sure-fire blockbusters. What else have audiences been offered? A repetitive diet of TV spinoffs (*Bewitched; The Dukes of Hazzard; The Honeymooners*); sequels and prequels (*Star Wars; The Exorcist; Batman; Herbie*); and remakes (*The Longest Yard; Flight of the Phoenix; Assault on Precinct 13; Charlie and the Chocolate Factory; The Bad News Bears; Dark Water* etc).

Such a long litany suggests a decadent culture feeding off itself – a concept which reaches its apotheosis in the syne-thespian: a computer generated simulacrum of an actor. We had a digitised Tom Hanks in multiple roles in the crushing *Polar Express*, and a reanimated Laurence Olivier in *Sky Captain and the World of Tomorrow*. In these films – and the hiply amoral comic book noir *Sin City* – digitally enhanced performers interact in computer generated worlds and ultimately blend with the scenery. In the animated *A Shark's Tale* 'stars' like Robert De Niro and Martin Scorsese lent their voices and personalities to a threadbare story in a sea of product placement and pop culture in-jokes; they themselves are no longer artists, but brands. When those brands try for sincerity – endorsing a politician, or campaigning for poverty relief, or rhapsodising over the new-found love of their life – the public's reaction is overwhelmingly cynical.

Unfortunately that cynicism extends to the few mainstream movies which ask (and sometimes deserve) to be taken seriously. Among the biggest flops of 2004 were two of the year's best Hollywood movies, *Kinsey* (total US gross: $10.2 million) and David O. Russell's wildly original philosophical screwball comedy *I Heart Huckabees* (total US gross $12.8 million). Both failed despite some strong reviews and an impressive roster of movie stars.

In 2005, neither of the summer's biggest box office disappointments were sequels, spin-offs or remakes. Whatever their relative merits, both Michael Bay's *The Island* and Ron Howard's *Cinderella Man* were original dramas attempting to address an adult audience. *The Island* was an intriguing (if clunky) science fiction thriller with Ewan McGregor and Scarlett Johansson discovering they are clones. It cost an estimated $120 million and made back just a tenth of that on its crucial first week.

Cinderella Man fared a little better, but the fallout may be more damaging. The filmmakers and the studio believed they had a hit on their hands with this one – strong reviews, big stars (Russell Crowe, Renee Zellweger), big Oscar potential and a fairytale underdog story about Depression-era boxer Jim Braddock – but the audience stayed away in droves.

At first glance the movie's $50 million US gross doesn't look too shoddy, but this is a film which cost nearly $90 million to shoot. Advertising expenditure would have been at least another $40 million. Prints and insurance would probably have cost another $20 million. And of course the cinema chains keep their share of that box office – something up to 50 per cent.

No wonder producer Brian Grazer said he felt like crying when the opening grosses came in – and things didn't get any better, not even after some theatres offered a money back guarantee. Grazer decided their timing was off – that summer was just the wrong season for a 'serious' film. He may or may not be right, but don't expect to see Oscar-calibre movies vying with the blockbusters next

summer. (The summer's surprise hit was an especially juvenile Marvel Comics' movie, *The Fantastic Four*.)

It is worth noting that cinemagoers now represent less than 15 per cent of worldwide revenues; home entertainment (basically DVD and TV sales) account for 85.8 per cent. As Edward Jay Epstein has written, this swing to the home audience has brought about a dramatic switch in the balance of power within the studios, with movie distribution arms now relegated well below home entertainment divisions. For the public, the most obvious effect is the shortening of the gap between a film's theatrical release and its appearance on DVD – a period that used to be six months, but is now routinely four, and sometimes shorter. (Director Steven Soderbergh has announced that his next film will be released simultaneously in cinemas, on pay TV, and on DVD.) Epstein points out that when the Hong Kong industry collapsed its video window in 2002, cinema attendance fell by 70 per cent. Cinema chains will have to adapt or die.

DIGITAL CINEMA UK

Strangely enough the United Kingdom is leading the way in embracing digital cinema, an innovation which may change the way films are distributed and programmed. In May 2005, the Film Council announced the creation of the world's first 'Digital Screen Network', an £11.7 million scheme to install digital projectors in 209 cinemas across Britain.

Digital projection dramatically decreases the costs associated with distributing 35mm film (about tenfold), and according to the Film Council the cinemas have made undertakings to screen a wider variety of specialised (i.e. non-Hollywood), classic and foreign language movies. In 2004, although foreign language films made up more than a third of films released (169 in total), they shared less than 5 per cent of the UK box office gross.

That announcement was followed in June with news that James Purnell MP, the Minister for Creative Industries, had ordered a 'stock take' of national film policy. The review will consider four key issues: attracting big budget films to the UK, supporting UK production, improving distribution and doing more for cultural film.

Somewhat controversially, the stock take was entrusted to John Woodward, CEO of the UK Film Council, and the man most responsible for shaping film policy over the last five years. Futhermore, tax relief for UK-based production was put outside Woodward's remit – after more than a year of indecision, in July 2005 the Treasury put forward for consultation new proposals, scrapping Section 42 but replacing it with more generous tax credit provisions than had been expected.

In the short term, there is no doubt that the prevailing uncertainty over tax relief has curtailed UK film production and derailed many potentially worthwhile projects (as well as many more dubious efforts): there were 40 fewer UK features made this year than last (133 in total). The Treasury's new plans were broadly welcomed by the industry, and if they work as planned should boost long-term UK production.

It was not, on the whole, a good year for British films, although as always there were a number of bright spots. Mike Leigh's *Vera Drake* dominated the BAFTAs with 11 nominations and three wins (Best Director, Costume Design and Best Actress – Imelda Staunton as the saintly backstreet abortionist). Leigh and Staunton were also nominated for Oscars, despite the film's controversial subject matter.

Curiously, almost all the more interesting British films were developed without a traditional screenplay: *Vera Drake,* Pawel Pawlikovski's *My Summer of Love,* Michael Winterbottom's sexually explicit *Nine Songs,* Ken Loach's *Ae Fond Kiss,* and Shane Meadows' *Dead Man's Shoes* were all developed through improvisation with the actors, finding their stories through workshops and extended rehearsal.

Audience figures for 2004 were put at 171 million, two per cent up on 2003, and the second highest in 32 years (2002 was a bumper year, with 175.9 million). As you would expect, box office receipts were also up, at £770 million, a four per cent increase on the previous year.

Officially, UK and UK co-productions made up just over 20 per cent of these earners (a 49 per cent increase on 2003). However, these statistics need closer scrutiny: the lion's share of the 'British' box office pie was shared by just Hollywood/UK co-productions: *Harry Potter and the Prisoner of Azkaban* (which alone took more than £46 million); *Bridget Jones: The Edge of Reason* (£36 million); and the not particularly British-feeling *Troy* (£18 million). The biggest homegrown hit was the zombie comedy *Shaun of the Dead* (£6.69 million). Top of the UK box office chart was the animated family film *Shrek 2* (£48.10 million).

The impact of the London bombings will likely hurt figures for 2005, but if the UK is to sustain its 20 per cent market share, that will be down almost entirely to the latest adventures of Harry Potter (*Harry Potter and the Goblet of Fire* is due on 18 November), and such co-productions as *The Hitchhiker's Guide to the Galaxy, Charlie and the Chocolate Factory* and *Kingdom of Heaven.* There are also high expectations for *The Chronicles of Narnia,* a December 2005 release.

LITERATURE

NEW FICTION

The London bombings in July made some of the year's novels seem prophetic. *Incendiary* (Chatto) by Chris Cleave is narrated by a woman whose husband and son are killed in a huge terrorist bomb blast at the new Emirates Stadium in Highbury, north London. It had already been the subject of a film deal and sold for substantial sums abroad, before it was published, with chilling timeliness, in July. There were also some unjustifiable accusations of 'cashing in' when the publication of Malorie Blackman's young adult novel *Checkmate* (Doubleday), the resolution of a trilogy (preceded by *Noughts and Crosses* and *Knife Edge*), brought sales of the three up to 300,000 copies. *Checkmate* told the story of a teenage girl groomed by a manipulative and murderous uncle to be a suicide bomber. The consciousness-raising series, which posits a society in which black people (the Crosses) are the ruling class and white people (the Noughts) are the underclass, had been, over its three volumes, the object of growing word-of-mouth success, and the recipient of book awards.

The first Man Booker International Prize was awarded, not for a single book, but for a body of work. A shortlist of 18 writers, including five Nobel laureates, was drawn up by the three judges: John Carey, Alberto Manguel and Azar Nafisi. Among the contenders were Nahgib Mahfouz, Ian McEwan, Margaret Atwood, Milan Kundera, Gunter Grass, Philip Roth, John Updike and Muriel Spark (though not Nobel laureates Toni Morrison, V S Naipaul or J M Coetzee). To the surprise of many, the £60,000 award went to the Albanian writer Ismail Kadare, now living in Paris, much of whose work published in English had been translated from French, although originally written in Albanian. His lifetime's work demonstrated the importance of writing and of free speech under an oppressive regime.

Also a surprise was the winner of the Impac Award, the world's most lucrative literary prize for a single work of fiction. Edward P. Jones' *The Known World*, published in the UK by Harper Perennial, was selected from a shortlist of ten books from many countries – of which the most familiar to a UK readership were Damon Galgut's *The Good Doctor* and Shirley Hazzard's Orange-shortlisted *The Great Fire* – to win the €100,000 (£66,000) prize. Jones's book, which had also won a Pulitzer Prize, is a story of slavery, set in Manchester County, Virginia.

Alan Hollinghurst's *The Line of Beauty* (Picador) won the 2004 Man Booker Prize, relating in elegant prose the story of a gay graduate living in the house of a Thatcherite MP in London in the 1980s, at the moment of the emergence of Aids. Among the shortlisted books, David Mitchell's *Cloud Atlas* (Sceptre), with its multiple narratives from different periods of history, also enjoyed enthusiastic support from readers who were to vote it the Richard and Judy Book Club Best Read of the Year.

The judges of the 2005 Man Booker Prize thought that it had been an exceptional year for contemporary British and Commonwealth literature, perhaps even 'one of the strongest since the prize was founded in 1969'. The longlist of 18 books announced in August reflected this: there were new novels from Ian McEwan (*Saturday*, Cape),

Salman Rushdie (*Shalimar the Clown*, Cape), J. M. Coetzee (*Slow Man*, Secker) and Kazuo Ishiguro (*Never Let Me Go*, Faber), all of them previous Booker winners, as well as from such admired authors as John Banville (*The Sea*, Picador), Julian Barnes (*Arthur & George*, Cape), Zadie Smith (*On Beauty*, Hamish Hamilton), Ali Smith (*The Accidental*, Hamish Hamilton), Hilary Mantel (*Beyond Black*, Fourth Estate) and Dan Jacobson (*All for Love*, Hamish Hamilton). The first novel on the longlist, its title most enjoyed by the media, was *A Short History of Tractors in Ukrainian* (Viking) by Marina Lewycka, which had also been shortlisted for the Orange Prize and appeared in the 'Page Turners' selection (*see* below). It tells the story of two feuding sisters of Ukrainian descent living in Peterborough, who lay aside their differences to save their widowed father from remarriage to a voluptuous Ukrainian gold-digger.

There was controversy over Ian McEwan's *Saturday* when the London Evening Standard 'threw the publication of the novel into chaos' by breaking its embargo. The newspaper paid undisclosed compensation to publisher Jonathan Cape. The novel is set on the day of the anti-Iraq War protest, and follows Perowne, a surgeon whose comfortable life comes under threat during the course of the day.

The 2004 Man Booker and Orange Prize winners competed for the first time on the Whitbread novel shortlist. Hollinghurst's *The Line of Beauty* and Andrea Levy's *Small Island* (Headline) were both in contention. The category was won by Levy, who went on to scoop the Whitbread Book of the Year prize, an unprecedented double. Levy's book is the charming and eye-opening tale of Jamaicans in the first wave of immigration to Britain in 1945. Geraldine McCaughrean's *Not the End of the World* (Oxford University Press), which sees Noah's flood from the point of view of the women (and some of the animals) on the ark, won the Whitbread Children's Novel category, beating Meg Rossoff's post-apocalyptic love story for young adults *How I Live Now* (Puffin). Rossoff's novel, winner of the Guardian Children's Fiction Prize, made a breakthrough by being one of the three shortlisted titles of the new 2005 Orange Prize for New Writers – a remarkable achievement for a book originally written for children. The prize, for a first novel, was won by Diana Evans, for *26a*, of which Boyd Tonkin, literary editor of *The Independent*, said 'the great Neasden novel has arrived . . . Evans' Neasden of the 1980s becomes a place of mystery, fantasy, joy and melancholy.'

The tenth annual Orange Prize for Fiction was won by American-born author Lionel Shriver, for her seventh novel *We Need to Talk about Kevin* (Serpent's Tail), the narrative of the mother of a psychotic boy who is responsible for a Columbine-style massacre, and whom she was never able to love. Its two Hitchcockian twists found favour with the judges, but 'a touch of sentimentality at the end' meant it only just pipped to the Prize British author Jane Gardam's *Old Filth* (Chatto), the life story of a judge who was born in Malaya, educated in England, and practised in the Far East, hence his nickname: 'Failed in London, Try Hong Kong'.

One million copies of Gabriel Garcia Marquez's new

novel, his first for ten years, *Memories of My Melancholy Whores*, went on sale in October 2004 in the Spanish-speaking world. A story of amorous passion rediscovered in old age, with a 90-year-old narrator, it was published by Cape in the UK the following autumn.

The fastest-selling book of the year, and, indeed the fastest-selling book ever, was J. K. Rowling's sixth novel, *Harry Potter and the Half-Blood Prince* (Bloomsbury), which was published at midnight on the night of 15–16 July, and launched with an event for eighty children at Edinburgh Castle. Rowling was interviewed only by children, representing the world's press. The book sold 3.1 million copies in the first week, although after this enormous first surge of sales, purchases slowed down. At 607 pages, slightly shorter than *Harry Potter and the Order of the Phoenix*, it was felt to be more tightly written than its predecessor, and received largely favourable reviews. Harry, in the Lower Sixth, finds love and loses another friend.

The Da Vinci Code (Corgi) by Dan Brown, a fictional mystery about conspiracies in the Catholic Church, broke records by reaching sales approaching 3 million, of which 1.6 million were in paperback between March and December 2004. This and his reissued backlist book, *Angels and Demons,* dominated the bestseller lists for most of the year. Brown's books were ousted from the top places by a very few books: Patricia Cornwell's latest thriller, *Trace* (Time Warner) – but only for a week – Martina Cole's *The Graft* (Headline) and Maeve Binchy's *Nights of Rain and Stars* (Orion), though none held sway for long. *The Da Vinci Code* took the Book of the Year award at the book industry's sales-motivated British Book Awards.

Other bestselling fiction of the year included *Lovers and Liars* by Josephine Cox (HarperCollins), *The Last Juror* by John Grisham (Arrow), Audrey Niffenegger's *The Time Traveler's Wife* (Vintage), Danielle Steel's *Ransom* (Corgi), Marian Keyes' *The Other Side of the Story* (Penguin) and Jane Green's *The Other Woman* (Penguin).

The 7 July London bombings caused the ceremony for the presentation of the CILIP Carnegie Medal for a children's book, planned for 8 July, to be postponed until the Youth Libraries Group conference in the autumn. The winner, defeating such luminaries as Eva Ibbotson (*The Star of Kazan,* Macmillan) and Philip Pullman (*The Scarecrow and the Servant,* Doubleday), was a first book – filmmaker Frank Cottrell Boyce's novel of his own film, *Millions* (Macmillan), the tale of two newly motherless brothers, one of whom is obsessed with saints, who find a fortune in notes on the eve of a currency change to the Euro, and have to decide how or whether to spend it. The winner of the CILIP Greenaway award for an illustrated children's book was Chris Riddell, for his lavish edition of *Gulliver's Travels* (Walker), which featured a satirical image of Tony Blair as a politician who had forgotten his promises.

NON-FICTION SUCCESSES

Non-fiction bestsellers included chef Jamie Oliver's *Jamie's Dinners* (Michael Joseph) and Michael Palin's travelogue *Himalaya* (Weidenfeld), both boosted by the authors' screen popularity. Also helped by a television programme was Gillian McKeith's *You Are What You Eat* (Michael Joseph), which sold 72,500 in a week in August 2004 and went on to sell more than 190,000 copies. The newspaper-led craze for the Japanese number puzzles, Sudoku, made sales of volumes of the puzzles overtake those of books of any other genre.

Actor Sheila Hancock's account of her life with her late husband, actor John Thaw, *The Two of Us* (Bloomsbury), sold 7,500 copies even before its official publication, at the end of 2004, and went on to be a huge Christmas bestseller; Hancock received the Author of the Year Award at the British Book Awards.

Jane Fonda's autobiography *My Life So Far* was published in May 2005 by Ebury, and at the same time actor Goldie Hawn told her personal story in *A Lotus Grows in the Mud* (Bantam Press). Radio presenter John Peel had written 50,000 words of his autobiography when he died in November 2004. Publisher Transworld had paid £1.6 million in April 2003 for the book, and publication went ahead in October 2005 with extra biographical material. Popular at his personal appearances was the former leader of the Conservative party William Hague, promoting his biography, *William Pitt the Younger* (HarperCollins), the British Book Awards History Book of the Year. In December 2004 the runner Kelly Holmes published her diary of the Athens Olympics, at which she won two gold medals, *My Olympic Ten Days,* and buyers flocked to her signings. The same publisher, Virgin, produced a second Holmes book in June 2005: an autobiography, *Black White and Gold,* tabloid interest in which concentrated on the revelation of an episode of self-harming in her youth. The marriage of Prince Charles and Camilla Parker Bowles triggered the publication of *Camilla and Charles: The Love Story* by Camilla's biographer Caroline Graham (Blake Publishing), to be followed by Gyles Brandreth's *Charles and Camilla: Portrait of an Affair* (Century), in October 2005.

The appalling destruction on Boxing Day 2004 of the Asian Tsunami inspired a fund-raising book, *New Beginnings* (Bloomsbury), to which 16 popular authors, from Stephen King to Vikram Seth, Margaret Atwood to Joanna Trollope, contributed new pieces of writing. It was published with a huge print run in March, with the entire cover price of £5 going to charity. Mary Archer, wife of Jeffrey Archer, lost a court battle to prevent publication in May of *Mary Archer* (Simon & Schuster), a biography by Margaret Crick, the wife of Jeffrey's biographer Michael Crick. The sex, paternity and visa scandal that caused the resignation of Home Secretary David Blunkett led to the rushed modification of his biography by Stephen Pollard, which had been years in the writing and was published by Hodder in December 2004.

Notable non-fiction also included *Mao: The Untold Story* (Cape) by Jung Chang and her husband Jon Halliday, who assembled, as never before, evidence of Mao Zedong's appalling crimes. The winner of the Samuel Johnson Prize for Non-Fiction was Jonathan Coe (whose novel *The Rotters' Club* was televised this year). Coe won the Prize with *Like a Fiery Elephant* (Picador), his biography of the writer B. S. Johnson, who committed suicide in the 1970s.

2005 saw the 70th anniversary of the Penguin paperback, celebrated with an exhibition of Penguin book jackets at the Victoria and Albert Museum and an accompanying volume, *Penguin by Design: A Cover Story,* with the republishing of 70 slim books by Penguin authors, sold at £1.50 each, and with the publication of Jeremy Lewis's biography of the man responsible, Allen Lane.

NEW INITIATIVES AND GROWING READERSHIP

It was a year of unprecedented scrutiny of the library service, with reports of falling book borrowings; several public criticisms of management from Tim Coates of

Libri, self-appointed scourge of the service (who nominated himself in May as the man to lead a radical overhaul); the publication of a Department for Culture, Media and Sport Select Committee inquiry chaired by Sir Gerald Kaufman MP; and, after the May election, the appointment of a new, and obviously committed, Libraries Minister in David Lammy. Meanwhile libraries were working in a new partnership with publishers to grow readership, and such library-centred reading initiatives as a promotion tied to the Channel 4 chat show Richard and Judy, the Summer Reading Challenge (which encouraged 300,000 children to read six books over the summer holidays) and reading groups sponsored by telecommunications company Orange, went from strength to strength.

Bestselling children's author Jacqueline Wilson was appointed the new Children's Laureate in May 2005, offering opportunities to use her notable ambassadorial skills and her exceptional, crowd-pulling rapport with children over the next two years of her tenure; she hoped to turn more children into readers and bring books into homes where they did not feature. Her prolific output was praised by the judges for: 'tackling deep emotions and harsh realities in a clear, simple and entertaining child's voice to which enormous numbers of children respond. She offers them hope, empathy and humour.' Meanwhile the pressure from the last Laureate, Michael Morpurgo (Allen Lane's son-in-law), to persuade schools to inculcate a love of literature, bore fruit in December 2004 with the publication of a landmark Ofsted report about the importance of teaching children the pleasures of reading, *Reading for Purpose and Pleasure*. Also this year, Philip Pullman was one of two recipients of the Astrid Lindgren Memorial Award, the world's largest award for children's and youth literature, worth a total of over €550,000 and presented in Sweden.

An initiative by Gail Rebuck, Chief Executive of the Random House Group, targeted reluctant readers by inviting popular, established authors to write short books, of 15–20,000 words, using simple vocabulary to engage this audience. Eight Quick Reads, at £2.99 each, were to be launched on World Book Day 2006, with eight more to follow in May for summer reading. Among those who joined in were: Ruth Rendell, Minette Walters, Hunter Davies, Maeve Binchy, Joanna Trollope, Val McDermid and Marian Keyes. A £1 Quick Reads token was to be distributed by the DfES to every adult enrolled on a literacy course. Quick Reads would be supported by the BBC as part of a three- to five-year literacy campaign launched in October 2005, targeting 12 million emergent readers aged between 25 and 54, and called RaW ('Reading and Writing: read more, write better').

In spring 2005 BBC1 launched a new book club project, 'Page Turners', on daytime television, in which celebrities championed 24 contemporary books selected by a panel including authors Fay Weldon and Marian Keyes. The choice was a good sampler of the popular and interesting books of the year, including non-fiction: from Bob Dylan's autobiographical *Chronicles: Volume One* (Simon & Schuster) to Nigella Lawson's book about cooking for celebratory occasions, *Feast* (Chatto); from Simon Barnes's surprise success *How to Be A Bad Birdwatcher* (Short Books) to a life of Leonardo da Vinci, *Flights of the Mind* by Charles Nicholl (Penguin); the Whitbread-winning children's book, Geraldine McCaughrean's *Not the End of the World;* popular fiction such as Ian Rankin's *Fleshmarket Close* (Orion), the British Book Awards crime thriller of the year, and highbrow reads such as Kazuo Ishiguro's *Never Let Me Go* (Faber). It also included some newcomers who had commanded attention and received notable praise, such as Chimamanda Ngozi Adichie's first novel *Purple Hibiscus* (Fourth Estate), an Orange-shortlisted title about political brutality and domestic violence in the adolescence of a Nigerian girl, and *The Icarus Girl* (Bloomsbury) by Helen Oyeyemi, written while the author was still studying for A-levels, about a child of mixed English and Nigerian parentage who meets her dangerous double.

Macmillan introduced a controversial initiative called New Writing, offering selected aspiring writers publication of their books, with no advance paid, but with a royalty of 20 per cent on net receipts. The chosen books would be minimally edited, and marketed only in a generic promotion. Some commentators, including agents as well as author Hari Kunzru, thought this venture was improper and exploitative, and likely to damage the existing system of author payments. Macmillan argued that the books would be very hard to publish and market under any other circumstances, and that this list at least gave their authors a chance of a readership. Macmillan would lose money on the venture, but gain broader access to new talent. The strategy was an acknowledgement that the claim that publishers rarely overlook work of real quality is flawed. Fifty manuscripts a day from hopeful authors began to arrive at the publisher's offices.

Finally this was the year the internet search engine Google announced its innovative Google Print, a plan to scan all the volumes of five of the world's major libraries onto the internet, causing extensive controversy over copyright and the potential damage to the publishing industry. At the time of publication the debate continued, with the Association of American Publishers requesting a six-month moratorium on the scanning of copyrighted books until the firm satisfactorily answered fundamental questions.

MUSIC

CLASSICAL MUSIC

LONDON

During the 2004–5 season, the South Bank Centre celebrated two of the great 20th century-born English composers as they both reached their 70th birthday. A festival dedicated to the work of Sir Harrison Birtwistle – 'Birtwistle Games: A Celebration of Harrison Birtwistle' – took place in October and November 2004, and a festival of the music of fellow-composer Sir Peter Maxwell Davies – 'Max: Peter Maxwell Davies, a Musician of Our Time' – in April 2005. They became fellow students at the Royal Northern College of Music and from there went on to become two of the most important British composers of our generation. 'Birtwistle Games' included London premieres of The Second Mrs Kong (semi-staged) and Night's Black Bird, and also the first British performance of the complete Orpheus Elegies. Other composers represented included Ligeti, Messiaen, Pierre de Manchicourt, Feldman and a world premiere by former Birtwistle student Kawai Shiu. The work by Shiu, a recent student of Birtwistle, was a South Bank Centre commission. Artists included the Philharmonia Orchestra, London Sinfonietta, BBC Symphony Orchestra, Endymion, New London Consort, the Arditti Quartet, Nash Ensemble, BBC Singers and the Choir of Westminster Abbey. Sir Peter Maxwell Davies was recently appointed Master of the Queen's Music, and the South Bank Centre and Royal Academy of Music put together a festival for April 2005 celebrating his work. The festival opened with music theatre works Miss Donnithorne's Maggot and Vesalii Icones performed by champions of the repertoire Psappha. Other highlights included the world premieres of A Dance on the Hill and Naxos Quartet No. 6. Artists included the City of London Sinfonia, Endymion, London Sinfonietta, Westminster Cathedral Choir and the Philharmonia Orchestra.

Since the Corporation of London's £7million investment in the Barbican Hall's refurbishment, the Centre has established new partnerships with top-ranking musicians and orchestras. The 'Great Performers 2004–5' season assembled a most impressive line-up of international performers, including debuts from Natalie Dessay and the Berliner Philharmoniker, continuing Bernard Haitink's 75th birthday celebrations, plus concerts with Cecilia Bartoli, Daniel Barenboim, Mariss Jansons with the Royal Concertgebouw Orchestra and Valery Gergiev with the Mariinsky Opera (formerly known as Kirov). In a new venture, the Barbican co-commissioned its first fully staged opera production with William Christie's Les Arts Florissants.

'Mostly Mozart', London's vibrant summer festival, returned to the Barbican for its third year. Set up to attract new audiences to classical music, 'Mostly Mozart' in its first year drew 60 per cent newcomers to the Barbican, the following year 52 per cent. The festival has become an important platform for young, up-and-coming artists to be profiled on a major London stage. Starting with Mozart's Requiem on the opening night, the festival presented a varied programme of works by Mozart and other composers, concluding with Beethoven's monumental 9th Symphony. Artists included Harry Christophers and the Sixteen, soprano Gillian Keith, mezzo soprano Alice Coote and pianist Freddy Kempf with his Kempf Trio (for Beethoven's Triple Concerto). Each concert in 'Mostly Mozart' allowed more than one young soloist to shine. Emmanuel Pahud (a rare example of EMI signing up a solo flautist) performed Mozart's 2nd Flute Concerto, Janine Jansen the 5th Violin Concerto, Andrew Marriner (principal clarinettist with the London Symphony Orchestra (LSO)) the Clarinet Concerto and Gianluca Cascioli (the piano phenomenon who has already performed with Muti, Abbado and Rostropovich) the 21st Piano Concerto K467. Pianists Steven Osborne and Paul Lewis teamed up for Mozart's delightful Double Piano Concerto K365. Natalie Clein, who at 16 won the BBC Young Musician of the Year Competition in 1994, performed Boccherini's Cello Concerto in E. Catrin Finch, the Royal Harpist to HRH The Prince of Wales, innovatively transposed Mozart's Piano Concerto K414 as a Harp Concerto.

The London Sinfonietta's 2004–5 season presented great diversity, paying tribute to composers the ensemble has long championed, as well as venturing into new territory, collaborating with different artists and finding fresh ways to experience contemporary music. The ensemble performed in festivals dedicated to Harrison Birtwistle and Peter Maxwell Davies (see above) and George Benjamin's pick of composers from around the world alongside commissions from Sam Hayden and Unsuk Chin. The ensemble continued its residency at the Concertgebouw Bruges. The acclaimed collaboration with Warp Records continued with tour dates abroad, and cutting-edge material from Radiohead's Jonny Greenwood and Thom Yorke heard at Ether 2005.

The London Sinfonietta returned to the Queen Elizabeth Hall (QEH) for Benedict Mason's Chaplin Operas, a live score performed alongside three classic Charlie Chaplin films: Easy Street, The Adventurer and The Immigrant. The ensemble's second day focused on works by Simon Holt and David Sawer, and in February workshops, concerts and compositions were presented by Blue Touch Paper participants past and present: Mary Bellamy, Anna Meredith and Tansy Davies. Another event showcasing young talent was Young Brits, the first of two BBC invitation concerts at LSO St Luke's, featuring the world premiere of Sam Hayden's London Sinfonietta commission. In the second, young conductor Ilan Volkov assembled a programme around the music of Helmut Lachenmann.

Festivals in the QEH rounded off the 2004–5 London season, the first dedicated to Peter Maxwell Davies at 70. Oliver Knussen conducted his choice of Maxwell Davies' most emotionally compelling works, and the UK premiere of De Assumtione Beatae Maria Virginis. In May, George Benjamin curated a series of three concerts with the London Sinfonietta and Arditti Quartet. Featuring the world premiere of Cantatrix Sopranica, a London Sinfonietta commission from Grawemeyer award-winner Unsuk Chin, and a new commission from Swedish composer Karin Rehnqvist, alongside Gérard Grisey's hugely acclaimed final work and pieces by Hans Abrahamsen and Franco Donatoni.

In the first week of June 2005, the BBC Radio 3 broadcasted the complete works of Beethoven, from the juvenile Piano Trios to the climactic String Quartet in F major, Opus 135. The BBC Philharmonic played the symphony cycle with chief conductor Gianandrea Noseda over two weekends at the Bridgewater Hall, Manchester – remarkably, the first time the city had heard the complete set in almost half a century (the last was conducted by Sir John Barbirolli in 1958–9). These concerts were aired on Radio 3 and 'streamed' for a week on its website. Anyone could download a set for free. It took only five minutes on broadband for Symphonies One to Eight, and ten for the momentous Ninth. So radical is this departure from all prior conventions of broadcasting and distributing works of music that the consequences were uncalculated. No one could have known if ten or ten million people would download the Beethoven symphonies in the event, it was 1.4 million, and whether this would form the cornerstone for a new habit of hoarding classical music, a surrogate for record buying.

OUTSIDE LONDON

Sage Gateshead, a £70m music centre designed by Foster and Partners, opened on 17 December 2004. It won the biggest lottery grant in the country outside London – £47m – and is the latest and most ambitious of Gateshead's confident wedge of new landmarks, alongside the Baltic art gallery and the Millennium Bridge. Beneath the curvaceous carapace it houses two concert halls, a rehearsal hall, bars, restaurants and education facilities. The Sage is expected to have a £12m annual turnover and its ambition for world significance rests partly on the claim that the larger of its halls, which seats 1,700, will be one of the world's great concert venues. Sage celebrated the opening by making tickets available free of charge for the first weekend. Artists involved in the opening weekend included the orchestra of the Sage Gateshead, Northern Sinfonia with music director Thomas Zehetmair, new-wave rock band and Warp Records' new signing Maximo Park, world renowned Northumbrian smallpipes player Kathryn Tickell, jazz pianist Alex Wilson and soul singer Juliet Roberts, funk revivalists New Mastersounds, saxophonist Andy Sheppard, and contemporary classical musicians the David Paul Jones Quartet.

The City of Birmingham Symphony Orchestra's (CBSO) 2004–5 season featured a rich mixture of music from Beethoven to Gershwin. In Sakari Oramo's seventh season as music director of the CBSO, he was joined by over 100 visiting artists and conductors. The major theme running through this season was the influence 'music of black origin' has on Western classical music. The orchestra also launched its Stravinsky cycle, a series of concerts encompassing Stravinsky's complete works which will take place over the next four years and includes a collaboration between the CBSO and Birmingham Royal Ballet to stage all Stravinsky's ballets. In January the CBSO performed Holst's *The Planets* including an eighth planet – *Pluto* – composed by Colin Matthews. In February the CBSO and Chorus joined in the celebrations marking the centenary of Sir Michael Tippett's birth with a performance of his most famous work, *A Child of Our Time.*

The Birmingham Contemporary Music Group's (BCMG) 2004–5 season began with with four new works composed by James MacMillan, John Croft, Simon Holt and John Woolrich and also by BCMG players in Peter Wiegold's 'Invisible Cities' programme. The season continued with UK premieres of pieces by Louis Andriessen and the young Scot Stuart MacRae. Song and story was a theme running throughout the season, with a starry line-up of singers including Anu Komsi, Mary King and Loré Lixenberg performing music from this century and last, and storyteller Vayu Naidu continuing her ground-breaking collaboration with Judith Weir, fusing music and words in new ways to tell epic tales from across the globe. Other guest artists included Sakari Oramo, Oliver Knussen and Susanna Mälkki and the virtuoso contemporary pianist Nicolas Hodges played the recent piano concerto by US grand master Elliott Carter, a concerto completed in his 94th year.

FESTIVALS

With 23 world premieres, 35 UK premieres and 4 new commissions, the Huddersfield Contemporary Music Festival (HCMF) 2004 was again a remarkable success. Along with a number of overseas performers who made their UK debuts, HCMF welcomed visits by Kevin Volans, Richard Ayres, Rebecca Saunders, Richard Rijnvos, Howard Skempton and Sir Peter Maxwell Davies. As ever, the Festival balanced its international perspective with providing opportunities to the best and most creative British and international artists. Many of these composers were from the younger generation, and their fresh outlook on composition was inspiring to all who heard it. The festival included a collaboration between the Italian Alter Ego ensemble and sound artist Scanner, performing and then remixing the works of Salvatore Sciarrino – a project to which Sciarrino himself gave his blessing – and the 'silent music' of Jonathan Burrows and Matteo Fargion's enchanting choreographed piece *Both Sitting Duet.* HCMF also provided a rare opportunity to hear five of the greatest international jazz improvisers on stage together, saxophone legend Evan Parker was joined by his regular trio partners Barry Guy and Paul Lytton, alongside improvising electronics duo Furt (composer Richard Barrett and Paul Obermayer). A fusion of Arabic lyricism, dance grooves and electronics was also provided by the charismatic Tunisian artist Dhafer Youssef, who appeared with a line-up of inspiring musicians that included Eivind Aarset and Arve Henriksen.

Other highlights included the British Music Information Centre Cutting Edge Tour of adventurous new Anglo-Belgian group Plus Minus; the Ives Ensemble who performed a programme of UK premieres by Gerald Barry, Luc Ferrari and others; the UK premiere of Richard Rijnvos' landmark cycle of works, *Block Beuys,* inspired by artist Joseph Beuys; the long awaited return of musikFabrik, the acclaimed contemporary music ensemble from Cologne; UK debut of brilliant young Austrian composer-pianist Thomas Larcher; a welcome return for young vocal ensemble/choir EXAUDI, specialising in contemporary repertoire; Festival favourites, Ensemble Recherche, brought an exquisite programme of music by Rebecca Saunders and Georg Friedrich Haas; and Rolf Hind and Nicolas Hodges – Britain's two leading interpreters of contemporary piano repertoire in a two-piano concert that included world premieres by David Sawer and Rebecca Saunders.

The Edinburgh International Festival had to ask for an emergency £600,000 funding bail-out earlier this year after its income from ticket sales fell from £2,237,000 in 2003 to £1,745,000 in 2004, a fall of almost £500,000. The Festival also faced losses at the Hub, its main centre which it owns and operates, of £120,000. The £5 nights were blamed for the loss and the programme for the 2005 festival was consequently conservative. Highlights included a five-concert residency with the Bamberg Symphony Orchestra under the direction of Jonathan Nott, a production of *Swan Lake* by American Pennsylvania Ballet with the Russian Tchaikovsky Symphony Orchestra of Moscow Radio conducted by Vladimir Fedoseyev, and a British staged premiere of John Adams' opera *The Death of Klinghoffer*.

The 2005 series of Promenade Concerts in London, under the directorship of Nicholas Kenyon, remained one of the largest music festivals anywhere, with over 70 concerts at the Albert Hall. As well as being broadcast live on BBC Radio 3 every evening, each concert was audio-streamed onto the internet. In addition a selection of concerts were shown on BBC Television, and on the BBC's digital TV channel, BBC4, and video-streamed onto an interactive website. As always the Proms attracted some of the biggest names in the classical music world, and an eclectic selection of renowned musicians performed for the first time, from the Spanish tenor Placido Domingo to the legendary sitar player Ravi Shankar. Each year the Proms explores different themes, as a way of bringing together music which spans many centuries and different styles. This year there were three main themes running through the festival: 'The Sea', 'Fairy Tales', and a number of composer anniversaries. To celebrate the 'Year of the Sea', 200 years after the Battle of Trafalgar, Sir John Eliot Gardiner conducted Haydn's *Nelson' Mass*, Sir Charles Mackerras conducted Gilbert & Sullivan's *HMS Pinafore*, Esa-Pekka Salonen marked the centenary of Debussy's *La mer*, and other seascapes flowed throughout the season, from Vaughan Williams' *A Sea Symphony* to Britten's 'Four Sea Interludes' from *Peter Grimes*. Among the great popularisers of fairy tales was the Danish writer and poet, Hans Christian Andersen. Born 200 years ago, Andersen has inspired composers from Stravinsky and Zemlinsky to Bent Sorensen, who wrote a new work on *The Little Mermaid*. Purcell's *The Fairy Queen* and Mendelssohn's *A Midsummer Night's Dream* led the season's fairy dance which included music drawing on a wide spectrum of folkloric traditions. Michael Tippett, one of the most inspirational composers of our time, would have been 100 this year; among several other major works, his *A Child of Our Time* marks the anniversary of the end of World War II. Other anniversaries – from Tallis and Carissimi to Rawsthorne and Lambert, Berg and Berio – were also celebrated.

OTHER NEWS

The Arts Council England has long offered ethnic minorities a path into the white-dominated societies of the West, whether in theatre, movies or popular music, but has decided to speed things up by introducing affirmative action to culture. Specifically, it wants the 1,100 cultural organisations that receive its help to employ minorities, to present black, Asian and other ethnic art, and to reach out to minorities unaccustomed to attending cultural events. Further, it has given the initiative teeth by linking its continuing financial support to adoption and execution of what it calls 'racial equality action plans'. Until now, while the council's beneficiaries have included ethnic minorities engaged in artistic activities, most of its annual budget of £412 million, has gone to mainstream theatre, dance, opera and classical music (major museums are supported directly by the government). Never before has the council tried to dictate quite so specifically how this money should be spent

A UK businessman, John Barker, spent £100,000 to hire the Royal Philharmonic to play for his girlfriend. He decided to repay his girlfriend Heather Axelson for nursing him through illness and knowing her love of classical music, he searched high and low for a concert hall playing her favourite piece, Janácek's *Sinfonietta*. He could not find one, so he splashed out £100,000 on booking the Royal Philharmonic Orchestra to play it at London's Royal Festival Hall. He also paid for violinist Nicola Benedetti, the BBC Young Musician of the Year, to take the lead role. The rest of the cost went towards booking a conductor, concert organiser and advertising for the event.

Boosey & Hawkes, the private equity-backed classical music publisher, has begun talks with its banks about a refinancing deal after a 73 per cent increase in profits in the past two years. The company, which has sold off its loss-making musical instruments business, is now focusing purely on exploiting its large catalogue of classical music rights that include the estates of Rachmaninoff, Stravinsky and Prokofiev. The company, led by John Minch has also been developing symphonic productions of popular musicals. It persuaded the English National Opera to stage Leonard Bernstein's *On the Town*, which opened at the Coliseum, and has begun talks with two music majors, Warner Music and Universal, to exploit their back catalogues of musicals. It also has the rights to the work of Aaron Copland, the popular American composer. Boosey & Hawkes was taken off the stock market in October 2003 when it was bought by HgCapital, which paid £44.3 million and assumed £31.1 million of debt. Since then the company's earnings have risen from £3 million in 2003 to £5.2 million last year.

AWARDS AND COMPETITIONS

ROYAL PHILHARMONIC SOCIETY MUSIC AWARDS
Presented at the Dorchester Hotel, London, on 11 May 2005 the awards, in 13 categories, honoured musicians, composers, writers, broadcasters and inspirational arts organisations for their work in 2004. This year's ceremony was hosted by BBC Radio 3's Stephanie Hughes, with awards presented by conductor Sir Andrew Davis. The keynote speech was given by theatre director Jude Kelly. The Royal Opera House was a big winner on the night, with three awards: its music director Antonio Pappano won the Conductor Award; the Singer Award went to Ben Heppner for his 'towering performance' in the title role of *Peter Grimes* and composer Thomas Adès was awarded the Award for Large-scale Composition for *The Tempest*. Opera North triumphed over the Royal Opera House in the Opera and Music Theatre category, with *Eight Little Greats*, its acclaimed series of short, rarely staged operas. Manchester's Hallé Orchestra took the Ensemble Award, the jury commenting: 'The revival of the Hallé under Mark Elder is one of the great success stories of British classical music.' Edward Gardner, 30-year-old music director of Glyndebourne Touring Opera, and until recently, assistant conductor to Elder at the Hallé, won the Award for Young Artists. Pianist Pierre-Laurent Aimard's 'adventurous commitment to 20th century and contemporary music' was rewarded with the Award for Instrumentalist.

The RPS Music Awards also recognised the wealth of extraordinary work taking place beyond the traditional concert hall. Birmingham Contemporary Music Group won the Award for Audience Development for its tours of contemporary classical music to rural village halls in Shropshire (a programme which has played to full and enthusiastic houses for the past five years). The Education Award went to 'Operaction Hackney: On London Fields', a ground-breaking project involving over 700 people, in which the Hackney Music Development Trust devised and produced a new community opera celebrating Hackney's history and diversity. The Award for Creative Communication, a new award which recognises the contribution of words and images, across all media, in furthering the understanding of classical music was awarded to director John Bridcut for *Britten's Children* (Mentorn for BBC), a 'touching revelatory film [which] explored one aspect of a composer's life in great depth, avoiding the temptation of sensationalism'. Composer Howard Skempton was a popular choice as winner of the Chamber Scale Composition category for his string quartet *Tendrils*. The passing of one of the 20th century's musical giants was marked with the award of the Festival and Series category to the South Bank Centre, Royal Academy of Music and London Sinfonietta for *Omaggio*, a season centred on the work of Luciano Berio (and planned with the composer shortly before his death). The RPS Gold Medal Award went to Sir Charles Mackerras, 'one of the great musicians of our age as a conductor and scholar who has illuminated a vast range of familiar and less well-known repertoire and who has maintained the highest musical standards throughout his varied and distinguished career'. Sir Charles Mackerras, who turns 80 later in 2005, is only the 91st recipient of the RPS Gold Medal Award

The UK's PRS Foundation launched a £50,000 New Music Award touted as the 'Turner Prize for Music'. Rather than rewarding an existing work, the award goes to support a yet-to-be-created music project. Jem Finer, a founding member of the Irish rock band The Pogues, was the inaugural winner with his project titled *Score for a Hole in the Ground*. He will dig a shaft with bowls of different sizes suspended within; as rain falls, it will cause the bowls to ring and change their timbre as they fill and spill water into the bowls below. The resulting sound will be carried 20 feet above the surface by a brass horn. He has until September 2006 to present his work. The other finalists were composer Terry Mann, who proposed recording every cathedral bell in the UK for a piece of installation art, and composer and producer Craig Vear, who wanted to capture live sounds from a buoy off the coast of south-western England and then feed them into an installation at the National Maritime Museum Cornwall. The judges for the award included percussionist Evelyn Glennie, film composer Anne Dudley, comedian Stewart Lee, BBC host Verity Sharp, and Aniruddha Das of the electronica group Asian Dub Foundation.

GRAMOPHONE AWARDS 2004
Mandarin Hotel, London – 1 October 2004
Record of the Year – Mozart *Le nozze di Figaro*. Soloists; Ghent Collegium Vocale; Cocerto Köln / René Jacobs. Harmonia Mundi
Best of Category (Early Music) – Gibbons *Consorts for Viols*. Phantasm with Asaka Morikawa and Susanna Pell
Best of Category (Concerto) – Grieg. Schumann *Piano Concertos*. Leif Ove Andsnes *pf* Berlin Philharmonic Orchestra/ Mariss Jansons. EMI
Best of Category (Baroque Vocal) – Vivaldi *Vespri Solenni per la Festa dell'Assunzione di Maria Vergine*. Gemma Bertagnolli, Roberta Invernizzi, Anna Simboli *sops* Sara

Mingardo *contr* Gianluca Ferrarini *ten* Matteo Bellotto *bar* Antonio de Secondi *vn* Concerto Italiano/Rinaldo Alessandrini. Naïve Opus
Best of Category (Orchestral) – Bax *The Symphonies*. BBC Philharmonic Orchestra/Vernon Handley. Chandos
Artist of the Year – Magdalena Kozená
Lilfetime Achievement – The LSO
Classic FM Listeners' Choice – Bryn Terfel
Special Achievement Award – Peter Alward
Label of the Year – Telarc

THE CLASSICAL BRIT AWARDS 2005
Royal Albert Hall, London – 25th May 2005
Female Artist of the Year – Marin Alsop
Male Artist of the Year – Bryn Terfel
Album of the Year – The Sixteen/Harry Christophers: *Renaissance*
Contemporary Music Award – John Adams: *On The Transmigration of Souls and Road Movies*.
NS&I Album of the Year – Katherine Jenkins: *Second Nature*
Soundtrack Composer Award – John Williams: *Harry Potter and the Prisoner of Azkaban*
Critics Award – Stephen Hough/Dallas SO/Andrew Litton: *Rachmaninov: Piano Concertos*
Oustanding Contribution to Music – Sir James Galway

POP MUSIC

A FORCE FOR GOOD
This year, the great and good of British pop music united on two occasions for charity in events that recalled those of 20 years earlier. In November, more than 50 artists gathered in London's Abbey Road studio to speedily record a new version of Band Aid's 1984 chart-topper, *Do They Know It's Christmas*. Organised once again by Sir Bob Geldof and Midge Ure to raise funds for famine relief in Africa, Band Aid 20's updated effort included contributions from Robbie Williams, Sir Paul McCartney and Coldplay's Chris Martin alongside a host of middle-order bands such as The Thrills and Travis. U2's frontman, Bono, the one participant involved in both Band Aids, reprised his line from the original. While the record's artistic merits were questionable, *Do They Know It's Christmas* secured the coveted festive number one spot and sold over a million copies in December, swiftly becoming 2004's best-selling single and generating millions of pounds for charity.

With characteristic vigour, Geldof then galvanised the UK in preparation for Live 8, a huge, free, all-day concert on the scale of 1985's historic Live Aid event, held in London's Hyde Park on Saturday, 2 July. Staged in conjunction with a handful of international charities, notably Make Poverty History, Live 8 aimed to pressure world leaders meeting in Scotland for the G8 summit to cancel the debt owed by the world's poorest countries to the world's wealthiest nations. Simultaneous Live 8 concerts performed by scores of the world's leading pop and rock acts took place in the other G8 countries – in Philadelphia, Berlin, Paris, Rome, Tokyo, Toronto and Moscow – and at the Eden Project in St. Austell, Cornwall. On 6 July, a further Live 8 concert was held at Murrayfield Stadium in Edinburgh, close to the G8 summit. Some 200,000 free tickets for the London extravaganza were allocated through a £1.50 text-message lottery, although 15,000 VIPs paid £799-a-head to enjoy corporate hospitality from within a 'golden circle' situated between the stage and the rest of the crowd. The glittering bill included special performances by Madonna, Robbie Williams, Sting, Annie Lennox, The Who, REM, Coldplay, Scissor Sisters, Elton John and Snoop Dogg, among others. Geldof persuaded rock legends Pink Floyd to reform for the event, while the opening performance of The Beatles' *Sergeant Pepper's Lonely Hearts Club Band* by Sir Paul McCartney and U2 became the first time the song had ever been played live by a Beatle. The track was made available to buy online mere hours after its performance, selling 20,000 downloads in two weeks.

The concert was broadcast live by the BBC across its television, radio and online networks. Eight hours of coverage on BBC1 averaged 7.8 million viewers, which is less than the average figure for a popular soap like *EastEnders*. Robbie Williams' lively set proved the biggest draw, attracting 9.6 million. However, 14.6 million page impressions were recorded on the BBC's Live 8 site over the weekend, a record for a music site, while the BBC's Live 8 mobile phone site received 112,000 hits. It is estimated that over 1 million attended all ten concerts around the world and that anywhere between 2 billion and 4 billion watched or listened to the shows at some point during the day. Regardless of their charitable intent, a number of Live 8's flagship acts saw their back catalogue sales dramatically increase throughout July. HMV reported that sales of Pink Floyd's *Echoes: The Best Of Pink Floyd* and The Who's *Then And Now* rose by 1,343 per cent and 863 per cent respectively. Albums by former Eurythmics singer Annie Lennox, Dido and Razorlight also benefited from the exposure. Fittingly, the top-selling music DVD of 2004 was *Live Aid*, a three-disc set featuring all the action from the 1985 event in Wembley Stadium. Yet the impact of Live 8 diminished in the wake of the terrorist bombings in London five days later.

THE BIG HITTERS

Coldplay, the mild-mannered British rock band led by Chris Martin, husband of actor Gwyneth Paltrow, returned in June with their solid third album, *X&Y*, to blanket adulation. Likeably self-deprecating, Martin often apologised in interviews for his group's extraordinary success as *X&Y* sold 4.5 million copies worldwide in two months, including a million in the UK where it spent five weeks at number one. The album topped charts in 32 countries, lasting three weeks at number one in the USA, a major achievement for a British act. Coldplay headlined a muddy Glastonbury Festival at the end of June before embarking on a sold-out tour of the globe's stadia. U2's 11th album, *How To Dismantle An Atomic Bomb*, cemented their position as the world's biggest rock outfit, entering charts at number one in 25 countries and shifting 8.5 million copies in eight months. Bolstered by a lavish marketing campaign, their single *Vertigo* was the UK's leading download in 2004 and Apple even produced a limited-edition U2 iPod. In September, singer Bono spoke about poverty in Africa at the Labour Party conference in Brighton.

It was an encouraging year here for new acts too, with Keane and Scissor Sisters each selling well over two million copies of their debut albums, *Hopes And Fears* and *Scissor Sisters*. A well-heeled, rosy-cheeked trio from Kent, Keane's billowy guitar-free MOR pop cleaned up in Coldplay's absence, winning them two BRIT Awards. Camp New York disco troupe Scissor Sisters thrilled festival crowds and record-buyers alike with flamboyant shows and infectious party tunes. In November, the band

penned Kylie Minogue's electro-pop comeback single, *I Believe In You*, and later romped to victory at the BRITS with three Awards, including Best International Group. They've yet to repeat their success in the USA.

A former British Army officer who served in Kosovo, 26-year-old James Blunt made for an unlikely pop star but this charismatic singer-songwriter was one of the success stories of 2005. *Back To Bedlam*, a debut LP of lovelorn power ballads, would win few prizes for innovation but crept to the top of the charts and remained there in July, having sold 900,000 copies. Joss Stone, the teenage soul sensation from Devon, managed to translate her Stateside success back home with her second album of ersatz blues, *Mind, Body & Soul*, performing well. She scooped BRITs for Best British Female and Best Urban Act. Another high-profile teenage songbird, Welsh soprano Charlotte Church, underwent a pop makeover in keeping with her headline-grabbing antics but her over-produced debut, *Tissues And Issues*, failed to convince her desired audience.

The big guns of alternative rock, Green Day, Oasis and The White Stripes, blazed back this year with decent albums that sold over half-a-million each. Dance music continued to wane with few new or established electronic acts capturing the public's imagination, although greatest hits compilations from dancefloor favourites Basement Jaxx (*The Singles*) and Faithless (*Forever Faithless*), which both sold 650,000, bucked this trend. Meanwhile, Gorillaz, the acclaimed cartoon band involving Blur's creative force Damon Albarn, returned with million-selling second album *Demon Days*, an inventive hotchpotch of rap, pop and rock designed to appeal to small children and ageing hipsters. Amid much fanfare, Gwen Stefani, the No Doubt singer, released her debut solo album in November. *Love Angel Music Baby* was an astute pop confection polished to near perfection by an array of songwriters and producers, chalking up 850,000 sales in the UK alone. Stefani's fashion line, LAMB, was soon to follow. Released the same month, US rapper Eminem's fourth LP in six years, *Encore*, showed the star was running out of ideas – and targets – and in July rumours circulated about his retirement, despite *Encore* notching 1.2 million sales here. His colleague, 50 Cent, served up *The Massacre*, another moronic but invariably popular collection of lunk-headed hip-hop.

THE FRANZ FERDINAND EFFECT

The remarkable international success this year of Glasgow's art-rock quartet Franz Ferdinand, whose eponymous debut album won the Mercury Music Prize in 2004 and sold a million copies in the USA, ensured the fortunes of a number of like-minded new British bands who emerged in their slipstream. Traditionally the darlings of music titles like the *New Musical Express*, fashionably edgy young groups such as Kasabian, Razorlight, Kaiser Chiefs and Bloc Party rapidly became mainstream concerns as younger music fans developed an insatiable appetite for the classic combination of sweaty gigs, heart-throb singers and melodic indie rock. Happy-go-lucky Leeds five-piece Kaiser Chiefs' ascent, boosted by sing-along hits *I Predict A Riot* and *Oh My God*, saw their *Employment* debut sell more than 600,000 in the UK, while angst-ridden London quartet Bloc Party's *Silent Alarm* LP took off in the USA, shifting 750,000 copies worldwide.

In contrast, The Killers, a Las Vegas pop band modelled on '80s new romantics Duran Duran, repeatedly toured their tuneful *Hot Fuss* debut across the UK. Their toil proved lucrative however, as the album went on to sell 1.2

million here, securing them a prestigious Live 8 slot. It was similarly hard to avoid London's Razorlight, the success of whose *Up All Night* debut owed much to the attention-seeking exploits of narcissistic frontman Johnny Borrell. His former east London sparring partners, The Libertines, released their second eponymous LP in August to great acclaim only to split up months later due to irreconcilable differences between the group's two mercurial songwriters, Carl Barat and Peter Doherty. Painted as a doomed romantic, Doherty's addiction to hard drugs, lengthening criminal record, and on-off relationship with supermodel Kate Moss made him a fixture in the tabloid press and celebrity gossip weeklies. His post-Libertines band, Babyshambles, lived up to their name, playing a succession of disastrous gigs, if they even bothered to turn up at all.

THE SINGLES MARKET

This new wave of British rock also contributed to a revival in fortunes of the seven-inch single in the UK, with Babyshambles, Kaiser Chiefs and Franz Ferdinand all releasing top-selling singles on this cherished format. According to the British Phonographic Industry, annual sales of the seven-inch approached 1.4 million, a 64 per cent improvement year-on-year and the best 12 months for the format since 1998. Overall, it was another year of major change for the UK singles market. In April, sales of legal music downloads were added to the official UK singles chart for the first time. As sales of singles from shops declined, so the number of downloads sold on the net increased. Now a standard format used by record companies, more than 10 million downloads were sold in the UK during the first half of 2005 – almost twice the amount for the whole of 2004. Apple's iTunes service reported annual sales of 5 billion downloads worldwide as demand for its iPod and other mp3 players continued. Other download services submitting sales to the official UK chart include Napster, MyCokeMusic, Bleep, easyMusic and Karma Download.

The introduction of downloads has altered the make-up of the Top 40. Acts are more likely to remain and grow in the charts rather than entering one week and disappearing without a trace the next, a practice that some believed had devalued the hit parade. Many music fans who stopped buying physical singles are now keen on downloading. Single-buying from shops is mostly left to teenage girls who prefer pop acts such as McFly and Westlife, while the majority of downloaders are male and more mature with rock-based tastes. Although under-25s purchase 39 per cent of CD singles, they account for just seven per cent of download sales.

Plans are also afoot to include sales of mobile phone ringtones in the Top 40. However, this did not prevent one of the UK's most popular – and irritating – ringtones, a version of '80s dance hit *Axel F* by Crazy Frog, becoming number one in May, selling in excess of 450,000 copies across all formats. Television adverts featuring the computer-generated road-racing amphibian's products reportedly had to be withdrawn after TV bosses complained that viewers automatically switched channels when the Crazy Frog appeared. Another popular download and chart-topper in 2005 was a new version of *(Is This The Way To) Amarillo* by veteran crooner Tony Christie and comedian Peter Kay, proving that in pop, the silly season lasts all year round.

AWARDS

BRIT AWARDS 2005
British Male: The Streets
British Female: Joss Stone
British Group: Franz Ferdinand
British Album: Keane, *Hopes And Fears*
British Single: Will Young, *Your Game*
British Breakthrough Act: Keane
Brits25 Best Song: Robbie Williams, *Angels*
British Live Act: Muse
International Male: Eminem
International Female: Gwen Stefani
International Group: Scissor Sisters
International Album: Scissor Sisters, *Scissor Sisters*
International Breakthrough Act: Scissor Sisters
Outstanding contribution to music: Bob Geldof
Rock Act: Franz Ferdinand
Pop Act: McFly
British Urban Act: Joss Stone

MERCURY MUSIC PRIZE 2004
Franz Ferdinand, *Franz Ferdinand*

NME AWARDS 2005
Best British Band: The Libertines
Best Album: Franz Ferdinand, *Franz Ferdinand*
Best Live Band: Muse
Best New Band: Razorlight
Best Solo Artist: Graham Coxon
Best Track: Franz Ferdinand, *Take Me Out*
Best International Band: The Killers
Best Video: Green Day, *American Idiot*
Best Radio Show: Zane Lowe, Radio 1

OPERA

Antonio Pappano, Covent Garden's music director, displayed his wide operatic sympathies during the season. Scheduled to conduct new productions of the first two operas in a cycle of *Der Ring des Nibelungen,* Massenet's *Werther* and Verdi's *Un ballo in maschera* as well as a revival of *Otello,* he also took on, at very short notice, another Verdi opera, *La forza del destino,* that he had never conducted before. The Royal Opera, wishing to tempt the Italian maestro Riccardo Muti back to Covent Garden, offered to import whichever production from La Scala that Muti preferred. He chose Hugo de Ana's *La forza del destino,* whose heavy sets needed minor alterations to fit the Garden stage and to comply with safety regulations.

Muti refused to countenance these alterations and when Covent Garden insisted, walked out. In the event, Pappano's conducting and the orchestral playing were among the major pleasures of the performance. Another great pleasure was the magnificent singing of the chorus, trained by Renato Balsadonna, who took over as chorus master from Terry Edwards at the beginning of the season. Chorus and orchestra were also in top form in *Un ballo in maschera.* The director, Mario Martone, chose the Boston version of the libretto, updating it to the time of the American Civil War, which worked surprisingly well, despite a few anachronisms.

It would be unfair to judge Keith Warner's production of Wagner's *Ring* when only half-finished, but Bryn Terfel's first Wotan showed great promise vocally and an interesting interpretation of the role. Again, Pappano's stylistic affinity with the score amazed, as it had done with Massenet's *Werther* earlier in the season. The world premiere of Lorin Maazel's *1984,* adapted from George Orwell's novel, was something of a damp squib. A clever production by Robert Lepage and a magnificent set designed by Carl Fillion, plus excellent performances from Simon Keenlyside as Winston and Richard Margison as O'Brien, could not hide the derivative nature of the score, conducted by Maazel himself.

At the Linley studio theatre the centenary of the birth of Sir Michael Tippett was celebrated with an interesting production of *The Knot Garden* (in the chamber version). The Royal Opera will mark the event later in 2005 with a new production of *The Midsummer Marriage,* premiered, like all Tippett's operas, at Covent Garden. Also at the Linley, Music Theatre Wales gave the world premiere of Nigel Osborne's *The Piano Tuner,* with a libretto by Amanda Holden based on the novel by Daniel Mason: in the late 19th century a piano tuner goes out to Burma to tune the piano of a British doctor, with unexpected results.

English National Opera completed its *Ring* cycle with performances of *Siegfried* and *Twilight of the Gods* in Phyllida Lloyd's controversial but to my mind very interesting production. The presence of Richard Berkeley-Steele as Siegfried and Kathleen Broderick as Brünnhilde, both of whom not merely sang splendidly but actually *looked* their roles was an enormous advantage. At the end, Brünnhilde spectacularly brought down Valhalla as a suicide bomber. Whether this *Ring* is ever given as a cycle hangs in the balance; conductor Paul Daniel leaves as music director at the end of the season. His successor has

been announced as Oleg Caetani. Daniel also conducted the two parts of Berlioz' *The Trojans,* given in one evening and a revival of Berg's *Lulu* with Lisa Saffer repeating her triumph in the title role.

ENO marked the Tippett centenary with a staging of the oratorio *A Child of our Time,* which despite its continuing relevance is not really dramatic. Handel's *Jephtha* is also an oratorio, but though this story is dramatic, Katie Mitchell's production (originally staged by Welsh National Opera) was too fussy. Musically however, it was excellent, with Mark Padmore a most compelling Jephtha and the very young Sarah Tynan quite riveting as Iphis. A new production (ENO's first) by David McVicar of Mozart's *La clemenza di Tito* was a great success, while a revival of Tchaikovsky's *Eugene Onegin,* with Gerald Finley singing the title role for the first time, gave great pleasure.

But the triumph of the season was undoubtedly the production, directed by Jude Kelly and choreographed by Stephen Mears, of Leonard Bernstein's *On the Town,* not performed in London since 1963. The size of the Coliseum stage allowed a much larger cast than on that occasion, with nine principal singers and 46 chorus and dancers, while Simon Lee, the conductor, reverted to Bernstein's original score, removing Broadway additions by other hands and re-instating some original numbers. The singers, from opera (including Willard White and Andrew Shore in small roles) and from musicals, belted out the stunning songs with tremendous enthusiasm, while the dancing, if not quite of Gene Kelly standard, was exceptionally good. The 17 scheduled performances were all sold out, and three more were fitted into the programme.

Leeds Grand Theatre, home of Opera North, closed for restoration and refurbishment at the end of February 2005. The Assembly Rooms adjacent to the theatre are also being restored, which will provide space for smaller scale productions and educational projects. In the months before the closure, Richard Farnes, the company's new music director, conducted new productions of Puccini's *Manon Lescaut* and Mozart's *Don Giovanni,* both of which were praised, in particular for the orchestral playing.

A new production of Kurt Weill's *One Touch of Venus,* with lyrics by Ogden Nash and book by S. J. Perelman, first staged on Broadway in 1943, was conducted by James Holmes and directed by Tim Albery. It joined the repertory in December 2004 and, together with *Don Giovanni* and a revival of Rossini's *The Thieving Magpie,* toured to eight of Opera North's usual venues while the Grand Theatre was closed. Finally, a new, semi-staged production of Bartok's *Duke Bluebeard's Castle,* conducted by Farnes, was given in concert halls in five different cities. Bluebeard was sung by John Tomlinson, who was knighted in the Queen's Birthday Honours, and Judith by Sally Burgess.

Scottish Opera (SO), although its financial position has been stabilised, has had to sell the Theatre Royal, Glasgow, purchased in 1975, to the Ambassador Theatre Group (ATG). Scottish Opera will continue to perform in the theatre, but ATG will own and manage it. Richard Jarman, general director of Scottish Opera from 1991 to

1997, was appointed interim general director on the resignation of the Chief Executive, Christopher Barron, in May 2005. Richard Armstrong, music director of SO for the last eleven years, left at the end of the season, and a new music director was being sought.

Armstrong conducted SO's contribution to the Tippett centenary, a new production of *The Knot Garden*, directed and designed by Antony McDonald. A new staging of Bartok's *Duke Bluebeard's Castle*, in a double bill with Schoenberg's *Erwartung*, was also conducted by Armstrong. The company returned to the Edinburgh Festival with the first British staging of *The Death of Klinghoffer* by the American composer John Adams. This was first performed in 1991 in Brussels, and is based on a real event, the hijacking of cruise liner the *Achille Laura* by terrorists and the subsequent murder of one of the passengers, a disabled man in a wheel chair.

Welsh National Opera (WNO) finally moved into its new home in the recently opened Wales Millennium Centre, Cardiff Bay. The season opened in September 2004 at the New Theatre, Cardiff, with a new production of Richard Strauss' *Ariadne auf Naxos* conducted by Carlo Rizzi, who returned to WNO as music director on the resignation last season of Tugan Sokhiev. Rizzi was music director from 1992 to 2001. The new production of Gluck's *Iphigénie en Tauride* was also staged at the New Theatre, and together with *Ariadne* and a revival of *Turandot*, was taken on an extended tour.

The first performance in the Millennium Centre, a revival of *La traviata* conducted by Rizzi, took place on 18 February 2005. The first new production, the following night, was of Berg's *Wozzeck*, staged by Richard Jones and conducted by Vladimir Jurowski. This was followed by revivals of *Cavalleria rusticana* and *Pagliacci* (performed by WNO on its original opening in April 1946), with Welsh tenor Dennis O'Neill as both Turiddu and Canio. The final new production of the season was Dominic Cooke's staging of *The Magic Flute*. A concert performance of Tchaikovsky's *Iolanta*, conducted by Vassily Sinaisky and premiered in Swansea, was also given in London at the BBC Proms in the Royal Albert Hall.

Glyndebourne Festival Opera offered two new productions in 2005. First came Rossini's *La Cenerentola*, splendidly conducted by Vladimir Jurowski, the music director, and staged by Peter Hall with due acknowledgement of the dark side of the Cinderella story. There was plenty of jokes, but the underlying cruelty of the Baron and his daughters toward Cenerentola was not glossed over. The second new production, Handel's *Giulio Cesare*, was directed by David McVicar, with William Christie conducting the Orchestra of the Age of Enlightenment. This was sheer delight from beginning to end, with a production that flitted between the centuries but was basically just pre-1914. A ravishing performance of Cleopatra by American soprano Danielle de Niese and Christie's wonderful command of Handelian style added to the enjoyment.

Garsington Opera also opened with Rossini, in this case *Le Comte Ory*. This was followed by *Arabella,* in the Richard Strauss series that Garsington has been pursuing. The third of the productions, all new, was *Le nozze di Figaro,* directed by John Cox, whose sensibility to Mozart ensured a stylish performance. The last act, set in the garden of the Almaviva chateau and surrounded by the real garden of Garsington Manor, was magical. Leonard Ingrams, owner of the Manor and founder of Garsington Opera, died suddenly on 27 July 2005.

Another country house opera, Grange Park, featured Donizetti's *Maria Stuarda,* staged by Stephen Langridge. In the central scene (according to Schiller), Queen Elizabeth I confronts Mary, Queen of Scots at Fotheringhay. The Tower of London Festival presented another Donizettian slice of British history with *Anna Bolena,* which was staged a few yards from the place where the real Anne Boleyn was executed.

The Opera Group, in collaboration with the vocal ensemble I Fagiolini, presented a new comic opera, *The Birds,* with music by Ed Hughes and text, after Aristophanes, by Glyn Maxwell. The first performance was given at St Andrew's Church, Holborn, as part of the 2005 City of London Festival, and the opera was then taken to Cheltenham Festival, Warwick Festival, Oxford and the Buxton Festival. Buxton also staged a new children's opera by Ian McQueen, *Hollow Hill,* set in a cave in the Peak District, as well as a production of *The Knot Garden* by Music Theatre Wales and Nicolai's *The Merry Wives of Windsor.*

The BBC Proms gave Covent Garden's *Die Walküre,* with Placido Domingo making his Prom debut as Siegmund, a magnificent performance by all concerned, received with delirious joy by the audience. Other Prom operas included Welsh National Opera's *Iolanta* and Glyndebourne's *Giulio Cesare,* as already mentioned, and Purcell's *Fairy Queen,* Stravinsky's *Le Rossignol* and the premiere of *The Little Mermaid* by Bent Sorensen, based on Hans Andersen's story. Edinburgh International Festival included a light French opera, Messager's *L'Amour manqué,* as well as Scottish Opera's *Death of Klinghoffer* and concert performances of Wagner's *Tristan und Isolde,* a double bill of *Ariadne auf Naxos* with Mozart's *Zaide* and a rare Rossini tragic opera, *Adelaide di Borgogna.*

GONE BUT NOT FORGOTTEN

The British soprano Ruth Packer died on 12 January 2005 aged 94. She sang Helmwige in *Die Walküre* conducted by Sir Thomas Beecham at Covent Garden in 1939. During and after the Second World War she sang with the Carl Rosa Opera Company. Her large repertory included Violetta in *La traviata,* Amelia in *A Masked Ball,* Leonora in *Il trovatore,* Santuzza in *Cavalleria rusticana,* Antonia in *The Tales of Hoffmann,* Senta in *The Flying Dutchman* and Elisabeth in *Tannhäuser.* In 1951 she created Sybil at the premiere of George Lloyd's *John Socman.* With Welsh National Opera she sang Abigaille in *Nabucco* and Elena in *The Sicilian Vespers.* After retiring from the stage she taught at the Royal College of Music; among her pupils were Dame Gwyneth Jones and Dame Anne Evans.

June Bronhill, the Australian soprano who sang for many years with Sadler's Wells (now English National) Opera, died on 25 January, aged 75. She joined the company in 1954 and among her roles were Gilda in *Rigoletto,* the Queen of Night in *The Magic Flute,* the title roles of Flotow's *Martha* and of Janacek's *The Cunning Little Vixen* and Zerbinetta in *Ariadne on Naxos.* She was also highly successful as a singer of operetta, as Hanna Glawari in *The Merry Widow* (which she sang over 200 times), Adele in *Die Fledermaus,* Eurydice in Offenbach's *Orpheus in the Underworld* and many others. In 1959 she sang the title role of Donizetti's *Lucia di Lammermoor* at Covent Garden.

Una Hale, another Australian soprano, died on 4 March 2005, aged 82. She sang with the Carl Rosa Opera Company in roles such as Violetta in *La traviata,* Mimi in

La Bohème and Marguerite in *Faust,* then made her debut at Covent Garden in 1954 as Micaela in *Carmen.* She sang there until 1963, and was much admired as the Countess in *The Marriage of Figaro,* Liu in *Turandot,* Madame Lidoine in Poulenc's *The Carmelites,* Eva in *Die Meistersinger von Nuremberg,* Ellen Orford in *Peter Grimes* and the Marschallin in *Der Rosenkavalier.*

The British conductor Meredith Davies, who died on 9 March 2005, was originally an organist and choral conductor, but in 1960 he was invited to join the English Opera Group (EOG), for whom he conducted Britten's *Rape of Lucretia, A Midsummer Night's Dream, Albert Herring, The Turn of the Screw* and *Let's Make an Opera.* With EOG he also conducted the first performances of Malcolm Williamson's *English Eccentrics* (1964) and Lennox Berkeley's *Castaway* (1967). Meanwhile he had conducted Britten's *Peter Grimes* both at Covent Garden and at Sadler's Wells, and in 1965 he conducted Britten's *Billy Budd* at Covent Garden. In 1979 he became Principal of Trinity College of Music in London, where he started an opera school. His many recordings included Vaughan Williams' *Riders on the Sea* and *Sir John in Love,* and Frederick Delius' *A Village, Romeo and Juliet* and *Fennimore and Gerda.*

Theodor Uppman, the American baritone who died on 17 March 2005, aged 83, was best known in the UK as the first Billy Budd, which he sang at the premiere of Britten's opera at Covent Garden on 1 December 1951. He also sang the first US performance on NBC Television the following year, and continued to sing Billy until 1970, retaining his youthful-sounding voice and handsome appearance.

Dr Stanley Sadie, who died on 21 March 2005, aged 74, was a musical scholar and critic who specialised in the 18th century, in particular of the works of Handel and Mozart; he wrote prolifically on those and many other subjects, but is best known for his editorship, over more than two decades, of *The New Grove Dictionary of Music and Musicians* (1980), *The New Grove Dictionary of Opera* (1992) and of the second edition of *New Grove* (2001).

Stella Chitty, who died on 17 June 2005, was employed at Covent Garden for nearly half a century. She became assistant stage manager for the opera company in 1950, deputy stage manager in 1958, and stage manager in 1964. Though she did not much care for 18th-century operas and preferred the Romantic works of Verdi and Wagner, she was particularly fond of two 20th-century works: Britten's *Billy Budd,* which received its world premiere in 1951 conducted by the composer, and Berg's *Wozzeck,* given its British stage premiere at Covent Garden in 1952, conducted by Erich Kleiber. Chitty particularly admired Erich's son, Carlos Kleiber, who conducted, as his father had done many years previously, *Der Rosenkavalier.* Another favourite was Carlo Maria Giulini, who conducted the superb production by Luchino Visconti of Verdi's *Don Carlos* in 1958. She got on well with music directors Georg Solti, Colin Davis and Bernard Haitink, as well as directors such as Visconti, Franco Zeffirelli, and Götz Friedrich, whose complicated production of the *Ring* cycle, designed by Josef Sloboda, tested the abilities of Chitty and her staff to their limits. She managed tours by the Royal Opera to South Korea and Japan and to Los Angeles for the Olympic Games. She retired from stage management in 1993 but continued another four years as relief house manager.

PRODUCTIONS

In the summaries of company activities shown below, the dates in brackets indicate the year that the current production entered the repertory.

ROYAL OPERA
Founded 1946
Royal Opera House, Covent Garden, London WC2E 9DD

PRODUCTIONS FROM THE REPERTORY: *The Greek Passion* (2000), *Così fan tutte* (1995), *Faust* (2004), *La rondine* (2002), *Turandot* (1984), *La traviata* (1994), *Die Zauberflöte* (2003), *Madama Butterfly* (2003), *Rigoletto* (2001), *La bohème* (1974), *Otello* (1987), *Mitridate, re di Ponto* (1991).

NEW PRODUCTIONS: *La gioconda* (Ponchielli), 6 September 2004. Conductor, Antonio Pappano; concert performance. Violeta Urmana (Gioconda), Marcello Giordani (Enzo), Alexandru Agache (Barnaba), Mariana Pentcheva (Laura), Eric Halfvarson (Alvise), Jill Grove (La Cieca)

Werther (Massenet), 20 September 2004. Conductor, Antonio Pappano; director, Benoit Jacquot; set designer, Charles Edwards; costume designer, Christian Gasc. Marcelo Alvarez (Werther), Ruxandra Donose (Charlotte), Ludovic Tezier (Albert), Sally Matthews (Sophie), Jonathan Veira (Le Bailli)

La forza del destino (Verdi), 16 October 2004. Conductor, Antonio Pappano; director/designer, Hugo de Ana. Violeta Urmana (Leonora), Salvatore Licitra (Don Alvaro), Ambrogio Maestri (Don Carlo), Ferruccio Furlanetto (Padre Guardiano), Roberto de Candia (Fra Melitone), Luciana D'Intino (Preziosilla), Brindley Sherrat (Marchese di Calatrava)

Don Pasquale (Donizetti), 27 November 2004. Conductor, Bruno Campanella; director, Jonathan Miller; designer, Isabella Bywater. Simone Alaimo (Don Pasquale), Juan Diego Florez (Ernesto), Tatiana Lisnic (Norina), Alessandro Corbelli (Doctor Malatesta)

Das Rheingold (Wagner), 18 December 2004. Conductor, Antonio Pappano; director, Keith Warner; set designer, Stefanos Lazaridis; costume designer, Marie-Jeanne Lecca. Bryn Terfel (Wotan), Philip Langridge (Loge), Gunter von Kannen (Alberich), Rosalind Plowriight (Fricka), Jane Henschel (Erda), Gerhad Siegel (Mime), Franz-Josef Selig (Fasolt), Philip Ens (Fafner), Emily Magee (Freia), Willi Hartmann (Froh)

Die Walküre (Wagner), 5 March 2005. Conductor, Antonio Pappano; director, Keith Warner; set designer; Stefanos Lazaridis; costume designer, Marie-Jeanne Lecca. Lisa Gasteen (Brünnhilde), Bryn Terfel (Wotan), Katarina Dalayman (Sieglinde), Jorma Silvasti (Siegmund), Rosalind Plowright (Fricka), Stephen Milling (Hunding)

Un ballo in maschera (Verdi), 12 April 2005. Conductor, Antonio Pappano; director, Mario Martone; set designer, Sergio Tramonti; costume designer, Bruno Schwengel. Marcelo Alvarez (Gustavo), Karita Mattila (Amelia), Thomas Hampson (Anckarstroem), Camilla Tilling (Oscar), Elisabetta Fiorillo (Madame Arvidson)

1984 (Maazel), 3 May 2005, world premiere. Conductor, Lorin Maazel; director Robert Lepage; set designer, Carl Fillion; costume designer, Yasmina Giguere. Simon Keenlyside (Winston), Nancy Gustafson (Julia), Richard Margison (O'Brien), Lawrence Brownlee (Symes), Diana Damrau (Gym Teacher/Old Hag)

Il Turco in Italia (Rossini), 28 May 2005. Conductor,

Adam Fischer; directors, Patrice Caurier and Moshe Leiser; set designer, Christophe Forey; costume designer, Agostino Cavalca. Cecilia Bartoli (Fiorilla), Ildebrando D'Arcangelo (Selim), Alessandro Corbelli (Don Geronio), Thomas Allen (Prosdocimo), Barry Banks (Don Narciso)

ENGLISH NATIONAL OPERA
Founded 1931
London Coliseum, St Martin's Lane, London WC2N 4BS

PRODUCTIONS FROM THE REPERTORY: *The Trojans* (2003), *Don Giovanni* (2001), *Falstaff* (1997), *Semele* (1999), *The Barber of Seville* (1987), *Lulu* (2002), *Cosi fan tutte* (2002), *Eugene Onegin* (1994)

NEW PRODUCTIONS: *Siegfried* (Wagner), 6 November 2004. Conductor, Paul Daniel; director, Phyllida Lloyd; designer, Richard Hudson. Richard Berkely-Steele (Siegfried), Kathleen Broderick (Brünnhilde), Robert Hayward (Wanderer), John Graham-Hall (Mime), Patricia Bardon (Erda), Andrew Shore (Alberich)
The Pirates of Penzance (Sullivan), 4 December 2004. Conductor, Mark Shanahan; director, Elijah Moshinsky; set designer, Michael Yeargan; costume designer, Anne Tilby. Richard Suart (Major-General Stanley), Karl Daymond (Sergeant of Police), Jean Rigby (Ruth), Mark Wilde (Frederic), Victoria Joyce (Mabel)
A Child of our Time (Tippett), 21 January 2005. Conductor, Martyn Brabbins; director, Jonathan Kent, designer, Paul Brown. Susan Gritton, Sara Fulgoni, Timothy Robinson, Brindley Sherratt
La clemenza di Tito (Mozart), 5 February 2005. Conductor, Roland Boer; director, David McVicar; designer, Yannis Thavoris. Paul Nilon (Tito), Emma Bell (Vitellia), Sarah Connolly (Sesto), Sally Matthews (Servillia), Christine Rice (Annio), Neal Davies (Publio)
On the Town (Bernstein), 10 March 2005. Conductor, Simon Lee; director, Jude Kelly; choreographer, Stephen Mear; designer, Robert Jones. Willard W. White (Workman 1), Tim Howar (Ozzie), Adam Garcia (Chip), Aaron Lazar (Gabey), Helen Anker (Ivy Smith), Caroline O'Connor (Hildy), Lucy Schaufer (Claire de Loone), Sylvia Syms (Madame Maude P. Dilly), Janine Duvitski (Lucy Schmeeler), Andrew Shore (Judge Pitkin)
Twilight of the Gods (Wagner), 2 April 2005. Conductor, Paul Daniel; director, Phyllida Lloyd; designer, Richard Hudson. Kathleen Broderick (Brünnhilde), Richard Berkeley-Steele (Siegfried), Gidon Saks (Hagen), Claire Weston (Gutrune), Iain Paterson (Gunther), Sara Fulgoni (Waltraute), Andrew Shore (Alberich)
Jephtha (Handel), 12 May 2005. Conductor, Nicholas Kraemer; director, Katie Mitchell; designer, Vicki Mortimer. Mark Padmore (Jephtha), Susan Bickley (Storge), Sarah Tynan (Iphis), Robin Blaze (Hamor), Neal Davies (Zebul), Sarah-Jane Davies (Angel)

OPERA NORTH
Founded 1978
Grand Theatre, 40 New Briggate, Leeds LS1 6NU

PRODUCTION FROM THE REPERTORY: *The Thieving Magpie* (1992)

NEW PRODUCTIONS: *Orfeo ed Euridice* (Gluck), 7 September 2004. Conductor, Nicholas Kok; director/set designer/choreographer, Emio Greco/Peter C. Scholten; costume designer, Clifford Portier. Daniel Taylor (Orfeo), Isabel Monar (Euridice), Claire Ormshaw (Amor)

Manon Lescaut (Puccini), 23 September 2004. Conductor, Richard Farnes; director, Daniel Slater; designer, Robert Innes Hopkins. Natalia Dercho (Manon), Hugh Smith (Chevalier des Grieux), Christopher Purves (Lescaut), Brian Bannatyne-Scott (Geronte), Gordon Wilson (Edmondo)
Così fan tutte (Mozart), 7 October 2004. Conductor, Yves Abel; director, Tim Albery; designer, Tobias Hoheisal. Malin Bystrom (Fiordiligi), Ann Taylor (Dorabella), Claire Wild (Despina), Iain Paton (Ferrando), Roderick Williams (Guglielmo), Peter Savidge (Don Alfonso)
One Touch of Venus (Kurt Weill), 8 December 2004. Conductor, James Holmes; director, Tim Albery; set designer, Antony Macdonald; costume designer, Emma Ryott. Karen Coker (Venus), Christianne Tisdale (Molly), Loren Geeting (Rodney Hatch), Ron Li Paz (Whitelaw Savory)
Don Giovanni (Mozart), 15 January 2005. Conductor, Richard Farnes; director, Olivia Fuchs; designer, Niki Turner. Roderick Williams (Don Giovanni), Gerard O'Connor (Commendatore), Susannah Glanville (Donna Anna), Iain Paton (Don Ottavio), Gisella Allen (Donna Elvira), Andrew Foster-Williams (Leporello), Kim-Marie Woodhouse (Zerlina), Wyn Pencarreg (Masetto)
Duke Bluebeard's Castle (Bartok), 27 May 2005. Conductor, Richard Farnes; director, Giles Havergal (semi-staged performance). John Tomlinson (Bluebeard), Sally Burgess (Judith)
Performances were given at the Grand Theatre, Leeds and on tour in Newcastle, Salford Quays, Nottingham, Hull, Sheffield, Norwich and Belfast.

SCOTTISH OPERA
Founded 1962
39 Elmbank Crescent, Glasgow G2 4PT

PRODUCTIONS FROM THE REPERTORY: *Tosca* (1980), *Hansel and Gretel* (2000), *Fidelio* (1994)

NEW PRODUCTIONS: *Duke Bluebeard's Castle* (Bartok), 8 October 2004. Conductor, Richard Armstrong; director, André Engel; set designer, Nicky Rieti; costume designer, Dominique Mueller. Michele Kalmandi (Bluebeard), Andrea Szanto (Judith)
Erwartung (Schoenberg), 8 October 2004. Conductor, Richard Armstrong; director, André Engel; set designer, Nicky Rieti; costume designer, Dominique Mueller. Renate Bele (The Woman)
The Knot Garden (Tippett), 19 January 2005. Conductor, Richard Armstrong; director/designer, Antony McDonald. Peter Savidge (Mangus), Jane Irwin (Thea), Hilton Marlton (Dov), Derrick Parker (Mel), Rachel Nicholls (Flora), Andrew Shore (Faber), Rachel Hynes (Denise)
Semele (Handel), 19 February 2005. Conductor, Christian Curnyn; director/designer, Yannis Kokkos. Lisa Milne (Semele), Jeremy Ovenden (Jupiter), Susan Blickley (Ino/Juno), Michael George (Cadmus/Somnus), Arnos Zlotnik (Athamas), Kate Royal (Iris)
The Death of Klinghoffer (John Adams), 23 August 2005. Conductor, Edward Gardner; director, Anthony Neilson; designer, Miriam Bluether. Jonathan Summers (Klinghoffer), Andrew Shroeder (The Captain), Kamel Boutros (Mamoud), Darren Abrahams (Molgi), Catherine Wyn-Rogers (Marilyn Klinghoffer)
Performances were given at the Theatre Royal, Glasgow and the Edinburgh Festival Theatre. The revival

of *Hansel and Gretel* was toured to Stirling, Aberdeen, Forfar, Ayr, Kelso, Inverness, Portree and Wick

WELSH NATIONAL THEATRE
Founded 1946
Wales Millenium Centre, Bute Place, Cardiff Bay CF10 5AL

PRODUCTIONS FROM THE REPERTORY: *Iphigénie en Tauride* (1992), *Turandot* (1994), *La traviata* (2004), *Cavalleria rusticana* and *Pagliacci* (1996), *Rigoletto* (2001)

NEW PRODUCTIONS: *Ariadne auf Naxos* (R. Strauss), 11 September 2004. Conductor, Carlo Rizzi; director, Neil Armfield; designer, Dale Ferguson. Janice Watson (Ariadne), Katarzyna Dondalska (Zerbinetta), Alice Coote (Composer), Peter Hoare (Bacchus), D'Arcy Bleiker (Harleqin)

Wozzeck (Berg), 19 February 2005. Conductor, Vladimir Jurowski; director, Richard Jones; set designer, Paul Steinberg; costume designer, Buki Shiff. Christopher Purves (Wozzeck), Gun-Brit Barkmin (Marie), Peter Hoare (Captain), Peter Svenson (Drum Major), Clive Bayley (Doctor)

The Magic Flute (Mozart), 14 May 2005. Conductor, Jean-Yves Ossonce; director, Dominic Cooke; set designer, Julian Crouch; costume designer, Kevin Pollard. Peter Wedd (Tamino), Rebecca Evans (Pamina), Teddy Tahu Rhodes (Papageno), Katarzyna Dondalska (Queen of Night), Brindley Sheratt (Sarastro)

Performances were given at the New Theatre, Cardiff (2004), the Wales Millennium Centre, Cardiff Bay (2005) and on tour in Swansea, Belfast, Oxford, Southampton, Llandudno, Birmingham, Liverpool, Bristol, Milton Keynes and Plymouth

GLYNDEBOURNE FESTIVAL OPERA
Founded 1934
Glyndebourne, Lewes, East Sussex BN8 5UU

The Festival ran from 19 May to 28 August 2005. *Die Zauberflote* (2004), *The Bartered Bride* (1999), *Otello* (2001) and *Flight* (1998) were revived.

NEW PRODUCTIONS: *La Cenerentola* (Rossini), 19 May 2005. Conductor, Vladimir Jurowski; director, Peter Hall; set designer, Hildegard Bechtler; costume designer, Moritz Junge. Ruxandra Donose (Cenerentola), Maxim Mironov (Don Ramiro), Simone Alberghini (Dandini), Luciano di Pasquale (Don Magnifico), Nathan Berg (Alidoro), Raquela Sheeran (Clorinda), Lucia Cirillo (Tisbe)

Giulio Cesare (Handel), 3 July 2005. Conductor, William Christie; director, David McVicar; set designer, Robert Jones; costume designer, Brigitte Reiffenstuel. Sarah Connolly (Giulio Cesare), Danielle de Niese (Cleopatra), Patricia Bardon (Cornelia), Angelika Kirchschlager (Sesto), Christopher Maltman (Achilla), Christophe Dumaux (Tolomeo)

GLYNDEBOURNE TOURING OPERA
Le nozze di Figaro (2000), *La Cenerentola* (2005) and *Tangier Tattoo* (a new opera by John Lunn) were performed from 11 October to 17 December 2005 at Glyndebourne, Woking, Norwich, Milton Keynes, Plymouth, Stoke-on-Trent, Oxford and Edinburgh

GARSINGTON OPERA
Founded 1989
Garsington Manor, Oxford OX44 9DH

The season ran from 11 June to 9 July 2005.

NEW PRODUCTIONS: *Le Comte Ory* (Rossini), 11 June 2005. Conductor, David Parry; director, Rupert Goold; designer, Laura Hopkins. Juanita Lascarro (Comtesse Adele), Victoria Simmons (Isolier), Anne-Marie Owens (Ragonde), Colin Lee (Comte Ory), Miljenko Turk (Raimbaud), Dean Robinson (Tutor)

Arabella (R. Strauss), 14 June 2005. Conductor, Elgar Howarth; director/designer, David Fielding. Orla Boylan (Arabella), Cora Burggraaf (Zdenka), Jeffrey Lloyd-Roberts (Matteo), Peter Coleman-Wright (Mandryka),

Le nozze di Figaro (Mozart), 26 June 2005. Conductor, Jane Glover; director, John Cox; designer, Robert Perdziola. D'Arcy Bleiker (Figaro), Lucy Crowe (Susanna), Julian Tovey (Count), Sarah-Jane Davies (Countess), Doreen Curran (Cherubino), Jennifer Rhys-Davies (Marcellina), Aled Hall (Don Basilio), Lynton Black (Doctor Bartolo)

ENGLISH TOURING OPERA
Founded 1980 as OPERA 80
La Bohème (Puccini) and *The Cunning Little Vixen* (Janacek) were toured to Hackney, Kendal, Runcorn, Canterbury, Cheltenham, Cambridge, High Wycombe, Snape Maltings, Exeter and Lincoln between 14 October and 1 December 2004.

Mary, Queen of Scots (Donizetti) and *Così fan tutte* (Mozart) were toured to Hackney, Cambridge, Crawley, Snape Maltings, Exeter, Truro, Poole, Sheffield, Reading, Malvern, Blackpool, Wolverhampton and York between 11 March and 10 May 2005

PARLIAMENT

The Parliamentary year was somewhat unusual with the prospect of a general election being called in May 2005 affecting much of the legislative business in the session. The issue of Iraq had not gone away but in Parliamentary terms was less prominent. Similarly the issue of Europe, and particularly the new EU constitution, was ever present but seemed more subdued, proving to be almost a non-issue in the election. The position of Prime Minister Tony Blair as leader of his party looked secure – even though at one stage his pre-election Commons majority of 167 was reduced to just 14 (on the Prevention of Terrorism Bill) – helped perhaps by his announcement (September 2004) that he intended to stand down after serving one more term as prime minister. As for his political opponents, Conservative Leader Michael Howard announced after the party's third election defeat that he would step down once a satisfactory method of choosing his successor had been agreed – leading to a plethora of potential candidates throwing their hats into the ring; and Liberal Democrat leader Charles Kennedy with his party winning 62 seats in the election, seemed to have done enough to see off his critics (although many had thought the party would do even better, especially against Conservatives in target seats). The issues of asylum and immigration and combating international terrorism were at the forefront of the legislative programme and the terrorist attacks in London obviously dominated the last few weeks before the summer recess. Significantly, after the election, for the first time in history, Labour became the largest single party in the House of Lords.

PRE-CONFERENCE SESSION
As usual, MPs returned for the short pre-conference session of Parliament in September 2004. On 7 September, responding to an Urgent Notice Question from Father of the House Tam Dalyell (Lab), Defence Minister Adam Ingram updated MPs on the military situation of the multinational force in Iraq, developing a security partnership with the Iraqi interim government and the Iraqi security forces. Foreign Secretary Jack Straw then updated MPs on developments in Beslan – 'what happened was simply evil beyond reason and excuse' – and in the Sudan where 'we must do everything we can to ensure that that vast country can at long last enjoy peace and stability.' On 8 September the Conservatives instigated debates on pensions policy and then on Hospital-Acquired Infection, issues they were to make central to their election policy in the following year. On 9 September MPs debated the draft European Constitutional Treaty, which had been agreed at the EU Council summit meeting in June. Jack Straw felt 'the European constitution is a necessary counterpart to the enlargement of the European Union.' He refused to be drawn on the possible reaction of the government if the promised referendum on the constitution returned a 'no' vote. Conservative Foreign Affairs spokesperson Michael Ancram called it 'not only an integrating constitution but an unnecessary one.'

On 13 September Minister for Local Government Nick Raynsford announced that following a critical report from the Electoral Commission, the proposed all-postal referendums on Regional Assemblies in the North-West and Yorkshire and the Humber would be postponed, although the ballot in the North-East would go ahead as planned on 4 November. The Children's Bill (Lords), having completed its passage through the Lords, received an unopposed Second Reading in the Commons, although 72 Opposition MPs voted against the programme motion in protest against the lack of time set aside for detailed debate in Committee. Home Secretary David Blunkett came to the House at 10.15 p.m. to make a statement about a security breach at Buckingham Palace. On 14 September International Development Secretary Hilary Benn made a statement on Hurricane Ivan, the devastation it had caused in the Caribbean and the help that the government had offered. On 15 September MPs debated all stages of the Hunting Bill, a bill to outlaw hunting with dogs identical to that which had received its Third Reading in the Commons on 3 July 2003, which had only been re-introduced under the Parliament Act the previous week. Feelings were running high in the Chamber at the use of this process but after an animated debate the Procedure Motion approving the one day consideration was passed by 309 votes to 157, a government majority of 152. During the Second Reading debate itself proceedings were suspended by the Speaker for twenty minutes when eight protestors gained entry to the House and three of them entered the Chamber and disrupted proceedings. In the event the Second Reading was passed by 356 votes to 166, a government majority of 190, and the Third Reading by 339 votes to 155, a government majority of 184. In a statement to the House Speaker Michael Martin outlined his plans to ensure that such an incident could not be repeated. The Bill had an unopposed Second Reading in the Lords on 12 October after nearly nine hours of debate. Environment Minister Lord Whitty urged peers to take 'proper note' of the views of the House of Commons: 'the ball is in the court, in this House, of those who have supported hunting in its present form to offer a way forward, or alternatively to accept the Bill as it now stands, if we are not to provoke the use of the Parliament Act'. Had peers voted against, the government could have used the Parliament Act to force the Bill onto the statute book. Labour Peer Baroness Mallalieu said banning hunting would not resolve the issue but would instead create a 'running sore.' 'The Prime Minister says that he still wants a compromise and so I believe do we in this Parliament, because a nation which is divided is in no-one's interests.' She urged the Lords to 'work constructively to return a bill to the Commons based on a framework which Rural Affairs Minister Alun Michael felt was right, a regulatory bill'. They took the opportunity to progress to the Committee Stage, where they could seek to amend it. At the first day of Committee consideration on 26 October Peers voted for an amendment moved by Labour Peer Lord Donoughue for licensed hunts instead of a full ban by 322 votes to 72. At Report Stage on 11 November they passed another amendment moved by Lord Donoughue that there should be no new limits on hunting before November 2007 by 175 votes to 49. Third Reading in the Lords was passed on 15 November. On 16 November the Commons overturned all the Lords amendments to the Bill with majorities in excess of 170 and sent the amended Bill back to the Lords. The Lords insisted on most of their amendments on 17 November with majorities in excess of 100. On 18 November the Commons again overturned the Lords amendments and sent the Bill back to the Upper House. When they still insisted on their amendment on the commencement date by a majority of 39, the Speaker invoked the Parliament Act at 9.01 p.m. to force the Bill through.

On 16 September two government bills (Public Audit (Wales) and Employment Relations) gained Royal Assent.

SPILL-OVER SESSION

Returning after the party conferences on 11 October, MPs took the Second Reading of the Mental Capacity Bill (designed to empower, protect and support people who lack mental capacity and give legal force to 'living wills', where people want medical treatment withheld if they become severely incapacitated) which had been considered in draft form the previous autumn. Junior Constitutional Affairs Minister David Lammy thought it would help 'those who care for people who lack mental capacity to understand more fully and more clearly their legal rights and responsibilities.' The Second Reading was passed by 326 votes to 62, a government majority of 264. Those voting against were led by former Conservative Party Leader Iain Duncan-Smith, who felt that the Bill did not deal fully with the issue of euthanasia and the concept of futile treatment, including assisted food and fluids and their withdrawal. The Bill was carried over into the following session and several amendments were introduced at Third Reading on 14 December in an attempt to meet some of these concerns. An amendment moved by Iain Duncan-Smith to ensure the bill did not allow decisions aimed at causing death was defeated by 297 to 203, with some 34 Labour MPs voting against the government and up to 100 more abstaining. The government avoided defeat when David Lammy referred to a letter from the Lord Chancellor Lord Falconer to the Catholic Archbishop of Cardiff, the Most Reverend Peter Smith, pledging that the Bill was not meant to authorise any decision where the motive is to kill as opposed to the relief or prevention of suffering, or ending treatment where the patient is in an irreversible coma. Discussion was reduced to a farce when David Lammy initially refused to show backbenchers the letter and eventually he was forced to read out the full text, five minutes before the vote was due to take place. Third Reading was passed by 354 votes to 118, a government majority of 236. The next day (15 December) at Prime Minister's Questions (PMQs) Tony Blair defended the handling of the Bill: 'at the House of Lords stage we will table amendments that will make it absolutely clear that while the Bland judgment will remain in being, we will not in any shape or form countenance the deliberate killing of people.' The Bill was considered in the Lords with Second Reading on 10 January and Third Reading on 24 March. The Bill received Royal Assent on 7 April.

On 12 October Jack Straw made a statement covering the execution of Kenneth Bigley in Iraq the previous week and the report of the Iraq Survey Group on Iraq's weapons of mass destruction (WMD), which had concluded that by the mid-1990s Iraq was essentially free of WMD. He concluded that 'I do not accept, even with hindsight, that we were wrong to act as we did in the circumstances that we faced at the time . . . although we can now plainly see that some of the intelligence was

wrong, I continue to believe that the judgements we made and the actions we took were right.' Speaking for the Conservatives, Junior Foreign Affairs spokesperson Gary Streeter said he and the British people had hoped the government would make 'a full explanation and a full apology – not an apology for the intelligence but an apology for the way in which the government conveyed the intelligence to the country.' Liberal Democrat Foreign Affairs spokesperson Sir Menzies Campbell felt the report proved the true objective of the war – regime change, 'illegal under international law.' Labour MP Robin Cook, who had resigned from the government over the war, said the report 'comprehensively demonstrates that there was no immediate threat from Iraq.'

The Civil Partnership Bill (Lords) to give gay couples the same rights as married ones, which had been amended in the Lords before the summer recess against the government's wishes, was given a Second Reading by 426 votes to 49, a government majority of 377. Deputy Minister for Equality and Women Jacqui Smith pledged to overturn Lords amendments extending the rights to family members and carers – this was duly amended in Committee. Junior Scottish Minister Anne McGuire announced that same-sex couples would in future benefit from the deceased partner's public services pensions. At Remaining Stages in the Commons on 11 November Conservative MP Edward Leigh proposed an amendment calling for brothers and sisters living together for at least 12 years to get the same rights over property and pensions that are being proposed for gay couples in the Bill. This was rejected by 381 votes to 74. Third Reading was passed by 389 votes to 47. The Bill received Royal Assent on 18 November.

On 18 October Defence Secretary Geoff Hoon made a statement about the deployment of UK forces in Iraq, confirming that the USA had requested a limited number of UK ground forces to be made available to relieve US forces to allow them in turn to participate in further operations elsewhere in Iraq. A response would be given later in the week. He stressed that this was a military request and not some sort of political request, linked to the presidential elections in the USA. Returning to the House on 21 October Geoff Hoon confirmed that the government had accepted the US request for assistance and that a force of some 850 soldiers, mainly Black Watch, would be deployed for 'a very limited and specified period of time, lasting weeks rather than months.' Conservative Defence spokesperson Nicholas Soames supported the deployment but was concerned at 'the exceptionally shabby way' in which the Black Watch had been treated over this. Liberal Democrat Defence spokesperson Paul Keetch was not able to support the redeployment: 'British troops should remain in the British sector, under British command.' Labour MP John Denham, who had also resigned from the government over the war, accepted that 'the decision was not made for political reasons but . . . it will carry a political cost.' Also on 18 October Education and Skills Secretary Charles Clarke made a statement on the reform of education and training for 14- to 19-year-olds following the publication of the final report from Mike Tomlinson, recommending the introduction of a diploma that would replace, over time, all existing academic and vocational qualifications. He promised a White Paper in the New Year with detailed proposals in response from the government. Conservative Education spokesperson Tim Collins looked for an 'unequivocal and final ruling out of the abolition of GCSEs and A-Levels', whilst Liberal Democrat Education spokesperson Phil Wills welcomed the concept of the new diploma.

On 26 October David Blunkett answered an Urgent Notice Question from Shadow Home Secretary David Davies on EU Immigration and Asylum Policy following confusion arising from reports of the EU Justice and Home Affairs Council meeting the day before. He confirmed that the agreement was that on external borders the UK 'would support collaboration but not control organised from Brussels' and on processing arrangements 'individual nations would retain control over decisions.' David Davies felt that 'as usual the government have returned claiming a victory. In truth they are trying to cover up a surrender with serious consequences for Britain's future ability to control its own borders.' The Commons then approved six motions drawn up by the Procedure Committee concerning the workings of the House, including making permanent the arrangements for the programming of bills and deferred divisions and the removal of references to strangers. These three reforms were all disputed by the Opposition. On 28 October David Blunkett answered an Urgent Notice Question from Conservative MP Douglas Hogg on reform of the laws of murder – he had intended to make an announcement on the establishment of a review in the Third Reading debate on the Domestic Violence, Crime and Victims Bill the previous night but, due to the programme motion the debate had not taken place and he apologised for the fact that a premature press release had been issued by his department. Despite his apology Douglas Hogg felt this was 'contrary to Mr Speaker's repeated instructions to Ministers.'

The School Transport Bill to enable Local Education Authorities to pilot school transport schemes received a Second Reading by 248 votes to 130, a government majority of 118. Opposition parties expressed concern that there were no safeguards to prevent Local Authorities charging a fee for something they had provided free for six decades. The Bill was carried over to the next session and later dropped due to the election.

The Gambling Bill, which would tighten the regulation of gambling but would also allow for super-casinos to be opened in the UK, had its Second Reading in the Commons on 1 November. Second Reading was passed by 286 votes to 212, a government majority of 84, with some 29 Labour MPs voting against. Culture Secretary Tessa Jowell said the plans to overhaul the laws would protect the 'weak and the vulnerable' and she had offered two concessions – local councils could be obliged to consult people on whether they wanted a super-casino in their area and action would be taken to prevent casinos getting planning permission 'through the back door' by closing a loophole in planning rules. She also promised more research on addiction before the Bill became law, but said there would be no cap on the number of new casinos. Conservative Culture spokesperson John Whittingdale argued 'What the government is proposing to do is introduce a kind of casino never before seen in this country. Their proposals open the door to a very large number coming into the hearts of our towns and cities.' Liberal Democrat Culture spokesperson Don Foster said his party would vote against the plans 'because it did not control the introduction of super-casinos.' The Bill was carried over to the next session. On 3 November MPs approved changes to Members' Allowances and Parliamentary Pensions.

On 8 November Prime Minister Tony Blair reported on the outcome of the European Council meeting in Brussels the previous weekend. The meeting 'underlined the importance to Britain of maintaining both a strong relationship with the USA and a strong place in the Councils of the European Union – both partnerships are vital to the British national interest and it will remain the policy of this government at least to nurture both.' Conservative leader Michael Howard felt the meeting had been 'a huge lost opportunity' and called for the Prime Minister to put a date on the referendum on the proposed European Constitution 'so the people can have their say.' Liberal Democrat leader Charles Kennedy asked for an assurance that 'irrespective of what might happen in referendums that may precede one here, the government will proceed with a referendum, come what may, in this country.' Deputy Prime Minister John Prescott then made a statement on the outcome of the Regional Assembly referendum in the North-East, which had seen the proposals rejected by 78 per cent of the electorate. The planned referendums in the North-West and Yorkshire and the Humber would not now go ahead. Conservative Local Government spokesperson Caroline Spelman thought the 'whole exercise has been humiliating for the government and expensive for the taxpayer.'

On 9 November David Blunkett made a statement on the publication of a White Paper on the second phase of the government's police reform agenda: 'our proposals embody reform for a purpose: to reduce crime and anti-social behaviour; to build safer and more secure communities; to reinforce respect for the law; to protect law-abiding citizens; and to provide a customer-focused service using modern technology to underpin neighbourhood policing.' David Davies felt 'there is precious little. . .to reassure our concerned and committed police force or to inspire the confidence of the worried citizens of this country.' Liberal Democrat Home Affairs spokesperson Mark Oaten wondered how it would all be funded. On 10 November Transport Secretary Alistair Darling made a statement on the train derailment at Ufton in Berkshire, when seven people were killed. A Rail Safety and Standards Board inquiry had been started into the incident.

On 15 November Northern Ireland Secretary Paul Murphy made a statement on developments in Northern Ireland and his decision to 'despecify' the Ulster Defence Association, following their re-affirmation that they would desist from all military activity. On 16 November Health Secretary John Reid published a White Paper on Public Health, which 'promotes the opportunity for healthy living in a manner and scale unseen before. . .it begins the transformation of our health care away from just a national treatment system for illness towards a true national health service.' Conservative Health spokesperson Andrew Lansley felt 'all the government can offer is gimmicks and a nanny state.' Liberal Democrat Health spokesperson Paul Burstow thought the government 'lack the courage to take the necessary action to deal with the wide range of public health threats posed in this country.' Parliament was prorogued and the 2003–4 session was brought to an end on 18 November at 9.59 p.m., after long periods of suspended sittings whilst the row over the Hunting Bill was played out. That Bill and five other government bills gained Royal Assent (including the Housing Bill and the Pensions Bill).

NEW SESSION (2004–5)

The 2004–5 session of Parliament was opened by the Queen's Speech on 23 November, later than usual, and contained proposals for thirty-two bills for the session (including three carried over from the last session and eight bills that would be introduced in draft), despite the fact that this was expected to be the last session of this Parliament, with an election widely likely to be called in the spring. The bills would 'focus on making Britain more secure – within national borders, within local neighbourhoods and within homes – in a changing world . . . and would reinforce the government's belief in the bargain between citizens and society: with the rights enjoyed as citizens balanced by responsibilities to one another.' In the ensuing debate Tony Blair felt the programme was 'strong on economic opportunity, strong on the nation's security and fair in helping all people whatever their background to fulfil their potential to the full.' Whilst welcoming some of the individual proposals in the speech, Michael Howard's reaction was 'haven't we heard it all before? . . . All we get from the government is more rhetoric, more promises and more talk . . . but this government will never turn talk into action.' Charles Kennedy, who tabled an amendment to the debate on the speech regretting the lack of legislation to clarify the prerogative powers of the Prime Minister and the role of Parliament on matters of war and peace, was also able to support some measures, although he was also 'relieved to say that the government show no temptation to steal our language or the philosophy that lies behind it . . . I am talking about an instinctively Liberal approach to the problems of the day . . . backed up by principles, as opposed to the instinctive reaction towards an illiberal partial solution to a much more complicated set of problems.' On 1 December after six days of debate the Liberal Democrat amendment was defeated by 443 votes to 68, a government majority of 375; the Speech itself was approved by 295 votes to 200, a government majority of 95.

On 29 November Jack Straw made a statement on the outcome of the presidential election in Ukraine and also on developments in the Middle East – in Iran with the issue of their nuclear programme, in Iraq with the conference at Sharm al-Sheikh and in Israel with the forthcoming Palestinian elections. On 30 November Armed Forces Minister Adam Ingram made a statement about the disclosure of Surrey Police papers listing allegations of inappropriate behaviour at Deepcut Army Barracks, and said he would be setting up a further review to be headed by a fully independent figure.

On 2 December, later than in previous years, Chancellor of the Exchequer Gordon Brown presented his Pre-Budget Report in which he forecast UK economic growth of 3.25 per cent in 2004 and between 3 and 3.5 per cent in 2005. This would meet his 'golden rule'. His new borrowing forecast for 2003–4 was £35 billion, £2.5 billion less than the £37.5 billion predicted in March's Budget with the figure falling to £31 billion by 2005–6, up by £2 billion from March's Budget. Inflation would be 1.75 per cent in 2005 and 2 per cent in the years to follow. He also announced the scrapping of the fuel duty increase, pledged an extra £105 million for the fight against terrorism, an extra £1 billion to help local authorities to hold down council tax bills, and money for more nursery places and for paid maternity leave to be extended from six to nine months. He hailed the longest period of growth in UK industrial history but denied he was 'gloating'. He concluded 'stability is the foundation: more investment not less; now and into the next Parliament; opportunity not just for some but for all and a progressive Britain we can be proud of.' Shadow Chancellor Oliver Letwin called him 'Sir Wastealot', and

felt 'the tide is going out on the Chancellor's credibility. He is spending, borrowing and taxing so much because he is not getting value for taxpayer's money.' Liberal Democrat Economic Affairs spokesperson Vincent Cable suggested 'the Chancellor has offered the economics of complacency . . . there are serious challenges ahead from the falling dollar and from the rapid downturn in the UK housing market and rising personal debt. But they have not been confronted.' Following the statement Local Government Minister Nick Raynsford gave details of the Local Government Finance Settlement for 2005–6 with total support of £60.1 billion, an increase of 6.2 per cent. He also indicated that the government was prepared to take tougher capping action against Local Authorities that introduced excessive council tax increases. Conservative Local Government spokesperson Eric Pickles called it 'a dawn raid masquerading as a strategy.' Liberal Democrat Local Government spokesperson Edward Davey asked whether 'he would list the cuts being made elsewhere to fund this attempt to massage council tax downwards before the election.'

On 6 December Work and Pensions Secretary Alan Johnson gave the details of the annual benefits uprating and welfare reform measures from the Pre-Budget Report, with most national insurance benefits rising by the Retail Price Index – 3.1 per cent and most income-related benefits rising by the Rossi index – 1 per cent, giving pension rates from April 2005 of £82.05 for single pensioner and £131.20 for couples. The Railways Bill, which would wind up the Strategic Rail Authority, give enhanced powers to the devolved administrations in Wales, Scotland and London and hand responsibility for safety to the Office of the Rail Regulator was given a Second Reading by 321 votes to 124, a government majority of 197. After Committee consideration the Bill had its Remaining Stages in the Commons on 27 January and received Royal Assent on 6 April.

On 7 December the Serious Organised Crime and Police Bill, which would create a new agency to tackle drug trafficking, people smuggling and criminal gangs but also included the creation of a new offence of incitement to religious hatred to protect faith groups from attack, was given an unopposed Second Reading; the Opposition voted against the programme motion. After Committee consideration the Bill had its Remaining Stages in the Commons on 7 February before going to the Lords. In the trade-off before the election, the government agreed to drop the section on religious hatred in order to save the rest of the Bill. It received Royal Assent on 7 April.

On 8 December the Commissioners for Revenue and Customs Bill, implementing the recommendations of the O'Donnell review and merging the Inland Revenue and HM Customs & Excise, had an unopposed Second Reading. It also received Royal Assent on 7 April. On 9 December Northern Ireland Secretary Paul Murphy made a statement on the publication by the Prime Minister and the Irish Taoiseach of proposals for a comprehensive agreement in relation to the political process in Northern Ireland; he outlined a series of statements which would have been published in sequence by the governments and the other relevant organisations if there had been an overall agreement, stating 'the issue now . . . is about confidence and trust between the parties.' Ulster Unionist leader David Trimble broadly welcomed the proposals but stated that he felt the requests that were being made for photographs to confirm IRA decommissioning were 'reasonable.'

On 16 December Defence Secretary Geoff Hoon made a statement on the future structure of the Army designed to 'develop a more deployable, agile and flexible force.' The infantry would be organised into large regiments with the consequential merging of many traditional local and regional regiments but 'the move to larger, multi-battalion regiments is the only way in which to structure the infantry for the long-term . . . and deliver an army fit for the challenge of the 21st century.' Conservative Foreign Affairs spokesperson Michael Ancram called it 'a dark day for our armed forces. It is an even darker day for the proud regiments that the government seek to scrap . . . and a day of shame for this discredited and ineffective Defence Secretary.' Liberal Democrat Defence spokesperson Paul Keetch agreed that there was 'a price to be paid for more high-tech equipment. Today, four battalions of the Army have paid that price and we believe it is not a price worth paying.'

On 20 December the new Home Secretary Charles Clarke (who had replaced David Blunkett after his resignation from the government on 16 December) responded to an Urgent Notice Question from Liberal Democrat Home Affairs spokesperson David Heath on the legislative consequences of the House of Lords judgment that the detention without trial of aliens held in HMP Belmarsh under the anti-terrorism laws was unlawful. The government would look carefully at the judgment and report back to the House but he reiterated that 'it is Parliament that must decide how best we deal with this country's security issues.' Tony Blair then made a statement on the outcome of the European Council meeting in Brussels the previous weekend, which had discussed accession negotiations, including those for Turkey, to begin in October 2005: 'if evidence is needed of the benefits of positive engagement and leadership in Europe, here it is.' Michael Howard hoped that by the time of the forthcoming UK presidency of the EU 'Britain has a government with the courage and conviction to put the case for the kind of Europe that the British people want to see.' The House then paid tribute to the retiring Serjeant-at-Arms Sir Michael Cummins.

One of the most contentious of the government's proposed bills, the Identity Cards Bill, received its Second Reading. Home Secretary Charles Clarke said 'the principle is right . . . the legislation is a critically important development in the security of this country.' Conservative Home Affairs spokesperson David Davis said his Party had reservations but would vote for the Bill 'to allow full scrutiny to take place'. Liberal Democrat spokesperson Mark Oaten feared 'this will be one of the most unpopular measures that we have seen in this Parliament.' Second Reading was passed by 385 votes to 93, a government majority of 292. Nineteen Labour MPs and 10 Conservative MPs voted with the Liberal Democrats to oppose the measure. After Committee scrutiny the Bill returned for Remaining Stages on 10 February, the day after Prime Minister Tony Blair said during PMQs that introduction of identity cards to protect the UK against crime and terrorism 'is long overdue . . . I don't think it is wrong or a breach of anyone's civil liberties.' Official Conservative policy was to abstain and Third Reading was passed by 224 votes to 64, a government majority of 160. Nineteen Labour MPs and 11 Tories rebelled against their Whips. The Bill then went to the Lords for Second Reading on 21 March. The measure was dropped due to the election.

In the House of Lords, the Constitutional Reform Bill, carried over from the previous session, received its Third Reading, endorsing their decision to maintain the post of Lord Chancellor, which they had inserted in July against the government's wishes and other amendments they had added. Second Reading in the Commons on 17 January was passed by 329 votes to 126, a government majority of 202. During Committee consideration the government overturned the defeats in the Lords and Third Reading on 1 March was passed by 280 votes to 118, a government majority of 162. On consideration of Commons Amendments in the Lords on 15 March Peers inflicted two defeats on the government – they voted by 215 to 199 to insist that Lord Chancellor must be a member of the Upper House and later insisted by a majority of 14 that the job should go to a lawyer. On 16 March the Commons overturned these by 256 votes to 109, a government majority of 147. On 21 March Peers insisted on their two amendments by majorities of 12 in both votes. In the event in order to get the Bill on the Statute Book the government conceded the points and the Bill received Royal Assent on 24 March. Before both Houses rose for the Christmas recess on 21 December the Attorney-General Lord Goldsmith made a statement in the Lords on the review of infant death syndrome cases, with some 29 cases having been identified as causing concern and referred to the Criminal Cases Review Commission.

Returning after the Christmas recess on 10 January Tony Blair made a statement on the Asian Tsunami on Boxing Day and the government's response. The number of confirmed British deaths was 51, with a further 402 missing presumed dead and some 871 unaccounted for. The government had pledged £75 million to the immediate humanitarian response. Mr Blair also raised the issue of the problems of Africa: 'if we were, as a result of the strength of our sentiment towards the victims of the tsunami, to turn that same sentiment into action on Africa, perhaps those whose faith has been shaken by the monstrous consequences of the event that we have witnessed would have it renewed. There could be no greater good to come out of it.' The Second Reading of the Clean Neighbourhoods and Environment Bill to enhance the powers of local authorities, allowing them to move abandoned cars immediately and close off alleyways where trouble-makers congregate, was approved by 356 votes to 151, a government majority of 204. After Committee consideration the Bill had its Remaining Stages in the Commons on 21 February and was sent to the Lords. It received Royal Assent on 7 April.

On 11 January the Commons faced no fewer than four oral statements: firstly Environment Minister Alun Michael responded to an Urgent Notice Question from Labour MP Sir Gerald Kaufman on the government's policy towards applications in the courts for injunctions to delay or to prevent the commencement of the Hunting Act 2004. 'We are confident that the Hunting Act is valid and rightly fulfils the will of the elected Chamber of Parliament. We are confident that the result of the court hearing will uphold that view and do so soon, providing certainty for everyone on all sides of the debate.' Foreign Secretary Jack Straw then made a statement on the return to the UK of the last four British citizens detained at Guantanamo Bay 'in the next few weeks . . . throughout the period of detention of British nationals in Guantanamo Bay, the government have sought to balance the need to safeguard the interests of Britons detained overseas with our duty to meet the threat from international terrorism.' Northern Ireland Secretary Paul Murphy then brought MPs up to date on developments in Northern Ireland and the suspected involvement of the Provisional IRA in the major robbery at the Northern Bank in Belfast just before Christmas and possible government sanctions as a result. Finally Environment Minister Elliot Morley made a statement on the serious flooding in Northern England and the assistance offered by the government. MPs then gave an unoppposed Second Reading to the Road Safety Bill, dropped due to the election. On 12 January Elliot Morley answered an Urgent Notice Question from SNP MP Pete Wishart on the severe weather conditions in Scotland and Northern Ireland and the government's response. The twenty MPs successful in the ballot for Private Members' Bills presented their bills but, due to the election, none progressed to the Statute Book. The Child Benefit Bill received an unopposed Second Reading, with Third Reading on 3 February, and after consideration in the Lords gained Royal Assent on 24 March. On 13 January the Consumer Credit Bill received an unopposed Second Reading with Third Reading on 3 March. Although welcomed by all parties, the Bill was dropped due to the election.

On 24 January Deputy Prime Minister John Prescott made a statement on the publication of the government's five year strategy 'Sustainable Communities: Homes for All', pledging the government would 'provide more homes to buy or rent through responsible growth; continue to improve the social housing stock; promote greater home ownership; and give more people a share in their home.' Conservative Housing spokesperson Caroline Spelman felt the announcement was 'a fudge and a hastily assembled compromise that will do little to help the increasing number of people who are priced out of the housing market. If ever there was a case of too little, too late, this is it.' Liberal Democrat spokesperson Edward Davey also thought 'the strategy falls far short of the new approach that Britain's families need.' The Third Reading of the Gambling Bill, carried over from the previous session, was passed by 236 votes to 38, with 22 Labour MPs voting against the government. A Conservative motion to limit the number of super-casinos to four had earlier been defeated by 271 votes to 131. In the Lords on 10 March Peers defeated the government by agreeing a series of amendments moved by Conservative Peer Baroness Buscombe by 123 votes to 105. With the election looming Culture Secretary Tessa Jowell struck a deal with the Conservatives to save the Bill, by agreeing to scale down plans for eight super-casinos to just one and so the Bill received Royal Assent on 7 April. On 26 January Home Secretary Charles Clarke made a statement on the future of the immigration powers in Part 4 of the Anti-Terrorism, Crime and Security Act 2001 and given the rulings of the Law Lords, the decision to replace them with a new system of control orders – 'I am, of course, well aware that the proposals I am making today represent a very substantial increase in the executive powers of the state in relation to British citizens who we fear are preparing for terrorist activities . . . but I believe that the need for us to protect ourselves against the threat justifies the changes I propose.' David Davies and Mark Oaten pledged the qualified support of their parties.

On 31 January Foreign Secretary Jack Straw made a statement on Iraq covering the crash of an RAF C-130 Hercules aircraft in which ten UK service personnel were killed and on the outcome of the elections: 'yesterday, the Iraqi people in their millions showed their wish to embrace freedom and to shape the future destiny of their country. I know that the whole House and our country stand behind them as they pursue that historic endeavour.' Shadow Foreign Secretary Michael Ancram agreed that 'yesterday's vote was good for Iraq, the Middle East and

freedom.' On 2 February Work and Pensions Secretary Alan Johnson made a statement on the publication of the government's five-year strategy 'Opportunity and Security Throughout Life' and the reform of the benefits system: 'its goal is genuine inclusion – stamping out the discrimination and disadvantage that prevents people from fulfilling their true potential.' Whilst agreeing the need for reform, Conservative Work and Pensions spokesperson David Willetts wondered 'whether, after eight years in office, the government have really learnt the lessons of their failure to reform welfare in the past.'

On 3 February Jack Straw made a statement on the publication of a White Paper on the prospects in the European Union for the coming six months, covering three main areas: 'enhancing prosperity across Europe and in this country; working together to tackle common threats to our security; and preparations for the United Kingdom's presidency of the EU in the second half of this year . . . we are confident about Britain's future in Europe and determined to continue shaping that future in the interests of businesses and individuals across the United Kingdom.' Michael Ancram questioned the need for the statement 'particularly as the Foreign Secretary had nothing new to say. Is not the reason that the government are involved in a taxpayer-subsidised propaganda exercise to try to sell the new EU to the country in advance of the forthcoming referendum and general election?'

On 7 February Home Secretary Charles Clarke made a statement on the publication of government's five year asylum strategy – 'this is a major programme to build on the foundations that we have laid by creating a system which will be, and which will be seen to be, transparent and fair to all. It is a practical and systematic response to the real problems of asylum and immigration. It will provide a simple and robust system for economic migration. It will tighten our rules for permanent settlement to ensure that those who stay bring benefit to the UK. It represents real determination to eliminate illegal entry, illegal working, asylum abuse and people-trafficking gangs, who, through their heinous crimes, gain most from the failures of our system.' David Davies called it 'the latest headline-grabbing initiative from a panic stricken government in the run-up to a general election. We have heard it all before; why should we believe any of it now?' Mark Oaten feared that 'there is now a bidding war taking place on immigration and asylum between the government and the official Opposition.' On 8 February Conservative MP Jonathan Sayeed was suspended from the House for a period of two weeks following a report from the Standards and Privileges Committee into allegations that he had abused Parliamentary privilege in respect of his association with English Manner Limited. He also had the Party Whip removed for a month until 8 March. On 23 March he made a personal statement to the House apologising both for his conduct and his response to the Committee report and did not in the event contest the general election.

On 9 February Health Secretary John Reid made a statement on financial allocations to Primary Care Trusts in the National Health Service amounting to £64 billion in 2006–7, an increase of 9.2 per cent. He stated: 'the biggest ever investment in our national health service, the fairest ever distribution of resources and a massive programme of continued reform by staff will together give the increased capacity and diversity of provision that will offer patients faster access to better quality health services than ever before, all free at the point of need under a Labour government.' Conservative Health spokesperson Andrew Lansley thought the government was 'promising money tomorrow while the NHS has deficits today. We could clear the deficit if the billions eaten up in bureaucracy . . . The Department of Health is imposing costs on the NHS with no idea of the effects.' Liberal Democrat Health spokesperson Paul Burstow welcomed the statement but feared 'the devil is in the detail.' The European Union Bill to enable the United Kingdom to ratify the EU Constitutional Treaty, and to decide that ratification can take place only if there is a positive vote in a United Kingdom referendum, received its Second Reading by 345 votes to 130, a government majority of 215. The Bill made no further progress and was dropped in the run up to the election.

PREVENTION OF TERRORISM BILL

After the half-term recess on 22 February Home Secretary Charles Clarke made a statement on the introduction of the Prevention of Terrorism Bill, promised in his statement on 26 January and 'designed to meet the Law Lords' criticism that the previous legislation was both disproportionate and discriminatory . . . we must have the capacity to protect our people now and in the future. It would be the gravest dereliction of duty to wait until we have suffered a terrorist outrage here, and then respond only after the event. I am not prepared to take a risk of that kind, and I hope the House will join me in that.' David Davies was unable to support the measure fully: 'I do not underestimate the difficulty of the problem facing the Home Secretary. I accept that there are no easy answers, and as far as I am aware, nobody is saying that we should do nothing. However, I have to tell him that I believe that he has settled on the wrong answers, which will sacrifice essential and long-standing British principles of liberty and justice in a way that is unlikely materially to enhance the security of our people – indeed, which may act to reduce that security.' Mark Oaten also felt: 'These judgments are all about the balance between the principles of justice and maintaining security. The proposals that the government have outlined today get that balance wrong and that is why we cannot support them.' At Second Reading on 23 February an Opposition reasoned amendment declining a Second Reading was defeated by 316 votes to 216, a government majority of 100; Second Reading itself was passed by 309 votes to 23, a government majority of 76. Some 32 Labour MPs voted against the government. In the Remaining Stages debate on 28 February Charles Clarke offered to amend the Bill in the Lords so that he would have to apply to a judge for a house arrest control order. This led to accusations that instead of MPs being able to debate the amendments tabled, the House had been 'hijacked' by this change of heart but it did ensure the defeat of a cross-party amendment to have all decisions on measures to control suspects made by judges by 267 votes to 253, a government majority of 14. Some 62 Labour MPs voted against the government but not all Conservative and Liberal Democrat MPs (including leader Charles Kennedy) turned up to vote – if they had all voted against, the amendment would have got through. Third Reading was passed by 272 votes to 219, a government majority of 53, and the Bill passed to the Lords, where it had its Second Reading (traditionally unopposed) on 1 March. On 2 March at PMQs Tony Blair rejected a Conservative compromise offer to insert a sunset clause into the Bill, which would have forced ministers to revisit it in November, in return for their support. At the first day of Lords Committee consideration on 3 March

Conservative spokesperson Lord Kingsland said while he did not 'like what the government was doing', his party had given 'an undertaking' to get the bill through. Backbench Conservative Peer the Earl of Onslow hoped the government would not get the 'rotten, rotten stinking bill' through but in the end Peers approved government amendments on transferring house arrest powers from politicians to judges. On the second day of Committee on 7 March Peers approved an amendment moved by Liberal Democrat Peer Lord Goodhart to give greater powers to the courts by 249 votes to 119, a majority against the government of 130. At Report Stage on 8 March the government suffered a series of defeats: an amendment moved by Lord Kingsland to list all restraints on the face of the Bill was passed by 256 votes to 129 (majority against the government of 127); an amendment moved by Lady Saltoun of Abernathy (Cross Bencher) on treatment of those under house arrest was passed by 241 votes to 139 (majority of 202); the inclusion of a sunset clause moved by Lord Kingsland was passed by 297 votes to 110 (majority 187); another Lord Kingsland amendment to give the Lord Chief Justice more powers over control orders was passed by 232 votes to 130 (majority 102); and another Lord Kingsland amendment to ensure the whole process complied with the European Convention on Human Rights was passed by 173 votes to 110 (majority 63). On 9 March in the Commons the government overturned these defeats comfortably with majorities in excess of 100, although some 37 Labour MPs voted against the government on the amendment calling for a higher burden of proof for control orders. The Lords then considered the Commons reasons on 10 March – a Parliamentary day that was to go on until 7.52 p.m. on the following day (although in Parliamentary terms this was still 10 March!), with the Bill passing between the two Houses, both of which sat all night. The Lords stood firm over three main issues: the sunset clause; demands for a group of senior politicians (from the Privy Council) to review the law; and for a higher standard of proof to be used before the proposed control orders are issued.

The Bill returned to the Commons in the early hours of the following morning and Home Office Minister Hazel Blears offered some minor concessions but refused to back down on the three key amendments put forward by the Lords, voting to overturn the Peers' amendments again. The Bill returned to the Lords in the afternoon and as the debate began Lord Chancellor Lord Falconer announced that the Conservatives had agreed not to pursue the need for a Privy Council review of the Bill, but Peers again voted to defy the Commons, supporting the other amendments: on the burden of proof for the control orders and on the sunset clause. Back in the Commons Prime Minister Tony Blair announced he would give MPs the chance to review the law in a year's time, whilst denying an accusation from Michael Howard that this represents a 'sunset clause in all but name'. This move succeeded in ending the deadlock between the two Houses. After more than 30 hours of debate, the Bill returned to the Lords where it was finally passed. It received the Royal Assent shortly after 7.30 p.m.

Also on 22 February Northern Ireland Secretary Paul Murphy made a statement on developments in Northern Ireland. In light of the Northern Bank robbery, he was considering financial sanctions against Sinn Fein and would bring them forward if satisfactory answers were not received from Sinn Fein within a week. On 23 February Education and Skills Secretary Ruth Kelly made an announcement of a White Paper on the reform of education for 14 to 19-year olds, responding fully to the Tomlinson report. 'There are some who argue that to transform opportunities for our children, we should scrap the current system of GCSEs and A-levels. I do not agree. We will not transform opportunities by abolishing what is good, what works and what is recognised by employers, universities, pupils and parents. We must build on what is good in the system, and reform and replace what is not working. In my reforms, there will be a relentless focus on the basics.' Conservative Education spokesperson Tim Collins agreed that A-levels and GCSEs should remain but thought 'the Secretary of State chose to listen to members of the Number 10 policy unit rather than to her department or to outside advice. She has thrown away the chance to get substantial agreement across party and the education sector. She will not now be remembered as a great reformer. This was her first big test. She has flunked it.' Liberal Democrat Education spokesperson Phil Willis said 'I always try to begin on occasions such as this by welcoming something in the statement, but to be perfectly honest that has been quite difficult today.'

On 2 March Culture Secretary Tessa Jowell made a statement on the future of the BBC, publishing a Green Paper 'A Strong BBC, Independent of Government'. She promised to 'secure a BBC that belongs to its licence fee payers and embodies the values that the British people want . . . a BBC that promotes citizenship and builds our civil society; that promotes education and learning; that is dedicated to creativity and cultural excellence; that celebrates our nations, regions and communities; that brings the world to the UK and the UK to the world; and that is strong, independent and securely at the heart of British broadcasting for ten more years.' Conservative Culture spokesperson John Whittingdale felt this consisted of 'a number of largely cosmetic changes to the structure and oversight of the BBC. It appears that once again, the BBC has successfully fought off all proposals for substantial or immediate change.' Liberal Democrat Culture spokesperson Don Foster welcomed the proposals 'which contain most of the provisions that we seek, to ensure that the BBC is strong, independent, and well and securely funded.' The Conservatives held two debates on council tax and Hospital-Acquired Infection, which would be major issues in the coming election.

On 10 March Leader of the House of Commons Peter Hain introduced a motion to suspend allowances paid to Members who had chosen not to take up their seats (ie Sinn Fein MPs) for twelve months. Conservative amendments to make the motion tougher were rejected but the motion itself was welcomed by nearly all MPs and was passed without division.

On 14 March International Development Secretary Hilary Benn made a statement on the report of the Commission for Africa published the previous week. He said that 'we can no longer claim that we did not know about the condition of Africa or what to do to help it to change its future. Our challenge now is to do it. If we fail to act . . . those who will come after us will ask how it was that people who were so aware of the suffering and so capable of responding chose to look away. If, however, we do act, we will help to build a safer, more secure and more just world.' Tackling the issue would be one of the priorities of the UK presidency of the G8. The report was welcomed by all parties.

BUDGET 2005

On 16 March Chancellor Gordon Brown presented his ninth Budget statement, which put the economy firmly at the heart of the forthcoming election campaign. His economic forecast included an inflation target of 1.75 per cent this year and 2 per cent in 2006 and beyond; growth for 2004 was 3.1 per cent, as forecast, and he predicted growth of 3 to 3.5 per cent in 2004–5 and 2.5 to 3 per cent the following year; interest rates were the lowest for 35 years and employment the highest ever; borrowing was forecast at £34 billion for 2004–5, £32 billion for 2005–6 and £29 billion for 2006–7. Key fiscal measures included: the stamp duty threshold doubled to £120,000; Inheritance Tax threshold to rise to £275,000 this year, £285,000 next year and then to £300,000; petrol duty inflation rise postponed until 1 September due to high oil prices; freezes on corporation tax, capital gains tax, air passenger tax, insurance premium tax, climate change levy, aggregates levy and company car levy; tax breaks on ISAs extended until 2010; personal income tax allowance to be raised in line with inflation; 100 per cent VAT refund for renovations to religious buildings to be extended by three years. Specifically for pensioners there would be: a council tax refund of £200; free local bus travel from next year and Pension Credit to rise by 13 per cent by 2008, in line with earnings. Specifically for children there would be: Child Tax Credit to rise by 13 per cent, in line with earnings, over next three years; Child benefit for the first child up 50 pence; help promised for early learning in every area for all children who need it; refund VAT incurred by local councils on children's centres; re-building programme for primary schools increased by £650m by 2010; five-year, £1.5 billion programme to renovate and renew further education colleges; and investment in the three-year programme for IT capital in schools to be raised to £1.67 billion. He also announced an extra £400 million for defence spending. He opened his speech by saying that 'Britain is today experiencing the longest period of sustained economic growth since records began in 1701. And the foundation of this Budget is our determination to maintain British stability and growth.' Remaining in upbeat mood he concluded 'stability the foundation; investment not cuts; every child the best start in life; and a Budget for Britain's hard-working families and pensioners.'

Michael Howard called it a 'vote now pay later Budget' and thought 'this government and this Chancellor have run out of solutions to the problems Britain faces . . . their only answer is to tax, to spend and to waste.' Charles Kennedy felt the Chancellor had failed to tackle the 'fundamental unfairness' in the tax system – 'how can it be right in Britain today that the poorest 20 per cent pay more in tax, as a proportion of their income, than the richest 20 per cent?' and he also criticised both the Chancellor and the Conservatives for failing to address the 'ticking bomb' of council tax revaluation. The Labour Chairman of the Treasury Select Committee John McFall welcomed the Budget but raised concerns over the UK's skills base, tax avoidance and the challenges posed by the emerging Chinese economy. After four days of debate Shadow Chancellor Oliver Letwin said 'this Budget debate will be remembered for the Chancellor's dodgy arithmetic. It will be remembered as the time when the Chancellor yet again locked himself into spending plans that the nation could not afford. It will be remembered as the time when the Chancellor yet again failed to set out any coherent plan for giving people in this country value for money.' The various Budget resolutions were approved without division. The Finance Bill containing the Budget proposals was only published on 24 March and with the imminent election, all stages of an agreed, much truncated Bill (some 66 Clauses were dropped) were taken in the Commons on 6 April and in the Lords on 7 April, when the Bill received Royal Assent

On 22 March Education and Skills Secretary Ruth Kelly made a statement on the next stage of the government's skills agenda with the publication of a Skills White Paper, focusing on ambitions for adult skills. 'Skills benefit all of society. If we tackle the challenges that face us, we shall have a real opportunity to make a fundamental change for the better – for individuals, for employers and for the country.' Tim Collins was disappointed: 'we heard the usual: vague words, empty aspirations and promises to do better next time. Meanwhile, British employers face real and growing difficulties. It is time to get a grip, and time to get on with the work.' Foreign Secretary Jack Straw updated the House on the aftermath of the Indian Ocean Tsunami, with 95 British citizens confirmed dead and a further 78 missing presumed dead. On 23 March Local Government Minister Nick Raynsford made a statement on Council Tax for 2005–6 and proposed government action against those authorities that had set excessive budgets. The average council tax increase in England would be 4.1 per cent. Nine authorities had been identified as setting excessive budgets and had been given 21 days in which to respond.

On 24 March Foreign Secretary Jack Straw answered an Urgent Notice Question from Shadow Attorney General Dominic Grieve on the Attorney-General's apparent change of opinion on the legality of the military action in Iraq as revealed in a letter from Elizabeth Wilmshurst. It remained the position of the government that Law Officers' advice should not be published. Prime Minister Tony Blair then reported back on the outcome of the European Council held in Brussels that week, which had failed to reach agreement on the Services Directive: 'the issue that underlies the debate about the Services Directive is the future of the European social model. Some, notably France, believe that that model would remain in its existing form. Some, like Britain, believe firmly in Europe's social dimension but wanted it updated to take account of modern economic reality . . . It is a debate that we can win. But to win we have to participate, fully, wholeheartedly, with self-confidence and belief; we must not marginalise Britain, reducing it to the role of spectator. The policy of this government is clear: to be at the centre of the debate, not the margins.'

Returning from the Easter recess on 4 April, with speculation rife about the confirming of the date of the general election, MPs and Peers paid tribute to former Prime Minister Lord Callaghan, who had died in the recess. On 5 April Tony Blair named 5 May as the date of the election and a period of hectic horse trading began with the opposition parties over the government's outstanding legislative programme, before the Prorogation of Parliament on 7 April. On 5 April Local Government Minister Nick Raynsford made a statement on the judgment in respect of allegations of postal fraud in the Birmingham wards of Bordesley Green and Ashton, which had declared the elections void. With the impending election the government was taking further steps to reinforce the safeguards against any potential fraud so that public confidence in the electoral system would not be undermined. Conservative Constitutional

Affairs spokesperson Oliver Heald echoed the judge's reported remarks that the government was 'not only complacent but in denial'. And Liberal Democrat spokesperson Edward Davey felt that 'if Ministers do not act, the stench of this shoddy affair might be the one issue that drives them from office.' After two days of hectic debates to finish proceedings on those bills which could be completed, Parliament met for Prorogation on 7 April. Some 14 bills gained Royal Assent (but nine bills were dropped including the Identity Cards and the Consumer Credit Bills) and the 2004–5 session of Parliament and the fifty third Parliament were brought to a close.

In the May 5 election Labour was returned to power with majority reduced from 167 to 67.

NEW PARLIAMENT

The 2005–6 session of Parliament was opened by the Queen's Speech on 17 May with proposals for forty-four bills, many of which were those lost in the previous session by the calling of the election (plus seven that would be introduced in draft). The session would last for some eighteen months (until October 2006). The bills had a theme of 'Reform and Respect . . . focus on radical public service renewal, aimed at achieving an irreversible widening of opportunity in Britain and a determination to tackle crime and disorder – moving Britain forward through greater reform and mutual respect . . . It reflects the priorities of the British people and begins the implementation of the manifesto on which the government was elected.' In the ensuing debate Prime Minister Tony Blair, on his historic third term victory, felt this programme showed 'the government's renewed energy, purpose and ambition to build on the achievements so far and to move faster and further in the direction that the country wants, in our public services, in reform of our welfare state and in tackling crime and antisocial behaviour. That is what the country voted for.' Michael Howard, who had announced that he would be standing down as Leader of the Conservative Party later in the year, congratulated the Prime Minister on his election victory but added 'it is time to reward people who do the right thing – the people who play by the rules, work hard and take responsibility for themselves and their families. It is also time to restore respect in our society: to tackle the yob culture head on, to restore discipline in schools and to ensure that the punishment fits the crime. The Prime Minister talks about these things, so for the sake of our country, I hope that his actions will finally match his words. If they do, we will support him, but whatever happens, this party will hold him to account for the promises that he has made to the British people.'

Charles Kennedy warned: 'there is a need for the Liberal voice to be heard in party politics, in Parliament and in public on many of the issues that face us today. The Labour government won only a marginal mandate, but they want to introduce illiberal measures. They can be assured that they will receive a Liberal response from those on these benches – and that that will be good for the quality of our politics as a whole.' After six days of debate the speech was approved by 322 votes to 246, a government majority of 76.

Returning from the Whitsun recess on 6 June Foreign Secretary Jack Straw made a statement on the EU Constitutional Treaty following the 'no' votes in France and the Netherlands and the resulting postponement of the Second Reading of the European Union Bill (to allow for a referendum in the UK) – 'it remains our view that the constitution represents a sensible new set of rules for the enlarged European Union. We reserve completely the right to bring back for consideration the Bill providing for a UK referendum should circumstances change, but we see no point in doing so at this moment.' Conservative Foreign Affairs spokesperson Liam Fox regretted the decision to put off the UK referendum: 'rejection by the British people would bring an end to this wretched process. The loss of the constitution is not a crisis for the people of Europe, it is an opportunity. The crisis is a crisis of leadership. While our government dither about what to do, people in boardrooms up and down this country are trying to make investment decisions, and they want clarity and certainty.' On 7 June the Finance Bill, containing those elements dropped before the election, received an unopposed Second Reading in the Commons. Clauses were considered in Committee of the Whole House on 13 June and Third Reading was passed on 6 July. The Lords considered the Bill on 19 July and it gained Royal Assent on 20 July. On 9 June the re-introduced Consumer Credit Bill had an unopposed Second Reading on the Commons.

On 14 June the re-introduced National Lottery Bill had its Second Reading in the Commons by 290 votes to 197, a government majority of 93. On 15 June Welsh Secretary Peter Hain made a statement on the publication of a White Paper 'Better Governance for Wales' with proposals to review and improve the workings of the Welsh Assembly six years after devolution, in response to the Richards Commission. It included plans to alter the regional list system to prevent individuals from simultaneously being candidates in constituency elections and eligible for election from party lists. 'It will provide a reformed structure that is more accountable, more participatory and more effective, giving more powers to the Assembly and leading to better governance for a better Wales.' Conservative Welsh Affairs spokesperson Bill Wiggin called this aspect 'most spiteful' and Liberal Democrat spokesperson Lembit Opik felt the proposal 'looks to other parties as if he is seeking to arrange matters in a way that favours his own party and potentially disadvantages others?'

On 20 June Prime Minister Tony Blair made a statement on the outcome of the European Council held in Brussels on 16–17 June, which concentrated on the consequences of the 'no' votes in the referendums in France & the Netherlands and on the financial perspectives, the budgetary ceilings for the European Union for 2007–13. It had been agreed that on the constitutional treaty 'it is sensible to have a period of reflection, in which crucial questions as to Europe's future direction are debated.' As for the budget, the UK had 'wanted a commitment to a comprehensive reassessment of the structure of the EU budget' but the review offered by the Luxembourg presidency 'was inadequate.' Michael Howard said 'if the PM uses Britain's presidency to take a lead in Europe, arguing for a more flexible and more accountable EU with powers returned to the nation states, we will support him every inch of the way.' Charles Kennedy felt that 'those of us in the fundamentally pro-European camp feel a degree of pessimism about the present state of affairs.' On 21 June Attorney-General Lord Goldsmith made a statement on the government's intention to implement Section 43 of Criminal Justice Act 2003, allowing for trials without jury in serious and complex fraud cases, with a view to bringing it into force in January 2006. In the Commons Shadow Solicitor-General Dominic Grieve accused the government of being 'flagrantly in breach of the assurances they gave to the House as to how they would proceed with this matter.'

Liberal Democrat spokesperson David Heath pledged that 'Liberal Democrats will resist the loss and erosion of jury trial, whether that is done by primary or secondary legislation.' In the Commons the Racial and Religious Hatred Bill, which introduces the new offences to outlaw incitement to religious hatred that had to be dropped from the Serious Organised Crime and Police Act before the election, had its Second Reading. Shadow Home Secretary David Davis said the bill was 'too general, too wide, too vague, too dangerous' and it was questionable that it would protect the minorities it sought to help. Liberal Democrat Home Affairs spokesperson Alistair Carmichael said the government was 'playing fast and loose' with freedom of religion and freedom of expression and warned that 'once lost [it] will never be easily regained'. Second Reading was passed by 303 votes to 247, a government majority of 56 (three Labour MPs had voted for an Opposition amendment to the Bill, which had been defeated by 303 votes to 246, a majority of 57). After Committee consideration the Bill received a Third Reading in the Commons on 11 July by 301 votes to 229, a majority of 72. An Opposition amendment (supported by a handful of Labour backbenchers) to outlaw religious hatred as a pretext for stirring up hatred against a racial group was defeated by 291 votes to 233, a government majority of 58. The Bill was expected to face stiff opposition in the Lords after the summer recess.

On 22 June Paymaster-General Dawn Primarolo made a statement on the operation of the Tax Credits system and the reports from the Parliamentary Ombudsman, the Citizen's Advice Bureau and the Adjudicator on the failings of the system. She thought that the policy itself was the 'best way to deal with society's responsibility to help with the costs of bringing up children and tackling child poverty' and that the department had 'already taken measures to act on each of the major administrative issues raised.' Shadow Chancellor George Osborne felt that 'the chaotic system of tax credits is having a devastating impact on the lives of some of Britain's poorest families. Do not they and Britain deserve better?' and Liberal Democrat Shadow Chancellor David Laws said 'is not the truth that the Tax Credits system has been in chaos and that Ministers have persistently been in denial about the extent of the problems, and that they still seem to be in denial?' The twenty MPs who had been successful in the ballot for Private Member's Bills presented their bills for First Reading.

On 27 June Home Secretary Charles Clarke made a statement on the return of failed asylum seekers to Zimbabwe, with 57 Zimbabwean nationals on hunger strike in UK holding centres, reiterating that the Home Office assessed cases on their individual merits. On 28 June the reintroduced Identity Cards Bill to allow the creation of a national identity card scheme had its Second Reading in the Commons. Home Secretary Charles Clarke said ID cards would help counter, not create, a 'big brother society' and he offered to place a cap on the price of the cards but did not announce a figure. David Davis said Labour's legacy would be 'surveillance from cradle to grave'. Liberal Democrat spokesperson Mark Oaten said the plans would not help fight terrorism and that 'this identity tax will haunt Tony Blair in the same way the Poll Tax became Mrs Thatcher's legacy.' In the event the Second Reading was passed by 314 votes to 283, a government majority of 31. Some 20 Labour MPs voted against the government and Labour MP David Taylor voted both for and against as a protest. The Bill then went into Committee. On 30 June Foreign Secretary Jack Straw announced the publication of a White Paper on the prospects for the European Union for the next six months, when the UK would hold the presidency – 'throughout our presidency and beyond, the government will maintain Britain's place as a leading European power, helping to shape the EU's future direction in our interests and in the interests of the European Union as a whole.' Liam Fox felt 'despite all the talk, all we have had today is the same old centralising direction, with a bit of new rhetoric. This is a momentous time for the EU. For all their talk, our government have failed in the task of leadership' and junior Liberal Democrat Foreign Affairs spokesperson Nick Clegg thought 'in the EU the trick is to translate words into action.'

On 5 July Transport Secretary Alistair Darling made a statement on the Transport Innovation Fund and detailed how the government would take forward the development of a national road pricing scheme. This was followed by the unopposed Second Reading of the Immigration, Asylum and Nationality Bill. On 6 July, with the Prime Minister already having left for the G8 Summit in Gleneagles and the Culture Secretary at the ceremony in Singapore, Foreign Secretary Jack Straw made a late (7 p.m.) statement on the award of the 2012 Olympic Games to London, to a celebratory House. A Bill would be introduced to set the statutory framework that was needed for the Games. On 7 July the mood of the House changed entirely with the Speaker suspending the House for 20 minutes before Home Secretary Charles Clarke made a statement on the terrorist incidents in central London. With a developing situation he could not give a conclusive account but wanted to keep the House as fully informed as possible. He announced that the Prime Minister would be returning from Gleneagles to chair a COBRA meeting later that day. David Davies said 'this morning's explosions were acts of almost unspeakable depravity and wickedness, planned with the deliberate intention of taking innocent life and the whole House condemns them utterly.' Later that evening there was a row in the Chamber when Respect MP George Galloway accused Junior Defence Minister Adam Ingram of attacking him during his wind up speech in a defence debate – 'a foul-mouthed, deliberately timed, last-10-second smear by the thug at the Dispatch Box.'

On 11 July Prime Minister Tony Blair made two statements to MPs. Firstly on the terrorist attacks in London the previous week. The number of confirmed dead was 52 with some 56 more still in hospital. 'The whole House, I know, will want to state our feelings strongly. We express our revulsion at this murderous carnage of the innocent. We send our deep and abiding sympathy and prayers to the victims and their families. We are united in our determination that our country will not be defeated by such terror, but will defeat it and emerge from this horror with our values, our way of life, our tolerance and respect for others, undiminished. I should also like us to record our heartfelt thanks to, and admiration for, our emergency services . . . Together, we will ensure that, though terrorists can kill, they will never destroy the way of life that we share and value, which we will defend with such strength of belief and conviction that it will be to us and not to the terrorists that victory will belong.'

Michael Howard echoed those sentiments and concluded: 'our citizens and our government have responded in a way of which we can all be proud. In the days ahead, that spirit of defiance, resolution and determination should not be lost. We owe it to the victims

of last Thursday's bombs to remember that terrorists should never profit from their embrace of evil.'

Charles Kennedy also associated himself with the Prime Minister's remarks adding 'a mature parliamentary democracy must react as exactly that in the light of such events. We have heard measured and determined statements from the government and the Prime Minister over the past few days, and the whole country is grateful for that. As long as the government continue to adopt that tone and approach, they deserve and will certainly receive wholehearted support.' The Prime Minister then turned to the G8 Summit in Gleneagles, which had concentrated on Africa and Climate Change: 'some will be disappointed with aspects of the G8 summit. However, on any realistic basis, on the two hardest issues on the international agenda, there was progress, and in the case of Africa, immense progress. We now have to build on that, using our EU presidency.' Michael Howard congratulated the Prime Minister on what he achieved at the summit. Charles Kennedy offered similar sentiments: 'it was a considerable achievement to produce a coherent communiqué from the G8 members, given everything else that properly demanded his attention and presence.' On 13 July the Commons finally agreed the membership of the Select Committees for this session after an unprecedented delay in selection, which had caused various arguments especially as there had been no Liaison Committee to examine the Prime Minister before the G8 summit or the UK took on the presidency of the EU. The motions also included proposals to pay the Chairmen of Standing Committees.

On 18 July the business of both Houses was cancelled and MPs and Peers paid tribute to former Prime Minister Sir Edward Heath, who died over the weekend. On 19 July the Crossrail Bill, a hybrid bill to allow for the construction of the railway was given a Second Reading by 394 votes to 24, a majority of 370. On 20 July Home Secretary Charles Clarke updated MPs on developments on the London terror attacks. Fifty-six people were confirmed dead and 27 remained in hospital. He outlined the proposals he had for new counter terrorism legislation to be brought forward as soon as practicable when the House returned from the summer recess. It would create three new offences: 'the first of these criminalises acts preparatory to terrorism in order to ensure that early intervention does not mean that those responsible, who may be planning very serious terrorist crimes, should escape prosecution. . .The second proposed new offence focuses on indirect incitement to terrorism . . . Indirect incitement, when it is done with the intention of inciting others to commit acts of terrorism – that is an important qualification – will become a criminal offence. Thirdly, the Bill will deal with the giving and receiving of terrorist training . . . The Bill will also make a number of other amendments to existing legislation.' Opposition parties welcomed the moves but also said that they would wish to scrutinise the detail when it was published; as Mark Oaten put it: 'it is our firm view that good legislation needs good debate and scrutiny by parliamentarians. The Liberal Democrats will play our part in that process, but we do so from the firm belief that all parties should work together on these measures to send the terrorists the strongest possible signal that parties committed to democracy in this country are determined to join together to defeat them.'

On the final day before the summer recess, 21 July, Junior Defence Minister Don Touhig replied to an Urgent Notice Question from Liberal Democrat MP Alistair

Carmichael on plans for defence modernisation, which MPs accused the government of trying to sneak out by a written statement on the last day before the recess. Mr Carmichael felt 'it beggars belief that this information was to be put before Parliament in a written statement. That was surely an abuse of process'; Conservative Defence spokesperson Gerald Howarth echoed the sentiment: 'I regard it as a gross discourtesy to Parliament that these important announcements about defence contracts and the restructuring of the Royal Air Force are being sneaked out by way of six ministerial written statements on the last day before the long summer recess'. Liberal Democrat Defence spokesperson Bob Russell went as far as to say 'thank you, Mr Speaker, for ensuring that a Minister was brought here to explain the consequences of one of today's 65 written statements. In the past week, there have been 156 written statements; last week, there were 34. A charitable person might say that the government were anxious to convey information to Hon. Members as soon as possible. However, it is possible that there is an ulterior motive. Perhaps in the last week before a recess, written statements should all be subject to recall.' Conservative MP Tony Baldry made a personal statement to the House following a critical report from the Committee on Standards and Privileges concerning 'inadvertent' breaches of the Code of Conduct. The London Olympic Bill received an unopposed Second Reading. Parliament then rose for the summer recess until 10 October, and would not be returning for a session in September as normal (barring a recall of Parliament) as building work in the Palace of Westminster, including the installation of a permanent security screen in the Chamber, would make that difficult.

PUBLIC ACTS OF PARLIAMENT

The date stated after each Act is the date on which it came into effect.

Sustainable and Secure Buildings Act 2004 c 22 (various dates, some to be appointed) makes provision in relation to matters connected with buildings.

Public Audit (Wales) Act 2004 c 23 (various dates, some to be appointed) confers further functions on the Auditor General for Wales; makes provision about the audit of accounts of public bodies in Wales and related matters; makes provision about economy, efficiency and effectiveness in relation to public bodies and registered social landlords in Wales; and for connected purposes.

Employment Relations Act 2004 c 24 (various dates, some to be appointed) amends the law relating to the recognition of trade unions and taking industrial action; makes provision about means of voting in ballots under the Trade Union and Labour Relations (Consolidation) Act 1992; amends provisions of that Act relating to rights of members and non-members of trade unions and makes other provision about rights of trade union members, employees and workers; and for connected purposes.

Horserace Betting and Olympic Lottery Act 2004 c 25 (various dates, some to be appointed) makes provision for the sale of the Tote; the abolition of the horserace betting levy system; the establishment of National Lottery games designed to raise money in connection with the hosting by London of the Olympic Games in 2012; and for connected purposes.

Christmas Day (Trading) Act 2004 c 26 (day to be appointed) prohibits the opening of large shops on Christmas Day and restricts the loading or unloading of goods at such shops on Christmas Day.

Companies (Audit, Investigations and Community Enterprise) Act 2004 c 27 (various dates, some to be appointed) amends the law relating to company auditors and accounts, to the provision that may be made in respect of certain liabilities incurred by a company's officers, and to company investigations; provides for community interest companies; and for connected purposes.

Domestic Violence, Crime and Victims Act 2004 c 28 (day to be appointed) amends the Family Law Act 1996 Part 4, the Protection from Harassment Act 1997 and the Protection from Harassment (Northern Ireland) Order 1997; makes provision about homicide; makes common assault an arrestable offence; provides for the payment of surcharges by offenders; for alternative verdicts; and for a procedure under which a jury tries only sample counts on an indictment; and for connected purposes.

Highways (Obstruction by Body Corporate) Act 2004 c 29 (January 15, 2005) applies the Highways Act 1980 s 314 to offences under ss 137 and 137ZA.

Human Tissue Act 2004 c 30 (various dates, some to be appointed) makes provision with respect to activities involving human tissue; about the transfer of human remains from certain museum collections; and for connected purposes.

Children Act 2004 c 31 (various dates, some to be appointed) makes provision for the establishment of a Children's Commissioner; about services provided to and for children and young people by local authorities and other persons; in relation to Wales about advisory and support services relating to family proceedings; about private fostering, child minding and day care, adoption review panels, the defence of reasonable punishment, the making of grants as respects children and families, child safety orders, the Children's Commissioner for Wales, the publication of material relating to children involved in certain legal proceedings and the disclosure by the Inland Revenue of information relating to children.

Armed Forces (Pensions and Compensation) Act 2004 c 32 (day to be appointed) makes new provision for establishing pension and compensation schemes for the armed or reserve forces; amends the Pensions Appeal Tribunals Act 1943; provides for the transfer of the property, rights and liabilities of the Royal Patriotic Fund Corporation to a registered charity; and for connected purposes.

Civil Partnership Act 2004 c 33 (various dates, some to be appointed) makes provision for and in connection with civil partnership.

Housing Act 2004 c 34 (various dates, some to be appointed) makes provision about housing conditions; regulates houses in multiple occupation and certain other residential accommodation; makes provision for home information packs in connection with the sale of residential properties; about secure tenants and the right to buy; and for connected purposes.

Pensions Act 2004 c 35 (various dates, some to be appointed) makes provision relating to pensions and financial planning for retirement and provision relating to entitlement to bereavement payments; and for connected purposes.

Civil Contingencies Act 2004 c 36 (various dates, some to be appointed) makes provision about civil contingencies.

Hunting Act 2004 c 37 (February 18, 2005) makes provision about hunting wild mammals with dogs; prohibits hare coursing; and for connected purposes.

Consolidated Fund (No. 2) Act 2004 c 38 (December 16, 2004) authorises the use of resources for the service of the years ending March 31, 2005 and March 31, 2006; applies certain sums out of the Consolidated Fund to the service of the years ending with March 31, 2005 and March 31, 2006.

Electoral Registration (Northern Ireland) Act 2005 c 1 (February 24, 2005) makes provision about the registration of electors in Northern Ireland in cases where required information is not provided.

Prevention of Terrorism Act 2005 c 2 (various dates) provides for the making against individuals involved in terrorism-related activity of orders imposing obligations on them for purposes connected with preventing or restricting their further involvement in such activity; makes provision about appeals and other proceedings relating to such orders; and for connected purposes.

Appropriation Act 2005 c 3 (March 17, 2005) authorises

the use of resources for the service of the years ending with March 31, 2004 and March 31, 2005 and applies certain sums out of the Consolidated Fund to the service of the years ending with March 31, 2004 and March 31, 2005; and appropriates the supply authorised in this Session of Parliament for the service of the years ending with March 31, 2004 and March 31, 2005.

Constitutional Reform Act 2005 c 4 (various dates, some to be appointed) makes provision for modifying the office of Lord Chancellor, and the functions of that office; establishes a Supreme Court of the United Kingdom, and abolishes the appellate jurisdiction of the House of Lords; about the jurisdiction of the Judicial Committee of the Privy Council and the judicial functions of the President of the Council; and about the judiciary, their appointment and discipline; and for connected purposes.

Income Tax (Trading and Other Income) Act 2005 c 5 (April 6, 2005) restates, with minor changes, certain enactments relating to income tax on trading income, property income, savings and investment income and certain other income; and for connected purposes. (This Act is part of the 'Re-Write project' which is designed to put tax provisions into user-friendly language.)

Child Benefit Act 2005 c 6 (April 10, 2006) makes provision for, and in connection with, altering the descriptions of persons in respect of whom a person may be entitled to child benefit.

Finance Act 2005 c 7 (April 7, 2005)
grants certain duties, alters others, and amends the law relating to the National Debt and the Public Revenue, and makes further provision in connection with finance.

Appropriation (No. 2) Act 2005 c 8 (April 7, 2005) appropriates the supply authorised in this Session of Parliament for the service of the year ending with March 31, 2006.

Mental Capacity Act 2005 c 9 (various dates, some to be appointed) makes new provision relating to persons who lack capacity; establishes a superior court of record called the Court of Protection in place of the office of the Supreme Court called by that name; makes provision in connection with the Convention on the International Protection of Adults signed at the Hague on 13th January 2000; and for connected purposes.

Public Services Ombudsman (Wales) Act 2005 c 10 (day to be appointed) establishes and makes provision about the office and functions of Public Services Ombudsman for Wales; and about compensation; abolishes the Commission for Local Administration in Wales and the offices of Welsh Administration Ombudsman, Health Service Commissioner for Wales and Social Housing Ombudsman for Wales; and for connected purposes.

Commissioners for Revenue and Customs Act 2005 c 11 (day to be appointed) makes provision for the appointment of Commissioners to exercise functions presently vested in the Commissioners of Inland Revenue and the Commissioners of Customs and Excise; for the establishment of a Revenue and Customs Prosecutions Office; and for connected purposes.

Inquiries Act 2005 c 12 (day to be appointed) makes provision about the holding of inquiries.

Disability Discrimination Act 2005 c 13 (various dates, some to be appointed) amends the 1995 Act; and for connected purposes.

Railways Act 2005 c 14 (day or days to be appointed) amends the law relating to the provision and regulation of railway services; and for connected purposes.

Serious Organised Crime and Police Act 2005 c 15 (various dates, some to be appointed) provides for the establishment and functions of the Serious Organised Crime Agency; makes provision about investigations, prosecutions, offenders and witnesses in criminal proceedings and the protection of persons involved in investigations or proceedings; make further provision for combating crime and disorder; and for connected purposes.

Clean Neighbourhoods and Environment Act 2005 c 16 (various dates, some to be appointed) amends the Crime and Disorder Act 1998 s 6; makes provision for the gating of certain minor highways; in relation to abandoned vehicles and the removal and disposal of vehicles; relating to litter and refuse, graffiti, fly-posting and the display of advertisements; relating to the control of dogs and amends the law relating to stray dogs; and for various other purposes connected with neighbourhoods and the environment.

Drugs Act 2005 c 17 (various dates, some to be appointed) makes provision in connection with controlled drugs and for the making of orders to supplement anti-social behaviour orders in cases where behaviour is affected by drug misuse or other prescribed factors.

Education Act 2005 c 18 (various dates, some to be appointed) makes provision about the inspection of schools, child minding, day care, and nursery education; about the training of persons who work in schools and other persons who teach, about the supply of personal information for purposes related to education and about the attendance of children at educational provision outside schools; and for connected purposes.

Gambling Act 2005 c 19 (day or days to be appointed) makes provision about gambling.

International Organisations Act 2005 c 20 (various dates, some to be appointed) makes provision about privileges, immunities and facilities in connection with certain international organisations.

Appropriation (No 3) Act 2005 c 21 (July 20, 2005) authorises the use of resources for the service of the year ending with March 31, 2006 and applies certain sums out of the Consolidated Fund to the service of the year ending with March 31, 2006; appropriates the supply authorised in this Session of Parliament for the service of the year ending with March 31, 2006; and repeals certain Consolidated Fund and Appropriation Acts.

Finance (No. 2) Act 2005 c 22 (July 20, 2005) grants certain duties, alters others duties, and amends the law relating to the National Debt and the Public Revenue, and makes further provision in connection with finance.

WHITE PAPERS

This section provides an outline of a selection of White Papers that have been published in the last year. For further information visit www.official-documents.co.uk or www.parliament.uk. Alternatively, visit the websites of individual government departments – *see* Government Departments section.

Building Communities, Beating Crime was presented to Parliament by the Secretary of State for the Home Department in November 2004 and sets out the second phase of the government's police reform agenda. The Paper contains three broad objectives: to spread policing to every community in the form of dedicated neighbourhood teams made up of officers and community support officers (CSOs); to further modernise the police workforce, reduce bureaucracy and introduce new powers for CSOs; and to embed a responsive customer service culture to provide citizens with greater scope to determine how their communities are policed.

Choosing Health: Making Healthy Choices Easier was presented to Parliament in November 2004 by the Secretary of State for Health. This Paper outlines the government's plans to help consumers make healthier choices, to protect people's health from the actions of others, and to recognise the importance of emotional and physical development for the young. Six priorities for action were established: reduce the number of smokers; reduce obesity and improve diet and nutrition; increase exercise; encourage and support sensible drinking; improve sexual health; and improve mental health.

Two *Sustainable Communities* White Papers were presented to Parliament by the Deputy Prime Minister and First Secretary of State in January 2005. *Homes for All* is a five-year plan to provide more homes to buy or rent through responsible growth. The government aims to do this by improving the social housing stock, promoting greater home ownership, and allowing council and housing association tenants to buy a stake in their home. *People, Places and Prosperity* is also a five-year plan. This Paper outlines the government's strategy to provide people with more input into the way their community is run, and its intention to work at the appropriate level (whether through the town, city or council hall) so that local government delivers the best possible services to the community. Tackling disadvantage will also be a priority, as will a strategic approach to regional planning.

Five-Year Strategy: Opportunity and Security Throughout Life was presented to Parliament in February 2005 by the Secretary of State for Work and Pensions. The Paper sets out the government's aim of achieving an 80 per cent employment rate by helping those traditionally defined as outside the labour market into work. It proposes to do this through supporting children and families (especially lone parents), helping those on incapacity benefits to return to work, and breaking down the barriers that prevent disabled people, older workers and ethnic minorities from realising their ambitions in the workplace.

Treaty Establishing a Constitution for Europe – Commentary was presented to Parliament in February 2005 by the Secretary of State for Foreign and Commonwealth Affairs, in response to a request from the European Scrutiny Committee of the House of Lords for an annotated analysis of the new Treaty. The Paper explains the Treaty and how it relates to previous treaties, and details the changes it would make to the EU's powers.

Controlling Our Borders: Making Migration Work for Britain – A Five-Year Strategy for Asylum and Immigration was presented to Parliament by the Secretary of State for the Home Department in February 2005. This Paper details the next stage of the government's reform of the immigration and asylum processes, including: the introduction of a skill-based points system, and of English language tests for those who wish to stay permanently; the implementation of fully integrated pre-entry, border and in-country controls; the detention of more failed asylum seekers and fast-track processing of all unfounded asylum claims.

14–19 Education and Skills was presented to Parliament in February 2005 by the Secretary of State for Education and Skills, in response to the report delivered in October 2004 by the Working Group on 14–19 Reform. The Paper outlines the government's plan to reform secondary and post-secondary education with the objective that all young people continue some form of learning until at least the age of 18. Proposals include providing a sound grounding in the core subjects of English and mathematics, and the option of vocational learning.

Skills: Getting on in Business, Getting on at Work was presented to Parliament by the Secretary of State for Education and Skills in March 2005. This Paper expands upon the National Skills Strategy, published in July 2003, and focuses on the next phase of reform in equipping adults with the skills needed to fulfil their personal and professional ambitions. The government plans to work in partnership with employers when designing and delivering training for adults; supply individuals with better guidance on further qualifications; help all adults gain the functional skills of literacy, language and numeracy; and tackle the obstacles that people face in gaining fair access to training and jobs.

SCIENCE AND DISCOVERY

MESSENGER TO MERCURY

Launched on a Delta 2 rocket from Cape Canaveral on 3 August 2004, NASA's Messenger spacecraft is destined to provide our first close-up views of Mercury since the Mariner 10 fly-by mission of 1974–5. Messenger will take several years to reach the Solar System's innermost planet, undergoing a series of 'gravitational slingshot' manoeuvres involving passages close to Earth, Venus and Mercury itself. The first encounter with Mercury, in January 2008, is expected to yield much new information.

Messenger (MErcury Surface Space Environment GEochemistry and Ranging) will become the first spacecraft to orbit Mercury, in 2011. From its highly elliptical 12-hour near-polar orbit, Messenger will undertake two 6-month mapping cycles covering the entire planet (only about 45 per cent of the surface was imaged by Mariner 10), and conduct measurements of Mercury's magnetosphere and extremely tenuous atmosphere.

T. REX GROWTH CYCLE RECONSTRUCTED

A new understanding of the life cycle of *Tyrannosaurus rex* has emerged from studies of annual growth rings in well preserved fossil bone samples from North America. Findings reported in *Nature* in August 2004 by Gregory M. Erickson (Florida State University) and co-workers show that *T. rex* attained most of its massive size (up to 5600 kg/12,300 lb) in a four-year growth spurt in its teenage years. During this interval, individuals had a projected growth rate of 2.1 kg (4.6 lb) per day. Thereafter, little or no further growth occurred; *T. rex* was fully mature at between 18 and 19 years old.

The study was based on 20 specimens of *Tyrannosauridae* skeletons from four related species. Seven of the skeletons were from *T. rex,* ranging in age at death from two to 28 years. Measurements of annual growth rings were taken from non weight-bearing bones such as ribs, avoiding complications resulting from distortion by the animal's own bulk. These results show that, at least for *T. rex,* great size was attained rapidly during a brief early stage of life, rather than being the result of sustained, continuous growth.

'BRAIN SCAN' CLARIFIES *ARCHAEOPTERYX* FLIGHT ABILITY

Widely accepted as an evolutionary link between dinosaurs and birds, *Archaeopteryx* is one of the most celebrated fossils, dating back to the late Jurassic period around 147 million years ago. *Archaeopteryx* shows feathered wings and a wishbone characteristic of birds, together with reptilian features liked toothed jaws and a tail. Seven examples have been recovered from limestone deposits in southern Germany, the first of these (discovered in 1861) being kept at London's Natural History Museum. A research team led by the Museum's Angela Milner has conducted detailed analysis on the braincase and inner ear structure of the London *Archaeopteryx* fossil.

It has been a matter of debate as to whether *Archaeopteryx* was capable of bird-like powered flight, or if it used its wings for gliding in the manner of a flying squirrel as has been proposed for the feathered dinosaur *Microraptor gui* (reported in early 2003) from 124–128 million years ago. X-ray computer tomography (CT) scanning of the *Archaeopteryx* braincase has allowed three dimensional reconstruction of the fossil's brain, from which the researchers were able to conclude that it was sufficiently large and well-developed to allow powered flight. The measured brain volume of 1.4 ml for the partial available sample leads to a proposed total of 1.6 ml – three times the volume in an equivalent-sized reptile. Enlargement of the parts of the brain involved in vision bears close resemblance to the structure of modern avian brains. Further evidence for powered flight in *Archaeopteryx* comes from study of the inner ear structures, essential for balance and co-ordination. These were found to be closer to those of birds than to modern-day reptiles. The findings, published in *Nature* in August 2004, suggest that powered flight in the earliest birds followed quickly upon the development of feathers: with an essentially avian, as opposed to reptilian, brain, *Archaeopteryx* was equipped to fly rather than simply glide.

GREENLAND CORE CHARTS ICE AGE ONSET

A new ice core from north-central Greenland provides an insight into conditions in the North Atlantic region during the onset of the most recent major ice age 120,000 years ago. An international collaboration involving scientists from nine countries, the North Greenland Ice Core Project (NGRIP) began work in 1996, drilling through a 3085 metre depth of ice to reach bedrock in July 2003. Preliminary results were published in September 2004.

As a result of geothermal heating, the final 45 metres of the core were in the form of liquid water. Melting at the deepest level has, however, preserved the record of annual snow deposits, later compressed to ice, in the overlying layers. Scientists have been able to more clearly trace year-by-year conditions in the NGRIP core than in the GRIP and GISP2 cores obtained from southern Greenland in the early 1990s; in contrast with these, the lowest parts of the NGRIP core have not undergone compression or folding resulting from contact with the bedrock.

The NGRIP core provides a record extending from the warm Eemian period, through the onset of the Ice Age, and up to the current, Holocene epoch (from the end of the Ice Age 10,000 years ago). Conditions in the late Eemian period were apparently stable and warm, with global temperatures about 5°C above those found today: modellers see this as a good analogy for a globally-warmed Earth, providing clues as to how climate may develop in the future.

From analysis of oxygen isotope ratios in air bubbles trapped in the annual ice deposits, scientists have reconstructed the temperature changes occurring in Greenland at the end of the Eemian and into the Ice Age. Cooling was found to have occurred gradually, over an interval of perhaps 5000 years, following which there were more rapid temperature fluctuations. Even during the Ice Age, there appear to have been interludes where temperatures rose by as much as 10°C over timescales of a few decades. The broad conclusion is that, initially at least, a future ice age will follow a slow deterioration in climate, rather than arriving abruptly.

The occurrence of liquid water below the ice at the NGRIP site (75.1°N, 42.3°W) also opens up the possibility of a northern hemisphere 'cold deep biosphere' analogous to that at Lake Vostok in the Antarctic – a likely subject for future investigation by researchers seeking microbial communities, which should have been isolated from the surface environment for an extremely long time.

GENERAL RELATIVITY PASSES ANOTHER TEST

One of the predictions to emerge from Einstein's theory of General Relativity is the phenomenon of 'frame dragging', wherein a large spinning mass such as the Earth should distort space-time in its immediate vicinity. A consequence of this is that a body in orbit around the mass will have its position altered from that predicted by purely Newtonian physics. Also described as a 'gravitomagnetic' phenomenon, frame dragging is more correctly known as the Lense-Thirring effect after a pair of scientists who described it in 1918, two years after Einstein first published his theory.

Studies of the motions of satellites in low-Earth orbit offer the possibility of gathering evidence for frame dragging. Confirmatory observations have been reported by Ignazio Ciufolini (Universita di Lecce, Italy) and Erricos Pavlis (University of Maryland, USA). Launched in 1976 and 1992 respectively, the Laser Geodynamics satellites LAGEOS and LAGEOS II have been subject to over 100 million laser-ranging measurements from more than 50 ground stations. According to Ciufolini and Pavlis, the *nodes,* where the planes of the satellites' highly-inclined orbits intersect that of Earth's equator, are dragged forward by 1.9 metres per year as a result of the Lense-Thirring effect. This is within 10 per cent of the predicted value.

The high level of accuracy in measuring frame dragging in the LAGEOS experiment comes from greatly-improved mapping of Earth's gravitational field by the twin GRACE (Gravity Recovery and Climate Environment) satellites launched by NASA in 2002. Scientists expect to make still more precise determinations of the frame dragging effect with NASA's Gravity Probe B satellite, which was launched into a 640 km altitude polar orbit in April 2004. Gravity Probe B contains a set of four solid quartz gyroscopes, described as the most perfect spheres ever manufactured. Measurements of the directional drift in the gyroscopes' spin are expected to test theoretically-predicted frame dragging to within 1 per cent accuracy, with first results anticipated in late 2005.

DECODING THE CHICKEN

The chicken became the first agricultural animal to have its entire DNA sequence (genome) deciphered, with the publication of a detailed draft version in December 2004. The work was carried out by the International Chicken Genome Sequencing Consortium, based on a single in-bred female of *Gallus gallus,* the red jungle fowl which is the ancestor of the various domesticated lines. Availability of the chicken genome sequence bridges a gap in studies of vertebrate evolution. In the laboratory, the chicken is an important model organism in studies of vertebrate development, and in understanding human genetic diseases such as muscular dystrophy and epilepsy.

The chicken genome comprises 1.06 billion basepairs (1.06 Gb) of DNA, about one-third the size of mammalian genomes. This is arranged in 38 chromosomes, plus two sex chromosomes. In contrast with the mammalian situation, much avian DNA is found in microchromosomes, containing between five and 20 million basepairs of material. Analysis of the sequence predicts between 20,000 and 23,000 genes.

Comparisons between the chicken and human genomes suggest that we diverged from the last common ancestor around 310 million years ago (divergence between human and mouse, for example, occurred more recently, around 75 million years ago). Genes specific for production of feathers and scales – lost from mammals – can be identified in the *Gallus gallus* genome. Perhaps one of the more surprising findings was that genes for olfaction are well-represented: chickens have a better sense of smell than was previously assumed.

The red jungle fowl genome sequence has been compared with three domesticated lines – broiler, layer and Chinese silkie – revealing a total of 2.8 million single nucleotide polymorphisms (SNPs; changes at the level of a single base), roughly one for every thousand basepairs of DNA. Tying these to individual genetic traits should be informative, and their abundance suggests that most SNPs arose before domestication of the chicken, believed to have occurred in Asia between 7,400 and 10,000 years ago.

BOVINE GENOME COMPLETED

An international project to determine the entire bovine DNA sequence took a major step towards completion in early October 2004 with the deposition in public databases of a first draft version. Biomedical and agricultural researchers now have access to the *Bos taurus* genome derived from the DNA of a Hereford cow known as L1 Dominette 01449. In common with previously-sequenced mammalian genomes, that of the cow contains roughly 3 billion basepairs of DNA.

It is hoped that availability of the completed bovine genome sequence will lead to improvements in milk and meat production. Comparative sequencing at a less intensive level is planned for other breeds, including Holstein, Jersey, Angus, Limousin, Norwegian Red and Brahman.

TYCHO'S STAR SUPERNOVA COMPANION IDENTIFIED

Type Ia supernovae occur in close binary star systems in which one member has more rapidly expended its hydrogen 'fuel' through nuclear reactions than its partner, becoming a carbon- and oxygen-rich white dwarf. Drawing in material from the less-evolved companion star's extended atmosphere, the white dwarf eventually accumulates sufficient mass to exceed the critical Chandrasekhar Limit of 1.4 solar masses, and as a result explodes as a supernova. Since the mechanism leading to type Ia supernovae always results in an explosion occurring at the same mass, these each have the same absolute luminosity, and astronomers have used them as 'standard candles' to measure the distances of host galaxies and, in turn, determine that the overall expansion of the Universe is accelerating (a consequence of the so-called 'dark energy').

The most recent type Ia supernova seen in our galaxy, Milky Way, occurred in 1572 in the constellation of Cassiopeia, and is known commonly as Tycho's Star after the renowned Danish astronomer Tycho Brahe who studied it. First seen in November 1572, the supernova became as bright as the planet Venus, and remained visible to the naked eye until March 1574. The supernova remnant is a strong source of radio waves and X-rays.

While the white dwarf star is completely destroyed in a type Ia supernova, the companion may survive, being ejected from the scene of the explosion and retaining its original orbital velocity. An international team led by Pilar Ruiz-Lapuente (University of Barcelona, Spain) has undertaken a search for the companion involved in Tycho's star. A candidate, named 'Tycho G', has been identified at an angular distance of 2.6 arc-seconds south of the supernova remnant's centre, well within the 9.1 arc-second maximum theoretical radius for a companion. The motion of Tycho G is three times as rapid as that of other stars in the same general region of the Galaxy, 10,000 light years away.

Surprisingly, Tycho G has a spectral class of G0 to G2, similar to our Sun. Tycho G has much the same surface temperature and luminosity as the Sun. On the basis of past models for the binary systems in which type Ia supernovae occur, astronomers might have expected to find cooler, giant star with more extended outer envelope. Confirmation of Tycho G as the companion to the white dwarf whose demise was witnessed as the 'new' star of 1572 may hinge on future spectral analysis which could reveal the presence of contaminating ejecta in its atmosphere.

Large numbers of supernovae continue to be discovered in external galaxies by systematic 'patrol' programmes, including some operated by amateur astronomers.

ANOTHER BRANCH TO THE HUMAN FAMILY TREE

A new hominin species, remains of which have been found in a limestone cave at Liang Bua in the eastern Indonesian island of Flores, has revealed further details of the complexity of human evolution. The discovery, made in September 2003, was reported in two papers in the 28 October 2004 issue of *Nature*, describing the findings of a team led by Peter Brown and Mike Morwood from the University of New England, Armidale, Australia.

Homo floresiensis (Flores Man) was remarkable for its small size. The partial skeleton (designated LB1) indicates a height of only one metre, leading the researchers to initially think it was that of a child. Wear on the teeth, and closed cranial sutures, however, are more consistent with the skeleton being that of a 30-year-old female. Anatomical features are consistent with an upright gait, and although the brain capacity (380 cc) is much smaller than in other species, the facial structure and dentition are indicative of *Homo* lineage. *Homo floresiensis* may have had a body mass up to 36 kg.

Charred animal bones found in association with the *H. floresiensis* remains suggest the use of fire, and stone tools have also been recovered from the cave. The LB1 skeleton has been reliably dated to 18,000 years ago. Partial remains of further individuals at the site show that *H. floresiensis* was extant 38,000 years ago, and the oldest specimens push the date back to between 74,000 and 95,000 years before present. The researchers speculate that, like *Homo sapiens*, Flores Man was a descendant of *Homo erectus*, evolving in isolation following dispersal from Africa 200,000 years ago. The small stature of *H. floresiensis* is a typical mammalian evolutionary response (island dwarfism) to an isolated environment in which the pressures of natural selection are low.

Homo floresiensis may have been extant as recently as 13,000 years ago, outliving the Neanderthals (which died out 28,000 years ago) and existing alongside early *Homo*

sapiens, although there is no evidence for interaction between the two species. It is possible that the remains of other parallel branches in Man's evolutionary history await discovery.

PIGEON NAVIGATION MAGNETIC LINK STRENGTHENED

The ability of homing pigeons to find their way back to roost has long been a subject for scientific speculation. While visual clues such as local landmarks are clearly very important, some workers have theorised that pigeons (and other birds) may be able to navigate by sensing Earth's magnetic field. Evidence in support of this idea has been provided by experiments conducted by Cordula Mora and colleagues at the University of Auckland in New Zealand.

Mora *et al* trained four experienced racing pigeons to jump on to a platform at one end of a tunnel in the presence of an artificially-induced magnetic field, or an identical platform at the other end in the field's absence. The birds' ability to correctly decide which platform to use was impaired when small powerful magnets were attached to the base of their beaks, or when local anaesthetic was applied to their olfactory cavities. Severing the trigeminal nerve which carries sensory information from the beak to the brain also impaired the pigeons' ability to correctly respond to the presence or absence of a magnetic field.

The researchers conclude that something in the upper beak – perhaps crystals of magnetite – is responsible for the ability of homing pigeons to detect variations in the local magnetic field, and this may indeed be an important part of birds' navigational sense.

DINOSAUR-EATING CRETACEOUS MAMMAL

The Yixian Formation in northeastern China has been a rich source of dinosaur fossils. A couple of further discoveries in the region have shed new light on early mammalian evolution, and challenge the prevailing view that the earliest mammals were nocturnal shrew-like creatures, foraging for seeds and nuts in the face of dominant predatory dinosaurs.

Mammals first appeared around 180 million years ago. Fossils of a now-extinct quadruped mammal lineage, *Repenomamus,* have been found in the Cretaceous period Yixian Formation dating back to 128 million years ago. *Repenomamus robustus* was a small animal about half a metre long with a projected weight of 4–6 kg. Rather more substantial was *R.giganticus,* which could have weighed as much as 12–14 kg. Both species had short legs, and an overall body structure likened to that of the modern Tasmanian Devil. Their dentition pattern and strong jaw suggests that *Repenomamus* were carnivores.

Further strong evidence for a carnivorous lifestyle comes from the most intact *R. robustus* skeleton yet uncovered. Under the ribcage, at the position of the animal's stomach, remains of a young *Psittacosaurus* (a herbivorous small dinosaur) were found. This had been disrupted into small pieces, some of the bones retaining their original articulation – consistent with the dinosaur having been swallowed in chunks (the jaw structure of *R. robustus* was unsuited to mastication).

Whether *R. robustus* was a hunter or scavenger is unresolved (the latter is considered less likely by analogy with most modern mammals), but these findings open up a new view on early mammal lifestyles; clearly, in at least some cases, mammals competed with dinosaurs for survival more successfully than was previously believed.

MODEL POINTS TO HUMAN INFLUENCE IN 2003 HEATWAVE

The summer of 2003 was exceptionally hot and dry across Europe, particularly during the period from August 1–15. In light of current concerns regarding global warming, research into a possible link to man-made influences such as increased levels of greenhouse gases like carbon dioxide is of particular interest. A report published in *Nature* by Peter Stott (UK Met. Office Hadley Centre for Climate Prediction and Research) with Daithi Stone and Myles Allen (University of Oxford) suggests that, for the first time, a likely anthropogenic signature is present in climate data for summer 2003.

Stott *et al* used the HadCM3 climate to predict likely weather conditions in the presence and absence of anthropogenic factors. While a hot summer like that experienced in 2003 is not impossible in the absence of human factors, the finding – at a confidence level of 90% – is that anthropogenic factors make such a heatwave four times more likely.

Summer temperatures in Europe during 2003 exceeded the 1961–90 mean by an average of 2.3°C. The model predicts that by 2040 more than half of all summers could be warmer than that of 2003. If borne out, this prediction could have serious implications: the 2003 heatwave is believed to have caused a significant increase in mortality – particularly among the elderly – in Italy, Germany and France.

TITAN REVEALED

After a seven-year journey from launch in 1997, the European Space Agency (ESA) Huygens probe landed on the surface of Saturn's major satellite Titan on 14 January 2005. Attached to the Cassini spacecraft for the long cruise through interplanetary space, Huygens was released on Christmas Day 2004. It entered Titan's atmosphere twenty days later, taking 2 hours 37 minutes to descend to the surface, braked by atmospheric friction from its initial velocity of 22,500 km/h, and was then further slowed by parachutes to make a relatively soft landing at 5 m/s. The 2.7-metre diameter probe weighed 31.8 kg.

Titan is the only satellite in the Solar System to possess a substantial atmosphere, composed mainly of nitrogen. Previous Earth-based studies and results from the Voyager spacecraft in the 1980s revealed a global abundance of methane in Titan's atmosphere. At high altitude, the action of solar radiation produces a photochemical haze, shrouding Titan's surface from view.

Once below the haze layer, the Huygens probe was able to image Titan's surface with the Descent Image-Spectral Radiometer (DISR) instrument. This revealed narrow, branching run-off channels, indicative of liquid flow on Titan. At the surface temperature of −180°C, the channels have been carved by the action of methane, rather than water. Over Titan as a whole, methane takes a role equivalent to that of water on Earth in the satellite's 'hydrological' cycle, driving processes of erosion and evaporation and precipitation. Methane rain and clouds are present. Winds at the surface are weak, but at an altitude of 120 km, Huygens encountered wind-speeds of 430 km/h.

Prior to the Huygens landing, much speculation surrounded the possibility of hydrocarbon (methane or ethane) seas on Titan; at the probe landing site, there is no sign of these, though some dark features recorded using DISR may be large pools from which methane has recently evaporated. Dark organic material precipitating from the atmosphere accumulates in the bottom of run-off channels, making these more prominent.

Substantial quantities of methane are apparently locked up in Titan's topsoil. Huygens landed on material with a consistency similar to wet sand and with a surface crust: the heat generated by impact released some of the trapped methane. The probe sank some 10–15 centimetres into the soil on landing.

Huygens' Surface Science Package (SSP) relayed data to the Cassini spacecraft, in orbit around Saturn, for 70 minutes after landing. Perhaps the most striking image from the mission shows the landing site, in a field of small 'pebbles' – in this case comprised of dirty ice; at the low temperatures in the outer Solar System, water behaves like rock – possibly in a dry river-bed. The Gas Chromatograph and Mass Spectrometer (GCMS) instrument recorded the presence of the argon isotope ^{40}Ar, a signal of cryovolcanic activity involving water and ammonia.

The highly successful Huygens mission ended once Cassini was lost over the horizon in line of sight for radio communication. Much has been learned about the enigmatic Titan, the most distant body on which a lander has been placed, and analysis of the data will continue for years to come. Some scientists are already clamouring for follow-up missions, possibly even with rover vehicles similar to those used to such great effect in the exploration of Mars.

MORE SCIENCE AT SATURN

The 5.7 tonne NASA Cassini spacecraft which carried the Huygens probe has, meanwhile, continued its own highly-successful exploration of Saturn and its satellites following insertion into orbit around the ringed planet on 1 July 2004. The Huygens results have been, and will continue to be, augmented by close passages to Titan, allowing infrared mapping of surface features. In February 2005, Cassini revealed the presence of a large (440 km diameter) impact crater on Titan. The spacecraft has also revealed complex layering in Titan's atmosphere.

On 9 March 2005, Cassini made a close (500 km) fly-by of Enceladus, imaging the satellite's grooved and cratered surface in unprecedented detail. Unexpectedly, Enceladus was found to possess a significant water vapour atmosphere, revealed through its interaction with Saturn's magnetosphere. With a diameter of only 500 km, Enceladus is too small to retain its atmosphere over long periods of time; the implication is, therefore, that this has to be continuously replenished by volcanic activity, geysers, or other mechanisms of gas release from the satellite. Rhea, with a diameter of 1530 km the second-largest of Saturn's satellites, has also been imaged in detail, showing a heavily-cratered surface with possible ice cliffs.

Some of the mission's most remarkable results so far have come from the Iapetus encounter on 31 December 2004, at a distance of 123,000 km. The 1400-km diameter satellite has a dark hemisphere, leading in the direction of its orbital motion around Saturn, and a lighter trailing side. Wispy structure imaged by Cassini in the dark material suggest that this was deposited on the surface, rather than extruded from Iapetus' interior. A ridge of mountains was discovered, extending along the equator for 1300 km (a third of Iapetus' circumference), and at points reaching heights of 20 km, taller than Mars' volcanic peak Olympus Mons.

Study of the famous ring system shows little change in overall structure since the 1980–1 Voyager encounters. Small-scale changes, however, point to the rings' relative youth, consistent with the idea that they resulted from disruption of a satellite or other small body passing close to Saturn within the past few hundreds of millions of years.

The planet is surrounded by a cloud of hydrogen to a distance of 2.6 million km, with a smaller cloud of oxygen closer in: this tenuous envelope results from dissociation of water molecules following collisions between small icy bodies in the rings.

Saturn itself has been studied by Cassini's instruments, confirming that, like Jupiter, the planet has powerful lightning storms in its atmosphere. Storm systems with wind-speeds up to 1800 km/h have been imaged.

Cassini's mission is scheduled to continue until at least 2008 (a total of 45 orbits around Saturn), with several more close fly-bys expected to reveal much more about this distant world and its icy satellites. The results already obtained represent a considerable step forward, and the mission is widely hailed as a resounding success.

MALARIA VACCINE QUEST CONTINUES

Malaria remains a major world health problem, with an estimated 2.2 billion people exposed to the disease. A study of global distribution of the most serious form, caused by the protozoan parasite *Plasmodium falciparum,* published in *Nature* in March 2005, suggests that over 500 million clinical episodes occurred in 2002 – 50 per cent more than previously estimated by the World Health Organisation. Most cases (about 70 per cent) occurred in sub-Saharan Africa, but a significant proportion (25 per cent) were in south-east Asia. The risk of death following an attack is greatest for those in poor African countries.

Efforts to produce an effective malaria vaccine continue. Results so far with 'subunit' vaccines, using isolated *P. falciparum* proteins produced by recombinant DNA biotechnological methods, have been disappointing. However, another approach based on genetically-manipulated attenuated parasites, has given some encouraging results in studies using the rodent malaria *P. berghei.*

Plasmodium species have a complex life cycle. In humans, infection follows injection of sporozoites from the salivary glands of *Anopheles* mosquitoes when they feed on the host's blood. Sporozoites invade liver cells, undergoing morphological changes which result in merozoites that are capable, in turn, of invading red blood cells. A vaccine capable of preventing sporozoite invasion would limit the risks of malarial infection. Experiments as long ago as the 1940s showed that inoculation with irradiated sporozoites was effective in reducing infection. Irradiated sporozoites are delivered to liver cells, but do not go on to produce full-blown infection. Proteins essential to stimulating the immune response are, however, present on the surface of sporozoite-containing liver cells. A vaccine based on irradiated sporozoites is, unfortunately, unfeasible due to the risk of even a small number surviving intact.

An alternative approach developed by Ann-Kristin Mueller (Heidelberg University School of Medicine) and colleagues exploits the availability of the recently-completed Plasmodium genome sequence. Expression profiling studies were used to identify genes active only in the early stages of the parasite's development in the mammalian host. Among these, UIS3 (Upregulated in Infective Sporozoites 3) was found to be essential for early liver-stage development following invasion. UIS3 encodes a small membrane protein of as-yet undetermined function. Studies in rats showed that sporozoites of

genetically modified *P. berghei* in which the UIS3 gene was deleted could successfully invade liver cells, but were unable to develop into later, blood-invasive forms.

In mice, the attenuated *P. berghei* conferred immunity against subsequent infection with genetically intact, wild-type sporozoites, effective for at least two months; long-term immunity is dependent on continued expression of parasite proteins on liver cell membranes.

The *P. berghei* UIS3 gene has an equivalent in the human parasite *P. falciparum,* and these results offer the hope that an attenuated, live malaria vaccine could be developed in the future. Several problems remain, however, not least the difficulty of producing the genetically modified sporozoites in sufficient quantity for large-scale vaccination programmes.

SCIENTISTS INVESTIGATE DECEMBER 2004 EARTHQUAKE AND TSUNAMI

Geophysical events surrounding the 26 December 2004 earthquake that caused the tsunami which brought about devastation and enormous loss of life in coastal regions around the Indian Ocean, have been closely studied by scientists. The earthquake measured 9.3 on the Richter scale, making it the largest since that in Prince William Sound, Alaska, in 1964.

Earthquakes occur most commonly in areas where tectonic plates – 'rafts' of Earth's crust which move slowly over the underlying semi-fluid mantle – collide. One (oceanic) plate is usually forced below the other (continental), a process called subduction. Jerky motions of the subducting plate lead to earthquakes and a folding of the crust. The December 2004 earthquake resulted from a sudden lurch northwards of the Indian plate as this continues to be subducted below the Burma microplate. Measurements indicate that some of the Islands carried along by the Indian plate may have moved their position by up to 20 metres. Sonar measurements of the seafloor, obtained from HMS *Scott,* reveal a new deep ocean trench and several new ridges where the crust has 'crumpled'; rock- and mud-slides from existing ridges are also evident.

The earthquake had its epicentre just west of Aceh, Indonesia, at a depth of about 35 km below the seafloor. The initial shock involved three abrupt movements of the sea floor over an interval of a few seconds, causing the Burma microplate to spring upwards violently by about ten metres. This movement displaced water in the overlying ocean to produce a long, low-amplitude wave radiating from the epicentre at about 900 km/h. As it reached shallower water, the wave reared up in amplitude, with catastrophic consequences in Indonesia and Thailand within an hour of the earthquake, and later for Sri Lanka and parts of southern India, and eventually for Somalia in eastern Africa.

A second earthquake, reaching 7.5 on the Richter scale, occurred north-west of the first about four hours later. The overall result has been a rupture in the Earth's crust over a faultline some 1200 km long. Geophysicists believe this has dissipated much of the stress which has been building up along the fault since the previous major earthquakes along it in 1833. It remains a matter of concern, however, that stress may remain on two large faults to the south.

The major loss of life resulting from the tsunami has led to calls for an early warning system in the Indian Ocean, similar to that in the Pacific. Buoys could be used to detect any post-earthquake wave while this is still in deep water, perhaps allowing evacuation of endangered coastal regions. It is hoped that study of the 2004 event will allow more reliable tsunami forecasting in the future. As demonstrated by a Richter scale 8.7 event with an epicentre off north Sumatra on 28 March 2005, not every undersea earthquake necessarily triggers a major tsunami, but there is a clear desire to better understand the process in the hope that any future disaster can be averted as far as possible.

MARS ROVERS ROLL ON

The NASA Mars Exploration Rovers *Spirit* and *Opportunity* have far exceeded their projected working lifetimes since landing successfully on the Red Planet in January 2004. Originally expected to operate for a nominal 90 days, the Rovers survived the harsh local winter conditions at their respective landing sites at Gusev Crater and Meridiani Planum on opposite sides of Mars, and continue to provide new and interesting data well over a year after their solar panels were expected to become too laden with dust to provide sufficient power. Indeed, mission scientists have been pleasantly surprised to find that the power generation efficiency of the solar panels has actually recovered, following the anticipated initial decline. Some mechanism – perhaps electrostatic, or simply the action of Martian surface winds – appears to have cleared the solar panels of dust. The Rovers' missions have been extended until at least September 2006, but mechanical failures will eventually bring these to an end: *Spirit,* for example, has one 'dragging' wheel.

Results from *Spirit* and *Opportunity* have spectacularly confirmed the past existence of bodies of standing water on the Martian surface, a finding given acclaim as the discovery of the year by the American journal *Science* in its review of 2004. Ever since the 1971 Mariner 9 orbiter mission, scientists have been aware of water outflow features on Mars' surface, but the extent and longevity of larger past bodies of water on the planet has been controversial. In the Columbia Hills, some 3–4 km east of its landing site, *Spirit* has been used to investigate rock outcrops showing layering, strongly suggestive of sedimentary processes which can only have occurred in a lake or shallow sea. Fine layering has also been found in rocks at the 20–30 metre wide Eagle Crater, and the larger (100–150 metre) Endurance Crater nearby by *Opportunity,* evidence that this part of Meridiani Planum was under water 3–4 billion years ago. How long the water was present remains a matter of debate: some scientists think it may have been there for at least 250,000 years, and that the northern hemisphere of Mars could have been covered by a vast ocean.

In late December 2004, *Opportunity* was directed to inspect the area where its ejected heat shield came down. During this exploration, a half-metre diameter iron meteorite was found lying on the Martian surface nearby – the first such discovery on a planet other than Earth.

EVIDENCE FOR RECENT MARTIAN WATER

While *Spirit* and *Opportunity* have been spectacularly successful in exploring Mars on the surface, NASA's orbiting Mars Global Surveyor and Mars Odyssey, and ESA's Mars Express, have also continued their missions, returning a wealth of detailed images and other data. The detection, with Mars Express' Planetary Fourier Spectrometer, of trace quantities (10 parts per billion) of methane in the Martian atmosphere adds to the ongoing debate as to whether the planet may harbour life: the methane could be of microbial origin, but volcanic or even cometary sources can also account for its presence, and most scientists are sceptical of this as a biological signature.

The High Resolution Stereo Camera (HRSC) aboard Mars Express has provided evidence of volcanic activity having occurred as recently as two million years ago. Associated with this are clear signs of comparatively recent glacial activity due to water released by eruptions within the past five million years – showing that not all water-related features on Mars are very ancient. HRSC images show a region on the Elysium plain in which a North Sea sized body of water was released then froze. Structures believed to be ice floes, covered in volcanic ash and thus insulated against evaporation and sublimation in the tenuous Martian atmosphere, are clearly visible. Mars Odyssey results have already shown the presence of water ice as permafrost on the planet, and in its next phase of the operation Mars Express will further map this using the Mars Advanced Radar for Subsurface and Ionospheric Sounding (MARSIS) instrument.

HUMAN X CHROMOSOME SEQUENCE

Published in March 2005, the work of a multinational research team has led to a largely complete sequence of the human X chromosome. Totalling 155 million basepairs of DNA, the X chromosome encodes 1098 identified genes. Large quantities of repeated sequence presented some difficulties; 14 gaps remain, but 99.3 per cent of the chromosome sequence has been reliably determined.

In mammals, sex is determined by the X and Y chromosomes. Males have one (maternal) X and one (paternal) Y chromosome, while females have two X chromosomes. The X and Y chromosomes are believed to have arisen as independent genetic elements (autosomes) around 300 million years ago. Over evolutionary time, the Y chromosome has decreased in size, now containing fewer than a hundred functional genes.

Early in female development, expression and binding of a large RNA (encoded by the *XIST* gene) leads to permanent inactivation of one copy of the X chromosome in a given cell line – this may be either the paternal or maternal X, resulting in a mixture (mosaic). Patterns of gene expression in females have been studied using a mouse cell system, into which human X chromosomes can be introduced. An investigation by Laura Carrel (Pennsylvania State University) and Huntington F. Willard (Duke University), using skin cells from 40 women donors, revealed that *XIST* silencing permanently turns off 75 per cent of X chromosome genes in the inactivated copy, but that 15 per cent escape this effect (meaning that, in females, these genes are expressed at twice the levels found in males, who have only a single copy). For the remaining 10 per cent of genes, expression levels varied from individual to individual.

Inactivation by *XIST* may be reinforced by repetitive sequences in the X chromosome DNA, and appears to be most effective for those genes with the longest evolutionary history.

Given the significance of clinical disorders specific to the X chromosome in males (haemophilia and Duchenne muscular dystrophy are among several X-linked diseases), availability of a more complete DNA sequence and improved understanding of gene expression patterns represent important steps forward. Evolutionary biologists are also keen to compare the human X chromosome with those of other species.

BACK TO THE MOON THE SLOW WAY

ESA's SMART-1 spacecraft, launched on an Ariane 5 rocket in September 2003, finally entered the Moon's gravitational sphere on 15 November 2004 (two months earlier than originally scheduled) following a long series of outwards-spiralling orbits around Earth. Designed principally to test new technology, SMART-1 uses a xenon gas propulsion system powered by solar panels. SMART-1 used 59 kg out of its 82 kg propellant reserves in getting to the Moon, leaving plenty for subsequent manoeuvres. These will insert the spacecraft into an elliptical 300 × 3000 km polar orbit, with its lowest point (perilune) over the Moon's southern hemisphere. Imaging and geological mapping will be carried out in a mission which has now been extended until August 2006. One aim is to verify the presence of water ice deposits in permanently-shaded craters at the Moon's south pole, first indicated by NASA's Clementine probe in 1994. With a relatively small launch mass of 367 kg, SMART-1 has already been a success in proving the usefulness of ion propulsion for long interplanetary cruises, and as a test-bed for miniaturised instrumentation.

GIANT STELLAR OUTBURST

At 21 30 GMT on 27 December 2004, detectors aboard several astronomical satellites recorded the most intense gamma ray burst ever witnessed. The source was a rapidly rotating neutron star (a supernova remnant) at an estimated distance of 50,000 light years in our galaxy, lying in the direction of the constellation Sagittarius. SGR 1806-20 is one of four known *magnetars*; such stars are among the most strongly magnetised objects in the universe. Its designation indicates its nature as a Soft Gamma Ray Repeater, producing frequent X- and gamma ray bursts.

The extremely intense December 2004 gamma ray burst is believed to have resulted from a catastrophic collapse of the star's outer crust, leading in turn to a sudden, major rearrangement of its magnetic field. Measurements obtained from the RHESSI (Reuven Ramaty High Energy Solar Spectroscopic Imager) and INTEGRAL (International Gamma-Ray Astrophysics Laboratory) satellites show that during the first 0.2 second of the burst, SGR 1806-20 leased as much energy as the Sun does in 250,000 years. The burst was preceded (142 seconds earlier) by a smaller event, and had a long declining tail lasting for 380 seconds. Oscillations in the burst's tail showed the known 7.56 seconds rotation period of the star. Increased activity had been noted since March 2004, perhaps suggesting a build-up towards the December event.

The gamma ray burst also briefly affected Earth's ionosphere. A sudden ionospheric disturbance was detected by enhanced VHF radio reception.

Described as a once-in-a-lifetime event of its kind, the 27 December 27 2004 SGR 1806-20 has already been the subject of numerous scientific papers. Astronomers will be keeping the object under close scrutiny in times ahead.

STEM CELL BREAKTHROUGHS BRING THERAPEUTIC CLONING CLOSER

Embryonic stem (ES) cells, which have the ability and can be chemically-induced to differentiate to produce a range of tissue types, are seen by many as a possible great step forward in the treatment of diseases. Replacement of damaged tissue with patient-specific cells grown from ES cells could, for example, eventually be developed as an effective treatment for some forms of spinal injury or diabetes. Growth of ES cells for these purposes would involve a process of 'therapeutic cloning', where a donor oocyte (egg cell) has its nucleus replaced by that of a cell

from the patient, and is then chemically stimulated to develop as a blastocyst. After five days, ES cells can be harvested and cultured.

The cloning procedure is not without its difficulties, but work by Woo Suk Hwang and Shin Yong Moon of Seoul National University, South Korea, reported in *Science* in May 2005, indicates significant progress. Previous work, using 'spare' oocytes available after infertility treatment, yielded only a single successful nuclear transfer in 200 attempts. In the new research, this has been improved to one success in 20 attempts. An important factor appears to be the age of the oocyte donor, greatest success being found with those from women aged under 30 years. Hwang and Moon *et al* introduced skin cell nuclei from 11 patients, affected variously by spinal cord injury, juvenile diabetes and congenital hypogammaglobulinaemia, via their process of Somatic Cell Nuclear Transfer (SCNT). The resulting ES cells were shown to be pluripotent (capable of development into a variety of tissue types), have normal chromosomes, and to be immunologically compatible with the patients – this last a vital requirement for transplantation.

Important progress has also been made by the South Korean workers in using human, rather than mouse, feeder cells in the propagation of ES cell lines. Some animal products (for example foetal calf serum, collagenase and trypsin) are still required, but elimination of these reduces the likelihood of xenograft contamination.

ES cells derived from patients carrying a genetic defect will, of course, be of no value in treatment. Such cell lines can, however, be studied to allow more detailed understanding of genetic diseases. Anticipated future developments may allow repair or replacement of defective genes at cellular level, producing 'corrected' lines for transplantation back to the patient.

In the United States, ethical barriers currently forbid federally funded research on ES cell lines produced later than August 2001, but polls show increasing public support in the USA for the therapeutic use of ES cells. A May 2005 vote in the House of Representatives, favouring the lifting of restrictions, offers some hope to American researchers. If passed at Senate level, however, the decision to allow such work is still subject to presidential veto.

SLIME MOULD SEQUENCE

The slime mould *Dictyostelium discoideum* has, for over half a century, been a widely used model organism for laboratory studies of cell motility and differentiation. Found naturally in habitats such as forest floors where it feeds on bacteria and yeasts, *Dictyostelium* can exist as a unicellular form, or as a multicellular 'social amoeba'. Under conditions of nutrient starvation, cells within the multicellular form undergo specific alterations to produce a fruiting body structure comprising a ball of spores supported by a stalk.

Concentrated efforts to decipher the *Dictyostelium* genome began in 1998, leading to publication of a greater than 95 per cent complete version in May 2005. Distributed over six chromosomes, *D. discoideum* has a total genome of 34 million basepairs of DNA, containing a large number of repeats. A predicted 12,500 proteins are encoded, similar to the total expected for multicellular eukaryotes; the complexity is higher than that of yeasts, for example. In evolutionary terms, *Dictyostelium* appears to have diverged from the animal-fungal eukaryotic lineage after the animal-plant divergence occurred.

THEATRE

THE CHANGING FORTUNES OF WEST END MUSICALS

There's nothing like a rousing musical for lifting people's spirits and last year saw three spectacular productions injecting new life into a troubled West End. The tide turned as high seat prices, crumbling buildings, lack of leg room, inadequate air conditioning, overpriced drinks, a scarcity of female toilets, and the hated booking fee didn't stop people queuing as soon as booking opened to buy tickets for *The Producers, Mary Poppins* and *Billy Elliot the Musical.* As a result, 2004 turned out to be a bumper year for the West End with a 3 per cent rise in audiences on the previous year and a 6 per cent rise in income.

The Producers, which opened in New York in 2001, took its time to cross the Atlantic but proved well worth the wait. Mel Brooks adapted and expanded his 1968 cult film in which Max Bialystock, the Broadway producer, and his new accountant, Leo Bloom, indulge in a showbiz scam based on Bialystock's improbable calculation that there are ways of making a flop more lucrative than a hit. The show they choose to produce is *Springtime for Hitler,* a celebration of the life of the German leader and guaranteed to be a tasteless disaster. In London, Richard Dreyfuss – not well known for his singing and dancing - was initially cast in the role of Bialystock. Just before the show opened at the Theatre Royal Drury Lane, however, Dreyfuss appeared on *The Frank Skinner Show* on TV and warned viewers that the show was unlikely to be up to scratch until after Christmas, several months after the opening. Dreyfuss was clearly feeling the physical strain of rehearsals and complained that director Susan Stroman was demanding more than he could possibly give. The real producers did not appreciate his comments. A week later his departure from the show was announced and Nathan Lane, the original Max on Broadway, was persuaded to replace him, to the joy of those who had already seen Lane in New York.

Lane and Lee Evans as the goofy accountant, Bloom, proved perfect partners in a show which is determinedly old-fashioned in its love of corny jokes and long-legged beauties, and politically incorrect in finding Nazis and gays equally funny. The pair had worked together before on the film *Mouse Hunt* and Max's feigned, over-the-top heart attack response to Bloom's innocent enquiry about how much money the producer would be investing in his own production was a show-stopping moment. There were other delights: the chorus of old ladies on zimmer frames; Conleth Hill as the cross-dressing, terrible director forced to step in and play Hitler in his own production; and a racing pigeon that gave a Nazi salute. Altogether they put the comedy back into the musical genre that has become very serious in the last twenty years.

The Producers caters for adults. *Mary Poppins* is more of a show for children, although one scary scene meant that it was not recommended for those under seven. This was the dream project of producer Cameron Mackintosh, who first showed an interest in acquiring the stage rights of P. L. Travers' books fifteen years ago. Losing out then, he finally persuaded Travers to give him the go-ahead in 1996. Mackintosh's challenge was to stay true to the books and yet not to disappoint those who love the 1964 Disney film with Julie Andrews, which is a good deal more sentimental than its source. Julian Fellowes, who won an Oscar for the script of *Gosford Park,* was asked to write the book, and composer George Stiles and the lyricist Anthony Drewe were brought in to adapt the Disney songs to fit the stage show and also to write new ones of their own. Richard Eyre, one-time artistic director of the National Theatre and responsible for the National's glorious production of *Guys and Dolls* directed, Bob Crowley designed, and Matthew Bourne and Stephen Mear were the outstanding choreographers. Laura Michelle Kelly, who, like Julie Andrews before her, had made her mark as Eliza Doolittle in *My Fair Lady,* was cast as Mary Poppins. The team came up with a musical that dwelt on a dysfunctional family that desperately needed the healing powers of their strange and unpredictable nanny. Two worlds were created. One in which a man must put childish things aside to go to the office and earn enough to pay for his family's needs; in which appearances must be upheld; and children seen and not heard. And another, in which imagination rules: putty coloured statues wriggle their hips; fathers fly kites with their children; and chimney sweeps and market traders are far better company than their social superiors. David Haig as Mr Banks was outstanding as the bank manager who still fears his nanny of twenty years ago – the formidable and villainous Miss Andrews, who in an unequal battle with Mary Poppins is forced to drink her own brimstone and treacle. Kelly's Mary Poppins slid up the banisters and magically produced a bed and a coat stand out of her black bag. In a spectacular climax, she and the children leapt among the chimney pots and Gavin Lee's Bert tap danced upside down across the top of the proscenium arch while singing *Step in Time.* Finally, her job done, Mary Poppins floated away above the heads of the audience waved off by the children.

These days it's more common for a film to be turned into a stage show – as in the case of *Mary Poppins* – rather than the other way round. It's unusual, however, for the original creative team to do both. But when Elton John saw the film of *Billy Elliot* at Cannes, he was eager to work with scriptwriter Lee Hall and director Stephen Daldry on transforming their film into a musical. *Billy Elliot* is the story of a young boy from a mining background in the north-east, whose mother has recently died, whose father and brother are miners, and who quite by chance discovers a talent for dance. Against the backdrop of the miners' strike in the early 1980s, he is encouraged by his dance teacher to apply for a place at the Royal Ballet School in London. Hall and John created a very British musical, which contrasted the communal values of the miners as they fight for their jobs with Billy's very individual talent. The production was complicated by the fact that no child is allowed to perform more than three times a week. So it was essential to find three young boys with the spectacular dancing and acting skills needed to carry the burden of a major show. In addition, as there are other children in the show and because of the need to accommodate the different dancing styles and musical range of the different boys, it was decided to create three different companies of twenty. Since each child is only allowed to play for six months, a school was set up in Leeds in order to track down and train further performers for the future. In the stage show, Billy's need for self-expression and the doomed struggle of the miners were skilfully woven together, most especially when the miners and police merged into the dancing class where Haydn Gwynne as the disillusioned teacher struggled to put a group of podgy, untalented girls through their paces. Elton John's score draws powerfully on union anthems, hymns and northern folk songs. The show suggests that everyone needs to express themselves; even Ann Emery's grandma shook an ancient leg while heaping abuse on her dead husband.

In such a year, Andrew Lloyd Webber's musical version of Wilkie Collins's 19th-century novel *The Woman in White* struggled for attention at the Palace. The young playwright Charlotte Jones was asked to adapt the novel, which is exceptionally long with a complicated plot full of melodramatic twists. She cleverly filleted the novel, making a central character out of Marian, noted for her spirit and intelligence rather than her beauty – Collins gives her a moustache – and played onstage by Maria Friedman. Collins' tale hinges on a dastardly plan by a young man and his accomplice to steal his wife's inheritance and have her locked up in an asylum. Sharing some similarities with *The Phantom of the Opera,* Lloyd Webber's music and David Zippel's lyrics had plenty to recommend them, and Michael Crawford in an inflated costume excelled as the villainous Italian Count Fosco who always travelled with his menagerie of rats. The major problem of Trevor Nunn's production was the set by William Dudley, which exploited revolutionary computer imaging in order to sweep the characters from one location to the next. Used in moderation it might have been effective but, endlessly on the move, it managed to make some members of the audience feel decidedly queasy.

In June, *Guys and Dolls* brought Ewan McGregor back to the stage in the role of Sky Masterson, much to the delight of his fans. Michael Grandage's production at the Piccadilly was very different and on a smaller scale than Richard Eyre's famous 1982 production at the National but in many ways just as effective. The hoods' suits were scruffier and the Hot Box seedier. Jane Krakowski made a delightful Miss Adelaide desperately trying to get Douglas Hodge's panicky Nathan Detroit to the altar. Rob Ashford's choreography was sensational, especially when the gamblers, who came in all shapes and sizes, played their card game beneath the sidewalk while pirouetting and leaping as if trying to give Billy Elliot a run for his money.

In a bumper year for musicals, Victoria Wood adapted *Acorn Antiques* for the stage with Julie Walters returning to play Mrs Overall. Ticket prices set a new record but Wood and Walters' fans were not to be deterred. There was also a landmark event when the first musical based on a British black experience transferred from the Theatre Royal Stratford East to Shaftesbury Avenue. Loosely inspired by *Love's Labour's Lost* with book and music by Paul Sirett and Paul Joseph, it described the experiences of a group of West Indian immigrants who arrive in London with high hopes and discover that they are not quite as welcome as they had anticipated. The combination of ska music and some fine performances made it a triumph for Stratford East and its policy of nurturing musical writers based on contemporary street music.

HOLLYWOOD SPARKLE

While the musicals thrived, straight plays didn't have such an easy ride. Producers continued to look to America to provide the stars to give them a sporting chance at the box office. Christian Slater appeared in the hugely successful *One Flew over the Cuckoo's Nest.* Holly Hunter was less fortunate in the strangely named *By the Bog of Cats* and *Friends* star David Schwimmer failed to make much impact in Neil LaBute's strangely subdued *Some Girl(s).* It was entirely fitting, however, that shortly after the death of Arthur Miller, one of the playwriting giants of the 20th century, the award-winning Broadway production of *Death of a Salesman* arrived in London with a cast headed by Brian Dennehy. He was an unusual Willy Loman, the deluded salesman who buys so fervently into the American dream, in that he is more often than not played by a small man – Dustin Hoffman and Warren Mitchell have both excelled in the role in the past. Dennehy, however, is huge. The contrast between his physical strength and his mental delusions made his collapse all the more powerful. Out of the West End at the Almeida, Gael Garcia Bernal appeared in Rufus Norris's production of *Blood Wedding* by the Spanish playwright, Lorca. It's a difficult play which combines symbolic characters such as the Moon and Death with the realism of a wedding at which a local married man, played by Bernal, runs away with the bride with disastrous results. The production was sold out before it opened because of Bernal's reputation, but he proved to have little presence on stage and was outclassed by the rest of the cast, who responded to a production which for once managed to marry the different styles successfully.

HOMEGROWN STARS

But a homegrown star headed the most unexpected hit in the West End. Derek Jacobi played the King of Spain in Michael Grandage's production of Schiller's *Don Carlos,* a transfer from the Sheffield Crucible and Grandage's final production there as artistic director. Schiller's 18th-century play portrays a clash between revolutionary idealism and catholic conservatism but in Grandage's hands it came across as an exciting, gripping thriller. Jacobi was fascinating as the isolated king who violently rejects his son's pleas to be trusted. He was in steely, magnificent form, easily able to dominate his poisonous ministers but not totally invulnerable. Christopher Oram's imposing sombre set was pierced by Paule Constable's lighting, which streamed through the high, barred windows without ever penetrating the corners where treacherous plots were hatched.

Where there were no stars, the West End invariably leaned on the imagination and talent of the subsidised theatre. *Hedda Gabler,* first seen at the Almeida, was given a tight production by Richard Eyre in which Eve Best played the driven, unhappy Hedda. *Losing Louis* by Simon Mendes da Costa made its mark at Hampstead before fitting in comfortably at the Trafalgar Studio where the comedy about fathers and sons, success and failure, settled in for a comfortable run with Alison Steadman and David Horovitch in leading roles.

SPACEY AND THE OLD VIC

At the Old Vic, Kevin Spacey launched his first season as artistic director. The actor first appeared at the famous theatre in the Cut in *The Iceman Cometh* in 1998. He fell in love with the building and its history, made a substantial donation and was invited to join the board. As the theatre struggled to find a role for itself – there were rumours that it would be turned into a lap dancing venue – Spacey decided to take on the running of the building himself with the full backing of the board. He was taking on a huge task as the Old Vic is not subsidised and vast sums had to be raised. The TV executive David Liddiment was brought in as executive director. When others expressed doubts, Spacey insisted that he was fully committed to the project although he always made it clear that he had no intention of giving up his film career. From the Old Vic's point of view it's important that he doesn't since it's the films that give him the star status that attracts people to the theatre.

The season opened with a Dutch play *Cloaca* by Maria Goos, a playwright unknown in Britain, directed by Spacey himself. The play's title, meaning 'sewer', came to haunt Spacey's unremarkable production. The cast of Hugh Bonneville, Stephen Tompkinson, Neil Pearson and Adrian Lukis couldn't make much of a tiresome tale of the men's midlife crises. Then, when Spacey went off to fulfil his long-cherished project of making a film about the life of Bobby Darin, Sean Mathias and Ian McKellen moved in to present *Aladdin,* a Christmas panto, which was big on charm and short on spectacle but made fascinating by McKellen's relish of his cross-dressing role as the Dame. But then the season ran aground again with Dennis McIntyre's *National Anthems* in which Spacey had appeared in the US as a young actor. Once again his choice of script, which seemed very dated, failed to connect with a British audience in spite of a brilliant performance by Spacey as the fantasist who visits a materialistic couple who find his behaviour unnerving. Even *The Philadelphia Story,* which seemed like a banker, failed to please the critics. Memories of the film clouded the stage as Spacey took the Cary Grant role and Jennifer Ehle played Katharine Hepburn. Matters weren't improved when Spacey left shortly after the play opened to take part in another film, leaving Adrian Lukis with the unenviable task of replacing him. But if Spacey has struggled in his first season to build a bridge between his own culture and that of London, he may have better luck in the autumn when he will play Richard II in Trevor Nunn's production of Shakespeare's play. It also has to be said that theatregoers remained loyal and complained on the internet that Spacey was being given too hard a time.

OTHER LONDON PRODUCTIONS

In the wake of the Iraq War and the events of September 11th, London theatre has become increasingly political. This can take the form of going back to the Greeks, who knew only too well about the bloodiness and corruption of war, or of new work with a political theme, or of the increasingly popular verbatim theatre – theatre drawn from factual events and using the words of those involved. David Hare's *Stuff Happens* was a mix of the last two, and a major event at the National Theatre. Scrupulously directed by Nicholas Hytner, Hare's play looked at the sequences of events in the West leading up to the war in Iraq. It recreated the conversations that took place in the White House, the UN and Downing Street as Bush, Rumsfeld and Cheney pushed for a military solution and Blair tried to persuade them to obtain the backing of the UN first. Nobody comes out of it well. Colin Powell is shown as having the best understanding of how the rest of the world views the US but he fails to pursue his case. Most interestingly, Bush is not presented as a fool but as a cunning adroit operator who keeps his cards close to his chest. It would be safe to say that most members of the

audience at the National Theatre were not in favour of the Iraq War but if they came hoping to laugh at the politicians, they discovered a much more serious, balanced piece that was only occasionally satirical.

By comparison, Tim Robbins' *Embedded* was a comic strip that seemed increasingly dated and childish. *My Name is Rachel Corrie* at the Royal Court was based on the edited diaries and emails of the 23-year-old American woman who was killed by an Israeli bulldozer in Palestine in 2003. The production by Alan Rickman, with Megan Dodds as Corrie proved so powerful in the Theatre Upstairs that it is planned to bring it down to the main house in the autumn. The Royal Court also staged Out of Joint's production of *Talking to Terrorists,* a sweeping account of those involved in terrorism from the people who commit the atrocities to those who pick up the pieces. It opened in the same week that a series of bombs in London killed over fifty people. For very good and understandable reasons, writer Robin Soans, director Max Stafford-Clark and his company of actors were only ever able to speak to ex-terrorists who inevitably felt that they were fighting against injustice. After the bomb outrages of July, however, it seemed that it would be better to talk to those in danger of being swayed by al-Qa'eda (assuming that it was responsible for the bombs) rather than al-Qa'eda itself, whose members seem to be fuelled by an irrational hatred.

At the Tricycle, the home of meticulously presented tribunal theatre, Nicolas Kent and Richard Norton-Taylor filleted months and months of evidence that had been given to the Saville Enquiry, charged with investigating what happened on Bloody Sunday in 1972 when 13 people were killed. Once again the production showed that there's nothing like the experience of sharing with others the details of the most crucial investigations of the last few years over a single evening.

Joe Penhall's *Dumb Show* could also come under the heading of political theatre in that it was an attack on the tabloid press. A comedian whose career and marriage are tottering perilously on the edge falls into the sweet, sticky tentacles of a pair of tabloid hacks. Douglas Hodge played the comedian, his crumpled face the perfect picture of a gullible man who has never grown up and is eager to be in the limelight. Penhall doesn't agree with those who say that the red tops' revelations are just harmless fun. But underscoring his play is the fact that the demands of the newspapers, stars and public are all intertwined.

Many of these productions were preaching to the converted. While that can lead to a certain complacency, there were worrying signs of a determination by a variety of religious groups to condemn freedom of speech on stage. The tour of *Jerry Springer the Opera* was postponed because of protests from the Christian right who had objected vociferously when the show was televised. Birmingham Rep, which has a good record in involving all the different communities that make up the city, ran into trouble when it presented *Behzti* by Gurpreet Kaur Bhatti, a young Sikh writer. The script was shown to local Sikh leaders in advance who were appalled by its presentation of sexual abuse in the Sikh place of worship. For reasons of public safety, the run was cancelled when a demonstration of 400 protesters tried to storm the theatre. Some theatres offered to stage the production instead but the playwright withheld her consent. Nicholas Hytner, the National Theatre's artistic director, called on everyone to stand firmly by the principle of free speech. The government failed to take such a stand, pleading instead for the feelings of a minority community to be understood. Others pointed out that Kaur Bhatti, as a young female Sikh, was a member of a more minority group than Sikhs as a whole.

SHAKESPEARE PLAYS

Shakespeare proliferated as ever. Although, oddly, the RSC had a greater success with Shakespeare's contemporaries at Stratford than it did with the man himself. Many RSC Shakespeare productions have been of interest, but none has really caught the imagination. Still, the company managed to pay off its £2.8m deficit, and announced ambitious plans to stage an international season presenting all of Shakespeare's plays next year. Three productions of *Macbeth* hit London within weeks of each other. At the Almeida, Simon Russell Beale gave an intensely intelligent interior performance as the bloody Scotsman but was let down by a production that moved at a snail's pace. In complete contrast, Max Stafford-Clark for Out of Joint took over first the Arcola and then Wilton's Music Hall for a promenade production set in Africa. The production drew on some of that continent's bloodiest wars and also on the superstitions that send men into battle wearing women's wigs. Danny Sapani played Macbeth as an Idi Amin character egged on by his white wife. In contrast, the RSC production by Dominic Cook at the Albery was relatively conventional.

It's some time now since the RSC left the Barbican and, following the success of the arts centre's international seasons, there are plenty of people wanting to fill the space. Much anticipated was Deborah Warner's production of *Julius Caesar* with Ralph Fiennes as Mark Antony, Simon Russell Beale improbably cast as 'the lean and hungry' Cassius, and a mix of local people and professionals playing the Roman crowd. Big cast plays are rare these days for reasons of cost and there was a real excitement when over a hundred people rushed down the massive marble steps and onto the stage. But for once the intensely moving second half of the play overshadowed the first as the conspirators were forced to confront their failures and prepared to kill themselves.

A new theatre was opened based, like Shakespeare's Globe, on the open-staged intimacy of the original Globe but without the intrusive pillars. Down in Kingston, Peter Hall has been invited to be artistic director of the new Rose, which will link up with Kingston University to run courses as well as produce plays – provided the necessary funds can be raised. In a brave move, Hall brought his production of *As You Like It* to the unfinished space to give audiences and critics a taste of the building. The production, headed by Hall's own daughter, Rebecca, as Rosalind, had been much-praised elsewhere but struggled to adapt to such an intimate relationship with the audience.

Another *As You Like It* opened later in the year in the West End, set in France in the 1940s with Helen McCrory as a heart-stopping Rosalind and tabloid favourite Sienna Miller as Celia. This was a Young Vic production, which is on walkabout while its own theatre is being rebuilt. Shakespeare's Globe had an eccentric season, Mark Rylance's last as artistic director. *The Tempest* in particular was hard to follow since it was staged with just three people. Kathryn Hunter's production of *Pericles* was better received but suffered a blow when Corin Redgrave, who was playing Pericles as an old man, fell ill and had to be replaced.

It was the National, which was otherwise not quite so invincible this year, that came up with the most satisfying Shakespearean productions. Nicholas Hytner directed the two parts of *Henry IV,* making full use of the Olivier's stage to present Shakespeare's richly detailed portrait of an England still suffering the lingering consequences of civil war, in which Prince Hal is torn between two fathers: his real father, the disapproving, guilt-ridden King; and the irresponsible but life-enhancing Falstaff. Performed as part of the Travelex £10 season, scenic budgets were tight but the production was cast to the hilt with John Wood as a wonderful Shallow longingly recalling his mis spent youth, David Bradley as the acid king, Matthew MacFadyen as his unresponsive son, and David Harewood as a rather mature but impressively fiery Hotspur. Most anticipated, however, was Michael Gambon as Falstaff who cut an absurd figure – as round as he was tall, a feather cap on his head and a filthy vest on his body. Gambon never sentimentalised a man who claims the credit for Hotspur's death, sends the weak into battle and is last seen in Part One robbing the corpses of their purses. At the same time, unlike the King, Falstaff's face lit up whenever Hal appeared. It was an epic production of a state of the nation play, which opened just as that same nation was heading to the polls to settle its state today.

THEATRE AWARDS

CRITICS' CIRCLE AWARDS

Best New Play – *The History Boys* by Alan Bennett

Best Musical – *The Producers* by Mel Brooks/Thomas Meehan

Best Director – Rufus Norris for *Festen*

Best Designer – Christopher Oram for *Suddenly Last Summer*

Best Actor – Richard Griffiths for *The History Boys*

Best Actress – Victoria Hamilton for *Suddenly Last Summer*

Most Promising Playwright – Rebecca Lenkiewicz for *The Night Season*

Most Promising Newcomer – Eddie Redmayne for *The Goat, or Who is Sylvia?*

Best Shakespearean Performance – Paul Rhys for *Measure for Measure*

EVENING STANDARD AWARDS

Best Play – *The History Boys* by Alan Bennett

Best Actor – Richard Griffiths for *The History Boys*

Best Actress – Victoria Hamilton for *Suddenly Last Summer*

Best Musical – *The Producers* by Mel Brooks/Thomas Meehan

Best Director – Rufus Norris for *Festen*

Best Designer – Ian MacNeil (set), Jean Kalman (lighting), Paul Arditti (sound) for *Festen*

Outstanding Newcomer – Eddie Redmayne for *The Goat, or Who is Sylvia?*

Special Award – The National Theatre; Harold Pinter; Dame Judi Dench

LAURENCE OLIVIER AWARDS

Best New Play – *The History Boys* by Alan Bennett

Best New Musical –*The Producers* by Mel Brooks/Thomas Meehan

Outstanding Musical Production – *Grand Hotel* by Luther Davis/Robert Wright/George Forrest/Maury Yeston

Best Revival – *Hamlet* by William Shakespeare (Old Vic)

Best Director – Nicholas Hytner for *The History Boys*

Best Designer – Giles Cadle for *His Dark Materials*

Best Lighting Designer – Paule Constable for *His Dark Materials*

Best Sound Design – Mick Potter for *The Woman in White*

Best Choreography – Matthew Bourne/Stephen Mear for *Mary Poppins*

Best Costume Designer – Deirdre Clancey for *All's Well That Ends Well*

Best Actor – Richard Griffiths for *The History Boys*

Best Actress – Clare Higgins for *Hecuba*

Best Supporting Performance – Amanda Harris for *Othello*

Best Actor in a Musical – Nathan Lane for *The Producers*

Best Actress in a Musical – Laura Michelle Kelly for *Mary Poppins*

Best Supporting Performance in a Musical – Conleth Hill for *The Producers*

Outstanding Achievement – Andrew Scott for *A Girl in a Car with a Man*

Special Award – Alan Bennett

WEATHER

JULY 2004

From the 1st to the 4th an area of low pressure drifted across the north of the United Kingdom, giving cyclonic conditions to many parts of England and Wales and bringing some mixed weather. There was 42.4 mm of rain recorded at Boscombe Down in Wiltshire on the 2nd. Another area of low pressure affected southern England on the 4th giving further showery rain, locally heavy and thundery. The 5th and 6th saw high pressure from the west to give most places long sunny periods. Central London recorded a temperature of 25°C on the 6th. From the 7th to the 11th a deepening area of low pressure gave some wet, windy and sometimes thundery weather. This was followed by a showery north-westerly air stream. Wittering near Peterborough recorded 108 mm on the 8th. Gusts in exposed parts of south-west England and South Wales exceeded 60 mph. From the 12th to the 18th a ridge of high pressure developed across the south of the country and more settled conditions followed. A frontal wave developed on the northern flank of the high on the 14th giving rather cloudy and sometimes wet conditions, especially across Wales. The front and its associated waves then spread east on the 17th to give East Anglia and south-east England some heavy and thundery rain. Holbeach in Lincolnshire recorded 25.2 mm in one hour in a heavy shower on the 18th. The 19th to the 23rd saw a fairly diverse pressure pattern which then became established giving some warm sunny spells, but also a scattering of showers, some heavy and thundery; Scampton in Lincolnshire recorded 28.6 mm of rain in just one hour on the 22nd. A high of 27.6°C was reached in central London and Charlwood on the 22nd. Weakening weather fronts drifted into the high from the north at first, giving cloudier and occasionally wet conditions, especially further north. Later in the month the high began to drift eastwards, drawing up some very warm and humid air from the Continent. Central London reached 30.1°C on the 29th, the warmest day of the month.

AUGUST 2004

It was generally sunny on the 1st except in eastern coastal regions, where low cloud and mist was persistent. On the 3rd, 42.4 mm of rain was recorded at High Wycombe in Buckinghamshire in an hour. Temperatures rose on the 7th and 8th – 31.5°C was recorded in Central London and at Northolt respectively, while eastern coasts again had misty low cloud. The hot weather culminated in some warm, sultry nights and at Marham in Norfolk a minimum of 21.9°C was recorded on the morning of the 9th, the warmest night there since at least 1957. Slow-moving fronts and troughs gave an unsettled period during the second week, with prolonged heavy thundery rain or heavy thundery showers. Wittering in West Sussex recorded 90.8 mm on the 10th. The 14th was fine in most places but this was only a temporary respite as Atlantic fronts edging into south-western parts on the 15th heralded another unsettled period. Rain pushed north-east overnight into the 16th followed by some torrential thundery downpours. On the 16th there was devastation in Boscastle in North Cornwall due to severe flooding and

at nearby Otterham 200.4 mm of rain fell in 24 hours. Lesnewth near Boscastle had 64.8 mm of rain in an hour. On the 17th the far west of Cornwall had heavy rain with 58 mm in three hours at Camborne and 31.6 mm in an hour at Culdrose. From the 18th to the 29th low pressure dominated with temperatures generally close to average. Northern England had heavy rain overnight into the 20th and there were thundery showers at Bedford where 41.8 mm of rain was reported. North-west England bore the brunt of the heavy rain on the 25th with 41.6 mm of rain recorded at Manchester Hulme. There were a few drier days, notably the 25th and 28th, while fronts cleared south-east during the 27th. West to north-west winds following in the wake of a low on the 28th brought cooler conditions. The 30th and 31st were rather cool in many places with fresh winds and some showers in the east.

SEPTEMBER 2004

From the 1st to the 5th fine weather was predominant with most parts largely dry and reasonably sunny. On the 5th Cardiff reached 28.6°C, their warmest September day since records began in 1895. The exception to the sunny weather was low cloud and occasional drizzle on western coasts and hills. It was dull and cloudy across northern England and Wales as far south as the Wash, and overnight the cloudy conditions and patchy drizzle extended south. Bright or sunny spells developed on each of the following few days only for low cloud, mist and fog to reform overnight. With the exception of some patchy drizzle (mainly overnight) most parts remained largely dry. However, thundery showers developed across Cornwall on the evening of the 9th, bringing a more unsettled spell of weather. The 10th to the 14th saw more unsettled conditions across England and Wales. Heavy rain, thundery in places, affected Wales and more southern counties during the morning. Despite the rather cloudy skies it was generally warm and locally very warm in the north and east with Keswick reaching 23.3°C. A mixture of clear, sunny spells and showers affected most parts over the following days with occasionally more persistent bands of rain sweeping across the country. The rainfall was particularly heavy across the Welsh mountains on the 12th, with 41.4 mm recorded at Capel Curig in Gwynedd. The 15th and 16th saw a brief respite from the showers with many parts seeing dry weather with sunny spells. Later on the 16th, further rain pushed across more western parts, an indication of more unsettled weather to come. It was rather cloudy through the 17th and 18th with outbreaks of rain and drizzle and some heavier pulses of rain pushed south-eastwards on the 18th. Showers were a feature of the weather from the 19th to the 24th and although some bands pushed eastwards, western parts bore the brunt. Capel Curig in Gwynedd recorded 58 mm of rain on the 19th. It was also windy from the 18th to 23rd with gusts of 55 knots across northern England on the 20th. Despite the unsettled weather it remained rather warm in the south with Wisley recording 21.9°C on the 23rd. With the exception of the 26th, when it was largely dry with clear or sunny spells, skies were overcast through the rest of this period.

Weather fronts brought bands of rain across the country and thundery showers developed on one such weather front across Lincolnshire and Norfolk on the evening of the 28th. Thundery showers also developed across East Anglia and Lincolnshire on the 30th as another weather front cleared eastwards.

OCTOBER 2004

The month began with wet and often very windy weather affecting all areas. Capel Curig in Gwynedd recorded 77.2 mm of rain, with gusts of 58 knots on the 4th. Heavy showers with thunder occurred over North Wales, Merseyside and Norfolk late in the afternoon of the 5th. From the 7th to the 11th the weather settled down as high pressure built across the area, giving 10 hours of sunshine at Hunstanton on the 10th. However low pressure over Biscay started to drift northwards on the 8th, bringing rain into the far south-west on the 9th. The 12th to the 19th saw numerous low pressure areas developing across England and Wales giving some torrential rain in places. Heathrow had 34 mm of rain on the 14th and there was a tornado during the early hours of the morning at Horsham in West Sussex. A slight respite occurred on the 18th, but more rain spread into the south-west during the 19th. From the 20th to the 26th low pressure remained in control with a number of frontal systems moving across the area. It was particularly wet over southern England on the 20th with thunderstorms in places, and over Wales on the 22nd and 23rd, with Capel Curig in Gwynedd recording 65.2 mm of rain on the 22nd and Sennybridge – 40 mm on the 23rd. On the 25th, strong winds affected many areas with gusts of 60 knots at Mumbles and 40–50 knots across southern England. The 27th to the 29th was dominated by a deep area of low pressure centred to the west and south-west of Cornwall. Its central pressure fell on the 27th, bringing severe gales to Devon, Cornwall and South Wales. Gusts of 59 knots were reported from Brixham on the 27th and a tornado occurred at Swanage on the 28th. Heavy rain, spring tides and gale-force south to south-easterly winds brought flooding to many coastal areas of Cornwall, Devon and Dorset. High pressure built in across England and Wales to give a quieter end to the month, however with light winds and clear skies overnight, dense fog patches developed in places.

NOVEMBER 2004

The 1st to the 11th saw a mild start to the month with high pressure in charge. Despite this, an active weather front affected the far south on the 2nd, giving some heavy rain. The high gradually drifted east into the Continent, allowing a weather front to spread south-east across all parts on the 4th. High pressure became established once again, allowing local air frost to develop in the south on the night of the 5th. From the 12th to the 17th the high receded west, allowing a cold front to sweep south across the country. Pressure then built once again, allowing some very sunny days and quite sharp overnight frost. Westerly winds helped to establish milder conditions later in the period. A much colder Arctic airflow developed on the 18th as a succession of fronts spread south and winds swung into the north. Gusty winds and a very sharp temperature drop were experienced on passage of the fronts. Heavy rain readily turned to snow over southern high ground as well as lower ground in the north. Significant snow fell as far south as the Chilterns and 5 cm of lying snow was reported at Cottesmore in Rutland and Wittering in Cambridgeshire. Thereafter it remained cold, but sunny, with some wintry showers and overnight frost patches. As milder air spread in from the west on the 21st, freezing rain became a hazard over the Pennines and eastern England. There was some disruption to transport, with black ice reported across some routes in Cumbria. There was also a marked temperature contrast across the region during the morning. Marham in Norfolk recorded minus 7°C, while Culdrose in Cornwall recorded 11°C in the much milder air. Towards the end of the month conditions generally became quieter and more settled. Weak weather fronts gave patchy rain and drizzle, but there was also some sunshine, as well as overnight mist and fog to finish the month.

DECEMBER 2004

The month began with sunny spells for many areas and Newquay in Cornwall logged 6.6 hours of sunshine on the 1st. However, the temperature only reached 3°C at Shoreham in West Sussex on the 3rd, as coastal fog became a feature. From the 4th to the 8th temperatures recovered for a few days as the wind turned more westerly, and at Torquay in Devon the temperature reached 13.6°C on the 4th. A weak front brought dull and drizzly weather to central England and Wales on the 7th, and southern parts on the 8th. From the 9th to the 13th high pressure over the Continent was close enough to keep most places dry but a weak warm front brought some drizzle to North Wales on the 11th. By the 13th it was cold in south-east England and at High Wycombe in Buckinghamshire the maximum temperature was only 0.7°C. From the 14th to the 17th the wind turned to the west or south-west, bringing milder temperatures. Shap Fell in Cumbria logged 40.8 mm of rain on the 14th. A small but deep low pressure centre quickly crossed southern parts on the 17th, bringing strong winds; gusts of up to 70 knots were logged at Berry Head in Devon and 67 knots at Lee-on-Solent in Hampshire. Showers early on the 18th gave way to a slow-moving band of rain that gradually retreated back south on the 19th. The 20th started with a sharp frost in places with Benson in Oxfordshire and Topcliffe in North Yorkshire recording minus 7°C. There was some rain or sleet in many areas on the 20th and one to two hours of snow over northern England in the afternoon. It briefly turned milder on the 22nd and 23rd. A cold front that cleared the south-east on the 24th was followed by showers and that turned wintry over Wales and western England. The 25th was a cold day and further snow showers fed in across north-west England, the Midlands and also across south-west England and south-west Wales as troughs developed. Many places were sunny on the 26th but remained cold. At Buxton in Derbyshire the maximum temperature reached was only 0.6°C. Wet weather spread across Wales and western parts on the 27th, clearing the south-east in the early hours of the 28th. As it cleared there was some hail, squally winds and another sharp drop in temperature. Much milder weather closed the year although it remained rather cold in the south-east on the 29th.

JANUARY 2005

The 1st was mild with highs generally around 10 to 12°C and there was plenty of dry and sunny weather on the 2nd and 3rd. Torquay recorded 7.2 hours of sun on the 2nd with Cromer in Norfolk recording 6.1 hours on the 3rd. It was very unsettled from the 4th to the 12th with spells of windy weather for most parts. On the 4th, gusts of 40–50 knots were widely reported, while Capel Curig recorded 26 mm of rain. The 6th saw the return of windy weather for the north and west with gusts of 54 knots at Redesdale in Northumberland. Northern and western parts recorded very wet weather on the 7th with over 100 mm of rain at both Capel Curig and Shap Fell in Cumbria. A further 81 mm fell at Shap Fell on the 8th, with the prolonged wet spell leading to flooding in Carlisle. On the 8th a gust of 88 knots was recorded at St Bees Head in Cumbria and it was also windy further south and east with strong gusts at Marham in Norfolk and Luton in Bedfordshire. Although not as strong, the windy weather continued from the 9th through to the 12th. From the 13th to the 16th a more settled spell of weather prevailed. Southern and eastern parts enjoyed some sunshine but also had to endure some overnight frosts. Further north and west, skies were cloudier with outbreaks of rain and drizzle, particularly over coasts and hills. From the 17th to the 22nd the ridge of high pressure moved away eastward with a series of Atlantic depressions and the associated weather fronts bringing a return of more unsettled weather. Thunder was associated with one such weather front as it crossed on the 18th, with the precipitation turning to snow showers over northern England. There was further wintry precipitation across Wales on the 21st, while rain also turned to sleet and snow across the high ground of central southern England on the 22nd. It was windy at times throughout this period with gusts of 50–60 knots around western coasts. The 23rd to the 27th saw a build-up of pressure to the west of the United Kingdom that brought a return of more settled weather to most parts. However, the northerly flow brought a wintry mix of showers to eastern coastal counties. There were frequent snow showers across eastern Kent on the 25th with reports of 3–4 cm of lying snow around Dover and Folkestone. However, the snow petered out from the 28th as a high pressure block, fed by mild air, dominated the weather.

FEBRUARY 2005

The beginning of the month saw high pressure centred to the west of Ireland and temperatures at Cardiff rose to 14°C as a result. From the 5th to the 6th a cold front pushed into Wales and south-west England and some local thunderstorms were reported over Devon and Cornwall. From the 7th to the 8th a ridge of high pressure from Scandinavia brought some welcome sunshine to eastern areas, Hunstanton in Norfolk recorded 8.6 hours on the 7th and Weymouth in Dorset saw 8.3 hours on the 8th. It also brought the first frost of the month to south-east England and East Anglia. The 9th to the 12th saw a more unsettled spell of weather with Capel Curig in Gwynedd recording 33 mm of rain during the day on the 9th and 63.2 mm on the 11th. Some exceptionally mild air on the night of the 11th to the 12th gave south-east England one of its warmest February nights on record, the temperature only falling to 11.9°C in London. However, with the passage of a cold front the 13th to the 17th saw strong north-westerly winds. Wintry showers started to affect eastern counties of England but this petered out on the 15th as a ridge of high pressure came in from the south-west. The temperature on the night of the 15th to the 16th fell to minus 6.4°C at Redesdale Camp in Northumberland. On the 18th, Arctic air brought snow to many places, especially the eastern counties of England. Fylingdales in North Yorkshire reported 8 cm of snow on the morning of the 21st and daytime temperatures only reached 0.8°C at Buxton in Derbyshire on the 22nd. From the 23rd to the 25th blizzard conditions occurred over eastern England bringing 20–30 cm of snow over

the Pennines. By the morning of the 24th there was 37 cm of lying snow at Boltshope Park in Northumberland and 50 cm by the morning of the 25th. During this period South Wales and the West Country remained dry with spells of sunshine. From the 26th to the 28th the cold weather continued with further snowfall over eastern and central areas of England. Up to 15 cm of snow fell in parts of Kent during the night of the 27th to the 28th and air temperatures that night fell to minus 9.5°C at Redhill in Surrey.

MARCH 2005

The first week of March was cold and wintry with winds blowing in mainly from the north or north-east. There were frequent outbreaks of snow, giving some significant accumulations, mainly over the hills and mountains in the north, as well as across parts of East Anglia, Kent, Sussex and Surrey. There was 40 cm of snow reported at Boltshope Park in Northumberland, much of which fell in February, while there were drifts of up to 30 cm over the Downs in south-east England. Some significant transport disruption as well as school closures occurred across the Kent and Sussex area, which saw its snowiest March for at least ten years. Even central London had temporary slight accumulations of snow on the morning of the 4th. Sharp overnight frosts were recorded, especially where there was snow cover. Western parts were generally milder, drier and brighter with over ten hours of sunshine recorded at Torquay in Devon on the 6th. From the 9th to the 13th the prolonged cold spell, which started in mid-February, began to turn milder and temperatures slowly recovered to near average. The 14th to 20th saw a mild and damp Atlantic south-westerly airstream set in, bringing some wet weather, especially across the Welsh and Cumbrian hills and mountains. Capel Curig in Gwynedd recorded over 26 mm of rain on the 14th, while Shap Fell in Cumbria recorded 36 mm on the 15th into the 16th. An area of high pressure then settled across the south of England on the 18th, bringing a period a dry, sunny and warm weather to many areas. However, some coastal regions saw some misty low cloud as well as thick sea fog. This led to a notable contrast in maximum temperatures on the 19th, with 21.6°C recorded at Wisley in Surrey, but only 8°C at Portland Bill in Dorset. Overnight frost was very localised. The 21st to the 31st saw a return to more unsettled weather. It generally remained mild, especially early in the period, with winds blowing from the south or south-west. Rain or showers affected many areas, giving some places their first significant rainfall of the year. Quite a few locations reported around 26 mm of rain during the closing days of the month. Thundery showers were reported across parts of East Anglia on the 26th, while Exmouth in Devon recorded around 35 mm of rain on the 29th into the 30th. Despite the changeable theme, parts of the south coast experienced some fine sunny weather over the Easter holiday weekend. Some coastal areas continued to be affected by low cloud and mist, especially in the east, and this led to rather chilly daytime temperatures. Some dense fog patches developed across inland parts overnight, mainly in eastern districts.

APRIL 2005

From the 1st to the 3rd a ridge of high pressure affected the southern half of the UK, with most parts experiencing dry and sunny weather. From the 4th to the 6th a weather front pushed south-eastwards, bringing showers across much of northern England, Wales and the Midlands. A weather front and associated rain pushed eastwards overnight, finally clearing the east coast around mid-afternoon on the 6th. Showers developed in its wake, some heavy with hail and thunder but in the south, showers were isolated. The 7th and 8th saw a further weather front pushing eastwards outbreaks of rain, sleet and snow. Temperatures fell and Benson in Oxfordshire reached minus 5.2°C on the night of the 8th. From the 9th to the 12th a more settled period dominated and during the 9th a ridge of high pressure extended eastwards across the southern half of the UK. In the north and west it was cloudier with some coastal fog. From the 13th to the 16th a low pressure centre drifted slowly eastwards. A further low developed across northern England on the 16th and this brought unsettled weather with showers or longer periods of rain, some locally heavy and thundery. It was particularly wet across northern England with Newcastle recording 35.4 mm on the 16th. The weather remained fine across southern and eastern parts on the 17th. However, weather fronts and associated rain spread slowly across western parts during the day and across other parts overnight. The rain cleared north-eastwards during the 18th with sunny weather following, but an arc of thundery showers pushed north-east across south Wales and southern England during the early hours of the 19th with thundery showers spreading across the rest of Wales, the Midlands and parts of East Anglia during the day. From the 20th to the 22nd the weather front in the north pushed slowly south and east, finally dissipating over Cornwall on the 21st. Drier sunny weather followed across most parts with temperatures warm inland. However, with an easterly wind developing it was rather cool on the east coast. The 23rd to the 27th saw an unsettled spell for southern parts with showers and bands of rain edging slowly northwards. Exmouth in Devon recorded 40.7 mm. For northern parts this period was more settled with clear spells by night and bright or sunny periods by day. However, the rain in the south transferred north-east during the 26th and heavy showers developed. From the 28th to the 30th rain cleared from most parts early on but a trailing weather front kept the far south cloudy and damp. Elsewhere it was generally fine, warm and sunny. However showers developed across western parts overnight into the 30th and further heavy and thundery showers developed across central and eastern England during the night of the 30th.

MAY 2005

The month began with heavy rain across North Wales, the Midlands, East Anglia and Lincolnshire. A band of showers reached Cornwall at dawn on the 2nd and spread north-east to exit north-east England in the evening. On the 3rd, thundery showers again moved from south-west England into Lincolnshire. On the 4th, a cold front cleared south-eastwards with some showery rain. The 5th started chilly with a temperature of minus 0.9°C at Redhill in Surrey and there was a widespread ground frost across southern areas. The 6th was a mixed day with sunny spells in most places except Cornwall and west Devon which saw some low cloud and drizzle. Some showery rain spread into northern districts later. This rain cleared the south overnight, but not before giving some heavy rain in places, as a small low centre tracked south-east. All parts then had a rather cold and breezy day with sunny spells and showers on the 7th with some thunder and hail. There were further showers on the 8th and 9th, again with hail and thunder in places, but south-west England, the south coast and South Wales stayed mainly

dry. There were some showers across eastern counties as a trough spread south and by the 11th a high was established, giving many areas a couple of dry and largely sunny days. Pressure was falling to the south and a chilly easterly wind picked up across southern England. Culdrose in Cornwall recorded a gust of 41 knots on both the 12th and the 13th and the temperature only reached 10°C at Cromer on the 13th. There were some showers across North Wales in the morning on the 17th and north-east England by the afternoon. Low pressure dominated the weather from the 19th to the 23rd. Rain in the south-west early on the 19th had spread to most places by dawn. On the 23rd it was showery, especially in the west and north. Shap Fell in Cumbria recorded 19.6 mm of rain whilst the south-eastern parts of England were largely dry and bright. Western and southern coasts had misty low cloud and some drizzle on the 25th as a warm front moved north-east, but it gave very little rain elsewhere. A weakening cold front in the west on the 26th cleared the south-east in the evening and then another warm front moved north on the 27th. Warm southerly winds on the 27th saw temperatures in central London reach 31.9°C, the highest May temperature in the UK since 1947. A cold front brought fresher weather on the 28th but most places were dry with sunny spells. Winds were lighter the following day and much of the country stayed dry for the remainder.

JUNE 2005

The first few days of the month were unsettled with southern and western coasts experiencing mist and fog, while cold fronts brought locally heavy and thundery rain across England and Wales. Showery rain affected north-east England on the 4th, bringing 36 mm to Boulmer in Northumberland. From the 7th to 13th high pressure developed across the country, bringing largely fine and dry conditions with plenty of sunshine, with Newquay in Cornwall recording over 15 hours of sunshine on the 9th. However, the clear nights saw temperatures drop and Benson in Oxfordshire broke its June minimum temperature record with a low of minus 0.3°C early on the 7th. Towards the end of this period the high began to move away west, allowing a cold front to spread south to give a cool and showery northerly airstream. From the 14th to the 16th, low pressure brought a return to more changeable conditions with plenty of cloud and rain across East Anglia. High pressure returned to the UK on the 17th and south-easterly winds, coming off a very warm Continent, brought a hot spell with temperatures reaching a scorching 33.1°C in central London on the 19th. As the high pressure slipped away eastwards on the 19th, thundery showers developed across North Wales and into north-east England. There were torrential downpours with hail, leading to flash flooding in places, especially across Yorkshire. Hawnby in North Yorkshire recorded an exceptional 60 mm in just one hour. The Azores high built across the south of the United Kingdom from the 21st to the 23rd bringing more fine and largely dry conditions. Eastbourne in East Sussex recorded over 15 hours of sunshine on the 23rd, while Gravesend in Kent recorded a high of 32.1°C on the same day. Dorset had a few thundery showers during the evening of the 23rd. From the 24th to 26th pressure fell across England and Wales, giving some very unsettled and thundery weather. The start of the Glastonbury Festival in Somerset was hampered by flooding on the 24th. On the same day, Teignmouth in Devon recorded 52 mm of rain. The closing stages of the month were marked by an initial ridge of high pressure soon breaking down from the south, to give yet more wet weather. Heavy and thundery showers moved north across England and Wales on the 28th giving some torrential downpours and frequent lightning. East Anglia and Essex continued to see the thunderstorms into the 29th. There were also reports of flooding near Padstow in Cornwall on the afternoon of the 29th.

AVERAGE AND GENERAL MONTHLY VALUES 2004–2005 (JUNE)

	Rainfall (mm)				Temperature (°C)				Bright Sunshine (hrs per day)			
	1961–90	2003	2004	2005	1961–90	2003	2004	2005	1961–90	2003	2004	2005
ENGLAND AND WALES												
January	77	84	124	68	3.8	4.2	4.9	5.7	1.6	2.35	1.60	1.82
February	55	39	56	50	3.8	3.7	5.0	4.0	2.4	3.47	3.07	2.48
March	63	39	51	53	5.6	7.2	6.2	6.7	3.5	5.56	3.51	2.55
April	53	43	80	76	7.7	9.3	9.1	8.6	4.9	6.42	4.46	5.00
May	56	73	46	45	10.9	11.6	11.7	11.0	6.2	5.96	6.58	7.07
June	58	67	58	56	13.9	15.5	14.9	15.0	6.4	7.13	6.63	6.70
July	56	76	69		15.7	17.0	15.4		6.0	5.57	5.35	
August	68	18	150		15.6	17.7	17.1		6.0	6.70	5.61	
September	70	37	66		13.6	14.0	14.4		4.5	5.53	5.19	
October	77	58	149		10.7	8.9	10.3		3.2	4.20	3.09	
November	81	100	53		6.6	7.9	7.5		2.2	2.25	1.60	
December	82	100	69		4.7	4.8	5.3		1.5	1.68	1.68	
YEAR	796	734	971		9.4	10.2	10.2		4.0	4.70	4.0	
SCOTLAND												
January	117	167	208	240	3.1	2.6	3.4	4.4	1.3	1.22	0.97	1.06
February	78	57	104	110	3.1	2.7	3.1	3.0	2.4	3.18	3.06	2.21
March	94	86	93	108	4.6	5.7	4.8	5 6	3.2	4.88	3.71	2.80
April	60	58	121	113	6.5	8.0	7.5	6.7	4.8	5.94	3.41	5.40
May	67	139	59	115	9.3	9.1	9.9	8.3	5.6	4.58	6.18	6.34
June	67	79	122	105	12.1	13	12.1	12.4	5.6	5.55	4.04	4.79
July	74	80	76		13.6	14.8	12.8		4.9	4.46	4.27	
August	92	46	188		13.5	14.4	14.5		4.9	5.88	4.75	
September	111	85	175		11.5	11.5	11.7		3.5	3.84	3.98	
October	120	78	204		9.1	6.8	7.7		2.6	3.44	1.97	
November	118	160	121		5.3	6.4	6.0		1.7	1.94	1.42	
December	115	168	192		3.9	3.2	4.4		1.0	1.03	1.08	
YEAR	1113	1203	1663		7.9	8.2	8.1		3.5	3.82	3.24	

Source: Data provided by the Met Office

WIND FORCE MEASURES

The *Beaufort Scale* of wind force has been accepted internationally and is used in communicating weather conditions. Devised originally by Admiral Sir Francis Beaufort in 1805, it now consists of the numbers 0–17, each representing a certain strength or velocity of wind at 10 m (33 ft) above ground in the open.

Scale no.	Wind Force	mph	knots
0	Calm	1	1
1	Light air	1–3	1–3
2	Slight breeze	4–7	4–6
3	Gentle breeze	8–12	7–10
4	Moderate breeze	13–18	11–16
5	Fresh breeze	19–24	17–21
6	Strong breeze	25–31	22–27
7	High wind	32–38	28–33
8	Gale	39–46	34–40
9	Strong gale	47–54	41–47
10	Whole gale	55–63	48–55
11	Storm	64–72	56–63
12	Hurricane	73–82	64–71
13	–	83–92	72–80
14	–	93–103	81–89
15	–	104–114	90–99
16	–	115–125	100–108
17	–	126–136	109–118

TEMPERATURE RAINFALL AND SUNSHINE

At selected climatological reporting stations, July 2004–June 2005 and calendar year 2004

Ht   height (in metres) of station above mean sea level
°C   mean air temperature
Rain total monthly rainfall
Sun   monthly total (hours)

	Ht	July 2004 °C	Rain mm	Sun hrs	August 2004 °C	Rain mm	Sun hrs	September 2004 °C	Rain mm	Sun hrs	October 2004 °C	Rain mm	Sun hrs
	m												
Lerwick	82	11.8	38.8	137.1	13.6	121.2	194.9	11.3	94.4	136.7	8.8	126.4	62.3
Stornoway	15	13.2	59.4	122.5	14.6	96.8	147.3	12.1	131.0	118.0	9.1	143.6	50.7
Dyce	65	13.8	51.8	160.9	15.1	94.4	166.3	13.0	24.0	181.3	9.5	145.0	71.9
Eskdalemuir	242	13.2	68.2	129.5	15.1	309.0	147.7	11.9	222.6	99.4	8.0	227.0	65.8
Aldergrove	68	14.2	57.0	132.7	15.8	87.0	137.2	13.6	75.0	107.6	8.9	106.4	72.7
Bingley	64	14.2	41.9	–	16.0	69.9	–	12.8	38.4	–	8.7	119.4	–
Valley	10	15.1	41.4	154.9	17.1	87.6	173.1	15.1	84.6	138.4	11.3	141.0	106.5
Coleshill	–	15.9	55.0	–	17.8	155.6	–	14.8	41.0	–	10.4	88.0	–
Skegness	6	16.2	82.8	184.7	17.6	89.8	174.2	14.7	38.9	169.2	11.3	106.3	102.3
Bristol	42	16.5	49.4	153.9	18.0	95.0	176.0	15.6	0.0	156.1	11.2	122.8	92.4
St Mawgan	103	15.3	77.6	169.2	17.0	116.8	210.1	15.5	50.0	157.2	11.5	153.4	135.7
Hastings	45	16.9	42.4	232.7	18.6	95.3	236.2	16.2	30.2	181.5	12.7	85.2	133.0

	November 2004 °C	Rain mm	Sun hrs	December 2004 °C	Rain mm	Sun hrs	The Year 2004 °C	Rain mm	Sun hrs	January 2005 °C	Rain mm	Sun hrs	February 2005 °C	Rain mm	Sun hrs
Lerwick	5.9	138.3	32.5	5.5	153.7	23.8	8.1	104.4	97.1	4.4	194.2	23.7	3.8	117.3	70.5
Stornoway	7.4	117.8	31.3	6.1	136.4	17.2	9.1	91.8	86.4	5.7	160.2	23.9	4.5	84.8	53.2
Dyce	6.9	52.0	57.9	4.9	33.4	66.0	9.2	65.2	121.1	5.4	43.1	51.8	4.1	54.5	82.0
Eskdalemuir	5.6	88.5	46.3	3.8	171.0	43.3	8.2	147.4	95.4	4.3	312.0	41.2	2.9	126.8	83.5
Aldergrove	8.1	39.2	36.2	5.8	68.0	44.3	9.7	62.9	104	5.8	54.7	41.0	4.4	60.0	64.4
Bingley	6.5	34.8	–	4.4	51.2	–	9.0	66.3	–	4.7	84.0	–	3.0	56.4	–
Valley	9.5	72.2	31.8	7.5	70.4	46.7	10.9	67.7	102.8	7.6	39.2	56.4	5.4	44.0	79.6
Coleshill	7.6	35.0	–	5.4	15.4	–	10.5	59.3	–	5.8	16.2	–	4.2	50.8	–
Skegness	7.9	37.0	39.5	5.2	22.4	73.1			–	5.9	15.5	49.8	4.5	43.4	–
Bristol	8.3	37.8	45.9	6.0	58.0	52.3	11.2	57.9	123.0	6.6	46.0	60.1	4.8	27.8	63.8
St Mawgan	9.9	43.2	62.4	7.9	70.9	58.8	11.3	75.7	152.7	7.8	58.8	52.3	5.3	41.0	105.3
Hastings	9.0	38.3	64.2	6.6	57.4	64.5	11.6	53.3	162	6.8	26.7	87.9	4.8	26.5	100.4

	March 2005 °C	Rain mm	Sun hrs	April 2005 °C	Rain mm	Sun hrs	May 2005 °C	Rain mm	Sun hrs	June 2005 °C	Rain mm	Sun hrs
Lerwick	4.7	121.9	87.7	6.5	71.1	128.3	7.3	80.7	169.7	10.2	95.4	135.0
Stornoway	6.6	99.0	88.4	7.7	112.7	156.9	8.5	51.0	168.9	11.9	92.8	101.1
Dyce	6.2	51.4	87.7	7.5	58.3	176.1	9.3	64.4	213.8	13.4	43.4	160.8
Eskdalemuir	5.5	96.8	77.2	6.8	123.0	150.7	8.6	169.6	185.1	12.6	91.6	133.1
Aldergrove	7.3	37.8	89.2	8.0	56.0	133.1	10.0	81.8	169.8	14.5	73.4	120.5
Bingley	5.6	23.8	–	7.2	118.7	–	10.1	47.6	–	14.2	46.0	–
Valley	8.0	42.8	111.3	9.1	101.0	126.6	11.1	33.0	221.1	14.6	18.8	184.5
Coleshill	7.0	38.8	–	9.2	26.2	–	11.6	31.4	–	15.2	84.6	–
Skegness	6.9	34.3	–	8.9	45.9	132.4	–					
Bristol	7.5	62.4	71.6	9.8	53.0	131.1	12.2	37.8	193.3	16.3	62.0	205.4
St Mawgan	8.2	47.8	114.6	9.5	95.2	181.2	11.0	40.4	202.4	15.4	46.4	215.4
Hastings	6.7	42.4	110.4	9.7	44.7	184.8	12.1	40.7	240.0	16.2	33.2	247.7

METEOROLOGICAL OBSERVATIONS LONDON (HEATHROW)

Temperature maxima and minima cover the 24-hour period 9 – 9 h; mean wind speed is 10 m above ground; rainfall is for the 24 hours starting on 9 h on the day of entry; sunshine is for the 24 hours. *Source:* Data provided by the Met Office

JULY 2004

Day		Temperature Max °C	Min °C	Wind knots	Rain mm	Sun hrs
Day	1	20.1	11.2	12.5	4.4	9.0
	2	19.2	11.9	13.1	3.2	6.3
	3	20.0	11.7	15.2	0.4	11.0
	4	18.1	11.7	8.5	Trace	4.6
	5	21.3	9.3	5.4	0.0	13.6
	6	23.7	11.1	5.2	0.0	10.4
	7	22.1	13.2	12.0	12.6	2.7
	8	18.9	12.2	6.5	2.2	2.8
	9	19.2	11.2	7.4	0.0	3.9
	10	18.4	10.0	7.0	3.6	8.5
	11	18.4	11.2	6.9	0.0	2.5
	12	18.7	12.3	5.9	Trace	1.8
	13	21.1	10.0	6.6	1.2	8.9
	14	22.1	13.1	10.4	Trace	2.3
	15	24.0	15.0	10.0	1.0	2.4
	16	24.0	17.0	9.8	Trace	4.9
	17	24.6	16.0	7.6	0.4	4.5
	18	22.6	16.2	7.9	Trace	3.0
	19	22.8	10.8	6.2	0.0	9.5
	20	24.7	13.0	6.6	8.6	6.9
	21	22.7	16.5	8.6	Trace	1.2
	22	26.7	15.0	6.1	Trace	2.9
	23	25.5	14.9	7.4	0.0	14.2
	24	24.5	13.2	9.3	0.0	11.4
	25	23.7	12.7	9.6	Trace	4.7
	26	22.9	15.7	6.5	0.0	4.7
	27	24.3	13.9	3.7	0.0	8.2
	28	27.3	13.5	5.4	0.0	7.7
	29	29.9	16.0	7.3	Trace	6.9
	30	25.5	17.4	5.6	0.0	11.0
	31	28.0	15.2	4.3	0.0	9.1

AUGUST 2004

Day		Temperature Max °C	Min °C	Wind knots	Rain mm	Sun hrs
Day	1	26.7	16.6	6.7	0.0	10.2
	2	28.1	15.2	7.5	Trace	8.6
	3	27.9	18.5	4.7	16.8	2.3
	4	28.1	15.2	3.5	Trace	13.0
	5	27.3	18.8	4.4	15.8	1.9
	6	27.6	15.6	5.8	0.0	13.1
	7	n/a	15.4	5.2	0.0	14.2
	8	n/a	18.5	8.7	Trace	8.7
	9	22.9	n/a	5.0	7.4	0.0
	10	25.4	17.7	5.5	0.2	7.9
	11	24.9	16.4	7.0	1.2	7.1
	12	24.2	17.6	9.5	5.0	8.6
	13	22.9	14.7	7.8	4.4	2.9
	14	24.2	16.4	4.9	0.0	3.9
	15	24.2	15.3	7.0	Trace	3.3
	16	21.7	15.9	9.2	2.2	3.5
	17	23.5	15.0	9.0	7.2	8.9
	18	23.8	16.6	10.9	6.2	6.7
	19	22.6	14.9	11.3	1.8	7.9
	20	21.5	14.5	10.2	2.4	8.0
	21	20.5	10.9	6.3	0.0	10.8
	22	22.0	12.7	6.9	8.4	6.0
	23	21.3	14.3	10.2	5.4	5.6
	24	22.6	15.3	10.8	9.0	6.6
	25	21.1	13.8	7.5	10.0	6.9
	26	21.6	12.5	9.0	3.4	8.5
	27	21.1	14.3	9.8	0.8	1.4
	28	20.0	11.5	5.7	Trace	6.8
	29	19.0	11.9	10.2	0.2	1.3
	30	20.2	12.1	10.0	Trace	10.7
	31	20.3	9.4	4.5	0.0	8.0

SEPTEMBER 2004

Day		Temperature Max °C	Min °C	Wind knots	Rain mm	Sun hrs
Day	1	21.6	9.7	4.3	0.0	11.9
	2	24.4	12.3	4.3	0.0	10.0
	3	26.1	13.4	4.8	0.0	10.7
	4	26.2	13.7	3.5	0.0	11.8
	5	27.7	15.1	4.1	0.0	11.5
	6	25.7	15.1	8.7	0.0	8.9
	7	24.7	16.9	10.3	0.0	7.2
	8	23.7	13.4	9.6	0.0	11.7
	9	25.1	15.4	7.3	1.6	9.5
	10	21.3	14.8	7.4	Trace	1.1
	11	22.2	16.1	15.8	Trace	8.0
	12	19.4	11.0	15.6	4.6	4.6
	13	19.3	14.1	14.3	3.4	5.6
	14	19.2	11.5	14.7	0.2	7.2
	15	18.5	8.8	7.2	0.0	10.3
	16	19.5	7.1	8.1	Trace	9.8
	17	20.1	13.2	11.6	0.4	0.0
	18	20.8	15.5	12.0	1.2	4.1
	19	17.3	8.7	9.8	Trace	4.4
	20	19.5	13.8	18.0	1.8	2.0
	21	16.7	9.9	14.1	0.0	8.7
	22	18.6	11.3	14.1	0.4	0.5
	23	20.7	15.8	11.6	1.0	6.4
	24	15.4	8.5	6.0	Trace	7.4
	25	15.3	5.3	6.8	0.6	0.2
	26	20.7	10.0	8.2	Trace	3.9
	27	20.7	12.8	7.6	Trace	0.7
	28	19.1	13.9	10.3	Trace	1.7
	29	16.2	13.1	4.5	1.4	0.0
	30	19.5	13.8	6.8	2.2	2.9

OCTOBER 2004

Day		Temperature Max °C	Min °C	Wind knots	Rain mm	Sun hrs
Day	1	16.7	10.0	6.4	1.4	0.1
	2	18.4	9.3	10.9	3.6	4.0
	3	16.7	10.1	9.3	13.6	0.2
	4	17.0	12.7	11.4	Trace	6.2
	5	17.8	7.6	10.8	0.2	3.3
	6	15.5	8.9	11.3	2.0	8.2
	7	15.6	7.5	6.2	0.0	7.5
	8	15.6	7.4	5.6	0.0	4.2
	9	14.9	8.3	9.8	0.0	3.6
	10	16.1	9.8	11.5	0.0	3.6
	11	13.9	9.0	10.0	0.8	6.3
	12	14.0	10.6	10.9	1.6	0.0
	13	15.9	9.6	8.0	34.4	2.5
	14	13.9	9.3	7.7	2.6	3.0
	15	10.9	7.9	6.3	2.2	0.2
	16	11.5	8.0	5.3	0.6	0.1
	17	13.0	6.3	8.0	0.2	2.1
	18	13.7	7.5	5.6	Trace	7.0
	19	15.5	4.1	7.0	5.6	0.3
	20	17.3	9.3	10.0	8.6	0.1
	21	16.1	8.3	17.7	Trace	9.0
	22	16.2	11.4	15.9	Trace	1.1
	23	16.6	14.0	15.3	10.8	0.1
	24	17.9	14.0	12.2	2.8	2.1
	25	14.4	11.7	15.4	0.0	7.3
	26	14.4	5.6	4.8	0.0	5.8
	27	14.0	5.5	11.5	3.2	0.0
	28	16.6	9.5	10.2	2.4	5.0
	29	14.9	10.2	9.7	Trace	0.3
	30	16.7	9.7	3.8	0.0	3.4
	31	13.9	10.1	5.2	0.0	4.6

NOVEMBER 2004

Day	Temperature Max °C	Min °C	Wind knots	Rain mm	Sun hrs
1	12.8	8.0	6.0	2.6	0.1
2	11.9	9.5	6.3	0.8	0.0
3	15.0	9.9	5.9	0.2	3.2
4	13.6	9.0	6.5	Trace	5.0
5	11.9	4.3	6.9	Trace	0.4
6	12.5	7.4	5.6	0.4	0.1
7	11.8	9.4	4.0	1.6	0.0
8	12.7	9.1	5.5	1.0	0.1
9	10.4	8.1	5.7	4.4	0.1
10	10.6	5.3	8.0	Trace	6.9
11	11.2	4.8	5.3	0.2	6.0
12	14.4	6.3	8.2	0.4	2.9
13	7.9	2.4	6.2	0.2	8.4
14	10.2	−0.5	4.3	0.0	8.1
15	10.2	2.0	7.3	0.0	0.0
16	12.9	6.8	7.0	Trace	0.6
17	13.9	9.5	14.2	3.4	1.5
18	11.0	8.9	10.6	6.2	0.0
19	5.7	1.0	5.3	0.0	5.3
20	5.2	−0.2	4.0	2.2	0.0
21	12.6	2.2	7.7	0.6	0.0
22	13.9	5.2	11.8	Trace	2.8
23	12.2	9.9	4.4	Trace	0.0
24	11.3	9.3	4.4	Trace	0.0
25	11.4	8.3	5.3	0.2	1.0
26	13.2	7.4	6.6	1.2	2.1
27	9.8	7.4	5.9	2.4	0.0
28	7.3	6.2	6.7	1.6	0.5
29	8.9	5.8	5.1	0.0	5.6
30	9.4	2.1	3.5	Trace	0.1

DECEMBER 2004

Day	Temperature Max °C	Min °C	Wind knots	Rain mm	Sun hrs
1	7.0	1.3	4.8	0.0	0.1
2	6.8	1.2	3.4	0.0	1.3
3	6.0	2.3	4.3	Trace	0.0
4	10.1	2.1	3.7	0.0	0.7
5	10.7	5.8	5.0	0.0	0.0
6	11.7	8.4	7.0	0.0	1.2
7	9.3	3.2	2.5	Trace	0.0
8	9.5	6.4	2.9	Trace	0.0
9	7.5	3.9	3.7	Trace	3.4
10	6.7	4.2	3.9	0.0	0.0
11	8.3	−0.7	3.0	Trace	4.0
12	6.1	0.7	8.8	0.0	0.0
13	7.1	1.2	3.0	0.2	0.0
14	10.5	1.3	7.4	Trace	0.0
15	12.3	6.8	8.6	0.6	0.6
16	11.5	9.2	12.8	3.4	1.9
17	7.1	6.2	11.2	13.0	1.1
18	7.7	0.9	8.6	12.0	0.0
19	6.3	3.5	8.7	0.0	5.6
20	6.2	−2.7	5.7	0.2	1.0
21	7.8	0.2	4.4	6.6	0.0
22	12.1	1.3	10.8	0.4	0.2
23	12.7	7.8	16.0	0.0	2.5
24	11.1	7.6	14.3	0.2	0.3
25	4.8	1.3	7.4	0.0	2.4
26	4.6	−2.8	4.5	0.0	5.7
27	8.2	−2.5	6.2	9.8	4.0
28	6.9	−1.3	11.3	Trace	7.0
29	11.3	1.6	7.5	Trace	2.6
30	13.0	2.2	8.0	Trace	1.0
31	12.6	8.5	9.4	Trace	1.6

JANUARY 2005

Day	Temperature Max °C	Min °C	Wind knots	Rain mm	Sun hrs
1	12.0	5.1	13.0	1.0	0.1
2	7.9	3.3	13.1	0.0	7.0
3	10.3	3.8	12.2	Trace	1.8
4	11.5	5.9	14.7	1.4	0.0
5	9.1	1.9	9.8	0.2	0.0
6	12.8	3.9	11.7	Trace	1.7
7	14.4	5.9	22.3	3.0	2.4
8	8.9	8.0	21.4	0.2	5.9
9	13.3	6.0	13.4	0.2	0.0
10	12.3	7.5	14.4	2.6	0.0
11	12.9	7.4	13.4	1.0	0.0
12	9.4	6.2	14.0	0.0	6.4
13	8.3	1.7	7.1	0.0	5.8
14	9.0	1.0	7.0	Trace	5.2
15	9.8	3.7	7.2	Trace	0.7
16	12.5	3.3	7.9	Trace	1.9
17	10.5	4.7	13.7	3.2	0.0
18	7.2	2.1	13.9	0.2	4.2
19	11.7	2.1	10.7	Trace	2.8
20	12.8	4.9	17.0	0.8	0.0
21	8.8	4.6	9.4	Trace	1.2
22	6.7	0.8	4.5	0.6	2.7
23	6.2	0.9	7.6	Trace	8.1
24	4.9	1.6	9.5	0.2	4.5
25	5.5	2.3	7.8	Trace	2.0
26	5.4	−0.1	6.0	0.2	5.1
27	7.4	1.5	6.4	3.6	0.0
28	7.8	5.2	10.7	2.6	0.0
29	7.5	4.5	5.3	Trace	0.4
30	8.3	5.5	5.4	0.0	0.2
31	10.4	2.3	7.2	0.6	2.0

FEBRUARY 2005

Day	Temperature Max °C	Min °C	Wind knots	Rain mm	Sun hrs
1	9.2	7.0	5.7	0.2	0.2
2	8.4	5.9	5.6	Trace	0.1
3	10.7	3.2	3.8	Trace	0.0
4	9.8	6.7	4.5	0.0	0.0
5	7.1	4.8	6.9	0.4	0.6
6	9.5	4.9	6.5	0.0	0.7
7	7.9	1.6	3.1	0.8	3.4
8	9.2	3.1	4.0	0.0	1.4
9	10.6	3.9	10.3	0.2	0.1
10	11.6	8.4	14.8	3.6	0.0
11	12.3	5.5	6.9	1.8	0.0
12	13.5	6.1	18.0	2.4	4.6
13	6.8	2.3	14.1	0.2	4.7
14	6.9	2.7	10.0	Trace	2.8
15	7.2	2.1	8.5	0.0	6.5
16	4.6	2.4	5.0	0.0	0.0
17	6.5	−0.2	3.0	3.0	0.0
18	9.0	2.8	7.0	0.4	1.5
19	6.2	2.8	8.3	Trace	8.0
20	4.9	−0.7	8.8	0.4	3.9
21	5.7	0.9	8.2	2.0	3.8
22	4.9	0.5	9.3	0.4	3.9
23	3.6	−0.8	7.9	0.2	2.0
24	2.7	0.7	8.1	1.5	0.0
25	3.3	−0.7	6.2	1.0	0.9
26	5.4	−0.2	6.0	0.8	0.6
27	3.9	−0.4	8.4	Trace	6.7
28	3.8	−4.7	5.9	0.4	6.0

MARCH 2005

		Temperature Max °C	Min °C	Wind knots	Rain mm	Sun hrs
Day	1	5.9	−1.0	7.5	3.8	0.2
	2	4.0	1.4	8.8	1.6	0.0
	3	4.7	−1.0	9.8	0.4	8.5
	4	8.0	−4.8	6.9	2.4	1.7
	5	6.5	−0.6	9.1	0.8	5.6
	6	4.3	−1.7	7.4	0.0	5.1
	7	7.5	−1.6	5.8	Trace	0.3
	8	8.1	2.3	5.6	Trace	0.0
	9	8.3	4.9	4.3	Trace	0.0
	10	9.3	3.9	4.5	Trace	1.2
	11	9.9	3.5	12.9	4.0	1.3
	12	8.5	1.9	9.2	0.0	7.5
	13	7.5	−1.4	6.7	0.0	2.8
	14	10.2	0.9	6.9	Trace	1.4
	15	12.4	3.6	11.1	Trace	0.3
	16	18.6	8.1	14.8	0.2	3.9
	17	18.9	11.3	12.8	0.0	9.3
	18	19.0	8.8	7.8	0.0	8.2
	19	20.1	6.1	4.3	0.0	9.6
	20	12.8	9.3	7.8	0.0	0.1
	21	16.0	6.3	8.3	1.8	2.1
	22	14.7	10.1	10.5	2.8	0.3
	23	17.1	8.0	8.1	3.2	5.3
	24	16.3	9.7	8.3	0.0	3.3
	25	15.9	8.5	4.3	0.0	4.6
	26	16.0	6.1	4.2	0.6	7.1
	27	10.6	8.0	5.5	0.0	0.0
	28	14.9	6.0	3.3	0.0	7.0
	29	9.5	6.6	8.1	21.0	0.0
	30	11.2	7.4	5.0	1.0	0.0
	31	11.1	8.7	5.7	Trace	0.0

APRIL 2005

		Temperature Max °C	Min °C	Wind knots	Rain mm	Sun hrs
Day	1	15.7	8.3	4.7	0.0	5.5
	2	18.3	8.5	6.4	0.0	7.2
	3	19.4	7.1	8.6	Trace	8.5
	4	12.1	10.2	7.3	0.6	0.2
	5	12.4	3.8	10.3	0.4	4.3
	6	13.9	7.5	15.4	3.6	4.2
	7	13.6	6.7	14.0	1.2	7.7
	8	8.6	4.0	9.6	0.2	2.8
	9	11.3	−1.2	10.0	Trace	7.3
	10	16.3	5.2	7.2	0.0	7.6
	11	17.2	5.5	5.0	0.0	11.1
	12	15.0	5.4	7.9	2.6	2.1
	13	12.8	7.0	7.3	0.2	1.2
	14	11.8	6.7	6.1	Trace	2.5
	15	9.8	2.9	4.1	1.8	0.0
	16	10.3	1.9	3.8	0.0	2.7
	17	15.3	1.2	6.8	4.8	9.8
	18	15.3	7.7	10.5	2.6	8.2
	19	14.8	4.2	7.5	Trace	6.4
	20	11.2	4.6	3.8	0.0	1.6
	21	15.3	5.7	6.6	0.0	10.1
	22	17.7	4.9	8.8	Trace	10.5
	23	14.4	8.2	6.3	0.2	0.0
	24	16.1	6.2	6.8	4.2	4.4
	25	12.6	8.2	4.5	2.8	0.2
	26	15.5	7.3	9.0	2.0	4.6
	27	15.6	6.9	9.8	2.6	9.3
	28	14.9	8.3	11.0	0.2	0.2
	29	19.0	9.3	6.2	Trace	9.4
	30	21.5	12.8	6.2	Trace	3.4

MAY 2005

		Temperature Max °C	Min °C	Wind knots	Rain mm	Sun hrs
Day	1	23.4	14.1	7.6	0.6	8.2
	2	21.3	13.3	8.6	0.4	9.3
	3	18.1	11.3	10.1	3.2	5.3
	4	11.8	11.1	7.2	Trace	0.4
	5	18.5	3.3	8.1	Trace	4.8
	6	17.2	9.5	10.1	1.6	10.2
	7	14.9	9.5	12.5	0.2	10.4
	8	15.2	4.5	8.6	1.6	11.6
	9	13.1	4.4	5.3	Trace	7.4
	10	12.9	3.8	6.3	0.4	7.9
	11	13.1	2.5	6.2	0.0	7.9
	12	15.3	3.9	10.8	0.0	12.8
	13	16.9	7.6	12.3	0.0	6.9
	14	15.2	6.6	9.4	0.0	1.5
	15	18.4	2.7	4.5	0.0	12.1
	16	16.7	7.9	7.3	2.8	1.5
	17	12.9	4.5	5.0	0.0	9.4
	18	15.6	4.9	7.7	0.4	4.1
	19	14.6	9.5	9.6	5.2	0.1
	20	19.1	12.4	12.5	0.4	5.6
	21	16.8	9.1	11.1	2.4	6.1
	22	16.5	9.8	13.0	Trace	7.5
	23	17.8	7.3	12.3	0.2	11.5
	24	18.7	10.1	13.2	0.2	5.1
	25	22.2	10.7	9.0	Trace	3.1
	26	24.4	n/a	8.0	Trace	6.0
	27	30.7	13.6	7.5	0.0	13.7
	28	20.9	14.9	14.3	0.0	11.9
	29	17.2	8.7	4.1	Trace	2.2
	30	18.6	9.9	6.1	0.2	10.9
	31	20.3	8.3	5.5	Trace	12.9

JUNE 2005

		Temperature Max °C	Min °C	Wind knots	Rain mm	Sun hrs
Day	1	16.7	10.6	7.9	1.4	0.1
	2	19.5	13.6	10.2	0.0	0.4
	3	22.3	12.3	8.6	11.2	6.7
	4	20.1	11.7	14.7	Trace	6.8
	5	18.7	11.7	10.6	Trace	1.4
	6	16.9	13.0	6.7	0.0	1.0
	7	18.2	5.8	5.3	0.0	14.6
	8	21.4	7.2	4.3	0.0	15.3
	9	22.9	9.3	3.8	Trace	8.8
	10	19.7	14.6	6.4	0.0	4.0
	11	17.7	7.0	4.4	0.2	6.6
	12	19.7	11.1	8.2	Trace	3.8
	13	19.9	5.9	9.6	0.0	13.0
	14	20.7	8.3	10.3	2.0	6.8
	15	21.5	11.5	11.9	0.8	5.6
	16	20.5	13.3	11.3	0.4	1.3
	17	26.4	15.1	9.1	Trace	6.9
	18	29.9	16.4	7.0	0.0	14.4
	19	n/a	17.9	7.0	Trace	15.0
	20	27.7	n/a	4.9	0.0	5.7
	21	26.1	15.4	6.5	0.0	13.1
	22	28.7	14.6	5.5	0.0	15.1
	23	n/a	15.9	4.5	0.0	12.7
	24	25.3	18.0	5.2	7.8	5.2
	25	18.8	16.8	7.3	Trace	0.0
	26	21.1	12.9	7.4	0.0	5.7
	27	26.2	12.1	5.9	0.0	14.8
	28	27.3	14.4	9.5	5.0	6.5
	29	25.9	15.3	7.1	1.0	7.9
	30	19.6	15.1	9.8	2.8	0.1

SPORTS RESULTS

For 2006 sports fixtures, *see* pages 13–14

ALPINE SKIING

WORLD CUP 2004–5
Lenzerheide, Switzerland, March

MEN
Downhill: Michael Walchhofer (Austria), 681 points
Slalom: Benjamin Raich (Austria), 552 points
Giant Slalom: Benjamin Raich (Austria), 423 points
Super Giant Slalom: Bode Miller (USA), 470 points
Overall: Bode Miller (USA), 1,648 points

WOMEN
Downhill: Renata Götschl (Austria), 567 points
Slalom: Tanja Poutiainen (Finland), 570 points
Giant Slalom: Tanja Poutiainen (Finland), 461 points
Super Giant Slalom: Michaela Dorfmeister (Austria), 493 points
Overall: Anja Paerson (Sweden), 1,359 points

WORLD CHAMPIONSHIPS 2005
Bormio and Santa Caterina, Italy, January

MEN
Downhill: Bode Miller (USA)
Slalom: Benjamin Raich (Austria)
Giant Slalom: Hermann Maier (Austria)
Super Giant Slalom: Bode Miller (USA)
Combined: Benjamin Raich (Austria)

WOMEN
Downhill: Janica Kostelic (Croatia)
Slalom: Janica Kostelic (Croatia)
Giant Slalom: Anja Paerson (Sweden)
Super Giant Slalom: Anja Paerson (Sweden)
Combined: Janica Kostelic (Croatia)

AMERICAN FOOTBALL

AFC Championship 2004: New England Patriots beat Pittsburgh Steelers 41–27
NFC Championship 2004: Philadelphia Eagles beat Atlanta Falcons 27–10
XXXIX Superbowl 2005 (Jacksonville, 6 February): New England Patriots beat Philadelphia Eagles 24–21

ANGLING

NATIONAL COARSE CHAMPIONSHIPS 2005
Division: 1
Individual winner: Simon Fry
Team winners: Starlets AS

Division: 2
Individual winner: Darren Mulheir
Team winners: Thorne and District

Division: 3
Individual winner: Shaun Coaten
Team winners: Telford
Ladies' Championship: Julie Abbott

ASSOCIATION FOOTBALL

LEAGUE COMPETITIONS 2004–5

ENGLAND AND WALES
Premiership
1. Chelsea, 95 points;
2. Arsenal, 83 points;
3. Manchester United, 77 points;
Relegated: Crystal Palace, Norwich City, Southampton

Championship
1. Sunderland, 94 points;
2. Wigan Athletic, 87 points;
Play-off winner and third promotion place: West Ham United
Relegated: Gillingham, Nottingham Forest, Rotherham United

League 1
1. Luton Town, 98 points;
2. Hull City, 86 points;
Play-off winner and third promotion place: Sheffield Wednesday
Relegated: Torquay United, Wrexham, Peterborough United, Stockport County

League 2
1. Yeovil Town, 83 points;
2. Scunthorpe United, 80 points;
3. Swansea City, 80 points;
Play-off winner and fourth promotion place: Southend United
Relegated: Kidderminster Harriers, Cambridge United

Football Conference
1. Barnet, 86 points;
Play-off winner and second promotion place: Carlisle United

League of Wales
1. TNS, 78 points;
2. Rhyl, 74 points;
3. Bangor City, 67 points

Women's Premier League National Division
1. Arsenal, 48 points;
2. Charlton Athletic, 41 points;
3. Everton, 37 points

SCOTLAND
Premier Division
1. Rangers, 93 points;
2. Celtic, 92 points,
Relegated: Dundee

Division 1
1. Falkirk, 75 points;
2. St Mirren, 60 points;
Relegated: Partick Thistle, Raith Rovers

Division 2
1. Brechin City, 72 points;
2. Stranraer, 63 points;
Relegated: Arbroath, Berwick Rangers

Division 3
1. Gretna, 98 points;
2. Peterhead, 78 points;
Bottom: East Stirling

NORTHERN IRELAND
Irish League Premier Division
1. Glentoran, 74 points; 2. Linfield, 72 points; 3. Portadown, 58 points

REPUBLIC OF IRELAND
Premier Division:
1. Shelbourne, 68 points; 2. Cork City, 65 points; 3. Bohemians, 60 points

FRANCE
Ligue 1: 1. Lyon, 79 points; 2. Lille, 67 points; 3. Monaco, 63 points

GERMANY
Bundesliga 1: 1. Bayern Munich, 77 points; 2. Schalke 04, 63 points; 3. Werder Bremen, 59 points

ITALY
Serie A: 1. Juventus, 83 points; 2. Milan, 78 points; 3. Internazionale, 71 points

NETHERLANDS
Eredivisie: 1. PSV, 87 points; 2. Ajax, 77 points; 3. AZ, 64 points

SPAIN
Primera Division: 1. Barcelona, 83 points; 2. Real Madrid, 77 points; 3. Villarreal, 62 points

CUP COMPETITIONS

ENGLAND
FA Cup final 2005: Arsenal beat Manchester United 5–4 on penalties (0–0 aet)
League Cup final 2005: Chelsea beat Liverpool 3–2 aet *(Score after 90 minutes: 1–1)*
LDV Trophy 2005: Wrexham beat Southend United 2–0
FA Vase final 2005: Didcot Town beat AFC Sudbury 3–2
FA Trophy final 2005: Grays Athletic beat Hucknall Town 6–5 on penalties (1–1 aet)
Community Shield 2005: Chelsea beat Arsenal 2–1

WOMEN
Women's FA Cup final 2005: Charlton Athletic beat Everton 1–0
Women's Premier League Cup final 2005: Arsenal beat Charlton Athletic 3–0
Women's Community Shield 2005: Charlton Athletic beat Arsenal 1–0

WALES
FA Wales Cup final 2005: TNS beat Carmarthen Town 1–0
FA Wales Premier Cup final 2005: Swansea City beat Wrexham 2–1

SCOTLAND
Scottish Cup final 2005: Celtic beat Dundee United 1–0
League Cup final 2005: Rangers beat Motherwell 5–1

NORTHERN IRELAND
Irish Cup final 2005: Portadown beat Larne 5–1

EUROPE
European Champions League final 2005: Liverpool beat Milan 3–2 on penalties (3–3 aet)
UEFA Cup final 2005: CSKA Moscow beat Sporting Lisbon 3–1
European Super Cup final 2005: Liverpool beat CSKA Moscow 3–1 aet *(score after 90 minutes: 1–1)*

WORLD FOOTBALLER OF THE YEAR
2004 – Ronaldinho (Brazil)
2003 – Zinedine Zidane (France)
2002 – Ronaldo (Brazil)
2001 – Luis Figo (Portugal)
2000 – Zinedine Zidane (France)
1999 – Rivaldo (Brazil)
1998 – Zinedine Zidane (France)
1997 – Ronaldo (Brazil)
1996 – Ronaldo (Brazil)
1995 – George Weah (Liberia)
1994 – Romario (Brazil)
1993 – Roberto Baggio (Italy)
1992 – Marco van Basten (Netherlands)

ATHLETICS

EUROPEAN CROSS-COUNTRY CHAMPIONSHIPS
Held at Heringsdorf, Germany, 12 December 2004

SENIOR MEN	(9,640m)	min. sec.
Individual:	Sergei Lebid (Ukraine)	27 31
Team:	France	28 pts

JUNIOR MEN	(5,640m)	
Individual:	Barnabas Bene (Hungary)	16 18
Team:	Russia	42 pts

SENIOR WOMEN	(5,640m)	
Individual:	Hayley Yelling (Great Britain)	18 06
Team:	Portugal	38 pts

JUNIOR WOMEN	(3,640m)	
Individual:	Binnaz Uslu (Turkey)	11 33
Team:	Romania	51 pts

ENGLISH NATIONAL CROSS-COUNTRY CHAMPIONSHIPS
Held at Birmingham, 19 February 2005

SENIOR MEN	(12km)	min. sec.
Individual:	Glynn Tromans (Coventry Godiva)	37 53
Team:	Salford	188pts

JUNIOR MEN	(9km)	
Individual:	Keith Gerrard (Manx)	31 50
Team:	Aldershot Farnham	74 pts

SENIOR WOMEN	(8km)	
Individual:	Hayley Yelling (Windsor Slough Eton Hounslow)	28 21
Team:	Bristol & West	55 pts

JUNIOR WOMEN (5km)		min. sec.
Individual:	Laura Kenney (Royal Sutton Coldfield)	18 53
Team:	Aldershot Farnham	132 pts

AAA INDOOR CHAMPIONSHIPS
Held at Sheffield, 12–13 February 2005

MEN
60m	Jason Gardener (Wessex)	6.60
200m	Paul Hession (Ireland)	21.01
400m	David Gillick (Ireland)	46.45
800m	James McIlroy (Windsor Slough Eton Hounslow)	1:47.94
1,500m	Neil Speaight (Belgrave)	3:45.87
3,000m	Mohamed Farah (Aldershot Farnham)	7:56.86
60mH	Allan Scott (Shaftesbury Barnet)	7.58

		metres
HJ	Rob Mitchell (Sale)	2.20
PV	Ashley Swain (Southampton)	5.25
LJ	Nathan Morgan (Birchfield)	7.96
TJ	Phillips Idowu (Belgrave)	17.30
SP	Emeka Udechuku (Woodford Green)	17.64

WOMEN
60m	Jeanette Kwakye (Woodford Green)	7.27
200m	Susan Deacon (Edinburgh SH)	23.67
400m	Kim Wall (Basingstoke)	53.45
800m	Jenny Meadows (Wigan)	2:04.43
1,500m	Hayley Ovens (Edinburgh SH)	4:19.11
3,000m	Jo Pavey (Exeter)	8:50.28
60mH	Sarah Claxton (Woodford Green)	7.96

		metres
HJ	Susan Jones (Trafford)	1.90
PV	Janine Whitlock (Trafford)	4.25
LJ	Jade Johnson (HHH)	6.50
TJ	Taneisha Scanlon (Ireland)	13.28
SP	Jo Duncan (Woodford Green)	15.27

EUROPEAN INDOOR CHAMPIONSHIPS
Held at Madrid, Spain, 4–6 March 2005

MEN
60m	Jason Gardener (Great Britain)	6.55
200m	Tobias Unger (Germany)	20.53
400m	David Gillick (Ireland)	46.30
800m	Dmitri Bogdanov (Russia)	1:48.61
1,500m	Ivan Heshko (Ukraine)	3:36.70
3,000m	Alistair Cragg (Ireland)	7:46.32
60mH	Ladji Doucouré (France)	7.50
4 x 400m	France	3:07.90

		metres
HJ	Stefan Holm (Sweden)	2.40
PV	Igor Pavlov (Russia)	5.90
LJ	Joan Lino Martinez (Spain)	8.37
TJ	Igor Spasovkhodski (Russia)	17.20
SP	Joachim Olsen (Denmark)	21.19
Heptathlon	Roman Sebrle (Czech Rep)	6,232 pts

WOMEN
60m	Kim Gevaert (Belgium)	7.16
200m	Ivet Lalova (Bulgaria)	22.91
400m	Svetlana Pospelova (Russia)	50.41

800m	Larisa Chzao (Russia)	1:59.97
1,500m	Elena Iagar (Romania)	4:03.09
3,000m	Lidia Chojecka (Poland)	8:43.76
60mH	Susanna Kallur (Sweden)	7.80
4 x 400m	Russia	3:28.00

		metres
HJ	Anna Chicherova (Russia)	2.01
PV	Yelena Isinbayeva (Russia)	4.90
LJ	Naide Gomes (Portugal)	6.70
TJ	Viktoriya Gurova (Russia)	14.74
SP	Nadyezhda Ostapchuk (Belarus)	19.37
Pentathlon	Carolina Kluft (Sweden)	4,948 pts

IAAF WORLD CROSS-COUNTRY CHAMPIONSHIPS
Held at St Galmier, France, 19–20 March 2005

SENIOR MEN	(12.02km)	min.	sec.
Individual:	Kenenisa Bekele (Ethiopia)	35	06
Team:	Ethiopia	24 pts	

SENIOR MEN	(4.2km)		
Individual:	Kenenisa Bekele (Ethiopia)	11	33
Team:	Ethiopia	23 pts	

JUNIOR MEN	(8.1km)		
Individual:	Augustine Choge (Kenya)	23	59
Team:	Kenya	10 pts	

SENIOR WOMEN (8.1km)			
Individual:	Tirunesh Dibaba (Ethiopia)	26	34
Team:	Ethiopia	16 pts	

SENIOR WOMEN (4.2km)			
Individual:	Tirunesh Dibaba (Ethiopia)	13	15
Team:	Ethiopia	18 pts	

JUNIOR WOMEN (6.15km)			
Individual:	Gelete Burika (Ethiopia)	20	12
Team:	Kenya	16 pts	

LONDON MARATHON
Held in London, 17 April 2005

		hr	min.	sec.
MEN	Martin Lel (Kenya)	2	07	26
WOMEN	Paula Radcliffe (Great Britain)	2	17	42

IAAF WORLD RACE WALKING CUP
Held at Naumburg, Germany, 1–2 May 2004

MEN		hr	min.	sec.
20km				
Individual:	Jefferson Perez (Ecuador)	1	18	42
Team:	China	18 pts		
50km				
Individual:	Aleksei Voyevodin (Russia)	3	42	44
Team:	Russia	8 pts		

WOMEN				
20km				
Individual:	Yelena Nikolayeva (Russia)	1	27	24
Team:	China	18 pts		

EUROPEAN CUP SUPER LEAGUE
Held at Florence, Italy, 17–19 June 2005

MEN		min.	sec.
100m	Ronald Pognon (France)		10.06
200m	Christian Malcolm (Great Britain)		20.15
400m	Marc Raquil (France)		45.80
800m	Antonio Reina (Spain)	1	46.11
1,500m	Juan Carlos Higuero (Spain)	3	41.72
3,000m	Jesus Espana (Spain)	8	16.48
5,000m	Juan Carlos de la Ossa (Spain)	13	30.97
3,000mSt	Antonio Jiminez (Spain)	8	20.17
110mH	Ladji Doucouré (France)		13.16
400mH	Naman Keita (France)		48.77
4 × 100m	Great Britain		38.67
4 × 400m	Great Britain	3	00.51

		metres
High Jump	Alexei Dimitrik (Russia)	2.30
Pole Vault	Giuseppe Gibilisco (Italy)	5.80
Long Jump	Nils Winter (Germany)	8.06
Triple Jump	Charles Friedek (Germany)	17.20
Shot	Ralf Bartels (Germany)	20.76
Discus	Mario Pestano (Spain)	66.29
Hammer	Szymon Ziolkowski (Poland)	79.14
Javelin	Mark Frank (Germany)	82.38

Points: Germany 113; France 104; Italy 98; Poland 94.5; Russia 88; Spain 86.5; Great Britain 70; Czech Republic 63

WOMEN		min.	sec.
100m	Christine Arron (France)		11.09
200m	Christine Arron (France)		22.84
400m	Natalya Antyukh (Russia)		50.67
800m	Maria Cioncan (Romania)	2	00.88
1,500m	Yuliya Chizhenko (Russia)	4	06.76
3,000m	Yelena Zadorozhnaya (Russia)	8	57.08
5,000m	Liliya Shobukhova (Russia)	15	01.15
3,000mSt	Cristina Casandra (Romania)	9	35.95
100mH	Linda Khodadin (France)		12.73
400mH	Anna Jeswien (Poland)		54.90
4 × 100m	Russia		42.73
4 × 400m	Russia	3	23.56

		metres
High Jump	Tatyana Kivimagi (Russia)	1.98
Pole Vault	Anna Rogowska (Poland)	4.60
Long Jump	Irina Simagina (Russia)	6.76
Triple Jump	Anna Pyatykh (Russia)	14.70
Shot	Olga Ryabinkina (Russia)	19.65
Discus	Franka Dietzsch (Germany)	64.38
Hammer	Kamila Skolimowska (Poland)	72.38
Javelin	Steffi Nerius (Germany)	64.59

Points: Russia 131.5; Poland 94; Germany 93; France 90.5; Ukraine 86; Romania 85; Italy 77; Greece 62

AAA CHAMPIONSHIPS
Held at Manchester, 9–10 July 2005

MEN		min.	sec.
100m	Jason Gardener (Bath & Wessex)		10.26
200m	Christian Malcolm (Cardiff)		20.65
400m	Tim Benjamin (Belgrave)		45.52
800m	Tim Bayley (Belgrave)	1	48.54
1,500m	Nick McCormick (Morpeth)	3	37.05
5,000m	Mark Carroll (Ireland)	13	48.90
10,000m*	Barnabas Kosgei (Kenya)	28	33.74
3,000mSt	Andrew Lemoncello (Fife)	8	33.93
110mH	Allan Scott (Shaftesbury Barnet)		13.62
400mH	Matt Elias (Cardiff)		49.67

		metres
High Jump	Ben Challenger (Belgrave)	2.27
Pole Vault	Nick Buckfield (Crawley)	5.50
Long Jump	Greg Rutherford (Milton Keynes)	7.79
Triple Jump	Nathan Douglas (Oxford City)	17.64
Shot	Carl Myerscough (Blackpool & Fylde)	20.27
Discus	Carl Myerscough (Blackpool & Fylde)	58.48
Hammer	Andy Frost (Woodford Green)	72.09
Javelin	Nick Nieland (Shaftesbury Barnet)	78.30
Decathlon**	Ben Hazell (Basingstoke & MH)	7,193 pts

WOMEN		min.	sec.
100m	Laura Turner (Harrow)		11.55
200m	Dawn Fraser (Croydon)		23.36
400m	Dawn Fraser (Croydon)		51.27
800m	Susan Scott (Glasgow)	2	02.97
1,500m	Helen Clitheroe (Preston)	4	08.29
5,000m	Hayley Yelling (WSE & H)	15	45.67
10,000m*	Kathy Butler (WSE & H)	31	46.53
3,000mSt	Tina Brown (Coventry)	10	01.57
100mH	Sarah Claxton (Woodford Green)		12.96
400mH	Nicola Sanders (WSE & H)		55.61

		metres
High Jump	Susan Jones (Trafford)	1.86
Pole Vault	Janine Whitlock (Trafford)	4.20
Long Jump	Kelly Sotherton (Birchfield)	6.48
Triple Jump	Taniesha Scanlon (Ireland)	13.30
Shot	Julie Dunkley (Shaftesbury Barnet)	16.14
Discus	Philippa Roles (Sale)	57.01
Hammer	Shirley Webb (Trafford)	66.60
Javelin	Goldie Sayers (Belgrave)	57.99
Heptathlon**	Kate Brewingon (Hav M)	5,041 pts

* Held at Watford, 11 June 2005
** Held at Hexham, 11–12 June 2005

WORLD ATHLETICS FINAL
Held at Monte Carlo, Monaco, 9–10 September 2005

MEN		min	sec
100m	Marc Burns (Trinidad)		10.00
200m	Tyson Gay (USA)		19.96
400m	Tyree Washington (USA)		44.51
800m	Wilfred Bungei (Kenya)	1	47.05
1,500m	Ivan Heshko (Ukraine)	3	33.50
3,000m	Bernard Lagat (USA)	7	38.00
5,000m	Sileshi Sihine (Ethiopia)	13	39.40
3,000mSt	Paul Koech (Kenya)	8	07.91
110mH	Allan Johnson (USA)		13.09
400mH	Bershawn Jackson (USA)		48.05

		metres
High Jump	Victor Moya (Cuba)	2.35
Pole Vault	Brad Walker (USA)	5.86
Long Jump	Dwight Phillips (USA)	8.46
Triple Jump	Yoandri Betanzos (Cuba)	17.46
Shot	Adam Nelson (USA)	21.92
Discus	Virgilijus Alekna (Lithuania)	67.64
Hammer*	Ivan Tikhon (Belarus)	81.70
Javelin	Tero Pitkamaki (Finland)	91.33

WOMEN		min	sec
100m	Veronica Campbell (Jamaica)		10.92
200m	Allyson Felix (USA)		22.27
400m	Sanya Richards (USA)		49.52
800m	Zulia Calatayud (Cuba)	1	59.07

1,500m	Maryam Jamal (Bahrain)	3	59.35
3,000m	Meseret Defar (Ethiopia)	8	47.26
5,000m	Meseret Defar (Ethiopia)	14	45.87
3,000mSt	Dorcus Inzikuru (Uganda)	9	21.80
100mH	Michelle Perry (USA)		12.54
400mH	Lashinda Demus (USA)		53.37

		metres
High Jump	Kajsa Bergquist (Sweden)	2.00
Pole Vault	Yelena Isinbayeva (Russia)	4.74
Long Jump	Tatyana Kotova (Russia)	6.83
Triple Jump	Hrysopiyi Devtzki (Greece)	14.89
Shot	Nadezhda Ostapchuk (Belarus)	20.44
Discus	Natalya Sadova (Russia)	63.40
Hammer*	Yipsi Moreno (Cuba)	74.75
Javelin	Osleidys Menendez (Cuba)	67.24

* Held at Szombathely, Hungary, 3 September

IAAF WORLD CHAMPIONSHIPS
Held at Helsinki, Finland, 6–14 August 2005

MEN		hr	min.	sec.
100m	Justin Gatlin (USA)			9.88
200m	Justin Gatlin (USA)			20.04
400m	Jeremy Wariner (USA)			43.93
800m	Rashid Ramzi (Bahrain)		1	44.24
1,500m	Rashid Ramzi (Bahrain)		3	37.88
5,000m	Benjamin Limo (Kenya)		13	32.55
10,000m	Kenenisa Bekele (Ethiopia)		27	08.33
Marathon	Jaouad Gharib (Morocco)	2	10	10
3,000 St	Saif Saaeed Shaheen (Qatar)		8	13.31
110mH	Ladji Doucouré (France)			13.07
400mH	Bershawn Jackson (USA)			47.30
4 x 100m	France			38.08
4 x 400m	United States		2	56.91
20km Walk	Jefferson Perez (Ecuador)	1	18	35
50km Walk	Sergei Kirdyapkin (Russia)	3	38	08

		metres
High Jump	Yuri Krymarenko (Ukraine)	2.32
Pole Vault	Rene Blom (Netherlands)	5.80
Long Jump	Dwight Phillips (USA)	8.60
Triple Jump	Walter Davis (USA)	17.57
Shot	Adam Nelson (USA)	21.73
Discus	Virglijus Alekna (Lithuania)	70.17
Hammer	Ivan Tikhon (Belarus)	83.89
Javelin	Arrus Varnik (Estonia)	87.17
Decathlon	Brian Clay (USA)	8,732 pts

WOMEN		hr	min.	sec.
100m	Lauryn Williams (USA)			10.93
200m	Allyson Felix (USA)			22.16
400m	Tonique Williams-Darling (Bahamas)			49.55
800m	Zulia Catalayud (Cuba)		1	58.82
1,500m	Tatyana Tomashova (Russia)		4	00.35
5,000m	Tirunesh Dibaba (Ethiopia)		14	38.59
10,000m	Tirunesh Dibaba (Ethiopia)		30	24.02
Marathon	Paula Radcliffe (GBR)	2	20	57
3,000mSt	Dorcus Inzikuru (Uganda)		9	18.24
100mH	Michelle Perry (USA)			12.66
400mH	Yuliya Pechonkina (Russia)			52.90
4 x 100m	United States			41.78
4 x 400m	Russia		3	20.95
20km Walk	Olimpiada Ivanova (Russia)	1	25	41

		metres
High Jump	Kajsa Bergquist (Sweden)	2.02
Pole Vault	Yelena Isinbayeva (Russia)	5.01
Long Jump	Tianna Madison (USA)	6.89
Triple Jump	Trecia Smith (Jamaica)	15.11
Shot	Nadezhda Ostapchuk (Belarus)	20.51
Discus	Franka Dietzsch (Germany)	66.56
Hammer	Olga Kuzenkova (Russia)	75.10
Javelin	Osleidys Menendez (Cuba)	71.70
Heptathlon	Carolina Kluft (Sweden)	6,887 pts

BADMINTON

WORLD CHAMPIONSHIPS 2005
Los Angeles, USA, August

Men's Singles: Taufik Hidayat (Indonesia), beat Lin Dan (China), 2–0
Ladies' Singles: Xingfang Xie (China), beat Ning Zhang (China), 2–1
Men's Doubles: Tony Gunawan and Howard Bach (USA), beat Candra Wijaya and Sigit Budiarto (Indonesia), 2–1
Ladies' Doubles: Wei Yang and Jiewen Zhang (China), beat Ling Gao and Sui Huang (China), 2–0
Mixed Doubles: Nova Widianto and Lilyana Natsir (Indonesia), beat Zhongbo Xie and Yawen Zhang (China), 2–1

ENGLISH NATIONAL CHAMPIONSHIPS 2005
Manchester, February

Men's Singles: Aamir Ghaffar beat Nicholas Kidd 2–0
Ladies' Singles: Elizabeth Cann beat Tracey Hallam 2–0
Men's Doubles: Simon Archer and Anthony Clark beat Robert Blair and Nathan Robertson 2–0
Ladies' Doubles: Gail Emms and Donna Kellogg beat Ella Tripp and Jo Wright 2–0
Mixed Doubles: Nathan Robertson and Gail Emms beat Robert Blair and Natalie Munt 2–0

SCOTTISH NATIONAL CHAMPIONSHIPS 2005
Perth, February

Men's Singles: Craig Goddard beat Bruce Flockhart 2–1
Ladies' Singles: Yuan Wemyss beat Susan Hughes 2–0
Men's Doubles: David Gilmour and Craig Robertson beat Graham Simpson and Graeme Smith 2–0
Ladies' Doubles: Sandra Watt and Yuan Wemyss beat Michelle Douglas and Kirsten McEwan-Miller 2–0
Mixed Doubles: Andrew Bowman and Kirsten McEwan-Miller beat Craig Robertson and Sandra Watt 2–1

ALL-ENGLAND CHAMPIONSHIPS 2005
Birmingham, March

Men's Singles: Hong Chen (China), beat Dan Lin (China), 2–1
Ladies' Singles: Xingfang Xie (China), beat Ning Zhang (China), 2–0
Men's Doubles: Yun Cai and Haifeng Fu (China), beat Lars Paaske and Jonas Rasmussen (Denmark), 2–0
Ladies' Doubles: Ling Gao and Sui Huang (China), beat Yili Wei and Tingting Zhao (China), 2–0
Mixed Doubles: Nathan Robertson and Gail Emms (Great Britain), beat Thomas Laybourn and Kamilla Rytter Juhl (Denmark), 2–0

BASEBALL

American League Championship Series 2004: Boston Red Sox beat New York Yankees 4–3
National League Championship Series 2004: St Louis Cardinals beat Houston Astros 4–3
World Series 2004: Boston Red Sox beat St Louis Cardinals 4–0

BASKETBALL

BRITISH

MEN
BBL Championship Final 2005: Newcastle Eagles beat Chester Jets 78–75
BBL Trophy Final 2005: Newcastle Eagles beat Brighton Bears 85–60
BBL Cup Final 2005: Brighton Bears beat Scottish Rocks 90–74
BBL Champions 2004–5: Chester Jets

WOMEN
EBL Division 1 2004–05: Rhondda Rebels
EBL Division 1 Play-off final 2004–05: Rhondda Rebels beat Sheffield Hatters 64–58
National Cup: Rhondda Rebels beat Sheffield Hatters 78–63

NORTH AMERICA – NATIONAL BASKETBALL LEAGUE (NBA)
Eastern Conference final 2005: Detroit Pistons beat Miami Heat 4–3
Western Conference final 2005: San Antonio Spurs beat Phoenix Suns 4–1
NBA final 2005: San Antonio Spurs beat Detroit Pistons 4–3

BOWLS – OUTDOOR

BRITISH ISLES CHAMPIONSHIPS 2005
Ayr, July

Singles: Ireland beat Scotland 21–18
Pairs: Guernsey beat Scotland 30–19
Triples: England beat Scotland 19–18
Fours: Scotland beat Jersey 16–14

ENGLISH NATIONAL CHAMPIONSHIPS 2005
Worthing, August

MEN
Singles: Middlesex 'A' beat Nottinghamshire 'A' 21–11
Pairs: Warwickshire 'A' beat Yorkshire 'B' 24–9
Triples: Wiltshire 'A' beat Cornwall 'A' 19–16
Fours: Berkshire 'A' beat Hampshire 'B' 18–17
Middleton Cup (Inter-County Championship), final 2005: Cumbria beat Oxfordshire 126–115

BOWLS – INDOOR

WORLD CHAMPIONSHIPS 2005
Norfolk, January

Men's Singles: Paul Foster (Scotland), beat John Price (Wales), 1–0
Women's Singles: Ellen Falkner (England), beat Caroline Brown (Scotland), 2–1

Men's Pairs: Mervyn King (England), and Kelvin Kerkow (Australia), beat Greg Harlow (England), and Jonathan Ross (Ireland), 2–0
Mixed Pairs: Carol Ashby (England), and John Price (Wales), beat Michelle Barlow (England), and Robert Weale (Wales), 2–1

BRITISH ISLES INDOOR BOWLS CHAMPIONSHIPS 2005
Belfast, March

Singles: Darren Burnett (Scotland), beat Jeremy Henry (Ireland), 21–15
Pairs: Ireland beat Channel Islands 24–23
Triples: Scotland beat Wales 24–8
Fours: England beat Ireland 31–14

ENGLISH NATIONAL CHAMPIONSHIPS 2005
Melton Mowbray, April

Singles: Andy Thomson beat Bill Hobart 21–11
Pairs: Nottingham beat Exonia 20–16
Triples: Lincoln beat Mid Gloucestershire 21–9
Fours: City of Ely beat Newquay 25–5
Liberty Trophy (Inter-County Championship), final: Norfolk CIBA beat Kent CIBA 110–106
Champion of Champions 2004–05: Graham Shadwell beat Paul Bennett 21–16

BOXING

PROFESSIONAL BOXING
as at 1 September 2005

WORLD BOXING COUNCIL (WBC), CHAMPIONS
Heavy: Vitali Klitschko (Germany)
Cruiser: Jean-Marc Mormeck (France)
Light-heavy: Tomasz Adamek (Poland)
Super-middle: Markus Beyer (Germany)
Middle: Jermain Taylor (USA)
Super-welter: Ricardo Mayorga (Nicaragua)
Welter: Zab Judah (USA)
Super-light: Floyd Mayweather (USA)
Light: Diego Corrales (USA)
Super-feather: Marco Antonio Barrera (Mexico)
Feather: Injin Chi (Korea)
Super-bantam: Oscar Larios (Mexico)
Bantam: Hozumi Hasegawa (Japan)
Super-fly: Masamori Tokuyama (Japan)
Fly: Pongsaklek Wonjongkam (Thailand)
Light-fly: Eric Ortiz (Mexico)
Straw: Eagle Kyowa (Japan)

WORLD BOXING ASSOCIATION (WBA), CHAMPIONS
Heavy: John Ruiz (USA)
Cruiser: Jean-Marc Mormeck (France)
Light-heavy: Fabrice Tiozzo (France)
Super-middle: Mikel Kessler (Denmark)
Middle: Jermain Taylor (USA)
Super-welter: Alejandro Garcia (Mexico)
Welter: Zab Judah (USA)
Super-light: Carlos Maussa (Columbia)
Light: Juan Diaz (USA)
Super-feather: Vicente Mosquera (Panama)
Feather: Juan Manuel Marquez (Mexico)
Super-bantam: Mahyar Monshipour (France)
Bantam: Wladimir Sidorenko (Ukraine)
Super-fly: Martin Castillo (Mexico)
Fly: Lorenzo Parra (Venezuela)
Light-fly: Roberto Vasques (Panama)
Straw: Yukata Niida (Japan)

WORLD BOXING ORGANISATION (WBO), CHAMPIONS
Heavy: Lamon Brewster (USA)
Cruiser: Johnny Nelson (England)
Light-heavy: Zsolt Erdei (Hungary)
Super-middle: Joe Calzaghe (Wales)
Middle: Jermain Taylor (USA)
Super-welter: Daniel Santos (Puerto Rico)
Welter: Antonio Margarito (Mexico)
Super-light: Miguel Cotto (Puerto Rico)
Light: Diego Corrales (USA)
Super-feather: Jorge Barrios (Argentina)
Feather: Scott Harrison (England)
Super-bantam: *vacant*
Bantam: Ratanachai Sor Vorapin (Thailand)
Super-fly: Fernando Montiel (Mexico)
Fly: Omar Narvaez (Argentina)
Light-fly: Hugo Cazarez (Mexico)
Straw: Ivan Calderon (Puerto Rico)

INTERNATIONAL BOXING FEDERATION (IBF),
CHAMPIONS
Heavy: Chris Byrd (USA)
Cruiser: O'Neill Bell (USA)
Light-heavy: Clinton Woods (England)
Super-middle: Jeff Lacy (USA)
Middle: Jermain Taylor (USA)
Super-welter: Roman Karmazin (Russia)
Welter: Zab Judah (USA)
Super-light: Ricky Hatton (England)
Light: Leavander Johnson (USA)
Super-feather: Robbie Peden (USA)
Feather: *vacant*
Super-bantam: Isreal Vasquez (Mexico)
Bantam: Rafael Marquez (Mexico)
Super-fly: Luis Perez (Nicaragua)
Fly: Vic Darchinian (Argentina)
Light-fly: Will Grigsby (USA)
Straw: Muhamad Rachman (Indonesia)

BRITISH CHAMPIONS
Heavy: Matt Skelton
Cruiser: Mark Hobson
Light-heavy: Peter Oboh
Super-middle: Carl Froch
Middle: Scott Dann
Light-middle: Jamie Moore
Welter: Michael Jennings
Light-welter: Junior Witter
Light: Graham Earl
Super-feather: Alex Arthur
Feather: Nicky Cook
Super-bantam: Michael Hunter
Bantam: Martin Power
Fly: *vacant*

CHESS

European Championship 2005 (Warsaw, June–July): Liviu-Dieter Nisipeanu (Romania)

CRICKET

TEST SERIES

ENGLAND V. SOUTH AFRICA
Port Elizabeth (17–21 December 2004): England beat South Africa by 7 wickets. South Africa 337 and 229; England 425 and 145–3.

Durban (26–30 December 2004): England drew with South Africa. England 139 and 570–7; South Africa 332 and 290–8.
Cape Town (2–6 January 2005): South Africa beat England by 196 runs. South Africa 441 and 222–8; England 163 and 304.
Johannesburg (13–17 January 2005): England beat South Africa by 77 runs. England 441–8 and 332–9; South Africa 419 and 247.
Centurion (21–25 January 2005): England drew with South Africa. South Africa 247 and 296–6; England 359 and 73–4.

ENGLAND V. BANGLADESH
Lord's (26–30 May 2005): England beat Bangladesh by an innings and 261 runs. Bangladesh 108 and 159; England 528–3.
Riverside (3–7 June 2005): England beat Bangladesh by an innings and 27 runs. Bangladesh 104 and 316; England 447–3.

ENGLAND V. AUSTRALIA
Lord's (21–25 July 2005): Australia beat England by 239 runs. Australia 190 and 384; England 155 and 180.
Edgbaston (4–8 August 2005): England beat Australia by 2 runs. England 407 and 182; Australia 308 and 279.
Old Trafford (11–15 August 2005): England drew with Australia. England 444 and 280–6; Australia 302 and 371–9.
Trent Bridge (25–29 August 2005): England beat Australia by 3 wickets. England 477 and 129–7; Australia 218 and 387.
Oval (8–12 September 2005): England drew with Australia. England 373 and 335; Australia 367 and 4–0.

ONE-DAY INTERNATIONALS

ENGLAND V. ZIMBABWE
Harare (28 November 2004): England beat Zimbabwe by 5 wickets. Zimbabwe 195; England 197–5.
Harare (1 December 2004): England beat Zimbabwe by 161 runs. England 263–6; Zimbabwe 102.
Bulawayo (4 December 2004): England beat Zimbabwe by 8 wickets. Zimbabwe 238–7; England 239–2.
Bulawayo (5 December 2004): England beat Zimbabwe by 74 runs. England 261–6; Zimbabwe 187.

ENGLAND V. SOUTH AFRICA
Johannesburg (30 January 2005): England beat South Africa by 26 runs (*Duckworth-Lewis*). South Africa 175–9; England 103–3.
Bloemfontein (2 February 2005): South Africa drew with England. England 270–5; South Africa 270–8.
Port Elizabeth (4 February 2005): South Africa beat England by 3 wickets. England 267–8; South Africa 270–7.
Cape Town (6 February 2005): South Africa beat England by 108 runs. South Africa 291–5; England 183.
East London (9 February 2005): South Africa beat England by 7 runs. South Africa 311–7; England 304–8.
Durban (11 February 2005): No result. South Africa 211; England 7–2.
Centurion (13 February 2005): South Africa beat England by 3 wickets. England 240; South Africa 241–7.

NATWEST SERIES
The Oval (16 June 2005): England beat Bangladesh by 10 wickets. Bangladesh 190; England 192–0.

Sophia Gardens (18 June 2005): Bangladesh beat Australia by 5 wickets. Australia 249–5; Bangladesh 250–5.

Bristol (19 June 2005): England beat Australia by 3 wickets. Australia 252–9; England 253–7

Trent Bridge (21 June 2005): England beat Bangladesh by 168 runs. England 391–4; Bangladesh 223.

Riverside (23 June 2005): Australia beat England by 57 runs. Australia 266–5; England 209–9.

Old Trafford (25 June 2005): Australia beat Bangladesh by 10 wickets. Bangladesh 139; Australia 140–0.

Headingley (26 June 2005): England beat Bangladesh by 5 wickets. Bangladesh 208–7; England 209–5.

Edgbaston (28 June 2005): No result. Australia 261–9; England 37–1.

Canterbury (30 June 2005): Australia beat Bangladesh by 6 wickets. Bangladesh 250–8; Australia 254–4.

Final: Lord's (2 July 2005): England tied with Australia. Australia 196; England 196–9.

NATWEST CHALLENGE

Headingley (7 July 2005): England beat Australia by 9 wickets. Australia 219–7; England 221–1.

Lord's (10 July 2005): Australia beat England by 7 wickets. England 223–8; Australia 224–3.

Oval (12 July 2005): Australia beat England by 8 wickets. England 228–7; Australia 229–2.

ENGLAND AND WALES DOMESTIC
COMPETITIONS 2005

County Championship: see Stop Press

National League: see Stop Press

C & G Trophy final: Hampshire beat Warwickshire by 18 runs. Hampshire 290; Warwickshire 272.

Twenty20 Cup final: Somerset beat Lancashire by 7 wickets. Lancashire 114–8; Somerset 118–3.

OTHER INTERNATIONAL DOMESTIC
CHAMPIONSHIPS

Australia: Pura Cup final 2004–05: New South Wales beat Queensland by 1 wicket. Queensland 102 and 268; New South Wales 188 and 183–9. *ING Cup final 2004–05:* Tasmania beat Queensland by 7 wickets. Queensland 246–7; Tasmania 247–3.

Bangladesh: National League 2004–05: Dhaka Division 43 points. *National One-Day League 2004–05:* Rajshahi Division 16 points.

India: Irani Trophy 2004–05: Rest of India beat Mumbai by 290 runs. Rest of India 314 and 378; Mumbai 198 and 204. *Ranji Trophy Elite final 2004–05:* Punjab drew with Railways. Railways wins the trophy. Railways 355 and 471; Punjab 309 and 137–4. *Ranji Trophy One-Day Competition 2004–05:* Tamil Nadu tied with Uttar Pradesh. Trophy shared. Tamil Nadu 248; Uttar Pradesh 248. *Deodhar Trophy 2004–05:* North Zone, 14 points. *Duleep Trophy final 2004–05:* Central Zone beat North Zone by 9 wickets. North Zone 104 and 169. Central Zone 133 and 142–1.

New Zealand: State Championship final 2004–05: Auckland beat Wellington by 7 wickets. Wellington 235 and 297; Auckland 325 and 209–3. *State Shield final 2004–05:* Northern Districts beat Central Districts by 20 runs. Northern Districts 190–9; Central Districts 170.

Pakistan: ABN-AMRO Cup final 2004–05: Lahore Region beat Sialkot Region by 95 runs. Lahore Region 278–5; Sialkot Region 183. *ABN-AMRO Patron's Cup final 2004–05:* Water and Power Development Authority beat Pakistan International Airlines by 36 runs. Water and Power Development Authority 288–9; Pakistan International Airlines 252. *ABN-AMRO Patron's Trophy final 2004–05:* Habib Bank drew with Pakistan International Airlines. Habib Bank 444; Pakistan International Airlines 154–3. *ABN-AMRO Twenty–20 Cup final 2004–05:* Faisalabad Wolves beat Karachi Dolphins by 2 wickets. Karachi Dolphins 158–7; Faisalabad Wolves 159–8. *Quaid-e-Azam Trophy final 2004–05:* Faisalabad Region drew with Peshawar Region. Faisalabad Region 226 and 217–9; Peshawar Region 279 and 83–0.

South Africa: SuperSport Series final 2004–05: Eagles drew with Dolphins. Series shared. Eagles 334 and 345–9; Dolphins 612–8. *Standard Bank Cup final 2004–05:* Eagles beat Titans by 7 wickets. Titans 258–5; Eagles 259–3. *UCB Provincial Cup final 2004–5:* Griqualand West beat Border by 7 wickets. Border 240 and 151; Griqualand West 184 and 208–3. *UCB Provincial Shield final 2004–5:* Free State beat Boland by 5 wickets. Boland 277–7; Free State 281–5. *Standard Bank Pro20 Series final 2004–05:* Titans beat Warriors by 8 wickets. Warriors 121; Titans 125–2.

Sri Lanka: Inter-Provincial Tournament final 2004–05: North Central Province beat Central Province by 60 runs. North Central Province 175 and 221; Central Province 202 and 134. *Premier League Tournament final 2004–05:* Colts Cricket Club drew with Burgher Recreation Club. Colts Cricket Club wins tournament. Colts Cricket Club 374 and 162–5; Burgher Recreation Club 178. *Twenty20 Cup final 2004:* Chilaw Marians beat Colts by 103 runs. Chilaw Marians 227–6; Colts 124.

West Indies: Carib Beer Cup final 2004–05: Jamaica beat Leeward Islands by 8 wickets. Leeward Islands 180 and 442; Jamaica 372 and 252–2. *Regional Tournament final 2004–5:* Trinidad and Tobago beat Guyana by 4 wickets. Guyana 160; Trinidad and Tobago 161–6.

Zimbabwe: Logan Cup 2004–05: Mashonaland. *Inter-Provincial One-Day Competition 2004–05:* Matabeleland, 12.

CURLING

EUROPEAN CHAMPIONSHIPS 2004
Sofia, Bulgaria, December

Men's final: Germany beat Sweden 8–7

Women's final: Sweden beat Switzerland 9–4

MEN'S WORLD CHAMPIONSHIPS 2005
Victoria, Canada, April

Final: Canada beat Scotland 11–4

WOMEN'S WORLD CHAMPIONSHIPS 2005
Paisley, Scotland, March

Final: Sweden beat USA 10–4

CYCLING

BRITISH NATIONAL ROAD RACE
CHAMPIONSHIPS 2005
Newport, June

MEN
Road Race: Roger Hammond

WOMEN
Road Race: Nicole Cooke

WORLD ROAD CYCLING CHAMPIONSHIPS 2004
Verona, Italy, September–October

MEN
Elite Time Trial (46.75km): Michael Rogers (Australia), 57:30.12
Road Race (265.5km): Oscar Freire Gomez (Spain), 6hr 57:15

WOMEN
Elite Time Trial (24.05km): Karin Thurig (Switzerland), 30:53.65
Road Race (132.75km): Judith Arndt (Germany), 3hr 44:38

GIRO D'ITALIA 2005: Paolo Savoldelli (Italy)
TOUR DE FRANCE 2005: Lance Armstrong (USA)
TOUR OF BRITAIN 2005: Nick Nuyens (Belgium)
TOUR OF SPAIN 2005 (September 18): Roberto Heras (Spain)

WORLD TRACK CHAMPIONSHIPS 2005
Los Angeles, USA, March

MEN
Points race: Volodymyr Rybin (Ukraine)
Olympic Sprint: Chris Hoy, Jason Queally, Jamie Staff (Great Britain)
1km Time Trial: Theo Bos (Netherlands)
Individual Pursuit: Robert Bartko (Germany)
Scratch Race: Alex Rasmussen (Denmark)
Keirin: Teun Mulder (Netherlands)
Team Pursuit: Steven Cummings, Robert Hayles, Paul Manning, Christopher Newton (Great Britain)
Madison: Mark Cavendish and Robert Hayles (Great Britain)
Sprint: Rene Wolff (Germany)

WOMEN
Keirin: Clara Sanchez (France)
Individual Pursuit: Katie Mactier (Australia)
Points Race: Vera Carrara (Italy)
Sprint: Victoria Pendleton (Great Britain)
Scratch: Olga Slyusareva (Russia)
500m Time Trial: Natallia Tsylinskaya (Belarus)

DARTS

BDO World Championship 2005: Raymond van Barneveld (Netherlands), beat Martin Adams (England), 6–2
PDC World Championship 2005: Phil Taylor (England), beat Mark Dudbridge (England), 7–4

EQUESTRIANISM

Badminton Horse Trials 2005: Pippa Funnell (Great Britain), on Primmore's Pride
British Open Horse Trials 2005 (Gatcombe Park): William Fox-Pitt (Great Britain), on Moon Man
Burghley Horse Trials 2005: William Fox-Pitt (Great Britain), on Ballincoola

ETON FIVES

Amateur Championship (Kinnaird Cup), final 2005: J. Toop and M. Wiseman beat T. Dunbar and P. Dunbar 3–1
Alan Barber Cup final 2005: Old Olavians beat Old Harrovians 2–1

County Championship final 2005: Kent beat Suffolk 2–1
Schools' Championship 2005: Highgate (M. R. Little and A. A. O'Callaghan), beat Shrewsbury (T. W. P. Cox and B. J. Alderson), 3–2
Preparatory Schools' Tournament 2005: Highgate 2 (M. Korav and C. Most), beat Highgate 1 (T. Cooling and H. Hatchwell), 2–1

FENCING

BRITISH CHAMPIONSHIPS 2005
RAF Cosford, July

MEN
Individual Foil: Jamie Kenber
Individual Epée: Chris Howser
Individual Sabre: Alex O'Connell
Team Foil: Salle Paul 'A'
Team Epée: Haverstock 'A'
Team Sabre: Brentwood

WOMEN
Individual Foil: Camille Datoo
Individual Epée: Kate Allenby
Individual Sabre: Chrystall Nicoll
Team Foil: Salle Paul 'A'
Team Epée: Haverstock 'A'
Team Sabre: Swash and Buckle 'A'

GOLF (MEN)

THE MAJOR CHAMPIONSHIPS 2005
US Masters (Augusta, 7–10 April): Tiger Woods (USA), 276
US Open (Pinehurst No.2, 16–19 June): Michael Campbell (New Zealand), 280
The Open (Old Course, St Andrews, 14–17 July): Tiger Woods (USA), 274
US PGA Championship (Baltusrol, New Jersey, 11–14 August): Phil Mickelson (USA), 276

WORLD RANKINGS
(as at 1 September 2005)

1. Tiger Woods (USA); 2. Vijay Singh (Fiji); 3. Phil Mickelson (USA); 4. Ernie Els (South Africa); 5. Retief Goosen (South Africa)

EUROPEAN TOUR ORDER OF MERIT
(as at 1 September 2005)

1. Michael Campbell (New Zealand); 2. Retief Goosen (South Africa); 3. Colin Montgomerie (Scotland); 4. Angel Cabrera (Argentina); 5. Thomas Bjorn (Denmark)

PGA EUROPEAN TOUR 2004
WGC Championship (Mount Juliet Conrad, USA): Ernie Els (South Africa), 270
Dunhill Links Championship (Old Course, St Andrews, Scotland): Stephen Gallagher (Scotland), 269
Mallorca Classic (Pula): Sergio Garcia (Spain), 268
World Match Play Championship (Wentworth, England): Ernie Els (South Africa)
Open de Madrid (Club de Campo): Richard Sterne (South Africa), 266
Volvo Masters Andalucia (Valderrama): Ian Poulter (England), 277
WGC World Cup (Real Club De Golf De Sevilla, Spain): England (Luke Donald and Paul Casey), 257

PGA EUROPEAN TOUR 2005
China Open (Shanghai Silport): Stephen Dodd (Wales), 276
Hong Kong Open (Hong Kong): Miguel Angel Jiménez (Spain), 266
Dunhill Championship (Leopold Creek, South Africa): Charl Schwartzel (South Africa), 281
South African Airways Open (Durban): Tim Clark (South Africa), 273
Caltex Masters (Laguna National, Singapore): Nick Dougherty (England), 270
Heineken Classic (Royal Melbourne, Australia): Craig Parry (Australia), 270
New Zealand Open (Gulf Harbour): Niclas Fasth (Sweden), 266
Malaysian Open (Saujana): Thongchai Jaidee (Thailand), 267
WGC – Accenture Match Play (La Costa, USA): David Toms (USA)
Dubai Desert Classic (Emirates): Ernie Els (South Africa), 269
Qatar Masters (Doha): Ernie Els (South Africa), 276
TCL Classic (Yalong Bay, China): Paul Casey (England), 266
Indonesia Open (Cengkareng): Thaworn Wiratchant (Thailand), 255
Open de Portugal (Quinta da Marinha): Paul Broadhurst (England), 271
Madeira Island Open (Santo da Serra): Robert-Jan Derksen (Netherlands), 275
Open de Espana en Andalucia (San Roque): Peter Hanson (Sweden), 280
Johnnie Walker Classic (Pine Valley, Australia): Adam Scott (Australia), 270
Asian Open (Shanghai Pudong, China): Ernie Els (South Africa), 262
Italian Open (Castello di Tolcinasco): Steve Webster (England), 270
British Masters (Forest of Arden, England): Thomas Björn (Denmark), 282
Irish Open (Carton House): Stephen Dodd (Wales), 279
BMW Championship (Wentworth, England): Angel Cabrera (Argentina), 273
Wales Open (Celtic Manor): Miguel Angel Jiménez (Spain), 262
Dutch Open (Hilversumsche): Gonzalo Fernandez-Castan (Spain), 269
Aa St Omer Open (Aa St Omer, France): Joakim Bäckström (Sweden), 280
Open de France (Le Golf National): Jean-Francois Remesy (France), 273
European Open (K Club, Ireland): Kenneth Ferrie (England), 285
Scottish Open (Loch Lomond): Tim Clark (South Africa), 265
Players Championship of Europe (Gut Kaden, Germany): Niclas Fasth (Sweden), 274
Scandinavian Masters (Kungsängen, Sweden): Mark Hensby (Australia), 262
Johnnie Walker Championship (Gleneagles, Scotland): Emanuele Canonica (Italy), 281
Russian Open (Le Meridien, Moscow): Mikael Lundberg (Sweden), 273
WGC NEC Invitational (Firestone, USA): Tiger Woods (USA), 274
BMW International Open (München Nord-Eichenried, Germany): David Howell (England), 265
Omega European Masters (Crans-sur-Sierre): Sergio Garcia (Spain), 270

German Masters (Gut larchenhof): Retief Goosen (South Africa), 268
Seve Trophy: see Stop Press

AMATEUR CHAMPIONSHIPS
British Amateur Championship 2005 (St Andrews): Brian McElhinney
English Amateur Championship 2005 (Bronborough): Paul Waring
Welsh Amateur Championship 2005 (Prestatyn): Carl Wakely
Scottish Amateur Championship 2005 (Southerness): Glenn Campbell
Brabazon Trophy (English Open Strokeplay) 2005 (Royal Birkdale): Lloyd Saltman, 278
Welsh Open Strokeplay 2005 (Royal St Davids): Robert Dinwiddie, 268
Scottish Open Strokeplay 2005 (Royal Aberdeen): Robert Dinwiddie, 281
Irish Amateur Open Championship 2005 (Carton House): Richie Ramsay, 283
Lytham Trophy 2005 (Royal Lytham Golf Club): Gary Lockerbie, 276
Irish Amateur Close Championship 2005 (Westport): Rory McIlroy
Walker Cup (Chicago, USA): USA beat Great Britain and Northern Ireland 12½–11½

GOLF (WOMEN)

THE MAJOR CHAMPIONSHIPS 2005
Kraft Nabisco Championship (Mission Hills Country Club, USA): Annika Sorenstam (Sweden), 273
US Women's Open (Cherry Hills): Birdie Kim (Korea), 287
McDonalds LPGA Championship (Bulle Rock, USA): Annika Sorenstam (Sweden), 277
Weetabix Women's British Open (Royal Birkdale, England): Jeong Jang (Korea), 272

EUROPEAN LPGA TOUR 2004
Catalonia Ladies' Masters' (Sant Cugat): Karine Icher (France), 190

EUROPEAN LPGA TOUR ORDER OF MERIT 2004
1. Laura Davies (England); 2. Trish Johnson (England); 3. Stephanie Arricau (France); 4. Karine Icher (France); 5. Asa Gottmo (Sweden)

EUROPEAN LPGA TOUR 2005
Samsung Ladies' Masters (Laguna National, Singapore): Bo Bae Song (Korea), 206
Women's World Cup of Golf (Fancourt, South Africa): Ai Miyazato and Rui Kitada (Japan), 289
ANZ Ladies' Masters (Royal Pines, Australia): Karrie Webb (Australia), 272
Thailand Ladies' Open (Alpine): Shani Waugh (Australia), 282
Tenerife Ladies' Open (Costa Adeje): Ludivine Kreutz (France), 277
Open de Espana Femenino (Panoramica): Iben Tinning (Denmark), 273
Austrian Ladies' Open (Fohrenwald-Wiener): Federica Piovano (Italy), 272
Ladies' Italian Open (Parco de' Medici): Iben Tinning (Denmark), 271
Open de France Dames (Le Golf d'Arras): Veronica Zorzi (Italy), 276
Ladies' Open of Portugal (Gramacho Pestana): Cecilia Ekelundh (Sweden), 210

Ladies' English Open (Chart Hills): Maria Hjorth (Sweden), 204

Ladies' Central European Open – Hungary (Old Lake): Ludivine Kreutz (France), 199

Evian Masters (Evian Masters, France): Paula Creamer (USA), 273

Scandinavian TPC (Barseback): Annika Sorenstam (Sweden), 284

Wales Ladies' Championship of Europe (Machynys Peninsula): Kirsty Taylor (England), 274

Ladies' Finnish Masters (Helsinki): Lisa Holm Sorensen (Denmark), 140

Nykredit Masters (Helsinki): Iben Tinning (Denmark), 273

Dutch Ladies' Open (Kennemer): Virginia Lagoutte (France), 215

Catalonia Masters (Platja de Pals): *see* Stop Press

Solheim Cup (Crooked Stick, USA): The USA beat Europe by 15½ to 12½

AMATEUR CHAMPIONSHIPS 2005

British Open Championship (Littlestone): Louise Stahle (Sweden)

British Open Amateur Strokeplay Championship (Nairn): Heather Macrae (Scotland), 288

Scottish Open Strokeplay Championship (Troon): Martina Gillen (Ireland), 215 (won play-off at the first hole)

Scottish Close Amateur Championship (Cruden Bay): Fiona Lockhart (Scotland)

English Close Amateur Championship (Burnham and Berrow): Felicity Johnson (England)

English Strokeplay Championship: Laura Eastwood (England), 287

Welsh Open Strokeplay (Pyle and Kenfig): Henni Brockway (England), 218

Irish Open Strokeplay Championship: Tara Delaney (Ireland), 219

GREYHOUND RACING

2004
Oaks (Wimbledon): Tidyplayroom
St Leger (Wimbledon): Roxholme Girl
Television Trophy (Wimbledon): Double Take
Pall Mall Stakes (Oxford): Tims Crow

2005
The Derby (Wimbledon): Westmead Hawk
Television Trophy (Wimbledon): Ericas Equity

GYMNASTICS

EUROPEAN CHAMPIONSHIPS 2005
Debrecen, Hungary, June

MEN
Overall Champion: Marinez Rafael (Spain)
Individual Apparatus Champions
 Floor: Marian Dragulescu (Romania)
 Pommel Horse: Krisztian Berki (Hungary)
 Still Rings: Andrea Coppolino (Italy)
 Vault: Evgeni Sapronenko (Latvia)
 Parallel Bars: Manuel Carballo (Spain)
 High Bar: Fabian Hambüchen (Germany)

WOMEN
Overall Champion: Marine Debauve (France)
Individual Apparatus Champions
 Floor: Isabelle Severino (France)
 Beam: Catalina Ponor (Romania)
 Vault: Francesca Benolli (Italy)
 Assymetric Bars: Emilie Lepennec (France)

BRITISH WOMEN'S CHAMPIONSHIPS 2005
Guildford, July

Overall Champion: Elizabeth Tweddle
Individual Apparatus Champions
 Floor: Elizabeth Tweddle
 Beam: Elizabeth Tweddle
 Vault: Elizabeth Tweddle
 Assymetric Bars: Elizabeth Tweddle

HOCKEY

MEN
English Hockey League 2004–5: Premier Division 1: Cannock 57 points; Premier Division 2: East Grinstead 50 points; Premier Division 3: Holcombe 56 points
Cup 2004–5: Cannock beat Loughborough 2–0
County Championship: Warwickshire beat Suffolk 4–2

WOMEN
English Hockey League 2004–5: Premier Division 1: Leicester 53 points; Premier Division 2: Old Loughtonians 57 points; Premier Division 3: Bradford 52 points
Cup 2004–5: Fyffes Leicester beat Clifton 2–0

HORSE RACING

THE FLAT
THE CLASSICS
ONE THOUSAND GUINEAS
(1814), Rowley Mile, Newmarket, for three-year-old fillies

Year	Winner	Betting	Owner	Jockey	Trainer	No. of Runners
2001	Ameerat	11–1	Sheikh Ahmed Al Maktoum	P. Robinson	M. A. Jarvis	15
2002	Kazzia	14–1	Godolphin	L. Dettori	Saeed bin Suroor	17
2003	Russian Rhythm	12–1	Cheveley Park Stud	K. Fallon	Sir Michael Stoute	19
2004	Attraction	11–2	Duke of Roxburghe	K. Darley	M. Johnston	16
2005	Virginia Waters	12–1	Mrs S. Magnier and M. Tabor	K. Fallon	A. O'Brien	20

THE OAKS

(1779), Epsom, 1 mile and about 4 f, for three-year-old fillies

Year	Winner	Betting	Owner	Jockey	Trainer	No. of Runners
2001	Imagine	3–1	Mrs. J Magnier	M. Kinane	A. O'Brien	12
2002	Kazzia	100–30	Godolphin	L. Dettori	S. bin Suroor	14
2003	Casual Look	10–1	W. Farish III	M. Dwyer	A. Balding	15
2004	Ouija Board	7–2	Lord Derby	K. Fallon	E. Dunlop	7
2005	Eswarah	11–4	Sheikh Hamdan Al Maktoum	R. Hills	M. Jarvis	12

ST LEGER

(1776), Doncaster, 1 mile and about 6 f, for three-year-olds

Year	Winner	Betting	Owner	Jockey	Trainer	No. of Runners
2001	Milan	13–8	–	M. Kinane	A. O'Brien	10
2002	Bollin Eric	7–1	Sir Neil and Lady Westbrook	K. Darley	T. Easterby	8
2003	Brian Boru	5–4	Sir Neil and Lady Westbrook	J. Spencer	A. O'Brien	8
2004	Rule Of Law	3–1	Godolphin	K. McEvoy	Saeed Bin Suroor	9
2005	Scorpion	10–11	Ballydoyle	L. Dettori	A.O'Brien	6

TWO THOUSAND GUINEAS

(1809), Rowley Mile, Newmarket, for three-year-olds

Year	Winner	Betting	Owner	Jockey	Trainer	No. of Runners
2001	Golan	11–1	Lord Weinstock	K. Fallon	Sir Michael Stoute	18
2002	Rock of Gibraltar	9–1	Sir Alex Ferguson	J. Murtagh	A. O'Brien	22
2003	Refuse To Bend	9–2	Moyglare Stud Farms	P. Smullen	D. Weld	20
2004	Haafhd	11–2	Sheikh Hamdan Al Maktoum	B. Hills	R. Hills	14
2005	Footstepsinthesand	13–2	Mrs S. Magnier and M. Tabor	K. Fallon	A. O'Brien	19

THE DERBY

(1780), Epsom, 1 mile and about 4 f, for three-year-olds

The first winner was Sir Charles Bunbury's Diomed in 1780. The owners with the record number of winners are Lord Egremont, who won in 1782, 1804, 1805, 1807, 1826 (also won five Oaks); and the late Aga Khan, who won in 1930, 1935, 1936, 1948, 1952. Other winning owners are: Duke of Grafton (1802, 1809, 1810, 1815); Mr J. Bowes (1835, 1843, 1852, 1853); Sir J. Hawley (1851, 1858, 1859, 1868); the 1st Duke of Westminster (1880, 1882, 1886, 1899); and Sir Victor Sassoon (1953, 1957, 1958, 1960).
The Derby was run at Newmarket in 1915–18 and 1940–5.

Year	Winner	Betting	Owner	Jockey	Trainer	No. of Runners
2001	Galileo	11–4	Mrs. John Magnier	M. Kinane	A. O'Brien	12
2002	High Chaparral	7–2	Michael Tabor	J. Murtagh	A. O'Brien	12
2003	Kris Kin	6–1	Saeed Suhail	K. Fallon	Sir Michael Stoute	20
2004	North Light	7–2	Exors of the late Lord Weinstock	K. Fallon	Sir Michael Stoute	14
2005	Motivator	3–1	Royal Ascot Racing Club	J. Murtagh	M. Bell	13

RESULTS

CAMBRIDGESHIRE HANDICAP
(1839), Newmarket, 1 mile

2001	I Cried For You (6y), M. Fenton
2002	Beauchamp Pilot (4y), E. Ahern
2003	Chivalry (4y), G. Duffield
2004	Spanish Don (6y), L. Keniry

PRIX DE L'ARC DE TRIOMPHE
(1920), Longchamp, 1 mile, 4 f

2001	Sakhee (4y), L. Dettori
2002	Marienbard (5y), L. Dettori
2003	Dalakhani (3y), C. Soumillon
2004	Bago (3y), T. Gillet

CESAREWITCH
(1839), Newmarket, 2 miles and about 2 f

2001	Distant Prospect, M. Dwyer
2002	Miss Fara, R. Moore
2003	Landing Light (8y), P. Eddery
2004	Contact Dancer (5y), R. Ffrench

CHAMPION STAKES
(1877), Newmarket, 1 mile, 2 f

2001	Nayef (3y), R. Hills
2002	Storming Home (4y), M. Hills
2003	Rakti (4y), P. Robinson
2004	Haafhd (3y), R. Hills

BREEDERS CUP CLASSIC
(1984), Various tracks, USA, 1 mile and 2 f

2001	Tiznow (4y), C. McCarron
2002	Volponi (4y), J. Santos
2003	Pleasantly Perfect (5y), A. Solis
2004	Ghostzapper (4y), J. Castellano

DUBAI WORLD CUP
(1957), Dubai, 1 mile and 2 f

2001	Captain Steve (4y), J. D. Bailey
2002	Street Cry (4y), J. D. Bailey
2003	Moon Ballad (4y), L. Dettori
2004	Roses In May (5y), J. Velazquez

LINCOLN HANDICAP
(1965), Doncaster, 1 mile

2002	Nimello (6y), J. Fortune
2003	Pablo (4y), M. Hills
2004	Babodana (4y), P. Robinson
2005	Stream Of Gold (4y), R. Winston

JOCKEY CLUB STAKES
(1894), Newmarket, 2 miles, 24 yds

2002	Marienbard (5y), J. Spencer
2003	Warrsan (5y), P. Robinson
2004	Gamut (5y), K. Fallon
2005	Alkaased (5y), J. Fortune

PRIX DU JOCKEY CLUB
(1836), Chantilly, 1½ miles, for three-year-olds

2002	Sulamani, T. Thulliez
2003	Dalakhani, C. Soumillon
2004	Blue Canari, T. Thulliez
2005	Shamardal, L. Dettori

ASCOT GOLD CUP
(1807), Ascot, 2 miles and about 4 f

2002	Royal Rebel (6y), J. P. Murtagh
2003	Mr Dinos, (4y), K. Fallon
2004	Papineau, (4y), L. Dettori
2005	Westerner (6y), O. Peslier

IRISH DERBY
(1866), Curragh, 1½ miles, for three-year-olds

2002	High Chaparral, M. Kinane
2003	Alamshar, J. P. Murtagh
2004	Grey Swallow, P. Smullen
2005	Hurricane Run, K. Fallon

ECLIPSE STAKES
(1886), Sandown, 1 mile and about 2 f

2002	Hawk Wing (3y), M. J. Kinane
2003	Falbrav, (5y), D. Netherlands
2004	Refuse To Bend (4y), L. Dettori
2005	Oratorio (3y), K. Fallon

KING GEORGE VI AND QUEEN ELIZABETH DIAMOND
STAKES
(1952), Ascot, 1 mile and about 4 f

2002	Golan, K. Fallon
2003	Alamshar (3y), J. P. Murtagh
2004	Doyen (4y), L. Dettori
2005	Azamour (4yr), M. J. Kinane

GOODWOOD CUP
(1812), Goodwood, about 2 miles

2002	Jardines Lookout (5y), M. J. Kinane
2003	Persian Punch (10y), M. Dwyer
2004	Darasim (6y), J. Fanning
2005	Distinction (6y), M. J. Kinane

STATISTICS
WINNING FLAT OWNERS 2004

Godolphin	£4,146,844
Hamdan Al Maktoum	£1,621,073
Cheveley Park Stud	£1,091,994
Ballymacoll Stud	£913,912
K. Abdulla	£821,133
Maktoum Al Maktoum	£721,672
Sheikh Mohammed	£624,568
Elite Racing Club	£544,452
Duke of Roxburghe	£487,018
Sheikh Ahmed Al Maktoum	£464,569

WINNING FLAT TRAINERS 2004

Saeed bin Suroor	£4,146,844
Sir Michael Stoute	£2,776,052
M. Johnston	£2,323,100
M. R. Channon	£1,579,066
B. W. Hills	£1,468,788
R. Hannon	£1,331,156
M. A. Jarvis	£1,218,323
J. H. M. Gosden	£1,134,772
J. R. Fanshawe	£1,134,753
J. L. Dunlop	£1,113,473

WINNING FLAT SIRES 2004

	Races won	Stakes
Sadler's Wells by Northern Dancer	54	£2,587,850
Danehill by Danzig	15	£1,880,457
Pivotal by Polar Falcon	50	£1,250,959
Efisio by Formidable	60	£1,108,246
Kingmambo by Mr Prospector	26	£1,069,973
Barathea by Sadler's Wells	57	£1,001,591
Selkirk by Sharpen Up	65	£943,547
Machiavellian by Mr Prospector	60	£930,562
Polar Falcon by Nureyev	58	£816,659
Cape Cross by Green Desert	56	£809,821

WINNING FLAT JOCKEYS 2004

	1st	2nd	3rd	Unpl.	Total mts
K. Fallon	200	166	136	607	1,109
L. Dettori	195	132	89	434	850
S. Sanders	165	119	87	631	1,002
D. Holland	152	137	137	752	1,178
R. L. Moore	132	125	107	644	1,008
N. Callan	126	117	103	684	1,030
R. Winston	114	105	114	675	1,008
A. Culhane	111	104	108	725	1,048
E. Ahern	111	99	108	698	1,016
P. Hanagan	101	70	100	558	829

NATIONAL HUNT

HENNESSY GOLD CUP
(1957), Newbury, 3 miles and about 2½ f

2001	What's Up Boys, P. Flynn
2002	Gingembre (8y), A. Thornton
2003	Strong Flow (6y), R. Walsh
2004	Celestial Gold (6y), T. Murphy

TINGLE CREEK CHASE
(1957), Sandown, 2 miles (held at Cheltenham in 2000)

2001	Flagship Uberalles (7y), R. Widger
2002	Cenkos (8y), R. Walsh
2003	Moscow Flyer (9y), B. Geraghty
2004	Moscow Flyer (10y), B. Geraghty

KING GEORGE VI CHASE
(1937), Kempton, about 3 miles

2001	Florida Pearl (9y), A. Maguire
2002	Best Mate (7y), A. P. McCoy
2003	Edredon Bleu (11y), J. Culloty
2004	Kicking King (6y), B. Geraghty

CHAMPION HURDLE
(1927), Cheltenham, 2 miles and about ½ f

2002	Hors La Loi III (7y), D. Gallagher
2003	Rooster Booster (9y), R. Johnson
2004	Hardy Eustace (7y), C. O'Dwyer
2005	Hardy Eustace (8y), C. O'Dwyer

QUEEN MOTHER CHAMPION CHASE
(1959), Cheltenham, about 2 miles

2002	Flagship Uberalles (8y), R. Johnson
2003	Moscow Flyer (9y), B. Geraghty
2004	Azertyuiop (8y), R. Walsh
2005	Moscow Flyer (11y), B. Geraghty

CHELTENHAM GOLD CUP
(1924), 3 miles and about 2½ f

2002	Best Mate (7y), J. Culloty
2003	Best Mate (8y), J. Culloty
2004	Best Mate (9y), J. Culloty
2005	Kicking King (7y), B. Geraghty

GRAND NATIONAL
(1837), Liverpool, 4 miles and about 4 f

2002	Bindaree (8y), J. Culloty
2003	Monty's Pass (10y), B. Geraghty
2004	Amberleigh House (12y), G. Lee
2005	Hedgehunter (9y), R. Walsh

BETFRED GOLD CUP
(1957), Sandown, 3 miles and about 5 f

2002	Bounce Back, A. P. McCoy
2003	Ad Hoc (9y), R. Walsh
2004	Puntal (8y), D. Howard
2005	Jack High (10y), G. Cotter

STATISTICS

WINNING NATIONAL HUNT TRAINERS 2004–5

M. C. Pipe	£2,613,666
P. F. Nicholls	£2,557,665
P. J. Hobbs	£1,448,363
J. Howard Johnson	£1,188,521
Jonjo O'Neill	£839,242
Miss V. Williams	£818,672
N. A. Twiston Davis	£753,978
A. King	£738,940
N. J. Henderson	£695,642
Mrs S. J. Smith	£660,896

WINNING NATIONAL HUNT JOCKEYS 2004–5

	1st	2nd	3rd	Unpl.	Total mts
A. P. McCoy	200	144	92	385	821
T. J. Murphy	143	90	73	387	693
R. Johnson	135	111	100	468	814
A. Dobbin	115	82	66	333	596
G. Lee	100	87	71	312	570
R. Thornton	97	85	70	384	636
R. Walsh	81	57	45	128	311
C. Llewellyn	72	54	48	356	530
P. J. Brennan	67	59	56	335	517
M. A. Fitzgerald	65	63	59	338	525

The above statistics have been provided by *Timeform*, publishers of the *Racehorses* and *Chasers and Hurdlers* annuals

ICE HOCKEY

MEN'S WORLD CHAMPIONSHIPS 2005
Innsbruck, Austria, May

Final: Czech Republic beat Canada 3–0

WOMEN'S WORLD CHAMPIONSHIPS 2005
May, Linkoping, Sweden, May

Final: USA beat Canada 3–1

DOMESTIC COMPETITIONS
Elite League Champions 2004–05: Coventry Blaze
Play-off Champions 2005: Coventry Blaze
Challenge Cup Final 2005: Coventry Blaze beat Cardiff
   Devils 11–5

NATIONAL HOCKEY LEAGUE
The 2004–5 season was cancelled after players and the NHL failed to agree salary arrangements.

ICE SKATING

BRITISH FIGURE SKATING CHAMPIONSHIPS 2004
Sheffield, December

Men: John Hamer
Women: Jenna McCorkell
Ice Dance: Sinead Kerr and John Kerr

EUROPEAN CHAMPIONSHIPS 2005
Turin, Italy, January

Men: Yevgeni Plushenko (Russia)
Women: Irina Slutskaya (Russia)
Pairs: Tatiana Totmianina and Maxim Marinin (Russia)
Ice Dance: Tatiana Navka and Roman Kostomarov (Russia)

WORLD CHAMPIONSHIPS 2005
Moscow, Russia, March

Men: Stephane Lambiel (Switzerland)
Women: Irina Slutskaya (Russia)
Pairs: Tatiana Totmianina and Maxim Marinin (Russia)
Ice Dance: Tatiana Navka and Roman Kostomarov (Russia)

JUDO

EUROPEAN CHAMPIONSHIPS 2005
Rotterdam, Netherlands, May

MEN
Heavyweight (over 100kg): Alexander Mikhaylin (Russia)
Light-heavyweight (100kg): Christophe Humbert (France)
Middleweight (90kg): David Alarza (Spain)
Welterweight (81kg): Ole Bischof (Germany)
Lightweight (73kg): Akos Braun (Hungary)
Junior Lightweight (66kg): Elchin Ismaylov (Azerbaijan)
Bantamweight (60kg): Armen Nazaryan (Armenia)

WOMEN
Heavyweight (over 78kg): Karina Bryant (Great Britain)
Light-heavyweight (78kg): Celine Lebrun (France)
Middleweight (70kg): Edith Bosch (Netherlands)
Welterweight (63kg): Elisabeth Willeboordse
  (Netherlands)
Lightweight (57kg): Olga Sonina (Russia)
Junior Lightweight (52kg): Ilse Heylen (Belgium)
Bantamweight (48kg): Alina Alexandra Dumitru (Romania)

MOTORCYCLING

500CC GRAND PRIX 2004
Qatari (Losail): Sete Gibernau (Spain), Honda
Malaysian (Sepang): Valentino Rossi (Italy), Yamaha
Australian (Phillip Island): Valentino Rossi (Italy), Yamaha
Valencian (Valencia): Valentino Rossi (Italy), Yamaha

Riders' Championship 2004: 1. Valentino Rossi (Italy),
  Yamaha, 304 pts; 2. Sete Gibernau (Spain), Honda,
  257 pts; 3. Max Biaggi (Italy), Honda, 217 pts

500CC GRAND PRIX 2005
Spanish (Jerez): Valentino Rossi (Italy), Yamaha
Portuguese (Estoril): Alex Barros (Brazil), Honda
Chinese (Shanghai): Valentino Rossi (Italy), Yamaha
French (Le Mans): Valentino Rossi (Italy), Yamaha
Italian (Mugello): Valentino Rossi (Italy), Yamaha
Catalunyan (Barcelona): Valentino Rossi (Italy), Yamaha
Dutch (Assen): Valentino Rossi (Italy), Yamaha
USA (Laguna Seca): Nicky Hayden (USA), Honda
British (Donington Park): Valentino Rossi (Italy), Yamaha
German (Sachsenring): Valentino Rossi (Italy), Yamaha
Czech Republic (Brno): Valentino Rossi (Italy), Yamaha
Japanese (Motegi): Louis Capirossi (Italy). Ducati
Malaysian (Sepang): *see* Stop Press

250CC GRAND PRIX 2004
Qatari (Losail): Sebastian Porto (Argentina), Aprilia
Malaysian (Sepang): Daniel Pedrosa (Spain), Honda
Australian (Phillip Island): Sebastian Porto (Argentina),
  Aprilia
Valencian (Valencia): Daniel Pedrosa (Spain), Honda

Riders' Championship 2004: 1. Daniel Pedrosa (Spain),
  Honda, 317 pts; 2. Sebastian Porto (Argentina), Aprilia,
  256 pts; 3. Randy De Puniet (France), Aprilia, 214 pts

250CC GRAND PRIX 2005
Spanish (Jerez): Daniel Pedrosa (Spain), Honda
Portuguese (Estoril): Casey Stoner (Australia), Aprilia
Chinese (Shanghai): Casey Stoner (Australia), Aprilia
French (Le Mans): Daniel Pedrosa (Spain), Honda
Italian (Mugello): Daniel Pedrosa (Spain), Honda
Catalunyan (Barcelona): Daniel Pedrosa (Spain), Honda
Dutch (Assen): Sebastian Porto (Argentina), Aprilia
British (Donington Park): Randy De Puniet (France),
  Aprilia
German (Sachsenring): Daniel Pedrosa (Spain), Honda
Czech Republic (Brno): Daniel Pedrosa (Spain), Honda
Japanese (Motegi): Hiroshi Aoyama (Japan), Honda
Malaysian (Sepang): *see* Stop Press

125CC GRAND PRIX 2004
Qatari (Losail): Jorge Lorenzo (Spain), Derbi
Malaysian (Sepang): Casey Stoner (Australia), KTM
Australian (Phillip Island): Andrea Dovisioso (Italy),
  Honda
Valencian (Valencia): Hector Barbera (Spain), Aprilia
Riders' Championship 2004: 1. Andrea Dovisioso (Italy),
  Honda, 293 pts; 2. Hector Barbera (Spain),
  Aprilia, 202 pts; 3. Roberto Locatelli (Italy), Aprilia,
  192 pts.

125CC GRAND PRIX 2005
Spanish (Jerez): Marco Simoncelli (Italy), Aprilia
Portuguese (Estoril): Mika Kallio (Finland), KTM
Chinese (Shanghai): Mattia Pasini (Italy), Aprilia
French (Le Mans): Thomas Luthi (Switzerland), Honda
Italian (Mugello): Gabor Talmacsi (Hungary), KTM
Catalunyan (Barcelona): Mattia Pasini (Italy), Aprilia
Dutch (Assen): Gabor Talmacsi (Hungary), KTM
British (Donington Park): Julian Simon (Spain), KTM
German (Sachsenring): Mika Kallio (Finland), KTM
Czech Republic (Brno): Thomas Luthi (Switzerland),
  Honda
Japanese (Motegi): Mika Kallio (Finland), KTM
Malaysian (Sepang): *see* Stop Press
Senior TT 2005, Isle of Man: John McGuinness
  (England), Yamaha
Junior TT 2005, Isle of Man: Ian Lougher (Scotland),
  Honda

WORLD SUPERBIKES 2004
Italy (Imola): Race 1 – Régis Laconi (France), Ducati;
  Race 2 – Régis Laconi (France), Ducati
France (Magny Cours): Race 1 – James Toseland (Great
  Britain), Ducati; Race 2 – Noriyuki Haga (Japan),
  Ducati
Riders' World Championship 2004: 1. James Toseland
  (Great Britain), 336 points; 2. Régis Laconi (France),
  327 points; 3. Noriyuki Haga (Japan), 299 points.

WORLD SUPERBIKES 2005
Qatar (Losail): Race 1 – Troy Corser (Australia), Suzuki;
  Race 2 – Yukio Kagayama (Japan), Suzuki
Australia (Phillip Island): Race 1 – Troy Corser (Australia),
  Suzuki; Race 2 – Troy Corser (Australia), Suzuki
Spain (Valencia): Race 1 – Troy Corser (Australia), Suzuki;
  Race 2 – Troy Corser (Australia), Suzuki
Italy (Monza): Race 1 – Troy Corser (Australia), Suzuki;
  Race 2 – Chris Vermeulen (Australia), Honda
Great Britain (Silverstone): Race 1 – Régis Laconi (France),
  Ducati; Race 2 – James Toseland (Great Britain), Ducati
San Marino (Misano Adriatico): Race 1 – Régis Laconi
  (France), Ducati; Race 2 – Régis Laconi (France),
  Ducati

Czech Republic (Brno): Race 1 – Troy Corser (Australia),
Suzuki; Race 2 – Noriyuki Haga (Japan), Yamaha
Europe (Brands Hatch): Race 1 – Troy Corser (Australia),
Suzuki; Race 2 – Noriyuki Haga (Japan), Yamaha
Netherlands (Assen): Race 1 – Chris Vermeulen (Australia),
Honda; Race 2 – Chris Vermeulen (Australia), Honda
Germany (Lausitz): Race 1 – Chris Vermeulen (Australia),
Honda; Race 2 – Chris Vermeulen (Australia), Honda

MOTOR RACING

FORMULA ONE GRAND PRIX 2004
Italian (Monza): Rubens Barrichello (Brazil), Ferrari
Chinese (Shanghai): Rubens Barrichello (Brazil), Ferrari
Japanese (Suzuka): Michael Schumacher (Germany),
Ferrari
Brazilian (Interlagos): Juan Pablo Montoya (Columbia),
Williams
Drivers' World Championship 2004: 1. Michael
Schumacher (Germany), Ferrari, 148 points; 2. Rubens
Barrichello (Brazil), Ferrari, 114 points; 3. Jenson
Button (Great Britain), BAR Honda, 85 points.
Constructors' World Championship 2004: 1. Ferrari, 262
points; 2. BAR Honda, 119 points; 3. Renault, 105
points.

FORMULA ONE GRAND PRIX 2005
Australian (Melbourne): Giancarlo Fisichella (Italy),
Renault
Malaysian (Sepang): Fernando Alonso (Spain), Renault
Bahraini (Sakhir): Fernando Alonso (Spain), Renault
San Marinese (Imola): Fernando Alonso (Spain), Renault
Spanish (Barcelona): Kimi Raikkonen (Finland), McLaren
Monégasque (Monte Carlo): Kimi Raikkonen (Finland),
McLaren
European (Nurburgring): Fernando Alonso (Spain),
Renault
Canadian (Montreal): Kimi Raikkonen (Finland), McLaren
United States (Indianapolis): Michael Schumacher
(Germany), Ferrari
French (Magny Cours): Fernando Alonso (Spain), Renault
British (Silverstone): Juan Pablo Montoya (Columbia),
McLaren
German (Hockenheim): Fernando Alonso (Spain), Renault
Hungarian (Hungaroring): Kimi Raikkonen (Finland),
McLaren
Turkish (Istanbul): Kimi Raikkonen (Finland), McLaren
Italian (Monza): Juan Pablo Montoya (Columbia), McLaren
Belgium (Spa): Kimi Raikkonen (Finland), McLaren
Brazilian (Interlagos, 25 September): *see* Stop Press

INDIANAPOLIS 500 2005: Dan Wheldon (Great Britain),
Andretti Green

LE MANS 24-HOUR RACE 2004: J. J. Lehto, Tom
Kristensen and Marco Werner (Audi)

MOTOR RALLYING

WORLD RALLY CHAMPIONSHIPS
2004
Great Britain: Petter Solberg (Norway), Subaru
Italy: Petter Solberg (Norway), Subaru
France: Markko Martin (Estonia), Ford
Spain: Markko Martin (Estonia), Ford
Australia: Sébastien Loeb (France), Citroën
Drivers' World Championship 2004: Sébastien Loeb
(France), 118 points
Manufacturers' World Championship 2004: Citroën, 188
points

2005
Monte Carlo: Sébastien Loeb (France), Citroën
Sweden: Petter Solberg (Norway), Subaru
Mexico: Petter Solberg (Norway), Subaru
New Zealand: Sébastien Loeb (France), Citroën
Italy: Sébastien Loeb (France), Citroën
Cyprus: Sébastien Loeb (France), Citroën
Turkey: Sébastien Loeb (France), Citroën
Acropolis: Sébastien Loeb (France), Citroën
Argentina: Sébastien Loeb (France), Citroën
Finland: Marcus Gronholm (Finland), Peugeot
Germany: Sébastien Loeb (France), Citroën
Great Britain: Petter Solberg (Norway), Subaru

DAKAR RALLY 2005
Cars: Stephane Peterhansel (France), Mitsubishi
Motorcycles: Cyril Despres (France), KTM
Trucks: Firdaus Kabirov (Russia), Kamaz

NETBALL

Inter-County Championship 2005: Bedfordshire
National Clubs League Championship 2005: Hucclecote
English Counties League Championship 2005: Bedfordshire
Super Cup final 2005: London Tornadoes beat
Birmingham University Blaze 53–44

NORDIC EVENTS

BIATHLON WORLD CHAMPIONSHIPS 2005
Hochfilzen, Austria, March

MEN
10km Sprint: Ole Einar Bjoerndalen (Norway), 24min.
37.50sec.
12.5km Pursuit: Ole Einar Bjoerndalen (Norway), 36min.
41.44sec.
15km Mass Start: Ole Einar Bjoerndalen (Norway), 40min.
51.99sec.
20km Individual: Roman Dostal (Czech Republic), 1hr.
0min. 24.50sec.
4 × 7.5km Relay: Norway, 1hr. 21min. 59.21sec.

WOMEN
7.5km Sprint: Uschi Disl (Germany), 21min. 58.60sec.
10km Pursuit: Uschi Disl (Germany), 33min. 32.54sec.
12.5km Mass Start: Gro Istad-Kristiansen (Norway),
41min. 40.36sec.
15km Individual: Andrea Henkel (Germany), 52min.
37.50sec.
4 × 6km Relay: Russian 1hr. 13min. 44.45sec.

BIATHLON WORLD CUP 2004–05
MEN
Overall: Ole Einar Bjoerndalen (Norway)

WOMEN
Overall: Sandrine Bailly (France)

NORDIC WORLD CHAMPIONSHIPS 2005
Obersdorf, Germany, February

CROSS-COUNTRY

Men
15km: Pietro Pillar Cottrer (Italy)
30km: Frode Estil (Norway)

Double Pursuit: Vincent Vittoz (France)
Sprint: Vassili Rotchev (Russia)
Team: Norway
Team Sprint: Norway

Women
10km: Katerina Neumannova (Czech Republic)
30km: Marit Bjoergen (Norway)
Double Pursuit: Julija Tchepalova (Russia)
Sprint: Emelie Oehrstig (Sweden)
Team: Norway
Team Sprint: Norway

SKI JUMPING
Large Hill: Janne Ahonen (Finland)
Normal Hill: Rok Benkovic (Slovenia)
Team Large Hill: Austria
Team Normal Hill: Austria

NORDIC COMBINED
Sprint: Ronny Ackermann (Germany)
Gundersen: Ronny Ackermann (Germany)
Team: Norway

NORDIC WORLD CUP 2004–5

CROSS-COUNTRY
Men: Axel Teichman (Germany), 584 points
Women: Marit Bjoergen (Norway), 1,320 points

SKI JUMPING
Janne Ahonen (Finland), 1,715 points

NORDIC COMBINED
Hannu Manninen (Finland), 1,466 points

POLO

Prince of Wales Trophy final 2005: Azzura beat Emerging 9–4
Queen's Cup final 2005: Dubai beat Black Bears 12–7
Warwickshire Cup final 2005: Black Bears beat Emlor 8–6
Gold Cup (British Open), final 2005: Dubai beat Black Bears 11–10
Coronation Cup final 2005: Australia beat England 8–7

RACKETS

Noel Bruce Cup final 2004: Marlborough beat Harrow 4–0
British Professional Singles Championship final 2005: Neil Smith beat Mark Hubbard 3–0
British Open Singles Championship final 2005: Guy Smith-Bingham beat Alex Titchener-Barrett 4–3
British Open Doubles Championship final 2005: Harry Foster and Mark Hue Williams beat Tim Cockroft & Guy Smith-Bingham 4–2
Amateur Singles Championship final 2004: Guy Smith-Bingham beat Rupert Owen-Browne 3–0
Amateur Doubles Championship final 2005: Tim Cockroft & Guy Smith-Bingham beat Guy Barker & Alister Robinson 4–3
World Singles Championship final 2005: Harry Foster beat Alister Robinson 7–5
World Doubles Championship final 2005: Guy Barker & Alister Robinson beat Tim Cockroft & Guy Smith-Bingham 7–4
The Foster Cup final 2004 (public schools' singles championship): Joe Bone *(Harrow)* beat Alex Hackett *(Radley)* 3–0

REAL TENNIS

British Professional Singles Championship final 2005 (19 September): *see* Stop Press
British Professional Doubles Championship final 2005: Mike Gooding and Nick Wood beat Robert Fahey and Danny Jones 3–1
British Open Singles Championship final 2005: Robert Fahey beat Ruaraidh Gunn 3–0
British Open Doubles Championship final 2005: Mike Gooding and Nick Wood beat Chris Bray and James Willcocks 3–0
Henry Leaf Cup final 2005 (public schools' old boys' doubles championship): Canford 1 beat Canford 2 2–0
European Open final 2005: Robert Fahey beat Nick Wood 3–0
World Doubles Championships final 2005: Robert Fahey and Kieron Booth beat Nick Wood and David Woodman 2–0
National League final 2005: Cambridge beat Oxford 2–1
Women's British Open Singles Championship final 2005: Charlotte Cornwallis beat Jo Iddles 2–0
Women's British Open Doubles Championship final 2005: Charlotte Cornwallis and Sue Haswell beat Jo Iddles and Jill Newby 2–0
Women's World Singles Championships final 2005: Charlotte Cornwallis beat Jo Iddles 2–1

ROWING

NATIONAL CHAMPIONSHIPS 2005
Holme Pierrepoint, July

MEN
Coxless pairs: Worcester RC 7:15.12
Coxed fours: Molesey BC 6:29.09
Coxless fours: Nautilus RC 6:28.79
Single sculls: Cantabrigian 7:37.81
Double sculls: Vesta RC/Thames Scullers' School 6:49.72
Quad sculls: Nautilus RC 6:13.16
Eights: Nautilus RC 6:10.32

WOMEN
Coxless pairs: Mortlake BC/Anglian BC/Alpha BC 7:55.91
Coxed fours: Thames RC 7:36.61
Coxless fours: Worcester RC/St Edwards RC/Gloucester RC/St Neots RC 7:18.40
Single sculls: Rebecca 8:05.19
Double sculls: Maidenhead RC/Molesey 8:00.24
Quad sculls: Nautilus RC 6:56.65
Eights: Nautilus RC 6:59.04

THE 151ST UNIVERSITY BOAT RACE
Putney–Mortlake, 4 miles 1 f, 180 yd, 27 March 2005

Oxford beat Cambridge by 2 lengths; 16min. 42sec.

Cambridge have won 78 times, Oxford 72 and there has been one dead heat. The record time is 16min. 19sec., rowed by Cambridge in 1998.

HENLEY ROYAL REGATTA 2005
Grand Challenge Cup: Dortmund Rowing Centre (Germany), beat Oxford Brookes University and Molesey BC by ⅔ length
Ladies' Challenge Plate: Cambridge University beat Leander Club by 1¼ lengths

Thames Challenge Cup: Henley RC beat Lady Elizabeth BC (Ireland), by 1 length

Temple Challenge Cup: Trinity College, Hartford (USA), beat Yale University (USA), by 3 lengths

Princess Elizabeth Challenge Cup: Eton College beat St Joseph's Prep School (USA), by 1 length

Remenham Challenge Cup: Thames RC 'A' beat Durham University and Leander Club by ¾ length

Stewards' Challenge Cup: Leander Club & Oxford University beat Victoria City RC (Canada), easily

Queen Mother Challenge Cup: AZS Szczecin & AZS Gorzow (Poland), beat Tideway Scullers' School & Leander Club by ¾ length

Visitors' Challenge Cup: National University of Ireland, Galway (Ireland), beat Oxford Brookes University by 1¼ lengths

Wyfold Challenge Cup: Army RC beat Thames RC 'A' by 1¾ lengths

Britannia Challenge Cup: Leander Club beat Thames RC easily

Fawley Challenge Cup: Sydney RC (Australia), beat Maidenhead RC & Newark RC by 1¾ lengths

Silver Goblets and Nickalls' Challenge Cup: R. P. Di Clementé, & D. Cech (South Africa), beat S. A. Frandsen & B. D. Williams by 4 lengths

Double Sculls Challenge Cup: M. J. Hunter & J. W. Lindsay-Fynn beat I. M. Snijders & A. F. Snijders (Netherlands), easily

Diamond Challenge Sculls: W. R. Allen (USA), beat C. M. Palmer by 3 lengths

Princess Royal Challenge Cup: R. Neykova (Bulgaria), beat F. M. Milne (Australia), by 2¾ lengths

Princess Grace Challenge Cup: TsSKA, Ukraine (Ukraine), beat Thames RC easily

Men's Quadruple Sculls: Commercial RC & Neptune RC (Ireland), beat Northwich RC & Dart-Totnes ARC by 1¼ lengths

OTHER ROWING EVENTS

Wingfield Sculls 2004: Matt Wells (University of London)

Oxford Torpids 2005: Men, Oriel; *Women*, New College

Oxford Summer Eights 2005: *Men*, Magdelen; *Women*, New College

Head of the River 2005: Men, Leander 1; *Women*, Leander

RUGBY FIVES

National Open Singles Championship final 2004: M. Cavanagh beat J. P. Toop

National Open Doubles Championship final 2005: H. Buchanan and R. A. Perry beat P. D. d'Ancona and B. R. Taberner

National Ladies' Singles Championship final 2004: C. Knowles beat P. B. Smith

National Ladies' Doubles Championship final 2005: C. Knowles and M. Whitehead beat D. Redmond and E. Seton

National Club Championship final 2005: Alleyn Old Boys beat Manchester YMCA

National Schools' Singles Champion 2005: J. Pendergrass (Loretto School)

National Schools' Doubles Champions 2005: W. Ellison and H. K. Mohammed (Winchester School)

Varsity Match 2005: Cambridge beat Oxford

RUGBY LEAGUE

Super League Grand Final 2004 (Old Trafford, 16 October): Leeds Rhinos beat Bradford Bulls 16–8

World Club Challenge 2004 (Elland Road, 4 February): Leeds Rhinos beat Canterbury Bulldogs 39–32

Challenge Cup final 2005 (Millennium Stadium, 27 August): Hull beat Leeds Rhinos 25–24

AMATEUR RUGBY LEAGUE 2004–5

National Conference League Premier Division Grand Final Champions: Leigh Miners Rangers; *Division One*: Shaw Cross Sharks; *Division Two*: Ince Rose Bridge

National Cup final: Wath Brow Hornets beat Skirlaugh 16–6

Varsity Match 2005: Cambridge beat Oxford 17–16

RUGBY UNION

SIX NATIONS CHAMPIONSHIP 2005

5 February	Paris	France 16 Scotland 9
	Cardiff	Wales 11 England 9
6 February	Rome	Italy 17 Ireland 28
12 February	Rome	Italy 8 Wales 38
	Edinburgh	Scotland 13 Ireland 40
13 February	London	England 17 France 18
26 February	Edinburgh	Scotland 18 Italy 10
	Paris	France 18 Wales 24
27 February	Dublin	Ireland 19 England 13
12 March	Dublin	Ireland 19 France 26
	London	England 39 Italy 7
13 March	Edinburgh	Scotland 22 Wales 46
19 March	Rome	Italy 13 France 56
	Cardiff	Wales 32 Ireland 20
	London	England 43 Scotland 22

Final standings: 1. Wales, 10 points; 2. France, 8 points; 3. Ireland, 6 points; 4. England, 4 points; 5. Scotland, 2 points; 6. Italy, 0 points

NEW ZEALAND V BRITISH AND IRISH LIONS 2005

First Test (Christchurch, 25 June): New Zealand 21 British and Irish Lions 3

Second Test (Wellington, 2 July): New Zealand 48 British and Irish Lions 18

Third Test (Auckland, 9 July): New Zealand 38 British and Irish Lions 19

EUROPEAN COMPETITIONS 2004–5

Heineken European Cup final 2005: Toulouse beat Stade Francais 18–12

Parker Pen Cup 2005: Sale beat Pau 27–3

Parker Pen Shield 2005: Auch beat Worcester 23–10

DOMESTIC COMPETITIONS 2004–5

ENGLAND

Zurich Premiership: Leicester, 78 points

Championship final: Wasps beat Leicester 39–14

National League: *Division 1*, Bristol, 105 points; *Division 2*, Doncaster, 106 points; *Division 3* (North), Halifax, 112 points; (South), Barking, 116 points

Powergen Cup final: Leeds beat Bath 20–12

Challenge Shield final: Bedford beat Plymouth 14–13

Tetley's County Championship final: Devon beat Lancashire 22–16

Tetley's County Shield: Hertfordshire beat North Midlands 20–13

123rd Varsity Match: Oxford beat Cambridge 18–11

CELTIC

Celtic League: Neath-Swansea Ospreys, 76 points
Celtic Cup final 2005: Munster beat Llanelli Scarlets
   27–16

SCOTLAND

Scottish Premier League: Division 1, Glasgow Hawks, 97
   points; *Division 2,* Stirling County, 102 points; *Division
   3,* Cartha QP, 75 points.
Scottish Cup final 2005: Boroughmuir beat Dundee HSFP
   39–25

WALES

Welsh Premiership: Neath, 81 points
Welsh National League: Division 1, Maesteg, 74 points
Konica Minolta Cup final: Llanelli beat Pontypridd
   25–24

IRELAND

All Ireland League: Division 1, Shannon, 51 points;
   Division 2, UL Bohemian, 59 points; *Division 3,*
   Greystones, 71 points

SHOOTING

**136TH NATIONAL RIFLE ASSOCIATION
IMPERIAL MEETING**
Bisley, July 2005

Queen's Prize: J. A. M. Paton, 300.40 v-bulls
Grand Aggregate: J. C. Underwood, 693.83 v-bulls
Prince of Wales Prize: P. B. Bromley, 75.12 v-bulls
St George's Vase: J. H. Messer, 150.27 v-bulls
All Comers' Aggregate: J. H. Messer, 372.48 v-bulls
Kolapore Cup: Great Britain, 1,189.180 v-bulls
Chancellor's Trophy: Oxford, 1,155.112 v-bulls
Musketeers Cup: University of London 'A', 592.72 v-bulls
County Long-Range Championship: London, 575.43
   v-bulls
Mackinnon Challenge Cup: England, 1,169.131 v-bulls
The Albert: C. N. Tremlett, 217.24 v-bulls
Hopton Challenge Cup: C. N. Tremlett, 994.119 v-bulls

SNOOKER

2004–5
Welsh Open (Cardiff): Ronnie O'Sullivan (England), beat
   Stephen Hendry (Scotland), 9–8
British Open (Brighton): John Higgins (Scotland), beat
   Stephen Maguire (Scotland), 9–6
UK Championship (York): Stephen Maguire (Scotland),
   beat David Gray (England), 10–1
Masters (Wembley): Ronnie O'Sullivan (England), beat
   John Higgins (Scotland), 10–3
China Open (Beijing): Ding Junhui (China), beat Stephen
   Hendry (Scotland), 9–5
Malta Cup (Malta): Stephen Hendry (Scotland), beat
   Graeme Dott (Scotland), 9–7
Irish Masters (Dublin): Ronnie O'Sullivan (England), beat
   Matthew Stevens (England), 10–8
Grand Prix (Preston): Ronnie O'Sullivan (England), beat
   Ian McCulloch (England), 9–5
Northern Ireland Trophy (Belfast): Matthew Stevens
   (England), beat Stephen Hendry (Scotland), 9–7
World Championship (Sheffield): Shaun Murphy
   (England), beat Matthew Stevens (England), 18–16

SPEED SKATING

EUROPEAN CHAMPIONSHIPS 2005
Heerenveen, Netherlands, January

MEN
500 metres: Mark Tuitert (Netherlands), 36.08sec
1,500 metres: Jochem Uytdehaage (Netherlands), 1min
   47.45sec
5,000 metres: Eskil Ervik (Norway), 6min 23.40sec
10,000 metres: Oystein Grodum (Norway), 13min
   06.81sec
Overall: Jochem Uytdehaage (Netherlands), 150.997
   points

WOMEN
500 metres: Anni Friesinger (Germany), 39.36sec
1,500 metres: Anni Friesinger (Germany), 1min 57.39sec
3,000 metres: Anni Friesinger (Germany), 4min 08.72sec
5,000 metres: Claudia Pechstein (Germany), 7min 02.76sec
Overall: Anni Friesinger (Germany), 162.530 points

WORLD CHAMPIONSHIPS 2005
Inzell, Germany, March

MEN
500 metres: Joji Kato (Japan), 1min. 11.42sec. (aggregate
   of two legs)
1,000 metres: Even Wetten (Norway), 1min 10.10sec
1,500 metres: Rune Stordal (Norway), 1min. 50.69sec.
5,000 metres: Chad Hedrick (USA), 6min. 25.61sec.
10,000 metres: Bob De Jong (Netherlands), 13min.
   25.64sec.
Team pursuit: Netherlands 3min. 52.83sec.

WOMEN
500 metres: Manli Wang (China), 1min. 17.210sec.
   (aggregate of two legs)
1,000 metres: Barbara De Loor (Netherlands), 1min 18.
   24sec
1,500 metres: Cindy Klassen (Canada), 1min. 58.49sec.
3,000 metres: Cindy Klassen (Canada), 4min. 10.37sec.
5,000 metres: Anni Friesinger (Germany), 7min. 18.32sec.
Team pursuit: Germany 3min. 05.81sec.

WORLD SHORT TRACK CHAMPIONSHIPS 2005
Beijing, China, March

MEN
500 metres: Francois-Louis Tremblay (Canada), 42.106sec.
1,000 metres: Apolo Anton Ohno (USA), 1min 30sec.
1,500 metres: Hyun-Soo Ahn (Korea), 2min. 14.3sec.
3,000 metres: Apolo Anton Ohno (USA), 5min. 13.7sec.
5,000 metres relay: Canada 6min. 39.9sec.
Overall: Hyun-Soo Ahn (Korea)

WOMEN
500 metres: Yang A Yang (China), 45.038sec.
1,000 metres: Eun-Kyung Choi (Korea), 1min. 31sec.
1,500 metres: Sun-Yu Jin (Korea), 2min. 20.4sec.
3,000 metres: Yun-Mi Kang (Korea), 5min. 21sec.
3,000 metres relay: Canada 4min. 20.7sec.
Overall: Sun-Yu Jin (Korea)

**EUROPEAN SHORT TRACK CHAMPIONSHIPS
2005**
Turin, Italy, January

MEN
500 metres: Fabio Carta (Italy), 43.010sec.
1,000 metres: Nicola Franceschina (Italy), 1min 33.751sec.
1,500 metres: Arian Nachbar (Germany), 2min. 22.210sec.
3,000 metres: Pieter Gysel (Belgium), 5min. 06.515sec.
5,000 metres relay: Germany 7min. 07.874sec.
Overall: Fabio Carta (Italy)

WOMEN
500 metres: Tatiana Borodulina (Russia), 45.840sec.
1,000 metres: Evgenia Radanova (Bulgaria), 1min.
    39.273sec.
1,500 metres: Evgenia Radanova (Bulgaria), 2min.
    26.542sec.
3,000 metres: Tatiana Borodulina (Russia), 5min.
    56.036sec.
3,000 metres relay: Russia 4min. 26.415sec.
Overall: Tatiana Borodulina (Russia)

SQUASH RACKETS

MEN
World Doubles Championship final 2004: Byron Davis and
    Cameron White (Australia), beat Ritwik Bhattacharya
    and Saurav Ghosal (India), 3–1
European Team Championship final 2005: England beat
    France 4–0
European Individual Championships final 2005: Gregory
    Gaultier (France), beat Jan Koukal (Czech Republic), 3–0
British Open final 2004: David Palmer (Australia), beat
    Amr Shabana (Egypt), 3–1
British National Championship final 2005: Lee Beachill
    (England), beat James Willstrop (England), 3–0

WOMEN
World Doubles Championship final 2004: Natalie Grinham
    and Rachel Grinham (Australia), beat Louise Crome
    and Lara Petera (New Zealand), 3–0
European Team Championship final 2005: England beat
    Netherlands 2–1
European Individual Championships final 2005: Vanessa
    Atkinson (Netherlands), beat Linda Elriani (England),
    3–0
British Open final 2004: Rachel Grinham (Australia), beat
    Natalie Grainger (USA), 3–1
British National Championship final 2005: Linda Elriani
    (England), beat Alison Waters (England), 3–0

SWIMMING

WORLD CHAMPIONSHIPS 2005
Montreal, Canada, July

MEN
50 metres freestyle: Roland Schoeman (South Africa),
    21.69
100 metres freestyle: Filippo Magnini (Italy), 48.12
200 metres freestyle: Michael Phelps (USA), 1:45.20
400 metres freestyle: Grant Hackett (Australia), 3:42.91
800 metres freestyle: Grant Hackett (Australia), 7:38.65
1,500 metres freestyle: Grant Hackett (Australia), 14:42.58
4 × 100 metres freestyle relay: United States, 3:13.77
4 × 200 metres freestyle relay: United States, 7:06.58
50 metres backstroke: Aristeidis Grigoriadis (Greece), 24.95
100 metres backstroke: Aaron Peirsol (USA), 53.62
200 metres backstroke: Aaron Peirsol (USA), 1:54.66
50 metres breaststroke: Mark Warnecke (Germany), 27.63
100 metres breaststroke: Brendan Hansen (USA), 59.37

200 metres breaststroke: Brendan Hansen (USA), 2:09.85
50 metres butterfly: Roland Schoeman (South Africa),
    22.96
100 metres butterfly: Ian Crocker (USA), 50.40
200 metres butterfly: Pawel Korzeniowski (Poland),
    1:55.02
200 metres medley: Michael Phelps (USA), 1:56.68
400 metres medley: Laszio Cseh (Hungary), 4:09.63
4 × 100 metres medley relay: United States, 3:31.85

WOMEN
50 metres freestyle: Lisbeth Lenton (Australia), 24.59
100 metres freestyle: Jodie Henry (Australia), 54.18
200 metres freestyle: Solenne Figues (France), 1:58.60
400 metres freestyle: Laure Manaudou (France), 4:06.44
800 metres freestyle: Kate Ziegler (USA), 8:25.31
1,500 metres freestyle: Kate Ziegler (USA), 16:00.41
4 × 100 metres freestyle relay: Australia, 3:37.32
4 × 200 metres freestyle relay: United States, 7:53.70
50 metres backstroke: Giaan Rooney (Australia), 28.63
100 metres backstroke: Kirsty Coventry (Zimbabwe),
    1:00.24
200 metres backstroke: Kirsty Coventry (Zimbabwe),
    2:08.52
50 metres breaststroke: Jade Edmistone (Australia), 30.45
100 metres breaststroke: Leisel Jones (Australia), 1:06.25
200 metres breaststroke: Leisel Jones (Australia), 2:21.72
50 metres butterfly: Danni Miatke (Australia), 26.11
100 metres butterfly: Jessicah Schipper (Australia), 57.23
200 metres butterfly: Otylia Jedrzejczak (Poland), 2:05.61
200 metres medley: Katie Hoff (USA), 2:10.41
400 metres medley: Katie Hoff (USA), 4:36.07
4 × 100 metres medley relay: Australia, 3:57.47

BRITISH CHAMPIONSHIPS 2004
Sheffield, August

MEN
50 metres freestyle: Simon Burnett, 22.12
100 metres freestyle: Simon Burnett, 48.68
200 metres freestyle: Simon Burnett, 1:46.59
400 metres freestyle: David Davies, 3:50.66
1,500 metres freestyle: David Davies, 14:59.20
50 metres backstroke: Liam Tancock, 25.17
100 metres backstroke: Liam Tancock, 55.12
200 metres backstroke: Gregor Tait, 2:00.10
50 metres breaststroke: Chris Cook, 27.82
100 metres breaststroke: Chris Cook, 1:00.70
200 metres breaststroke: Kris Gilchrist, 2:14.51
50 metres butterfly: Mark Foster, 24.08
100 metres butterfly: Michael Rock, 54.26
200 metres butterfly: Matthew Bowe, 1:59.21
200 metres medley: Gregor Tait, 2:02.20
400 metres medley: David Carry, 4:19.15

WOMEN
50 metres freestyle: Lisa Chapman, 25.75
100 metres freestyle: Melanie Marshall, 55.50
200 metres freestyle: Melanie Marshall, 1:59.86
400 metres freestyle: Joanne Jackson, 4:09.43
800 metres freestyle: Rebecca Cooke, 8:30.51
50 metres backstroke: Katy Sexton, 29.14
100 metres backstroke: Katy Sexton, 1:01.46
200 metres backstroke: Katy Sexton, 2:12.28
50 metres breaststroke: Kate Haywood, 31.70
100 metres breaststroke: Kate Haywood, 1:08.91
200 metres breaststroke: Kerry Buchan, 2:30.02
50 metres butterfly: Rosalind Brett, 27.30

100 metres butterfly: Terri Dunning, 1:00.95
200 metres butterfly: Jessica Dickons, 2:12.67
200 metres medley: Terri Dunning, 2:16.73
400 metres medley: Rebecca Cooke, 4:45.52

TABLE TENNIS

WORLD CHAMPIONSHIPS 2005
Shanghai, China, April–May

Men's Singles: Liqin Wang (China), beat Lin Ma (China), 4–2
Women's Singles: Yining Zhang (China), beat Yah Guo (China), 4–2
Men's Doubles: Linghui Kong and Hao Wang (China), beat Timo Boll and Christian Suss (Germany), 4–1
Women's Doubles: Nan Wang and Yining Zhang (China), beat Yue Guo and Jianfeng Niu (China), 4–1
Mixed Doubles: Yue Guo and Liqin Wang (China), beat Yang Bai and Guozheng Liu (China), 4–3

EUROPEAN CHAMPIONSHIPS 2005
Aarhus, Denmark, March–April

Men's Singles: Vladimir Samsonov (Belarus), beat Jean-Michel Saive (Begium), 4–1
Women's Singles: Liu Jia (Austria), beat Mihaela Steff (Romania), 4–0
Men's Doubles: Werner Schlager and Karl Jindrak (Austria), beat Vladimir Samsonov (Belarus), and Kalinkos Kreanga (Greece), 4–2
Women's Doubles: Michaela Steff (Romania), and Tamara Boros (Croatia), beat Kritztina Toth and Csilia Batorfi (Hungary), 4–0
Mixed Doubles: Aleksander Karakasevic (Serbia), and Ruta Garkauskaite-Budiene (Lithuania) beat Viktoria Pavlovich (Belarus), Weixing Chen (Austria), 4–1

ENGLISH NATIONAL CHAMPIONSHIPS 2005
Sheffield, March

Men's Singles: Alan Cooke (Derbys), beat Alex Perry (Devon), 4–2
Women's Singles: Helen Lower (Staffs), beat Andrea Holt (Lancs), 4–0
Men's Doubles: Alex Perry (Devon), and Terry Young (Berks), beat Bryn Drinkhall (Coventry), and Andrew Rushton (Lancs), 3–0
Women's Doubles: Natalie Bawden (Essex), and Helen Lower (Staffs), beat Kelly Sibley (Wales), and Georgina Walker (Notts), 3–0
Mixed Doubles: Helen Lower (Staffs), and Alex Perry (Devon), beat Kelly Sibley (Wales), and Paul Drinkhall (Coventry), 3–2

TENNIS

AUSTRALIAN OPEN CHAMPIONSHIPS 2005
Melbourne, 17–30 January

Men's Singles: Marat Safin (Russia), beat Lleyton Hewitt (Australia), 1–6, 6–3, 6–4, 6–4
Women's Singles: Serena Williams (USA), beat Lindsay Davenport (USA), 2–6, 6–3, 6–0
Men's Doubles: Wayne Black and Kevin Ullyett (Zimbabwe), beat Bob Bryan and Mike Bryan (USA), 6–4, 6–4
Women's Doubles: Svetlana Kuznetsova (Russia), & Alicia Molik (Australia), beat Lindsay Davenport and Corina Morariu (USA), 6–3, 6–4
Mixed Doubles: Samantha Stosur and Scott Draper (Australia), beat Liezel Huber (South Africa), and Kevin Ullyett (Zimbabwe), 6–2, 2–6, 7–6

FRENCH OPEN CHAMPIONSHIP 2005
Paris, 23 May–5 June

Men's Singles: Rafael Nadal (Spain), beat Mariano Puerta (Argentina), 6–7, 6–3, 6–1, 7–5
Women's Singles: Justine Henin-Hardenne (Belgium), beat Mary Pierce (France), 6–1, 6–1
Men's Doubles: Jonas Bjorkman (Sweden), and Max Mirnyi (Belarus), beat Bob Bryan and Mike Bryan (USA), 2–6, 6–1, 6–4
Women's Doubles: Virginia Ruano Pascual (Spain), & Paola Suarez (Argentina), beat Cara Black (Zimbabwe), and Liezel Huber (South Africa), 4–6, 6–3, 6–3
Mixed Doubles: Daniela Hantuchova (Slovakia), and Fabrice Santoro (France), beat Martina Navratilova (USA), and Leander Paes (India), 3–6, 6–3, 6–2

ALL-ENGLAND CHAMPIONSHIPS 2005
Wimbledon, 21 June–4 July

Men's Singles: Roger Federer (Switzerland), beat Andy Roddick (USA), 6–2, 7–6, 6–4
Women's Singles: Venus Williams (USA), beat Lindsay Davenport (USA), 4–6, 7–6, 9–7
Men's Doubles: Stephen Huss (Australia), and Wesley Moodie (South Africa), beat Bob Bryan and Mike Bryan (USA), 7–6, 6–3, 6–7, 6–3
Women's Doubles: Cara Black (Zimbabwe), and Liezel Huber (South Africa), beat Svetlana Kuznetzova (Russia), and Amelie Mauresmo (France), 6–2, 6–1
Mixed Doubles: Mary Pierce (France), and Mahesh Bhupathi (India), beat Tatiana Perebiynis (Ukraine), and Paul Hanley (Australia), 6–4, 6–2

US OPEN CHAMPIONSHIPS 2004
New York, 29 August–11 September

Men's Singles: Roger Federer (Switzerland) beat Andre Agassi (USA) 6–3, 2–6, 7–6, 6–1
Women's Singles: Kim Clijsters (Belgium) beat Mary Pierce (France) 6–3, 6–1
Men's Doubles: Bob Bryan and Mike Bryan (USA) beat Jonas Bjorkman (Sweden) and Max Mirnyi (Belarus) 6–1, 6–4
Women's Doubles: Lisa Raymond (USA) and Samantha Stosur (Australia) beat Elena Dementieva (Russia) and Flavia Pennetta (Italy) 6–2, 5–7, 6–3
Mixed Doubles: Daniela Hantuchova (Slovakia) and Mahesh Bhupathi (India) beat Katarina Srebotnik (Slovenia) and Nenad Zimonjic (Serbia and Montenegro) 6–4, 6–2

TEAM CHAMPIONSHIPS
Davis Cup final 2004: Spain beat USA 3–2
Federation Cup final 2004: Russia beat France 3–2

SPORTS RECORDS

ATHLETICS WORLD RECORDS
AS AT SEPTEMBER 2005

All the world records given below have been accepted by the International Amateur Athletic Federation except those marked with an asterisk* which are awaiting homologation. Fully automatic timing to 1/100th second is mandatory up to and including 400 metres. For distances up to and including 10,000 metres, records will be accepted to 1/100th second if timed automatically, and to 1/10th if hand timing is used.

MEN'S EVENTS

TRACK EVENTS	hr.	min.	sec.
100 metres			9.77
Asafa Powell, Jamaica, 2005			
200 metres			19.32
Michael Johnson, USA, 1996			
400 metres			43.18
Michael Johnson, USA, 1999			
800 metres		1	41.11
Wilson Kipketer, Denmark, 1997			
1,000 metres		2	11.96
Noah Ngeny, Kenya, 1999			
1,500 metres		3	26.00
Hicham El Guerrouj, Morocco, 1998			
1 mile		3	43.13
Hicham El Guerrouj, Morocco, 1999			
2,000 metres		4	44.79
Hicham El Guerrouj, Morocco, 1999			
3,000 metres		7	20.67
Daniel Komen, Kenya, 1996			
5,000 metres		12	37.35
Kenenisa Bekele, Ethiopia, 2004			
10,000 metres		26	17.53
Kenenisa Bekele, Ethiopia, 2005			
20,000 metres		56	55.6
Arturo Barrios, Mexico, 1991			
21,101 metres (13 miles 196 yards 1 foot)	1	00	00.0
Arturo Barrios, Mexico, 1991			
25,000 metres	1	13	55.8
Toshihiko Seko, Japan, 1981			
30,000 metres	1	29	18.8
Toshihiko Seko, Japan, 1981			
Marathon	2	04	55
Paul Tergat, Kenya, 2003			
110 metres hurdles (3 ft 6 in)			12.91
Colin Jackson, GB, 1993 and Liu Xiang, China, 2004			
400 metres hurdles (3 ft 0 in)			46.78
Kevin Young, USA, 1992			
3,000 metres steeplechase		7	53.63
Saif Saaeed Shaheen, Qatar, 2004			

RELAYS		min.	sec.
4 × 100 metres			37.40
USA, 1992, 1993			
4 × 200 metres		1	18.68
Santa Monica TC, 1994			
4 × 400 metres		2	54.20
USA, 1998			
4 × 800 metres		7	03.89
GB, 1982			
4 × 1,500 metres		14	38.8
Federal Republic of Germany, 1977			

FIELD EVENTS	metres	ft	in
High jump	2.45	8	0½
Javier Sotomayor, Cuba, 1993			
Pole vault	6.14	20	1¾
Sergei Bubka, Ukraine, 1994			
Long jump	8.95	29	4½
Mike Powell, USA, 1991			
Triple jump	18.29	60	0¼
Jonathan Edwards, GB, 1995			
Shot	23.12	75	10¼
Randy Barnes, USA, 1990			
Discus	74.08	243	0
Jürgen Schult, GDR, 1986			
Hammer	86.74	284	7
Yuriy Sedykh, USSR, 1986			
Javelin	98.48	323	1
Jan Zelezny, Czech Rep., 1996			
Decathlon†	9,026 points		
Roman Sebrle, Czech Rep., 2001			

† Ten events comprising 100 m, long jump, shot, high jump, 400 m, 110 m hurdles, discus, pole vault, javelin, 1500 m

WALKING (TRACK)	hr.	min.	sec.
20,000 metres	1	17	25.6
Bernard Segura, Mexico, 1994			
29,572 metres (18 miles 660 yards)	2	00	00.0
Maurizio Damilano, Italy, 1992			
30,000 metres	2	01	44.1
Maurizio Damilano, Italy, 1992			
50,000 metres	3	40	57.9
Thierry Toutain, France, 1996			

WOMEN'S EVENTS

TRACK EVENTS	hr.	min.	sec.
100 metres			10.49
Florence Griffith-Joyner, USA, 1988			
200 metres			21.34
Florence Griffith-Joyner, USA, 1988			
400 metres			47.60
Marita Koch, GDR, 1985			
800 metres		1	53.28
Jarmila Kratochvilova, Czechoslovakia, 1983			
1,500 metres		3	50.46
Qu Yunxia, China, 1993			
1 mile		4	12.56
Svetlana Masterkova, Russia, 1996			
3,000 metres		8	06.11
Wang Junxia, China, 1993			
5,000 metres		14	24.68
Elvan Abeylegesse, Turkey, 2004			
10,000 metres		29	31.78
Wang Junxia, China, 1993			
Marathon	2	15	25
Paula Radcliffe, GB, 2003			
100 metres hurdles (2 ft 9 in)			12.21
Yordanka Donkova, Bulgaria, 1988			

		min.	sec.
400 metres hurdles (2 ft 6 in)			52.34
Yulia Pechonkina, Russia, 2003			
3,000 metres steeplechase		9	01.59
Gulnara Samitova, Russia, 2004			

RELAYS		min.	Sec.
4 × 100 metres			41.37
GDR, 1985			
4 × 200 metres		1	27.46
USA, 2000			
4 × 400 metres		3	15.17
USSR, 1988			
4 × 800 metres		7	50.17
USSR, 1984			

FIELD EVENTS	metres	ft	in
High jump	2.09	6	10¼
Stefka Kostadinova, Bulgaria, 1987			
Pole vault	5.01*	16	5¼
Yelena Isinbayeva, Russia, 2005			
Long jump	7.52	24	8¼
Galina Chistiakova, USSR, 1988			
Triple jump	15.50	50	10¼
Inessa Kravets, Ukraine, 1995			
Shot	22.63	74	3
Natalya Lisovskaya, USSR, 1987			
Discus	76.80	252	0
Gabriele Reinsch, GDR, 1988			
Hammer	77.06	252	10
Tatyana Lysenko, Russia, 2005			
Javelin (new implement in 1999)	71.70	235	3
Osleidys Menendez, Cuba, 2005			
Heptathlon†		7,291 points	
Jackie Joyner-Kersee, USA, 1988			

† Seven events comprising 100 m hurdles, shot, high jump, 200 m, long jump, javelin, 800 m

ATHLETICS NATIONAL (UK) RECORDS
AS AT SEPTEMBER 2005

Records set anywhere by athletes eligible to represent Great Britain and Northern Ireland

MEN

TRACK EVENTS	hr.	min.	sec.
100 metres			9.87
Linford Christie, 1993 and			
Dwain Chambers, 2002			
200 metres			19.87
John Regis, 1994			
400 metres			44.36
Iwan Thomas, 1997			
800 metres		1	41.73
Sebastian Coe, 1981			
1,000 metres		2	12.18
Sebastian Coe, 1981			
1,500 metres		3	29.67
Sebastian Coe, 1985			
1 mile		3	46.32
Steve Cram, 1985			
2,000 metres		4	51.39
Steve Cram, 1985			
3,000 metres		7	32.79
David Moorcroft, 1982			
5,000 metres	13		00.41
David Moorcroft, 1982			

	hr.	min.	sec.
10,000 metres		27	18.14
Jon Brown, 1998			
20,000 metres		57	28.7
Carl Thackery, 1990			
20,855 metres	1	00	00.0
Carl Thackery, 1990			
25,000 metres	1	15	22.6
Ron Hill, 1965			
30,000 metres	1	31	30.4
Jim Alder, 1970			
Marathon	2	07	13
Steve Jones, 1985			
3,000 metres steeplechase		8	07.96
Mark Rowland, 1988			
110 metres hurdles			12.91
Colin Jackson, 1993			
400 metres hurdles			47.82
Kriss Akabusi, 1992			

RELAYS		min.	sec.
4 × 100 metres			37.73
GB team, 1999			
4 × 200 metres		1	21.29
GB team, 1989			
4 × 400 metres		2	56.60
GB team, 1996			
4 × 800 metres		7	03.89
GB team, 1982			

FIELD EVENTS	metres	ft	in
High jump	2.37	7	9¼
Steve Smith, 1993			
Pole vault	5.80	19	0¼
Nick Buckfield, 1998			
Long jump	8.27	27	1¾
Chris Tomlinson, 2002			
Triple jump	18.29	60	0¼
Jonathan Edwards, 1995			
Shot	21.92	71	11
Carl Myerscough, 2003			
Discus	66.64	218	8
Perris Wilkins, 1998			
Hammer	77.54	254	5
Martin Girvan, 1984			
Javelin	91.46	300	1
Steve Backley, 1992			
Decathlon		8,847 points	
Daley Thompson, 1984			

WALKING (TRACK)	hr.	min.	sec.
20,000 metres	1	23	26.5
Ian McCombie, 1990			
30,000 metres	2	19	18
Christopher Maddocks, 1984			
50,000 metres	4	05	44.6
Paul Blagg, 1990			
26,037 metres (16 miles 315 yards)	2	00	00.0
Ron Wallwork, 1971			

WOMEN

TRACK EVENTS	hr.	min.	sec.
100 metres			11.10
Kathy Cook, 1981			
200 metres			22.10
Kathy Cook, 1984			
400 metres			49.43
Kathy Cook, 1984			
800 metres		1	56.21
Kelly Holmes, 1995			

1,500 metres		3	57.90	
Kelly Holmes, 2004				
1 mile		4	17.57	
Zola Budd, 1985				
3,000 metres		8	22.20	
Paula Radcliffe, 2002				
5,000 metres		14	29.11*	
Paula Radcliffe, 2004				
10,000 metres		30	01.09	
Paula Radcliffe, 2002				
Marathon	2	15	25	
Paula Radcliffe, 2003				
100 metres hurdles			12.80	
Angela Thorp, 1996				
400 metres hurdles			52.74	
Sally Gunnell, 1993				
3,000 metres steeplechase		9	48.57*	
Tina Brown, 2005				

	min.	sec.
RELAYS		
4 × 100 metres		42.43
GB team, 1980		
4 × 200 metres	1	31.57
GB team, 1977		
4 × 400 metres	3	22.01
GB team, 1991		
4 × 800 metres	8	23.8
GB team, 1971		

	metres	ft	in
FIELD EVENTS			
High jump	1.95	6	4¾
Diana Elliott, 1982			
Susan Jones, 2001			
Pole vault	4.47	14	8
Janine Whitlock, 2002			
Long jump	6.90	22	7¾
Beverley Kinch, 1983			
Triple jump	15.15	49	8½
Ashia Hansen, 1997			
Shot	19.36	63	6¼
Judy Oakes, 1988			
Discus	67.48	221	5
Margaret Ritchie, 1981			
Hammer	68.93	226	1
Lorraine Shaw, 2001			
Javelin (new implement)	64.87	212	9
Kelly Morgan, 2002			
Heptathlon		6,831 points	
Denise Lewis, 2000			

*Awaiting ratification

SWIMMING WORLD RECORDS
AS AT SEPTEMBER 2005

	min.	sec.
MEN		
50 metres freestyle		21.64
Alexander Popov, Russia		
100 metres freestyle		47.84
Pieter van den Hoogenband, Netherlands		
200 metres freestyle	1	44.06
Ian Thorpe, Australia		
400 metres freestyle	3	40.08
Ian Thorpe, Australia		
800 metres freestyle	7	38.66
Grant Hackett, Australia		
1,500 metres freestyle	14	34.56
Grant Hackett, Australia		
50 metres breaststoke		27.18
Oleg Lisogor, Ukraine		

100 metres breaststroke		59.30
Brendan Hansen, USA		
200 metres breaststroke	2	09.04
Brendan Hansen, USA		
50 metres butterfly		22.96
Roland Schoeman, South Africa		
100 metres butterfly		50.76
Ian Crocker, USA		
200 metres butterfly	1	53.93
Michael Phelps, USA		
50 metres backstroke		24.80
Thomas Rupprath, Germany		
100 metres backstroke		53.17
Aaron Peirsol, USA		
200 metres backstroke	1	54.66
Aaron Peirsol, USA		
200 metres medley	1	55.94
Michael Phelps, USA		
400 metres medley	4	08.26
Michael Phelps, USA		
4 × 100 metres freestyle relay	3	13.17
South Africa		
4 × 200 metres freestyle relay	7	04.66
Australia		
4 × 100 metres medley relay	3	30.68
USA		

	min.	sec.
WOMEN		
50 metres freestyle		24.13
Inge de Bruin, Netherlands		
100 metres freestyle		53.52
Jodie Henry, Australia		
200 metres freestyle	1	56.64
Franziska van Almsick, Germany		
400 metres freestyle	4	03.85
Janet Evans, USA		
800 metres freestyle	8	16.22
Janet Evans, USA		
1,500 metres freestyle	15	52.10
Janet Evans, USA		
50 metres breaststroke		30.40
Jade Edminstone, Australia		
100 metres breaststroke	1	06.20
Jessica Hardy, USA		
200 metres breaststroke	2	21.72
Leisel Jones, Australia		
50 metres butterfly		25.57
Anna-Karin Kammerling, Sweden		
100 metres butterfly		56.61
Inge de Bruin, Netherlands		
200 metres butterfly	2	05.61
Otylia Jedrzejczak, Poland		
50 metres backstroke		28.19
Janine Pietsch, Germany		
100 metres backstroke		59.58
Natalie Coughlin, USA		
200 metres backstroke	2	06.62
Krisztina Egerszegi, Hungary		
200 metres medley	2	09.72
Wu Yanyan, China		
400 metres medley	4	33.59
Yana Klochkova, Ukraine		
4 × 100 metres freestyle relay	3	35.94
Australia		
4 × 200 metres freestyle relay	7	53.42
USA		
4 × 100 metres medley relay	3	57.32
Australia		

ASSOCIATION FOOTBALL

WORLD CUP WINNERS
First held 1930

YEAR	HOST	WINNER
1930	Uruguay	Uruguay
1934	Italy	Italy
1938	France	Italy
1950	Brazil	Uruguay
1954	Switzerland	West Germany
1958	Sweden	Brazil
1962	Chile	Brazil
1966	England	England
1970	Mexico	Brazil
1974	West Germany	West Germany
1978	Argentina	Argentina
1982	Spain	Italy
1986	Mexico	Argentina
1990	Italy	West Germany
1994	USA	Brazil
1998	France	France
2002	Korea/Japan	Brazil

LEAGUE CHAMPIONS since 1980
First held 1889

YEAR	WINNER
1980	Liverpool
1981	Aston Villa
1982	Liverpool
1983	Liverpool
1984	Liverpool
1985	Everton
1986	Liverpool
1987	Everton
1988	Liverpool
1989	Arsenal
1990	Liverpool
1991	Arsenal
1992	Leeds United
1993	Manchester United
1994	Manchester United
1995	Blackburn Rovers
1996	Manchester United
1997	Manchester United
1998	Arsenal
1999	Manchester United
2000	Manchester United
2001	Manchester United
2002	Arsenal
2003	Manchester United
2004	Arsenal
2005	Chelsea

FA CUP WINNERS since 1980
First held 1872

YEAR	WINNER
1980	West Ham United
1981	Tottenham Hotspur
1982	Tottenham Hotspur
1983	Manchester United
1984	Everton
1985	Manchester United
1986	Liverpool
1987	Coventry
1988	Wimbledon
1989	Liverpool
1990	Manchester United
1991	Tottenham Hotspur
1992	Liverpool
1993	Arsenal
1994	Manchester United
1995	Everton
1996	Manchester United
1997	Chelsea
1998	Arsenal
1999	Manchester United
2000	Chelsea
2001	Liverpool
2002	Arsenal
2003	Arsenal
2004	Manchester United
2005	Arsenal

ATHLETICS

LONDON MARATHON MEN'S WINNERS
First held 1981

YEAR	WINNER
1981	Dick Beardsley (USA)
	Inge Simonson (Norway)
1982	Hugh Jones (GB)
1983	Mike Gratton (GB)
1984	Charlie Spedding (GB)
1985	Steve Jones (GB)
1986	Toshihiko Seko (Japan)
1987	Hiromi Taniguchi (Japan)
1988	Henrik Jorgensen (Denmark)
1989	Douglas Wakiihuri (Kenya)
1990	Allister Hutton (GB)
1991	Yakov Tolstikov (EUN)
1992	Antonio Pinto (Portugal)
1993	Eamonn Martin (GB)
1994	Dionicio Ceron (Mexico)
1995	Dionicio Ceron (Mexico)
1996	Dionicio Ceron (Mexico)
1997	Antonio Pinto (Portugal)
1998	Abel Anton (Spain)
1999	Abdelkader el Mouaziz (Morocco)
2000	Antonio Pinto (Portugal)
2001	Abdelkader el Mouaziz (Morocco)
2002	Khalid Khannouchi (US)
2003	Gezahegne Abera (Ethiopia)
2004	Evans Rutto (Kenya)
2005	Martin Lel (Kenya)

LONDON MARATHON WOMEN'S WINNERS
First held 1981

YEAR	WINNER
1981	Joyce Smith (GB)
1982	Joyce Smith (GB)
1983	Grete Waitz (Norway)
1984	Ingrid Kristiansen (Norway)
1985	Ingrid Kristiansen (Norway)
1986	Grete Waitz (Norway)
1987	Ingrid Kristiansen (Norway)
1988	Ingrid Kristiansen (Norway)
1989	Veronique Marot (GB)
1990	Wanda Panfil (Poland)
1991	Rosa Mota (Portugal)
1992	Katrin Dorre (Germany)
1993	Katrin Dorre (Germany)
1994	Katrin Dorre (Germany)
1995	Malgorzata Sobanska (Poland)
1996	Liz McColgan (GB)
1997	Joyce Chepchumba (Kenya)
1998	Catherina McKiernan (Ireland)

1999	Joyce Chepchumba (Kenya)
2000	Tegla Loroupe (Kenya)
2001	Deratu Tulu (Ethiopia)
2002	Paula Radcliffe (GB)
2003	Paula Radcliffe (GB)
2004	Margaret Okayo (Kenya)
2005	Paula Radcliffe (GB)

CRICKET
WORLD CUP WINNERS
First held 1975

YEAR	WINNER
1975	West Indies
1979	West Indies
1983	India
1987	Australia
1992	Pakistan
1996	Sri Lanka
1999	Australia
2003	Australia

COUNTY CHAMPIONS since 1980
First held 1864

YEAR	WINNER
1980	Middlesex
1981	Nottinghamshire
1982	Middlesex
1983	Essex
1984	Essex
1985	Middlesex
1986	Essex
1987	Nottinghamshire
1988	Worcestershire
1989	Worcestershire
1990	Middlesex
1991	Essex
1992	Essex
1993	Middlesex
1994	Warwickshire
1995	Warwickshire
1996	Leicestershire
1997	Glamorgan
1998	Leicestershire
1999	Surrey
2000	Surrey
2001	Yorkshire
2002	Surrey
2003	Sussex
2004	Warwickshire
2005	Nottinghamshire

GOLF

THE OPEN CHAMPIONS since 1980
First held 1860. Played over 72 holes since 1892

YEAR	WINNER
1980	Tom Watson (USA)
1981	Bill Rogers (USA)
1982	Tom Watson (USA)
1983	Tom Watson (USA)
1984	Severiano Ballesteros (Spain)
1985	Sandy Lyle (GB)
1986	Greg Norman (Australia)
1987	Nick Faldo (GB)
1988	Severiano Ballesteros (Spain)
1989	Mark Calcavecchia (USA)
1990	Nick Faldo (GB)
1991	Ian Baker-Finch (Australia)
1992	Nick Faldo (GB)
1993	Greg Norman (Australia)
1994	Nick Price (Zimbabwe)
1995	John Daly (USA)
1996	Tom Lehman (USA)
1997	Justin Leonard (USA)
1998	Mark O'Meara (USA)
1999	Paul Lawrie (GB)
2000	Tiger Woods (USA)
2001	David Duval (USA)
2002	Ernie Els (South Africa)
2003	Ben Curtis (USA)
2004	Todd Hamilton (USA)
2005	Tiger Woods (USA)

RYDER CUP WINNERS since 1951
First held 1927. Played over 2 days 1927–61; over 3 days 1963 to date

YEAR	WINNER
1951	USA
1953	USA
1955	USA
1957	Great Britain
1959	USA
1961	USA
1963	USA
1965	USA
1967	USA
1969	Match drawn
1971	USA
1973	USA
1975	USA
1977	USA
1979	USA
1981	USA
1983	USA
1985	Great Britain and Europe
1987	Great Britain and Europe
1989	Match drawn
1991	USA
1993	USA
1995	Europe
1997	Europe
1999	USA
2002	Europe
2004	Europe

US OPEN CHAMPIONS since 1980
First held 1895

YEAR	WINNER
1980	Jack Nicklaus (USA)
1981	David Graham (Australia)
1982	Tom Watson (USA)
1983	Larry Nelson (USA)
1984	Fuzzy Zoeller (USA)
1985	Andy North (USA)
1986	Raymond Floyd (USA)
1987	Scott Simpson (USA)
1988	Curtis Strange (USA)
1989	Curtis Strange (USA)
1990	Hale Irwin (USA)
1991	Payne Stewart (USA)
1992	Tom Kite (USA)
1993	Lee Janzen (USA)
1994	Ernie Els (South Africa)
1995	Corey Pavin (USA)
1996	Steve Jones (USA)
1997	Ernie Els (South Africa)

1998	Lee Janzen (USA)
1999	Payne Stewart (USA)
2000	Tiger Woods (USA)
2001	Retief Goosen (South Africa)
2002	Tiger Woods (USA)
2003	Jim Furyk (USA)
2004	Retief Goosen (South Africa)
2005	Michael Campbell (New Zealand)

US MASTERS CHAMPIONS since 1980
First held 1934

YEAR	WINNER
1980	Severiano Ballesteros (Spain)
1981	Tom Watson (USA)
1982	Craig Stadler (USA)
1983	Severiano Ballesteros (Spain)
1984	Ben Crenshaw (USA)
1985	Bernhard Langer (W. Germany)
1986	Jack Nicklaus (USA)
1987	Larry Mize (USA)
1988	Sandy Lyle (GB)
1989	Nick Faldo (GB)
1990	Nick Faldo (GB)
1991	Ian Woosnam (GB)
1992	Fred Couples (USA)
1993	Bernhard Langer (Germany)
1994	José María Olazábal (Spain)
1995	Ben Crenshaw (USA)
1996	Nick Faldo (GB)
1997	Tiger Woods (USA)
1998	Mark O'Meara (USA)
1999	José María Olazábal (Spain)
2000	Vijay Singh (Fiji)
2001	Tiger Woods (USA)
2002	Tiger Woods (USA)
2003	Mike Weir (Canada)
2004	Phil Mickelson (USA)
2005	Tiger Woods (USA)

HORSE RACING

GRAND NATIONAL WINNERS since 1980
The Grand National was first run in 1839

YEAR	WINNING HORSE
1980	Ben Nevis
1981	Aldaniti
1982	Grittar
1983	Corbiere
1984	Hallo Dandy
1985	Last Suspect
1986	West Tip
1987	Maori Venture
1988	Rhyme 'N' Reason
1989	Little Polveir
1990	Mr Frisk
1991	Seagram
1992	Party Politics
1993	*Race declared void*
1994	Miinnehoma
1995	Royal Athlete
1996	Rough Quest
1997	Lord Gyllene
1998	Earth Summit
1999	Bobbyjo
2000	Papillon
2001	Red Marauder
2002	Bindaree
2003	Monty's Pass

2004	Amberleigh House
2005	Hedgehunter

DERBY WINNERS since 1980
The Derby was first run in 1780

YEAR	WINNING HORSE
1980	Henbit
1981	Shergar
1982	Golden Fleece
1983	Teenoso
1984	Secreto
1985	Slip Anchor
1986	Shahrastani
1987	Reference Point
1988	Kahyasi
1989	Nashwan
1990	Quest for Fame
1991	Generous
1992	Dr Devious
1993	Commander In Chief
1994	Erhaab
1995	Lammtarra
1996	Shaamit
1997	Benny The Dip
1998	High Rise
1999	Oath
2000	Sinndar
2001	Galileo
2002	High Chaparral
2003	Kris Kin
2004	North Light
2005	Motivator

MOTOR RACING

FORMULA ONE WORLD CHAMPIONS since 1980
First held 1950

YEAR	WINNER
1980	Alan Jones (Australia)
1981	Nelson Piquet (Brazil)
1982	Keke Rosberg (Finland)
1983	Nelson Piquet (Brazil)
1984	Niki Lauda (Austria)
1985	Alain Prost (France)
1986	Alain Prost (France)
1987	Nelson Piquet (Brazil)
1988	Ayrton Senna (Brazil)
1989	Alain Prost (France)
1990	Ayrton Senna (Brazil)
1991	Ayrton Senna (Brazil)
1992	Nigel Mansell (GB)
1993	Alain Prost (France)
1994	Michael Schumacher (Germany)
1995	Michael Schumacher (Germany)
1996	Damon Hill (GB)
1997	Jacques Villeneuve (Canada)
1998	Mika Hakkinen (Finland)
1999	Mika Hakkinen (Finland)
2000	Michael Schumacher (Germany)
2001	Michael Schumacher (Germany)
2002	Michael Schumacher (Germany)
2003	Michael Schumacher (Germany)
2004	Michael Schumacher (Germany)
2005	Fernando Alonso (Spain)

ROWING

THE UNIVERSITY BOAT RACE since 1980
First held 1829
1829–2005: Cambridge 78 wins, Oxford 72; one dead heat (1877)

YEAR	WINNER
1980	Oxford
1981	Oxford
1982	Oxford
1983	Oxford
1984	Oxford
1985	Oxford
1986	Cambridge
1987	Oxford
1988	Oxford
1989	Oxford
1990	Oxford
1991	Oxford
1992	Oxford
1993	Cambridge
1994	Cambridge
1995	Cambridge
1996	Cambridge
1997	Cambridge
1998	Cambridge
1999	Cambridge
2000	Oxford
2001	Oxford
2002	Oxford
2003	Oxford
2004	Cambridge
2005	Oxford

RUGBY LEAGUE

WORLD CUP WINNERS
First held 1954

YEAR	WINNER
1954	Great Britain
1957	Australia
1960	Great Britain
1968	Australia
1970	Australia
1972	Great Britain
1975	Australia
1977	Australia
1988	Australia
1992	Australia
1995	Australia
2000	Australia

CHALLENGE CUP WINNERS since 1980
First held 1897

YEAR	WINNER
1980	Hull Kingston Rovers
1981	Widnes
1982	Hull
1983	Featherstone Rovers
1984	Widnes
1985	Wigan
1986	Castleford
1987	Halifax
1988	Wigan
1989	Wigan
1990	Wigan
1991	Wigan
1992	Wigan
1993	Wigan
1994	Wigan
1995	Wigan
1996	St Helens
1997	St Helens
1998	Sheffield
1999	Leeds
2000	Bradford
2001	St Helens
2002	Wigan Warriors
2003	Bradford Bulls
2004	St Helens
2005	Hull

RUGBY UNION

WORLD CUP WINNERS
First held 1987

YEAR	WINNER
1987	New Zealand
1991	Australia
1995	South Africa
1999	Australia
2003	England

FOUR/FIVE/SIX NATIONS CHAMPIONS since 1980
First held 1883

YEAR	WINNER
1980	England
1981	France
1982	Ireland
1983	France/Ireland
1984	Scotland
1985	Ireland
1986	France/Scotland
1987	France
1988	Wales/France
1989	France
1990	Scotland
1991	England
1992	England
1993	France
1994	Wales
1995	England
1996	England
1997	France
1998	France
1999	Scotland
2000	England
2001	England
2002	France
2003	England
2004	France
2005	Wales

SNOOKER

WORLD PROFESSIONAL CHAMPIONS since 1980
First held 1927

YEAR	WINNER
1980	Cliff Thorburn (Canada)
1981	Steve Davis (England)
1982	Alex Higgins (N. Ireland)
1983	Steve Davis (England)
1984	Steve Davis (England)
1985	Dennis Taylor (N. Ireland)
1986	Joe Johnson (England)

1987	Steve Davis (England)
1988	Steve Davis (England)
1989	Steve Davis (England)
1990	Stephen Hendry (Scotland)
1991	John Parrott (England)
1992	Stephen Hendry (Scotland)
1993	Stephen Hendry (Scotland)
1994	Stephen Hendry (Scotland)
1995	Stephen Hendry (Scotland)
1996	Stephen Hendry (Scotland)
1997	Ken Doherty (Ireland)
1998	John Higgins (Scotland)
1999	Stephen Hendry (Scotland)
2000	Mark Williams (Wales)
2001	Ronnie O'Sullivan (England)
2002	Peter Ebdon (England)
2003	Mark Williams (Wales)
2004	Ronnie O'Sullivan (England)
2005	Sean Murphy (England)

TENNIS

WIMBLEDON MEN'S SINGLES CHAMPIONS since 1980

First held 1877

YEAR	WINNER
1980	Bjorn Borg (Sweden)
1981	John McEnroe (USA)
1982	Jimmy Connors (USA)
1983	John McEnroe (USA)
1984	John McEnroe (USA)
1985	Boris Becker (W. Germany)
1986	Boris Becker (W. Germany)
1987	Pat Cash (Australia)
1988	Stefan Edberg (Sweden)
1989	Boris Becker (W. Germany)
1990	Stefan Edberg (Sweden)
1991	Michael Stich (Germany)
1992	Andre Agassi (USA)
1993	Pete Sampras (USA)
1994	Pete Sampras (USA)
1995	Pete Sampras (USA)

1996	Richard Krajicek (Netherlands)
1997	Pete Sampras (USA)
1998	Pete Sampras (USA)
1999	Pete Sampras (USA)
2000	Pete Sampras (USA)
2001	Goran Ivanisevic (Croatia)
2002	Lleyton Hewitt (Australia)
2003	Roger Federer (Switzerland)
2004	Roger Federer (Switzerland)
2005	Roger Federer (Switzerland)

WIMBLEDON WOMEN'S SINGLES CHAMPIONS since 1980

First held 1884

YEAR	WINNER
1980	Evonne Cawley (Australia)
1981	Chris Evert Lloyd (USA)
1982	Martina Navratilova (USA)
1983	Martina Navratilova (USA)
1984	Martina Navratilova (USA)
1985	Martina Navratilova (USA)
1986	Martina Navratilova (USA)
1987	Martina Navratilova (USA)
1988	Steffi Graf (W. Germany)
1989	Steffi Graf (W. Germany)
1990	Martina Navratilova (USA)
1991	Steffi Graf (Germany)
1992	Steffi Graf (Germany)
1993	Steffi Graf (Germany)
1994	Conchita Martinez (Spain)
1995	Steffi Graf (Germany)
1996	Steffi Graf (Germany)
1997	Martina Hingis (Switzerland)
1998	Jana Novotna (Czech Republic)
1999	Lindsay Davenport (USA)
2000	Venus Williams (USA)
2001	Venus Williams (USA)
2002	Serena Williams (USA)
2003	Serena Williams (USA)
2004	Maria Sharapova (Russia)
2005	Venus Williams (USA)

TIME AND SPACE

ASTRONOMY

The following pages give astronomical data for each month of the year 2006. There are four pages of data for each month. All data are given for 0h Greenwich Mean Time (GMT), i.e. at the midnight at the beginning of the day named. This applies also to data for the months when British Summer Time is in operation (for dates, *see* below).

The astronomical data are given in a form suitable for observation with the naked eye or with a small telescope. These data do not attempt to replace the *Astronomical Almanac* for professional astronomers.

A fuller explanation of how to use the astronomical data is given on pages 1279–81.

CALENDAR FOR EACH MONTH

The calendar for each month comprises dates of general interest plus the dates of birth or death of well-known people. For key religious, civil and legal dates *see* page 9. For details of flag-flying days *see* page 23. For royal birthdays *see* pages 23 and 24–5. Public holidays are given in italics. *See* also pages 10 and 11.

Fuller explanations of the various calendars can be found under Time Measurement and Calendars (pages 1289–304).

The zodiacal signs through which the Sun is passing during each month are illustrated. The date of transition from one sign to the next, to the nearest hour, is given under Astronomical Phenomena.

JULIAN DATE

The Julian date on 2006 January 0.0 is 2453735.5. To find the Julian date for any other date in 2006 (at 0h GMT), add the day-of-the-year number on the extreme right of the calendar for each month to the Julian date for January 0.0.

SEASONS

The seasons are defined astronomically as follows:

Spring from the vernal equinox to the summer solstice
Summer from the summer solstice to the autumnal equinox
Autumn from the autumnal equinox to the winter solstice
Winter from the winter solstice to the vernal equinox

The seasons in 2006 are:

Northern Hemisphere

Vernal equinox	March 20d 18h GMT
Summer solstice	June 21d 12h GMT
Autumnal equinox	September 23d 04h GMT
Winter solstice	December 22d 00h GMT

Southern Hemisphere

Autumnal equinox	March 20d 18h GMT
Winter solstice	June 21d 12h GMT
Vernal equinox	September 23d 04h GMT
Summer solstice	December 22d 00h GMT

The longest day of the year, measured from sunrise to sunset, is at the summer solstice. The longest day in the United Kingdom will fall on 21 June in 2006.

The shortest day of the year is at the winter solstice. The shortest day in the United Kingdom will fall on 22 December in 2006.

The equinox is the point at which day and night are of equal length all over the world.

In popular parlance, the seasons in the northern hemisphere comprise the following months:

Spring	March, April, May
Summer	June, July, August
Autumn	September, October, November
Winter	December, January, February

BRITISH SUMMER TIME

British Summer Time is the legal time for general purposes during the period in which it is in operation (*see also* pages 1283–4). During this period, clocks are kept one hour ahead of Greenwich Mean Time. The hour of changeover is 01h Greenwich Mean Time. The duration of Summer Time in 2006 is from March 26 01h GMT to October 29 01h GMT.

JANUARY 2006

FIRST MONTH, 31 DAYS. *Janus*, god of the portal, facing two ways, past and future

1	Sunday	Harriet Brooks b. 1876. Heinrich Hertz d. 1894	1

2	Monday	Isaac Asimov b. 1920. Léon Teisserenc de Bort d. 1913	week 1 day 2
3	Tuesday	J. R. R. Tolkien b. 1892. Jeremiah Horrocks d. 1641	3
4	Wednesday	Louis Braille b. 1809. Erwin Schrödinger d. 1961	4
5	Thursday	King Camp Gillette b. 1855. Ernest Shackleton d. 1922	5
6	Friday	James Fitzmaurice b. 1898. Gregor Mendel d. 1884	6
7	Saturday	Johann Philipp Reis b. 1834. Vladimir Prelog d. 1998	7
8	Sunday	Stephen Hawking b. 1942. Galileo Galilei d. 1642	8

9	Monday	Vladimir Steklov b. 1864. Kenichi Fukui d. 1998	week 2 day 9
10	Tuesday	The world's first underground railway opens to passengers in London 1863	10
11	Wednesday	Albert Hofmann b. 1906. Isidor Isaac Rabi d. 1988	11
12	Thursday	Sergey Korolev b. 1907. Pierre de Fermat d. 1665	12
13	Friday	The National Geographic Society is founded in Washington DC 1888	13
14	Saturday	Shannon Lucid b. 1943. Kurt Gödel d. 1978	14
15	Sunday	The Soviet Union launches the Soyuz 5 spacecraft 1969	15

16	Monday	Douglas Mawson, Alistair Forbes Mackay and Tannatt William Edgeworth David reach the magnetic South Pole 1909	week 3 day 16
17	Tuesday	Benjamin Franklin b. 1706. Clyde Tombaugh d. 1997	17
18	Wednesday	Jacob Bronowski b. 1908. Adolf Butenandt d. 1995	18
19	Thursday	James Watt b. 1736. Henri Regnault d. 1878	19
20	Friday	Col. Edwin 'Buzz' Aldrin b. 1930. Dmitry Mendeleyev d. 1907	20
21	Saturday	Concorde's first commercial flights take off simultaneously from London and Paris 1976	21
22	Sunday	Lev Landau b. 1908. Queen Victoria d. 1901	22

23	Monday	David Hilbert b. 1862. Claude Chappe d. 1805	week 4 day 23
24	Tuesday	Desmond Morris b. 1928. Winston Churchill d. 1965	24
25	Wednesday	Robert Boyle b. 1627. Stephen Cole Kleene d. 1994	25
26	Thursday	Ancel Keys b. 1904. Edward Jenner d. 1823	26
27	Friday	Lewis Carroll b. 1832. Thomas Crapper d. 1910	27
28	Saturday	Johannes Hevelius b. 1611. King Henry VIII d. 1547	28
29	Sunday	Linda Buck b. 1947. Fritz Haber d. 1934	29

30	Monday	Douglas Engelbart b. 1925. Orville Wright d. 1948	week 5 day 30
31	Tuesday	Rudolf Mössbauer b. 1929. Guy Fawkes d. 1606	31

ASTRONOMICAL PHENOMENA

d	h	
1	12	Venus in conjunction with Moon. Venus 7°N.
4	15	Earth at perihelion (147 million km.)
8	19	Mars in conjunction with Moon. Mars 1°S.
14	00	Venus in inferior conjunction
15	15	Saturn in conjunction with Moon. Saturn 4°S.
17	16	Venus in conjunction with Mercury. Venus 8°N.
20	05	Sun's longitude 300°; ≈≈
23	18	Jupiter in conjunction with Moon. Jupiter 4°N.
26	22	Mercury in superior conjunction
27	23	Saturn at opposition
28	02	Venus in conjunction with Moon. Venus 12°N.
29	18	Mercury in conjunction with Moon. Mercury 2°N.

MINIMA OF ALGOL

d	h	d	h	d	h
3	08.0	14	19.2	26	06.5
6	04.8	17	16.1	29	03.4
9	01.6	20	12.9		
11	22.4	23	09.7		

CONSTELLATIONS

The following constellations are near the meridian at

d	h		d	h
December	1	24	January	16	21
December	16	23	February	1	20
January	1	22	February	15	19

Draco (below the Pole), Ursa Minor (below the Pole), Camelopardus, Perseus, Auriga, Taurus, Orion, Eridanus and Lepdus

THE MOON

Phases, Apsides and Node	d	h	m
☽ First Quarter	6	18	56
○ Full Moon	14	09	48
☾ Last Quarter	22	15	14
● New Moon	29	14	15

Perigee (361,766km)	1	22	41
Apogee (405,858km)	17	18	57
Perigee (357,784km)	30	07	45

Mean longitude of ascending node on January 1, 9°

THE SUN

s.d. 16'.3

Day	Right Ascension			Dec.		Equation of time		Rise 52°		Rise 56°		Transit		Set 52°		Set 56°		Sidereal time			Transit of first point of Aries		
	h	m	s	°	'	m	s	h	m	h	m	h	m	h	m	h	m	h	m	s	h	m	s
1	18	45	21	23	02	−3	19	8	08	8	31	12	04	15	59	15	36	6	42	01	17	15	09
2	18	49	45	22	57	−3	47	8	08	8	31	12	04	16	00	15	37	6	45	58	17	11	13
3	18	54	10	22	51	−4	15	8	08	8	31	12	04	16	01	15	39	6	49	55	17	07	17
4	18	58	34	22	46	−4	43	8	08	8	30	12	05	16	03	15	40	6	53	51	17	03	21
5	19	02	58	22	39	−5	10	8	07	8	30	12	05	16	04	15	41	6	57	48	16	59	25
6	19	07	21	22	32	−5	37	8	07	8	29	12	06	16	05	15	43	7	01	44	16	55	29
7	19	11	44	22	25	−6	03	8	07	8	29	12	06	16	06	15	44	7	05	41	16	51	33
8	19	16	07	22	17	−6	29	8	06	8	28	12	07	16	08	15	46	7	09	37	16	47	37
9	19	20	28	22	09	−6	54	8	06	8	27	12	07	16	09	15	47	7	13	34	16	43	41
10	19	24	50	22	01	−7	19	8	05	8	26	12	08	16	10	15	49	7	17	30	16	39	45
11	19	29	10	21	52	−7	43	8	04	8	25	12	08	16	12	15	51	7	21	27	16	35	49
12	19	33	30	21	42	−8	07	8	04	8	25	12	08	16	13	15	52	7	25	24	16	31	54
13	19	37	50	21	32	−8	30	8	03	8	24	12	09	16	15	15	54	7	29	20	16	27	58
14	19	42	09	21	22	−8	52	8	02	8	23	12	09	16	16	15	56	7	33	17	16	24	02
15	19	46	27	21	11	−9	14	8	01	8	21	12	09	16	18	15	58	7	37	13	16	20	06
16	19	50	45	21	00	−9	35	8	00	8	20	12	10	16	20	16	00	7	41	10	16	16	10
17	19	55	01	20	49	−9	55	7	59	8	19	12	10	16	21	16	02	7	45	06	16	12	14
18	19	59	18	20	37	−10	15	7	58	8	18	12	10	16	23	16	04	7	49	03	16	08	18
19	20	03	33	20	25	−10	34	7	57	8	16	12	11	16	24	16	05	7	52	59	16	04	22
20	20	07	48	20	12	−10	52	7	56	8	15	12	11	16	26	16	07	7	56	56	16	00	26
21	20	12	02	19	59	−11	09	7	55	8	14	17	11	16	28	16	09	8	00	53	15	56	30
22	20	16	15	19	45	−11	26	7	54	8	12	12	12	16	30	16	12	8	04	49	15	52	34
23	20	20	28	19	32	−11	42	7	53	8	11	12	12	16	31	16	14	8	08	46	15	48	38
24	20	24	40	19	18	−11	57	7	52	8	09	12	12	16	33	16	16	8	12	42	15	44	43
25	20	28	51	19	03	−12	12	7	50	8	08	12	12	16	35	16	18	8	16	39	15	40	47
26	20	33	01	18	48	−12	26	7	49	8	06	12	13	16	37	16	20	8	20	35	15	36	51
27	20	37	10	18	33	−12	38	7	48	8	04	12	13	16	38	16	22	8	24	32	15	32	55
28	20	41	19	18	17	−12	51	7	46	8	02	12	13	16	40	16	24	8	28	28	15	28	59
29	20	45	27	18	02	−13	02	7	45	8	01	12	13	16	42	16	26	8	32	25	15	25	03
30	20	49	34	17	45	−13	12	7	43	7	59	12	13	16	44	16	28	8	36	22	15	21	07
31	20	53	40	17	29	−13	22	7	42	7	57	12	13	16	46	16	31	8	40	18	15	17	11

DURATION OF TWILIGHT (in minutes)

Latitude	52°	56°	52°	56°	52°	56°	52°	56°
	1 January		11 January		21 January		31 January	
Civil	41	47	40	45	38	43	37	41
Nautical	84	96	82	93	80	90	78	87
Astronomical	125	141	123	138	120	134	117	130

THE NIGHT SKY

Mercury is unsuitably placed for observation as it passes through superior conjunction on the 26th.

Venus, its magnitude fading from −4.4 to −4.1, is a brilliant object low in the south-western sky in the early evenings just after sunset, at the at the beginning of the month. This evening apparition will last for about ten days before the planet becomes too close to the Sun for observation. However Venus passes rapidly through inferior conjunction late on the 13th when it is 5.5 degrees north of the ecliptic. On the following morning the planet becomes visible again, magnitude −4.1, very low in the south-eastern sky shortly before sunrise. Its apparent diameter of 62 arcseconds must be near its maximum possible value as the Earth is not far from perihelion and Venus's orbit is nearly circular.

Mars continues to be visible as an evening object in the south-western quadrant of the sky and still above the horizon until well after midnight. During the month its magnitude fades from −0.6 to +0.2. Mars remains in the constellation of Aries throughout January. Mars will be seen in the vicinity of the Moon, just past First Quarter, on the evenings of the 7th and 8th.

Jupiter is a brilliant object in the south-eastern quadrant of the sky before dawn, magnitude −1.9. On the mornings of the 23rd and 24th the Moon, at Last Quarter, is near the planet. A few days before the middle of the month Jupiter passes about 0.8 degrees north of the wide naked-eye double star Alpha Librae. The two components are separated by about 3 arcminutes and have magnitudes of 5.15 and 2.75.

Saturn, magnitude −0.2, reaches opposition on the 27th and is therefore visible throughout the hours of darkness. It is near the Full Moon on the night of the 14th/15th. It is in the western part of the constellation of Cancer moving slowly retrograde in the direction of the Beehive cluster, Praesepe. The rings are now closing, and as a result, the planet is not quite as bright as it was in the previous two oppositions. The south pole is presented towards the Earth, but the far side of the rings no longer appears clear of the body of the planet.

THE MOON

Day	RA h	RA m	Dec. °	Hor. par.	Semi-diam. '	Sun's Co-long. °	PA of Br. Limb °	Ph. %	Age d	Rise 52° h	Rise 52° m	Rise 56° h	Rise 56° m	Transit h	Transit m	Set 52° h	Set 52° m	Set 56° h	Set 56° m
1	19	40	−26.4	60.5	16.5	284	282	1	0.9	9	52	10	21	13	32	17	22	16	54
2	20	44	−22.7	60.6	16.5	296	264	5	1.9	10	19	10	40	14	32	18	58	18	38
3	21	43	−17.5	60.5	16.5	308	255	12	2.9	10	37	10	51	15	27	20	31	20	19
4	22	38	−11.4	60.1	16.4	321	250	20	3.9	10	52	10	59	16	17	22	00	21	55
5	23	30	−4.8	59.6	16.2	333	247	30	4.9	11	04	11	05	17	05	23	25	23	27
6	0	20	+1.9	59.0	16.1	345	247	41	5.9	11	15	11	11	17	52	—	—	—	—
7	1	09	+8.4	58.3	15.9	357	248	52	6.9	11	27	11	17	18	39	0	49	0	57
8	1	59	+14.4	57.6	15.7	9	250	63	7.9	11	41	11	25	19	27	2	12	2	26
9	2	50	+19.6	57.0	15.5	21	255	73	8.9	11	59	11	36	20	18	3	36	3	57
10	3	43	+23.7	56.5	15.4	34	260	82	9.9	12	23	11	54	21	11	4	57	5	26
11	4	38	+26.7	55.9	15.2	46	268	89	10.9	12	58	12	22	22	05	6	14	6	49
12	5	34	+28.2	55.5	15.1	58	277	94	11.9	13	45	13	06	22	59	7	19	7	58
13	6	31	+28.3	55.1	15.0	70	290	98	12.9	14	46	14	09	23	52	8	09	8	46
14	7	26	+26.9	54.7	14.9	82	325	100	13.9	15	57	15	26	—	—	8	45	9	17
15	8	18	+24.3	54.4	14.8	94	68	100	14.9	17	11	16	48	0	43	9	10	9	35
16	9	08	+20.7	54.2	14.8	106	94	98	15.9	18	26	18	09	1	29	9	28	9	46
17	9	54	+16.3	54.1	14.7	118	104	94	16.9	19	39	19	28	2	13	9	41	9	54
18	10	39	+11.3	54.0	14.7	131	109	89	17.9	20	50	20	44	2	54	9	52	10	00
19	11	21	+5.9	54.1	14.7	143	112	82	18.9	22	00	21	59	3	34	10	02	10	04
20	12	03	+0.3	54.3	14.8	155	113	74	19.9	23	11	23	15	4	13	10	10	10	09
21	12	45	−5.4	54.7	14.9	167	113	66	20.9	—	—	—	—	4	52	10	20	10	13
22	13	29	−11.0	55.3	15.1	179	112	56	21.9	0	24	0	34	5	34	10	31	10	19
23	14	15	−16.3	56.0	15.2	191	109	46	22.9	1	40	1	57	6	18	10	44	10	26
24	15	05	−21.0	56.8	15.5	203	105	36	23.9	3	01	3	25	7	07	11	03	10	38
25	16	00	−24.9	57.7	15.7	216	99	27	24.9	4	25	4	57	8	02	11	31	10	59
26	17	00	−27.5	58.7	16.0	228	92	18	25.9	5	46	6	25	9	02	12	14	11	35
27	18	04	−28.5	59.6	16.2	240	83	10	26.9	6	54	7	34	10	06	13	19	12	39
28	19	10	−27.5	60.4	16.5	252	71	4	27.9	7	44	8	18	11	10	14	44	14	11
29	20	15	−24.6	61.0	16.6	264	49	1	28.9	8	17	8	43	12	13	16	20	15	57
30	21	18	−19.9	61.3	16.7	277	286	0	0.4	8	40	8	57	13	12	17	58	17	43
31	22	16	−13.9	61.2	16.7	289	257	3	1.4	8	56	9	06	14	06	19	33	19	25

MERCURY

Day	RA h	RA m	Dec. °	Diam. "	Phase %	Transit h	Transit m	5° high 52° h	5° high 52° m	5° high 56° h	5° high 56° m
1	17	41	−23.5	5	92	11	00	8	02	8	39
3	17	54	−23.8	5	93	11	05	8	10	8	48
5	18	07	−24.1	5	94	11	11	8	17	8	56
7	18	21	−24.2	5	95	11	16	8	24	9	04
9	18	34	−24.2	5	96	11	22	8	30	9	10
11	18	48	−24.2	5	97	11	28	8	35	9	15
13	19	02	−24.1	5	97	11	34	8	40	9	19
15	19	16	−23.9	5	98	11	40	8	44	9	22
17	19	29	−23.6	5	99	11	46	8	47	9	24
19	19	43	−23.2	5	99	11	52	8	49	9	24
21	19	57	−22.7	5	99	11	58	8	51	9	24
23	20	12	−22.0	5	100	12	04	15	18	14	46
25	20	26	−21.3	5	100	12	11	15	30	15	00
27	20	40	−20.5	5	100	12	17	15	43	15	15
29	20	54	−19.6	5	100	12	23	15	56	15	30
31	21	08	−18.6	5	99	12	29	16	10	15	46

VENUS

Day	RA h	RA m	Dec. °	Diam. "	Phase %	Transit h	Transit m	5° high 52° h	5° high 52° m	5° high 56° h	5° high 56° m
1	20	08	−17.8	58	6	13	23	9	39	10	02
6	19	58	−17.0	61	3	12	53	9	04	9	26
11	19	46	−16.3	62	1	12	21	8	28	8	48
16	19	33	−15.8	62	1	11	49	7	52	8	11
21	19	21	−15.4	61	2	11	17	7	18	7	37
26	19	12	−15.3	58	6	10	49	6	49	7	08
31	19	07	−15.4	54	10	10	25	6	25	6	44

MARS

Day	RA h	RA m	Dec. °	Diam. "	Phase %	Transit h	Transit m	5° high 52° h	5° high 52° m	5° high 56° h	5° high 56° m
1	2	33	+16.6	12	92	19	48	2	44	2	55
6	2	38	+17.1	11	91	19	34	2	33	2	44
11	2	44	+17.6	11	91	19	20	2	22	2	34
16	2	51	+18.2	10	90	19	07	2	12	2	24
21	2	58	+18.7	10	90	18	55	2	03	2	16
26	3	06	+19.3	9	90	18	44	1	55	2	08
31	3	15	+19.9	9	89	18	33	1	47	2	01

SUNRISE AND SUNSET

	London 0° 05'	51° 30'		Bristol 2° 35'	51° 28'		Birmingham 1° 55'	52° 28'		Manchester 2° 15'	53° 28'		Newcastle 1° 37'	54° 59'		Glasgow 4° 14'	55° 52'		Belfast 5° 56'	54° 35'	
	h m	h m	h m	h m	h m	h m	h m	h m	h m	h m	h m	h m	h m	h m
1	8 06	16 02	8 16	16 12	8 18	16 04	8 25	16 00	8 31	15 49	8 47	15 54	8 46	16 09
2	8 06	16 03	8 16	16 13	8 18	16 05	8 25	16 01	8 31	15 50	8 47	15 55	8 46	16 10
3	8 06	16 04	8 16	16 14	8 18	16 07	8 25	16 03	8 31	15 51	8 47	15 56	8 46	16 11
4	8 06	16 05	8 15	16 15	8 18	16 08	8 24	16 04	8 30	15 53	8 46	15 58	8 45	16 12
5	8 05	16 06	8 15	16 17	8 17	16 09	8 24	16 05	8 30	15 54	8 46	15 59	8 45	16 14
6	8 05	16 08	8 15	16 18	8 17	16 10	8 23	16 06	8 29	15 55	8 45	16 01	8 44	16 15
7	8 04	16 09	8 14	16 19	8 17	16 12	8 23	16 08	8 29	15 57	8 45	16 02	8 44	16 16
8	8 04	16 10	8 14	16 20	8 16	16 13	8 22	16 09	8 28	15 58	8 44	16 04	8 43	16 18
9	8 04	16 12	8 13	16 22	8 15	16 14	8 22	16 11	8 28	16 00	8 43	16 05	8 43	16 19
10	8 03	16 13	8 13	16 23	8 15	16 16	8 21	16 12	8 27	16 01	8 42	16 07	8 42	16 21
11	8 02	16 14	8 12	16 25	8 14	16 17	8 20	16 14	8 26	16 03	8 42	16 08	8 41	16 23
12	8 02	16 16	8 12	16 26	8 14	16 19	8 20	16 15	8 25	16 05	8 41	16 10	8 40	16 24
13	8 01	16 17	8 11	16 28	8 13	16 20	8 19	16 17	8 24	16 06	8 40	16 12	8 39	16 26
14	8 00	16 19	8 10	16 29	8 12	16 22	8 18	16 18	8 23	16 08	8 39	16 14	8 38	16 28
15	7 59	16 20	8 09	16 31	8 11	16 24	8 17	16 20	8 22	16 10	8 38	16 16	8 37	16 29
16	7 59	16 22	8 08	16 32	8 10	16 25	8 16	16 22	8 21	16 12	8 36	16 17	8 36	16 31
17	7 58	16 24	8 08	16 34	8 09	16 27	8 15	16 24	8 20	16 14	8 35	16 19	8 35	16 33
18	7 57	16 25	8 07	16 35	8 08	16 28	8 14	16 25	8 19	16 15	8 34	16 21	8 34	16 35
19	7 56	16 27	8 06	16 37	8 07	16 30	8 13	16 27	8 18	16 17	8 33	16 23	8 33	16 36
20	7 55	16 29	8 05	16 39	8 06	16 32	8 12	16 29	8 16	16 19	8 31	16 25	8 32	16 38
21	7 54	16 30	8 03	16 40	8 05	16 34	8 11	16 31	8 15	16 21	8 30	16 27	8 30	16 40
22	7 52	16 32	8 02	16 42	8 04	16 35	8 09	16 32	8 14	16 23	8 28	16 29	8 29	16 42
23	7 51	16 34	8 01	16 44	8 02	16 37	8 08	16 34	8 12	16 25	8 27	16 31	8 28	16 44
24	7 50	16 35	8 00	16 45	8 01	16 39	8 07	16 36	8 11	16 27	8 25	16 33	8 26	16 46
25	7 49	16 37	7 59	16 47	8 00	16 41	8 05	16 38	8 09	16 29	8 24	16 35	8 25	16 48
26	7 47	16 39	7 57	16 49	7 58	16 43	8 04	16 40	8 08	16 31	8 22	16 37	8 23	16 50
27	7 46	16 41	7 56	16 51	7 57	16 44	8 02	16 42	8 06	16 33	8 21	16 39	8 22	16 52
28	7 45	16 42	7 55	16 52	7 56	16 46	8 01	16 44	8 04	16 35	8 19	16 42	8 20	16 54
29	7 43	16 44	7 53	16 54	7 54	16 48	7 59	16 46	8 03	16 37	8 17	16 44	8 18	16 56
30	7 42	16 46	7 52	16 56	7 53	16 50	7 58	16 48	8 01	16 39	8 15	16 46	8 17	16 58
31	7 40	16 48	7 50	16 58	7 51	16 52	7 56	16 50	7 59	16 41	8 13	16 48	8 15	17 00

JUPITER

Day	RA		Dec.		Transit		5° high			
							52°		56°	
	h	m	°	'	h	m	h	m	h	m
1	14	44.8	−14	47	8	02	3	58	4	16
11	14	50.8	−15	13	7	28	3	28	3	46
21	14	56.1	−15	35	6	54	2	56	3	15
31	15	00.4	−15	52	6	19	2	23	2	42

Diameters – equatorial 35″ polar 32″

SATURN

Day	RA		Dec.		Transit		5° high			
							52°		56°	
	h	m	°	'	h	m	h	m	h	m
1	8	50.2	+18	22	2	08	19	01	18	48
11	8	47.3	+18	35	1	26	18	17	18	05
21	8	44.2	+18	48	0	43	17	34	17	21
31	8	40.8	+19	02	0	01	16	50	16	36

Diameters – equatorial 20″ polar 18″
Rings – major axis 46″ minor axis 15″

URANUS

Day	RA		Dec.		Transit		10° high			
							52°		56°	
	h	m	°	'	h	m	h	m	h	m
1	22	38.7	−9	22	15	54	19	54	19	38
11	22	40.2	−9	13	15	16	19	18	19	01
21	22	41.9	−9	03	14	39	18	41	18	25
31	22	43.8	−8	51	14	01	18	05	17	49

Diameter 4″

NEPTUNE

Day	RA		Dec.		Transit		10° high			
							52°		56°	
	h	m	°	'	h	m	h	m	h	m
1	21	13.9	−16	12	14	30	17	42	17	13
11	21	15.3	−16	06	13	52	17	05	16	37
21	21	16.7	−16	00	13	14	16	28	16	00
31	21	18.2	−15	53	12	36	15	51	15	23

Diameter 2″

 **FEBRUARY 2006**

SECOND MONTH, 28 or 29 DAYS. *Februa*, Roman festival of Purification

1	*Wednesday*	The Columbia space shuttle disintegrates, killing all seven astronauts on board 2003	32
2	*Thursday*	Alfred Brehm b. 1829. Bertrand Russell d. 1970	33
3	*Friday*	Elizabeth Blackwell b. 1821. Frank Oppenheimer d. 1985	34
4	*Saturday*	Charles Lindbergh b. 1902. Hendrik Lorentz d. 1928	35
5	*Sunday*	John Boyd Dunlop b. 1840. Ludwig Binswanger d. 1966	36

6	*Monday*	William Murphy b. 1892. Salvador Luria d. 1991	week 6 day 37
7	*Tuesday*	Alfred Worden b. 1932. Secondo Campini d. 1980	38
8	*Wednesday*	Chester Carlson b. 1906. John von Neumann d. 1957	39
9	*Thursday*	Daniel Bernoulli b. 1700. Herbert Simon d. 2001	40
10	*Friday*	John Enders b. 1897. Wilhelm Conrad Röntgen d. 1923	41
11	*Saturday*	Thomas Edison b. 1847. Léon Foucault d. 1868	42
12	*Sunday*	Charles Darwin b. 1809. Christopher Clavius d. 1612	43

13	*Monday*	John Hunter b. 1728. Rudjer Boscovich d. 1787	week 7 day 44
14	*Tuesday*	Christopher Sholes b. 1819. Capt. James Cook d. 1779	45
15	*Wednesday*	Roger Chaffee b. 1935. Richard Feynman d. 1988	46
16	*Thursday*	Francis Galton b. 1822. John Garand d. 1974	47
17	*Friday*	René Laënnec b. 1781. Jan Swammerdam d. 1680	48
18	*Saturday*	Alessandro Volta b. 1745. Robert Oppenheimer d. 1967	49
19	*Sunday*	Nicolaus Copernicus b. 1473. André Cournand d. 1988	50

20	*Monday*	Ludwig Boltzmann b. 1844. Solomon Asch d. 1996	week 8 day 51
21	*Tuesday*	Henrik Dam b. 1895. Frederick Banting d. 1941	52
22	*Wednesday*	Frank P. Ramsey b. 1903. Charles Lyell d. 1875	53
23	*Thursday*	Carl Menger b. 1840. Carl Friedrich Gauss d. 1855	54
24	*Friday*	Steve Jobs b. 1955. Robert Fulton d. 1815	55
25	*Saturday*	Henry Watson b. 1827. Glenn Seaborg d. 1999	56
26	*Sunday*	Giulio Natta b. 1903. Richard Gatling d. 1903	57

27	*Monday*	Charles Best b. 1899. Konrad Lorenz d. 1989	week 9 day 58
28	*Tuesday*	James Watson and Francis Crick announce their discovery of the structure of DNA 1953	59

ASTRONOMICAL PHENOMENA

d h
- 3 09 Venus at stationary point
- 5 21 Mars in conjunction with Moon. Mars 2°S.
- 6 06 Neptune in conjunction
- 11 17 Saturn in conjunction with Moon. Saturn 4°S.
- 17 15 Venus at greatest brilliancy
- 18 19 Sun's longitude 330° $\mathcal{H}$
- 20 05 Jupiter in conjunction with Moon. Jupiter 5°N.
- 24 05 Mercury at greatest elongation E. 18°
- 25 00 Venus in conjunction with Moon. Venus 10°N.

MINIMA OF ALGOL

d	h	d	h	d	h
1	00.2	12	11.5	23	22.7
3	21.0	15	08.3	26	19.6
6	17.8	18	05.1		
9	14.6	21	01.9		

CONSTELLATIONS

The following constellations are near the meridian at

	d	h		d	h
January	1	24	February	15	21
January	16	23	March	1	20
February	1	22	March	16	19

Draco (below the Pole), Camelopardus, Auriga, Taurus, Gemini, Orion, Canis Minor, Monoceros, Lepus, Canis Major and Puppis

THE MOON

Phases, Apsides and Node	d	h	m
☽ First Quarter	5	06	29
○ Full Moon	13	04	44
☾ Last Quarter	21	07	17
● New Moon	28	00	31

Apogee (406,352 km)	14	00	30
Perigee (356,883km)	27	20	19

Mean longitude of ascending node on February 1, 7°

THE SUN

s.d. 16′.2

Day	Right Ascension			Dec.		Equation of time		Rise 52°		Rise 56°		Transit		Set 52°		Set 56°		Sidereal time			Transit of first point of Aries		
	h	m	s	°	′	m	s	h	m	h	m	h	m	h	m	h	m	h	m	s	h	m	s
1	20	57	46	17	12	−13	31	7	40	7	55	12	14	16	48	16	33	8	44	15	15	13	15
2	21	01	50	16	55	−13	39	7	39	7	53	12	14	16	49	16	35	8	48	11	15	09	19
3	21	05	54	16	38	−13	46	7	37	7	51	12	14	16	51	16	37	8	52	08	15	05	23
4	21	09	57	16	20	−13	53	7	35	7	49	12	14	16	53	16	39	8	56	04	15	01	28
5	21	13	59	16	02	−13	58	7	34	7	47	12	14	16	55	16	41	9	00	01	14	57	32
6	21	18	00	15	44	−14	03	7	32	7	45	12	14	16	57	16	44	9	03	57	14	53	36
7	21	22	01	15	25	−14	07	7	30	7	43	12	14	16	59	16	46	9	07	54	14	49	40
8	21	26	00	15	06	−14	10	7	28	7	41	12	14	17	01	16	48	9	11	51	14	45	44
9	21	29	59	14	47	−14	12	7	27	7	39	12	14	17	02	16	50	9	15	47	14	41	48
10	21	33	57	14	28	−14	14	7	25	7	37	12	14	17	04	16	52	9	19	44	14	37	52
11	21	37	55	14	08	−14	14	7	23	7	35	12	14	17	06	16	55	9	23	40	14	33	56
12	21	41	51	13	49	−14	14	7	21	7	32	12	14	17	08	16	57	9	27	37	14	30	00
13	21	45	47	13	29	−14	13	7	19	7	30	12	14	17	10	16	59	9	31	33	14	26	04
14	21	49	42	13	08	−14	12	7	17	7	28	12	14	17	12	17	01	9	35	30	14	22	08
15	21	53	36	12	48	−14	09	7	15	7	26	12	14	17	14	17	03	9	39	26	14	18	13
16	21	57	29	12	27	−14	06	7	13	7	23	12	14	17	15	17	06	9	43	23	14	14	17
17	22	01	22	12	07	−14	03	7	11	7	21	12	14	17	17	17	08	9	47	20	14	10	21
18	22	05	14	11	46	−13	58	7	09	7	19	12	14	17	19	17	10	9	51	16	14	06	25
19	22	09	06	11	24	−13	53	7	07	7	16	12	14	17	21	17	12	9	55	13	14	02	29
20	22	12	56	11	03	−13	47	7	05	7	14	12	14	17	23	17	14	9	59	09	13	58	33
21	22	16	46	10	41	−13	41	7	03	7	12	12	14	17	25	17	17	10	03	06	13	54	37
22	22	20	36	10	20	−13	34	7	01	7	09	12	13	17	27	17	19	10	07	02	13	50	41
23	22	24	25	9	58	−13	26	6	59	7	07	12	13	17	28	17	21	10	10	59	13	46	45
24	22	28	13	9	36	−13	18	6	57	7	04	12	13	17	30	17	23	10	14	55	13	42	49
25	22	32	01	9	13	−13	09	6	55	7	02	12	13	17	32	17	25	10	18	52	13	38	53
26	22	35	48	8	51	−12	59	6	53	6	59	12	13	17	34	17	27	10	22	49	13	34	58
27	22	39	34	8	29	−12	49	6	51	6	57	12	13	17	36	17	29	10	26	45	13	31	02
28	22	43	20	8	06	−12	39	6	48	6	55	12	13	17	38	17	32	10	30	42	13	27	06

DURATION OF TWILIGHT (in minutes)

Latitude	52°	56°	52°	56°	52°	56°	52°	56°
	1 February		11 February		21 February		31 February	
Civil	37	41	35	39	34	38	34	37
Nautical	77	86	75	83	74	81	73	80
Astronomical	117	130	114	126	113	124	112	124

THE NIGHT SKY

Mercury is visible as an evening object during the second half of the month, low above the south-western horizon around the end of evening civil twilight. During this period the magnitude of Mercury fades from −1.1 to +0.5, so it is at its brightest before it reaches greatest eastern elongation (18 degrees) on the 24th. This evening apparition will be the most suitable one of the year for observers in the latitudes of the British Isles.

Venus attains its greatest brilliancy (magnitude −4.6) on the 17th, and completely dominates the south-eastern sky in the early mornings before dawn. Venus appears as a slender crescent and thus is a beautiful sight in a small telescope. During February the phase increases noticeably as the apparent diameter decreases. On the mornings of the 24th and 25th Venus is in the same part of the sky as the waning crescent Moon. This is a good opportunity to detect the planet in the early morning daylight. The Moon is passing well south of the planet and, even at closest approach around midday on the 24th, the two bodies will still be about ten degrees apart.

Mars, its magnitude fading from +0.2 to +0.7 during the month, is still visible as an evening object in the western sky. Early in the month the planet moves from Aries into Taurus and during the second half of February it will be seen passing between the Hyades and the Pleiades. At that time it is only slightly brighter than Aldebaran. During the evening of the 5th the First Quarter Moon will be seen passing less than 1 degree above Mars.

Jupiter, magnitude −2.1, continues to be visible as a brilliant object in the south-eastern sky in the mornings. The waning gibbous Moon is near the planet on the 19th and 20th.

Saturn, only just past opposition, is still available for observation for the greater part of the night. As soon as it gets dark enough in the evenings it is visible in the eastern sky. It continues to retrograde slowly in Cancer, passing about 1 degree south of the well-known Beehive open cluster, named Praesepe, early in February. Saturn's magnitude is −0.2. Early on the 11th the waxing gibbous Moon passes 3 degrees north of the planet.

Zodiacal Light. The evening cone may be observed stretching up from the western horizon, along the ecliptic, after the end of twilight, from the 15th to the end of the month. This faint phenomenon is only visible under good conditions and in the absence of both moonlight and artificial lighting.

THE MOON

Day	RA h m	Dec. °	Hor. par.	Semi-diam. ′	Sun's Co-long.	PA of Br. Limb °	Ph. %	Age d	Rise 52° h m	Rise 56° h m	Transit h m	Set 52° h m	Set 56° h m
1	23 11	−7.1	60.8	16.6	301	250	9	2.4	9 09	9 13	14 57	21 03	21 02
2	0 03	−0.1	60.2	16.4	313	247	16	3.4	9 21	9 19	15 46	22 31	22 36
3	0 54	+6.8	59.4	16.2	325	247	26	4.4	9 33	9 25	16 35	23 57	—
4	1 45	+13.1	58.6	16.0	337	249	36	5.4	9 47	9 33	17 24	—	0 09
5	2 37	+18.6	57.7	15.7	350	252	47	6.4	10 03	9 43	18 14	1 23	1 42
6	3 30	+23.1	56.9	15.5	2	257	58	7.4	10 26	9 58	19 07	2 47	3 13
7	4 25	+26.3	56.2	15.3	14	263	68	8.4	10 57	10 22	20 01	4 06	4 40
8	5 21	+28.1	55.6	15.1	26	269	77	9.4	11 40	11 01	20 55	5 14	5 54
9	6 17	+28.5	55.0	15.0	38	277	84	10.4	12 37	11 58	21 48	6 09	6 48
10	7 12	+27.5	54.6	14.9	50	284	91	11.4	13 45	13 12	22 39	6 48	7 22
11	8 05	+25.2	54.3	14.8	63	292	96	12.4	14 58	14 33	23 26	7 16	7 43
12	8 55	+21.8	54.1	14.7	75	304	99	13.4	16 13	15 54	—	7 35	7 55
13	9 42	+17.5	54.0	14.7	87	348	100	14.4	17 27	17 14	0 11	7 49	8 04
14	10 27	+12.6	54.0	14.7	99	95	99	15.4	18 38	18 31	0 53	8 01	8 10
15	11 10	+7.2	54.0	14.7	111	108	97	16.4	19 49	19 47	1 33	8 10	8 14
16	11 52	+1.6	54.1	14.8	123	112	93	17.4	20 59	21 02	2 12	8 19	8 19
17	12 34	−4.1	54.4	14.8	135	114	88	18.4	22 11	22 19	2 51	8 28	8 23
18	13 17	−9.7	54.7	14.9	148	113	81	19.4	23 26	23 40	3 31	8 38	8 28
19	14 01	−15.0	55.2	15.0	160	111	73	20.4	—	—	4 14	8 50	8 34
20	14 49	−19.9	55.8	15.2	172	108	63	21.4	0 44	1 05	5 00	9 06	8 43
21	15 41	−24.0	56.6	15.4	184	103	53	22.4	2 05	2 33	5 51	9 28	8 59
22	16 38	−26.9	57.5	15.7	196	97	43	23.4	3 25	4 02	6 46	10 03	9 26
23	17 38	−28.5	58.4	15.9	208	90	32	24.4	4 37	5 18	7 46	10 55	10 14
24	18 42	−28.3	59.3	16.2	221	82	22	25.4	5 34	6 12	8 49	12 09	11 31
25	19 46	−26.2	60.2	16.4	233	74	13	26.4	6 14	6 44	9 52	13 39	13 10
26	20 49	−22.3	60.9	16.6	245	67	6	27.4	6 41	7 02	10 52	15 16	14 56
27	21 49	−16.9	61.3	16.7	257	57	2	28.4	6 59	7 13	11 48	16 53	16 42
28	22 46	−10.3	61.4	16.7	269	346	0	29.4	7 14	7 21	12 42	18 28	18 23

MERCURY

Day	RA h m	Dec. °	Diam. ″	Phase %	Transit h m	5° high 52° h m	56° h m
1	21 15	−18.1	5	99	12 32	16 17	15 54
3	21 29	−16.9	5	99	12 38	16 32	16 11
5	21 43	−15.7	5	98	12 44	16 46	16 27
7	21 57	−14.3	5	96	12 50	17 01	16 44
9	22 10	−12.9	5	94	12 56	17 16	17 00
11	22 23	−11.4	5	91	13 01	17 30	17 17
13	22 36	−9.8	6	88	13 06	17 44	17 32
15	22 49	−8.2	6	83	13 11	17 58	17 48
17	23 01	−6.6	6	78	13 14	18 10	18 02
19	23 12	−5.0	6	71	13 17	18 21	18 14
21	23 21	−3.5	7	63	13 19	18 31	18 25
23	23 30	−2.1	7	54	13 17	18 38	18 33
25	23 36	−0.8	7	45	13 17	18 42	18 38
27	23 41	+0.2	8	36	13 13	18 43	18 40
29	23 44	+1.0	8	27	13 07	18 40	18 38
31	23 44	+1.5	9	19	12 59	18 34	18 32

VENUS

Day	RA h m	Dec. °	Diam. ″	Phase %	Transit h m	5° high 52° h m	56° h m
1	19 06	−15.4	53	11	10 20	6 21	6 40
6	19 07	−15.6	49	15	10 01	6 03	6 22
11	19 11	−15.8	45	20	9 46	5 49	6 09
16	19 19	−16.1	42	24	9 34	5 39	5 59
21	19 29	−16.2	38	28	9 26	5 31	5 52
26	19 42	−16.3	35	32	9 19	5 25	5 46
31	19 57	−16.2	33	36	9 15	5 20	5 40

MARS

Day	RA h m	Dec. °	Diam. ″	Phase %	Transit h m	5° high 52° h m	56° h m
1	3 17	+20.0	9	89	18 31	1 46	2 00
6	3 26	+20.6	8	89	18 20	1 39	1 54
11	3 36	+21.2	8	89	18 10	1 32	1 48
16	3 46	+21.7	8	89	18 01	1 26	1 42
21	3 56	+22.2	7	89	17 52	1 20	1 37
26	4 07	+22.7	7	89	17 43	1 14	1 31
31	4 18	+23.2	7	89	17 34	1 08	1 26

SUNRISE AND SUNSET

	London				Bristol				Birmingham				Manchester				Newcastle				Glasgow				Belfast			
	0° 05'		51° 30'		2° 35'		51° 28'		1° 55'		52° 28'		2° 15'		53° 28'		1° 37'		54° 59'		4° 14'		55° 52'		5° 56'		54° 35'	
d	h	m	h	m	h	m	h	m	h	m	h	m	h	m	h	m	h	m	h	m	h	m	h	m	h	m	h	m
1	7	39	16	50	7	49	17	00	7	49	16	54	7	54	16	51	7	58	16	43	8	12	16	50	8	13	17	02
2	7	37	16	51	7	47	17	01	7	48	16	56	7	53	16	53	7	56	16	45	8	10	16	52	8	11	17	04
3	7	36	16	53	7	46	17	03	7	46	16	57	7	51	16	55	7	54	16	47	8	08	16	55	8	10	17	06
4	7	34	16	55	7	44	17	05	7	45	16	59	7	49	16	57	7	52	16	50	8	06	16	57	8	08	17	08
5	7	33	16	57	7	42	17	07	7	43	17	01	7	47	16	59	7	50	16	52	8	04	16	59	8	06	17	10
6	7	31	16	59	7	41	17	09	7	41	17	03	7	46	17	01	7	48	16	54	8	02	17	01	8	04	17	12
7	7	29	17	00	7	39	17	11	7	39	17	05	7	44	17	03	7	46	16	56	8	00	17	03	8	02	17	14
8	7	27	17	02	7	37	17	12	7	37	17	07	7	42	17	05	7	44	16	58	7	58	17	05	8	00	17	17
9	7	26	17	04	7	36	17	14	7	36	17	09	7	40	17	07	7	42	17	00	7	55	17	08	7	58	17	19
10	7	24	17	06	7	34	17	16	7	34	17	11	7	38	17	09	7	40	17	02	7	53	17	10	7	56	17	21
11	7	22	17	08	7	32	17	18	7	32	17	13	7	36	17	11	7	38	17	04	7	51	17	12	7	54	17	23
12	7	20	17	10	7	30	17	20	7	30	17	15	7	34	17	13	7	36	17	06	7	49	17	14	7	52	17	25
13	7	18	17	11	7	28	17	22	7	28	17	16	7	32	17	15	7	34	17	08	7	47	17	16	7	50	17	27
14	7	16	17	13	7	26	17	23	7	26	17	18	7	30	17	17	7	32	17	11	7	45	17	19	7	48	17	29
15	7	15	17	15	7	24	17	25	7	24	17	20	7	28	17	19	7	29	17	13	7	42	17	21	7	46	17	31
16	7	13	17	17	7	23	17	27	7	22	17	22	7	26	17	21	7	27	17	15	7	40	17	23	7	43	17	33
17	7	11	17	19	7	21	17	29	7	20	17	24	7	24	17	23	7	25	17	17	7	38	17	25	7	41	17	35
18	7	09	17	21	7	19	17	31	7	18	17	26	7	22	17	25	7	23	17	19	7	35	17	27	7	39	17	37
19	7	07	17	22	7	17	17	32	7	16	17	28	7	20	17	27	7	20	17	21	7	33	17	29	7	37	17	39
20	7	05	17	24	7	15	17	34	7	14	17	30	7	17	17	29	7	18	17	23	7	31	17	32	7	34	17	41
21	7	03	17	26	7	13	17	36	7	12	17	32	7	15	17	31	7	16	17	25	7	28	17	34	7	32	17	43
22	7	01	17	28	7	11	17	38	7	10	17	33	7	13	17	33	7	14	17	27	7	26	17	36	7	30	17	45
23	6	59	17	30	7	09	17	40	7	08	17	35	7	11	17	35	7	11	17	29	7	23	17	38	7	28	17	47
24	6	57	17	31	7	06	17	41	7	05	17	37	7	09	17	37	7	09	17	31	7	21	17	40	7	25	17	50
25	6	54	17	33	7	04	17	43	7	03	17	39	7	06	17	39	7	06	17	34	7	19	17	42	7	23	17	52
26	6	52	17	35	7	02	17	45	7	01	17	41	7	04	17	41	7	04	17	36	7	16	17	45	7	21	17	54
27	6	50	17	37	7	00	17	47	6	59	17	43	7	02	17	43	7	02	17	38	7	14	17	47	7	18	17	56
28	6	48	17	39	6	58	17	49	6	57	17	45	7	00	17	45	6	59	17	40	7	11	17	49	7	16	17	58

JUPITER

Day	RA		Dec.		Transit		5° high			
							52°		56°	
	h	m	°	'	h	m	h	m	h	m
1	15	00.8	−15	53	6	16	2	19	2	39
11	15	04.1	−16	05	5	40	1	44	2	05
21	15	06.2	−16	12	5	02	1	08	1	28
31	15	07.0	−16	14	4	24	0	30	0	50

Diameters – equatorial 38" polar 35"

SATURN

Day	RA		Dec.		Transit		5° high			
							52°		56°	
	h	m	°	'	h	m	h	m	h	m
1	8	40.5	+19	03	23	52	7	03	7	16
11	8	37.2	+19	16	23	09	6	22	6	35
21	8	34.2	+19	28	22	27	5	41	5	54
31	8	31.7	+19	38	21	45	5	00	5	13

Diameters – equatorial 20" polar 18"
Rings – major axis 46" minor axis 15"

URANUS

Day	RA		Dec.		Transit		10° high			
							52°		56°	
	h	m	°	'	h	m	h	m	h	m
1	22	44.0	−8	50	13	58	18	01	17	45
11	22	46.0	−8	38	13	20	17	25	17	09
21	22	48.1	−8	25	12	43	16	49	16	34
31	22	50.3	−8	12	12	06	16	13	15	58

Diameter 4"

NEPTUNE

Day	RA		Dec.		Transit		10° high			
							52°		56°	
	h	m	°	'	h	m	h	m	h	m
1	21	18.4	−15	52	12	32	9	17	9	45
11	21	19.9	−15	45	11	54	8	38	9	06
21	21	21.3	−15	39	11	16	8	00	8	27
31	21	22.8	−15	32	10	39	7	21	7	48

Diameter 2"

MARCH 2006

THIRD MONTH, 31 DAYS. *Mars*, Roman god of battle

1	*Wednesday*	Archer Martin b. 1910. Jacobus Henricus van 't Hoff d. 1911	60
2	*Thursday*	The British Commonwealth Trans-Antarctic Expedition completes the first surface crossing of the South Pole 1958	61
3	*Friday*	Alexander Graham Bell b. 1847. Gerhard Herzberg d. 1999	62
4	*Saturday*	Hans Eysenck b. 1916. Charles Sherrington d. 1952	63
5	*Sunday*	James Tobin b. 1918. Pierre-Simon Laplace d. 1827	64

6	*Monday*	Dmitry Mendeleyev unveils his periodic table 1869	week 10 day 65
7	*Tuesday*	John Herschel b. 1792. E. M. Purcell d. 1997	66
8	*Wednesday*	Otto Hahn b. 1879. John Ericsson d. 1889	67
9	*Thursday*	Yury Gagarin b. 1934. Max Delbrück d. 1981	68
10	*Friday*	Val Logsdon Fitch b. 1923. William Henry Bragg d. 1942	69
11	*Saturday*	Nicolaas Bloembergen b. 1920. Alexander Fleming d. 1955	70
12	*Sunday*	Gustav Kirchhoff b. 1824. Ragnar Granit d. 1991	71

13	*Monday*	The German astronomer William Herschel discovers the planet Uranus 1781	week 11 day 72
14	*Tuesday*	Albert Einstein b. 1879. George Eastman d. 1932	73
15	*Wednesday*	John Snow b. 1813. Joseph Bazalgette d. 1891	74
16	*Thursday*	Georg Ohm b. 1789. John Macleod d. 1935	75
17	*Friday*	Walter Hess b. 1881. Irène Joliot-Curie d. 1956	76
18	*Saturday*	Cosmonaut Aleksey Leonov becomes the first person to walk in space 1965	77
19	*Sunday*	Frédéric Joliot-Curie b. 1900. Louis de Broglie d. 1987	78

20	*Monday*	Erwin Neher b. 1944. Isaac Newton d. 1727	week 12 day 79
21	*Tuesday*	Jean Fourier b. 1768. Giovanni Arduino d. 1795	80
22	*Wednesday*	Robert Millikan b. 1868. Hilda Geiringer von Mises d. 1973	81
23	*Thursday*	Erich Fromm b. 1900. Friedrich von Hayek d. 1992	82
24	*Friday*	Walter Baade b. 1893. Auguste Piccard d. 1962	83
25	*Saturday*	Christiaan Huygens discovers Saturn's largest moon, which was named Titan in 1847, 1655	84
26	*Sunday*	*British Summer Time commences.* Christian Anfinsen b. 1916..	85

27	*Monday*	Otto Wallach b. 1847. Wilhelm Beer d. 1850	week 13 day 86
28	*Tuesday*	Corneille Heymans b. 1892. William Giauque d. 1982	87
29	*Wednesday*	John Vane b. 1927. Emanuel Swedenborg d. 1772	88
30	*Thursday*	Anaesthesia is used for the first time during an operation, in Georgia, USA 1842	89
31	*Friday*	René Descartes b. 1596. Emil von Behring d. 1917	90

ASTRONOMICAL PHENOMENA

d	h	
1	04	Mercury in conjunction with Moon. Mercury 3°N.
1	11	Uranus in conjunction
2	20	Mercury at stationary point
4	18	Jupiter at stationary point
6	06	Mars in conjunction with Moon. Mars 3°S.
10	20	Saturn in conjunction with Moon. Saturn 4°S.
12	03	Mercury in inferior conjunction
19	11	Jupiter in conjunction with Moon. Jupiter 5°N.
20	18	Sun's longitude 0° ♈
25	07	Venus at greatest elongation W.47°
25	14	Mercury at stationary point
26	02	Venus in conjunction with Moon. Venus 5°N.
27	18	Mercury in conjunction with Moon. Mercury 2°N.
29	10	Total eclipse of Sun (*see* page 1278)
29	13	Pluto at stationary point

MINIMA OF ALGOL

d	h	d	h	d	h
1	16.4	13	03.7	24	15.0
4	13.2	16	00.5	27	11.8
7	10.0	18	21.3	30	08.6
10	06.9	21	18.1		

CONSTELLATIONS

The following constellations are near the meridian at

	d	h		d	h
February	1	24	March	16	21
February	15	23	April	1	20
March	1	22	April	15	19

Cepheus (below the Pole), Camelopardus, Lybx, Gemini, Cancer, Leo, Canis Minor, Hydra, Monoceros, Canis Major and Puppis

THE MOON

Phases, Apsides and Node		d	h	m
☽	First Quarter	6	20	16
○	Full Moon	14	23	35
☾	Last Quarter	22	19	10
●	New Moon	29	10	15

	d	h	m
Apogee (406,292 km)	13	01	31
Perigee (359,160 km)	28	07	06

Mean longitude of ascending node on March 1, 6°

THE SUN

s.d. 16'.1

Day	Right Ascension			Dec.		Equation of time		Rise 52°		Rise 56°		Transit		Set 52°		Set 56°		Sidereal time			Transit of first point of Aries		
	h	m	s	°	'	m	s	h	m	h	m	h	m	h	m	h	m	h	m	s	h	m	s
1	22	47	06	−7	43	−12	28	6	46	6	52	12	12	17	39	17	34	10	34	38	13	23	10
2	22	50	51	−7	21	−12	16	6	44	6	49	12	12	17	41	17	36	10	38	35	13	19	14
3	22	54	35	−6	58	−12	04	6	42	6	47	12	12	17	43	17	38	10	42	31	13	15	18
4	22	58	19	−6	35	−11	51	6	40	6	44	12	12	17	45	17	40	10	46	28	13	11	22
5	23	02	03	−6	11	−11	38	6	37	6	42	12	12	17	47	17	42	10	50	24	13	07	26
6	23	05	46	−5	48	−11	25	6	35	6	39	12	11	17	48	17	44	10	54	21	13	03	30
7	23	09	28	−5	25	−11	11	6	33	6	37	12	11	17	50	17	46	10	58	18	12	59	34
8	23	13	11	−5	02	−10	56	6	31	6	34	12	11	17	52	17	49	11	02	14	12	55	38
9	23	16	52	−4	38	−10	42	6	28	6	32	12	11	17	54	17	51	11	06	11	12	51	43
10	23	20	34	−4	15	−10	27	6	26	6	29	12	10	17	55	17	53	11	10	07	12	47	47
11	23	24	15	−3	51	−10	11	6	24	6	26	12	10	17	57	17	55	11	14	04	12	43	51
12	23	27	56	−3	28	−9	55	6	22	6	24	12	10	17	59	17	57	11	18	00	12	39	55
13	23	31	36	−3	04	−9	39	6	19	6	21	12	10	18	01	17	59	11	21	57	12	35	59
14	23	35	16	−2	40	−9	23	6	17	6	19	12	09	18	02	18	01	11	25	53	12	32	03
15	23	38	56	−2	17	−9	06	6	15	6	16	12	09	18	04	18	03	11	29	50	12	28	07
16	23	42	36	−1	53	−8	49	6	12	6	13	12	09	18	06	18	05	11	33	47	12	24	11
17	23	46	15	−1	29	−8	32	6	10	6	11	12	08	18	08	18	07	11	37	43	12	20	15
18	23	49	54	−1	06	−8	14	6	08	6	08	12	08	18	09	18	09	11	41	40	12	16	19
19	23	53	33	−0	42	−7	57	6	06	6	05	12	08	18	11	18	11	11	45	36	12	12	23
20	23	57	12	−0	18	−7	39	6	03	6	03	12	08	18	13	18	13	11	49	33	12	08	28
21	0	00	51	+0	05	−7	21	6	01	6	00	12	07	18	15	18	15	11	53	29	12	04	32
22	0	04	29	+0	29	−7	04	5	59	5	58	12	07	18	16	18	17	11	57	26	12	00	36
23	0	08	08	+0	53	−6	46	5	56	5	55	12	07	18	18	18	20	12	01	22	11	56	40
24	0	11	47	+1	17	−6	28	5	54	5	52	12	06	18	20	18	22	12	05	19	11	52	44
25	0	15	25	+1	40	−6	10	5	52	5	50	12	06	18	21	18	24	12	09	16	11	48	48
26	0	19	04	+2	04	−5	51	5	49	5	47	12	06	18	23	18	26	12	13	12	11	44	52
27	0	22	42	+2	27	−5	33	5	47	5	44	12	05	18	25	18	28	12	17	09	11	40	56
28	0	26	20	+2	51	−5	15	5	45	5	42	12	05	18	27	18	30	12	21	05	11	37	00
29	0	29	59	+3	14	−4	57	5	42	5	39	12	05	18	28	18	32	12	25	02	11	33	04
30	0	33	38	+3	38	−4	39	5	40	5	36	12	05	18	30	18	34	12	28	58	11	29	08
31	0	37	16	+4	01	−4	21	5	38	5	34	12	04	18	32	18	36	12	32	55	11	25	13

DURATION OF TWILIGHT (in minutes)

Latitude	52°	56°	52°	56°	52°	56°	52°	56°
	1 March		11 March		21 March		31 March	
Civil	34	37	34	37	34	37	34	38
Nautical	73	80	73	80	74	81	75	84
Astronomical	112	124	113	125	115	128	120	135

THE NIGHT SKY

Mercury, magnitude +1, may only be detected very low above the western horizon for a very short while around the end of evening civil twilight for the first two days of the month. On the 12th it passes through inferior conjunction.

Venus, magnitude −4.5, continues to be visible as a brilliant object in the morning skies, low above the east-south-eastern horizon, but only for about an hour before sunrise. On the 25th Venus reaches its greatest western elongation (47 degrees).

Mars remains visible in the south-western sky, in the evenings, and still visible up to midnight even by the end of the month. Its magnitude fades during March from +0.8 to +1.2. On the evening of the 5th the Moon, near First Quarter, passes 2 degrees north of the planet. Mars is in Taurus, passing 7 degrees north of Aldebaran on the 10th.

Jupiter is still visible as a brilliant morning object, magnitude −2.3. By the middle of the month it has started to become visible low above the east-south-eastern horizon before midnight. On the 4th Jupiter reaches its first stationary point and commences its retrograde motion. The waning gibbous Moon passes south of Jupiter on the night of the 18th/19th.

Saturn, magnitude +0.1, continues to be visible as an evening object in the south western sky in the evenings. The planet is in the vicinity of the waxing gibbous Moon on the 10th. Saturn is in Cancer. The rings of Saturn present a beautiful spectacle to the observer armed with a small telescope. The diameter of the minor axis is now 15 arcseconds, rather less than the polar diameter of the planet itself. The rings were last at their maximum opening in 2002 and will next appear edge-on in 2009.

Zodiacal Light. The evening cone may be observed stretching up from the western horizon, along the ecliptic, after the end of twilight, from the 17th to the 30th. This faint phenomenon is only visible under good conditions and in the absence of both moonlight and artificial lighting.

THE MOON

Day	RA h	RA m	Dec. °	Hor. par. ′	Semi-diam. ′	Sun's Co-long. °	PA of Br. Limb °	Ph. %	Age d	Rise 52° h	Rise 52° m	Rise 56° h	Rise 56° m	Transit h	Transit m	Set 52° h	Set 52° m	Set 56° h	Set 56° m
1	23	40	− 3.2	61.2	16.7	282	250	1	1.0	7	27	7	27	13	33	20	00	20	02
2	0	33	+ 4.0	60.7	16.5	294	246	6	2.0	7	39	7	34	14	23	21	30	21	39
3	1	25	+10.9	59.9	16.3	306	246	13	3.0	7	52	7	40	15	14	22	59	23	16
4	2	19	+16.9	59.0	16.1	318	249	21	4.0	8	07	7	49	16	06	—	—	—	—
5	3	13	+22.0	58.0	15.8	330	253	31	5.0	8	27	8	02	17	00	0	28	0	52
6	4	09	+25.7	57.1	15.6	343	258	41	6.0	8	56	8	23	17	54	1	52	2	24
7	5	06	+27.9	56.2	15.3	355	265	52	7.0	9	35	8	56	18	50	3	06	3	45
8	6	03	+28.7	55.5	15.1	7	272	62	8.0	10	28	9	48	19	44	4	07	4	47
9	6	59	+28.0	54.9	15.0	19	278	71	9.0	11	34	10	58	20	35	4	51	5	27
10	7	52	+25.9	54.5	14.8	31	284	79	10.0	12	46	12	18	21	24	5	21	5	51
11	8	43	+22.8	54.2	14.8	43	290	86	11.0	14	01	13	40	22	09	5	43	6	05
12	9	31	+28.7	54.0	14.7	56	294	92	12.0	15	15	15	00	22	52	5	58	6	14
13	10	16	+13.9	54.0	14.7	68	298	96	13.0	16	27	16	18	23	32	6	10	6	21
14	10	59	+ 8.6	54.0	14.7	80	303	99	14.0	17	38	17	34	—		6	20	6	26
15	11	41	+ 3.0	54.1	14.8	92	35	100	15.0	18	49	18	50	0	12	6	28	6	30
16	12	23	− 2.7	54.3	14.8	104	114	99	16.0	20	01	20	07	0	51	6	37	6	34
17	13	06	− 8.4	54.6	14.9	116	116	96	17.0	21	15	21	27	1	31	6	47	6	38
18	13	50	−13.8	55.0	15.0	128	114	92	18.0	22	31	22	50	2	12	6	58	6	44
19	14	37	−18.8	55.4	15.1	141	111	86	19.0	23	51	—	—	2	57	7	12	6	52
20	15	28	−23.1	56.0	15.3	153	107	78	20.0	—	—	0	17	3	46	7	32	7	05
21	16	22	−26.4	56.6	15.4	165	101	69	21.0	1	11	1	45	4	39	8	01	7	26
22	17	21	−28.3	57.3	15.6	177	95	59	22.0	2	25	3	06	5	36	8	45	8	05
23	18	22	−28.6	58.1	15.8	189	88	48	23.0	3	27	4	07	6	36	9	48	9	08
24	19	24	−27.2	58.9	16.0	202	80	37	24.0	4	11	4	45	7	37	11	09	10	36
25	20	25	−24.1	59.7	16.3	214	74	26	25.0	4	42	5	07	8	36	12	41	12	17
26	21	24	−19.3	60.3	16.4	226	68	17	26.0	5	03	5	20	9	32	14	16	14	00
27	22	21	−13.3	60.8	16.6	238	65	9	27.0	5	19	5	29	10	26	15	50	15	41
28	23	15	− 6.5	61.0	16.6	250	63	3	28.0	5	32	5	36	11	17	17	22	17	21
29	0	08	+ 0.7	61.0	16.6	263	65	0	29.0	5	44	5	42	12	08	18	53	18	59
30	1	01	+ 7.8	58.2	16.5	275	239	0	0.6	5	56	5	48	12	59	20	25	20	37
31	1	55	+14.4	60.0	16.3	287	243	4	1.6	6	10	5	56	13	52	21	57	22	17

MERCURY

Day	RA h	RA m	Dec. °	Diam. ″	Phase %	Transit h	Transit m	5° high 52° h	5° high 52° m	5° high 56° h	5° high 56° m
1	23	44	+1.0	8	27	13	07	18	40	18	38
3	23	44	+1.5	9	19	12	59	18	34	18	32
5	23	42	+1.7	9	12	12	49	18	23	18	21
7	23	38	+1.5	10	7	12	37	18	10	18	07
9	23	33	+1.0	10	3	12	23	17	53	17	51
11	23	27	+0.3	11	1	12	09	17	35	17	31
13	23	20	−0.6	11	1	11	54	6	32	6	36
15	23	13	−1.6	11	2	11	40	6	23	6	28
17	23	07	−2.6	11	5	11	26	6	15	6	20
19	23	02	−3.6	11	8	11	14	6	07	6	14
21	22	59	−4.5	11	12	11	03	6	01	6	08
23	22	57	−5.2	10	17	10	54	5	55	6	03
25	22	57	−5.8	10	21	10	46	5	50	5	59
27	22	58	−6.2	10	25	10	39	5	46	5	54
29	23	00	−6.5	9	29	10	34	5	42	5	51
31	23	04	−6.6	9	34	10	30	5	38	5	47

VENUS

Day	RA h	RA m	Dec. °	Diam. ″	Phase %	Transit h	Transit m	5° high 52° h	5° high 52° m	5° high 56° h	5° high 56° m
1	19	51	−16.3	34	35	9	16	5	22	5	42
6	20	07	−16.1	31	38	9	13	5	17	5	38
11	20	25	−15.8	29	41	9	10	5	13	5	32
16	20	43	−15.3	28	44	9	09	5	08	5	27
21	21	02	−14.5	26	47	9	09	5	03	5	21
26	21	22	−13.6	24	50	9	09	4	57	5	14
31	21	43	−12.5	23	52	9	10	4	51	5	06

MARS

Day	RA h	RA m	Dec. °	Diam. ″	Phase %	Transit h	Transit m	5° high 52° h	5° high 52° m	5° high 56° h	5° high 56° m
1	4	13	+23.0	7	89	17	38	1	11	1	28
6	4	25	+23.4	7	90	17	29	1	05	1	23
11	4	36	+23.8	7	90	17	21	0	59	1	18
16	4	48	+24.2	6	90	17	13	0	54	1	13
21	5	00	+24.5	6	90	17	06	0	48	1	07
26	5	12	+24.7	6	90	16	58	0	42	1	02
31	5	25	+24.9	6	91	16	51	0	36	0	56

SUNRISE AND SUNSET

	London 0° 05′ 51° 30′				Bristol 2° 35′ 51° 28′				Birmingham 1° 55′ 52° 28′				Manchester 2° 15′ 53° 28′				Newcastle 1° 37′ 54° 59′				Glasgow 4° 14′ 55° 52′				Belfast 5° 56′ 54° 35′			
	h	m	h	m	h	m	h	m	h	m	h	m	h	m	h	m	h	m	h	m	h	m	h	m	h	m	h	m
1	6	46	17	40	6	56	17	50	6	55	17	46	6	57	17	46	6	57	17	42	7	09	17	51	7	14	18	00
2	6	44	17	42	6	54	17	52	6	52	17	48	6	55	17	48	6	54	17	44	7	06	17	53	7	11	18	02
3	6	42	17	44	6	52	17	54	6	50	17	50	6	53	17	50	6	52	17	46	7	04	17	55	7	09	18	04
4	6	39	17	46	6	49	17	56	6	48	17	52	6	50	17	52	6	50	17	48	7	01	17	57	7	06	18	06
5	6	37	17	47	6	47	17	57	6	46	17	54	6	48	17	54	6	47	17	50	6	59	17	59	7	04	18	08
6	6	35	17	49	6	45	17	59	6	43	17	56	6	46	17	56	6	45	17	52	6	56	18	01	7	01	18	10
7	6	33	17	51	6	43	18	01	6	41	17	57	6	43	17	58	6	42	17	54	6	54	18	04	6	59	18	12
8	6	31	17	53	6	41	18	03	6	39	17	59	6	41	18	00	6	40	17	56	6	51	18	06	6	57	18	14
9	6	28	17	54	6	38	18	04	6	36	18	01	6	39	18	02	6	37	17	58	6	48	18	08	6	54	18	16
10	6	26	17	56	6	36	18	06	6	34	18	03	6	36	18	03	6	35	18	00	6	46	18	10	6	52	18	17
11	6	24	17	58	6	34	18	08	6	32	18	05	6	34	18	05	6	32	18	02	6	43	18	12	6	49	18	19
12	6	22	17	59	6	32	18	09	6	30	18	06	6	31	18	07	6	30	18	04	6	41	18	14	6	47	18	21
13	6	19	18	01	6	29	18	11	6	27	18	08	6	29	18	09	6	27	18	06	6	38	18	16	6	44	18	23
14	6	17	18	03	6	27	18	13	6	25	18	10	6	27	18	11	6	25	18	08	6	35	18	18	6	42	18	25
15	6	15	18	05	6	25	18	15	6	23	18	12	6	24	18	13	6	22	18	10	6	33	18	20	6	39	18	27
16	6	13	18	06	6	23	18	16	6	20	18	13	6	22	18	15	6	20	18	12	6	30	18	22	6	37	18	29
17	6	10	18	08	6	20	18	18	6	18	18	15	6	19	18	16	6	17	18	14	6	28	18	24	6	34	18	31
18	6	08	18	10	6	18	18	20	6	16	18	17	6	17	18	18	6	14	18	16	6	25	18	26	6	32	18	33
19	6	06	18	11	6	16	18	21	6	13	18	19	6	14	18	20	6	12	18	18	6	22	18	28	6	29	18	35
20	6	04	18	13	6	14	18	23	6	11	18	21	6	12	18	22	6	09	18	20	6	20	18	30	6	27	18	37
21	6	01	18	15	6	11	18	25	6	08	18	22	6	10	18	24	6	07	18	22	6	17	18	32	6	24	18	39
22	5	59	18	16	6	09	18	26	6	06	18	24	6	07	18	26	6	04	18	24	6	15	18	34	6	22	18	41
23	5	57	18	18	6	07	18	28	6	04	18	26	6	05	18	28	6	02	18	26	6	12	18	36	6	19	18	43
24	5	54	18	20	6	04	18	30	6	01	18	28	6	02	18	29	5	59	18	28	6	09	18	38	6	17	18	45
25	5	52	18	22	6	02	18	32	5	59	18	29	6	00	18	31	5	57	18	29	6	07	18	40	6	14	18	47
26	5	50	18	23	6	00	18	33	5	57	18	31	5	57	18	33	5	54	18	31	6	04	18	43	6	12	18	48
27	5	48	18	25	5	58	18	35	5	54	18	33	5	55	18	35	5	52	18	33	6	01	18	45	6	09	18	50
28	5	45	18	27	5	55	18	37	5	52	18	35	5	53	18	37	5	49	18	35	5	59	18	47	6	07	18	52
29	5	43	18	28	5	53	18	38	5	50	18	36	5	50	18	39	5	46	18	37	5	56	18	49	6	04	18	54
30	5	41	18	30	5	51	18	40	5	47	18	38	5	48	18	40	5	44	18	39	5	54	18	51	6	02	18	56
31	5	38	18	32	5	49	18	42	5	45	18	40	5	45	18	42	5	41	18	41	5	51	18	53	5	59	18	58

JUPITER

Day	RA		Dec.		Transit		5° high			
								52°		56°
	h	m	°	′	h	m	h	m	h	m
1	15	07.0	−16	14	4	32	0	38	0	58
11	15	06.8	−16	11	3	52	23	54	0	18
21	15	05.5	−16	04	3	11	23	12	23	32
31	15	02.9	−15	52	2	30	22	29	22	49

Diameters – equatorial 41″ polar 39″

SATURN

Day	RA		Dec.		Transit		5° high			
								52°		56°
	h	m	°	′	h	m	h	m	h	m
1	8	32.1	+19	36	21	54	5	08	5	22
11	8	30.0	+19	44	21	12	4	27	4	41
21	8	28.5	+19	50	20	32	3	47	4	01
31	8	27.7	+19	53	19	32	3	07	3	21

Diameters – equatorial 20″ polar 18″
Rings – major axis 44″ minor axis 15″

URANUS

Day	RA		Dec.		Transit		10° high			
								52°		56°
	h	m	°	′	h	m	h	m	h	m
1	22	49.9	−8	14	12	13	8	06	8	21
11	22	52.0	−8	01	11	36	7	28	7	43
21	22	54.1	−7	48	10	59	6	49	7	04
31	22	56.1	−7	36	10	22	6	11	6	25

Diameter 4″

NEPTUNE

Day	RA		Dec.		Transit		10° high			
								52°		56°
	h	m	°	′	h	m	h	m	h	m
1	21	22.5	−15	33	10	46	7	29	7	56
11	21	23.9	−15	27	10	08	6	50	7	17
21	21	25.1	−15	21	9	30	6	11	6	38
31	21	26.3	−15	16	8	52	5	32	5	59

Diameter 2″

APRIL 2006

FOURTH MONTH, 30 DAYS. *Aperire*, to open; Earth opens to receive seed.

1	*Saturday*	William Harvey b. 1578. Charles Drew d. 1950	91
2	*Sunday*	George Spencer-Brown b. 1923. Samuel Morse d. 1872	92
3	*Monday*	The world's first mobile telephone call is placed in New York 1973	week 14 day 93
4	*Tuesday*	Denton Cooley, a surgeon in Texas, implants the first artificial heart 1969	94
5	*Wednesday*	Joseph Lister b. 1827. Hermann Muller d. 1967	95
6	*Thursday*	James Watson b. 1928. Jules Bordet d. 1961	96
7	*Friday*	The unmanned Mars Odyssey spacecraft is launched from Cape Canaveral, Florida 1942	97
8	*Saturday*	Melvin Calvin b. 1911. Daniel Bovet d. 1992	98
9	*Sunday*	Isambard Kingdom Brunel b. 1806. Michel Chevreul d. 1889	99
10	*Monday*	Samuel Hahnemann b. 1755. Joseph Lagrange d. 1813	week 15 day 100
11	*Tuesday*	Andrew Wiles b. 1953. Luther Burbank d. 1926	101
12	*Wednesday*	Otto Meyerhof b. 1884. George Wald d. 1997	102
13	*Thursday*	Robert Watson-Watt b. 1892. Henry de la Beche d. 1855	103
14	*Friday*	Christiaan Huygens b. 1629. Emmy Noether d. 1935	104
15	*Saturday*	Johannes Stark b. 1874. Arthur Aikin d. 1854	105
16	*Sunday*	Wilbur Wright b. 1867. George Hill d. 1914	106
17	*Monday*	Giovanni Riccioli b. 1598. Samuel Morey d. 1843	week 16 day 107
18	*Tuesday*	Joseph Goldstein b. 1940. Justus von Liebig d. 1873	108
19	*Wednesday*	Richard von Mises b. 1883. Pierre Curie d. 1906	109
20	*Thursday*	Karl Müller b. 1927. Karl Braun d. 1918	110
21	*Friday*	Michel Rolle b. 1652. John Maynard Keynes d. 1946	111
22	*Saturday*	Robert Barany b. 1876. Emilio Segrè d. 1989	112
23	*Sunday*	Max Planck b. 1858. William Shakespeare d. 1616	113
24	*Monday*	The Hubble space telescope is launched by the space shuttle Discovery 1990	week 17 day 114
25	*Tuesday*	Wolfgang Pauli b. 1900. Anders Celsius d. 1744	115
26	*Wednesday*	Charles Richter b. 1900. Carl Bosch d. 1940	116
27	*Thursday*	Philip Abelson b. 1913. Karl Pearson d. 1936	117
28	*Friday*	Eugene Shoemaker b. 1928. Arthur Schawlow d. 1999	118
29	*Saturday*	Harold C. Urey b. 1893. William Eccles d. 1966	119
30	*Sunday*	Claude Shannon b. 1916. Robert FitzRoy d. 1865	120

ASTRONOMICAL PHENOMENA

d h
3 19 Mars in conjunction with Moon. Mars 4°S.
5 13 Saturn at stationary point
7 01 Saturn in conjunction with Moon. Saturn 4°S.
8 19 Mercury at greatest elongation W.28°.
15 13 Jupiter in conjunction with Moon. Jupiter 5°N.
20 05 Sun's longitude 30° ♉
24 14 Venus in conjunction with Moon. Venus 0°.4 N.
26 05 Mercury in conjunction with Moon. Mercury 4°S.

MINIMA OF ALGOL

d	h	d	h	d	h
2	05.4	13	16.7	25	04.0
5	02.2	16	13.5	28	00.8
7	23.1	19	10.3	30	21.6
10	19.9	22	07.2		

CONSTELLATIONS

The following constellations are near the meridian at

	d	h		d	h
March	1	24	April	15	21
March	16	23	May	1	20
April	1	22	May	16	19

Cepheus (below the Pole), Cassiopeia (below the Pole), Ursa Major, Leo Minor, Leo, Sextans, Hydra and Crater

THE MOON

Phases, Apsides and Node	d	h	m
☽ First Quarter	5	12	01
○ Full Moon	13	16	40
☾ Last Quarter	21	03	28
● New Moon	27	19	44
Apogee (405,579 km)	9	13	10
Perigee (363,714 km)	25	10	25

Mean longitude of ascending node on April 1, 4°

THE SUN

s.d. 16'.0

Day	Right Ascension			Dec. +		Equation of time		Rise 52°		Rise 56°		Transit		Set 52°		Set 56°		Sidereal time			Transit of First point of Aries		
	h	m	s	°	'	m	s	h	m	h	m	h	m	h	m	h	m	h	m	s	h	m	s
1	0	40	55	4	24	−4	03	5	35	5	31	12	04	18	33	18	38	12	36	51	11	21	17
2	0	44	34	4	47	−3	46	5	33	5	29	12	04	18	35	18	40	12	40	48	11	17	21
3	0	48	12	5	10	−3	28	5	31	5	26	12	03	18	37	18	42	12	44	45	11	13	25
4	0	51	51	5	33	−3	10	5	29	5	23	12	03	18	39	18	44	12	48	41	11	09	29
5	0	55	31	5	56	−2	53	5	26	5	21	12	03	18	40	18	46	12	52	38	11	05	33
6	0	59	10	6	19	−2	36	5	24	5	18	12	02	18	42	18	48	12	56	34	11	01	37
7	1	02	49	6	42	−2	19	5	22	5	16	12	02	18	44	18	50	13	00	31	10	57	41
8	1	06	29	7	04	−2	02	5	19	5	13	12	02	18	45	18	52	13	04	27	10	53	45
9	1	10	09	7	27	−1	45	5	17	5	10	12	02	18	47	18	54	13	08	24	10	49	49
10	1	13	49	7	49	−1	29	5	15	5	08	12	01	18	49	18	56	13	12	20	10	45	53
11	1	17	30	8	11	−1	13	5	13	5	05	12	01	18	51	18	58	13	16	17	10	41	58
12	1	21	10	8	33	−0	57	5	10	5	03	12	01	18	52	19	00	13	20	14	10	38	02
13	1	24	51	8	55	−0	41	5	08	5	00	12	01	18	54	19	02	13	24	10	10	34	06
14	1	28	32	9	17	−0	26	5	06	4	58	12	00	18	56	19	04	13	28	07	10	30	10
15	1	32	14	9	38	−0	11	5	04	4	55	12	00	18	57	19	06	13	32	03	10	26	14
16	1	35	56	10	00	+0	04	5	02	4	53	12	00	18	59	19	08	13	36	00	10	22	18
17	1	39	38	10	21	+0	18	4	59	4	50	12	00	19	01	19	10	13	39	56	10	18	22
18	1	43	21	10	42	+0	32	4	57	4	48	11	59	19	03	19	13	13	43	53	10	14	26
19	1	47	04	11	03	+0	45	4	55	4	45	11	59	19	04	19	15	13	47	49	10	10	30
20	1	50	48	11	24	+0	58	4	53	4	43	11	59	19	06	19	17	13	51	46	10	06	34
21	1	54	32	11	44	+1	11	4	51	4	40	11	59	19	08	19	19	13	55	43	10	02	38
22	1	58	16	12	05	+1	23	4	49	4	38	11	59	19	09	19	21	13	59	39	9	58	43
23	2	02	01	12	25	+1	35	4	47	4	35	11	58	19	11	19	23	14	03	36	9	54	47
24	2	05	46	12	45	+1	46	4	45	4	33	11	58	19	13	19	25	14	07	32	9	50	51
25	2	09	32	13	04	+1	56	4	43	4	31	11	58	19	14	19	27	14	11	29	9	46	55
26	2	13	19	13	24	+2	07	4	41	4	28	11	58	19	16	19	29	14	15	25	9	42	59
27	2	17	06	13	43	+2	16	4	39	4	26	11	58	19	18	19	31	14	19	22	9	39	03
28	2	20	53	14	02	+2	26	4	37	4	23	11	58	19	20	19	33	14	23	18	9	35	07
29	2	24	41	14	21	+2	34	4	35	4	21	11	57	19	21	19	35	14	27	15	9	31	11
30	2	28	29	14	40	+2	42	4	33	4	19	11	57	19	23	19	37	14	31	12	9	27	15

DURATION OF TWILIGHT (in minutes)

Latitude	52°	56°	52°	56°	52°	56°	52°	56°
	1 April		11 April		21 April		31 April	
Civil	34	38	35	39	37	42	39	44
Nautical	76	84	79	89	83	96	89	106
Astronomical	120	136	127	147	137	165	152	204

THE NIGHT SKY

Mercury, although it reaches greatest western elongation (28 degrees) on the 8th, only one day before aphelion, is unsuitably placed for observation.

Venus is still visible as a brilliant object in the morning sky before dawn, magnitude −4.2. However, it will only be visible, low above the east-south-eastern horizon for a short while before sunrise. The waning crescent Moon is very near to the planet on the morning of the 24th.

Mars continues to be visible in the western sky in the evenings, and even by the end of the month should still be observable for a short while after midnight. The waxing crescent Moon is near the planet on the evenings of the 2nd and 3rd. Mars moves from Taurus into Gemini during April, while its magnitude fades from +1.2 to +1.5.

Jupiter will be coming to opposition early in May and thus it is now visible for the greater part of the hours of darkness. Its magnitude is −2.5. Jupiter is moving slowly retrograde in the constellation of Libra, and passes north of Alpha Librae again at the end of the month. On the night of the 14th/15th the Moon, just after Full, passes about 6 degrees south of the planet.

Saturn, magnitude +0.3, is still visible as an evening object in the constellation of Cancer, though only visible in the early part of the evening. On the 5th of April it reaches its first stationary point and then it begins its retrograde motion. The Moon, near First Quarter, is in the vicinity of the planet on the evenings of the 5th and 6th.

THE MOON

Day	RA h	RA m	Dec. °	Hor. Par. ′	Semi-diam. ′	Sun's Co-Long. °	PA of Br. Limb °	Ph. %	Age d	Rise 52° h	Rise 52° m	Rise 56° h	Rise 56° m	Transit h	Transit m	Set 52° h	Set 52° m	Set 56° h	Set 56° m
1	2	50	+20.1	59.2	16.1	299	248	9	2.6	6	29	6	07	14	46	23	26	23	55
2	3	48	+24.4	58.2	15.9	311	253	17	3.6	6	54	6	24	15	42	—	—	—	—
3	4	46	+27.3	57.3	15.6	324	260	26	4.6	7	29	6	52	16	39	0	48	1	25
4	5	45	+28.6	56.4	15.4	336	267	35	5.6	8	18	7	38	17	36	1	57	2	37
5	6	42	+28.4	55.6	15.2	348	274	45	6.6	9	21	8	43	18	29	2	48	3	26
6	7	37	+26.7	55.0	15.0	0	280	55	7.6	10	32	10	01	19	20	3	24	3	56
7	8	29	+23.8	54.5	14.9	12	285	64	8.6	11	47	11	23	20	06	3	48	4	13
8	9	18	+19.9	54.2	14.8	25	290	73	9.6	13	02	12	45	20	50	4	06	4	24
9	10	04	+15.3	54.1	14.7	37	293	81	10.6	14	15	14	04	21	31	4	18	4	31
10	10	47	+10.1	54.1	14.7	49	295	88	11.6	15	26	15	20	22	10	4	29	4	36
11	11	30	+4.6	54.2	14.8	61	295	93	12.6	16	37	16	36	22	49	4	38	4	41
12	12	12	−1.1	54.4	14.8	73	294	97	13.6	17	48	17	53	23	29	4	47	4	45
13	12	54	−6.9	54.7	14.9	85	286	100	14.6	19	02	19	12	—	—	4	56	4	49
14	13	39	−12.5	55.1	15.0	98	142	100	15.6	20	19	20	35	0	11	5	06	4	54
15	14	25	−17.6	55.5	15.1	110	120	98	16.6	21	38	22	02	0	55	5	20	5	02
16	15	16	−22.1	56.0	15.2	122	113	95	17.6	22	59	23	31	1	43	5	38	5	13
17	16	09	−25.7	56.5	15.4	134	106	89	18.6	—	—	—	—	2	35	6	04	5	31
18	17	07	−27.9	57.0	15.5	146	99	82	19.6	0	16	0	55	3	31	6	43	6	04
19	18	07	−28.7	57.5	15.7	159	92	73	20.6	1	21	2	02	4	30	7	40	6	59
20	19	08	−27.7	58.1	15.8	171	85	63	21.6	2	10	2	46	5	29	8	54	8	19
21	20	08	−25.0	58.7	16.0	183	78	52	22.6	2	44	3	12	6	27	10	20	9	53
22	21	06	−20.9	59.2	16.1	195	72	40	23.6	3	07	3	27	7	23	11	51	11	33
23	22	02	−15.4	59.7	16.3	207	68	29	24.6	3	24	3	37	8	16	13	22	13	11
24	22	55	−9.1	60.1	16.4	220	66	19	25.6	3	38	3	45	9	06	14	52	14	47
25	23	47	−2.2	60.3	16.4	232	66	11	26.6	3	50	3	51	9	56	16	21	16	23
26	0	39	+4.9	60.2	16.4	244	68	5	27.6	4	02	3	57	10	45	17	50	17	59
27	1	32	+11.6	60.0	16.3	256	78	1	28.6	4	15	4	04	11	36	19	21	19	38
28	2	26	+17.7	59.5	16.2	268	199	0	0.2	4	31	4	13	12	30	20	53	21	17
29	3	23	+22.7	58.9	16.0	281	241	2	1.2	4	53	4	27	13	26	22	21	22	53
30	4	22	+26.3	58.1	15.8	293	252	6	2.2	5	23	4	50	14	24	23	38	—	—

MERCURY

Day	RA h	RA m	Dec. °	Diam. ″	Phase %	Transit h	Transit m	5° high 52° h	5° high 52° m	5° high 56° h	5° high 56° m
1	23	06	−6.6	9	35	10	28	5	36	5	45
3	23	11	−6.4	9	39	10	26	5	33	5	41
5	23	17	−6.2	8	43	10	24	5	29	5	38
7	23	24	−5.8	8	46	10	23	5	26	5	34
9	23	31	−5.3	8	49	10	23	5	23	5	30
11	23	39	−4.6	7	52	10	23	5	19	5	27
13	23	48	−3.9	7	55	10	24	5	16	5	23
15	23	57	−3.1	7	58	10	25	5	13	5	19
17	0	06	−2.1	7	61	10	27	5	10	5	15
19	0	16	−1.1	7	63	10	29	5	07	5	11
21	0	27	0.0	6	66	10	32	5	04	5	07
23	0	38	+1.1	6	69	10	35	5	00	5	03
25	0	49	+2.4	6	71	10	38	4	57	4	59
27	1	01	+3.7	6	74	10	42	4	55	4	55
29	1	13	+5.1	6	77	10	46	4	52	4	51
31	1	25	+6.5	6	80	10	51	4	49	4	47

VENUS

Day	RA h	RA m	Dec. °	Diam. ″	Phase %	Transit h	Transit m	5° high 52° h	5° high 52° m	5° high 56° h	5° high 56° m
1	21	47	−12.3	23	53	9	10	4	50	5	05
6	22	07	−10.9	22	55	9	11	4	43	4	56
11	22	28	−9.5	21	58	9	12	4	35	4	47
16	22	49	−7.8	20	60	9	13	4	27	4	37
21	23	10	−6.1	19	62	9	14	4	18	4	27
26	23	31	−4.2	18	64	9	16	4	10	4	17
31	23	52	−2.2	17	66	9	17	4	01	4	06

MARS

Day	RA h	RA m	Dec. °	Diam. ″	Phase %	Transit h	Transit m	5° high 52° h	5° high 52° m	5° high 56° h	5° high 56° m
1	5	27	+24.9	6	91	16	49	0	34	0	55
6	5	40	+25.0	6	91	16	42	0	28	0	49
11	5	52	+25.1	5	91	16	35	0	21	0	42
16	6	05	+25.1	5	92	16	28	0	14	0	35
21	6	18	+25.0	5	92	16	21	0	07	0	27
26	6	31	+24.9	5	92	16	14	23	57	0	19
31	6	43	+24.6	5	93	16	07	23	49	0	11

SUNRISE AND SUNSET

	London 0°05'	51°30'	Bristol 2°35'	51°28'	Birmingham 1°55'	52°28'	Manchester 2°15'	53°28'	Newcastle 1°37'	54°59'	Glasgow 4°14'	55°52'	Belfast 5°56'	54°35'
	h m	h m	h m	h m	h m	h m	h m	h m	h m	h m	h m	h m	h m	h m
1	5 36	18 33	5 46	18 43	5 43	18 42	5 43	18 44	5 39	18 43	5 48	18 55	5 56	19 00
2	5 34	18 35	5 44	18 45	5 40	18 43	5 41	18 46	5 36	18 45	5 46	18 57	5 54	19 02
3	5 32	18 37	5 42	18 47	5 38	18 45	5 38	18 48	5 34	18 47	5 43	18 59	5 52	19 04
4	5 29	18 38	5 39	18 48	5 36	18 47	5 36	18 49	5 31	18 49	5 40	19 01	5 49	19 06
5	5 27	18 40	5 37	18 50	5 33	18 49	5 33	18 51	5 29	18 51	5 38	19 03	5 47	19 08
6	5 25	18 42	5 35	18 52	5 31	18 50	5 31	18 53	5 26	18 53	5 35	19 05	5 44	19 10
7	5 23	18 43	5 33	18 53	5 29	18 52	5 29	18 55	5 24	18 55	5 33	19 07	5 42	19 11
8	5 21	18 45	5 31	18 55	5 26	18 54	5 26	18 57	5 21	18 57	5 30	19 09	5 39	19 13
9	5 18	18 47	5 28	18 57	5 24	18 56	5 24	18 59	5 19	18 59	5 28	19 11	5 37	19 15
10	5 16	18 48	5 26	18 58	5 22	18 57	5 21	19 00	5 16	19 01	5 25	19 13	5 34	19 17
11	5 14	18 50	5 24	19 00	5 20	18 59	5 19	19 02	5 14	19 03	5 22	19 15	5 32	19 19
12	5 12	18 52	5 22	19 02	5 17	19 01	5 17	19 04	5 11	19 05	5 20	19 17	5 29	19 21
13	5 09	18 53	5 20	19 03	5 15	19 03	5 14	19 06	5 09	19 06	5 17	19 19	5 27	19 23
14	5 07	18 55	5 17	19 05	5 13	19 04	5 12	19 08	5 06	19 08	5 15	19 21	5 24	19 25
15	5 05	18 57	5 15	19 07	5 11	19 06	5 10	19 09	5 04	19 10	5 12	19 23	5 22	19 27
16	5 03	18 58	5 13	19 08	5 08	19 08	5 08	19 11	5 01	19 12	5 10	19 25	5 20	19 29
17	5 01	19 00	5 11	19 10	5 06	19 09	5 05	19 13	4 59	19 14	5 07	19 27	5 17	19 31
18	4 59	19 02	5 09	19 12	5 04	19 11	5 03	19 15	4 57	19 16	5 05	19 29	5 15	19 32
19	4 57	19 03	5 07	19 13	5 02	19 13	5 01	19 17	4 54	19 18	5 02	19 31	5 13	19 34
20	4 55	19 05	5 05	19 15	5 00	19 15	4 58	19 19	4 52	19 20	5 00	19 33	5 10	19 36
21	4 52	19 07	5 03	19 17	4 57	19 16	4 56	19 20	4 50	19 22	4 57	19 35	5 08	19 38
22	4 50	19 08	5 00	19 18	4 55	19 18	4 54	19 22	4 47	19 24	4 55	19 37	5 06	19 40
23	4 48	19 10	4 58	19 20	4 53	19 20	4 52	19 24	4 45	19 26	4 53	19 39	5 03	19 42
24	4 46	19 12	4 56	19 22	4 51	19 22	4 50	19 26	4 43	19 28	4 50	19 41	5 01	19 44
25	4 44	19 13	4 54	19 23	4 49	19 23	4 47	19 28	4 40	19 30	4 48	19 43	4 59	19 46
26	4 42	19 15	4 52	19 25	4 47	19 25	4 45	19 29	4 38	19 32	4 45	19 45	4 57	19 48
27	4 40	19 17	4 50	19 27	4 45	19 27	4 43	19 31	4 36	19 34	4 43	19 47	4 54	19 50
28	4 38	19 18	4 48	19 28	4 43	19 29	4 41	19 33	4 34	19 36	4 41	19 49	4 52	19 52
29	4 36	19 20	4 47	19 30	4 41	19 30	4 39	19 35	4 31	19 38	4 39	19 51	4 50	19 53
30	4 35	19 22	4 45	19 32	4 39	19 32	4 37	19 37	4 29	19 40	4 36	19 53	4 48	19 55

JUPITER

Day	RA		Dec.		Transit		5° high 52°		56°	
	h	m	°	′	h	m	h	m	h	m
1	15	02.6	−15	51	2	25	22	24	22	44
11	14	58.9	−15	35	1	42	21	40	21	59
21	14	54.5	−15	15	0	59	20	54	21	13
31	14	49.6	−14	54	0	14	20	07	20	25

Diameters – equatorial 44″ polar 41″

SATURN

Day	RA		Dec.		Transit		5° high 52°		56°	
	h	m	°	′	h	m	h	m	h	m
1	8	27.7	+19	53	19	48	3	03	3	17
11	8	27.7	+19	53	19	08	2	24	2	38
21	8	28.5	+19	50	18	30	1	45	1	59
31	8	30.0	+19	45	17	52	1	07	1	21

Diameters – equatorial 19″ polar 17″
Rings – major axis 42″ minor axis 15″

URANUS

Day	RA		Dec.		Transit		10° high 52°		56°	
	h	m	°	′	h	m	h	m	h	m
1	22	56.3	−7	35	10	18	6	07	6	21
11	22	58.2	−7	24	9	40	5	28	5	42
21	22	59.9	−7	13	9	03	4	49	5	04
31	23	01.4	−7	04	8	25	4	11	4	25

Diameter 4″

NEPTUNE

Day	RA		Dec.		Transit		10° high 52°		56°	
	h	m	°	′	h	m	h	m	h	m
1	21	26.4	−15	16	8	48	5	28	5	55
11	21	27.3	−15	11	8	10	4	49	5	16
21	21	28.1	−15	08	7	31	4	10	4	37
31	21	28.7	−15	05	6	52	3	31	3	58

Diameter 2″

 MAY 2006

FIFTH MONTH, 31 DAYS. *Maia*, goddess of growth and increase

1	*Monday*	Santiago Ramón y Cajal b. 1852. Gabriel Lamé d. 1870	week 18 day 121
2	*Tuesday*	Elijah McCoy b. 1844. Leonardo da Vinci d. 1519	122
3	*Wednesday*	Alfred Kastler b. 1902. Lev Pontryagin d. 1988	123
4	*Thursday*	Thomas Huxley b. 1825. Edward Kendall d. 1972	124
5	*Friday*	Cathleen Morawetz b. 1923. Jean Astruc d. 1766	125
6	*Saturday*	Sigmund Freud b. 1856. Alexander von Humboldt d. 1859	126
7	*Sunday*	Edwin Land b. 1909. Allan Cormack d. 1998	127
8	*Monday*	H. Robert Horvitz b. 1947. Henry Whitehead d. 1960	week 19 day 128
9	*Tuesday*	Manfred Eigen b. 1927. Albert Michelson d. 1931	129
10	*Wednesday*	USS *Triton*, a nuclear submarine, completes the first underwater circumnavigation of the globe 1960	130
11	*Thursday*	Antony Hewish b. 1924. Odd Hassel d. 1981	131
12	*Friday*	Dorothy Crowfoot Hodgkin b. 1910. Edme Mariotte d. 1684	132
13	*Saturday*	Ronald Ross b. 1857. Cyrus McCormick d. 1884	133
14	*Sunday*	The USA's first space station is launched; Skylab spent over six years orbiting Earth 1973	134
15	*Monday*	The United Kingdom tests its first hydrogen bomb on Christmas Atoll in the Pacific Ocean 1957	week 20 day 135
16	*Tuesday*	Ilya Mechnikov b. 1845. Frederick Hopkins d. 1947	136
17	*Wednesday*	Joseph Norman Lockyer b. 1836. Alexis Clairault d. 1765	137
18	*Thursday*	Bertrand Russell b. 1872. Alphonse Laveran d. 1922	138
19	*Friday*	Max Perutz b. 1914. Joseph Larmor d. 1942	139
20	*Saturday*	William Hewlett b. 1913. Philipp Lenard d. 1947	140
21	*Sunday*	Andrey Sakharov b. 1921. Geoffrey de Havilland d. 1965	141
22	*Monday*	Herbert Brown b. 1912. Alfred Hershey d. 1997	week 21 day 142
23	*Tuesday*	John Bardeen b. 1908. Augustin Cauchy d. 1857	143
24	*Wednesday*	Samuel Morse sends the first electric telegram from Washington DC to Baltimore 1844	144
25	*Thursday*	Igor Sikorsky b. 1889. Frank Dyson d. 1939	145
26	*Friday*	Abraham de Moivre b. 1667. Edward Sabine d. 1883	146
27	*Saturday*	John Cockcroft b. 1897. Robert Koch d. 1910	147
28	*Sunday*	Stanley Prusiner b. 1942. Ilya Prigogine d. 2003	148
29	*Monday*	Edmund Hillary and Tenzing Norgay reach the summit of Mount Everest 1953	week 22 day 149
30	*Tuesday*	Julius Axelrod b. 1912. Leo Szilard d. 1964	150
31	*Wednesday*	Jay Miner b. 1932. James Rainwater d. 1986	151

ASTRONOMICAL PHENOMENA

d h
2 11 Mars in conjunction with Moon. Mars 4°S.
4 10 Saturn in conjunction with Moon. Saturn 4°S.
4 15 Jupiter at opposition
12 13 Jupiter in conjunction with Moon. Jupiter 5°N.
18 20 Mercury in superior conjunction
21 05 Sun's longitude 60° ♊
22 13 Neptune at stationary point
24 06 Venus in conjunction with Moon. Venus 4°S.
28 02 Mercury in conjunction with Moon. Mercury 3°S.
31 05 Mars in conjunction with Moon. Mars 3°S.
31 23 Saturn in conjunction with Moon. Saturn 3°S.

MINIMA OF ALGOL

Algol is inconveniently situated for observation during May

CONSTELLATIONS

The following constellations are near the meridian at

	d	h		d	h
April	1	24	May	16	21
April	15	23	June	1	20
May	1	22	June	15	19

Cepheus (below the Pole), Cassiopeia (below the Pole), Ursa Minor, Ursa Major, Canes Venatici, Coma Berenices, Bootes, Leo, Virgo, Crater, Corvus and Hydra

THE MOON

Phases, Apsides and Node		d	h	m
☽	First Quarter	5	05	13
○	Full Moon	13	06	51
☾	Last Quarter	20	09	21
●	New Moon	27	05	26

Apogee (404,610 km)	7	06	43
Perigee (368,577 km)	22	15	16

Mean longitude of ascending node on May 1, 3°

THE SUN

s.d. 15′.8

Day	Right Ascension			Dec. +		Equation of time		Rise 52°		Rise 56°		Transit		Set 52°		Set 56°		Sidereal time			Transit of first point of Aries		
	h	m	s	°	′	m	s	h	m	h	m	h	m	h	m	h	m	h	m	s	h	m	s
1	2	32	18	14	58	+2	50	4	31	4	17	11	57	19	25	19	39	14	35	08	9	23	19
2	2	36	07	15	16	+2	57	4	29	4	14	11	57	19	26	19	41	14	39	05	9	19	23
3	2	39	57	15	34	+3	04	4	27	4	12	11	57	19	28	19	43	14	43	01	9	15	28
4	2	43	48	15	52	+3	10	4	25	4	10	11	57	19	30	19	45	14	46	58	9	11	32
5	2	47	39	16	09	+3	15	4	23	4	08	11	57	19	31	19	47	14	50	54	9	07	36
6	2	51	30	16	26	+3	20	4	21	4	06	11	57	19	33	19	49	14	54	51	9	03	40
7	2	55	23	16	43	+3	25	4	20	4	03	11	57	19	34	19	51	14	58	47	8	59	44
8	2	59	15	17	00	+3	29	4	18	4	01	11	56	19	36	19	53	15	02	44	8	55	48
9	3	03	08	17	16	+3	32	4	16	3	59	11	56	19	38	19	55	15	06	41	8	51	52
10	3	07	02	17	32	+3	35	4	14	3	57	11	56	19	39	19	57	15	10	37	8	47	56
11	3	10	56	17	47	+3	37	4	13	3	55	11	56	19	41	19	59	15	14	34	8	44	00
12	3	14	51	18	03	+3	39	4	11	3	53	11	56	19	43	20	01	15	18	30	8	40	04
13	3	18	47	18	18	+3	40	4	10	3	51	11	56	19	44	20	03	15	22	27	8	36	08
14	3	22	43	18	33	+3	40	4	08	3	49	11	56	19	46	20	04	15	26	23	8	32	13
15	3	26	39	18	47	+3	40	4	06	3	48	11	56	19	47	20	06	15	30	20	8	28	17
16	3	30	37	19	01	+3	40	4	05	3	46	11	56	19	49	20	08	15	34	16	8	24	21
17	3	34	34	19	15	+3	39	4	03	3	44	11	56	19	50	20	10	15	38	13	8	20	25
18	3	38	33	19	28	+3	37	4	02	3	42	11	56	19	52	20	12	15	42	10	8	16	29
19	3	42	32	19	42	+3	34	4	01	3	40	11	56	19	53	20	14	15	46	06	8	12	33
20	3	46	31	19	54	+3	32	3	59	3	39	11	57	19	55	20	15	15	50	03	8	08	37
21	3	50	31	20	07	+3	28	3	58	3	37	11	57	19	56	20	17	15	53	59	8	04	41
22	3	54	32	20	19	+3	24	3	57	3	36	11	57	19	58	20	19	15	57	56	8	00	45
23	3	58	33	20	31	+3	20	3	55	3	34	11	57	19	59	20	21	16	01	52	7	56	49
24	4	02	34	20	42	+3	14	3	54	3	32	11	57	20	00	20	22	16	05	49	7	52	53
25	4	06	37	20	53	+3	09	3	53	3	31	11	57	20	02	20	24	16	09	45	7	48	58
26	4	10	39	21	04	+3	03	3	52	3	30	11	57	20	03	20	25	16	13	42	7	45	02
27	4	14	43	21	14	+2	56	3	51	3	28	11	57	20	04	20	27	16	17	39	7	41	06
28	4	18	46	21	24	+2	49	3	50	3	27	11	57	20	05	20	29	16	21	35	7	37	10
29	4	22	50	21	34	+2	41	3	49	3	26	11	57	20	07	20	30	16	25	32	7	33	14
30	4	26	55	21	43	+2	33	3	48	3	24	11	58	20	08	20	32	16	29	28	7	29	18
31	4	31	00	21	52	+2	25	3	47	3	23	11	58	20	09	20	33	16	33	25	7	25	22

DURATION OF TWILIGHT (in minutes)

Latitude	52°	56°	52°	56°	52°	56°	52°	56°
	1 May		11 May		21 May		31 May	
Civil	39	44	41	48	44	53	46	57
Nautical	89	106	97	120	106	141	115	187
Astronomical	152	204	176	TAN	TAN	TAN	TAN	TAN

THE NIGHT SKY

Mercury is not suitably placed for observation as it passes through superior conjunction on the 18th.

Venus, magnitude −4.1, is still a splendid object in the early mornings before sunrise, though still only visible, low above the eastern horizon, for a short while before dawn.

Mars is still visible as an evening object in the western sky, though no longer visible after midnight, even at the beginning of the month. Its magnitude is +1.6. On the 1st, and again on the 30th, the thin waxing crescent Moon will be seen passing about 3 degrees north of the planet. Mars is moving eastwards in Gemini, and during the second part of the month will be seen passing south of the Twins, Castor and Pollux, before entering the constellation of Cancer at the end of May.

Jupiter, magnitude −2.5, reaches opposition on the 4th and is therefore available for observation throughout the hours of darkness, crossing the meridian at midnight. The planet continues to move slowly retrograde in the constellation of Libra. The Full Moon passes about 5 degrees south of Jupiter on the night of the 11th/12th. The four Galilean satellites are readily observable with a small telescope or even a good pair of binoculars provided that they are held rigidly.

Saturn, magnitude +0.4, is still visible in the western sky in the early evenings, in the constellation of Cancer. By the middle of the month it is no longer visible after midnight. On the late evening of the 3rd, and again on the 31st, the waxing crescent Moon will be seen passing 3 degrees north of the planet.

THE MOON

Day	R.A. h	R.A. m	Dec. °	Hor. Par. '	Semi-diam. '	Sun's Co-Long. °	PA of Bright Limb °	Ph. %	Age d	Rise 52° h	Rise 52° m	Rise 56° h	Rise 56° m	Transit h	Transit m	Set 52° h	Set 52° m	Set 56° h	Set 56° m
1	5	22	+28.2	57.3	15.6	305	260	13	3.2	6	07	5	28	15	23	—	—	0	17
2	6	21	+28.5	56.5	15.4	317	268	20	4.2	7	05	6	26	16	19	0	39	1	18
3	7	19	+27.3	55.7	15.2	330	275	29	5.2	8	15	7	41	17	12	1	22	1	56
4	8	12	+24.7	55.1	15.0	342	281	38	6.2	9	30	9	04	18	00	1	51	2	18
5	9	03	+21.1	54.6	14.9	354	286	48	7.2	10	46	10	27	18	45	2	11	2	31
6	9	49	+16.7	54.3	14.8	6	290	58	8.2	12	00	11	47	19	28	2	25	2	40
7	10	34	+11.7	54.2	14.8	18	293	67	9.2	13	12	13	04	20	08	2	37	2	46
8	11	16	+6.2	54.2	14.8	31	294	75	10.2	14	22	14	20	20	47	2	46	2	51
9	11	58	+0.6	54.4	14.8	43	294	83	11.2	15	33	15	36	21	26	2	55	2	55
10	12	41	−5.2	54.7	14.9	55	292	90	12.2	16	46	16	54	22	07	3	04	2	59
11	13	25	−10.8	55.1	15.0	67	288	95	13.2	18	02	18	16	22	50	3	14	3	04
12	14	11	−16.1	55.6	15.2	79	279	98	14.2	19	21	19	42	23	38	3	27	3	11
13	15	01	−20.9	56.2	15.3	92	239	100	15.2	20	43	21	12	—	—	3	43	3	21
14	15	54	−24.8	56.7	15.4	104	129	99	16.2	22	03	22	40	0	29	4	07	3	37
15	16	52	−27.4	57.2	15.6	116	109	97	17.2	23	14	23	54	1	25	4	42	4	05
16	17	52	−28.5	57.7	15.7	128	98	92	18.2	—	—	—	—	2	24	5	34	4	53
17	18	54	−27.9	58.1	15.8	140	90	85	19.2	0	08	0	46	3	24	6	44	6	07
18	19	55	−25.6	58.5	15.9	152	82	76	20.2	0	46	1	17	4	23	8	08	7	38
19	20	53	−21.8	58.9	16.0	165	75	66	21.2	1	12	1	35	5	19	9	37	9	16
20	21	49	−16.6	59.1	16.1	177	71	55	22.2	1	31	1	46	6	11	11	06	10	53
21	22	41	−10.6	59.3	16.2	189	68	43	23.2	1	45	1	54	7	01	12	34	12	27
22	23	32	−4.0	59.5	16.2	201	66	32	24.2	1	57	2	00	7	49	14	00	14	00
23	0	23	+2.8	59.5	16.2	214	67	22	25.2	2	08	2	06	8	37	15	26	15	33
24	1	13	+9.5	59.4	16.2	226	70	13	26.2	2	21	2	12	9	26	16	54	17	07
25	2	06	+15.6	59.1	16.1	238	75	6	27.2	2	35	2	20	10	18	18	24	18	44
26	3	01	+20.9	58.7	16.0	250	86	2	28.2	2	54	2	32	11	12	19	53	20	21
27	3	59	+25.0	58.2	15.9	263	135	0	29.2	3	20	2	50	12	09	21	15	21	51
28	4	58	+27.6	57.6	15.7	275	238	1	0.8	3	57	3	21	13	08	22	24	23	04
29	5	59	+28.5	56.9	15.5	287	258	4	1.8	4	50	4	10	14	06	23	15	23	52
30	6	57	+27.8	56.2	15.3	299	268	9	2.8	5	56	5	20	15	01	23	50	—	—
31	7	53	+25.6	55.6	15.1	312	276	15	3.8	7	11	6	42	15	52	—	—	0	20

MERCURY

Day	R.A. h	R.A. m	Dec. °	Diam. "	Phase %	Transit h	Transit m	5° high 52° h	5° high 52° m	5° high 56° h	5° high 56° m
1	1	25	+6.5	6	80	10	51	4	49	4	47
3	1	38	+8.0	6	83	10	57	4	47	4	44
5	1	52	+9.5	5	86	11	02	4	45	4	40
7	2	06	+11.0	5	89	11	09	4	43	4	37
9	2	21	+12.6	5	91	11	16	4	42	4	34
11	2	36	+14.1	5	94	11	23	4	41	4	32
13	2	52	+15.7	5	97	11	31	4	40	4	30
15	3	08	+17.2	5	98	11	40	4	41	4	29
17	3	25	+18.7	5	100	11	50	4	42	4	29
19	3	43	+20.0	5	100	11	59	4	44	4	29
21	4	01	+21.3	5	99	12	10	19	35	19	52
23	4	19	+22.4	5	98	12	20	19	52	20	10
25	4	38	+23.4	5	95	12	31	20	08	20	27
27	4	56	+24.2	5	92	12	41	20	23	20	43
29	5	14	+24.8	5	88	12	51	20	37	20	57
31	5	31	+25.2	6	83	13	00	20	48	21	10

VENUS

Day	RA h	RA m	Dec. °	Diam. "	Phase %	Transit h	Transit m	5° high 52° h	5° high 52° m	5° high 56° h	5° high 56° m
1	23	52	−2.2	17	66	9	17	4	01	4	06
6	0	13	−0.2	17	68	9	18	3	51	3	55
11	0	34	+1.9	16	70	9	20	3	42	3	44
16	0	56	+4.0	16	71	9	21	3	33	3	33
21	1	17	+6.1	15	73	9	23	3	24	3	23
26	1	39	+8.1	15	75	9	25	3	16	3	13
31	2	01	+10.2	14	76	9	28	3	08	3	03

MARS

Day	RA h	RA m	Dec. °	Diam. "	Phase %	Transit h	Transit m	5° high 52° h	5° high 52° m	5° high 56° h	5° high 56° m
1	6	43	+24.6	5	93	16	07	23	49	0	11
6	6	56	+24.4	5	93	16	01	23	40	0	02
11	7	09	+24.0	5	93	15	54	23	31	23	50
16	7	22	+23.6	5	94	15	47	23	22	23	40
21	7	35	+23.1	5	94	15	40	23	12	23	29
26	7	48	+22.6	4	94	15	33	23	01	23	18
31	8	00	+22.0	4	95	15	26	22	51	23	07

SUNRISE AND SUNSET

	London 0° 05' 51° 30'		Bristol 2° 35' 51° 28'		Birmingham 1° 55' 52° 28'		Manchester 2° 15' 53° 28'		Newcastle 1° 37' 54° 59'		Glasgow 4° 14' 55° 52'		Belfast 5° 56' 54° 35'	
d	h m	h m	h m	h m	h m	h m	h m	h m	h m	h m	h m	h m	h m	h m
1	4 33	19 23	4 43	19 33	4 37	19 34	4 35	19 38	4 27	19 41	4 34	19 55	4 46	19 57
2	4 31	19 25	4 41	19 35	4 35	19 35	4 33	19 40	4 25	19 43	4 32	19 57	4 44	19 59
3	4 29	19 27	4 39	19 36	4 33	19 37	4 31	19 42	4 23	19 45	4 30	19 59	4 41	20 01
4	4 27	19 28	4 37	19 38	4 31	19 39	4 29	19 44	4 21	19 47	4 27	20 01	4 39	20 03
5	4 25	19 30	4 35	19 40	4 29	19 41	4 27	19 46	4 18	19 49	4 25	20 03	4 37	20 05
6	4 24	19 31	4 34	19 41	4 27	19 42	4 25	19 47	4 16	19 51	4 23	20 05	4 35	20 07
7	4 22	19 33	4 32	19 43	4 26	19 44	4 23	19 49	4 14	19 53	4 21	20 07	4 33	20 08
8	4 20	19 35	4 30	19 45	4 24	19 46	4 21	19 51	4 12	19 55	4 19	20 09	4 31	20 10
9	4 18	19 36	4 28	19 46	4 22	19 47	4 19	19 53	4 10	19 57	4 17	20 11	4 29	20 12
10	4 17	19 38	4 27	19 48	4 20	19 49	4 18	19 54	4 08	19 58	4 15	20 13	4 28	20 14
11	4 15	19 39	4 25	19 49	4 19	19 50	4 16	19 56	4 07	20 00	4 13	20 15	4 26	20 16
12	4 13	19 41	4 24	19 51	4 17	19 52	4 14	19 58	4 05	20 02	4 11	20 17	4 24	20 18
13	4 12	19 42	4 22	19 52	4 15	19 54	4 12	19 59	4 03	20 04	4 09	20 19	4 22	20 19
14	4 10	19 44	4 20	19 54	4 14	19 55	4 11	20 01	4 01	20 06	4 07	20 21	4 20	20 21
15	4 09	19 45	4 19	19 55	4 12	19 57	4 09	20 03	3 59	20 08	4 05	20 23	4 18	20 23
16	4 07	19 47	4 18	19 57	4 11	19 58	4 07	20 04	3 58	20 09	4 03	20 24	4 17	20 25
17	4 06	19 48	4 16	19 58	4 09	20 00	4 06	20 06	3 56	20 11	4 02	20 26	4 15	20 26
18	4 05	19 50	4 15	20 00	4 08	20 02	4 04	20 08	3 54	20 13	4 00	20 28	4 13	20 28
19	4 03	19 51	4 13	20 01	4 06	20 03	4 03	20 09	3 53	20 14	3 58	20 30	4 12	20 30
20	4 02	19 53	4 12	20 03	4 05	20 05	4 01	20 11	3 51	20 16	3 56	20 32	4 10	20 31
21	4 01	19 54	4 11	20 04	4 03	20 06	4 00	20 12	3 49	20 18	3 55	20 33	4 09	20 33
22	3 59	19 56	4 09	20 05	4 02	20 07	3 59	20 14	3 48	20 19	3 53	20 35	4 07	20 34
23	3 58	19 57	4 08	20 07	4 01	20 09	3 57	20 15	3 46	20 21	3 52	20 37	4 06	20 36
24	3 57	19 58	4 07	20 08	4 00	20 10	3 56	20 17	3 45	20 23	3 50	20 38	4 04	20 38
25	3 56	20 00	4 06	20 09	3 58	20 12	3 55	20 18	3 44	20 24	3 49	20 40	4 03	20 39
26	3 55	20 01	4 05	20 11	3 57	20 13	3 53	20 20	3 42	20 26	3 47	20 42	4 02	20 41
27	3 54	20 02	4 04	20 12	3 56	20 14	3 52	20 21	3 41	20 27	3 46	20 43	4 01	20 42
28	3 53	20 03	4 03	20 13	3 55	20 16	3 51	20 22	3 40	20 29	3 45	20 45	3 59	20 43
29	3 52	20 05	4 02	20 14	3 54	20 17	3 50	20 24	3 39	20 30	3 43	20 46	3 58	20 45
30	3 51	20 06	4 01	20 16	3 53	20 18	3 49	20 25	3 37	20 31	3 42	20 48	3 57	20 46
31	3 50	20 07	4 00	20 17	3 52	20 19	3 48	20 26	3 36	20 33	3 41	20 49	3 56	20 47

JUPITER

Day	R.A. h m	Dec. ° '	Transit h m	5° high 52° h m	5° high 56° h m
1	14 49.6	−14 54	0 14	4 17	3 59
11	14 44.6	−14 32	23 26	3 35	3 17
21	14 39.8	−14 11	22 42	2 53	2 36
31	14 35.5	−13 53	21 58	2 12	1 55

Diameters – equatorial 44″ polar 42″

SATURN

Day	R.A. h m	Dec. ° '	Transit h m	5° high 52° h m	5° high 56° h m
1	8 30.0	+19 45	17 52	1 07	1 21
11	8 32.2	+19 38	17 15	0 29	0 43
21	8 35.0	+19 28	16 38	23 48	0 05
31	8 38.3	+19 16	16 03	23 11	23 24

Diameters – equatorial 18″ polar 16″
Rings – major axis 40″ minor axis 13″

URANUS

Day	R.A. h m	Dec. ° '	Transit h m	10° high 52° h m	10° high 56° h m
1	23 01.4	−7 04	8 25	4 11	4 25
11	23 02.6	−6 57	7 47	3 32	3 46
21	23 03.7	−6 51	7 09	2 53	3 07
31	23 04.4	−6 47	6 30	2 14	2 28

Diameter 4″

NEPTUNE

Day	R.A. h m	Dec. ° '	Transit h m	10° high 52° h m	10° high 56° h m
1	21 28.7	−15 05	6 52	3 31	3 58
11	21 29.0	−15 04	6 13	2 52	3 18
21	21 29.2	−15 03	5 34	2 13	2 39
31	21 29.1	−15 04	4 55	1 34	2 00

Diameter 2″

JUNE 2006

SIXTH MONTH, 30 DAYS. *Junius*, Roman gens (family)

1	Thursday	William Knowles b. 1917. Werner Forssmann d. 1979	152
2	Friday	Clair Patterson b. 1922. John Stevens d. 1943	153
3	Saturday	Otto Loewi b. 1873. Archibald Hill d. 1977	154
4	Sunday	Heinrich Wieland b. 1877. Maurice Fréchet d. 1973	155
5	Monday	The Montgolfier Brothers demonstrate their hot air balloon in public for the first time 1783	week 23 day 156
6	Tuesday	Manfred Sakel b. 1900. Carl Jung d. 1961	157
7	Wednesday	Philipp Lenard b. 1862. Alan Turing d. 1954	158
8	Thursday	Francis Crick b. 1916. John Scott Russell d. 1882	159
9	Friday	Elizabeth Garrett Anderson b. 1836. Camille Guérin d. 1961	160
10	Saturday	Laszlo and Georg Biro file a patent for their ballpoint pen 1943	161
11	Sunday	Jacques Cousteau b. 1910. Daniel Kirkwood d. 1895	162
12	Monday	Fritz Lipmann b. 1899. Karl von Frisch d. 1982	week 24 day 163
13	Tuesday	John Nash b. 1928. Georg von Bekesy d. 1972	164
14	Wednesday	Alois Alzheimer b. 1864. John Logie Baird d. 1946	165
15	Thursday	Benjamin Franklin proves that lightning is electrical when he deliberately flies a kite during a storm 1752	166
16	Friday	Georg Wittig b. 1897. Wernher von Braun d. 1977	167
17	Saturday	François Jacob b. 1920. Thomas Kuhn d. 1996	168
18	Sunday	Dudley Herschbach b. 1932. Paul Karrer d. 1971	169
19	Monday	Aage Bohr b. 1922. Joseph Banks d. 1820	week 25 day 170
20	Tuesday	Frederick Hopkins b. 1861. Erwin Chargaff d. 2002	171
21	Wedesday	Siméon Poisson b. 1781. William Morgan d. 1994	172
22	Thursday	Hermann Minkowski b. 1864. Ilya Frank d. 1990	173
23	Friday	Vint Cerf b. 1943. Jonas Salk d. 1995	174
24	Saturday	Victor Hess b. 1883. Willy Ley d. 1969	175
25	Sunday	Walther Nernst b. 1864. Ernest Walton d. 1995	176
26	Monday	Lord Kelvin b. 1824. Karl Landsteiner d. 1943	week 26 day 177
27	Tuesday	Hans Spemann b. 1869. Sophie Germain d. 1831	178
28	Wednesday	Maria Göppert-Mayer b. 1906. Vannevar Bush d. 1974	179
29	Thursday	George Ellery Hale b. 1868. Thomas Addison d. 1860	180
30	Friday	Paul Berg b. 1926. William Oughtred d. 1660	181

ASTRONOMICAL PHENOMENA

d h

8	16	Jupiter in conjunction with Moon. Jupiter 4°N.
16	17	Pluto at opposition
18	06	Saturn in conjunction with Mars. Saturn 0°.6 s.
19	08	Uranus at stationary point
20	20	Mercury at greatest elongation E.25°
21	12	Sun's longitude 90° ♋
23	01	Venus in conjunction with Moon. Venus 6°S.
27	16	Mercury in conjunction with Moon. Mercury 5°S.
28	12	Saturn in conjunction with Moon. Saturn 3°S.
28	23	Mars in conjunction with Moon. Mars 2°S.

MINIMA OF ALGOL

Algol is inconveniently situated for observation during June

CONSTELLATIONS

The following constellations are near the meridian at

	d	h		d	h
May	1	24	June	15	21
May	16	23	July	1	20
June	1	22	July	16	19

Cassiopeia (below the Pole), Ursa Minor, Draco, Ursa Major, Canes Venatici, Bootes, Corona, Serpens, Virgo and Libra

THE MOON

Phases, Apsides and Node	d	h	m
☽ First Quarter	3	23	06
○ Full Moon	11	18	03
☾ Last Quarter	18	14	08
● New Moon	25	16	05
Apogee (404,120 km)	4	01	39
Perigee (368,886 km)	16	17	06

Mean longitude of ascending node on June 1, 1°

THE SUN

s.d. 15'.8

Day	Right Ascension			Dec. +		Equation of time		Rise 52°		Rise 56°		Transit		Set 52°		Set 56°		Sidereal time			Transit of first point of Aries		
	h	m	s	°	'	m	s	h	m	h	m	h	m	h	m	h	m	h	m	s	h	m	s
1	4	35	05	22	00	+2	16	3	46	3	22	11	58	20	10	20	34	16	37	21	7	21	26
2	4	39	11	22	09	+2	07	3	45	3	21	11	58	20	11	20	36	16	41	18	7	17	30
3	4	43	17	22	16	+1	57	3	45	3	20	11	58	20	12	20	37	16	45	14	7	13	34
4	4	47	24	22	24	+1	47	3	44	3	19	11	58	20	13	20	38	16	49	11	7	09	38
5	4	51	31	22	30	+1	37	3	43	3	18	11	58	20	14	20	39	16	53	08	7	05	43
6	4	55	38	22	37	+1	26	3	43	3	18	11	59	20	15	20	40	16	57	04	7	01	47
7	4	59	45	22	43	+1	15	3	42	3	17	11	59	20	16	20	42	17	01	01	6	57	51
8	5	03	53	22	49	+1	04	3	42	3	16	11	59	20	17	20	43	17	04	57	6	53	55
9	5	08	01	22	54	+0	53	3	41	3	15	11	59	20	18	20	43	17	08	54	6	49	59
10	5	12	09	22	59	+0	41	3	41	3	15	11	59	20	19	20	44	17	12	50	6	46	03
11	5	16	18	23	04	+0	29	3	40	3	14	12	00	20	19	20	45	17	16	47	6	42	07
12	5	20	26	23	08	+0	17	3	40	3	14	12	00	20	20	20	46	17	20	43	6	38	11
13	5	24	35	23	11	+0	05	3	40	3	14	12	00	20	21	20	47	17	24	40	6	34	15
14	5	28	44	23	15	-0	08	3	40	3	13	12	00	20	21	20	47	17	28	37	6	30	19
15	5	32	53	23	18	-0	20	3	39	3	13	12	00	20	22	20	48	17	32	33	6	26	23
16	5	37	03	23	20	-0	33	3	39	3	13	12	01	20	22	20	49	17	36	30	6	22	27
17	5	41	12	23	22	-0	46	3	39	3	13	12	01	20	23	20	49	17	40	26	6	18	32
18	5	45	22	23	24	-0	59	3	39	3	13	12	01	20	23	20	50	17	44	23	6	14	36
19	5	49	31	23	25	-1	12	3	39	3	13	12	01	20	23	20	50	17	48	19	6	10	40
20	5	53	41	23	26	-1	25	3	39	3	13	12	02	20	24	20	50	17	52	16	6	06	44
21	5	57	51	23	26	-1	38	3	40	3	13	12	02	20	24	20	50	17	56	13	6	02	48
22	6	02	00	23	26	-1	51	3	40	3	13	12	02	20	24	20	51	18	00	09	5	58	52
23	6	06	10	23	26	-2	04	3	40	3	14	12	02	20	24	20	51	18	04	06	5	54	56
24	6	10	20	23	25	-2	17	3	41	3	14	12	02	20	24	20	51	18	08	02	5	51	00
25	6	14	29	23	24	-2	30	3	41	3	14	12	03	20	24	20	51	18	11	59	5	47	04
26	6	18	39	23	22	-2	43	3	41	3	15	12	03	20	24	20	51	18	15	55	5	43	08
27	6	22	48	23	20	-2	56	3	42	3	15	12	03	20	24	20	50	18	19	52	5	39	12
28	6	26	57	23	18	-3	09	3	42	3	16	12	03	20	24	20	50	18	23	48	5	35	17
29	6	31	06	23	15	-3	21	3	43	3	17	12	03	20	24	20	50	18	27	45	5	31	21
30	6	35	15	23	12	-3	33	3	44	3	17	12	04	20	23	20	49	18	31	42	5	27	25

DURATION OF TWILIGHT (in minutes)

Latitude	52°	56°	52°	56°	52°	56°	52°	56°
	1 June		11 June		21 June		31 June	
Civil	46	58	48	61	49	63	48	61
Nautical	116	TAN	124	TAN	127	TAN	124	TAN
Astronomical	TAN	TAN	TAN	TAN	TAN	TAN	TAN	TAN

THE NIGHT SKY

Mercury reaches greatest eastern elongation on the 20th and is an evening object for the first three weeks of the month. However the long evening twilight, coupled with the fact its maximum altitude above the west-north-west horizon at the time of end of evening civil twilight is never more than about 7 degrees, will be a serious hindrance to observation. On the 1st its magnitude is −0.8 but this has faded to +0.6 by the 21st.

Venus, magnitude −4.0, continues to be visible as a splendid object in the early morning skies, low above the eastern horizon before dawn. Each morning it becomes visible for a little longer as the month progresses. This effect is the result of the planet's northward movement in declination which more than offsets the fact that it is slowly moving in towards the Sun. The waning crescent Moon is near the planet on the mornings of the 22nd and 23rd.

Mars, magnitude +1.8, continues to be visible as an evening object, low in the western sky as soon as it is dark. Around the middle of the month it will be seen passing south of the well-known Beehive Cluster (Praesepe). However it is now coming towards the end of its evening apparition and it will be lost to view in the gathering twilight before the end of June.

Jupiter, magnitude −2.4, continues to be visible in the south-western sky in the evenings, in the constellation of Libra. The waxing gibbous Moon is near the planet on the evenings of the 7th and 8th.

Saturn, magnitude +0.4, continues to be visible low in the western sky in the early evenings, though it is no longer an easy object to detect in the lengthening twilight, and is unlikely to be seen after the first three weeks of the month. Mars passes 0.5 degrees north of Saturn on 18 June, while Saturn passes about one degree south of Praesepe again early in June.

THE MOON

Day	R.A.		Dec.	Hor. Par.	Semi-diam.	Sun's Co-Long.	PA of Br. Limb	Ph.	Age	Rise				Transit		Set			
										52°		56°				52°		56°	
	h	m	°	'	'	°	°	%	d	h	m	h	m	h	m	h	m	h	m
1	8	45	+22.3	55.0	15.0	324	283	23	4.8	8	28	8	06	16	39	0	14	0	37
2	9	34	+18.0	54.6	14.9	336	287	32	5.8	9	43	9	28	17	23	0	30	0	47
3	10	19	+13.2	54.4	14.8	348	291	41	6.8	10	56	10	46	18	03	0	43	0	54
4	11	02	+7.9	54.3	14.8	0	293	50	7.8	12	07	12	03	18	43	0	53	1	00
5	11	44	+2.3	54.3	14.8	13	293	60	8.8	13	17	13	18	19	22	1	03	1	04
6	12	26	−3.4	54.6	14.9	25	293	69	9.8	14	28	14	34	20	02	1	11	1	08
7	13	09	−9.0	55.0	15.0	37	291	78	10.8	15	42	15	54	20	44	1	21	1	13
8	13	55	−14.5	55.5	15.1	49	288	85	11.8	17	00	17	18	21	29	1	33	1	19
9	14	43	−19.4	56.1	15.3	61	282	92	12.8	18	21	18	47	22	19	1	47	1	28
10	15	36	−23.6	56.8	15.5	74	273	96	13.8	19	43	20	17	23	14	2	08	1	41
11	16	32	−26.7	57.4	15.6	86	252	99	14.8	21	00	21	39	—	—	2	38	2	04
12	17	33	−28.3	58.0	15.8	98	150	100	15.8	22	02	22	41	0	13	3	24	2	45
13	18	36	−28.2	58.6	16.0	110	103	98	16.8	22	46	23	19	1	14	4	30	3	51
14	19	38	−26.2	59.0	16.1	122	89	94	17.8	23	16	23	40	2	15	5	52	5	20
15	20	39	−22.7	59.3	16.1	135	80	87	18.8	23	37	23	54	3	13	7	22	6	59
16	21	36	−17.7	59.4	16.2	147	73	78	19.8	23	52	—	—	4	08	8	53	8	38
17	22	29	−11.8	59.4	16.2	159	69	68	20.8	—	—	0	02	4	59	10	21	10	13
18	23	21	−5.3	59.4	16.2	171	67	57	21.8	0	05	0	09	5	47	11	48	11	46
19	0	11	+1.4	59.2	16.1	183	67	45	22.8	0	16	0	15	6	35	13	13	13	17
20	1	00	+8.0	58.9	16.1	196	68	34	23.8	0	28	0	21	7	22	14	38	14	49
21	1	52	+14.2	58.6	16.0	208	71	24	24.8	0	41	0	28	8	12	16	05	16	23
22	2	45	+19.6	58.3	15.9	220	76	15	25.8	0	58	0	38	9	04	17	32	17	58
23	3	41	+24.0	57.8	15.8	232	83	8	26.8	1	20	0	54	9	59	18	56	19	30
24	4	39	+26.9	57.4	15.6	245	95	3	27.8	1	53	1	18	10	56	20	10	20	48
25	5	38	+28.3	56.8	15.5	257	119	1	28.8	2	39	2	00	11	54	21	07	21	45
26	6	37	+28.1	56.3	15.3	269	222	0	0.3	3	40	3	02	12	50	21	48	22	21
27	7	34	+26.4	55.7	15.2	281	263	2	1.3	4	52	4	20	13	43	22	16	22	41
28	8	28	+23.4	55.2	15.1	294	276	6	2.3	6	09	5	45	14	32	22	35	22	54
29	9	17	+19.4	54.8	14.9	306	283	11	3.3	7	26	7	08	15	17	22	49	23	02
30	10	04	+14.6	54.5	14.8	318	288	18	4.3	8	40	8	28	15	59	23	00	23	08

MERCURY

Day	R.A.		Dec.	Diam.	Phase	Transit		5° high			
								52°		56°	
	h	m	°	"	%	h	m	h	m	h	m
1	5	40	+25.3	6	81	13	05	20	54	21	15
3	5	56	+25.5	6	76	13	13	21	03	21	24
5	6	12	+25.5	6	71	13	21	21	10	21	31
7	6	27	+25.4	6	67	13	28	21	15	21	37
9	6	41	+25.2	6	62	13	34	21	19	21	40
11	6	54	+24.8	7	58	13	39	21	22	21	42
13	7	07	+24.4	7	54	13	43	21	22	21	42
15	7	18	+23.8	7	50	13	46	21	22	21	40
17	7	28	+23.2	8	46	13	48	21	20	21	38
19	7	38	+22.6	8	42	13	50	21	17	21	34
21	7	46	+21.9	8	39	13	50	21	13	21	29
23	7	53	+21.2	9	35	13	49	21	07	21	23
25	7	59	+20.5	9	31	13	47	21	01	21	15
27	8	04	+19.8	9	28	13	43	20	54	21	07
29	8	08	+19.1	10	24	13	39	20	45	20	58
31	8	11	+18.5	10	21	13	33	20	36	20	48

VENUS

Day	R.A.		Dec.	Diam.	Phase	Transit		5° high			
								52°		56°	
	h	m	°	"	%	h	m	h	m	h	m
1	2	06	+10.6	14	76	9	28	3	06	3	01
6	2	28	+12.5	14	78	9	31	2	59	2	52
11	2	51	+14.3	13	79	9	34	2	52	2	44
16	3	14	+16.1	13	81	9	38	2	47	2	36
21	3	38	+17.6	13	82	9	42	2	42	2	30
26	4	02	+19.0	12	84	9	47	2	39	2	25
31	4	27	+20.3	12	85	9	52	2	37	2	22

MARS

Day	R.A.		Dec.	Diam.	Phase	Transit		5° high			
								52°		56°	
	h	m	°	"	%	h	m	h	m	h	m
1	8	03	+21.9	4	95	15	25	22	48	23	05
6	8	16	+21.2	4	95	15	18	22	37	22	53
11	8	28	+20.5	4	95	15	10	22	26	22	40
16	8	41	+19.7	4	96	15	03	22	14	22	28
21	8	53	+18.9	4	96	14	56	22	02	22	14
26	9	05	+18.0	4	96	14	49	21	49	22	01
31	9	18	+17.1	4	96	14	41	21	36	21	47

SUNRISE AND SUNSET

	London				Bristol				Birmingham				Manchester				Newcastle				Glasgow				Belfast			
	0°05′		51°30′		2°35′		51°28′		1°55′		52°28′		2°15′		53°28′		1°37′		54°59′		4°14′		55°52′		5°56′		54°35′	
d	h	m	h	m	h	m	h	m	h	m	h	m	h	m	h	m	h	m	h	m	h	m	h	m	h	m	h	m
1	3	49	20	08	3	59	20	18	3	51	20	20	3	47	20	27	3	35	20	34	3	40	20	50	3	55	20	49
2	3	48	20	09	3	58	20	19	3	50	20	21	3	46	20	28	3	34	20	35	3	39	20	52	3	54	20	50
3	3	48	20	10	3	58	20	20	3	50	20	23	3	45	20	30	3	33	20	36	3	38	20	53	3	53	20	51
4	3	47	20	11	3	57	20	21	3	49	20	24	3	45	20	31	3	33	20	38	3	37	20	54	3	52	20	52
5	3	46	20	12	3	56	20	22	3	48	20	25	3	44	20	32	3	32	20	39	3	36	20	55	3	52	20	53
6	3	46	20	13	3	56	20	23	3	48	20	26	3	43	20	33	3	31	20	40	3	35	20	56	3	51	20	54
7	3	45	20	14	3	55	20	24	3	47	20	26	3	43	20	34	3	30	20	41	3	35	20	57	3	50	20	55
8	3	45	20	15	3	55	20	24	3	47	20	27	3	42	20	35	3	30	20	42	3	34	20	58	3	50	20	56
9	3	44	20	15	3	54	20	25	3	46	20	28	3	41	20	35	3	29	20	43	3	33	20	59	3	49	20	57
10	3	44	20	16	3	54	20	26	3	46	20	29	3	41	20	36	3	29	20	44	3	33	21	00	3	49	20	58
11	3	43	20	17	3	54	20	27	3	45	20	30	3	41	20	37	3	28	20	44	3	32	21	01	3	48	20	59
12	3	43	20	17	3	53	20	27	3	45	20	30	3	40	20	38	3	28	20	45	3	32	21	02	3	48	21	00
13	3	43	20	18	3	53	20	28	3	45	20	31	3	40	20	38	3	27	20	46	3	32	21	03	3	47	21	00
14	3	43	20	19	3	53	20	28	3	45	20	32	3	40	20	39	3	27	20	47	3	31	21	03	3	47	21	01
15	3	43	20	19	3	53	20	29	3	44	20	32	3	40	20	40	3	27	20	47	3	31	21	04	3	47	21	02
16	3	42	20	20	3	53	20	29	3	44	20	33	3	39	20	40	3	27	20	48	3	31	21	05	3	47	21	02
17	3	42	20	20	3	53	20	30	3	44	20	33	3	39	20	40	3	27	20	48	3	31	21	05	3	47	21	03
18	3	42	20	20	3	53	20	30	3	44	20	33	3	39	20	41	3	27	20	49	3	31	21	05	3	47	21	03
19	3	43	20	21	3	53	20	31	3	44	20	34	3	39	20	41	3	27	20	49	3	31	21	06	3	47	21	03
20	3	43	20	21	3	53	20	31	3	44	20	34	3	40	20	41	3	27	20	49	3	31	21	06	3	47	21	04
21	3	43	20	21	3	53	20	31	3	45	20	34	3	40	20	42	3	27	20	49	3	31	21	06	3	47	21	04
22	3	43	20	21	3	53	20	31	3	45	20	34	3	40	20	42	3	27	20	50	3	31	21	07	3	47	21	04
23	3	43	20	22	3	54	20	31	3	45	20	35	3	40	20	42	3	28	20	50	3	32	21	07	3	48	21	04
24	3	44	20	22	3	54	20	31	3	45	20	35	3	41	20	42	3	28	20	50	3	32	21	07	3	48	21	04
25	3	44	20	22	3	54	20	32	3	46	20	35	3	41	20	42	3	28	20	50	3	32	21	07	3	48	21	04
26	3	44	20	22	3	55	20	31	3	46	20	35	3	41	20	42	3	29	20	50	3	33	21	07	3	49	21	04
27	3	45	20	22	3	55	20	31	3	47	20	34	3	42	20	42	3	29	20	49	3	33	21	06	3	49	21	04
28	3	45	20	21	3	56	20	31	3	47	20	34	3	43	20	42	3	30	20	49	3	34	21	06	3	50	21	04
29	3	46	20	21	3	56	20	31	3	48	20	34	3	43	20	41	3	31	20	49	3	35	21	06	3	51	21	03
30	3	47	20	21	3	57	20	31	3	48	20	34	3	44	20	41	3	31	20	49	3	35	21	05	3	51	21	03

JUPITER

Day	RA		Dec.		Transit		5° high			
							52°		56°	
	h	m	°	′	h	m	h	m	h	m
1	14	35.1	−13	51	21	54	2	07	1	50
11	14	31.7	−13	37	21	11	1	26	1	10
21	14	29.3	−13	28	20	30	0	45	0	29
31	14	28.0	−13	25	19	49	0	05	23	45

Diameters – equatorial 42″ polar 40″

SATURN

Day	RA		Dec.		Transit		5° high			
							52°		56°	
	h	m	°	′	h	m	h	m	h	m
1	8	38.7	+19	14	15	59	23	07	23	20
11	8	42.6	+19	00	15	24	22	30	22	43
21	8	46.8	+18	44	14	48	21	53	22	06
31	8	51.4	+18	26	14	14	21	17	21	30

Diameters – equatorial 17″ polar 15″
Rings – major axis 38″ minor axis 12″

URANUS

Day	RA		Dec.		Transit		10° high			
							52°		56°	
	h	m	°	′	h	m	h	m	h	m
1	23	04.4	−6	47	6	26	2	10	2	24
11	23	04.9	−6	44	5	47	1	31	1	45
21	23	05.0-	−6	44	5	08	0	52	1	05
31	23	04.8	−6	46	4	28	0	12	0	26

Diameter 4″

NEPTUNE

Day	RA		Dec.		Transit		10° high			
							52°		56°	
	h	m	°	′	h	m	h	m	h	m
1	21	29.1	−15	04	4	51	1	30	1	56
11	21	28.8	−15	05	4	11	0	50	1	16
21	21	28.3	−15	08	3	32	0	11	0	37
31	21	27.6	−15	11	2	52	23	27	23	54

Diameter 2″

JULY 2006

SEVENTH MONTH, 31 DAYS. *Julius* Caesar, formerly *Quintilis*, fifth month of Roman pre-Julian calendar

1	Saturday	The Wallace-Darwin theory of evolution is presented to the Linnaean Society in London 1858	182
2	Sunday	Richard Axel b. 1946. Thomas Harriot d. 1621	183

3	Monday	Jesse Douglas b. 1897. André Citroën d. 1935	week 27 day 184
4	Tuesday	Gerard Debreu b. 1921. Marie Curie d. 1934	185
5	Wednesday	James Mirrlees b. 1936. Albrecht Kossel d. 1927	186
6	Thursday	Hugo Theorell b. 1903. Regiomontanus d. 1476	187
7	Friday	Work begins on the Boulder Dam (now known as Hoover Dam) on the border of Arizona and Nevada 1930	188
8	Saturday	Igor Tamm b. 1895. Robert Woodward d. 1979	189
9	Sunday	Pyotr Kapitsa b. 1894. Paul Broca d. 1880	190

10	Monday	Owen Chamberlain b. 1920. Frank Schlesinger d. 1943	week 28 day 191
11	Tuesday	Aleksandr Prokhorov b. 1916. Simon Newcomb d. 1909	192
12	Wednesday	William Osler b. 1849. Jean Picard d. 1682	193
13	Thursday	John Dee b. 1527. Gabriel Lippmann d. 1921	194
14	Friday	Mariner 4 spacecraft takes the first close-up photographs of Mars 1965	195
15	Saturday	Bertram Brockhouse b. 1918. Emil Fischer d. 1919	196
16	Sunday	Frits Zernike b. 1888. Ilya Mechnikov d. 1916	197

17	Monday	Georges Lemaître b. 1894. James Lighthill d. 1998	week 29 day 198
18	Tuesday	Roald Hoffmann b. 1937. Henry Farman d. 1958	199
19	Wednesday	Rosalyn Yalow b. 1921. Francis Balfour d. 1882	200
20	Thursday	Gerd Binnig b. 1947. Guglielmo Marconi d. 1937	201
21	Friday	Jean Picard b. 1620. Edward B. Lewis d. 2004	202
22	Saturday	Selman Waksman b. 1888. Giuseppe Piazzi d. 1826	203
23	Sunday	Walter H. Schottky b. 1886. William Ramsay d. 1916	204

24	Monday	Joseph Nicollet b. 1786. James Chadwick d. 1974	week 30 day 205
25	Tuesday	Rosalind Franklin b. 1920. Charles Macintosh d. 1843	206
26	Wednesday	Isaac Babbitt b. 1799. Gottlob Frege d. 1925	207
27	Thursday	Johann Bernoulli b. 1667. Theodor Kocher d. 1917	208
28	Friday	Charles Perrine b. 1867. Allvar Gullstrand d. 1930	209
29	Saturday	Heinz Fraenkel-Conrat b. 1910. Vladimir Zworykin d. 1982	210
30	Sunday	Regnier de Graaf b. 1641. John Milne d. 1913	211

31	Monday	Theobald Smith b. 1859. Hendrik van de Hulst d. 2000	week 31 day 212

ASTRONOMICAL PHENOMENA

d h
4 00 Earth at aphelion (152 million km.)
4 20 Mercury at stationary point
5 23 Jupiter in conjunction with Moon. Jupiter 4° N.
6 07 Jupiter at stationary point
18 07 Mercury in inferior conjunction
22 23 Sun's longitude 120° ♌
23 00 Venus in conjunction with Moon. Venus 6° S.
24 09 Mercury in conjunction with Moon. Mercury 9° S.
26 02 Saturn in conjunction with Moon. Saturn 3° S.
27 18 Mars in conjunction with Moon. Mars 1° S.
29 01 Mercury at stationary point

MINIMA OF ALGOL

d	h	d	h	d	h
2	23.5	14	10.8	25	22.0
5	20.3	17	07.6	28	18.8
8	17.1	20	04.4	31	15.6
11	14.0	23	01.2		

CONSTELLATIONS

The following constellations are near their meridian at

d	h		d	h
June	1	24	July	16	21
June	15	23	August	1	20
July	1	22	August	16	19

Ursa Minor, Draco, Coruna, Hercules, Lyra, Serpens, Ophiuchus, Libra, Scorpius and Sagittarius

THE MOON

Phases, Apsides and Node	d	h	m
☽ First Quarter	3	16	37
○ Full Moon	11	03	02
☾ Last Quarter	17	19	13
● New Moon	25	04	31

Apogee (404,484 km)	1	20	14
Perigee (364,268 km)	13	17	40
Apogee (405,436 km)	29	13	09

Mean longitude of ascending node on July 1, 359°

THE SUN

Day	Right Ascension			Dec. +		Equation of time		Rise 52°		Rise 56°		Transit		Set 52°		Set 56°		Sidereal time			Transit of first point of Aries		
	h	m	s	°	′	m	s	h	m	h	m	h	m	h	m	h	m	h	m	s	h	m	s
1	6	39	23	23	08	−3	45	3	44	3	18	12	04	20	23	20	49	18	35	38	5	23	29
2	6	43	31	23	04	−3	56	3	45	3	19	12	04	20	23	20	49	18	39	35	5	19	33
3	6	47	39	22	59	−4	08	3	46	3	20	12	04	20	22	20	48	18	43	31	5	15	37
4	6	51	47	22	54	−4	19	3	46	3	21	12	04	20	22	20	47	18	47	28	5	11	41
5	6	55	54	22	49	−4	29	3	47	3	22	12	05	20	21	20	47	18	51	24	5	07	45
6	7	00	01	22	43	−4	40	3	48	3	23	12	05	20	21	20	46	18	55	21	5	03	49
7	7	04	07	22	37	−4	50	3	49	3	24	12	05	20	20	20	45	18	59	17	4	59	53
8	7	08	13	22	31	−4	59	3	50	3	25	12	05	20	20	20	44	19	03	14	4	55	57
9	7	12	19	22	24	−5	09	3	51	3	26	12	05	20	19	20	43	19	07	11	4	52	01
10	7	16	24	22	17	−5	17	3	52	3	28	12	05	20	18	20	42	19	11	07	4	48	06
11	7	20	29	22	09	−5	26	3	53	3	29	12	05	20	17	20	41	19	15	04	4	44	10
12	7	24	34	22	01	−5	34	3	54	3	30	12	06	20	16	20	40	19	19	00	4	40	14
13	7	28	38	21	53	−5	41	3	55	3	32	12	06	20	15	20	39	19	22	57	4	36	18
14	7	32	41	21	44	−5	48	3	56	3	33	12	06	20	15	20	38	19	26	53	4	32	22
15	7	36	44	21	35	−5	54	3	58	3	35	12	06	20	14	20	36	19	30	50	4	28	26
16	7	40	47	21	25	−6	00	3	59	3	36	12	06	20	12	20	35	19	34	46	4	24	30
17	7	44	49	21	15	−6	06	4	00	3	38	12	06	20	11	20	34	19	38	43	4	20	34
18	7	48	51	21	05	−6	11	4	01	3	39	12	06	20	10	20	32	19	42	40	4	16	38
19	7	52	52	20	55	−6	15	4	03	3	41	12	06	20	09	20	31	19	46	36	4	12	42
20	7	56	52	20	44	−6	19	4	04	3	42	12	06	20	08	20	29	19	50	33	4	08	46
21	8	00	52	20	32	−6	23	4	05	3	44	12	06	20	07	20	28	19	54	29	4	04	51
22	8	04	52	20	21	−6	26	4	07	3	46	12	06	20	05	20	26	19	58	26	4	00	55
23	8	08	51	20	09	−6	28	4	08	3	47	12	06	20	04	20	24	20	02	22	3	56	59
24	8	12	49	19	56	−6	30	4	10	3	49	12	07	20	03	20	23	20	06	19	3	53	03
25	8	16	47	19	44	−6	31	4	11	3	51	12	07	20	01	20	21	20	10	15	3	49	07
26	8	20	44	19	31	−6	32	4	12	3	53	12	07	20	00	20	19	20	14	12	3	45	11
27	8	24	40	19	17	−6	32	4	14	3	54	12	07	19	58	20	17	20	18	09	3	41	15
28	8	28	36	19	04	−6	31	4	15	3	56	12	07	19	57	20	16	20	22	05	3	37	19
29	8	32	32	18	50	−6	30	4	17	3	58	12	06	19	55	20	14	20	26	02	3	33	23
30	8	36	26	18	36	−6	28	4	18	4	00	12	06	19	54	20	12	20	29	58	3	29	27
31	8	40	20	18	21	−6	26	4	20	4	02	12	06	19	52	20	10	20	33	55	3	25	31

DURATION OF TWILIGHT (in minutes)

Latitude	52°	56°	52°	56°	52°	56°	52°	56°
	1 July		11 July		21 July		31 July	
Civil	48	61	47	58	44	53	42	49
Nautical	124	TAN	117	TAN	107	146	98	123
Astronomical	TAN	TAN	TAN	TAN	TAN	TAN	182	TAN

THE NIGHT SKY

Mercury is more than 15 degrees from the Sun at the beginning of the month and again at the end. In between it passes rapidly through inferior conjunction on the 18th. However its magnitude is so faint at either end of July that it will be impossible to detect Mercury with the naked-eye against the bright twilight background.

Venus is still visible as a brilliant object in the eastern morning skies before sunrise. By about 03h the planet is visible low in the east-north-east. Its magnitude −4.0. Venus passes 4 degrees north of Aldebaran on the 2nd. The waning crescent Moon passes north of the planet on the morning of the 22nd.

Mars is no longer suitably placed for observation and in fact it will not be possible to see Mars again until next year.

Jupiter, magnitude −2.2, is still visible as a brilliant object in the south-western sky in the evenings. On the 6th it reaches its second stationary point and resumes its direct motion. The waxing gibbous Moon is near the planet on the evenings of the 4th and 5th.

Saturn has now been lost in the long evening twilight and will not be seen again until next month.

Twilight. Reference to the section above shows that astronomical twilight lasts all night for a period around the summer solstice (i.e. in June and July), even in southern England. Under these conditions the sky never gets completely dark as the Sun is always less than 18 degrees below the horizon.

THE MOON

Day	R.A. h	R.A. m	Dec. °	Hor. Par. '	Semi-diam. '	Sun's Co-Long. °	PA of Br. Limb °	Ph. %	Age d	Rise 52° h	Rise 52° m	Rise 56° h	Rise 56° m	Transit h	Transit m	Set 52° h	Set 52° m	Set 56° h	Set 56° m
1	10	48	+9.4	54.3	14.8	330	291	26	5.3	9	52	9	45	16	39	23	10	23	13
2	11	30	+3.9	54.2	14.8	343	293	34	6.3	11	02	11	01	17	18	23	18	23	17
3	12	12	−1.7	54.3	14.8	355	293	44	7.3	12	12	12	16	17	57	23	28	23	22
4	12	54	−7.4	54.6	14.9	7	293	53	8.3	13	24	13	33	18	37	23	38	23	27
5	13	38	−12.8	55.0	15.0	19	291	63	9.3	14	39	14	54	19	21	23	51	23	34
6	14	25	−17.9	55.6	15.2	32	287	72	10.3	15	58	16	20	20	08	—	—	23	45
7	15	15	−22.3	56.4	15.4	44	282	80	11.3	17	19	17	49	21	00	0	08	—	—
8	16	10	−25.8	57.1	15.6	56	275	88	12.3	18	39	19	16	21	57	0	34	0	03
9	17	09	−27.9	58.0	15.8	68	266	94	13.3	19	48	20	28	22	58	1	12	0	34
10	18	12	−28.4	58.7	16.0	80	251	98	14.3	20	40	21	16	—	—	2	10	1	30
11	19	16	−27.1	59.4	16.2	93	192	100	15.3	21	16	21	44	0	01	3	27	2	52
12	20	18	−24.0	59.9	16.3	105	96	99	16.3	21	41	22	00	1	02	4	57	4	31
13	21	18	−19.3	60.1	16.4	117	79	95	17.3	21	58	22	11	1	59	6	31	6	13
14	22	14	−13.4	60.2	16.4	129	72	89	18.3	22	12	22	18	2	53	8	04	7	53
15	23	07	−6.8	60.0	16.4	141	68	80	19.3	22	24	22	24	3	44	9	33	9	29
16	23	58	0.0	59.7	16.3	153	66	70	20.3	22	35	22	30	4	32	11	00	11	03
17	0	49	+6.8	59.3	16.2	166	67	59	21.3	22	48	22	37	5	20	12	26	12	35
18	1	40	+13.1	58.8	16.0	178	69	48	22.3	23	03	22	46	6	09	13	53	14	08
19	2	32	+18.7	58.2	15.9	190	73	37	23.3	23	23	22	59	7	00	15	19	15	43
20	3	27	+23.2	57.7	15.7	202	78	27	24.3	23	52	23	20	7	53	16	44	17	15
21	4	24	+26.5	57.1	15.6	215	85	18	25.3	—	—	23	54	8	49	18	00	18	38
22	5	22	+28.2	56.6	15.4	227	93	10	26.3	0	33	—	—	9	46	19	02	19	41
23	6	21	+28.4	56.1	15.3	239	103	5	27.3	1	28	0	49	10	42	19	47	20	22
24	7	18	+27.0	55.6	15.2	251	116	2	28.3	2	37	2	02	11	36	20	19	20	47
25	8	12	+24.4	55.2	15.0	264	166	0	29.3	3	52	3	25	12	26	20	40	21	01
26	9	02	+20.6	54.8	14.9	276	265	1	0.8	5	10	4	49	13	13	20	56	21	11
27	9	50	+16.0	54.5	14.8	288	282	3	1.8	6	25	6	11	13	56	21	07	21	17
28	10	34	+10.9	54.2	14.8	300	289	7	2.8	7	37	7	29	14	36	21	17	21	22
29	11	17	+5.4	54.1	14.7	313	292	13	3.8	8	48	8	45	15	15	21	26	21	26
30	11	59	−0.2	54.1	14.7	325	294	20	4.8	9	58	10	00	15	54	21	35	21	30
31	12	40	−5.8	54.2	14.8	337	294	28	5.8	11	08	11	16	16	33	21	44	21	35

MERCURY

Day	R.A. h	R.A. m	Dec. °	Diam. "	Phase %	Transit h	Transit m	5° high 52° h	5° high 52° m	5° high 56° h	5° high 56° m
1	8	11	+18.5	10	21	13	33	20	36	20	48
3	8	12	+17.9	10	18	13	26	20	25	20	37
5	8	12	+17.4	11	14	13	18	20	14	20	26
7	8	11	+16.9	11	11	13	09	20	02	20	13
9	8	08	+16.6	11	8	12	58	19	50	20	00
11	8	05	+16.3	12	6	12	47	19	37	19	47
13	8	01	+16.1	12	4	12	34	19	24	19	34
15	7	55	+16.1	12	2	12	21	19	10	19	21
17	7	50	+16.1	12	1	12	08	18	57	19	08
19	7	44	+16.2	12	1	11	54	5	04	4	54
21	7	39	+16.5	11	2	11	42	4	50	4	39
23	7	35	+16.8	11	4	11	30	4	36	4	25
25	7	31	+17.2	11	6	11	19	4	23	4	11
27	7	29	+17.6	10	9	11	09	4	11	3	59
29	7	29	+18.0	10	13	11	01	4	00	3	48
31	7	30	+18.4	9	18	10	55	3	51	3	38

VENUS

Day	R.A. h	R.A. m	Dec. °	Diam. "	Phase %	Transit h	Transit m	5° high 52° h	5° high 52° m	5° high 56° h	5° high 56° m
1	4	27	+20.3	12	85	9	52	2	37	2	22
6	4	52	+21.3	12	86	9	58	2	36	2	20
11	5	18	+22.0	12	87	10	03	2	37	2	21
16	5	44	+22.5	11	88	10	10	2	40	2	23
21	6	10	+22.8	11	90	10	16	2	45	2	28
26	6	36	+22.8	11	91	10	22	2	52	2	34
31	7	02	+22.5	11	92	10	29	3	00	2	43

MARS

Day	R.A. h	R.A. m	Dec. °	Diam. "	Phase %	Transit h	Transit m	5° high 52° h	5° high 52° m	5° high 56° h	5° high 56° m
1	9	18	+17.1	4	96	14	41	21	36	21	47
6	9	30	+16.1	4	97	14	33	21	23	21	33
11	9	42	+15.1	4	97	14	26	21	10	21	19
16	9	54	+14.0	4	97	14	18	20	57	21	05
21	10	06	+12.9	4	98	14	10	20	43	20	50
26	10	18	+11.8	4	98	14	02	20	29	20	35
31	10	29	+10.6	4	98	13	55	20	15	20	20

SUNRISE AND SUNSET

	London 0°05' 51°30'		Bristol 2°35' 51°28'		Birmingham 1°55' 52°28'		Manchester 2°15' 53°28'		Newcastle 1°37' 54°49'		Glasgow 4°14' 55°52'		Belfast 5°56' 54°35'	
d	h m	h m	h m	h m	h m	h m	h m	h m	h m	h m	h m	h m	h m	h m
1	3 47	20 21	3 57	20 31	3 49	20 34	3 44	20 41	3 32	20 48	3 36	21 05	3 52	21 03
2	3 48	20 20	3 58	20 30	3 50	20 33	3 45	20 40	3 33	20 48	3 37	21 04	3 53	21 02
3	3 49	20 20	3 59	20 30	3 51	20 33	3 46	20 40	3 34	20 47	3 38	21 04	3 54	21 02
4	3 49	20 20	4 00	20 29	3 51	20 32	3 47	20 39	3 35	20 47	3 39	21 03	3 54	21 01
5	3 50	20 19	4 00	20 29	3 52	20 32	3 48	20 39	3 35	20 46	3 40	21 03	3 55	21 01
6	3 51	20 18	4 01	20 28	3 53	20 31	3 49	20 38	3 36	20 45	3 41	21 02	3 56	21 00
7	3 52	20 18	4 02	20 28	3 54	20 30	3 50	20 38	3 38	20 45	3 42	21 01	3 57	20 59
8	3 53	20 17	4 03	20 27	3 55	20 30	3 51	20 37	3 39	20 44	3 43	21 00	3 59	20 58
9	3 54	20 17	4 04	20 26	3 56	20 29	3 52	20 36	3 40	20 43	3 44	20 59	4 00	20 58
10	3 55	20 16	4 05	20 26	3 57	20 28	3 53	20 35	3 41	20 42	3 46	20 58	4 01	20 57
11	3 56	20 15	4 06	20 25	3 58	20 27	3 54	20 34	3 42	20 41	3 47	20 57	4 02	20 56
12	3 57	20 14	4 07	20 24	3 59	20 27	3 55	20 33	3 43	20 40	3 48	20 56	4 03	20 55
13	3 58	20 13	4 08	20 23	4 01	20 26	3 56	20 32	3 45	20 39	3 49	20 55	4 05	20 54
14	3 59	20 12	4 09	20 22	4 02	20 25	3 58	20 31	3 46	20 38	3 51	20 54	4 06	20 52
15	4 00	20 11	4 11	20 21	4 03	20 24	3 59	20 30	3 47	20 36	3 52	20 52	4 07	20 51
16	4 02	20 10	4 12	20 20	4 04	20 22	4 00	20 29	3 49	20 35	3 54	20 51	4 09	20 50
17	4 03	20 09	4 13	20 19	4 05	20 21	4 01	20 28	3 50	20 34	3 55	20 50	4 10	20 49
18	4 04	20 08	4 14	20 18	4 07	20 20	4 03	20 27	3 52	20 33	3 57	20 48	4 11	20 48
19	4 05	20 07	4 16	20 17	4 08	20 19	4 04	20 25	3 53	20 31	3 58	20 47	4 13	20 46
20	4 07	20 06	4 17	20 16	4 09	20 18	4 06	20 24	3 55	20 30	4 00	20 45	4 14	20 45
21	4 08	20 05	4 18	20 14	4 11	20 16	4 07	20 23	3 56	20 28	4 02	20 44	4 16	20 43
22	4 09	20 03	4 19	20 13	4 12	20 15	4 09	20 21	3 58	20 27	4 03	20 42	4 17	20 42
23	4 11	20 02	4 21	20 12	4 14	20 14	4 10	20 20	4 00	20 25	4 05	20 41	4 19	20 40
24	4 12	20 01	4 22	20 11	4 15	20 12	4 12	20 18	4 01	20 24	4 07	20 39	4 21	20 39
25	4 13	19 59	4 24	20 09	4 17	20 11	4 13	20 17	4 03	20 22	4 08	20 37	4 22	20 37
26	4 15	19 58	4 25	20 08	4 18	20 09	4 15	20 15	4 05	20 20	4 10	20 35	4 24	20 36
27	4 16	19 56	4 26	20 06	4 19	20 08	4 16	20 14	4 06	20 19	4 12	20 34	4 26	20 34
28	4 18	19 55	4 28	20 05	4 21	20 06	4 18	20 12	4 08	20 17	4 14	20 32	4 27	20 32
29	4 19	19 53	4 29	20 03	4 23	20 05	4 19	20 10	4 10	20 15	4 16	20 30	4 29	20 30
30	4 21	19 52	4 31	20 02	4 24	20 03	4 21	20 09	4 11	20 13	4 17	20 28	4 31	20 29
31	4 22	19 50	4 32	20 00	4 26	20 01	4 23	20 07	4 13	20 11	4 19	20 26	4 32	20 27

JUPITER

Day	R.A.		Dec.		Transit		5° high			
									52°	56°
	h	m	°	'	h	m	h m		h m	h m
1	14	28.0	−13	25	19	49	0 05		23 45	
11	14	27.9	−13	27	19	10	23 22		23 05	
21	14	29.0	−13	35	18	32	22 43		22 26	
31	14	31.2	−13	48	17	55	22 04		21 47	

Diameters − equatorial 39″ polar 37″

SATURN

Day	R.A.		Dec.		Transit		5° high			
									52°	56°
	h	m	°	'	h	m	h m		h m	h m
1	8	51.4	+18	26	14	14	21 17		21 30	
11	8	56.3	+18	07	13	39	20 41		20 53	
21	9	01.3	+17	47	13	05	20 04		20 16	
31	9	06.4	+17	25	12	31	19 28		19 40	

Diameters − equatorial 16″ polar 15″
Rings − major axis 37″ minor axis 11″

URANUS

Day	R.A.		Dec.		Transit		10° high			
									52°	56°
	h	m	°	'	h	m	h m		h m	h m
1	23	04.8	−6	46	4	28	0 12		0 26	
11	23	04.3	−6	49	3	49	23 29		23 43	
21	23	03.6	−6	54	3	09	22 49		23 03	
31	23	02.6	−7	01	2	28	22 10		22 24	

Diameter 4″

NEPTUNE

Day	R.A.		Dec.		Transit		5° high			
									52°	56°
	h	m	°	'	h	m	h m		h m	h m
1	21	27.6	−15	11	2	52	23 27		23 54	
11	21	26.8	−15	15	2	11	22 48		23 14	
21	21	25.9	−15	20	1	31	22 08		22 35	
31	21	24.9	−15	25	0	51	21 28		21 55	

Diameter 2″

AUGUST 2006

EIGHTH MONTH, 31 DAYS. *Augustus*, formerly *Sextilis*, sixth month of Roman pre-Julian calendar

1	Tuesday	George de Hevesy b. 1885. Tadeus Reichstein d. 1996	week 31 day 213
2	Wednesday	Leopold Gmelin b. 1788. Louis Blériot d. 1936	214
3	Thursday	Koichi Tanaka b. 1959. Emile Berliner d. 1929	215
4	Friday	William Rowan Hamilton b. 1805. Walther Flemming d. 1905	216
5	Saturday	Wassily Leontief b. 1906. Heinrich Wieland d. 1957	217
6	Sunday	The first of only two atomic bombs ever to be used in warfare is dropped on Hiroshima, Japan 1945	218

7	Monday	Carl Ritter b. 1779. Jöns Jacob Berzelius d. 1848	week 32 day 219
8	Tuesday	Roger Penrose b. 1931. Edgar Douglas Adrian d. 1977	220
9	Wednesday	Thomas Telford b. 1757. John Fields d. 1932	221
10	Thursday	Arne Tiselius b. 1902. Robert Goddard d. 1945	222
11	Friday	James Herrick b. 1861. Macedonio Melloni d. 1854	223
12	Saturday	Otto Struve b. 1897. George Stephenson d. 1848	224
13	Sunday	Anders Angstrom b. 1814. Florence Nightingale d. 1910	225

14	Monday	Ernest Just b. 1883. Paul Sabatier d. 1941	week 33 day 226
15	Tuesday	Leslie Comrie b. 1893. Sune Bergstrom d. 2004	227
16	Wednesday	Wendell Stanley b. 1904. Jean-Martin Charcot d. 1893	228
17	Thursday	In London, Bridget Driscoll becomes the first person to be killed in a car accident when she is hit at 4 mph 1896	229
18	Friday	Brook Taylor b. 1685. Richard Synge d. 1994	230
19	Saturday	Philo Farnsworth b. 1906. Linus Pauling d. 1994	231
20	Sunday	Roger Sperry b. 1913. Fred Hoyle d. 2001	232

21	Monday	Charles Frédéric Gerhardt b. 1816. Harald Sverdrup d. 1957	week 34 day 233
22	Tuesday	Charles Jenkins b. 1867. Paul Ewald d. 1985	234
23	Wednesday	Sarah Whiting b. 1847. Charles-Augustin de Coulomb d. 1806	235
24	Thursday	Albert Claude b. 1899. Rudolf Clausius d. 1888	236
25	Friday	Hans Krebs b. 1900. Henri Becquerel d. 1908	237
26	Saturday	Albert Sabin b. 1906. Frederick Reines d. 1998	238
27	Sunday	The first flight of a jet aircraft (Heinkel He 178) takes place in Germany 1939	239

28	Monday	George Whipple b. 1878. Giulio Racah d. 1965	week 35 day 240
29	Tuesday	Charles Kettering b. 1876. Christian Schönbein d. 1868	241
30	Wednesday	Ernest Rutherford b. 1871. Wilhelm Wien d. 1928	242
31	Thursday	H. David Politzer b. 1949. Frank Macfarlane Burnet b. 1985.	243

ASTRONOMICAL PHENOMENA

d	h	
2	09	Jupiter in conjunction with Moon. Jupiter 5° N.
7	00	Mercury at greatest elongation W.19°
7	12	Saturn in conjunction
11	05	Neptune at opposition
21	01	Saturn in conjunction with Mercury. Saturn 0°.5 S.
22	05	Venus in conjunction with Moon. Venus 3° S.
22	16	Saturn in conjunction with Moon. Saturn 2° S.
22	23	Mercury in conjunction with Moon. Mercury 2° S.
23	06	Sun's longitude 150° ♍
25	13	Mars in conjunction with Moon. Mars 0°.5 N.
27	00	Saturn in conjunction with Venus. Saturn 0°.01 S.
29	22	Jupiter in conjunction with Moon. Jupiter 5°N.

MINIMA OF ALGOL

d	h	d	h	d	h
3	12.4	14	23.7	26	10.9
6	09.2	17	20.5	29	07.7
9	06.1	20	17.3		
12	02.9	23	14.1		

CONSTELLATIONS

The following constellations are near their meridian at

	d	h		d	h
July	1	24	August	16	21
July	16	23	September	1	20
August	1	22	September	15	19

Draco, Hercules, Lyra, Cygnus, Sagitta, Ophiuchus, Serpens, Aquila and Sagittarius

THE MOON

Phases, Apsides and Node		d	h	m
☽	First Quarter	2	08	46
○	Full Moon	9	10	54
☾	Last Quarter	16	01	51
●	New Moon	23	19	10
☽	First Quarter	31	22	56

Perigee (359,737 km)	10	18	33
Apogee (406,286 km)	26	01	34

Mean longitude of ascending node on August 1, 358°

THE SUN

s.d. 15′.8

Day	Right Ascension			Dec. +		Equation of time		Rise 52°		Rise 56°		Transit		Set 52°		Set 56°		Sidereal time			Transit of first point of Aries		
	h	m	s	°	′	m	s	h	m	h	m	h	m	h	m	h	m	h	m	s	h	m	s
1	8	44	14	18	06	−6	23	4	21	4	03	12	06	19	50	20	08	20	37	51	3	21	35
2	8	48	07	17	51	−6	19	4	23	4	05	12	06	19	49	20	06	20	41	48	3	17	40
3	8	51	59	17	36	−6	14	4	24	4	07	12	06	19	47	20	04	20	45	45	3	13	44
4	8	55	51	17	20	−6	10	4	26	4	09	12	06	19	45	20	02	20	49	41	3	09	48
5	8	59	42	17	04	−6	04	4	28	4	11	12	06	19	43	20	00	20	53	38	3	05	52
6	9	03	32	16	48	−5	58	4	29	4	13	12	06	19	42	19	58	20	57	34	3	01	56
7	9	07	22	16	31	−5	51	4	31	4	15	12	06	19	40	19	55	21	01	31	2	58	00
8	9	11	11	16	14	−5	44	4	32	4	17	12	06	19	38	19	53	21	05	27	2	54	04
9	9	14	59	15	57	−5	36	4	34	4	19	12	06	19	36	19	51	21	09	24	2	50	08
10	9	18	47	15	40	−5	27	4	36	4	21	12	05	19	34	19	49	21	13	20	2	46	12
11	9	22	35	15	22	−5	18	4	37	4	23	12	05	19	32	19	46	21	17	17	2	42	16
12	9	26	22	15	05	−5	08	4	39	4	25	12	05	19	30	19	44	21	21	14	2	38	20
13	9	30	08	14	47	−4	58	4	40	4	27	12	05	19	28	19	42	21	25	10	2	34	25
14	9	33	54	14	28	−4	47	4	42	4	28	12	05	19	26	19	40	21	29	07	2	30	29
15	9	37	39	14	10	−4	36	4	44	4	30	12	05	19	24	19	37	21	33	03	2	26	33
16	9	41	24	13	51	−4	24	4	45	4	32	12	04	19	22	19	35	21	37	00	2	22	37
17	9	45	08	13	32	−4	11	4	47	4	34	12	04	19	20	19	32	21	40	56	2	18	41
18	9	48	51	13	13	−3	59	4	48	4	36	12	04	19	18	19	30	21	44	53	2	14	45
19	9	52	35	12	53	−3	45	4	50	4	38	12	04	19	16	19	28	21	48	49	2	10	49
20	9	56	17	12	34	−3	31	4	52	4	40	12	03	19	14	19	25	21	52	46	2	06	53
21	10	00	00	12	14	−3	17	4	53	4	42	12	03	19	12	19	23	21	56	43	2	02	57
22	10	03	41	11	54	−3	02	4	55	4	44	12	03	19	10	19	20	22	00	39	1	59	01
23	10	07	23	11	34	−2	47	4	57	4	46	12	03	19	08	19	18	22	04	36	1	55	05
24	10	11	04	11	13	−2	32	4	58	4	48	12	02	19	05	19	15	22	08	32	1	51	10
25	10	14	44	10	53	−2	15	5	00	4	50	12	02	19	03	19	13	22	12	29	1	47	14
26	10	18	24	10	32	−1	59	5	02	4	52	12	02	19	01	19	10	22	16	25	1	43	18
27	10	22	04	10	11	−1	42	5	03	4	54	12	02	18	59	19	08	22	20	22	1	39	22
28	10	25	43	9	50	−1	25	5	05	4	56	12	01	18	57	19	05	22	24	18	1	35	26
29	10	29	22	9	29	−1	07	5	06	4	58	12	01	18	54	19	03	22	28	15	1	31	30
30	10	33	01	9	08	−0	49	5	08	5	00	12	01	18	52	19	00	22	32	12	1	27	34
31	10	36	39	8	46	−0	31	5	10	5	02	12	00	18	50	18	58	22	36	08	1	23	38

DURATION OF TWILIGHT (in minutes)

Latitude	52°	56°	52°	56°	52°	56°	52	56°
	1 August		11 August		21 August		31 August	
Civil	41	49	39	45	37	42	35	40
Nautical	97	121	90	107	84	97	79	90
Astronomical	179	TAN	154	210	139	168	128	148

THE NIGHT SKY

Mercury, after the first few days of the month, becomes a morning object and remains visible as such for about a fortnight. It may be detected low above the east-north-east horizon around the time of beginning of morning civil twilight. During this period its magnitude brightens from +0.8 to −1.2. It will be noticed that Mercury is at its brightest after it reaches greatest western elongation (19 degrees) on the 7th.

Venus, magnitude −3.9, is still visible as a splendid morning object above the east-north-east horizon well before dawn. However it is no longer rising as early as it did in July. By the end of the month it will not be visible until well after 04h. The waning crescent Moon passes 2 degrees north of the planet on the 22nd.

Mars remains unsuitably placed for observation.

Jupiter, magnitude −2.0, is still a brilliant object in the south-western skies in the evenings. The Moon, near First Quarter, passes 5 degrees south of the planet on the evening of the 1st, and again on the 29th.

Saturn passes through conjunction on the 7th and therefore is not available for observation at first. However it is just possible that, under very good conditions, keen-sighted observers could detect the planet as a morning object, on the last few days of the month, low above the east-north-east horizon, before the sky gets too bright at sunrise. If Venus can be seen on the morning of the 27th then, with only slight optical aid, Saturn, which will be only 0.2 degrees to the right of Venus, may be located. Saturn's magnitude is +0.3. Saturn passes from Cancer into Leo at the very end of the month.

Neptune is at opposition on the 11th, in the constellation of Capricornus. It is not visible to the naked-eye since its magnitude is +7.8.

Meteors. The maximum of the famous Perseid meteor shower occurs on the evening of the 12th and will be best seen from the late evening onwards, though there will be severe interference from moonlight.

THE MOON

Day	R.A. h	R.A. m	Dec. °	Hor. Par. '	Semi-diam. '	Suns Co-Long. °	PA of Br. Limb °	Ph. %	Age d	Rise 52° h	Rise 52° m	Rise 56° h	Rise 56° m	Transit h	Transit m	Set 52° h	Set 52° m	Set 56° h	Set 56° m
1	13	23	−11.3	54.5	14.9	349	292	37	6.8	12	21	12	34	17	15	21	56	21	41
2	14	08	−16.4	55.0	15.0	2	290	47	7.8	13	37	13	57	17	59	22	11	21	50
3	14	56	−21.0	55.6	15.2	14	286	56	8.8	14	56	15	23	18	48	22	32	22	04
4	15	49	−24.8	56.4	15.4	26	281	66	9.8	16	16	16	51	19	42	23	03	22	27
5	16	45	−27.4	57.2	15.6	38	274	76	10.8	17	30	18	10	20	40	23	50	23	10
6	17	46	−28.6	58.2	15.8	50	266	84	11.8	18	30	19	09	21	42	—	—	—	—
7	18	49	−28.0	59.1	16.1	63	258	92	12.8	19	13	19	45	22	44	0	58	0	19
8	19	52	−25.5	59.9	16.3	75	247	97	13.8	19	42	20	05	23	44	2	24	1	52
9	20	54	−21.3	60.5	16.5	87	224	100	14.8	20	02	20	18	—	—	3	58	3	36
10	21	52	−15.7	60.9	16.6	99	89	100	15.8	20	17	20	26	0	41	5	34	5	20
11	22	48	−9.2	60.9	16.6	111	71	96	16.8	20	30	20	33	1	34	7	07	7	01
12	23	41	−2.1	60.7	16.5	123	67	91	17.8	20	42	20	39	2	25	8	38	8	39
13	0	33	+4.9	60.3	16.4	136	66	83	18.8	20	54	20	45	3	15	10	08	10	15
14	1	25	+11.6	59.7	16.3	148	67	73	19.8	21	09	20	53	4	05	11	37	11	51
15	2	19	+17.6	58.9	16.1	160	70	62	20.8	21	28	21	05	4	56	13	06	13	27
16	3	14	+22.5	58.2	15.8	172	75	51	21.8	21	53	21	23	5	49	14	32	15	02
17	4	11	+26.0	57.4	15.6	185	80	40	22.8	22	30	21	53	6	45	15	52	16	29
18	5	09	+28.1	56.7	15.5	197	87	30	23.8	23	21	22	41	7	41	16	59	17	39
19	6	07	+28.6	56.1	15.3	209	94	21	24.8	—	—	23	49	8	38	17	48	18	26
20	7	04	+27.6	55.6	15.1	221	102	13	25.8	0	26	—	—	9	32	18	23	18	54
21	7	58	+25.2	55.1	15.0	233	109	7	26.8	1	39	1	09	10	23	18	46	19	10
22	8	50	+21.7	54.7	14.9	246	116	3	27.8	2	56	2	34	11	10	19	03	19	21
23	9	37	+17.3	54.4	14.8	258	127	1	28.8	4	12	3	56	11	53	19	16	19	28
24	10	22	+12.3	54.2	14.8	270	249	0	0.2	5	25	5	15	12	34	19	26	19	33
25	11	05	+6.9	54.0	14.7	282	289	1	1.2	6	36	6	32	13	14	19	35	19	37
26	11	47	+1.3	54.0	14.7	295	294	4	2.2	7	46	7	47	13	52	19	44	19	41
27	12	29	−4.4	54.0	14.7	307	295	9	3.2	8	56	9	02	14	31	19	53	19	45
28	13	11	−9.9	54.2	14.8	319	294	15	4.2	10	08	10	19	15	12	20	03	19	50
29	13	55	−15.1	54.5	14.8	331	293	23	5.2	11	22	11	39	15	55	20	16	19	57
30	14	41	−19.8	54.9	15.0	344	289	31	6.2	12	39	13	03	16	41	20	34	20	08
31	15	31	−23.8	55.5	15.1	356	285	41	7.2	13	57	14	29	17	32	20	59	20	27

MERCURY

Day	R.A. h	R.A. m	Dec. °	Diam. "	Phase %	Transit h	Transit m	5° high 52° h	5° high 52° m	5° high 56° h	5° high 56° m
1	7	31	+18.6	9	21	10	52	3	47	3	34
3	7	35	+19.0	8	26	10	48	3	41	3	28
5	7	40	+19.3	8	33	10	46	3	37	3	23
7	7	48	+19.6	8	40	10	46	3	35	3	21
9	7	57	+19.7	7	47	10	48	3	36	3	22
11	8	07	+19.7	7	55	10	51	3	39	3	25
13	8	19	+19.5	6	62	10	55	3	44	3	30
15	8	33	+19.2	6	70	11	01	3	52	3	38
17	8	47	+18.7	6	77	11	08	4	01	3	48
19	9	02	+18.0	6	83	11	15	4	12	4	00
21	9	18	+17.1	5	88	11	23	4	25	4	14
23	9	33	+16.1	5	93	11	31	4	39	4	28
25	9	49	+15.0	5	96	11	38	4	53	4	44
27	10	05	+13.7	5	98	11	46	5	08	5	00
29	10	20	+12.3	5	99	11	53	5	23	5	16
31	10	35	+10.8	5	100	12	00	18	21	18	27

VENUS

Day	R.A. h	R.A. m	Dec. °	Diam. "	Phase %	Transit h	Transit m	5° high 52° h	5° high 52° m	5° high 56° h	5° high 56° m
1	7	08	+22.4	11	92	10	30	3	02	2	45
6	7	34	+21.8	11	93	10	37	3	12	2	56
11	8	00	+20.9	11	94	10	43	3	24	3	08
16	8	25	+19.8	10	94	10	49	3	36	3	22
21	8	50	+18.4	10	95	10	54	3	50	3	37
26	9	15	+16.8	10	96	10	59	4	04	3	53
31	9	40	+15.1	10	97	11	04	4	19	4	09

MARS

Day	R.A. h	R.A. m	Dec. °	Diam. "	Phase %	Transit h	Transit m	5° high 52° h	5° high 52° m	5° high 56° h	5° high 56° m
1	10	32	+10.4	4	98	13	53	20	12	20	17
6	10	43	+9.2	4	98	13	45	19	58	20	02
11	10	55	+7.9	4	98	13	37	19	44	19	47
16	11	07	+6.7	4	99	13	29	19	29	19	31
21	11	19	+5.4	4	99	13	21	19	15	19	16
26	11	30	+4.1	4	99	13	13	19	00	19	00
31	11	42	+2.8	4	99	13	05	18	46	18	45

SUNRISE AND SUNSET

	London				Bristol				Birmingham				Manchester				Newcastle				Glasgow				Belfast			
	0°05'		51°30'		2°35'		51°28'		1°55'		52°28'		2°15'		53°28'		1°37'		54°59'		4°14'		55°52'		5°56'		54°35'	
d	h	m	h	m	h	m	h	m	h	m	h	m	h	m	h	m	h	m	h	m	h	m	h	m	h	m	h	m
1	4	24	19	49	4	34	19	59	4	27	20	00	4	24	20	05	4	15	20	09	4	21	20	24	4	34	20	25
2	4	25	19	47	4	35	19	57	4	29	19	58	4	26	20	03	4	17	20	08	4	23	20	22	4	36	20	23
3	4	27	19	45	4	37	19	55	4	30	19	56	4	28	20	02	4	18	20	06	4	25	20	20	4	38	20	21
4	4	28	19	44	4	38	19	53	4	32	19	55	4	29	20	00	4	20	20	04	4	27	20	18	4	39	20	19
5	4	30	19	42	4	40	19	52	4	34	19	53	4	31	19	58	4	22	20	02	4	29	20	16	4	41	20	17
6	4	31	19	40	4	41	19	50	4	35	19	51	4	33	19	56	4	24	20	00	4	31	20	14	4	43	20	15
7	4	33	19	38	4	43	19	48	4	37	19	49	4	34	19	54	4	26	19	57	4	32	20	12	4	45	20	13
8	4	34	19	37	4	45	19	46	4	38	19	47	4	36	19	52	4	28	19	55	4	34	20	10	4	46	20	11
9	4	36	19	35	4	46	19	45	4	40	19	45	4	38	19	50	4	29	19	53	4	36	20	07	4	48	20	09
10	4	38	19	33	4	48	19	43	4	42	19	43	4	39	19	48	4	31	19	51	4	38	20	05	4	50	20	07
11	4	39	19	31	4	49	19	41	4	43	19	41	4	41	19	46	4	33	19	49	4	40	20	03	4	52	20	05
12	4	41	19	29	4	51	19	39	4	45	19	39	4	43	19	44	4	35	19	47	4	42	20	01	4	54	20	03
13	4	42	19	27	4	52	19	37	4	47	19	37	4	45	19	42	4	37	19	45	4	44	19	58	4	56	20	00
14	4	44	19	25	4	54	19	35	4	48	19	35	4	46	19	40	4	39	19	42	4	46	19	56	4	57	19	58
15	4	45	19	23	4	56	19	33	4	50	19	33	4	48	19	38	4	41	19	40	4	48	19	54	4	59	19	56
16	4	47	19	21	4	57	19	31	4	52	19	31	4	50	19	36	4	42	19	38	4	50	19	51	5	01	19	54
17	4	49	19	19	4	59	19	29	4	53	19	29	4	52	19	33	4	44	19	36	4	52	19	49	5	03	19	52
18	4	50	19	17	5	00	19	27	4	55	19	27	4	53	19	31	4	46	19	33	4	54	19	47	5	05	19	49
19	4	52	19	15	5	02	19	25	4	57	19	25	4	55	19	29	4	48	19	31	4	56	19	44	5	07	19	47
20	4	53	19	13	5	03	19	23	4	58	19	23	4	57	19	27	4	50	19	29	4	58	19	42	5	08	19	45
21	4	55	19	11	5	05	19	21	5	00	19	21	4	59	19	25	4	52	19	26	5	00	19	39	5	10	19	42
22	4	57	19	09	5	07	19	19	5	02	19	18	5	00	19	22	4	54	19	24	5	02	19	37	5	12	19	40
23	4	58	19	07	5	08	19	17	5	03	19	16	5	02	19	20	4	55	19	21	5	03	19	34	5	14	19	38
24	5	00	19	05	5	10	19	15	5	05	19	14	5	04	19	18	4	57	19	19	5	05	19	32	5	16	19	35
25	5	01	19	02	5	11	19	12	5	07	19	12	5	06	19	15	4	59	19	17	5	07	19	29	5	18	19	33
26	5	03	19	00	5	13	19	10	5	08	19	10	5	07	19	13	5	01	19	14	5	09	19	27	5	19	19	30
27	5	05	18	58	5	15	19	08	5	10	19	07	5	09	19	11	5	03	19	12	5	11	19	24	5	21	19	28
28	5	06	18	56	5	16	19	06	5	12	19	05	5	11	19	09	5	05	19	09	5	13	19	22	5	23	19	26
29	5	08	18	54	5	18	19	04	5	13	19	03	5	13	19	06	5	07	19	07	5	15	19	19	5	25	19	23
30	5	09	18	52	5	19	19	01	5	15	19	01	5	14	19	04	5	09	19	04	5	17	19	17	5	27	19	21
31	5	11	18	49	5	21	18	59	5	17	18	58	5	16	19	02	5	10	19	02	5	19	19	14	5	29	19	18

JUPITER

Day	R.A.		Dec.		Transit		5° high			
							52°		56°	
	h	m	°	'	h	m	h	m	h	m
1	14	31.5	−13	50	17	51	22	00	21	43
11	14	34.8	−14	09	17	15	21	22	21	05
21	14	39.1	−14	31	16	40	20	45	20	27
31	14	44.3	−14	57	16	06	20	08	19	50

Diameters – equatorial 36″ polar 33″

SATURN

Day	R.A.		Dec.		Transit		5° high			
							52°		56°	
	h	m	°	'	h	m	h	m	h	m
1	9	06.9	+17	23	12	27	5	30	5	18
11	9	12.1	+17	02	11	53	4	58	4	46
21	9	17.2	+16	40	11	19	4	25	4	15
31	9	22.2	+16	18	10	45	3	53	3	43

Diameters – equatorial 16″ polar 15″
Rings – major axis 37″ minor axis 10″

URANUS

Day	R.A.		Dec.		Transit		5° high			
							52°		56°	
	h	m	°	'	h	m	h	m	h	m
1	23	02.5	−7	01	2	24	22	06	22	20
11	23	01.3	−7	09	1	44	21	26	21	40
21	22	59.9	−7	18	1	03	20	46	21	00
31	22	58.5	−7	27	0	22	20	06	20	21

Diameter 4″

NEPTUNE

Day	R.A.		Dec.		Transit		5° high			
							52°		56°	
	h	m	°	'	h	m	h	m	h	m
1	21	24.8	−15	25	0	47	4	05	3	38
11	21	23.7	−15	30	0	06	3	24	2	57
21	21	22.6	−15	35	23	22	2	43	2	16
31	21	21.6	−15	40	22	42	2	02	1	35

Diameter 2″

SEPTEMBER 2006

NINTH MONTH, 30 DAYS. *Septem* (seven), seventh month of Roman pre-Julian calendar

1	*Friday*	Francis Aston b. 1877. Luis Alvarez d. 1988	244
2	*Saturday*	Frederick Soddy b. 1877. Barbara McClintock d. 1992	245
3	*Sunday*	Carl Anderson b. 1905. Martin Heinrich Rathke d. 1860	246

4	*Monday*	Stanford Moore b. 1913. Albert Schweitzer d. 1965	week 36 day 247
5	*Tuesday*	Eugen Goldstein b. 1850. Johann Georg Hagen d. 1930	248
6	*Wednesday*	Susumu Tonegawa b. 1939. Frederick Abel d. 1902	249
7	*Thursday*	John Cornforth b. 1917. Edwin McMillan d. 1991	250
8	*Friday*	Derek Barton b. 1918. Peter Pallas d. 1811	251
9	*Saturday*	Luigi Galvani b. 1737. Paul Flory d. 1985	252
10	*Sunday*	Stephen Jay Gould b. 1941. Felix Bloch d. 1983	253

11	*Monday*	Carl Zeiss b. 1816. Norman Bowen d. 1956	week 37 day 254
12	*Tuesday*	Four teenagers discover paleolithic artwork on the walls of caves at Lascaux in south-west France 1940	255
13	*Wednesday*	Andrew Noble b. 1831. August Krogh d. 1949	256
14	*Thursday*	The Soviet Union's Luna 2 becomes the first spacecraft to land on the Moon 1959	257
15	*Friday*	Murray Gell-Mann b. 1929. Alfred Blalock d. 1964	258
16	*Saturday*	Nicolas Desmarest b. 1725. Gabriel Fahrenheit d. 1736	259
17	*Sunday*	Marquis de Condorcet b. 1743. Antoine-Laurent de Jussieu d. 1836	260

18	*Monday*	Siegfried Marcus b. 1831. Hippolyte Fizeau d. 1896	week 38 day 261
19	*Tuesday*	James Alexander b. 1888. Ole Romer d. 1710	262
20	*Wednesday*	James Dewar b. 1842. Paul Erdos d. 1996	263
21	*Thursday*	Charles Nicolle b. 1866. Robert L. Forward d. 2002	264
22	*Friday*	Michael Faraday b. 1791. Vincenzo Viviani d. 1703	265
23	*Saturday*	Robert Bosch b. 1861. Jean Chacornac d. 1873	266
24	*Sunday*	Severo Ochoa b. 1905. Hans Geiger d. 1945	267

25	*Monday*	Thomas Morgan b. 1866. Nikolay Semyonov d. 1986	week 39 day 268
26	*Tuesday*	Barnes Wallis b. 1887. August Möbius d. 1868	269
27	*Wednesday*	SMART-1, the European Space Agency's first mission to the Moon, is launched from French Guiana 2003	270
28	*Thursday*	Seymour Cray b. 1925. John Chapman d. 1979	271
29	*Friday*	Enrico Fermi b. 1901. Rudolf Diesel d. 1913	272
30	*Saturday*	Johann Deisenhofer b. 1943. André Lwoff d. 1994	273

ASTRONOMICAL PHENOMENA

d h

1 05 Mercury in superior conjunction
4 23 Pluto at stationary point
5 11 Uranus at opposition
7 19 Partial eclipse of Moon (*see* page 1278)
15 19 Mars in conjunction with Mercury. Mars 0°.1 N.
19 04 Saturn in conjunction with Moon. Saturn 2°S.
21 15 Venus in conjunction with Moon. Venus 0°.8 N.
22 12 Annular eclipse of Sun (*see* page 1278)
23 04 Sun's longitude 180° ♎
23 09 Mars in conjunction with Moon. Mars 2°N.
24 02 Mercury in conjunction with Moon. Mercury 2°N.
26 13 Jupiter in conjunction with Moon. Jupiter 5°N.

MINIMA OF ALGOL

d	h	d	h	d	h
1	04.5	12	15.8	24	03.0
4	01.3	15	12.6	26	23.8
6	22.2	18	09.4	29	20.6
9	19.0	21	06.2		

CONSTELLATIONS

The following constellations are near their meridian at

	d	h		d	h
August	1	24	September	15	21
August	16	23	October	1	20
September	1	22	October	16	19

Draco, Cepheus, Lyra, Cygnus, Vulpecula, Sagitta, Delphinus, Equuleus, Aquila, Aquarius and Capricornus

THE MOON

Phases, Apsides and Node	d	h	m
○ Full Moon	7	18	42
☾ Last Quarter	14	11	15
● New Moon	22	11	45
☽ First Quarter	30	11	04

Perigee (357,173km)	8	03	10
Apogee (406,497km)	22	05	37

Mean longitude of ascending node on September 1, 356°

THE SUN

s.d. 15'.9

Day	Right Ascension			Dec.		Equation of time		Rise 52°		Rise 56°		Transit		Set 52°		Set 56°		Sidereal time			Transit of first point of Aries		
	h	m	s	°	'	m	s	h	m	h	m	h	m	h	m	h	m	h	m	s	h	m	s
1	10	40	17	+8	24	−0	12	5	11	5	04	12	00	18	48	18	55	22	40	05	1	19	42
2	10	43	54	+8	03	+0	07	5	13	5	06	12	00	18	45	18	52	22	44	01	1	15	46
3	10	47	31	+7	41	+0	26	5	15	5	08	11	59	18	43	18	50	22	47	58	1	11	50
4	10	51	08	+7	19	+0	46	5	16	5	10	11	59	18	41	18	47	22	51	54	1	07	55
5	10	54	45	+6	57	+1	06	5	18	5	12	11	59	18	39	18	45	22	55	51	1	03	59
6	10	58	21	+6	34	+1	26	5	19	5	14	11	58	18	36	18	42	22	59	47	1	00	03
7	11	01	57	+6	12	+1	47	5	21	5	15	11	58	18	34	18	39	23	03	44	0	56	07
8	11	05	33	+5	50	+2	07	5	23	5	17	11	58	18	32	18	37	23	07	41	0	52	11
9	11	09	09	+5	27	+2	28	5	24	5	19	11	57	18	29	18	34	23	11	37	0	48	15
10	11	12	45	+5	04	+2	49	5	26	5	21	11	57	18	27	18	31	23	15	34	0	44	19
11	11	16	20	+4	42	+3	10	5	28	5	23	11	57	18	25	18	29	23	19	30	0	40	23
12	11	19	56	+4	19	+3	31	5	29	5	25	11	56	18	22	18	26	23	23	27	0	36	27
13	11	23	31	+3	56	+3	52	5	31	5	27	11	56	18	20	18	24	23	27	23	0	32	31
14	11	27	06	+3	33	+4	14	5	32	5	29	11	56	18	18	18	21	23	31	20	0	28	35
15	11	30	41	+3	10	+4	35	5	34	5	31	11	55	18	15	18	18	23	35	16	0	24	40
16	11	34	17	+2	47	+4	56	5	36	5	33	11	55	18	13	18	16	23	39	13	0	20	44
17	11	37	52	+2	24	+5	18	5	37	5	35	11	55	18	11	18	13	23	43	09	0	16	48
18	11	41	27	+2	00	+5	39	5	39	5	37	11	54	18	08	18	10	23	47	06	0	12	52
19	11	45	02	+1	37	+6	00	5	41	5	39	11	54	18	06	18	08	23	51	03	0	08	56
20	11	48	37	+1	14	+6	22	5	42	5	41	11	53	18	04	18	05	23	54	59	0	05	00
21	11	52	13	+0	51	+6	43	5	44	5	43	11	53	18	01	18	02	23	58	56	0 / 23	01 / 57	04 / 08
22	11	55	48	+0	27	+7	04	5	46	5	45	11	53	17	59	18	00	0	02	52	23	53	12
23	11	59	24	+0	04	+7	25	5	47	5	47	11	52	17	57	17	57	0	06	49	23	49	16
24	12	02	59	−0	19	+7	46	5	49	5	49	11	52	17	54	17	54	0	10	45	23	45	20
25	12	06	35	−0	43	+8	07	5	50	5	51	11	52	17	52	17	52	0	14	42	23	41	25
26	12	10	11	−1	06	+8	28	5	52	5	53	11	51	17	50	17	49	0	18	38	23	37	29
27	12	13	47	−1	30	+8	48	5	54	5	55	11	51	17	47	17	46	0	22	35	23	33	33
28	12	17	23	−1	53	+9	09	5	55	5	57	11	51	17	45	17	44	0	26	32	23	29	37
29	12	21	00	−2	16	+9	29	5	57	5	59	11	50	17	43	17	41	0	30	28	23	25	41
30	12	24	36	−2	40	+9	49	5	59	6	00	11	50	17	40	17	38	0	34	25	23	21	45

DURATION OF TWILIGHT (in minutes)

Latitude	52°	56°	52°	56°	52°	56°	52°	56
	1 September		11 September		21 September		31 September	
Civil	35	39	34	38	34	37	34	37
Nautical	79	89	76	85	74	82	73	80
Astronomical	127	147	120	136	116	129	113	125

THE NIGHT SKY

Mercury passes through superior conjunction on the 1st and remains unsuitably placed for observation throughout the month.

Venus, magnitude −3.9, remains a brilliant object low above the eastern horizon before dawn. However, by the end of the month, observers are very unlikely to be able to see it for more than about ten minutes or so before the planet is lost in the glare of the rising Sun.

Mars continues to be unsuitably placed for observation.

Jupiter continues to be visible in the early evenings, magnitude −1.8, though it will only be low in the south-western sky for a short while after sunset. For the third time this year Jupiter passes near Alpha Librae, this time on about the 10th. The waxing crescent Moon is in the vicinity of the planet on the evenings of the 25th and 26th.

Saturn, magnitude +0.5, continues to be visible as a very difficult morning object in the south-eastern quadrant of the sky gradually pulling away from the Sun and getting more easily detectable during the month. The planet is moving slowly direct in Leo. The waning crescent Moon will be seen close to the planet on the morning of the 19th.

Uranus is at opposition on the 5th in the constellation of Aquarius. Uranus is barely visible to the naked-eye as its magnitude is +5.7, but it is readily located with only small optical aid.

Zodiacal Light. The morning cone may be observed stretching up from the eastern horizon, along the ecliptic, before the beginning of morning twilight, from the beginning of the month until the 6th, and again after the 20th. This faint phenomenon is only visible under good conditions and in the absence of both moonlight and artificial lighting.

THE MOON

Day	R.A. h	R.A. m	Dec. °	Hor. Par. '	Semi-diam. '	Sun's Co-Long. °	PA of Br. Limb °	Ph. %	Age d	Rise 52° h	Rise 52° m	Rise 56° h	Rise 56° m	Transit h	Transit m	Set 52° h	Set 52° m	Set 56° h	Set 56° m
1	16	26	−26.8	56.2	15.3	8	279	51	8.2	15	12	15	51	18	27	21	38	20	59
2	17	23	−28.5	57.1	15.6	20	272	61	9.2	16	17	16	58	19	25	22	35	21	54
3	18	24	−28.5	58.0	15.8	32	265	71	10.2	17	06	17	42	20	25	23	51	23	15
4	19	26	−26.9	59.0	16.1	45	258	81	11.2	17	41	18	08	21	25	—	—	—	—
5	20	27	−23.4	59.9	16.3	57	251	89	12.2	18	04	18	24	22	23	1	20	0	54
6	21	27	−18.4	60.7	16.5	69	245	95	13.2	18	22	18	34	23	18	2	55	2	38
7	22	23	−12.2	61.2	16.7	81	239	99	14.2	18	36	18	41	—	—	4	31	4	21
8	23	18	− 5.2	61.4	16.7	93	79	100	15.2	18	48	18	48	0	11	6	05	6	02
9	0	12	+ 2.1	61.3	16.7	105	64	98	16.2	19	00	18	54	1	02	7	37	7	41
10	1	05	+ 9.2	60.8	16.6	118	64	93	17.2	19	14	19	01	1	54	9	10	9	20
11	2	00	+15.7	60.1	16.4	130	67	85	18.2	19	31	19	12	2	46	10	42	11	01
12	2	56	+21.2	59.3	16.2	142	71	76	19.2	19	55	19	27	3	41	12	14	12	40
13	3	54	+25.3	58.4	15.9	154	76	66	20.2	20	28	19	52	4	37	13	39	14	14
14	4	54	+27.8	57.5	15.7	166	83	55	21.2	21	15	20	35	5	35	14	52	15	32
15	5	53	+28.7	56.6	15.4	179	90	45	22.2	22	16	21	38	6	33	15	48	16	27
16	6	51	+28.0	55.9	15.2	191	97	35	23.2	23	28	22	56	7	38	16	27	17	00
17	7	46	+25.9	55.3	15.1	203	103	25	24.2	—	—	—	—	8	20	16	53	17	19
18	8	38	+22.7	54.8	14.9	215	108	17	25.2	0	44	0	19	9	08	17	11	17	31
19	9	26	+18.5	54.4	14.8	227	112	11	26.2	2	00	1	42	9	52	17	25	17	38
20	10	11	+13.6	54.2	14.8	240	115	5	27.2	3	14	3	02	10	34	17	36	17	44
21	10	55	+ 8.3	54.0	14.7	252	117	2	28.2	4	26	4	19	11	14	17	45	17	48
22	11	37	+ 2.7	53.9	14.7	264	115	0	29.2	5	36	5	35	11	52	17	53	17	52
23	12	18	− 3.0	54.0	14.7	276	303	0	0.5	6	46	6	50	12	31	18	02	17	56
24	13	00	− 8.6	54.1	14.7	289	299	2	1.5	7	57	8	06	13	11	18	12	18	01
25	13	44	−13.9	54.3	14.8	301	297	6	2.5	9	10	9	25	13	53	18	24	18	07
26	14	30	−18.7	54.6	14.9	313	293	11	3.5	10	26	10	48	14	38	18	40	18	17
27	15	18	−22.9	55.0	15.0	325	289	18	4.5	11	43	12	13	15	26	19	02	18	32
28	16	11	−26.1	55.5	15.1	337	283	26	5.5	12	59	13	36	16	19	19	35	18	57
29	17	06	−28.1	56.2	15.3	350	277	35	6.5	14	07	14	48	17	15	20	23	19	42
30	18	05	−28.7	56.9	15.5	2	270	45	7.5	15	00	15	39	18	13	21	29	20	51

MERCURY

Day	R.A. h	R.A. m	Dec. °	Diam. "	Phase %	Transit h	Transit m	5° high 52° h	5° high 52° m	5° high 56° h	5° high 56° m
1	10	42	+10.1	5	100	12	04	18	21	18	25
3	10	56	+ 8.6	5	100	12	10	18	19	18	22
5	11	10	+ 7.0	5	99	12	16	18	17	18	19
7	11	24	+ 5.4	5	99	12	22	18	14	18	15
9	11	37	+ 3.8	5	98	12	27	18	11	18	11
11	11	50	+ 2.3	5	97	12	31	18	08	18	06
13	12	02	+ 0.7	5	95	12	36	18	04	18	01
15	12	14	− 0.8	5	94	12	40	18	01	17	56
17	12	26	− 2.4	5	93	12	44	17	57	17	51
19	12	38	− 3.9	5	92	12	48	17	52	17	45
21	12	49	− 5.3	5	90	12	51	17	48	17	40
23	13	00	− 6.8	5	89	12	54	17	43	17	34
25	13	11	− 8.2	5	87	12	57	17	39	17	28
27	13	22	− 9.5	5	86	13	00	17	34	17	21
29	13	33	−10.8	5	84	13	03	17	29	17	15
31	13	43	−12.1	5	83	13	06	17	24	17	09

VENUS

Day	R.A. h	R.A. m	Dec. °	Diam. "	Phase %	Transit h	Transit m	5° high 52° h	5° high 52° m	5° high 56° h	5° high 56° m
1	9	45	+14.7	10	97	11	05	4	22	4	13
6	10	09	+12.7	10	97	11	09	4	37	4	30
11	10	33	+10.6	10	98	11	13	4	52	4	47
16	10	56	+ 8.3	10	98	11	17	5	07	5	04
21	11	19	+ 5.9	10	99	11	20	5	23	5	22
26	11	42	+ 3.5	10	99	11	24	5	39	5	39
31	12	05	+ 1.0	10	99	11	27	5	55	5	57

MARS

Day	R.A. h	R.A. m	Dec. °	Diam. "	Phase %	Transit h	Transit m	5° high 52° h	5° high 52° m	5° high 56° h	5° high 56° m
1	11	44	+2.6	4	99	13	03	18	43	18	41
6	11	56	+1.3	4	99	12	55	18	28	18	26
11	12	08	0.0	4	100	12	48	18	13	18	10
16	12	20	−1.4	4	100	12	40	17	59	17	54
21	12	32	−2.7	4	100	12	32	17	44	17	38
26	12	44	−4.0	4	100	12	24	17	29	17	22
31	12	56	−5.3	4	100	12	17	17	15	17	07

SUNRISE AND SUNSET

d	London 0°05'	51°30'	Bristol 2°35'	51°28'	Birmingham 1°55'	52°28'	Manchester 2°15'	53°28'	Newcastle 1°37'	54°59'	Glasgow 4°14'	55°52'	Belfast 5°56'	54°35'
	h m	h m	h m	h m	h m	h m	h m	h m	h m	h m	h m	h m	h m	h m
1	5 13	18 47	5 23	18 57	5 18	18 56	5 18	18 59	5 12	18 59	5 21	19 12	5 30	19 16
2	5 14	18 45	5 24	18 55	5 20	18 54	5 19	18 57	5 14	18 57	5 23	19 09	5 32	19 13
3	5 16	18 43	5 26	18 53	5 22	18 51	5 21	18 54	5 16	18 54	5 25	19 06	5 34	19 11
4	5 17	18 40	5 27	18 50	5 23	18 49	5 23	18 52	5 18	18 52	5 27	19 04	5 36	19 08
5	5 19	18 38	5 29	18 48	5 25	18 47	5 25	18 50	5 20	18 49	5 29	19 01	5 38	19 06
6	5 20	18 36	5 31	18 46	5 27	18 44	5 26	18 47	5 22	18 47	5 31	18 59	5 40	19 03
7	5 22	18 34	5 32	18 44	5 28	18 42	5 28	18 45	5 23	18 44	5 33	18 56	5 41	19 01
8	5 24	18 31	5 34	18 41	5 30	18 40	5 30	18 42	5 25	18 42	5 35	18 53	5 43	18 58
9	5 25	18 29	5 35	18 39	5 31	18 37	5 32	18 40	5 27	18 39	5 37	18 51	5 45	18 56
10	5 27	18 27	5 37	18 37	5 33	18 35	5 33	18 37	5 29	18 37	5 38	18 48	5 47	18 53
11	5 28	18 25	5 38	18 34	5 35	18 33	5 35	18 35	5 31	18 34	5 40	18 46	5 49	18 51
12	5 30	18 22	5 40	18 32	5 36	18 30	5 37	18 33	5 33	18 32	5 42	18 43	5 50	18 48
13	5 32	18 20	5 42	18 30	5 38	18 28	5 39	18 30	5 35	18 29	5 44	18 40	5 52	18 46
14	5 33	18 18	5 43	18 28	5 40	18 26	5 40	18 28	5 37	18 26	5 46	18 38	5 54	18 43
15	5 35	18 15	5 45	18 25	5 41	18 23	5 42	18 25	5 38	18 24	5 48	18 35	5 56	18 41
16	5 36	18 13	5 46	18 23	5 43	18 21	5 44	18 23	5 40	18 21	5 50	18 32	5 58	18 38
17	5 38	18 11	5 48	18 21	5 45	18 19	5 46	18 20	5 42	18 19	5 52	18 30	6 00	18 36
18	5 40	18 08	5 50	18 18	5 46	18 16	5 47	18 18	5 44	18 16	5 54	18 27	6 01	18 33
19	5 41	18 06	5 51	18 16	5 48	18 14	5 49	18 15	5 46	18 14	5 56	18 24	6 03	18 31
20	5 43	18 04	5 53	18 14	5 50	18 11	5 51	18 13	5 48	18 11	5 58	18 22	6 05	18 28
21	5 44	18 01	5 54	18 11	5 51	18 09	5 53	18 11	5 50	18 08	6 00	18 19	6 07	18 26
22	5 46	17 59	5 56	18 09	5 53	18 07	5 54	18 08	5 51	18 06	6 02	18 16	6 09	18 23
23	5 48	17 57	5 58	18 07	5 55	18 04	5 56	18 06	5 53	18 03	6 04	18 14	6 11	18 20
24	5 49	17 55	5 59	18 05	5 57	18 02	5 58	18 03	5 55	18 01	6 06	18 11	6 12	18 18
25	5 51	17 52	6 01	18 02	5 58	18 00	6 00	18 01	5 57	17 58	6 08	18 09	6 14	18 15
26	5 52	17 50	6 02	18 00	6 00	17 57	6 01	17 58	5 59	17 56	6 10	18 06	6 16	18 13
27	5 54	17 48	6 04	17 58	6 02	17 55	6 03	17 56	6 01	17 53	6 12	18 03	6 18	18 10
28	5 56	17 45	6 06	17 55	6 03	17 52	6 05	17 53	6 03	17 50	6 13	18 01	6 20	18 08
29	5 57	17 43	6 07	17 53	6 05	17 50	6 07	17 51	6 05	17 48	6 15	17 58	6 22	18 05
30	5 59	17 41	6 09	17 51	6 07	17 48	6 08	17 49	6 07	17 45	6 17	17 55	6 24	18 03

JUPITER

Day	R.A.		Dec.		Transit		5° high 52°		56°	
	h	m	°	'	h	m	h	m	h	m
1	14	44.9	−15	00	16	03	20	05	19	46
11	14	51.0	−15	29	15	29	19	28	19	09
21	14	57.7	−16	01	14	57	18	52	18	32
31	15	05.1	−16	33	14	25	18	17	17	56

Diameters – equatorial 33" polar 31"

SATURN

Day	R.A.		Dec.		Transit		5° high 52°		56°	
	h	m	°	'	h	m	h	m	h	m
1	9	22.7	+16	15	10	41	3	50	3	39
11	9	27.4	+15	54	10	07	3	17	3	07
21	9	32.0	+15	34	9	32	2	44	2	35
31	9	36.2	+15	15	8	57	2	11	2	01

Diameters – equatorial 17" polar 15"
Rings – major axis 38" minor axis 9"

URANUS

Day	R.A.		Dec.		Transit		10° high 52°		56°	
	h	m	°	'	h	m	h	m	h	m
1	22	58.3	−7	27	0	18	4	30	4	16
11	22	56.8	−7	37	23	33	3	48	3	34
21	22	55.4	−7	46	22	53	3	07	2	52
31	22	54.0	−7	54	22	12	2	25	2	10

Diameter 4"

NEPTUNE

Day	R.A.		Dec.		Transit		10° high 52°		56°	
	h	m	°	'	h	m	h	m	h	m
1	21	21.5	−15	41	22	38	1	58	1	31
11	21	20.6	−15	45	21	57	1	17	0	50
21	21	19.7	−15	49	21	17	0	37	0	09
31	21	19.1	−15	52	20	37	23	52	23	24

Diameter 2"

OCTOBER 2006

TENTH MONTH, 31 DAYS. *Octo* (eighth), eighth month of Roman pre-Julian calendar

1	*Sunday*	William Boeing b. 1881. Walter Cannon d. 1945	274
2	*Monday*	Jack Parsons b. 1914. Svante Arrhenius d. 1927	week 40 day 275
3	*Tuesday*	Charles J. Pedersen b. 1904. Edouard Lucas d. 1891	276
4	*Wednesday*	The Soviet Union launches Sputnik 1, the first man-made satellite, into orbit around the Earth 1957	277
5	*Thursday*	Peyton Rous b. 1879. Maurice Wilkins d. 2004	278
6	*Friday*	Thor Heyerdahl b. 1914. Benjamin Peirce d. 1880	279
7	*Saturday*	Niels Bohr b. 1885. Harvey Cushing d. 1939	280
8	*Sunday*	Ejnar Hertzsprung b. 1873. Sergey Chaplygin d. 1942	281
9	*Monday*	Max von Laue b. 1879. Pieter Zeeman d. 1943	week 41 day 282
10	*Tuesday*	William Lassell discovers Triton, Neptune's largest moon 1846	283
11	*Wednesday*	Lewis Fry Richardson b. 1881. James Prescott Joule d. 1889	284
12	*Thursday*	Arthur Harden b. 1865. Max Wertheimer d. 1943	285
13	*Friday*	Peter Barlow b. 1776. William Hopkins d. 1866	286
14	*Saturday*	W. Edwards Deming b. 1900. Martin Ryle d. 1984	287
15	*Sunday*	Asaph Hall b. 1829. Konrad Bloch d. 2000	288
16	*Monday*	Albrecht von Haller b. 1708. William S. Gosset d. 1937	week 42 day 289
17	*Tuesday*	Johann Friedrich Meckel b. 1781. Jacques Hadamard d. 1963	290
18	*Wednesday*	The British Broadcasting Company, later to become the British Broadcasting Corporation (BBC), is founded 1922	291
19	*Thursday*	Auguste Lumière b. 1862. Charles Wheatstone d. 1875	292
20	*Friday*	Christopher Wren b. 1632. Paul Dirac d. 1984	293
21	*Saturday*	Alfred Nobel b. 1833. Waclaw Sierpinski d. 1969	294
22	*Sunday*	Karl Jansky b. 1905. Elvin M. Jellinek d. 1963	295
23	*Monday*	Gilbert N. Lewis b. 1875. Edward Adelbert Doisy d. 1986	week 43 day 296
24	*Tuesday*	Edmund Taylor Whittaker b. 1873. Tycho Brahe d. 1601	297
25	*Wednesday*	Evariste Galois b. 1811. Evangelista Torricelli d. 1647	298
26	*Thursday*	Lewis Boss b. 1846. Alfred Tarski d. 1983	299
27	*Friday*	Marcellin Berthelot b. 1827. Lise Meitner d. 1968	300
28	*Saturday*	Bill Gates b. 1955. John Wallis d. 1703	301
29	*Sunday*	*British Summer Time ends.* Robert Grant Aitken d. 1951	302
30	*Monday*	Gerhard Domagk b. 1895. Gustav Ludwig Hertz d. 1975	week 44 day 303
31	*Tuesday*	John Pople b. 1925. Lord Rosse d. 1867	304

ASTRONOMICAL PHENOMENA

d	h	
16	16	Saturn in conjunction with Moon. Saturn 2°S.
17	04	Mercury at greatest elongation E.25°
22	02	Venus in conjunction with Moon. Venus 4°N.
22	06	Mars in conjunction with Moon. Mars 3°N.
22	15	Jupiter in conjunction with Mercury. Jupiter 4° N.
23	07	Mars in conjunction
23	13	Sun's longitude 210° ♏
24	06	Jupiter in conjunction with Moon. Jupiter 5° N.
24	07	Mercury in conjunction with Moon. Mercury 1° N.
25	06	Mars in conjunction with Venus. Mars 0°.7 S.
27	18	Venus in superior conjunction
28	19	Mercury at stationary point
29	08	Neptune at stationary point
31	03	Jupiter in conjunction with Mercury. Jupiter 3° N.

MINIMA OF ALGOL

d	h	d	h	d	h
2	17.4	14	04.7	25	15.9
5	14.3	17	01.5	28	12.8
8	11.1	19	22.3	31	09.6
11	07.9	22	19.1		

CONSTELLATIONS

The following constellations are near their meridian at

	d	h		d	h
September	1	24	October	16	21
September	15	23	November	1	20
October	1	22	November	15	19

Ursa Major (below the Pole), Cepheus, Cassiopeia, Cygnus, Lacerta, Andromeda, Pegasus, Capricornus, Aquarius and Piscis Austrinus

THE MOON

Phases, Apsides and Node	d	h	m
○ Full Moon	7	03	13
☾ Last Quarter	14	00	26
● New Moon	22	05	14
☽ First Quarter	29	21	25
Perigee (357,415 km)	6	14	19
Apogee (406,053 km)	19	09	47

Mean longitude of ascending node on October 1, 355°

THE SUN

s.d. 16′.1

Day	Right Ascension			Dec.		Equation of time		Rise 52°		Rise 56°		Transit		Set 52°		Set 56°		Sidereal time			Transit of first point of Aries		
	h	m	s	°	′	m	s	h	m	h	m	h	m	h	m	h	m	h	m	s	h	m	s
1	12	28	13	3	03	+10	08	6	01	6	03	11	50	17	38	17	36	0	38	21	23	17	49
2	12	31	50	3	26	+10	28	6	02	6	04	11	49	17	36	17	33	0	42	18	23	13	53
3	12	35	28	3	49	+10	47	6	04	6	06	11	49	17	33	17	31	0	46	14	23	09	57
4	12	39	05	4	13	+11	05	6	06	6	08	11	49	17	31	17	28	0	50	11	23	06	01
5	12	42	44	4	36	+11	24	6	07	6	10	11	48	17	29	17	25	0	54	07	23	02	06
6	12	46	22	4	59	+11	42	6	09	6	12	11	48	17	26	17	23	0	58	04	22	58	10
7	12	50	01	5	22	+12	00	6	11	6	15	11	48	17	24	17	20	1	02	01	22	54	14
8	12	53	40	5	45	+12	17	6	12	6	16	11	48	17	22	17	18	1	05	57	22	50	18
9	12	57	20	6	08	+12	34	6	14	6	19	11	47	17	20	17	15	1	09	54	22	46	22
10	13	01	00	6	30	+12	50	6	16	6	21	11	47	17	17	17	12	1	13	50	22	42	26
11	13	04	40	6	53	+13	06	6	17	6	23	11	47	17	15	17	10	1	17	47	22	38	30
12	13	08	21	7	16	+13	22	6	19	6	25	11	47	17	13	17	07	1	21	43	22	34	34
13	13	12	03	7	38	+13	37	6	21	6	27	11	46	17	11	17	05	1	25	40	22	30	38
14	13	15	45	8	01	+13	51	6	23	6	29	11	46	17	09	17	02	1	29	36	22	26	42
15	13	19	28	8	23	+14	05	6	24	6	31	11	46	17	06	17	00	1	33	33	22	22	46
16	13	23	11	8	45	+14	19	6	26	6	33	11	46	17	04	16	57	1	37	30	22	18	51
17	13	26	55	9	07	+14	31	6	28	6	35	11	45	17	02	16	55	1	41	26	22	14	55
18	13	30	39	9	29	+14	44	6	30	6	37	11	45	17	00	16	52	1	45	23	22	10	59
19	13	34	24	9	51	+14	55	6	31	6	39	11	45	16	58	16	50	1	49	19	22	07	03
20	13	38	10	10	13	+15	06	6	33	6	41	11	45	16	56	16	48	1	53	16	22	03	07
21	13	41	56	10	34	+15	16	6	35	6	43	11	45	16	54	16	45	1	57	12	21	59	11
22	13	45	43	10	55	+15	26	6	37	6	45	11	44	16	52	16	43	2	01	09	21	55	15
23	13	49	31	11	17	+15	35	6	38	6	47	11	44	16	50	16	40	2	05	05	21	51	19
24	13	53	19	11	38	+15	43	6	40	6	50	11	44	16	47	16	38	2	09	02	21	47	23
25	13	57	08	11	58	+15	51	6	42	6	52	11	44	16	45	16	36	2	12	59	21	43	27
26	14	00	58	12	19	+15	57	6	44	6	54	11	44	16	43	16	33	2	16	55	21	39	31
27	14	04	48	12	40	+16	04	6	46	6	56	11	44	16	42	16	31	2	20	52	21	35	36
28	14	08	39	13	00	+16	09	6	47	6	58	11	44	16	40	16	29	2	24	48	21	31	40
29	14	12	31	13	20	+16	14	6	49	7	00	11	44	16	38	16	26	2	28	45	21	27	44
30	14	16	24	13	40	+16	18	6	51	7	02	11	44	16	36	16	24	2	32	41	21	23	48
31	14	20	17	13	59	+16	21	6	53	7	04	11	44	16	34	16	22	2	36	38	21	19	52

DURATION OF TWILIGHT (in minutes)

Latitude	52°	56°	52°	56°	52°	56°	52°	56
	1 October		11 October		21 October		31 October	
Civil	34	37	34	37	34	38	35	39
Nautical	73	80	73	80	74	81	75	83
Astronomical	113	125	112	124	113	124	114	126

THE NIGHT SKY

Mercury remains unobservable to those in the British Isles even though it reaches greatest eastern elongation (25 degrees) on the 17th.

Venus, magnitude −3.9, remains a splendid morning object, but only very low above the eastern horizon shortly before dawn. It is coming to the end of its period of visibility and after the first week of the month it becomes too close to the Sun to be detected. On the 27th Venus passes slowly through superior conjunction and will not be visible again until it reappears in the evenings at the very end of the year.

Mars passes through conjunction on the 23rd and therefore remains too close to the Sun for observation throughout October.

Jupiter is now coming towards the end of its period of evening visibility and can only be seen low in the south-western sky shortly after sunset, but only for about the first week of the month. Its magnitude is −1.8.

Saturn, magnitude +0.5, is still visible in the eastern sky in the early mornings. It is continuing its direct motion in the constellation of Leo, towards Regulus, though it will not actually go past that star until next August. The waning crescent Moon passes only 1 degree north of Saturn on the morning of the 16th.

THE MOON

Day	R.A. h	R.A. m	Dec. °	Hor. Par. '	Semi-diam. '	Sun's Co-Long. °	PA of Br. Limb °	Ph. %	Age d	Rise 52° h	Rise 52° m	Rise 56° h	Rise 56° m	Transit h	Transit m	Set 52° h	Set 52° m	Set 56° h	Set 56° m
1	19	05	−27.6	57.8	15.7	14	263	56	8.5	15	39	16	11	19	11	22	51	22	20
2	20	04	−24.9	58.6	16.0	26	257	67	9.5	16	06	16	29	20	08	—	—	23	59
3	21	03	−20.6	59.5	16.2	38	251	77	10.5	16	25	16	41	21	02	0	21	—	—
4	21	59	−15.0	60.3	16.4	51	247	86	11.5	16	40	16	49	21	55	1	54	1	40
5	22	53	−8.5	60.9	16.6	63	245	93	12.5	16	53	16	56	22	46	3	27	3	20
6	23	47	−1.3	61.3	16.7	75	247	98	13.5	17	05	17	02	23	38	4	59	4	59
7	0	41	+6.0	61.3	16.7	87	285	100	14.5	17	18	17	09	—	—	6	32	6	39
8	1	35	+12.9	61.0	16.6	99	56	99	15.5	17	34	17	18	0	31	8	07	8	21
9	2	32	+19.0	60.4	16.5	111	64	95	16.5	17	55	17	31	1	26	9	42	10	04
10	3	31	+23.8	59.6	16.2	124	71	88	17.5	18	24	17	52	2	23	11	14	11	45
11	4	32	+27.1	58.7	16.0	136	78	80	18.5	19	07	18	28	3	23	12	36	13	14
12	5	34	+28.6	57.7	15.7	148	85	71	19.5	20	04	19	25	4	22	13	41	14	20
13	6	34	+28.4	56.8	15.5	160	92	61	20.5	21	15	20	40	5	20	14	26	15	02
14	7	31	+26.6	56.0	15.3	172	99	50	21.5	22	31	22	04	6	15	14	57	15	25
15	8	24	+23.6	55.3	15.1	184	104	40	22.5	23	48	23	28	7	05	15	18	15	39
16	9	14	+19.6	54.7	14.9	197	109	31	23.5	—	—	—	—	7	50	15	33	15	48
17	10	00	+14.9	54.4	14.8	209	112	23	24.5	1	03	0	49	8	33	15	45	15	54
18	10	44	+9.7	54.1	14.7	221	114	15	25.5	2	15	2	07	9	13	15	54	15	59
19	11	26	+4.2	54.0	14.7	233	114	9	26.5	3	25	3	22	9	52	16	03	16	03
20	12	07	−1.5	54.0	14.7	245	112	4	27.5	4	35	4	37	10	31	16	12	16	07
21	12	49	−7.1	54.1	14.7	258	106	1	28.5	5	46	5	53	11	10	16	21	16	12
22	13	33	−12.6	54.3	14.8	270	63	0	29.5	6	59	7	12	11	52	16	33	16	18
23	14	18	−17.6	54.6	14.9	282	311	1	0.8	8	14	8	34	12	36	16	47	16	26
24	15	06	−21.9	54.9	15.0	294	298	3	1.8	9	32	9	58	13	24	17	07	16	40
25	15	58	−25.4	55.3	15.1	306	290	7	2.8	10	48	11	23	14	15	17	37	17	02
26	16	53	−27.7	55.8	15.2	319	282	14	3.8	11	58	12	38	15	10	18	20	17	40
27	17	51	−28.6	56.3	15.4	331	275	21	4.8	12	56	13	36	16	07	19	20	18	40
28	18	50	−27.9	57.0	15.5	343	267	30	5.8	13	39	14	13	17	04	20	35	20	02
29	19	48	−25.7	57.6	15.7	355	260	40	6.8	14	08	14	35	17	59	22	00	21	35
30	20	45	−22.0	58.3	15.9	7	255	51	7.8	14	29	14	48	18	53	23	28	23	11
31	21	40	−16.9	59.1	16.1	20	250	62	8.8	14	45	14	57	19	44	—	—	—	—

MERCURY

Day	R.A. h	R.A. m	Dec. °	Diam. "	Phase %	Transit h	Transit m	5° high 52° h	5° high 52° m	5° high 56° h	5° high 56° m
1	13	43	−12.1	5	83	13	06	17	24	17	09
3	13	54	−13.3	6	81	13	08	17	19	17	02
5	14	04	−14.5	6	79	13	10	17	14	16	56
7	14	14	−15.6	6	77	13	12	17	09	16	49
9	14	24	−16.6	6	74	13	14	17	04	16	43
11	14	33	−17.6	6	72	13	16	16	59	16	36
13	14	42	−18.5	6	69	13	17	16	54	16	29
15	14	51	−19.3	6	66	13	18	16	49	16	23
17	14	59	−20.0	7	62	13	18	16	44	16	16
19	15	07	−20.6	7	58	13	17	16	39	16	10
21	15	14	−21.2	7	54	13	16	16	33	16	03
23	15	19	−21.6	7	49	13	14	16	28	15	57
25	15	24	−21.8	8	43	13	10	16	23	15	51
27	15	27	−21.9	8	37	13	04	16	17	15	45
29	15	28	−21.8	9	30	12	57	16	11	15	40
31	15	27	−21.4	9	23	12	47	16	05	15	35

VENUS

Day	R.A. h	R.A. m	Dec. °	Diam. "	Phase %	Transit h	Transit m	5° high 52° h	5° high 52° m	5° high 56° h	5° high 56° m
1	12	05	+1.0	10	99	11	27	5	55	5	57
6	12	28	−1.5	10	100	11	30	6	11	6	15
11	12	51	−4.0	10	100	11	33	6	27	6	34
16	13	14	−6.5	10	100	11	37	6	44	6	53
21	13	37	−8.9	10	100	11	40	7	01	7	13
26	14	01	−11.2	10	100	11	44	7	19	7	33
31	14	25	−13.4	10	100	11	49	7	37	7	53

MARS

Day	R.A. h	R.A. m	Dec. °	Diam. "	Phase %	Transit h	Transit m	5° high 52° h	5° high 52° m	5° high 56° h	5° high 56° m
1	12	56	−5.3	4	100	12	17	7	18	7	26
6	13	08	−6.6	4	100	12	09	7	17	7	27
11	13	20	−7.9	4	100	12	02	7	17	7	28
16	13	33	−9.2	4	100	11	55	7	17	7	29
21	13	45	−10.4	4	100	11	47	7	18	7	31
26	13	58	−11.7	4	100	11	41	7	18	7	32
31	14	11	−12.9	4	100	11	34	7	18	7	34

SUNRISE AND SUNSET

d	London 0°05' 51°30' h m	h m	Bristol 2°35' 51°28' h m	h m	Birmingham 1°55' 52°28' h m	h m	Manchester 2°15' 53°28' h m	h m	Newcastle 1°37' 54°59' h m	h m	Glasgow 4°14' 55°52' h m	h m	Belfast 5°56' 54°35' h m	h m
1	6 01	17 39	6 11	17 49	6 08	17 45	6 10	17 46	6 08	17 43	6 19	17 53	6 26	18 00
2	6 02	17 36	6 12	17 46	6 10	17 43	6 12	17 44	6 10	17 40	6 21	17 50	6 27	17 58
3	6 04	17 34	6 14	17 44	6 12	17 41	6 14	17 41	6 12	17 38	6 23	17 48	6 29	17 55
4	6 05	17 32	6 15	17 42	6 13	17 38	6 16	17 39	6 14	17 35	6 25	17 45	6 31	17 53
5	6 07	17 29	6 17	17 39	6 15	17 36	6 17	17 37	6 16	17 33	6 27	17 42	6 33	17 50
6	6 09	17 27	6 19	17 37	6 17	17 34	6 19	17 34	6 18	17 30	6 29	17 40	6 35	17 48
7	6 10	17 25	6 20	17 35	6 19	17 31	6 21	17 32	6 20	17 28	6 31	17 37	6 37	17 45
8	6 12	17 23	6 22	17 33	6 20	17 29	6 23	17 29	6 22	17 25	6 33	17 35	6 39	17 43
9	6 14	17 21	6 24	17 31	6 22	17 27	6 25	17 27	6 24	17 23	6 35	17 32	6 41	17 40
10	6 15	17 18	6 25	17 28	6 24	17 25	6 26	17 25	6 26	17 20	6 37	17 30	6 42	17 38
11	6 17	17 16	6 27	17 26	6 26	17 22	6 28	17 22	6 28	17 18	6 39	17 27	6 44	17 36
12	6 19	17 14	6 29	17 24	6 27	17 20	6 30	17 20	6 30	17 15	6 41	17 24	6 46	17 33
13	6 20	17 12	6 30	17 22	6 29	17 18	6 32	17 18	6 32	17 13	6 43	17 22	6 48	17 31
14	6 22	17 10	6 32	17 20	6 31	17 16	6 34	17 15	6 34	17 10	6 45	17 19	6 50	17 28
15	6 24	17 08	6 34	17 18	6 33	17 13	6 36	17 13	6 35	17 08	6 48	17 17	6 52	17 26
16	6 26	17 05	6 36	17 15	6 34	17 11	6 37	17 11	6 37	17 06	6 50	17 14	6 54	17 24
17	6 27	17 03	6 37	17 13	6 36	17 09	6 39	17 09	6 39	17 03	6 52	17 12	6 56	17 21
18	6 29	17 01	6 39	17 11	6 38	17 07	6 41	17 06	6 41	17 01	6 54	17 10	6 58	17 19
19	6 31	16 59	6 41	17 09	6 40	17 05	6 43	17 04	6 43	16 59	6 56	17 07	7 00	17 17
20	6 32	16 57	6 42	17 07	6 42	17 03	6 45	17 02	6 45	16 56	6 58	17 05	7 02	17 14
21	6 34	16 55	6 44	17 05	6 43	17 00	6 47	17 00	6 47	16 54	7 00	17 02	7 04	17 12
22	6 36	16 53	6 46	17 03	6 45	16 58	6 49	16 58	6 49	16 52	7 02	17 00	7 06	17 10
23	6 38	16 51	6 48	17 01	6 47	16 56	6 50	16 55	6 51	16 49	7 04	16 58	7 08	17 08
24	6 39	16 49	6 49	16 59	6 49	16 54	6 52	16 53	6 53	16 47	7 06	16 55	7 10	17 05
25	6 41	16 47	6 51	16 57	6 51	16 52	6 54	16 51	6 55	16 45	7 08	16 53	7 12	17 03
26	6 43	16 45	6 53	16 55	6 52	16 50	6 56	16 49	6 58	16 43	7 10	16 51	7 14	17 01
27	6 45	16 43	6 55	16 53	6 54	16 48	6 58	16 47	6 59	16 40	7 12	16 48	7 16	16 59
28	6 46	16 41	6 56	16 51	6 56	16 46	7 00	16 45	7 02	16 38	7 15	16 46	7 18	16 57
29	6 48	16 39	6 58	16 49	6 58	16 44	7 02	16 43	7 04	16 36	7 17	16 44	7 20	16 54
30	6 50	16 37	7 00	16 47	7 00	16 42	7 04	16 41	7 06	16 34	7 19	16 42	7 22	16 52
31	6 52	16 36	7 02	16 46	7 02	16 40	7 06	16 39	7 08	16 32	7 21	16 39	7 24	16 50

JUPITER

Day	R.A. h m	Dec. ° '	Transit h m	5° high 52° h m	56° h m
1	15 05.1	−16 33	14 25	18 17	17 56
11	15 13.0	−17 06	13 53	17 41	17 20
21	15 21.3	−17 40	13 22	17 07	16 44
31	15 30.0	−18 12	12 52	16 32	16 08

Diameters – equatorial 32" polar 30"

SATURN

Day	R.A. h m	Dec. ° '	Transit h m	5° high 52° h m	56° h m
1	9 36.2	+15 15	8 57	2 11	2 01
11	9 40.0	+14 57	8 21	1 37	1 28
21	9 43.4	+14 42	7 45	1 02	0 53
31	9 46.2	+14 30	7 08	0 27	0 18

Diameters – equatorial 17" polar 15"
Rings – major axis 39" minor axis 9"

URANUS

Day	R.A. h m	Dec. ° '	Transit h m	10° high 52° h m	56° h m
1	22 54.0	−7 54	22 12	2 25	2 10
11	22 52.8	−8 01	21 31	1 44	1 29
21	22 51.8	−8 07	20 51	1 03	0 48
31	22 51.0	−8 11	20 11	0 22	0 07

Diameter 4"

NEPTUNE

Day	R.A. h m	Dec. ° '	Transit h m	10° high 52° h m	56° h m
1	21 19.1	−15 52	20 37	23 52	23 24
11	21 18.6	−15 55	19 58	23 12	22 44
21	21 18.3	−15 56	19 18	22 33	22 04
31	21 18.2	−15 56	18 39	21 53	21 25

Diameter 2"

NOVEMBER 2006

ELEVENTH MONTH, 30 DAYS. *Novem* (nine), ninth month of Roman pre-Julian calendar

1	*Wednesday*	Greenwich Mean Time is adopted as the standard against which the world's time zones are set 1884	305
2	*Thursday*	George Boole b. 1815. Peter Debye d. 1966	306
3	*Friday*	Daniel Rutherford b. 1749. Aleksandr Lyapunov d. 1918	307
4	*Saturday*	The entrance to Tutankhamun's tomb is discovered by the British archaeologist Howard Carter 1922	308
5	*Sunday*	J. B. S. Haldane b. 1892. Jan Oort d. 1992	309

6	*Monday*	Alois Senefelder b. 1771. Claude-Louis Berthollet d. 1822	week 45 day 310
7	*Tuesday*	Chandrasekhara Venkata Raman b. 1888. Alfred Russel Wallace d. 1913	311
8	*Wednesday*	Hermann Rorschach b. 1884. George Peacock d. 1858	312
9	*Thursday*	Benjamin Banneker b. 1731. Chaim Weizmann d. 1952	313
10	*Friday*	Igor Novikov b. 1935. Walter S. Sutton d. 1916	314
11	*Saturday*	Vesto Slipher b. 1875. Artturi Ilmari Virtanen d. 1973	315
12	*Sunday*	Portuguese neurologist Egas Moriz performs the world's first lobotomy 1935	316

13	*Monday*	Tim Berners-Lee, the British inventor of the World Wide Web, writes the first known web page 1990	week 46 day 317
14	*Tuesday*	Henri Dutrochet b. 1776. Nicolas-Louis Vauquelin d. 1829	318
15	*Wednesday*	Michel Chasles b. 1793. Johannes Kepler d. 1630	319
16	*Thursday*	Eugenio Beltrami b. 1835. Daniel Nathans d. 1999	320
17	*Friday*	Stanley Cohen b. 1922. Herman Hollerith d. 1929	321
18	*Saturday*	Louis-Jacques-Mandé Daguerre b. 1787. Gustav Theodor Fechner d. 1887	322
19	*Sunday*	Yuan Lee b. 1936. William Siemens d. 1883	323

20	*Monday*	Russia launches the first module of the International Space Station from Kazakhstan 1998	week 47 day 324
21	*Tuesday*	Thomas Edison announces his invention of the phonograph, a machine for recording and replaying sound 1877	325
22	*Wednesday*	Wiley Post b. 1898. Arthur Stanley Eddington d. 1944	326
23	*Thursday*	John Wallis b. 1616. Walter Reed d. 1902	327
24	*Friday*	Charles Darwin publishes the first edition of *The Origin of Species* 1859	328
25	*Saturday*	Nikolay Vavilov b. 1887. Henri Coanda d. 1972	329
26	*Sunday*	Norbert Wiener b. 1894. Thomas Andrews d. 1885	330

27	*Monday*	Lars Onsager b. 1976. Abraham de Moivre d. 1754	week 48 day 331
28	*Tuesday*	Luke Howard b. 1772. Mary Somerville d. 1872	332
29	*Wednesday*	Ernest William Brown b. 1866. John Wyatt d. 1766	333
30	*Thursday*	Nils Gustaf Dalén b. 1869. Marcello Malpighi d. 1694	334

ASTRONOMICAL PHENOMENA

d	h	
7	17	Venus in conjunction with Mercury. Venus 1° N.
8	22	Mercury in inferior conjunction (transit)
11	15	Mars in conjunction with Mercury. Mars 0°.6 S.
13	02	Saturn in conjunction with Moon. Saturn 1° S.
15	21	Jupiter in conjunction with Venus. Jupiter 0°.4 N.
18	00	Mercury at stationary point
19	09	Mercury in conjunction with Moon. Mercury 6° N.
20	04	Mars in conjunction with Moon. Mars 4° N.
20	06	Uranus at stationary point
21	00	Jupiter in conjunction with Moon. Jupiter 5° N.
21	11	Venus in conjunction with Moon. Venus 5° N.
21	23	Jupiter in conjunction
22	11	Sun's longitude 240° ♐
25	13	Mercury at greatest elongation W.20°

MINIMA OF ALGOL

d	h	d	h	d	h
3	06.4	14	17.6	26	04.9
6	03.2	17	14.5	29	01.7
9	00.0	20	11.3		
11	20.8	23	08.1		

CONSTELLATIONS

The following constellations are near their meridian at

	d	h		d	h
October	1	24	November	15	21
October	16	23	December	1	20
November	1	22	December	16	19

Ursa Major (below the Pole), Cepheus, Cassiopeia, Andromeda, Pegasus, Pisces, Acquarius and Cetus

THE MOON

Phases, Apsides and Node		d	h	m
○	Full Moon	5	12	58
☾	Last Quarter	12	17	45
●	New Moon	20	22	18
☽	First Quarter	28	06	29

	d	h	m
Perigee (360,610 km)	3	23	56
Apogee (405,160 km)	15	23	26

Mean longitude of ascending node on November 1, 353°

THE SUN

s.d. 16′.2

Day	Right Ascension			Dec.		Equation of time		Rise 52°		Rise 56°		Transit		Set 52°		Set 56°		Sidereal time			Transit of first point of Aries		
	h	m	s	°		m	s	h	m	h	m	h	m	h	m	h	m	h	m	s	h	m	s
1	14	24	11	14	19	+16	23	6	54	7	07	11	44	16	32	16	20	2	40	34	21	15	56
2	14	28	06	14	38	+16	25	6	56	7	09	11	44	16	30	16	18	2	44	31	21	12	00
3	14	32	02	15	57	+16	26	6	58	7	11	11	44	16	28	16	16	2	48	28	21	08	04
4	14	35	58	15	16	+16	26	7	00	7	13	11	44	16	27	16	13	2	52	24	21	04	08
5	14	39	56	15	34	+16	25	7	02	7	15	11	44	16	25	16	11	2	56	21	21	00	12
6	14	43	54	15	52	+16	23	7	03	7	17	11	44	16	23	16	09	3	00	17	20	56	16
7	14	47	53	16	10	+16	21	7	05	7	19	11	44	16	21	16	07	3	04	14	20	52	21
8	14	51	53	16	28	+16	18	7	07	7	21	11	44	16	20	16	05	3	08	10	20	48	25
9	14	55	53	16	45	+16	13	7	09	7	24	11	44	16	18	16	03	3	12	07	20	44	29
10	14	59	55	17	02	+16	08	7	11	7	26	11	44	16	17	16	01	3	16	03	20	40	33
11	15	03	57	17	19	+16	03	7	12	7	28	11	44	16	15	16	00	3	20	00	20	36	37
12	15	08	01	17	36	+15	56	7	14	7	30	11	44	16	13	15	58	3	23	57	20	32	41
13	15	12	05	17	52	+15	48	7	16	7	32	11	44	16	12	15	56	3	27	53	20	28	45
14	15	16	10	18	08	+15	40	7	18	7	34	11	44	16	10	15	54	3	31	50	20	24	49
15	15	20	16	18	23	+15	31	7	19	7	36	11	45	16	09	15	52	3	35	46	20	20	53
16	15	24	22	18	39	+15	20	7	21	7	38	11	45	16	08	15	51	3	39	43	20	16	57
17	15	28	30	18	54	+15	09	7	23	7	40	11	45	16	06	15	49	3	43	39	20	13	01
18	15	32	38	19	08	+14	58	7	25	7	42	11	45	16	05	15	47	3	47	36	20	09	05
19	15	36	48	19	22	+14	45	7	26	7	44	11	45	16	04	15	46	3	51	32	20	05	10
20	15	40	58	19	36	+14	31	7	28	7	46	11	46	16	03	15	44	3	55	29	20	01	14
21	15	45	09	19	50	+14	17	7	30	7	48	11	46	16	01	15	43	3	59	26	19	57	18
22	15	49	20	20	03	+14	02	7	31	7	50	11	46	16	00	15	41	4	03	22	19	53	22
23	15	53	33	20	16	+13	46	7	33	7	52	11	46	15	59	15	40	4	07	19	19	49	26
24	15	57	46	20	28	+13	29	7	35	7	54	11	47	15	58	15	39	4	11	15	19	45	30
25	16	02	00	20	41	+13	11	7	36	7	56	11	47	15	57	15	38	4	15	12	19	41	34
26	16	06	15	20	52	+12	53	7	38	7	58	11	47	15	56	15	36	4	19	08	19	37	38
27	16	10	31	21	04	+12	34	7	39	8	00	11	48	15	55	15	35	4	23	05	19	33	42
28	16	14	47	21	14	+12	14	7	41	8	01	11	48	15	55	15	34	4	27	01	19	29	46
29	16	19	04	21	25	+11	54	7	42	8	03	11	48	15	54	15	33	4	30	58	19	25	50
30	16	23	22	21	35	+11	33	7	44	8	05	11	49	15	53	15	32	4	34	55	19	21	55

DURATION OF TWILIGHT (in minutes)

Latitude	52°	56°	52°	56°	52°	56°	52°	56
	1 November		11 November		21 November		31 November	
Civil	36	40	37	41	38	43	40	45
Nautical	75	84	78	87	80	90	82	93
Astronomical	115	127	117	130	120	134	123	138

THE NIGHT SKY

Mercury passes through inferior conjunction on the 8th, and an actual transit occurs, though it cannot be observed from the British Isles (see page 1270). By the middle of the month it has become visible as a morning object low above the south-eastern horizon around the beginning of morning civil twilight. Its magnitude brightens from +1.0 to −0.6 during its period of visibility. It will be noticed that Mercury is at its brightest after it reaches greatest western elongation (20 degrees) on the 25th. For observers in northern temperate latitudes this will be the most favourable morning apparition of the year.

Venus is on the far side of the Sun and is unsuitably placed for observation throughout the month.

Mars continues to be unsuitably placed for observation.

Jupiter passes through conjunction on the 21st and therefore is not suitably placed for observation.

Saturn, magnitude +0.4, is still visible as a morning object in the south-eastern quadrant of the sky. By the end of the month it may be seen rising slightly north of east well before midnight. Saturn is moving very slowly direct in the constellation of Leo. On the morning of the 12th the Moon, at Last Quarter, will be seen passing only 1 degree north of the planet.

Meteors. Although the Leonids do not usually produce a brilliant display there has been considerable activity during the last few years. The peak of any activity will occur around the 17th but is not likely to produce a spectacular display.

THE MOON

Day	R.A. h	R.A. m	Dec. °	Hor. Par. '	Semi-diam. '	Sun's Co-Long. °	PA of Br. Limb °	Ph. %	Age d	Rise 52° h	Rise 52° m	Rise 56° h	Rise 56° m	Transit h	Transit m	Set 52° h	Set 52° m	Set 56° h	Set 56° m
1	22	33	−10.9	59.7	16.3	32	247	73	9.8	14	59	15	04	20	34	0	57	0	48
2	23	25	− 4.2	60.3	16.4	44	247	83	10.8	15	11	15	10	21	23	2	26	2	23
3	0	17	+ 2.9	60.7	16.5	56	248	91	11.8	15	23	15	17	22	14	3	56	4	00
4	1	10	+ 9.9	60.8	16.6	68	253	97	12.8	15	37	15	25	23	08	5	28	5	38
5	2	06	+16.3	60.7	16.5	80	274	99	13.8	15	55	15	36	—	—	7	02	7	20
6	3	04	+21.7	60.2	16.4	92	40	100	14.8	16	20	15	53	0	04	8	37	9	04
7	4	06	+25.7	59.6	16.2	105	66	97	15.8	16	57	16	21	1	04	10	07	10	42
8	5	08	+28.0	58.8	16.0	117	77	92	16.8	17	49	17	09	2	05	11	23	12	02
9	6	11	+28.5	57.9	15.8	129	86	85	17.8	18	56	18	19	3	06	12	19	12	56
10	7	11	+27.2	57.0	15.5	141	94	76	18.8	20	13	19	43	4	04	12	56	13	27
11	8	07	+24.5	56.1	15.3	153	101	67	19.8	21	32	21	09	4	57	13	21	13	45
12	8	59	+20.8	55.4	15.1	165	106	57	20.8	22	48	22	32	5	45	13	39	13	56
13	9	46	+16.2	54.8	14.9	178	110	48	21.8	—	—	23	52	6	30	13	52	14	03
14	10	31	+11.1	54.4	14.8	190	112	38	22.8	0	02	—	—	7	11	14	02	14	09
15	11	14	+ 5.6	54.2	14.8	202	113	29	23.8	1	13	1	08	7	50	14	11	14	13
16	11	55	0.0	54.1	14.7	214	113	21	24.8	2	23	2	23	8	29	14	20	14	17
17	12	37	− 5.6	54.2	14.8	226	112	14	25.8	3	33	3	38	9	08	14	30	14	22
18	13	20	−11.1	54.4	14.8	238	108	8	26.8	4	45	4	56	9	49	14	40	14	28
19	14	05	−16.2	54.7	14.9	251	102	4	27.8	5	59	6	17	10	32	14	54	14	35
20	14	53	−20.8	55.1	15.0	263	86	1	28.8	7	17	7	41	11	19	15	13	14	47
21	15	44	−24.5	55.5	15.1	275	3	0	0.1	8	35	9	07	12	10	15	39	15	07
22	16	39	−27.1	56.0	15.2	287	299	1	1.1	9	48	10	27	13	05	16	18	15	40
23	17	37	−28.4	56.4	15.4	299	283	5	2.1	10	51	11	31	14	02	17	14	16	34
24	18	36	−28.0	56.9	15.5	312	273	10	3.1	11	38	12	14	14	59	18	25	17	51
25	19	35	−26.1	57.4	15.6	324	265	17	4.1	12	11	12	39	15	55	19	48	19	21
26	20	32	−22.7	57.9	15.8	336	258	26	5.1	12	34	12	55	16	49	21	15	20	55
27	21	27	−18.0	58.4	15.9	348	253	36	6.1	12	51	13	05	17	39	22	41	22	29
28	22	19	−12.4	58.8	16.0	0	249	47	7.1	13	05	13	13	18	28	—	—	—	—
29	23	10	− 6.0	59.2	16.1	12	247	58	8.1	13	17	13	19	19	16	0	07	0	02
30	0	00	+ 0.8	59.6	16.2	25	247	69	9.1	13	29	13	25	20	04	1	33	1	34

MERCURY

Day	R.A. h	R.A. m	Dec. °	Diam. "	Phase %	Transit h	Transit m	5° high 52° h	5° high 52° m	5° high 56° h	5° high 56° m
1	15	25	−21.2	9	19	12	42	16	01	15	32
3	15	21	−20.4	10	12	12	28	15	54	15	27
5	15	13	−19.4	10	6	12	13	15	47	15	22
7	15	05	−18.2	10	1	11	56	8	14	8	37
9	14	55	−16.8	10	0	11	38	7	47	8	08
11	14	45	−15.4	10	2	11	22	7	21	7	40
13	14	38	−14.1	9	7	11	07	6	58	7	16
15	14	32	−13.2	9	15	10	54	6	40	6	56
17	14	30	−12.6	9	24	10	44	6	27	6	42
19	14	30	−12.4	8	33	10	37	6	19	6	34
21	14	33	−12.5	8	43	10	33	6	15	6	30
23	14	38	−12.8	7	51	10	30	6	14	6	30
25	14	44	−13.4	7	59	10	29	6	17	6	33
27	14	53	−14.1	6	66	10	30	6	22	6	39
29	15	02	14.9	6	71	10	31	6	28	6	47
31	15	12	−15.8	6	76	10	33	6	36	6	56

VENUS

Day	R.A. h	R.A. m	Dec. °	Diam. "	Phase %	Transit h	Transit m	5° high 52° h	5° high 52° m	5° high 56° h	5° high 56° m
1	14	30	−13.9	10	100	11	49	15	58	15	40
6	14	54	−15.9	10	100	11	54	15	49	15	29
11	15	19	−17.8	10	100	12	00	15	42	15	19
16	15	45	−19.5	10	100	12	06	15	36	15	09
21	16	11	−21.0	10	100	12	12	15	31	15	01
26	16	37	−22.2	10	99	12	19	15	28	14	55
31	17	04	−23.1	10	99	12	26	15	27	14	51

MARS

Day	R.A. h	R.A. m	Dec. °	Diam. "	Phase %	Transit h	Transit m	5° high 52° h	5° high 52° m	5° high 56° h	5° high 56° m
1	14	14	−13.1	4	100	11	33	7	18	7	35
6	14	27	−14.3	4	100	11	26	7	19	7	37
11	14	40	−15.4	4	100	11	20	7	20	7	39
16	14	54	−16.4	4	100	11	14	7	21	7	42
21	15	08	−17.5	4	100	11	08	7	22	7	45
26	15	22	−18.4	4	100	11	02	7	23	7	47
31	15	36	−19.3	4	100	10	57	7	24	7	50

SUNRISE AND SUNSET

	London 0°05′		51°30′		Bristol 2°35′		51°28′		Birmingham 1°55′		52°28′		Manchester 2°15′		53°28′		Newcastle 1°37′		54°59′		Glasgow 4°14′		55°52′		Belfast 5°56′		54°35′	
	h	m	h	m	h	m	h	m	h	m	h	m	h	m	h	m	h	m	h	m	h	m	h	m	h	m	h	m
1	6	53	16	34	7	03	16	44	7	03	16	38	7	08	16	37	7	10	16	30	7	23	16	37	7	26	16	48
2	6	55	16	32	7	05	16	42	7	05	16	36	7	10	16	35	7	12	16	28	7	25	16	35	7	28	16	46
3	6	57	16	30	7	07	16	40	7	07	16	35	7	11	16	33	7	14	16	26	7	27	16	33	7	30	16	44
4	6	59	16	28	7	09	16	38	7	09	16	33	7	13	16	31	7	16	16	23	7	29	16	31	7	32	16	42
5	7	01	16	27	7	10	16	37	7	11	16	31	7	15	16	29	7	18	16	22	7	32	16	29	7	34	16	40
6	7	02	16	25	7	12	16	35	7	13	16	29	7	17	16	27	7	20	16	20	7	34	16	27	7	36	16	38
7	7	04	16	23	7	14	16	33	7	14	16	28	7	19	16	26	7	22	16	18	7	36	16	25	7	38	16	36
8	7	06	16	22	7	16	16	32	7	16	16	26	7	21	16	24	7	24	16	16	7	38	16	23	7	40	16	34
9	7	08	16	20	7	17	16	30	7	18	16	24	7	23	16	22	7	26	16	14	7	40	16	21	7	42	16	33
10	7	09	16	19	7	19	16	29	7	20	16	23	7	25	16	20	7	28	16	12	7	42	16	19	7	44	16	31
11	7	11	16	17	7	21	16	27	7	22	16	21	7	27	16	19	7	30	16	10	7	44	16	17	7	46	16	29
12	7	13	16	16	7	23	16	26	7	24	16	19	7	29	16	17	7	32	16	09	7	46	16	15	7	48	16	27
13	7	15	16	14	7	24	16	24	7	25	16	18	7	30	16	15	7	34	16	07	7	48	16	13	7	50	16	26
14	7	16	16	13	7	26	16	23	7	27	16	16	7	32	16	14	7	36	16	05	7	50	16	12	7	52	16	24
15	7	18	16	11	7	28	16	21	7	29	16	15	7	34	16	12	7	38	16	03	7	52	16	10	7	54	16	22
16	7	20	16	10	7	30	16	20	7	31	16	14	7	36	16	11	7	40	16	02	7	54	16	08	7	55	16	21
17	7	21	16	09	7	31	16	19	7	32	16	12	7	38	16	09	7	42	16	00	7	57	16	07	7	57	16	19
18	7	23	16	07	7	33	16	17	7	34	16	11	7	40	16	08	7	44	15	59	7	59	16	05	7	59	16	18
19	7	25	16	06	7	35	16	16	7	36	16	10	7	41	16	07	7	46	15	57	8	01	16	03	8	01	16	16
20	7	26	16	05	7	36	16	15	7	38	16	08	7	43	16	05	7	48	15	56	8	03	16	02	8	03	16	15
21	7	28	16	04	7	38	16	14	7	39	16	07	7	45	16	04	7	50	15	54	8	04	16	01	8	05	16	14
22	7	30	16	03	7	40	16	13	7	41	16	06	7	47	16	03	7	51	15	53	8	06	15	59	8	07	16	12
23	7	31	16	02	7	41	16	12	7	43	16	05	7	49	16	02	7	53	15	52	8	08	15	58	8	09	16	11
24	7	33	16	01	7	43	16	11	7	44	16	04	7	50	16	01	7	55	15	51	8	10	15	56	8	10	16	10
25	7	34	16	00	7	44	16	10	7	46	16	03	7	52	15	59	7	57	15	49	8	12	15	55	8	12	16	09
26	7	36	15	59	7	46	16	09	7	48	16	02	7	54	15	58	7	59	15	48	8	14	15	54	8	14	16	08
27	7	38	15	58	7	47	16	08	7	49	16	01	7	55	15	58	8	00	15	47	8	16	15	53	8	16	16	07
28	7	39	15	57	7	49	16	07	7	51	16	00	7	57	15	57	8	02	15	46	8	18	15	52	8	17	16	06
29	7	41	15	56	7	50	16	06	7	52	15	59	7	58	15	56	8	04	15	45	8	19	15	51	8	19	16	05
30	7	42	15	56	7	52	16	06	7	54	15	58	8	00	15	55	8	05	15	44	8	21	15	50	8	21	16	04

JUPITER

Day	R.A.		Dec.		Transit		5° high			
							52°		56°	
	h	m	°	′	h	m	h	m	h	m
1	15	30.9	−18	16	12	49	9	09	9	32
11	15	39.8	−18	47	12	18	8	42	9	07
21	15	49.0	−19	18	11	48	8	16	8	41
31	15	58.2	−19	46	11	18	7	49	8	16

Diameters – equatorial 31″ polar 29″

SATURN

Day	R.A.		Dec.		Transit		5° high			
							52°		56°	
	h	m	°	′	h	m	h	m	h	m
1	9	46.4	+14	29	7	05	0	23	0	15
11	9	48.6	+14	20	6	28	23	43	23	35
21	9	50.0	+14	14	5	50	23	06	22	57
31	9	50.8	+14	13	5	11	22	27	22	19

Diameters – equatorial 18″ polar 16″
Rings– major axis 41″ minor axis 9″

URANUS

Day	R.A.		Dec.		Transit		10° high			
							52°		56°	
	h	m	°	′	h	m	h	m	h	m
1	22	51.0	−8	11	20	07	0	18	0	03
11	22	50.9	−8	14	19	27	23	34	23	19
21	22	50.4	−8	14	18	48	22	55	22	40
31	22	50.5	−8	13	18	09	22	16	22	01

Diameter 4″

NEPTUNE

Day	R.A.		Dec.		Transit		10° high			
							52°		56°	
	h	m	°	′	h	m	h	m	h	m
1	21	18.2	−15	56	18	35	21	49	21	21
11	21	18.4	−15	56	17	55	21	10	20	42
21	21	18.8	−15	54	17	17	20	32	20	03
31	21	19.4	−15	51	16	38	19	53	19	25

Diameter 2″

DECEMBER 2006

TWELFTH MONTH, 31 DAYS. *Decem* (ten), tenth month of Roman pre-Julian calendar

1	*Friday*	Martin Rodbell b. 1925. George Everest d. 1866	335
2	*Saturday*	George Minot b. 1885. Gerardus Mercator d. 1594	336
3	*Sunday*	Ellen Swallow Richards b. 1842. Lewis Thomas d. 1993	337
4	*Monday*	Frank Press b. 1924. Charles Richet d. 1935	week 49 day 338
5	*Tuesday*	Werner Heisenberg b. 1901. Gaspard Bauhin d. 1624	339
6	*Wednesday*	Joseph-Louis Gay-Lussac b. 1778. Robert Esnault-Pelterie d. 1957	340
7	*Thursday*	NASA launches Apollo 17, the sixth and last mission to land on the Moon 1972	341
8	*Friday*	Jan Ingenhousz b. 1730. Hermann Weyl d. 1955	342
9	*Saturday*	Grace Murray Hopper b. 1906. Carl Culmann d. 1881	343
10	*Sunday*	Ada Lovelace b. 1815. Thomas Johann Seebeck d. 1831	344
11	*Monday*	Max Born b. 1882. Johann Daniel Titius d. 1796	week 50 day 345
12	*Tuesday*	Erasmus Darwin b. 1731. Andrew Taylor Still d. 1917	346
13	*Wednesday*	Johann von Lamont b. 1805. David John Wheeler d. 2004	347
14	*Thursday*	Max Planck presents his quantum theory to the German Physical Society in Berlin 1900	348
15	*Friday*	Gustave Eiffel b. 1832. Charles Stanhope d. 1816	349
16	*Saturday*	Johann Wilhelm Ritter b. 1776. Hellmuth Walter d. 1980	350
17	*Sunday*	Willard Frank Libby b. 1908. Johannes Nicolaus Bronsted d. 1947	351
18	*Monday*	J. J. Thomson b. 1856. Nathan Rosen d. 1995	week 51 day 352
19	*Tuesday*	Charles-Julien Brianchon b. 1783. Paul Langevin d. 1946	353
20	*Wednesday*	Robert Jemison Van de Graaff b. 1901. Emil Artin d. 1962	354
21	*Thursday*	I. S. Bowen b. 1898. Nikolaas Tinbergen d. 1988	355
22	*Friday*	Srinivasa Ramanujan b. 1887. Jean-Victor Poncelet d. 1867	356
23	*Saturday*	Axel Fredrik Cronstedt b. 1722. Gerard Kuiper d. 1973	357
24	*Sunday*	William Hayward Pickering b. 1910. William John Macquorn Rankine d. 1872	358
25	*Monday*	Ernst Ruska b. 1906. Vladimir Belousov d. 1990	week 52 day 359
26	*Tuesday*	Pierre and Marie Curie announce their discovery of radium 1898	360
27	*Wednesday*	HMS *Beagle* sets sail from Plymouth with a young Charles Darwin on board 1831	361
28	*Thursday*	Maarten Schmidt b. 1929. Johannes Rydberg d. 1919	362
29	*Friday*	Charles Goodyear b. 1800. Leopold Kronecker d. 1891	363
30	*Saturday*	John N. Bahcall b. 1934. Jan Baptista van Helmont d. 1644	364
31	*Sunday*	Andreas Vesalius b. 1514. Aleksandr Popov d. 1905	365

ASTRONOMICAL PHENOMENA

d h
6 04 Saturn at stationary point
10 02 Mars in conjunction with Mercury. Mars 1° S.
10 12 Saturn in conjunction with Moon. Saturn 1° S.
10 17 Jupiter in conjunction with Mercury. Jupiter 0°.1 S.
11 16 Jupiter in conjunction with Mars. Jupiter 0°.8 N.
18 15 Pluto in conjunction
18 19 Jupiter in conjunction with Moon. Jupiter 6° N.
19 02 Mars in conjunction with Moon. Mars 5° N.
19 18 Mercury in conjunction with Moon. Mercury 5° N.
21 16 Venus in conjunction with Moon. Venus 4° N.
22 00 Sun's longitude 270° ♑

MINIMA OF ALGOL

d	h	d	h	d	h
1	22.5	13	09.8	24	21 1
4	19.4	16	06.6	27	17.9
7	16.2	19	03.4	30	14.7
10	13.0	22	00.3		

CONSTELLATIONS

The following constellations are near their meridian at

	d	h		d	h
November	1	24	January	1	20
December	16	21	December	1	22
November	15	23	January	16	19

Ursa Major (below the Pole), Ursa Minor (below the Pole), Cassiopeia, Andromeda, Perseus, Triangulum, Aries, Taurus, Cetus and Eridanus

THE MOON

Phases, Apsides and Node	d	h	m
○ Full Moon	5	00	25
☾ Last Quarter	12	14	32
● New Moon	20	14	01
☽ First Quarter	27	14	48
Perigee (365,947 km)	2	00	14
Apogee (404,379 km)	13	18	57
Perigee (370,360 km)	28	02	22

Mean longitude of ascending node on December 1, 351°

THE SUN

s.d. 16′.3

Day	Right Ascension			Dec. −		Equation of time		Rise 52°		Rise 56°		Transit		Set 52°		Set 56°		Sidereal time			Transit of first point of Aries		
	h	m	s	°	′	m	s	h	m	h	m	h	m	h	m	h	m	h	m	s	h	m	s
1	16	27	40	21	45	+11	11	7	45	8	07	11	49	15	52	15	31	4	38	51	19	17	59
2	16	31	59	21	54	+10	49	7	47	8	08	11	49	15	52	15	30	4	42	48	19	14	03
3	16	36	18	22	03	+10	26	7	48	8	10	11	50	15	51	15	29	4	46	44	19	10	07
4	16	40	38	22	11	+10	02	7	49	8	11	11	50	15	51	15	29	4	50	41	19	06	11
5	16	44	59	22	19	+9	38	7	51	8	13	11	51	15	50	15	28	4	54	37	19	02	15
6	16	49	20	22	27	+9	13	7	52	8	14	11	51	15	50	15	27	4	58	34	18	58	19
7	16	53	42	22	34	+8	48	7	53	8	16	11	51	15	49	15	27	5	02	30	18	54	23
8	16	58	05	22	41	+8	22	7	54	8	17	11	52	15	49	15	26	5	06	27	18	50	27
9	17	02	27	22	47	+7	56	7	56	8	18	11	52	15	49	15	26	5	10	24	18	46	31
10	17	06	51	22	53	+7	29	7	57	8	20	11	53	15	49	15	26	5	14	20	18	42	35
11	17	11	14	22	58	+7	02	7	58	8	21	11	53	15	48	15	25	5	18	17	18	38	40
12	17	15	39	23	03	+6	35	7	59	8	22	11	54	15	48	15	25	5	22	13	18	34	44
13	17	20	03	23	07	+6	07	8	00	8	23	11	54	15	48	15	25	5	26	10	18	30	48
14	17	24	28	23	11	+5	38	8	01	8	24	11	55	15	48	15	25	5	30	06	18	26	52
15	17	28	53	23	15	+5	10	8	02	8	25	11	55	15	48	15	25	5	34	03	18	22	56
16	17	33	19	23	18	+4	41	8	02	8	26	11	56	15	49	15	25	5	38	00	18	19	00
17	17	37	45	23	21	+4	12	8	03	8	27	11	56	15	49	15	25	5	41	56	18	15	04
18	17	42	11	23	23	+3	42	8	04	8	28	11	57	15	49	15	25	5	45	53	18	11	08
19	17	46	37	23	24	+3	13	8	05	8	28	11	57	15	49	15	26	5	49	49	18	07	12
20	17	51	03	23	25	+2	43	8	05	8	29	11	58	15	50	15	26	5	53	46	18	03	16
21	17	55	29	23	26	+2	13	8	06	8	30	11	58	15	50	15	26	5	57	42	17	59	20
22	17	59	56	23	26	+1	43	8	06	8	30	11	59	15	51	15	27	6	01	39	17	55	24
23	18	04	22	23	26	+1	13	8	07	8	31	11	59	15	51	15	28	6	05	35	17	51	29
24	18	08	49	23	26	+0	43	8	07	8	31	12	00	15	52	15	28	6	09	32	17	47	33
25	18	13	15	23	24	+0	13	8	07	8	31	12	00	15	53	15	29	6	13	29	17	43	37
26	18	17	42	23	23	−0	17	8	08	8	31	12	01	15	53	15	30	6	17	25	17	39	41
27	18	22	08	23	21	−0	46	8	08	8	32	12	01	15	54	15	31	6	21	22	17	35	45
28	18	26	34	23	18	−1	16	8	08	8	32	12	01	15	55	15	31	6	25	18	17	31	49
29	18	31	00	23	15	−1	45	8	08	8	32	12	02	15	56	15	32	6	29	15	17	27	53
30	18	35	26	23	11	−2	14	8	08	8	32	12	02	15	57	15	33	6	33	11	17	23	57
31	18	39	51	23	07	−2	43	8	08	8	32	12	03	15	58	15	35	6	37	08	17	20	01

DURATION OF TWILIGHT (in minutes)

Latitude	52°	56°	52°	56°	52°	56°	52°	56
	1 December		11 December		21 December		31 December	
Civil	40	45	41	47	41	47	41	47
Nautical	82	93	84	96	85	97	84	96
Astronomical	123	138	125	141	126	142	125	141

THE NIGHT SKY

Mercury, magnitude −0.6, continues to be visible in the mornings for the first week or ten days of the month, when it may be seen low above the south-eastern horizon around the time of beginning of morning civil twilight.

Venus remains too close to the Sun for observation for the first three weeks of the month but then becomes visible low above the south-western horizon for a very short while after sunset. Its magnitude is −3.9. By chance Mercury and Venus are both at aphelion on the 27th at 21h.

Mars continues to be unsuitably placed for observation.

Jupiter, magnitude −1.7, becomes a brilliant morning object as it emerges from the morning twilight after the first fortnight of the month, when it may be seen low in the south-eastern sky for a short while before sunrise.

The planet moves eastwards from Libra into Scorpius at the beginning of the month. The thin waning crescent Moon will be seen near Jupiter on the morning of the 18th.

Saturn, magnitude +0.3, can now be seen in the south-eastern quadrant of the sky from the late evening onwards, crossing the meridian well before sunrise. On the 6th it reaches its first stationary point and then moves slowly retrograde, in Leo. Around midnight on the 9th/10th the waning gibbous Moon will be seen about 5 degrees above the planet.

Meteors. The maximum of the well known Geminid meteor shower occurs during the early morning of the 14th, though there will be a little interference by moonlight from the waning crescent Moon, rising shortly after 01h.

THE MOON

Day	R.A.		Dec.	Hor. Par.	Semi-diam.	Sun's Co-Long.	PA of Br. Limb	Ph.	Age	Rise 52°		Rise 56°		Transit		Set 52°		Set 56°	
	h	m	°	'	'	°	°	%	d	h	m	h	m	h	m	h	m	h	m
1	0	51	+7.6	59.8	16.3	37	249	79	10.1	13	41	13	32	20	55	3	00	3	08
2	1	44	+14.0	59.9	16.3	49	253	88	11.1	13	57	13	41	21	48	4	30	4	45
3	2	40	+19.7	59.8	16.3	61	260	94	12.1	14	18	13	55	22	45	6	03	6	25
4	3	39	+24.2	59.5	16.2	73	275	98	13.1	14	49	14	17	23	46	7	34	8	05
5	4	41	+27.2	59.0	16.1	85	350	100	14.1	15	33	14	55	—	—	8	57	9	35
6	5	44	+28.4	58.4	15.9	97	68	99	15.1	16	35	15	56	0	48	10	04	10	42
7	6	46	+27.8	57.7	15.7	110	85	95	16.1	17	49	17	16	1	48	10	50	11	24
8	7	45	+25.6	56.9	15.5	122	95	89	17.1	19	09	18	44	2	44	11	21	11	48
9	8	39	+22.1	56.1	15.3	134	102	82	18.1	20	29	20	10	3	36	11	42	12	03
10	9	29	+17.6	55.5	15.1	146	107	74	19.1	21	45	21	33	4	23	11	57	12	11
11	10	16	+12.6	54.9	15.0	158	110	65	20.1	22	57	22	51	5	06	12	09	12	17
12	10	59	+7.2	54.5	14.9	170	113	56	21.1	—	—	—	—	5	46	12	18	12	22
13	11	41	+1.6	54.3	14.8	182	113	46	22.1	0	08	0	07	6	25	12	27	12	26
14	12	23	−4.0	54.2	14.8	195	113	37	23.1	1	18	1	21	7	04	12	36	12	31
15	13	05	−9.5	54.3	14.8	207	111	28	24.1	2	28	2	37	7	44	12	47	12	36
16	13	49	−14.7	54.6	14.9	219	108	20	25.1	3	42	3	56	8	26	12	59	12	43
17	14	36	−19.5	55.0	15.0	231	104	13	26.1	4	58	5	19	9	12	13	16	12	53
18	15	27	−23.5	55.5	15.1	243	97	7	27.1	6	16	6	45	10	01	13	39	13	09
19	16	21	−26.4	56.1	15.3	256	86	3	28.1	7	33	8	09	10	55	14	13	13	37
20	17	19	−28.1	56.7	15.4	268	59	1	29.1	8	41	9	21	11	52	15	04	14	24
21	18	18	−28.2	57.3	15.6	280	311	0	0.4	9	34	10	12	12	51	16	12	15	35
22	19	19	−26.7	57.8	15.7	292	276	2	1.4	10	13	10	43	13	49	17	33	17	04
23	20	18	−23.5	58.2	15.9	304	263	7	2.4	10	39	11	01	14	44	19	01	18	40
24	21	14	−19.0	58.6	16.0	316	256	14	3.4	10	58	11	13	15	37	20	29	20	15
25	22	07	−13.5	58.9	16.0	329	251	22	4.4	11	12	11	21	16	26	21	56	21	49
26	22	58	−7.2	59.0	16.1	341	248	32	5.4	11	24	11	28	17	14	23	21	23	20
27	23	48	−0.5	59.2	16.1	353	246	43	6.4	11	36	11	34	18	01	—	—	—	—
28	0	38	+6.1	59.2	16.1	5	247	54	7.4	11	48	11	40	18	49	0	46	0	51
29	1	29	+12.5	59.2	16.1	17	249	66	8.4	12	02	11	48	19	40	2	12	2	24
30	2	23	+18.3	59.1	16.1	29	253	76	9.4	12	20	11	59	20	34	3	41	4	01
31	3	19	+23.0	58.9	16.0	42	259	85	10.4	12	46	12	17	21	32	5	11	5	38

MERCURY

Day	R.A.		Dec.	Diam.	Phase	Transit		5° high 52°		5° high 56°	
	h	m	°	"	%	h	m	h	m	h	m
1	15	12	−15.8	6	76	10	33	6	36	6	56
3	15	22	−16.7	6	80	10	36	6	45	7	07
5	15	33	−17.6	6	84	10	40	6	55	7	18
7	15	45	−18.5	5	86	10	43	7	05	7	30
9	15	57	−19.4	5	89	10	47	7	15	7	42
11	16	09	−20.2	5	91	10	52	7	26	7	54
13	16	21	−21.0	5	92	10	56	7	37	8	07
15	16	34	−21.7	5	94	11	01	7	47	8	19
17	16	47	−22.3	5	95	11	06	7	58	8	31
19	17	00	−22.9	5	96	11	12	8	08	8	43
21	17	13	−23.4	5	97	11	17	8	18	8	55
23	17	27	−23.8	5	97	11	23	8	27	9	06
25	17	40	−24.2	5	98	11	28	8	36	9	16
27	17	54	−24.5	5	99	11	34	8	44	9	25
29	18	08	−24.6	5	99	11	40	8	52	9	34
31	18	22	−24.7	5	99	11	46	8	59	9	41

VENUS

Day	R.A.		Dec.	Diam.	Phase	Transit		5° high 52°		5° high 56°	
	h	m	°	"	%	h	m	h	m	h	m
1	17	04	−23.1	10	99	12	26	15	27	14	51
6	17	31	−23.8	10	99	12	34	15	29	14	51
11	17	59	−24.1	10	98	12	41	15	34	14	55
16	18	26	−24.2	10	98	12	49	15	42	15	02
21	18	54	−23.9	10	98	12	57	15	53	15	14
26	19	21	−23.3	10	97	13	04	16	06	15	30
31	19	48	−22.5	10	97	13	12	16	21	15	48

MARS

Day	R.A.		Dec.	Diam.	Phase	Transit		5° high 52°		5° high 56°	
	h	m	°	"	%	h	m	h	m	h	m
1	15	36	−19.3	4	100	10	57	7	24	7	50
6	15	51	−20.1	4	99	10	52	7	26	7	53
11	16	05	−20.9	4	99	10	47	7	27	7	56
16	16	20	−21.6	4	99	10	42	7	27	7	59
21	16	36	−22.2	4	99	10	37	7	28	8	01
26	16	51	−22.7	4	99	10	33	7	28	8	02
31	17	06	−23.2	4	99	10	29	7	28	8	03

SUNRISE AND SUNSET

d	London 0°05' 51°30' h m	h m	Bristol 2°35' 51°28' h m	h m	Birmingham 1°55' 52°28' h m	h m	Manchester 2°15' 53°28' h m	h m	Newcastle 1°37' 54°59' h m	h m	Glasgow 4°14' 55°52' h m	h m	Belfast 5°56' 54°35' h m	h m
1	7 43	15 55	7 53	16 05	7 55	15 58	8 01	15 54	8 07	15 43	8 23	15 49	8 22	16 03
2	7 45	15 54	7 55	16 04	7 57	15 57	8 03	15 53	8 09	15 43	8 24	15 48	8 24	16 02
3	7 46	15 54	7 56	16 04	7 58	15 56	8 04	15 53	8 10	15 42	8 26	15 47	8 25	16 01
4	7 47	15 53	7 57	16 03	7 59	15 56	8 06	15 52	8 12	15 41	8 27	15 46	8 27	16 01
5	7 49	15 53	7 59	16 03	8 01	15 55	8 07	15 52	8 13	15 41	8 29	15 46	8 28	16 00
6	7 50	15 52	8 00	16 03	8 02	15 55	8 09	15 51	8 15	15 40	8 30	15 45	8 30	16 00
7	7 51	15 52	8 01	16 02	8 03	15 55	8 10	15 51	8 16	15 40	8 32	15 45	8 31	15 59
8	7 52	15 52	8 02	16 02	8 04	15 54	8 11	15 50	8 17	15 39	8 33	15 44	8 32	15 59
9	7 53	15 52	8 03	16 02	8 06	15 54	8 12	15 50	8 18	15 39	8 34	15 44	8 33	15 58
10	7 55	15 51	8 04	16 02	8 07	15 54	8 13	15 50	8 20	15 38	8 36	15 43	8 35	15 58
11	7 56	15 51	8 05	16 01	8 08	15 54	8 15	15 50	8 21	15 38	8 37	15 43	8 36	15 58
12	7 57	15 51	8 06	16 01	8 09	15 54	8 16	15 49	8 22	15 38	8 38	15 43	8 37	15 58
13	7 58	15 51	8 07	16 01	8 10	15 54	8 17	15 49	8 23	15 38	8 39	15 43	8 38	15 58
14	7 58	15 51	8 08	16 01	8 11	15 54	8 18	15 49	8 24	15 38	8 40	15 43	8 39	15 58
15	7 59	15 51	8 09	16 02	8 12	15 54	8 19	15 50	8 25	15 38	8 41	15 43	8 40	15 58
16	8 00	15 52	8 10	16 02	8 13	15 54	8 19	15 50	8 26	15 38	8 42	15 43	8 41	15 58
17	8 01	15 52	8 11	16 02	8 13	15 54	8 20	15 50	8 27	15 38	8 43	15 43	8 41	15 58
18	8 02	15 52	8 11	16 02	8 14	15 54	8 21	15 50	8 27	15 38	8 44	15 43	8 42	15 58
19	8 02	15 52	8 12	16 03	8 15	15 55	8 22	15 50	8 28	15 39	8 44	15 44	8 43	15 59
20	8 03	15 53	8 13	16 03	8 15	15 55	8 22	15 51	8 29	15 39	8 45	15 44	8 44	15 59
21	8 03	15 53	8 13	16 03	8 16	15 55	8 23	15 51	8 29	15 40	8 46	15 44	8 44	15 59
22	8 04	15 54	8 14	16 04	8 16	15 56	8 23	15 52	8 30	15 40	8 46	15 45	8 45	16 00
23	8 04	15 54	8 14	16 04	8 17	15 57	8 24	15 52	8 30	15 41	8 47	15 45	8 45	16 00
24	8 05	15 55	8 15	16 05	8 17	15 57	8 24	15 53	8 31	15 41	8 47	15 46	8 45	16 01
25	8 05	15 56	8 15	16 06	8 18	15 58	8 24	15 54	8 31	15 42	8 47	15 47	8 46	16 02
26	8 05	15 56	8 15	16 06	8 18	15 59	8 25	15 54	8 31	15 43	8 47	15 48	8 46	16 03
27	8 06	15 57	8 16	16 07	8 18	15 59	8 25	15 55	8 31	15 44	8 48	15 48	8 46	16 03
28	8 06	15 58	8 16	16 08	8 18	16 00	8 25	15 56	8 32	15 45	8 48	15 49	8 46	16 04
29	8 06	15 59	8 16	16 09	8 18	16 01	8 25	15 57	8 32	15 45	8 48	15 50	8 46	16 05
30	8 06	16 00	8 16	16 10	8 18	16 02	8 25	15 58	8 32	15 46	8 48	15 51	8 46	16 06
31	8 06	16 01	8 16	16 11	8 18	16 03	8 25	15 59	8 31	15 48	8 48	15 52	8 46	16 07

JUPITER

Day	R.A. h m	Dec. ° '	Transit h m	5° high 52° h m	56° h m
1	15 58.2	−19 46	11 18	7 49	8 16
11	16 07.4	−20 12	10 48	7 22	7 50
21	16 16.5	−20 36	10 18	6 55	7 23
31	16 25.4	−20 57	9 47	6 27	6 57

Diameters − equatorial 31″ polar 29″

SATURN

Day	R.A. h m	Dec. ° '	Transit h m	5° high 52° h m	56° h m
1	9 50.8	+14 13	5 11	22 27	22 19
11	9 50.9	+14 14	4 32	21 48	21 39
21	9 50.2	+14 20	3 52	21 07	20 59
31	9 48.9	+14 29	3 11	20 26	20 17

Diameters − equatorial 19″ polar 17″
Rings − major axis 43″ minor axis 9″

URANUS

Day	R.A. h m	Dec. ° '	Transit h m	10° high 52° h m	56° h m
1	22 50.5	−8 13	18 09	22 16	22 01
11	22 51.0	−8 09	17 30	21 38	21 22
21	22 51.8	−8 04	16 51	21 00	20 45
31	22 52.9	−7 57	16 13	20 22	20 07

Diameter 4″

NEPTUNE

Day	R.A. h m	Dec. ° '	Transit h m	10° high 52° h m	56° h m
1	21 19.4	−15 51	16 38	19 53	19 25
11	21 20.2	−15 47	15 59	19 15	18 47
21	21 21.2	−15 43	15 21	18 38	18 10
31	21 22.4	−15 37	14 43	18 00	17 33

Diameter 2″

RISING AND SETTING TIMES

TABLE 1. SEMI-DIURNAL ARCS (HOUR ANGLES AT RISING/SETTING)

Dec.	Latitude												Dec.
	0°	10°	20°	30°	40°	45°	50°	52°	54°	56°	58°	60°	
	h m	h m	h m	h m	h m	h m	h m	h m	h m	h m	h m	h m	
0°	6 00	6 00	6 00	6 00	6 00	6 00	6 00	6 00	6 00	6 00	6 00	6 00	0°
1°	6 00	6 01	6 01	6 02	6 03	6 04	6 05	6 05	6 06	6 06	6 06	6 07	1°
2°	6 00	6 01	6 03	6 05	6 07	6 08	6 10	6 10	6 11	6 12	6 13	6 14	2°
3°	6 00	6 02	6 04	6 07	6 10	6 12	6 14	6 15	6 17	6 18	6 19	6 21	3°
4°	6 00	6 03	6 06	6 09	6 13	6 16	6 19	6 21	6 22	6 24	6 26	6 28	4°
5°	6 00	6 04	6 07	6 12	6 17	6 20	6 24	6 26	6 28	6 30	6 32	6 35	5°
6°	6 00	6 04	6 09	6 14	6 20	6 24	6 29	6 31	6 33	6 36	6 39	6 42	6°
7°	6 00	6 05	6 10	6 16	6 24	6 28	6 34	6 36	6 39	6 42	6 45	6 49	7°
8°	6 00	6 06	6 12	6 19	6 27	6 32	6 39	6 41	6 45	6 48	6 52	6 56	8°
9°	6 00	6 06	6 13	6 21	6 31	6 36	6 44	6 47	6 50	6 54	6 59	7 04	9°
10°	6 00	6 07	6 15	6 23	6 34	6 41	6 49	6 52	6 56	7 01	7 06	7 11	10°
11°	6 00	6 08	6 16	6 26	6 38	6 45	6 54	6 58	7 02	7 07	7 12	7 19	11°
12°	6 00	6 09	6 18	6 28	6 41	6 49	6 59	7 03	7 08	7 13	7 20	7 26	12°
13°	6 00	6 09	6 19	6 31	6 45	6 53	7 04	7 09	7 14	7 20	7 27	7 34	13°
14°	6 00	6 10	6 21	6 33	6 48	6 58	7 09	7 14	7 20	7 27	7 34	7 42	14°
15°	6 00	6 11	6 22	6 36	6 52	7 02	7 14	7 20	7 27	7 34	7 42	7 51	15°
16°	6 00	6 12	6 24	6 38	6 56	7 07	7 20	7 26	7 33	7 41	7 49	7 59	16°
17°	6 00	6 12	6 26	6 41	6 59	7 11	7 25	7 32	7 40	7 48	7 57	8 08	17°
18°	6 00	6 13	6 27	6 43	7 03	7 16	7 31	7 38	7 46	7 55	8 05	8 17	18°
19°	6 00	6 14	6 29	6 46	7 07	7 21	7 37	7 45	7 53	8 03	8 14	8 26	19°
20°	6 00	6 15	6 30	6 49	7 11	7 25	7 43	7 51	8 00	8 11	8 22	8 36	20°
21°	6 00	6 16	6 32	6 51	7 15	7 30	7 49	7 58	8 08	8 19	8 32	8 47	21°
22°	6 00	6 16	6 34	6 54	7 19	7 35	7 55	8 05	8 15	8 27	8 41	8 58	22°
23°	6 00	6 17	6 36	6 57	7 23	7 40	8 02	8 12	8 23	8 36	8 51	9 09	23°
24°	6 00	6 18	6 37	7 00	7 28	7 46	8 08	8 19	8 31	8 45	9 02	9 22	24°
25°	6 00	6 19	6 39	7 02	7 32	7 51	8 15	8 27	8 40	8 55	9 13	9 35	25°
26°	6 00	6 20	6 41	7 05	7 37	7 57	8 22	8 35	8 49	9 05	9 25	9 51	26°
27°	6 00	6 21	6 43	7 08	7 41	8 03	8 30	8 43	8 58	9 16	9 39	10 08	27°
28°	6 00	6 22	6 45	7 12	7 46	8 08	8 37	8 52	9 08	9 28	9 53	10 28	28°
29°	6 00	6 22	6 47	7 15	7 51	8 15	8 45	9 01	9 19	9 41	10 10	10 55	29°
30°	6 00	6 23	6 49	7 18	7 56	8 21	8 54	9 11	9 30	9 55	10 30	12 00	30°
35°	6 00	6 28	6 59	7 35	8 24	8 58	9 46	10 15	10 58	12 00	12 00	12 00	35°
40°	6 00	6 34	7 11	7 56	8 59	9 48	12 00	12 00	12 00	12 00	12 00	12 00	40°
45°	6 00	6 41	7 25	8 21	9 48	12 00	12 00	12 00	12 00	12 00	12 00	12 00	45°
50°	6 00	6 49	7 43	8 54	12 00	12 00	12 00	12 00	12 00	12 00	12 00	12 00	50°
55°	6 00	6 58	8 05	9 42	12 00	12 00	12 00	12 00	12 00	12 00	12 00	12 00	55°
60°	6 00	7 11	8 36	12 00	12 00	12 00	12 00	12 00	12 00	12 00	12 00	12 00	60°
65°	6 00	7 29	9 25	12 00	12 00	12 00	12 00	12 00	12 00	12 00	12 00	12 00	65°
70°	6 00	7 56	12 00	12 00	12 00	12 00	12 00	12 00	12 00	12 00	12 00	12 00	70°
75°	6 00	8 45	12 00	12 00	12 00	12 00	12 00	12 00	12 00	12 00	12 00	12 00	75°
80°	6 00	12 00	12 00	12 00	12 00	12 00	12 00	12 00	12 00	12 00	12 00	12 00	80°

TABLE 2. CORRECTION FOR REFRACTION AND SEMI-DIAMETER

	m	m	m	m	m	m	m	m	m	m	m	m	m
0°	3	3	4	4	4	5	5	5	6	6	6	7	0°
10°	3	3	4	4	4	5	5	6	6	6	7	7	10°
20°	4	4	4	4	5	5	6	7	7	8	8	9	20°
25°	4	4	4	5	5	6	7	8	8	9	11	13	25°
30°	4	4	4	5	6	7	8	9	11	14	21	—	30°

NB: Regarding Table 1. If latitude and declination are of the same sign, take out the respondent directly. If they are of opposite signs, subtract the respondent from 12h.

Table 1 gives the complete range of declinations in case any user wishes to calculate semi-diurnal arcs for bodies other than the Sun and Moon.

Example:

Lat.	Dec.	Semi-diurnal arc
+52°	+20°	7h 51m
+52°	−20°	4h 09m

SUNRISE AND SUNSET

The local mean time of sunrise or sunset may be found by obtaining the hour angle from Table 1 and applying it to the time of transit. The hour angle is negative for sunrise and positive for sunset. A small correction to the hour angle, which always has the effect of increasing it numerically, is necessary to allow for the Sun's semi-diameter (16') and for refraction (34'); it is obtained from Table 2. The resulting local mean time may be converted into the standard time of the country by taking the difference between the longitude of the standard meridian of the country and that of the place, adding it to the local mean time if the place is west of the standard meridian, and subtracting it if the place is east.

Example – Required the New Zealand Mean Time (12h fast on GMT) of sunset on May 23 at Auckland, latitude 36° 50' S. (or minus), longitude 11h 39m E. Taking the declination as +20°.6 (page 1245), we find

	h	m
New Zealand Standard Time	+ 12	00
Longitude	− 11	39
Longitudinal Correction	+ 0	21
Tabular entry for Lat. 30° and Dec. 20°, opposite signs	+ 5	11
Proportional part for 6° 50' of Lat.	−	15
Proportional part for 0°.6 of Dec.	−	2
Correction (Table 2)	+	4
Hour angle	4	58
Sun transits (page 1245)	11	57
Longitudinal correction	+	21
New Zealand Mean Time	17	16

MOONRISE AND MOONSET

It is possible to calculate the times of moonrise and moonset using Table 1, though the method is more complicated because the apparent motion of the Moon is much more rapid and also more variable than that of the Sun.

TABLE 3. LONGITUDE CORRECTION

X	40m	45m	50m	55m	60m	65m	70m
A							
h	m	m	m	m	m	m	m
1	2	2	2	2	3	3	3
2	3	4	4	5	5	5	6
3	5	6	6	7	8	8	9
4	7	8	8	9	10	11	12
5	8	9	10	11	13	14	15
6	10	11	13	14	15	16	18
7	12	13	15	16	18	19	20
8	13	15	17	18	20	22	23
9	15	17	19	21	23	24	26
10	17	19	21	23	25	27	29
11	18	21	23	25	28	30	32
12	20	23	25	28	30	33	35
13	22	24	27	30	33	35	38
14	23	26	29	32	35	38	41
15	25	28	31	34	38	41	44
16	27	30	33	37	40	43	47
17	28	32	35	39	43	46	50
18	30	34	38	41	45	49	53
19	32	36	40	44	48	51	55
20	33	38	42	46	50	54	58
21	35	39	44	48	53	57	61
22	37	41	46	50	55	60	64
23	38	43	48	53	58	62	67
24	40	45	50	55	60	65	70

The parallax of the Moon, about 57', is near to the sum of the semi-diameter and refraction but has the opposite effect on these times. It is thus convenient to neglect all three quantities in the method outlined below.

Notation

ϕ	= latitude of observer
λ	= longitude of observer (measured positively towards the west)
T_{-1}	= time of transit of Moon on previous day
T_0	= time of transit of Moon on day in question
T_1	= time of transit of Moon on following day
δ_0	= approximate declination of Moon
δ_R	= declination of Moon at moonrise
δ_S	= declination of Moon at moonset
h_0	= approximate hour angle of Moon
h_R	= hour angle of Moon at moonrise
h_S	= hour angle of Moon at moonset
t_R	= time of moonrise
t_S	= time of moonset

Method

1. With arguments ϕ, δ_0 enter Table 1 on page 1276 to determine h_0 where h_0 is negative for moonrise and positive for moonset.

2. Form approximate times from
$$t_R = T_0 + \lambda + h_0$$
$$t_S = T_0 + \lambda + h_0$$

3. Determine δ_R, δ_S for times t_R, t_S respectively.

4. Re-enter Table 1 on page 1266 with
(a) arguments ϕ, δ_R to determine h_R
(b) arguments ϕ, δ_S to determine h_S

5. Form $t_R = T_0 + \lambda + h_R + AX$
$\quad\quad t_S = T_0 + \lambda + h_S + AX$

where $A = (\lambda + h)$

and $\quad X = (T_0 - T_{-1})$ if $(\lambda + h)$ is negative
$\quad\quad\quad X = (T_1 - T_0)$ if $(\lambda + h)$ is positive

AX is the respondent in Table 3.

Example – To find the times of moonrise and moonset at Vancouver ($\phi = +49°$, $\lambda = +8h\ 12m$) on 2006 August 13. The starting data (page 1252) are

T_{-1} = 2h 25m
T_0 = 3h 15m
T_1 = 4h 05m
δ_0 = +6°

1. h_0 = 6h 28m
2. Approximate values
t_R = 13d 03h 15m + 8h 12m + (−6h 28m)
= 13d 04h 59m
t_S = 13d 03h 15m + 8h 12m + (+6h 28m)
= 13d 17h 55m
3. δ_R = +6°.2
δ_S = +9°.9
4. h_R = − 6h 29m
h_S = +6h 47m
5. t_R = 13d 03h 15m + 8h 12m + (−6h 29m) + 3m
= 13d 05h 01m
t_S = 13d 03h 15m + 8h 12m + (+6h 47m) + 31m
= 13d 18h 45m

To get the LMT of the phenomenon the longitude is subtracted from the GMT thus:

Moonrise = 13d 05h 01m − 8h 12m = 12d 20h 49m
Moonset = 13d 18h 45m − 8h 12m = 13d 10h 33m

ECLIPSES 2006

ECLIPSES

During 2006 there will be three eclipses, two of the Sun and one of the Moon. (Penumbral eclipses are not mentioned in this section as they are so difficult to observe).

1. A total eclipse of the Sun on March 29 is visible as a partial eclipse from the extreme east of Brazil, the Atlantic Ocean, Africa (except the southwest), Iceland, northeast Greenland, the Arctic Ocean, Europe, Asia (except the east, and southern India). The partial phase begins at 07h 37m and ends at 12h 46m.

The track of the central line starts in the extreme eastern part of Brazil, crosses the Atlantic Ocean, passes through Ghana, Togo, Benin, Nigeria, Niger, extreme northwest Chad, Libya, extreme northwest Egypt, Turkey, Georgia, and southern Russia, before ending in Kazakhstan. Totality begins at 8h 34m and ends at 11h 48m. The maximum duration of totality is 4m 07s. At Greenwich the partial eclipse begins at 09h 45m and ends at 11h 22m: at maximum 28 per cent of the Sun is obscured. From Edinburgh the partial eclipse begins at 09h 55m and ends at 11h 16m: at maximum 20 per cent of the Sun is obscured.

2. A partial eclipse of the Moon on September 7 is visible from the western Pacific Ocean, Australasia, Asia, Africa, Europe, Antarctica, Iceland, and eastern Brazil. The eclipse begins at 18h 05m and ends at 19h 38m. At maximum 19 per cent of the Moon's disk is obscured.

3. An annual eclipse of the Sun on September 22 is visible as a partial eclipse from Central and South America, the Atlantic Ocean, west and south Africa, southern Madagascar, and Antarctica. The partial phase begins at 08h 40m and ends at 14h 40m. The path of annularity starts in Guyana, crosses Surinam, French Guiana and ends in the south Atlantic Ocean. Annularity begins at 09h 48m and ends at 13h 31m. The maximum duration is 07m 09s.

TRANSIT

A transit of Mercury across the face of the Sun occurs on November 8. The beginning is visible from Bermuda, the Americas, Hawaii, and New Zealand. The end is visible from Hawaii, Australasia and extreme eastern Asia. It begins at 19h 12m and ends at 24h 08m. Although times vary slightly depending on the observer's position, the differences from the times above are not likely to be much more than about one minute.

POSITIONS OF STARS

The positions of heavenly bodies on the celestial sphere are defined by two co-ordinates, right ascension and declination, which are analogous to longitude and latitude on the surface of the Earth. If we imagine the plane of the terrestrial equator extended indefinitely, it will cut the celestial sphere in a great circle known as the celestial equator. Similarly the plane of the Earth's orbit, when extended, cuts in the great circle called the ecliptic. The two intersections of these circles are known as the First Point of Aries and the First Point of Libra. If from any star a perpendicular is drawn to the celestial equator, the length of this perpendicular is the star's declination. The arc, measured eastwards along the equator from the First Point of Aries to the foot of this perpendicular, is the

right ascension. An alternative definition of right ascension is that it is the angle at the celestial pole (where the Earth's axis, if prolonged, would meet the sphere) between the great circles to the First Point of Aries and to the star.

The plane of the Earth's equator has a slow movement, so that our reference system for right ascension and declination is not fixed. The consequent alteration in these quantities from year to year is called precession. In right ascension it is an increase of about 3 seconds a year for equatorial stars, and larger or smaller changes in either direction for stars near the poles, depending on the right ascension of the star. In declination it varies between $+20''$ and $-20''$ according to the right ascension of the star.

A star or other body crosses the meridian when the sidereal time is equal to its right ascension. The altitude is then a maximum, and may be deduced by remembering that the altitude of the elevated pole is numerically equal to the latitude, while that of the equator at its intersection with the meridian is equal to the co-latitude, or complement of the latitude.

Thus in London (lat. 51° 30′) the meridian altitude of Sirius is found as follows:

	°	′
Altitude of equator	38	30
Declination south	16	43
Difference	21	47

The altitude of Capella (Dec. $+46°$ 00′) at lower transit is:

	°	′
Altitude of pole	51	30
Polar distance of star	44	00
Difference	7	30

The brightness of a heavenly body is denoted by its magnitude. Omitting the exceptionally bright stars Sirius and Canopus, the twenty brightest stars are of the first magnitude, while the faintest stars visible to the naked eye are of the sixth magnitude. The magnitude scale is a precise one, as a difference of five magnitudes represents a ratio of 100 to 1 in brightness. Typical second magnitude stars are Polaris and the stars in the belt of Orion. The scale is most easily fixed in memory by comparing the stars with Norton's *Star Atlas*. The stars Sirius and Canopus and the planets Venus and Jupiter are so bright that their magnitudes are expressed by negative numbers. A small telescope will show stars down to the ninth or tenth magnitude, while stars fainter than the twentieth magnitude may be photographed by long exposures with the largest telescopes.

MEAN AND SIDEREAL TIME

The length of a sidereal day in mean time is 23h 56m 04s.09. Hence 1h MT = 1h+9ˢ.86 ST and 1h ST = 1h−9ˢ.83 MT.

To convert an interval of mean time to the corresponding interval of sidereal time, enter the acceleration table with the given mean time (taking the hours and the minutes and seconds separately) and add the acceleration obtained to the given mean time. To convert an interval of sidereal time to the corresponding interval of mean time, take out the retardation for the given sidereal time and subtract.

Acceleration							Retardation					
h	m	s	m	s	s		h	m	s	m	s	s
1	0	10	0	00			1	0	10	0	00	
2	0	20	3	02	0		2	0	20	3	03	0
3	0	30	9	07	1		3	0	29	9	09	1
4	0	39	15	13	2		4	0	39	15	15	2
5	0	49	21	18	3		5	0	49	21	21	3
6	0	59	27	23	4		6	0	59	27	28	4
7	1	09	33	28	5		7	1	09	33	34	5
8	1	19	39	34	6		8	1	19	39	40	6
9	1	29	45	39	7		9	1	28	45	46	7
10	1	39	51	44	8		10	1	38	51	53	8
11	1	48	57	49	9		11	1	48	57	59	9
12	1	58	60	00	10		12	1	58	60	00	10
13	2	08					13	2	08			
14	2	18					14	2	18			
15	2	28					15	2	27			
16	2	38					16	2	37			
17	2	48					17	2	47			
18	2	57					18	2	57			
19	3	07					19	3	07			
20	3	17					20	3	17			
21	3	27					21	3	26			
22	3	37					22	3	36			
23	3	47					23	3	46			
24	3	57					24	3	56			

The columns for the minutes and seconds of the argument are in the form known as critical tables. To use these tables, find in the appropriate left-hand column the two entries between which the given number of minutes and seconds lies, the quantity in the right-hand column between these two entries is the required acceleration or retardation. Thus the acceleration for 11m 26s (which lies between the entries 9m 07s and 15m 13s) is 2s. If the given number of minutes and seconds is a tabular entry, the required acceleration or retardation is the entry in the right-hand column above the given tabular entry, e.g. the retardation for 45m 46s is 7s.

Example – Convert 14h 27m 35s from ST to MT

	h	m	s
Given ST	14	27	35
Retardation for 14h		2	18
Retardation for 27m 35s			5
Corresponding MT	14	25	12

For further explanation, *see* pages 1281–2.

EXPLANATION OF ASTRONOMICAL DATA

Positions of the heavenly bodies are given only to the degree of accuracy required by amateur astronomers for setting telescopes, or for plotting on celestial globes or star atlases. Where intermediate positions are required, linear interpolation may be employed.

Definitions of the terms used cannot be given here. They must be sought in astronomical literature and textbooks.

A special feature has been made of the times when the various heavenly bodies are visible in the British Isles. Since two columns, calculated for latitudes 52° and 56°, are devoted to risings and settings, the range 50° to 58° can be covered by interpolation and extrapolation. The times given in these columns are Greenwich Mean Times for the meridian of Greenwich. An observer west of this meridian must add his/her longitude (in time) and vice versa.

In accordance with the usual convention in astronomy, + and − indicate respectively north and south latitudes or declinations.

All data are, unless otherwise stated, for 0h Greenwich Mean Time (GMT), i.e. at the midnight at the beginning of the day named. Allowance must be made for British Summer Time during the period that this is in operation.

PAGE ONE OF EACH MONTH

The calendar for each month is explained on page 1227.

Under the heading Astronomical Phenomena will be found particulars of the more important conjunctions of the Sun, Moon and planets with each other, and also the dates of other astronomical phenomena of special interest.

Times of Minima of Algol are approximate times of the middle of the period of diminished light.

The Constellations listed each month are those that are near the meridian at the beginning of the month at 22h local mean time. Allowance must be made for British Summer Time if necessary. The fact that any star crosses the meridian 4m earlier each night or 2h earlier each month may be used, in conjunction with the lists given each month, to find what constellations are favourably placed at any moment. The table preceding the list of constellations may be extended indefinitely at the rate just quoted.

The principal phases of the Moon are the GMTs when the difference between the longitude of the Moon and that of the Sun is 0°, 90°, 180° or 270°. The times of perigee and apogee are those when the Moon is nearest to, and farthest from, the Earth, respectively. The nodes or points of intersection of the Moon's orbit and the ecliptic make a complete retrograde circuit of the ecliptic in about 19 years. From a knowledge of the longitude of the ascending node and the inclination, whose value does not vary much from 5°, the path of the Moon among the stars may be plotted on a celestial globe or star atlas.

PAGE TWO OF EACH MONTH

The Sun's semi-diameter, in arc, is given once a month.

The right ascension and declination (Dec.) is that of the true Sun. The right ascension of the mean Sun is obtained by applying the equation of time, with the sign given, to the right ascension of the true Sun, or, more easily, by applying 12h to the Sidereal Time. The direction in which the equation of time has to be applied in different problems is a frequent source of confusion and error. Apparent Solar Time is equal to the Mean Solar Time plus the Equation of Time. For example, at 12h GMT on August 8 the Equation of Time is −5m 40s and thus at 12h Mean Time on that day the Apparent Time is 12h − 5m 40s = 11h 54m 20s.

The Greenwich Sidereal Time at 0h and the Transit of the First Point of Aries (which is really the mean time when the sidereal time is 0h) are used for converting mean time to sidereal time and vice versa.

The GMT of transit of the Sun at Greenwich may also be taken as the local mean time (LMT) of transit in any longitude. It is independent of latitude. The GMT of transit in any longitude is obtained by adding the longitude to the time given if west, and vice versa.

LIGHTING-UP TIME

The legal importance of sunrise and sunset is that the Road Vehicles Lighting Regulations 1989 (SI 1989 No. 1796) make the use of front and rear position lamps on vehicles compulsory during the period between sunset and sunrise. Headlamps on vehicles are required to be used during the hours of darkness on unlit roads or whenever visibility is seriously reduced. The hours of darkness are defined in these regulations as the period between half an hour after sunset and half an hour before sunrise.

In all laws and regulations 'sunset' refers to the local sunset, i.e. the time at which the Sun sets at the place in question. This common-sense interpretation has been upheld by legal tribunals. Thus the necessity for providing for different latitudes and longitudes, as already described, is evident.

SUNRISE AND SUNSET

The times of sunrise and sunset are those when the Sun's upper limb, as affected by refraction, is on the true horizon of an observer at sea-level. Assuming the mean refraction to be 34', and the Sun's semi-diameter to be 16', the time given is that when the true zenith distance of the Sun's centre is 90°+34'+16' or 90° 50', or, in other words, when the depression of the Sun's centre below the true horizon is 50'. The upper limb is then 34' below the true horizon, but is brought there by refraction. An observer on a ship might see the Sun for a minute or so longer, because of the dip of the horizon, while another viewing the sunset over hills or mountains would record an earlier time. Nevertheless, the moment when the true zenith distance of the Sun's centre is 90° 50' is a precise time dependent only on the latitude and longitude of the place, and independent of its altitude above sea-level, the contour of its horizon, the vagaries of refraction or the small seasonal change in the Sun's semi-diameter; this moment is suitable in every way as a definition of sunset (or sunrise) for all statutory purposes. (For further information, see footnote on page 1281.)

TWILIGHT

Light reaches us before sunrise and continues to reach us for some time after sunset. The interval between darkness and sunrise or sunset and darkness is called twilight. Astronomically speaking, twilight is considered to begin or end when the Sun's centre is 18° below the horizon, as no light from the Sun can then reach the observer. As thus defined twilight may last several hours; in high latitudes at the summer solstice the depression of 18° is not reached, and twilight lasts from sunset to sunrise.

The need for some sub-division of twilight is met by dividing the gathering darkness into four stages.

(1) *Sunrise or Sunset*, defined as above
(2) *Civil twilight*, which begins or ends when the Sun's centre is 6° below the horizon. This marks the time when operations requiring daylight may commence or must cease. In England it varies from about 30 to 60 minutes after sunset and the same interval before sunrise
(3) *Nautical twilight*, which begins or ends when the Sun's centre is 12° below the horizon. This marks the time when it is, to all intents and purposes, completely dark
(4) *Astronomical twilight*, which begins or ends when the Sun's centre is 18° below the horizon. This marks theoretical perfect darkness. It is of little practical importance, especially if nautical twilight is tabulated

To assist observers the durations of civil, nautical and astronomical twilights are given at intervals of ten days. The beginning of a particular twilight is found by subtracting the duration from the time of sunrise, while the end is found by adding the duration to the time of sunset. Thus the beginning of astronomical twilight in latitude 52°, on the Greenwich meridian, on March 11 is found as 06h 24m − 113m = 04h 31m and similarly the end of civil twilight as 17h 57m +34m = 18h 31m. The

letters TAN (twilight all night) are printed when twilight lasts all night.

Under the heading The Night Sky will be found notes describing the position and visibility of the planets and other phenomena.

PAGE THREE OF EACH MONTH

The Moon moves so rapidly among the stars that its position is given only to the degree of accuracy that permits linear interpolation. The right ascension (RA) and declination (Dec.) are geocentric, i.e. for an imaginary observer at the centre of the Earth. To an observer on the surface of the Earth the position is always different, as the altitude is always less on account of parallax, which may reach 1°.

The lunar terminator is the line separating the bright from the dark part of the Moon's disk. Apart from irregularities of the lunar surface, the terminator is elliptical, because it is a circle seen in projection. It becomes the full circle forming the limb, or edge, of the Moon at New and Full Moon. The selenographic longitude of the terminator is measured from the mean centre of the visible disk, which may differ from the visible centre by as much as 8°, because of libration.

Instead of the longitude of the terminator the Sun's selenographic co-longitude (Sun's co-long.) is tabulated. It is numerically equal to the selenographic longitude of the morning terminator, measured eastwards from the mean centre of the disk. Thus its value is approximately 270° at New Moon, 360° at First Quarter, 90° at Full Moon and 180° at Last Quarter.

The Position Angle (PA) of the Bright Limb is the position angle of the midpoint of the illuminated limb, measured eastwards from the north point on the disk. The Phase column shows the percentage of the area of the Moon's disk illuminated; this is also the illuminated percentage of the diameter at right angles to the line of cusps. The terminator is a semi-ellipse whose major axis is the line of cusps, and whose semi-minor axis is determined by the tabulated percentage; from New Moon to Full Moon the east limb is dark, and vice versa.

The times given as moonrise and moonset are those when the upper limb of the Moon is on the horizon of an observer at sea-level. The Sun's horizontal parallax (Hor. par.) is about 9", and is negligible when considering sunrise and sunset, but that of the Moon averages about 57'. Hence the computed time represents the moment when the true zenith distance of the Moon is 90° 50' (as for the Sun) minus the horizontal parallax. The time required for the Sun or Moon to rise or set is about four minutes (except in high latitudes). See also page 1277 and footnote on page 1281.

The GMT of transit of the Moon over the meridian of Greenwich is given; these times are independent of latitude but must be corrected for longitude. For places in the British Isles it suffices to add the longitude if west, and vice versa. For other places a further correction is necessary because of the rapid movement of the Moon relative to the stars. The entire correction is conveniently determined by first finding the west longitude λ of the place. If the place is in west longitude, λ is the ordinary west longitude; if the place is in east longitude λ is the complement to 24h (or 360°) of the longitude and will be greater than 12h (or 180°). The correction then consists of two positive portions, namely λ and the fraction $\lambda/24$ (or $\lambda°/360$) multiplied by the difference between consecutive transits. Thus for Christchurch, New Zealand, the longitude is 11h 31m east, so λ = 12h 29m and the fraction $\lambda/24$ is 0.52. The transit on the local date 22 May 2006 is found as follows:

		d	h	m
GMT of transit at Greenwich	May	21	07	01
λ			12	29
$0.52 \times (6h\ 53m - 6h\ 05m)$				25
GMT of transit at Christchurch		21	19	55
Corr. to NZ Standard Time			12	00
Local standard time of transit	May	22	07	55

As is evident, for any given place the quantities λ and the correction to local standard time may be combined permanently, being here 24h 29m.

Positions of Mercury are given for every second day, and those of Venus and Mars for every fifth day; they may be interpolated linearly. The diameter (Diam.) is given in seconds of arc. The phase is the illuminated percentage of the disk. In the case of the inner planets this approaches 100 at superior conjunction and 0 at inferior conjunction. When the phase is less than 50 the planet is crescent-shaped or horned; for greater phases it is gibbous. In the case of the exterior planet Mars, the phase approaches 100 at conjunction and opposition, and is a minimum at the quadratures.

Since the planets cannot be seen when on the horizon, the actual times of rising and setting are not given; instead, the time when the planet has an apparent altitude of 5° has been tabulated. If the time of transit is between 00h and 12h the time refers to an altitude of 5° above the eastern horizon; if between 12h and 24h, to the western horizon. The phenomenon tabulated is the one that occurs between sunset and sunrise. The times given may be interpolated for latitude and corrected for longitude, as in the case of the Sun and Moon.

PAGE FOUR OF EACH MONTH

The GMTs of sunrise and sunset for seven cities, whose adopted positions in longitude (W.) and latitude (N.) are given immediately below the name, may be used not only for these phenomena, but also for lighting-up times (*see* pages 1279–80 for a fuller explanation).

The particulars for the four outer planets resemble those for the planets on Page Three of each month, except that, under Uranus and Neptune, times when the planet is 10° high instead of 5° high are given; this is because of the inferior brightness of these planets. The diameters given for the rings of Saturn are those of the major axis (in the plane of the planet's equator) and the minor axis respectively. The former has a small seasonal change due to the slightly varying distance of the Earth from Saturn,

SUNRISE, SUNSET, MOONRISE AND MOONSET

The tables have been constructed for the meridian of Greenwich and for latitudes 52° and 56°. They give Greenwich Mean Time (GMT) throughout the year. To obtain the GMT of the phenomenon as seen from any other latitude and longitude in the British Isles, first interpolate or extrapolate for latitude by the usual rules of proportion. To the time thus found, the longitude (expressed in time) is to be added if west (as it usually is in Great Britain) or subtracted if east. If the longitude is expressed in degrees and minutes of arc, it must be converted to time at the rate of $1° = 4m$ and $15' = 1m$. A method of calculating rise and set time for other places in the world is given on page 1277

The GMT at which the planet transits the Greenwich meridian is also given. The times of transit are to be corrected to local meridians in the usual way, as already described.

but the latter varies from zero when the Earth passes through the ring plane every 15 years to its maximum opening half-way between these periods. The rings were last open at their widest extent (and Saturn at its brightest) in 2002; this will occur again in 2017. The Earth passed through the ring plane in 1995–6 and will do so again in 2009.

TIME

From the earliest ages, the natural division of time into recurring periods of day and night has provided the practical time-scale for the everyday activities of the human race. Indeed, if any alternative means of time measurement is adopted, it must be capable of adjustment so as to remain in general agreement with the natural time-scale defined by the diurnal rotation of the Earth on its axis. Ideally the rotation should be measured against a fixed frame of reference; in practice it must be measured against the background provided by the celestial bodies. If the Sun is chosen as the reference point, we obtain Apparent Solar Time, which is the time indicated by a sundial. It is not a uniform time but is subject to variations which amount to as much as a quarter of an hour in each direction. Such wide variations cannot be tolerated in a practical time-scale, and this has led to the concept of Mean Solar Time in which all the days are exactly the same length and equal to the average length of the Apparent Solar Day.

The positions of the stars in the sky are specified in relation to a fictitious reference point in the sky known as the First Point of Aries (or the Vernal Equinox). It is therefore convenient to adopt this same reference point when considering the rotation of the Earth against the background of the stars. The time-scale so obtained is known as Apparent Sidereal Time.

GREENWICH MEAN TIME

The daily rotation of the Earth on its axis causes the Sun and the other heavenly bodies to appear to cross the sky from east to west. It is convenient to represent this relative motion as if the Sun really performed a daily circuit around a fixed Earth. Noon in Apparent Solar Time may then be defined as the time at which the Sun transits across the observer's meridian. In Mean Solar Time, noon is similarly defined by the meridian transit of a fictitious Mean Sun moving uniformly in the sky with the same average speed as the true Sun. Mean Solar Time observed on the meridian of the transit circle telescope of the Royal Observatory at Greenwich is called Greenwich Mean Time (GMT). The mean solar day is divided into 24 hours and, for astronomical and other scientific purposes, these are numbered 0 to 23, commencing at midnight. Civil time is usually reckoned in two periods of 12 hours, designated a.m. (*ante meridiem*, i.e. before noon) and p.m. (*post meridiem*, i.e. after noon), although the 24 hour clock is increasingly being used.

UNIVERSAL TIME

Before 1925 January 1, GMT was reckoned in 24 hours commencing at noon; since that date it has been reckoned from midnight. To avoid confusion in the use of the designation GMT before and after 1925, since 1928 astronomers have tended to use the term Universal Time (UT) or Weltzeit (WZ) to denote GMT measured from Greenwich Mean Midnight.

In precision work it is necessary to take account of small variations in Universal Time. These arise from small irregularities in the rotation of the Earth. Observed astronomical time is designated UT0. Observed time corrected for the effects of the motion of the poles (giving rise to a 'wandering' in longitude) is designated UT1. There is also a seasonal fluctuation in the rate of rotation of the Earth arising from meteorological causes, often called the annual fluctuation. UT1 corrected for this effect is designated UT2 and provides a time-scale free from short-period fluctuations. It is still subject to small secular and irregular changes.

APPARENT SOLAR TIME

As mentioned above, the time shown by a sundial is called Apparent Solar Time. It differs from Mean Solar Time by an amount known as the Equation of Time, which is the total effect of two causes which make the length of the apparent solar day non-uniform. One cause of variation is that the orbit of the Earth is not a circle but an ellipse, having the Sun at one focus. As a consequence, the angular speed of the Earth in its orbit is not constant; it is greatest at the beginning of January when the Earth is nearest the Sun.

The other cause is due to the obliquity of the ecliptic; the plane of the equator (which is at right angles to the axis of rotation of the Earth) does not coincide with the ecliptic (the plane defined by the apparent annual motion of the Sun around the celestial sphere) but is inclined to it at an angle of 23° 26'. As a result, the apparent solar day is shorter than average at the equinoxes and longer at the solstices. From the combined effects of the components due to obliquity and eccentricity, the equation of time reaches its maximum values in February (−14 minutes) and early November (+16 minutes). It has a zero value on four dates during the year, and it is only on these dates (approximately April 15, June 14, September 1 and December 25) that a sundial shows Mean Solar Time.

SIDEREAL TIME

A sidereal day is the duration of a complete rotation of the Earth with reference to the First Point of Aries. The term sidereal (or 'star') time is a little misleading since the time-scale so defined is not exactly the same as that which would be defined by successive transits of a selected star, as there is a small progressive motion between the stars and the First Point of Aries due to the precession of the Earth's axis. This makes the length of the sidereal day shorter than the true period of rotation by 0.008 seconds. Superimposed on this steady precessional motion are small oscillations (nutation), giving rise to fluctuations in apparent sidereal time amounting to as much as 1.2 seconds. It is therefore customary to employ Mean Sidereal Time, from which these fluctuations have been removed. The conversion of GMT to Greenwich sidereal time (GST) may be performed by adding the value of the GST at 0h on the day in question (page two of each month) to the GMT converted to sidereal time using the table on page 1279.

Example – To find the GST at August 8d 02h 41m 11s GMT

	h	m	s
GST at 0h	21	05	27
GMT	2	41	11
Acceleration for 2h			20
Acceleration for 41m 11s			7
Sum = GST =	23	47	05

If the observer is not on the Greenwich meridian then his/her longitude, measured positively westwards from Greenwich, must be subtracted from the GST to obtain Local Sidereal Time (LST). Thus, in the above example, an observer 5h east of Greenwich, or 19h west, would find the LST as 4h 47m 05s.

EPHEMERIS TIME

An analysis of observations of the positions of the Sun, Moon and planets taken over an extended period is used in preparing ephemerides. (An ephemeris is a table giving the apparent position of a heavenly body at regular intervals of time, e.g. one day or ten days, and may be used to compare current observations with tabulated positions.) Discrepancies between the positions of heavenly bodies observed over a 300-year period and their predicted positions arose because the time-scale to which the observations were related was based on the assumption that the rate of rotation of the Earth is uniform. It is now known that this rate of rotation is variable. A revised time-scale, Ephemeris Time (ET), was devised to bring the ephemerides into agreement with the observations.

The second of ET is defined in terms of the annual motion of the Earth in its orbit around the Sun (1/31556925.9747 of the tropical year for 1900 January 0d 12h ET). The precise determination of ET from astronomical observations is a lengthy process as the requisite standard of accuracy can only be achieved by averaging over a number of years.

In 1976 the International Astronomical Union adopted Terrestrial Dynamical Time (TDT), a new dynamical time-scale for general use whose scale unit is the SI second (*see* Atomic Time, below). TDT was renamed Terrestrial Time (TT) in 1991. ET is now of little more than historical interest.

TERRESTRIAL TIME

The uniform time system used in computing the ephemerides of the solar system is Terrestrial Time (TT), which has replaced ET for this purpose. Except for the most rigorous astronomical calculations, it may be assumed to be the same as ET. During 2006 the estimated difference TT − UT is about 65 seconds.

ATOMIC TIME

The fundamental standards of time and frequency must be defined in terms of a periodic motion adequately uniform, enduring and measurable. Progress has made it possible to use natural standards, such as atomic or molecular oscillations. Continuous oscillations are generated in an electrical circuit, the frequency of which is then compared or brought into coincidence with the frequency characteristic of the absorption or emission by the atoms or molecules when they change between two selected energy levels. Since the 13th General Conference on Weights and Measures in October 1967, the unit of time, the second, has been defined in the International System of units (SI) as 'the duration of 9 192 631 770 periods of the radiation corresponding to the transition between the two hyperfine levels of the ground state of the caesium-133 atom.'

In the UK, the national time scale is maintained by the National Physical Laboratory (NPL), using an ensemble of atomic clocks based on either caesium or hydrogen atoms. In addition the NPL (along with several other national laboratories) has constructed and operates a caesium fountain primary frequency standard, which utilises the cooling of caesium atoms by laser light to determine the duration of the SI second at the highest attainable level of accuracy. Caesium fountain primary standards typically achieve an accuracy of around 1 part in 1,000 000 000 000 000, which is equivalent to one second in 30 million years.

Timekeeping worldwide is based on two closely related atomic time scales that are established through international collaboration. International Atomic Time (TAI) is formed by combining the readings of more than 250 atomic clocks located in about 55 institutes and was set close to the astronomically-based Universal Time (UT) near the beginning of 1958. It was formally recognised in 1971 and since 1988 January 1 has been maintained by the International Bureau of Weights and Measures (BIPM). Civil time in almost all countries is now based on Co-ordinated Universal Time (UTC), which differs from TAI by an integer number of seconds and was designed to make both atomic time and UT available with accuracy appropriate for most users. On 1 January 1972 UTC was set to be exactly 10 seconds behind TAI, and since then the UTC time-scale has been adjusted by the insertion (or, in principle, omission) of leap seconds in order to keep it within ±0.9 s of UT. These leap seconds are introduced, when necessary, at the same instant throughout the world, either at the end of December or at the end of June. The last leap second occurred at 0h UTC on 1 January 1999, and was the 22nd leap second. All leap seconds so far have been positive, with 61 seconds in the final minute of the UTC month. The time 23h 59m 60s UTC is followed one second later by 0h 0m 00s of the first day of the following month. Notices concerning the insertion of leap seconds are issued by the International Earth Rotation Service (IERS) at the Observatoire de Paris.

The computation of UTC is carried out monthly by the BIPM and takes place in three stages. First, a weighted average known as Echelle Atomique Libre (EAL) is calculated from all of the contributing atomic clocks. In the second stage, TAI is generated by applying small corrections, derived from the results contributed by primary frequency standards, to the scale interval of EAL to maintain its value close to that of the SI second. Finally, UTC is formed from TAI by the addition of an integer number of seconds. The results are published monthly in the BIPM Circular T in the form of offsets at 5-day intervals between UTC and the time scales of contributing organisations.

RADIO TIME-SIGNALS

UTC is made generally available through time-signals and standard frequency broadcasts such as MSF in the UK, CHU in Canada and WWV and WWVH in the USA. These are based on national time-scales that are maintained in close agreement with UTC and provide traceability to the national time-scale and to UTC. The markers of seconds in the UTC scale coincide with those of TAI.

To disseminate the national time-scale in the UK, special signals are broadcast by the National Physical Laboratory radio station at Rugby (call-sign MSF). The signals are controlled from a caesium beam atomic frequency standard and consist of a precise frequency carrier of 60 kHz which is switched off, after being on for at least half a second, to mark every second. The first second of the minute begins with a period of 500 ms with the carrier switched off, to serve as a minute marker. In the other seconds the carrier is always off for at least one tenth of a second at the start and then it carries an on-off code giving the British clock time and date, together with

information identifying the start of the next minute. Changes to and from summer time are made following government announcements. Leap seconds are inserted as announced by the IERS and information provided by them on the difference between UTC and UT is also signalled. Other broadcast signals in the UK include the BBC six pips signal, the BT Timeline ('speaking clock'), the NPL Truetime service for computers, and a coded time-signal on the BBC 198 kHz transmitters which is used for timing in the electricity supply industry. From 1972 January 1 the six pips on the BBC have consisted of five short pips from second 55 to second 59 (six pips in the case of a leap second) followed by one lengthened pip, the start of which indicates the exact minute. From 1990 February 5 these signals have been controlled by the BBC with seconds markers referenced to the satellite-based US navigation system GPS (Global Positioning System) and time and day referenced to the MSF transmitter. Formerly they were generated by the Royal Greenwich Observatory. The BT Timeline is compared daily with the National Physical Laboratory caesium beam atomic frequency standard at the Rugby radio station. The NPL Truetime service is directly connected to the national time scale.

Accurate timing may also be obtained from the signals of international navigation systems such as the ground-based Omega, or the satellite-based American GPS or Russian GLONASS systems.

STANDARD TIME

Since 1880 the standard time in Britain has been Greenwich Mean Time (GMT); a statute that year enacted that the word 'time' when used in any legal document relating to Britain meant, unless otherwise specifically stated, the mean time of the Greenwich meridian. Greenwich was adopted as the universal meridian on 13 October 1884. A system of standard time by zones is used world-wide, standard time in each zone differing from that of the Greenwich meridian by an integral number of hours, either fast or slow. The large territories of the USA and Canada are divided into zones approximately 7.5° on either side of central meridians.

Variations from the standard time of some countries occur during part of the year; they are decided annually and are usually referred to as Summer Time or Daylight Saving Time.

At the 180th meridian the time can be either 12 hours fast on Greenwich Mean Time or 12 hours slow, and a change of date occurs. The internationally recognised date or calendar line is a modification of the 180th meridian, drawn so as to include islands of any one group on the same side of the line, or for political reasons. The line is indicated by joining up the following co-ordinates:

Lat.	Long.	Lat.	Long.
90° S.	180°	48° N.	180°
51° S.	180°	53° N.	170° E.
45° S.	172.5° W.	65.5° N.	169° W.
15° S.	172.5° W.	68° N.	169° W.
5° S.	180°	90° N.	180°

Changes to the date line would require an international conference.

BRITISH SUMMER TIME

In 1916 an Act ordained that during a defined period of that year the legal time for general purposes in Great Britain should be one hour in advance of Greenwich

Mean Time. The Summer Time Acts 1922 and 1925 defined the period during which Summer Time was to be in force, stabilising practice until the Second World War.

During World War 2 (1941–5) and in 1947 Double Summer Time (two hours in advance of Greenwich Mean Time) was used for the period in which ordinary Summer Time would have been in force. During these years clocks were also kept one hour in advance of Greenwich Mean Time in the winter. After the war, ordinary Summer Time was invoked each year from 1948–68.

Between 1968 October 27 and 1971 October 31 clocks were kept one hour ahead of Greenwich Mean Time throughout the year. This was known as British Standard Time.

The most recent legislation is the Summer Time Act 1972, which enacted that 'the period of summer time for the purposes of this Act is the period beginning at two o'clock, Greenwich mean time, in the morning of the day after the third Saturday in March or, if that day is Easter Day, the day after the second Saturday in March, and ending at two o'clock, Greenwich mean time, in the morning of the day after the fourth Saturday in October.'

The duration of Summer Time can be varied by Order in Council and in recent years alterations have been made to synchronise the period of Summer Time in Britain with that used in Europe. The rule for 1981–94 defined the period of Summer Time in the UK as from the last Sunday in March to the day following the fourth Saturday in October and the hour of changeover was altered to 01h Greenwich Mean Time.

There was no rule for the dates of Summer Time between 1995–7. Since 1998 the 9th European Parliament and Council Directive on Summer Time has harmonised the dates on which Summer Time begins and ends across member states as the last Sundays in March and October respectively. Under the Directive Summer Time begins and ends at 01hr Greenwich Mean Time in each member state. Amendments to the Summer Time Act to implement the Directive came into force on 11 March 2002.

The duration of Summer Time in 2006 is:

March 26 01h GMT to October 29 01h GMT

MEAN REFRACTION

Alt.		Ref.	Alt.		Ref.	Alt.		Ref.
°	′	′	°	′	′	°	′	′
1	20	21	3	12	13	7	54	6
1	30	20	3	34	12	9	27	5
1	41	19	4	00	11	11	39	4
1	52	18	4	30	10	15	00	3
2	05	17	5	06	9	20	42	2
2	19	16	5	50	8	32	20	1
2	35	15	6	44	7	62	17	0
2	52	14	7	54		90	00	
3	12							

The refraction table is in the form of a critical table (*see* page 1279)

ASTRONOMICAL CONSTANTS

Solar parallax	8″.794
Astronomical unit	149597870 km
Precession for the year 2006	50″.291
Precession in right ascension	3ˢ.075
Precession in declination	20″.043
Constant of nutation	9″.202
Constant of aberration	20″.496
Mean obliquity of ecliptic (2006)	23° 26′ 18″
Moon's equatorial hor. parallax	57′ 02″.70
Velocity of light in vacuo per second	299792.5 km
Solar motion per second	20.0 km
Equatorial radius of the Earth	6378.140 km
Polar radius of the Earth	6356.755 km
North galactic pole (IAU standard)	
	RA 12h 49m (1950.0). Dec. +27°.4 N.
Solar apex	RA 18h 06m Dec.+30°

Length of year (in mean solar days)

Tropical	365.24219
Sidereal	365.25636
Anomalistic (perihelion to perihelion)	365.25964
Eclipse	346.62000

Length of month (mean values)	d	h	m	s
New Moon to New	29	12	44	02.9
Sidereal	27	07	43	11.5
Anomalistic (perigee to perigee)	27	13	18	33.2

THE EARTH

The shape of the Earth is that of an oblate spheroid or solid of revolution whose meridian sections are ellipses not differing much from circles, whilst the sections at right angles are circles. The length of the equatorial axis is about 12,756 km, and that of the polar axis is 12,714 km. The mean density of the Earth is 5.5 times that of water, although that of the surface layer is less. The Earth and Moon revolve about their common centre of gravity in a lunar month; this centre in turn revolves round the Sun in a plane known as the ecliptic, that passes through the Sun's centre. The Earth's equator is inclined to this plane at an angle of 23.4°. This tilt is the cause of the seasons. In mid-latitudes, and when the Sun is high above the Equator, not only does the high noon altitude make the days longer, but the Sun's rays fall more directly on the Earth's surface; these effects combine to produce summer. In equatorial regions the noon altitude is large throughout the year, and there is little variation in the length of the day. In higher latitudes the noon altitude is lower, and the days in summer are appreciably longer than those in winter.

The average velocity of the Earth in its orbit is 30 km a second. It makes a complete rotation on its axis in about 23h 56m of mean time, which is the sidereal day. Because of its annual revolution round the Sun, the rotation with respect to the Sun, or the solar day, is more than this by about four minutes (*see* page 1282). The extremity of the axis of rotation, or the North Pole of the Earth, is not rigidly fixed, but wanders over an area roughly 20 metres in diameter.

ELEMENTS OF THE SOLAR SYSTEM

Orb	Mean distance from Sun (Earth = 1)	Mean distance from Sun km 10⁶	Sidereal period days	Synodic period days	Incl. of orbit to ecliptic °	Incl. of orbit to ecliptic ′	Diameter km	Mass (Earth = 1)	Period of rotation on axis days
Sun	—	—	—	—	—		1,392,530	332,946	25–35*
Mercury	0.39	58	88.0	116	7	00	4,879	0.0553	58.646
Venus	0.72	108	224.7	584	3	24	12,104	0.8150	243.019r
Earth	1.00	150	365.3	—	—		12,756e	1.0000	0.997
Mars	1.52	228	687.0	780	1	51	6,794e	0.1074	1.026
Jupiter	5.20	778	4,332.6	399	1	18	142,984e / 133,708p	317.89	0.410e
Saturn	9.54	1427	10,759.2	378	2	29	120,536e / 108,728p	95.18	0.426e
Uranus	19.18	2870	30,684.6	370	0	46	51,118e	14.54	0.718r
Neptune	30.06	4497	60,191.0	367	1	46	49,528e	17.15	0.671
Pluto	39.80	5954	91,708.2	367	17	09	2,302	0.002	6.387

e equatorial, p polar, r retrograde, * depending on latitude

THE SATELLITES

Name		Star mag.	Mean distance from primary km	Sidereal period of revolution d
EARTH				
I	Moon	—	384,400	27.322
MARS				
I	Phobos	11	9,378	0.319
II	Deimos	12	23,459	1.262
JUPITER				
XVI	Metis	17	127,960	0.295
XV	Adrastea	19	128,980	0.298
V	Amalthea	14	181,300	0.498
XIV	Thebe	16	221,900	0.675
I	Io	5	421,600	1.769
II	Europa	5	670,900	3.552
III	Ganymede	5	1,070,000	7.155
IV	Callisto	6	1,883,000	16.689
XIII	Leda	20	11,165,000	240.92
VI	Himalia	15	11,460,000	250.57
X	Lysithea	18	11,717,000	259.20
VII	Elara	17	11,741,000	259.64
XII	Ananke	19	21,276,000	629.77r
XI	Carme	18	23,404,000	734.17r
VIII	Pasiphae	17	23,624,000	743.68r
IX	Sinope	18	23,939,000	758.90r
SATURN				
XVIII	Pan	20	133,583	0.575
XV	Atlas	18	137,640	0.602
XVI	Prometheus	16	139,353	0.613
XVII	Pandora	16	141,700	0.629
XI	Epimetheus	15	151,422	0.695
X	Janus	14	151,472	0.695
I	Mimas	13	185,520	0.942
II	Enceladus	12	238,020	1.370
III	Tethys	10	294,660	1.888
XIII	Telesto	19	294,660	1.888
XIV	Calypso	19	294,660	1.888
IV	Dione	10	377,400	2.737
XII	Helene	18	377,400	2.737
V	Rhea	10	527,040	4.518
VI	Titan	8	1,221,850	15.945

Name		Star mag.	Mean distance from primary km	Sidereal period of revolution d
SATURN				
VII	Hyperion	14	1,464,100	21.277
VIII	Iapetus	11	3,560,800	79.330
IX	Phoebe	16	12,944,300	550.48r
URANUS				
VI	Cordelia	24	49,750	0.335
VII	Orphelia	24	53,760	0.376
VIII	Bianca	23	59,170	0.435
IX	Cressida	22	61,780	0.464
X	Desdemona	22	62,660	0.474
XI	Juliet	21	64,360	0.493
XII	Portia	21	66,100	0.513
XIII	Rosalind	22	69,930	0.558
XIV	Belinda	22	75,260	0.624
XV	Puck	20	86,000	0.762
V	Miranda	16	129,900	1.413
I	Ariel	14	190,900	2.520
II	Umbriel	15	266,000	4.144
III	Titania	14	436,300	8.706
IV	Oberon	14	583,600	13.463
XVI	Caliban	22	7,231,000	579.93
XX	Stephano	24	8,004,000	677.36
XVII	Sycorax	21	12,179,000	1,288.30
XVIII	Prospero	23	16,256,000	1,978.29
XIX	Setebos	23	17,418,000	2,225.21
NEPTUNE				
III	Naiad	25	48,230	0.294
IV	Thalassa	24	50,070	0.311
V	Despina	23	52,530	0.335
VI	Galatea	22	61,950	0.429
VII	Larissa	22	73,550	0.555
VIII	Proteus	20	117,650	1.122
I	Triton	13	354,760	5.877
II	Nereid	19	5,513,400	360.136
PLUTO				
I	Charon	17	19,600	6.387

Currently the total number of satellites of the outer planets are: Jupiter 63, Saturn 31, Uranus 28, Neptune 13, Pluto 1.

TERRESTRIAL MAGNETISM

The Earth's main magnetic field corresponds approximately to that of a very strong small bar magnet near the centre of the Earth, but with appreciable smooth spatial departures. The origin of the main field is generally ascribed to electric currents associated with fluid motions in the Earth's core. As a result not only does the main field vary in strength and direction from place to place, but also with time. Superimposed on the main field are local and regional anomalies whose magnitudes may in places approach that of the main field; these are due to the influence of mineral deposits in the Earth's crust. A small proportion of the field is of external origin, mostly associated with electric currents in the ionosphere. The configuration of the external field and the ionisation of the atmosphere depend on the incident particle and radiation flux from the Sun. There are, therefore, short-term and non-periodic as well as diurnal, 27-day, seasonal and 11-year periodic changes in the magnetic field, dependent upon the position of the Sun and the degree of solar activity.

A magnetic compass points along the horizontal component of a magnetic line of force. These lines of force converge on the 'magnetic dip-poles', the places where the Earth's magnetic field is vertical. These poles move with time, and their present approximate adopted mean positions are 83.7° N., 120.8° W. and 64.5° S., 137.8° E.

There is also a 'magnetic equator', at all points of which the vertical component of the Earth's magnetic field is zero and a magnetised needle remains horizontal. This line runs between 2° and 12° north of the geographical equator in Asia and Africa, turns sharply south off the west African coast, and crosses South America through Brazil, Bolivia and Peru; it re-crosses the geographical equator in mid-Pacific.

Reference has already been made to secular changes in the Earth's field. The following table indicates the changes in magnetic declination (or variation of the compass). Declination is the angle in the horizontal plane between the direction of true north and that in which a magnetic compass points. Similar, though much smaller, changes have occurred in 'dip' or magnetic inclination. Secular changes differ throughout the world. Although the London observations suggest a cycle with a period of several hundred years, an exact repetition is unlikely.

London			Greenwich		
1580	11°	15' E.	1900	16°	29' W.
1622	5°	56' E.	1925	13°	10' W.
1665	1°	22' W.	1950	9°	07' W.
1730	13°	00' W.	1975	6°	39' W.
1773	21°	09' W.	1998	3°	32' W.
1850	22°	24' W.			

In order that up-to-date information on declination may be available, many governments publish magnetic charts on which there are lines (isogonic lines) passing through all places at which specified values of declination will be found at the date of the chart.

In the British Isles, isogonic lines now run approximately north-east to south-west. Though there are considerable local deviations due to geological causes, a rough value of magnetic declination may be obtained by assuming that at 50° N. on the meridian of Greenwich, the value in 2006 is 1° 40' west and allowing an increase of 13' for each degree of latitude northwards and one of 27' for each degree of longitude westwards. For example, at 53° N., 5° W., declination will be about 1°40' + 39' + 135', i.e. 4° 34' west. The average annual change at the present time is about 11' decrease.

The number of magnetic observatories is about 180, irregularly distributed over the globe. There are three in Great Britain, run by the British Geological Survey: at Hartland, north Devon; at Eskdalemuir, Dumfries and Galloway; and at Lerwick, Shetland Islands. The following are some recent annual mean values of the magnetic elements for Hartland.

Year	Declination West ° '	Dip or inclination ° '	Horizontal intensity nanoTesla (nT)	Vertical intensity nT
1960	9 58.8	66 43.9	18707	43504
1965	9 30.1	66 34.0	18872	43540
1970	9 06.5	66 26.1	19033	43636
1975	8 32.3	66 17.0	19212	43733
1980	7 43.8	66 10.3	19330	43768
1985	6 56.1	66 07.9	19379	43796
1990	6 15.0	66 09.7	19539	43896
1995	5 33.2	66 07.3	19457	43951
2000	4 43.6	66 06.9	19508	44051
2004	4 05.5	66 06.2	19563	44154

As well as navigation at sea, in the air and on land by compass the oil industry depends on the Earth's magnetic field as a directional reference. They use magnetic survey tools when drilling well-bores and require accurate estimates of the local magnetic field, taking into account the crustal and external fields.

MAGNETIC STORMS

Occasionally, sometimes with great suddenness, the Earth's magnetic field is subject for several hours to marked disturbance. During a severe storm in October 2003 the declination at Eskdalemuir changed by over 5° in six minutes. In many instances such disturbances are accompanied by widespread displays of aurorae, marked changes in the incidence of cosmic rays, an increase in the reception of 'noise' from the Sun at radio frequencies, and rapid changes in the ionosphere and induced electric currents within the Earth which adversely affect satellite operations, telecommunications and electric power transmission systems. The disturbances are caused by changes in the stream of ionised particles which emanates from the Sun and through which the Earth is continuously passing. Some of these changes are associated with visible eruptions on the Sun, usually in the region of sun-spots. There is a marked tendency for disturbances to recur after intervals of about 27 days, the apparent period of rotation of the Sun on its axis, which is consistent with the sources being located on particular areas of the Sun.

ARTIFICIAL SATELLITES

Since the beginning of the Space Age, *Whitaker's Almanack* has given details of every successful satellite launch. This edition gives details of all successful launches that have taken place since the last edition. To consider the orbit of an artificial satellite, it is best to imagine that one is looking at the Earth from a distant point in space. The Earth would then be seen to be rotating about its axis inside the orbit described by the rapidly revolving satellite. The inclination of a satellite orbit to the Earth's equator (which generally remains almost constant throughout the satellite's lifetime) gives at once the maximum range of latitudes over which the satellite passes. Thus a satellite whose orbit has an inclination of 53° will pass overhead all latitudes between 53° S. and 53° N., but would never be seen in the zenith of any place nearer the poles than these latitudes. If we consider a particular place on the earth, whose latitude is less than the inclination of the satellite's orbit, then the Earth's rotation carries this place first under the northbound part of the orbit and then under the southbound part of the orbit, these two occurrences being always less than 12 hours apart for satellites moving in direct orbits (i.e. to the east). (For satellites in retrograde orbits, the words 'northbound' and 'southbound' should be interchanged in the preceding statement.) As the value of the latitude of the observer increases and approaches the value of the inclination of the orbit, so this interval gets shorter until (when the latitude is equal to the inclination) only one overhead passage occurs each day.

OBSERVATION OF SATELLITES

The regression of the orbit around the Earth causes alternate periods of visibility and invisibility, though this is of little concern to the radio or radar observer. To the visual observer the following cycle of events normally occurs (though the cycle may start in any position): invisibility, morning observations before dawn, invisibility, evening observations after dusk, invisibility, morning observations before dawn, and so on. With reasonably high satellites and for observers in high latitudes around the summer solstice, the evening observations follow the morning observations without interruption as sunlight passing over the polar regions can still illuminate satellites which are passing over temperate latitudes at local midnight. At the moment all satellites rely on sunlight to make them visible, though a satellite with a flashing light has been suggested for a future launching. The observer must be in darkness or twilight in order to make any useful observations. (For durations of twilight, and sunrise and sunset times, *see* page two of each month.)

Some of the satellites are visible to the naked eye and much interest has been aroused by the spectacle of a bright satellite disappearing into the Earth's shadow. The event is even more interesting telescopically as the disappearance occurs gradually as the satellite traverses the Earth's penumbral shadow, and during the last few seconds before the eclipse is complete the satellite may change colour (in suitable atmospheric conditions) from yellow to red. This is because the last rays of sunlight are refracted through the denser layers of our atmosphere before striking the satellite.

Some satellites rotate about one or more axes so that a periodic variation in brightness is observed. This was particularly noticeable in several of the Soviet satellites.

Satellite research has provided some interesting results, including a revised value of the Earth's oblateness (1/298.2), and the discovery of the Van Allen radiation belts.

LAUNCHINGS

Apart from their names, e.g. Cosmos 6 Rocket, the satellites are also classified according to their date of launch. Thus 1961 α refers to the first satellite launching of 1961. A number following the Greek letter indicated the relative brightness of the satellites put in orbit. From the beginning of 1963 the Greek letters were replaced by numbers and the numbers by roman letters e.g. 1963–01A. For all satellites successfully injected into orbit the following table gives the designation and names of the main objects, the launch date and some initial orbital data. These are the inclination to the equator (*i*), the nodal period of revolution (*P*), and the apogee and perigee heights.

Although most of the satellites launched are injected into orbits less than 1,000 km high, there are an increasing number of satellites in geostationary orbits, i.e. where the orbital inclination is zero, the eccentricity close to zero, and the period of revolution is 1436.1 minutes. Thus the satellite is permanently situated over the equator at one selected longitude at a mean height of 35,786 km. This geostationary band is crowded. In one case there are six television satellites (Astra 2, 5, 6, 7, 1H and 2C) orbiting within a few tens of kilometres of each other. In the sky they appear to be separated by only a few arcminutes.

In 1997 a number of *Iridium* satellites were launched into high inclination orbits. These are owned by the mobile telephone company Cellnet. For visual observers, these satellites have the interesting characteristic that the large aerials they carry can, when in exactly the right orientation with respect to the Sun and the observer, give off a 'flare' in brightness which can on occasion attain a magnitude of −6, much brighter than Venus. The flare can be visible to the naked eye for nearly a minute.

The Russian Space Station, Mir, 1986–17A, which was launched in 1986 was successfully de-orbited on March 23 2001. The re-entry was carried out in several stages, the first small burn to lower the orbit occurring at 00h 33m. The main de-orbit burn began at 05h 07m, which lowered the perigee height to <80km. At 05h 50m observers in Fiji saw multiple bright re-entry bodies in the sky. The impact area was at about W. 160°, S. 40°. During its 15 years in orbit it had been visited by 111 spacecraft. The record for the longest spaceflight was set by Valeriy Polyakov in 1994–5 who spent 437 days in Mir.

The new International Space Station ISS, 1998–67A, is currently being assembled in an orbit of similar size and inclination to Mir. It will become even brighter as more parts are added to it. When passing over Britain it can appear to be almost as bright as Jupiter on favourable transits, though only visible for four or five minutes on each pass.

ARTIFICIAL SATELLITE LAUNCHES

Designation 2004–	Satellite	Launch date	P m	i °	Apogee km	Perigee km
006	ROSETTA, rocket	Mar. 2	No elements available			
007	MBSAT, rocket	Mar. 13	630.4	24.9	35788	162
008	EUTELSAT W3A, tank	Mar. 15	701.8	12.7	35722	3842
009	NAVSTAR 54 (USA 177), rocket, rocket	Mar. 20	718.0	55.1	20277	20089
010	RADUGA 1–7, platform, rocket, rocket, rocket, rocket	Mar. 27	1329.9	0.0	35056	32306
011	SUPERBIRD 6, rocket, rocket,	Apr. 16	2857.6	25.6	119532	1124
012	TANSUO 1, NAXING 1	Apr. 18	96.3	97.6	619	543
013	SOYUZ-TMA 4, rocket	Apr. 19	91.8	51.6	371	355
014	GP-B, rocket	Apr. 20	97.6	90.0	645	641
015	EXPRESS AM-11, platform, rocket	Apr. 26	1429.2	0.0	35713	35591
016	DIRECTV-7S, rocket	May 4	628.8	0.0	35719	149
017	AMC-11 (GE-11), rocket	May 19	1436.0	0.0	35792	35778
018	ROCSAT 2, rocket	May 20	102.8	99.1	891	887
019	PROGRESS-M 49, rocket	May 25	91.8	51.6	367	359
020	COSMOS 2405, rocket	May 28	92.8	65.0	417	405
021	COSMOS 2406, rocket	Jun. 10	102.1	71.0	865	847
022	INTELSAT 1002, rocket	Jun. 16	710.4	23.7	35805	4187
023	NAVSTAR 55 (USA 178), rocket rocket	Jun. 23	720.1	55.0	20360	20108
024	APSTAR 5 (TELSTAR 18), rocket	Jun. 29	386.1	0.0	21643	729
025	APRIZESAT-2, CELESTIS, DEMETER, SAUDICOMSAT 1, SAUDICOMSAT 2, SAUDISAT 3, APRIZESAT-1, UNISAT 3, AMSAT ECHO	Jun. 29	100.3	98.3	852	696
026	AURA, rocket	Jul. 15	98.3	98.2	681	673
027	ANIK F2, rocket	Jul. 18	696.0	6.9	38664	610
028	COSMOS 2409, rocket	Jul. 22	104.6	83.0	1006	950
029	DOUBLE STAR	Jul. 25	695.1	90.1	38566	662
030	MESSENGER, rocket, rocket (for Mercury fly-by between 2008–2011)	Aug. 3	87.8	32.5	2530	2202
031	AMAZONAS, rocket	Aug. 4	1198.0	1.1	35802	26170
032	PROGRESS-M 50, rocket	Aug. 11	89.9	51.6	277	259
033	FSW-3, rocket	Aug. 29	91.1	63.0	492	166
034	USA 179, rocket	Aug. 31	280.4	57.4	15369	257
035	SJ-6A, SJ-6B, rocket	Sep. 8	96.6	97.7	603	593
036	GSAT 3, rocket	Sep. 20	1426.6	0.1	35611	35591
037	COSMOS 2408, 2409, rocket	Sep. 24	115.6	82.5	1496	1470
038	COSMOS 2410, rocket	Sep. 24	89.9	67.2	327	211
039	FSW-3 3, rocket	Sep. 27	89.7	63.0	320	204
040	SOYUZ-TMA 5, rocket	Oct. 14	91.7	51.6	364	352
041	AMC-15, rocket	Oct. 14	1436.1	0.0	35792	35780
042	FENGYUN 2C, rocket	Oct. 19	1436.0	0.8	35790	35780
043	EXPRESS AM-1, rocket, platform, rocket	Oct. 29	1438.5	0.1	35868	35798
044	JB-3, rocket	Nov. 6	94.1	97.3	482	472
045	NAVSTAR 56 (USA-180), rocket, rocket	Nov. 6	356.4	39.1	20386	160
046	TANSUO 2, rocket	Nov. 18	98.8	98.2	711	695
047	SWIFT, rocket	Nov. 20	96.6	20.6	604	584
048	AMC-16, rocket	Dec. 17	721.5	18.0	35716	4820
049	HELIOS-2A, NANOSAT-1, ESSAIM 1–4, PARASOL, rocket	Dec. 18	98.0	98.1	665	665
050	USA 181	Dec. 21	1044.6	13.5	36416	19036
051	PROGRESS M51, rocket	Dec. 23	91 6	51.6	354	350
052	SICH-1N, rocket, COSMOS 2412	Dec. 24	93.7	82.6	632	280
053	COSMOS 2413, 2411, 2412, rocket, rocket, platform	Dec. 26	675.7	64.8	19152	19108
001	DEEP IMPACT, rocket, rocket	Jan. 12	No elements available			
002	COSMOS 2414, rocket, TATIANA	Jan. 20	103.8	83.0	967	909

TIME MEASUREMENT AND CALENDARS

MEASUREMENTS OF TIME

Measurements of time are based on the time taken by the earth to rotate on its axis (day); by the moon to revolve round the earth (month); and by the earth to revolve round the sun (year). From these, which are not commensurable, certain average or mean intervals have been adopted for ordinary use.

THE DAY

The day begins at midnight and is divided into 24 hours of 60 minutes, each of 60 seconds. The hours are counted from midnight up to 12 noon (when the sun crosses the meridian), and these hours are designated a.m. *(ante meridiem)*; and again from noon up to 12 midnight, which hours are designated p.m. *(post meridiem)*, except when the 24-hour reckoning is employed. The 24-hour reckoning ignores a.m. and p.m., numbering the hours 0 to 23 from midnight.

Colloquially the 24 hours are divided into day and night, day being the time while the sun is above the horizon (including the four stages of twilight defined in the Astronomy section). Day is subdivided into morning, the early part of daytime, ending at noon; afternoon, from noon to about 6 p.m.; and evening, which may be said to extend from 6 p.m. until midnight. Night begins at the close of astronomical twilight (*see* the Astronomy section) and extends beyond midnight to sunrise the next day.

The names of the days are derived from Old English translations or adaptations of the Roman titles.

Sunday	Sun	Sol
Monday	Moon	Luna
Tuesday	Tiw/Tyr (god of war)	Mars
Wednesday	Woden/Odin	Mercury
Thursday	Thor	Jupiter
Friday	Frigga/Freyja (goddess of love)	Venus
Saturday	Saeternes	Saturn

THE MONTH

The month in the ordinary calendar is approximately the twelfth part of a year, but the lengths of the different months vary from 28 (or 29) days to 31.

THE YEAR

The equinoctial or tropical year is the time that the earth takes to revolve round the sun from equinox to equinox, i.e. 365.24219 mean solar days, or 365 days 5 hours 48 minutes and 45 seconds.

The calendar year usually consists of 365 days but a year containing 366 days is called bissextile (*see* Roman calendar) or leap year, one day being added to the month of February so that a date 'leaps over' a day of the week. In the Roman calendar the day that was repeated was the sixth day before the beginning of March, the equivalent of 24 February.

A year is a leap year if the date of the year is divisible by four without remainder, unless it is the last year of the century. The last year of a century is a leap year only if its number is divisible by 400 without remainder, e.g. the years 1800 and 1900 had only 365 days but the year 2000 had 366 days.

THE SOLSTICE

A solstice is the point in the tropical year at which the sun attains its greatest distance, north or south, from the Equator. In the northern hemisphere the furthest point north of the Equator marks the summer solstice and the furthest point south the winter solstice.

The date of the solstice varies according to locality. For example, if the summer solstice falls on 21 June late in the day by Greenwich time, that day will be the longest of the year at Greenwich though it may be by only a second, but it will fall on 22 June, local date, in Japan, and so 22 June will be the longest day there. The date of the solstice is also affected by the length of the tropical year, which is 365 days 6 hours less about 11 minutes 15 seconds. If a solstice happens late on 21 June in one year, it will be nearly six hours later in the next (unless the next year is a leap year), i.e. early on 22 June, and that will be the longest day.

This delay of the solstice does not continue because the extra day in leap year brings it back a day in the calendar. However, because of the 11 minutes 15 seconds mentioned above, the additional day in leap year brings the solstice back too far by 45 minutes, and the time of the solstice in the calendar is earlier, in a four-year pattern, as the century progresses. The last year of a century is in most cases not a leap year, and the omission of the extra day puts the date of the solstice later by about six hours too much. Compensation for this is made by the fourth centennial year being a leap year. The solstice has become earlier in date throughout the last century and, because the year 2000 was a leap year, the solstice will get earlier still throughout the 21st century.

The date of the winter solstice, the shortest day of the year, is affected by the same factors as the longest day.

At Greenwich the sun sets at its earliest by the clock about ten days before the shortest day. The daily change in the time of sunset is due in the first place to the sun's movement southwards at this time of the year, which diminishes the interval between the sun's transit and its setting. However, the daily decrease of the Equation of Time causes the time of apparent noon to be continuously later day by day, which to some extent counteracts the first effect. The rates of the change of these two quantities are not equal or uniform; their combination causes the date of earliest sunset to be 12 or 13 December at Greenwich. In more southerly latitudes the effect of the movement of the sun is less, and the change in the time of sunset depends on that of the Equation of Time to a greater degree, and the date of earliest sunset is earlier than it is at Greenwich, e.g. on the Equator it is about 1 November.

THE EQUINOX

The equinox is the point at which the sun crosses the Equator and day and night are of equal length all over the world. This occurs in March and September.

DOG DAYS

The days about the heliacal rising of the Dog Star, noted from ancient times as the hottest period of the year in the northern hemisphere, are called the Dog Days. Their incidence has been variously calculated as depending on the Greater or Lesser Dog Star (Sirius or Procyon) and their duration has been reckoned as from 30 to 54 days. A generally accepted period is from 3 July to 15 August.

CHRISTIAN CALENDAR

In the Christian chronological system the years are distinguished by cardinal numbers before or after the birth of Christ, the period being denoted by the letters BC (Before Christ) or, more rarely, AC *(Ante Christum)*, and AD *(Anno Domini* – In the Year of Our Lord). The correlative dates of the epoch are the fourth year of the 194th Olympiad, the 753rd year from the foundation of Rome, AM 3761 in Jewish chronology, and the 4714th year of the Julian period. The actual date of the birth of Christ is somewhat uncertain.

The system was introduced into Italy in the sixth century. Though first used in France in the seventh century, it was not universally established there until about the eighth century. It has been said that the system was introduced into England by St Augustine (AD 596), but it was probably not generally used until some centuries later. It was ordered to be used by the Bishops at the Council of Chelsea (AD 816).

THE JULIAN CALENDAR

In the Julian calendar (adopted by the Roman Empire in 45 BC) all the centennial years were leap years, and for this reason towards the close of the 16th century there was a difference of ten days between the tropical and calendar years; the equinox fell on 11 March of the calendar, whereas at the time of the Council of Nicaea (AD 325), it had fallen on 21 March. In 1582 Pope Gregory ordained that 5 October should be called 15 October and that of the end-century years only the fourth should be a leap year.

THE GREGORIAN CALENDAR

The Gregorian calendar was adopted by Italy, France, Spain and Portugal in 1582, by Prussia, the Roman Catholic German states, Switzerland, Holland and Flanders on 1 January 1583, by Poland in 1586, Hungary in 1587, the Protestant German and Netherland states and Denmark in 1700, and by Great Britain and Dominions (including the North American colonies) in 1752, by the omission of eleven days (3 September being reckoned as 14 September). Sweden omitted the leap day in 1700 but observed leap days in 1704 and 1708, and reverted to the Julian calendar by having two leap days in 1712; the Gregorian calendar was adopted in 1753 by the omission of eleven days (18 February being reckoned as 1 March). Japan adopted the calendar in 1872, China in 1912, Bulgaria in 1915, Turkey and Soviet Russia in 1918, Yugoslavia and Romania in 1919, and Greece in 1923.

In the same year that the change was made in England from the Julian to the Gregorian calendar, the beginning of the new year was also changed from 25 March to 1 January.

THE ORTHODOX CHURCHES

Some Orthodox Churches still use the Julian reckoning but the majority of Greek Orthodox Churches and the Romanian Orthodox Church have adopted a modified 'New Calendar', observing the Gregorian calendar for fixed feasts and the Julian for movable feasts.

The Orthodox Church year begins on 1 September. There are four fast periods and, in addition to Pascha (Easter), twelve great feasts, as well as numerous commemorations of the saints of the Old and New Testaments throughout the year.

THE DOMINICAL LETTER

The dominical letter is one of the letters A–G which are used to denote the Sundays in successive years. If the first day of the year is a Sunday the letter is A; if the second, B; the third, C; and so on. A leap year requires two letters, the first for 1 January to 29 February, the second for 1 March to 31 December.

EPIPHANY

The feast of the Epiphany, commemorating the manifestation of Christ, later became associated with the offering of gifts by the Magi. The day was of great importance from the time of the Council of Nicaea (AD 325), as the primate of Alexandria was charged at every Epiphany feast with the announcement in a letter to the churches of the date of the forthcoming Easter. The day was also of importance in Britain as it influenced dates, ecclesiastical and lay, e.g. Plough Monday, when work was resumed in the fields, fell on the Monday in the first full week after Epiphany.

LENT

The Teutonic word *Lent*, which denotes the fast preceding Easter, originally meant no more than the spring season; but from Anglo-Saxon times at least it has been used as the equivalent of the more significant Latin term Quadragesima, meaning the 'forty days' or, more literally, the fortieth day. Ash Wednesday is the first day of Lent, which ends at midnight before Easter Day.

PALM SUNDAY

Palm Sunday, the Sunday before Easter and the beginning of Holy Week, commemorates the triumphal entry of Christ into Jerusalem and is celebrated in Britain (when palm is not available) by branches of willow gathered for use in the decoration of churches on that day.

MAUNDY THURSDAY

Maundy Thursday is the day before Good Friday, the name itself being a corruption of *dies mandati* (day of the mandate) when Christ washed the feet of the disciples and gave them the mandate to love one another.

EASTER DAY

Easter Day is the first Sunday after the full moon which happens on, or next after, the 21st day of March; if the full moon happens on a Sunday, Easter Day is the Sunday after.

This definition is contained in an Act of Parliament (24 Geo. II c. 23) and explanation is given in the preamble to the Act that the day of full moon depends on certain tables that have been prepared. These tables are summarised in the early pages of the Book of Common Prayer. The moon referred to is not the real moon of the heavens, but a hypothetical moon on whose 'full' the date of Easter depends, and the lunations of this 'calendar' moon consist of twenty-nine and thirty days alternately, with certain necessary modifications to make the date of its full agree as nearly as possible with that of the real moon, which is known as the Paschal Full Moon.

A FIXED EASTER

In 1928 the House of Commons agreed to a motion for the third reading of a bill proposing that Easter Day shall, in the calendar year next but one after the commencement of the Act and in all subsequent years, be the first Sunday after the second Saturday in April. Easter would thus fall on the second or third Sunday in April, i.e. between 9 and 15 April (inclusive). A clause in the Bill provided that before it shall come into operation, regard shall be had to any opinion expressed officially by the various Christian churches. Efforts by the World Council of Churches to secure a unanimous choice of date for Easter by its member churches have so far been unsuccessful.

ROGATION DAYS

Rogation Days are the Monday, Tuesday and Wednesday preceding Ascension Day and from the fifth century were observed as public fasts with solemn processions and supplications. The processions were discontinued as religious observances at the Reformation, but survive in the ceremony known as 'beating the parish bounds'. Rogation Sunday is the Sunday before Ascension Day.

EMBER DAYS

The Ember Days at the four seasons are the Wednesday,

Friday and Saturday (a) before the third Sunday in Advent, (b) before the second Sunday in Lent, and (c) before the Sundays nearest to the festivals of St Peter and of St Michael and All Angels.

TRINITY SUNDAY

Trinity Sunday is eight weeks after Easter Day, on the Sunday following Pentecost (Whit Sunday). Subsequent Sundays are reckoned in the Book of Common Prayer calendar of the Church of England as 'after Trinity'.

Thomas Becket (1118–70) was consecrated Archbishop of Canterbury on the Sunday after Whit Sunday and his first act was to ordain that the day of his consecration should be held as a new festival in honour of the Holy Trinity. This observance spread from Canterbury throughout the whole of Christendom.

MOVABLE FEASTS TO THE YEAR 2035

Year	Ash Wednesday	Easter	Ascension	Pentecost (Whit Sunday)	Advent Sunday
2006	1 March	16 April	25 May	4 June	3 December
2007	21 February	8 April	17 May	27 May	2 December
2008	6 February	23 March	1 May	11 May	30 November
2009	25 February	12 April	21 May	31 May	29 November
2010	17 February	4 April	13 May	23 May	28 November
2011	9 March	24 April	2 June	12 June	27 November
2012	22 February	8 April	17 May	27 May	2 December
2013	13 February	31 March	9 May	19 May	1 December
2014	5 March	20 April	29 May	8 June	30 November
2015	18 February	5 April	14 May	24 May	29 November
2016	10 February	27 March	5 May	15 May	27 November
2017	1 March	16 April	25 May	4 June	3 December
2018	14 February	1 April	10 May	20 May	2 December
2019	6 March	21 April	30 May	9 June	1 December
2020	26 February	12 April	21 May	31 May	29 November
2021	17 February	4 April	13 May	23 May	28 November
2022	2 March	17 April	26 May	5 June	27 November
2023	22 February	9 April	18 May	28 May	3 December
2024	14 February	31 March	9 May	19 May	1 December
2025	5 March	20 April	29 May	8 June	30 November
2026	18 February	5 April	14 May	24 May	29 November
2027	10 February	28 March	6 May	16 May	28 November
2028	1 March	16 April	25 May	4 June	3 December
2029	14 February	1 April	10 May	20 May	2 December
2030	6 March	21 April	30 May	9 June	1 December
2031	26 February	13 April	22 May	1 June	30 November
2032	11 February	28 March	6 May	16 May	28 November
2033	2 March	17 April	26 May	5 June	27 November
2034	22 February	9 April	18 May	28 May	3 December
2035	7 February	25 March	3 May	13 May	2 December

NOTES

Ash Wednesday (first day in Lent) can fall at earliest on 4 February and at latest on 10 March

Mothering Sunday (fourth Sunday in Lent) can fall at earliest on 1 March and at latest on 4 April

Easter Day can fall at earliest on 22 March and at latest on 25 April

Ascension Day is forty days after Easter Day and can fall at earliest on 30 April and at latest on 3 June

Pentecost (Whit Sunday) is seven weeks after Easter and can fall at earliest on 10 May and at latest on 13 June

Trinity Sunday is the Sunday after Whit Sunday

Corpus Christi falls on the Thursday after Trinity Sunday

Sundays after Pentecost – there are not less than 18 and not more than 23

Advent Sunday is the Sunday nearest to 30 November

EASTER DAYS AND DOMINICAL LETTERS 1500 TO 2035

Dates up to and including 1752 are according to the Julian calendar. For dominical letters in leap years, *see* note below

		1500–1599	1600–1699	1700–1799	1800–1899	1900–1999	2000–2035
March							
d	22	1573	1668	1761	1818		
e	23	1505/16	1600	1788	1845/56	1913	2008
f	24		1611/95	1706/99		1940	
g	25	1543/54	1627/38/49	1722/33/44	1883/94	1951	2035
A	26	1559/70/81/92	1654/65/76	1749/58/69/80	1815/26/37	1967/78/89	
b	27	1502/13/24/97	1608/87/92	1785/96	1842/53/64	1910/21/32	2005/16
c	28	1529/35/40	1619/24/30	1703/14/25	1869/75/80	1937/48	2027/32
d	29	1551/62	1635/46/57	1719/30/41/52	1807/12/91	1959/64/70	
e	30	1567/78/89	1651/62/73/84	1746/55/66/77	1823/34	1902/75/86/97	
f	31	1510/21/32/83/94	1605/16/78/89	1700/71/82/93	1839/50/61/72	1907/18/29/91	2002/13/24
April							
g	1	1526/37/48	1621/32	1711/16	1804/66/77/88	1923/34/45/56	2018/29
A	2	1553/64	1643/48	1727/38	1809/20/93/99	1961/72	
b	3	1575/80/86	1659/70/81	1743/63/68/74	1825/31/36	1904/83/88/94	
c	4	1507/18/91	1602/13/75/86/97	1708/79/90	1847/58	1915/20/26/99	2010/21
d	5	1523/34/45/56	1607/18/29/40	1702/13/24/95	1801/63/74/85/96	1931/42/53	2015/26
e	6	1539/50/61/72	1634/45/56	1729/35/40/60	1806/17/28/90	1947/58/69/80	
f	7	1504/77/88	1667/72	1751/65/76	1822/33/44	1901/12/85/96	
g	8	1509/15/20/99	1604/10/83/94	1705/87/92/98	1849/55/60	1917/28	2007/12
A	9	1531/42	1615/26/37/99	1710/21/32	1871/82	1939/44/50	2023/34
b	10	1547/58/69	1631/42/53/64	1726/37/48/57	1803/14/87/98	1955/66/77	
c	11	1501/12/63/74/85/96	1658/69/80	1762/73/84	1819/30/41/52	1909/71/82/93	2004
d	12	1506/17/28	1601/12/91/96	1789	1846/57/68	1903/14/25/36/98	2009/20
e	13	1533/44	1623/28	1707/18	1800/73/79/84	1941/52	2031
f	14	1555/60/66	1639/50/61	1723/34/45/54	1805/11/16/95	1963/68/74	
g	15	1571/82/93	1655/66/77/88	1750/59/70/81	1827/38	1900/06/79/90	2001
A	16	1503/14/25/36/87/98	1609/20/82/93	1704/75/86/97	1843/54/65/76	1911/22/33/95	2006/17/28
b	17	1530/41/52	1625/36	1715/20	1808/70/81/92	1927/38/49/60	2022/33
c	18	1557/68	1647/52	1731/42/56	1802/13/24/97	1954/65/76	
d	19	1500/79/84/90	1663/74/85	1747/67/72/78	1829/35/40	1908/81/87/92	
e	20	1511/22/95	1606/17/79/90	1701/12/83/94	1851/62	1919/24/30	2003/14/25
f	21	1527/38/49	1622/33/44	1717/28	1867/78/89	1935/46/57	2019/30
g	22	1565/76	1660	1739/53/64	1810/21/32	1962/73/84	
A	23	1508	1671		1848	1905/16	2000
b	24	1519	1603/14/98	1709/91	1859		2011
c	25	1546	1641	1736	1886	1943	

No dominical letter is placed against the intercalary day 29 February but since it is still counted as a weekday and given a name, the series of letters moves back one day every leap year after intercalation. Thus, a leap year beginning with the dominical letter C will change to a year with the dominical letter B on 1 March

HINDU CALENDAR

The Hindu calendar is a luni-solar calendar of twelve months, each containing 29 days, 12 hours. Each month is divided into a light fortnight (Shukla or Shuddha) and a dark fortnight (Krishna or Vadya) based on the waxing and waning of the moon. In most parts of India the month starts with the light fortnight, i.e. the day after the new moon, although in some regions it begins with the dark fortnight, i.e. the day after the full moon.

The new year begins in the month of Chaitra (March/April) and ends in the month of Phalgun (March). The twelve months, Chaitra, Vaishakh, Jyeshtha, Ashadh, Shravan, Bhadrapad, Ashvin, Kartik, Margashirsh, Paush, Magh and Phalgun, have Sanskrit names derived from twelve asterisms (constellations). There are regional variations to the names of the months but the Sanskrit names are understood throughout India.

Every lunar month must have a solar transit and is termed pure (shuddha). The lunar month without a solar transit is impure (mala) and called an intercalary month. An intercalary month occurs approximately every 32 lunar months, whenever the difference between the Hindu year of 360 lunar days (354 days 8 hours solar time) and the 365 days 6 hours of the solar year reaches the length of one Hindu lunar month (29 days 12 hours).

The leap month may be added at any point in the Hindu year. The name given to the month varies according to when it occurs but is taken from the month immediately following it. There is no leap month in 2006.

The days of the week are called Raviwar (Sunday), Somawar (Monday), Mangalwar (Tuesday), Budhawar (Wednesday), Guruwar (Thursday), Shukrawar (Friday) and Shaniwar (Saturday). The names are derived from the Sanskrit names of the Sun, the Moon and five planets, Mars, Mercury, Jupiter, Venus and Saturn.

Most fasts and festivals are based on the lunar calendar but a few are determined by the apparent movement of the Sun, e.g. Sankranti and Pongal (in southern India), which are celebrated on 14/15 January to mark the start of the Sun's apparent journey northwards and a change of season.

Festivals celebrated throughout India are Chaitra (the New Year), Raksha-bandhan (the renewal of the kinship bond between brothers and sisters), Navaratri (a nine-night festival dedicated to the goddess Parvati), Dasara (the victory of Rama over the demon army), Diwali (a festival of lights), Makara Sankranti, Shivaratri (dedicated to Shiva), and Holi (a spring festival).

Regional festivals are Durga-puja (dedicated to the goddess Durga (Parvati)), Sarasvati-puja (dedicated to the goddess Sarasvati), Ganesh Chaturthi (worship of Ganesh on the fourth day (Chaturthi) of the light half of Bhadrapad), Ramanavami (the birth festival of the god Rama) and Janmashtami (the birth festival of the god Krishna).

The main festivals celebrated in Britain are Navaratri, Dasara, Durga-puja, Diwali, Holi, Sarasvati-puja, Ganesh Chaturthi, Raksha-bandhan, Ramanavami and Janmashtami.

For dates of the main festivals in 2006, *see* page 9.

JEWISH CALENDAR

The story of the Flood in the Book of Genesis indicates the use of a calendar of some kind and that the writers recognised thirty days as the length of a lunation. However, after the diaspora, Jewish communities were left in considerable doubt as to the times of fasts and festivals. This led to the formation of the Jewish calendar as used today. It is said that this was done in AD 358 by Rabbi Hillel II, though some assert that it did not happen until much later.

The calendar is luni-solar, and is based on the lengths of the lunation and of the tropical year as found by Hipparchus (*c*.120 BC), which differ little from those adopted at the present day. The year AM 5766 (2005–2006) is the 9th year of the 304th Metonic (Minor or Lunar) cycle of 19 years and the 26th year of the 206th Solar (or Major) cycle of 28 years since the Era of the Creation. Jews hold that the Creation occurred at the time of the autumnal equinox in the year known in the Christian calendar as 3760 BC (954 of the Julian period). The epoch or starting point of Jewish chronology corresponds to 7 October 3761 BC. At the beginning of each solar cycle, the Tekufah of Nisan (the vernal equinox) returns to the same day and to the same hour.

The hour is divided into 1080 minims, and the month between one new moon and the next is reckoned as 29 days, 12 hours, 793 minims. The normal calendar year, called a Regular Common year, consists of 12 months of 30 days and 29 days alternately. Since 12 months such as these comprise only 354 days, in order that each of them shall not diverge greatly from an average place in the solar year, a 13th month is occasionally added after the fifth month of the civil year (which commences on the first day of the month Tishri), or as the penultimate month of the ecclesiastical year (which commences on the first day of the month Nisan). The years when this happens are called Embolismic or leap years.

Of the 19 years that form a Metonic cycle, seven are leap years; they occur at places in the cycle indicated by the numbers 3, 6, 8, 11, 14, 17 and 19, these places being chosen so that the accumulated excesses of the solar years should be as small as possible.

A Jewish year is of one of the following six types:

Minimal Common	353 days
Regular Common	354 days
Full Common	355 days
Minimal Leap	383 days
Regular Leap	384 days
Full Leap	385 days

The Regular year has alternate months of 30 and 29 days. In a Full year, whether common or leap, Marcheshvan, the

second month of the civil year, has 30 days instead of 29; in Minimal years Kislev, the third month, has 29 instead of 30. The additional month in leap years is called Adar I and precedes the month called Adar in Common years. Adar II is called Adar Sheni in leap years, and the usual Adar festivals are kept in Adar Sheni. Adar I and Adar II always have 30 days, but neither this, nor the other variations mentioned, is allowed to change the number of days in the other months, which still follow the alternation of the normal twelve.

These are the main features of the Jewish calendar, which must be considered permanent because as a Jewish law it cannot be altered except by a great Sanhedrin.

The Jewish day begins between sunset and nightfall. The time used is that of the meridian of Jerusalem, which is 2h 21m in advance of Greenwich Mean Time. Rules for the beginning of sabbaths and festivals were laid down for the latitude of London in the 18th century and hours for nightfall are now fixed annually by the Chief Rabbi.

JEWISH CALENDAR 5766–7

AM 5766 (766) is a Regular Common year of 12 months, 50 sabbaths and 354 days.

Month (first day)	AM 5766	AM 5767
Tishri 1 (30)	4 October 2005	23 September 2006
Marcheshvan 1 (29)	3 November	23 October
Kislev 1 (30)	2 December	22 November
Tebet 1 (29)	1 January 2006	22 December
Shebat 1 (30)	30 January	
Adar 1 (29)	1 March	
Adar 2	—	
Nisan 1 (30)	30 March	
Iyar 1 (29)	29 April	
Sivan 1 (30)	28 May	
Tammuz 1 (29)	27 June	
Ab 1 (30)	26 July	
Elul 1 (29)	25 August	

*Known as Adar Rishon in leap years
†Known as Adar Sheni in leap years

JEWISH FASTS AND FESTIVALS

For dates of principal festivals in 2006, *see* page 9.

Tishri 1–2	Rosh Hashanah (New Year)
Tishri 3	*Fast of Gedaliah
Tishri 10	Yom Kippur (Day of Atonement)
Tishri 15–21	Succoth (Feast of Tabernacles)
Tishri 21	Hoshana Rabba
Tishri 22	Shemini Atseret (Solemn Assembly)
Tishri 23	Simchat Torah (Rejoicing of the Law)
Kislev 25	Chanucah (Dedication of the Temple) begins
Tebet 10	Fast of Tebet
†*Adar* 13	§Fast of Esther
†*Adar* 14	Purim
†*Adar* 15	Shushan Purim
Nisan 15–22	Pesach (Passover)
Sivan 6–7	Shavuot (Feast of Weeks)
Tammuz 17	*Fast of Tammuz
Ab 9	*Fast of Ab

*If these dates fall on the sabbath the fast is kept on the following day
†Adar Sheni in leap years
§This fast is observed on Adar 11 (or Adar Sheni 11 in leap years) if Adar 13 falls on a Sabbath

THE MUSLIM CALENDAR

The Muslim era is dated from the *Hijrah*, or flight of the Prophet Muhammad from Mecca to Medina, the corresponding date of which in the Julian calendar is 16 July AD 622. The lunar *hijri* calendar is used principally in Iran, Egypt, Malaysia, Pakistan, Mauritania, various Arab states and certain parts of India. Iran uses the solar *hijri* calendar as well as the lunar *hijri* calendar. The dating system was adopted about AD 639, commencing with the first day of the month Muharram.

The lunar calendar consists of twelve months containing an alternate sequence of 30 and 29 days, with the intercalation of one day at the end of the twelfth month at stated intervals in each cycle of 30 years. The object of the intercalation is to reconcile the date of the first day of the month with the date of the actual new moon.

Some adherents still take the date of the evening of the first physical sighting of the crescent of the new moon as that of the first of the month. If cloud obscures the moon the present month may be extended to 30 days, after which the new month will begin automatically regardless of whether the moon has been seen. (Under religious law a month must have less than 31 days.) This means that the beginning of a new month and the date of religious festivals can vary from the published calendars.

In each cycle of 30 years, 19 years are common and contain 354 days, and 11 years are intercalary (leap years) of 355 days, the latter being called *kabisah*. The mean length of the Hijrah years is 354 days 8 hours 48 minutes and the period of mean lunation is 29 days 12 hours 44 minutes.

To ascertain if a year is common or kabisah, divide it by 30: the quotient gives the number of completed cycles and the remainder shows the place of the year in the current cycle. If the remainder is 2, 5, 7, 10, 13, 16, 18, 21, 24, 26 or 29, the year is kabisah and consists of 355 days.

MUSLIM CALENDAR 1426–28

Hijrah 1426 AH (remainder 16) is a kabisah year, 1427 AH (remainder 17) is a common year. 1428 AH (remainder 18 is a kabisah year. Calendar dates below are estimates based on calculations of moon phases.

Month (Length)	1426–7 AH	1427–8 AH
Dhu'l-Qa'da (30)	2 December	22 November
Dhu'l-Hijjah (29 or 30)	1 January 2006	22 December
Muharram (30)	31 January	20 January 2007
Safar (29)	2 March	19 February
Rabi' I (30)	31 March	20 March
Rabi' II (29)	30 April	19 April
Jumada I (30)	29 May	18 May
Jumada II (29)	28 June	17 June
Rajab (30)	27 July	16 July
Sha'ban (29)	26 August	15 August
Ramadân (30)	24 September	13 September
Shawwâl (29)	24 October	13 October

MUSLIM FESTIVALS

Ramadan is a month of fasting for all Muslims because it is the month in which the revelation of the *Qur'an* (Koran) began. During Ramadan Muslims abstain from food, drink and sexual pleasure from dawn until after sunset throughout the month.

The two major festivals are *Id al-Fitr* and *Id al-Adha*. Id al-Fitr marks the end of the Ramadan fast and is celebrated on the day after the sighting of the new moon of the following month. Id al-Adha, the festival of sacrifice (also known as the great festival), celebrates the submission of the Prophet Ibrahim (Abraham) to God. Id al-Adha falls on the tenth day of Dhul-Hijjah, coinciding with the day when those on *hajj* (pilgrimage to Mecca) sacrifice animals.

Other days accorded special recognition are:

Muharram 1	New Year's Day
Muharram 10	Ashura (the day Prophet Noah left the Ark and Prophet Moses was saved from Pharaoh (Sunni), the death of the Prophet's grandson Husain (Shi'ite))
Rabi'u-l-Awwal (Rabi' I) 12	Mawlid al-Nabi (birthday of the Prophet Muhammad)
Rajab 27	Laylat al-Isra' wa'l-Mi'raj (The Night of Journey and Ascension)
Ramadân One of the odd-numbered nights in the last 10 of the month	Laylat al-Qadr (Night of Power)
Dhu'l-Hijjah 10	Id al-Adha (Festival of Sacrifice)

THE SIKH CALENDAR

The Sikh calendar is a lunar calendar of 365 days divided into 12 months. The length of the months varies between 29 and 32 days.

There are no prescribed feast days and no fasting periods. The main celebrations are Baisakhi Mela (the new year and the anniversary of the founding of the Khalsa), Diwali Mela (festival of light), Hola Mohalla Mela (a spring festival held in the Punjab), and the Gurupurabs (anniversaries associated with the ten Gurus). For dates of the major celebrations in 2006, *see* page 9.

THAI CALENDAR

Thailand adopted the Suriyakati calendar, a modified version of the Gregorian calendar (Suriyakati) during the reign of King Rama V in 1888, using 1 April as the first day of the year. In 1940, the date of the new year was changed to 1 January. The years are counted from the beginning of the Buddhist era (BE), which is calculated to have commenced upon the death of the Lord Buddha, which is taken to have occurred in BC 543, so AD 2006 is BE 2549. The Chinese system of associating years with one of twelve animals is also in use in Thailand. The Chantarakati lunar calendar is used to determine religious holidays; the new year begins on the first day of the waxing moon in November or, if there is a leap month, in December.

CIVIL AND LEGAL CALENDAR

THE HISTORICAL YEAR

Before 1752, two calendar systems were used in England. The civil or legal year began on 25 March and the historical year on 1 January. Thus the civil or legal date 24 March 1658 was the same day as the historical date 24 March 1659; a date in that portion of the year is written as 24 March 165 8/9, the lower figure showing the historical year.

THE NEW YEAR

In England in the seventh century, and as late as the 13th, the year was reckoned from Christmas Day, but in the 12th century the Church in England began the year with the feast of the Annunciation of the Blessed Virgin ('Lady Day') on 25 March and this practice was adopted generally in the 14th century. The civil or legal year in the British Dominions (exclusive of Scotland) began with Lady Day until 1751. But in and since 1752 the civil year has begun with 1 January. New Year's Day in Scotland was changed from 25 March to 1 January in 1600.

Elsewhere in Europe, 1 January was adopted as the first day of the year by Venice in 1522, German states in 1544, Spain, Portugal and the Roman Catholic Netherlands in 1556, Prussia, Denmark and Sweden in 1559, France in 1564, Lorraine in 1579, the Protestant Netherlands in 1583, Russia in 1725, and Tuscany in 1751.

REGNAL YEARS

Regnal years are the years of a sovereign's reign and each begins on the anniversary of his or her accession, e.g. regnal year 55 of the present Queen begins on 6 February 2006.

The system was used for dating Acts of Parliament until 1962. The Summer Time Act 1925, for example, is quoted as 15 and 16 Geo. V c. 64, because it became law in the parliamentary session which extended over part of both of these regnal years. Acts of a parliamentary session during which a sovereign died were usually given two year numbers, the regnal year of the deceased sovereign and the regnal year of his or her successor, e.g. those passed in 1952 were dated 16 Geo. VI and 1 Elizabeth II. Since 1962 Acts of Parliament have been dated by the calendar year.

QUARTER AND TERM DAYS

Holy days and saints days were the usual means in early times for setting the dates of future and recurrent appointments. The quarter days in England and Wales are the feast of the Nativity (25 December), the feast of the Annunciation (25 March), the feast of St John the Baptist (24 June) and the feast of St Michael and All Angels (29 September).

The term days in Scotland are Candlemas (the feast of the Purification), Whitsunday, Lammas (Loaf Mass), and Martinmas (St Martin's Day). These fell on 2 February, 15 May, 1 August and 11 November respectively. However, by the Term and Quarter Days (Scotland) Act 1990, the dates of the term days were changed to 28 February (Candlemas), 28 May (Whitsunday), 28 August (Lammas) and 28 November (Martinmas).

RED-LETTER DAYS

Red-letter days were originally the holy days and saints days indicated in early ecclesiastical calendars by letters printed in red ink. The days to be distinguished in this way were approved at the Council of Nicaea in AD 325.

These days still have a legal significance, as judges of the Queen's Bench Division wear scarlet robes on red-letter days falling during the law sittings. The days designated as red-letter days for this purpose are:

Holy and saints days
The Conversion of St Paul, the Purification, Ash Wednesday, the Annunciation, the Ascension, the feasts of St Mark, SS Philip and James, St Matthias, St Barnabas, St John the Baptist, St Peter, St Thomas, St James, St Luke, SS Simon and Jude, All Saints, St Andrew.

Civil calendar (for dates, *see* page 9)
The anniversaries of The Queen's accession, The Queen's birthday and The Queen's coronation, The Queen's official birthday, the birthday of the Duke of Edinburgh, the birthday of the Prince of Wales, St David's Day and Lord Mayor's Day.

PUBLIC HOLIDAYS

Public holidays are divided into two categories, common law and statutory. Common law holidays are holidays 'by habit and custom'; in England, Wales and Northern Ireland these are Good Friday and Christmas Day.

Statutory public holidays, known as bank holidays, were first established by the Bank Holidays Act 1871. They were, literally, days on which the banks (and other public institutions) were closed and financial obligations due on that day were payable the following day. The legislation currently governing public holidays in the UK, which is the Banking and Financial Dealings Act 1971, stipulates the days that are to be public holidays in England, Wales, Scotland and Northern Ireland.

Certain holidays (indicated by * below) are granted annually by royal proclamation, either throughout the UK or in any place in the UK. The public holidays are:

England and Wales
*New Year's Day
Good Friday
Easter Monday
*The first Monday in May
The last Monday in May
The last Monday in August
26 December, if it is not a Sunday
27 December when 25 or 26 December is a Sunday

Scotland
New Year's Day, or if it is a Sunday, 2 January
2 January, or if it is a Sunday, 3 January
Good Friday
The first Monday in May
*The last Monday in May
The first Monday in August
Christmas Day, or if it is a Sunday, 26 December
*Boxing Day – if Christmas Day falls on a Sunday, 26 December is given in lieu and an alternative day is given for Boxing Day

Northern Ireland
*New Year's Day
17 March, or if it is a Sunday, 18 March
Easter Monday
*The first Monday in May
The last Monday in May
*12 July, or if it is a Sunday, 13 July
The last Monday in August
26 December, if it is not a Sunday
27 December if 25 or 26 December is a Sunday

For dates of public holidays in 2006 and 2007, *see* pages 10–11.

CHRONOLOGICAL CYCLES AND ERAS

SOLAR (OR MAJOR) CYCLE

The solar cycle is a period of twenty-eight years in any corresponding year of which the days of the week recur on the same day of the month.

METONIC (LUNAR, OR MINOR) CYCLE

In 432 BC, Meton, an Athenian astronomer, found that 235 lunations are very nearly, though not exactly, equal in duration to 19 solar years and so after 19 years the phases of the Moon recur on the same days of the month (nearly). The dates of full moon in a cycle of 19 years were inscribed in figures of gold on public monuments in Athens, and the number showing the position of a year in the cycle is called the golden number of that year.

JULIAN PERIOD

The Julian period was proposed by Joseph Scaliger in 1582. The period is 7980 Julian years, and its first year coincides with the year 4713 BC. The figure of 7980 is the product of the number of years in the solar cycle, the Metonic cycle and the cycle of the Roman indiction (28 × 19 × 15).

ROMAN INDICTION
The Roman indiction is a period of fifteen years, instituted for fiscal purposes about AD 300.

EPACT
The epact is the age of the calendar Moon, diminished by one day, on 1 January, in the ecclesiastical lunar calendar.

CHINESE CALENDAR
A lunar calendar was the sole calendar in use in China until 1911, when the government adopted the new (Gregorian) calendar for official and most business activities. The Chinese tend to follow both calendars, the lunar calendar playing an important part in personal life, e.g. birth celebrations, festivals, marriages; and in rural villages the lunar calendar dictates the cycle of activities, denoting the change of weather and farming activities.

The lunar calendar is used in Hong Kong, Singapore, Malaysia, Tibet and elsewhere in south-east Asia. The calendar has a cycle of 60 years. The new year begins at the first new moon after the sun enters the sign of Aquarius, i.e. the new year falls between 21 January and 19 February in the Gregorian calendar.

Each year in the Chinese calendar is associated with one of 12 animals: the rat, the ox, the tiger, the rabbit, the dragon, the snake, the horse, the goat or sheep, the monkey, the chicken or rooster, the dog, and the pig.

The date of the Chinese new year and the astrological sign for the years 2006–2009 are:

2006	29 January	Dog
2007	18 February	Pig
2008	7 February	Rat
2009	26 January	Ox

COPTIC CALENDAR
In the Coptic calendar, which is used in parts of Egypt and Ethiopia, the year is made up of 12 months of 30 days each, followed, in general, by five complementary days. Every fourth year is an intercalary or leap year and in these years there are six complementary days. The intercalary year of the Coptic calendar immediately precedes the leap year of the Julian calendar. The era is that of Diocletian or the Martyrs, the origin of which is fixed at 29 August AD 284 (Julian date).

INDIAN ERAS
In addition to the Muslim reckoning, other eras are used in India. The Saka era of southern India, dating from 3 March AD 78, was declared the national calendar of the Republic of India with effect from 22 March 1957, to be used concurrently with the Gregorian calendar. As revised, the year of the new Saka era begins at the spring equinox, with five successive months of 31 days and seven of 30 days in ordinary years, and six months of each length in leap years. The year AD 2006 is 1928 of the revised Saka era.

The year AD 2006 corresponds to the following years in other eras:

Year 2063 of the Vikram Samvat era
Year 1413 of the Bengali San era
Year 1182 of the Kollam era
Vedanga Jyotisa year 2 of the five-yearly cycle (387th cycle of Paitamah Siddhanta)

Year 6007 of the Kaliyuga era
Year 2548 of the Buddha Nirvana era

JAPANESE CALENDAR
The Japanese calendar is essentially the same as the Gregorian calendar, the years, months and weeks being of the same length and beginning on the same days as those of the Gregorian calendar. The numeration of the years is different, based on a system of epochs or periods, each of which begins at the accession of an Emperor or other important occurrence. The method is not unlike the British system of regnal years, except that each year of a period closes on 31 December. The Japanese chronology begins about AD 650 and the three latest epochs are defined by the reigns of Emperors, whose actual names are not necessarily used:

Epoch
Taisho 1 August 1912 to 25 December 1926
Showa 26 December 1926 to 7 January 1989
Heisei 8 January 1989

The year Heisei 17 begins on 1 January 2005.

The months are known as First Month, Second Month, etc., First Month being equivalent to January. The days of the week are Nichiyobi (Sun-day), Getsuyobi (Moon-day), Kayobi (Fire-day), Suiyobi (Water-day), Mokuyobi (Wood-day), Kinyobi (Metal-day), Doyobi (Earth-day).

THE MASONIC YEAR
Two dates are quoted in warrants, dispensations, etc., issued by the United Grand Lodge of England, those for the current year being expressed as *Anno Domini* 2006–*Anno Lucis* 6006. This *Anno Lucis* (year of light) is based on the Book of Genesis 1:3, the 4000-year difference being derived, in modified form, from *Ussher's Notation*, published in 1654, which places the Creation of the World in 4004 BC.

OLYMPIADS
Ancient Greek chronology was reckoned in Olympiads, cycles of four years corresponding with the periodic Olympic Games held on the plain of Olympia in Elis once every four years. The intervening years were the first, second, etc., of the Olympiad, which received the name of the victor at the Games. The first recorded Olympiad is that of Choroebus, 776 BC.

ZOROASTRIAN CALENDAR
Zoroastrians, followers of the Iranian prophet Zarathushtra (known to the Greeks as Zoroaster) are mostly to be found in Iran and in India, where they are known as Parsees.

The Zoroastrian era dates from the coronation of the last Zoroastrian Sasanian king in AD 631. The Zoroastrian calendar is divided into twelve months, each comprising 30 days, followed by five holy days of the Gathas at the end of each year to make the year consist of 365 days.

In order to synchronise the calendar with the solar year of 365 days, an extra month was intercalated once every 120 years. However, this intercalation ceased in the 12th century and the New Year, which had fallen in the spring, slipped back to August. Because intercalation ceased at different times in Iran and India, there was one month's difference between the calendar followed in Iran (Kadmi calendar) and that followed by the Parsees (Shenshai calendar). In 1906 a group of Zoroastrians decided to bring the calendar back in line with the seasons again and restore the New Year to 21 March each year (Fasli calendar).

The Shenshai calendar (New Year in August) is mainly used by Parsees. The Fasli calendar (New Year, 21 March) is mainly used by Zoroastrians living in Iran, in the Indian subcontinent, or away from Iran.

THE ROMAN CALENDAR

Roman historians adopted as an epoch the foundation of Rome, which is believed to have happened in the year 753 BC. The ordinal number of the years in Roman reckoning is followed by the letters AUC *(ab urbe condita)*, so that the year 2006 is 2759 AUC (MMDCCLIX). The calendar that we know has developed from one said to have been established by Romulus using a year of 304 days divided into ten months, beginning with March. To this Numa added January and February, making the year consist of 12 months of 30 and 29 days alternately, with an additional day so that the total was 355. It is also said that Numa ordered an intercalary month of 22 or 23 days in alternate years, making 90 days in eight years, to be inserted after 23 February.

However, there is some doubt as to the origination and the details of the intercalation in the Roman calendar. It is certain that some scheme of this kind was inaugurated and not fully carried out, for in the year 46 BC Julius Caesar found that the calendar had been allowed to fall into some confusion. He sought the help of the Egyptian astronomer Sosigenes, which led to the construction and adoption (45 BC) of the Julian calendar, and, by a slight alteration, to the Gregorian calendar now in use. The year 46 BC was made to consist of 445 days and is called the Year of Confusion.

In the Roman (Julian) calendar the days of the month were counted backwards from three fixed points, or days, and an intervening day was said to be so many days before the next coming point, the first and last being counted. These three points were the Kalends, the Nones, and the Ides. Their positions in the months and the method of counting from them will be seen in the table below. The year containing 366 days was called *bissextillis annus*, as it had a doubled sixth day *(bissextus dies)* before the March Kalends on 24 February – *ante diem sextum Kalendas Martias*, or a.d. VI Kal. Mart.

Present days of the month	*March, May, July, October have thirty-one days*		*January, August, December have thirty-one days*		*April, June, September, November have thirty days*		*February has twenty-eight days, and in leap year twenty-nine*	
1	Kalendis		Kalendis		Kalendis		Kalendis	
2	VI		IV	ante	IV	ante	IV	ante
3	V	ante	III	Nonas	III	Nonas	III	Nonas
4	IV	Nonas	pridie Nonas		pridie Nonas		pridie Nonas	
5	III		Nonis		Nonis		Nonis	
6	pridie Nonas		VIII		VIII		VIII	
7	Nonis		VII		VII		VII	
8	VIII		VI	ante	VI	ante	VI	ante
9	VII		V	Idus	V	Idus	V	Idus
10	VI	ante	IV		IV		IV	
11	V	Idus	III		III		III	
12	IV		pridie Idus		pridie Idus		pridie Idus	
13	III		Idibus		Idibus		Idibus	
14	pridie Idus		XIX		XVIII		XVI	
15	Idibus		XVIII		XVII		XV	
16	XVII		XVII		XVI		XIV	
17	XVI		XVI		XV		XIII	
18	XV		XV		XIV		XII	
19	XIV		XIV		XIII		XI	
20	XIII		XIII		XII	ante Kalendas	X	ante Kalendas
21	XII		XII	ante Kalendas	XI	(of the month	IX	Martias
22	XI	ante Kalendas	XI	(of the month	X	following)	VIII	
23	X	(of the month	X	following)	IX		VII	
24	IX	following)	IX		VIII		*VI	
25	VIII		VIII		VII		V	
26	VII		VII		VI		IV	
27	VI		VI		V		III	
28	V		V		IV		pridie Kalendas	
29	IV		IV		III		Martias	
30	III		III		pridie Kalendas			
31	pridie Kalendas (Aprilis, Iunias, Sextilis, Novembris)		pridie Kalendas (Februarias, Septembris, Ianuarias)		(Maias, Quinctilis, Octobris, Decembris)		*(repeated in leap year)	

CALENDAR FOR ANY YEAR 1780–2040

To select the correct calendar for any year between 1780 and 2040, consult the index below

*leap year

1780 N*	1813 K	1846 I	1879 G	1912 D*	1945 C	1978 A	2011 M
1781 C	1814 M	1847 K	1880 J*	1913 G	1946 E	1979 C	2012 B*
1782 E	1815 A	1848 N*	1881 M	1914 I	1947 G	1980 F*	2013 E
1783 G	1816 D*	1849 C	1882 A	1915 K	1948 J*	1981 I	2014 G
1784 J*	1817 G	1850 E	1883 C	1916 N*	1949 M	1982 K	2015 I
1785 M	1818 I	1851 G	1884 F*	1917 C	1950 A	1983 M	2016 L*
1786 A	1819 K	1852 J*	1885 I	1918 E	1951 C	1984 B*	2017 A
1787 C	1820 N*	1853 M	1886 K	1919 G	1952 F*	1985 E	2018 C
1788 F*	1821 C	1854 A	1887 M	1920 J*	1953 I	1986 G	2019 E
1789 I	1822 E	1855 C	1888 B*	1921 M	1954 K	1987 I	2020 H*
1790 K	1823 G	1856 F*	1889 E	1922 A	1955 M	1988 L*	2021 K
1791 M	1824 J*	1857 I	1890 G	1923 C	1956 B*	1989 A	2022 M
1792 B*	1825 M	1858 K	1891 I	1924 F*	1957 E	1990 C	2023 A
1793 E	1826 A	1859 M	1892 L*	1925 I	1958 G	1991 E	2024 D*
1794 G	1827 C	1860 B*	1893 A	1926 K	1959 I	1992 H*	2025 G
1795 I	1828 F*	1861 E	1894 C	1927 M	1960 L*	1993 K	2026 I
1796 L*	1829 I	1862 G	1895 E	1928 B*	1961 A	1994 M	2027 K
1797 A	1830 K	1863 I	1896 H*	1929 E	1962 C	1995 A	2028 N*
1798 C	1831 M	1864 L*	1897 K	1930 G	1963 E	1996 D*	2029 C
1799 E	1832 B*	1865 A	1898 M	1931 I	1964 H*	1997 G	2030 E
1800 G	1833 E	1866 C	1899 A	1932 L*	1965 K	1998 I	2031 G
1801 I	1834 G	1867 E	1900 C	1933 A	1966 M	1999 K	2032 J*
1802 K	1835 I	1868 H*	1901 E	1934 C	1967 A	2000 N*	2033 M
1803 M	1836 L*	1869 K	1902 G	1935 E	1968 D*	2001 C	2034 A
1804 B*	1837 A	1870 M	1903 I	1936 H*	1969 G	2002 E	2035 C
1805 E	1838 C	1871 A	1904 L*	1937 K	1970 I	2003 G	2036 F*
1806 G	1839 E	1872 D*	1905 A	1938 M	1971 K	2004 J*	2037 I
1807 I	1840 H*	1873 G	1906 C	1939 A	1972 N*	2005 M	2038 K
1808 L*	1841 K	1874 I	1907 E	1940 D*	1973 C	2006 A	2039 M
1809 A	1842 M	1875 K	1908 H*	1941 G	1974 E	2007 C	2040 B*
1810 C	1843 A	1876 N*	1909 K	1942 I	1975 G	2008 F*	
1811 E	1844 D*	1877 C	1910 M	1943 K	1976 J*	2009 I	
1812 H*	1845 G	1878 E	1911 A	1944 N*	1977 M	2010 K	

A

	January	February	March
Sun.	1 8 15 22 29	5 12 19 26	5 12 19 26
Mon.	2 9 16 23 30	6 13 20 27	6 13 20 27
Tue.	3 10 17 24 31	7 14 21 28	7 14 21 28
Wed.	4 11 18 25	1 8 15 22	1 8 15 22 29
Thur.	5 12 19 26	2 9 16 23	2 9 16 23 30
Fri.	6 13 20 27	3 10 17 24	3 10 17 24 31
Sat.	7 14 21 28	4 11 18 25	4 11 18 25

	April	May	June
Sun.	2 9 16 23 30	7 14 21 28	4 11 18 25
Mon.	3 10 17 24	1 8 15 22 29	5 12 19 26
Tue.	4 11 18 25	2 9 16 23 30	6 13 20 27
Wed.	5 12 19 26	3 10 17 24 31	7 14 21 28
Thur.	6 13 20 27	4 11 18 25	1 8 15 22 29
Fri.	7 14 21 28	5 12 19 26	2 9 16 23 30
Sat.	1 8 15 22 29	6 13 20 27	3 10 17 24

	July	August	September
Sun.	2 9 16 23 30	6 13 20 27	3 10 17 24
Mon.	3 10 17 24 31	7 14 21 28	4 11 18 25
Tue.	4 11 18 25	1 8 15 22 29	5 12 19 26
Wed.	5 12 19 26	2 9 16 23 30	6 13 20 27
Thur.	6 13 20 27	3 10 17 24 31	7 14 21 28
Fri.	7 14 21 28	4 11 18 25	1 8 15 22 29
Sat.	1 8 15 22 29	5 12 19 26	2 9 16 23 30

	October	November	December
Sun.	1 8 15 22 29	5 12 19 26	3 10 17 24 31
Mon.	2 9 16 23 30	6 13 20 27	4 11 18 25
Tue.	3 10 17 24 31	7 14 21 28	5 12 19 26
Wed.	4 11 18 25	1 8 15 22 29	6 13 20 27
Thur.	5 12 19 26	2 9 16 23 30	7 14 21 28
Fri.	6 13 20 27	3 10 17 24	1 8 15 22 29
Sat.	7 14 21 28	4 11 18 25	2 9 16 23 30

EASTER DAYS

March 26	1815, 1826, 1837, 1967, 1978, 1989
April 2	1809, 1893, 1899, 1961
April 9	1871, 1882, 1939, 1950, 2023, 2034
April 16	1786, 1797, 1843, 1854, 1865, 1911
	1922, 1933, 1995, 2006, 2017
April 23	1905

B (LEAP YEAR)

	January	February	March
Sun.	1 8 15 22 29	5 12 19 26	4 11 18 25
Mon.	2 9 16 23 30	6 13 20 27	5 12 19 26
Tue.	3 10 17 24 31	7 14 21 28	6 13 20 27
Wed.	4 11 18 25	1 8 15 22 29	7 14 21 28
Thur.	5 12 19 26	2 9 16 23	1 8 15 22 29
Fri.	6 13 20 27	3 10 17 24	2 9 16 23 30
Sat.	7 14 21 28	4 11 18 25	3 10 17 24 31

	April	May	June
Sun.	1 8 15 22 29	6 13 20 27	3 10 17 24
Mon.	2 9 16 23 30	7 14 21 28	4 11 18 25
Tue.	3 10 17 24	1 8 15 22 29	5 12 19 26
Wed.	4 11 18 25	2 9 16 23 30	6 13 20 27
Thur.	5 12 19 26	3 10 17 24 31	7 14 21 28
Fri.	6 13 20 27	4 11 18 25	1 8 15 22 29
Sat.	7 14 21 28	5 12 19 26	2 9 16 23 30

	July	August	September
Sun.	1 8 15 22 29	5 12 19 26	2 9 16 23 30
Mon.	2 9 16 23 30	6 13 20 27	3 10 17 24
Tue.	3 10 17 24 31	7 14 21 28	4 11 18 25
Wed.	4 11 18 25	1 8 15 22 29	5 12 19 26
Thur.	5 12 19 26	2 9 16 23 30	6 13 20 27
Fri.	6 13 20 27	3 10 17 24 31	7 14 21 28
Sat.	7 14 21 28	4 11 18 25	1 8 15 22 29

	October	November	December
Sun.	7 14 21 28	4 11 18 25	2 9 16 23 30
Mon.	1 8 15 22 29	5 12 19 26	3 10 17 24 31
Tue.	2 9 16 23 30	6 13 20 27	4 11 18 25
Wed.	3 10 17 24 31	7 14 21 28	5 12 19 26
Thur.	4 11 18 25	1 8 15 22 29	6 13 20 27
Fri.	5 12 19 26	2 9 16 23 30	7 14 21 28
Sat.	6 13 20 27	3 10 17 24	1 8 15 22 29

EASTER DAYS

April 1	1804, 1888, 1956, 2040
April 8	1792, 1860, 1928, 2012
April 22	1832, 1984

C

	January	February	March
Sun.	7 14 21 28	4 11 18 25	4 11 10 25
Mon.	1 8 15 22 29	5 12 19 26	5 12 19 26
Tue.	2 9 16 23 30	6 13 20 27	6 13 20 27
Wed.	3 10 17 24 31	7 14 21 28	7 14 21 28
Thur.	4 11 18 25	1 8 15 22	1 8 15 22 29
Fri.	5 12 19 26	2 9 16 23	2 9 16 23 30
Sat.	6 13 20 27	3 10 17 24	3 10 17 24 31

	April	May	June
Sun.	1 8 15 22 29	6 13 20 27	3 10 17 24
Mon.	2 9 16 23 30	7 14 21 28	4 11 18 25
Tue.	3 10 17 24	1 8 15 22 29	5 12 19 26
Wed.	4 11 18 25	2 9 16 23 30	6 13 20 27
Thur.	5 12 19 26	3 10 17 24 31	7 14 21 28
Fri.	6 13 20 27	4 11 18 25	1 8 15 22 29
Sat.	7 14 21 28	5 12 19 26	2 9 16 23 30

	July	August	September
Sun.	1 8 15 22 29	5 12 19 26	2 9 16 23 30
Mon.	2 9 16 23 30	6 13 20 27	3 10 17 24
Tue.	3 10 17 24 31	7 14 21 28	4 11 18 25
Wed.	4 11 18 25	1 8 15 22 29	5 12 19 26
Thur.	5 12 19 26	2 9 16 23 30	6 13 20 27
Fri.	6 13 20 27	3 10 17 24 31	7 14 21 28
Sat.	7 14 21 28	4 11 18 25	1 8 15 22 29

	October	November	December
Sun.	7 14 21 28	4 11 18 25	2 9 16 23 30
Mon.	1 8 15 22 29	5 12 19 26	3 10 17 24 31
Tue.	2 9 16 23 30	6 13 20 27	4 11 18 25
Wed.	3 10 17 24 31	7 14 21 28	5 12 19 26
Thur.	4 11 18 25	1 8 15 22 29	6 13 20 27
Fri.	5 12 19 26	2 9 16 23 30	7 14 21 28
Sat.	6 13 20 27	3 10 17 24	1 8 15 22 29

EASTER DAYS
March 25	1883, 1894, 1951, 2035
April 1	1866, 1877, 1923, 1934, 1945, 2018, 2029
April 8	1787, 1798, 1849, 1855, 1917, 2007
April 15	1781, 1827, 1838, 1900, 1906, 1979, 1990, 2001
April 22	1810, 1821, 1962, 1973

E

	January	February	March
Sun.	6 13 20 27	3 10 17 24	3 10 17 24 31
Mon.	7 14 21 28	4 11 18 25	4 11 18 25
Tue.	1 8 15 22 29	5 12 19 26	5 12 19 26
Wed.	2 9 16 23 30	6 13 20 27	6 13 20 27
Thur.	3 10 17 24 31	7 14 21 28	7 14 21 28
Fri.	4 11 18 25	1 8 15 22	1 8 15 22 29
Sat.	5 12 19 26	2 9 16 23	2 9 16 23 30

	April	May	June
Sun.	7 14 21 28	5 12 19 26	2 9 16 23 30
Mon.	1 8 15 22 29	6 13 20 27	3 10 17 24
Tue.	2 9 16 23 30	7 14 21 28	4 11 18 25
Wed.	3 10 17 24	1 8 15 22 29	5 12 19 26
Thur.	4 11 18 25	2 9 16 23 30	6 13 20 27
Fri.	5 12 19 26	3 10 17 24 31	7 14 21 28
Sat.	6 13 20 27	4 11 18 25	1 8 15 22 29

	July	August	September
Sun.	7 14 21 28	4 11 18 25	1 8 15 22 29
Mon.	1 8 15 22 29	5 12 19 26	2 9 16 23 30
Tue.	2 9 16 23 30	6 13 20 27	3 10 17 24
Wed.	3 10 17 24 31	7 14 21 28	4 11 18 25
Thur.	4 11 18 25	1 8 15 22 29	5 12 19 26
Fri.	5 12 19 26	2 9 16 23 30	6 13 20 27
Sat.	6 13 20 27	3 10 17 24 31	7 14 21 28

	October	November	December
Sun.	6 13 20 27	3 10 17 24	1 8 15 22 29
Mon.	7 14 21 28	4 11 18 25	2 9 16 23 30
Tue.	1 8 15 22 29	5 12 19 26	3 10 17 24 31
Wed.	2 9 16 23 30	6 13 20 27	4 11 18 25
Thur.	3 10 17 24 31	7 14 21 28	5 12 19 26
Fri.	4 11 18 25	1 8 15 22 29	6 13 20 27
Sat.	5 12 19 26	2 9 16 23 30	7 14 21 28

EASTER DAYS
March 24	1799
March 31	1782, 1793, 1839, 1850, 1861, 1907
	1918, 1929, 1991, 2002, 2013
April 7	1822, 1833, 1901, 1985
April 14	1805, 1811, 1895, 1963, 1974
April 21	1867, 1878, 1889, 1935, 1946, 1957, 2019, 2030

D (LEAP YEAR)

	January	February	March
Sun.	7 14 21 28	4 11 18 25	3 10 17 24 31
Mon.	1 8 15 22 29	5 12 19 26	4 11 18 25
Tue.	2 9 16 23 30	6 13 20 27	5 12 19 26
Wed.	3 10 17 24 31	7 14 21 28	6 13 20 27
Thur.	4 11 18 25	1 8 15 22 29	7 14 21 28
Fri.	5 12 19 26	2 9 16 23	1 8 15 22 29
Sat.	6 13 20 27	3 10 17 24	2 9 16 23 30

	April	May	June
Sun.	7 14 21 28	5 12 19 26	2 9 16 23 30
Mon.	1 8 15 22 29	6 13 20 27	3 10 17 24
Tue.	2 9 16 23 30	7 14 21 28	4 11 18 25
Wed.	3 10 17 24	1 8 15 22 29	5 12 19 26
Thur.	4 11 18 25	2 9 16 23 30	6 13 20 27
Fri.	5 12 19 26	3 10 17 24 31	7 14 21 28
Sat.	6 13 20 27	4 11 18 25	1 8 15 22 29

	July	August	September
Sun.	7 14 21 28	4 11 18 25	1 8 15 22 29
Mon.	1 8 15 22 29	5 12 19 26	2 9 16 23 30
Tue.	2 9 16 23 30	6 13 20 27	3 10 17 24
Wed.	3 10 17 24 31	7 14 21 28	4 11 18 25
Thur.	4 11 18 25	1 8 15 22 29	5 12 19 26
Fri.	5 12 19 26	2 9 16 23 30	6 13 20 27
Sat.	6 13 20 27	3 10 17 24 31	7 14 21 28

	October	November	December
Sun.	6 13 20 27	3 10 17 24	1 8 15 22 29
Mon.	7 14 21 28	4 11 18 25	2 9 16 23 30
Tue.	1 8 15 22 29	5 12 19 26	3 10 17 24 31
Wed.	2 9 16 23 30	6 13 20 27	4 11 18 25
Thur.	3 10 17 24 31	7 14 21 28	5 12 19 26
Fri.	4 11 18 25	1 8 15 22 29	6 13 20 27
Sat.	5 12 19 26	2 9 16 23 30	7 14 21 28

EASTER DAYS
March 24	1940
March 31	1872, 2024
April 7	1844, 1912, 1996
April 14	1816, 1968

F (LEAP YEAR)

	January	February	March
Sun.	6 13 20 27	3 10 17 24	2 9 16 23 30
Mon.	7 14 21 28	4 11 18 25	3 10 17 24 31
Tue.	1 8 15 22 29	5 12 19 26	4 11 18 25
Wed.	2 9 16 23 30	6 13 20 27	5 12 19 26
Thur.	3 10 17 24 31	7 14 21 28	6 13 20 27
Fri.	4 11 18 25	1 8 15 22 29	7 14 21 28
Sat.	5 12 19 26	2 9 16 23	1 8 15 22 29

	April	May	June
Sun.	6 13 20 27	4 11 18 25	1 8 15 22 29
Mon.	7 14 21 28	5 12 19 26	2 9 16 23 30
Tue.	1 8 15 22 29	6 13 20 27	3 10 17 24
Wed.	2 9 16 23 30	7 14 21 28	4 11 18 25
Thur.	3 10 17 24	1 8 15 22 29	5 12 19 26
Fri.	4 11 18 25	2 9 16 23 30	6 13 20 27
Sat.	5 12 19 26	3 10 17 24 31	7 14 21 28

	July	August	September
Sun.	6 13 20 27	3 10 17 24 31	7 14 21 28
Mon.	7 14 21 28	4 11 18 25	1 8 15 22 29
Tue.	1 8 15 22 29	5 12 19 26	2 9 16 23 30
Wed.	2 9 16 23 30	6 13 20 27	3 10 17 24
Thur.	3 10 17 24 31	7 14 21 28	4 11 18 25
Fri.	4 11 18 25	1 8 15 22 29	5 12 19 26
Sat.	5 12 19 26	2 9 16 23 30	6 13 20 27

	October	November	December
Sun.	5 12 19 26	2 9 16 23 30	7 14 21 28
Mon.	6 13 20 27	3 10 17 24	1 8 15 22 29
Tue.	7 14 21 28	4 11 18 25	2 9 16 23 30
Wed.	1 8 15 22 29	5 12 19 26	3 10 17 24 31
Thur.	2 9 16 23 30	6 13 20 27	4 11 18 25
Fri.	3 10 17 24 31	7 14 21 28	5 12 19 26
Sat.	4 11 18 25	1 8 15 22 29	6 13 20 27

EASTER DAYS
March 23	1788, 1856, 2008
April 6	1828, 1980
April 13	1884, 1952, 2036
April 20	1924

G

	January	February	March
Sun.	5 12 19 26	2 9 16 23	2 9 16 23 30
Mon.	6 13 20 27	3 10 17 24	3 10 17 24 31
Tue.	7 14 21 28	4 11 18 25	4 11 18 25
Wed.	1 8 15 22 29	5 12 19 26	5 12 19 26
Thur.	2 9 16 23 30	6 13 20 27	6 13 20 27
Fri.	3 10 17 24 31	7 14 21 28	7 14 21 28
Sat.	4 11 18 25	1 8 15 22	1 8 15 22 29

	April	May	June
Sun.	6 13 20 27	4 11 18 25	1 8 15 22 29
Mon.	7 14 21 28	5 12 19 26	2 9 16 23 30
Tue.	1 8 15 22 29	6 13 20 27	3 10 17 24
Wed.	2 9 16 23 30	7 14 21 28	4 11 18 25
Thur.	3 10 17 24	1 8 15 22 29	5 12 19 26
Fri.	4 11 18 25	2 9 16 23 30	6 13 20 27
Sat.	5 12 19 26	3 10 17 24 31	7 14 21 28

	July	August	September
Sun.	6 13 20 27	3 10 17 24 31	7 14 21 28
Mon.	7 14 21 28	4 11 18 25	1 8 15 22 29
Tue.	1 8 15 22 29	5 12 19 26	2 9 16 23 30
Wed.	2 9 16 23 30	6 13 20 27	3 10 17 24
Thur.	3 10 17 24 31	7 14 21 28	4 11 18 25
Fri.	4 11 18 25	1 8 15 22 29	5 12 19 26
Sat.	5 12 19 26	2 9 16 23 30	6 13 20 27

	October	November	December
Sun.	5 12 19 26	2 9 16 23 30	7 14 21 28
Mon.	6 13 20 27	3 10 17 24	1 8 15 22 29
Tue.	7 14 21 28	4 11 18 25	2 9 16 23 30
Wed.	1 8 15 22 29	5 12 19 26	3 10 17 24 31
Thur.	2 9 16 23 30	6 13 20 27	4 11 18 25
Fri.	3 10 17 24 31	7 14 21 28	5 12 19 26
Sat.	4 11 18 25	1 8 15 22 29	6 13 20 27

EASTER DAYS
March 23 — 1845, 1913
March 30 — 1823, 1834, 1902, 1975, 1986, 1997
April 6 — 1806, 1817, 1890, 1947, 1958, 1969
April 13 — 1800, 1873, 1879, 1941, 2031
April 20 — 1783, 1794, 1851, 1862, 1919, 1930, 2003, 2014, 2025

I

	January	February	March
Sun.	4 11 18 25	1 8 15 22	1 8 15 22 29
Mon.	5 12 19 26	2 9 16 23	2 9 16 23 30
Tue.	6 13 20 27	3 10 17 24	3 10 17 24 31
Wed.	7 14 21 28	4 11 18 25	4 11 18 25
Thur.	1 8 15 22 29	5 12 19 26	5 12 19 26
Fri.	2 9 16 23 30	6 13 20 27	6 13 20 27
Sat.	3 10 17 24 31	7 14 21 28	7 14 21 28

	April	May	June
Sun.	5 12 19 26	3 10 17 24 31	7 14 21 28
Mon.	6 13 20 27	4 11 18 25	1 8 15 22 29
Tue.	7 14 21 28	5 12 19 26	2 9 16 23 30
Wed.	1 8 15 22 29	6 13 20 27	3 10 17 24
Thur.	2 9 16 23 30	7 14 21 28	4 11 18 25
Fri.	3 10 17 24	1 8 15 22 29	5 12 19 26
Sat.	4 11 18 25	2 9 16 23 30	6 13 20 27

	July	August	September
Sun.	5 12 19 26	2 9 16 23 30	6 13 20 27
Mon.	6 13 20 27	3 10 17 24 31	7 14 21 28
Tue.	7 14 21 28	4 11 18 25	1 8 15 22 29
Wed.	1 8 15 22 29	5 12 19 26	2 9 16 23 30
Thur.	2 9 16 23 30	6 13 20 27	3 10 17 24
Fri.	3 10 17 24 31	7 14 21 28	4 11 18 25
Sat.	4 11 18 25	1 8 15 22 29	5 12 19 26

	October	November	December
Sun.	4 11 18 25	1 8 15 22 29	6 13 20 27
Mon.	5 12 19 26	2 9 16 23 30	7 14 21 28
Tue.	6 13 20 27	3 10 17 24	1 8 15 22 29
Wed.	7 14 21 28	4 11 18 25	2 9 16 23 30
Thur.	1 8 15 22 29	5 12 19 26	3 10 17 24 31
Fri.	2 9 16 23 30	6 13 20 27	4 11 18 25
Sat.	3 10 17 24 31	7 14 21 28	5 12 19 26

EASTER DAYS
March 22 — 1818
March 29 — 1807, 1891, 1959, 1970
April 5 — 1795, 1801, 1863, 1874, 1885, 1931, 1942, 1953, 2015, 2026, 2037
April 12 — 1789, 1846, 1857, 1903, 1914, 1925, 1998, 2009
April 19 — 1829, 1835, 1981, 1987

H (LEAP YEAR)

	January	February	March
Sun.	5 12 19 26	2 9 16 23	1 8 15 22 29
Mon.	6 13 20 27	3 10 17 24	2 9 16 23 30
Tue.	7 14 21 28	4 11 18 25	3 10 17 24 31
Wed.	1 8 15 22 29	5 12 19 26	4 11 18 25
Thur.	2 9 16 23 30	6 13 20 27	5 12 19 26
Fri.	3 10 17 24 31	7 14 21 28	6 13 20 27
Sat.	4 11 18 25	1 8 15 22 29	7 14 21 28

	April	May	June
Sun.	5 12 19 26	3 10 17 24 31	7 14 21 28
Mon.	6 13 20 27	4 11 18 25	1 8 15 22 29
Tue.	7 14 21 28	5 12 19 26	2 9 16 23 30
Wed.	1 8 15 22 29	6 13 20 27	3 10 17 24
Thur.	2 9 16 23 30	7 14 21 28	4 11 18 25
Fri.	3 10 17 24	1 8 15 22 29	5 12 19 26
Sat.	4 11 18 25	2 9 16 23 30	6 13 20 27

	July	August	September
Sun.	5 12 19 26	2 9 16 23 30	6 13 20 27
Mon.	6 13 20 27	3 10 17 24 31	7 14 21 28
Tue.	7 14 21 28	4 11 18 25	1 8 15 22 29
Wed.	1 8 15 22 29	5 12 19 26	2 9 16 23 30
Thur.	2 9 16 23 30	6 13 20 27	3 10 17 24
Fri.	3 10 17 24 31	7 14 21 28	4 11 18 25
Sat.	4 11 18 25	1 8 15 22 29	5 12 19 26

	October	November	December
Sun.	4 11 18 25	1 8 15 22 29	6 13 20 27
Mon.	5 12 19 26	2 9 16 23 30	7 14 21 28
Tue.	6 13 20 27	3 10 17 24	1 8 15 22 29
Wed.	7 14 21 28	4 11 18 25	2 9 16 23 30
Thur.	1 8 15 22 29	5 12 19 26	3 10 17 24 31
Fri.	2 9 16 23 30	6 13 20 27	4 11 18 25
Sat.	3 10 17 24 31	7 14 21 28	5 12 19 26

EASTER DAYS
March 29 — 1812, 1964
April 5 — 1896
April 12 — 1868, 1936, 2020
April 19 — 1840, 1908, 1992

J (LEAP YEAR)

	January	February	March
Sun.	4 11 18 25	1 8 15 22 29	7 14 21 28
Mon.	5 12 19 26	2 9 16 23	1 8 15 22 29
Tue.	6 13 20 27	3 10 17 24	2 9 16 23 30
Wed.	7 14 21 28	4 11 18 25	3 10 17 24 31
Thur.	1 8 15 22 29	5 12 19 26	4 11 18 25
Fri.	2 9 16 23 30	6 13 20 27	5 12 19 26
Sat.	3 10 17 24 31	7 14 21 28	6 13 20 27

	April	May	June
Sun.	4 11 18 25	2 9 16 23 30	6 13 20 27
Mon.	5 12 19 26	3 10 17 24 31	7 14 21 28
Tue.	6 13 20 27	4 11 18 25	1 8 15 22 29
Wed.	7 14 21 28	5 12 19 26	2 9 16 23 30
Thur.	1 8 15 22 29	6 13 20 27	3 10 17 24
Fri.	2 9 16 23 30	7 14 21 28	4 11 18 25
Sat.	3 10 17 24	1 8 15 22 29	5 12 19 26

	July	August	September
Sun.	4 11 18 25	1 8 15 22 29	5 12 19 26
Mon.	5 12 19 26	2 9 16 23 30	6 13 20 27
Tue.	6 13 20 27	3 10 17 24 31	7 14 21 28
Wed.	7 14 21 28	4 11 18 25	1 8 15 22 29
Thur.	1 8 15 22 29	5 12 19 26	2 9 16 23 30
Fri.	2 9 16 23 30	6 13 20 27	3 10 17 24
Sat.	3 10 17 24 31	7 14 21 28	4 11 18 25

	October	November	December
Sun.	3 10 17 24 31	7 14 21 28	5 12 19 26
Mon.	4 11 18 25	1 8 15 22 29	6 13 20 27
Tue.	5 12 19 26	2 9 16 23 30	7 14 21 28
Wed.	6 13 20 27	3 10 17 24	1 8 15 22 29
Thur.	7 14 21 28	4 11 18 25	2 9 16 23 30
Fri.	1 8 15 22 29	5 12 19 26	3 10 17 24 31
Sat.	2 9 16 23 30	6 13 20 27	4 11 18 25

EASTER DAYS
March 28 — 1880, 1948, 2032
April 4 — 1920
April 11 — 1784, 1852, 2004
April 18 — 1824, 1976

K

	January	February	March
Sun.	3 10 17 24 31	7 14 21 28	7 14 21 28
Mon.	4 11 18 25	1 8 15 22	1 8 15 22 29
Tue.	5 12 19 26	2 9 16 23	2 9 16 23 30
Wed.	6 13 20 27	3 10 17 24	3 10 17 24 31
Thur.	7 14 21 28	4 11 18 25	4 11 18 25
Fri.	1 8 15 22 29	5 12 19 26	5 12 19 26
Sat.	2 9 16 23 30	6 13 20 27	6 13 20 27

	April	May	June
Sun.	4 11 18 25	2 9 16 23 30	6 13 20 27
Mon.	5 12 19 26	3 10 17 24 31	7 14 21 28
Tue.	6 13 20 27	4 11 18 25	1 8 15 22 29
Wed.	7 14 21 28	5 12 19 26	2 9 16 23 30
Thur.	1 8 15 22 29	6 13 20 27	3 10 17 24
Fri.	2 9 16 23 30	7 14 21 28	4 11 18 25
Sat.	3 10 17 24	1 8 15 22 29	5 12 19 26

	July	August	September
Sun.	4 11 18 25	1 8 15 22 29	5 12 19 26
Mon.	5 12 19 26	2 9 16 23 30	6 13 20 27
Tue.	6 13 20 27	3 10 17 24 31	7 14 21 28
Wed.	7 14 21 28	4 11 18 25	1 8 15 22 29
Thur.	1 8 15 22 29	5 12 19 26	2 9 16 23 30
Fri.	2 9 16 23 30	6 13 20 27	3 10 17 24
Sat.	3 10 17 24 31	7 14 21 28	4 11 18 25

	October	November	December
Sun.	3 10 17 24 31	7 14 21 28	5 12 19 26
Mon.	4 11 18 25	1 8 15 22 29	6 13 20 27
Tue.	5 12 19 26	2 9 16 23 30	7 14 21 28
Wed.	6 13 20 27	3 10 17 24	1 8 15 22 29
Thur.	7 14 21 28	4 11 18 25	2 9 16 23 30
Fri.	1 8 15 22 29	5 12 19 26	3 10 17 24 31
Sat.	2 9 16 23 30	6 13 20 27	4 11 18 25

EASTER DAYS
March 28	1869, 1875, 1937, 2027
April 4	1790, 1847, 1858, 1915, 1926, 1999, 2010, 2021
April 11	1819, 1830, 1841, 1909, 1971, 1982, 1993
April 18	1802, 1813, 1897, 1954, 1965
April 25	1886, 1943, 2038

M

	January	February	March
Sun.	2 9 16 23 30	6 13 20 27	6 13 20 27
Mon.	3 10 17 24 31	7 14 21 28	7 14 21 28
Tue.	4 11 18 25	1 8 15 22	1 8 15 22 29
Wed.	5 12 19 26	2 9 16 23	2 9 16 23 30
Thur.	6 13 20 27	3 10 17 24	3 10 17 24 31
Fri.	7 14 21 28	4 11 18 25	4 11 18 25
Sat.	1 8 15 22 29	5 12 19 26	5 12 19 26

	April	May	June
Sun.	3 10 17 24	1 8 15 22 29	5 12 19 26
Mon.	4 11 18 25	2 9 16 23 30	6 13 20 27
Tue.	5 12 19 26	3 10 17 24 31	7 14 21 28
Wed.	6 13 20 27	4 11 18 25	1 8 15 22 29
Thur.	7 14 21 28	5 12 19 26	2 9 16 23 30
Fri.	1 8 15 22 29	6 13 20 27	3 10 17 24
Sat.	2 9 16 23 30	7 14 21 28	4 11 18 25

	July	August	September
Sun.	3 10 17 24 31	7 14 21 28	4 11 18 25
Mon.	4 11 18 25	1 8 15 22 29	5 12 19 26
Tue.	5 12 19 26	2 9 16 23 30	6 13 20 27
Wed.	6 13 20 27	3 10 17 24 31	7 14 21 28
Thur.	7 14 21 28	4 11 18 25	1 8 15 22 29
Fri.	1 8 15 22 29	5 12 19 26	2 9 16 23 30
Sat.	2 9 16 23 30	6 13 20 27	3 10 17 24

	October	November	December
Sun.	2 9 16 23 30	6 13 20 27	4 11 18 25
Mon.	3 10 17 24 31	7 14 21 28	5 12 19 26
Tue.	4 11 18 25	1 8 15 22 29	6 13 20 27
Wed.	5 12 19 26	2 9 16 23 30	7 14 21 28
Thur.	6 13 20 27	3 10 17 24	1 8 15 22 29
Fri.	7 14 21 28	4 11 18 25	2 9 16 23 30
Sat.	1 8 15 22 29	5 12 19 26	3 10 17 24 31

EASTER DAYS
March 27	1785, 1842, 1853, 1910, 1921, 2005
April 3	1825, 1831, 1983, 1994
April 10	1803, 1814, 1887, 1898, 1955, 1966, 1977, 2039
April 17	1870, 1881, 1927, 1938, 1949, 2022, 2033
April 24	1791, 1859, 2011

L (LEAP YEAR)

	January	February	March
Sun.	3 10 17 24 31	7 14 21 28	6 13 20 27
Mon.	4 11 18 25	1 8 15 22 29	7 14 21 28
Tue.	5 12 19 26	2 9 16 23	1 8 15 22 29
Wed.	6 13 20 27	3 10 17 24	2 9 16 23 30
Thur.	7 14 21 28	4 11 18 25	3 10 17 24 31
Fri.	1 8 15 22 29	5 12 19 26	4 11 18 25
Sat.	2 9 16 23 30	6 13 20 27	5 12 19 26

	April	May	June
Sun.	3 10 17 24	1 8 15 22 29	5 12 19 26
Mon.	4 11 18 25	2 9 16 23 30	6 13 20 27
Tue.	5 12 19 26	3 10 17 24 31	7 14 21 28
Wed.	6 13 20 27	4 11 18 25	1 8 15 22 29
Thur.	7 14 21 28	5 12 19 26	2 9 16 23 30
Fri.	1 8 15 22 29	6 13 20 27	3 10 17 24
Sat.	2 9 16 23 30	7 14 21 28	4 11 18 25

	July	August	September
Sun.	3 10 17 24 31	7 14 21 28	4 11 18 25
Mon.	4 11 18 25	1 8 15 22 29	5 12 19 26
Tue.	5 12 19 26	2 9 16 23 30	6 13 20 27
Wed.	6 13 20 27	3 10 17 24 31	7 14 21 28
Thur.	7 14 21 28	4 11 18 25	1 8 15 22 29
Fri.	1 8 15 22 29	5 12 19 26	2 9 16 23 30
Sat.	2 9 16 23 30	6 13 20 27	3 10 17 24

	October	November	December
Sun.	2 9 16 23 30	6 13 20 27	4 11 18 25
Mon.	3 10 17 24 31	7 14 21 28	5 12 19 26
Tue.	4 11 18 25	1 8 15 22 29	6 13 20 27
Wed.	5 12 19 26	2 9 16 23 30	7 14 21 28
Thur.	6 13 20 27	3 10 17 24	1 8 15 22 29
Fri.	7 14 21 28	4 11 18 25	2 9 16 23 30
Sat.	1 8 15 22 29	5 12 19 26	3 10 17 24 31

EASTER DAYS
March 27	1796, 1864, 1932, 2016
April 3	1836, 1904, 1988
April 17	1808, 1892, 1960

N (LEAP YEAR)

	January	February	March
Sun.	2 9 16 23 30	6 13 20 27	5 12 19 26
Mon.	3 10 17 24 31	7 14 21 28	6 13 20 27
Tue.	4 11 18 25	1 8 15 22 29	7 14 21 28
Wed.	5 12 19 26	2 9 16 23	1 8 15 22 29
Thur.	6 13 20 27	3 10 17 24	2 9 16 23 30
Fri.	7 14 21 28	4 11 18 25	3 10 17 24 31
Sat.	1 8 15 22 29	5 12 19 26	4 11 18 25

	April	May	June
Sun.	2 9 16 23 30	7 14 21 28	4 11 18 25
Mon.	3 10 17 24	1 8 15 22 29	5 12 19 26
Tue.	4 11 18 25	2 9 16 23 30	6 13 20 27
Wed.	5 12 19 26	3 10 17 24 31	7 14 21 28
Thur.	6 13 20 27	4 11 18 25	1 8 15 22 29
Fri.	7 14 21 28	5 12 19 26	2 9 16 23 30
Sat.	1 8 15 22 29	6 13 20 27	3 10 17 24

	July	August	September
Sun.	2 9 16 23 30	6 13 20 27	3 10 17 24
Mon.	3 10 17 24 31	7 14 21 28	4 11 18 25
Tue.	4 11 18 25	1 8 15 22 29	5 12 19 26
Wed.	5 12 19 26	2 9 16 23 30	6 13 20 27
Thur.	6 13 20 27	3 10 17 24 31	7 14 21 28
Fri.	7 14 21 28	4 11 18 25	1 8 15 22 29
Sat.	1 8 15 22 29	5 12 19 26	2 9 16 23 30

	October	November	December
Sun.	1 8 15 22 29	5 12 19 26	3 10 17 24 31
Mon.	2 9 16 23 30	6 13 20 27	4 11 18 25
Tue.	3 10 17 24 31	7 14 21 28	5 12 19 26
Wed.	4 11 18 25	1 8 15 22 29	6 13 20 27
Thur.	5 12 19 26	2 9 16 23 30	7 14 21 28
Fri.	6 13 20 27	3 10 17 24	1 8 15 22 29
Sat.	7 14 21 28	4 11 18 25	2 9 16 23 30

EASTER DAYS
March 26	1780
April 2	1820, 1972
April 9	1944
April 16	1876, 2028
April 23	1848, 1916, 2000

GEOLOGICAL TIME

The earth is thought to have come into existence approximately 4,600 million years ago, but for nearly half this time, the Archean era, it was uninhabited. Life is generally believed to have emerged in the succeeding Proterozoic era. The Archean and the Proterozoic eras are often together referred to as the Precambrian.

Although primitive forms of life, e.g. algae and bacteria, existed during the Proterozoic era, it is not until the strata of Palaeozoic rocks is reached that abundant fossilised remains appear.

Since the Precambrian, there have been three great geological eras:

PALAEOZOIC ('ancient life')
c. 542–*c.* 251 million years ago
Cambrian – Mainly sandstones, slate and shales; limestones in Scotland. Shelled fossils and invertebrates, e.g. trilobites and brachiopods appear, as do the earliest known vertebrates (jawless fish)
Ordovician – Mainly shales and mudstones, e.g. in north Wales; limestones in Scotland. First fishes
Silurian – Shales, mudstones and some limestones, found mostly in Wales and southern Scotland
Devonian – Old red sandstone, shale, limestone and slate, e.g. in south Wales and the West Country
Carboniferous–Coal-bearing rocks, millstone grit, limestone and shale. First traces of land-living life
Permian – Marls, sandstones and clays. First reptile fossils

There were two great phases of mountain building in the Palaeozoic era: the Caledonian, characterised in Britain by NE–SW lines of hills and valleys; and the later Hercyian, widespread in west Germany and adjacent areas, and in Britain exemplified in E.–W. lines of hills and valleys.

The end of the Palaeozoic era was marked by the extensive glaciations of the Permian period in the southern continents and the decline of amphibians. It was succeeded by an era of warm conditions.

MESOZOIC ('middle forms of life')
c. 251–*c.* 65.5 million years ago
Triassic – Mostly sandstone, e.g. in the West Midlands; primitive mammals appear
Jurassic–Mainly limestones and clays, typically displayed in the Jura mountains, and in England in a NE–SW belt from Lincolnshire and the Wash to the Severn and the Dorset coast
Cretaceous – Mainly chalk, clay and sands, e.g. in Kent and Sussex

Giant reptiles were dominant during the Mesozoic era, but it was at this time that marsupial mammals first appeared, as well as *Archaeopteryx lithographica*, the earliest known species of bird. Coniferous trees and flowering plants also developed during the era and, with the birds and the mammals, were the main species to survive into the Cenozoic era. The giant reptiles became extinct.

CENOZOIC ('recent life')
from *c.* 65.5 million years ago
Palaeocene ⎤   The emergence of new forms of life,
Eocene ⎦   including existing species; primates appear
Oligocene – Fossils of a few still existing species
Miocene – Fossil remains show a balance of existing and extinct species

Pliocene – Fossil remains show a majority of still existing species
Pleistocene – The majority of remains are those of still existing species
Holocene–The present, post-glacial period. Existing species only, except for a few exterminated by man.

In the last 23 million years, from the Miocene through the Pliocene periods, the Alpine-Himalayan and the circum-Pacific phases of mountain building reached their climax. During the Pleistocene period ice-sheets repeatedly locked up masses of water as land ice; its weight depressed the land, but the locking-up of the water lowered the sea-level by 100–200 metres. The glaciations and interglacials of the Ice Age are difficult to date and classify, but recent scientific opinion considers the Pleistocene period to have begun approximately 1.64 million years ago. The last glacial retreat, merging into the Holocene period, was 10,000 years ago.

HUMAN DEVELOPMENT

Any consideration of the history of mankind must start with the fact that all members of the human race belong to one species of animal, i.e. *Homo sapiens*, the definition of a species being in biological terms that all its members can interbreed. As a species of mammal it is possible to group man with other similar types, known as the primates. Amongst these is found a sub-group, the apes, which includes, in addition to man, the chimpanzees, gorillas, orang-utans and gibbons. All lack a tail, have shoulder blades at the back, and a Y-shaped chewing pattern on the surface of their molars, as well as showing the more general primate characteristics of four incisors, a thumb which is able to touch the fingers of the same hand, and finger and toe nails instead of claws. The factors available to scientific study suggest that human beings have chimpanzees and gorillas as their nearest relatives in the animal world. However, there remains the possibility that there once lived creatures, now extinct, which were closer to modern man than the chimpanzees and gorillas, and which shared with modern man the characteristics of having flat faces (i.e. the absence of a pronounced muzzle), being bipedal, and possessing large brains.

There are two broad groups of extinct apes recognised by specialists. The ramapithecines, the remains of which, mainly jaw fragments, have been found in east Africa, Asia, and Turkey. They lived about 14 to 8 million years ago, and from the evidence of their teeth it seems they chewed more in the manner of modern man than the other presently living apes. The second group, the australopithecines, have left more numerous remains amongst which sub-groups may be detected, although the geographic spread is limited to south and east Africa. Living between 5 and 1.5 million years ago, they were closer relatives of modern man to the extent that they walked upright, did not have an extensive muzzle and had similar types of pre-molars. The first australopithecine remains were recognised at Taung in South Africa in 1924 and named *Australopithecus africanus*, dating to 2.8 to 2.3 million years ago. The most impressive discovery was made at Hadar, Ethiopia, in 1974 when about half a skeleton of *Australopithecus afarensis*, known as 'Lucy', was found. Some 3.2 million years ago, 'Lucy' certainly walked upright.

Also in east Africa, especially at Olduvai Gorge in Tanzania, between 1.9 and 1.8 million years ago, lived a hominid group which not only walked upright, had a flat face, and a large brain case, but also made simple pebble and flake stone tools. On present evidence these habilines seem to have been the first people to make tools, however crude. This facility is related to the larger brain size and human beings are the only animals to make implements to be used in other processes. These early pebble tool users, because of their distinctive characteristics, have been grouped as a separate sub-species, now extinct, of the genus *Homo* and are known as *Homo habilis*.

The use of fire, again a human characteristic, is associated with another group of extinct hominids whose remains, about a million years old, are found in south and east Africa, China, Indonesia, north Africa and Europe. Mastery of the techniques of making fire probably helped the colonisation of the colder northern areas and in this respect the site of Vertesszollos in Hungary is of particular importance. *Homo ergaster* in Africa and *Homo erectus* in Asia are the names given to this group of fossils and they relate to a number of famous individual discoveries, e.g. Solo Man, Heidelberg Man, and especially Peking Man who lived at the cave site at Choukoutien which has yielded evidence of fire and burnt bone.

The well-known group Neanderthal Man, or *Homo neanderthalensis*, is an extinct form of man who lived between about 230,000 and 28,000 years ago, thus spanning the last Ice Age. Indeed, its ability to adapt to the cold climate on the edge of the ice-sheets is one of its characteristic features, the remains being found only in Europe, Asia and the Middle East. Complete neanderthal skeletons were found during excavations at Tabun in Israel, together with evidence of tool-making and the use of fire. Distinguished by very large brains, it seems that neanderthal man was the first to develop recognisable social customs, especially deliberate burial rites. Why the neanderthals became extinct is not clear but it may be connected with the climatic changes at the end of the Ice Ages, which would have seriously affected their food supplies; possibly they became too specialised for their own good.

The shin bone of Boxgrove Man found in 1993 – *Homo heidelbergensis* – and the Swanscombe skull are the best known human fossil remains found in England. Some specialists see Swanscombe Man (or, more probably, woman) as best grouped together with the Steinheim skull from Germany, seeing both as a separate sub-species. There is too little evidence as yet on which to form a final judgement.

Modern Man, *Homo sapiens* had evolved to our present physical condition and had colonised much of the world by about 40,000 years ago. There are many previously distinguished individual specimens, e.g. Cromagnon Man, which may now be grouped together as *Homo sapiens*. It was modern man who spread to the American continent by crossing the landbridge between Siberia and Alaska and thence moved south through North America and into South America. Equally it is modern man who over the last 40,000 years has been responsible for the major developments in technology, art and civilisation generally.

One of the problems for those studying fossil man is the lack in many cases of sufficient quantities of fossil bone for analysis. It is important that theories should be tested against evidence, rather than the evidence being made to fit the theory. The Piltdown hoax of 1912 (and not fully exposed until the 1970s) is a well-known example of 'fossils' being forged to fit what was seen in some quarters as the correct theory of man's evolution.

The discovery of the structure of DNA in 1953 has come to have a profound effect upon the study of human evolution. For example, it was claimed in 1987 that a common ancestor of all human beings was a person who lived in Africa some 200,000 years ago, thus encouraging the 'out of Africa' theory of hominid migration from east Africa to the Middle East and then throughout the world. There is no doubt that the studies based on DNA have vast potential to elucidate further the course of human evolution.

CULTURAL DEVELOPMENT

The Eurocentric bias of early archaeologists meant that the search for a starting point for the development and transmission of cultural ideas, especially by migration, trade and warfare, concentrated unduly on Europe and the Near East. The Three Age system, whereby pre-history was divided into a Stone Age, a Bronze Age and an Iron Age, was devised by Christian Thomsen, curator of the National Museum of Denmark in the early 19th century, to facilitate the classification of the museum's collections. The descriptive adjectives referred to the materials from which the implements and weapons were made and came to be regarded as the dominant features of the societies to which they related. The refinement of the Three Age system once dominated archaeological thought and remains a generally accepted concept in the popular mind. However, it is now seen by archaeologists as an inadequate model for human development.

Common sense suggests that there were no complete breaks between one so-called Age and another, any more than contemporaries would have regarded 1485 as a complete break between medieval and modern English history. Nor can the Three Age system be applied universally. In some areas it is necessary to insert a Copper Age, while in Africa south of the Sahara there would seem to be no Bronze Age at all; in Australia, Old Stone Age societies survived, while in South America, New Stone Age communities existed into modern times. The civilisations in other parts of the world clearly invalidate a Eurocentric theory of human development.

The concept of the 'Neolithic revolution', associated with the domestication of plants and animals, was a development of particular importance in the human cultural pattern. It reflected change from the primitive hunter/gatherer economies to a more settled agricultural way of life and therefore, so the argument goes, made possible the development of urban civilisation. However, it can no longer be argued that this 'revolution' took place only in one area from which all development stemmed. Though it appears that the cultivation of wheat and barley was first undertaken, together with the domestication of cattle and goats/sheep in the Fertile Crescent (the area bounded by the rivers Tigris and Euphrates), there is evidence that rice was first deliberately planted and pigs domesticated in south-east Asia, maize first cultivated in Central America and llamas first domesticated in South America. It has been recognised in recent years that cultural changes can take place independently of each other in different parts of the world at different rates and different times. There is no need for a general diffusionist theory.

Although scholars will continue to study the particular societies which interest them, it may be possible to obtain a reliable chronological framework, against which the cultural development of any particular area may be set. The development and refinement of radio-carbon dating and other scientific methods of producing absolute chronologies is enabling the cross-referencing of societies to be undertaken. As the techniques of dating become more rigorous in application and the number of scientifically obtained dates increases, the attainment of an absolute chronology for prehistoric societies throughout the world comes closer to being achieved.

GEOLOGICAL TIME

Era	Period	Epoch	Date ended*	Evolutionary stages
Cenozoic	Quaternary	Holocene	0.01	Man
Cenozoic	Quaternary	Pleistocene	1.81	Man
Cenozoic	Tertiary	Pliocene	5.33	Man
Cenozoic	Tertiary	Miocene	23.0	Man
Cenozoic	Tertiary	Oligocene	33.9	Man
Cenozoic	Tertiary	Eocene	55.8	Man
Cenozoic	Tertiary	Palaeocene	65.5	Man
Mesozoic	Cretaceous		145.5	
Mesozoic	Jurassic		199.6	First birds
Mesozoic	Triassic		251.0	First mammals
Palaeozoic	Permian		299.0	First reptiles
Palaeozoic	Carboniferous		359.2	First amphibians and insects
Palaeozoic	Devonian		416.0	
Palaeozoic	Silurian		443.7	
Palaeozoic	Ordovician		488.3	First fishes
Palaeozoic	Cambrian		542.0	First invertebrates
Precambrian			4,560.0	First primitive life forms e.g. algae and bacteria

* Millions of years ago

TIDAL PREDICTIONS

CONSTANTS

The constant tidal difference may be used in conjunction with the time of high water at a standard port shown in the predictions data below to find the time of high water at any of the ports or places listed.

These tidal differences are very approximate and should be used only as a guide to the time of high water at the places below. More precise local data should be obtained for navigational and other nautical purposes.

All data allow high water time to be found in Greenwich Mean Time: this applies to data for the months when British Summer Time is in operation and the hour's time difference should be allowed for. Ports marked * are in a different time zone and the standard time zone difference also needs to be added/subtracted to give local time.

EXAMPLE

Required time of high water at Stranraer at 2 January 2006

Appropriate time of high water at Greenock	
Afternoon tide 2 January	1400hrs
Tidal difference	− 0020hrs
High water at Stranraer	1340hrs

The columns headed 'Springs' and 'Neaps' show the height, in metres, of the tide above datum for mean high water springs and mean high water neaps respectively.

Port		Diff.		Springs	Neaps
		h	m	m	m
Aberdeen	Leith	−1	19	4.4	3.4
*Antwerp	London	+0	50	5.8	4.8
(Prosperpolder)					
Ardrossan	Greenock	−0	15	3.2	2.6
Avonmouth	London	−6	45	12.2	9.8
Ayr	Greenock	−0	25	3.0	2.5
Barrow (Docks)	Liverpool	0	00	9.3	7.1
Belfast	London	−2	47	3.5	3.0
Blackpool	Liverpool	−0	10	8.9	7.0
*Boulogne	London	−2	44	8.9	7.2
*Calais	London	−2	04	7.2	5.9
*Cherbourg	London	−6	00	6.4	5.0
Cobh	Liverpool	−5	55	4.2	3.2
Cowes	London	−2	38	4.2	3.5
Dartmouth	London	+4	25	4.9	3.8
*Dieppe	London	−3	03	9.3	7.3
Douglas, IoM	Liverpool	−0	04	6.9	5.4
Dover	London	−2	52	6.7	5.3
Dublin	London	−2	05	4.1	3.4
Dun Loaghaire	London	−2	10	4.1	3.4
*Dunkirk	London	−1	54	6.0	4.9
Fishguard	Liverpool	−4	01	4.8	3.4
Fleetwood	Liverpool	0	00	9.2	7.3
*Flushing	London	−0	15	4.7	3.9
Folkestone	London	−3	04	7.1	5.7
Galway	Liverpool	−6	08	5.1	3.9
Glasgow	Greenock	+0	26	4.7	4.0
Harwich	London	−2	06	4.0	3.4
*Le Havre	London	−3	55	7.9	6.6
Heysham	Liverpool	+0	05	9.4	7.4

Port		Diff.		Springs	Neaps
Holyhead	Liverpool	−0	50	5.6	4.4
*Hook of Holland	London	−0	01	2.1	1.7
Hull (Albert Dock)	London	−7	40	7.5	5.8
Immingham	London	−8	00	7.3	5.8
Larne	London	−2	40	2.8	2.5
Lerwick	Leith	−3	48	2.2	1.6
Londonderry	London	−5	37	2.7	2.1
Lowestoft	London	−4	25	2.4	2.1
Margate	London	−1	53	4.8	3.9
Milford Haven	Liverpool	−5	08	7.0	5.2
Morecambe	Liverpool	+0	07	9.5	7.4
Newhaven	London	−2	46	6.7	5.1
Oban	Greenock	+5	43	4.0	2.9
*Ostend	London	−1	32	5.1	4.2
Plymouth	London	+4	05	5.5	4.4
Portland	London	+5	09	2.1	1.4
Portsmouth	London	−2	38	4.7	3.8
Ramsgate	London	−2	32	5.2	4.1
Richmond Lock	London	+1	00	4.9	3.7
Rosslare Harbour	Liverpool	−5	24	1.9	1.4
Rosyth	Leith	+0	09	5.8	4.7
*Rotterdam	London	+1	45	2.0	1.7
St Helier	London	+4	48	11.0	8.1
St Malo	London	+4	27	12.2	9.2
St Peter Port	London	+4	54	9.3	7.0
Scrabster	Leith	−6	06	5.0	4.0
Sheerness	London	−1	19	5.8	4.7
Shoreham	London	−2	44	6.3	4.9
Southampton	London	−2	54	4.5	3.7
(1st high water)					
Spurn Head	London	−8	25	6.9	5.5
Stornoway	Liverpool	−4	16	4.8	3.7
Stranraer	Greenock	−0	20	3.0	2.4
Stromness	Leith	−5	26	3.6	2.7
Swansea	London	−7	35	9.5	7.2
Tees (River Entrance)	Leith	+1	09	5.5	4.3
Tilbury	London	−0	49	6.4	5.4
Tobermory	Liverpool	−5	11	4.4	3.3
Tyne River	London	−10	30	5.0	3.9
(North Shields)					
Ullapool	Leith	−7	40	5.2	3.9
Walton-on-the-Naze	London	−2	10	4.2	3.4
Wick	Leith	−3	26	3.5	2.8
Zeebrugge	London	−0	55	4.8	3.9

PREDICTIONS

The following data are daily predictions of the time and height of high water at London Bridge, Liverpool, Greenock and Leith. The time of the data is Greenwich Mean Time; this applies also to data for the months when British Summer Time is in operation and the hour's time difference should be allowed for. The datum of predictions for each port shows the difference of height, in metres from Ordnance data (Newlyn).

JANUARY 2006   *High Water*   GMT

Datum of Predictions: LONDON BRIDGE 3.20m below · LIVERPOOL 4.93m below · GREENOCK 1.62m below · LEITH 2.90m below

Day	London Bridge hr m	ht	hr m	ht	Liverpool hr m	ht	hr m	ht	Greenock hr m	ht	hr m	ht	Leith hr m	ht	hr m	ht
SU 1	02 12	6.9	14 39	7.1	11 53	9.5	—	—	00 52	3.3	13 17	3.6	03 06	5.6	15 17	5.5
M 2	02 58	6.9	15 29	7.1	00 21	9.3	12 42	9.6	01 44	3.3	14 00	3.7	03 53	5.7	16 02	5.6
TU 3	03 45	6.8	16 19	7.1	01 11	9.3	13 31	9.7	02 34	3.3	14 44	3.7	04 40	5.6	16 48	5.6
W 4	04 31	6.8	17 08	7.0	02 00	9.2	14 20	9.6	03 23	3.3	15 29	3.7	05 29	5.5	17 37	5.5
TH 5	05 18	6.7	17 58	6.9	02 49	8.9	15 10	9.3	04 12	3.3	16 16	3.7	06 21	5.3	18 28	5.4
F 6	06 05	6.6	18 50	6.6	03 39	8.6	16 02	9.0	05 01	3.2	17 07	3.6	07 16	5.1	19 26	5.2
SA 7	06 58	6.5	19 46	6.4	04 34	8.2	16 58	8.5	05 51	3.1	18 02	3.4	08 17	4.8	20 32	5.0
SU 8	07 57	6.3	20 47	6.1	05 36	7.8	18 02	8.1	06 43	3.0	19 04	3.2	09 21	4.7	21 41	4.8
M 9	09 01	6.2	21 49	6.0	06 46	7.6	19 13	7.9	07 42	3.0	20 26	3.1	10 25	4.6	22 50	4.7
TU 10	10 07	6.1	22 51	6.0	07 57	7.7	20 24	8.0	09 01	3.0	21 49	3.1	11 30	4.6	23 57	4.8
W 11	11 13	6.1	23 50	6.1	08 59	8.0	21 24	8.2	10 11	3.1	22 53	3.1	12 31	4.8	—	—
TH 12	12 13	6.3	—	—	09 50	8.4	22 14	8.4	11 04	3.2	23 46	3.1	00 58	4.8	13 24	4.9
F 13	00 43	6.3	13 08	6.5	10 34	8.7	22 58	8.6	11 49	3.4	—	—	01 50	4.9	14 09	5.1
SA 14	01 32	6.4	13 57	6.6	11 14	8.9	23 37	8.7	00 34	3.1	12 30	3.5	02 33	5.0	14 48	5.2
SU 15	02 14	6.5	14 41	6.6	11 51	9.0	—	—	01 17	3.1	13 08	3.5	03 11	5.1	15 24	5.2
M 16	02 51	6.5	15 19	6.6	00 12	8.7	12 26	9.0	01 55	3.1	13 44	3.6	03 46	5.1	15 58	5.2
TU 17	03 22	6.4	15 52	6.5	00 47	8.7	13 00	9.0	02 30	3.1	14 18	3.6	04 19	5.1	16 30	5.2
W 18	03 51	6.4	16 23	6.5	01 20	8.6	13 34	8.9	03 02	3.0	14 51	3.5	04 53	5.0	17 03	5.1
TH 19	04 21	6.4	16 55	6.5	01 54	8.5	14 08	8.7	03 35	3.0	15 25	3.5	05 28	4.9	17 38	5.0
F 20	04 54	6.4	17 30	6.5	02 28	8.3	14 44	8.5	04 09	3.0	16 01	3.4	06 06	4.8	18 14	4.9
SA 21	05 30	6.3	18 09	6.4	03 05	8.1	15 22	8.3	04 45	3.0	16 39	3.3	06 46	4.6	18 54	4.7
SU 22	06 10	6.2	18 52	6.2	03 46	7.8	16 06	7.9	05 24	2.9	17 21	3.2	07 30	4.5	19 39	4.6
M 23	06 57	6.0	19 42	6.0	04 37	7.5	17 02	7.6	06 08	2.8	18 09	3.0	08 22	4.4	20 38	4.4
TU 24	07 56	5.8	20 42	5.8	05 41	7.3	18 09	7.5	07 01	2.7	19 07	2.9	09 22	4.3	21 51	4.3
W 25	09 05	5.7	21 53	5.7	06 55	7.3	19 22	7.5	08 12	2.7	20 21	2.9	10 30	4.4	23 07	4.4
TH 26	10 22	5.8	23 09	5.9	08 08	7.7	20 35	7.9	09 40	2.8	21 46	2.9	11 38	4.6	—	—
F 27	11 39	6.1	—	—	09 11	8.3	21 38	8.4	10 45	3.0	22 55	3.0	00 17	4.7	12 42	4.8
SA 28	00 15	6.3	12 44	6.5	10 05	8.9	22 33	8.9	11 35	3.3	23 53	3.2	01 18	5.1	13 35	5.1
SU 29	01 10	6.6	13 39	6.9	10 55	9.4	23 23	9.3	12 20	3.5	—	—	02 09	5.4	14 21	5.4
M 30	01 59	6.9	14 29	7.2	11 43	9.8	—	—	00 47	3.2	13 06	3.6	02 55	5.7	15 04	5.7
TU 31	02 46	7.0	15 18	7.3	00 11	9.6	12 30	10.1	01 38	3.3	13 50	3.8	03 40	5.8	15 48	5.9

FEBRUARY 2006   *High Water*   GMT

Day	London Bridge hr m	ht	hr m	ht	Liverpool hr m	ht	hr m	ht	Greenock hr m	ht	hr m	ht	Leith hr m	ht	hr m	ht
W 1	03 31	7.1	16 05	7.3	00 58	9.7	13 16	10.1	02 26	3.3	14 34	3.8	04 24	5.8	16 32	5.9
TH 2	04 15	7.1	16 51	7.3	01 42	9.6	14 01	10.0	03 09	3.4	15 16	3.9	05 10	5.7	17 17	5.8
F 3	04 58	7.1	17 35	7.1	02 26	9.3	14 16	9.7	03 49	3.4	15 58	3.8	05 57	5.4	18 05	5.6
SA 4	05 40	7.0	18 19	6.8	03 09	8.9	15 31	9.1	04 27	3.3	16 41	3.6	06 45	5.1	18 56	5.3
SU 5	06 23	6.8	19 05	6.4	03 55	8.3	16 20	8.5	05 07	3.2	17 25	3.4	07 39	4.8	19 56	4.9
M 6	07 11	6.4	19 56	6.0	04 48	7.7	17 20	7.8	05 50	3.1	18 15	3.1	08 40	4.5	21 07	4.6
TU 7	08 12	6.0	21 01	5.6	05 58	7.3	18 40	7.3	06 40	2.9	19 19	2.8	09 47	4.3	22 24	4.4
W 8	09 32	5.7	22 15	5.4	07 29	7.2	20 07	7.3	07 46	2.8	21 43	2.7	11 02	4.3	23 46	4.4
TH 9	10 52	5.7	23 26	5.6	08 43	7.6	21 14	7.7	09 48	2.9	22 52	2.9	12 17	4.5	—	—
F 10	12 00	6.0	—	—	09 38	8.1	22 04	8.1	10 50	3.1	23 42	3.0	00 56	4.6	13 16	4.8
SA 11	00 26	6.0	12 56	6.3	10 23	8.5	22 46	8.4	11 37	3.2	—	—	01 47	4.8	14 01	5.0
SU 12	01 16	6.3	13 44	6.6	11 01	8.8	23 23	8.7	00 26	3.0	12 18	3.4	02 26	5.0	14 37	5.1
M 13	01 59	6.5	14 25	6.7	11 36	9.0	23 56	8.8	01 06	3.0	12 55	3.4	02 58	5.1	15 09	5.2
TU 14	02 35	6.5	15 00	6.7	12 08	9.1	—	—	01 41	3.0	13 28	3.4	03 27	5.1	15 39	5.3
W 15	03 06	6.5	15 30	6.6	00 27	8.8	12 40	9.1	02 12	3.0	13 58	3.4	03 56	5.1	16 08	5.3
TH 16	03 33	6.4	15 58	6.5	00 57	8.8	13 10	9.0	02 38	3.0	14 27	3.4	04 26	5.1	16 37	5.3
F 17	04 00	6.4	16 27	6.6	01 27	8.8	13 40	8.9	03 04	3.0	14 59	3.4	04 58	5.0	17 08	5.2
SA 18	04 28	6.5	16 59	6.6	01 57	8.7	14 11	8.8	03 32	3.1	15 32	3.4	05 32	4.9	17 40	5.0
SU 19	05 01	6.5	17 35	6.6	02 28	8.5	14 44	8.5	04 02	3.0	16 07	3.3	06 08	4.8	18 15	4.8
M 20	05 40	6.5	18 15	6.4	03 03	8.1	15 24	8.1	04 35	2.9	16 45	3.2	06 47	4.6	18 58	4.6
TU 21	06 25	6.3	19 02	6.1	03 48	7.7	16 17	7.7	05 11	2.8	17 28	3.0	07 33	4.4	19 52	4.4
W 22	07 21	5.9	19 59	5.7	04 51	7.3	17 29	7.3	05 58	2.7	18 24	2.8	08 32	4.3	21 08	4.3
TH 23	08 28	5.6	21 09	5.5	06 13	7.1	18 54	7.2	07 09	2.6	19 42	2.7	09 49	4.2	22 39	4.3
F 24	09 47	5.6	22 36	5.6	07 42	7.4	20 21	7.6	09 04	2.6	21 30	2.7	11 11	4.4	—	—
SA 25	11 22	5.9	23 56	6.0	08 55	8.1	21 28	8.3	10 24	2.9	22 49	2.9	00 00	4.6	12 23	4.7
SU 26	12 32	6.5	—	—	09 51	8.9	22 21	9.0	11 17	3.2	23 46	3.1	01 04	5.1	13 18	5.1
M 27	00 54	6.6	13 26	7.0	10 40	9.6	23 08	9.5	12 04	3.4	—	—	01 54	5.5	14 03	5.5
TU 28	01 43	6.9	14 14	7.3	11 26	10.1	23 53	9.8	00 36	3.2	12 49	3.6	02 38	5.8	14 45	5.9

MARCH 2006   *High Water*   GMT

Datum of Predictions: LONDON BRIDGE 3.20m below · LIVERPOOL 4.93m below · GREENOCK 1.62m below · LEITH 2.90m below

Day	LONDON BRIDGE hr	m	ht	hr	m	ht	LIVERPOOL hr	m	ht	hr	m	ht	GREENOCK hr	m	ht	hr	m	ht	LEITH hr	m	ht	hr	m	ht
W 1	02	27	7.2	15	00	7.5	12	10	10.3	—		—	01	23	3.3	13	34	3.8	03	20	5.9	15	27	6.0
TH 2	03	10	7.3	15	43	7.4	00	36	9.9	12	54	10.3	02	05	3.4	14	16	3.9	04	02	5.9	16	10	6.1
F 3	03	51	7.3	16	25	7.3	01	18	9.8	13	37	10.1	02	42	3.4	14	57	3.9	04	45	5.7	16	54	5.9
SA 4	04	31	7.3	17	05	7.1	01	58	9.5	14	19	9.7	03	17	3.4	15	35	3.8	05	28	5.4	17	40	5.6
SU 5	05	11	7.1	17	43	6.8	02	38	9.0	15	01	9.0	03	52	3.4	16	14	3.6	06	14	5.1	18	30	5.2
M 6	05	51	6.9	18	21	6.3	03	19	8.4	15	46	8.2	04	29	3.3	16	55	3.3	07	03	4.7	19	28	4.8
TU 7	06	34	6.4	19	01	5.9	04	06	7.7	16	44	7.4	05	10	3.1	17	41	3.0	08	02	4.4	20	39	4.4
W 8	07	30	5.9	19	55	5.4	05	15	7.1	18	12	6.9	05	58	2.9	18	39	2.6	09	12	4.2	21	59	4.2
TH 9	09	01	5.4	21	39	5.1	06	59	6.9	19	49	6.9	06	59	2.8	21	41	2.6	10	32	4.2	23	31	4.2
F 10	10	33	5.5	23	00	5.4	08	21	7.3	20	55	7.4	09	23	2.7	22	41	2.7	11	57	4.4	—		—
SA 11	11	41	5.9	—		—	09	16	7.9	21	44	7.9	10	31	3.0	23	26	2.9	00	44	4.5	12	58	4.7
SU 12	00	02	5.9	12	35	6.3	10	00	8.4	22	23	8.4	11	17	3.1	—		—	01	31	4.7	13	40	4.9
M 13	00	53	6.3	13	21	6.7	10	38	8.8	22	58	8.7	00	05	3.0	11	57	3.2	02	06	4.9	14	15	5.1
TU 14	01	34	6.6	13	59	6.8	11	12	9.0	23	30	8.8	00	42	3.0	12	32	3.3	02	35	5.0	14	45	5.2
W 15	02	11	6.6	14	32	6.7	11	43	9.0	—		—	01	14	3.0	13	03	3.3	03	01	5.1	15	13	5.3
TH 16	02	41	6.5	15	01	6.6	00	00	8.9	12	13	9.0	01	43	3.0	13	30	3.3	03	28	5.2	15	41	5.3
F 17	03	08	6.4	15	29	6.5	00	29	8.9	12	42	9.0	02	06	3.0	13	59	3.3	03	56	5.2	16	11	5.2
SA 18	03	34	6.4	15	57	6.6	00	57	8.9	13	11	8.9	02	29	3.1	14	31	3.3	04	27	5.1	16	41	5.2
SU 19	04	03	6.5	16	29	6.6	01	26	8.8	13	41	8.8	02	56	3.1	15	05	3.3	05	00	5.0	17	14	5.1
M 20	04	37	6.6	17	05	6.6	01	56	8.6	14	15	8.5	03	25	3.1	15	40	3.2	05	35	4.9	17	51	4.9
TU 21	05	17	6.5	17	45	6.4	02	31	8.3	14	55	8.1	03	56	3.0	16	17	3.1	06	14	4.7	18	36	4.7
W 22	06	03	6.3	18	32	6.0	03	16	7.9	15	49	7.6	04	29	2.9	17	00	2.9	07	00	4.5	19	33	4.4
TH 23	06	59	6.0	19	28	5.7	04	20	7.4	17	05	7.1	05	13	2.7	17	58	2.7	07	58	4.3	20	49	4.3
F 24	08	06	5.6	20	38	5.4	05	48	7.1	18	41	7.1	06	26	2.6	19	26	2.6	09	20	4.2	22	21	4.4
SA 25	09	30	5.5	22	12	5.5	07	23	7.5	20	09	7.6	08	37	2.6	21	24	2.7	10	48	4.4	23	42	4.7
SU 26	11	11	5.9	23	36	6.0	08	36	8.2	21	12	8.4	10	01	2.9	22	37	2.9	12	00	4.8	—		—
M 27	12	17	6.6	—		—	09	31	9.0	22	02	9.1	10	54	3.2	23	29	3.1	00	43	5.1	12	54	5.2
TU 28	00	32	6.6	13	08	7.1	10	19	9.7	22	46	9.6	11	42	3.4	—		—	01	32	5.5	13	39	5.6
W 29	01	19	7.0	13	53	7.4	11	04	10.1	23	29	9.8	00	15	3.2	12	28	3.6	02	14	5.7	14	21	5.9
TH 30	02	02	7.3	14	36	7.5	11	47	10.2	—		—	00	58	3.3	13	12	3.7	02	55	5.8	15	04	6.0
F 31	02	44	7.4	15	17	7.4	00	10	9.9	12	30	10.1	01	36	3.4	13	54	3.8	03	36	5.8	15	48	6.0

APRIL 2006   *High Water*   GMT

Day	LONDON BRIDGE hr	m	ht	hr	m	ht	LIVERPOOL hr	m	ht	hr	m	ht	GREENOCK hr	m	ht	hr	m	ht	LEITH hr	m	ht	hr	m	ht
SA 1	03	25	7.4	15	56	7.2	00	51	9.7	13	11	9.8	02	11	3.4	14	34	3.7	04	18	5.6	16	33	5.8
SU 2	04	05	7.3	16	34	6.9	01	30	9.4	13	52	9.3	02	46	3.5	15	13	3.6	05	01	5.4	17	20	5.5
M 3	04	45	7.1	17	09	6.6	02	08	8.9	14	33	8.6	03	21	3.5	15	51	3.4	05	45	5.0	18	10	5.0
TU 4	05	27	6.7	17	44	6.3	02	48	8.3	15	18	7.9	03	58	3.4	16	32	3.1	06	33	4.7	19	07	4.6
W 5	06	12	6.3	18	23	5.8	03	33	7.7	16	15	7.2	04	38	3.2	17	20	2.8	07	30	4.4	20	13	4.3
TH 6	07	08	5.7	19	12	5.4	04	40	7.1	17	44	6.7	05	27	3.0	18	24	2.5	08	40	4.2	21	28	4.1
F 7	08	38	5.4	21	00	5.1	06	23	6.9	19	16	6.8	06	30	2.8	21	14	2.5	09	58	4.1	22	55	4.1
SA 8	10	06	5.5	22	27	5.4	07	43	7.2	20	21	7.2	08	14	2.7	22	12	2.7	11	19	4.3	—		—
SU 9	11	10	5.9	23	29	5.8	08	41	7.7	21	09	7.8	09	56	2.9	22	54	2.8	00	11	4.4	12	22	4.6
M 10	12	03	6.3	—		—	09	26	8.2	21	49	8.2	10	44	3.0	23	32	2.9	00	58	4.6	13	06	4.8
TU 11	00	19	6.2	12	48	6.6	10	05	8.5	22	25	8.6	11	23	3.1	—		—	01	32	4.8	13	41	5.0
W 12	01	02	6.5	13	26	6.7	10	40	8.8	22	57	8.8	00	07	3.0	11	58	3.1	02	01	5.0	14	12	5.2
TH 13	01	38	6.5	13	59	6.7	11	12	8.9	23	28	8.9	00	40	3.0	12	28	3.1	02	28	5.1	14	41	5.2
F 14	02	11	6.5	14	29	6.6	11	42	8.9	23	57	8.9	01	08	3.0	12	57	3.2	02	56	5.2	15	12	5.3
SA 15	02	40	6.4	14	59	6.5	12	12	8.9	—		—	01	32	3.0	13	29	3.2	03	26	5.2	15	43	5.3
SU 16	03	10	6.4	15	31	6.5	00	27	8.9	12	44	8.9	01	57	3.1	14	05	3.2	03	58	5.2	16	17	5.2
M 17	03	43	6.5	16	05	6.6	00	59	8.8	13	19	8.7	02	26	3.2	14	41	3.2	04	32	5.1	16	55	5.1
TU 18	04	21	6.6	16	42	6.5	01	34	8.7	13	57	8.5	02	57	3.2	15	19	3.1	05	09	5.0	17	37	4.9
W 19	05	03	6.5	17	24	6.3	02	14	8.4	14	43	8.1	03	30	3.1	16	00	3.0	05	51	4.8	18	26	4.7
TH 20	05	52	6.3	18	11	6.0	03	04	8.0	15	40	7.6	04	06	3.0	16	49	2.8	06	40	4.6	19	25	4.5
F 21	06	49	6.0	19	09	5.7	04	10	7.5	16	57	7.2	04	55	2.8	17	57	2.6	07	41	4.4	20	40	4.4
SA 22	07	59	5.7	20	22	5.5	05	35	7.4	18	28	7.3	06	17	2.7	19	32	2.6	09	02	4.4	22	03	4.5
SU 23	09	26	5.7	21	53	5.7	07	01	7.7	19	47	7.8	08	13	2.7	21	07	2.7	10	25	4.6	23	17	4.8
M 24	10	51	6.2	23	07	6.2	08	09	8.4	20	46	8.5	09	32	3.0	22	13	2.9	11	32	4.9	—		—
TU 25	11	52	6.7	—		—	09	05	9.0	21	36	9.0	10	28	3.2	23	03	3.1	00	16	5.1	12	26	5.3
W 26	00	04	6.7	12	42	7.1	09	54	9.5	22	21	9.4	11	16	3.4	23	47	3.2	01	05	5.4	13	13	5.6
TH 27	00	52	7.1	13	27	7.3	10	39	9.8	23	03	9.6	12	03	3.5	—		—	01	48	5.6	13	57	5.8
F 28	01	36	7.3	14	10	7.3	11	23	9.8	23	44	9.6	00	28	3.3	12	48	3.6	02	29	5.6	14	42	5.8
SA 29	02	19	7.3	14	50	7.2	12	06	9.7	—		—	01	07	3.4	13	32	3.5	03	11	5.6	15	28	5.7
SU 30	03	02	7.2	15	29	7.0	00	24	9.4	12	48	9.4	01	43	3.4	14	14	3.5	03	54	5.5	16	15	5.5

MAY 2006   *High Water*   GMT

	LONDON BRIDGE				LIVERPOOL				GREENOCK				LEITH			
	* Datum of Predictions 3.20m below				* Datum of Predictions 4.93m below				* Datum of Predictions 1.62m below				* Datum of Predictions 2.90m below			
	hr	m	hr	m	hr	m	hr	m	hr	m	hr	m	hr	m	hr	m
		ht		ht		ht		ht		ht		ht		ht		ht
M 1	03 45	7.1	16 06	6.7	01 03	9.1	13 29	8.9	02 19	3.5	14 54	3.4	04 37	5.3	17 03	5.2
TU 2	04 27	6.9	16 42	6.5	01 43	8.7	14 11	8.4	02 56	3.5	15 35	3.2	05 21	5.0	17 53	4.9
W 3	05 11	6.5	17 18	6.2	02 23	8.3	14 56	7.8	03 34	3.4	16 19	3.0	06 09	4.7	18 46	4.6
TH 4	05 58	6.2	17 58	5.9	03 09	7.8	15 50	7.2	04 15	3.2	17 11	2.7	07 04	4.5	19 44	4.3
F 5	06 52	5.8	18 48	5.6	04 10	7.3	17 05	6.8	05 04	3.0	18 15	2.6	08 07	4.3	20 47	4.1
SA 6	08 04	5.5	20 07	5.3	05 36	7.1	18 26	6.8	06 04	2.8	19 40	2.5	09 16	4.2	21 55	4.1
SU 7	09 22	5.5	21 39	5.4	06 52	7.2	19 31	7.1	07 19	2.8	21 13	2.6	10 24	4.3	23 06	4.3
M 8	10 26	5.8	22 43	5.7	07 52	7.5	20 24	7.6	08 50	2.8	22 05	2.7	11 27	4.5	—	—
TU 9	11 20	6.1	23 36	6.0	08 42	7.9	21 07	8.0	09 53	2.9	22 48	2.8	00 02	4.5	12 17	4.7
W 10	12 05	6.4	—	—	09 24	8.2	21 46	8.4	10 37	3.0	23 26	2.9	00 43	4.7	12 57	4.8
TH 11	00 21	6.3	12 46	6.5	10 02	8.5	22 21	8.6	11 13	3.0	—	—	01 18	4.9	13 34	5.0
F 12	01 01	6.4	13 23	6.6	10 36	8.6	22 54	8.8	00 01	3.0	11 48	3.0	01 51	5.0	14 09	5.1
SA 13	01 38	6.4	13 58	6.6	11 11	8.7	23 27	8.9	00 32	3.0	12 24	3.1	02 24	5.1	14 45	5.2
SU 14	02 14	6.5	14 34	6.6	11 46	8.8	—	—	01 01	3.1	13 02	3.1	02 58	5.2	15 21	5.2
M 15	02 50	6.5	15 10	6.6	00 02	8.9	12 24	8.8	01 31	3.2	13 43	3.1	03 34	5.2	16 00	5.2
TU 16	03 30	6.6	15 48	6.6	00 40	8.9	13 05	8.7	02 04	3.2	14 25	3.1	04 11	5.2	16 42	5.1
W 17	04 13	6.6	16 29	6.5	01 22	8.7	13 50	8.5	02 40	3.3	15 09	3.0	04 52	5.1	17 28	5.0
TH 18	04 59	6.5	17 13	6.3	02 09	8.5	14 40	8.2	03 17	3.2	15 57	2.9	05 37	4.9	18 20	4.9
F 19	05 51	6.4	18 03	6.1	03 03	8.3	15 39	7.8	04 00	3.1	16 55	2.8	06 29	4.8	19 19	4.7
SA 20	06 49	6.1	19 01	5.9	04 06	8.0	16 48	7.6	04 57	3.0	18 05	2.7	07 29	4.7	20 27	4.7
SU 21	07 57	6.0	20 13	5.8	05 19	7.9	18 05	7.6	06 15	2.9	19 20	2.7	08 43	4.7	21 40	4.7
M 22	09 13	6.1	21 29	6.0	06 31	8.1	19 15	7.9	07 44	2.9	20 33	2.8	09 57	4.8	22 47	4.8
TU 23	10 22	6.3	22 35	6.3	07 37	8.4	20 15	8.3	08 59	3.0	21 38	2.9	11 02	5.0	23 46	5.0
W 24	11 22	6.7	23 33	6.7	08 36	8.8	21 08	8.7	09 59	3.2	22 31	3.0	11 58	5.2	—	—
TH 25	12 14	6.9	—	—	09 28	9.1	21 55	9.0	10 51	3.3	23 18	3.1	00 37	5.2	12 50	5.4
F 26	00 25	6.9	13 02	7.0	10 17	9.3	22 40	9.2	11 40	3.3	—	—	01 24	5.3	13 39	5.5
SA 27	01 14	7.0	13 46	7.0	11 03	9.3	23 22	9.2	00 01	3.2	12 28	3.3	02 08	5.4	14 27	5.5
SU 28	02 00	7.1	14 28	6.9	11 47	9.1	—	—	00 42	3.3	13 14	3.3	02 51	5.4	15 15	5.4
M 29	02 46	7.0	15 09	6.7	00 02	9.1	12 30	8.9	01 21	3.4	13 59	3.2	03 35	5.3	16 02	5.3
TU 30	03 32	6.8	15 47	6.5	00 43	8.9	13 12	8.6	02 00	3.5	14 42	3.1	04 18	5.2	16 48	5.1
W 31	04 16	6.6	16 23	6.4	01 23	8.6	13 53	8.3	02 38	3.5	15 25	3.0	05 02	5.0	17 34	4.9

JUNE 2006   *High Water*   GMT

	LONDON BRIDGE				LIVERPOOL				GREENOCK				LEITH			
TH 1	04 59	6.4	17 00	6.2	02 05	8.4	14 36	7.9	03 17	3.4	16 10	2.9	05 47	4.8	18 20	4.7
F 2	05 42	6.2	17 40	6.1	02 49	8.0	15 22	7.5	03 57	3.3	16 59	2.8	06 35	4.6	19 09	4.5
SA 3	06 27	6.0	18 25	5.9	03 38	7.7	16 16	7.2	04 42	3.1	17 52	2.7	07 28	4.5	20 00	4.3
SU 4	07 19	5.8	19 20	5.7	04 37	7.4	17 20	7.1	05 34	3.0	18 47	2.7	08 25	4.4	20 55	4.2
M 5	08 17	5.7	20 27	5.5	05 44	7.3	18 27	7.1	06 32	2.9	19 45	2.6	09 23	4.3	21 51	4.2
TU 6	09 20	5.7	21 37	5.6	06 48	7.4	19 26	7.3	07 33	2.8	20 49	2.7	10 20	4.4	22 47	4.4
W 7	10 20	5.9	22 40	5.8	07 45	7.6	20 18	7.7	08 37	2.8	21 50	2.7	11 15	4.5	23 41	4.5
TH 8	11 15	6.1	23 34	6.0	08 35	7.8	21 03	8.1	09 37	2.9	22 40	2.8	12 07	4.6	—	—
F 9	12 03	6.3	—	—	09 19	8.1	21 44	8.4	10 27	2.9	23 22	2.9	00 30	4.7	12 55	4.8
SA 10	00 23	6.2	12 49	6.5	10 02	8.4	22 23	8.7	11 12	3.0	—	—	01 14	4.9	13 40	5.0
SU 11	01 08	6.4	13 31	6.6	10 44	8.6	23 03	8.8	00 00	3.0	11 57	3.0	01 56	5.0	14 23	5.1
M 12	01 52	6.6	14 13	6.7	11 27	8.7	23 45	9.0	00 36	3.1	12 42	3.1	02 35	5.2	15 05	5.2
TU 13	02 36	6.7	14 56	6.7	12 11	8.8	—	—	01 13	3.2	13 29	3.1	03 15	5.2	15 48	5.3
W 14	03 21	6.8	15 39	6.6	00 29	9.0	12 59	8.8	01 51	3.4	14 18	3.0	03 56	5.3	16 32	5.3
TH 15	04 08	6.8	16 23	6.6	01 16	9.0	13 47	8.7	02 31	3.4	15 08	3.0	04 40	5.3	17 20	5.3
F 16	04 57	6.7	17 09	6.5	02 06	9.0	14 37	8.6	03 14	3.3	16 00	3.0	05 27	5.2	18 10	5.2
SA 17	05 48	6.6	17 58	6.4	02 58	8.8	15 31	8.3	04 00	3.3	16 56	2.9	06 17	5.1	19 05	5.0
SU 18	06 43	6.5	18 52	6.3	03 54	8.6	16 28	8.1	04 54	3.2	17 53	2.9	07 13	5.0	20 06	4.9
M 19	07 43	6.3	19 53	6.2	04 54	8.5	17 32	7.9	05 57	3.1	18 50	2.9	08 18	4.9	21 11	4.8
TU 20	08 47	6.3	20 58	6.2	05 58	8.3	18 39	7.9	07 07	3.0	19 49	2.8	09 26	4.9	22 15	4.8
W 21	09 51	6.3	22 02	6.3	07 03	8.3	19 44	8.0	08 23	3.0	20 55	2.8	10 33	4.9	23 16	4.8
TH 22	10 51	6.4	23 04	6.4	08 08	8.4	20 43	8.3	09 32	3.1	22 00	2.9	11 35	5.0	—	—
F 23	11 47	6.5	—	—	09 08	8.5	21 36	8.5	10 33	3.1	22 54	3.0	00 13	4.9	12 35	5.0
SA 24	00 00	6.5	12 40	6.6	10 01	8.6	22 23	8.7	11 27	3.1	23 42	3.1	01 06	5.0	13 29	5.1
SU 25	00 58	6.7	13 28	6.7	10 50	8.7	23 07	8.8	12 18	3.1	—	—	01 54	5.1	14 19	5.2
M 26	01 49	6.7	14 13	6.6	11 35	8.7	23 48	8.9	00 25	3.2	13 07	3.1	02 39	5.2	15 06	5.2
TU 27	02 37	6.7	14 56	6.6	12 17	8.6	—	—	01 06	3.3	13 53	3.0	03 22	5.2	15 50	5.1
W 28	03 23	6.7	15 34	6.5	00 28	8.8	12 57	8.5	01 46	3.4	14 36	3.0	04 03	5.2	16 31	5.1
TH 29	04 04	6.6	16 09	6.4	01 07	8.7	13 35	8.3	02 23	3.4	15 16	2.9	04 43	5.1	17 11	4.9
F 30	04 42	6.5	16 43	6.3	01 46	8.6	14 12	8.2	03 01	3.4	15 55	2.9	05 22	5.0	17 50	4.8

JULY 2006   *High Water*   GMT

	LONDON BRIDGE *Datum of Predictions 3.20m below				LIVERPOOL *Datum of Predictions 4.93m below				GREENOCK *Datum of Predictions 1.62m below				LEITH *Datum of Predictions 2.90m below			
	hr	m	hr	m	hr	m	hr	m	hr	m	hr	m	hr	m	hr	m
SA 1	05 18	6.3	17 18	6.3	02 24	8.4	14 51	8.0	03 38	3.3	16 36	2.9	06 02	4.9	18 30	4.6
SU 2	05 55	6.2	17 56	6.2	03 05	8.1	15 31	7.7	04 17	3.2	17 17	2.8	06 45	4.7	19 14	4.5
M 3	06 35	6.1	18 39	6.0	03 48	7.9	16 17	7.5	04 58	3.1	18 00	2.8	07 31	4.6	20 01	4.4
TU 4	07 21	5.9	19 29	5.8	04 37	7.6	17 11	7.3	05 45	3.0	18 45	2.7	08 22	4.5	20 53	4.3
W 5	08 14	5.8	20 28	5.7	05 33	7.4	18 14	7.2	06 36	2.9	19 36	2.7	09 19	4.4	21 49	4.3
TH 6	09 15	5.8	21 34	5.6	06 35	7.4	19 19	7.4	07 35	2.8	20 38	2.7	10 19	4.4	22 48	4.4
F 7	10 20	5.8	22 44	5.8	07 39	7.5	20 19	7.7	08 42	2.8	21 50	2.7	11 21	4.4	23 47	4.6
SA 8	11 23	6.1	23 48	6.1	08 39	7.8	21 11	8.2	09 49	2.8	22 48	2.9	12 22	4.6	—	—
SU 9	12 19	6.4	—	—	09 34	8.1	21 59	8.6	10 47	2.9	23 34	3.0	00 43	4.8	13 17	4.9
M 10	00 44	6.4	13 10	6.6	10 25	8.5	22 46	8.9	11 39	3.0	—	—	01 33	5.0	14 06	5.1
TU 11	01 35	6.7	13 57	6.8	11 14	8.7	23 32	9.2	00 17	3.2	12 31	3.0	02 18	5.2	14 51	5.4
W 12	02 24	6.9	14 43	6.8	12 03	8.9	—	—	00 59	3.3	13 23	3.1	03 01	5.4	15 35	5.5
TH 13	03 12	7.0	15 29	6.9	00 19	9.4	12 51	9.1	01 41	3.4	14 14	3.1	03 43	5.5	16 20	5.6
F 14	04 00	7.1	16 13	6.9	01 07	9.5	13 38	9.1	02 24	3.5	15 04	3.1	04 27	5.6	17 05	5.6
SA 15	04 47	7.0	16 58	6.8	01 55	9.5	14 24	9.0	03 07	3.5	15 51	3.1	05 12	5.6	17 53	5.4
SU 16	05 35	6.9	17 43	6.8	02 43	9.4	15 11	8.8	03 51	3.5	16 36	3.1	06 00	5.5	18 43	5.2
M 17	06 24	6.7	18 29	6.7	03 32	9.1	16 00	8.5	04 38	3.4	17 22	3.1	06 50	5.3	19 38	5.0
TU 18	07 16	6.5	19 21	6.5	04 24	8.7	16 55	8.0	05 28	3.3	18 08	3.0	07 48	5.1	20 38	4.7
W 19	08 14	6.2	20 21	6.3	05 23	8.2	17 59	7.7	06 26	3.1	18 58	2.9	08 56	4.9	21 43	4.6
TH 20	09 16	6.0	21 28	6.0	06 31	7.9	19 14	7.6	07 38	3.2	20 00	2.8	10 08	4.7	22 49	4.6
F 21	10 20	5.9	22 40	6.0	07 47	7.8	20 25	7.8	09 14	2.8	21 31	2.8	11 21	4.7	23 56	4.7
SA 22	11 23	6.0	23 48	6.1	08 56	7.9	21 25	8.1	10 29	2.9	22 39	3.0	12 30	4.8	—	—
SU 23	12 22	6.2	—	—	09 54	8.2	22 14	8.5	11 27	3.0	23 30	3.1	00 57	4.9	13 29	4.9
M 24	00 48	6.4	13 16	6.4	10 43	8.4	22 58	8.7	12 18	3.0	—	—	01 48	5.0	14 17	5.0
TU 25	01 41	6.6	14 02	6.6	11 26	8.5	23 37	8.9	00 15	3.2	13 05	3.0	02 32	5.2	14 58	5.1
W 26	02 28	6.8	14 44	6.6	12 04	8.6	—	—	00 56	3.3	13 47	3.0	03 11	5.2	15 35	5.1
TH 27	03 10	6.7	15 20	6.6	00 14	8.9	12 39	8.6	01 33	3.4	14 24	2.9	03 47	5.3	16 09	5.1
F 28	03 46	6.6	15 51	6.5	00 48	8.9	13 12	8.5	02 08	3.4	14 57	2.9	04 20	5.3	16 42	5.0
SA 29	04 18	6.5	16 20	6.5	01 22	8.8	13 44	8.5	02 41	3.4	15 29	2.9	04 54	5.2	17 16	5.0
SU 30	04 48	6.5	16 50	6.4	01 55	8.7	14 17	8.3	03 13	3.4	16 01	3.0	05 28	5.1	17 52	4.8
M 31	05 20	6.4	17 23	6.4	02 29	8.5	14 51	8.1	03 46	3.3	16 34	2.9	06 03	4.9	18 31	4.7

AUGUST 2006   *High Water*   GMT

	LONDON BRIDGE				LIVERPOOL				GREENOCK				LEITH			
TU 1	05 55	6.3	18 00	6.3	03 05	8.2	15 28	7.9	04 22	3.2	17 10	2.9	06 42	4.8	19 13	4.6
W 2	06 35	6.2	18 42	6.1	03 46	7.9	16 13	7.5	05 02	3.1	17 51	2.8	07 26	4.6	20 01	4.4
TH 3	07 23	5.9	19 35	5.8	04 37	7.5	17 10	7.3	05 49	2.9	18 39	2.7	08 21	4.4	20 58	4.3
F 4	08 20	5.7	20 39	5.6	05 40	7.3	18 22	7.2	06 47	2.8	19 39	2.6	09 29	4.3	22 03	4.3
SA 5	09 28	5.6	21 54	5.6	06 53	7.2	19 40	7.4	07 59	2.7	21 02	2.7	10 43	4.3	23 12	4.4
SU 6	10 45	5.8	23 17	5.9	08 10	7.5	20 47	8.0	09 22	2.7	22 20	2.8	11 55	4.5	—	—
M 7	11 55	6.1	—	—	09 17	8.0	21 42	8.4	10 33	2.9	23 14	3.1	00 18	4.7	12 59	4.9
TU 8	00 26	6.4	12 52	6.6	10 12	8.5	22 31	9.1	11 31	3.0	23 59	3.3	01 15	5.0	13 50	5.3
W 9	01 21	6.8	13 41	6.9	11 02	9.0	23 18	9.6	12 23	3.1	—	—	02 01	5.3	14 35	5.6
TH 10	02 10	7.1	14 27	7.0	11 48	9.3	—	—	00 43	3.4	13 14	3.2	02 43	5.6	15 18	5.8
F 11	02 57	7.3	15 11	7.1	00 04	9.9	12 34	9.5	01 27	3.6	14 02	3.2	03 24	5.8	16 00	5.8
SA 12	03 42	7.3	15 53	7.1	00 50	10.0	13 18	9.5	02 10	3.7	14 46	3.3	04 07	6.0	16 44	5.8
SU 13	04 27	7.2	16 35	7.1	01 34	10.0	14 01	9.4	02 52	3.7	15 26	3.3	04 50	5.9	17 29	5.6
M 14	05 11	7.1	17 17	7.1	02 19	9.7	14 44	9.1	03 33	3.7	16 04	3.3	05 36	5.8	18 16	5.3
TU 15	05 54	6.8	17 58	6.9	03 04	9.2	15 28	8.6	04 14	3.6	16 42	3.2	06 26	5.5	19 07	5.0
W 16	06 40	6.4	18 44	6.6	03 52	8.6	16 18	8.0	04 57	3.4	17 24	3.1	07 22	5.1	20 05	4.7
TH 17	07 31	6.0	19 41	6.1	04 49	7.9	17 22	7.4	05 46	3.1	18 11	3.0	08 32	4.7	21 13	4.5
F 18	08 35	5.6	20 57	5.7	06 05	7.3	18 51	7.2	06 49	2.8	19 09	2.8	09 50	4.5	22 27	4.4
SA 19	09 51	5.5	22 24	5.6	07 37	7.2	20 14	7.5	09 20	2.7	21 09	2.8	11 13	4.5	23 45	4.6
SU 20	11 03	5.6	23 37	5.9	08 50	7.6	21 15	8.0	10 33	2.8	22 28	3.0	12 31	4.6	—	—
M 21	12 06	6.0	—	—	09 44	8.0	22 03	8.5	11 25	3.0	23 18	3.2	00 50	4.8	13 27	4.9
TU 22	00 37	6.4	12 59	6.4	10 29	8.4	22 43	8.8	12 10	3.0	—	—	01 39	5.0	14 09	5.0
W 23	01 27	6.7	13 44	6.7	11 08	8.6	23 20	9.0	00 01	3.3	12 51	3.1	02 19	5.2	14 43	5.1
TH 24	02 11	6.9	14 24	6.8	11 43	8.7	23 53	9.1	00 40	3.4	13 27	3.0	02 53	5.3	15 14	5.2
F 25	02 48	6.9	14 58	6.7	12 14	8.7	—	—	01 15	3.4	13 59	3.0	03 23	5.4	15 42	5.2
SA 26	03 20	6.7	15 26	6.5	00 23	9.0	12 44	8.7	01 46	3.4	14 28	3.0	03 53	5.4	16 11	5.2
SU 27	03 47	6.6	15 52	6.5	00 53	8.9	13 13	8.7	02 14	3.4	14 54	3.1	04 22	5.3	16 43	5.1
M 28	04 14	6.5	16 19	6.5	01 22	8.8	13 42	8.6	02 44	3.4	15 20	3.1	04 54	5.2	17 16	5.0
TU 29	04 43	6.5	16 49	6.5	01 53	8.6	14 12	8.4	03 16	3.4	15 50	3.1	05 27	5.1	17 52	4.9
W 30	05 16	6.5	17 24	6.4	02 25	8.4	14 45	8.1	03 49	3.3	16 23	3.0	06 04	4.9	18 31	4.7
TH 31	05 54	6.3	18 06	6.2	03 03	8.0	15 27	7.7	04 26	3.1	17 00	2.9	06 46	4.6	19 16	4.5

SEPTEMBER 2006   *High Water*   GMT

	LONDON BRIDGE * Datum of Predictions 3.20m below				LIVERPOOL * Datum of Predictions 4.93m below				GREENOCK * Datum of Predictions 1.62m below				LEITH * Datum of Predictions 2.90m below			
	hr	m ht	hr	m ht	hr	m ht	hr	m ht	hr	m ht	hr	m ht	hr	m ht	hr	m ht
F 1	06 38	6.0	18 57	5.9	03 53	7.5	16 23	7.3	05 09	2.9	17 45	2.8	07 38	4.4	20 11	4.3
SA 2	07 33	5.7	20 00	5.6	05 00	7.1	17 40	7.1	06 06	2.7	18 50	2.6	08 49	4.2	21 24	4.3
SU 3	08 41	5.5	21 16	5.5	06 24	7.0	19 11	7.3	07 27	2.6	20 24	2.7	10 13	4.3	22 43	4.4
M 4	10 07	5.5	22 53	5.7	07 55	7.4	20 29	8.0	09 08	2.7	21 56	2.9	11 34	4.6	23 56	4.7
TU 5	11 33	6.0	—	—	09 04	8.0	21 25	8.7	10 28	2.9	22 52	3.2	12 39	5.0	—	—
W 6	00 10	6.4	12 32	6.5	09 57	8.7	22 13	9.4	11 22	3.1	23 39	3.4	00 52	5.1	13 30	5.4
TH 7	01 04	6.9	13 19	6.9	10 43	9.3	22 58	9.9	12 10	3.2	—	—	01 38	5.5	14 13	5.8
F 8	01 50	7.3	14 03	7.2	11 27	9.6	23 42	10.2	00 23	3.6	12 55	3.3	02 19	5.9	14 54	5.9
SA 9	02 35	7.5	14 45	7.3	12 10	9.8	—	—	01 07	3.7	13 38	3.4	03 00	6.1	15 35	6.0
SU 10	03 18	7.4	15 26	7.3	00 25	10.3	12 52	9.7	01 50	3.8	14 17	3.4	03 42	6.2	16 18	5.9
M 11	04 00	7.3	16 07	7.3	01 09	10.1	13 33	9.5	02 31	3.8	14 53	3.5	04 27	6.1	17 01	5.6
TU 12	04 40	7.1	16 48	7.2	01 52	9.7	14 14	9.1	03 10	3.8	15 29	3.5	05 13	5.8	17 47	5.3
W 13	05 20	6.8	17 30	6.9	02 36	9.1	14 56	8.5	03 49	3.6	16 06	3.4	06 04	5.4	18 37	5.0
TH 14	06 00	6.3	18 15	6.5	03 23	8.3	15 44	7.9	04 30	3.3	16 47	3.3	07 01	5.0	19 36	4.6
F 15	06 42	5.9	19 10	6.0	04 21	7.5	16 51	7.3	05 17	3.0	17 35	3.1	08 13	4.6	20 48	4.4
SA 16	07 44	5.4	20 38	5.5	05 50	7.0	18 33	7.0	06 20	2.7	18 35	2.9	09 34	4.3	22 07	4.4
SU 17	09 25	5.2	22 09	5.5	07 26	7.0	19 56	7.4	09 26	2.7	20 44	2.8	11 02	4.4	23 28	4.5
M 18	10 40	5.5	23 19	5.9	08 33	7.4	20 54	8.0	10 25	2.9	22 08	3.1	12 20	4.6	—	—
TU 19	11 42	6.0	—	—	09 24	8.0	21 40	8.5	11 09	3.1	22 57	3.3	00 32	4.8	13 11	4.9
W 20	00 15	6.5	12 34	6.5	10 05	8.4	22 19	8.9	11 48	3.1	23 38	3.4	01 18	5.1	13 48	5.0
TH 21	01 03	6.8	13 17	6.8	10 41	8.7	22 54	9.0	12 23	3.2	—	—	01 55	5.3	14 18	5.2
F 22	01 44	7.0	13 56	6.8	11 14	8.8	23 25	9.1	00 15	3.4	12 57	3.2	02 26	5.4	14 45	5.2
SA 23	02 18	6.9	14 29	6.7	11 44	8.9	23 54	9.0	00 48	3.4	13 27	3.2	02 54	5.4	15 11	5.3
SU 24	02 48	6.7	14 57	6.5	12 11	8.9	—	—	01 16	3.4	13 53	3.2	03 22	5.4	15 39	5.3
M 25	03 13	6.6	15 22	6.4	00 21	9.0	12 39	8.8	01 44	3.4	14 16	3.2	03 52	5.4	16 10	5.2
TU 26	03 39	6.5	15 48	6.4	00 50	8.9	13 08	8.7	02 14	3.4	14 42	3.3	04 24	5.3	16 42	5.1
W 27	04 08	6.6	16 20	6.5	01 20	8.7	13 38	8.5	02 47	3.4	15 12	3.3	04 58	5.1	17 17	5.0
TH 28	04 41	6.5	16 57	6.5	01 53	8.4	14 12	8.3	03 21	3.3	15 44	3.2	05 36	4.9	17 55	4.8
F 29	05 19	6.4	17 40	6.3	02 33	8.0	14 55	7.9	03 57	3.1	16 18	3.1	06 20	4.7	18 40	4.6
SA 30	06 03	6.1	18 33	6.0	03 24	7.5	15 53	7.4	04 39	2.9	17 01	2.9	07 15	4.5	19 37	4.4

OCTOBER 2006   *High Water*   GMT

	LONDON BRIDGE				LIVERPOOL				GREENOCK				LEITH			
SU 1	06 57	5.7	19 36	5.7	04 35	7.1	17 14	7.1	05 37	2.7	18 09	2.8	08 25	4.3	20 52	4.3
M 2	08 05	5.4	20 52	5.5	06 06	7.0	18 48	7.4	07 09	2.6	19 55	2.8	09 50	4.4	22 17	4.5
TU 3	09 33	5.5	22 33	5.8	07 39	7.5	20 05	8.1	08 58	2.8	21 28	3.0	11 11	4.7	23 29	4.9
W 4	11 04	6.0	23 48	6.5	08 44	8.2	21 01	8.9	10 12	3.0	22 26	3.3	12 14	5.2	—	—
TH 5	12 03	6.6	—	—	09 33	8.9	21 49	9.6	11 03	3.2	23 14	3.5	00 25	5.3	13 04	5.5
F 6	00 40	7.0	12 51	7.0	10 18	9.5	22 34	10.1	11 47	3.4	23 59	3.7	01 11	5.7	13 47	5.8
SA 7	01 26	7.4	13 35	7.3	11 01	9.8	23 17	10.3	12 28	3.5	—	—	01 53	6.0	14 27	6.0
SU 8	02 08	7.5	14 17	7.4	11 43	9.9	—	—	00 43	3.8	13 08	3.5	02 35	6.2	15 09	6.0
M 9	02 50	7.4	14 59	7.4	00 00	10.2	12 24	9.8	01 27	3.9	13 46	3.6	03 19	6.2	15 51	5.8
TU 10	03 30	7.2	15 41	7.3	00 44	9.9	13 05	9.5	02 09	3.8	14 22	3.7	04 05	6.0	16 35	5.6
W 11	04 10	7.0	16 24	7.1	01 27	9.4	13 46	9.0	02 49	3.7	14 59	3.7	04 54	5.7	17 21	5.3
TH 12	04 47	6.7	17 08	6.8	02 10	8.8	14 28	8.5	03 28	3.6	15 37	3.6	05 46	5.3	18 11	5.0
F 13	05 25	6.3	17 55	6.4	02 58	8.1	15 16	7.9	04 10	3.3	16 19	3.5	06 46	4.8	19 11	4.6
SA 14	06 04	5.9	18 54	5.9	03 58	7.3	16 24	7.3	05 00	3.0	17 08	3.2	07 55	4.5	20 24	4.4
SU 15	06 59	5.4	20 21	5.5	05 28	6.9	18 02	7.1	06 11	2.7	18 11	3.0	09 10	4.3	21 39	4.4
M 16	08 54	5.2	21 43	5.6	06 56	6.9	19 21	7.4	09 01	2.7	19 46	3.0	10 32	4.3	22 55	4.5
TU 17	10 09	5.5	22 48	5.9	08 01	7.4	20 20	7.9	09 56	2.9	21 31	3.1	11 47	4.5	23 58	4.8
W 18	11 08	6.0	23 43	6.4	08 50	7.9	21 06	8.3	10 38	3.1	22 23	3.3	12 38	4.8	—	—
TH 19	11 59	6.4	—	—	09 31	8.3	21 46	8.7	11 14	3.2	23 05	3.4	00 44	5.0	13 15	5.0
F 20	00 29	6.7	12 43	6.6	10 08	8.7	22 22	8.9	11 48	3.3	23 42	3.4	01 21	5.2	13 45	5.1
SA 21	01 09	6.8	13 22	6.7	10 41	8.8	22 53	9.0	12 21	3.3	—	—	01 53	5.3	14 12	5.2
SU 22	01 43	6.8	13 55	6.6	11 11	8.9	23 22	9.0	00 14	3.4	12 52	3.3	02 23	5.4	14 39	5.3
M 23	02 13	6.7	14 25	6.5	11 39	8.9	23 51	8.9	00 43	3.3	13 18	3.3	02 54	5.4	15 08	5.3
TU 24	02 40	6.6	14 54	6.4	12 08	8.9	—	—	01 14	3.3	13 43	3.4	03 26	5.3	15 40	5.3
W 25	03 09	6.6	15 24	6.5	00 22	8.8	12 40	8.8	01 47	3.4	14 12	3.4	04 00	5.2	16 13	5.2
TH 26	03 40	6.6	16 00	6.5	00 56	8.7	13 14	8.7	02 23	3.3	14 43	3.4	04 37	5.1	16 49	5.1
F 27	04 15	6.5	16 40	6.5	01 34	8.4	13 53	8.4	03 00	3.3	15 17	3.3	05 18	5.0	17 29	4.9
SA 28	04 54	6.4	17 26	6.4	02 17	8.1	14 40	8.1	03 39	3.1	15 53	3.2	06 05	4.8	18 16	4.7
SU 29	05 39	6.2	18 20	6.1	03 11	7.6	15 40	7.7	04 25	3.0	16 38	3.1	07 01	4.6	19 14	4.6
M 30	06 33	5.8	19 22	5.8	04 21	7.3	16 56	7.5	05 29	2.8	17 49	2.9	08 08	4.5	20 27	4.5
TU 31	07 41	5.6	20 39	5.7	05 48	7.2	18 20	7.7	07 00	2.8	19 26	3.0	09 27	4.6	21 49	4.7

NOVEMBER 2006   *High Water*   GMT

	LONDON BRIDGE * Datum of Predictions 3.20m below						LIVERPOOL * Datum of Predictions 4.93m below						GREENOCK * Datum of Predictions 1.62m below						LEITH * Datum of Predictions 2.90m below					
	hr	m	ht	hr	m	ht	hr	m	ht	hr	m	ht	hr	m	ht	hr	m	ht	hr	m	ht	hr	m	ht
W 1	09	08	5.7	22	08	6.0	07	11	7.7	19	33	8.3	08	32	2.9	20	53	3.1	10	42	4.8	22	58	5.0
TH 2	10	29	6.1	23	17	6.5	08	14	8.3	20	31	8.9	09	42	3.1	21	55	3.4	11	44	5.2	23	54	5.3
F 3	11	30	6.6	—	—		09	05	8.9	21	22	9.5	10	34	3.3	22	47	3.6	12	34	5.5	—	—	
SA 4	00	11	7.0	12	21	7.0	09	51	9.4	22	09	9.9	11	19	3.4	23	34	3.7	00	42	5.7	13	20	5.7
SU 5	00	58	7.3	13	07	7.3	10	35	9.7	22	54	10.0	12	00	3.5				01	28	5.9	14	02	5.8
M 6	01	42	7.4	13	52	7.4	11	18	9.7	23	38	9.9	00	21	3.8	12	40	3.6	02	14	6.0	14	44	5.8
TU 7	02	24	7.3	14	37	7.3	12	00	9.6				01	06	3.8	13	19	3.7	03	01	6.0	15	28	5.7
W 8	03	04	7.1	15	22	7.2	00	22	9.6	12	42	9.3	01	50	3.7	13	58	3.8	03	49	5.8	16	13	5.5
TH 9	03	44	6.8	16	08	7.0	01	06	9.1	13	24	9.0	02	32	3.6	14	37	3.8	04	40	5.5	16	59	5.3
F 10	04	22	6.5	16	55	6.7	01	51	8.6	14	07	8.5	03	15	3.4	15	17	3.7	05	32	5.2	17	49	5.0
SA 11	05	00	6.2	17	43	6.3	02	39	8.0	14	55	8.1	04	00	3.2	15	59	3.6	06	28	4.8	18	47	4.7
SU 12	05	41	5.9	18	38	5.9	03	34	7.4	15	54	7.6	04	53	3.0	16	48	3.4	07	28	4.5	19	53	4.5
M 13	06	32	5.6	19	46	5.7	04	47	7.0	17	13	7.3	06	00	2.8	17	47	3.2	08	32	4.4	21	00	4.5
TU 14	08	00	5.4	20	59	5.6	06	07	7.1	18	29	7.4	07	33	2.8	18	57	3.1	09	39	4.3	22	05	4.5
W 15	09	21	5.5	22	03	5.8	07	12	7.2	19	32	7.6	08	58	2.9	20	21	3.1	10	46	4.4	23	06	4.6
TH 16	10	23	5.8	22	58	6.1	08	06	7.6	20	23	8.0	09	49	3.0	21	32	3.2	11	44	4.6	23	58	4.8
F 17	11	16	6.1	23	46	6.3	08	51	8.1	21	07	8.3	10	31	3.2	22	21	3.2	12	28	4.8	—	—	
SA 18	12	03	6.3	—	—		09	30	8.4	21	45	8.5	11	10	3.3	23	02	3.3	00	40	5.0	13	04	4.9
SU 19	00	28	6.5	12	44	6.4	10	06	8.7	22	20	8.7	11	46	3.3	23	37	3.3	01	18	5.1	13	36	5.1
M 20	01	05	6.6	13	22	6.5	10	39	8.8	22	53	8.8	12	18	3.4				01	54	5.2	14	08	5.2
TU 21	01	39	6.6	13	57	6.5	11	12	8.9	23	27	8.8	00	11	3.3	12	48	3.4	02	29	5.2	14	42	5.3
W 22	02	13	6.6	14	32	6.5	11	45	9.0	—	—		00	48	3.3	13	18	3.5	03	06	5.3	15	16	5.3
TH 23	02	47	6.6	15	09	6.6	00	03	8.8	12	22	8.9	01	26	3.3	13	50	3.5	03	43	5.2	15	52	5.3
F 24	03	22	6.6	15	50	6.6	00	42	8.7	13	01	8.8	02	06	3.3	14	25	3.5	04	23	5.2	16	30	5.2
SA 25	04	00	6.6	16	33	6.6	01	25	8.5	13	45	8.7	02	48	3.2	15	02	3.5	05	06	5.1	17	12	5.1
SU 26	04	41	6.4	17	21	6.5	02	12	8.3	14	35	8.5	03	33	3.1	15	43	3.4	05	54	5.0	18	00	5.0
M 27	05	27	6.3	18	14	6.3	03	05	8.0	15	31	8.3	04	24	3.0	16	32	3.3	06	47	4.9	18	55	4.9
TU 28	06	19	6.1	19	13	6.1	04	08	7.7	16	36	8.1	05	26	2.9	17	36	3.2	07	49	4.8	20	00	4.8
W 29	07	24	5.9	20	23	6.0	05	19	7.6	17	46	8.2	06	38	2.9	18	52	3.2	08	59	4.7	21	14	4.9
TH 30	08	40	6.0	21	37	6.1	06	32	7.8	18	55	8.4	07	50	3.0	20	12	3.2	10	08	4.9	22	23	5.0

DECEMBER 2006   *High Water*   GMT

	LONDON BRIDGE						LIVERPOOL						GREENOCK						LEITH					
F 1	09	53	6.2	22	44	6.4	07	39	8.2	19	59	8.7	09	00	3.1	21	22	3.3	11	11	5.0	23	23	5.2
SA 2	10	57	6.5	23	41	6.7	08	36	8.6	20	56	9.1	10	00	3.2	22	21	3.5	12	05	5.2	—	—	
SU 3	11	53	6.8	—	—		09	27	9.0	21	48	9.3	10	50	3.3	23	13	3.5	00	18	5.4	12	55	5.4
M 4	00	32	6.9	12	45	7.0	10	14	9.3	22	37	9.4	11	36	3.5	—	—		01	10	5.6	13	41	5.5
TU 5	01	19	7.0	13	34	7.1	10	59	9.4	23	23	9.4	00	04	3.6	12	19	3.6	02	01	5.6	14	27	5.6
W 6	02	03	6.9	14	23	7.1	11	43	9.4	—	—		00	53	3.5	13	00	3.7	02	50	5.6	15	12	5.5
TH 7	02	46	6.8	15	11	6.9	00	08	9.2	12	26	9.2	01	40	3.5	13	41	3.8	03	39	5.5	15	57	5.4
F 8	03	27	6.6	15	58	6.8	00	53	8.9	13	08	9.0	02	25	3.4	14	21	3.8	04	28	5.3	16	43	5.3
SA 9	04	06	6.5	16	43	6.6	01	36	8.6	13	51	8.7	03	09	3.3	15	02	3.7	05	16	5.1	17	29	5.1
SU 10	04	44	6.3	17	27	6.4	02	19	8.2	14	35	8.4	03	53	3.2	15	44	3.6	06	03	4.9	18	19	4.9
M 11	05	23	6.1	18	11	6.2	03	05	7.8	15	21	8.1	04	41	3.1	16	29	3.5	06	52	4.6	19	11	4.7
TU 12	06	06	6.0	18	57	5.9	03	55	7.5	16	14	7.8	05	32	3.0	17	17	3.4	07	42	4.5	20	07	4.6
W 13	06	57	5.8	19	49	5.8	04	54	7.2	17	15	7.5	06	25	2.9	18	10	3.2	08	36	4.3	21	04	4.5
TH 14	08	00	5.6	20	48	5.7	06	00	7.2	18	20	7.4	07	22	2.9	19	06	3.1	09	31	4.3	22	00	4.5
F 15	09	11	5.6	21	50	5.7	07	05	7.3	19	23	7.6	08	27	2.9	20	08	3.0	10	28	4.4	22	57	4.5
SA 16	10	16	5.7	22	49	5.9	08	01	7.6	20	18	7.8	09	34	3.0	21	16	3.0	11	23	4.5	23	52	4.6
SU 17	11	14	5.9	23	41	6.1	08	50	8.0	21	06	8.1	10	28	3.1	22	14	3.1	12	15	4.7	—	—	
M 18	12	05	6.1	—	—		09	32	8.3	21	49	8.3	11	12	3.2	23	02	3.1	00	42	4.8	13	01	4.9
TU 19	00	28	6.4	12	51	6.4	10	12	8.6	22	29	8.6	11	49	3.3	23	45	3.2	01	28	4.9	13	43	5.1
W 20	01	11	6.5	13	34	6.5	10	51	8.9	23	10	8.7	12	24	3.4	—	—		02	10	5.1	14	22	5.2
TH 21	01	52	6.7	14	16	6.7	11	30	9.0	23	52	8.8	00	28	3.2	12	59	3.5	02	51	5.2	15	00	5.3
F 22	02	32	6.7	14	59	6.8	12	11	9.1	—	—		01	13	3.2	13	35	3.5	03	31	5.3	15	38	5.4
SA 23	03	12	6.7	15	44	6.8	00	35	8.9	12	55	9.2	01	58	3.2	14	14	3.6	04	12	5.4	16	17	5.4
SU 24	03	53	6.6	16	29	6.8	01	20	8.8	13	40	9.2	02	43	3.2	14	54	3.6	04	55	5.3	17	00	5.4
M 25	04	35	6.6	17	16	6.7	02	06	8.7	14	28	9.1	03	29	3.2	15	37	3.6	05	41	5.3	17	45	5.3
TU 26	05	20	6.5	18	05	6.6	02	55	8.6	15	17	8.9	04	17	3.1	16	23	3.5	06	30	5.1	18	34	5.2
W 27	06	07	6.4	18	58	6.4	03	47	8.3	16	11	8.7	05	08	3.1	17	16	3.4	07	24	5.0	19	30	5.1
TH 28	07	02	6.3	19	57	6.2	04	45	8.0	17	11	8.5	06	01	3.0	18	15	3.3	08	26	4.8	20	35	5.0
F 29	08	07	6.2	21	02	6.1	05	51	7.9	18	17	8.3	06	57	3.0	19	23	3.2	09	32	4.7	21	48	4.9
SA 30	09	16	6.1	22	09	6.1	07	01	7.9	19	27	8.3	08	04	3.0	20	46	3.2	10	37	4.8	22	57	4.9
SU 31	10	25	6.2	—	—		08	10	8.1	—	—		09	22	3.0	—	—		11	40	4.9	—	—	

GENERAL REFERENCE

WEIGHTS AND MEASURES

SI UNITS

The Système International d'Unités (SI) is an international and coherent system of units devised to meet all known needs for measurement in science and technology. The system was adopted by the eleventh Conférence Générale des Poids et Mesures (CGPM) in 1960. A comprehensive description of the system is given in *SI The International System of Units* (HMSO). The British Standards describing the essential features of the International System of Units are *Specifications for SI units and recommendations for the use of their multiples and certain other units* (BS 5555:1993) and *Conversion Factors and Tables* (BS 350, Part 1:1974).

The system consists of seven base units and the derived units formed as products or quotients of various powers of the base units. Together the base units and the derived units make up the coherent system of units. In the UK the SI base units, and almost all important derived units, are realised at the National Physical Laboratory and disseminated through the National Measurement System.

BASE UNITS

metre (m) = unit of length
kilogram (kg) = unit of mass
second (s) = unit of time
ampere (A) = unit of electric current
kelvin (K) = unit of thermodynamic temperature
mole (mol) = unit of amount of substance
candela (cd) = unit of luminous intensity

DERIVED UNITS

For some of the derived SI units, special names and symbols exist; those approved by the CGPM are as follows:

hertz (Hz) = unit of frequency
newton (N) = unit of force
pascal (Pa) = unit of pressure, stress
joule (J) = unit of energy, work, quantity of heat
watt (W) = unit of power, radiant flux
coulomb (C) = unit of electric charge, quantity of electricity
volt (V) = unit of electric potential, potential difference, electromotive force
farad (F) = unit of electric capacitance
ohm (Ω) = unit of electric resistance
siemens (S) = unit of electric conductance
weber (Wb) = unit of magnetic flux
tesla (T) = unit of magnetic flux density
henry (H) = unit of inductance
degree Celsius (°C) = unit of Celsius temperature
lumen (lm) = unit of luminous flux
lux (lx) = unit of illuminance
becquerel (Bq) = unit of activity (of a radionuclide)
gray (Gy) = unit of absorbed dose, specific energy imparted, kerma, absorbed dose index
sievert (Sv) = unit of dose equivalent, dose equivalent index
radian (rad) = unit of plane angle
steradian (sr) = unit of solid angle

Other derived units are expressed in terms of base units.

Some of the more commonly used derived units are the following:

Unit of area = square metre (m^2)
Unit of volume = cubic metre (m^3)
Unit of velocity = metre per second ($m\ s^{-1}$)
Unit of acceleration = metre per second squared ($m\ s^{-2}$)
Unit of density = kilogram per cubic metre ($kg\ m^{-3}$)
Unit of momentum = kilogram metre per second ($kg\ m\ s^{-1}$)
Unit of magnetic field strength = ampere per metre ($A\ m^{-1}$)
Unit of surface tension = newton per metre ($N\ m^{-1}$)
Unit of dynamic viscosity = pascal second (Pa s)
Unit of heat capacity = joule per kelvin ($J\ K^{-1}$)
Unit of specific heat capacity = joule per kilogram kelvin ($J\ kg^{-1}\ K^{-1}$)
Unit of heat flux density, irradiance = watt per square metre ($W\ m^{-2}$)
Unit of thermal conductivity = watt per metre kelvin ($W\ m^{-1}\ K^{-1}$)
Unit of electric field strength = volt per metre ($V\ m^{-1}$)
Unit of luminance = candela per square metre ($cd\ m^{-2}$)

SI PREFIXES

Decimal multiples and submultiples of the SI units are indicated by SI prefixes. These are as follows:

multiples	*submultiples*
yotta (Y) $\times 10^{24}$	deci (d) $\times 10^{-1}$
zetta (Z) $\times 10^{21}$	centi (c) $\times 10^{-2}$
exa (E) $\times 10^{18}$	milli (m) $\times 10^{-3}$
peta (P) $\times 10^{15}$	micro (μ) $\times 10^{-6}$
tera (T) $\times 10^{12}$	nano (n) $\times 10^{-9}$
giga (G) $\times 10^{9}$	pico (p) $\times 10^{-12}$
mega (M) $\times 10^{6}$	femto (f) $\times 10^{-15}$
kilo (k) $\times 10^{3}$	atto (a) $\times 10^{-18}$
hecto (h) $\times 10^{2}$	zepto (z) $\times 10^{-21}$
deca (da) $\times 10$	yocto (y) $\times 10^{-24}$

METRIC UNITS

The metric primary standards are the metre as the unit of measurement of length, and the kilogram as the unit of measurement of mass. Other units of measurement are defined by reference to the primary standards.

MEASUREMENT OF LENGTH

Kilometre (km) = 1000 metres
Metre (m) is the length of the path travelled by light in vacuum during a time interval of 1/299 792 458 of a second
Decimetre (dm) = 1/10 metre
Centimetre (cm) = 1/100 metre
Millimetre (mm) = 1/1000 metre

MEASUREMENT OF AREA

Hectare (ha) = 100 ares
Decare = 10 ares
Are (a) = 100 square metres
Square metre = a superficial area equal to that of a square each side of which measures one metre
Square decimetre = 1/100 square metre

Square centimetre = 1/100 square decimetre
Square millimetre = 1/100 square centimetre

MEASUREMENT OF VOLUME
Cubic metre (m^3) = a volume equal to that of a cube each
    edge of which measures one metre
Cubic decimetre = 1/1000 cubic metre
Cubic centimetre (cc) = 1/1000 cubic decimetre
Hectolitre = 100 litres
Litre = a cubic decimetre
Decilitre = 1/10 litre
Centilitre = 1/100 litre
Millilitre = 1/1000 litre

MEASUREMENT OF CAPACITY
Hectolitre (hl) = 100 litres
Litre (l or L) = a cubic decimetre
Decilitre (dl) = 1/10 litre
Centilitre (cl) = 1/100 litre
Millilitre (ml) = 1/1000 litre

MEASUREMENT OF MASS OR WEIGHT
Tonne (t) = 1000 kilograms
Kilogram (kg) is equal to the mass of the international
    prototype of the kilogram
Hectogram (hg) = 1/10 kilogram
Gram (g) = 1/1000 kilogram
*Carat (metric) = 1/5 gram
Milligram (mg) = 1/1000 gram

* Used only for transactions in precious stones or pearls

METRICATION IN THE UK
The European Council Directive 80/181/EEC, as
amended by Council Directive 89/617/EEC, relates to
the use of units of measurement for economic, public
health, public safety or administrative purposes in the
member states of the European Union. The provisions of
the directives were incorporated into British law by the
Weights and Measures Act 1985 (Metrication)
(Amendment) Order 1994 and the Units of Measurement
Regulations 1994; these instruments amended the
Weights and Measures Act 1985. Parallel statutory rules
amending Northern Ireland weights and measures
legislation were made in May 1995.

The general effect of the 1994 and 1995 legislation is to
end the use of imperial units of measurement for trade,
replacing them with metric units. Imperial units can,
however, be used in addition to metric units, as
supplementary indications.

IMPERIAL UNITS

The imperial primary standards are the yard as the unit of
measurement of length and the pound as the unit of
measurement of mass. Other units of measurement are
defined by reference to the primary standards. Most of
these units are no longer authorised for use in trade in the
UK – see below.

MEASUREMENT OF LENGTH
Mile = 1760 yards
Furlong = 220 yards
Chain = 22 yards
Yard (yd) = 0.9144 metre
Foot (ft) = 1/3 yard
Inch (in) = 1/36 yard

MEASUREMENT OF AREA
Square mile = 640 acres
Acre = 4840 square yards
Rood = 1210 square yards
Square yard (sq. yd) = a superficial area equal to that of a
    square each side of which measures one yard
Square foot (sq. ft) = 1/9 square yard
Square inch (sq. in) = 1/144 square foot

MEASUREMENT OF VOLUME
Cubic yard = a volume equal to that of a cube each edge of
    which measures one yard
Cubic foot = 1/27 cubic yard
Cubic inch = 1/1728 cubic foot

MEASUREMENT OF CAPACITY
Bushel = 8 gallons
Peck = 2 gallons
Gallon (gal) = 4.54609 cubic decimetres
Quart (qt) = 1/4 gallon
*Pint (pt) = 1/2 quart
Gill = 1/4 pint
*Fluid ounce (fl oz) = 1/20 pint
Fluid drachm = 1/8 fluid ounce
Minim (min) = 1/60 fluid drachm

MEASUREMENT OF MASS OR WEIGHT
Ton = 2240 pounds
Hundredweight (cwt) = 112 pounds
Cental = 100 pounds
Quarter = 28 pounds
Stone = 14 pounds
*Pound (lb) = 0.453 592 37 kilogram
*Ounce (oz) = 1/16 pound
*†Ounce troy (oz tr) = 12/175 pound
Dram (dr) = 1/16 ounce
Grain (gr) = 1/7000 pound
Pennyweight (dwt) = 24 grains
Ounce apothecaries' = 480 grains
Drachm (ʒ1) = 1/8 ounce apothecaries'
Scruple (ɜ1) = 1/3 drachm

* Units of measurement still authorised for use for trade in the
UK

† Used only for transactions in gold, silver or other precious
metals, and articles made therefrom

PHASING-OUT OF IMPERIAL UNITS IN THE UK
Since 1965 the United Kingdom has been adopting
metric weights and measures in response to the adoption
of metric units as the international system of
measurement. Since 1 January 2000, goods sold loose by
weight (mainly fresh foods) are required to be sold in
grams and kilograms, and fathoms (for marine
navigation), fluid ounces and pints (for beer, cider, water,
lemonade and fruit juice), and therms (for gas supply) are
unauthorised units of measurement. Retailers can
continue to display the price per imperial unit alongside
the price per metric unit. Consumers can continue to
express in ounces and pounds the quantity they wish to
buy. Retailers will weigh out the equivalent quantity in
grams and kilograms. The Weights and Measures Units of
Measurement Regulations 1995 (Statutory Instrument
1995 No. 1804) require that metric units should be used
for all economic, public health, public safety and
administrative purposes.

Units of measurement authorised for use in specialised fields are:

Unit	Field of application
Inch	
Foot	Road traffic signs, distance and
Yard	speed measurement
Mile	
Pint	Dispense of draught beer or cider in returnable containers
Acre	Land registration
Troy ounce	Transactions in precious metals

MEASUREMENT OF ELECTRICITY

Units of measurement of electricity are defined by the Weights and Measures Act 1985 as follows:

ampere (A) = that constant current which, if maintained in two straight parallel conductors of infinite length, of negligible circular cross-section and placed 1 metre apart in vacuum, would produce between these conductors a force equal to 2 x 10^{-7} newton per metre of length

ohm (Ω) = the electric resistance between two points of a conductor when a constant potential difference of 1 volt, applied between the two points, produces in the conductor a current of 1 ampere, the conductor not being the seat of any electromotive force

volt (V) = the difference of electric potential between two points of a conducting wire carrying a constant current of 1 ampere when the power dissipated between these points is equal to 1 watt

watt (W) = the power which in one second gives rise to energy of 1 joule

kilowatt (kW) = 1000 watts

megawatt (MW) = one million watts

WATER AND LIQUOR MEASURES

1 cubic foot = 62.32 lb
1 gallon = 10 lb
1 cubic cm = 1 gram
1000 cubic cm = 1 litre; 1 kilogram
1 cubic metre = 1000 litres; 1000 kg; 1 tonne
An inch of rain on the surface of an acre (43560 sq. ft) = 3630 cubic ft = 100.992 tons
Cisterns: A cistern 4 × 2½ feet and 3 feet deep will hold brimful 186.963 gallons, weighing 1869.63 lb in addition to its own weight

WATER FOR SHIPS
Kilderkin = 18 gallons
Barrel = 36 gallons
Puncheon = 72 gallons
Butt = 110 gallons
Tun = 210 gallons

BOTTLES OF WINE
Traditional equivalents in standard champagne bottles:
Magnum = 2 bottles
Jeroboam = 4 bottles
Rehoboam = 6 bottles
Methuselah = 8 bottles
Salmanazar = 12 bottles
Balthazar = 16 bottles
Nebuchadnezzar = 20 bottles

A quarter of a bottle is known as a *nip*
An eighth of a bottle is known as a *baby*

ANGULAR AND CIRCULAR MEASURES

60 seconds (") = 1 minute (')
60 minutes = 1 degree (°)
90 degrees = 1 right angle or quadrant
Diameter of circle × 3.1416 = circumference
Diameter squared × 0.7854 = area of circle
Diameter squared × 3.1416 = surface of sphere
Diameter cubed × 0.523 = solidity of sphere
One degree of circumference × 57.3 = radius*
Diameter of cylinder × 3.1416; product by length or height, gives the surface
Diameter squared × 0.7854; product by length or height, gives solid content

*Or, one radian (the angle subtended at the centre of a circle by an arc of the circumference equal in length to the radius) = 57.3 degrees

MILLION, BILLION, ETC.

Value in the UK

Million	thousand × thousand	10^6
*Billion	million × million	10^{12}
Trillion	million × billion	10^{18}
Quadrillion	million × trillion	10^{24}

Value in the USA

Million	thousand × thousand	10^6
*Billion	thousand × million	10^9
Trillion	million × million	10^{12}
Quadrillion	million × billion US	10^{15}

* The US usage of billion (i.e. 10^9) is increasingly common, and is now universally used by statisticians

NAUTICAL MEASURES

DISTANCE
Distance at sea is measured in nautical miles. The British standard nautical mile was 6080 feet but this measure has been obsolete since 1970 when the international nautical mile of 1852 metres was adopted by the Hydrographic Department of the Ministry of Defence. The cable (600 feet or 100 fathoms) was a measure approximately one-tenth of a nautical mile. Such distances are now expressed in decimal parts of a sea mile or in metres.

Soundings at sea were recorded in fathoms (6 feet). Depths are now expressed in metres on Admiralty charts.

SPEED
Speed is measured in nautical miles per hour, called knots. A ship moving at the rate of 30 nautical miles per hour is said to be doing 30 knots.

Knots	m.p.h.	knots	m.p.h.
1	1.1515	9	10.3636
2	2.3030	10	11.5151
3	3.4545	15	17.2727
4	4.6060	20	23.0303
5	5.7575	25	28.7878
6	6.9090	30	34.5454
7	8.0606	35	40.3030
8	9.2121	40	46.0606

TONNAGE

Under the Merchant Shipping Act 1854, the tonnage of UK-registered vessels was measured in tons of 100 cubic feet. The need for a universal method of measurement led to the adoption of the International Convention on Tonnage Measurements of Ships 1969, which measures, in cubic metres, all the internal spaces of a vessel for the gross tonnage and those of the cargo compartments for the net tonnage. The convention has applied since July 1982 to new ships, ships which needed to be remeasured because of substantial alterations, and ships whose owners requested remeasurement. On 18 July 1994 the convention became mandatory.

DISTANCE OF THE HORIZON

The limit of distance to which one can see varies with the height of the spectator. The greatest distance at which an object on the surface of the sea, or of a level plain, can be seen by a person whose eyes are at a height of five feet from the same level is nearly three miles. At a height of 20 feet the range is increased to nearly six miles, and an approximate rule for finding the range of vision for small heights is to increase the square root of the number of feet that the eye is above the level surface by a third of itself. The result is the distance of the horizon in miles, but is slightly in excess of that in the table below, which is computed by a more precise formula. The table may be used conversely to show the distance of an object of given height that is just visible from a point on the surface of the earth or sea. Refraction is taken into account both in the approximate rule and in the table.

Height in feet	Range in miles
5	2.9
20	5.9
50	9.3
100	13.2
500	29.5
1,000	41.6
2,000	58.9
3,000	72.1
4,000	83.3
5,000	93.1
20,000	186.2

TEMPERATURE SCALES

The SI (International System) unit of temperature is the kelvin, which is defined as the fraction $1/273.16$ of the temperature of the triple point of water (i.e. where ice, water and water vapour are in equilibrium). The zero of the Kelvin scale is the absolute zero of temperature. The freezing point of water is 273.15 K and the boiling point (as adopted in the International Temperature Scale of 1990) is 373.124 K.

The Celsius scale (formerly centigrade) is defined by subtracting 273.15 from the Kelvin temperature. The Fahrenheit scale is related to the Celsius scale by the relationships:

temperature $°F = (\text{temperature } °C \times 1.8) + 32$
temperature $°C = (\text{temperature } °F - 32) \div 1.8$

It follows from these definitions that the freezing point of water is 0°C and 32°F. The boiling point is 99.974°C and 211.953°F.

The temperature of the human body varies from person to person and in the same person can be affected by a variety of factors. In most people body temperature varies between 36.5°C and 37.2°C (97.7–98.9°F).

Conversion between scales

°C	°F	°C	°F	°C	°F
100	212	60	140	20	68
99	210.2	59	138.2	19	66.2
98	208.4	58	136.4	18	64.4
97	206.6	57	134.6	17	62.6
96	204.8	56	132.8	16	60.8
95	203	55	131	15	59
94	201.2	54	129.2	14	57.2
93	199.4	53	127.4	13	55.4
92	197.6	52	125.6	12	53.6
91	195.8	51	123.8	11	51.8
90	194	50	122	10	50
89	192.2	49	120.2	9	48.2
88	190.4	48	118.4	8	46.4
87	188.6	47	116.6	7	44.6
86	186.8	46	114.8	6	42.8
85	185	45	113	5	41
84	183.2	44	111.2	4	39.2
83	181.4	43	109.4	3	37.4
82	179.6	42	107.6	2	35.6
81	177.8	41	105.8	1	33.8
80	176	40	104	Zero	32
79	174.2	39	102.2	−1	30.2
78	172.4	38	100.4	−2	28.4
77	170.6	37	98.6	−3	26.6
76	168.8	36	96.8	−4	24.8
75	167	35	95	−5	23
74	165.2	34	93.2	−6	21.2
73	163.4	33	91.4	−7	19.4
72	161.6	32	89.6	−8	17.6
71	159.8	31	87.8	−9	15.8
70	158	30	86	−10	14
69	156.2	29	84.2	−11	12.2
68	154.4	28	82.4	−12	10.4
67	152.6	27	80.6	−13	8.6
66	150.8	26	78.8	−14	6.8
65	149	25	77	−15	5
64	147.2	24	75.2	−16	3.2
63	145.4	23	73.4	−17	1.4
62	143.6	22	71.6	−18	0.4
61	141.8	21	69.8	−19	−2.2

PAPER MEASURES

Printing Paper		*Writing Paper*	
516 sheets	= 1 ream	480 sheets	= 1 ream
2 reams	= 1 bundle	20 quires	= 1 ream
5 bundles	= 1 bale	24 sheets	= 1 quire

INTERNATIONAL PAPER SIZES

The basis of the international series of paper sizes is a rectangle having an area of one square metre, the sides of which are in the proportion of $1:\sqrt{2}$. The proportions $1:\sqrt{2}$ have a geometrical relationship, the side and diagonal of any square being in this proportion. The effect of this arrangement is that if the area of the sheet of paper is doubled or halved, the shorter side and the longer side of the new sheet are still in the same proportion $1:\sqrt{2}$. This feature is useful where photographic enlargement or reduction is used, as the proportions remain the same.

Description of the A series is by capital A followed by a

figure. The basic size has the description A0 and the higher the figure following the letter, the greater is the number of sub-divisions and therefore the smaller the sheet. Half A0 is A1 and half A1 is A2. Where larger dimensions are required the A is preceded by a figure. Thus 2A means twice the size A0; 4A is four times the size of A0.

SUBSIDIARY SERIES

B sizes are sizes intermediate between any two adjacent sizes of the A series. There is a series of C sizes which is used much less. A is for magazines and books, B for posters, wall charts and other large items, C for envelopes particularly where it is necessary for an envelope (in C series) to fit into another envelope. The size recommended for business correspondence is A4.

Long sizes (DL) are obtainable by dividing any appropriate sizes from the two series above into three, four or eight equal parts parallel with the shorter side in such a manner that the proportion of $1 : \sqrt{2}$ is not maintained, the ratio between the longer and the shorter sides being greater than $\sqrt{2} : 1$. In practice long sizes should be produced from the A series only.

It is an essential feature of these series that the dimensions are of the trimmed or finished size.

A SERIES

	mm		mm
A0	841 × 1189	A6	105 × 148
A1	594 × 841	A7	74 × 105
A2	420 × 594	A8	52 × 74
A3	297 × 420	A9	37 × 52
A4	210 × 297	A10	26 × 37
A5	148 × 210		

B SERIES

	mm		mm
B0	1000 × 1414	B6	125 × 176
B1	707 × 1000	B7	88 × 125
B2	500 × 707	B8	62 × 88
B3	353 × 500	B9	44 × 62
B4	250 × 353	B10	31 × 44
B5	176 × 250		

C SERIES | | **DL** | |
	mm		mm
C4	324 × 229	DL	110 × 220
C5	229 × 162		
C6	114 × 162		

CONVERSION TABLES FOR WEIGHTS AND MEASURES

Bold figures equal units of either of the columns beside them; thus: 1 cm = 0.394 inches and 1 inch = 2.540 cm

LENGTH — AREA — VOLUME — WEIGHT (MASS)

Centimetres		Inches	Square cm		Square in	Cubic cm		Cubic in	Kilograms		Pounds
2.540	1	0.394	6.452	1	0.155	16.387	1	0.061	0.454	1	2.205
5.080	2	0.787	12.903	2	0.310	32.774	2	0.122	0.907	2	4.409
7.620	3	1.181	19.355	3	0.465	49.161	3	0.183	1.361	3	6.614
10.160	4	1.575	25.806	4	0.620	65.548	4	0.244	1.814	4	8.819
12.700	5	1.969	32.258	5	0.775	81.936	5	0.305	2.268	5	11.023
15.240	6	2.362	38.710	6	0.930	98.323	6	0.366	2.722	6	13.228
17.780	7	2.756	45.161	7	1.085	114.710	7	0.427	3.175	7	15.432
20.320	8	3.150	51.613	8	1.240	131.097	8	0.488	3.629	8	17.637
22.860	9	3.543	58.064	9	1.395	147.484	9	0.549	4.082	9	19.842
25.400	10	3.937	64.516	10	1.550	163.871	10	0.610	4.536	10	22.046
50.800	20	7.874	129.032	20	3.100	327.742	20	1.220	9.072	20	44.092
76.200	30	11.811	193.548	30	4.650	491.613	30	1.831	13.608	30	66.139
101.600	40	15.748	258.064	40	6.200	655.484	40	2.441	18.144	40	88.185
127.000	50	19.685	322.580	50	7.750	819.355	50	3.051	22.680	50	110.231
152.400	60	23.622	387.096	60	9.300	983.226	60	3.661	27.216	60	132.277
177.800	70	27.559	451.612	70	10.850	1147.097	70	4.272	31.752	70	154.324
203.200	80	31.496	516.128	80	12.400	1310.968	80	4.882	36.287	80	176.370
228.600	90	35.433	580.644	90	13.950	1474.839	90	5.492	40.823	90	198.416
254.000	100	39.370	645.160	100	15.500	1638.710	100	6.102	45.359	100	220.464

Metres		Yards	Square m		Square yd	Cubic m		Cubic yd	Metric tonnes		Tons (UK)
0.914	1	1.094	0.836	1	1.196	0.765	1	1.308	1.016	1	0.984
1.829	2	2.187	1.672	2	2.392	1.529	2	2.616	2.032	2	1.968
2.743	3	3.281	2.508	3	3.588	2.294	3	3.924	3.048	3	2.953
3.658	4	4.374	3.345	4	4.784	3.058	4	5.232	4.064	4	3.937
4.572	5	5.468	4.181	5	5.980	3.823	5	6.540	5.080	5	4.921
5.486	6	6.562	5.017	6	7.176	4.587	6	7.848	6.096	6	5.905
6.401	7	7.655	5.853	7	8.372	5.352	7	9.156	7.112	7	6.889
7.315	8	8.749	6.689	8	9.568	6.116	8	10.464	8.128	8	7.874
8.230	9	9.843	7.525	9	10.764	6.881	9	11.772	9.144	9	8.858
9.144	10	10.936	8.361	10	11.960	7.646	10	13.080	10.161	10	9.842
18.288	20	21.872	16.723	20	23.920	15.291	20	26.159	20.321	20	19.684
27.432	30	32.808	25.084	30	35.880	22.937	30	39.239	30.481	30	29.526
36.576	40	43.745	33.445	40	47.840	30.582	40	52.318	40.642	40	39.368
45.720	50	54.681	41.806	50	59.799	38.228	50	65.398	50.802	50	49.210
54.864	60	65.617	50.168	60	71.759	45.873	60	78.477	60.963	60	59.052
64.008	70	76.553	58.529	70	83.719	53.519	70	91.557	71.123	70	68.894
73.152	80	87.489	66.890	80	95.679	61.164	80	104.636	81.284	80	78.737
82.296	90	98.425	75.251	90	107.639	68.810	90	117.716	91.444	90	88.579
91.440	100	109.361	83.613	100	119.599	76.455	100	130.795	101.605	100	98.421

Kilometres		Miles	Hectares		Acres	Litres		Gallons	Metric tonnes		Tons (US)
1.609	1	0.621	0.405	1	2.471	4.546	1	0.220	0.907	1	1.102
3.219	2	1.243	0.809	2	4.942	9.092	2	0.440	1.814	2	2.205
4.828	3	1.864	1.214	3	7.413	13.638	3	0.660	2.722	3	3.305
6.437	4	2.485	1.619	4	9.844	18.184	4	0.880	3.629	4	4.409
8.047	5	3.107	2.023	5	12.355	22.730	5	1.100	4.536	5	5.521
9.656	6	3.728	2.428	6	14.826	27.276	6	1.320	5.443	6	6.614
11.265	7	4.350	2.833	7	17.297	31.822	7	1.540	6.350	7	7.716
12.875	8	4.971	3.327	8	19.769	36.368	8	1.760	7.257	8	8.818
14.484	9	5.592	3.642	9	22.240	40.914	9	1.980	8.165	9	9.921
16.093	10	6.214	4.047	10	24.711	45.460	10	2.200	9.072	10	11.023
32.187	20	12.427	8.094	20	49.421	90.919	20	4.400	18.144	20	22.046
48.280	30	18.641	12.140	30	74.132	136.379	30	6.599	27.216	30	33.069
64.374	40	24.855	16.187	40	98.842	181.839	40	8.799	36.287	40	44.092
80.467	50	31.069	20.234	50	123.555	227.298	50	10.999	45.359	50	55.116
96.561	60	37.282	24.281	60	148.263	272.758	60	13.199	54.431	60	66.139
112.654	70	43.496	28.328	70	172.974	318.217	70	15.398	63.503	70	77.162
128.748	80	49.710	32.375	80	197.684	363.677	80	17.598	72.575	80	88.185
144.841	90	55.923	36.422	90	222.395	409.137	90	19.798	81.647	90	99.208
160.934	100	62.137	40.469	100	247.105	454.596	100	21.998	90.719	100	110.231

Key:

6 — atomic number
Carbon — name of element
C — chemical number
12.01 — atomic mass

Main Periodic Table

Group	IA (Alkali metals)	IIA (Alkaline earth metals)	Transition metals →					VIII			IB	IIB	IIIA	IVA	VA	VIA	VIIA	Noble gases
			III B	IV B	V B	VI B	VII B											
1	1 Hydrogen **H** 1.01																	2 Helium **He** 4.00
2	3 Lithium **Li** 6.94	4 Beryllium **Be** 9.01											5 Boron **B** 10.81	6 Carbon **C** 12.01	7 Nitrogen **N** 14.01	8 Oxygen **O** 16.00	9 Fluorine **F** 19.00	10 Neon **Ne** 20.18
3	11 Sodium **Na** 22.99	12 Magnesium **Mg** 24.31											13 Aluminium **Al** 26.98	14 Silicon **Si** 28.09	15 Phosphorus **P** 30.97	16 Sulphur **S** 32.07	17 Chlorine **Cl** 35.45	18 Argon **Ar** 39.95
4	19 Potassium **K** 39.10	20 Calcium **Ca** 40.08	21 Scandium **Sc** 44.96	22 Titanium **Ti** 47.88	23 Vanadium **V** 50.94	24 Chromium **Cr** 52.00	25 Manganese **Mn** 54.95	26 Iron **Fe** 55.85	27 Cobalt **Co** 58.93	28 Nickel **Ni** 58.70	29 Copper **Cu** 63.55	30 Zinc **Zn** 65.39	31 Gallium **Ga** 69.72	32 Germanium **Ge** 72.61	33 Arsenic **As** 74.92	34 Selenium **Se** 78.96	35 Bromine **Br** 79.904	36 Krypton **Kr** 83.80
5	37 Rubidium **Rb** 85.47	38 Strontium **Sr** 87.62	39 Yttrium **Y** 88.91	40 Zirconium **Zr** 91.22	41 Niobium **Nb** 92.91	42 Molybdenum **Mo** 95.94	43 Technetium **Tc** 97.91	44 Ruthenium **Ru** 101.07	45 Rhodium **Rh** 102.91	46 Palladium **Pd** 106.4	47 Silver **Ag** 107.87	48 Cadmium **Cd** 112.41	49 Indium **In** 114.82	50 Tin **Sn** 118.71	51 Antimony **Sb** 121.74	52 Tellurium **Te** 127.60	53 Iodine **I** 126.9045	54 Xenon **Xe** 131.29
6	55 Caesium **Cs** 132.91	56 Barium **Ba** 137.33	57 Lanthanum **La** 138.91 (Lanthanide series, see below)	72 Hafnium **Hf** 178.49	73 Tantalum **Ta** 180.94	74 Tungsten **W** 183.85	75 Rhenium **Re** 186.21	76 Osmium **Os** 190.23	77 Iridium **Ir** 192.22	78 Platinum **Pt** 195.08	79 Gold **Au** 196.97	80 Mercury **Hg** 200.59	81 Thallium **Tl** 204.38	82 Lead **Pb** 207.2	83 Bismuth **Bi** 208.98	84 Polonium **Po** 209	85 Astatine **At** 210	86 Radon **Rn** 222.02
7	87 Francium **Fr** 223.02	88 Radium **Ra** 226.03	89 Actinium **Ac** 227.03 (Actinide series, see below)	104 Rutherfordium **Rf** 261.12	105 Dubnium **Db** 262.11	106 Seaborgium **Sg** 236.12	107 Bohrium **Bh** 262	108 Hassium **Hs** 265	109 Meitnerium **Mt** 266	110 Darmstadtium **Ds** 269	111 Unununium **Uuu** 272	112 Ununbium **Uub** 277	114 Ununquadium **Uuq** 289					

Non-metals are to the upper right of the stepped line; metals to the left.

Rare earth elements — Lanthanide series

57 Lanthanum **La** 138.91	58 Cerium **Ce** 140.12	59 Praseodymium **Pr** 140.91	60 Neodymium **Nd** 144.24	61 Promethium **Pm** 144.91	62 Samarium **Sm** 150.36	63 Europium **Eu** 151.96	64 Gadolinium **Gd** 157.25	65 Terbium **Tb** 158.93	66 Dysprosium **Dy** 162.50	67 Holmium **Ho** 164.93	68 Erbium **Er** 167.26	69 Thulium **Tm** 168.93	70 Ytterbium **Yb** 173.04	71 Lutetium **Lu** 174.97

Actinide series

89 Actinium **Ac** 227.03	90 Thorium **Th** 232.04	91 Protactinium **Pa** 231.04	92 Uranium **U** 238.03	93 Neptunium **Np** 237.05	94 Plutonium **Pu** 244.06	95 Americium **Am** 243.06	96 Curium **Cm** 247.07	97 Berkelium **Bk** 247	98 Californium **Cf** 251.08	99 Einsteinium **Es** 252.08	100 Fermium **Fm** 257.10	101 Mendelevium **Md** 258.10	102 Nobelium **No** 259.10	103 Lawrencium **Lr** 260.11

The Periodic Table arranges the elements into horizontal rows (periods) and vertical columns (groups) according to their atomic number. The elements in a group all have similar properties; across each period, atoms are electropositive (form positive ions) to the left and electronegative to the right. The earliest version of the periodic table was devised in 1869 by Dmitriy Mendeleyev, who predicted the existence of several elements from gaps in the table.

ABBREVIATIONS AND ACRONYMS

A

AA	Alcoholics Anonymous
	Automobile Association
AAA	Amateur Athletic Association
ABA	Amateur Boxing Association
abbr(ev)	abbreviation
ABM	anti-ballistic missile
abr	abridged
ac	alternating current
a/c	account
AC	*(ante Christum)* before Christ
	Companion, Order of Australia
ACAS	Advisory, Conciliation and Arbitration Service
ACT	Australian Capital Territory
AD	*(anno Domini)* in the year of our Lord
ADB	Asian Development Bank
ADC	Aide-de-Camp
ADC (P)	Personal ADC to The Queen
adj	adjective
Adj	Adjutant
ad lib	*(ad libitum)* at pleasure
Adm	Admiral
adv	adverb
AE	Air Efficiency Award
AEM	Air Efficiency Medal
AFC	Air Force Cross
AFM	Air Force Medal
AG	Adjutant-General
	Attorney-General
AGM	air-to-ground missile
	annual general meeting
AH	*(anno Hegirae)* in the year of the Hegira
AI	artificial intelligence
Aids	acquired immune deficiency syndrome
AIM	Alternative Investment Market
alt	altitude
a.m.	*(ante meridiem)* before noon
AM	*(anno mundi)* in the year of the world
	amplitude modulation
amp	ampere
	amplifier
AMU	Arab Maghreb Union
ANC	African National Congress
anon	anonymous
Anzac	Australian and New Zealand Army Corps
AO	Air Officer
	Officer, Order of Australia
AOC	Air Officer Commanding
AONB	Area of Outstanding Natural Beauty
APEC	Asia Pacific Economic Co-operation
APR	annual percentage rate
AS	Anglo-Saxon

ASA	Advertising Standards Authority
	Amateur Swimming Association
asap	as soon as possible
ASEAN	Association of South East Asian Nations
ASH	Action on Smoking and Health
ASLEF	Associated Society of Locomotive Engineers and Firemen
ASLIB	Association for Information Management
ATC	Air Training Corps
AUC	*(ab urbe condita)* in the year from the foundation of Rome
	(anno urbis conditae) in the year of the founding of the city
AUT	Association of University Teachers
AV	audio-visual
	Authorised Version *(of Bible)*
AVR	Army Volunteer Reserve
AWOL	absent without (official) leave

B

b	born
	bowled
BA	Bachelor of Arts
BAA	British Airports Authority
	British Astronomical Association
BAF	British Athletics Federation
BAFTA	British Academy of Film and Television Arts
BAS	Bachelor in Agricultural Science
	British Antarctic Survey
BBA	British Bankers' Association
BBC	British Broadcasting Corporation
BBSRC	Biotechnology and Biological Sciences Research Council
BC	before Christ
	Borough Council
	British Columbia
BCH (D)	Bachelor of (Dental) Surgery
BCL	Bachelor of Civil Law
BCOM	Bachelor of Commerce
BD	Bachelor of Divinity
BDA	British Dental Association
BDS	Bachelor of Dental Surgery
BED	Bachelor of Education
BEM	British Empire Medal
BENG	Bachelor of Engineering

BFI	British Film Institute
BFPO	British Forces Post Office
BLIT	Bachelor of Literature
BLITT	Bachelor of Letters
BM	Bachelor of Medicine
	British Museum
BMA	British Medical Association
BMI	body mass index
BMUS	Bachelor of Music
BNFL	British Nuclear Fuels
BOTB	British Overseas Trade Board
Bp	Bishop
BPHARM	Bachelor of Pharmacy
BPHIL	Bachelor of Philosophy
bpm	beats per minute
Br(it)	Britain
	British
Brig	Brigadier
BSC	Bachelor of Science
BSE	bovine spongiform encephalopathy
BSI	British Standards Institution
BST	British Summer Time
Bt	Baronet
BTEC	Business and Technology Education Council
Btu	British thermal unit
BVMS	Bachelor of Veterinary Medicine and Surgery

C

c	*(circa)* about
C	Celsius
	centigrade
CA	chartered accountant *(Scotland)*
CAA	Civil Aviation Authority
CAB	Citizens' Advice Bureau
CAD	computer-aided design
CADW	Ancient Monuments Board for Wales
Cantab	(of) Cambridge
Cantuar:	of Canterbury *(Archbishop)*
CAP	Common Agricultural Policy
Capt	Captain
Caricom	Caribbean Community and Common Market
Carliol:	of Carlisle *(Bishop)*
CB	Companion, Order of the Bath
CBE	Commander, Order of the British Empire
CBI	Confederation of British Industry
CBSS	Council of the Baltic Sea States
CC	Chamber of Commerce
	Companion, Order of Canada
	City Council
	County Council
	County Court

CCC	County Cricket Club	C of E	Church of England	DL	Deputy Lieutenant
CCF	Combined Cadet Force	COI	Central Office of	DLIT	Doctor of Literature
CCTA	City Colleges for		Information	DLITT	Doctor of Letters
	Technology and the Arts	Col	Colonel	DM	Deutsche Mark
CCHEM	chartered chemist	Con.	Conservative	DMUS	Doctor of Music
CD	Civil Defence	*cons.*	consecrated	DNA	deoxyribonucleic acid
	compact disc	Cpl	Corporal	DNB	*Dictionary of National*
	Corps Diplomatique	CPM	Colonial Police Medal		*Biography*
Cdr	Commander	CPRE	Council for the Protection	do	*(ditto)* the same
Cdre	Commodore		of Rural England	DoH	Department of Health
CDS	Chief of the Defence Staff	CPS	Crown Prosecution	DOS	disk operating system
CE	Common (or Christian)		Service	DPH or	Doctor of Philosophy
	Era	CPVE	Certificate of Pre-	DPHIL	
	civil engineer		Vocational Education	DPP	Director of Public
CENG	chartered engineer	CRE	Commission for Racial		Prosecutions
CERN	European Organisation for		Equality	Dr	Doctor
	Nuclear Research	CSA	Child Support Agency	DRC	Disability Rights
Cestr:	of Chester *(Bishop)*	CSI	Companion, Order of the		Commission
CET	Central European Time		Star of India	DSC	Distinguished Service
	Common External Tariff	CVO	Commander, Royal		Cross
cf	*(confer)* compare		Victorian Order		Doctor of Science
CF	Chaplain to the Forces			DSM	Distinguished Service
CFC	chlorofluorocarbon	**D**			Medal
CGC	Conspicuous Gallantry			DSO	Companion,
	Cross	d	*(denarius)* penny		Distinguished Service
CGEOL	chartered geologist	DBE	Dame Commander, Order		Order
CGI	computer generated		of the British Empire	DTI	Department of Trade and
	imagery	dc	direct current		Industry
CGM	Conspicuous Gallantry	DC	District Council	DTP	desk-top publishing
	Medal		District of Columbia	Dunelm:	of Durham *(Bishop)*
cgs	centimetre-gramme-	DCA	Department for	DV	*(Deo volente)* God willing
	second *(system)*		Constitutional Affairs	DVD	digital versatile disc
	Chief of General Staff	DCB	Dame Commander, Order	DVLA	Driver and Vehicle
CH	Companion of Honour		of the Bath		Licensing Agency
CHB/M	Bachelor/Master of	D CH	*(Doctor Chirurgiae)* Doctor	DWI	Drinking Water
	Surgery		of Surgery		Inspectorate
CI	Channel Islands	DCL	Doctor of Civil Law	DWP	Department for Work and
	The Imperial Order of the	DCM	Distinguished Conduct		Pensions
	Crown of India		Medal		
CIA	Central Intelligence	DCMG	Dame Commander, Order	**E**	
	Agency		of St Michael and St		
CICA	Conference on Interaction		George	E	east
	and Confidence Building	DCMS	Department for Culture,	Ebor:	of York *(Archbishop)*
	Measures in Asia		Media and Sport	EBRD	European Bank for
	Criminal Injuries	DCVO	Dame Commander, Royal		Reconstruction and
	Compensation Authority		Victorian Order		Development
CICAP	Criminal Injuries	DD	Doctor of Divinity	EC	European Community
	Compensation Appeals	DDS	Doctor of Dental Surgery	ECG	electrocardiogram
	Panel	DDT	dichlorodiphenyl	ECGD	Export Credits Guarantee
Cicestr:	of Chichester *(Bishop)*		trichloroethane		Department
CID	Criminal Investigation	del	*(delineavit)* he/she drew it	ECOWAS	Economic Community of
	Department	DEFRA	Department of the		West African States
CIE	Companion, Order of the		Environment, Food and	ECSC	European Coal and Steel
	Indian Empire		Rural Affairs		Community
cif	cost, insurance and freight	DFC	Distinguished Flying	ECU	European Currency Unit
C-in-C	Commander-in-Chief		Cross	ED	Efficiency Decoration
CIPFA	Chartered Institute of	DfES	Department for Education	EEC	European Economic
	Public Finance and		and Skills		Community
	Accountancy	DFID	Department for	EEG	electroencephalogram
CIS	Commonwealth of		International	EFA	European Fighter Aircraft
	Independent States		Development	EFTA	European Free Trade
CJD	Creutzfeld-Jakob disease	DFM	Distinguished Flying		Association
CLJ	Commander, Order of St		Medal	eg	*(exempli gratia)* for the sake
	Lazarus of Jerusalem	DfT	Department for Transport		of example
CM	*(Chirurgiae Magister)*	DG	*(Dei gratia)* by the grace of	EIB	European Investment
	Master of Surgery		God		Bank
CMG	Companion, Order of St		Director General	EMS	European Monetary
	Michael and St George	DHA	District Health Authority		System
CND	Campaign for Nuclear	DIP ED	Diploma in Education	EMU	European Monetary
	Disarmament	DIP HE	Diploma in Higher		Union
c/o	care of		Education	EOC	Equal Opportunities
CO	Commanding Officer	DJ	disc jockey		Commission

EPSRC   Engineering and Physical Sciences Research Council

ER   *(Elizabetha Regina)* Queen Elizabeth

ERM   exchange rate mechanism

ERNIE   electronic random number indicator equipment

ESA   European Space Agency

ESP   extra-sensory perception

ESRC   Economic and Social Research Council

ETA   *Euzkadi ta Askatasuna* (Basque separatist organisation)

et al   *(et alibi)* and elsewhere *(et alii)* and others

etc   *(et cetera)* and the other things/and so forth

et seq   *(et sequentia)* and the following

EU   European Union

Euratom   European Atomic Energy Community

Exon: of Exeter *(Bishop)*

F

ƒ   *(forte)* loud

F   Fahrenheit Fellow of

FA   Football Association

FANY   First Aid Nursing Yeomanry

FAO   Food and Agriculture Organisation *(UN)* for the attention of

FAQ   frequently asked questions

FBA   Fellow, British Academy

FBAA   Fellow, British Association of Accountants and Auditors

FBI   Federal Bureau of Investigation

FBU   Fire Brigades Union

FCO   Foreign and Commonwealth Office

FIMGT   Fellow, Institute of Management

FBS   Fellow, Botanical Society

FC   Football Club

FCA   Fellow, Institute of Chartered Accountants in England and Wales

FCCA   Fellow, Chartered Association of Certified Accountants

FCGI   Fellow, City and Guilds of London Institute

FCIA   Fellow, Corporation of Insurance Agents

FCIARB   Fellow, Chartered Institute of Arbitrators

FCIB   Fellow, Chartered Institute of Bankers Fellow, Corporation of Insurance Brokers

FCIBSE   Fellow, Chartered Institution of Building Services Engineers

FCII   Fellow, Chartered Insurance Institute

FCIPS   Fellow, Chartered Institute of Purchasing and Supply

FCIS   Fellow, Institute of Chartered Secretaries and Administrators

FCIT   Fellow, Chartered Institute of Transport

FCMA   Fellow, Chartered Institute of Management Accountants

FCO   Foreign and Commonwealth Office

FCP   Fellow, College of Preceptors

FD   *(Fidei Defensor)* Defender of the Faith

FE   further education

fec   *(fecit)* made this

ff   *(fecerunt)* made this (pl) folios following

ƒƒ   *(fortissimo)* very loud

FFA   Fellow, Faculty of Actuaries *(Scotland)* Fellow, Institute of Financial Accountants

FFAS   Fellow, Faculty of Architects and Surveyors

FFCM   Fellow, Faculty of Community Medicine

FFPHM   Fellow, Faculty of Public Health Medicine

FGS   Fellow, Geological Society

FHS   Fellow, Heraldry Society

FHSM   Fellow, Institute of Health Service Management

FIA   Fellow, Institute of Actuaries

FIBIOL   Fellow, Institute of Biology

FICE   Fellow, Institution of Civil Engineers

FICS   Fellow, Institution of Chartered Shipbrokers

FIEE   Fellow, Institution of Electrical Engineers

FIERE   Fellow, Institution of Electronic and Radio Engineers

FIFA   International Association Football Federation

FIM   Fellow, Institute of Metals

FIMM   Fellow, Institution of Mining and Metallurgy

FINSTF   Fellow, Institute of Fuel

FINSTP   Fellow, Institute of Physics

FIQS   Fellow, Institute of Quantity Surveyors

FIS   Fellow, Institute of Statisticians

FJI   Fellow, Institute of Journalists

FLA   Fellow, Library Association

FLS   Fellow, Linnean Society

FM   Field Marshal frequency modulation

fo   folio

FO   Flying Officer

fob   free on board

FPHS   Fellow, Philosophical Society

FRAD   Fellow, Royal Academy of Dancing

FRAES   Fellow, Royal Aeronautical Societ

FRAI   Fellow, Royal Anthropological Institute

FRAM   Fellow, Royal Academy of Music

FRAS   Fellow, Royal Asiatic Society Fellow, Royal Astronomical Society

FRBS   Fellow, Royal Botanic Society Fellow, Royal Society of British Sculptors

FRCA   Fellow, Royal College of Anaesthetists

FRCGP   Fellow, Royal College of General Practitioners

FRCM   Fellow, Royal College of Music

FRCO   Fellow, Royal College of Organists

FRCOG   Fellow, Royal College of Obstetricians and Gynaecologists

FRCP   Fellow, Royal College of Physicians, London

FRCPATH   Fellow, Royal College of Pathologists

FRCPE *or* FRCPEd   Fellow, Royal College of Physicians, Edinburgh

FRCPI   Fellow, Royal College of Physicians, Ireland

FRCPSYCH   Fellow, Royal College of Psychiatrists

FRCR   Fellow, Royal College of Radiologists

FRCS   Fellow, Royal College of Surgeons of England

FRCSE *or* FRCSED   Fellow, Royal College of Surgeons of Edinburgh

FRCSGLAS   Fellow, Royal College of Physicians and Surgeons of Glasgow

FRCSI   Fellow, Royal College of Surgeons in Ireland

FRCVS   Fellow, Royal College of Veterinary Surgeons

FRECONS   Fellow, Royal Economic Society

FRENG   Fellow, Royal Academy of Engineering

FRGS   Fellow, Royal Geographical Society

FRHISTS   Fellow, Royal Historical Society

FRHS   Fellow, Royal Horticultural Society

FRIBA   Fellow, Royal Institute of British Architects

FRICS   Fellow, Royal Institution of Chartered Surveyors

FRMETS   Fellow, Royal Meteorological Society

FRMS   Fellow, Royal Microscopical Society

FRNS   Fellow, Royal Numismatic Society

FRPHARMS	Fellow, Royal Pharmaceutical Society	GMB	General, Municipal, Boilermakers and Allied Trades Union	**I**
FRPS	Fellow, Royal Photographic Society	GMT	Greenwich Mean Time	I	Island
FRS	Fellow, Royal Society	GNI	gross national income	IAAS	Incorporated Association of Architects and Surveyors
FRSA	Fellow, Royal Society of Arts	GNP	gross national product		
		GNVQ	General National Vocational Qualification	IAEA	International Atomic Energy Agency
FRSC	Fellow, Royal Society of Chemistry	GOC	General Officer Commanding	IATA	International Air Transport Association
FRSE	Fellow, Royal Society of Edinburgh	GP	General Practitioner	ibid	*(ibidem)* in the same place
FRSH	Fellow, Royal Society of Health	Gp Capt	Group Captain	IBRD	International Bank for Reconstruction and Development
FRSL	Fellow, Royal Society of Literature	GSA	Girls' Schools Association		
		GST	Greenwich Sidereal Time	ICAO	International Civil Aviation Organisation
FRTPI	Fellow, Royal Town Planning Institute			ICBM	inter-continental ballistic missile
FSA	Fellow, Society of Antiquaries	**H**		ICFTU	International Confederation of Free Trade Unions
	Financial Services Authority	HAC	Honourable Artillery Company		
	Food Standards Agency	HB	His Beatitude	ICJ	International Court of Justice
FSS	Fellow, Royal Statistical Society	HBM	Her/His Britannic Majesty('s)	ICRC	International Committee of the Red Cross
FSVA	Fellow, Incorporated Society of Valuers and Auctioneers	HCF	highest common factor Honorary Chaplain to the Forces	id	*(idem)* the same
				IDA	International Development Association
FT	*Financial Times*	HE	Her/His Excellency		
FTI	Fellow, Textile Institute		higher education	IDD	International direct dialling
FTII	Fellow, Chartered Institute of Taxation		His Eminence	ie	*(id est)* that is
FZS	Fellow, Zoological Society	HGV	heavy goods vehicle	IEA	International Energy Agency
		HH	Her/His Highness Her/His Honour His Holiness	IFA	independent financial advisor
G		HIM	Her/His Imperial Majesty	IFAD	International Fund for Agricultural Development
GATT	General Agreement on Tariffs and Trade	HIV	human immunodeficiency virus	IFC	International Finance Corporation
GBE	Dame/Knight Grand Cross, Order of the British Empire	HJS	*(hic jacet sepultus)* here lies buried	ILO	International Labour Office/Organisation
GC	George Cross	HM	Her/His Majesty('s)	ILR	Independent Local Radio
GCB	Dame/Knight Grand Cross, Order of the Bath	HMAS	Her/His Majesty's Australian Ship	IMF	International Monetary Fund
GCC	Gulf Co-operation Council	HMC	Headmasters' Conference	IMO	International Maritime Organisation
GCHQ	Government Communications Headquarters	HMI	Her/His Majesty's Inspector	Inc	Incorporated
		HML	Her/His Majesty's Lieutenant	incog	*(incognito)* unknown, unrecognised
GCIE	Knight Grand Commander, Order of the Indian Empire	HMS	Her/His Majesty's Ship	INLA	Irish National Liberation Army
		HMSO	Her/His Majesty's Stationery Office		
GCLJ	Knight Grand Cross, Order of St Lazarus of Jerusalem	HNC	Higher National Certificate	in loc	*(in loco)* in its place
		HND	Higher National Diploma	Inmarsat	International Maritime Satellite Organisation
GCMG	Dame/Knight Grand Cross, Order of St Michael and St George	Hon	Honorary Honourable	INRI	*(Iesus Nazarenus Rex Iudaeorum)* Jesus of Nazareth, King of the Jews
		hp	horse power		
GCSE	General Certificate of Secondary Education	HP	hire purchase	inst	*(instant)* current month
GCSI	Knight Grand Commander, Order of the Star of India	HQ	Headquarters	Intelsat	International Telecommunications Satellite Organisation
		HR	human resources		
		HRH	Her/His Royal Highness	Interpol	International Criminal Police Organisation
GCVO	Dame/Knight Grand Cross, Royal Victorian Order	HRT	hormone replacement therapy	IOC	International Olympic Committee
		HSE	Health and Safety Executive	IoM	Isle of Man
GDP	gross domestic product		*(hic sepultus est)* here lies buried	IOU	I owe you
Gen	General			IoW	Isle of Wight
GHQ	General Headquarters	HSH	Her/His Serene Highness	IQ	intelligence quotient
GLA	Greater London Authority	HST	Hubble Space Telescope	IRA	Irish Republican Army
GM	George Medal genetically modified	HTML	hypertext mark-up language	IRC	International Red Cross
		HTTP	hypertext transfer protocol		
		HWM	high water mark		

Is	Islands	LD	Liberal Democrat	MCC	Marylebone Cricket Club
ISA	individual savings account	LDS	Licentiate in Dental	MCH(D)	Master of (Dental) Surgery
ISBN	International Standard		Surgery	MD	Managing Director
	Book Number	LEA	Local Education Authority		Doctor of Medicine
ISO	Imperial Service Order	LHD	*(Literarum Humaniorum*	MDS	Master of Dental Surgery
	International Standards		*Doctor)* Doctor of Humane	ME	Middle English
	Organisation		Letters/Literature		Myalgic
ISSN	International Standard	Lib	Liberal		Encephalomyelitis
	Serial Number	Lic	*(Licenciado)* lawyer	MEC	Member of Executive
ISP	Internet service provider		*(Spanish)*		Council
IT	information technology	lit	literary	MED	Master of Education
ITN	Independent Television	Lit Hum	*(Literae Humaniores)* classics	mega	one million times
	News		course, Oxford University	MEP	Member of the European
ITU	International	LITT D	Doctor of Letters		Parliament
	Telecommunication Union	LJ	Lord Justice	MFH	Master of Foxhounds
ITV	Independent Television	LLB	Bachelor of Laws	Mgr	Monsignor
IVF	in vitro fertilisation	LLD	Doctor of Laws	MI	Military Intelligence
		LLM	Master of Laws	micro	one-millionth part
J		LMS	local management in	milli	one-thousandth part
			schools	min	minimum
J	Judge	LMSSA	Licentiate in Medicine and	MLA	Member of Legislative
	Justice		Surgery, Society of		Assembly
JP	Justice of the Peace		Apothecaries	MLC	Member of Legislative
		loc cit	*(loco citato)* in the place		Council
K			cited	MLITT	Master of Letters
		log	logarithm	Mlle	Mademoiselle
KBE	Knight Commander,	Londin:	of London *(Bishop)*	MLR	minimum lending rate
	Order of the British	Long	longitude	MM	Military Medal
	Empire	LRT	London Regional	Mme	Madame
KCB	Knight Commander,		Transport	MMR	measles, mumps and
	Order of the Bath	LS	*(loco sigilli)* place of the		rubella (vaccine)
KCIE	Knight Commander,		seal	MN	Merchant Navy
	Order of the Indian	LSA	Licentiate of Society of	MO	Medical Officer/Orderly
	Empire		Apothecaries	MoD	Ministry of Defence
KCLJ	Knight Commander,	LSC	Learning and Skills	MoT	Ministry of Transport
	Order of St Lazarus of		Council	MP	Member of Parliament
	Jerusalem		Legal Services		Military Police
KCMG	Knight Commander,		Commission	mph	miles per hour
	Order of St Michael and St	Lsd	*(librae, solidi, denarii)*	MPHIL	Master of Philosophy
	George		pounds, shillings and	MR	Master of the Rolls
KCSI	Knight Commander,		pence	MRC	Medical Research Council
	Order of the Star of India	LSE	London School of	MRSA	Methicillin-Resistant
KCVO	Knight Commander,		Economics and Political		Staphylococcus Aureus
	Royal Victorian Order		Science	MS	Master of Surgery
KG	Knight of the Garter	LST	Local Sidereal Time		manuscript *pl* (MSS)
KGB	(Komitet Gosudarstvennoi	Lt	Lieutenant		multiple sclerosis
	Bezopasnosti) Committee	LTA	Lawn Tennis Association	MSC	Master of Science
	of State Security (USSR)	Ltd	Limited (liability)	MSP	Member of Scottish
kHz	kilohertz	LVO	Lieutenant, Royal		Parliament
KLJ	Knight, Order of St		Victorian Order	Mus B/D	Bachelor/Doctor of Music
	Lazarus of Jerusalem	LW	long wave	MV	merchant vessel
ko	knock out (boxing)	LWM	low water mark		motor vessel
KP	Knight, Order of St			MVO	Member, Royal Victorian
	Patrick	**M**			Order
KStJ	Knight, Order of St John			MW	medium wave
	of Jerusalem	M	Member	MWA	Member of the Welsh
Kt	Knight		Monsieur		Assembly
KT	Knight of the Thistle	MA	Master of Arts		
kV	kilovolt	Maj	Major	**N**	
kW	kilowatt	maj	majority		
kWh	kilowatt hour	max	maximum	N	north
		MB	*(Medicinae Baccalaureus)*	n/a	not applicable
L			Bachelor of Medicine		not available
		MBA	Master of Business	NAAFI	Navy, Army and Air Force
L	Liberal		Administration		Institutes
Lab	Labour	MBC	Metropolitan Borough	NAFTA	North American Free
Lat	Latitude		Council		Trade Agreement
lbw	leg before wicket	MBE	Member, Order of the	NASA	National Aeronautics and
lc	lower case *(printing)*		British Empire		Space Administration
LCJ	Lord Chief Justice	MBO	management buy-out	NASUWT	National Association of
LCM	least/lowest common	MC	Master of Ceremonies		Schoolmasters/Union of
	multiple		Military Cross		Women Teachers

NATO	North Atlantic Treaty Organisation	OECD	Organisation for Economic Co-operation and Development	PG	parental guidance
NB	New Brunswick			PGA	Professional Golfers Association
	(nota bene) note well	OED	*Oxford English Dictionary*	PGCE	Postgraduate Certificate of Education
NCIS	National Criminal Intelligence Service	Ofcom	Office of Communications		
		Ofgem	Office of Gas and Electricity Markets	PHD	Doctor of Philosophy
NCO	non-commissioned officer			PHLS	Public Health Laboratory Service
NDPB	non-departmental public body	OFM	Order of Friars Minor *(Franciscans)*	PIF	Pacific Islands Forum
NEB	New English Bible	Ofreg	Office for the Regulation of Electricity and Gas	pl	plural
nem con	*(nemine contradicente)* no one contradicting			PLA	Port of London Authority
		Ofsted	Office for Standards in Education	PLC	public limited company
NERC	Natural Environment Research Council			PLO	Palestine Liberation Organisation
		OFT	Office of Fair Trading		
nes	not elsewhere specified	Ofwat	Office of Water Services	p.m.	*(post meridiem)* after noon
NESTA	National Endowment for Science, Technology and the Arts	OHMS	On Her/His Majesty's Service	PM	Prime Minister
					post mortem
		ohp	overhead projector	PMRAFNS	Princess Mary's Royal Air Force Nursing Service
NFT	National Film Theatre	OIC	Organisation of the Islamic Conference		
NFU	National Farmers' Union			PO	petty officer
NHS	National Health Service	OM	Order of Merit		pilot officer
NI	National Insurance	ono	or near offer		post office
	Northern Ireland	ONS	Office for National Statistics		postal order
no	*(numero)* number			POW	prisoner of war
non seq	*(non sequitur)* it does not follow	op	*(opus)* work	pp	pages
		OP	opposite prompt side *(of theatre)*		*(per procurationem)* by proxy
Norvic:	of Norwich *(Bishop)*				
NP	Notary Public		Order of Preachers *(Dominicans)*	PPARC	Particle Physics and Astronomy Research Council
NRA	National Rifle Association				
NS	New Style *(calendar)*		out of print *(books)*		
	Nova Scotia	op cit	*(opere citato)* in the work cited	PPS	Parliamentary Private Secretary
NSPCC	National Society for the Prevention of Cruelty to Children				
		OPEC	Organisation of Petroleum Exporting Countries	PR	proportional representation
NSW	New South Wales	OPRAF	Office of Passenger Rail Franchising		public relations
NT	National Theatre			PRA	President of the Royal Academy
	National Trust	OPS	Office of Public Service		
	New Testament	ORR	Office of the Rail Regulator	Pres	president
	Northern Territory			pro tem	*(pro tempore)* for the time being
NUJ	National Union of Journalists	OS	Old Style *(calendar)*		
			Ordnance Survey	prox	*(proximo)* next month
NUM	National Union of Mineworkers	OSA	Order of St Augustine	PRS	President of the Royal Society
		OSB	Order of St Benedict		
NUS	National Union of Students	OSCE	Organisation for Security and Co-operation in Europe	PRSE	President of the Royal Society of Edinburgh
NUT	National Union of Teachers			PS	*(postscriptum)* postscript
		OStJ	Officer, Order of St John of Jerusalem	PSBR	public sector borrowing requirement
NVQ	National Vocational Qualification				
		OT	Old Testament	psc	passed staff college
NWT	Northwest Territory	OTC	Officers' Training Corps	PSV	public service vehicle
NZ	New Zealand	Oxon	(of) Oxford Oxfordshire	PTA	Parent-Teacher Association
O				Pte	Private
		P		PTO	please turn over
OAP	old age pension(er)			PVC	polyvinyl chloride
OAPEC	Organisation of Arab Petroleum Exporting Countries	p	page		
		p	*(piano)* softly	**Q**	
		PA	personal assistant		
OAS	Organisation of American States		Press Association	QARANC	Queen Alexandra's Royal Army Nursing Corps
			public address *(system)*		
OAU	Organisation of African Unity	PAYE	pay as you earn	QARNNS	Queen Alexandra's Royal Naval Nursing Service
		pc	*(per centum)* in the hundred		
Ob *or* obit	died	PC	personal computer	QBD	Queen's Bench Division
OBE	Officer, Order of the British Empire		Police Constable	QC	Queen's Counsel
			politically correct	QED	*(quod erat demonstrandum)* which was to be proved
OC	Officer Commanding		Privy Counsellor		
ODA	Overseas Development Administration	PDA	personal digital assistant	QGM	Queen's Gallantry Medal
		PDSA	People's Dispensary for Sick Animals	QHC	Queen's Honorary Chaplain
ODPM	Office of the Deputy Prime Minister				
		PE	physical education	QHDS	Queen's Honorary Dental Surgeon
OE	Old English	Petriburg:	of Peterborough *(Bishop)*		
	omissions excepted	PFI	Private Finance Initiative		

QHNS	Queen's Honorary Nursing Sister	Rep	representative Republican	RSVP	*(répondez, s'il vous plaît)* please reply
QHP	Queen's Honorary Physician	Rev(d)	Reverend	RSW	Royal Scottish Society of Painters in Watercolours
QHS	Queen's Honorary Surgeon	RFU	Rugby Football Union		
		RGN	Registered General Nurse		
Qld	Queensland	RGS	Royal Geographical Society	Rt Hon	Right Honourable
QMG	Quartermaster General			RTPI	Royal Town Planning Institute
QPM	Queen's Police Medal	RHA	Regional Health Authority		
QS	quarter sessions	RHS	Royal Horticultural Society	RU	Rugby Union
	Queen's Scholar			RUC	Royal Ulster Constabulary
QSO	quasi-stellar object (quasar)	RI	Rhode Island	RV	Revised Version *(of Bible)*
			Royal Institute of Painters in Watercolours	RWS	Royal Water Colour Society
	Queen's Service Order		Royal Institution	RYS	Royal Yacht Squadron
quango	quasi-autonomous non-governmental organisation	RIBA	Royal Institute of British Architects	**S**	
qv	*(quod vide)* which see	RIP	*(requiescat in pace)* may he/she rest in peace	s	second
R		RIR	Royal Irish Regiment		*(solidus)* shilling
		RL	Rugby League	S	south
r.	*(recto)* on the right-hand page	RM	Registered Midwife	SA	Salvation Army
			Royal Marines		South Africa
R	*(Regina)* Queen	RMA	Royal Military Academy		South America
	(Rex) King	RMN	Registered Mental Nurse		South Australia
RA	Royal Academy/ Academician	RMT	National Union of Rail, Maritime and Transport Workers	SAARC	South Asian Association for Regional Co-operation
	Royal Artillery			SAE	stamped addressed envelope
R&B	rhythm and blues	RN	Royal Navy		
R&D	research and development	RNIB	Royal National Institute for the Blind	Salop	Shropshire
RAC	Royal Armoured Corps			SARS	Severe Acute Respiratory Syndrome
	Royal Automobile Club	RNID	Royal National Institute for the Deaf		
RADA	Royal Academy of Dramatic Art			Sarum:	of Salisbury (Bishop)
		RNLI	Royal National Lifeboat Institution	SAS	Special Air Service
RADC	Royal Army Dental Corps			SBS	Special Boat Service
RAE	Royal Aerospace Establishment	RNMH	Registered Nurse for the Mentally Handicapped		Small Business Service
				ScD	Doctor of Science
RAEC	Royal Army Educational Corps	RNR	Royal Naval Reserve	SCM	State Certified Midwife
		RNVR	Royal Naval Volunteer Reserve	SDLP	Social Democratic and Labour Party
RAES	Royal Aeronautical Society	RNXS	Royal Naval Auxiliary Service	SEAQ	Stock Exchange Automated Quotations system
RAF	Royal Air Force				
RAM	random-access memory	RNZN	Royal New Zealand Navy		
	Royal Academy of Music	ROC	Royal Observer Corps	SEN	special educational needs
		Roffen:	of Rochester *(Bishop)*		State Enrolled Nurse
RAMC	Royal Army Medical Corps	ROI	Royal Institute of Oil Painters	SERPS	State Earnings Related Pension Scheme
RAN	Royal Australian Navy	ROM	read-only memory	SFO	Serious Fraud Office
RAOC	Royal Army Ordnance Corps	RoSPA	Royal Society for the Prevention of Accidents	SHMIS	Society of Headmasters and Headmistresses of Independent Schools
RAPC	Royal Army Pay Corps	RP	Royal Society of Portrait Painters		
RAVC	Royal Army Veterinary Corps			SI	*(Système International d'Unités)* International System of Units
		RPA	Rural Payments Agency		
RBG	Royal Botanic Garden	rpm	revolutions per minute		
RBS	Royal Society of British Sculptors	RRC	Lady of Royal Red Cross		statutory instrument
		RSA	Royal Scottish Academician	sic	so written
RC	Red Cross			Sig	signature
	Roman Catholic		Royal Society of Arts		Signor
RCM	Royal College of Music	RSC	Royal Shakespeare Company	SJ	Society of Jesus *(Jesuits)*
RCN	Royal Canadian Navy			SLD	Social and Liberal Democrats
RCT	Royal Corps of Transport	RSCN	Registered Sick Children's Nurse		
RD	refer to drawer *(banking)*				
	Royal Naval and Royal Marine Forces Reserve Decoration	RSE	Royal Society of Edinburgh	**T**	
		RSM	Regimental Sergeant Major	TA	Territorial Army
	Rural Dean			TB	tuberculosis
RDI	Royal Designer for Industry	RSPB	Royal Society for the Protection of Birds	TCCB	Test and County Cricket Board
RE	Religious Education	RSPCA	Royal Society for the Prevention of Cruelty to Animals	TD	Territorial Decoration
	Royal Engineers			TEC	Training and Enterprise Council
REM	rapid eye movement				
REME	Royal Electrical and Mechanical Engineers	RSV	Revised Standard Version *(of Bible)*	TEFL	teaching English as a foreign language

temp	temperature	UNHCR	United Nations High	VSO	Voluntary Service
	temporary employee		Commissioner for		Overseas
TES	*Times Educational*		Refugees	VTOL	vertical take-off and
	Supplement	UNICEF	United Nations Children's		landing *(aircraft)*
T&G	Transport and General		Fund		
	Workers' Union	UNIDO	United Nations Industrial	**W**	
THES	*Times Higher Education*		Development		
	Supplement		Organisation	W	website
TLS	*Times Literary Supplement*	Unita	National Union for the		west
TNT	trinitrotoluene *(explosive)*		Total Independence of	WCC	World Council of
trans.	translated		Angola		Churches
trs	transpose *(printing)*	UNPO	Unrepresented Nations	WEA	Workers' Educational
TRH	Their Royal Highnesses		and Peoples Organisation		Association
TT	Tourist Trophy *(motorcycle*	UPU	Universal Postal Union	WEU	Western European Union
	races)	US(A)	United States (of America)	WFTU	World Federation of Trade
	tuberculin tested	USDAW	Union of Shop,		Unions
TUC	Trades Union Congress		Distributive and Allied	WHO	World Health
			Workers		Organisation
U		USM	Unlisted Securities Market	WI	West Indies
		USSR	Union of Soviet Socialist		Women's Institute
U	Unionist		Republics	Winton:	of Winchester *(Bishop)*
UAE	United Arab Emirates	UTC	co-ordinated universal	WIPO	World Intellectual
uc	upper case *(printing)*		time system		Property Organisation
UC	Unitary Council	UVF	Ulster Volunteer Force	WMD	weapons of mass
UCAS	Universities and				destruction
	Colleges Admissions	**V**		WMO	World Meteorological
	Service				Organisation
UCATT	Union of Construction,	v	*(versus)* against	WO	Warrant Officer
	Allied Trades and	v.	*(verso)* on the left-hand	WRAC	Women's Royal Army
	Technicians		page		Corps
UCL	University College	VA	Vicar Apostolic	WRAF	Women's Royal Air Force
	London		Victoria and Albert Order	WRNS	Women's Royal Naval
UDA	Ulster Defence	VAD	Voluntary Aid Detachment		Service
	Association		*(nursing)*	WRVS	Women's Royal Voluntary
UDI	Unilateral Declaration of	V&A	Victoria and Albert		Service
	Independence		Museum	WS	Writer to the Signet
UDR	Ulster Defence Regiment	VAT	value added tax	WTO	World Trade Organisation
UEFA	Union of European	VC	Victoria Cross	WWW	World Wide Web
	Football Associations	VCR	video cassette recorder	WYSIWYG	what you see is what you
UFF	Ulster Freedom Fighters	VD	venereal disease		get
UFO	unidentified flying		Volunteer Officers'		
	object		Decoration	**Y**	
UHF	ultra-high frequency	VDU	visual display unit		
UKAEA	UK Atomic Energy	Ven	Venerable	YMCA	Young Men's Christian
	Authority	VHF	very high frequency		Association
UN	United Nations	VIP	very important person	YWCA	Young Women's Christian
UNESCO	United Nations	VRD	Royal Naval Volunteer		Association
	Educational, Scientific and		Reserve Officers'		
	Cultural Organisation		Decoration		

INDEX

STOP PRESS

CHANGES SINCE PAGES WENT TO PRESS

PARLIAMENT

A parliamentary by-election prompted by the death of Robin Cook, MP for the Scottish constituency of Livingston, was held on 29 September. Labour candidate Jim Devine won with 12,319 votes, a majority of 2,680 (9.09 per cent).

LAW COURTS AND OFFICES

Lord Justice of Appeal, The Rt. Hon. Sir Jonathan Mance, was appointed a Lord of Appeal in Ordinary (under the Appellate Jurisdiction Act 1876), with the style and title of Baron Mance.

EUROPEAN UNION

On 4 October the EU officially opened accession talks with Turkey and Croatia after diplomatic deadlocks were resolved with both countries.

COUNTRIES OF THE WORLD – SEPTEMBER 2005

AFGHANISTAN

27. The interior minister Ali Ahmad Jalali announced he would resign, citing personal reasons.

EGYPT

27. Egyptian president Hosni Mubarak was sworn into office for a fifth term.

POLAND

25. The legislative election was won by the centre-right Law and Justice Party (PiS) with 155 seats in the *Sejm*. The Civic Platform (PO) came in second place with 133 seats; negotiations to form a coalition government were expected to take place within weeks. The leader of the PiS, Jaroslaw Kaczynski, announced he would not assume the role of prime minister if his brother Lech wins the presidential vote in October.

EVENTS OF THE YEAR – SEPTEMBER 2005

NORTHERN IRELAND AFFAIRS

26. John de Chastelain, the retired Canadian general responsible for overseeing the decommissioning process, announced that the IRA had put the last of its weapons beyond use.

THE AMERICAS

1. In the wake of Hurricane Katrina the US government announced an additional 10,000 national guard troops would be deployed to New Orleans in an attempt to restore order as looting and gun-battles broke out in the city. Reports from the New Orleans Convention Centre described scenes of chaos and violence as food and water supplies ran out; several bodies were spotted outside the building. **2.** President Bush admitted that the relief effort was 'not acceptable' as the security situation in New Orleans deteriorated. Members of congress passed a $10.5 billion emergency aid package. **3.** In the USA, Chief Justice of the Supreme Court William H. Renquist died aged 80.

EUROPE

25. In Switzerland, a national referendum was held on plans to open the country's job market to workers from the ten newest EU countries; a 56 per cent majority voted yes.

SPORTS RESULTS

CRICKET

County Championship Cricket 2005: Division 1, Nottinghamshire, 236 points; *Relgated,* Surrey, 180.5 points; Gloucestershire, 104 points; Glamorgan, 88.5 points

Division 2, Promoted, Lancashire, 212 points; Durham, 205 points; Yorkshire, 200.5 points

National One Day League: Division 1, Essex, 56 points; *Relegated:* Gloucestershire, 26 points; Worcestershire, 22 points; Hampshire 22 points

Division 2, Promoted, Sussex, 54 points; Durham, 52 points; Warwickshire, 44 points

GOLF

Seve Trophy (The Wynyard, England): Great Britain and Ireland beat Continental Europe 16½–11½

Catalonia Masters (El Golf Platja de Pals, Spain): Karine Icher (France), 207

MOTOR CYCLING

Grand Prix 2005

Malaysia (Sepang): *500cc,* Loris Capirossi (Italy), Ducati

250cc, Casey Stoner (Australia), Aprilia

125cc, Thomas Luthi (Switzerland), Honda

MOTOR RACING

Brazilian Formula One Grand Prix 2005 (Interlagos): Juan Pablo Montoya (Columbia), McLaren

REAL TENNIS

British Professional Singles Championship Final 2005: Steve Virgona (Australia) beat Rod Fahey (Australia) 6–2, 1–6, 3–6, 6–4, 1–0 retired